The Harper Single Volume American Literature

The Harper Single Volume American Literature

THIRD EDITION

Donald McQuade ► University of California, Berkeley
General Editor

Robert Atwan ► Seton Hall University

Martha Banta ► University of California, Los Angeles

Justin Kaplan ► Cambridge, Massachusetts

David Minter ► Rice University

Robert Stepto ► Yale University

Cecelia Tichi ► Vanderbilt University

Helen Vendler ► Harvard University

LONGMAN

An imprint of Addison Wesley Longman, Inc.

New York • Reading, Massachusetts • Menlo Park, California • Harlow, England
Don Mills, Ontario • Sydney • Mexico City • Madrid • Amsterdam

Development Editor: Marlane Miriello
Marketing Manager: John Holdcroft
Supplements Editor: Donna Campion
Project Coordination and Text Design: Ruttle, Shaw & Wetherill, Inc.
Cover Design Manager: Nancy Danahy
Cover Designer: Kay Petronio
Cover Art: © Romare Bearden Foundation/Licensed by VAGA, New York, NY; *front cover:* Detail from "The
Block" by Romare Bearden, 1971; *back cover:* "The Block" by Romare Bearden, 1971.
Full Service Production Manager: Joseph Vella
Senior Print Buyer: Hugh Crawford
Photo Researcher: Julie Tesser
Electronic Page Makeup: Ruttle, Shaw & Wetherill, Inc.
Printer and Binder: Quebecor World–Taunton
Cover Printer: The Lehigh Press, Inc.

For permission to use copyrighted material, grateful acknowledgment is made to the copyright holders on
pp. 2845–2850, which are hereby made part of this copyrighted page.

Library of Congress Cataloging-in-Publication Data

The Harper single volume American literature / Donald McQuade,
general editor . . . [et al.]. — 3rd ed.
    p. cm.
    "Single volume."
    Includes bibliographical references and index.
    ISBN 0-321-01269-0
    1. American literature.   2. United States — Literary collections.
I. McQuade, Donald.
    PS507 .H227 1999
    810.8 — dc21

                    98-36994
                     CIP
                     Rev.

Harper is a registered trademark of HarperCollins Publishers Inc. Used under license.

Please visit our website at http://longman.awl.com

ISBN 0-321-012690

Contents

257   The Literature of the New Republic, 1776–1836

Introduction

1289   The Literature of an Expanding Nation, 1865–1912

1863   The Literature of a New Century, 1912–1945

Preface

This third edition of *The Harper Single Volume American Literature* (previously *The Harper American Literature, Compact Edition*) reaffirms and invigorates its editors' commitment to provide students with the most comprehensive and reliable introduction to the diversity and depth of American literature. This thoroughly revised edition reflects what we have learned from our classroom experiences using the text and our discussions with students, as well as from our conversations with scores of instructors across the country who have worked successfully with the first two editions.

In developing this new edition, we have taken great care to seek out—and respond to—the instructional interests and needs of individual faculty and, in doing so, to build a consensus toward a comprehensive collection of American literature for use in different pedagogical settings. Drawing on a detailed analysis of a remarkable range of course descriptions and a thorough survey and review process, we have reorganized this third edition to reflect the changing patterns of reading assigned in the one-semester course in American literature, and we have developed each of the seven periods out of a matrix of selections that are consistently taught in this course.

Reorganization and New Period Headings

Responding to the instructional requests of our colleagues, we have integrated our presentation of twentieth-century literature. Where poetry and prose were previously divided—into a series of six sections from 1912 to the present—we have now interwoven these traditions into a single chronological order, trimmed the number of sections to two, and redesignated them "The Literature of a New Century" and "The Literature Since Midcentury." This more direct and accessible restructuring enables instructors to teach together the writings of several authors—such as T. S. Eliot and Mary Oliver—who have written noteworthy poetry and prose. "The Literature of a New Century" and "The Literature Since Midcentury" also invite readers to appreciate more readily the continuum of literary themes and styles throughout the twentieth century without encountering artificial breaks in the chronology.

The instructional aims of each of the seven sections in *The Harper Single Volume American Literature* are reinforced by "Cultural Portfolios," a series of pedagogically supportive groupings of brief literary selections, letters, journal entries, cultural artifacts, and artwork collected under headings designating both historical periods and significant literary movements.

The Literature of the New World
> Cultural Portfolio: The European Conquest of America

The Literature of Colonial America
> Cultural Portfolio: The Witchcraft Trials
> Cultural Portfolio: The Ways of the Native Americans

The Literature of the New Republic
> Cultural Portfolio: Slavery, Freedom, and Identity
> Cultural Portfolio: Asserting a National Language and Literature

The Literature of the American Renaissance
> Cultural Portfolio: Nature's Nation

The Literature of an Expanding Nation
> Cultural Portfolio: The New Immigrants
> Cultural Portfolio: Oral Traditions and Turn-of-the-Century Literature

The Literature of a New Century
> Cultural Portfolio: The Harlem Renaissance
> Cultural Portfolio: The Southern Renaissance

American Literature Since Midcentury
> Cultural Portfolio: Who Is an American Writer?

We have designed each cultural portfolio to offer assisted invitations to instructors to teach literature through the cultural and historical themes that influenced our national literature and thereby to enhance their students' appreciation of the interdependence of writers' lives, works, and cultural backgrounds.

This new edition of *The Harper Single Volume American Literature* also features an expanded program of artwork and illustrations, strategically interspersed throughout to highlight especially significant literary themes and issues. These images include early maps, architecture, portraits of writers and covers of famous first editions, landscape paintings, and documentary photos dating back to as early as Mathew Brady's famous photographs of the Civil War.

A Wide and Diverse Range of American Literature

This edition of *The Harper Single Volume American Literature* reprints many of the most widely recognized American literary classics. Yet we want these classics to reflect more than an attenuated literary tradition, one too often dismissed as elitist. We believe that America's literary classics can—and should—exemplify what the scholar Nathan Huggins calls a "pluralistic realism." No collection of American literature can be complete unless it includes a wide range of distinctive voices, including those of women, African Americans, Asian Americans, Native Americans, and the various cultures of Spanish-speaking Americans. In our selections, headnote essays, and section introductions, we blend these works of diverse literary and cultural merit with other, more traditional selections so that these new voices can be heard as more than simply statistical responses or intellectual concessions to contemporary propriety.

A Broad Range of Teaching Options

The Harper Single Volume American Literature refines as well as reinforces our commitment to our original ideas. For example, this edition further enriches and extends the representation of America's dramatic tradition. Included in this edition are Susan Keating Glaspell's *Trifles*, Eugene O'Neill's *The Emperor Jones*, Tennessee Williams's *The Glass Menagerie*, and Tony Kushner's *Angels in America: Millennium Approaches*. In addition, we have featured in the final cultural portfolio, "Who Is an American Writer?," an instructionally self-contained excerpt from *Sarita*, by the Cuban American playwright Maria Irene Fornes.

Previous editions pioneered diversity among collections of American literature, and this third edition upholds its leadership among single-volume anthologies. Additional, and diverse, selections of the highest quality increase our representation of the aesthetic, regional, ethnic, racial, and gender riches of American poetry and prose. We have strengthened what was our groundbreaking representation of literature reflecting the complexity and variety of Native American, African American, Asian American, and different Hispanic American cultural traditions. This edition includes, to note but a few examples, Reginald McKnight's "The Kind of Light That Shines on Texas," showing how a young African American child in a predominantly white town learns the complexities of racial hatred and redemption; Tony Kushner's award-winning play about gay rights, *Angels in America: Millennium Approaches*; and ample selections from the work of such distinguished women writers as Susan Howe, a poet of the L-A-N-G-U-A-G-E movement, known for her experimentation in avant-garde style and form, Gish Jen, the celebrated Chinese American writer of fiction, and Maria Irene Fornes, the outstanding Cuban American playwright. And with the addition of the "Cultural Portfolios," we now present more focused and sustained attention to the historical and cultural contexts within which these poems, stories, plays, and essays appear. In a similar vein, this third edition also features an added emphasis on regional—and especially Southern—literature. In effect, this edition offers an even more effective instructional synthesis of recognized literary classics and lesser-known, but significant, works that continue to reshape America's literary traditions.

In response to instructors' requests for more attention to literature since 1945, we present here a greater diversity of styles, themes, and literary approaches as well as increase our in-depth coverage of each writer—especially poets, each of whom is now represented by a minimum of four works. The many new writers and selections in the contemporary period include, for example, Susan Howe, who appears on our pages for the first time with her long poetic sequence, "Thorow." Audre Lorde's poetry also graces the pages of this single-volume edition for the first time, and Mary Oliver's poetry appears alongside a newer prose work, "Owls." James Baldwin is represented by both a story, "Sonny's Blues," and an essay, "Letter to My Nephew on the One-Hundredth Anniversary of the Emancipation." Leslie Marmon Silko appears with two stories, "Storyteller," and "Lullaby." Other especially noteworthy additions to this section, "The Literature Since Midcentury," are Alice Walker's "Everyday Use," Martin Luther King, Jr.'s "Letter from Birmingham Jail," Sandra Cisneros's "Barbie-Q," Gish Jen's "Hot Times at the Hot Line," Louise Erdrich's "Lulu's Boys," and Tony Kushner's masterful play, *Angels in America: Millennium Approaches*.

Related Voices

Building on the editorial principle of establishing productive literary connections featured in previous editions, we have increased the number of major selections paired with supporting texts, and accentuated the ways in which each pair will expand students' awareness of ongoing literary influence and dialogues. Among the many examples are Emma Willard's "On Female Education," which accompanies Abigail Adams' letter to John Adams on the rights and treatment of women in the new republic; a newspaper account and photo of the famous black female abolitionist Sojourner Truth, placed immediately after the publication of Sarah and Angelina Grimké's "Appeal to Christian Women of the South"; a collection of literary, documentary, political, and propagandizing texts to accompany Rebecca Harding Davis's *Life in the Iron Mills;* a newspaper account by William Dean Howells, entitled "On Deciding to Publish 'The Yellow Wallpaper'," which follows the early radical feminist story "The Yellow Wallpaper"; and, accompanying the twentieth-century poet Robert Hayden's "A Letter to Phillis Wheatley," a letter by this famous slave and poet of the eighteenth century.

Broadening and Redefining an American Classic

The new edition broadens the restrictive notion of what constitutes an American classic. We include, for example, a representative selection of Native American oral and written literatures, stretching from the oral poetry of the sixteenth century to the fiction and poetry of contemporary writers. In doing so, we seek to show how celebrated and less-heralded works of literature illumine each other and enable us to appreciate the diverse achievements that have shaped a distinctively American culture. For "major" and "minor" figures alike, our consistent editorial aim has been to preserve the writer's living complexity, his or her verbal struggles with the challenges of shaping a self, modifying a genre, extending a literary tradition, or enriching a cultural context—as these are reflected in individual compositions.

A Continued Commitment to Excellence and Diversity

This edition of *The Harper Single Volume American Literature* continues to express its editors' commitment to what is now a nearly 150-year-old tradition of collections of American literature. From the publication in 1855 of Evert A. and George L. Duyckinck's two-volume *Cyclopaedia of American Literature*, readers wanting to explore what the Duyckincks called "the literary biography of America" have had ready access to what each succeeding generation judged the literature most worthy of its collective attention. Yet *The Harper Single Volume American Literature* was the first comprehensive gathering and reassessment of American literature to achieve the goal announced in the Duyckinck preface and subsequently endorsed by the editors of virtually every collection of American literature—"to bring together in one book convenient for perusal and reference . . . memorials and records of the writers of the country and their works, from the earliest period to the present day." What distinguishes *The Harper Single Volume American Literature* from its predecessors and competitors is its commitment to presenting fully both the excellence and the breadth of American literature, its thematic and stylistic range as well as its geographical and ethnic diversity. To this end, we have worked to extend the conventional boundaries of the American literary tradition.

Prior to the publication of the first edition of this text in 1987, virtually every collection of American literature began either with a generous selection of Puritan writings or, in fewer instances, with Captain John Smith and his engaging account of the early years of the Virginia colony. Such beginnings ignored a wealth of compelling literature written in and about America long before the first settlements at either Roanoke Island or Plymouth Plantation—from the compelling creation myths of Native Americans to Cabeza de Vaca's harrowing sixteenth-century narrative of his struggles to survive along the southeast coast of what is now Texas. To displace the narrow, northeastern, Puritan bias of currently available texts, *The Harper Single Volume American Literature* continues to open with a generous sampling of presettlement writing. "The Literature of the New World" maps out new approaches to the important cultural forces that have helped shape American life.

This edition further extends America's literary tradition in another significant direction. Its final section, "The Literature Since Midcentury," devotes sustained attention to our most recent—and eloquent—writers of fiction, poetry, and drama, far beyond the mid-1960s boundaries set by editors of nearly all other collections. Sampling the work of such important contemporary writers of fiction as Toni Morrison, Louise Erdrich, Bobbie Ann Mason, Maxine Hong Kingston, Sandra Cisneros, and Gish Jen, poets Michael S. Harper, Rita Dove, Joy Harjo, Jorie Graham, Alberto Rios, Li-Young Lee, and Cathy Song—to name but a few many fresh and already celebrated voices—will enable readers to explore unexpected dimensions of American literature.

The Most Comprehensive Regathering and Reassessment of American Literature

These distinctive sections, "The Literature of the New World" and "The Literature Since Midcentury," enlarge our presentation of American literary history. The earliest of our texts dates from 1492, the latest from 1996. We also reprint important but neglected works by classic writers, as well as important works by such neglected writers as Abigail Adams and Harriet Beecher Stowe. Throughout this edition, the contributing editors aim to present the most comprehensive regathering and reassessment ever of America's literary tradition, including but extending beyond classic works. For example, we have framed a representation of Paul Laurence Dunbar's poetry by the debate between Booker T. Washington and W. E. B. Du Bois over how the race and the nation must deal with the tragic consequences of "double consciousness" (divisions within the psyche of African Americans) and "the problem of the color line" (divisions between African Americans and whites).

The Harper Single Volume American Literature also features new views of traditional writers. To highlight the importance of Emily Dickinson's and Walt Whitman's poetic visions and accomplishments and to provide instructors with greater pedagogical flexibility, we provide generous selections from their work, including a liberal selection from Dickinson's letters. We have revised the previous edition to reflect America's literary traditions, refreshed by bold and practical innovations. Indicative of its editors' continued commitment to presenting the ethnic and geographic diversity of American literature, the writings of Native Americans take their place in authentic, scholarly texts, not accounts from popular newspapers. So too, edition allows instructors to provide their students with broader access to regional writing in their courses. We have included, for example, a sampling of southern writing from the pre-Revolutionary era through the antebellum South and beyond.

Faithful to America's literary traditions, and responsible to their many voices, *The Harper Single Volume American Literature* continues to provide a just and full representation of the literary achievements of American women and minority writers. We have revised the section entitled "The Literature of an Expanding Nation" to include far greater attention to the range and depth of our representation of the highly gendered hue and cry raised at the turn of the century, including Kate Chopin, Charlotte Perkins Gilman, Edith Wharton, and Zitkala Ša (Gertrude Simmons Bonnin).

In addition to the most teachable of Henry James's fiction and nonfiction prose, we have reprinted an engaging selection from Alice James's piquant, poignant diary. We have also strengthened our representation of such writers as Zora Neale Hurston and Stephen Crane, adding to Crane's most famous story several of his most powerful poems—dark cries of an angry young man working out in short verse form his ironic resistance to cosmic injustice and the absurdities of fate. In a similar vein, we have enriched our representation of late-nineteenth-century writers to include such figures as Edith Wharton and Susan Keating Glaspell. The selections in this section emphasize the sense of change that swept late-nineteenth-century America—of singularly new social relationships; of a self radically reformed into something unrecognizable and perhaps not wholly unified; of the furious surge of technology; of historical events that extended past one's neighborhood or hometown into the national and global arenas; of problems and prospects from the 1890s that resemble what Americans experience in the late 1990s.

We have revised and expanded the number of poets in "The Literature of a New Century" to feature the works of two major women poets—H. D. (Hilda Doolittle) and Edna St. Vincent Millay. In addition, we have reprinted a generous sampling of several major statements on poetry and/or the poet's vocation from Robert Frost, Wallace Stevens, T. S. Eliot, and Langston Hughes. We also have revised "The Literature Since Midcentury" to offer significant—and new—representation of writers born since 1950, especially those of color. We have expanded this section to include more poems by each poet; among them are a recent Nobel laureate (Derek Walcott, 1992), a recent winner of the Pulitzer Prize for poetry (Mary Oliver, 1992), and a poet laureate (Rita Dove).

By offering fresh perspectives on the work of America's literary masters and significant new voices, we provide evidence of the ways in which American literature helped shape, and in turn was influenced by, American culture during each period in its history. Throughout, we have taken special care to provide readers with ready access to unexpected and inviting selections without overburdening overcrowded reading schedules. We hope that inquisitive readers will be prompted to explore further the works, careers, and interconnections that give American literature its inexhaustible richness.

Criteria for Selection

Committed to offering a broader range in the characteristic modes of America's most prominent literary figures, we established the following criteria to guide us in presenting the work of each writer: the literary merits of a particular selection, its significance in American literary history, its reflection of the range and depth of the writer's accomplishments, its connections to other themes and styles, and its power to document the literary values of the culture within which the writer works. Most often, we represent American writers by their most important work and by a sampling of other literary performances that show them engaging significant cultural issues.

Introductions to the Cultural Backgrounds of American Literature

A perennial problem of any collection of American literature is a structure that appears to isolate careers and periods without adequate attention to the interactions of these lives, works, and times. *The Harper Single Volume American Literature* represents a concerted effort to weave selections, footnotes, author headnotes, and period introductions into a unified approach to American literature and the culture that informs it. In this volume, we seek not only to celebrate the classics of American literature and to locate neglected works of special literary merit, but also to suggest the many ways in which these works are enmeshed in a particular social and cultural context. We have designed the seven period introductions to show how major American writers were shaped by, influential in, and responsive to their times—to offer a memorable view of the cultural immediacy of a period, what Gertrude Stein calls "the continuous present."

Each introduction focuses on the prevailing circumstances and competitions American writers faced in each period. What was it like for writers to work at different moments in American cultural history? Were writers peripheral or central figures in examining the major issues and crises of their eras? What major developments occurred in the related arts? What was the taste of the reading public in each period? What, more generally, was the state of language, literacy, and public discourse? The answers to these and similar questions create vivid images of how writers lived and worked in their times.

Each period introduction highlights relevant American literary issues, cultural materials, and personalities. A short list of suggested further reading, arranged chronologically, follows the introduction to each historical period.

An Informative Headnote to Each Author

A brief informative essay introduces each writer represented in this edition. These headnote essays provide biographical details and the specific literary context for each writer's work. A major purpose of these headnotes is to show writers writing. In them, we trace the shape of an author's career and address the question of that writer's place in American literary history. We also consider how each writer feeds on, recoils from, or is in conflict with a particular literary, social, political, or cultural environment. At once biographical, contextual, and analytical, these essays counter the tendency to view writers in isolation from one another, by placing their contributions in the context of the main thematic and stylistic traditions of American literature. We designed the headnote essays to be informative enough to free our readers from the need for additional secondary sources before they read, but suggestions for further reading assist those who want to explore further the life and work of a particular author.

An Unobtrusive Editorial Presence

We have taken great care to provide reliable and readable texts, editing or modernizing only as needed (principally in spelling and punctuation). We have aimed to maintain the flavor of the original while making it accessible to contemporary readers. We note special textual problems and give the date of first publication at the end of each selection, preceded by the date of composition, if known. Footnotes, which are kept to a judicious minimum, explain obscure references, biblical and classical allusions, foreign words, and phrases having special or archaic meanings. We avoid interpretive footnotes. We have tried in every way possible to create conditions for reading that will enable students to discover and develop the integrity of their own responses with the support of their instructors.

We present this third edition of *The Harper Single Volume American Literature* as the most comprehensive single-volume collection ever assembled for the purpose of understanding—and reconstructing—American literary history. But we also intend it to be a flexible instructional resource. Because it contains virtually all the primary and supporting material required for instructional use and leisurely reading, this edition enables instructors and students to concentrate on the literary merits of significant American writing. Readers will find in these pages new forms, subjects, themes, and styles—each the product of a distinctive American literary imagination.

Donald McQuade
General Editor

Acknowledgments

The publication of the third edition of *The Harper Single Volume American Literature* represents the collaborative efforts of numerous professionals. In many ways its final shape challenges the accuracy of the century-old American adage, first recorded in Henry Ward Beecher's *Proverbs from Plymouth Pulpit* (1887): "It is not the going out of port, but the coming in, that determines the success of a voyage." The contributing editors of this edition would like to acknowledge those who contributed to this ambitious undertaking at both ends.

The first edition of the text could not have been launched without the vision and imaginative intelligence of John J. McDermott, Distinguished Professor of Philosophy at Texas A & M University, who helped articulate the need for a substantially different collection of American writing. His generous advice and rich understanding of American culture have proven invaluable throughout the project's development. Helene Brewer, Professor Emerita of American literature at Queens College, CUNY, served as a limitless resource during the early phases of shaping this collection. John Frederick Nims, University of Illinois at Chicago, and Joseph F. Trimmer, Ball State University, made significant contributions to the project's early development.

Many of our colleagues have offered incisive readings and helpful suggestions for improving the project. For their thoughtful critiques and helpful suggestions of this edition, we would especially like to thank the following: Mukhtar Ali Asani, Virginia Tech University; Howard Bahr, Motlow State Community College; Stuart Bloodworth, Motlow State Community College; James M. Boehnlein, University of Dayton; Heather Bouwman, University of Illinois, Urbana-Champaign; Seth Bovey, Louisiana State University-Alexandria; Patrick W. Bryant, Georgia State University; Stephanie Buchanan, University of Texas at Austin; Donna Burney, Howard Payne University; Marcia H. Cassell, East Tennessee State University; Tom Chase, Linn-Benton Community College; Linda Costanzo Cahir, Centenary College; Charlene Taylor Evans, Texas Southern University; Judith Halden-Sullivan, State University of West Virginia; Faye W. Hardiman, Georgia State University; Lisa Hammond Rashley, Michigan State University; Stephen Hecox, University of Nevada, Reno; Gary Hoppenstand, Michigan State University; George Kerrick, Middle Tennessee State University; J. Michael King, Radford University; John Leonard, Charleston Southern University; Cristine Levendusky, Emory University; Wayne Lesser, University of Texas at Austin; Drema P. Lipscomb, University of Rochester; Lisa M. Siefker Long, Middle Tennessee State University; Susan Lurie, Rice University; Ivan Melada, University of New Mexico; John Michael, University of Rochester; Bruce Michelson, University of Illinois, Urbana-Champaign; Norbert F. Nunes, Massachusetts Bay Community

College; Robert B. Olafson, Eastern Washington University; Jeanette Palmer, Motlow State Community College; Erin Redfield, Louisiana State University-Alexandria; Gary Richards, University of New Orleans; Chris Roberts, Clark State Community College; Linda F. Selzer, Pennsylvania State University; Lois Schmidt, Hibbing Community College; Gayle Smith, Pennsylvania State University-Worthington Scranton; Jack Solomon, California State University-Northridge; John Snider, Montana State University Northern; Mark Walter, William Jewell College; Marta Werner, Georgia State University; and Rosemary Whitaker, Colorado State University.

In addition, we would like to acknowledge our many colleagues across the country who served as reviewers of previous editions: Robert Abrams, University of Washington; Alida Allison, San Diego State University; Stephen Carl Arch, Michigan State University; Deborah Barker, Colorado State University; Art Bervin, Linn-Benton Community College; James Boehnlein, University of Dayton; Seth Bovey, Louisiana State University-Alexandria; Charles E. Bressler, Houghton College; Ludger Brinker, Macomb Community College; Robert Brinkmeier, University of Mississippi; Matthew J. Bruccoli, University of South Carolina; Bruce Burgett, University of Wisconsin-Madison; William Cain, Wellesley College; John Clendenning, California State University-Northridge; Stanley Corkin, University of Cincinnati; Pattie Cowell, Colorado State University; John J. Covolo, Lakeland Community College; George W. Crandell, Auburn University; Mary Cross, Fairleigh Dickinson University; Charles Crow, Bowling Green State University; Thomas M. Davis, Kent State University; Jean DeMarr, Indiana State University, Terre Haute; Peter W. Dowell, Emory College; Steven Fink, The Ohio State University; Robert E. Fleming, University of New Mexico; Elinor C. Flewellen, Santa Barbara City College; Joseph Flora, University of North Carolina at Chapel Hill; Phyllis Frus, Vanderbilt University; Arthur Geffen, University of Minnesota; Charles Genthe, California State University; Joan R. Griffin, Metropolitan State College-Denver; Mike Grimwood, North Carolina State University; Beverly Haviland, Vassar College; William Hedge, Goucher College; Robert J. Higgs, East Tennessee State University; Helen Hogan, Tarrant County Junior College South; Bruce Holland, University of Akron; John R. Holt, Centenary College; Donald C. Irving, Grinnell College; Shelley Jackson, University of Maryland; James Karman, California State University, Chico; Jan Kilby, Texas Lutheran College; Susan Koprince, University of North Dakota; Virginia Kouidis, Auburn University; David Larson, Cleveland State University; Jerome Loving, Texas A & M University; Chris MacGowan, The College of William and Mary; Tom Mack, University of South Carolina-Aiken; Janet Madden, El Camino Community College District; Julian Mason, University of North Carolina at Charlotte; Hubert H. McAlexander, University of Georgia; Dorothy Jean McIver, University of South Alabama; Robin McNallie, James Madison Unviersity; David Mesher, San Jose State University; Bruce Michelson, University of Illinois at Urbana-Champaign; Patrick Morrow, Auburn University; Jonathan Morse, University of Hawaii at Manoa; Merritt Moseley, University of North Carolina-Ashville; Betty Murnan-Smith, University of Wisconsin Center-Waukesha County; Lisa Myers, University of Pennsylvania; Rudolph Nelson, University of Albany; Cameron Nickels, James Madison University; Charles O'Neill, St. Thomas Aquinas College; Michael Oriad, Oregon State University; John Orr, Fullerton College; Ralph H. Orth, University of Vermont; Jeanette Palmer, Motlow State Community College; J. Daniel Patterson, The University of Southwestern Louisiana; Joyce Pettis, North

Carolina State University; Diane Quantic, Wichita State University; Jarold Ramsey, University of Rochester; Kenneth Roemer, University of Texas-Arlington; Robert T. Rhode, Northern Kentucky University; Judith Saunders, Marist College; Gary Scharnhorst, University of New Mexico; Ann Semel, St. Mary's University; Kathryn Shanley, Cornell University; Frank Shuffelton, University of Rochester; Mary J. Stone, Oregon State University; William E. Stupp, Richlan College; Arnold Tew, Cleveland State University; John W. Treel, Marshall University; Dawn Trouard, University of Akron; Albert J. von Frank, Washington State University, Pullman; Cheryl Walker, Scripps College; Jeffrey Walker, Penn State University; Elaine Ware, Middle Tennessee State University; Lonnie L. Willis, Boise State University.

We would also like to acknowledge our colleagues who offered thoughtful suggestions that helped shape the original project: Daniel Aaron, Harvard University; Maurice Bassan, San Francisco State University; Calvin Bedient, University of California at Los Angeles; Frank Bergon, Vassar College; Dennis Berthold, Texas A & M University; Lynn Z. Bloom, University of Connecticut, Storrs; Virginia W. Brumbach, Eastfield College; Louis J. Budd, Duke University; Lawrence Buell, Harvard University; Bonnie Costello, Radcliffe College; Michael Dunne, Middle Tennessee State University; Kathy Early, Middlesex County College; Emory Elliott, University of California at Riverside; Suzanne Ferguson, Case Western Reserve University; Steven Fink, The Ohio State University; Benjamin Franklin Fisher IV, University of Mississippi; Michael T. Gilmore, Brandeis University; James Goodwin, University of California at Los Angeles; Robert C. Grayson, Southeast Missouri State University; Malcom Griffith, University of Washington; Phillip F. Gura, University of North Carolina at Chapel Hill; William Howarth, Princeton University; J. G. Jannsen, Arizona State University; Donald Kartiganer, University of Washington; Merrill Lewis, Western Washington University; John S. Mann, Western Illinois University; Terence Martin, Indiana University; Lee Mitchell, Princeton University; James Moore, Mount San Antonio College; Elsa Nettels, College of William and Mary; Sarah Emily Newton, California State University, Chico; Thornton H. Parsons, Syracuse University; David Perkins, Harvard University; Marjorie Perloff, Stanford University; Robert L. Phillips, Mississippi State University; Donald Pizer, Tulane University; Joel Porte, Cornell University; Carolyn Porter, University of California, Berkeley; John Reardon, Miami University, Ohio; Louis D. Rubin, University of North Carolina at Chapel Hill; Henry M. Sayre, Oregon State University; Richard Schramm, University of Utah; Dorothy U. Seyler, Northern Virginia Community College; Frank Shuffelton, University of Rochester; Ellen Hurt Smith, Stetson University; Haskell Springer, University of Kansas; William T. Stafford, Purdue University; Eric J. Sundquist, Northwestern University; David O. Tomlinson, U.S. Naval Academy; Darwin T. Turner, University of Iowa; Emily S. Watts, University of Illinois at Urbana-Champaign; Robert P. Weeks, University of Michigan; Michael West, University of Pittsburgh; Ann Woodlief, Virginia Connonwealth University; Larzer Ziff, Johns Hopkins University.

We are grateful to the following colleagues and friends for their many helpful suggestions and generous encouragement: Daniel Aaron, Harvard University; Max Apple, Rice Univeristy; Helene Atwan; Anne Bernays; Joe Cuomo, Queens College, CUNY; Joan Feinberg; Joseph A. Finder; Steven Fink, The Ohio State University; Sally Fitzgerald; Bruce Forer; Reginald Gibbons, Northwestern University; William Howarth, Princeton University; Dennis Huston, Rice University; Richard Hutson,

University of California, Berkeley; Walter Isle, Rice University; William P. Kelly, Queens College; Bridget Gellert Lyons, Rutgers University; Robert B. Lyons, Queens College, CUNY; Lucy Maddox, Georgetown University; Rosemary Magee, Emory University; Wendy Martin, Claremont Graduate School; Larry McMurtry; Susanne B. McQuade; Caroline Minter; Terry Munisteri, Rice University; Carol Oles, California State University, Chico; Genaro Padilla, University of California, Berkeley; Louise Penner, Rice University; Marie Ponsot, Queens College, CUNY; Carolyn Porter, University of California, Berkeley; Edward Quinn, City College, CUNY; Harold Schechter, Queens College, CUNY; Nancy Sommers, Harvard University; Donald Stone, Queens College, CUNY; William Vesterman, Rutgers University; William P. Wilson, Queens College, CUNY; Hertha Wong, University of California, Berkeley; and Thomas Wortham, University of California at Los Angeles.

We are also indebted to Frederick Buell, Queens College, CUNY; Eileen O'Malley Callahan, University of California at Berkeley; Andrew J. Furer, University of California, Berkeley; and Sook Mee Hahn, University of California at Berkeley; their imaginative intelligence, critical acumen, and patient understanding made this a far more teachable book than it otherwise would have been. Elissa Weaver, University of Chicago, provided what are at once highly reliable and readable new translations of materials relating to Columbus's voyages. Wallace Chafe, University of California at Santa Barbara; Russ Hall; William C. Sturtevant, Smithsonian Institution and Hertha Wong, University of California, Berkeley helped strengthen our representation of Native American literature, as did the work of Paula Gunn Allen, University of California at Los Angeles, and her colleagues on the Modern Language Association's Commission on the Languages and Literature of America. Sally McLendon, Hunter College, CUNY, contributed immeasurably to our efforts to call greater attention to the eloquence and significance of Native American oral and written literatures. H. Barbara Weinberg, Curator of American Painting at the Metropolitan Museum of New York, served as an extraordinary resource for exploring the interrelations of American literature and art. Her command of American art history made each edition of the text more attractive as well as more responsive to the interplay of artistic forces in our culture.

For their invaluable research and editorial assistance in preparing various editions of the text, we continue to be grateful to: Jill Anderson, Rutgers University; Dianne Armstrong, University of California at Los Angeles; Michael Arnold, Rutgers University; Trudy Baltz; James Barszcz; Stephanie Bobo, Boston University; Ruth Burke, University of California at Los Angeles; Eileen O'Malley Callahan, University of California, Berkeley; Carolyn Denard, Kennesaw College; Francis P. J. DiCesare II; Nora Elias, University of California at Los Angeles; JoEllen Fisherkeller, New York University; Jeannette Gilkerson, University of California at Los Angeles; Gaspar Gonzalez, Yale University; David Harris; Ken Houghton, University of California at San Diego; Karen Johnson, Indiana University-Purdue University, Indianapolis; Jane Morris, Vanderbilt University; Marise McDermott, Virginia McDermott, Tara McDermott, Terry Munisteri, Rice University; Lisa McGill, Sharon Palmer, Yale University; Laura Parkington, Seton Hall University; John Pearson, Boston University; Louise Penner, Rice University; Allison Piepmeyer, Vanderbilt University; Sandy Qualls, Emory University; Anthony Shipps, Indiana University; Elizabeth Smith, CUNY Graduate Center; and Errol Somay, New York Public Library; Michelle

Stephens, Yale University; Jo Taylor, Emory University; Bryce Traister, University of Western Ontario; John Utz, Yale University; Willene Van Blair, University of California at Los Angeles; Chansonette Wedemeyer, University of California, Berkeley; David Wheeler; Cynthia Young, Yale University; and especially Sook Mee Hahn and Nadia Nurhussein, University of California, Berkeley and Nancy Leroy, Yale University.

We would also like to express our appreciation to the staffs at the libraries of Boston, Columbia, Emory, Harvard, Indiana, Princeton, Rice, Seton Hall, and Vanderbilt Universities; the University of California, Berkeley; the University of California at Los Angeles; the Bienecke Manuscript and Rare Book Library at Yale University; as well as the South Orange, New Jersey Public Library.

This third edition of *The Harper Single Volume American Literature* has benefited immeasurably from the contributions of Anne Marie Welsh, whose intellectual presence is evident in several headnotes, section introductions, and cultural portfolios. Two outstanding teachers, Gary Richards of the University of New Orleans and Cristine Levendusky of Emory University, generously took the lead in preparing the cultural portfolios entitled "Oral Traditions and Turn-of-the-Century Literature," and "The New Immigrants," respectively. We are grateful for their contributions.

We believe that the instructor's manual that accompanies the edition is an invaluable pedagogical aid for helping students to respond more effectively—in class discussions and in papers—to the breadth and depth of American literary history represented in this collection. For preparing such engaging and insightful views of the new material for the instructor's manual, we would like to thank Heather Bouwman, and for the previous edition of the text's instructor's manual, we would like to thank: Charlene Taylor Evans, Texas Southern University; Andrew J. Furer, Harvard University; Andrea Kwasny, University of Arkansas at Little Rock; Jack Roberts, St. Thomas Aquinas College; James Schramer, Youngstown State University; Karen F. Stein, University of Rhode Island; Bryce Traister, Western Ontario University; and Colin Wells, Rutgers University.

Our continuing thanks go to the skillful and gracious professionals at Addison Wesley Longman, Inc. This new edition could not have been published without the support of Lisa Moore, its editor. Without her commitment to *The Harper Single Volume American Literature*, to the principles underlying it, and to each of its contributing editors, this edition would not have made it into print. We are also grateful to Roth Wilkofsky, Vice President and General Manager, for his personal interest as well as his principled and continued support of this project. We would also like to acknowledge the first-rate professional assistance of Lois Lombardo, Peg Markow, and Joe Vella in the production of this edition.

We are especially indebted to Marlane Miriello, who kept the project on course with an admirable blend of intelligence, diligence, common sense, and good will and who coordinated the editorial process with remarkable energy, exactness, and unfailing good humor as well as uncommon graciousness and unflappable patience.

We would like to thank Megan Schumacher and Alison Ellis, who managed acquiring the rights to reprint thousands of pages of material. Ruttle, Shaw & Wetherill, Inc. directed the flow of these several thousand pages of manuscript and page proofs—under tight deadlines—with professionalism, good cheer, and genuine concern for the excellence of the project.

With affection and admiration, we often have invoked Philip Leininger, the sponsoring editor of the original edition, during the course of our deliberations aimed at continuing to reexamine—and reconstruct—the literary heritages of the United States.

We trust that all those who contributed to putting *The Harper Single Volume American Literature* in print will endorse Ralph Waldo Emerson's notion that "the reward of a thing well done is to have it done."

The Harper Single Volume American Literature

John White
Indians Fishing
watercolor, 1585.
British Museum, London
(Courtesy of the Trustees of the British Museum)

The Literature of the New World

The Discoveries of America

America has had many discoverers. The first arrived some 12,000 years ago (some scholars argue much earlier), when Stone Age hunters from Asia crossed the land bridge that is now the Bering Strait. These groups presumably became the earliest inhabitants of the New World, spreading gradually across North and South America. The theory of the Bering Strait migrations, however, does not go undisputed. Some Native Americans believe—as the creation stories in this first section reveal—that their people always lived in the Americas. The literature of the New World thus begins with Native American creation narratives; this is especially appropriate since the Judeo-Christian creation account from the Book of Genesis pervades the European exploration literature. On either side in this entangled and culturally diverse literary landscape we encounter the question of origins.

Archaeological evidence and a few persuasive literary texts also suggest that early in the eleventh century, some five hundred years before Columbus, a Viking crew led by Leif Eriksson sailed across present-day Davis Strait, explored Baffin Island and Labrador, and set up camp sites in Newfoundland, though no one is certain whether this is the place that Eriksson named "Vinland." The Norse made a few subsequent attempts at colonization but they were discouraged by skirmishes with native inhabitants. The literary works which contain these accounts, known as the Icelandic or Norse sagas, represent the earliest depictions of the New World in European literature (see Cultural Portfolio "The European Conquest of America").

At 2:00 A.M., Friday, October 12, 1492, Christopher Columbus undeniably made the first recorded discovery of America. Yet his reputation as *the* discoverer of the New World is somewhat tainted; he never understood *what* it was he had actually found. Hoping to discover a route, not a region, Columbus set sail from Spain on August 3, 1492, the very day that other ships were removing Jews from Spanish territory. Like navigators before him, he sought to find a convenient sea passage to the Orient and commercial access to the opulent world that Marco Polo described so vividly in his famous thirteenth century account of an overland journey to the court of Kublai Khan. From the moment Columbus first spotted the island of Guanahani—which he promptly renamed San Salvador—he was certain that his grand calculation had been correct: He had reached the east by sailing west. He was so convinced of this that throughout the four voyages he made to the New World between 1492 and 1502 he saw and interpreted everything—every plant, animal, mineral, place, and person he encountered—within the context of his having successfully reached Asia. To Washington Irving, Columbus was a man "predisposed to be deceived." The world he found was truly new, yet he persisted in seeing it as old.

Columbus's grand illusion derived ultimately from a mental picture of the earth that he pieced together from his reading of the prophetic books of the Bible, Marco Polo, and the famous ancient geographer Ptolemy. In brief, Columbus's dream of sailing directly west to Asia depended on what could be called the "small-earth theory." In his mathematically oriented *Geography* (ca. 150 A.D.), Ptolemy had grossly underestimated the size of the earth and had greatly extended Asia's eastern coast. This world image fitted in nicely with Marco Polo's speculations concerning the position of Japan, which Columbus—accepting Polo's location—estimated lay only 2,760 miles from Portugal. (The actual distance is well over 12,000 miles.) Columbus reinforced his calculations with quotations from the Old Testament prophets. In the apocryphal Book of Esdras (2:6) he read that the earth consists of six parts land and only one part water, a ratio that he believed would result in a short sea voyage. And in the Book of Ezekiel (5:5) he read that Jerusalem had been placed at the center of the world, a location that led him during his third voyage to conclude that he had approached the "Terrestrial Paradise," the original Garden of Eden.

Not only did Columbus derive an image of the world from the prophetic books, but he also wrote his own *Book of Prophecies*. In it he saw his career as the fulfillment of Isaiah 11:10–12: "And he shall set up an ensign for the nations." In 1502 Columbus wrote: "In carrying out this Enterprise of the Indies, neither reason, nor mathematics nor maps were any use to me: fully accomplished were the words of Isaiah." By his fourth voyage Columbus had sailed beyond geography into a vast, visionary world, wandering, as Irving put it, "in lands of his imagination." It was a geography in which every new observation, every new discovery, was made to fit into a single overarching theory—the belief that he had discovered a passage to India.

Native American Literature: First Encounters

In the nearly five centuries that have passed since Christopher Columbus accidentally discovered America and opened unbounded vistas for the literature of the New World, the response of European emigrants to America to the people they found there has fluctuated greatly, often moving rapidly between the extremes of trying ruthlessly to eliminate or mindlessly to glorify the Native American population. Within these extremes, the colonists persisted in their efforts to assimilate each Native American group within their nation's cultural heritage.

Europeans found Columbus's discovery of the New World as bewildering as it was unexpected. Samuel Eliot Morison, the distinguished biographer of Columbus, notes that "when discovered it [America] was not wanted, and most of the exploration for the next fifty years was done in the hope of getting through or around it." Columbus's reports on his voyages, for example, underscore his conviction that he had accomplished what he had set out to do: discover a shorter route to the East Indies. And because he could not adjust his expectations to the reality he confronted in the New World, Columbus insisted on calling the people he found there Indians, as though they were the people of the Near East he had sailed west to find. Columbus had discovered America, but not its people.

Generations of European explorers and colonists repeated Columbus's efforts to reinvent America and its inhabitants. Europeans dealt with the unrelenting novelty of their experiences with this newfound land and the people who inhabited it by reconstituting those experiences according to a more readily accessible and familiar cultural framework. As the historian Edmundo O'Gorman has noted, "The native cultures of the newly found lands could not be recognized and respected in their own right, as an original way of realizing human ideals and values, but only for the meaning they might have in relation to Christian European culture." America was invented, O'Gorman suggests, "in the image of its inventor," by those who could not free themselves from inherited European cultural perspectives and values. As a result, the distinctive nature of Native American culture was, to use William Carlos Williams's terms (from *In the American Grain*), "lost in chaos of borrowed titles, many of them inappropriate, under which the true character lies hid."

Perhaps the most striking fact about Native American literature is the cultural diversity that it represents. At the time of Columbus's voyages, more than 350 distinct, mutually unintelligible Native American languages were spoken in the area that is now the United States—and nearly half of these languages are still spoken in contemporary America. Literally thousands of distinct political and social groups were spread across the land. Given this range of identities, no single image of the Native American people can accurately capture the complexity of their culture. Yet historically, convenient stereotypes have dominated the nation's view of Native Americans: naked, mysterious, gullible creatures or noble savages; cigar-store props and dime-novel caricatures on the warpath or resilient, loyal companions of white-horsed heroes; and, more recently, soft-spoken wise men with drug-induced access to fundamental knowledge. Over the course of five centuries, Native Americans have come to be isolated geographically and culturally, relegated to the lowly status of the "other," with relatively few opportunities to posit the richness and complexity of their individual and collective voices in the cultural consciousness of the nation within whose boundaries they live.

The literature of Native Americans has been transmitted primarily through oral traditions. Skills in oratory are highly valued, in part because most North American tribes govern themselves through participatory democracy. Research conducted since the late nineteenth century reveals a number of highly developed oral literary forms—including ceremonial and popular songs, prayers, incantations, and mythic narratives—each with its own characteristic style and art in each Native American language. Yet because this literature is based on Native American cultural assumptions, it has traditionally been regarded as the province of anthropology rather than literary studies. Much like Puritan sermons and explorers' narratives, these texts, although culturally interesting, have not been considered part of the belles lettres tradition. Closer examination suggests that the literary features of these Native American texts are consistent with the stylistic qualities, including repetition and rhythmic patterning, of the great oral tradition of European literature dating back to classical antiquity. Like its European counterpart, the Native American literary oral tradition has articulated important states of individual consciousness while helping to reinforce a sense of community within each language group.

The confrontation between European and Native American cultures in the New World is amply reported from colonial points of view. Spanish, English, and French explorers and missionaries have left graphic narratives of their efforts to "civilize" and convert the New World's population. Relatively few voices remain, however, to represent reliably the Native American perspective on these same events. Most eyewitness accounts survive through secondhand and thirdhand translations. Many suffer to an indeterminate extent by being "screened" by a colonial sensibility. Like Powhatan's speech printed here, the surviving text may well reflect more what their white audiences thought, or hoped, Native Americans had said than what they did in fact say. In other instances, such as Mayan responses to the Spanish conquest, Native American authors had to master the language of their conquerors in order to preserve the anguish of their people.

Since the late nineteenth century, an increasing amount of indigenous oral literature has been transcribed by Native Americans in their own languages as well as in English and is increasingly available to be read. As a result, accurate texts of Native American literature can be included in the American literary tradition with greater confidence and frequency. The texts presented here illustrate the varying forms of literature that distinguished the conquered from the conqueror in the New World. These texts help us appreciate not only how each side discovered the "other" that neither knew but also how vibrant the Native American oral tradition has remained.

How the New World Became America

Credit for the discovery of America as a distinctly new region of the earth is often, though not without controversy, awarded to the Florentine navigator Amerigo Vespucci. In 1501, sailing to Brazil under the Portuguese flag, Vespucci noted that "we arrived at a new land which . . . we observed to be a continent." When his *Mundus Novus* (*The New World*) appeared in 1503, it received far wider circulation than anything Columbus had written. Vespucci was imbued with a deeper spirit of the Renaissance than Columbus, whose views in many respects resembled the views of such medieval travelers as Marco Polo. Vespucci doubted Ptolemy's accuracy. Like his family's friend Leonardo da Vinci, Vespucci maintained that observation was a more trustworthy guide than authority.

Vespucci secured his reputation as the discoverer of the New World by claiming in his next published work that he had found the South American continent during a 1497 voyage. Clearly he fabricated this early voyage to get around the fact that Columbus had set foot on—though not convincingly identified—the Paria peninsula of Venezuela on his third voyage in 1498. Thus Vespucci promoted himself not only as the first explorer to recognize the existence of a new world, but also as the first to discover its mainland. The following passage describes his first Brazilian voyage in 1502:

> Now we come to the reasoning animals. We found all the earth inhabited by people completely nude, men as well as women, without covering their shame. They have bodies well proportioned, white in color with black hair, and little or no beard. I tried very hard to understand their life and customs because for 27 days I ate and slept with them, and that which I learned of them follows:
>
> They have no laws or faith, and live according to nature. They do not recognize the immortality of the soul, they have among them no private property, because everything is common; they have no boundaries of kingdoms and provinces, and no king! They obey nobody, each is lord unto himself; no justice, no gratitude, which to them is unnecessary because it is not part of their code. They live in common in houses made like very large cabins; and for people who have no iron or other metal, it is possible to say that their cabins are truly wonderful, for I have seen houses which are 200 *passi* long and 30 wide and artfully made by craftsmen, and in one of these houses were 500 or perhaps 600 souls. They slept in nets [hammocks] woven of cotton, exposed to the air without any other covering; they eat seated on the ground; their food is roots of herbs and many good fruits, an infinity of fish and great quantities of shellfish; crabs, oysters, lobsters, crayfish, and many other things which the sea produces. The meat which they eat commonly is human flesh, as shall be told. When they can have other flesh of animals and birds they eat that too but they do not hunt for it much because they have no dogs and their land is very full of woods which are filled with fierce wild beasts, so they do not ordinarily enter the woods unless with a crowd of people.[1]

When an obscure German geographer, Martin Waldseemüller, came across Vespucci's work while preparing an edition of Ptolemy, he decided that this new land ought to bear the name of its finder: "[Europe, Africa, and Asia] have been more widely explored, and another, fourth part has been discovered by Americus Vesputius . . . , and I do not see why anyone should rightly forbid naming it Amerigo, land of Americus as it were, after its discoverer Americus, a man of acute genius, or America, inasmuch as both Europe and Asia have received their names from women." The geographer then took the liberty of writing the word *America* across the new territory on his 1507 world map. Despite numerous objections (the Spanish and Portuguese continued to refer to the New World as "the Indies" until the eighteenth century), and despite Waldseemüller's own change of mind, the name stuck. Ralph Waldo Emerson thought it "strange" that Vespucci had "managed in this lying world to supplant Columbus and baptize half the earth with his own dishonest name."

Vespucci's writings and Waldseemüller's geography convinced Europeans that something was drastically amiss with Columbus's version of the world. Here was no string of Asian islands but a newly discovered continent, a fourth part of the world. Ptolemy's influential map required serious revision; the world was not what everyone supposed. As Vespucci cautiously admitted: "Let it be said in a whisper, experience is certainly worth more than theory."

---

[1] Amerigo Vespucci (1502), on his first Brazilian voyage (translated by S. E. Morison).

Theodore Galle (after Jan van der Street)
The Arrival of Vespucci in the New World
engraving, 1600.
(Reproduced from the Collections of the Library of Congress)

A Literature of Experience

As a central issue of Renaissance thought, the conflict between experience and theory, between modern observation and ancient authority, understandably left its mark on the literature of exploration. The discovery of the New World was itself a product of the Renaissance: Leonardo da Vinci drew his designs for a flying machine in the same year Columbus claimed San Salvador for Spain. *Experience* became a key word of intellectual discourse: "To me it seems," da Vinci wrote, "that all sciences are vain and full of errors that are not born of Experience, mother of all certainty, and that are not tested by Experience." The tension between experience and authority informed all of the arts and sciences of the time. In geography the conflict was dramatized by two sorts of maps—the theoretical maps of the entire world (*mappi mundi*) elaborately devised by learned academicians and the practical cruising charts (*portolanos*) made from the direct experience of working navigators. The early mariners and explorers constantly found themselves confronted by a discrepancy between what the big maps led them to expect and what was actually there.

By means of the *portolanos*, generations of mariners gradually pieced together a precise outline of the known world, especially the heavily traveled Mediterranean. Closely related to the practical coastal chart was the written record of assorted observations and experiences navigators kept during a voyage. Known in Greek as a *periplus* ("sailing around"), such navigational records go back to the fifth century B.C. A *periplus* eventually came to signify the narrative of a voyage around a coastline.

Henry David Thoreau, a voluminous reader, alludes in *Walden* to one of the most famous of these, *The Periplus of Hanno*. The classical *periplus* clearly served as an important model of composition for the early explorers of the New World and subsequently left its mark on the great nineteenth-century voyage literature of Cooper, Poe, Thoreau, Twain, and Melville. Ezra Pound in the *Cantos* also saw the form as a literary plunge into direct experience: "periplum, not as land looks on a map / but as sea bord seen by men sailing."

One of the finest and most polished examples of coastal voyage writing is Giovanni da Verrazano's "Letter to the King," the record of his 1524 journey up the North American seaboard from North Carolina to Maine. Verrazano's, too, is primarily a voyage of confounded expectations. Like Columbus, he starts out theoretically: "My intention on this voyage was to reach Cathay and the extreme eastern coast of Asia." His expectations, however, forced him to recognize a new version of the globe:

> My intention on this voyage was to reach Cathay and the extreme eastern coast of Asia, but I did not expect to find such an obstacle of new land as I have found; and if for some reason I did expect to find it, I estimated there would be some strait to get through to the Eastern Ocean. This was the opinion of all the ancients, who certainly believed that our Western Ocean was joined to the Eastern Ocean of India without any land in between. Aristotle supports this theory by arguments of various analogies, but this opinion is quite contrary to that of the moderns, and has been proven false by experience. Nevertheless, land has been found by modern man which was unknown to the ancients, another world with respect to the one they knew, which appears to be larger than our Europe, than Africa, and almost larger than Asia, if we estimate its size correctly. . . . and if the territorial area of this [new] land corresponds in size to its maritime shore, there is no doubt that it is larger than Asia. In this way we find that the extension of the land is much greater than the ancients believed, and contrary to the Mathematicians who considered that there was less land than water,[2] we have proven it by experience to be the reverse.[3]

Verrazano's narrative prefigures one of the dominant themes of American literature and philosophy—the experiential challenge to an authoritative theoretical framework, or as the cultural philosopher John J. McDermott states it, "the dominance of the 'experience' over any conceptual anticipation of 'how things should be.' "

Another feature of Verrazano's narrative that would occupy a preeminent place in subsequent American literature is his emphasis on the idyllic landscape of the New World. Borrowing from the title of a popular Renaissance romance and ultimately from Virgil's *Eclogues*, Verrazano baptized Virginia's Accomack peninsula "Arcadia." For Renaissance writers Arcadia represented a lovely natural landscape comfortably inhabited by shepherds who live—mainly for love and song—in hardy simplicity. This highly conventionalized ideal, known as the pastoral, evolved into a cultural attitude that not only shaped the American writer's response to the natural world but also led to a persistent devaluation of civilized society in favor of a return to simpler ways of

[2] And contrary to the biblical reference in the first book of the prophet Esdras, which claims that the ratio of earth to water is six to one.

[3] From *Letter to the King* (1524). *The Voyages of Giovanni Verrazano, 1524–1528*, ed. L. Wroth; trans. S. Tarrow, 1970.

life. As the critic Leo Marx noted in *The Machine in the Garden,* his study of the pastoral ideal in America, the central theme of a remarkably large number of books is the "withdrawal from society into an idealized landscape."

America and the Pastoral Ideal

Literary pastoral had long symbolized the European dream of a Golden Age, and with the discovery of the New World that dream seemed for a brief moment in history to have come true. It seemed, at last, that an actual physical world did indeed exist uncorrupted by man and resembling the original state of nature. Columbus on his third voyage thought that he had literally come near to the Terrestrial Paradise. Later explorers, possessing a less biblical sense of geography, would still see the primeval American landscape as offering the possibility for another earthly paradise. This view dominated most descriptions of the new land. Thus the great French essayist Montaigne would write of the inhabitants of America, "I think that what we have seen of these people with our own eyes surpasses not only the pictures with which poets have illustrated the golden age, and all their attempts to draw mankind in the state of happiness, but the ideas and the very aspirations of philosophers as well." In his "Ode to the Virginia Voyage," the English poet Michael Drayton succinctly expressed the general enthusiasm for the new Golden Age, calling Virginia "Earth's only paradise." One hundred years later the American writer Robert Beverley would say of the same region that it "did still seem to retain the virgin Purity and Plenty of the First Creation, and the People their Primitive Innocence."

For nearly all the early explorers, the vision of the Golden Age was also a vision of actual gold. All other motives for exploration—the investigation of new regions, the religious conversion of native populations, the discovery of previously unknown natural phenomena—were secondary compared to the acquisition of gold and silver. "We came here to serve God," said the conquistador Bernal Diaz, "and also to get rich." Columbus never ceased quizzing native chieftains about gold, and the repeated failure of all the first explorers to find precious metals severely dampened the initial European enthusiasm for the new land. After all, what good was this New World if it were poorer than the old one? What was the point in financing expedition after expedition if all that could be brought back were colorful birds, strange plants, and poor naked people? If no wealth could be found, then this entire New World amounted to no more than the "obstacle" Verrazano found it to be—a vast and useless mass of land inconveniently blocking the way to the fabulous Indies. The search for gold, not geographical curiosity, stimulated the earliest penetrations into the North American wilderness.

During the period of inland exploration, the pastoral ideal had little to do with what we now think of as the wilderness. The conventional landscape of pastoral poetry and romance took the form of a gentle, bountiful, and orderly garden, the type of landscape the early explorers would have recognized as a standard feature of Renaissance painting. An appreciation of such landscapes was more the result of an acquired taste for certain picturesque configurations of natural scenery than of a direct encounter with vast and impenetrable forests. Verrazano possessed a trained eye for the details of a landscape and could make careful discriminations among various "styles" of scenery. As he crossed north, he grew less enthusiastic about the land and its people. He found the northern forests too "dense" and—perhaps assuming some connection between environment and human nature—the inhabitants "barbarous."

For the first explorers and settlers, *wilderness* had highly pejorative connotations. The word conjured up medieval images of bestiality, malevolence, and the horrors of hell. From the deck of the *Mayflower* in 1620, William Bradford looked out on a "hideous and desolate wilderness, full of wild beasts and wild men." He saw a landscape far removed from any comfortable pastoral ideal:

> For summer being done, all things stand upon them with a weatherbeaten face; and the whole country, full of woods and thickets, represented a wild and savage hue. If they looked behind them, there was the mighty ocean which they had passed, and was now as a main bar and gulf to separate them from all the civil parts of the world.

Nonetheless, by the end of the eighteenth century, the wilderness came to possess a decidedly positive value. By the era of Cooper and Thoreau, it would replace the cultivated garden as the ideal American landscape.

Survival and Rebirth

Survival in the wilderness—the central action of so many exploration narratives—would become a recurring theme of both popular and classic American literature. Out of the confrontation with the wilderness emerged a new type of hero: tough, self-reliant, experienced, in contact with life at its most elemental levels. We can trace the origins of this new heroic personality in such early exploration texts as *The Narrative of Alvar Núñez Cabeza de Vaca* (1542), one of the great documents in the literature of human endurance. Cabeza de Vaca's story is the harrowing account of how four shipwrecked men managed to keep themselves alive while wandering for eight years through the hard country of the Texas Gulf. Like many American survival and captivity tales, Cabeza de Vaca's narrative culminates in a spiritual rebirth—the survivors in this case literally saving themselves by becoming faith healers among the various Indian communities they encountered.

The connection between physical survival and spiritual rebirth is best expressed by the explorer who more than any other typified the new American hero—Captain John Smith. "It is a happy thing to be born to strength, wealth and honor," Smith wrote, "but that which is got by prowess and magnanimity is the truest luster; and those can the best distinguish content, that have escaped most honorable dangers; as if, out of every extremity, he found himself now born to a new life."

In Smith's vigorous writing, the idea of experience takes on new significance. Experience is important not only as a method of testing a theory but also a supreme value in and for itself. Experiences become cumulative and hierarchical. The hero has many experiences—the more extreme the better.

Though Smith's numerous accounts of the New World contain a few Edenic overtones ("And then the Country of Massachusetts, which is the Paradise of all those parts"), his Arcadia is mainly a utilitarian utopia. His descriptions seem pastoral insofar as they are textured with an imagery of natural abundance. Despite the abundance of resources, the new land required, Smith continually emphasized, discipline and hard work to forge out of the raw resources an independent subsistence. The bitter experiences Smith eventually suffered in Virginia left him skeptical of the "golden promises" that made colonists "slaves in hopes of recompenses." Instead of the lure of gold, Smith held out to future settlers the lure of fish. Men, women, and children, he promised more extravagantly than usual, "with a small hook and line, by angling may take divers sorts of excellent fish at their pleasures; and is it not pretty sport to pull up two pense, six pense, and twelve pense, as fast as you can haul and vere [pay out] a line." Throughout his writing, Smith scornfully dismissed the possibility of gold and silver mines and underscored—in terms Benjamin Franklin a century later could hardly disagree with—the inevitable convertibility of labor into wealth.

Smith wrote his books and pamphlets primarily to attract potential colonists to America. Like such earlier promotional efforts as Thomas Hariot's *A briefe and true report of the new found land of Virginia* (1588), Smith's writing stressed the "incredible abundance" of the New World. Smith, however, went a step further by promoting the land as a means to individual well-being, liberty, and improved social status. In his books we find the earliest formulations of what would become a prevailing image of America: an open society where someone without benefit of family connections, inheritance, or formal education can by virtue of hard work alone enjoy a happy, independent, and prosperous life. The role Smith played in the "invention" of America may be far more important than the part he played in its discovery.

Toward a Pluralistic Culture

With Captain John Smith, the English language and the American experience became inseparably united. For that reason Smith has often been called the first writer in American literature. Yet it is important to remember that initially the English participated only minimally in the colonization of the New World. While Smith struggled with a disorganized band of lazy colonists in Jamestown to erect a dingy fort, Spain and France had already created a New World literature. French influence extended throughout Canada, the Northeast, and the Midwest. By the mid-eighteenth century, Spain controlled everything west of the Mississippi and south of the Oregon country as well as Florida and territories south of Tennessee. The Dutch, too, made a considerable effort at colonizing the New World, controlling Manhattan Island along with the rich and beautiful Hudson Valley.

A cultural pluralism characterized the New World from the start. Long before Smith reached Virginia, an African slave named Estevan ("Stephen") had journeyed far into the wilderness of New Mexico. Estevan, a Moor from Morocco, was one of the four shipwrecked men whose eight years of wandering through the Texas Gulf country was reported by Cabeza de Vaca (see p. 48). As the men slowly found their way to Mexico City, they heard stories about prosperous towns to the North. In 1539, the viceroy of Mexico, hoping to duplicate Pizarro's recent conquest of Peru, appointed Estevan as head of a scouting party to prepare the way for the major expedition in search of the mythic "Seven Cities of Cibola" that Francisco de Coronado would undertake the following year. Estevan knew the region and had presumably acquired skills in translation and diplomacy during his years of wandering and intermittent captivity. When he reached the first of the reputed seven cities, Hawikuh (which turned out to be a poor village near the present New Mexico-Arizona border), Estevan somehow offended the Zuni rulers and he was sentenced to death (see p. 34). His execution did not deter the 1540 Coronado expedition, however, which explored the Colorado River region and the Great Plains. Although Coronado failed to find the riches of Peru, his journey remains the most extensive early foray into the interior of what would become the United States.

The Spanish presence in the American South and Southwest considerably precedes the English and French exploration and colonization of the North and Northeast. By the time Captain John Smith abandoned Jamestown, the Spanish had established a number of settled communities in the Southwest. "We Americans," wrote Walt Whitman in an 1883 letter commemorating the three hundred and thirty-third anniversary of Santa Fe, New Mexico,

> have yet to really learn our own antecedents, and sort them, to unify them. They will be found ampler as has been supposed, and in widely different sources. Thus far, impress'd by New England writers and schoolmasters, we tacitly abandon ourselves to the notion that our United States have been fashioned from the British Islands only—which is a very great mistake.

Exploration writing did not end with Captain John Smith but evolved into an American literary tradition as men and women like William Bradford, Mary Rowlandson, William Byrd, Daniel Boone, Thomas Jefferson, and William Bartram conducted their various errands into the wilderness. America, as Thoreau reminds us in *The Maine Woods,* always seems in the process of being discovered. The sheer wonder of discovery, in fact, may be the Age of Exploration's most durable legacy to American literature. Steeped in the writings of the great discoverers and explorers, major American authors, from Washington Irving and James Fenimore Cooper to Willa Cather, Hart Crane, and William Carlos Williams, repeatedly beheld a world that was excitingly and inexhaustibly new. The inescapable fact of that newness may be what is most essentially American about American literature.

Further Reading:

J. Fiske, *Discovery of America,* 2 vols., 1893.
F. J. Turner, *The Frontier in American History,* 1920.
H. N. Smith, *The Virgin Land,* 1950.
R. W. B. Lewis, *The American Adam,* 1955.
E. O'Gorman, *The Invention of America,* 1961.
C. L. Sanford, *The Quest for Paradise: Europe and the American Moral Imagination,* 1961.
L. Marx, *The Machine in the Garden: Technology and the Pastoral Ideal in America,* 1964.
H. M. Jones, *O Strange New World,* 1964.
J. J. McDermott, *The American Angle of Vision,* 1966.
R. Nash, *Wilderness and the American Mind,* 1967, 1973.
S. Greenblatt, *Marvelous Possessions,* 1991.
S. Greenblatt, ed., *New World Encounters,* 1992.
J. S. Romm, *The Edges of the Earth in Ancient Thought,* 1992.

S. E. Morison, *The European Discovery of America: The Northern Voyages,* 1971, and *The Southern Voyages,* 1974.
E. Page, *American Genesis,* 1973.
R. Slotkin, *Regeneration Through Violence: The Mythology of the American Frontier, 1600–1860,* 1973.
J. Seelye, *Prophetic Waters: The River in Early American Life and Literature,* 1977.
W. Franklin, *Discoverers, Explorers, Settlers: The Diligent Writers of Early America,* 1979.
F. Turner, *Beyond Geography: The Western Spirit Against the Wilderness,* 1980.
T. Todorov, *The Conquest of America,* 1984.
H. Thomas, *Conquest,* 1993.
S. Cavell, *This New Yet Unapproachable America,* 1989.

W. C. Spengemann, *A Mirror for Americanists,* 1989.
P. Lauter, *Canons and Contexts,* 1991.
J. Rogozinski, *A Brief History of the Caribbean,* 1994.

H. Diaz Polanco, *Indigenous Peoples in Latin America,* 1997.

Native American Literature:

For comprehensive studies of the history and literature of Native Americans, see. H. E. Driver, *Indians of North America,* 1961.
W. T. Hagan, *American Indians,* 1961.
R. H. Pearch, *The Savages of America: A Study of the Indian and the Idea of Civilization,* 2d ed., 1965.
D. McNickle, *Native American Tribalism,* 1973.
W. E. Washburn, *The Indian in America,* 1975.
Handbook of North American Indians, ed. W. C. Sturtevant, 20 vols. Planned, 1978–.
D. Hymes, *In Vain I Tried to Tell You: Essays in Native American Ethnopoetics,* 1981.
K. Kroeber, *American Indian Literature: Texts and Interpretations,* 1981.
A. Rosenstiel, *Red and White: Indian Views of the White Man, 1492–1982,* 1983.

Studies in American Indian Literature, ed. Paula Gunn Allen, 1983.
For Native American material in "The Literature of the New World," see E. O'Gorman, *The Invention of America,* 1961.
R. Drinnon, *Facing West,* 1980.
D. Tedlock, *The Spoken Word and the Work of Interpretation,* 1983.
T. Todorov, *The Conquest of America,* 1984.
D. Buhane, *The Navajo Creation Story,* 1985.
B. Swann and A. Krupat, *Essays on Native American Literature,* 1987.
M. Leon Portilla, *The Broken Spears,* 1992.

Native American Narratives

All Native American groups possess a body of narratives that can be called myths because of the central role they play in articulating religious experience and organizing ethical, moral, and social behavior. The myths also relate to Native American rituals and ceremonies. Just as the Christian mass or communion service reenacts a critical section of the Gospel (the Last Supper) and the Jewish Passover seder recalls central acts in the book of Exodus, Native American rituals and ceremonies frequently refer to and reenact important sections of myths.

Myths also had—and continue to have—an educational function, much as Bible stories are the basis of moral instruction in Christian Sunday schools. (In Native American societies, children's instruction took place primarily in the home, usually at night, and often during the winter season.)

In all their roles, Native American myths might best be understood as resembling dramatic performances. Virtually every component of the narrative includes direct speech, sometimes without apparent reason. In actual performance, the narrator would enact the scene, taking on different voices and gestures for different characters. Such a well-formed oral narrative may seem slow or awkward when written down in the form usually reserved for fiction, but in performance it would be absorbing. Moreover, like theater, the performance of oral literature can be expected to vary with the narrator, audience, setting, and time period.

A Bering Strait Eskimo Creation Account

Printed here are the beginning episodes of a Bering Strait Eskimo creation myth collected in Alaska between 1877 and 1881 by Edward William Nelson. The elderly man who told the tale remembered having learned the text from an old man who came from the Bering Strait. Nelson's source also remembered that when the man from Bering Strait "finished the tales on the third evening, he would pour a cup of water on the floor and say: 'Drink well, spirits of those of whom I have told.' "

The Bering Sea Eskimos occupy the lowland regions of western Alaska, between the Bering Straits and the Aleutian Islands. Unlike the Native Americans of the eastern Arctic and Greenland, Bering Strait Eskimos live in large, permanent villages with sizable log and sod houses during the winter and in plank houses during the summer. They eat a diet of stored fish, game, and berries, much like their Indian neighbors to the south on the Northwest coast. During the winter months they hold large festivals and dramatized ceremonies with masks and elaborate theatrical effects, the primary purpose of which is "to propitiate the spirits controlling the universe and bring success in hunting."

In their elegantly illustrated description of Bering Sea Eskimo life, William W. Fitzhugh and Susan A. Kaplan offer the following explanation of the cultural and religious importance of the Raven: "Spiritual transformation, symbolized by Man's first encounter with his maker, Raven, was at the heart of Bering Sea Eskimo life and culture. When an animal died its *inua* inhabited the form of an unborn animal of the same or similar species. Therefore, man needed to deal respectfully with animals and objects so as not to displease their *inuas*."

Further Reading:

W. W. Fitzhugh and S. A. Kaplan, *Inua: Spirit World of the Bering Sea Eskimos*, 1982.

W. C. Sturtevant, gen. ed., *Handbook of North American Indians* and D. Damas, ed., vol. 5, *Arctic*, 1984.

Text:

18th Annual Report, Part 1, Bureau of American Ethnology, 1896–1897.

from The Time When There Were No People on the Earth Plain

It was in the time when there were no people on the earth plain. During four days the first man lay coiled up in the pod of a beach-pea. On the fifth day he stretched out his feet and burst the pod, falling to the ground, where he stood up, a full-grown man. He looked about him, and then moved his hands and arms, his neck and legs, and examined himself curiously. Looking back, he saw the pod from which he had fallen, still hanging to the vine, with a hole in the lower end, out of which he had dropped. Then he looked about him again and saw that he was getting farther away from his starting place, and that the ground moved up and down under his feet and seemed very soft. After a while he had an unpleasant feeling in his stomach, and he stooped down to take some water into his mouth from a small pool at his feet. The water ran down into his stomach and he felt better. When he looked up again he saw approaching, with a waving motion, a dark object which came on until just in front of him, when it stopped, and, standing on the ground, looked at him. This was a raven, and, as soon as it stopped, it raised one of its wings, pushed up its beak, like a mask, to the top of its head, and changed at once into a man. Before he raised his mask Raven had stared at the man, and after it was raised he stared more than ever, moving about from side to side to obtain a better view. At last he said: "What are you? Whence did you come? I have never seen anything like you." Then Raven looked at Man, and was still more surprised to find that this strange new being was so much like himself in shape.

Then he told Man to walk away a few steps, and in astonishment exclaimed again: "When did you come? I have never seen anything like you before." To this Man replied: "I came from the pea-pod." And he pointed to the plant from which he came. "Ah!" exclaimed Raven, "I made that vine, but did not know that anything like you would ever come from it. Come with me to the high ground over there; this ground I made later, and it is still soft and thin, but it is thicker and harder there."

In a short time they came to the higher land, which was firm under their feet. Then Raven asked Man if he had eaten anything. The latter answered that he had taken some soft stuff into him at one of the pools. "Ah!" said Raven, "you drank some water. Now wait for me here."

Then he drew down the mask over his face, changing again into a bird, and flew far up into the sky where he disappeared. Man waited where he had been left until the fourth day, when Raven returned, bringing four berries in his claws. Pushing up his mask, Raven became a man again and held out two salmonberries and two hearthberries, saying, "Here is what I have made for you to eat. I also wish them to be plentiful over the earth. Now eat them." Man took the berries and placed them in his mouth one after the other and they satisfied his hunger, which had made him feel uncomfortable. Raven then led Man to a small creek near by and left him while he went to the water's edge and molded a couple of pieces of clay into the form of a pair of mountain sheep, which he held in his hand, and when they became dry he called Man to show him what he had done. Man thought they were very pretty, and Raven told him to close his eyes. As soon as Man's eyes were closed Raven drew down his mask and waved his wings four times over the images, when they became endowed with life and bounded away as full-grown mountain sheep. Raven then raised his mask and told Man to look. When Man saw the sheep moving away, full of life, he cried out with pleasure. Seeing how pleased Man was, Raven said, "If these animals are numerous, perhaps people will wish very much to get them." And Man said he thought they would. "Well," said Raven, "it will be better for them to have their home among the high cliffs, so that every one can not kill them, and there only shall they be found."

Then Raven made two animals of clay which he endowed with life as before, but as they were dry only in spots when they were given life, they remained brown and white, and so originated the tame reindeer with mottled coat. Man thought these were very handsome, and Raven told him that they would be very scarce. In the same way a pair of wild reindeer were made and permitted to get dry and white only on their bellies, then they were given life; in consequence, to this day the belly of the wild reindeer is the only white part about it. Raven told Man that these animals would be very common, and people would kill many of them.

"You will be very lonely by yourself," said Raven. "I will make you a companion." He then went to a spot some distance from where he had made the animals, and looking now and then at Man, made an image very much like him. Then he fastened a lot of fine water grass on the back of the head for hair, and after the image had dried in his hands, he waved his wings over it as before and a beautiful young woman arose and stood beside Man. "There," cried Raven, "is a companion for you," and he led them back to a small knoll near by.

In those days there were no mountains far or near, and the sun never ceased shining brightly; no rain ever fell and no winds blew. When they came to the knoll, Raven showed the pair how to make a bed in the dry moss, and they slept there very warmly; Raven drew down his mask and slept near by in the form of a bird. Waking before the others, Raven went back to the creek and made a pair each of sticklebacks, graylings, and blackfish. When these were swimming about in the water, he called Man to see them. When the latter looked at them and saw the sticklebacks swim up the stream with a wriggling motion he was so surprised that he raised his hand suddenly and the fish darted away. Raven then showed him the graylings and told him that they would be found in clear mountain streams, while the sticklebacks would live along the seacoast and that both would be good for food. Next the shrew-mouse was made, Raven saying that it would not be good for food but would enliven the ground and prevent it from seeming barren and cheerless.

In this way, Raven continued for several days making birds, fishes, and animals showing them to Man, and explaining their uses.

1899

Seneca Account

"The Story-Telling Stone" is one of the finest illustrations of the power of stories to captivate both individuals and communities. As this myth dramatically portrays, the enchantment of stories can easily sidetrack us from day-to-day obligations and can illuminate our lives and heritage.

The Seneca, a nation of North American Indians who called themselves "The People of the Stone," inhabited what is now western New York State between Seneca Lake and the Genesee River. They belonged to the Iroquois Confederacy. The Seneca eventually became a powerful force in the Five Nations, one of the most important political organizations in American Indian history. During the Revolutionary War, under the famous leadership of Joseph Brant, they fought on the side of the British. The age of this myth is unknown; it was first transcribed in the nineteenth century.

The Story-Telling Stone

In that eastern lake country where the long spine of the Appalachians yawns seaward there was a domain of dense forests interspersed with flat meadowlands of good soil in which the people could supplement the harvest of the hunt with yields of maize and melon. It was a strong land, deeply etched by seasonal changes, and it demanded strong people to live in it. Such were the Five Nations of the Iroquois. One of the nations, the Seneca, told a story of a time when their land had spoken to them of itself, of its past, of a world that had existed long before the people had come to live here. This is what they said.

It was very long ago. In a Seneca village there lived a boy whose parents had both died when he was but a few weeks old. A woman who had been a relation of the parents took the boy to raise as her own and gave him the name Poyeshaon, which means "Orphan."

The little boy grew quickly and well. He was active and keen-minded, and it was not long before his foster mother saw that he could begin helping her with the business of living. One day she called him to her and gave him a bow and arrows, saying as she did so, "It is time for you to learn to hunt. Tomorrow morning take these into the woods and kill all the birds you can."

That evening the woman shelled corn and parched the kernels in hot ashes. She rolled these up in a piece of buckskin and the next morning gave them to Poyeshaon on his way out. Her words reminded him that a good hunter always has a happy home.

The boy traveled into the woods. Before noon he had shot a good number of birds, and so he sat down to rest and eat his parched corn. Then in the afternoon he worked back toward the village while the woods shadows deepened and stretched. When he arrived, his foster mother praised him warmly.

The next day the woman sent the boy out again. Again he rested at noon, eating his corn in a small clearing with his string of birds beside him. And again he returned at evening with a goodly number. His foster mother thanked him and told him that now he had begun to help with the business of living. He felt happy at this and determined to become so good a hunter that soon he would be allowed to go after big game.

Each day he went out, farther and farther into the great forest. And each evening he returned with a longer string of birds until finally he was forced to pack them in bundles on his back. His happy foster mother now had enough to give away to her relations.

On the tenth day Poyeshaon hunted a part of the woods he had never seen. As he took aim at a bird, the sinew that bound the feathers of his arrow loosened and the boy lowered his bow to make repairs. There was a clearing just ahead, and in its midst a high, smooth stone, round and with a flat top. The boy scrambled up to this natural seat, lay his string of birds beside him, and began to retie the sinew. Just as he was rearranging the feathers along the shafts, he heard a voice right next to him. "Shall I tell you stories?" it asked. Poyeshaon looked up expecting to see a man standing there in the clearing, but there was no one. He clambered around the rock and looked behind it, but he seemed alone. So he sat down again and resumed his work. Again the voice spoke, right under him, it seemed: "Shall I tell you stories?" The boy looked up quickly but could see no one. But this time he determined to watch carefully to see who was fooling him, and so when the voice spoke again, asking its question, he found that it came from the stone. It was the stone that had been speaking to him.

"What is that?" he asked. "What does it mean to tell 'stories'?"

"It is telling what happened long ago," the stone replied. "If you'll give me your birds, I'll tell you stories."

"You may have them all," Poyeshaon said quickly, and then he put his head down in a listening attitude and waited. Now the stone began, telling one story of the long ago and then another one as soon as that was finished. The boy sat atop the stone in the woods clearing until nightfall, when the stone said, "We'll rest now. Come again tomorrow, and if any should ask where all your birds are, tell them that you have killed so many that now you have to go a long way to find even a few." As he went homeward through the gloom, the boy was able to shoot a few birds and give these to his foster mother along with the excuse.

The next morning he took his pouch of corn, his bow and arrows, and went into the woods. But his mind was on the stories, not the birds, and he shot only those that lighted on his way to the stone in the clearing. When he got there, he put the birds on the stone and called out, "I've come! Here are the birds. Now begin again." And the stone did this, telling story after story until it stopped at dusk. On the way home the boy looked for birds, but it was late and he could find only a few.

That night his foster mother told her neighbors that there was something strange about Poyeshaon. When he had first hunted he had been very successful, but now, though he was in the woods from morning to night, he brought back but five or six birds. Perhaps he threw the others away, she thought, or else gave them to an animal. Or maybe he just idled his time away and did not hunt. She hired an older boy to follow Poyeshaon to find out what he was up to.

So the next morning the hired boy took his bow and arrows as if to hunt and followed Poyeshaon into the woods, keeping out of sight and observing that Poyeshaon killed a good many birds. Then about the middle of the morning, Poyeshaon suddenly stopped hunting and ran toward the east as fast as he could. The hired boy followed until he came to a clearing and saw Poyeshaon climb atop a large round stone and sit down. As he crept nearer, the hired boy heard talking but could see no one to whom Poyeshaon might be speaking. So he went boldly up to him and asked, "What are you doing here?"

"Hearing stories."

"What are 'stories'?" the other asked.

"They are tellings of things that happened long ago. Put your birds here on the stone and say, 'I've come to hear stories.' " The hired boy did so, and the stone began again and continued until sundown, the two boys sitting silent in the clearing with their heads down, listening hard.

When they got back to the village with but a few birds, the hired boy explained to the foster mother that he had followed Poyeshaon for a while and then had spoken to him. "After that we hunted together," he said, "but we couldn't find many birds."

The next morning the older boy told his mother that he was going hunting with Poyeshaon. "It's good fun to hunt with him," he said, and off they went. By the middle of the morning each had a good string of birds, and then they hurried with these to the clearing.

"We have come!" they called to the stone. "Here are our birds. Now tell us stories." And the stone commenced, one after another, the boys listening with their heads down, until at dusk the stone said, "We'll rest until tomorrow." The boys returned to the village, but as before, they had little to show for their day-long hunt.

Several days went by in this way until at last the foster mother said to herself, "These boys kill more birds than they bring home." And she hired two men to follow the boys when they went into the woods the morning after. The men watched the boys hunting eastward until each had a good string of birds. Then they stopped hunting and hurried to a clearing where the men saw them climb a large stone and sit there listening to a man's voice.

"Let's go there and find out who is talking to them," one of the watchers said, and they stepped quickly into the clearing.

"What are you doing here, boys?" they asked. The boys were startled, but Poyeshaon spoke up quickly, saying that they must tell no one. The men agreed, and then Poyeshaon directed them to climb the stone and sit with them.

Then he said to the stone. "Go on with the story. We are all listening." So there were four of them now, sitting with their heads down as the stone told a story and then another and another. When it was almost night the stone finished.

"Tomorrow," it said, "all the people in the village must come and listen to my stories. Tell the chief to send everyone, and let each bring something for me to eat. And you must clear away the brush so that the people may sit on the ground near me."

That night Poyeshaon related the stone's instructions to the chief, who sent a runner to give the message to each family in the village. Early on the morrow all the people followed Poyeshaon into the woods, carrying with them bread and meat as gifts for the stone.

When the gifts had been deposited and the people quietly seated in the clearing, the stone spoke to them: "Now I will tell you stories of long ago. There was a world before this one, and the stories I am going to tell happened in that world. Some of you will remember every word I say; some will remember part of my words; and some will forget them all. I think this will be the way, but each must do the best he can. Hereafter, you must tell these stories to one another. Now listen!" The people bent their heads, and the stone went on until nightfall. Then it told the people to come again in the morning bearing gifts.

The next morning as the people gathered again in the clearing and deposited their gifts, they found that those they had left the day before were gone. When all was quiet the stone began to speak and continued until sundown. And this time it said, "Come again tomorrow. Tomorrow I will finish the stories of long ago."

Early in the morning the people gathered around the stone, and when it was quiet the stone began again. It went on into the afternoon, and then it said, "I have finished! You must keep these stories as long as the world lasts. Tell them to your children and your grandchildren, generation after generation. One person will remember them better than another. And when you go to a man or woman who knows these stories well, take something along to pay for them, bread or meat, or whatever you have. You must keep these things up. I have spoken!"

So it has been from that time to this. From the stone the Seneca learned all they know of the world before this one. That must be why they are called The People of the Stone.

Cultural Portfolio
The European Conquest of America

The arrival of European ships on October 12, 1492, put an end to the isolated existence of the Caribbean people and permanently altered the course of history. Within a few decades, successive waves of explorers and colonists slaughtered, raped, and exploited indigenous populations who were poorly equipped to resist the bearded, white strangers invading their bays, inlets, and high plateaus. Spears, arrows, wood, and human agility proved no match against guns, cannon, steel, and horses. Many native communities were wiped out and a way of life stripped of its local character and traditions. In the islands, the Spanish would soon rely on slave labor to send profitable supplies of gold, sugar, coffee, and tobacco (new human "necessities") to European markets. On the mainland, in 1521, only seventeen years after Columbus had returned from his final voyage, Cortés (with the help of native allies) would capture Mexico City in what the historian J. M. Roberts calls "one of the most dramatic tales of the whole history of imperialism." The center of Aztec civilization, Mexico City (or Tenochtitlán, as the Aztecs called it), was at the time of its conquest one of the world's largest and most culturally complex cities.

The native populations never recovered from the assault on their world, which in 1507 (the same year Leonardo da Vinci painted the Mona Lisa) a German mapmaker named "America" in honor of one of the earliest explorers. In some regions, the native inhabitants were massacred, in others, displaced from their land. Enslavement was common: as early as 1493, Columbus sent back to Spain five hundred slaves captured in Hispaniola (now Haiti and the Dominican Republic). Normally, the slaves were confined to labor in the islands themselves, but when the Spanish saw how rapidly the natives were dying, they began importing African slaves to fill their places. The first African slaves to be brought to the "new world" arrived in Santo Domingo (Hispaniola) in 1501. As the twentieth-century Argentinian poet Jorge Luis Borges wrote: "In 1517 Friar Bartolomé de las Casas took pity on the Indians who were languishing in the arduous hells of the Antillean gold mines and proposed to the emperor, Charles V, the importation of black people to languish in the arduous hells of the Antillean gold mines."

The most lethal weapons by far in the European conquest of America were not muskets but microbes—what the Carolina Algonquians called "invisible bullets." Many native populations were decimated by European and African diseases they had never before experienced, such as smallpox, cholera, yellow fever, malaria, typhus, tuberculosis, measles, influenza, and even the common cold. The fatal epidemics, however, cannot be viewed apart from the circumstances of colonization. The epidemics were often ignited by the crowded conditions of forced labor and relocation. All told, the combination of slavery, disease, captivity, and brutality exacted a heavy toll throughout the Americas. Friar Bartolomé de las Casas, for example, estimated that in 1492 the native population of Hispaniola stood between 3 to 4 million; in 1509, an official Spanish census showed 60,000, and by 1548, after several slave revolts, the native population of the Caribbean's once most populated island had fallen drastically to under 500. Although no one can be sure of the pre-Columbian population figures, one thing is certain: by the end of the sixteenth century, the major Caribbean groups—the peaceful Arawaks and the more militant Caribs—had been virtually annihilated.

Almost all extant accounts of this era (especially the maps) reflect a European perspective. So does the commonly used terminology—such words as *Indian, discovery,* and *new world* have left an indelible mark on subsequent historical discourse. The word *exploration* itself can frequently mask such related activities as invasion, looting, and slave raiding. Even *conquest* can be double-edged, since European monarchs believed they possessed a legal right of conquest over pagan territories. Reading the European narratives and documents of the era thus demands close attention to cultural biases and distortions of vocabulary; we often need to read against the grain, to see viewpoints and hear voices that are submerged or appear only at the periphery of the texts. Furthermore, not all reports of native populations were hostile or dehumanizing, and thus some European texts can help us reconstruct authentic pre-Columbian social and cultural perspectives better than others.

Still, there is another story. A sufficient number of native documents, picto-glyphic texts, and oral accounts tell the victims' saga of invasion, enslavement, sickness, and defeat. As the body of this earliest literature grows through archaeological and archival research, we will begin to get a fuller picture of the conquest and be able to see the catastrophic events through native eyes. In light of this heterogeneous material, readers will be less inclined—as they once were—to begin the study of American literature with merely the works of a small band of Pilgrim and Puritan colonists who settled the rocky coast of New England in the early seventeenth century.

Aside from their historical value, the wide range of native expression and the exploration narratives challenges traditional notions of American literature. What do we mean by American literature in the first place? Is it simply a branch of English literature? How do we decide who is an "American" writer and who isn't? Does a bilingual Mexican-American citizen of the United States, who lives in Texas and publishes poetry in Spanish belong to American literature? Or is American literature exclusively defined by the English language? Should we exclude from American literature all writing that appeared prior to the official formation of the United States? If so, should we then exclude colonial works and writing that grew out of regions and territories not yet admitted to statehood? These are only a few fundamental issues stimulated by a careful consideration of the multi-ethnic writings that originated in response to the era of European exploration and conquest. Many of these questions are complicated by the custom of calling "The United States of America" simply "America."

Walt Whitman in 1883 had already understood how geographically and ethnically diverse the culture and literature of the United States truly were. He was also among the first to celebrate the contributions of "our aboriginal or Indian population." "As America," he wrote, "from its many far-back sources and current supplies, develops, adapts, entwines, faithfully identifies its own—are we to see it cheerfully accepting and using all the contributions of foreign lands from the whole outside globe—and then rejecting the only ones distinctively its own—the autochthonic [native] ones?" With critical attention increasingly focused on literary inclusivity and diversity, such "far-back" materials will surely play a significant part in helping to redefine and renew our concept of "American" literature.

A Skirmish with the Skraelings

The earliest account of a violent encounter between Europeans and inhabitants of the New World appears in an Icelandic saga that narrates the Norse discovery and aborted colonization of Vinland (probably in present-day Newfoundland) in the early years of the eleventh century. Ethnologists remain uncertain about the identity of the "Skraelings"— they may be Eskimo natives similar to those the Norse encountered in their previous colonization of Greenland, or they might even be native Americans who journeyed north each summer. The word *Skraeling* can roughly be translated as *savage, wretch,* or *barbarian.* Although the Icelandic sagas are more literary and mythic than factual, there is sufficient archaeological evidence to support the narrative's historical plausibility. Subsequent colonizing attempts were thwarted by the Skraelings, whose continued resistance eventually forced the Norse to abandon their western settlements.

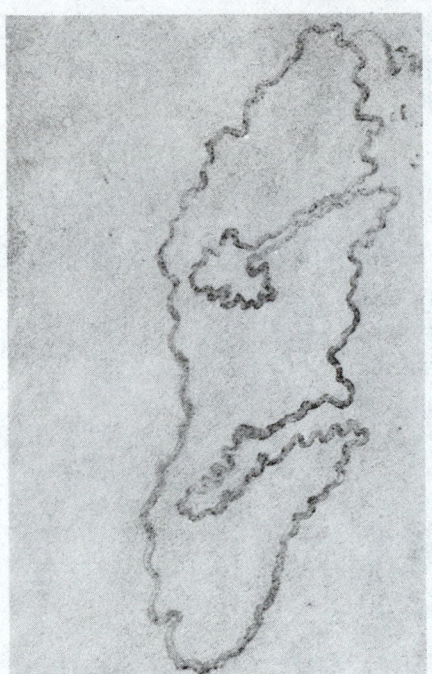

Vinland Map
An inscription above this map, made by a Swiss Monk about 1440 and rediscovered in 1957, states that Vinland was discovered and named by the Norse explorers Bjarni Herjolfsson and Leif Eriksson. The upper two inlets penetrating the island may be the strait leading to Hudson Bay; the lower one the Gulf of the St. Lawrence River. Some skeptics believe the map to be a twentieth century forgery. ink on parchment, origin disputed; possibly c. 1440. (The Beinecke Rare Book and Manuscript Library, Yale University)

from *The Saga of the Greenlanders**

Transcribed by Magnus Magnusson and Hermann Palsson

Next summer Thorvald [Leif Eriksson's brother] sailed east with his ship and then north along the coast. They ran into a fierce gale off a headland and were driven ashore; the keel was shattered and they had to stay there for a long time while they repaired the ship.

Thorvald said to his companions, 'I want to erect the old keel here on the headland, and call the place *Kjalarness.*'

They did this and then sailed away eastward along the coast. Soon they found themselves at the mouth of two fjords, and sailed up to the promontory that jutted out between them; it was heavily wooded. They moored the ship alongside and put out the gangway, and Thorvald went ashore with all his men.

'It is beautiful here,' he said. 'Here I should like to make my home.'

On their way back to the ship they noticed three humps on the sandy beach just in from the headland. When they went closer they found that these were three skin-boats [canoes made of hide instead of bark], with three men under each of them. Thorvald and his men divided forces and captured all of them except one, who escaped in his boat. They killed the other eight and returned to the headland, from which they scanned the surrounding country. They could make out a number of humps farther up the fjord and concluded that these were settlements.

* Author unknown.

John White
*View of the Village
of Secoton*, ca. 1585
John White was the first
Englishman to paint the
people and the natural life
of the American continent.
(Courtesy of the Trustees
of the British Museum)

Then they were overwhelmed by such a heavy drowsiness that they could not stay awake, and they all fell asleep—until they were awakened by a voice that shouted, 'Wake up, Thorvald, and all you men, if you want to stay alive! Get to your ship with all your company and get away as fast as you can!'

A great swarm of skin-boats was then heading towards them down the fjord.

Thorvald said, 'We shall set up breastworks on the gunwales and defend ourselves as best we can, but fight back as little as possible.'

They did this. The Skraelings shot at them for a while, and then turned and fled as fast as they could.

Thorvald asked his men if any of them were wounded; they all replied that they were unhurt.

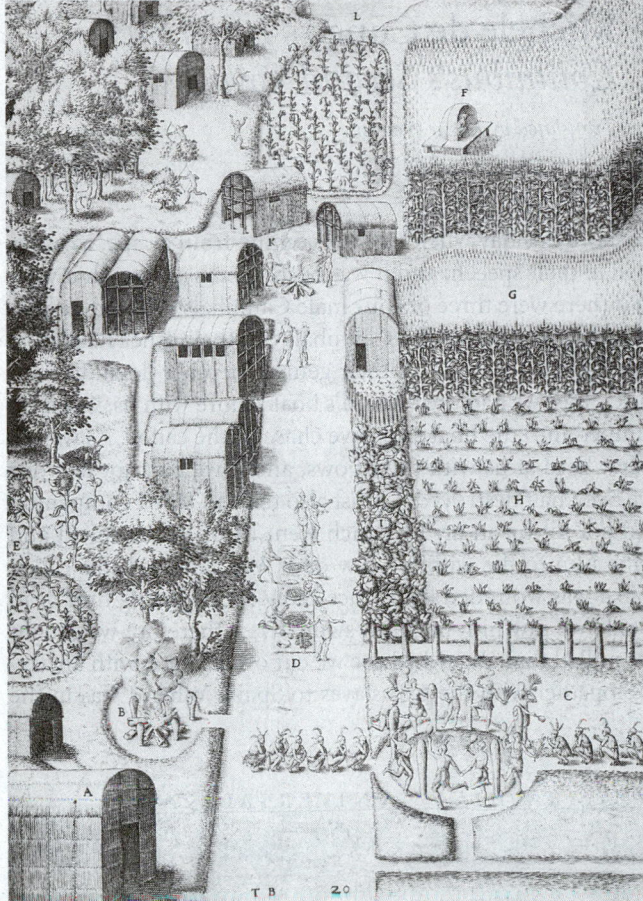

Theodor de Bry
*Engraving of
Secoton Village,* 1590
When de Bry published
Hariot's *Brief and True Report of . . . Virginia* (1590),
he included engravings of
White's watercolors, idealized reconstructions that
lured Europeans to the new
world for centuries.
(Courtesy of the Trustees of
the British Museum)

'I have a wound in the armpit,' said Thorvald. 'An arrow flew up between the gunwale and my shield, under my arm—here it is. This will lead to my death.

'I advise you now to go back as soon as you can. But first I want you to take me to the headland I thought so suitable for a home. I seem to have hit on the truth when I said that I would settle there for a while. Bury me there and put crosses at my head and feet, and let the place be called *Krossaness* for ever afterwards.'

Rape in the Virgin Islands

No official record or ship's log of Columbus's second voyage (1493) to the New World has survived. Columbus was, however, accompanied by one of his aristocratic friends, Michele de Cuneo, who left us a sexually graphic and disturbing personal report of a violent episode in the Virgin Islands. Columbus named the Virgin Islands after the Catholic legend of St. Ursula and the 11,000 virgin martyrs of Cologne. (A fuller version of de Cuneo's narrative appears on pp. 41–44.)

from Michele de Cuneo's *Letter on Columbus's Second Voyage*

Translated by Elissa Weaver

We had anchored and gone ashore one day when we saw, coming from a cape, a canoe, that is, a boat, for so it is called in their speech, and it was beating oars as though it were a well-armed brigantine. On it there were three or four male Cannibals with two female Cannibals and two captured Indian slaves—so the Cannibals call their other neighbors from those other islands; they had also just cut off their genital member down to their belly and so they were still sick. Since we had the captain's boat ashore with us, when we saw this canoe we quickly jumped into the boat and gave chase to the canoe. As we approached it, the Cannibals shot hard at us with their bows, and if we had not had our Pavian shields we would have been half destroyed. I must also tell you that a companion who had a shield in his hand got hit by an arrow which went through the shield and into his chest 3 inches causing him to die within a few days. We captured this canoe with all the men. One Cannibal was wounded by a lance-blow and thinking him dead we left him in the sea. Suddenly we saw him begin to swim away; therefore we caught him and with a long hook we pulled him aboard where we cut off his head with an axe. We sent the other Cannibals together with the two slaves to Spain. When I was in the

TYPVS COSMOGRAPHICVS VNIVERSALIS.

SIM. GRYNÆUS.   NOVUS ORBIS.
BASILEÆ   1532.

Johann Huttich (after Hans Holbein the Younger)
Novus Orbus Regionum
Basle, 1532
(Reproduced from the Collections of the Library of Congress)

boat, I took a beautiful Cannibal girl and the admiral gave her to me. Having her in my room and she being naked as is their custom, I began to want to amuse myself with her. Since I wanted to have my way with her and she was not willing, she worked me over so badly with her nails that I wished I had never begun. To get to the end of the story, seeing how things were going, I got a rope and tied her up so tightly that she made unheard of cries which you wouldn't have believed. At the end, we got along so well that, let me tell you, it seemed she had studied at a school for whores. The admiral named the cape on that island the Cape of the Arrow for the man who was killed by the arrow.

The Mysterious Strangers

In August 1521, Don Hernando Cortés captured and destroyed the magnificent Aztec capital of Tenochtitlán (now Mexico City). More than 240,000 Aztecs were killed during the protracted battle. When the Spanish first arrived two years earlier, the Aztecs thought the Europeans were gods returning from beyond the sea. The best-known eyewitness account of the expedition was written by one of Cortés's junior officers, Bernal Díaz, some fifty years after the event in *The Conquest of New Spain*. But we also learn of the fall of the Aztec civilization from a number of native sources. While the Spanish fleet was still on the coast, the Aztec king, Motecuhzoma (or, as it was once spelled, Montezuma), sent messengers to bring Cortés welcoming gifts and to learn what they could about the mysterious strangers. The Aztec account, portraying the conquerors from the perspective of a people who had no knowledge of horses, armor, and guns, is reflected in Bernal Díaz's recollection of the same event.

from *Broken Spears: The Aztec Account of the Conquest of Mexico**

Translated by Angel Maria Eavibayk and Lysander Kemp

Aztec Account of the Arrival of Cortés

When the sacrifice was finished, the messengers reported to the king. They told him how they had made the journey, and what they had seen, and what food the strangers ate. Motecuhzoma was astonished and terrified by their report, and the description of the strangers' food astonished him above all else.

He was also terrified to learn how the cannon roared, how its noise resounded, how it caused one to faint and grow deaf. The messengers told him: "A thing like a ball of stone comes out of its entrails: it comes out shooting sparks and raining fire. The smoke that comes out with it has a pestilent odor, like that of rotten mud. This odor penetrates

* Author unknown.

even to the brain and causes the greatest discomfort. If the cannon is aimed against a mountain, the mountain splits and cracks open. If it is aimed against a tree, it shatters the tree into splinters. This is a most unnatural sight, as if the tree had exploded from within."

The messengers also said: "Their trappings and arms are all made of iron. They dress in iron and wear iron casques on their heads. Their swords are iron; their bows are iron; their shields are iron; their spears are iron. Their deer carry them on their backs wherever they wish to go. These deer, our lord, are as tall as the roof of a house.

"The strangers' bodies are completely covered, so that only their faces can be seen. Their skin is white, as if it were made of lime. They have yellow hair, though some of them have black. Their beards are long and yellow, and their moustaches are also yellow. Their hair is curly, with very fine strands.

"As for their food, it is like human food. It is large and white, and not heavy. It is something like straw, but with the taste of a cornstalk, of the pith of a cornstalk. It is a little sweet, as if it were flavored with honey; it tastes of honey, it is sweet-tasting food.

"Their dogs are enormous, with flat ears and long, dangling tongues. The color of their eyes is a burning yellow; their eyes flash fire and shoot off sparks. Their bellies are hollow, their flanks long and narrow. They are tireless and very powerful. They bound here and there, panting, with their tongues hanging out. And they are spotted like an ocelot."

When Motecuhzoma heard this report, he was filled with terror. It was as if his heart had fainted, as if it had shriveled. It was as if he were conquered by despair.

---

from Bernal Díaz, *The Conquest of New Spain*

Translated by J. M. Cohen

Spanish Account of the Arrival of Cortés

It appears that Tendile [one of the Aztec messengers; a governor] brought with him some of those skilled painters they have in Mexico, and that he gave them instructions to make realistic full-length portraits of Cortés and all his captains and soldiers, also to draw the ships, sails, and horses, Doña Marina and Aguilar,[1] and even the two greyhounds. The cannon and cannon-balls, and indeed the whole of our army, were faithfully portrayed, and the drawings were taken to Montezuma.

Cortés ordered our gunners to load the lombards with a big charge of powder, so that they should make a great noise when fired, and told Pedro de Alvarado that all his horsemen must be ready with little bells tied to their breastplates, to gallop in

---

[1] Cortés's translators; see "Doña Marina" on p. 30.

front of Montezuma's servants. He too mounted his horse. 'It would be a good thing,' he said, 'if we could gallop on these dunes. But they will see that even on foot we get stuck in the sand. Let us go down to the beach when the tide is low and gallop there two by two.' And he put all the horsemen under the command of Pedro de Alvarado [one of the captains], whose sorrel mare was a great runner and very quick on the rein.

The display was carried out in the presence of the two ambassadors, and in order that they should see the shot leave the guns Cortés pretended that he wished to speak to them and some other *Caciques* [chiefs] again, just before the cannon was fired. As it was very still at that moment, the balls resounded with a great din as they went over the forest. The two governors and the rest of the Indians were frightened by this strange happening, and ordered their painters to paint it, so that Montezuma might see. It appears that one of our soldiers had a helmet that was half-gilt but somewhat rusty. This Tendile noticed, and being of a more inquiring disposition than his fellow *Cacique*, he asked if he might see it, since it was like one that they possessed which had been left them by their ancestors of the race from which they sprang and placed on the head of their god Huichilobos [Huitzilopochti, god of war]. He said that his master Montezuma would like to see this helmet, and it was given to him. Cortés said, however, that as he wished to know whether the gold of their country was the same as the gold we find in our rivers, they might send it back filled with grains of gold, as a present for our great Emperor. After this Tendile took his leave of us all, and after many protestations of regard on Cortés' part, promised to return very promptly with a reply. After his departure we discovered that Tendile was not only an important man of affairs but the most active of Montezuma's servants. He went with all haste, and gave his master a complete account of events, showing him the pictures which had been painted and the present that Cortés had sent him, which is said to have astonished Montezuma, who accepted it with great satisfaction. And when he compared the helmet with that of his god Huichilobos, he was convinced that we were of that race which, according to the prophecies of his ancestors, would come to rule the land.

The Beginning of Sickness

The following transcription of what was originally an oral poem dates back to the earliest years of contact between the Mayan people and the Spanish conquistadores. The Maya are natives of Central America; the majority settled in what is now the Yucatán, Guatemala, and western Honduras. They were able to maintain many aspects of their indigenous culture despite being forced to adapt to the influence of their conquerors. Soon after the Spanish con-

quest, for example, many Maya learned to translate their language into Spanish. They then proceeded to record Mayan history and culture in what quickly became the venerated *Book of Chilam Balam of Chumayel*, from which "The Beginning of Sickness" is drawn. The poem uses the traditional repetition of oral literature to contrast life before the arrival of the Spanish with the consequences of the conquistadores' presence in the New World.

from *The Book of Chilam Balam of Chumayel**

Translated by R. Roys

Then they adhered to their reason.
There was no sin;
in the holy faith their lives were passed.
There was then no sickness;
they had then no aching bones;   5
they had then no high fever;
they had then no smallpox;
they had then no burning chest;
they had then no abdominal pains;
they had then no consumption;   10
they had then no headache.
At that time the course of humanity was orderly.
The foreigners made it otherwise when they arrived here.
They brought shameful things when they came . . .
this was the cause of our sickness also.   15
There were no more lucky days for us;
we had no sound judgment.
At the end of our loss of vision,
and of our shame,
everything shall be revealed.   20

Doña Marina

Cortés's party included one of the most important female figures of the exploration era. The Aztecs called her La Malinche, the Spanish Doña Marina. The daughter of a prominent Gulf Coast family, she could speak local dialects, the Aztec language, and Mayan. Her decision to follow Cortés and serve as a translator proved invaluable to the conquerors. She teamed up with a shipwrecked Spaniard, Jerónimo de Águilar, who had learned Mayan in captivity. Their procedure sheds some light on the linguistic complexity behind the conquest: Doña Marina would translate what the Aztecs said into Mayan and then Águilar would translate the Mayan into Spanish. The fascinating Doña Marina, who learned Spanish quickly and converted to Catholicism, plays a prominent role throughout both the Aztec and Spanish accounts. Her participation went far beyond the role of a translator. Aware of all the warring factions in Mexico, she was able to help Cortés turn internal feuds to his own advantage. She also made it known to Cortés that the Aztecs thought he might be their returned god, Quetzalcoatl. In the following passage from Bernal Díaz's *The Conquest of New Spain*, Doña Marina uncovers a plot to ambush the Spaniards in the town of Cholula as they made their way, against Montezuma's wishes, to Mexico City. According to Díaz, Doña Marina became Cortés's mistress, gave birth to a son, and later married a Spanish gentleman. Without her political and linguistic abilities, the Mexican capital may have never been captured.

* Author unknown.

from Bernal Díaz, *The Conquest of New Spain*

Translated by J. M. Cohen

That night we were on the alert and under arms, with our horses saddled and bridled. Though it was always our custom to keep a good watch, we had more sentinels and patrols than usual, for we felt certain that all the companies, Mexican and Cholulan, would attack us that night.

Now a certain old Indian woman, a *Cacique*'s [chief's] wife who knew all about the plot and the trap that had been prepared, came secretly to Doña Marina, having noticed that she was a young woman and handsome and rich, and advised her to come to her house if she wanted to escape with her life, because that night or next day we should all be killed, by command of the great Montezuma. The plan was, she said, that the Cholulans and Mexicans should join forces, and that none of us should be left alive except those who were to be taken bound to Mexico. But knowing of this, and feeling some commiseration for Doña Marina, the old woman had come to tell her she had better collect her possessions and come to her house, where she would marry her to her son, the brother of another youth who accompanied her.

When Doña Marina heard her story, she said to the old woman, with her usual quickwittedness: 'Oh, mother, I am indeed grateful to you for telling me this! I would come with you at once, but I have no one here whom I can trust to carry my clothes and golden jewels, of which I have plenty. Wait here a little, mother, I implore you, you and your son, and we will set out tonight. For now, as you see, these *Teules* [gods or demons, i.e., the Spaniards] are on the watch, and would hear us.'

The old woman believed what she had said and remained chatting with her. Doña Marina asked her how they were going to kill us all, and how, when, and where the plot had been made. And the old woman told her exactly what the *papas* [priests] had told us. Then Doña Marina asked her: 'Seeing that the business is so secret, how did you come to know about it?' She answered that her husband had told her, for he was captain of one of the clans in the city, and as captain he was now out with the warriors under his command, giving them orders to join up with the great Montezuma's companies in the ravines, where she thought they were already assembling in expectation of our departure, with the intention of killing us there. As for the plot, she had known about it for three days, since they had sent her husband a gilded drum from Mexico, and rich cloaks and golden jewels to three other captains, as an inducement to bring us bound to their lord Montezuma. When Doña Marina heard this, she concealed her feelings from the old woman and said: 'I am indeed glad that this son of yours to whom you want to marry me is an important person—we have been talking a long while, and I do not want them to notice us; so wait here, mother, and I will begin to bring my possessions, because I cannot carry everything out at once. You and your son, my brother, must look after them, and then we shall be able to go.' The old woman believed all she said, and she and her son sat down to rest.

Doña Marina burst into the room where Cortés was and told him all about her conversation with the Indian woman. Our Captain ordered the old woman to be brought before him, and questioned her about these treasons and plots; and she told him exactly the same story as he had heard from the *papas*. He then put a guard on her so that she should not escape.

A Beautiful People

Not all first encounters were hostile. As he explored the coast of North America in 1524, the Florentine navigator Giovanni da Verrazano met with numerous native American people. The following report narrates one such encounter; the land is very likely present-day Newport, Rhode Island, and the people the Wampanoag, the same group who a century later would befriend the Pilgrims and who would also be nearly wiped out by disease. One of the most literary of the early explorers, Verrazano was deeply influenced by the classics, especially Virgil's pastoral poetry.

---

from Giovanni da Verrazano, *Letter to the King*

Translated by S. Tarrow

We reached another land xv [15] leagues from the island, where we found an excellent harbor; before entering it, we saw about xx [20] boats full of people who came around the ship uttering various cries of wonderment. They did not come nearer than fifty paces, but stopped to look at the structure of our ship, our persons, and our clothes; then all together they raised a loud cry which meant that they were joyful. We reassured them somewhat by imitating their gestures, and they came near enough for us to throw them a few little bells and mirrors and many trinkets, which they took and looked at, laughing, and then they confidently came on board ship. Among them were two kings, who were as beautiful of stature and build as I can possible describe. The first was about xxxx [40] years old, the other a young man of xxiv [24], and they were dressed thus: the older man had on his naked body a stag skin, skillfully worked like damask with various embroideries; the head was bare, the hair tied back with various bands, and around the neck hung a wide chain decorated with many different-colored stones. The young man was dressed in almost the same way. These people are the most beautiful and have the most civil customs that we have found on this voyage. They are taller than we are; they are a bronze color, some tending more toward whiteness, others to a tawny color; the face is clear-cut; the hair is long and black, and they take great pains to decorate it; the eyes are black and alert, and their manner is sweet and gentle, very like the manner of the ancients. I shall not speak to Your Majesty of the other parts of the body, since they have all the proportions belonging to any well-built man. Their women are just as shapely and beautiful; very gracious, of attractive manner and pleasant appearance; their customs and behavior follow womanly custom as far as befits human nature; they go nude except for a stag skin embroidered like the men's, and some wear rich lynx skins on their arms; their bare heads are decorated with various ornaments made of braids of their own hair which hang down over their breasts on either side. Some have other hair arrangements such as the women of Egypt and Syria wear, and these women are older and have been joined in wedlock. Both men and women have various trinkets hanging from their ears as the Orientals do; and we saw

Edward Hicks
Peaceable Kingdom
oil on canvas, ca. 1834
(National Gallery of Art, Washington, D.C., Gift of
Edgar William and Bernice Chrysler Garbisch)

that they had many sheets of worked copper which they prize more than gold. They do not value gold because of its color; they think it the most worthless of all, and rate blue and red above all other colors. The things we gave them that they prized the most were little bells, blue crystals, and other trinkets to put in the ear or around the neck. They did not appreciate cloth of silk and gold, nor even of any other kind, nor did they care to have them; the same was true for metals like steel and iron, for many times when we showed them some of our arms, they did not admire them, nor ask for them, but merely examined the workmanship. They did the same with mirrors, they would look at them quickly, and then refuse them, laughing. They are very generous and give away all they have. We made great friends with them, and one day before we entered the harbor with the ship, when we were lying at anchor one league out to sea because of unfavorable weather, they came out to the ship with a great number of their boats; they had painted and decorated their faces with various colors, showing us that it was a sign of happiness. They brought us some of their food, and showed us by signs where we should anchor in the port for the ship's safety, and then accompanied us all the way until we dropped anchor.

The Death of Estevan

One of the first expeditions into the American southwest was led by an African slave, a Moor, who is known only by his first name, Estevan (Stephen). One of the four survivors of an ill-fated attack on Florida, Estevan spent eight years wandering the Gulf Coast before finding his way to Mexico City (for an account of his survival, see *The Narrative of Alvar Núñez Cabeza de Vaca* on pp. 48–53).

In 1539, Estevan was sent north with an Italian friar on a scouting mission to find the fabled "Seven Cities of Cibola" that Coronado would attempt to conquer a year later. What happened when Estevan reached the first of the reputedly wealthy cities (a crowded Zuni village near the present Mexico-Arizona border) is reported by one of Coronado's soldiers, Pedro de Casteñeda.

from Pedro de Casteñeda, *The Narrative of the Expedition of Coronado*

Translated by G. P. Winship

After Estevan had left the friars, he thought he could get all the reputation and honor himself, and that if he should discover those settlements with such famous high houses, alone, he would be considered bold and courageous. So he proceeded with the people who had followed him, and attempted to cross the wilderness which lies between the country he had passed through and Cibola. [. . .] Estevan reached Cibola loaded with the large quantity of turquoises they had given him and some beautiful women whom the Indians who followed him and carried his things were taking with them and had given him. These had followed him from all the settlements he had passed, believing that under his protection they could traverse the whole world without any danger. But as the people in this country were more intelligent than those who followed Estevan, they lodged him in a little hut they had outside their village, and the older men and the governors heard his story and took steps to find out the reason he had come to that country. For three days they made inquiries about him and held a council. The account which the negro gave them of two white men who were following him, sent by a great lord, who knew about the things in the sky, and how these were coming to instruct them in divine matters, made them think that he must be a spy or a guide from some nations who wished to come and conquer them, because it seemed to them unreasonable to say that the people were white in the country from which he came and that he was sent by them, he being black. Besides these other reasons, they thought it was hard of him to ask them for turquoises and women, and so they decided to kill him. They did this, but they did not kill any of those who went with him, although they kept some young fellows and let the others, about sixty persons, return freely to their own country. As these, who were badly scared, were returning in flight, they happened to come upon the friars in the desert sixty leagues from Cibola, and told them the sad news, which frightened them so much that they would not even trust these folks who had been with the negro, but opened the packs they were carrying and gave away everything they had except the holy vestments for saying mass. They returned from here by double marches, prepared for anything, without seeing any more of the country except what the Indians told them.

Invisible Bullets

One of the most scholarly visitors to the New World was Thomas Hariot, a prominent Oxford mathematician and astronomer. In 1583, he arrived at Roanoke Island in Virginia with a small colonizing expedition financed by Sir Walter Raleigh that hoped to find ways to profit from the new land. After his return to England, Hariot published a pamphlet—part scientific and part promotional—detailing the geography, natural resources, peoples, and cultures of the region. *A brief and true report* *of the new found land of Virginia* (1588) is the first published book about America written in English by an English eyewitness. Hariot soon noticed that many of the Native Americans his party came in contact with rapidly developed incurable illnesses. Knowing nothing of microbes and immunity, his own superstitions led him to think that only those groups that tried to trick the English with a "subtle device" (an underhanded strategem) fell victims of the "invisible bullets."

---

from Thomas Hariot, *A Brief and True Report of the New Found Land of Virginia*

One other rare and strange accident, leaving others, will I mention before I end, which moved the whole country that either knew or heard of us to have us in wonderful admiration.

There was no town where we had any subtle device practiced against us (we leaving it unpunished or not revenged because we sought by all means possible to win them by gentleness) but that within a few days after our departure from every such town, the people began to die very fast and many in short space: in some towns about twenty, in some forty, in some sixty, and in one six score, which in truth was very many in respect of their numbers. This happened in no place that we could learn but where we had been, where they used some practice [trick] against us, and after such time. This disease [was] also so strange that they neither knew what it was nor how to cure it. The like, by report of the oldest men in the country, never happened before, time out of mind: a thing specially observed by us as also by the natural inhabitants themselves.

Insomuch that when some of the inhabitants which were our friends, and especially the *Wiroans Wingina*, had observed such effects in four or five towns to follow their wicked practices, they were persuaded that it was the work of our God through our means, and that we by him might kill and slay whom we would without weapons and not come near them. [. . .]

This marvelous accident in all the country wrought so strange opinions of us, that some people could not tell whether to think us gods or men, and the rather because that all the space of their sickness, there was no man of ours known to die or that was specially sick. They noted also that we had no women amongst us [and] neither did we care for any of theirs.

Some therefore were of the opinion that we were not born of women, and therefore not mortal, but that we were men of an old generation many years past then risen again to immortality.

Some would likewise seem to prophesy that there were more of our generation yet to come, to kill theirs and take their places, as some thought the purpose was by that which was already done.

Those that were immediately to come after us they imagined to be in the air, yet invisible and without bodies, and that they by our entreaty and for the love of us did make the people to die in that sort as they did by shooting invisible bullets into them.

To confirm this opinion, their physicians to excuse their ignorance in curing the disease, would not be ashamed to say—but [would] earnestly make the simple people believe—that the strings of blood that they sucked out of the sick bodies were the strings wherewithal the invisible bullets were tied and cast.

Christopher Columbus
1451–1506

Between 1492 and 1502, Christopher Columbus, convinced that the world was much smaller than it is and that the Orient could be easily reached by sailing west, made four voyages to the New World. On the first journey, on October 12, 1492, he discovered the island of San Salvador, and from there he went on to find the Bahamas, Cuba, and Haiti (he named the island Hispaniola). Though he discovered none of the riches that Marco Polo had spoken about so glowingly, he nevertheless returned to Spain confident that he had indeed reached the East. He was so certain that he had found the Indies that he named the people of the islands "Indians."

During the voyage, Columbus kept a daily journal that, like so many other original documents of these expeditions, is now lost. Our information concerning the first voyage comes from an abstract made of Columbus's journal by the Spanish historian Bartolome de Las Casas. The abstract puts Columbus's observations into the third person, except when Las Casas thought the admiral's words should be left intact (these are noted by quotation marks). Otherwise, the abstract appears to retain all the essential facts of the journey.

Columbus set out on his second voyage in September 1493. Though he discovered Puerto Rico, Jamaica, parts of Cuba, the Virgin Islands, and the Lesser Antilles, the expedition proved to be a financial disaster: still no gold or silver, still no fabulous cities. Of this voyage there is neither a journal nor an abstract. An aristocratic friend of Columbus's, however, accompanied him on the expedition and left an informal account. Michele de Cuneo's record of the journey shows how quickly relations between the Europeans and the natives deteriorated. His cold-blooded narrative of the skirmish in which Columbus's crew surprised a band of Carib men and women near St. Croix represents the first documented battle between the Old World and the New. It prefigures the many disastrous encounters that would occur between the two worlds for centuries.

On the third voyage, which departed in May 1498, Columbus discovered Trinidad and the Spanish Main and came very close to finding the Amazon. He set foot on the South American continent, but, believing it an island, sailed up to Cuba, which he ironically thought must be the mainland, the gateway to the land of the Great Khan. While sailing in the Gulf of Paria, off the coast of Venezuela, Columbus formed a fantastic theory, which he set out in his journals and in a formal letter to the queen and king of Spain. He imagined that the earth was not perfectly round but rather pear-shaped and that he had approached its highest point. Here was to be found the original Garden of Eden, the "Terrestrial Paradise."

A great navigator but a poor administrator, Columbus was eventually relieved of his governorship in the New World. He had not found riches, nor had he been able to establish a peaceful, successful colony. Arrested by a special delegation, Columbus was returned to Spain in chains. Frustrated, his mind turning more and more to visionary goals, he immersed himself in the prophetic books of the Bible and attempted to prove to the Crown that Spain was destined to liberate Jerusalem from Islam. To provide the finances for this religious goal, Columbus made yet another voyage to the New World, this time searching for a passage through the newly discovered islands. On this journey, though he discovered Honduras, Nicaragua, Costa Rica, Panama, and Colombia, he never found the illusory passage (none would exist until the opening of the Panama Canal in 1914). Throughout the trip, Columbus encountered fierce storms, smashed vessels, mutiny, and madness. He spent an entire year marooned in a small cove off Jamaica; physically ill and profoundly disillusioned, he dreamed of Cathay and recorded the voices he heard from heaven. He miraculously made it back to Spain in November 1504, and for the remaining year and a half of his life wrote report after report insisting on his great accomplishment—his discovery that the Malay peninsula could be reached by sailing west. He died never realizing the magnificence of what he actually did find.

Further Reading:

W. Irving, *A History of the Life and Voyages of Christopher Columbus*, 1828.

S. E. Morison, *Admiral of the Ocean Sea: A Life of Christopher Columbus*, 1942.

B. Landstrom, *Columbus*, 1966.

E. Bradford, *Christopher Columbus*, 1973.

K. Sale, *The Conquest of Paradise*, 1990.

F. Fernandez-Armesto, *Columbus*, 1991.

J. N. Wilford, *The Mysterious History of Columbus*, 1991.

V. I. J. Flint, *The Imaginative Landscape of Christopher Columbus*, 1992.

Text:

Journals and Other Documents on the Life and Voyages of Christopher Columbus, ed. S. E. Morison, 1963.

The First Voyage: The West Indies *

[October 12, 1492]

Friday, 12 October

At two hours after midnight appeared the land,[1] at a distance of 2 leagues. They handed all sails and set the *treo,* which is the mainsail without bonnets, and lay-to waiting for daylight Friday, when they arrived at an island of the Bahamas that was called in the Indians' tongue *Guanahaní.* Presently they saw naked people, and the Admiral went ashore in his barge, and Martín Alonso Pinzón and Vicente Yáñez, his brother, who was captain of the *Niña,* followed. The Admiral broke out the royal standard, and the captains [displayed] two banners of the Green Cross, which the Admiral flew on all the vessels as a signal, with an F and a Y,[2] one at one arm of the cross and the other on the other, and over each letter his or her crown.

Once ashore they saw very green trees, many streams, and fruits of different kinds. The Admiral called to the two captains and to the others who jumped ashore and to Rodrigo de Escobedo, secretary of the whole fleet, and to Rodrigo Sánchez of Segovia, and said that they should bear faith and witness how he before them all was taking, as in

---

* From *The Journal of the First Voyage.* The first printed version of the *Journal* appeared in 1825. It was first translated into English in 1827. The present translation is by Samuel Eliot Morison.

[1] San Salvador.

[2] For Ferdinand and Isabella, the king and queen of Spain. (Isabella is spelled in Spanish with a *Y.*)

fact he took, possession of the said island for the King and Queen, their Lord and Lady, making the declarations that are required, as is set forth at length in the testimonies which were there taken down in writing. Presently there gathered many people of the island. What follows are the formal words of the Admiral, in his Book of the First Navigation and Discovery of these Indies:[3]

"I," says he, "in order that they might develop a very friendly disposition towards us, because I knew that they were a people who could better be freed and converted to our Holy Faith by love than by force, gave to some of them red caps and to others glass beads, which they hung on their necks, and many other things of slight value, in which they took much pleasure. They remained so much our [friends] that it was a marvel, later they came swimming to the ships' boats in which we were, and brought us parrots and cotton thread in skeins and darts and many other things, and we swopped them for other things that we gave them, such as little glass beads and hawks' bells.[4] Finally they traded and gave everything they had, with good will; but it appeared to me that these people were very poor in everything. They all go quite naked as their mothers bore them; and also the women, although I didn't see more than one really young girl. All that I saw were young men, none of them more than 30 years old, very well built, of very handsome bodies and very fine faces; the hair coarse, almost like the hair of a horse's tail, and short, the hair they wear over their eyebrows, except for a hank behind that they wear long and never cut. Some of them paint themselves black (and they are of the color of the Canary Islanders, neither black nor white), and others paint themselves white, and some red, and others with what they find. And some paint their faces, others the body, some the eyes only, others only the nose. They bear no arms, nor know thereof; for I showed them swords and they grasped them by the blade and cut themselves through ignorance. They have no iron. Their darts are a kind of rod without iron, and some have at the end a fish's tooth and others, other things. They are generally fairly tall and good looking, well built. I saw some who had marks of wounds on their bodies, and made signs to them to ask what it was, and they showed me that people of other islands which are near came there and wished to capture them, and they defended themselves. And I believed and now believe that people do come here from the mainland to take them as slaves. They ought to be good servants and of good skill, for I see that they repeat very quickly whatever was said to them. I believe that they would easily be made Christians, because it seemed to me that they belonged to no religion. I, please Our Lord, will carry off six of them at my departure to Your Highnesses, that they may learn to speak. I saw no animal of any kind in this island, except parrots." All these are the words of the Admiral.

[October 13, 1492]

Saturday, 13 October

At the time of daybreak there came to the beach many of these men, all young men, as I have said, and all of good stature, very handsome people. Their hair is not kinky but straight and coarse like horsehair; the whole forehead and head is very broad, more so than [in] any other race that I have yet seen, and the eyes very handsome and not small.

---

[3] Title of Columbus's original journal.
[4] Tiny bells used in falconry; these had proved, along with other trifles, popular with African natives.

They themselves are not at all black, but of the color of the Canary Islanders; nor should anything else be expected, because this is on the same latitude as the island of Ferro in the Canaries.[5] The legs of all, without exception, are very straight and [they have] no paunch, but are very well proportioned. They came to the ship in dug-outs which are fashioned like a long boat from the trunk of a tree, and all in one piece, and wonderfully made (considering the country), and so big that in some came 40 or 50 men, and others smaller, down to some in which but a single man came. They row with a thing like a baker's peel[6] and go wonderfully, and if they capsize all begin to swim and right it and bail it out with calabashes[7] that they carry. They brought skeins of spun cotton, and parrots, and darts, and other trifles that would be tedious to describe, and give all for whatever is given to them. And I was attentive and worked hard to know if there was any gold, and saw that some of them wore a little piece hanging from a thing like a needle case which they have in the nose; and by signs I could understand that, going to the S, or doubling the island to the S, there was a king there who had great vessels of it and possessed a lot. I urged them to go there, and later saw that they were not inclined to the journey. I decided to wait until tomorrow afternoon and then depart to the SW, since, as many of them informed me, there should be land to the S, SW, and NW, and that they of the NW used to come to fight them many times; and so also to go to the SW to search for gold and precious stones. This island is very big[8] and very level; and the trees very green, and many bodies of water, and a very big lake in the middle, but no mountain, and the whole of it so green that it is a pleasure to gaze upon, and this people are very docile, and from their longing to have some of our things, and thinking that they will get nothing unless they give something, and not having it, they take what they can, and soon swim off. But all that they have, they give for whatever is given to them, even bartering for pieces of broken crockery and glass. I even saw 16 skeins of cotton given for three *ceitis* of Portugal, which is [equivalent to] a *blanca* of Castile,[9] and in them there was more than an *arroba*[10] of spun cotton. This I should have forbidden and would not have allowed anyone to take anything, except that I had ordered it all taken for Your Highnesses if there was any there in abundance. It is grown in this island; but from the short time I couldn't say for sure; and also here is found the gold that they wear hanging from the nose. But, to lose no time, I intend to go and see if I can find the Island of Çipango.[11] Now, as it was night, all went ashore in their dugouts.

[October 14, 1492]

Sunday, 14 October

"When day was breaking I ordered the ship's gig and the caravels' barges to be readied, and I went along the coast of the island to the NNE, to see the other side, which was the eastern side, what there was there, and also to see the villages; and soon I saw two or

---

[5] Columbus accepted Aristotle's theory that people and things from the same latitude are similar.

[6] This was the first time that Europeans had seen canoe paddles.

[7] Gourds.

[8] About sixteen nautical miles long and seven wide.

[9] Fractions of a cent.

[10] About twenty-five pounds.

[11] Japan; following Marco Polo's report, Columbus thought the island of Japan was approximately fifteen hundred miles from the Asian continent.

three, and the people who all came to the beach, shouting and giving thanks to God. Some brought us water, others, other things to eat. Others, when they saw that I didn't care to go ashore, plunged into the sea swimming, and came out, and we understood that they asked us if we had come from the sky. And one old man got into the boat, and others shouted in loud voices to all, men and women, 'Come and see the men who come from the sky, bring them food and drink.' Many came and many women, each with something, giving thanks to God, throwing themselves on the ground, they raised their hands to the sky, and then shouted to us to come ashore; but I was afraid to, from seeing a great reef of rocks which surrounded the whole of this island, and inside it was deep water and a harbor to hold all the ships in Christendom, and the entrance of it very narrow. It's true that inside this reef there are some shoal spots, but the sea moves no more than within a well. In order to see all this I kept going this morning, that I might give an account of all to Your Highnesses, and also [to see] where there might be a fortress; and I saw a piece of land which is formed like an island, although it isn't one (and on it there are six houses), the which could in two days be made an island, although I don't see that it would be necessary, because these people are very unskilled in arms, as Your Highnesses will see from the seven that I caused to be taken to carry them off to learn our language and return; unless Your Highnesses should order them all to be taken to Castile or held captive in the same island, for with 50 men they could all be subjected and made to do all that one wished. And, moreover, next to said islet are groves of trees the most beautiful that I have seen, and as green and leafy as those of Castile in the months of April and May; and much water. I inspected all that harbor, and then returned to the ship and made sail, and saw so many islands that I could not decide where to go first; and those men whom I had captured made signs to me that they were so many that they could not be counted, and called by their names more than a hundred. Finally I looked for the biggest,[12] and decided to go there, and so I did, and it is probably distant from this island of San Salvador 5 leagues, and some of them more, some less. All are very level, without mountains, and very fertile, and all inhabited, and they make war on one another, although these are very simple people and very fine figures of men."

1492/1825

The Second Voyage:
The Cannibals*

[October 28, 1495]

In the name of Jesus and of his glorious mother Mary from whom all good things come. On the 25th of September, 1493, we left Cadiz under 17 sails and all in good order—15

---

[12] Rum Cay.

* No official journal or abstract of the second voyage has survived. This account was written by Michele de Cuneo, an aristocratic

friend who accompanied Columbus on the expedition. The translation here was prepared especially for this volume by Professor Elissa Weaver of the University of Chicago.

square and 2 lateen sails—and on the 2nd of October we anchored at the Grand Canary Island; the following night we set sail and on the 5th we anchored at Gomera, one of the Canary Islands; and it would take too long to tell you about the glorious reception we were given, the rounds fired by cannons and flame-throwers, all ordered by the lady who governs the island and with whom our admiral was once somewhat in love.[1] Here we refreshed ourselves as much as we needed and on October 10th we set out on our voyage, but due to unfavorable weather we stayed around the Canary Islands three days. On the morning of October 13th, a Sunday, we left the Island of Ferro [Hierro], the last of the Canaries and we headed southwest. On the 25th of October, the eve of Saints Simon and Jude, at approximately 1600 we hit a storm of such force you wouldn't believe it and we thought our time was up. It lasted all night and 'til day and was so bad we couldn't see one another; at the end, as it pleased God, we found each other, and on November 3rd, a Sunday, we sighted land—five unknown islands. Our admiral named the first Santo Domingo since it was discovered on the Lord's day; the second he called Santa Maria la Gallante out of love for his ship, which was called Maria la Gallante. These two were not very large islands; nevertheless the admiral mapped them. If I remember correctly, it took us 22 days to get from the Island of Ferro to Santa Maria la Gallante, but I think one could well make the trip in 16 days of good wind.

On the island of Santa Maria la Gallante we got water and wood. The island is uninhabited even though it's full of trees and plains. We set sail from there that day and arrived at a large island inhabited by Cannibals,[2] who fled immediately to the mountains when they saw us. We landed on this island and stayed about 6 days since eleven of our men, who had banded together in order to steal, went 5 or 6 miles into the deserted area by such a route that when they wanted to return, they were unable to find their way, even though they were all sailors and could follow the sun, which they couldn't see well for the thick and full woods. When the admiral saw that these men had not returned and were nowhere to be found, he sent 200 men divided into 4 squadrons with trumpets, horns and lanterns, but even they were unable to find the lost men, and there was a time when we were more worried about the 200 men than the others before them. But, as it pleased God, the 200 returned with great difficulty and greater hunger; we judged that the eleven had been eaten by the Cannibals as they are wont to do. However, after 5 or 6 days, the eleven men, as it pleased God, when there remained little hope of ever finding them, built a fire on a cape; seeing the fire, we judged it to be them and we sent a boat and in that way recovered them. Had it not been that an old woman showed them the way back with gestures they'd have been done for since we had planned to set sail on the following day.

On that island we took 12 very beautiful and fat females about 15 or 16 years old and 2 boys of the same age whose genital member had been cut off down to their belly; and we judged that this had been done to keep them from mixing with their women or at least to fatten them and then eat them. These boys and girls had been picked by the Cannibals for us to send to Spain to the king as an exhibit. The admiral named this island Santa Maria di Guadalupe.[3]

---

[1] Although Cuneo is the only source of this information, Columbus apparently had fallen in love with the woman who ruled the island of Gomera.

[2] In the original manuscript the word is *Cam-balli*; it means either "Carib Indians" or "cannibals."

[3] Guadeloupe, named after the famous Spanish shrine.

We set sail from this island of Santa Maria di Guadalupe, the Island of Cannibals, on November 10th and on the 14th we reached another beautiful and fertile island[4] of Cannibals and we came to a very beautiful port. When the Cannibals caught sight of us they fled, as the others had, to the mountains and abandoned their houses where we went and took what we liked. In these few days we found many islands where we didn't disembark, but others where we did—for the night. When we didn't leave the ship we kept it tied, and this we did so we wouldn't travel on and out of fear of running aground. Because these islands were closely adjoining, the admiral called them the Eleven Thousand Virgins,[5] and the previous one, Santa Croce.

We had anchored and gone ashore one day when we saw, coming from a cape, a canoe, that is, a boat, for so it is called in their speech, and it was beating oars as though it were a well-armed brigantine. On it there were three or four male Cannibals with two female Cannibals and two captured Indian slaves—so the Cannibals call their other neighbors from those other islands; they had also just cut off their genital member down to their belly and so they were still sick. Since we had the captain's boat ashore with us, when we saw this canoe we quickly jumped into the boat and gave chase to the canoe. As we approached it, the Cannibals shot hard at us with their bows, and if we had not had our Pavian shields[6] we would have been half destroyed. I must also tell you that a companion who had a shield in his hand got hit by an arrow which went through the shield and into his chest 3 inches causing him to die within a few days. We captured this canoe with all the men. One Cannibal was wounded by a lance-blow and thinking him dead we left him in the sea. Suddenly we saw him begin to swim away; therefore we caught him and with a long hook we pulled him aboard where we cut off his head with an axe. We sent the other Cannibals together with the two slaves to Spain. When I was in the boat, I took a beautiful Cannibal girl and the admiral gave her to me. Having her in my room and she being naked as is their custom, I began to want to amuse myself with her. Since I wanted to have my way with her and she was not willing, she worked me over so badly with her nails that I wished I had never begun. To get to the end of the story, seeing how things were going, I got a rope and tied her up so tightly that she made unheard of cries which you wouldn't have believed. At the end, we got along so well that, let me tell you, it seemed she had studied at a school for whores. The admiral named the cape on that island the Cape of the Arrow for the man who was killed by the arrow.

On the 14th of November we set sail from the island in bad weather. On the 19th we anchored at a large and beautiful island of Indians called, in their language, Boluchen, which the admiral named St. John the Baptist.[7] As we sailed these 5 days both on the right and on the left we saw many islands all of which the admiral has had clearly mapped. At the island mentioned above we stopped to refresh ourselves and on the 21st we sailed; on the 25th, in the name of God, we anchored at Hispaniola,[8] an island discovered earlier by the admiral, where we went ashore at an excellent port called Monte Christo. In these few days we had more bad weather and we saw about 10 islands. We

---

[4] Now St. Croix.

[5] The Virgin Islands, named for the legend of St. Ursula and the 11,000 virgin martyrs of Cologne.

[6] Large, rectangular shields from the northern Italian city of Pavia.

[7] Now Puerto Rico.

[8] The large island that Columbus called Hispaniola is the present-day Haiti and the Dominican Republic.

judged the distance from the island of Santo Domingo to Monte Christo to be 300 leagues. We were not able to keep a straight course for the shallows.

On the 27th of November we set sail to go to Monte Santo where the admiral on his last voyage left 38 men, and that same night we anchored at that very place.[9] On the 28th we went ashore, where we found all of our above-mentioned men dead and still stretched out there on the ground; their eyes were gone and we judged they had been eaten since when the Cannibals decapitate someone they immediately take out his eyes and eat them. They could have been dead 15 to 20 days. We were with the ruler of the place whose name was Goachanari, who, with tears running down his chest, and his men likewise, told us that the ruler of the mountain area named Goacanaboa had come with 3 thousand men and killed them together with some of their own people and robbed them out of spite. We found none of the things the admiral had left there, and having heard this story, we took it to be true. We spent 10 days on this business and on the 8th of December we left the place since it was not healthful because of its swamps, and we went to another place on the same island to an excellent port where we went ashore. There we built 200 houses which are small, like the huts we build at home for hunting birds, and they are covered with grass.

When we had built the settlement[10] for ourselves, the inhabitants of the island, who lived between one and two leagues from us, came to visit, as though we were brothers, saying that we were men of God come down from the sky, and many stood in awe watching us. They brought us some of their food to eat and we gave them some of ours since they behaved like brothers. And here we arrive at the end of our voyage, although I will say more below of another voyage I made later with the admiral when he decided to find terra firma; but now we will speak of other things and first about the search for gold on the island of Hispaniola.

1495/1885

The Third Voyage: The Terrestrial Paradise*

[October 18, 1498]

When I sailed from Spain to the Indies I found immediately on passing 100 leagues west of the Azores a very considerable change in the sky and the stars, and in the temperature of the air and in the waters of the sea. I took great pains in putting this to the test. I found that, from north to south, passing the said islands by the said 100 leagues, the compass needles, which hitherto had varied northeasterly, now varied a full point to the NW. On reaching that line it was as if someone had transported a hill thither.

[9] The fortress of Navidad, which Columbus had constructed on his first voyage.

[10] Isabella, the first European attempt at a permanent settlement in the New World.

* The first printed version of this text appeared in 1825. It was printed again in 1892–1894. The latter is the version used as the basis for this translation by Samuel Eliot Morison.

Moreover, I found the sea full of a certain weed,[1] resembling little pine branches and heavily laden with fruit like that of the mastic. It is so thick that on the First Voyage I thought that it was a shoal and that the ship would run aground. But until we reached this line we did not come upon a single branch. When we got there, moreover, I found the sea very calm and smooth and although the wind was strong, it never got rough. Furthermore, beyond the said line, towards the west, I found the weather to be very mild and unchanging in character, winter or summer. When I was there I discovered that the North Star described a circle, with a diameter of 5°, and when the Guards are in the Right [E] Arm, the star is at its lowest elevation, and it continues to rise until it reaches Left [W] Arm; then it has 5° [elevation]. From that point it sinks until it once more returns to Right Arm.

On this [Third] Voyage . . . as soon as I succeeded in attaining this line [100 leagues W of the Azores] I immediately found the temperature very mild, and the further forward I went the more it increased; but I did not find the stars consistent with this. I found that, as night fell, I observed the North Star at an altitude of 5°, and then the Guards were at "head"; and afterwards at midnight I observed the Star 10° high, and at daybreak at 15° with the Guards at "feet." I found the smoothness of the sea conformed to this, but not the gulfweed. I was much amazed by this business of the North Star, and hence for many nights I "shot" it with the quadrant very carefully. But I always found that the plumb-bob and line hit the same point [on the scale]. I regard this as something new, and mayhap it will be concluded that in this little space the sky changes so much.

I have always read that the world, both land and water, was spherical, as the authority and researches of Ptolemy and all the others who have written on this subject demonstrate and prove, as do the eclipses of the moon and other experiments that are made from east to west, and the elevation of the North Star from north to south. But I have seen this discrepancy, as I have said. I am compelled, therefore, to come to this view of the world: I have found that it does not have the kind of sphericity described by the authorities, but that it has the shape of a pear, which is all very round, except at the stem, which is rather prominent, or that it is as if one had a very round ball, on one part of which something like a woman's teat were placed, this part with the stem being the uppermost and nearest to the sky, lying below the equinoctial line in this ocean sea, at the end of the East. I mean by the end of the East the point where its land and islands terminate. To confirm this I cite all the arguments written above about the line which passes from north to south 100 leagues west of the Azores. For in crossing this to the westward the vessels keep rising gradually toward the sky and then enjoy milder weather; and the needle varied a point on account of this mildness. The farther and higher we went, the more the needle varied towards the NW. This elevation is responsible for the variation of the circle which the North Star describes with the Guards. The closer one comes to the equator, the higher they will rise and the greater the difference will be in the said stars and their orbits.

Ptolemy and the other scholars who have written about this world believed it spherical, thinking that this hemisphere was round like that in which they lived and which has its center in the island of Aryn,[2] which is below the equinoctial line between the

---

[1] Gulfweed.
[2] In ancient and medieval geography, a sacred Asian city thought to be the "umbilical" of the world; it divided East from West.

Arabian Gulf and the Persian Gulf; the circle passes over Cape St. Vincent in Portugal in the west and by Cangara and the Seres[3] in the east. In that hemisphere I see nothing that stands in the way of its being round, as they claim. But as for this other hemisphere I maintain that it is like a half of a very round pear which had a long stem, as I have said, or like a woman's teat on a round ball. So neither Ptolemy nor the others who wrote about the world had any information about this half, for it was altogether unknown. They merely based their opinion on the hemisphere in which they lived, which is round, as I have said above. And now that Your Highnesses have ordered navigation and search and discovery it is revealed very clearly. For during this voyage when I was 20 degrees N of the equinoctial line I was there in the latitude of Arguin[4] and those other lands, and the people there are black and the land thoroughly scorched. After I went to Cape Verde Islands [I noticed] that the people in those regions are much darker, and the farther south they are the closer they approach the extreme; so, on the parallel of Sierra Leone, where I was when the North Star at nightfall had an elevation of 5°, the people are extremely black, and, after I sailed westward there, [I met] extreme heat. Once the line of which I spoke was passed, I found the climate increasingly mild, to such a degree that when I made the island of Trinidad, where the North Star at night- fall also had an elevation of 5°, I found the temperature there and in the land of Gracia very mild, the ground and the trees being very green and as beautiful as the orchards of Valencia in April. The people there are of very handsome build and whiter than any others I have seen in the Indies. Their hair is very long and smooth. The people are more intelligent and have more ability, and they are not cowards. The sun was then in Virgo, above our heads and theirs.

All this comes from the very mild temperature which prevails there, and this in turn comes from its being the highest land in the world and the closest to the sky. I therefore assert that the world is not spherical but that it has this other shape which I have already described, and which is in the hemisphere where the Indies end and the Ocean Sea [be- gins], and its extremity is below the equator. And this view is greatly supported by the fact that the sun, when Our Lord first created it, was at the first point of the East,[5] and the first light was here in the Orient, here where the world is highest. Although Aristotle was of the opinion that the Antarctic pole or the land beneath it is the highest part of the world and nearest the sky, other wise men opposed him, saying that the highest part is beneath the Arctic pole. By this reasoning it appears that they believed that one part of the world must be higher and closer to the sky than the other, and they did not hit upon this view that it is beneath the equator, for the reason I have stated. This is not surprising, for no sound knowledge was available about this hemisphere, but only very vague information of uncertain character, for no one had ever gone, or been sent, to check on it until now, when Your Highnesses gave orders that the sea and land be ex- plored and discovered.

Holy Scripture testifies that Our Lord created the Terrestrial Paradise and planted in it the tree of life, and that a fountain sprang up there, from which flow the four principal rivers of the world: the Ganges in India, the Tigris and the Euphrates in [blank], which cut through a mountain range and form Mesopotamia and flow into Persia, and the

---

[3] Ancient name for China.
[4] Island off the west coast of Africa.   [5] Aryn. (See footnote 2.)

Nile, which rises in Ethiopia and empties into the sea at Alexandria. I do not find and have never found any Latin or Greek work which definitely locates the Terrestrial Paradise in this world,[6] nor have I seen it securely placed on any world map on the basis of proof. Some put it at the sources of the Nile in Ethiopia, but others have visited all these countries without finding evidence of it in the mildness of the sky, or in its height towards the sky, by which it might be understood that it was there, or that the waters of the flood, which had risen above, had penetrated to it. Some gentiles attempted to argue that it was in the Fortunate Islands, which are the Canaries, etc. St. Isidore, Bede, Strabo, the Master of Scholastic History, St. Ambrose, Scotus, and all dependable theologians, agree that the Terrestrial Paradise is in the east, etc.

I return to my discussion of the land of Gracia and the river and lake I found there, so large that it may better be called sea than lake; for a lake is a place containing water and if it is large it is called a sea, as in the case of the Sea of Galilee and the Dead Sea. I say that if this river does not originate in the Terrestrial Paradise, it comes and flows from a land of infinite size to the south, of which we have no knowledge as yet. But I am completely persuaded in my own mind that the Terrestrial Paradise is in the place I have described, and I rely upon the arguments and authorities above cited.

May it please Our Lord to grant Your Highnesses long life, health and leisure to be able to pursue this very noble Enterprise by which I think Our Lord is greatly served and Spain receives increase in dominion and all Christians are much consoled and pleased, for the name of Our Lord will here be preached. In all the lands which the vessels of Your Highnesses visit, and on every cape, I order a cross to be set up, and I inform all the people whom I find of the estate of Your Highnesses and how you are fixed in Spain. I tell them of our holy faith as best I can and of the dogma of our Holy Mother Church,[7] which has her members in the entire world: I tell them of the polity and nobility of all Christians, and of their faith in the Holy Trinity. May it please Our Lord to forgive the persons who reviled and do revile this most excellent Enterprise and who oppose and have opposed it so that it may not go forward, without considering how much honor and glory it is for the royal estate of Your Highnesses throughout the world. They know not what to say to malign it, except that it involves expense and that vessels have not been immediately dispatched laden with gold, without taking into account the shortness of time and the considerable difficulties that have been experienced here. They do not consider that in Castile, in the household of Your Highnesses, there are persons who each of them annually earn greater sums than it is necessary to expend on this enterprise. They likewise fail to note that no princes of Spain ever gained territory outside their borders save now, when Your Highnesses have an Other World here, by which our holy faith can be so greatly advanced and from which such great wealth can be drawn . . .

Thanks be to God.

1492/1825

---

[6] Columbus had assimilated a great deal of medieval thought concerning the exact location of the biblical Garden of Eden (i.e., the "Terrestrial Paradise").

[7] i.e., the Catholic church.

Alvar Núñez Cabeza de Vaca
ca. 1490–ca. 1557

In 1528 Pánfilo de Narváez led an expedition to establish a conquistadorial regime on the west coast of Florida. Beaten by the Florida wilderness and the unyielding Apalachee Indians, the expedition—the first overland journey on future United States soil—tried to escape to Mexico, but a gulf storm wrecked the Spaniard's makeshift boats near Galveston Island, Texas. Starvation, exposure, disease, and exhaustion reduced the original party of three hundred to four men: Cabeza de Vaca, Alonzo del Castillo, Andrés Dorantes, and his Moroccan slave, Estevan (or Estevanico). For the next eight years they wandered the Gulf Coast, where they lived mainly on prickly pears and were periodically taken into captivity by various Indian tribes. The four apparently managed to survive by assuming the role—reluctantly at first—of medicine men or shamans and practicing faith healing. The grisly account of their journey is the subject of the first North American captivity tale, *The Narrative of Alvar Núñez Cabeza de Vaca* (1542).

Contemporary psychologists have observed that hostages may gradually come to identify with their captors. Because of his many favorable experiences, Cabeza de Vaca retained a sympathetic—though nonetheless politically superior—attitude to the Indians, which was far different from most other conquistadores. He argued that "to bring all these people to Christianity and subjection to Your Imperial Majesty, they must be won by kindness, the only certain way." At journey's end, Cabeza de Vaca assures the party of friendly Indians who had accompanied him to the Spanish outposts that they need fear no harm. He is deceived, and his profound disappointment with his own people results in a dramatic psychological event that will recur throughout the literature of the New World: A tough-minded European explorer adrift in a vast alien land must suddenly confront not a mere loss of direction but a far more disorienting loss of identity.

Further Reading:

M. Bishop, *The Odyssey of Cabeza de Vaca*, 1933.
H. Long, *The Power Within Us*, 1944.
C. Hallenbeck, *Alvar Núñez Cabeza de Vaca: The Journey and Route . . .* , 1971.

J. B. Fernandez, *Alvar Núñez Cabeza de Vaca: The Forgotten Chronicler*, 1975.
P. Wild, *Alvar Núñez Cabeza de Vaca*, 1991.

Text:

Spanish Explorers in the Southern United States 1528–1543, ed. F. W. Hodge, trans. B. Smith, 1907.

from The Narrative of Alvar Núñez Cabeza de Vaca*

[The Faith Healers]

That same night of our arrival,[1] some Indians came to Castillo and told him that they had great pain in the head, begging him to cure them. After he made over them the sign of the cross, and commended them to God, they instantly said that all the pain had left, and went to their houses bringing us prickly pears,[2] with a piece of venison, a thing to us little known. As the report of Castillo's performances spread, many came to us that night sick, that we should heal them, each bringing a piece of venison, until the quantity became so great we knew not where to dispose of it. We gave many thanks to God, for every day went on increasing his compassion and his gifts. After the sick were attended to, they began to dance and sing, making themselves festive, until sunrise; and because of our arrival, the rejoicing was continued for three days.

When these were ended, we asked the Indians about the country farther on, the people we should find in it, and of the subsistence there. They answered us, that throughout all the region prickly-pear plants abounded; but the fruit was now gathered and all the people had gone back to their houses. They said the country was very cold, and there were few skins. Reflecting on this, and that it was already winter, we resolved to pass the season with these Indians.

Five days after our arrival, all the Indians went off, taking us with them to gather more prickly pears, where there were other peoples speaking different tongues. After walking five days in great hunger, since on the way was no manner of fruit, we came to a river[3] and put up our houses. We then went to seek the product of certain trees, which is like peas. As there are no paths in the country, I was detained some time. The others returned, and coming to look for them in the dark I got lost. Thank God I found a burning tree, and in the warmth of it I passed the cold of that night. In the morning, loading myself with sticks, and taking two brands with me, I returned to seek them. In this manner I wandered five days, ever with my fire and load; for if the wood had failed me where none could be found, as many parts are without any, though I might have sought sticks elsewhere, there would have been no fire to kindle them. This was all the protection I had against cold, while walking naked as I was born. Going to the low woods near the rivers, I prepared myself for the night, stopping in them before sunset. I made a hole in the ground and threw in fuel which the trees abundantly afforded, collected in good quantity from those that were fallen and dry. About the whole I made four fires, in the form of a cross, which I watched and made up from time to time. I also gathered some bundles of the coarse straw that there abounds, with which I covered myself in the hole. In this way I was sheltered at night from cold. On one occasion while

* Cabeza de Vaca composed his narrative in 1536, after reaching Mexico; it was first published in Spain in 1542.

[1] In 1534.

[2] The spiny, edible fruit of the flat-stemmed cactus.

[3] Probably the San Antonio.

I slept, the fire fell upon the straw, when it began to blaze so rapidly that notwithstand-ing the haste I made to get out of it, I carried some marks on my hair of the danger to which I was exposed. All this while I tasted not a mouthful, nor did I find anything I could eat. My feet were bare and bled a good deal. Through the mercy of God, the wind did not blow from the north in all this time, otherwise I should have died.

At the end of the fifth day I arrived on the margin of a river,[4] where I found the Indi-ans, who with the Christians, had considered me dead, supposing that I had been stung by a viper. All were rejoiced to see me, and most so were my companions. They said that up to that time they had struggled with great hunger, which was the cause of their not having sought me. At night, all gave me of their prickly pears, and the next morning we set out for a place where they were in large quantity, with which we satisfied our great craving, the Christians rendering thanks to our Lord that He had ever given us His aid. . . .

The next day morning, many Indians came, and brought five persons who had cramps and were very unwell. They came that Castillo might cure them. Each offered his bow and arrows, which Castillo received. At sunset he blessed them, commending them to God our Lord, and we all prayed to Him the best we could to send health; for that He knew there was no other means, than through Him, by which this people would aid us, so we could come forth from this unhappy existence. He bestowed it so merci-fully, that, the morning having come, all got up well and sound, and were as strong as though they never had a disorder. It caused great admiration, and inclined us to render many thanks to God our Lord, whose goodness we now clearly beheld, giving us firm hopes that He would liberate and bring us to where we might serve Him. For myself I can say that I ever had trust in His providence that He would lead me out from that captivity, and thus I always spoke of it to my companions.

The Indians having gone and taken their friends with them in health, we departed for a place at which others were eating prickly pears. These people are called Cuthalchuches[5] and Malicones, who speak different tongues. Adjoining them were others called Coayos and Susolas, who were on the opposite side, others called Atayos, who were at war with the Susolas, exchanging arrow shots daily. As through all the country they talked only of the wonders which God our Lord worked through us, per-sons came from many parts to seek us that we might cure them. At the end of the sec-ond day after our arrival, some of the Susolas came to us and besought Castillo that he would go to cure one wounded and others sick, and they said that among them was one very near his end. Castillo was a timid practitioner, most so in serious and dangerous cases, believing that his sins would weigh, and some day hinder him in performing cures. The Indians told me to go and heal them, as they liked me; they remembered that I had ministered to them in the walnut grove when they gave us nuts and skins, which occurred when I first joined the Christians. So I had to go with them, and Dorantes ac-companied me with Estevanico. Coming near their huts, I perceived that the sick man we went to heal was dead. Many persons were around him weeping, and his house was prostrate, a sign that the one who dwelt in it is no more. When I arrived I found his eyes rolled up, and the pulse gone, he having all the appearances of death, as they seemed to me and as Dorantes said. I removed a mat with which he was covered, and supplicated

---

[4] Presumably, the same river where they had set up shelters.

[5] These two groups were apparently south Texas Indians.

our Lord as fervently as I could, that He would be pleased to give health to him, and to the rest that might have need of it. After he had been blessed and breathed upon many times, they brought me his bow, and gave me a basket of pounded prickly pears.

The natives took me to cure many others who were sick of a stupor, and presented me two more baskets of prickly pears, which I gave to the Indians who accompanied us. We then went back to our lodgings. Those to whom we gave the fruit tarried, and returned at night to their houses, reporting that he who had been dead and for whom I wrought before them, had got up whole and walked, had eaten and spoken with them and that all to whom I had ministered were well and much pleased. This caused great wonder and fear, and throughout the land the people talked of nothing else. All to whom the fame of it reached, came to seek us that we should cure them and bless their children.

When the Cuthalchuches, who were in company with our Indians, were about to return to their own country, they left us all the prickly pears they had, without keeping one: they gave us flints of very high value there, a palm and a half in length, with which they cut. They begged that we would remember them and pray to God that they might always be well, and we promised to do so. They left, the most satisfied beings in the world, having given us the best of all they had.

We remained with the Avavares eight months, reckoned by the number of moons. In all this time people came to seek us from many parts, and they said that most truly we were children of the sun. Dorantes and the negro[6] to this time had not attempted to practise; but because of the great solicitation made by those coming from different parts to find us, we all became physicians, although in being venturous and bold to attempt the performance of any cure, I was the most remarkable. No one whom we treated, but told us he was left well; and so great was the confidence that they would become healed if we administered to them, they even believed that whilst we remained none of them could die. These and the rest of the people behind, related an extraordinary circumstance, and by the way they counted, there appeared to be fifteen or sixteen years since it occurred.

They said that a man wandered through the country whom they called Badthing; he was small of body and wore beard, and they never distinctly saw his features. When he came to the house where they lived, their hair stood up and they trembled. Presently a blazing torch shone at the door, when he entered and seized whom he chose, and giving him three great gashes in the side with a very sharp flint, the width of the hand and two palms in length, he put his hand through them, drawing forth the entrails, from one of which he would cut off a portion more or less, the length of a palm, and throw it on the embers. Then he would give three gashes to an arm, the second cut on the inside of an elbow, and would sever the limb. A little after this, he would begin to unite it, and putting his hands on the wounds, these would instantly become healed. They said that frequently in the dance he appeared among them, sometimes in the dress of a woman, at others in that of a man; that when it pleased him he would take a buhío, or house, and lifting it high, after a little he would come down with it in a heavy fall. They also stated that many times they offered him victuals, but that he never ate: they asked him whence he came and where was his abiding place, and he showed them a fissure in the earth and said that his house was there below. These things they told us of, we much

---

[6] Estevan, or Estevanico, mentioned previously.

laughed at and ridiculed; and they seeing our incredulity, brought to us many of those they said he had seized; and we saw the marks of the gashes made in the places according to the manner they had described. We told them he was an evil one, and in the best way we could, gave them to understand, that if they would believe in God our Lord, and become Christians like us, they need have no fear of him, nor would he dare to come and inflict those injuries, and they might be certain he would not venture to appear while we remained in the land. At this they were delighted and lost much of their dread. They told us that they had seen the Asturian and Figueroa with people farther along the coast, whom we had called those of the figs.

They are all ignorant of time, either by the sun or moon, nor do they reckon by the month or year; they better know and understand the differences of the seasons, when the fruits come to ripen, where the fish resort, and the position of the stars, at which they are ready and practised. By these we were ever well treated. We dug our own food and brought our loads of wood and water. Their houses and also the things we ate, are like those of the nation from which we came, but they suffer far greater want, having neither maize, acorns, nor nuts. We always went naked like them, and covered ourselves at night with deer-skins.

Of the eight months we were among this people, six we supported in great want, for fish are not to be found where they are. At the expiration of the time, the prickly pears began to ripen,[7] and I and the negro went, without these Indians knowing it, to others farther on, a day's journey distant, called Maliacones. At the end of three days, I sent him to bring Castillo and Dorantes, and they having arrived, we all set out with the Indians who were going to get the small fruit of certain trees on which they support themselves ten or twelve days whilst the prickly pears are maturing. They joined others called Arbadaos, whom we found to be very weak, lank, and swollen, so much so as to cause us great astonishment. We told those with whom we came, that we wished to stop with these people, at which they showed regret and went back by the way they came; so we remained in the field near the houses of the Indians, which when they observed, after talking among themselves they came up together, and each of them taking one of us by the hand, led us to their dwellings. Among them we underwent greater hunger than with the others; we ate daily not more than two handfuls of the prickly pears, which were green and so milky they burned our mouths. As there was lack of water, those who ate suffered great thirst. In our extreme want we bought two dogs, giving in exchange some nets, with other things, and a skin I used to cover myself.

I have already stated that throughout all this country we went naked, and as we were unaccustomed to being so, twice a year we cast our skins like serpents. The sun and air produced great sores on our breasts and shoulders, giving us sharp pain; and the large loads we had, being very heavy, caused the cords to cut into our arms. The country is so broken and thickset, that often after getting our wood in the forests, the blood flowed from us in many places, caused by the obstruction of thorns and shrubs that tore our flesh wherever we went. At times, when my turn came to get wood, after it had cost me much blood, I could not bring it out either on my back or by dragging. In these labors my only solace and relief were in thinking of the sufferings of our Redeemer, Jesus Christ, and in the blood He shed for me, in considering how much greater must have been the torment He sustained from the thorns, than that I there received.

---

[7] i.e., in the summer of 1535.

I bartered with these Indians in combs that I made for them and in bows, arrows, and nets. We made mats, which are their houses, that they have great necessity for; and although they know how to make them, they wish to give their full time to getting food, since when otherwise employed they are pinched with hunger. Sometimes the Indians would set me to scraping and softening skins; and the days of my greatest prosperity there, were those in which they gave me skins to dress. I would scrape them a very great deal and eat the scraps, which would sustain me two or three days. When it happened among these people, as it had likewise among others whom we left behind, that a piece of meat was given us, we ate it raw; for if we had put it to roast, the first native that should come along would have taken it off and devoured it; and it appeared to us not well to expose it to this risk; besides we were in such condition it would have given us pain to eat it roasted, and we could not have digested it so well as raw. Such was the life we spent there; and the meagre subsistence we earned by the matters of traffic which were the work of our hands.

1536/1542

Powhatan
d. 1618

The early contacts between Native Americans and Europeans on the America's East Coast duplicated the pattern on the West Coast—mistrust, violence, and dispersion. The Algonquian Confederacy stretched across tidewater Virginia from the Potomac River south to Albermarle Sound. For many years the leader of this confederacy was Powhatan, also known as Wahunsonacock. Late in 1608 the English colonists (including Captain John Smith) reluctantly followed the instructions of the Virginia royal council in England and offered to crown Powhatan a subject-king under James I as a gesture of recognition, friendship, and peace. Powhatan insisted that the English come to his village at Weremoco (now Gloucester County, Virginia), where he accepted a copper crown and gifts of a woolen robe and an English bedstead. Powhatan's refusal to bow to the king of England and his reciprocal gifts—his shoes and cloak—angered the English. This awkward exchange began a period of strained relations between the colonists and the Algonquians.

Captain John Smith made frequent trips up the Chicahominy River in the Virginia colony to trade for Algonquian corn. On one of these expeditions, Smith's party was attacked and captured by the Algonquians and taken to Weremoco on the York River, where Powhatan delivered some version of the speech printed here, transcribed by Smith. In it, Powhatan rebukes Smith and his retinue for wishing "to conquer more than to trade" and for their excesses in dealing with the Native Americans.

There is, however, no compelling evidence to verify that John Smith spoke Powhatan's language or that Powhatan spoke English. In fact, it is highly unlikely that any individual would have been fluent in both languages at this point in Virginia's history. While the basis for Smith's transcription remains uncertain, Powhatan's speech might well represent Smith's best estimate of what Powhatan had said—or of what he hoped he had said.

A fragile peace between the English and the Algonquians was maintained for several years, mostly through the marriage of Powhatan's daughter, Pocahontas, to the Englishman John Rolfe. But by the mid-seventeenth century the British and the Indian tribes that had converted to Christianity defeated and disbanded the Algonquian Confederacy in a series of bloody encounters. The Algonquians are now extinct.

Further Reading:

G. Sagard, *The Long Journey to the Country of the Hurons*, 1632, ed. G. M. Wrong, 1939.
S. Smith, *Powhatan: A Metrical Romance*, 1841.
N. B. Wood, *Lives of Famous Indian Chiefs*, 1906.

R. W. Andrews, *Indian Leaders Who Helped Shape America*, 1971.
C. Feest, "Virginia Algonquians," in *Handbook of North American Indians*, gen. ed. W. C. Sturtevant, vol. 15, ed. B. G. Trigger, 1978.

Text:

S. G. Drake, *Biography and History of the Indians of North America*, 1841.

Letter to Captain John Smith

I am now grown old, and must soon die; and the succession must descend, in order, to my brothers, *Opitchapan, Opekankanough,* and *Catataugh,* and then to my two sisters, and their two daughters. I wish their experience was equal to mine; and that your love to us might not be less than ours to you. Why should you take by force that from us which you can have by love? Why should you destroy us, who have provided you with food? What can you get by war? We can hide our provisions, and fly into the woods; and then you must consequently famish by wronging your friends. What is the cause of your jealousy? You see us unarmed, and willing to supply your wants, if you will come in a friendly manner, and not with swords and guns, as to invade an enemy. I am not so simple, as not to know it is better to eat good meat, lie well, and sleep quietly with my women and children; to laugh and be merry with the English; and, being their friend, to have copper, hatchets, and whatever else I want, than to fly from all, to lie cold in the woods, feed upon acorns, roots, and such trash, and to be so hunted, that I cannot rest, eat, or sleep. In such circumstances, my men must watch, and if a twig should but break, all would cry out, *"Here comes Capt. Smith"*; and so, in this miserable manner, to end my miserable life; and, Capt. Smith, this *might* be soon your fate too, through your rashness and unadvisedness. I, therefore, exhort you to peaceable councils; and, above all, I insist that the guns and swords, the cause of all our jealousy and uneasiness, be removed and sent away.

ca. 1609/1841

Captain John Smith
1580–1631

Captain John Smith entered the arena of North American exploration at a time when the romantic age of buccaneers and seadogs was giving way to the new, financially cautious policies of seventeenth-century colonization. Born into a moderately prosperous Lincolnshire family, Smith received a solid English grammar school education and, after a brief apprenticeship to a prominent merchant, enlisted at the age of fifteen to fight in the Netherlands. For ten years Smith pursued an adventurous military career that took him to Hungary, France, Germany, Spain, Austria, Rumania, Transylvania, Turkey, and North Africa. Toward the end of his life he wrote about these experiences in a brief autobiography, *The True Travels, Adventures, and Observations of Captain John Smith* (1630).

Upon his return to England, Smith—always eager for new adventures—joined the expedition that founded the Jamestown colony in 1607. An iron-willed disciplinarian, he tried almost single-handedly to keep a quarrelsome, inept, and frequently dissatisfied party intact. In his reports to his superiors Smith deplored the lack of skilled labor, complaining that too many of the colonists were "gentlemen" who found "not English cities, nor such fair houses, nor at their own wishes any of their accustomed dainties, with feather beds and down pillows, taverns and alehouses in every breathing place . . . For the country was to them a misery, a ruin, a death, a hell."

While at Jamestown, Smith conducted several short exploratory trips into the interior. During one of these journeys he was captured by Chesapeake Indians, who brought him to their king, Powhatan. As Smith many years later recounted the incident, he was condemned to death and then saved at the last minute by the timely intercession of Powhatan's favorite daughter, Pocahontas. Smith's failure to mention this dramatic episode in his first account of the Virginia expedition led a number of historians (beginning with Henry Adams) to consider the Pocahontas incident as mere fabricated afterthought. Yet, given Smith's promotional purposes at the time, it is quite possible that he wanted to omit any material that might scare off potential colonists. Whether true report or tall tale, Captain Smith's brief captivity and his hairbreadth escape has become one of the best-known passages in the literature of North American exploration.

Smith stayed on at Jamestown until the fall of 1609, when it was becoming clear that his efforts to bring effective management to the colony were futile. In 1614 he made another trip to North America, this time mapping out the coast of New England, a region he not only named but also fell so in love with that he ardently promoted its colonization in two important books, *A Description of New England* (1614) and *Advertisements for the Unexperienced Planters of New England, or Anywhere* (1631). The *Advertisements,* a list of "experienced memorandums" offering practical advice and theoretical suggestions on colonization, was addressed to the Puritan leaders who founded the Massachusetts Bay Colony in 1630. It was Smith's last work, and given the way he had been neglected during his final years, he would not have been surprised to find that most of his admonitions went unheeded.

Further Reading:

H. Adams, "Captain John Smith: Sometime
Governour in Virginia and Admirall of New
England," *North American Review,* January 1867.

B. Smith, *Captain John Smith: His Life and Legend,*
1953.

P. L. Barbour, *The Three Worlds of Captain John
Smith,* 1964.

E. H. Emerson, *Captain John Smith,* 1971.

A. T. Vaughan, *American Genesis: Captain John
Smith and the Founding of Virginia,* 1975.

F. Mossiker, *Pocahontas: The Life and Legend,* 1976.

J. A. L. Lemay, *The American Dream of Captain John
Smith,* 1991.

J. A. L. Lemay, *Did Pocahontas Save Captain John
Smith?,* 1992.

Text:

Travels and Works of Captain John Smith, ed.
E. Arber, 1884; reprinted with an introduction by
A. G. Bradley, 2 vols., 1910. Spelling and punctuation have been changed to conform to modern
usage.

The Generall Historie of Virginia, New England, and the Summer Isles

Book III

from *Chapter II [Captain Smith's Captivity]*

But our comedies never endured long without a tragedy; some idle exceptions being
muttered against Captain Smith[1] for not discovering the head of [the] Chickahominy
river and [being] taxed by the Council to be too slow in so worthy an attempt. The next
voyage he proceeded so far that with much labor by cutting of trees asunder he made
his passage; but when his barge could pass no farther, he left her in a broad bay out of
danger of shot, commanding none should go ashore till his return; himself with two
English and two savages went up higher in a canoe. But he was not long absent but his
men went ashore, whose want of government[2] gave both occasion and opportunity to
the savages to surprise one George Cassen, whom they slew, and much failed not to
have cut off the boat and all the rest.

Smith little dreaming of that accident, being got to the marshes at the river's head
twenty miles in the desert,[3] had his two men slain (as is supposed) sleeping by the canoe, while himself by fowling sought them victual; who finding he was beset with 200
savages, two of them he slew, still defending himself with the aid of a savage his guide,
whom he bound to his arm with his garters and used him as a buckler,[4] yet he[5] was shot
in his thigh a little, and had many arrows that stuck in his clothes but no great hurt, till
at last they took him prisoner.

When this news came to Jamestown, much was their sorrow for his loss, few expecting what ensued.

---

[1] The narrative is written in the third person.
Smith often incorporated the official reports
of others into his history; this section was
written by Smith and several members of his
party.

[2] Discipline.

[3] Wilderness.

[4] Shield.

[5] Smith.

Six or seven weeks[6] those barbarians kept him prisoner, many strange triumphs and conjurations they made of him, yet he so demeaned[7] himself amongst them as he not only diverted them from surprising the fort, but procured his own liberty, and got himself and his company such estimation amongst them, that those savages admired him more than their own *Quiyoughkasoucks.*[8]

The manner how they used and delivered him, is as follows.

The savages having drawn from George Cassen whither Captain Smith was gone, prosecuting that opportunity they followed him with 300 bowmen, conducted by the King of Pamunkey, who in divisions searching the turnings of the river found Robinson and Emry by the fireside; those they shot full of arrows and slew. Then finding the Captain, as is said, who used the savage that was his guide as his shield (three of them being slain and divers others so galled[9]) all the rest would not come near him. Thinking thus to have returned to his boat, regarding them, as he marched, more than his way, [he] slipped up to the middle in an oozy creek and his savage with him, yet durst they not come to him, till being near dead with cold, he threw away his arms. Then according to their composition[10] they drew him forth and led him to the fire where his men were slain. Diligently they chafed his benumbed limbs.

He demanding for their captain, they showed him Opechancanough, King of Pamunkey, to whom he gave a round ivory double compass dial. Much they marvelled at the playing of the fly[11] and needle, which they could see so plainly and yet not touch it because of the glass that covered them. But when he demonstrated by that globe-like jewel the roundness of the earth and skies, the sphere of the sun, moon, and stars, and how the sun did chase the night round about the world continually, the greatness of the land and sea, the diversity of nations, variety of complexions, and how we were to them antipodes,[12] and many other such like matters, they all stood as amazed with admiration.

Notwithstanding, within an hour after, they tied him to a tree, and as many as could stand about him prepared to shoot him; but the King holding up the compass in his hand, they all laid down their bows and arrows and in a triumphant manner led him to Orapakes,[13] where he was after their manner kindly feasted and well used.

Their order in conducting him was thus: Drawing themselves all in a file, the King in the midst had all their pieces and swords borne before him. Captain Smith was led after him by three great savages holding him fast by each arm, and on each side six went in file with their arrows nocked.[14] But arriving at the town (which was but only thirty or forty hunting houses made of mats, which they remove as they please, as we our tents) all the women and children staring to behold him, the soldiers first all in file performed the form of a *bissone*[15] so well as could be, and on each flank, officers as sergeants to see them keep their orders. A good time they continued this exercise and then cast themselves in a ring, dancing in such several postures and singing and yelling out such hellish notes and screeches; being strangely painted, every one his quiver of arrows and at his back a club, on his arm a fox or an otter's skin or some such matter for his vam-

---

[6] Actually, approximately the three weeks from December 16, 1607, to January 8, 1608.

[7] Behaved; conducted.

[8] In Smith's own glossary of Indian words, the term is defined as "petty Gods, and their affinities."

[9] Harassed; annoyed.

[10] Habits.

[11] Compass face, indicating directional points.

[12] Opposite poles.

[13] An Indian village.

[14] Readied.

[15] A military maneuver.

brace;[16] their heads and shoulders painted red with oil and pocones[17] mingled together, which scarlet-like color made an exceeding handsome show; each had his bow in his hand and the skin of a bird with her wings spread abroad,[18] dried, tied on his head, a piece of copper, a white shell, a long feather, with a small rattle growing at the tails of their snakes tied to it, or some such like toy.

All this while Smith and the King stood in the midst guarded, as before is said, and after three dances they all departed. Smith they conducted to a long house where thirty or forty tall fellows did guard him, and ere long more bread and venison was brought him than would have served twenty men. I think his stomach at that time was not very good; what he left they put in baskets and tied over his head. About midnight they set the meat again before him; all this time not one of them would eat a bit with him, till the next morning they brought him as much more, and then did they eat all the old and reserved the new as they had done the other, which made him think they would fat him to eat him. Yet in this desperate estate, to defend him from the cold, one Maocassater brought him his gown in requital of some beads and toys Smith had given him at his first arrival in Virginia.

Two days after, a man would have slain him (but that the guard prevented it) for the death of his son, to whom they conducted him to recover the poor man then breathing his last. Smith told them that at Jamestown he had a water[19] would do it, if they would let him fetch it, but they would not permit that, but made all the preparations they could to assault Jamestown, craving his advice, and for recompense he should have, life, liberty, land, and women. In part of a table book[20] he wrote his mind to them at the fort, what was intended, how they should follow that direction to affright the messengers, and without fail send him such things as he wrote for, and an inventory with them. The difficulty and danger he told the savages of, the mines, great guns, and other engines, exceedingly affrighted them, yet according to his request they went to Jamestown in as bitter weather as could be of frost and snow, and within three days returned with an answer.

But when they came to Jamestown, seeing men sally out as he had told them they would, they fled; yet in the night they came again to the same place where he had told them they should receive an answer and such things as he had promised them, which they found accordingly and with which they returned with no small expedition, to the wonder of them all that heard it, that he could either divine[21] or the paper could speak.

Then they led him to the Youghtanunds, the Mattapanients, the Payankatanks, the Nantaughtacunds, and Onawmanients upon the rivers of Rappahannock and Potomac, over all those rivers and back again by divers other several nations to the King's habitation at Pamunkey, where they entertained him with most strange and fearful conjurations:

> As if near led to hell,
> Amongst the devils to dwell.

---

[16] Forearm armor.
[17] Bloodroot.
[18] Spread out.
[19] A distilled alcoholic liquor, used medicinally.

[20] Notebook; tablet.
[21] Prophesy.

Not long after, early in a morning, a great fire was made in a long house and a mat spread on the one side as on the other; on the one they caused him to sit, and all the guard went out of the house, and presently came skipping in a great grim fellow all painted over with coal mingled with oil, and many snakes' and weasels' skins stuffed with moss, and all their tails tied together so as they met on the crown of his head in a tassel, and round about the tassel was a coronet of feathers, the skins hanging round about his head, back, and shoulders and in a manner covered his face, with a hellish voice, and a rattle in his hand. With most strange gestures and passions he began his invocation and environed the fire with a circle of meal; which done, three more such like devils came rushing in with the like antique[22] tricks, painted half black, half red, but all their eyes were painted white and some red strokes like Mutchatos[23] along their cheeks; round about him those fiends danced a pretty while, and then came in three more as ugly as the rest, with red eyes and white strokes over their black faces; at last they all sat down right against him, three of them on the one hand of the chief priest and three on the other. Then all with their rattles began a song; which ended, the chief priest laid down five wheat corns; then, straining his arms and hands with such violence that he sweat and his veins swelled, he began a short oration; at the conclusion they all gave a short groan and then laid down three grains more. After that, began their song again, and then another oration, ever laying down so many corns as before till they had twice encircled the fire; that done, they took a bunch of little sticks prepared for that purpose, continuing still their devotion, and at the end of every song and oration they laid down a stick betwixt the divisions of corn. Till night, neither he nor they did either eat or drink, and then they feasted merrily with the best provisions they could make. Three days they used this ceremony; the meaning whereof, they told him, was to know if he intended them well or no. The circle of meal signified their country, the circles of corn the bounds of the sea, and the sticks his country. They imagined the world to be flat and round, like a trencher,[24] and they in the midst.

After this they brought him a bag of gunpowder, which they carefully preserved till the next spring, to plant as they did their corn, because they would be acquainted with the nature of that seed.

Opitchapam, the King's brother, invited him to his house, where, with as many platters of bread, fowl, and wild beasts as did environ him, he bid him welcome, but not any of them would eat a bit with him but put up all the remainder in baskets.

At his return to Opechancanough's, all the King's women and their children flocked about him for their parts,[25] as a due by custom, to be merry with such fragments.

> But his waking mind in hideous dreams did
>   oft see wondrous shapes
>
> Of bodies strange, and huge in growth, and
>   of stupendous makes.

22 Ancient.
23 Mustaches.
24 Platter.
25 Gifts.

At last they brought him to Werowocomoco,[26] where was Powhatan, their Emperor. Here more than two hundred of those grim courtiers stood wondering at him, as [if] he had been a monster, till Powhatan and his train had put themselves in their greatest braveries.[27] Before a fire, upon a seat like a bedstead, he sat covered with a great robe made of Rarowcun[28] skins and all the tails hanging by. On either hand did sit a young wench of sixteen or eighteen years and along each side [of] the house, two rows of men and behind them as many women, with all their heads and shoulders painted red, many of their heads bedecked with the white down of birds; but every one with something, and a great chain of white beads about their necks.

At his entrance before the King, all the people gave a great shout. The Queen of Appomattoc[29] was appointed to bring him water to wash his hands, and another brought him a bunch of feathers, instead of a towel, to dry them; having feasted him after their best barbarous manner they could, a long consultation was held, but the conclusion was, two great stones were brought before Powhatan; then as many as could laid hands on him, dragged him to them, and thereon laid his head, and being ready with their clubs, to beat out his brains. Pocohontas, the King's dearest daughter, when no entreaty could prevail, got his head in her arms and laid her own upon his to save him from death,[30] whereat the Emperor was contented he should live to make him hatchets, and her bells, beads, and copper, for they thought him as well[31] of all occupations as themselves. For the King himself will make his own robes, shoes, bows, arrows, pots; plant, hunt, or do anything so well as the rest.

> They say he bore a pleasant show,
> But sure his heart was sad.
> For who can pleasant be, and rest,
> That lives in fear and dread:
> And having life suspected, doth
> It still suspected lead.

Two days after,[32] Powhatan, having disguised himself in the most fearfulest manner he could, caused Captain Smith to be brought forth to a great house in the woods and there upon a mat by the fire to be left alone. Not long after, from behind a mat that divided the house, was made the most dolefulest noise he ever heard; then Powhatan, more like a devil than a man, with some two hundred more as black as himself, came unto him and told him now they were friends, and presently he should go to Jamestown to send him two great guns and a grindstone for which he would give him the country of Capahowasick[33] and forever esteem him as his son Nantaquond.

So to Jamestown with twelve guides Powhatan sent him. That night they quartered in the woods, he still expecting (as he had done all this long time of his imprisonment)

---

[26] Chief's Town, Powhatan's home on the York River. This was on January 5, 1608.
[27] Costumes.
[28] Raccoon.
[29] Powhatan tribe on the James River.
[30] This may have been a custom among Indian

women, who then had a claim over the person they rescued.
[31] Capable.
[32] On January 7, 1608.
[33] A neighboring tribe.

every hour to be put to one death or other, for all their feasting. But almighty God (by His divine providence) had mollified the hearts of those stern barbarians with compassion. The next morning betimes they came to the fort, where Smith having used the savages with what kindness he could, he showed Rawhunt, Powhatan's trusty servant, two demiculverins[34] and a millstone to carry [to] Powhatan; they found them somewhat too heavy, but when they did see him discharge them, being loaded with stones, among the boughs of a great tree loaded with icicles, the ice and branches came so tumbling down that the poor savages ran away half dead with fear. But at last we regained some conference with them and gave them such toys and sent to Powhatan, his women, and children such presents as gave them in general full content.

1624

---

from A Description of New England

[*Growing Rich in the New World*]

I have not been so ill bred, but I have tasted of plenty and pleasure, as well as want and misery; nor does necessity yet, or occasion of discontent, force me to these endeavors; nor am I ignorant what small thanks I shall have for my pains, or that many would have the world imagine them to be of great judgement, that can but blemish these my designs,[1] by their witty objections and detractions. Yet (I hope) my reasons with my deeds, will so prevail with some, that I shall not want employment in these affairs, to make the most blind see his own senselessness and incredulity, hoping that gain will make them affect that which religion, charity and the common good cannot. It were but a poor device in me to deceive myself, much more the King and State, my friends and country, with these inducements: which seeing His Majesty hath given permission, I wish all sorts of worthy, honest, industrious spirits would understand, and if they desire any further satisfaction, I will do my best to give it, not to persuade them to go only, but go with them; not leave them there, but live with them there.

I will not say, but by ill providing and undue managing, such courses may be taken [that] may make us miserable enough. But if I may have the execution of what I have projected; if they want to eat, let them eat or never digest[2] me. If I perform what I say, I desire but that reward out of the gains [which] may suit my pains, quality and condition. And if I abuse you with my tongue, take my head for satisfaction. If any dislike at the year's end, defraying their charge, by my consent they should freely return, if God please to bless me from such accidents as are beyond my power in reason to prevent. For I am not so simple to think that ever any other motive than wealth will ever erect there a commonwealth or draw company from their ease and humors[3] at home to stay in New England to effect my purposes.

---

[34] Nine-foot cannon.
[1] i.e., his plans to colonize New England.

[2] Tolerate.
[3] Whims.

And lest any should think the toil might be insupportable, though these things may be had by labor and diligence, I assure myself there are those who delight extremely in vain pleasure, that take much more pains in England to enjoy it than I should do here [in New England] to gain wealth sufficient. And yet I think they should not have half such sweet content for our pleasure here is still gains; in England charges and loss. Here nature and liberty afford us that freely which in England we want, or it costs us dearly. What pleasure can be more than (being tired with any occasion ashore, in planting vines, fruits, or herbs, in contriving their own grounds, to the pleasure of their own minds, their fields, gardens, orchards, buildings, ships, and other works, &c) to recreate themselves before their own doors, in their own boats upon the sea, where man, woman, and child, with a small hook and line, by angling may take divers sorts of excellent fish at their pleasures? And is it not pretty sport to pull up two pence, six pence, and twelve pence as fast as you can haul and veer[4] a line? He is a very bad fisher [that] cannot kill in one day, with his hook and line, one, two, or three hundred cods, which dressed and dried, if they be sold there for ten shilling the hundred [pounds], though in England they will give more than twenty, may not both the servant, the master, and merchant be well content with this gain? If a man work but three days in seven he may get more than he can spend, unless he will be excessive. Now that carpenter, mason, gardener, tailor, smith, sailor, forgers,[5] or what other, may they not make this a pretty recreation, though they fish but an hour in the day, to take more than they eat in a week? Or if they will not eat it, because there is so much better choice, yet [they may] sell it or change it with the fishermen or merchants for anything they want. And what sport does yield a more pleasing content and less hurt or charge than angling with a hook and crossing the sweet air from isle to isle, over the silent streams of a calm sea? Wherein the most curious may find pleasure, profit, and content.

Thus, though all men be not fishers, yet all men, whatsoever, may in other matters do as well. For necessity does in these cases so rule a commonwealth, and each in their several functions, as their labors in their qualities, may be as profitable because there is a necessary mutual use of all.

For gentlemen, what exercise should more delight them than ranging daily those unknown parts, using fowling and fishing, for hunting and hawking? And yet you shall see the wild hawks give you some pleasure, in seeing them stoop[6] (six or seven after one another) an hour or two together at the schools of fish in the fair harbors, as those ashore [do] at a fowl, and never trouble nor torment yourselves with watching, mewing,[7] feeding, and attending them, nor kill a horse and man with running and crying, "See you not a hawk?" For hunting also, the woods, lakes and rivers afford not only chase sufficient for any that delight in that kind of toil or pleasure but such beast to hunt that besides the delicacy of their bodies for food, their skins are so rich as may well recompense thy daily labor with a Captain's pay.

For laborers, if those [in England] that sow hemp, rape,[8] turnips, parsnips, carrots, cabbage, and such like, give twenty, thirty, forty, fifty shilling yearly for an acre of ground, and meat, drink, and wages to use it and yet grow rich, when better or at least

---

[4] Let out.
[5] Metal workers.
[6] Swoop.

[7] Keeping in cages.
[8] Herb grown as a forage crop for hogs and sheep.

as good ground may be had [in New England] and cost nothing but labor, it seems strange to me any such should there grow poor.

My purpose is not to persuade children from their parents, men from their wives, nor servants from their masters; only such as with free consent may be spared. But that each parish or village, in city or country, that will but apparel[9] their fatherless children of thirteen or fourteen years of age, or young married people that have small wealth to live on, here by their labor may live exceedingly well. Provided always that first there be a sufficient power to command them, houses to receive them, means to defend them, and meet[10] provisions for them; for any place may be overlain,[11] and it is most necessary to have a fortress (ere this grow to practice) and sufficient masters (as carpenters, masons, fishers, fowlers, gardeners, husbandmen,[12] sawyers,[13] smiths, spinners, tailors, weavers, and such like) to take ten, twelve, or twenty, or as there is occasion, for apprentices. The masters by this may quickly grow rich; these apprentices their trades themselves to do the like, to a general and an incredible benefit for king and country, master and servant.

1616

[9] Prepare.
[10] Suitable.
[11] Overthrown.

[12] Farmers.
[13] Those who saw timber.

Alexander Anderson
Evening Amusements
woodcut c. 1820
(Print Collection. Miriam & Ira D. Wallach Division of Art, Prints and Photographs. The New York
Public Library. Astor, Lenox & Tilden Foundations.)

The Literature of Colonial America 1620–1776

A "Citty upon a Hill": New England

Colonial American literature was produced by men and women who first settled a rocky, sandy coastline that reaches into the Atlantic like a grappling hook. These Pilgrim and Puritan colonists aspired to be a "citty upon a hill," as the Massachusetts Puritan governor John Winthrop put it, though they coped at first with primitive conditions. In the 1600s they "forsooke a fruitful land, stately buildings, goodly gardens, orchards, dear friends, and near relations" to seek God's way in the "desert wilderness" of the New World.

The writings of the early explorers are multinational, but the literature of colonial America, north and south, in areas ultimately to become part of the United States, is principally English. It resulted from the tumultuous religious Reformation begun by Martin Luther (1483–1546) and spurred by the teachings of the French theologian John Calvin (1509–1564).

The Religious Background

By the late Middle Ages numerous Christians felt that the vital center of human life, the church, had strayed from its original mission and become corrupt. Protestant reformers argued that Scripture, not an institution or its trappings, was the essence of the Christian life. The authority of the pope came into question. As a result, in 1543, King Henry VIII formed the Church of England, a Protestant national church independent of Roman Catholicism and the pope. By English law citizens were required to obey its rules and observe its practices.

Thus, the monarch became the temporal authority with the church subject to the state. Conformity—or nonconformity—to established authority was a hallmark of this struggle. The nonconformists were called, scornfully at first, Puritans, for their efforts at purification. Some others, notably the Bradford group who migrated to Plymouth, Massachusetts, despaired of successful reforms and separated from the Church of England altogether. They took direction from the Bible (2 Corinthians 6:17): "Come out from among them and be ye separate, saith the Lord."

Meanwhile, Anglican church officials and agents of King James I (1566–1625) and of Charles I (1625–1649) made life difficult for all dissenters. "Nothing but the wide ocean and savage deserts," wrote the poet John Milton, "could hide and shelter . . . numbers of faithful and freeborn Englishmen . . . from the fury of the bishops."

One such group of "faithful and freeborn Englishmen" were the Plymouth Pilgrims, who represented a new kind of resident in America. Unlike the Jamestown colonists, the Pilgrims had no ambitions for riches. And they understood that a successful colony needed a sound financial basis, that it had to feed and sustain itself, and to be able to conduct trade. Since 1608 the Bradford group had lived in Holland, which afforded them religious freedom but "Dutchified" their lives. Fearing the loss of their cultural identity and religious intensity, they set sail on the *Mayflower* on September 16, 1620, with 149 aboard, forty-seven of them crewmen and officers. Their grim toll in that first American winter, when half of them died, can be traced in part to the two-month voyage on a diet deficient in fresh produce and to the cold and barren land where they settled.

Americans cherish the Pilgrims of the tiny Plymouth colony largely because of William Bradford's compelling account of it in *Of Plymouth Plantation* (1856), which he may have written in one of three "carved chairs" left in his will and doubtless transported on the *Mayflower*. Much more of our colonial literature, however, comes from the far less radical Puritan immigrants who arrived in a so-called Great Migration to the Massachusetts Bay Colony (1628–1643). They clustered in towns around current-day Boston and then extended into Connecticut and other parts of New England. Wherever they went, they and their descendants kept records of their experience in prose and verse.

The Puritans, like all immigrants to America, hoped to build a better life, one they defined largely in spiritual terms. Deploring the intractable corruption of the Church of England, they decided to build a church as pure as was humanly possible in New England. God seemed to direct them to do so through providential signs of catastrophe in their native land. King Charles I ascended to the English throne in 1625, a year in which the plague threatened London. He pressured Parliament to impose new, heavy taxes in a time of general high inflation and, in some trades, depression. In 1629 the king dissolved Parliament, stripping the populace of legislative representation.

Puritans like John Winthrop of Suffolk experienced these events personally. An attorney and landholder of high principles, he was dismayed by dishonesty at court and, though previously successful in his family's cloth trade, saw it sink in depression as prices rose and heavier taxes loomed. Mysteriously, he lost his attorney's license (perhaps for Puritan beliefs) and saw two friends imprisoned for tax resistance. Winthrop, a landholder with acreage planted in wheat, rye, and barley, was also a landlord responsible for his tenants and household servants, and a husband and father of seven children. He read God's message in this convergence of dire events and took drastic action. Within a year he arranged to transport his household and family to America to help build the spiritually exemplary "citty upon a hill."

The Voyage; the Landfall

At first these colonial immigrants lived in squalor brightened spiritually by their religious devotion and physically by the furnishings they managed to ship with them. Items like William Bradford's "six leather chairs," "great beer bowle," court cupboard, pewter dishes, and "red Turkey grogram suit of clothes" took up space below decks with the colony's supplies of firearms and ammunition, tools, and farming implements. In the Winthrop party, livestock (240 cattle, "about sixty horses") traveled in separate ships topside in open pens. Many animals died in the early spring Atlantic storms that made the colonists' shipboard lives miserable as well.

The sea voyage was a grim initiation for colonial living, especially for Puritan immigrants like the poet Anne Dudley Bradstreet, who was accustomed to certain middle-class comforts of the day. For three tempestuous months she—and many other women and children—slept in the stuffy "between-decks" area, with the main deck their roof, the ceiling of the cargo hold their floor. Bradstreet's husband and father, like the other men, slept in hammocks slung in every available space. The only heat came from the cooking stove, because the threat of fire prevented the use of candles or lanterns. Thus each day ended at sundown, when the passengers took to their beds.

Landfall presented its own complications. The *Arbella,* the flagship of the fleet, dropped anchor off the tiny, year-old settlement of Salem, Massachusetts, on June 12, 1630. "Some gentlemen and some of the women" were rowed ashore in shallops, and the scene before them must have looked like their own bleak futures. For Salem Plantation had, at most, forty dwellings, of which about a dozen were recognizable houses framed in oak and covered with pine boards roughly sawed or hewn with axes. Others were thatch-roofed cottages of one or two rooms with chimneys of logs or of wattle and daub (woven twigs and plaster) and windows of greased paper. The one "faire house," that of the Salem governor, had four rooms and an attic, a great central chimney of brick and fieldstone, a shingled roof, and probably small leaded windows of hand-blown, diamond-shaped panes of colored glass brought from England. Civilization itself was doubtless symbolized in that one house.

Yet the poet Anne Bradstreet, the diarist (and governor) Winthrop, and the writer of a notable historical letter, Thomas Dudley, could only have been sobered to see the wretched hovels of the less prosperous Salem colonists who lived in hillside excavations or in "English wigwams," described by one minister as "verie little and homely, made with small poles prick't into the ground and so bended and fastened at the tops and on the side, they are matted with boughs and covered with sedge and old mats." From Salem colonists, who according to glowing reports honored the newcomers with "a good venison pasty and good beer," came a grim story of overcrowding, of provisions in short supply, of such household necessities as soap produced by hand in the crudest fashion. No matter how spiritually elevated these Puritan writers and their fellow colonists felt, they knew the "city upon a hill" needed to do better. It was one thing for southern colonial writers a century later to satirize colonists for "belly-aches" from eating unripe fruit or to poke fun at their rustic lives in which "conversation's lost, and manners drowned." But Massachusetts Bay colonists intending to build a new Jerusalem hardly found such matters to be the grounds for humor. Salem, as Dudley confided, "pleased us not."

For the first years, nonetheless, living conditions remained primitive. Dudley, who was Anne Bradstreet's father, offers a valuable glimpse of the colonial writer at work. "In the throng of domestic [and public] business" he wrote a newsletter to the Lady Bridget, Countess of Lincoln, in March 1631 apologizing for written work that he suspected might suffer from interruption, distraction, and crude surroundings. "I have yet," he reported, "no table, nor other room to write in than by the fireside upon my knee, in this sharp winter; to which my family must have leave to resort, though they break good manners, and make me many times forget what I would say, and say what I would not." Dudley was not the only colonial writer to observe that as he wrote, the ink froze in his well.

Puritan Beliefs

What drove these New England colonists to put their lives on the line for an uncertain future? What thoughts sustained them and moved so many to write the histories and verses, the sermons and autobiographies that went far to shape the national identity of the people and the place that became the United States of America?

These Puritans and Pilgrims held in common one set of unshakable beliefs, most of which sound perplexing and harsh to modern Americans. They believed, first, that because Adam and Eve disobeyed God and fell from grace, all their heirs were also fallen and predestined to eternal punishment—except for an elect group redeemed by the suffering of Jesus Christ and chosen to be recipients of God's grace. They spoke of their doctrine in terms of covenants, the binding and solemn agreements made between two parties. In the Bible they discerned, first, a covenant of works made between God and Adam, who was to enjoy perpetual life in the Garden of Eden in return for total obedience to God. When Adam disobeyed, he committed the first or "original" sin, broke the covenant, fell from grace, and, together with Eve, was cast out of the Garden forever to toil in the world.

Later God made a second covenant, one of grace, with Abraham, whose children he promised to save unconditionally. The Puritans considered themselves descendants of Abraham, redeemed by Jesus Christ who was sent by God to show His mercy. These saved souls, an indeterminate but limited number called the "elect," were to be brought to a full consciousness of their condition by the ministry of the biblical word. The experience of saving grace was not usually swift or instantaneous, but slow and agonizing as the soul came into consciousness of its sin and worthlessness, often with the help of a minister's sermon; such awareness did not necessarily come in a church or meetinghouse. One New England immigrant, Thomas Shepard, got "dead drunk" on a Saturday night at college, awoke late "that Sabbath" with a hangover, and then "in shame and confusion . . . went out into the cornfields . . . where the Lord . . . did meet me with much sadness of heart and troubled my soul." It is no exaggeration to say that Puritan colonial literature arose from the private need to examine the inner life.

It is extremely difficult for modern readers to appreciate the attraction of such life and to understand why by 1642 some twenty thousand people had immigrated to New

England to enter into colonial life dominated by Puritan practices. It is helpful, perhaps, to be reminded that in England Puritanism reformulated the terms of society. On the basis of biblical (which is to say God's) authority, Puritanism found one person to be as good as another, no matter what that person's earthly social station was. Aristocracy might rule England, but Puritanism argued that the average man or woman might be one of God's elect and thus a spiritual aristocrat destined to inherit the heavens and the earth.

One article of faith especially connected Puritan spiritual life to the work of colonization. Writings from William Bradford and beyond show the conviction that the apocalyptic prophecy of the New Testament Book of Revelation was about to be fulfilled. Within the scheme of Christian history, the Puritans believed, the final events of earthly time were coming to a close. They had a method for determining this. Martin Luther had shown them how. Luther argued that historical events on earth matched the symbols in Revelation. These symbols thus became guides to the past and to the future. The difficulty lay in correlating biblical and earthly events accurately. In theological study the ministers were trained to interpret such biblical symbols as the ten-horned beast, the grapes of wrath, and the seven vials and to apply their meaning to such worldly events as war, plague, and royal oppression. To do so accurately was to know God's own timetable for the final events of human history. For according to Scripture, there would occur a period of severe earthly tumult and dissension, after which the Messiah, the Christ, would return to earth. At that point God would bind up Satan for one thousand years, the duration of the peaceful and harmonious millennium, to be followed by one final great battle that signified the end of the world and the eternal peace of the elect with God.

Puritan Literature

From the beginnings of settlement the Puritan and Pilgrim writers labored to justify American innovations to an English audience. Men like Thomas Dudley and women like his daughter Anne Bradstreet or her confrere Mary Rowlandson did not have much leisure to sit writing before the fire, even with makeshift lapboards in the icy depths of winter. Their literary record reflects ideals and hardships. Historical literature like Bradford's *Of Plymouth Plantation* (1856), Winthrop's *Journal* (1853), and such sermons as Jonathan Edwards's "Sinners in the Hands of an Angry God" (1741) testify to the New Englanders' urgent justification of socioreligious practices.

The American experience provided colonial writers with some disquieting subject matter. Chattel slavery, customarily associated with the South, existed in New England and mocked Puritan aspirations; in the late 1600s the worldly Puritan diarist Samuel Sewall wrote an antislavery tract. The Native Americans became another recurrent topic in colonial writing. Orthodox Puritan writers could not regard Indians with objective interest, since their stated goal of colonization was the conversion of these heathens to Christianity. Squanto's help to the Pilgrims seemed to be God's providence at work in the initial encounter between the English and the Indians. As the "heathens" soon became alarmed by the settlers' relentless encroachment on their lands, two uprisings occurred: the Pequot War (1635–1636), which Puritans considered God's test of their mettle, and the severe King Philip's War (1675), which seriously threatened English settlement and suggested to some that their city was failing.

Native Americans

Puritan relations with Native Americans became an important topic in narratives, autobiography, verse, and history. Mary Rowlandson's narrative, for instance, attempts to redeem her experience in captivity—and implicitly the pilgrimage of all white Christian New Englanders. Yet texts involving relations with the indigenous peoples were complex and filled with misunderstanding. A minority of Puritan colonists believed that the Native Americans were the remnants of one of the Ten Lost Tribes of Israel and therefore were Jews whom the Puritans felt obliged to try to convert to Christianity. A majority of the Puritan colonists, however, believed the "Barbarous Creatures," as Mary Rowlandson called the indigenous people, to be agents of Satan, embodiments of evil. The native peoples, on their part, regarded the natural world as an interrelational one in which humans, animals, plants, earth, water, rocks, sky, clouds—in sum, all matter—were bound together in sacred trust in kinship. The other-than-human beings held the same status as the human, and, as the Native American genesis narratives show, people and animals were subject to changes of form. Spiritual forces were sometimes benevolent, sometimes malevolent, but no such concept as land ownership or private property entered into Native American thought.

The Puritans, on the contrary, like their English counterparts in the South, believed themselves to be authorized by the biblical Book of Genesis to go forth and subdue the earth and take dominion over it as God's stewards. For them, land clearance, fencing, agriculture and artisanry in such work as metal smithing proved their legal right to possess New World property in a state of godly authorization. The tribal wars against them were understood as God's ways to test their strength and commitment, and also as Satan's exertion of evil. They had no concept of Native American social organization, spirituality or cultural practices, and for the most part looked down on the Indians, in the words of Daniel Gookin, as a "woeful, miserable, and deplorable" lot "that in sin hath reduced mankind into naturally, and especially as live without means of cultivating and civilizing . . . and not many degrees above beasts in matters of fact."

The Cultural Portfolio section on "The Ways of the Native Americans" reveals the efforts of English colonists to come to terms with peoples who seemed alien yet not altogether inhuman. Roger Williams's effort to decode the Indians' language and Robert Beverley's quasi-anthropological observations on Native Americans' social patterns mix with colonists' narratives of war-mongering, demonic Indians, and also with the remarkable narrative of Hannah Dustan, whose child was killed by Indians in King Philip's War and who, taken captive herself, fought back with a hatchet and took scalps of her own. Native Americans became a recurrent subject in early American literature, not only in seventeenth-century Puritan writings but in those of eighteenth-century plantation owners such as William Byrd of Westover and Thomas Jefferson.

Government Obedience

Internal trials and dissension were another important concern to the colonial writers, who felt that God tried them even as Satan worked to subvert them. It was one thing to decree an orderly society based, as Winthrop said, on "justice and mercy" but another to organize and sustain it. Puritan-Pilgrim culture was prone to superstition and intolerant of dissent, and by later standards it did not handle either well. Witchcraft and heresy were investigated and punished and were considered a legitimate preoccupation of writers seeking, in Puritan terms, to justify the ways of God to men.

Women

Dissension among the laity was especially painful for the Puritan community. In 1637 Anne Hutchinson, an influential parishioner of the prestigious Reverend John Cotton, proclaimed that the elect need not concern themselves with human law. She challenged the authenticity of civil and religious authority. One writer summarized the case against her: "The faithful ministers of Christ must have dung cast on their faces, and be no better than . . . opposers of Christ himself." Hutchinson's troubles were chronicled in Winthrop's *Journal* and in her trial transcript. She was brought to trial, found guilty, and, like Williams, banished from the Massachusetts Bay.

The treatment of Anne Hutchinson raises questions on the status of women in the literature of Puritan and colonial New England. It has been argued that a woman's domain was the family dwelling and its immediate surroundings, including milk houses, butteries, and cellars. The biblical model for the virtuous housewife was Bathsheba (Proverbs 31), exemplary for skills of household management and for charity. The colonial housewife was responsible for spinning, weaving and sewing, for making soap and preserving foodstuffs and beverages, such as cider, and overseeing the cooking and the laundering, especially of linens, and keeping household order. It has been noted that Mary Rowlandson survived her Indian captivity because she adroitly used the skills of a good housewife, sewing and knitting, for survival among captors in need of her needlework talents. A colonial woman also administered corporal punishment to children and any others in her charge, such as maids. If her husband was away temporarily, as Anne Bradstreet's Simon regularly was, tending to colonial business as governor, then she became a kind of "deputy husband" in the interim, relinquishing the role immediately after his return. The time-consuming occupations of household management left precious little time for a woman to write. Therefore Ann Bradstreet's accomplishment is all the more striking when set against her obligations. The woman who might attempt to influence events outside her domain, for instance the selection of a new minister, did so only indirectly.

Yet if Bathsheba provided the model of the virtuous housewife, the biblical Jael provided a quite different example—of the woman warriors as instanced in Hannah Dustan, who was just five days past childbirth when "Indian Salvages" captured her and marched her one hundred miles into the wilderness. Unlike captive Mary Rowlandson, who used her domestic talents to trade for life, Dustan "slew ten of the Indians, and returned with their scalps." The scriptural Jael (Judges V) had killed the army commander, Sisera, who tried to hide in her tent. So the Puritans had found their Jael. Hannah Dustan was hailed as a heroine by the leading Puritan clergymen who cited her deed as a sign from God that the New Israel, like the Old, would be saved and continue to find godly favor. Dustan, however, was not celebrated as a woman warrior but as a traditional wife and mother moved by egregious circumstances to act in an extraordinary way. Paradoxically, then, her deed reinforced her identity as an exemplary Puritan colonial wife and mother.

Colonial court records show yet another category of colonial woman. This type was cast as disturbing the social order. Court records show a number of women tried and punished for "disorderly violence," meaning unprovoked and random acts of assault on persons or property. It has been documented that political disobedience and riot in England were cause for the prosecution of women, and to some extent this pattern continued in America. Cases in which women hurled bricks at men, stoned and dismembered Indian captives, and destroyed neighbors' cornfields have been documented in the records of New England colonial towns.

Perhaps more disturbing to a patriarchal social order, however, was the example of Anne Hutchinson, whose story resonated well into the nineteenth century. Hutchinson's dissent was the transgression of gender boundaries by which worldly, magisterial, and ecclesiastical power relationships were maintained. Hutchinson's following at prayer meetings, in effect, provided her a "congregation" of her own, one that demonstrated the ability of a woman to interpret the word of God outside the structures of the church and its ministry. To read her trial transcript is virtually to hear the palpable relief on the part of Governor Winthrop and Reverend John Cotton at the critical moment when Hutchinson averred that God spoke directly to her. In Puritan terms, such a position was heresy and blasphemy. Thus Hutchinson was subject to conviction and punishment. Her case is an example of the delegitimation and criminalization that preserved the patriarchal Puritan status quo.

Subsequent generations have viewed Anne Hutchinson's brutal slaying by Indians on Long Island as an indication of Puritan harshness and have seen the execution and mutilation of Quakers in the same light. It is helpful to recall that the pluralistic America of the twentieth century was unlike anything the Puritans could have envisioned or desired. New Englanders fled a society they thought corrupted in spirit and circumstance and made tremendous personal sacrifices to live under what they understood to be God's direction. From their viewpoint, strict laws and orthodox practices were proper godly vigilance, not brutality, although it is understandable that a modern American might react negatively to them.

The colonists of the Great Migration and thereafter worked exhaustively to build their agricultural New Jerusalem. Some twenty years after the Winthrop group had looked at Salem in dismay, one colonist could boast that "this remote, rocky, barren, bushy, wild-woody wilderness . . . now through the mercy of Christ [has] become a second England for fertileness. In so short a space," he added, "that is indeed the wonder of the world."

A "Vale of Plenty": The South

Southern colonists did not come to America to found a city upon a hill. Their American dream was quite different. Captain John Smith's expression, "vale of plenty," captured the essence of the southern response to America. The vale, or valley, of plenty signified a fruitful garden, even a paradise, that could be attained with human effort. Two centuries of southern colonial writers saw their land as a natural paradise, not a howling wilderness. The Puritan might write of hardship in winter, but the southerner reports no such discomfort. In 1665 Robert Moray wrote an epistle describing life in the Carolinas:

> None can know the sweetness of it but he that tasts it. One ocular [visual] inspection, one aromatick smel of our woods, one hearing of the consert of our birds in those

woods would affect them more than 1000 reported stories let the authors be never so readible.

Southern colonists conceived of the good life in terms of a fertile valley that, industriously cultivated, could realistically become an American dream come true—as Robert Beverley put it, a "paradise improved." These colonists came from English villages and from cities like London and Bristol. Accordingly, they brought to America an ideal of English farm life and the Renaissance commitment to exploration and knowledge.

The colonial South included cultures of the Chesapeake Bay, Virginia, the Carolinas, and, in the eighteenth century, Georgia. The early southern writers were planters, merchants, artisans, and ministers, and they wrote in many forms, among them letters, personal journals, autobiographies, poems, sermons, and translations. Colonial southern writing enriched the national literature with satire, song, storytelling, and a spirit of exploration inherent in the English Renaissance. The southern ideal, expressed in literature and the fine arts, was that of country life. It was modeled on English farm life but intended to surpass it in the sylvan New World. Thus southern writers like Smith, Beverley, William Byrd II, and even the satirist Ebenezer Cooke elaborated the idea of America as a Canaan, a "vale" of plenty.

Southern colonists suffered the same shipboard travails as their counterparts in New England. Their justification for taking the land was similar to that of the Puritans. "We chanced in a lande," wrote Smith, "even as God made it, where we found only an idle, improvident, scattered people." Through two centuries the southerners negotiated treaties with that "scattered people" as they penetrated inland, cultivating the tobacco crop that depleted the richest soil, and which induced them to move on and to recruit workers—at first whites, then black slaves—for field cultivation. Southern colonists learned to expect harmful winter frosts but knew they could look forward to very long summers whose growing season averaged six to nine months. Daily life could be conducted in the outdoors in forms not possible in the North. Thus in 1705 Beverley could observe that "all their drudgeries of cookery, washing, dairies, etc., are performed in offices detached from the dwelling-houses, which by this means are kept cool and sweet."

The southern colonists, like those in the North, first constructed dwellings of mud and twigs, although even in 1608 or 1609 a visitor to Jamestown noticed that beautifully woven Indian mats decorated colonists' walls. In Maryland, as elsewhere, early colonists ate and slept on shipboard while they constructed a framed timber fort and built cottages onshore. By the 1660s brick kilns were in use in Jamestown and Henrico, Virginia, and bricklayers were at work constructing houses. Later in that century, and throughout the next, brickwork became decorative in checkerboard and diagonal patterns that were popular throughout the South. The simple, versatile, quickly constructed log house, which was introduced to Englishmen by Germans and Scandinavians, probably first appeared in America in the Carolinas. By the end of the colonial period, southern frontiersmen in western Virginia lived in it, as did some black slaves in "quarters" set at a distance from the main house.

Gardens complemented southern colonial houses at every socioeconomic level. They ranged from quadrangles of shrubs, flowers, and herbs to elaborate arrangements of terraces, mounds, ponds, and lakes modeled on English precedent but adapted to the new environment. Often decorative, edible, and medicinal vegetation was mixed together as ornamental gardens merged with the kitchen garden. And for some men and women interested in botany, medicine, and landscaping, the ornamental garden was a nursery and experiment station.

The legend of gracious southern living persists in twentieth-century movies and in the remaining eighteenth-century plantation houses and grounds open to tourists. Colonial texts document this quality of southern life as early as 1686, when a French traveler commented on his visit to Colonel William Fitzhugh's estate near Manannas, Virginia: "The Colonel's accommodations were . . . so ample that this company [of twenty] gave him no trouble at all; we were all supplied with beds . . . Col. Fitzhugh showed us the largest hospitality. He had store of good wine and other things to drink, and a frolic ensued."

Southern colonial life assumed its own social forms. If it lacked the visible community focal point of the meetinghouse, southerners were nonetheless joined together by waterways and rounds of visits. The men mustered for militia exercises at appointed times and places and attended sessions of court. Many families sojourned to Anglican and other church services. Even the roads themselves provided at times a forum for social life, as owners raced horses on them and wagered on the outcome.

Southern Intellectual Life

Southern colonial intellectual life in this agrarian culture was both broad and deep in spite of dispersed settlement patterns. Indian missionary work was one educational incentive, which John Brinsley, a Virginian, recognized in 1622 when he wrote that God had "ordained schooles of learning to be a principal means to reduce a barbarous people to civilitie." Formal education became a concern throughout the colonies. There were Jesuit schools in Catholic Maryland, a school for orphans founded in Georgia by the preacher George Whitefield, and a variety of private, parish, and tutorial schools elsewhere. The College of William and Mary, which Thomas Jefferson attended, was founded in 1693.

Religious life was richly varied in the colonial South. During the seventeenth century, the Anglican church (the Church of England) predominated, but Roman Catholics were appearing in all five southern colonies, as were various dissenters, including a few Puritans. With Lord Baltimore's founding of Maryland in 1634, Catholics had a colonial center. And Quaker missionaries were at work in Virginia in the mid-seventeenth century. After 1700, French and German Protestants, Lutherans, Baptists, and evangelical Presbyterians gained increasing religious influence in the South. They coexisted uneasily with the Anglican clergy, who overlooked the power of their evangelical fervor and so failed to take part in the religious movement known as the Great Awakening, a phenomenon in South and North alike.

Colonial writers of the South, like their northern counterparts, wrote much literature that was deliberately useful or purposeful. Such texts as Indian treaties, promotion tracts, sermons, and treatises on education or science or technology were intentionally utilitarian even though they all had aesthetic qualities. Yet an abundance of verse (elegies, pastoral poems, satires, ballads) and of journals, diaries, letters, essays, and autobiographies shows the powerful belletristic strain in writings of the region. It must be remembered as well that a literary tradition was in the making in the slave quarters. A growing population of black African slaves sang songs and kept alive the African folklore which, mingled with slaves' experience in the New World, would eventually find its way into formal writing in the nineteenth and twentieth centuries. Although some slaves learned to read and write (using these very skills in the eighteenth century to petition for their freedom), slaves by law were kept illiterate in the South and therefore had no opportunity in the colonial era to give written expression to their oral traditions. That flowering would have to wait a century. The record of extant southern literature of the seventeenth and eighteenth centuries is one principally of white writers.

Toward the Revolution: The Eighteenth Century

In 1726 the English bishop George Berkeley wrote a verse which American colonists, including Benjamin Franklin, liked to quote because it nourished confidence in the growth of American culture:

Westward the course of empire takes its way;
   The first four acts already past,
A fifth shall close the drama with the day;
   Time's noblest offspring is the last.

Berkeley's "Verses on the Prospect of Planting Arts and Learning in America" expressed the patriotic idea of a progressively westward-moving culture. Through the eighteenth century the idea of westward empire began to coincide with the concept of nationhood. The European movement known as the Enlightenment began to transform American thought and writing and to make possible the political and literary unification of the thirteen very different colonies.

The Enlightenment

In the eighteenth century scientists and philosophers posed serious challenge to the seventeenth-century mentality. As Sir Isaac Newton (1642–1727) formulated the laws of gravity and motion, John Locke (1633–1704) advanced the theory that knowledge is gained only by sensory perception. Newtonian thought embraced a pattern of ideas: that the universe is governed by immutable natural laws, that these laws constitute a harmonious system reflecting a benevolent and wise higher power, and that humankind desires to bring about a correspondingly harmonious, benevolent life on earth. Newton, a Christian, saw God as a cosmic geometrician. In so doing, he inadvertently fostered the Enlightenment idea of Deism, which weakened the power of traditional religious authority.

   The Deists, among them Benjamin Franklin, deduced the existence of God from the structure of the universe, not from the Bible. They rejected revealed religion and looked instead to the "simplicity of nature," which signified the "established order, and course of natural things." The scientist Robert Boyle, a follower of Newton, wrote that mathematical and mechanical principles were "the alphabet in which God wrote the world." By implication, human beings could comprehend the laws of the universe and, by the application of reason, arrange human affairs in a correspondingly rational, benevolent way. The Deists were less interested in theology than in the application of human reason to earthly problems. John Locke reinforced the position by emphasizing that individuals are not born with innate ideas of good or evil but that each is a blank slate or *tabula rasa* on which experience is inscribed to form character and personality. In eighteenth-century America, such Enlightenment ideas as the inevitability of progress, the efficacy of reason, and the perfectibility of man marked a distinct change in American literature. Concurrently, American writings were influenced by popular literary forms, including newspapers, and by social and religious patterns as well.

Living conditions in the colonies continued to vary in the eighteenth century. A well-off family would be likely to read colonial newspapers, twenty-six of which had been published weekly in 1765. They were literary, attempting to imitate the sophisticated style of English periodicals, especially the essays of Joseph Addison and Richard Steele.

Eighteenth-century booksellers, like many newspaper editors, depended on the professional classes for the bulk of their sales because books were terribly expensive. Personal libraries rarely exceeded twenty-five volumes and were dominated by the Bible, *The Pilgrim's Progress* (1678), sermons and tracts, almanacs, medical books, and practical and scientific treatises like *The Farmer's Companion* (1754) or Jared Eliot's *Essay on Field Husbandry* (1762).

Because the literacy rate was high (among white males, at least) in the South, the middle colonies, and especially New England, literary taste itself gradually became a value in colonial eighteenth-century America. Writers looked to the mother country for models, including those provided by Addison and Steele, John Dryden, Dr. Samuel Johnson, Jonathan Swift, and especially Alexander Pope, whose *Essay on Man* (1733–1734) went through forty-five American printings before the end of the century. Benjamin Franklin took full advantage of the exemplary lessons of these English figures, for he sought the approval of the American reading public. Consistently, his work addressed the subject of that virtue in a secular realm.

Jonathan Edwards and the Great Awakening

Religious life continued to be crucial to the colonial experience through the eighteenth century. Franklin's generation gave rise to a formidable theologian and metaphysician, Jonathan Edwards, whose thought and temperament so differed from Franklin's that it has become customary to view their careers as antithetical parts of the colonial mentality. Both men originated in Puritan New England and were deeply influenced by the scientific and philosophical writings of Newton and Locke. In Franklin those influences found expression in a progress-oriented, public-spirited ideology based on the religious assumptions of Deism, the Newtonian view of a God who did not participate directly in human affairs. In Edwards, however, Enlightenment thought led to a reformulation of Puritanism, with emphasis on the authenticity of feelings or affections as indices of God's disposition toward the individual. Love, said Edwards, "is not only one of the affections but it is the first and chief . . . and the fountain of all the affections."

Edward's stirring sermons placed him at the center of a series of religious revivals known as the Great Awakening, which was in large part a reaction against Deism and Newtonian science. Begun in the 1740s, this evangelical movement occurred in all colonies. It affected the Pennsylvania German Pietists, the Methodists, and the Baptists, Quakers, and Scotch-Irish Presbyterians in North Carolina, New Jersey, Connecticut, and Virginia. In several trips up and down the coast, the Methodist itinerant preacher George Whitefield (1714–1770) prayed that "grace in every heart might dwell," as the black poet Phillis Wheatley wrote in her elegy "On the Death of Rev. Mr. George Whitefield, 1770."

In 1740 Whitefield brought his evangelistic energies to New England, traveling west from Boston to Jonathan Edwards's Northampton, where he stayed with the Edwards family and preached in the parish church, moving Edwards to tears. Soon Edwards's own congregation—indeed the entire Holyoke Valley—was swept into the movement. Jonathan Edwards became its exponent. As a reader of John Locke in his student days, he understood the English philosopher's empiricism—yet Edwards saw in Lockean thought a potential antidote to the cold religiosity, which he felt had gradually corrupted the Puritan mission in the eighteenth century. He used Lockean thought to reaffirm Puritan doctrine, especially that of predestination.

The work of Edwards—in fact of all who participated in the Great Awakening—had significant implications for the American Revolution. The movement emphasized liberation from traditional authority and, in political terms, anticipated the eventual severance from England. Politically, the Great Awakening can be read as a struggle between the values of a distant, established authority and those of individuals in remote communities. It bred intercolonial communications and fostered collective resistance toward distant, more orthodox opponents.

Settlers and Skirmishes

The eighteenth century saw marked demographic changes in the American colonies, deriving from the Treaty of Utrecht (1713) in which the monarchies of England, France, Spain, and Holland agreed to renounce claims to each other's thrones and entered into commercial pacts. Temporarily, these pacts suppressed French and Spanish territorial designs and created a relatively stable Atlantic environment in which the colonies could undertake political and economic initiatives.

It is helpful to note the demographic changes in the decades before the Revolution. In 1713 English colonists comprised 90 percent of the population. During the next fifty years that proportion declined to less than 60 percent whereas the total colonial population increased fourfold. European colonists ventured to settle in the New World at a rate proportionally higher than at any previous time in American history. Germans found their way into Pennsylvania, western Maryland, Virginia, the Carolinas, and Georgia. Scotch-Irish settled from Maine to South Carolina in border areas, providing a buffer zone between settled habitations and the Indian-filled wilderness. By 1749 they accounted for nearly one-quarter of Pennsylvania's population. The French Protestants, the Huguenots, settled in the southern and middle colonies, while the Dutch established elaborate feudal estates in New York's Hudson Valley and controlled much of the colony's mercantile activity.

One-third to one-half of all white settlers who entered the New World before the Revolution arrived under contract ("indenture") for four to seven years' service in exchange for the costs of their transportation, food, clothing, and shelter. Most of these individuals and families fulfilled their contracts through work as field hands or household servants, though a few became artisans or teachers. Although a high mortality rate threatened this group, they were, technically at least, "free," when their period of bondage by contract ended. Not so the increasing slave population. Its numbers rose to upwards of one-half million by 1770, that is, 90 percent in the southern colonies. By the eve of the Revolution, African American slavery had developed into the "peculiar institution," with a century-long history of court cases that grappled with the contradictory views of slaves as property and as people. The virtues of freedom and of the free holding of land in a pluralistic society entered American literature in the writings of Franklin and, after the Revolution, in Michel Guillaume Jean de Crèvecoeur's *Letters from an American Farmer,* (c. 1774–1781/1782).

Intercolonial affairs did not proceed smoothly. The decades leading to the Revolution were fraught with tensions, even violence among the colonies and among ethnic and religious groups. For instance, fighting erupted between Connecticut and Pennsylvania in the 1750s over rival claims to Susquehanna land. And cities with large slave populations, like Charleston and New York, lived in continuous dread of riots and arson. Occasional labor insurrections, like that of the Greek and Italian immigrants in Florida in 1769, led to the virtual extinction of newly formed communities of the indentured. And Indian raids were a constant threat, especially during the French and Indian War (1756–1763).

In the decades leading up to the Revolutionary War, Britain found the colonists increasingly resistant to its policies, which often seemed capricious even to moderates. The Hat Act of 1732 and the Molasses Act of 1733, both unpopular measures to control colonial trade, had been countered with smuggling and commercial chicanery. The Stamp Act of 1765 met violent opposition. Tradesmen, artisans, and laborers joined in mass protests against the rather high tax levied on colonial newspapers, almanacs, advertisements, single-sheet or broadside publications, pamphlets, and legal documents. Colonial merchants agreed to boycott English goods, and the dissident "Sons of Liberty" intimidated or attacked British officials and destroyed their property.

When Parliament passed the Tea Act of 1773, colonial seaports united to prevent the unloading and sale of tea which, taxed by Britain, would still have been inexpensive to buy. The principle of unfair taxation, not the price of tea, was at issue when Samuel Adams's band of patriots disguised as Mohawks raided the British ships and dumped the tea chests into Boston Harbor. Immediately, other colonies applauded the gesture and decided to stage "tea parties" of their own. Since the following year, 1774, colonial relations with England had not improved, the first of two Continental Congresses convened at Philadelphia. The colonists would soon hear rhetoric like Thomas Paine's: in January 1776 he wrote, "Of more worth is one honest man to society, and in the sight of God, than all the crowned ruffians that ever lived."

Within months Thomas Jefferson would codify those sentiments in the Declaration of Independence, a document thematically characteristic of a new body of American literature. In one sense the ideals of "life, liberty, and the pursuit of happiness" were characteristic of the American Enlightenment and so place Jefferson and the signers of the declaration fully in their contemporary moment.

Yet the ideology of the American Revolution has a long foreground in colonial American literature. Specific to its own cultural and historical moment, indebted to Enlightenment, science, and religion, the last and latest writings of the American colonists also hark back as far as Captain John Smith's Jamestown and William Bradford's Plymouth. Writings from the "vale of plenty" and from the Puritan "city upon a hill" anticipate the literature of the American Revolution.

Further Reading:

S. Ahlstrom, *A Religious History of the American People*, 1972.

L. Ziff, *Puritanism in America: New Culture in a New World*, 1973.

H. May, *The Enlightenment in America*, 1976.

E. Emerson, *Puritanism in America, 1620–1750*, 1977.

S. Bercovitch, *The American Journal*, 1978.

R. Davis, *The Intellectual Life of the Colonial South*, 3 vols., 1978.

L. Ulrich, *Good Wives: Image and Reality in the Lives of Women in New England 1650–1750*, 1980.

J. Stilgoe, *Common Landscape of America, 1580–1845*, 1982.

W. Cronon, *Changes in the Land: Indians, Colonists, and the Ecology of New England*, 1983.

A. Lang, *Prophetic Woman: Anne Hutchinson and the Problem of Dissent in the Literature of New England*, 1987.

William Bradford
1590–1657

William Bradford is the writer synonymous with the Pilgrims, the *Mayflower,* and the first Thanksgiving. As a colonist, he was a governor engaged for more than thirty years in religious, social, and economic problems. His history of the New England pilgrims, *Of Plymouth Plantation*, stands as one of the major works of colonial literature. In it Bradford recorded the struggles of the Plymouth, Massachusetts, Pilgrims in language he called "a plain style, with singular regard unto the simple truth in all things." Bradford's history tells its readers of the mutual love and affection of the *Mayflower* group. It commends the heroism of individuals and laments the inevitable weaknesses of bad judgment, cowardice, and greed. Central to the work is the very question of the colonists' survival in the New World.

Bradford was born in Austerfield, Yorkshire, of modestly prosperous parents. After the boy's father died, Bradford's mother remarried, and William was raised by uncles and grandparents who taught him agriculture and animal husbandry. Unlike the numerous university-trained Puritan writers who moved in intellectual circles, Bradford prepared to become a farmer.

William's plans changed in his mid-teens, when he heard the sermons of Richard Clyfton and was so stirred by that, to the dismay of his family and the "scoff" of his neighbors, that he left home to join the Scrooby Pilgrims, who believed that the Church of England was so thoroughly corrupted that they had no alternative but to separate from it. These Pilgrims wanted to reform or purify their church. Their model was the Old Testament, with Scripture alone as their highest authority. By separating from the national church however, the Scrooby congregation committed treason and was thereafter an outlaw band.

The Scrooby Pilgrims' sojourn in the Netherlands may seem to be a detour on the way to America. In fact, they planned in 1607 to move to the Low Countries in order to find "freedom of religion for all men." Bradford went with them to Amsterdam in

1608 and on to Leyden in the following year. There they worshiped "God amongst themselves" while Bradford earned his living as a weaver and studied several languages, including Dutch, French, Latin, and Greek. Ten years passed, and the group saw itself aging and thinned by death. Fearful of dispersal, impoverished, and worried about the encroachment of Dutch ways into their lives and those of their children, the group decided to move again.

The Bradford party sailed on the *Mayflower* in September 1620 and reached Cape Code, Massachusetts, after a two-month voyage in crowded conditions and stormy weather. They decided to stay in New England, but because they lacked royal title to its land, they were vulnerable to charges that their officials lacked legal authority. The Bradford group thus formulated the Mayflower Compact, legitimating the "Civil Body Politick." It was the first New World document on democratic government. Bradford was one of the signers and soon became a colonial leader. Upon the death of John Carver, the Pilgrim governor, Bradford was elected to that office; he was reelected thirty times between 1621 and 1656.

Bradford's *Of Plymouth Plantation,* begun in 1630, shows more concern for spiritual wealth than for material expectations in America, which Bradford called a "roost" or "resting place." At several points he linked the Plymouth group to the Old Testament Israelites led by Moses. The Pilgrims, too, were a chosen people journeying through the wilderness in search of the Promised Land. They, like the Massachusetts Bay Puritans, anticipated the commencement of the Christian millennium, the harvest of the Lord characterized by "the Spirit of God and His grace" on earth. They understood the millennium to be a state of spiritual community and not a materialistic utopia. He thus wrote *Of Plymouth Plantation* to record God's providential work among the colonists and to remind readers that the Pilgrims must once again return to their original religious mission. Bradford's readers would surely have heard the language of Scripture in the rhythms and the references of his prose, for the Bible was his manual of style and rhetoric, as well as the record of God's truth.

Further Reading:
S. E. Morison, *Builders of the Bay Colony*, 1930, 1958.   G. Langdon, *Pilgrim Colony*, 1966.
B. Smith, *Bradford of Plymouth*, 1951.   K. Callrey, *The Mayflower*, 1974.

Text:
Of Plymouth Plantation, ed. S. E. Morison, 1952, 1959.

from Of Plymouth Plantation

And first of the occasion and inducements thereunto; the which, that I may truly unfold, I must begin at the very root and rise of the same. The which I shall endeavour to manifest in a plain style, with singular regard unto the simple truth in all things; at least as near as my slender judgment can attain the same.

Chapter IX: Of Their Voyage, and How They Passed the Sea; and of Their Safe Arrival at Cape Cod

September 6. These troubles being blown over, and now all being compact together in one ship, they put to sea again with a prosperous wind, which continued divers days together, which was some encouragement unto them; yet, according to the usual manner, many were afflicted with seasickness. And I may not omit here a special work of God's providence. There was a proud and very profane young man, one of the seamen, of a lusty, able body, which made him the more haughty; he would always be contemning the poor people in their sickness and cursing them daily with grievous execrations; and did not let to tell them that he hoped to help to cast half of them overboard before they came to their journey's end, and to make merry with what they had; and if he were by any gently reproved, he would curse and swear most bitterly. But it pleased God before they came half seas over, to smite this young man with a grievous disease, of which he died in a desperate manner, and so was himself the first that was thrown overboard. Thus his curses light on his own head, and it was an astonishment to all his fellows for they noted it to be the just hand of God upon him.

After they had enjoyed fair winds and weather for a season, they were encountered many times with cross winds and met with many fierce storms with which the ship was shroudly shaken, and her upper works made very leaky; and one of the main beams in the midships was bowed and cracked, which put them in some fear that the ship could not be able to perform the voyage. So some of the chief of the company, perceiving the mariners to fear the sufficiency of the ship as appeared by their mutterings, they entered into serious consultation with the master and other officers of the ship, to consider in time of the danger, and rather to return than to cast themselves into a desperate and inevitable peril. And truly there was great distraction and difference of opinion amongst the mariners themselves; fain would they do what could be done for their wages' sake (being now near half the seas over) and on the other hand they were loath to hazard their lives too desperately. But in examining of all opinions, the master and others affirmed they knew the ship to be strong and firm under water; and for the buckling of the main beam, there was a great iron screw the passengers brought out of Holland, which would raise the beam into his place; the which being done, the carpenter and master affirmed that with a post put under it, set firm in the lower deck and otherways bound, he would make it sufficient. And as for the decks and upper works, they would caulk them as well as they could, and though with the working of the ship they would not long keep staunch, yet there would otherwise be no great danger, if they did not overpress her with sails. So they committed themselves to the will of God and resolved to proceed.

In sundry of these storms the winds were so fierce and the seas so high, as they could not bear a knot of sail, but were forced to hull[1] for divers days together. And in one of them, as they thus lay at hull in a mighty storm, a lusty young man called John Howland, coming upon some occasion above the gratings was, with a seele[2] of the ship,

---

[1] To drift with the wind under short sail, typically in a storm.

[2] A roll or a pitch.

thrown into sea; but it pleased God that he caught hold of the topsail halyards which hung overboard and ran out at length. Yet he held his hold (though he was sundry fathoms under water) till he was hauled up by the same rope to the brim of the water, and then with a boat hook and other means got into the ship again and his life saved. And though he was something ill with it, yet he lived many years after and became a profitable member both in church and commonwealth. In all this voyage there died but one of the passengers, which was William Butten, a youth, servant to Samuel Fuller, when they drew near the coast.

But to omit other things (that I may be brief) after long beating at sea they fell with that land which is called Cape Cod; the which being made and certainly known to be it, they were not a little joyful. After some deliberation had amongst themselves and with the master of the ship, they tacked about and resolved to stand for the southward (the wind and weather being fair) to find some place about Hudson's River for their habitation.[3] But after they had sailed that course about half the day, they fell amongst dangerous shoals and roaring breakers, and they were so far entangled therewith as they conceived themselves in great danger; and the wind shrinking upon them withal, they resolved to bear up again for the Cape and thought themselves happy to get out of those dangers before night overtook them, as by God's good providence they did. And the next day they got into the Cape Harbor where they rid in safety.

A word or two by the way of this cape. It was thus first named by Captain Gosnold and his company, Anno 1602, and after by Captain Smith was called Cape James; but it retains the former name amongst seamen. Also, that point which first showed those dangerous shoals unto them they called Point Care, and Tucker's Terrour; but the French and Dutch to this day call it Malabar by reason of those perilous shoals and the losses they have suffered there.

Being thus arrived in a good harbor, and brought safe to land, they fell upon their knees and blessed the God of Heaven who had brought them over the vast and furious ocean, and delivered them from all the perils and miseries thereof, again to set their feet on the firm and stable earth, their proper element. And no marvel if they were thus joyful, seeing wise Seneca[4] was so affected with sailing a few miles on the coast of his own Italy, as he affirmed, that he had rather remain twenty years on his way by land than pass by sea to any place in a short time, so tedious and dreadful was the same unto him.

But here I cannot but stay and make a pause, and stand half amazed at this poor people's present condition; and so I think will the reader, too, when he well considers the same. Being thus passed the vast ocean, and a sea of troubles before in their preparation (as may be remembered by that which went before), they had now no friends to welcome them nor inns to entertain or refresh their weatherbeaten bodies; no houses or much less towns to repair to, to seek for succour. It is recorded in Scripture as a mercy to the Apostle and his shipwrecked company, that the barbarians showed them no small kindness in refreshing them, but these savage barbarians, when they met with them (as after will appear) were readier to fill their sides full of arrows than otherwise. And for the season it was winter, and they that know the winters of that country know

---

[3] The English were aware of Dutch claims to the area but did not honor those claims. The Pilgrims hoped to be the first to colonize the area, which the Dutch did not settle until six years later.

[4] Lucius Annaeus Seneca (ca. 4 B.C.–A.D. 65), Roman statesman and philosopher.

them to be sharp and violent, and subject to cruel and fierce storms, dangerous to travel to known places, much more to search an unknown coast. Besides, what could they see but a hideous and desolate wilderness, full of wild beasts and wild men—and what multitudes there might be of them they knew not. Neither could they, as it were, go up to the top of Pisgah[5] to view from this wilderness a more goodly country to feed their hopes; for which way soever they turned their eyes (save upward to the heavens) they could have little solace or content in respect of any outward objects. For summer being done, all things stand upon them with a weather-beaten face, and the whole country, full of woods and thickets, represented a wild and savage hue. If they looked behind them, there was the mighty ocean which they had passed and was now as a main bar and gulf to separate them from all the civil parts of the world. If it be said they had a ship to succour them, it is true; but what heard they daily from the master and company? But that with speed they should look out a place (with their shallop) where they would be, at some near distance; for the season was such as he would not stir from thence till a safe harbor was discovered by them, where they would be, and he might go without danger; and that victuals consumed apace but he must and would keep sufficient for themselves and their return. Yea, it was muttered by some that if they got not a place in time, they would turn them and their goods ashore and leave them. Let it also be considered what weak hopes of supply and succour they left behind them, that might bear up their minds in this sad condition and trials they were under; and they could not but be very small. It is true, indeed, the affections and love of their brethren at Leyden was cordial and entire towards them, but they had little power to help them or themselves; and how the case stood between them and the merchants at their coming away hath already been declared.

What could now sustain them but the Spirit of God and His grace? May not and ought not the children of these fathers rightly say: "Our fathers were Englishmen which came over this great ocean, and were ready to perish in this wilderness; but they cried unto the Lord, and He heard their voice and looked on their adversity,"[6] etc. "Let them therefore praise the Lord, because He is good: and His mercies endure forever." "Yea, let them which have been redeemed of the Lord, shew how He hath delivered them from the hand of the oppressor. When they wandered in the desert wilderness out of the way, and found no city to dwell in, both hungry and thirsty, their soul was overwhelmed in them. Let them confess before the Lord His loving-kindness and His wonderful works before the sons of men."[7]

Chapter X: Showing How They Sought Out a Place of Habitation; and What Befell Them Thereabout

Being thus arrived at Cape Cod the 11th of November, and necessity calling them to look out a place for habitation (as well as the master's and mariners' importunity); they having brought a large shallop with them out of England, stowed in quarters in the ship,

---

[5] Deuteronomy 33:34: "And Moses went up . . . to the top of Pisgah . . . and the Lord showed him all the land of Gilead . . . unto the utmost sea."

[6] Deuteronomy 26:5, 7.
[7] Psalm 107:1–5, 8.

they now got her out and set their carpenters to work to trim her up; but being much bruised and shattered in the ship with foul weather, they saw she would be long in mending. Whereupon a few of them tendered themselves to go by land and discover those nearest places, whilst the shallop was in mending; and the rather because as they went into that harbor there seemed to be an opening some two or three leagues off, which the master judged to be a river. It was conceived there might be some danger in the attempt, yet seeing them resolute, they were permitted to go, being sixteen of them well armed under the conduct of Captain Standish, having such instructions given them as was thought meet.

They set forth the 15th of November; and when they had marched about the space of a mile by the seaside, they espied five or six persons with a dog coming towards them, who were savages; but they fled from them and ran up into the woods, and the English followed them, partly to see if they could speak with them, and partly to discover if there might not be more of them lying in ambush. But the Indians seeing themselves thus followed, they again forsook the woods and ran away on the sands as hard as they could, so as they could not come near them but followed them by the track of their feet sundry miles and saw that they had come the same way. So, night coming on, they made their rendezvous and set out their sentinels, and rested in quiet that night; and the next morning followed their track till they had headed a great creek and so left the sands, and turned another way into the woods. But they still followed them by guess, hoping to find their dwellings; but they soon lost both them and themselves, falling into such thickets as were ready to tear their clothes and armor in pieces; but were most distressed for want of drink. But at length they found water and refreshed themselves, being the first New England water they drunk of, and was now in great thirst as pleasant unto them as wine or beer had been in foretimes.

Afterwards they directed their course to come to the other shore, for they knew it was a neck of land they were to cross over, and so at length got to the seaside and marched to this supposed river, and by the way found a pond of clear, fresh water, and shortly after a good quantity of clear ground where the Indians had formerly set corn, and some of their graves. And proceeding further they saw new stubble where corn had been set the same year; also they found where lately a house had been, where some planks and a great kettle was remaining, and heaps of sand newly paddled with their hands. Which, they digging up, found in them divers fair Indian baskets filled with corn, and some in ears, fair and good, of divers colours, which seemed to them a very goodly sight (having never seen any such before). This was near the place of that supposed river they came to seek, unto which they went and found it to open itself into two arms with a high cliff of sand in the entrance but more like to be creeks of salt water than any fresh, for aught they saw; and that there was good harborage for their shallop, leaving it further to be discovered by their shallop, when she was ready. So, their time limited them being expired, they returned to the ship lest they should be in fear of their safety; and took with them part of the corn and buried up the rest. And so, like the men from Eshcol, carried with them of the fruits of the land and showed their brethren; of which, and their return, they were marvelously glad and their hearts encouraged.

After this, the shallop being got ready, they set out again for the better discovery of this place, and the master of the ship desired to go himself. So there went some thirty men but found it to be no harbor for ships but only for boats. There was also found two of their houses covered with mats, and sundry of their implements in them, but the people were run away and could not be seen. Also there was found more of their corn and of their beans of various colours; the corn and beans they brought away, purposing to give them full satisfaction when they should meet with any of them as, about some six months afterward they did, to their good content.

And here is to be noted a special providence of God, and a great mercy to this poor people, that here they got seed to plant them corn the next year, or else they might have starved, for they had none nor any likelihood to get any till the season had been past, as the sequel did manifest. Neither is it likely they had had this, if the first voyage had not been made, for the ground was now all covered with snow and hard frozen; but the Lord is never wanting unto His in their greatest needs; let His holy name have all the praise.

The month of November being spent in these affairs, and much foul weather falling in, the 6th of December they sent out their shallop again with ten of their principal men and some seamen, upon further discovery, intending to circulate that deep bay of Cape Cod. The weather was very cold and it froze so hard as the spray of the sea lighting on their coats, they were as if they had been glazed. Yet that night betimes they got down into the bottom of the bay, and as they drew near the shore they saw some ten or twelve Indians very busy about something. They landed about a league or two from them, and had much ado to put ashore anywhere—it lay so full of flats. Being landed, it grew late and they made themselves a barricado with logs and boughs as well as they could in the time, and set out their sentinel and betook them to rest, and saw the smoke of the fire the savages made that night. When morning was come they divided their company, some to coast along the shore in the boat, and the rest marched through the woods to see the land, if any fit place might be for their dwelling. They came also to the place where they saw the Indians the night before, and found they had been cutting up a great fish like a grampus,[8] being some two inches thick of fat like a hog, some pieces whereof they had left by the way. And the shallop found two more of these fishes dead on the sands, a thing usual after storms in that place, by reason of the great flats of sand[9] that lie off.

So they ranged up and down all that day, but found no people, nor any place they liked. When the sun grew low, they hasted out of the woods to meet with their shallop, to whom they made signs to come to them into a creek hard by, the which they did at high water; of which they were very glad, for they had not seen each other all that day since the morning. So they made them a barricado as usually they did every night, with logs, stakes and thick pine boughs, the height of a man, leaving it open to leeward, partly to shelter them from the cold and wind (making their fire in the middle and lying round about it) and partly to defend them from any sudden assaults of the savages, if they should surround them; so being very weary, they betook them to rest. But about midnight they heard a hideous and great cry, and their sentinel called "Arm! arm!" So they bestirred them and stood to their arms and shot off a couple of muskets, and then the noise ceased. They concluded it was a company of wolves or such like wild beasts, for one of the seamen told them he had often heard such a noise in Newfoundland.

So they rested till about five of the clock in the morning; for the tide, and their purpose to go from thence, made them be stirring betimes. So after prayer they prepared for breakfast, and it being day dawning it was thought best to be carrying things down to the boat. But some said it was not best to carry the arms down, others said they would be the

---

[8] Large sea mammal related to whales, dolphins, and porpoises.

[9] i.e., sand bars

readier, for they had lapped them up in their coats from the dew; but some three or four would not carry theirs till they went themselves. Yet as it fell out, the water being not high enough, they laid them down on the bank side and came up to breakfast.

But presently, all on the sudden, they heard a great and strange cry, which they knew to be the same voices they heard in the night, though they varied their notes; and one of their company being abroad came running in and cried, "Men, Indians! Indians!" And withal, their arrows came flying amongst them. Their men ran with all speed to recover their arms, as by the good providence of God they did. In the meantime, of those that were there ready, two muskets were discharged at them, and two more stood ready in the entrance of their rendezvous but were commanded not to shoot till they could take full aim at them. And the other two charged again with all speed, for there were only four had arms there, and defended the barricado, which was first assaulted. The cry of the Indians was dreadful, especially when they saw their men run out of the rendezvous toward the shallop to recover their arms, the Indians wheeling about upon them. But some running out with coats of mail on, and cutlasses in their hands, they soon got their arms and let fly amongst them and quickly stopped their violence. Yet there was a lusty man, and no less valiant, stood behind a tree within half a musket shot, and let his arrows fly at them; he was seen [to] shoot three arrows, which were all avoided. He stood three shots of a musket, till one taking full aim at him and made the bark or splinters of the tree fly about his ears, after which he gave an extraordinary shriek and away they went, all of them. They left some to keep the shallop and followed them about a quarter of a mile and shouted once or twice, and shot off two or three pieces, and so returned. This they did that they might conceive that they were not afraid of them or any way discouraged.

Thus it pleased God to vanquish their enemies and give them deliverance; and by His special providence so to dispose that not any one of them were either hurt or hit, though their arrows came close by them and on every side [of] them; and sundry of their coats, which hung up in the barricado, were shot through and through. Afterwards they gave God solemn thanks and praise for their deliverance, and gathered up a bundle of their arrows and sent them into England afterward by the master of the ship, and called that place the First Encounter.

From hence they departed and coasted all along but discerned no place likely for harbor; and therefore hasted to a place that their pilot (one Mr. Coppin who had been in the country before) did assure them was a good harbor, which he had been in, and they might fetch it before night; of which they were glad for it began to be foul weather.

After some hours' sailing it began to snow and rain, and about the middle of the afternoon the wind increased and the sea became very rough, and they broke their rudder, and it was as much as two men could do to steer her with a couple of oars. But their pilot bade them be of good cheer for he saw the harbor; but the storm increasing, and night drawing on, they bore what sail they could to get in, while they could see. But herewith they broke their mast in three pieces and their sail fell overboard in a very grown sea, so as they had like to have been cast away. Yet by God's mercy they recovered themselves, and having the flood with them, struck into the harbor. But when it came to, the pilot was deceived in the place, and said the Lord be merciful unto them for his eyes never saw that place before; and he and the master's mate would have run her ashore in a cove full of breakers before the wind. But a lusty seaman which steered bade those which rowed, if they were men, about with her or else they were all cast away; the which they did with speed. So he bid them be of good cheer and row lustily, for there was a fair sound before them, and he doubted not but they should find one place or other where they might ride in safety. And though it was very dark and rained sore, yet in the end they got under the lee of a small island and remained there all that night in safety. But they knew not this to be an island till morning, but were divided in their minds; some would keep the boat for fear they might be amongst the Indians, others were so wet and cold they could not endure but got ashore, and with much ado got fire (all things being so wet); and the rest were glad to come to them, for after midnight the wind shifted to the northwest and it froze hard.

But though this had been a day and night of much trouble and danger unto them, yet God gave them a morning of comfort and refreshing (as usually He doth to His children) for the next day was a fair, sunshining day, and they found themselves to be on an island secure from the Indians, where they might dry their stuff, fix their pieces and rest themselves; and gave God thanks for His mercies in their manifold deliverances. And this being the last day of the week, they prepared there to keep the Sabbath.

On Monday they sounded the harbor and found it fit for shipping, and marched into the land and found divers cornfields and little running brooks, a place (as they supposed) fit for situation. At least it was the best they could find, and the season and their present necessity made them glad to accept of it. So they returned to their ship again with this news to the rest of their people, which did much comfort their hearts.

On the 15th of December they weighed anchor to go to the place they had discovered, and came within two leagues of it, but were fain to bear up again; but the 16th day, the wind came fair, and they arrived safe in this harbor. And afterwards took better view of the place, and resolved where to pitch their dwelling; and the 25th day began to erect the first house for common use to receive them and their goods.

from *Chapter XI: The Remainder of Anno 1620*

[The Mayflower Compact]

I shall a little return back, and begin with a combination made by them before they came ashore; being the first foundation of their government in this place. Occasioned partly by the discontented and mutinous speeches that some of the strangers amongst them had let fall from them in the ship: That when they came ashore they would use their own liberty, for none had power to command them, the patent they had being for Virginia and not for New England, which belonged to another government, with which the Virginia Company had nothing to do. And partly that such an act by them done, this their condition considered, might be as firm as any patent, and in some respects more sure.

The form was as followeth:

IN THE NAME OF GOD, AMEN.

We whose names are underwritten, the loyal subjects of our dread Sovereign Lord King James, by the Grace of God of Great Britain, France, and Ireland King, Defender of the Faith, etc.

Having undertaken, for the Glory of God and advancement of the Christian Faith and Honour of our King and Country, a Voyage to plant the First Colony in the Northern Parts of Virginia, do by these presents solemnly and mutually in the presence of God and one of another, Covenant and Combine ourselves together into a

Civil Body Politic, for our better ordering and preservation and furtherance of the ends aforesaid; and by virtue hereof to enact, constitute and frame such just and equal Laws, Ordinances, Acts, Constitutions and Offices, from time to time, as shall be thought most meet and convenient for the general good of the Colony, unto which we promise all due submission and obedience. In witness whereof we have hereunder subscribed our names at Cape Cod, the 11th of November, in the year of the reign of our Sovereign Lord King James, of England, France and Ireland the eighteenth, and of Scotland the fifty-fourth. Anno Domini 1620.

After this they chose, or rather confirmed, Mr. John Carver (a man godly and well approved amongst them) their Governor for that year. And after they had provided a place for their goods, or common store (which were long in unlading for want of boats, foulness of the winter weather and sickness of divers) and begun some small cottages for their habitation; as time would admit, they met and consulted of laws and orders, both for their civil and military government as the necessity of their condition did require, still adding thereunto as urgent occasion in several times, and as cases did require.

In these hard and difficult beginnings they found some discontents and murmurings arise amongst some, and mutinous speeches and carriages in other; but they were soon quelled and overcome by the wisdom, patience, and just and equal carriage of things, by the Governor and better part, which clave faithfully together in the main.

[The Starving Time]

But that which was most sad and lamentable was, that in two or three months' time half of their company died, especially in January and February, being the depth of winter, and wanting houses and other comforts; being infected with the scurvy and other diseases which this long voyage and their inaccommodate condition had brought upon them. So as there died some times two or three of a day in the foresaid time, that of 100 and odd persons, scarce fifty remained. And of these, in the time of most distress, there was but six or seven sound persons who to their great commendations, be it spoken, spared no pains night nor day, but with abundance of toil and hazard of their own health, fetched them wood, made them fires, dressed them meat, made their beds, washed their loathsome clothes, clothed and unclothed them. In a word, did all the homely and necessary offices for them which dainty and queasy stomachs cannot endure to hear named; and all this willingly and cheerfully, without any grudging in the least, showing herein their true love unto their friends and brethren; a rare example and worthy to be remembered. Two of these seven were Mr. William Brewster, their reverend Elder, and Myles Standish, their Captain and military commander, unto whom myself and many others were much beholden in our low and sick condition. And yet the Lord so upheld these persons as in this general calamity they were not at all infected either with sickness or lameness. And what I have said of these I may say of many others who died in this general visitation, and others yet living; that whilst they had health, yea, or any strength continuing, they were not wanting to any that had need of them. And I doubt not but their recompense is with the Lord.

But I may not here pass by another remarkable passage not to be forgotten. As this calamity fell among the passengers that were to be left here to plant, and were hasted ashore and made to drink water that the seamen might have the more beer, and one in his sickness desiring but a small can of beer, it was answered that if he were their own father he should have none. The disease began to fall amongst them also, so as almost half of their company died before they went away, and many of their officers and lustiest men, as the boatswain, gunner, three quartermasters, the cook and others. At which the Master was something strucken and sent to the sick ashore and told the Governor he should send for beer for them that had need of it, though he drunk water homeward bound.

But now amongst his company there was far another kind of carriage in this misery than amongst the passengers. For they that before had been boon companions in drinking and jollity in the time of their health and welfare, began now to desert one another in this calamity, saying they would not hazard their lives for them, they should be infected by coming to help them in their cabins; and so, after they came to lie by it, would do little or nothing for them but, "if they died, let them die." But such of the passengers as were yet aboard showed them what mercy they could, which made some of their hearts relent, as the boatswain (and some others) who was a proud young man and would often curse and scoff at the passengers. But when he grew weak, they had compassion on him and helped him; then he confessed he did not deserve it at their hands, he had abused them in word and deed. "Oh!" (saith he) "you, I now see, show your love like Christians indeed one to another, but we let one another lie and die like dogs." Another lay cursing his wife, saying if it had not been for her he had never come this unlucky voyage, and anon cursing his fellows, saying he had done this and that for some of them; he had spent so much and so much amongst them, and they were now weary of him and did not help him, having need. Another gave his companion all he had, if he died, to help him in his weakness; he went and got a little spice and made him a mess of meat once or twice. And because he died not so soon as he expected, he went amongst his fellows and swore the rogue would cozen him, he would see him choked before he made him any more meat; and yet the poor fellow died before morning.

[Indian Relations]

All this while the Indians came skulking about them, and would sometimes show themselves aloof off, but when any approached near them, they would run away; and once they stole away their tools where they had been at work and were gone to dinner. But about the 16th of March, a certain Indian came boldly amongst them and spoke to them in broken English, which they could well understand but marveled at it. At length they understood by discourse with him, that he was not of these parts, but belonged to the eastern parts where some English ships came to fish, with whom he was acquainted and could name sundry of them by their names, amongst whom he had got his language. He became profitable to them in acquainting them with many things concerning the state of the country in the east parts where he lived, which was afterwards profitable unto them; as also of the people here, of their names, number and strength, of their situation and distance from this place, and who was chief amongst them. His name was Samoset. He told them also of another Indian whose name was Squanto, a native of this place, who had been in England and could speak better English than himself.

Being, after some time of entertainment and gifts dismissed, a while after he came again, and five more with him, and they brought again all the tools that were stolen away before, and made way for the coming of their great Sachem, called Massasoit. Who, about four or five days after, came with the chief of his friends and other attendance, with the aforesaid Squanto. With whom, after friendly entertainment and some gifts given him, they made a peace with him (which hath now continued this 24 years) in these terms:

1. That neither he nor any of his should injure or do hurt to any of their people.
2. That if any of his did hurt to any of theirs, he should send the offender, that they might punish him.
3. That if anything were taken away from any of theirs, he should cause it to be restored; and they should do the like to his.
4. If any did unjustly war against him, they would aid him; if any did war against them, he should aid them.
5. He should send to his neighbours confederates to certify them of this, that they might not wrong them, but might be likewise comprised in the conditions of peace.
6. That when their men came to them, they should leave their bows and arrows behind them.

After these things he returned to his place called Sowams, some 40 miles from this place, but Squanto continued with them and was their interpreter and was a special instrument sent of God for their good beyond their expectation. He directed them how to set their corn, where to take fish, and to procure other commodities, and was also their pilot to bring them to unknown places for their profit, and never left them till he died. He was a native of this place, and scarce any left alive besides himself. He was carried away with divers others by one Hunt, a master of a ship, who thought to sell them for slaves in Spain. But he got away for England and was entertained by a merchant in London, and employed to Newfoundland and other parts, and lastly brought hither into these parts by one Mr. Dermer, a gentleman employed by Sir Ferdinando Gorges and others for discovery and other designs in these parts. Of whom I shall say something, because it is mentioned in a book set forth Anno 1622 by the President and Council for New England, that he made the peace between the savages of these parts and the English, of which this plantation, as it is intimated, had the benefit; but what a peace it was may appear by what befell him and his men.

This Mr. Dermer was here the same year that these people came, as appears by a relation written by him and given me by a friend, bearing date June 30, Anno 1620. And they came in November following, so there was but four months difference. In which relation to his honoured friend, he hath these passages of this very place:

I will first begin (saith he) with that place from whence Squanto or Tisquantum, was taken away; which in Captain Smith's map is called Plymouth; and I would that Plymouth had the like commodities. I would that the first plantation might here be seated, if there come to the number of 50 persons, or upward. Otherwise, Charlton, because there the savages are less to be feared. The Pocanockets, which live to the west of Plymouth, bear an inveterate malice to the English, and are of more strength than all the savages from thence to Penobscot. Their desire of revenge was occasioned by an Englishman, who having many of them on board, made a greater slaughter with their murderers and small shot when as (they say) they offered no injury on their parts. Whether they were English or no it may be doubted; yet they believe they were, for the French have so possessed them. For which cause Squanto cannot deny but they would have killed me when I was at Namasket, had he not entreated hard for me.

The soil of the borders of this great bay may be compared to most of the plantations which I have seen in Virginia. The land is of divers sorts, for Patuxet is a hardy but strong soil; Nauset and Satucket are for the most part a blackish and deep mould much like that where groweth the best tobacco in Virginia. In the bottom of that great bay is store of cod and bass or mullet, etc. But above all he commends Pocanocket for the richest soil, and much open ground fit for English grain, etc.

Massachusetts is about nine leagues from Plymouth, and situated in the midst between both, is full of islands and peninsulas, very fertile for the most part.

With sundry such relations which I forbear to transcribe, being now better known than they were to him.

He was taken prisoner by the Indians at Manamoyick, a place not far from hence, now well known. He gave them what they demanded for his liberty, but when they had got what they desired, they kept him still, and endeavoured to kill his men. But he was freed by seizing on some of them and kept them bound till they gave him a canoe's load of corn. Of which, see Purchas, lib. 9, fol. 1778. But this was Anno 1619.

After the writing of the former relation, he came to the Isle of Capawack (which lies south of this place in the way to Virginia) and the aforesaid Squanto with him, where he going ashore amongst the Indians to trade, as he used to do, was betrayed and assaulted by them, and all his men slain, but one that kept the boat. But himself got aboard very sore wounded, and they had cut off his head upon the cuddy of the boat, had not the man rescued him with a sword. And so they got away and made shift to get into Virginia where he died, whether of his wounds or the diseases of the country, or both together, is uncertain. By all which it may appear how far these people were from peace, and with what danger this plantation was begun, save as the powerful hand of the Lord did protect them.

These things were partly the reason why they kept aloof and were so long before they came to the English. Another reason as after themselves made known was how about three years before, a French ship was cast away at Cape Cod, but the men got ashore and saved their lives, and much of their victuals and other goods. But after the Indians heard of it, they gathered together from these parts and never left watching and dogging them till they got advantage and killed them all but three or four which they kept, and sent from one sachem to another to make sport with, and used them worse than slaves. Of which the aforesaid Mr. Dermer redeemed two of them; and they conceived this ship was now come to revenge it.

Also, as after was made known, before they came to the English to make friendship, they got all the Powachs[10] of the country, for three days together in a horrid and devilish manner, to curse and execrate them with their conjurations, which assembly and service they held in a dark and dismal swamp.

But to return. The spring now approaching, it pleased God the mortality began to cease amongst them, and the sick and lame recovered apace, which put as [it] were new life into them, though they had borne their sad affliction with much patience and contentedness as I think any people could do. But it was the Lord which upheld them, and had beforehand prepared them; many having long borne the yoke, yea from their youth. Many other smaller matters I omit, sundry of them having been already published in a journal made by one of the company, and some other passages of journeys

[10] Medicine men.

and relations already published, to which I refer those that are willing to know them more particularly.

And being now come to the 25th of March, I shall begin the year 1621. . . .

RELATED VOICES

The Life of William Bradford, Esq.

5. Here was Mr. Bradford, in the year 1621, unanimously chosen the governour of the plantation: the difficulties whereof were such, that if he had not been a person of more than ordinary piety, wisdom and courage, he must have sunk under them. He had, with a laudable industry, been laying up a treasure of experiences, and he had now occasion to use it: indeed, nothing but an *experienced* man could have been suitable to the necessities of the people. The potent nations of the Indians, into whose country they were come, would have cut them off, if the blessing of God upon *his* conduct had not quelled them; and if his prudence, justice and moderation had not over-ruled them, they had been ruined by their own distempers. One specimen of his demeanour is to this day particularly spoken of. A company of young fellows that were newly arrived, were very unwilling to comply with the governour's order for working abroad on the publick account; and therefore on Christmas-day, when he had called upon them, they excused themselves, with a pretence that it was against their conscience to *work* such a day. The governour gave them no answer, only that he would spare them till they were better informed; but by and by he found them all at *play* in the street, sporting themselves with various diversions; whereupon commanding the instruments of their games to be taken from them, he effectually gave them to understand, "*That it was against his conscience that they should play whilst others were at work:* and that if they had any devotion to the day, they should show it at home in the exercises of religion, and not in the streets with pastime and frolicks;" and this gentle reproof put a final stop to all such disorders for the future.

Cotton Mather, from Magnalia Christi Americana

John Winthrop
1588–1649

By birth and breeding, John Winthrop seems to have been destined to be a leader in Puritan colonial life. The son of an English country gentleman, Winthrop was married at eighteen and became steward and justice of the peace on his father's estate at Groton, to which he had returned after two years of legal studies at Trinity College, Cambridge University. The Winthrops were Puritans, and though John wrote of his "wild and dissolute youth," he found "some peace and comfort in God and his wayes" in his late teens, and thereafter his faith strengthened by degrees.

Winthrop began to consider emigration to the New World when political and religious conditions worsened in England. Under the reign of Archbishop Laud, ministers who refused strict adherence to all Anglican practices fell under suspicion or were silenced. Openly a Puritan, Winthrop lost his attorneyship. Everywhere the dreaded Roman Catholicism seemed on the rise. By spring 1629, Winthrop feared that "God will bringe some heavye Affliction upon this lande" in the form of political reprisals or natural disasters such as the plague. Yet he trusted that the Lord would "provide a shelter & a hidinge place for us and others."

The Lord's instrument seemed to be the new Massachusetts Bay Company, which elected Winthrop its first governor in 1629. He sailed for America the following year on the *Arbella,* the flagship vessel of a fleet carrying some seven hundred persons in a "Great Migration" that would soon bring twenty thousand settlers to New England. At sea on board the *Arbella,* Winthrop preached a now-classic sermon on the ideals of Christian charity that he felt must govern the colony in all its affairs. It was imperative, he argued, that the settlers form a commonwealth for the mutual benefit of all and that their society be able to withstand the scrutiny of a watchful world. In the Massachusetts Bay, Winthrop acted as governor or deputy governor for nearly twenty years, upholding the standards set in his "Model of Christian Charity." In practice his leadership was sought in trials of settlement, trade, property disputes, economic hard times, Indian wars, and the religious controversies that threatened to split the colony into warring camps. Winthrop's *Journal* was the record of these events and became, over time, a record by which to measure how close colonial New England came to being that model "citty upon a hill."

Further Reading:

R. Winthrop, *Life and Letters of John Winthrop,* 1864–1867.

S. E. Morison, *Builders of the Bay Colony,* 1930.

E. Morgan, *The Puritan Dilemma,* 1958.

D. Rutman, *Winthrop's Boston,* 1965.

S. Bercovitch, *Puritan Origins of the American Self,* 1975.

J. Lepore, *The Name of War,* 1998.

Texts:

"A Model of Christian Charity," *The Winthrop Papers,* ed. A. Forbes, 5 vols., 1929–1947.

The History of New England, ed. J. Savage, 2 vols., 1853, 1972.

---

from A Model of Christian Charity

Now the only way to avoide this shipwracke and to provide for our posterity is to followe the Counsell of Micah,[1] to doe Justly, to love mercy, to walke humbly with our God; for this end, wee must be knit together in this worke as one man, wee must entertaine each other in brotherly Affection, wee must be willing to abridge our selves of our superfluities for the supply of others necessities, wee must uphold a familiar Commerce

---

[1] Micah 6:8: ". . . and what doth the Lord require of thee, but to do justly and to love mercy, and to walk humbly with thy God?"

together in all meekness, gentleness, patience and liberallity, wee must delight in each other, make others Condicions our owne, rejoice together, mourne together, labour, and suffer together, allways haveing before our eyes our Commission and Community in the worke, our Community as members of the same body. Soe shall wee keepe the unity of the spirit in the bond of peace, the Lord will be our God and delight to dwell among us, as his owne people and will command a blessing upon us in all our ways, soe that wee shall see much more of his wisdom, power, goodnes and truth than formerly wee have beene acquainted with; wee shall finde that the God of Israell is among us, when ten of us shall be able to resist a thousand of our enemies, when hee shall make us a praise and glory, that men shall say of succeeding plantations: the lord make it like that of New England: for wee must Consider that wee shall be as a Citty upon a Hill,[2] the eyes of all people are uppon us; soe that if wee shall deale falsely with our god in this worke wee have undertaken and soe cause him to withdrawe his present help from us, wee shall be made a story and a byword through the world, wee shall open the mouths of enemies to speake evill of the ways of god and all professours for Gods sake; wee shall shame the faces of many of gods worthy servants, and cause their prayers to be turned into Cursses upon us till wee be consumed out of the good land whether wee are going: And to shutt up this discourse with that exhortation of Moses that faithfull servant of the Lord in his last farewell to Israell (Deut. 30).[3] Beloved there is now set before us life, and good, death and evill in that wee are Commaunded this day to love the Lord our God, and to love one another to walk in his ways and to keepe his Commaundements and his Ordinance, and his lawes, and the Articles of our Covenant with him that wee may live and be multiplied, and that the Lord our God may blesse us in the land whether wee go to possesse it: But if our heartes shall turne away soe that wee will not obey, but shall be seduced and worship other Gods our pleasures, and proffitts, and serve them; it is propounded unto us this day, wee shall surely perish out of the good Land whither wee passe over this vast Sea to possess it;

Therefore lett us choose life,[4]
   that wee, and our Seede,
     may live; by obeyeing his
  voice, and cleaving to him,
    for hee is our life, and
      our prosperity.

1838

---

2 Matthew 5:14–15: "Ye are the light of the world. A city that is set on a hill cannot be hid. Neither do men light a candle, and put it under a bushel, but on a candlestick; and it giveth light unto all that are in the house."

3 Deuteronomy 30:1–3: "And it shall come to pass, when all these things are come upon thee, the blessing and the curse, which I have set before thee, and thou shalt call them to mind among all the nations, whither the Lord thy God hath driven thee, And shalt return unto the Lord thy God, and shalt obey his voice according to all that I command thee this day, thou and thy children, with all thine heart, and with all thy soul; That then the Lord thy God will turn thy captivity, and have compassion upon thee, and will return and gather thee from all the nations, whither the Lord thy God hath scattered thee."

4 Deuteronomy 30:19: ". . . I have set before you life & death, blessing & cursing: therefore, choose life, that both thou & thy seed may live. . . ."

Anne Bradstreet
ca. 1612–1672

Anne Bradstreet was an English gentlewoman whose heart "rose" in revulsion at the sight of the New World. Yet she became the first significant poet in American literature precisely by capturing the essence of life as a Puritan and as a woman under colonial conditions. She "submitted," as she put it, to the "new world and new manners," though the transition was undeniably wrenching.

Anne Dudley was born in Northampton, England. Her father, Thomas, was then a financial officer in the household of the Earl of Lincoln. Anne called him her "guide," her "instructor," and "a magazine of history." Dudley evidently took unusual care with the education of his daughter, perhaps following one educator's advice to teach the "Abcie and primer" while "playing with [the little children] at dinners and suppers, or as they sit by the fire." Anne reported that at about age six or seven she was reading the Scriptures.

Young Anne Bradstreet's era was intellectually lively, as was her immediate environment in the household of the nobleman whose library was probably accessible to her. She evidently knew Sir Walter Raleigh's *History of the World* (1614), a study of the ancient kingdoms and dynasties emphasizing God's authority through every historical cycle. And she knew the poetry of Sir Philip Sidney, Edmund Spenser, and Michael Drayton, in addition to Robert Burton's *Anatomy of Melancholy* and Francis Bacon's *Essays*. She had probably read some Shakespeare, and she openly admired Joshua Sylvester's translation of Guillaume du Barta's *Divine Weeks and Works*. In addition, Anne knew John Foxe's *Actes and Monuments*, a Protestant martyrology, and countless contemporary Puritan tracts and pamphlets. But the girl's education came only in part from books. Her mind was doubtlessly sharpened from listening to the household debates and discussions of a distinguished company of Puritan intellectuals in the thick of intense religious controversy.

In the late 1620s, political conditions worsened for the Dudley family, because as Puritan employees of a Puritan nobleman they increasingly suffered from the king's disfavor. When Charles I began to prosecute retainers of Lord Lincoln, Anne's father fell under suspicion of harboring a fugitive. In 1630 the Dudley family sailed with the Winthrop party to Massachusetts.

Anne was sixteen at the time of the voyage and already the wife of Simon Bradstreet, a graduate of Emmanuel College, Cambridge, a university center of nonconformity. Anne had married the twenty-five-year-old steward, her father's assistant, about two years earlier. At the time of her wedding, Anne was recuperating from smallpox; her convalescence was perhaps lengthened by her earlier childhood bouts of rheumatic fever, and for the remainder of her life Anne Bradstreet's health was precarious. She was subject to lameness, fever, and fainting in a land rife with disease and death. It is understandable that the dominant images in her poems concern the human body, illness, and mortality.

The Bradstreets began Massachusetts life in Salem, but in spring 1631, resettled in Newton, now Cambridge. During the years of their marriage, Simon Bradstreet was often absent on colonial business. He was secretary to the Bay Company, its deputy governor, and in 1645 its governor. In 1661, with the restoration of the monarchy in England, he traveled there to renegotiate the charter of the Bay Company. Bradstreet's absences increased his wife's burdens.

Given her circumstances, it is astonishing that Anne Bradstreet could make time to write poetry and prose. The household relocations, the eight births and years of child rearing, domestic and social obligations, the sicknesses, cramped quarters, and the disapproval (as she recorded in one poem) of "each carping tongue/who says my hand a needle better fits"—any or all would have silenced a writer who was less driven than she. Yet she called poetry a "room of my own," and she worked at it until her death.

Bradstreet's writings fall into two groups. One is scholarly and monumental and concerns such subjects as the four elements and four humors (named for the ancient Greeks' belief that the world was composed of earth, air, fire, and water and that the human temperament was formed of warmth, cold, wet, and dry). Bradstreet likewise searched for cosmic themes when she wrote poetry of historical cycles she called the "ages of man" and the "four monarchies." In these four-part poems Anne Bradstreet most fully reveals her ambition to take her place among the English and French poets, all of them men.

Ironically, the second group of "domestic" poems and the *Contemplations* stand as Bradstreet's literary achievement. She is now most appreciated for the writings that convey her personal feelings about New England and family life. As a mother she writes of her "eight birds hatcht in one nest" and as a wife inscribes her love for Simon ("If ever man were lov'd by wife, than thee"). Her tone ranges from light irony, as when she calls the error-ridden text of *The Tenth Muse* an "ill-form'd offspring of my feeble brain," to the poignance of the poem occasioned by the burning of the Bradstreet house in 1666. Her elegies on the death of her grandchildren convey a deep sense of loss even as they evoke the solace of her religion. These poems exploit the tension between the individual's wishes and desires and the need to submit to God's will. Many of the poems were published in 1678, six years after her death.

Further Reading:

J. Piercy, *Anne Bradstreet*, 1965.

E. White, *Anne Bradstreet: The Tenth Muse*, 1971.

A. Stanford, *Anne Bradstreet: The Worldly Puritan*, 1974.

W. Martin, *An American Triptych*, 1984.

Text:

The Works of Anne Bradstreet, ed. J. Hensley, 1967.

The Prologue

1

To sing of wars, of captains, and of kings,
Of cities founded, commonwealths begun,
For my mean pen are too superior things:
Or how they all, or each their dates have run
Let poets and historians set these forth,   5
My obscure lines shall not so dim their worth.

2

But when my wond'ring eyes and envious heart
Great Bartas'[1] sugared lines do but read o'er,
Fool I do grudge the Muses did not part
'Twixt him and me that overfluent store;   10
A Bartas can do what a Bartas will
But simple I according to my skill.

3

From schoolboy's tongue no rhet'ric we expect,
Nor yet a sweet consort from broken strings,
Nor perfect beauty where's a main defect: 15
My foolish, broken, blemished Muse so sings,
And this to mend, alas, no art is able,
'Cause nature made it so irreparable.

4

Nor can I, like that fluent sweet tongued Greek,[2]
Who lisped at first, in future times speak plain.   20
By art he gladly found what he did seek,
A full requital of his striving pain.
Art can do much, but this maxim's most sure:
A weak or wounded brain admits no cure.

---

[1] Guillaume du Bartas (1544–1590), French poet.

[2] Demosthenes (385?–322 B.C.), Athenian orator.

5

I am obnoxious to each carping tongue   25
Who says my hand a needle better fits,
A poet's pen all scorn I should thus wrong,
For such despite they cast on female wits:
If what I do prove well, it won't advance,
They'll say it's stol'n, or else it was by chance.   30

6

But sure the antique Greeks were far more mild
Else of our sex, why feigned they those nine
And poesy made Calliope's[3] own child;
So 'mongst the rest they placed the arts divine:
But this weak knot they will full soon untie,   35
The Greeks did nought, but play the fools and lie.

7

Let Greeks be Greeks, and women what they are
Men have precedency and still excel,
It is but vain unjustly to wage war;
Men can do best, and women know it well.   40
Preeminence in all and each is yours;
Yet grant some small acknowledgement of ours.

8

And oh ye high flown quills that soar the skies,
And ever with your prey still catch your praise,
If e'er you deign these lowly lines your eyes,   45
Give thyme or parsley wreath, I ask no bays;[4]
This mean and unrefined ore of mine
Will make your glist'ring gold but more to shine.
1650

The Author to Her Book

Thou ill-formed offspring of my feeble brain,
Who after birth didst by my side remain,

---

[3] Calliope, the Muse of heroic poetry, was one   [4] Laurels.
of the nine Muses who presided over the arts
and sciences.

Till snatched from thence by friends, less wise
   than true,
Who thee abroad, exposed to public view,
Made thee in rags, halting to th' press to trudge,   5
Where errors were not lessened (all may judge).
At thy return my blushing was not small,
My rambling brat (in print) should mother call,
I cast thee by as one unfit for light,
Thy visage was so irksome in my sight;   10
Yet being mine own, at length affection would
Thy blemishes amend, if so I could:
I washed thy face, but more defects I saw,
And rubbing off a spot still made a flaw.
I stretched thy joints to make thee even feet,   15
Yet still thou run'st more hobbling than is meet;
In better dress to trim thee was my mind,
But nought save homespun cloth i' th' house I find.
In this array 'mongst vulgars may'st thou roam.
In critic's hands beware thou dost not come,   20
And take thy way where yet thou art not known;
If for thy father asked, say thou hadst none;
And for thy mother, she alas is poor,
Which caused her thus to send thee out of door.
1678

Before the Birth of One of Her Children

All things within this fading world hath end,
Adversity doth still our joys attend;
No ties so strong, no friends so dear and sweet,
But with death's parting blow is sure to meet.
The sentence past is most irrevocable,   5
A common thing, yet oh, inevitable.
How soon, my Dear, death may my steps attend,
How soon't may be thy lot to lose thy friend,
We both are ignorant, yet love bids me
These farewell lines to recommend to thee,   10
That when that knot's untied that made us one,
I may seem thine, who in effect am none.
And if I see not half my days that's due,
What nature would, God grant to yours and you;
The many faults that well you know I have   15
Let be interred in my oblivious grave;

If any worth or virtue were in me,
Let that live freshly in thy memory
And when thou feel'st no grief, as I no harms,
Yet love thy dead, who long lay in thine arms.   20
And when thy loss shall be repaid with gains
Look to my little babes, my dear remains.
And if thou love thyself, or loved'st me,
These O protect from step-dame's injury.
And if chance to thine eyes shall bring this verse,   25
With some sad sighs honour my absent hearse;
And kiss this paper for thy love's dear sake,
Who with salt tears this last farewell did take.
1867

To My Dear and Loving Husband

If ever two were one, then surely we.
If ever man were loved by wife, then thee;
If ever wife was happy in a man,
Compare with me, ye women, if you can.
I prize thy love more than whole mines of gold   5
Or all the riches that the East doth hold.
My love is such that rivers cannot quench,
Nor ought but love from thee, give recompense.
Thy love is such I can no way repay,
The heavens reward thee manifold, I pray.   10
Then while we live, in love let's so persevere
That when we live no more, we may live ever.
1867

In Memory of My Dear Grandchild Elizabeth Bradstreet, Who Deceased August, 1665, Being a Year and Half Old

[1]

Farewell dear babe, my heart's too much content,
Farewell sweet babe, the pleasure of mine eye,

Farewell fair flower that for a space was lent,
Then ta'en away unto eternity.
Blest babe, why should I once bewail thy fate,   5
Or sigh thy days so soon were terminate,
Sith thou art settled in an everlasting state.

[2]

By nature trees do rot when they are grown,
And plums and apples thoroughly ripe do fall,
And corn and grass are in their season mown,   10
And time brings down what is both strong and tall.
But plants new set to be eradicate,
And buds new blown to have so short a date,
Is by His hand alone that guides nature and fate.

1867

Here Follows Some Verses upon the Burning of Our House
July 10th, 1666

Copied Out of a Loose Paper

In silent night when rest I took
For sorrow near I did not look
I wakened was with thund'ring noise
And piteous shrieks of dreadful voice.
That fearful sound of "Fire!" and "Fire!"   5
Let no man know is my desire.
I, starting up, the light did spy,
And to my God my heart did cry
To strengthen me in my distress
And not to leave me succorless.   10
Then, coming out, beheld a space
The flame consume my dwelling place.
And when I could no longer look,
I blest His name that gave and took,
That laid my goods now in the dust.   15
Yea, so it was, and so 'twas just.
It was His own, it was not mine,
Far be it that I should repine;
He might of all justly bereft
But yet sufficient for us left.   20

When by the ruins oft I past
My sorrowing eyes aside did cast,
And here and there the places spy
Where oft I sat and long did lie:
Here stood that trunk, and there that chest,   25
There lay that store I counted best.
My pleasant things in ashes lie,
And them behold no more shall I.
Under thy roof no guest shall sit,
Nor at thy table eat a bit.   30
No pleasant tale shall e'er be told,
Nor things recounted done of old.
No candle e'er shall shine in thee,
Nor bridegroom's voice e'er heard shall be.
In silence ever shall thou lie,   35
Adieu, Adieu, all's vanity.
Then straight I 'gin my heart to chide,
And did thy wealth on earth abide?
Didst fix they hope on mold'ring dust?
The arm of flesh didst make thy trust?   40
Raise up thy thoughts above the sky
That dunghill mists away may fly.
Thou hast an house on high erect,
Framed by that mighty Architect,
With glory richly furnished,   45
Stands permanent though this be fled.
It's purchased and paid for too
By Him who hath enough to do.
A price so fast as is unknown
Yet by His gift is made thine own;   50
There's wealth enough, I need no more,
Farewell, my pelf,[1] farewell my store.
The world no longer let me love,
My hope and treasure lies above.

1867

---

[1] Disparaging term for money or riches.

To My Dear Children

This book by any yet unread,
I leave for you when I am dead,
That being gone, here you may find
What was your living mother's mind.
Make use of what I leave in love,
And God shall bless you from above.
                                                    A. B.

My dear children,

I, knowing by experience that the exhortations of parents take most effect when the speakers leave to speak, and those especially sink deepest which are spoke latest, and being ignorant whether on my death bed I shall have opportunity to speak to any of you, much less to all, thought it the best, whilst I was able, to compose some short matters (for what else to call them I know not) and bequeath to you, that when I am no more with you, yet I may be daily in your remembrance (although that is the least in my aim in what I now do), but that you may gain some spiritual advantage by my experience. I have not studied in this you read to show my skill, but to declare the truth, not to set forth myself, but the glory of God. If I had minded the former, it had been perhaps better pleasing to you, but seeing the last is the best, let it be best pleasing to you.

The method I will observe shall be this: I will begin with God's dealing with me from my childhood to this day.

In my young years, about 6 or 7 as I take it, I began to make conscience of my ways, and what I knew was sinful, as lying, disobedience to parents, etc., I avoided it. If at any time I was overtaken with the like evils, it was as a great trouble, and I could not be at rest 'till by prayer I had confessed it unto God. I was also troubled at the neglect of private duties though too often tardy that way. I also found much comfort in reading the Scriptures, especially those places I thought most concerned my condition, and as I grew to have more understanding, so the more solace I took in them.

In a long fit of sickness which I had on my bed I often communed with my heart and made my supplication to the most High who set me free from that affliction.

But as I grew up to be about 14 or 15, I found my heart more carnal, and sitting loose from God, vanity and the follies of youth take hold of me.

About 16, the Lord laid His hand sore upon me and smote me with the smallpox. When I was in my affliction, I besought the Lord and confessed my pride and vanity, and He was entreated of me and again restored me. But I rendered not to Him according to the benefit received.

After a short time I changed my condition and was married, and came into this country, where I found a new world and new manners, at which my heart rose. But after I was convinced it was the way of God, I submitted to it and joined to the church at Boston.

After some time I fell into a lingering sickness like a consumption together with a lameness, which correction I saw the Lord sent to humble and try me and do me good, and it was not altogether ineffectual.

It pleased God to keep me a long time without a child, which was a great grief to me and cost me many prayers and tears before I obtained one, and after him gave me many more of whom I now take the care, that as I have brought you into the world, and with great pains, weakness, cares, and fears brought you to this, I now travail in birth again of you till Christ be formed in you.

Among all my experiences of God's gracious dealings with me, I have constantly observed this, that He hath never suffered me long to sit loose from Him, but by one affliction or other hath made me look home, and search what was amiss; so usually thus it hath been with me that I have no sooner felt my heart out of order, but I have expected correction for it, which most commonly hath been upon my own person in sickness, weakness, pains, sometimes on my soul, in doubts and fears of God's displeasure and my sincerity towards Him; sometimes He hath smote a child with a sickness, sometimes chastened by losses in estate, and these times (through His great mercy) have been the times of my greatest getting and advantage; yea, I have found them the times when the Lord hath manifested the most love to me. Then have I gone to searching and have said with David, "Lord, search me and try me, see what ways of wickedness are in me, and lead me in the way ever-lasting," and seldom or never but I have found either some sin I lay under which God would have reformed, or some duty neglected which He would have performed, and by His help I have laid vows and bonds upon my soul to perform His righteous commands.

If at any time you are chastened of God, take it as thankfully and joyfully as in greatest mercies, for if ye be His, ye shall reap the greatest benefit by it. It hath been no small support to me in times of darkness when the Almighty hath hid His face from me that yet I have had abundance of sweetness and refreshment after affliction and more circumspection in my walking after I have been afflicted. I have been with God like an untoward child, that no longer than the rod has been on my back (or at least in sight) but I have been apt to forget Him and myself, too. Before I was afflicted, I went astray, but now I keep Thy statutes.

I have had great experience of God's hearing my prayers and returning comfortable answers to me, either in granting the thing I prayed for, or else in satisfying my mind without it, and I have been confident it hath been from Him, because I have found my heart through His goodness enlarged in thankfulness to Him.

I have often been perplexed that I have not found that constant joy in my pilgrimage and refreshing which I supposed most of the servants of God have, although He hath not left me altogether without the witness of His holy spirit, who hath oft given me His word and set to His seal that it shall be well with me. I have sometimes tasted of that hidden manna that the world knows not, and have set up my Ebenezer, and have resolved with myself that against such a promise, such tastes of sweetness, the gates of hell shall never prevail; yet have I many times sinkings and droopings, and not enjoyed that felicity that sometimes I have done. But when I have been in darkness and seen no light, yet have I desired to stay myself upon the Lord, and when I have been in sickness and pain, I have thought if the Lord would but lift up the light of His countenance upon me, although He ground me to powder, it would be but light to me; yea, oft have I thought were I in hell itself and could there find the love of God toward me, it would be a heaven. And could I have been in heaven without the love of God, it would have been a hell to me, for in truth it is the absence and presence of God that makes heaven or hell.

Many times hath Satan troubled me concerning the verity of the Scriptures, many times by atheism how I could know whether there was a God; I never saw any miracles to confirm me, and those which I read of, how did I know but they were feigned? That there is a God my reason would soon tell me by the wondrous works that I see, the vast frame of the heaven and the earth, the order of all things, night and day, summer and winter, spring and autumn, the daily providing for this great household upon the earth, the preserving and directing of all to its proper end. The consideration of these things would with amazement certainly resolve me that there is an Eternal Being. But how should I know He is such a God as I worship in Trinity, and such a Saviour as I rely upon? Though this hath thousands of times been suggested to me, yet God hath helped me over. I have argued thus with myself. That there is a God, I see. If ever this God hath revealed himself, it must be in His word, and this must be it or none. Have I not found that operation by it that no human invention can work upon the soul, hath not judgments befallen divers who have scorned and contemned it, hath it not been preserved through all ages maugre[1] all the heathen tyrants and all of the enemies who have opposed it? Is there any story but that which shows the beginnings of times, and how the world came to be as we see? Do we not know the prophecies in it fulfilled which could not have been so long foretold by any but God Himself?

When I have got over this block, then have I another put in my way, that admit this be the true God whom we worship, and that be his word, yet why may not the Popish religion be the right? They have the same God, the same Christ, the same word. They only interpret it one way, we another.

This hath sometimes stuck with me, and more it would, but the vain fooleries that are in their religion together with their lying miracles and cruel persecutions of the saints, which admit were they as they term them, yet not so to be dealt withal.

The consideration of these things and many the like would soon turn me to my own religion again.

But some new troubles I have had since the world has been filled with blasphemy and sectaries, and some who have been accounted sincere Christians have been carried away with them, that sometimes I have said, "Is there faith upon the earth?" and I have not known what to think; but then I have remembered the works of Christ that so it must be, and if it were possible, the very elect should be deceived. "Behold," saith our Saviour, "I have told you before." That hath stayed my heart, and I can now say, "Return, O my Soul, to thy rest, upon this rock Christ Jesus will I build my faith, and if I perish, I perish"; but I know all the Powers of Hell shall never prevail against it. I know whom I have trusted, and whom I have believed, and that He is able to keep that I have committed to His charge.

Now to the King, immortal, eternal and invisible, the only wise God, be honour, and glory for ever and ever, Amen.

This was written in much sickness and weakness, and is very weakly and imperfectly done, but if you can pick any benefit out of it, it is the mark which I aimed at.
1867

---

[1] Despite.

Cultural Portfolio
The Witchcraft Trials

Witchcraft was a commonly held belief in six-teenth- and seventeenth-century Europe. In England also a witch was defined as an individual committed to perform evil deeds in the world in the service of Satan. Often witches were identified by any strange mark on their bodies, known as a nipple where the devil would nurse. Witches were also understood to have "familiars" or animals who would perform evil deeds for the witches; sometimes the witches themselves were understood to take the form of animals.

In 1542 the English Parliament made witchcraft a capital offense. From that point on, witchcraft trials and executions were common. Between 1645 and 1647 England experienced its greatest witchcraft crisis: several hundred people were tried and hanged for being witches. Witchcraft accusations and trials in New England were very similar to those in England, although New England was slightly more active in its persecution of presumed witches. In New England 234 people were tried for being witches, and thirty-six were executed between 1647, when the first executions for witchcraft took place, and the end of the seventeenth century.

Many scholars have examined witchcraft as a phenomenon requiring explanation. Some scholars suggest that witchcraft accusations were prompted by economic motivations; if someone felt financially insecure, he or she might accuse someone more successful of being a witch. Other explanations for witchcraft focus on tensions within the Puritan community; a witch might be a neighbor who refused to be supportive of other neighbors. Still other explanations examine the gender inflections of witchcraft. In England and New England, 90 percent of accused witches were women, and even today, when we visualize witches, we generally see a woman. Perhaps witchcraft accusations were a way to monitor and punish improper female behavior, including female financial power.

It is important to remember that seventeenth-century New Englanders believed in the "Wonders of the Invisible World," as Cotton Mather titled a tract in which he documented the struggle of Christian colonists against the malevolent acts of witches. The metaphysical presence of demonic spirits was a tenet of belief in the New England colonies. Witchcraft was understood to be a way in which Satan sustained his ungodly battle for the souls of the righteous, and the New England Puritan witchcraft trials must be understood in this context.

In 1692 in Salem, north of Boston, an adolescent girl, Betty Parris, the daughter of a minister, grew hysterical when she thought she saw "a specter in the likeness of a coffin." When she and her cousin, Abigail, began to behave strangely, barking, writhing, and moaning, a physician diagnosed them as possessed by "the Evil Hand." Thus began New England's greatest witchcraft crisis. The church and its clergy seemed defenseless against Satan's infiltration of the righteous citizenry. The Parris's slave, a West Indian woman named Tituba, confessed, "The devil came to me and bid me serve him," and through succeeding months those accused were brought to trial under Massachusetts Chief Justice Stoughton and eight judges, including the great grandfather of Nathaniel Hawthorne. Being accused was often considered a sign of guilt, and prisoners were presumed guilty. Neighbor turned against neighbor, and many confessed.

In all, nineteen people were executed, and by the time the colonial governor, Sir William Phips, moved to put a stop to the trials and executions, 150 accused persons were imprisoned and awaiting trial. When the mass hysteria ended, some prominent figures, including Judge Samuel Sewall, publicly expressed regret for the parts they had played in sentencing innocent people to death. As Reverend Increase Mather wrote,

"I had rather judge a witch to be an honest woman, than judge an honest woman as a witch."

The Salem trials stand as one of the heinous events in American history. The episode provided the basis for dramatist Arthur Miller's *The Crucible* and Maryse Condé's novel, *I, Tituba* in the twentieth century and is the basis for the negative sociopolitical term, witch hunt.

Artist unknown
Punishments for witchcraft: hanging
ca. 1558–1618

from C. L'Estrange Ewen, *Witch Hunting
& Witch Trials: The Indictments for
Witchcraft from the Records of 1373
Assizes Held for the Home Circuit
A.D. 1559–1736*

Appendix II

The Discovery of Witches

compiled by Michael Dalton "partly out
of the book of discovery of the Witches that were
arraigned at Lancaster, anno 1612 before Sir James
Altham & Sir Edward Bromley, Judges of Assize
there, and partly out of M. Bernard's
Guide to Grand Jurymen."

1. These witches have ordinarily a familiar or spirit, which appeareth to them; sometimes in one shape, sometimes in another, as in the shape of a man, woman, boy, dog, cat, foal, fowl, hare, rat, toad, &c. And to these their spirits they give names, and they meet together to christen them (as they speak). *Ber.* 107, 113.

2. Their said familiar hath some big or little teat upon their body, and in some secret place, where he sucketh them. And besides their sucking, the Devil leaveth other marks upon their body, sometimes like a blue spot or red spot, like a flea biting; sometimes the flesh sunk in and hollow (all which for a time may be covered, yea taken away, but will come again, to their old form). And these the Devils marks be insensible, and being pricked will not bleed, and be often in their secretest parts, and therefore require diligent and careful search. *Ber.* 112, 219.

These first two are main points to discover and convict these witches; for they prove fully that those witches have a familiar, and made a league with the Devil. *Ber.* 60.

So likewise if the suspected be proved to have been heard to call upon their spirit, or to talk to them, or of them, or have offered them to others. So if they have been seen with their spirit, or seen to feed some thing secretly; these are proofs they have a familiar, &c.

The Confession of Agnes Waterhowse the xxvii daye of July in Anno 1566 at Chelmsforde before Justice Southcote and M. Gerard the quenes atturney.

Fyrst being demaunded whether that shee were gyltye or not gyltye upon her araynement of the murtheringe of a man, she confessed that she was gyltye, and then uppon the evidence geven agaynst her daughter Jone Waterhowse, she sayde that she hade a white Cat, and wylled her cat that he shuld destroy many of his neyghbours cattell, and also that he shoulde kyll a man, and so he dyd, and then after she must go ii or iii mile from her house, and then she toke thoughte howe to kepe her catte, then she and her catte concluded that he the sayde Catte wolde become a tode, and then she shuld kepe him in a close house and geve hym mylke, and so he wolde continue tyll she came home againe, and then being gone forth, her daughter having ben at a neyghbour's house there by, required of one Agnes Browne, of the age of xii yeres or more, a peece of breade and cheese, and the sayde Agnes saide that shee had none, and that she had not the key of the milkhouse dore, and then the sayde Jone went home and was angry with the said Agnes Browne and she saide that she remembred that her mother was wonte to go up and downe in her house and to call Sathan Sathan she sayde she wolde prove the like, and then she went up and downe the house and called Sathan, and then there came a black dogge to her and asked her what she would have, and then she said she was aferd and sayd, I wold have thee to make one Agnes Browne afrayde, and then he asked her what she wold give him and she saide she wold geve hym a red kock; and he said he wolde have none of that, and shee asked him what he wolde have then, and he sayde he wold have her body and soule, and so upon requeste and feare together she gave him her body and soule, and then sayde the quenes atturneye *Howe wylt thou do before God.* O My Lord, I trust God wyll have mercy upon mee, and then he saide *thou saiste well,* and then he departed from her, and then she saide that she herde that he made the sayde Agnes Browne a fearde.

from Cotton Mather, *Magnalia Christi Americana, Boston 1702*

The Witchcraft Trials in Salem

It is to be confessed and bewailed, that many inhabitants of New-England, and young people especially, had been led away with little *sorceries,* wherein they "did secretly those things that were not right against the Lord their God;" they would often cure hurts with *spells,* and practice detestable conjurations with *sieves,* and *keys,* and *pease,* and *nails,* and *horse-shoes,* and other implements, to learn the things for which they had a forbidden and impious curiosity. Wretched books had stoln into the land, wherein fools were instructed how to become able fortune-tellers: among which, I wonder that a blacker brand is not set upon that fortune-telling wheel, which that sham-scribler that goes under the letters of R. B.[1] has promised in his *"Delights for the Ingenious,"* as an *honest and pleasant recreation;* and by these books, the minds of many had been so poisoned, that they studied this *finer witchcraft;* until 'tis well if some of them were not betrayed into what is grosser, and more sensible and capital. Although these *diabolical divinations* are more ordinarily committed perhaps all over the *whole world,* than they are in the country of New-England, yet, that being a country devoted unto the worship and service of the Lord JESUS CHRIST above the *rest of the world,* HE signalized his vengeance against these wickednesses, with such extraordinary dispensations as have not been often seen in other places.

The *devils* which had been so played withal, and, it may be, by some few criminals more explicitly engaged and imployed, now broke in upon the country, after as astonishing a manner as was ever heard of. Some scores of people, first about Salem, the cen-

[1] Pseudonym for Nathaniel Crouch.

Artist unknown
Judith Philips, fortune teller and swindler
ca. 1558–1618
(This item is reproduced by permission of The Huntington Library, San Marino, California)

tre and first-born of all the towns in the colony, and afterwards in several other places, were arrestd with many *preternatural vexations* upon their bodies, and a variety of cruel torments, which were evidently inflicted from the *dæmons* of the *invisible world*. The people that were infected and infested with such dæmons, in a few days' time arrived unto such a *refining alteration* upon their eyes, that they could see their tormentors: they saw a *devil* of a little *stature,* and of a tawny *colour,* attended still with spectres that appeared in more humane circumstances.

These *tormentors* tendred unto the afflicted a *book,* requiring them to *sign* it, or to *touch* it at least, in token of their consenting to be listed in the service of the devil; which they refusing to do, the spectres under the command of that *blackman,* as they called him, would apply themselves to torture them with prodigious molestations.

The afflicted wretches were horribly *distorted* and *convulsed;* they were *pinched* black and blue: *pins* would be run every where in their flesh; they would be *scalded* until they had *blisters* raised on them; and a thousand other things before hundreds of witnesses were done unto them, evidently *preternatural:* for if it were *preternatural* to keep a rigid *fast* for *nine,* yea, for *fifteen* days together; or if it were *preternatural* to have one's hands *tyed* close together with a rope to be plainly seen, and then by *unseen hands* presently pulled up a great way from the earth before a croud of people; such *preternatural* things were endured by them.

But of all the preternatural things which befel these people, there were none more *unaccountable* than those wherein the prestigious dæmons would ever now and then cover the most *corporeal* things in the world with a *fascinating mist* of *invisibility.* As now; a person was cruelly assaulted by a spectre, that, she said, run at her with a *spindle,* though no body else in the room could see either the spectre or the spindle: at last, in her agonies, giving a snatch at the spectre, she pulled the *spindle* away; and it was no sooner got into her hand, but the other folks then present beheld that it was indeed a real, proper, iron spindle; which, when they locked up very safe, it was nevertheless by the *dæmons* taken away to do farther mischief.

Again, a person was haunted by a most abusive spectre, which came to her, she said, with a *sheet* about her, though seen to none but her self. After she had undergone a deal of teaze from the annoyance of the spectre, she gave a violent *snatch* at the sheet that was upon it; where-from she tore a corner, which in her hand immediately was beheld by all were present, a palpable corner of a sheet: and her father, which was now holding of her, *catched,* that he might *keep* what his daughter had so strangely seized; but the spectre had like to have wrung his hand off, by endeavouring to wrest it from him; however, he still held it, and several times this odd accident was renewed in the family. There wanted not the *oaths* of good credible people to these particulars.

Also, it is well known, that these wicked spectres did proceed so far as to steal several quantities of money from divers people, part of which individual money was dropt sometimes out of the air, before sufficient *spectators,* into the hands of the afflicted, while the spectres were urging them to subscribe their *covenant with death.* Moreover, *poisons* to the standers-by, wholly *invisibly,* were sometimes forced upon the afflicted; which when they have with much reluctancy swallowed, they have *swoln* presently, so that the common medicines for poisons have been found necessary to relieve them: yea, sometimes the spectres, in the *struggles,* have so dropt the poisons, that the standers-by have smelt them, and viewed them, and beheld the pillows of the miserable stained with them.

Yet more: the miserable have complained bitterly of *burning rags* run into their forceably distended *mouths;* and though nobody could see any such *clothes,* or indeed any *fires* in the chambers, yet presently the *scalds* were seen plainly by every body on the mouths of the complainers, and not only the *smell,* but the *smoke* of the burning sensibly filled the chambers.

Once more: the miserable exclaimed extreamly of *branding irons* heating at the fire on the hearth to mark them. Now, though the standers-by could see no irons, yet they could see distinctly the print of them in the ashes, and *smell* them too as they were carried by the *not-seen furies* unto the poor creatures for whom they were intended; and those poor creatures were thereupon so *stigmatized* with them, that they will bear the *marks* of them to their dying day. Nor are these the *tenth part* of the *prodigies* that fell out among the inhabitants of New-England.

Flashy people may burlesque these things, but when hundreds of the most sober people in a country where they have as much *mother-wit* certainly as the rest of mankind, know them to be *true,* nothing but the absurd and froward spirit of Sadducism[2] can question them. I have not yet mentioned so much as one thing that will not be justified, if it be required by the *oaths* of more considerate persons than any that can ridicule these odd *phænomena.* . . .

It was also found, that the flesh of the afflicted was often *bitten* at such a rate, that not only the *print of teeth* would be left on their flesh, but the very *slaver* of spittle too; and there would appear just such a *set of teeth* as was in the accused, even such as might be

---

[2] Sadducees denied the existence of spirits.

clearly distinguished from other peoples. And usually the afflicted went through a terrible deal of seeming difficulties from the tormenting spectres, and must be long waited on before they could get a breathing space from their *torments* to give in their testimonies.

Now, many good men took up an opinion, that the *providence* of God would not permit an innocent person to come under such a spectral representation; and that a concurrence of so many circumstances would prove an accused person to be in a *confederacy* with the dæmons thus afflicting of the neighbours; they judged that, except these things might amount unto a conviction, it would scarce be possible ever to *convict a witch:* and they had some *philosophical schemes of witchcraft,* and of the method and manner wherein *magical poisons* operate, which further supported them in their opinion. . . .

On the other part, there were many persons of great judgment, piety and experience, who from the beginning were very much dissatisfied at these proceedings; they feared lest the *devil* would get so far into the *faith* of the people, that for the sake of many *truths* which they might find him telling of them, they would come at length to believe all his *lies;* whereupon what a desolation of names—yea, and of lives also—would ensue, a man might, without much witchcraft, be able to prognosticate; and they feared, lest in such an extraordinary descent of wicked spirits from their high places upon us, there might such *principles* be taken up, as, when put into *practice,* would unavoidably cause the *righteous to perish with the wicked,* and procure the blood-shed of persons like the Gibeonites, whom some learned men suppose to be under a false pretence of witchcraft, by Saul exterminated.[3] . . . .

In fine, the country was in a dreadful *ferment,* and wise men foresaw a long train of dismal and bloody consequences. Hereupon they first advised that the afflicted might be kept asunder in the closest privacy; and one particular person, (whom I have cause to know,) in pursuance of this advice, offered himself singly to provide accommodations for any six of them, that so the success of more than ordinary *prayer* with *fasting* might, with *patience,* be *experienced,* before any other courses were taken.

And Sir William Phips arriving to his government, after this *ensnaring horrible storm* was begun, did consult the neighbouring ministers of the province, who made unto his Excellency and the council a return, (drawn up at their desire by Mr. Mather the younger, as I have been informed) wherein they declared:

> We judge, that in the prosecution of these and all such *witchcrafts,* there is need of a very critical and exquisite caution: lest by too much credulity for things received only upon the *devil's authority,* there be a door opened for a long train of miserable consequences, and Satan get an advantage over us; for we should not be ignorant of his devices.
>
> As in complaints upon *witchcrafts,* there may be matters of *enquiry,* which do not amount unto matters of *presumption;* and there may be matters of *presumption,* which yet may not be reckoned matters of *conviction;* so 'tis necessary that all proceedings thereabout be managed with an *exceeding tenderness* towards those that may be complained of: especially if they have been persons formerly of an *unblemished reputation.*
>
> When the *first enquiry* is made into the circumstances of such as may lye under any just suspicion of *witchcraft,* we could wish that there may be admitted as little as is possible of such *noise, company,* and *openness* as may too hastily expose them that are examined: and that there may nothing be used as a *test* for the trial of the suspected, the lawfulness whereof may be doubted among the people of God: but that the directions given by such judicious writers as Perkins and Bernard, be consulted in such a case.

---

[3] Samuel 21:1–6. Saul's reason for the execution
of the Gibeonites is a matter of speculation.

Presumptions, whereupon persons may be committed, and much more *convictions,* whereupon persons may be condemned as guilty of *witchcrafts,* ought certainly to be more considerable, than barely the *accused* person's being *represented* by a *spectre* to the afflicted: inasmuch as it is an undoubted and a notorious thing, that a dæmon may, by God's permission, appear even to ill purposes in the shape of an *innocent,* yea, and a *virtuous* man: nor can we esteem *alterations* made in the *sufferers,* by a *look* or *touch* of the accused, to be an infallible evidence of guilt: but frequently liable to be abused by the devil's *legerdemains.*[4]

We know not whether some *remarkable affronts* given to the *devils,* by our disbelieving of those testimonies whose whole force and strength is from *them* alone, may not put a period unto the progress of a direful calamity begun upon us, in the *accusation* of so many persons, whereof, we hope, some are yet *clear from the great transgression* laid unto their charge.

The ministers of the province also being jealous lest this counsel should not be duly followed, requested the President of Harvard-Colledge to compose and publish (which he did) some *cases of conscience* referring to these difficulties: in which treatise he did, with demonstrations of incomparable *reason* and *reading,* evince it, that Satan may appear in the shape of an innocent and a virtuous person, to afflict those that suffer by the *diabolical molestations:* and that the *ordeal* of the *sight,* and the *touch,* is not a conviction of a *covenant* with the devil, but liable to great exceptions against the *lawfulness,* as well as the *evidence* of it: and that either a free and fair *confession* of the criminals, or the oath of two credible persons proving such things against the person accused, as none but such as have a familiarity with the devil can know, or do, is necessary to the proof of the crime. . . .

In fine, the last courts that sate upon this *thorny business,* finding that it was impossible to penetrate into the whole meaning of the things that had happened, and that so many *unsearchable cheats* were interwoven into the *conclusion* of a mysterious business, which perhaps had not crept thereinto at the *beginning* of it, they *cleared* the accused as fast as they *tried* them; and within a little while the afflicted were most of them delivered out of their troubles also; and the land had peace restored unto it, by the "God of peace, treading Satan under foot." Erasmus, among other historians, does tell us, that at a town in Germany, a dæmon appeared on the top of a chimney, threatned that he would set the town on fire, and at length scattering some ashes abroad, the whole town was presently and horribly burnt unto the ground.

Sir William Phips now beheld such dæmons hideously scattering *fire* about the country, in the exasperations which the minds of men were on these things rising unto; and therefore when he had well canvased a *cause,* which perhaps might have puzzled the wisdom of the wisest men on earth to have managed, without any *error* in their administrations, he thought, if it would be any *error* at all, it would certainly be the *safest* for him to put a stop unto all future prosecutions, as far as it lay in him to do it.

He did so, and for it he had not only the printed acknowledgments of the New-Englanders, who publickly thanked him, "As one of the tribe of Zebulun, raised up from among themselves, and *spirited* as well as *commissioned* to be the *steers-man* of a vessel befogged in the *mare mortuum*[5] of witchcraft, who now so happily steered her course, that she escaped shipwrack, and was safely again moored under the Cape of *Good Hope;* and cut asunder the Circæan knot of enchantment, more difficult to be dissolved than the famous Gordian one of old."[6]

[4] Sleight-of-hand magic.
[5] Latin: "Dead Sea."
[6] In Greek myth, the enchantress Circe turned men into swine; the Gordian knot (tied by the ancient King Gordius of Phrygia) was cut rather than untied by Alexander the Great.

Artist unknown
Witch Feeding Familiars
ca. 1558–1618 (Courtesy of the Trustees of the British Museum)

from Samuel Sewall, *The Diary of Samuel Sewall*

April 11th 1692. Went to Salem, where, in the Meeting-house, the persons accused of Witchcraft were examined; was a very great Assembly; 'twas awfull to see how the afflicted persons were agitated. Mr. Noyes pray'd at the beginning, and Mr. Higginson concluded. [*In the margin*], Væ, Væ, Væ, Witchcraft. . . .

[*Augt. 19th 1692*] . . . This day [*in the margin,* Dolefull! Witchcraft] George Burrough, John Willard, Jnᵒ Procter, Martha Carrier and George Jacobs were executed at Salem, a very great number of Spectators being present. Mr. Cotton Mather was there, Mr. Sims, Hale, Noyes, Chiever, &c. All of them said they were innocent, Carrier and all. Mr. Mather says they all died by a Righteous Sentence. Mr. Burrough by his Speech, Prayer, protestation of his Innocence, did much move unthinking persons, which occasions their speaking hardly concerning his being executed. . . .

Monday, Sept. 19, 1692. About noon, at Salem, Giles Corey was press'd to death for standing Mute; much pains was used with him two days, one after another, by the Court and Capt. Gardner of Nantucket who had been of his acquaintance: but all in vain.

Sept. 20. Now I hear from Salem that about 18 years agoe, he was suspected to have stampd and press'd a man to death, but was cleared. Twas not remembred till Anne Putnam was told of it by said Corey's Spectre the Sabbath-day night before Execution. . . .

Nov. 22, 1692. I prayd that God would pardon all my Sinfull Wanderings, and direct me for the future. That God would bless the Assembly in their debates, and that would chuse and assist our Judges, &c., and save New England as to Enemies and Witchcrafts, and vindicate the late Judges, consisting wtih his Justice and Holiness, &c., with Fasting. . . .

1697. Copy of the Bill I put up on the Fast day; giving it to Mr. Willard as he pass'd by, and standing up at the reading of it, and bowing when finished; in the Afternoon.

Samuel Sewall, sensible of the reiterated strokes of God upon himself and family; and being sensible, that as to the Guilt contracted, upon the opening of the late Commission of Oyer and Terminer at Salem (to which the order for this Day relates) he is, upon many accounts, more concerned than any that he knows of, Desires to take the Blame and Shame of it, Asking pardon of Men, And especially desiring prayers that God, who has an Unlimited Authority, would pardon that Sin and all other his Sins; personal and Relative: And according to his infinite Benignity, and Soveraignty, Not Visit the Sin of him, or of any other, upon himself or any of his, nor upon the Land: But that He would powerfully defend him against all Temptations to Sin, for the future; and vouchsafe him the Efficacious, Saving Conduct of his Word and Spirit.

Anne Hutchinson's Trial

Anne Hutchinson was the key figure in the 1637 antinomian controversy. Subsequent generations have identified Hutchinson as a martyr to the cause of religious freedom and women's rights. Hutchinson, a housewife and the mother of twelve children, had been a parishioner of the Reverend John Cotton in Boston, England. One year after Cotton's departure for America, the Hutchinson family followed him. Mistress Hutchinson soon established herself as a valued nurse and midwife. In addition, as a devout and intellectually gifted woman she attracted a circle of some sixty women and men to "private conferences" on Mr. Cotton's sermons. Soon she broadened her discussions to include critical analyses of the teachings of other ministers.

As a partisan of Cotton and a sharp critic of his colleagues, Hutchinson put herself at the center of a theological controversy that concerned the part human beings could play in preparing their hearts to receive God's saving grace. This debate had already pitted Cotton against other powerful ministers. Therefore the widespread publicity of Anne Hutchinson's meetings made her the focus of dissension.

Finally brought to trial on charges of sedition, Hutchinson testified that she had received special divine revelation. In Puritan theology this was heresy and carried political implications as well. The individual who received divine guidance directly from God would not need the teaching of the scriptural word (in Latin, *nomen*) from the ministers. Nor would public officials like John Winthrop retain their authority, since they claimed that their power came from biblical injunctions. Hutchinson implicitly challenged the power of both church and state. Her minister, Cotton, joined all the others in condemning her.

She was banished by the Massachusetts General Court in November 1637 and moved to Rhode Island with a small band of her followers. She was later killed in an Indian raid. Yet Hutchinson remained in the American imagination. She was a major source for Hawthorne's character Hester in *The Scarlet Letter*. And her intellectual power anticipates that of Margaret Fuller, the mid-nineteenth-century writer and great conversationalist who was sometimes as disturbing to Ralph Waldo Emerson as Anne Hutchinson was to John Winthrop.

from The Antinomian Controversy*

Dep. gov. . . . . About three years ago we were all in peace. Mrs. Hutchinson from that time she came hath made a disturbance, and some that came over with her in the ship did inform me what she was as soon as she was landed. I being then in place dealt with the pastor and teacher of Boston and desired them to enquire of her, and then I was satisfied that she held nothing different from us, but within half a year after, she had

---

* Edited by David D. Hall.

vented divers of her strange opinions and had made parties in the country, and at length it comes that Mr. Cotton and Mr. Vane were of her judgment, but Mr. Cotton hath cleared himself that he was not of that mind, but now it appears by this woman's meeting that Mrs. Hutchinson hath so forestalled the minds of many by their resort to her meeting that now she hath a potent party in the country. Now if all these things have endangered us as from that foundation and if she in particular hath disparaged all our ministers in the land that they have preached a covenant of works, and only Mr. Cotton a covenant of grace, why this is not to be suffered, and therefore being driven to the foundation and it being found that Mrs. Hutchinson is she that hath depraved all the ministers and hath been the cause of what is fallen out, why we must take away the foundation and the building will fall. . . .

The next morning.

Gov. We proceeded the last night as far as we could in hearing of this cause of Mrs. Hutchinson. There were divers things laid to her charge, her ordinary meetings about religious exercises, her speeches in derogation of the ministers among us, and the weakning of the hands and hearts of the people towards them. Here was sufficient proof made of that which she was accused of in that point concerning the ministers and their ministry, as that they did preach a covenant of works when others did preach a covenant of grace, and that they were not able ministers of the new testament, and that they had not the seal of the spirit, and this was spoken not as was pretended out of private conference, but out of conscience and warrant from scripture alledged the fear of man is a snare and seeing God had given her a calling to it she would freely speak. Some other speeches she used, as that the letter of the scripture held forth a covenant of works, and this is offered to be proved by probable grounds. If there be anything else that the court hath to say they may speak. . . .

Mrs. H. If you please to give me leave I shall give you the ground of what I know to be true. Being much troubled to see the falseness of the constitution of the church of England, I had like to have turned separatist; whereupon I kept a day of solemn humiliation and pondering of the thing; this scripture was brought unto me—he that denies Jesus Christ to be come in the flesh is antichrist[1]—This I considered of and in considering found that the papists did not deny him to be come in the flesh, nor we did not deny him—who then was antichrist? Was the Turk antichrist only? The Lord knows that I could not open scripture; he must by his prophetical office open it unto me. So after that being unsatisfied in the thing, the Lord was pleased to bring this scripture out of the Hebrews.[2] He that denies the testament denies the testator, and in this did open unto me and give me to see that those which did not teach the new covenant had the spirit of antichrist, and upon this he did discover the ministry unto me and ever since. I bless the Lord, he hath let me see which was the clear ministry and which the wrong. Since that time I confess I have been more choice and he hath let me to distinguish between the voice of my beloved and the voice of Moses, the voice of John Baptist and the voice of antichrist, for all those voices are spoken of in scripture. Now if you do condemn me for speaking what in my conscience I know to be truth I must commit myself unto the Lord.

[1] 1 John 2:18.   [2] Hebrews 9:16.

Mr. Nowell. How do you know that that was the spirit?

Mrs. H. How did Abraham know that it was God that bid him offer his son, being a breach of the sixth commandment?

Dep. Gov. By an immediate voice.

Mrs. H. So to me by an immediate revelation.

Dep. Gov. How! an immediate revelation.

Mrs. H. By the voice of his own spirit to my soul. I will give you another scripture, Jer. 46. 27, 28—out of which the Lord shewed me what he would do for me and the rest of his servants.—But after he was pleased to reveal himself to me I did presently like Abraham run to Hagar.[3] And after that he did let me see the atheism of my own heart, for which I begged of the Lord that it might not remain in my heart, and being thus, he did shew me this (a twelvemonth after) which I told you of before. Ever since that time I have been confident of what he hath revealed unto me.

Obliter- ⎱ another place out of Daniel chap. 7. and he and for us all, wherein he shewed
ated   ⎰ me the sitting of the judgment and the standing of all high and low before the Lord and how thrones and kingdoms were cast down before him. When our teacher came to New-England it was a great trouble unto me, my brother Wheelwright being put by also. I was then much troubled concerning the ministry under which I lived, and then that place in the 30th of Isaiah was brought to my mind. Though the Lord give thee bread of adversity and water of affliction yet shall not thy teachers be removed into corners any more, but thine eyes shall see thy teachers. The Lord giving me this promise and they being gone there was none then left that I was able to hear, and I could not be at rest but I must come hither. Yet that place of Isaiah did much follow me, though the Lord give thee the bread of adversity and water of affliction. This place lying I say upon me then this place in Daniel[4] was brought unto me and did shew me that though I should meet with affliction yet I am the same God that delivered Daniel out of the lion's den, I will also deliver thee.—Therefore I desire you to look to it, for you see this scripture fulfilled this day and therefore I desire you that as you tender the Lord and the church and commonwealth to consider and look what you do. You have power over my body but the Lord Jesus hath power over my body and soul, and assure yourselves thus much, you do as much as in you lies to put the Lord Jesus Christ from you, and if you go on in this course you begin you will bring a curse upon you and your posterity, and the mouth of the Lord hath spoken it.

Dep. gov. What is the scripture she brings?

Mr. Stoughton. Behold I turn away from you.

Mrs. H. But now having seen him which is invisible I fear not what man can do unto me.

Gov. Daniel was delivered by miracle do you think to be deliver'd so too?

Mrs. H. I do here speak it before the court. I look that the Lord should deliver me by his providence. . . .

Gov. I am persuaded that the revelation she brings forth is delusion.

All the court but some two or three ministers cry out, we all believe it—we all believe it. . . .

Gov. The court hath already declared themselves satisfied concerning the things you hear, and concerning the troublesomeness of her spirit and the danger of her course

---

[3] *Abraham run to Hagar:* In Genesis 16:1-6, Abram (later Abraham) fathers a child with his concubine Hagar when his wife Sarai (later Sarah) cannot conceive.

[4] Daniel 6:4–5.

amongst us, which is not to be suffered. Therefore if it be the mind of the court that Mrs. Hutchinson for these things that appear before us is unfit for our society, and if it be the mind of the court that she shall be banished out of our liberties and imprisoned till she be sent away, let them hold up their hands.

All but three.

Those that are contrary minded hold up yours,

Mr. Coddington and Mr. Colborn, only.

Mr. Jennison.[5] I cannot hold up my hand one way or the other, and I shall give my reason if the court require it.

Gov. Mrs. Hutchinson, the sentence of the court you hear is that you are banished from out of our jurisdiction as being a woman not fit for our society, and are to be imprisoned till the court shall send you away.

Mrs. H. I desire to know wherefore I am banished?

Gov. Say no more, the court knows wherefore and is satisfied.

---

from John Winthrop's Journal*

[Examination of Mrs. Anne Hutchinson]

The wife of one William Dyer, a milliner in the New Exchange, a very proper and fair woman, and both of them notoriously infected with Mrs. Hutchinson's errors, and very censorious and troublesome, (she being of a very proud spirit, and much addicted to revelations,) had been delivered of [a] child some few months before, October 17, and the child buried, (being stillborn,) and viewed of none but Mrs. Hutchinson and the midwife, one Hawkins's wife, a rank familist also; and another woman had a glimpse of it, who, not being able to keep counsel, as the other two did, some rumor began to spread, that the child was a monster. One of the elders, hearing of it, asked Mrs. Hutchinson, when she was ready to depart; whereupon she told him how it was, and said she meant to have it chronicled,[1] but excused her concealing of it till then, (by advice, as she said, of Mr. Cotton,) which coming to the governor's knowledge, he called another of the magistrates and that elder, and sent for the midwife, and examined her about it. At first she confessed only, that the head was defective and misplaced, but being told that Mrs. Hutchinson had revealed all, and that he intended to have it taken up and viewed, she made this report of it, viz.: It was a woman child, stillborn, about two months before the just time, having life a few hours before; it came hiplings till she turned it; it was of ordinary bigness; it had a face, but no head, and the ears stood upon the shoulders and were like an ape's; it had no forehead, but over the eyes four horns,

---

[5] William Jennison, a deputy from Watertown to the General Court.

* Appeared in *History of New England, 1630–1649*, edited by James Kendall Hosmer, 1908.

[1] Public registration of births, marriages and deaths was maintained in the Bay colony with great care.

hard and sharp; two of them were above one inch long, the other two shorter; the eyes standing out, and the mouth also; the nose hooked upward; all over the breast and back full of sharp pricks and scales, like a thornback; the navel and all the belly, with the distinction of the sex, were where the back should be, and the back and hips before, where the belly should have been; behind, between the shoulders, it had two mouths, and in each of them a piece of red flesh sticking out; it had arms and legs as other children; but, instead of toes, it had on each foot three claws, like a young fowl, with sharp talons.

The governor speaking with Mr. Cotton about it, he told him the reason why he advised them to conceal it: 1. Because he saw a providence of God in it, that the rest of the women, which were coming and going in the time of her travail, should then be absent. 2. He considered, that, if it had been his own case, he should have desired to have had it concealed. 3. He had known other monstrous births, which had been concealed, and that he thought God might intend only the instruction of the parents, and such other to whom it was known, etc. The like apology he made for himself in public, which was well accepted.

(2.) (*April.*)] The governor, with advice of some other of the magistrates and of the elders of Boston, caused the said monster to be taken up, and though it were much corrupted, yet most of those things were to be seen, as the horns and claws, the scales, etc. When it died in the mother's body, (which was about two hours before the birth,) the bed whereon the mother lay did shake, and withal there was such a noisome savor, as most of the women were taken with extreme vomiting and purging, so as they were forced to depart; and others of them their children were taken with convulsions, (which they never had before nor after,) and so were sent for home, so as by these occasions it came to be concealed.

Another thing observable was, the discovery of it, which was just when Mrs. Hutchinson was cast out of the church. For Mrs. Dyer going forth with her, a stranger asked, what young woman it was. The others answered, it was the woman which had the monster. . . .

Mary Rowlandson
ca. 1637–ca. 1710/11

Mary Rowlandson became a best-selling author from the trauma of Indian attack and captivity. At sunrise in February 1676 she and her family fell victim to rampaging Indians who had banded together throughout New England in "King Philip's War," a desperate effort to regain tribal lands. The story of Mrs. Rowlandson's ordeal in captivity became a phenomenon in American publishing history. A *Narrative of the Captivity and Restoration of Mrs. Mary Rowlandson* (1682), was reprinted so many times that it ranks as one of the great best-sellers in all of American literature.

Little is known of Mary Rowlandson's early life. Like many Puritans, she was probably brought to New England in childhood by her father, the wealthy landholder John White, who settled in Lancaster, Massachusetts. Around 1656 Mary wed the Reverend Joseph Rowlandson, and for twenty years thereafter she lived the demanding life of a frontier housewife and mother of three children. In early summer 1675, Indian assaults began against the Massachusetts colonists, initiated by the *sachem* (chief) Philip, three of whose tribesmen had been executed in Plymouth. Word of the Indian uprising spread through the colony. The Rowlandsons and their neighbors, fearing attack, fortified their dwellings, but the Rowlandson house was one of twelve hundred houses to be burned in King Philip's War, and the child they lost was among three hundred casualties suffered by colonial families before the war ended in August 1676. Mary was held captive of Indians for eleven weeks, then ransomed for twenty pounds and reunited with her husband and two surviving children. In the following year the family moved to Wethersfield, Connecticut, where Reverend Rowlandson—and then Mary—died within months.

In her own colonial era, the *Narrative* was religious in purpose. It reassured its author and her readers that God might sorely test them with "many trials and afflictions" but would ultimately redeem them. Puritan writers saw the Indians as "Dregs and Lees of the Earth"—at worst Satan's emissaries, at best heathen. In this context, Indian hostility indicated God's attitude toward the colonists. Many Puritan settlers found in Mary Rowlandson's example the assurance that God's redemptive power worked beyond the atrocities of this Indian war, one that Puritans felt posed a serious threat to the English settlements in New England. Mrs. Rowlandson's captivity and release to freedom seemed to be an individual reenactment of the colonists' communal mission toward salvation. Its piety, heroism, and fortitude were exemplary.

Mrs. Rowlandson and her contemporaries would be horrified to know that her *Narrative* is the fountainhead of popular frontier and Wild West thrillers recycling the pattern of attack, captivity, and escape from exotic Indians in wild, unsettled country. She would also be puzzled to hear that her *Narrative* is a part of our literature of cross-cultural encounter, including the writings of James Fenimore Cooper, Herman Melville, Lydia Maria Child, and William Faulkner. The *Narrative* is the antecedent of an important American literary tradition in which individualism and nationalism merge.

Further Reading:

A. Keiser, *The Indian in American Literature*, 1933.
R. Pearce, *The Savages of America*, 1953.
R. Slotkin, *Regeneration Through Violence*, 1973.

A. Kolodny, *The Land Before Her*, 1984.
M. Breitwieser, *American Puritanism and the Defense of Mourning*, 1990.

Text:

Journeys in New Worlds: Early American Women's Narratives, ed. D. Shea, with an introduction by A. Lang, 1990.

A Narrative of the Captivity and Restoration of Mrs. Mary Rowlandson

On the tenth of February, 1675, came the *Indians* with great number upon Lancaster. Their first coming was about Sun-rising. Hearing the noise of some guns, we looked out; several Houses were burning, and the smoke ascending to Heaven. There were five persons taken in one House, the Father and the Mother, and a sucking Child, they knock'd on the head; the other two they took, and carried away alive. There were two others, who, being out of their Garrison upon some occasion, were set upon; one was knock'd on the head, the other escaped. Another there was, who, running along, was shot and wounded, and fell down; he begged of them his Life, promising them Money, (as they told me;) but they would not hearken to him, but knock'd him on the head, stripped him naked, and split open his Bowels. Another, seeing many of the *Indians* about his Barn, ventured and went out, but was quickly shot down. There were three others belonging to the same Garrison who were killed. The *Indians,* getting up upon the Roof of the Barn, had advantage to shoot down upon them over their Fortification. Thus these murtherous Wretches went on, burning and destroying before them.

At length they came and beset our own House, and quickly it was the dolefullest day that ever mine eyes saw. The House stood upon the edge of a Hill; some of the *Indians* got behind the Hill, others into the Barn, and others behind any thing that would shelter them; from all which Places they shot against the House, so that the Bullets seemed to fly like Hail; and quickly they wounded one Man among us, then another, and then a third. About two Hours (according to my observation in that amazing time) they had been about the House before they could prevail to fire it, (which they did with flax and Hemp, which they brought out of the Barn, and there being no Defence about the House, only two Flankers,[1] at two opposite Corners, and one of them not finished). They fired it once, and one ventured out and quenched it; but they quickly fired it again, and that took. Now is that dreadful Hour come that I have often heard of, (in the time of the War, as it was the Case of others,) but now mine Eyes see it. Some in our House were fighting for their Lives, others wallowing in their Blood; the House on fire over our Heads, and the bloody Heathen ready to knock us on the Head if we stirred out. Now might we hear Mothers and Children crying out for themselves and one another, *Lord, what shall we do?* Then I took my Children (and one of my Sisters, hers) to go forth and leave the House; but as soon as we came to the Door and appeared, the *Indians* shot so thick that the Bullets rattled against the House as if one had taken an handful of Stones and threw them; so that we were fain to give back. We had six stout Dogs belonging to our Garrison, but none of them would stir, though another time, if an *Indian* had come to the Door, they were ready to fly upon him, and tear him down. The Lord hereby would make us the more to acknowledge his Hand, and to see that our Help is always in him. But out we must go, the Fire increasing and coming along behind us roaring, and the *Indians* gaping before us with their Guns, Spears, and Hatchets to devour us. No sooner were we out of the House but my Brother-in-Law[2] (being before wounded, in defending the House, in or near the Throat) fell down dead, whereat the *Indians* scornfully shouted and hallowed, and were presently upon him, stripping off his Clothes. The Bullets flying thick, one went thorow my side, and the same (as would seem) thorow the Bowels and Hand of my dear Child in my Arms.[3] One of my eldest Sister's Children (named William) had then his Leg broken, which the *Indians* perceiving, they knock'd him on the head. Thus were we butchered by those merciless Hea-

---

[1] Projecting fortifications.
[2] Ensign John Divoll, husband of Rowlandson's youngest sister, Hannah.

[3] Sarah, age six.

then, standing amazed, with the Blood running down to our Heels. My elder sister,[4] being yet in the House, and seeing those woful Sights, the Infidels hauling Mothers one way and Children another, and some wallowing in their Blood, and her elder son telling her that (her Son) William was dead, and myself was wounded; she said, *And, Lord, let me die with them!* which was no sooner said but she was struck with a Bullet, and fell down dead over the Threshold. I hope she is reaping the Fruit of her good Labours, being faithful to the Service of God in her Place. In her younger years she lay under much trouble upon Spiritual accounts, till it pleased God to make that precious Scripture take hold of her Heart, *2 Cor.* xii. 9, *And he said unto me, My grace is sufficient for thee.* More than twenty years after, I have heard her tell how sweet and comfortable that Place was to her. But to return: the *Indians* laid hold of us, pulling me one way and the Children another, and said, *Come, go along with us.* I told them they would kill me. They answered, *If I were willing to go along with them, they would not hurt me.*

O the doleful Sight that now was to behold at this House! *Come, behold the works of the Lord, what desolation he has made in the earth.*[5] Of thirty seven Persons who were in this one House, none escaped either present Death or a bitter Captivity, save only one, who might say as he, *Job* i. 15, *And I only am escaped alone to tell the news.* There were twelve killed, some shot, some stabb'd with their Spears, some knock'd down with their Hatchets. When we are in prosperity, oh the Little that we think of such dreadful Sights; and to see our dear Friends and Relations lie bleeding out their Heart-blood upon the Ground! There was one who was chopped into the Head with a Hatchet, and stripp'd naked, and yet was crawling up and down. It was a solemn Sight to see so many Christians lying in their Blood, some here and some there, like a company of Sheep torn by Wolves; all of them stript naked by a company of hell-hounds, roaring, singing, ranting, and insulting, as if they would have torn our very hearts out; yet the Lord, by his Almighty power, preserved a number of us from death, for there were twenty-four of us taken alive; and carried Captive.

I had often before this said, that if the *Indians* should come, I should chuse rather to be killed by them than taken alive; but when it came to the trial my mind changed; their glittering Weapons so daunted my Spirit, that I chose rather to go along with those (as I may say) ravenous Bears, than that moment to end my daies. And that I may the better declare what happened to me during that grievous Captivity, I shall particularly speak of the several Removes we had up and down the Wilderness.

The first Remove.—Now away we must go with those Barbarous Creatures, with our bodies wounded and bleeding, and our hearts no less than our bodies. About a mile we went that night; up upon a hill, within sight of the Town, where they intended to lodge. There was hard by a vacant house; (deserted by the English before for fear of the *Indians;*) I asked them whether I might not lodge in the house that night? to which they answered, What, will you love *English-men* still? This was the dolefullest night that ever my eyes saw: oh the roaring, and singing, and dancing, and yelling of those black creatures in the night, which made the place a lively resemblance of hell! And as miserable

---

[4] Elizabeth, wife of Henry Kerley. Kerley was en route to Boston with Joseph Rowlandson at the time of the raid.

[5] Psalm 46:8. Like many of the biblical passages Rowlandson quotes, this one alludes to God's conquest of the heathen and closes with the injunction "Be still, and know that I am God: I will be exalted among the heathen, I will be exalted in the earth."

was the waste that was there made of Horses, Cattle, Sheep, Swine, Calves, Lambs, Roasting Pigs, and Fowls, (which they had plundered in the Town,) some roasting, some lying and burning, and some boyling, to feed our merciless Enemies; who were joyful enough, though we were disconsolate. To add to the dolefulness of the former day, and the dismalness of the present night, my thoughts ran upon my losses and sad bereaved condition. All was gone; my Husband gone, (at least separated from me, he being in the Bay; and, to add to my grief, the *Indians* told me they would kill him as he came homeward,) my Children gone, my Relations and Friends gone, our house and home, and all our comforts within door and without, all was gone, (except my life,) and I knew not but the next moment that might go too.

There remained nothing to me but one poor wounded Babe, and it seemed at present worse than death that it was in such a pitiful condition, bespeaking Compassion, and I had no refreshing for it, nor suitable things to revive it. Little do many think what is the savageness and brutishness of this barbarous Enemy, even those that seem to profess[6] more than others among them, when the *English* have fallen into their hands.

Those seven that were killed at Lancaster the summer before, upon a Sabbath-day, and the one that was afterward killed upon a week day, were slain and mangled in a barbarous manner by one-eyed John, and Marlberough's Praying *Indians*,[7] which Capt. Mosely[8] brought to Boston, as the *Indians* told me.

The second Remove.—But now (the next morning) I must turn my back upon the Town, and travel with them into the vast and desolate Wilderness, I know not whither. It is not my tongue or pen can express the sorrows of my heart and bitterness of my spirit that I had at this departure: but God was with me in a wonderful manner, carrying me along, and bearing up my Spirit, that it did not quite fail. One of the *Indians* carried my poor wounded Babe upon a horse: it went moaning all along, I shall die, I shall die! I went on foot after it, with sorrow that cannot be exprest. At length I took it off the horse, and carried it in my arms, till my strength failed, and I fell down with it. Then they set me upon a horse, with my wounded Child in my lap; and there being no Furniture upon the horse back; as we were going down a steep hill, we both fell over the horse's head, at which they, like inhuman creatures, laught, and rejoiced to see it, though I thought we should there have ended our dayes, as overcome with so many difficulties. But the Lord renewed my strength still, and carried me along, that I might see more of his power, yea, so much that I could never have thought of had I not experienced it.

After this it quickly began to Snow; and when night came on they stopt; and now down I must sit in the Snow, (by a little fire and a few boughs behind me,) with my sick Child in my lap; and calling much for water, being now (thorough the wound) fallen into a violent Fever; (my own wound also growing so stiff that I could scarce sit down or rise up;) yet so it must be, that I must sit all this cold winter night upon the cold snowy ground, with my sick Child in my arms, looking that every hour would be the last of its life; and having no Christian Friend near me, either to comfort or help me. Oh

---

6 That is, profess Christianity.
7 Rowlandson refers here to a raid on the outskirts of Lancaster the previous August led by "One-eyed" John Monoco, chief of the Nashaway Indians, and involving the Christian Indians who owned 150 acres in the

town of Marlborough, ten miles from Lancaster.
8 An ex-Jamaica privateer and a notorious Indian-hater, Samuel Mosely was one of the most popular and cruelest officers in the English army.

I may see the wonderful power of God, that my Spirit did not utterly sink under my affliction!—still the Lord upheld me with his gracious and merciful Spirit, and we were both alive to see the light of the next morning.

The third Remove.—The morning being come, they prepared to go on their way. One of the Indians got up upon a horse, and they set me up behind him, with my poor sick Babe in my lap. A very wearisome and tedious day I had of it; what with my own wound, and my Child's being so exceeding sick, and in a lamentable Condition with her wound. It may easily be judged what a poor feeble condition we were in, there being not the least crumb of refreshing that came within either of our mouths from Wednesday night to Saturday night, except only a little cold water. This day in the afternoon, about an hour by Sun, we came to the place where they intended, *viz.* an *Indian town* called Wenimesset,[9] Northward of Quabaug. When we were come, Oh the number of Pagans (now merciless Enemies) that there came about me, that I may say as *David,* Psal. xxvii. 13. *I had fainted, unless I had believed,*[10] &c. The next day was the Sabbath: I then remembered how careless I had been of God's holy time; how many Sabbaths I had lost and mispent, and how evilly I had walked in God's sight; which lay so close upon my Spirit, that it was easie for me to see how righteous it was with God to cut off the thread of my life, and cast me out of his presence for ever. Yet the Lord still shewed mercy to me, and upheld me; and as he wounded me with one hand, so he healed me with the other. This day there came to me one Robert Pepper, (a Man belonging to Roxbury,) who was taken in Capt. Beers his fight;[11] and had been now a considerable time with the *Indians;* and up with them almost as far as Albany, to see King Philip, as he told me, and was now very lately come with them into these parts. Hearing, I say, that I was in this *Indian* Town, he obtained leave to come and see me. He told me he himself was wounded in the Leg, at Capt. Beers his fight; and was not able sometime to go, but as they carried him, and that he took oaken leaves and laid to his wound, and through the blessing of God he was able to travel again. Then I took oaken leaves and laid to my side, and with the blessing of God it cured me also; yet before the cure was wrought, I may say as it is in *Psal.* xxxviii. 5, 6, *My wounds stink and are corrupt, I am troubled, I am bowed down greatly, I go mourning all the day long.* I sate much alone with a poor wounded Child in my lap, which mourned night and day, having nothing to revive the body or chear the Spirits of her; but, instead of that, sometimes one Indian would come and tell me one hour, And your Master will knock your Child in the head, and then a second, and then a third, Your Master will quickly knock your Child in the head.

This was the Comfort I had from them; miserable comforters are ye all, as he said. Thus nine dayes I sat upon my knees, with my babe in my lap, till my flesh was raw again. My child, being even ready to depart this sorrowful world, they bad me carry it

---

[9] The swamp stronghold of the Quabaug Indians, near New Braintree, Massachusetts.

[10] Once again the psalm enjoins patience: "I had fainted, unless I had believed to see the goodness of the Lord in the land of the living. Wait on the Lord: be of good courage, and he shall strengthen thine heart: wait, I say, on the Lord."

[11] Captain Richard Beers of Watertown was waylaid by Indians on September 3, 1675, while leading a party of thirty-six reinforcements to the garrison at Northfield. Beers and nineteen others were killed, Robert Pepper was taken captive, and the remainder escaped.

out to another Wigwam; (I suppose because they would not be troubled with such spectacles;) whither I went with a very heavy heart, and down I sate with the picture of death
in my lap. About two hours in the Night, my sweet Babe, like a Lamb, departed this life,
on Feb. 18, 1675 [1676] it being about six years and five months old. It was nine dayes
(from the first wounding) in this Miserable condition, without any refreshing of one nature or other, except a little cold water. I cannot but take notice how, at another time, I
could not bear to be in the room where any dead person was; but now the case is
changed; I must and could lye down by my dead Babe, side by side, all the night after. I
have thought since of the wonderful goodness of God to me, in preserving me so in the
use of my reason and senses in that distressed time, that I did not use wicked and violent
means to end my own miserable life. In the morning, when they understood that my
child was dead, they sent for me home to my Master's Wigwam; (by my Master, in this
writing, must be understood Quannopin, who was a Saggamore, and married King
Philip's wife's Sister; not that he first took me, but I was sold to him by another *Narrhaganset Indian,* who took me when first I came out of the Garrison). I went to take up my
dead Child in my arms to carry it with me, but they bid me let it alone; there was no resisting, but go I must and leave it. When I had been a while at my Master's wigwam, I
took the first opportunity I could get to go look after my dead child. When I came, I
asked them what they had done with it. They told me it was upon the hill; then they went
and shewed me where it was, where I saw the ground was newly digged, and there they
told me they had buried it; there I left that child in the Wilderness, and must commit it,
and myself also, in this wilderness condition, to Him who is above all. God having taken
away this dear child, I went to see my daughter Mary, who was at the same *Indian Town,*
at a Wigwam not very far off, though we had little liberty or opportunity to see one another: she was about ten years old, and taken from the door at first by a Praying *Indian,*
and afterward sold for a gun. When I came in sight she would fall a-weeping; at which
they were provoked, and would not let me come near her, but bade me be gone, which
was a heart-cutting word to me. I had one child dead, another in the wilderness I knew
not where, the third they would not let me come near to: *Me* (as he said) *have ye bereaved
of my children; Joseph is not, and Simeon is not, and ye will take Benjamin also, all these
things are against me.*[12] I could not sit still in this condition, but kept walking from one
place to another: and as I was going along, my heart was even overwhelmed with the
thoughts of my condition, and that I should have Children and a Nation which I knew
not ruled over them; whereupon I earnestly intreated the Lord that he would consider
my low estate, and shew me a token for good, and, if it were his blessed will, some sign
and hope of some relief: and indeed quickly the Lord answered, in some measure, my
poor Prayer; for, as I was going up and down, mourning and lamenting my condition,
my Son came to me, and asked me how I did. I had not seen him before since the destruction of the Town; and I knew not where he was till I was informed by himself, that
he was amongst a smaller parcel of *Indians,* whose place was about six miles off. With
tears in his eyes, he asked me whether his sister Sarah was dead, and told me he had seen
his Sister Mary; and prayed me that I would not be troubled in reference to himself. The
occasion of his coming to see me at this time was this: There was, as I said, about six

---

[12] Genesis 42:36.

miles from us a small Plantation of *Indians*, where it seems he had been during his Captivity; and at this time there were some Forces of the *Indians* gathered out of our company, and some also from them, (amongst whom was my Son's Master,) to go to assault and burn Medfield: in this time of the absence of his Master, his Dame brought him to see me. I took this to be some gracious Answer to my earnest and unfeigned desire. The next day, *viz.* to this, the *Indians* returned from Medfield, (all the Company, for those that belonged to the other smaller company came thorow the Town that now we were at). But before they came to us, Oh the outragious roaring and hooping that there was! They began their din about a mile before they came to us. By their noise and hooping, they signified how many they had destroyed; (which was at that time twenty-three). Those that were with us at home were gathered together as soon as they heard the hooping, and every time that the other went over their number, these at home gave a shout, that the very Earth rang again; and thus they continued till those that had been upon the expedition were come up to the Saggamore's Wigwam; and then, Oh the hideous insulting and triumphing that there was over some *English-men's* Scalps that they had taken (as their manner is) and brought with them! I cannot but take notice of the wonderful mercy of God to me in those afflictions, in sending me a Bible: one of the *Indians* that came from Medfield fight, and had brought some plunder; came to me, and asked me if I would have a Bible, he had got one in his Basket. I was glad of it, and asked him whether he thought the *Indians* would let me read. He answered, yes. So I took the Bible, and in that melancholy time it came into my mind to read first the 28th *Chapter* of *Deuteronomie*, which I did; and when I had read it, my dark heart wrought on this manner, that there was no mercy for me; that the blessings were gone, and the curses came in their room, and that I had lost my opportunity. But the Lord helped me to go on reading till I came to *Chap.* xxx, the seven first verses;[13] where I found there was mercy promised again, if we would return to him by repentance; and though we were scattered from one end of the earth to the other, yet the Lord would gather us together, and turn all those curses upon our Enemies. I do not desire to live to forget this Scripture, and what comfort it was to me.

Now the *Indians* began to talk of removing from this place, some one way and some another. There were now, besides myself, nine *English* Captives in this place, (all of them Children, except one Woman). I got an opportunity to go and take my leave of them; they being to go one way and I another. I asked them whether they were earnest

---

[13] "And it shall come to pass, when all these things are come upon thee, the blessing and the curse, which I have set before thee, and thou shalt call them to mind among all the nations, whither the Lord thy God hath driven thee, and shalt return unto the Lord thy God, and shalt obey his voice according to all that I command thee this day, thou and thy children, with all thine heart, and with all thy soul; that then the Lord thy God will turn thy captivity, and have compassion upon thee, and will return and gather thee from all the nations, whither the Lord thy God hath scattered thee. If any of thine be driven out unto the outmost parts of heaven, from thence will the Lord thy God gather thee, and from thence will he fetch thee: and the Lord thy God will bring thee into the land which thy fathers possessed, and thou shalt possess it; and he will do thee good, and multiply thee above thy fathers. And the Lord thy God will circumcise thine heart, and the heart of thy seed, to love the Lord thy God with all thine heart, and with all thy soul, that thou mayest live. And the Lord thy God will put all these curses upon thine enemies, and on them that hate thee, which persecuted thee" (Deuteronomy 30:1–7).

with God for deliverance; they all told me they did as they were able; and it was some comfort to me that the Lord stirred up Children to look to him. The Woman, *viz.* Goodwife Joslin, told me she should never see me again, and that she could find in her heart to run away. I wisht her not to run away by any means, for we were near thirty miles from any *English* Town, and she very big with Child, and had but one week to reckon; and another Child in her arms two years old; and bad rivers there were to go over, and we were feeble with our poor and coarse entertainment. I had my Bible with me; I pulled it out; and asked her whether she would read; we opened the Bible, and lighted on *Psal.* xxvii, in which Psalm we especially took notice of that, *ver. ult. Wait on the Lord, be of good courage, and he shall strengthen thine heart; wait, I say, on the Lord.*

   The fourth Remove.—And now must I part with that little company that I had. Here I parted from my daughter Mary, (whom I never saw again till I saw her in Dorchester, returned from Captivity,) and from four little Cousins and Neighbors, some of which I never saw afterward; the Lord only knows the end of them. Amongst them also was that poor woman beforementioned,[14] who came to a sad end, as some of the company told me in my travel: she having much grief upon her Spirit about her miserable condition, being so near her time, she would be often asking the Indians to let her go home; they, not being willing to that, and yet vexed with her importunity, gathered a great company together about her, and stript her naked, and set her in the midst of them; and when they had sung and danced about her (in their hellish manner) as long as they pleased; they knockt her on the head, and the child in her arms with her. When they had done that they made a fire, and put them both into it; and told the other Children that were with them, that if they attempted to go home, they would serve them in like manner. The Children said she did not shed one tear, but prayed all the while. But, to return to my own Journey,—we travelled about half a day, or a little more, and came to a desolate place in the Wilderness; where there were no Wigwams or Inhabitants before; we came about the middle of the afternoon to this place; cold, and wet, and snowy, and hungry, and weary, and no refreshing (for man) but the cold ground to sit on, and our poor *Indian cheer.*

   Heart-aking thoughts here I had about my poor Children, who were scattered up and down amongst the wild Beasts of the Forest: my head was light and dizzy, (either through hunger, or hard lodging, or trouble, or all together,) my knees feeble, my body raw by sitting double night and day, that I cannot express to man the affliction that lay upon my Spirit; but the Lord helped me at that time to express it to himself. I opened my Bible to read, and the Lord brought that precious Scripture to me, *Jer.* xxxi. 16, *Thus saith the Lord, refrain thy voice from weeping, and thine eyes from tears, for thy work shall be rewarded, and they shall come again from the land of the enemy.*[15] This was a sweet Cordial to me when I was ready to faint; many and many a time have I sate down and wept sweetly over this Scripture. At this place we continued about four days.

   The fifth Remove.—The occasion (as I thought) of their moving at this time was the *English Army,* its being near and following them; for they went as if they had gone for their lives for some considerable way; and then they made a stop, and chose out some of their stoutest men, and sent them back to hold the *English Army* in play whilst the rest escaped; and then, like Jehu,[16] they marched on furiously, with their old and with their

14 That is, Goodwife Joslin.   16 See 2 Kings 9:20.
15 These words are spoken to Rachel, who is
   mourning her lost children.

young: some carried their old decrepit Mothers, some carried one and some another. Four of them carried a great *Indian* upon a bier; but going through a thick Wood with him they were hindered, and could make no haste; whereupon they took him upon their backs, and carried him, one at a time, till we came to Bacquaug River. Upon a Friday, a little after noon, we came to this River. When all the Company was come up, and were gathered together, I thought to count the number of them; but they were so many, and being somewhat in motion, it was beyond my skill. In this travel, because of my wound, I was somewhat favoured in my load; I carried only my knitting-work, and two quarts of parched Meal. Being very faint, I asked my Mistress to give me one spoonful of the meal, but she would not give me a taste. They quickly fell to cutting dry trees, to make rafts to carry them over the River; and soon my turn came to go over. By the advantage of some brush, which they had laid upon the Raft to sit on; I did not wet my foot, (when many of themselves at the other end were mid-leg deep,) which cannot but be acknowledged as a favour of God to my weakened body, it being a very cold time. I was not before acquainted with such kind of doings or dangers.—*When thou passest through the waters I will be with thee, and through the rivers they shall not overflow thee.* Isai. xliii. 2. A certain number of us got over the river that night, but it was the night after the Sabbath before all the company was got over. On the Saturday they boyled an old Horse's leg, (which they had got,) and so we drank of the broth; as soon as they thought it was ready, and when it was almost all gone, they filled it up again.

The first week of my being among them I hardly eat any thing; the second week I found my stomach grow very faint for want of something; and yet 'twas very hard to get down their filthy trash; but the third week (though I could think how formerly my stomach would turn against this or that, and I could starve and die before I could eat such things, yet) they were pleasant and savoury to my taste. I was at this time knitting a pair of white Cotton Stockings for my Mistress; and I had not yet wrought upon the Sabbath-day: when the Sabbath came, they bade me go to work; I told them it was Sabbath-day, and desired them to let me rest, and told them I would do as much more to-morrow; to which they answered me, they would break my face. And here I cannot but take notice of the strange providence of God in preserving the Heathen: They were many hundreds, old and young, some sick and some lame; many had *Papooses* at their backs, the greatest number (at this time with us) were *Squaws;* and they travelled with all they had, bag and baggage, and yet they got over this River aforesaid; and on Monday they set their Wigwams on fire, and away they went: on that very day came the *English* Army after them to this River, and saw the smoke of their Wigwams; and yet this River put a stop to them. God did not give them courage or activity to go after us; we were not ready for so great a mercy as victory and deliverance; if we had been, God would have found out a way for the *English* to have passed this River, as well as for the *Indians*, with their *Squaws* and *Children,* and all their *Luggage.*—*Oh that my people had hearkened to me, and Israel had walked in my wayes, I should soon have subdued their Enemies, and turned my hand against their Adversaries,* Psal. lxxxi. 13, 14.

The sixth Remove.—On Monday (as I said) they set their Wigwams on fire and went away. It was a cold morning; and before us was a great Brook with Ice on it; some waded through it up to the knees and higher; but others went till they came to a Beaver-Dam, and I amongst them, where, thorough the good providence of God, I did not wet my foot. I went along that day mourning and lamenting, leaving farther my own Countrey, and travelling into the vast and howling Wilderness; and I understood something of Lot's Wife's Temptation,[17] when she looked back. We came that day to a great Swamp; by the side of which we took up our lodging that night. When I came to the brow of the hill that looked toward the Swamp, I thought we had been come to a great *Indian Town,* (though there were none but our own Company,) the *Indians* were as thick as the Trees; it seemed as if there had been a thousand Hatchets going at once: if one looked before one there was nothing but *Indians,* and behind one nothing but *Indians;* and so on either hand; I myself in the midst, and no Christian Soul near me, and yet how hath the Lord preserved me in safety! Oh the experience that I have had of the goodness of God to me and mine!

The seventh Remove.—After a restless and hungry night there, we had a wearisome time of it the next day. The Swamp by which we lay was, as it were, a deep Dungeon, and an exceeding high and steep hill before it. Before I got to the top of the hill, I thought my heart and legs and all would have broken and failed me; what through faintness and soreness of Body, it was a grievous day of Travel to me. As we went along, I saw a place where *English* Cattle had been; that was a comfort to me, such as it was. Quickly after that we came to an *English* path, which so took with me that I thought I could there have freely lyen down and died. That day, a little after noon, we came to Squaukheag; where the *Indians* quickly spread themselves over the deserted *English* Fields, gleaning what they could find; some pickt up Ears of Wheat that were crickled down; some found ears of *Indian Corn;* some found Ground-nuts, and others sheaves of wheat, that were frozen together in the Shock, and went to threshing of them out. Myself got two Ears of *Indian Corn;* and whilst I did but turn my back, one of them was stollen from me, which much troubled me. There came an *Indian* to them at that time with a Basket of *Horse-liver.* I asked him to give me a piece. What, (says he) can you eat Horse-liver? I told him I would try, if he would give me a piece; which he did; and I laid it on the coals to roast; but before it was half ready, they got half of it away from me; so that I was fain to take the rest, and eat it as it was, with the blood about my mouth, and yet a savory bit it was to me; for to the hungry soul every bitter thing is sweet. A solemn sight me thought it was to see whole fields of Wheat and *Indian Corn* forsaken and spoiled; and the remainders of them to be food for our merciless Enemies. That night we had a mess of Wheat for our supper.

The eighth Remove.—On the morrow morning we must go over the River, *i.e.* Connecticut, to meet with King Philip. Two Cannoos full they had carried over, the next turn I myself was to go; but as my foot was upon the Cannoo to step in, there was a sudden outcry among them, and I must step back; and, instead of going over the River, I must go four or five miles up the River farther northward. Some of the *Indians* ran one way, and some another. The cause of this rout was, as I thought, their espying some *English* Scouts who were thereabout.

In this travel up the River, about noon the Company made a stop, and sat down; some to eat, and others to rest them. As I sate amongst them, musing of things past, my Son Joseph unexpectedly came to me; we asked of each others welfare; bemoaning our doleful condition, and the change that had come upon us: we had Husband and Father,

---

[17] Lot's wife is turned into a pillar of salt when she disobeys God's command and looks back at the destruction of Sodom and Gomorrah (see Genesis 19).

and Children and Sisters, and Friends and Relations, and House and Home, and many Comforts of this life; but now we might say as *Job, Naked came I out of my mother's womb, and naked shall I return; the Lord gave, and the Lord hath taken away, blessed be the name of the Lord.* I asked him, whether he would read? he told me he earnestly desired it. I gave him my Bible, and he lighted upon that comfortable Scripture, *Psal.* cxviii. 17, 18, *I shall not die, but live, and declare the works of the Lord: the Lord hath chastened me sore, yet he hath not given me over to death.* Look here, *Mother,* (says he) did you read this? And here I may take occasion to mention one principal ground of my setting forth these few Lines; even as the Psalmist says, To declare the works of the Lord, and his wonderful power in carrying us along, preserving us in the Wilderness, while under the Enemies hand, and returning of us in safety again; and his goodness in bringing to my hand so many comfortable and suitable Scriptures in my distress. But, to Return: we travelled on till night, and, in the morning, we must go over the River to Philip's Crew. When I was in the Cannoo, I could not but be amazed at the numerous Crew of Pagans that were on the Bank on the other side. When I came ashore, they gathered all about me, I sitting alone in the midst; I observed they asked one another Questions, and laughed, and rejoyced over their Gains and Victories; then my heart began to faile; and I fell a-weeping; which was the first time, to my remembrance, that I wept before them. Although I had met with so much Affliction, and my heart was many times ready to break, yet could I not shed one tear in their sight; but rather had been all this while in a maze, and like one astonished; but now I may say, as *Psal.* cxxxvii. 1, *By the rivers of* Babylon, *there we sate down, yea we wept when we remembered Zion.* There one of them asked me, why I wept? I could hardly tell what to say; yet I answered, they would kill me: No, said he, none will hurt you. Then came one of them and gave me two spoonfuls of Meal to comfort me, and another gave me half a pint of Pease, which was more worth than many Bushels at another time. Then I went to see King Philip; he bade me come in and sit down, and asked me, whether I would smoak it? (an usual Compliment now-a-days amongst Saints and Sinners.) But this no way suited me; for though I had formerly used Tobacco, yet I had left it ever since I was first taken. *It seems to be a Bait the Devil layes to make men lose their precious time.* I remember with shame, how, formerly, when I had taken two or three Pipes, I was presently ready for another, such a bewitching thing it is; but I thank God he has now given me power over it; surely there are many who may be better imployed than to lye sucking a stinking Tobacco-pipe.

Now the *Indians* gather their Forces to go against North-hampton; over night one went about yelling and hooting to give notice of the design; whereupon they fell to boyling of Ground Nuts, and parching of Corn, (as many as had it) for their Provision; and, in the morning, away they went. During my abode in this place Philip spake to me to make a shirt for his Boy, which I did; for which he gave me a shilling; I offered the money to my Master, but he bade me keep it; and with it I bought a piece of Horse flesh. Afterwards I made a Cap for his Boy, for which he invited me to Dinner; I went, and he gave me a Pancake about as big as two fingers; it was made of parched Wheat, beaten and fryed in Bears grease, but I thought I never tasted pleasanter meat in my life. There was a Squaw who spake to me to make a shirt for her Sannup;[18] for which she gave me a piece of Bear. Another asked me to knit a pair of Stockings, for which she

---

[18] Algonquin for "husband."

gave me a quart of Pease. I boyled my Pease and Bear together, and invited my Master and Mistress to Dinner; but the proud Gossip,[19] because I served them both in one Dish, would eat nothing, except one bit that he gave her upon the point of his Knife. Hearing that my Son was come to this place, I went to see him, and found him lying flat upon the ground; I asked him how he could sleep so? he answered me, that he was not asleep, but at Prayer; and lay so, that they might not observe what he was doing. I pray God he may remember these things, now he is returned in safety. At this place (the Sun now getting higher) what with the beams and heat of the Sun, and the smoak of the Wigwams, I thought I should have been blind: I could scarce discern one Wigwam from another. There was here one Mary Thurston of Medfield, who, seeing how it was with me, lent me a Hat to wear; but as soon as I was gone, the Squaw (who owned that Mary Thurston) came running after me, and got it away again. Here there was a Squaw who gave me one spoonful of Meal; I put it in my Pocket to keep it safe; yet, notwithstanding, somebody stole it, but put five *Indian Corns* in the room of it; which Corns were the greatest Provision I had in my travel for one day.

The *Indians* returning from North-hampton, brought with them some Horses and Sheep, and other things which they had taken; I desired them that they would carry me to Albany upon one of those Horses, and sell me for Powder; for so they had sometimes discoursed. I was utterly hopeless of getting home on foot the way that I came. I could hardly bear to think of the many weary steps I had taken to come to this place.

The ninth Remove.—But instead of going either to Albany or homeward, we must go five miles up the River, and then go over it. Here we abode a while. Here lived a sorry *Indian,* who spake to me to make him a shirt; when I had done it, he would pay me nothing. But he living by the River side, where I often went to fetch water, I would often be putting him in mind, and calling for my pay; at last, he told me, if I would make another shirt, for a Papoos not yet born, he would give me a knife, which he did, when I had done it. I carried the knife in, and my Master asked me to give it him, and I was not a little glad that I had any thing that they would accept of, and be pleased with. When we were at this place, my Master's Maid came home; she had been gone three Weeks into the *Narrhaganset country* to fetch Corn, where they had stored up some in the ground; she brought home about a peck and half of Corn. This was about the time that their great Captain (Naananto)[20] was killed in the *Narrhaganset* Country.

My son being now about a mile from me, I asked liberty to go and see him; they bade me go, and away I went; but quickly lost myself, travelling over Hills and through Swamps, and could not find the way to him. And I cannot but admire at the wonderful power and goodness of God to me, in that though I was gone from home, and met with all sorts of *Indians,* and those I had no knowledge of, and there being no *Christian Soul* near me; yet not one of them offered the least imaginable miscarriage to me. I turned homeward again, and met with my Master; he shewed me the way to my Son: when I came to him I found him not well; and withal he had a Boyl on his side, which much troubled him; we bemoaned one another a while, as the Lord helped us, and then I returned again. When I was returned, I found myself as unsatisfied as I was before. I went

---

[19] A person, usually a woman, of light and trifling character.

[20] Better known as Canonchet, the "king" of the Narragansetts, Naananto was captured by the English on April 2, 1676.

up and down moaning and lamenting; and my spirit was ready to sink with the thoughts of my poor Children; my Son was ill, and I could not but think of his mournful looks; and no *Christian Friend* was near him to do any office of love for him, either for Soul or Body. And my poor Girl, I knew not where she was, nor whether she was sick or well, or alive or dead. I repaired under these thoughts to my Bible (my great comforter in that time) and that scripture came to my hand, *Cast thy burden upon the Lord, and he shall sustain thee.* Psal. lv. 22.

But I was fain to go and look after something to satisfie my hunger; and going among the Wigwams, I went into one, and there found a Squaw who shewed herself very kind to me, and gave me a piece of Bear. I put it into my pocket, and came home; but could not find an opportunity to broil it, for fear they would get it from me, and there it lay all that day and night in my stinking pocket. In the morning I went again to the same Squaw, who had a Kettle of Ground nuts boyling; I asked her to let me boyle my piece of Bear in her Kettle, which she did, and gave me some Ground nuts to eat with it, and I cannot but think how pleasant it was to me. I have seen Bear baked very handsomely amongst the *English,* and some liked it, but the thoughts that it was Bear made me tremble: but now that was savoury to me that one would think was enough to turn the stomach of a bruit Creature.

One bitter cold day I could find no room to sit down before the fire; I went out, and could not tell what to do, but I went into another Wigwam where they were also sitting round the fire; but the Squaw laid a skin for me, and bid me sit down; and gave me some Ground nuts, and bade me come again; and told me they would buy me if they were able; and yet these were Strangers to me that I never knew before.

The tenth Remove.—That day a small part of the Company removed about three quarters of a mile, intending farther the next day. When they came to the place where they intended to lodge, and had pitched their Wigwams; being hungry, I went again back to the place we were before at, to get something to eat, being incouraged by the Squaw's kindness who bade me come again; when I was there, there came an *Indian* to look after me; who, when he had found me, kickt me all along; I went home, and found Venison roasting that night, but they would not give me one bit of it. Sometimes I met with Favour, and sometimes with nothing but Frowns.

The eleventh Remove.—The next day in the morning they took their Travel, intending a dayes journey up the River; I took my load at my back, and quickly we came to wade over a River, and passed over tiresome and wearisome Hills. One Hill was so steep, that I was fain to creep up upon my knees; and to hold by the twigs and bushes to keep myself from falling backward. My head also was so light, that I usually reeled as I went, but I hope all those wearisome steps that I have taken are but a forwarding of me to the Heavenly rest. *I know, O Lord, that thy judgments are right, and that thou in faithfulness hast afflicted me.* Psal. cxix. 75.

The twelfth Remove.—It was upon a Sabbath-day morning that they prepared for their Travel. This morning, I asked my Master, whether he would sell me to my Husband? he answered, *Nux,*[21] which did much rejoyce my spirit. My Mistress, before we went, was gone to the burial of a *Papoos;* and returning, she found me sitting and reading in my Bible; she snatched it hastily out of my hand, and threw it out of doors; I ran out and catcht it up, and put it into my pocket, and never let her see it afterward. Then

---

[21] That is, yes.

they packed up their things to be gone, and gave me my load; I complained it was too heavy, whereupon she gave me a slap in the face, and bade me go; I lifted up my heart to God, hoping the Redemption was not far off; and the rather, because their insolency grew worse and worse.

But the thoughts of my going homeward (for so we bent our course) much cheared my Spirit, and made my burden seem light, and almost nothing at all. But (to my amazement and great perplexity) the scale was soon turned; for, when we had gone a little way, on a sudden my Mistress gives out she would go no further, but turn back again, and said I must go back again with her, and she called her Sannup, and would have had him gone back also, but he would not, but said, he would go on, and come to us again in three dayes. My Spirit was upon his (I confess) very impatient and almost outragious. I thought I could as well have died as went back. I cannot declare the trouble that I was in about it; but yet back again I must go. As soon as I had an opportunity, I took my Bible to read, and that quieting Scripture came to my hand, *Psal.* xlvi. 10, *Be still, and know that I am God,* which stilled my spirit for the present; but a sore time of trial I concluded I had to go through. My Master being gone, who seemed to me the best Friend that I had of an *Indian,* both in cold and hunger, and quickly so it proved; down I sat, with my Heart as full as it could hold, and yet so hungry, that I could not sit neither; but going out to see what I could find, and walking among the Trees, I found six Acorns and two Chesnuts, which were some refreshment to me. Towards night I gathered me some sticks for my own comfort, that I might not lye a Cold; but when we came to lye down, they bade me go out and lye somewhere else, for they had company (they said) come in more than their own; I told them I could not tell where to go, they bade me go look; I told them, if I went to another *Wigwam* they would be angry, and send me home again. Then one of the company drew his Sword, and told me he would run me through if I did not go presently. Then was I fain to stoop to this rude Fellow, and to go out in the Night, I knew not whither. Mine eyes have seen that fellow afterwards walking up and down in Boston, under the appearance of a *Friend-Indian,* and several others of the like Cut. I went to one *Wigwam,* and they told me they had no room; then I went to another, and they said the same: at last an old *Indian* bade me come to him, and his squaw gave me some Ground nuts, she gave me also something to lay under my head, and a good fire we had; and, through the good Providence of God, I had a comfortable lodging that Night. In the morning, another *Indian* bade me come at night, and he would give me six Ground nuts, which I did. We were at this place and time about two miles from Connecticut river. We went in the morning (to gather Ground nuts) to the River, and went back again at Night. I went with a great load at my back (for they, when they went, though but a little way, would carry all their trumpery with them) I told them the skin was off my back, but I had no other comforting answer from them than this, that it would be no matter if my Head were off too.

The thirteenth Remove.—Instead of going toward the Bay[22] (which was that I desired) I must go with them five or six miles down the River, into a mighty Thicket of Brush; where we abode almost a fortnight. Here one asked me to make a shirt for her Papoos, for which she gave me a mess of Broth, which was thickened with meal made of the Bark of a Tree; and to make it the better, she had put into it about a handful of Pease, and a few roasted Ground nuts. I had not seen my Son a pretty while, and here

[22] Massachusetts Bay Colony.

was an *Indian* of whom I made inquiry after him, and asked him when he saw him? he answered me, that such a time his Master roasted him; and that himself did eat a piece of him as big as his two fingers, and that he was very good meat: but the Lord upheld my Spirit under his discouragement; and I considered their horrible addictedness to ly-ing, and that there is not one of them that makes the least conscience of speaking the truth. In this place, on a cold night, as I lay by the fire, I removed a stick which kept the heat from me; a Squaw moved it down again, at which I lookt up, and she threw an handful of ashes in my eyes; I thought I should have been quite blinded and have never seen more; but lying down, the Water run out of my eyes, and carried the dirt with it, that, by the morning, I recovered my sight again. Yet upon this, and the like occasions, I hope it is not too much to say with *Job, Have pity upon me, have pity upon me, Oh ye my Friends, for the hand of the Lord has touched me.*[23] And here I cannot but remember how many times, sitting in their Wigwams, and musing on things past, I should suddenly leap up and run out, as if I had been at home, forgetting where I was, and what my con-dition was: but, when I was without, and saw nothing but Wilderness and Woods, and a company of barbarous Heathen; my mind quickly returned to me, which made me think of that spoken concerning *Sampson,* who said, *I will go out and shake myself as at other times, but he wist not that the Lord was departed from him.*[24] About this time I be-gan to think that all my hope of Restoration would come to nothing; I thought of the *English* Army, and hoped for their coming, and being retaken by them, but that failed. I hoped to be carried to Albany, as the *Indians* had discoursed, but that failed also. I thought of being sold to my Husband, as my Master spake; but, instead of that, my Master himself was gone, and I left behind; so that my spirit was now quite ready to sink. I asked them to let me go out and pick up some sticks, that I might get alone, and pour out my heart unto the Lord. Then also I took my Bible to read, but I found no comfort here neither; yet I can say, that in all my sorrows and afflictions, God did not leave me to have my impatience work towards himself, as if his ways were unrighteous; but I knew that he laid upon me less than I deserved. Afterward, before this doleful time ended with me, I was turning the leaves of my Bible, and the Lord brought to me some Scriptures which did a little revive me, as that, *Isaiah* lv. 8, *For my thoughts are not your thoughts, neither are your ways my ways, saith the Lord.* And also that, *Psal.* xxxvii. 5, *Commit thy way unto the Lord, trust also in him, and he shall bring it to pass.*

About this time they came yelping from Hadly, having there killed three *English-men,* and brought one Captive with them, *viz.* Thomas Read.[25] They all gathered about the poor Man, asking him many Questions. I desired also to go and see him; and when I came, he was crying bitterly; supposing they would quickly kill him; whereupon I asked one of them, whether they intended to kill him? he answered me, they would not: he be-ing a little cheared with that, I asked him about the welfare of my Husband; by which I certainly understood (though I suspected it before) that whatsoever the *Indians* told me respecting him was vanity and lies. Some of them told me he was dead, and they had killed him; some said he was Married again, and that the Governour wished him to

---

[23] Interestingly, the passage continues, "Oh that my words were now written! oh that they were printed in a book! that they were graven with an iron pen and lead in the rock forever! For I know that my redeemer liveth . . ." (Job 19:23–25).

[24] Judges 16:20.

[25] The soldier Thomas Read, captured at Hadley, escaped on May 15, 1676.

Marry; and told him he should have his choice, and that all perswaded him I was dead. So like were these barbarous creatures to him who was a liar from the beginning.[26]

As I was sitting once in the Wigwam here, Philip's Maid came in with the Child in her arms, and asked me to give her a piece of my Apron to make a flap[27] for it; I told her I would not: then my Mistress bade me give it, but still I said no. The Maid told me, if I would not give her a piece, she would tear a piece off it; I told her I would tear her Coat then: with that my Mistress rises up; and takes up a stick big enough to have killed me, and struck at me with it, but I stept out, and she struck the stick into the Mat of the Wigwam. But while she was pulling of it out, I ran to the Maid and gave her all my Apron, and so that storm went over.

Hearing that my Son was come to this place, I went to see him, and told him his Father was well, but very melancholy; he told me he was as much grieved for his Father as for himself; I wondred at his speech, for I thought I had enough upon my spirit in reference to myself, to make me mindless of my Husband and every one else; they being safe among their Friends. He told me also, that a while before, his Master (together with other *Indians*) were going to the *French* for Powder, but by the way the *Mohawks* met with them, and killed four of their Company, which made the rest turn back again; for which I desire that myself and he may bless the Lord; for it might have been worse with him, had he been sold to the *French,* than it proved to be in his remaining with the *Indians.*

I went to see an *English* Youth in this place, one John Gilberd,[28] of Springfield. I found him lying without doors, upon the ground; I asked him how he did? he told me he was very sick of a flux,[29] with eating so much blood. They had turned him out of the Wigwam, and with him an *Indian Papoos,* almost dead, (whose parents had been killed) in a bitter cold day, without fire or clothes: the young man himself had nothing on but his shirt and waistcoat; this sight was enough to melt a heart of flint. There they lay quivering in the Cold, the youth round like a dog; the *Papoos* stretcht out, with his eyes and nose and mouth full of dirt, and yet alive and groaning. I advised John to go and get to some fire; he told me he could not stand, but I perswaded him still, lest he should ly there and die; and with much ado I got him to a fire, and went myself home. As soon as I was got home, his Master's Daughter came after me, to know what I had done with the *English-man?* I told her I had got him to a fire in such a place. Now had I need to pray *Paul's* prayer, 2 *Thess.* iii. 2, *That we may be delivered from unreasonable and wicked men.* For her satisfaction I went along with her, and brought her to him; but, before I got home again, it was noised about that I was running away, and getting the *English* youth along with me; that, as soon as I came in, they began to rant and domineer; asking me where I had been? and what I had been doing? and saying they would knock me in the head; I told them I had been seeing the *English Youth;* and that I would not run away; they told me I lied, and taking up a Hatchet, they came to me, and said they would knock me down if I stirred out again; and so confined me to the Wigwam. Now may I say with *David,* 2 *Sam.* xxiv. 14, *I am in a great strait.* If I keep in, I must dye with hunger, and if I go out, I must be knockt in the head. This distressed condition held that day and half the next; and then the Lord remembered me, whose mercies are great.

---

[26] That is, Satan.
[27] Any piece of cloth fastened on only one side, hanging broad and loose; in this case, perhaps a bib.
[28] John Gilbert, a seventeen-year-old captive who later escaped.
[29] Dysentery.

Then came an *Indian* to me with a pair of Stockings which were too big for him, and he would have me ravel them out, and knit them fit for him. I shewed myself willing, and bid him ask my Mistress if I might go along with him a little way; she said yes, I might, but I was not a little refresht with that news, that I had my liberty again. Then I went along with him, and he gave me some roasted Ground nuts, which did again revive my feeble stomach.

Being got out of her sight, I had time and liberty again to look into my Bible, which was my guide by day, and my Pillow by night. Now that comfortable Scripture presented itself to me, *Isaiah liv. 7, For a small moment have I forsaken thee; but with great mercies will I gather thee.* Thus the Lord carried me along from one time to another; and made good to me this precious promise, and many others. Then my Son came to see me, and I asked his Master to let him stay a while with me, that I might comb his head, and look over him, for he was almost overcome with lice. He told me, when I had done, that he was very hungry, but I had nothing to relieve him; but bid him go into the Wigwams as he went along, and see if he could get any thing among them, which he did, and (it seems) tarried a little too long; for his Master was angry with him, and beat him, and then sold him. Then he came running to tell me he had a new Master, and that he had given him some Ground nuts already. Then I went along with him to his new Master, who told me he loved him; and he should not want. So his Master carried him away, and I never saw him afterward: till I saw him at Pascataqua, in Portsmouth.

That night they bade me go out of the Wigwam again; my Mistress's *Papoos* was sick, and it died that night; and there was one benefit in it, that there was more room. I went to a Wigwam, and they bade me come in, and gave me a skin to lye upon, and a mess of Venison and Ground nuts; which was a choice Dish among them. On the morrow they buried the *Papoos;* and afterward, both morning and evening, there came a company to mourn and howl with her; though I confess I could not much condole with them. Many sorrowful days I had in this place; often getting alone; *Like a Crane or a Swallow so did I chatter; I did mourn as a Dove, mine eyes fail with looking upward. Oh Lord, I am oppressed, undertake for me.* Isaiah xxxviii. 14. I could tell the Lord, as *Hezechiah,* ver. 3, *Remember now, O Lord, I beseech thee, how I have walked before thee in truth.*[30] Now had I time to examine all my wayes; my Conscience did not accuse me of unrighteousness toward one or other, yet I saw how in my walk with God I had been a careless creature. As *David* said, *Against thee, thee only have I sinned,*[31] and I might say, with the poor Publican, *God be merciful unto me a sinner.*[32] On the Sabbath days I could look upon the Sun, and think how People were going to the house of God to have their Souls refresht; and then home, and their bodies also; but I was destitute of both; and might say, as the poor Prodigal, *he would fain have filled his belly with the husks that the Swine did eat, and no man gave unto him.* Luke xv. 16. For I must say with him, *Father, I have sinned against Heaven, and in thy sight,* ver. 21. I remember how, on the night before and after the Sabbath, when my Family was about me, and Relations and Neighbours with us, we could pray and sing, and then refresh our bodies with the good creatures of God, and then have a comfortable Bed to ly down on; but, instead of all this, I had only a little Swill for the body, and then, like a Swine, must ly down on the Ground; I cannot express to man the sorrow that lay upon my Spirit, the Lord knows it. Yet that comfort-

---

[30] Isaiah 37:3.
[31] Psalm 51:4.

[32] Luke 18:13.

able Scripture would often come to my mind, *For a small moment have I forsaken thee, but with great mercies I will gather thee.*[33]

The fourteenth Remove.—Now must we pack up and be gone from this Thicket, bending our course towards the Bay-Towns. I having nothing to eat by the way this day, but a few crumbs of Cake, that an *Indian* gave my Girl the same day we were taken. She gave it me, and I put it into my pocket; there it lay till it was so mouldy (for want of good baking) that one could not tell what it was made of; it fell all to crumbs, and grew so dry and hard, that it was like little flints; and this refreshed me many times when I was ready to faint. It was in my thoughts when I put it into my mouth; that if ever I returned, I would tell the world what a blessing the Lord gave to such mean food. As we went along, they killed a *Deer,* with a young one in her; they gave me a piece of the fawn, and it was so young and tender, that one might eat the bones as well as the flesh, and yet I thought it very good. When night came on we sate down; it rained, but they quickly got up a Bark Wigwam, where I lay dry that night. I looked out in the morning, and many of them had lain in the rain all night. I saw by their Reeking. Thus the Lord dealt mercifully with me many times; and I fared better than many of them. In the morning they took the blood of the *Deer* and put it into the Paunch, and so boiled it: I could eat nothing of that; though they ate it sweetly; and yet they were so nice[34] in other things, that when I had fetcht water, and had put the Dish I dipt the water with into the Kettle of water which I brought, they would say they would knock me down; for they said it was a sluttish trick.

The fifteenth Remove.—We went on our travel, I having got one handful of Ground nuts for my support that day: they gave me my load, and I went on cheerfully, (with the thoughts of going homeward) having my burden more on my back than my spirit; we came to Baquaug River again that day, near which we abode a few days. Sometimes one of them would give me a Pipe, another a little Tobacco, another a little Salt; which I would change for a little Victuals. I cannot but think what a Wolvish appetite persons have in a starving condition; for many times, when they gave me that which was hot, I was so greedy, that I should burn my mouth, that it would trouble me hours after; and yet I should quickly do the same again. And after I was thoroughly hungry, I was never again satisfied; for though sometimes it fell out that I got enough, and did eat till I could eat no more, yet I was as unsatisfied as I was when I began. And now could I see that Scripture verified, (there being many Scriptures which we do not take notice of, or understand, till we are afflicted,) *Mic.* vi. 14, *Thou shalt eat and not be satisfied.* Now might I see more than ever before, the miseries that sin hath brought upon us. Many times I should be ready to run out against the Heathen, but that Scripture would quiet me again, *Amos* iii. 6, *Shall there be evil in the City and the Lord hath not done it?* The Lord help me to make a right improvement of his word, and that I might learn that great lesson, *Mic.* vi. 8, 9, *He hath shewed thee, O Man, what is good; and what doth the Lord require of thee but to do justly, and love mercy, and walk humbly with thy God? Hear ye the rod, and who hath appointed it.*

The sixteenth Remove.—We began this Remove with wading over Baquaug River. The Water was up to the knees, and the stream very swift, and so cold that I thought it would have cut me in sunder. I was so weak and feeble, that I reeled as I went along, and thought there I must end my days at last, after my bearing and getting through so many

---

[33] Isaiah 54:7.   [34] Fastidious, dainty.

difficulties. The *Indians* stood laughing to see me staggering along; but in my distress the Lord gave me experience of the truth and goodness of that promise, *Isai.* xliii. 2, *When thou passest thorough the waters, I will be with thee, and thorough the Rivers, they shall not overflow thee.* Then I sate down to put on my stockings and shoes, with the tears running down my eyes, and many sorrowful thoughts in my heart, but I gat up to go along with them. Quickly there came up to us an *Indian,* who informed them that I must go to Wachuset to my Master; for there was a Letter come from the Council[35] to the *Saggamores,*[36] about redeeming the Captives, and that there would be another in fourteen days, and that I must be there ready. My heart was so heavy before that I could scarce speak, or go in the path, and yet now so light that I could run. My strength seemed to come again, and to recruit my feeble knees and aking heart; yet it pleased them to go but one mile that night, and there we stayed two days. In that time came a company of *Indians* to us, near thirty, all on Horse back. My heart skipt within me, thinking they had been *English-men* at the first sight of them; for they were dressed in *English* Apparel, with Hats, white Neckcloths, and Sashes about their waists, and Ribbons upon their shoulders; but, when they came near, there was a vast difference between the lovely Faces of *Christians,* and the foul looks of those *Heathens;* which much damped my spirit again.

The seventeenth Remove.—A comfortable Remove it was to me, because of my hopes. They gave me my pack, and along we went cheerfully; but quickly my Will proved more than my strength; having little or no refreshing, my strength failed, and my spirits were almost quite gone. Now may I say as *David,* Psal. cix. 22, 23, 24, *I am poor and needy, and my heart is wounded within me. I am gone like the shadow when it declineth: I am tossed up and down like the Locust: my knees are weak through fasting, and my flesh faileth of fatness.* At night we came to an *Indian Town,* and the *Indians* sate down by a Wigwam discoursing, but I was almost spent, and could scarce speak. I laid down my load, and went into the Wigwam, and there sate an *Indian* boiling of *Horses feet:* (they being wont to eat the flesh first, and when the feet were old and dried, and they had nothing else, they would cut off the feet and use them.) I asked him to give me a little of his Broth, or Water they were boiling in: he took a Dish, and gave me one spoonful of Samp,[37] and bid me take as much of the Broth as I would. Then I put some of the hot water to the Samp, and drank it up, and my spirit came again. He gave me also a piece of the Ruffe or Ridding[38] of the small Guts, and I broiled it on the coals; and now may I say with *Jonathan, See, I pray you, how mine eyes have been enlightened, because I tasted a little of this honey,* 1 Sam. xiv. 29. Now is my Spirit revived again: though means be never so inconsiderable, yet if the Lord bestow his blessing upon them, they shall refresh both Soul and Body.

The eighteenth Remove.—We took up our packs, and along we went; but a wearisome day I had of it. As we went along I saw an *English-man* stript naked, and lying dead upon the ground, but knew not who it was. Then we came to another Indian Town, where we stayed all night: In this Town there were four *English Children,* Captives: and one of them my own Sister's: I went to see how she did, and she was well, considering her Captive condition. I would have tarried that night with her, but they that

---

[35] The Massachusetts Council.

[36] The heads or chiefs of the tribe.

[37] Porridge made from coarsely ground Indian corn.

[38] The refuse or waste portion.

owned her would not suffer it. Then I went to another Wigwam, where they were boiling Corn and Beans, which was a lovely sight to see; but I could not get a taste thereof. Then I went into another Wigwam, where there were two of the *English Children:* The Squaw was boiling horses feet; then she cut me off a little piece, and gave one of the *English Children* a piece also: Being very hungry, I had quickly eat up mine; but the Child could not bite it, it was so tough and sinewy, but lay sucking, gnawing, chewing, and slobbering it in the mouth and hand; then I took it of the Child, and eat it myself; and savoury it was to my taste.

That I may say as *Job,* chap. vi. 7, *The things that my Soul refused to touch are as my sorrowful meat.* Thus the Lord made that pleasant and refreshing which another time would have been an Abomination. Then I went home to my Mistress's Wigwam; and they told me I disgraced my Master with begging; and if I did so any more they would knock me on the head: I told them, they had as good knock me on the head as starve me to death.

The nineteenth Remove.—They said when we went out, that we must travel to Wachuset this day. But a bitter weary day I had of it; travelling now three dayes together, without resting any day between. At last, after many weary steps, I saw Wachusets hills, but many miles off. Then we came to a great Swamp; through which we travelled up to the knees in mud and water; which was heavy going to one tired before: Being almost spent, I thought I should have sunk down at last, and never got out; but I may say, as in *Psal.* xciv. 18, *When my foot slipped, thy mercy, O Lord, held me up.* Going along, having indeed my life, but little spirit, Philip, (who was in the Company) came up, and took me by the hand, and said, *Two weeks more, and you shall be Mistress again.* I asked him if he spake true? he answered, Yes, and quickly you shall come to your Master again; who had been gone from us three weeks. After many weary steps we came to Wachuset, where he was; and glad I was to see him. He asked me, when I washt me? I told him not this moneth; then he fetch me some water himself, and bid me wash, and gave me the Glass to see how I lookt, and bid his Squaw give me something to eat: So she gave me a mess of Beans and meat, and a little Ground-nut Cake. I was wonderfully revived with this favour shewed me, *Psal.* cvi. 46, *He made them also to be pitied of all those that carried them Captives.*

My Master had three Squaws; living sometimes with one, and sometimes with another: One, this old Squaw at whose Wigwam I was, and with whom my Master had been those three weeks: Another was Wettimore, with whom I had lived and served all this while: A severe and proud Dame she was; bestowing every day in dressing herself near as much time as any of the Gentry of the land; powdering her hair and painting her face, going with her Neck-laces, with Jewels in her ears, and bracelets upon her hands: When she had dressed herself, her Work was to make Girdles of Wampom[39] and Beads. The third Squaw was a younger one, by whom he had two Papooses. By that time I was refresht by the old Squaw, with whom my Master was, Wettimore's Maid came to call me home, at which I fell a weeping; then the old Squaw told me, to encourage me, that if I wanted victuals I should come to her, and that I should lye there in her Wigwam. Then I went with the Maid, and quickly came again and lodged there. The Squaw laid a Mat under me and a good Rugg over me; the first time I had any such Kindness shewed me. I understood that Wettimore thought, that if she should let me go and serve with

---

[39] That is, wampum, cylindrical beads made from shells and used as currency.

the old Squaw she would be in danger to lose not only my service, but the redemption-pay also: And I was not a little glad to hear this; being by it raised in my hopes, that in God's due time there would be an end of this sorrowful hour. Then came an *Indian,* and asked me to knit him three pair of Stockings for which I had a Hat and a silk Handkerchief. Then another asked me to make her a shift, for which she gave me an Apron.

Then came Tom and Peter,[40] with the second Letter from the Council about the Captives. Though they were *Indians,* I gat them by the hand, and burst out into tears; my heart was so full that I could not speak to them: But recovering myself, I asked them how my Husband did, and all my Friends and Acquaintance? they said, they were well, but very Melancholy. They brought me two Biskets and a pound of Tobacco; the Tobacco I quickly gave away; when it was all gone, one asked me to give him a pipe of Tobacco; I told him all was gone; then began he to rant and to threaten; I told him when my Husband came I would give him some: Hang him, Rogue, (says he) I will knock out his brains if he comes here. And then again, in the same breath, they would say, that if there should come an hundred without Guns they would do them no hurt. So unstable and like madmen they were: So that, fearing the worst, I durst not send to my Husband, though there were some thoughts of his coming to Redeem and fetch me, not knowing what might follow; for there was little more to trust them than to the Master they served. When the Letter was come, the Saggamores met to consult about the Captives; and called me to them to enquire how much my Husband would give to redeem me: When I came, I sate down among them, as I was wont to do, as their manner is: Then they bade me stand up, and said, they were the *General Court:* They bid me speak what I thought he would give. Now, knowing that all we had was destroyed by the *Indians,* I was in a great strait. I thought if I should speak of but little it would be slighted, and hinder the matter; if of a great Sum, I knew not where it would be procured; yet at a venture, I said *Twenty pounds,* yet desired them to take less; but they would not hear of that, but sent that message to Boston, that for *twenty pounds* I should be redeemed. It was a Praying *Indian* that wrote their Letter for them. There was another Praying *Indian,* who told me, that he had a Brother that would not eat Horse; his Conscience was so tender and scrupulous, (though as large as Hell for the destruction of poor *Christians*). Then he said, he read that Scripture to him, 2 *King.* vi. 25, *There was a famine in* Samaria, *and behold they besieged it, until an Ass's head was sold for four-score pieces of silver, and the fourth part of a Kab of Doves dung for five pieces of silver.* He expounded this place to his Brother, and shewed him that it was lawful to eat that in a Famine, which is not at another time. And now, says he, he will eat Horse with any *Indian* of them all. There was another Praying *Indian,* who, when he had done all the Mischief that he could, betrayed his own Father into the *Englishes* hands, thereby to purchase his own Life. Another Praying *Indian* was at Sudbury Fight, though, as he deserved, he was afterward hanged for it. There was another Praying *Indian,* so wicked and cruel, as to wear a string about his neck strung with *Christian* Fingers. Another Praying *Indian,* when they went to Sudbury Fight,[41] went with them, and his Squaw also with him, with

---

40 Tom Dublet (Nepanet) and Peter Conway (Tataquinea), Christian Indians of Nashoba village, were persuaded by Joseph Rowlandson and other clergymen to serve as messengers to the hostile sachems to ask about terms for the release of captives.

41 On April 18, 1676, Captain Samuel Wadsworth of Milton, Samuel Brocklebank of Rowley, and thirty other men were ambushed and slain at Sudbury.

her Papoos at her back: Before they went to that Fight, they got a company together to *Powaw:*[42] the manner was as followeth: There was one that kneeled upon a *Deer-skin*, with the Company round him in a Ring, who kneeled, striking upon the Ground with their hands and with sticks, and muttering or humming with their Mouths. Besides him who kneeled in the Ring, there also stood one with a Gun in his hand: Then he on the Deer-skin made a speech, and all manifested assent to it; and so they did many times together. Then they bade him with the Gun go out of the Ring, which he did; but when he was out they called him in again; but he seemed to make a stand; then they called the more earnestly, till he returned again. Then they all sang. Then they gave him two Guns, in either hand one. And so he on the Deer-skin began again; and at the end of every Sentence in his speaking they all assented, humming or muttering with their Mouths, and striking upon the Ground with their Hands. Then they bade him with the two Guns go out of the Ring again; which he did a little way. Then they called him in again, but he made a stand, so they called him with greater earnestness; but he stood reeling and wavering, as if he knew not whether he should stand or fall, or which way to go. Then they called him with exceeding great vehemency, all of them, one and another: after a little while, he turned in, staggering as he went, with his Arms stretched out; in either hand a Gun. As soon as he came in, they all sang and rejoyced exceedingly a while. And then he upon the Deer-skin made another speech, unto which they all assented in a rejoycing manner: And so they ended their business, and forthwith went to Sudbury Fight. To my thinking, they went without any scruple but that they should prosper and gain the Victory. And they went out not so rejoycing, but that they came home with as great a Victory. For they said they had killed two Captains and almost an hundred men. One *Englishman* they brought alive with them; and he said it was too true, for they had made sad work at Sudbury; as indeed it proved. Yet they came home without that rejoycing and triumphing over their Victory which they were wont to shew at other times; but rather like Dogs (as they say) which have lost their Ears: Yet I could not perceive that it was for their own loss of Men: they said they had not lost above five or six; and I missed none, except in one Wigwam. When they went, they acted as if the Devil had told them that they should gain the Victory; and now they acted as if the Devil had told them that they should have a fall: Whether it were so or no, I cannot tell, but so it proved; for quickly they began to fall, and so held on that Summer, till they came to utter ruine. They came home on a Sabbath day; and the Powaw that kneeled upon the Deer-skin came home (I may say without any abuse) as black as the Devil. When my Master came home, he came to me and bid me make a shirt for his Papoos of a Hollandlaced Pillowbeer.[43] About that time there came an *Indian* to me, and bade me come to his *Wigwam* at night, and he would give me some Pork and Groundnuts; which I did, and as I was eating, another *Indian* said to me, he seems to be your good Friend, but he killed two *English-men* at Sudbury, and there lye their Cloaths behind you: I looked behind me, and there I saw bloody Cloaths, with Bullet-holes in them: yet the Lord suffered not this Wretch to do me any hurt. Yea, instead of that, he many times refresht me: five or six times did he and his Squaw refresh my feeble Carcass. If I went to their *Wigwam* at any time, they would always give me something; and yet they

---

[42] That is, *powwow*, the term used by the English settlers to describe a feast, dance, or other event preliminary to a hunt or war ex-pedition. By extention, the term was used to identify a native priest or shaman.
[43] Pillowcase.

were strangers that I never saw before. Another *Squaw* gave me a piece of fresh Pork and a little Salt with it; and lent me her Frying pan to fry it in: and I cannot but remember what a sweet, pleasant, and delightful relish that bit had to me, to this day. So little do we prize common mercies when we have them to the full.

The twentieth Remove.—It was their usual manner to remove when they had done any mischief, lest they should be found out; and so they did at this time. We went about three or four miles, and there they built a great *Wigwam*, big enough to hold an hundred *Indians;* which they did in preparation to a great day of Dancing. They would say now amongst themselves, that the *Governour* would be so angry for his loss at Sudbury, that he would send no more about the Captives; which made me grieve and tremble. My Sister being not far from the place where we now were, and hearing that I was here, desired her Master let her come and see me, and he was willing to it, and would go with her; but she being ready before him, told him she would go before, and was come within a Mile or two of the place: Then he overtook her, and began to rant as if he had been mad, and made her go back again in the Rain; so that I never saw her till I saw her in Charlstown. But the Lord requited many of their ill-doings; for this *Indian,* her Master, was hanged after at Boston. The *Indians* now began to come from all quarters against the merry dancing day. Amongst some of them came one Goodwife Kettle:[44] I told her that my Heart was so heavy that it was ready to break: so is mine too, said she; but yet said, I hope we shall hear some good news shortly. I could hear how earnestly my Sister desired to see me, and I as earnestly desired to see her; and yet neither of us could get an opportunity. My Daughter was also now but about a Mile off; and I had not seen her in nine or ten Weeks, as I had not seen my Sister since our first taking. I earnestly desired them to let me go and see them: yea, I intreated, begged, and perswaded them but to let me see my Daughter; and yet so hard-hearted were they, that they would not suffer it. They made use of their Tyrannical Power whilst they had it: but through the Lord's wonderful mercy, their time now was but short.

On a Sabbath day, the Sun being about an hour high, in the Afternoon, came Mr John Hoar,[45] (the Council permitting him, and his own forward spirit inclining him) together with the two forementioned *Indians,* Tom and Peter, with the third letter from the Council. When they came near, I was abroad; though I saw them not, they presently called me in, and bade me sit down, and not stir. Then they catched up their Guns, and away they ran, as if an Enemy had been at hand; and the Guns went off apace. I manifested some great trouble, and they asked me what was the matter? I told them I thought they had killed the *English-man,* (for they had in the meantime informed me that an *English-man* was come;) they said No; they shot over his Horse, and under, and before his horse, and they pusht him this way and that way at their pleasure, shewing what they could do: Then they let them come to their Wigwams. I begged of them to let me see the *English-man,* but they would not; but there was I fain to sit their pleasure. When they had talked their fill with him, they suffered me to go to him. We asked each other of our welfare, and how my Husband did, and all my Friends? he told me they were all well, and would be glad to see me. Amongst other things which my Husband sent me, there came a pound of *Tobacco;* which I sold for nine shillings in Money: for many of the *Indians,* for

[44] Elizabeth Kettle and her three children were taken captive from the Rowlandson garrison.

[45] John Hoar was a Concord lawyer who aided Rowlandson in finding Nashobas willing to assist in the ransom negotiations.

want of *Tobacco,* smoaked *Hemlock* and *Ground-ivy.* It was a great mistake in any who thought I sent for *Tobacco:* for, through the favour of God, that desire was overcome. I now asked them, whether I should go home with Mr Hoar? they answered, No, one and another of them: and it being Night, we lay down with that Answer: in the Morning Mr Hoar invited the *Saggamores* to Dinner: but when we went to get it ready, we found that they had stollen the greatest part of the Provision Mr Hoar had brought out of the Bags in the Night. And we may see the wonderful power of God, in that one passage, in that when there was such a great number of the *Indians* together, and so greedy of a little good Food; and no *English* there, but Mr Hoar and myself; that there they did not knock us in the Head, and take what we had; there being, not only some Provision, but also Trading Cloth, a part of the twenty pounds agreed upon: But instead of doing us any mischief, they seemed to be ashamed of the Fact, and said, it were some *Matchit Indians*[46] that did it. O that we could believe that there is nothing too hard for God! God shewed his power over the Heathen in this, as he did over the hungry Lions when *Daniel* was cast into the Den. Mr Hoar called them betime to Dinner; but they ate very little, they being so busie in dressing themselves, and getting ready for their Dance; which was carried on by eight of them; four Men and four Squaws; my Master and Mistress being two. He was dressed in his Holland Shirt,[47] with great Laces sewed at the tail of it; he had his silver Buttons, his white Stockings, his Garters were hung round with shillings; and he had Girdles of *Wampom* upon his Head and Shoulders. She had a Kersey Coat,[48] and covered with Girdles of Wampom from the Loins and upward; her Arms, from her elbows to her Hands, were covered with Bracelets; there were handfuls of Neck-laces about her Neck, and several sorts of Jewels in her Ears: She had fine red Stockings and white Shoes, her Hair powdered, and her face painted Red, that was always before Black; and all the Dancers were after the same manner. There were two other singing and knocking on a Kettle for their Musick. They kept hopping up and down one after another, with a Kettle of Water in the midst, standing warm upon some Embers, to drink of when they were a-dry. They held on till it was almost night, throwing out Wampom to the standersby. At night I asked them again if I should go home? they all as one said, No, except my Husband would come for me. When we were lain down, my Master went out of the Wigwam, and by and by sent in an *Indian,* called James, the PRINTER,[49] who told Mr Hoar, that my Master would let me go home to-morrow, if he would let him have one pint of Liquors. Then Mr Hoar called his own *Indians,* Tom and Peter; and bid them all go and see whether he would promise it before them three; and if he would, he should have it; which he did, and had it. Then Philip smelling the business, called me to him, and asked me what I would give him to tell me some good news, and to speak a good word for me, that I might go home to-morrow? I told him I could not tell what to give him: I would give any thing I had, and asked him what he would have? He said, two Coats and twenty shillings in Money, and half a bushel of Seed-Corn and some Tobacco: I thanked him for his love; but I knew the good news as well as that crafty Fox. My Master, after he had had his Drink, quickly came ranting into the Wigwam again, and called for Mr Hoar, drinking to him, and saying he was a good man; and then again he would

---

46 Bad Indians.

47 A shirt made of linen from the Netherlands.

48 A coat made of coarse, narrow cloth, usually ribbed.

49 James the Printer (Wowaus) was a Christian Indian who was apprenticed to the Cambridge printer Samuel Green.

say, Hang him, Rogue. Being almost drunk, he would drink to him, and yet presently say he should be hanged. Then he called for me; I trembled to hear him, yet I was fain to go to him; and he drunk to me, shewing no incivility. He was the first *Indian* I saw drunk all the while that I was amongst them. At last his Squaw ran out, and he after her, round the Wigwam, with his money gingling at his knees: but she escaped him; but, having an old Squaw, he ran to her; and so, through the Lord's mercy, we were no more troubled with him that night: Yet I had not a comfortable night's rest; for I think I can say, I did not sleep for three nights together. The night before the Letter came from the Council, I could not rest, I was so full of fears and troubles, (God many times leaving us most in the dark when deliverance is nearest) yea, at this time I could not rest night nor day. The next night I was over-joyed, Mr Hoar being come, and that with such good Tydings. The third night I was even swallowed up with the thoughts of things; *viz.* that ever I should go home again; and that I must go, leaving my Children behind me in the Wilderness; so that sleep was now almost departed from mine eyes.

On Tuesday morning they called their General Court (as they stiled it) to consult and determine whether I should go home or no: And they all as one man did seemingly consent to it, that I should go home; except Philip, who would not come among them.

But before I go any further, I would take leave to mention a few remarkable passages of Providence; which I took special notice of in my afflicted time.

1. Of the fair opportunity lost in the long March, a little after the Fort-fight, when our *English* Army was so numerous, and in pursuit of the Enemy; and so near as to overtake several and destroy them; and the Enemy in such distress for Food, that our men might track them by their rooting in the Earth for Groundnuts, whilst they were flying for their lives: I say, that then our Army should want Provision, and be forced to leave their pursuit, and return homeward; and the very next week the Enemy came upon our Town like Bears bereft of their whelps, or so many ravenous Wolves, rending us and our Lambs to death. But what shall I say? God seemed to leave his People to themselves, and ordered all things for his own holy ends. *Shall there be evil in the City and the Lord hath not done it? They are not grieved for the affliction of Joseph, therefore they shall go captive with the first that go Captive. It is the Lord's doing, and it should be marvellous in our Eyes.*[50]

2. I cannot but remember how the *Indians* derided the slowness and dulness of the *English* Army in its setting out: For, after the desolations at Lancaster and Medfield, as I went along with them, they asked me when I thought the *English* Army would come after them? I told them I could not tell: it may be they will come in May, said they. Thus did they scoffe at us, as if the *English* would be a quarter of a Year getting ready.

3. Which also I have hinted before; when the *English* Army with new supplies were sent forth to pursue after the Enemy, and they understanding it; fled before them till they came to Baquaug River, where they forthwith went over safely: that that River should be impassable to the *English,* I cannot but admire to see the wonderful providence of God in preserving the Heathen for farther affliction to our poor Country. They could go in great numbers over, but the *English* must stop: God had an overruling hand in all those things.

4. It was thought, if their Corn were cut down, they would starve and die with hunger: and all their Corn that could be found was destroyed, and they driven from

[50] A fusion of Amos 3:6, Amos 6:6–7, and Psalm 118:23.

that little they had in store into the Woods in the midst of Winter; and yet how to admiration did the Lord preserve them for his holy ends, and the destruction of many still amongst the *English!* strangely did the Lord provide for them, that I did not see (all the time I was among them) one Man, or Woman, or Child, die with Hunger.

Though many times they would eat that that a hog or a dog would hardly touch, yet by that God strengthened them to be a scourge to his people.

Their chief and commonest food was Ground-nuts; they eat also Nuts and Acorns, Hartychoaks, Lilly-roots, Ground-beans, and several other weeds and roots that I know not.

They would pick up old bones, and cut them in pieces at the joynts, and if they were full of worms and magots, they would scald them over the fire to make the vermine come out; and then boyle them, and drink up the Liquor, and then beat the great ends of them in a Mortar, and so eat them. They would eat Horses guts and ears, and all sorts of wild birds which they could catch; also Bear, Venison, Beavers, Tortois, Frogs, Squirrels, Dogs, Skunks, Rattle-snakes; yea, the very Barks of Trees; besides all sorts of creatures and provision which they plundered from the *English.* I cannot but stand in admiration to see the wonderful power of God, in providing for such a vast number of our Enemies in the Wilderness, where there was nothing to be seen but from hand to mouth. Many times in the morning the generality of them would eat up all they had, and yet have some farther supply against they wanted. It is said, *Psal.* lxxxi. 13, 14, *Oh that my people had hearkened to me, and Israel had walked in my ways, I should soon have subdued their Enemies, and turned my hand against their adversaries.* But now our perverse and evil carriages in the sight of the Lord have so offended him; that, instead of turning his hand against them, the Lord feeds and nourishes them up to be a scourge to the whole land.

5. Another thing that I would observe is, the strange providence of God in turning things about when the *Indians were at the highest,* and the *English at the lowest.* I was with the Enemy eleven weeks and five days; and not one Week passed without the fury of the Enemy, and some desolation by fire and sword upon one place or other. They mourned (with their black faces) for their own losses; yet triumphed and rejoyced in their inhumane (and many times devlish cruelty) to the *English.* They would boast much of their Victories; saying, that in two hours time, they had destroyed such a Captain and his Company in such a place; and such a Captain and his Company in such a place; and such a Captain and his Company in such a place: and boast how many Towns they had destroyed, and then scoff, and say, they had done them a good turn to send them to Heaven so soon. Again they would say, this Summer they would knock all the Rogues in the head, or drive them into the Sea, or make them flie the Country: thinking surely, *Agag-like, The bitterness of death is past.*[51] Now the *Heathen* begin to think that all is their own, and the poor *Christians* hopes to fail (as to man) and now their eyes are more to God, and their hearts sigh heaven-ward; and to say in good earnest, *Help, Lord, or we perish;* when the Lord had brought his People to this, that they saw no help in any thing but himself; then he takes the quarrel into his own hand; and though they had made a pit (in their own imaginations) as deep as hell for the *Christians* that Summer; yet the Lord hurl'd themselves into it. And the Lord had not so many wayes before to preserve them, but now he hath as many to destroy them.

[51] See 1 Samuel 15:32.

But to return again to my going home; where we may see a remarkable change of Providence: At first they were all against it, except my Husband would come for me; but afterwards they assented to it, and seemed much to rejoyce in it; some asking me to send them some Bread, others some Tobacco, others shaking me by the hand, offering me a Hood and Scarf to ride in; not one moving hand or tongue against it. Thus hath the Lord answered my poor desires, and the many requests of others put up unto God for me. In my Travels an *Indian* came to me, and told me, if I were willing, he and his Squaw would run away, and go home along with me. I told him, No, I was not willing to run away, but desired to wait God's time, that I might go home quietly, and without fear. And now God hath granted me my desire. O the wonderful power of God that I have seen, and the experiences that I have had! I have been in the midst of those roaring Lions and Savage Bears, that feared neither God nor Man, nor the Devil, by night and day, alone and in company, sleeping all sorts together; and yet not one of them ever offered the least abuse or unchastity to me in word or action. Though some are ready to say I speak it for my own credit; but I speak it in the presence of God, and to his Glory. God's power is as great now, and as sufficient to save, as when he preserved *Daniel* in the Lions Den, or the three Children in the Fiery Furnace. I may well say, as he, *Psal.* cvii. 1, 2, *Oh give thanks unto the Lord, for he is good, for his mercy endureth for ever. Let the Redeemed of the Lord say so, whom he hath redeemed from the hand of the Enemy;* especially that I should come away in the midst of so many hundreds of Enemies quietly and peaceably, and not a Dog moving his tongue. So I took leave of them, and in coming along my heart melted into Tears, more than all the while I was with them, and I was almost swallowed up with the thoughts that ever I should go home again. About the Sun's going down, Mr Hoar and myself, and the two *Indians,* came to Lancaster; and a solemn sight it was to me. There had I lived many comfortable years amongst my Relations and Neighbours; and now not one *Christian* to be seen, nor one House left standing. We went on to a Farm-house that was yet standing, where we lay all night; and a comfortable lodging we had, though nothing but straw to lye on. The Lord preserved us in safety that night, and raised us again in the morning, and carried us along, that before noon we came to Concord. Now was I full of joy, and yet not without sorrow: joy to see such a lovely sight, so many *Christians* together, and some of them my Neighbours: There I met with my Brother, and my Brother-in-Law, who asked me, if I knew where his Wife was? Poor heart! he had helped to bury her, and knew it not; she being shot down by the house, was partly burnt: so that those who were at Boston at the desolation of the Town, and came back afterward, and buried the dead, did not know her. Yet I was not without sorrow, to think how many were looking and longing, and my own Children amongst the rest, to enjoy that deliverance that I had now received; and I did not know whether ever I should see them again. Being recruited with Food and Raiment, we went to Boston that day, where I met with my dear Husband; but the thoughts of our dear Children, one being dead, and the other we could not tell where, abated our comfort each in other. I was not before so much hemm'd in with the merciless and cruel *Heathen,* but now as much with pitiful, tender-hearted, and compassionate *Christians.* In that poor, and distressed, and beggarly condition, I was received in, I was kindly entertained in several houses; so much love I received from several, (some of whom I knew, and others I knew not,) that I am not capable to declare it. But the Lord knows them all by name: the Lord reward them sevenfold into their bosoms of his spirituals for their temporals. The twenty pounds, the price of my Redemption, was raised by some Boston Gentlewomen, and M. Usher,[52] whose bounty and religious charity I would not forget to make mention of. Then Mr Thomas Shepherd[53] of Charlstown received us into his House, where we continued eleven weeks; and a Father and Mother they were unto us. And many more tender-hearted Friends we met with in that place. We were now in the midst of love, yet not without much and frequent heaviness of heart for our poor Children and other Relations who were still in affliction.

The week following, after my coming in, the Governour and Council sent forth to the *Indians* again, and that not without success; for they brought in my Sister and Goodwife Kettle; their not knowing where our Children were was a sore trial to us still, and yet we were not without secret hopes that we should see them again. That which was dead lay heavier upon my spirit than those which were alive amongst the *Heathen*; thinking how it suffered with its wounds, and I was no way able to relieve it; and how it was buried by the *Heathen* in the Wilderness, from amongst all *Christians*. We were hurried up and down in our thoughts; sometimes we should hear a report that they were gone this way and sometimes that; and that they were come in in this place or that; we kept inquiring and listning to hear concerning them, but no certain news as yet. About this time the Council had ordered a day of publick *Thanksgiving;* though I thought I had still cause of mourning; and being unsettled in our minds, we thought we would ride toward the Eastward, to see if we could hear any thing concerning our Children. And as we were riding along (God is the wise disposer of all things) between Ipswich and Rowly we met with Mr William Hubbard,[54] who told us our Son Joseph was come in to Major Waldrens,[55] and another with him, which was my Sister's Son. I asked him how he knew it? he said, the Major himself told me so. So along we went till we came to Newbury; and their Minister being absent, they desired my Husband to Preach the *Thanksgiving* for them; but he was not willing to stay there that night, but would go over to Salisbury to hear farther, and come again in the morning; which he did, and Preached there that day. At night, when he had done, one came and told him that his Daughter was come in at Providence: here was mercy on both hands. Now hath God fulfilled that precious Scripture, which was such a comfort to me in my distressed condition. When my heart was ready to sink into the Earth, (my Children being gone I could not tell whither) and my knees trembled under me, and I was walking through the valley of the shadow of death; then the Lord brought, and now has fulfilled that reviving word unto me; *Thus saith the Lord, Refrain thy voice from weeping, and thy eyes from tears, for thy work shall be rewarded, saith the Lord, and they shall come again from the Land of the Enemy.*[56] Now we were between them, the one on the East, and the other on the West; our Son being nearest we went to him first, to Portsmouth; where we met with him, and with the Major also; who told us he had done what he could, but could not redeem him under seven pounds, which the good People thereabouts were pleased to pay. The Lord reward the Major and all the rest, though unknown to me, for their

[52] Probably Hezekiah Usher, a wealthy Boston bookseller and selectman, who died two weeks after Rowlandson's ransom.

[53] Son of the more famous Reverend Thomas Shepard (1605–1649), pastor of the church at Cambridge and one of the most prominent religious and intellectual leaders of New England.

[54] The Reverend William Hubbard of Ipswich was the author of *A Narrative of the Troubles with the Indians* (1677).

[55] Actually Major Richard Waldron of Dover, New Hampshire, notorious for the severity of his dealings with the Indians.

[56] Jeremiah 31:16.

labour of love. My Sister's Son was redeemed for four pounds, which the Council gave order for the payment of. Having now received one of our Children, we hastened towards the other; going back through Newbury, my Husband preached there on the Sabbath day; for which they rewarded him manifold.

On Monday we came to Charlstown; where we heard that the Governour of Road-Island had sent over for our Daughter to take care of her, being now within his Jurisdiction; which should not pass without our acknowledgments. But she being nearer Rehoboth than Road-Island, Mr. Newman[57] went over and took care of her, and brought her to his own house. And the goodness of God was admirable to us in our estate; in that he raised up compassionate Friends on every side to us; when we had nothing to recompence any for their love. The *Indians* were now gone that way, that it was apprehended dangerous to go to her; but the Carts which carried Provision to the *English* Army being guarded, brought her with them to Dorchester, where we received her safe; blessed be the Lord for it, *for great is his power, and he can do whatsoever seemeth him good.* Her coming in was after this manner: She was travelling one day with the *Indians* with her basket at her back; the company of *Indians* were got before her, and gone out of sight, all except one Squaw; she followed the Squaw till night, and then both of them lay down; having nothing over them but the Heavens, nor under them but the Earth. Thus she travelled three days together, not knowing whither she was going; having nothing to eat or drink but water and green *Hirtleberries.* At last they came into Providence, where she was kindly entertained by several of that Town. The *Indians* often said that I should never have her under twenty pounds; but now the Lord hath brought her in upon free cost, and given her to me the second time. The Lord make us a blessing indeed each to others. Now have I seen that Scripture also fulfilled, *Deut.* xxx. 4, 7, *If any of thine be driven out to the utmost parts of heaven, from thence will the Lord thy God gather thee, and from thence will he fetch thee. And the Lord thy God will put all these curses upon thine enemies, and on them which hate thee, which persecuted thee.* Thus hath the Lord brought me and mine out of that horrible pit, and hath set us in the midst of tender-hearted and compassionate Christians. 'Tis the desire of my soul that we may walk worthy of the mercies received, and which we are receiving.

Our Family being now gathered together, (those of us that were living) the South Church in Boston hired an house for us; then we removed from Mr. Shepards (those cordial Friends) and went to Boston, where we continued about three quarters of a year; Still the Lord went along with us, and provided graciously for us. I thought it somewhat strange to set up house-keeping with bare walls; but, as *Solomon* says, *Money answers all things,*[58] and that we had, through the benevolence of *Christian* Friends, some in this Town and some in that, and others, and some from England, that in a little time we might look and see the house furnished with love. The Lord hath been exceeding good to us in our low estate, in that when we had neither house nor home, nor other necessaries, the Lord so moved the hearts of these and those towards us; that we wanted neither food nor rayment for ourselves or ours, Prov. xviii. 24. *There is a Friend that sticketh closer than a Brother.* And how many such Friends have we found, and now living amongst! and truly such a Friend have we found him to be unto us, in whose house we lived, *viz.* Mr James Whitcomb,[59] a Friend unto us near hand and afar off.

---

[57] Noah Newman of Rehoboth.
[58] Ecclesiastes 10:19.

[59] James Whitcomb was a wealthy Bostonian, apparently active in the Indian slave trade.

I can remember the time, when I used to sleep quietly without workings in my thoughts, whole nights together; but now it is otherwise with me. When all are fast about me, and no eye open but His who ever waketh, my thoughts are upon things past, upon the awful dispensations of the Lord towards us; upon his wonderful power and might in carrying us through so many difficulties, in returning us in safety, and suffering none to hurt us. I remember in the night season, how the other day I was in the midst of thousands of enemies, and nothing but death before me; it was then hard work to persuade myself that ever I should be satisfied with bread again. But now we are fed with the finest of the Wheat, and (as I may so say) with honey out of the rock; instead of the husks, we have the fatted Calf; the thoughts of these things in the particulars of them, and of the love and goodness of God towards us, make it true of me, what *David* said of himself, *Psal.* vi. 6, *I water my couch with my tears.* Oh the wonderful power of God that mine eyes have seen, affording matter enough for my thoughts to run in, that when others are sleeping mine eyes are weeping.

I have seen the extreme vanity of this World; one hour I have been in health and wealth, wanting nothing; but the next hour in sickness, and wounds, and death, having nothing but sorrow and affliction.

Before I knew what affliction meant I was ready sometimes to wish for it. When I lived in prosperity; having the comforts of this World about me, my Relations by me, and my heart chearful; and taking little care for any thing; and yet seeing many (whom I preferred before myself) under many trials and afflictions, in sickness, weakness, poverty, losses, crosses, and cares of the World, I should be sometimes jealous least I should have my portion in this life; and that Scripture would come to my mind, *Heb.* xii 6, *For whom the Lord loveth he chasteneth, and scourgeth every Son whom he receiveth;* but now I see the Lord had his time to scourge and chasten me. The portion of some is to have their Affliction by drops, now one drop and then another; but the dregs of the Cup, the wine of astonishment, like a sweeping rain that leaveth no food, did the Lord prepare to be my portion. Affliction I wanted, and Affliction I had, full measure, (I thought) pressed down and running over; yet I see when God calls a person to any thing, and through never so many difficulties, yet he is fully able to carry them through, and make them see and say they have been gainers thereby. And I hope I can say in some measure as *David* did, *It is good for me that I have been afflicted.*[60] The Lord hath shewed me the vanity of these outward things, that they are the *vanity of vanities, and vexation of spirit,*[61] that they are but a shadow, a blast, a bubble, and things of no continuance; that we must rely on God himself, and our whole dependence must be upon him. If trouble from smaller matters begin to arise in me, I have something at hand to check myself with, and say when I am troubled, it was but the other day, that if I had had the world, I would have given it for my Freedom, or to have been a Servant to a *Christian.* I have learned to look beyond present and smaller troubles, and to be quieted under them, as *Moses* said, *Exod.* xiv. 13, *Stand still, and see the salvation of the Lord.*[62]

Finis

1682

---

[60] Psalm 119:71.
[61] Ecclesiastes 1:2, 14.
[62] The complete verse from Exodus reads: "And Moses said unto the people, Fear ye not, stand still, and see the salvation of the Lord, which he will show to you today; for the Egyptians whom ye have seen today, ye shall see them again no more forever."

RELATED VOICES

Hannah Dustan's Narrative

[*A Narrative of Notable Deliverance from Captivity.*]

On the fifteenth Day, of the last March, Hannah Dustan, of Haverhil, having lain in about a week, attended with her Nurse, Mary Ness, a widow, a body of terrible Indians drew near in the House where she lay, with designs to carry on the bloody Devastations, which they had begun upon the Neighborhood. Her husband, hastened from his Employments abroad, unto the Relief of his Distressed Family; and first bidding *Seven* of his *Eight* Children (which were from Two to *Seventeen* years of age,) to get away as fast as they could, unto some Garrison in the Town, he went in, to inform is Wife, of the horrible Distress now come upon them. Ere he could get up, the fierce *Indians* were got so near, that utterly despairing to do her any Service, he ran out after his Children; Resolving that on the Horse, which he had with him, he would Ride away, with *That,* which he would in this Extremity find his affections to pitch most upon, and leave the rest, unto the care of the Divine Providence. He overtook his Children, about Forty Rod from his Door; but then, such was the Agony of his Parental Affections, that he found it Impossible for him, to Distinguish any one of them from the Rest; wherefore he took up a Courageous Resolution, to Live & Dy with them All. A party of Indians came up with him; and now, though they fired at him, and he Fired at them, yet he manfully kept in the Reer of his *Little Army* of unarmed Children, while they March'd off, with the pace of a Child of Five years old; until, by the Singular Providence of God, he arrived Safe with them all, unto a place of Safety, about a Mile or two from his House. But his House must in the mean Time, have more dismal *Tradegies* acted at it. The Nurse, trying to Escape, with the New born Infant, fell into the hands of the formidable Salvages; & those furious Tawnies, coming in to the House, bid poor *Dustan,* to Rise immediately. Full of Astonishment, she did so; and Sitting down in the Chimney, with an heart full of most fearful Expectation, she saw the Raging Dragons riffle all that they could carry away: and set the House on Fire. About Nineteenth or Twenty *Indians,* now led these away, with about Half a score other, English *Captives:* but e're they had gone many Steps, they dash'd out the Brains of the Infant against a Tree, and several of the other *Captives,* as they begun to Tire in their sad Journey, were soon sent unto their long Home, but the Salvages would presently bury their Hatchets in their Brains, and leave their Carcases on the ground, for Birds & Beasts to feed upon. [Christians, A *Joshua* would have *Rent his Clothes, & fallen to the Earth on his Face,* and have *Humbled* himself Exceedingly upon the falling out of such doleful Ruines upon his Neighbours!] However, *Dustan* (with her Nurse,) notwithstanding her present Condition, Travelled that Night, about a Dozen Miles; and then kept up with their New Masters, in a long Travel of an Hundred and fifty Miles, more or less, within a few Dayes Ensuing; without any sensible Damage, in their Health, from the Hardships of their *Travel,* their *Lodging,* their *Diet,* and their many other Difficulties. These two poor Women, were now in the

Hands of those, *Whose Tender Mercies are Cruelty:* but the Good God, who hath all *Hearts* in *His own Hands,* heard the Sighs of *these Prisoners* unto Him, and gave them to find unexpected Favour, from the *Master,* who Laid claim unto them. That *Indian Family* consisted of Twelve persons, Two stout men, three women, and seven Children; and for the shame of many a *Prayerless Family* among our English, I must now publish what these poor women assure me; 'Tis *This;* In Obedience to the Instruction which the French have given them, they would have *Prayers* in their Family, no less than Thrice every Day; In the *Morning,* an *Noon,* and in the *Evening,* nor would they ordinarily let so much as a Child, Eat or Sleep, without first saying their *Prayers.* Indeed, these *Idolaters,* were like the rest of the whiter Brethren *Persecutors,* and would not Endure that these poor *Women* should Retire to their *English Prayers,* if they could hinder them. Nevertheless, the poor Women, had nothing but fervent *Prayers,* to make their Lives comfortable, or tolerable; and by being daily sent out, upon Business, they had opportunities together and asunder, to do like another *Hannah,* in *pouring out their Souls before the Lord:* Nor did their Praying Friends among our selves, forbear to *pour out* Supplications for them. Now, they could not observe it, without some wonder, that their Indian Master, sometimes, when he saw them Dejected, would say unto them; *What need you Trouble your self? If your God will have you Delivered, you shall be so!* And it seems, our God, would have it so to be!

This Indian Family, was now Travelling with these two Captive women, (& an English youth, taken from *Worcester,* last *September* was a Twelve month,) unto a Rendezveuze of Salvages, which they call a Town, somewhere beyond *Penacook;* and they still told these poor women, that when they came to this Town, they must be Strip't, & Scourged, and Run the Gantlet, through the whole Army of *Indians.* They said, this was the *Fashion,* when the Captives first came to a Town; and they decided, some of the faint hearted English which, they said, fainted and swooned away under the *Torments* of this Discipline. [Syrs, can we hear of these things befalling our Neighbours, & not *Humble* our selves before our God!] But on this Day se'night, while they were yet it may be, about an hundred and fifty miles from the Indian Town, a little before Break of Day, when the whole Crew was in a Dead Sleep, ('twill presently prove so!) One of these women took up a Resolution, to Imitate the Action of Jael upon Sisera[1], and being where she had not her *own Life* secured by any *Law* unto her, she thought she was not forbidden by any Law, to take away the *Life,* of the *Murderers,* by whom her *Child* had been butchered. She heartened the *Nurse,* and the *Youth,* to assist her, in this Enterprise; & they all furnishing themselves with *Hatchets* for the purpose, they struck such Home Blowes, upon the Heads of their *Sleeping Oppressors,* that e're they could any of them struggle into any effectual Resistance, at the Feat of those poor Prisoners, *They bowed, they fell, they lay down; at their feet they bowed, they fell; where they bowed, there they fell down. Dead.* Onely one *Squaw* Escaped sorely wounded from them, and one *Boy,* whom they Reserved Asleep, intending to bring him away with them, suddenly wak'd and stole away, from this Desolation.

---

[1] Jael, wife of a sheik, killed the fugitive army general, Sisera, with a tent-pin when he sought refuge in her private tent (Judges 4–5).

But cutting off the Scalps of the Ten Wretches, who had Enslav'd 'em, they are come off; and I perceive, that newly arriving among us, they are in the Assembly at this Time, to give Thanks unto, God their Savior.

[An Improvement of the foregoing Narrative.]

If we did now *Humble* our selves throughout the Land, who can say, whether the *Revenges on the Enemy,* thus Exemplified, would not proceed much rather unto the Quick Extirpation, or those *Bloody and Crafty men.*

However, I may not Conclude, until I have said Something unto YOU, that I see, now stand before the Lord, in this Assembly, the Subjects of such a Wonderful *Deliverance,* from your *Captivity;* a *Deliverance* which hath seen Signalized with such Unusual Circumstances. Words that are spoken in an *Ordinance* of the Lord Jesus Christ, carry with them a peculiar Efficacy and Authority. The Lord Jesus Christ, hath by a Surprising *Providence* of His, brought you this Day, to wait upon Him, in that Great *Ordinance* which is *His Power for the Salvation of our Souls.* Hear a Servant of the LORD JESUS CHRIST, in His Name, now Publickly & Solemnly calling upon you, to make a Right use of the *Deliverance,* wherewith He has Highly favored you. The *Use,* which you are to make of it, is, To *Humble* your selves before the Lord Exceedingly. As you have had the Extraordinary Judgments of God upon you, to *Humble* you, so, Except His Extraordinary *Mercies* do likewise *Humble* you, you do but Exceedingly *Abuse* them: *The Rich Goodness of God unto you, is to Lead you into Repentance!*

When you were Carried into Captivity, We did not say, *That you were greater Sinners,* than the rest that yet escape it. You are now Rescued from *Captivity,* and must not think, *That they are greater Sinners, who are Left behind in the most barbarous Hands imaginable.* No, you that have been under the *Mighty Hand of God,* are to *Humble* your selves, under that *Hand.* But it you do indeed so, I know, what you will do. You will seriously consider, What you shall render *to the Lord for all His Benefits?* And you will sincerely *Render* your very *Selves* unto the Lord: You are not now the Slaves of Indians, as you were a few Dayes ago; but if you continue Unhumbled, in your Sins, you will be the Slaves of *Devils;* and, Let me tell you, A Slavery to *Devils,* to be in *Their* Hands, is worse than to be in the Hands of *Indians!* I beseech you then, by the Mercies of God, that you present your selves unto the Lord Jesus Christ; Become the sincere servants of that Lord, who by

His *Blood* has brought you out of the *Dungeon,* wherein you were lately Languishing; *Oh! Deny not the Lord,* who has thus *Brought you* out of your Captivity. I tell you truly, the Lord Expects great Returns of *Humiliation,* of *Thankfulness,* and of *Obedience,* from you; and I therefore Leave with you, one Sentence of Scripture to be often thought upon; 'Tis That, in *Ezra* 9, 13, 14. *After all that is come upon us, for our Evil Deeds, seeing thou, our God, hast given us such Deliverance at this, should we again break thy Commandments, wouldest thou not be angry with us, till thou hadst Consumed us?*

Now, Let *all Consider what hath been said, and the Lord give us Understanding in all things!*

from Cotton Mather, Humiliations Followed with Deliverances

Cultural Portfolio
The Ways of the Native Americans

Early American settlers lived in close proximity to native tribes. However, the relationship between the settlers and the natives was rarely peaceful. The Pequot War (1635–1636) was the first major conflict between the Puritans and the Native Americans, and the later King Philip's War (1675) was so severe that it threatened English settlement and suggested to some Puritans that their city on a hill was failing. Puritan writers feared that "our Israel . . . a plante of Gods owne hand," as one versifier put it, was jeopardized by savages ("salvages"), and some used graphic, disturbing imagery to portray the violence inflicted by the native warriors. Some compared the native peoples to animals, signalling both their perception of the natives' lack of humanity and the Puritans' justification for their own acts of violence. Other settlers, such as Robert Beverley, write about more peaceful encounters with the Native Americans, documenting native culture and language in a way that suggests that native civilization is as viable as that of the English settlers. William Byrd and Roger Williams, and Thomas Jefferson too,

look at native societies from a somewhat more accepting perspective, portraying Native Americans as bizarre people worthy of examination. They also, however, emphasize native barbarity, describing them, in Byrd's words, as creatures of "ingenious malice and cruelty."

The selections that follow show a range of viewpoints, from Roger Williams's efforts to decode the Narragansett language to facilitate trade and communication to Thomas Jefferson's speculation on whether the climate and soil of North America had retarded the civilizing process and left the native peoples in a backward state—even as Jefferson reproduced Chief Logan's speech on whites' murderous injustices to his people in the Ohio area and the necessary tribal retaliation. Curiosity, hostility, righteousness, fear and anxiety mix in the voices that follow. As Mary Rowlandson's captivity narrative has been increasingly interesting to contemporary readers, these texts indicate the range and persistence of engagement in the topic of nonwhite groups indigenous to America.

Native Americans of the Plains
Painted buffalo hide found by Lewis and Clark in 1805. Depicts 44 warriors on foot and 20 mounted with bows and arrows, lances, and the firearms that show evidence of white trade, in a battle between the Mandans and enemy tribesmen.
ca. 1797
(Peabody Museum, Harvard University. Photo by Hillel Burger)

from Robert Beverley, *The History and Present State of Virginia, 1705*

from Book III: Of the Indians, Their Religion, Laws, and Customs, in War and Peace

from *Chap. I: Of the Persons of the Indians, and Their Dress*

1. The *Indians* are of the middling and largest stature of the *English:* They are straight and well proportion'd, having the cleanest and most exact Limbs in the World: They are so perfect in their outward frame, that I never heard of one single *Indian,* that was either dwarfish, crooked, bandy-legg'd, or otherwise misshapen. But if they have any such practices among them, as the *Romans* had, of exposing such Children till they dyed, as were weak and misshapen at their Birth, they are very shy of confessing it, and I could never yet learn that they had.

Their Colour, when they are grown up, is a Chestnut brown and tawny; but much clearer in their Infancy. Their Skin comes afterwards to harden and grow blacker, by greasing and Sunning themselves. They have generally coal-black Hair, and very black Eyes, which are most commonly grac'd with that sort of Squint which many of the *Jews* are observ'd to have. Their Women are generally Beautiful, possessing an un-common delicacy of Shape and Features, and wanting no Charm, but that of a fair Complexion.

2. The Men wear their Hair cut after several fanciful Fashions, sometimes greas'd, and sometimes painted. The Great Men, or better sort, preserve a long Lock behind for distinction. They pull their Beards up by the roots with a Muscle-shell; and both Men and Women do the same by the other parts of their Body for Cleanliness sake. The Women wear the Hair of the Head very long, either hanging at their Backs, or brought before in a single Lock, bound up with a Fillet of Peak, or Beads; sometimes also they wear it neatly tyed up in a Knot behind. It is commonly greased, and shining black, but never painted.

The People of Condition of both Sexes, wear a sort of Coronet on their Heads, from 4 to 6 inches broad, open at the top, and composed of Peak, or Beads, or else of both interwoven together, and workt into Figures, made by a nice mixture of the Colours. Sometimes they wear a Wreath of Dyed Furrs; as likewise Bracelets on their Necks and Arms. The Common People go bareheaded, only sticking large shining Feathers about their Heads, as their fancies lead them.

from *Chap. II: Of the Marriages Amongst the Indians, and Management of Their Children*

6. The *Indians* have their solemnities of Marriage, and esteem the Vows made at that time as most sacred and inviolable. Notwithstanding, they allow both the Man and the Wife to part upon disagreement; yet so great is the disreputation of a Divorce, that Marry'd people, to avoid the Character of Inconstant and Ungenerous, very rarely let their Quarrels proceed to a Separation. However, when it does so happen, they reckon all the ties of Matrimony dissolv'd, and each hath the liberty of marrying another. But Infidelity is accounted the most unpardonable of all Crimes in either of the Parties, as long as the Contract continues.

In these Separations, the Children go, according to the affection of the Parent, with the one or the other; for Children are not reckon'd a Charge among them, but rather Riches, according to the blessing of the Old Testament; and if they happen to differ about dividing their Children, their method is then, to part them equally, allowing the Man the first choice. . . .

8. The manner of the *Indians* treating their young Children is very strange, for instead of keeping them warm, at their first entry into the World, and wrapping them up, with I don't know how many Cloaths, according to our fond custom; the first thing they do, is to dip the Child over Head and Ears in cold Water, and then to bind it naked to a convenient Board, having a hole fitly plac'd for evacuation; but they always put Cotton, Wool, Furr, or other soft thing, for the Body to rest easy on, between the Child and the Board. In this posture they keep it several months, till the Bones begin to harden, the Joynts to knit, and the Limbs to grow strong; and then they let it loose from the Board, suffering it to crawl about, except when they are feeding, or playing with it.

While the Child is thus at the Board, they either lay it flat on its back, or set it leaning on one end, or else hang it up by a string fasten'd to the upper end of the Board for that purpose. The Child and Board being all this while carry'd about together. As our Women undress their Children to clean them and shift their Linnen, so they do theirs to wash and grease them. . . .

from *Chap. III: Of the Towns, Buildings and Fortifications of the Indians*

10. The manner the *Indians* have of building their Houses, is very slight and cheap; when they would erect a *Wigwang,* which is the *Indian* name for a House, they stick Saplins into the ground by one end, and bend the other at the top, fastening them together by strings made of fibrous Roots, the rind of Trees, or of the green Wood of the white Oak, which will rive into Thongs. The smallest sort of these Cabbins are conical like a Bee-hive; but the larger are built in an oblong form, and both are cover'd with the Bark of Trees, which will rive off into great flakes. Their Windows are little holes left open for the passage of the Light, which in bad weather they stop with Shutters of the same Bark, opening the Leeward Windows for Air an Light. Their Chimney, as among the true-Born *Irish,* is a little hole in the top of the House, to let out the Smoak, having no sort of Funnel, or any thing within, to confine the Smoke from ranging through the whole Roof of the Cabbins, if the vent will not let it out fast enough. The Fire is always made in the middle of the Cabbin. Their Door is a Pendent Mat, when they are near home; but when they go abroad, they barricado it with great Logs of Wood set against the Mat, which are sufficient to keep out Wild Beasts. There's never more than one Room in a House, except in some Houses of State, or Religion, where the Partition is made only by Mats, and loose Poles.

11. Their Houses or Cabbins, as we call them, are by this ill method of Building, continually Smoaky, when they have Fire in them; but to ease that inconvenience, and to make the Smoak less troublesome to their Eyes, they generally burn Pine, or Lightwood, (that is, the fat knots of dead Pine) the Smoak of which does no offend the Eyes, but smuts the Skin exceedingly, and is perhaps another occasion of the darkness of their Complexion.

1705

from Roger Williams, *A Key into the Language of America, 1643*

Direction for the use of the Language.

3. It is framed chiefly after the Narroganset dialects, because most spoken in the Countrey, and (with attending to the variation of peoples and dialects) it will be of great use in all parts of the Countrey.
4. Whatever your occasion bee either of Travell, Discourse, Trading, etc. . . .

CHAP. VII.

Of their Persons and parts of body.

Uppaquontup.	The head.
Nuppaquontup.	My head.
Wefheck.	The hayre.
Wuchechepúnnock.	A great bunch of hayre bound up behind.
Múppacuck.	A long locke.

Yet some cut their haire round, and some as low and as short as the sober *English;* yet I never saw any so to forget nature itselfe in such excessive length and monstrous fashion, as to the shame of the *English* Nation, I now (with griefe) see my Countrey-men in England are degenerated unto.

In the braine their opinion is, that the soule . . . keeps her chiefe seat and residence. . . .

For the temper of the braine is quick apprehensions and accurate judgements (to say no more) the most high and sovereign God and Creator, hath not made them inferiour to *Europeans.*

The *Manquanoges,* or *Men-eaters,* that live two or three miles West from us, make a delicious monstrous dish of the head and brains of their enemies; which yet is no barre (when the time shall approach) against Gods call, and their repentance and (who knowes but) greater love to the Lord Jesus? Great sinners forgiven love much.

Mscattuck.	*The fore-head.*
Naskeéfuck-quash.	*Eye,* or *eyes.*
Tiyùsh kusskeefuck-quash?	*Can you not see,* or *where are your eyes?*
Wuchaun.	*The nostrills.*
Wuttovwog, guish.	*Eare, eares.*
Wutrone.	*The mouth.*
Wéenat.	*The tongue.*
Wépit-teash.	Tooth, teeth.
Pummaumpiteùnck.	The tooth-ake.
Wunnaks.	*The bellie.*
Apòme, Apòmash.	*The thigh, the thighs.*
Mohcónt, tash.	A legge, legs.

Wussete, tash	A foot, feet
Wunnicheganash.	The toes.
Tou wuttinsin.	What manner of man?
Tou núckquaque.	Of what bignesse?
Womcésu.	White.
Mowessu, & Suckesu.	Blacke, or swarsith.

Hence they call a *Blackamore* (themselves are tawnie, by the Sunne and their annoyntings, yet they are borne white:)

Suckautacone.	A cole blacke man.

For, *Suski* is black, and *Wautacome,* one that weares clothes, whence *English, Dutch, French, Scotch,* they call *Wautaconaueg,* or *Coatmen.*

Of Discourse and News.

Minioquesu.	*Weake.*
Cumminiocquese.	*Weake you are.*
Qunnaúqussu.	*A tall man.*
Qunnauqussitchick.	*Tall men.*
Tiaquónqussu.	*Low and short.*
Tiaquonqussichick.	*Men of lowe stature.*
Wunnêtu-wock.	*Proper and personall.*

The generall Observations from the parts of the bodie.
Nature knowes no difference between *Europe* and *Americans* in blood, birth, bodies, &c. God having of one blood made all mankind.

---

from William Byrd, *History of the Dividing Line*

[The Great Dismal Swamp]

And now I mention the northern Indians, it may not be improper to take notice of their implacable hatred to those of the south. Their wars are everlasting, without any peace, enmity being the only inheritance among them that descends from father to son, and either party will march a thousand miles to take their revenge upon such hereditary enemies. . . .

'Tis amazing to see their sagacity in discerning the track of a human foot, even amongst dry leaves, which to our shorter sight is quite undiscoverable. If by one or more of those signs they be able to find out the camp of any southern Indians, they squat down in some thicket and keep themselves hush and snug till it is dark; then, creeping up softly, they approach near enough to observe all the motions of the enemy. And about two o'clock in the morning, when they conceive them to be in a profound sleep, for they never keep watch and ward, pour in a volley upon them, each singling out his man. The moment they have discharged their pieces they rush in with their tomahawks and make sure work of all that are disabled. Sometime, when they find the enemy asleep round their little fire, they first pelt them with little stones to wake them, and when they get up, fire in upon them, being in that posture a better mark than when prostrate on the ground.

They that are killed of the enemy or disabled, they scalp: that is, they cut the skin all round the head just below the hair, and then, clapping their feet to the poor mortal's shoulders, pull the scalp off clean and carry it home in triumph, being as proud of those trophies as the Jews used to be of the foreskins of the Philistines. This way of scalping was practiced by the ancient Scythians, who used these hairy scalps as towels at home and trappings for their horses when they went abroad. They also made cups of their enemies' skulls, in which they drank prosperity to their country and confusion to all their foes.

The prisoners they happen to take alive in these expeditions generally pass their time very scurvily. They put them to all the tortures that ingenious malice and cruelty can invent. And (what shows the baseness of the Indian temper in perfection) they never fail to treat those with greatest inhumanity that have distinguished themselves most by their bravery, and if he be a war captain, they do him the honor to roast him alive and distribute a collop to all that had a share in stealing the victory. Though who can reproach the poor Indians for this, when Homer makes his celebrated hero, Achilles, drag the body of Hector at the tail of his chariot for having fought gallantly in defense of his country?[1] Nor was Alexander the Great, with all his famed generosity, less inhuman to the brave Tyrians, two thousand of which he ordered to be crucified in cold blood for no other fault but for having defended their city most courageously against him during a siege of seven months.[2] And what was still more brutal, he dragged———alive at the tail of his chariot through all the streets, for defending the town with so much vigor.

They are very cunning in finding out new ways to torment their unhappy captives, though, like those of hell, their usual method is by fire. Sometimes they barbecue them over live coals, taking them off every now and then to prolong their misery; at other times they will stick sharp pieces of lightwood all over their bodies and, setting them on fire, let them burn down into the flesh to the very bone. And when they take a stout fellow that they believe able to endure a great deal, they will tear all the flesh off his bones with red-hot pincers. While these and suchlike barbarities are practicing, the victors are so far from being touched with tenderness and compassion that they dance and sing round these wretched mortals, showing all the marks of pleasure and jollity. And if such cruelties happen to be executed in their towns, they employ their children in tormenting the prisoners, in order to extinguish in them betimes all sentiments of humanity. In the meantime, while these poor wretches are under the anguish of all this inhuman treatment, they disdain so much as to groan, sigh, or show the least sign of dismay or concern so much as in their looks; on the contrary, they make it a point of honor all the time to soften their features and look as pleased as if they were in the actual enjoyment of some delight; and if they never sang before in their lives, they will be sure to be melodious on this sad and dismal occasion. So prodigious a degree of passive valor in the In-

---

[1] In Homer's *Iliad*, Achilles killed Hector during the battle of Troy and dragged his body around the walls of the city.

[2] Alexander the Great fought Tyrian resistance for seven months. When Tyre fell in 332 B.C., Alexander slaughtered thousands of Tyrians.

dians is the more to be wondered at, because in all articles of danger they are apt to behave like cowards. And what is still more surprising, the very women discover on such occasions as great fortitude and contempt, both of pain and death, as the gallantest of their men can do. . . .

In the evening we examined our friend Bearskin concerning the religion of his country, and he explained it to us without any of that reserve to which his nation is subject. He told us he believed there was one supreme god, who had several subaltern deities under him. And that this master god made the world a long time ago. That he told the sun, the moon, and stars their business in the beginning, which they, with good looking-after, have faithfully performed ever since. That the same power that made all things at first has taken care to keep them in the same method and motion ever since. He believed that God had formed many worlds before he formed this, but that those worlds either grew old and ruinous or were destroyed for the dishonesty of the inhabitants. That God is very just and very good, ever well pleased with those men who possess those godlike qualities. That he takes good people into his safe protection, makes them very rich, fills their bellies plentifully, preserves them from sickness and from being surprised or overcome by their enemies. But all such as tell lies and cheat those they have dealings with he never fails to punish with sickness, poverty, and hunger and, after all that, suffers them to be knocked on the head and scalped by those that fight against them.

He believed that after death both good and bad people are conducted by a strong guard into a great road, in which departed souls travel together for some time till at a certain distance this road forks into two paths, the one extremely level and the other stony and mountainous. Here the good are parted from the bad by a flash of lightning, the first being hurried away to the right, the other to the left. The right-hand road leads to a charming, warm country, where the spring is everlasting and every month is May; and as the year is always in its youth, so are the people, and particularly the women are bright as stars and never scold. That in this happy climate there are deer, turkeys, elks, and buffaloes innumerable, perpetually fat and gentle, while the trees are loaded with delicious fruit quite throughout the four seasons. That the soil brings forth corn spontaneously, without the curse of labor, and so very wholesome that none who have the happiness to eat of it are ever sick, grow old, or die. Near the entrance into this blessed land sits a venerable old man on a mat richly woven, who examines strictly all that are brought before him, and if they have behaved well, the guards are ordered to open the crystal gate and let them enter into the land of delight. The left-hand path is very rugged and uneven, leading to a dark and barren country where it is always winter. The ground is the whole year round covered with snow, and nothing is to be seen upon the trees but icicles. All the people are hungry yet have not a morsel of anything to eat except a bitter kind of potato, that gives them the dry gripes and fills their whole body with loathsome ulcers that stink and are insupportably painful. Her all the women are old and ugly, having claws like a panther with which they fly upon the men that slight their passion. For it seems these haggard old furies are intolerably fond and expect a vast deal of cherishing. They talk much and exceedingly shrill, giving exquisite pain to the drum of the ear, which in that place of the torment is so tender that every sharp note wounds it to the quick. At the end of this path sits a dreadful old woman on a monstrous toadstool, whose head is covered with rattlesnakes instead of tresses, with glaring white eyes that strike a terror unspeakable into all that behold her. This hag pronounces sentence of woe upon all the miserable wretches that hold up their hands at her tribunal. After this they are delivered over to huge turkey buzzards, like harpies, that fly away with them to the place above-mentioned. Here, after they have been tormented a certain number of years according to their several degrees of guilt, they are again driven back into this world to try if they will mend their manners and merit a place the next time in the regions of bliss.

This was the substance of Bearskin's religion and was as much to the purpose as could be expected from a mere state of nature, without one glimpse of revelation or philosophy. It contained, however, the three great articles of natural religion: the belief of a god, the moral distinction betwixt good and evil, and the expectation of rewards and punishments in another world. Indeed, the Indian notion of a future happiness is a little gross and sensual, like Mahomet's Paradise.[3] But how can it be otherwise in a people that are contented with Nature as they find her and have no other lights but what they receive from purblind tradition?

---

from Thomas Jefferson, *Notes on the State of Virginia*

[On North American Indians]

The Indian of North America being more within our reach, I can speak of him somewhat from my own knowledge, but more from the information of others better acquainted with him, and on whose truth and judgment I can rely. From these sources I am able to say, in contradiction to this representation, that he is neither more defective in ardor, nor more impotent with his female, than the white reduced to the same diet and exercise: that he is brave, when an enterprize depends on bravery; education with him making the point of honor consist in the destruction of an enemy by stratagem, and in the preservation of his own person free from injury; or perhaps this is nature; while it is education which teaches us to honor force more than finesse; that he will defend himself against an host of enemies, always chusing to be killed, rather than to surrender; though it be to the whites, who he knows will treat him well: that in other situations also he meets death with more deliberation, and endures tortures with a firmness unknown almost to religious enthusiasm with us: that he is affectionate to his children, careful of them, and indulgent in the extreme: that his affections comprehend his other connections, weakening, as with us, from circle to circle, as they recede from the center: that his friendships are strong and faithful to the uttermost extremity: that his sensibility is keen, even the warriors weeping most bitterly on the loss of their children, though in general they endeavour to appear superior to human events: that his vivacity and activity of mind is equal to ours in the same situation; hence his eagerness for hunting, and for games of chance. The women are submitted to unjust drudgery. This I believe is the case with every barbarous people. With such, force is law. The stronger sex therefore imposes on the weaker. It is civilization alone which replaces women in the enjoyment of their natural equality. That first teaches us to subdue the selfish passions, and to respect those rights in others which we value in ourselves. Were we in equal barbarism, our females would be equal drudges. The man with them is less strong than with us, but

---

[3] *Mahomet's Paradise:* the Islamic afterlife involves a paradise of beautiful women for the faithful.

their woman stronger than ours; and both for the same obvious reason; because our man and their woman is habituated to labour, and formed by it. With both races the sex which is indulged with ease is least athletic. An Indian man is small in the hand and wrist for the same reason for which a sailor is large and strong in the arms and shoulders, and a porter in the legs and thighs.—They raise fewer children than we do. The causes of this are to be found, not in a difference of nature, but of circumstances. The women very frequently attending the men in their parties of war and of hunting, childbearing becomes extremely inconvenient to them. It is said, therefore, that they have learnt the practice of procuring abortion by the use of some vegetable; and that it even extends to prevent conception for a considerable time after. During these parties they are exposed to numerous hazards, to excessive exertions, to the greatest extremities of hunger. Even at their homes the nation depends for food, through a certain part of every year, on the gleanings of the forest: that is, they experience a famine once in every year. With all animals, if the female be badly fed, or not fed at all, her young perish: and if both male and female be reduced to like want, generation becomes less active, less productive. To the obstacles then of want and hazard, which nature has opposed to the multiplication of wild animals, for the purpose of restraining their numbers within certain bounds, those of labour and of voluntary abortion are added with the Indian. No wonder then if they multiply less than we do. Where food is regularly supplied, a single farm will shew more of cattle, than a whole country of forests can of buffaloes. The same Indian women, when married to white traders, who feed them and their children plentifully and regularly, who exempt them from excessive drudgery, who keep them stationary and unexposed to accident, produce and raise as many children as the white women. Instances are known, under these circumstances, of their rearing a dozen children. An inhuman practice once prevailed in this country of making slaves of the Indians. (This practice commenced with the Spaniards with the first discovery of America). It is a fact well known with us, that the Indian women so enslaved produced and raised as numerous families as either the whites or blacks among whom they lived.—It has been said, that Indians have less hair than the whites, except on the head. But this is a fact of which fair proof can scarcely be had. With them it is disgraceful to be hairy on the body. They say it likens them to hogs. They therefore pluck the hair as fast as it appears. But the traders who marry their women, and prevail on them to discontinue this practice, say, that nature is the same with them as with the whites. Nor, if the fact be true, is the consequence necessary which has been drawn from it. Negroes have notoriously less hair than the whites; yet they are more ardent. But if cold and moisture be the agents of nature for diminishing the races of animals, how comes she all at once to suspend their operation as to the physical man of the new world, whom the Count acknowledges to be "about the same size as the man of our hemisphere,[1] and to let loose their influence on his moral faculties? How has this combination of the elements and other physical causes, so contrary to the enlargement of animal nature in this new world, these obstacles to the developement and formation of great germs," been arrested and suspended, so as to permit the human body to acquire its just dimensions, and by what inconceivable process has their action been directed on his mind alone? To judge of the truth of this, to form a just estimate of their genius and mental powers, more facts are wanting, and great allowance to be made for those circumstances of their

---

[1] Count de Buffon, a well-respected French naturalist.

situation which call for a display of particular talents only. This done, we shall probably find that they are formed in mind as well as in body, on the same module with the "Homo sapiens Europæus." The principles of their society forbidding all compulsion, they are to be led to duty and to enterprize by personal influence and persuasion. Hence eloquence in council, bravery and address in war, become the foundations of all consequence with them. To these acquirements all their faculties are directed. Of their bravery and address in war we have multiplied proofs, because we have been the subjects on which they were exercised. Of their eminence in oratory we have fewer examples, because it is displayed chiefly in their own councils. Some, however, we have of very superior lustre. I may challenge the whole orations of Demosthenes and Cicero,[2] and of any more eminent orator, if Europe has furnished more eminent, to produce a single passage, superior to the speech of Logan, a Mingo chief, to Lord Dunmore, when governor of this state. . . .

[Jefferson then quotes Chief Logan's speech on the murder of his family by white soldiers avenging a robbery by Indians:]

"I appeal to any white man to say, if ever he entered Logan's cabin hungry, and he gave him not meat; if ever he came cold and naked, and he clothed him not. During the course of the last long and bloody war, Logan remained idle in his cabin, an advocate for peace. Such was my love for the whites, that my countrymen pointed as they passed, and said, 'Logan is the friend of white men.' I had even thought to have lived with you, but for the injuries of one man. Col. Cresap, the last spring, in cold blood, and unprovoked, murdered all the relations of Logan, not sparing even my women and children. There runs not a drop of my blood in the veins of any living creature. This called on me for revenge. I have sought it: I have killed many; I have fully glutted my vengeance. For my country, I rejoice at the beams of peace. But do not harbour a thought that mine is the joy of fear. Logan never felt fear. He will not turn on his heel to save his life. Who is there to mourn for Logan?—Not one."

Before we condemn the Indians of this continent as wanting genius, we must consider that letters have not yet been introduced among them. . . .

Having given a sketch of our . . . Man of America, . . . aboriginal and emigrant, I will proceed. . . .

---

[2] *Demosthenes and Cicero:* Demosthenes (382 B.C.–322 B.C.) was a great Greek orator, and Cicero (106 B.C.–45 B.C.) was a great Roman orator and statesman.

Edward Taylor
ca. 1642–1729

Edward Taylor's poems were virtually hidden in a manuscript book for more than two centuries. Their discovery and publication in 1939 brought Taylor to light as colonial America's foremost poet, though information about his life remains incomplete.

Taylor was born in Sketchley, England, near Leicestershire, during the turmoil of the English Civil War. As a farmer's son educated by a nonconformist schoolmaster, he grew up during the rise of Oliver Cromwell, the defeat of the armies of King Charles I, who was put to death, and the establishment of the Puritan Holy Commonwealth. It is possible that Taylor attended Cambridge University for a time, although official records are lacking. Taylor became a schoolmaster, but his career was cut short by the restoration of the English monarch in 1660. Taylor's unwillingness to comply with the Act of Uniformity, which required annual acceptance of communion at the Anglican ceremony, forced him to forfeit his position. In 1668 Taylor sailed for America and was admitted to Harvard College where he studied theology with advanced standing in the class of 1671, accepting a call to the sparsely settled western Massachusetts community of Westfield. None of Taylor's parishioners, however, knew that their minister's spiritual preparation took an unusual turn. At age forty-two Taylor embarked on a series of intensely private poems, the *Preparatory Meditations,* each one an integral part of his preparation to receive and to administer the sacrament of communion. Although Taylor wrote more than forty thousand lines of poetry during his life, these poems are considered to be his finest, in part because they show the tensions of a mind simultaneously feeling and thinking out the human relationship to the Creator in vivid figures of speech.

Taylor's *Preparatory Meditations* show his familiarity with the metaphysical tradition of such poets as George Herbert, Francis Quarles, and the Catholic poet Richard Crashaw. Their work showed the forging of wit and passion. It emphasized playful language, such as puns, and elaborate imagery. For Taylor and other Puritans, God's messages could be divined in such wordplay. Taylor's poetic images come from several sources, first among them the Bible, especially the sensuous Song of Songs. But Taylor also used poetic figures from the activities of everyday life, such as the weaving and farming he knew from his English boyhood, and from the conditions of western Massachusetts, where, he wrote, "little save Rusticity is." Taylor's poetry has been called "wilderness baroque," bringing elements of the unexpected into an ordered and formal structure that elicits an "earthly enjoyment of things divine."

Apart from the *Preparatory Meditations,* Taylor wrote miscellaneous occasional poems whose images reveal his apprehension of detail and whose themes are those of an orthodox Puritan. His interest in natural science is evident in "Upon a Spider Catching a Fly," in which he carefully traces the movement of the satanic spider. Taylor's best-known long poem bears the lengthy title *Gods Determinations touching his Elect: and the Elects Combat in their Conversion and coming up to God in Christ together with the Comfortable Effects thereof.* Known simply as *Gods Determinations,* the poem is based on the medieval debate literature, including the morality plays that Taylor might have seen in boyhood. Taylor died in his eighty-eighth year, requesting his heirs not to publish his poetry. That request was honored, but in 1937 Taylor's leather manuscript book, containing some four hundred pages, was found in the Yale University Library. The publication of a substantial selection from that book in 1939 established Taylor, the poet of "wilderness baroque," as a major figure in colonial American literature.

Further reading:

N. Grabo, *Edward Taylor*, 1962.

D. Stanford, *Edward Taylor*, 1965.

W. Scheick, *The Will and the Word: The Poetry of Edward Taylor*, 1974.

K. Keller, *The Example of Edward Taylor*, 1975.

Text:

The Poems of Edward Taylor, ed. D. Stanford, 1960.

N. Grabo, 1962.

---

from Preparatory Meditations

Meditation 8 (First Series): [I kening through Astronomy Divine]

Joh. 6.51. I am the Living Bread.

I kening[1] through Astronomy Divine
    The World's bright Battlement, wherein I spy
A Golden Path my Pensill cannot line,
    From that bright Throne unto my Threshold ly.
    And while my puzzled thoughts about it pore   5
    I finde the Bread of Life in't at my doore.

When that this Bird of Paradise put in
    This Wicker Cage (my Corps) to tweedle praise
Had peckt the Fruite forbad: and so did fling
    Away its Food; and lost its golden dayes;   10
    It fell into Celestiall Famine sore:
    And never could attain a morsell more.

Alas! alas! Poore Bird, what wilt thou doe?
    The Creatures field no food for Souls e're gave.
And if thou knock at Angells dores they show   15
    An Empty Barrell: they no soul bread have.

---

[1] Discovering.

Alas! Poore Bird, the Worlds White Loafe is done.
And cannot yield thee here the smallest Crumb.

In this sad state, Gods Tender Bowells[2] run
    Out streams of Grace: And he to end all strife   20
The Purest Wheate in Heaven, his deare-dear Son
    Grinds, and kneads up into this Bread of Life.
    Which Bread of Life from Heaven down came and stands
    Disht on thy Table up by Angells Hands.

Did God mould up this Bread in Heaven, and bake,   25
    Which from his Table came, and to thine goeth?
Doth he bespeake thee thus, This Soule Bread take.
    Come Eate thy fill of this thy God's White Loafe?
    Its Food too fine for Angells, yet come, take
    And Eate thy fill. Its Heavens Sugar Cake.   30

What Grace is this knead in this Loafe? This thing
    Souls are but petty things it to admire.
Yee Angells, help: This fill would to the brim
    Heav'ns whelm'd-down Chrystall meele Bowle, yea and higher.
    This Bread of Life dropt in thy mouth, doth Cry.   35
    Eate, Eate me, Soul, and thou shalt never dy.

1939

Preface to God's Determinations

Infinity, when all things it beheld
In Nothing, and of Nothing all did build,
Upon what Base was fixt the Lath, wherein
He turn'd this Globe, and riggalld it so trim?[1]
Who blew the Bellows of his Furnace Vast?   5
Or held the Mould wherein the world was Cast?
Who laid its Corner Stone? Or whose Command?
Where stand the Pillars upon which it stands?
Who Lac'de and Fillitted the earth so fine,
With Rivers like green Ribbons Smaragdine?[2]   10
Who made the Sea's its Selvedge,[2] and it locks
Like a Quilt Ball within a Silver Box?
Who Spread its Canopy? Or Curtains Spun?
Who in this Bowling Alley bowld the Sun?

---

[2] The bowels were supposedly the seat of pity
  and tenderness.

[1] Made ringed marks.

[2] Border.

Who made it always when it rises set   15
To go at once both down, and up to get?
Who th'Curtain rods made for this Tapistry?
Who hung the twinckling Lanthorns in the Sky?
Who? who did this? or who is he? Why, know
Its Onely Might Almighty this did doe.   20
His hand hath made this noble worke which Stands
His Glorious Handywork not made by hands.
Who spake all things from nothing; and with ease
Can speake all things to nothing, if he please.
Whose Little finger at his pleasure Can   25
Out mete ten thousand worlds with halfe a Span:
Whose Might Almighty can by half a looks
Root up the rocks and rock the hills by th'roots.
Can take this mighty World up in his hande,
And shake it like a Squitchen[3] or a Wand.   30
Whose single Frown will make the Heavens shake
Like as an aspen leafe the Winde makes quake.
Oh! what a might is this Whose single frown
Doth shake the world as it would shake it down?
Which All from Nothing fet,[4] from Nothing, All: 35
Hath All on Nothing set, lets Nothing fall.
Gave All to nothing Man indeed, whereby
Through nothing man all might him Glorify.
In Nothing then imbosst the brightest Gem
More pretious than all pretiousness in them.   40
But Nothing man did throw down all by Sin:
And darkened that lightsom Gem in him.
    That now his Brightest Diamond is grown
    Darker by far than any Coalpit Stone.
1939

Huswifery

Make me, O Lord, thy Spining Wheele compleate.
  Thy Holy Worde my Distaff[1] make for mee.
Make mine Affections[2] thy Swift Flyers neate
  And make my Soule thy holy Spoole to bee.
My Conversation make to be thy Reele   5
And reele the yarn thereon spun of thy
    Wheele.

---

[3] A slip of branch cut for grafting.
[4] Fetched.
[1] The distaff holds the fibers of wool, which are twisted into threads by the revolving flyers and then wound onto the spool.
[2] Religious feelings.

Make me thy Loome then, knit therein this Twine:
And make thy Holy Spirit, Lord, winde quills:[3]
Then weave the Web thyselfe. The yarn is fine.
Thine Ordinances make my Fulling Mills.[4]   10
Then dy the same in Heavenly Colours
Choice,
All pinkt[5] with Varnisht[6] Flowers of Paradise.

Then cloath therewith mine Understanding, Will,
Affections, Judgment, Conscience, Memory
My Words, and Actions, that their shine may fill   15
My wayes with glory and thee glorify.
Then mine apparell shall display before yee
That I am Cloathd in Holy robes for glory.

1937

William Byrd
1674–1744

William Byrd of Westover, Virginia, called "one of the state's great gentlemen" was a lawyer, planter, writer, and public official. Like similar aristocrats of his time, he was a dilettante who pursued science and writing as hobbies and considered himself to be knowledgeable in medicine, often prescribing for members of his household. Some of his speculations and observations on Native Americans are reflected in his *History of the Dividing Line* (see Cultural Portfolio "The Ways of the Indians"), a narrative of the Virginia-North Carolina boundary line survey of 1728, in which he led the Virginia party. Byrd was the son of one of Virginia's wealthiest planters. He was educated in England, where he befriended leading dramatists, wrote satirical poetry, and also was invited to join the Royal Society, comprised of leading scientific minds of the day. Throughout his adult life, Byrd remained in correspondence with British intellectuals. Byrd's diary, selections from which follow, was composed in shorthand and not published until after his death. It shows Byrd to be a ribald wit, a household manager, and a patriarch with robust sexual appetites.

Further Reading:

M. Tinling, ed., *The Correspondence of the Three William Byrds 1684–1776*, 1977.
P. Marambaud, *William Byrd of Westover*, 1971.

L. B. Wright, ed., *The Prose Works of William Byrd*, 1966.

Texts:
William Byrd: His Secret Diary for the Years 1709–1712, eds. Louis B. Wright and Marion Tinling, 1963

---

[3] Bobbins to hold the thread.
[4] Mills in which cloth is cleansed and stiffened.
[5] Decorated.
[6] Shining.

William Byrd: His Secret Diary for the Years 1709–1712

June 1710

25. I rose at 6 o'clock and found myself a little hot and therefore I took a vomit of infused ipecac, which worked but moderately. I neglected to say my prayers. I ate some toast and canary for breakfast. I could not go to church nor would my wife leave me but I sent several letters to people there. After church Will Randolph came over and told me his father was better. I ate poached eggs for dinner. In the afternoon I found myself a little better and then Will Randolph went away and my wife and I took a walk and met Mr. C-s who came home with us and told us of the unkindness of Mrs. Harrison. I was so tired with walking that I could not hold open my eyes. My people could not find the negro woman but found her hoe by the church land. I neglected to say my prayers but had indifferent health, humor, and thoughts; God send me better. This morning the hogshead of molasses looked above half out.

26. I rose about 6 o'clock and took a purge [of p-l-c-ch] which worked very extremely. I neglected to say my prayers, for which God forgive me. I had eight stools and my fundament was swelled with a sharp humor and very sore. I drank some water gruel. They began to reap this day. I read a chapter in Hebrew. I ate some boiled chicken for dinner. In the afternoon I took a nap which refreshed me a little. The violence of the purge gave me the piles extremely. . . . Mr. Gee came to see me and in the evening Mr. Bland came up in his shallop from Williamsburg and expected to find cargo but I told him it was not come. . . .

27. I lay in bed till 9 o'clock because of the piles, and read a chapter in Hebrew and some Greek in the Testament. I said my prayers and ate milk and [m-l-y] for breakfast. My wife anointed my fundament with tobacco oil and balsam of saltpeter mixed together. It was very much swelled and very painful so that I could not sit nor stand. I settled my closet. . . . About 4 o'clock Mrs. Anderson, Colonel Hill, and Mr. Anderson came to see me and condoled my sore backside and advised me to use linseed oil made hot. As soon as they were gone I tried their medicine and soon after went to bed, but was in exceeding pain so that I was forced to take an opiate and could hardly sleep with that. . . .

28. I lay abed till 10 o'clock and read some letters which Mr. Mumford brought me. Then I read some news. I said a short prayer and ate boiled milk and [m-l-y] for breakfast. My wife anointed my bum with hot linseed oil which had done it some good. However it was not easy yet. Captain Broadwater brought over my sister Brayne's two children who were much below my expectation, being very ordinary. I thanked him for his kindness to the children. About 12 o'clock came Captain Burbydge and Mr. J—, who both dined here. I ate fish for dinner. In the afternoon the company went away. I went to bed early and had my breech anointed. The negro woman was found again that they thought had drowned herself. I said a short prayer. . . .

30. . . . I wrote a letter to Mr. Perry to desire him to send Mr. Bland's goods by the fall fleet. My bum was better, thank God, and I was well again. I ate roast mutton for dinner. In the afternoon the sloop came from Appomattox with tobacco and the other sloop from the ship with my goods and Mr. Bland and Mr. Mumford went aboard to

part them between them and in the evening they made an end. I ate some bread and butter for supper. In the evening I said a short prayer and had good health, good thoughts, and good humor, thank God. I gave my wife a flourish. My cousin Betty Harrison was here this evening and told us Colonial Harrison was very ill of a fever. . . .

July 1710

25. . . . My wife was out of humor this evening for nothing, which I bore very well and was willing to be reconciled. . . .

26. . . . In the evening my wife and I took a walk about the plantation and were good friends. Mr. C-s went to Mrs. Harrison's. I said my prayers and had good health, good thoughts, and good humor, thanks be to God Almighty. I gave my wife a flourish.

27. . . . Colonial Hill came this morning and stayed about an hour. Then came Colonel Randolph who was just recovered of a dangerous sickness. My sloop came from Sandy Point and I sent more tobacco on board Captain Bradby. . . .

28. . . . In the afternoon my wife and I had a little quarrel because she moved my letters. Captain Burbydge came to see us and told me my great sloop was come round. I sent ten hogsheads more on board him. I walked with him some part of the way towards Mrs. Harrison's. When we came home my wife was pleased to be out of humor. . . .

30. . . . I read a sermon in Dr. Tillotson and then took a little [nap]. I ate fish for dinner. In the afternoon my wife and I had a little quarrel which I reconciled with a flourish. Then she read a sermon in Dr. Tillotson to me. It is to be observed that the flourish was performed on the billiard table. I read a little Latin. In the evening we took a walk about the plantation. I neglected to say my prayers but had good health, good thoughts, and good humor, thanks be to God. This month there were many people sick of fever and pain in their heads; perhaps this might be caused by the cold weather which we had this month, which was indeed the coldest that ever was known in July in this country. Several of my people have been sick, but none died, thank God.

31. . . . My daughter was taken sick of a fever this morning and I gave her a vomit which worked very well and brought away great curds out of her stomach and made her well again. My people were all well again, thank God. I went to the store and unpacked some things. About 12 o'clock Captain Burbydge and Captain Broadwater came over. The first went away to Colonel Randolph's; the other stayed to dine with us. I ate hashed mutton for dinner. In the afternoon Dick Randolph came from Williamsburg and brought me the bad news that much of my wine was run out. God's will be done. In the evening Mrs. Harrison and her daughter came over. . . .

August, 1710

2. . . . My daughter was worse this morning and my wife gave her another vomit of tartar emetic which worked much both up and down. She continued very ill all day and was not sensible. . . .

4. I rose at 5 o'clock and found my daughter very ill, so that I sent for Dr. Cocke. I read a chapter in Hebrew and a little Greek in Thucydides. I said my prayers but ate no breakfast, I was so concerned for my daughter. I read French but could not keep my mind steady. Mr. Anderson came to the next house and would not be so kind as to call to see the child. I ate some minced veal for dinner. In the afternoon I took a little [nap]

and then read more French. I sent for Dr. Cocke, but a gust hindered him from coming and me from taking a walk. In the evening my daughter began to be better and had a sort of a looseness which abated her distemper. . . .

5. . . . About 10 o'clock the Doctor came but found the child in no danger. Dr. Bowman came to tell me that my negro boy which he had was too big for him to manage, and therefore desired me to send for him, which I did. The Doctor ordered the child oil of bitters drunk three times a day. About 10 o'clock Mr. Anderson and his wife and Mrs. Harrison came to see us. I scolded at Mr. Anderson for not coming to see the child, but I was satisfied with his excuse. . . .

6. . . . Mrs. John Stith sent my wife some grapes. The Doctor took part of them. The child was much better and [I] gave the Doctor four pieces of gold and desired him to accept of them. He went away about 9 o'clock. About 11 o'clock I went to church and heard a sermon from Mr. Anderson. . . . I gave my wife a flourish on the couch in the library.

8. . . . The child had rested very ill tonight and drank abundance of water. However she had little fever and was hungry. Colonel Hill and Mr. Anderson called here on their way over the river. About 10 o'clock Captain Burbydge came with his boat and I went with him over the river to choose burgesses for Prince George. When we came there we found abundance of people met together and about 2 o'clock they chose Colonel Hardiman and Robin Bolling. I stayed there till 5 o'clock and then went to Mrs. Harrison's where we found Major Burwell. . . .

9. . . . I paid the builder of my sloop £60 which was £10 more than I agreed for. I settled my public accounts. My daughter was better, thank God, but was a little bloated. I was very much out of humor for nothing by reason of the weather or my constitution. I ate boiled lamb for dinner. In the afternoon I read some French. Mr. Salle came and told me that my coaler had the ague and that my shoemaker was sick at his own house. I drank some syllabub and after that ate some beef with him for supper. . . .

March 1711

29. I rose about 7 o'clock and neglected to say my prayers. The Governor made me a compliment and would permit me to go with him no farther but the Doctor endeavored to persuade me to it. About 9 o'clock I ate boiled beef for breakfast. About 10 I took leave of the Governor and when I had seen him [to] Pamunkey River, I and the gentlemen with me returned and had one of the Major's sons for our guide as far as Mr. Fleming's where we drank abundance of cider but we could not see his pretty daughters because they were gone to a meeting. Mr. Fleming himself went with us to show us the way to the bridge where I took leave of the gentlemen that had been with me to wait on the Governor and I rode by myself home, where I arrived about 9 o'clock and found all well, thank God Almighty. I gave Mrs. Russell an account of the Governor's health and of his journey and that the Doctor was to ride on her horse because he had foundered his own which she was very sorry for. In the evening we drank a bottle of mead and I ate some toast. My gray horse carried me this journey very well and so did Ch-s-r which Bannister rode for he had taken good care of them. I said my prayers and had good health, good thoughts, and good humor, thank God Almighty. I rogered my wife with vigor.

30. I rose about 6 o'clock and read two chapters in Hebrew and some Greek in Lucian. I said my prayers and ate boiled milk for breakfast. My wife and I paid all possible respect to Mrs. Russell and I entertained her as well as I could and her conversation was very agreeable. The women drank tea but I drank none with them. About 11 o'clock

came Captain Posford and we settled the freight at £12 per ton and I engaged for 100 hogsheads. He told me that Captain Stith was better. He stayed with us at dinner and I ate fish which made me very dry. In the afternoon the Captain went away and I wrote my journal. About 4 o'clock I drank some coffee with the women and talked with them till the evening. Then I took a walk about the plantation. At night we drank a bottle of cider and talked till about 9 o'clock and then the ladies went to bed. I said my prayers and had good health, good thoughts, and good humor, thank God Almighty. I rogered my wife again.

31. I rose about 6 o'clock and read two chapters in Hebrew and some Greek in Lucian. I said my prayers and ate boiled milk for breakfast. My wife told me of the misfortunes of Mrs. Dunn—that her husband had beat her, and that she had complained to Mr. Gee of it, who made Mr. Dunn swear that he would never beat her again; that he threatened to kill her and abused her extremely and told her he would go from her. I was sorry to hear it and told my wife if he did go from her she might come here. I read some news till dinner. I ate boiled beef for dinner. In the afternoon we made a cold tincture. In the evening I took a long walk about the plantation. At night we drank a bottle of French wine. I said my prayers and had good health, good thoughts, and good humor, thank God Almighty. Mrs. Russell has good sense and very good breeding but can hardly forbear being hysterical, notwithstanding it is with good manners.

April 1711

29. . . . I settled all my affairs and then went to Mr. Bland's to take my leave, which I did about 9 o'clock. Then I rode to my sister Custis' and found them pretty well, only my sister was melancholy. I comforted her as well as I could and then took a walk with my sister and brother in the orchard. About one o'clock Dr. Cocke came from Williamsburg and soon after we went to dinner and I ate boiled beef. In the afternoon we sat and talked till 3 o'clock and then I took my leave and went to Green Spring, and the Doctor returned home. I found a great deal of company with Colonel Ludwell who went away in the evening and we took a walk and romped with the girls at night. I ate some partridge and about 10 went to bed. I said a short prayer and had good health, good thoughts, and good humor, thank God Almighty. I had wicked inclinations to Mistress Sarah Taylor.

30. . . . I took my leave about 6 o'clock and found it very cold. I met with nothing extraordinary in my journey and got home about 11 o'clock and found all well, only my wife was melancholy. We took a walk in the garden and pasture. We discovered that by the contrivance of Nurse and Anaka Prue got in at the cellar window and stole some strong beer and cider and wine. I turned Nurse away upon it and punished Anaka. I ate some fish for dinner. In the afternoon I caused Jack and John to be whipped for drinking at John [Cross] all last Sunday. In the evening I took a walk about the plantation and found things in good order. . . . The weather was very cold for the season. I gave my wife a powerful flourish and gave her great ecstasy and refreshment. . . .

October 1711

29. . . . About 9 o'clock I went to wait on the Governor but he was not at home and I walked after him to the new house and found him there and saw several of the Governor's contrivances, and particularly that for hanging the arms. About 11 o'clock I came

with the Governor to court where we sat till about 3 and then I went up stairs and danced my dance and wrote a letter to England. Then I returned to court where we stayed till about 5 and then I went home with the Governor and ate venison for dinner and then drank a bottle till 8 o'clock. Then we went to the coffeehouse, where we played at cards till 10 and I won 25 shillings. Then I returned home and I committed manual uncleanness, for which God forgive me. I neglected to say my prayers but had good health, good humor, but indifferent thoughts.

30. . . . About 10 o'clock I went to court where I sat till about 2 and then went up stairs and danced my dance and wrote a letter to England. Then I returned into court where we sat till about 5. Then I went with the Governor to dinner and found the weather very cold. I ate venison pasty for dinner and then we drank a bottle till 8 o'clock. Afterwards we went to the coffeehouse where I played at piquet and won 5 shillings. In the evening Colonel Smith and Colonel Carter were at Marot's and somebody cast a brick from the street into the room which narrowly missed Colonel Carter. . . .

31. . . . About 10 o'clock I went to court where I sat till about 3 and then I went up stairs and danced my dance and wrote a letter to England. About 4 I returned to court and we sat till past 5. Then we went to dine at Marot's and I ate roast veal for dinner. About 8 o'clock we went to the coffeehouse and I had not been there half an hour before Eugene came and told me that my wife was at my lodgings. I instantly went home and found her there. She told me all was well at home, thank God, this morning. I neglected to say my prayers but had good health, good thoughts, and good humor, thank God Almighty. I rogered my wife. The weather was very cold. . . .

November 1711

22. . . . Mr. Bland came to see me and told me he would go about the dividing of old Colonel Parke's land as we desired. About 11 I went to the capitol where I found the Governor, who had letters from the Governor of North Carolina which gave a terrible account of the state of Carolina. He had also a letter from the Baron by which he had a relation of his being taken with Mr. Lawson by the Indians and of Mr. Lawson's murder. The House of Burgesses brought their address of thanks to which the Governor answered them that he would thank them when he saw them act with as little self interest as he had done. About 3 o'clock we went to dinner and I ate some roast goose. Then I took a walk to the Governor's new house with Frank W-l-s and then returned to the coffeehouse where I lost 12 pounds 10 shillings and about 10 o'clock returned home very much out of humor to think myself such a fool. . . .

23. . . . About 10 o'clock I went to the capitol where I danced my dance and then wrote in my journal. It was very cold this morning. About 11 o'clock I went to the coffeehouse where the Governor also came and from thence we went to the capitol and read the bill concerning ports the first time. We stayed till 3 o'clock and then went to dinner to Marot's but could get none there and therefore Colonel Lewis and I dined with Colonel Duke and I ate broiled chicken for dinner. After dinner we went to Colonel Carter's room where we had a bowl of punch of French brandy and oranges. We talked very lewdly and were almost drunk and in that condition we went to the coffeehouse and played at dice and I lost £12. We stayed at the coffeehouse till almost 4 o'clock in the morning talking with Major Harrison. Then I went to my lodging, where I committed uncleanness, for which I humbly beg God Almighty's pardon.

24. I rose about 8 o'clock and read a chapter in Hebrew and some Greek in Homer. I said my prayers and ate boiled milk for breakfast. Colonel Carter and several others came to my lodgings to laugh at me for my disorder last night. About 10 I went to the coffeehouse and drank some tea and then we went to the President's and read the law about probate and administration. Then I went to the capitol and danced my dance and wrote in my journal and read Italian. This day I make a solemn resolution never at once to lose more than 50 shillings and to spend less time in gaming, and I beg the God Almighty to give me grace to keep so good a resolution if it be His holy will. . . .

Jonathan Edwards
1703–1758

Jonathan Edwards was a soft-spoken Puritan mystic and intellectual who ranged boldly in thought and writing; he is best known for a sermon that depicts sinners dangling by a spider's filament over "hell's wide gaping mouth." Edwards was born in East Windsor, Connecticut, the sole son among ten daughters of the Reverend Timothy Edwards and Esther Stoddard, herself the daughter of the renowned Puritan minister Solomon Stoddard. Tutored at home by his gifted parents, Edwards entered Yale at the age of thirteen. As his college diary shows, Edwards, like Benjamin Franklin, was determined to improve himself and "never to lose one moment of time." He graduated in 1720. In 1727, in his mid-twenties, Edwards became his grandfather's assistant minister at the church in Northampton, Massachusetts. (That July he married Sarah Pierrepont, the granddaughter of the illustrious Puritan minister Thomas Hooker.) Edwards's grandfather had presided over his congregation with a sense of the value of compromise.

Edwards proved to be very different from his predecessor. Well aware of the contemporary ecumenical spirit of things, Edwards asserted that these newer "reasonable" moderations of Puritan doctrine were "repugnant to the design and tenor of the gospel." Edwards championed the orthodox Puritanism of the founders in the face of the new "free and catholick" temper of the times. His Northampton sermons and other writings over the next few years fortified that position. Above all, Edwards wished to move his congregation beyond a mere cerebral grasp of doctrine. His reading of the philosopher John Locke reinforced his belief that intellectual comprehension of religious ideas was insufficient. Instead, the individual must be moved actually to experience the doctrinal truth. It was the difference, Edwards wrote, between knowing the word *fire* and being burned. As Edwards wrote, "People do not need to have their heads stored so much as their hearts touched."

From 1735 the hearts of the Northampton congregation were indeed touched in an unusual religious revival in which Edwards played a vital part. Soon the revival spread throughout the Connecticut River valley, bringing much word-of-mouth attention to Edwards and his congregation. Though their revival ran its course in two years, the evangelical fervor of the Northampton awakening anticipated the much larger Great Awakening which preoccupied the American colonies from New England to Georgia in the 1740s.

In large part Edwards's religious beliefs were the outcome of his mystical conversion experience in his youth in which he experienced knowledge of God's grace. He later described it in his *Personal Narrative,* in terms so appreciative of the natural world that he sounds to some like a Romantic writer. Believing, however, in the absolute supremacy of God, Edwards saw revivalism as an opportunity to authenticate his faith and to restore Puritanism to its original strength. To this end he delivered the sulphurous sermon titled "Sinners in the Hands of an Angry God," which remains the best-known sermon in American history. It was designed specifically to awaken the congregation to a sense of their sinfulness, and it bears the stamp of his major concerns: that raised affections are visible signs, that mere human efforts to achieve salvation are futile, and that God alone is the omnipotent judge.

Edwards made Northampton a renowned center of orthodoxy and revived spirituality, but by the mid-1740s affairs between the minister and his congregation were moving toward crisis. A backlash developed over the excesses of the Great Awakening and its itinerant preachers, whose "beastly brayings" Edwards himself deplored. Amid controversy, Edwards was forced to resign. Without public rancor he preached his farewell sermon in 1750.

In the following year Edwards assumed the duties of a frontier minister to whites and Indians in Stockbridge, a remote western Massachusetts mission. There Edwards wrote his greatest philosophical works, including *Freedom of the Will* (1754), *The Doctrine of Original Sin Defended* (1758), and *The Nature of True Virtue* (1765). These works examine the nature and place of free will in a predetermined universe and explore the relation between virtue and religious affections. The publication of these works brought Edwards renewed attention from scholars and intellectuals, who invited him to become the president of Princeton University. He arrived with his family amid an outbreak of smallpox. In 1758, after less than two months in office, Edwards died from an adverse reaction to a smallpox inoculation, for which he had volunteered. He is revered as an American philosopher of originality and a literary stylist of subtlety and power.

Further Reading:

T. H. Johnson, *The Printed Writings of Jonathan Edwards, 1703–1758,* 1940, 1970.
O. Winslow, *Jonathan Edwards,* 1940.
P. Miller, *Jonathan Edwards,* 1949.

A. Aldridge, *Jonathan Edwards,* 1964.
C. Cherry, *The Theology of Jonathan Edwards,* 1966.
E. Griffin, *Jonathan Edwards,* 1971.

Text:
Images or Shadows of Divine Things, ed. P. Miller, 1948.

---

from Personal Narrative

I had a variety of concerns and exercises about my soul from my childhood; but had two more remarkable seasons of awakening,[1] before I met with that change by which I was brought to those new dispositions, and that new sense of things, that I have since had. The first time was when I was a boy, some years before I went to college, at a time

---

[1] Religious enlivening.

of remarkable awakening in my father's congregation. I was then very much affected for many months, and concerned about the things of religion, and my soul's salvation; and was abundant in duties. I used to pray five times a day in secret, and to spend much time in religious talk with other boys; and used to meet with them to pray together. I experienced I know not what kind of delight in religion. My mind was much engaged in it, and had much self-righteous pleasure; and it was my delight to abound in religious duties. I with some of my schoolmates joined together, and built a booth in a swamp, in a very retired spot, for a place of prayer. And besides, I had particular secret places of my own in the woods, where I used to retire by myself; and was from time to time much affected. My affections[2] seemed to be lively and easily moved, and I seemed to be in my element when engaged in religious duties. And I am ready to think, many are deceived with such affections, and such a kind of delight as I then had in religion, and mistake it for grace.

But in process of time, my convictions and affections wore off; and I entirely lost all those affections and delights and left off secret prayer, at least as to any constant perfor-mance of it; and returned like a dog to his vomit,[3] and went on in the ways of sin. In-deed I was at times very uneasy, especially towards the latter part of my time at college, when it pleased God to seize me with the pleurisy, in which He brought me nigh to the grave, and shook me over the pit of hell. And yet, it was not long after my recovery, be-fore I fell again into my old ways of sin. But God would not suffer me to go on with any quietness; I had great and violent inward struggles, till, after many conflicts with wicked inclinations, repeated resolutions, and bonds that I laid myself under by a kind of vows to God, I was brought wholly to break off all former wicked ways, and all ways of known outward sin; and to apply myself to seek salvation, and practice many religious duties; but without that kind of affection and delight which I had formerly experienced. My concern now wrought more by inward struggles and conflicts, and self-reflections. I made seeking my salvation the main business of my life. But yet, it seems to me I sought after a miserable manner; which has made me sometimes since to question, whether ever it issued in that which was saving; being ready to doubt, whether such miserable seeking ever succeeded. I was indeed brought to seek salvation in a manner that I never was before; I felt a spirit to part with all things in the world, for an interest in Christ. My concern continued and prevailed, with many exercising thoughts and inward struggles; but yet it never seemed to be proper to express that concern by the name of terror.

From my childhood up, my mind had been full of objections against the doctrine of God's sovereignty, in choosing whom He would to eternal life, and rejecting whom He pleased; leaving them eternally to perish, and be everlastingly tormented in hell. It used to appear like a horrible doctrine to me. But I remember the time very well, when I seemed to be convinced, and fully satisfied, as to this sovereignty of God, and His jus-tice in thus eternally disposing of men, according to His sovereign pleasure. But I never could give an account how, or by what means, I was thus convinced, not in the least imagining at the time, nor a long time after, that there was any extraordinary influence of God's Spirit in it; but only that now I saw further, and my reason apprehended the justice and reasonableness of it. However, my mind rested in it; and it put an end to all those cavils and objections. And there has been a wonderful alteration in my mind, with respect to the doctrine of God's sovereignty, from that day to this; so that I scarce ever

---

[2] Religious feelings.   [3] See Proverbs 26:11.

have found so much as the rising of an objection against it, in the most absolute sense, in God's showing mercy to whom He will show mercy, and hardening whom He will.[4] God's absolute sovereignty and justice, with respect to salvation and damnation, is what my mind seems to rest assured of, as much as of anything that I see with my eyes; at least it is so at times. But I have often, since that first conviction, had quite another kind of sense of God's sovereignty than I had then. I have often since had not only a conviction, but a delightful conviction. The doctrine has very often appeared exceeding pleasant, bright, and sweet. Absolute sovereignty is what I love to ascribe to God. But my first conviction was not so.

The first instance that I remember of that sort of inward, sweet delight in God and divine things that I have lived much in since, was on reading those words, 1 Timothy 1:17, *Now unto the King eternal, immortal, invisible, the only wise God, be honor and glory forever and ever, Amen.* As I read the words, there came into my soul, and was as it were diffused through it, a sense of the glory of the Divine Being; a new sense, quite different from anything I ever experienced before. Never any words of Scripture seemed to me as these words did. I thought within myself, how excellent a Being that was, and how happy I should be, if I might enjoy that God, and be rapt[5] up to him in heaven, and be as it were swallowed up in him forever! I kept saying, and as it were singing over these words of Scripture to myself; and went to pray to God that I might enjoy Him, and prayed in a manner quite different from what I used to do; with a new sort of affection. But it never came into my thought that there was anything spiritual, or of a saving nature, in this.

From about that time, I began to have a new kind of apprehensions and ideas of Christ, and the work of redemption, and the glorious way of salvation by Him. An inward, sweet sense of these things, at times, came into my heart; and my soul was led away in pleasant views and contemplations of them. And my mind was greatly engaged to spend my time in reading and meditating on Christ, on the beauty and excellency of His person, and the lovely way of salvation by free grace in Him. I found no books so delightful to me, as those that treated of these subjects. Those words, Canticles[6] 2:1, used to be abundantly with me, *I am the Rose of Sharon, and the lily of the valleys.* The words seemed to me sweetly to represent the loveliness and beauty of Jesus Christ. The whole book of Canticles used to be pleasant to me, and I used to be much in reading it, about that time; and found, from time to time, an inward sweetness, that would carry me away, in my contemplations. This I know not how to express otherwise, than by a calm, sweet abstraction of soul from all the concerns of this world; and sometimes a kind of vision, or fixed ideas and imaginations, of being alone in the mountains, or some solitary wilderness, far from all mankind, sweetly conversing with Christ, and wrapped and swallowed up in God. The sense I had of divine things would often of a sudden kindle up, as it were, a sweet burning in my heart; an ardor of soul, that I know not how to express.

Not long after I first began to experience these things, I gave an account to my father of some things that had passed in my mind. I was pretty much affected by the discourse we had together; and when the discourse was ended, I walked abroad alone, in a solitary place in my father's pasture, for contemplation. And as I was walking there, and looking

---

[4] See Romans 9:18.   [6] The biblical Song of Solomon.
[5] Lifted.

up on the sky and clouds, there came into my mind so sweet a sense of the glorious *majesty* and *grace* of God, that I know not how to express. I seemed to see them both in a sweet conjunction; majesty and meekness joined together; it was a sweet and gentle, and holy majesty; and also a majestic meekness; an awful sweetness; a high, and great, and holy gentleness.

After this my sense of divine things gradually increased, and became more and more lively, and had more of that inward sweetness. The appearance of every thing was altered; there seemed to be, as it were, a calm, sweet cast, or appearance of divine glory, in almost everything. God's excellency, His wisdom, His purity and love, seemed to appear in every thing; in the sun, and moon, and stars; in the clouds and blue sky; in the grass, flowers, trees; in the water, and all nature; which used greatly to fix my mind. I often used to sit and view the moon for a long time; and in the day spent much time in viewing the clouds and sky, to behold the sweet glory of God in these things; in the meantime, singing forth, with a low voice, my contemplations of the Creator and Redeemer. And scarce anything, among all the works of nature, was so sweet to me as thunder and lightning; formerly, nothing had been so terrible to me. Before, I used to be uncommonly terrified with thunder, and to be struck with terror when I saw a thunder storm rising; but now, on the contrary, it rejoiced me. I felt God, so to speak, at the first appearance of a thunder storm; and used to take the opportunity, at such times, to fix myself in order to view the clouds, and see the lightnings play, and hear the majestic and awful voice of God's thunder, which oftentimes was exceedingly entertaining, leading me to sweet contemplations of my great and glorious God. While thus engaged, it always seemed natural to me to sing, or chant forth my meditations; or, to speak my thoughts in soliloquies with a singing voice.

I felt then great satisfaction, as to my good state; but that did not content me. I had vehement longings of soul after God and Christ, and after more holiness, wherewith my heart seemed to be full, and ready to break; which often brought to my mind the words of the Psalmist, Psalms 119:20: *My soul breaketh for the longing that it hath.* I often felt a mourning and lamenting in my heart, that I had not turned to God sooner, that I might have had more time to grow in grace. My mind was greatly fixed on divine things; almost perpetually in the contemplation of them. I spent most of my time in thinking of divine things, year after year; often walking alone in the woods, and solitary places, for meditation, soliloquy, and prayer, and converse with God; and it was always my manner, at such times, to sing forth my contemplations. I was almost constantly in ejaculatory prayer, wherever I was. Prayer seemed to be natural to me, as the breath by which the inward burnings of my heart had vent. The delights which I now felt in the things of religion, were of an exceeding different kind from those before mentioned, that I had when a boy; and what I then had no more notion of, than one born blind has of pleasant and beautiful colors. They were of a more inward, pure, soul-animating and refreshing nature. Those former delights never reached the heart; and did not arise from any sight of the divine excellency of the things of God; or any taste of the soul-satisfying and life-giving good there is in them. . . .

I very frequently used to retire into a solitary place, on the banks of Hudson's river, at some distance from the city, for contemplation on divine things, and secret converse with God; and had many sweet hours there. Sometimes Mr. Smith and I walked there together, to converse on the things of God; and our conversation used to turn much on the advancement of Christ's kingdom in the world, and the glorious things that God would accomplish for his church in the latter days. I had then, and at other times, the greatest delight in the holy Scriptures, of any book whatsoever. Oftentimes in reading it, every word seemed to touch my heart. I felt a harmony between something in my heart, and those sweet and powerful words. I seemed often to see so much light exhibited by every sentence, and such a refreshing food communicated, that I could not get along in reading; often dwelling long on one sentence, to see the wonders contained in it; and yet almost every sentence seemed to be full of wonders. . . .

Sometimes, only mentioning a single word caused my heart to burn within me; or only seeing the name of Christ, or the name of some attribute of God. And God has appeared glorious to me, on account of the Trinity. It has made me have exalting thoughts of God, that He subsists in three persons; Father, Son, and Holy Ghost. The sweetest joys and delights I have experienced, have not been those that have arisen from a hope of my own good estate; but in a direct view of the glorious things of the gospel. When I enjoy this sweetness, it seems to carry me above the thoughts of my own estate; it seems at such times a loss that I cannot bear, to take off my eye from the glorious pleasant object I behold without me, to turn my eye in upon myself, and my own good estate.

My heart has been much on the advancement of Christ's kingdom in the world. The histories of the past advancement of Christ's kingdom have been sweet to me. When I have read histories of past ages, the pleasantest thing in all my reading has been, to read of the kingdom of Christ being promoted. And when I have expected, in my reading, to come to any such thing, I have rejoiced in the prospect, all the way as I read. And my mind has been much entertained and delighted with the Scripture promises and prophecies, which relate to the future glorious advancement of Christ's kingdom upon earth.

I have sometimes had a sense of the excellent fulness of Christ, and His meetness and suitableness as a Saviour, whereby He has appeared to me, far above all, the chief of ten thousands.[7] His blood and atonement have appeared sweet, and His righteousness sweet; which was always accompanied with ardency of spirit; and inward strugglings, and breathings, and groanings that cannot be uttered to be emptied of myself, and swallowed up in Christ. . . .

I have greatly longed of late, for a broken heart, and to lie low before God; and, when I ask for humility, I cannot bear the thoughts of being no more humble than other Christians. It seems to me, that though their degrees of humility may be suitable for them, yet it would be a vile self-exaltation in me, not to be the lowest in humility of all mankind. Others speak of their longing to be "humbled to the dust"; that may be a proper expression for them, but I always think of myself, that I ought, and it is an expression that has long been natural for me to use in prayer, "to lie infinitely low before God." And it is affecting to think, how ignorant I was, when a young Christian, of the bottomless, infinite depths of wickedness, pride, hypocrisy, and deceit, left in my heart.

I have a much greater sense of my universal, exceeding dependence on God's grace and strength, and mere good pleasure, of late, than I used formerly to have; and have experienced more of an abhorrence of my own righteousness. The very thought of any joy arising in me, on any consideration of my own amiableness, performances, or experiences, or any goodness of heart or life, is nauseous and detestable to me. And yet I am greatly afflicted with a proud and self-righteous spirit, much more sensibly than I used

---

[7] Song of Solomon 5:10: "My beloved is . . . chiefest among ten thousand."

to be formerly. I see that serpent rising and putting forth its head continually, everywhere, all around me.

Though it seems to me, that, in some respects, I was a far better Christian, for two or three years after my first conversion, than I am now; and lived in a more constant delight and pleasure; yet, of late years, I have had a more full and constant sense of the absolute sovereignty of God, and a delight in that sovereignty; and have had more of a sense of the glory of Christ, as a Mediator revealed in the gospel. On one Saturday night, in particular, I had such a discovery of the excellency of the gospel above all other doctrines, that I could not but say to myself, "This is my chosen light, my chosen doctrine;" and of Christ, "This is my chosen Prophet." It appeared sweet, beyond all expression, to follow Christ, and to be taught, and enlightened, and instructed by Him; to learn of Him, and live to Him. Another Saturday night, (*January, 1739*) I had such a sense, how sweet and blessed a thing it was to walk in the way of duty; to do that which was right and meet to be done, and agreeable to the holy mind of God; that it caused me to break forth into a kind of loud weeping, which held me some time, so that I was forced to shut myself up, and fasten the doors. I could not but, as it were, cry out, "How happy are they which do that which is right in the sight of God! They are blessed indeed, they are the happy ones!" I had, at the same time, a very affecting sense, how meet and suitable it was that God should govern the world, and order all things according to His own pleasure; and I rejoiced in it, that God reigned, and that His will was done.

1765

Sinners in the Hands of an Angry God

Their foot shall slide in due time.
Deuteronomy 32:35

In this verse is threatened the vengeance of God on the wicked unbelieving Israelites, that were God's visible people, and lived under means of grace;[1] and that notwithstanding all God's wonderful works that He had wrought towards that people, yet remained, as is expressed verse 28, void of counsel, having no understanding in them; and that, under all the cultivations of heaven, brought forth bitter and poisonous fruit; as in the two verses next preceding the text.

The expression that I have chosen for my text, *their foot shall slide in due time*, seems to imply the following things relating to the punishment and destruction that these wicked Israelites were exposed to.

1. That they are always exposed to destruction, as one that stands or walks in slippery places is always exposed to fall. This is implied in the manner of their destruction's coming upon them, being represented by their foot's sliding. The same is expressed,

---

[1] According to God's covenant with Abraham (Genesis 17–18), the chosen people would receive God's grace and be saved. In Puritan thought Jesus' atonement fulfilled the covenant with Abraham, which restored the possibility of salvation previously lost through the sin of Adam and Eve.

Psalm 73:18: "Surely thou didst set them in slippery places: thou castedst them down into destruction."

2. It implies that they were always exposed to sudden, unexpected destruction. As he that walks in slippery places is every moment liable to fall, he cannot foresee one moment whether he shall stand or fall the next; and when he does fall, he falls at once, without warning, which is also expressed in that Psalm 73:18–19: "Surely thou didst set them in slippery places: thou castedst them down into destruction. How are they brought into desolation as in a moment."

3. Another thing implied is that they are liable to fall of *themselves,* without being thrown down by the hand of another, as he that stands or walks on slippery ground needs nothing but his own weight to throw him down.

4. That the reason why they are not fallen already, and do not fall now, is only that God's appointed time is not come. For it is said that when that due time or appointed time comes, their foot shall slide. Then they shall be left to fall, as they are inclined by their own weight. God will not hold them up in these slippery places any longer but will let them go; and then, at that very instant, they shall fall into destruction; as he that stands on such slippery declining ground on the edge of a pit that he cannot stand alone, when he is let go he immediately falls and is lost.

The observation from the words that I would now insist upon is this.

There is nothing that keeps wicked men at any one moment out of hell, but the mere pleasure of God.

Benjamin Franklin
1706–1790

Eighteenth-century America produced a number of strong, versatile personalities, but none with the creative range of Benjamin Franklin. A summary of his career reads like one of Walt Whitman's catalogs of occupations: printer, publisher, journalist, essayist, scientist, philosopher, merchant, educator, inventor, politician, diplomat.

Franklin was born in Boston in 1706, the fifteenth child of a soap and candle maker. The early "poverty" in which he claims to have been raised may be more accurate than the "obscurity." As a respected member of the Boston community and the prestigious Old South Church, Josiah Franklin numbered among his friends many leading Boston figures. Showing signs of precocity, Franklin was sent to the Boston Grammar School, where he characteristically rose to the head of his class. The expenses of the large Franklin family, however, prevented his continuing in a college preparatory curriculum, and he was removed to a private school established to teach future tradesmen the necessary skills of "writing and arithmetic." At ten, Franklin left school altogether to help in the family business, but disliking it, was officially apprenticed two years later to his half brother James, who had recently set up a printing shop in Boston. Franklin made, as he says, "great progress" in this trade and particularly enjoyed the access it gave him to books and booksellers.

In 1722, the year after his brother founded the iconoclastic *New England Courant,* Franklin wrote a series of humorous essays in the vein of Addison and Steele's popular *Spectator Papers* and submitted them to the *Courant* under a pseudonym, "Mrs. Silence Dogood." After the fourteenth "Dogood" paper, Franklin let his brother in on the author's identity, but this disclosure added to a growing tension between master and apprentice. The relationship ended bitterly the next year; Franklin violated the terms of indenture and ran off to begin a new life in Philadelphia.

He found work in Samuel Keimer's small, ill-equipped printing shop but did not stay long. The governor of Pennsylvania, Sir William Keith, at the suggestion of Franklin's brother-in-law, decided to assist the young printer by sponsoring a trip to London, but when he reached London, Franklin learned that he could not rely on Keith's promises. Undaunted, he quickly found employment in a famous London printing house, where by day he perfected his craft and by evening made the acquaintance of some noted writers, scientists, and philosophers.

Franklin returned to Philadelphia in 1726 and began working as a merchant's clerk. When his employer died the following year, he had little choice than to go back to Keimer's printing shop. He determined to make a success of himself by adhering to a meticulous schedule of work and self-improvement and by methodically attending to every detail of daily existence with a rigor that would have pleased his Puritan forebears. Over the next three years, Franklin purchased and revitalized a newspaper (*The Pennsylvania Gazette*), opened a stationer's shop, and was appointed public printer of Pennsylvania. In 1730 he married Deborah Read, whom he had first noticed the day he made his awkward entrance into Philadelphia as a runaway apprentice. With her, Franklin had three children. The first (Francis, b. 1732) died of smallpox as a child; the two others (Sarah and William) lived into adulthood. Between 1733 and 1744 he founded a fire company, established America's first circulating library, was appointed deputy postmaster general of the colonies, launched a magazine, organized the American Philosophical Society, invented the popular Franklin stove, and drew up a proposal for what would become the University of Pennsylvania.

In 1732 Franklin began *Poor Richard's Almanac,* a somewhat parodic annual compendium of weather predictions, folk wisdom, poetic snippets, recipes, medical advice, proverbs, moral anecdotes, and useful information on how to make money and save time for people who had little of either.

By 1748 Franklin had made enough money to leave the management of his various businesses in other hands so that he could concentrate his energies in two areas, science and politics. He had begun conducting experiments in electricity in 1746, and five years later the first of many editions of *Experiments and Observations on Electricity* was published in London. Franklin had an eye for the theatrical side of science; in the summer of 1752 he performed highly publicized kite experiments, which established the electrical nature of lightning and ensured his election to the Royal Society of London.

From his proposal for colonial unification at the Albany Congress in 1754 to his stirring speech at the Constitutional Convention in 1787, Franklin played a pivotal role in the struggle for colonial independence and the building of a new nation. In 1755 and 1756 he lent his business skills to help General Braddock obtain transportation and supplies during the French and Indian War. As a colonel of militia, he supervised the construction of forts in Pennsylvania. Between 1757 and 1762 he served as agent for the Province of Pennsylvania in London. In Philadelphia, in 1775, Franklin served as a delegate to the Second Continental Congress and as a member of the committee appointed to draft the Declaration of Independence. In 1776, Franklin sailed for Paris as a congressional minister to the Court of Louis XVI, where he secured crucial support for his homeland. He charmed Parisian society with his wit and warmth, and in 1781 was again sent to France to negotiate a peace treaty with Great Britain. He resigned his diplomatic post in 1785 and returned to Philadelphia. where he served in the state government before being elected president of the Pennsylvania Society for the Abolition of Slavery and a delegate to the Constitutional Convention. In 1788, "afflicted with almost constant and grievous pain," he retired altogether from public life.

On his second visit to England, during a leisurely week in August 1771, Franklin began his memoirs. Personal and political difficulties interrupted the work, and an uncompleted *Autobiography* passed through a number of unauthorized and unreliable editions until the original manuscript was discovered in France in 1868. Franklin's *Autobiography* transformed the rags-to-riches theme into world myth.

Further Reading:

B. Granger, *Benjamin Franklin: An American Man of Letters*, 1964.
R. F. Sayre, *The Examined Life*, 1964.
A. O. Aldridge, *Benjamin Franklin: Philosopher and Man*, 1965.
C. Lopez and E. W. Herbert, *The Private Franklin: The Man and His Family*, 1975.
A. B. Tourtellot, *Benjamin Franklin: The Boston Years*, 1977.

R. W. Clark, *Benjamin Franklin: A Biography*, 1983.
M. R. Breitweiler, *Cotton Mather and Benjamin Franklin: The Price of Representative Personality*, 1985.
O. Seavey, *Becoming Benjamin Franklin: The Autobiography and the Life*, 1988.
M. Warner, *Letters of the Republic*, 1990.
J. A. L. Lemay, ed., *Reappraising Benjamin Franklin*, 1992.

Texts:

The Autobiography of Benjamin Franklin, ed. L. W. Labaree et al., 1964.
Other selections prior to 1773 are from *The Papers of Benjamin Franklin*, ed. L. W. Labaree et al., 21 vols., 1959–1978.

All remaining selections are from *The Writings of Benjamin Franklin*, ed. A. H. Smyth, 10 vols., 1905–1907.
(Some inconsistencies in spelling have been silently corrected.)

The Autobiography

from Part One

Twyford,[1] at the Bishop of St. Asaph's 1771.

Dear Son,[2]

I have ever had a Pleasure in obtaining any little Anecdotes of my Ancestors. You may remember the Enquiries I made among the Remains of my Relations when you were with me in England; and the Journey I took for that purpose.[3] Now imagining it

---

[1] Country home near Winchester, England, of Franklin's friend Jonathan Shipley, bishop of St. Asaph.
[2] William Franklin, royal governor of New Jersey.
[3] During a tour of England in 1758, they searched out the home of their ancestors.

may be equally agreeable to you to know the Circumstances of *my* Life, many of which you are yet unacquainted with; and expecting a Weeks uninterrupted Leisure in my present Country Retirement, I sit down to write them for you. To which I have besides some other Inducements. Having emerg'd from the Poverty and Obscurity in which I was born and bred, to a State of Affluence and some Degree of Reputation in the World, and having gone so far thro' Life with a considerable Share of Felicity, the conducing Means I made use of, which, with the Blessing of God, so well succeeded, my Posterity may like to know, as they may find some of them suitable to their own Situations, and therefore fit to be imitated. That Felicity, when I reflected on it, has induc'd me sometimes to say, that were it offer'd to my Choice, I should have no Objection to a Repetition of the same Life from its Beginning, only asking the Advantage Authors have in a second Edition to correct some Faults of the first. So would I if I might, besides corr[ectin]g the Faults, change some sinister Accidents and Events of it for others more favourable, but tho' this were deny'd, I should still accept the Offer. However, since such a Repetition is not to be expected, the next Thing most like living one's Life over again, seems to be a *Recollection* of that Life; and to make that Recollection as durable as possible, the putting it down in Writing. Hereby, too, I shall indulge the Inclination so natural in old Men, to be talking of themselves and their own past Actions, and I shall indulge it, without being troublesome to others who thro' respect to Age might think themselves oblig'd to give me a Hearing, since this may be read or not as any one pleases. And lastly, (I may as well confess it, since my Denial of it will be believ'd by no body) perhaps I shall a good deal gratify my own *Vanity.* Indeed I scarce ever heard or saw the introductory Words, *Without Vanity I may say,* &c. but some vain thing immediately follow'd. Most People dislike Vanity in others whatever Share they have of it themselves, but I give it fair Quarter wherever I meet with it, being persuaded that it is often productive of Good to the Possessor and to others that are within his Sphere of Action: And therefore in many Cases it would not be quite absurd if a Man were to thank God for his Vanity among the other Comforts of Life. . . .

And now I speak of thanking God, I desire with all Humility to acknowledge, that I owe the mention'd Happiness of my past Life to his kind Providence, which led me to the Means I us'd and gave them Success. My Belief of this, induces me to *hope,* tho' I must not *presume,* that the same Goodness will still be exercis'd towards me in continuing that Happiness, or in enabling me to bear a fatal Reverse, which I may experience as others have done, the Complexion of my future Fortune being known to him only: and in whose Power it is to bless to us even our Afflictions.

The Notes one of my Uncles (who had the same kind of Curiosity in collecting Family Anecdotes) once put into my Hands, furnish'd me with several Particulars relating to our Ancestors. From these Notes I learnt that the Family had liv'd in the same Village, Ecton in Northamptonshire, for 300 Years, and how much longer he knew not (perhaps from the Time when the Name *Franklin* that before was the Name of an Order of People,[4] was assum'd by them for a Surname, when others took Surnames all over the Kingdom). (Here a Note)[5] on a Freehold of about 30 Acres, aided by the Smith's Business which had continued in the Family till his Time, the eldest Son being always

---

[4] In feudal England, *franklin* was a term for a middle-class property owner.

[5] Omitted by Franklin.

bred to that Business. A Custom which he and my Father both followed as to their eldest Sons. When I search'd the Register at Ecton, I found an Account of their Births, Marriages and Burials, from the Year 1555 only, there being no Register kept in that Parish at any time preceding. By that Register I perceiv'd that I was the youngest Son of the youngest Son for 5 Generations back.

My Grandfather Thomas, who was born in 1598, lived at Ecton till he grew too old to follow Business longer, when he went to live with his Son John, a Dyer at Banbury in Oxfordshire, with whom my Father serv'd an Apprenticeship. There my Grandfather died and lies buried. We saw his Gravestone in 1758. His eldest Son Thomas liv'd in the House at Ecton, and left it with the Land to his only Child, a Daughter, who with her Husband, one Fisher of Wellingborough sold it to Mr. Isted, now Lord of the Manor there. My Grandfather had 4 Sons that grew up, viz. Thomas, John, Benjamin and Josiah. I will give you what Account I can of them at this distance from my Papers, and if they are not lost in my Absence, you will among them find many more Particulars. Thomas was bred a Smith under his Father, but being ingenious, and encourag'd in Learning (as all his Brothers like wise were) by an Esquire Palmer then the principal Gentleman in that Parish, he qualify'd for the Business of Scrivener,[6] became a considerable Man in the County Affairs, was a chief Mover of all publick Spirited Undertakings, for the County, or Town of Northampton and his own Village, of which many Instances were told us at Ecton and he was much taken Notice of and patroniz'd by the then Lord Halifax. He died in 1702, Jan. 6, old Stile, just 4 Years to a Day before I was born.[7] The Account we receiv'd of his Life and Character from some old People at Ecton, I remember struck you, as something extraordinary from its Similarity to what you knew of mine. Had he died on the same Day, you said one might have suppos'd a Transmigration.

John was bred a Dyer, I believe of Woollens. Benjamin, was bred a Silk Dyer, serving an Apprenticeship at London. He was an ingenious Man, I remember him well, for when I was a Boy he came over to my Father in Boston, and lived in the House with us some Years. He lived to a great Age. His Grandson Samuel Franklin now lives in Boston. He left behind him two Quarto Volumes, M.S. of his own Poetry, consisting of little occasional Pieces address'd to his Friends and Relations, of which the following sent to me, is a Specimen. (Here insert it.)[8] He had form'd a Shorthand of his own, which he taught me, but never practising it I have now forgot it. I was nam'd after this Uncle, there being a particular Affection between him and my Father. He was very pious, a great Attender of Sermons of the best Preachers, which he took down in his Shorthand and had with him many Volumes of them. He was also much of a Politician, too much perhaps for his Station. There fell lately into my Hands in London a Collection he had made of all the principal Pamphlets relating to Publick Affairs from 1641 to 1717. Many of the Volumes are wanting, as appears by the Numbering, but there still remains 8 Vols. Folio, and 24 in 4to and 8vo.[9] A Dealer in old Books met with them,

---

[6] A professional writer, often responsible for legal documents.

[7] Because of astronomical inaccuracies, the Julian ("Old Style") calendar was replaced by the Gregorian ("New Style") calendar in 1752. An act of Parliament advanced the calendar eleven days, thus shifting Franklin's birth date from January 6, 1706, to January 17, 1706.

[8] Omitted by Franklin.

[9] Traditional designations of book sizes.

and knowing me by my sometimes buying of him, he brought them to me. It seems my Uncle must have left them here when he went to America, which was above 50 Years since. There are many of his Notes in the Margins.

This obscure Family of ours was early in the Reformation, and continu'd Protestants thro' the Reign of Queen Mary,[10] when they were sometimes in Danger of Trouble on Account of their Zeal against Popery. They had got an English Bible, and to conceal and secure it, it was fastned open with Tapes under and within the Frame of a Joint Stool. When my Great Great Grandfather read in it to his Family, he turn'd up the Joint Stool upon his Knees, turning over the Leaves then under the Tapes. One of the Children stood at the Door to give Notice if he saw the Apparitor coming, who was an Officer of the Spiritual Court. In that Case the Stool was turn'd down again upon its feet, when the Bible remain'd conceal'd under it as before. This Anecdote I had from my Uncle Benjamin. The Family continu'd all of the Church of England till about the End of Charles the 2ds Reign,[11] when some of the Ministers that had been outed for Nonconformity,[12] holding Conventicles[13] in Northamptonshire, Benjamin and Josiah adher'd to them, and so continu'd all their Lives. The rest of the Family remain'd with the Episcopal Church.

Josiah, my Father, married young, and carried his Wife with three Children unto New England, about 1682.[14] The Conventicles having been forbidden by Law, and frequently disturbed, induced some considerable Men of his Acquaintance to remove to that Country, and he was prevail'd with to accompany them thither, where they expected to enjoy their Mode of Religion with Freedom. By the same Wife he had 4 Children more born there, and by a second Wife ten more, in all 17, of which I remember 13 sitting at one time at his Table, who all grew up to be Men and Women, and married. I was the youngest Son and the youngest Child but two, and was born in Boston, N. England.

My Mother the 2d Wife was Abiah Folger, a Daughter of Peter Folger, one of the first Settlers of New England,[15] of whom honourable mention is made by Cotton Mather, in his Church History of that Country, (entitled Magnalia Christi Americana) as a *godly learned Englishman*, if I remember the words rightly. I have heard that he wrote sundry small occasional Pieces, but only one of them[16] was printed which I saw now many Years since. It was written in 1675, in the homespun Verse of that Time and People, and address'd to those then concern'd in the Government there. It was in favour of Liberty of Conscience, and in behalf of the Baptists, Quakers, and other Sectaries, that had been under Persecution; ascribing the Indian Wars and other Distresses, that had befallen the Country to that Persecution, as so many Judgments of God, to punish so heinous an Offence; and exhorting a Repeal of those uncharitable Laws. The whole appear'd to me as written with a good deal of Decent Plainness and manly Freedom. The six last concluding Lines I remember, tho' I have forgotten the two first of the Stanza, but the

---

[10] A Roman Catholic, she reigned from 1553 to 1558.

[11] Charles II ruled from 1660 to 1685.

[12] They were ousted from the Church of England for refusing to read the prayer book.

[13] Secret religious meetings.

[14] Actually, 1683.

[15] The Folgers were a prominent Nantucket, Massachusetts, family.

[16] *A Looking Glass for the Times, or the Former Spirit of New England Revived in This Generation* (Boston, 1676).

Purport of them was that his Censures proceeded from *Goodwill,* and therefore he would be known as the Author,

> because to be a Libeller, (says he)
>   I hate it with my Heart.
> From Sherburne Town[17] where now I dwell,
>   My Name I do put here,
> Without Offence, your real Friend,
>   It is Peter Folgier.

My elder Brothers were all put Apprentices to different Trades. I was put to the Grammar School at Eight Years of Age, my Father intending to devote me as the Tithe[18] of his Sons to the Service of the Church. My early Readiness in learning to read (which must have been very early, as I do not remember when I could not read) and the Opinion of all his Friends that I should certainly make a good Scholar, encourag'd him in this Purpose of his. My Uncle Benjamin too approv'd of it, and propos'd to give me all his Shorthand Volumes of Sermons I suppose as a Stock to set up with, if I would learn his Character.[19] I continu'd however at the Grammar School not quite one Year, tho' in that time I had risen gradually from the Middle of the Class of that Year to be the Head of it, and farther was remov'd into the next Class above it, in order to go with that into the third at the End of the Year. But my Father in the mean time, from a View of the Expence of a College Education which, having so large a Family, he could not well afford, and the mean Living many so educated were afterwards able to obtain, Reasons that he gave to his Friends in my Hearing, altered his first Intention, took me from the Grammar School, and sent me to a School for Writing and Arithmetic kept by a then famous Man, Mr. Geo. Brownell, very successful in his Profession generally, and that by mild encouraging Methods. Under him I acquired fair Writing pretty soon, but I fail'd in the Arithmetic, and made no Progress in it.

At Ten Years old, I was taken home to assist my Father in his Business, which was that of a Tallow Chandler and Sope-Boiler. A Business he was not bred to, but had assumed on his Arrival in New England and on finding his Dying Trade would not maintain his Family, being in little Request. Accordingly I was employed in cutting Wick for the Candles, filling the Dipping Mold, and the Molds for cast Candles, attending the Shop, going of Errands, &c. I dislik'd the Trade and had a strong Inclination for the Sea; but my Father declar'd against it; however, living near the Water, I was much in and about it, learnt early to swim well, and to manage Boats, and when in a Boat or Canoe with other Boys I was commonly allow'd to govern, especially in any case of Difficulty; and upon other Occasions I was generally a Leader among the Boys, and sometimes led them into Scrapes, of which I will mention one Instance, as it shows an early projecting public Spirit, tho' not then justly conducted. There was a Salt Marsh that bounded part of the Mill Pond, on the Edge of which at Highwater, we us'd to stand to fish for Minews. By much Trampling, we had made it a mere Quagmire. My Proposal was to build a Wharff there fit for us to stand upon, and I show'd my Comrades a large Heap

---

[17] Franklin's note: "In the Island of Nantucket."

[18] A contribution of the tenth part of one's income to the church; Franklin was the tenth son.

[19] The shorthand method.

of Stones which were intended for a new House near the Marsh, and which would very well suit our Purpose. Accordingly in the Evening when the Workmen were gone, I assembled a Number of my Playfellows, and working with them diligently like so many Emmets,[20] sometimes two or three to a Stone, we brought them all away and built our little Wharff. The next Morning the Workmen were surpriz'd at Missing the Stones; which were found in our Wharff; Enquiry was made after the Removers; we were discovered and complain'd of; several of us were corrected by our Fathers; and tho' I pleaded the Usefulness of the Work, mine convinc'd me that nothing was useful which was not honest. . . .

I continu'd thus employ'd in my Father's Business for two Years, that is till I was 12 Years old; and my Brother John, who was bred to that Business having left my Father, married and set up for himself at Rhodeisland, there was all Appearance that I was destin'd to supply his Place and be a Tallow Chandler. But my Dislike to the Trade continuing, my Father was under Apprehensions that if he did not find one for me more agreable, I should break away and get to Sea, as his Son Josiah had done to his great Vexation. He therefore sometimes took me to walk with him, and see Joiners, Bricklayers, Turners, Braziers, &c. at their Work, that he might observe my Inclination, and endeavour to fix it on some Trade or other on Land. It has ever since been a Pleasure to me to see good Workmen handle their Tools; and it has been useful to me, having learnt so much by it, as to be able to do little Jobs my self in my House, when a Workman could not readily be got; and to construct little Machines for my Experiments while the Intention of making the Experiment was fresh and warm in my Mind. My Father at last fix'd upon the Cutler's Trade, and my Uncle Benjamin's Son Samuel who was bred to that Business in London being about that time establish'd in Boston, I was sent to be with him some time on liking. But his Expectations of a Fee with me displeasing my Father, I was taken home again.

From a Child I was fond of Reading, and all the little Money that came into my Hands was ever laid out in Books. Pleas'd with the Pilgrim's Progress,[21] my first Collection was of John Bunyan's Works, in separate little Volumes. I afterwards sold them to enable me to buy R. Burton's[22] Historical Collections; they were small Chapmen's Books and cheap, 40 or 50 in all. My Father's little Library consisted chiefly of Books in polemic Divinity, most of which I read, and have since often regretted, that at a time when I had such a Thirst for Knowledge, more proper Books had not fallen in my Way, since it was now resolv'd I should not be a Clergyman. Plutarch's Lives[23] there was, in which I read abundantly, and I still think that time spent to great Advantage. There was also a Book of Defoe's, called an Essay on Projects,[24] and another of Dr. Mather's, call'd Essays to do Good[25] which perhaps gave me a Turn of Thinking that had an Influence on some of the principal future Events of my Life.

---

[20] Ants.

[21] John Bunyan's best-known work, published in 1678.

[22] A pseudonym of Nathaniel Crouch, who "melted down the best . . . English histories into twelve penny books, which are filled with wonders, rarities, and curiosities" (*Dictionary of National Biography*).

[23] *Parallel Lives,* the Greek historian Plutarch's series of forty-six paired biographies.

[24] Published in 1697, *Essay Upon Projects* suggested several civic and fiscal improvements.

[25] Published in 1710, *Bonifacius, an Essay upon the Good* inspired a number of Franklin's civic and moral endeavors.

This Bookish Inclination at length determin'd my Father to make me a Printer, tho' he had already one Son, (James) of that Profession. In 1717 my Brother James return'd from England with a Press and Letters to set up his Business in Boston. I lik'd it much better than that of my Father, but still had a Hankering for the Sea. To prevent the apprehended Effect of such an Inclination, my Father was impatient to have me bound to my Brother. I stood out some time, but at last was persuaded and signed the Indentures, when I was yet but 12 Years old. I was to serve as an Apprentice till I was 21 Years of Age, only I was to be allow'd Journeyman's Wages during the last Year. In a little time I made great Proficiency in the Business, and became a useful Hand to my Brother. I now had Access to better Books. An Acquaintance with the Apprentices of Booksellers, enabled me sometimes to borrow a small one, which I was careful to return soon and clean. Often I sat up in my Room reading the greatest Part of the Night, when the Book was borrow'd in the Evening and to be return'd early in the Morning lest it should be miss'd or wanted. And after some time an ingenious Tradesman Mr. Matthew Adams who had a pretty Collection of Books, and who frequented our Printing House, took Notice of me, invited me to his Library, and very kindly lent me such Books as I chose to read. I now took a Fancy to Poetry, and made some little Pieces. My Brother, thinking it might turn to account encourag'd me, and put me on composing two occasional Ballads. One was called the *Light House Tragedy,* and contain'd an Account of the drowning of Capt. Worthilake with his Two Daughters; the other was a Sailor Song on the Taking of *Teach* or Blackbeard the Pirate.[26] They were wretched Stuff, in the Grubstreet Ballad Stile, and when they were printed he sent me about the Town to sell them. The first sold wonderfully, the Event being recent, having made a great Noise. This flatter'd my Vanity. But my Father discourag'd me, by ridiculing my Performances, and telling me Verse-makers were generally Beggars; so I escap'd being a Poet, most probably a very bad one. But as Prose Writing has been of great Use to me in the Course of my Life, and was a principal Means of my Advancement, I shall tell you how in such a Situation I acquir'd what little Ability I have in that Way.

There was another Bookish Lad in the Town, John Collins by Name, with whom I was intimately acquainted. We sometimes disputed, and very fond we were of Argument, and very desirous of confuting one another. Which disputacious Turn, by the way, is apt to become a very bad Habit, making People often extreamly disagreable in Company, by the Contradiction that is necessary to bring it into Practice, and thence, besides souring and spoiling the Conversation, is productive of Disgusts and perhaps Enmities where you may have occasion for Friendship. I had caught it by reading my Father's Books of Dispute about Religion. Persons of good Sense, I have since observ'd, seldom fall into it, except Lawyers, University Men, and Men of all Sorts that have been bred at Edinborough. A Question was once some how or other started between Collins and me, of the Propriety of educating the Female Sex in Learning, and their Abilities for Study. He was of Opinion that it was improper; and that they were naturally unequal to it. I took the contrary Side, perhaps a little for Dispute sake. He was naturally more eloquent, had a ready Plenty of Words, and sometimes as I thought bore me down more by his Fluency than by the Strength of his Reasons. As we parted without settling the

---

[26] These two were written in November 1718. The full texts of Franklin's ballads have not been found.

Point, and were not to see one another again for some time, I sat down to put my Arguments in Writing, which I copied fair and sent to him. He answer'd and I reply'd. Three or four Letters of a Side had pass'd, when my Father happen'd to find my Papers, and read them. Without entring into the Discussion, he took occasion to talk to me about the Manner of my Writing, observ'd that tho' I had the Advantage of my Antagonist in correct Spelling and pointing[27] (which I ow'd to the Printing House) I fell far short in elegance of Expression, in Method and in Perspicuity, of which he convinc'd me by several Instances. I saw the Justice of his Remarks, and thence grew more attentive to the *Manner* in Writing, and determin'd to endeavour at Improvement.

About this time I met with an odd Volume of the Spectator.[28] It was the third. I had never before seen any of them. I bought it, read it over and over, and was much delighted with it. I thought the Writing excellent, and wish'd if possible to imitate it. With that View, I took some of the Papers, and making short Hints of the Sentiment in each Sentence, laid them by a few Days, and then without looking at the Book, try'd to compleat the Papers again, by expressing each hinted Sentiment at length and as fully as it had been express'd before, in any suitable Words, that should come to hand.

Then I compar'd my Spectator with the Original, discover'd some of my Faults and corrected them. But I found I wanted a Stock of Words or a Readiness in recollecting and using them, which I thought I should have acquir'd before that time, if I had gone on making Verses, since the continual Occasion for Words of the same Import but of different Length, to suit the Measure, or of different Sound for the Rhyme, would have laid me under a constant Necessity of searching for Variety, and also have tended to fix that Variety in my Mind, and make me Master of it. Therefore I took some of the Tales and turn'd them into Verse: And after a time, when I had pretty well forgotten the Prose, turn'd them back again. I also sometimes jumbled my Collections of Hints into Confusion, and after some Weeks, endeavour'd to reduce them into the best Order, before I began to form the full Sentences, and compleat the Paper. This was to teach me Method in the Arrangement of Thoughts. By comparing my work afterwards with the original, I discover'd many faults and amended them; but I sometimes had the Pleasure of Fancying that in certain Particulars of small Import, I had been lucky enough to improve the Method or the Language and this encourag'd me to think I might possibly in time come to be a tolerable English Writer, of which I was extreamly ambitious.

My Time for these Exercises and for Reading, was at Night, after Work or before Work began in the Morning; or on Sundays, when I contriv'd to be in the Printing House alone, evading as much as I could the common Attendance on publick Worship, which my Father used to exact of me when I was under his Care: and which indeed I still thought a Duty; tho' I could not, as it seemed to me, afford the Time to practise it.

When about 16 Years of Age, I happen'd to meet with a Book, written by one Tryon, recommending a Vegetable Diet.[29] I determined to go into it. My Brother being yet unmarried, did not keep House, but boarded himself and his Apprentices in another Family. My refusing to eat Flesh occasioned an Inconveniency, and I was frequently chid for my singularity. I made my self acquainted with Tryon's Manner of preparing some of

---

[27] Punctuating.

[28] An enormously influential London literary daily (1711–1712) conducted by Joseph Addison and Richard Steele.

[29] Thomas Tryon's *The Way to Health, Long Life and Happiness, or a Discourse of Temperance* (1691).

his Dishes, such as Boiling Potatoes or Rice, making Hasty Pudding, and a few others, and then propos'd to my Brother, that if he would give me Weekly half the Money he paid for my Board I would board my self. He instantly agreed to it, and I presently found that I could save half what he paid me. This was an additional Fund for buying Books: but I had another Advantage in it. My Brother and the rest going from the Printing House to their Meals, I remain'd there alone, and dispatching presently my light Repast, (which often was no more than a Bisket or a Slice of Bread, a Handful of Raisins or a Tart from the Pastry Cook's, and a Glass of Water) had the rest of the Time till their Return, for Study, in which I made the greater Progress from that greater Clearness of Head and quicker Apprehension which usually attend Temperance in Eating and Drinking. And now it was that being on some Occasion made asham'd of my Ignorance in Figures, which I had twice failed in learning when at School, I took Cocker's Book of Arithmetick,[30] and went thro' the whole by my self with great Ease. I also read Seller's and Sturmy's Books of Navigation,[31] and became acquainted with the little Geometry they contain, but never proceeded far in that Science. And I read about this Time Locke on Human Understanding, and the Art of Thinking by Messrs. du Port Royal.[32]

While I was intent on improving my Language, I met with an English Grammar (I think it was Greenwood's)[33] at the End of which there were two little Sketches of the Arts of Rhetoric and Logic, the latter finishing with a Specimen of a Dispute in the Socratic Method. And soon after I procur'd Xenophon's Memorable Things of Socrates,[34] wherein there are many Instances of the same Method. I was charm'd with it, adopted it, dropt my abrupt Contradiction, and positive Argumentation, and put on the humble Enquirer and Doubter. And being then, from reading Shaftsbury and Collins,[35] become a real Doubter in many Points of our Religious Doctrine, I found this Method safest for my self and very embarassing to those against whom I used it, therefore I took a Delight in it, practis'd it continually and grew very artful and expert in drawing People even of superior Knowledge into Concessions the Consequences of which they did not foresee, entangling them in Difficulties out of which they could not extricate themselves, and so obtaining Victories that neither my self nor my Cause always deserved.

I continu'd this Method some few Years, but gradually left it, retaining only the Habit of expressing my self in Terms of modest Diffidence, never using when I advance any thing that may possibly be disputed, the Words, *Certainly, undoubtedly,* or any others that give the Air of Positiveness to an Opinion; but rather say, I conceive, or I apprehend a Thing to be so or so, It appears to me, or I should think it so or so for such and such Reasons, or I imagine it to be so, or it is so if I am not mistaken. This Habit I believe has been of great Advantage to me, when I have had occasion to inculcate my Opinions and persuade Men into Measures that I have been from time to time engag'd in promoting. And as the chief Ends of Conversation are to *inform,* or to be *informed,* to

---

[30] Edward Cocker (1631–1675) wrote several books on arithmetic.

[31] John Seller's *An Epitome of the Art of Navigation* (1681); Samuel Sturmy's *The Mariner's Magazine;* or *Sturmy's Mathematical and Practical Arts* (1669).

[32] John Locke's *Essay Concerning Human Understanding* (1690) and *Logic: Or the Art of Thinking* by Antoine Arnauld and Pierre Nicole (1662; English trans. 1687).

[33] James Greenwood's *An Essay Towards a Practical English Grammar* (1711).

[34] Translated by Edward Bysshe (1712).

[35] Anthony Ashley Cooper, third earl of Shaftesbury (1671–1713); Anthony Collins (1676–1729).

please or to *persuade,* I wish wellmeaning sensible Men would not lessen their Power of doing Good by a Positive assuming Manner that seldom fails to disgust, tends to create Opposition, and to defeat every one of those Purposes for which Speech was given us, to wit, giving or receiving Information, or Pleasure: For if you would *inform,* a positive dogmatical Manner in advancing your Sentiments, may provoke Contradiction and prevent a candid Attention. If you wish Information and Improvement from the Knowledge of others and yet at the same time express your self as firmly fix'd in your present Opinions, modest sensible Men, who do not love Disputation, will probably leave you undisturb'd in the Possession of your Error; and by such a Manner you can seldom hope to recommend your self in *pleasing* your Hearers, or to persuade those whose Concurrence you desire. Pope says, judiciously,

> Men should be taught as if you taught them not,
> And things unknown propos'd as things forgot,

farther recommending it to us,

> To speak tho' sure, with seeming Diffidence.[36]

And he might have coupled with this Line that which he has coupled with another, I think less properly,

> For Want of Modesty is Want of Sense.

If you ask why, *less properly,* I must repeat the Lines;

> Immodest Words admit of *no* Defence;
> *For* Want of Modesty is Want of Sense.[37]

Now is not *Want of Sense* (where a Man is so unfortunate as to want it) some Apology for his *Want of Modesty?* and would not the Lines stand more justly thus?

> Immodest Words admit *but this* Defence,
> That Want of Modesty is Want of Sense.

This however I should submit to better Judgments.

My Brother had in 1720 or 21, begun to print a Newspaper. It was the second that appear'd in America, and was called *The New England Courant.* The only one before it, was *The Boston News Letter.*[38] I remember his being dissuaded by some of his Friends

---

[36] Alexander Pope (1688–1744), *An Essay on Criticism* (1711), ll. 574–575, 567.

[37] Franklin quotes, although inaccurately, from Wentworth Dillon, fourth earl of Roscommon (1633?–1685), *Essay on Translated Verse* (1684), ll. 113–114. These lines frequently were credited to Pope.

[38] *The New England Courant* was the fourth. *The Boston News Letter,* established April 24, 1704, was the first continuously published newspaper in the colonies. The earliest newspaper to appear, *Publick Occurrences* (September 25, 1690), lasted only one issue.

from the Undertaking, as not likely to succeed, one Newspaper being in their Judgment enough for America. At this time 1771 there are not less than five and twenty. He went on however with the Undertaking, and after having work'd in composing the Types and printing off the Sheets I was employ'd to carry the Papers thro' the Streets to the Customers. He had some ingenious Men among his Friends who amus'd themselves by writing little Pieces for this Paper, which gain'd it Credit, and made it more in Demand; and these Gentlemen often visited us. Hearing their Conversations, and their Accounts of the Approbation their Papers were receiv'd with, I was excited to try my Hand among them. But being still a Boy, and suspecting that my Brother would object to printing any Thing of mine in his Paper if he knew it to be mine, I contriv'd to disguise my Hand, and writing an anonymous Paper I put it in at Night under the Door of the Printing House. It was found in the Morning and communicated to his Writing Friends when they call'd in as usual. They read it, commented on it in my Hearing, and I had the exquisite Pleasure, of finding it met with their Approbation, and that in their different Guesses at the Author none were named but Men of some Character among us for Learning and Ingenuity.

I suppose now that I was rather lucky in my Judges: And that perhaps they were not really so very good ones as I then esteem'd them. Encourag'd however by this, I wrote and convey'd in the same Way to the Press several more Papers,[39] which were equally approv'd, and I kept my Secret till my small Fund of Sense for such Performances was pretty well exhausted, and then I discovered it; when I began to be considered a little more by my Brother's Acquaintance, and in a manner that did not quite please him, as he thought, probably with reason, that it tended to make me too vain. And perhaps this might be one Occasion of the Differences that we frequently had about this Time. Tho' a Brother, he considered himself as my Master, and me as his Apprentice; and accordingly expected the same Services from me as he would from another; while I thought he demean'd me too much in some he requir'd of me, who from a Brother expected more Indulgence. Our Disputes were often brought before our Father, and I fancy I was either generally in the right, or else a better Pleader, because the Judgment was generally in my favour: But my Brother was passionate and had often beaten me, which I took extreamly amiss; and thinking my Apprenticeship very tedious, I was continually wishing for some Opportunity of shortening it. . . .[40]

At length a fresh Difference arising between my Brother and me, I took upon me to assert my Freedom . . . in me to take this Advantage, and this I therefore reckon one of the first Errata[41] of my Life: But the Unfairness of it weigh'd little with me, when under the Impressions of Resentment, for the Blows his Passion too often urg'd him to bestow upon me. Tho' he was otherwise not an ill-natur'd Man: Perhaps I was too saucy and provoking.

When he found I would leave him, he took care to prevent my getting Employment in any other Printing-House of the Town, by going round and speaking to every Master, who accordingly refus'd to give me Work. . . . My Father now siding with my

---

[39] Franklin's fourteen letters, published under the pseudonym "Silence Dogood" in *The New England Courant* between April 12 and October 8, 1722.

[40] Franklin's note: "I fancy his harsh and tyrannical Treatment of me, might be a means of impressing me with that Aversion to arbitrary Power that has stuck to me thro' my whole Life."

[41] Plural of Latin *erratum*: "errors."

Brother, I was sensible that if I attempted to go openly, Means would be used to prevent me. My Friend Collins therefore undertook to manage a little for me. He agreed with the Captain of a New York Sloop for my Passage, under the Notion of my being a young Acquaintance of his that had got a naughty Girl with Child, whose Friends would compel me to marry her, and therefore I could not appear or come away publickly. So I sold some of my Books to raise a little Money, Was taken on board privately, and as we had a fair Wind in three Days I found my self in New York near 300 Miles from home, a Boy of but 17, without the least Recommendation to or Knowledge of any Person in the Place, and with very little Money in my Pocket.

My Inclinations for the Sea, were by this time worne out, or I might now have gratify'd them. But having a Trade, and supposing my self a pretty good Workman, I offer'd my Service to the Printer of the Place, old Mr. Wm. Bradford,[42] (who had been the first Printer in Pensilvania, but remov'd from thence upon the Quarrel of Geo. Keith).[43] He could give me no Employment, having little to do, and Help enough already: But, says he, my Son[44] at Philadelphia has lately lost his principal Hand, Aquila Rose, by Death. If you go thither I believe he may employ you. Philadelphia was 100 Miles farther. I set out, however, in a Boat for Amboy, leaving my Chest and Things to follow me round by Sea. In crossing the Bay we met with a Squall that tore our rotten Sails to pieces, prevented our getting into the Kill,[45] and drove us upon Long Island. In our Way a drunken Dutchman, who was a Passenger too, fell over board; when he was sinking I reach'd thro' the Water to his shock Pate and drew him up so that we got him in again. His Ducking sober'd him a little, and he went to sleep, taking first out of his Pocket a Book which he desir'd I would dry for him. It prov'd to be my old favourite Author Bunyan's Pilgrim's Progress in Dutch, finely printed on good Paper with copper Cuts, a Dress better than I had ever seen it wear in its own Language. I have since found that it has been translated into most of the Languages of Europe, and suppose it has been more generally read than any other Book except perhaps the Bible. Honest John was the first that I know of who mix'd Narration and Dialogue, a Method of Writing very engaging to the Reader, who in the most interesting Parts finds himself as it were brought into the Company, and present at the Discourse. Defoe in his Cruso, his Moll Flanders, Religious Courtship, Family Instructor, and other Pieces, has imitated it with Success. And Richardson has done the same in his Pamela, &c.[46]

When we drew near the Island we found it was at a Place where there could be no Landing, there being a great Surff on the stony Beach. So we dropt Anchor and swung round towards the Shore. Some People came down to the Water Edge and hallow'd to us, as we did to them. But the Wind was so high and the Surff so loud, that we could not hear so as to understand each other. There were Canoes on the Shore, and we made Signs and hallow'd that they should fetch us, but they either did not understand us, or thought it impracticable. So they went away, and Night coming on, we had no Remedy

---

[42] William Bradford (1663–1752), one of the chief printers in the colonies at the time.

[43] George Keith (1638–1716), a controversial Quaker leader.

[44] Andrew Bradford (1686–1742), who in 1719 published *The American Mercury,* the first newspaper printed in Pennsylvania.

[45] Narrow channel separating Staten Island, New York, from New Jersey.

[46] Samuel Richardson's *Pamela, or Virtue Rewarded* (1740), became the first novel published in the colonies when Franklin reprinted it in 1744.

but to wait till the Wind should abate, and in the mean time the Boatman and I concluded to sleep if we could, and so crouded into the Scuttle with the Dutchman who was still wet, and the Spray beating over the Head of our Boat, leak'd thro' to us, so that we were soon almost as wet as he. In this Manner we lay all Night with very little Rest. But the Wind abating the next Day, we made a Shift to reach Amboy before Night, having been 30 Hours on the Water without Victuals, or any Drink but a Bottle of filthy Rum: The Water we sail'd on being salt.

In the Evening I found my self very feverish, and went in to Bed. But having read somewhere that cold Water drank plentifully was good for a Fever, I follow'd the Prescription, sweat plentifully most of the Night, my Fever left me, and in the Morning crossing the Ferry, I proceeded on my Journey, on foot, having 50 Miles to Burlington,[47] where I was told I should find Boats that would carry me the rest of the Way to Philadelphia.

It rain'd very hard all the Day, I was thoroughly soak'd and by Noon a good deal tir'd, so I stopt at a poor Inn, where I staid all Night, beginning now to wish I had never left home. I cut so miserable a Figure too, that I found by the Questions ask'd me I was suspected to be some runaway Servant, and in danger of being taken up on that Suspicion. However I proceeded the next Day, and walking in the Evening by the Side of the River a Boat came by, which I found was going towards Philadelphia, with several People in her. They took me in, and as there was no Wind, we row'd all the Way; and about Midnight not having yet seen the City, some of the Company were confident we must have pass'd it, and would row no farther, the others knew not where we were, so we put towards the Shore, got into a Creek, landed near an old Fence with the Rails of which we made a Fire, the Night being cold, in October, and there we remain'd till Daylight. Then one of the Company knew the Place to be Cooper's Creek a little above Philadelphia, which we saw as soon as we got out of the Creek, and arriv'd there about 8 or 9 a Clock, on the Sunday morning, and landed at the Market street Wharff.[48]

I have been the more particular in this Description of my Journey, and shall be so of my first Entry into that City, that you may in your Mind compare such unlikely Beginnings with the Figure I have since made there. I was in my Working Dress, my best Cloaths being to come round by Sea. I was dirty from my Journey; my Pockets were stuff'd out with Shirts and Stockings; I knew no Soul, nor where to look for Lodging. I was fatigu'd with Travelling, Rowing and Want of Rest. I was very hungry, and my whole Stock of Cash consisted of a Dutch Dollar and about a Shilling in Copper. The latter I gave the People of the Boat for my Passage, who at first refus'd it on Account of my Rowing; but I insisted on their taking it, a Man being sometimes more generous when he has but a little Money than when he has plenty, perhaps thro' Fear of being thought to have but little.

Then I walk'd up the Street, gazing about, till near the Market House I met a Boy with Bread. I had made many a Meal on Bread, and inquiring where he got it, I went immediately to the Baker's he directed me to in second Street; and ask'd for Bisket, intending such as we had in Boston, but they it seems were not made in Philadelphia, then I ask'd for a threepenny Loaf, and was told they had none such: so not considering or knowing the Difference of Money and the greater Cheapness nor the Names of his Bread, I bad him give me three penny worth of any sort. He gave me accordingly three

---

47 Town in western New Jersey.
48 The landing took place sometime in October 1723.

great Puffy Rolls. I was surpriz'd at the Quantity, but took it, and having no room in my Pockets, walk'd off, with a Roll under each Arm, and eating the other. Thus I went up Market Street as far as fourth Street, passing by the Door of Mr. Read, my future Wife's Father, when she standing at the Door saw me, and thought I made as I certainly did a most awkward ridiculous Appearance. Then I turn'd and went down Chestnut Street and part of Walnut Street, eating my Roll all the Way, and coming round found my self again at Market Street Wharff, near the Boat I came in, to which I went for a Draught of the River Water, and being fill'd with one of my Rolls, gave the other two to a Woman and her Child that came down the River in the Boat with us and were waiting to go farther. Thus refresh'd I walk'd again up the Street, which by this time had many clean dress'd People in it who were all walking the same Way; I join'd them, and thereby was led into the great Meeting House of the Quakers near the Market. I sat down among them, and after looking round a while and hearing nothing said, being very drowzy thro' Labour and want of Rest the preceding Night, I fell fast asleep, and continu'd so till the Meeting broke up, when one was kind enough to rouse me. This was therefore the first House I was in or slept in, in Philadelphia. . . .

Then I made my self as tidy as I could, and went to Andrew Bradford the Printer's. I found in the Shop the old Man his Father, whom I had seen at New York, and who travelling on horse back had got to Philadelphia before me. He introduc'd me to his Son, who receiv'd me civilly, gave me a Breakfast, but told me he did not at present want a Hand, being lately supply'd with one. But there was another Printer in town lately set up, one Keimer,[49] who perhaps might employ me; if not, I should be welcome to lodge at his House, and he would give me a little Work to do now and then till fuller Business should offer.

The old Gentleman said, he would go with me to the new Printer: and when we found him, Neighbour, says Bradford, I have brought to see you a young Man of your Business, perhaps you may want such a One. He ask'd me a few Questions, put a Composing Stick in my Hand to see how I work'd, and then said he would employ me soon, tho' he had just then nothing for me to do. And taking old Bradford whom he had never seen before, to be one of the Towns People that had a Good Will for him, enter'd into a Conversation on his present Undertaking and Prospects; while Bradford not discovering[50] that he was the other Printer's Father, on Keimer's saying he expected soon to get the greatest Part of the Business into his own Hands, drew him on by artful Questions and starting little Doubts, to explain all his Views, what interest he rely'd on, and in what manner he intended to proceed. I who stood by and heard all, saw immediately that one of them was a crafty old Sophister, and the other a mere Novice. Bradford left me with Keimer, who was greatly surpriz'd when I told him who the old Man was.

Keimer's Printing House I found, consisted of an old shatter'd Press, and one small worn-out Fount of English,[51] which he was then using himself, composing in it an Elegy on Aquila Rose before-mentioned, an ingenious young Man of excellent Character much respected in the Town, Clerk of the Assembly, and a pretty Poet. Keimer made

---

[49] Samuel Keimer (ca. 1688–1742) had deserted his wife in London and come to Philadelphia the year before in order to establish himself as a printer. At the time Franklin met him, Keimer was in his midthirties. After failing at the printer's trade, he left Philadelphia in 1730.

[50] Disclosing.

[51] A "fount," or font, of type contains the complete alphabet of single letters cast in the same size and design. "English" was an oversized, and hence cumbersome, typeface.

Verses, too, but very indifferently. He could not be said to write them, for his Manner was to compose them in the Types directly out of his Head; so there being no Copy, but one Pair of Cases, and the Elegy likely to require all the Letter, no one could help him. I endeavour'd to put his Press (which he had not yet us'd, and of which he understood nothing) into Order fit to be work'd with; and promising to come and print off his Elegy as soon as he should have got it ready, I return'd to Bradford's who gave me a little job to do for the present, and there I lodged and dieted. A few Days after Keimer sent for me to print off the Elegy.[52] And now he had got another Pair of Cases,[53] and a Pamphlet to reprint, on which he set me to work.

These two Printers I found poorly qualified for their Business. Bradford had not been bred to it, and was very illiterate; and Keimer tho' something of a Scholar, was a mere Compositor, knowing nothing of Presswork. He had been one of the French Prophets[54] and could act their enthusiastic Agitations. At this time he did not profess any particular Religion, but something of all on occasion; was very ignorant of the World, and had, as I afterwards found, a good deal of the Knave in his Composition. He did not like my Lodging at Bradford's while I work'd with him. He had a House indeed, but without Furniture, so he could not lodge me: But he got me a Lodging at Mr. Read's before-mentioned, who was the Owner of his House. And my Chest and Clothes being come by this time, I made rather a more respectable Appearance in the Eyes of Miss Read, than I had done when she first happen'd to see me eating my Roll in the Street.

I began now to have some Acquaintance among the young People of the Town, that were Lovers of Reading with whom I spent my Evenings very pleasantly and gaining Money by my Industry and Frugality, I lived very agreably, forgetting Boston as much as I could, and not desiring that any there should know where I resided, except my Friend Collins who was in my Secret, and kept it when I wrote to him. At length an Incident happened that sent me back again much sooner than I had intended.

I had a Brother-in-law, Robert Holmes,[55] Master of a Sloop, that traded between Boston and Delaware. He being at New Castle 40 Miles below Philadelphia, heard there of me, and wrote me a Letter, mentioning the Concern of my Friends in Boston at my abrupt Departure, assuring me of their Goodwill to me, and that every thing would be accommodated to my Mind if I would return, to which he exhorted me very earnestly. I wrote an Answer to his Letter, thank'd him for his Advice, but stated my Reasons for quitting Boston fully, and in such a Light as to convince him I was not so wrong as he had apprehended.

Sir William Keith Governor of the Province,[56] was then at New Castle, and Capt. Holmes happening to be in Company with him when my Letter came to hand, spoke to him of me, and show'd him the Letter. The Governor read it, and seem'd surpriz'd when he was told my Age. He said I appear'd a young Man of promising Parts, and therefore should be encouraged: The Printers at Philadelphia were wretched ones, and if I would set up there, he made no doubt I should succeed; for his Part, he would pro-

---

[52] A single-leaf broadside, sold by Keimer for twopence.

[53] Trays of type.

[54] Sect of French Protestant refugees in England in 1706. Subject to trances and revelations, its members proclaimed the imminent coming of a messianic kingdom.

[55] Holmes, married to Franklin's sister Mary, was captain of a ship.

[56] Sir William Keith (1680–1749) was governor of Pennsylvania from 1717 to 1726.

cure me the publick Business, and do me every other Service in his Power. This my Brother-in-Law afterwards told me in Boston. But I knew as yet nothing of it; when one Day Keimer and I being at Work together near the Window, we saw the Governor and another Gentleman (which prov'd to be Col. French, of New Castle) finely dress'd, come directly across the Street to our House, and heard them at the Door. Keimer ran down immediately, thinking it a Visit to him. But the Governor enquir'd for me, came up, and with a Condescension and Politeness I had been quite unus'd to, made me many Compliments, desired to be acquainted with me, blam'd me kindly for not having made my self known to him when I first came to the Place, and would have me away with him to the Tavern where he was going with Col. French to taste as he said some excellent Madeira. I was not a little surpriz'd, and Keimer star'd like a Pig poison'd. I went however with the Governor and Col. French, to a Tavern the Corner of Third Street, and over the Madeira he propos'd my Setting up my Business, laid before me the Probabilities of Success, and both he and Col. French assur'd me I should have their Interest and Influence in procuring the Publick Business of both Governments. On my doubting whether my Father would assist me in it, Sir William said he would give me a Letter to him, in which he would state the Advantages, and he did not doubt of prevailing with him. So it was concluded I should return to Boston in the first Vessel with the Governor's Letter recommending me to my Father. In the mean time the Intention was to be kept secret, and I went on working with Keimer as usual, the Governor sending for me now and then to dine with him, a very great Honour I thought it, and conversing with me in the most affable, familiar, and friendly manner imaginable.

About the End of April 1724. a little Vessel offer'd for Boston. I took Leave of Keimer as going to see my Friends. The Governor gave me an ample Letter, saying many flattering things of me to my Father, and strongly recommending the Project of my setting up at Philadelphia, as a Thing that must make my Fortune. We struck on a Shoal in going down the Bay and sprung a Leak, we had a blustring time at Sea, and were oblig'd to pump almost continually, at which I took my Turn. We arriv'd safe however at Boston in about a Fortnight. I had been absent Seven Months and my Friends had heard nothing of me; for my Br. Holmes was not yet return'd; and had not written about me. My unexpected Appearance surpriz'd the Family; all were however very glad to see me and made me Welcome, except my Brother. I went to see him at his Printing-House: I was better dress'd than ever while in his Service, having a genteel new Suit from Head to foot, a Watch, and my Pockets lin'd with near Five Pounds Sterling in Silver. He receiv'd me not very frankly, look'd me all over, and turn'd to his Work again. The Journey-Men were inquisitive where I had been, what sort of a Country it was, and how I lik'd it? I prais'd it much, and the happy Life I led in it; expressing strongly my Intention of returning to it; and one of them asking what kind of Money we had there, I produc'd a handful of Silver and spread it before them, which was a kind of Raree-Show[57] they had not been us'd to, Paper being the Money of Boston. Then I took an Opportunity of letting them see my Watch: and lastly, (my Brother still grum and sullen) I gave them a Piece of Eight[58] to drink and took my Leave. This Visit of mine offended him extreamly. For when my Mother some time after spoke to him of a Reconciliation, and of her Wishes to see us on good Terms together, and that we might live for the future as

---

[57] Small street show.
[58] Spanish dollar. The term "piece of eight" has a parallel in the contemporary expression "two bits," meaning a quarter of a dollar.

Brothers, he said, I had insulted him in such a Manner before his People that he could never forget or forgive it. In this however he was mistaken.

My Father receiv'd the Governor's Letter with some apparent Surprize; but said little of it to me for some Days; when Capt. Holmes returning, he show'd it to him, ask'd if he knew Keith, and what kind of a Man he was: Adding his Opinion that he must be of small Discretion, to think of setting a Boy up in Business who wanted yet 3 Years of being at Man's Estate. Holmes said what he could in favour of the Project; but my Father was clear in the Impropriety of it; and at last gave a flat Denial to it. Then he wrote a civil Letter to Sir William thanking him for the Patronage he had so kindly offered me, but declining to assist me as yet in Setting up, I being in his Opinion too young to be trusted with the Management of a Business so important, and for which the Preparation must be so expensive.

My Friend and Companion Collins, who was a Clerk at the Post-Office, pleas'd with the Account I gave him of my new Country, determin'd to go thither also: And while I waited for my Fathers Determination,[59] he set out before me by Land to Rhodeisland, leaving his Books which were a pretty Collection of Mathematicks and Natural Philosophy, to come with mine and me to New York where he propos'd to wait for me. My Father, tho' he did not approve Sir William's Proposition was yet pleas'd that I had been able to obtain so advantageous a Character from a Person of such Note where I had resided, and that I had been so industrious and careful as to equip my self so handsomely in so short a time: therefore seeing no Prospect of an Accommodation between my Brother and me, he gave his Consent to my Returning again to Philadelphia, advis'd me to behave respectfully to the People there, endeavour to obtain the general Esteem, and avoid lampooning and libelling to which he thought I had too much Inclination; telling me, that by steady Industry and a prudent Parsimony, I might save enough by the time I was One and Twenty to set me up, and that if I came near the Matter he would help me out with the rest. This was all I could obtain, except some small Gifts as Tokens of his and my Mother's Love, when I embark'd again for New-York, now with their Approbation and their Blessing.

The Sloop putting in at Newport, Rhodeisland, I visited my Brother John, who had been married and settled there some Years. He received me very affectionately, for he always lov'd me. A Friend of his, one Vernon, having some Money due to him in Pensilvania, about 35 Pounds Currency, desired I would receive it for him, and keep it till I had his Directions what to remit it in. Accordingly he gave me an Order. This afterwards occasion'd me a good deal of Uneasiness. At Newport we took in a Number of Passengers for New York: Among which were two young Women, Companions, and a grave, sensible Matron-like Quaker-Woman with her Attendants. I had shown an obliging readiness to do her some little Services which impress'd her I suppose with a degree of Good-will towards me. Therefore when she saw a daily growing Familiarity between me and the two Young Women, which they appear'd to encourage, she took me aside and said, Young Man, I am concern'd for thee, as thou has no Friend with thee, and seems not to know much of the World, or of the Snares Youth is expos'd to; depend upon it those are very bad Women, I can see it in all their Actions, and if thee art not upon thy Guard, they will draw thee into some Danger: they are Strangers to thee, and I advise thee in a friendly Concern for thy Welfare, to have no Acquaintance with them.

[59] Decision.

As I seem'd at first not to think so ill of them as she did, she mention'd some Things she had observ'd and heard that had escap'd my Notice; but now convinc'd me she was right. I thank'd her for her kind Advice, and promis'd to follow it. When we arriv'd at New York, they told me where they liv'd, and invited me to come and see them: but I avoided it. And it was well I did: For the next Day, the Captain miss'd a Silver Spoon and some other Things that had been taken out of his Cabbin, and knowing that these were a Couple of Strumpets, he got a Warrant to search their Lodgings, found the stolen Goods, and had the Thieves punish'd. So tho' we had escap'd a sunken Rock which we scrap'd upon in the Passage, I thought this Escape of rather more Importance to me.

At New York I found my Friend Collins, who had arriv'd there some Time before me. We had been intimate from Children, and had read the same Books together. But he had the Advantage of more time for reading, and Studying and a wonderful Genius for Mathematical Learning in which he far outstript me. While I liv'd in Boston most of my Hours of Leisure for Conversation were spent with him, and he continu'd a sober as well as an industrious Lad; was much respected for his Learning by several of the Clergy and other Gentlemen, and seem'd to promise making a good Figure in Life: but during my Absence he had acquir'd a Habit of Sotting with Brandy; and I found by his own Account and what I heard from others, that he had been drunk every day since his Arrival at New York, and behav'd very oddly. He had gam'd too and lost his Money, so that I was oblig'd to discharge[60] his Lodgings, and defray his Expences to and at Philadelphia: Which prov'd extreamly inconvenient to me. The then Governor of N York, Burnet,[61] Son of Bishop Burnet hearing from the Captain that a young Man, one of his Passengers, had a great many Books, desired he would bring me to see him. I waited upon him accordingly, and should have taken Collins with me but that he was not sober. The Governor treated me with great Civility, show'd me his Library, which was a very large one, and we had a good deal of Conversation about Books and Authors. This was the second Governor who had done me the Honour to take Notice of me, which to a poor Boy like me was very pleasing.

We proceeded to Philadelphia. I received on the Way Vernon's Money, without which we could hardly have finish'd our Journey. Collins wish'd to be employ'd in some Counting House; but whether they discover'd his Dramming by his Breath, or by his Behaviour, tho' he had some Recommendations, he met with no Success in any Application, and continu'd Lodging and Boarding at the same House with me and at my Expence. Knowing I had that Money of Vernon's he was continually borrowing of me, still promising Repayment as soon as he should be in Business. At length he had got so much of it, that I was distress'd to think what I should do, in case of being call'd on to remit it. His Drinking continu'd about which we sometimes quarrel'd, for when a little intoxicated he was very fractious. Once in a Boat on the Delaware with some other young Men, he refused to row in his Turn: I will be row'd home, says he. We will not row you, says I. You must or stay all Night on the Water, says he, just as you please. The others said, Let us row; what signifies it? But my Mind being soured with his other Conduct, I continu'd to refuse. So he swore he would make me row, or throw me overboard; and coming along stepping on the Thwarts towards me, when he came up and struck at me I clapt my Hand under his Crutch,[62] and rising pitch'd him head-fore-

---

60 Pay for.

61 William Burnet (1688–1729) served as
   governor from 1720 to 1728.

62 Crotch.

most into the River. I knew he was a good Swimmer, and so was under little Concern about him; but before he could get round to lay hold of the Boat, we had with a few Strokes pull'd her out of his Reach. And ever when he drew near the Boat, we ask'd if he would row, striking a few Strokes to slide her away from him. He was ready to die with Vexation, and obstinately would not promise to row; however seeing him at last beginning to tire, we lifted him in; and brought him home dripping wet in the Evening. We hardly exchang'd a civil Word afterwards; and a West India Captain who had a Commission to procure a Tutor for the Sons of a Gentleman at Barbadoes, happening to meet with him, agreed to carry him thither. He left me then, promising to remit me the first Money he should receive in order to discharge the Debt. But I never heard of him after.

The Breaking into this Money of Vernon's was one of the first great Errata of my Life. And this Affair show'd that my Father was not much out in his Judgment when he suppos'd me too young to manage Business of Importance. But Sir William, on reading his Letter, said he was too prudent. There was great Difference in Persons, and Discretion did not always accompany Years, nor was Youth always without it. And since he will not set you up, says he, I will do it my self. Give me an Inventory of the Things necessary to be had from England, and I will send for them. You shall repay me when you are able; I am resolv'd to have a good Printer here, and I am sure you must succeed. This was spoken with such an Appearance of Cordiality, that I had not the least doubt of his meaning what he said. I had hitherto kept the Proposition of my Setting up a Secret in Philadelphia, and I still kept it. Had it been known that I depended on the Governor, probably some Friend that knew him better would have advis'd me not to rely on him, as I afterwards heard it as his known Character to be liberal of Promises which he never meant to keep. Yet unsolicited as he was by me, how could I think his generous Offers insincere? I believ'd him one of the best Men in the World.

I presented him an Inventory of a little Printing House, amounting by my Computation to about £100 Sterling. He lik'd it, but ask'd me if my being on the Spot in England to chuse the Types and see that every thing was good of the kind, might not be of some Advantage. Then, says he, when there, you may make Acquaintances and establish Correspondencies in the Bookselling and Stationary Way. I agreed that this might be advantageous. Then says he, get yourself ready to go with Annis;[63] which was the annual Ship, and the only one at that Time usually passing between London and Philadelphia. But it would be some Months before Annis sail'd, so I continu'd working with Keimer, fretting about the Money Collins had got from me, and in daily Apprehensions of being call'd upon by Vernon, which however did not happen for some Years after.

I believe I have omitted mentioning that in my first Voyage from Boston, being becalm'd off Block Island,[64] our People set about catching Cod and hawl'd up a great many. Hitherto I had stuck to my Resolution of not eating animal Food; and on this Occasion, I consider'd with my Master Tryon, the taking every Fish as a kind of unprovok'd Murder, since none of them had or ever could do us any Injury that might justify the Slaughter. All this seem'd very reasonable. But I had formerly been a great Lover of Fish, and when this came hot out of the Frying Pan, it smelt admirably well. I balanc'd some time between Principle and Inclination: till I recollected, that when the Fish were

---

[63] Captain Thomas Annis, master of the "annual Ship" that sailed between Philadelphia and England.

[64] Ten miles off the coast of Rhode Island.

opened, I saw smaller Fish taken out of their Stomachs: then thought I, if you eat one another, I don't see why we mayn't eat you. So I din'd upon Cod very heartily and continu'd to eat with other People, returning only now and then occasionally to a vegetable Diet. So convenient a thing it is to be a *reasonable Creature,* since it enables one to find or make a Reason for every thing one has a mind to do.

Keimer and I liv'd on a pretty good familiar Footing and agreed tolerably well: for he suspected nothing of my Setting up. He retain'd a great deal of his old Enthusiasms, and lov'd Argumentation. We therefore had many Disputations. I us'd to work him so with my Socratic Method, and had trapann'd[65] him so often by Questions apparently so distant from any Point we had in hand, and yet by degrees led to the Point, and brought him into Difficulties and Contradictions that at last he grew ridiculously cautious, and would hardly answer me the most common Question, without asking first, *What do you intend to infer from that?* However it gave him so high an Opinion of my Abilities in the Confuting Way, that he seriously propos'd my being his Colleague in a Project he had of setting up a new Sect. He was to preach the Doctrines, and I was to confound all Opponents. When he came to explain with me upon the Doctrines, I found several Conundrums which I objected to unless I might have my Way a little too, and introduce some of mine. Keimer wore his Beard at full Length, because somewhere in the Mosaic Law it is said, *thou shalt not mar the Corners of thy Beard.*[66] He likewise kept the seventh day Sabbath; and these two Points were Essentials with him. I dislik'd both, but agreed to admit them upon Condition of his adopting the Doctrine of using no animal Food. I doubt, says he, my Constitution will not bear that. I assur'd him it would, and that he would be the better for it. He was usually a great Glutton, and I promis'd my self some Diversion in half-starving him. He agreed to try the Practice if I would keep him Company. I did so and we held it for three Months. We had our Victuals dress'd and brought to us regularly by a Woman in the Neighbourhood, who had from me a List of 40 Dishes to be prepar'd for us at different times, in all which there was neither Fish Flesh nor Fowl, and the whim suited me the better at this time from the Cheapness of it, not costing us above 18*d.*[67] Sterling each, per Week. I have since kept several Lents most strictly, Leaving the common Diet for that, and that for the common, abruptly, without the least Inconvenience: So that I think there is little in the Advice of making those Changes by easy Gradations. I went on pleasantly, but poor Keimer suffer'd grievously, tir'd of the Project, long'd for the Flesh Pots of Egypt, and order'd a roast Pig. He invited me and two Women Friends to dine with him, but it being brought too soon upon table, he could not resist the Temptation, and ate it all up before we came.

I had made some Courtship during this time to Miss Read. I had a great Respect and Affection for her, and had some Reason to believe she had the same for me: but as I was about to take a long Voyage, and we were both very young, only a little above 18. it was thought most prudent by her Mother to prevent our going too far at present, as a Marriage if it was to take place would be more convenient after my Return, when I should be as I expected set up in my Business. Perhaps too she thought my Expectations not so wellfounded as I imagined them to be.

---

[65] Trapped.
[66] Leviticus 19:27: "Ye shall not round the corners of your heads, neither shalt thou mar the corners of thy beard."

[67] Small *d* is an abbreviation for the British penny (plural: pence).

My chief Acquaintances at this time were, Charles Osborne, Joseph Watson, and James Ralph;[68] All Lovers of Reading. The two first were Clerks to an eminent Scrivener or Conveyancer[69] in the Town, Charles Brogden;[70] the other was Clerk to a Merchant. Watson was a pious sensible young Man, of great Integrity. The others rather more lax in their Principles of Religion, particularly Ralph, who as well as Collins had been unsettled by me, for which they both made me suffer. Osborne was sensible, candid, frank, sincere, and affectionate to his Friends; but in litterary Matters too fond of Criticising. Ralph, was ingenious, genteel in his Manners, and extreamly eloquent; I think I never knew a prettier Talker. Both of them great Admirers of Poetry, and began to try their Hands in little Pieces. Many pleasant Walks we four had together on Sundays into the Woods near Skuylkill,[71] where we read to one another and conferr'd on what we read.

Ralph was inclin'd to pursue the Study of Poetry, not doubting but he might become eminent in it and make his Fortune by it, alledging that the best Poets must when they first began to write, make as many Faults as he did. Osborne dissuaded him, assur'd him he had no Genius for Poetry, and advis'd him to think of nothing beyond the Business he was bred to; that in the mercantile way tho' he had no Stock, he might by his Diligence and Punctuality recommend himself to Employment as a Factor,[72] and in time acquire wherewith to trade on his own Account. I approv'd the amusing one's self with Poetry now and then, so far as to improve one's Language, but no farther. On this it was propos'd that we should each of us at our next Meeting produce a Piece of our own Composing, in order to improve by our mutual Observations, Criticisms and Corrections. As Language and Expression was what we had in View, we excluded all Considerations of Invention, by agreeing that the Task should be a Version of the 18th Psalm, which describes the Descent of a Deity. When the Time of our Meeting drew nigh, Ralph call'd on me first, and let me know his Piece was ready. I told him I had been busy, and having little Inclination had done nothing. He then show'd me his Piece for my Opinion; and I much approv'd it, as it appear'd to me to have great Merit. Now, says he, Osborne never will allow the least Merit in any thing of mine, but makes 1000 Criticisms out of mere Envy. He is not so jealous of you. I wish therefore you would take this Piece, and produce it as yours. I will pretend not to have had time, and so produce nothing: We shall then see what he will say to it. It was agreed, and I immediately transcrib'd it that it might appear in my own hand. We met. Watson's Performance was read: there were some Beauties in it: but many Defects. Osborne's was read: it was much better. Ralph did it Justice, remark'd some Faults, but applauded the Beauties. He himself had nothing to produce. I was backward, seem'd desirous of being excus'd, had not had sufficient Time to correct; &c. but no Excuse could be admitted, produce I must. It was read and repeated; Watson and Osborne gave up the Contest; and join'd in applauding it immoderately. Ralph only made some Criticisms and propos'd some Amendments, but I defended my Text. Osborne was against Ralph, and told him he was no better a Critic than Poet; so he dropt the Argument. As they two went home together, Osborne express'd himself still more strongly in favour of what he thought my Production, having restrain'd himself before as he said, lest I should think it Flattery.

[68] James Ralph (d. 1762). A failure as a poet, Ralph achieved success as a political writer in England. Upon Franklin's return to London in 1757, Ralph helped him prepare propaganda for the colonies.

[69] One who drafts property deeds and leases.
[70] Charles Brockden.
[71] The Schuylkill River in Philadelphia.
[72] Business representative.

But who would have imagin'd, says he, that Franklin had been capable of such a Performance; such Painting, such Force! such Fire! he has even improv'd the Original! In his common Conversation, he seems to have no Choice of Words; he hesitates and blunders; and yet, good God, how he writes! When we next met, Ralph discover'd the Trick, we had plaid him, and Osborne was a little laught at. This Transaction fix'd Ralph in his Resolution of becoming a Poet. I did all I could to dissuade him from it, but He continued scribbling Verses, till Pope cur'd him.[73] He became however a pretty good Prose Writer. More of him hereafter.

But as I may not have occasion again to mention the other two, I shall just remark here, that Watson died in my Arms a few Years after, much lamented, being the best of our Set. Osborne went to the West Indies, where he became an eminent Lawyer and made Money, but died young. He and I had made a serious Agreement, that the one who happen'd first to die, should if possible make a friendly Visit to the other, and acquaint him how he found things in that Separate State. But he never fulfill'd his Promise.

The Governor, seeming to like my Company, had me frequently to his House; and his setting me up was always mention'd as a fix'd thing. I was to take with me Letters recommendatory to a Number of his Friends, besides the Letter of Credit to furnish me with the necessary Money for purchasing the Press and Types, Paper, &c. For these Letters I was appointed to call at different times, when they were to be ready, but a future time was still named. Thus we went on till the Ship whose Departure too had been several times postponed was on the Point of sailing. Then when I call'd to take my Leave and Receive the Letters, his Secretary, Dr. Bard, came out to me and said the Governor was extreamly busy, in writing, but would be down at Newcastle[74] before the Ship, and there the Letters would be delivered to me.

Ralph, tho' married and having one Child, had determined to accompany me in this Voyage. It was thought he intended to establish a Correspondence, and obtain Goods to sell on Commission. But I found afterwards, that thro' some Discontent with his Wifes Relations, he purposed to leave her on their Hands, and never return again. Having taken leave of my Friends, and interchang'd some Promises with Miss Read, I left Philadelphia in the Ship, which anchor'd at Newcastle. The Governor was there. But when I went to his Lodging, the Secretary came to me from him with the civillest Message in the World, that he could not then see me being engag'd in Business of the utmost Importance; but should send the Letters to me on board, wish'd me heartily a good Voyage and a speedy Return, &c. I return'd on board, a little puzzled, but still not doubting.

Mr. Andrew Hamilton,[75] a famous Lawyer of Philadelphia, had taken Passage in the same Ship for himself and Son: and with Mr. Denham[76] a Quaker Merchant, and Messrs. Onion and Russel Masters of an Iron Work in Maryland, had engag'd the Great Cabin; so that Ralph and I were forc'd to take up with a Birth in the Steerage:[77] And none on board knowing us, were considered as ordinary Persons. But Mr. Hamilton

---

[73] Ralph was attacked by Alexander Pope in the second edition of the *Dunciad* (III. 159–160): "Silence, ye Wolves! while Ralph to Cynthia howls, / And makes Night hideous—Answer him, ye Owls."

[74] In Delaware.

[75] Andrew Hamilton (ca. 1678–1741), father of James Hamilton (1710–1783), who served as governor of Pennsylvania four times between 1748 and 1773.

[76] Thomas Denham (d. 1728), Philadelphia merchant and later a benefactor to Franklin.

[77] Cheapest accommodations on a ship, located in the stern near the rudder.

and his Son (it was James, since Governor) return'd from New Castle to Philadelphia, the Father being recall'd by a great Fee to plead for a seized Ship. And just before we sail'd Col. French coming on board, and showing me great Respect, I was more taken Notice of, and with my Friend Ralph invited by the other Gentlemen to come into the Cabin, there being now Room. Accordingly we remov'd thither.

Understanding that Col. French had brought on board the Governor's Dispatches, I ask'd the Captain for those Letters that were to be under my Care. He said all were put into the Bag together; and he could not then come at them; but before we landed in England, I should have an Opportunity of picking them out. So I was satisfy'd for the present, and we proceeded on our Voyage. We had a sociable Company in the Cabin, and lived uncommonly well, having the Addition of all Mr. Hamilton's Stores, who had laid in plentifully. In this Passage Mr. Denham contracted a Friendship for me that continued during his Life. The voyage was otherwise not a pleasant one, as we had a great deal of bad Weather.

When we came into the Channel, the Captain kept his word with me, and gave me an Opportunity of examining the Bag for the Governor's Letters. I found none upon which my Name was put, as under my Care; I pick'd out 6 or 7 that by the Hand writing I thought might be the promis'd Letters, especially as one of them was directed to Basket the King's Printer, and another to some Stationer. We arriv'd in London the 24th of December, 1724. I waited upon the Stationer who came first in my way, delivering the Letter as from Gov. Keith. I don't know such a Person, says he: but opening the Letter, O, this is from Riddlesden,[78] I have lately found him to be a compleat Rascal, and I will have nothing to do with him, nor receive any Letters from him. So putting the Letter into my Hand, he turn'd on his Heel and left me to serve some Customer. I was surprized to find these were not the Governor's Letters. And after recollecting and comparing Circumstances, I began to doubt his Sincerity. I found my Friend Denham, and opened the whole Affair to him. He let me into Keith's Character, told me there was not the least Probability that he had written any Letters for me, that no one who knew him had the smallest Dependance on him, and he laught at the Notion of the Governor's giving me a Letter of Credit, having as he said no Credit to give. On my expressing some Concern about what I should do: he advis'd me to endeavour getting some Employment in the Way of my Business. Among the Printers here, says he, you will improve yourself; and when you return to America, you will set up to greater Advantage.

We both of us happen'd to know, as well as the Stationer, that Riddlesden the attorney, was a very Knave. He had half ruin'd Miss Read's Father by drawing him in to be bound for him.[79] By his Letter it appear'd, there was a secret Scheme on foot to the Prejudice of Hamilton, (Suppos'd to be then coming over with us,) and that Keith was concern'd in it with Riddlesden. Denham, who was a Friend of Hamilton's, thought he ought to be acquainted with it. So when he arriv'd in England, which was soon after, partly from Resentment and Ill-Will to Keith and Riddlesden, and partly from Good Will to him: I waited on him, and gave him the Letter. He thank'd me cordially, the Information being of Importance to him. And from that time he became my Friend, greatly to my Advantage afterwards on many Occasions.

---

[78] William Riddlesden, a well-known Maryland swindler and con artist.

[79] Read's "ruin" came about through a contract that held him legally responsible for Riddlesden's debts.

But what shall we think of a Governor's playing such pitiful Tricks, and imposing so grossly on a poor ignorant Boy! It was a Habit he had acquired. He wish'd to please every body; and having little to give, he gave Expectations. He was otherwise an ingenious sensible Man, a pretty good Writer, and a good Governor for the People, tho' not for his Constituents the Proprietaries, whose Instructions he sometimes disregarded. Several of our best Laws were of his Planning, and pass'd during his Administration.

Ralph and I were inseparable Companions. We took Lodgings together in Little Britain at 3*s*. 6*d*. per Week, as much as we could then afford. He found some Relations, but they were poor and unable to assist him. He now let me know his Intentions of remaining in London, and that he never meant to return to Philadelphia. He had brought no Money with him, the whole he could muster having been expended in paying his Passage. I had 15 Pistoles:[80] So he borrowed occasionally of me, to subsist while he was looking out for Business. He first endeavoured to get into the Playhouse, believing himself qualify'd for an Actor; but Wilkes,[81] to whom he apply'd, advis'd him candidly not to think of that Employment, as it was impossible he should succeed in it. Then he propos'd to Roberts, a Publisher in Paternoster Row,[82] to write for him a Weekly Paper like the Spectator, on certain Conditions, which Roberts did not approve. Then he endeavour'd to get Employment as a Hackney writer[83] to copy for the Stationers[84] and Lawyers about the Temple:[85] but could find no Vacancy.

I immediately got into Work at Palmer's then a famous Printing House in Bartholomew Close; and here I continu'd near a Year. I was pretty diligent; but spent with Ralph a good deal of my Earnings in going to Plays and other Places of Amusement. We had together consum'd all my Pistoles, and now just rubb'd on from hand to mouth. He seem'd quite to forget his Wife and Child, and I by degrees my Engagements with Miss Read, to whom I never wrote more than one Letter, and that was to let her know I was not likely soon to return. This was another of the great Errata of my Life, which I should wish to correct if I were to live it over again. In fact, by our Expences, I was constantly kept unable to pay my Passage.

At Palmer's I was employ'd in composing for the second Edition of Woollaston's Religion of Nature.[86] Some of his Reasonings not appearing to me well-founded, I wrote a little metaphysical Piece, in which I made Remarks on them. It was entitled, *A Dissertation on Liberty and Necessity, Pleasure and Pain*. I inscrib'd it to my Friend Ralph. I printed a small Number. It occasion'd my being more consider'd by Mr. Palmer, as a young Man of some Ingenuity, tho' he seriously expostulated with me upon the Principles of my Pamphlet which to him appear'd abominable. My printing this Pamphlet was another Erratum.[87]

[80] Pistole: Spanish gold coin worth just under one English pound.

[81] Robert Wilks (1665?–1732), prominent London actor.

[82] Street that served as one of the centers for the London printing business.

[83] Hired writer who worked out of a horse-drawn cab called a "hackney." (The term *hack writer* derives therefrom.)

[84] Printers and sellers of legal forms.

[85] Group of buildings that comprised the center for the London legal profession.

[86] Actually the third edition of *The Religion of Nature Delineated* (1722), a treatise on morality as derived from observations of nature by the Anglican clergyman and schoolmaster William Wollaston.

[87] This pamphlet (1725) subjected Franklin to charges of atheism by its denial of the existence of vice and virtue. Franklin soon afterward burned all but one of the copies. Only four copies are known to exist today.

While I lodg'd in Little Britain I made an Acquaintance with one Wilcox a Bookseller, whose Shop was at the next Door. He had an immense Collection of secondhand Books. Circulating Libraries were not then in Use; but we agreed that on certain reasonable Terms which I have now forgotten, I might take, read and return any of his Books. This I esteem'd a great Advantage, and I made as much use of it as I could.

My pamphlet by some means falling into the Hands of one Lyons, a Surgeon, Author of a Book intituled *The Infallibility of Human Judgment,* it occasioned an Acquaintance between us; he took great Notice of me, call'd on me often, to converse on those Subjects, carried me to the Horns a pale Ale-House in ——— Lane, Cheapside, and introduc'd me to Dr. Mandevile, Author of the Fable of the Bees[88] who had a Club there, of which he was the Soul, being a most facetious entertaining Companion. Lyons too introduc'd me, to Dr. Pemberton, at Batson's Coffee House,[89] who promis'd to give me an Opportunity some time or other of seeing Sir Isaac Newton, of which I was extreamly desirous; but this never happened.

I had brought over a few Curiosities among which the principal was a Purse made of the Asbestos, which purifies by Fire. Sir Hans Sloane heard of it, came to see me, and invited me to his House in Bloomsbury Square, where he show'd me all his Curiosities, and persuaded me to let him add that to the Number, for which he paid me handsomely.

In our House there lodg'd a young Woman; a Millener, who I think had a Shop in the Cloisters. She had been genteelly bred, was sensible and lively, and of most pleasing Conversation. Ralph read Plays to her in the Evenings, they grew intimate, she took another Lodging, and he follow'd her. They liv'd together some time, but he being still out of Business, and her Income not sufficient to maintain them with her Child, he took a Resolution of going from London, to try for a Country School, which he thought himself well qualify'd to undertake, as he wrote an excellent Hand, and was a Master of Arithmetic and Accounts. This however he deem'd a Business below him, and confident of future better Fortune when he should be unwilling to have it known that he once was so meanly employ'd, he chang'd his Name, and did me the Honour to assume mine. For I soon after had a Letter from him, acquainting me, that he was settled in a small Village in Berkshire, I think it was, where he taught reading and writing to 10 or a dozen Boys at 6 pence each per Week, recommending Mrs. T. to my Care, and desiring me to write to him directing for Mr. Franklin Schoolmaster at such a Place. He continu'd to write frequently, sending me large Specimens of an Epic Poem, which he was then composing, and desiring my Remarks and Corrections. These I gave him from time to time, but endeavour'd rather to discourage his Proceeding. One of Young's Satires was then just publish'd. I copy'd and sent him a great Part of it, which set in a strong Light the Folly of pursuing the Muses with any Hope of Advancement by them.[90] All was in vain. Sheets of the Poem continu'd to come by every Post. In the mean time Mrs. T. having on his Account lost her Friends and Business, was often in Distresses, and us'd to send for me, and borrow what I could spare to help her out of them. I grew fond of her Company, and be-

---

[88] Bernard Mandeville's *Fable of the Bees* (1714) argued that the greedy self-pursuits of the individual ultimately benefited society. Although the treatise was viciously attacked by moralists for its cynicism, it nevertheless was widely read and went through numerous reprints. Mandeville was an im-portant source for James Madison's arguments in *The Federalist,* Number 10. (See p. 344)

[89] A favorite meeting place of physicians.

[90] This reference is probably to *Love of Fame, the Universal Passion* (1725), by Edward Young (1683–1765).

ing at this time under no Religious Restraints, and presuming on my Importance to her, I attempted Familiarities, (another Erratum) which she repuls'd with a proper Resentment, and acquainted him with my Behaviour. This made a Breach between us, and when he return'd again to London, he let me know he thought I had cancel'd all the Obligations he had been under to me. So I found I was never to expect his Repaying me what I lent to him or advanc'd for him. This was however not then of much Consequence, as he was totally unable. And in the Loss of his Friendship I found my self reliev'd from a Burthen. I now began to think of getting a little Money beforehand; and expecting better Work, I left Palmer's to work at Watts's near Lincoln's Inn Fields, a still greater Printing House. Here I continu'd all the rest of my Stay in London.

At my first Admission into this Printing House, I took to working at Press, imagining I felt a Want of the Bodily Exercise I had been us'd to in America, where Presswork is mix'd with Composing. I drank only Water; the other Workmen, near 50 in Number, were great Guzzlers of Beer. On occasion I carried up and down Stairs a large Form of Types[91] in each hand, when others carried but one in both Hands. They wonder'd to see from this and several Instances that the Water-American as they call'd me was *stronger* than themselves who drank *strong* Beer. We had an Alehouse Boy who attended always in the House to supply the Workmen. My Companion at the Press, drank every day a Pint before Breakfast, a Pint at Breakfast with his Bread and Cheese; a Pint between Breakfast and Dinner; a Pint at Dinner; a Pint in the Afternoon about Six o'Clock, and another when he had done his Day's-Work. I thought it a detestable Custom. But it was necessary, he suppos'd, to drink *strong* Beer that he might be *strong* to labour. I endeavour'd to convince him that the Bodily Strength afforded by Beer could only be in proportion to the Grain or Flour of the Barley dissolved in the Water of which it was made; that there was more Flour in a Penny-worth of Bread, and therefore if he would eat that with a Pint of Water, it would give him more strength than a Quart of Beer. He drank on however, and had 4 or 5 Shillings to pay out of his Wages every Saturday Night for that muddling Liquor; an Expence I was free from. And thus these poor Devils keep themselves always under. . . .

Watts after some Weeks desiring to have me in the Composing Room, I left the Pressmen. A new *Bienvenu*[92] or Sum for Drink, being 5*s.*, was demanded of me by the Compositors. I thought it an Imposition, as I had paid below. The Master thought so too, and forbad my Paying it. I stood out two or three Weeks, was accordingly considered as an Excommunicate, and had so many little Pieces of private Mischief done me, by mixing my Sorts, transposing my Pages, breaking my Matter,[93] &c. &c. if I were ever so little out of the Room, and all ascrib'd to the Chapel Ghost, which they said ever haunted those not regularly admitted, that notwithstanding the Master's Protection, I found myself oblig'd to comply and pay the Money; convinc'd of the Folly of being on ill Terms with those one is to live with continually. I was now on a fair Footing with them, and soon acquir'd considerable Influence. I propos'd some reasonable Alterations in their Chapel[94] Laws, and carried them against all Opposition. From my Example a great Part of them, left their muddling Breakfast of Beer and Bread and Cheese,

---

[91] Pages of type, set and secured in a metal frame or "chase."

[92] French: "welcome."

[93] Sorts: letters from the same font or style of type; Matter: a body of lines set into pages.

[94] Franklin's note: "A Printing House is always called a Chappel by the Workmen."

finding they could with me be supply'd from a neighbouring House with a large Porringer of hot Water-gruel, sprinkled with Pepper, crumb'd with Bread, and a Bit of Butter in it, for the Price of a Pint of Beer, viz, three halfpence. This was a more comfortable as well as cheaper Breakfast, and kept their Heads clearer. Those who continu'd
sotting with Beer all day, were often, by not paying, out of Credit at the Alehouse, and
us'd to make Interest with me to get Beer, *their Light,* as they phras'd it, *being out.* I
watch'd the Pay table on Saturday Night, and collected what I stood engag'd for them,
having to pay some times near Thirty Shillings a Week on their Accounts. This, and my
being esteem'd a pretty good Riggite, that is a jocular verbal Satyrist, supported my
Consequence in the Society. My constant Attendance, (I never making a St. Monday),[95]
recommended me to the Master; and my uncommon Quickness at Composing, occasion'd my being put upon all Work of Dispatch which was generally better paid. So I
went on now very agreably. . . .

Thus I spent about 18 Months in London. Most Part of the Time, I work'd hard at
my Business, and spent but little upon my self except in seeing Plays and in Books. My
Friend Ralph had kept me poor. He owed me about 27 Pounds; which I was now never
likely to receive; a great Sum out of my small Earnings. I lov'd him notwithstanding, for
he had many amiable Qualities. Tho' I had by no means improv'd my Fortune. But I
had pick'd up some very ingenious Acquaintance whose Conversation was of great Advantage to me, and I had read considerably.

We sail'd from Gravesend on the 23d of July 1726. For the Incidents of the Voyage, I
refer you to my Journal, where you will find them all minutely related. Perhaps the most
important Part of that Journal is the *Plan* to be found in it which I formed at Sea, for
regulating my future Conduct in Life.[96] It is the more remarkable, as being form'd when
I was so young, and yet being pretty faithfully adhered to quite thro' to old Age. We
landed in Philadelphia the 11th of October, where I found sundry Alterations. Keith was
no longer Governor, being superceded by Major Gordon:[97] I met him walking the
Streets as a common Citizen. He seem'd a little asham'd at seeing me, but pass'd without saying any thing. I should have been as much asham'd at seeing Miss Read, had not
her Friends, despairing with Reason of my Return, after the Receipt of my Letter, persuaded her to marry another, one Rogers, a Potter, which was done in my Absence.
With him however she was never happy, and soon parted from him, refusing to cohabit
with him, or bear his Name It being now said that he had another Wife. He was a worthless Fellow tho' an excellent Workman which was the Temptation to her Friends. He got
into Debt, and ran away in 1727 or 28. Went to the West Indies, and died there. Keimer
had got a better House, a Shop well supply'd with Stationary, plenty of new Types, a
number of Hands tho' none good, and seem'd to have a great deal of Business. . . .

But however serviceable I might be, I found that my Services became every Day of
less Importance, as the other Hands improv'd in the Business. And when Keimer paid
my second Quarter's Wages, he let me know that he felt them too heavy, and thought I
should make an Abatement. He grew by degrees less civil, put on more of the Master,
frequently found Fault, was captious and seem'd ready for an Out-breaking. I went on
nevertheless with a good deal of Patience, thinking that his incumber'd Circumstances

[95] I.e., never absent from work on Monday because of weekend revelry or observance of a
Saint's day (holiday).

[96] Only the "Journal" of the voyage survives;
the "Plan" has been lost.

[97] Patrick Gordon (1644–1736), governor of
Pennsylvania from 1726 to 1736.

were partly the Cause. At length a Trifle snapt our Connexion. For a great Noise happening near the Courthouse, I put my Head out of the Window to see what was the Matter. Keimer being in the Street look'd up and saw me, call'd out to me in a loud Voice and angry Tone to mind my Business, adding some reproachful Words, that nettled me the more for their Publicity, all the Neighbours who were looking out on the same Occasion being Witnesses how I was treated. He came up immediately into the Printing-House, continu'd the Quarrel, high Words pass'd on both Sides, he gave me the Quarter's Warning we had stipulated, expressing a Wish that he had not been oblig'd to so long a Warning: I told him his Wish was unnecessary for I would leave him that Instant; and so taking my Hat walk'd out of Doors . . .

Before I enter upon my public Appearance in Business it may be well to let you know the then State of my Mind, with regard to my Principles and Morals, that you may see how far those influenc'd the future Events of my Life. My Parents had early given me religious Impressions, and brought me through my Childhood piously in the Dissenting Way. But I was scarce 15 when, after doubting by turns of several Points as I found them disputed in the different Books I read, I began to doubt of Revelation it self. Some Books against Deism fell into my Hands; they were said to be the Substance of Sermons preached at Boyle's Lectures.[98] It happened that they wrought an Effect on me quite contrary to what was intended by them: For the Arguments of the Deists which were quoted to be refuted, appeared to me much stronger than the Refutations. In short I soon became a thorough Deist. . . .

We had not been long return'd to Philadelphia, before the New Types arriv'd from London. We settled with Keimer, and left him by his Consent before he heard of it. We found a House to hire near the Market, and took it. To lessen the Rent, (which was then but £24 a Year tho' I have since known it let for 70) we took in Tho' Godfrey a Glazier[99] and his Family, who were to pay a considerable Part of it to us, and we to board with them. We had scarce opened our Letters and put our Press in Order, before George House, an Acquaintance of Mine, brought a Country-man to us; whom he had met in the Street enquiring for a Printer. All our Cash was now expended in the Variety of Particulars we had been obliged to procure and this Countryman's Five Shillings being our first Fruits, and coming so seasonably, gave me more Pleasure than any Crown[100] I have since earn'd; and from the Gratitude I felt towards House, has made me often more ready than perhaps I should otherwise have been to assist young Beginners. . . .

I should have mention'd before, that in the Autumn of the preceding Year I had form'd most of my ingenious Acquaintance into a Club for mutual Improvement, which we call'd the Junto.[101] We met on Friday Evenings. The Rules I drew up requir'd that every Member in his Turn should produce one or more Queries on any Point of Morals, Politics or Natural Philosophy, to be discuss'd by the Company, and once in three Months produce and read an Essay of his own Writing on any Subject he pleased. Our Debates were to be under the Direction of a President, and to be conducted in the sincere Spirit of Enquiry after Truth, without Fondness for Dispute, or Desire of Victory; and to prevent Warmth all Expressions of Positiveness in Opinion, or of direct

---

[98] Series of lectures defending Christianity against skeptics, established by the chemist Robert Boyle (1627–1691).

[99] One who sets glass panes in windows and doors.

[100] A five-shilling coin.

[101] Small group or clique (from the Spanish *junta*).

Contradiction, were after some time made contraband and prohibited under small pecuniary Penalties. . . .

And the club . . . was the best School of Philosophy, Morals and Politics that then existed in the Province; for our Queries which were read the Week preceding their Discussion, put us on Reading with Attention upon the several Subjects, that we might speak more to the purpose: and here too we acquired better Habits of Conversation, every thing being studied in our Rules which might prevent our disgusting each other. From hence the long Continuance of the Club, which I shall have frequent Occasion to speak farther of hereafter; But my giving this Account of it here, is to show something of the Interest I had, every one of these exerting themselves in recommending Business to us. . . .

And this Industry visible to our Neighbours began to give us Character and Credit . . . I began now gradually to pay off the Debt I was under for the Printing-House. In order to secure my Credit and Character as a Tradesman, I took care not only to be in *Reality* Industrious and frugal, but to avoid all *Appearances* of the Contrary. I drest plainly; I was seen at no Places of idle Diversion; I never went out a-fishing or shooting; a Book, indeed, sometimes debauch'd me from my Work; but that was seldom, snug, and gave no Scandal: and to show that I was not above my Business, I sometimes brought home the Paper I purchas'd at the Stores, thro' the Streets on a Wheelbarrow. Thus being esteem'd an industrious thriving young Man, and paying duly for what I bought, the Merchants who imported Stationary solicited my Custom, others propos'd supplying me with Books, and I went on swimmingly. In the mean time Keimer's Credit and Business declining daily, he was at last forc'd to sell his Printing-house to satisfy his Creditors. He went to Barbadoes, and there lived some Years, in very poor Circumstances. . . .

Having turn'd my Thoughts to Marriage, I look'd round me, and made Overtures of Acquaintance in other Places; but soon found that the Business of a Printer being generally thought a poor one, I was not to expect Money with a Wife[102] unless with such a one, as I should not otherwise think agreable. In the mean time, that hard-to-be-govern'd Passion of Youth, had hurried me frequently into Intrigues with low Women that fell in my Way, which were attended with some Expence and great Inconvenience, besides a continual Risque to my Health by a Distemper which of all Things I dreaded, tho' by great good Luck I escaped it.[103]

A friendly Correspondence as Neighbours and old Acquaintances, had continued between me and Mrs. Read's family, who all had a Regard for me from the time of my first Lodging in their House. I was often invited there and consulted in their Affairs, wherein I sometimes was of service. I pity'd poor Miss Read's unfortunate Situation, who was generally dejected, seldom chearful, and avoided Company. I consider'd my Giddiness and Inconstancy when in London as in a great degree the Cause of her Unhappiness; tho' the Mother was good enough to think the Fault more her own than mine, as she had prevented our Marrying before I went thither, and persuaded the other Match in my Absence. Our mutual Affection was revived, but there were now great Objections to our Union. That Match was indeed look'd upon as invalid, a preceding Wife being said to be living in England; but this could not easily be prov'd, be-

---

[102] During this time the financial considerations of a proposed marriage far outweighed romantic ones. Hence, Franklin's monetary expectations were not out of the ordinary.

[103] Franklin is referring to syphilis.

cause of the Distance. And tho' there was a Report of his Death, it was not certain. Then tho' it should be true, he had left many Debts which his Successor might be call'd on to pay. We ventured however, over all these Difficulties, and I [took] her to wife Sept. 1. 1730.[104] None of the inconveniencies happened that we had apprehended, she prov'd a good and faithful Helpmate, assisted me much by attending the Shop, we throve together, and have ever mutually endeavour'd to make each other happy. Thus I corrected that great *Erratum* as well as I could.

About this Time our Club Meeting, not at a Tavern, but in a little Room of Mr. Grace's set apart for that Purpose; a Proposition was made by me that since our Books were often referr'd to in our Disquisitions upon the Queries, it might be convenient to us to have them all together where we met, that upon Occasion they might be consulted; and by thus clubbing our Books to a common Library, we should, while we lik'd to keep them together, have each of us the Advantage of using the Books of all the other Members, which would be nearly as beneficial as if each owned the whole. It was lik'd and agreed to, and we fill'd one End of the Room with such Books as we could best spare. The Number was not so great as we expected; and tho' they had been of great Use, yet some Inconveniencies occurring for want of due Care of them, the Collection after about a Year was separated, and each took his Books home again.

And now I set on foot my first Project of a public Nature, that for a Subscription Library. I drew up the Proposals, got them put into Form by our great Scrivener Brockden, and by the help of my Friends in the Junto, procur'd Fifty Subscribers of 40s. each to begin with and 10s. a Year for 50 Years, the Term our Company was to continue. We afterwards obtain'd a Charter, the Company being increas'd to 100. This was the Mother of all the N American Subscription Libraries now so numerous.[105] It is become a great thing itself, and continually increasing. These Libraries have improv'd the general Conversation of the Americans, made the common Tradesmen and Farmers as intelligent as most Gentlemen from other Countries, and perhaps have contributed in some degree to the Stand so generally made throughout the Colonies in Defence of their Privileges.[106]

Thus far was written with the Intention express'd in the Beginning and therefore contains several little family Anecdotes of no Importance to others.[107] What follows was written many Years after in compliance with the Advice contain'd in these Letters, and accordingly intended for the Publick. The Affairs of the Revolution occasion'd the Interruption. . . .

[104] Lacking evidence that her first husband, the missing John Rogers, was either dead or practicing bigamy, Deborah was legally still Rogers's spouse and could not re-marry. (The punishment for bigamy was thirty-nine lashes in public and life imprisonment.) However, Deborah's family and all their friends quickly recognized the "difficulties" of the situation and thereafter accepted this "common law" marriage as adequate, and the Franklins' two children were regarded as legitimate. In the absence of divorce or annulment laws, such arrangements were not uncommon. Deborah Read Franklin died in 1774.

[105] The Library Company of Philadelphia was the first subscription library in North America, although a good many public or semipublic collections (most of them small and oriented to religion) existed long before 1731.

[106] Franklin, writing in 1771, here refers to the growing colonial protests against British "tyranny," which were to culminate in revolution a few years later.

[107] Because of the Revolution, Franklin was now estranged from his Loyalist son William, to whom he had originally addressed the opening of the *Autobiography*.

Part Two: Continuation of the Account of My Life.

Begun at Passy[108] 1784

It is some time since I receiv'd the above Letters, but I have been too busy till now to think of complying with the Request they contain. It might too be much better done if I were at home among my Papers, which would aid my Memory and help to ascertain Dates. But my Return being uncertain, and having just now a little Leisure, I will endeavour to recollect and write what I can; if I live to get home, it may there be corrected and improv'd.[109]

Not having any Copy here of what is already written, I know not whether an Account is given of the means I used to establish the Philadelphia publick Library, which from a small Beginning is now become so considerable, though I remember to have come down to near the Time of that Transaction, 1730. I will therefore begin here, with an Account of it, which may be struck out if found to have been already given.

At the time I establish'd my self in Pensylvania, there was not a good Bookseller's Shop in any of the Colonies to the Southward of Boston. In New-York and Philadelphia the Printers were indeed Stationers, they sold only Paper, &c., Almanacks, Ballads, and a few common School Books. Those who lov'd Reading were oblig'd to send for their Books from England. The Members of the Junto had each a few. We had left the Ale-house where we first met, and hired a Room to hold our Club in. I propos'd that we should all of us bring our Books to that Room, where they would not only be ready to consult in our Conferences, but become a common Benefit, each of us being at Liberty to borrow such as he wish'd to read at home. This was accordingly done, and for some time contented us. Finding the Advantage of this little Collection, I propos'd to render the Benefit from Books more common by commencing a Public Subscription Library. I drew a Sketch of the Plan and Rules that would be necessary, and got a skilful Conveyancer, Mr. Charles Brockden to put the whole in Form of Articles of Agreement to be subscribed; by which each Subscriber engag'd to pay a certain Sum down for the first Purchase of Books and an annual Contribution for encreasing them. So few were the Readers at that time in Philadelphia, and the Majority of us so poor, that I was not able with great Industry to find more than Fifty Persons, mostly young Tradesmen, willing to pay down for this purpose Forty Shillings each, and Ten Shillings per Annum. On this little Fund we began. The Books were imported. The Library was open one Day in the Week for lending them to the Subscribers, on their Promisory Notes to pay Double the Value if not duly returned. The Institution soon manifested its Utility, was imitated by other Towns and in other Provinces, the Librarys were augmented by Donations, Reading became fashionable, and our People having no publick Amusements to divert their Attention from Study became better acquainted with Books, and in a few Years were observ'd by Strangers to be better instructed and more intelligent than People of the same Rank generally are in other Countries. . . .

We have an English Proverb that says,

---

[108] Suburb of Paris where Franklin stayed while serving as negotiator for the United States during the writing of the Treaty of Paris.

[109] The Treaty of Peace with Britain was signed in Paris on September 3, 1783.

Franklin asked Congress for leave to come home, but he remained as minister until succeeded by Thomas Jefferson in May 1785. He left Paris for America that July. Franklin was seventy-eight years old when he wrote this part of the *Autobiography*.

> He that would thrive
> Must ask his Wife;

it was lucky for me that I had one as much dispos'd to Industry and Frugality as my self. She assisted me chearfully in my Business, folding and stitching Pamphlets, tending Shop, purchasing old Linen Rags for the Paper-makers, &c. &c. We kept no idle Servants, our Table was plain and simple, our Furniture of the cheapest. For instance my Breakfast was a long time Bread and Milk, (no Tea) and I ate it out of a twopenny earthen Porringer[110] with a Pewter Spoon. But mark how Luxury will enter Families, and make a Progress, in Spite of Principle. Being call'd one Morning to Breakfast, I found it in a China Bowl with a Spoon of Silver. They had been bought for me without my Knowledge by my Wife, and had cost her the enormous Sum of three and twenty Shillings, for which she had no other Excuse or Apology to make, but that she thought her Husband deserv'd a Silver Spoon and China Bowl as well as any of his Neighbours. This was the first Appearance of Plate[111] and China in our House, which afterwards in a Course of Years as our Wealth encreas'd augmented gradually to several Hundred Pounds in Value.

I had been religiously educated as a Presbyterian; and tho' some of the Dogmas of that Persuasion, such as the Eternal Decrees of God, Election, Reprobation, &c. appear'd to me unintelligible, others doubtful, and I early absented myself from the Public Assemblies of the Sect, Sunday being my Studying-Day, I never was without some religious Principles; I never doubted, for instance, the Existance of the Deity, that he made the World, and govern'd it by his Providence; that the most acceptable Service of God was the doing Good to Man; that our Souls are immortal; and that all Crime will be punished and Virtue rewarded either here or hereafter; these I esteem'd the Essentials of every Religion, and being to be found in all the Religions we had in our Country I respected them all, tho' with different degrees of Respect as I found them more or less mix'd with other Articles which without any Tendency to inspire, promote or confirm Morality, serv'd principally to divide us and make us unfriendly to one another. This Respect to all, with an Opinion that the worst had some good Effects, induc'd me to avoid all Discourse that might tend to lessen the good Opinion another might have of his own Religion; and as our Province increas'd in People and new Places of worship were continually wanted, and generally erected by voluntary Contribution, my Mite for such purpose, whatever might be the Sect, was never refused.[112] . . .

It was about this time that I conceiv'd the bold and arduous Project of arriving at moral Perfection.[113] I wish'd to live without committing any Fault at any time; I would conquer all that either Natural Inclination, Custom, or Company might lead me into. As I knew, or thought I knew, what was right and wrong, I did not see why I might not *always* do the one and avoid the other. But I soon found I had undertaken a Task of more Difficulty than I had imagined. While my *Attention was taken up* in guarding against one Fault, I was often surpriz'd by another. Habit took the Advantage of Inattention. Inclination was sometimes too strong for Reason. I concluded at length, that the mere speculative Conviction that it was our Interest to be compleatly virtuous, was not sufficient to

---

[110] Porridge bowl.
[111] Silver.
[112] In 1788 Franklin was one of the largest donors to the erection of a synagogue for the Jewish population of Philadelphia.

[113] Franklin had at one time planned to write a book on moral improvement.

prevent our Slipping, and that the contrary Habits must be broken and good ones acquired and established, before we can have any Dependance on a steady uniform Rectitude of Conduct. For this purpose I therefore contriv'd the following Method.

In the various Enumerations of the moral Virtues I had met with in my Reading, I found the Catalogue more or less numerous, as different Writers included more or fewer Ideas under the same Name. Temperance, for Example, was by some confin'd to Eating and Drinking, while by others it was extended to mean the moderating every other Pleasure, Appetite, Inclination or Passion, bodily or mental, even to our Avarice and Ambition. I propos'd to myself, for the sake of Clearness, to use rather more Names with fewer Ideas annex'd to each, than a few Names with more Ideas; and I included under Thirteen Names of Virtues all that at that time occurr'd to me as necessary or desirable, and annex'd to each a short Precept, which fully express'd the Extent I gave to its Meaning.

These Names of Virtues with their Precepts were

1. TEMPERANCE.

Eat not to Dulness. Drink not to Elevation.

2. SILENCE.

Speak not but what may benefit others or yourself. Avoid trifling Conversation.

3. ORDER.

Let all your Things have their Places. Let each Part of your Business have its Time.

4. RESOLUTION.

Resolve to perform what you ought. Perform without fail what you resolve.

5. FRUGALITY.

Make no Expence but to do good to others or yourself: i.e. Waste nothing.

6. INDUSTRY.

Lose no Time. Be always employ'd in something useful. Cut off all unnecessary Actions.

7. SINCERITY.

Use no hurtful Deceit. Think innocently and justly; and, if you speak, speak accordingly.

8. JUSTICE.

Wrong none, by doing Injuries or omitting the Benefits that are your Duty.

9. MODERATION.

Avoid Extreams. Forbear resenting Injuries so much as you think they deserve.

10. CLEANLINESS.

Tolerate no Uncleanness in Body, Cloaths or Habitation.

11. TRANQUILITY.

Be not disturbed at Trifles, or at Accidents common or unavoidable.

12. CHASTITY.

Rarely use Venery but for Health or Offspring; Never to Dulness, Weakness, or the Injury of your own or another's Peace or Reputation.

13. HUMILITY.

Imitate Jesus and Socrates.

My Intention being to acquire the *Habitude* of all these Virtues, I judg'd it would be well not to distract my Attention by attempting the whole at once, but to fix it on one of them at a time, and when I should be Master of that, then to proceed to another, and so on till I should have gone thro' the thirteen. And as the previous Acquisition of some might facilitate the Acquisition of certain others, I arrang'd them with that View as they stand above. *Temperance* first, as it tends to procure that Coolness and Clearness of Head, which is so necessary where constant Vigilance was to be kept up, and Guard maintained, against the unremitting Attraction of ancient Habits, and the Force of perpetual Temptations. This being acquir'd and establish'd, *Silence* would be more easy, and my Desire being to gain Knowledge at the same time that I improv'd in Virtue, and considering that in Conversation it was obtain'd rather by the use of the Ears than of the Tongue, and therefore wishing to break a Habit I was getting into of Prattling, Punning and Joking, which only made me acceptable to trifling Company, I gave *Silence* the second Place. This, and the next, *Order,* I expected would allow me more Time for attending to my Project and my Studies; RESOLUTION, once become habitual, would keep me firm in my Endeavours to obtain all the subsequent Virtues; *Frugality* and *Industry,* by freeing me from my remaining Debt, and producing Affluence, Art and Independance, would make more easy the Practice of *Sincerity* and *Justice,* &c. &c. Conceiving then that agreable to the Advice of Pythagoras[114] in his Golden Verses daily Examination would be necessary, I contriv'd the following Method for conducting that Examination.

I made a little Book in which I allotted a Page for each of the Virtues. I rul'd each Page with red Ink, so as to have seven Columns, one for each Day of the Week, marking

---

[114] Greek philosopher and mathematician (sixth century B.C.). Franklin intended to insert the appropriate verse: "Let sleep not close your eyes till you have thrice examined the transactions of the day: where have I strayed, what have I done, what good have I omitted?"

Form of the Pages

		S	M	T	W	T	F	S
TEMPERANCE								
Eat not to Dulness. Drink not to Elevation.								
	T							
	S	••	•		•		•	
	O	•	•	•		•	•	•
	R			•			•	
	F		•			•		
	I			•				
	S							
	J							
	M							
	Cl.							
	T							
	Ch.							
	H							

each Column with a Letter for the Day. I cross'd these Columns with thirteen red Lines, marking the Beginning of each Line with the first Letter of one of the Virtues, on which Line and in its proper Column I might mark by a little black Spot every Fault I found upon Examination to have been committed respecting that Virtue upon that Day.

I determined to give a Week's strict Attention to each of the Virtues successively. Thus in the first Week my great Guard was to avoid every the least Offence against Temperance, leaving the other Virtues to their ordinary Chance, only marking every Evening the Faults of the Day. Thus if in the first Week I could keep my first Line marked T clear of Spots, I suppos'd the Habit of that Virtue so much strengthen'd and its opposite weaken'd, that I might venture extending my Attention to include the next, and for the following Week keep both Lines clear of Spots. Proceeding thus to the last, I could go thro' a Course compleat in Thirteen Weeks, and four Courses in a Year. And like him who having a Garden to weed, does not attempt to eradicate all the bad Herbs at once, which would exceed his Reach and his Strength, but works on one of the Beds at a time, and having accomplish'd the first proceeds to a Second; so I should have, (I hoped) the encouraging Pleasure of seeing on my Pages the Progress I made in Virtue, by clearing successively my Lines of their Spots, till in the End by a Number of Courses, I should be happy in viewing a clean Book after a thirteen Weeks daily Examination.

This my little Book had for its Motto these Lines from Addison's *Cato;*

Here will I hold: If there is a Pow'r above us,
(And that there is, all Nature cries aloud
Thro' all her Works) he must delight in Virtue,
And that which he delights in must be happy.[115]

---

[115] Joseph Addison, *Cato, a Tragedy* (1713),
Act V, Sc. i, ll. 15–18.

Another from Cicero.

O Vitœ Philosophia Dux! O Virtutum indagatrix, expultrixque vitiorum! Unus dies bene, et ex preceptis tuis actus, peccanti immortalitati est anteponendus.[116]

Another from the Proverbs of Solomon speaking of Wisdom or Virtue;

Length of Days is in her right hand, and in her Left Hand Riches and Honours; Her Ways are Ways of Pleasantness, and all her Paths are Peace.

III, 16, 17.

And conceiving God to be the Fountain of Wisdom, I thought it right and necessary to solicit his Assistance for obtaining it; to this End I form'd the following little Prayer, which was prefix'd to my Tables of Examination; for daily Use.

O Powerful Goodness! bountiful Father! merciful Guide! Increase in me that Wisdom which discovers my truest Interests; Strengthen my Resolutions to perform what that Wisdom dictates. Accept my kind Offices to thy other Children, as the only Return in my Power for thy continual Favours to me.

I us'd also sometimes a little Prayer which I took from Thomson's Poems. viz

> Father of Light and Life, thou Good supreme,
> O teach me what is good, teach me thy self!
> Save me from Folly, Vanity and Vice,
> From every low Pursuit, and fill my Soul
> With Knowledge, conscious Peace, and Virtue pure,
> Sacred, substantial, neverfading Bliss![117]

The Precept of *Order* requiring that *every Part of my Business should have its allotted Time*, one Page in my little Book contain'd the following Scheme of Employment for the Twenty-four Hours of a natural Day,

I enter'd upon the Execution of this Plan for Self Examination, and continu'd it with occasional Intermissions for some time. I was surpriz'd to find myself so much fuller of Faults than I had imagined, but I had the Satisfaction of seeing them diminish. To avoid the Trouble of renewing now and then my little Book, which by scraping out the Marks on the Paper of old Faults to make room for new Ones in a new Course, became full of Holes: I transferr'd my Tables and Precepts to the Ivory Leaves of a Memorandum Book, on which the Lines were drawn with red Ink that made a durable Stain, and on those Lines I mark'd my Faults with a black Lead Pencil, which Marks I could easily wipe out with a wet Sponge. After a while I went thro' one Course only in a year, and

---

[116] Marcus Tullius Cicero, *Tusculan Disputations*, V, ii, 5: "O philosophy, guide of life! O seeker out of virtues and expeller of vices! [Here Franklin omitted several lines from the original.] One day lived well, and according to thy precepts, is to be preferred to an eternity of sin."

[117] James Thomson, *The Seasons* (1726), "Winter," ll. 218–223.

afterwards only one in several Years, till at length I omitted them entirely, being employ'd in Voyages and Business abroad with a Multiplicity of Affairs, that interfered, but I always carried my little Book with me.

My Scheme of ORDER, gave me the most Trouble, and I found, that tho' it might be practicable where a Man's Business was such as to leave him the Disposition of his Time, that of a Journey-Man Printer for instance, it was not possible to be exactly observ'd by a Master, who must mix with the World, and often receive People of Business at their own Hours. *Order* too, with regard to Places for Things, Papers, &c. I found extreamly difficult to acquire. I had not been early accustomed to *Method,* and having an exceeding good Memory, I was not so sensible of the Inconvenience attending Want of Method. This Article therefore cost me so much painful Attention and my Faults in it vex'd me so much, and I made so little Progress in Amendment, and had such frequent Relapses, that I was almost ready to give up the Attempt, and content my self with a faulty Character in that respect. Like the Man who in buying an Ax of a Smith my neighbour, desired to have the whole of its Surface as bright as the Edge; the Smith consented to grind it bright for him if he would turn the Wheel. He turn'd while the Smith press'd the broad Face of the Ax hard and heavily on the Stone, which made the Turning of it very fatiguing. The Man came every now and then from the Wheel to see how the Work went on; and at length would take his Ax as it was without farther Grinding. No, says the Smith, Turn on, turn on; we shall have it bright by and by; as yet 'tis only speckled. Yes, says the Man; but—*I think I like a speckled Ax best.* And I believe this may have been the Case with many who having for want of some such Means as I employ'd found the Difficulty of obtaining good, and breaking bad Habits, in other Points of Vice and Virtue, have given up the Struggle, and concluded that *a speckled Ax was best.* For something that pretended to be Reason was every now and then suggesting to me, that such extream Nicety as I exacted of my self might be a kind of Foppery in Morals, which if it were known would make me ridiculous; that a perfect Character might be attended with the Inconvenience of being envied and hated; and that a benevolent Man should allow a few Faults in himself, to keep his Friends in Countenance.

In truth I found myself incorrigible with respect to *Order;* and now I am grown old, and my Memory bad, I feel very sensibly the want of it. But on the whole, tho' I never arrived at the Perfection I had been so ambitious of obtaining, but fell far short of it, yet I was by the Endeavour a better and a happier Man than I otherwise should have been, if I had not attempted it; As those who aim at perfect Writing by imitating the engraved Copies, tho' they never reach the wish'd for Excellence of those Copies, their Hand is mended by the Endeavour, and is tolerable while it continues fair and legible.

And it may be well my Posterity should be informed, that to this little Artifice, with the Blessing of God, their Ancestor ow'd the constant Felicity of his Life down to his 79th Year in which this is written. What Reverses may attend the Remainder is in the Hand of Providence: But if they arrive the Reflection on past Happiness enjoy'd ought to help his Bearing them with more Resignation. To *Temperance* he ascribes his long-continu'd Health, and what is still left to him of a good Constitution. To *Industry* and *Frugality* the early Easiness of his Circumstances, and Acquisition of his Fortune, with all that Knowledge which enabled him to be an useful Citizen, and obtain'd for him some Degree of Reputation among the Learned. To *Sincerity* and *Justice* the Confidence of his Country, and the honourable Employs it conferr'd upon him. And to the joint Influence of the whole Mass of the Virtues, even in the imperfect State he was able to acquire them, all that

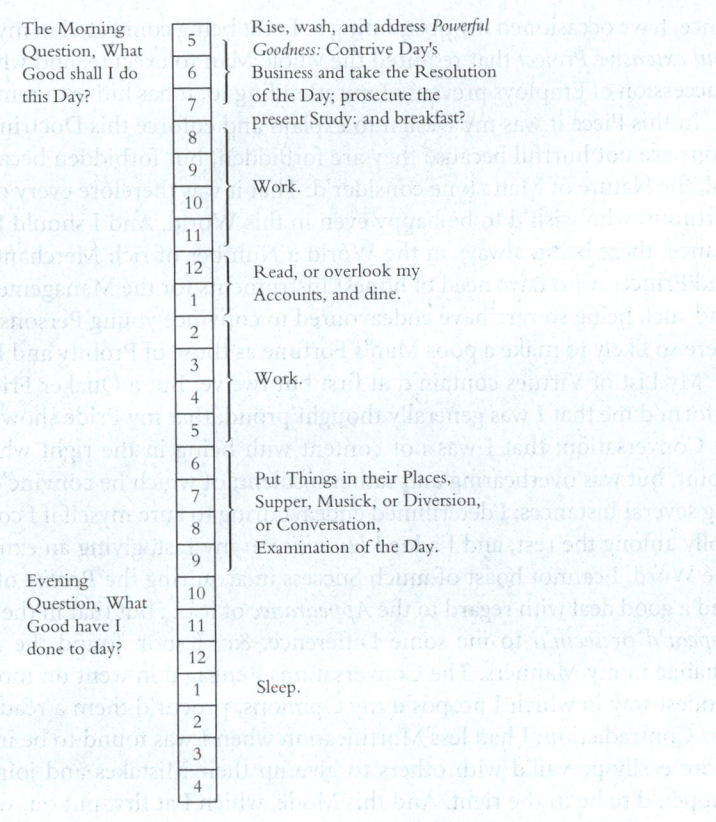

The Morning
Question, What
Good shall I do
this Day?

5	Rise, wash, and address *Powerful*
6	*Goodness:* Contrive Day's
7	Business and take the Resolution
	of the Day; prosecute the
	present Study: and breakfast?
8	
9	
10	Work.
11	
12	Read, or overlook my
1	Accounts, and dine.
2	
3	Work.
4	
5	
6	Put Things in their Places,
7	Supper, Musick, or Diversion,
8	or Conversation,
9	Examination of the Day.

Evening
Question, What
Good have I
done to day?

10	
11	
12	
1	Sleep.
2	
3	
4	

Evenness of Temper, and that Chearfulness in Conversation which makes his Company still sought for, and agreable even to his younger Acquaintance. I hope therefore that some of my Descendants may follow the Example and reap the Benefit.

It will be remark'd that, tho' my Scheme was not wholly without Religion there was in it no Mark of any of the distinguishing Tenets of any particular Sect. I had purposely avoided them; for being fully persuaded of the Utility and Excellency of my Method, and that it might be serviceable to People in all Religions, and intending some time or other to publish it, I would not have any thing in it that should prejudice any one of any Sect against it. I purposed writing a little Comment on each Virtue, in which I would have shown the Advantages of possessing it, and the Mischiefs attending its opposite Vice; and I should have called my Book the ART *of Virtue,* because it would have shown the *Means* and *Manner* of obtaining Virtue, which would have distinguish'd it from the mere Exhortation to be good, that does not instruct and indicate the Means; but is like the Apostle's Man of verbal Charity, who only, without showing to the Naked and the Hungry *how* or where they might get Cloaths or Victuals, exhorted them to be fed and clothed. *James* II, 15, 16.

But it so happened that my Intention of writing and publishing this Comment was never fulfilled. I did indeed, from time to time put down short Hints of the Sentiments, Reasonings, &c. to be made use of in it; some of which I have still by me: But the necessary close Attention to private Business in the earlier part of Life, and public Business since, have occasioned my postponing it. For it being connected in my Mind with a *great and extensive Project* that required the whole Man to execute, and which an unforeseen Succession of Employs prevented my attending to, it has hitherto remain'd unfinish'd.

In this Piece it was my Design to explain and enforce this Doctrine, that vicious Actions are not hurtful because they are forbidden, but forbidden because they are hurtful, the Nature of Man alone consider'd: That it was therefore every one's Interest to be virtuous, who wish'd to be happy even in this World. And I should from this Circumstance, there being always in the World a Number of rich Merchants, Nobility, States and Princes, who have need of honest Instruments for the Management of their Affairs, and such being so rare have endeavoured to convince young Persons, that no Qualities were so likely to make a poor Man's Fortune as those of Probity and Integrity.

My List of Virtues contain'd at first but twelve: But a Quaker Friend having kindly inform'd me that I was generally thought proud; that my Pride show'd itself frequently in Conversation; that I was not content with being in the right when discussing any Point, but was overbearing and rather insolent; of which he convinc'd me by mentioning several Instances; I determined endeavouring to cure myself if I could of this Vice or Folly among the rest, and I added *Humility* to my List, giving an extensive Meaning to the Word. I cannot boast of much Success in acquiring the *Reality* of this Virtue; but I had a good deal with regard to the *Appearance* of it. . . . but that in the present case there *appear'd* or *seem'd* to me some Difference, &c. I soon found the Advantage of this Change in my Manners. The Conversations I engag'd in went on more pleasantly. The modest way in which I propos'd my Opinions, procur'd them a readier Reception and less Contradiction; I had less Mortification when I was found to be in the wrong, and I more easily prevail'd with others to give up their Mistakes and join with me when I happen'd to be in the right. And this Mode, which I at first put on, with some violence to natural Inclination, became at length so easy and so habitual to me, that perhaps for these Fifty Years past no one has ever heard a dogmatical Expression escape me. And to this Habit (after my Character of Integrity) I think it principally owing, that I had early so much Weight with my Fellow Citizens, when I proposed new Institutions, or Alterations in the old; and so much Influence in public Councils when I became a Member. For I was but a bad Speaker, never eloquent, subject to much Hesitation in my choice of Words, hardly correct in Language, and yet I generally carried my Points.

In reality there is perhaps no one of our natural Passions so hard to subdue as *Pride.* Disguise it, struggle with it, beat it down, stifle it, mortify it as much as one pleases, it is still alive, and will every now and then peep out and show itself. You will see it perhaps often in this History. For even if I could conceive that I had compleatly overcome it, I should probably by [be] proud of my Humility.

Thus far written at Passy 1784

1784/1818

from Poor Richard Improved, 1758*

[Father Abraham's Speech; or The Way to Wealth]

Courteous Reader,

I have heard that nothing gives an Author so great Pleasure, as to find his Works respectfully quoted by other learned Authors. This Pleasure I have seldom enjoyed; for tho' I have been, if I may say it without Vanity, an *eminent Author* of Almanacks annually now a full Quarter of a Century, my Brother Authors in the same Way, for what Reason I know not, have ever been very sparing in their Applauses; and no other Author has taken the least Notice of me, so that did not my Writings produce me some solid *Pudding,* the great Deficiency of *Praise* would have quite discouraged me.

I concluded at length, that the People were the best Judges of my Merit; for they buy my Works; and besides, in my Rambles, where I am not personally known, I have frequently heard one or other of my Adages repeated, with, *as Poor Richard says,* at the End on't; this gave me some Satisfaction, as it showed not only that my Instructions were regarded, but discovered likewise some Respect for my Authority; and I own, that to encourage the Practice of remembering and repeating those wise Sentences, I have sometimes *quoted myself* with great Gravity.

---

* Franklin's note from the *Autobiography,* Part III: "In 1732 I first published my Almanack, under the Name of *Richard Saunders;* it was continu'd by me about 25 Years, commonly call'd *Poor Richard's* Almanack. I endeavour'd to make it both entertaining and useful, and it accordingly came to be in such Demand that I reap'd considerable Profit from it, vending annually near ten Thousand. And observing that it was generally read, scarce any Neighbourhood in the Province being without it, I consider'd it as a proper Vehicle for conveying Instruction among the common People, who bought scarce any other Books. I therefore filled all the little Spaces that occurr'd between the Remarkable Days in the Calendar, with Proverbial Sentences, chiefly such as inculcated Industry and Frugality, as the Means of procuring Wealth and thereby securing Virtue, it being more difficult for a Man in Want to act always honestly, as (to use here one of those Proverbs) *it is hard for an empty Sack to stand upright.* These Proverbs, which contained the Wisdom of many Ages and Nations, I assembled and form'd into a connected Discourse prefix'd to the Almanack of 1757, as the Harangue of a wise old Man to the People attending an Auction. The bringing all these scatter'd Counsels thus into a Focus, enabled them to make greater Impression. The Piece being universally approved was copied in all the Newspapers of the Continent, reprinted in Britain on a Broadside to be stuck up in Houses, two Translations were made of it in French, and great Numbers bought by the Clergy and Gentry to distribute gratis among their poor Parishioners and Tenants. In Pennsylvania, as it discouraged useless Expence in foreign Superfluities, some thought it had its share of Influence in producing that growing Plenty of Money which was observable for several Years after its Publication. . . ."

In 1748 Franklin enlarged his successful *Poor Richard's Almanack* and changed its title to *Poor Richard Improved.* For the 1758 edition, the twenty-sixth and last prepared under his supervision, Franklin invented the character Father Abraham, "a plain clean old Man, with white Locks," who in a long speech distills all of the aphoristic wisdom relating to hard work, prudence, and thrift contained in the earlier versions of the *Almanack.* This enormously popular preface, variously known as *Father Abraham's Speech* and *The Way to Wealth,* went through at least 145 printings before the end of the eighteenth century.

Judge then how much I must have been gratified by an Incident I am going to relate to you. I stopt my Horse lately where a great Number of People were collected at a Vendue of Merchant Goods. The Hour of Sale not being come, they were conversing on the Badness of the Times, and one of the Company call'd to a plain clean old Man, with white Locks, *Pray, Father Abraham, what think you of the Times? Won't these heavy Taxes quite ruin the Country? How shall we be ever able to pay them? What would you advise us to?*—Father Abraham stood up, and reply'd, If you'd have my Advice, I'll give it you in short, for a *Word to the Wise is enough,* and *many Words won't fill a Bushel,* as *Poor Richard says.* They join'd in desiring him to speak his Mind, and gathering round him, he proceeded as follows;

"Friends, says he, and Neighbours, the Taxes are indeed very heavy, and if those laid on by the Government were the only Ones we had to pay, we might more easily discharge them; but we have many others, and much more grievous to some of us. We are taxed twice as much by our *Idleness,* three times as much by our *Pride,* and four times as much by our *Folly,* and from these Taxes the Commissioners cannot ease or deliver us by allowing an Abatement. However let us hearken to good Advice, and something may be done for us; *God helps them that help themselves,* as Poor Richard says, in his Almanack of 1733.

It would be thought a hard Government that should tax its People one tenth Part of their *Time,* to be employed in its Service. But *Idleness* taxes many of us much more, if we reckon all that is spent in absolute *Sloth,* or doing of nothing, with that which is spent in idle Employments or Amusements, that amount to nothing. *Sloth,* by bringing on Diseases, absolutely shortens Life. *Sloth, like Rust, consumes faster than Labour wears, while the used Key is always bright,* as Poor Richard says. But *dost thou love Life, then do not squander Time, for that's the Stuff Life is made of,* as Poor Richard says. How much more than is necessary do we spend in Sleep! forgetting that *The sleeping Fox catches no Poultry,* and that *there will be sleeping enough in the Grave,* as Poor Richard says. If Time be of all Things the most precious, *wasting Time* must be, as Poor Richard says, *the greatest Prodigality,* since, as he elsewhere tells us, *Lost Time is never found again;* and what we call *Time-enough, always proves little enough:* Let us then be up and be doing, and doing to the Purpose; so by Diligence shall we do more with less Perplexity. *Sloth makes all Things difficult, but Industry all easy,* as Poor Richard says; and *He that riseth late, must trot all Day, and shall scarce overtake his Business at Night.* While *Laziness travels so slowly, that Poverty soon overtakes him,* as we read in Poor Richard, who adds, *Drive thy Business, let not that drive thee;* and *Early to Bed, and early to rise, makes a Man healthy, wealthy and wise.*

So what signifies *wishing* and *hoping* for better Times. We may make these Times better if we bestir ourselves. *Industry need not wish,* as Poor Richard says, and *He that lives upon Hope will die fasting. There are no Gains, without Pains;* then *Help Hands, for I have no Lands,* or if I have, they are smartly taxed. And, as Poor Richard likewise observes, *He that hath a Trade hath an Estate,* and *He that hath a Calling hath an Office of Profit and Honour;* but then the *Trade* must be worked at, and the *Calling* well followed, or neither the *Estate,* nor the *Office,* will enable us to pay our Taxes. If we are industrious we shall never starve; for, as Poor Richard says, *At the working Man's House Hunger looks in, but dares not enter.* Nor will the Bailiff nor the Constable enter, for *Industry pays Debts, while Despair encreaseth them,* says Poor Richard. What though you have found no Treasure, nor has any rich Relation left you a Legacy, *Diligence is the Mother of*

Good luck, as Poor Richard says, and *God gives all Things to Industry.* Then *plough deep, while Sluggards sleep, and you shall have Corn to sell and to keep,* says Poor Dick. Work while it is called To-day, for you know not how much you may be hindered To-morrow, which makes Poor Richard say, *One To-day is worth two To-morrows;* and farther, *Have you somewhat to do To-morrow, do it To-day.* If you were a Servant, would you not be ashamed that a good Master should catch you idle? Are you then your own Master, *be ashamed to catch yourself idle,* as Poor Dick says. When there is so much to be done for yourself, your Family, your Country, and your gracious King, be up by Peep of Day; *Let not the Sun look down and say, Inglorious here he lies.* Handle your Tools without Mittens; remember that *the Cat in Gloves catches no Mice,* as Poor Richard says. 'Tis true there is much to be done, and perhaps you are weak handed, but stick to it steadily, and you will see great Effects, for *constant Dropping wears away Stones,* and by *Diligence and Patience the Mouse ate in two the Cable;* and *little Strokes fell great Oaks,* as Poor Richard says in his Almanack, the Year I cannot just now remember.

Methinks I hear some of you say, *Must a Man afford himself no Leisure?* I will tell thee, my Friend, what Poor Richard says, *Employ thy Time well if thou meanest to gain Leisure;* and, *since thou art not sure of a Minute, throw not away an Hour.* Leisure, is Time for doing something useful; this Leisure the diligent Man will obtain, but the lazy Man never; so that, as Poor Richard says, a *Life of Leisure and a Life of Laziness are two Things.* Do you imagine that Sloth will afford you more Comfort than Labour? No, for as Poor Richard says, *Trouble springs from Idleness, and grievous Toil from needless Ease. Many without Labour, would live by their WITS only, but they break for want of Stock.* Whereas Industry gives Comfort, and Plenty, and Respect: *Fly Pleasures, and they'll follow you. The diligent Spinner has a large Shift;*[1] and *now I have a Sheep and a Cow, every Body bids me Good morrow;* all which is well said by Poor Richard.

But with our Industry, we must likewise be *steady, settled* and *careful,* and oversee our own Affairs *with our own Eyes,* and not trust too much to others; for, as Poor Richard says,

> I never saw an oft removed Tree,
> Nor yet an oft removed Family,
> That throve so well as those that settled be.

And again, *Three Removes*[2] *is as bad as a Fire;* and again, *Keep thy Shop, and thy Shop will keep thee;* and again, *If you would have your Business done, go; If not, send.* And again,

> He that by the Plough would thrive,
> Himself must either hold or drive.

And again, *The Eye of a Master will do more Work than both his Hands;* and again, *Want of Care does us more Damage than Want of Knowledge;* and again, *Not to oversee Workmen, is to leave them your Purse open.* Trusting too much to others Care is the Ruin of many; for, as the Almanack says, *In the Affairs of this World, Men are saved, not by Faith, but by the Want of it;* but a Man's own Care is profitable; for, saith Poor Dick, *Learning is to the Studious, and Riches to the Careful,* as well as *Power to the Bold,* and

---

[1] Wardrobe.   [2] Moves.

Heaven to the Virtuous. And farther, *If you would have a faithful Servant, and one that you like, serve yourself.* And again, he adviseth to Circumspection and Care, even in the smallest Matters, because sometimes *a little Neglect may breed great Mischief;* adding, *For want of a Nail the Shoe was lost; for want of a Shoe the Horse was lost; and for want of a Horse the Rider was lost,* being overtaken and slain by the Enemy, all for want of Care about a Horse-shoe Nail.

So much for Industry, my Friends, and Attention to one's own Business; but to these we must add *Frugality,* if we would make our *Industry* more certainly successful. A Man may, if he knows not how to save as he gets, *keep his Nose all his Life to the Grindstone,* and die not worth a *Groat*[3] at last. *A fat Kitchen makes a lean Will,* as Poor Richard says; and,

> Many Estates are spent in the Getting,
> Since Women for Tea forsook Spinning and Knitting,
> And Men for Punch forsook Hewing and Splitting.

If you would be wealthy, says he, in another Almanack, *think of Saving as well as of Getting: the Indies have not made Spain rich, because her* Outgoes *are greater than her* Incomes. Away then with your expensive Follies, and you will not have so much Cause to complain of hard Times, heavy Taxes, and chargeable Families; for, as Poor Dick says,

> Women and Wine, Game and Deceit,
> Make the Wealth small, and the Wants great.

And farther, *What maintains one Vice, would bring up two Children.* You may think perhaps, That a *little* Tea, or a *little* Punch now and then, Diet a *little* more costly, Clothes a *little* finer, and a *little* Entertainment now and then, can be no *great* Matter; but remember what Poor Richard says, *Many a Little makes a Mickle;*[4] and farther, *Beware of little Expences; a small Leak will sink a great Ship;* and again, *Who Dainties love, shall Beggars prove;* and moreover, *Fools make Feasts, and wise Men eat them.*

Here you are all got together at this Vendue of *Fineries* and *Knicknacks.* You call them *Goods,* but if you do not take Care, they will prove *Evils* to some of you. You expect they will be sold *cheap,* and perhaps they may for less than they cost; but if you have no Occasion for them, they must be *dear* to you. Remember what Poor Richard says, *Buy what thou hast no Need of, and ere long thou shalt sell thy Necessaries.* And again, *At a great Pennyworth pause a while:* He means, that perhaps the Cheapness is *apparent* only, and not *real;* or the Bargain, by straitning thee in thy Business, may do thee more Harm than Good. For in another Place he says, *Many have been ruined by buying good Pennyworths.* Again, Poor Richard says, *'Tis foolish to lay out Money in a Purchase of Repentance;* and yet this Folly is practised every Day at Vendues, for want of minding the Almanack. *Wise Men,* as Poor Dick says, *learn by others Harms, Fools scarcely by their own;* but, *Felix quem faciunt aliena Pericula cautum.*[5] Many a one, for the Sake of Finery on the Back, have gone with a hungry Belly, and half starved their Families; *Silks and Sattins, Scarlet and Velvets,* as Poor Richard says, *put out the Kitchen Fire.* These are not the *Necessaries* of Life; they can scarcely be called the *Conveniencies,* and yet only be-

---

[3] About four pence.
[4] Lot.

[5] Latin: "They are fortunate who have been made wary by the misfortunes of others."

cause they look pretty, how many *want* to *have* them. The *artificial* Wants of Mankind thus become more numerous than the *natural;* and, as Poor Dick says, *For one* poor *Person, there are an hundred* indigent. By these, and other Extravagancies, the Genteel are reduced to Poverty, and forced to borrow of those whom they formerly despised, but who through *Industry* and *Frugality* have maintained their Standing; in which Case it appears plainly, that a *Ploughman on his Legs is higher than a Gentleman on his Knees,* as Poor Richard says. Perhaps they have had a small Estate left them, which they knew not the Getting of; they think *'tis Day, and will never be Night;* that a little to be spent out of *so much,* is not worth minding; *(a Child and a Fool,* as Poor Richard says, *imagine Twenty Shillings and Twenty Years can never be spent)* but, *always taking out of the Meal-tub, and never putting in, soon comes to the Bottom;* then, as Poor Dick says, *When the Well's dry, they know the Worth of Water.* But this they might have known before, if they had taken his Advice; *If you would know the Value of Money, go and try to borrow some;* for, *he that goes a borrowing goes a sorrowing;* and indeed so does he that lends to such People, when he goes *to get it in again.* Poor Dick farther advises, and says,

> Fond *Pride of Dress,* is sure a very Curse;
> E'er *Fancy* you consult, consult your Purse.

And again, *Pride is as loud a Beggar as Want, and a great deal more saucy.* When you have bought one fine Thing you must buy ten more, that your Appearance may be all of a Piece; but Poor Dick says, *'Tis easier to suppress the first Desire, than to satisfy all that follow it.* And 'tis as truly Folly for the Poor to ape the Rich, as for the Frog to swell, in order to equal the Ox.

> Great Estates may venture more,
> But little Boats should keep near Shore.

'Tis however a Folly soon punished; for *Pride that dines on Vanity sups on Contempt,* as Poor Richard says. And in another Place, *Pride breakfasted with Plenty, dined with Poverty, and supped with Infamy.* And after all, of what Use is this *Pride of Appearance,* for which so much is risked, so much is suffered? It cannot promote Health, or ease Pain; it makes no Increase of Merit in the Person, it creates Envy, it hastens Misfortune.

> What is a Butterfly? At best
> He's but a Caterpillar drest.
> The gaudy Fop's his Picture just,

as Poor Richard says.

But what Madness must it be to *run in Debt* for these Superfluities! We are offered, by the Terms of this Vendue, *Six Months Credit;* and that perhaps has induced some of us to attend it, because we cannot spare the ready Money, and hope now to be fine without it. But, ah, think what you do when you run in Debt; *You give to another Power over your Liberty.* If you cannot pay at the Time, you will be ashamed to see your Creditor; you will be in Fear when you speak to him; you will make poor pitiful sneaking Excuses, and by Degrees come to lose your Veracity, and sink into base downright lying; for, as Poor Richard says, *The second Vice is Lying, the first is running in Debt.* And again, to the same Purpose, *Lying rides upon Debt's Back.* Whereas a freeborn Englishman ought not to be ashamed or afraid to see or speak to any Man living. But Poverty often deprives a Man of all Spirit and Virtue: *'Tis hard for an empty Bag to stand upright,* as Poor Richard truly says. What would you think of that Prince, or that Government, who should issue an Edict forbidding you to dress like a Gentleman or a Gentlewoman, on Pain of Imprisonment or Servitude? Would you not say, that you are free, have a Right to dress as you please, and that such an Edict would be a Breach of your Privileges, and such a Government tyrannical? And yet you are about to put yourself under that Tyranny when you run in Debt for such Dress! Your Creditor has Authority at his Pleasure to deprive you of your Liberty, by confining you in Goal for Life, or to sell you for a Servant, if you should not be able to pay him! When you have got your Bargain, you may, perhaps, think little of Payment; but *Creditors,* Poor Richard tells us, *have better Memories than Debtors;* and in another Place says, *Creditors are a superstitious Sect, great Observers of set Days and Times.* The Day comes round before you are aware, and the Demand is made before you are prepared to satisfy it. Or if you bear your Debt in Mind, the Term which at first seemed so long, will, as it lessens, appear extreamly short. *Time* will seem to have added Wings to his Heels as well as Shoulders. *Those have a short Lent,* saith Poor Richard, *who owe Money to be paid at Easter.* Then since, as he says, *The Borrower is a Slave to the Lender, and the Debtor to the Creditor,* disdain the Chain, preserve your Freedom; and maintain your Independency: Be *industrious* and *free;* be *frugal* and *free.* At present, perhaps, you may think yourself in thriving Circumstances, and that you can bear a little Extravagance without Injury; but,

> For Age and Want, save while you may;
> No Morning Sun lasts a whole Day,

as Poor Richard says. Gain may be temporary and uncertain, but ever while you live, Expence is constant and certain; and *'tis easier to build two Chimnies than to keep one in Fuel,* as Poor Richard says. So *rather go to Bed supperless than rise in Debt.*

> Get what you can, and what you get hold;
> 'Tis the Stone that will turn all your Lead into Gold,

as Poor Richard says. And when you have got the Philosopher's Stone,[6] sure you will no longer complain of bad Times, or the Difficulty of paying Taxes.

This Doctrine, my Friends, is *Reason* and *Wisdom;* but after all, do not depend too much upon your own *Industry,* and *Frugality,* and *Prudence,* though excellent Things, for they may all be blasted without the Blessing of Heaven; and therefore ask that Blessing humbly, and be not uncharitable to those that at present seem to want it, but comfort and help them. Remember Job suffered, and was afterwards prosperous.

And now to conclude, *Experience keeps a dear School, but Fools will learn in no other, and scarce in that;* for it is true, *we may give Advice, but we cannot give Conduct,* as Poor Richard says: However, remember this, *They that won't be counselled, can't be helped,* as

---

[6] In alchemy, the substance that was thought to turn base metals into gold.

Poor Richard says: And farther, That *if you will not hear Reason, she'll surely rap your Knuckles.*

Thus the old Gentleman ended his Harangue. The People heard it, and approved the Doctrine, and immediately practised the contrary, just as if it had been a common Sermon; for the Vendue opened, and they began to buy extravagantly, notwithstanding all his Cautions, and their own Fear of Taxes. I found the good Man had thoroughly studied my Almanacks, and digested all I had dropt on those Topicks during the Course of Five-and-twenty Years. The frequent Mention he made of me must have tired any one else, but my Vanity was wonderfully delighted with it, though I was conscious that not a tenth Part of the Wisdom was my own which he ascribed to me, but rather the *Gleanings* I had made of the Sense of all Ages and Nations. However, I resolved to be the better for the Echo of it; and though I had at first determined to buy Stuff for a new Coat, I went away resolved to wear my old One a little longer. *Reader,* if thou wilt do the same, thy Profit will be as great as mine. I am, as ever, Thine to serve thee,   RICHARD SAUNDERS.[7] July 7, 1757.
1757/1758

---

from Information to Those Who Would Remove to America*

Many Persons in Europe, having directly or by Letters, express'd to the Writer of this, who is well acquainted with North America, their Desire of transporting and establishing themselves in that Country; but who appear to have formed, thro' Ignorance, mistaken Ideas and Expectations of what is to be obtained there; he thinks it may be useful, and prevent inconvenient, expensive, and fruitless Removals and Voyages of improper Persons, if he gives some clearer and truer Notions of that part of the World, than appear to have hitherto prevailed.

He finds it is imagined by Numbers, that the Inhabitants of North America are rich, capable of rewarding, and dispos'd to reward, all sorts of Ingenuity; that they are at the same time ignorant of all the Sciences, and, consequently, that Strangers, possessing Talents in the Belles-Lettres, fine Arts, &c., must be highly esteemed, and so well paid, as to become easily rich themselves; that there are also abundance of profitable Offices to be disposed of, which the Natives are not qualified to fill; and that, having few Persons of Family among them, Strangers of Birth must be greatly respected, and of course easily obtain the best of those Offices, which will make all their Fortunes; that the Governments too, to encourage Emigrations from Europe, not only pay the Expence of personal Transportation, but give Lands gratis to Strangers, with Negroes to work for them, Utensils of Husbandry, and Stocks of Cattle. These are all wild Imaginations; and

---

[7] Franklin used the name of a well-known seventeenth-century London almanac writer.
* Title of pirated edition published in 1784.

Franklin later that year published the pamphlet under the title *Advice to Such as Would Remove to America.*

those who go to America with Expectations founded upon them will surely find themselves disappointed.

The Truth is, that though there are in that Country few People so miserable as the Poor of Europe, there are also very few that in Europe would be called rich; it is rather a general happy Mediocrity that prevails. There are few great Proprietors of the Soil, and few Tenants; most People cultivate their own Lands, or follow some Handicraft or Merchandise; very few rich enough to live idly upon their Rents or Incomes, or to pay the high Prices given in Europe for Paintings, Statues, Architecture, and the other Works of Art, that are more curious than useful. Hence the natural Geniuses, that have arisen in America with such Talents, have uniformly quitted that Country for Europe, where they can be more suitably rewarded. It is true, that Letters and Mathematical Knowledge are in Esteem there, but they are at the same time more common than is apprehended; there being already existing nine Colleges or Universities, viz. four in New England, and one in each of the Provinces of New York, New Jersey, Pensilvania, Maryland, and Virginia, all furnish'd with learned Professors; besides a number of smaller Academies; these educate many of their Youth in the Languages, and those Sciences that qualify men for the Professions of Divinity, Law, or Physick. Strangers indeed are by no means excluded from exercising those Professions; and the quick Increase of Inhabitants everywhere gives them a Chance of Employ, which they have in common with the Natives. Of civil Offices, or Employments, there are few; no superfluous Ones, as in Europe; and it is a Rule establish'd in some of the States, that no Office should be so profitable as to make it desirable. The 36th Article of the Constitution of Pennsilvania, runs expressly in these Words; "As every Freeman, to preserve his Independence, (if he has not a sufficient Estate) ought to have some Profession, Calling, Trade, or Farm, whereby he may honestly subsist, there can be no Necessity for, nor Use in, establishing Offices of Profit; the usual Effects of which are Dependance and Servility, unbecoming Freemen, in the Possessors and Expectants; Faction, Contention, Corruption, and Disorder among the People. Wherefore, whenever an Office, thro' Increase of Fees or otherwise, becomes so profitable, as to occasion many to apply for it, the Profits ought to be lessened by the Legislature."

These Ideas prevailing more or less in all the United States, it cannot be worth any Man's while, who has a means of Living at home, to expatriate himself, in hopes of obtaining a profitable civil Office in America; and, as to military Offices, they are at an End with the War, the Armies being disbanded. Much less is it adviseable for a Person to go thither, who has no other Quality to recommend him but his Birth. In Europe it has indeed its Value; but it is a Commodity that cannot be carried to a worse Market than that of America, where people do not inquire concerning a Stranger, *What is he?* but, *What can he do?* If he has any useful Art, he is welcome; and if he exercises it, and behaves well, he will be respected by all that know him; but a mere Man of Quality, who, on that Account, wants to live upon the Public, by some Office or Salary, will be despis'd and disregarded. The Husbandman is in honor there, and even the Mechanic, because their Employments are useful. The People have a saying, that God Almighty is himself a Mechanic, the greatest in the Univers; and he is respected and admired more for the Variety, Ingenuity, and Utility of his Handyworks, than for the Antiquity of his Family. They are pleas'd with the Observation of a Negro, and frequently mention it, that *Boccarorra* (meaning the White men) *make de black man workee, make de Horse workee, make de Ox workee, make ebery ting workee; only de Hog. He, de hog, no workee; he eat, he drink, he walk about, he go to sleep when he please, he libb like a Gentleman.* According to these Opinions of the Americans, one of them would think himself more oblig'd to a Genealogist, who could prove for him that his Ancestors and Relations for ten Generations had been Ploughmen, Smiths, Carpenters, Turners, Weavers, Tanners, or even Shoemakers, and consequently that they were useful Members of Society; than if he could only prove that they were Gentlemen, doing nothing of Value, but living idly on the Labour of others, mere *fruges consumere nati,*[1] and otherwise *good for nothing,* till by their Death their Estates, like the Carcass of the Negro's Gentleman-Hog, come to be *cut up.*

With regard to Encouragements for Strangers from Government, they are really only what are derived from good Laws and Liberty. Strangers are welcome, because there is room enough for them all, and therefore the old Inhabitants are not jealous of them; the Laws protect them sufficiently, so that they have no need of the Patronage of Great Men; and every one will enjoy securely the Profits of his Industry. But, if he does not bring a Fortune with him, he must work and be industrious to live. One or two Years' residence gives him all the Rights of a Citizen; but the government does not at present, whatever it may have done in former times, hire People to become Settlers, by Paying their Passages, giving Land, Negroes, Utensils, Stock, or any other kind of Emolument whatsoever. In short, America is the Land of Labour, and by no means what the English call *Lubberland,* and the French *Pays de Cocagne,* where the streets are said to be pav'd with half-peck Loaves, the Houses til'd with Pancakes, and where the Fowls fly about ready roasted, crying, *Come eat me!*[2] . . .

1784

Native Americans and the Myth of the Noble Savage

Our world has just discovered another world (and who will guarantee us that it is the last of its brothers, since the daemons, the sibyls, and we ourselves have up to now been ignorant of this one?) no less great, full, and well-limbed than itself, yet so new and so infantile that it is still being taught its A B C; not fifty years ago it knew neither letters, nor weights and measures, nor clothes, nor wheat, nor vines. It was still quite naked at the breast, and lived only on what its nursing mother provided. If we are right to infer the end of our world, and that poet is right about the youth of his own age, this other world will only be coming into the light when ours is leaving it. The universe will fall into paralysis; one member will be crippled, the other in full vigor.

I am much afraid that we shall have very greatly hastened the decline and ruin of this new world by our contagion, and that we will have sold it our opinions and our arts very dear. It was an infant world; yet we have not whipped it and subjected it to our discipline by the advantage of our natural valor and strength, nor won it over by our justice and goodness, nor subjugated it by our magnanimity. Most of the responses

---

[1] Franklin's note: "Born Merely to eat up the corn.—Watts"

[2] The text continues with a description of "the kind of Persons to whom an Emigration to America may be advantageous."

of these people and most of our dealings with them show that they were not at all behind us in natural brightness of mind and pertinence. . . .

How easy it would have been to make good use of souls so fresh, so famished to learn, and having, for the most part, such fine natural beginnings! On the contrary, we took advantage of their ignorance and inexperience to incline them the more easily toward treachery, lewdness, avarice, and every sort of inhumanity and cruelty, after the example and pattern of our ways. Who ever set the utility of commerce and trading at such a price? So many cities razed, so many nations exterminated, so many millions of people put to the sword, and the richest and most beautiful part of the world turned upside down, for the traffic in pearls and pepper! Base and mechanical victories! Never did ambition, never did public enmities, drive men against one another to such horrible hostilities and such miserable calamities.

Michel de Montaigne, "Of Coaches" (1585–1588)

Those that scaped the fire were slain with the sword, some hewed to pieces, others run through with their rapiers, so as they were quickly dispatched and very few escaped. It was conceived they thus destroyed about 400 at this time. It was a fearful sight to see them thus frying in the fire and the streams of blood quenching the same, and horrible was the stink and scent thereof; but the victory seemed a sweet sacrifice, and they gave the praise thereof to God, who had wrought so wonderfully for them, thus to enclose their enemies in their hands and give them so speedy a victory over so proud and insulting an enemy.

William Bradford, on the burning of a Pequot village,
Of Plymouth Plantation (1637)

I should think it requisite that convenient tracts of land should be set out to them; and that by plain and natural boundaries, as much as may be—as lakes, rivers, mountains, rocks—upon which for any Englishman to encroach should be accounted a crime.

Samuel Sewall, letter to Sir William Ashurst (May 3, 1700)

You will do well to try to inoculate the Indians by means of blankets in which smallpox patients have slept, as well as by every other method that can serve to extirpate this execrable race. I should be very glad if your scheme of hunting them down by dogs could take effect.

General Jeffery Amherst, letter (1732)

Men no sooner began to set a Value upon each other and know what Esteem was, than each laid claim to it, and it was no longer safe for any Man to refuse it to another. Hence the first Duties of Civility and Politeness, even among Savages; and hence every voluntary Injury became an Affront, as besides the Mischief, which resulted from it as an Injury, the Party offended was sure to find in it a Contempt for his Person more intolerable than the Mischief itself. It is thus that every Man, punishing the Contempt expressed for him by others in proportion to the value set upon himself, the Effects of Revenge become terrible, and Men learned to be sanguinary and cruel. Such precisely was the Degree attained by most of the savage Nations with whom we are acquainted. And it is for want of sufficiently distinguishing Ideas, and observing at how great a Distance these People were from the first state of Nature, that so many Authors have hastily concluded that Man is naturally cruel, and requires a regular System of Police to be reclaimed; whereas nothing can be more gentle than him in his primitive State, when placed by Nature at an equal Distance from the Stupidity of Brutes, and the pernicious good Sense of civilized Man. . . .

The more we reflect on this State, the more convinced we shall be, that it was the least subject of any to Revolutions, the best for Man, and that nothing could have drawn him out of it but some fatal Accident, which, for the public good, should never have happened. The Example of the Savages, most of whom have been found in this Condition, seems to confirm that Mankind was formed ever to remain in it, that this Condition is the real Youth of the World, and that all ulterior Improvements have been so many Steps, in Appearance towards the Perfection of Individuals, but in Fact towards the Decrepitness of the Species.

> Jean-Jacques Rousseau, *Discourse upon the Origin and Foundation of the Inequality Among Mankind* (1755)

Unhappy people! to have lived in such times, and by such neighbors! We have seen that they would have been safer among the ancient heathens with whom the rites of hospitality were sacred. They would have been considered as guests of the public, and the religion of the country would have operated in their favor. But our frontier people call themselves Christians! They would have been safer if they had submitted to the Turks.

> Benjamin Franklin, *A Narrative of the Late Massacres in Lancaster County* (1764), [written soon after the murder of several Conestoga Indians by Scotch-Irish settlers in Pennsylvania]

I have had frequent opportunities to observe moral dispositions in the men we call savages, that would do much honour to the most civilized European.

> Pierre Marie François de Pages, *Travels Round the World in the Years 1767–1771*

Seneca and Cherokee Oral History

No sooner had Europeans encountered coastal-dwelling Native Americans than many Indian people quickly ceased to exist. Within twenty years of Columbus's first having sighted America on October 12, 1492, the entire native population of Hispaniola (now Santo Domingo) was eliminated. Powhatan's Algonquin Confederacy had disappeared within fifty years of his speech to Captain John Smith.

Native American groups living considerably inland, such as the Iroquois, the Cherokee, and the Creek, were far more fortunate. Several generations passed before the number of European emigrants on the coast became so large that the adventurous were encouraged to strike out for the frontier. During this period of colonial expansion, several large inland groups of Native Americans had the opportunity to adjust physically to the new diseases the Europeans had carried with them (such as

Thomas Easterly
Keokuk or The Watchful Fox
daguerreotype, 1847
(The Smithsonian Institution)

measles, smallpox, and whooping cough) as well as to adjust culturally, economically, and socially to the implications of permanent white settlement in North America. In addition, interior groups such as the Iroquois, the Cherokee, and the Creek were able to maintain a far more independent stance in response to the different European factions competing for dominance in the region. These Native Americans were able to play off the various European powers, especially the French and the English, against each other.

While the coastal Indians were alternately fighting off and trying to make peace with various European colonial groups, the inland tribes continued to be preoccupied with intertribal relations. But the introduction of European goods complicated

George Catlin
Woman Who Lives in a Bear's Den
oil on canvas, 1832
(National Museum of American Art, Washington, D.C./Art Resource, NY)

matters. The Indians found themselves increasingly caught up in the fur trade in order to satisfy their initial desire, and subsequent need, for those goods. For example, the northern Iroquois tribes of the Five Nations, in what is now northern New York State, not only participated in the fur trade as primary suppliers but also served increasingly as brokers between neighboring Indian groups and the Europeans. They maintained this position through the political and military power of the Iroquois League. Before 1680 they had conquered all of the tribes on their immediate borders and aimed their military prowess against the more distant Illinois, Catawba, and Cherokee tribes. For nearly one hundred years the Iroquois and Cherokee continued to conduct small-scale raids on each other. As James Mooney notes in *Myths of the Cherokee,* "The great object of every Iroquois boy [was] to go against the Cherokee as soon as he was old enough to take the war path."

The journey from Iroquois country to the Cherokee frontier took more than five days "for a rapidly traveling war party" from what is now western New York State along "the Great Indian War Path" to Virginia, Kentucky, northern Tennessee, and North Carolina and on to the Creek territory in what is now Alabama. Mooney observes that "as the distance was too great for large expeditions, the war consisted chiefly of a series of individual exploits, a single Cherokee often going hundreds of miles to strike a blow, which was surely to be retaliated by the warriors to the north." The two narratives printed here offer different perspectives on such skirmishes and reveal something of the Native American ritual and folklore that surround war. The first selection represents Senecan oral history, the second Cherokee.

Cherokee oral tradition reports that the war was finally brought to an end by an Iroquois delegation sent to the Cherokee to propose a general alliance of southern and western tribes. A formal peace treaty was arranged by Sir William Johnson, the British agent for the Mohawk, in 1768.

Further Reading:
A. F. C. Wallace, *The Death and Rebirth of the Seneca*, 1970.
W. C. Sturtevant, gen. ed., *Handbook of North American Indians*, and B. G. Trigger, ed., vol. 15, *Northeast*, 1978.

Text:
Myths of the Cherokees, 19th Annual Report of the Bureau of American Ethnology, Part 1, 1897–98, J. Mooney, 1900.

The Unseen Helpers

Ganogwioeoñ, a war chief of the Seneca, led a party against the Cherokee. When they came near the first town he left his men outside and went in alone. At the first house he found an old woman and her granddaughter. They did not see him, and he went into the house and hid himself under some wood. When darkness came on he heard the old woman say, "Maybe Ganogwioeoñ is near; I'll close the door." After a while he heard them going to bed. When he thought they were asleep he went into the house. The fire had burned down low, but the girl was still awake and saw him. She was about to scream, when he said, "I am Ganogwioeoñ. If you scream I'll kill you. If you keep quiet I'll not hurt you." They talked together, and he told her that in the morning she must bring the chief's daughter to him. She promised to do it, and told him where he should wait. Just before daylight he left the house.

In the morning the girl went to the chief's house and said to his daughter, "Let's go out together for wood." The chief's daughter got ready and went with her, and when they came to the place where Ganogwioeoñ was hiding he sprang out and killed her,[1] but did not hurt the other girl. He pulled off the scalp and gave such a loud scalp yell that all the warriors in the town heard it and came running out after him. He shook the scalp at them and then turned and ran. He killed the first one that came up, but when he tried to shoot the next one the bow broke and the Cherokee got him.

They tied him and carried him to the two women of the tribe who had the power to decide what should be done with him. Each of these women had two snakes tattooed on her lips, with their heads opposite each other, in such a way that when she opened her mouth the two snakes opened their mouths also. They decided to burn the soles of his feet until they were blistered, then to put grains of corn under the skin and to chase him with clubs until they had beaten him to death.

They stripped him and burnt his feet. Then they tied a bark rope around his waist, with an old man to hold the other end, and made him run between two lines of people, and with clubs in their hands. When they gave the word to start Ganogwioeoñ pulled the rope away from the old man and broke through the line and ran until he had left them all out of sight. When night came he crawled into a hollow log. He was naked and unarmed, with his feet in a pitiful condition, and thought he could never get away.

He heard footsteps on the leaves outside and thought his enemies were upon him. The footsteps came up to the log and some one said to another, "This is our friend." Then the stranger said to Ganogwioeoñ, "You think you are the same as dead, but it is not so. We will take care of you. Stick out your feet." He put out his feet from the log and felt something licking them. After a while the voice said, "I think we have licked his feet enough. Now we must crawl inside the log and lie on each side of him to keep him warm." They crawled in beside him. In the morning they crawled out and told him to stick out his feet again. They licked them again and then said to him, "Now we have done all we can do this time. Go on until you come to the place where you made a bark shelter a long time ago, and under the bark you will find something to help you." Ganogwioeoñ crawled out of the log, but they were gone. His feet were better now and he could walk comfortably. He went on until about noon, when he came to the bark shelter, and under it he found a knife, an awl, and a flint, that his men had hidden there two years before. He took them and started on again.

Toward evening he looked around until he found another hollow tree and crawled into it to sleep. At night he heard the footsteps and voices again. When he put out his feet again, as the strangers told him to do, they licked his feet as before and then crawled in and lay down on each side of him to keep him warm. Still he could not see them. In the morning after they went out they licked his feet again and said to him, "At noon you will find food." Then they went away.

Ganogwioeoñ crawled out of the tree and went on. At noon he came to a burning log, and near it was a dead bear, which was still warm, as if it had been killed only a short time before. He skinned the bear and found it very fat. He cut up the meat and roasted as much as he could eat or carry. While it was roasting he scraped the skin and rubbed rotten wood dust on it to clean it until he was tired. When night came he lay down to sleep. He heard the steps and the voices again and one said, "Well, our friend is

---

[1] The Iroquois believed that killing a woman required greater courage because the attacker had to penetrate a village to do so.

lying down. He has plenty to eat, and it does not seem as if he is going to die. Let us lick his feet again." When they had finished they said to him, "You need not worry any more now. You will get home all right." Before it was day they left him.

When morning came he put the bearskin around him like a shirt, with the hair outside, and started on again, taking as much of the meat as he could carry. That night his friends came to him again. They said, "Your feet are well, but you will be cold," so they lay again on each side of him. Before daylight they left, saying, "About noon you will find something to wear." He went on and about midday he came to two young bears just killed. He skinned them and dressed the skins, then roasted as much meat as he wanted, and lay down to sleep. In the morning he made leggings of the skins, took some of the meat, and started on.

His friends came again the next night and told him that in the morning he would come upon something else to wear. As they said, about noon he found two fawns just killed. He turned the skins and made himself a pair of moccasins, then cut some of the meat, and traveled on until evening, when he made a fire and had supper.

That night again he heard the steps and voices, and one said, "My friend, very soon now you will reach home safely and find your friends all well. Now we will tell you why we have helped you. Whenever you went hunting you always gave the best part of the meat to us and kept only the smallest part for yourself. For that we are thankful and help you. In the morning you will see us and know who we are."[2]

In the morning when he woke up they were still there—two men as he thought—but after he had said the last words to them and started on, he turned again to look, and one was a white wolf and the other a black wolf. That day he reached home.
1900

Hemp-Carrier

On the southern slope of the ridge, along the trail from Robbinsville to Valley river, in Cherokee county, North Carolina, are the remains of a number of stone cairns. The piles are leveled now, but thirty years ago the stones were still heaped up into pyramids, to which every Cherokee who passed added a stone. According to the tradition these piles marked the graves of a number of women and children of the tribe who were surprised and killed on the spot by a raiding party of the Iroquois shortly before the final peace between the two Nations. As soon as the news was brought to the settlements on Hiwassee and Cheowa[1] a party was made under Talé tanigí skĭ, "Hemp-carrier," to follow and take vengeance on the enemy. Among others of the party was the father of the noted chief Tsunú lăhuñ skĭ or Junaluska, who died on Cheowa about 1855.

For days they followed the trail of the Iroquois across the Great Smoky mountains, through forests and over rivers, until they finally tracked them to their very town in the

---

[2] Ganogwioeoñ is apparently a member of the wolf clan, whose totemic figure protects him here. The Iroquois always left a portion of their hunting for their totemic animal. Thus the wolf protects him here.

[1] Rivers running through Tennessee and North Carolina.

far northern Seneca country. On the way they met another war party headed for the south, and the Cherokee killed them all and took their scalps. When they came near the Seneca town it was almost night, and they heard shouts in the townhouse, where the women were dancing over the fresh Cherokee scalps. The avengers hid themselves near the spring, and as the dancers came down to drink the Cherokee silently killed one and another until they had counted as many scalps as had been taken on Cheowa, and still the dancers in the townhouse never thought that enemies were near. Then said the Cherokee leader, "We have covered the scalps of our women and children. Shall we go home now like cowards, or shall we raise the war whoop and let the Seneca know that we are men?" "Let them come, if they will," said his men; and they raised the scalp yell of the Cherokee. At once there was an answering shout from the townhouse, and the dance came to a sudden stop. The Seneca warriors swarmed out with ready gun and hatchet, but the nimble Cherokee were off and away. There was a hot pursuit in the darkness, but the Cherokee knew the trails and were light and active runners, and managed to get away with the loss of only a single man. The rest got home safely, and the people were so well pleased with Hemp-carrier's bravery and success that they gave him seven wives.[2]

1900

Samson Occom
1723–1792

Missionaries conducted most of the training of Native Americans in English during the colonial period. Samson Occom was a product of such efforts and one of the first Native Americans to publish in English. A member of the Mohegan (or Mohican) tribe that, along with the Pequot, settled in southeastern Connecticut, Occom was one of the first students of the celebrated Congregational minister Eleazar Wheelock. In 1749 Occom moved to eastern Long Island to set up a church and school for the Montauk Indians. He was formally ordained in 1759. In 1766 he traveled to England to raise funds to establish what became Dartmouth College.

On September 2, 1772, Samson Occom preached a sermon at the execution of Moses Paul, a thirty-year-old Mohegan who had been convicted of murder and sentenced to be hanged. Paul had served in the colonial militia and on board various frigates and commercial ships. In inviting Occom to preach at his execution, Moses Paul "earnestly wishes," Occom noted, "that his untimely End, may be a means of detering others, from following those sinful Practices, which has made him so public an Example for his Sin and Folly." The following excerpts from Occom's fiery sermon on "the wages of sin" and the self-inflicted frightful consequences of Indian drunkenness recall the religious and rhetorical traditions of Jonathan Edwards's "Sinners in the Hands of an Angry God" and also reveal Occom's self-consciousness about his audience—both the Indian Moses Paul and the white colonists who had come to witness his execution.

---

[2] Seven is the Cherokee ritual number.

The sermon, the earliest extant by a Native American, quickly received widespread attention. Within a few years it had been reprinted nineteen times, making it a best-seller on the eve of the American Revolution and launching Occom's career as a noted public figure. Occom also composed a good deal of church music, much of which is gathered in his volume *A Choice Collection of Hymns and Spiritual Songs* (1774). A highly respected figure in both religious and educational circles, Samson Occom died in 1792, having devoted himself for years to the success of Dartmouth College.

Further Reading:

W. D. Love, *Samson Occom and the Christian Indians of New England*, 1899.

H. Blodgett, *Samson Occom*, 1935.

Text:

A Sermon Preached at the Execution of Moses Paul, an Indian, 1772.

---

from A Sermon, Preached at the Execution of Moses Paul, an Indian*

The Preface

The world is already full of books; and the people of God are abundantly furnished with excellent books upon divine subjects; and it seems, that every subject has been written upon over and over again: and the people in very deed have had precept upon precept, line upon line, here a little and there a little; and so in the whole, they have much, yea, very much, they have enough and more than enough. And when I come to consider these things, I am ready to say with myself, What folly and madness is it in me to suffer any thing of mine to appear in print, to expose my ignorance to the world.

It seems altogether unlikely that my performance will do any manner of service in the world, since the most excellent writings of worthy and learned men are disregarded. But there are two or three considerations that have induced me to be willing, to suffer my broken hints to appear in the world. One is, that the books that are in the world are written in very high and refined language; and the sermons that are delivered every sabbath in general, are in a very high and lofty stile, so that the common people understand but little of them. But I think they can't help understanding my talk; it is common, plain, every day talk: little children may understand me. And poor Negroes may plainly and fully understand my meaning; and it may be of service to them. Again, it may in a particular manner be serviceable to my poor kindred the Indians. Further, as it comes from an uncommon quarter, it may induce people to read it, because it is from an In-

---

* The title page of the first edition reads: "A SERMON, Preached at the Execution of *Moses Paul*, An INDIAN, Who was executed at *New-Haven*, on the 2d of *September*, 1772, for the MURDER of Mr. MOSES COOK, Late of *Water-* *bury*, on the 7th of *December*, 1771. Preached at the Desire of said PAUL. By SAMSON OCCOM, Minister of the Gospel and Missionary to the INDIANS."

dian. Lastly, God works where and when he pleases, and by what instruments he sees fit, and he can and has used weak and unlikely instruments to bring about his great work.

It was a stormy and very uncomfortable day, when the following discourse was delivered, and about one half of it was not delivered, as it was written, and now it is a little altered and enlarged in some places.

Introduction

By the melancholy providence of God, and at the earnest desire and invitation of the poor condemned criminal, I am here before this great concourse of people at this time, to give the last discourse to the poor miserable object who is to be executed this day before your eyes, for the due reward of his folly and madness, and enormous wickedness. It is an unwelcome task to me to speak upon such an occasion; but since it is the desire of the poor man himself, who is to die a shameful death this day, in conscience I cannot deny him; I must endeavor to do the great work the dying man requests.

I conclude that this great concourse of people have come together to see the execution of justice upon this poor Indian, and I suppose the biggest part of you look upon yourselves christians, and as such I hope you will demean yourselves; and that you will have suitable commiseration towards this poor object. Tho' you can't in justice pray for his life to be continued in this world, yet you can pray earnestly for the salvation of his poor soul, consistently with the mind of God: Let this be therefore the fervent exercise of our souls: for this is the last day we have to pray for him. As for you, that don't regard religion, it cannot be expected, that you will put up one petition for this miserable creature: yet I would intreat you seriously to consider the frailty of corrupt nature, and behave yourselves as becomes rational creatures.

And in a word, let us all be suitably affected with the melancholy occasion of this day, knowing that we are all dying creatures, and accountable unto God. Though this poor condemned creature will in a few minutes know more than all of us, either in unutterable joy, or in inconceivable wo, yet we shall certainly know as much as he, in a few days.

The sacred words that I have chosen to speak from upon this undesirable occasion, are found written in the Epistle of St. PAUL to the

ROMANS VI. 23.

For the wages of sin is death, but the gift of God is eternal life through Jesus Christ our Lord.

[from *The Sermon*]

Death is called the King of Terrors, and it ought to be the subject of every man and woman's thoughts daily; because it is that unto which they are liable every moment of their lives: and therefore, it cannot be unseasonable to think, speak and hear of it at any time, and especially on this mournful occasion; for we must all come to it, how soon we cannot tell; whether we are prepared or not prepared, ready or not ready, whether death is welcome or not welcome, we must feel the force of it; whether we concern ourselves with death or not, it will concern itself with us. Seeing that this is the case with every one of us, what manner of persons ought we to be in all holy conversation, and godliness; how ought men to exert themselves in preparation for death continually for they know not what a day or an hour may bring forth, with respect to them. But, alas! according to the appearance of mankind in general, death is the least tho't of. They go on from day to day, as if they were to live here forever, as if this was the only life. They contrive, rack their inventions, disturb their rest, and even hazard their lives in all manner of dangers, both by sea and land; yea, they leave no stone unturned that they may live in the world, & at the same time have little or no contrivance to die well: God and their souls are neglected, and heaven & eternal happiness are disregarded; Christ and his religion are despised—yet most of these very men intend to be happy when they come to die, not considering that there must be great preparation in order to die well. Yea there is no [one] so fit to live as those that are fit to die; those that are not fit to die are not fit to live. Life & death are nearly connected; we generally own that it is a great and solemn thing to die. If this be true, then it is a great and solemn thing to live; for as we live, so we shall die. But I say again, how little do mankind realize these things? They are busy about the things of this world as if there was no death before them. . . ./.

The next thing I shall consider, is the actual death of the body, or separation between soul and body. At the cessation of natural life, there is an end of all the enjoyments of this life; there is no more joy nor sorrow; no more hope nor fear, as to the body; no more contrivance and carrying on any business; no more merchandizing and trading; no more farming; no more buying and selling; no more building of any kind, no more contrivance at all to live in the world; no more flatteries nor frowns from the world; no more honour nor reproach; no more praise; no more good report, nor evil report; no more learning of any trades arts or sciences in the world; no more sinful pleasures, they are all at an end; recreations visiting, tavern hunting, music, and dancing, chambering, and carousing, playing at dice and cards, or any game whatsoever; cursing and swearing; and profaning the holy name of God, drunkenness, fighting, debauchery, lying and cheating, in this world must cease forever. Not only so, but they must bid an eternal farewell to all the world: bid farewell to all their beloved sins and pleasures; and the places and possessions, that knew them once, shall know them no more forever. And further, they must bid adieu to all sacred and divine things. They are obliged to leave the bible, and all the ordinances thereof; and to bid farewell to preachers, and all sermons and all christian people, and christian conversation; they must bid a long farewell to sabbaths and seasons, and opportunities to worship; yea, an eternal farewell to all mercy and all hope; an eternal farewell to God the Father, Son and Holy Ghost, and adieu to heaven and all happiness, to saints and all the inhabitants of the upper world. At your leisure please to read the destruction of Babylon; you will find it written in the 18th of the Revelations.

On the other hand, the poor departed soul must take up in lodging in sorrow, wo and misery, in the lake that burns with fire and brimstone, where the worm dieth not, and the fire is not quenched; where a multitude of frightful deformed devils dwell, and the damned ghosts of Adam's race; where darkness, horror and despair reigns, or where hope never comes, and where poor guilty naked souls will be tormented with exquisite torments, even the wrath of the Almighty poured out upon their damned souls; the smoke of their torments ascending up forever and ever; their mouths and nostrils streaming forth with living fire; and hellish groans, cries and shrieks all around them, and merciless devils upbraiding them for their folly and madness, and tormenting them incessantly. And there they must endure the most unsatiable, fruitless desire, and the most overwhelming shame and confusion, and the most horrible fear, and the most doleful sorrow, and the most racking despair. When they call their flaming eyes to heaven, with Dives in torments, they behold an angry GOD, whose eyes are as a flaming fire, and they are struck with ten thousand darts of pain; and the sight of the happiness of the saints above, adds to their pains and aggravates their misery. And when they reflect upon their past folly and madness in neglecting the great salvation in their day, it will pierce them with ten thousand inconceivable torments: it will as it were enkindle their hell afresh; and it will cause them to curse themselves bitterly, and curse the day in which they were born, and curse their parents that were the instruments of their being in the world; yea, they will curse, bitterly curse, and with that very God that gave them their being, to be in the same condition with them in hell torments. This is what is called the second death, and it is the last death, and an eternal death to a guilty fool.

And O eternity, eternity, eternity! Who can measure it? Who can count the years thereof? Arithmetic must fail, the thoughts of men and angels are drowned in it; how shall we describe eternity? To what shall we compare it? Were it possible to employ a fly to carry off this globe by the small particles thereof, and to carry them to such a distance that it would return once in ten thousand years for another particle, and so continue till it has carried off all this globe, and framed them together in some unknown space, till it has made just such a world as this is: after all eternity would remain the same unexhausted duration. Thus must be the unavoidable portion of all impenitent sinners, let them be who they will, great or small, honorable or ignoble, rich or poor, bond or free. Negroes, Indians, English or of what nations soever, all that die in their sins, must go to hell together, for the wages of sin is death. . . .

I have now gone thro' what I proposed from my text. And I shall now make some application of the whole.

First on the criminal in particular and then to the auditory in general.

My poor unhappy brother Moses;

As it was your own desire that I should preach to you this last discourse, so I shall speak plainly to you—You are the bone of my bone, and flesh of my flesh. You are an Indian, a despised creature, but you have despised yourself; yea you have despised God more; you have trodden under foot his authority; you have despised his commands and precepts: and now, as God says, be sure your sins will find you out. And now, poor Moses, your sins have found you out, and they have overtaken you this day; the day of your death is now come; the king of terrors is at hand; you have but a very few moments to breathe in this world.—The just law of man and the holy laws of Jehovah, call aloud for the destruction of your mortal life; God says, "Whoso sheddeth man's blood, by man shall his blood be shed." This is the ancient decree of heaven, and it is to be executed by man; nor have you the least gleam of hope of escape, for the unalterable sentence is past; the terrible day of execution is come; the unwelcome guard is about you; and the fatal instruments of death are now made ready; your coffin and your grave, your last lodging are open ready to receive you.

Alas! poor Moses, now you know by sad, by woful experience, the living truth of our text, that the wages of sin is death. You have been already dead; yea, twice dead: by nature spiritually dead. And since the awful sentence of death has been passed upon you, you have been dead to all the pleasures of this life; or all the pleasures, lawful or unlawful, have been dead to you: And death, which is the wages of sin, is standing even on this side of your grave ready to put a final period to your mortal life; and just beyond the grave, eternal death awaits your poor soul; and devils are ready to drag your miserable soul down to their bottomless den, where everlasting wo and horror reigns; the place is filled with doleful shrieks, howls and groans of the damned. Oh! to what a miserable, forlorn, and wretched condition has your extravagant folly and wickedness bro't you! i.e. if you did in your sins. And O! what manner of repentance ought you to manifest! How ought your heart to bleed for what you have done! How ought you to prostrate your soul before a bleeding God! And under self-condemnation, cry out, Ah Lord, ah Lord, what have I done?—Whatever partiality, injustice and error there may be among the judges of the earth, remember that you have deferred a thousand deaths, and a thousand hells, by reason of your sins, at the hands of a holy God. Should God come out against you in strict justice, alas! what could you say for yourself? For you have been brought up under the bright sun-shine, and plain, and loud sound of the gospel; and you have had a good education; you can read and write well; and God has given you a good natural understanding: and therefore your sins are so much more aggravated.— You have not sinned in such an ignorant manner as others have done; but you have sinned with both your eyes open as it were, under the light even the glorious light of the gospel of the Lord Jesus Christ.—You have sinned against the light of your own conscience, against your knowledge and understanding; you have sinned against the pure and holy laws of God, and the just laws of men; you have sinned against heaven and earth; you have sinned against all the mercies and goodness of God; you have sinned against the whole bible, against the old and new testament; you have sinned against the blood of Christ, which is the blood of the everlasting covenant. O poor Moses, see what you have done! and now repent, repent, I say again repent; see how the blood you shed cries against you, and the Avenger of blood is at your heels. O fly, fly to the blood of the Lamp of God for the pardon of all your aggravated sins.

But let us now turn to a more pleasant theme.—Though you have been a great sinner, a heaven-daring sinner; yet hark and hear the joyful sound from heaven, even from the King of kings, and Lord of lords; that the gift of God is eternal life, through Jesus Christ our Lord.—It is a free gift, and offered to the greatest sinners, and upon their true repentance towards God and faith in the Lord Jesus Christ, they shall be welcome to the life which we have spoken of; it is offered upon free terms. He that hath no money may come; he that hath no righteousness, no goodness, may come; the call is to poor undone sinners; the call is not to the righteous, but sinners calling them to repentance.—Hear the voice of the Sun of the Most High God, Come unto me all ye that labour and are heavy laden, and I will give you rest. This is a call, a gracious call to you poor Moses, under your present burdens and distresses. And Christ alone has a right to call sinners to himself. It would be presumptuous for a mighty angel to call a poor sinner in this manner; and were it possible for you to apply to all God's creatures, they would with one voice tell you, that it was not in them to help you. Go to all the means of grace, they would prove miserable helps without Christ himself. Yea, apply to all the ministers of the gospel in the world, they would all say, that it was not in them, but would only prove as indexes, to point out to you, the Lord Jesus Christ, the only Saviour of sinners of mankind. Yea, go to all the angels in heaven, they would do the same. Yes, go to God the father himself, without Christ, he cou'd not help you, to speak after the manner of men, he would also point to the Lord Jesus Christ, and say this is my beloved son, in whom I am well pleased, hear ye him. Thus you see, poor Moses that there is none in heaven, or on earth, that can help you, but Christ; he alone has power to save, and to give life.— God the eternal Father appointed him, chose him, authorized, and fully commissioned him to save sinners. He came down from heaven into this lower world, and became as one of us, and stood in our room. He was the second Adam. And as God demanded correct obedience of the first Adam; the second fulfil'd it; and as the first sinned, and incurred the wrath and anger of God, the second endured it; he suffered in our room. As he became sin for us, he was a man of sorrows, and acquainted with grief, all our strifes were laid upon him; yea, he was finally condemned, because we were under condemnation; and at last was executed and put to death, for our sins; was lifted up between the heaven and the earth, and was crucified on the accursed tree; his blessed hands and feet were fastened there;—there he died a shameful and ignominious death: there he finished the great work of our redemption: there his heart's blood was shed for our cleansing; there he fully satisfied the divine justice of God, for penitent, believing sinners, though they have been the chief of sinners—O Moses! this is good news to you, in this last day of your life; here is a crucified Saviour at hand for your sins; his blessed hands are outstretched, all in a gore of blood for you. This is the only Saviour, an Almighty Saviour, just such as you stand in infinite and perishing need of. O, poor Moses! hear the dying prayer of a gracious Saviour on the accursed tree—Father forgive them for they know not what they do. This was a prayer for his enemies and murderers; and it is for you, if you will only repent and believe in him. O why will you die eternally, poor Moses, since Christ has died for sinners? Why will you go to hell from beneath a bleeding Saviour as it were? This is the day of your execution, yet it is the accepted time, it is the day of salvation if you will now believe in the Lord Jesus Christ. Must Christ follow you into the prison by his servants, and there intreat you to accept of eternal life, and will you refuse it? and must he follow you even to the gallows, and there beseech you to accept of him, and will you refuse him? Shall he be crucified by your gallows, as it were, and will you regard him not? O, poor Moses, now believe on the Lord Jesus Christ with all your heart, and thou shalt be saved eternally. Come just as you are with all your sins and abominations, with all your filthiness, with all your blood-guiltiness, with all your condemnation, and lay hold as the hope set before you this day. This is the last day of salvation with your soul; you will be beyond the bounds of mercy in a few minutes more. O, what a joyful day would it be if you would now openly believe in and receive the Lord Jesus Christ; it would be the beginning of heavenly days with your poor soul; instead of a melancholy day, it would be a wedding day to your soul: it would cause the very angels in heaven to rejoice, and the saints on earth to be glad; it would cause the angels to come down from the realms above, and wait hovering about your gallows, ready to convey your soul to the heavenly mansions, there to take the possession of eternal glory and happiness, and join the heavenly choirs in singing the songs of Moses and the Lamb: there to set down forever with Abraham, Isaac and Jacob in the kingdom of God's glory; and your shame and guilt shall be forever banished from the place, and all sorrow and fear forever fly away, and tears be wip'd from your face; and there shall you forever admire the astonishing and amazing and infinite mercy of God in Christ Jesus, in pardoning such a monstrous sinner as you have been; there you will claim the highest note of praise, for the riches of free grace in Christ Jesus. But if you will not accept of a Saviour so freely offered to you in this last day of your life, you must make this very day bid farewell to God the Father, Son and Holy Ghost, to heaven and all the saints and angels that are there; and you must bid all the saints in this lower world an eternal farewell, and even the whole world. And so I must leave you in the hands of God; and I must turn to the whole auditory.

Sirs, We may plainly see, from what we have heard, and from the miserable object before us, into what a doleful condition sin has brought mankind, even into a state of death and misery. We are by nature as certainly under sentence of death from God, as this miserable man is, by the just determination of man; and we are all dying creatures, and we are, or ought to be sensible of it; and this is the dreadful fruit of sin. O let us then fly from all appearance of sin; let us fight against it with all our might; let us repent and turn to our God, and believe in the Lord Jesus Christ, that we may live forever; let us all prepare for death for we know not how soon, nor how suddenly we may be called out of the world. . . .

I shall now address myself to the Indians, my brethren and kindred according to the flesh.

My poor kindred,

You see the woful consequences of sin, by freeing this our poor miserable country-man now before us, who is to die this day for his sins and great wickedness. And it was the sin of drunkenness that has brought this destruction and untimely death upon him. There is a dreadful ire denounced from the Almighty against drunkards; and it is this sin, this abominable, this beastly and accursed sin of drunkenness, that has stript us of every desirable comfort in this life; by this we are poor, miserable and wretched; by this sin we have no name of credit in the world among polite nations; for this sin we are de-spised in the world, and it is all right and just, for we despise ourselves more; and if we don't regard ourselves, who will regard us? And it is for our sins and especially for that accursed, that most devilish sin of drunkenness that we suffer every day. For the love of strong drink we spend all that we have, and every thing we can get. By this sin we can't have comfortable houses, nor any thing comfortable in our houses; neither food nor raiment, nor decent utensils. We are obliged to put up with any sort of shelter just to screen us from the severity of the weather; and we go about with very mean, ragged and dirty clothes, almost naked. And we are half-starved, for most of the time obliged to pick up any thing to eat.—And our poor children are suffering every day for want of the accessories of life; they are very often crying for want of food, and we have nothing to give them; and in the cold weather they are shivering and crying, being pinched with cold—All this for the love of strong drink. And this is not all the misery and evil we bring on ourselves in this world; but when we are intoxicated with strong drink, we drown our rational powers, by which we are distinguished from the brutal creation; we un-man ourselves, and bring ourselves not only level with the beasts of the field, but seven degrees beneath them; yea, we bring ourselves level with the devils; I don't know but we make ourselves worse than devils, for I never heard of drunken devils.

My poor kindred, do consider what a dreadful abominable sin drunkenness is. God made us men, and we chose to be beasts and devils; God made us rational creatures, and we chose to be fools. Do consider further, and behold a drunkard, and see how he looks, when he has drowned his reason; how deformed and shameful does he appear? He dis-figures every part of him, both soul and body, which was made after the image of God. He appears with awful deformity, and his whole visage is dis-figured; if he at-tempts to speak he cannot bring out his words distinct, so as to be understood, if he walks he reels and staggers to and for, and tumbles down. And see how he behaves, he is now laughing, and then he is crying; he is singing, and the next minute he is mourning; and is all love to every one, and soon he is raging, and for fighting, and killing all before him, even the nearest and the dearest relations and friends: Yes, nothing is too bad for a drunken man to do. He will do that, which we would not do for the world, in his right mind; he may lie with his own father or daughter as Lot did.

Further, when a person is drunk, he is just good for nothing in the world; he is of no service to himself, to his family, to his neighbors, or his country; and how much more unfit is he to serve God; yet he is just fit for the service of the devil.

Again, a man in drunkenness is in all manner of dangers, he may be killed by his fellow-man, by wild beasts, and tame beasts; he may fall into the fire, into the water, or into a ditch; or he may fall down as he walks along, and break his bones or his neck; and he may cut himself with edge-tools.—Further, if he has any money or any thing valuable, he may lose it all, or may be robb'd, or he may make a foolish bargain, and be cheated out of all he has.

I believe you know the truth of what I have just now said, many of you by sad experience; yet you will go on still in your drunkenness. Though you have been cheated over and over again, and you have lost your substance by drunkenness, yet you will venture to go on in this most destructive sin. O fools when will ye be wise?—We all know the truth of what I have been saying, by what we have seen and heard of drunken deaths. How many have been drowned in our rivers, and how many frozen to death in the winter seasons! yet drunkards go on without fear and consideration: Alas, alas! What will become of all such drunkards? Without doubt they must all go to hell, except they truly repent and turn to God. Drunkenness is so common amongst us, that even our young men, (and what is still more shocking) young women are not ashamed to get drunk. Our young men will get drunk as soon as they will eat when they are hungry.—It is generally esteemed amongst men, more abominable for a woman to be drunk than a man; and yet there is nothing more common amongst us than female drunkards. Women ought to be more modest than men; the holy scriptures recommend modesty to women in particular;—but drunken women have no modesty at all. It is more intolerable for a woman to get drunk. If we consider further, that she is in great danger of falling into the hands of the sons of Belial,[1] or wicked men, and being shamefully treated by them.

And here I cannot but observe, we find in sacred writ, a wo against men who put their bottles to their neighbours mouth to make them drunk, that they may see their nakedness: and no doubt there are such devilish men now in our days, as there were in the days of old.

And to conclude, consider my poor kindred, you that are drunkards, into what a miserable condition you have brought yourselves. There is a dreadful wo thundering against you every day, and the Lord says, That drunkards shall not inherit the kingdom of heaven.

And now let me exhort you all to break off from your drunkenness by a gospel repentance, and believe on the Lord Jesus and you shall be saved. Take warning by this doleful sight before us, and by all the dreadful judgments that have befallen poor drunkards. O let us all reform our lives, and live as becomes dying creatures, in time to come. Let us be persuaded that we are accountable creatures to God, and we must be called to an account in a few days. You that have been careless all your days, now awake to righteousness, and be concerned for your poor never-dying souls. Fight against all sins, and especially the sin that easily besets you, and behave in time to come as becomes rational creatures; and above all things, receive and believe on the Lord Jesus Christ, and you shall have eternal life; and when you come to die, your souls will be received into heaven, there to be with the Lord Jesus in eternal happiness, with all the saints in glory; which, GOD of his infinite mercy great, through Jesus Christ our Lord.

AMEN.

1772/1772

---

[1] Satanic personification of wickedness and godliness; in John Milton's *Paradise Lost,* one of the fallen angels who rebelled against God.

Phillis Wheatley
ca. 1754–1784

A frail but precious child who "had no other covering than a quantity of dirty carpet about her" stood among the "small Negroes" offered for sale in Boston, 1761. Susannah Wheatley, the wife of a prosperous Boston tailor, purchased this young girl "for a trifle" and gave her, as was the custom, a Christian first name. Although her roots are obscure, Phillis Wheatley was judged "from the circumstance of shedding her front teeth" to be approximately seven years of age at the time of her sale, and more certainly to be the kidnap victim of slave traders who used northern cities to dispose of those Africans who remained after the "strong and hearty" were sold at more lucrative southern markets.

Phillis Wheatley quickly revealed "uncommon intelligence" and within sixteen months at the Wheatley house had mastered English, astronomy, geography, and history, as well as the most knotty passages from the Scriptures. The Wheatley family encouraged Phillis's formidable talents, tutored her in classical languages and literatures, exempted her from the usual domestic labors, removed her from the company of other African Americans, and gradually turned her into a curiosity in New England's intellectual circles. A brilliant conversationalist, she frequently accompanied her owners on their social rounds of Boston but invariably declined "the seat offered her at their board, and, requesting that a sidetable might be laid for her, dined modestly apart from the rest of the company." Given such circumstances, Phillis Wheatley spent most of her life isolated from both African Americans and whites, enthralled only by the companionship of British poetry, most notably Alexander Pope's heroic couplets.

Writing "originally for the Amusement of the Author," she filled all her leisure moments with poetry, published her first verse at thirteen, and soon won the praise of such prominent figures as Thomas Hutchinson, the last colonial governor of Massachusetts. Fame followed the publication in 1770 of her widely reprinted broadside poem on the death of "the celebrated Divine, and eminent Servant of Jesus Christ, the late Reverend, and Pious George Whitefield," the remarkably popular preacher-missionary.

In her nineteenth year, Phillis Wheatley crossed the Atlantic as a celebrated writer bound for London and a meeting with the Countess of Huntingdon, Whitefield's patron. This "sooty prodigy" from Boston soon became the "Sable Muse" of London. Voltaire acclaimed her, Franklin visited her, and the Lord Mayor of London and the Earl of Dartmouth honored her with special editions of *Paradise Lost* and Smollett's translation of *Don Quixote*. But in the midst of plans to present her to King George III, Phillis had to return to America to care for her sickly mistress. When she left London, Phillis Wheatley carried with her copies of her recently printed *Poems on Various Subjects, Religious and Moral* (1773), the first published volume by an African American. The circulation of a book of poems by a nineteen-year-old slave was regarded as so unusual that Wheatley's work, dedicated to the Countess of Huntingdon, had to be prefaced by the testimony of eighteen prestigious Bostonians, certifying the poems' authenticity. As Richard Wright, the twentieth-century African

American novelist, reminds us, "Before the webs of slavery had so tightened as to snare nearly all Negroes in our land, one was freed by accident to give in clear, bell-like limpid cadence the hope of freedom in the New World."

At the onset of the American Revolution, Phillis fled with the Wheatley family to Providence, where she addressed a letter and poem "To His Excellency General Washington." Responding four months later, Washington hailed "this new instance" of Wheatley's "genius" and, at the risk of "imputation of vanity," sent the poem to Thomas Paine to be published in his *Pennsylvania Magazine*.

In the years following, Phillis Wheatley gained her freedom upon the death of the Wheatleys, married a free African American, John Peters, and bore three children, all of whom died in childhood. Destitute, in failing health, and suffering from the unaccustomed burdens of menial work at "a common negro boarding-house," Wheatley tried to reverse her misfortune by advertising a three-hundred-page volume of "Poems & Letters on various subjects, dedicated to the Right Hon. Benjamin Franklin Esq." For want of subscribers, the project never appeared, and Phillis Wheatley, once the best-known colonial poet in England, died in obscurity in 1784.

Further Reading:

M. M. Odell, *Memoir*, 1834.
W. D. Jordon, *White over Black: American Attitude Toward the Negro, 1550–1812*, 1968.
S. Graham, *The Story of Phillis Wheatley*, 1969.
M. A. Richmond, *Bid the Vassal Soar*, 1974.
W. Robinson, *Phillis Wheatley*, 1975.
S. E. Ogude, *Genius in Bondage: A Study of the Origins of African Literature in English*, 1983.

W. H. Robinson, *Phillis Wheatley and Her Writings*, 1984.
A. T. McCluskey, ed., *Women of Color: Perspectives on Feminism and Identity*, 1985.
M. A. Richmond, *Phillis Wheatley*, 1988.

Text:

The Poems of Phillis Wheatley, ed. J. D. Mason, 1966.

On the Death of the Rev. Mr. George Whitefield, 1770*

Hail, happy saint, on thine immortal throne,
Possest of glory, life, and bliss unknown;
We hear no more the music of thy tongue,
Thy wonted auditories cease to throng.
Thy sermons in unequall'd accents flow'd,   5
And ev'ry bosom with devotion glow'd;
Thou didst in strains of eloquence refin'd
Inflame the heart, and captivate the mind.

* Whitefield (1714–1770), an English disciple of John Wesley, was the most popular revivalist of the eighteenth century. Whitefield, who frequently visited the United States, died in Massachusetts. This, Wheatley's first published poem, brought her international acclaim.

Unhappy we the setting sun deplore,
So glorious once, but ah! it shines no more.   10

Behold the prophet in his tow'ring flight!
He leaves the earth for heav'n's unmeasur'd height,
And worlds unknown receive him from our sight.
There *Whitefield* wings with rapid course his way,
And sails to *Zion*[1] through vast seas of day.   15
Thy pray'rs, great saint, and thine incessant cries
Have pierc'd the bosom of thy native skies.
Thou moon hast seen, and all the stars of light,
How he has wrestled with his God by night.
He pray'd that grace in ev'ry heart might dwell,   20
He long'd to see *America* excel;
He charg'd its youth that ev'ry grace divine
Should with full lustre in their conduct shine;
That Saviour, which his soul did first receive,
The greatest gift that ev'n a God can give,   25
He freely offer'd to the num'rous throng,
That on his lips with list'ning pleasure hung.

"Take him, ye wretched, for your only good,
"Take him ye starving sinners, for your good;
"Ye thirsty, come to this life-giving stream,   30
"Ye preachers, take him for your joyful theme;
"Take him my dear *Americans,* he said,
"Be your complaints on his kind bosom laid:
"Take him, ye *Africans,* he longs for you,
"*Impartial Saviour* is his title due: 35
"Wash'd in the fountain of redeeming blood,
"You shall be sons, and kings, and priests to God."

"Great *Countess,*[2] we *Americans* revere
Thy name, and mingle in thy grief sincere;
New England deeply feels, the *Orphans* mourn,   40
Their more than father will no more return.

But, though arrested by the hand of death,
Whitefield no more exerts his lab'ring breath,
Yet let us view him in th' eternal skies,
Let ev'ry heart to this bright vision rise;   45
While the tomb safe retains its sacred trust,
Till life divine re-animates his dust.
1770/1773

---

[1] God's heavenly city.
[2] Selina Shirley Hastings (1707–1791), whom
Phillis Wheatley visited in 1773, was George

Whitefield's patron and an ardent member
of the Methodist church.

On Being Brought from Africa to America

'Twas mercy brought me from my *Pagan* land,
Taught my benighted soul to understand
That there's a God, that there's a *Saviour* too:
Once I redemption neither sought nor knew.
Some view our sable race with scornful eye,   5
"Their colour is a diabolic die."
Remember, *Christians*, *Negroes*, black as *Cain*,[1]
May be refin'd, and join th' angelic train.
1773/1773

To S. M. a Young African Painter, on Seeing His Works*

To show the lab'ring bosom's deep intent,
And thought in living characters to paint,
When first thy pencil did those beauties give,
And breathing figures learnt from thee to live,
How did those prospects give my soul delight,   5
A new creation rushing on my sight?
Still, wond'rous youth! each noble path pursue,
On deathless glories fix thine ardent view:
Still may the painter's and the poet's fire
To aid thy pencil, and thy verse conspire!   10
And may the charms of each seraphic theme
Conduct thy footsteps to immortal fame!
High to the blissful wonders of the skies
Elate thy soul, and raise thy wishful eyes.
Thrice happy, when exalted to survey   15
That splendid city, crown'd with endless day,
Whose twice six gates[1] on radiant hinges ring:
Celestial *Salem*[2] blooms in endless spring.

---

[1] Cain slew his brother, Abel, and for doing so was marked by God (Genesis 4:1–15). This mark is sometimes interpreted as the origin of the Negro.

* Probably Scipio Moorhead, a Boston slave of the Reverend John Moorhead.

[1] Revelation 21:12 represents the walls of heavenly Jerusalem by twelve gates.
[2] Jerusalem (in heaven).

Calm and serene thy moments glide along,
And may the muse inspire each future song!   20
Still, with the sweets of contemplation bless'd,
May peace with balmy wings your soul invest!
But when these shades of time are chas'd away,
And darkness ends in everlasting day,
On what seraphic pinions shall we move,   25
And view the landscapes in the realms above?
There shall thy tongue in heav'nly murmurs flow,
And there my muse with heav'nly transport glow:
No more to tell of *Damon's*[3] tender sighs,
Or rising radiance of *Aurora's*[4] eyes,   30
For nobler themes demand a nobler strain,
And purer language on th' ethereal plain.
Cease, gentle muse! the solemn gloom of night
Now seals the fair creation from my sight.
1773

To His Excellency General Washington*

SIR,
I Have taken the freedom to address your Excellency in the enclosed poem, and entreat
your acceptance, though I am not insensible of its inaccuracies. Your being appointed
by the Grand Continental Congress to be Generalissimo of the armies of North America, together with the fame of your virtues, excite sensations not easy to suppress. Your
generosity, therefore, I presume, will pardon the attempt. Wishing your Excellency all
possible success in the great cause you are so generously engaged in. I am,
                    Your Excellency's most obedient humble servant,
                              PHILLIS WHEATLEY.

Providence, Oct. 26, 1775.
His Excellency Gen. Washington.

Celestial choir!
enthron'd in
realms of light,
Columbia's[1] scenes of glorious toils I write.

---

[3] Damon: in classical mythology, a shepherd
singer who pledged his life for his condemned friend Pythias.
[4] Aurora: goddess of the dawn in Roman myth.
* Washington responded to Wheatley, prais-

ing her poetical elegance and inviting her to
visit him in Cambridge, Massachusetts.
[1] American poets had been referring to America as Columbia since 1761.

While freedom's cause her anxious breast alarms,
She flashes dreadful in refulgent arms.
See mother earth her offspring's fate bemoan,   5
And nations gaze at scenes before unknown!
See the bright beams of heaven's revolving light
Involved in sorrows and the veil of night!
　　The goddess comes, she moves divinely fair,
Olive and laurel binds her golden hair: 10
Wherever shines this native of the skies,
Unnumber'd charms and recent graces rise.
　　Muse! bow propitious while my pen relates
How pour her armies through a thousand gates,
As when Eolus[2] heaven's fair face deforms,   15
Enwrapp'd in tempest and a night of storms;
Astonish'd ocean feels the wild uproar,
The refluent surges beat the sounding shore;
Or thick as leaves in Autumn's golden reign,
Such, and so many, moves the warrior's train.   20
In bright array they seek the work of war,
Where high unfurl'd the ensign waves in air.
Shall I to Washington their praise recite?
Enough thou know'st them in the fields of fight.
Thee, first in peace and honours,—we demand   25
The grace and glory of thy martial band.
Fam'd for thy valour, for thy virtues more,
Hear every tongue thy guardian aid implore!
　　One century scarce perform'd its destined round,
When Gallic powers Columbia's fury found;[3]   30
And so may you, whoever dares disgrace
The land of freedom's heaven-defended race!
Fix'd are the eyes of nations on the scales,
For in their hopes Columbia's arm prevails.
Anon Britannia droops the pensive head,   35
While round increase the rising hills of dead.
Ah! cruel blindness to Columbia's state!
Lament thy thirst of boundless power too late.
　　Proceed, great chief, with virtue on thy side,
Thy ev'ry action let the goddess guide.   40
A crown, a mansion, and a throne that shine,
With gold unfading, WASHINGTON! be thine.
1775/1776

---

[2] In Roman myth Aeolus is god of the winds.
[3] In the French & Indian Wars, which continued for nearly fifty years and which are said
to have begun with King William's War
(1689–1697) and Queen Anne's War
(1702–1703).

RELATED VOICES

Notes on the State of Virginia, 1787

[On Phillis Wheatley]

. . . But never yet could I find that a black had uttered a thought above the level of plain narration; never see even an elementary trait of painting or sculpture. In music they are more generally gifted than the whites with accurate ears for tune and time, and they have been found capable of imagining a small catch.[1] Whether they will be equal to the composition of a more extensive run of melody, or of complicated harmony, is yet to be proved. Misery is often the parent of the most affecting touches in poetry. Among the blacks is misery enough, God knows, but no poetry. Love is the peculiar oestrum [desire] of the poet. Their love is ardent, but it kindles the senses only, not the imagination. Religion indeed has produced a Phyllis Whately [Phillis Wheatley]; but it could not produce a poet. The compositions published under her name are below the dignity of criticism.

Thomas Jefferson, from Writings

---

[1] The instrument proper to them is the Banjar, which they brought hither from Africa, and which is the original of the guitar, its chords being precisely the four lower chords of the guitar.

Washington Allston
The Poor Author and the Rich Bookseller
oil on canvas, 1811
(Museum of Fine Arts, Boston
Bequest of Charles Sprague Sargent, 1927)

The Literature of the
New Republic
1776–1836

The Declaration of Independence proclaimed the political freedom of the American colonies and launched their self-conscious quest for a national identity. Americans quickly found themselves grappling with many momentous issues, not the least of them being, to borrow the title of Michel-Guillaume Jean de Crèvecoeur's celebrated essay, "What is an American?" Along with that overarching question came several other related issues that were debated for the next century: Did America possess a unique, distinctive culture? Was there such a thing as an American language? Did an authentic American literature exist? That such issues were debated is not at all surprising given the colonies' newly won independence from England, but they even continued to be public concerns for many decades after the new nation had been founded.

The founding of the American republic hardly seemed auspicious in literary terms. Most literary historians have tended to dismiss the period between 1776 and 1836, as one put it, "as a sort of blank space between the Revolution and the mature work of Irving, Bryant and Cooper." Another judged the writers of the new republic "blind sailors navigating the Dead Sea of Federalist Pessimism." Yet between 1776 and 1836, American writers expressed the essential features of a distinctive national literature: for the first time, they consciously, though anxiously, asserted their autonomy, sought workable alternatives to servile imitation of

English neoclassical models, and abandoned the traditional literary expressions of Enlightenment social consciousness in favor of greater individuality in more spontaneous forms commensurate with the powerful presence of the American landscape. This period also saw produced the early writings of such notable American literary figures as Edgar Allen Poe, Nathaniel Hawthorne, and Ralph Waldo Emerson, as well as the major works of Washington Irving, James Fenimore Cooper, and William Cullen Bryant.

More important, however, American writers in the years between 1776 and 1836 articulated the literary values that would define much of subsequent American literary history—indigenous values that would find their fullest expression in the years after 1836. The literature of the new republic constitutes this nation's first comprehensive attempt to establish an independent literary identity. Controversy, anxiety, false starts, numerous obstacles, and impressive accomplishments characterize this quest.

The Literature of Persuasion

When the American colonists' grievances against British rule erupted into the Revolutionary War, the most widely circulated forms of colonial literature were travel narratives, religious journals, and political tracts, as well as poetry and occasional essays highly derivative in their structures and themes from British models. To be sure, a growing number of young writers—including Philip Freneau, Hugh Henry Brackenridge, Noah Webster, Joel Barlow, Timothy Dwight, and John Trumbull—sought to express what Freneau and Brackenridge called, in their 1771 Princeton University commencement ode, "the Rising Glory of America." Yet these same writers—and scores of less celebrated figures—postponed their literary ambitions and put their pens in the service of securing political independence. As the notable literary historian Moses Coit Tyler explained, the Revolutionary War "drove out the tranquil forms of literature and encouraged more aggressive and partisan literary efforts."

Writers seemed to be everywhere, aggressively addressing the pressing issues of the time. In no other period of American literary history would writers so passionately involve themselves with so strong a sense of public responsibility in such crucial public debates. As Thomas Paine noted in *The American Crisis*, writers had the power "to make a world happy—to teach mankind the art of being so—to exhibit, on the theater of the universe, a character hitherto unknown—and to have, as it were, a new creation entrusted to our hands." And with that power came a sense of moral leadership. The obligation of American writers, Joel Barlow argued, was to "excite emulation through the kingdoms of the earth, and meliorate the condition of the human race." With such noble goals, American writers posted their patriotic ballads and broadsides in the streets and recited or sang them in local taverns and meeting halls. Their satires on the political controversies and caricatures of the leading personalities on both sides of the Atlantic contended for the shrinking space in newspapers whose pulp and rag content had increasingly been diverted to support the escalating war.

The popular literature of the American Revolution consisted principally of first-hand narratives of legendary campaigns, such as a raw recruit's heroic life at the end of a gun barrel or in a prisoner-of-war camp. Modeled to a large extent on the Indian captivity narratives popular in the late seventeenth and early eighteenth centuries, this campaign literature, often borrowing battle accounts, invariably substituted patriotic lessons for the moral conclusions of their predecessors.

The most pervasive and influential form of writing during the Revolutionary period was the political pamphlet, with the redoubtable Thomas Paine its master. Political pamphlets and essays were so widely distributed that American writing immediately before, during, and after the war might well be called "the literature of persuasion." Pamphlets, however, gradually yielded to the increasing number of newspapers and magazines that appeared at the turn of the century, only to resurface in the mid-nineteenth century during the heated public debate over slavery and secession.

Making Thirteen Clocks Tick Together

By and large, for both rich and poor, to live in the newly formed United States was to live in an economically and culturally "underdeveloped" country, whose standards of living and cultural taste depended almost exclusively on British goods and styles—whether in business, clothing, household furnishings, painting, architecture, periodicals, or heroic couplets. Independently minded Americans repeatedly complained about the new nation's economic and cultural subservience. De Crèvecoeur, the French aristocrat successfully transplanted to the American frontier, complained about the number of shops stocked with British products and calculated that at least "one fifth of all our labors every year is laid out in English commodities." Thomas Jefferson, even more bitterly, regarded his fellow Virginia planters as little more than "a species of property annexed to certain mercantile houses in London." In economic terms, the original thirteen states remained for many years more closely tied to England than to each other. The lure of materialism frequently tested America's commitment to idealistic principles. In matters of goods and services, most Americans subscribed, however reluctantly, to the notion that British is better. Socially, the new nation could hardly be described as a homogeneous democracy replete with egalitarian impulses. In the aftermath of America's Declaration of Independence and its defeat of the British in the Revolutionary War, many former colonists became extremely concerned about whether the newly formed confederation of thirteen states could ever properly be called a nation, since state allegiances seemed more important in determining self-identity than the notion of being an "American."

A slowly emerging economic and social hierarchy was increasingly evident—in classes ranging from quasi-aristocratic landholders to slaves and indentured servants, and from artisans and merchants boosting profits in coastal commercial centers to resolutely self-sufficient men and women pushing the wilderness farther southward and westward. Sectional rivalries and prejudices also abounded. In 1813 John Adams wrote disconsolately to a friend, "How shall we cure that distemper of State vanity?"

No religion or national system of education unified the citizenry. The variety of religious affiliations (including, among other sects, Catholics, Huguenots, Unitarians, Presbyterians, and Lutherans) only increased factionalism among Americans. Opposing political tendencies, regional interests, cultural diversity, and broad-based philosophical and religious tensions characterized much of the public life in the new nation. Nowhere were these traits more amply evident than in the debate over the function and powers of a central government.

In 1787 the thirteen states, some quite reluctantly, sent delegates to take up the matter of a constitution, a document that would define the fundamental principles of the new nation, determine the powers and duties of the government, guarantee certain rights to the people, and codify the laws of the land. Draft in hand, these representatives returned home to weigh public support for ratification. Many Americans could see no point in abandoning the Articles of Confederation—which had entrusted nearly total sovereignty to the states and claimed no political authority over individuals. An equally large number of Americans, having fought to free themselves from the restraints of one powerful central authority, were wary of establishing another of their own.

To promote the Constitution in New York and in other reluctant states, Alexander Hamilton of New York, James Madison of Virginia, and John Jay of New York published a series of eighty-five letters in a New York newspaper in 1787 and 1788 under the collective pseudonym "Publius." These letters, given the title *The Federalist* when they were first collected in a volume in 1788, endorsed the principle of an indivisible union of states coordinated by a strong central government. *The Federalist* served as a tough-minded argument that gave meaning and justification to the Constitution and helped ensure its adoption. Yet, in another sense, *The Federalist* also contributed significantly to developing a national literature. In its discussion of the distinctions between "federal" and "national" and its predisposition to expect the worst and demand the best from human nature, *The Federalist* also helped define the polarities of the American character, establishing themes and a tone central to much of later American literature. As an expression of this crucial debate over whether a strong central government was at once indispensable to the new nation's survival as well as compatible with individual liberty, *The Federalist* constitutes the United States' first classic literary text.

Cultivating New Meanings

The debate over the nature and extent of a federal government's powers reverberated in virtually every aspect of American culture. One important example can be found in the concerted effort, led by the young Noah Webster, to purify and standardize the American language. Webster envisioned an America "peopled with a hundred millions of men, *all speaking the same language.*" His *Dissertations on the English Language* (1789) attempted to establish a uniform set of principles "for the rules of pronunciation in our language," just as his speller had done so much to regularize American orthography. Webster hoped, in effect, to do for the English language what the Puritan experiment in the New World had attempted to do for religion—to set an American example for purifying what had become corrupt in Europe.

Webster's interest in linguistic reform was decidedly conservative. "In the few instances in which I write words a little differently from the present usage," he explained, "I do *not* innovate, but *reject innovation.* When I write *fether, lether, and mold,* I do nothing more than reduce the words to their original orthography, no other being used in our earliest English books." Searching for what he called a "primitive etymological orthography" that would "call back the language to the purity of former times," Webster envisioned a language spoken and written in America that would set the standard for enlightened discourse at home and abroad.

When Webster published his *American Dictionary of the English Language* in 1828, he had not fundamentally changed his position on the purity of the American language, but he had softened it considerably. He recognized that differences between American and British English were traceable less to vocal variations than to basic differences in the respective institutions and customs of each nation. (In addition, as H. L. Mencken later noted in his classic three-volume study *The American Language* (1919; 1974), more "Americanisms" (a word coined by John Witherspoon in 1781) entered the language between the American Revolution and 1800 than at any other time before the mid-nineteenth-century rush to the West.) In drawing on numerous examples from American writers for his definitions, Webster apparently had become satisfied with explaining such distinctions with the skill of a lexicographer rather than continuing to call for reforms in spelling and usage.

Yet the issues Webster had raised about orthography would persist in American literature into the twentieth century, stretching well beyond his search for etymological purity to Walt Whitman's unusual spellings and usages, as well as to Emily Dickinson's pronunciation (implied by her rhyme schemes) and Ezra Pound's abbreviations ("sd" and "thro," for example). In a curious way, the efforts of these three writers proved consistent with Webster's original purpose: to make words look more like they were spoken, to emphasize, in effect, the distinctive nature of an American literary voice.

The Quest for Literary Independence

The new nation's reliance on the English language and a lingering attraction to the cultural tradition deflated the initial and widespread expectation among Americans that their political freedom would result in an equally independent literary and cultural identity. Several other factors heightened the new nation's collective anxiety about its cultural identity both in the present and in the future. One highly controversial proposition, promoted by the French naturalist and theologian Georges Louis Le Clerc de Buffon (1707–1788), asserted that the human race had degenerated in the Western Hemisphere, an assertion rebuked by Thomas Jefferson in his *Notes on the State of Virginia* (1785) and attacked in a March 1787 editorial in *American Museum* magazine. The United States, the editors advised, ought "to explode the European creed, that we are infantile in our acquisitions, and savage in our manners, because we are inhabitants of a new world, lately occupied by a race of savages." More widespread—and accurate—was the conviction among many American writers that they could not establish an indigenous identity until they had developed both the language and the intellectual structures adequate to express the distinctive qualities of American experience.

Much of the nation's creative energy in its earliest years focused on securing economic and political stability. John Quincy Adams spoke for the vast majority when he noted how difficult it was "to be a man of business and a man of rime." More important, the United States lacked an audience sizable and interested enough to support writers and artists. Philip Freneau advised the would-be writer to "graft his authorship upon some other calling." Few writers in the early years of the new republic had the financial resources to devote themselves full-time to cultivating their art. Henry Wadsworth Longfellow's father urged his son to explore another calling because "there is not wealth and munificence enough in this country to afford sufficient encouragement and patronage to merely literary men." The sense of public responsibility and moral leadership that American writers had so vigorously exercised during the earliest years of the new nation was gradually yielding in the early decades of the nineteenth century to a sense of isolation, if not alienation. In this respect, the period between 1776 and 1836 reflects a growing anti-intellectual strain in American society that ever since has set writers apart from their fellow citizens.

Cultural, political, and legal obstacles discouraged all but the most resolute writers. Many cultivated citizens feared that the principles of democracy would reduce cultural standards to the least common denominator, thereby producing, in the reigning logic of the time, a mediocre literary tradition. About this concern the influential magazine *Boston Anthology* bellowed in an 1807 editorial: "The spirit of democracy blasts everything beautiful in nature and corrodes everything in art." The lack of an adequate copyright law also discouraged native literary talent. Without enforceable protection for writers, American printers found it far easier to reprint, at far greater profit, already successful British books than to publish—at far greater risk—the works of American authors.

With American bookstores filled with English and continental models well into the second decade of the nineteenth century, American writers in the new republic continued to feel the pressure to imitate the prevailing forms of literary expression rather than to invent new ones to accommodate what was gradually being recognized as the unrelenting originality of American experience. The most notable writers during the first decades of the new nation—including Philip Freneau, Hugh Henry Brackenridge, Noah Webster, and especially Joel Barlow, Timothy Dwight, and John Trumbull, who came to be known as the "Connecticut Wits"—adapted the major features of imported neoclassical forms to American subjects. In their shared interest in preserving literary decorum and restraint, working within traditional literary forms, especially those with epic and satiric purposes, and associating America with classical Greece and Rome, these writers strove to demonstrate that America was capable of inspiring its own versions of literary grandeur.

The predominance of neoclassical elements in the literature of the new republic also reflects both a lingering sense of American cultural inferiority among these writers and a concern that cultural anarchy might be a legacy of the American Revolution. Their reverence for tradition, their interest in learned rather than spontaneous forms of literary expression, and their readiness to conform artistically suggest that writers were quite willing—and prepared—to legislate national standards for both the new nation's political and literary experiences. They were eager advocates of an orderly search for national cultural identity and would willingly have assumed the role of moral monitors of the new nation's progress.

Westward the Course of Empire

By any standard, the applied, creative, and imaginative arts in the early years of the new republic would have struck most cultivated Europeans as impoverished. From the English point of view, the United States could boast of no Addison and Steele; no Pope, Swift, Richardson, Johnson, Burke, or Hume; no Byron, Keats, or Shelley, who were the admired young writers of that time. Writing in his later years, Benjamin Franklin wondered why a "petty island" like England "should enjoy in every Neighbourhood, more sensible, virtuous, and elegant Minds, than we can collect in ranging one hundred Leagues in our vast Forests." Yet Franklin at least had patriotic convention on his side when he added: "But, 'tis said, the Arts delight to travel Westward." At the center of American cultural development in the first few decades following the Revolution was a powerful, optimistic idea: the course of empire was inexorably moving westward.

Franklin did not dwell on the fact, however, that as the arts headed westward, a large percentage of American artistic and professional talent—painters, musicians, physicians, lawyers, and ministers—headed eastward to England and the continent for study and training. The two finest painters of the period, John Singleton Copley (1738–1815) and Benjamin West (1738–1820), both traveled from colonial America to England to secure their professional reputations.

Professional prospects seemed as dim for drama, playwrights, and actors in post-Revolutionary America. The first play written by an American and acted by a professional American company, Thomas Godfrey's *Prince of Parthia*, was not staged until 1767. Long afterward, New England still continued to legislate against plays as "dangerous to the soul" and as a "great and unnecessary" expense, a diversion that discouraged industry and frugality, and an entertainment which increased "immorality, impiety, and a contempt for religion." Actors discovered more receptive audiences in the southern states, where a few resident companies managed to earn a modest living in the more densely populated cities.

What little American drama there was in the new nation consisted primarily of adaptations of European models reworked to satisfy American thematic interests. Royall Tyler's *The Contrast* (1787) is the best-known American play of this period. Its focus on the distinctions between native dignity and foreign affectation earned it a special place in the limited repertoire of American theater companies. Later, such writers as William Dunlap (1766–1839) and John Howard Payne (1791–1852) dramatized historical subjects and nationalistic sentiments to small but appreciative audiences, Dunlap in *André* (1798) and Payne in *Brutus* (1818). In the early decades of the new republic, the theater faced popular indifference and lacked institutional support.

Printing and the Reading Public

As a major industrial art, printing served as one of the clearest indications of the cultural lag that characterized the relationship of American and British arts, crafts, and trades into the early years of the nineteenth century. In 1776 well over one hundred printing presses were at work throughout the new nation. Yet a printing press in itself represented the merest beginning of a trade. It was in the best interests of British suppliers to continue the colonial policy of keeping American printers dependent on run-down, secondhand equipment and materials. Type, always difficult to obtain, remained prohibitively expensive after the Revolutionary War. Better quality paper and ink had never been available to the American colonists in sufficient amounts. Naturally, the Revolution did little to change that fact. The inadequacies of American printing were widely known and lamented. In 1779 the elderly Benjamin Franklin, serving as the American representative at the French court, wryly observed when sent a batch of Boston newspapers that the paper and typography were of such poor quality that "if you should ever have any secrets that you should wish to be well kept, get them printed in these papers."

In the first several decades following the Revolution, newspapers continued as the staple of the American printing trade. As such, their cultural content continued to reflect the economic and literary dependencies of their printer-publishers. The contents of most American newspapers left little doubt that a relatively small, affluent class of readers determined the papers' interests, style, tone, and subscription base.

Since newspapers provided one of the major outlets for the new republic's literary efforts, the space accorded literature in those pages was one reliable measure of their importance to the general public in the new nation. Newspapers contained a fair measure of poetry, a few occasional essays, and a scattering of literary reviews and notices. Yet newspaper columns in the new republic featured more profitable, less intellectually demanding enterprises: a scattering of social announcements, a generous sampling of political reports from local and congressional sources as well as foreign dispatches, a wealth of advertisements and lists of cargo arrivals, along with editorial commentary and thinly disguised satire. From their odes to their ads, most newspapers in the new republic were addressed to social groupings roughly designated in those presociology days as "the better sort" (the gentry and the upper ranks of professional classes) and "the middle sort" (independent farmers, artisans, schoolteachers, and the lower ranks of the professions). "The meaner sort" (laborers, seamen, and indentured servants), those whom Alexander Hamilton called "the great beast," did not find a place in the network of public communications until the introduction of the so-called "Penny Press" in the late 1820s and early 1830s.

After the Revolutionary War, more papers gradually began to adopt the principle advocated by Massachusetts printer Isaiah Thomas—that journalism ought to be "popular" and written in a style that would express "common sense in common language." Thomas promoted his own *Massachusetts Spy* (founded in 1770) as one that could be read by "mechanics and other classes of people who had not much time to spare from business." Thomas's confidence that newspapers could reach "the meaner sort" had been bolstered by an upward trend in reading and writing skills that moved closer to nearly universal literacy among American white males by the beginning of the nineteenth century. In New England the legacy of Calvinism, the policy of compulsory education, and the ideology of self-improvement resulted in the highest rate of literacy in the new republic. In the middle and southern colonies, the relatively high literacy rate among European immigrants counterbalanced the lower percentage of literate native white males and helped extend reading and writing skills beyond only the wealthy and socially prominent.

The market for American newspapers developed rapidly in the early decades of the new republic. In 1785 approximately seventy-five newspapers were being printed in the United States. Five years later, that number had climbed to nearly one hundred. By 1820 technical improvements and the beginnings of industrialization had helped increase the total to 508. By 1830, such developments as steam and cylinder presses helped to more than double that number. Nearly every town in America—and several fairly remote frontier settlements—could boast of its own printing press.

But the ever-increasing number of newspapers in print was offset by the limited circulation of each. Even taking into account the rather high reader-per-copy ratio (estimated in the early years of the new nation to be well over twenty), the reading public for newspapers still represented in post-Revolutionary America a surprisingly small portion of the total reading public. The new nation was demonstrating a consistent cultural feature of modern societies: populations grow literate faster than they develop the habit of reading.

In many respects, the book market presented even greater problems for American printers than did newspaper circulations. Given the technical difficulties and production costs they continued to face after the Revolution, American printers could only occasionally afford to tie up their presses with books, and even then the quality of their products could hardly compete with the handsome editions routinely manufactured in England. But whether domestic or imported, books remained too expensive for most Americans' modest standard of living. A single volume of any writer's work would have cost an American laborer a sizable portion of a week's wages. Even for the fairly affluent, books were regarded as luxuries. With the introduction of such mechanical improvements as the Columbia iron press in 1807 and other more efficient printing methods, cheaper printed matter eventually found its way into the homes of the poor, but even then, as James Fenimore Cooper observed, such reading material usually consisted of little more than "a fragment of a Bible, *Pilgrim's Progress,* and an almanac that was four years old."

Regardless of their size and owner's profession, personal libraries in the first few decades following the Revolution were still dominated by the Puritan legacy of what Cotton Mather had called "devout and useful Books." The Bible, *Pilgrim's Progress, The Book of Common Prayer,* sermons, theological tracts, and such didactic staples as *The Practice of Piety* and *The Whole Duty of Man* lined many of the shelves in the growing number of bookshops squeezed into the bustling commercial districts of coastal cities. While Americans still seemed absorbed in reflection about their own spiritual welfare, they also seemed increasingly interested in broadening their experiences and cultivating the vast amount of untitled land that stretched farther and farther westward.

Frontiers of Literature

When Thomas Jefferson's purchase of the Louisiana Territory in 1803 doubled the area of the United States and opened the prospect of expansion to the Pacific, countless Americans were drawn by the large stretches of land available to anyone who wanted them. Not everyone, of course, could afford to develop this land or even, in some areas, to get to it; but many of those who could, did so.

With so much of its territory unsettled, and with a population so rich in individual and collective spontaneity, vision, and energy, the United States promised to be, to use the literary historian Perry Miller's phrase, "nature's nation." Space was rapidly replacing time as the single most crucial factor in American life, and it would soon dominate American literature as well. The land itself had become the new nation's most precious commodity and its greatest source for literary subjects and locations. The land, and the sense of "place" it engendered, had come to serve as the locus for American vision and aspiration.

Scores of early-nineteenth-century pioneer diaries and journals recorded the dramatic nature of unprecedented experiences along the ever-expanding southern and western frontiers. Gradually, however, as settlers transformed freshly cut clearings into towns, Americans with more literary aspirations began to turn out with increasing frequency a newly appropriate subject for literature—personal accounts of life west of the Alleghenies. Timothy Flint's renditions of backwoods America helped chart what remains the most legendary part of our national consciousness and encouraged even more ambitious and extravagant literary efforts. More widely publicized literary excursions, including those of Washington Irving and James Fenimore Cooper, drew even greater attention to the American frontier, especially among readers in coastal cities. Broadening the nation's literary horizon had become a fact of cultural life in the new republic.

As new populations cleared more land and pushed the frontier farther southward and westward, the settlers' interest in the literature of the frontier remained secondary to their need for practical books. Guides to virtually every aspect of frontier life began to compete vigorously with political and religious titles. Backwoods peddlers had to create more places among their assorted wares for copies of various guides to farming and everyday life along the frontier. As white settlers pushed back the wilderness and displaced greater numbers of Native Americans, books about Indians also appeared with greater frequency, with such self-explanatory titles as *The American Savage: How He May Be Tamed by the Weapons of Civilization.* Yet at the same time that white settlers drove more and more Native Americans from their land and appropriated their knowledge of agriculture and medicine, the broader American reading public continued to be fascinated with what were known as captivity narratives—harrowing accounts of the narrator's capture, imprisonment, torture, and inevitable escape from Indian captors. Eventually, these narratives gave way to the equally heroic exploits of such legendary frontier figures as Daniel Boone and Davy Crockett. The popularity of these frontier stories gave rise to what became the even more celebrated tradition of the tall tale and local-color fiction in late-nineteenth-century American literature.

Because land was now the new nation's principal commodity, and its cultivation a chief occupation, ownership disputes proved inevitable. Books on law were accordingly carted out to frontier settlements, where doctors, ministers, and occasionally the settlers themselves had to compensate for the shortage of lawyers in adjudicating conflicting claims. Even more specialized books dealing with, for example, medicine, agriculture, or horsemanship could be found nestled among the piles of outdated almanacs in backwoods cabins. The almanac undisputedly reigned as the new nation's best-seller and served as the chief instrument for reaching what one writer called "the solidarity dwellings of the poor and illiterate, where the studied ingenuity of the learned writers never comes." Combined with the increasing sales of guides to domesticating the frontier, the almanac set what is still an enduring standard for America's dedication to self-made success.

Often there were not enough books to satisfy the American public's interest in self-improvement. Even if there were, many Americans could not afford them. The spread of subscription libraries offered one ingenious solution to this predicament. Beginning in 1731 when Benjamin Franklin organized the Library Company of Philadelphia, subscription libraries recruited members who paid fees to be put toward the purchase of books, which then circulated among the subscribers. At the outbreak of the Revolution, sixty-four subscription libraries, dedicated to "the promotion of knowledge and virtue," had been established, with the borrowing time sensibly determined by the length of the book, the user's distance from the library, and the fee charged. In the years following the Revolution, public circulating libraries flourished and exerted considerable influence on the cultural life of the new republic. Reading

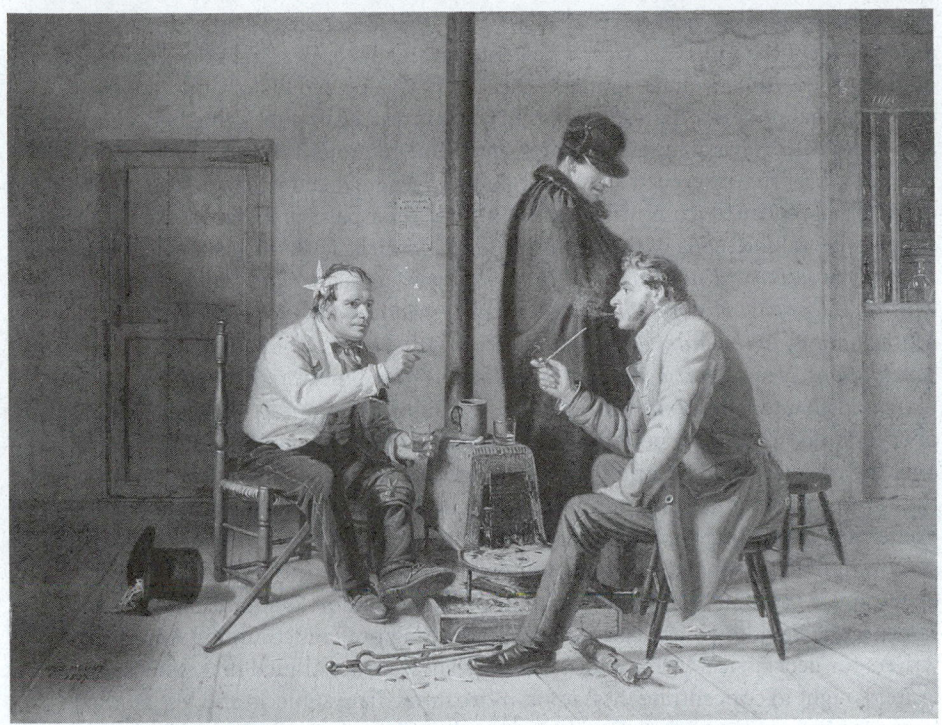

William Sidney Mount
The Long Story (Tough Story)
oil on panel, 1837
(The Corcoran Gallery of Art, Washington, D.C.)

was gradually becoming a democratic practice, no longer an activity restricted by virtue of education to the upper class in urban settings.

The Prospects of an American Literature

Despite a formidable list of circumstances and problems that had impaired the development of an American literature, writers and readers in the early nineteenth century could find several reasons to be encouraged about the cultural prospects of the new republic. In his monumental nine-volume study of the period, *History of the United States of America During the Administrations of Jefferson and Madison* (1889), Henry Adams observed:

> The average American was more intelligent than the average European, and was becoming every year still more active-minded as the new movement of society caught him up and swept him through a life of more varied experiences. On all sides the national mind responded to its stimulants. Deficient as the American was in the machinery of higher instruction; remote and poor, unable by any exertion to acquire the training, the capital, or even the elementary textbooks he needed for a fair development of his natural powers—his native energy and ambition already responded to the spur applied to them.

Nowhere were these "varied experiences" and "native energy and ambition" more amply evident than in the scores of new magazines that appeared in the first few decades of the new republic. Frank Luther Mott, a respected historian of the trade, estimates that no fewer than seventy-one periodicals began publishing between 1786 and 1800, with "several hundred more" appearing between 1800 and 1830. Most were relatively brief (few exceeded sixty-four pages in length), and nearly all relied initially on material reprinted from British sources to fill their pages inexpensively. Yet their subtitles reveal the scope of their interests: the *Massachusetts Magazine* billed itself as a *Monthly Museum of Knowledge and Rational Entertainment. Containing, Poetry, Musick, Biography, History, Physick, Geography, Morality, Criticism, Philosophy, Mathematicks, Agriculture, Architecture, Chymistry, Novels, Tales, Romances, Translations, News, Marriages, Deaths, Meteorological Observations, &c., &c.*

In addition to being compendiums, as one publication put it, of "useful knowledge of every kind," American periodicals also served as the principal forum for the debate over the prospects of developing a truly indigenous American literature. Each issue of the *North American Review,* founded in 1815 as the first American journal devoted exclusively to printing American material, abounded with calls for American writers to stop imitating British and continental literary models. The most vocal advocates of a distinctively national literature—including William Tudor, Walter Channing, and James Kirke Paulding—criticized the still prevailing preference among American writers for neoclassical forms and standards. These critics argued that American writers ought to concentrate instead on more immediate subjects and less studied forms for literary expression. Condemning what Channing called "the Literary Delinquency of America," these critics recognized in American scenery, history, and social relations suitable and untapped resources for literary distinction. Other critics, including R. H. Dana, Sr., and Francis Calley Gray, encouraged American literary independence, but at a much slower pace and without either excluding foreign examples or sacrificing literary standards.

James Kirke Paulding remained the most eloquent and hopeful voice among the periodical essayists' campaign for literary independence. In his essay "National Literature" (1819–1820), he noted that American writers had "debased the genius of this new world by making it the ape and the tributary of that of the old" and observed that the new nation had overlooked its own "rich resources, and sponged upon the exhausted treasury of our impoverished neighbors." American literary independence, Paulding claimed, would not be secure until the American writer freed himself from "a habit of servile imitation." The message was clear: American writers must fathom their own distinctive experiences before they could create a national literature equal to expressing those experiences in indigenous terms.

The Makings of American Literature

The basic ingredients of an independent national literature were in place: ambitious writers, suitable subjects, and an increasing number of printing presses, newspapers, magazines, book shops, schools, and libraries. All that remained was to make that literature distinctively American. "It does not follow because many books are written by persons born in America," Margaret Fuller cautioned several years later, "that there exists an American literature. Books which imitate or represent the thought and life of

Europe do not constitute an American literature. Before such can exist, an original idea must animate this nation and fresh currents must call into life fresh thoughts along its shores." By the late 1820s, Americans could point with pride to the publication of, among other notable works, Washington Irving's *Sketch Book* (1819–1820), William Cullen Bryant's *Poems* (1821), three of James Fenimore Cooper's "Leather-Stocking Tales" (*The Pioneers,* 1823; *The Last of the Mohicans,* 1826; and *The Prairie,* 1827), Edgar Allan Poe's *Tamerlane and Other Poems* (1827), and Noah Webster's *American Dictionary* (1828). Ample evidence of America's literary progress could also be seen in the increasing number of writers who devoted themselves exclusively to their craft as well as in the growing interest in literary theory and controversy. The prominence of the so-called Knickerbocker School, the most famous group of writers in the early decades of the new republic, added luster to the American literary scene and helped turn New York into the literary matrix of the early nineteenth century, outshining Philadelphia, just as that city had in turn overshadowed Boston. However, the writers identified with the Knickerbocker group—including, among others, James Kirke Paulding, Fitz-Greene Halleck, John Howard Payne, Washington Irving, and, for a time, William Cullen Bryant and James Fenimore Cooper—were closer geographically than in aesthetic principle. Yet however loosely associated, these writers did avow the same interest in exploring American subjects and themes.

Self-consciousness about the irrepressible novelty of American experience proved to be the new nation's greatest literary resource. With, as Timothy Dwight observed, no "ancient castles, ruined abbeys, and fine pictures" to re-create in literature, American writers sought new modes and styles to express their nation's unprecedented experiences in the natural world. The land and the limitless experiences it generated had become an "experiment," a word first used in an American context. "Men are like plants," Crèvecoeur observed; they are as different as "the peculiar soil and exposition in which they grow." And with no sense of failure to inhibit them, Americans in the early decades of the new republic were free to explore their indigenous experience. The extraordinary discoveries in botany recorded in William Bartram's *Travels Through North and South Carolina, Georgia, East and West Florida* (1791), for example, not only increased the nation's understanding of the natural world but also provided many prominent American poets of the time (including Philip Freneau and William Cullen Bryant) with reliable yet exotic views of American nature.

Novelty and experimentation, which were everywhere apparent in daily American experience, surfaced at first only intermittently in the nation's characteristic literary forms. Imitating imported literary methods still dominated poetic expression throughout the period, including the works of its two major poets, Philip Freneau and William Cullen Bryant. Both Freneau and the renowned Bryant, who vehemently denounced those who "do not praise a thing until [they] see the seal of transatlantic approbation upon it," found it far easier to admire indigenous American subjects than to render them in distinctive American terms.

The familiar essay met much the same fate as poetry in the hands of American writers during the early republic. Most newspapers featured essay series, many written under such delightful pseudonyms as "The Prompter" (Noah Webster), "Tomo Cheeki" and "Robert Slender" (Philip Freneau), "Oliver Oldstyle" (Joseph Dennie), and "Jonathan Oldstyle" (from the pen of the master of the genre, Washington Irving). Despite the essay's use as the principal means to decry British influence on American literature, most American writers regularly invoked Addison and Steele as their literary precedent, just as American reviewers relied on their English counterparts to set the standards for witty and incisive commentary on cultural and social affairs.

During this same period, however, two groups that had rarely posited their voices in colonial American literature began to express their individual and collective interests and sensibilities. Women and African Americans made significant gains as writers and readers during the years between 1776 and 1836. For African Americans, a class deliberately kept uneducated in the new republic, learning to read and write was largely a matter of fortitude, luck, or subterfuge. But in March 1827, John B. Russwurm, the first African American college graduate (Bowdoin, 1826), and Samuel Cornish founded *Freedom's Journal* in New York City. This, the nation's first newspaper owned and edited by African Americans, aimed to serve both to inform "our brethren in the different states of this great confederacy" and to conciliate what the editors hoped would be a large white audience. In its attention to "useful knowledge of every kind," "moral and religious improvement," and "civil rights," *Freedom's Journal* succeeded admirably in its announced purpose: "to plead our own cause." It also contributed to the nature of the debate over abolition.

Women had from childhood on traditionally been discriminated against in colonial America. They hardly received any formal education. Despite the urgings of Abigail Adams and other prominent women, the Revolution and its aftermath did little to improve their lot. For women in the new nation, literacy continued to be determined, principally, by their class. Women who read, enjoyed mainly fiction. Thus, the development of the American novel depended to a large extent on a female readership.

Sentimental novels were among the most popular forms of fiction in the new republic. Highly didactic, these novels—including William Hill Brown's *Power of Sympathy* (1799) and Susannah Rowson's *Charlotte Temple: A Tale of Truth* (1791)—featured an epistolary style derived primarily from Samuel Richardson. The prefaces to these novels emphasized moral messages and disclaimers; Brown explained, for example, that he wrote *The Power of Sympathy* to "expose the dangerous Consequences of Seduction and to set forth the advantages of female Education." Yet such prominent figures as Thomas Jefferson, Timothy Dwight, and Noah Webster severely criticized American novelists in the new republic for corrupting impressionable young women with fanciful accounts of contemporary life. A fairly widespread belief held, in the words of one critic, that novels "lead onto a path of vice," "inflame the passions and corrupt the heart," "pollute the imaginations of young women and likewise give them false ideas of life."

Other popular fictional forms of the time were the historical romances influenced primarily by Sir Walter Scott and the satiric novel. *The Algerine Captive* (1797) by Royall Tyler and *Modern Chivalry* (1792) by Hugh Henry Brackenridge remain the best known, with Brackenridge among the first authors to incorporate American materials and current events into their work, including the Whiskey Rebellion, the American Constitution, and the French Revolution. Charles Brockden Brown's Gothic novels—including *Weiland* (1798), *Edgar Huntly* (1799), and *Arthur Mervyn* (1799–1800)—also enjoyed wide readership. The American writer must "examine objects with his own eyes," Brown exhorted. He must "employ European models merely for the improvement of his taste" and draw on "all that is genuine and peculiar in the scene before him" to create literature equivalent to his sources. The irony of

John Quidor
The Return of Rip Van Winkle
oil on canvas, 1829
(National Gallery of Art, Washington, D.C., Andrew Mellon Collection)

Brown's work, like that of each of the other novelists in the new republic, is its dependence on English and continental sources. Yet these fictional forms also introduce characters, settings, and themes that would be developed more elaborately in the later fiction of Irving, Cooper, Poe, Hawthorne, and Melville.

European Models and the American Landscape

The careers of Washington Irving and James Fenimore Cooper span the period of America's self-conscious quest for an independent literary identity. Their writings most clearly illustrate the major tension in the literature of the new republic: eager but anxious responses to the lure of literary nationalism set off against assurances of working within traditional European models. Their writings also underscore the principal literary issues in the new republic: the writer's identity in a society preoccupied with material progress; the literary consequences of America's absorption in the present and the future and its neglect of the past; and, above all, the writer's need to create an *American* time and place where the imagination could flourish. For Irving this would be colonial Sleepy Hollow. For Cooper it was the unspoiled, dense woods of the frontier as well as the open stretches of the sea, the same regions depicted in the new American landscape painting led by Thomas Cole. Later writers, including

Hawthorne, Thoreau, Twain, Crane, and Faulkner, created their own distinctive versions of a specifically American historical context, but Irving and Cooper first grappled with the issue in a way that made the nature of both the literary problem and its solution luminously clear.

Irving helped American writers discover the literary potential of the past by adapting Europe's rich cultural heritage to American settings. Cooper shared Irving's interest in the literary possibilities of history and opened two additional prospects for American literature: the frontier and life at sea. Cooper's "Leather-Stocking Tales" played a significant role in establishing the frontier as the principal shaping influence on nineteenth-century and much of twentieth-century American literature and turned Natty Bumppo into the American archetype of individual freedom and self-reliance. Cooper's backwoodsman served as the fictional forerunner of countless legendary mountain men and cowboys, America's purest examples of self-expression in the wilderness.

The irony of Cooper's and Irving's accomplishments is that in both cases they were nurtured principally during the authors' extended stays in Europe. Irving's and Cooper's familiar essays, stories, novels, and social criticism, adapted largely from European sources, form a compendium of American literary taste in the first half of the nineteenth century—moving in Irving's case from neoclassical wit and satire to Romantic interest in atmosphere and sentiment, and in the case of Cooper from an interest in the traditional novel of manners to the broader brushstrokes of painting mythic American landscapes populated with legendary characters. The diversity (their willingness to explore multiple aspects of experience), the dynamism (their constant growth as writers), and the organic unity of their writings (their interest in the whole as much as the part), along with their commitment to extolling a strong sense of individuality, independence and introspection in the face of the powerful rawness of the American landscape, place Irving and Cooper at the beginning of what would become a long tradition of Romantic writing in American literature, a tradition that would have its fullest expression in the great flowering of the American Renaissance. At the end of "The American Scholar" (1837), Ralph Waldo Emerson proclaimed that Americans "will walk on our own feet; we will work with our own hands; we will speak our own minds." The writers of the new republic laid the foundation that enabled Emerson to declare the symbolic birth of a truly distinctive American literature with such confidence.

Further Reading:

H. Adams, *The History of the United States of America During the Administrations of Jefferson and Madison*, 8 vols., 1884–1901.

M. Ellis, *Joseph Dennie and His Circle*, 1915.

V. W. Brooks, *The Flowering of New England*, 1936.

L. Howard, *The Connecticut Wits*, 1943.

H. M. Jones, *O Strange New World: American Culture, the Formative Years*, 1952.

H. H. Clark, *Transitions in American Literary History*, 1953.

B. T. Spencer, *The Quest for Nationality*, 1957.

D. Boorstin, *The Americans: The Colonial Experience*, 1958.

M. Cunliffe, *The Nation Takes Shape*, 1959.

R. B. Nye, *The Cultural Life of the New Nation*, 1960.

L. P. Simpson, *The Federalist Literary Mind*, 1962.

C. L. Sanford, *Quest for America 1810–1824*, 1964.

D. Boorstin, *The Americans: The National Experience*, 1965.

G. Dangerfield, *The Awakening of American Nationalism, 1815–1828*, 1965.

W. Hedges, *Washington Irving: An American Study, 1802–1832*, 1965.

J. T. Main, *The Social Structure of Revolutionary America*, 1965.

P. Miller, *The Life of the Mind in America: From the Revolution to the Civil War*, 1965.

R. E. Spiller, *The American Literary Revolution*, 1967.

W. Charvat, *The Profession of Authorship in America, 1800–1870*, ed. M. J. Bruccoli, 1968.

H. Petter, *The Early American Novel*, 1971.

L. Simpson, *The Man of Letters in New England and the South*, 1973.
L. J. Friedman, *Inventors of the Promised Land*, 1975.
H. F. May, *The Enlightenment in America*, 1976.
K. Silverman, *Cultural History of the American Revolution*, 1976.
S. Bercovitch, *The Puritan Origins of the American Self*, 1978.
M. Kammen, *A Season of Youth: The American Revolution and the Historical Imagination*, 1978.
J. Ellis, *After the Revolution*, 1979.

E. Elliott, *Revolutionary Writers: Literature and Authority in the New Republic, 1725–1810*, 1982.
J. Fliegelman, *Prodigals and Pilgrims: The American Revolution Against Patriarchal Authority*, 1982.
R. Ferguson, *Law and Letters in American Culture*, 1984.
R. H. Wiebe, *The Opening of American Society*, 1984.
L. Buell, *New England Literary Culture: From Revolution Through Renaissance*, 1986.
M. Warner, *The Letters of the Republic*, 1990.
L. Ziff, *Writing in the New Nation*, 1991.

Thomas Jefferson
1743–1826

Thomas Jefferson's literary life is intertwined with his life as diplomat, statesman, architect, environmental planner, scientist, politician, and theorist of education. Jefferson embodies the eighteenth-century ideal of a gentleman, yet he became an American paradox, an aristocrat who was also a democrat and slaveholder.

Jefferson was born in central Virginia near the future sites of Monticello and the University of Virginia. His father's estate, Shadwell, was at that time near the frontier. Therefore, Peter Jefferson, a farmer and surveyor, taught his son also Indian lore and mapmaking, which perhaps established the basis for Jefferson's eventual interests in anthropological study and in design. At age five Jefferson was sent to an English school some fifty miles distant and at ten was enrolled in a Latin school for training in classical language and literature. In 1760 he entered the College of William and Mary, where he had the "great good fortune," as he put it, "to be instructed by Dr. William Small, then Professor of Mathematics, a man who, Jefferson wrote, "probably fixed the destinies of my life."

After graduation in 1762, Jefferson began to study law, and to absorb the principles of republicanism. He shed the orthodox, conservative Anglican heritage and embraced Deism, which provided the model of the Creator to be emulated in building a new republic. He became aware of the Scottish Common Sense school, from which he came to believe that the moral sense is one's highest faculty and is equally present to all, a view he later expressed in the Declaration of Independence.

Jefferson was admitted to the bar in 1767 and practiced law while taking advantage of the cultural opportunities of Williamsburg, which was a colonial capital as well as a college town. He learned the violin, attended theatrical performances, and began collecting the books that proliferated into a library of about ten thousand volumes, which later became the basis for the Library of Congress. He doubtlessly learned to participate in the polished, urbane conversation of the colonial aristocracy, although Jefferson never was skilled at public speaking.

Jefferson entered Virginia politics in 1769, when he was elected to the legislative House of Burgesses. In those years he also began the construction of Monticello (the estate would not be complete for some forty years). The design for Monticello was

Jefferson's own, and has been called "classical with American elements." Jefferson's interest in design continued into his presidential years, when he took part in the plan for the nation's Capitol, and into his so-called retirement, when he designed the campus and buildings (and the curriculum) of the University of Virginia at Charlottesville.

In 1772 Jefferson married Martha Wayles Skelton, a wealthy, slaveholding widow. Within a year their first child, a daughter, was born. The couple had six children, including a son, but only two daughters lived to adulthood. Jefferson was deeply bereaved when his wife died after ten years of marriage.

Pre-Revolutionary politics proved irresistible. In 1774 Jefferson attended the newly formed Continental Congress and won respect for his clear style and moderate tone in a pamphlet that defended colonial rights, *A Summary View of the Rights of British America.* By 1776, with events of the Revolution moving swiftly, Jefferson was one of a committee appointed to draft a document announcing the severance of the colonies from England. Though the committee and the Congress edited the draft, the Declaration of Independence was Jefferson's. He considered the document "an expression of the American mind." Its ideals were compatible with Jefferson's work in Virginia to establish religious freedom by law and thus to separate church and state. These two achievements meant so much to him that he included them, together with his fathering of the University of Virginia, in the epitaph he wrote and left behind at his death.

During the Revolutionary War years, Jefferson served as governor of Virginia, narrowly escaping British capture. In 1783 he was elected to Congress and became minister to France, where he served for five years. He was a member of Washington's cabinet, vice president under John Adams, and then president for two terms beginning in 1801. Jefferson envisioned the United States as a self-sufficient, agrarian nation and enacted his vision of its future in the Louisiana Purchase (1803), persuading Congress to sponsor the expedition of Meriwether Lewis and William Clark to explore and map the new territory. Jefferson's presidency marked the beginning of the democratic plain style in politics. The chief executive lived at a boarding house, rejected all outward signs of wealth or pomp (including ornamental shoe buckles), and was known to receive visitors in his slippers. After his presidency he withdrew from public life.

Evidence suggests that the "bosom" of Jefferson's family included a thirty-eight-year relationship with a slave woman, Sally Hemings, who was a quadroon, the half sister of Jefferson's deceased wife. Social attitudes of the time would have made marital legitimation of the relationship impossible, no matter how much both parties might have wished otherwise. The affair, together with Jefferson's keeping of slaves, has raised charges of hypocrisy against him and has remained troubling to scholars and analysts. It must be pointed out, however, that Jefferson attempted to outlaw slavery in his original draft of the Declaration of Independence and that as president he worked successfully for the enactment of a law banning the further importation of slaves.

Jefferson's literary achievement is a part of his public life. His *Notes on the State of Virginia* (1785), a work of natural science, was occasioned by a query by the Marquis de Barbé-Marois, who posed a set of questions concerning the geography, social history, and ecology of Virginia. Jefferson took the opportunity not only to respond to the questions but also to rebut the widely held European view that America was an unhealthy place that was causing the degeneration of its species. Jefferson's book won him the apology of the famous French naturalist Georges Louis Le Clerc de Buffon. Jefferson's varied writings—from letters to political documents and geography—show that literature embraces wide-ranging forms that remain vital in the hands of a skilled practitioner.

Further Reading:

A. Koch, *The Philosophy of Thomas Jefferson*, 1943.
D. Malone, *Jefferson and His Time*, 5 vols., 1948–1974.
D. Boorstin, *The Lost World of Thomas Jefferson*, 1948.
M. Peterson, *Thomas Jefferson and the New Nation*, 1970.

F. Brodie, *Thomas Jefferson: An Intimate History*, 1974.
G. Wills, *Inventing America*, 1978.
W. Bottorff, *Thomas Jefferson*, 1979.

Texts:

"The Declaration of Independence," *Papers of Thomas Jefferson*, 18 vols., ed. J. Boyd, 1950–1971.
Notes on the State of Virginia, ed. W. Peden, 1955.

The Adams-Jefferson Letters, ed. L. Cappon, 1959.
Writings of Thomas Jefferson, 10 vols., ed. P. Ford, 1892–1899.

The Declaration of Independence as Adopted by Congress

In Congress July 4, 1776

The Unanimous Declaration of the Thirteen United States of America

When in the Course of human events, it becomes necessary for one people to dissolve the political bands which have connected them with another, and to assume among the powers of the earth, the separate and equal station to which the Laws of Nature and of Nature's God entitle them, a decent respect to the opinions of mankind requires that they should declare the causes which impel them to the separation. We hold these truths to be self-evident, that all men are created equal, that they are endowed by their Creator with certain unalienable Rights, that among these are Life, Liberty and the pursuit of Happiness. That to secure these rights, Governments are instituted among Men, deriving their just powers from the consent of the governed, That whenever any Form of Government becomes destructive of these ends, it is the Right of the People to alter or to abolish it, and to institute new Government, laying its foundation on such principles and organizing its powers in such form, as to them shall seem most likely to effect their Safety and Happiness. Prudence, indeed, will dictate that Governments long established should not be changed for light and transient causes; and accordingly all experience hath shewn, that mankind are more disposed to suffer, while evils are sufferable, than to right themselves by abolishing the forms to which they are accustomed. But when a long train of abuses and usurpations, pursuing invariably the same Object evinces a design to reduce them under absolute Despotism, it is their right, it is their duty, to throw off such Government, and to provide new Guards for their future security. Such has been the patient sufferance of these Colonies; and such is now the necessity which constrains them to alter their former Systems of Government. The history of the present King of Great Britain is a history of repeated injuries and usurpations, all having in direct object the establishment of an absolute Tyranny over these States. To prove this, let Facts be submitted to a candid world. He has refused his Assent to Laws, the most wholesome and necessary for the public good. He has forbidden his Governors to pass Laws of immediate and pressing importance, unless suspended in their operation till his Assent should be obtained; and when so suspended, he has utterly neglected to attend to them. He has refused to pass other Laws for the accommodation of large districts of people, unless those people would relinquish the right of Representation in the Legislature, a right inestimable to them and formidable to tyrants only. He has called together legislative bodies at places unusual, uncomfortable, and distant from the depository of their public Records, for the sole purpose of fatiguing them into compliance with his measures. He has dissolved Representative Houses repeatedly, for opposing with manly firmness his invasions on the rights of the people. He has refused for a long time, after such dissolutions, to cause others to be elected; whereby the Legislative powers, incapable of Annihilation, have returned to the People at large for their exercise; the State remaining in the mean time exposed to all the dangers of invasion from without, and convulsions within. He has endeavoured to prevent the population of these States; for that purpose obstructing the Laws for Naturalization of Foreigners; refusing to pass others to encourage their migrations hither, and raising the conditions of new Appropriations of Lands. He has obstructed the Administration of Justice, by refusing his Assent to Laws for establishing Judiciary powers. He has made Judges dependent on his Will alone, for the tenure of their offices, and the amount and payment of their salaries. He has erected a multitude of New Offices, and sent hither swarms of Officers to harrass our people, and eat out their substance. He has kept among us, in times of peace, standing Armies without the Consent of our legislatures. He has affected to render the Military independent of and superior to the Civil power. He has combined with others to subject us to a jurisdiction foreign to our constitution, and unacknowledged by our laws; giving his Assent to their Acts of pretended Legislation: For Quartering large bodies of armed troops among us: For protecting them, by a mock Trial, from punishment for any Murders which they should commit on the Inhabitants of these States: For cutting off our Trade with all parts of the world: For imposing Taxes on us without our Consent: For depriving us in many cases of the benefits of Trial by Jury: For transporting us beyond Seas to be tried for pretended offences: For abolishing the free System of English Laws in a neighbouring Province, establishing therein an Arbitrary government, and enlarging its Boundaries so as to render it at once an example and fit instrument for introducing the same absolute rule into these Colonies: For taking away our Charters, abolishing our most valuable Laws, and altering fundamentally the Forms of our Governments: For suspending our own Legislatures, and declaring themselves invested with power to legislate for us in all cases whatsoever. He has abdicated Government here, by declaring us out of his Protection and waging War against us. He has plundered our seas, ravaged our Coasts, burnt our towns, and destroyed the Lives of our people. He is at this time transporting large Armies of foreign Mercenaries to compleat the works of death, desolation and tyranny, already begun with circumstances of Cruelty & perfidy scarcely paralleled in the most barbarous ages, and totally unworthy the Head of a civilized nation. He has constrained our fellow Citizens taken Captive on the high Seas to bear Arms against their Country, to become the executioners of their friends and Brethren, or to fall themselves by their Hands. He has excited domestic insurrections amongst us, and has endeavoured to bring on the inhabitants of our frontiers, the merciless Indian Savages, whose known rule of warfare, is an undistinguished destruction of all ages, sexes and conditions. In every stage of these Oppressions We have Petitioned for Redress in the most humble terms: Our repeated Petitions have been answered only by repeated injury. A Prince, whose character is thus marked by every act which may define a Tyrant, is unfit to be the ruler of a free people. Nor have We been wanting in attentions to our Brittish brethren. We have warned them from time to time of attempts by their legislature to extend an unwarrantable jurisdiction over us. We have reminded them of the circumstances of our emigration and settlement here. We have appealed to their native justice and magnanimity, and we have conjured them by the ties of our common kindred to disavow these usurpations, which, would inevitably interrupt our connections and correspondence. They too have been deaf to the voice of justice and of consanguinity. We must, therefore, acquiesce in the necessity, which denounces our Separation, and hold them, as we hold the rest of mankind, Enemies in War, in Peace Friends.

We, therefore, the Representatives of the United States of America, in General Congress, Assembled, appealing to the Supreme Judge of the world for the rectitude of our intentions, do, in the Name, and by Authority of the good People of these Colonies, solemnly publish and declare, That these United Colonies are, and of Right ought to be Free and Independent States; that they are Absolved from all Allegiance to the British Crown, and that all political connection between them and the State of Great Britain, is and ought to be totally dissolved; and that as Free and Independent States, they have full Power to levy War, conclude Peace, contract Alliances, establish Commerce, and to do all other Acts and Things which Independent States may of right do. And for the support of this Declaration, with a firm reliance on the protection of divine Providence, we mutually pledge to each other our Lives, our Fortunes and our sacred Honor.

1776

Notes on the State of Virginia

from **Query V: Cascades**

[Natural Bridge]

The *Natural Bridge*, the most sublime of Nature's works, though not comprehended under the present head, must not be pretermitted.[1] It is on the ascent of a hill, which seems to have been cloven through its length by some great convulsion. The fissure, just at the bridge, is, by some admeasurements, 270 feet deep, by others only 205. It is about 45 feet wide at the bottom, and 90 feet at the top; this of course determines the length of the bridge, and its height from the water. Its breadth in the middle, is about 60 feet, but more at the ends, and the thickness of the mass at the summit of the arch, about 40 feet. A part of this thickness is constituted by a coat of earth, which gives growth to many large trees. The residue, with the hill on both sides, is one solid rock of limestone. The arch approaches the Semi-elliptical form; but the larger axis of the ellipsis, which would

---

[1] i.e., although not a cascade, the natural bridge must not be omitted.

be the cord of the arch, is many times longer than the (semi-axis which gives its height.) Though the sides of this bridge are provided in some parts with a parapet of fixed rocks, yet few men have resolution to walk to them and look over into the abyss. You involuntarily fall on your hands and feet, creep to the parapet and peep over it. Looking down from this height about a minute, gave me a violent head ach. (This painful sensation is relieved by a short, but pleasing view of the Blue ridge along the fissure downwards, and upwards by that of the Short hills, which, with the Purgatory mountain is a divergence from the North ridge; and, descending then to the valley below, the sensation becomes delightful in the extreme. It is impossible for the emotions, arising from the sublime, to be felt beyond what they are here: so beautiful an arch, so elevated, so light, and springing, as it were, up to heaven, the rapture of the Spectator is really indiscribable! The fissure continues deep and narrow and, following the margin of the stream upwards about three eights of a mile you arrive at a limestone cavern, less remarkable, however, for height and extent than those before described. Its entrance into the hill is but a few feet above the bed of the stream.) This bridge is in the county of Rockbridge, to which it has given name, and affords a public and commodious passage over a valley, which cannot be crossed elsewhere for a considerable distance. The stream passing under it is called Cedar creek. It is a water of James river, and sufficient in the driest seasons to turn a grist-mill, though its fountain is not more than two miles above. . . .

from Query VI: Productions Mineral, Vegetable and Animal

[Rebuttal to Count Buffon]

The opinion advanced by the Count de Buffon,[2] is 1. That the animals common both to the old and new world, are smaller in the latter. 2. That those peculiar to the new, are on a smaller scale. 3. That those which have been domesticated in both, have degenerated in America: and 4. That on the whole it exhibits fewer species. And the reason he thinks is, that the heats of America are less; that more waters are spread over its surface by nature, and fewer of these drained off by the hand of man. In other words, that heat is friendly, and moisture adverse to the production and developement of large quadrupeds. . . .

Hitherto I have considered this hypothesis as applied to brute animals only, and not in its extension to the man of America, whether aboriginal or transplanted. It is the opinion of Mons. de Buffon that the former furnishes no exception to it: "Although the savage of the new world is about the same height as man in our world, this does not suffice for him to constitute an exception to the general fact that all living nature has become smaller on that continent. The savage is feeble, and has small organs of generation; he has neither hair nor beard, and no ardor whatever for his female; although swifter than the European because he is better accustomed to running, he is, on the other hand, less strong in body; he is also less sensitive, and yet more timid and cowardly; he has no vivacity, no activity of mind; the activity of his body is less an exercise, a voluntary motion, than a necessary action caused by want; relieve him of hunger and thirst, and you deprive him of the active principle of all his movements; he will rest stupidly upon his legs or lying down entire days. There is no need for seeking further the cause of the iso-

---

[2] Georges Louis Leclerc de Buffon (1707–1788), French author of the multivolume *Natural History,* which argued that the American environment was conducive to the degeneration of species and thus unsuited to civilized life.

lated mode of life of these savages and their repugnance for society: the most precious spark of the fire of nature has been refused to them; they lack ardor for their females, and consequently have no love for their fellow men; not knowing this strongest and most tender of all affections, their other feelings are also cold and languid; they love their parents and children but little; the most intimate of all ties, the family connection, binds them therefore but loosely together; between family and family there is no tie at all; hence they have no communion, no commonwealth, no state of society. Physical love constitues their only morality; their heart is icy, their society cold, and their rule harsh. They look upon their wives only as servants for all work, or as beasts of burden, which they load without consideration with the burden of their hunting, and which they compel without mercy, without gratitude, to perform tasks which are often beyond their strength. They have only few children, and they take little care of them. Everywhere the original defect appears: they are indifferent because they have little sexual capacity, and this indifference to the other sex is the fundamental defect which weakens their nature, prevents its development, and—destroying the very germs of life—uproots society at the same time. Man is here no exception to the general rule. Nature, by refusing him the power of love, has treated him worse and lowered him deeper than any animal." An afflicting picture indeed, which, for the honor of human nature, I am glad to believe has no original. Of the Indian of South America I know nothing; for I would not honor with the appelation of knowledge, what I derive from the fables published of them. These I believe to be just as true as the fables of Æsop. This belief is founded on what I have seen of man, white, red, and black, and what has been written of him by authors, enlightened themselves, and writing amidst an enlightened people. The Indian of North America being more within our reach, I can speak of him somewhat from my own knowledge, but more from the information of others better acquainted with him, and on whose truth and judgment I can rely. From these sources I am able to say, in contradiction to this representation, that he is neither more defective in ardor, nor more impotent with his female, than the white reduced to the same diet and exercise: that he is brave, when an enterprize depends on bravery; education with him making the point of honor consist in the destruction of an enemy by stratagem, and in the preservation of his own person free from injury; or perhaps this is nature; while it is education which teaches us to honor force more than finesse; that he will defend himself against an host of enemies, always chusing to be killed, rather than to surrender, though it be to the whites, who he knows will treat him well: that in other situations also he meets death with more deliberation, and endures tortures with a firmness unknown almost to religious enthusiasm with us: that he is affectionate to his children, careful of them, and indulgent in the extreme: that his affections comprehend his other connections, weakening, as with us, from circle to circle, as they recede from the center: that his friendships are strong and faithful to the uttermost extremity: that his sensibility is keen, even the warriors weeping most bitterly on the loss of their children, though in general they endeavour to appear superior to human events: that his vivacity and activity of mind is equal to ours in the same situation; hence his eagerness for hunting, and for games of chance. The women are submitted to unjust drudgery. This I believe is the case with every barbarous people. With such, force is law. The stronger sex therefore imposes on the weaker. It is civilization alone which replaces women in the enjoyment of their natural equality. That first teaches us to subdue the selfish passions, and to respect those rights in others which we value in ourselves. Were we in equal barbarism, our females would be equal drudges. The man with them is less strong than with us, but their woman stronger than ours; and both for the same obvious reason; because our man and their woman is habituated to labour, and formed by it. With both races the sex which is indulged with ease is least athletic. An Indian man is small in the hand and wrist for the same reason for which a sailor is large and strong in the arms and shoulders, and a porter in the legs and thighs.—They raise fewer children than we do. The causes of this are to be found, not in a difference of nature, but of circumstance. The women very frequently attending the men in their parties of war and of hunting, child-bearing becomes extremely inconvenient to them. It is said, therefore, that they have learnt the practice of procuring abortion by the use of some vegetable; and that it even extends to prevent conception for a considerable time after. During these parties they are exposed to numerous hazards, to excessive exertions, to the greatest extremities of hunger. Even at their homes the nation depends for food, through a certain part of every year, on the gleanings of the forest: that is, they experience a famine once in every year. With all animals, if the female be badly fed, or not fed at all, her young perish: and if both male and female be reduced to like want, generation becomes less active, less productive. To the obstacles then of want and hazard, which nature has opposed to the multiplication of wild animals, for the purpose of restraining their numbers within certain bounds, those of labour and of voluntary abortion are added with the Indian. No wonder then if they multiply less than we do. Where food is regularly supplied, a single farm will shew more of cattle, than a whole country of forests can of buffaloes. The same Indian women, when married to white traders, who feed them and their children plentifully and regularly, who exempt them from excessive drudgery, who keep them stationary and unexposed to accident, produce and raise as many children as the white women. Instances are known, under these circumstances, of their rearing a dozen children. . . .

Before we condemn the Indians of this continent as wanting genius,[3] we must consider that letters[4] have not yet been introduced among them. Were we to compare them in their present state with the Europeans North of the Alps, when the Roman arms and arts first crossed those mountains, the comparison would be unequal, because, at that time, those parts of Europe were swarming with numbers; because numbers produce emulation, and multiply the chances of improvement, and one improvement begets another. Yet I may safely ask, How many good poets, how many able mathematicians, how many great inventors in arts or sciences, had Europe North of the Alps then produced? And it was sixteen centuries after this before a Newton could be formed. I do not mean to deny, that there are varieties in the race of man, distinguished by their powers both of body and mind. I believe there are, as I see to be the case in the races of other animals. I only mean to suggest a doubt, whether the bulk and faculties of animals depend on the side of the Atlantic on which their food happens to grow, or which furnishes the elements of which they are compounded? Whether nature has enlisted herself as a Cis[5] or Trans-Atlantic partisan? I am induced to suspect, there has been more eloquence than sound reasoning displayed in support of this theory; that it is one of those cases where the judgment has been seduced by a glowing pen: and whilst I render every tribute of honor and esteem to the celebrated Zoologist, who has added, and is still adding, so many precious things to the treasures of science, I must doubt whether in this instance he has not cherished error also, by lending her for a moment his vivid imagination and bewitching language.

[3] Mental capacity and ability.
[4] Learning or knowledge.

[5] On the near side (i.e., European).

So far the Count de Buffon has carried this new theory of the tendency of nature to belittle her productions on this side of the Atlantic. Its application to the race of whites, transplanted from Europe, remained for the Abbé Raynal.[6] "One must be astonished (he says) that America has not yet produced one good poet, one able mathematician, one man of genius in a single art or a single science." "America has not yet produced one good poet." When we shall have existed as a people as long as the Greeks did before they produced a Homer, the Romans a Virgil, the French a Racine and Voltaire, the English a Shakespeare and Milton, should this reproach be still true, we will enquire from what unfriendly causes it has proceeded, that the other countries of Europe and quarters of the earth shall not have inscribed any name in the roll of poets. But neither has America produced "one able mathematician, one man of genius in a single art or a single science." In war we have produced a Washington, whose memory will be adored while liberty shall have votaries, whose name will triumph over time, and will in future ages assume its just station among the most celebrated worthies of the world, when that wretched philosophy shall be forgotten which would have arranged him among the degeneracies of nature. In physics we have produced a Franklin, than whom no one of the present age has made more important discoveries, nor has enriched philosophy with more, or more ingenious solutions of the phænomena of nature. We have supposed Mr. Rittenhouse[7] second to no astronomer living: that in genius he must be the first, because he is self-taught. As an artist he has exhibited as great a proof of mechanical genius as the world has ever produced. He has not indeed made a world; but he has by imitation approached nearer its Maker than any man who has lived from the creation to this day. As in philosophy and war, so in government, in oratory, in painting, in the plastic art, we might shew that America, though but a child of yesterday, has already given hopeful proofs of genius, as well of the nobler kinds, which arouse the best feelings of man, which call him into action, which substantiate his freedom, and conduct him to happiness, as of the subordinate, which serve to amuse him only. We therefore suppose, that this reproach is as unjust as it is unkind; and that, of the geniuses which adorn the present age, America contributes its full share. For comparing it with those countries, where genius is most cultivated, where are the most excellent models for art, and scaffoldings for the attainment of science, as France and England for instance, we calculate thus. The United States contain three millions of inhabitants; France twenty millions; and the British islands ten. We produce a Washington, a Franklin, a Rittenhouse. France then should have half a dozen in each of these lines, and Great-Britain half that number, equally eminent. It may be true, that France has: we are but just becoming acquainted with her, and our acquaintance so far gives us high ideas of the genius of her inhabitants. It would be injuring too many of them to name particularly a Voltaire, a Buffon, the constellation of Encyclopedists,[8] the Abbé Raynal himself, &c. &c. We therefore have reason to believe she can produce her full quota of genius. The present war having so long cut off all communication with Great-Britain, we are not able to make a fair estimate of the state of science in that country. The spirit in which she wages war is the only sample before our eyes, and that does not seem the legitimate

---

[6] Guillaume Thomas François Raynal (1713–1796), French writer who concurred with Buffon that the American environment was degenerative.

[7] David Rittenhouse (1732–1796), American astronomer who built orreries, or models of the solar system.

[8] Such figures as Denis Diderot (1713–1784), who contributed to the French *Encyclopédie* (1751–1771).

offspring either of science or of civilization. The sun of her glory is fast descending to the horizon. Her philosophy has crossed the Channel, her freedom the Atlantic, and herself seems passing to that awful dissolution, whose issue is not given human foresight to scan.

Abigail Adams
1744–1818

John Adams's frequent and prolonged absences resulted not only in Abigail Adams's uncommon self-sufficiency but also in her voluminous, rich correspondence with her husband; with her son John Quincy, who later served as sixth president of the United States; and with numerous political leaders in the new republic. The "long and cruel separations" attended her husband John's many years of public service: as a Massachusetts delegate to the Continental Congress, as a negotiator of the Treaty of Paris, as the American joint commissioner at the court of France, as the nation's first vice president, and as the second president of the United States. Abigail's letters constitute one of the most incisive private commentaries on the public events that crowded the new nation's history.

Abigail Smith Adams was the second of three daughters born to Reverend William Smith and Elizabeth Quincy, parents who could trace their distinguished lineages back through the pages of Cotton Mather's *Magnalia Christi Americana*. She entered, as did all eighteenth-century women, a world indifferent to the education of females. In a letter dated 1817, she observed:

> My early education did not partake of the opportunities which the present days offer, and which even our common country schools now afford. I never was sent to any school. I was always sick. Female education, in the best families, went no further than writing and arithmetic; in some few and rare instances, music and dancing.

Under the tutelage of her grandmother, who offered a "happy method of mixing instruction and amusement," young Abigail became a practiced letter writer early on and read widely among English poets and essayists, developing an especially high regard for Addison and Steele's *Spectator* papers.

In 1764 she married John Adams, despite some resistance from her family, who regarded this lawyer son of a small farmer as beneath their own social and professional standing. As her husband traveled more frequently to participate in the political controversies that led to the American Revolution, Abigail endured the prolonged silences of late eighteenth-century mail and took on increasingly more responsibility for her family's well-being: cultivating a farm, managing the finances, ordering and selling goods from abroad, discussing current prices, and arguing over local and national politics.

Armed with an independent and imaginative intelligence, she vigorously expressed her ideas on a wide range of subjects, most particularly on women's rights. Her letters reveal her longing for an American declaration of independence, and she was one of the first Americans to perceive the implications of the Revolution for African Americans and women. She insisted that wives ought to be freed from the absolute legal authority husbands held over their lives: "If particular care and attention is not paid to the ladies, we are determined to foment a rebellion, and will not hold ourselves bound by any laws in which we have no voice or representation." Abigail Adams remained steadfast in the counsel she offered her husband: She was determined to strengthen women's roles in American culture and politics. Her own wide reading is evident in the many literary and biblical allusions that punctuate her correspondence, especially in her letters detailing the progress of the Revolutionary War while her husband was abroad.

Soon after the war, Abigail Adams joined her husband in France for the American trade negotiations. Her correspondence during this period is filled with trenchant observations on European manners and customs as well as revealing glimpses of the social behavior of some of the leading American representatives, including Benjamin Franklin and Thomas Jefferson. The Adams family returned to the United States in 1788 and to John Adams's election as vice president. The presidency followed in 1797, and it was not until 1801 that the family settled permanently in their home at Braintree (now Quincy), Massachusetts, where Abigail lived in retirement until her death from typhoid fever in 1818.

Further Reading:

J. Whitney, *Abigail Adams*, 1947.
L. Withey, *Dearest Friend: A Life of Abigail Adams*, 1981.
P. L. Levin, *Abigail Adams: A Biography*, 1987.
P. C. Nagel, *The Adams Women: Abigail and Louisa Adams*, 1987.

A. Osborne, *Abigail Adams*, 1989.
E. B. Gelles, *Portia: The World of Abigail Adams*, 1992.

Texts:

Letters of Mrs. Adams, the Wife of John Adams, ed. C. F. Adams, 2 vols., 1840.
Familiar Letters of John Adams and His Wife Abigail Adams, During the Revolution, ed. C. F. Adams, 1876.

The Book of Abigail and John: Selected Letters of the Adams Family, 1762–1784, ed., L. H. Butterfield et al., 1975.
See also *New Letters, 1788–1801*, ed. S. Mitchell, 1947.

Letter to John Adams

[March 31, 1776: The Passion for Liberty]

. . . I desire you would Remember the Ladies, and be more generous and favourable to them than your ancestors. Do not put such unlimited power into the hands of the Husbands. Remember all Men would be tyrants if they could. If perticuliar care and attention is not paid to the Laidies we are determined to foment a Rebellion, and will not hold ourselves bound by any Laws in which we have no voice, or Representation.

That your Sex are Naturally Tyrannical is a Truth so thoroughly established as to admit of no dispute, but such of you as wish to be happy willingly give up the harsh title of Master for the more tender and endearing one of Friend. Why then, not put it out of the power of the vicious and the Lawless to use us with cruelty and indignity with impunity. Men of Sense in all Ages abhor those customs which treat us only as the vassals of your Sex. Regard us then as Beings placed by providence under your protection and in immitation of the Supreem Being make use of that power only for our happiness.
1776/1876

RELATED VOICES

On Female Education

In calling on my patriotic countrymen, to effect so noble an object, the consideration of national glory, should not be overlooked. Ages have rolled away;—barbarians have trodden the weaker sex beneath their feet;—tyrants have robbed us of the present light of heaven, and fain would take its future also. Nations, calling themselves polite, have made us the fancied idols of ridiculous worship, and we have repaid them with ruin for their folly. But where is that wise and heroic country, which has considered, that our rights are sacred, though we cannot defend them? that tho' a weaker, we are an essential part of the body politic, whose corruption or improvement must affect the whole? and which, having thus considered, has sought to give us by education, that rank in the scale of being, to which our importance entitles us? History shows not that country. It shows many, whose legislatures have sought to improve their various vegetable productions, and their breeds of useful brutes; but none, whose public councils have made it an object of their deliberations, to improve the character of their women. Yet though history lifts not her finger to such a one, anticipation does. She points to a nation, which having thrown off the shackles of authority and precedent, shrinks not from schemes of improvement, because other nations have never attempted them; but, which, in its pride of independence, would rather lead than follow, in the march of human improvement: a nation, wise and magnanimous to plan, enterprising to undertake, and rich in resources to execute. Does not every American exult that this country is his own? And who knows how great and good a race of men, may yet arise from the forming hand of mothers, enlightened by the bounty of that beloved country, to defend her liberties, to plan her future improvement, and to raise her to unparalleled glory.

Emma Willard, "An Address to . . . the Legislature of
New York Proposing a Plan for Improving Female Education"
(1819)

Thomas Paine
1737–1809

The son of a Thetford corsetmaker, Thomas Paine had twice fled the Quaker environment of his youth before settling in London, resuming his father's trade, and filling himself with all the science and political philosophy his considerable intellectual curiosity could gather. In 1760 Paine experienced the first in a series of adversities: the death of his wife in childbirth during the first year of their marriage. He was later fired twice from his job collecting excise taxes, worked briefly—and unhappily—as a teacher in Kensington, married someone with whom he apparently never lived, and took over his father's failing business. Before long, Paine was reduced to posting the following announcement in the local British newspaper: "To be sold by auction, on Thursday the 14th of April, and following day, all the household furniture, stock in trade and other effects of Thomas Paine." Such indignities would pursue Thomas Paine all his life. His own repeated misfortunes make more appreciable his fundamental commitment "to meliorate the situation of mankind."

Within six months of his arrival in America, Paine could proudly report to his friend Benjamin Franklin that, despite never having "published a syllable" in England, his numerous topical essays on slavery, unhappy marriages, dueling, inventions, and the rights of the "Female Sex" had helped nearly triple the circulation of the *Pennsylvania Magazine, or American Museum,* the journal he edited and gradually converted into an important popular advocate of independence. He had entered a new world of political turmoil, yet the populace's attachment to Britain was, as he noted, "obstinate." Like the majority of Americans, Paine regarded the dispute with England "as a kind of law suit, in which I supposed, the parties would find a way either to decide or settle it. I had no thoughts of independence or arms." But these sentiments shifted radically with the outbreak of hostilities at Lexington and Concord.

On January 10, 1776, at the encouragement of Dr. Benjamin Rush, Paine published *Common Sense.* Within three months, the pamphlet had sold more than one hundred thousand copies, an extraordinary number in an age when most works were published by subscription, with sales averaging well below one thousand. His bold and simple argument rallied a scattered citizenry to the cause of freedom and exerted considerable influence on the new nation's emerging political philosophy.

Paine's conviction that "those who expect to reap the blessings of freedom must . . . undergo the fatigue of supporting it" led him to enlist in the Revolutionary forces, serving as aide-de-camp to General Nathanael Greene. Witnessing the loss of New York and joining the retreat to Newark, Paine wrote the first of the *American Crisis* letter-pamphlets ("These are the times that try men's souls"), a text that George Washington ordered read to all the troops. Over the next seven years, Paine published thirteen essays in the series, along with three supplementary pieces. Each helped bolster the sagging spirits of the ill-fitted troops and firm the resolve of an occasionally diffident population.

After a brief stint in western Pennsylvania soliciting the support of the Indians in the Revolutionary cause, Paine was elected secretary of the Congressional Committee on Foreign Affairs in April 1777. He held this post until his disclosure of secret information he knew would save Congress the expense of profiteering loans from France. Once again beset by dwindling finances, Paine drifted in and out of various jobs and causes. He supported Robert Morris's efforts to start what is now the Bank of America; he traveled to France to secure additional relief for the Continental Army; he drafted the first legislative act of emancipation while serving as clerk of the Pennsylvania assembly. In 1783 he moved to Bordentown, New Jersey, and devoted himself to invention. He produced, among other items, a smokeless candle and developed a model for an iron bridge without piers. But in 1787, when he could not muster enough capital to finance his projects, he once again left for France.

Paine traveled frequently to England over the next few years and oversaw the construction of the first bridge built under the patent the British government had awarded him. He visited Paris in 1790 to observe the French Revolution and quickly became enmeshed in the political debate it inspired. In 1791 he drafted the first part of *The Rights of Man* as a defense of the French cause in response to Edmund Burke's *Reflections on the Late Revolution in France*. In Paine's view, "every age and generation must be free to act for itself *in all cases* as the ages and generations which preceded it. The vanity and presumption of governing beyond the grave is the most ridiculous and insolent of all tyrannies." Charged with sedition in England, Paine fled to France in 1792, where he was made an honorary citizen, represented Calais at the French Convention, and helped draft that nation's constitution. But his opposition to the execution of Louis XVI landed him in prison for ten months. Before being led away, Paine gave to Joel Barlow, the American poet and journalist, the first part of *The Age of Reason*, a Deist tract that attacked Christianity and praised the virtues of both an impersonal God and the common people.

Paine was released from prison through the efforts of James Monroe, the American ambassador, in whose home Paine lived for the next eighteen months. In ill health and bitter about his neglect while in prison, Paine wrote the second part of *The Age of Reason*, published numerous essays denouncing the Federalists in America, and formulated "agrarian justice," a radical proposal for the democratization of wealth. Banished from England, imprisoned in France, and branded an "infidel" in America, Paine could take some solace in an earlier declaration:

> I speak an open and disinterested language, dictated by no passion but that of humanity. . . . Independence is my happiness, and I view things as they are, without regard to place or purpose; my country is the world, and my religion is to do good.

His altruistic sense of the world included humanitarian views of capital punishment, labor reform, and pensions. His vision culminated in the prospect of a league of nations to foster disarmament.

Thomas Paine returned to the United States in 1802 and spent his last seven years adjusting to new political and social circumstances. Insulted and harassed because of his religious writings, Paine suffered one final round of ignominy: He was not allowed to vote; he was humiliated on his deathbed by the local clergy and barred from burial in a Quaker cemetery. Ten years after his death, Paine's body was exhumed and returned to England to be displayed as a symbol of social reform. His bones, which eventually disappeared, were reported to have been auctioned off as a curiosity.

Paine's criticism of the Bible (Theodore Roosevelt called him a "filthy little atheist") long distracted readers from recognizing Paine's importance as a writer. His humanitarian impulses shaped much of the new nation's thinking about tyranny, justice, equality, and the natural rights of the individual. And his determination to offer a willing audience a plain, simple, vigorous, and forthright version of eighteenth-century liberal thought made Paine one of the most persuasive writers in America's struggle for independence.

Further Reading:

M. D. Conway, *The Life of Thomas Paine*, 2 vols., 1892.

J. Dos Passos, *The Living Thoughts of Thomas Paine*, 1940.

L. Gurko, *Tom Paine, Freedom's Apostle*, 1957.

A.O. Aldridge, *Man of Reason: The Life of Thomas Paine*, 1959.

D. Hawke, *Paine*, 1974.

A. O. Aldridge, *Thomas Paine's American Ideology*, 1984.

I. Dyck, ed., *Citizen of the World: Essays on Thomas Paine*, 1987.

A. J. Ayer, *Thomas Paine*, 1988.

G. Claeys, *Thomas Paine: Social and Political Thought*, 1989.

J. D. Wilson, *Thomas Paine*, 1989.

Text:

The Writings of Thomas Paine, ed. M. D. Conway, 4 vols., 1894–1896.

---

from Common Sense*

Introduction

Perhaps the sentiments contained in the following pages, are not *yet* sufficiently fashionable to procure them general Favor; a long Habit of not thinking a Thing *wrong*, gives it a superficial appearance of being *right*, and raises at first a formidable outcry in defence of Custom. But the Tumult soon subsides. Time makes more Converts than Reason.

As a long and violent abuse of power is generally the means of calling the right of it in question, (and in matters too which might never have been thought of, had not the sufferers been aggravated into the inquiry,) and as the King of England hath undertaken in his *own right*, to support the Parliament in what he calls *Theirs*, and as the good People of this Country are grievously oppressed by the Combination, they have an undoubted privilege to enquire into the Pretensions of both, and equally to reject the Usurpation of *either*.

In the following Sheets, the Author hath studiously avoided every thing which is personal among ourselves. Compliments as well as censure to individuals make no part thereof. The wise and the worthy need not the triumph of a Pamphlet; and those whose sentiments are injudicious or unfriendly will cease of themselves, unless too much pains is bestowed upon their conversions.

---

* The complete title is *Common Sense: Addressed to the Inhabitants of America on the Following Interesting Subjects: viz.: I. Of the origin and design of government in general; with concise remarks on the English constitu-* *tion. II. Of monarchy and hereditary succession. III. Thoughts on the present state of American affairs. IV. Of the present ability of America; with some miscellaneous reflections.*

The cause of America is in a great measure the cause of all mankind. Many circumstances have, and will arise, which are not local, but universal, and through which the principles of all lovers of mankind are affected, and in the event of which their affections are interested. The laying a country desolate with fire and sword, declaring war against the natural rights of all mankind, and extirpating the defenders thereof from the face of the earth, is the concern of every man to whom nature hath given the power of feeling; of which class, regardless of party censure, is

THE AUTHOR.

Thoughts on the Present State of American Affairs

In the following pages I offer nothing more than simple facts, plain arguments, and common sense: and have no other preliminaries to settle with the reader, than that he will divest himself of prejudice and prepossession, and suffer his reason and his feelings to determine for themselves: that he will put on, or rather that he will not put off, the true character of a man, and generously enlarge his views beyond the present day.

Volumes have been written on the subject of the struggle between England and America. Men of all ranks have embarked in the controversy, from different motives, and with various designs; but all have been ineffectual, and the period of debate is closed. Arms as the last resource decide the contest; the appeal was the choice of the King, and the Continent has accepted the challenge.

It hath been reported of the late Mr. Pelham[1] (who tho' an able minister was not without his faults) that on his being attacked in the House of Commons on the score that his measures were only of a temporary kind, replied, *"they will last my time."* Should a thought so fatal and unmanly possess the Colonies in the present contest, the name of ancestors will be remembered by future generations with detestation.

The Sun never shined on a cause of greater worth. 'Tis not the affair of a City, a County, a Province, or a Kingdom; but of a Continent—of at least one eighth part of the habitable Globe. 'Tis not the concern of a day, a year, or an age; posterity are virtually involved in the contest, and will be more or less affected even to the end of time, by the proceedings now. Now is the seed-time of Continental union, faith and honour. The least fracture now will be like a name engraved with the point of a pin on the tender rind of a young oak; the wound would enlarge with the tree, and posterity read it in full grown characters.

By referring the matter from argument to arms, a new æra for politics is struck—a new method of thinking hath arisen. All plans, proposals, &c. prior to the nineteenth of April, *i.e.* to the commencement of hostilities,[2] are like the almanacks of the last year; which tho' proper then, are superceded and useless now. Whatever was advanced by the advocates on either side of the question then, terminated in one and the same point, viz. a union with Great Britain; the only difference between the parties was the method of effecting it; the one proposing force, the other friendship; but it hath so far happened that the first hath failed, and the second hath withdrawn her influence.

---

[1] British prime minister (1743–1754).
[2] At Lexington, Massachusetts, the first armed conflict of the American Revolution began as the "minutemen" defended their ammunition stores against the British on April 19, 1775.

As much hath been said of the advantages of reconciliation, which, like an agreeable dream, hath passed away and left us as we were, it is but right that we should examine the contrary side of the argument, and enquire into some of the many material injuries which these Colonies sustain, and always will sustain, by being connected with and dependent on Great-Britain. To examine that connection and dependence, on the principles of nature and common sense, to see what we have to trust to, if separated, and what we are to expect, if dependant.

I have heard it asserted by some, that as America has flourished under her former connection with Great-Britain, the same connection is necessary towards her future happiness, and will always have the same effect. Nothing can be more fallacious than this kind of argument. We may as well assert that because a child has thrived upon milk, that it is never to have meat, or that the first twenty years of our lives is to become a precedent for the next twenty. But even this is admitting more than is true; for I answer roundly, that America would have flourished as much, and probably much more, had no European power taken any notice of her. The commerce by which she hath enriched herself are the necessaries of life, and will always have a market while eating is the custom of Europe.

But she has protected us, say some. That she hath engrossed us is true, and defended the Continent at our expense as well as her own, is admitted; and she would have defended Turkey from the same motive, *viz.* for the sake of trade and dominion.

Alas! we have been long led away by ancient prejudices and made large sacrifices to superstition. We have boasted the protection of Great Britain, without considering, that her motive was *interest* not *attachment;* and that she did not protect us from *our enemies* on *our account;* but from *her enemies* on *her own account,* from those who had no quarrel with us on any *other account,* and who will always be our enemies on the *same account.* Let Britain waive her pretensions to the Continent, or the Continent throw off the dependance, and we should be at peace with France and Spain, were they at war with Britain. The miseries of Hanover's[3] last war ought to warn us against connections.

It hath lately been asserted in parliament, that the Colonies have no relation to each other but through the Parent Country, *i.e.* that Pennsylvania and the Jerseys,[4] and so on for the rest, are sister Colonies by the way of England; this is certainly a very roundabout way of proving relationship, but it is the nearest and only true way of proving enmity (or enemyship, if I may so call it.) France and Spain never were, nor perhaps ever will be, our enemies as *Americans,* but as our being the *subjects of Great Britain.*

But Britain is the parent country, say some. Then the more shame upon her conduct. Even brutes do not devour their young, nor savages make war upon their families; Wherefore, the assertion, if true, turns to her reproach; but it happens not to be true, or only partly so, and the phrase *parent* or *mother country* hath been jesuitically adopted by the King and his parasites, with a low papistical design of gaining an unfair bias on the credulous weakness of our minds. Europe, and not England, is the parent country of America. This new World hath been the asylum for the persecuted lovers of civil and re-

---

[3] Britain's King George III was a descendant of the Prussian House of Hanover; here Paine refers to the Seven Years' War (1756–1763), which originally engaged Prussia and Austria and expanded to include all major European powers. Although Britain was favored in the war settlement, American losses in the French and Indian campaigns were severe.

[4] At the time the colony was sectioned into East and West Jersey.

ligious liberty from *every part* of Europe. Hither have they fled, not from the tender embraces of the mother, but from the cruelty of the monster; and it is so far true of England, that the same tyranny which drove the first emigrants from home, pursues their descendants still.

In this extensive quarter of the globe, we forget the narrow limits of three hundred and sixty miles (the extent of England) and carry our friendship on a larger scale; we claim brotherhood with every European Christian, and triumph in the generosity of the sentiment.

It is pleasant to observe by what regular gradations we surmount the force of local prejudices, as we enlarge our acquaintance with the World. A man born in any town in England divided into parishes, will naturally associate most with his fellow parishioners (because their interests in many cases will be common) and distinguish him by the name of *neighbour;* if he meet him but a few miles from home, he drops the narrow idea of a street, and salutes him by the name of *townsman;* if he travel out of the county and meet him in any other, he forgets the minor divisions of street and town, and calls him *countryman, i.e. countyman:* but if in their foreign excursions they should associate in France, or any other part of *Europe,* their local remembrance would be enlarged into that of *Englishmen.* And by a just parity of reasoning, all Europeans meeting in America, or any other quarter of the globe, are *countrymen;* for England, Holland, Germany, or Sweden, when compared with the whole, stand in the same places on the larger scale, which the divisions of street, town, and county do on the smaller ones; Distinctions too limited for Continental minds. Not one third of the inhabitants, even of this province[5] are of English descent. Wherefore, I reprobate the phrase of Parent or Mother Country applied to England only, as being false, selfish, narrow and ungenerous.

But, admitting that we were all of English descent, what does it amount to? Nothing. Britain, being now an open enemy, extinguishes every other name and title: and to say that reconciliation is our duty, is truly farcical. The first king of England, of the present line (William the Conqueror) was a Frenchman, and half the peers of England are descendants from the same country; wherefore, by the same method of reasoning, England ought to be governed by France.

Much hath been said of the united strength of Britain and the Colonies, that in conjunction they might bid defiance to the world: But this is mere presumption; the fate of war is uncertain, neither do the expressions mean any thing; for this continent would never suffer itself to be drained of inhabitants, to support the British arms in either Asia, Africa, or Europe.

Besides, what have we to do with setting the world at defiance? Our plan is commerce, and that, well attended to, will secure us the peace and friendship of all Europe; because it is the interest of all Europe to have America a free port. Her trade will always be a protection, and her barrenness of gold and silver secure her from invaders.

I challenge the warmest advocate for reconciliation to show a single advantage that this continent can reap by being connected with Great Britain. I repeat the challenge; not a single advantage is derived. Our corn will fetch its price in any market in Europe, and our imported goods must be paid for by them where we will.

But the injuries and disadvantages which we sustain by that connection, are without number; and our duty to mankind at large, as well as to ourselves, instruct us to re-

---

[5] Pennsylvania.

nounce the alliance: because, any submission to, or dependance on, Great Britain, tends directly to involve this Continent in European wars and quarrels, and set us at variance with nations who would otherwise seek our friendship, and against whom we have neither anger nor complaint. As Europe is our market for trade, we ought to form no partial connection with any part of it. It is the true interest of America to steer clear of European contentions, which she never can do, while, by her dependance on Britain, she is made the makeweight in the scale of British politics.

Europe is too thickly planted with Kingdoms to be long at peace, and whenever a war breaks out between England and any foreign power, the trade of America goes to ruin, *because of her connection with Britain.* The next war may not turn out like the last,[6] and should it not, the advocates for reconciliation now will be wishing for separation then, because neutrality in that case would be a safer convoy than a man of war. Everything that is right or reasonable pleads for separation. The blood of the slain, the weeping voice of nature cries. 'TIS TIME TO PART. Even the distance at which the Almighty hath placed England and America is a strong and natural proof that the authority of the one over the other, was never the design of Heaven. The time likewise at which the Continent was discovered, adds weight to the argument, and the manner in which it was peopled, encreases the force of it. The Reformation was preceded by the discovery of America: As if the Almighty graciously meant to open a sanctuary to the persecuted in future years, when home should afford neither friendship nor safety.

The authority of Great Britain over this continent, is a form of government, which sooner or later must have an end: And a serious mind can draw no true pleasure by looking forward, under the painful and positive conviction that what he calls "the present constitution" is merely temporary. As parents, we can have no joy, knowing that this government is not sufficiently lasting to ensure any thing which we may bequeath to posterity: And by a plain method of argument, as we are running the next generation into debt, we ought to do the work of it, otherwise we use them meanly and pitifully. In order to discover the line of our duty rightly, we should take our children in our hand, and fix our station a few years farther into life; that eminence will present a prospect which a few present fears and prejudices conceal from our sight.

Though I would carefully avoid giving unnecessary offence, yet I am inclined to believe, that all those who espouse the doctrine of reconciliation, may be included within the following descriptions.

Interested men, who are not to be trusted, weak men who *cannot* see, prejudiced men who will not see, and a certain set of moderate men who think better of the European world than it deserves; and this last class, by an ill-judged deliberation, will be the cause of more calamities to this Continent than all the other three.

It is the good fortune of many to live distant from the scene of present sorrow; the evil is not sufficiently brought to their doors to make them feel the precariousness with which all American property is possessed. But let our imaginations transport us a few moments to Boston; that seat of wretchedness will teach us wisdom, and instruct us for ever to renounce a power in whom we can have no trust.[7] The inhabitants of that un-

---

[6] At the conclusion of the Seven Years' War, Britain was given all the French territory in North America through the Treaty of Paris (1763).

[7] Boston was blockaded for six months under British military occupation.

fortunate city who but a few months ago were in ease and affluence, have now no other alternative than to stay and starve, or turn out to beg. Endangered by the fire of their friends if they continue within the city, and plundered by the soldiery if they leave it, in their present situation they are prisoners without the hope of redemption, and in a general attack for their relief they would be exposed to the fury of both armies.

Men of passive tempers look somewhat lightly over the offences of Great Britain, and, still hoping for the best, are apt to call out, *Come, come, we shall be friends again for all this.* But examine the passions and feelings of mankind: bring the doctrine of reconciliation to the touchstone of nature, and then tell me whether you can hereafter love, honour, and faithfully serve the power that hath carried fire and sword into your land? If you cannot do all these, then are you only deceiving yourselves, and by your delay bringing ruin upon posterity. Your future connection with Britain, whom you can neither love nor honour, will be forced and unnatural, and being formed only on the plan of present convenience, will in a little time fall into a relapse more wretched than the first. But if you say, you can still pass the violations over, then I ask, hath your house been burnt? Hath your property been destroyed before your face? Are your wife and children destitute of a bed to lie on, or bread to live on? Have you lost a parent or a child by their hands, and yourself the ruined and wretched survivor? If you have not, then you are not a judge of those who have. But if you have, and can still shake hands with the murderers, then are you unworthy the name of husband, father, friend, or lover, and whatever may be your rank or title in life, you have the heart of a coward, and the spirit of a sycophant.

This is not inflaming or exaggerating matters, but trying them by those feelings and affections which nature justifies, and without which we should be incapable of discharging the social duties of life, or enjoying the felicities of it. I mean not to exhibit horror for the purpose of provoking revenge, but to awaken us from fatal and unmanly slumbers, that we may pursue determinately some fixed object. 'Tis not in the power of Britain or of Europe to conquer America, if she doth not conquer herself by delay and timidity. The present winter is worth an age if rightly employed, but if lost or neglected the whole Continent will partake of the misfortune; and there is no punishment which that man doth not deserve, be he who, or what, or where he will, that may be the means of sacrificing a season so precious and useful.

'Tis repugnant to reason, to the universal order of things, to all examples from former ages, to suppose that this Continent can long remain subject to any external power. The most sanguine in Britain doth not think so. The utmost stretch of human wisdom cannot, at this time, compass a plan, short of separation, which can promise the continent even a year's security. Reconciliation is *now* a fallacious dream. Nature hath deserted the connection, and art cannot supply her place. For, as Milton wisely expresses, "never can true reconcilement grow where wounds of deadly hate have pierced so deep."[8]

A government of our own is our natural right: and when a man seriously reflects on the precariousness of human affairs, he will become convinced, that it is infinitely wiser and safer, to form a constitution of our own in a cool deliberate manner, while we have it in our power, than to trust such an interesting event to time and chance. If we omit it

---

8 John Milton, *Paradise Lost*, IV, 98–99.

now, some Massanello[9] may hereafter arise, who, laying hold of popular disquietudes, may collect together the desperate and the discontented, and by assuming to themselves the powers of government, finally sweep away the liberties of the Continent like a deluge. Should the government of America return again into the hands of Britain, the tottering situation of things will be a temptation for some desperate adventurer to try his fortune; and in such a case, what relief can Britain give? Ere she could hear the news, the fatal business might be done; and ourselves suffering like the wretched Britons under the oppression of the Conqueror. Ye that oppose independance now, ye know not what ye do: ye are opening a door to eternal tyranny, by keeping vacant the seat of government. There are thousands and tens of thousands, who would think it glorious to expel from the Continent, that barbarous and hellish power, which hath stirred up the Indians and the Negroes to destroy us; the cruelty hath a double guilt, it is dealing brutally by us, and treacherously by them.

To talk of friendship with those in whom our reason forbids us to have faith, and our affections wounded thro' a thousand pores instruct us to detest, is madness and folly. Every day wears out the little remains of kindred between us and them; and can there be any reason to hope, that as the relationship expires, the affection will encrease, or that we shall agree better when we have ten times more and greater concerns to quarrel over than ever?

Ye that tell us of harmony and reconciliation, can ye restore to us the time that is past? Can ye give to prostitution its former innocence? neither can ye reconcile Britain and America. The last cord now is broken, the people of England are presenting addresses against us. There are injuries which nature cannot forgive; she would cease to be nature if she did. As well can the lover forgive the ravisher of his mistress, as the Continent forgive the murders of Britain. The Almighty hath implanted in us these unextinguishable feelings for good and wise purposes. They are the Guardians of his Image in our hearts. They distinguish us from the herd of common animals. The social compact would dissolve, and justice be extirpated from the earth, or have only a casual existence were we callous to the touches of affection. The robber and the murderer would often escape unpunished, did not the injuries which our tempers sustain, provoke us into justice.

O! ye that love mankind! Ye that dare oppose not only the tyranny but the tyrant, stand forth! Every spot of the old world is overrun with oppression. Freedom hath been hunted round the Globe. Asia and Africa have long expelled her. Europe regards her like a stranger, and England hath given her warning to depart. O! receive the fugitive, and prepare in time an asylum for mankind.

1776

---

[9] Paine's note: "Thomas Anello, otherwise Massanello, a fisherman of Naples who after spiriting up his countrymen in the public marketplace, against the oppression of the Spaniards, to whom the place was then subject, prompted them to revolt, and in the space of a day became King."

from The American Crisis

Number 1

These are the times that try men's souls. The summer soldier and the sunshine patriot will, in this crisis, shrink from the service of their country; but he that stands it *now*, deserves the love and thanks of man and woman. Tyranny, like hell, is not easily conquered; yet we have this consolation with us, that the harder the conflict, the more glorious the triumph. What we obtain too cheap, we esteem too lightly: it is dearness only that gives every thing its value. Heaven knows how to put a proper price upon its goods; and it would be strange indeed if so celestial an article as FREEDOM should not be highly rated. Britain, with an army to enforce her tyranny, has declared that she has a right (*not only to* TAX) but "to BIND *us in* ALL CASES WHATSOEVER,"[1] and if being *bound in that manner,* is not slavery, then is there not such a thing as slavery upon earth. Even the expression is impious; for so unlimited a power can belong only to God.

Whether the independence of the continent was declared too soon, or delayed too long, I will not now enter into as an argument; my own simple opinion is, that had it been eight months earlier, it would have been much better. We did not make a proper use of last winter, neither could we, while we were in a dependant state. However, the fault, if it were one, was all our own;[2] we have none to blame but ourselves. But no great deal is lost yet. All that Howe[3] has been doing for this month past, is rather a ravage than a conquest, which the spirit of the Jerseys,[4] a year ago, would have quickly repulsed, and which time and a little resolution will soon recover.

I have as little superstition in me as any man living, but my secret opinion has ever been, and still is, that God Almighty will not give up a people to military destruction, or leave them unsupportedly to perish, who have so earnestly and so repeatedly sought to avoid the calamities of war, by every decent method which wisdom could invent. Neither have I so much of the infidel in me, as to suppose that He has relinquished the government of the world, and given us up to the care of devils; and as I do not, I cannot see on what grounds the king of Britain can look up to heaven for help against us: a common murderer, a highwayman, or a house-breaker, has as good a pretence as he.

'Tis surprising to see how rapidly a panic will sometimes run through a country. All nations and ages have been subject to them: Britain has trembled like an ague at the report of a French fleet of flat bottomed boats; and in the fourteenth century[5] the whole English army, after ravaging the kingdom of France, was driven back like men petrified with fear; and this brave exploit was performed by a few broken forces collected and headed by a woman, Joan of Arc. Would that heaven might inspire some Jersey maid to spirit up her countrymen, and save her fair fellow sufferers from ravage and ravishment! Yet panics, in some cases, have their uses; they produce as much good as hurt.

---

[1] The quotation is from an English parliamentary act of 1776.

[2] Paine's note, a quotation from his *Common Sense* (1776): "The present winter is worth an age, if rightly employed; but if lost or neglected, the whole continent will partake of the evil; and there is no punishment that man does not deserve, be he who, or what, or where he will, that may be the means of sacrificing a season so precious and useful."

[3] British general.

[4] The colony was composed of East Jersey and West Jersey.

[5] Actually the fifteenth century.

Their duration is always short; the mind soon grows through them, and acquires a firmer habit than before. But their peculiar advantage is, that they are the touchstones of sincerity and hypocrisy, and bring things and men to light, which might otherwise have lain forever undiscovered. In fact, they have the same effect on secret traitors, which an imaginary apparition would have upon a private murderer. They sift out the hidden thoughts of man, and hold them up in public to the world. Many a disguised tory has lately shown his head, that shall penitentially solemnize with curses the day on which Howe arrived upon the Delaware.

As I was with the troops at Fort Lee, and marched with them to the edge of Pennsylvania, I am well acquainted with many circumstances, which those who live at a distance know but little or nothing of. Our situation there was exceedingly cramped, the place being a narrow neck of land between the North River[6] and the Hackensack. Our force was inconsiderable, being not one fourth so great as Howe could bring against us. We had no army at hand to have relieved the garrison, had we shut ourselves up and stood on our defence. Our ammunition, light artillery, and the best part of our stores, had been removed, on the apprehension that Howe would endeavor to penetrate the Jerseys, in which case Fort Lee could be of no use to us; for it must occur to every thinking man, whether in the army or not, that these kind of field forts are only for temporary purposes, and last in use no longer than the enemy directs his force against the particular object, which such forts are raised to defend. Such was our situation and condition at Fort Lee on the morning of the 20th of November, when an officer arrived with information that the enemy with 200 boats had landed about seven miles above: Major General [Nathaniel] Green, who commanded the garrison, immediately ordered them under arms, and sent express to General Washington at the town of Hackensack, distant by the way of the ferry = six miles. Our first object was to secure the bridge over the Hackensack, which laid up the river between the enemy and us, about six miles from us, and three from them. General Washington arrived in about three quarters of an hour, and marched at the head of the troops towards the bridge, which place I expected we should have a brush for; however, they did not choose to dispute it with us, and the greatest part of our troops went over the bridge, the rest over the ferry, except some which passed at a mill on a small creek, between the bridge and the ferry, and made their way through some marshy grounds up to the town of Hackensack, and there passed the river. We brought off as much baggage as the wagons could contain, the rest was lost. The simple object was to bring off the garrison, and march them on till they could be strengthened by the Jersey or Pennsylvania militia, so as to be enabled to make a stand. We staid four days at Newark, collected our out-posts with some of the Jersey militia, and marched out twice to meet the enemy, on being informed that they were advancing, though our numbers were greatly inferior to theirs. Howe, in my little opinion, committed a great error in generalship in not throwing a body of forces off from Staten Island through Amboy, by which means he might have seized all our stores at Brunswick, and intercepted our march into Pennsylvania; but if we believe the power of hell to be limited, we must likewise believe that their agents are under some providential controul.

I shall not now attempt to give all the particulars of our retreat to the Delaware; suffice it for the present to say, that both officers and men, though greatly harassed and

---

[6] The Hudson.

fatigued, frequently without rest, covering, or provision, the inevitable consequences of a long retreat, bore it with a manly and martial spirit. All their wishes centered in one, which was, that the country would turn out and help them to drive the enemy back. Voltaire has remarked that king William[7] never appeared to full advantage but in difficulties and in action; the same remark may be made on General Washington, for the character fits him. There is a natural firmness in some minds which cannot be unlocked by trifles, but which, when unlocked, discovers a cabinet of fortitude; and I reckon it among those kind of public blessings, which we do not immediately see, that God hath blessed him with uninterrupted health, and given him a mind that can even flourish upon care.

I shall conclude this paper with some miscellaneous remarks on the state of our affairs; and shall begin with asking the following question, Why is it that the enemy have left the New-England provinces, and made these middle ones the seat of war? The answer is easy: New-England is not infested with tories, and we are. I have been tender in raising the cry against these men, and used numberless arguments to show them their danger, but it will not do to sacrifice a world either to their folly or their baseness. The period is now arrived, in which either they or we must change our sentiments, or one or both must fall. And what is a tory? Good God! what is he? I should not be afraid to go with a hundred whigs against a thousand tories, were they to attempt to get into arms. Every tory is a coward; for servile, slavish, self-interested fear is the foundation of toryism; and a man under such influence, though he may be cruel, never can be brave.

But, before the line of irrecoverable separation be drawn between us, let us reason the matter together: Your conduct is an invitation to the enemy, yet not one in a thousand of you has heart enough to join him. Howe is as much deceived by you as the American cause is injured by you. He expects you will all take up arms, and flock to his standard, with muskets on your shoulders. Your opinions are of no use to him, unless you support him personally, for 'tis soldiers, and not tories, that he wants.

I once felt all that kind of anger, which a man ought to feel, against the mean principles that are held by the tories: a noted one, who kept a tavern at Amboy, was standing at his door, with as pretty a child in his hand, about eight or nine years old, as I ever saw, and after speaking his mind as freely as he thought was prudent, finished with this unfatherly expression, *"Well! give me peace in my day."* Not a man lives on the continent but fully believes that a separation must some time or other finally take place, and a generous parent should have said, *"If there must be trouble, let it be in my day, that my child may have peace;"* and this single reflection, well applied, is sufficient to awaken every man to duty. Not a place upon earth might be so happy as America. Her situation is remote from all the wrangling world, and she has nothing to do but to trade with them. A man can distinguish himself between temper and principle, and I am as confident, as I am that God governs the world, that America will never be happy till she gets clear of foreign dominion. Wars, without ceasing, will break out till that period arrives, and the continent must in the end be conqueror; for though the flame of liberty may sometimes cease to shine, the coal can never expire.

America did not, nor does not want force; but she wanted a proper application of that force. Wisdom is not the purchase of a day, and it is no wonder that we should err

---

[7] William III, king of England from 1689 to 1702.

at the first setting off. From an excess of tenderness, we were unwilling to raise an army, and trusted our cause to the temporary defence of a well-meaning militia. A summer's experience has now taught us better; yet with those troops, while they were collected, we were able to set bounds to the progress of the enemy, and, thank God! they are again assembling. I always considered militia as the best troops in the world for a sudden exertion, but they will not do for a long campaign. Howe, it is probable, will make an attempt on this city;[8] should he fail on this side the Delaware, he is ruined: if he succeeds, our cause is not ruined. He stakes all on his side against a part on ours; admitting he succeeds, the consequence will be, that armies from both ends of the continent will march to assist their suffering friends in the middle states; for he cannot go everywhere, it is impossible. I consider Howe as the greatest enemy the tories have; he is bringing a war into their country, which, had it not been for him and partly for themselves, they had been clear of. Should he now be expelled, I wish with all the devotion of a Christian, that the names of whig and tory may never more be mentioned; but should the tories give him encouragement to come, or assistance if he come, I as sincerely wish that our next year's arms may expel them from the continent, and the congress appropriate their possessions to the relief of those who have suffered in well-doing. A single successful battle next year will settle the whole. America could carry on a two years war by the confiscation of the property of disaffected persons, and be made happy by their expulsion. Say not that this is revenge, call it rather the soft resentment of a suffering people, who, having no object in view but the *good* of *all,* have staked their *own all* upon a seemingly doubtful event. Yet it is folly to argue against determined hardness; eloquence may strike the ear, and the language of sorrow draw forth the tear of compassion, but nothing can reach the heart that is steeled with prejudice.

Quitting this class of men, I turn with the warm ardor of a friend to those who have nobly stood, and are yet determined to stand the matter out: I call not upon a few, but upon all: not on *this* state or *that* state, but on *every* state: up and help us; lay your shoulders to the wheel; better have too much force than too little, when so great an object is at stake. Let it be told to the future world, that in the depth of winter, when nothing but hope and virtue could survive, that the city and the country, alarmed at one common danger, came forth to meet and to repulse it. Say not that thousands are gone, turn out your tens of thousands; throw not the burden of the day upon Providence, but *"show your faith by your works,"*[9] that God may bless you. It matters not where you live, or what rank of life you hold, the evil or the blessing will reach you all. The far and the near, the home counties and the back, the rich and the poor, will suffer or rejoice alike. The heart that feels not now, is dead: the blood of his children will curse his cowardice, who shrinks back at a time when a little might have saved the whole, and made *them* happy. I love the man that can smile in trouble, that can gather strength from distress, and grow brave by reflection. 'Tis the business of little minds to shrink; but he whose heart is firm, and whose conscience approves his conduct, will pursue his principles unto death. My own line of reasoning is to myself as straight and clear as a ray of light. Not all the treasures of the world, so far as I believe, could have induced me to support an offensive war, for I think it murder; but if a thief breaks into my house, burns and

---

[8] Philadelphia.
[9] James 2:18.

destroys my property, and kills or threatens to kill me, or those that are in it, and to "*bind me in all cases whatsoever*"[10] to his absolute will, am I to suffer it? What signifies it to me, whether he who does it is a king or a common man; my countryman or not my countryman; whether it be done by an individual villain, or an army of them? If we reason to the root of things we shall find no difference; neither can any just cause be assigned why we should punish in the one case and pardon in the other. Let them call me rebel, and welcome, I feel no concern from it; but I should suffer the misery of devils, were I to make a whore of my soul by swearing allegiance to one whose character is that of a sottish, stupid, stubborn, worthless, brutish man. I conceive likewise a horrid idea in receiving mercy from a being, who at the last day shall be shrieking to the rocks and mountains to cover him, and fleeing with terror from the orphan, the widow, and the slain of America.

There are cases which cannot be overdone by language, and this is one. There are persons, too, who see not the full extent of the evil which threatens them; they solace themselves with hopes that the enemy, if he succeed, will be merciful. It is the madness of folly, to expect mercy from those who have refused to do justice; and even mercy, where conquest is the object, is only a trick of war; the cunning of the fox is as murderous as the violence of the wolf, and we ought to guard equally against both. Howe's first object is, partly by threats and partly by promises, to terrify or seduce the people to deliver up their arms and receive mercy. The ministry recommended the same plan to Gage,[11] and this is what the tories call making their peace, "*a peace which passeth all understanding*" *indeed!*[12] A peace which would be the immediate forerunner of a worse ruin than any we have yet thought of. Ye men of Pennsylvania, do reason upon these things! Were the back counties to give up their arms, they would fall an easy prey to the Indians, who are all armed: this perhaps is what some tories would not be sorry for. Were the home counties to deliver up their arms, they would be exposed to the resentment of the back counties, who would then have it in their power to chastise their defection at pleasure. And were any one state to give up its arms, *that* state must be garrisoned by all Howe's army of Britons and Hessians to preserve it from the anger of the rest. Mutual fear is the principal link in the chain of mutual love, and woe be to that state that breaks the compact. Howe is mercifully inviting you to barbarous destruction, and men must be either rogues or fools that will not see it. I dwell not upon the vapours of imagination; I bring reason to your ears, and, in language as plain as A, B, C, hold up truth to your eyes.

I thank God, that I fear not. I see no real cause for fear. I know our situation well, and can see the way out of it. While our army was collected, Howe dared not risk a battle; and it is no credit to him that he decamped from the White Plains, and waited a mean opportunity to ravage the defenceless Jerseys; but it is great credit to us, that, with a handful of men, we sustained an orderly retreat for near an hundred miles, brought off our ammunition, all our field pieces, the greatest part of our stores, and had four rivers to pass. None can say that our retreat was precipitate, for we were near three weeks in performing it, that the country[13] might have time to come in. Twice we marched back to meet the enemy, and remained out till dark. The sign of fear was not

---

[10] See footnote 1.

[11] A commander of British forces from 1763 to 1775.

[12] A play on Philippians 4:7.

[13] i.e., local volunteers.

seen in our camp, and had not some of the cowardly and disaffected inhabitants spread false alarms through the country, the Jerseys had never been ravaged. Once more we are again collected and collecting; our new army at both ends of the continent is recruiting fast, and we shall be able to open the next campaign with sixty thousand men, well armed and clothed. This is our situation, and who will may know it. By perseverance and fortitude we have the prospect of a glorious issue; by cowardice and submission, the sad choice of a variety of evils—a ravaged country—a depopulated city—habitations without safety, and slavery without hope—our homes turned into barracks and bawdy-houses for Hessians, and a future race to provide for, whose fathers we shall doubt of. Look on this picture and weep over it! and if there yet remains one thoughtless wretch who believes it not, let him suffer it unlamented.

COMMON SENSE.

1776

Michel-Guillaume Jean de Crèvecoeur
1735–1813

"What then is the American, this new man?" With that question a Jesuit-trained, English-educated, aristocratic Frenchman who had adopted New York as his native ground began one of the earliest inquiries into a relatively new psychosocial phenomenon, the American identity.

The question suited the personality of the man who asked it. Himself an amalgam of identities, Michel-Guillaume Jean de Crèvecoeur was born near Caen, in Normandy, in 1735. He received a Jesuit education, completed his studies in England, and then, at nineteen, left for Canada, where he served as an officer and cartographer under General Montcalm. After Wolfe defeated the French at Quebec in 1759, Crèvecoeur resigned his commission and traveled extensively through the British colonies. He finally settled down in New York, where in 1765 he took out citizenship papers, purchased a large farm in Orange County, married a woman from Yonkers, had three children, and immersed himself physically and philosophically in the role of "a simple American farmer." Presumably to assure himself of his new identity, he decided to go by the English name Hector St. John, though he was never consistent about what he called himself: "J. Hector St. John (a Pennsylvanian farmer)" appears on the title page of his first book, and throughout his career he used various combinations of his real and assumed names.

The American Revolution interrupted a pattern of life that Crèvecoeur rhapsodically described as one of idyllic agrarian self-sufficiency. Partisans are not noted for their tolerance of mixed identities during times of political crisis, and Crèvecoeur, who attempted to remain neutral, found himself suspected by both sides. His rural tranquility shattered by the war, his life in danger, he resolved to leave the country. After months of anxious waiting and a few more months in a British prison in

New York City, Crèvecoeur obtained permission in 1780 to sail with one of his children for Europe. He took with him manuscripts he had worked on during his early travels and his farming days. In 1782 a London publisher brought out *Letters from an American Farmer,* a series of twelve epistolary essays, all but one of which Crèvecoeur had composed before the Revolution. The *Letters* were an immediate success, and Crèvecoeur became a popular figure in Parisian literary circles, where, according to the fashionable primitivism of the time, he was referred to as "an American savage." An advertisement appended to the *Letters* promised a second series, but in 1783 Crèvecoeur accepted a position in New York City as French consul to New York, Connecticut, and New Jersey. The second series of letters remained unpublished until the 1920s, when they were rediscovered and brought out as *Sketches of Eighteenth-Century America.* Revealing more clearly than in previous writings his Tory leanings and advocating highly restrictive trade policies, the sequel of letters had probably been suppressed once Crèvecoeur had assumed his new diplomatic position.

When Crèvecoeur returned to America in 1783, he found his wife dead, his farm destroyed by an allied attack of Loyalists and Indians, and his children in the care of a Boston family. Recovering his children, he moved to New York City, where he established headquarters and worked at continuing friendly diplomatic relations between his two countries. He also contributed medical and agricultural articles to journals and is credited with having introduced alfalfa to the United States. He made another trip to Paris to prepare a second edition of the *Letters,* then, after serving as consul for three more years, left America permanently in 1790. In 1801 he published in French a three-volume travel book on America, *Le Voyage dans la haute Pennsylvanie et dans l'état de New-York,* which he camouflaged as merely his edited translation of an anonymous, deteriorated English manuscript discovered in Copenhagen. Crèvecoeur died in Normandy in 1813.

Like many late-eighteenth-century writers, Crèvecoeur wrote glowingly of nature and the values of an agrarian economy. His enticing descriptions of a simple rural life based on a domestic economy of "ample subsistence" had the unfortunate promotional effect of luring many people into frontier conditions that little resembled the author's Orange County plantation. "I used to admire my head off," said D. H. Lawrence of Crèvecoeur's world, "before I tiptoed into the Wilds and saw the shacks of the Homesteaders." But if Crèvecoeur sometimes cheats on the side of sentimentality when it comes to providing an accurate account of rural benefits and New World opportunities, he could, as *Sketches of Eighteenth-Century America* shows, also write quite convincingly of rural hardships and the ordinary tasks of agricultural life. The set of sketches collected as "Thoughts of an American Farmer on Various Rural Subjects" offers one of the most vivid accounts we have of everyday life in a small, late-eighteenth-century farm community.

Although Crèvecoeur wrote most effectively when he was being least promotional and least theoretical, he nevertheless remains best known for his investigations into the American character. He concludes his most famous essay with a case study (omitted here) of a single immigrant whose history answers the essay's central question, "What is an American?" Given Crèvecoeur's versatility, his pragmatic buoyancy, his capacity for multiple loyalties, and his self-reliance and self-inventiveness, he might just as well have appended his own biography as the answer to that still intriguing question.

Further Reading:
J. P. Mitchell, *St. Jean de Crèvecoeur*, 1916.
T. Philbrick, *St. John de Crèvecoeur*, 1970.

G. W. Allen and R. Asselineau, *St. John de Crève-coeur: The Life of an American Farmer*, 1987.

Text:
Letters from an American Farmer, ed. W. B. Trent, 1904.
See also *Crèvecoeur's 18th-Century Travels in Pennsylvania and New York,* ed. P. G. Adams, 1962.

Letters from an American Farmer, ed. A. E. Stone, 1963.
Journey into Northern Pennsylvania and the State of New York, ed. C. S. Bostelmann, 1964.

Letters from an American Farmer

from ***Letter III: What Is an American?***

I wish I could be acquainted with the feelings and thoughts which must agitate the heart and present themselves to the mind of an enlightened Englishman, when he first lands on this continent. He must greatly rejoice that he lived at a time to see this fair country discovered and settled; he must necessarily feel a share of national pride, when he views the chain of settlements which embellishes these extended shores. When he says to himself, this is the work of my countrymen, who, when convulsed by factions, afflicted by a variety of miseries and wants, restless and impatient, took refuge here. They brought along with them their national genius, to which they principally owe what liberty they enjoy, and what substance they possess. Here he sees the industry of his native country displayed in a new manner, and traces in their works the embrios of all the arts, sciences, and ingenuity which flourish in Europe. Here he beholds fair cities, substantial villages, extensive fields, an immense country filled with decent houses, good roads, orchards, meadows, and bridges, where an hundred years ago all was wild, woody and uncultivated! What a train of pleasing ideas this fair spectacle must suggest; it is a prospect which must inspire a good citizen with the most heartfelt pleasure. The difficulty consists in the manner of viewing so extensive a scene. He is arrived on a new continent; a modern society offers itself to his contemplation, different from what he had hitherto seen. It is not composed, as in Europe, of great lords who possess every thing, and of a herd of people who have nothing. Here are no aristocratical families, no courts, no kings, no bishops, no ecclesiastical dominion, no invisible power giving to a few a very visible one; no great manufacturers employing thousands, no great refinements of luxury. The rich and the poor are not so far removed from each other as they are in Europe. Some few towns excepted, we are all tillers of the earth, from Nova Scotia to West Florida. We are a people of cultivators, scattered over an immense territory, communicating with each other by means of good roads and navigable rivers, united by the silken bands of mild government, all respecting the laws, without dreading their power, because they are equitable. We are all animated with the spirit of an industry which is unfettered and unrestrained, because each person works for himself. If he travels through our rural districts he views not the hostile castle, and the haughty mansion, contrasted with the clay-built hut and miserable cabbin, where cattle and men help to keep each other warm, and dwell in meanness, smoke, and indigence. A pleasing uniformity of decent competence appears throughout our habitations. The meanest of our log-houses is a dry and comfortable habitation. Lawyer or merchant are the fairest titles our towns afford; that of a farmer is the only appellation of the rural inhabitants of our country. It must take some time ere he can reconcile himself to our dictionary, which is but short in words of dignity, and names of honour. There, on a Sunday, he sees a congregation of respectable farmers and their wives, all clad in neat homespun, well mounted, or riding in their own humble waggons. There is not among them an esquire, saving the unlettered magistrate. There he sees a parson as simple as his flock, a farmer who does not riot on the labour of others. We have no princes, for whom we toil, starve, and bleed: we are the most perfect society now existing in the world. Here man is free as he ought to be; nor is this pleasing equality so transitory as many others are. Many ages will not see the shores of our great lakes replenished with inland nations, nor the unknown bounds of North America entirely peopled. Who can tell how far it extends? Who can tell the millions of men whom it will feed and contain? for no European foot has as yet travelled half the extent of this mighty continent!

The next wish of this traveller will be to know whence came all these people? they are a mixture of English, Scotch, Irish, French, Dutch, Germans, and Swedes. From this promiscuous breed, that race now called Americans have arisen. The eastern provinces must indeed be excepted, as being the unmixed descendents of Englishmen. I have heard many wish that they had been more intermixed also: for my part, I am no wisher, and think it much better as it has happened. They exhibit a most conspicuous figure in this great and variegated picture; they too enter for a great share in the pleasing perspective displayed in these thirteen provinces. I know it is fashionable to reflect on them, but I respect them for what they have done; for the accuracy and wisdom with which they have settled their territory; for the decency of their manners; for their early love of letters; their ancient college,[1] the first in this hemisphere; for their industry; which to me who am but a farmer, is the criterion of everything. There never was a people, situated as they are, who with so ungrateful a soil have done more in so short a time. Do you think that the monarchical ingredients which are more prevalent in other governments, have purged them from all foul stains? Their histories assert the contrary.

In this great American asylum, the poor of Europe have by some means met together, and in consequence of various causes; to what purpose should they ask one another what countrymen they are? Alas, two thirds of them had no country. Can a wretch who wanders about, who works and starves, whose life is a continual scene of sore affliction or pinching penury; can that man call England or any other kingdom his country? A country that had no bread for him, whose fields procured him no harvest, who met with nothing but the frowns of the rich, the severity of the laws, with jails and punishments; who owned not a single foot of the extensive surface of this planet? No! urged by a variety of motives, here they came. Every thing has tended to regenerate them; new laws, a new mode of living, a new social system; here they are become men: in Europe they were as so many useless plants, wanting vegetative mould, and refreshing showers; they withered, and were mowed down by want, hunger, and war; but now by the power of transplantation, like all other plants they have taken root and flourished! Formerly they were not numbered in any civil lists of their country, except in

---

[1] Harvard, founded in 1636.

those of the poor; here they rank as citizens. By what invisible power has the surprising metamorphosis been performed? By that of the laws and that of their industry. The laws, the indulgent laws, protect them as they arrive, stamping on them the symbol of adoption; they receive ample rewards for their labours; these accumulated rewards procure them lands; those lands confer on them the title of freemen, and to that title every benefit is affixed which men can possibly require. This is the great operation daily performed by our laws. From whence proceed these laws? From our government. Whence the government? It is derived from the original genius and strong desire of the people ratified and confirmed by the crown. This is the great chain which links us all, this is the picture which every province exhibits, Nova Scotia excepted. There the crown has done all;[2] either there were no people who had genius, or it was not much attended to: the consequence is, that the province is very thinly inhabited indeed; the power of the crown in conjunction with the musketos has prevented men from settling there. Yet some parts of it flourished once, and it contained a mild harmless set of people. But for the fault of a few leaders, the whole were banished. The greatest political error the crown ever committed in America, was to cut off men from a country which wanted nothing but men!

What attachment can a poor European emigrant have for a country where he had nothing? The knowledge of the language, the love of a few kindred as poor as himself, were the only cords that tied him: his country is now that which gives him land, bread, protection, and consequence: *Ubi panis ibi patria,*[3] is the motto of all emigrants. What then is the American, this new man? He is either an European, or the descendant of an European, hence that strange mixture of blood, which you will find in no other country. I could point out to you a family whose grandfather was an Englishmen, whose wife was Dutch, whose son married a French woman, and whose present four sons have now four wives of different nations. *He* is an American, who leaving behind him all his ancient prejudices and manners, receives new ones from the new mode of life he has embraced, the new government he obeys, and the new rank he holds. He becomes an American by being received in the broad lap of our great *Alma Mater.* Here individuals of all nations are melted into a new race of men, whose labours and posterity will one day cause great changes in the world. Americans are the western pilgrims, who are carrying along with them that great mass of arts, sciences, vigour, and industry which began long since in the east; they will finish the great circle. The Americans were once scattered all over Europe; here they are incorporated into one of the finest systems of population which has ever appeared, and which will hereafter become distinct by the power of the different climates they inhabit. The American ought therefore to love this country much better than that wherein either he or his forefathers were born. Here the rewards of his industry follow with equal steps the progress of his labour; his labour is founded on the basis of nature, *self-interest;* can it want a stronger allurement? Wives and children, who before in vain demanded of him a morsel of bread, now, fat and frolicsome, gladly help their father to clear those fields whence exuberant crops are to arise to feed and to clothe them all; without any part being claimed, either by a despotic prince, a rich abbot, or a mighty lord. Here religion demands but little of him; a small

---

[2] In 1755 the English banished thousands of French settlers from Nova Scotia.

[3] Latin: "Where bread is, there is one's country."

voluntary salary to the minister, and gratitude to God; can he refuse these? The American is a new man, who acts upon new principles; he must therefore entertain new ideas, and form new opinions. From involuntary idleness, servile dependence, penury, and useless labour, he has passed to toils of a very different nature, rewarded by ample subsistence.—This is an American.

British America is divided into many provinces, forming a large association, scattered along a coast 1500 miles extent and about 200 wide. This society I would fain examine, at least such as it appears in the middle provinces; if it does not afford that variety of tinges and gradations which may be observed in Europe, we have colours peculiar to ourselves. For instance, it is natural to conceive that those who live near the sea, must be very different from those who live in the woods; the intermediate space will afford a separate and distinct class.

Men are like plants; the goodness and flavour of the fruit proceeds from the peculiar soil and exposition in which they grow. We are nothing but what we derive from the air we breathe, the climate we inhabit, the government we obey, the system of religion we profess, and the nature of our employment. Here you will find but few crimes; these have acquired as yet no root among us. I wish I were able to trace all my ideas; if my ignorance prevents me from describing them properly, I hope I shall be able to delineate a few of the outlines, which are all I propose.

Those who live near the sea, feed more on fish than on flesh, and often encounter that boisterous element. This renders them more bold and enterprising; this leads them to neglect the confined occupations of the land. They see and converse with a variety of people; their intercourse with mankind becomes extensive. The sea inspires them with a love of traffic, a desire of transporting produce from one place to another; and leads them to a variety of resources which supply the place of labour. Those who inhabit the middle settlements, by far the most numerous, must be very different; the simple cultivation of the earth purifies them, but the indulgences of the government, the soft remonstrances of religion, the rank of independent freeholders, must necessarily inspire them with sentiments, very little known in Europe among people of the same class. What do I say? Europe has no such class of men; the early knowledge they acquire, the early bargains they make, give them a great degree of sagacity. As freemen they will be litigious; pride and obstinacy are often the cause of law suits; the nature of our laws and governments may be another. As citizens it is easy to imagine, that they will carefully read the newspapers, enter into every political disquisition, freely blame or censure governors and others. As farmers they will be careful and anxious to get as much as they can, because what they get is their own. As northern men they will love the chearful cup. As Christians, religion curbs them not in their opinions; the general indulgence leaves every one to think for themselves in spiritual matters; the laws inspect our actions, our thoughts are left to God. Industry, good living, selfishness, litigiousness, country politics, the pride of freemen, religious indifference, are their characteristics. If you recede still farther from the sea, you will come into more modern settlements; they exhibit the same strong lineaments, in a ruder appearance. Religion seems to have still less influence, and their manners are less improved.

Now we arrive near the great woods, near the last inhabited districts; there men seem to be placed still farther beyond the reach of government, which in some measure leaves them to themselves. How can it pervade every corner; as they were driven there by misfortunes, necessity of beginnings, desire of acquiring large tracks of land, idleness, frequent want of economy, ancient debts; the reunion of such people does not afford a very pleasing spectacle. When discord, want of unity and friendship; when either drunkenness or idleness prevail in such remote districts; contention, inactivity, and wretchedness must ensue. There are not the same remedies to these evils as in a long established community. The few magistrates they have, are in general little better than the rest; they are often in a perfect state of war; that of man against man, sometimes decided by blows, sometimes by means of the law; that of man against every wild inhabitant of these venerable woods, of which they are come to dispossess them. There men appear to be no better than carnivorous animals of a superior rank, living on the flesh of wild animals when they can catch them, and when they are not able, they subsist on grain. He who would wish to see America in its proper light, and have a true idea of its feeble beginnings and barbarous rudiments, must visit our extended line of frontiers where the last settlers dwell, and where he may see the first labours of settlement, the mode of clearing the earth, in all their different appearances; where men are wholly left dependent on their native tempers, and on the spur of uncertain industry, which often fails when not sanctified by the efficacy of a few moral rules. There, remote from the power of example, and check of shame, many families exhibit the most hideous parts of our society. They are a kind of forlorn hope, preceding by ten or twelve years the most respectable army of veterans which come after them. In that space, prosperity will polish some, vice and the law will drive off the rest, who uniting again with others like themselves will recede still farther; making room for more industrious people, who will finish their improvements, convert the loghouse into a convenient habitation, and rejoicing that the first heavy labours are finished, will change in a few years that hitherto barbarous country into a fine fertile, well regulated district. Such is our progress, such is the march of the Europeans toward the interior parts of this continent. In all societies there are off-casts; this impure part serves as our precursors or pioneers; my father himself was one of that class, but he came upon honest principles, and was therefore one of the few who held fast; by good conduct and temperance, he transmitted to me his fair inheritance, when not above one in fourteen of his contemporaries had the same good fortune.[4]

Forty years ago this smiling country was thus inhabited; it is now purged, a general decency of manners prevails throughout, and such has been the fate of our best countries.

Exclusive of those general characteristics, each province has its own, founded on the government, climate, mode of husbandry, customs, and peculiarity of circumstances. Europeans submit insensibly to these great powers, and become, in the course of a few generations, not only Americans in general, but either Pennsylvanians, Virginians, or provincials under some other name. Whoever traverses the continent must easily observe those strong differences, which will grow more evident in time. The inhabitants of Canada, Massachuset, the middle provinces, the southern ones will be as different as their climates; their only points of unity will be those of religion and language.

As I have endeavoured to shew you how Europeans become Americans; it may not be disagreeable to shew you likewise how the various Christian sects introduced, wear out, and how religious indifference becomes prevalent. When any considerable number of a particular sect happen to dwell contiguous to each other, they immediately erect a temple, and there worship the Divinity agreeably to their own peculiar ideas. Nobody

---

[4] Part of Crèvecoeur's disguise; his father had never been to America.

disturbs them. If any new sect springs up in Europe, it may happen that many of its professors will come and settle in America. As they bring their zeal with them, they are at liberty to make proselytes if they can, and to build a meeting and to follow the dictates of their consciences; for neither the government nor any other power interferes. If they are peaceable subjects, and are industrious, what is it to their neighbours how and in what manner they think fit to address their prayers to the Supreme Being? But if the sectaries are not settled close together, if they are mixed with other denominations, their zeal will cool for want of fuel, and will be extinguished in a little time. Then the Americans become as to religion, what they are as to country, allied to all. In them the name of Englishman, Frenchman, and European is lost, and in like manner, the strict modes of Christianity as practised in Europe are lost also. This effect will extend itself still farther hereafter, and though this may appear to you as a strange idea, yet it is a very true one. I shall be able perhaps hereafter to explain myself better, in the meanwhile, let the following example serve as my first justification.

Let us suppose you and I to be travelling; we observe that in this house, to the right, lives a Catholic, who prays to God as he has been taught, and believes in transubstantiation; he works and raises wheat, he has a large family of children, all hale and robust; his belief, his prayers offend nobody. About one mile farther on the same road, his next neighbour may be a good honest plodding German Lutheran, who addresses himself to the same God, the God of all, agreeably to the modes he has been educated in, and believes in consubstantiation; by so doing he scandalizes nobody; he also works in his fields, embellishes the earth, clears swamps, &c. What has the world to do with his Lutheran principles? He persecutes nobody, and nobody persecutes him, he visits his neighbours, and his neighbours visit him. Next to him lives a seceder, the most enthusiastic of all sectaries; his zeal is hot and fiery, but separated as he is from others of the same complexion, he has no congregation of his own to resort to, where he might cabal and mingle religious pride with worldly obstinacy. He likewise raises good crops, his house is handsomely painted, his orchard is one of the fairest in the neighbourhood. How does it concern the welfare of the country, or of the province at large, what this man's religious sentiments are, or really whether he has any at all? He is a good farmer, he is a sober, peaceable, good citizen: William Penn himself would not wish for more. This is the visible character, the invisible one is only guessed at, and is nobody's business. Next again lives a Low Dutchman, who implicitly believes the rules laid down by the synod of Dort. He conceives no other idea of a clergyman than that of a hired man; if he does his work well he will pay him the stipulated sum; if not he will dismiss him, and do without his sermons, and let his church be shut up for years. But notwithstanding this coarse idea, you will find his house and farm to be the neatest in all the country; and you will judge by his waggon and fat horses, that he thinks more of the affairs of this world than of those of the next. He is sober and laborious, therefore he is all he ought to be as to the affairs of this life; as for those of the next, he must trust to the great Creator. Each of these people instruct their children as well as they can, but these instructions are feeble compared to those which are given to the youth of the poorest class in Europe. Their children will therefore grow up less zealous and more indifferent in matters of religion than their parents. The foolish vanity, or rather the fury of making Proselytes, is unknown here; they have no time, the seasons call for all their attention, and thus in a few years, this mixed neighbourhood will exhibit a strange religious medley, that will be neither pure Catholicism nor pure Calvinism. A very perceptible indifference even in the first generation, will become apparent; and it may happen that the daughter of the Catholic will marry the son of the seceder, and settle by themselves at a distance from their parents. What religious education will they give their children? A very imperfect one. If there happens to be in the neighbourhood any place of worship, we will suppose a Quaker's meeting; rather than not shew their fine clothes, they will go to it, and some of them may perhaps attach themselves to that society. Others will remain in a perfect state of indifference; the children of these zealous parents will not be able to tell what their religious principles are, and their grandchildren still less. The neighbourhood of a place of worship generally leads them to it, and the action of going thither, is the strongest evidence they can give of their attachment to any sect. The Quakers are the only people who retain a fondness for their own mode of worship; for be they ever so far separated from each other, they hold a sort of communion with the society, and seldom depart from its rules, at least in this country. Thus all sects are mixed as well as all nations; thus religious indifference is imperceptibly disseminated from one end of the continent to the other; which is at present one of the strongest characteristics of the Americans. Where this will reach no one can tell, perhaps it may leave a vacuum fit to receive other systems. Persecution, religious pride, the love of contradiction, are the food of what the world commonly calls religion. These motives have ceased here: zeal in Europe is confined; here it evaporates in the great distance it has to travel; there it is a grain of powder inclosed, here it burns away in the open air, and consumes without effect.

But to return to our back settlers. I must tell you, that there is something in the proximity of the woods, which is very singular. It is with men as it is with the plants and animals that grow and live in the forests; they are entirely different from those that live in the plains. I will candidly tell you all my thoughts but you are not to expect that I shall advance any reasons. By living in or near the woods, their actions are regulated by the wildness of the neighbourhood. The deer often come to eat their grain, the wolves to destroy their sheep, the bears to kill their hogs, the foxes to catch their poultry. This surrounding hostility, immediately puts the gun into their hands; they watch these animals, they kill some; and thus by defending their property, they soon become professed hunters; this is the progress; once hunters, farewell to the plough. The chase renders them ferocious, gloomy, and unsociable; a hunter wants no neighbour, he rather hates them, because he dreads the competition. In a little time their success in the woods makes them neglect their tillage. They trust to the natural fecundity of the earth, and therefore do little; carelessness in fencing, often exposes what little they sow to destruction; they are not at home to watch; in order therefore to make up the deficiency, they go oftener to the woods. That new mode of life brings along with it a new set of manners, which I cannot easily describe. These new manners being grafted on the old stock, produce a strange sort of lawless profligacy, the impressions of which are indelible. The manners of the Indian natives are respectable, compared with this European medley. Their wives and children live in sloth and inactivity; and having no proper pursuits, you may judge what education the latter receive. Their tender minds have nothing else to contemplate but the example of their parents; like them they grow up a mongrel breed, half civilized, half savage, except nature stamps on them some constitutional propensities. That rich, that voluptuous sentiment is gone that struck them so forcibly; the possession of their freeholds no longer conveys to their minds the same pleasure and pride. To all these reasons you must add, their lonely situation, and you cannot imagine what an effect on manners the great distances they live from each other has! Consider one of the last settlements in it's first view: of what is it composed? Europeans who have not that sufficient share of knowledge they ought to have, in order to prosper; people who have suddenly passed from oppression, dread of government, and fear of laws, into the unlimited freedom of the woods. This sudden change must have a very great effect on most men, and on that class particularly. Eating of wild meat, whatever you may think, tends to alter their temper; though all the proof I can adduce, is, that I have seen it: and having no place of worship to resort to, what little society this might afford, is denied them. The Sunday meetings, exclusive of religious benefits, were the only social bonds that might have inspired them with some degree of emulation in neatness. Is it then surprising to see men thus situated, immersed in great and heavy labours, degenerate a little? It is rather a wonder the effect is not more diffusive. The Moravians and the Quakers are the only instances in exception to what I have advanced. The first never settle singly, it is a colony of the society which emigrates; they carry with them their forms, worship, rules, and decency: the others never begin so hard, they are always able to buy improvements, in which there is a great advantage, for by that time the country is recovered from its first barbarity. Thus our bad people are those who are half cultivators and half hunters; and the worst of them are those who have degenerated altogether into the hunting state. As old ploughmen and new men of the woods, as Europeans and new made Indians, they contract the vices of both; they adopt the moroseness and ferocity of a native, without his mildness, or even his industry at home. If manners are not refined, at least they are rendered simple and inoffensive by tilling the earth; all our wants are supplied by it, our time is divided between labour and rest, and leaves none for the commission of great misdeeds. As hunters it is divided between the toil of the chase, the idleness of repose, or the indulgence of inebriation. Hunting is but a licentious idle life, and if it does not always pervert good dispositions; yet, when it is united with bad luck, it leads to want: want stimulates that propensity to rapacity and injustice, too natural to needy men, which is the fatal gradation. After this explanation of the effects which follow by living in the woods, shall we yet vainly flatter ourselves with the hope of converting the Indians? We should rather begin with converting our back-settlers; and now if I dare mention the name of religion, its sweet accents would be lost in the immensity of these woods. Men thus placed, are not fit either to receive or remember its mild instructions; they want temples and ministers, but as soon as men cease to remain at home, and begin to lead an erratic life, let them be either tawny or white, they cease to be its disciples.

Thus have I faintly and imperfectly endeavoured to trace our society from the sea to our woods! yet you must not imagine that every person who moves back, acts upon the same principles, or falls into the same degeneracy. Many families carry with them all their decency of conduct, purity of morals, and respect of religion; but these are scarce, the power of example is sometimes irresistible. Even among these back-settlers, their depravity is greater or less, according to what nation or province they belong. Were I to adduce proofs of this, I might be accused of partiality. If there happens to be some rich intervals, some fertile bottoms, in those remote districts, the people will there prefer tilling the land to hunting, and will attach themselves to it; but even on these fertile spots you may plainly perceive the inhabitants to acquire a great degree of rusticity and selfishness.

It is in consequence of this straggling situation, and the astonishing power it has on manners, that the back-settlers of both the Carolinas, Virginia, and many other parts, have been long a set of lawless people; it has been even dangerous to travel among them. Government can do nothing in so extensive a country, better it should wink at these irregularities, than that it should use means inconsistent with its usual mildness. Time will efface those stains: in proportion as the great body of population approaches them they will reform, and become polished and subordinate. Whatever has been said of the four New England provinces, no such degeneracy of manners has ever tarnished their annals; their back-settlers have been kept within the bounds of decency, and government, by means of wise laws, and by the influence of religion. What a detestable idea such people must have given to the natives of the Europeans! They trade with them, the worst of people are permitted to do that which none but persons of the best characters should be employed in. They get drunk with them, and often defraud the Indians. Their avarice, removed from the eyes of their superiors, knows no bounds; and aided by a little superiority of knowledge, these traders deceive them, and even sometimes shed blood. Hence those shocking violations, those sudden devastations which have so often stained our frontiers, when hundreds of innocent people have been sacrificed for the crimes of a few. It was in consequence of such behaviour, that the Indians took the hatchet against the Virginians in 1774. Thus are our first steps trod, thus are our first trees felled, in general, by the most vicious of our people; and thus the path is opened for the arrival of a second and better class, the true American freeholders; the most respectable set of people in this part of the world: respectable for their industry, their happy independence, the great share of freedom they possess, the good regulation of their families, and for extending the trade and the dominion of our mother country.

Europe contains hardly any other distinctions but lords and tenants; this fair country alone is settled by freeholders, the possessors of the soil they cultivate, members of the government they obey, and the framers of their own laws, by means of their representatives. This is a thought which you have taught me to cherish; our difference from Europe, far from diminishing, rather adds to our usefulness and consequence as men and subjects. Had our forefathers remained there, they would only have crouded it, and perhaps prolonged those convulsions which had shook it so long. Every industrious European who transports himself here, may be compared to a sprout growing at the foot of a great tree; it enjoys and draws but a little portion of sap; wrench it from the parent roots, transplant it, and it will become a tree bearing fruit also. Colonists are therefore entitled to the consideration due to the most useful subjects; a hundred families barely existing in some parts of Scotland, will here in six years, cause an annual exportation of 10,000 bushels of wheat: 100 bushels being but a common quantity for an industrious family to sell, if they cultivate good land. It is here then that the idle may be employed, the useless become useful, and the poor become rich; but by riches I do not mean gold and silver, we have but little of those metals; I mean a better sort of wealth, cleared lands, cattle, good houses, good cloaths, and an increase of people to enjoy them.

There is no wonder that this country has so many charms, and presents to Europeans so many temptations to remain in it. A traveller in Europe becomes a stranger as soon as he quits his own kingdom; but it is otherwise here. We know, properly speaking, no strangers; this is every person's country; the variety of our soils, situations, climates, governments, and produce, hath something which must please every body. No sooner does an European arrive, no matter of what condition, than his eyes are opened upon the fair prospect; he hears his language spoke, he retraces many of his own country manners, he perpetually hears the names of families and towns with which he is acquainted; he sees happiness and prosperity in all places disseminated; he meets with hospitality, kindness, and plenty every where; he beholds hardly any poor, he seldom hears of punishments and executions; and he wonders at the elegance of our towns, those miracles of industry and freedom. He cannot admire enough our rural districts, our convenient roads, good taverns, and our many accommodations; he involuntarily loves a country where every thing is so lovely. When in England, he was a mere Englishman; here he stands on a larger portion of the globe, not less than its fourth part, and may see the productions of the north, in iron and naval stores; the provisions of Ireland, the grain of Egypt, the indigo, the rice of China. He does not find, as in Europe, a crouded society, where every place is over-stocked; he does not feel that perpetual collision of parties, that difficulty of beginning, that contention which oversets so many. There is room for every body in America; has he any particular talent, or industry? he exerts it in order to procure a livelihood, and it succeeds. Is he a merchant? the avenues of trade are infinite; is he eminent in any respect? he will be employed and respected. Does he love a country life? pleasant farms present themselves; he may purchase what he wants, and thereby become an American farmer. Is he a labourer, sober and industrious? he need not go many miles, nor receive many informations before he will be hired, well fed at the table of his employer, and paid four or five times more than he can get in Europe. Does he want uncultivated lands? thousands of acres present themselves, which he may purchase cheap. Whatever be his talents or inclinations, if they are moderate, he may satisfy them. I do not mean that every one who comes will grow rich in a little time; no, but he may procure an easy, decent maintenance, by his industry. Instead of starving he will be fed, instead of being idle he will have employment; and these are riches enough for such men as come over here. The rich stay in Europe, it is only the middling and the poor that emigrate. Would you wish to travel in independent idleness, from north to south, you will find easy access, and the most chearful reception at every house; society without ostentation, good cheer without pride, and every decent diversion which the country affords, with little expence. It is no wonder that the European who has lived here a few years, is desirous to remain; Europe with all its pomp, is not to be compared to this continent, for men of middle stations, or labourers.

An European, when he first arrives, seems limited in his intentions, as well as in his views; but he very suddenly alters his scale; two hundred miles formerly appeared a very great distance, it is now but a trifle; he no sooner breathes our air than he forms schemes, and embarks in designs he never would have thought of in his own country. There the plenitude of society confines many useful ideas, and often extinguishes the most laudable schemes which here ripen into maturity. Thus Europeans become Americans.

But how is this accomplished in that croud of low, indigent people, who flock here every year from all parts of Europe? I will tell you; they no sooner arrive than they immediately feel the good effects of that plenty of provisions we possess: they fare on our best food, and are kindly entertained; their talents, character, and peculiar industry are immediately inquired into; they find countrymen every where disseminated, let them come from whatever part of Europe. Let me select one as an epitome of the rest; he is hired, he goes to work, and works moderately; instead of being employed by a haughty person, he finds himself with his equal, placed at the substantial table of the farmer, or else at an inferior one as good; his wages are high, his bed is not like that bed of sorrow on which he used to lie: if he behaves with propriety, and is faithful, he is caressed, and becomes as it were a member of the family. He begins to feel the effects of a sort of resurrection; hitherto he had not lived, but simply vegetated; he now feels himself a man, because he is treated as such; the laws of his own country had overlooked him in his insignificancy; the laws of this cover him with their mantle. Judge what an alteration there must arise in the mind and thoughts of this man; he begins to forget his former servitude and dependence, his heart involuntarily swells and glows; this first swell inspires him with those new thoughts which constitute an American. What love can he entertain for a country where his existence was a burthen to him; if he is a generous good man, the love of this new adoptive parent will sink deep into his heart. He looks around, and sees many a prosperous person, who but a few years before was as poor as himself. This encourages him much, he begins to form some little scheme, the first, alas, he ever formed in his life. If he is wise he thus spends two or three years, in which time he acquires knowledge, the use of tools, the modes of working the lands, felling trees, &c. This prepares the foundation of a good name, the most useful acquisition he can make. He is encouraged, he has gained friends; he is advised and directed, he feels bold, he purchases some land; he gives all the money he has brought over, as well as what he has earned, and trusts to the God of harvests for the discharge of the rest. His good name procures him credit. He is now possessed of the deed, conveying to him and his posterity the fee simple[5] and absolute property of two hundred acres of land, situated on such a river. What an epocha in this man's life! He is become a freeholder, from perhaps a German boor—he is now an American, a Pennsylvanian, an English subject. He is naturalized, his name is enrolled with those of the other citizens of the province. Instead of being a vagrant, he has a place of residence; he is called the inhabitant of such a county, or of such a district, and for the first time in his life counts for something; for hitherto he has been a cypher. I only repeat what I have heard many say, and no wonder their hearts should glow, and be agitated with a multitude of feelings, not easy to describe. From nothing to start into being; from a servant to the rank of a master; from being the slave of some despotic prince, to become a free man, invested with lands, to which every municipal blessing is annexed! What a change indeed! It is in consequence of that change that he becomes an American. This great metamorphosis has a double effect, it extinguishes all his European prejudices, he forgets that mechanism of subordination, that servility of disposition which poverty had taught him; and sometimes he is apt to forget too much, often passing from one extreme to the other. If he is a good man, he forms schemes of future prosperity, he proposes to educate his children better than he has been educated himself; he thinks of future modes of conduct, feels an ardor to labour he never felt before. Pride steps in and leads him to every thing that the laws do not forbid: he respects them; with a heart-felt gratitude he looks toward the east, toward that insular government from whose wisdom all his new felicity is derived, and under whose wings and protection he now lives. These reflections constitute him the good man and the good subject. Ye poor Europeans, ye, who sweat, and work for the great—ye, who are obliged to give so many sheaves to the church, so many to your lords, so many to your government, and have hardly any left for yourselves—ye, who are held in less estimation than favourite hunters or useless lap dogs—ye, who only

---

[5] Full legal possession.

breathe the air of nature, because it cannot be withheld from you; it is here that ye can conceive the possibility of those feelings I have been describing; it is here the laws of naturalization invite every one to partake of our great labours and felicity, to till un-rented, untaxed lands! Many, corrupted beyond the power of amendment, have brought with them all their vices, and disregarding the advantages held to them, have gone on in their former career of iniquity, until they have been overtaken and punished by our laws. It is not every emigrant who succeeds; no, it is only the sober, the honest, and industrious: happy those to whom this transition has served as a powerful spur to labour, to prosperity, and to the good establishment of children, born in the days of their poverty; and who had no other portion to expect but the rags of their parents, had it not been for their happy emigration. Others again, have been led astray by this en-chanting scene; their new pride, instead of leading them to the fields, has kept them in idleness; the idea of possessing lands is all that satisfies them—though surrounded with fertility, they have mouldered away their time in inactivity, misinformed husbandry, and ineffectual endeavours. How much wiser, in general, the honest Germans than al-most all other Europeans; they hire themselves to some of their wealthy landsmen, and in that apprenticeship learn every thing that is necessary. They attentively consider the prosperous industry of others, which imprints in their minds a strong desire of possess-ing the same advantages. This forcible idea never quits them, they launch forth, and by dint of sobriety, rigid parsimony, and the most persevering industry, they commonly succeed. Their astonishment at their first arrival from Germany is very great—it is to them a dream; the contrast must be powerful indeed; they observe their countrymen flourishing in every place; they travel through whole counties where not a word of Eng-lish is spoken; and in the names and the language of the people, they retrace Germany. They have been an useful acquisition to this continent, and to Pennsylvania in particu-lar; to them it owes some share of its prosperity: to their mechanical knowledge and pa-tience, it owes the finest mills in all America, the best teams of horses, and many other advantages. The recollection of their former poverty and slavery never quits them as long as they live.

The Scotch and the Irish might have lived in their own country perhaps as poor, but enjoying more civil advantages, the effects of their new situation do not strike them so forcibly, nor has it so lasting an effect. From whence the difference arises I know not, but out of twelve families of emigrants of each country, generally seven Scotch will suc-ceed, nine German, and four Irish. The Scotch are frugal and laborious, but their wives cannot work so hard as German women, who on the contrary vie with their husbands, and often share with them the most severe toils of the field, which they understand bet-ter. They have therefore nothing to struggle against, but the common casualties of na-ture. The Irish do not prosper so well; they love to drink and to quarrel; they are liti-gious, and soon take to the gun, which is the ruin of everything; they seem beside to labour under a greater degree of ignorance in husbandry than the others; perhaps it is that their industry had less scope, and was less exercised at home. I have heard many re-late, how the land was parcelled out in that kingdom; their ancient conquest has been a great detriment to them, by over-setting their landed property. The lands possessed by a few, are leased down *ad infinitum,* and the occupiers often pay five guineas an acre. The poor are worse lodged there than any where else in Europe; their potatoes, which are easily raised, are perhaps an inducement to laziness: their wages are too low and their whisky too cheap.

There is no tracing observations of this kind, without making at the same time very great allowances, as there are every where to be found, a great many exceptions. The Irish themselves, from different parts of that kingdom, are very different. It is difficult to account for this surprising locality, one would think on so small an island an Irishman must be an Irishman: yet it is not so, they are different in their aptitude to, and in their love of labour.

The Scotch on the contrary are all industrious and saving; they want nothing more than a field to exert themselves in, and they are commonly sure of succeeding. The only difficulty they labour under is, that technical American knowledge which requires some time to obtain; it is not easy for those who seldom saw a tree, to conceive how it is to be felled, cut up, and split into rails and posts.

As I am fond of seeing and talking of prosperous families, I intend to finish this letter by relating to you the history of an honest Scotch Hebridean, who came here in 1774, which will shew you in epitome, what the Scotch can do, wherever they have room for the exertion of their industry. Whenever I hear of any new settlement, I pay it a visit once or twice a year, on purpose to observe the different steps each settler takes, the gradual improvements, the different tempers of each family, on which their prosperity in a great nature depends; their different modifications of industry, their ingenuity, and contrivance; for being all poor, their life requires sagacity and prudence. In an evening I love to hear them tell their stories, they furnish me with new ideas; I sit still and listen to their ancient misfortunes, observing in many of them a strong degree of gratitude to God, and the government. Many a well meant sermon have I preached to some of them. When I found laziness and inattention to prevail, who could refrain from wishing well to these new countrymen; after having under gone so many fatigues. Who could withhold good advice? What a happy change it must be, to descend from the high, sterile, bleak lands of Scotland, where everything is barren and cold, to rest on some fertile farms in these middle provinces! Such a transition must have afforded the most pleasing satisfaction.

The following dialogue passed at an out-settlement, where I lately paid a visit:

Well, friend, how do you do now; I am come fifty odd miles on purpose to see you; how do you go on with your new cutting and slashing? Very well, good Sir, we learn the use of the axe bravely, we shall make it out; we have a belly full of victuals every day, our cows run about, and come home full of milk, our hogs get fat of themselves in the woods: Oh, this is a good country! God bless the king, and William Penn; we shall do very well by and by, if we keep our healths. Your loghouse looks neat and light, where did you get these shingles? One of our neighbours is a New-England man, and he shewed us how to split them out of chestnut-trees. Now for a barn, but all in good time, here are fine trees to build with. Who is to frame it, sure you don't understand that work yet? A countryman of ours who has been in America these ten years, offers to wait for his money until the second crop is lodged in it. What did you give for your land? Thirty-five shillings per acre, payable in seven years. How many acres have you got? An hundred and fifty. That is enough to begin with; is not your land pretty hard to clear? Yes, Sir, hard enough, but it would be harder still if it was ready cleared, for then we should have no timber, and I love the woods much; the land is nothing without them. Have not you found out any bees yet? No, Sir; and if we had we should not know what to do with them. I will tell you by and by. You are very kind. Farewell, honest man, God prosper you; whenever you travel toward ———, enquire for J.S. he will entertain you kindly, provided you bring him good tidings from your family and farm. In this manner I often visit them, and carefully examine their houses, their modes of ingenuity, their different ways; and make them all relate all they know, and describe all they feel. These are scenes which I believe you would willingly share with me. I well remember your philanthropic turn of mind. Is it not better to contemplate under these humble roofs, the rudiments of future wealth and population, than to behold the accumulated bundles of litigious papers in the office of a lawyer? To examine how the world is gradually settled, how the howling swamp is converted into a pleasing meadow, the rough ridge into a fine field; and to hear the chearful whistling, the rural song, where there was no sound heard before, save the yell of the savage, the screech of the owl, or the hissing of the snake? Here an European, fatigued with luxury, riches, and pleasures, may find a sweet relaxation in a series of interesting scenes, as affecting as they are new. England, which now contains so many domes, so many castles, was once like this; a place woody and marshy; its inhabitants, now the favourite nation for arts and commerce, were once painted like our neighbours. The country will flourish in its turn, and the same observations will be made which I have just delineated. Posterity will look back with avidity and pleasure, to trace, if possible, the area of this or that particular settlement.

Pray, what is the reason that the Scots are in general more religious, more faithful, more honest, and industrious than the Irish? I do not mean to insinuate national reflections, God forbid! It ill becomes any man, and much less an American; but as I know men are nothing of themselves, and that they owe all their different modifications either to government or other local circumstances, there must be some powerful causes which constitute this great national difference.

Agreeable to the account which severale Scotchmen have given me of the north of Britain, of the Orkneys, and the Hebride Islands, they seem, on many accounts, to be unfit for the habitation of men; they appear to be calculated only for great sheep pastures. Who then can blame the inhabitants of these countries for transporting themselves hither? This great continent must in time absorb the poorest part of Europe; and this will happen in proportion as it becomes better known; and as war, taxation, oppression, and misery increase there. The Hebrides appear to be fit only for the residence of malefactors, and it would be much better to send felons there than either to Virginia or Maryland. What a strange compliment has our mother country paid to two of the finest provinces in America! England has entertained in that respect very mistaken ideas; what was intended as a punishment, is become the good fortune of several; many of those who have been transported as felons, are now rich, and strangers to the stings of those wants that urged them to violations of the law: they are become industrious, exemplary, and useful citizens. The English government should purchase the most northern and barren of those islands; it should send over to us the honest, primitive Hebrideans, settle them here on good lands, as a reward for their virtue and ancient poverty; and replace them with a colony of her wicked sons. The severity of the climate, the inclemency of the seasons, the sterility of the soil, the tempestuousness of the sea, would afflict and punish enough. Could there be found a spot better adapted to retaliate the injury it had received by their crimes? Some of those islands might be considered as the hell of Great Britain, where all evil spirits should be sent. Two essential ends would be answered by this simple operation. The good people, by emigration, would be rendered happier; the bad ones would be placed where they ought to be. In a few years the dread of being sent to that wintry region would have a much stronger effect, than that of transportation.—This is no place of punishment; were I a poor hopeless, bread-less Englishman, and not restrained by the power of shame, I should be very thankful for the passage. It is of very little importance how, and in what manner an indigent man arrives; for if he is but sober, honest, and industrious, he has nothing more to ask of heaven. Let him go to work, he will have opportunities enough to earn a comfortable support, and even the means of procuring some land; which ought to be the utmost wish of every person who has health and hands to work. I knew a man who came to this country, in the literal sense of the expression, stark naked; I think he was a Frenchman, and a sailor on board an English man of war. Being discontented, he had stripped him-self and swam ashore; where finding clothes and friends, he settled afterwards at Mara-neck, in the county of Chester, in the province of New-York: he married and left a good farm to each of his sons. I knew another person who was but twelve years old when he was taken on the frontiers of Canada, by the Indians; at his arrival at Albany he was purchased by a gentleman, who generously bound him apprentice to a taylor. He lived to the age of ninety, and left behind him a fine estate and a numerous family, all well settled; many of them I am acquainted with.—Where is then the industrious European who ought to despair?

After a foreigner from any part of Europe is arrived, and become a citizen; let him devoutly listen to the voice of our great parent, which says to him, "Welcome to my shores, distressed European; bless the hour in which thou didst see my verdant fields, my fair navigable rivers, and my green mountains!—If thou wilt work, I have bread for thee; if thou wilt be honest, sober, and industrious, I have greater rewards to confer on thee—ease and independence. I will give thee fields to feed and cloath thee; a comfort-able fire-side to sit by, and tell thy children by what means thou has prospered; and a decent bed to repose on. I shall endow thee beside with the immunities of a freeman. If thou wilt carefully educate thy children, teach them gratitude to God, and reverence to that government, that philanthropic government, which has collected here so many men and made them happy. I will also provide for thy progeny; and to every good man this ought to be the most holy, the most powerful, the most earnest wish he can possibly form, as well as the most consolatory prospect when he dies. Go thou and work and till; thou shalt prosper, provided thou be just, grateful and industrious." . . .

Oloudah Equiano (Gustavus Vassa) 1745–1801

Gustavus Vassa's *Narrative* reminds us that not all colonial American writings represent the New World as a pastoral Eden, as a New English Israel of the chosen people, or (in John Adams's term) as a "grand Design in Providence for the illumination of all mankind." Vassa's America is a slave state encountered through "the violence of the African trader, the pestilential stench of a Guinea [slave] ship, and the lash and lust of a brutal and unrelenting overseer." Vassa's *Narrative,* published in England, understandably was recognized on both sides of the Atlantic as a valuable antislavery polemic.

Vassa was born in Benin, west of the lower Niger River in western Africa. At age eleven he was kidnapped, enslaved, and sold repeatedly to different African tribal families. Reaching the coast, he saw "the sea and a slave ship" and succumbed to the most brutal treatment of his young life as a captive of "nominal Christians" transporting their human cargo to America. For a time Vassa served on a Virginia plantation; from there he was sold to a British naval officer, who helped to educate him. Subsequently he became the slave of a Philadelphia merchant and worked on vessels bound for the West Indies. His last owner helped him purchase his freedom, after which Vassa traveled as a ship's steward, became converted to Methodism, and settled permanently in England to work for the abolition of slavery. In 1790 Vassa presented to Parliament a petition calling for the end of the slave trade.

The Interesting Narrative of the Life of Oloudah Equiano, or Gustavus Vassa was published in two volumes in London in 1789. In the next five years, eight editions of this successful work appeared. In its own day the Narrative interested some readers as an exciting travel book, others as an antislavery tract. In American literature it is a minority report on human rights. Held for comparison against the Declaration of Independence and Paine's Common Sense, it becomes a scathing commentary on the gulf between American ideals and actualities.

Further Reading:
Equiano's Travels, ed. P. Edwards, 1966.
Cavalcade: Negro American Writing from 1760 to the
    Present, ed. A. Davis and S. Redding, 1971.

Text:
The Interesting Narrative of the Life of Oloudah
    Equiano, or Gustavus Vassa, 2 vols., 1789.

The Interesting Narrative of the Life of Oloudah Equiano

Chapter II: Kidnapping and Enslavement

I hope the reader will not think I have trespassed on his patience in introducing myself to him, with some account of the manners and customs of my country. They had been implanted in me with great care, and made an impression on my mind which time could not erase, and which all the adversity and variety of fortune I have since experienced served only to rivet and record; for, whether the love of one's country be real or imaginary, or a lesson of reason, or an instinct of nature, I still look back with pleasure on the first scenes of my life, though that pleasure has been for the most part mingled with sorrow.

I have already acquainted the reader with the time and place of my birth. My father, besides many slaves, had a numerous family, of which seven lived to grow up, including myself and a sister, who was the only daughter. As I was the youngest of the sons, I became, of course, the greatest favorite with my mother, and was always with her; and she used to take particular pains to form my mind. I was trained up from my earliest years in the arts of agriculture and war: my daily exercise was shooting and throwing javelins; and my mother adorned me with emblems, after the manner of our greatest warriors. In this way I grew up till I was turned the age of eleven, when an end was put to my happiness in the following manner:—Generally, when the grown people in the neighborhood were gone far in the fields to labour, the children assembled together in some of the neighbors' premises to play; and commonly some of us used to get up a tree to look out for any assailant or kidnapper that might come upon us; for they sometimes took those opportunities of our parents' absence, to attack and carry off as many as they could seize. One day, as I was watching at the top of a tree in our yard, I saw one of those people come into the yard of our next neighbor but one, to kidnap, there being many stout young people in it. Immediately, on this, I gave the alarm of the rogue, and he was surrounded by the stoutest of them, who entangled him with cords, so that he could not escape till some of the grown people came and secured him.

But alas! ere long, it was my fate to be thus attacked, and to be carried off, when none of our grown people were nigh. One day, when all our people were gone out to their works as usual, and only I and my dear sister were left to mind the house, two men and a woman got over our walls, and in a moment seized us both; and without giving us time to cry out, or make resistance, they stopped our mouths and ran off with us into the nearest wood. Here they tied our hands, and continued to carry us as far as they could, till night came on, when we reached a small house, where the robbers halted for refreshment, and spent the night. We were then unbound, but were unable to take any food; and, being quite overpowered by fatigue and grief, our only relief was some sleep, which allayed our misfortune for a short time. The next morning we left the house, and continued traveling all the day. For a long time we had kept the woods, but at last we came in to a road which I believed I knew. I now had some hopes of being delivered; for we had advanced but a little way when I discovered some people at a distance, on which I began to cry out for their assistance; but my cries had no other effect than to make them tie me faster and stop my mouth, and then they put me into a large sack. They also stopped my sister's mouth and tied her hands; and in this manner we proceeded till we were out of the sight of these people.—When we went to rest the following night they offered us some victuals, but we refused them; and the only comfort we had was in being in one another's arms all that night, and bathing each other with our tears.

But alas! we were soon deprived of even the small comfort of weeping together. The next day proved a day of greater sorrow than I had yet experienced; for my sister and I were then separated, while we lay clasped in each other's arms: it was in vain that we besought them not to part us; she was torn from me, and immediately carried away, while I was left in a state of distraction not to be described. I cried and grieved continually; and for several days did not eat any thing but what they forced into my mouth. At length, after many days traveling, during which I had often changed masters, I got into the hands of a chieftain, in a very pleasant country. This man had two wives and some children, and they all used me extremely well, and did all they could to comfort me; particularly the first wife, who was something like my mother. Although I was a great many days journey from my father's house, yet these people spoke exactly the same language with us. This first master of mine, as I may call him, was a smith, and my principal employment was working his bellows, which was the same kind as I had seen in my vicinity. They were in some respects not unlike the stoves here in gentlemen's kitchens; and were covered over with leather; and in the middle of that leather a stick was fixed, and a person stood up, and worked it, in the same manner as is done to pump water out of a cask with a hand pump. I believe it was gold he worked, for it was of a lovely bright yellow colour, and was worn by the women on their wrists and ancles. I was there I suppose about a month, and they at last used to trust me some little distance from the house. This liberty I used in embracing every opportunity to inquire the way to my own home: and I also sometimes, for the same purpose, went with the maidens, in the cool of the evenings, to bring pitchers of water from the springs for the use of the house.

I had also remarked where the sun rose in the morning, and set in the evening, as I had travelled along; and I had observed that my father's house was towards the rising of the sun. I therefore determined to seize the first opportunity of making my escape, and to shape my course for that quarter; for I was quite oppressed and weighed down by grief after my mother and friends; and my love of liberty, ever great, was strengthened by the mortifying circumstance of not daring to eat with the free-born children, although I was mostly their companion.—While I was projecting my escape one day, an unlucky event happened, which quite disconcerted my plan, and put an end to my hopes. I used to be sometimes employed in assisting an elderly woman slave to cook and take care of the poultry; and one morning while I was feeding some chickens, I happened to toss a small pebble at one of them, which hit it on the middle, and directly killed it. The old slave, having soon after missed the chicken, inquired after it; and on my relating the accident, (for I told her the truth, because my mother would never suffer me to tell a lie), she flew into a violent passion, threatened that I should suffer for it; and, my master being out, she immediately went and told her mistress what I had done. This alarmed me very much, and I expected an instant flogging, which to me was uncommonly dreadful; for I had seldom been beaten at home.

I therefore resolved to fly; and accordingly I ran into a thicket that was hard by, and hid myself in the bushes. Soon afterwards my mistress and the slave returned, and, not seeing me, they searched all the house, but not finding me, and I not making answer when they called to me, they thought I had run away, and the whole neighborhood was raised in the pursuit of me. In that part of the country (as well as ours) the houses and villages were skirted with woods or shrubberies, and the bushes were so thick, that a man could readily conceal himself in them, so as to elude the strictest search. The neighbors continued the whole day looking for me, and several times many of them came within a few yards of the place where I lay hid. I expected every moment, when I heard a rustling among the trees, to be found out, and punished by my master; but they never discovered me, though they were often so near that I even heard their conjectures as they were looking about for me; and I now learned from them that any attempt to return home would be hopeless. Most of them supposed I had fled towards home; but the distance was so great, and the way so intricate, that they thought I could never reach it, and that I should be lost in the woods. When I heard this I was seized with a violent panic, and abandoned myself to despair. Night too began to approach, and aggravated all my fears. I had before entertained hopes of getting home, and had determined when it should be dark to make the attempt; but I was now convinced that it was fruitless, and began to consider that, if possibly I could escape all other animals, I could not those of the human kind; and that, not knowing the way, I must perish in the woods.—Thus was I like the hunted deer:

—"Ev'ry leaf, and ev'ry whisp'ring breath
 "Convey'd a foe, and ev'ry foe a death."

I heard frequent rustlings among the leaves; and being pretty sure they were snakes, I expected every instant to be stung by them.—This increased my anguish; and the horror of my situation became now quite insupportable. I at length quitted the thicket, very faint and hungry, for I had not eaten or drank anything all the day, and crept to my master's kitchen, from whence I set out at first, and which was an open shed, and laid myself down in the ashes with an anxious wish for death to relieve me from all my pains. I was scarcely awake in the morning, when the old woman slave, who was the first up, came to light the fire, and saw me in the fireplace. She was very much surprised to see me, and could scarcely believe her own eyes. She now promised to intercede for me, and went for her master, who soon after came, and having lightly reprimanded me, ordered me to be taken care of, and not ill treated.

Soon after this my master's only daughter and child by his first wife sickened and died, which affected him so much that for some time he was almost frantic, and really would have killed himself, had he not been watched and prevented. However, in a small time afterwards he recovered and I was again sold. I was now carried to the left of the sun's rising, through many dreary wastes and dismal woods, amidst the hideous roaring of wild beasts.—The people I was sold to used to carry me very often, when I was tired, either on their shoulders or on their backs. I saw many convenient well-built sheds along the road, at proper distances, to accommodate the merchants and travellers, who lay in those buildings along with their wives, who often accompany them; and they always go well armed.

From the time I left my own nation I always found somebody that understood me till I came to the sea coast. The languages of different nations did not totally differ, nor were they so copious as those of the Europeans, particularly the English. They were therefore easily learned; and while I was journeying thus through Africa, I acquired two or three different tongues. In this manner I had been travelling for a considerable time, when one evening to my great surprise, whom should I see brought to the house where I was but my dear sister? As soon as she saw me she gave a loud shriek, and ran into my arms. I was quite overpowered: neither of us could speak, but, for a considerable time, clung to each other in mutual embraces, unable to do anything but weep. Our meeting affected all who saw us; and indeed I must acknowledge, in honour of those sable destroyers of human rights, that I never met with any ill treatment, or saw any offered to their slaves, except tying them, when necessary to keep them from running away. When these people knew we were brother and sister, they indulged us to be together; and the man, to whom I supposed we belonged, lay with us, he in the middle, while she and I held one another by the hands across his breast all night; and thus for awhile we forgot our misfortunes in the joy of being together; but even this small comfort was soon to have an end; for scarcely had the fatal morning appeared, when she was again torn from me for ever! I was now more miserable, if possible, than before. The small relief which her presence gave me from pain was gone, and the wretchedness of my situation was redoubled by my anxiety after her fate, and my apprehensions lest her sufferings should be greater than mine, when I could not be with her to alleviate them. Yes, thou dear partner of my childish sports! thou sharer of my joys and sorrows! happy should I have ever esteemed myself to encounter every misery for you, and to procure your freedom by the sacrifice of my own! Though you were early forced from my arms, your image has been always rivetted in my heart, from which neither *time nor fortune* have been able to remove it: so that, while the thoughts of your suffering have dampened my prosperity, they have mingled with adversity and increased its bitterness.—To that Heaven which protects the weak from the strong, I commit the care of your innocence and virtues, if they have not already received their full reward, and if your youth and delicacy have not long since fallen victims to the violence of the African trader, the pestilential stench of a Guinea ship, the seasoning in the European colonies, or the lash and lust of a brutal and unrelenting overseer.

I did not long remain after my sister. I was again sold, and carried through a number of places, till after travelling a considerable time, I came to a town called Tinmah, in the most beautiful country I had yet seen in Africa. It was extremely rich, and there were many rivulets which flowed through it, and supplied a large pond in the centre of the town, where the people washed. Here I first saw and tasted cocoa nuts, which I thought superior to any nuts I had ever tasted before; and the trees which were loaded were also interspersed among the houses, which had commodious shades adjoining, and were in the same manner as ours, the insides being neatly plastered and whitewashed. Here I also saw and tasted for the first time, sugar cane. Their money consisted of little white shells, the size of the finger nail. I was sold here for one hundred and seventy-two of them, by a merchant who lived and brought me there. I had been about two or three days at his house, when a wealthy widow, a neighbor of his, came there one evening, and brought with her an only son, a young gentleman about my own age and size. Here they saw me; and having taken a fancy to me, I was bought of the merchant, and went home with them. Her house and premises were situated close to one of those rivulets I have mentioned, and were the finest I ever saw in Africa: they were very extensive, and she had a number of slaves to attend her. The next day I was washed and perfumed, and when meal time came, I was led into the presence of my mistress, and ate and drank before her with her son. This filled me with astonishment; and I could scarce help expressing my surprise that the young gentleman should suffer me, who was bound, to eat with him who was free; and not only so, but that he would not at any time either eat or drink till I had taken first, because I was the eldest, which was agreeable to our custom. Indeed, everything here, and all their treatment of me, made me forget that I was a slave. The language of these people resembled ours so nearly, that we understood each other perfectly. They had also the same customs as we. There were likewise slaves daily to attend us, while my young master and I, with other boys, sported with our darts and bows and arrows, as I had been used to do at home. In this resemblance to my former happy state, I passed about two months; and I now began to think I was to be adopted into the family, and was beginning to be reconciled to my situation, and to forget by degrees my misfortunes, when all at once the delusion vanished; for, without the least previous knowledge, one morning early, while my dear master and companion was still asleep, I was awakened out of my reverie to fresh sorrow, and hurried away even amongst the uncircumcised.[1]

Thus at the very moment I dreamed of the greatest happiness, I found myself most miserable; and it seemed as if fortune wished to give me this taste of joy only to render the reverse more poignant.—The change I now experienced, was as painful as it was

---

[1] i.e., he was treated as a person of low esteem.

sudden and unexpected. It was a change indeed, from a state of bliss to a scene which is inexpressible by me, as it discovered to me an element I had never before beheld, and till then had no idea of, and wherein such instances of hardship and cruelty occurred, as I can never reflect on but with horror.

All the nations and people I had hitherto passed through, resembled our own in their manners, customs and language; but I came at length to a country, the inhabitants of which differed from us in all those particulars. I was very much struck with this difference, especially when I came among a people who did not circumcise, and ate without washing their hands. They cooked also in iron pots, and had European cutlasses and cross bows, which were unknown to us, and fought with their fists among themselves. Their women were not so modest as ours, for they ate and drank, and slept with their men. But, above all, I was amazed to see no sacrifices or offerings among them. In some of these places the people ornamented themselves with scars, and likewise filed their teeth very sharp. They wanted sometimes to ornament me in the same manner, but I would not suffer them; hoping that I might some time be among a people who did not thus disfigure themselves, as I thought they did. At last I came to the banks of a large river which was covered with canoes, in which the people appeared to live with their household utensils, and provisions of all kinds. I was beyond measure astonished at this, as I had never before seen any water larger than a pond or a rivulet: and my surprise was mingled with no small fear when I was put into one of these canoes, and we began to paddle and move along the river. We continued going on thus till night, when we came to land, and made fires on the banks, each family by themselves; some dragged their canoes on shore, others stayed and cooked in theirs, and laid in them all night. Those on the land had mats, of which they made tents, some in the shape of little houses; in these we slept; and after the morning meal, we embarked again and proceeded as before. I was often very much astonished to see some of the women, as well as the men, jump into the water, dive to the bottom, come up again, and swim about.—— Thus I continued to travel, sometimes by land, sometimes by water, through different countries and various nations, till, at the end of six or seven months after I had been kidnapped, I arrived at the sea coast. It would be tedious and uninteresting to relate all the incidents which befell me during this journey, and which I have not yet forgotten; of the various hands I passed through, and the manners and customs of all the different people among whom I lived. I shall therefore only observe, that in all the places where I was, the soil was exceedingly rich; the pumpkins, eadas, plaintains, yams, etc., were in great abundance, and of incredible size. There were also vast quantities of different gums, though not used for any purpose, and every where a great deal of tobacco. The cotton even grew quite wild, and there was plenty of red-wood. I saw no mechanics whatever in all the way, except such as I have mentioned. The chief employment in all these countries was agriculture, and both the males and females, as with us, were brought up to it, and trained in the arts of war.

The first object which saluted my eyes when I arrived on the coast, was the sea, and a slave ship, which was then riding at anchor, and waiting for its cargo. These filled me with astonishment, which was soon converted into terror, when I was carried on board. I was immediately handled, and tossed up to see if I were sound, by some of the crew; and I was now persuaded that I had gotten into a world of bad spirits, and that they were going to kill me. Their complexions, too, differing so much from ours, their long hair, and the language they spoke, (which was very different from any I had ever heard) united to confirm me in this belief. Indeed, such were the horrors of my views and fears at the moment, that, if ten thousand worlds had been my own, I would have freely parted with them all to have exchanged my condition with that of the meanest slave in my own country. When I looked round the ship too, and saw a large furnace of copper boiling, and a multitude of black people of every description chained together, every one of their countenances expressing dejection and sorrow, I no longer doubted of my fate; and quite overpowered with horror and anguish, I fell motionless on the deck and fainted. When I recovered a little, I found some black people about me, who I believed were some of those who had brought me on board, and had been receiving their pay; they talked to me in order to cheer me, but all in vain. I asked them if we were not to be eaten by those white men with horrible looks, red faces and long hair. They told me I was not: and one of the crew brought me a small portion of spirituous liquor in a wine glass, but, being afraid of him, I would not take it out of his hand. One of the blacks, therefore, took it from him and gave it to me, and I took a little down my palate, which, instead of reviving me, as they thought it would, threw me into the greatest consternation at the strange feeling it produced, having never tasted any such liquor before. Soon after this, the blacks who brought me on board went off, and left me abandoned to despair.

I now saw myself deprived of all chance of returning to my native country, or even the least glimpse of hope of gaining the shore, which I now considered as friendly; and I even wished for my former slavery in preference to my present situation, which was filled with horrors of every kind, still heightened by my ignorance of what I was to undergo. I was not long suffered to indulge my grief; I was soon put down under the decks, and there I received such a salutation in my nostrils as I had never experienced in my life: so that, with the loathsomeness of the stench and crying together, I became so sick and low that I was not able to eat, nor had I the least desire to taste any thing. I now wished for the last friend, death, to relieve me; but soon, to my grief, two of the white men offered me eatables; and, on my refusing to eat, one of them held me fast by the hands, and laid me across, I think the windlass, and tied my feet, while the other flogged me severely. I had never experienced any thing of this kind before, and although not being used to the water, I naturally feared that element the first time I saw it, yet, nevertheless, could I have got over the nettings, I would have jumped over the side, but I could not; and besides, the crew used to watch us very closely who were not chained down to the decks, lest we should leap into the water; and I have seen some of these poor African prisoners most severely cut, for attempting to do so, and hourly whipped for not eating. This indeed was often the case with myself. In a little time after, amongst the poor chained men, I found some of my own nation, which in a small degree gave ease to my mind. I inquired of these what was to be done with us? They gave me to understand, we were to be carried to these white people's country to work for them. I then was a little revived, and thought, if it were no worse than working, my situation was not so desperate; but still I feared I should be put to death, the white people looked and acted, as I thought, in so savage a manner; for I had never seen among any people such instances of brutal cruelty; and this not only shown towards us blacks, but also to some of the whites themselves. One white man in particular I saw, when we were permitted to be on deck, flogged so unmercifully with a large rope near the foremast, that he died in consequence of it; and they tossed him over the side as they would have done a brute. This made me fear these people the more; and I expected nothing less than to be treated in the same manner. I could not help expressing my fears and apprehensions to some of my countrymen; I asked them if these people had no country, but lived in this hollow place? (the ship) they told me they did not, but came from a distant one. "Then," said I, "how comes it in all our country we never heard of them?" They told me because they lived so very far off. I then asked where were their women? had they any like themselves? I was told they had. "And why," said I, "do we not see them?" They answered, because they were left behind. I asked how the vessel could go? they told me they could not tell; but that there was cloth put upon the masts by the help of the ropes I saw, and then the vessel went on; and the white men had some spell or magic they put in the water when they liked in order to stop the vessel. I was exceedingly amazed at this account, and really thought they were spirits. I therefore wished much to be from amongst them, for I expected they would sacrifice me; but my wishes were vain, for we were so quartered that it was impossible for any of us to make our escape.

While we stayed on the coast I was mostly on deck; and one day, to my great astonishment, I saw one of these vessels coming in with the sails up. As soon as the whites saw it, they gave a great shout, at which we were amazed; and the more so, as the vessel appeared larger by approaching nearer. At last, she came to an anchor in my sight, and when the anchor was let go, I and my countrymen who saw it, were lost in astonishment to observe the vessel stop—and were now convinced it was done by magic. Soon after this the other ship got her boats out, and they came on board of us, and the people of both ships seemed very glad to see each other.—Several of the strangers also shook hands with us black people, and made motions with their hands, signifying, I suppose, we were to go to their country, but we did not understand them.

At last, when the ship we were in, had got in all her cargo, they made ready with many fearful noises, and we were all put under deck, so that we could not see how they managed the vessel. But this disappointment was the least of my sorrow. The stench of the hold while we were on the coast was so intolerably loathsome, that it was dangerous to remain there for any time, and some of us had been permitted to stay on the deck for the fresh air; but now that the whole ship's cargo were confined together, it became absolutely pestilential. The closeness of the place, and the heat of the climate, added to the number in the ship, which was so crowded that each had scarcely room to turn himself, almost suffocated us. This produced copious perspirations, so that the air soon became unfit for respiration, from a variety of loathsome smells, and brought on a sickness among the slaves, of which many died—thus falling victims to the improvident avarice, as I may call it, of their purchasers. This wretched situation was again aggravated by the falling of the chains, now become insupportable; and the filth of the necessary tubs, into which the children often fell, and were almost suffocated. The shrieks of the women, and the groans of the dying, rendered the whole a scene of horror almost inconceivable. Happily perhaps, for myself, I was soon reduced so low here that it was thought necessary to keep me almost always on deck; and from my extreme youth I was not put in fetters. In this situation I expected every hour to share the fate of my companions, some of whom were almost daily brought upon the deck at the point of death, which I began to hope would soon put an end to my miseries. Often did I think many of the inhabitants of the deep much more happy than myself. I envied them the freedom they enjoyed, and as often wished I could change my condition for theirs. Every circumstance I met with, served only to render my state more painful, and heightened my apprehensions, and my opinion of the cruelty of the whites.

One day they had taken a number of fishes; and when they had killed and satisfied themselves with as many as they thought fit, to our astonishment, who were on deck, rather than give any of them to us to eat, as we expected, they tossed the remaining fish into the sea again, although we begged and prayed for some as well as we could, but in vain; and some of my countrymen, being pressed by hunger, took an opportunity, when they thought no one saw them, of trying to get a little privately; but they were discovered, and the attempt procured them some very severe floggings. One day, when we had a smooth sea and moderate wind, two of my wearied countrymen who were chained together, (I was near them at the time,) preferring death to such a life of misery, somehow made through the nettings and jumped into the sea: immediately, another quite dejected fellow, who, on account of his illness, was suffered to be out of irons, also followed their example; and I believe many more would very soon have done the same, if they had not been prevented by the ship's crew, who were instantly alarmed. Those of us that were the most active, were in a moment put down under the deck, and there was such a noise and confusion amongst the people of the ship as I never heard before, to stop her and get the boat out to go after the slaves. However, two of the wretched were drowned, but they got the other, and afterwards flogged him unmercifully, for thus attempting to prefer death to slavery. In this manner we continued to undergo more hardships than I can now relate, hardships which are inseparable from this accursed trade. Many a time we were near suffocation from the want of fresh air, which we were often without for whole days together. This and the stench of the necessary tubs, carried off many.

During our passage, I first saw flying fishes, which surprised me very much; they used frequently to fly across the ship, and many of them fell on the deck. I also now first saw the use of the quadrant; I had often with astonishment seen the mariners make observations with it, and I could not think what it meant. They at last took notice of my surprise; and one of them, willing to increase it, as well as to gratify my curiosity, made me one day look through it. The clouds appeared to me to be land, which disappeared as they passed along. This heightened my wonder; and I was now more persuaded than ever, that I was in another world, and that every thing about me was magic. At last, we came in sight of the island of Barbadoes, at which the whites on board gave a great shout, and made many signs of joy to us. We did not know what to think of this; but as the vessel drew nearer, we plainly saw the harbor, and other ships of different kinds and sizes, and we soon anchored amongst them, off Bridgetown. Many merchants and planters now came on board, though it was in the evening. They put us in separate parcels, and examined us attentively. They also made us jump, and pointed to the land, signifying we were to go there. We thought by this, we should be eaten by these ugly men, as they appeared to us; and, when soon after we were all put down under the deck again, there was much dread and trembling among us, and nothing but bitter cries to be heard all the night from these apprehensions, insomuch that at last the white people got some old slaves from the land to pacify us. They told us we were not to be eaten, but to work, and were soon to go on land, where we should see many of our country people. This report eased us much. And sure enough, soon after we were landed, there came to us Africans of all languages.

We were conducted immediately to the merchant's yard, where we were all pent up together, like so many sheep in a fold, without regard to sex or age. As every object was new to me, everything I saw filled me with surprise. What struck me first, was that the houses were built with bricks and stories, and in every other respect different from those I had seen in Africa; but I was still more astonished on seeing people on horseback. I did not know what this could mean; and, indeed, I thought these people were full of nothing but magical arts. While I was in this astonishment, one of my fellow-prisoners spoke to a countryman of his, about the horses, who said they were the same kind they had in their country. I understood them, though they were from a distant part of Africa; and I thought it odd I had not seen any horses there; but afterwards, when I came to converse with different Africans, I found they had many horses amongst them, and much larger than those I then saw.

We were not many days in the merchant's custody, before we were sold after their usual manner, which is this:—On a signal given, (as the beat of a drum,) the buyers rush at once into the yard where the slaves are confined, and make choice of that parcel they like best. The noise and clamor with which this is attended, and the eagerness visible in the countenance of the buyers, serve not a little to increase the apprehension of terrified Africans, who may well be supposed to consider them as the ministers of that destruction to which they think themselves devoted. In this manner, without scruple, are relations and friends separated, most of them never to see each other again. I remember in the vessel in which I was brought over, in the men's apartment, there were several brothers, who, in the sale, were sold in different lots; and it was very moving on this occasion, to see and hear their cries at parting. O, ye nominal Christians! might not an African ask you—Learned you this from your God, who says unto you, Do unto all men as you would men should do unto you? Is it not enough that we are torn from our country and friends, to toil for your luxury and lust of gain? Must every tender feeling be likewise sacrificed to your avarice? Are the dearest friends and relations, now rendered more dear by their separation from their kindred, still to be parted from each other, and thus prevented from cheering the gloom of slavery, with the small comfort of being together, and mingling their sufferings and sorrows? Why are parents to lose their children, brothers their sisters, or husbands their wives? Surely, this is a new refinement in cruelty, which, while it has no advantage to atone for it, thus aggravates distress, and adds fresh horrors even to the wretchedness of slavery.

1789

Cultural Portfolio
Slavery, Freedom, and Identity

Over the course of the sixteenth and seventeenth centuries, the slave trade swelled from a mere trickle to an immense flood. As early as 1518, slaves were being imported to the West Indies, particularly to Hispaniola, which is now Haiti. By 1540 ten thousand Africans a year endured the notorious Middle Passage across the Atlantic, and by the end of the sixteenth century there were already nearly a million black slaves there.

A slave ship landed to the north, in the Virginia colony of the American mainland, probably as early as 1619. Though at first some Africans were treated similarly to white indentured servants, by 1705, Robert Beverley in his *History of the Present State of Virginia* reported a clear distinction between servants and slaves.

The slave trip fell into three parts. On the Gold Coast–Niger area of West Africa, slaves were first either bought from "dealers," captured like prisoners of war, or abducted singly or in groups. Near the water's edge, they were held captive in slave "factories" guarded by white men with muskets. Once the "cargo" was procured, the voyage from Africa to the New World took from fifteen days to four months. The Africans who survived the treacherous Middle Passage were sold, or "distributed" on the American shores.

The horrors of the Middle Passage are now well documented. Heads were shaved and clothing removed before the sailing. Men were shackled while the women were left free and at the mercy of the sailors. Savage beatings met those who attempted suicide by jumping overboard. Africans of both sexes were "danced," a form of exercise enforced by a cat o' nine tails. Eventually, overcrowding on board resulted in a high death rate from disease.

Yet these people certainly were not savages, as some earlier American scholars believed. Nor were they, as Thomas Jefferson wrote, completely other than the Europeans, with physical and moral "differences" innately "fixed in nature."

Mythology, folk tales, proverbs, poetry, and sculpture were highly evolved in the sections of West Africa from which the majority of the enslaved emerged. Music was the most developed of their arts; its polyrhythmic complexity was as sophisticated as any compositional structure in the world. The beat of those West African drums was allowed to continue in the Catholic-dominated West Indies where the African was generally considered a human being. But in the Protestant-settled lands of America, the drumbeat was soon silenced, for the instrument that played for dancing could also communicate revolutionary messages.

With the increase in the slave population, there also came more stringent laws to govern them. And so, for 160 years the African American slaves remained in official bondage. Rebellions and insurrections were frequent. Even plots to burn both Boston and New York were discovered in the early 1700s. One of the more effective insurrections at Stono, a plantation west of Charleston, was called the Cato conspiracy. There slaves killed two guards, stole arms and ammunition, and escaped toward freedom in Florida. As a result, even stricter regulations against assembly and communication by drum were passed in South Carolina and elsewhere.

Because of these strictures, the principal sources of information on the African American experience in colonial America were written by whites. Plantation inventories, diaries, letters, laws, documents, and court records give the "official" picture. Because of their frequent dislocations and their exclusion from education, few slaves wrote of their experiences. With the exception of such rare autobiographical writing in fugitive slave journals, eighteenth-century African American culture was almost exclusively oral; that culture survives in such communal activities as songs, hymns, and dances.

It was not until the eve of the Revolution that African American literature, known principally through the poetry of Phillis Wheatley, gained the attention of white colonists. And it was not until 1827 that "Freedom's Journal," the nation's first newspaper edited for and by African Americans, was published and disseminated.

While Samuel Adams was drafting polemical essays condemning the English Parliament's suppression of the colonist's "natural rights," while Thomas Paine was urging the colonists to take up arms "to reap the blessings of freedom," a group of African American slaves petitioned the Massachusetts governor and assembly to recognize their legal claims.

Adams and Paine failed to include the "natural rights" of African Americans when they demanded such liberties for Americans of European origin. But some white colonists, such as Samuel Sewall, did question the slave system and "the Vast Weight that is built upon it." Sewall already then stated that all men are made of "One Blood" and as "coheirs of Adam," have "equal Right unto Liberty and all the other outward Comforts of Life."

The African American petitioners in Massachusetts wrote that they too were a "freeborn Pepel and have never forfeited this Blessing by aney compact or agreement whatever." They appealed to the legislator's charity and humanitarian impulses by describing the abuses they had suffered. Their petitions are eloquent briefs for personal and political freedom. Their call for a "Natural and Unaliable Right" to liberty and for the privileges and immunities of "free and natural born subjects" anticipates both the language and the sentiment of the Declaration of Independence.

Patrick Reason, African American engraver
Kneeling Slave
engraving, 1835
(Moorland Spingarn Research Center, Howard University)

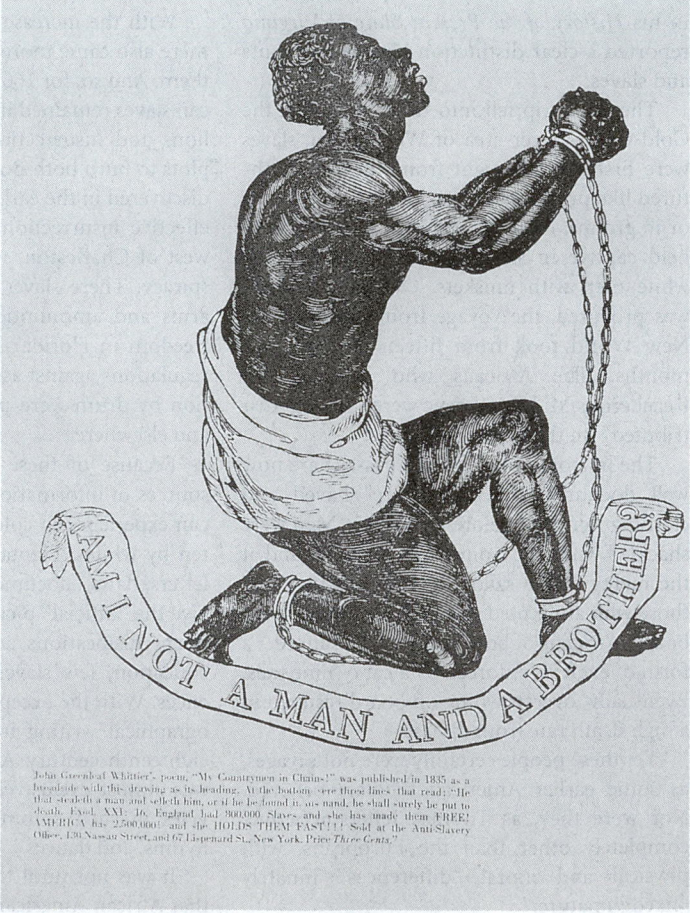

John Greenleaf Whittier's poem, "My Countrymen in Chains!" was published in 1835 as a broadside with this drawing as its heading. At the bottom are three lines that read: "He that stealeth a man and selleth him, or if he be found in his hand, he shall surely be put to death. Exod. XXI: 16. England had 800,000 Slaves and she has made them FREE! AMERICA has 2,500,000! and she HOLDS THEM FAST!!! Sold at the Anti-Slavery Office, 130 Nassau Street, and 67 Liespenard St., New York. Price *Three Cents.*"

from Samuel Sewall, *The Diary of Samuel Sewall*

The Selling of Joseph

A Memorial

Forasmuch as Liberty *is in real value next unto* Life: *None ought to part with it themselves, or deprive others of it, but upon most mature Consideration.*

The Numerousness of Slaves at this day in the Province, and the Uneasiness of them under their Slavery, hath put many upon thinking whether the Foundation of it be firmly and well laid; so as to sustain the Vast Weight that is built upon it. It is most certain that all Men, as they are the Sons of *Adam,* are Coheirs; and have equal Right unto Liberty, and all other outward Comforts of Life. *God hath given the Earth* [with all its Commodities] *unto the Sons of Adam, Psal* 115.16. *And hath made of One Blood, all Nations of Men, for to dwell on all the face of the Earth, and hath determined the Times before appointed, and the bounds of their habitation: That they should seek the Lord. Forasmuch then as we are the Offspring of GOD &c. Act* 17.26, 27, 29. Now although the Title given by the last ADAM, doth infinitely better Mens Estates, respecting GOD and themselves; and grants them a most beneficial and inviolable Lease under the Broad Seal of Heaven, who were before only Tenants at Will: Yet through the Indulgence of GOD to our First Parents after the Fall, the outward Estate of all and every of their Children, remains the same, as to one another. . . .

It is likewise most lamentable to think, how in taking Negros out of *Africa,* and Selling of them here, That which GOD ha's joyned together men do boldly rend asunder; Men from their Country, Husbands from their Wives, Parents from their Children. How horrible is the Uncleanness, Mortality, if not Murder, that the Ships are guilty of that bring great Crouds of these miserable Men, and Women. Methinks, when we are bemoaning the barbarous Usage of our Friends and Kinsfolk in *Africa:* it might not be unseasonable to enquire whether we are not culpable in forcing the *Africans* to become Slaves amongst our selves. . . .

It is Observable that the *Israelites* were strictly forbidden the buying, or selling one another for Slaves. *Levit.* 25. 39. 46. *Jer.* 34. 8......22. And GOD gaged His Blessing in lieu of any loss they might conceipt they suffered thereby. *Deut.* 15. 18. And since the partition Wall is broken down, inordinate Self love should likewise be demolished. GOD expects that Christians should be of a more Ingenuous and benign frame of spirit. Christians should carry it to all the World, as the *Israelites* were to carry it one towards another. And for men obstinately to persist in holding their Neighbours and Brethren under the Rigor of perpetual Bondage, seems to be no proper way of gaining Assurance that God ha's given them Spiritual Freedom. Our Blessed Saviour ha's altered the Measures of the ancient Love-Song, and set it to a most Excellent New Tune, which all ought to be ambitious of Learning. *Matt.* 5. 43, 44. *John* 13. 34. These *Ethiopians,* as black as they are; seeing they are the Sons and Daughters of the First *Adam,* the Brethren and Sisters of the Last ADAM, and the Offspring of GOD; They ought to be treated with a Respect agreeable.

Runaway Slave Poster
1849
(State Historical Society of Wisconsin)

Eastman Johnson, *Old Kentucky Home (Negro Life in the South)*
oil on canvas, 1859
(The New-York Historical Society)

William Sidney Mount
The Power of Music
oil on canvas, 1847
(The Cleveland Museum of Art, Leonard C. Hanna, Jr. Fund 1991.110)

from Benjamin Franklin, *An Address to the Public*

from the Pennsylvania Society for Promoting the Abolition of Slavery, and the Relief of Free Negroes Unlawfully Held in Bondage

It is with peculiar satisfaction we assure the friends of humanity, that, in prosecuting the design of our association, our endeavours have proved successful, far beyond our most sanguine expectations.

Encouraged by this success, and by the daily progress of that luminous and benign spirit of liberty, which is diffusing itself throughout the world, and humbly hoping for the continuance of the divine blessing on our labours, we have ventured to make an important addition to our original plan, and do therefore earnestly solicit the support and assistance of all who can feel the tender emotions of sympathy and compassion, or relish the exalted pleasure of beneficence.

Slavery is such an atrocious debasement of human nature, that its very extirpation, if not performed with solicitous care, may sometimes open a source of serious evils.

The unhappy man, who has long been treated as a brute animal, too frequently sinks beneath the common standard of the human species. The galling chains, that bind his body, do also fetter his intellectual faculties, and impair the social affections of his heart. Accustomed to move like a mere machine, by the will of a master, reflection is suspended; he has not the power of choice; and reason and conscience have but little influence over his conduct, because he is chiefly governed by the passion of fear. He is poor and friendless; perhaps worn out by extreme labour, age, and disease.

Under such circumstances, freedom may often prove a misfortune to himself, and prejudicial to society.

Attention to emancipated black people, it is therefore to be hoped, will become a branch of our national policy; but, as far as we contribute to promote this emancipation, so far that attention is evidently a serious duty incumbent on us, and which we mean to discharge to the best of our judgment and abilities.

To instruct, to advise, to qualify those, who have been restored to freedom, for the exercise and enjoyment of civil liberty, to promote in them habits of industry, to furnish them with employments suited to their age, sex, talents, and other circumstances, and to procure their children an education calculated for their future situation in life; these are the great outlines of the annexed plan, which we have adopted, and which we conceive will essentially promote the public good, and the happiness of these our hitherto too much neglected fellow-creatures.

A plan so extensive cannot be carried into execution without considerable pecuniary resources, beyond the present ordinary funds of the Society. We hope much from the generosity of enlightened and benevolent freemen, and will gratefully receive any donations or subscriptions for this purpose, which may be made to our treasurer, James Starr, or to James Pemberton, chairman of our committee of correspondence.

Signed, by order of the Society,

B.FRANKLIN, *President.*

Philadelphia, 9th of November, 1789
1789/1789

from Thomas Jefferson, *Notes on the State of Virginia*

On the Traits of Blacks

The first difference which strikes us is that of colour. Whether the black of the negro resides in the reticular membrane between the skin and scarf-skin, or in the scarf-skin itself; whether it proceeds from the colour of the blood, the colour of the bile, or from that of some other secretion, the difference is fixed in nature, and is as real as if its seat and cause were better known to us. And is this difference of no importance? Is it not the foundation of a greater or less share of beauty in the two races? Are not the fine mixtures of red and white, the expressions of every passion by

William Sidney Mount
The Banjo Player
oil on canvas, 1856
(The Museums at Stonybrook)

greater or less suffusions of colour in the one, preferable to that eternal monotony, which reigns in the countenances, that immoveable veil of black which covers all the emotions of the other race? Add to these, flowing hair, a more elegant symmetry of form, their own judgment in favour of the whites, declared by their preference of them, as uniformly as is the preference of the Oran-ootan for the black women over those of his own species. The circumstance of superior beauty, is thought worthy attention in the propagation of our horses, dogs, and other domestic animals; why not in that of man? Besides those of colour, figure, and hair, there are other physical distinctions proving a difference of race. They have less hair on the face and body. They secrete less by the kidnies, and more by the glands of the skin, which gives them a very strong and disagreeable odour. This greater degree of transpiration renders them more tolerant of heat, and less so of cold, than the whites. Perhaps too a difference of structure in the pulmonary apparatus, which a late ingenious experimentalist has discovered to be the principal regulator of animal heat, may have disabled them from extricating, in the act of inspiration, so much of that fluid from the outer air, or obliged them in expiration, to part with more of it. They seem to require less sleep. A black, after hard labour through the day, will be induced by the slightest amusement to sit up till midnight, or later, though knowing he must be out with the first dawn of the morning. They are at least as brave, and more adventuresome. But this may perhaps proceed from a want of forethought, which prevents their seeing a danger till it be present. When present, they do not go through it with more coolness or steadiness than the whites. They are more ardent after their female: but love seems with them to be more an eager desire, than a tender delicate mixture of sentiment and sensation. Their griefs are transient. Those numberless afflictions, which render it doubtful whether heaven has given life to us in mercy or in wrath, are less felt, and sooner forgotten with them. In general, their existence appears to participate more of sensation than reflection. To this must be ascribed their disposition to sleep when abstracted from their diversions, and unemployed in labour. An animal whose body is at rest, and who does not reflect, must be disposed to sleep of course. Comparing them by their faculties of memory, reason, and imagination, it appears to me, that in memory they are equal to the whites; in reason much inferior, and I think one could scarcely be found capable of tracing and comprehending the investigations of Euclid; and that in imagination they are dull, tasteless, and anomalous. It would be unfair to follow them to Africa for this investigation. We will consider them here, on the same stage with the whites, and where the facts are not apocryphal on which a judgment is to be formed. It will be right to make great allowances for the difference of condition, of education, of conversation, of the sphere in which they move. Many millions of them have been brought to, and born in America. Most of them indeed have been confined to tillage, to their own homes, and their own society: yet many have been so situated, that they might have availed themselves of the conversation of their masters; many have been brought up to the handicraft arts, and from that circumstance have always been associated with the whites. Some have been liberally educated, and all have lived in countries where the arts and sciences are cultivated to a considerable degree, and have had before their eyes samples of the best works from abroad.

from *Black Petitions for Freedom*

To his Excellency Thomas Hutch[inson Gov]ernor of said Prov[i]nce, to the Honorable his Majestys Council, [and to the] Honourable House of Representatives in General Court assembled June 1773.

The Petition of us the subscribers in behalf of all thous who by divine Permission are held in a state of slavery, within the bowels of a free Country, Humbly sheweth,—

    That your Petitioners apprehend they have in comon with other men a naturel right to be free and without molestation to injoy such Property as thay may acquire by their industry, or by any other means not detrimental to their fellow men and that no person can have any just claim to their services unless. . . .

1773/1773

> To his Excellency Thomas Gage Esq Captain General and Governor in Chief in and over this Province. To the Honourable his Majestys Council and the Honourable House of Representatives in General Court assembled may 25 177——[1]

The Petition of a Grate Number of Blackes of this Province who by divine permission are held in a state of Slavery within the bowels of a free and christian Country

Humbly Shewing

That your Petitioners apprehind we have in common with all other men a naturel right to our freedoms without Being depriv'd of them by our fellow men as we are a freeborn Pepel and have never forfeited this Blessing by aney compact or agreement whatever. But we were unjustly dragged by the cruel hand of power from our dearest frinds and sum of us stolen from the bosoms of our tender Parents and from a Populous Pleasant and plentiful country and Brought hither to be made slaves for Life in a Christian land. Thus we are deprived of every thing that hath a tendency to make life even tolerable, the endearing ties of husband and wife we are strangers to for we are no longer man and wife then our masters or mestreses thinkes proper marred or onmarred. Our children are also taken from us by force and sent maney miles from us wear we seldom or ever see them again there to be made slaves of for Life which sumtimes is vere short by Reson of Being dragged from their mothers Breest Thus our Lives are imbittered to us on these accounts By our deplorable situation we are rendered incapable of shewing our obedience to Almighty God how can a slave perform the duties of a husband to a wife or parent to his child How can a husband leave master and work and cleave to his wife. How can the wife submit themselves to there husbands in all things. How can the child obey thear parents in all things. There is a grat number of us sencear . . . members of the Church of Christ how can the master and the slave be said to fulfil that command Live in love let Brotherly Love contuner and abound Beare yea onenothers Bordenes How can the master be said to Beare my Borden when he Beares me down whith the Have chanes of slavery and operson against my will and how can we fulfill our parte of duty to him whilst in this condition and as we cannot searve our God as we ought whilst in this situation Nither can we reap an equal benefet from the laws of the Land which doth not justifi but condemns Slavery or if there had bin aney Law to hold us in Bondege we are Humbely of the Opinion ther never was aney to inslave our children for life when Born in a free Countrey. We therfor Bage your Excellency and Honours will give this its deu weight and consideration and that you will accordingly cause an act of the legislative to be pessed that we may obtain our Natural right our freedoms and our children be set at lebety at the yeare of Twenty one for whoues sekes more petequeley your Petitioners is in Duty ever to Pray.

1774/1774

---

[1] The last numeral has been changed several times in the manuscript, but the date should be 1774.

To his Excellency Thomas Gage Governor:—
To the Honourable His Majesty's Council, and the
Honourable House of Representatives of the Province
of the Massachusetts Bay in General Court assembled,
June—Anno Domini 1774.

The Petition of us the Subscribers, in behalf of all those, who, by divine permission, are held in a State of *Slavery* within the Bowels of a Free Country.

Humbly Sheweth

That your petitioners apprehend, they have in common with other men, a natural right to be free, and without molestation, to enjoy such property, as they may acquire by their industry, or by any other means not detrimental to their fellow men; and that no person can have any just claim to their services unless by the laws of the land they have forfeited them, or by voluntary compact become servants; neither of which is our case; but we were dragged by the cruel hand of power, some of us from our dearest connections, and others stolen from the bosoms of tender parents and brought hither to be enslaved. Thus are we deprived of every thing that has a tendency to make life even tol[erable.] . . . We are informed, there is no law of this Province, whereby our masters can claim our services, mere custom is the tyrant that keeps us in bondage, and deprives us of that use of the law, which our fellow men, who we believe under God are no better than us, are entitled to and do enjoy. We do not claim rigid justice, but as we are deserving like other men, of some compensation for all our toils and sufferings; we would therefore in addition to our prayer, that all of us, excepting such as are now infirm through age, or otherways unable to support themselves, may be liberated and made free men of this community, and be entitled to all the privileges and immunities of its free and natural born subjects. Further humbly ask that your Excellency and Honours would be pleased to give and grant to us some part of the unimproved land, belonging to the province, for a settlement, that each of us may there quietly sit down under his own fig tree [and enjoy] the fruits of his labour. . . .

1774/1774

To the Honorable Counsel & House of [Representa]tives
for the State of Massachusitte Bay in General Court
assembled, Jan. 13, 1777.

The petition of A Great Number of Blackes detained in a State of slavery in the Bowels of a free & Christian Country Humbly shuwith that your Petitioners apprehend that thay have in Common with all other men a Natural and Unaliable Right to that freedom which the Grat Parent of the Unavers hath Bestowed equalley on all menkind and which they have Never forfuted by any Compact or agreement whatever—but thay wher Unjustly Dragged by the hand of cruel Power from their Derest friends and sum of them Even torn from the Embraces of their tender Parents—from A popolous Pleasant and plentiful contry and in violation of Laws of Nature and off Nations and in defiance of all the tender feelings of humanity Brough hear Either to Be sold Like Beast of Burthen & Like them Condemnd to Slavery for Life—Among A People Profesing the mild Religion of Jesus A people Not Insensible of the Secrets of Rationable Being Nor without spirit to Resent the unjust endeavours of others to Reduce them to a state of

Bondage and Subjection your honouer Need not to be informed that A Life of Slavery Like that of your petioners Deprived of Every social privilege of Every thing Requiset to Render Life Tolable is far worse then Nonexistance.

[In imitat]ion of the Lawdable Example of the Good People of these States your petiononers have Long and Patiently waited the Evnt of petition after petition By them presented to the Legislative Body of this state and cannot but with Grief Reflect that their Sucess hath ben but too similar they Cannot but express their Astonishment that It has Never Bin Consirdered that Every Principle from which Amarica has Acted in the Cours of their unhappy Deficultes with Great Briton Pleads Stronger than A thousand arguments in favowrs of your petioners they therfor humble Beseech your honours to give this petion its due weight & consideration and cause an act of the Legislatur to be past Wherby they may Be Restored to the Enjoyments of that which is the Naturel Right of all men—and their Children who wher Born in this Land of Liberty may not be heald as Slaves after they arrive at the age of Twenty one years so may the Inhabitance of thes Stats No longer chargeable with the inconsistancey of acting themselves the part which they condem and oppose in others Be prospered in their present Glorious struggle for Liberty and have those Blessing to them, &c.

1777/1777

Robert S. Duncanson, African American painter
Blue Hole, Flood Waters, Little Miami River
oil on canvas, 1851
(Gift of Norbert Heerman and Arthur Helbig/Cincinnati Art Museum)

from **The American Museum; or, Repository of Ancient and Modern Fugitive Pieces, Prose and Poetical, May 1789***

Prose description of the Engraving "Plan of an African Ship's Lower Deck"

"The annexed plate represents the lower deck of an African ship of one hundred and ninety-seven tons of burden, with the slaves stowed on it, in the proportion of not quite one to a Ton.

In the men's apartment, the space allowed to each is six feet in length, by fifteen inches in breadth. The boys are allowed five feet by fourteen inches. The women, five feet ten inches, by fifteen inches; and the girls, four feet by one foot each. The perpendicular height between decks is five feet eight inches.

The men are fastened together, two and two, by handcuffs on their wrists, and by irons riveted on their legs. They are brought up on the main deck every day, about eight o'clock, and as each pair ascend, a strong chain, fastened by ring bolts to the deck, is passed through their shackles; a precaution absolutely necessary to prevent insurrections. In this state, if the weather is favorable, they are permitted to remain about one-third part of twenty-four hours, and during this interval they are fed, and their apartment below is cleaned; but when the weather is bad, even those indulgences cannot be granted them, and they are only permitted to come up in small companies, of about ten at a time, to be fed, where, after remaining a quarter of an hour, each mess is obliged to give place to the next in rotation.

It may perhaps be conceived, from the crowded state in which the slaves appear in the plate, that an unusual and exaggerated instance has been produced; this, however, is so far from being the case, that no ship, if her intended cargo can be procured, ever carries a less number than one to a ton, and the usual practice has been to carry nearly double that number. . . . The *Brooks of Liverpool*, a capital ship, from which the [accompanying] sketch was proportioned, did, in one voyage, actually carry six hundred and nine slaves, which is more than double the number that appear in the plate. The mode of stowing them was as follows: platforms, or wide shelves, were erected between the decks, extending so far from the sides towards the middle of the vessel, as to be capable of containing four additional rows of slaves, by which means the perpendicular height between each tier, after allowing for the beams and platforms, was reduced to two feet six inches, so that they could not even sit in an erect posture; besides which, in the men's apartment, instead of four rows, five were stowed, by placing the heads of one between the legs of another. All the horrors of this situation are still multiplied in the smaller vessels."

* Author unknown.

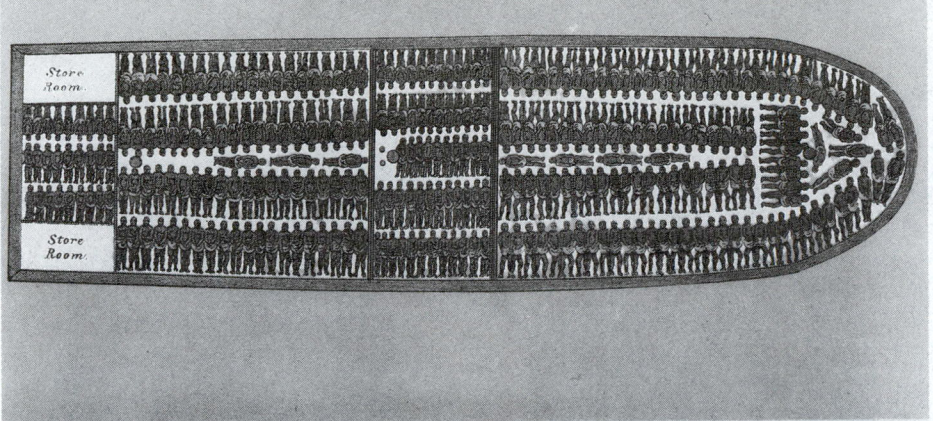

THE LOWER DECK OF A GUINEA-MAN IN THE LAST CENTURY.

Anonymous (American engraver), *Plan of an African Ship's Lower Deck*, 1789.
Engraving, 4 3/8 x 13 1/4 inches.
Published in *The American Museum; or, Repository of Ancient and Modern Fugitive Pieces, Prose and Poetical*, V, no. 5, May 1789.
lithograph, 1789
(Corbis-Bettmann)

from Michel-Guillaume Jean de Crèvecoeur, *Letters from an American Farmer*

Letter IX: Charleston Slave

The following scene will I hope account for these melancholy reflections, and apologize for the gloomy thoughts with which I have filled this letter: my mind is, and always has been, oppressed since I became a witness to it. I was not long since invited to dine with a planter who lived three miles from ———, where he then resided. In order to avoid the heat of the sun, I resolved to go on foot, sheltered in a small path, leading through a pleasant wood. I was leisurely travelling along, attentively examining some peculiar plants which I had collected, when all at once I felt the air strongly agitated; though the day was perfectly calm and sultry. I immediately cast my eyes toward the cleared ground, from which I was but at a small distance, in order to see whether it was not occasioned by a sudden shower; when at that instant a sound resembling a deep rough voice, uttered, as I thought, a few inarticulate monosyllables. Alarmed and surprized, I precipitately looked all round, when I perceived at about six rods distance something resembling a cage, suspended to the limbs of a tree; all the branches of which appeared covered with large birds of prey, fluttering about, and anxiously endeavouring to perch on the cage. Actuated by an involuntary motion of my hands, more than by any design

Caesar, one of 21,329 slaves listed in the state of New York in 1790. Among the last slaves in the state to be freed when, on July 4, 1827, a state emancipation act went into effect.
daguerreotype, ca. 1852
(The New York Historical Society)

of my mind, I fired at them; they all flew to a short distance, with a most hideous noise: when, horrid to think and painful to repeat, I perceived a negro, suspended in the cage, and left there to expire! I shudder when I recollect that the birds had already picked out his eyes, his cheek bones were bare; his arms had been attacked in several places, and his body seemed covered with a multitude of wounds. From the edges of the hollow sockets and from the lacerations with which he was disfigured, the blood slowly dropped, and tinged the ground beneath. No sooner were the birds flown, than swarms of insects covered the whole body of this unfortunate wretch, eager to feed on his mangled flesh and to drink his blood. I found myself suddenly arrested by the power of affright and terror; my nerves were convulsed; I trembled, I stood motionless, involuntarily contemplating the fate of this negro, in all its dismal latitude. The living spectre, though deprived of his eyes, could still distinctly hear, and in his uncouth dialect begged me to give him some water to allay his thirst. Humanity herself would have recoiled back with horror; she would have balanced whether to lessen such reliefless distress, or mercifully with one blow to end this dreadful scene of agonizing torture! Had I had a ball in my gun, I certainly should have despatched him; but finding myself unable to perform so kind an office, I sought, though trembling, to relieve him as well as I could. A shell ready fixed to a pole, which had been used by some negroes, presented itself to me; I filled it with water, and with trembling hands I guided it to the quivering lips of the wretched sufferer. Urged by the irresistible power of thirst, he endeavoured to meet it, as he instinctively guessed its approach by the noise it made in passing through the bars of the cage. "Tanke, you white man, tanke you, pute some poyson and give me." How long have you been hanging there? I asked him. "Two days, and me no die; the birds, the birds; aaah me!" Oppressed with the reflections which this shocking spectacle afforded me, I mustered strength enough to walk away, and soon reached the house at which I intended to dine. There I heard that the reason for this slave being thus punished, was on account of his having killed the overseer of the plantation. They told me that the laws of self-preservation rendered such executions necessary; and supported the doctrine of slavery with the arguments generally made use of to justify the practice; with the repetition of which I shall not trouble you at present.

Adieu.

1774–1781/1782

The Federalist

On October 27, 1787, a month after the Federal Convention presented for individual state ratification a new constitution to replace the six-year-old Articles of Confederation, the first of a series of eighty-five incisively argued political essays defending the new document appeared in a New York newspaper. Signed "Publius" and explicitly addressed "to the People of New York," the essay, written by Alexander Hamilton (1757–1804), established immediately the topic and tone of the series: to persuade the citizens of New York by means of careful "deliberation" that their personal liberty and security as well as the future prosperity of the entire country depended on a strong central government, which only the immediate adoption of the proposed Constitution could provide. Although the Constitution required only the approval of nine states for ratification, its supporters felt that anything short of unanimity would cause a serious breach among the states, one that would inevitably lead to dangerous alliances among themselves and with foreign nations. Hamilton especially felt that New York, led by its governor, George Clinton, a powerful advocate of local sovereignty, represented a key state in the impending battle for ratification.

"Publius" became a collective pseudonym shortly after the first essay as Hamilton enlisted the help of two other partisans: John Jay (1745–1829), the affluent, conservative New York attorney who eventually served as a Supreme Court Justice and later as governor of New York, and the young though politically seasoned Virginian James Madison (1751–1836), who, more than any other delegate to the convention, had been responsible for the overall design of the Constitution and who would later serve as fourth president of the United States. Since Jay had held the office of secretary of foreign affairs under the Articles of Confederation and had helped negotiate the Treaty of Paris, his diplomatic experiences lent impressive support to his essays on international relations. Because of poor health, however, Jay was able to contribute only five essays to the series; after the fifth paper it became, with one exception, exclusively the labor of Hamilton and Madison.

A native of the West Indies, Alexander Hamilton completed his studies at Columbia (then called King's College), served on Washington's staff during the Revolution, and afterward established a highly successful law practice in New York City. At the Constitutional Convention, which he attended sporadically, Hamilton argued strenuously for an energetic central government headed by a powerful executive. An outspoken proponent of business interests and industrialization, Hamilton, as the first secretary of the treasury, brilliantly engineered a fiscal policy that gave the floundering new nation the foreign credibility and domestic assurance it needed to survive. When in January 1790, only a year and a half after the final *Federalist* essay went to press, Hamilton submitted to Congress his "Report on the Public Credit," his chief political opponent had become Publius's other half, James Madison. By then, the Constitution ratified and the machinery of the new administration in operation, Madison was thinking and acting more sectionally as a Virginian and less, as Hamilton liked to put it, "continentally" as an American.

But in 1787 Publius's "split personality" could be seen only in a few inconsistencies and disparate emphases, tensions forgivable and easily overlooked in the steadily accumulating output of penetrating political analysis. Composed hastily and under too much pressure, the papers could hardly offer systematic coverage of all the principles of constitutional government. Nevertheless, given the strains of collaboration and deadlines, Publius achieved a remarkably high-minded level of political discourse and an admirable degree of theoretical complexity. The man who would in a few years become Hamilton's fiercest enemy, Thomas Jefferson, considered *The Federalist* "the best commentary on the principles of government, which ever was written" and later made the book required reading for all students at the University of Virginia. What was conceived primarily as a popular series of campaign tracts to influence a relatively small group of voters eventually became, by virtue of its articulation and political discernment, one of the central documents of American government, a necessary supplement to all historical and judicial interpretations of the Constitution.

At the center of Publius's argument, as the opening paper makes clear, is the desire for a strong Union and the belief that a new constitution must supersede the totally inadequate Articles of Confederation. What may seem obvious today, it is important to remember, was not so obvious then. A country that had recently gone through a debilitating war to shake off the political and economic impositions of one strong government was hardly eager to adopt another to replace it. The Constitutional Convention itself, moreover, was viewed by many citizens (especially in New York and Virginia) as unauthorized and extralegal, a fairly open conspiracy among a small group of reactionary, propertied people who, in their enthusiasm to "form a more perfect union," would undoubtedly perpetuate an aristocracy of the wealthy and influential.

Another objection that serious, well-informed citizens raised against the Constitution was that no republic, certainly no democracy, could be maintained in a country as geographically diverse and extensive as their own. In general, objections to the Constitution varied according to the degree of local suspicions and local power. The main task Publius faced throughout the papers was to convince a skeptical public that a strong central government was not only possible and indispensable for security and survival but also that, more important, it was compatible with individual liberty.

In Publius's papers, as in all significant political discourse, definitions and distinctions play a crucial role. In fact, the very title given to the series after the individual essays had been collected in May 1788, *The Federalist*, caused considerable confusion. Those who supported the Articles of Confederation argued that *they* were the real Federalists and contended that Publius had coopted the term.

In an earlier paper Madison had confronted another result of the "confusion of names," the important distinctions between a republic and a democracy. Language, he acknowledges in yet another paper, is a "cloudy medium" in which the science of politics and the complex institutions it attempts to delineate are continually being trapped in "obscurity."

For Hamilton and Madison, the intellectual confusions brought about by vague and inaccurate definitions and the emotional confusions resulting from "intemperance of expression" presented formidable obstacles to both good government and good writing; Publius seldom indulges in rhetorical flourishes. In fact, the vocabulary of "passion" (one of the key words of *The Federalist*) is throughout the series closely associated with the "animosity," "violence," and "disease" generated by the "factions" that Madison examines in the celebrated tenth paper. In their exacting style and dispassionate designs, Publius's essays, always lucid, often ironic, tough-mindedly predisposed to expect the worst and demand the best from human nature, represent the consummate expression of one of America's most consequential political programs and philosophies.

Further Reading:

G. Dietze, *The Federalist: A Classic on Federalism and Free Government,* 1960.

J. C. Miller, *The Federalist Era,* 1960.

G. Wood, *The Creation of the American Republic, 1776–1787,* 1969.

G. Mace, *Locke, Hobbes, and the Federalist Papers,* 1979.

D. Epstein, *The Political Theory of the Federalist,* 1984.

A. Furtwangler, *The Authority of Publius: A Reading of the Federalist Papers,* 1984.

G. W. Carey, *The Federalist: Design for a Constitutional Republic,* 1989.

Text:
The Federalist, ed. J. E. Cooke, 1961.

The Federalist

No. 10 [James Madison]

November 22, 1787

To the People of the State of New York.

Among the numerous advantages promised by a well constructed Union, none deserves to be more accurately developed than its tendency to break and control the violence of faction. The friend of popular governments, never finds himself so much alarmed for their character and fate, as when he contemplates their propensity to this dangerous vice. He will not fail therefore to set a due value on any plan which, without violating the principles to which he is attached, provides a proper cure for it. The instability, injustice and confusion introduced into the public councils, have in truth been the mortal diseases under which popular governments have every where perished; as they continue to be the favorite and fruitful topics from which the adversaries to liberty derive their most specious declamations. The valuable improvements made by the American Constitutions on the popular models, both ancient and modern, cannot certainly be too much admired; but it would be an unwarrantable partiality, to contend that they have as effectually obviated the danger on this side as was wished and expected. Complaints are every where heard from our most considerate and virtuous citizens, equally the friends of public and private faith, and of public and personal liberty; that our governments are too unstable; that the public good is disregarded in the conflicts of rival parties; and that measures are too often decided, not according to the rules of justice, and the rights of the minor party; but by the superior force of an interested and over-bearing majority. However anxiously we may wish that these complaints had no foundation, the evidence of known facts will not permit us to deny that they are in some degree true. It will be found indeed, on a candid review of our situation, that some of the distresses under which we labor, have been erroneously charged on the operation of our governments; but it will be found, at the same time, that other causes will not alone account for many of our heaviest misfortunes; and particularly, for that prevailing and increasing distrust of public engagements, and alarm for private rights, which are echoed from one end of the continent to the other. These must be chiefly, if not wholly, effects of the unsteadiness and injustice, with which a factious spirit has tainted our public administrations.

By a faction I understand a number of citizens, whether amounting to a majority or minority of the whole, who are united and actuated by some common impulse of passion, or of interest, adverse to the rights of other citizens, or to the permanent and aggregate interests of the community.

There are two methods of curing the mischiefs of faction: the one, by removing its causes; the other, by controling its effects.

There are again two methods of removing the causes of faction: the one by destroying the liberty which is essential to its existence; the other, by giving to every citizen the same opinions, the same passions, and the same interests.

It could never be more truly said than of the first remedy, that it is worse than the disease. Liberty is to faction, what air is to fire, an aliment[1] without which it instantly expires. But it could not be a less folly to abolish liberty, which is essential to political life, because it nourishes faction, than it would be to wish the annihilation of air, which is essential to animal life, because it imparts to fire its destructive agency.

The second expedient is as impracticable, as the first would be unwise. As long as the reason of man continues fallible, and he is at liberty to exercise it, different opinions will be formed. As long as the connection subsists between his reason and his self-love, his opinions and his passions will have a reciprocal influence on each other; and the former will be objects to which the latter will attach themselves. The diversity in the faculties of men from which the rights of property originate, is not less an insuperable obstacle to a uniformity of interests. The protection of these faculties is the first object of Government. From the protection of different and unequal faculties of acquiring property, the possession of different degrees and kinds of property immediately results: and from the influence of these on the sentiments and views of the respective proprietors, ensues a division of the society into different interests and parties.

The latent causes of faction are thus sown in the nature of man; and we see them every where brought into different degrees of activity, according to the different circumstances of civil society. A zeal for different opinions concerning religion, concerning Government and many other points, as well of speculation as of practice; an attachment to different leaders ambitiously contending for pre-eminence and power; or to persons of other descriptions whose fortunes have been interesting to the human passions, have in turn divided mankind into parties, inflamed them with mutual animosity, and rendered them much more disposed to vex and oppress each other, than to co-operate for their common good. So strong is this propensity of mankind to fall into mutual animosities, that where no substantial occasion presents itself, the most frivolous and fanciful distinctions have been sufficient to kindle their unfriendly passions, and excite their most violent conflicts. But the most common and durable source of factions, has been the various and unequal distribution of property. Those who hold, and those who are without property, have ever formed distinct interests in society. Those who are creditors, and those who are debtors, fall under a like discrimination. A landed interest, a manufacturing interest, a mercantile interest, a monied interest, with

---

[1] Nutriment.

many lesser interests, grow up of necessity in civilized nations, and divide them into different classes, actuated by different sentiments and views. The regulation of these various and interfering interests forms the principal task of modern Legislation, and involves the spirit of party and faction in the necessary and ordinary operations of Government.

No man is allowed to be a judge in his own cause; because his interest would certainly bias his judgment, and, not improbably, corrupt his integrity. With equal, nay with greater reason, a body of men, are unfit to be both judges and parties, at the same time; yet, what are many of the most important acts of legislation, but so many judicial determinations, not indeed concerning the rights of single persons, but concerning the rights of large bodies of citizens; and what are the different classes of legislators, but advocates and parties to the causes which they determine? Is a law proposed concerning private debts? It is a question to which the creditors are parties on one side, and the debtors on the other. Justice ought to hold the balance between them. Yet the parties are and must be themselves the judges; and the most numerous party, or, in other words, the most powerful faction must be expected to prevail. Shall domestic manufactures be encouraged, and in what degree, by restrictions on foreign manufactures? are questions which would be differently decided by the landed and the manufacturing classes; and probably by neither, with a sole regard to justice and the public good. The apportionment of taxes on the various descriptions of property, is an act which seems to require the most exact impartiality; yet, there is perhaps no legislative act in which greater opportunity and temptation are given to a predominant party, to trample on the rules of justice. Every shilling with which they over-burden the inferior number, is a shilling saved to their own pockets.

It is in vain to say, that enlightened statesmen will be able to adjust these clashing interests, and render them all subservient to the public good. Enlightened statesmen will not always be at the helm: Nor, in many cases, can such an adjustment be made at all, without taking into view indirect and remote considerations, which will rarely prevail over the immediate interest which one party may find in disregarding the rights of another, or the good of the whole.

The inference to which we are brought, is, that the *causes* of faction cannot be removed; and that relief is only to be sought in the means of controling its *effects*.

If a faction consists of less than a majority, relief is supplied by the republican principle, which enables the majority to defeat its sinister views by regular vote: It may clog the administration, it may convulse the society; but it will be unable to execute and mask its violence under the forms of the Constitution. When a majority is included in a faction, the form of popular government on the other hand enables it to sacrifice to its ruling passion or interest, both the public good and the rights of other citizens. To secure the public good, and private rights, against the danger of such a faction, and at the same time to preserve the spirit and the form of popular government, is then the great object to which our enquiries are directed: Let me add that it is the great desideratum,[2] by which alone this form of government can be rescued from the opprobrium under which it has so long labored, and be recommended to the esteem and adoption of mankind.

---

[2] Necessary goal.

By what means is this object attainable? Evidently by one of two only. Either the existence of the same passion or interest in a majority at the same time, must be prevented; or the majority, having such co-existent passion or interest, must be rendered, by their number and local situation, unable to concert and carry into effect schemes of oppression. If the impulse and the opportunity be suffered to coincide, we well know that neither moral nor religious motives can be relied on as an adequate control. They are not found to be such on the injustice and violence of individuals, and lose their efficacy in proportion to the number combined together; that is, in proportion as their efficacy becomes needful.

From this view of the subject, it may be concluded, that a pure Democracy, by which I mean, a Society, consisting of a small number of citizens, who assemble and administer the Government in person, can admit of no cure for the mischiefs of faction. A common passion or interest will, in almost every case, be felt by a majority of the whole; a communication and concert results from the form of Government itself; and there is nothing to check the inducements to sacrifice the weaker party, or an obnoxious individual. Hence it is, that such Democracies have ever been spectacles of turbulence and contention; have ever been found incompatible with personal security, or the rights of property; and have in general been as short in their lives, as they have been violent in their deaths. Theoretic politicians, who have patronized this species of Government, have erroneously supposed, that by reducing mankind to a perfect equality in their political rights, they would, at the same time, be perfectly equalized and assimilated in their possessions, their opinions, and their passions.

A Republic, by which I mean a Government in which the scheme of representation takes place, opens a different prospect, and promises the cure for which we are seeking. Let us examine the points in which it varies from pure Democracy, and we shall comprehend both the nature of the cure, and the efficacy which it must derive from the Union.

The two great points of difference between a Democracy and a Republic are, first, the delegation of the Government, in the latter, to a small number of citizens elected by the rest: secondly, the greater number of citizens, and greater sphere of country, over which the latter may be extended.

The effect of the first difference is, on the one hand to refine and enlarge the public views, by passing them through the medium of a chosen body of citizens, whose wisdom may best discern the true interest of their country, and whose patriotism and love of justice, will be least likely to sacrifice it to temporary or partial considerations. Under such a regulation, it may well happen that the public voice pronounced by the representatives of the people, will be more consonant to the public good, than if pronounced by the people themselves convened for the purpose. On the other hand, the effect may be inverted. Men of factious tempers, of local prejudices, or of sinister designs, may by intrigue, by corruption or by other means, first obtain the suffrages,[3] and then betray the interests of the people. The question resulting is, whether small or extensive Republics are most favorable to the election of proper guardians of the public weal:[4] and it is clearly decided in favor of the latter by two obvious considerations.

[3] Support of the voters.
[4] Well-being.

In the first place it is to be remarked that however small the Republic may be, the Representatives must be raised to a certain number, in order to guard against the cabals of a few; and that however large it may be, they must be limited to a certain number, in order to guard against the confusion of a multitude. Hence the number of Representatives in the two cases, not being in proportion to that of the Constituents, and being proportionally greatest in the small Republic, it follows, that if the proportion of fit characters, be not less, in the large than in the small Republic, the former will present a greater option, and consequently a greater probability of a fit choice.

In the next place, as each Representative will be chosen by a greater number of citizens in the large than in the small Republic, it will be more difficult for unworthy candidates to practise with success the vicious arts, by which elections are too often carried; and the suffrages of the people being more free, will be more likely to centre on men who possess the most attractive merit, and the most diffusive and established characters.

It must be confessed, that in this, as in most other cases, there is a mean, on both sides of which inconveniences will be found to lie. By enlarging too much the number of electors, you render the representative too little acquainted with all their local circumstances and lesser interests; as by reducing it too much, you render him unduly attached to these, and too little fit to comprehend and pursue great and national objects. The Federal Constitution forms a happy combination in this respect; the great and aggregate interests being referred to the national, the local and particular, to the state legislatures.

The other point of difference is, the greater number of citizens and extent of territory which may be brought within the compass of Republican, than of Democratic Government; and it is this circumstance principally which renders factious combinations less to be dreaded in the former, than in the latter. The smaller the society, the fewer probably will be the distinct parties and interests composing it; the fewer the distinct parties and interests, the more frequently will a majority be found of the same party; and the smaller the number of individuals composing a majority, and the smaller the compass within which they are placed, the more easily will they concert and execute their plans of oppression. Extend the sphere, and you take in a greater variety of parties and interests; you make it less probable that a majority of the whole will have a common motive to invade the rights of other citizens; or if such a common motive exists, it will be more difficult for all who feel it to discover their own strength, and to act in unison with each other. Besides other impediments, it may be remarked, that where there is a consciousness of unjust or dishonorable purposes, communication is always checked by distrust, in proportion to the number whose concurrence is necessary.

Hence it clearly appears, that the same advantage, which a Republic has over a Democracy, in controling the effects of faction, is enjoyed by a large over a small Republic—is enjoyed by the Union over the States composing it. Does this advantage consist in the substitution of Representatives, whose enlightened views and virtuous sentiments render them superior to local prejudices, and to schemes of injustice? It will not be denied, that the Representation of the Union will be most likely to possess these requisite endowments. Does it consist in the greater security afforded by a greater variety of parties, against the event of any one party being able to outnumber and oppress the rest? In an equal degree does the encreased variety of parties, comprised within the Union, encrease this security. Does it, in fine, consist in the greater obstacles opposed to the concert and accomplishment of the secret wishes of an unjust and interested majority? Here, again, the extent of the Union gives it the most palpable advantage.

The influence of factious leaders may kindle a flame within their particular States, but will be unable to spread a general conflagration through the other States: a religious sect, may degenerate into a political faction in a part of the Confederacy: but the variety of sects dispersed over the entire face of it, must secure the national Councils against any danger from that source: a rage for paper money, for an abolition of debts, for an equal division of property, or for any other improper or wicked project, will be less apt to pervade the whole body of the Union, than a particular member of it; in the same proportion as such a malady is more likely to taint a particular county or district, than an entire State.

In the extent and proper structure of the Union, therefore, we behold a Republican remedy for the diseases most incident to Republican Government. And according to the degree of pleasure and pride, we feel in being Republicans, ought to be our zeal in cherishing the spirit, and supporting the character of Federalists.

PUBLIUS.[5]

1787/1787

Philip Freneau
1752–1832

When Philip Freneau died in 1832 on the side of a snow-swept road in the rural stretches of New Jersey, he was far removed from the center of the political and ideological controversies that dominated the earliest years of the new republic. Once heralded as the most forceful literary voice in the American Revolution, he was later considered too radical for many political tastes and was finally regarded as simply unfashionable. His disillusionment with the course of American politics and the drift of his own career ferried him back and forth between satire and solitude.

The son of a prosperous woman of Scottish ancestry and a French Huguenot émigré, Philip Freneau was born into comfortable circumstances in New York City on January 2, 1752. The eldest of five children, Freneau stayed behind to study the classics and the English poets when the family moved to Mount Pleasant, a thousand-acre tract in New Jersey modeled on an elaborate southern plantation and the site to which Freneau would intermittently retreat from economic misfortune and political combat. At the urging of his father, Freneau prepared for the ministry, and at the age of sixteen he enrolled as a second-year student at the College of New Jersey (later Princeton), where he was a classmate of James Madison and Hugh Henry Brackenridge and a friend of Aaron Burr. He collaborated with Brackenridge on an unfinished novel, *Father Bombo's Pilgrimage to Mecca in Arabia,* and on "A Poem on the Rising Glory of America," read as the commencement ode in 1771. Freneau's commitment to a vision

---

[5] Publius was the pseudonym of the writers of the *Federalist* and was known to be such by most eighteenth-century readers.

of America's future inspired him to record indigenous experiences, although ones that, at least for his generation, were best expressed in the forms of "heav'nly Pope" and "godlike Addison."

After college, Freneau worked briefly in education for less than a year as Brackenridge's assistant at the Somerset Academy in Maryland. Freneau proceeded to study theology for two years before gravitating to New York, where he wrote a series of popular attacks on the British presence in the colonies. Discouraged by the political controversy his poetry had occasioned, Freneau left New York in 1776 for a two-year stay in the West Indies. But the increasing tempo of Revolutionary activities drew him home. He was captured and released by the British en route and joined the New Jersey militia when he reached the United States.

Freneau devoted himself completely to the Revolutionary cause. He ran supplies through British naval blockades and contributed patriotic verse to Brackenridge's newly formed *United States Magazine*. In 1780 Freneau was again captured at sea, but this time he was imprisoned aboard British ships in New York harbor. Within a year of his release, Freneau published "The Prison Ship," a popular broadside recording his mistreatment at the hands of his captors. He then traveled to Philadelphia to help edit the strongly anti-British *Freeman's Journal*.

After a brief stint as a postal clerk at the end of the war and a new round of disheartening squabbles in Pennsylvania politics, Freneau withdrew to the seclusion of nearly seven years of work at sea. He served as the captain of coastal vessels and published a great deal of satirical, fanciful, and humorous verse in the newspapers of the ports he plied. The growing popularity of his poetry lured him ashore, and in 1790 he settled in New York, married Eleanor Forman, and, inspired by the politics of Jefferson and other prominent Republicans of the time, established the *National Gazette* in Philadelphia as a virulent response to the Federalist political and economic policies of Alexander Hamilton and John Adams.

A yellow fever epidemic, poor advertising revenue, and unbridled attacks on his Republican editorials drove Freneau from Philadelphia in 1793. He retired to Mount Pleasant for nearly a year but returned to public life as publisher of another newspaper, the *Jersey Chronicle*. When that venture failed, he launched yet another, the *Time-Piece and Literary Companion*, which focused, he announced, on "literary amusements and an abridgement of the most interesting intelligence foreign and domestic." Despite an unusually large number of female contributors who "gave freely of their sentimental lyrics and sprightly letters," the journal overplayed Freneau's public-spirited but sneering editorials on the federal government and fell victim to the sedition law. Retreating once again to Mount Pleasant, Freneau penned a series of humorous essays for the Philadelphia *Aurora* in the guise of Robert Slender, a rustic sage far removed from political controversy. By 1800 Freneau had settled into discreet obscurity and returned to a life at sea. He surfaced again at the outbreak of the War of 1812, but with much of his vituperative energy drained.

Freneau published five volumes of poetry in his lifetime. In each, the intensity of his poems on the splendor of the American landscape often competed with self-conscious political satires on British subjects. Yet Freneau always maintained his commitment to explore native themes in colloquial terms. "The Wild Honey Suckle" (1786) and "The Indian Burying Ground" (1788), printed more than a decade before Wordsworth and Coleridge's *Lyrical Ballads,* are perhaps the best testaments to that interest.

The unpretentious characters that populate Freneau's essays and journalism ("The Pilgrim," "Tomo-Cheeki, the Creek Indian," and "Hezakiah Salem," the defrocked Yankee deacon) express his sensitivity to the philosophical, social, and economic issues that preoccupied American society in the first decades of the new nation. Freneau anticipated William Cullen Bryant's preoccupation with lush poetic landscapes, Ralph Waldo Emerson's insistent individualism, and Walt Whitman's embrace of the commonplace in America. Freneau's writing helped expand the field and introduced complexities into American themes.

Further Reading:

L. Leary, *That Rascal Freneau: A Study in Literary Failure,* 1941, 1964.

N. F. Adkins, *Philip Freneau and the Cosmic Enigma: The Religious and Philosophical Speculations of an American Poet,* 1949.

J. Axelrad, *Philip Freneau: Champion of Democracy,* 1967.

P. Marsh, *The Works of Philip Freneau: A Critical Study,* 1968.

M. Bowden, *Philip Freneau,* 1976.

R. Vitzthum, *Land and Sea: The Lyric Poetry of Philip Freneau,* 1978.

J. R. Hiltner, *The Newspaper Verse of Philip Freneau,* 1986.

Texts:

"On Mr. Paine's Rights of Man" from *Poems of Freneau,* ed. H. H. Clark, 1929.

All others from *The Poems of Philip Freneau,* ed. F. L. Pattee, 3 vols., 1902–1907.

On the Emigration to America and Peopling the Western Country

To western woods, and lonely plains,
Palemon[1] from the crowd departs,
Where Nature's wildest genius reigns,
To tame the soil, and plant the arts—
What wonders there shall freedom show,   5
What mighty states successive grow!

From Europe's proud, despotic shores
Hither the stranger takes his way,
And in our new found world explores
A happier soil, a milder sway,   10
Where no proud despot holds him down,
No slaves insult him with a crown.

What charming scenes attract the eye,
On wild Ohio's savage stream!

---

[1] Character in Chaucer's "Knight's Tale" (in *The Canterbury Tales*) who has come to represent any person setting out on a journey.

There Nature reigns, whose works outvie   15
The boldest pattern art can frame;
There ages past have rolled away,
And forests bloomed but to decay.

From these fair plains, these rural seats,
So long concealed, so lately known,   20
The unsocial Indian far retreats,
To make some other clime his own,
When other streams, less pleasing, flow,
And darker forests round him grow.

Great Sire[2] of floods! Whose varied wave   25
Through climes and countries takes its way,
To whom creating Nature gave
Ten thousand streams to swell thy sway!
No longer shall they useless prove,
Nor idly through the forests rove;   30

Nor longer shall your princely flood
From distant lakes be swelled in vain,
Nor longer through a darksome wood
Advance, unnoticed, to the main,
Far other ends, the heavens decree—   35
And commerce plans new freights for thee.

While virtue warms the generous breast,
There heaven-born freedom shall reside,
Nor shall the voice of war molest,
Nor Europe's all-aspiring pride—   40
There Reason shall new laws devise,
And order from confusion rise.

Forsaking kings and regal state,
With all their pomp and fancied bliss,
The traveller owns, convinced though late,   45
No realm so free, so blest as this—
The east is half to slaves consigned,
Where kings and priests enchain the mind.

O come the time, and haste the day,
When man shall man no longer crush,   50
When Reason shall enforce her sway,
Nor these fair regions raise our blush,

---

[2] Freneau's note: "Mississippi."

Where still the African complains,
And mourns his yet unbroken chains.

Far brighter scenes a future age,   55
The muse predicts, these States will hail,
Whose genius may the world engage,
Whose deeds may over death prevail,
And happier systems bring to view,
Than all the eastern sages knew.   60
1784/1785

The Wild Honey Suckle

Fair flower, that dost so comely grow,
Hid in this silent, dull retreat,
Untouched thy honied blossoms blow,
Unseen thy little branches greet:
    No roving foot shall crush thee here,   5
    No busy hand provoke a tear.

By Nature's self in white arrayed,
She bade thee shun the vulgar eye,
And planted here the guardian shade,
And sent soft waters murmuring by;   10
    Thus quietly thy summer goes,
    Thy days declining to repose.

Smit with those charms, that must decay,
I grieve to see your future doom;
They died—nor were those flowers more gay,   15
The flowers that did in Eden bloom;
    Unpitying frosts, and Autumn's power
    Shall leave no vestige of this flower.

From morning suns and evening dews
At first thy little being came: 20
If nothing once, you nothing lose,
For when you die you are the same;
    The space between, is but an hour,
    The frail duration of a flower.
1786

The Indian Burying Ground

In spite of all the learned have said,
    I still my old opinion keep;
The posture, that we give the dead,
    Points out the soul's eternal sleep.

Not so the ancients of these lands—   5
    The Indian, when from life released,
Again is seated with his friends,
    And shares again the joyous feast.[1]

His imaged birds, and painted bowl,
    And venison, for a journey dressed,   10
Bespeak the nature of the soul,
    Activity, that knows no rest.

His bow, for action ready bent,
    And arrows, with a head of stone,
Can only mean that life is spent,   15
    And not the old ideas gone.

Thou, stranger, that shalt come this way,
    No fraud upon the dead commit—
Observe the swelling turf, and say
    They do not lie, but here they sit.   20

Here still a lofty rock remains,
    On which the curious eye may trace
(Now wasted, half, by wearing rains)
    The fancies of a ruder race.

Here still an aged elm aspires,   25
    Beneath whose far-projecting shade
(And which the shepherd still admires)
    The children of the forest played!

There oft a restless Indian queen
    (Pale Shebah,[2] with her braided hair)   30

---

[1] Freneau's note: "The North American Indians bury their dead in a sitting posture; decorating the corpse with wampum, the images of birds, quadrupeds, &c: And (if that of a warrior) with bows, arrows, tomhawks [sic], and other military weapons."

[2] The Queen of Sheba, legendary for her beauty and wisdom. (See I Kings 10 and 2 Chronicles 9.)

And many a barbarous form is seen
    To chide the man that lingers there.

By midnight moons, o'er moistening dews;
    In habit for the chase arrayed,
The hunter still the deer pursues,   35
    The hunter and the deer, a shade!

And long shall timorous fancy see
    The painted chief, and pointed spear,
And Reason's self shall bow the knee
    To shadows and delusions here.   40
1787

On Mr. Paine's Rights of Man*

Thus briefly sketched the sacred RIGHTS OF MAN,
How inconsistent with the ROYAL PLAN!
Which for itself exclusive honour craves,
Where some are masters born, and millions slaves.
With what contempt must every eye look down   5
On that base, childish bauble called a *crown*,
The gilded bait, that lures the crowd, to come,
Bow down their necks, and meet a slavish doom;
The source of half the miseries men endure,
The quack that kills them, while it seems to cure.   10
    Roused by the REASON of his manly page,
Once more shall PAINE a listening world engage:
From Reason's source, a bold reform he brings,
In raising up *mankind*, he pulls down *kings*,
Who, source of discord, patrons of all wrong,   15
On blood and murder have been fed too long:
Hid from the world, and tutored to be base,
The curse, the scourge, the ruin of our race,
Theirs' was the task, a dull designing few,
To shackle beings that they scarcely knew,   20
Who made this globe the residence of slaves,
And built their thrones on systems formed by
    knaves

* Thomas Paine (1737–1809) had supported
the French Revolution in *The Rights of Man*
(1791).

—Advance, bright years, to work their final fall,
And haste the period that shall crush them all.
    Who, that has read and scann'd the historic page   25
But glows, at every line, with kindling rage,
To see by them the rights of men aspersed,
Freedom restrain'd, and Nature's law reversed,
Men, ranked with beasts, by monarchs *will'd* away,
And bound young fools, or madmen to obey: 30
Now driven to wars, and now oppressed at home,
Compelled in crowds o'er distant seas to roam,
From India's climes the plundered prize to bring
To glad the strumpet, or to glut the king.
    COLUMBIA,[1] hail! Immortal be thy reign: 35
Without a king, we till the smiling plain;
Without a king, we trace the unbounded sea,
And traffic round the globe, through each degree;
Each foreign clime our honour'd flag reveres,
Which asks no monarch, to support the STARS: 40
Without a *king*, the laws maintain their sway,
While honour bids each generous heart obey.
Be ours the task the ambitious to restrain,
And this great lesson teach—that kings are vain;
That warring realms to certain ruin haste,   45
That kings subsist by war, and wars are waste:
So shall our nation, form'd on Virtue's plan,
Remain the guardian of the Rights of Man,
A vast Republic, famed through every clime,
Without a king, to see the end of time.   50
1791

Native Americans and "Westward the Course of Empire"

Some Views of an Other

It may be regarded as certain, that not a foot of land will ever be taken from the Indians, without their own consent. The sacredness of their rights is felt by all thinking persons in America as much as in Europe.

Thomas Jefferson (1786)

---

[1] America.

The utmost good faith shall always be observed toward the Indians; their lands and property shall never be taken from them without their consent; and in their property, rights, and liberty they never shall be invaded or disturbed unless in just and lawful wars authorized by Congress; but laws founded in justice and humanity shall, from time to time, be made for preventing wrongs being done to them and for preserving peace and friendship with them.

> Northwest Ordinance (July 13, 1787)

The tribes which occupied the countries now constituting the Eastern states were annihilated or have melted away to make room for the whites. The waves of population and civilization are rolling to the westward, and we now propose to acquire the countries occupied by the red men of the South and West by a fair exchange, and, at the expense of the United States, to send them to a land where their existence may be prolonged and perhaps made perpetual.

> President Andrew Jackson, Message to Congress
> (December 6, 1830)

In the whole history of the incipient settlement of our country, not one solitary instance of an attempt to settle an unoccupied tract, claimed by the natives, is to be found, which was not succeeded by all the revolting details of Indian warfare. It is of little importance to inquire, which party was the aggressor. The natives were not sufficient civilians to distinguish between the right of empire and the right of soil. . . . Our industry, fixed residences, modes, laws, institutions, schools, religion, rendered an union with them as incompatible as with animals of another nature. . . . In the unchangeable order of things, two such races can not exist together, each preserving its co-ordinate identity. Either this great continent, in the order of Providence, should have remained in the occupancy of half a million of savages, engaged in everlasting conflicts of their peculiar warfare with each other, or it must have become, as it has, the domain of civilized millions.

> Timothy Flint, Indian Wars of the West (1833)

A crime is projected that confounds our understandings by its magnitude—a crime that really deprives us as well as the Cherokees of a country, for how could we call the conspiracy that should crush these poor Indians our government, or the land that was cursed by their parting and dying imprecations our country, any more? You, sir, will bring down that renowned chair in which you sit into infamy if your seal is set to this instrument of perfidy; and the name of this nation, hitherto the sweet omen of religion and liberty, will stink to the world.

> Ralph Waldo Emerson, letter to President Martin Van Buren
> on the removal of the Cherokee Indians (April 23, 1838)

It is too often the case, that civilized beings sojourning among savages soon come to regard them with disdain and contempt. But though in many cases this feeling is almost natural, it is not defensible; and it is wholly wrong. Why should we contemn them? Because we are better than they? Assuredly not; . . . Who can swear, that among the naked British barbarians sent to Rome to be stared at more than 1500 years ago, the ancestor of Bacon might not have been found? . . . We are all of us—Anglo-Saxons,

Dyaks, and Indians—sprung from one head, and made in one image. And if we regret this brotherhood now, we shall be forced to join hands hereafter. A misfortune is not a fault; and good luck is not meritorious. The savage is born a savage; and the civilized being but inherits his civilization, nothing more.

Herman Melville, review of Francis Parkman's *The California and Oregon Trail* (1849)

William Apess
1798–?

William Apess was abandoned by his Native American mother and half-white father soon after the family moved from his birthplace near Colrain, Massachusetts, to the two small Pequot reservations near Colchester, Connecticut. By the age of five, William had been beaten so often and so severely by his alcoholic grandfather that his recovery depended on the town's charity for a year. From the age of six he was "bound out" to successive sets of foster parents, the first Baptists, the second Presbyterians. They provided him with six years of formal schooling but left him no freer from verbal and physical abuse than before.

At the age of fifteen Apess fled from his latest guardians and wandered between New York and New England before joining the U.S. Army, on a drunken whim, as a drummer boy. Reclassified as an infantry soldier during the War of 1812, Apess deserted. Quickly recaptured, he served for more than two years.

At the end of the War of 1812 Apess began several years' work at odd jobs in northern New York State and Canada before returning to the Pequot reservation near Groton, Connecticut, where he spent the next few years hiring himself out to local farmers. By the early 1820s Apess was regularly preaching the Gospel to Native American and white audiences. His success apparently angered the local preachers, and he soon found himself what he called an "outcast from society." He married, and over the next few years supported his wife and several children by farming and working as a tavern keeper. Gradually he returned to preaching and between 1826 and 1829 traveled throughout New England ministering to Native American, African American, and white church groups.

Apess published a brief autobiography, *A Son of the Forest,* in 1829, the first Native American autobiography published in book form. A second, enlarged edition, in 1831, gave increasing room to Apess's belief that Christ had died for *all* people. "If black or red skins, or any other skin of color is disgraceful to God, it appears that [God] has disgraced himself a great deal—for he has made fifteen colored people to one white, and placed them upon the earth." His autobiography also includes an impassioned brief for the use of the term *Native Americans*. According to Kim McQuaid, the author of one useful biographical account of Apes, *A Son of the Forest* set the standard for many Native American autobiographies later in the nineteenth century. Several generations were to find inspiration in the story of Apess's life. In his struggles they recognized the possibility of Native American dignity and accomplishment in a period when all signs pointed to the removal of their peoples from the new nation's culture, its conscience, and its future.

By the mid-1830s, Apess had become a celebrated preacher, an advocate of Indian rights, and a social reformer, especially among the Mashpee tribe of southeastern Massachusetts, among whom he and his family had settled. In 1836 he published a comprehensive study of the rights of Native Americans and their relations with white Americans, titled *Eulogy on King Philip* in honor of the legendary seventeenth-century Native American hero who had driven white settlers from tribal lands in New England. Within a few years of the book's controversial publication, Apess had withdrawn from public view, ironically an example himself of the "vanishing race" that he so vigorously defended and that he helped to maintain as a vibrant part of American culture.

Further Reading:

E. S. Bates, "William Apess," *Dictionary of American Biography*, vol. 1, 1928.

F. P. Prucha, *American Indian Policy in the Formative Years, 1790–1834*, 1962.

K. McQuaid, "William Apess, Pequot: An Indian Reformer in the Jackson Era," *New England Quarterly*, 1977.

B. O'Connell, ed., *On Our Ground: The Complete Writings of William Apess, A Pequot*, 1992.

Text:

A Son of the Forest, 1829.

A Son of the Forest

from **Chapter 1**

William Apes, the author of the following narrative, was born in the town of Colereign, Massachusetts, on the thirty-first of January, in the year of our Lord seventeen hundred and ninety-eight. My grandfather was a white man, and married a female attached to the royal family of Philip,[1] king of the Pequod tribe of Indians, so well known in that part of American history, which relates to the wars between the whites and the natives. My grandmother was, if I am not misinformed, the king's granddaughter, and a fair and beautiful woman. This statement is given not with a view of appearing great, in the estimation of others—what I would ask, is *royal* blood—the blood of a king is no better than that of the subject—we are in fact but one family; we are all the descendants of one great progenitor—Adam. I would not boast of my extraction, as I consider myself nothing more than a worm of the earth.

---

[1] King Philip, the son of Massasoit and chief of the Wampanoag Indians. The reference here is to King Philip's War (1675–1676), the most deadly of Indian conflicts in New England. The Pequot Indians are an Algonquin tribe of southeastern Connecticut.

I have given the above account of my origin, with the simple view of narrating the truth as I have received it; and under the settled conviction that I must render an account at the last day, to the sovereign Judge of all men, for every word contained in this little book. . . .

from *Chapter 2*

. . . I thought it disgraceful to be called an Indian;[2] it was considered as a slur upon an oppressed and scattered nation, and I have often been led to inquire where the whites received this word, which they so often threw as an opprobrious epithet at the sons of the forest. I could not find it in the bible, and therefore concluded, that it was a word imported for the special purpose of degrading us. At other times I thought it was derived from the term in-gen-uity. But the proper term which ought to be applied to our nation, to distinguish it from the rest of the human family, is that of *"Natives"*—and I humbly conceive that the natives of this country are the only people under heaven who have a just title to the name, inasmuch as we are the only people who retain the original complexion of our father Adam. Notwithstanding my thoughts on this matter, so completely was I weaned from the interests and affections of my brethren, that a mere threat of being sent away among the Indians into the dreary woods, had a much better effect in making me obedient to the commands of my superiors, than any corporeal punishment that they ever inflicted. I had received a lesson in the unnatural treatment of my own relations, which could not be effaced; and I thought that if those who should have loved and protected me, treated me with such unkindness, surely I had no reason to expect mercy or favour at the hands of those who knew me in no other relation than that of a cast-off member of the tribe. A threat, of the kind alluded to, invariably produced obedience on my part, so far as I understood the nature of the command.

I cannot perhaps give a better idea of the dread which prevaded my mind on seeing any of my brethren of the forest, than by relating the following occurrence. One day several of the family went into the woods to gather berries, taking me with them. We had not been out long before we fell in with a company of white females, on the same errand—their complexion was, to say, the least, as *dark* as that of the natives. This circumstance filled my mind with terror, and I broke from the party with my utmost speed, and I could not muster courage enough to look behind until I had reached home. By this time my imagination had pictured out a tale of blood, and as soon as I regained breath sufficient to answer the questions which my master asked, I informed him that we had met a body of the natives in the woods, but what had become of the party I could not tell. Notwithstanding the manifest incredibility of my tale of terror, Mr. Furman was agitated; my very appearance was sufficient to convince him that I had been terrified by something, and summoning the remainder of the family, he sallied out in quest of the absent party, whom he found searching for me among the bushes. The whole mystery was soon unravelled. It may be proper for me here to remark, that the great fear I entertained of my brethren, was occasioned by the many stories I had heard of their cruelty towards the whites—how they were in the habit of killing and scalping men, women and children. But the whites did not tell me that they were in a great ma-

---

[2] Apes, whose father was of mixed blood, was brought up among Europeans—first by his white grandfather, a drinker who physically abused his grandchildren, then by the Furmans, a poor laboring couple.

jority of instances the aggressors—that they had imbrued their hands in the life blood of my brethren, driven them from their once peaceful and happy homes—that they introduced among them the fatal and exterminating diseases of civilized life. If the whites had told me how cruel they had been to the "poor Indian," I should have apprehended as much harm from them.

Shortly after this occurrence I relapsed into my former bad habits—was fond of the company of the boys, and in a short time lost in a great measure that spirit of obedience which had made me the favourite of my mistress. I was easily led astray, and, once in particular, I was induced by a boy, (my senior by five or six years) to assist him in his depredations on a water melon patch belonging to one of the neighbours. But we were found out, and my companion in wickedness led me deeper in sin, by persuading me to deny the crime laid to our charge. I obeyed him to the very letter, and when accused, flatly denied knowing any thing of the matter. The boasted courage of the boy, however, began to fail as soon as he saw danger thicken, and he confessed it as strongly as he had denied it. The man from whom we had pillaged the melons threatened to send us to Newgate, but he relented. The story shortly afterward reached the ears of the good Mrs. Furman, who talked seriously to me about it. She told me that I could be sent to prison for it—that I had done wrong, and gave me a great deal of wholesome advice. This had a much better effect than forty floggings—it sunk so deep into my mind that the impression can never be effaced.

I now went on without difficulty for a few months, when I was assailed by fresh and unexpected troubles. One of the girls belonging to the house had taken some offence at me, and declared she would be revenged. The better to effect this end, she told Mr. Furman that I had not only threatened to kill her, but had actually pursued her with a knife, whereupon he came to the place where I was working and began to whip me severely. I could not tell for what. I told him I had done no harm, to which he replied, "I will learn you, you Indian dog, how to chase people with a knife." I told him I had not, but he would not believe me, and continued to whip me for a long while. But the poor man soon found out his error, as *after* he had flogged me, he undertook to investigate the matter, when to his amazement he discovered it was nothing but fiction, as all the children assured him that I did no such thing. He regretted being so hasty—but I saw wherein the great difficulty consisted, if I had not denied the melon affair, he would have believed me, but as I had uttered an untruth about that, it was natural for him to think that the person who will tell one lie, will not scruple at two. For a long while after this circumstance transpired, I did not associate with my companions.

1829

Washington Irving
1783–1859

Washington Irving's life spans virtually all of American history and culture from the Revolution to the Civil War. Celebrated both at home and abroad as the dean of American letters, Irving lived to see his writings translated into twelve languages and printed in more than fifty different editions. His essays and sketches earned the respect of Europe's leading intellectuals and the praise of such prominent English writers as Coleridge, Byron, Scott, and Dickens. The influential London *Athenaeum* credited Irving with having declared America's literary independence. He was universally regarded, in the words of the Victorian novelist William Makepeace Thackeray, as "the first Ambassador whom the New World of Letters sent to the Old."

Washington Irving was born in New York's lower Manhattan in April 1783, a few days before Congress ratified the preliminary treaty ending the Revolutionary War; he was named after the war's most prominent hero. The youngest of eleven children, Irving grew up in a home bristling with Federalist sentiments and Calvinist principles; his father, a Scottish hardware merchant, is said to have "led the children to believe all pleasures were wicked." His relatively brief formal schooling took place in the city's private academies, but his more enduring education occurred along the city's streets and piers listening to merchants and seamen weave homespun tales of adventure and romance.

Washington Irving took a very early interest in writing and, much like Benjamin Franklin before him, modeled his first work on the familiar essays of Addison and Steele's *Spectator*. His first published writing, printed over the signature "Jonathan, Oldstyle, Gent.," earned Irving modest critical attention. The pseudonym Irving used in these essays—a combination of the British nickname for American patriots and the name of the calendar abandoned by England and the colonies in 1752—reflects the lifelong tension he felt between the lure of literary nationalism and a reliance on European cultural forms.

Irving had studied law, but in 1803 he eagerly interrupted his work as a law clerk to travel through the frontier of upper New York State and eastern Canada. The threat of tuberculosis prompted Irving's family to send him to Europe in 1804. In Rome he met the American painter Washington Allston and flirted with the idea of taking up art. He returned to the United States not only in better health but also with greater sensitivity to American provincialism. He was admitted to the New York bar in 1806, but, practiced in a desultory fashion, preferring to spend his time cultivating his interests in current political and cultural affairs and nurturing his friendships with several like-minded young well-to-do and well-read bachelors intent on displaying their wit and sophistication in New York's taverns and literary circles.

The spirit of this group is best represented in Irving's first major literary venture, *Salmagundi; or, the Whim-Whams and Opinions of Launcelot Langstaff, Esq., and Others* (1807–1808). Published in collaboration with his brother William and James Kirke Paulding, this series of twenty pocket-sized pamphlets developed into a delightful intellectual potpourri of social criticism, literary reviews, and lampoons of the latest trends in politics and the theater.

Salmagundi quickly became the gravitational center of a literary circle that eventually became known as the Knickerbocker school; William Cullen Bryant and James Fenimore Cooper were also identified with this "school." In virtually every case, however, the association of these writers was more geographic than aesthetic. But as soon as Washington Irving had published Diedrich Knickerbocker's *History of New York* (1809), the label would prove hard to escape.

A History of New York, from the Beginning of the World to the End of the Dutch Dynasty, by Diedrich Knickerbocker brought Irving extraordinary financial success, earning several thousand dollars in royalties at a time when nearly all authors had to underwrite the costs of publishing their work. Irving also enjoyed international acclaim; Sir Walter Scott praised the work in what undoubtedly were then extravagant terms: "I have never read anything so closely resembling the style of Dean Swift, as the annals of Diedrich Knickerbocker."

Irving remained a Federalist in politics and culture throughout his life. His critics accused him of being a dandy and an Anglophile whose American identity as a writer was more a matter of birth than sensibility. Yet Irving's early work had dealt directly— and most often satirically—with the issue most central to an American writer's identity, the absence of a native cultural tradition.

What might be called the second phase of Irving's career began in 1815 with his second trip to Europe. He remained there for the next seventeen years. Ostensibly, Irving had traveled to Europe to help manage the Liverpool office of his family's importing business, but within three years, the business had collapsed into bankruptcy and Irving had decided to gamble on making a living as a writer.

Irving's years in Europe regenerated his creative energies and he resolved to adapt Europe's rich cultural heritage to American settings. The principal expression of this interest was *The Sketch Book* (1819–1820), a compendium of gracefully written familiar essays nostalgically surveying the traditions of English life ("The Christmas Dinner," "A Sunday in London," "Westminster Abbey"), along with six chapters on American scenes, including an essay on "Traits of Indian Character" and two Americanized renditions of European folktales, "Rip Van Winkle" and "The Legend of Sleepy Hollow." Published in several installments, *The Sketch Book* captured unprecedented international attention for an American work; although he was viewed slightly condescendingly by the English (as an American who writes as though he were English), he was lionized as a figure of national pride in the United States.

"Rip Van Winkle" and "The Legend of Sleepy Hollow" also highlight concerns fundamental to appreciating American literary history: the role of the imagination in a society devoted to material progress, the marginal identity of the artist in American life, the sense of loss implicit in America's commitment to the present and future while neglecting the past, and the urgent need to establish a specifically American historical context. At the same time, *The Sketch Book* expresses the American writer's need to create what the critic Richard Poirier has called "a world elsewhere," a place (in this case Sleepy Hollow) where and a time (colonial America) when the imagination might flourish. Later American writers would locate this "world" in colonial Salem (Nathaniel Hawthorne), Walden Pond (Henry David Thoreau), the boundless ocean (Herman Melville), the splendid Mississippi (Mark Twain), and Yoknapatawpha County (William Faulkner), to name but a few.

Washington Irving spent the early 1820s searching the Continent for additional literary material, all the while enjoying the literary status afforded him in London, Paris, Dresden, and Vienna. When challenged to explain whether his protracted absence from the United States indicated that he had renounced his native land, Irving replied, "I am endeavouring to serve my country. Whatever I have written has been written with the feelings and published as the writing of an American. Is that renouncing my country? How else am I to serve my country—by coming home and begging an office of it: which I should not have the kind of talent or the business habits requisite to fill?—If I can do any good in this world it is with my pen."

The final phase of Irving's career began with his triumphant return to the United States. He brought with him an honorary degree from Oxford, the medal of the Royal Society of Literature, and an international reputation unprecedented for an American writer. Soon after his arrival, he set out for a tour of the American South and West. The diary of his adventurous experiences on the Oklahoma frontier formed the basis for his autobiographical narrative *A Tour of the Prairies,* printed as the first volume of *The Crayon Miscellany* (1835). The book marks another significant shift in Irving's work, from the detached cynicism of Jonathan Oldstyle and the reserve of Geoffrey Crayon to direct authorial participation in *A Tour.* The later portions of *A Tour* may be seen as Irving's own dramatic initiation into what are often the violent rituals of establishing a distinctively American identity.

Irving settled in New York for the decade following his western tour. He published two additional books based on this trip: *Astoria* (1836), an account of John Jacob Astor's fur-trading empire, and *The Adventures of Captain Bonneville, U.S.A.* (1837). He declined invitations to run for election as mayor of New York City and later to serve as secretary of the navy under President Van Buren. But Irving did return to Europe in 1842 as minister to Spain, the first in a line of literary figures—including James Russell Lowell, Nathaniel Hawthorne, Bret Harte, and William Dean Howells—to serve their country as foreign ministers. After three years in Spain, Irving spent a year in London negotiating a diplomatic resolution to the Oregon question. He returned to the United States in 1846 and spent his last years at Sunnyside, his country retreat near Tarrytown, New York, to enjoy his literary preeminence and to continue writing.

Preoccupied with biography during his final years, Irving published a study of the English writer Oliver Goldsmith in 1840 and the two-volume *Mahomet and His Successors* in 1849 and 1850. In 1859, the year he died, Irving completed a massive five-volume biography of George Washington. He regarded the project as something of a prose epic and as an opportunity for America to re-create a distinguished past for itself worthy of its imagined future greatness.

Washington Irving's career as a writer paralleled the new nation's as a culture. His literary career reflects both the cultural anxiety of the new republic and its growing self-assurance in the years immediately preceding the Civil War. In this respect, Irving's work illustrates with striking clarity the early struggle of American culture to establish its autonomy. Many prominent American writers in the nineteenth century, from James Fenimore Cooper to Henry James, claimed that America lacked subject matter suitable for literature. Yet, as Irving's work suggests, the problem was not as much the paucity of American experience as it was that such experience was resistant to the European forms imposed on it. As Irving eventually discovered, the literary models available to American writers in the early decades of the nineteenth century were inappropriate—or inadequate—to the experiences they were expected to transform. This problem often left the literature of the new republic either fragmented or derivative. Irving's struggles with this problem illustrate rather than resolve America's efforts to establish cultural independence. Years before James Fenimore Cooper, Nathaniel Hawthorne, and Henry James investigated the nature of the American identity, Washington Irving recognized the artistic problems implicit in forging a distinctively new American perspective from inherited English traditions. Despite the derivative nature of a good deal of Irving's writing, he helped develop the American short story and secured the legitimacy of American authorship. Irving's work remains not only a hallmark of the new nation's literary tastes but also a projection of new patterns of vision responsive to a new cultural context. His anxieties as a writer offer an enlightening introduction to the cultural preoccupations of the new republic, and his accomplishments remain a harbinger of the literary achievements of the American Renaissance.

Further Reading:

V. W. Brooks, *The World of Washington Irving*, 1944.
S. T. Williams, *Biography of Washington Irving*, 1935, 1979.
E. Wagenknecht, *Washington Irving: Moderation Displayed*, 1962.
L. Leary, *Irving*, 1963.
W. L. Hedges, *Washington Irving: An American Study, 1802–1832*, 1965.
D. Ringe, *The Pictorial Mode: Space and Time in the Art of Bryant, Irving, and Cooper*, 1971.
A. B. Myer, *Washington Irving: A Tribute*, 1972.
M. Roth, *Comedy and America: The Lost World of Washington Irving*, 1976.

A. B. Myer, *A Century of Commentary on the Works of Washington Irving*, 1976.
H. Springer, *Washington Irving: A Reference Guide*, 1976.
S. Browdin, ed., *The Old and New World Romanticism of Washington Irving*, 1986.
J. Rubin-Dorsky, *Adrift in the Old World: The Psychological Pilgrimage of Washington Irving*, 1988.
R. M. Aderman, ed., *Critical Essays on Washington Irving*, 1990.
P. Anteleyes, *Tales of Adventurous Enterprise: Washington Irving and the Poetics of Western Expansion*, 1990.

Text:
The Works of Washington Irving, 1860.
The 28-volume definitive edition of Washington Irving's writing, edited by H. Pochman, H. Klein-feld, and R. Rust, has been published (1969–1990) by the University of Wisconsin Press under the title *The Complete Works of Washington Irving*.

---

from The Sketch Book*

The Author's Account of Himself

> *"I am of this mind with Homer, that as the snaile that crept out of her shel was turned eftsoons into a toad, and thereby was forced to make a stoole to sit on; so the traveller that stragleth from his owne country is in a short time transformed into so monstrous a shape, that he is faine to alter his mansion with his manners, and to live where he can, not where he would."*
>
> Lyly's *Euphues*[1]

I was always fond of visiting new scenes, and observing strange characters and manners. Even when a mere child I began my travels, and made many tours of discovery into foreign parts and unknown regions of my native city, to the frequent alarm of my parents,

---

* This essay and two others were originally published in 1819–1820 as *The Sketch Book of Geoffrey Crayon, Gent.*, which incorporates an adopted pseudonym for Irving. *The Sketch Book* was later revised and expanded to include thirty-two tales and sketches.
[1] From *Euphues and his England* (1580), a prose romance by John Lyly (1554?–1606).

and the emolument of the town-crier. As I grew into boyhood, I extended the range of my observations. My holiday afternoons were spent in rambles about the surrounding country. I made myself familiar with all its places famous in history or fable. I knew every spot where a murder or robbery had been committed, or a ghost seen. I visited the neighboring villages, and added greatly to my stock of knowledge, by noting their habits and customs, and conversing with their sages and great men. I even journeyed one long summer's day to the summit of the most distant hill, whence I stretched my eye over many a mile of terra incognita,[2] and was astonished to find how vast a globe I inhabited.

This rambling propensity strengthened with my years. Books of voyages and travels became my passion, and in devouring their contents, I neglected the regular exercises of the school. How wistfully would I wander about the pierheads in fine weather, and watch the parting ships, bound to distant climes—with what longing eyes would I gaze after their lessening sails, and waft myself in imagination to the ends of the earth!

Further reading and thinking, though they brought this vague inclination into more reasonable bounds, only served to make it more decided. I visited various parts of my own country; and had I been merely a lover of fine scenery, I should have felt little desire to seek elsewhere its gratification, for on no country have the charms of nature been more prodigally lavished. Her mighty lakes, like oceans of liquid silver; her mountains, with their bright aerial tints; her valleys, teeming with wild fertility; her tremendous cataracts, thundering in their solitudes; her boundless plains, waving with spontaneous verdure; her broad deep rivers, rolling in solemn silence to the ocean; her trackless forests, where vegetation puts forth all its magnificence; her skies, kindling with the magic of summer clouds and glorious sunshine;—no, never need an American look beyond his own country for the sublime and beautiful of natural scenery.

But Europe held forth the charms of storied and poetical association. There were to be seen the masterpiece of art, the refinements of highly-cultivated society, the quaint peculiarities of ancient and local custom. My native country was full of youthful promise: Europe was rich in the accumulated treasures of age. Her very ruins told the history of times gone by, and every mouldering stone was a chronicle. I longed to wander over the scenes of renowned achievement—to tread, as it were, in the footsteps of antiquity—to loiter about the ruined castle—to meditate on the falling tower—to escape, in short, from the common-place realities of the present, and lose myself among the shadowy grandeurs of the past.

I had, beside all this, an earnest desire to see the great men of the earth. We have, it is true, our great men in America: not a city but has an ample share of them. I have mingled among them in my time, and been almost withered by the shade into which they cast me; for there is nothing so baleful to a small man as the shade of a great one, particularly the great man of a city. But I was anxious to see the great men of Europe; for I had read in the works of various philosophers, that all animals degenerated in America, and man among the number.[3] A great man of Europe, thought I, must therefore be as superior to a great man of America, as a peak of the Alps to a highland of the Hudson; and in this idea I was confirmed, by observing the comparative importance and swelling magnitude of many English travellers among us, who, I was assured, were very

2 Latin: "unknown land."
3 Georges Louis Leclerc de Buffon (1707–1788), a French naturalist, concluded that the American environment would cause the physical degeneration of European emigrants.

little people in their own country. I will visit this land of wonders, thought I, and see the gigantic race from which I am degenerated.

It has been either my good or evil lot to have my roving passion gratified. I have wandered through different countries, and witnessed many of the shifting scenes of life. I cannot say that I have studied them with the eye of a philosopher; but rather with the sauntering gaze with which humble lovers of the picturesque stroll from the window of one print-shop to another; caught sometimes by the delineations of beauty, sometimes by the distortions of caricature, and sometimes by the loveliness of landscape. As it is the fashion for modern tourists to travel pencil in hand, and bring home their portfolios filled with sketches, I am disposed to get up a few for the entertainment of my friends. When, however, I look over the hints and memorandums I have taken down for the purpose, my heart almost fails me at finding how my idle humor has led me aside from the great objects studied by every regular traveller who would make a book. I fear I shall give equal disappointment with an unlucky landscape painter, who had travelled on the continent, but, following the bent of his vagrant inclination, had sketched in nooks, and corners, and by-places. His sketch-book was accordingly crowded with cottages, and landscapes, and obscure ruins; but he had neglected to paint St. Peter's, or the Coliseum; the cascade of Terni,[4] or the bay of Naples; and had not a single glacier or volcano in his whole collection.

Rip Van Winkle[5]

A posthumous writing of Diedrich Knickerbocker

> *By Woden,[6] God of Sacons,*
> *From whence comes Wensday, that is Wodensday.*
> *Truth is a thing that ever I will keep*
> *Unto thylke day in which I creep into*
> *My sepulchre—*
>
> Cartwright[7]

[The following Tale was found among the papers of the late Diedrich Knickerbocker, an old gentleman of New York, who was very curious in the Dutch history of the province, and the manners of the descendants from its primitive settlers. His historical researches, however, did not lie so much among books as among men; for the former are lamentably scanty on his favorite topics; whereas he found the old burghers, and still more their wives, rich in that legendary lore, so invaluable to true history. Whenever, therefore, he happened upon a genuine Dutch family, snugly shut up in its low-roofed farmhouse, under a spreading sycamore, he looked upon it as a little clasped volume of black-letter,[8] and studied it with the zeal of a book-worm.

---

4 Famous waterfalls in central Italy.
5 "Rip Van Winkle" and "The Legend of Sleepy Hollow" are adaptations of German folk legends.
6 In Norse mythology, supreme god and creator.

7 From *The Ordinary* (1651) by English playwright William Cartwright (1611–1643).
8 Typeface used in early printed books, now called Gothic or Old English.

The result of all these researches was a history of the province during the reign of the Dutch governors, which he published some years since. There have been various opinions as to the literary character of his work, and, to tell the truth, it is not a whit better than it should be. Its chief merit is its scrupulous accuracy, which indeed was a little questioned on its first appearance, but has since been completely established; and it is now admitted into all historical collections, as a book of unquestionable authority.

The old gentleman died shortly after the publication of his work, and now that he is dead and gone, it cannot do much harm to his memory to say that his time might have been much better employed in weightier labors. He, however, was apt to ride his hobby his own way; and though it did now and then kick up the dust a little in the eyes of his neighbors, and grieve the spirit of some friends, for whom he felt the truest deference and affection; yet his errors and follies are remembered "more in sorrow than in anger,"[9] and it begins to be suspected, that he never intended to injure or offend. But however his memory may be appreciated by critics, it is still held dear by many folk, whose good opinion is well worth having; particularly by certain biscuit-bakers, who have gone so far as to imprint his likeness on their new-year cakes; and have thus given him a chance for immortality, almost equal to the being stamped on a Waterloo Medal,[10] or a Queen Anne's Farthing.][11]

Whoever has made a voyage up the Hudson must remember the Kaatskill[12] mountains. They are a dismembered branch of the great Appalachian family, and are seen away to the west of the river, swelling up to a noble height, and lording it over the surrounding country. Every change of season, every change of weather, indeed, every hour of the day, produces some change in the magical hues and shapes of these mountains, and they are regarded by all the good wives, far and near, as perfect barometers. When the weather is fair and settled, they are clothed in blue and purple, and print their bold outlines on the clear evening sky; but, sometimes, when the rest of the landscape is cloudless, they will gather a hood of gray vapors about their summits, which, in the last rays of the setting sun, will glow and light up like a crown of glory.

At the foot of these fairy mountains, the voyager may have descried the light smoke curling up from a village, whose shingle-roofs gleam among the trees, just where the blue tints of the upland melt away into the fresh green of the nearer landscape. It is a little village, of great antiquity, having been founded by some of the Dutch colonists, in the early times of the province, just about the beginning of the government of the good Peter Stuyvesant,[13] (may he rest in peace!) and there were some of the houses of the original settlers standing within a few years, built of small yellow bricks brought from Holland, having latticed windows and gable fronts, surmounted with weather-cocks.

In that same village, and in one of these very houses (which, to tell the precise truth, was sadly time-worn and weather-beaten), there lived many years since, while the country was yet a province of Great Britain, a simple good-natured fellow, of the name of Rip Van Winkle. He was a descendant of the Van Winkles who figured so gallantly in

---

[9] Shakespeare's *Hamlet,* Act I, Sc. ii, l. 232.
[10] The Waterloo Medal was minted after the British defeat of Napoleon in 1815.
[11] Farthing: English coin of small value.

[12] The Catskills in southeastern New York.
[13] Last governor of the Dutch province of New Netherlands (1647–1664).

the chivalrous days of Peter Stuyvesant, and accompanied him to the siege of Fort Christina.[14] He inherited, however, but little of the martial character of his ancestors. I have observed that he was a simple good-natured man; he was, moreover, a kind neighbor, and an obedient hen-pecked husband. Indeed, to the latter circumstance might be owing that meekness of spirit which gained him such universal popularity; for those men are most apt to be obsequious and conciliating abroad, who are under the discipline of shrews at home. Their tempers, doubtless, are rendered pliant and malleable in the fiery furnace of domestic tribulation; and a curtain lecture[15] is worth all the sermons in the world for teaching the virtues of patience and long-suffering. A termagant wife may, therefore, in some respects, be considered a tolerable blessing; and if so, Rip Van Winkle was thrice blessed.

Certain it is, that he was a great favorite among all the good wives of the village, who, as usual, with the amiable sex, took his part in all family squabbles; and never failed, whenever they talked those matters over in their evening gossipings, to lay all the blame on Dame Van Winkle. The children of the village, too, would shout with joy whenever he approached. He assisted at their sports, made their playthings, taught them to fly kites and shoot marbles, and told them long stories of ghosts, witches, and Indians. Whenever he went dodging about the village, he was surrounded by a troop of them, hanging on his skirts, clambering on his back, and playing a thousand tricks on him with impunity; and not a dog would bark at him throughout the neighborhood.

The great error in Rip's composition was an insuperable aversion to all kinds of profitable labor. It could not be from the want of assiduity or perseverance; for he would sit on a wet rock, with a rod as long and heavy as a Tartar's lance, and fish all day without a murmur, even though he should not be encouraged by a single nibble. He would carry a fowling-piece on his shoulder for hours together, trudging through woods and swamps, and up hill and down dale, to shoot a few squirrels or wild pigeons. He would never refuse to assist a neighbor even in the roughest toil, and was a foremost man at all country frolics for husking Indian corn, or building stone-fences; the women of the village, too, used to employ him to run their errands, and to do such little odd jobs as their less obliging husbands would not do for them. In a word Rip was ready to attend to anybody's business but his own; but as to doing family duty, and keeping his farm in order, he found it impossible.

In fact, he declared it was of no use to work on his farm; it was the most pestilent little piece of ground in the whole country; every thing about it went wrong, and would go wrong, in spite of him. His fences were continually falling to pieces; his cow would either go astray, or get among the cabbages; weeds were sure to grow quicker in his fields than anywhere else; the rain always made a point of setting in just as he had some out-door work to do; so that though his patrimonial estate had dwindled away under his management, acre by acre, until there was little more left than a mere patch of Indian corn and potatoes, yet it was the worst conditioned farm in the neighborhood.

His children, too, were as ragged and wild as if they belonged to nobody. His son Rip, an urchin begotten in his own likeness, promised to inherit the habits, with the old

[14] Peter Stuyvesant (1592–1672) led Dutch forces in defeating the Swedish colonists at Fort Christina on the Delaware in 1655.

[15] Tirade delivered by an angry wife from behind her bed curtains.

clothes of his father. He was generally seen trooping like a colt at his mother's heels, equipped in a pair of his father's cast-off galligaskins, which he had much ado to hold up with one hand, as a fine lady does her train in bad weather.

Rip Van Winkle, however, was one of those happy mortals, of foolish, well-oiled dispositions, who take the world easy, eat white bread or brown, whichever can be got with least thought or trouble, and would rather starve on a penny than work for a pound. If left to himself, he would have whistled life away in perfect contentment; but his wife kept continually dinning in his ears about his idleness, his carelessness, and the ruin he was bringing on his family. Morning, noon, and night, her tongue was incessantly going, and every thing he said or did was sure to produce a torrent of household eloquence. Rip had but one way of replying to all lectures of the kind, and that, by frequent use, had grown into a habit. He shrugged his shoulders, shook his head, cast up his eyes, but said nothing. This, however, always provoked a fresh volley from his wife; so that he was fain to draw off his forces, and take to the outside of the house—the only side which, in truth, belongs to a hen-pecked husband.

Rip's sole domestic adherent was his dog Wolf, who was as much hen-pecked as his master; for Dame Van Winkle regarded them as companions in idleness, and even looked upon Wolf with an evil eye, as the cause of his master's going so often astray. True it is, in all points of spirit befitting an honorable dog, he was as courageous an animal as ever scoured the woods—but what courage can withstand the everduring and all-besetting terrors of a woman's tongue? The moment Wolf entered the house his crest fell, his tail drooped to the ground, or curled between his legs, he sneaked about with a gallows air, casting many a sidelong glance at Dame Van Winkle, and at the least flourish of a broomstick or ladle, he would fly to the door with yelping precipitation.

Times grew worse and worse with Rip Van Winkle as years of matrimony rolled on; a tart temper never mellows with age, and a sharp tongue is the only edged tool that grows keener with constant use. For a long while he used to console himself, when driven from home, by frequenting a kind of perpetual club of the sages, philosophers, and other idle personages of the village; which held its sessions on a bench before a small inn, designated by a rubicund portrait of His Majesty George the Third. Here they used to sit in the shade through a long lazy summer's day, talking listlessly over village gossip, or telling endless sleepy stories about nothing. But it would have been worth any statesman's money to have heard the profound discussions that sometimes took place, when by chance an old newspaper fell into their hands from some passing traveller. How solemnly they would listen to the contents, as drawled out by Derrick Van Bummel, the schoolmaster, a dapper learned little man, who was not to be daunted by the most gigantic word in the dictionary; and how sagely they would deliberate upon public events some months after they had taken place.

The opinions of this junto[16] were completely controlled by Nicholas Vedder, a patriarch of the village, and landlord of the inn, at the door of which he took his seat from morning till night, just moving sufficiently to avoid the sun and keep in the shade of a large tree; so that the neighbors could tell the hour by his movements as accurately as by a sun-dial. It is true he was rarely heard to speak, but smoked his pipe incessantly. His adherents, however (for every great man has his adherents), perfectly understood him,

---

[16] Committee or caucus.

and knew how to gather his opinions. When any thing that was read or related displeased him, he was observed to smoke his pipe vehemently, and to send forth short, frequent and angry puffs; but when pleased, he would inhale the smoke slowly and tranquilly, and emit it in light and placid clouds; and sometimes, taking the pipe from his mouth, and letting the fragrant vapor curl about his nose, would gravely nod his head in token of perfect approbation.

From even this stronghold the unlucky Rip was at length routed by his termagant wife, who would suddenly break in upon the tranquillity of the assemblage and call the members all to naught; nor was that august personage, Nicholas Vedder himself, sacred from the daring tongue of this terrible virago, who charged him outright with encouraging her husband in habits of idleness.

Poor Rip was at last reduced almost to despair; and his only alternative, to escape from the labor of the farm and clamor of his wife, was to take gun in hand and stroll away into the woods. Here he would sometimes seat himself at the foot of a tree, and share the contents of his wallet[17] with Wolf, with whom he sympathized as a fellow-sufferer in persecution. "Poor Wolf," he would say, "thy mistress leads thee a dog's life of it; but never mind, my lad, whilst I live thou shalt never want a friend to stand by thee!" Wolf would wag his tail, look wistfully in his master's face, and if dogs can feel pity I verily believe he reciprocated the sentiment with all his heart.

In a long ramble of the kind on a fine autumnal day, Rip had unconsciously scrambled to one of the highest parts of the Kaatskill mountains. He was after his favorite sport of squirrel shooting, and the still solitudes had echoed and reechoed with the reports of his gun. Panting and fatigued, he threw himself, late in the afternoon, on a green knoll, covered with mountain herbage, that crowned the brow of a precipice. From an opening between the trees he could overlook all the lower country for many a mile of rich woodland. He saw at a distance the lordly Hudson, far, far below him, moving on its silent but majestic course, with the reflection of a purple cloud, or the sail of a lagging bark, here and there sleeping on its glassy bosom, and at last losing itself in the blue highlands.

On the other side he looked down into a deep mountain glen, wild, lonely, and shagged, the bottom filled with fragments from the impending cliffs, and scarcely lighted by the reflected rays of the setting sun. For some time Rip lay musing on this scene; evening was gradually advancing; the mountains began to throw their long blue shadows over the valleys; he saw that it would be dark long before he could reach the village, and he heaved a heavy sigh when he thought of encountering the terrors of Dame Van Winkle.

As he was about to descend, he heard a voice from a distance, hallooing, "Rip Van Winkle! Rip Van Winkle!" He looked round, but could see nothing but a crow winging its solitary flight across the mountain. He thought his fancy must have deceived him, and turned again to descend, when he heard the same cry ring through the still evening air; "Rip Van Winkle! Rip Van Winkle!"—at the same time Wolf bristled up his back, and giving a low growl, skulked to his master's side, looking fearfully down into the glen. Rip now felt a vague apprehension stealing over him; he looked anxiously in the same direction, and perceived a strange figure slowly toiling up the rocks, and bending

[17] Here, knapsack.

under the weight of something he carried on his back. He was surprised to see any human being in this lonely and unfrequented place, but supposing it to be some one of the neighborhood in need of his assistance, he hastened down to yield it.

On nearer approach he was still more surprised at the singularity of the stranger's appearance. He was a short square-built old fellow, with thick bushy hair, and a grizzled beard. His dress was of the antique Dutch fashion—a cloth jerkin strapped round the waist—several pair of breeches, the outer one of ample volume, decorated with rows of buttons down the sides, and bunches at the knees. He bore on his shoulder a stout keg, that seemed full of liquor, and made signs for Rip to approach and assist him with the load. Though rather shy and distrustful of this new acquaintance, Rip complied with his usual alacrity; and mutually relieving one another, they clambered up a narrow gully, apparently the dry bed of a mountain torrent. As they ascended, Rip every now and then heard long rolling peals, like distant thunder, that seemed to issue out of a deep ravine, or rather cleft, between lofty rocks, toward which their rugged path conducted. He paused for an instant, but supposing it to be the muttering of one of those transient thunder-showers which often take place in mountain heights, he proceeded. Passing through the ravine, they came to a hollow, like a small amphitheatre, surrounded by perpendicular precipices, over the brinks of which impending trees shot their branches, so that you only caught glimpses of the azure sky and the bright evening cloud. During the whole time Rip and his companion had labored on in silence; for though the former marvelled greatly what could be the object of carrying a keg of liquor up this wild mountain, yet there was something strange and incomprehensible about the unknown, that inspired awe and checked familiarity.

On entering the amphitheatre, new objects of wonder presented themselves. On a level spot in the centre was a company of odd-looking personages playing at nine-pins. They were dressed in a quaint outlandish fashion; some wore short doublets, others jerkins, with long knives in their belts, and most of them had enormous breeches, of similar style with that of the guide's. Their visages, too, were peculiar: one had a large beard, broad face, and small piggish eyes: the face of another seemed to consist entirely of nose, and was surmounted by a white sugar-loaf hat, set off with a little red cock's tail. They all had beards, of various shapes and colors. There was one who seemed to be the commander. He was a stout old gentleman, with a weather-beaten countenance; he wore a laced doublet, broad belt and hanger,[18] high crowned hat and feather, red stockings, and high-heeled shoes, with roses[19] in them. The whole group reminded Rip of the figures in an old Flemish painting, in the parlor of Dominic[20] Van Shaick, the village parson, and which had been brought over from Holland at the time of the settlement.

What seemed particularly odd to Rip was, that though these folks were evidently amusing themselves, yet they maintained the gravest faces, the most mysterious silence, and were, withal, the most melancholy party of pleasure he had ever witnessed. Nothing interrupted the stillness of the scene but the noise of the balls, which, whenever they were rolled, echoed along the mountains like rumbling peals of thunder.

As Rip and his companion approached them, they suddenly desisted from their play, and stared at him with such fixed statue-like gaze, and such strange, uncouth, lack-

---

[18] Short, curved sword worn at the side.
[19] Rosettes.
[20] Pastor.

lustre countenances, that his heart turned within him, and his knees smote together. His companion now emptied the contents of the keg into large flagons, and made signs to him to wait upon the company. He obeyed with fear and trembling; they quaffed the liquor in profound silence, and then returned to their game.

By degrees Rip's awe and apprehension subsided. He even ventured, when no eye was fixed upon him, to taste the beverage, which he found had much of the flavor of excellent Hollands.[21] He was naturally a thirsty soul, and was soon tempted to repeat the draught. One taste provoked another; and he reiterated his visits to the flagon so often that at length his senses were overpowered, his eyes swam in his head, his head gradually declined, and he fell into a deep sleep.

On waking, he found himself on the green knoll whence he had first seen the old man of the glen. He rubbed his eyes—it was a bright sunny morning. The birds were hopping and twittering among the bushes, and the eagle was wheeling aloft, and breasting the pure mountain breeze. "Surely," thought Rip, "I have not slept here all night." He recalled the occurrences before he fell asleep. The strange man with a keg of liquor—the mountain ravine—the wild retreat among the rocks—the wobegone party at nine-pins—the flagon—"Oh! that flagon! that wicked flagon!" thought Rip—"what excuse shall I make to Dame Van Winkle!"

He looked round for his gun, but in place of the clean well-oiled fowling-piece, he found an old firelock lying by him, the barrel incrusted with rust, the lock falling off, and the stock worm-eaten. He now suspected that the grave roysters of the mountain had put a trick upon him, and, having dosed him with liquor, had robbed him of his gun. Wolf, too, had disappeared, but he might have strayed away after a squirrel or partridge. He whistled after him and shouted his name, but all in vain; the echoes repeated his whistle and shout, but no dog was to be seen.

He determined to revisit the scene of the last evening's gambol, and if he met with any of the party, to demand his dog and gun. As he rose to walk, he found himself stiff in the joints, and wanting in his usual activity. "These mountain beds do not agree with me," thought Rip, "and if this frolic should lay me up with a fit of the rheumatism, I shall have a blessed time with Dame Van Winkle." With some difficulty he got down into the glen: he found the gully up which he and his companion had ascended the preceding evening; but to his astonishment a mountain stream was now foaming down it, leaping from rock to rock, and filling the glen with babbling murmurs. He, however, made shift to scramble up its sides, working his toilsome way through thickets of birch, sassafras, and witchhazel, and sometimes tripped up or entangled by the wild grapevines that twisted their coils or tendrils from tree to tree, and spread a kind of network in his path.

At length he reached to where the ravine had opened through the cliffs to the amphitheatre; but no traces of such opening remained. The rocks presented a high impenetrable wall over which the torrent came tumbling in a sheet of feathery foam, and fell into a broad deep basin, black from the shadows of the surrounding forest. Here, then, poor Rip was brought to a stand. He again called and whistled after his dog; he was only answered by the cawing of a flock of idle crows, sporting high in the air about a dry tree that overhung a sunny precipice; and who, secure in their elevation, seemed to look down and scoff at the poor man's perplexities. What was to be done? the morning was passing away, and Rip felt famished for want of his breakfast. He grieved to give up his

---

[21] Dutch gin.

dog and gun; he dreaded to meet his wife; but it would not do to starve among the mountains. He shook his head, shouldered the rusty firelock, and, with a heart full of trouble and anxiety, turned his steps homeward.

As he approached the village he met a number of people, but none whom he knew, which somewhat surprised him, for he had thought himself acquainted with every one in the country round. Their dress, too, was of a different fashion from that to which he was accustomed. They all stared at him with equal marks of surprise, and whenever they cast their eyes upon him, invariably stroked their chins. The constant recurrence of this gesture induced Rip, involuntarily, to do the same, when, to his astonishment, he found his beard had grown a foot long!

He had now entered the skirts of the village. A troop of strange children ran at his heels, hooting after him, and pointing at his gray beard. The dogs, too, not one of which he recognized for an old acquaintance, barked at him as he passed. The very village was altered; it was larger and more populous. There were rows of houses which he had never seen before, and those which had been his familiar haunts had disappeared. Strange names were over the doors—strange faces at the windows—every thing was strange. His mind now misgave him; he began to doubt whether both he and the world around him were not bewitched. Surely this was his native village, which he had left but the day before. There stood the Kaatskill mountains—there ran the silver Hudson at a distance—there was every hill and dale precisely as it had always been—Rip was sorely perplexed—"That flagon last night," thought he, "has addled my poor head sadly!"

It was with some difficulty that he found the way to his own house, which he approached with silent awe, expecting every moment to hear the shrill voice of Dame Van Winkle. He found the house gone to decay—the roof fallen in, the windows shattered, and the doors off the hinges. A half-starved dog that looked like Wolf was sulking about it. Rip called him by name, but the cur snarled, showed his teeth, and passed on. This was an unkind cut indeed—"My very dog," sighed poor Rip, "has forgotten me!"

He entered the house, which, to tell the truth, Dame Van Winkle had always kept in neat order. It was empty, forlorn, and apparently abandoned. This desolateness overcame all his connubial fears—he called loudly for his wife and children—the lonely chambers rang for a moment with his voice, and then all again was silence.

He now hurried forth, and hastened to his old resort, the village inn—but it too was gone. A large rickety wooden building stood in its place, with great gaping windows, some of them broken and mended with old hats and petticoats, and over the door was painted, "the Union Hotel, by Jonathan Doolittle." Instead of the great tree that used to shelter the quiet little Dutch inn of yore, there now was reared a tall naked pole, with something on the top that looked like a red night-cap, and from it was fluttering a flag, on which was a singular assemblage of stars and stripes—all this was strange and incomprehensible.[22] He recognized on the sign, however, the ruby face of King George, under which he had smoked so many a peaceful pipe; but even this was singularly metamorphosed. The red coat was changed for one of blue and buff,[23] a sword was held in the hand instead of a sceptre, the head was decorated with a cocked hat, and underneath was painted in large characters, GENERAL WASHINGTON.

---

[22] The liberty cap and liberty pole were adopted as symbols of freedom during the French and American revolutions.

[23] Colors of the American army uniforms.

There was, as usual, a crowd of folk about the door, but none that Rip recollected. The very character of the people seemed changed. There was a busy, bustling, disputatious tone about it, instead of the accustomed phlegm and drowsy tranquillity. He looked in vain for the sage Nicholas Vedder, with his broad face, double chin, and fair long pipe, uttering clouds of tobacco-smoke instead of idle speeches; or Van Bummel, the schoolmaster, doling forth the contents of an ancient newspaper. In place of these, a lean, bilious-looking fellow, with his pockets full of handbills, was haranguing vehemently about rights of citizens—elections—members of congress—liberty—Bunker's Hill—heroes of seventy-six—and other words, which were a perfect Babylonish jargon[24] to the bewildered Van Winkle.

The appearance of Rip, with his long grizzled beard, his rusty fowling-piece, his uncouth dress, and an army of women and children at his heels, soon attracted the attention of the tavern politicians. They crowded around him, eyeing him from head to foot with great curiosity. The orator bustled up to him, and, drawing him partly aside, inquired "on which side he voted?" Rip stared in vacant stupidity. Another short but busy little fellow pulled him by the arm, and, rising on tiptoe, inquired in his ear, "Whether he was Federal or Democrat?"[25] Rip was equally at a loss to comprehend the question; when a knowing, self-important old gentleman, in a sharp cocked hat, made his way through the crowd, putting them to the right and left with his elbows as he passed, and planting himself before Van Winkle, with one arm akimbo, the other resting on his cane, his keen eyes and sharp hat penetrating, as it were, into his very soul, demanded in an austere tone, "what brought him to the election with a gun on his shoulder, and a mob at his heels, and whether he meant to breed a riot in the village?"—"Alas! gentlemen," cried Rip, somewhat dismayed, "I am a poor quiet man, a native of the place, and a loyal subject of the king, God bless him!"

Here a general shout burst from the by-standers—"A tory! a tory! a spy! a refugee! hustle him! away with him!" It was with great difficulty that the self-important man in the cocked hat restored order; and, having assumed a tenfold austerity of brow, demanded again of the unknown culprit, what he came there for, and whom he was seeking? The poor man humbly assured him that he meant no harm, but merely came there in search of some of his neighbors, who used to keep about the tavern.

"Well—who are they?—name them."

Rip bethought himself a moment, and inquired, "Where's Nicholas Vedder?"

There was a silence for a little while, when an old man replied, in a thin piping voice, "Nicholas Vedder! why, he is dead and gone these eighteen years! There was a wooden tombstone in the church-yard that used to tell all about him, but that's rotten and gone too."

"Where's Brom Dutcher?"

"Oh, he went off to the army in the beginning of the war; some say he was killed at the storming of Stony Point—others say he was drowned in a squall at the foot of Antony's Nose.[26] I don't know—he never came back again."

"Where's Van Bummel, the schoolmaster?"

---

[24] Reference to the "Confusion of Tongues" at the Tower of Babel (Genesis 11:1–9).

[25] Political parties of early America, respectively conservative and liberal.

[26] Mountain near West Point on the Hudson River.

"He went off to the wars too, was a great militia general, and is now in congress."

Rip's heart died away at hearing of these sad changes in his home and friends, and finding himself thus alone in the world. Every answer puzzled him too, by treating of such enormous lapses of time, and of matters which he could not understand: war—congress—Stony Point;—he had no courage to ask after any more friends, but cried out in despair, "Does nobody here know Rip Van Winkle?"

"Oh, Rip Van Winkle!" exclaimed two or three, "Oh, to be sure! that's Rip Van Winkle yonder, leaning against the tree."

Rip looked, and beheld a precise counterpart of himself, as he went up to the mountain: apparently as lazy, and certainly as ragged. The poor fellow was now completely confounded. He doubted his own identity, and whether he was himself or another man. In the midst of his bewilderment, the man in the cocked hat demanded who he was, and what was his name?

"God knows," exclaimed he, at his wit's end; "I'm not myself—I'm somebody else—that's me yonder—no—that's somebody else got into my shoes—I was myself last night, but I fell asleep on the mountain, and they've changed my gun, and every thing's changed, and I'm changed, and I can't tell what's my name, or who I am!"

The by-standers began now to look at each other, nod, wink significantly, and tap their fingers against their foreheads. There was a whisper, also, about securing the gun, and keeping the old fellow from doing mischief, at the very suggestion of which the self-important man in the cocked hat retired with some precipitation. At this critical moment a fresh comely woman pressed through the throng to get a peep at the gray-bearded man. She had a chubby child in her arms, which, frightened at his looks, began to cry. "Hush, Rip," cried she, "hush, you little fool; the old man won't hurt you." The name of the child, the air of the mother, the tone of her voice, all awakened a train of recollections in his mind. "What is your name, my good woman?" asked he.

"Judith Gardenier."

"And your father's name?"

"Ah, poor man, Rip Van Winkle was his name, but it's twenty years since he went away from home with his gun, and never has been heard of since—his dog came home without him; but whether he shot himself, or was carried away by the Indians, nobody can tell. I was then but a little girl."

Rip had but one question more to ask; but he put it with a faltering voice:

"Where's your mother?"

"Oh, she too had died but a short time since; she broke a blood-vessel in a fit of passion at a New-England peddler."

There was a drop of comfort, at least, in this intelligence. The honest man could contain himself no longer. He caught his daughter and her child in his arms. "I am your father!" cried he—"Young Rip Van Winkle once—old Rip Van Winkle now!—Does nobody know poor Rip Van Winkle?"

All stood amazed, until an old woman, tottering out from among the crowd, put her hand to her brow, and peering under it in his face for a moment, exclaimed, "Sure enough! it is Rip Van Winkle—it is himself! Welcome home again, old neighbor—Why, where have you been these twenty long years?"

Rip's story was soon told, for the whole twenty years had been to him but as one night. The neighbors stared when they heard it; some were seen to wink at each other, and put their tongues in their cheeks: and the self-important man in the cocked hat, who, when the alarm was over, had returned to the field, screwed down the corners of his mouth, and shook his head—upon which there was a general shaking of the head throughout the assemblage.

It was determined, however, to take the opinion of old Peter Vanderdonk, who was seen slowly advancing up the road. He was a descendant of the historian of that name,[27] who wrote one of the earliest accounts of the province. Peter was the most ancient inhabitant of the village, and well versed in all the wonderful events and traditions of the neighborhood. He recollected Rip at once, and corroborated his story in the most satisfactory manner. He assured the company that it was a fact, handed down from his ancestor the historian, that the Kaatskill mountains had always been haunted by strange beings. That it was affirmed that the great Hendrick Hudson,[28] the first discoverer of the river and country, kept a kind of vigil there every twenty years, with his crew of the Half-moon; being permitted in this way to revisit the scenes of his enterprise, and keep a guardian eye upon the river, and the great city called by his name.[29] That his father had once seen them in their old Dutch dresses playing at nine-pins in a hollow of the mountain; and that he himself had heard, one summer afternoon, the sound of their balls, like distant peals of thunder.

To make a long story short, the company broke up, and returned to the more important concerns of the election. Rip's daughter took him home to live with her; she had a snug, well-furnished house, and a stout cheery farmer for a husband, whom Rip recollected for one of the urchins that used to climb upon his back. As to Rip's son and heir, who was the ditto of himself, seen leaning against the tree, he was employed to work on the farm; but evinced an hereditary disposition to attend to any thing else but his business.

Rip now resumed his old walks and habits; he soon found many of his former cronies, though all rather the worse for the wear and tear of time; and preferred making friends among the rising generation, with whom he soon grew into great favor.

Having nothing to do at home, and being arrived at that happy age when a man can be idle with impunity, he took his place once more on the bench at the inn door, and was reverenced as one of the patriarchs of the village, and a chronicle of the old times "before the war." It was some time before he could get into the regular track of gossip, or could be made to comprehend the strange events that had taken place during his torpor. How that there had been a revolutionary war—that the country had thrown off the yoke of old England—and that, instead of being a subject of his Majesty George the Third, he was now a free citizen of the United States. Rip, in fact, was no politician; the changes of states and empires made but little impression on him; but there was one species of despotism under which he had long groaned, and that was—petticoat government. Happily that was at an end; he had got his neck out of the yoke of matrimony, and could go in and out whenever he pleased, without dreading the tyranny of Dame Van Winkle. Whenever her name was mentioned, however, he shook his head,

[27] Adriaen Van Der Donck (1620?–1655), Dutch lawyer and author of a history of New Netherlands (Amsterdam, 1655).
[28] English navigator Henry Hudson (d. 1611), employed by the Dutch to explore the river that now bears his name.
[29] The town of Hudson, New York.

shrugged his shoulders, and cast up his eyes; which might pass either for an expression of resignation to his fate, or joy at his deliverance.

He used to tell his story to every stranger that arrived at Mr. Doolittle's hotel. He was observed, at first, to vary on some points every time he told it, which was, doubtless, owing to his having so recently awaked. It at last settled down precisely to the tale I have related, and not a man, woman, or child in the neighborhood, but knew it by heart. Some always pretended to doubt the reality of it, and insisted that Rip had been out of his head, and that this was one point on which he always remained flighty. The old Dutch inhabitants, however, almost universally gave it full credit. Even to this day they never hear a thunderstorm of a summer afternoon about the Kaatskill, but they say Hendrick Hudson and his crew are at their game of nine-pins; and it is a common wish of all henpecked husbands in the neighborhood, when life hangs heavy on their hands, that they might have a quieting draught out of Rip Van Winkle's flagon.

Note

The foregoing Tale, one would suspect, had been suggested to Mr. Knickerbocker by a little German superstition about the Emperor Frederick *der Rothbart*,[30] and the Kypphaüser mountain: the subjoined note, however, which he had appended to the tale, shows that it is an absolute fact, narrated with his usual fidelity:

"The story of Rip Van Winkle may seem incredible to many, but nevertheless I give it my full belief, for I know the vicinity of our old Dutch settlements to have been very subject to marvellous events and appearances. Indeed, I have heard many stranger stories than this, in the villages along the Hudson; all of which were too well authenticated to admit of a doubt. I have even talked with Rip Van Winkle myself, who, when last I saw him, was a very venerable old man, and so perfectly rational and consistent on every other point, that I think no conscientious person could refuse to take this into the bargain; nay, I have seen a certificate on the subject taken before a country justice and signed with a cross, in the justice's own handwriting. The story, therefore, is beyond the possibility of doubt.

D.K."

The Legend of Sleepy Hollow

Found among the papers of the late Diedrich Knickerbocker

> *A pleasing land of drowsy head it was,*
> *Of dreams that wave before the half-shut eye;*
> *And of gay castles in the clouds that pass,*
> *For ever flushing round a summer sky.*

Castle of Indolence[31]

---

[30] Frederick Barbarossa (1123–1190), emperor of the Holy Roman Empire (1152–1190). Legend maintains that he is resting in a cave in the Kyffhauser Mountain in Germany until his country needs his rule. (*Barbarossa* and *der Rothbart* mean "red beard" in Latin and German, respectively.)

[31] By James Thomson (1700–1748), Scottish poet.

In the bosom of one of those spacious coves which indent the eastern shore of the Hudson, at that broad expansion of the river denominated by the ancient Dutch navigators the Tappan Zee,[32] and where they always prudently shortened sail, and implored the protection of St. Nicholas when they crossed, there lies a small market-town or rural port, which by some is called Greensburgh, but which is more generally and properly known by the name of Tarry Town. This name was given, we are told, in former days, by the good housewives of the adjacent country, from the inveterate propensity of their husbands to linger about the village tavern on market days. Be that as it may, I do not vouch for the fact, but merely advert to it, for the sake of being precise and authentic. Not far from this village, perhaps about two miles, there is a little valley, or rather lap of land, among high hills, which is one of the quietest places in the whole world. A small brook glides through it, with just murmur enough to lull one to repose; and the occasional whistle of a quail, or tapping of a woodpecker, is almost the only sound that ever breaks in upon the uniform tranquillity.

I recollect that, when a stripling, my first exploit in squirrel-shooting was in a grove of tall walnut-trees that shades one side of the valley. I had wandered into it at noon time, when all nature is peculiarly quiet, and was startled by the roar of my own gun, as it broke the Sabbath stillness around, and was prolonged and reverberated by the angry echoes. If ever I should wish for a retreat, whither I might steal from the world and its distractions, and dream quietly away the remnant of a troubled life, I know of none more promising than this little valley.

From the listless repose of the place, and the peculiar character of its inhabitants, who are descendants from the original Dutch settlers, this sequestered glen has long been known by the name of SLEEPY HOLLOW,[33] and its rustic lads are called the Sleepy Hollow Boys throughout all the neighboring country. A drowsy, dreamy influence seems to hang over the land, and to pervade the very atmosphere. Some say that the place was bewitched by a high German[34] doctor, during the early days of the settlement; others, that an old Indian chief, the prophet or wizard of his tribe, held his powwows there before the country was discovered by Master Hendrick Hudson.[35] Certain it is, the place still continues under the sway of some witching power, that holds a spell over the minds of the good people, causing them to walk in a continual reverie. They are given to all kinds of marvellous beliefs; are subject to trances and visions; and frequently see strange sights, and hear music and voices in the air. The whole neighborhood abounds with local tales, haunted spots, and twilight superstitions; stars shoot and meteors glare oftener across the valley than in any other part of the country, and the nightmare, with her whole nine fold,[36] seems to make it the favorite scene of her gambols.

The dominant spirit, however, that haunts this enchanted region, and seems to be commander-in-chief of all the powers of the air, is the apparition of a figure on horseback without a head. It is said by some to be the ghost of a Hessian trooper,[37] whose head had been carried away by a cannon-ball, in some nameless battle during the revolutionary war; and who is ever and anon seen by the country folk, hurrying along in the

---

[32] Expanse in the Hudson River in Tarrytown, New York.

[33] At Tarrytown.

[34] High German: from southern Germany.

[35] Henry Hudson.

[36] The demonic nightmare of folk legend had nine foals or imps.

[37] Mercenary from Hesse, Germany, hired by the British to fight in the American revolution.

gloom of night, as if on the wings of the wind. His haunts are not confined to the valley, but extend at times to the adjacent roads, and especially to the vicinity of a church at no great distance. Indeed, certain of the most authentic historians of those parts, who have been careful in collecting and collating the floating facts concerning this spectre, allege that the body of the trooper, having been buried in the church-yard, the ghost rides forth to the scene of battle in nightly quest of his head; and that the rushing speed with which he sometimes passes along the Hollow, like a midnight blast, is owing to his being belated, and in a hurry to get back to the church-yard before daybreak.[38]

Such is the general purport of this legendary superstition, which has furnished materials for many a wild story in that region of shadows; and the spectre is known, at all the country firesides, by the name of the Headless Horseman of Sleepy Hollow.

It is remarkable that the visionary propensity I have mentioned is not confined to the native inhabitants of the valley, but is unconsciously imbibed by every one who resides there for a time. However wide awake they may have been before they entered that sleepy region, they are sure, in a little time, to inhale the witching influence of the air, and begin to grow imaginative—to dream dreams, and see apparitions.

I mention this peaceful spot with all possible laud; for it is in such little retired Dutch valleys, found here and there embosomed in the great State of New-York, that population, manners, and customs, remain fixed; while the great torrent of migration and improvement, which is making such incessant changes in other parts of this restless country, sweeps by them unobserved. They are like those little nooks of still water which border a rapid stream; where we may see the straw and bubble riding quietly at anchor, or slowly revolving in their mimic harbor, undisturbed by the rush of the passing current. Though many years have elapsed since I trod the drowsy shades of Sleepy Hollow, yet I question whether I should not still find the same trees and the same families vegetating in its sheltered bosom.

In this by-place of nature, there abode, in a remote period of American history, that is to say, some thirty years since, a worthy wight of the name of Ichabod Crane; who sojourned, or, as he expressed it, "tarried," in Sleepy Hollow, for the purpose of instructing the children of the vicinity. He was a native of Connecticut; a State which supplies the Union with pioneers for the mind as well as for the forest, and sends forth yearly its legions of frontier woodsmen and country schoolmasters. The cognomen of Crane was not inapplicable to his person. He was tall, but exceedingly lank, with narrow shoulders, long arms and legs, hands that dangled a mile out of his sleeves, feet that might have served for shovels, and his whole frame most loosely hung together. His head was small, and flat at top, with huge ears, large green glassy eyes, and a long snipe nose, so that it looked like a weather-cock, perched upon his spindle neck, to tell which way the wind blew. To see him striding along the profile of a hill on a windy day, with his clothes bagging and fluttering about him, one might have mistaken him for the genius of famine descending upon the earth, or some scarecrow eloped from a cornfield.

His school-house was a low building of one large room, rudely constructed of logs; the windows partly glazed, and partly patched with leaves of old copy-books. It was most ingeniously secured at vacant hours, by a withe twisted in the handle of the door, and stakes set against the window shutters; so that, though a thief might get in with per-

[38] Reference to the superstition that spirits must return to their graves before dawn.

fect ease, he would find some embarrassment in getting out; an idea most probably borrowed by the architect, Yost Van Houten, from the mystery of an eel-pot.[39] The schoolhouse stood in a rather lonely but pleasant situation, just at the foot of a woody hill, with a brook running close by, and a formidable birch tree growing at one end of it. From hence the low murmur of his pupils' voices, conning over their lessons, might be heard in a drowsy summer's day, like the hum of a bee-hive; interrupted now and then by the authoritative voice of the master, in the tone of menace or command; or, peradventure, by the appalling sound of the birch, as he urged some tardy loiterer along the flowery path of knowledge. Truth to say, he was a conscientious man, and ever bore in mind the golden maxim, "Spare the rod and spoil the child."[40]—Ichabod Crane's scholars certainly were not spoiled.

I would not have it imagined, however, that he was one of those cruel potentates of the school, who joy in the smart[41] of their subjects; on the contrary, he administered justice with discrimination rather than severity; taking the burthen off the backs of the weak, and laying it on those of the strong. Your mere puny stripling, that winced at the least flourish of the rod, was passed by with indulgence; but the claims of justice were satisfied by inflicting a double portion on some little, tough, wrong-headed, broad-skirted Dutch urchin, who sulked and swelled and grew dogged and sullen beneath the birch. All this he called "doing his duty by their parents;" and he never inflicted a chastisement without following it by the assurance, so consolatory to the smarting urchin, that "he would remember it, and thank him for it the longest day he had to live."

When school hours were over, he was even the companion and playmate of the larger boys; and on holiday afternoons would convoy some of the smaller ones home, who happened to have pretty sisters, or good housewives for mothers, noted for the comforts of the cupboard. Indeed it behooved him to keep on good terms with his pupils. The revenue arising from his school was small, and would have been scarcely sufficient to furnish him with daily bread, for he was a huge feeder, and though lank, had the dilating powers of an anaconda;[42] but to help out his maintenance, he was, according to country custom in those parts, boarded and lodged at the houses of the farmers, whose children he instructed. With these he lived successively a week at a time; thus going the rounds of the neighborhood, with all his worldly effects tied up in a cotton handkerchief.

That all this might not be too onerous on the purses of his rustic patrons, who are apt to consider the costs of schooling a grievous burden, and schoolmasters as mere drones, he had various ways of rendering himself both useful and agreeable. He assisted the farmers occasionally in the lighter labors of their farms; helped to make hay; mended the fences; took the horses to water; drove the cows from pasture; and cut wood for the winter fire. He laid aside, too, all the dominant dignity and absolute sway with which he lorded it in his little empire, the school, and became wonderfully gentle and ingratiating. He found favor in the eyes of the mothers, by petting the children, particularly the youngest; and like the lion bold, which whilom[43] so magnanimously the

---

[39] Eel trap.

[40] From *Hudibras* (1664) by English poet Samuel Butler (1612–1680). The passage originates in Proverbs 13:24: "He that spareth his rod, hateth his son."

[41] Pain.

[42] Species of large snake capable of swallowing animals whole.

[43] Formerly.

lamb did hold,[44] he would sit with a child on one knee, and rock a cradle with his foot for whole hours together.

In addition to his other vocations, he was the singing-master of the neighborhood, and picked up many bright shillings by instructing the young folks in psalmody. It was a matter of no little vanity to him, on Sundays, to take his station in front of the church gallery, with a band of chosen singers; where, in his own mind, he completely carried away the palm from the parson. Certain it is, his voice resounded far above all the rest of the congregation; and there are peculiar quavers still to be heard in that church, and which may even be heard half a mile off, quite to the opposite side of the mill-pond, on a still Sunday morning, which are said to be legitimately descended from the nose of Ichabod Crane. Thus, by divers little make-shifts in that ingenious way which is commonly denominated "by hook and by crook,"[45] the worthy pedagogue got on tolerably enough, and was thought, by all who understood nothing of the labor of headwork, to have a wonderfully easy life of it.

The schoolmaster is generally a man of some importance in the female circle of a rural neighborhood; being considered a kind of idle gentlemanlike personage, of vastly superior taste and accomplishments to the rough country swains, and, indeed, inferior in learning only to the parson. His appearance, therefore, is apt to occasion some little stir at the tea-table of a farmhouse, and the addition of a supernumerary dish of cakes or sweetmeats, or, peradventure, the parade of a silver tea-pot. Our man of letters, therefore, was peculiarly happy in the smiles of all the country damsels. How he would figure among them in the churchyard, between services on Sundays! gathering grapes for them from the wild vines that overrun the surrounding trees; reciting for their amusement all the epitaphs on the tombstones; or sauntering, with a whole bevy of them, along the banks of the adjacent mill-pond; while the more bashful country bumpkins hung sheepishly back, envying his superior elegance and address.

From his half itinerant life, also, he was a kind of travelling gazette, carrying the whole budget of local gossip from house to house; so that his appearance was always greeted with satisfaction. He was, moreover, esteemed by the women as a man of great erudition, for he had read several books quite through, and was a perfect master of Cotton Mather's[46] history of New England Witchcraft, in which, by the way, he most firmly and potently believed.

He was, in fact, an odd mixture of small shrewdness and simple credulity. His appetite for the marvellous, and his powers of digesting it, were equally extraordinary; and both had been increased by his residence in this spellbound region. No tale was too gross or monstrous for his capacious swallow. It was often his delight, after his school was dismissed in the afternoon, to stretch himself on the rich bed of clover, bordering the little brook that whimpered by his school-house, and there con over old Mather's direful tales, until the gathering dusk of the evening made the printed page a mere mist before his eyes. Then, as he wended his way, by swamp and stream and awful woodland, to the farmhouse where he happened to be quartered, every sound of nature, at that

---

[44] The *New England Primer* represents the letter *L* with a lion and a lamb and the rhyme "The Lion Bold / The Lamb doth hold" (from Isaiah 11:6–9).

[45] From "Colyn Cloute" (1519?) by John Skelton (1460?–1529), English poet.

[46] Cotton Mather (1663–1728), author of *Memorable Providences Relating to Witchcraft* (1689) and *The Wonders of the Invisible World* (1693).

witching hour, fluttered his excited imagination: the moan of the whip-poor-will[47] from the hill-side; the boding cry of the tree-toad, that harbinger of storm; the dreary hooting of the screech-owl, or the sudden rustling in the thicket of birds frightened from their roost. The fire-flies, too, which sparkled most vividly in the darkest places, now and then startled him, as one of uncommon brightness would stream across his path; and if, by chance, a huge blockhead of a beetle came winging his blundering flight against him, the poor varlet was ready to give up the ghost, with the idea that he was struck with a witch's token. His only resource on such occasions, either to drown thought, or drive away evil spirits, was to sing psalm tunes;—and the good people of Sleepy Hollow, as they sat by their doors of an evening, were often filled with awe, at hearing his nasal melody, "in linked sweetness long drawn out,"[48] floating from the distant hill, or along the dusky road.

Another of his sources of fearful pleasure was to pass long winter evenings with the old Dutch wives, as they sat spinning by the fire, with a row of apples roasting and spluttering along the hearth, and listen to their marvellous tales of ghosts and goblins, and haunted fields, and haunted brooks, and haunted bridges, and haunted houses, and particularly of the headless horseman, or galloping Hessian of the Hollow, as they sometimes called him. He would delight them equally by his anecdotes of witchcraft, and of the direful omens and portentous sights and sounds in the air, which prevailed in the earlier times of Connecticut; and would frighten them wofully with speculations upon comets and shooting stars; and with the alarming fact that the world did absolutely turn round, and that they were half the time topsy-turvy!

But if there was a pleasure in all this, while snugly cuddling in the chimney corner of a chamber that was all of a ruddy glow from the crackling wood fire, and where, of course, no spectre dared to show his face, it was dearly purchased by the terrors of his subsequent walk homewards. What fearful shapes and shadows beset his path amidst the dim and ghastly glare of a snowy night!—With what wistful look did he eye every trembling ray of light streaming across the waste fields from some distant window!—How often was he appalled by some shrub covered with snow, which, like a sheeted spectre, beset his very path!—How often did he shrink with curdling awe at the sound of his own steps on the frosty crust beneath his feet; and dread to look over his shoulder, lest he should behold some uncouth being tramping close behind him!—and how often was he thrown into complete dismay by some rushing blast, howling among the trees, in the idea that it was the Galloping Hessian on one of his nightly scourings!

All these, however, were mere terrors of the night, phantoms of the mind that walk in darkness; and though he had seen many spectres in his time, and been more than once beset by Satan in divers shapes, in his lonely perambulations, yet daylight put an end to all these evils; and he would have passed a pleasant life of it, in despite of the devil and all his works, if his path had not been crossed by a being that causes more perplexity to mortal man than ghosts, goblins, and the whole race of witches put together, and that was—a woman.

Among the musical disciples who assembled, one evening in each week, to receive his instructions in psalmody, was Katrina Van Tassel, the daughter and only child of a

---

[47] Irving's note: "The whip-poor-will is a bird which is only heard at night. It receives its name from its note, which is thought to resemble those words."

[48] From "L'Allegro" (1632) by John Milton (1608–1674), English poet.

substantial Dutch farmer. She was a blooming lass of fresh eighteen; plump as a partridge; ripe and melting and rosy cheeked as one of her father's peaches, and universally famed, not merely for her beauty, but her vast expectations. She was withal a little of a coquette, as might be perceived even in her dress, which was a mixture of ancient and modern fashions, as most suited to set off her charms. She wore the ornaments of pure yellow gold, which her great-great-grandmother had brought over from Saardam;[49] the tempting stomacher[50] of the olden time; and withal a provokingly short petticoat, to display the prettiest foot and ankle in the country round.

Ichabod Crane had a soft and foolish heart towards the sex; and it is not to be wondered at, that so tempting a morsel soon found favor in his eyes; more especially after he had visited her in her paternal mansion. Old Baltus Van Tassel was a perfect picture of a thriving, contented, liberal-hearted farmer. He seldom, it is true, sent either his eyes or his thoughts beyond the boundaries of his own farm; but within those every thing was snug, happy, and well-conditioned. He was satisfied with his wealth, but not proud of it; and piqued himself upon the hearty abundance, rather than the style in which he lived. His stronghold was situated on the banks of the Hudson, in one of those green, sheltered, fertile nooks, in which the Dutch farmers are so fond of nestling. A great elm-tree spread its broad branches over it; at the foot of which bubbled up a spring of the softest and sweetest water, in a little well, formed of a barrel; and then stole sparkling away through the grass, to a neighboring brook, that bubbled along among alders and dwarf willows. Hard by the farmhouse was a vast barn, that might have served for a church; every window and crevice of which seemed bursting forth with the treasures of the farm; the flail was busily resounding within it from morning to night; swallows and martins skimmed twittering about the eaves; and rows of pigeons, some with one eye turned up, as if watching the weather, some with their heads under their wings, or buried in their bosoms, and others swelling, and cooing, and bowing about their dames, were enjoying the sunshine on the roof. Sleek unwieldy porkers were grunting in the repose and abundance of their pens; whence sallied forth, now and then, troops of sucking pigs, as if to snuff the air. A stately squadron of snowy geese were riding in an adjoining pond, convoying whole fleets of ducks; regiments of turkeys were gobbling through the farmyard, and guinea fowls fretting about it, like ill-tempered housewives, with their peevish discontented cry. Before the barn door strutted the gallant cock, that pattern of a husband, a warrior, and a fine gentleman, clapping his burnished wings, and crowing in the pride and gladness of his heart—sometimes tearing up the earth with his feet, and then generously calling his ever-hungry family of wives and children to enjoy the rich morsel which he had discovered.

The pedagogue's mouth watered, as he looked upon this sumptuous promise of luxurious winter fare. In his devouring mind's eye, he pictured to himself every roasting-pig running about with a pudding in his belly, and an apple in his mouth; the pigeons were snugly put to bed in a comfortable pie, and tucked in with a coverlet of crust; the geese were swimming in their own gravy; and the ducks pairing cosily in dishes, like snug married couples, with a decent competency of onion sauce. In the porkers he saw carved out the future sleek side of bacon, and juicy relishing ham; not a turkey but he

---

[49] Modern Zaandam, near Amsterdam.
[50] Decorated centerpiece of the bodice or
    waistband of a dress.

beheld daintily trussed up, with its gizzard under its wing, and, peradventure, a necklace of savory sausages; and even bright chanticleer himself lay sprawling on his back, in a side-dish, with uplifted claws, as if craving that quarter[51] which his chivalrous spirit disdained to ask while living.

As the enraptured Ichabod fancied all this, and as he rolled his great green eyes over the fat meadow-lands, the rich fields of wheat, of rye, of buckwheat, and Indian corn, and the orchards burthened with ruddy fruit, which surrounded the warm tenement of Van Tassel, his heart yearned after the damsel who was to inherit these domains, and his imagination expanded with the idea, how they might be readily turned into cash, and the money invested in immense tracts of wild land, and shingle palaces in the wilderness. Nay, his busy fancy already realized his hopes, and presented to him the blooming Katrina, with a whole family of children, mounted on the top of a wagon loaded with household trumpery, with pots and kettles dangling beneath; and he beheld himself bestriding a pacing mare, with a colt at her heels, setting out for Kentucky, Tennessee, or the Lord knows where.

When he entered the house the conquest of his heart was complete. It was one of those spacious farmhouses, with high-ridged, but lowly-sloping roofs, built in the style handed down from the first Dutch settlers; the low projecting eaves forming a piazza along the front, capable of being closed up in bad weather. Under this were hung flails, harness, various utensils of husbandry, and nets for fishing in the neighboring river. Benches were built along the sides for summer use; and a great spinning-wheel at one end, and a churn at the other, showed the various uses to which this important porch might be devoted. From this piazza the wondering Ichabod entered the hall, which formed the centre of the mansion and the place of usual residence. Here, rows of resplendent pewter, ranged on a long dresser, dazzled his eyes. In one corner stood a huge bag of wool ready to be spun; in another a quantity of linsey-woolsey just from the loom; ears of Indian corn, and strings of dried apples and peaches, hung in gay festoons along the walls, mingled with the gaud of red peppers; and a door left ajar gave him a peep into the best parlor, where the claw-footed chairs, and dark mahogany tables, shone like mirrors; and irons, with their accompanying shovel and tongs, glistened from their covert of asparagus tops; mock-oranges and conch-shells decorated the mantel-piece; strings of various colored birds' eggs were suspended above it: a great ostrich egg was hung from the centre of the room, and a corner cupboard, knowingly left open, displayed immense treasures of old silver and well-mended china.

From the moment Ichabod laid his eyes upon these regions of delight, the peace of his mind was at an end, and his only study was how to gain the affections of the peerless daughter of Van Tassel. In this enterprise, however, he had more real difficulties than generally fell to the lot of a knight-errant of yore, who seldom had any thing but giants, enchanters, fiery dragons, and such like easily-conquered adversaries, to contend with; and had to make his way merely through gates of iron and brass, and walls of adamant, to the castle keep, where the lady of his heart was confined; all which he achieved as easily as a man would carve his way to the centre of a Christmas pie; and then the lady gave him her hand as a matter of course. Ichabod, on the contrary, had to win his way to the heart of a country coquette, beset with a labyrinth of whims and caprices, which were

---

[51] Clemency.

for ever presenting new difficulties and impediments; and he had to encounter a host of fearful adversaries of real flesh and blood, the numerous rustic admirers, who beset every portal to her heart; keeping a watchful and angry eye upon each other, but ready to fly out in the common cause against any new competitor.

Among these the most formidable was a burly, roaring, roystering blade, of the name of Abraham, or, according to the Dutch abbreviation, Brom Van Brunt, the hero of the country round, which rang with his feats of strength and hardihood. He was broad-shouldered and double-jointed, with short curly black hair, and a bluff, but not un-pleasant countenance, having a mingled air of fun and arrogance. From his Herculean frame and great powers of limb, he had received the nickname of BROM BONES, by which he was universally known. He was famed for great knowledge and skill in horse-manship, being as dexterous on horseback as a Tartar.[52] He was foremost at all races and cock-fights; and, with the ascendency which bodily strength acquires in rustic life, was the umpire in all disputes, setting his hat on one side, and giving his decisions with an air and tone admitting of no gainsay or appeal. He was always ready for either a fight or a frolic; but had more mischief than ill-will in his composition; and, with all his over-bearing roughness, there was a strong dash of waggish good humor at bottom. He had three or four boon companions, who regarded him as their model, and at the head of whom he scoured the country, attending every scene of feud or merriment for miles round. In cold weather he was distinguished by a fur cap, surmounted with a flaunting fox's tail; and when the folks at a country gathering descried this well-known crest at a distance, whisking about among a squad of hard riders, they always stood by for a squall. Sometimes his crew would be heard dashing along past the farmhouses at mid-night, with whoop and halloo, like a troop of Don Cossacks;[53] and the old dames, star-tled out of their sleep, would listen for a moment till the hurry-scurry had clattered by, and then exclaim, "Ay, there goes Brom Bones and his gang!" The neighbors looked upon him with a mixture of awe, admiration, and good will; and when any madcap prank, or rustic brawl, occurred in the vicinity, always shook their heads, and warranted Brom Bones was at the bottom of it.

This rantipole[54] hero had for some time singled out the blooming Katrina for the object of his uncouth gallantries, and though his amorous toyings were something like the gentle caresses and endearments of a bear, yet it was whispered that she did not alto-gether discourage his hopes. Certain it is, his advances were signals for rival candidates to retire, who felt no inclination to cross a lion in his amours; insomuch, that when his horse was seen tied to Van Tassel's paling, on a Sunday night, a sure sign that his master was courting, or, as it is termed, "sparking," within, all other suitors passed by in de-spair, and carried the war into other quarters.

Such was the formidable rival with whom Ichabod Crane had to contend, and, con-sidering all things, a stouter man than he would have shrunk from the competition, and a wiser man would have despaired. He had, however, a happy mixture of pliability and perseverance in his nature; he was in form and spirit like a supple-jack[55]—yielding, but tough; though he bent, he never broke; and though he bowed beneath the slightest pressure, yet, the moment it was away—jerk! he was as erect, and carried his head as high as ever.

---

[52] Violent Asian warrior.
[53] Russian cavalry of the Don River area.

[54] Wild and reckless.
[55] A woody vine with strong, pliant stems.

To have taken the field openly against his rival would have been madness; for he was not a man to be thwarted in his amours, any more than that stormy lover, Achilles.[56] Ichabod, therefore, made his advances in a quiet and gently-insinuating manner. Under cover of his character of singing-master, he made frequent visits at the farmhouse; not that he had any thing to apprehend from the meddlesome interference of parents, which is so often a stumbling-block in the path of lovers. Balt Van Tassel was an easy indulgent soul; he loved his daughter better even than his pipe, and, like a reasonable man and an excellent father, let her have her way in every thing. His notable little wife, too, had enough to do to attend to her housekeeping and manage her poultry; for, as she sagely observed, ducks and geese are foolish things, and must be looked after, but girls can take care of themselves. Thus while the busy dame bustled about the house, or plied her spinning-wheel at one end of the piazza, honest Balt would sit smoking his evening pipe at the other, watching the achievements of a little wooden warrior, who, armed with a sword in each hand, was most valiantly fighting the wind on the pinnacle of the barn. In the mean time, Ichabod would carry on his suit with the daughter by the side of the spring under the great elm, or sauntering along in the twilight, that hour so favorable to the lover's eloquence.

I profess not to know how women's hearts are wooed and won. To me they have always been matters of riddle and admiration. Some seem to have but one vulnerable point, or door of access; while others have a thousand avenues, and may be captured in a thousand different ways. It is a great triumph of skill to gain the former, but a still greater proof of generalship to maintain possession of the latter, for the man must battle for his fortress at every door and window. He who wins a thousand common hearts is therefore entitled to some renown; but he who keeps undisputed sway over the heart of a coquette, is indeed a hero. Certain it is, this was not the case with the redoubtable Brom Bones; and from the moment Ichabod Crane made his advances, the interests of the former evidently declined; his horse was no longer seen tied at the palings on Sunday nights, and a deadly feud gradually arose between him and the preceptor of Sleepy Hollow.

Brom, who had a degree of rough chivalry in his nature, would fain have carried matters to open warfare, and have settled their pretensions to the lady, according to the mode of those most concise and simple reasoners, the knights-errant of yore—by single combat; but Ichabod was too conscious of the superior might of his adversary to enter the lists against him: he had overheard a boast of Bones, that he would "double the schoolmaster up, and lay him on a shelf of his own school-house;" and he was too wary to give him an opportunity. There was something extremely provoking in this obstinately pacific system; it left Brom no alternative but to draw upon the funds of rustic waggery in his disposition, and to play off boorish practical jokes upon his rival. Ichabod became the object of whimsical persecution to Bones, and his gang of rough riders. They harried his hitherto peaceful domains; smoked out his singing school, by stopping up the chimney; broke into the school-house at night, in spite of its formidable fastenings of withe and window stakes, and turned every thing topsy-turvy: so that the poor schoolmaster began to think all the witches in the country held their meetings there. But what

[56] In Homer's *Iliad* Achilles became furious when his captive love, Briseis, was taken from him by King Agamemnon.

was still more annoying, Brom took all opportunities of turning him into ridicule in presence of his mistress, and had a scoundrel dog whom he taught to whine in the most ludicrous manner, and introduced as a rival of Ichabod's to instruct her in psalmody.

In this way matters went on for some time, without producing any material effect on the relative situation of the contending powers. On a fine autumnal afternoon, Ichabod, in pensive mood, sat enthroned on the lofty stool whence he usually watched all the concerns of his little literary realm. In his hand he swayed a ferule, that sceptre of despotic power; the birch of justice reposed on three nails, behind the throne, a constant terror to evil doers; while on the desk before him might be seen sundry contraband articles and prohibited weapons, detected upon the persons of idle urchins; such as half-munched apples, popguns, whirligigs, fly-cages, and whole legions of rampant little paper game-cocks. Apparently there had been some appalling act of justice recently inflicted, for his scholars were all busily intent upon their books, or slyly whispering behind them with one eye kept upon the master; and a kind of buzzing stillness reigned throughout the school-room. It was suddenly interrupted by the appearance of a negro, in tow-cloth jacket and trowsers, a round-crowned fragment of a hat, like the cap of Mercury,[57] and mounted on the back of a ragged, wild, half-broken colt, which he managed with a rope by way of halter. He came clattering up to the school door with an invitation to Ichabod to attend a merry-making or "quilting frolic," to be held that evening at Mynheer Van Tassel's; and having delivered his message with that air of importance, and effort at fine language, which a negro is apt to display on petty embassies of the kind, he dashed over the brook, and was seen scampering away up the hollow, full of the importance and hurry of his mission.

All was now bustle and hubbub in the late quiet school-room. The scholars were hurried through their lessons, without stopping at trifles; those who were nimble skipped over half with impunity, and those who were tardy, had a smart application now and then in the rear, to quicken their speed, or help them over a tall word. Books were flung aside without being put away on the shelves, ink stands were overturned, benches thrown down, and the whole school was turned loose an hour before the usual time, bursting forth like a legion of young imps, yelping and racketing about the green, in joy at their early emancipation.

The gallant Ichabod now spent at least an extra half hour at his toilet, brushing and furbishing up his best, and indeed only suit of rusty black, and arranging his looks by a bit of broken looking-glass, that hung up in the school-house. That he might make his appearance before his mistress in the true style of a cavalier, he borrowed a horse from the farmer with whom he was domiciliated, a choleric old Dutchman, of the name of Hans Van Ripper, and, thus gallantly mounted, issued forth, like a knight-errant in quest of adventures. But it is meet I should, in the true spirit of romantic story, give some account of the looks and equipments of my hero and his steed. The animal he bestrode was a broken-down plough-horse, that had outlived almost every thing but his viciousness. He was gaunt and shagged, with a ewe neck and a head like a hammer; his rusty mane and tail were tangled and knotted with burrs; one eye had lost its pupil, and was glaring and spectral; but the other had the gleam of a genuine devil in it. Still he must have had fire and mettle in his day, if we may judge from the name he bore of Gunpowder. He had, in fact, been a favorite steed of his master's, the choleric Van Rip-

[57] The winged hat of Mercury, Roman messenger of the gods, is a symbol of speed.

per, who was a furious rider, and had infused, very probably, some of his own spirit into the animal; for, old and broken-down as he looked, there was more of the lurking devil in him than in any young filly in the country.

Ichabod was a suitable figure for such a steed. He rode with short stirrups, which brought his knees nearly up to the pommel of the saddle; his sharp elbows stuck out like grasshoppers'; he carried his whip perpendicularly in his hand, like a sceptre, and, as his horse jogged on, the motion of his arms was not unlike the flapping of a pair of wings. A small wool hat rested on the top of his nose, for so his scanty strip of forehead might be called; and the skirts of his black coat fluttered out almost to the horse's tail. Such was the appearance of Ichabod and his steed, as they shambled out of the gate of Hans Van Ripper, and it was altogether such an apparition as is seldom to be met with in broad daylight.

It was, as I have said, a fine autumnal day, the sky was clear and serene, and nature wore that rich and golden livery which we always associate with the idea of abundance. The forests had put on their sober brown and yellow, while some trees of the tenderer kind had been nipped by the frosts into brilliant dyes of orange, purple, and scarlet. Streaming files of wild ducks began to make their appearance high in the air; the bark of the squirrel might be heard from the groves of beech and hickory nuts, and the pensive whistle of the quail at intervals from the neighboring stubble-field.

The small birds were taking their farewell banquets. In the fulness of their revelry, they fluttered, chirping and frolicking, from bush to bush, and tree to tree, capricious from the very profusion and variety around them. There was the honest cock-robin, the favorite game of stripling sportsmen, with its loud querulous note; and the twittering blackbirds flying in sable clouds; and the golden-winged woodpecker, with his crimson crest, his broad black gorget,[58] and splendid plumage; and the cedar bird, with its red-tipt wings and yellow-tipt tail, and its little monteiro cap of feathers;[59] and the blue jay, that noisy coxcomb, in his gay light-blue coat and white under-clothes; screaming and chattering, nodding and bobbing and bowing, and pretending to be on good terms with every songster of the grove.

As Ichabod jogged slowly on his way, his eye, ever open to every symptom of culinary abundance, ranged with delight over the treasures of jolly autumn. On all sides he beheld vast store of apples; some hanging in oppressive opulence on the trees; some gathered into baskets and barrels for the market; others heaped up in rich piles for the cider-press. Farther on he beheld great fields of Indian corn, with its golden ears peeping from their leafy coverts, and holding out the promise of cakes and hasty pudding; and the yellow pumpkins lying beneath them, turning up their fair round bellies to the sun, and giving ample prospects of the most luxurious of pies; and anon he passed the fragrant buckwheat fields, breathing the odor of the bee-hive, and as he beheld them, soft anticipations stole over his mind of dainty slapjacks, well buttered, and garnished with honey or treacle, by the delicate little dimpled hand of Katrina Van Tassel.

Thus feeding his mind with many sweet thoughts and "sugared suppositions," he journeyed along the sides of a range of hills which look out upon some of the goodliest scenes of the mighty Hudson. The sun gradually wheeled his broad disk down into the west. The wide bosom of the Tappan Zee lay motionless and glassy, excepting that here

---

[58] Throat.
[59] i.e., a feathered plume resembling a hunting cap with flaps.

and there a gentle undulation waved and prolonged the blue shadow of the distant mountain. A few amber clouds floated in the sky, without a breath of air to move them. The horizon was of a fine golden tint, changing gradually into a pure apple green, and from that into the deep blue of the midheaven. A slanting ray lingered on the woody crests of the precipices that overhung some parts of the river, giving greater depth to the dark-gray and purple of their rocky sides. A sloop was loitering in the distance, dropping slowly down with the tide, her sail hanging uselessly against the mast; and as the reflection of the sky gleamed along the still water, it seemed as if the vessel was suspended in the air.

It was toward evening that Ichabod arrived at the castle of the Heer Van Tassel, which he found thronged with the pride and flower of the adjacent country. Old farmers, a spare leathern-faced race, in homespun coats and breeches, blue stockings, huge shoes, and magnificent pewter buckles. Their brisk withered little dames, in close crimped caps, long-waisted shortgowns, homespun petticoats, with scissors and pincushions, and gay calico pockets hanging on the outside. Buxom lasses, almost as antiquated as their mothers, excepting where a straw hat, a fine ribbon, or perhaps a white frock, gave symptoms of city innovation. The sons, in short square-skirted coats with rows of stupendous brass buttons, and their hair generally queued in the fashion of the times, especially if they could procure an eel-skin for the purpose, it being esteemed, throughout the country, as a potent nourisher and strengthener of the hair.

Brom Bones, however, was the hero of the scene, having come to the gathering on his favorite steed Daredevil, a creature, like himself, full of mettle and mischief, and which no one but himself could manage. He was, in fact, noted for preferring vicious animals, given to all kinds of tricks, which kept the rider in constant risk of his neck, for he held a tractable well-broken horse as unworthy of a lad of spirit.

Fain would I pause to dwell upon the world of charms that burst upon the enraptured gaze of my hero, as he entered the state parlor of Van Tassel's mansion. Not those of the bevy of buxom lasses, with their luxurious display of red and white; but the ample charms of a genuine Dutch country tea-table, in the sumptuous time of autumn. Such heaped-up platters of cakes of various and almost indescribable kinds, known only to experienced Dutch housewives! There was the doughty dough-nut, the tenderer oly koek,[60] and the crisp and crumbling cruller; sweet cakes and short cakes, ginger cakes and honey cakes, and the whole family of cakes. And then there were apple pies and peach pies and pumpkin pies; besides slices of ham and smoked beef; and moreover delectable dishes of preserved plums, and peaches, and pears, and quinces; not to mention broiled shad and roasted chickens; together with bowls of milk and cream, all mingled higgledy-piggledy, pretty much as I have enumerated them, with the motherly tea-pot sending up its clouds of vapor from the midst—Heaven bless the mark! I want breath and time to discuss this banquet as it deserves, and am too eager to get on with my story. Happily, Ichabod Crane was not in so great a hurry as his historian, but did ample justice to every dainty.

He was a kind and thankful creature, whose heart dilated in proportion as his skin was filled with good cheer; and whose spirits rose with eating as some men's do with drink. He could not help, too, rolling his large eyes round him as he ate, and chuckling with the possibility that he might one day be lord of all this scene of almost unimagin-

---

[60] "Oil cake," a delicate pastry fried in oil.

able luxury and splendor. Then, he thought, how soon he'd turn his back upon the old school-house; snap his fingers in the face of Hans Van Ripper, and every other niggardly patron, and kick any itinerant pedagogue out of doors that should dare to call him comrade!

Old Baltus Van Tassel moved about among his guests with a face dilated with content and good humor, round and jolly as the harvest moon. His hospitable attentions were brief, but expressive, being confined to a shake of the hand, a slap on the shoulder, a loud laugh, and a pressing invitation to "fall to, and help themselves."

And now the sound of the music from the common room, or hall, summoned to the dance. The musician was an old grayheaded negro, who had been the itinerant orchestra of the neighborhood for more than half a century. His instrument was as old and battered as himself. The greater part of the time he scraped on two or three strings, accompanying every movement of the bow with a motion of the head; bowing almost to the ground, and stamping with his foot whenever a fresh couple were to start.

Ichabod prided himself upon his dancing as much as upon his vocal powers. Not a limb, not a fibre about him was idle; and to have seen his loosely hung frame in full motion, and clattering about the room, you would have thought Saint Vitus[61] himself, that blessed patron of the dance, was figuring before you in person. He was the admiration of all the negroes; who, having gathered, of all ages and sizes, from the farm and the neighborhood, stood forming a pyramid of shining black faces at every door and window, gazing with delight at the scene, rolling their white eye-balls, and showing grinning rows of ivory from ear to ear. How could the flogger of urchins be otherwise than animated and joyous? the lady of his heart was his partner in the dance, and smiling graciously in reply to all his amorous oglings; while Brom Bones, sorely smitten with love and jealousy, sat brooding by himself in one corner.

When the dance was at an end, Ichabod was attracted to a knot of the sager folks, who, with old Van Tassel, sat smoking at one end of the piazza, gossiping over former times, and drawing out long stories about the war.

This neighborhood, at the time of which I am speaking, was one of those highly-favored places which abound with chronicle and great men. The British and American line had run near it during the war; it had, therefore, been the scene of marauding, and infested with refugees, cow-boys,[62] and all kinds of border chivalry. Just sufficient time had elapsed to enable each story-teller to dress up his tale with a little becoming fiction, and, in the indistinctness of his recollection, to make himself the hero of every exploit.

There was the story of Doffue Martling, a large blue-bearded Dutchman, who had nearly taken a British frigate with an old iron nine-pounder[63] from a mud breastwork, only that his gun burst at the sixth discharge. And there was an old gentleman who shall be nameless, being too rich a mynheer to be lightly mentioned, who, in the battle of Whiteplains,[64] being an excellent master of defence, parried a musket ball with a small sword, insomuch that he absolutely felt it whiz round the blade, and glance off at the hilt: in proof of which, he was ready at any time to show the sword, with the hilt a little bent. There were several more that had been equally great in the field, not one of whom but was persuaded that he had a considerable hand in bringing the war to a happy termination.

---

[61] Early Christian martyr invoked by victims of nervous disorders.

[62] Bands of pro-British guerilas operating near New York during the Revolution.

[63] Small cannon.

[64] Scene of George Washington's defeat by the British near New York City in 1776.

But all these were nothing to the tales of ghosts and apparitions that succeeded. The neighborhood is rich in legendary treasures of the kind. Local tales and superstitions thrive best in these sheltered long-settled retreats; but are trampled under foot by the shifting throng that forms the population of most of our country places. Besides, there is no encouragement for ghosts in most of our villages, for they have scarcely had time to finish their first nap, and turn themselves in their graves, before their surviving friends have travelled away from the neighborhood; so that when they turn out at night to walk their rounds, they have no acquaintance left to call upon. This is perhaps the reason why we so seldom hear of ghosts except in our long-established Dutch communities.

The immediate cause, however, of the prevalence of supernatural stories in these parts, was doubtless owing to the vicinity of Sleepy Hollow. There was a contagion in the very air that blew from that haunted region; it breathed forth an atmosphere of dreams and fancies infecting all the land. Several of the Sleepy Hollow people were present at Van Tassel's, and, as usual, were doling out their wild and wonderful legends. Many dismal tales were told about funeral trains, and mourning cries and wailings heard and seen about the great tree where the unfortunate Major André[65] was taken, and which stood in the neighborhood. Some mention was made also of the woman in white, that haunted the dark glen at Raven Rock, and was often heard to shriek on winter nights before a storm, having perished there in the snow. The chief part of the stories, however, turned upon the favorite spectre of Sleepy Hollow, the headless horseman, who had been heard several times of late, patrolling the country; and, it was said, tethered his horse nightly among the graves in the churchyard.

The sequestered situation of this church seems always to have made it a favorite haunt of troubled spirits. It stands on a knoll, surrounded by locust-trees and lofty elms, from among which its decent whitewashed walls shine modestly forth, like Christian purity beaming through the shades of retirement. A gentle slope descends from it to a silver sheet of water, bordered by high trees, between which, peeps may be caught at the blue hills of the Hudson. To look upon its grass-grown yard, where the sunbeams seem to sleep so quietly, one would think that there at least the dead might rest in peace. On one side of the church extends a wide woody dell, along which raves a large brook among broken rocks and trunks of fallen trees. Over a deep black part of the stream, not far from the church, was formerly thrown a wooden bridge; the road that led to it, and the bridge itself, were thickly shaded by overhanging trees, which cast a gloom about it, even in the daytime; but occasioned a fearful darkness at night. This was one of the favorite haunts of the headless horseman; and the place where he was most frequently encountered. The tale was told of old Brouwer, a most heretical disbeliever in ghosts, how he met the horseman returning from his foray into Sleepy Hollow, and was obliged to get up behind him; how they galloped over bush and brake, over hill and swamp, until they reached the bridge; when the horseman suddenly turned into a skeleton, threw old Brouwer into the brook, and sprang away over the tree-tops with a clap of thunder.

This story was immediately matched by a thrice marvellous adventure of Brom Bones, who made light of the galloping Hessian as an arrant jockey.[66] He affirmed that, on returning one night from the neighboring village of Sing Sing,[67] he had been overtaken by this midnight trooper; that he had offered to race with him for a bowl of punch,

---

[65] John André (1751–1780), captured and executed as a British spy.

[66] Fraud or cheat.

[67] Now known as Ossining, New York.

and should have won it too, for Daredevil beat the goblin horse all hollow, but, just as they came to the church-bridge, the Hessian bolted, and vanished in a flash of fire.

All these tales, told in that drowsy undertone with which men talk in the dark, the countenances of the listeners only now and then receiving a casual gleam from the glare of a pipe, sank deep in the mind of Ichabod. He repaid them in kind with large extracts from his invaluable author, Cotton Mather, and added many marvellous events that had taken place in his native State of Connecticut, and fearful sights which he had seen in his nightly walks about Sleepy Hollow.

The revel now gradually broke up. The old farmers gathered together their families in their wagons, and were heard for some time rattling along the hollow roads, and over the distant hills. Some of the damsels mounted on pillions behind their favorite swains, and their light-hearted laughter, mingling with the clatter of hoofs, echoed along the silent woodlands, sounding fainter and fainter until they gradually died away—and the late scene of noise and frolic was all silent and deserted. Ichabod only lingered behind, according to the custom of country lovers, to have a tête-à-tête with the heiress, fully convinced that he was now on the high road to success. What passed at this interview I will not pretend to say, for in fact I do not know. Something, however, I fear me, must have gone wrong, for he certainly sallied forth, after no very great interval, with an air quite desolate and chop-fallen.—Oh these women! these women! Could that girl have been playing off any of her coquettish tricks?—Was her encouragement of the poor pedagogue all a mere sham to secure her conquest of his rival?—Heaven only knows, not I!—Let it suffice to say, Ichabod stole forth with the air of one who had been sacking a hen-roost, rather than a fair lady's heart. Without looking to the right or left to notice the scene of rural wealth, on which he had so often gloated, he went straight to the stable, and with several hearty cuffs and kicks, roused his steed most uncourteously from the comfortable quarters in which he was soundly sleeping, dreaming of mountains of corn and oats, and whole valleys of timothy and clover.

It was the very witching time of night[68] that Ichabod, heavy-hearted and crest-fallen, pursued his travel homewards, along the sides of the lofty hills which rise above Tarry Town, and which he had traversed so cheerily in the afternoon. The hour was as dismal as himself. Far below him, the Tappan Zee spread its dusky and indistinct waste of waters, with here and there the tall mast of a sloop, riding quietly at anchor under the land. In the dead hush of midnight, he could even hear the barking of the watch dog from the opposite shore of the Hudson; but it was so vague and faint as only to give an idea of his distance from this faithful companion of man. Now and then, too, the long-drawn crowing of a cock, accidentally awakened, would sound far, far off, from some farm-house away among the hills—but it was like a dreaming sound in his ear. No signs of life occurred near him, but occasionally the melancholy chirp of a cricket, or perhaps the guttural twang of a bull-frog, from a neighboring marsh, as if sleeping uncomfortably, and turning suddenly in his bed.

All the stories of ghosts and goblins that he had heard in the afternoon, now came crowding upon his recollection. The night grew darker and darker; the stars seemed to sink deeper in the sky, and driving clouds occasionally hid them from his sight. He had never felt so lonely and dismal. He was, moreover, approaching the very place where

---

68 As described in Shakespeare's *Hamlet,* Act III, Sc. ii, l. 406.

many of the scenes of the ghost stories had been laid. In the centre of the road stood an enormous tulip-tree, which towered like a giant above all the other trees of the neighborhood, and formed a kind of landmark. Its limbs were gnarled, and fantastic, large enough to form trunks for ordinary trees, twisting down almost to the earth, and rising again into the air. It was connected with the tragical story of the unfortunate André, who had been taken prisoner hard by; and was universally known by the name of Major André's tree. The common people regarded it with a mixture of respect and superstition, partly out of sympathy for the fate of its ill-starred namesake, and partly from the tales of strange sights and doleful lamentations told concerning it.

As Ichabod approached this fearful tree, he began to whistle: he thought his whistle was answered—it was but a blast sweeping sharply through the dry branches. As he approached a little nearer, he thought he saw something white, hanging in the midst of the tree—he paused and ceased whistling; but on looking more narrowly, perceived that it was a place where the tree had been scathed by lightning, and the white wood laid bare. Suddenly he heard a groan—his teeth chattered and his knees smote against the saddle: it was but the rubbing of one huge bough upon another, as they were swayed about by the breeze. He passed the tree in safety, but new perils lay before him.

About two hundred yards from the tree a small brook crossed the road, and ran into a marshy and thickly-wooded glen, known by the name of Wiley's swamp. A few rough logs, laid side by side, served for a bridge over this stream. On that side of the road where the brook entered the wood, a group of oaks and chestnuts, matted thick with wild grapevines, threw a cavernous gloom over it. To pass this bridge was the severest trial. It was at this identical spot that the unfortunate André was captured, and under the covert of those chestnuts and vines were the sturdy yoemen concealed who surprised him. This has ever since been considered a haunted stream, and fearful are the feelings of the schoolboy who has to pass it alone after dark.

As he approached the stream his heart began to thump; he summoned up, however, all his resolution, gave his horse half a score of kicks in the ribs, and attempted to dash briskly across the bridge; but instead of starting forward, the perverse old animal made a lateral movement, and ran broadside against the fence. Ichabod, whose fears increased with the delay, jerked the reins on the other side, and kicked lustily with the contrary foot: it was all in vain; his steed started, it is true, but it was only to plunge to the opposite side of the road into a thicket of brambles and alder bushes. The schoolmaster now bestowed both whip and heel upon the starveling ribs of old Gunpowder, who dashed forward, snuffling and snorting, but came to a stand just by the bridge, with a suddenness that had nearly sent his rider sprawling over his head. Just at this moment a plashy tramp by the side of the bridge caught the sensitive ear of Ichabod. In the dark shadow of the grove, on the margin of the brook, he beheld something huge, misshapen, black and towering. It stirred not, but seemed gathered up in the gloom, like some gigantic monster ready to spring upon the traveller.

The hair of the affrighted pedagogue rose upon his head with terror. What was to be done? To turn and fly was now too late; and besides, what chance was there of escaping ghost or goblin, if such it was, which could ride upon the wings of the wind? Summoning up, therefore, a show of courage, he demanded in stammering accents—"Who are you?" He received no reply. He repeated his demand in a still more agitated voice. Still there was no answer. Once more he cudgelled the sides of the inflexible Gunpowder, and, shutting his eyes, broke forth with involuntary fervor into a psalm tune. Just then the shadowy object of alarm put itself in motion, and, with a scramble and a bound, stood at once in the middle of the road. Though the night was dark and dismal, yet the form of the unknown might now in some degree be ascertained. He appeared to be a horseman of large dimensions, and mounted on a black horse of powerful frame. He made no offer of molestation or sociability, but kept aloof on one side of the road, jogging along on the blind side of old Gunpowder, who had now got over his fright and waywardness.

Ichabod, who had no relish for this strange midnight companion, and bethought himself of the adventure of Brom Bones with the Galloping Hessian, now quickened his steed, in hopes of leaving him behind. The stranger, however, quickened his horse to an equal pace. Ichabod pulled up, and fell into a walk, thinking to lag behind—the other did the same. His heart began to sink within him; he endeavored to resume his psalm tune, but his parched tongue clove to the roof of his mouth, and he could not utter a stave. There was something in the moody and dogged silence of this pertinacious companion, that was mysterious and appalling. It was soon fearfully accounted for. On mounting a rising ground, which brought the figure of his fellow-traveller in relief against the sky, gigantic in height, and muffled in a cloak, Ichabod was horror-struck, on perceiving that he was headless!—but his horror was still more increased, on observing that the head, which should have rested on his shoulders, was carried before him on the pommel of the saddle: his terror rose to desperation; he rained a shower of kicks and blows upon Gunpowder, hoping, by a sudden movement, to give his companion the slip—but the spectre started full jump with him. Away then they dashed, through thick and thin; stones flying, and sparks flashing at every bound. Ichabod's flimsy garments fluttered in the air, as he stretched his long lank body away over his horse's head, in the eagerness of his flight.

They had now reached the road which turns off to Sleepy Hollow; but Gunpowder, who seemed possessed with a demon, instead of keeping up it, made an opposite turn, and plunged headlong down hill to the left. This road leads through a sandy hollow, shaded by trees for about a quarter of a mile, where it crosses the bridge famous in goblin story, and just beyond swells the green knoll on which stands the whitewashed church.

As yet the panic of the steed had given his unskilful rider an apparent advantage in the chase; but just as he had got half way through the hollow, the girths of the saddle gave way, and he felt it slipping from under him. He seized it by the pommel, and endeavored to hold it firm, but in vain; and had just time to save himself by clasping old Gunpowder round the neck, when the saddle fell to the earth, and he heard it trampled under foot by his pursuer. For a moment the terror of Hans Van Ripper's wrath passed across his mind—for it was his Sunday saddle; but this was no time for petty fears; the goblin was hard on his haunches; and (unskilful rider that he was!) he had much ado to maintain his seat; sometimes slipping on one side, sometimes on another, and sometimes jolted on the high ridge of his horse's back-bone, with a violence that he verily feared would cleave him asunder.

An opening in the trees now cheered him with the hopes that the church bridge was at hand. The wavering reflection of a silver star in the bosom of the brook told him that he was not mistaken. He saw the walls of the church dimly glaring under the trees beyond. He recollected the place where Brom Bones's ghostly competitor had disappeared. "If I can but reach that bridge," thought Ichabod, "I am safe."[69] Just then he

[69] Superstition maintained that evil spirits
could not cross water.

heard the black steed panting and blowing close behind him; he even fancied that he felt his hot breath. Another convulsive kick in the ribs, and old Gunpowder sprang upon the bridge; he thundered over the resounding planks; he gained the opposite side; and now Ichabod cast a look behind to see if his pursuer should vanish, according to rule, in a flash of fire and brimstone. Just then he saw the goblin rising in his stirrups, and in the very act of hurling his head at him. Ichabod endeavored to dodge the horrible missile, but too late. It encountered his cranium with a tremendous crash—he was tumbled headlong into the dust, and Gunpowder, the black steed, and the goblin rider, passed by like a whirlwind.

The next morning the old horse was found without his saddle, and with the bridle under his feet, soberly cropping the grass at his master's gate. Ichabod did not make his appearance at breakfast—dinner-hour came, but no Ichabod. The boys assembled at the school-house, and strolled idly about the banks of the brook; but no schoolmaster. Hans Van Ripper now began to feel some uneasiness about the fate of poor Ichabod, and his saddle. An inquiry was set on foot, and after diligent investigation they came upon his traces. In one part of the road leading to the church was found the saddle trampled in the dirt; the tracks of horses' hoofs deeply dented in the road, and evidently at furious speed, were traced to the bridge, beyond which, on the bank of a broad part of the brook, where the water ran deep and black, was found the hat of the unfortunate Ichabod, and close beside it a shattered pumpkin.

The brook was searched, but the body of the schoolmaster was not to be discovered. Hans Van Ripper, as executor of his estate, examined the bundle which contained all his worldly effects. They consisted of two shirts and a half; two stocks[70] for the neck; a pair or two of worsted stockings; an old pair of corduroy small-clothes; a rusty razor; a book of psalm tunes, full of dogs' ears; and a broken pitchpipe. As to the books and furniture of the school-house, they belonged to the community, excepting Cotton Mather's History of Witchcraft, a New England Almanac, and a book of dreams and fortune-telling; in which last was a sheet of foolscap much scribbled and blotted in several fruitless attempts to make a copy of verses in honor of the heiress of Van Tassel. These magic books and the poetic scrawl were forthwith consigned to the flames by Hans Van Ripper; who from that time forward determined to send his children no more to school; observing, that he never knew any good come of this same reading and writing. Whatever money the schoolmaster possessed, and he had received his quarter's pay but a day or two before, he must have had about his person at the time of his disappearance.

The mysterious event caused much speculation at the church on the following Sunday. Knots of gazers and gossips were collected in the churchyard, at the bridge, and at the spot where the hat and pumpkin had been found. The stories of Brouwer, of Bones, and a whole budget of others, were called to mind; and when they had diligently considered them all, and compared them with the symptoms of the present case, they shook their heads, and came to the conclusion that Ichabod had been carried off by the galloping Hessian. As he was a bachelor, and in nobody's debt, nobody troubled his head any more about him. The school was removed to a different quarter of the hollow, and another pedagogue reigned in his stead.

It is true, an old farmer, who had been down to New York on a visit several years after, and from whom this account of the ghostly adventure was received, brought home

---

[70] Stock: scarf or cravat.

the intelligence that Ichabod Crane was still alive; that he had left the neighborhood, partly through fear of the goblin and Hans Van Ripper, and partly in mortification at having been suddenly dismissed by the heiress; that he had changed his quarters to a distant part of the country; had kept school and studied law at the same time, had been admitted to the bar, turned politician, electioneered, written for the newspapers, and finally had been made a justice of the Ten Pound Court.[71] Brom Bones too, who shortly after his rival's disappearance conducted the blooming Katrina in triumph to the altar, was observed to look exceedingly knowing whenever the story of Ichabod was related, and always burst into a hearty laugh at the mention of the pumpkin; which led some to suspect that he knew more about the matter than he chose to tell.

The old country wives, however, who are the best judges of these matters, maintain to this day that Ichabod was spirited away by supernatural means; and it is a favorite story often told about the neighborhood round the winter evening fire. The bridge became more than ever an object of superstitious awe, and that may be the reason why the road has been altered of late years, so as to approach the church by the border of the mill-pond. The school-house being deserted, soon fell to decay, and was reported to be haunted by the ghost of the unfortunate pedagogue; and the ploughboy, loitering homeward of a still summer evening, has often fancied his voice at a distance, chanting a melancholy psalm tune among the tranquil solitudes of Sleepy Hollow.

Postscript Found in the Handwriting of Mr. Knickerbocker.

The preceding Tale is given, almost in the precise words in which I heard it related at a Corporation meeting of the ancient city of Manhattoes,[72] at which were present many of its sagest and most illustrious burghers. The narrator was a pleasant, shabby, gentlemanly old fellow, in pepper-and-salt clothes, with a sadly humorous face; and one whom I strongly suspected of being poor,—he made such efforts to be entertaining. When his story was concluded, there was much laughter and approbation, particularly from two or three deputy aldermen, who had been asleep the greater part of the time. There was, however, one tall, dry-looking old gentleman, with beetling eyebrows, who maintained a grave and rather severe face throughout: now and then folding his arms, inclining his head, and looking down upon the floor, as if turning a doubt over in his mind. He was one of your wary men, who never laugh, but upon good grounds—when they have reason and the law on their side. When the mirth of the rest of the company had subsided, and silence was restored, he leaned one arm on the elbow of his chair, and, sticking the other akimbo, demanded, with a slight but exceedingly sage motion of the head, and contraction of the brow, what was the moral of the story, and what it went to prove?

The story-teller, who was just putting a glass of wine to his lips, as a refreshment after his toils, paused for a moment, looked at his inquirer with an air of infinite deference, and, lowering the glass slowly to the table, observed, that the story was intended most logically to prove:—

"That there is no situation in life but has its advantages and pleasures—provided we will but take a joke as we find it:

---

[71] Limited to cases involving no more than £10.
[72] i.e., New York City.

"That, therefore, he that runs races with goblin troopers is likely to have rough riding of it.

"Ergo, for a country schoolmaster to be refused the hand of a Dutch heiress, is a certain step to high preferment in the state."

The cautious old gentleman knit his brows tenfold closer after this explanation, being sorely puzzled by the ratiocination of the syllogism; while, methought, the one in pepper-and-salt eyed him with something of a triumphant leer. At length, he observed, that all this was very well, but still he thought the story a little on the extravagant—there were one or two points on which he had his doubts.

"Faith, sir," replied the story-teller, "as to that matter, I don't believe one-half of it myself."

1819–1820

D.K.

Cultural Portfolio
Asserting a National Language and Literature

America's cultivation of a literary identity bore its first fruits in the careers of Washington Irving and James Fenimore Cooper. The self-conscious drive to assert a national character, however, began much sooner, certainly as early as 1781 in the dozen fictionalized missives of French-born Michel Guillaume Jean de Crèvecoeur's *Letters from an American Farmer*. Pointedly investigating the emerging American character, Crèvecoeur wrote: "The American is a new man who acts upon new principles; he must therefore entertain new ideas, and form new opinions." A new language and a new literature must emerge, Crèvecoeur and other pragmatic theorists concluded, to express such new ideas and opinions.

The self-conscious drive for literary independence began soon after in Royall Tyler's 1787 play, *The Contrast*. The Prologue to this first comedy written and produced in the new republic asks:

Why should our thoughts to distant
    countries roam
When each refinement may be found
    at home?

Then, with ebullient nationalism, the Prologue begs the audience for a lenient judgment of the play's faults; this is, after all, a conscious first attempt to initiate a new dramatic literature. Ironically, Tyler's work, like that of the earliest American fiction writers, both male and female, depended on English and continental sources for its form. In content, however, the play's thematic contrast between a stalwart American and a foppish imitator of British fashion, its recognizable types speaking native dialect, and its New York setting mark it as distinctively American and set it apart from continental models and subject matter.

The landscape of the new republic proved just as important a stimulus to the literary imagination as the evolving American mind and character. Essayist Walter Channing concluded in 1815 that because "our country" was so different from England, "our descriptions" could not be made in the language of that other nation. Language suited for the falls at London bridge, he claimed, was too tame to describe the mighty Niagara Falls, and words suitable for the gently flowing Thames could not reflect the "majesty of the Mississippi." Other advocates of a new American literature expressed similar arguments in such periodicals as the *North American Review*, founded in 1815. Although a half dozen writers debated the pace and degree to which American writers should throw off the neoclassical forms and standards of their literary ancestors, these essayists did agree on one point: American writers must study the new national character, the expansive new landscape, and their distinctive experiences of both in order to create a national literature truly reflective of indigenous life.

Noah Webster made the study of the developing American language his life's work. *The American Spelling Book* (1783) was the first of Webster's efforts to define a specifically American language. He wanted to remove the "odious" regionalisms of provincial dialects, to standardize pronunciation, and to establish democratic guidelines based on "general custom" and the "rule of speaking." In speeches, letters, essays, and pamphlets he also argued for a republic as independent in its language as in its politics, and as famous for its arts as for its arms.

Webster's *Compendious Dictionary of the English Language* (1806) was the first dictionary compiled in the United States to be insistently American. Seeing language as an instrument of national unity, Webster spent another twenty years in research, at last producing in his *An American Dictionary of the English Language* (1828) a linguistic declaration of independence. The work became standard and achieved such immense popularity his name soon became synonymous with dictionary.

These cultural seeds of a native language and literature took root in fertile cultural soil. By 1846 Margaret Fuller could write at length about "American Literature" and exercise her considerable critical skills on a large body of American poetry and prose.

Cooper, she wrote, may have had obvious plots, shallow thought, and poverty in the presentation of character, but he had "grandeur and originality in his sea-sketches, and has redeemed from oblivion our forest-scenery and the noble romance of the hunter-pioneer's life." These strengths, she wrote, have done much to redeem "these irrevocable beauties from the corrosive acid of a semi-civilized invasion."

Fuller argued that the genius of an American literature would rise even higher when the "fusion of races among us is more complete." The American language, she and other essayists already knew, was an evolving "hybrid" tongue, and its literature, the vigorous creation of an unprecedented mix of races.

---

from Noah Webster, *Dissertations on the English Language*

"A National Language"

A *national language* is a bond of *national union*. Every engine should be employed to render the people of this country *national;* to call their attachments home to their own country; and to inspire them with the pride of national character. However they may boast of Independence, and the freedom of their government, yet their *opinions* are not sufficiently independent; an astonishing respect for the arts and literature of their parent country, and a blind imitation of its manners, are still prevalent among the Americans. Thus an habitual respect for another country, deserved indeed and once laudable, turns their attention from their own interests, and prevents their respecting themselves. . . .

America is in a situation the most favorable for great reformations; and the present time is, in a singular degree, auspicious. The minds of men in this country have been awakened. New scenes have been, for many years, presenting new occasions for exertion; unexpected distresses have called forth the powers of invention; and the application of new expedients has demanded every possible exercise of wisdom and talents. Attention is roused; the mind expanded; and the intellectual faculties invigorated. Here men are prepared to receive improvements, which would be rejected by nations, whose habits have not been shaken by similar events.

Now is the time, and *this* the country, in which we may expect success, in attempting changes favorable to language, science and government. Delay, in the plan here proposed, may be fatal; under a tranquil general government, the minds of men may again sink into indolence; a national acquiescence in error will follow; and posterity be doomed to struggle with difficulties, which time and accident will perpetually multiply.

Let us then seize the present moment and establish a *national language,* as well as a national government. Let us remember that there is a certain respect due to the opinions of other nations. As an independent people, our reputation abroad demands that, in all things, we should be federal; be *national;* for if we do not respect *ourselves,* we may be assured that *other nations* will not respect us. In short, let it be impressed upon the mind of every American, that to neglect the means of commanding respect abroad, is treason against the character and dignity of a brave independent people.

1789

Illustration from Noah Webster's *American Spelling Book*
Fable I: Of the Boy that stole Apples
1789
(Public domain)

from Noah Webster, *American Spelling Book*

Of the Boy that stole Apples

AN old Man found a rude Boy upon one of his trees stealing Apples, and desired him to come down; but the young Sauce-box told him plainly he would not. Won't you? said the old Man, then I will fetch you down; so he pulled up some tufts of Grass, and threw at him; but this only made the Youngster laugh, to think the old Man should pretend to beat him down from the tree with grass only.

Well, well, said the old Man, if neither words nor grass will do, I must try what virtue there is in Stones; so the old man pelted him heartily with stones; which soon made the young Chap hasten down from the tree and beg the old Man's pardon.

Moral

If good words and gentle means will not reclaim the wicked, they must be dealt with in a more severe manner.

from Michel-Guillaume Jean de Crèvecoeur, *Letters from an American Farmer*

from Letter III: What Is an American?

In this great American asylum, the poor of Europe have by some means met together, and in consequence of various causes; to what purpose should they ask one another what countrymen they are? Alas, two thirds of them had no country. Can a wretch who wanders about, who works and starves, whose life is a continual scene of sore affliction or pinching penury; can that man call England or any other kingdom his country? A country that had no bread for him, whose fields procured him no harvest, who met with nothing but the frowns of the rich, the severity of the laws, with jails and punishments; who owned not a single foot of the extensive surface of this planet? No! urged by a variety of motives, here they came. Every thing has tended to regenerate them; new laws, a new mode of living, a new social system; here they are become men: in Europe they were as so many useless plants, wanting vegetative mould, and refreshing showers; they withered, and were mowed down by want, hunger, and war; but now by the power of transplantation, like all other plants they have taken root and flourished! Formerly they were not numbered in any civil lists of their country, except in those of the poor; here they rank as citizens. By what invisible power has the surprising metamorphosis been performed? By that of the laws and that of their industry. The laws, the indulgent laws, protect them as they arrive, stamping on them the symbol of adoption; they receive ample rewards for their labours; these accumulated rewards procure them lands; those lands confer on them the title of freemen, and to that title every benefit is affixed which men can possibly require. This is the great operation daily performed by our laws. From whence proceed these laws? From our government. Whence the government? It is derived from the original genius and strong desire of the people ratified and confirmed by the crown. This is the great chain which links us all, this is the picture which every province exhibits, Nova Scotia excepted. There the crown has done all;[1] either there were no people who had genius, or it was not much attended to: the consequence is, that the province is very thinly inhabited indeed; the power of the crown in conjunction with the musketos has prevented men from settling there. Yet some parts of it flourished once, and it contained a mild harmless set of people. But for the fault of a few leaders, the whole were banished. The greatest political error the crown ever committed in America, was to cut off men from a country which wanted nothing but men!

What attachment can a poor European emigrant have for a country where he had nothing? The knowledge of the language, the love of a few kindred as poor as himself, were the only cords that tied him: his country is now that which gives him land, bread, protection, and consequence: *Ubi panis ibi patria,*[2] is the motto of all emigrants. What then is the American, this new man? He is either an European, or the descendant of an European, hence that strange mixture of blood, which you will find in no other country. I could point out to you a family whose grandfather was an Englishman, whose wife was Dutch, whose son married a French woman, and whose present four sons have now four

---

[1] In 1755 the English banished thousands of French settlers from Nova Scotia.

[2] Latin: "Where bread is, there is one's country."

wives of different nations. *He* is an American, who leaving behind him all his ancient prejudices and manners, receives new ones from the new mode of life he has embraced, the new government he obeys, and the new rank he holds. He becomes an American by being received in the broad lap of our great *Alma Mater*. Here individuals of all nations are melted into a new race of men, whose labours and posterity will one day cause great changes in the world. Americans are the western pilgrims, who are carrying along with them that great mass of arts, sciences, vigour, and industry which began long since in the east; they will finish the great circle. The Americans were once scattered all over Europe; here they are incorporated into one of the finest systems of population which has ever appeared, and which will hereafter become distinct by the power of the different climates they inhabit. The American ought therefore to love this country much better than that wherein either he or his forefathers were born. Here the rewards of his industry follow with equal steps the progress of his labour; his labour is founded on the basis of nature, *self-interest*; can it want a stronger allurement? Wives and children, who before in vain demanded of him a morsel of bread, now, fat and frolicsome, gladly help their father to clear those fields whence exuberant crops are to arise to feed and to clothe them all; without any part being claimed, either by a despotic prince, a rich abbot, or a mighty lord. Here

Unidentified Artist
frontispiece and title-page of the
"Columbian Magazine"
engraving, 1787
(Library Company of Philadelphia)

Unidentified Artist
Washington Giving the Laws to America
engraving
(The New York Public Library)

religion demands but little of him; a small voluntary salary to the minister, and gratitude to God; can he refuse these? The American is a new man, who acts upon new principles; he must therefore entertain new ideas, and form new opinions. From involuntary idleness, servile dependence, penury, and useless labour, he has passed to toils of a very different nature, rewarded by ample subsistence.—This is an American.

---

from Walter Channing, *American Language and Literature*

The whole external character of our country is totally unlike that of England. Our descriptions, of course, which must, if we ever have a poetry, be made in the language of another country, can never be distinctive. They can never possess the peculiar claims which those of native individuality teem with; which are more beautiful to a foreigner because he is willing in reading them to heighten the beauties of an obscure passage by lending it the aid of his own imagination. How tame will his language sound who would describe Niagara in language fitted for the falls at London bridge, or attempt the majesty of the Mississippi in that which was made for the Thames?
1815

---

from James Kirke Paulding, *Salmagundi, Second Series, Saturday, August 19, 1820*

A National Literature

It has been often observed by such as have attempted to account for the scarcity of romantic fiction among our native writers, that the history of the country affords few materials for such works, and offers little in its traditionary lore to warm the heart or elevate the imagination. The remark has been so often repeated that it is now pretty generally received with perfect docility, as an incontrovertible truth, though it seems to me without the shadow of a foundation. It is in fact an observation that never did nor ever will apply to any nation, ancient or modern.

Wherever there are men, there will be materials for romantic adventure. In the misfortunes that befall them; in the sufferings and vicissitudes which are everywhere the lot of human beings; in the struggles to counteract fortune, and in the conflicts of the passions, in every situation of life, he who studies nature and draws his pictures from her rich and inexhaustible sources of variety, will always find enough of those characters and incidents which give a relish to works of fancy. The aid of superstition, the agency of ghosts, fairies, goblins, and all that antiquated machinery which till lately was confined to the nursery, is not necessary to excite our wonder or interest our feelings; although it is not the least of incongruities, that in an age which boasts of having by its

Francis Kearney (after Gideon Fairman)
American Literature and Fine Arts Rewarding Patriotism and Virtue
engraving, 1815
(Library Company of Philadelphia)

scientific discoveries dissipated almost all the materials of superstition, some of the most popular fictions should be founded upon a superstition which is now become entirely ridiculous, even among the ignorant.

The best and most perfect works of imagination appear to me to be those which are founded upon a combination of such characters as every generation of men exhibits, and such events as have often taken place in the world, and will again. Such works are only fictions, because the tissue of events which they record never perhaps happened in precisely the same train, and to the same number of persons, as are exhibited and associated in the relation. Real life is fraught with adventures, to which the wildest fictions scarcely afford a parallel; and it has this special advantage over its rival, that these events, however extraordinary, can always be traced to motives, actions, and passions, arising out of circumstances no way unnatural, and partaking of no impossible or supernatural agency.

Hence it is, that the judgment and the fancy are both equally gratified in the perusal of this class of fictions, if they are skilfully conducted; while in those which have nothing to recommend them but appeals to the agency of beings in whose existence nobody believes, and whose actions of course can have no alliance either with nature or probability, it is the imagination alone that is satisfied, and that only by the total subjection of every other faculty of the mind. . . .

That these materials have as yet been little more than partially interwoven into the few fictions which this country has given birth to, is not owing to their being inapplicable to that purpose, but to another cause entirely. We have been misled by bad models, or the suffrages of docile critics, who have bowed to the influence of rank and fashion, and given testimony in favour of works which their better judgment must have condemned. We have cherished a habit of looking to other nations for examples of every kind, and debased the genius of this new world by making it the ape and the tributary of that of the old. We have imitated where we might often have excelled; we have overlooked our own rich resources, and sponged upon the exhausted treasury of our empoverished neighbours; we were born rich, and yet have all our lives subsisted by borrowing. Hence it has continually occurred, that those who might have gone before had they chosen a new path, have been content to come last, merely by following the old track. Many a genius that could and would have attained an equal height, in some new and unexplored region of fancy, has dwindled into insignificance and contempt by stooping to track some inferior spirit, to whom fashion had assigned a temporary elevation. They ought to be told, that though fashion may give a momentary popularity to works that neither appeal to national attachments, domestic habits, or those feelings which are the same yesterday, today, forever, and everywhere, still it is not by imitation they can hope to equal any thing great. It appears to me that the young candidate for the prize of genius, in the regions of invention and fancy, has but one path open to fame. He cannot hope to wing his way above those immortal works that have stood the test of ages, and are now with one consent recognised as specimens beyond which the intellect of man is not permitted to soar. But a noble prize is yet within his grasp, and worthy of the most aspiring ambition.

James Fenimore Cooper
1789–1851

James Fenimore Cooper's life spans America's cultural transformation—from the new nation's anxious efforts to establish a distinctive cultural identity to its confident expression of a truly distinguished literary tradition in the mid-nineteenth-century "renaissance." In 1789, the year of Cooper's birth, American writers self-consciously struggled with the lag between the new republic's political and cultural independence. In 1851, the year of Cooper's death, American readers had already seen the publication of most of Ralph Waldo Emerson's essays and poems, Edgar Allan Poe's tales and verse, Nathaniel Hawthorne's *The Scarlet Letter* (1850) and *House of the Seven Gables* (1851), and Herman Melville's *Moby-Dick* (1851). Henry David Thoreau's *Walden* (1854) and Walt Whitman's *Leaves of Grass* (1855) would follow within a few years of Cooper's death.

Writing in 1831 as an author celebrated both in the United States and abroad, Cooper proposed a literary ambition that he had little difficulty satisfying: America's "mental independence is my object, and if I can go down to the grave with the reflection that I have done a little towards it, I shall have the consolation of knowing that I have not been useless in my generation." Cooper's accomplishments far exceeded his literary aims. He was the first novelist to explore and define American themes, settings, and characters. He launched several distinct genres in American fiction: the American novel of manners, the sea novel, the European-American novel, and, in the "Leather-Stocking" series, the novel of the mythic frontier. Cooper also helped establish what has become the American writer's traditional role as a social and cultural critic.

Cooper's father, Judge William Cooper, a prominent political leader (a two-term member of Congress) as well as a wealthy merchant and landowner, passed on his ardent Federalist beliefs to his son. He entered Yale at age thirteen, steeped in Shakespeare and the major eighteenth-century English poets. Within two years, Cooper had been summarily dismissed by Timothy Dwight, then the president, for rowdy behavior and dangerous pranks.

Sent to sea by his father after his dismissal from Yale, Cooper served for two years as a deckhand on a merchant ship before being commissioned a midshipman in the navy, where he labored for the next three years. He resigned his commission in 1811 shortly after his marriage to Susan Augusta De Lancey, the daughter of a wealthy New York family with lingering Tory sentiments. His father died soon after—from a blow to the head received during a political dispute. Cooper's inheritance included more than fifty thousand dollars as well as his father's political and social conservatism. Quickly settled into a life as a country gentleman, Cooper revealed little initial interest in pursuing a career as a writer.

Cooper never freed himself completely from the legacy of his accomplished and strong-willed father. Their relationship in many respects previews the persistent tension evident both in Cooper's writing and in his nation's culture—the conflicting lures of the desire for personal and cultural originality and the attraction toward established forms and inherited contexts. This dual anxiety is most readily felt in

Cooper's—and his nation's—attitudes toward the future: at once a celebratory anticipation and an overarching fear that undisciplined originality would lead to chaos.

Cooper plunged into a literary career at age thirty, when his wife urged him to act on his claim that he could write a better novel than the sentimental tale of rural English life he had been reading aloud to her.

Impatient with his own first efforts, Cooper destroyed those initial attempts but soon completed a full-length manuscript, *Precaution* (1820). A novel of manners in the tradition of Jane Austen, *Precaution* proved his point and left him with a lifelong urge to write. As Cooper later explained in *A Letter to His Countrymen* (1834):

> Accident first made me a writer, and the same accident gave a direction to my pen. Ashamed to have fallen into the track of imitation, I endeavored to repair the wrong done to my own views, by producing a work that should be purely American, and of which love of country should be the theme.

With the Revolutionary War as a backdrop, *The Spy* demonstrated Cooper's belief that American history could be a suitable setting for fiction. Within a year, the best-selling novel was reprinted in several editions, turned into a play, and translated into several languages. Cooper had suddenly become the most popular American writer in Europe.

The frontier of his childhood provided the setting for his third novel, *The Pioneers; or, The Sources of the Susquehanna*. Set in the Otsego Lake region during the decade following the Revolutionary War, *The Pioneers* became the first in what would become a series of five "Leather-Stocking Tales": *The Pioneers* (1823), *The Last of the Mohicans* (1826), *The Prairie* (1827), *The Pathfinder* (1840), and *The Deerslayer* (1841). (In relation to plot, the sequence is *The Deerslayer, The Last of the Mohicans, The Pathfinder, The Pioneers*, and *The Prairie*.) Deriving their collective title from their hero's nickname (based on his habit of wearing long deerskin leggings), the "Leather-Stocking Tales" trace the life, adventures, and death of Natty Bumppo and his Indian companions, most notably the chieftain Chingachgook. A simple character whose love of the wilderness and dislike of civilization's restraints remain consistent—and uncompromised—throughout the series, Natty Bumppo possesses the moral resolve, generosity, and resourcefulness that set the standard for American fictional heroes well into the twentieth century.

Following the publication of *The Pioneers*, Cooper's attention to American settings and characters promptly shifted from the wilderness to the sea. The first of what would be Cooper's eleven sea novels, *The Pilot* (1823) blended technical detail, memorable characters (such as Long Tom Coffin), and patriotic appeal to create yet another enormously successful novel—a fictional precedent whose influence Herman Melville and Joseph Conrad would later generously acknowledge. In the short span of three years, Cooper had opened three new territories for American fiction: the nation's past, its frontier, and its life at sea.

By the mid-1820s, James Fenimore Cooper (he added his mother's maiden name in 1826) had established a formidable reputation in American literary circles. The success of *The Pioneers* prompted Cooper to resume his account of the adventures of the frontier scout Natty Bumppo in *The Last of the Mohicans* (1826) and *The Prairie* (1827), completing the latter while traveling in Europe. Initially drawn to the Continent because of his own poor health, his interest in introducing his daughters to

Italian and French culture, and his eagerness to protect his royalties abroad, Cooper spent the next seven years there, based primarily in Lyons, where he served, often rather casually, as the American consul. During this period he also wrote several more novels, three of which—*The Red Rover* (1827), *The Wept of Wishton-Wish* (1829), and *The Water Witch* (1830)—focus on American history and life at sea.

While abroad, Cooper unhesitatingly defended American culture and democracy from attacks by cynical British commentators. Cooper responded to these critics in *Notions of the Americans* (1828), a series of fictional letters from a sophisticated European traveler to a member of a geographic society. The book, however, pleased neither the Americans, who were increasingly alienated both by Cooper's long absence and by his association with European aristocracy, nor the English, who preferred the America depicted in *The Pioneers*. Cooper's seven years in Europe also marked a serious shift in his writing—from his early, largely optimistic writing to his later, more broad-ranging and highly critical work. The moral champion of American life would soon become one of its fiercest critics.

Cooper had set out for Europe during the presidency of John Quincy Adams. He returned to a far different place: Jacksonian America. Repulsed by what he regarded as President Jackson's vulgar and narrow version of frontier democracy, Cooper argued strenuously for a return to American life led by an elite minority, principally the Christian agrarian gentlemen of his youth. He was quickly judged a reactionary by the same Americans he had idealized while living abroad; he received neither the warm reception nor the privileged treatment afforded Washington Irving when he had returned from Europe the year before.

Cooper envisioned an America in which democratic gentlemen would provide the leadership necessary to explore the full potential of the New World. These paragons would combine a respect for tradition with a commitment to democratic values and reasoned change. Their position would be achieved by merit rather than birth, by manifest quality rather than privilege. For Cooper, moderation and balance were cardinal virtues. In his vision, America would embody neither the common excesses of frontier democracy nor the traditional arrogance of European aristocracy. America would mature into a democracy in which the access afforded by social mobility would elevate the best people to positions of power. Sorely disappointed by what he considered to be the mediocrity of the Jacksonian democracy, Cooper launched a series of polemic salvos at American behavior and belief.

Charged by the press with being a Tory renegade, Cooper spent a good deal of the rest of his life defending himself in public and suing his detractors for libel. More often than not, he won. He spent a good portion of each year in Cooperstown, where he enjoyed the companionship and support of his daughter Susan, who also served as his amanuensis. During these years, Cooper's prodigious talents had also produced a wide and varied range of fiction and nonfiction. Despite the extraordinary range of his literary interests and accomplishments, Cooper's fame in his own day and his importance in American cultural history depended primarily, he realized, on the reception of his "Leather-Stocking Tales." He resumed the series with the publication of the fourth volume, *The Pathfinder,* in 1840 and concluded his treatment of Natty Bumppo in *The Deerslayer* (1841). The popularity of the "Leather-Stocking" series, their articulation of an American mythos, their progressive departure from overt social engagement, and their definition of the frontier as the primary fact of American history truly distinguished these novels as classics in American literature. Yet later generations of American writers, most notably Mark Twain in his widely read essay "Fenimore Cooper's Literary Offenses," ridiculed Cooper's handling of language, syntax, dialogue, plot, narrative pace, and characterization—especially his portrayal of women. As James Russell Lowell wryly noted in *A Fable for Critics* (1848): "The women he draws from one model don't vary, / All sappy as maples and flat as a prairie." Such criticism reduced the "Leather-Stocking" series to the status of elementary school texts by the turn of the twentieth century. Renewed attention to Cooper's social criticism in the 1920s gradually led to a reassessment of the "Leather-Stocking" novels.

Although Cooper did have considerable difficulty developing a style to express adequately the distinctiveness of his American subject matter in the "Leather-Stocking Tales," he did unfold several themes that quickly took on mythic importance in American literary history. Cooper used some of the major thematic concerns of the series—advancing a sense of both temporal order and the past's continued presence—to help give shape to American history at a time when our nation's historical consciousness seemed precarious and ephemeral. Cooper's depiction of the American land—and more particularly his ability to envision personal freedom in the unencumbered space stretching beyond the confines of institutional life—enabled his "Leather-Stocking Tales" to transcend the creakiness of his plots and the clumsiness of his language. As a cultural mediator between civilization and the wilderness, Natty Bumppo served as the metaphor for all that Cooper achieved—an image of an ideal, balanced existence that receded ceaselessly into the past. As Cooper explained in his preface to the "Leather-Stocking Tales," Natty Bumppo was "a fit subject to represent the better qualities of both conditions, without pushing either to extremes." As such, Natty Bumppo is a prototypical American hero, an antecedent of, for example, Melville's Ishmael, Twain's Huck Finn, Faulkner's Ike McCaslin, and Hemingway's protagonists.

The sense of loss that increasingly dominates each of the "Leather-Stocking" novels illustrated—much like Cooper's social criticism—the shifting national views on America's direction and destiny in the first half of the nineteenth century. The pervasive melancholy of late-eighteenth- and early-nineteenth-century literature, which essentially shaped Cooper's writing, ceased to be merely a borrowed rhetorical device in the course of the "Leather-Stocking" series and became instead a way to conceptualize a recurring image in American writing—a gradual diminution of an impossible vision of the land, one that nonetheless remained a powerful *imagined* alternative to material progress.

James Fenimore Cooper died on September 14, 1851, in Cooperstown, New York. Less than two weeks later a memorial service was held in New York City, at which Washington Irving presided and Daniel Webster and William Cullen Bryant spoke.

Cooper's life and work had already taken on mythic dimensions. The breadth of his interests and the range of his accomplishments set the standards for nineteenth-century American writers. He was the first American novelist to create an extensive body of work. His social criticism helped define issues central to American identity—qualities of leadership, standards of excellence, measures for minority and majority voices, and the like. And just as the "Leather-Stocking Tales" had returned American culture to a pristine origin that defined all that was to follow, so too did Cooper's writing create a foundation for the careers of later writers and the directions of our nation's literary canon.

Cooper's work articulated a compelling sense of the literary potential of American history—of the possibilities implicit in its past, of the tensions and contradictions inherent in its present, of the pressures exerted by its uncertain and unprecedented future. Cooper helped accelerate America's literary development by formulating thematic patterns, narrative structures, and prototypical characters and situations that later writers would return to again and again in their own efforts to come to terms with America's distinctive cultural identity.

Further Reading:

W. C. Bryant, "Discourse on the Life and Genius of Cooper," in *Memorial of James Fenimore Cooper*, 1852.

S. F. Cooper, *The Cooper Gallery*, 1865.

D. H. Lawrence, *Studies in Classic American Literature*, 1923.

H. W. Boynton, *James Fenimore Cooper*, 1931.

R. E. Spiller, *Fenimore Cooper: Critic of His Times*, 1931.

V. W. Brooks, *The World of Washington Irving*, 1950.

J. Grossman, *James Fenimore Cooper*, 1947, 1967.

H. N. Smith, *Virgin Land*, 1957.

M. Bewley, *The Eccentric Design*, 1959.

D. A. Ringe, *James Fenimore Cooper*, 1962.

L. Fiedler, *Love and Death in the American Novel*, 1966.

R. Slotkin, *Regeneration Through Violence: The Mythology of the American Frontier, 1600–1860*, 1973.

H. D. Peck, *A World by Itself: The Pastoral Moment in Cooper's Fiction*, 1977.

S. Railton, *Fenimore Cooper: A Study of His Life and Imagination*, 1979.

W. Franklin, *The New World of James Fenimore Cooper*, 1982.

W. P. Kelly, *Plotting America's Past: Fenimore Cooper and the Leatherstocking Tales*, 1984.

P. Fisher, *Hard Facts*, 1985.

R. Clark, ed., *James Fenimore Cooper: New Critical Essays*, 1985.

J. Tompkins, *Sensational Designs: The Cultural Work of American Fiction*, 1985.

W. Motley, *The American Abraham: James Fenimore Cooper and the Frontier Patriarch*, 1987.

R. S. Levine, *Conspiracy and Romance: Studies in Brockden Brown, Cooper, Hawthorne, and Melville*, 1989.

C. H. Adams, "The Guardian of the Law": Authority and Identity in James Fenimore Cooper, 1990.

R. E. Long, *James Fenimore Cooper*, 1990.

G. Rans, *Cooper's Leather-Stocking Tales: A Secular Reading*, 1991.

Texts:

Notions of the Americans: Picked Up by a Travelling Bachelor, 1828.

The American Democrat, with an introduction by H. L. Mencken, 1956.

Cooper's Novels, 1859–1861.

The definitive edition of the works of James Fenimore Cooper, edited by James F. Beard, is being published by the State University of New York Press. See also *The Letters and Journals of James Fenimore Cooper*, ed. J. F. Beard, 6 vols., 1960–1968.

Preface to *The Leather-Stocking Tales**

This series of Stories, which has obtained the name of "The Leather-Stocking Tales," has been written in a very desultory and inartificial manner. The order in which the several books appeared was essentially different from that in which they would have been presented to the world, had the regular course of their incidents been consulted. In "The Pioneers," the first of the series written, the Leather-Stocking is represented as already old, and driven from his early haunts in the forest, by the sound of the axe and

---

* Written especially for a complete edition of *The Leather-Stocking Tales* that appeared in 1850.

the smoke of the settler. "The Last of the Mohicans," the next book in the order of pub-lication, carried the readers back to a much earlier period in the history of our hero, representing him as middle-aged, and in the fullest vigor of manhood. In "The Prairie," his career terminates, and he is laid in his grave. There, it was originally the intention to leave him, in the expectation that, as in the case of the human mass, he would soon be forgotten. But a latent regard for this character induced the author to resuscitate him in "The Pathfinder," a book that was not long after succeeded by "The Deerslayer," thus completing the series as it now exists.

While the five books that have been written were originally published in the order just mentioned, that of the incidents insomuch as they are connected with the career of their principal character, is, as has been stated, very different. Taking the life of the Leather-Stocking as a guide, "The Deerslayer" should have been the opening book, for in that work he is seen just emerging into manhood; to be succeeded by "The Last of the Mohicans," "The Pathfinder," "The Pioneers," and "The Prairie." This arrangement embraces the order of events, though far from being that in which the books at first ap-peared. "The Pioneers" was published in 1822;[1] "The Deerslayer" in 1841; making the interval between them nineteen years. Whether these progressive years have had a ten-dency to lessen the value of the last-named book, by lessening the native fire of its au-thor, or of adding somewhat in the way of improved taste and a more matured judg-ment, is for others to decide.

If anything from the pen of the writer of these romances is at all to outlive himself, it is, unquestionably, the series of "The Leather-Stocking Tales." To say this is not to pre-dict a very lasting reputation for the series itself, but simply to express the belief it will outlast any, or all, of the works from the same hand.

It is undeniable that the desultory manner in which "The Leather-Stocking Tales" were written has, in a measure, impaired their harmony, and otherwise lessened their interest. This is proved by the fate of the two books last published, though probably the two most worthy an enlightened and cultivated reader's notice. If the facts could be as-certained, it is probable the result would show that of all those (in America, in particu-lar) who have read the three first books of the series, not one in ten has a knowledge of the existence even of the two last. Several causes have tended to produce this result. The long interval of time between the appearance of "The Prairie" and that of "The Pathfinder" was itself a reason why the later books of the series should be overlooked. There was no longer novelty to attract attention, and the interest was materially im-paired by the manner in which events were necessarily anticipated, in laying the last of the series first before the world. With the generation that is now coming on the stage this fault will be partially removed by the edition contained in the present work, in which the several tales will be arranged solely in reference to their connection with each other.

The author has often been asked if he had any original in his mind, for the character of Leather-Stocking. In a physical sense, different individuals known to the writer in early life certainly presented themselves as models, through his recollections; but in a moral sense this man of the forest is purely a creation. The idea of delineating a charac-ter that possessed little of civilization but its highest principles as they are exhibited in the uneducated, and all of savage life that is not incompatible with these great rules of

[1] *The Pioneers* did not appear until February 1823.

conduct, is perhaps natural to the situation in which Natty was placed. He is too proud of his origin to sink into the condition of the wild Indian, and too much a man of the woods not to imbibe as much as was at all desirable from his friends and companions. In a moral point of view it was the intention to illustrate the effect of seed scattered by the wayside. To use his own language, his "gifts" were "white gifts," and he was not disposed to bring on them discredit. On the other hand, removed from nearly all the temptations of civilized life, placed in the best associations of that which is deemed savage, and favorably disposed by nature to improve such advantages, it appeared to the writer that his hero was a fit subject to represent the better qualities of both conditions, without pushing either to extremes.

There was no violent stretch of the imagination, perhaps, in supposing one of civilized associations in childhood retaining many of his earliest lessons amid the scenes of the forest. Had these early impressions, however, not been sustained by continued though casual connection with men of his own color, if not of his own caste, all our information goes to show he would soon have lost every trace of his origin. It is believed that sufficient attention was paid to the particular circumstances in which this individual was placed, to justify the picture of his qualities that has been drawn. The Delawares early attracted the attention of the missionaries, and were a tribe unusually influenced by their precepts and example. In many instances they became Christians, and cases occurred in which their subsequent lives gave proof of the efficacy of the great moral changes that had taken place within them.

A leading character in a work of fiction has a fair right to the aid which can be obtained from a poetical view of the subject. It is in this view, rather than in one more strictly circumstantial, that Leather-Stocking has been drawn. The imagination has no great task in portraying to itself a being removed from the every-day inducements to err which abound in civilized life, while he retains the best and simplest of his early impressions; who sees God in the forest; hears him in the winds; bows to him in the firmament that o'ercanopies all; submits to his sway in a humble belief of his justice and mercy—in a word, a being who finds the impress of the Deity in all the works of nature, without any of the blots produced by the expedients, and passion, and mistakes of man. This is the most that has been attempted in the character of Leather-Stocking. Had this been done without any of the drawbacks of humanity, the picture would have been, in all probability, more pleasing than just. In order to preserve the *vraisemblable*,[2] therefore, traits derived from the prejudices, tastes, and even the weaknesses of his youth, have been mixed up with these higher qualities and longings, in a way, it is hoped, to represent a reasonable picture of human nature, without offering to the spectator a "monster of goodness."

It has been objected to these books that they give a more favorable picture of the red man than he deserves. The writer apprehends that much of this objection arises from the habits of those who have made it. One of his critics, on the appearance of the first work in which Indian character was portrayed, objected that its "characters were Indians of the school of Heckewelder,[3] rather than of the school of nature." These words quite probably contain the substance of the true answer to the objection. Heckewelder

---

[2] French: "verisimilitude." In a literary sense, realism.

[3] John Gottlieb Heckewelder (1743–1823), pioneer Moravian missionary among the Indians.

was an ardent, benevolent missionary, bent on the good of the red man, and seeing in him one who had the soul, reason, and characteristics of a fellow-being. The critic is understood to have been a very distinguished agent of the government, one very familiar with Indians, as they are seen at the councils to treat for the sale of their lands, where little or none of their domestic qualities come in play, and where, indeed, their evil passions are known to have the fullest scope. As just would it be to draw conclusions of the general state of American society from the scenes of the capital, as to suppose that the negotiating of one of these treaties is a fair picture of Indian life.

It is the privilege of all writers of fiction, more particularly when their works aspire to the elevation of romances, to present the *beau-idéal*[4] of their characters to the reader. This it is which constitutes poetry, and to suppose that the red man is to be represented only in the squalid misery or in the degraded moral state that certainly more or less belongs to his condition, is, we apprehend, taking a very narrow view of an author's privileges. Such criticism would have deprived the world of even Homer.

1850

The Deerslayer

Chapter VII
The Commencement of a Career in Forest Exploits

"Clear, placid Leman! Thy contrasted lake
With the wild world I dwelt in, is a thing
Which warns me, with its stillness, to forsake
Earth's troubled waters for a purer spring.
This quiet sail is as a noiseless wing
To waft me from distraction: once I loved
Torn ocean's roar, but thy soft murmuring
Sounds sweet as if a sister's voice reproved,
  That I with stern delights should e'er have been so
  moved."[1]
   Byron.

Day had fairly dawned before the young man, whom we have left in the situation described in the last chapter, again opened his eyes. This was no sooner done than he started up and looked about him with the eagerness of one who suddenly felt the importance of accurately ascertaining his precise position. His rest had been deep and undisturbed; and when he awoke, it was with a clearness of intellect and a readiness of

---

[4] French: "highest form of beauty."
[1] *Childe Harold's Pilgrimage* (Canto III, stanza 85), by George Gordon, Lord Byron (1788–1824).

resources that were much needed at that particular moment. The sun had not risen, it is true, but the vault of heaven was rich with the winning softness that "brings and shuts the day," while the whole air was filled with the carols of birds, the hymns of the feathered tribe. These sounds first told Deerslayer the risks he ran. The air—for wind it could scarce be called—was still light, it is true, but it had increased a little in the course of the night, and as the canoes were mere feathers on the water, they had drifted twice the expected distance; and, what was still more dangerous, had approached so near the base of the mountain, that here rose precipitously from the eastern shore, as to render the carols of the birds plainly audible. This was not the worst. The third canoe had taken the same direction, and was slowly drifting toward a point where it must inevitably touch, unless turned aside by a shift of wind or human hands. In other respects, nothing presented itself to attract attention or to awaken alarm. The castle stood on its shoal, nearly abreast of the canoes, for the drift had amounted to miles in the course of the night, and the ark lay fastened to its piles, as both had been left so many hours before.

As a matter of course, Deerslayer's attention was first given to the canoe ahead. It was already quite near the point, and a very few strokes of the paddle sufficed to tell him that it must touch before he could possibly overtake it. Just at this moment, too, the wind inopportunely freshened, rendering the drift of the light craft much more rapid and certain. Feeling the impossibility of preventing a contact with the land, the young man wisely determined not to heat himself with unnecessary exertions; but first looking to the priming of his piece, he proceeded slowly and warily toward the point, taking care to make a little circuit, that he might be exposed on only one side as he approached.

The canoe adrift, being directed by no such intelligence, pursued its proper way and grounded on a small sunken rock, at the distance of three or four yards from the shore. Just at that moment, Deerslayer had got abreast of the point and turned the bows of his own boat to the land; first casting loose his tow, that his movements might be unencumbered. The canoe hung an instant on the rock; then it rose a hair's-breadth on an almost imperceptible swell of the water, swung round, floated clear, and reached the strand. All this the young man noted, but it neither quickened his pulses nor hastened his hand. If any one had been lying in wait for the arrival of the waif, he must be seen, and the utmost caution in approaching the shore became indispensable; if no one was in ambush, hurry was unnecessary. The point being nearly diagonally opposite to the Indian encampment, he hoped the last, though the former was not only possible, but probable; for the savages were prompt in adopting all the expedients of their particular modes of warfare, and quite likely had many scouts searching the shores for craft to carry them off to the castle. As a glance at the lake from any height or projection would expose the smallest object on its surface, there was little hope that either of the canoes could pass unseen; and Indian sagacity needed no instruction to tell which way a boat or a log would drift, when the direction of the wind was known. As Deerslayer drew nearer and nearer to the land, the stroke of his paddle grew slower, his eye became more watchful, and his ears and nostrils almost dilated with the effort to detect any lurking danger. 'Twas a trying moment for a novice, nor was there the encouragement which even the timid sometimes feel, when conscious of being observed and commended. He was entirely alone, thrown on his own resources, and was cheered by no friendly eye, emboldened by no encouraging voice. Notwithstanding all these circumstances, the most experienced veteran in forest warfare could not have behaved better. Equally free from recklessness and hesitation, his advance was marked by a sort of philosophical prudence, that appeared to render him superior to all motives but those which were best calculated to effect his purpose. Such was the commencement of a career in forest exploits, that afterward rendered this man, in his way, and under the limits of his habits and opportunities, as renowned as many a hero whose name has adorned the pages of works more celebrated than legends simple as ours can ever become.

When about a hundred yards from the shore, Deerslayer rose in the canoe, gave three or four vigorous strokes with the paddle, sufficient of themselves to impel the bark to land, and then quickly laying aside the instrument of labor, he seized that of war. He was in the very act of raising the rifle, when a sharp report was followed by the buzz of a bullet that passed so near his body as to cause him involuntarily to start. The next instant Deerslayer staggered and fell his whole length in the bottom of the canoe. A yell—it came from a single voice—followed, and an Indian leaped from the bushes upon the open area of the point, bounding toward the canoe. This was the moment the young man desired. He rose on the instant and levelled his own rifle at his uncovered foe; but his finger hesitated about pulling the trigger on one whom he held at such a disadvantage. This little delay, probably, saved the life of the Indian, who bounded back into the cover as swiftly as he had broken out of it. In the mean time Deerslayer had been swiftly approaching the land, and his own canoe reached the point just as his enemy disappeared. As its movements had not been directed, it touched the shore a few yards from the other boat; and though the rifle of his foe had to be loaded, there was not time to secure his prize and to carry it beyond danger before he would be exposed to another shot. Under the circumstances, therefore, he did not pause an instant, but dashed into the woods and sought a cover.

On the immediate point there was a small open area, partly in native grass and partly beach, but a dense fringe of bushes lined its upper side. This narrow belt of dwarf vegetation passed, one issued immediately into the high and gloomy vaults of the forest. The land was tolerably level for a few hundred feet, and then it rose precipitously in a mountain-side. The trees were tall, large, and so free from underbrush that they resembled vast columns, irregularly scattered, upholding a dome of leaves. Although they stood tolerably close together, for their ages and size, the eye could penetrate to considerable distances; and bodies of men, even, might have engaged beneath their cover with concert and intelligence.

Deerslayer knew that his adversary must be employed in reloading, unless he had fled. The former proved to be the case, for the young man had no sooner placed himself behind a tree than he caught a glimpse of the arm of the Indian, his body being concealed by an oak, in the very act of forcing the leathered bullet home. Nothing would have been easier than to spring forward and decide the affair by a close assault on his unprepared foe; but every feeling of Deerslayer revolted at such a step, although his own life had just been attempted from a cover. He was yet unpractised in the ruthless expedients of savage warfare, of which he knew nothing except by tradition and theory, and it struck him as an unfair advantage to assail an unarmed foe. His color had heightened, his eye frowned, his lips were compressed, and all his energies were collected and ready; but, instead of advancing to fire, he dropped his rifle to the usual position of a sportsman in readiness to catch his aim, and muttered to himself, unconscious that he was speaking:

"No, no—that may be red-skin warfare, but it's not a Christian's gifts. Let the miscreant charge, and then we'll take it out like men; for the canoe he *must* not and *shall* not have. No, no; let him have time to load, and God will take care of the right!"

All this time the Indian had been so intent on his own movements that he was even ignorant that his enemy was in the wood. His only apprehension was, that the canoe would be recovered and carried away before he might be in readiness to prevent it. He had sought the cover from habit, but was within a few feet of the fringe of bushes, and could be at the margin of the forest in readiness to fire in a moment. The distance between him and his enemy was about fifty yards, and the trees were so arranged by nature that the line of sight was not interrupted, except by the particular trees behind which each party stood.

His rifle was no sooner loaded than the savage glanced around him, and advanced incautiously as regarded the real, but stealthily as respected the fancied position of his enemy, until he was fairly exposed. Then Deerslayer stepped from behind his own cover and hailed him.

"This-a-way, red-skin; this-a-way, if you're looking for me," he called out. "I'm young in war, but not so young as to stand on an open beach to be shot down like an owl by daylight. It rests on yourself whether it's peace or war atween us; for my gifts are white gifts, and I'm not one of them that thinks it valiant to slay human mortals singly in the woods."

The savage was a good deal startled by this sudden discovery of the danger he ran. He had a little knowledge of English, however, and caught the drift of the other's meaning. He was also too well schooled to betray alarm, but, dropping the butt of his rifle to the earth with an air of confidence, he made a gesture of lofty courtesy. All this was done with the ease and self-possession of one accustomed to consider no man his superior. In the midst of this consummate acting, however, the volcano that raged within caused his eyes to glare and his nostrils to dilate like those of some wild beast that is suddenly prevented from taking the fatal leap.

"Two canoe," he said, in the deep guttural tones of his race, holding up the number of fingers he mentioned, by way of preventing mistakes; "one for you—one for me."

"No, no, Mingo,[2] that will never do. You own neither; and neither shall you have, as long as I can prevent it. I know it's war atween your people and mine, but that's no reason why human mortals should slay each other like savage creatur's that meet in the woods; go your way, then, and leave me to go mine. The world is large enough for us both; and when we meet fairly in battle, why, the Lord will order the fate of each of us."

"Good!" exclaimed the Indian; "my brother missionary—great talk; all about Manitou."[3]

"Not so—not so, warrior. I'm not good enough for the Moravians,[4] and am too good for most of the other vagabonds that preach about in the woods. No, no, I'm only a hunter, as yet, though afore the peace is made, 'tis like enough there'll be occasion to strike a blow at some of your people. Still, I wish it to be done in fair fight, and not in a quarrel about the ownership of a miserable canoe."

---

[2] Slang term for an Iroquois or Sioux brave.
[3] One of the great spirits that rule nature.

[4] Early sect of devout European missionaries who preached among the Indians.

"Good! My brother very young—but he very wise. Little warrior—great talker. Chief, sometimes, in council."

"I don't know this, nor do I say it, Injin," returned Deerslayer, coloring a little at the ill-concealed sarcasm of the other's manner; "I look forward to a life in the woods, and I only hope it may be a peaceable one. All young men must go on the war-path when there's occasion, but war isn't needfully massacre. I've seen enough of the last, this very night, to know that Providence frowns on it; and I now invite you to go your own way, while I go mine; and hope that we may part fri'nds."

"Good! My brother has two scalp—grey hair under t'other. Old wisdom—young tongue."

Here the savage advanced with confidence, his hand extended, his face smiling, and his whole bearing denoting amity and respect. Deerslayer met his offered friendship in a proper spirit, and they shook hands cordially, each endeavoring to assure the other of his sincerity and desire to be at peace.

"All have his own," said the Indian; "my canoe, mine; your canoe, your'n. Go look; if your'n, you keep; if mine, I keep."

"That's just, red-skin; though you must be wrong in thinking the canoe your property. Howsever, seein' is believin', and we'll go down to the shore, where you may look with your own eyes; for it's likely you'll object to trustin' altogether to mine."

The Indian uttered his favorite exclamation of "good!" and then they walked side by side toward the shore. There was no apparent distrust in the manner of either, the Indian moving in advance, as if he wished to show his companion that he did not fear turning his back to him. As they reached the open ground the former pointed toward Deerslayer's boat, and said emphatically:

"No mine—pale-face canoe. *This* red-man's. No want other man's canoe—want his own."

"You're wrong, red-skin, you're altogether wrong. This canoe was left in old Hutter's keeping, and is his'n according to all law, red or white, till its owner comes to claim it. Here's the seats and the stitching of the bark to speak for themselves. No man ever know'd an Injin to turn off such work."

"Good! My brother little ole—big wisdom. Injin no make him. White man's work."

"I'm glad you think so, for holding out to the contrary might have made ill blood atween us; every one having a right to take possession of his own. I'll just shove the canoe out of reach of dispute at once, as the quickest way of settling difficulties."

While Deerslayer was speaking he put a foot against the end of the light boat, and giving a vigorous shove, he sent it out into the lake a hundred feet or more, where, taking the true current, it would necessarily float past the point and be in no further danger of coming ashore. The savage started at this ready and decided expedient, and his companion saw that he cast a hurried and fierce glance at his own canoe, or that which contained the paddles. The change of manner, however, was but momentary, and then the Iroquois resumed his air of friendliness and a smile of satisfaction.

"Good!" he repeated, with stronger emphasis than ever. "Young head, old mind. Know how to settle quarrel. Farewell, brother. He go to house in water—muskrat house—Injin go to camp; tell chiefs no find canoe."

Deerslayer was not sorry to hear this proposal, for he felt anxious to join the females, and he took the offered hand of the Indian very willingly. The parting words were friendly, and, while the red-man walked calmly toward the wood, with the rifle in the hollow of his arm, without once looking back in uneasiness or distrust, the white man moved toward the remaining canoe, carrying his piece in the same pacific manner, it is true, but keeping his eyes fastened on the movements of the other. This distrust, however, seemed to be altogether uncalled for, and as if ashamed to have entertained it, the young man averted his look and stepped carelessly up to his boat. Here he began to push the canoe from the shore and to make his other preparations for departing. He might have been thus employed a minute, when, happening to turn his face toward the land, his quick and certain eye told him at a glance the imminent jeopardy in which his life was placed. The black, ferocious eyes of the savage were glancing on him, like those of the crouching tiger, through a small opening in the bushes, and the muzzle of his rifle seemed already to be opening in a line with his own body.

Then, indeed, the long practice of Deerslayer, as a hunter, did him good service. Accustomed to fire with the deer on the bound, and often when the precise position of the animal's body had in a manner to be guessed at, he used the same expedients here. To cock and poise his rifle were the acts of a single moment and a single motion; then, aiming almost without sighting, he fired into the bushes where he knew a body ought to be, in order to sustain the appalling countenance which alone was visible. There was not time to raise the piece any higher or to take a more deliberate aim. So rapid were his movements that both parties discharged their pieces at the same instant, the concussions mingling in one report. The mountains, indeed, gave back but a single echo. Deerslayer dropped his piece and stood, with head erect, steady as one of the pines in the calm of a June morning, watching the result; while the savage gave the yell that has become historical for its appalling influence leaped through the bushes and came bounding across the open ground, flourishing a tomahawk. Still Deerslayer moved not, but stood with his unloaded rifle fallen against his shoulders, while, with a hunter's habits, his hands were mechanically feeling for the powder-horn and charger. When about forty feet from his enemy, the savage hurled his keen weapon; but it was with an eye so vacant and a hand so unsteady and feeble that the young man caught it by the handle as it was flying past him. At that instant the Indian staggered and fell his whole length on the ground.

"I know'd it—I know'd it!" exclaimed Deerslayer, who was already preparing to force a fresh bullet into his rifle; "I know'd it must come to this, as soon as I had got the range from the creatur's eyes. A man sights suddenly and fires quick when his own life's in danger; yes, I know'd it would come to this. I was about the hundredth part of a second too quick for him, or it might have been bad for me! The riptyle's bullet has just grazed my side—but, say what you will for or ag'in 'em, a red-skin is by no means as sartain with powder and ball as a white man. Their gifts don't seem to lie that-a-way. Even Chingachgook,[5] great as he is in other matters, isn't downright deadly with the rifle."

By this time the piece was reloaded, and Deerslayer, after tossing the tomahawk into the canoe, advanced to his victim, and stood over him, leaning on his rifle, in melancholy attention. It was the first instance in which he had seen a man fall in battle—it

[5] A young Mohican chief of the larger Delaware tribe, he is also Deerslayer's Indian "blood-brother." Natty Bumppo was orphaned at an early age and was partially raised by the Delaware Indians. Chingachgook plays a significant role in both *The Deerslayer* and *The Last of the Mohicans*.

was the first fellow-creature against whom he had ever seriously raised his own hand. The sensations were novel; and regret, with the freshness of our better feelings, mingled with his triumph. The Indian was not dead, though shot directly through the body. He lay on his back motionless, but his eyes, now full of consciousness, watched each action of his victor—as the fallen bird regards the fowler—jealous of every movement. The man probably expected the fatal blow which was to precede the loss of his scalp; or perhaps he anticipated that this latter act of cruelty would precede his death. Deerslayer read his thoughts; and he found a melancholy satisfaction in relieving the apprehensions of the helpless savage.

"No, no, red-skin," he said; "you've nothing more to fear from me. I am of a Christian stock, and scalping is not of my gifts. I'll just make sartain of your rifle and then come back and do you what service I can. Though here I can't stay much longer, as the crack of three rifles will be apt to bring some of your devils down upon me."

The close of this was said in a sort of a soliloquy, as the young man went in quest of the fallen rifle. The piece was found where its owner had dropped it, and was immediately put into the canoe. Laying his own rifle at its side, Deerslayer then returned and stood over the Indian again.

"All inmity atween you and me's at an ind, red-skin," he said; "and you may set your heart at rest on the score of the scalp or any further injury. My gifts are white, as I've told you; and I hope my conduct will be white also!"

Could looks have conveyed all they meant, it is probable Deerslayer's innocent vanity on the subject of color would have been rebuked a little; but he comprehended the gratitude that was expressed in the eyes of the dying savage, without in the least detecting the bitter sarcasm that struggled with the better feeling.

"Water!" ejaculated the thirsty and unfortunate creature; "give poor Injun water."

"Aye, water you shall have, if you drink the lake dry. I'll just carry you down to it, that you may take your fill. This is the way, they tell me, with all wounded people—water is their greatest comfort and delight."

So saying, Deerslayer raised the Indian in his arms, and carried him to the lake. Here he first helped him to take an attitude in which he could appease his burning thirst; after which he seated himself on a stone and took the head of his wounded adversary in his own lap and endeavored to soothe his anguish in the best manner he could.

"It would be sinful in me to tell you your time hadn't come, warrior," he commenced, "and therefore I'll not say it. You've passed the middle age already, and, considerin' the sort of lives ye lead, your days have been pretty well filled. The principal thing now is to look forward to what comes next. Neither red-skin nor pale-face, on the whole, calculates much on sleepin' forever; but both expect to live in another world. Each has his gifts, and will be judged by 'em, and, I suppose, you've thought these matters over enough, not to stand in need of sarmons when the trial comes. You'll find your happy hunting-grounds, if you've been a just Injin; if an onjust, you'll meet your desarts in another way. I've my own idees about these things; but you're too old and exper'enced to need any explanations from one as young as I."

"Good!" ejaculated the Indian, whose voice retained its depth even as life ebbed away; "young head—ole wisdom!"

"It's sometimes a consolation, when the ind comes, to know that them we've harmed, or *tried* to harm, forgive us. I suppose natur' seeks this relief, by way of getting a pardon on 'arth; as we never can know whether He pardons, who is all in all, till judgment itself comes. It's soothing to know that *any* pardon at such times; and that, I conclude, is the secret. Now, as for myself, I overlook altogether your designs ag'in my life; first, because no harm came of 'em; next, because it's your gifts and natur' and trainin', and I ought not to have trusted you at all; and, finally and chiefly, because I can bear no ill-will to a dying man, whether heathen or Christian. So put your heart at ease, so far as I'm consarned; you know best what other matters ought to trouble you, or what ought to give you satisfaction in so trying a moment."

It is probable that the Indian had some of the fearful glimpses of the unknown state of being which God in mercy seems at times to afford to all the human race; but they were necessarily in conformity with his habits and prejudices. Like most of his people, and like too many of our own, he thought more of dying in a way to gain applause among those he left than to secure a better state of existence hereafter. While Deerslayer was speaking, his mind was a little bewildered, though he felt that the intention was good; and when he had done, a regret passed over his spirit that none of his own tribe were present to witness his stoicism under extreme bodily suffering, and the firmness with which he met his end. With the high innate courtesy that so often distinguishes the Indian warrior before he becomes corrupted by too much intercourse with the worst class of the white men, he endeavored to express his thankfulness for the other's good intentions, and to let him understand that they were appreciated.

"Good!" he repeated, for this was an English word much used by the savages— "good—young head; young *heart*, too. *Old* heart tough; no shed tear. Hear Indian when he die, and no want to lie—what he call him?"

"Deerslayer is the name I bear now, though the Delawares have said that when I get back from this war-path, I shall have a more manly title, provided I can 'arn one."

"That good name for boy—poor name for warrior. He get better quick. No fear *there*"—the savage had strength sufficient, under the strong excitement he felt, to raise a hand and tap the young man on his breast—"eye sartain—finger lightning—aim, death— great warrior soon. No Deerslayer—Hawkeye—Hawkeye—Hawkeye. Shake hand."

Deerslayer—or Hawkeye, as the youth was then first named, for in after years he bore the appellation throughout all that region—Deerslayer took the hand of the savage, whose last breath was drawn in that attitude, gazing in admiration at the countenance of a stranger, who had shown so much readiness, skill, and firmness, in a scene that was equally trying and novel. When the reader remembers it is the highest gratification an Indian can receive to see his enemy betray weakness, he will be better able to appreciate the conduct which had extorted so great a concession at such a moment.

"His spirit has fled!" said Deerslayer, in a suppressed, melancholy voice. "Ah's me! Well, to this we must all come, sooner or later; and he is happiest, let his skin be of what color it may, who is best fitted to meet it. Here lies the body of no doubt a brave warrior, and the soul is already flying toward its heaven or hell, whether that be a happy hunting-ground, a place scant of game; regions of glory, according to Moravian doctrine, or flames of fire! So it happens, too, as regards other matters! Here have old Hutter and Hurry Harry got themselves into difficulty, if they hav'n't got themselves into torment and death, and all for a bounty that luck offers to me in what many would think a lawful and suitable manner. But not a farthing of such money shall cross my hand. White I was born, and white will I die; clinging to color to the last, even though the King's Majesty, his governors, and all his councils, both at home and in the Colonies, forget from what they come, and where they hope to go, and all for a little advantage in warfare. No, no—warrior, hand of mine shall never molest your scalp, and so your soul may rest in peace on the p'int of making a decent appearance, when the body comes to join it, in your own land of spirits."

Deerslayer arose as soon as he had spoken. Then he placed the body of the dead man in a sitting posture, with its back against the little rock, taking the necessary care to prevent it from falling or in any way settling into an attitude that might be thought unseemly by the sensitive, though wild, notions of a savage. When this duty was performed, the young man stood gazing at the grim countenance of his fallen foe, in a sort of melancholy abstraction. As was his practice, however, a habit gained by living so much alone in the forest, he then began again to give utterance to his thoughts and feelings aloud.

"I didn't wish your life, red-skin," he said, "but you left me no choice atween killing or being killed. Each party acted according to his gifts, I suppose, and blame can light on neither. You were treacherous, according to your natur' in war, and I was a little oversightful, as I'm apt to be in trusting others. Well, this is my first battle with a human mortal, though it's not likely to be the last. I have fou't most of the creatur's of the forest, such as bears, wolves, painters,[6] and catamounts,[7] but this is the beginning with the red-skins. If I was Injin born, now, I might tell of this, or carry in the scalp, and boast of the expl'ite afore the whole tribe; or, if my inimy had only been even a bear, 'twould have been nat'ral and proper to let everybody know what had happened; but I don't well see how I'm to let even Chingachgook into this secret, so long as it can be done only by boasting with a white tongue. And why should I wish to boast of it a'ter all? It's slaying a human, although he was a savage; and how do I know that he was a just Injin; and that he has not been taken away suddenly to anything but happy hunting-grounds. When it's onsartain whether good or evil has been done, the wisest way is not to be boastful—still, I *should* like Chingachgook to know that I haven't discredited the Delawares or my training!"

Part of this was uttered aloud, while part was merely muttered between the speaker's teeth; his more confident opinions enjoying the first advantage, while his doubts were expressed in the latter mode. Soliloquy and reflection received a startling interruption, however, by the sudden appearance of a second Indian on the lake shore, a few hundred yards from the point. This man, evidently another scout, who had probably been drawn to the place by the reports of the rifles, broke out of the forest with so little caution that Deerslayer caught a view of his person before he was himself discovered. When the latter event did occur, as was the case a moment later, the savage gave a loud yell, which was answered by a dozen voices from different parts of the mountain-side. There was no longer any time for delay; in another minute the boat was quitting the shore under long and steady sweeps of the paddle.

As soon as Deerslayer believed himself to be at a safe distance, he ceased his efforts, permitting the little bark to drift, while he leisurely took a survey of the state of things. The canoe first sent adrift was floating before the air, quite a quarter of a mile above him, and a little nearer to the shore than he wished, now that he knew more of the savages were so near at hand. The canoe shoved from the point was within a few yards of him, he having directed his own course toward it on quitting the land. The dead Indian lay in

---

[6] Panthers.
[7] Lynxes or cougars.

grim quiet where he had left him, the warrior who had shown himself from the forest had already vanished, and the woods themselves were as silent and seemingly deserted as the day they came fresh from the hands of their great Creator. This profound stillness, however, lasted but a moment. When time had been given to the scouts of the enemy to reconnoitre, they burst out of the thicket upon the naked point, filling the air with yells of fury at discovering the death of their companion. These cries were immediately succeeded by shouts of delight when they reached the body and clustered eagerly around it. Deerslayer was a sufficient adept in the usages of the natives to understand the reason of the change. The yell was the customary lamentation at the loss of a warrior, the shout a sign of rejoicing that the conqueror had not been able to secure the scalp; the trophy without which a victory is never considered complete. The distance at which the canoes lay probably prevented any attempts to injure the conqueror, the American Indian, like the panther of his own woods, seldom making any effort against his foe unless tolerably certain it is under circumstances that may be expected to prove effective.

As the young man had no longer any motive to remain near the point, he prepared to collect his canoes, in order to tow them off to the castle. That nearest was soon in tow, when he proceeded in quest of the other, which was all this time floating up the lake. The eye of Deerslayer was no sooner fastened on this last boat, than it struck him that it was nearer to the shore than it would have been had it merely followed the course of the gentle current of air. He began to suspect the influence of some unseen current in the water, and he quickened his exertions, in order to regain possession of it before it could drift into a dangerous proximity to the woods. On getting nearer, he thought that the canoe had a perceptible motion through the water, and, as it lay broadside to the air, that this motion was taking it toward the land. A few vigorous strokes of the paddle carried him still nearer, when the mystery was explained. Something was evidently in motion on the off-side of the canoe or that which was furthest from himself, and closer scrutiny showed that it was a naked human arm. An Indian was lying in the bottom of the canoe, and was propelling it slowly, but certainly, to the shore, using his hand as a paddle. Deerslayer understood the whole artifice at a glance. A savage had swum off to the boat while he was occupied with his enemy on the point, got possession, and was using these means to urge it to the shore.

Satisfied that the man in the canoe could have no arms, Deerslayer did not hesitate to dash close alongside of the retiring boat, without deeming it necessary to raise his own rifle. As soon as the wash of the water, which he made in approaching, became audible to the prostrate savage, the latter sprang to his feet, and uttered an exclamation that proved how completely he was taken by surprise.

"If you've enj'yed yourself enough in that canoe, redskin," Deerslayer coolly observed, stopping his own career in sufficient time to prevent an absolute collision between the two boats—"if you've enj'yed yourself enough in that canoe, you'll do a prudent act by taking to the lake ag'in. I'm reasonable in these matters, and don't crave your blood, though there's them about that would look upon you more as a due-bill for the bounty than a human mortal.[8] Take to the lake this minute, afore we get to hot words."

The savage was one of those who did not understand a word of English, and he was indebted to the gestures of Deerslayer, and to the expression of an eye that did not often

---

8 At the time, the British were offering an attractive premium for Indian scalps.

deceive, for an imperfect comprehension of his meaning. Perhaps, too, the sight of the rifle that lay so near the hand of the white man quickened his decision. At all events, he crouched like a tiger about to take his leap, uttered a yell, and the next instant his naked body disappeared in the water. When he rose to take breath, it was at the distance of several yards from the canoe, and the hasty glance he threw behind him denoted how much he feared the arrival of a fatal messenger from the rifle of his foe. But the young man made no indication of any hostile intention. Deliberately securing the canoe to the others, he began to paddle from the shore; and by the time the Indian reached the land, and had shaken himself, like a spaniel on quitting the water, his dreaded enemy was already beyond rifle-shot on his way to the castle. As was so much his practice, Deerslayer did not fail to soliloquize on what had just occurred, while steadily pursuing his course toward the point of destination.

"Well, well"—he commenced—" 'twould have been wrong to kill a human mortal without an object. Scalps are of no account with me, and life is sweet, and ought not to be taken marcilessly by them that have white gifts. The savage was a Mingo, it's true; and I make no doubt he is, and will be as long as he lives, a ra'al riptyle and vagabond; but that's no reason I should forget my gifts and color. No, no—let him go; if ever we meet ag'in, rifle in hand, why then 'twill be seen which has the stoutest heart and the quickest eye. Hawkeye! That's not a bad name for a warrior, sounding much more manful and valiant than Deerslayer! 'Twouldn't be a bad title to begin with, and it has been fairly 'arned. If 'twas Chingachgook, now, he might go home and boast of his deeds, and the chiefs would name him Hawkeye in a minute; but it don't become white blood to brag, and 'tisn't easy to see how the matter can be known unless I do. Well, well—everything is in the hands of Providence; this affair as well as another; I'll trust to that for getting my desarts in all things."

Having thus betrayed what might be termed his weak spot, the young man continued to paddle in silence, making his way diligently, and as fast as his tows would allow him, toward the castle. By this time the sun had not only risen, but it had appeared over the eastern mountains, and was shedding a flood of glorious light on this as yet unchristened sheet of water. The whole scene was radiant with beauty; and no one unaccustomed to the ordinary history of the woods would fancy it had so lately witnessed incidents so ruthless and barbarous. As he approached the building of old Hutter, Deerslayer thought, or rather *felt,* that its appearance was in singular harmony with all the rest of the scene. Although nothing had been consulted but strength and security, the rude, massive logs, covered with their rough bark, the projecting roof, and the form, would contribute to render the building picturesque in almost any situation, while its actual position added novelty and piquancy to its other points of interest.

When Deerslayer drew nearer to the castle, however, objects of interest presented themselves that at once eclipsed any beauties that might have distinguished the scenery of the lake, and the site of the singular edifice. Judith and Hetty stood on the platform before the door, Hurry's door-yard, awaiting his approach with manifest anxiety; the former, from time to time, taking a survey of his person and of the canoes through the old ship's spy-glass that has been already mentioned. Never probably did this girl seem more brilliantly beautiful than at that moment; the flush of anxiety and alarm increasing her color to its richest tints, while the softness of her eyes, a charm that even poor Hetty shared with her, was deepened by intense concern. Such, at least, without pausing or pretending to analyze motives, or to draw any other very nice distinctions between

cause and effect, were the opinions of the young man, as his canoes reached the side of the ark, where he carefully fastened all three before he put his foot on the platform.
1841

The Pioneers

Chapter XXXIII
Not Guilty with a Clean Conscience

Fetch here the stocks, ho!
You stubborn ancient knave, you reverend braggart,
We'll teach you![1]
            Lear

The long days and early sun of July allowed time for a gathering of the interested, before the little bell of the academy announced that the appointed hour had arrived for administering right to the wronged, and punishment to the guilty. Ever since the dawn of day, the highways and woodpaths that, issuing from the forests, and winding along the sides of the mountains, centered in Templeton, had been thronged with equestrians and footmen, bound to the haven of justice. There was to be seen a well-clad yeoman, mounted on a sleek, switch-tailed steed, ambling along the highway, with his red face elevated in a manner that said, "I have paid for my land, and fear no man;" while his bosom was swelling with the pride of being one of the grand inquest for the county. At his side rode a companion, his equal in independence of feeling, perhaps, but his inferior in thrift, as in property and consideration. This was a professed dealer in lawsuits,—a man whose name appeared in every calendar,—whose substance, gained in the multifarious expedients of a settler's changeable habits, was wasted in feeding the harpies[2] of the courts. He was endeavoring to impress the mind of the grand juror with the merits of a cause now at issue. Along with these was a pedestrian, who, having thrown a rifle frock over his shirt, and placed his best wool hat above his sunburnt visage, had issued from his retreat in the woods by a footpath, and was striving to keep company with the others, on his way to hear and to decide the disputes of his neighbors, as a petit juror.[3] Fifty similar little knots of countrymen might have been seen, on that morning, journeying toward the shire-town on the same errand.

By ten o'clock the streets of the village were filled with busy faces; some talking of their private concerns, some listening to a popular expounder of political creeds; and others gaping in at the open stores, admiring the finery, or examining scythes, axes, and such other manufactures as attracted their curiosity or excited their admiration. A few women were in the crowd, most carrying infants, and followed, at a lounging, listless

---

[1] Shakespeare's King Lear, Act II, Sc. ii, ll. 129–131.
[2] Mythological predatory monsters having the heads and torsos of women and the tails, wings, and talons of birds.
[3] Member of a civil jury.

gait, by their rustic lords and masters. There was one young couple, in whom connubial love was yet fresh, walking at a respectful distance from each other; while the swain directed the timid steps of his bride, by a gallant offering of a thumb!

At the first stroke of the bell, Richard issued from the door of the "Bold Dragoon," flourishing a sheathed sword, that he was fond of saying his ancestors had carried in one of Cromwell's victories, and crying, in an authoritative tone, to "clear the way for the court." The order was obeyed promptly, though not servilely, the members of the crowd nodding familiarly to the members of the procession as it passed. A party of constables with their staves followed the Sheriff, preceding Marmaduke, and four plain, grave-looking yeomen, who were his associates on the bench. There was nothing to distinguish these subordinate judges from the better part of the spectators, except gravity, which they affected a little more than common, and that one of their number was attired in an old-fashioned military coat, with skirts that reached no lower than the middle of his thighs, and bearing two little silver epaulettes, not half so big as a modern pair of shoulder-knots. This gentleman was a colonel of the militia, in attendance on a courtmartial, who found leisure to steal a moment from his military to attend to his civil jurisdiction; but this incongruity excited neither notice nor comment. Three or four clean-shaved lawyers followed, as meekly as if they were lambs going to the slaughter. One or two of their number had contrived to obtain an air of scholastic gravity by wearing spectacles. The rear was brought up by another posse of constables, and the mob followed the whole into the room where the court held its sittings.

The edifice was composed of a basement of squared logs, perforated here and there with small grated windows, through which a few wistful faces were gazing at the crowd without. Among the captives were the guilty, downcast countenances of the counterfeiters, and the simple but honest features of the Leather-stocking. The dungeons were to be distinguished, externally, from the debtors' apartments only by the size of the apertures, the thickness of the grates, and by the heads of the spikes that were driven into the logs as a protection against the illegal use of edge-tools. The upper story was of framework, regularly covered with boards, and contained one room decently fitted up for the purposes of justice. A bench, raised on a narrow platform to the height of a man above the floor, and protected in front by a light railing, ran along one of its sides. In the centre was a seat, furnished with rude arms, that was always filled by the presiding judge. In front, on a level with the floor of the room, was a large table covered with green baize, and surrounded by benches; and at either of its ends were rows of seats, rising one over the other, for jury boxes. Each of these divisions was surrounded by a railing. The remainder of the room was an open square, appropriated to the spectators.

When the judges were seated, the lawyers had taken possession of the table, and the noise of moving feet had ceased in the area, the proclamations were made in the usual form, the jurors were sworn, the charge was given, and the court proceeded to hear the business before them.

We shall not detain the reader with a description of the captious discussions that occupied the court for the first two hours. Judge Temple had impressed on the jury, in his charge, the necessity for despatch on their part, recommending to their notice, from motives of humanity, the prisoners in the jail, as the first objects of their attention. Accordingly, after the period we have mentioned had elapsed, the cry of the officer to "clear the way for the grand jury," announced the entrance of that body. The usual forms were observed, when the foreman handed up to the bench two bills, on both of which the Judge observed, at the first glance of his eye, the name of Nathaniel Bumppo. It was a leisure moment with the court; some low whispering passed between the bench and the Sheriff, who gave a signal to his officers, and in a very few minutes the silence that prevailed was interrupted by a general movement in the outer crowd; when presently the Leather-Stocking made his appearance, ushered into the criminal's bar under the custody of two constables. The hum ceased, the people closed into the open space again, and the silence soon became so deep, that the hard breathing of the prisoner was audible.

Natty was dressed in his buckskin garments, without his coat, in place of which he wore only a shirt of coarse linen-check, fastened at his throat by the sinew of a deer, leaving his red neck and weather-beaten face exposed and bare. It was the first time that he had ever crossed the threshold of a court of justice, and curiosity seemed to be strongly blended with his personal feelings. He raised his eyes to the bench, thence to the jury-boxes, the bar, and the crowd without, meeting everywhere looks fastened on himself. After surveying his own person, as searching the cause of this unusual attraction, he once more turned his face around the assemblage, and opened his mouth in one of his silent and remarkable laughs.

"Prisoner, remove your cap," said Judge Temple.

The order was either unheard or unheeded.

"Nathaniel Bumppo, be uncovered," repeated the Judge.

Natty started at the sound of his name, and raising his face earnestly toward the bench, he said—

"Anan!"

Mr. Lippet arose from his seat at the table, and whispered in the ear of the prisoner; when Natty gave him a nod of assent, and took the deerskin covering from his head.

"Mr. District Attorney," said the Judge, "the prisoner is ready; we wait for the indictment."

The duties of public prosecutor were discharged by Dirck Van der School, who adjusted his spectacles, cast a cautious look around him at his brethren of the bar, which he ended by throwing his head aside so as to catch one glance over the glasses, when he proceeded to read the bill aloud. It was the usual charge for an assault and battery on the person of Hiram Doolittle, and was couched in the ancient language of such instruments, especial care having been taken by the scribe not to omit the name of a single offensive weapon known to the law. When he had done, Mr. Van der School removed his spectacles, which he closed and placed in his pocket, seemingly for the pleasure of again opening and replacing them on his nose. After this revolution was repeated once or twice, he handed the bill over to Mr. Lippet, with a cavalier air, that said as much as "Pick a hole in that if you can."

Natty listened to the charge with great attention, leaning forward toward the reader with an earnestness that denoted his interest; and when it was ended, he raised his tall body to the utmost, and drew a long sigh. All eyes were turned to the prisoner, whose voice was vainly expected to break the stillness of the room.

"You have heard the presentment that the grand jury have made, Nathaniel Bumppo," said the Judge; "what do you plead to the charge?"

The old man dropped his head for a moment in a reflecting attitude, and then raising it, he laughed before he answered—

"That I handled the man a little rough or so, is not to be denied; but that there was occasion to make use of all the things that the gentleman has spoken of, is downright untrue. I am not much of a wrestler, seeing that I'm getting old; but I was out among the Scotch-Irishers[4]—let me see—it must have been as long ago as the first year of the old war—"

"Mr. Lippet, if you are retained for the prisoner," interrupted Judge Temple, "instruct your client how to plead; if not, the court will assign him counsel."

Aroused from studying the indictment by this appeal, the attorney got up, and after a short dialogue with the hunter in a low voice, he informed the court that they were ready to proceed.

"Do you plead guilty or not guilty?" said the Judge.

"I may say not guilty with a clean conscience," returned Natty; "for there's no guilt in doing what's right; and I'd rather died on the spot, than had him put foot in the hut at that moment."

Richard started at this declaration, and bent his eyes significantly on Hiram, who returned the look with a slight movement of his eyebrows.

"Proceed to open the cause, Mr. District Attorney," continued the Judge. "Mr. Clerk, enter the plea of not guilty."

After a short opening address from Mr. Van der School, Hiram was summoned to the bar to give his testimony. It was delivered to the letter, perhaps, but with all that moral coloring which can be conveyed under such expressions as, "thinking no harm," "feeling it my bounden duty as a magistrate," and "seeing that the constable was back'ard in the business." When he had done, and the district attorney declined putting any further interrogatories, Mr. Lippet arose, with an air of keen investigation, and asked the following questions:

"Are you a constable of this county, sir?"

"No, sir," said Hiram, "I'm only a justice-peace."

"I ask you, Mr. Doolittle, in the face of this court, putting it to your conscience and your knowledge of the law, whether you had any right to enter that man's dwelling?"

"Hem!" said Hiram, undergoing a violent struggle between his desire for vengeance and his love of legal fame; "I do suppose—that in—that is—strict law—that supposing—maybe I hadn't a real—lawful right;—but as the case was—and Billy was so back'ard—I thought I might come for'ard in the business."

"I ask you again, sir," continued the lawyer, following up his success, "whether this old, this friendless old man, did or did not repeatedly forbid your entrance?"

"Why, I must say," said Hiram, "that he was considerable cross-grained; not what I call clever, seeing that it was only one neighbor wanting to go into the house of another."

"Oh! then you own it was only meant for a neighborly visit on your part, and without the sanction of law. Remember, gentlemen, the words of the witness, 'one neighbor wanting to enter the house of another.' Now, sir, I ask you if Nathaniel Bumppo did not again and again order you not to enter?"

"There was some words passed between us," said Hiram, "but I read the warrant to him aloud."

"I repeat my question; did he tell you not to enter his habitation?"

---

4 Group of early settlers of mixed Scottish
and Irish lineage who fought in the British-
Indian wars.

"There was a good deal passed betwixt us—but I've the warrant in my pocket; maybe the court would wish to see it?"

"Witness," said Judge Temple, "answer the question directly; did or did not the prisoner forbid your entering his hut?"

"Why, I some think—"

"Answer without equivocation," continued the Judge, sternly.

"He did."

"And did you attempt to enter after this order?"

"I did; but the warrant was in my hand."

"Proceed, Mr. Lippet, with your examination."

But the attorney saw that the impression was in favor of his client, and, waving his hand with a supercilious manner, as if unwilling to insult the understanding of the jury with any further defence, he replied—

"No, sir; I leave it for your honor to charge; I rest my case here."

"Mr. District Attorney," said the Judge, "have you anything to say?"

Mr. Van der School removed his spectacles, folded them, and replacing them once more on his nose, eyed the other bill which he held in his hand, and then said, looking at the bar over the top of his glasses—

"I shall rest the prosecution here, if the court please."

Judge Temple arose and began the charge.

"Gentlemen of the jury," he said, "you have heard the testimony, and I shall detain you but a moment. If an officer meet with resistance in the execution of a process he has an undoubted right to call any citizen to his assistance; and the acts of such assistant come within the protection of the law. I shall leave you to judge, gentlemen, from the testimony, how far the witness in this prosecution can be so considered, feeling less reluctance to submit the case thus informally to your decision, because there is yet another indictment to be tried, which involves heavier charges against the unfortunate prisoner."

The tone of Marmaduke was mild and insinuating, and as his sentiments were given with such apparent impartiality, they did not fail of carrying due weight with the jury. The grave-looking yeomen who composed this tribunal, laid their heads together for a few minutes, without leaving the box, when the foreman arose, and after the forms of the court were duly observed, he pronounced the prisoner to be—

"Not guilty."

"You are acquitted of this charge, Nathaniel Bumppo," said the Judge.

"Anan!" said Natty.

"You are found not guilty of striking and assaulting Mr. Doolittle."

"No, no, I'll not deny but that I took him a little roughly by the shoulders," said Natty, looking about him with great simplicity, "and that I—"

"You are acquitted," interrupted the Judge, "and there is nothing further to be said or done in the matter."

A look of joy lighted up the features of the old man, who now comprehended the case, and placing his cap eagerly on his head again, he threw up the bar of his little prison, and said feelingly—

"I must say this for you, Judge Temple, that the law has not been so hard on me as I dreaded. I hope God will bless you for the kind things you've done to me this day."

But the staff of the constable was opposed to his egress, and Mr. Lippet whispered a few words in his ear, when the aged hunter sank back into his place, and, removing his cap, stroked down the remnants of his gray and sandy locks, with an air of mortification mingled with submission.

"Mr. District Attorney," said Judge Temple, affecting to busy himself with his minutes, "proceed with the second indictment."

Mr. Van der School took great care that no part of the presentment, which he now read, should be lost on his auditors. It accused the prisoner of resisting the execution of a search-warrant, by force of arms, and particularized, in the vague language of the law, among a variety of other weapons, the use of the rifle. This was indeed a more serious charge than an ordinary assault and battery, and a corresponding degree of interest was manifested by the spectators in its result. The prisoner was duly arraigned, and his plea again demanded. Mr. Lippet had anticipated the answers of Natty, and in a whisper advised him how to lead. But the feelings of the old hunter were awakened by some of the expressions of the indictment, and, forgetful of his caution, he exclaimed—

" 'Tis a wicked untruth; I crave no man's blood. Them thieves, the Iroquois, won't say it to my face, that I ever thirsted after man's blood. I have fou't as a soldier that feared his Maker and his officer, but I never pulled trigger on any but a warrior that was up and awake. No man can say that I ever struck even a Mingo in his blanket. I believe there's some who thinks there's no God in a wilderness!"

"Attend to your plea, Bumppo," said the Judge; "you hear that you are accused of using your rifle against an officer of justice? are you guilty or not guilty?"

By this time the irritated feelings of Natty had found vent; and he rested on the bar for a moment, in a musing posture, when he lifted his face, with his silent laugh, and, pointing to where the wood-chopper stood, he said—

"Would Billy Kirby be standing there, d'ye think, if I had used the rifle?"

"Then you deny it," said Mr. Lippet; "you plead not guilty?"

"Sartain," said Natty; "Billy knows that I never fired at all. Billy, do you remember the turkey last winter? ah! me! that was better than common firing; but I can't shoot as I used to could."

"Enter the plea of not guilty," said Judge Temple, strongly affected by the simplicity of the prisoner.

Hiram was again sworn, and his testimony given on the second charge. He had discovered his former error, and proceeded more cautiously than before. He related very distinctly, and for the man, with amazing terseness, the suspicion against the hunter, the complaint, the issuing of the warrant, and the swearing in of Kirby; all of which, he affirmed, were done in due form of law. He then added the manner in which the constable had been received; and stated distinctly, that Natty had pointed the rifle at Kirby, and threatened his life, if he attempted to execute his duty. All this was confirmed by Jotham, who was observed to adhere closely to the story of the magistrate. Mr. Lippet conducted an artful cross-examination of these two witnesses, but after consuming much time, was compelled to relinquish the attempt to obtain any advantage, in despair.

At length the district attorney called the wood-chopper to the bar. Billy gave an extremely confused account of the whole affair, although he evidently aimed at the truth, until Mr. Van der School aided him, by asking some direct questions:—

"It appears from examining the papers, that you demanded admission into the hut legally; so you were put in bodily fear by his rifle and threats?"

"I didn't mind them that, man," said Billy, snapping his fingers; "I should be a poor stick to mind old Leather-Stocking."

"But I understood you to say (referring to your previous words (as delivered here in court) in the commencement of your testimony) that you thought he meant to shoot you?"

"To be sure I did; and so would you too, squire, if you had seen the chap dropping a muzzle that never misses, and cocking an eye that has a natural squint by long practice. I thought there would be a dust on't, and my back was up at once; but Leather-Stocking gi'n up the skin, and so the matter ended."

"Ah! Billy," said Natty, shaking his head, "'twas a lucky thought in me to throw out the hide, or there might have been blood spilt; and I'm sure, if it had been yourn, I should have mourn'd it sorely the little while I have to stay."

"Well, Leather-Stocking," returned Billy, facing the prisoner with a freedom and familiarity that utterly disregarded the presence of the court, "as you are on the subject, it may be that you've no—"

"Go on with your examination, Mr. District Attorney."

That gentleman eyed the familiarity between his witness and the prisoner with manifest disgust, and indicated to the court that he was done.

"Then you didn't feel frightened, Mr. Kirby?" said the counsel for the prisoner.

"Me! no," said Billy, casting his eyes over his own huge frame with evident self-satisfaction; "I'm not to be skeared so easy."

"You look like a hardy man; where were you born, sir?"

"Varmount state; 'tis a mountaynious place, but there's a stiff soil, and it's pretty much wooded with beech and maple."

"I have always heard so," said Mr. Lippet, soothingly. "You have been used to the rifle yourself, in that country?"

"I pull the second best trigger in this county. I knock under to Natty Bumppo there, sin' he shot the pigeon."

Leather-Stocking raised his head, and laughed again, when he abruptly thrust out a wrinkled hand, and said—

"You're young yet, Billy, and hav'n't seen the matches that I have; but here's my hand; I bear no malice to you, I don't."

Mr. Lippet allowed this conciliatory offering to be accepted, and judiciously paused, while the spirit of peace was exercising its influence over the two; but the Judge interposed his authority.

"This is an improper place for such dialogues," he said.

"Proceed with your examination of this witness, Mr. Lippet, or I shall order the next."

The attorney started, as if unconscious of any impropriety, and continued—

"So you settled the matter with Natty amicably on the spot, did you?"

"He gi'n me the skin, and I didn't want to quarrel with an old man; for my part, I see no such mighty matter in shooting a buck!"

"And you parted friends? and you would never have thought of bringing the business up before a court, hadn't you been subpœnaed?"

"I don't think I should; he gi'n the skin, and I didn't feel a hard thought, though Squire Doolittle got some affronted."

"I have done, sir," said Mr. Lippet, probably relying on the charge of the Judge, as he again seated himself, with the air of a man who felt that his success was certain.

When Mr. Van der School arose to address the jury, he commenced by saying—

"Gentlemen of the jury, I should have interrupted the leading questions put by the prisoner's counsel (by leading questions I mean telling him what to say), did I not feel confident that the law of the land was superior to any advantages (I mean legal advantages) which he might obtain by his art. The counsel for the prisoner, gentlemen, has endeavored to persuade you, in opposition to your own good sense, to believe that pointing a rifle at a constable (elected or deputed) is a very innocent affair; and that society (I mean the commonwealth, gentlemen) shall not be endangered thereby. But let me claim your attention, while we look over the particulars of this heinous offence." Here Mr. Van der School favored the jury with an abridgment of the testimony, recounted in such a manner as utterly to confuse the faculties of his worthy listeners. After this exhibition he closed as follows:—"And now, gentlemen, having thus made plain to your senses the crime of which this unfortunate man has been guilty (unfortunate both on account of his ignorance and his guilt), I shall leave you to your own consciences; not in the least doubting that you will see the importance (notwithstanding the prisoner's counsel (doubtless relying on your former verdict) wishes to appear so confident of success) of punishing the offender, and asserting the dignity of the laws."

It was now the duty of the Judge to deliver his charge. It consisted of a short, comprehensive summary of the testimony, laying bare the artifice of the prisoner's counsel, and placing the facts in so obvious a light, that they could not well be misunderstood. "Living as we do, gentlemen," he concluded, "on the skirts of society, it becomes doubly necessary to protect the ministers of the law. If you believe the witnesses, in their construction of the acts of the prisoner, it is your duty to convict him; but if you believe that the old man, who this day appears before you, meant not to harm the constable, but was acting more under the influence of habit than by the instigations of malice, it will be your duty to judge him, but to do it with lenity."

As before, the jury did not leave their box; but, after a consultation of some little time, their foreman arose, and pronounced the prisoner—

"Guilty."

There was but little surprise manifested in the court room at this verdict, as the testimony, the greater part of which we have omitted, was too clear and direct to be passed over. The judges seemed to have anticipated this sentiment, for a consultation was passing among them also, during the deliberation of the jury, and the preparatory movements of the "bench" announced the coming sentence.

"Nathaniel Bumppo," commenced the Judge, making the customary pause.

The old hunter, who had been musing again, with his head on the bar, raised himself, and cried, with a prompt, military tone—

"Here."

The Judge waved his hand for silence, and proceeded—

"In forming their sentence, the court have been governed as much by the consideration of your ignorance of the laws, as by a strict sense of the importance of punishing such outrages as this of which you have been found guilty. They have therefore passed over the obvious punishment of whipping on the bare back, in mercy to your years; but as the dignity of the law requires an open exhibition of the consequences of your crime, it is ordered, that you be conveyed from this room to the public stocks, where you are to be confined for one hour; that you pay a fine to the state of one hundred dollars; and that you be imprisoned in the jail of this county for one calendar month, and furthermore, that your imprisonment do not cease until the said fine shall be paid. I feel it my duty, Nathaniel Bumppo—"

"And where should I get the money?" interrupted the Leather-Stocking, eagerly; "where should I get the money? you'll take away the bounty on the painters,[5] because I cut the throat of a deer; and how is an old man to find so much gold or silver in the woods? No, no, judge: think better of it, and don't talk of shutting me up in a jail for the little time I have to stay."

"If you have anything to urge against the passing of the sentence, the court will yet hear you," said the Judge, mildly.

"I have enough to say ag'in it," cried Natty, grasping the bar on which his fingers were working with a convulsed motion. "Where am I to get the money? Let me out into the woods and hills, where I've been used to breathe the clear air, and though I'm three-score and ten, if you've left game enough in the country, I'll travel night and day but I'll make you up the sum afore the season is over. Yes, yes—you see the reason of the thing, and the wickedness of shutting up an old man, that has spent his days, as one may say, where he could always look into the windows of heaven."

"I must be governed by the law—"

"Talk not to me of law, Marmaduke Temple," interrupted the hunter. "Did the beast of the forest mind your laws, when it was thirsty and hungering for the blood of your own child! She was kneeling to her God for a greater favor than I ask, and he heard her; and if you now say no to my prayers, do you think he will be deaf?"

"My private feelings must not enter into—"

"Hear me, Marmaduke Temple," interrupted the old man, with melancholy earnestness, "and hear reason. I've travelled these mountains when you was no judge, but an infant in your mother's arms; and I feel as if I had a right and a privilege to travel them ag'in afore I die. Have you forgot the time that you come on to the lake-shore, when there wasn't even a jail to lodge in; and didn't I give you my own bear-skin to sleep on, and the fat of a noble buck to satisfy the cravings of your hunger? Yes, yes—you thought it no sin then to kill a deer! And this I did, though I had no reason to love you, for you had never done anything but harm to them that loved and sheltered me. And now, will you shut me up in your dungeons to pay me for my kindness? A hundred dollars! where should I get the money? No, no—there's them that says hard things of you, Marmaduke Temple, but you an't so bad as to wish to see an old man die in a prison, because he stood up for the right. Come, friend, let me pass; it's long sin' I've been used to such crowds, and I crave to be in the woods ag'in. Don't fear me, Judge—I bid you not to fear me; for if there's beaver enough left on the streams, or the buckskins will sell for a shilling a-piece, you shall have the last penny of the fine. Where are ye, pups! come away, dogs! come away! we have a grievous toil to do for our years, but it shall be done—yes, yes, I've promised it, and it shall be done!"

It is unnecessary to say, that the movement of the Leather-Stocking was again intercepted by the constable; but before he had time to speak, a bustling in the crowd, and a loud hem, drew all eyes to another part of the room.

Benjamin had succeeded in edging his way through the people, and was now seen balancing his short body, with one foot in a window and the other on a railing of the jurybox. To the amazement of the whole court, the steward was evidently preparing to

5 Panthers.

speak. After a good deal of difficulty, he succeeded in drawing from his pocket a small bag, and then found utterance.

"If-so-be," he said, "that your honor is agreeable to trust the poor fellow out on another cruise among the beasts, here's a small matter that will help to bring down the risk, seeing that there's just thirty-five of your Spaniards[6] in it; and I wish, from the bottom of my heart, that they was raal British guineas,[7] for the sake of the old boy. But 'tis as it is; and if Squire Dickens will just be so good as to overhaul this small bit of an account, and take enough from the bag to settle the same, he's welcome to hold on upon the rest, till such time as the Leather-Stocking can grapple with them said beaver, or, for that matter, forever, and no thanks asked."

As Benjamin concluded, he thrust out the wooden register of his arrears to the "Bold Dragon" with one hand, while he offered his bag of dollars with the other. Astonishment at this singular interruption produced a profound stillness in the room, which was only interrupted by the Sheriff, who struck his sword on the table, and cried—

"Silence!"

"There must be an end to this," said the Judge, struggling to overcome his feelings. "Constable, lead the prisoner to the stocks. Mr. Clerk, what stands next on the calendar?"

Natty seemed to yield to his destiny, for he sank his head on his chest, and followed the officer from the court-room in silence. The crowd moved back for the passage of the prisoner, and when his tall form was seen descending from the outer door, a rush of the people to the scene of his disgrace followed.

1823

The Prairie

Chapter XXXIV
I Die, as I Have Lived

—Methought I heard a voice.[1]
Shakespeare

The watercourses were at their height, and the boat went down the swift current like a bird. The passage proved prosperous and speedy. In less than a third of the time that would have been necessary for the same journey by land, it was accomplished by the favor of those rapid rivers. Issuing from one stream into another, as the veins of the human body communicate with the larger channels of life, they soon entered the grand artery of the western waters, and landed safely at the very door of the father of Inez.

The joy of Don Augustin, and the embarrassment of the worthy father Ignatius, may be imagined. The former wept and returned thanks to Heaven; the latter returned thanks and did not weep. The mild provincials were too happy to raise any questions on the character of so joyful a restoration; and, by a sort of general consent, it soon became

---

[6] Spanish dollars.
[7] Guinea: British coin worth about £1.

[1] *Macbeth*, Act II, Sc. ii, l. 35.

to be an admitted opinion that the bride of Middleton had been kidnapped by a villain, and that she was restored to her friends by human agency. There were, as respects this belief, certainly a few sceptics, but then they enjoyed their doubts in private, with that species of sublimated and solitary gratification that a miser finds in gazing at his growing, but useless hoards.

In order to give the worthy priest something to employ his mind, Middleton made him the instrument of uniting Paul and Ellen. The former consented to the ceremony, because he found that all his friends laid great stress on the matter; but shortly after, he led his bride into the plains of Kentucky, under the pretence of paying certain customary visits to sundry members of the family of Hover. While there, he took occasion to have the marriage properly solemnized by a justice of the peace of his acquaintance, in whose ability to forge the nuptial chain he had much more faith than in that of all the gownsmen[2] within the pale of Rome. Ellen, who appeared conscious that some extraordinary preventives might prove necessary to keep one of so erratic a temper as her partner, within the proper matrimonial boundaries, raised no objections to these double knots, and all parties were content.

The local importance Middleton had acquired, by his union with the daughter of so affluent a proprietor as Don Augustin, united to his personal merit, attracted the attention of the government. He was soon employed in various situations of responsibility and confidence, which both served to elevate his character in the public estimation, and to afford the means of patronage. The bee-hunter was among the first of those to whom he saw fit to extend his favor. It was far from difficult to find situations suited to the abilities of Paul, in the state of society that existed three-and-twenty years ago in those regions. The efforts of Middleton and Inez, in behalf of her husband, were warmly and sagaciously seconded by Ellen, and they succeeded, in process of time, in working a great and beneficial change in his character. He soon became a landholder, then a prosperous cultivator of the soil, and shortly after a town-officer. By that progressive change in fortunes, which in the republic is often seen to be so singularly accompanied by a corresponding improvement in knowledge and self-respect, he went on, from step to step, until his wife enjoyed the maternal delight of seeing her children placed far beyond the danger of returning to that state from which both their parents had issued. Paul is actually at this moment a member of the lower branch of the legislature of the State where he has long resided; and he is even notorious for making speeches that have a tendency to put that deliberative body in good humor, and which, as they are based on great practical knowledge suited to the condition of the country, possess a merit that is much wanted in many more subtle and fine-spun theories, that are daily heard in similar assemblies, to issue from the lips of certain instinctive politicians. But all these happy fruits were the results of much care, and of a long period of time. Middleton, who fills, with a credit better suited to the difference in their educations, a seat in a far higher branch of legislative authority, is the source from which we have derived most of the intelligence necessary to compose our legend. In addition to what he has related of Paul, and of his own continued happiness, he has added a short narrative of what took place on a subsequent visit to the prairies, with which, as we conceive it a suitable termination to what has gone before, we shall judge it wise to conclude our labors.

---

[2] i.e., ministers or priests.

In the autumn of the year that succeeded the season in which the preceding events occurred, the young man, still in the military service, found himself on the waters of the Missouri, at a point not far remote from the Pawnee towns. Released from any immediate calls of duty, and strongly urged to the measure by Paul, who was in his company, he determined to take horse, and cross the country to visit the partisan, and to inquire into the fate of his friend the trapper. As his train was suited to his functions and rank, the journey was effected, with the privations and hardships that are the accompaniments to all travelling in a wild, but without any of those dangers and alarms that marked his former passage through the same regions. When within a proper distance, he despatched an Indian runner, belonging to a friendly tribe, to announce the approach of himself and party, continuing his route at a deliberate pace, in order that the intelligence might, as was customary, precede his arrival. To the surprise of the travellers, their message was unanswered. Hour succeeded hour, and mile after mile was passed, without bringing either the signs of an honorable reception, or the more simple assurances of a friendly welcome. At length the cavalcade, at whose head rode Middleton and Paul, descended from the elevated plain, on which they had long been journeying, to a luxuriant bottom, that brought them to the level of the village of the Loups. The sun was beginning to fall, and a sheet of golden light was spread over the placid plain, lending to its even surface those glorious tints and hues, that the human imagination is apt to conceive, form the embellishment of still more imposing scenes. The verdure of the year yet remained, and herds of horses and mules were grazing peacefully in the vast natural pasture, under the keeping of vigilant Pawnee boys. Paul pointed out among them the well-known form of Asinus, sleek, fat, and luxuriating in the fulness of content, as he stood with reclining ears and closed eyelids, seemingly musing on the exquisite nature of his present indolent enjoyment.

The route of the party led them at no great distance from one of those watchful youths who was charged with a trust heavy as the principal wealth of his tribe. He heard the trampling of the horses, and cast his eye aside, but instead of manifesting curiosity or alarm, his look instantly returned whence it had been withdrawn, to the spot where the village was known to stand.

"There is something remarkable in all this," muttered Middleton, half offended at what he conceived to be not only a slight to his rank, but offensive to himself personally; "yonder boy has heard of our approach, or he would not fail to notify his tribe; and yet he scarcely deigns to favor us with a glance. Look to your arms, men; it may be necessary to let these savages feel our strength."

"Therein, Captain, I think you're in an error," returned Paul: "if honesty is to be met on the prairies at all, you will find it in our old friend Hard-Heart; neither is an Indian to be judged of by the rules of a white. See! we are not altogether slighted, for here comes a party at last to meet us, though it is a little pitiful as to show and numbers."

Paul was right in both particulars. A group of horsemen were at length seen wheeling round a little copse, and advancing across the plain directly toward them. The advance of this party was slow and dignified. As it drew nigh, the partisan of the Loups was seen at its head, followed by a dozen younger warriors of his tribe. They were all unarmed, nor did they even wear any of those ornaments or feathers, which are considered testimonials of respect to the guest an Indian receives, as well as evidence of his own importance.

The meeting was friendly, though a little restrained on both sides. Middleton, jealous of his own consideration, no less than of the authority of his government, suspected some undue influence on the part of the agents of the Canadas; and, as he was determined to maintain the authority of which he was the representative, he felt himself constrained to manifest a hauteur[3] that he was far from feeling. It was not so easy to penetrate the motives of the Pawnees. Calm, dignified, and yet far from repulsive, they set an example of courtesy, blended with reserve, that many a diplomatist of the most polished court might have striven in vain to imitate.

In this manner the two parties continued their course to the town. Middleton had time during the remainder of the ride, to revolve in his mind all the probable reasons which his ingenuity could suggest for this strange reception. Although he was accompanied by a regular interpreter, the chiefs made their salutations in a manner that dispensed with his services. Twenty times the Captain turned his glance on his former friend, endeavoring to read the expression of his rigid features. But every effort and all conjectures proved equally futile. The eye of Hard-Heart was fixed, composed, and a little anxious; but as to every other emotion, impenetrable. He neither spoke himself, nor seemed willing to invite discourse in his visitors: it was therefore necessary for Middleton to adopt the patient manners of his companions, and to await the issue for the explanation.

When they entered the town, its inhabitants were seen collected in an open space, where they were arranged with the customary deference to age and rank. The whole formed a large circle, in the centre of which were perhaps a dozen of the principal chiefs. Hard-Heart waved his hand as he approached, and, as the mass of bodies opened he rode through, followed by his companions. Here they dismounted; and as the beasts were led apart, the strangers found themselves environed by a thousand grave, composed, but solicitous faces.

Middleton gazed about him in growing concern, for no cry, no song, no shout welcomed him among a people, from whom he had so lately parted with regret. His uneasiness, not to say apprehensions, was shared by all his followers. Determination and stern resolution began to assume the place of anxiety in every eye, as each man silently felt for his arms, and assured himself that his several weapons were in a state for service. But there was no answering symptom of hostility on the part of their hosts. Hard-Heart beckoned for Middleton and Paul to follow, leading the way toward the cluster of forms that occupied the centre of the circle. Here the visitors found a solution of all the movements which had given them so much reason for apprehension.

The trapper was placed on a rude seat, which had been made, with studied care, to support his frame in an upright and easy attitude. The first glance of the eye told his former friends, that the old man was at length called upon to pay the last tribute of nature. His eye was glazed, and apparently as devoid of sight as of expression. His features were a little more sunken and strongly marked than formerly; but there, all change, so far as exterior was concerned, might be said to have ceased. His approaching end was not to be ascribed to any positive disease, but had been a gradual and mild decay of the physical powers. Life, it is true, still lingered in his system; but it was as if at times entirely ready to depart, and then it would appear to reanimate the sinking form, reluctant to give up the possession of a tenement that had never been corrupted by vice or undermined by disease. It would have been no violent fancy to have imagined that the spirit fluttered about the placid lips of the old woodsman, reluctant to depart from a shell that had so long given it an honest and honorable shelter.

[3] Haughtiness.

His body was placed so as to let the light of the setting sun fall full upon the solemn features. His head was bare, the long, thin locks of gray fluttering lightly in the evening breeze. His rifle lay upon his knee, and the other accoutrements of the chase were placed at his side, within reach of his hand. Between his feet lay the figure of a hound, with its head crouching to the earth, as if it slumbered; and so perfectly easy and natural was its position, that a second glance was necessary to tell Middleton he saw only the skin of Hector, stuffed, by Indian tenderness and ingenuity, in a manner to represent the living animal. His own dog was playing at a distance with the child of Tachechana and Mahtoree. The mother herself stood at hand, holding in her arms a second offspring, that might boast of a parentage no less honorable than that which belonged to the son of Hard-Heart. Le Balafré was seated nigh the dying trapper, with every mark about his person that the hour of his own departure was not far distant. The rest of those immediately in the centre were aged men, who had apparently drawn near in order to observe the manner in which a just and fearless warrior would depart on the greatest of his journeys.

The old man was reaping the rewards of a life remarkable for temperance and activity, in a tranquil and placid death. His vigor in a manner endured to the very last. Decay, when it did occur, was rapid, but free from pain. He had hunted with the tribe in the spring, and even throughout most of the summer; when his limbs suddenly refused to perform their customary offices. A sympathizing weakness took possession of all his faculties; and the Pawnees believed that they were going to lose, in this unexpected manner, a sage and counsellor whom they had begun both to love and respect. But, as we have already said, the immortal occupant seemed unwilling to desert its tenement. The lamp of life flickered, without becoming extinguished. On the morning of the day on which Middleton arrived, there was a general reviving of the powers of the whole man. His tongue was again heard in wholesome maxims, and his eye from time to time recognized the persons of his friends. It merely proved to be a brief and final intercourse with the world, on the part of one who had already been considered, as to mental communion, to have taken his leave of it forever.

When he had placed his guests in front of the dying man, Hard-Heart, after a pause, that proceeded as much from sorrow as decorum, leaned a little forward, and demanded—

"Does my father hear the words of his son?"

"Speak," returned the trapper, in tones that issued from his chest, but which were rendered awfully distinct by the stillness that reigned in the place. "I am about to depart from the village of the Loups, and shortly shall be beyond the reach of your voice."

"Let the wise chief have no cares for his journey," continued Hard-Heart, with an earnest solicitude that led him to forget, for the moment, that others were waiting to address his adopted parent; "a hundred Loups shall clear his path from briers."

"Pawnee, I die, as I have lived, a Christian man!" resumed the trapper, with a force of voice that had the same startling effect on his hearers as is produced by the trumpet, when its blast rises suddenly and freely on the air, after its obstructed sounds have been heard struggling in the distance: "as I came into life so will I leave it. Horses and arms are not needed to stand in the presence of the Great Spirit of my people. He knows my color, and according to my gifts will He judge my deeds."

"My father will tell my young men how many Mingoes he has struck, and what acts of valor and justice he has done, that they may know how to imitate him."

"A boastful tongue is not heard in the heaven of a white man!" solemnly returned the old man. "What I have done He has seen. His eyes are always open. That which has been well done will He remember; wherein I have been wrong will He not forget to chastise, though He will do the same in mercy. No, my son; a Pale-face may not sing his own praises, and hope to have them acceptable before his God!"

A little disappointed, the young partisan stepped modestly back, making way for the recent comers to approach. Middleton took one of the meagre hands of the trapper, and struggling to command his voice, he succeeded in announcing his presence.

The old man listened like one whose thoughts were dwelling on a very different subject; but when the other had succeeded in making him understand that he was present, an expression of joyful recognition passed over his faded features.

"I hope you have not so soon forgotten those whom you so materially served!" Middleton concluded. "It would pain me to think my hold on your memory was so light."

"Little that I have ever seen is forgotten," returned the trapper; "I am at the close of many weary days, but there is not one among them all that I could wish to overlook. I remember you, with the whole of your company; ay, and your gran'ther, that went before you. I am glad that you have come back upon these plains, for I had need of one who speaks the English, since little faith can be put in the traders of these regions. Will you do a favor to an old and dying man?"

"Name it," said Middleton; "it shall be done."

"It is a far journey to send such trifles," resumed the old man, who spoke at short intervals, as strength and breath permitted, "a far and weary journey is the same; but kindnesses and friendships are things not to be forgotten. There is a settlement among the Otsego hills—"

"I know the place," interrupted Middleton, observing that he spoke with increasing difficulty; "proceed to tell me what you would have done."

"Take this rifle, and pouch, and horn, and send them to the person whose name is graven on the plates of the stock,—a trader cut the letters with his knife,—for it is long that I have intended to send him such a token of my love!"

"It shall be so. Is there more that you could wish?"

"Little else have I to bestow. My traps I give to my Indian son; for honestly and kindly has he kept his faith. Let him stand before me."

Middleton explained to the chief what the trapper had said, and relinquished his own place to the other.

"Pawnee," continued the old man, always changing his language to suit the person he addressed, and not unfrequently according to the ideas he expressed, "it is a custom of my people for the father to leave his blessing with the son before he shuts his eyes forever. This blessing I give to you; take it; for the prayers of a Christian man will never make the path of a just warrior to the blessed prairies either longer or more tangled. May the God of a white man look on your deeds with friendly eyes, and may you never commit an act that shall cause Him to darken His face. I know not whether we shall ever meet again. There are many traditions concerning the place of Good Spirits. It is not for one like me, old and experienced though I am, to set up my opinion against a nation's. You believe in the blessed prairies, and I have faith in the sayings of my fathers. If both are true our parting will be final; but if it should prove that the same meaning is hid under different words, we shall yet stand together, Pawnee, before the face of your Wahcondah, who will then be no other than my God. There is much to be said in favor of both religions, for each seems suited to its own people, and no doubt it was so intended. I fear I have not altogether followed the gifts of my color, inasmuch as I find it a little painful to give up forever the use of the rifle, and the comforts of the chase. But then the fault has been my own, seeing that it could not have been His. Ay, Hector," he continued, leaning forward a little, and feeling for the ears of the hound, "our parting has come at last, dog, and it will be a long hunt. You have been an honest, and a bold, and a faithful hound. Pawnee, you cannot slay the pup on my grave, for where a Christian dog falls there he lies forever; but you can be kind to him after I am gone, for the love you bear his master."

"The words of my father are in my ears," returned the young partisan, making a grave and respectful gesture of assent.

"Do you hear what the chief has promised, dog?" demanded the trapper, making an effort to attract the notice of the insensible effigy of his hound. Receiving no answering look, nor hearing any friendly whine, the old man felt for the mouth, and endeavored to force his hand between the cold lips. The truth then flashed upon him, although he was far from perceiving the whole extent of the deception. Falling back in his seat, he hung his head, like one who felt a severe and unexpected shock. Profiting by this momentary forgetfulness, two young Indians removed the skin with the same delicacy of feeling that had induced them to attempt the pious fraud.

"The dog is dead!" muttered the trapper, after a pause of many minutes; "a hound has his time as well as a man; and well has he filled his days! Captain," he added, making an effort to wave his hand for Middleton, "I am glad you have come; for though kind, and well meaning according to the gifts of their color, these Indians are not the men to lay the head of a white man in his grave. I have been thinking, too, of this dog at my feet; it will not do to set forth the opinion that a Christian can expect to meet his hound again; still there can be little harm in placing what is left of so faithful a servant nigh the bones of his master."

"It shall be as you desire."

"I'm glad you think with me in this matter. In order, then, to save labor, lay the pup at my feet; or for that matter, put him side by side. A hunter need never be ashamed to be found in company with his dog!"

"I charge myself with your wish."

The old man made a long, and apparently a musing pause. At times he raised his eyes wistfully, as if he would again address Middleton, but some innate feeling appeared always to suppress his words. The other, who observed his hesitation, inquired in a way most likely to encourage him to proceed whether there was aught else that he could wish to have done.

"I am without kith or kin in the wide world!" the trapper answered: "when I am gone there will be an end of my race. We have never been chiefs; but honest, and useful in our way I hope it cannot be denied we have always proved ourselves. My father lies buried near the sea, and the bones of his son will whiten on the prairie—"

"Name the spot, and your remains shall be placed by the side of your father," interrupted Middleton.

"Not so, not so, Captain. Let me sleep where I have lived—beyond the din of the settlements! Still I see no need why the grave of an honest man should be hid, like a Redskin in his ambushment. I paid a man in the settlements to make and put a graven stone at the head of my father's resting-place. It was of the value of twelve beaverskins, and cunningly and curiously was it carved! Then it told to all comers that the body of such a

Christian lay beneath; and it spoke of his manner of life, of his years, and of his honesty. When we had done with the Frenchers in the old war I made a journey to the spot, in order to see that all was rightly performed, and glad I am to say, the workman had not forgotten his faith."

"And such a stone you would have at your grave?"

"I! no, no, I have no son but Hard-Heart, and it is little that an Indian knows of white fashions and usages. Besides, I am his debtor already, seeing it is so little I have done since I have lived in his tribe. The rifle might bring the value of such a thing—but then I know it will give the boy pleasure to hang the piece in his hall, for many is the deer and the bird that he has seen it destroy. No, no, the gun must be sent to him whose name is graven on the lock!"

"But there is one who would gladly prove his affection in the way you wish; he who owes you not only his own deliverance from so many dangers, but who inherits a heavy debt of gratitude from his ancestors. The stone shall be put at the head of your grave."

The old man extended his emaciated hand, and gave the other a squeeze of thanks.

"I thought you might be willing to do it, but I was backward in asking the favor," he said, "seeing that you are not of my kin. Put no boastful words on the same, but just the name, the age, and the time of the death, with something from the holy book; no more, no more. My name will then not be altogether lost on 'arth; I need no more."

Middleton intimated his assent, and then followed a pause that was only broken by distant and broken sentences from the dying man. He appeared now to have closed his accounts with the world, and to await merely for the final summons to quit it. Middleton and Hard-Heart placed themselves on the opposite sides of his seat, and watched with melancholy solicitude, the variations of his countenance. For two hours there was no very sensible alteration. The expression of his faded and time-worn features was that of a calm and dignified repose. From time to time he spoke, uttering some brief sentence in the way of advice, or asking some simple questions concerning those in whose fortunes he took a friendly interest. During the whole of that solemn and anxious period each individual of the tribe kept his place, in the most self-restrained patience. When the old man spoke, all bent their heads to listen; and when his words were uttered, they seemed to ponder on their wisdom and usefulness.

As the flame drew nigher to the socket his voice was hushed, and there were moments when his attendants doubted whether he still belonged to the living. Middleton, who watched each wavering expression of his weather-beaten visage, with the interest of a keen observer of human nature, softened by the tenderness of personal regard, fancied he could read the workings of the old man's soul in the strong lineaments of his countenance. Perhaps what the enlightened soldier took for the delusion of mistaken opinion did actually occur—for who has returned from that unknown world to explain by what forms, and in what manner, he was introduced into its awful precincts? Without pretending to explain what must ever be a mystery to the quick, we shall simply relate facts as they occurred.

The trapper had remained nearly motionless for an hour. His eyes alone had occasionally opened and shut. When opened, his gaze seemed fastened on the clouds which hung around the western horizon, reflecting the bright colors, and giving form and loveliness to the glorious tints of an American sunset. The hour—the calm beauty of the season—the occasion, all conspired to fill the spectators with solemn awe. Suddenly, while musing on the remarkable position in which he was placed, Middleton felt the hand which he held grasp his own with incredible power, and the old man, supported on either side by his friends, rose upright to his feet. For a moment he looked about him, as if to invite all in presence to listen (the lingering remnant of human frailty), and then, with a fine military elevation of the head, and with a voice that might be heard in every part of that numerous assembly, he pronounced the word—

"Here!"

A movement so entirely unexpected, and the air of grandeur and humility which were so remarkably united in the mien of the trapper, together with the clear and uncommon force of his utterance, produced a short period of confusion in the faculties of all present. When Middleton and Hard-Heart, each of whom had involuntarily extended a hand to support the form of the old man, turned to him again, they found that the subject of their interest was removed forever beyond the necessity of their care. They mournfully placed the body in its seat, and Le Balafré arose to announce the termination of the scene to the tribe. The voice of the old Indian seemed a sort of echo from that invisible world to which the meek spirit of the trapper had just departed.

"A valiant, a just, and a wise warrior, has gone on the path which will lead him to the blessed grounds of his people!" he said. "When the voice of the Wahcondah called him, he was ready to answer. Go, my children; remember the just chief of the Pale-faces, and clear your own tracks from briers!"

The grave was made beneath the shade of some noble oaks. It has been carefully watched to the present hour by the Pawnees of the Loup, and is often shown to the traveller and the trader as a spot where a just white man sleeps. In due time the stone was placed at its head, with the simple inscription which the trapper had himself requested. The only liberty taken by Middleton was to add—*"May no wanton hand ever disturb his remains!"*

1827

Sarah Grimké
(1792–1873)

Angelina Grimké
(1805–1879)

Angelina Grimké writes as a woman from a prominent Southern family who had obviously experienced slavery firsthand; her *Appeal to the Christian Women of the South* (1836) attempts to show that slavery is un-American as well as un-Christian. Both women were extremely pious, and their appeals against slavery are grounded in the Christian faith: "Slavery is a crime against God and man" writes Angelina; "I [appeal] to your sense of duty as Christian women." She traces the role of women throughout the Bible, concluding that "the heart of man will bend under moral suasion" and that, that being the case, it falls to women everywhere to put an end to slavery.

The Grimké sisters were the daughters of a wealthy, aristocratic South Carolina family; Robert Barnwell Rhett was their cousin. Born into Charleston's elite, both women rejected their family's Episcopalianism and fashionable social life to join the Society of Friends (Quakers), and both eventually came to resent the Friends' equivocations on matters of slavery and abolition.

Originally, the Grimkés were concerned only about slavery and abolition, and they spoke to small women's groups. They moved to lecture platforms, first addressing only women but, later, mixed audiences. The opposition to their speaking in public was so strong that they began to address women's rights as well as abolition.

Angelina Grimké's more important titles include *Appeal to the Christian Women of the South* (1836), *Appeal to the Women of the Nominally Free States* (1837), and *Letters to Catharine E. Beecher in Reply to an Essay on Slavery and Abolitionism* (1838), which denounced gradualism in the ending of slavery. Sarah's important works include *Epistle to the Clergy of the Southern States* (1836) and *Letters on the Equality of the Sexes and the Condition of Woman* (1838). In addition, Angelina and Sarah Grimké, along with Angelina's husband, the abolitionist Theodore Weld, gathered the interviews printed in the influential *American Slavery as It Is: Testimony of a Thousand Witnesses* (1839). Harriet Beecher Stowe drew heavily on this work when writing *Uncle Tom's Cabin.*

The Grimké sisters died in Hyde Park, Massachusetts, Sarah in 1873 and Angelina in 1879.

Further Reading:

C. H. Birney, *The Grimké Sisters: Sarah and Angelina Grimké, the First American Advocates of Abolition and Woman's Rights*, 1970.

G. Lerner, *The Grimké Sisters from South Carolina: Rebels Against Slavery*, 1967.

K. D. Lumpkin, *The Emancipation of Angelina Grimké*, 1974.

Text:

The Public Years of Sarah and Angelina Grimké: Selected Writings, 1835–1839, ed. L. Ceplair, 1989.

Appeal to the Christian Women of the South*

... Be not afraid then to read my appeal; it is *not* written in the heat of passion or prejudice, but in that solemn calmness which is the result of conviction and duty. It is true, I am going to tell you unwelcome truths, but I mean to speak those *truths in love,* and remember Solomon says, "faithful are the *wounds* of a friend." I do not believe the time has yet come when *Christian women* "will not endure sound doctrine," even on the subject of slavery, if it is spoken to them in tenderness and love, therefore I now address *you.*

* (New York: [American Anti-Slavery Society], 1836; New York: Arno and *New York Times,* 1969).

To all of you then, known or unknown, relatives or strangers, (for you are all *one* in Christ,) I would speak. I have felt for you at this time, when unwelcome light is pouring in upon the world on the subject of slavery; light which even Christians would exclude, if they could, from our country, or at any rate from the southern portion of it, saying, as its rays strike the rock bound coasts of New England and scatter their warmth and radiance over her hills and valleys, and from thence travel onward over the Palisades of the Hudson, and down the soft flowing waters of the Delaware and gild the waves of the Potomac, "hitherto shalt thou come and no further"; I know that even professors of His name who has been emphatically called the "Light of the world" would, if they could, build a wall of adamant around the Southern States whose top might reach unto heaven, in order to shut out the light which is bounding from mountain to mountain and from the hills to the plains and valleys beneath, through the vast extent of our Northern States. But believe me, when I tell you, their attempts will be as utterly fruitless as were the efforts of the builders of Babel; and why? Because moral, like natural light, is so extremely subtle in its nature as to overleap all human barriers, and laugh at the puny efforts of man to control it. All the excuses and palliations of this system must inevitably be swept away, just as other "refuges of lies" have been, by the irresistible torrent of a rectified public opinion. "The *supporters* of the slave system," says Jonathan Dymond in his admirable work on the Principles of Morality,[1] "will *hereafter* be regarded with the *same* public feeling, as he who was an advocate for the slave trade *now is.*" It will be, and that very soon, clearly perceived and fully acknowledged by all the virtuous and the candid, that in *principle* it is as sinful to hold a human being in bondage who has been born in Carolina, as one who has been born in Africa. All that sophistry of argument which has been employed to prove, that although it is sinful to send to Africa to procure men and women as slaves, who have never been in slavery, that still, it is not sinful to keep those in bondage who have come down by inheritance, will be utterly overthrown. We must come back to the good old doctrine of our forefathers who declared to the world, "this self evident truth that *all* men are created equal, and that they have certain *inalienable* rights among which are life, *liberty,* and the pursuit of happiness." It is even a greater absurdity to suppose a man can be legally born a slave under *our free Republican* Government, than under the petty despotisms of barbarian Africa. If then, we have no right to enslave an African, surely we can have none to enslave an American; if it is a self evident truth that *all* men, every where and of every color are born equal, and have an *inalienable right to liberty,* then it is equally true that *no* man can be born a slave, and no man can ever *rightfully* be reduced to *involuntary* bondage and held as a slave, however fair may be the claim of his master or mistress through will and title-deeds. . . .

But perhaps you will be ready to query, why appeal to *women* on this subject? *We* do not make the laws which perpetuate slavery. *No* legislative power is vested in *us; we* can do nothing to overthrow the system, even if we wished to do so. To this I reply, I know you do not make the laws, but I also know that *you are the wives and mothers, the sisters*

---

[1] Jonathan Dymond (1796–1828), a British Quaker moralist, published *An Enquiry into the Accordancy of War with the Principles of Christianity* . . . in 1823 and founded a peace society in Exeter in 1825. *Essays on the principles of morality, and on the private and political rights of mankind* was published posthumously in England in 1829. The sisters edited a version of it with notes by Thomas S. Grimké (Philadelphia, Pa.: Ashmead, 1834).

and daughters of those who do; and if you really suppose *you* can do nothing to overthrow slavery, you are greatly mistaken. You can do much in every way: four things I will name. 1st. You can read on this subject. 2d. You can pray over this subject. 3d. You can speak on this subject. 4th. You can *act* on this subject. I have not placed reading before praying because I regard it more important, but because, in order to pray aright, we must understand what we are praying for; it is only then we can "pray with the understanding and the spirit also."

1. Read then on the subject of slavery. Search the Scriptures daily, whether the things I have told you are true. Other books and papers might be a great help to you in this investigation, but they are not necessary, and it is hardly probable that your Committees of Vigilance[2] will allow you to have any other. The *Bible* then is the book I want you to read in the spirit of inquiry, and the spirit of prayer. Even the enemies of Abolitionists, acknowledge that their doctrines are drawn from it. . . .

2. Pray over this subject. When you have entered into your closets, and shut to the doors, then pray to your father, who seeth in secret, that he would open your eyes to see whether slavery is *sinful,* and if it is, that he would enable you to bear a faithful, open and unshrinking testimony against it, and to do whatsoever your hands find to do, leaving the consequences entirely to him, who still says to us whenever we try to reason away duty from the fear of consequences, *"What is that to thee, follow thou me."* Pray also for that poor slave, that he may be kept patient and submissive under his hard lot, until God is pleased to open the door of freedom to him without violence or bloodshed. Pray too for the master that his heart may be softened, and he made willing to acknowledge, as Joseph's brethren did, "Verily we are guilty concerning our brother," before he will be compelled to add in consequence of Divine judgment, "therefore is all this evil come upon us." Pray also for all your brethren and sisters who are laboring in the righteous cause of Emancipation in the Northern States, England and the world. There is great encouragement for prayer in these words of our Lord. "Whatsoever ye shall ask the Father *in my name,* he *will give* it to you"—Pray then without ceasing, in the closet and the social circle.

3. Speak on this subject. It is through the tongue, the pen, and the press, that truth is principally propagated. Speak then to your relatives, your friends, your acquaintances on the subject of slavery; be not afraid if you are conscientiously convinced it is *sinful,* to say so openly, but calmly, and to let your sentiments be known. If you are served by the slaves of others, try to ameliorate their condition as much as possible; never aggravate their faults, and thus add fuel to the fire of anger already kindled in a master and mistress's bosom; remember their extreme ignorance, and consider them as your Heavenly Father does the *less* culpable on this account, even when they do wrong things. Discountenance *all* cruelty to them, all starvation, all corporal chastisement; these may brutalize and *break* their spirits, but will never bond them to willing, cheerful obedience. If possible, see that they are comfortably and *seasonably* fed, whether in the house or the field; it is unreasonable and cruel to expect slaves to wait for their breakfast until eleven o'clock, when they rise at five or six. Do all you can, to induce their owners to clothe them well, and to allow them many little indulgences which would contribute to their comfort. Above all, try to persuade your husband, father, brothers and sons, that

---

[2] Self-appointed groups of southern white males organized to confiscate what Southerners termed "incendiary" (i.e. abolitionist) literature and generally suppress antislavery speech.

slavery is a crime against God and man, and that it is a great sin to keep *human beings* in such abject ignorance; to deny them the privilege of learning to read and write. The Catholics are universally condemned, for denying the Bible to the common people, but, *slaveholders must not* blame them, for *they* are doing the *very same thing,* and for the very same reason, neither of these systems can bear the light which bursts from the pages of that Holy Book. And lastly, endeavour to inculcate submission on the part of the slaves, but whilst doing this be faithful in pleading the cause of the oppressed. . . .

4. Act on this subject. Some of you *own* slaves yourselves. If you believe slavery is *Sinful,* set them at liberty, "undo the heavy burdens and let the oppressed go free." If they wish to remain with you, pay them wages, if not let them leave you. Should they remain teach them, and have them taught the common branches of an English education; they have minds and those minds, *ought to be improved.* So precious a talent as intellect, never was given to be wrapt in a napkin and buried in the earth. It is the *duty* of all, as far as they can, to improve their own mental faculties, because we are commanded to love God with *all our minds,* as well as with all our hearts, and we commit a great sin, if we *forbid or prevent* that cultivation of the mind in others, which would enable them to perform this duty. Teach your servants then to read &c, and encourage them to believe it is their *duty* to learn, if it were only that they might read the Bible.

But some of you will say, we can neither free our slaves nor teach them to read, for the laws of our state forbid it. Be not surprised when I say such wicked laws *ought to be no barrier* in the way of your duty, and I appeal to the Bible to prove this position. . . .

But some of you may say, if we do free our slaves, they will be taken up and sold, therefore there will be no use in doing it. Peter and John might just as well have said, we will not preach the gospel, for if we do, we shall be taken up and put in prison, therefore there will be no use in our preaching. *Consequences,* my friends, belong no more to *you,* than they did to these apostles. Duty is ours and events are God's. If you think slavery is sinful, all *you* have to do is to set your slaves at liberty, do all you can to protect them, and in humble faith and fervent prayer, commend them to your common Father. He can take care of them. . . .

But you will perhaps say, such a course of conduct would inevitably expose us to great suffering. Yes! my christian friends, I believe it would, but this will *not* excuse you or any one else for the neglect of *duty.* . . .

But you may say we are *women,* how can *our* hearts endure persecution? And why not? Have not *women* stood up in all the dignity and strength of moral courage to be the leaders of the people, and to bear a faithful testimony for the truth whenever the providence of God has called them to do so? Are there no *women* in that noble army of martyrs who are now singing the song of Moses and the Lamb? Who led out the women of Israel from the house of bondage, striking the timbrel, and singing the song of deliverance on the banks of that sea whose waters stood up like walls of crystal to open a passage for their escape? It was a *woman;* Miriam, the prophetess, the sister of Moses and Aaron. Who went up with Barak to Kadesh to fight against Jabin, King of Canaan, into whose hand Israel had been sold because of their iniquities? It was a *woman!* . . .

Yes, *women* suffered under the ten persecutions of heathen Rome, with the most unshrinking constancy and fortitude; not all the entreaties of friends, nor the claims of new born infancy, nor the cruel threats of enemies could make *them* sprinkle one grain of incense upon the altars of Roman idols. Come now with me to the beautiful valleys of Piedmont. Whose blood stains the green sward, and decks the wild flowers with colors not their own, and smokes on the sword of persecuting France? It is *woman's,* as well as man's? Yes, *women* were accounted as sheep for the slaughter, and were cut down as the tender saplings of the wood.

But time would fail me, to tell of all those hundreds and thousands of *women*, who perished in the Low countries of Holland, when Alva's[3] sword of vengeance was unsheathed against the Protestants, when the Catholic Inquisitions of Europe became the merciless executioners of vindictive wrath, upon those who dared to worship God, instead of bowing down in unholy adoration before "my Lord God the *Pope*," and when England, too, burnt her Ann Ascoes[4] at the stake of martyrdom. Suffice it to say, that the Church, after having been driven from Judea to Rome, and from Rome to Piedmont, and from Piedmont to England, and from England to Holland, at last stretched her fainting wings over the dark bosom of the Atlantic, and found on the shores of a great wilderness, a refuge from tyranny and oppression—as she thought, but *even here,* (the warm blush of shame mantles my cheeks as I write it,) *even there,* woman was beaten and banished, imprisoned, and hung upon the gallows, a trophy to the Cross.

And what, I would ask in conclusion, have *women* done for the great and glorious cause of Emancipation? Who wrote that pamphlet which moved the heart of Wilberforce[5] to pray over the wrongs, and his tongue to plead the cause of the oppressed African? It was a *woman,* Elizabeth Heyrick. Who labored assiduously to keep the sufferings of the slave continually before the British public? They were *women.* And how did they do it? By their needles, paint brushes and pens, by speaking the truth, and petitioning Parliament for the abolition of slavery. And what was the effect of their labors? Read it in the Emancipation bill[6] of Great Britain. Read it, in the present state of her West India Colonies. Read it, in the impulse which has been given to the cause of freedom in the United States of America. Have English women then done so much for the negro, and shall American women do nothing? Oh no! Already are there sixty female Anti-Slavery Societies in operation. These are doing just what the English women did, telling the story of the colored man's wrongs, praying for his deliverance, and presenting his kneeling image constantly before the public eye on bags and needle-books, card-racks, pen-wipers, pin-cushions, &c. Even the children of the north are inscribing on their handy work, "May the points of our needles prick the slaveholder's conscience." Some of the reports of these Societies exhibit not only considerable talent, but a deep sense of religious duty, and a determination to persevere through evil as well as good report, until every scourge, and every shackle, is buried under the feet of the manumitted slave. . . .

Northern women may labor to produce a correct public opinion at the North, but if Southern women sit down in listless indifference and criminal idleness, public opinion cannot be rectified and purified at the South. It is manifest to every reflecting mind,

---

3 Fernando, third duke of Alba (1507–1582), commanded Charles V's army in a vain attempt to stamp out Lutheranism from Germany and then led the equally unsuccessful effort to crush Protestantism in the Spanish Netherlands.

4 Anne Askew was burnt, with three men, on July 16, 1546, for refusing to accept the doctrine of transubstantiation.

5 William Wilberforce (1759–1833), a British philanthropist and reformer who led the fight to end the slave trade and slavery in the British Empire.

6 Parliament, on August 29, 1833, passed a bill, to take effect eleven months hence, freeing slave children under the age of six, and holding the other slaves in an apprenticeship system (six years for field hands, four years for others). Slaveowners were paid twenty million pounds in compensation. Antigua and Bermuda waived the apprenticeship system, and the other colonies so abused it that the act was amended on April 11, 1838, ending the apprenticeship system as of August 1 of that year.

that slavery must be abolished; the era in which we live, and the light which is over-spreading the whole world on this subject, clearly show that the time cannot be distant when it will be done. Now there are only two ways in which it can be effected, by moral power or physical force, and it is for *you* to choose which of these you prefer. . . .

My object has been to arouse *you,* as the wives and mothers, the daughters and sisters, of the South, to a sense of your duty as *women,* and as Christian women, on that great subject, which has already shaken our country, from the St. Lawrence and the lakes, to the Gulf of Mexico, and from the Mississippi to the shores of the Atlantic; *and will continue mightily to shake it,* until the polluted temple of slavery fall and crumble into ruin. . . .

Can you not, my friends, understand the signs of the time; do you not see the sword of retributive justice hanging over the South, or are you still slumbering at your posts? . . .

The *women of the South can overthrow* this horrible system of oppression and cruelty, licentiousness and wrong. . . . Such appeals to your legislatures would be irresistible, for there is something in the heart of man which *will bend under moral suasion.* There is a swift witness for truth in his bosom, which *will respond to truth* when it is uttered with calmness and dignity. If you could obtain but six signatures to such a petition in only one state, I would say, send up that petition, and be not in the least discouraged by the scoffs and jeers of the heartless, or the resolution of the house to lay it on the table. It will be a great thing if the subject can be introduced into your legislatures in any way, even by *women,* and *they* will be the most likely to introduce it there in the best possible manner, as a matter of *morals* and *religion,* not of expediency or politics. You may petition, too, the different ecclesiastical bodies of the slave states. Slavery must be attacked with the whole power of truth and the sword of the spirit. You must take it up on *Christian* ground, and fight against it with Christian weapons, whilst your feet are shod with the preparation of the gospel of peace. And *you are now* loudly called upon by the cries of the widow and the orphan, to arise and gird yourselves for this great moral conflict, with the whole armour of righteousness upon the right hand and on the left.

RELATED VOICES

Woman's Rights Convention

One of the most unique and interesting speeches of the Convention was made by Sojourner Truth, an emancipated slave. It is impossible to transfer it to paper, or convey any adequate idea of the effect it produced upon the audience. Those only can appreciate it who saw her powerful form, her whole-souled, earnest gestures, and listened to her strong and truthful tones. She came forward to the platform and addressing the President said with great simplicity:

May I say a few words? Receiving an affirmative answer, she proceeded; I want to say a few words about this matter. I am a woman's rights. I have as much muscle as any man, and can do as much work as any man. I have plowed and reaped and husked and chopped and mowed, and can any man do more than that? I have heard much about the sexes being equal; I can carry as much as any man, and can eat as much too, if I can get it. I am as strong as any man that is now. As for intellect, all I can say is, if woman have a pint and man a quart—why can't she have her little pint full? You need not be afraid to give us our rights for fear we will take too much,—for we can't take more than our pint'll hold. The poor men seem to be all in confusion, and don't know what to do. Why children, if you have woman's rights give it to her and you will feel better. You will have your own rights, and they wont be so much trouble. I can't read, but I can hear. I have heard the bible and have learned that Eve caused man to sin. Well if woman upset the world, do give her a chance to set it right side up again. The Lady has spoken about Jesus, how he never spurned woman from him, and she was right. When Lazarus died, Mary and Martha came to him with faith and love and besought him to raise their brother. And Jesus wept—and Lazarus came forth. And how came Jesus into the world? Through God who created him and woman who bore him. Man, where is your part? But the woman are coming up blessed be God and a few of the men are coming up with them. But man is in a tight place, the poor slave is on him, woman is coming on him, and he is surely between a hawk and a buzzard.

Sojourner Truth as reported in The Anti-Slavery Bugle, June 21, 1851 (v.6, no. 41)

Unidentified photographer
With her name describing her life, the traveling preacher and one-time slave Sojourner Truth became a well known activist for the rights of women and African Americans. In this photograph—one of many she had made for publicity purposes during her life—she is shown wearing traveling clothes, and her right hand, which was missing the index finger, is visible.
(Sophia Smith Collection, Women's History Archive, Smith College)

William Cullen Bryant
1794–1878

William Cullen Bryant's popular image haunts his poetry. The classroom portrait of this legendary patriarch of American verse, with a chiseled old face and deep-set eyes peering out from behind bushy eyebrows and a long, flowing white beard, solemnly oversaw generations of American schoolchildren dutifully reciting "Thanatopsis" and "To a Waterfowl." His publications span the administrations of seventeen presidents, from Thomas Jefferson to Rutherford B. Hayes. Yet the definitive edition of Bryant's poems consists of but two relatively small volumes: meditative, restrained, full of dignified serenity and pleasure in nature, Bryant's early work reveals few youthful flaws, his last efforts few signs of his eighty-three years.

William Cullen Bryant was born in Cummington, a small town in western Massachusetts's Berkshire Mountains. His mother, a hardy Calvinist descendant of the Pilgrim John Alden, made the following brief entry in her diary for November 3, 1794: "Stormy, wind N.E. Churned. Seven in the evening a son was born." His father, a doctor, encouraged him to read widely in the family's modest but well-chosen library of English and classical literature.

Privately educated by country ministers, as was the custom in rural New England, Bryant began writing poetry at eight years of age and, supported by his father, had his first work published as an anonymous "Youth of Thirteen." *The Embargo; or, Sketches of the Times* (1808) is a Federalist satire on the policies of President Jefferson, whom Bryant came to admire years later. The poem's vitriolic couplets testify both to Bryant's youthful poetic tendencies and to the still reigning influence of Alexander Pope on American verse. He studied law privately and was admitted to the Massachusetts bar in 1814. He wrote a great deal of poetry during those early years of practicing law, and he also served as town clerk of Great Barrington, where in 1821 he married Fanny Fairchild. His *Poems* were published in the same year. Bryant was eager to settle in Boston, but his father discouraged him, noting that there were too many lawyers there already.

In 1825 Bryant moved to New York, where he edited a magazine, the *New York Review*, and became part of a literary group that came to be known as the Knickerbocker school and included Washington Irving and James Fenimore Cooper. In 1826 he signed on as the assistant editor of the New York *Evening Post*, and from 1829 to his death in 1878 he served as its editor in chief. An inveterate traveler, Bryant made several trips to Europe and the American frontier (to visit his pioneer brothers) and lengthy visits to Canada, Mexico, and the Caribbean. But New York remained his home and writing his central activity for the rest of his life.

Although Bryant spent more than fifty years there, New York seems to have had little impact on either his character or his poetry. Never quite as urbane as Washington Irving, Bryant maintained the austerity of a New England winter in his life and work. He rarely allowed himself, as he notes in "The Poet," the luxury of "burning words" or "impassioned thought." Bryant's lifelong interest in the classics and his familiarity with the leading eighteenth-century Neoclassical English poets who wrote on nature and melancholy, especially those in the "Graveyard school," most notably Thomson, Blair, Young, and Gray, is never more apparent than in "Thanatopsis," first published in the newly established *North American Review* in 1817. Recalling the circumstances, one of the editors, Richard Henry Dana, Sr., later wrote:

> Going into town one day while assisting E. T. Channing (now Professor) in the *North American Review* [1817], he read to me a couple of pieces of poetry which had just been sent to the *Review*—the "Thanatopsis" and "The Inscription for the Entrance to a Wood." While C—— was reading one of them, I broke out, saying, "That was never written on this side of the water"—and naturally enough, considering what American poetry had been up to that moment.

Bryant, like many of his contemporaries, was absorbed in the issues surrounding American literary nationalism. He vigorously opposed the lingering tendency of many Americans who "do not praise a thing until [they] see the seal of transatlantic approbation upon it." He insisted that America was "a rich and varied field for literature." Yet, like his counterparts in the art world, particularly his "kindred spirits" in what came to be known as the Hudson River school, Bryant was more successful at introducing indigenous American subjects than in treating them in distinctively American terms.

His literary criticism, however, stands as one of the earliest efforts in the new nation to study poetry systematically. From his *Lectures on Poetry* (delivered in 1825 but published posthumously in 1884) to his essay "Poets and Poetry of the English Language" (printed as the introduction to his anthology, *A Library of Poetry and Song*, in 1871), Bryant consistently focused on the original, imaginative, moral, and didactic properties of poetry. Bryant sought "a luminous style" in his verse, and in reading him we ought to keep in mind his own guidelines for writing it:

> The elements of poetry lie in natural objects, in the vicissitudes of human life, in the emotions of the human heart, and the relations of man to man. He who can present them in combinations and lights which at once affect the mind with a deep sense of their truth and beauty is the poet for his own age and the ages that succeed him. . . . The metaphysician, the subtle thinker, the dealer in abstruse speculations, whatever his skill in versification, misapplies it when he abandons the more convenient form of prose, and perplexes himself with the attempt to express his ideas in poetic numbers.

More than two-thirds of Bryant's poems focus on the natural world. In this respect, his repeated reading of Wordsworth as a youth had a profound impact on his verse. Dana describes the nature of the influence: "He said that, upon opening the book, a thousand springs seemed to gush up at once in his heart, and the face of Nature, of a sudden, to change into a strange freshness and life." Bryant's enthusiasm for Wordsworth's verse had waned noticeably by the time they finally met in England in 1845, yet Bryant's vision of nature, like Wordsworth's, remains stately; both write with considerable self-control, emotional distance, and purity of line. And, revealing the influence of Wordsworth, Bryant is the first major American poet to celebrate what would soon become the Romantic tradition of recognizing divine splendor in nature's beauty and taking personal solace from it. In this respect, Bryant spent much of his life using nature and poetry as tools to create a religion to sustain himself.

Nearly all of Bryant's poetry that claims our attention was written before 1840, when the pressures of editing a major newspaper in one of the nation's largest cities allowed him little time to write verse.

Bryant knew that there was but a small audience for poetry in the early decades of nineteenth-century America and that, as he told Dana, "no man makes money by it. . . . The taste for it is something old-fashioned; the march of the age is in another direction; mankind are occupied with politics, railroads, and steamboats." Not surprisingly, Bryant's became one of the most respected voices in nineteenth-century American journalism, and his incisive editorials tackled virtually every important issue of the the time. His opinions counted in every public cause, and his presence was felt in innumerable acts of community planning and service.

Bryant's literary efforts in his last few decades focused primarily on translating the *Iliad* (1870) and the *Odyssey* (1872), editing Shakespeare, celebrating American history and literature, and eulogizing the deaths of the nation's leading writers; he remained an extremely popular poet, despite the long intervals between his volumes. By the time of his death in 1878, Bryant had become such a prominent figure in New York intellectual and political circles that the city's flags flew at half mast, its shops draped in black.

Bryant's importance in American literature can be considered in the appraisals of his more distinguished contemporaries. Edgar Allan Poe called Bryant "full of the aristocracy of intellect." Ralph Waldo Emerson praised Bryant as "always original—a true painter of the face of the country, and of the sentiment of his own people. . . . It is his proper praise that he first, and he only, made known to mankind our northern landscape—its summer splendor, its autumn russet, its winter lights and glooms." Yet Walt Whitman offers the most expansive version of Bryant's achievement:

Bryant pulsing the first interior verse-throbs of a mighty world—bard of the river and the wood, ever conveying a taste of open air . . . always lurkingly fond of threnodies— beginning and ending his long career with chants of death . . . touching the highest universal truth, enthusiasms, duties—morals as grim and eternal, if not as stormy and fateful, as anything in Aeschylus.

Further Reading:

P. Godwin, *The Life and Works of William Cullen Bryant*, 2 vols., 1883.

J. Bigelow, *William Cullen Bryant*, 1890.

W. A. Bradley, *William Cullen Bryant*, 1905.

A. Nevins, *The Evening Post: A Century of Journalism*, 1922.

T. McDowell, ed., *Bryant*, 1935.

H. H. Peckham, *Gotham Yankee: A Biography of William Cullen Bryant*, 1950.

C. S. Johnson, *Politics and a Bellyful: The Journalistic Career of William Cullen Bryant*, 1962.

A. McLean, *William Cullen Bryant*, 1964.

C. Brown, *William Cullen Bryant*, 1972.

N. Krapf, ed., *Under Open Sky: Poets on William Cullen Bryant*, 1986.

Text:

The Poetical Works of William Cullen Bryant, ed. P. Godwin, 2 vols., 1883.

Thanatopsis*

To him who in the love of Nature holds
Communion with her visible forms, she speaks
A various language; for his gayer hours
She has a voice of gladness, and a smile
And eloquence of beauty, and she glides   5
Into his darker musings, with a mild
And healing sympathy, that steals away
Their sharpness, ere he is aware. When thoughts
Of the last bitter hour come like a blight
Over thy spirit, and sad images   10
Of the stern agony, and shroud, and pall,
And breathless darkness, and the narrow house,
Make thee to shudder, and grow sick at heart;—
Go forth, under the open sky, and list
To Nature's teachings, while from all around—   15
Earth and her waters, and the depths of air—
Comes a still voice.—

                 Yet a few days, and thee
The all-beholding sun shall see no more
In all his course; nor yet in the cold ground,
Where thy pale form was laid, with many tears,   20
Nor in the embrace of ocean, shall exist
Thy image. Earth, that nourished thee, shall claim
Thy growth, to be resolved to earth again,
And, lost each human trace, surrendering up
Thine individual being, shalt thou go   25
To mix for ever with the elements,
To be a brother to the insensible rock
And to the sluggish clod, which the rude swain
Turns with his share,[1] and treads upon. The oak
Shall send his roots abroad, and pierce thy mould.   30

    Yet not to thine eternal resting-place
Shalt thou retire alone, nor couldst thou wish
Couch more magnificent. Thou shalt lie down
With patriarchs of the infant world—with kings,
The powerful of the earth—the wise, the good,   35
Fair forms, and hoary seers of ages past,
All in one mighty sepulchre. The hills
Rock-ribbed and ancient as the sun,—the vales
Stretching in pensive quietness between;
The venerable woods—rivers that move   40

---

* Greek: "Meditation on Death."   [1] Plowshare.

In majesty, and the complaining brooks
That make the meadows green; and, poured round all,

Old Ocean's gray and melancholy waste,—
Are but the solemn decorations all
Of the great tomb of man. The golden sun,   45
The planets, all the infinite host of heaven,
Are shining on the sad abodes of death,
Through the still lapse of ages. All that tread
The globe are but a handful to the tribes
That slumber in its bosom.—Take the wings   50
Of morning, pierce the Barcan wilderness,[2]
Or lose thyself in the continuous woods
Where rolls the Oregon,[3] and hears no sound,
Save his own dashings—yet the dead are there:
And millions in those solitudes, since first   55
The flight of years began, have laid them down
In their last sleep—the dead reign there alone.
So shalt thou rest, and what if thou withdraw
In silence from the living, and no friend
Take note of thy departure? All that breathe   60
Will share thy destiny. The gay will laugh
When thou art gone, the solemn brood of care
Plod on, and each one as before will chase
His favorite phantom; yet all these shall leave
Their mirth and their employments, and shall come   65
And make their bed with thee. As the long train
Of ages glides away, the sons of men,
The youth in life's fresh spring, and he who goes
In the full strength of years, matron and maid,
The speechless babe, and the gray-headed man—   70
Shall one by one be gathered to thy side,
By those, who in their turn shall follow them.

So live, that when thy summons comes to join
The innumerable caravan, which moves
To that mysterious realm, where each shall take   75
His chamber in the silent halls of death,
Thou go not, like the quarry-slave at night,
Scourged to his dungeon, but, sustained and soothed
By an unfaltering trust, approach thy grave,
Like one who wraps the drapery of his couch   80
About him, and lies down to pleasant dreams.
ca. 1814/1817; 1821

---

[2] The desert of Barca in northeast Libya.
[3] Indian name for what is now the Columbia
River.

To a Waterfowl

Whither, midst falling dew,
    While glow the heavens with the last steps of day,
Far, through their rosy depths, dost thou pursue
    Thy solitary way?

    Vainly the fowler's eye   5
Might mark thy distant flight to do thee wrong,
As, darkly painted on the crimson sky,
    Thy figure floats along.

    Seek'st thou the plashy brink
Of weedy lake, or marge of river wide,   10
Or where the rocking billows rise and sink
    On the chafed ocean-side?

    There is a Power whose care
Teaches thy way along that pathless coast—
The desert and illimitable air—   15
    Lone wandering, but not lost.

    All day thy wings have fanned,
At that far height, the cold, thin atmosphere,
Yet stoop not, weary, to the welcome land,
    Though the dark night is near.   20

    And soon that toil shall end;
Soon shalt thou find a summer home, and rest,
And scream among thy fellows; reeds shall bend,
    Soon, o'er thy sheltered nest.

    Thou'rt gone, the abyss of heaven   25
Hath swallowed up thy form; yet, on my heart
Deeply has sunk the lesson thou hast given,
    And shall not soon depart.

    He who, from zone to zone,
Guides through the boundless sky thy certain flight,   30
In the long way that I must tread alone,
    Will lead my steps aright.

1815/1818; 1821

The Prairies*

These are the gardens of the Desert,[1] these
The unshorn fields, boundless and beautiful,
For which the speech of England has no name[2]—
The Prairies. I behold them for the first,
And my heart swells, while the dilated sight   5
Takes in the encircling vastness. Lo! they stretch,
In airy undulations, far away,
As if the ocean, in his gentlest swell,
Stood still, with all his rounded billows fixed,
And motionless forever.—Motionless?—   10
No—they are all unchained again. The clouds
Sweep over with their shadows, and, beneath,
The surface rolls and fluctuates to the eye;
Dark hollows seem to glide along and chase
The sunny ridges. Breezes of the South!   15
Who toss the golden and the flame-like flowers,
And pass the prairie-hawk that, poised on high,
Flaps his broad wings, yet moves not—ye have played
Among the palms of Mexico and vines
Of Texas, and have crisped the limpid brooks   20
That from the fountains of Sonora[3] glide
Into the calm Pacific—have ye fanned
A nobler or a lovelier scene than this?
Man hath no power in all this glorious work:
The hand that built the firmament hath heaved   25
And smoothed these verdant swells, and sown their slopes
With herbage, planted them with island groves,
And hedged them round with forests. Fitting floor
For this magnificent temple of the sky—
With flowers whose glory and whose multitude   30
Rival the constellations! The great heavens
Seem to stoop down upon the scene in love,—
A nearer vault, and of a tenderer blue,
Than that which bends above our eastern hills.

As o'er the verdant waste I guide my steed,   35
Among the high rank grass that sweeps his sides
The hollow beating of his footstep seems
A sacrilegious sound. I think of those

---

* Written after Bryant's first view of the
prairies of Illinois in 1832.
[1] In the early nineteenth century, the Great
Plains of the American West were considered the "Great American Desert."

[2] The word *prairie* was adopted from the
French explorers' term *la prairie*, meaning
"meadow."
[3] State in northwest Mexico.

Upon whose rest he tramples. Are they here—
The dead of other days?—and did the dust   40
Of these fair solitudes once stir with life
And burn with passion? Let the mighty mounds[4]
That overlook the rivers, or that rise
In the dim forest crowded with old oaks,
Answer. A race, that long has passed away,   45
Built them;—a disciplined and populous race
Heaped, with long toil, the earth, while yet the Greek
Was hewing the Pentelicus[5] to forms
Of symmetry, and rearing on its rock
The glittering Parthenon. These ample fields   50
Nourished their harvests, here their herds were fed,
When haply by their stalls the bison lowed,
And bowed his manèd shoulder to the yoke.
All day this desert murmured with their toils,
Till twilight blushed, and lovers walked, and wooed   55
In a forgotten language, and old tunes,
From instruments of unremembered form,
Gave the soft winds a voice. The red man came—
The roaming hunter tribes, warlike and fierce,
And the mound-builders vanished from the earth.   60
The solitude of centuries untold
Has settled where they dwelt. The prairie-wolf
Hunts in their meadows, and his fresh-dug den
Yawns by my path. The gopher mines the ground
Where stood their swarming cities. All is gone;   65
All—save the piles of earth that hold their bones,
The platforms where they worshipped unknown gods,
The barriers which they builded from the soil
To keep the foe at bay—till o'er the walls
The wild beleaguerers broke, and, one by one,   70
The strongholds of the plain were forced, and heaped
With corpses. The brown vultures of the wood
Flocked to those vast uncovered sepulchres,
And sat unscared and silent at their feast.
Haply some solitary fugitive,   75
Lurking in marsh and forest, till the sense
Of desolation and of fear became
Bitterer than death, yielded himself to die.
Man's better nature triumphed then. Kind words
Welcomed and soothed him; the rude conquerors   80
Seated the captive with their chiefs; he chose
A bride among their maidens, and at length
Seemed to forget—yet ne'er forgot—the wife

---

[4] Indian burial earthworks ascribed to a vanished race of ancient "mound builders."

[5] Greek Mt. Pentelikon, the site from which
marble was quarried for the Parthenon.

Of his first love, and her sweet little ones,
Butchered, amid their shrieks, with all his race.   85

  Thus change the forms of being. Thus arise
Races of living things, glorious in strength,
And perish, as the quickening breath of God
Fills them, or is withdrawn. The red man, too,
Has left the blooming wilds he ranged so long,   90
And, nearer to the Rocky Mountains, sought
A wilder hunting-ground. The beaver builds
No longer by these streams, but far away,
On waters whose blue surface ne'er gave back
The white man's face—among Missouri's springs,   95
And pools whose issues swell the Oregon[6]—
He rears his little Venice. In these plains
The bison feeds no more. Twice twenty leagues
Beyond remotest smoke of hunter's camp,
Roams the majestic brute, in herds that shake   100
The earth with thundering steps—yet here I meet
His ancient footprints stamped beside the pool.

  Still this great solitude is quick with life.
Myriads of insects, gaudy as the flowers
They flutter over, gentle quadrupeds,   105
And birds, that scarce have learned the fear of man,
Are here, and sliding reptiles of the ground,
Startlingly beautiful. The graceful deer
Bounds to the wood at my approach. The bee,
A more adventurous colonist than man,   110
With whom he came across the eastern deep,
Fills the savannas with his murmurings,
And hides his sweets, as in the golden age,
Within the hollow oak. I listen long
To his domestic hum, and think I hear   115
The sound of that advancing multitude
Which soon shall fill these deserts. From the ground
Comes up the laugh of children, the soft voice
Of maidens, and the sweet and solemn hymn
Of Sabbath worshippers. The low of herds   120
Blends with the rustling of the heavy grain
Over the dark brown furrows. All at once
A fresher wind sweeps by, and breaks my dream,
And I am in the wilderness alone.
1832/1833

---

6 The Columbia River.

George Caleb Bingham
Daniel Boone Escorting Settlers Through the Cumberland Gap
oil on canvas, 1851–1852
(Collection, Washington University Gallery of Art, St. Louis)

The Literature of the American Renaissance 1836–1865

"Who Reads an American Book?"

Could literature and art, as defined by colonial standards, thrive in the new nation? Were they appropriate to the special political, social, and economic conditions Americans found and in turn created? How could the language and literary models of England be naturalized to these conditions? Was there a cultural counterpart to political independence? These were some of the issues confronting the men and women who became the writers of the American Renaissance.

"We have no distinct class of literati in our country," Thomas Jefferson had noted. "Every man is engaged in some industrious pursuit. . . . Few therefore of those who are qualified have leisure to write." Former President John Quincy Adams declared "that literature was, and in its nature must always be, aristocratic; that democracy of numbers and literature were self-contradictory." Democratic nations, said Alexis de Tocqueville after visiting Jacksonian America in 1831, "will habitually prefer the useful to the beautiful, and they will require that the beautiful should be useful." Americans were newspaper readers, he said, and they relied on newspapers to "maintain civilization." "The universal equality of conditions spreads a monotonous tint over all society," said his traveling companion, the novelist Gustave de Beaumont; he warned Europeans not to "look for poetry, literature, or fine arts in this country." When one of the proprietors of the *North American Review* first read young William Cullen Bryant's blank verse, Wordsworthian "Thanatopsis" (1817), a poem subsequently hailed as the finest yet written in America, he assumed the author was British: "No one on this side of the Atlantic is capable of writing such verse."

Washington Irving and James Fenimore Cooper, both successful professional men of letters, believed they had overcome cultural and economic obstacles likely to discourage other native writers. Americans were supposedly too busy making money and taming the wilderness to have leisure for literary reading, but with a few notable exceptions, chiefly the work of Irving and Cooper, most of the books they did read were written in England. This was partly due to a shortsighted Copyright Act, passed by the First Congress in 1790, that granted protection only to citizens or residents of the United States. All others were fair game for "pirates," publishers of unauthorized editions. The act's implicit rejection of international copyright encouraged American book, magazine, and newspaper publishers to favor foreign authors, whose work they could get for nothing and reprint cheaply, thereby neglecting or exploiting native authors, to whom they had to pay royalties or fees.

As yet without the annals, traditions, and associations that nurtured Old World writers, the United States offered its own writers a "poverty of materials," Cooper said. "The weakest hand can extract a spark from the flint, but it would baffle the strength of a giant to attempt kindling a flame with a pudding-stone." Yet Cooper had a shrewd sense of the future. "The literature of the United States is a subject of the highest interest to the civilized world," he wrote, "for when it does begin to be felt, it will be felt with a force, a directness, and a common sense in its application, that has never yet been known. . . . I think the time for the experiment is getting near."

John L. O'Sullivan launched his grandly titled *United States Magazine and Democratic Review* in 1837 with a declaration of purpose: "The vital principle of our literature must be democracy. . . . All history is to be rewritten; political science and the whole scope of moral truth have to be reconsidered in the light of the democratic principle." Following its "manifest destiny," a resounding slogan that O'Sullivan coined, messianic "Young America" was "to overspread the continent allotted by Providence for the free development of our yearly multiplying millions" and also lead the world to salvation by the road of republicanism. In ideology as well as religion this was an evangelical age. "We Americans are the peculiar, chosen people—the Israel of our times," Herman Melville wrote in 1850. "We bear the ark of the liberties of the world. . . . In our youth is our strength; in our inexperience, our wisdom." Writing in praise of Hawthorne's *Mosses from an Old Manse,* he declared that "men not very much inferior to Shakespeare are this day being born on the banks of the Ohio."

Similar grandiose sentiments were voiced all through the period. They were undoubtedly good for morale, but they were not necessarily good for literature and criticism. "It is now the fashion to extol everything American," Cooper observed. "The country is filled, today, with the most profound provincial self-admiration." "We are becoming boisterous and arrogant in the pride of a too speedily assumed literary freedom," said Edgar Allan Poe. "We get up a hue and cry about the necessity of encouraging native writers of merit—we blindly fancy that we can accomplish this by indiscriminate puffing of good, bad, and indifferent . . . and thus often find ourselves involved in the gross paradox of liking a stupid book the better, because, sure enough, its stupidity is American." Poe was a universalist rather than a nationalist. He developed a body of literary theory that drew on many European sources, and he was to have a considerable posthumous reputation in England and Europe, particularly among Charles Baudelaire and the French Symbolists. As editor he anticipated the great magazine-reading audience that arrived in full force only after the Civil War. As poet and fiction writer he courted popularity—and from time to time won it to a spectacular degree. During the later 1840s Poe's raven, the dusky phantom of his most popular poem, was so celebrated that it appeared to vie with the American bald eagle for the title of national bird.

In *Kavanagh: A Tale* (1849), Henry Wadsworth Longfellow satirized the rant of the "Young America" movement. "We want a national literature commensurate with our mountains and rivers," one of his characters announces. "We want a national literature altogether shaggy and unshorn, that shall shake the earth, like a herd of buffaloes, thundering over the prairies!" It was clear that something more than bluster and false analogies was called for if the country were to have a culture in keeping with its political character. "It does not follow because many books are written by persons born in America that there exists an American literature," Margaret Fuller wrote in 1846. "Before such can exist, an original idea must animate this nation and fresh currents of life must call into life fresh thoughts along its shores."

There were several main issues in this ongoing discussion. One, whether America provided a favorable cultural climate for writers, artists, and intellectuals, was to be debated again and again, after the Civil War and especially during the 1920s. But a second issue, whether America was capable of making a literature of its own fit to stand with the literatures of the Old World, simply ceased to exist. Two native poetic geniuses flourishing around midcentury, Walt Whitman and Emily Dickinson, had proved this point.[1] As for broad popularity, Harriet Beecher Stowe and Henry Wadsworth Longfellow alone offered a sufficient rejoinder to the English wit Sydney Smith's gibe, "In the four quarters of the globe, who reads an American book?" London bookshops in 1852 displayed twenty different editions of *Uncle Tom's Cabin*. By 1856 this novel had sold nearly a million copies in the British Isles, had been translated into every European language, and was on its way to achieving a global popularity second only to that of the Bible. As for Longfellow, "No other poet has anything like your vogue," Hawthorne wrote to him from England in 1855, when Longfellow published *The Song of Hiawatha*, a long poem with an Ojibway Indian hero but written in the manner and meters of the Finnish national epic, *Kalevala*. On publication day in 1858, Londoners bought some ten thousand copies of Longfellow's *The Courtship of Miles Standish*, another excursion into national legend.

A wondrous half decade, 1850–1855, saw the publication of Hawthorne's *The Scarlet Letter* and *The House of the Seven Gables*, Melville's *Moby-Dick* and *Pierre*, Thoreau's *Walden*, and Whitman's *Leaves of Grass*. Like all significant and lasting art, they are autonomous, self-contained, self-justifying, and even to some extent self-generated. Still, neither Hawthorne's books nor those of Melville, Thoreau, and

---

[1] Emily Dickinson's poems, written mainly during the early 1860s, were not published until several years after her death in 1886.

Whitman could have emerged from any other country in any other century, nor did they happen overnight or in a vacuum. They rest on a substrate of many other American books of the period, some of them now reemerging from noncanonical status to critical recognition. "It takes a great deal of history to produce a little literature," Henry James was to say. "It needs a complex social machinery to set a writer in motion."

A Revolution in Consciousness

"There are always two parties," Ralph Waldo Emerson wrote, "the party of the Past and the party of the Future; the Establishment and the Movement." For Emerson and other New England writers and thinkers around the middle third of the nineteenth century, Transcendentalism was part of an ongoing revolution in consciousness. "The mind had become aware of itself," he wrote. Like the Reverend Theodore Parker, another prominent spokesman, Emerson claimed that Transcendentalism was not a concerted party or movement at all but a loose confederation of compatible souls. Having imbibed a distillate of Kant, Goethe, Coleridge, Wordsworth, Carlyle, and other philosophical and literary idealists, the Transcendentalists set about their business in a characteristically self-reliant way. Embroiled in a doctrinal controversy over Holy Communion, Emerson went through a personal crisis and resigned from the Unitarian ministry to follow a career as writer and lecturer. Parker continued in the ministry but exhausted himself in debates and reforms. Margaret Fuller published the first major American feminist treatise, *Woman in the Nineteenth Century,* in 1845; the following year she went to Europe as foreign correspondent for Horace Greeley's *New York Tribune* and committed herself to the cause of Italian nationalism. Thoreau built his hut at Walden Pond, was jailed for refusing to pay a poll tax, and preached civil disobedience.

Transcendentalism had only a scant organizational existence. It began as an informal "club," first convened in 1836. It generated *The Dial,* a quarterly journal of "literature, philosophy, and religion," edited by Fuller and Emerson, which lasted only four years (1840–1844), never reached a circulation of over three hundred, and was frequently ridiculed for unballasted flights into the empyrean. And it inspired two experiments in cooperative living and high thinking near Boston: Brook Farm (1841–1847) and Fruitlands (1843). Yet, out of all proportion to these evidences, Transcendentalism, especially as channeled through Emerson, generated a significant reexamination of values even in those who derided it. Reversing the European historical order, the Transcendental "reformation," announcing a gospel of spiritual self-sufficiency, came before the literary "renaissance," an awakening, maturation, and release of radical energies.

The Transcendentalists set themselves against what they considered to be the materialism, rationalism, conformity, and played-out liberalism of American religion and society. The social reformer William Henry Channing recalled the movement as inspiring "a vague yet exalting conception of the godlike nature of the human spirit" and "a pilgrimage from the idolatrous world of creeds and rituals to the temple of the Living God in the soul." Ideas of God, right and wrong, and immortality were not matters of doctrine or theology but, according to Parker, "facts of consciousness given by the instinctive action of human nature itself." The Transcendentalists contemplated the actualities of life in the street, the mill, the farmhouse, and the marketplace and aimed to restore to the humblest persons and pursuits a measure of poetry, religious impulse, mystery, surprise, joy, and dread and a sense of wonder and oneness with the universe. "I have taught one doctrine," Emerson said, "the infinitude of the private man." "All Souls' Day" had dawned: Each and every person was at once priest, church, and Bible, "a part of eternity and immensity, a god walking in flesh." "So we saunter toward the Holy Land," Thoreau wrote, "till one day the sun shall shine more brightly than ever he has done, shall perchance shine into our minds and hearts, and light up our whole lives with a great awakening light, as warm and serene and golden as on a bankside in autumn."

Transcendentalism arrived as social and religious protest. The conservative theologian Andrews Norton denounced it as "the latest form of infidelity," an unassisted and therefore arrogant attempt to attain assurance "concerning the unseen, the eternal, the great objects of religion." By the 1870s much of Transcendentalism's radical force had become diluted, dissipated, and factional. Although Transcendentalism, as Emerson articulated it during the 1830s and 1840s, deplored materialism, Emerson ended up buttressing the cult of success. "Money is, in its effects and laws, as beautiful as roses," he said. "Property keeps the accounts of the world, and is always moral." After the Civil War, princes of industry and finance quoted his advice, "Hitch your wagon to a star," and installed him in the pantheon of American practical philosophers along with Benjamin Franklin. A religious, ethical, and aesthetic response to nationalism, a homegrown counterpart of European romanticism with elements drawn from Eastern philosophy, this "latest form of infidelity" proved to be the animating force without which, as Margaret Fuller said, there could be no "American literature."

Three decisive Emerson statements—*Nature* (1836), *The American Scholar* (1837), and his 1838 address to the Harvard Divinity School—served as a Declaration of Independence for the spirit, intellect, and imagination. The homeliest trifle bristled with the polarity of material and spiritual truth; the writer was seer and sayer, "eye" and "I"; language was the hinge of the seen and the unseen, and all the world was a text to be read, studied, and rewritten. "Oregon and Texas are yet unsung," said Emerson. He awaited the arrival of native geniuses possessing "nerve and dagger" and a "tyrannous" command of "our incomparable materials." "America is a poem in our eyes; its ample geography dazzles the imagination, and it will not wait long for metres." Eventually Walt Whitman had the last word in the debate over nationalism and culture. "The United States themselves," he announced in 1855, "are essentially the greatest poem."

In major respects, the literature of the American Renaissance was "a language experiment," as Whitman once described *Leaves of Grass*, a grappling with the transcendency of words. But it was also a series of inspired explorations of the theme of solitude and, correspondingly, of society. Tocqueville had warned, "Not only does democracy make each man forget his ancestors, but it hides his descendants and separates his contemporaries from them; it throws him back upon himself alone and threatens in the end to confine him entirely within the solitude of his own heart." "Instead of the social existence which all shared, was now separation," Emerson said. "Every one for himself; driven to find all his resources, hopes, rewards, society and deity within himself." This was as true of Thoreau in his cabin at Walden as it was of

Melville's Ishmael aboard the *Pequod*. As Poe recognized, solitude also generated claustrophobia.

"Incomparable Materials"

The period of the American Renaissance is framed by two upheavals, the Panic of 1837 and the Civil War, and by the emergence of two political leaders, Andrew Jackson and Abraham Lincoln, each of whom was widely perceived as representing the will of the people and the spirit of the frontier. The saturnalia of Jackson's first inauguration in 1829, a riot of drunkenness, bloody noses, and broken White House crystal and china, seemed to mark an end to patrician presidency. The "great democratic God," Melville wrote in *Moby-Dick,* had plucked Old Hickory from the backwoods of Tennessee, hurled him upon a warhorse, and thundered him "higher than a throne." Yet for all the swirl, boil, and social ferment associated with Jacksonian democracy, to some contemporary observers the 1830s seemed peculiarly prosaic, a falling-off from the heroic age of the founders. A revolutionary nation was becoming middle-class. "Public and private avarice make the air we breathe thick and fat," Emerson said. "The mind of this country, taught to aim at low objects, eats upon itself." The celebrated "age of the common man" saw growing concentrations of wealth in the hands of a tiny percentage of the population. It was also an age of urban slums, wage slavery, and other inequities connected with the shift from an agrarian to an industrial economy. At New Orleans in 1815, Jackson defeated the British. In the White House two decades later, the first of the log-cabin presidents, he defeated the eastern banking interests only to see the country plunge into business failures and unemployment. The Panic of 1837 initiated the worst depression the United States had yet known.

Abraham Lincoln exercised unprecedented executive authority during a civil war far bloodier and longer than anyone had foreseen. Midway through the war, Whitman described Lincoln:

> He has a face like a hoosier Michael Angelo, so awful ugly it becomes beautiful, with its strange mouth, its deep cut, cris-cross lines, and its doughnut complexion. . . . He has shown, I sometimes think, an almost supernatural tact in keeping the ship afloat at all, with head steady, not only not going down, and now certain not to, but with proud and resolute spirit, and flag flying in sight of the world, menacing and high as ever.

Lincoln's "idiomatic western genius," as Whitman called it, was above all conspicuous in his spoken and written prose, a supple middle style that was lofty and colloquial, beautiful and homely, and always got to the point. Lincoln's prose showed that the basic forms of American humor, including the tall tale and the anecdote, were appropriate in statecraft as well as in literature.

In the years between these two presidencies, the face, form, and fiber of the United States underwent enormous change. Pushed by poverty, famine, and overcrowding at home and pulled by the promise of limitless opportunity in America, great waves of newcomers arrived from Ireland, Western Europe, and Scandinavia to settle in the cities, clear the wilderness, work the farms, build the canals and railroads. They created new opportunities and new labor needs that in turn attracted other immigrants. Meanwhile, especially in New York and New England in the 1840s and after, a riptide of movement from the country to the city, from the barn to the mill, drained villages and townships. Farmhouses stood empty, cleared land reverted to forest, and some regions, as Melville noted, looked as if they had been "depopulated by plague and war." When Jackson left office in 1837 the population was 16 million. By 1865 it was 36 million, having grown by about 35 percent each decade. What sorts of readers would these new millions be, and what sorts of writers could meet their needs? Whitman believed that "to have great poets, there must be great audiences, too."

An Improving Spirit

The abolition of slavery was the most vigorous and portentous reform issue of the period. It drew militant support from other reform causes, notably the women's rights movement, given official identity in 1848 at the Seneca Falls (New York) Convention. The Quaker poet John Greenleaf Whittier told his fellow abolitionists, the southerners Sarah and Angelina Grimké, he feared "the cause of the poor and miserable slave" was being weakened by its association with women's rights, which he described as "a selfish crusade against some paltry grievance of your own." Nevertheless, the alliance was powerful evidence of an improving spirit that affected nearly every aspect of American life, from the care of the blind, the deaf, and the insane to municipal sanitation, the prevention of drunkenness, and the salvation of souls.

In 1837, the year of a great financial panic, Massachusetts established America's first state board of education and appointed as its secretary Horace Mann. He believed that the public elementary school, "the greatest discovery ever made by man," could prevent life in the open society from becoming a series of "gladiatorial contests." Under Mann and other reformers in the field, public education—a democratic dream that had appeared to be fading because it was expensive to provide as a service and humiliating to receive as a charity—became a significant cause. By midcentury, attendance in public systems that went from the infant grades through high school was growing faster than the population as a whole. Higher education, however, remained beyond the reach of all but a relative few (the estimated college enrollment was 27,000 in 1850, 56,000 in 1860). Along with a literacy rate significantly higher than that of the British Isles came a familiarity with certain basic texts (the Bible, Shakespeare, Dickens, and John Bunyan's *Pilgrim's Progress*, for example) that would seem quite remarkable today.

For the developing readership of the period, the debating society and the lyceum were available, potent agencies of higher education. Debaters in cities, towns, and villages addressed themselves to such topics as the pros and cons of slavery, capital punishment, and unrestricted immigration; the role of the arts and sciences in a democracy and of genetic and social factors in the formation of character; the achievements of Napoleon Bonaparte; and the relative merits of Queen Elizabeth and Mary, Queen of Scots. Tocqueville noted that the habit of public argument acquired in these societies left its mark on the native character: "An American cannot converse, but he can discuss. He speaks to you as if he was addressing a meeting."

The New Englander Josiah Holbrook described the lyceum system (which he founded in 1826) as a national network of "associations of Adults for Mutual Education." Arriving in remote settlements with the locomotive and the depot, lyceum lecture courses took their place in the civic order alongside the church, the schoolhouse, the courtroom, the saloon, and the jail. Citizens bought series or single tickets to hear evening talks on the North American Indian, the lives of Mohammed and Oliver Cromwell, the productive cycle of the honeybee, causes of the American Revolution, the sun, the education of children, and the capacity of the human mind for culture and improvement. "There was the real impression," Edward Everett Hale recalled, "that the kingdom of heaven was to be brought in by teaching people what were the relations of acids to alkalies, and what was the derivation of the word 'cordwainer.' If only we knew enough, it was thought, we should be wise enough to keep out of the fire, and we should not be burned." Lyceum lectures also served a social purpose in towns that lacked other secular entertainments: They enabled young men and women to mingle in semidarkened halls. During its heyday as a distinctive institution of American life, the lyceum educated a generation and a half of readers, offered a forum for debate on such important reform issues as women's rights, temperance, and the abolition of slavery, and also provided writers and intellectuals with a source of income.

"Self-Made or Never Made"

An era of self-trust, self-improvement, and perfectionism in general offered many attractive ways of bringing in the kingdom of heaven. In the nineteenth as well as the twentieth century, the United States was world haven not only for immigrants and refugees from European oppression but also for schemes promising social and individual happiness, among them phrenology, or the science of mind, a European import. One of its founders, Johann Kaspar Spurzheim, was hailed as a messiah when he arrived in America in 1832 and was mourned accordingly when he was buried there the same year. His truth, such as it was, marched on for three decades.

In the phrenological scheme of things, each intellectual faculty had a specific location in the brain and could be measured by corresponding bumps on the skull; "secretiveness," "amativeness," "benevolence," and other traits were as palpable and distinct as onions, turnips, and potatoes in a sack. These homely propositions had an electrifying corollary. In the words of Orson Squire Fowler, the leading American popularizer of phrenology, "the exercise of particular mental faculties . . . causes the exercise, and consequent enlargement, of corresponding portions of the brain." One could "elevate" faculties that had been diagnosed deficient, "depress" those that were too prominent, and presumably arrive near, if not at, a state of perfection in personality, temperament, and ability. Fowler's motto was "self-made or never made."

Phrenology turned out to be a benevolent, infinitely attractive fantasy, with no footing in either fact or theory, and in the hands of shabby practitioners plying their trade along the frontier it eventually declined into simple quackery. If nothing else, the great science of mind offered the promise, Theodore Parker said, of "leading men to study the constitution of man more wisely than before." Poe claimed phrenology had achieved "the majesty of a science, and as a science ranks among the most important which can engage the attention of thinking beings." Horace Mann, as wholly serious as when confronting slavery, ignorance, profanity, or drunkenness, said phrenology was "the guide of philosophy, and the handmaid of Christianity," an opinion shared by Horace Greeley, William Cullen Bryant, Henry Ward Beecher, and others of comparable eminence. Emerson and Webster had their bumps read; so did Whitman,

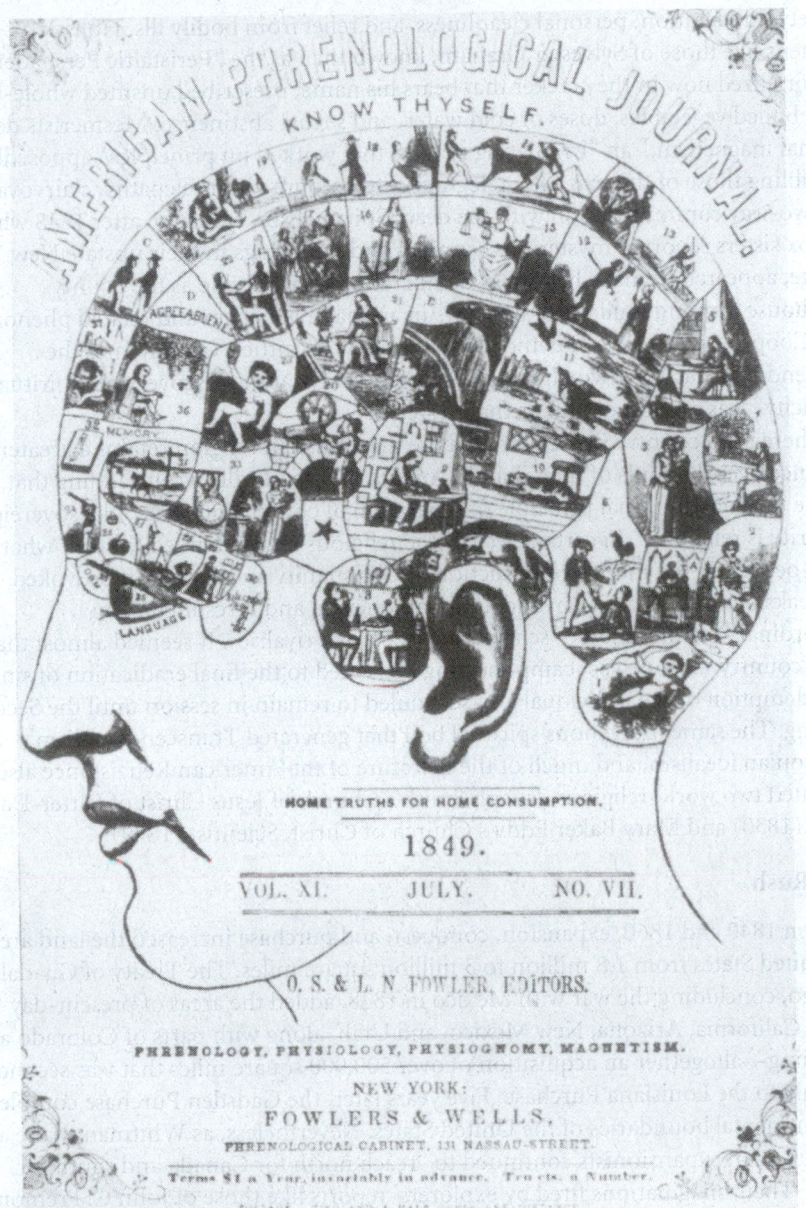

American Phrenological Journal
July 1949
(Harvard College Library)

who was thereby confirmed in his mission to become the poet of America. Even in his old age he said, "I probably have not got by the phrenology stage yet."

In its heyday phrenology also energized a variety of other approaches to self-improvement and well-being. "Hydropathy," or water cure, offered an avenue to sobriety, moderation, personal cleanliness, and relief from bodily ills. Holistic regimens like those of Sylvester Graham, known then as the "Peristaltic Persuader" and memorialized now in the cracker that bears his name, prescribed unsifted whole-wheat flour, boiled vegetables, doses of cold water, and sexual abstinence. Mesmerists dealt in "animal magnetism," an "irradiating power" that worked on principles supposedly resembling those of the magnetic telegraph and accounted for telepathy, clairvoyance, and two-way communication with the dead. Spiritualism, epidemic after 1848 when the Fox sisters reported mysterious rappings and knockings in their upstate New York cottage, appeared to make heaven as democratic and accessible as the county courthouse. Among millions of believers in animal magnetism and related phenomena were Cooper, Irving, Poe, Hawthorne, Longfellow, Whittier, Greeley, and the Reverend Thomas Wentworth Higginson, who said that the discovery of "spiritual electricity" was as momentous as that of steam.

"There is no country in the world where the Christian religion retains a greater influence over the souls of men than in America," Tocqueville wrote, adding that, despite the constitutional principle of separation of church and state, "the sovereign authority is religious." In certain sectors the religious revival tended to scant what might be seen as the moral contradiction of Christianity and slavery; it provoked outbreaks of virulent nativism and anti-Catholicism, and it resulted in an extraordinary proliferation of schisms and sectarian rivalries. It seemed almost that the entire country was one vast camp meeting dedicated to the final eradication of sin and the redemption of the individual and scheduled to remain in session until the Second Coming. The same indigenous spiritual boil that generated Transcendentalism, Emersonian idealism, and much of the literature of the American Renaissance also generated two world religions, Joseph Smith's Church of Jesus Christ of Latter-Day Saints (1830) and Mary Baker Eddy's Church of Christ, Scientist (1879).

Gold Rush

Between 1840 and 1860, expansion, conquest, and purchase increased the land area of the United States from 1.8 million to 3 million square miles. The Treaty of Guadalupe Hidalgo, concluding the war with Mexico in 1848, added the areas of present-day Texas, California, Arizona, New Mexico, and Utah, along with parts of Colorado and Wyoming—altogether an acquisition of over 500,000 square miles that was second in size only to the Louisiana Purchase. Five years later, the Gadsden Purchase completed the continental boundaries of the United States. Nevertheless, as Whitman wrote after the Civil War, expansionists continued to "reach north for Canada and south for Cuba." Their imaginations fired by explorers' reports like those of John C. Frémont, the most effective publicist of the trans-Mississippi West, thousands of young men left city and farm jobs, packed up their families, and set out along the Santa Fe, Oregon, and California trails.

Continental space, seemingly limitless, shaped the vision of writers and artists by demanding corresponding qualities of amplitude, grandeur, and reverence. But the fulfillment of manifest destiny also raised questions about where America was going. Whitman said, "It is as if we were somehow being endow'd with a vast and more and more thoroughly-appointed body, and then left with little or no soul." The discovery of California gold in January 1848, just nine days before the signing of the Treaty of Guadalupe Hidalgo, appeared to many patriots to be something more than Yankee luck. It was a providential event, a confirmation of national grace and mission. Although this gold lay under their feet and ready to their hands, patriotic logic ran, it had not been revealed to the Indians, Spaniards, and Mexicans who occupied the land for two centuries before it became a part of Protestant America. Now the existence of a great treasure had been discovered, quite accidentally, by a man from New Jersey, James Marshall, overseeing the construction of a sawmill on the south fork of the American River. "My eye was caught by something shining in the bottom of a ditch. . . . I reached my hand down and picked it up; it made my heart thump, for I was certain it was gold. The piece was about half the size and shape of a pea. Then I saw another." After President Polk verified the extent of the finds in his 1848 message to Congress, California gold fever supplanted the "Oregon fever" of a few years earlier, and a new wave of emigrants traveled west by way of Cape Horn (a fifteen-thousand-mile voyage), the Isthmus of Panama, and the overland trails.

"Instead of being rich, I am ruined," said John Sutter, on whose property Marshall made his find. Marauders and squatters killed Sutter's cattle; his workers ran off to become prospectors while his wheat rotted in the fields and his tannery and mills stood idle; strangers preempted his mining claims. "By this sudden discovery of the gold, all my great plans were destroyed. Had I succeeded with my mills and manufactories for a few years before the gold was discovered, I should have been the richest citizen on the Pacific shore; but it had to be different." Marshall was another casualty and ended up working as a gardener. For him and Sutter, as well as for the many thousand prospectors who never struck it rich and were happy just to return home alive, the gold rush (like B. Traven's novel and John Huston's film, *The Treasure of the Sierra Madre*) proved to be a native version of Chaucer's tale about three revelers who quarreled over gold and killed one another. But the gold rush was also a peculiarly apt fable of America in transition. "I know of no more startling development of the morality of trade and all the modes of getting a living than the rush to California affords," Thoreau wrote in his journal. "Of what significance is . . . a world that will rush to the lottery of California gold-digging—to live by luck, to get the means of commanding the labor of others less lucky, *i.e.* slaveholding, without contributing any value to society? . . . Going to California. It is only three thousand miles nearer to hell."

Railroad Iron

California promoters had invoked the preclassical example of Jason's Argonauts and the golden fleece to suggest that the gold rush was a return to an Arcadian age of adventure. Thoreau, Mark Twain, and other social critics thought of the gold rush as a dividing line between America's own Arcadian age—in idealized retrospect a time of pastoral peace, agrarian self-sufficiency, and communal rectitude—and the industrial age of cities and machines, steam, electricity, steel, and big business. Gone was what the English journalist Harriet Martineau had called "a sweet temper diffused like sunshine over the land." For a glorious year and a half (April 1860–October 1861) pony express riders, buckskin-clad heroes armed with Colt six-shooters and eighteen-inch knives, carried mail nearly two thousand miles in eight days between Sacramento, California, and St. Joseph, Missouri, but the entire venture was little more than a romantic rear-guard action, "a flash of unreal fantasy," in Mark Twain's words. Outmoded by the telegraph and steam locomotive, the age's most conspicuous symbols and agencies of change, the pony express passed into American folklore. By the end of the 1860s, travelers rode coast-to-coast in the sleeping and dining luxury of George Pullman's Palace Cars.

"Railroad iron is a magician's rod in its power to evoke the sleeping energies of land and water," Emerson said. "Readers of poetry see the factory-village and the railway, and fancy that the poetry of the landscape is broken up by these; for these works of art are not yet consecrated in their reading; but the poet sees them fall within the great Order not less than the beehive or the spider's geometrical web." By the end of the period, the number of miles of track in operation (thirty-five thousand) had grown by a factor of twenty-six, which opened the prairies for agricultural use. Railroading was America's first billion-dollar industry and provided the pattern for other gigantic concentrations of capital. Literature and the facts of industry may have been compatible, as Emerson claimed, but what did these facts mean?

"Railroad iron" opened the wilderness but also preserved it by putting up obstacles to agriculture along the right-of-way. "Punctual as a Star," the locomotive was, in Emily Dickinson's words, both "docile and omnipotent"; its "horrid, hooting stanza" broke the primal silence, interrupted meditation, and itself became the subject of meditation. "Type of the modern—emblem of motion and power-pulse of the continent," Whitman wrote, "Fierce-throated beauty!" Hawthorne described the locomotive as looking "much more like a sort of mechanical demon, that would hurry us to the infernal regions, than a laudable contrivance for smoothing our way to the Celestial City."

Impending Crisis

Whether the new industrial age represented progress or destruction was one of several ambiguities writers of the period had to confront. They were as divided here as they were in their responses to the other contradictions—social, economic, political, and moral—of American life around the middle of the century. The freest nation on earth, inspired by dreams of a just and perfect society, maintained the institution of slavery, denied women the vote and other legal rights, and harried its aboriginal population toward extinction through chicanery, forced removals, and broken treaties.

Torn between humanitarian and expedient principles, many Americans detested slavery but at the same time despaired of finding a fair or peaceful way of putting an end to it. For the most part, the writers of New England and the middle states had as muddled a comprehension of the South, based on little or no firsthand experience, as their southern counterparts had of the North. Each group accused the other of fanaticism and monomania and fell back on unexamined stereotypes: The South was a violent, backward, culturally barren region ruled by King Cotton and his Lords of the Lash, while the North was culturally tyrannical, obsessed with trade and stirring up blood violence between slaves and masters. Moreover, within each loosely defined opposed faction there were, in turn, differences almost as extreme as those existing between the factions themselves.

At one end of the northern spectrum stood the abolitionist poet John Greenleaf Whittier. His single-mindedness was tempered by Quaker pacifism, while William Lloyd Garrison's abolitionist zeal—he denounced the U.S. Constitution as a "Covenant with Death and an Agreement with Hell"—made him as ardent a secessionist as any fire-eating counterpart in the South. During the 1830s and 1840s,

Emerson remained evasive on the great issue of the day: "What right have I to speak of slavery? Are we not *all* slaves?" (This meshed with the antiabolitionist argument that the white wage slaves—the indentured servants—of the North and industrialized England were infinitely worse off than the African American chattel slaves of the Cotton Kingdom.) Hawthorne and Melville (despite the marked sympathy for African Americans the latter showed in his novels) shunned reform causes and mass initiatives in general. Longfellow withdrew into genial isolation.

The historian Francis Parkman represented the other extreme of northern opinion and spoke for many southerners as well: "For my part, I would see every slave knocked on the head before I would see the Union go to pieces, and would include in the sacrifice as many abolitionists as could be conveniently brought together." This was the fundamental position that Lowell, a hot abolitionist earlier, arrived at just before the war and that Whitman, self-annointed bard of the Union and democracy, maintained even during the war.

Writers in the South, less visible as a group, in part because of their dependence on northern readers and publishing outlets, were also less vocal as a group, but they were spread along the same broad spectrum of opinion. The Charleston romancer William Gilmore Simms, the most prolific and popular writer of the South, and James De Bow, professor of political economy at the University of Louisiana, shared the familiar antebellum dream that a great civilization, like that of ancient Greece, could be raised on a foundation of human bondage. Meanwhile, Hinton Rowan Helper of North Carolina, a failed prospector in the Gold Rush who had become an out-and-out negrophobe, was urging abolition on the grounds that black slavery depressed the market for white labor and kept the South poor and backward. His populist, superficially progressive, but bitterly racist tract, *The Impending Crisis of the South* (1857), suppressed in some slave states and widely circulated by abolitionists in the North, may have been as effective in arousing sectional antagonism as *Uncle Tom's Cabin*. Fierce and uncompromising, the fire-eating Simms tried to promote his antithetic gospel of slavery to northern lecture audiences in 1856. Another Charlestonian, the poet Henry Timrod, was an apologist for slavery and "the laureate of the Confederacy" only with the utmost reluctance—he had tried to stay above sectional issues. Maryland novelist and politician John Pendleton Kennedy, Poe's friend and patron, wrote and lectured against secession. Like that of the North, the southern literary and intellectual community did not speak with one voice on the underlying issues of the Civil War.

The Missouri Compromise (1820), an attempt to establish geographical and political balance between free states and slave states, had offered the promise of domestic tranquillity while evading the basic moral issue involved. Nevertheless, Jefferson heard in its terms "a fire-bell" tolling "the knell of the Union." After half a generation of silence this bell began to toll again with increasing frequency. In November 1837, two months after Emerson called on "the American scholar" to speak his own mind and look to self-trust, a mob in Alton, Illinois, murdered Elijah Lovejoy, editor of the *Observer,* an abolitionist newspaper. The antislavery cause had its first martyr in a line that would end with Captain John Brown. Wendell Phillips's tribute to Lovejoy at a public meeting in Boston's Faneuil Hall belonged in a tradition of abolitionist oratory that eventually included Theodore Parker, Senator Charles Sumner, the Reverend Henry Ward Beecher, Frederick Douglass, and Henry Thoreau.

The slavery issue surfaced again in the Mexican War, "essentially a war of false pretenses," Lowell said at the time, which would result in "widening the boundaries and so prolonging the life of slavery."

The Wilmot Proviso (1846), an attempt to outlaw slavery in any territory acquired from Mexico, revealed the peculiarly complex and contradictory makeup of the Free Soil movement, an amalgam of conscience, self-interest, and racism. The author of the proviso, David Wilmot, a hitherto inconspicuous Democratic member of Congress from Pennsylvania, had "no morbid sympathy for the slave," he said, only a desire to protect white men from "the disgrace which association with negro slavery brings upon free labor." His position scarcely differed from Helper's.

On these issues Whitman exemplifies the hesitancies that afflicted other writers of the period. Although he was an ardent Free-Soiler, editor and publisher of the Brooklyn *Freeman,* a weekly newspaper dedicated to opposing "under all circumstances the addition to the Union, in future, of a single inch of *slave land,*" Whitman denounced abolitionism because, in his opinion, it was fanatical, defied the law of the land, and, at a time when "United States" was still a plural noun, as in "these United States," jeopardized the sacred constitutional pact. Like Emerson, Thoreau, Parker, and many other writers (with the conspicuous exception of Melville) who accepted "scientific" doctrines of the day, Whitman also believed that African Americans were genetically unsuited for assimilation into American life. "Nature has set an impassable seal against it," he declared in an 1850s editorial. His day-to-day social policy and conduct were no different from those of most northerners, abolitionists included, who deplored slavery but at the same time denied even free African Americans the most rudimentary civil rights. "You loathe them as you would a snake or a toad, yet you are indignant at their wrongs," St. Clare, a Louisiana planter, says to his New England cousin in Harriet Beecher Stowe's novel, *Uncle Tom's Cabin.* "You would not have them abused; but you don't want to have anything to do with them yourselves. You would send them to Africa, out of your sight and smell, and then send a missionary or two to do up all the self-denial of elevating them compendiously." Like her brother Henry Ward Beecher, Theodore Parker, and other antislavery radicals, Mrs. Stowe believed that the ultimate solution to an intolerable race problem was African American colonization in a more tropical part of the world than the North American continent.

Bitter congressional debates over Henry Clay's "Omnibus Bill" (1850) and the Kansas-Nebraska Act (1854) created further dismay and confusion for northern liberals. Among their deposed heroes was Daniel Webster, a man of outstanding intellect and character; according to the phrenologists, his skull (twenty-five inches around) was to common skulls "what the great dome of St. Peter's is to the small cupolas at its side." On the Senate floor in March 1850, Webster, faced, as he believed, with the momentous choice of preserving the Union or countenancing secession, threw his support to Clay's compromise resolutions. In the bitter aftermath of Webster's speech, Parker said, "There is no such life of crime long enough to prepare a man for such a pitch of depravity." The poet Whittier, too, aired criticism: "When faith is lost, when honor dies, / The man is dead." In the poem, Webster is the biblical Ichabod, a name meaning, "the glory is departed."

The most inflammatory of the compromise measures that Webster supported, the Fugitive Slave Law made the federal government the enforcing agency of southern property claims and created a corps of federal slave catchers to penetrate the asylums and underground railroads of the North. "This filthy enactment," Emerson wrote in his journal, "was made in the nineteenth century by men who could read and write. I will not obey it, by God." Under the Fugitive Slave Law, which had also triggered Mrs. Stowe's famous novel, President Franklin Pierce dispatched a government cutter and federal troops, armed with loaded rifles and fixed bayonets, to Boston in June 1854 to ensure the return of Anthony Burns, a runaway slave, to his owner in Virginia. The rendition of Burns left Thoreau "with the sense of having suffered a vast and indefinite loss," he said in his July 4 address, *Slavery in Massachusetts*. "I did not know at first what ailed me. At last it occurred to me that what I had lost was a country. . . . We have used up all our inherited freedom. If we would save our lives, we must fight for them." This was his version of the same "higher law" that Captain John Brown invoked in October 1859 when, hoping to raise a slave insurrection in Virginia, he led his attack on the federal arsenal at Harpers Ferry and again, a month and a half later, when he mounted the scaffold to die "for God's eternal truth." Devoutly antislavery northerners believed, as Emerson put it, that Brown made "the gallows glorious like the Cross." "He is not Old Brown any longer," Thoreau said; "he is an angel of light." For Melville and Whitman, Brown's execution was also a "meteor" that aroused "forebodings," "portent" of the cataclysmic four-year Civil War.

"I saw an open field," Ulysses Grant was to write of the Battle of Shiloh (April 6–7, 1862), "over which the Confederates had made repeated charges the day before, so covered with dead that it would have been possible to walk across the clearing, in any direction, without a foot touching the ground." Until Shiloh, Grant, "as well as thousands of other citizens, believed that the rebellion against the Government would collapse suddenly and soon." The Civil War was to rage on for three more years and in the end claim more than half a million lives. "When Lilacs Last in the Dooryard Bloom'd," Whitman's great poem of mourning for Abraham Lincoln, shot five days after General Robert E. Lee surrendered his army at Appomattox Courthouse in Virginia, was also a dirge for the entire nation, North and South.

Further Reading:
D. H. Lawrence, *Studies in Classic American Literature*, 1923.
C. Rourke, *American Humor*, 1931.
V. Brooks, *The Flowering of New England, 1815–1865*, 1936.
F. O. Matthiessen, *American Renaissance*, 1941.
V. Brooks, *The Times of Melville and Whitman*, 1947.
The Transcendentalists, ed. P. Miller, 1950.
H. N. Smith, *Virgin Land*, 1950.
R. W. B. Lewis, *The American Adam*, 1955.
C. Bode, *The Anatomy of Popular Culture, 1840–1861*, 1959.
E. Wilson, *Patriotic Gore*, 1962.
L. Marx, *The Machine in the Garden*, 1964.
D. Boorstin, *The Americans: The National Experience*, 1965.

J. A. Hawgood, *America's Western Frontiers*, 1967.
D. Aaron, *The Unwritten War*, 1973.
P. Miller, *The Raven and the Whale*, 1973.
R. B. Nye, *Society and Culture in America, 1830–1860*, 1974.
G. B. Forgie, *Patricide in the House Divided*, 1979.
J. T. Irwin, *American Hieroglyphics*, 1980.
B. Novak, *Nature and Culture: American Landscape Painting, 1825–1875*, 1980.
L. Ziff, *Literary Democracy*, 1981.
J. R. Stilgoe, *Metropolitan Corridor*, 1983.
D. S. Reynolds, *Beneath the American Renaissance*, 1988.
L. Buell, *The Environmental Imagination*, 1995.

John Pendleton Kennedy
(1795–1870)

John Pendleton Kennedy is best known for his writings on early Virginia. He concentrated on past Virginia culture, rather than on the more diffuse southern culture as a whole, and is considered to be the originator of the southern plantation legend. His novel *Swallow Barn* (1832) is often considered the first really important plantation novel, and certainly influenced later writers who sought to portray the South, not as it was, but as they wished it had been. Kennedy's work is different from that of Thomas Nelson Page in that he actually wrote about plantation life and society during the antebellum era; his nostalgia has a vastly different tone than Page's more mythicized portrayal of Virginia culture. Nevertheless, Kennedy subscribes to many of the same views as Page, often painting his characters more as stereotypes than as actual human beings (negroes could "never become a happier people than I find them here [Virginia]"). His novel, then, can be recognized as an early "novel of manners," but one which seeks to preserve the "local differences" which are rapidly being lost rather than to merely present the social behaviors of the time.

The son of a prosperous merchant, Kennedy was born on October 25, 1795, in Baltimore, Maryland. Kennedy fought in the War of 1812, participating in the battles of Bladensburg and North Point. A Whig, he served as a member of the Maryland House of Representatives from 1840–1844, and he also participated in state politics in the House of Delegates. Kennedy served as Millard Fillmore's secretary of the navy from 1852–1853. A unionist, Kennedy opposed secession, did not defend slavery (his tone on the matter in *Swallow Barn* is fairly dispassionate), and voted for Abraham Lincoln in 1864. He numbered Edgar Allan Poe among his friends, and actively supported his career.

Kennedy's earliest important work is *Swallow Barn; or, A Sojourn in the Old Dominion,* which was published under the pseudonym Mark Littleton in 1832. As a novel, it is somewhat disjointed, moving back and forth between sketches that are mere character sketches and chapters that actually further the plot. This work accurately reflects the distrust of plantation owners of the world—particularly the northern world—outside of their home; all weaknesses aside, *Swallow Barn* gives a true portrait of agrarian political sentiment of the time. Kennedy's other works include *Horse-Shoe Robinson* (1835), *Rob of the Bowl* (1838), *Quodlibet* (1840), a pro-Whig political satire, and *Memoirs of the Life of William Wirt* (1842). Kennedy also wrote pamphlets and political articles for the press, including the *National Intelligencer*. His *A Defense of the Whigs* (1844) denounced the political defection of John Tyler.

Kennedy died on August 18, 1870, in Newport, Rhode Island. He had long given up his literary career for one in business, but his works remained in print for years afterward (*Horse-Shoe Robinson* was last printed in 1937, over a century after its original publication).

Further Reading:

C. H. Bohner, *John Pendleton Kennedy, Gentleman
  from Baltimore,* 1961.
R. B. Davis, *Literature and Society in Early Virginia,
  1608–1840,* 1973.

E. M. Gwathmey, *John Pendleton Kennedy,* 1931.
J. V. Ridgely, *John Pendleton Kennedy,* 1966.

Text:

Swallow Barn; or, A Sojourn in the Old Dominion,
  1853. Introduction by Lucinda H. MacKethan.

Swallow Barn

II: *A Country Gentleman*

The master of this lordly domain is Frank Meriwether. He is now in the meridian of
life—somewhere about forty-five. Good cheer and an easy temper tell well upon him.
The first has given him a comfortable, portly figure, and the latter a contemplative turn
of mind, which inclines him to be lazy and philosophical.

He has some right to pride himself on his personal appearance, for he has a handsome face, with a dark blue eye and a fine intellectual brow. His head is growing scant of
hair on the crown, which induces him to be somewhat particular in the management of
his locks in that locality, and these are assuming a decided silvery hue.

It is pleasant to see him when he is going to ride to the Court House on business occasions. He is then apt to make his appearance in a coat of blue broadcloth, astonishingly glossy, and with an unusual amount of plaited ruffle strutting through the folds of
a Marseilles waistcoat. A worshipful finish is given to this costume by a large straw hat,
lined with green silk. There is a magisterial fulness in his garments which betokens condition in the world, and a heavy bunch of seals, suspended by a chain of gold, jingles as
he moves, pronouncing him a man of superfluities.

It is considered rather extraordinary that he has never set up for Congress: but the
truth is, he is an unambitious man, and has a great dislike to currying favor—as he calls
it. And, besides, he is thoroughly convinced that there will always be men enough in Virginia willing to serve the people, and therefore does not see why he should trouble his
head about it. Some years ago, however, there was really an impression that he meant to
come out. By some sudden whim, he took it into his head to visit Washington during the
session of Congress, and returned, after a fortnight, very seriously distempered with politics. He told curious anecdotes of certain secret intrigues which had been discovered in
the affairs of the capital, gave a clear insight into the views of some deep-laid combinations, and became, all at once, painfully florid in his discourse, and dogmatical to a degree that made his wife stare. Fortunately, this orgasm soon subsided, and Frank relapsed into an indolent gentleman of the opposition; but it had the effect to give a much
more decided cast to his studies, for he forthwith discarded the "Richmond Whig" from
his newspaper subscription, and took to "The Enquirer," like a man who was not to be
disturbed by doubts. And as it was morally impossible to believe all that was written on

both sides, to prevent his mind from being abused, he from this time forward took a stand against the re-election of Mr. Adams to the Presidency, and resolved to give an implicit faith to all alleged facts which set against his administration. The consequence of this straight-forward and confiding deportment was an unexpected complimentary notice of him by the Executive of the State. He was put into the commission of the peace, and having thus become a public man against his will, his opinions were observed to undergo some essential changes. He now thinks that a good citizen ought neither to solicit nor decline office; that the magistracy of Virginia is the sturdiest pillar which supports the fabric of the Constitution; and that the people, "though in their opinions they may be mistaken, in their sentiments they are never wrong;"—with some such other dogmas as, a few years ago, he did not hold in very good repute. In this temper, he has of late embarked on the millpond of county affairs, and notwithstanding his amiable character and his doctrinary republicanism, I am told he keeps the peace as if he commanded a garrison, and administers justice like a Cadi.

He has some claim to supremacy in this last department; for during three years he smoked segars in a lawyer's office in Richmond, which enabled him to obtain a bird's-eye view of Blackstone and the Revised Code. Besides this, he was a member of a Law Debating Society, which ate oysters once a week in a cellar; and he wore, in accordance with the usage of the most promising law students of that day, six cravats, one over the other, and yellow-topped boots, by which he was recognized as a blood of the metropolis. Having in this way qualified himself to assert and maintain his rights, he came to his estate, upon his arrival at age, a very model of landed gentlemen. Since that time his avocations have had a certain literary tincture; for having settled himself down as a married man, and got rid of his superfluous foppery, he rambled with wonderful assiduity through a wilderness of romances, poems, and dissertations, which are now collected in his library, and, with their battered blue covers, present a lively type of an army of continentals at the close of the war, or a hospital of invalids. These have all, at last, given way to the newspapers—a miscellaneous study very attractive and engrossing to country gentlemen. This line of study has rendered Meriwether a most perilous antagonist in the matter of legislative proceedings.

A landed proprietor, with a good house and a host of servants, is naturally a hospitable man. A guest is one of his daily wants. A friendly face is a necessary of life, without which the heart is apt to starve, or a luxury without which it grows parsimonious. Men who are isolated from society by distance, feel these wants by an instinct, and are grateful for the opportunity to relieve them. In Meriwether, the sentiment goes beyond this. It has, besides, something dialectic in it. His house is open to every body, as freely almost as an inn. But to see him when he has had the good fortune to pick up an intelligent, educated gentleman,—and particularly one who listens well!—a respectable, assentatious stranger!—All the better if he has been in the Legislature, or better still, if in Congress. Such a person caught within the purlieus of Swallow Barn, may set down one week's entertainment as certain—inevitable, and as many more as he likes—the more the merrier. He will know something of the quality of Meriwether's rhetoric before he is gone.

Then again, it is very pleasant to see Frank's kind and considerate bearing towards his servants and dependents. His slaves appreciate this, and hold him in most affectionate reverence, and, therefore, are not only contented, but happy under his dominion.

Meriwether is not much of a traveller. He has never been in New England, and very seldom beyond the confines of Virginia. He makes now and then a winter excursion to

Richmond, which, I rather think, he considers as the centre of civilization; and towards autumn, it is his custom to journey over the mountain to the Springs, which he is obliged to do to avoid the unhealthy season in the tide-water region. But the upper country is not much to his taste, and would not be endured by him if it were not for the crowds that resort there for the same reason which operates upon him; and I may add,—though he would not confess it—for the opportunity this concourse affords him for discussion of opinions.

He thinks lightly of the mercantile interest, and, in fact, undervalues the manners of the large cities generally. He believes that those who live in them are hollow-hearted and insincere, and wanting in that substantial intelligence and virtue, which he affirms to be characteristic of the country. He is an ardent admirer of the genius of Virginia, and is frequent in his commendation of a toast in which the state is compared to the mother of the Gracchi:—indeed, it is a familiar thing with him to speak of the aristocracy of talent as only inferior to that of the landed interest,—the idea of a freeholder inferring to his mind a certain constitutional preeminence in all the virtues of citizenship, as a matter of course.

The solitary elevation of a country gentleman, well to do in the world, begets some magnificent notions. He becomes as infallible as the Pope; gradually acquires a habit of making long speeches; is apt to be impatient of contradiction, and is always very touchy on the point of honor. There is nothing more conclusive than a rich man's logic any where, but in the country, amongst his dependents, it flows with the smooth and unresisted course of a full stream irrigating a meadow, and depositing its mud in fertilizing luxuriance. Meriwether's sayings, about Swallow Barn, import absolute verity. But I have discovered that they are not so current out of his jurisdiction. Indeed, every now and then, we have quite obstinate discussions when some of the neighboring potentates, who stand in the same sphere with Frank, come to the house; for these worthies have opinions of their own, and nothing can be more dogged than the conflict between them. They sometimes fire away at each other with a most amiable and unconvinceable hardihood for a whole evening, bandying interjections, and making bows, and saying shrewd things with all the courtesy imaginable. But for unextinguishable pertinacity in argument, and utter impregnability of belief, there is no disputant like your country-gentleman who reads the newspapers. When one of these discussions fairly gets under weigh, it never comes to an anchor again of its own accord;—it is either blown out so far to sea as to be given up for lost, or puts into port in distress for want of documents,—or is upset by a call for the boot-jack and slippers—which is something like the previous question in Congress.

If my worthy cousin be somewhat over-argumentative as a politician, he restores the equilibrium of his character by a considerate coolness in religious matters. He piques himself upon being a high-churchman, but is not the most diligent frequenter of places of worship, and very seldom permits himself to get into a dispute upon points of faith. If Mr. Chub, the Presbyterian tutor in the family, ever succeeds in drawing him into this field, as he occasionally has the address to do, Meriwether is sure to fly the course; he gets puzzled with scripture names, and makes some odd mistakes between Peter and Paul, and then generally turns the parson over to his wife, who, he says, has an astonishing memory.

He is somewhat distinguished as a breeder of blooded horses; and, ever since the celebrated race between Eclipse and Henry, has taken to this occupation with a renewed zeal, as a matter affecting the reputation of the state. It is delightful to hear him expatiate upon the value, importance, and patriotic bearing of this employment, and to listen to all his technical lore touching the mystery of horse-craft. He has some fine colts in training, which are committed to the care of a pragmatical old negro, named Carey, who, in his reverence for the occupation, is the perfect shadow of his master. He and Frank hold grave and momentous consultations upon the affairs of the stable, in such a sagacious strain of equal debate, that it would puzzle a spectator to tell which was the leading member in the council. Carey thinks he knows a great deal more upon the subject than his master, and their frequent intercourse has begot a familiarity in the old negro which is almost fatal to Meriwether's supremacy. The old man feels himself authorized to maintain his positions according to the freest parliamentary form, and sometimes with a violence of asseveration that compels his master to abandon his ground, purely out of faint-heartedness. Meriwether gets a little nettled by Carey's doggedness, but generally turns it off in a laugh. I was in the stable with him, a few mornings after my arrival, when he ventured to expostulate with the venerable groom upon a professional point, but the controversy terminated in its customary way. "Who sot you up, Master Frank, to tell me how to fodder that 'ere cretur, when I as good as nursed you on my knee?"

"Well, tie up your tongue, you old mastiff," replied Frank, as he walked out of the stable, "and cease growling, since you will have it your own way;"—and then, as we left the old man's presence, he added, with an affectionate chuckle—"a faithful old cur, too, that snaps at me out of pure honesty; he has not many years left, and it does no harm to humor him!"

1853

Ralph Waldo Emerson
1803–1882

Ralph Waldo Emerson has been such an original and pervasive presence in nineteenth- and twentieth-century American culture that most Americans know something about the spirit and substance of his writing, even if they have never deliberately read a line of his work. In voluminous journals, lectures, essays, and poems, Emerson articulated principles that have become central to defining traditional American values: self-reliance, individual authority and responsibility, a resolute optimism, moral idealism, the veneration of experience, and a worshipful return to nature. Emerson's expression of these fundamental principles in America's collective identity has been quoted, endorsed, and adapted by so many generations of writers and public figures that their familiarity may well reduce our appreciation of just how original these ideas were when Emerson expressed them. As the inheritors of a literary legacy nourished on a schoolroom diet of Emerson's most epigrammatic lines, contemporary readers must rediscover the range, freshness, complexity, and elasticity of his writing. The challenge in reading Emerson is to recover the originality of his now-familiar ideas.

Emerson was born in 1803 and grew up in a family whose heritage included nine successive generations of notable New England ministers. His father, a well-known Unitarian preacher, died when Ralph Waldo was eight, leaving him, his mother, and four brothers with little more than pride in a family name that filled several chapters in local church history. With the encouragement of his resilient and inventive mother, Ruth Haskins, the support of his Puritanical stepgrandfather, the Reverend Ezra Ripley, and the stern guidance of his strong-willed aunt, Mary Moody Emerson, Ralph Waldo entered Harvard at the age of fourteen. There he began keeping what quickly became extensive journals.

Emerson's performance at Harvard was not particularly distinguished. He graduated in 1821, thirty-ninth in a class of fifty-nine. After several unsettling years teaching, Emerson enrolled in the Harvard Divinity School and prepared to carry on the family tradition by studying to be a Unitarian minister. Emerson's studies, interrupted by spells of weak eyesight and his own unconventional thinking, proceeded slowly. As he dispassionately noted some years later, "Had they examined me, they would never have passed me."

Within a few years, however, Emerson had married an aspiring poet, Ellen Tucker, and had settled into a successful life as the pastor of Boston's Second Church, where Increase and Cotton Mather had preached more than a century earlier. There he attracted considerable attention for his eloquent and unorthodox sermons. This period of what he called "uninterrupted prosperity" included an honorary membership in Phi Beta Kappa, appointment as chaplain of the Massachusetts Senate, and election to the Boston School Committee. But this period of contentment was short-lived. By 1831 his wife had died, his brother Edward's health had deteriorated rapidly, and his doubts about his own ministry had increased greatly. Impatient with the ceremonial rituals and institutional structures and pressures of the church, Emerson began to seek more direct and immediate access to religious experience. In Emerson's view, the Unitarian church had become far too negative and rational—"corpse-cold," as he called it; Emerson sought more intuitive, personally revelatory religious experiences. In late October 1832 Emerson resigned his pastorate, having decided that he could no longer in good conscience administer Communion.

On Christmas Day in 1832 Emerson sailed for Europe and spent the next 10 months on the Continent and in England. Emerson returned to Massachusetts in 1833 and began a lecture series with such titles as "Human Life," "The Present Age," and "Human Culture." While his reputation as an orator earned him considerable attention, his $1,200 annual income from Ellen Tucker's estate—approximately two-thirds of his earnings as a minister—freed him from the financial concerns.

After a brief courtship filled with the "most agreeable recollections," Emerson married Lydia Jackson in 1835 and settled into a comfortable life in a large plain white frame house ("Coolidge Castle," or "Bush," as it came to be known), where they remained until fire destroyed it in 1872. Soon after their marriage, Emerson began a lifelong practice of calling his wife "Lidian," to avoid the New England pronunciation that slips an *r* sound between words that end and begin with a vowel. Occasionally, he traveled in the Northeast and out to the western frontier to lecture.

Only rarely did Emerson draw the same large crowds that came to hear the most popular politicians, reformers, phrenologists, and mesmerists of the mid-nineteenth century, yet he always cut an imposing figure behind the lectern. Emerson the lecturer was as ambitious as he was dynamic. "A lecture is a new literature," he noted in his journals, "which leaves aside all tradition, time, place, circumstance, & addresses an assembly as mere human beings. . . . It has never been done well. It is an organ of sublime power." Emerson prepared rigorously for his lectures. He drew primarily on his extensive journals (his "savings bank," as he called them) for both subjects and phrasing. Once Emerson had settled on a subject for a lecture, he would work through his journals (he created an index for easier reference) in search of appropriate entries. Characteristically, he then rewrote these entries and blended them into a final draft. He later recast the most successful of his lectures into essays. In effect, Emerson used his lectures to field-test his ideas before committing them to print.

Emerson's first major publication was *Nature* (1836), which earned him a modest profit and considerable attention in the United States and abroad. *Nature* provides the theoretical underpinnings for developing what became an indigenous American literature in the nineteenth century. Emerson builds into his essay a strikingly bold proposition: to substitute nature for what was generally regarded to be the new nation's lack of a distinctive cultural heritage.

In Emerson's view, nature—the land itself—should be the source for articulating and developing a unique American cultural identity. Like his counterparts in art—most notably the painter Thomas Cole, who figured so prominently in the Hudson River school—Emerson revered nature and saw in America the finest expression of what has been called "Nature's nation." In contrast to the many Americans, Emerson and Cole venerated nature not for the economic but for the spiritual and artistic opportunities inherent in it. For Emerson and Cole, nature would replace the Bible as the greatest spiritual text, capable of being read by anyone.

Emerson returned to Harvard in 1837 as the keynote speaker on Phi Beta Kappa Day. His address on that occasion, "The American Scholar," urged his audience to break with the past and to concentrate on recognizing and developing the enormous cultural potential of their own experience. Emerson hoped to formulate a set of distinctive principles for American experience, a forward-looking philosophy based on spontaneous action, creative intuition, and self-reliance. Like most of his writing, "The American Scholar" is explicitly inspirational. To be the representative American, the scholar must be self-reliant—full enough of self-trust to be open to any experience and patient enough to "relinquish display and immediate fame." The "true scholar," Emerson declared, doesn't lead a repetitive, derivative life but looks insistently and carefully at the present; refusing to be cut off from the world of action, the scholar relies on the creative power of intuition rather than on the treatises of others to map out the "resounding tumult" of experience. Emerson closed by proclaiming America's literary independence: "We have listened too long to the courtly muses of Europe. . . . We shall walk on our own feet, we will work with our own hands, we will speak our own minds."

"The American Scholar" produced, according to Emerson's close friend Bronson Alcott, a mixture of "confusion, consternation, surprise, and wonder." For Oliver Wendell Holmes, then a prominent young physician, the address represented nothing less than America's "intellectual Declaration of Independence." The distinguished literary critic James Russell Lowell, recalling his undergraduate days at Harvard, offered perhaps the most comprehensive view of the lecture's significance:

The Puritan revolt had made us ecclesiastically and the Revolution politically independent, but we were socially and intellectually moored to English thought, till Emerson cut the cable and gave us a chance at the dangers and glories of blue water. . . . His oration before the Phi Beta Kappa Society at Cambridge, some thirty years ago, was an event without any former parallel in our literary annals.

No longer, Emerson asserted, would there be a hierarchy of meaning. No longer would "quality" be abstract. For Emerson, quality resided in the texture of experience. In this respect, much of late-nineteenth- and twentieth-century literature, art, and popular culture can be said to have its symbolic birth in "The American Scholar." Consider, for example, Emerson's influence on the work of such divergent figures as Walt Whitman, William James, Robert Frost, William Carlos Williams, F. Scott Fitzgerald, Willa Cather, Gertrude Stein, A. R. Ammons, Frederick Law Olmsted, Louis Sullivan, Frank Lloyd Wright, and innumerable others.

Emerson's increasing reputation as a lecturer put him at the center of a small group of disaffected intellectuals who met frequently—though not on any regular schedule—to exchange ideas. Dubbed the "Transcendentalists" by their detractors (principally because they were reported to have spent so much time discussing Immanuel Kant's "transcendental" philosophy), the group included, among others, Margaret Fuller, Theodore Parker, Orestes Brownson, Bronson Alcott, Elizabeth Peabody, George Ripley, Frederic Henry Hedge, and Christopher Cranch. Mostly young and Boston bred, these feisty radical thinkers tackled the most pressing issues of the time and endorsed, with varying degrees of zeal, the major efforts at moral reform—most notably abolition, the temperance movement, and women's rights.

The most appreciable public result of their discussions was *The Dial*, an intellectual miscellany published between 1840 and 1844 and edited at various times by Margaret Fuller, George Ripley, and Emerson. Because more than half the participants in the Transcendentalists' conversations had trained for the Unitarian ministry, their discussions naturally drifted toward the religious controversies of the day. These occasions invariably provided Emerson with frequent opportunities to test his own ideas about religion. During one of these meetings, Emerson is known to have said:

> The Puritans came here in revolt against forms. Why should they have kept any, then? . . . Is *any* form necessary? Do we need any gift or foreign force? Can we not be self-sustaining? See this divinity of daisies around us. Can we not be level to them? What need is there of miracles? That Jesus lived purely was his strong argument.

These are substantially the same points that Emerson developed in a controversial address to the senior class at the Harvard Divinity School in the summer of 1838, a lecture that dramatically affected the remainder of his life.

The Divinity School address challenged the church's assumption that "the age of inspiration is dead." He identified Jesus and the prophets as "holy bards," discounted the importance of miracles, redefined *good* and *evil,* and urged these fledgling ministers to cast aside conformity, to free themselves from the authority of the church. They must help their parishioners "to love God without mediator or veil." Hoping to stir these ministers to recognize that their preaching had to be "rammed with life,"

Emerson instead was roundly condemned as a heretic by the Divinity School faculty and effectively banned from speaking at Harvard for the next thirty years.

Emerson's two volumes of essays, published in 1841 and 1844, respectively, provide ample evidence with which to trace his distinctively American mind. Yet his ideas grew and changed over the span of nearly fifty years of lecturing and writing. He often modified his thinking and occasionally shifted it dramatically. In his later years, for example, he tempered much of his earlier, occasionally extravagant optimism. Recursive in his early essays, his thinking tended to be linear in later ones. Throughout his essays, however, Emerson steadfastly resisted the complacency of attaching himself to any single, narrow, categorical view of experience; "to define is to confine," he noted.

His thinking has a democratic ring to it—open to any influence, receptive to change and growth. Emerson's ideas can develop over the course of a single essay or over the length of his career precisely because he resists fixing or even limiting the significance of a thought. He seeks to make the movement of thought in each of his sentences and paragraphs analogous to the flow of the natural world—to the point where the mind "insures an order of expression which is the order of nature itself." Thinking and writing are organic for Emerson; his essays characteristically proceed by association rather than by logic. They reflect the way his mind actually works: moving from impression to impression, from association to association, always enlarging the context and broadening the range of experience. As Emerson's mind moves in a tangled web of observation, discovery, allusion, aphorism, and quotation, his essays become aggregates of sentences and paragraphs—a collection of insights. In this respect, a sentence in Emerson's essays generally carries the weight of what in other writers would be a paragraph. Like nineteenth-century American culture itself, Emerson's essays seem to have little patience with a single idea. Flashes of truth and moments of insight encourage a sense of surprise and intellectual discovery in his readers.

By the mid-1840s Emerson was spending more and more of his time on the road as one of the most respected members of what was known as the Lyceum movement, an association formed to offer general instruction to adults through a network of lectures and concerts. He was by no means successful everywhere he lectured. In the West, especially, he found difficult traveling conditions, primitive lodgings, and cantankerous and occasionally rowdy audiences more accustomed to humorous tall tales than to intellectual speculation. Yet Emerson's lectures, despite occasionally confused or unflattering responses, drew large audiences virtually everywhere. The moral and personal values Emerson advocated—especially the basic belief that each individual has "a greater possibility"—had enormous appeal to the average American in the 1840s.

Emerson lectured extensively in England in 1847 and 1848, spent more time with his friend Carlyle, and took copious notes for what became *Representative Men* (1850) and *English Traits* (1856), the latter a detailed, witty, insightful, and occasionally startled look at British culture. These works suggest just how empirical and skeptical Emerson had grown in the years following his first two collections of essays. The death of his six-year-old son, Waldo, in 1842 had deeply affected him, and although he had tried to "justify" the child's death in his essay "Experience" and in the poem "Threnody," Emerson clearly had begun to moderate his optimism. By the late 1840s he seemed willing to accept the painful realities of particular places, times, and events. He had also become slightly more aristocratic, even fateful, about the average

American's potential. By the time he published *English Traits,* Emerson's style had become more factual and reportorial. He now observed the world from a more detached point of view.

A renowned international figure by the 1850s, Emerson spent much of his time resisting involvement in the public controversies of the day. "I do not often speak to public questions," he announced. "They are odious and hurtful, and it seems like meddling or leaving your work." He preferred to cultivate the interior landscape of what Thoreau called "home cosmography." There were exceptions, of course: He opposed racial and social injustice, slavery, the removal of the Cherokee Nation from Georgia in the late 1830s, U.S. involvement in the Mexican War, and the Fugitive Slave Law. The epigraph to his journal for 1837 puts his views on public issues most succinctly: "I write the laws, / Not plead a cause."

The Emerson house in Concord became a port of call for virtually every major American writer of the time. His last years were devoted to being "the representative American." Too old to participate in the Civil War, Emerson became absorbed in the rhetoric surrounding it and wrote movingly about the Emancipation Proclamation and the death of Lincoln. Regarded as a sage in the United States and abroad, Emerson spent much of his time lecturing and trying to compensate for what he believed was America's "bad name for superficialness." In the years following the Civil War he grew increasingly impatient with his own failing health and eventually needed the help of both his daughter, Ellen, and James Cabot, his authorized biographer and literary executor, to see him through his lecturing and publishing commitments. It may well have been the accidental burning of "Coolidge House" in 1872 that precipitated Emerson's decline. Facing the loss of important papers and the disarray of so many others, he began to lose his memory and slipped into senility. His memory gone and his ability to perform publicly irreparably impaired, Emerson slowly settled into dying. On April 27, 1882, Concord's church bells rang seventy-nine times, proclaiming his life and announcing his death.

Perhaps the most appropriate epitaph for Emerson's life had been offered unceremoniously years before his death. In the early summer of 1848, near the end of his very successful—and controversial—lecture tour of Great Britain, a letter from a disconsolate reader appeared in a London newspaper, requesting that the admission price of Emerson's lectures be reduced so that the poorer classes could hear him speak. "Emerson," the letter writer observed, "is a phenomenon whose like is not in the world, and to miss him is to lose an important part of the Nineteenth century."

Further Reading:

O. W. Holmes, *Ralph Waldo Emerson,* 1885.

J. Cabot, *A Memoir of Ralph Waldo Emerson,* 2 vols., 1887.

V. W. Brooks, *The Life of Emerson,* 1932.

R. Rusk, *The Life of Ralph Waldo Emerson,* 1949, 1957.

V. Hopkins, *Spires of Form,* 1951.

S. Paul, *Emerson's Angle of Vision,* 1952.

F. Carpenter, *The Emerson Handbook,* 1953.

S. Whicher, *Freedom and Fate,* 1953, 1959.

K. W. Cameron, ed., *Emerson's Workshop: An Analysis of His Reading in Periodicals Through 1836,* 1964.

R. Poirier, *A World Elsewhere,* 1966.

K. W. Cameron, ed., *Emerson Among His Contemporaries,* 1967.

W. Harding, *Emerson's Library,* 1967.

J. Porte, *Emerson and Thoreau: Transcendentalists in Conflict,* 1967.

L. Buell, *Literary Transcendentalism,* 1973.

H. H. Waggoner, *Emerson as Poet,* 1974.

S. Bercovitch, *The Puritan Origin of the American Self,* 1975.

D. Porter, *Emerson and Literary Change,* 1978.

R. A. Yoder, *Emerson and the Orphic Poet in America,* 1978.

J. Porte, *Representative Man: Ralph Waldo Emerson in His Time,* 1979.

G. W. Allen, *Waldo Emerson,* 1981.

B. Packer, *Emerson's Fall,* 1982.

D. Robinson, *Apostle of Culture: Emerson as Preacher and Lecturer,* 1982.

D. Yannela, *Ralph Waldo Emerson,* 1982.

R. E. Burkholder and J. Myerson, eds., *Critical Essays on Ralph Waldo Emerson,* 1983.

J. McAleer, *Ralph Waldo Emerson: Days of Encounter,* 1984.

J. Ellison, *Emerson's Romantic Style,* 1984.

H. Bloom, ed., *Ralph Waldo Emerson,* 1985.

D. Van Leer, *Emerson's Epistemology: The Argument of the Essays,* 1986.

R. Poirier, *The Renewal of Literature: Emersonian Reflections,* 1987.

J. Steele, *The Representation of the Self in the American Renaissance,* 1987.

E. Barish, *Emerson, The Roots of Prophecy,* 1989.

S. Cavell, *Conditions Handsome and Unhandsome: The Constitution of Emersonian Perfectionism,* 1990.

D. L. Gelpi, *Endless Seeker: The Religious Quest of Ralph Waldo Emerson,* 1991.

M. Gonnaud, *An Uneasy Solitude: Individual and Society in the Work of Ralph Waldo Emerson,* 1991.

R. Poirier, *Poetry and Pragmatism,* 1992.

L. Buell, ed., *Ralph Waldo Emerson: A Collection of Critical Essays,* 1993.

R. Richardson, *Emerson: The Mind on Fire,* 1995.

Texts:

"Nature," "The American Scholar," the Divinity School address, and "Self-reliance," from *The Collected Works of Ralph Waldo Emerson,* vol. 1, ed. R. E. Spiller and A. R. Ferguson, 1971, and vol. 2, ed. J. Slater, A. R. Ferguson, and J. F. Carr, 1979.

See also *The Early Lectures of Ralph Waldo Emerson,* 3 vols., ed. S. Whicher et al., 1959–1971.

All poetry from *The Complete Works of Ralph Waldo Emerson,* ed. E. W. Emerson, 1903–1904.

"The Poet" and "Experience" from *Essays, Second Series,* 1844.

See also *The Journals of Ralph Waldo Emerson,* 10 vols., ed. E. W. Emerson and W. Forbes, 1909–1914, and *The Journals and Miscellaneous Notebooks of Ralph Waldo Emerson,* ed. W. Gilman, 16 vols., 1960–1982.

See also *Emerson's Literary Criticism,* ed. E. W. Carlson, 1979.

RELATED VOICES

The Supremacy of Mind over Matter

There is a class of persons who desire a reform in the prevailing philosophy of the day. These are called Transcendentalists, because they believe in an order of truths which transcends the sphere of the external sense. Their leading idea is the supremacy of mind over matter. Hence they maintain that the truth of religion does not depend on tradition, nor historical facts, but has an unerring witness in the soul. There is a light, they believe, which enlighteneth every man that cometh into the world; there is a faculty in all—the most degraded, the most ignorant, the most obscure—to perceive spiritual truth when distinctly presented; and the ultimate appeal on all moral questions is not to a jury of scholars, a hierarchy of divines, or the prescriptions of a creed, but to the common sense of the human race.

George Ripley, letter to the Church on Purchase Street
(1840)

Nature*

A subtle chain of countless rings
The next unto the farthest brings;
The eye reads omens where it goes,
And speaks all languages the rose;
And, striving to be man, the worm
Mounts through all the spires of form.[1]

Introduction

Our age is retrospective. It builds the sepulchres of the fathers. It writes biographies, histories, and criticism. The foregoing generations beheld God and nature face to face; we, through their eyes. Why should not we also enjoy an original relation to the universe? Why should not we have a poetry and philosophy of insight and not of tradition, and a religion by revelation to us, and not the history of theirs? Embosomed for a season in nature, whose floods of life stream around and through us, and invite us, by the powers they supply, to action proportioned to nature, why should we grope among the dry bones of the past, or put the living generation into masquerade out of its faded wardrobe? The sun shines to-day also. There is more wool and flax in the fields. There are new lands, new men, new thoughts. Let us demand our own works and laws and worship.

Undoubtedly we have no questions to ask which are unanswerable. We must trust the perfection of the creation so far as to believe that whatever curiosity the order of things has awakened in our minds, the order of things can satisfy. Every man's condition is a solution in hieroglyphic to those inquiries he would put. He acts it as life, before he apprehends it as truth. In like manner, nature is already, in its forms and tendencies, describing its own design. Let us interrogate the great apparition that shines so peacefully around us. Let us inquire, to what end is nature?

All science has one aim, namely, to find a theory of nature. We have theories of races and of functions, but scarcely yet a remote approach to an idea of creation. We are now so far from the road to truth, that religious teachers dispute and hate each other, and speculative men are esteemed unsound and frivolous. But to a sound judgment, the most abstract truth is the most practical. Whenever a true theory appears, it will be its own evidence. Its test is, that it will explain all phenomena. Now many are thought not only unexplained but inexplicable; as language, sleep, madness, dreams, beasts, sex.

Philosophically considered, the universe is composed of Nature and the Soul. Strictly speaking, therefore, all that is separate from us, all which Philosophy distinguishes as the NOT ME, that is, both nature and art, all other men and my own body,

---

* Emerson's first major work and the first proclamation of New England Transcendentalism.

[1] The first edition of "Nature" in 1836 had as its motto a quote from the Roman philosopher Plotinus: "Nature is but an image or imitation of wisdom, the last thing of the soul; nature being a thing which doth only do, but not know." In the 1849 edition, Emerson's epigraphic poem was substituted, supporting Darwin's concept of evolutionary progress.

must be ranked under this name, NATURE. In enumerating the values of nature and casting up their sum, I shall use the word in both senses—in its common and in its philosophical import. In inquiries so general as our present one, the inaccuracy is not material; no confusion of thought will occur. *Nature,* in the common sense, refers to essences unchanged by man; space, the air, the river, the leaf. *Art* is applied to the mixture of his will with the same things, as in a house, a canal, a statue, a picture. But his operations taken together are so insignificant, a little chipping, baking, patching, and washing, that in an impression so grand as that of the world on the human mind, they do not vary the result.

I

To go into solitude, a man needs to retire as much from his chamber as from society. I am not solitary whilst I read and write, though nobody is with me. But if a man would be alone, let him look at the stars. The rays that come from those heavenly worlds will separate between him and what he touches. One might think the atmosphere was made transparent with this design, to give man, in the heavenly bodies, the perpetual presence of the sublime. Seen in the streets of cities, how great they are! If the stars should appear one night in a thousand years, how would men believe and adore; and preserve for many generations the remembrance of the city of God which had been shown! But every night come out these envoys of beauty, and light the universe with their admonishing smile.

The stars awaken a certain reverence, because though always present, they are inaccessible; but all natural objects make a kindred impression, when the mind is open to their influence. Nature never wears a mean appearance. Neither does the wisest man extort her secret, and lose his curiosity by finding out all her perfection. Nature never became a toy to a wise spirit. The flowers, the animals, the mountains, reflected the wisdom of his best hour, as much as they had delighted the simplicity of his childhood.

When we speak of nature in this manner, we have a distinct but most poetical sense in the mind. We mean the integrity of impression made by manifold natural objects. It is this which distinguishes the stick of timber of the wood-cutter from the tree of the poet. The charming landscape which I saw this morning is indubitably made up of some twenty or thirty farms. Miller owns this field, Locke that, and Manning the woodland beyond. But none of them owns the landscape. There is a property in the horizon which no man has but he whose eye can integrate all the parts, that is, the poet. This is the best part of these men's farms, yet to this their warranty-deeds give no title.

To speak truly, few adult persons can see nature. Most persons do not see the sun. At least they have a very superficial seeing. The sun illuminates only the eye of the man, but shines into the eye and the heart of the child. The lover of nature is he whose inward and outward senses are still truly adjusted to each other; who has retained the spirit of infancy even into the era of manhood. His intercourse with heaven and earth becomes part of his daily food. In the presence of nature a wild delight runs through the man, in spite of real sorrows. Nature says—he is my creature, and maugre all his impertinent griefs, he shall be glad with me. Not the sun or the summer alone, but every hour and season yields its tribute of delight; for every hour and change corresponds to and authorizes a different state of the mind, from breathless noon to grimmest midnight. Nature is a setting that fits equally well a comic or a mourning piece. In good health, the air is a cordial of incredible virtue. Crossing a bare common, in snow puddles, at twilight, under a clouded sky, without having in my thoughts any occurrence of special good fortune, I have enjoyed a perfect exhilaration. I am glad to the brink of fear. In the woods, too, a man casts off his years, as the snake his slough, and at what period soever of life is always a child. In the woods is perpetual youth. Within these plantations of God, a decorum and sanctity reign, a perennial festival is dressed, and the guest sees not how he should tire of them in a thousand years. In the woods, we return to reason and faith. There I feel that nothing can befall me in life—no disgrace, no calamity (leaving me my eyes), which nature cannot repair. Standing on the bare ground—my head bathed by the blithe air and uplifted into infinite space—all mean egotism vanishes. I become a transparent eyeball; I am nothing; I see all; the currents of the Universal Being circulate through me; I am part or parcel of God. The name of the nearest friend sounds then foreign and accidental: to be brothers, to be acquaintances, master or servant, is then a trifle and a disturbance. I am the lover of uncontained and immortal beauty. In the wilderness, I find something more dear and connate than in streets or villages. In the tranquil landscape, and especially in the distant line of the horizon, man beholds somewhat as beautiful as his own nature.

The greatest delight which the fields and woods minister is the suggestion of an occult relation between man and the vegetable. I am not alone and unacknowledged. They nod to me, and I to them. The waving of the boughs in the storm is new to me and old. It takes me by surprise, and yet is not unknown. Its effect is like that of a higher thought or a better emotion coming over me, when I deemed I was thinking justly or doing right.

Yet it is certain that the power to produce this delight does not reside in nature, but in man, or in a harmony of both. It is necessary to use these pleasures with great temperance. For nature is not always tricked[2] in holiday attire, but the same scene which yesterday breathed perfume and glittered as for the frolic of the nymphs is overspread with melancholy to-day. Nature always wears the colors of the spirit. To a man laboring under calamity, the heat of his own fire hath sadness in it. Then there is a kind of contempt of the landscape felt by him who has just lost by death a dear friend. The sky is less grand as it shuts down over less worth in the population.

II: Commodity

Whoever considers the final cause of the world will discern a multitude of uses that enter as parts into that result. They all admit of being thrown into one of the following classes: Commodity; Beauty; Language; and Discipline.

Under the general name of commodity, I rank all those advantages which our senses owe to nature. This, of course, is a benefit which is temporary and mediate,[3] not ultimate, like its service to the soul. Yet although low, it is perfect in its kind, and is the only use of nature which all men apprehend. The misery of man appears like childish petulance, when we explore the steady and prodigal provision that has been made for his support and delight on this green ball which floats him through the heavens. What angels invented these splendid ornaments, these rich conveniences, this ocean of air above, this ocean of water beneath, this firmament of earth between? this zodiac of

2 Clad.
3 In between.

lights, this tent of dropping clouds, this striped coat of climates, this fourfold year? Beasts, fire, water, stones, and corn serve him. The field is at once his floor, his work-yard, his play-ground, his garden, and his bed.

> "More servants wait on man
> Than he'll take notice of."[4]

Cycles of nature

Nature, in its ministry to man, is not only the material, but is also the process and the re-sult. All the parts incessantly work into each other's hands for the profit of man. The wind sows the seed; the sun evaporates the sea; the wind blows the vapor to the field; the ice, on the other side of the planet, condenses rain on this; the rain feeds the plant; the plant feeds the animal; and thus the endless circulations of the divine charity nourish man.

The useful arts are reproductions or new combinations by the wit of man, of the same natural benefactors. He no longer waits for favoring gales, but by means of steam, he realizes the fable of Aeolus's bag,[5] and carries the two and thirty winds in the boiler of his boat. To diminish friction, he paves the road with iron bars,[6] and, mounting a coach with a ship-load of men, animals, and merchandise behind him, he darts through the country, from town to town, like an eagle or a swallow through the air. By the ag-gregate of these aids, how is the face of the world changed, from the era of Noah to that of Napoleon! The private poor man hath cities, ships, canals, bridges, built for him. He goes to the post-office, and the human race run on his errands; to the book-shop, and the human race read and write of all that happens for him; to the court-house, and na-tions repair his wrongs. He sets his house upon the road, and the human race go forth every morning, and shovel out the snow, and cut a path for him.

But there is no need of specifying particulars in this class of uses. The catalogue is endless, and the examples so obvious, that I shall leave them to the reader's reflection, with the general remark, that this mercenary benefit is one which has respect to a far-ther good. A man is fed, not that he may be fed, but that he may work.

III: Beauty

A nobler want of man is served by nature, namely, the love of Beauty.

The ancient Greeks called the world χο´σμος,[7] beauty. Such is the constitution of all things, or such the plastic power of the human eye, that the primary forms, as the sky, the mountain, the tree, the animal, give us a delight *in and for themselves;* a pleasure arising from outline, color, motion, and grouping. This seems partly owing to the eye itself. The eye is the best of artists. By the mutual action of its structure and of the laws of light, perspective is produced, which integrates every mass of objects, of what charac-ter soever, into a well colored and shaded globe, so that where the particular objects are mean and unaffecting, the landscape which they compose is round and symmetrical. And as the eye is the best composer, so light is the first of painters. There is no object so

---

[4] From "Man" by the English poet George Herbert (1593–1633).

[5] Aeolus, a god in Homer's *Odyssey,* gave Odysseus "a mighty bag" of bottled winds. Inquisitive sailors opened this bag and re-leased a tumultuous storm.

[6] Railroad tracks.

[7] Greek: "beauty" in the sense of the complex-ity of the universe expressed as orderly and harmonious.

foul that intense light will not make beautiful. And the stimulus it affords to the sense, and a sort of infinitude which it hath, like space and time, make all matter gay. Even the corpse has its own beauty. But besides this general grace diffused over nature, almost all the individual forms are agreeable to the eye, as is proved by our endless imitations of some of them, as the acorn, the grape, the pine-cone, the wheat-ear, the egg, the wings and forms of most birds, the lion's claw, the serpent, the butterfly, sea-shells, flames, clouds, buds, leaves, and the forms of many trees, as the palm.

For better consideration, we may distribute the aspects of Beauty in a threefold manner.

1.   First, the simple perception of natural forms is a delight. The influence of the forms and actions in nature is so needful to man, that, in its lowest functions, it seems to lie on the confines of commodity and beauty. To the body and mind which have been cramped by noxious work or company, nature is medicinal and restores their tone. The tradesman, the attorney comes out of the din and craft of the street and sees the sky and the woods, and is a man again. In their eternal calm, he finds himself. The health of the eye seems to demand a horizon. We are never tired, so long as we can see far enough.

But in other hours, Nature satisfies by its loveliness, and without any mixture of corporeal benefit. I see the spectacle of morning from the hilltop over against my house, from daybreak to sunrise, with emotions which an angel might share. The long slender bars of cloud float like fishes in the sea of crimson light. From the earth, as a shore, I look out into that silent sea. I seem to partake its rapid transformations; the active enchantment reaches my dust, and I dilate and conspire with the morning wind. How does Nature deify us with a few and cheap elements! Give me health and a day, and I will make the pomp of emperors ridiculous. The dawn is my Assyria;[8] the sunset and moonrise my Paphos,[9] and unimaginable realms of faerie; broad noon shall be my England of the senses and the understanding; the night shall be my Germany of mystic philosophy and dreams.[10]

Not less excellent, except for our less susceptibility in the afternoon, was the charm, last evening, of a January sunset. The western clouds divided and subdivided themselves into pink flakes modulated with tints of unspeakable softness, and the air had so much life and sweetness that it was a pain to come within doors. What was it that nature would say? Was there no meaning in the live repose of the valley behind the mill, and which Homer or Shakespeare could not re-form for me in words? The leafless trees become spires of flame in the sunset, with the blue east for their background, and the stars of the dead calices[11] of flowers, and every withered stem and stubble rimed with frost, contribute something to the mute music.

The inhabitants of cities suppose that the country landscape is pleasant only half the year. I please myself with the graces of the winter scenery, and believe that we are as much touched by it as by the genial influences of summer. To the attentive eye, each moment of the year has its own beauty, and in the same field, it beholds, every hour, a

---

[8] Ancient Near Eastern empire, emblematic of magnificence.

[9] Ancient city of Cyprus, distinguished for its worship of Aphrodite, Greek goddess of love and beauty.

[10] The rational empiricism of English philosophers, such as Hume, and the "common sense" school of thought are contrasted to the idealism of German philosophers, such as Kant.

[11] External, leafy parts of flowers.

picture which was never seen before and which shall never be seen again. The heavens change every moment, and reflect their glory or gloom on the plains beneath. The state of the crop in the surrounding farms alters the expression of the earth from week to week. The succession of native plants in the pastures and roadsides, which make the silent clock by which time tells the summer hours, will make even the divisions of the day sensible to a keen observer. The tribes of birds and insects, like the plants punctual to their time, follow each other, and the year has room for all. By watercourses, the variety is greater. In July, the blue pontederia or pickerel-weed blooms in large beds in the shallow parts of our pleasant river,[12] and swarms with yellow butterflies in continual motion. Art cannot rival this pomp of purple and gold. Indeed the river is a perpetual gala, and boasts each month a new ornament.

But this beauty of Nature which is seen and felt as beauty, is the least part. The shows of day, the dewy morning, the rainbow, mountains, orchards in blossom, stars, moonlight, shadows in still water, and the like, if too eagerly hunted, become shows merely, and mock us with their unreality. Go out of the house to see the moon, and 't is mere tinsel; it will not please as when its light shines upon your necessary journey. The beauty that shimmers in the yellow afternoons of October, who ever could clutch it? Go forth to find it, and it is gone; 't is only a mirage as you look from the windows of diligence.

2.   The presence of a higher, namely, of the spiritual element is essential to its perfection. The high and divine beauty which can be loved without effeminacy, is that which is found in combination with the human will. Beauty is the mark God sets upon virtue. Every natural action is graceful. Every heroic act is also decent, and causes the place and the bystanders to shine. We are taught by great actions that the universe is the property of every individual in it. Every rational creature has all nature for his dowry and estate. It is his, if he will. He may divest himself of it; he may creep into a corner, and abdicate his kingdom, as most men do, but he is entitled to the world by his constitution. In proportion to the energy of his thought and will, he takes up the world into himself. "All those things for which men plough, build, or sail, obey virtue;" said Sallust.[13] "The winds and waves," said Gibbon, "are always on the side of the ablest navigators."[14] So are the sun and moon and all the stars of heaven. When a noble act is done—perchance in a scene of great natural beauty; when Leonidas[15] and his three hundred martyrs consume one day in dying, and the sun and moon come each and look at them once in the steep defile of Thermopylae; when Arnold Winkelried,[16] in the high Alps, under the shadow of the avalanche, gathers in his side a sheaf of Austrian spears to break the line for his comrades; are not these heroes entitled to add the beauty of the scene to the beauty of the deed? When the bark of Columbus nears the shore of America; before it the beach lined with savages, fleeing out of all their huts of cane; the sea behind; and the purple mountains of the Indian Archipelago around, can we separate the

---

[12] The Concord River.

[13] From *The Conspiracy of Catiline* by the Roman historian Gaius Sallustius Crispus (86–35 B.C.).

[14] From *The Decline and Fall of the Roman Empire* (1788) by Edward Gibbon (1737–1794), English historian.

[15] King Leonidas and three hundred fellow Spartans died while defending the pass at

Thermopylae against the Persian army in 480 B.C.

[16] Swiss hero who exposed himself to the spears of the Austrians in the Battle of Sempach (1386). When the Austrians had exhausted their supply, Winkelried defeated them and proclaimed Swiss independence.

man from the living picture? Does not the New World clothe his form with her palm-groves and savannahs as fit drapery? Ever does natural beauty steal in like air, and envelop great actions. When Sir Harry Vane[17] was dragged up the Tower-hill,[18] sitting on a sled, to suffer death as the champion of the English laws, one of the multitude cried out to him, "You never sate on so glorious a seat!" Charles II, to intimidate the citizens of London, caused the patriot Lord Russell[19] to be drawn in an open coach through the principal streets of the city on his way to the scaffold. "But," his biographer says, "the multitude imagined they saw liberty and virtue sitting by his side." In private places, among sordid objects, an act of truth or heroism seems at once to draw to itself the sky as its temple, the sun as its candle. Nature stretches out her arms to embrace man, only let his thoughts be of equal greatness. Willingly does she follow his steps with the rose and the violet, and bend her lines of grandeur and grace to the decoration of her darling child. Only let his thoughts be of equal scope, and the frame will suit the picture. A virtuous man is in unison with her works, and makes the central figure of the visible sphere. Homer, Pindar, Socrates, Phocion,[20] associate themselves fitly in our memory with the geography and climate of Greece. The visible heavens and earth sympathize with Jesus. And in common life whosoever has seen a person of powerful character and happy genius, will have remarked how easily he took all things along with him—the persons, the opinions, and the day, and nature became ancillary to a man.

3.   There is still another aspect under which the beauty of the world may be viewed, namely, as it becomes an object of the intellect. Beside the relation of things to virtue, they have a relation to thought. The intellect searches out the absolute order of things as they stand in the mind of God, and without the colors of affection. The intellectual and the active powers seem to succeed each other, and the exclusive activity of the one generates the exclusive activity of the other. There is something unfriendly in each to the other, but they are like the alternate periods of feeding and working in animals; each prepares and will be followed by the other. Therefore does beauty, which, in relation to actions, as we have seen, comes unsought, and comes because it is unsought, remain for the apprehension and pursuit of the intellect; and then again, in its turn, of the active power. Nothing divine dies. All good is eternally reproductive. The beauty of nature reforms itself in the mind, and not for barren contemplation, but for new creation.

All men are in some degree impressed by the face of the world; some men even to delight. This love of beauty is Taste. Others have the same love in such excess, that, not content with admiring, they seek to embody it in new forms. The creation of beauty is Art.

The production of a work of art throws a light upon the mystery of humanity. A work of art is an abstract or epitome of the world. It is the result or expression of nature, in miniature. For although the works of nature are innumerable and all different, the result or the expression of them all is similar and single. Nature is a sea of forms radically alike and even unique. A leaf, a sunbeam, a landscape, the ocean, make an analogous impression on the mind. What is common to them all—that perfectness and

---

[17] English Puritan (1613–1662) executed for opposing the restoration of Charles II.

[18] Hill next to the Tower of London where executions for treason took place.

[19] William Russell (1639–1683), executed for cooperating with a plot to overthrow Charles II.

[20] Homer: Greek epic poet (fl. 850? B.C.); Pindar: Greek poet (522?–443 B.C.); Socrates: Greek philosopher (470?–399 B.C.); Phocion: Athenian general and statesman (402?–317 B.C.).

harmony, is beauty. The standard of beauty is the entire circuit of natural forms—the totality of nature; which the Italians expressed by defining beauty "il più nell' uno."[21] Nothing is quite beautiful alone; nothing but is beautiful in the whole. A single object is only so far beautiful as it suggests this universal grace. The poet, the painter, the sculptor, the musician, the architect, seek each to concentrate this radiance of the world on one point, and each in his several work to satisfy the love of beauty which stimulates him to produce. Thus is Art a nature passed through the alembic of man. Thus in art does Nature work through the will of a man filled with the beauty of her first works.

The world thus exists to the soul to satisfy the desire of beauty. This element I call an ultimate end. No reason can be asked or given why the soul seeks beauty. Beauty, in its largest and profoundest sense, is one expression for the universe. God is the all-fair. Truth, and goodness, and beauty, are but different faces of the same All. But beauty in nature is not ultimate. It is the herald of inward and eternal beauty, and is not alone a solid and satisfactory good. It must stand as a part, and not as yet the last or highest expression of the final cause of Nature.

IV: Language

Language is a third use which Nature subserves to man. Nature is the vehicle of thought, and in a simple, double, and three-fold degree.

1. Words are signs of natural facts.
2. Particular natural facts are symbols of particular spiritual facts.
3. Nature is the symbol of spirit.

1. Words are signs of natural facts. The use of natural history is to give us aid in supernatural history; the use of the outer creation, to give us language for the beings and changes of the inward creation. Every word which is used to express a moral or intellectual fact, if traced to its root, is found to be borrowed from some material appearance. *Right* means *straight; wrong* means *twisted; Spirit* primarily means *wind; transgression,* the crossing of a *line; supercilious,* the *raising of the eyebrow.* We say the *heart* to express emotion, the *head* to denote thought; and *thought* and *emotion* are words borrowed from sensible things, and now appropriated to spiritual nature. Most of the process by which this transformation is made, is hidden from us in the remote time when language was framed; but the same tendency may be daily observed in children. Children and savages use only nouns or names of things, which they convert into verbs, and apply to analogous mental acts.

2. But this origin of all words that convey a spiritual import—so conspicuous a fact in the history of language—is our least debt to nature. It is not words only that are emblematic; it is things which are emblematic. Every natural fact is a symbol of some spiritual fact. Every appearance in nature corresponds to some state of the mind, and that state of the mind can only be described by presenting that natural appearance as its picture. An enraged man is a lion, a cunning man is a fox, a firm man is a rock, a learned man is a torch. A lamb is innocence; a snake is subtle spite; flowers express to us the delicate affections. Light and darkness are our familiar expression for knowledge

---

[21] Italian: "the many in one."

and ignorance; and heat for love. Visible distance behind and before us, is respectively our image of memory and hope.

Who looks upon a river in a meditative hour and is not reminded of the flux of all things? Throw a stone into the stream, and the circles that propagate themselves are the beautiful type of all influence. Man is conscious of a universal soul within or behind his individual life, wherein, as in a firmament, the natures of Justice, Truth, Love, Freedom, arise and shine. This universal soul he calls Reason: it is not mine, or thine, or his, but we are its; we are its property and men. And the blue sky in which the private earth is buried, the sky with its eternal calm, and full of everlasting orbs, is the type of Reason. That which intellectually considered we call Reason, considered in relation to nature, we call Spirit. Spirit is the Creator. Spirit hath life in itself. And man in all ages and countries embodies it in his language as the FATHER.

It is easily seen that there is nothing lucky or capricious in these analogies, but that they are constant, and pervade nature. These are not the dreams of a few poets, here and there, but man is an analogist, and studies relations in all objects. He is placed in the centre of beings, and a ray of relation passes from every other being to him. And neither can man be understood without these objects, nor these objects without man. All the facts in natural history taken by themselves, have no value, but are barren, like a single sex. But marry it to human history, and it is full of life. Whole floras, all Linnæus' and Buffon's[22] volumes, are dry catalogues of facts; but the most trivial of these facts, the habit of a plant, the organs, or work, or noise of an insect, applied to the illustration of a fact in intellectual philosophy, or in any way associated to human nature, affects us in the most lively and agreeable manner. The seed of a plant—to what affecting analogies in the nature of man is that little fruit made use of, in all discourse, up to the voice of Paul, who calls the human corpse a seed—"It is sown a natural body; it is raised a spiritual body."[23] The motion of the earth round its axis and round the sun, makes the day and the year. These are certain amounts of brute light and heat. But is there no intent of an analogy between man's life and the seasons? And do the seasons gain no grandeur or pathos from that analogy? The instincts of the ant are very unimportant considered as the ant's; but the moment a ray of relation is seen to extend from it to man, and the little drudge is seen to be a monitor, a little body with a mighty heart, then all its habits, even that said to be recently observed, that it never sleeps, become sublime.

Because of this radical correspondence between visible things and human thoughts, savages, who have only what is necessary, converse in figures. As we go back in history, language becomes more picturesque, until its infancy, when it is all poetry; or all spiritual facts are represented by natural symbols. The same symbols are found to make the original elements of all languages. It has moreover been observed, that the idioms of all languages approach each other in passages of the greatest eloquence and power. And as this is the first language, so is it the last. This immediate dependence of language upon nature, this conversion of an outward phenomenon into a type of somewhat in human life, never loses its power to affect us. It is this which gives that piquancy to the conversation of a strong-natured farmer or backwoodsman, which all men relish.

[22] Linnæus: Carolus Linnæus (1707–1778), Swedish botanist; Buffon: Georges Louis Leclerc, comte de Buffon (1707–1788), French naturalist.

[23] See 1 Corinthians 15:44.

A man's power to connect his thought with its proper symbol, and so to utter it, depends on the simplicity of his character, that is, upon his love of truth and his desire to communicate it without loss. The corruption of man is followed by the corruption of language. When simplicity of character and the sovereignty of ideas is broken up by the prevalence of secondary desires—the desire of riches, of pleasure, of power, and of praise—and duplicity and falsehood take place of simplicity and truth, the power over nature as an interpreter of the will is in a degree lost; new imagery ceases to be created, and old words are perverted to stand for things which are not; a paper currency is employed, when there is no bullion in the vaults. In due time the fraud is manifest, and words lose all power to stimulate the understanding or the affections. Hundreds of writers may be found in every long-civilized nation who for a short time believe and make others believe that they see and utter truths, who do not of themselves clothe one thought in its natural garment, but who feed unconsciously on the language created by the primary writers of the country, those, namely, who hold primarily on nature.

But wise men pierce this rotten diction and fasten words again to visible things; so that picturesque language is at once a commanding certificate that he who employs it is a man in alliance with truth and God. The moment our discourse rises above the ground line of familiar facts and is inflamed with passion or exalted by thought, it clothes itself in images. A man conversing in earnest, if he watch his intellectual processes, will find that a material image more or less luminous arises in his mind, contemporaneous with every thought, which furnishes the vestment of the thought. Hence, good writing and brilliant discourse are perpetual allegories. This imagery is spontaneous. It is the blending of experience with the present action of the mind. It is proper creation. It is the working of the Original Cause through the instruments he has already made.

These facts may suggest the advantage which the country-life possesses, for a powerful mind, over the artificial and curtailed life of cities. We know more from nature than we can at will communicate. Its light flows into the mind evermore, and we forget its presence. The poet, the orator, bred in the woods, whose senses have been nourished by their fair and appeasing changes, year after year, without design and without heed— shall not lose their lesson altogether, in the roar of cities or the broil of politics. Long hereafter, amidst agitation and terror in national councils—in the hour of revolution— these solemn images shall reappear in their morning lustre, as fit symbols and words of the thoughts which the passing events shall awaken. At the call of a noble sentiment, again the woods wave, the pines murmur, the river rolls and shines, and the cattle low upon the mountains, as he saw and heard them in his infancy. And with these forms, the spells of persuasion, the keys of power are put into his hands.

3.   We are thus assisted by natural objects in the expression of particular meanings. But how great a language to convey such pepper-corn[24] informations! Did it need such noble races of creatures, this profusion of forms, this host of orbs in heaven, to furnish man with the dictionary and grammar of his municipal speech? Whilst we use this grand cipher to expedite the affairs of our pot and kettle, we feel that we have not yet put it to its use, neither are able. We are like travellers using the cinders of a volcano to roast their eggs. Whilst we see that it always stands ready to clothe what we would say, we cannot avoid the question whether the characters are not significant of themselves. Have

[24] Unimportant.

mountains, and waves, and skies, no significance but what we consciously give them when we employ them as emblems of our thoughts? The world is emblematic. Parts of speech are metaphors, because the whole of nature is a metaphor of the human mind. The laws of moral nature answer to those of matter as face to face in a glass. "The visible world and the relation of its parts, is the dial plate of the invisible."[25] The axioms of physics translate the laws of ethics. Thus, "the whole is greater than its part;" "reaction is equal to action;" "the smallest weight may be made to lift the greatest, the difference of weight being compensated by time;" and many the like propositions, which have an ethical as well as physical sense. These propositions have a much more extensive and universal sense when applied to human life, than when confined to technical use.

In like manner, the memorable words of history and the proverbs of nations consist usually of a natural fact, selected as a picture or parable of a moral truth. Thus: A rolling stone gathers no moss; A bird in the hand is worth two in the bush; A cripple in the right way will beat a racer in the wrong; Make hay while the sun shines; 'Tis hard to carry a full cup even; Vinegar is the son of wine; The last ounce broke the camel's back; Long-lived trees make roots first—and the like. In their primary sense these are trivial facts, but we repeat them for the value of their analogical import. What is true of proverbs, is true of all fables, parables, and allegories.

This relation between the mind and matter is not fancied by some poet, but stands in the will of God, and so is free to be known by all men. It appears to men, or it does not appear. When in fortunate hours we ponder this miracle, the wise man doubts if at all other times he is not blind and deaf;

> "Can such things be,
> And overcome us like a summer's cloud,
> Without our special wonder?"[26]

for the universe becomes transparent, and the light of higher laws than its own shines through it. It is the standing problem which has exercised the wonder and the study of every fine genius since the world began; from the era of the Egyptians and the Brahmins to that of Pythagoras, of Plato, of Bacon, of Leibnitz, of Swedenborg.[27] There sits the Sphinx[28] at the road-side, and from age to age, as each prophet comes by, he tries his fortune at reading her riddle. There seems to be a necessity in spirit to manifest itself in

---

[25] Quoted from the philosopher Emanuel Swedenborg (1688–1772) (see note 27 below).

[26] Shakespeare's *Macbeth*, Act III, Sc. iv, ll. 110–112.

[27] Teachings that influenced Emerson's interpretations of the universe. Egyptian and Brahmin mystics taught transmigration of the soul. Pythagoras (sixth century B.C.) believed in the infinite recurrence of phenomena. Plato (428–347 B.C.) fostered the idealism of Western philosophy. Francis Bacon

(1561–1626), British founder of inductive science, believed in religious mysticism. Gottfried Wilhelm von Leibnitz (1646–1716) was a German mathematician and idealist philosopher. Emanuel Swedenborg (1688–1772) was the Swedish religious mentor whom Emerson characterized as "the mystic" in *Representative Men*.

[28] According to Greek mythology, this monster killed anyone who failed to answer her riddle.

material forms; and day and night, river and storm, beast and bird, acid and alkali, preëxist in necessary Ideas in the mind of God, and are what they are by virtue of preceding affections in the world of spirit. A Fact is the end or last issue of spirit. The visible creation is the terminus or the circumference of the invisible world. "Material objects," said a French philosopher,[29] "are necessarily kinds of *scoriæ*[30] of the substantial thoughts of the Creator, which must always preserve an exact relation to their first origin; in other words, visible nature must have a spiritual and moral side."

This doctrine is abstruse, and though the images of "garment," "scoriæ," "mirror," etc., may stimulate the fancy, we must summon the aid of subtler and more vital expositors to make it plain. "Every scripture is to be interpreted by the same spirit which gave it forth,"[31] is the fundamental law of criticism. A life in harmony with Nature, the love of truth and of virtue, will purge the eyes to understand her text. By degrees we may come to know the primitive sense of the permanent objects of nature, so that the world shall be to us an open book, and every form significant of its hidden life and final cause.

A new interest surprises us, whilst, under the view now suggested, we contemplate the fearful extent and multitude of objects; since "every object rightly seen, unlocks a new faculty of the soul."[32] That which was unconscious truth, becomes, when interpreted and defined in an object, a part of the domain of knowledge—a new weapon in the magazine of power.

V: Discipline

In view of the significance of nature, we arrive at once at a new fact, that nature is a discipline. This use of the world includes the preceding uses, as parts of itself.

Space, time, society, labor, climate, food, locomotion, the animals, the mechanical forces, give us sincerest lessons, day by day, whose meaning is unlimited. They educate both the Understanding and the Reason. Every property of matter is a school for the understanding—its solidity or resistance, its inertia, its extension, its figure, its divisibility. The understanding adds, divides, combines, measures, and finds nutriment and room for its activity in this worthy scene. Meantime, Reason transfers all these lessons into its own world of thought, by perceiving the analogy that marries Matter and Mind.

1. Nature is a discipline of the understanding in intellectual truths. Our dealing with sensible objects is a constant exercise in the necessary lessons of difference, of likeness, of order, of being and seeming, of progressive arrangement; of ascent from particular to general; of combination to one end of manifold forces. Proportioned to the importance of the organ to be formed, is the extreme care with which its tuition is provided—a care pretermitted in no single case. What tedious training, day after day, year after year, never ending, to form the common sense; what continual reproduction of annoyances, inconveniences, dilemmas; what rejoicing over us of little men; what disputing of prices, what reckonings of interest—and all to form the Hand of the

---

[29] Guillaume Oegger in *The True Messiah* (1829).

[30] Slag from the melting of metals.

[31] Quoted from the English Quaker George Fox (1624–1691).

[32] From a compendium of literary criticism and philosophy, *Aids to Reflection* (1825), by Samuel Taylor Coleridge (1772–1834).

mind—to instruct us that "good thoughts are no better than good dreams, unless they be executed!"[33]

The same good office is performed by Property and its filial systems of debt and credit. Debt, grinding debt, whose iron face the widow, the orphan, and the sons of genius fear and hate—debt, which consumes so much time, which so cripples and disheartens a great spirit with cares that seem so base, is a preceptor whose lessons cannot be foregone, and is needed most by those who suffer from it most. Moreover, property, which has been well compared to snow—"if it fall level to-day, it will be blown into drifts to-morrow," is the surface action of internal machinery, like the index on the face of a clock. Whilst now it is the gymnastics of the understanding, it is hiving, in the foresight of the spirit, experience in profounder laws.

The whole character and fortune of the individual are affected by the least inequalities in the culture of the understanding; for example, in the perception of differences. Therefore is Space, and therefore Time, that man may know that things are not huddled and lumped, but sundered and individual. A bell and a plough have each their use, and neither can do the office of the other. Water is good to drink, coal to burn, wool to wear; but wool cannot be drunk, nor water spun, nor coal eaten. The wise man shows his wisdom in separation, in gradation, and his scale of creatures and of merits is as wide as nature. The foolish have no range in their scale, but suppose every man is as every other man. What is not good they call the worst, and what is not hateful, they call the best.

In like manner, what good heed Nature forms in us! She pardons no mistakes. Her yea is yea, and her nay, nay.

The first steps in Agriculture, Astronomy, Zoölogy (those first steps which the farmer, the hunter, and the sailor take), teach that Nature's dice are always loaded; that in her heaps and rubbish are concealed sure and useful results.

How calmly and genially the mind apprehends one after another the laws of physics! What noble emotions dilate the mortal as he enters into the councils of the creation, and feels by knowledge the privilege to BE! His insight refines him. The beauty of nature shines in his own breast. Man is greater that he can see this, and the universe less, because Time and Space relations vanish as laws are known.

Here again we are impressed and even daunted by the immense Universe to be explored. "What we know is a point to what we do not know."[34] Open any recent journal of science, and weigh the problems suggested concerning Light, Heat, Electricity, Magnetism, Physiology, Geology, and judge whether the interest of natural science is likely to be soon exhausted.

Passing by many particulars of the discipline of nature, we must not omit to specify two.

The exercise of the Will, or the lesson of power, is taught in every event. From the child's successive possession of his several senses up to the hour when he saith, "Thy will be done!"[35] he is learning the secret that he can reduce under his will not only particular events but great classes, nay, the whole series of events, and so conform all facts to his character. Nature is thoroughly mediate. It is made to serve. It receives the dominion of

---

[33] From "Of Great Place" in the *Essays* (1625) of Sir Francis Bacon (1561–1626).
[34] Quotation attributed to English theologian and moralist Bishop Joseph Butler (1692–1752).
[35] Matthew 6:10; 26:42.

man as meekly as the ass on which the Saviour rode.[36] It offers all its kingdoms to man as the raw material which he may mould into what is useful. Man is never weary of working it up. He forges the subtle and delicate air into wise and melodious words, and gives them wing as angels of persuasion and command. One after another his victorious thought comes up with and reduces all things, until the world becomes at last only a realized will—the double of the man.

2. Sensible objects conform to the premonitions of Reason and reflect the conscience. All things are moral; and in their boundless changes have an unceasing reference to spiritual nature. Therefore is nature glorious with form, color, and motion; that every globe in the remotest heaven, every chemical change from the rudest crystal up to the laws of life, every change of vegetation from the first principle of growth in the eye of a leaf, to the tropical forest and antediluvian coal-mine, every animal function from the sponge up to Hercules, shall hint or thunder to man the laws of right and wrong, and echo the Ten Commandments. Therefore is Nature ever the ally of Religion: lends all her pomp and riches to the religious sentiment. Prophet and priest, David, Isaiah, Jesus, have drawn deeply from this source. This ethical character so penetrates the bone and marrow of nature, as to seem the end for which it was made. Whatever private purpose is answered by any member or part, this is its public and universal function, and is never omitted. Nothing in nature is exhausted in its first use. When a thing has served an end to the uttermost, it is wholly new for an ulterior service. In God, every end is converted into a new means. Thus the use of commodity, regarded by itself, is mean and squalid. But it is to the mind an education in the doctrine of Use, namely, that a thing is good only so far as it serves; that a conspiring of parts and efforts to the production of an end is essential to any being. The first and gross manifestation of this truth is our inevitable and hated training in values and wants, in corn and meat.

It has already been illustrated, that every natural process is a version of a moral sentence. The moral law lies at the centre of nature and radiates to the circumference. It is the pith and marrow of every substance, every relation, and every process. All things with which we deal, preach to us. What is a farm but a mute gospel? The chaff and the wheat, weeds and plants, blight, rain, insects, sun—it is a sacred emblem from the first furrow of spring to the last stack which the snow of winter overtakes in the fields. But the sailor, the shepherd, the miner, the merchant, in their several resorts, have each an experience precisely parallel, and leading to the same conclusion: because all organizations are radically alike. Nor can it be doubted that this moral sentiment which thus scents the air, grows in the grain, and impregnates the waters of the world, is caught by man and sinks into his soul. The moral influence of nature upon every individual is that amount of truth which it illustrates to him. Who can estimate this? Who can guess how much firmness the sea-beaten rock has taught the fisherman? How much tranquillity has been reflected to man from the azure sky, over whose unspotted deeps the winds forevermore drive flocks of stormy clouds, and leave no wrinkle or stain? How much industry and providence and affection we have caught from the pantomime of brutes? What a searching preacher of self-command is the varying phenomenon of Health!

Herein is especially apprehended the unity of Nature—the unity in variety—which meets us everywhere. All the endless variety of things make an identical impression.

---

[36] Matthew 21:5: "Behold thy king cometh
   unto thee, meek, and sitting upon an ass."

Xenophanes[37] complained in his old age, that, look where he would, all things hastened back to Unity. He was weary of seeing the same entity in the tedious variety of forms. The fable of Proteus[38] has a cordial truth. A leaf, a drop, a crystal, a moment of time, is related to the whole, and partakes of the perfection of the whole. Each particle is a microcosm, and faithfully renders the likeness of the world.

Not only resemblances exist in things whose analogy is obvious, as when we detect the type of the human hand in the flipper of the fossil saurus,[39] but also in objects wherein there is great superficial unlikeness. Thus architecture is called "frozen music," by De Staël and Goethe.[40] Vitruvius[41] thought an architect should be a musician. "A Gothic church," said Coleridge,[42] "is a petrified religion." Michael Angelo maintained, that, to an architect, a knowledge of anatomy is essential. In Haydn's oratorios,[43] the notes present to the imagination not only motions, as of the snake, the stag, and the elephant, but colors also; as the green grass. The law of harmonic sounds reappears in the harmonic colors. The granite is differenced in its laws only by the more or less of heat from the river that wears it away. The river, as it flows, resembles the air that flows over it; the air resembles the light which traverses it with more subtile currents; the light resembles the heat which rides with it through Space. Each creature is only a modification of the other; the likeness in them is more than the difference, and their radical law is one and the same. A rule of one art, or a law of one organization, holds true throughout nature. So intimate is this Unity, that, it is easily seen, it lies under the undermost garment of Nature, and betrays its source in Universal Spirit. For it pervades Thought also. Every universal truth which we express in words, implies or supposes every other truth. *Omne verum vero consonat.*[44] It is like a great circle on a sphere, comprising all possible circles; which, however, may be drawn and comprise it in like manner. Every such truth is the absolute Ens[45] seen from one side. But it has innumerable sides.

The central Unity is still more conspicuous in actions. Words are finite organs of the infinite mind. They cannot cover the dimensions of what is in truth. They break, chop, and impoverish it. An action is the perfection and publication of thought. A right action seems to fill the eye, and to be related to all nature. "The wise man, in doing one thing, does all; or, in the one thing he does rightly, he sees the likeness of all which is done rightly."[46]

Words and actions are not the attributes of brute nature. They introduce us to the human form, of which all other organizations appear to be degradations. When this appears among so many that surround it, the spirit prefers it to all others. It says, "From such as this have I drawn joy and knowledge; in such as this have I found and beheld myself; I will speak to it; it can speak again; it can yield me thought already formed and

[37] Greek philosopher of the sixth century B.C.

[38] God of Greek fable who could assume various forms.

[39] Extinct reptiles.

[40] De Staël: French writer Anne Louise Germaine (1766–1817), baronne de Staël; Goethe: German poet Johann Wolfgang von Goethe (1749–1832).

[41] Roman architect Marcus Vitruvius Pollio (first century B.C.).

[42] From "A Lecture on the General Characteristics of the Gothic Mind in the Middle Ages" in *Literary Remains* (1836) by Samuel Taylor Coleridge.

[43] Choral music of Austrian composer Franz Joseph Haydn (1732–1809).

[44] Latin: "Every truth agrees with every other truth."

[45] A name for "abstract being" in Latin philosophy.

[46] Quote from Goethe's *Wilhelm Meister's Travels* (1821, 1829).

alive." In fact, the eye—the mind—is always accompanied by these forms, male and female; and these are incomparably the richest informations of the power and order that lie at the heart of things. Unfortunately every one of them bears the marks as of some injury; is marred and superficially defective. Nevertheless, far different from the deaf and dumb nature around them, these all rest like fountain-pipes on the unfathomed sea of thought and virtue whereto they alone, of all organizations, are the entrances.

It were a pleasant inquiry to follow into detail their ministry to our education, but where would it stop? We are associated in adolescent and adult life with some friends, who, like skies and waters, are coextensive with our idea; who, answering each to a certain affection of the soul, satisfy our desire on that side; whom we lack power to put at such focal distance from us, that we can mend or even analyze them. We cannot choose but love them. When much intercourse with a friend has supplied us with a standard of excellence, and has increased our respect for the resources of God who thus sends a real person to outgo our ideal; when he has, moreover, become an object of thought, and, whilst his character retains all its unconscious effect, is converted in the mind into solid and sweet wisdom—it is a sign to us that his office is closing, and he is commonly withdrawn from our sight in a short time.

VI: Idealism

Thus is the unspeakable but intelligible and practicable meaning of the world conveyed to man, the immortal pupil, in every object of sense. To this one end of Discipline, all parts of nature conspire.

A noble doubt perpetually suggests itself—whether this end be not the Final Cause of the Universe; and whether nature outwardly exists. It is a sufficient account of that Appearance we call the World, that God will teach a human mind, and so makes it the receiver of a certain number of congruent sensations, which we call sun and moon, man and woman, house and trade. In my utter impotence to test the authenticity of the report of my senses, to know whether the impressions they make on me correspond with outlying objects, what difference does it make, whether Orion[47] is up there in heaven, or some god paints the image in the firmament of the soul? The relations of parts and the end of the whole remaining the same, what is the difference, whether land and sea interact, and worlds revolve and intermingle without number or end—deep yawning under deep, and galaxy balancing galaxy, throughout absolute space—or whether, without relations of time and space, the same appearances are inscribed in the constant faith of man? Whether nature enjoy a substantial existence without, or is only in the apocalypse of the mind, it is alike useful and alike venerable to me. Be it what it may, it is ideal to me so long as I cannot try the accuracy of my senses.

The frivolous make themselves merry with the Ideal theory, as if its consequences were burlesque; as if it affected the stability of nature. It surely does not. God never jests with us, and will not compromise the end of nature by permitting any inconsequence in its procession. Any distrust of the permanence of laws would paralyze the faculties of man. Their permanence is sacredly respected, and his faith therein is perfect. The wheels and springs of man are all set to the hypothesis of the permanence of nature. We are not built like a ship to be tossed, but like a house to stand. It is a natural conse-

---

[47] Constellation of stars.

quence of this structure, that so long as the active powers predominate over the reflective, we resist with indignation any hint that nature is more short-lived or mutable than spirit. The broker, the wheelwright, the carpenter, the tollman, are much displeased at the intimation.

But whilst we acquiesce entirely in the permanence of natural laws, the question of the absolute existence of nature still remains open. It is the uniform effect of culture on the human mind, not to shake our faith in the stability of particular phenomena, as of heat, water, azote; but to lead us to regard nature as phenomenon, not a substance; to attribute necessary existence to spirit; to esteem nature as an accident and an effect.

To the senses and the unrenewed understanding, belongs a sort of instinctive belief in the absolute existence of nature. In their view man and nature are indissolubly joined. Things are ultimates, and they never look beyond their sphere. The presence of Reason mars this faith. The first effort of thought tends to relax this despotism of the senses which binds us to nature as if we were a part of it, and shows us nature aloof, and, as it were, afloat. Until this higher agency intervened, the animal eye sees, with wonderful accuracy, sharp outlines and colored surfaces. When the eye of Reason opens, to outline and surface are at once added grace and expression. These proceed from imagination and affection, and abate somewhat of the angular distinctness of objects. If the Reason be stimulated to more earnest vision, outlines and surfaces become transparent, and are no longer seen; causes and spirits are seen through them. The best moments of life are these delicious awakenings of the higher powers, and the reverential withdrawing of nature before its God.

Let us proceed to indicate the effects of culture.

1. Our first institution in the Ideal philosophy is a hint from Nature herself.

Nature is made to conspire with spirit to emancipate us. Certain mechanical changes, a small alteration in our local position, apprizes us of a dualism. We are strangely affected by seeing the shore from a moving ship, from a balloon, or through the tints of an unusual sky. The least change in our point of view gives the whole world a pictorial air. A man who seldom rides, needs only to get into a coach and traverse his own town, to turn the street into a puppet-show. The men, the women—talking, running, bartering, fighting—the earnest mechanic, the lounger, the beggar, the boys, the dogs, are unrealized at once, or, at least, wholly detached from all relation to the observer, and seen as apparent, not substantial beings. What new thoughts are suggested by seeing a face of country quite familiar, in the rapid movement of the railroad car! Nay, the most wonted objects (make a very slight change in the point of vision), please us most. In a camera obscura,[48] the butcher's cart, and the figure of one of our own family amuse us. So a portrait of a well-known face gratifies us. Turn the eyes upside down, by looking at the landscape through your legs, and how agreeable is the picture, though you have seen it any time these twenty years!

In these cases, by mechanical means, is suggested the difference between the observer and the spectacle—between man and nature. Hence arises a pleasure mixed with awe; I may say, a low degree of the sublime is felt, from the fact, probably, that man is hereby apprized that whilst the world is a spectacle, something in himself is stable.

---

[48] Chamber into which an image is projected onto a wall; forerunner of the modern camera.

2.   In a higher manner the poet communicates the same pleasure. By a few strokes he delineates, as on air, the sun, the mountain, the camp, the city, the hero, the maiden, not different from what we know them, but only lifted from the ground and afloat before the eye. He unfixes the land and the sea, makes them revolve around the axis of his primary thought, and disposes them anew. Possessed himself by a heroic passion, he uses matter as symbols of it. The sensual man conforms thoughts to things; the poet conforms things to his thoughts. The one esteems nature as rooted and fast; the other, as fluid, and impresses his being thereon. To him, the refractory world is ductile and flexible; he invests dust and stones with humanity, and makes them the words of the Reason. The Imagination may be defined to be the use which the Reason makes of the material world. Shakspeare possesses the power of subordinating nature for the purposes of expression, beyond all poets. His imperial muse tosses the creation like a bauble from hand to hand, and uses it to embody any caprice of thought that is uppermost in his mind. The remotest spaces of nature are visited, and the farthest sundered things are brought together, by a subtile spiritual connection. We are made aware that magnitude of material things is relative, and all objects shrink and expand to serve the passion of the poet. Thus in his sonnets, the lays of birds, the scents and dyes of flowers he finds to be the *shadow* of his beloved; time, which keeps her from him, is his *chest*; the suspicion she has awakened, is her *ornament*;

> The ornament of beauty is Suspect,
> A crow which flies in heaven's sweetest air.[49]

His passion is not the fruit of chance; it swells, as he speaks, to a city, or a state.

> No, it was builded far from accident;
> It suffers not in smiling pomp, nor falls
> Under the brow of thralling discontent;
> It fears not policy, that heretic,
> That works on leases of short numbered hours,
> But all alone stands hugely politic.[50]

In the strength of his constancy, the Pyramids seem to him recent and transitory. The freshness of youth and love dazzles him with its resemblance to morning;

> Take those lips away
> Which so sweetly were forsworn;
> And those eyes,—the break of day,
> Lights that do mislead the morn.[51]

The wild beauty of this hyperbole, I may say in passing, it would not be easy to match in literature.

This transfiguration which all material objects undergo through the passion of the poet—this power which he exerts to dwarf the great, to magnify the small—might be

---

[49] Shakespeare, *Sonnets*, LXX, ll. 3–4.
[50] Shakespeare, *Sonnets*, CXXIV, ll. 5–11.

[51] Shakespeare, *Measure for Measure*, Act IV, Sc. i, ll. 1–4.

illustrated by a thousand examples from his Plays. I have before me the Tempest, and will cite only these few lines.

> ARIEL. The strong based promontory
> Have I made shake, and by the spurs plucked up
> The pine and cedar.

Prospero calls for music to soothe the frantic Alonzo, and his companions;

> A solemn air, and the best comforter
> To an unsettled fancy, cure thy brains
> Now useless, boiled within thy skull.

Again;

> The charm dissolves apace,
> And, as the morning steals upon the night,
> Melting the darkness, so their rising senses
> Begin to chase the ignorant fumes that mantle
> Their clearer reason.
>   Their understanding
> Begins to swell: and the approaching tide
> Will shortly fill the reasonable shores
> That now lie foul and muddy.[52]

The perception of real affinities between events (that is to say, of *ideal* affinities, for those only are real), enables the poet thus to make free with the most imposing forms and phenomena of the world, and to assert the predominance of the soul.

3. Whilst thus the poet animates nature with his own thoughts, he differs from the philosopher only herein, that the one proposes Beauty as his main end; the other Truth. But the philosopher, not less than the poet, postpones the apparent order and relations of things to the empire of thought. "The problem of philosophy," according to Plato, "is, for all that exists conditionally, to find a ground unconditioned and absolute."[53] It proceeds on the faith that a law determines all phenomena, which being known, the phenomena can be predicted. That law, when in the mind, is an idea. Its beauty is infinite. The true philosopher and the true poet are one, and a beauty, which is truth, and a truth, which is beauty, is the aim of both. Is not the charm of one of Plato's or Aristotle's definitions strictly like that of the Antigone of Sophocles? It is, in both cases, that a spiritual life has been imparted to nature; that the solid seeming block of matter has been pervaded and dissolved by a thought; that this feeble human being has penetrated the vast masses of nature with an informing soul, and recognized itself in their harmony, that is, seized their law. In physics, when this is attained, the memory disburthens itself of its cumbrous catalogues of particulars, and carries centuries of observation in a single formula.

---

[52] Shakespeare, *The Tempest*, Act V, Sc. i, ll. 46–48, 58–60, 64–68, 79–82. Prospero, not Ariel, speaks the opening lines.

[53] Quotation from Plato's *Republic*, Book V. Emerson uses an abridged rendering from Coleridge's *The Friend* (1818).

Thus even in physics, the material is degraded before the spiritual. The astronomer, the geometer, rely on their irrefragable analysis, and disdain the results of observation. The sublime remark of Euler[54] on his law of arches, "This will be found contrary to all experience, yet is true;" had already transferred nature into the mind, and left matter like an outcast corpse.

4.   Intellectual science has been observed to beget invariably a doubt of the existence of matter. Turgot[55] said, "He that has never doubted the existence of matter, may be assured he has no aptitude for metaphysical inquiries." It fastens the attention upon immortal necessary uncreated natures, that is, upon Ideas; and in their presence we feel that the outward circumstance is a dream and a shade. Whilst we wait in this Olympus of gods, we think of nature as an appendix to the soul. We ascend into their region, and know that these are the thoughts of the Supreme Being. "These are they who were set up from everlasting, from the beginning, or ever the earth was. When he prepared the heavens, they were there; when he established the clouds above, when he strengthened the fountains of the deep. Then they were by him, as one brought up with him. Of them took he counsel."[56]

Their influence is proportionate. As objects of science they are accessible to few men. Yet all men are capable of being raised by piety or by passion, into their region. And no man touches these divine natures, without becoming, in some degree, himself divine. Like a new soul, they renew the body. We become physically nimble and lightsome; we tread on air; life is no longer irksome, and we think it will never be so. No man fears age or misfortune or death in their serene company, for he is transported out of the district of change. Whilst we behold unveiled the nature of Justice and Truth, we learn the difference between the absolute and the conditional or relative. We apprehend the absolute. As it were, for the first time, *we exist.* We become immortal, for we learn that time and space are relations of matter; that with a perception of truth or a virtuous will they have no affinity.

5.   Finally, religion and ethics, which may be fitly called the practice of ideas, or the introduction of ideas into life, have an analogous effect with all lower culture, in degrading nature and suggesting its dependence on spirit. Ethics and religion differ herein; that the one is the system of human duties commencing from man; the other, from God. Religion includes the personality of God; Ethics does not. They are one to our present design. They both put nature under foot. The first and last lesson of religion is, "The things that are seen, are temporal; the things that are unseen, are eternal."[57] It puts an affront upon nature. It does that for the unschooled, which philosophy does for Berkeley and Viasa.[58] The uniform language that may be heard in the churches of the most ignorant sects is—"Contemn the unsubstantial shows of the world; they are vanities, dreams, shadows, unrealities; seek the realities of religion." The devotee flouts nature. Some theosophists have arrived at a certain hostility and indignation towards mat-

---

[54] Swiss mathematician Leonhard Euler (1707–1783).

[55] French statesman and economist Robert Jacques Turgot (1727–1781).

[56] Abbreviated version of Proverbs 8:23, 27, 28, 30.

[57] See 2 Corinthians 4:18.

[58] Berkeley: George Berkeley (1685–1753), English churchman and philosophical idealist; Viyasa: proverbial Hindu philosopher.

ter, as the Manichean[59] and Plotinus.[60] They distrusted in themselves any looking back to these flesh-pots of Egypt.[61] Plotinus was ashamed of his body. In short, they might all say of matter, what Michael Angelo said of external beauty, "It is the frail and weary weed, in which God dresses the soul which he has called into time."[62]

It appears that motion, poetry, physical and intellectual science, and religion, all tend to affect our convictions of the reality of the external world. But I own there is something ungrateful in expanding too curiously the particulars of the general proposition, that all culture tends to imbue us with idealism. I have no hostility to nature, but a child's love to it. I expand and live in the warm day like corn and melons. Let us speak her fair. I do not wish to fling stones at my beautiful mother, nor soil my gentle nest. I only wish to indicate the true position of nature in regard to man, wherein to establish man all right education tends; as the ground which to attain is the object of human life, that is, of man's connection with nature. Culture inverts the vulgar view of nature, and brings the mind to call that apparent which it uses to call real, and that real which it uses to call visionary. Children, it is true, believe in the external world. The belief that it appears only, is an afterthought, but with culture this faith will as surely arise on the mind as did the first.

The advantage of the ideal theory over the popular faith is this, that it presents the world in precisely that view which is most desirable to the mind. It is, in fact, the view which Reason, both speculative and practical, that is, philosophy and virtue, take. For seen in the light of thought, the world always is phenomenal; and virtue subordinates it to the mind. Idealism sees the world in God. It beholds the whole circle of persons and things, of actions and events, of country and religion, not as painfully accumulated, atom after atom, act after act, in an aged creeping Past, but as one vast picture which God paints on the instant eternity for the contemplation of the soul. Therefore the soul holds itself off from a too trivial and microscopic study of the universal tablet. It respects the end too much to immerse itself in the means. It sees something more important in Christianity than the scandals of ecclesiastical history or the niceties of criticism; and, very incurious concerning persons or miracles, and not at all disturbed by chasms of historical evidence, it accepts from God the phenomenon, as it finds it, as the pure and awful form of religion in the world. It is not hot and passionate at the appearance of what it calls its own good or bad fortune, at the union or opposition of other persons. No man is its enemy. It accepts whatsoever befalls, as part of its lesson. It is a watcher more than a doer, and it is a doer, only that it may the better watch.

VII: Spirit

It is essential to a true theory of nature and of man, that it should contain[63] somewhat progressive. Uses that are exhausted or that may be, and facts that end in the statement, cannot be all that is true of this brave lodging wherein man is harbored, and wherein all

---

[59] A disciple of Manes, third-century Christian sage who theorized that the evil of the body exists in duality with the goodness of the soul.

[60] Roman Neoplatonic philosopher (205?–?270).

[61] See Exodus 16:2–3.

[62] Michelangelo, *Sonnet* 51.

[63] Remain.

his faculties find appropriate and endless exercise. And all the uses of nature admit of being summed in one, which yields the activity of man an infinite scope. Through all its kingdoms, to the suburbs and outskirts of things, it is faithful to the cause whence it had its origin. It always speaks of Spirit. It suggests the absolute. It is a perpetual effect. It is a great shadow pointing always to the sun behind us.

The aspect of Nature is devout. Like the figure of Jesus, she stands with bended head, and hands folded upon the breast. The happiest man is he who learns from nature the lesson of worship.

Of that ineffable essence which we call Spirit, he that thinks most, will say least. We can foresee God in the coarse, and, as it were, distant phenomena of matter; but when we try to define and describe himself, both language and thought desert us, and we are as helpless as fools and savages. That essence refuses to be recorded in propositions, but when man has worshipped him intellectually, the noblest ministry of nature is to stand as the apparition of God. It is the organ through which the universal spirit speaks to the individual, and strives to lead back the individual to it.

When we consider Spirit, we see that the views already presented do not include the whole circumference of man. We must add some related thoughts.

Three problems are put by nature to the mind: What is matter? Whence is it? and Whereto? The first of these questions only, the ideal theory answers. Idealism saith: matter is a phenomenon, not a substance. Idealism acquaints us with the total disparity between the evidence of our own being and the evidence of the world's being. The one is perfect; the other, incapable of any assurance; the mind is a part of the nature of things; the world is a divine dream, from which we may presently awake to the glories and certainties of day. Idealism is a hypothesis to account for nature by other principles than those of carpentry and chemistry. Yet, if it only deny the existence of matter, it does not satisfy the demands of the spirit. It leaves God out of me. It leaves me in the splendid labyrinth of my perceptions, to wander without end. Then the heart resists it, because it balks the affections in denying substantive being to men and women. Nature is so pervaded with human life that there is something of humanity in all and in every particular. But this theory makes nature foreign to me, and does not account for that consanguinity which we acknowledge to it.

Let it stand then, in the present state of our knowledge, merely as a useful introductory hypothesis, serving to apprize us of the eternal distinction between the soul and the world.

But when, following the invisible steps of thoughts, we come to inquire, Whence is matter? and Whereto? many truths arise to us out of the recesses of consciousness. We learn that the highest is present to the soul of man; that the dread universal essence, which is not wisdom, or love, or beauty, or power, but all in one, and each entirely, is that for which all things exist, and that by which they are; that spirit creates; that behind nature, throughout nature, spirit is present; one and not compound it does not act upon us from without, that is, in space and time, but spiritually, or through ourselves: therefore, that spirit, that is, the Supreme Being, does not build up nature around us, but puts it forth through us, as the life of the tree puts forth new branches and leaves through the pores of the old. As a plant upon the earth, so a man rests upon the bosom of God; he is nourished by unfailing fountains, and draws at his need inexhaustible power. Who can set bounds to the possibilities of man? Once inhale the upper air, being admitted to behold the absolute natures of justice and truth, and we learn that man has access to the entire mind of the Creator, is himself the creator in the finite. This view, which admonishes me where the sources of wisdom and power lie, and points to virtue as to

> "The golden key
> Which opes the palace of eternity,"[64]

carries upon its face the highest certificate of truth, because it animates me to create my own world through the purification of my soul.

The world proceeds from the same spirit as the body of man. It is a remoter and inferior incarnation of God, a projection of God in the unconscious. But it differs from the body in one important respect. It is not, like that, now subjected to the human will. Its serene order is inviolable by us. It is, therefore, to us, the present expositor of the divine mind. It is a fixed point whereby we may measure our departure. As we degenerate, the contrast between us and our house is more evident. We are as much strangers in nature as we are aliens from God. We do not understand the notes of birds. The fox and the deer run away from us; the bear and tiger rend us. We do not know the uses of more than a few plants, as corn and the apple, the potato and the vine. Is not the landscape, every glimpse of which hath a grandeur, a face of him? Yet this may show us what discord is between man and nature, for you cannot freely admire a noble landscape if laborers are digging in the field hard by. The poet finds something ridiculous in his delight until he is out of the sight of men.

VIII: Prospects

In inquiries respecting the laws of the world and the frame of things, the highest reason is always the truest. That which seems faintly possible, it is so refined, is often faint and dim because it is deepest seated in the mind among the eternal verities. Empirical science is apt to cloud the sight, and by the very knowledge of functions and processes to bereave the student of the manly contemplation of the whole. The savant becomes unpoetic. But the best read naturalist who lends an entire and devout attention to truth, will see that there remains much to learn of his relation to the world, and that it is not to be learned by any addition or subtraction or other comparison of known quantities, but is arrived at by untaught sallies of the spirit, by a continual self-recovery, and by entire humility. He will perceive that there are far more excellent qualities in the student than preciseness and infallibility; that a guess is often more fruitful than an indisputable affirmation, and that a dream may let us deeper into the secret of nature than a hundred concerted experiments.

For the problems to be solved are precisely those which the physiologist and the naturalist omit to state. It is not so pertinent to man to know all the individuals of the animal kingdom, as it is to know whence and whereto is this tyrannizing unity in his constitution, which evermore separates and classifies things, endeavoring to reduce the

[64] John Milton, *Comus*, ll. 13–14.

most diverse to one form. When I behold a rich landscape, it is less to my purpose to recite correctly the order and superposition of the strata, than to know why all thought of multitude is lost in a tranquil sense of unity. I cannot greatly honor minuteness in details, so long as there is no hint to explain the relation between things and thoughts; no ray upon the *metaphysics* of conchology, of botany, of the arts, to show the relation of the forms of flowers, shells, animals, architecture, to the mind, and build science upon ideas. In a cabinet of natural history,[65] we become sensible of a certain occult recognition and sympathy in regard to the most unwieldy and eccentric form of beast, fish, and insect. The American who has been confined, in his own country, to the sight of buildings designed after foreign models, is surprised on entering York Minster[66] or St. Peter's at Rome, by the feeling that these structures are imitations also—faint copies of an invisible archetype. Nor has science sufficient humanity, so long as the naturalist overlooks that wonderful congruity which subsists between man and the world; of which he is lord, not because he is the most subtile inhabitant, but because he is its head and heart, and finds something of himself in every great and small thing, in every mountain stratum, in every new law of color, fact of astronomy, or atmospheric influence which observation or analysis lays open. A perception of this mystery inspires the muse of George Herbert, the beautiful psalmist of the seventeenth century. The following lines are part of his little poem on Man.

> Man is all symmetry,
> Full of proportions, one limb to another,
>   And all to all the world besides.
>   Each part may call the farthest, brother;
> For head with foot hath private amity,
>   And both with moons and tides.
>
> Nothing hath got so far
> But man hath caught and kept it as his prey;
>   His eyes dismount the highest star:
>   He is in little all the sphere.
> Herbs gladly cure our flesh, because that they
>   Find their acquaintance there.
>
>   For us, the winds do blow,
> The earth doth rest, heaven move, and fountains flow;
>   Nothing we see, but means our good,
>   As our delight, or as our treasure;
> The whole is either our cupboard of food,
>   Or cabinet of pleasure.
>
>   The stars have us to bed:
> Night draws the curtain; which the sun withdraws.
>   Music and light attend our head.
>   All things unto our flesh are kind,

---

[65] i.e., display case of biological specimens.
[66] Stately cathedral at York, England.

In their descent and being; to our mind,
   In their ascent and cause.

   More servants wait on man
Than he'll take notice of. In every path,
   He treads down that which doth befriend him
   When sickness makes him pale and wan.
Oh mighty love! Man is one world, and hath
   Another to attend him.[67]

The perception of this class of truths makes the attraction which draws men to science, but the end is lost sight of in attention to the means. In view of this half-sight of science, we accept the sentence of Plato, that "poetry comes nearer to vital truth than history." Every surmise and vaticination of the mind is entitled to a certain respect, and we learn to prefer imperfect theories, and sentences which contain glimpses of truth, to digested systems which have no one valuable suggestion. A wise writer will feel that the ends of study and composition are best answered by announcing undiscovered regions of thought, and so communicating, through hope, new activity to the torpid spirit.

I shall therefore conclude this essay with some traditions of man and nature, which a certain poet[68] sang to me; and which, as they have always been in the world, and perhaps reappear to every bard, may be both history and prophecy.

"The foundations of man are not in matter, but in spirit. But the element of spirit is eternity. To it, therefore, the longest series of events, the oldest chronologies are young and recent. In the cycle of the universal man, from whom the nown individuals proceed, centuries are points, and all history is but the epoch of one degradation.

"We distrust and deny inwardly our sympathy with nature. We own and disown our relation to it, by turns. We are like Nebuchadnezzar, dethroned, bereft of reason, and eating grass like an ox.[69] But who can set limits to the remedial force of spirit?

"A man is a god in ruin. When men are innocent, life shall be longer, and shall pass into the immortal as gently as we awake from dreams. Now, the world would be insane and rabid, if these disorganizations should last for hundreds of years. It is kept in check by death and infancy. Infancy is the perpetual Messiah, which comes into the arms of fallen men, and pleads with them to return to paradise.

"Man is the dwarf of himself. Once he was permeated and dissolved by spirit. He filled nature with his overflowing currents. Out from him sprang the sun and moon; from man the sun, from woman the moon. The laws of his mind, the periods of his actions externized themselves into day and night, into the year and the seasons. But, having made for himself this huge shell, his waters retired; he no longer fills the veins and veinlets; he is shrunk to a drop. He sees that the structure still fits him, but fits him colossally. Say, rather, once it fitted him, now it corresponds to him from far and on high. He adores timidly his own work. Now is man the follower of the sun, and woman

---

[67] Stanzas 1–4 and 6 of "Man" (1633) by George Herbert (1593–1633), English poet.

[68] Perhaps Emerson himself, or Bronson Alcott (1799–1888), New England Transcendentalist and author of *Orphic Sayings* (1840).

[69] See Daniel 4:24–33. Nebuchadnezzar became irrational, "was driven from men, and did eat grass as oxen."

the follower of the moon. Yet sometimes he starts in his slumber, and wonders at himself and his house, and muses strangely at the resemblance betwixt him and it. He perceives that if his law is still paramount, if still he have elemental power, if his word is sterling yet in nature, it is not conscious power, it is not inferior but superior to his will. It is instinct." Thus my Orphic[70] poet sang.

At present, man applies to nature but half his force. He works on the world with his understanding alone. He lives in it and masters it by a penny-wisdom; and he that works most in it is but a half-man, and whilst his arms are strong and his digestion good, his mind is imbruted, and he is a selfish savage. His relation to nature, his power over it, is through the understanding, as by manure; the economic use of fire, wind, water, and the mariner's needle; steam, coal, chemical agriculture; the repairs of the human body by the dentist and the surgeon. This is such a resumption of power as if a banished king should buy his territories inch by inch, instead of vaulting at once into his throne. Meantime, in the thick darkness, there are not wanting gleams of a better light—occasional examples of the action of man upon nature with his entire force—with reason as well as understanding. Such examples are, the traditions of miracles in the earliest antiquity of all nations; the history of Jesus Christ; the achievements of a principle, as in religious and political revolutions, and in the abolition of the slave-trade; the miracles of enthusiasm,[71] as those reported of Swedenborg, Hohenlohe, and the Shakers;[72] many obscure and yet contested facts, now arranged under the name of Animal Magnetism;[73] prayer; eloquence; self-healing; and the wisdom of children. These are examples of Reason's momentary grasp of the sceptre; the exertions of a power which exists not in time or space, but an instantaneous in-streaming causing power. The difference between the actual and the ideal force of man is happily figured by the schoolmen, in saying, that the knowledge of man is an evening knowledge, *vespertina cognitio*, but that of God is a morning knowledge, *matutina cognitio*.[74]

The problem of restoring to the world original and eternal beauty is solved by the redemption of the soul. The ruin or the blank that we see when we look at nature, is in our own eye. The axis of vision is not coincident with the axis of things, and so they appear not transparent but opaque. The reason why the world lacks unity, and lies broken and in heaps, is because man is disunited with himself. He cannot be a naturalist until he satisfies all the demands of the spirit. Love is as much its demand as perception. Indeed, neither can be perfect without the other. In the uttermost meaning of the words thought is devout, and devotion is thought. Deep calls unto deep.[75] But in actual life, the marriage is not celebrated. There are innocent men who worship God after the tradition of

---

[70] i.e., characteristic of mystic doctrines ascribed to Orpheus, poet of Greek mythology.

[71] Divine hysteria.

[72] Swedenborg: see note 27 above; Hohenlohe: Leopold Emmerich, German prince of Hohenlohe-Waldenberg-Schillingfurst (1794–1849), Catholic bishop and writer; Shakers: those affiliated with the millenial church, which had its inception in England in 1747 and which was renowned for its frenzied dancing and prophetic manifestations in services.

[73] Hypnosis.

[74] Latin phrases attributable to academic philosophers of the Middle Ages, particularly St. Augustine and St. Thomas Aquinas.

[75] Psalm 42:7.

their fathers, but their sense of duty has not yet extended to the use of all their faculties. And there are patient naturalists, but they freeze their subject under the wintry light of the understanding. Is not prayer also a study of truth—a sally of the soul into the unfound infinite? No man ever prayed heartily without learning something. But when a faithful thinker, resolute to detach every object from personal relations and see it in the light of thought, shall, at the same time, kindle science with the fire of the holiest affections, then will God go forth anew into the creation.

It will not need, when the mind is prepared for study, to search for objects. The invariable mark of wisdom is to see the miraculous in the common. What is a day? What is a year? What is summer? What is woman? What is a child? What is sleep? To our blindness, these things seem unaffecting. We make fables to hide the baldness of the fact and conform it, as we say, to the higher law of the mind. But when the fact is seen under the light of an idea, the gaudy fable fades and shrivels. We behold the real higher law. To the wise, therefore, a fact is true poetry, and the most beautiful of fables. These wonders are brought to our own door. You also are a man. Man and woman and their social life, poverty, labor, sleep, fear, fortune, are known to you. Learn that none of these things is superficial, but that each phenomenon has its roots in the faculties and affections of the mind. Whilst the abstract question occupies your intellect, nature brings it in the concrete to be solved by your hands. It were a wise inquiry for the closet, to compare, point by point, especially at remarkable crises in life, our daily history with the rise and progress of ideas in the mind.

So shall we come to look at the world with new eyes. It shall answer the endless inquiry of the intellect—What is truth? and of the affections—What is good? by yielding itself passive to the educated Will. Then shall come to pass what my poet said: "Nature is not fixed but fluid. Spirit alters, moulds, makes it. The immobility or bruteness of nature is the absence of spirit; to pure spirit it is fluid, it is volatile, it is obedient. Every spirit builds itself a house, and beyond its house a world, and beyond its world a heaven. Know then that the world exists for you. For you is the phenomenon perfect. What we are, that only can we see. All that Adam had, all that Cæsar could, you have and can do. Adam called his house, heaven and earth; Cæsar called his house, Rome; you perhaps call yours, a cobbler's trade; a hundred acres of ploughed land; or a scholar's garret. Yet line for line and point for point your dominion is as great as theirs, though without fine names. Build therefore your own world. As fast as you conform your life to the pure idea in your mind, that will unfold its great proportions. A correspondent revolution in things will attend the influx of the spirit. So fast will disagreeable appearances, swine, spiders, snakes, pests, mad-houses, prisons, enemies, vanish; they are temporary and shall be no more seen. The sordor and filths of nature, the sun shall dry up and the wind exhale. As when the summer comes from the south the snowbanks melt and the face of the earth becomes green before it, so shall the advancing spirit create its ornaments along its path, and carry with it the beauty it visits and the song which enchants it; it shall draw beautiful faces, warm hearts, wise discourse, and heroic acts, around its way, until evil is no more seen. The kingdom of man over nature, which cometh not with observation—a dominion such as now is beyond his dream of God—he shall enter without more wonder than the blind man feels who is gradually restored to sight."

1836

The American Scholar*

MR. PRESIDENT AND GENTLEMEN:

I greet you on the recommencement of our literary year.[1] Our anniversary is one of hope, and, perhaps, not enough of labor. We do not meet for games of strength or skill, for the recitation of histories, tragedies, and odes, like the ancient Greeks; for parliaments of love and poesy, like the Troubadours;[2] nor for the advancement of science, like our contemporaries in the British and European capitals. Thus far, our holiday has been simply a friendly sign of the survival of the love of letters amongst a people too busy to give to letters any more. As such it is precious as the sign of an indestructible instinct. Perhaps the time is already come when it ought to be, and will be, something else; when the sluggard intellect of this continent will look from under its iron lids and fill the postponed expectation of the world with something better than the exertions of mechanical skill. Our day of dependence, our long apprenticeship to the learning of other lands, draws to a close. The millions that around us are rushing into life, cannot always be fed on the sere remains of foreign harvests. Events, actions arise, that must be sung, that will sing themselves. Who can doubt that poetry will revive and lead in a new age, as the star in the constellation Harp,[3] which now flames in our zenith, astronomers announce, shall one day be the polestar[4] for a thousand years?

In this hope I accept the topic which not only usage but the nature of our association seem to prescribe to this day—the AMERICAN SCHOLAR. Year by year we come up hither to read one more chapter of his biography. Let us inquire what light new days and events have thrown on his character and his hopes.

It is one of those fables which out of an unknown antiquity convey an unlooked-for wisdom, that the gods, in the beginning, divided Man into men, that he might be more helpful to himself;[5] just as the hand was divided into fingers, the better to answer its end.

The old fable covers a doctrine ever new and sublime; that there is One Man—present to all particular men only partially, or through one faculty; and that you must take the whole society to find the whole man. Man is not a farmer, or a professor, or an engineer, but he is all. Man is priest, and scholar, and statesman, and producer, and soldier. In the *divided* or social state these functions are parcelled out to individuals, each of whom aims to do his stint of the joint work, whilst each other performs his. The fable implies that the individual, to possess himself, must sometimes return from his own labor to embrace all the other laborers. But, unfortunately, this original unit, this fountain of power, has been so distributed to multitudes, has been so minutely subdivided and peddled out, that it is spilled into drops, and cannot be gathered. The state of society is one in which the members have suffered amputation from the trunk, and strut

---

* This essay was first printed as a pamphlet entitled *Man Thinking: An Oration Delivered Before the Phi Beta Kappa Society, at Cambridge, August 31, 1837.* Emerson retitled it "The American Scholar" in *Essays* (1841) in order to address all students and anyone else committed to thought.

[1] The customary college year, beginning in September.

[2] Courtly poets of southern France in the twelfth and thirteenth centuries.

[3] The constellation referred to is Lyra, which includes the bright star Vega.

[4] The earth's axis points toward the North Star.

[5] The fable recalled by Emerson is from Plato's *Symposium.*

about so many walking monsters—a good finger, a neck, a stomach, an elbow, but never a man.

Man is thus metamorphosed into a thing, into many things. The planter, who is Man sent out into the field to gather food, is seldom cheered by any idea of the true dignity of his ministry. He sees his bushel and his cart, and nothing beyond, and sinks into the farmer, instead of Man on the farm. The tradesman scarcely ever gives an ideal worth to his work, but is ridden by the routine of his craft, and the soul is subject to dollars. The priest becomes a form; the attorney a statute-book; the mechanic a machine; the sailor a rope of the ship.

In this distribution of functions the scholar is the delegated intellect. In the right state he is *Man Thinking*. In the degenerate state, when the victim of society, he tends to become a mere thinker, or still worse, the parrot of other men's thinking.

In this view of him, as Man Thinking, the theory of his office is contained. Him Nature solicits with all her placid, all her monitory pictures; him the past instructs; him the future invites. Is not indeed every man a student, and do not all things exist for the student's behoof? And, finally, is not the true scholar the only true master? But the old oracle said, "All things have two handles: beware of the wrong one." In life, too often, the scholar errs with mankind and forfeits his privilege. Let us see him in his school, and consider him in reference to the main influences he receives.

I.   The first in time and the first in importance of the influences upon the mind is that of nature. Every day, the sun; and, after sunset, Night and her stars. Ever the winds blow; ever the grass grows. Every day, men and women, conversing—beholding and beholden. The scholar is he of all men whom this spectacle most engages. He must settle its value in his mind. What is nature to him? There is never a beginning, there is never an end, to the inexplicable continuity of this web of God, but always circular power returning into itself. Therein it resembles his own spirit, whose beginning, whose ending, he never can find—so entire, so boundless. Far too as her splendors shine, system on system shooting like rays, upward, downward, without centre, without circumference—in the mass and in the particle, Nature hastens to render account of herself to the mind. Classification begins. To the young mind every thing is individual, stands by itself. By and by, it finds how to join two things and see in them one nature; then three, then three thousand; and so, tyrannized over by its own unifying instinct, it goes on tying things together, diminishing anomalies, discovering roots running under ground whereby contrary and remote things cohere and flower out from one stem. It presently learns that since the dawn of history there has been a constant accumulation and classifying of facts. But what is classification but the perceiving that these objects are not chaotic, and are not foreign, but have a law which is also a law of the human mind? The astronomer discovers that geometry, a pure abstraction of the human mind, is the measure of planetary motion. The chemist finds proportions and intelligible method throughout matter; and science is nothing but the finding of analogy, identity, in the most remote parts. The ambitious soul sits down before each refractory fact; one after another reduces all strange constitutions, all new powers, to their class and their law, and goes on forever to animate the last fibre of organization, the outskirts of nature, by insight.

Thus to him, to this schoolboy under the bending dome of day, is suggested that he and it proceed from one root; one is leaf and one is flower; relation, sympathy, stirring in every vein. And what is that root? Is not that the soul of his soul? A thought too bold;

a dream too wild. Yet when this spiritual light shall have revealed the law of more earthly natures—when he has learned to worship the soul, and to see that the natural philosophy that now is, is only the first gropings of its gigantic hand, he shall look forward to an ever expanding knowledge as to a becoming creator. He shall see that nature is the opposite of the soul, answering to it part for part. One is seal and one is print. Its beauty is the beauty of his own mind. Its laws are the laws of his own mind. Nature then becomes to him the measure of his attainments. So much of nature as he is ignorant of, so much of his own mind does he not yet possess. And, in fine, the ancient precept, "Know thyself," and the modern precept, "Study nature," become at last one maxim.

II.   The next great influence[6] into the spirit of the scholar is the mind of the Past—in whatever form, whether of literature, of art, of institutions, that mind is inscribed. Books are the best type of the influence of the past, and perhaps we shall get at the truth—learn the amount of this influence more conveniently—by considering their value alone.

The theory of books is noble. The scholar of the first age received into him the world around; brooded thereon; gave it the new arrangement of his own mind, and uttered it again. It came into him life; it went out from him truth. It came to him shortlived actions; it went out from him immortal thoughts. It came to him business; it went from him poetry. It was dead fact; now, it is quick[7] thought. It can stand, and it can go. It now endures, it now flies, it now inspires. Precisely in proportion to the depth of mind from which it issued, so high does it soar, so long does it sing.

Or, I might say, it depends on how far the process had gone, of transmuting life into truth. In proportion to the completeness of the distillation, so will the purity and imperishableness of the product be. But none is quite perfect. As no air-pump can by any means make a perfect vacuum, so neither can any artist entirely exclude the conventional, the local, the perishable from his book, or write a book of pure thought, that shall be as efficient, in all respects, to a remote posterity, as to contemporaries, or rather to the second age. Each age, it is found, must write its own books; or rather, each generation for the next succeeding. The books of an older period will not fit this.

Yet hence arises a grave mischief. The sacredness which attaches to the act of creation, the act of thought, is transferred to the record. The poet chanting was felt to be a divine man: henceforth the chant is divine also. The writer was a just and wise spirit: henceforward it is settled the book is perfect; as love of the hero corrupts into worship of his statue. Instantly the book becomes noxious: the guide is a tyrant. The sluggish and perverted mind of the multitude, slow to open to the incursions of Reason, having once so opened, having once received this book, stands upon it, and makes an outcry if it is disparaged. Colleges are built on it. Books are written on it by thinkers, not by Man Thinking; by men of talent, that is, who start wrong, who set out from accepted dogmas, not from their own sight of principles. Meek young men grow up in libraries, believing it their duty to accept the views which Cicero, which Locke, which Bacon[8] have

---

[6] Inflowing, from the Latin verb *influere.*
[7] Active or living.
[8] Cicero: Marcus Tullius Cicero (106–43 B.C.), Roman statesman and orator; Locke: John

Locke (1632–1704), English philosopher and political thinker; Bacon: Sir Francis Bacon (1561–1626), English statesman and pioneer of inductive science.

given; forgetful that Cicero, Locke, and Bacon were only young men in libraries when they wrote these books.

Hence, instead of Man Thinking, we have the bookworm. Hence the book-learned class, who value books, as such; not as related to nature and the human constitution, but as making a sort of Third Estate[9] with the world and the soul. Hence the restorers of readings, the emendators, the bibliomaniacs of all degrees.

Books are the best of things, well used; abused, among the worst. What is the right use? What is the one end which all means go to effect? They are for nothing but to inspire. I had better never see a book than to be warped by its attraction clean out of my own orbit, and made a satellite instead of a system. The one thing in the world, of value, is the active soul. This every man is entitled to; this every man contains within him, although in almost all men obstructed and as yet unborn. The soul active sees absolute truth and utters truth, or creates. In this action it is genius; not the privilege of here and there a favorite, but the sound estate of every man. In its essence it is progressive. The book, the college, the school of art, the institution of any kind, stop with some past utterance of genius. This is good, say they—let us hold by this. They pin me down. They look backward and not forward. But genius looks forward: the eyes of man are set in his forehead, not in his hindhead: man hopes: genius creates. Whatever talents may be, if the man create not, the pure efflux of the Deity is not his; cinders and smoke there may be, but not yet flame. There are creative manners, there are creative actions, and creative words; manners, actions, words, that is, indicative of no custom or authority, but springing spontaneous from the mind's own sense of good and fair.

On the other part, instead of being its own seer, let it receive from another mind its truth, though it were in torrents of light, without periods of solitude, inquest, and self-recovery, and a fatal disservice is done. Genius is always sufficiently the enemy of genius by over-influence. The literature of every nation bears me witness. The English dramatic poets have Shakspearized now for two hundred years.

Undoubtedly there is a right way of reading, so it be sternly subordinated. Man Thinking must not be subdued by his instruments. Books are for the scholar's idle times. When he can read God directly, the hour is too precious to be wasted in other men's transcripts of their readings. But when the intervals of darkness come, as come they must—when the sun is hid and the stars withdraw their shining—we repair to the lamps which were kindled by their ray, to guide our steps to the East again, where the dawn is. We hear, that we may speak. The Arabian proverb says, "A fig tree, looking on a fig tree, becometh fruitful."

It is remarkable, the character of the pleasure we derive from the best books. They impress us with the conviction that one nature wrote and the same reads. We read the verses of one of the great English poets, of Chaucer, of Marvell, of Dryden, with the most modern joy—with a pleasure, I mean, which is in great part caused by the abstraction of all *time* from their verses. There is some awe mixed with the joy of our surprise, when this poet, who lived in some past world, two or three hundred years ago, says that which lies close to my own soul, that which I also had well-nigh thought and said. But for the evidence thence afforded to the philosophical doctrine of the identity of all

---

[9] Analogous to the third of three separate estates or classes that feudal Europe acknowledged: the clergy, the nobility, and the common people.

minds, we should suppose some preëstablished harmony, some foresight of souls that were to be, and some preparation of stores for their future wants, like the fact observed in insects, who lay up food before death for the young grub they shall never see.

I would not be hurried by any love of system, by any exaggeration of instincts, to underrate the Book. We all know, that as the human body can be nourished on any food, though it were boiled grass and the broth of shoes, so the human mind can be fed by any knowledge. And great and heroic men have existed who had almost no other information than by the printed page. I only would say that it needs a strong head to bear that diet. One must be an inventor to read well. As the proverb says, "He that would bring home the wealth of the Indies, must carry out the wealth of the Indies." There is then creative reading as well as creative writing. When the mind is braced by labor and invention, the page of whatever book we read becomes luminous with manifold allusion. Every sentence is doubly significant, and the sense of our author is as broad as the world. We then see, what is always true, that as the seer's hour of vision is short and rare among heavy days and months, so is its record, perchance, the least part of his volume. The discerning will read, in his Plato or Shakspeare, only that least part—only the authentic utterances of the oracles; all the rest he rejects, were it never so many times Plato's and Shakspeare's.

Of course there is a portion of reading quite indispensable to a wise man. History and exact science he must learn by laborious reading. Colleges, in like manner, have their indispensable office—to teach elements. But they can only highly serve us when they aim not to drill, but to create; when they gather from far every ray of various genius to their hospitable halls, and by the concentrated fires, set the hearts of their youth on flame. Thought and knowledge are natures in which apparatus and pretension avail nothing. Gowns and pecuniary foundations, though of towns of gold, can never countervail the least sentence or syllable of wit. Forget this, and our American colleges will recede in their public importance, whilst they grow richer every year.

III.   There goes in the world a notion that the scholar should be a recluse, a valetudinarian—as unfit for any handiwork or public labor as a penknife for an axe. The so-called "practical men" sneer at speculative men, as if, because they speculate or *see*, they could do nothing. I have heard it said that the clergy—who are always, more universally than any other class, the scholars of their day—are addressed as women; that the rough, spontaneous conversation of men they do not hear, but only a mincing and diluted speech. They are often virtually disfranchised; and indeed there are advocates for their celibacy. As far as this is true of the studious classes, it is not just and wise. Action is with the scholar subordinate, but it is essential. Without it he is not yet man. Without it thought can never ripen into truth. Whilst the world hangs before the eye as a cloud of beauty, we cannot even see its beauty. Inaction is cowardice, but there can be no scholar without the heroic mind. The preamble of thought, the transition through which it passes from the unconscious to the conscious, is action. Only so much do I know, as I have lived. Instantly we know whose words are loaded with life, and whose not.

The world—this shadow of the soul, or *other me*—lies wide around. Its attractions are the keys which unlock my thoughts and make me acquainted with myself. I run eagerly into this resounding tumult. I grasp the hands of those next me, and take my place in the ring to suffer and to work, taught by an instinct that so shall the dumb abyss be vocal with speech. I pierce its order; I dissipate its fear; I dispose of it within the circuit of my expanding life. So much only of life as I know by experience, so much of the wilderness have I vanquished and planted, or so far have I extended my being, my dominion. I do not see how any man can afford, for the sake of his nerves and his nap, to spare any action in which he can partake. It is pearls and rubies to his discourse. Drudgery, calamity, exasperation, want, are instructors in eloquence and wisdom. The true scholar grudges every opportunity of action past by, as a loss of power. It is the raw material out of which the intellect moulds her splendid products. A strange process too, this by which experience is converted into thought, as a mulberry leaf is converted into satin.[10] The manufacture goes forward at all hours.

The actions and events of our childhood and youth are now matters of calmest observation. They lie like fair pictures in the air. Not so with our recent actions—with the business which we now have in hand. On this we are quite unable to speculate. Our affections as yet circulate through it. We no more feel or know it than we feel the feet, or the hand, or the brain of our body. The new deed is yet a part of life—remains for a time immersed in our unconscious life. In some contemplative hour it detaches itself from the life like a ripe fruit, to become a thought of the mind. Instantly it is raised, transfigured; the corruptible has put on incorruption.[11] Henceforth it is an object of beauty, however base its origin and neighborhood. Observe too the impossibility of antedating this act. In its grub state, it cannot fly, it cannot shine, it is a dull grub. But suddenly, without observation, the selfsame thing unfurls beautiful wings, and is an angel of wisdom. So is there no fact, no event, in our private history, which shall not, sooner or later, lose its adhesive, inert form, and astonish us by soaring from our body into the empyrean. Cradle and infancy, school and playground, the fear of boys, and dogs, and ferrules, the love of little maids and berries, and many another fact that once filled the whole sky, are gone already; friend and relative, profession and party, town and country, nation and world, must also soar and sing.

Of course, he who has put forth his total strength in fit actions has the richest return of wisdom. I will not shut myself out of this globe of action, and transplant an oak into a flowerpot, there to hunger and pine; nor trust the revenue of some single faculty, and exhaust one vein of thought, much like those Savoyards,[12] who, getting their livelihood by carving shepherds, shepherdesses, and smoking Dutchmen,[13] for all Europe, went out one day to the mountain to find stock, and discovered that they had whittled up the last of their pine trees. Authors we have, in numbers, who have written out their vein, and who, moved by a commendable prudence, sail for Greece or Palestine, follow the trapper into the prairie, or ramble round Algiers, to replenish their merchantable stock.

If it were only for a vocabulary, the scholar would be covetous of action. Life is our dictionary. Years are well spent in country labors; in town; in the insight into trades and manufactures; in frank intercourse with many men and women; in science; in art; to the one end of mastering in all their facts a language by which to illustrate and embody our perceptions. I learn immediately from any speaker how much he has already lived, through the poverty or the splendor of his speech. Life lies behind us as the quarry from whence we get tiles and copestones for the masonry of to-day. This is the

---

10 i.e., silk, which is produced by silkworms feeding on mulberry leaves.

11 1 Corinthians 15:53: "For this corruptible must put on incorruption, and this mortal must put on immortality."

12 Residents of Savoy, now a province of France.

13 i.e., pipes.

way to learn grammar. Colleges and books only copy the language which the field and the work-yard made.

But the final value of action, like that of books, and better than books, is that it is a resource. That great principle of Undulation in nature, that shows itself in the inspiring and expiring of the breath; in desire and satiety; in the ebb and flow of the sea; in day and night; in heat and cold; and, as yet more deeply ingrained in every atom and every fluid, is known to us under the name of Polarity—these "fits of easy transmission and reflection," as Newton[14] called them, are the law of nature because they are the law of spirit.

The mind now thinks, now acts, and each fit reproduces the other. When the artist has exhausted his materials, when the fancy no longer paints, when thoughts are no longer apprehended and books are a weariness—he has always the resources to *live*. Character is higher than intellect. Thinking is the function. Living is the functionary. The stream retreats to its source. A great soul will be strong to live, as well as strong to think. Does he lack organ or medium to impart his truths? He can still fall back on this elemental force of living them. This is a total act. Thinking is a partial act. Let the grandeur of justice shine in his affairs. Let the beauty of affection cheer his lowly roof. Those "far from fame," who dwell and act with him, will feel the force of his constitution in the doings and passages of the day better than it can be measured by any public and designed display. Time shall teach him that the scholar loses no hour which the man lives. Herein he unfolds the sacred germ of his instinct, screened from influence. What is lost in seemliness is gained in strength. Not out of those on whom systems of education have exhausted their culture, comes the helpful giant to destroy the old or to build the new, but out of unhandselled[15] savage nature; out of terrible Druids and Berserkers[16] come at last Alfred[17] and Shakspeare.

I hear therefore with joy whatever is beginning to be said of the dignity and necessity of labor to every citizen. There is virtue yet in the hoe and the spade, for learned as well as for unlearned hands. And labor is everywhere welcome; always we are invited to work; only be this limitation observed, that a man shall not for the sake of wider activity sacrifice any opinion to the popular judgments and modes of action.

I have now spoken of the education of the scholar by nature, by books, and by action. It remains to say somewhat of his duties.

They are such as become Man Thinking. They may all be comprised in self-trust. The office of the scholar is to cheer, to raise, and to guide men by showing them facts amidst appearances. He plies the slow, unhonored, and unpaid task of observation. Flamsteed and Herschel,[18] in their glazed observatories, may catalogue the stars with the praise of all men, and the results being splendid and useful, honor is sure. But he, in his private observatory, cataloguing obscure and nebulous stars of the human mind, which as yet no man has thought of as such—watching days and months sometimes for a few facts; correcting still his old records; must relinquish display and immediate fame. In the long period of his preparation he must betray often an ignorance and shiftless-

---

[14] From *Optics* by Sir Isaac Newton (1642–1727), English mathematician and philosopher.

[15] Ungrateful.

[16] Respectively, barbaric Celts and uncivilized warriors of Norse mythology.

[17] Alfred (849–901), king of the West Saxons, who instituted English laws and fostered literacy.

[18] John Flamsteed (1646–1719) and Sir Frederick William Herschel (1738–1822), prominent English astronomers.

ness in popular arts, incurring the disdain of the able who shoulder him aside. Long he must stammer in his speech; often forego the living for the dead. Worse yet, he must accept—how often!—poverty and solitude. For the ease and pleasure of treading the old road, accepting the fashions, the education, the religion of society, he takes the cross of making his own, and, of course, the self-accusation, the faint heart, the frequent uncertainty and loss of time, which are the nettles and tangling vines in the way of the self-relying and self-directed; and the state of virtual hostility in which he seems to stand to society, and especially to educated society. For all this loss and scorn, what offset? He is to find consolation in exercising the highest functions of human nature. He is one who raises himself from private considerations and breathes and lives on public and illustrious thoughts. He is the world's eye. He is the world's heart. He is to resist the vulgar prosperity that retrogrades ever to barbarism, by preserving and communicating heroic sentiments, noble biographies, melodious verse, and the conclusions of history. Whatsoever oracles the human heart, in all emergencies, in all solemn hours, has uttered as its commentary on the world of actions—these he shall receive and impart. And whatsoever new verdict Reason from her inviolable seat pronounces on the passing men and events of to-day—this he shall hear and promulgate.

These being his functions, it becomes him to feel all confidence in himself, and to defer never to the popular cry. He and he only knows the world. The world of any moment is the merest appearance. Some great decorum, some fetish of a government, some ephemeral trade, or war, or man, is cried up by half mankind and cried down by the other half, as if all depended on this particular up or down. The odds are that the whole question is not worth the poorest thought which the scholar has lost in listening to the controversy. Let him not quit his belief that a popgun is a popgun, though the ancient and honorable of the earth affirm it to be the crack of doom. In silence, in steadiness, in severe abstraction, let him hold by himself; add observation to observation, patient of neglect, patient of reproach, and bide his own time—happy enough if he can satisfy himself alone that this day he has seen something truly. Success treads on every right step. For the instinct is sure, that prompts him to tell his brother what he thinks. He then learns that in going down into the secrets of his own mind he has descended into the secrets of all minds. He learns that he who has mastered any law in his private thoughts, is master to that extent of all men whose language he speaks, and of all into whose language his own can be translated. The poet, in utter solitude remembering his spontaneous thoughts and recording them, is found to have recorded that which men in crowded cities find true for them also. The orator distrusts at first the fitness of his frank confessions, his want of knowledge of the persons he addresses, until he finds that he is the complement of his hearers; that they drink his words because he fulfils for them their own nature; the deeper he dives into his privatest, secretest presentiment, to his wonder he finds this is the most acceptable, most public, and universally true. The people delight in it; the better part of every man feels, This is my music; this is myself.

In self-trust all the virtues are comprehended. Free should the scholar be—free and brave. Free even to the definition of freedom, "without any hindrance that does not arise out of his own constitution." Brave; for fear is a thing which a scholar by his very function puts behind him. Fear always springs from ignorance. It is a shame to him if his tranquillity, amid dangerous times, arise from the presumption that like children and women his is a protected class; or if he seek a temporary peace by the diversion of his thoughts from politics or vexed questions, hiding his head like an ostrich in the flowering bushes, peeping into microscopes, and turning rhymes, as a boy whistles to keep his courage up. So is the danger a danger still; so is the fear worse. Manlike let him turn and face it. Let him look into its eye and search its nature, inspect its origin—see the whelping of this lion—which lies no great way back; he will then find in himself a perfect comprehension of its nature and extent; he will have made his hands meet on the other side, and can henceforth defy it and pass on superior. The world is his who can see through its pretension. What deafness, what stone-blind custom, what over-grown error you behold is there only by sufferance—by your sufferance. See it to be a lie, and you have already dealt it its mortal blow.

Yes, we are the cowed—we the trustless. It is a mischievous notion that we are come late into nature; that the world was finished a long time ago. As the world was plastic and fluid in the hands of God, so it is ever to so much of his attributes as we bring to it. To ignorance and sin, it is flint. They adapt themselves to it as they may; but in propor-tion as a man has any thing in him divine, the firmament flows before him and takes his signet and form. Not he is great who can alter matter, but he who can alter my state of mind. They are the kings of the world who give the color of their present thought to all nature and all art, and persuade men by the cheerful serenity of their carrying the mat-ter, that this thing which they do is the apple which the ages have desired to pluck, now at last ripe, and inviting nations to the harvest. The great man makes the great thing. Wherever Macdonald sits, there is the head of the table.[19] Linnaeus makes botany the most alluring of studies, and wins it from the farmer and the herb-woman; Davy, chemistry; and Cuvier,[20] fossils. The day is always his who works in it with serenity and great aims. The unstable estimates of men crowd to him whose mind is filled with a truth, as the heaped waves of the Atlantic follow the moon.

For this self-trust, the reason is deeper than can be fathomed—darker than can be enlightened. I might not carry with me the feeling of my audience in stating my own be-lief. But I have already shown the ground of my hope, in adverting to the doctrine that man is one. I believe man has been wronged; he has wronged himself. He has almost lost the light that can lead him back to his prerogatives. Men are become of no account. Men in history, men in the world of to-day, are bugs, are spawn, and are called "the mass" and "the herd." In a century, in a millennium, one or two men; that is to say, one or two approximations to the right state of every man. All the rest behold in the hero or the poet their own green and crude being—ripened; yes, and are content to be less, so *that* may attain to its full stature. What a testimony, full of grandeur, full of pity, is borne to the demands of his own nature, by the poor clansman, the poor partisan, who rejoices in the glory of his chief. The poor and the low find some amends to their im-mense moral capacity, for their acquiescence in a political and social inferiority. They are content to be brushed like flies from the path of a great person, so that justice shall be done by him to that common nature which it is the dearest desire of all to see en-larged and glorified. They sun themselves in the great man's light, and feel it to be their own element. They cast the dignity of man from their downtrod selves upon the shoul-ders of a hero, and will perish to add one drop of blood to make that great heart beat, those giant sinews combat and conquer. He lives for us, and we live in him.

---

[19] Emerson's version of a proverb of the time.
[20] Linnaeus: Swedish botanist Carolus Lin-naeus (1707–1778); Davy: English chemist

Sir Humphrey Davy (1778–1829); Cuvier: French naturalist Georges Cuvier (1769–1832).

Men, such as they are, very naturally seek money or power; and power because it is as good as money—the "spoils," so called, "of office." And why not? for they aspire to the highest, and this, in their sleep-walking, they dream is highest. Wake them and they shall quit the false good and leap to the true, and leave governments to clerks and desks. This revolution is to be wrought by the gradual domestication of the idea of Culture. The main enterprise of the world for splendor, for extent, is the upbuilding of a man. Here are the materials strewn along the ground. The private life of one man shall be a more illustrious monarchy, more formidable to its enemy, more sweet and serene in its influence to its friend, than any kingdom in history. For a man, rightly viewed, comprehendeth the particular natures of all men. Each philosopher, each bard, each actor has only done for me, as by a delegate, what one day I can do for myself. The books which once we valued more than the apple of the eye, we have quite exhausted. What is that but saying that we have come up with the point of view which the universal mind took through the eyes of one scribe; we have been that man, and have passed on. First, one, then another, we drain all cisterns, and waxing greater by all these supplies, we crave a better and more abundant food. The man has never lived that can feed us ever. The human mind cannot be enshrined in a person who shall set a barrier on any one side to this unbounded, unboundable empire. It is one central fire, which, flaming now out of the lips of Etna,[21] lightens the capes of Sicily, and now out of the throat of Vesuvius,[22] illuminates the towers and vineyards of Naples. It is one light which beams out of a thousand stars. It is one soul which animates all men.

But I have dwelt perhaps tediously upon this abstraction of the Scholar. I ought not to delay longer to add what I have to say of nearer reference to the time and to this country.

Historically, there is thought to be a difference in the ideas which predominate over successive epochs, and there are data for marking the genius of the Classic, of the Romantic, and now of the Reflective or Philosophical age. With the views I have intimated of the oneness or the identity of the mind through all individuals, I do not much dwell on these differences. In fact, I believe each individual passes through all three. The boy is a Greek; the youth, romantic; the adult, reflective. I deny not, however, that a revolution in the leading idea may be distinctly enough traced.

Our age is bewailed as the age of Introversion. Must that needs be evil? We, it seems, are critical; we are embarrassed with second thoughts; we cannot enjoy any thing for hankering to know whereof the pleasure consists; we are lined with eyes; we see with our feet; the time is infected with Hamlet's unhappiness—

"Sicklied o'er with the pale cast of thought."[23]

It is so bad then? Sight is the last thing to be pitied. Would we be blind? Do we fear lest we should outsee nature and God, and drink truth dry? I look upon the discontent of the literary class as a mere announcement of the fact that they find themselves not in the state of mind of their fathers, and regret the coming state as untried; as a boy dreads the water before he has learned that he can swim. If there is any period one would desire to be born in, is it not the age of Revolution; when the old and the new stand side by

---

[21] Active volcano in Sicily.
[22] Volcano in Italy.

[23] Shakespeare's *Hamlet*, Act III, Sc. i, l. 85.

side and admit of being compared; when the energies of all men are searched by fear and by hope; when the historic glories of the old can be compensated by the rich possibilities of the new era? This time, like all times, is a very good one, if we but know what to do with it.

I read with some joy of the auspicious signs of the coming days, as they glimmer already through poetry and art, through philosophy and science, through church and state.

One of these signs is the fact that the same movement which effected the elevation of what was called the lowest class in the state, assumed in literature a very marked and as benign an aspect. Instead of the sublime and beautiful, the near, the low, the common, was explored and poetized. That which had been negligently trodden under foot by those who were harnessing and provisioning themselves for long journeys into far countries, is suddenly found to be richer than all foreign parts. The literature of the poor, the feelings of the child, the philosophy of the street, the meaning of household life, are the topics of the time. It is a great stride. It is a sign—is it not?—of new vigor when the extremities are made active, when currents of warm life run into the hands and the feet. I ask not for the great, the remote, the romantic; what is doing in Italy or Arabia; what is Greek art, or Provencal minstrelsy;[24] I embrace the common, I explore and sit at the feet of the familiar, the low. Give me insight into to-day, and you may have the antique and future worlds. What would we really know the meaning of? The meal in the firkin; the milk in the pan; the ballad in the street; the news of the boat; the glance of the eye; the form and the gait of the body; show me the ultimate reason of these matters; show me the sublime presence of the highest spiritual cause lurking, as always it does lurk, in these suburbs and extremities of nature; let me see every trifle bristling with the polarity that ranges it instantly on an eternal law; and the shop, the plough, and the ledger referred to the like cause by which light undulates and poets sing; and the world lies no longer a dull miscellany and lumber-room,[25] but has form and order; there is no trifle, there is no puzzle, but one design unites and animates the farthest pinnacle and the lowest trench.

This idea has inspired the genius of Goldsmith, Burns, Cowper, and, in a newer time, of Goethe, Wordsworth, and Carlyle. This idea they have differently followed and with various success. In contrast with their writing, the style of Pope, of Johnson, of Gibbon, looks cold and pedantic. This writing is blood-warm. Man is surprised to find that things near are not less beautiful and wondrous than things remote. The near explains the far. The drop is a small ocean. A man is related to all nature. This perception of the worth of the vulgar is fruitful in discoveries. Goethe, in this very thing the most modern of the moderns, has shown us, as none ever did, the genius of the ancients.

There is one man of genius who has done much for this philosophy of life, whose literary value has never yet been rightly estimated; I mean Emanuel Swedenborg.[26] The most imaginative of men, yet writing with the precision of a mathematician, he endeavored to engraft a purely philosophical Ethics on the popular Christianity of his time. Such an attempt of course must have difficulty which no genius could surmount. But he saw and showed the connection between nature and the affections of the soul. He pierced the emblematic or spiritual character of the visible, audible, tangible word.

[24] The troubadors of the late Middle Ages established Provence in southeast France as a cultural center.

[25] Room for storage.

[26] Swedish scientist and theologian (1688–1772).

Especially did his shade-loving muse hover over and interpret the lower parts of nature; he showed the mysterious bond that allies moral evil to the foul material forms, and has given in epical parables a theory of insanity, of beasts, of unclean and fearful things.

Another sign of our times, also marked by an analogous political movement, is the new importance given to the single person. Every thing that tends to insulate the individual—to surround him with barriers of natural respect, so that each man shall feel the world is his, and man shall treat with man as a sovereign state with a sovereign state—tends to true union as well as greatness. "I learned," said the melancholy Pestalozzi,[27] "that no man in God's wide earth is either willing or able to help any other man." Help must come from the bosom alone. The scholar is that man who must take up into himself all the ability of the time, all the contributions of the past, all the hopes of the future. He must be an university of knowledges. If there be one lesson more than another which should pierce his ear, it is, The world is nothing, the man is all; in yourself is the law of all nature, and you know not yet how a globule of sap ascends; in yourself slumbers the whole of Reason; it is for you to know all; it is for you to dare all. Mr. President and Gentlemen, this confidence in the unsearched might of man belongs, by all motives, by all prophecy, by all preparation, to the American Scholar. We have listened too long to the courtly muses of Europe. The spirit of the American free-man is already suspected to be timid, imitative, tame. Public and private avarice make the air we breathe thick and fat. The scholar is decent, indolent, complaisant. See already the tragic consequence. The mind of this country, taught to aim at low objects, eats upon itself. There is no work for any but the decorous and the complaisant. Young men of the fairest promise, who begin life upon our shores, inflated by the mountain winds, shined upon by all the stars of God, find the earth below not in unison with these, but are hindered from action by the disgust which the principles on which business is managed inspire, and turn drudges, or die of disgust, some of them suicides. What is the remedy? They did not yet see, and thousands of young men as hopeful now crowding to the barriers for the career do not yet see, that if the single man plant himself indomitably on his instincts, and there abide, the huge world will come round to him. Patience—patience; with the shades of all the good and great for company; and for solace the perspective of your own infinite life; and for work the study and the communication of principles, the making those instincts prevalent, the conversion of the world. Is it not the chief disgrace in the world, not to be an unit; not to be reckoned one character; not to yield that peculiar fruit which each man was created to bear, but to be reckoned in the gross, in the hundred, or the thousand, of the party, the section, to which we belong; and our opinion predicted geographically, as the north, or the south? Not so, brothers and friends—please God, ours shall not be so. We will walk on our own feet; we will work with our own hands; we will speak our own minds. The study of letters shall be no longer a name for pity, for doubt, and for sensual indulgence. The dread of man and the love of man shall be a wall of defence and a wreath of joy around all. A nation of men will for the first time exist, because each believes himself inspired by the Divine Soul which also inspires all men.

1837

---

[27] Swiss educational theorist Johann Heinrich Pestalozzi (1746–1826).

RELATED VOICES

Our Intellectual Declaration of Independence

Out of the West comes a clear utterance, clearly recognizable as a *man's* voice, and I *have* a kinsman and brother: God be thanked for it! I could have *wept* to read that speech; the clear high melody of it went tingling through my heart. . . . My brave Emerson!

Thomas Carlyle (1837)

This grand oration was our intellectual Declaration of Independence. . . . No listener ever forgot that Address, and among all the noble utterances of the speaker it may be questioned if one ever contained more truth in language more like that of immediate inspiration.

Oliver Wendell Holmes (1885)

We were socially and intellectually moored to English thought, till Emerson cut the cable and gave us a chance at the dangers and glories of blue water. . . . His oration before the Phi Beta Kappa Society at Cambridge, some thirty years ago, was an event without any former parallel in our literary annals.

James Russell Lowell (1871)

Responses to Emerson's *The American Scholar.*

An Address*

In this refulgent summer, it has been a luxury to draw the breath of life. The grass grows, the buds burst, the meadow is spotted with fire and gold in the tint of flowers. The air is full of birds, and sweet with the breath of the pine, the balm-of-Gilead,[1] and the new hay. Night brings no gloom to the heart with its welcome shade. Through the transparent darkness the stars pour their almost spiritual rays. Man under them seems a young child, and his huge globe a toy. The cool night bathes the world as with a river, and prepares his eyes again for the crimson dawn. The mystery of nature was never displayed more happily. The corn and the wine have been freely dealt to all creatures, and the never-broken silence with which the old bounty goes forward has not yielded yet one word of explanation. One is constrained to respect the perfection of this world in which our senses converse. How wide; how rich; what invitation from every property it

---

* Soon after it was delivered, Emerson's lecture was published as *An Address Delivered Before the Senior Class in Divinity College, Cambridge, Sunday Evening 15 July 1838.* His criticism of traditional Christianity so offended the religious establishment at Harvard that he was not invited to speak there again for 30 years.

[1] Fragrant evergreen tree.

gives to every faculty of man! In its fruitful soils; in its navigable sea; in its mountains of metal and stone; in its forests of all woods; in its animals; in its chemical ingredients; in the powers and path of light, heat, attraction and life, it is well worth the pith and heart of great men to subdue and enjoy it. The planters, the mechanics, the inventors, the astronomers, the builders of cities, and the captains, history delights to honor.

But when the mind opens and reveals the laws which traverse the universe and make things what they are, then shrinks the great world at once into a mere illustration and fable of this mind. What am I? and What is? asks the human spirit with a curiosity new-kindled, but never to be quenched. Behold these outrunning laws, which our imperfect apprehension can see tend this way and that, but not come full circle. Behold these infinite relations, so like, so unlike; many, yet one. I would study, I would know, I would admire forever. These works of thought have been the entertainments of the human spirit in all ages.

A more secret, sweet, and overpowering beauty appears to man when his heart and mind open to the sentiment of virtue. Then he is instructed in what is above him. He learns that his being is without bound; that to the good, to the perfect, he is born, low as he now lies in evil and weakness. That which he venerates is still his own, though he has not realized it yet. *He ought.* He knows the sense of that grand word, though his analysis fails to render account of it. When in innocency or when by intellectual perception he attains to say—"I love the Right; Truth is beautiful within and without for evermore. Virtue, I am thine; save me; use me; thee will I serve, day and night, in great, in small, that I may be not virtuous, but virtue;" then is the end of the creation answered, and God is well pleased.

The sentiment of virtue is a reverence and delight in the presence of certain divine laws. It perceives that this homely game of life we play, covers, under what seem foolish details, principles that astonish. The child amidst his baubles is learning the action of light, motion, gravity, muscular force; and in the game of human life, love, fear, justice, appetite, man, and God, interact. These laws refuse to be adequately stated. They will not be written out on paper, or spoken by the tongue. They elude our persevering thought; yet we read them hourly in each other's faces, in each other's actions, in our own remorse. The moral traits which are all globed into every virtuous act and thought—in speech we must sever, and describe or suggest by painful enumeration of many particulars. Yet, as this sentiment is the essence of all religion, let me guide your eye to the precise objects of the sentiment, by an enumeration of some of those classes of facts in which this element is conspicuous.

The intuition of the moral sentiment is an insight of the perfection of the laws of the soul. These laws execute themselves. They are out of time, out of space, and not subject to circumstance. Thus in the soul of man there is a justice whose retributions are instant and entire. He who does a good deed is instantly ennobled. He who does a mean deed is by the action itself contracted. He who puts off impurity, thereby puts on purity. If a man is at heart just, then in so far is he God; the safety of God, the immortality of God, the majesty of God do enter into that man with justice. If a man dissemble, deceive, he deceives himself, and goes out of acquaintance with his own being. A man in the view of absolute goodness, adores, with total humility. Every step so downward, is a step upward. The man who renounces himself, comes to himself.

See how this rapid intrinsic energy worketh everywhere, righting wrongs, correcting appearances, and bringing up facts to a harmony with thoughts. Its operation in life, though slow to the senses, is at last as sure as in the soul. By it a man is made the Providence to himself, dispensing good to his goodness, and evil to his sin. Character is always known. Thefts never enrich; alms never impoverish; murder will speak out of stone walls. The least admixture of a lie—for example, the taint of vanity, any attempt to make a good impression, a favorable appearance—will instantly vitiate the effect. But speak the truth, and all nature and all spirits help you with unexpected furtherance. Speak the truth, and all things alive or brute are vouchers, and the very roots of the grass underground there do seem to stir and move to bear you witness. See again the perfection of the Law as it applies itself to the affections, and becomes the law of society. As we are, so we associate. The good, by affinity, seek the good; the vile, by affinity, the vile. Thus of their own volition, souls proceed into heaven, into hell.

These facts have always suggested to man the sublime creed that the world is not the product of manifold power, but of one will, of one mind; and that one mind is everywhere active, in each ray of the star, in each wavelet of the pool; and whatever opposes that will is everywhere balked and baffled, because things are made so, and not otherwise. Good is positive. Evil is merely privative, not absolute: it is like cold, which is the privation of heat. All evil is so much death or nonentity. Benevolence is absolute and real. So much benevolence as a man hath, so much life hath he. For all things proceed out of this same spirit, which is differently named love, justice, temperance, in its different applications, just as the ocean receives different names on the several shores which it washes. All things proceed out of the same spirit, and all things conspire with it. Whilst a man seeks good ends, he is strong by the whole strength of nature. In so far as he roves from these ends, he bereaves himself of power, or auxiliaries; his being shrinks out of all remote channels, he becomes less and less, a mote, a point, until absolute badness is absolute death.

The perception of this law of laws awakens in the mind a sentiment which we call the religious sentiment, and which makes our highest happiness. Wonderful is its power to charm and to command. It is a mountain air. It is the embalmer of the world. It is myrrh and storax, and chlorine and rosemary. It makes the sky and the hills sublime, and the silent song of the stars is it. By it is the universe made safe and habitable, not by science or power. Thought may work cold and intransitive in things, and find no end or unity; but the dawn of the sentiment of virtue on the heart, gives and is the assurance that Law is sovereign over all natures; and the worlds, time, space, eternity, do seem to break out into joy.

This sentiment is divine and deifying. It is the beatitude of man. It makes him illimitable. Through it, the soul first knows itself. It corrects the capital mistake of the infant man, who seeks to be great by following the great, and hopes to derive advantages *from another*—by showing the fountain of all good to be in himself, and that he, equally with every man, is an inlet into the deeps of Reason. When he says, "I ought;" when love warms him; when he chooses, warned from on high, the good and great deed; then, deep melodies wander through his soul from Supreme Wisdom. Then he can worship, and be enlarged by his worship; for he can never go behind this sentiment. In the sublimest flights of the soul, rectitude is never surmounted, love is never outgrown.

This sentiment lies at the foundation of society, and successively creates all forms of worship. The principle of veneration never dies out. Man fallen into superstition, into sensuality, is never quite without the visions of the moral sentiment. In like manner, all the expressions of this sentiment are sacred and permanent in proportion to their purity. The expressions of this sentiment affect us more than all other compositions. The sentences of the oldest time, which ejaculate this piety, are still fresh and fragrant. This thought dwelled always deepest in the minds of men in the devout and contemplative East; not alone in Palestine, where it reached its purest expression, but in Egypt, in Persia, in India, in China. Europe has always owed to oriental genius its divine impulses. What these holy bards said, all sane men found agreeable and true. And the unique impression of Jesus upon mankind, whose name is not so much written as ploughed into the history of this world, is proof of the subtle virtue of this infusion.

Meantime, whilst the doors of the temple stand open, night and day, before every man, and the oracles of this truth cease never, it is guarded by one stern condition; this, namely, it is an intuition. It cannot be received at second hand. Truly speaking, it is not instruction, but provocation, that I can receive from another soul. What he announces, I must find true in me, or reject; and on his word, or as his second, be he who he may, I can accept nothing. On the contrary, the absence of this primary faith is the presence of degradation. As is the flood, so is the ebb. Let this faith depart, and the very words it spake and the things it made become false and hurtful. Then falls the church, the state, art, letters, life. The doctrine of the divine nature being forgotten, a sickness infects and dwarfs the constitution. Once man was all; now he is an appendage, a nuisance. And because the indwelling Supreme Spirit cannot wholly be got rid of, the doctrine of it suffers this perversion, that the divine nature is attributed to one or two persons, and denied to all the rest, and denied with fury. The doctrine of inspiration is lost; the base doctrine of the majority of voices usurps the place of the doctrine of the soul. Miracles, prophecy, poetry, the ideal life, the holy life, exist as ancient history merely; they are not in the belief, nor in the aspiration of society; but, when suggested, seem ridiculous. Life is comic or pitiful as soon as the high ends of being fade out of sight, and man becomes near-sighted, and can only attend to what addresses the senses.

These general views, which, whilst they are general, none will contest, find abundant illustration in the history of religion, and especially in the history of the Christian church. In that, all of us have had our birth and nurture. The truth contained in that, you, my young friends, are now setting forth to teach. As the Cultus, or established worship of the civilized world, it has great historical interest for us. Of its blessed words, which have been the consolation of humanity, you need not that I should speak. I shall endeavor to discharge my duty to you on this occasion, by pointing out two errors in its administration, which daily appear more gross from the point of view we have just now taken.

Jesus Christ belonged to the true race of prophets. He saw with open eye the mystery of the soul. Drawn by its severe harmony, ravished with its beauty, he lived in it, and had his being there. Alone in all history he estimated the greatness of man. One man was true to what is in you and me. He saw that God incarnates himself in man, and evermore goes forth anew to take possession of his World. He said, in this jubilee of sublime emotion, 'I am divine. Through me, God acts; through me, speaks. Would you see God, see me; or see thee, when thou also thinkest as I now think.' But what a distortion did his doctrine and memory suffer in the same, in the next, and the following ages! There is no doctrine of the Reason which will bear to be taught by the Understanding.[2] The understanding caught this high chant from the poet's lips, and said, in

---

[2] Throughout his works, Emerson uses "Reason" to mean knowledge derived from intuition and "Understanding" to mean knowledge derived from logic.

the next age, 'This was Jehovah come down out of heaven. I will kill you, if you say he was a man.' The idioms of his language and the figures of his rhetoric have usurped the place of his truth; and churches are not built on his principles, but on his tropes. Christianity became a Mythus,[3] as the poetic teaching of Greece and of Egypt, before. He spoke of miracles; for he felt that man's life was a miracle, and all that man doth, and he knew that this daily miracle shines as the character ascends. But the word Miracle, as pronounced by Christian churches, gives a false impression; it is Monster. It is not one with the blowing clover and the falling rain.

He felt respect for Moses and the prophets, but no unfit tenderness at postponing their initial revelations to the hour and the man that now is; to the eternal revelation in the heart. Thus was he a true man. Having seen that the law in us is commanding, he would not suffer it to be commanded. Boldly, with hand, and heart, and life, he declared it was God. Thus is he, as I think, the only soul in history who has appreciated the worth of man.

1. In this point of view we become sensible of the first defect of historical Christianity. Historical Christianity has fallen into the error that corrupts all attempts to communicate religion. As it appears to us, and as it has appeared for ages, it is not the doctrine of the soul, but an exaggeration of the personal, the positive, the ritual. It has dwelt, it dwells, with noxious exaggeration about the *person* of Jesus. The soul knows no persons. It invites every man to expand to the full circle of the universe, and will have no preferences but those of spontaneous love. But by this eastern monarchy of a Christianity, which indolence and fear have built, the friend of man is made the injurer of man. The manner in which his name is surrounded with expressions which were once sallies of admiration and love, but are now petrified into official titles, kills all generous sympathy and liking. All who hear me, feel that the language that describes Christ to Europe and America is not the style of friendship and enthusiasm to a good and noble heart, but is appropriated and formal—paints a demigod, as the Orientals or the Greeks would describe Osiris or Apollo.[4] Accept the injurious impositions of our early catechetical instruction,[5] and even honesty and self-denial were but splendid sins, if they did not wear the Christian name. One would rather be

"A pagan, suckled in a creed outworn,"[6]

than to be defrauded of his manly right in coming into nature and finding not names and places, not land and professions, but even virtue and truth foreclosed and monopolized. You shall not be a man even. You shall not own the world; you shall not dare and live after the infinite Law that is in you, and in company with the infinite Beauty which heaven and earth reflect to you in all lovely forms; but you must subordinate your nature to Christ's nature; you must accept our interpretations, and take his portrait as the vulgar draw it.

That is always best which gives me to myself. The sublime is excited in me by the great stoical doctrine, Obey thyself. That which shows God in me, fortifies me. That

---

[3] Deliberately promoted cult.
[4] Osiris: Egyptian fertility god; Apollo: Greek god of the sun.
[5] Technique of religious instruction employing dogmatic questions and answers.

[6] From the sonnet "The World Is Too Much with Us" (1807) by William Wordsworth (1770–1850).

which shows God out of me, makes me a wart and a wen. There is no longer a necessary reason for my being. Already the long shadows of untimely oblivion creep over me, and I shall decrease forever.

The divine bards are the friends of my virtue, of my intellect, of my strength. They admonish me that the gleams which flash across my mind are not mine, but God's; that they had the like, and were not disobedient to the heavenly vision.[7] So I love them. Noble provocations go out from them, inviting me to resist evil; to subdue the world; and to Be. And thus, by his holy thoughts, Jesus serves us, and thus only. To aim to convert a man by miracles is a profanation of the soul. A true conversion, a true Christ, is now, as always, to be made by the reception of beautiful sentiments. It is true that a great and rich soul, like his, falling among the simple, does so preponderate, that, as his did, it names the world. The world seems to them to exist for him, and they have not yet drunk so deeply of his sense as to see that only by coming again to themselves, or to God in themselves, can they grow for evermore. It is a low benefit to give me something; it is a high benefit to enable me to do somewhat of myself. The time is coming when all men will see that the gift of God to the soul is not a vaunting, overpowering, excluding sanctity, but a sweet, natural goodness, a goodness like thine and mine, and that so invites thine and mine to be and to grow.

The injustice of the vulgar tone of preaching is not less flagrant to Jesus than to the souls which it profanes. The preachers do not see that they make his gospel not glad, and shear him of the locks of beauty and the attributes of heaven. When I see a majestic Epaminondas,[8] or Washington; when I see among my contemporaries a true orator, an upright judge, a dear friend; when I vibrate to the melody and fancy of a poem; I see beauty that is to be desired. And so lovely, and with yet more entire consent of my human being, sounds in my ear the severe music of the bards that have sung of the true God in all ages. Now do not degrade the life and dialogues of Christ out of the circle of this charm, by insulation and peculiarity. Let them lie as they befell, alive and warm, part of human life and the landscape and the cheerful day.

2. The second defect of the traditionary and limited way of using the mind of Christ is a consequence of the first; this, namely; that the Moral Nature, that Law of laws whose revelations introduce greatness—yea, God himself—into the open soul, is not explored as the fountain of the established teaching in society. Men have come to speak of the revelation as somewhat long ago given and done, as if God were dead. The injury to faith throttles the preacher; and the goodliest of institutions becomes an uncertain and inarticulate voice.

It is very certain that it is the effect of conversation with the beauty of the soul, to beget a desire and need to impart to others the same knowledge and love. If utterance is denied, the thought lies like a burden on the man. Always the seer is a sayer. Somehow his dream is told; somehow he publishes it with solemn joy: sometimes with pencil on canvas, sometimes with chisel on stone, sometimes in towers and aisles of granite, his soul's worship is builded; sometimes in anthems of indefinite music; but clearest and most permanent, in words.

The man enamored of this excellency becomes its priest or poet. The office is coeval with the world. But observe the condition, the spiritual limitation of the office. The

---

[7] See Acts 26:19: "I was not disobedient unto the heavenly vision."

[8] Greek statesman and general instrumental in ending Sparta's dominance in Greece.

spirit only can teach. Not any profane man, not any sensual, not any liar, not any slave can teach, but only he can give, who has; he only can create, who is. The man on whom the soul descends, through whom the soul speaks, alone can teach. Courage, piety, love, wisdom, can teach; and every man can open his door to these angels, and they shall bring him the gift of tongues. But the man who aims to speak as books enable, as synods use, as the fashion guides, and as interest commands, babbles. Let him hush.

To this holy office you propose to devote yourselves. I wish you may feel your call in throbs of desire and hope. The office is the first in the world. It is of that reality that it cannot suffer the deduction of any falsehood. And it is my duty to say to you that the need was never greater of new revelation than now. From the views I have already expressed, you will infer the sad conviction, which I share, I believe, with numbers, of the universal decay and now almost death of faith in society. The soul is not preached. The Church seems to totter to its fall, almost all life extinct. On this occasion, any complaisance would be criminal which told you, whose hope and commission it is to preach the faith of Christ, that the faith of Christ is preached.

It is time that this ill-suppressed murmur of all thoughtful men against the famine of our churches; this moaning of the heart because it is bereaved of the consolation, the hope, the grandeur that come alone out of the culture of the moral nature—should be heard through the sleep of indolence, and over the din of routine. This great and perpetual office of the preacher is not discharged. Preaching is the expression of the moral sentiment in application to the duties of life. In how many churches, by how many prophets, tell me, is man made sensible that he is an infinite Soul; that the earth and heavens are passing into his mind; that he is drinking forever the soul of God? Where now sounds the persuasion, that by its very melody imparadises my heart, and so affirms its own origin in heaven? Where shall I hear words such as in elder ages drew men to leave all and follow—father and mother, house and land, wife and child?[9] Where shall I hear these august laws of moral being so pronounced as to fill my ear, and I feel ennobled by the offer of my uttermost action and passion? The test of the true faith, certainly, should be its power to charm and command the soul, as the laws of nature control the activity of the hands—so commanding that we find pleasure and honor in obeying. The faith should blend with the light of rising and of setting suns, with the flying cloud, the singing bird, and the breath of flowers. But now the priest's Sabbath has lost the splendor of nature; it is unlovely; we are glad when it is done; we can make, we do make, even sitting in our pews, a far better, holier, sweeter, for ourselves.

Whenever the pulpit is usurped by a formalist, then is the worshipper defrauded and disconsolate. We shrink as soon as the prayers begin, which do not uplift, but smite and offend us. We are fain to wrap our cloaks about us, and secure, as best we can, a solitude that hears not. I once heard a preacher who sorely tempted me to say I would go to church no more. Men go, thought I, where they are wont to go, else had no soul entered the temple in the afternoon. A snow-storm was falling around us. The snow-storm was real, the preacher merely spectral, and the eye felt the sad contrast in looking at him, and then out of the window behind him into the beautiful meteor of the snow. He had lived in vain. He had no one word intimating that he had laughed or wept, was married

---

[9] See Matthew 19:28–29: "And Jesus said unto them, . . . every one that hath forsaken houses, or brethren, or sisters, or father, or mother, or wife, or children, or lands, for my name's sake, shall receive an hundredfold, and shall inherit everlasting life."

or in love, had been commended, or cheated, or chagrined. If he had ever lived and acted, we were none the wiser for it. The capital secret of his profession, namely, to convert life into truth, he had not learned. Not one fact in all his experience had he yet imported into his doctrine. This man had ploughed and planted and talked and bought and sold; he had read books; he had eaten and drunken; his head aches, his heart throbs; he smiles and suffers; yet was there not a surmise, a hint, in all the discourse, that he had ever lived at all. Not a line did he draw out of real history. The true preacher can be known by this, that he deals out to the people his life—life passed through the fire of thought. But of the bad preacher, it could not be told from his sermon what age of the world he fell in; whether he had a father or a child; whether he was a freeholder or a pauper; whether he was a citizen or a countryman; or any other fact of his biography. It seemed strange that the people should come to church. It seemed as if their houses were very unentertaining, that they should prefer this thoughtless clamor. It shows that there is a commanding attraction in the moral sentiment, that can lend a faint tint of light to dulness and ignorance coming in its name and place. The good hearer is sure he has been touched sometimes; is sure there is somewhat to be reached, and some word that can reach it. When he listens to these vain words, he comforts himself by their relation to his remembrance of better hours, and so they clatter and echo unchallenged.

I am not ignorant that when we preach unworthily, it is not always quite in vain. There is a good ear, in some men, that draws supplies to virtue out of very indifferent nutriment. There is poetic truth concealed in all the commonplaces of prayer and of sermons, and though foolishly spoken, they may be wisely heard; for each is some select expression that broke out in a moment of piety from some stricken or jubilant soul, and its excellency made it remembered. The prayers and even the dogmas of our church are like the zodiac of Denderah[10] and the astronomical monuments of the Hindoos, wholly insulated from anything now extant in the life and business of the people. They mark the height to which the waters once rose. But this docility is a check upon the mischief from the good and devout. In a large portion of the community, the religious service gives rise to quite other thoughts and emotions. We need not chide the negligent servant. We are struck with pity, rather, at the swift retribution of his sloth. Alas for the unhappy man that is called to stand in the pulpit, and *not* give bread of life. Everything that befalls, accuses him. Would he ask contributions for the missions, foreign or domestic? Instantly his face is suffused with shame, to propose to his parish that they should send money a hundred or a thousand miles, to furnish such poor fare as they have at home and would do well to go the hundred or the thousand miles to escape. Would he urge people to a godly way of living; and can he ask a fellow-creature to come to Sabbath meetings, when he and they all know what is the poor uttermost they can hope for therein? Will he invite them privately to the Lord's Supper?[11] He dares not. If no heart warm this rite, the hollow, dry, creaking formality is too plain, than that he can face a man of wit and energy and put the invitation without terror. In the street, what has he to say to the bold village blasphemer? The village blasphemer sees fear in the face, form, and gait of the minister.

---

[10] Ancient city in Egypt and place of worship of the goddess Hathor, where a zodiacal table is displayed in an ancient ruined temple.

[11] In 1832 Emerson decided to resign as minister of the Second Church of Boston after losing faith in the special graces of the sacrament of Holy Communion.

Let me not taint the sincerity of this plea by any oversight of the claims of good men. I know and honor the purity and strict conscience of numbers of the clergy. What life the public worship retains, it owes to the scattered company of pious men, who minister here and there in the churches, and who, sometimes accepting with too great tenderness the tenet of the elders, have not accepted from others, but from their own heart, the genuine impulses of virtue, and so still command our love and awe, to the sanctity of character. Moreover, the exceptions are not so much to be found in a few eminent preachers, as in the better hours, the truer inspirations of all—nay, in the sincere moments of every man. But, with whatever exception, it is still true that tradition characterizes the preaching of this country; that it comes out of the memory, and not out of the soul; that it aims at what is usual, and not at what is necessary and eternal; that thus historical Christianity destroys the power of preaching, by withdrawing it from the exploration of the moral nature of man; where the sublime is, where are the resources of astonishment and power. What a cruel injustice it is to that Law, the joy of the whole earth, which alone can make thought dear and rich; that Law whose fatal sureness the astronomical orbits poorly emulate; that it is travestied and depreciated, that it is behooted and behowled, and not a trait, not a word of it articulated. The pulpit in losing sight of this Law, loses its reason, and gropes after it knows not what. And for want of this culture the soul of the community is sick and faithless. It wants nothing so much as a stern, high, stoical, Christian discipline, to make it know itself and the divinity that speaks through it. Now man is ashamed of himself; he skulks and sneaks through the world, to be tolerated, to be pitied, and scarcely in a thousand years does any man dare to be wise and good, and so draw after him the tears and blessings of his kind.

Certainly there have been periods when, from the inactivity of the intellect on certain truths, a greater faith was possible in names and persons. The Puritans in England and America found in the Christ of the Catholic Church and in the dogmas inherited from Rome, scope for their austere piety and their longings for civil freedom. But their creed is passing away, and none arises in its room. I think no man can go with his thoughts about him into one of our churches, without feeling that what hold the public worship had on men is gone, or going. It has lost its grasp on the affection of the good and the fear of the bad. In the country, neighborhoods, half parishes are *signing off*, to use the local term. It is already beginning to indicate character and religion to withdraw from the religious meetings. I have heard a devout person, who prized the Sabbath, say in bitterness of heart, "On Sundays, it seems wicked to go to church." And the motive that holds the best there is now only a hope and a waiting. What was once a mere circumstance, that the best and the worst men in the parish, the poor and the rich, the learned and the ignorant, young and old, should meet one day as fellows in one house, in sign of an equal right in the soul, has come to be a paramount motive for going thither.

My friends, in these two errors, I think, I find the causes of a decaying church and a wasting unbelief. And what greater calamity can fall upon a nation than the loss of worship? Then all things go to decay. Genius leaves the temple to haunt the senate or the market. Literature becomes frivolous. Science is cold. The eye of youth is not lighted by the hope of other worlds, and age is without honor. Society lives to trifles, and when men die we do not mention them.

And now, my brothers, you will ask, What in these desponding days can be done by us? The remedy is already declared in the ground of our complaint of the Church. We have contrasted the Church with the Soul. In the soul then let the redemption be sought. Wherever a man comes, there comes revolution. The old is for slaves. When a man comes, all books are legible, all things transparent, all religions are forms. He is religious. Man is the wonderworker. He is seen amid miracles. All men bless and curse. He saith yea and nay, only. The stationariness of religion; the assumption that the age of inspiration is past, that the Bible is closed; the fear of degrading the character of Jesus by representing him as a man; indicate with sufficient clearness the falsehood of our theology. It is the office of a true teacher to show us that God is, not was; that He speaketh, not spake. The true Christianity—a faith like Christ's in the infinitude of men—is lost. None believeth in the soul of man, but only in some man or person old and departed. Ah me! no man goeth alone. All men go in flocks to this saint or that poet, avoiding the God who seeth in secret. They cannot see in secret; they love to be blind in public. They think society wiser than their soul, and know not that one soul, and their soul, is wiser than the whole world. See how nations and races flit by on the sea of time and leave no ripple to tell where they floated or sunk, and one good soul shall make the name of Moses, or of Zeno, or of Zoroaster,[12] reverend forever. None assayeth the stern ambition to be the Self of the nation and of nature, but each would be an easy secondary to some Christian scheme, or sectarian connection, or some eminent man. Once leave your own knowledge of God, your own sentiment, and take secondary knowledge, as St. Paul's, or George Fox's, or Swedenborg's,[13] and you get wide from God with every year this secondary form lasts, and if, as now, for centuries—the chasm yawns to that breadth, that men can scarcely be convinced there is in them anything divine.

Let me admonish you, first of all, to go alone; to refuse the good models, even those which are sacred in the imagination of men, and dare to love God without mediator or veil. Friends enough you shall find who will hold up to your emulation Wesleys and Oberlins,[14] Saints and Prophets. Thank God for these good men, but say, 'I also am a man.' Imitation cannot go above its model. The imitator dooms himself to hopeless mediocrity. The inventor did it because it was natural to him, and so in him it has a charm. In the imitator something else is natural, and he bereaves himself of his own beauty, to come short of another man's.

Yourself a newborn bard of the Holy Ghost, cast behind you all conformity, and acquaint men at first hand with Deity. Look to it first and only, that fashion, custom, authority, pleasure, and money, are nothing to you—are not bandages over your eyes, that you cannot see—but live with the privilege of the immeasurable mind. Not too anxious to visit periodically all families and each family in your parish connection—when you meet one of these men or women, be to them a divine man; be to them thought and virtue; let their timid aspirations find in you a friend; let their trampled instincts be genially tempted out in your atmosphere; let their doubts know that you have doubted, and their wonder feel that you have wondered. By trusting your own heart,

[12] Zeno: Greek philosopher Zeno of Citium (ca. 334–262 B.C.), founder of Stoicism; Zoroaster: religious reformer of ancient Persia (ca. 628–552 B.C.) and founder of Zoroastrianism.

[13] George Fox: English founder (1624–1691), of the Society of Friends (Quakers); Swedenborg: Emanuel Swedenborg (1688–1722), Swedish philosopher and theologian.

[14] Wesley: English preacher John Wesley (1703–1791) or his brother Charles (1707–1788), founders of Methodism; Oberlin: Lutheran preacher Jean Frederic Oberlin (1740–1826), innovator in children's education.

you shall gain more confidence in other men. For all our penny-wisdom, for all our soul-destroying slavery to habit, it is not to be doubted that all men have sublime thoughts; that all men value the few real hours of life; they love to be heard; they love to be caught up into the vision of principles. We mark with light in the memory the few interviews we have had, in the dreary years of routine and of sin, with souls that made our souls wiser; that spoke what we thought; that told us what we knew; that gave us leave to be what we inly were. Discharge to men the priestly office, and, present or absent, you shall be followed with their love as by an angel.

And, to this end, let us not aim at common degrees of merit. Can we not leave, to such as love it, the virtue that glitters for the commendation of society, and ourselves pierce the deep solitudes of absolute ability and worth? We easily come up to the standard of goodness in society. Society's praise can be cheaply secured, and almost all men are content with those easy merits; but the instant effect of conversing with God will be to put them away. There are persons who are not actors, not speakers, but influences; persons too great for fame, for display; who disdain eloquence; to whom all we call art and artist, seems too nearly allied to show and by-ends, to the exaggeration of the finite and selfish, and loss of the universal. The orators, the poets, the commanders encroach on us only as fair women do, by our allowance and homage. Slight them by preoccupation of mind, slight them, as you can well afford to do, by high and universal aims, and they instantly feel that you have right, and that it is in lower places that they must shine. They also feel your right; for they with you are open to the influx of the all-knowing Spirit, which annihilates before its broad noon the little shades and gradations of intelligence in the compositions we call wiser and wisest.

In such high communion let us study the grand strokes of rectitude: a bold benevolence, an independence of friends, so that not the unjust wishes of those who love us shall impair our freedom, but we shall resist for truth's sake the freest flow of kindness, and appeal to sympathies far in advance; and—what is the highest form in which we know this beautiful element—a certain solidity of merit, that has nothing to do with opinion, and which is so essentially and manifestly virtue, that it is taken for granted that the right, the brave, the generous step will be taken by it, and nobody thinks of commending it. You would compliment a coxcomb doing a good act, but you would not praise an angel. The silence that accepts merit as the most natural thing in the world, is the highest applause. Such souls, when they appear, are the Imperial Guard of Virtue, the perpetual reserve, the dictators of fortune. One needs not praise their courage—they are the heart and soul of nature. O my friends, there are resources in us on which we have not drawn. There are men who rise refreshed on hearing a threat; men to whom a crisis which intimidates and paralyzes the majority—demanding not the faculties of prudence and thrift but comprehension, immovableness, the readiness of sacrifice—comes graceful and beloved as a bride. Napoleon said of Massena,[15] that he was not himself until the battle began to go against him; then, when the dead began to fall in ranks around him, awoke his powers of combination, and he put on terror and victory as a robe. So it is in rugged crises, in unwearieable endurance, and in aims which put sympathy out of question that the angel is shown. But these are heights that we can scarce remember and look up to without contrition and shame. Let us thank God that such things exist.

---

[15] André Massena (1758–1817), marshal of
Napoleon's empire.

And now let us do what we can to rekindle the smouldering, nigh quenched fire on the altar. The evils of the church that now is are manifest. The question returns, What shall we do? I confess, all attempts to project and establish a Cultus with new rites and forms, seem to me vain. Faith makes us, and not we it, and faith makes its own forms. All attempts to contrive a system are as cold as the new worship introduced by the French to the goddess of Reason—to-day, pasteboard and filigree, and ending to-morrow in madness and murder. Rather let the breath of new life be breathed by you through the forms already existing. For if once you are alive, you shall find they shall become plastic and new. The remedy to their deformity is first, soul, and second, soul, and evermore, soul. A whole popedom[16] of forms one pulsation of virtue can uplift and vivify. Two inestimable advantages Christianity has given us; first the Sabbath, the jubilee of the whole world, whose light dawns welcome alike into the closet of the philosopher, into the garret of toil, and into prison-cells, and everywhere suggests, even to the vile, the dignity of spiritual being. Let it stand forevermore, a temple, which new love, new faith, new sight shall restore to more than its first splendor to mankind. And secondly, the institution of preaching—the speech of man to men—essentially the most flexible of all organs, of all forms. What hinders that now, everywhere, in pulpits, in lecture-rooms, in houses, in fields, wherever the invitation of men or your own occasions lead you, you speak the very truth, as your life and conscience teach it, and cheer the waiting, fainting hearts of men with new hope and new revelation?

I look for the hour when that supreme Beauty which ravished the souls of those Eastern men, and chiefly of those Hebrews, and through their lips spoke oracles to all time, shall speak in the West also. The Hebrew and Greek Scriptures contain immortal sentences, that have been bread of life to millions. But they have no epical integrity; are fragmentary; are not shown in their order to the intellect. I look for the new Teacher that shall follow so far those shining laws that he shall see them come full circle; shall see their rounding complete grace; shall see the world to be the mirror of the soul; shall see the identity of the law of gravitation with purity of heart; and shall show that the Ought, that Duty, is one thing with Science, with Beauty, and with Joy.

1838

Self-Reliance

"Ne te quæsiveris extra."[1]

"Man is his own star; and the soul that can
Render an honest and a perfect man,
Commands all light, all influence, all fate;
Nothing to him falls early or too late.
Our acts our angels are, or good or ill,

---

[16] i.e., inflexible hierarchy.
[1] Latin: "Do not seek outside yourself."

Our fatal shadows that walk by us still."
Epilogue to Beaumont and Fletcher's
Honest Man's Fortune[2]

Cast the bantling[3] *on the rocks,*
Suckle him with the she-wolf's teat;
Wintered with the hawk and fox,
Power and speed be hands and feet.[4]

I read the other day some verses written by an eminent painter[5] which were original and not conventional. The soul always hears an admonition in such lines, let the subject be what it may. The sentiment they instil is of more value than any thought they may contain. To believe your own thought, to believe that what is true for you in your private heart, is true for all men,—that is genius. Speak your latent conviction and it shall be the universal sense; for the inmost in due time becomes the outmost,—and our first thought is rendered back to us by the trumpets of the Last Judgment. Familiar as the voice of the mind is to each, the highest merit we ascribe to Moses, Plato, and Milton, is that they set at naught books and traditions, and spoke not what men wrote but what they thought. A man should learn to detect and watch that gleam of light which flashes across his mind from within, more than the lustre of the firmament of bards and sages. Yet he dismisses without notice his thought, because it is his. In every work of genius we recognize our own rejected thoughts: they come back to us with a certain alienated majesty. Great works of art have no more affecting lesson for us than this. They teach us to abide by our spontaneous impression with good-humored inflexibility then most when the whole cry of voices is on the other side. Else, to-morrow a stranger will say with masterly good sense precisely what we have thought and felt all the time, and we shall be forced to take with shame our own opinion from another.

There is a time in every man's education when he arrives at the conviction that envy is ignorance; that imitation is suicide; that he must take himself for better, for worse, as his portion; that though the wide universe is full of good, no kernel of nourishing corn can come to him but through his toil bestowed on that plot of ground which is given to him to till. The power which resides in him is new in nature, and none but he knows what that is which he can do, nor does he know until he has tried. Not for nothing one face, one character, one fact makes much impression on him, and another none. This sculpture in the memory is not without preëstablished harmony. The eye was placed where one ray should fall, that it might testify of that particular ray. We but half express ourselves, and are ashamed of that divine idea which each of us represents. It may be safely trusted as proportionate and of good issues, so it be faithfully imparted, but God will not have his work made manifest by cowards. A man is relieved and gay when he has put his heart into his work and done his best; but what he has said or done other-

---

[2] Elizabethan playwrights Francis Beaumont (1584–1616) and John Fletcher (1579–1625) were authors of *Honest Man's Fortune* (1647).

[3] Infant.

[4] Emerson's own verses.

[5] Most likely the American painter and poet Washington Allston (1779–1843).

wise, shall give him no peace. It is a deliverance which does not deliver. In the attempt his genius deserts him; no muse befriends; no invention, no hope.

Trust thyself: every heart vibrates to that iron string. Accept the place the divine Providence has found for you; the society of your contemporaries, the connexion of events. Great men have always done so and confided themselves childlike to the genius of their age, betraying their perception that the absolutely trustworthy was seated at their heart, working through their hands, predominating in all their being. And we are now men, and must accept in the highest mind the same transcendent destiny; and not minors and invalids in a protected corner, not cowards fleeing before a revolution, but guides, redeemers, and benefactors, obeying the Almighty effort, and advancing on Chaos and the Dark.

What pretty oracles nature yields us on this text in the face and behavior of children, babes and even brutes. That divided and rebel mind, that distrust of a sentiment because our arithmetic has computed the strength and means opposed to our purpose, these have not. Their mind being whole, their eye is as yet unconquered, and when we look in their faces, we are disconcerted. Infancy conforms to nobody: all conform to it, so that one babe commonly makes four or five out of the adults who prattle and play to it. So God has armed youth and puberty and manhood no less with its own piquancy and charm, and made it enviable and gracious and its claims not to be put by, if it will stand by itself. Do not think the youth has no force because he cannot speak to you and me. Hark! in the next room his voice is sufficiently clear and emphatic. It seems he knows how to speak to his contemporaries. Bashful or bold, then, he will know how to make us seniors very unnecessary.

The nonchalance of boys who are sure of a dinner, and would disdain as much as a lord to do or say aught to conciliate one, is the healthy attitude of human nature. A boy is in the parlour what the pit[6] is in the playhouse; independent, irresponsible, looking out from his corner on such people and facts as pass by, he tries and sentences them on their merits, in the swift summary way of boys, as good, bad, interesting, silly, eloquent, troublesome. He cumbers himself never about consequences, about interests: he gives an independent, genuine verdict. You must court him: he does not court you. But the man is, as it were, clapped into jail by his consciousness. As soon as he has once acted or spoken with eclat, he is a committed person, watched by the sympathy or the hatred of hundreds whose affections must now enter into his account. There is no Lethe[7] for this. Ah, that he could pass again into his neutrality! Who can thus avoid all pledges, and having observed, observe again from the same unaffected, unbiassed, unbribable, unaffrighted innocence, must always be formidable. He would utter opinions on all passing affairs, which being seen to be not private but necessary, would sink like darts into the ear of men, and put them in fear.

These are the voices which we hear in solitude, but they grow faint and inaudible as we enter into the world. Society everywhere is in conspiracy against the manhood of every one of its members. Society is a joint-stock company in which the members agree for the better securing of his bread to each shareholder, to surrender the liberty and cul-

---

[6] Least expensive section of older theaters, where the audience was often clamorous and unrestrained.

[7] River in Greek mythology that causes forgetfulness.

ture of the eater. The virtue in most request is conformity. Self-reliance is its aversion. It loves not realities and creators, but names and customs.

Whoso would be a man must be a nonconformist. He who would gather immortal palms must not be hindered by the name of goodness, but must explore if it be goodness. Nothing is at last sacred but the integrity of your own mind. Absolve you to yourself, and you shall have the suffrage of the world. I remember an answer which when quite young I was prompted to make to a valued adviser who was wont to importune me with the dear old doctrines of the church. On my saying, What have I to do with the sacredness of traditions, if I live wholly from within? my friend suggested—"But these impulses may be from below, not from above." I replied, "They do not seem to me to be such; but if I am the Devil's child, I will live then from the Devil." No law can be sacred to me but that of my nature. Good and bad are but names very readily transferable to that or this; the only right is what is after my constitution, the only wrong what is against it. A man is to carry himself in the presence of all opposition as if everything were titular and ephemeral but he. I am ashamed to think how easily we capitulate to badges and names, to large societies and dead institutions. Every decent and well-spoken individual affects and sways me more than is right. I ought to go upright and vital, and speak the rude truth in all ways. If malice and vanity wear the coat of philanthropy, shall that pass? If an angry bigot assumes this bountiful cause of Abolition, and comes to me with his last news from Barbadoes,[8] why should I not say to him, "Go love thy infant; love thy wood-chopper: be good-natured and modest: have that grace; and never varnish your hard, uncharitable ambition with this incredible tenderness for black folk a thousand miles off. Thy love afar is spite at home." Rough and graceless would be such greeting, but truth is handsomer than the affectation of love. Your goodness must have some edge to it—else it is none. The doctrine of hatred must be preached as the counteraction of the doctrine of love when that pules and whines. I shun father and mother and wife and brother, when my genius calls me. I would write on the lintels of the door-post, *Whim.*[9] I hope it is somewhat better than whim at last, but we cannot spend the day in explanation. Expect me not to show cause why I seek or why I exclude company. Then, again, do not tell me, as a good man did to-day, of my obligation to put all poor men in good situations. Are they *my* poor? I tell thee, thou foolish philanthropist, that I grudge the dollar, the dime, the cent I give to such men as do not belong to me and to whom I do not belong. There is a class of persons to whom by all spiritual affinity I am bought and sold; for them I will go to prison, if need be; but your miscellaneous popular charities; the education at college of fools; the building of meeting-houses to the vain end to which many now stand; alms to sots; and the thousandfold Relief Societies;—though I confess with shame I sometimes succumb and give the dollar, it is a wicked dollar which by and by I shall have the manhood to withhold.

Virtues are in the popular estimate rather the exception than the rule. There is the man *and* his virtues. Men do what is called a good action, as some piece of courage or charity, much as they would pay a fine in expiation of daily non-appearance on parade.

---

[8] In 1834 slavery was officially abolished on this island (Barbados) in the British West Indies.

[9] i.e., for rejecting a family in order to obey a divine command (Matthew 10:34–37). See Exodus 12:17, in which God tells Moses to mark the "upper door post" and "two side posts" with blood so that God would not include those inside when he came to "smite all the firstborn in the land of Egypt, both man and beast."

Their works are done as an apology or extenuation of their living in the world,—as invalids and the insane pay a high board. Their virtues are penances. I do not wish to expiate, but to live. My life is for itself and not for a spectacle. I much prefer that it should be of a lower strain, so it be genuine and equal, than that it should be glittering and unsteady. I wish it to be sound and sweet, and not to need diet and bleeding.[10] I ask primary evidence that you are a man, and refuse this appeal from the man to his actions. I know that for myself it makes no difference whether I do or forbear those actions which are reckoned excellent. I cannot consent to pay for a privilege where I have intrinsic right. Few and mean as my gifts may be, I actually am, and do not need for my own assurance or the assurance of my fellows any secondary testimony.

What I must do, is all that concerns me, not what the people think. This rule, equally arduous in actual and in intellectual life, may serve for the whole distinction between greatness and meanness. It is the harder, because you will always find those who think they know what is your duty better than you know it. It is easy in the world to live after the world's opinion; it is easy in solitude to live after our own; but the great man is he who in the midst of the crowd keeps with perfect sweetness the independence of solitude.

The objection to conforming to usages that have become dead to you, is, that it scatters your force. It loses your time and blurs the impression of your character. If you maintain a dead church, contribute to a dead Bible-Society, vote with a great party either for the Government or against it, spread your table like base housekeepers,—under all these screens, I have difficulty to detect the precise man you are. And, of course, so much force is withdrawn from your proper life. But do your work, and I shall know you. Do your work, and you shall reinforce yourself. A man must consider what a blindman's-buff is this game of conformity. If I know your sect, I anticipate your argument. I hear a preacher announce for his text and topic the expediency of one of the institutions of his church. Do I not know beforehand that not possibly can he say a new and spontaneous word? Do I not know that with all this ostentation of examining the grounds of the institution, he will do no such thing? Do I not know that he is pledged to himself not to look but at one side,—the permitted side, not as a man, but as a parish minister? He is a retained attorney, and these airs of the bench are the emptiest affectation. Well, most men have bound their eyes with one or another handkerchief, and attached themselves to some one of these communities of opinion. This conformity makes them not false in a few particulars, authors of a few lies, but false in all particulars. Their every truth is not quite true. Their two is not the real two, their four not the real four: so that every word they say chagrins us, and we know not where to begin to set them right. Meantime nature is not slow to equip us in the prison-uniform of the party to which we adhere. We come to wear one cut of face and figure, and acquire by degrees the gentlest asinine expression. There is a mortifying experience in particular which does not fail to wreck itself also in the general history; I mean "the foolish face of praise,"[11] the forced smile which we put on in company where we do not feel at ease in answer to conversation which does not interest us. The muscles, not spontaneously moved, but moved by a low usurping wilfulness, grow tight about the outline of the face with the most disagreeable sensation.

[10] Bloodletting.
[11] Alexander Pope, "Epistle to Dr. Arbuthnot,"
    l. 212.

For nonconformity the world whips you with its displeasure. And therefore a man must know how to estimate a sour face. The bystanders look askance on him in the public street or in the friend's parlor. If this aversation had its origin in contempt and resistance like his own, he might well go home with a sad countenance; but the sour faces of the multitude, like their sweet faces, have no deep cause, but are put on and off as the wind blows, and a newspaper directs. Yet is the discontent of the multitude more formidable than that of the senate and the college. It is easy enough for a firm man who knows the world to brook the rage of the cultivated classes. Their rage is decorous and prudent, for they are timid as being very vulnerable themselves. But when to their feminine rage the indignation of the people is added, when the ignorant and the poor are aroused, when the unintelligent brute force that lies at the bottom of society is made to growl and mow,[12] it needs the habit of magnanimity and religion to treat it godlike as a trifle of no concernment.

The other terror that scares us from self-trust is our consistency; a reverence for our past act or word, because the eyes of others have no other data for computing our orbit than our past acts, and we are loath to disappoint them.

But why should you keep your head over your shoulder? Why drag about this corpse of your memory, lest you contradict somewhat you have stated in this or that public place? Suppose you should contradict yourself; what then? It seems to be a rule of wisdom never to rely on your memory alone, scarcely even in acts of pure memory, but to bring the past for judgment into the thousand-eyed present, and live ever in a new day. In your metaphysics you have denied personality to the Deity: yet when the devout motions of the soul come, yield to them heart and life, though they should clothe God with shape and color. Leave your theory as Joseph his coat in the hand of the harlot,[13] and flee.

A foolish consistency is the hobgoblin of little minds, adored by little statesmen and philosophers and divines. With consistency a great soul has simply nothing to do. He may as well concern himself with his shadow on the wall. Speak what you think now in hard words, and to-morrow speak what to-morrow thinks in hard words again, though it contradict every thing you said to-day.—'Ah, so you shall be sure to be misunderstood.'—Is it so bad then to be misunderstood? Pythagoras[14] was misunderstood, and Socrates, and Jesus, and Luther, and Copernicus,[15] and Galileo,[16] and Newton, and every pure and wise spirit that ever took flesh. To be great is to be misunderstood.

I suppose no man can violate his nature. All the sallies of his will are rounded in by the last of his being as the inequalities of Andes and Himmaleh[17] are insignificant in the curve of the sphere. Nor does it matter how you gauge and try him. A character is like an acrostic or Alexandrian stanza;[18]—read it forward, backward, or across, it still spells the same thing. In this pleasing contrite wood-life which God allows me, let me record day

---

[12] Archaic for "grimace."

[13] In Genesis 39:12, Potiphar's wife tempted Joseph by grabbing his garment and asking him to sleep with her, whereupon Joseph fled, leaving the garment behind.

[14] Greek mathematician (sixth century B.C.) and mystic philosopher.

[15] Polish astronomer (1473–1543) who proposed the current theory of the solar system, which was rejected in his lifetime.

[16] Galileo Galilei (1564–1642), Italian astronomer and physicist who endorsed Copernicus's theories and as a result was tried by the Inquisition of the Catholic church.

[17] Mountains in Asia bordering China and India (now Himalayas).

[18] Palindrome, or statement that can be read the same forward and backward.

by day my honest thought without prospect or retrospect, and, I cannot doubt, it will be found symmetrical, though I mean it not, and see it not. My book should smell of pines and resound with the hum of insects. The swallow over my window should interweave that thread or straw he carried in his bill into my web also. We pass for what we are. Character teaches above our wills. Men imagine that they communicate their virtue or vice only by overt actions and do not see that virtue or vice emit a breath every moment.

There will be an agreement in whatever variety of actions, so they be each honest and natural in their hour. For of one will, the actions will be harmonious, however unlike they seem. These varieties are lost sight of at a little distance, at a little height of thought. One tendency unites them all. The voyage of the best ship is a zigzag line of a hundred tacks. See the line from a sufficient distance, and it straightens itself to the average tendency. Your genuine action will explain itself and will explain your other genuine actions. Your conformity explains nothing. Act singly, and what you have already done singly, will justify you now. Greatness appeals to the future. If I can be firm enough today to do right and scorn eyes, I must have done so much right before, as to defend me now. Be it how it will, do right now. Always scorn appearances, and you always may. The force of character is cumulative. All the foregone days of virtue work their health into this. What makes the majesty of the heroes of the senate and the field, which so fills the imagination? The consciousness of a train of great days and victories behind. They shed an united light on the advancing actor. He is attended as by a visible escort of angels. That is it which throws thunder into Chatham's[19] voice, and dignity into Washington's[20] port,[21] and America into Adams's[22] eye. Honor is venerable to us because it is no ephemeris. It is always ancient virtue. We worship it to-day, because it is not of to-day. We love it and pay it homage, because it is not a trap for our love and homage, but is self-dependent, self-derived, and therefore of an old immaculate pedigree, even if shown in a young person.

I hope in these days we have heard the last of conformity and consistency. Let the words be gazetted[23] and ridiculous henceforward. Instead of the gong for dinner, let us hear a whistle from the Spartan fife.[24] Let us never bow and apologize more. A great man is coming to eat at my house. I do not wish to please him: I wish that he should wish to please me. I will stand here for humanity, and though I would make it kind, I would make it true. Let us affront and reprimand the smooth mediocrity and squalid contentment of the times, and hurl in the face of custom, and trade, and office, the fact which is the upshot of all history, that there is a great responsible Thinker and Actor working wherever a man works; that a true man belongs to no other time or place, but is the centre of things. Where he is, there is nature. He measures you, and all men, and all events. Ordinarily every body in society reminds us of somewhat else or of some other person. Character, reality, reminds you of nothing else; it takes place of the whole creation. The man must be so much that he must make all circumstances indifferent.

---

[19] Chatham: William Pitt (1708–1778), earl of Chatham, English orator and statesman.
[20] Washington: George Washington (1732–1799), first American president.
[21] Demeanor.
[22] Adams: Revolutionary War patriot Samuel Adams (1722–1803); John Adams (1735–1826), second president; John Quincy Adams (1767–1848), sixth president.
[23] i.e., let an announcement be made of their public dismissal.
[24] The Spartans were noted for their strict discipline.

Every true man is a cause, a country, and an age; requires infinite spaces and numbers and time fully to accomplish his design;—and posterity seem to follow his steps as a train of clients. A man Cæsar is born, and for ages after, we have a Roman Empire. Christ is born, and millions of minds so grow and cleave to his genius, that he is confounded with virtue and the possible of man. An institution is the lengthened shadow of one man; as, Monachism, of the Hermit Antony; the Reformation, of Luther; Quakerism of Fox; Methodism, of Wesley; Abolition, of Clarkson.[25] Scipio,[26] Milton called "the height of Rome;" and all history resolves itself very easily into the biography of a few stout and earnest persons.

Let a man then know his worth, and keep things under his feet. Let him not peep or steal, or skulk up and down with the air of a charity-boy, a bastard, or an interloper, in the world which exists for him. But the man in the street finding no worth in himself which corresponds to the force which built a tower or sculptured a marble god, feels poor when he looks on these. To him a palace, a statue, or a costly book have an alien and forbidding air, much like a gay equipage, and seem to say like that, "Who are you, sir?" Yet they all are his, suitors for his notice, petitioners to his faculties that they will come out and take possession. The picture waits for my verdict: it is not to command me, but I am to settle its claims to praise. That popular fable of the sot who was picked up dead drunk in the street, carried to the duke's house, washed and dressed and laid in the duke's bed, and, on his waking, treated with all obsequious ceremony like the duke, and assured that he had been insane, owes its popularity to the fact, that it symbolizes so well the state of man, who is in the world a sort of sot, but now and then wakes up, exercises his reason, and finds himself a true prince.

Our reading is mendicant and sycophantic. In history, our imagination plays us false. Kingdom and lordship, power and estate are a gaudier vocabulary than private John and Edward in a small house and common day's work: but the things of life are the same to both: the sum total of both is the same. Why all this deference to Alfred, and Scanderbeg, and Gustavus?[27] Suppose they were virtuous: did they wear out virtue? As great a stake depends on your private act to-day, as followed their public and renowned steps. When private men shall act with original views, the lustre will be transferred from the actions of kings to those of gentlemen.

The world has been instructed by its kings, who have so magnetized the eyes of nations. It has been taught by this colossal symbol the mutual reverence that is due from man to man. The joyful loyalty with which men have everywhere suffered the king, the noble, or the great proprietor to walk among them by a law of his own, make his own scale of men and things, and reverse theirs, pay for benefits not with money but with honor, and represent the Law in his person, was the hieroglyphic by which they obscurely signified their consciousness of their own right and comeliness, the right of every man.

---

[25] Antony: St. Anthony (ca. 250–350) originated Christian monasticism; Fox: George Fox (1624–1691) founded the Society of Friends in England; Wesley: John Wesley (1703–1791) fostered Methodism; Clarkson: Thomas Clarkson (1760–1846) advocated abolition in England.

[26] Roman general (237–183 B.C.) who conquered Carthage.

[27] Alfred: Alfred the Great (849–899), king of England; Scanderbeg: national hero of Albania (1403?–1468); Gustavus: Gustavus Adolphus (1594–1632), king of Sweden.

The magnetism which all original action exerts is explained when we inquire the reason of self-trust. Who is the Trustee? What is the aboriginal Self on which a universal reliance may be grounded? What is the nature and power of that science-baffling star, without parallax,[28] without calculable elements, which shoots a ray of beauty even into trivial and impure actions, if the least mark of independence appear? The inquiry leads us to that source, at once the essence of genius, of virtue, and of life, which we call Spontaneity or Instinct. We denote this primary wisdom as Intuition, whilst all later teachings are tuitions. In that deep force, the last fact behind which analysis cannot go, all things find their common origin. For the sense of being which in calm hours rises, we know not how, in the soul, is not diverse from things, from space, from light, from time, from man, but one with them, and proceeds obviously from the same source whence their life and being also proceed. We first share the life by which things exist, and afterwards see them as appearances in nature, and forget that we have shared their cause. Here is the fountain of action and of thought. Here are the lungs of that inspiration which giveth man wisdom, and which cannot be denied without impiety and atheism. We lie in the lap of immense intelligence, which makes us receivers of its truth and organs of its activity. When we discern justice, when we discern truth, we do nothing of ourselves, but allow a passage to its beams. If we ask whence this comes, if we seek to pry into the soul that causes, all philosophy is at fault. Its presence or its absence is all we can affirm. Every man discriminates between the voluntary acts of his mind, and his involuntary perceptions, and knows that to his involuntary perceptions a perfect faith is due. He may err in the expression of them, but he knows that these things are so, like day and night, not to be disputed. My wilful actions and acquisitions are but roving;—the idlest reverie, the faintest native emotion, command my curiosity and respect. Thoughtless people contradict as readily the statement of perceptions as of opinions, or rather much more readily; for, they do not distinguish between perception and notion. They fancy that I choose to see this or that thing. But perception is not whimsical, but fatal. If I see a trait, my children will see it after me, and in course of time, all mankind,—although it may chance that no one has seen it before me. For my perception of it is as much a fact as the sun.

The relations of the soul to the divine spirit are so pure that it is profane to seek to interpose helps. It must be that when God speaketh, he should communicate not one thing, but all things; should fill the world with his voice; should scatter forth light, nature, time, souls, from the centre of the present thought; and new date and new create the whole. Whenever a mind is simple, and receives a divine wisdom, old things pass away,—means, teachers, texts, temples fall; it lives now and absorbs past and future into the present hour. All things are made sacred by relation to it,—one as much as another. All things are dissolved to their centre by their cause, and in the universal miracle petty and particular miracles disappear. If, therefore, a man claims to know and speak of God, and carries you backward to the phraseology of some old mouldered nation in another country, in another world, believe him not. Is the acorn better than the oak which is its fullness and completion? Is the parent better than the child into whom he

---

[28] Apparent change in the direction of an object caused by a change in the position from which it is seen. Emerson may well be using "without parallax" to mean "without an observational position."

has cast his ripened being? Whence then this worship of the past? The centuries are conspirators against the sanity and authority of the soul. Time and space are but physiological colors which the eye makes, but the soul is light; where it is, is day; where it was, is night; and history is an impertinence and an injury, if it be anything more than a cheerful apologue or parable of my being and becoming.

Man is timid and apologetic; he is no longer upright; he dares not say 'I think,' 'I am,' but quotes some saint or sage. He is ashamed before the blade of grass or the blowing rose. These roses under my window make no reference to former roses or to better ones; they are for what they are; they exist with God to-day. There is no time to them. There is simply the rose; it is perfect in every moment of its existence. Before a leaf-bud has burst, its whole life acts; in the full-blown flower, there is no more; in the leafless root, there is no less. Its nature is satisfied, and it satisfies nature, in all moments alike. But man postpones or remembers; he does not live in the present, but with reverted eye laments the past, or, heedless of the riches that surround him, stands on tiptoe to foresee the future. He cannot be happy and strong until he too lives with nature in the present, above time.

This should be plain enough. Yet see what strong intellects dare not yet hear God himself, unless he speak the phraseology of I know not what David, or Jeremiah, or Paul.[29] We shall not always set so great a price on a few texts, on a few lives. We are like children who repeat by rote the sentences of grandames and tutors, and, as they grow older, of the men of talents and character they chance to see,—painfully recollecting the exact words they spoke; afterwards, when they come into the point of view which those had who uttered these sayings, they understand them, and are willing to let the words go; for, at any time, they can use words as good, when occasion comes. If we live truly, we shall see truly. It is as easy for the strong man to be strong, as it is for the weak to be weak. When we have new perception, we shall gladly disburden the memory of its hoarded treasures as old rubbish. When a man lives with God, his voice shall be as sweet as the murmur of the brook and the rustle of the corn.

And now at last the highest truth on this subject remains unsaid; probably, cannot be said; for all that we say is the far off remembering of the intuition. That thought, by what I can now nearest approach to say it, is this. When good is near you, when you have life in yourself, it is not by any known or accustomed way; you shall not discern the foot-prints of any other; you shall not see the face of man; you shall not hear any name;—the way, the thought, the good shall be wholly strange and new. It shall exclude example and experience. You take the way from man, not to man. All persons that ever existed are its forgotten ministers. Fear and hope are alike beneath it. There is somewhat low even in hope. In the hour of vision, there is nothing that can be called gratitude, nor properly joy. The soul raised over passion beholds identity and eternal causation, perceives the self-existence of Truth and Right, and calms itself with knowing that all things go well. Vast spaces of nature, the Atlantic Ocean, the South Sea,—long intervals of time, years, centuries,—are of no account. This which I think and feel underlay every former state of life and circumstances, as it does underlie my present, and what is called life, and what is called death.

Life only avails, not the having lived. Power ceases in the instant of repose; it resides in the moment of transition from a past to a new state, in the shooting of the gulf, in the darting to an aim. This one fact the world hates, that the soul *becomes;* for, that forever

---

[29] The three biblical authors.

degrades the past, turns all riches to poverty, all reputation to a shame, confounds the saint with the rogue, shoves Jesus and Judas equally aside. Why then do we prate of self-reliance? Inasmuch as the soul is present, there will be power not confident but agent. To talk of reliance, is a poor external way of speaking. Speak rather of that which relies, because it works and is. Who has more obedience than I, masters me, though he should not raise his finger. Round him I must revolve by the gravitation of spirits. We fancy it rhetoric when we speak of eminent virtue. We do not yet see that virtue is Height, and that a man or a company of men plastic and permeable to principles, by the law of nature must overpower and ride all cities, nations, kings, rich men, poets, who are not.

This is the ultimate fact which we so quickly reach on this as on every topic, the resolution of all into the ever blessed ONE. Self-existence is the attribute of the Supreme Cause, and it constitutes the measure of good by the degree in which it enters into all lower forms. All things real are so by so much virtue as they contain. Commerce, husbandry, hunting, whaling, war, eloquence, personal weight, are somewhat, and engage my respect as examples of its presence and impure action. I see the same law working in nature for conservation and growth. Power is in nature the essential measure of right. Nature suffers nothing to remain in her kingdoms which cannot help itself. The genesis and maturation of a planet, its poise and orbit, the bended tree recovering itself from the strong wind, the vital resources of every animal and vegetable, are demonstrations of the self-sufficing, and therefore self-relying soul.

Thus all concentrates; let us not rove; let us sit at home with the cause. Let us stun and astonish the intruding rabble of men and books and institutions by a simple declaration of the divine fact. Bid the invaders take the shoes from off their feet, for God is here within.[30] Let our simplicity judge them, and our docility to our own law demonstrate the poverty of nature and fortune beside our native riches.

But now we are a mob. Man does not stand in awe of man, nor is his genius admonished to stay at home, to put itself in communication with the internal ocean, but it goes abroad to beg a cup of water of the urns of other men. We must go alone. I like the silent church before the service begins, better than any preaching. How far off, how cool, how chaste the persons look, begirt each one with a precinct or sanctuary. So let us always sit. Why should we assume the faults of our friend, or wife, or father, or child, because they sit around our hearth, or are said to have the same blood? All men have my blood, and I have all men's. Not for that will I adopt their petulance or folly, even to the extent of being ashamed of it. But your isolation must not be mechanical, but spiritual, that is, must be elevation. At times the whole world seems to be in conspiracy to importune you with emphatic trifles. Friend, client, child, sickness, fear, want, charity, all knock at once at thy closet door and say,—"Come out unto us." But keep thy state; come not into their confusion. The power men possess to annoy me, I give them by a weak curiosity. No man can come near me but through my act. "What we love that we have, but by desire we bereave ourselves of the love."

If we cannot at once rise to the sanctities of obedience and faith, let us at least resist our temptations; let us enter into the state of war, and wake Thor and Woden,[31]

---

[30] See Exodus 3:5, in which God says to Moses: "Put off thy shoes from off thy feet, for the place whereon thou standest is holy ground."

[31] Thor and Woden (Odin) are gods of preeminent power in Norse mythology.

courage and constancy, in our Saxon breasts. This is to be done in our smooth times by speaking the truth. Check this lying hospitality and lying affection. Live no longer to the expectation of these deceived and deceiving people with whom we converse. Say to them, O father, O mother, O wife, O brother, O friend, I have lived with you after appearances hitherto. Henceforward I am the truth's. Be it known unto you that henceforward I obey no law less than the eternal law. I will have no covenants but proximities. I shall endeavor to nourish my parents, to support my family, to be the chaste husband of one wife,—but these relations I must fill after a new and unprecedented way. I appeal from your customs. I must be myself. I cannot break myself any longer for you, or you. If you can love me for what I am, we shall be the happier. If you cannot, I will still seek to deserve that you should. I will not hide my tastes or aversions. I will so trust that what is deep is holy, that I will do strongly before the sun and moon whatever inly rejoices me, and the heart appoints. If you are noble, I will love you; if you are not, I will not hurt you and myself by hypocritical attentions. If you are true, but not in the same truth with me, cleave to your companions; I will seek my own. I do this not selfishly, but humbly and truly. It is alike your interest and mine and all men's, however long we have dwelt in lies, to live in truth. Does this sound harsh to-day? You will soon love what is dictated by your nature as well as mine, and if we follow the truth, it will bring us out safe at last.—But so you may give these friends pain. Yes, but I cannot sell my liberty and my power, to save their sensibility. Besides, all persons have their moments of reason when they look out into the region of absolute truth; then will they justify me and do the same thing.

The populace think that your rejection of popular standards is a rejection of all standard, and mere antinomianism;[32] and the bold sensualist will use the name of philosophy to gild his crimes. But the law of consciousness abides. There are two confessionals, in one or the other of which we must be shriven. You may fulfil your round of duties by clearing yourself in the *direct,* or, in the *reflex* way. Consider whether you have satisfied your relations to father, mother, cousin, neighbor, town, cat, and dog; whether any of these can upbraid you. But I may also neglect this reflex standard, and absolve me to myself. I have my own stern claims and perfect circle. It denies the name of duty to many offices that are called duties. But if I can discharge its debts, it enables me to dispense with the popular code. If any one imagines that this law is lax, let him keep its commandment one day.

And truly it demands something godlike in him who has cast off the common motives of humanity, and has ventured to trust himself for a taskmaster. High be his heart, faithful his will, clear his sight, that he may in good earnest be doctrine, society, law to himself, that a simple purpose may be to him as strong as iron necessity is to others.

If any man consider the present aspects of what is called by distinction *society,* he will see the need of these ethics. The sinew and heart of man seem to be drawn out, and we are become timorous desponding whimperers. We are afraid of truth, afraid of fortune, afraid of death, and afraid of each other. Our age yields no great and perfect persons. We want men and women who shall renovate life and our social state, but we see that most natures are insolvent, cannot satisfy their own wants, have an ambition out of all proportion to their practical force, and do lean and beg day and night continually. Our housekeeping is mendicant, our arts, our occupations, our marriages, our religion we

[32] Resistance to religious and moral laws.

have not chosen, but society has chosen for us. We are parlor soldiers. We shun the rugged battle of fate, where strength is born.

If our young men miscarry in their first enterprizes, they lose all heart. If the young merchant fails, men say he is *ruined.* If the finest genius studies at one of our colleges, and is not installed in an office within one year afterwards in the cities or suburbs of Boston or New York, it seems to his friends and to himself that he is right in being disheartened and in complaining the rest of his life. A sturdy lad from New Hampshire or Vermont, who in turn tries all the professions, who *teams it, farms it, peddles,* keeps a school, preaches, edits a newspaper, goes to Congress, buys a township, and so forth, in successive years, and always, like a cat, falls on his feet, is worth a hundred of these city dolls. He walks abreast with his days, and feels no shame in not 'studying a profession,' for he does not postpone his life, but lives already. He has not one chance, but a hundred chances. Let a Stoic[33] open the resources of man, and tell men they are not leaning willows, but can and must detach themselves; that with the exercise of self-trust, new powers shall appear; that a man is the word made flesh,[34] born to shed healing to the nations, that he should be ashamed of our compassion, and that the moment he acts from himself, tossing the laws, the books, idolatries, and customs out of the window, we pity him no more but thank and revere him,—and that teacher shall restore the life of man to splendor, and make his name dear to all History.

It is easy to see that a greater self-reliance must work a revolution in all the offices and relations of men; in their religion; in their education; in their pursuits; their modes of living; their association; in their property; in their speculative views.

1. In what prayers do men allow themselves! That which they call a holy office, is not so much as brave and manly. Prayer looks abroad and asks for some foreign addition to come through some foreign virtue, and loses itself in endless mazes of natural and supernatural, and mediatorial and miraculous. Prayer that craves a particular commodity,—any thing less than all good,—is vicious. Prayer is the contemplation of the facts of life from the highest point of view. It is the soliloquy of a beholding and jubilant soul. It is the spirit of God pronouncing his works good.[35] But prayer as a means to effect a private end, is meanness and theft. It supposes dualism and not unity in nature and consciousness. As soon as the man is at one with God, he will not beg. He will then see prayer in all action. The prayer of the farmer kneeling in his field to weed it, the prayer of the rower kneeling with the stroke of his oar, are true prayers heard throughout nature, though for cheap ends. Caratach, in Fletcher's *Bonduca,*[36] when admonished to inquire the mind of the god Audate, replies,—

> "His hidden meaning lies in our endeavors,
> Our valors are our best gods."

Another sort of false prayers are our regrets. Discontent is the want of self-reliance: it is infirmity of will. Regret calamities, if you can thereby help the sufferer; if not, attend

---

[33] Ancient Greek philosophers who professed passionless independence and submission to natural law.

[34] John 1:14: "And the word was made flesh, and dwelt among us . . . full of grace and truth."

[35] Genesis 1:31: "And God saw everything that he had made, and, behold, *it was* very good."

[36] Drama by Elizabethan playwright John Fletcher (1579–1625). The lines Emerson cites are slightly misquoted.

your own work, and already the evil begins to be repaired. Our sympathy is just as base. We come to them who weep foolishly, and sit down and cry for company, instead of imparting to them truth and health in rough electric shocks, putting them once more in communication with their own reason. The secret of fortune is joy in our hands. Welcome evermore to gods and men is the self-helping man. For him all doors are flung wide: him all tongues greet, all honors crown, all eyes follow with desire. Our love goes out to him and embraces him, because he did not need it. We solicitously and apologetically caress and celebrate him, because he held on his way and scorned our disapprobation. The gods love him because men hated him. "To the persevering mortal," said Zoroaster,[37] "the blessed Immortals are swift."

As men's prayers are a disease of the will, so are their creeds a disease of the intellect. They say with those foolish Israelites, "Let not God speak to us, lest we die. Speak thou, speak any man with us, and we will obey."[38] Everywhere I am hindered of meeting God in my brother, because he has shut his own temple doors, and recites fables merely of his brother's, or his brother's brother's God. Every new mind is a new classification. If it prove a mind of uncommon activity and power, a Locke, a Lavoisier, a Hutton, a Bentham, a Fourier,[39] it imposes its classification on other men, and lo! a new system. In proportion to the depth of the thought, and so to the number of the objects it touches and brings within reach of the pupil, is his complacency. But chiefly is this apparent in creeds and churches, which are also classifications of some powerful mind acting on the elemental thought of Duty, and man's relation to the Highest. Such is Calvinism, Quakerism, Swedenborgianism. The pupil takes the same delight in subordinating every thing to the new terminology, as a girl who has just learned botany in seeing a new earth and new seasons thereby. It will happen for a time, that the pupil will find his intellectual power has grown by the study of his master's mind. But in all unbalanced minds, the classification is idolized, passes for the end, and not for a speedily exhaustible means, so that the walls of the system blend to their eye in the remote horizon with the walls of the universe; the luminaries of heaven seem to them hung on the arch their master built. They cannot imagine how you aliens have any right to see,—how you can see; "It must be somehow that you stole the light from us." They do not yet perceive, that light, unsystematic, indomi-table, will break into any cabin, even into theirs. Let them chirp awhile and call it their own. If they are honest and do well, presently their neat new pinfold[40] will be too strait and low, will crack, will lean, will rot and vanish, and the immortal light, all young and joyful, million-orbed, million-colored, will beam over the universe as on the first morning.

2. It is for want of self-culture that the superstition of Travelling, whose idols are Italy, England, Egypt, retains its fascination for all educated Americans. They who made England, Italy, or Greece venerable in the imagination, did so by sticking fast where

---

[37] Persian prophet of the sixth century B.C.

[38] Anxious words of the Hebrews to Moses, after God had given him the Ten Commandments. (See Exodus 20:19.)

[39] Locke: John Locke (1632–1704), English philosopher who heralded a theory of knowledge; Lavoisier: Antoine Laurent Lavoisier (1743–1794), who initiated advances in chemistry; Hutton: James Hutton (1726–1797), pioneer in geology; Bentham: Jeremy Bentham (1748–1832), who originated practical doctrines for law and government; Fourier: François Marie Charles Fourier (1772–1837), who pioneered in sociology.

[40] Fenced yard for holding animals.

they were, like an axis of the earth. In manly hours, we feel that duty is our place. The soul is no traveller: the wise man stays at home, and when his necessities, his duties, on any occasion call him from his house, or into foreign lands, he is at home still, and shall make men sensible by the expression of his countenance, that he goes the missionary of wisdom and virtue, and visits cities and men like a sovereign, and not like an interloper or a valet.

I have no churlish objection to the circumnavigation of the globe, for the purposes of art, of study, and benevolence, so that the man is first domesticated, or does not go abroad with the hope of finding somewhat greater than he knows. He who travels to be amused, or to get somewhat which he does not carry, travels away from himself, and grows old even in youth among old things. In Thebes, in Palmyra,[41] his will and mind have become old and dilapidated as they. He carries ruins to ruins.

Travelling is a fool's paradise. Our first journeys discover to us the indifference of places. At home I dream that at Naples, at Rome, I can be intoxicated with beauty, and lose my sadness. I pack my trunk, embrace my friends, embark on the sea, and at last wake up in Naples, and there beside me is the stern Fact, the sad self, unrelenting, identical, that I fled from. I seek the Vatican, and the palaces. I affect to be intoxicated with sights and suggestions, but I am not intoxicated. My giant goes with me wherever I go.

3. But the rage of travelling is a symptom of a deeper unsoundness affecting the whole intellectual action. The intellect is vagabond, and our system of education fosters restlessness. Our minds travel when our bodies are forced to stay at home. We imitate; and what is imitation but the travelling of the mind? Our houses are built with foreign taste; our shelves are garnished with foreign ornaments; our opinions, our tastes, our faculties, lean, and follow the Past and the Distant. The soul created the arts wherever they have flourished. It was in his own mind that the artist sought his model. It was an application of his own thought to the thing to be done and the conditions to be observed. And why need we copy the Doric or the Gothic model? Beauty, convenience, grandeur of thought, and quaint expression are as near to us as to any, and if the American artist will study with hope and love the precise thing to be done by him, considering the climate, the soil, the length of the day, the wants of the people, the habit and form of the government, he will create a house in which all these will find themselves fitted, and taste and sentiment will be satisfied also.

Insist on yourself; never imitate. Your own gift you can present every moment with the cumulative force of a whole life's cultivation; but of the adopted talent of another, you have only an extemporaneous, half possession. That which each can do best, none but his Maker can teach him. No man yet knows what it is, nor can, till that person has exhibited it. Where is the master who could have taught Shakspeare? Where is the master who could have instructed Franklin, or Washington, or Bacon, or Newton? Every great man is a unique. The Scipionism[42] of Scipio is precisely that part he could not borrow. Shakspeare will never be made by the study of Shakspeare. Do that which is assigned you, and you cannot hope too much or dare too much. There is at this moment for you an utterance brave and grand as that of the colossal chisel of Phidias,[43] or trowel of the Egyptians, or the pen of Moses, or Dante, but different from all these. Not possi-

---

[41] Thebes; Palmyra: ancient cities in Egypt and Syria, respectively.
[42] i.e., Scipio's essence.

[43] Renowned Greek sculptor of the fifth century B.C.

bly will the soul all rich, all eloquent, with thousand-cloven tongue, deign to repeat itself; but if you can hear what these patriarchs say, surely you can reply to them in the same pitch of voice: for the ear and the tongue are two organs of one nature. Abide in the simple and noble regions of thy life, obey thy heart, and thou shalt reproduce the Foreworld again.

4. As our Religion, our Education, our Art look abroad, so does our spirit of society. All men plume themselves on the improvement of society, and no man improves.

Society never advances. It recedes as fast on one side as it gains on the other. It undergoes continual changes: it is barbarous, it is civilized, it is christianized, it is rich, it is scientific; but this change is not amelioration. For every thing that is given, something is taken. Society acquires new arts and loses old instincts. What a contrast between the well-clad, reading, writing, thinking American, with a watch, a pencil, and a bill of exchange in his pocket, and the naked New Zealander, whose property is a club, a spear, a mat, and an undivided twentieth of a shed to sleep under. But compare the health of the two men, and you shall see that the white man has lost his aboriginal strength. If the traveller tell us truly, strike the savage with a broad axe, and in a day or two the flesh shall unite and heal as if you struck the blow into soft pitch, and the same blow shall send the white to his grave.

The civilized man has built a coach, but has lost the use of his feet. He is supported on crutches, but lacks so much support of muscle. He has a fine Geneva watch, but he fails of the skill to tell the hour by the sun. A Greenwich nautical almanac he has, and so being sure of the information when he wants it, the man in the street does not know a star in the sky. The solstice he does not observe; the equinox he knows as little; and the whole bright calendar of the year is without a dial in his mind. His note-books impair his memory; his libraries overload his wit; the insurance office increases the number of accidents; and it may be a question whether machinery does not encumber; whether we have not lost by refinement some energy, by a christianity entrenched in establishments and forms, some vigor of wild virtue. For every stoic was a stoic; but in Christendom where is the Christian?

There is no more deviation in the moral standard than in the standard of height or bulk. No greater men are now than ever were. A singular equality may be observed between the great men of the first and of the last ages; nor can all the science, art, religion and philosophy of the nineteenth century avail to educate greater men than Plutarch's[44] heroes, three or four and twenty centuries ago. Not in time is the race progressive. Phocion, Socrates, Anaxagoras, Diogenes, are great men, but they leave no class.[45] He who is really of their class will not be called by their name, but will be his own man, and, in his turn the founder of a sect. The arts and inventions of each period are only its costume, and do not invigorate men. The harm of the improved machinery may compensate its good. Hudson and Behring accomplished so much in their fishing-boats, as to astonish Parry and Franklin, whose equipment exhausted the resources of science and art.[46] Galileo, with an opera-glass, discovered a more splendid series of celestial phe-

---

[44] Plutarch: Greek biographer (46?–?120) who recorded the lives of famous Romans and Greeks.

[45] All "great men" cited here were Greek philosophers of the third and fourth centuries B.C.

[46] Hudson: English navigator Henry Hudson (d. 1611); Behring: Dutch navigator Vitus Jonassen Bering (1680–1741); Parry and Franklin: English arctic explorers Sir William Edward Parry (1790–1855) and Sir John Franklin (1786–1847).

nomena than any one since. Columbus found the New World in an undecked boat. It is curious to see the periodical disuse and perishing of means and machinery which were introduced with loud laudation, a few years or centuries before. The great genius returns to essential man. We reckoned the improvements of the art of war among the triumphs of science, and yet Napoleon conquered Europe by the Bivouac, which consisted of falling back on naked valor, and disencumbering it of all aids. The Emperor held it impossible to make a perfect army, says Las Cases,[47] "without abolishing our arms, magazines, commissaries, and carriages, until in imitation of the Roman custom, the soldier should receive his supply of corn, grind it in his hand-mill, and bake his bread himself."

Society is a wave. The wave moves onward, but the water of which it is composed, does not. The same particle does not rise from the valley to the ridge. Its unity is only phenomenal. The persons who make up a nation to-day, next year die, and their experience with them.

And so the reliance on Property, including the reliance on governments which protect it, is the want of self-reliance. Men have looked away from themselves and at things so long, that they have come to esteem the religious, learned, and civil institutions, as guards of property, and they deprecate assaults on these, because they feel them to be assaults on property. They measure their esteem of each other, by what each has, and not by what each is. But a cultivated man becomes ashamed of his property, out of new respect for his nature. Especially he hates what he has, if he see that it is accidental,— came to him by inheritance, or gift, or crime; then he feels that it is not having; it does not belong to him, has no root in him, and merely lies there, because no revolution or no robber takes it away. But that which a man is, does always by necessity acquire, and what the man acquires is living property, which does not wait the beck of rulers, or mobs, or revolutions, or fire, or storm, or bankruptcies, but perpetually renews itself wherever the man breathes. "Thy lot or portion of life," said the Caliph Ali,[48] "is seeking after thee; therefore be at rest from seeking after it." Our dependence on these foreign goods leads us to our slavish respect for numbers. The political parties meet in numerous conventions; the greater the concourse, and with each new uproar of announcement, The delegation from Essex![49] The Democrats from New Hampshire! The Whigs of Maine! the young patriot feels himself stronger than before by a new thousand of eyes and arms. In like manner the reformers summon conventions, and vote and resolve in multitude. Not so, O friends! will the God deign to enter and inhabit you, but by a method precisely the reverse. It is only as a man puts off all foreign support, and stands alone, that I see him to be strong and to prevail. He is weaker by every recruit to his banner. Is not a man better than a town? Ask nothing of men, and in the endless mutation, thou only firm column must presently appear the upholder of all that surrounds thee. He who knows that power is inborn, that he is weak because he has looked for good out of him and elsewhere, and so perceiving, throws himself unhesitatingly on his thought, instantly rights himself, stands in the erect position, commands his limbs, works miracles; just as a man who stands on his feet is stronger than a man who stands on his head.

---

[47] French historian Comte Emmanuel Augustin de las Cases (1766–1842).
[48] Ali-ibn-abn-Talib (600?–661), fourth Muslem caliph of Mecca.

[49] County in Massachusetts.

So use all that is called Fortune. Most men gamble with her, and gain all, and lose all, as her wheel rolls. But do thou leave as unlawful these winnings, and deal with Cause and Effect, the chancellors of God. In the Will work and acquire, and thou hast chained the wheel of Chance, and shalt sit hereafter out of fear from her rotations. A political victory, a rise of rents, the recovery of your sick, or the return of your absent friend, or some other favorable event, raises your spirits, and you think good days are preparing for you. Do not believe it. Nothing can bring you peace but yourself. Nothing can bring you peace but the triumph of principles.

1841

The Poet

A moody child and wildly wise
Pursued the game with joyful eyes,
Which chose, like meteors, their way,
And rived the dark with private ray:
They overleapt the horizon's edge,
Searched with Apollo's privilege;
Through man, and woman, and sea, and star,
Saw the dance of nature forward far;
Through worlds, and races, and terms, and times,
Saw musical order, and pairing rhymes.[1]

Olympian bards who sung
Divine ideas below,
Which always find us young,
And always keep us so.[2]

Those who are esteemed umpires of taste, are often persons who have acquired some knowledge of admired pictures or sculptures, and have an inclination for whatever is elegant; but if you inquire whether they are beautiful souls, and whether their own acts are like fair pictures, you learn that they are selfish and sensual. Their cultivation is local, as if you should rub a log of dry wood in one spot to produce fire, all the rest remaining cold. Their knowledge of the fine arts is some study of rules and particulars, or some limited judgment of color or form, which is exercised for amusement or for show. It is a proof of the shallowness of the doctrine of beauty, as it lies in the minds of our amateurs, that men seem to have lost the perception of the instant dependence of form upon soul. There is no doctrine of forms in our philosophy. We were put into our bodies, as fire is put into a pan, to be carried about; but there is no accurate adjustment between the spirit and the organ, much less is the latter the germination of the former. So in regard to other forms, the intellectual men do not believe in any essential depen-

---

[1] From Emerson's unfinished poem "The Poet," published posthumously.

[2] From Emerson's "Ode to Beauty."

dence of the material world on thought and volition. Theologians think it a pretty air-castle to talk of the spiritual meaning of a ship or a cloud, of a city or a contract, but they prefer to come again to the solid ground of historical evidence; and even the poets are contented with a civil and conformed manner of living, and to write poems from the fancy, at a safe distance from their own experience. But the highest minds of the world have never ceased to explore the double meaning, or, shall I say, the quadruple, or the centuple, or much more manifold meaning, of every sensuous fact: Orpheus, Empedocles, Heraclitus, Plato, Plutarch, Dante, Swedenborg,[3] and the masters of sculpture, picture, and poetry. For we are not pans and barrows, nor even porters of the fire and torch-bearers, but children of the fire, made of it, and only the same divinity transmuted, and at two or three removes, when we know least about it. And this hidden truth, that the fountains when all this river of Time, and its creatures, floweth, are intrinsically ideal and beautiful, draws us to the consideration of the nature and functions of the Poet, or the man of Beauty, to the means and materials he uses, and to the general aspect of the art in the present time.

The breadth of the problem is great, for the poet is representative. He stands among partial men for the complete man, and apprises us not of his wealth, but of the commonwealth. The young man reveres men of genius, because, to speak truly, they are more himself than he is. They receive of the soul as he also receives, but they more. Nature enhances her beauty, to the eye of loving men, from their belief that the poet is beholding her shows at the same time. He is isolated among his contemporaries, by truth and by his art, but with this consolation in his pursuits, that they will draw all men sooner or later. For all men live by truth, and stand in need of expression. In love, in art, in avarice, in politics, in labor, in games, we study to utter our painful secret. The man is only half himself, the other half is his expression.

Notwithstanding this necessity to be published, adequate expression is rare. I know not how it is that we need an interpreter; but the great majority of men seem to be minors, who have not yet come into possession of their own, or mutes, who cannot report the conversation they have had with nature. There is no man who does not anticipate a supersensual utility in the sun, and stars, earth, and water. These stand and wait to render him a peculiar service. But there is some obstruction, or some excess of phlegm in our constitution, which does not suffer them to yield the due effect. Too feeble fall the impressions of nature on us to make us artists. Every touch should thrill. Every man should be so much an artist, that he could report in conversation what had befallen him. Yet, in our experience, the rays or appulses[4] have sufficient force to arrive at the senses, but not enough to reach the quick, and compel the reproduction of themselves in speech. The poet is the person in whom these powers are in balance, the man without impediment, who sees and handles that which others dream of, traverses the whole scale of experience, and its representatives of man, in virtue of being the largest power to receive and to impart.

For the Universe has three children, born at one time, which reappear, under different names, in every system of thought, whether they be called cause, operation, and

---

[3] Emerson refers here, respectively, to a mythical Greek poet, Greek philosophers of the fifth, sixth, and fourth centuries b.c., a Greek biographer of the first century, an Italian poet of the Middle Ages, and a Swedish mystical scientist of the eighteenth century.

[4] Potent energies.

effect; or, more poetically, Jove, Pluto, Neptune; or, theologically, the Father, the Spirit, and the Son; but which we will call here, the Knower, the Doer, and the Sayer. These stand respectively for the love of truth, for the love of good, and for the love of beauty. These three are equal. Each is that which he is essentially, so that he cannot be surmounted or analyzed, and each of these three has the power of the others latent in him, and his own patent.

The poet is the sayer, the namer, and represents beauty. He is a sovereign, and stands on the centre. For the world is not painted, or adorned, but is from the beginning beautiful; and God has not made some beautiful things, but Beauty is the creator of the universe. Therefore the poet is not any permissive potentate, but is emperor in his own right. Criticism is infested with a cant of materialism, which assumes that manual skill and activity is the first merit of all men, and disparages such as say and do not, overlooking the fact, that some men, namely, poets, are natural sayers, sent into the world to the end of expression, and confounds them with those whose province is action, but who quit it to imitate the sayers. But Homer's words are as costly and admirable to Homer, as Agamemnon's victories are to Agamemnon. The poet does not wait for the hero or the sage, but, as they act and think primarily, so he writes primarily what will and must be spoken, reckoning the others, though primaries also, yet, in respect to him, secondaries and servants; as sitters or models in the studio of a painter, or as assistants who bring building materials to an architect.

For poetry was all written before time was, and whenever we are so finely organized that we can penetrate into that region where the air is music, we hear those primal warblings, and attempt to write them down, but we lose ever and anon a word, or a verse, and substitute something of our own, and thus miswrite the poem. The men of more delicate ear write down these cadences more faithfully, and these transcripts, though imperfect, become the songs of the nations. For nature is as truly beautiful as it is good, or as it is reasonable, and must as much appear, as it must be done, or be known. Words and deeds are quite indifferent modes of the divine energy. Words are also actions, and actions are a kind of words.

The sign and credentials of the poet are, that he announces that which no man foretold. He is the true and only doctor;[5] he knows and tells; he is the only teller of news, for he was present and privy to the appearance which he describes. He is a beholder of ideas, and an utterer of the necessary and causal. For we do not speak now of men of poetical talents, or of industry and skill in metre, but of the true poet. I took part in a conversation the other day, concerning a recent writer of lyrics, a man of subtle mind, whose head appeared to be a music-box of delicate tunes and rhythms, and whose skill, and command of language, we could not sufficiently praise. But when the question arose, whether he was not only a lyrist, but a poet, we were obliged to confess that he is plainly a contemporary, not an eternal man. He does not stand out of our low limitations, like a Chimborazo[6] under the line, running up from the torrid base through all the climates of the globe, with belts of the herbage of every latitude on its high and mottled sides; but this genius is the landscape-garden of a modern house, adorned with fountains and statues, with well-bred men and women standing and sitting in the walks

[5] In the traditional Latin sense, teacher.
[6] Mountain in Ecuador located below the equator.

and terraces. We hear, through all the varied music, the ground-tone of conventional life. Our poets are men of talents who sing, and not the children of music. The argument is secondary, the finish of the verses is primary.

For it is not metres, but a metre-making argument, that makes a poem,—a thought so passionate and alive, that, like the spirit of a plant or an animal, it has an architecture of its own, and adorns nature with a new thing. The thought and the form are equal in the order of time, but in the order of genesis the thought is prior to the form. The poet has a new thought: he has a whole new experience to unfold; he will tell us how it was with him, and all men will be the richer in his fortune. For, the experience of each new age requires a new confession, and the world seems always waiting for its poet. I remember, when I was young, how much I was moved one morning by tidings that genius had appeared in a youth who sat near me at table. He had left his work, and gone rambling none knew whither, and had written hundreds of lines, but could not tell whether that which was in him was therein told: he could tell nothing but that all was changed,—man, beast, heaven, earth, and sea. How gladly we listened! how credulous! Society seemed to be compromised. We sat in the aurora of a sunrise which was to put out all the stars. Boston seemed to be at twice the distance it had the night before, or was much farther than that. Rome,—what was Rome? Plutarch and Shakspeare were in the yellow leaf,[7] and Homer no more should be heard of. It is much to know that poetry has been written this very day, under this very roof, by your side. What! that wonderful spirit has not expired! these stony moments are still sparkling and animated! I had fancied that the oracles were all silent, and nature had spent her fires, and behold! all night, from every pore, these fine auroras have been streaming. Every one has some interest in the advent of the poet, and no one knows how much it may concern him. We know that the secret of the world is profound, but who or what shall be our interpreter, we know not. A mountain ramble, a new style of face, a new person, may put the key into our hands. Of course, the value of genius to us is in the veracity of its report. Talent may frolic and juggle; genius realizes and adds. Mankind, in good earnest, have availed so far in understanding themselves and their work, that the foremost watchman on the peak announces his news. It is the truest word ever spoken, and the phrase will be the fittest, most musical, and the unerring voice of the world for that time.

All that we call sacred history attests that the birth of a poet is the principal event in chronology. Man, never so often deceived, still watches for the arrival of a brother who can hold him steady to a truth, until he has made it his own. With what joy I begin to read a poem, which I confide in as an inspiration! And now my chains are to be broken; I shall mount above these clouds and opaque airs in which I live,—opaque, though they seem transparent,—and from the heaven of truth I shall see and comprehend my relations. That will reconcile me to life, and renovate nature, to see trifles animated by a tendency, and to know what I am doing. Life will no more be a noise; now I shall see men and women, and know the signs by which they may be discerned from fools and satans. This day shall be better than my birth-day: then I became an animal: now I am invited into the science of the real. Such is the hope, but the fruition is postponed. Oftener it falls, that this winged man, who will carry me into the heaven, whirls me into the

---

[7] *Macbeth,* Act V, Sc. iii, ll. 22–23: "I have lived long enough. My way of life is fallen into the sere, the yellow leaf."

clouds, then leaps and frisks about with me from cloud to cloud, still affirming that he is bound heavenward; and I, being myself a novice, am slow in perceiving that he does not know the way into the heavens, and is merely bent that I should admire his skill to rise, like a fowl or a flying fish, a little way from the ground or the water; but the all-piercing, all-feeding, and ocular air of heaven, that man shall never inhabit. I tumble down again soon into my old nooks, and lead the life of exaggerations as before, and have lost my faith in the possibility of any guide who can lead me thither where I would be.

But leaving these victims of vanity, let us, with new hope, observe how nature, by worthier impulses, has ensured the poet's fidelity to his office of announcement and affirming, namely, by the beauty of things, which becomes a new, and higher beauty, when expressed. Nature offers all her creatures to him as a picture-language. Being used as a type, a second wonderful value appears in the object, far better than its old value, as the carpenter's stretched cord, if you hold your ear close enough, is musical in the breeze. "Things more excellent than every image," says Jamblichus,[8] "are expressed through images." Things admit of being used as symbols, because nature is a symbol, in the whole, and in every part. Every line we can draw in the sand, has expression; and there is no body without its spirit or genius. All form is an effect of character; all condition, of the quality of the life; all harmony, of health; (and, for this reason, a perception of beauty should be sympathetic, or proper only to the good.) The beautiful rests on the foundations of the necessary. The soul makes the body, as the wise Spenser teaches:—

> "So every spirit, as it is most pure,
>   And hath in it the more of heavenly light,
>   So it the fairer body doth procure
>   To habit in, and it more fairly dight,
>   With cheerful grace and amiable sight.
>   For, of the soul, the body form doth take,
>   For soul is form, and doth the body make."[9]

Here we find ourselves, suddenly, not in a critical speculation, but in a holy place, and should go very warily and reverently. We stand before the secret of the world, there where Being passes into Appearance, and Unity into Variety.

The Universe is the externisation of the soul. Wherever the life is, that bursts into appearance around it. Our science is sensual, and therefore superficial. The earth, and the heavenly bodies, physics, and chemistry, we sensually treat, as if they were self-existent; but these are the retinue of that Being we have. "The mighty heaven," said Proclus,[10] "exhibits, in its transfigurations, clear images of the splendor of intellectual perceptions; being moved in conjunction with the unapparent periods of intellectual natures." Therefore, science always goes abreast with the just elevation of the man, keeping step with religion and metaphysics; or, the state of science is an index of our self-knowledge. Since everything in nature answers to a moral power, if any phenomenon remains brute and dark, it is that the corresponding faculty in the observer is not yet active.

No wonder, then, if these waters be so deep, that we hover over them with a religious

---

[8] Philosopher of the fourth century who advocated Neoplatonism, a religious mysticism drawing on elements of Greek philosophy.

[9] From "An Hymn in Honor of Beauty"

(1596) by English poet Edmund Spenser (1552?–1599).

[10] Greek Neoplatonic philosopher (411–485).

regard. The beauty of the fable proves the importance of the sense; to the poet, and to all others; or, if you please, every man is so far a poet as to be susceptible of these enchantments of nature: for all men have the thoughts whereof the universe is the celebration. I find that the fascination resides in the symbol. Who loves nature? Who does not? Is it only poets, and men of leisure and cultivation, who live with her? No; but also hunters, farmers, grooms, and butchers, though they express their affection in their choice of life, and not in their choice of words. The writer wonders what the coachman or the hunter values in riding, in horses, and dogs. It is not superficial qualities. When you talk with him, he holds these at as slight a rate as you. His worship is sympathetic; he has no definitions, but he is commanded in nature, by the living power which he feels to be there present. No imitation, or playing of these things, would content him; he loves the earnest of the northwind, of rain, of stone, and wood, and iron. A beauty not explicable, is dearer than a beauty which we can see to the end of. It is nature the symbol, nature certifying the supernatural, body overflowed by life, which he worships, with coarse, but sincere rites.

The inwardness, and mystery, of this attachment, drives men of every class to the use of emblems. The schools of poets, and philosophers, are not more intoxicated with their symbols, than the populace with theirs. In our political parties, compute the power of badges and emblems. See the great ball which they roll from Baltimore to Bunker hill![11] In the political processions, Lowell goes in a loom, and Lynn in a shoe, and Salem in a ship.[12] Witness the cider-barrel, the log-cabin, the hickory-stick, the palmetto, and all the cognizances of party. See the power of national emblems. Some stars, lilies, leopards, a crescent, a lion, an eagle, or other figure, which came into credit God knows how, on an old rag of bunting, blowing in the wind, on a fort, at the ends of the earth, shall make the blood tingle under the rudest, or the most conventional exterior. The people fancy they hate poetry, and they are all poets and mystics!

Beyond this universality of the symbolic language, we are apprised of the divineness of this superior use of things, whereby the world is a temple, whose walls are covered with emblems, pictures, and commandments of the Deity, in this, that there is no fact in nature which does not carry the whole sense of nature; and the distinctions which we make in events, and in affairs, of low and high, honest and base, disappear when nature is used as a symbol. Thought makes every thing fit for use. The vocabulary of an omniscient man would embrace words and images excluded from polite conversation. What would be base, or even obscene, to the obscene, becomes illustrious, spoken in a new connexion of thought. The piety of the Hebrew prophets purges their grossness. The circumcision is an example of the power of poetry to raise the low and offensive. Small and mean things serve as well as great symbols. The meaner the type by which a law is expressed, the more pungent it is, and the more lasting in the memories of men: just as we choose the smallest box, or case, in which any needful utensil can be carried. Bare lists of words are found suggestive, to an imaginative and excited mind; as it is related of Lord Chatham,[13] that he was accustomed to read in Bailey's Dictionary, when he was

[11] Allusion to a political gimmick used by the 1840 campaign supporters of W. H. Harrison: "Keep the ball a-rolling."
[12] The towns of Lowell, Lynn, and Salem, Massachusetts, are represented by their major products.

[13] William Pitt (1708–1778), earl of Chatham, was a powerfully eloquent English statesman.

preparing to speak in Parliament. The poorest experience is rich enough for all the purposes of expressing thought. Why covet a knowledge of new facts? Day and night, house and garden, a few books, a few actions, serve us as well as would all trades and all spectacles. We are far from having exhausted the significance of the few symbols we use. We can come to use them yet with a terrible simplicity. It does not need that a poem should be long. Every word was once a poem. Every new relation is a new word. Also, we use defects and deformities to a sacred purpose, so expressing our sense that the evils of the world are such only to the evil eye. In the old mythology, mythologists observe, defects are ascribed to divine natures, as lameness to Vulcan, blindness to Cupid, and the like, to signify exuberances.

For, as it is dislocation and detachment from the life of God, that makes things ugly, the poet, who re-attaches things to nature and the Whole,—re-attaching even artificial things, and violations of nature, to nature, by a deeper insight,—disposes very easily of the most disagreeable facts. Readers of poetry see the factory-village, and the railway, and fancy that the poetry of the landscape is broken up by these; for these works of art are not yet consecrated in their reading; but the poet sees them fall within the great Order not less than the bee-hive, or the spider's geometrical web. Nature adopts them very fast into her vital circles, and the gliding train of cars she loves like her own. Besides, in a centred mind, it signifies nothing how many mechanical inventions you exhibit. Though you add millions, and never so surprising, the fact of mechanics has not gained a grain's weight. The spiritual fact remains unalterable, by many or by few particulars; as no mountain is of any appreciable height to break the curve of the sphere. A shrewd country-boy goes to the city for the first time, and the complacent citizen is not satisfied with his little wonder. It is not that he does not see all the fine houses, and know that he never saw such before, but he disposes of them as easily as the poet finds place for the railway. The chief value of the new fact, is to enhance the great and constant fact of Life, which can dwarf any and every circumstance, and to which the belt of wampum, and the commerce of America, are alike.

The world being thus put under the mind for verb and noun, the poet is he who can articulate it. For, though life is great, and fascinates, and absorbs,—and though all men are intelligent of the symbols through which it is named,—yet they cannot originally use them. We are symbols, and inhabit symbols; workman, work, and tools, words and things, birth and death, all are emblems; but we sympathize with the symbols, and, being infatuated with the economical uses of things, we do not know that they are thoughts. The poet, by an ulterior intellectual perception, gives them a power which makes their old use forgotten, and puts eyes, and a tongue, into every dumb and inanimate object. He perceives the independence of the thought on the symbol, the stability of the thought, the accidency and fugacity of the symbol. As the eyes of Lyncæus[14] were said to see through the earth, so the poet turns the world to glass, and shows us all things in their right series and procession. For, through that better perception, he stands one step nearer to things, and sees the flowing or metamorphosis; perceives that thought is multiform; that within the form of every creature is a force impelling it to ascend into a higher form; and, following with his eyes the life, uses the forms which express that life, and so his speech flows with the flowing of nature. All the facts of the an-

[14] In Greek myth, the sailor with the keenest eye.

imal economy, sex, nutriment, gestation, birth, growth, are symbols of the passage of
the world into the soul of man, to suffer there a change, and reappear, a new and higher
fact. He uses forms according to the life, and not according to the form. This is true science. The poet alone knows astronomy, chemistry, vegetation, and animation, for he
does not stop at these facts, but employs them as signs. He knows why the plain, or
meadow of space, was strown with these flowers we call suns, and moons, and stars;
why the great deep is adorned with animals, with men, and gods; for, in every word he
speaks he rides on them as the horses of thought.

By virtue of this science the poet is the Namer, or Language-maker, naming things
sometimes after their appearance, sometimes after their essence, and giving to every
one its own name and not another's, thereby rejoicing the intellect, which delights in
detachment or boundary. The poets made all the words, and therefore language is the
archives of history, and, if we must say it, a sort of tomb of the muses. For, though the
origin of most of our words is forgotten, each word was at first a stroke of genius, and
obtained currency, because for the moment it symbolized the world to the first speaker
and to the hearer. The etymologist finds the deadest word to have been once a brilliant
picture. Language is fossil poetry. As the limestone of the continent consists of infinite
masses of the shells of animalcules, so language is made up of images, or tropes, which
now, in their secondary use, have long ceased to remind us of their poetic origin. But
the poet names the thing because he sees it, or comes one step nearer to it than any
other. This expression, or naming, is not art, but a second nature, grown out of the first,
as a leaf out of a tree. What we call nature, is a certain self-regulated motion, or change;
and nature does all things by her own hands, and does not leave another to baptise her,
but baptises herself; and this through the metamorphosis again. I remember that a certain poet[15] described it to me thus:

Genius is the activity which repairs the decays of things, whether wholly or partly of a
material and finite kind. Nature, through all her kingdoms, insures herself. Nobody
cares for planting the poor fungus: so she shakes down from the gills of one agaric
countless spores, any one of which, being preserved, transmits new billions of spores to-
morrow or next day. The new agaric of this hour has a chance which the old one had
not. This atom of seed is thrown into a new place, not subject to the accidents which destroyed its parent two rods off. She makes a man; and having brought him to ripe age,
she will no longer run the risk of losing this wonder at a blow, but she detaches from
him a new self, that the kind may be safe from accidents to which the individual is exposed. So when the soul of the poet has come to ripeness of thought, she detaches and
sends away from it its poems or songs,—a fearless, sleepless, deathless progeny, which is
not exposed to the accidents of the weary kingdom of time: a fearless, vivacious offspring, clad with wings (such was the virtue of the soul out of which they came), which
carry them fast and far, and infix them irrecoverably into the hearts of men. These
wings are the beauty of the poet's soul. The songs, thus flying immortal from their mortal parent, are pursued by clamorous flights of censures, which swarm in far greater
numbers, and threaten to devour them; but these last are not winged. At the end of a
very short leap they fall plump down, and rot, having received from the souls out of

[15] Presumably this is a droll reference to
Emerson himself.

which they came no beautiful wings. But the melodies of the poet ascend, and leap, and pierce into the deeps of infinite time.

So far the bard taught me, using his freer speech. But nature has a higher end, in the production of new individuals, than security, namely, *ascension,* or, the passage of the soul into higher forms. I knew, in my younger days, the sculptor who made the statue of the youth which stands in the public garden. He was, as I remember, unable to tell directly, what made him happy, or unhappy, but by wonderful indirections he could tell. He rose one day, according to his habit, before the dawn, and saw the morning break, grand as the eternity out of which it came, and, for many days after, he strove to express this tranquillity, and, lo! his chisel had fashioned out of marble the form of a beautiful youth, Phosphorus,[16] whose aspect is such, that, it is said, all persons who look on it become silent. The poet also resigns himself to his mood, and that thought which agitated him is expressed, but *alter idem,*[17] in a manner totally new. The expression is organic, or, the new type which things themselves take when liberated. As, in the sun, objects paint their images on the retina of the eye, so they, sharing the aspiration of the whole universe, tend to paint a far more delicate copy of their essence in his mind. Like the metamorphosis of things into higher organic forms, is their change into melodies. Over everything stands its dæmon, or soul, and, as the form of the thing is reflected by the eye, so the soul of the thing is reflected by a melody. The sea, the mountain-ridge, Niagara, and every flower-bed, pre-exist, or super-exist, in pre-cantations,[18] which sail like odors in the air, and when any man goes by with an ear sufficiently fine, he overhears them, and endeavors to write down the notes, without diluting or depraving them. And herein is the legitimation of criticism, in the mind's faith, that the poems are a corrupt version of some text in nature, with which they ought to be made to tally. A rhyme in one of our sonnets should not be less pleasing than the iterated nodes of a sea-shell, or the resembling difference of a group of flowers. The pairing of the birds is an idyl, not tedious as our idyls are; a tempest is a rough ode, without falsehood or rant: a summer, with its harvest sown, reaped, and stored, is an epic song, subordinating how many admirably executed parts. Why should not the symmetry and truth that modulate these, glide into our spirits, and we participate the invention of nature?

This insight, which expresses itself by what is called Imagination, is a very high sort of seeing, which does not come by study, but by the intellect being where and what it sees, by sharing the path, or circuit of things through forms, and so making them translucid to others. The path of things is silent. Will they suffer a speaker to go with them? A spy they will not suffer; a lover, a poet, is the transcendency of their own nature,—him they will suffer. The condition of true naming, on the poet's part, is his resigning himself to the divine aura which breathes through forms, and accompanying that.

It is a secret which every intellectual man quickly learns, that, beyond the energy of his possessed and conscious intellect, he is capable of a new energy (as of an intellect doubled on itself), by abandonment to the nature of things; that, beside his privacy of power as an individual man, there is a great public power, on which he can draw, by unlocking, at all risks, his human doors, and suffering the ethereal tides to roll and circulate through him: then he is caught up into the life of the Universe, his speech is thun-

---

[16] "Light-bearing," a mythical Greek god associated with the morning star.

[17] Latin: "the same yet not identical."

[18] Incantations that are foretelling.

der, his thought is law, and his words are universally intelligible as the plants and animals. The poet knows that he speaks adequately, then, only when he speaks somewhat wildly, or, "with the flower of the mind;" not with the intellect, used as an organ, but with the intellect released from all service, and suffered to take its direction from its celestial life; or, as the ancients were wont to express themselves, not with intellect alone, but with the intellect inebriated by nectar. As the traveller who has lost his way, throws his reins on his horse's neck, and trusts to the instinct of the animal to find his road, so must we do with the divine animal who carries us through this world. For if in any manner we can stimulate this instinct, new passages are opened for us into nature, the mind flows into and through things hardest and highest, and the metamorphosis is possible.

This is the reason why bards love wine, mead, narcotics, coffee, tea, opium, the fumes of sandal-wood and tobacco, or whatever other species of animal exhilaration. All men avail themselves of such means as they can, to add this extraordinary power to their normal powers; and to this end they prize conversation, music, pictures, sculpture, dancing, theatres, travelling, war, mobs, fires, gaming, politics, or love, or science, or animal intoxication, which are several coarser or finer *quasi*-mechanical substitutes for the true nectar, which is the ravishment of the intellect by coming nearer to the fact. These are auxiliaries to the centrifugal tendency of a man, to his passage out into free space, and they help him to escape the custody of that body in which he is pent up, and of that jail-yard of individual relations in which he is enclosed. Hence a great number of such as were professionally expressors of Beauty, as painters, poets, musicians, and actors, have been more than others wont to lead a life of pleasure and indulgence; all but the few who received the true nectar; and, as it was a spurious mode of attaining freedom, as it was an emancipation not into the heavens, but into the freedom of baser places, they were punished for that advantage they won, by a dissipation and deterioration. But never can any advantage be taken of nature by a trick. The spirit of the world, the great calm presence of the creator, comes not forth to the sorceries of opium or of wine. The sublime vision comes to the pure and simple soul in a clean and chaste body. That is not an inspiration which we owe to narcotics, but some counterfeit excitement and fury. Milton says, that the lyric poet may drink wine and live generously, but the epic poet, he who shall sing of the gods, and their descent unto men, must drink water out of a wooden bowl.[19] For poetry is not 'Devil's wine,' but God's wine. It is with this as it is with toys. We fill the hands and nurseries of our children with all manner of dolls, drums, and horses, withdrawing their eyes from the plain face and sufficing objects of nature, the sun, and moon, the animals, the water, and stones, which should be their toys. So the poet's habit of living should be set on a key so low and plain, that the common influences should delight him. His cheerfulness should be the gift of the sunlight; the air should suffice for his inspiration, and he should be tipsy with water. That spirit which suffices quiet hearts, which seems to come forth to such from every dry knoll of sere grass, from every pine-stump, and half-imbedded stone, on which the dull March sun shines, comes forth to the poor and hungry, and such as are of simple taste. If thou fill thy brain with Boston and New York, with fashion and covetousness, and wilt stimulate thy jaded senses with wine and French coffee, thou shalt find no radiance of wisdom in the lonely waste of the pinewoods.

[19] Restated from "Sixth Latin Elegy," a poem
    by John Milton.

If the imagination intoxicates the poet, it is not inactive in other men. The metamorphosis excites in the beholder an emotion of joy. The use of symbols has a certain power of emancipation and exhilaration for all men. We seem to be touched by a wand, which makes us dance and run about happily, like children. We are like persons who come out of a cave or cellar into the open air. This is the effect on us of tropes, fables, oracles, and all poetic forms. Poets are thus liberating gods. Men have really got a new sense, and found within their world, another world, or nest of worlds; for, the metamorphosis once seen, we divine that it does not stop. I will not now consider how much this makes the charm of algebra and the mathematics, which also have their tropes, but it is felt in every definition; as, when Aristotle defines *space* to be an immovable vessel, in which things are contained;—or, when Plato defines a *line* to be a flowing point; or, *figure* to be bound of solid; and many the like. What a joyful sense of freedom we have, when Vitruvius[20] announces the old opinion of artists, that no architect can build any house well, who does not know something of anatomy. When Socrates, in Charmides,[21] tells us that the soul is cured of its maladies by certain incantations, and that these incantations are beautiful reasons, from which temperance is generated in souls; when Plato calls the world an animal; and Timæus[22] affirms that the plants also are animals; or affirms a man to be a heavenly tree, growing with his root, which is his head, upward; and, as George Chapman, following him, writes,—

> "So in our tree of man, whose nervie root
> Springs in his top;"[23]

when Orpheus speaks of hoariness as "that white flower which marks extreme old age;" when Proclus calls the universe the statue of the intellect; when Chaucer, in his praise of "Gentilesse,"[24] compares good blood in mean condition to fire, which, though carried to the darkest house betwixt this and the mount of Caucasus, will yet hold its natural office, and burn as bright as if twenty thousand men did it behold, when John saw, in the apocalypse, the ruin of the world through evil, and the stars fall from heaven, as the figtree casteth her untimely fruit;[25] when Æsop reports the whole catalogue of common daily relations through the masquerade of birds and beasts;—we take the cheerful hint of the immortality of our essence, and its versatile habit and escapes, as when the gypsies say, "it is in vain to hang them, they cannot die."

The poets are thus liberating gods. The ancient British bards had for the title of their order, "Those who are free throughout the world." They are free, and they make free. An imaginative book renders us much more service at first, by stimulating us through its tropes, than afterward, when we arrive at the precise sense of the author. I think nothing is of any value in books, excepting the transcendental and extraordinary. If a man is inflamed and carried away by his thought, to that degree that he forgets the authors and the public, and heeds only this one dream, which holds him like an insanity, let me read his paper, and you may have all the arguments and histories and criticism.

[20] Roman architect and writer.
[21] Dialogue of Plato.
[22] Another dialogue of Plato.
[23] Excerpt from George Chapman's (1559?–?1634) dedication to his translation of Homer.

[24] In "The Wife of Bath's Tale" by Geoffrey Chaucer.
[25] See Revelation 6:13.

All the value which attaches to Pythagoras, Paracelsus, Cornelius Agrippa, Cardan, Kepler, Swedenborg, Schelling, Oken,[26] or any other who introduces questionable facts into his cosmogony, as angels, devils, magic, astrology, palmistry, mesmerism, and so on, is the certificate we have of departure from routine, and that here is a new witness. That also is the best success in conversation, the magic of liberty, which puts the world, like a ball, in our hands. How cheap even the liberty then seems; how mean to study, when an emotion communicates to the intellect the power to sap and upheave nature: how great the perspective! nations, times, systems, enter and disappear, like threads in tapestry of large figure and many colors; dream delivers us to dream, and, while the drunkenness lasts, we will sell our bed, our philosophy, our religion, in our opulence.

There is good reason why we should prize this liberation. The fate of the poor shepherd, who, blinded and lost in the snowstorm, perishes in a drift within a few feet of his cottage door, is an emblem of the state of man. On the brink of the waters of life and truth, we are miserably dying. The inaccessibleness of every thought but that we are in, is wonderful. What if you come near to it,—you are as remote, when you are nearest, as when you are farthest. Every thought is also a prison; every heaven is also a prison. Therefore we love the poet, the inventor, who in any form, whether in an ode, or in an action, or in looks and behavior, has yielded us a new thought. He unlocks our chains, and admits us to a new scene.

This emancipation is dear to all men, and the power to impart it, as it must come from greater depth and scope of thought, is a measure of intellect. Therefore all books of the imagination endure, all which ascend to that truth, that the writer sees nature beneath him, and uses it as his exponent. Every verse or sentence, possessing this virtue, will take care of its own immortality. The religions of the world are the ejaculations of a few imaginative men.

But the quality of the imagination is to flow, and not to freeze. The poet did not stop at the color, or the form, but read their meaning; neither may he rest in this meaning, but he makes the same objects exponents of his new thought. Here is the difference betwixt the poet and the mystic, that the last nails a symbol to one sense, which was a true sense for a moment, but soon becomes old and false. For all symbols are fluxional; all language is vehicular and transitive, and is good, as ferries and horses are, for conveyance, not as farms and houses are, for homestead. Mysticism consists in the mistake of an accidental and individual symbol for an universal one. The morning-redness happens to be the favorite meteor to the eyes of Jacob Behmen,[27] and comes to stand to him for truth and faith; and he believes should stand for the same realities to every reader. But the first reader prefers as naturally the symbol of a mother and child, or a gardener and his bulb, or a jeweller polishing a gem. Either of these, or of a myriad more, are equally good to the person to whom they are significant. Only they must be held lightly,

---

[26] All of the following were dedicated to theoretical speculation. Pythagoras: Greek mathematician and mystic philosopher (sixth century B.C.); Paracelsus: Swiss alchemist Philippus Paracelsus (1493–1541); Cornelius Agrippa: German physician (1486?–1535); Cardan: Italian mathematician Jerome Cardan (1501–1576); Kepler: German astronomer Johannes Kepler (1571–1630); Swedenborg: Swedish philosopher and religious writer Emanuel Swedenborg (1688–1772); Schelling: German philosopher Freidrich von Schelling (1775–1854); Oken: German naturalist Lorenz Oken (1779–1851).

[27] German theosophist and mystic (1575–1624).

and be very willingly translated into the equivalent terms which others use. And the mystic must be steadily told,—All that you say is just as true without the tedious use of that symbol as with it. Let us have a little algebra, instead of this trite rhetoric,—universal signs, instead of these village symbols,—and we shall both be gainers. The history of hierarchies seems to show, that all religious error consisted in making the symbol too stark and solid, and, at last, nothing but an excess of the organ of language.

Swedenborg, of all men in the recent ages, stands eminently for the translator of nature into thought. I do not know the man in history to whom things stood so uniformly for words. Before him the metamorphosis continually plays. Everything on which his eye rests, obeys the impulses of moral nature. The figs become grapes whilst he eats them. When some of his angels affirmed a truth, the laurel twig which they held blossomed in their hands. The noise which, at a distance, appeared like gnashing and thumping, on coming nearer was found to be the voice of disputants. The men, in one of his visions, seen in heavenly light, appeared like dragons, and seemed in darkness; but, to each other, they appeared as men, and, when the light from heaven shone into their cabin, they complained of the darkness, and were compelled to shut the window that they might see.

There was this perception in him, which makes the poet or seer, an object of awe and terror, namely, that the same man, or society of men, may wear one aspect to themselves and their companions, and a different aspect to higher intelligences. Certain priests, whom he describes as conversing very learnedly together, appeared to the children, who were at some distance, like dead horses: and many the like misappearances. And instantly the mind inquires, whether these fishes under the bridge, yonder oxen in the pasture, those dogs in the yard, are immutably fishes, oxen, and dogs, or only so appear to me, and perchance to themselves appear upright men; and whether I appear as a man to all eyes. The Bramins and Pythagoras propounded the same question, and if any poet has witnessed the transformation, he doubtless found it in harmony with various experiences. We have all seen changes as considerable in wheat and caterpillars. He is the poet, and shall draw us with love and terror, who sees, through the flowing vest, the firm nature, and can declare it.

I look in vain for the poet whom I describe. We do not, with sufficient plainness, or sufficient profoundness, address ourselves to life, nor dare we chaunt our own times and social circumstance. If we filled the day with bravery, we should not shrink from celebrating it. Time and nature yield us many gifts, but not yet the timely man, the new religion, the reconciler, whom all things await. Dante's praise is, that he dared to write his autobiography in colossal cipher, or into universality. We have yet had no genius in America, with tyrannous eye, which knew the value of our incomparable materials, and saw, in the barbarism and materialism of the times, another carnival of the same gods whose picture he so much admires in Homer; then in the middle age; then in Calvinism. Banks and tariffs, the newspaper and caucus, methodism and unitarianism, are flat and dull to dull people, but rest on the same foundations of wonder as the town of Troy, and the temple of Delphos, and are as swiftly passing away. Our logrolling, our stumps[28] and their politics, our fisheries, our Negroes, and Indians, our boats, and our repudiations, the wrath of rogues, and the pusillanimity of honest men, the northern trade, the southern planting, the western clearing, Oregon, and Texas, are yet unsung. Yet America is a poem in our eyes; its ample geography dazzles the imagination, and it

[28] Political deceptions; public speaking.

will not wait long for metres. If I have not found that excellent combination of gifts in my countrymen which I seek, neither could I aid myself to fix the idea of the poet by reading now and then in Chalmers's[29] collection of five centuries of English poets. These are wits, more than poets, though there have been poets among them. But when we adhere to the ideal of the poet, we have our difficulties even with Milton and Homer. Milton is too literary, and Homer too literal and historical.

But I am not wise enough for a national criticism, and must use the old largeness a little longer, to discharge my errand from the muse to the poet concerning his art.

Art is the path of the creator to his work. The paths, or methods, are ideal and eternal, though few men ever see them, not the artist himself for years, or for a lifetime, unless he come into the conditions. The painter, the sculptor, the composer, the epic rhapsodist, the orator, all partake one desire, namely, to express themselves symmetrically and abundantly, not dwarfishly and fragmentarily. They found or put themselves in certain conditions, as, the painter and sculptor before some impressive human figures; the orator, into the assembly of the people; and the others, in such scenes as each has found exciting to his intellect; and each presently feels the new desire. He hears a voice, he sees a beckoning. Then he is apprised, with wonder, what herds of dæmons hem him in. He can no more rest; he says, with the old painter, "By God, it is in me, and must go forth of me." He pursues a beauty, half seen, which flies before him. The poet pours out verses in every solitude. Most of the things he says are conventional, no doubt; but by and by he says something which is original and beautiful. That charms him. He would say nothing else but such things. In our way of talking, we say, "That is yours, this is mine;" but the poet knows well that it is not his; that it is as strange and beautiful to him as to you; he would fain hear the like eloquence at length. Once having tasted this immortal ichor, he cannot have enough of it, and, as an admirable creative power exists in these intellections, it is of the last importance that these things get spoken. What a little of all we know is said! What drops of all the sea of our science are baled up! and by what accident it is that these are exposed, when so many secrets sleep in nature! Hence the necessity of speech and song; hence these throbs and heart-beatings in the orator, at the door of the assembly, to the end, namely, that thought may be ejaculated as Logos, or Word.

Doubt not, O poet, but persist. Say, "It is in me, and shall out." Stand there, baulked and dumb, stuttering and stammering, hissed and hooted, stand and strive, until, at last, rage draw out of thee that *dream*-power which every night shows thee is thine own; a power transcending all limit and privacy, and by virtue of which a man is the conductor of the whole river of electricity. Nothing walks, or creeps, or grows, or exists, which must not in turn arise and walk before him as exponent of his meaning. Comes he to that power, his genius is no longer exhaustible. All the creatures, by pairs and by tribes, pour into his mind as into a Noah's ark, to come forth again to people a new world. This is like the stock of air for our respiration, or for the combustion of our fireplace, not a measure of gallons, but the entire atmosphere if wanted. And therefore the rich poets, as Homer, Chaucer, Shakspeare, and Raphael, have obviously no limits to their works, except the limits of their lifetime, and resemble a mirror carried through the street, ready to render an image of every created thing.

---

[29] Scottish journalist and biographer Alexander Chalmers (1759–1834) compiled an extensive collection of English poetry (1810).

O poet! a new nobility is conferred in groves and pastures, and not in castles, or by the sword-blade, any longer. The conditions are hard, but equal. Thou shalt leave the world, and know the muse only. Thou shalt not know any longer the times, customs, graces, politics, or opinions of men, but shalt take all from the muse. For the time of towns is tolled from the world by funereal chimes, but in nature the universal hours are counted by succeeding tribes of animals and plants, and by growth of joy on joy. God wills also that thou abdicate a manifold and duplex life, and that thou be content that others speak for thee. Others shall be thy gentlemen, and shall represent all courtesy and worldly life for thee; others shall do the great and resounding actions also. Thou shalt lie close hid with nature, and canst not be afforded to the Capitol or the Exchange. The world is full of renunciations and apprenticeships, and this is thine: thou must pass for a fool and a churl for a long season. This is the screen and sheath in which Pan[30] has protected his well-beloved flower, and thou shalt be known only to thine own, and they shall console thee with tenderest love. And thou shalt not be able to rehearse the names of thy friends in thy verse, for an old shame before the holy ideal. And this is the reward: that the ideal shall be real to thee, and the impressions of the actual world shall fall like summer rain, copious, but not troublesome, to thy invulnerable essence. Thou shalt have the whole land for thy park and manor, the sea for thy bath and navigation, without tax and without envy; the woods and the rivers thou shalt own; and thou shalt possess that wherein others are only tenants and boarders. Thou true land-lord! sea-lord! air-lord! Wherever snow falls, or water flows, or birds fly, wherever day and night meet in twilight, wherever the blue heaven is hung by clouds, or sown with stars, wherever are forms with transparent boundaries, wherever are outlets into celestial space, wherever is danger, and awe, and love, there is Beauty, plenteous as rain, shed for thee, and though thou shouldest walk the world over, thou shalt not be able to find a condition inopportune or ignoble.

1844

Experience*

The lords of life, the lords of life,—
I saw them pass,
In their own guise,
Like and unlike,
Portly and grim,
Use and Surprise,
Surface and Dream,
Succession swift, and spectral Wrong,
Temperament without a tongue,

---

[30] God of the woods and fields in Greek mythology.

* This essay appeared in January 1842, shortly after the death of Emerson's young son Waldo.

And the inventor of the game
Omnipresent without name;—
Some to see, some to be guessed,
They marched from east to west:
Little man, least of all,
Among the legs of his guardians tall,
Walked about with puzzled look:—
Him by the hand dear nature took;
Dearest nature, strong and kind,
Whispered, "Darling, never mind!
Tomorrow they will wear another face,
The founder thou! these are thy race!"[1]

Where do we find ourselves? In a series[2] of which we do not know the extremes, and believe that it has none. We wake and find ourselves on a stair; there are stairs below us, which we seem to have ascended; there are stairs above us, many a one, which go upward and out of sight. But the Genius[3] which, according to the old belief, stands at the door by which we enter, and gives us the lethe[4] to drink, that we may tell no tales, mixed the cup too strongly, and we cannot shake off the lethargy now at noonday. Sleep lingers all our lifetime about our eyes, as night hovers all day in the boughs of the fir-tree. All things swim and glitter. Our life is not so much threatened as our perception. Ghost-like we glide through nature, and should not know our place again. Did our birth fall in some fit of indigence and frugality in nature, that she was so sparing of her fire and so liberal of her earth, that it appears to us that we lack the affirmative principle, and though we have health and reason, yet we have no superfluity of spirit for new creation? We have enough to live and bring the year about, but not an ounce to impart or to invest. Ah that our Genius were a little more of a genius! We are like millers on the lower levels of a stream, when the factories above them have exhausted the water. We too fancy that the upper people must have raised their dams.

If any of us knew what we were doing, or where we are going, then when we think we best know! We do not know today whether we are busy or idle. In times when we thought ourselves indolent, we have afterwards discovered, that much was accomplished, and much was begun in us. All our days are so unprofitable while they pass, that 'tis wonderful where or when we ever got anything of this which we call wisdom, poetry, virtue. We never got it on any dated calendar day. Some heavenly days must have been intercalated somewhere, like those that Hermes won with dice of the Moon, that Osiris[5] might be born. It is said, all martyrdoms looked mean when they were suffered. Every ship is a romantic object, except that we sail in. Embark, and the romance quits our vessel, and hangs on every other sail in the horizon. Our life looks trivial, and

---

[1] The epigraph is Emerson's.

[2] In mathematics, a sequence of terms.

[3] Personal guardian spirit.

[4] Water from Lethe, the mythic river of forgetfulness.

[5] In Plutarch's *Morals,* the mythological sun god Cronus declared that his wife, Rhea, could not give birth to her lover's child on any day of the year. Because Hermes won five new days for the calendar by shooting dice with the Moon, Rhea was nevertheless able to deliver Osiris, the highest Egyptian divinity.

we shun to record it. Men seem to have learned of the horizon the art of perpetual re-treating and reference. "Yonder uplands are rich pasturage, and my neighbor has fertile meadow, but my field," says the querulous farmer, "only holds the world together." I quote another man's saying; unluckily, that other withdraws himself in the same way, and quotes me. 'Tis the trick of nature thus to degrade today; a good deal of buzz, and somewhere a result slipped magically in. Every roof is agreeable to the eye, until it is lifted; then we find tragedy and moaning women, and hard-eyed husbands, and deluges of lethe, and the men ask, "What's the news?" as if the old were so bad. How many indi-viduals can we count in society? how many actions? how many opinions? So much of our time is preparation, so much is routine, and so much retrospect, that the pith of each man's genius contracts itself to a very few hours. The history of literature—take the net result of Tiraboschi, Warton, or Schlegel,[6]—is a sum of very few ideas, and of very few original tales,—all the rest being variation of these. So in this great society wide lying around us, a critical analysis would find very few spontaneous actions. It is almost all custom and gross sense. There are even few opinions, and these seem organic in the speakers, and do not disturb the universal necessity.

What opium is instilled into all disaster! It shows formidable as we approach it, but there is at last no rough rasping friction, but the most slippery sliding surfaces. We fall soft on a thought. *Ate Dea*[7] is gentle,

"Over men's heads walking aloft,
   With tender feet treading so soft."[8]

People give and bemoan themselves, but it is not half so bad with them as they say. There are moods in which we court suffering, in the hope that here, at least, we shall find reality, sharp peaks and edges of truth. But it turns out to be scene-painting and counterfeit. The only thing grief has taught me, is to know how shallow it is. That, like all the rest, plays about the surface, and never introduces me into the reality, for contact with which, we would even pay the costly price of sons and lovers. Was it Boscovich[9] who found out that bodies never come in contact? Well, souls never touch their objects. An innavigable sea washes with silent waves between us and the things we aim at and converse with. Grief too will make us idealists. In the death of my son, now more than two years ago, I seem to have lost a beautiful estate,—no more. I cannot get it nearer to me. If tomorrow I should be informed of the bankruptcy of my principal debtors, the loss of my property would be a great inconvenience to me, perhaps, for many years; but it would leave me as it found me,—neither better nor worse. So is it with this calamity: it does not touch me: some thing which I fancied was a part of me, which could not be torn away without tearing me, nor enlarged without enriching me, falls off from me, and leaves no scar. It was caducous. I grieve that grief can teach me nothing, nor carry

---

[6] All literary historians. Tiraboschi: Italian Girolamo Tiraboschi (1731–1794); Warton: British Thomas Warton (1728–1790); Schlegel: German philosopher Friedrich von Schlegel (1772–1829) or his brother August Wilhelm von Schlegel (1767–1845).

[7] Greek goddess of mischief and reckless folly.
[8] Homer's *Iliad,* XIX, 92–93.
[9] Ruggiero Giuseppe Boscovich (1711–1787), Italian physicist who developed a molecular theory of matter.

me one step into real nature. The Indian who was laid under a curse, that the wind should not blow on him, nor water flow to him, nor fire burn him,[10] is a type of us all. The dearest events are summer-rain, and we the Para coats[11] that shed every drop. Nothing is left us now but death. We look to that with a grim satisfaction, saying, there at least is reality that will not dodge us.

I take this evanescence and lubricity of all objects, which lets them slip through our fingers then when we clutch hardest, to be the most unhandsome part of our condition. Nature does not like to be observed, and likes that we should be her fools and play-mates. We may have the sphere for our cricket-ball, but not a berry for our philosophy. Direct strokes she never gave us power to make; all our blows glance, all our hits are accidents. Our relations to each other are oblique and casual.

Dream delivers us to dream, and there is no end to illusion. Life is a train of moods like a string of beads, and, as we pass through them, they prove to be many-colored lenses which paint the world their own hue, and each shows only what lies in its focus. From the mountain you see the mountain. We animate what we can, and we see only what we animate. Nature and books belong to the eyes that see them. It depends on the mood of the man, whether he shall see the sunset or the fine poem. There are always sunsets, and there is always genius; but only a few hours so serene that we can relish nature or criticism. The more or less depends on structure or temperament. Temperament is the iron wire on which the beads are strung. Of what use is fortune or talent to a cold and defective nature? Who cares what sensibility or discrimination a man has at some time shown, if he falls asleep in his chair? or if he laugh and giggle? or if he apologize? or is affected with egotism? or thinks of his dollar? or cannot go buy food? or has gotten a child in his boyhood? Of what use is genius, if the organ is too convex or too concave, and cannot find a focal distance within the actual horizon of human life? Of what use, if the brain is too cold or too hot, and the man does not care enough for results, to stimulate him to experiment, and hold him up in it? or if the web is too finely woven, too irritable by pleasure and pain, so that life stagnates from too much reception, without due outlet? Of what use to make heroic vows of amendment, if the same old law-breaker is to keep them? What cheer can the religious sentiment yield, when that is suspected to be secretly dependent on the seasons of the year, and the state of the blood? I knew a witty physician who found theology in the biliary duct, and used to affirm that if there was disease in the liver, the man became a Calvinist, and if that organ was sound, he became a Unitarian.[12] Very mortifying is the reluctant experience that some unfriendly excess or imbecility neutralizes the promise of genius. We see young men who owe us a new world, so readily and lavishly they promise, but they never acquit the debt; they die young and dodge the account: or if they live, they lose themselves in the crowd.

Temperament also enters fully into the system of illusions, and shuts us in a prison of glass which we cannot see. There is an optical illusion about every person we meet. In

[10] See The Curse of Kehama (1810) by English poet Robert Southey (1774–1843).
[11] Then a term for rubber coats.
[12] The Calvinist interpretation of Original Sin is viewed here as the psychosomatic display of a bodily disease. Unitarians do not believe that humankind is damned eternally but instead hold that we have spiritual autonomy.

truth, they are all creatures of given temperament, which will appear in a given character, whose boundaries they will never pass: but we look at them, they seem alive, and we presume there is impulse in them. In the moment it seems impulse; in the year, in the lifetime, it turns out to be a certain uniform tune which the revolving barrel of the music-box must play. Men resist the conclusion in the morning, but adopt it as the evening wears on, that temper prevails over everything of time, place, and condition, and is inconsumable in the flames of religion. Some modifications the moral sentiment avails to impose, but the individual texture holds its dominion, if not to bias the moral judgments, yet to fix the measure of activity and of enjoyment.

I thus express the law as it is read from the platform of ordinary life, but must not leave it without noticing the capital exception. For temperament is a power which no man willingly hears any one praise but himself. On the platform of physics, we cannot resist the contracting influences of so-called science. Temperament puts all divinity to rout. I know the mental proclivity of physicians. I hear the chuckle of the phrenologists. Theoretic kidnappers and slave-drivers, they esteem each man the victim of another, who winds him round his finger by knowing the law of his being, and by such cheap signboards as the color of his beard, or the slope of his occiput, reads the inventory of his fortunes and character. The grossest ignorance does not disgust like this impudent knowingness. The physicians say, they are not materialists; but they are:—Spirit is matter reduced to an extreme thinness: O *so* thin!—But the definition of *spiritual* should be, *that which is its own evidence.* What notions do they attach to love! what to religion! One would not willingly pronounce these words in their hearing, and give them the occasion to profane them. I saw a gracious gentleman who adapts his conversation to the form of the head of the man he talks with! I had fancied that the value of life lay in its inscrutable possibilities; in the fact that I never know, in addressing myself to a new individual, what may befall me. I carry the keys of my castle in my hand, ready to throw them at the feet of my lord, whenever and in what disguise soever he shall appear. I know he is in the neighborhood hidden among vagabonds. Shall I preclude my future, by taking a high seat, and kindly adapting my conversation to the shape of heads? When I come to that, the doctors shall buy me for a cent.—"But, sir, medical history; the report to the Institute; the proven facts!"—I distrust the facts and the inferences. Temperament is the veto or limitation-power in the constitution, very justly applied to restrain an opposite excess in the constitution, but absurdly offered as a bar to original equity. When virtue is in presence, all subordinate powers sleep. On its own level, or in view of nature, temperament is final. I see not, if one be once caught in this trap of so-called sciences, any escape for the man from the links of the chain of physical necessity. Given such an embryo, such a history must follow. On this platform, one lives in a sty of sensualism, and would soon come to suicide. But it is impossible that the creative power should exclude itself. Into every intelligence there is a door which is never closed, through which the creator passes. The intellect, seeker of absolute truth, or the heart, lover of absolute good, intervenes for our succor, and at one whisper of these high powers, we awake from ineffectual struggles with this nightmare. We hurl it into its own hell, and cannot again contract ourselves to so base a state.

The secret of the illusoriness is in the necessity of a succession of moods or objects. Gladly we would anchor, but the anchorage is quicksand. This onward trick of nature is too strong for us: *Pero si muove.*[13] When, at night, I look at the moon and stars, I seem stationary, and they to hurry. Our love of the real draws us to permanence, but health of body consists in circulation, and sanity of mind in variety or facility of association. We need change of objects. Dedication to one thought is quickly odious. We house with the insane, and must humor them; then conversation dies out. Once I took such delight in Montaigne,[14] that I thought I should not need any other book; before that, in Shakspeare; then in Plutarch;[15] then in Plotinus;[16] at one time in Bacon;[17] afterwards in Goethe;[18] even in Bettine;[19] but now I turn the pages of either of them languidly, whilst I still cherish their genius. So with pictures; each will bear an emphasis of attention once, which it cannot retain, though we fain would continue to be pleased in that manner. How strongly I have felt of pictures, that when you have seen one well, you must take your leave of it; you shall never see it again. I have had good lessons from pictures, which I have since seen without emotion or remark. A deduction must be made from the opinion, which even the wise express of a new book or occurrence. Their opinion gives me tidings of their mood, and some vague guess at the new fact, but is nowise to be trusted as the lasting relation between that intellect and that thing. The child asks, "Mamma, why don't I like the story as well as when you told it me yesterday?" Alas, child, it is even so with the oldest cherubim of knowledge. But will it answer thy question to say, Because thou wert born to a whole, and this story is a particular? The reason of the pain this discovery causes us (and we make it late in respect to works of art and intellect), is the plaint of tragedy which murmurs from it in regard to persons, to friendship and love.

That immobility and absence of elasticity which we find in the arts, we find with more pain in the artist. There is no power of expansion in men. Our friends early appear to us as representatives of certain ideas, which they never pass or exceed. They stand on the brink of the ocean of thought and power, but they never take the single step that would bring them there. A man is like a bit of Labrador spar,[20] which has no lustre as you turn it in your hand, until you come to a particular angle; then it shows deep and beautiful colors. There is no adaptation or universal applicability in men, but each has his special talent, and the mastery of successful men consists in adroitly keeping themselves where and when that turn shall be oftenest to be practised. We do what we must, and call it by the best names we can, and would fain have the praise of having intended the result which ensues. I cannot recall any form of man who is not superfluous sometimes. But is not this pitiful? Life is not worth the taking, to do tricks in.

Of course, it needs the whole society, to give the symmetry we seek. The parti-colored wheel must revolve very fast to appear white. Something is learned too by conversing with so much folly and defect. In fine, whoever loses, we are always of the gaining

---

[13] Italian: "Still, it moves." Galileo's response after the Roman Catholic church forced him to retract his theory that the earth revolves around the sun.

[14] French essayist Michel de Montaigne (1533–1592).

[15] Greek biographer (A.D. 46?–?120).

[16] Roman philosopher (A.D. 205?–?270)

[17] English literary statesman (1561–1626).

[18] German poet and dramatist (1749–1832).

[19] German author Elizabeth ("Bettine") von Arnim (1785–1859).

[20] Crystalline rock.

party. Divinity is behind our failures and follies also. The plays of children are nonsense, but very educative nonsense. So it is with the largest and solemnest things, with commerce, government, church, marriage, and so with the history of every man's bread, and the ways by which he is to come by it. Like a bird which alights nowhere, but hops perpetually from bough to bough, is the Power which abides in no man and in no woman, but for a moment speaks from this one, and for another moment from that one.

But what help from these fineries or pedantries? What help from thought? Life is not dialectics. We, I think, in these times, have had lessons enough of the futility of criticism. Our young people have thought and written much on labor and reform, and for all that they have written, neither the world nor themselves have got on a step. Intellectual tasting of life will not supersede muscular activity. If a man should consider the nicety of the passage of a piece of bread down his throat, he would starve. At Education-Farm,[21] the noblest theory of life sat on the noblest figures of young men and maidens, quite powerless and melancholy. It would not rake or pitch a ton of hay; it would not rub down a horse; and the men and maidens it left pale and hungry. A political orator wittily compared our party promises to western roads, which opened stately enough, with planted trees on either side, to tempt the traveller, but soon became narrow and narrower, and ended in a squirrel-track, and ran up a tree. So does culture with us; it ends in head-ache. Unspeakably sad and barren does life look to those, who a few months ago were dazzled with the splendor of the promise of the times. "There is now no longer any right course of action, nor any self-devotion left among the Iranis."[22] Objections and criticism we have had our fill of. There are objections to every course of life and action, and the practical wisdom infers an indifferency, from the omnipresence of objection. The whole frame of things preaches indifferency. Do not craze yourself with thinking, but go about your business anywhere. Life is not intellectual or critical, but sturdy. Its chief good is for well-mixed people who can enjoy what they find, without question. Nature hates peeping, and our mothers speak her very sense when they say, "Children, eat your victuals, and say no more of it." To fill the hour,—that is happiness; to fill the hour, and leave no crevice for a repentance or an approval. We live amid surfaces, and the true art of life is to skate well on them. Under the oldest mouldiest conventions, a man of native force prospers just as well as in the newest world, and that by skill of handling and treatment. He can take hold anywhere. Life itself is a mixture of power and form, and will not bear the least excess of either. To finish the moment, to find the journey's end in every step of the road, to live the greatest number of good hours, is wisdom. It is not the part of men, but of fanatics, or of mathematicians, if you will, to say, that, the shortness of life considered, it is not worth caring whether for so short a duration we were sprawling in want, or sitting high. Since our office is with moments, let us husband them. Five minutes of today are worth as much to me, as five minutes in the next millennium. Let us be poised, and wise, and our own, today. Let us treat the men and women well: treat them as if they were real: perhaps they are. Men live in their fancy, like drunkards whose hands are too soft and tremulous for successful labor. It is a tempest of fancies, and the only ballast I know, is a respect to the present hour. Without any shadow of doubt, amidst this vertigo of shows and politics, I settle

21 Transcendentalist commune, more widely known as Brook Farm.

22 From *Desatir*, ancient Persian writings attributed to Zoroaster (sixth century B.C.).

myself ever the firmer in the creed, that we should not postpone and refer and wish, but do broad justice where we are, by whomsoever we deal with, accepting our actual companions and circumstances, however humble or odious, as the mystic officials to whom the universe has delegated its whole pleasure for us. If these are mean and malignant, their contentment, which is the last victory of justice, is a more satisfying echo to the heart, than the voice of poets and the casual sympathy of admirable persons. I think that however a thoughtful man may suffer from the defects and absurdities of his company, he cannot without affectation deny to any set of men and women, a sensibility to extraordinary merit. The coarse and frivolous have an instinct of superiority, if they have not a sympathy, and honor it in their blind capricious way with sincere homage.

The fine young people despise life, but in me, and in such as with me are free from dyspepsia, and to whom a day is a sound and solid good, it is a great excess of politeness to look scornful and to cry for company. I am grown by sympathy a little eager and sentimental, but leave me alone, and I should relish every hour and what it brought me, the potluck of the day, as heartily as the oldest gossip in the bar-room. I am thankful for small mercies. I compared notes with one of my friends who expects everything of the universe, and is disappointed when anything is less than the best, and I found that I begin at the other extreme, expecting nothing, and am always full of thanks for moderate goods. I accept the clangor and jangle of contrary tendencies. I find my account in sots and bores also. They give a reality to the circumjacent picture, which such a vanishing meteorous appearance can ill spare. In the morning I awake, and find the old world, wife, babes, and mother, Concord and Boston, the dear old spiritual world, and even the dear old devil not far off. If we will take the good we find, asking no questions, we shall have heaping measures. The great gifts are not got by analysis. Everything good is on the highway. The middle region of our being is the temperate zone. We may climb into the thin and cold realm of pure geometry and lifeless science, or sink into that of sensation. Between these extremes is the equator of life, of thought, of spirit, of poetry,—a narrow belt. Moreover, in popular experience, everything good is on the highway. A collector peeps into all the picture-shops of Europe, for a landscape of Poussin, a crayon-sketch of Salvator;[23] but the Transfiguration, the Last Judgment, the Communion of St. Jerome,[24] and what are as transcendent as these, are on the walls of the Vatican, the Uffizi,[25] or the Louvre, where every footman may see them; to say nothing of nature's pictures in every street, of sunsets and sunrises every day, and the sculpture of the human body never absent. A collector recently bought at public auction, in London, for one hundred and fifty-seven guineas,[26] an autograph of Shakspeare: but for nothing a school-boy can read Hamlet, and can detect secrets of highest concernment yet unpublished therein. I think I will never read any but the commonest books,—the Bible, Homer, Dante, Shakspeare, and Milton. Then we are impatient of so public a life and planet, and run hither and thither for nooks and secrets. The imagination delights in the woodcraft of Indians, trappers, and bee-hunters. We fancy that we are strangers, and not so intimately domesticated in the planet as the wild man, and the wild beast

---

23 Poussin: French classical painter Nicholas Poussin (1594–1665); Salvator: Italian painter Salvator Rosa (1615–1673), renowned for his exotic landscapes.
24 Respectively, paintings of Raphael, Michelangelo, and Domenichino.
25 Renowned museum in Florence.
26 Guinea: British coin worth slightly more than one pound.

and bird. But the exclusion reaches them also; reaches the climbing, flying, gliding, feathered and four-footed man. Fox and woodchuck, hawk and snipe, and bittern, when nearly seen, have no more root in the deep world than man, and are just such superficial tenants of the globe. Then the new molecular philosophy shows astronomical interspaces betwixt atom and atom, shows that the world is all outside: it has no inside.

The mid-world is best. Nature, as we know her, is no saint. The lights of the church, the ascetics, Gentoos[27] and Grahamites,[28] she does not distinguish by any favor. She comes eating and drinking and sinning. Her darlings, the great, the strong, the beautiful, are not children of our law, do not come out of the Sunday School, nor weigh their food, nor punctually keep the commandments. If we will be strong with her strength, we must not harbor such disconsolate consciences, borrowed too from the consciences of other nations. We must set up the strong present tense against all the rumors of wrath, past or to come. So many things are unsettled which it is of the first importance to settle,—and, pending their settlement, we will do as we do. Whilst the debate goes forward on the equity of commerce, and will not be closed for a century or two, New and Old England may keep shop. Law of copyright and international copyright is to be discussed,[29] and, in the interim, we will sell our books for the most we can. Expediency of literature, reason of literature, lawfulness of writing down a thought, is questioned; much is to say on both sides, and, while the fight waxes hot, thou, dearest scholar, stick to thy foolish task, add a line every hour, and between whiles add a line. Right to hold land, right of property, is disputed, and the conventions convene, and before the vote is taken, dig away in your garden, and spend your earnings as a waif or godsend to all serene and beautiful purposes. Life itself is a bubble and a skepticism, and a sleep within a sleep. Grant it, and as much more as they will,—but thou, God's darling! heed thy private dream: thou wilt not be missed in the scorning and skepticism: there are enough of them: stay there in thy closet, and toil, until the rest are agreed what to do about it. Thy sickness, they say, and thy puny habit, require that thou do this or avoid that, but know that thy life is a flitting state, a tent for a night, and do thou, sick or well, finish that stint. Thou art sick, but shalt not be worse, and the universe, which holds thee dear, shall be the better.

Human life is made up of the two elements, power and form, and the proportion must be invariably kept, if we would have it sweet and sound. Each of these elements in excess makes a mischief as hurtful as its defect. Everything runs to excess: every good quality is noxious, if unmixed, and, to carry the danger to the edge of ruin, nature causes each man's peculiarity to superabound. Here, among the farms, we adduce the scholars as examples of this treachery. They are nature's victims of expression. You who see the artist, the orator, the poet, too near, and find their life no more excellent than that of mechanics or farmers, and themselves victims of partiality, very hollow and haggard, and pronounce them failures,—not heroes, but quacks,—conclude very reasonably, that these arts are not for man, but are disease. Yet nature will not bear you out. Irresistible nature made men such, and makes legions more of such, every day. You love the boy reading in a book, gazing at a drawing, or a cast: yet what are these millions who

---

[27] Hindu sect.
[28] Vegetarian followers of Sylvester Graham (1794–1851), whose food faddism is paid tribute in the Graham cracker.

[29] The U.S. Congress passed an international copyright law in 1891.

read and behold, but incipient writers and sculptors? Add a little more of that quality which now reads and sees, and they will seize the pen and chisel. And if one remembers how innocently he began to be an artist, he perceives that nature joined with his enemy. A man is a golden impossibility. The line he must walk is a hair's breadth. The wise through excess of wisdom is made a fool.

How easily, if fate would suffer it, we might keep forever these beautiful limits, and adjust ourselves, once for all, to the perfect calculation of the kingdom of known cause and effect. In the street and in the newspapers, life appears so plain a business, that manly resolution and adherence to the multiplication-table through all weathers, will insure success. But ah! presently comes a day, or is it only a half-hour, with its angel-whispering,—which discomfits the conclusions of nations and of years! Tomorrow again, everything looks real and angular, the habitual standards are reinstated, common sense is as rare as genius,—is the basis of genius, and experience is hands and feet to every enterprise;—and yet, he who should do his business on this understanding, would be quickly bankrupt. Power keeps quite another road than the turnpikes of choice and will, namely, the subterranean and invisible tunnels and channels of life. It is ridiculous that we are diplomatists, and doctors, and considerate people: there are no dupes like these. Life is a series of surprises, and would not be worth taking or keeping, if it were not. God delights to isolate us every day, and hide from us the past and the future. We would look about us, but with grand politeness he draws down before us an impenetrable screen of purest sky, and another behind us of purest sky. "You will not remember," he seems to say, "and you will not expect." All good conversation, manners, and action, come from a spontaneity which forgets usages, and makes the moment great. Nature hates calculators; her methods are saltatory and impulsive. Man lives by pulses; our organic movements are such; and the chemical and ethereal agents are undulatory and alternate; and the mind goes antagonizing on, and never prospers but by fits. We thrive by casualties. Our chief experiences have been casual. The most attractive class of people are those who are powerful obliquely, and not by the direct stroke: men of genius, but not yet accredited: one gets the cheer of their light, without paying too great a tax. Theirs is the beauty of the bird, or the morning light, and not of art. In the thought of genius there is always a surprise; and the moral sentiment is well called "the newness," for it is never other; as new to the oldest intelligence as to the young child,—"the kingdom that cometh without observation."[30] In like manner, for practical success, there must not be too much design. A man will not be observed in doing that which he can do best. There is a certain magic about his properest action, which stupefies your powers of observation, so that though it is done before you, you wist not of it. The art of life has a pudency, and will not be exposed. Every man is an impossibility, until he is born; every thing impossible, until we see a success. The ardors of piety agree at last with the coldest skepticism,—that nothing is of us or our works,—that all is of God. Nature will not spare us the smallest leaf of laurel. All writing comes by the grace of God, and all doing and having. I would gladly be moral, and keep due metes and bounds, which I dearly love, and allow the most to the will of man, but I have set my heart on honesty in this chapter, and I can see nothing at last, in success or failure, than more or less of vital force supplied from the Eternal. The results of life are uncalculated and uncalculable. The years teach much which the days never know. The

---

[30] See Luke 17:20.

persons who compose our company, converse, and come and go, and design and execute many things, and somewhat comes of it all, but an unlooked for result. The individual is always mistaken. He designed many things, and drew in other persons as coadjutors, quarrelled with some or all, blundered much, and something is done; all are a little advanced, but the individual is always mistaken. It turns out somewhat new, and very unlike what he promised himself.

The ancients, struck with this irreducibleness of the elements of human life to calculation, exalted Chance into a divinity, but that is to stay too long at the spark,—which glitters truly at one point,—but the universe is warm with the latency of the same fire. The miracle of life which will not be expounded, but will remain a miracle, introduces a new element. In the growth of the embryo, Sir Everard Home,[31] I think, noticed that the evolution was not from one central point, but coactive from three or more points. Life has no memory. That which proceeds in succession might be remembered, but that which is coexistent, or ejaculated from a deeper cause, as yet far from being conscious, knows not its own tendency. So is it with us, now skeptical, or without unity, because immersed in forms and effects all seeming to be of equal yet hostile value, and now religious, whilst in the reception of spiritual law. Bear with these distractions, with this coetaneous growth of the parts: they will one day be *members,* and obey one will. On that one will, on that secret cause, they nail our attention and hope. Life is hereby melted into an expectation or a religion. Underneath the inharmonious and trivial particulars, is a musical perfection, the Ideal journeying always with us, the heaven without rent or seam. Do but observe the mode of our illumination. When I converse with a profound mind, or if at any time being alone I have good thoughts, I do not at once arrive at satisfactions, as when, being thirsty, I drink water, or go to the fire, being cold: no! but I am at first apprised of my vicinity to a new and excellent region of life. By persisting to read or to think, this region gives further sign of itself, as it were in flashes of light, in sudden discoveries of its profound beauty and repose, as if the clouds that covered it parted at intervals, and showed the approaching traveller the inland mountains, with the tranquil eternal meadows spread at their base, whereon flocks graze, and shepherds pipe and dance. But every insight from this realm of thought is felt as initial, and promises a sequel. I do not make it; I arrive there, and behold what was there already. I make! O no! I clap my hands in infantine joy and amazement, before the first opening to me of this august magnificence, old with the love and homage of innumerable ages, young with the life of life, the sunbright Mecca of the desert. And what a future it opens! I feel a new heart beating with the love of the new beauty. I am ready to die out of nature, and be born again into this new yet unapproachable America I have found in the West.

> "Since neither now nor yesterday began
>   These thoughts, which have been ever, nor yet can
>   A man be found who their first entrance knew."[32]

If I have described life as a flux of moods, I must now add, that there is that in us which changes not, and which ranks all sensations and states of mind. The conscious-

---

[31] Scottish surgeon (1756–1832).
[32] Translation of lines 455–457 from Sophocles' *Antigone.*

ness in each man is a sliding scale, which identifies him now with the First Cause, and now with the flesh of his body; life above life, in infinite degrees. The sentiment from which it sprung determines the dignity of any deed, and the question ever is, not, what you have done or forborne, but, at whose command you have done or forborne it.

Fortune, Minerva,[33] Muse, Holy Ghost,—these are quaint names, too narrow to cover this unbounded substance. The baffled intellect must still kneel before this cause, which refuses to be named,—ineffable cause, which every fine genius has essayed to represent by some emphatic symbol, as, Thales by water, Anaximenes by air, Anaxagoras[34] by (Νοῦς) thought, Zoroaster[35] by fire, Jesus and the moderns by love: and the metaphor of each has become a national religion. The Chinese Mencius[36] has not been the least successful in his generalization. "I fully understand language," he said, "and nourish well my vast-flowing vigor."—"I beg to ask what you call vast-flowing vigor?"—said his companion. "The explanation," replied Mencius, "is difficult. This vigor is supremely great, and in the highest degree unbending. Nourish it correctly, and do it no injury, and it will fill up the vacancy between heaven and earth. This vigor accords with and assists justice and reason, and leaves no hunger."—In our more correct writing, we give to this generalization the name of Being, and thereby confess that we have arrived as far as we can go. Suffice it for the joy of the universe, that we have not arrived at a wall, but at interminable oceans. Our life seems not present, so much as prospective; not for the affairs on which it is wasted, but as a hint of this vast-flowing vigor. Most of life seems to be mere advertisement of faculty: information is given us not to sell ourselves cheap; that we are very great. So, in particulars, our greatness is always in a tendency or direction, not in an action. It is for us to believe in the rule, not in the exception. The noble are thus known from the ignoble. So in accepting the leading of the sentiments, it is not what we believe concerning the immortality of the soul, or the like, but *the universal impulse to believe,* that is the material circumstance, and is the principal fact in the history of the globe. Shall we describe this cause as that which works directly? The spirit is not helpless or needful of mediate organs. It has plentiful powers and direct effects. I am explained without explaining, I am felt without acting, and where I am not. Therefore all just persons are satisfied with their own praise. They refuse to explain themselves, and are content that new actions should do them that office. They believe that we communicate without speech, and above speech, and that no right action of ours is quite unaffecting to our friends, at whatever distance; for the influence of action is not to be measured by miles. Why should I fret myself, because a circumstance has occurred, which hinders my presence where I was expected? If I am not at the meeting, my presence where I am, should be as useful to the commonwealth of friendship and wisdom, as would be my presence in that place. I exert the same quality of power in all places. Thus journeys the mighty Ideal before us; it never was known to fall into the rear. No man ever came to an experience which was satiating, but his good is tidings of a better. Onward and onward! In liberated moments, we know that a

---

[33] Roman goddess of wisdom.
[34] Thales, Anaximenes, and Anaxagoras, respectively, were Greek philosophers of the seventh, sixth, and fifth centuries B.C.

[35] In sixth-century Persia, Zoroaster preached fire or light worship.
[36] Confucian philosopher Meng-Tse (third century B.C.).

new picture of life and duty is already possible; the elements already exist in many minds around you, of a doctrine of life which shall transcend any written record we have. The new statement will comprise the skepticisms, as well as the faiths of society, and out of unbeliefs a creed shall be formed. For, skepticisms are not gratuitous or lawless, but are limitations of the affirmative statement, and the new philosophy must take them in, and make affirmations outside of them, just as much as it must include the oldest beliefs.

It is very unhappy, but too late to be helped, the discovery we have made, that we exist. That discovery is called the Fall of Man. Ever afterwards, we suspect our instruments. We have learned that we do not see directly, but mediately, and that we have no means of correcting these colored and distorting lenses which we are, or of computing the amount of their errors. Perhaps these subject-lenses have a creative power; perhaps there are no objects. Once we lived in what we saw; now, the rapaciousness of this new power, which threatens to absorb all things, engages us. Nature, art, persons, letters, religions,—objects, successively tumble in, and God is but one of its ideas. Nature and literature are subjective phenomena; every evil and every good thing is a shadow which we cast. The street is full of humiliations to the proud. As the fop contrived to dress his bailiffs in his livery, and make them wait on his guests at table, so the chagrins which the bad heart gives off as bubbles, at once take form as ladies and gentlemen in the street, shopmen or barkeepers in hotels, and threaten or insult whatever is threatenable and insultable in us. 'Tis the same with our idolatries. People forget that it is the eye which makes the horizon, and the rounding mind's eye which makes this or that man a type or representative of humanity with the name of hero or saint. Jesus the "providential man," is a good man on whom many people are agreed that these optical laws shall take effect. By love on one part, and by forbearance to press objection on the other part, it is for a time settled, that we will look at him in the centre of the horizon, and ascribe to him the properties that will attach to any man so seen. But the longest love or aversion has a speedy term. The great and crescive self, rooted in absolute nature, supplants all relative existence, and ruins the kingdom of mortal friendship and love. Marriage (in what is called the spiritual world) is impossible, because of the inequality between every subject and every object. The subject is the receiver of Godhead, and at every comparison must feel his being enhanced by that cryptic might. Though not in energy, yet by presence, this magazine[37] of substance cannot be otherwise than felt: nor can any force of intellect attribute to the object the proper deity which sleeps or wakes forever in every subject. Never can love make consciousness and ascription equal in force. There will be the same gulf between every me and thee, as between the original and the picture. The universe is the bride of the soul. All private sympathy is partial. Two human beings are like globes, which can touch only in a point, and, whilst they remain in contact, all other points of each of the spheres are inert; their turn must also come, and the longer a particular union lasts, the more energy of appetency[38] the parts not in union acquire.

Life will be imaged, but cannot be divided nor doubled. Any invasion of its unity would be chaos. The soul is not twin-born, but the only begotten, and though revealing itself as child in time, child in appearance, is of a fatal and universal power, admitting

---

[37] Stored supply.
[38] Being propelled toward unity.

no co-life. Every day, every act betrays the ill-concealed deity. We believe in ourselves, as we do not believe in others. We permit all things to ourselves, and that which we call sin in others, is experiment for us. It is an instance of our faith in ourselves, that men never speak of crime as lightly as they think: or, every man thinks a latitude safe for himself, which is nowise to be indulged to another. The act looks very differently on the inside, and on the outside; in its quality, and in its consequences. Murder in the murderer is no such ruinous thought as poets and romancers will have it; it does not unsettle him, or fright him from his ordinary notice of trifles: it is an act quite easy to be contemplated, but in its sequel, it turns out to be a horrible jangle and confounding of all relations. Especially the crimes that spring from love, seem right and fair from the actor's point of view, but, when acted, are found destructive of society. No man at last believes that he can be lost, nor that the crime in him is as black as in the felon. Because the intellect qualifies in our own case the moral judgments. For there is no crime to the intellect. That is antinomian or hypernomian,[39] and judges law as well as fact. "It is worse than a crime, it is a blunder," said Napoleon, speaking the language of the intellect. To it, the world is a problem in mathematics or the science of quantity, and it leaves out praise and blame, and all weak emotions. All stealing is comparative. If you come to absolutes, pray who does not steal? Saints are sad, because they behold sin, (even when they speculate,) from the point of view of the conscience, and not of the intellect; a confusion of thought. Sin seen from the thought, is a diminution or *less:* seen from the conscience or will, it is pravity or *bad.* The intellect names it shade, absence of light, and no essence. The conscience must feel it as essence, essential evil. This it is not: it has an objective existence, but no subjective.

Thus inevitably does the universe wear our color, and every object fall successively into the subject itself. The subject exists, the subject enlarges; all things sooner or later fall into place. As I am, so I see; use what language we will, we can never say anything but what we are; Hermes, Cadmus,[40] Columbus, Newton, Buonaparte; are the mind's ministers. Instead of feeling a poverty when we encounter a great man, let us treat the new comer like a travelling geologist, who passes through our estate, and shows us good slate, or limestone, or anthracite, in our brush pasture. The partial action of each strong mind in one direction, is a telescope for the objects on which it is pointed. But every other part of knowledge is to be pushed to the same extravagance, ere the soul attains her due sphericity. Do you see that kitten chasing so prettily her own tail? If you could look with her eyes, you might see her surrounded with hundreds of figures performing complex dramas, with tragic and comic issues, long conversations, many characters, many ups and downs of fate,—and meantime it is only puss and her tail. How long before our masquerade will end its noise of tamborines, laughter, and shouting, and we shall find it was a solitary performance?—A subject and an object,—it takes so much to make the galvanic circuit complete, but magnitude adds nothing. What imports it whether it is Kepler[41] and the sphere; Columbus and America; a reader and his book; or puss with her tail?

---

[39] Against or above the control of law.
[40] Creative pioneers: Hermes, Greek god who invented the lyre; Cadmus, mythic founder of the Thebans, who brought the alphabet to Greece.

[41] German physicist and astronomer Johannes Kepler (1571–1630), who pioneered the discovery of the laws of planetary motion.

It is true that all the muses and love and religion hate these developments, and will find a way to punish the chemist, who publishes in the parlor the secrets of the laboratory. And we cannot say too little of our constitutional necessity of seeing things under private aspects, or saturated with our humors. And yet is the God the native of these bleak rocks. That need makes in morals the capital virtue of self-trust. We must hold hard to this poverty, however scandalous, and by more vigorous self-recoveries, after the sallies of action, possess our axis more firmly. The life of truth is cold, and so far mournful; but it is not the slave of tears, contritions, and perturbations. It does not attempt another's work, nor adopt another's facts. It is a main lesson of wisdom to know your own from another's. I have learned that I cannot dispose of other people's facts; but I possess such a key to my own, as persuades me against all their denials, that they also have a key to theirs. A sympathetic person is placed in the dilemma of a swimmer among drowning men, who all catch at him, and if he give so much as a leg or a finger, they will drown him. They wish to be saved from the mischiefs of their vices, but not from their vices. Charity would be wasted on this poor waiting on the symptoms. A wise and hardy physician will say, *Come out of that,* as the first condition of advice.

In this our talking America, we are ruined by our good nature and listening on all sides. This compliance takes away the power of being greatly useful. A man should not be able to look other than directly and forthright. A preoccupied attention is the only answer to the importunate frivolity of other people: an attention, and to an aim which makes their wants frivolous. This is a divine answer, and leaves no appeal, and no hard thoughts. In Flaxman's[42] drawing of the Eumenides of Æschylus, Orestes supplicates Apollo, whilst the Furies sleep on the threshold. The face of the god expresses a shade of regret and compassion, but calm with the conviction of the irreconcilableness of the two spheres. He is born into other politics, into the eternal and beautiful. The man at his feet asks for his interest in turmoils of the earth, into which his nature cannot enter. And the Eumenides there lying express pictorially this disparity. The god is surcharged with his divine destiny.

Illusion, Temperament, Succession, Surface, Surprise, Reality, Subjectiveness,—these are threads on the loom of time, these are the lords of life. I dare not assume to give their order, but I name them as I find them in my way. I know better than to claim any completeness for my picture. I am a fragment, and this is a fragment of me. I can very confidently announce one or another law, which throws itself into relief and form, but I am too young yet by some ages to compile a code. I gossip for my hour concerning the eternal politics. I have seen many fair pictures not in vain. A wonderful time I have lived in. I am not the novice I was fourteen, nor yet seven years ago. Let who will ask, where is the fruit? I find a private fruit sufficient. This is a fruit,—that I should not ask for a rash effect from meditations, counsels, and the hiving of truths. I should feel it pitiful to demand a result on this town and county, an overt effect on the instant month and year. The effect is deep and secular as the cause. It works on periods in which mortal lifetime is lost. All I know is reception; I am and I have: but I do not get, and when I have fancied I had gotten anything, I found I did not. I worship with wonder the great Fortune.

[42] Flaxman: British artist John Flaxman (1755–1826), illustrator of the scene mentioned from *The Eumenides* by Aeschylus (525–456 B.C.).

My reception has been so large, that I am not annoyed by receiving this or that super-abundantly. I say to the Genius, if he will pardon the proverb, *In for a mill, in for a million.* When I receive a new gift, I do not macerate my body to make the account square, for, if I should die, I could not make the account square. The benefit overran the merit the first day, and has overran the merit ever since. The merit itself, so-called, I reckon part of the receiving.

Also, that hankering after an overt or practical effect seems to me an apostasy. In good earnest, I am willing to spare this most unnecessary deal of doing. Life wears to me a visionary face. Hardest, roughest action is visionary also. It is but a choice between soft and turbulent dreams. People disparage knowing and the intellectual life, and urge doing. I am very content with knowing, if only I could know. That is an august entertainment, and would suffice me a great while. To know a little, would be worth the expense of this world. I hear always the law of Adrastia,[43] "that every soul which had acquired any truth, should be safe from harm until another period."[44]

I know that the world I converse with in the city and in the farms, is not the world I *think.* I observe that difference, and shall observe it. One day, I shall know the value and law of this discrepance. But I have not found that much was gained by manipular attempts to realize the world of thought. Many eager persons successively make an experiment in this way, and make themselves ridiculous. They acquire democratic manners, they foam at the mouth, they hate and deny. Worse, I observe, that, in the history of mankind, there is never a solitary example of success,—taking their own tests of success. I say this polemically, or in reply to the inquiry, why not realize your world? But far be from me the despair which prejudges the law by a paltry empiricism,—since there never was a right endeavor, but it succeeded. Patience and patience, we shall win at the last. We must be very suspicious of the deceptions of the element of time. It takes a good deal of time to eat or to sleep, or to earn a hundred dollars, and a very little time to entertain a hope and an insight which becomes the light of our life. We dress our garden, eat our dinners, discuss the household with our wives, and these things make no impression, are forgotten next week; but in the solitude to which every man is always returning, he has a sanity and revelations, which in his passage into new worlds he will carry with him. Never mind the ridicule, never mind the defeat: up again, old heart!—it seems to say,—there is victory yet for all justice; and the true romance which the world exists to realize, will be the transformation of genius into practical power.

1844

---

[43] Nemesis, Greek goddess of retribution or destiny.
[44] From Plato's *Phaedrus.*

Concord Hymn*

Sung at the completion of the Battle Monument,
July 4, 1837

By the rude bridge that arched the flood,
   Their flag to April's breeze unfurled,
Here once the embattled farmers stood
   And fired the shot heard round the world.

The foe long since in silence slept;   5
   Alike the conqueror silent sleeps;
And Time the ruined bridge has swept
   Down the dark stream which seaward creeps.

On this green bank, by this soft stream,
   We set to-day a votive stone;   10
That memory may their deed redeem,
   When, like our sires, our sons are gone.

Spirit, that made those heroes dare
   To die, and leave their children free,
Bid Time and Nature gently spare   15
   The shaft we raise to them and thee.
1837

The Rhodora†

On being asked, whence is the flower?

In May, when sea-winds pierced our solitudes,
I found the fresh Rhodora in the woods,
Spreading its leafless blooms in a damp nook,
To please the desert and the sluggish brook.
The purple petals, fallen in the pool,   5
Made the black water with their beauty gay;

---

* This poem was first printed in a pamphlet
distributed at the dedication of the monument commemorating the battles of Lexington and Concord (April 19, 1775) in the
American Revolutionary War.

† Shrub similar to the rhododendron found in
New England.

Here might the red-bird come his plumes to cool,
And court the flower that cheapens his array.
Rhodora! if the sages ask thee why
This charm is wasted on the earth and sky,   10
Tell them, dear, that if eyes were made for seeing,
Then Beauty is its own excuse for being:
Why thou wert there, O rival of the rose!
I never thought to ask, I never knew:
But, in my simple ignorance, suppose   15
The self-same Power that brought me there brought you.
1834/1839

Each and All

Little thinks, in the field, yon red-cloaked clown[1]
Of thee from the hill-top looking down;
The heifer that lows in the upland farm,
Far-heard, lows not thine ear to charm;
The sexton, tolling his bell at noon,   5
Deems not that great Napoleon
Stops his horse, and lists with delight,
Whilst his files sweep round yon Alpine height;
Nor knowest thou what argument
Thy life to thy neighbor's creed has lent.   10
All are needed by each one;
Nothing is fair or good alone.
I thought the sparrow's note from heaven,
Singing at dawn on the alder bough;
I brought him home, in his nest, at even;   15
He sings the song, but it cheers not now,
For I did not bring home the river and sky;—
He sang to my ear,—they sang to my eye.
The delicate shells lay on the shore;
The bubbles of the latest wave   20
Fresh pearls to their enamel gave,
And the bellowing of the savage sea
Greeted their safe escape to me.
I wiped away the weeds and foam,
I fetched my sea-born treasures home;   25
But the poor, unsightly, noisome things
Had left their beauty on the shore

---

[1] Rustic; peasant.

With the sun and the sand and the wild uproar.
The lover watched his graceful maid,
As 'mid the virgin train she strayed,   30
Nor knew her beauty's best attire
Was woven still by the snow-white choir.
At last she came to his hermitage,
Like the bird from the woodlands to the cage;—
The gay enchantment was undone,   35
A gentle wife, but fairy none.
Then I said, 'I covet truth;
Beauty is unripe childhood's cheat;
I leave it behind with the games of youth:'—
As I spoke, beneath my feet   40
The ground-pine curled its pretty wreath,
Running over the club-moss burrs;
I inhaled the violet's breath;
Around me stood the oaks and firs;
Pine-cones and acorns lay on the ground;   45
Over me soared the eternal sky,
Full of light and of deity;
Again I saw, again I heard,
The rolling river, the morning bird;—
Beauty through my senses stole;   50
I yielded myself to the perfect whole.
1839

Hamatreya*

Bulkeley, Hunt, Willard, Hosmer, Meriam, Flint,[1]
Possessed the land which rendered to their toil
Hay, corn, roots, hemp, flax, apples, wool and wood.
Each of these landlords walked amidst his farm,
Saying, ' 'Tis mine, my children's and my name's.   5
How sweet the west wind sounds in my own trees!
How graceful climb those shadows on my hill!
I fancy these pure waters and the flags[2]
Know me, as does my dog: we sympathize;
And, I affirm, my actions smack of the soil.'   10
Where are these men? Asleep beneath their grounds:

---

* A derivation of *Maitreya*, the Hindu god
named in the sacred *Vishnu Purana*. Also
possibly a Greek interpretation of "earth-
mother."

[1] Family names of the first settlers of Concord,
Massachusetts.
[2] Wild irises.

And strangers, fond as they, their furrows plough.
Earth laughs in flowers, to see her boastful boys
Earth-proud, proud of the earth which is not theirs;
Who steer the plough, but cannot steer their feet   15
Clear of the grave.
They added ridge to valley, brook to pond,
And sighed for all that bounded their domain;
'This suits me for a pasture; that's my park;
We must have clay, lime, gravel, granite-ledge,   20
And misty lowland, where to go for peat.
The land is well,—lies fairly to the south.
'Tis good, when you have crossed the sea and back,
To find the sitfast acres where you left them.'
Ah! the hot owner sees not Death, who adds   25
Him to his land, a lump of mould the more.
Hear what the Earth says:—

   EARTH-SONG

   'Mine and yours;
   Mine, not yours.
   Earth endures;   30
   Stars abide—
   Shine down in the old sea;
   Old are the shores;
   But where are old men?
   I who have seen much,   35
   Such have I never seen.

   'The lawyer's deed
   Ran sure,
   In tail,[3]
   To them, and to their heirs   40
   Who shall succeed,
   Without fail,
   Forevermore.

   'Here is the land,
   Shaggy with wood,   45
   With its old valley,
   Mound and flood.
   But the heritors?—

---

[3] As in *entail,* the legal designation of an inheritance to specific descendants.

Fled like the flood's foam.
The lawyer, and the laws,   50
And the kingdom,
Clean swept herefrom.

'They called me theirs,
Who so controlled me;
Yet every one   55
Wished to stay, and is gone,
How am I theirs,
If they cannot hold me,
But I hold them?'
When I heard the Earth-song   60
I was no longer brave;
My avarice cooled
Like lust in the chill of the grave.

1847

Days

Daughters of Time, the hypocritic Days,
Muffled and dumb like barefoot dervishes,
And marching single in an endless file,
Bring diadems and fagots in their hands.
To each they offer gifts after his will,   5
Bread, kingdoms, stars, and sky that holds them all.
I, in my pleached garden, watched the pomp,
Forgot my morning wishes, hastily
Took a few herbs and apples, and the Day
Turned and departed silent. I, too late,   10
Under her solemn fillet saw the scorn.

1857

Cultural Portfolio
Nature's Nation

In his first major publication *Nature* (1836), Ralph Waldo Emerson attempted to define the individual's relation to nature so that the American land could become the basis for the new nation's distinctive culture identity. Emerson, and such contemporaries in the visual arts as painter Thomas Cole, viewed nature not as a place to be developed and exploited for financial gain, but as a source of spiritual solace and artistic inspiration. For these artists and writers, landscape embodied a major theme: the deep opposition between virgin, Edenic nature and the encroachments of economic expansion and development.

James Fenimore Cooper and Nathaniel Hawthorne had already extolled the sense of individuality and introspection triggered by the powerful rawness of the American landscape. Thus they launched the long tradition of Romantic literature that came to its fullest expression in the work of Emerson and other writers of the American Renaissance. Emerson called American "a poem in our eyes; its ample geography dazzles the imagination and it will not wait long for metres."

Thomas Cole created landscapes that were vehicles for elevated, even sublime feelings about nature and its transience. In America, unlike Europe, there was no continuity between nature and culture because the new nation was all nature, if fitfully riddled with destructive intrusions for commercial development. Cole, like Emerson, turned this fact to his artistic advantage. Writing in 1835, Cole relished the truth that American nature was not encumbered by other artists' visions. "The Painter of American scenery," he concluded, "has indeed privileges superior to any other; all nature here is new to Art. No Tivoli's, Terni's, Mont Blanc's, . . . hackneyed & worn by the daily pencils of hundreds, but virgin forest, lakes & waterfalls feast his eye with new delights, fill his portfolio with their features of beauty . . . because they had been preserved untouched from the time of creation for his heaven-favored pencil."

When Cole left for Italy in 1830, his friend, the poet William Cullen Bryant, begged him to remember the Edenic American landscape which, even as he wrote, was vanishing: "Lone lakes—savannas where the bison roves—/ Rocks rich with summer garlands—solemn streams—/Skies, where the desert eagle wheels and screams—/Spring bloom and autumn blaze of boundless groves."

Emerson's analysis in *Nature* is more finely wrought than such emotion-laden appreciations: He goes beyond the obvious beauty of nature to anatomize the spiritual element in landscape, the intellectual satisfactions the natural order affords, and the call to individualism and idealism which nature makes to those who reverse it. Twenty years later, in 1855, poet Walt Whitman could still declare: "The United States themselves are the greatest poem."

In fact, however, westward expansion was permanently changing that landscape, as booming business in logging, mining, and most of all, railroading used the wilderness for profit. Painter Alfred Bierstadt capitalized on the uniqueness of the American West, creating luminous panoramas of expansionist scenes: the grandeur of the Rocky Mountains; the glory of a Plains sunset; the miraculous passage beyond Donner Lake in the Sierra Nevada; the awe-inspiring domes of Yosemite. Among Bierstadt's generous customers were the magnates of development who were taming the very wilderness the painter so grandly depicted.

When the transcontinental railroad was completed in 1869, the vice president of the Central Pacific Railroad, Collis Huntington, commissioned Bierstadt to create a 6-by-10 foot canvas commemorating the landscape where construction difficulties had been overcome. Developers in "Nature's nation" were so intent on profiting from the land they were destroying that, with the backing of Northern Pacific Railroad directors, geologist Dr. Ferdinand Hayden, lobbied Congress to set aside Yellowstone as a national park, or what art critic Robert Hughes, recently called "a museum of American sublimity."

Albert Bierstadt
Among the Sierra Nevada Mountains, California
oil on canvas, 1868
(National Museum of American Art,
Washington, D.C./Art Resource, N.Y.)

In 1872, Ulysses Grant signed into law an act of Congress that protected all 35,000 square miles of the Yellowstone area in perpetuity; the act and its representation in a virtuosic Thomas Moran painting launched a new and profitable era of wilderness tourism.

But in another way, Emerson, who extolled the singularity of the inspiring American scene, was proved right. Some aspects of American nature proved too large, too raw to be directly depicted in literature or the visual arts. When Moran tried to paint the Grand Canyon of Colorado, like every other landscape painter before and since, critic Hughes concluded, he was de-feated. Not even Moran could solve the principal problem of painting so vast a natural phenomenon, the lack of any scale that related to the human and thus might place the imaginative viewer within that noble scene. In some areas, still, American has remained "nature's nation" where, as Emerson wrote "the best read naturalist who lends an entire and devout attention to truth, will see that there remains much to learn of his relation to the world, and that it is not to be learned by any addition or subtraction or other comparison of known quantities, but is arrived at by untaught sallies of the spirit, by a continual self-recovery, and by entire humility."

from Thomas Cole, *Essay on American Scenery*

A Fitting Place to Speak of God

Perhaps the most impressive characteristic of American scenery is its wilderness.

It is the most distinctive because in civilized Europe the primitive features of scenery have long since been destroyed or modified—the extensive forests that once overshadowed a great part of it have been felled—rugged mountains have been smoothed, and impetuous rivers turned from their courses to accommodate the tastes and necessities of a dense population—the once tangled wood is now a grassy lawn; the turbulent brook a navigable stream—crags that could not be removed have been crowned with towers, and the rudest valleys tamed by the plough.

And to this cultivated state our western world is fast approaching; but nature is still predominant, and there are those who regret that with the improvements of cultivation the sublimity of the wilderness should pass away: for those scenes of solitude from which the hand of nature has never been lifted, affect the mind with a more deep toned emotion than aught which the hand of man has touched. Amid them the consequent associations are of God the creator—theyare his undefiled works, and the mind is cast into the contemplation of eternal things.

Thomas Cole
Home in the Woods
1847
(Reynolds House, Museum of American Art, Winston-Salem, N.C.)

Asher Durand
Kindred Spirits
1849
(Collection of The New York Public Library.
Astor, Lenox & Tilden Foundations)

from Ralph Waldo Emerson, _Nature_

The noblest ministry of nature is to stand as the apparition of God. It is the organ through which the universal spirit speaks to the individual, and strives to lead back the individual to it.

from Ralph Waldo Emerson, _Circles_

We can never see Christianity from the catechism—from the pastures, from a boat in the pond, from amidst the songs of wood-birds, we possibly may.

from James Brooks, _The Knickerbocker_

God has promised us a renowned existence, if we will but deserve it. He speaks this promise in the sublimity of Nature. It resounds all along the crags of the Alleghenies. It is uttered in the thunder of Niagara. It is heard in the roar of two oceans, from the great Pacific to the rocky ramparts of the Bay of Fundy. His finger has written it in the broad expanse of our Inland Seas, and traced it out by the Mighty Father of Waters! The august TEMPLE in which we dwell was built for lofty purposes. Oh! that we may consecrate it to LIBERTY and CONCORD, and be found fit worshippers within its holy wall!

from Henry David Thoreau, *The Maine Woods*

[Primeval, Untamed, and Forever Untameable Nature]

Perhaps I most fully realized that this was primeval, untamed, and forever untameable Nature, or whatever else men call it, while coming down this part of the mountain. We were passing over "Burnt Lands," burnt by lightning, perchance, though they showed no recent marks of fire, hardly so much as a charred stump, but looked rather like a natural pasture for the moose and deer, exceedingly wild and desolate, with occasional strips of timber crossing them, and low poplars springing up, and patches of blueberries here and there. I found myself traversing them familiarly, like some pasture run to waste, or partially reclaimed by main; but when I reflected what man, what brother or sister or kinsman of our race made it and claimed it, I expected the proprietor to rise up and dispute my passage. It is difficult to conceive of a region uninhabited by man. We habitually presume his presence and influence everywhere. And yet we have not seen pure Nature, unless we have seen her thus vast, and drear, and inhuman, though in the midst of cities. Nature was here something savage and awful, though beautiful. I looked with awe at the ground I trod on, to see what the Powers had made there, the form and fashion and material of their work. This was that Earth of which we have heard, made out of Chaos and Old Night. Here was no man's garden, but the unhandselled globe. It was not lawn, nor pasture, nor mead, nor woodland, nor lea, nor arable, nor wasteland. It was the fresh and natural surface of the planet Earth, as it was made forever and ever,—to be the dwelling of man, we say,—so Nature made it, and man may use it if he can. Man was not to be associated with it. It was Matter, vast, terrific,—not his Mother Earth that we have heard of, not for him to tread on, or be buried in,—no, it were being too familiar even to let his bones lie there—the home this of Necessity and Fate. There was there felt the presence of a force not bound to be kind to man. It was a place for heathenism and superstitious rites,—to be inhabited by men nearer of kin to the rocks and to wild animals than we. We walked over it with a certain awe, stopping from time to time to pick the blueberries which grew there, and had a smart and spicy taste. Perchance where *our* wild pines stand, and leaves lie on their forest floor in Concord, there were once reapers, and husbandmen planted grain; but here not even the surface had been scarred by man, but it was a specimen of what God saw fit to make this world. What is it to be admitted to a museum, to see a myriad of particular things, compared with being shown some star's surface, some hard matter in its home! I stand in awe of my body, this matter to which I am bound has become so strange to me. I fear not spirits, ghosts, of which I am one,—*that* my body might,—but I fear bodies, I tremble to meet them. What is this Titan that has possession of me? Talk of mysteries—Think of our life in nature,—daily to be shown matter, to come in contact with it,—rocks, trees, wind on our cheeks! the *solid* earth! the *actual* world! the *common sense! Contact! Contact! Who* are we? *where* are we?

1848/1864

from James Fenimore Cooper, *The Pioneers*

Commonly selecting one of the most noble, for the first trial of his power, he would approach it with a listless air, whistling a low tune; and wielding his ax, with a certain flourish, not unlike the salutes of a fencing master, he would strike a light blow into the bark, and measure his distance. The pause that followed was ominous of the fall of the forest, which had flourished there for centuries. The heavy and brisk blows that he struck were soon succeeded by the thundering report of the tree, as it came, first cracking and threatening . . . finally meeting the ground with a shock but little inferior to an earthquake. From that moment the sounds of the ax were ceaseless, while the falling of the trees was like a distant cannonading. . . . [Eventually] the jobber would collect together his implements of labor, like the heaps of timber, and march away, under the blaze of the prostrate forest, like the conqueror of some city, who, having first prevailed over his adversary, applies the torch as the finishing blow to his conquest.

George Inness
The Lackawanna Valley
oil on canvas
(Gift of Mrs. Huttleston Rogers 1945, National Gallery of Art, Washington, D.C.)

Alexander Gardner, *View Near Fort Harker, Kansas;* from series: Kansas-Pacific Railroad photograph, 1867 (George Eastman House)

Emanuel Gottlieb Leutze, *Westward the Course of Empire Takes Its Way* (Mural Study U.S. Capitol) oil on canvas, 1861 (National Museum of American Art, Washington, D.C./Art Resource, N.Y.)

Henry David Thoreau
1817–1862

Thoreau was a determined man. He may not have always recognized exactly what form his life would take, but he knew that he was meant to serve. As an avid student of what words signify once one cuts through the surface, he responded fully to the demands placed on him by "vocation"—the voice that calls someone out of the crowd to perform a sacred duty to the world.

To trace Thoreau's life and his writing career is to realize what "growing up in Concord" meant in the fertile, fervid years prior to the Civil War, particularly to one of the young people who had been born, as Emerson put it, with "knives in their brains." Thoreau spent his forty-four years listening to the sounds of the voice that led him toward his destiny. This attentiveness made him kin to a number of his New England contemporaries, especially those loosely grouped under the label Transcendentalists. But Thoreau felt compelled to follow a somewhat different drummer than the one followed by Ralph Waldo Emerson, Bronson Alcott, William Ellery Channing, or Margaret Fuller.

Any review of the checkered annals of Thoreau's aspirations, disappointments, and achievements makes clear how this man failed in the sight of many of his contemporaries, those relative few who had even heard of him. Such a review of his life also suggests why he is now considered one of America's major literary figures; it indicates that the myth of the man in the woods—the lonely rebel of Walden Pond—is less interesting and provocative than the reality that lies behind that misty cult figure.

Thoreau was born and raised in Concord, Massachusetts, the only hometown boy among the band of men and women later associated with that small but enormously influential New England village. In the parlance of the success stories that have piqued the American imagination since Benjamin Franklin's *Autobiography,* the Thoreau family was "poor but honest." One of the ways the Thoreaus got along was by making lead pencils in a family-circle factory, the kind of work that was being eased out of existence by the Industrial Revolution. The talent for entrepreneurship that made Thoreau an adroit maker of good pencils gave him pause once when he realized how easy it would be for him to corner the local cranberry market and become not so poor or so honest. His experiences in basic economics helped spur him to try other experiments in spiritual coinage. It became urgent for him to discover alternatives to the habits of buying and selling that he believed would ruin the American character.

But first Thoreau had to educate himself. Like Benjamin Franklin, Herman Melville, and Mark Twain (to name a few of the self-educated men of American literature), Thoreau learned that true education meant immersion in the world, whether or not he always liked what he found there. Thoreau started out, however, as a Harvard man. At the age of sixteen, he became one of the poor but diligent young men who, like Emerson a few years before, worked their way through the college. Thoreau's student essays are dutiful and a bit plodding, but they show early signs of his talent for seeing things from his distinctive point of view, one that would continue to puzzle conventional minds throughout his lifetime. Upon graduation in 1837, he returned to

Concord—as he always did after forays away from home. He taught briefly but soon resigned that post rather than do what was expected of local schoolmasters: inflict bodily punishment on erring students. Four years of running a private school with his older brother John followed. John's illness and death put an end to Thoreau's interest in teaching in the institutional sense. He would remain a teacher all his days, but he had to find other ways to instruct, just as he had to find other means of working so that he could live well, rather than living wretchedly in order to work.

Emerson's house and mind were good places for Thoreau to continue his tutelage in the demands of the spirit. Between 1841 and 1843 he lived with the Emerson family as a handyman. He also lived with the ideas Emerson provided the Transcendentalist Club, a group that met to talk about social and personal reforms. However, the most crucial event in Thoreau's life occurred in 1845, the year he moved two miles out of Concord to live in a one-room hut erected beside Walden Pond on land Emerson had loaned him. But experiences other than Harvard and the Emersons had been readying Thoreau for that maturing time by the pond. They helped him to decide which voices he must use to persuade his listeners to the message of challenge and joy he felt compelled to declare.

Speaking in a classroom had not sufficed for Thoreau. His contemporaries found ready audiences for their ideas by lecturing before local groups, so he began to try his hand at this popular form of public address. Thoreau's audiences wanted either to be instructed with the kind of nature lore he drew from the walks in the woods he had been making since he was a child or to be amused by familiar Yankee wit, the kind that was simultaneously exaggeration and understatement. Thoreau provided both the lore and the wit in his lectures, but also something more, and this was not so readily accepted. His audiences did not care to be told that they were fools for having resigned themselves to living stupid, wasted lives, but this was precisely what Thoreau most wanted to tell them. Somehow he had to find ways to make his often harsh home truths palatable to the people he most wished to affect.

By the mid-1840s Thoreau had found a means to win over his audiences. He told them of his travels through the New England landscape, offered them brief essays on a life lived honestly and close to the nub, shucked free of the unnecessary "thingness" that weighed down their materialistic society. Out of a two-week canoe excursion that Thoreau and his brother had taken in 1839 came the experiences of the book *A Week on the Concord and Merrimack Rivers.* Thoreau's only previous experience at writing had been the essays and poems that Emerson printed in *The Dial,* the journal that he and Margaret Fuller edited, along with a piece placed in a Boston journal and "Paradise (to Be) Regained" and "The Landlord," both of which he sold to New York editors during his brief stay on Staten Island in 1843 while tutoring the children of Emerson's brother. These events came in quick succession, and the early 1840s were busy and instructive years for Thoreau's career. Just at this point, Thoreau walked out of Concord to the hut by Walden Pond and set up housekeeping; it was a day he considered symbolically apt for his first major undertaking as a writer: Independence Day, 1845.

Thoreau went into the woods to live the Walden life; while there, he stored up thoughts and experiences he would use when he left the pond in the early autumn of 1847 to begin the long process of writing his masterwork, *Walden.* But the initial reason he settled into the hut was to write *A Week on the Concord and Merrimack Rivers.* Recent scholarship indicates that not only did Thoreau consistently attempt throughout his career to adjust the specialness of his ideas and his literary manner to the expectations of potential reading audiences, but also that *A Week* was itself an important venture in the conversion of his ideas into a literary style that would have the greatest possible appeal. A grab-bag affair whose parts constitute less than a discernible whole, *A Week* was Thoreau's calculated effort to please as wide a reading audience as possible while winning them to a new way of thinking about the diverse worlds, both natural and mental they had the power to make their own. Of the thousand copies of the book Thoreau had printed in 1849, approximately two hundred were sold. Writing *A Week* at Walden Pond was a failed experiment in the most obvious sense. But what Thoreau learned about addressing his audience from that failure was of the utmost value when it came time to write his next full-length book.

Walden: or, Life in the Woods, published in 1854, is what we remember best about Thoreau. The book was slow in coming into its final form. Thoreau spent five years reworking the material he had gathered into his journals during the Walden years of 1845 to 1847. He tinkered and copied, rewrote and recopied. With extreme consciousness of effort, he mastered a language of spontaneity. With great seriousness, he pointed up the wit of his observations concerning the absurdities of the country's social conditions. When at last the book was published, his friends responded to its several levels of mysticism and social theory. Too many took Thoreau's remarks too literally. *Walden* was liked, but not greatly, and it received relatively little critical attention. Thoreau's masterwork, so many years in the making, had to wait almost eighty years more—until the 1930s—before people recognized how advanced his program for the good life was.

Thoreau left Walden Pond in 1847 because he had "several more lives to live and could not spare any more for that one." Those other lives, of involvement with social and literary matters, together with "that one" of the man "on vacation" at Walden, resulted in the activities that occupied him through the fifteen years he had yet to live, giving him the ideas and energies he expended on the writing that lay ahead.

Thoreau said he scorned the need to travel far. Unlike the young Richard Henry Dana, Herman Melville, or the men who were just then setting out for the California gold fields, Thoreau insisted that the best traveling is done while staying home, exploring the cosmography of the imagination. Yet Thoreau made three forays into Maine, where he encountered forests and mountains far rawer than anything he could see in the gentler areas around Concord. Thoreau dealt with the life of the spirit, but he also kept close account of events that were shaking the American social and political system to its foundation: the Fugitive Slave Act, utopian reform plans for communal living and socialistic societies, the Mexican-American War, John Brown's raid on the Harpers Ferry arsenal, the underground railroad, the effects of the new telegraph and increased newspaper circulation, the coming to New England of the Irish immigrants and the changes in the landscape caused by the railroads they were hired to construct, the marketing of everything from blocks of pond ice for chilling the drinks of urban Bostonians to the wild berries whose flavor vanished the moment they were picked for shipment from their native hillsides. Thoreau took note of these events, wrote about them all, and participated directly in several: calling his neighbors together after John Brown's capture to read them his lecture in praise of the man's heroic acts on behalf of the slaves, conveying African Americans over the Underground Railroad on their run toward freedom, and refusing to pay local taxes that supported the Mexican-American War effort.

Thoreau said he was happiest alone, yet he was frequently in contact with the

Concord-Boston group that included Emerson, Fuller, Hawthorne, Alcott, and Ellery Channing. He made a special trip to New Jersey to meet Walt Whitman; he visited with others, such as the Canadian woodcutter Alek Therion, on his walks through the woods and to the surrounding farms. He spent many hours as "servant to Admetus" (an allusion to the Greek myth of the poet-god Apollo, who lived among mortals by doing menial tasks for a local ruler), and he earned the wealth of his observations. Thoreau was also in touch with newspaper editors and book publishers whom he tried to interest in his works, as well as with the men who arranged his lecturing engagements that took him as far afield as Philadelphia and Bangor. Thoreau lived so busy a life, filled with so many activities that kept him in almost constant give-and-take with the everyday world, that it might seem surprising he had time for solitary meditations on the simplified life dedicated to contemplating eternal and universal truths.

Thoreau's health began to decline as early as 1855. By May 1862 he was dead of tuberculosis. Emerson stood over his grave outside Concord and delivered a eulogy that praised Thoreau's exceptional character but also lamented that he had failed to be all he should have been. These comments were based on Emerson's own expectations, colored by the on-again, off-again relationship of admiration and disappointment shared by the older man and his prickly younger friend. That scene by Thoreau's graveside represents what continued to happen in the years following his death as his status was taken under consideration by some of the more influential reputation makers of the period. John Greenleaf Whittier, Oliver Wendell Holmes, and James Russell Lowell, among others, sniped at Thoreau for having been surly, self-conscious, antagonistic, and without humor; that is, for personality traits that assumed more importance in their minds than the form his life's work as a writer had taken.

Thoreau's personal force had not been totally ignored during his lifetime, either as a writer or a thinker. The abrasive urgency of his self-appointed role as prophet and the pawky intelligence of his writing style made it impossible for his essays to be met altogether by silence or dismissal. Immediately after his death, however, it was easier to give approval to Thoreau by taming him, by reducing him to the pupil who had stood in the shadow cast by Emerson. Some tried to convert him into a nature writer who provided nice descriptions of woodland walks. Others turned him into the anecdotist of quaint bits of New England history. By the end of the century, however, Thoreau was taken up as a social reformer by the English Fabians and by Mahatma Ghandi in India, who focused on the same lessons in passive resistance that Martin Luther King, Jr., was to use in the American civil rights struggles. By the 1960s and 1970s Thoreau's image had been reshaped yet again. Many elected to make him the defiant loner and social anarchist, the mindless nature boy, or the dedicated environmentalist. The general effect of these manipulations continued to be reductive. Those who used Thoreau for their own purposes were often incapable of recognizing the critical eye and the sharp tongue he would have turned on their own slack minds and wayward doings.

Recent scholarship has reassessed the quality of Thoreau's prose style and analyzed the conscious adjustments he made in his writing so that what he wanted to say could be brought into line with what his audiences wanted to read. Older views of Thoreau as naturalist and social philosopher, and as the eccentric favored by the current taste for psychobiographies, are now supplemented by appraisals of his forceful literary imagination. Hitherto neglected writings—including the journals, *A Week,* and such essays as "Wild Apples"—are the subject of the appraisals they deserve.

None of these newer evaluations threatens the place of *Walden.* It remains secure as one of the American masterworks. What is gained, however, in going beyond the conventional views of Thoreau is a better appreciation of how exactly he responded to the "voice" that pointed him toward his special vocation as a writer. The recent emphasis in the criticism points up the literary means he used to present the fact that we live perilously and paradoxically between heaven and earth—between "the higher laws" and "brute neighbors."

The many discrepancies Thoreau found in the world parallel his own nature. Both as a man and as a writer, he tried to convert the jagged connections of the world of human society into the seamless cosmic whole of nature's universe. He portrayed the aspirations of our dual selves, which go to the bottom of ponds and to the heights of stars. Thoreau realized the hazardous terms by which our duality comes into conjunction with the universe. We are instructed to live in the exact nick of time, lest we fall outside the fateful rhythms set up for our lives. We must be fully awake in order to escape the seep of the spirit into the dead weight of an exclusively material system. We have to simplify the acts of our daily doings while relishing the array of meanings that lie in the sacred "texts" found in the natural world. We are encouraged to go to inner frontiers where facts are "confronted"—traveling far while staying home. Thoreau's writings provide a list of all the things he believed we must be concerned with because they were what mattered the most to him: how, without "marriage," to have the perfect friendship between one person and another or between the dual selves that lie within each person's nature; how to evoke the sense of social crisis without singing an ode of dejection; how to appeal to religious sensibilities while keeping free of the accepted Christian conventions of doctrine; how to achieve self-pride in the midst of self-doubts; how to attempt to live a model life without appearing to be an egoist and how to write in the autobiographical mode even when the facts make one seem the village fool; how to balance the carnal, "woodchuck" needs of our physical nature with a desire for chastity of spirit; how to insist on the primacy of the present and the value of the future; how to replace the past while using the wisdom of ancient scriptures; how to convey common sense by the uncommon means of language; and, most of all, how to celebrate the unique attributes of the true American democrat who must aspire to live in the heavens yet acknowledge the muddy depths and demands of the everyday world.

Further Reading:

H. Canby, *Thoreau,* 1939, 1968.

L. Shanley, *The Making of Walden,* 1957.

S. Paul, *The Shores of America: Thoreau's Inward Journey,* 1958.

W. Harding, *Thoreau Handbook,* 1959; rev., 1980. *Thoreau: A Collection of Critical Essays,* ed. S. Paul, 1962.

J. Porte, *Emerson and Thoreau, Transcendentalists in Conflict,* 1966.

R. Bridgman, *Dark Thoreau,* 1982.

W. Howarth, *The Book of Concord,* 1982.

R. Richardson, *Henry David Thoreau: Life of the Mind,* 1986.

F. Garber, "Henry David Thoreau," *Columbia Literary History of the United States,* 1988.

L. Neufeldt, *The Economist: Henry Thoreau and Enterprise,* 1989.

L. Buell, "The Thoreauvian Pilgrimage," *American Literature* 61 (1989), 175–99.

R. Sattlemeyer, " 'When He Became My Enemy': Emerson and Thoreau," *New England Quarterly* 62 (1989), 187–204.

H. Peck, *Thoreau's Morning Work,* 1990.

S. Fink, *Prophet in the Marketplace,* 1992.

Texts:

Walden and "Resistance to Civil Government" from *The Writings of Henry D. Thoreau,* 12 vols., 1971–1992.

See also *The Writings of Henry David Thoreau* (Walden Edition), 20 vols., 1906.

Walden*

Economy

When I wrote the following pages, or rather the bulk of them, I lived alone, in the woods, a mile from any neighbor, in a house which I had built myself, on the shore of Walden Pond, in Concord, Massachusetts, and earned my living by the labor of my hands only. I lived there two years and two months. At present I am a sojourner in civilized life again.

I should not obtrude my affairs so much on the notice of my readers if very particular inquiries had not been made by my townsmen concerning my mode of life, which some would call impertinent, though they do not appear to me at all impertinent, but, considering the circumstances, very natural and pertinent. Some have asked what I got to eat; if I did not feel lonesome; if I was not afraid; and the like. Others have been curious to learn what portion of my income I devoted to charitable purposes; and some, who have large families, how many poor children I maintained. I will therefore ask those of my readers who feel no particular interest in me to pardon me if I undertake to answer some of these questions in this book. In most books, the *I,* or first person, is omitted; in this it will be retained; that, in respect to egotism, is the main difference. We commonly do not remember that it is, after all, always the first person that is speaking. I should not talk so much about myself if there were any body else whom I knew as well. Unfortunately, I am confined to this theme by the narrowness of my experience. Moreover, I, on my side, require of every writer, first or last, a simple and sincere account of his own life, and not merely what he has heard of other men's lives; some such account as he would send to his kindred from a distant land; for if he has lived sincerely, it must have been in a distant land to me. Perhaps these pages are more particularly addressed to poor students. As for the rest of my readers, they will accept such portions as apply to them. I trust that none will stretch the seams in putting on the coat, for it may do good service to him whom it fits.

I would fain say something, not so much concerning the Chinese and Sandwich Islanders[1] as you who read these pages, who are said to live in New England; something about your condition, especially your outward condition or circumstances in this world, in this town, what it is, whether it is necessary that it be as bad as it is, whether it cannot be improved as well as not. I have travelled a good deal in Concord; and every where, in shops, and offices, and fields, the inhabitants have appeared to me to be doing

---

* *Walden* was published in 1854, seven years after Thoreau left his hut by the pond. While living at Walden Pond, Thoreau wrote *A Week on the Concord and Merrimack Rivers* and portions of *Walden.* He continued revising the latter between 1849 and 1854.

[1] Natives of what are now the Hawaiian Islands.

penance in a thousand remarkable ways. What I have heard of Brahmins[2] sitting exposed to four fires and looking in the face of the sun; or hanging suspended, with their heads downward, over flames; or looking at the heavens over their shoulders "until it becomes impossible for them to resume their natural position, while from the twist of the neck nothing but liquids can pass into the stomach;" or dwelling, chained for life, at the foot of a tree; or measuring with their bodies, like caterpillars, the breadth of vast empires; or standing on one leg on the tops of pillars,—even these forms of conscious penance are hardly more incredible and astonishing than the scenes which I daily witness. The twelve labors of Hercules[3] were trifling in comparison with those which my neighbors have undertaken; for they were only twelve, and had an end; but I could never see that these men slew or captured any monster or finished any labor. They have no friend Iolas to burn with a hot iron the root of the hydra's head, but as soon as one head is crushed, two spring up.

I see young men, my townsmen, whose misfortune it is to have inherited farms, houses, barns, cattle, and farming tools; for these are more easily acquired than got rid of. Better if they had been born in the open pasture and suckled by a wolf, that they might have seen with clearer eyes what field they were called to labor in. Who made them serfs of the soil? Why should they eat their sixty acres, when man is condemned to eat only his peck of dirt? Why should they begin digging their graves as soon as they are born? They have got to live a man's life, pushing all these things before them, and get on as well as they can. How many a poor immortal soul have I met well nigh crushed and smothered under its load, creeping down the road of life, pushing before it a barn seventy-five feet by forty, its Augean stables[4] never cleansed, and one hundred acres of land, tillage, mowing, pasture, and wood-lot! The portionless, who struggle with no such unnecessary inherited encumbrances, find it labor enough to subdue and cultivate a few cubic feet of flesh.

But men labor under a mistake. The better part of the man is soon ploughed into the soil for compost. By a seeming fate, commonly called necessity, they are employed, as it says in an old book, laying up treasures which moth and rust will corrupt and thieves break through and steal.[5] It is a fool's life, as they will find when they get to the end of it, if not before. It is said that Deucalion and Pyrrha[6] created men by throwing stones over their heads behind them:—

> Inde genus durum sumus, experiensque laborum,
> Et documenta damus qua simus origine nati.[7]

Or, as Raleigh rhymes it in his sonorous way,—

---

[2] Hindus of the highest caste.

[3] In classic myth, the hero Hercules was set to perform twelve arduous tasks. Among these was the slaying of the nine-headed monster Hydra, which he was able to do with the help of his companion Iolas. Iolas seared the stumps of each of Hydra's heads as Hercules cut them off, so they could not grow back.

[4] Stables in which three-thousand oxen had been kept for thirty years by King Augeas; it was one of Hercules' labors to clean them.

[5] Thoreau paraphrases from Matthew 6:19, from "the old book (the Bible)."

[6] Survivors of a great flood, Deucalion and Pyrrha in classic myth repopulated the earth by throwing stones over their shoulders which were transformed into men and women.

[7] *Metamorphoses*, Book I, by Ovid (43 B.C.–A.D. 17?).

> "From thence our kind hard-hearted is, enduring pain and care,
> Approving that our bodies of a stony nature are."[8]

So much for a blind obedience to a blundering oracle, throwing the stones over their heads behind them, and not seeing where they fell.

Most men, even in this comparatively free country, through mere ignorance and mistake, are so occupied with the factitious cares and superfluously coarse labors of life that its finer fruits cannot be plucked by them. Their fingers, from excessive toil, are too clumsy and tremble too much for that. Actually, the laboring man has not leisure for a true integrity day by day; he cannot afford to sustain the manliest relations to men; his labor would be depreciated in the market. He has no time to be any thing but a machine. How can he remember well his ignorance—which his growth requires—who has so often to use his knowledge? We should feed and clothe him gratuitously sometimes, and recruit him with our cordials, before we judge of him. The finest qualities of our nature, like the bloom on fruits, can be preserved only by the most delicate handling. Yet we do not treat ourselves nor one another thus tenderly.

Some of you, we all know, are poor, find it hard to live, are sometimes, as it were, gasping for breath. I have no doubt that some of you who read this book are unable to pay for all the dinners which you have actually eaten, or for the coats and shoes which are fast wearing or are already worn out, and have come to this page to spend borrowed or stolen time, robbing your creditors of an hour. It is very evident what mean and sneaking lives many of you live, for my sight has been whetted by experience; always on the limits,[9] trying to get into business and trying to get out of debt, a very ancient slough, called by the Latins, *æs alienum,* another's brass,[10] for some of their coins were made of brass; still living, and dying, and buried by this other's brass; always promising to pay, promising to pay, to-morrow, and dying to-day, insolvent; seeking to curry favor, to get custom, by how many modes, only not state-prison offences; lying, flattering, voting, contracting yourselves into a nutshell of civility, or dilating into an atmosphere of thin and vaporous generosity, that you may persuade your neighbor to let you make his shoes, or his hat, or his coat, or his carriage, or import his groceries for him; making yourselves sick, that you may lay up something against a sick day, something to be tucked away in an old chest, or in a stocking behind the plastering, or, more safely, in the brick bank; no matter where, no matter how much or how little.

I sometimes wonder that we can be so frivolous, I may almost say, as to attend to the gross but somewhat foreign form of servitude called Negro Slavery, there are so many keen and subtle masters that enslave both north and south. It is hard to have a southern overseer; it is worse to have a northern one; but worst of all when you are the slave-driver of yourself. Talk of a divinity in man! Look at the teamster on the highway, wending to market by day or night; does any divinity stir within him? His highest duty to fodder and water his horses! What is his destiny to him compared with the shipping interests? Does not he drive for Squire Make-a-stir? How godlike, how immortal, is he? See how he cowers and sneaks, how vaguely all the day he fears, not being immortal nor divine,

---

[8] From *The History of the World* (1614) by Sir Walter Raleigh (1552?–1618), English explorer, historian, poet, and courtier.

[9] In matters of credit.

[10] Someone else's money.

but the slave and prisoner of his own opinion of himself, a fame won by his own deeds. Public opinion is a weak tyrant compared with our own private opinion. What a man thinks of himself, that it is which determines, or rather indicates, his fate. Self-emancipation even in the West Indian provinces of the fancy and imagination,—what Wilberforce[11] is there to bring that about? Think, also, of the ladies of the land weaving toilet[12] cushions against the last day, not to betray too green an interest in their fates! As if you could kill time without injuring eternity.

The mass of men lead lives of quiet desperation. What is called resignation is confirmed desperation. From the desperate city you go into the desperate country, and have to console yourself with the bravery of minks and muskrats. A stereotyped but unconscious despair is concealed even under what are called the games and amusements of mankind. There is no play in them, for this comes after work. But it is a characteristic of wisdom not to do desperate things.

When we consider what, to use the words of the catechism,[13] is the chief end of man, and what are the true necessaries and means of life, it appears as if men had deliberately chosen the common mode of living because they preferred it to any other. Yet they honestly think there is no choice left. But alert and healthy natures remember that the sun rose clear. It is never too late to give up our prejudices. No way of thinking or doing, however ancient, can be trusted without proof. What every body echoes or in silence passes by as true to-day may turn out to be falsehood to-morrow, mere smoke of opinion, which some had trusted for a cloud that would sprinkle fertilizing rain on their fields. What old people say you cannot do you try and find that you can. Old deeds for old people, and new deeds for new. Old people did not know enough once, perchance, to fetch fresh fuel to keep the fire a-going; new people put a little dry wood under a pot,[14] and are whirled round the globe with the speed of birds, in a way to kill old people, as the phrase is. Age is no better, hardly so well, qualified for an instructor as youth, for it has not profited so much as it has lost. One may almost doubt if the wisest man has learned any thing of absolute value by living. Practically, the old have no very important advice to give the young, their own experience has been so partial, and their lives have been such miserable failures, for private reasons, as they must believe; and it may be that they have some faith left which belies that experience, and they are only less young than they were. I have lived some thirty years on this planet, and I have yet to hear the first syllable of valuable or even earnest advice from my seniors. They have told me nothing, and probably cannot tell me any thing, to the purpose. Here is life, an experiment to a great extent untried by me; but it does not avail me that they have tried it. If I have any experience which I think valuable, I am sure to reflect that this my Mentors said nothing about.

One farmer says to me, "You cannot live on vegetable food solely, for it furnishes nothing to make bones with;" and so he religiously devotes a part of his day to supplying his system with the raw material of bones; walking all the while he talks behind his oxen, which, with vegetable-made bones, jerk him and his lumbering plough

[11] William Wilberforce (1759–1833), English philanthropist and abolitionist.

[12] Boudoir, dressing room.

[13] The Westminster Catechism, printed in the *New England Primer*, the book of instruction for children in the New England colonies, stated that the chief purpose of human existence "is to glorify God and to enjoy him forever."

[14] Locomotive steam boiler.

along in spite of every obstacle. Some things are really necessaries of life in some circles, the most helpless and diseased, which in others are luxuries merely, and in others still are entirely unknown.

The whole ground of human life seems to some to have been gone over by their predecessors, both the heights and the valleys, and all things to have been cared for. According to Evelyn,[15] "the wise Solomon prescribed ordinances for the very distances of trees; and the Roman prætors have decided how often you may go into your neighbor's land to gather the acorns which fall on it without trespass, and what share belongs to that neighbor." Hippocrates[16] has even left directions how we should cut our nails; that is, even with the ends of the fingers, neither shorter nor longer. Undoubtedly the very tedium and ennui which presume to have exhausted the variety and the joys of life are as old as Adam. But man's capacities have never been measured; nor are we to judge of what he can do by any precedents, so little has been tried. Whatever have been thy failures hitherto, "be not afflicted, my child, for who shall assign to thee what thou hast left undone?"[17]

We might try our lives by a thousand simple tests; as, for instance, that the same sun which ripens my beans illumines at once a system of earths like ours. If I had remembered this it would have prevented some mistakes. This was not the light in which I hoed them. The stars are the apexes of what wonderful triangles! What distant and different beings in the various mansions of the universe are contemplating the same one at the same moment! Nature and human life are as various as our several constitutions. Who shall say what prospect life offers to another? Could a greater miracle take place than for us to look through each other's eyes for an instant? We should live in all the ages of the world in an hour; ay, in all the worlds of the ages. History, Poetry, Mythology!—I know of no reading of another's experience so startling and informing as this would be.

The greater part of what my neighbors call good I believe in my soul to be bad, and if I repent of any thing, it is very likely to be my good behavior. What demon possessed me that I behaved so well? You may say the wisest thing you can, old man,—you who have lived seventy years, not without honor of a kind,—I hear an irresistible voice which invites me away from all that. One generation abandons the enterprises of another like stranded vessels.

I think that we may safely trust a good deal more than we do. We may waive just so much care of ourselves as we honestly bestow elsewhere. Nature is as well adapted to our weakness as to our strength. The incessant anxiety and strain of some is a well nigh incurable form of disease. We are made to exaggerate the importance of what work we do; and yet how much is not done by us! or, what if we had been taken sick? How vigilant we are! determined not to live by faith if we can avoid it; all the day long on the alert, at night we unwillingly say our prayers and commit ourselves to uncertainties. So thoroughly and sincerely are we compelled to live, reverencing our life, and denying the possibility of change. This is the only way, we say; but there are as many ways as there can be drawn radii from one centre. All change is a miracle to contemplate; but it is a

---

[15] John Evelyn (1620–1706), best known for his diaries, but also the author of *Sylva* (1644), a book on the growing of trees.

[16] Greek physician (460?–377 B.C.).

[17] From the *Vishnu Purana*, a Hindu sacred text.

miracle which is taking place every instant. Confucius[18] said, "To know that we know what we know, and that we do not know what we do not know, that is true knowledge." When one man has reduced a fact of the imagination to be a fact to his understanding, I foresee that all men will at length establish their lives on that basis.

Let us consider for a moment what most of the trouble and anxiety which I have referred to is about, and how much it is necessary that we be troubled or, at least, careful. It would be some advantage to live a primitive and frontier life, though in the midst of an outward civilization, if only to learn what are the gross necessaries of life and what methods have been taken to obtain them; or even to look over the old daybooks of the merchants, to see what it was that men most commonly bought at the stores, what they stored, that is, what are the grossest groceries. For the improvements of ages have had but little influence on the essential laws of man's existence; as our skeletons, probably, are not to be distinguished from those of our ancestors.

By the words, *necessary of life,* I mean whatever, of all that man obtains by his own exertions, has been from the first, or from long use has become, so important to human life that few, if any, whether from savageness, or poverty, or philosophy, ever attempt to do without it. To many creatures there is in this sense but one necessary of life, Food. To the bison of the prairie it is a few inches of palatable grass, with water to drink; unless he seeks the Shelter of the forest or the mountain's shadow. None of the brute creation requires more than Food and Shelter. The necessaries of life for man in this climate may, accurately enough, be distributed under the several heads of Food, Shelter, Clothing, and Fuel; for not till we have secured these are we prepared to entertain the true problems of life with freedom and a prospect of success. Man has invented, not only houses, but clothes and cooked food; and possibly from the accidental discovery of the warmth of fire, and the consequent use of it, at first a luxury, arose the present necessity to sit by it. We observe cats and dogs acquiring the same second nature. By proper Shelter and Clothing we legitimately retain our own internal heat; but with an excess of these, or of Fuel, that is, with an external heat greater than our own internal, may not cookery properly be said to begin? Darwin, the naturalist, says of the inhabitants of Tierra del Fuego,[19] that while his own party, who were well clothed and sitting close to a fire, were far from too warm, these naked savages, who were farther off, were observed, to his great surprise, "to be streaming with perspiration at undergoing such a roasting." So, we are told, the New Hollander[20] goes naked with impunity, while the European shivers in his clothes. Is it impossible to combine the hardiness of these savages with the intellectualness of the civilized man? According to Liebig,[21] man's body is a stove, and food the fuel which keeps up the internal combustion in the lungs. In cold weather we eat more, in warm less. The animal heat is the result of a slow combustion, and disease and death take place when this is too rapid; or for want of fuel, or from some defect in the draught, the fire goes out. Of course the vital heat is not to be confounded with fire; but so much for analogy. It appears, therefore, from the above list, that the expression, *animal life,* is nearly synonymous with the expression, *animal*

---

[18] From *The Analects,* II, 17, by the Chinese philosopher Confucius (ca. 551–479 B.C.).

[19] Charles Darwin (1809–1882) described this archipelago near the southern tip of South America in his *Journal of Researches* (1839).

[20] Aboriginal Australian.

[21] The German chemist Justus von Liebig (1803–1873).

heat; for while Food may be regarded as the Fuel which keeps up the fire within us,—and Fuel serves only to prepare that Food or to increase the warmth of our bodies by addition from without,—Shelter and Clothing also serve only to retain the *heat* thus generated and absorbed.

The grand necessity, then, for our bodies, is to keep warm, to keep the vital heat in us. What pains we accordingly take, not only with our Food, and Clothing, and Shelter, but with our beds, which are our night-clothes, robbing the nests and breasts of birds to prepare this shelter within a shelter, as the mole has its bed of grass and leaves at the end of its burrow! The poor man is wont to complain that this is a cold world; and to cold, no less physical than social, we refer directly a great part of our ails. The summer, in some climates, makes possible to man a sort of Elysian life.[22] Fuel, except to cook his Food, is then unnecessary; the sun is his fire, and many of the fruits are sufficiently cooked by its rays; while Food generally is more various, and more easily obtained, and Clothing and Shelter are wholly or half unnecessary. At the present day, and in this country, as I find by my own experience, a few implements, a knife, an axe, a spade, a wheelbarrow, & c., and for the studious, lamplight, stationery, and access to a few books, rank next to necessaries, and can all be obtained at a trifling cost. Yet some, not wise, go to the other side of the globe, to barbarous and unhealthy regions, and devote themselves to trade for ten or twenty years, in order that they may live,—that is, keep comfortably warm,—and die in New England at last. The luxuriously rich are not simply kept comfortably warm, but unnaturally hot;[23] as I implied before, they are cooked, of course *à la mode*.[24]

Most of the luxuries, and many of the so called comforts of life, are not only not indispensable, but positive hinderances to the elevation of mankind. With respect to luxuries and comforts, the wisest have ever lived a more simple and meager life than the poor. The ancient philosophers, Chinese, Hindoo, Persian, and Greek, were a class than which none has been poorer in outward riches, none so rich in inward. We know not much about them. It is remarkable that *we* know so much of them as we do. The same is true of the more modern reformers and benefactors of their race. None can be an impartial or wise observer of human life but from the vantage ground of what *we* should call voluntary poverty. Of a life of luxury the fruit is luxury, whether in agriculture, or commerce, or literature, or art. There are nowadays professors of philosophy, but not philosophers. Yet it is admirable to profess because it was once admirable to live. To be a philosopher is not merely to have subtle thoughts, nor even to found a school, but so to love wisdom as to live according to its dictates, a life of simplicity, independence, magnanimity, and trust. It is to solve some of the problems of life, not only theoretically, but practically. The success of great scholars and thinkers is commonly a courtier-like success, not kingly, not manly. They make shift to live merely by conformity, practically as their fathers did, and are in no sense the progenitors of a nobler race of men. But why do men degenerate ever? What makes families run out? What is the nature of the luxury which enervates and destroys nations? Are we sure that there is none of it in our own lives? The philosopher is in advance of his age even in the outward form of his life. He is not fed, sheltered, clothed, warmed, like his contemporaries. How can a man be a philosopher and not maintain his vital heat by better methods than other men?

---

[22] i.e., as fine a life as that enjoyed by the inhabitants of the paradise described in Greek myth.

[23] With central heating.

[24] In high style.

When a man is warmed by the several modes which I have described, what does he want next? Surely not more warmth of the same kind, as more and richer food, larger and more splendid houses, finer and more abundant clothing, more numerous incessant and hotter fires, and the like. When he has obtained those things which are necessary to life, there is another alternative than to obtain the superfluities; and that is, to adventure on life now, his vacation from humbler toil having commenced. The soil, it appears, is suited to the seed, for it has sent its radicle[25] downward, and it may now send its shoot upward also with confidence. Why has man rooted himself thus firmly in the earth, but that he may rise in the same proportion into the heavens above?—for the nobler plants are valued for the fruit they bear at last in the air and light, far from the ground, and are not treated like the humbler esculents, which, though they may be biennials, are cultivated only till they have perfected their root, and often cut down at top for this purpose, so that most would not know them in their flowering season.

I do not mean to prescribe rules to strong and valiant natures, who will mind their own affairs whether in heaven or hell, and perchance build more magnificently and spend more lavishly than the richest, without ever impoverishing themselves, not knowing how they live,—if, indeed, there are any such, as has been dreamed; nor to those who find their encouragement and inspiration in precisely the present condition of things, and cherish it with the fondness and enthusiasm of lovers,—and, to some extent, I reckon myself in this number; I do not speak to those who are well employed, in whatever circumstances, and they know whether they are well employed or not;—but mainly to the mass of men who are discontented, and idly complaining of the hardness of their lot or of the times, when they might improve them. There are some who complain most energetically and inconsolably of any, because they are, as they say, doing their duty. I also have in my mind that seemingly wealthy, but most terribly impoverished class of all, who have accumulated dross, but know not how to use it, or get rid of it, and thus have forged their own golden or silver fetters.

If I should attempt to tell how I have desired to spend my life in years past, it would probably surprise those of my readers who are somewhat acquainted with its actual history; it would certainly astonish those who know nothing about it. I will only hint at some of the enterprises which I have cherished.

In any weather, at any hour of the day or night, I have been anxious to improve the nick of time, and notch it on my stick too; to stand on the meeting of two eternities, the past and future, which is precisely the present moment; to toe that line. You will pardon some obscurities, for there are more secrets in my trade than in most men's, and yet not voluntarily kept, but inseparable from its very nature. I would gladly tell all that I know about it, and never paint "No Admittance" on my gate.

I long ago lost a hound, a bay horse, and a turtledove, and am still on their trail. Many are the travellers I have spoken concerning them, describing their tracks and what calls they answered to. I have met one or two who had heard the hound, and the tramp of the horse, and even seen the dove disappear behind a cloud, and they seemed as anxious to recover them as if they had lost them themselves.

To anticipate, not the sunrise and the dawn merely, but, if possible, Nature herself! How many mornings, summer and winter, before yet any neighbor was stirring about

---

[25] Root.

his business, have I been about mine! No doubt, many of my townsmen have met me returning from this enterprise, farmers starting for Boston in the twilight, or wood-choppers going to their work. It is true, I never assisted the sun materially in his rising, but, doubt not, it was of the last importance only to be present at it.

So many autumn, ay, and winter days, spent outside the town, trying to hear what was in the wind, to hear and carry it express! I well-nigh sunk all my capital in it, and lost my own breath into the bargain, running in the face of it. If it had concerned either of the political parties, depend upon it, it would have appeared in the Gazette[26] with the earliest intelligence.[27] At other times watching from the observatory of some cliff or tree, to telegraph any new arrival; or waiting at evening on the hill-tops for the sky to fall, that I might catch something, though I never caught much, and that, manna-wise,[28] would dissolve again in the sun.

For a long time I was reporter to a journal,[29] of no very wide circulation, whose editor has never yet seen fit to print the bulk of my contributions, and, as is too common with writers, I got only my labor for my pains. However, in this case my pains were their own reward.

For many years I was self-appointed inspector of snow storms and rain storms, and did my duty faithfully; surveyor, if not of highways, then of forest paths and all across-lot routes, keeping them open, and ravines bridged and passable at all seasons, where the public heel had testified to their utility.

I have looked after the wild stock of the town, which give a faithful herdsman a good deal of trouble by leaping fences; and I have had an eye to the unfrequented nooks and corners of the farm; though I did not always know whether Jonas or Solomon worked in a particular field to-day; that was none of my business. I have watered the red huckle-berry, the sand cherry and the nettle tree, the red pine and the black ash, the white grape and the yellow violet, which might have withered else in dry seasons.

In short, I went on thus for a long time, I may say it without boasting, faithfully minding my business, till it became more and more evident that my townsmen would not after all admit me into the list of town officers, nor make my place a sinecure with a moderate allowance. My accounts, which I can swear to have kept faithfully, I have, indeed, never got audited, still less accepted, still less paid and settled. However, I have not set my heart on that.

Not long since, a strolling Indian went to sell baskets at the house of a well-known lawyer in my neighborhood. "Do you wish to buy any baskets?" he asked. "No, we do not want any," was the reply. "What!" exclaimed the Indian as he went out the gate, "do you mean to starve us?" Having seen his industrious white neighbors so well off,—that the lawyer had only to weave arguments, and by some magic wealth and standing followed, he had said to himself; I will go into business; I will weave baskets; it is a thing which I can do. Thinking that when he had made the baskets he would have done his part, and then it would be the white man's to buy them. He had not discovered that it was necessary for him to make it worth the other's while to buy them, or at least make

---

[26] The weekly newspaper of Concord.
[27] News.
[28] Exodus 16 recounts the time that manna, a food given to the Israelites on their journey out of Egypt, melted in the sun.

[29] Thoreau wrote on different occasions for *The Dial, The Democratic Review,* and other magazines, and at all times faithfully "reported" his activities and thoughts to his own journals.

him think that it was so, or to make something else which it would be worth his while to buy. I too had woven a kind of basket of a delicate texture, but I had not made it worth any one's while to buy them. Yet not the less, in my case, did I think it worth my while to weave them, and instead of studying how to make it worth men's while to buy my baskets, I studied rather how to avoid the necessity of selling them. The life which men praise and regard as successful is but one kind. Why should we exaggerate any one kind at the expense of the others?

Finding that my fellow-citizens were not likely to offer me any room in the court house, or any curacy or living any where else, but I must shift for myself, I turned my face more exclusively than ever to the woods, where I was better known. I determined to go into business at once, and not wait to acquire the usual capital, using such slender means as I had already got. My purpose in going to Walden Pond was not to live cheaply nor to live dearly there, but to transact some private business[30] with the fewest obstacles; to be hindered from accomplishing which for want of a little common sense, a little enterprise and business talent, appeared not so sad as foolish.

I have always endeavored to acquire strict business habits; they are indispensable to every man. If your trade is with the Celestial Empire,[31] then some small counting house on the coast, in some Salem harbor, will be fixture enough. You will export such articles as the country affords, purely native products, much ice and pine timber and a little granite, always in native bottoms. These will be good ventures. To oversee all the details yourself in person; to be at once pilot and captain, and owner and underwriter; to buy and sell and keep the accounts; to read every letter received, and write or read every letter sent; to superintend the discharge of imports night and day; to be upon many parts of the coast almost at the same time;—often the richest freight will be discharged upon a Jersey shore;[32]—to be your own telegraph, unweariedly sweeping the horizon, speaking all passing vessels bound coastwise; to keep up a steady despatch of commodities, for the supply of such a distant and exorbitant market; to keep yourself informed of the state of the markets, prospects of war and peace every where, and anticipate the tendencies of trade and civilization,—taking advantage of the results of all exploring expeditions, using new passages and all improvements in navigation;—charts to be studied, the position of reefs and new lights and buoys to be ascertained, and ever, and ever, the logarithmic tables to be corrected, for by the error of some calculator the vessel often splits upon a rock that should have reached a friendly pier,—there is the untold fate of La Perouse;[33]—universal science to be kept pace with, studying the lives of all great discoverers and navigators, great adventurers and merchants, from Hanno and the Phœnicians[34] down to our day; in fine, account of stock to be taken from time to time, to know how you stand. It is a labor to task the faculties of a man,—such problems of profit and loss, of interest, of tare and tret,[35] and gauging of all kinds in it, as demand a universal knowledge.

---

[30] To complete his first book, *A Week on the Concord and Merrimack Rivers* (1849).

[31] China.

[32] New Jersey.

[33] Jean François de Gallup, count de la Perouse (1741–1788), French explorer lost somewhere in the South Pacific.

[34] Hanno was a Carthaginian explorer of the fifth century B.C.; the ancient Phoenicians were also famous for their voyages into uncharted waters.

[35] Calculations of weight.

I have thought that Walden Pond would be a good place for business, not solely on account of the railroad and the ice trade; it offers advantages which it may not be good policy to divulge; it is a good port and a good foundation. No Neva[36] marshes to be filled; though you must every where build on piles of your own driving. It is said that a flood-tide, with a westerly wind, and ice in the Neva, would sweep St. Petersburg from the face of the earth.

As this business was to be entered into without the usual capital, it may not be easy to conjecture where those means, that will still be indispensable to every such undertaking, were to be obtained. As for Clothing, to come at once to the practical part of the question, perhaps we are led oftener by the love of novelty, and a regard for the opinions of men, in procuring it, than by a true utility. Let him who has work to do recollect that the object of clothing is, first, to retain the vital heat, and secondly, in this state of society, to cover nakedness, and he may judge how much of any necessary or important work may be accomplished without adding to his wardrobe. Kings and queens who wear a suit but once, though made by some tailor or dressmaker to their majesties, cannot know the comfort of wearing a suit that fits. They are no better than wooden horses to hang the clean clothes on. Every day our garments become more assimilated to ourselves, receiving the impress of the wearer's character, until we hesitate to lay them aside, without such delay and medical appliances and some such solemnity even as our bodies. No man ever stood the lower in my estimation for having a patch in his clothes; yet I am sure that there is greater anxiety, commonly, to have fashionable, or at least clean and unpatched clothes, than to have a sound conscience. But even if the rent is not mended, perhaps the worst vice betrayed is improvidence. I sometimes try my acquaintances by such tests as this;—who could wear a patch, or two extra seams only, over the knee? Most behave as if they believed that their prospects for life would be ruined if they should do it. It would be easier for them to hobble to town with a broken leg than with a broken pantaloon. Often if an accident happens to a gentleman's legs, they can be mended; but if a similar accident happens to the legs of his pantaloons, there is no help for it; for he considers, not what is truly respectable, but what is respected. We know but few men, a great many coats and breeches. Dress a scarecrow in your last shift, you standing shiftless by, who would not soonest salute the scarecrow? Passing a cornfield the other day, close by a hat and coat on a stake, I recognized the owner of the farm. He was only a little more weather-beaten than when I saw him last. I have heard of a dog that barked at every stranger who approached his master's premises with clothes on, but was easily quieted by a naked thief. It is an interesting question how far men would retain their relative rank if they were divested of their clothes. Could you, in such a case, tell surely of any company of civilized men, which belonged to the most respected class? When Madam Pfeiffer,[37] in her adventurous travels round the world, from east to west, had got so near home as Asiatic Russia, she says that she felt the necessity of wearing other than a travelling dress, when she went to meet the authorities, for she "was now in a civilized country, where —— people are judged of by their clothes." Even in our democratic New England towns the accidental possession of wealth, and its manifestation in dress and equipage alone, obtain for the possessor al-

---

[36] River in Russia near the site of St. Petersburg.

[37] Ida Reyer Pfeiffer (1797–1858), Austrian writer of travel books, such as *A Woman's Journey Round the World* (1852).

most universal respect. But they who yield such respect, numerous as they are, are so far heathen, and need to have a missionary sent to them. Beside, clothes introduced sewing, a kind of work which you may call endless; a woman's dress, at least, is never done.

A man who has at length found something to do will not need to get a new suit to do it in; for him the old will do, that has lain dusty in the garret for an indeterminate period. Old shoes will serve a hero longer than they have served his valet,—if a hero ever has a valet—bare feet are older than shoes, and he can make them do. Only they who go to soirées and legislative halls must have new coats, coats to change as often as the man changes in them. But if my jacket and trousers, my hat and shoes, are fit to worship God in, they will do; will they not? Who ever saw his old clothes,—his old coat, actually worn out, resolved into its primitive elements, so that it was not a deed of charity to bestow it on some poor boy, by him perchance to be bestowed on some poorer still, or shall we say richer, who could do with less? I say, beware of all enterprises that require new clothes, and not rather a new wearer of clothes. If there is not a new man, how can the new clothes be made to fit? If you have any enterprise before you, try it in your old clothes. All men want, not something to *do with,* but something to *do,* or rather something to *be.* Perhaps we should never procure a new suit, however ragged or dirty the old, until we have so conducted, so enterprised or sailed in some way, that we feel like new men in the old, and that to retain it would be like keeping new wine in old bottles.[38] Our moulting season, like that of the fowls, must be a crisis in our lives. The loon retires to solitary ponds to spend it. Thus also the snake casts its slough, and the caterpillar its wormy coat, by an internal industry and expansion; for clothes are but our outmost cuticle and mortal coil. Otherwise we shall be found sailing under false colors, and be inevitably cashiered at last by our own opinion, as well as that of mankind.

We don garment after garment, as if we grew like exogenous plants by addition without. Our outside and often thin and fanciful clothes are our epidermis or false skin, which partakes not of our life, and may be stripped off here and there without fatal injury; our thicker garments, constantly worn, are our cellular integument, or cortex; but our shirts are our liber or true bark, which cannot be removed without girdling and so destroying the man. I believe that all races at some seasons wear something equivalent to the shirt. It is desirable that a man be clad so simply that he can lay his hands on himself in the dark, and that he live in all respects so compactly and preparedly, that, if an enemy take the town, he can, like the old philosopher, walk out the gate empty-handed without anxiety. While one thick garment is, for most purposes, as good as three thin ones, and cheap clothing can be obtained at prices really to suit customers; while a thick coat can be bought for five dollars, which will last as many years, thick pantaloons for two dollars, cowhide boots for a dollar and a half a pair, a summer hat for a quarter of a dollar, and a winter cap for sixty-two and a half cents, or a better be made at home at a nominal cost, where is he so poor that, clad in such a suit, *of his own earning,* there will not be found wise men to do him reverence?

When I ask for a garment of a particular form, my tailoress tells me gravely, "They do not make them so now," not emphasizing the "They" at all, as if she quoted an authority as impersonal as the Fates,[39] and I find it difficult to get made what I want, sim-

---

[38] Allusion to Matthew 9:17.
[39] In classic myth, the goddesses who determine men's destinies.

ply because she cannot believe that I mean what I say, that I am so rash. When I hear this oracular sentence, I am for a moment absorbed in thought, emphasizing to myself each word separately that I may come at the meaning of it, that I may find out by what degree of consanguinity *They* are related to *me,* and what authority they may have in an affair which affects me so nearly; and, finally, I am inclined to answer her with equal mystery, and without any more emphasis of the "they,"—"It is true, they did not make them so recently, but they do now." Of what use this measuring of me if she does not measure my character, but only the breadth of my shoulders, as it were a peg to hang the coat on? We worship not the Graces,[40] nor the Parcæ,[41] but Fashion. She spins and weaves and cuts with full authority. The head monkey[42] at Paris puts on a traveller's cap, and all the monkeys in America do the same. I sometimes despair of getting any thing quite simple and honest done in this world by the help of men. They would have to be passed through a powerful press first, to squeeze their old notions out of them, so that they would not soon get upon their legs again, and then there would be some one in the company with a maggot in his head, hatched from an egg deposited there nobody knows when, for not even fire kills these things, and you would have lost your labor. Nevertheless, we will not forget that some Egyptian wheat is said to have been handed down to us by a mummy.[43]

On the whole, I think that it cannot be maintained that dressing has in this or any country risen to the dignity of an art. At present men make shift to wear what they can get. Like shipwrecked sailors, they put on what they can find on the beach, and at a little distance, whether of space or time, laugh at each other's masquerade. Every generation laughs at the old fashions, but follows religiously the new. We are amused at beholding the costume of Henry VIII., or Queen Elizabeth,[44] as much as if it was that of the King and Queen of the Cannibal Islands. All costume off a man is pitiful or grotesque. It is only the serious eye peering from and the sincere life passed within it, which restrain laughter and consecrate the costume of any people. Let Harlequin be taken with a fit of the colic and his trappings will have to serve that mood too. When the soldier is hit by a cannon ball rags are as becoming as purple.

The childish and savage taste of men and women for new patterns keeps how many shaking and squinting through kaleidoscopes that they may discover the particular figure which this generation requires to-day. The manufacturers have learned that this taste is merely whimsical. Of two patterns which differ only by a few threads more or less of a particular color, the one will be sold readily, the other lie on the shelf, though it frequently happens that after the lapse of a season the latter becomes the most fashionable. Comparatively, tattooing is not the hideous custom which it is called. It is not barbarous merely because the printing is skin-deep and unalterable.

I cannot believe that our factory system is the best mode by which men may get clothing. The condition of the operatives is becoming every day more like that of the English; and it cannot be wondered at, since, as far as I have heard or observed, the principal object is, not that mankind may be well and honestly clad, but, unquestionably, that the corporations may be enriched. In the long run men hit only what they aim at. Therefore, though they should fail immediately, they had better aim at something high.

---

40 Greek deities of beauty, happiness, and brilliance.
41 Roman goddesses of destiny.
42 Dictator of fashion.

43 i.e., sprung from seeds sealed within an Egyptian tomb.
44 Tudor king (1509–1547) and queen (1558–1603) of England.

As for a Shelter, I will not deny that this is now a necessary of life, though there are instances of men having done without it for long periods in colder countries than this. Samuel Laing[45] says that "The Laplander in his skin dress, and in a skin bag which he puts over his head and shoulders, will sleep night after night on the snow——in a degree of cold which would extinguish the life of one exposed to it in any woollen clothing." He had seen them asleep thus. Yet he adds, "They are not hardier than other people." But, probably, man did not live long on the earth without discovering the convenience which there is in a house, the domestic comforts, which phrase may have originally signified the satisfactions of the house more than of the family; though these must be extremely partial and occasional in those climates where the house is associated in our thoughts with winter or the rainy season chiefly, and two thirds of the year, except for a parasol, is unnecessary. In our climate, in the summer, it was formerly almost solely a covering at night. In the Indian gazettes a wigwam was the symbol of a day's march, and a row of them cut or painted on the bark of a tree signified that so many times they had camped. Man was not made so large limbed and robust but that he must seek to narrow his world, and wall in a space such as fitted him. He was at first bare and out of doors; but though this was pleasant enough in serene and warm weather, by daylight, the rainy season and the winter, to say nothing of the torrid sun, would perhaps have nipped his race in the bud if he had not made haste to clothe himself with the shelter of a house. Adam and Eve, according to the fable, wore the bower before other clothes. Man wanted a home, a place of warmth, or comfort, first of physical warmth, then the warmth of the affections.

We may imagine a time when, in the infancy of the human race, some enterprising mortal crept into a hollow in a rock for shelter. Every child begins the world again, to some extent, and loves to stay out doors, even in wet and cold. It plays house, as well as horse, having an instinct for it. Who does not remember the interest with which when young he looked at shelving rocks, or any approach to a cave? It was the natural yearning of that portion of our most primitive ancestor which still survived in us. From the cave we have advanced to roofs of palm leaves, of bark and boughs, of linen woven and stretched, of grass and straw, of boards and shingles, of stones and tiles. At last, we know not what it is to live in the open air, and our lives are domestic in more senses than we think. From the hearth to the field is a great distance. It would be well perhaps if we were to spend more of our days and nights without any obstruction between us and the celestial bodies, if the poet did not speak so much from under a roof, or the saint dwell there so long. Birds do not sing in caves, nor do doves cherish their innocence in dovecots.

However, if one designs to construct a dwelling house, it behooves him to exercise a little Yankee shrewdness, lest after all he find himself in a workhouse, a labyrinth without a clew, a museum, an almshouse, a prison, or a splendid mausoleum instead. Consider first how slight a shelter is absolutely necessary. I have seen Penobscot Indians,[46] in this town, living in tents of thin cotton cloth, while the snow was nearly a foot deep around them, and I thought that they would be glad to have it deeper to keep out the wind. Formerly, when how to get my living honestly, with freedom left for my proper pursuits, was a question which vexed me even more than it does now, for unfortunately

[45] In his book *Journal of a Residence in Norway* (1837).

[46] Thoreau visited northern Maine and became acquainted with members of the Penobscot tribe at that time.

I am become somewhat callous, I used to see a large box by the railroad, six feet long by three wide, in which the laborers locked up their tools at night, and it suggested to me that every man who was hard pushed might get such a one for a dollar, and, having bored a few auger holes in it, to admit the air at least, get into it when it rained and at night, and hook down the lid, and so have freedom in his love, and in his soul be free. This did not appear the worst, nor by any means a despicable alternative. You could sit up as late as you pleased, and, whenever you got up, go abroad without any landlord or house-lord dogging you for rent. Many a man is harassed to death to pay the rent of a larger and more luxurious box who would not have frozen to death in such a box as this. I am far from jesting. Economy is a subject which admits of being treated with levity, but it cannot so be disposed of. A comfortable house for a rude and hardy race, that lived mostly out of doors, was once made here almost entirely of such materials as Nature furnished ready to their hands. Gookin,[47] who was superintendent of the Indians subject to the Massachusetts Colony, writing in 1674, says, "The best of their houses are covered very neatly, tight and warm, with barks of trees, slipped from their bodies at those seasons when the sap is up, and made into great flakes, with pressure of weighty timber, when they are green. . . . The meaner sort are covered with mats which they make of a kind of bulrush, and are also indifferently tight and warm, but not so good as the former. . . . Some I have seen, sixty or a hundred feet long and thirty feet broad. . . . I have often lodged in their wigwams, and found them as warm as the best English houses." He adds, that they were commonly carpeted and lined within with well-wrought embroidered mats, and were furnished with various utensils. The Indians had advanced so far as to regulate the effect of the wind by a mat suspended over the hole in the roof and moved by a string. Such a lodge was in the first instance constructed in a day or two at most, and taken down and put up in a few hours; and every family owned one, or its apartment in one.

In the savage state every family owns a shelter as good as the best, and sufficient for its coarser and simpler wants; but I think that I speak within bounds when I say that, though the birds of the air have their nests, and the foxes their holes,[48] and the savages their wigwams, in modern civilized society not more than one half the families own a shelter. In the large towns and cities, where civilization especially prevails, the number of those who own a shelter is a very small fraction of the whole. The rest pay an annual tax for this outside garment of all, become indispensable summer and winter, which would buy a village of Indian wigwams, but now helps to keep them poor as long as they live. I do not mean to insist here on the disadvantage of hiring compared with owning, but it is evident that the savage owns his shelter because it costs so little, while the civilized man hires his commonly because he cannot afford to own it; nor can he, in the long run, any better afford to hire. But, answers one, by merely paying this tax the poor civilized man secures an abode which is a palace compared with the savage's. An annual rent of from twenty-five to a hundred dollars, these are the country rates, entitles him to the benefit of the improvements of centuries, spacious apartments, clean paint and paper, Rumford fireplace,[49] back plastering,[50] Venetian blinds, copper pump, spring lock, a commodious cellar, and many other things. But how happens it that he who is said to enjoy these things is so commonly a *poor* civilized man, while the savage,

[47] Daniel Gookin (1612–1687) wrote *Historical Collections of the Indians in New England.*

[48] Reference to Matthew 8:20.

[49] Smokeless stove invented by Count Rumford (1753–1814).

[50] Insulation.

who has them not, is rich as a savage? If it is asserted that civilization is a real advance in the condition of man,—and I think that it is, though only the wise improve their advantages,—it must be shown that it has produced better dwellings without making them more costly; and the cost of a thing is the amount of what I will call life which is required to be exchanged for it, immediately or in the long run. An average house in this neighborhood costs perhaps eight hundred dollars, and to lay up this sum will take from ten to fifteen years of the laborer's life, even if he is not encumbered with a family;—estimating the pecuniary value of every man's labor at one dollar a day, for if some receive more, others receive less;—so that he must have spent more than half his life commonly before *his* wigwam will be earned. If we suppose him to pay a rent instead, this is but a doubtful choice of evils. Would the savage have been wise to exchange his wigwam for a palace on these terms?

It may be guessed that I reduce almost the whole advantage of holding this superfluous property as a fund in store against the future, so far as the individual is concerned, mainly to the defraying of funeral expenses. But perhaps a man is not required to bury himself. Nevertheless this points to an important distinction between the civilized man and the savage; and, no doubt, they have designs on us for our benefit, in making the life of a civilized people an *institution*, in which the life of the individual is to a great extent absorbed, in order to preserve and perfect that of the race. But I wish to show at what a sacrifice this advantage is at present obtained, and to suggest that we may possibly so live as to secure all the advantage without suffering any of the disadvantage. What mean ye by saying that the poor ye have always with you, or that the fathers have eaten sour grapes, and the children's teeth are set on edge?[51]

"As I live, saith the Lord God, ye shall not have occasion any more to use this proverb in Israel."

"Behold all souls are mine; as the soul of the father, so also the soul of the son is mine: the soul that sinneth it shall die."[52]

When I consider my neighbors, the farmers of Concord, who are at least as well off as the other classes, I find that for the most part they have been toiling twenty, thirty, or forty years, that they may become the real owners of their farms, which commonly they have inherited with encumbrances, or else bought with hired money,—and we may regard one third of that toil as the cost of their houses,—but commonly they have not paid for them yet. It is true, the encumbrances sometimes outweigh the value of the farm, so that the farm itself becomes one great encumbrance, and still a man is found to inherit it, being well acquainted with it, as he says. On applying to the assessors, I am surprised to learn that they cannot at once name a dozen in the town who own their farms free and clear. If you would know the history of these homesteads, inquire at the bank where they are mortgaged. The man who has actually paid for his farm with labor on it is so rare that every neighbor can point to him. I doubt if there are three such men in Concord. What has been said of the merchants, that a very large majority, even ninety-seven in a hundred, are sure to fail, is equally true of the farmers. With regard to the merchants, however, one of them says pertinently that a great part of their failures are not genuine pecuniary failures, but merely failures to fulfil their engagements, because it is inconvenient; that is, it is the moral character that breaks down. But this puts

[51] Reference to John 12:8 and Ezekiel 18:2.
[52] Ezekiel 18:3–4.

an infinitely worse face on the matter, and suggests, beside, that probably not even the other three succeed in saving their souls, but are perchance bankrupt in a worse sense than they who fail honestly. Bankruptcy and repudiation are the spring-boards from which much of our civilization vaults and turns its somersets, but the savage stands on the unelastic plank of famine. Yet the Middlesex Cattle Show[53] goes off here with *éclat* annually, as if all the joints of the agricultural machine were suent.[54]

The farmer is endeavoring to solve the problem of livelihood by a formula more complicated than the problem itself. To get his shoestrings he speculates in herds of cattle. With consummate skill he has set his trap with a hair spring to catch comfort and independence, and then, as he turned away, got his own leg into it. This is the reason he is poor; and for a similar reason we are all poor in respect to a thousand savage comforts, though surrounded by luxuries. As Chapman sings,—

> "The false society of men—
>   —for earthly greatness
> All heavenly comforts rarefies to air."[55]

And when the farmer has got his house, he may not be the richer but the poorer for it, and it be the house that has got him. As I understand it, that was a valid objection urged by Momu[56] against the house which Minerva[57] made, that she "had not made it movable, by which means a bad neighborhood might be avoided;" and it may still be urged, for our houses are such unwieldy property that we are often imprisoned rather than housed in them; and the bad neighborhood to be avoided is our own scurvy selves. I know one or two families, at least, in this town, who, for nearly a generation, have been wishing to sell their houses in the outskirts and move into the village, but have not been able to accomplish it, and only death will set them free.

Granted that the *majority* are able at last either to own or hire the modern house with all its improvements. While civilization has been improving our houses, it has not equally improved the men who are to inhabit them. It has created palaces, but it was not so easy to create noblemen and kings. And *if the civilized man's pursuits are no worthier than the savage's, if he is employed the greater part of his life in obtaining gross necessaries and comforts merely, why should he have a better dwelling than the former?*

But how do the poor *minority* fare? Perhaps it will be found, that just in proportion as some have been placed in outward circumstances above the savage, others have been degraded below him. The luxury of one class is counterbalanced by the indigence of another. On the one side is the palace, on the other are the almshouse and "silent poor."[58] The myriads who built the pyramids to be the tombs of the Pharaohs were fed on garlic, and it may be were not decently buried themselves. The mason who finishes the cornice of the palace returns at night perchance to a hut not so good as a wigwam. It is a mistake to suppose that, in a country where the usual evidences of civilization exist, the

---

[53] Annual agricultural fair held in Concord.
[54] Properly functioning.
[55] From *Caesar and Pompey* (1631), Act V, Sc. i, ll. 210, 212–213, by George Chapman, English poet, dramatist, and translator (1559?–1634).

[56] God of mockery in classic myth.
[57] Handicrafts was one of the skills for which the Greek goddess acted as patron.
[58] Those who conceal their poverty.

condition of a very large body of the inhabitants may not be as degraded as that of savages. I refer to the degraded poor, not now to the degraded rich. To know this I should not need to look farther than to the shanties which every where border our railroads, that last improvement in civilization; where I see in my daily walks human beings living in sties, and all winter with an open door, for the sake of light, without any visible, often imaginable, wood pile, and the forms of both old and young are permanently contracted by the long habit of shrinking from cold and misery, and the development of all their limbs and faculties is checked. It certainly is fair to look at that class by whose labor the works which distinguish this generation are accomplished. Such too, to a greater or less extent, is the condition of the operatives of every denomination in England, which is the great workhouse of the world. Or I could refer you to Ireland,[59] which is marked as one of the white or enlightened spots on the map. Contrast the physical condition of the Irish with that of the North American Indian, or the South Sea Islander, or any other savage race before it was degraded by contact with the civilized man. Yet I have no doubt that that people's rulers are as wise as the average of civilized rulers. Their condition only proves what squalidness may consist with civilization. I hardly need refer now to the laborers in our Southern States who produce the staple exports of this country, and are themselves a staple production of the South. But to confine myself to those who are said to be in *moderate* circumstances.

Most men appear never to have considered what a house is, and are actually though needlessly poor all their lives because they think that they must have such a one as their neighbors have. As if one were to wear any sort of coat which the tailor might cut out for him, or, gradually leaving off palmleaf hat or cap of woodchuck skin, complain of hard times because he could not afford to buy him a crown! It is possible to invent a house still more convenient and luxurious than we have, which yet all would admit that man could not afford to pay for. Shall we always study to obtain more of these things, and not sometimes to be content with less? Shall the respectable citizen thus gravely teach, by precept and example, the necessity of the young man's providing a certain number of superfluous glow-shoes,[60] and umbrellas, and empty guest chambers for empty guests, before he dies? Why should not our furniture be as simple as the Arab's or the Indian's? When I think of the benefactors of the race, whom we have apotheosized as messengers from heaven, bearers of divine gifts to man, I do not see in my mind any retinue at their heels, any car-load of fashionable furniture. Or what if I were to allow—would it not be a singular allowance?—that our furniture should be more complex than the Arab's, in proportion as we are morally and intellectually his superiors! At present our houses are cluttered and defiled with it, and a good housewife would sweep out the greater part into the dust hole, and not leave her morning's work undone. Morning work! By the blushes of Aurora[61] and the music of Memnon,[62] what should be man's *morning work* in this world? I had three pieces of limestone on my desk, but I was terrified to find that they required to be dusted daily, when the furniture of my mind was all undusted still, and I threw them out the window in disgust. How, then, could I

---

[59] That is, Ireland in the grip of the potato famine of the 1840s.

[60] Overshoes.

[61] Goddess of dawn in classic myth.

[62] Gigantic statue of an ancient Egyptian king that emitted musical sounds when struck by the morning light.

have a furnished house? I would rather sit in the open air, for no dust gathers on the grass, unless where man has broken ground.

It is the luxurious and dissipated who set the fashions which the herd so diligently follow. The traveller who stops at the best houses, so called, soon discovers this, for the publicans presume him to be a Sardanapalus,[63] and if he resigned himself to their tender mercies he would soon be completely emasculated. I think that in the railroad car we are inclined to spend more on luxury than on safety and convenience, and it threatens without attaining these to become no better than a modern drawing room, with its divans, and ottomans, and sunshades, and a hundred other oriental things, which we are taking west with us, invented for the ladies of the harem and the effeminate natives of the Celestial Empire, which Jonathan[64] should be ashamed to know the names of. I would rather sit on a pumpkin and have it all to myself, than be crowded on a velvet cushion. I would rather ride on earth in an ox cart with a free circulation, than go to heaven in the fancy car of an excursion train and breathe a *malaria* all the way.

The very simplicity and nakedness of man's life in the primitive ages imply this advantage at least, that they left him still but a sojourner in nature. When he was refreshed with food and sleep he contemplated his journey again. He dwelt, as it were, in a tent in this world, and was either threading the valleys, or crossing the plains, or climbing the mountain tops. But lo! men have become the tools of their tools. The man who independently plucked the fruits when he was hungry is become a farmer; and he who stood under a tree for shelter, a housekeeper. We now no longer camp as for a night, but have settled down on earth and forgotten heaven. We have adopted Christianity merely as an improved method of *agri*-culture. We have built for this world a family mansion, and for the next a family tomb. The best works of art are the expression of man's struggle to free himself from this condition, but the effect of our art is merely to make this low state comfortable and that higher state to be forgotten. There is actually no place in this village for a work of *fine* art, if any had come down to us, to stand, for our lives, our houses and streets, furnish no proper pedestal for it. There is not a nail to hang a picture on, nor a shelf to receive the bust of a hero or a saint. When I consider how our houses are built and paid for, or not paid for, and their internal economy managed and sustained, I wonder that the floor does not give way under the visitor while he is admiring the gewgaws upon the mantel-piece, and let him through into the cellar, to some solid and honest though earthy foundation. I cannot but perceive that this so called rich and refined life is a thing jumped at, and I do not get on in the enjoyment of the *fine* arts which adorn it, my attention being wholly occupied with the jump; for I remember that the greatest genuine leap, due to human muscles alone, on record, is that of certain wandering Arabs, who are said to have cleared twenty-five feet on level ground. Without factitious support, man is sure to come to earth again beyond that distance. The first question which I am tempted to put to the proprietor of such great impropriety is, Who bolsters you? Are you one of the ninety-seven who fail? or of the three who succeed? Answer me these questions, and then perhaps I may look at your bawbles and find them ornamental. The cart before the horse is neither beautiful nor useful. Before

[63] Ruler of Assyria, whose kingdom was destroyed in the ninth century B.C.; known for his immorality and decadent behavior.

[64] A Yankee or American.

we can adorn our houses with beautiful objects the walls must be stripped, and our lives must be stripped, and beautiful housekeeping and beautiful living be laid for a foundation: now, a taste for the beautiful is most cultivated out of doors, where there is no house and no housekeeper.

Old Johnson,[65] in his "Wonder-Working Providence," speaking of the first settlers of this town, with whom he was contemporary, tells us that "they burrow themselves in the earth for their first shelter under some hillside, and, casting the soil aloft upon timber, they make a smoky fire against the earth, at the highest side." They did not "provide them houses," says he, "till the earth, by the Lord's blessing, brought forth bread to feed them," and the first year's crop was so light that "they were forced to cut their bread very thin for a long season." The secretary of the Province of New Netherland,[66] writing Dutch, in 1650, for the information of those who wished to take up land there, states more particularly, that "those in New Netherland, and especially in New England, who have no means to build farm houses at first according to their wishes, dig a square pit in the ground, cellar fashion, six or seven feet deep, as long and as broad as they think proper, case the earth inside with wood all round the wall, and line the wood with the bark of trees or something else to prevent the caving in of the earth; floor this cellar with plank, and wainscot it overhead for a ceiling, raise a roof of spars clear up, and cover the spars with bark or green sods, so that they can live dry and warm in these houses with their entire families for two, three, and four years, it being understood that partitions are run through those cellars which are adapted to the size of the family. The wealthy and principal men in New England, in the beginning of the colonies, commenced their first dwelling houses in this fashion for two reasons; firstly, in order not to waste time in building, and not to want food the next season; secondly, in order not to discourage poor laboring people whom they brought over in numbers from Fatherland. In the course of three or four years when the country became adapted to agriculture, they built themselves handsome houses, spending on them several thousands."

In this course which our ancestors took there was a show of prudence at least, as if their principle were to satisfy the more pressing wants first. But are the more pressing wants satisfied now? When I think of acquiring for myself one of our luxurious dwellings, I am deterred, for, so to speak, the country is not yet adapted to *human* culture, and we are still forced to cut our *spiritual* bread far thinner than our forefathers did their wheaten. Not that all architectural ornament is to be neglected even in the rudest periods; but let our houses first be lined with beauty, where they come in contact with our lives, like the tenement of the shellfish, and not overlaid with it. But, alas! I have been inside one or two of them, and know what they are lined with.

Though we are not so degenerate but that we might possibly live in a cave or a wigwam or wear skins today, it certainly is better to accept the advantages, though so dearly bought, which the invention and industry of mankind offer. In such a neighborhood as this, boards and shingles, lime and bricks, are cheaper and more easily obtained than suitable caves, or whole logs, or bark in sufficient quantities, or even well-tempered clay

---

[65] Edward Johnson (1598–1672), author of *Wonder-Working Providence of Sion's Saviour in New England* (1654), account of early Puritan settlement.

[66] Later the colony of New York. The quotation that follows is taken from *The Documentary History of the State of New-York* (1850–1851).

or flat stones. I speak understandingly on this subject, for I have made myself acquainted with it both theoretically and practically. With a little more wit we might use these materials so as to become richer than the richest now are, and make our civilization a blessing. The civilized man is a more experienced and wiser savage. But to make haste to my own experiment.

Near the end of March, 1845, I borrowed an axe and went down to the woods by Walden Pond, nearest to where I intended to build my house, and began to cut down some tall arrowy white pines, still in their youth, for timber. It is difficult to begin without borrowing, but perhaps it is the most generous course thus to permit your fellowmen to have an interest in your enterprise. The owner of the axe, as he released his hold on it, said that it was the apple of his eye; but I returned it sharper than I received it. It was a pleasant hillside where I worked, covered with pine woods, through which I looked out on the pond, and a small open field in the woods where pines and hickories were springing up. The ice in the pond was not yet dissolved, though there were some open spaces, and it was all dark colored and saturated with water. There were some slight flurries of snow during the days that I worked there; but for the most part when I came out on to the railroad, on my way home, its yellow sand heap stretched away gleaming in the hazy atmosphere, and the rails shone in the spring sun, and I heard the lark and pewee and other birds already come to commence another year with us. They were pleasant spring days, in which the winter of man's discontent[67] was thawing as well as the earth, and the life that had lain torpid began to stretch itself. One day, when my axe had come off and I had cut a green hickory for a wedge, driving it with a stone, and had placed the whole to soak in a pond hole in order to swell the wood, I saw a striped snake run into the water, and he lay on the bottom, apparently without inconvenience, as long as I staid there, or more than a quarter of an hour; perhaps because he had not yet fairly come out of the torpid state. It appeared to me that for a like reason men remain in their present low and primitive condition; but if they should feel the influence of the spring of springs arousing them, they would of necessity rise to a higher and more ethereal life. I had previously seen the snakes in frosty mornings in my path with portions of their bodies still numb and inflexible, waiting for the sun to thaw them. On the 1st of April it rained and melted the ice, and in the early part of the day, which was very foggy, I heard a stray goose groping about over the pond and cackling as if lost, or like the spirit of the fog.

So I went on for some days cutting and hewing timber, and also studs and rafters, all with my narrow axe, not having many communicable or scholar-like thoughts, singing to myself,—

> Men say they know many things;
> But lo! they have taken wings,—
> The arts and sciences,
> And a thousand appliances;
> The wind that blows
> Is all that any body knows.[68]

[67] Paraphrase from *Richard III*, Act I, Sc. i, l. 1.
[68] Thoreau's own verses.

I hewed the main timbers six inches square, most of the studs on two sides only, and the rafters and floor timbers on one side, leaving the rest of the bark on, so that they were just as straight and much stronger than sawed ones. Each stick was carefully mortised or tenoned by its stump, for I had borrowed other tools by this time. My days in the woods were not very long ones; yet I usually carried my dinner of bread and butter, and read the newspaper in which it was wrapped, at noon, sitting amid the green pine boughs which I had cut off, and to my bread was imparted some of their fragrance, for my hands were covered with a thick coat of pitch. Before I had done I was more the friend than the foe of the pine tree, though I had cut down some of them, having become better acquainted with it. Sometimes a rambler in the wood was attracted by the sound of my axe, and we chatted pleasantly over the chips which I had made.

By the middle of April, for I made no haste in my work, but rather made the most of it, my house was framed and ready for the raising. I had already bought the shanty of James Collins, an Irishman who worked on the Fitchburg Railroad, for boards. James Collins' shanty was considered an uncommonly fine one. When I called to see it he was not at home. I walked about the outside, at first unobserved from within, the window was so deep and high. It was of small dimensions, with a peaked cottage roof, and not much else to be seen, the dirt being raised five feet all around as if it were a compost heap. The roof was the soundest part, though a good deal warped and made brittle by the sun. Door-sill there was none, but a perennial passage for the hens under the door board. Mrs. C. came to the door and asked me to view it from the inside. The hens were driven in by my approach. It was dark, and had a dirt floor for the most part, dank, clammy, and aguish, only here a board and there a board which would not bear removal. She lighted a lamp to show me the inside of the roof and the walls, and also that the board floor extended under the bed, warning me not to step into the cellar, a sort of dust hole two feet deep. In her own words, they were "good boards overhead, good boards all around, and a good window,"—of two whole squares originally, only the cat had passed out that way lately. There was a stove, a bed, and a place to sit, an infant in the house where it was born, a silk parasol, gilt-framed looking-glass, and a patent new coffee mill nailed to an oak sapling, all told. The bargain was soon concluded, for James had in the mean while returned. I to pay four dollars and twenty-five cents to-night, he to vacate at five tomorrow morning, selling to nobody else meanwhile: I to take possession at six. It were well, he said, to be there early, and anticipate certain indistinct but wholly unjust claims on the score of ground rent and fuel. This he assured me was the only encumbrance. At six I passed him and his family on the road. One large bundle held their all,—bed, coffee-mill, looking-glass, hens,—all but the cat, she took to the woods and became a wild cat, and, as I learned afterward, trod in a trap set for woodchucks, and so became a dead cat at last.

I took down this dwelling the same morning, drawing the nails, and removed it to the pond side by small cartloads, spreading the boards on the grass there to bleach and warp back again in the sun. One early thrush gave me a note or two as I drove along the woodland path. I was informed treacherously by a young Patrick[69] that neighbor Seeley, an Irishman, in the intervals of the carting, transferred the still tolerable, straight, and drivable nails, staples, and spikes to his pocket, and then stood when I came back to pass the time of day, and look freshly up, unconcerned, with spring thoughts, at the

---

[69] Irishman.

devastation; there being a dearth of work, as he said. He was there to represent specta-tordom, and help make this seemingly insignificant event one with the removal of the gods of Troy.[70]

I dug my cellar in the side of a hill sloping to the south, where a woodchuck had for-merly dug his burrow, down through sumach and blackberry roots, and the lowest stain of vegetation, six feet square by seven deep, to a fine sand where potatoes would not freeze in any winter. The sides were left shelving, and not stoned; but the sun having never shone on them, the sand still keeps its place. It was but two hours' work. I took particular pleasure in this breaking of ground, for in almost all latitudes men dig into the earth for an equable temperature. Under the most splendid house in the city is still to be found the cellar where they store their roots as of old, and long after the super-structure has disappeared posterity remark its dent in the earth. The house is still but a sort of porch at the entrance of a burrow.

At length, in the beginning of May, with the help of some of my acquaintances, rather to improve so good an occasion for neighborliness than from any necessity, I set up the frame of my house. No man was ever more honored in the character of his rais-ers than I. They are destined, I trust, to assist at the raising of loftier structures one day. I began to occupy my house on the 4th of July, as soon as it was boarded and roofed, for the boards were carefully feather-edged and lapped, so that it was perfectly impervious to rain; but before boarding I laid the foundation of a chimney at one end, bringing two cartloads of stones up the hill from the pond in my arms. I built the chimney after my hoeing in the fall, before a fire became necessary for warmth, doing my cooking in the mean while out of doors on the ground, early in the morning: which mode I still think is in some respects more convenient and agreeable than the usual one. When it stormed before my bread was baked, I fixed a few boards over the fire, and sat under them to watch my loaf, and passed some pleasant hours in that way. In those days, when my hands were much employed, I read but little, but the least scraps of paper which lay on the ground, my holder, or tablecloth, afforded me as much entertainment, in fact an-swered the same purpose as the Iliad.[71]

It would be worth the while to build still more deliberately than I did, considering, for instance, what foundation a door, a window, a cellar, a garret, have in the nature of man, and perchance never raising any superstructure until we found a better reason for it than our temporal necessities even. There is some of the same fitness in a man's building his own house that there is in a bird's building its own nest. Who knows but if men constructed their dwellings with their own hands, and provided food for them-selves and families simply and honestly enough, the poetic faculty would be universally developed, as birds universally sing when they are so engaged? But alas! we do like cow-birds and cuckoos, which lay their eggs in nests which other birds have built, and cheer no traveller with their chattering and unmusical notes. Shall we forever resign the plea-sure of construction to the carpenter? What does architecture amount to in the experi-ence of the mass of men? I never in all my walks came across a man engaged in so sim-

---

[70] In Greek legend, Troy was safe as long as the statue of the goddess Pallas Athena re-mained in her temple; during the Trojan War the Greeks stole the statue, supposedly making their later victory possible.

[71] Homer's epic poem about the fall of Troy.

ple and natural an occupation as building his house. We belong to the community. It is not the tailor alone who is the ninth part of a man;[72] it is as much the preacher, and the merchant, and the farmer. Where is this division of labor to end? and what object does it finally serve? No doubt another *may* also think for me; but it is not therefore desirable that he should do so to the exclusion of my thinking for myself.

True, there are architects so called in this country, and I have heard of one at least possessed with the idea of making architectural ornaments have a core of truth, a necessity, and hence a beauty, as if it were a revelation to him. All very well perhaps from his point of view, but only a little better than the common dilettantism. A sentimental reformer in architecture, he began at the cornice, not at the foundation. It was only how to put a core of truth within the ornaments, that every sugar plum in fact might have an almond or caraway seed in it,—though I hold that almonds are most wholesome without the sugar,—and not how the inhabitant, the indweller, might build truly within and without, and let the ornaments take care of themselves. What reasonable man ever supposed that ornaments were something outward and in the skin merely,—that the tortoise got his spotted shell, or the shellfish its mother-o'-pearl tints, by such a contract as the inhabitants of Broadway their Trinity Church?[73] But a man has no more to do with the style of architecture of his house than a tortoise with that of its shell: nor need the soldier be so idle as to try to paint the precise *color* of his virtue on his standard. The enemy will find it out. He may turn pale when the trial comes. This man seemed to me to lean over the cornice and timidly whisper his half truth to the rude occupants who really knew it better than he. What of architectural beauty I now see, I know has gradually grown from within outward, out of the necessities and character of the indweller, who is the only builder,—out of some unconscious truthfulness, and nobleness, without ever a thought for the appearance; and whatever additional beauty of this kind is destined to be produced will be preceded by a like unconscious beauty of life. The most interesting dwellings in this country, as the painter knows, are the most unpretending, humble log huts and cottages of the poor commonly; it is the life of the inhabitants whose shells they are, and not any peculiarity in their surfaces merely, which makes them *picturesque;* and equally interesting will be the citizen's suburban box, when his life shall be as simple and as agreeable to the imagination, and there is as little straining after effect in the style of his dwelling. A great proportion of architectural ornaments are literally hollow, and a September gale would strip them off, like borrowed plumes, without injury to the substantials. They can do without *architecture* who have no olives nor wines in the cellar. What if an equal ado were made about the ornaments of style in literature, and the architects of our bibles spent as much time about their cornices as the architects of our churches do? So are made the *belles-lettres* and the *beaux-arts* and their professors. Much it concerns a man, forsooth, how a few sticks are slanted over him or under him, and what colors are daubed upon his box. It would signify somewhat, if, in any earnest sense, *he* slanted them and daubed it; but the spirit having departed out of the tenant, it is of a piece with constructing his own coffin,—the architecture of the grave, and "carpenter" is but another name for "coffin-maker." One man says, in his despair or indifference to life, take up a handful of the earth at your feet, and

---

[72] According to the old saying, which recognizes that those who make our clothes contribute to our being.

[73] Ornate Gothic-style church built in New York City (1839–1846).

paint your house that color. Is he thinking of his last and narrow house?[74] Toss up a copper[75] for it as well. What an abundance of leisure he must have! Why do you take up a handful of dirt? Better paint your house your own complexion; let it turn pale or blush for you. An enterprise to improve the style of cottage architecture! When you have got my ornaments ready I will wear them.

Before winter I built a chimney, and shingled the sides of my house, which were already impervious to rain, with imperfect and sappy shingles made of the first slice of the log, whose edges I was obliged to straighten with a plane.

I have thus a tight shingled and plastered house, ten feet wide by fifteen long, and eight-feet posts, with a garret and a closet, a large window on each side, two trap doors, one door at the end, and a brick fireplace opposite. The exact cost of my house, paying the usual price for such materials as I used, but not counting the work, all of which was done by myself, was as follows; and I give the details because very few are able to tell exactly what their houses cost, and fewer still, if any, the separate cost of the various materials which compose them:—

Boards, ...	$ 8 03 1/2,	mostly shanty boards.
Refuse shingles for roof and sides, ...	4 00	
Laths, ...	1 25	
Two second-hand windows with glass	2 43	
One thousand old brick, ...	4 00	
Two casks of lime, ...	2 40	That was high.
Hair, ...	0 31	More than I needed.
Mantle-tree iron, ...	0 15	
Nails, ...	3 90	
Hinges and screws, ...	0 14	
Latch, ...	0 10	
Chalk, ...	0 01	
Transportation, ...	1 40	} I carried a good part on my back.
In all, ...	$28 12 1/2	

These are all the materials excepting the timber stones and sand, which I claimed by squatter's right. I have also a small wood-shed adjoining, made chiefly of the stuff which was left after building the house.

I intend to build me a house which will surpass any on the main street in Concord in grandeur and luxury, as soon as it pleases me as much and will cost me no more than my present one.

I thus found that the student who wishes for a shelter can obtain one for a lifetime at an expense not greater than the rent which he now pays annually. If I seem to boast more than is becoming, my excuse is that I brag for humanity rather than for myself; and my shortcomings and inconsistencies do not affect the truth of my statement. Notwithstanding much cant and hypocrisy,—chaff which I find it difficult to separate from my wheat, but for which I am as sorry as any man,—I will breathe freely and stretch myself

---

74 i.e., coffin.
75 Coin used in payment to Charon, who fer- ried the dead across the river Styx in classic myth.

in this respect, it is such a relief to both the moral and physical system; and I am resolved that I will not through humility become the devil's attorney.[76] I will endeavor to speak a good word for the truth. At Cambridge College[77] the mere rent of a student's room, which is only a little larger than my own, is thirty dollars each year, though the corporation had the advantage of building thirty-two side by side and under one roof, and the occupant suffers the inconvenience of many and noisy neighbors, and perhaps a residence in the fourth story. I cannot but think that if we had more true wisdom in these respects, not only less education would be needed, because, forsooth, more would already have been acquired, but the pecuniary expense of getting an education would in a great measure vanish. Those conveniences which the student requires at Cambridge or elsewhere cost him or somebody else ten times as great a sacrifice of life as they would with proper management on both sides. Those things for which the most money is demanded are never the things which the student most wants. Tuition, for instance, is an important item in the term bill, while for the far more valuable education which he gets by associating with the most cultivated of his contemporaries no charge is made. The mode of founding a college is, commonly, to get up a subscription of dollars and cents, and then following blindly the principles of a division of labor to its extreme, a principle which should never be followed but with circumspection,—to call in a contractor who makes this a subject of speculation, and he employs Irishmen or other operatives actually to lay the foundations, while the students that are to be are said to be fitting themselves for it; and for these oversights successive generations have to pay. I think that it would be *better than this,* for the students, or those who desire to be benefited by it, even to lay the foundation themselves. The student who secures his coveted leisure and retirement by systematically shirking any labor necessary to man obtains but an ignoble and unprofitable leisure, defrauding himself of the experience which alone can make leisure fruitful. "But," says one, "you do not mean that the students should go to work with their hands instead of their heads?" I do not mean that exactly, but I mean something which he might think a good deal like that; I mean that they should not *play* life, or *study* it merely, while the community supports them at this expensive game, but earnestly *live* it from beginning to end. How could youths better learn to live than by at once trying the experiment of living? Methinks this would exercise their minds as much as mathematics. If I wished a boy to know something about the arts and sciences, for instance, I would not pursue the common course, which is merely to send him into the neighborhood of some professor, where any thing is professed and practised but the art of life;—to survey the world through a telescope or a microscope, and never with his natural eye; to study chemistry, and not learn how his bread is made, or mechanics, and not learn how it is earned; to discover new satellites to Neptune, and not detect the motes in his eyes, or to what vagabond he is a satellite himself; or to be devoured by the monsters that swarm all around him, while contemplating the monsters in a drop of vinegar. Which would have advanced the most at the end of a month,—the boy who had made his own jack-knife from the ore which he had dug and smelted, reading as much as would be necessary for this,—or the boy who had attended the lectures on metallurgy at the Institute in the

---

[76] Official appointed to Roman Catholic courts to probe any weaknesses in the cases of persons put forward for sainthood.

[77] Harvard College; Thoreau was a graduate in 1837.

mean while, and had received a Rodgers' penknife[78] from his father? Which would be most likely to cut his fingers?—To my astonishment I was informed on leaving college that I had studied navigation!—why, if I had taken one turn down the harbor I should have known more about it. Even the *poor* student studies and is taught only *political* economy, while that economy of living which is synonymous with philosophy is not even sincerely professed in our colleges. The consequence is, that while he is reading Adam Smith, Ricardo, and Say,[79] he runs his father in debt irretrievably.

As with our colleges, so with a hundred "modern improvements"; there is an illusion about them; there is not always a positive advance. The devil goes on exacting compound interest to the last for his early share and numerous succeeding investments in them. Our inventions are wont to be pretty toys, which distract our attention from serious things. They are but improved means to an unimproved end, an end which it was already but too easy to arrive at; as railroads lead to Boston or New York. We are in great haste to construct a magnetic telegraph from Maine to Texas; but Maine and Texas, it may be, have nothing important to communicate. Either is in such a predicament as the man who was earnest to be introduced to a distinguished deaf woman, but when he was presented, and one end of her ear trumpet was put into his hand, had nothing to say. As if the main object were to talk fast and not to talk sensibly. We are eager to tunnel under the Atlantic and bring the old world some weeks nearer to the new; but perchance the first news that will leak through into the broad, flapping American ear will be that the Princess Adelaide[80] has the whooping cough. After all, the man whose horse trots a mile in a minute does not carry the most important messages; he is not an evangelist, nor does he come round eating locusts and wild honey.[81] I doubt if Flying Childers[82] ever carried a peck of corn to mill.

One says to me, "I wonder that you do not lay up money; you love to travel; you might take the cars and go to Fitchburg[83] to-day and see the country." But I am wiser than that. I have learned that the swiftest traveller is he that goes afoot. I say to my friend, Suppose we try who will get there first. The distance is thirty miles; the fare ninety cents. That is almost a day's wages. I remember when wages were sixty cents a day for laborers on this very road. Well, I start now on foot, and get there before night; I have travelled at that rate by the week together. You will in the mean while have earned your fare, and arrive there some time to-morrow, or possibly this evening, if you are lucky enough to get a job in season. Instead of going to Fitchburg, you will be working here the greater part of the day. And so, if the railroad reached round the world, I think that I should keep ahead of you; and as for seeing the country and getting experience of that kind, I should have to cut your acquaintance altogether.

Such is the universal law, which no man can ever outwit, and with regard to the railroad even we may say it is as broad as it is long. To make a railroad round the world available to all mankind is equivalent to grading the whole surface of the planet. Men have an indistinct notion that if they keep up this activity of joint stocks and spades long enough all will at length ride somewhere, in next to no time, and for nothing; but though

---

[78] Made by Joseph Rodgers, cutlery maker from Sheffield, England.

[79] Adam Smith, David Ricardo, and Jean Baptiste Léon Say, eighteenth-century economists.

[80] Sister of Louis-Phillipe, king of France, she lived 1771–1847.

[81] What sustained John the Baptist while living in the wilderness (Matthew 3:4).

[82] Well-known racehorse of the eighteenth century.

[83] Small town near Concord; end of the railroad line that passed by Walden Pond.

a crowd rushes to the depot, and the conductor shouts "All aboard!" when the smoke is blown away and the vapor condensed, it will be perceived that a few are riding, but the rest are run over,—and it will be called, and will be, "A melancholy accident." No doubt they can ride at last who shall have earned their fare, that is, if they survive so long, but they will probably have lost their elasticity and desire to travel by that time. This spending of the best part of one's life earning money in order to enjoy a questionable liberty during the least valuable part of it, reminds me of the Englishman who went to India to make a fortune first, in order that he might return to England and live the life of a poet. He should have gone up garret at once. "What!" exclaim a million Irishmen starting up from all the shanties in the land, "is not this railroad which we have built a good thing?" Yes, I answer, *comparatively* good, that is, you might have done worse; but I wish, as you are brothers of mine, that you could have spent your time better than digging in this dirt.

Before I finished my house, wishing to earn ten or twelve dollars by some honest and agreeable method, in order to meet my unusual expenses, I planted about two acres and a half of light and sandy soil near it chiefly with beans, but also a small part with potatoes, corn, peas, and turnips. The whole lot contains eleven acres, mostly growing up to pines and hickories, and was sold the preceding season for eight dollars and eight cents an acre. One farmer said that it was "good for nothing but to raise cheeping squirrels on." I put no manure on this land, not being the owner, but merely a squatter, and not expecting to cultivate so much again, and I did not quite hoe it all once. I got out several cords of stumps in ploughing, which supplied me with fuel for a long time, and left small circles of virgin mould, easily distinguishable through the summer by the greater luxuriance of the beans there. The dead and for the most part unmerchantable wood behind my house, and the driftwood from the pond, have supplied the remainder of my fuel. I was obliged to hire a team and a man for the ploughing, though I held the plough myself. My farm outgoes for the first season were, for implements, seed, work, &c., $14 72 1/2. The seed corn was given me. This never costs any thing to speak of, unless you plant more than enough. I got twelve bushels of beans, and eighteen bushels of potatoes, beside some peas and sweet corn. The yellow corn and turnips were too late to come to any thing. My whole income from the farm was

	$23 44
Deducting the outgoes, ...	14 72 1/2,
there are left, ...	$ 8 71 1/2,

beside produce consumed and on hand at the time this estimate was made of the value of $4 50,—the amount on hand much more than balancing a little grass which I did not raise. All things considered, that is, considering the importance of a man's soul and of to-day, notwithstanding the short time occupied by my experiment, nay, partly even because of its transient character, I believe that that was doing better than any farmer in Concord did that year.

The next year I did better still, for I spaded up all the land which I required, about a third of an acre, and I learned from the experience of both years, not being in the least awed by many celebrated works on husbandry, Arthur Young[84] among the rest, that if

[84] English author (1741–1820) of works on husbandry.

one would live simply and eat only the crop which he raised, and raise no more than he ate, and not exchange it for an insufficient quantity of more luxurious and expensive things, he would need to cultivate only a few rods of ground, and that it would be cheaper to spade up that than to use oxen to plough it, and to select a fresh spot from time to time than to manure the old, and he could do all his necessary farm work as it were with his left hand at odd hours in the summer; and thus he would not be tied to an ox, or horse, or cow, or pig, as at present. I desire to speak impartially on this point, and as one not interested in the success or failure of the present economical and social arrangements. I was more independent than any farmer in Concord, for I was not anchored to a house or farm, but could follow the bent of my genius, which is a very crooked one, every moment. Beside being better off than they already, if my house had been burned or my crops had failed, I should have been nearly as well off as before.

I am wont to think that men are not so much the keepers of herds as herds are the keepers of the men, the former are so much the freer. Men and oxen exchange work; but if we consider necessary work only, the oxen will be seen to have greatly the advantage, their farm is so much the larger. Man does some of his part of the exchange work in his six weeks of haying, and it is no boy's play. Certainly no nation that lived simply in all respects, that is, no nation of philosophers, would commit so great a blunder as to use the labor of animals. True, there never was and is not likely soon to be a nation of philosophers, nor am I certain it is desirable that there should be. However, *I* should never have broken a horse or bull and taken him to board for any work he might do for me, for fear I should become a horse-man or a herds-man merely; and if society seems to be the gainer by so doing, are we certain that what is one man's gain is not another's loss, and that the stable-boy has equal cause with his master to be satisfied? Granted that some public works would not have been constructed without this aid, and let man share the glory of such with the ox and horse; does it follow that he could not have accomplished works yet more worthy of himself in that case? When men begin to do, not merely unnecessary or artistic, but luxurious and idle work, with their assistance, it is inevitable that a few do all the exchange work with the oxen, or, in other words, become the slaves of the strongest. Man thus not only works for the animal within him, but, for a symbol of this, he works for the animal without him. Though we have many substantial houses of brick or stone, the prosperity of the farmer is still measured by the degree to which the barn overshadows the house. This town is said to have the largest houses for oxen cows and horses hereabouts, and it is not behindhand in its public buildings; but there are very few halls for free worship or free speech in this county. It should not be by their architecture, but why not even by their power of abstract thought, that nations should seek to commemorate themselves? How much more admirable the Bhagvat-Geeta[85] than all the ruins of the East! Towers and temples are the luxury of princes. A simple and independent mind does not toil at the bidding of any prince. Genius is not a retainer to any emperor, nor is its material silver, or gold, or marble, except to a trifling extent. To what end, pray, is so much stone hammered? In Arcadia,[86] when I was there, I did not see any hammering stone. Nations are possessed with an insane ambition to perpetuate the memory of themselves by the amount of hammered stone they leave. What if equal pains were taken to smooth and polish their manners? One piece of

[85] A sacred text of the Hindus, the *Bhagavad Gita.*
[86] Region in Greek myth where men supposedly lived in pastoral happiness. (Thoreau visited it only by means of his imagination.)

good sense would be more memorable than a monument as high as the moon. I love better to see stones in place. The grandeur of Thebes was a vulgar grandeur. More sensible is a rod of stone wall that bounds an honest man's field than a hundred-gated Thebes[87] that has wandered farther from the true end of life. The religion and civilization which are barbaric and heathenish build splendid temples; but what you might call Christianity does not. Most of the stone a nation hammers goes toward its tomb only. It buries itself alive. As for the Pyramids, there is nothing to wonder at in them so much as the fact that so many men could be found degraded enough to spend their lives constructing a tomb for some ambitious booby, whom it would have been wiser and manlier to have drowned in the Nile, and then given his body to the dogs. I might possibly invent some excuse for them and him, but I have no time for it. As for the religion and love of art of the builders, it is much the same all the world over, whether the building be an Egyptian temple or the United States Bank. It costs more than it comes to. The mainspring is vanity, assisted by the love of garlic and bread and butter. Mr. Balcom, a promising young architect, designs it on the back of his Vitruvius,[88] with hard pencil and ruler, and the job is let out to Dobson & Sons, stonecutters. When the thirty centuries begin to look down on it, mankind begin to look up at it. As for your high towers and monuments, there was a crazy fellow once in this town who undertook to dig through to China, and he got so far that, as he said, he heard the Chinese pots and kettles rattle; but I think that I shall not go out of my way to admire the hole which he made. Many are concerned about the monuments of the West and the East,—to know who built them. For my part, I should like to know who in those days did not build them,—who were above such trifling. But to proceed with my statistics.

By surveying, carpentry, and day-labor of various other kinds in the village in the mean while, for I have as many trades as fingers, I had earned $13 34. The expense of food for eight months, namely, from July 4th to March 1st, the time when these estimates were made, though I lived there more than two years,—not counting potatoes, a little green corn, and some peas, which I had raised, nor considering the value of what was on hand at the last date, was

Rice,	$1 73 1/2	
Molasses,	1 73	Cheapest form of the saccharine.
Rye meal,	1 04 3/4	
Indian meal,	0 99 3/4	Cheaper than rye.
Pork,	0 22	
Flour	0 88	} Costs more than Indian meal, both money and trouble.
Sugar,	0 80	
Lard,	0 65	
Apples,	0 25	
Dried apple,	0 22	} All experiments which failed.
Sweet potatoes,	0 10	
One pumpkin,	0 6	
One watermelon,	0 2	
Salt,	0 3	

---

[87] City in ancient Egypt whose walls had 100 gates.

[88] Roman writings on architecture by Vitruvius (first century B.C.).

Yes, I did eat $8 74, all told; but I should not thus unblushingly publish my guilt, if I did not know that most of my readers were equally guilty with myself, and that their deeds would look no better in print. The next year I sometimes caught a mess of fish for my dinner, and once I went so far as to slaughter a woodchuck which ravaged my bean-field,—effect his transmigration, as a Tartar[89] would say,—and devour him, partly for experiment's sake; but though it afforded me a momentary enjoyment, notwithstanding a musky flavor, I saw that the longest use would not make that a good practice, however it might seem to have your woodchucks ready dressed by the village butcher.

Clothing and some incidental expenses within the same dates, though little can be inferred from this item, amounted to

$8 40 3/4

Oil and some household utensils, ... 2 00

So that all the pecuniary outgoes, excepting for washing and mending, which for the most part were done out of the house, and their bills have not yet been received,—and these are all and more than all the ways by which money necessarily goes out in this part of the world,—were

House, ... $28 12 1/2
Farm one year, ... 14 72 1/2
Food eight months, ... 8 74
Clothing, &c., eight months, ... 8 40 3/4
Oil, &c., eight months, ... 2 00

In all, ... $61 99 3/4

I address myself now to those of my readers who have a living to get. And to meet this I have for farm produce sold

$23 44

Earned by day-labor, ... 13 34

In all, ... $36 78,

which subtracted from the sum of the outgoes leaves a balance of $25 21 3/4 on the one side,—this being very nearly the means with which I started, and the measure of expenses to be incurred,—and on the other, beside the leisure and independence and health thus secured, a comfortable house for me as long as I choose to occupy it.

These statistics, however accidental and therefore uninstructive they may appear, as they have a certain completeness, have a certain value also. Nothing was given me of which I have not rendered some account. It appears from the above estimate, that my food alone cost me in money about twenty-seven cents a week. It was, for nearly two years after this, rye and Indian meal without yeast, potatoes, rice, a very little salt pork, molasses, and salt, and my drink water. It was fit that I should live on rice, mainly, who

[89] Native of Russian Asia; the Tartars held that
after death their souls passed into other
bodies.

loved so well the philosophy of India. To meet the objections of some inveterate cav-
illers, I may as well state, that if I dined out occasionally, as I always had done, and I
trust shall have opportunities to do again, it was frequently to the detriment of my domestic arrangements. But the dining out, being, as I have stated, a constant element,
does not in the least affect a comparative statement like this.

I learned from my two years' experience that it would cost incredibly little trouble to
obtain one's necessary food, even in this latitude; that a man may use as simple a diet as
the animals, and yet retain health and strength. I have made a satisfactory dinner, satisfactory on several accounts, simply off a dish of purslane *(Portulaca oleracea)* which I
gathered in my cornfield, boiled and salted. I give the Latin on account of the savoriness
of the trivial name. And pray what more can a reasonable man desire, in peaceful times,
in ordinary noons, than a sufficient number of ears of green sweet-corn boiled, with the
addition of salt? Even the little variety which I used was a yielding to the demands of appetite, and not of health. Yet men have come to such a pass that they frequently starve,
not for want of necessaries, but for want of luxuries; and I know a good woman who
thinks that her son lost his life because he took to drinking water only.

The reader will perceive that I am treating the subject rather from an economic than
a dietetic point of view, and he will not venture to put my abstemiousness to the test
unless he has a well-stocked larder.

Bread I at first made of pure Indian meal and salt, genuine hoe-cakes, which I baked
before my fire out of doors on a shingle or the end of a stick of timber sawed off in
building my house; but it was wont to get smoked and to have a piny flavor. I tried flour
also; but have at last found a mixture of rye and Indian meal most convenient and
agreeable. In cold weather it was no little amusement to bake several small loaves of this
in succession, tending and turning them as carefully as an Egyptian his hatching eggs.
They were a real cereal fruit which I ripened, and they had to my senses a fragrance like
that of other noble fruits, which I kept in as long as possible by wrapping them in
cloths. I made a study of the ancient and indispensable art of bread-making, consulting
such authorities as offered, going back to the primitive days and first invention of the
unleavened kind, when from the wildness of nuts and meats men first reached the mildness and refinement of this diet, and travelling gradually down in my studies through
that accidental souring of the dough which, it is supposed, taught the leavening process,
and through the various fermentations thereafter, till I came to "good, sweet, wholesome bread," the staff of life. Leaven, which some deem the soul of bread, the *spiritus*[90]
which fills its cellular tissue, which is religiously preserved like the vestal fire,[91]—some
precious bottle-full, I suppose, first brought over in the May-flower, did the business
for America, and its influence is still rising, swelling, spreading, in cerealian[92] billows
over the land,—this seed I regularly and faithfully procured from the village, till at
length one morning I forgot the rules, and scalded my yeast; by which accident I discovered that even this was not indispensable,—for my discoveries were not by the synthetic
but analytic process,—and I have gladly omitted it since, though most housewives
earnestly assured me that safe and wholesome bread without yeast might not be, and elderly people prophesied a speedy decay of the vital forces. Yet I find it not to be an essential ingredient, and after going without it for a year am still in the land of the living;

[90] Latin: "breath of life."
[91] Sacred flame of the ancient Romans.

[92] Wordplay in reference to *cerulean,* the color blue.

and I am glad to escape the trivialness of carrying a bottle-full in my pocket, which would sometimes pop and discharge its contents to my discomfiture. It is simpler and more respectable to omit it. Man is an animal who more than any other can adapt himself to all climates and circumstances. Neither did I put any sal soda, or other acid or alkali, into my bread. It would seem that I made it according to the recipe which Marcus Porcius Cato[93] gave about two centuries before Christ. "Panem depsticium sic facito. Manus mortariumque bene lavato. Farinam in mortarium indito, aquæ paulatim addito, subigitoque pulchre. Ubi bene subegeris, defingito, coquitoque sub testu." Which I take to mean—"Make kneaded bread thus. Wash your hands and trough well. Put the meal into the trough, add water gradually, and knead it thoroughly. When you have kneaded it well, mould it, and bake it under a cover," that is, in a baking-kettle. Not a word about leaven. But I did not always use this staff of life. At one time, owing to the emptiness of my purse, I saw none of it for more than a month.

Every New Englander might easily raise all his own breadstuffs in this land of rye and Indian corn, and not depend on distant and fluctuating markets for them. Yet so far are we from simplicity and independence that, in Concord, fresh and sweet meal is rarely sold in the shops, and hominy and corn in a still coarser form are hardly used by any. For the most part the farmer gives to his cattle and hogs the grain of his own producing, and buys flour, which is at least no more wholesome, at a greater cost, at the store. I saw that I could easily raise my bushel or two of rye and Indian corn, for the former will grow on the poorest land, and the latter does not require the best, and grind them in a hand-mill, and so do without rice and pork; and if I must have some concentrated sweet, I found by experiment that I could make a very good molasses either of pumpkins or beets, and I knew that I needed only to set out a few maples to obtain it more easily still, and while these were growing I could use various substitutes beside those which I have named, "For," as the Forefathers sang,—

> "we can make liquor to sweeten our lips
> Of pumpkins and parsnips and walnut-tree chips."

Finally, as for salt, that grossest of groceries, to obtain this might be a fit occasion for a visit to the seashore, or, if I did without it altogether, I should probably drink the less water. I do not learn that the Indians ever troubled themselves to go after it.

Thus I could avoid all trade and barter, so far as my food was concerned, and having a shelter already, it would only remain to get clothing and fuel. The pantaloons which I now wear were woven in a farmer's family,—thank Heaven there is so much virtue still in man; for I think the fall from the farmer to the operative as great and memorable as that from the man to the farmer;—and in a new country fuel is an encumbrance. As for a habitat, if I were not permitted still to squat, I might purchase one acre at the same price for which the land I cultivated was sold—namely, eight dollars and eight cents. But as it was, I considered that I enhanced the value of the land by squatting on it.

There is a certain class of unbelievers who sometimes ask me such questions as, if I think that I can live on vegetable food alone; and to strike at the root of the matter at once,—for the root is faith,—I am accustomed to answer such, that I can live on board

---

[93] Roman statesman (234–149 B.C.), from whose *De Agricultura* the recipe is taken.

nails. If they cannot understand that, they cannot understand much that I have to say. For my part, I am glad to hear of experiments of this kind being tried; as that a young man tried for a fortnight to live on hard, raw corn on the ear, using his teeth for all mortar. The squirrel tribe tried the same and succeeded. The human race is interested in these experiments, though a few old women who are incapacitated for them, or who own their thirds in mills,[94] may be alarmed.

My furniture, part of which I made myself, and the rest cost me nothing of which I have not rendered an account, consisted of a bed, a table, a desk, three chairs, a looking-glass three inches in diameter, a pair of tongs and andirons, a kettle, a skillet, and a frying-pan, a dipper, a wash-bowl, two knives and forks, three plates, one cup, one spoon, a jug for oil, a jug for molasses, and a japanned lamp. None is so poor that he need sit on a pumpkin. That is shiftlessness. There is a plenty of such chairs as I like best in the village garrets to be had for taking them away. Furniture! Thank God, I can sit and I can stand without the aid of a furniture warehouse. What man but a philosopher would not be ashamed to see his furniture packed in a cart and going up country exposed to the light of heaven and the eyes of men, a beggarly account of empty boxes? That is Spaulding's furniture. I could never tell from inspecting such a load whether it belonged to a so called rich man or a poor one; the owner always seemed poverty-stricken. Indeed, the more you have of such things the poorer you are. Each load looks as if it contained the contents of a dozen shanties; and if one shanty is poor, this is a dozen times as poor. Pray, for what do we *move* ever but to get rid of our furniture, our *exuviæ;*[95] at last to go from this world to another newly furnished, and leave this to be burned? It is the same as if all these traps were buckled to a man's belt, and he could not move over the rough country where our lines are cast without dragging them,—dragging his trap. He was a lucky fox that left his tail in the trap. The muskrat will gnaw his third leg off to be free. No wonder man has lost his elasticity. How often he is at a dead set![96] "Sir, if I may be so bold, what do you mean by a dead set?" If you are a seer, whenever you meet a man you will see all that he owns, ay, and much that he pretends to disown, behind him, even to his kitchen furniture and all the trumpery which he saves and will not burn, and he will appear to be harnessed to it and making what headway he can. I think that the man is at a dead set who has got through a knot hole or gateway where his sledge load of furniture cannot follow him. I cannot but feel compassion when I hear some trig,[97] compact-looking man, seemingly free, all girded and ready, speak of his "furniture," as whether it is insured or not. "But what shall I do with my furniture?" My gay butterfly is entangled in a spider's web then. Even those who seem for a long while not to have any, if you inquire more narrowly you will find have some stored in somebody's barn. I look upon England to-day as an old gentleman who is travelling with a great deal of baggage, trumpery which has accumulated from long housekeeping, which he has not the courage to burn; great trunk, little trunk, bandbox and bundle. Throw away the first three at least. It would surpass the powers of a well man nowadays to take up his bed and walk, and I should certainly advise a sick one to lay down his bed and run. When I have met an immigrant tottering under a bundle which contained his all,—looking like

---

[94] Toothless old women or those who own the traditional third of the estate left them upon their husbands' deaths and have invested in mills that do their grinding for them.

[95] Latin: "discards."

[96] At a dead end; immobile.

[97] Spruce.

an enormous wen which had grown out of the nape of his neck,—I have pitied him, not because that was his all, but because he had all *that* to carry. If I have got to drag my trap, I will take care that it be a light one and do not nip me in a vital part. But perchance it would be wisest never to put one's paw into it.

I would observe, by the way, that it costs me nothing for curtains, for I have no gazers to shut out but the sun and moon, and I am willing that they should look in. The moon will not sour milk nor taint meat of mine, nor will the sun injure my furniture or fade my carpet, and if he is sometimes too warm a friend, I find it still better economy to retreat behind some curtain which nature has provided, than to add a single item to the details of housekeeping. A lady once offered me a mat, but as I had no room to spare within the house, nor time to spare within or without to shake it, I declined it, preferring to wipe my feet on the sod before my door. It is best to avoid the beginnings of evil.

Not long since I was present at the auction of a deacon's effects, for his life had not been ineffectual:—

"The evil that men do lives after them."[98]

As usual, a great proportion was trumpery which had begun to accumulate in his father's day. Among the rest was a dried tapeworm. And now, after lying half a century in his garret and other dust holes, these things were not burned; instead of a *bonfire*, or purifying destruction of them, there was an *auction*,[99] or increasing of them. The neighbors eagerly collected to view them, bought them all, and carefully transported them to their garrets and dust holes, to lie there till their estates are settled, when they will start again. When a man dies he kicks the dust.

The customs of some savage nations might, perchance, be profitably imitated by us, for they at least go through the semblance of casting their slough annually; they have the idea of the thing, whether they have the reality or not. Would it not be well if we were to celebrate such a "busk," or "feast of first fruits," as Bartram[100] describes to have been the custom of the Mucclasse Indians? "When a town celebrates the busk," says he, "having previously provided themselves with new clothes, new pots, pans, and other household utensils and furniture, they collect all their worn out clothes and other despicable things, sweep and cleanse their houses, squares, and the whole town, of their filth, which with all the remaining grain and other old provisions they cast together into one common heap, and consume it with fire. After having taken medicine, and fasted for three days, all the fire in the town is extinguished. During this fast they abstain from the gratification of every appetite and passion whatever. A general amnesty is proclaimed; all malefactors may return to their town.—"

"On the fourth morning, the high priest, by rubbing dry wood together, produces new fire in the public square, from whence every habitation in the town is supplied with the new and pure flame."

They then feast on the new corn and fruits and dance and sing for three days, "and the four following days they receive visits and rejoice with their friends from neighboring towns who have in like manner purified and prepared themselves."

---

[98] From Shakespeare's *Julius Caesar*, Act III, Sc. ii, l. 81.

[99] The original Latin meant "an increase"; modern usage applies to the raising of the cost of an item by bidding.

[100] William Bartram (1739–1823), American naturalist and travel writer.

The Mexicans also practised a similar purification at the end of every fifty-two years, in the belief that it was time for the world to come to an end.

I have scarcely heard of a truer sacrament, that is, as the dictionary defines it, "outward and visible sign of an inward and spiritual grace," than this, and I have no doubt that they were originally inspired directly from Heaven to do thus, though they have no biblical record of the revelation.

For more than five years I maintained myself thus solely by the labor of my hands, and I found, that by working about six weeks in a year, I could meet all the expenses of living. The whole of my winters, as well as most of my summers, I had free and clear for study. I have thoroughly tried school-keeping, and found that my expenses were in proportion, or rather out of proportion, to my income, for I was obliged to dress and train, not to say think and believe, accordingly, and I lost my time into the bargain. As I did not teach for the good of my fellow-men, but simply for a livelihood, this was a failure. I have tried trade; but I found that it would take ten years to get under way in that, and that then I should probably be on my way to the devil. I was actually afraid that I might by that time be doing what is called a good business. When formerly I was looking about to see what I could do for a living, some sad experience in conforming to the wishes of friends being fresh in my mind to tax my ingenuity, I thought often and seriously of picking huckleberries; that surely I could do, and its small profits might suffice,—for my greatest skill has been to want but little,—so little capital it required, so little distraction from my wonted moods, I foolishly thought. While my acquaintances went unhesitatingly into trade or the professions, I contemplated this occupation as most like theirs; ranging the hills all summer to pick the berries which came in my way, and thereafter carelessly dispose of them; so, to keep the flocks of Admetus.[101] I also dreamed that I might gather the wild herbs, or carry evergreens to such villagers as loved to be reminded of the woods, even to the city, by hay-cart loads. But I have since learned that trade curses every thing it handles; and though you trade in messages from heaven, the whole curse of trade attaches to the business.

As I preferred some things to others, and especially valued my freedom, as I could fare hard and yet succeed well, I did not wish to spend my time in earning rich carpets or other fine furniture, or delicate cookery, or a house in the Grecian or the Gothic style just yet. If there are any to whom it is no interruption to acquire these things, and who know how to use them when acquired, I relinquish to them the pursuit. Some are "industrious," and appear to love labor for its own sake, or perhaps because it keeps them out of worse mischief; to such I have at present nothing to say. Those who would not know what to do with more leisure than they now enjoy, I might advise to work twice as hard as they do,—work till they pay for themselves, and get their free papers.[102] For myself I found that the occupation of a day-laborer was the most independent of any, especially as it required only thirty or forty days in a year to support one. The laborer's day ends with the going down of the sun, and he is then free to devote himself to his chosen pursuit, independent of his labor; but his employer, who speculates from month to month, has no respite from one end of the year to the other.

---

[101] To pass a time of servitude, as the god Apollo once did in the service of King Admetus.

[102] To end their period of indenturedness by working off their debts.

In short, I am convinced, both by faith and experience, that to maintain one's self on this earth is not a hardship but a pastime, if we will live simply and wisely; as the pursuits of the simpler nations are still the sports of the more artificial. It is not necessary that a man should earn his living by the sweat of his brow, unless he sweats easier than I do.

One young man of my acquaintance, who has inherited some acres, told me that he thought he should live as I did, *if he had the means.* I would not have any one adopt *my* mode of living on any account; for, beside that before he has fairly learned it I may have found out another for myself, I desire that there may be as many different persons in the world as possible; but I would have each one be very careful to find out and pursue *his own* way, and not his father's or his mother's or his neighbor's instead. The youth may build or plant or sail, only let him not be hindered from doing that which he tells me he would like to do. It is by a mathematical point only that we are wise, as the sailor or the fugitive slave keeps the polestar[103] in his eye; but that is sufficient guidance for all our life. We may not arrive at our port within a calculable period, but we would preserve the true course.

Undoubtedly, in this case, what is true for one is truer still for a thousand, as a large house is not more expensive than a small one in proportion to its size, since one roof may cover, one cellar underlie, and one wall separate several apartments. But for my part, I preferred the solitary dwelling. Moreover, it will commonly be cheaper to build the whole yourself than to convince another of the advantage of the common wall; and when you have done this, the common partition, to be much cheaper, must be a thin one, and that other may prove a bad neighbor, and also not keep his side in repair. The only coöperation which is commonly possible is exceedingly partial and superficial; and what little true coöperation there is, is as if it were not, being a harmony inaudible to men. If a man has faith he will coöperate with equal faith every where; if he has not faith, he will continue to live like the rest of the world, whatever company he is joined to. To coöperate, in the highest as well as the lowest sense, means *to get our living together.* I heard it proposed lately that two young men should travel together over the world, the one without money, earning his means as he went, before the mast and behind the plough, the other carrying a bill of exchange in his pocket. It was easy to see that they could not long be companions or coöperate, since one would not *operate* at all. They would part at the first interesting crisis in their adventures. Above all, as I have implied, the man who goes alone can start today; but he who travels with another must wait till that other is ready, and it may be a long time before they get off.

But all this is very selfish, I have heard some of my townsmen say. I confess that I have hitherto indulged very little in philanthropic enterprises. I have made some sacrifices to a sense of duty, and among others have sacrificed this pleasure also. There are those who have used all their arts to persuade me to undertake the support of some poor family in the town; and if I had nothing to do,—for the devil finds employment for the idle,—I might try my hand at some such pastime as that. However, when I have thought to indulge myself in this respect, and lay their Heaven under an obligation by maintaining certain poor persons in all respects as comfortably as I maintain myself,

[103] The North Star, which guides him toward
   freedom in Canada.

and have even ventured so far as to make them the offer, they have one and all unhesitatingly preferred to remain poor. While my townsmen and women are devoted in so many ways to the good of their fellows, I trust that one at least may be spared to other and less humane pursuits. You must have a genius for charity as well as for any thing else. As for Doing-good, that is one of the professions which are full. Moreover, I have tried it fairly, and, strange as it may seem, am satisfied that it does not agree with my constitution. Probably I should not consciously and deliberately forsake my particular calling to do the good which society demands of me, to save the universe from annihilation; and I believe that a like but infinitely greater steadfastness elsewhere is all that now preserves it. But I would not stand between any man and his genius; and to him who does this work, which I decline, with his whole heart and soul and life, I would say, Persevere, even if the world call it doing evil, as it is most likely they will.

I am far from supposing that my case is a peculiar one; no doubt many of my readers would make a similar defence. At doing something,—I will not engage that my neighbors shall pronounce it good,—I do not hesitate to say that I should be a capital fellow to hire; but what that is, it is for my employer to find out. What *good* I do, in the common sense of that word, must be aside from my main path, and for the most part wholly unintended. Men say, practically, Begin where you are and such as you are, without aiming mainly to become of more worth, and with kindness aforethought go about doing good. If I were to preach at all in this strain, I should say rather, Set about being good. As if the sun should stop when he had kindled his fires up to the splendor of a moon or a star of the sixth magnitude, and go about like a Robin Goodfellow,[104] peeping in at every cottage window, inspiring lunatics, and tainting meats, and making darkness visible, instead of steadily increasing his genial heat and beneficence till he is of such brightness that no mortal can look him in the face, and then, and in the mean while too, going about the world in his own orbit, doing it good, or rather, as a truer philosophy has discovered, the world going about him getting good. When Phaeton,[105] wishing to prove his heavenly birth by his beneficence, had the sun's chariot but one day, and drove out of the beaten track, he burned several blocks of houses in the lower streets of heaven, and scorched the surface of the earth, and dried up every spring, and made the great desert of Sahara, till at length Jupiter hurled him headlong to the earth with a thunderbolt, and the sun, through grief at his death, did not shine for a year.

There is no odor so bad as that which arises from goodness tainted. It is human, it is divine, carrion. If I knew for a certainty that a man was coming to my house with the conscious design of doing me good, I should run for my life, as from that dry and parching wind of the African deserts called the simoom, which fills the mouth and nose and ears and eyes with dust till you are suffocated, for fear that I should get some of his good done to me,—some of its virus mingled with my blood. No,—in this case I would rather suffer evil the natural way. A man is not a good *man* to me because he will feed me if I should be starving, or warm me if I should be freezing, or pull me out of a ditch if I should ever fall into one. I can find you a Newfoundland dog that will do as much. Philanthropy is not love for one's fellow-man in the broadest sense. Howard[106] was no

---

[104] In folklore, the elf who plays tricks; associated with Puck.

[105] Apollo's son, and thereby the son of the sun.

[106] John Howard (1726?–1790), English leader in prison reform.

doubt an exceedingly kind and worthy man in his way, and has his reward; but, comparatively speaking, what are a hundred Howards to *us*, if their philanthropy do not help *us* in our best estate, when we are most worthy to be helped? I never heard of a philanthropic meeting in which it was sincerely proposed to do any good to me, or the like of me.

The Jesuits[107] were quite balked by those Indians who, being burned at the stake, suggested new modes of torture to their tormentors. Being superior to physical suffering, it sometimes chanced that they were superior to any consolation which the missionaries could offer; and the law to do as you would be done by fell with less persuasiveness on the ears of those, who, for their part, did not care how they were done by, who loved their enemies after a new fashion, and came very near freely forgiving them all they did.

Be sure that you give the poor the aid they most need, though it be your example which leaves them far behind. If you give money, spend yourself with it, and do not merely abandon it to them. We make curious mistakes sometimes. Often the poor man is not so cold and hungry as he is dirty and ragged and gross. It is partly his taste, and not merely his misfortune. If you give him money, he will perhaps buy more rags with it. I was wont to pity the clumsy Irish laborers who cut ice on the pond, in such mean and ragged clothes, while I shivered in my more tidy and somewhat more fashionable garments, till, one bitter cold day, one who had slipped into the water came to my house to warm him, and I saw him strip off three pairs of pants and two pairs of stockings ere he got down to the skin, though they were dirty and ragged enough, it is true, and that he could afford to refuse the *extra* garments which I offered him, he had so many *intra* ones.[108] This ducking was the very thing he needed. Then I began to pity myself, and I saw that it would be a greater charity to bestow on me a flannel shirt than a whole slop-shop on him. There are a thousand hacking at the branches of evil to one who is striking at the root, and it may be that he who bestows the largest amount of time and money on the needy is doing the most by his mode of life to produce that misery which he strives in vain to relieve. It is the pious slave-breeder devoting the proceeds of every tenth slave[109] to buy a Sunday's liberty for the rest. Some show their kindness to the poor by employing them in their kitchens. Would they not be kinder if they employed themselves there? You boast of spending a tenth part of your income in charity; may be you should spend the nine tenths so, and done with it. Society recovers only a tenth part of the property then. Is this owing to the generosity of him in whose possession it is found, or to the remissness of the officers of justice?

Philanthropy is almost the only virtue which is sufficiently appreciated by mankind. Nay, it is greatly overrated; and it is our selfishness which overrates it. A robust poor man, one sunny day here in Concord, praised a fellow-townsman to me, because, as he said, he was kind to the poor; meaning himself. The kind uncles and aunts of the race are more esteemed than its true spiritual fathers and mothers. I once heard a reverend lecturer on England, a man of learning and intelligence, after enumerating her scientific, literary, and political worthies, Shakspeare, Bacon, Cromwell, Milton, Newton, and others, speak next of her Christian heroes, whom, as if his profession required it of him, he elevated to a place far above all the rest, as the greatest of the great. They were

---

[107] Roman Catholic religious order, the Society of Jesus; one of its concerns was to convert Indians to Christianity.

[108] *Extra:* "outer"; *intra:* "inner."

[109] In the custom of the tithe, churchgoers give one-tenth of their income to support the church's good works.

Penn, Howard, and Mrs. Fry.[110] Every one must feel the falsehood and cant of this. The last were not England's best men and women; only, perhaps, her best philanthropists.

I would not subtract any thing from the praise that is due to philanthropy, but merely demand justice for all who by their lives and works are a blessing to mankind. I do not value chiefly a man's uprightness and benevolence, which are, as it were, his stem and leaves. Those plants of whose greenness withered we make herb tea for the sick, serve but a humble use, and are most employed by quacks. I want the flower and fruit of a man; that some fragrance be wafted over from him to me, and some ripeness flavor our intercourse. His goodness must not be a partial and transitory act, but a constant superfluity, which costs him nothing and of which he is unconscious. This is a charity that hides a multitude of sins. The philanthropist too often surrounds mankind with the remembrance of his own cast-off griefs as an atmosphere, and calls it sympathy. We should impart our courage, and not our despair, our health and ease, and not our disease, and take care that this does not spread by contagion. From what southern plains[111] comes up the voice of wailing? Under what latitudes reside the heathen to whom we would send light? Who is that intemperate and brutal man whom we would redeem? If any thing ail a man, so that he does not perform his functions, if he have a pain in his bowels even,—for that is the seat of sympathy,[112]—he forthwith sets about reforming—the world. Being a microcosm himself, he discovers, and it is a true discovery, and he is the man to make it,—that the world has been eating green apples; to his eyes, in fact, the globe itself is a great green apple, which there is danger awful to think of that the children of men will nibble before it is ripe; and straightway his drastic philanthropy seeks out the Esquimaux[113] and the Patagonian,[114] and embraces the populous Indian and Chinese villages; and thus, by a few years of philanthropic activity, the powers in the mean while using him for their own ends, no doubt, he cures himself of his dyspepsia, the globe acquires a faint blush on one or both of its cheeks, as if it were beginning to be ripe, and life loses its crudity and is once more sweet and wholesome to live. I never dreamed of any enormity greater than I have committed. I never knew, and never shall know, a worse man than myself.

I believe that what so saddens the reformer is not his sympathy with his fellows in distress, but, though he be the holiest son of God, is his private ail. Let this be righted, let the spring come to him, the morning rise over his couch, and he will forsake his generous companions without apology. My excuse for not lecturing against the use of tobacco is, that I never chewed it; that is a penalty which reformed tobacco-chewers have to pay; though there are things enough I have chewed, which I could lecture against. If you should ever be betrayed into any of these philanthropies, do not let your left hand know what your right hand does, for it is not worth knowing.[115] Rescue the drowning and tie your shoe-strings. Take your time, and set about some free labor.

Our manners have been corrupted by communication with the saints. Our hymn-books resound with a melodious cursing of God and enduring him forever. One would

---

[110] Like John Howard, the Quakers William Penn (1644–1718) and Elizabeth Fry (1780–1845) were active reformers of social ills.

[111] Slave states.

[112] That compassion found its source in the bowels was an age-old notion.

[113] Eskimo.

[114] From the nethermost region of South America.

[115] See Matthew 6:3.

say that even the prophets and redeemers had rather consoled the fears than confirmed the hopes of man. There is nowhere recorded a simple and irrepressible satisfaction with the gift of life, any memorable praise of God. All health and success does me good, however far off and withdrawn it may appear; all disease and failure helps to make me sad and does me evil, however much sympathy it may have with me or I with it. If, then, we would indeed restore mankind by truly Indian, botanic, magnetic, or natural means, let us first be as simple and well as Nature ourselves, dispel the clouds which hang over our own brows, and take up a little life into our pores. Do not stay to be an overseer of the poor, but endeavor to become one of the worthies of the world.

I read in the Gulistan, or Flower Garden, of Sheik Sadi of Shiraz,[116] that "They asked a wise man, saying; Of the many celebrated trees which the Most High God has created lofty and umbrageous, they call none azad, or free, excepting the cypress, which bears no fruit; what mystery is there in this? He replied; Each has its appropriate produce, and appointed season, during the continuance of which it is fresh and blooming, and during their absence dry and withered; to neither of which states is the cypress exposed, being always flourishing; and of this nature are the azads, or religious independents.—Fix not thy heart on that which is transitory; for the Dijlah, or Tigris, will continue to flow through Bagdad after the race of caliphs is extinct: if thy hand has plenty, be liberal as the date tree; but if it affords nothing to give away, be an azad, or free man, like the cypress."

Complemental Verses

The Pretensions of Poverty[117]

"Thou dost presume too much, poor needy wretch,
　To claim a station in the firmament,
　Because thy humble cottage, or thy tub,
　Nurses some lazy or pedantic virtue
　In the cheap sunshine or by shady springs,
　With roots and pot-herbs; where thy right hand,
　Tearing those humane passions from the mind,
　Upon whose stocks fair blooming virtues flourish,
　Degradeth nature, and benumbeth sense,
　And, Gorgon-like, turns active men to stone.
　We not require the dull society
　Of your necessitated temperance,
　Or that unnatural stupidity
　That knows nor joy nor sorrow; nor your forc'd
　Falsely exalted passive fortitude
　Above the active. This low abject brood,
　That fix their seats in mediocrity,
　Become your servile minds; but we advance

---

[116] Persian poet of the thirteenth century.
[117] The English poet Thomas Carew (1595?–1645) wrote this poem, which was included in *Coelum Brittannicum* (1661). Thoreau added the title.

Such virtues only as admit excess,
Brave, bounteous acts, regal magnificence,
All-seeing prudence, magnanimity
That knows no bound, and that heroic virtue
For which antiquity hath left no name,
But patterns only, such as Hercules,
Achilles, Theseus. Back to thy loath'd cell;
And when thou seest the new enlightened sphere,
Study to know but what those worthies were."
                                            T. CAREW

Where I Lived, and What I Lived For

At a certain season of our life we are accustomed to consider every spot as the possible
site of a house. I have thus surveyed the country on every side within a dozen miles of
where I live. In imagination I have bought all the farms in succession, for all were to be
bought, and I knew their price. I walked over each farmer's premises, tasted his wild apples, discoursed on husbandry with him, took his farm at his price, at any price, mort-
gaging it to him in my mind; even put a higher price on it,—took every thing but a deed
of it,—took his word for his deed, for I dearly love to talk,—cultivated it, and him too
to some extent, I trust, and withdrew when I had enjoyed it long enough, leaving him to
carry it on. This experience entitled me to be regarded as a sort of real-estate broker by
my friends. Wherever I sat, there I might live, and the landscape radiated from me accordingly. What is a house but a *sedes*, a seat?—better if a country seat. I discovered
many a site for a house not likely to be soon improved, which some might have thought
too far from the village, but to my eyes the village was too far from it. Well, there I
might live, I said; and there I did live, for an hour, a summer and a winter life; saw how
I could let the years run off, buffet the winter through, and see the spring come in. The
future inhabitants of this region, wherever they may place their houses, may be sure
that they have been anticipated. An afternoon sufficed to lay out the land into orchard
woodlot and pasture, and to decide what fine oaks or pines should be left to stand before the door, and whence each blasted tree could be seen to the best advantage; and
then I let it lie, fallow perchance, for a man is rich in proportion to the number of
things which he can afford to let alone.

My imagination carried me so far that I even had the refusal of several farms,—the
refusal was all I wanted,—but I never got my fingers burned by actual possession. The
nearest that I came to actual possession was when I bought the Hollowell Place, and had
begun to sort my seeds, and collected materials with which to make a wheelbarrow to
carry it on or off with; but before the owner gave me a deed of it, his wife—every man
has such a wife—changed her mind and wished to keep it, and he offered me ten dollars
to release him. Now, to speak the truth, I had but ten cents in the world, and it surpassed my arithmetic to tell, if I was that man who had ten cents, or who had a farm, or
ten dollars, or all together. However, I let him keep the ten dollars and the farm too, for
I had carried it far enough; or rather, to be generous, I sold him the farm for just what I
gave for it, and, as he was not a rich man, made him a present of ten dollars, and still
had my ten cents, and seeds, and materials for a wheelbarrow left. I found thus that I
had been a rich man without any damage to my poverty. But I retained the landscape,

and I have since annually carried off what it yielded without a wheelbarrow. With respect to landscapes,—

> "I am monarch of all I *survey*,
>   My right there is none to dispute."[118]

I have frequently seen a poet withdraw, having enjoyed the most valuable part of a farm, while the crusty farmer supposed that he had got a few wild apples only. Why, the owner does not know it for many years when a poet has put his farm in rhyme, the most admirable kind of invisible fence, has fairly impounded it, milked it, skimmed it, and got all the cream, and left the farmer only the skimmed milk.

The real attractions of the Hollowell farm, to me, were; its complete retirement, being about two miles from the village, half a mile from the nearest neighbor, and separated from the highway by a broad field; its bounding on the river, which the owner said protected it by its fogs from frosts in the spring, though that was nothing to me; the gray color and ruinous state of the house and barn, and the dilapidated fences, which put such an interval between me and the last occupant; the hollow and lichen-covered apple trees, gnawed by rabbits, showing what kind of neighbors I should have; but above all, the recollection I had of it from my earliest voyages up the river, when the house was concealed behind a dense grove of red maples, through which I heard the house-dog bark. I was in haste to buy it, before the proprietor finished getting out some rocks, cutting down the hollow apple trees, and grubbing up some young birches which had sprung up in the pasture, or, in short, had made any more of his improvements. To enjoy these advantages I was ready to carry it on; like Atlas,[119] to take the world on my shoulders,—I never heard what compensation he received for that,—and do all those things which had no other motive or excuse but that I might pay for it and be unmolested in my possession of it; for I knew all the while that it would yield the most abundant crop of the kind I wanted if I could only afford to let it alone. But it turned out as I have said.

All that I could say, then, with respect to farming on a large scale, (I have always cultivated a garden,) was, that I had had my seeds ready. Many think that seeds improve with age. I have no doubt that time discriminates between the good and the bad; and when at last I shall plant, I shall be less likely to be disappointed. But I would say to my fellows, once for all, As long as possible live free and uncommitted. It makes but little difference whether you are committed to a farm or the county jail.

Old Cato, whose "De Re Rustica"[120] is my "Cultivator," says, and the only translation I have seen makes sheer nonsense of the passage, "When you think of getting a farm, turn it thus in your mind, not to buy greedily; nor spare your pains to look at it, and do not think it enough to go round it once. The oftener you go there the more it will please you, if it is good." I think I shall not buy greedily, but go round and round it as long as I live, and be buried in it first, that it may please me the more at last.

---

[118] Thoreau, a part-time surveyor, chose to emphasize the word *survey* when quoting from "Verses Supposed to be Written by Alexander Selkirk" by William Cowper (1731–1800).

[119] In classic myth, the giant who bore the world on his shoulders.

[120] Marcus Porcius Cato (234–149 B.C.), author of a work on agriculture (160? B.C.) that is sometimes given this name.

The present was my next experiment of this kind, which I purpose to describe more at length; for convenience, putting the experience of two years into one. As I have said, I do not propose to write an ode to dejection, but to brag as lustily as chanticleer in the morning, standing on his roost, if only to wake my neighbors up.

When first I took up my abode in the woods, that is, began to spend my nights as well as days there, which, by accident, was on Independence Day, or the fourth of July, 1845, my house was not finished for winter, but was merely a defence against the rain, without plastering or chimney, the walls being of rough weather-stained boards, with wide chinks, which made it cool at night. The upright white hewn studs and freshly planed door and window casings gave it a clean and airy look, especially in the morning, when its timbers were saturated with dew, so that I fancied that by noon some sweet gum would exude from them. To my imagination it retained throughout the day more or less of this auroral character, reminding me of a certain house on a mountain which I had visited the year before. This was an airy and unplastered cabin, fit to entertain a travelling god, and where a goddess might trail her garments. The winds which passed over my dwelling were such as sweep over the ridges of mountains, bearing the broken strains, or celestial parts only, of terrestrial music. The morning wind forever blows, the poem of creation is uninterrupted; but few are the ears that hear it. Olympus[121] is but the outside of the earth every where.

The only house I had been the owner of before, if I except a boat, was a tent, which I used occasionally when making excursions in the summer, and this is still rolled up in my garret; but the boat, after passing from hand to hand, has gone down the stream of time. With this more substantial shelter about me, I had made some progress toward settling in the world. This frame, so slightly clad, was a sort of crystallization around me, and reacted on the builder. It was suggestive somewhat as a picture in outlines. I did not need to go out doors to take the air, for the atmosphere within had lost none of its freshness. It was not so much within doors as behind a door where I sat, even in the rainiest weather. The Harivansa[122] says, "An abode without birds is like a meat without seasoning." Such was not my abode, for I found myself suddenly neighbor to the birds; not by having imprisoned one, but having caged myself near them. I was not only nearer to some of those which commonly frequent the garden and the orchard, but to those wilder and more thrilling songsters of the forest which never, or rarely, serenade a villager,—the wood-thrush, the veery, the scarlet tanager, the field-sparrow, the whippoorwill, and many others.

I was seated by the shore of a small pond, about a mile and a half south of the village of Concord and somewhat higher than it, in the midst of an extensive wood between that town and Lincoln, and about two miles south of that our only field known to fame, Concord Battle Ground;[123] but I was so low in the woods that the opposite shore, half a mile off, like the rest, covered with wood, was my most distant horizon. For the first week, whenever I looked out on the pond it impressed me like a tarn high up on the side of a mountain, its bottom far above the surface of other lakes, and, as the sun arose, I saw it throwing off its nightly clothing of mist, and here and there, by degrees, its soft ripples, or its smooth reflecting surface was revealed, while the mists, like ghosts, were

[121] Mountain abode of the Greek gods.
[122] Fifth century Hindu religious epic.
[123] Where one of the opening battles of the American Revolution was fought, on April 19, 1775.

stealthily withdrawing in every direction into the woods, as at the breaking up of some nocturnal conventicle. The very dew seemed to hang upon the trees later into the day than usual, as on the sides of mountains.

This small lake was of most value as a neighbor in the intervals of a gentle rain storm in August, when, both air and water being perfectly still, but the sky overcast, mid-afternoon had all the serenity of evening, and the wood-thrush sang around, and was heard from shore to shore. A lake like this is never smoother than at such a time; and the clear portion of the air above it being shallow and darkened by clouds, the water, full of light and reflections, becomes a lower heaven itself so much the more important. From a hill top near by, where the wood had been recently cut off, there was a pleasing vista southward across the pond, through a wide indentation in the hills which form the shore there, where their opposite sides sloping toward each other suggested a stream flowing out in that direction through a wooded valley, but stream there was none. That way I looked between and over the near green hills to some distant and higher ones in the horizon, tinged with blue. Indeed, by standing on tiptoe I could catch a glimpse of some of the peaks of the still bluer and more distant mountain ranges in the north-west, those true-blue coins from heaven's own mint, and also of some portion of the village. But in other directions, even from this point, I could not see over or beyond the woods which surrounded me. It is well to have some water in your neighborhood, to give buoyancy to and float the earth. One value even of the smallest well is, that when you look into it you see that earth is not continent but insular. This is as important as that it keeps butter cool. When I looked across the pond from this peak toward the Sudbury meadows, which in time of flood I distinguished elevated perhaps by a mirage in their seething valley, like a coin in a basin, all the earth beyond the pond appeared like a thin crust insulated and floated even by this small sheet of intervening water, and I was reminded that this on which I dwelt was but *dry land*.

Though the view from my door was still more contracted, I did not feel crowded or confined in the least. There was pasture enough for my imagination. The low shrub-oak plateau to which the opposite shore arose, stretched away toward the prairies of the West and the steppes of Tartary,[124] affording ample room for all the roving families of men. "There are none happy in the world but beings who enjoy freely a vast horizon,"—said Damodara,[125] when his herds required new and larger pastures.

Both place and time were changed, and I dwelt nearer to those parts of the universe and to those eras in history which had most attracted me. Where I lived was as far off as many a region viewed nightly by astronomers. We are wont to imagine rare and delectable places in some remote and more celestial corner of the system, behind the constellation of Cassiopeia's Chair, far from noise and disturbance. I discovered that my house actually had its site in such a withdrawn, but forever new and unprofaned, part of the universe. If it were worth the while to settle in those parts near to the Pleiades or the Hyades, to Aldebaran or Altair,[126] then I was really there, or at an equal remoteness from the life which I had left behind, dwindled and twinkling with as fine a ray to my nearest neighbor, and to be seen only in moonless nights by him. Such was that part of creation where I had squatted;—

[124] In Russian Asia.
[125] Hindu god mentioned in the *Harivansa;* another name for Krishna.

[126] Stars and constellations.

> "There was a shepherd that did live,
> And held his thoughts as high
>   As were the mounts whereon his flocks
>   Did hourly feed him by."

What should we think of the shepherd's life if his flocks always wandered to higher pastures than his thoughts?

Every morning was a cheerful invitation to make my life of equal simplicity, and I may say innocence, with Nature herself. I have been as sincere a worshipper of Aurora[127] as the Greeks. I got up early and bathed in the pond; that was a religious exercise, and one of the best things which I did. They say that characters were engraven on the bathing tub of king Tching-thang[128] to this effect: "Renew thyself completely each day; do it again, and again, and forever again." I can understand that. Morning brings back the heroic ages. I was as much affected by the faint hum of a mosquito making its invisible and unimaginable tour through my apartment at earliest dawn, when I was sitting with door and windows open, as I could be by any trumpet that ever sang of fame. It was Homer's requiem; itself an Iliad and Odyssey in the air, singing its own wrath and wanderings. There was something cosmical about it; a standing advertisement, till forbidden, of the everlasting vigor and fertility of the world. The morning, which is the most memorable season of the day, is the awakening hour. Then there is least somnolence in us; and for an hour, at least, some part of us awakes which slumbers all the rest of the day and night. Little is to be expected of that day, if it can be called a day, to which we are not awakened by our Genius, but by the mechanical nudgings of some servitor, are not awakened by our own newly-acquired force and aspirations from within, accompanied by the undulations of celestial music, instead of factory bells, and a fragrance filling the air—to a higher life than we fell asleep from; and thus the darkness bear its fruit, and prove itself to be good, no less than the light. That man who does not believe that each day contains an earlier, more sacred, and auroral hour than he has yet profaned, has despaired of life, and is pursuing a descending and darkening way. After a partial cessation of his sensuous life, the soul of man, or its organs rather, are reinvigorated each day, and his Genius[129] tries again what noble life it can make. All memorable events, I should say, transpire in morning time and in a morning atmosphere. The Vedas[130] say, "All intelligences awake with the morning." Poetry and art, and the fairest and most memorable of the actions of men, date from such an hour. All poets and heroes, like Memnon, are the children of Aurora, and emit their music at sunrise. To him whose elastic and vigorous thought keeps pace with the sun, the day is a perpetual morning. It matters not what the clocks say or the attitudes and labors of men. Morning is when I am awake and there is a dawn in me. Moral reform is the effort to throw off sleep. Why is it that men give so poor an account of their day if they have not been slumbering? They are not such poor calculators. If they had not been overcome with drowsiness they would have performed something. The millions are awake enough for physical labor; but only one in a million is awake enough for effective intellectual exertion, only

127 Although Thoreau refers to Aurora as a Greek goddess (of the dawn), that was the Roman name for her.

128 The lines, taken from the tub of the Chinese monarch who founded the Shang dynasty (1766–1122 B.C.), are from a gloss of Confucius' *The Great Learning*.

129 Guardian spirit.

130 Religious text of the Hindus.

one in a hundred millions to a poetic or divine life. To be awake is to be alive. I have never yet met a man who was quite awake. How could I have looked him in the face?

We must learn to reawaken and keep ourselves awake, not by mechanical aids, but by an infinite expectation of the dawn, which does not forsake us in our soundest sleep. I know of no more encouraging fact than the unquestionable ability of man to elevate his life by a conscious endeavor. It is something to be able to paint a particular picture, or to carve a statue, and so to make a few objects beautiful; but it is far more glorious to carve and paint the very atmosphere and medium through which we look, which morally we can do. To affect the quality of the day, that is the highest of arts. Every man is tasked to make his life, even in its details, worthy of the contemplation of his most elevated and critical hour. If we refused, or rather used up, such paltry information as we get, the oracles would distinctly inform us how this might be done.

I went to the woods because I wished to live deliberately, to front only the essential facts of life, and see if I could not learn what it had to teach, and not, when I came to die, discover that I had not lived. I did not wish to live what was not life, living is so dear; nor did I wish to practise resignation, unless it was quite necessary. I wanted to live deep and suck out all the marrow of life, to live so sturdily and Spartanlike as to put to rout all that was not life, to cut a broad swath and shave close, to drive life into a corner, and reduce it to its lowest terms, and, if it proved to be mean, why then to get the whole and genuine meanness of it, and publish its meanness to the world; or if it were sublime, to know it by experience, and be able to give a true account of it in my next excursion. For most men, it appears to me, are in a strange uncertainty about it, whether it is of the devil or of God, and have *somewhat hastily* concluded that it is the chief end of man here to "glorify God and enjoy him forever."

Still we live meanly, like ants; though the fable tells us that we were long ago changed into men;[131] like pygmies we fight with cranes;[132] it is error upon error, and clout upon clout, and our best virtue has for its occasion a superfluous and evitable wretchedness. Our life is frittered away by detail. An honest man has hardly need to count more than his ten fingers, or in extreme cases he may add his ten toes, and lump the rest. Simplicity, simplicity, simplicity! I say, let your affairs be as two or three, and not a hundred or a thousand; instead of a million count half a dozen, and keep your accounts on your thumb nail. In the midst of this chopping sea of civilized life, such are the clouds and storms and quicksands and thousand-and-one items to be allowed for, that a man has to live, if he would not founder and go to the bottom and not make his port at all, by dead reckoning,[133] and he must be a great calculator indeed who succeeds. Simplify, simplify. Instead of three meals a day, if it be necessary eat but one; instead of a hundred dishes, five; and reduce other things in proportion. Our life is like a German Confederacy,[134] made up of petty states, with its boundary forever fluctuating, so that even a German cannot tell you how it is bounded at any moment. The nation itself, with all its so called internal improvements, which, by the way, are all external and superficial, is

131 In a classic myth Zeus transformed ants into men for the purpose of repopulating a plague-devastated land.
132 The Trojans were likened to cranes that fought with pygmies in the *Iliad,* Book III.
133 A system for navigating a ship at sea without the aid of the sun and stars.

134 Germany, as Thoreau knew it during his lifetime, was an unstable grouping of states; only in 1871 was it brought together into a national unit by Bismarck.

just such an unwieldy and overgrown establishment, cluttered with furniture and tripped up by its own traps, ruined by luxury and heedless expense, by want of calculation and a worthy aim, as the million households in the land; and the only cure for it as for them is in a rigid economy, a stern and more than Spartan simplicity of life and elevation of purpose. It lives too fast. Men think that it is essential that the *Nation* have commerce, and export ice, and talk through a telegraph, and ride thirty miles an hour, without a doubt, whether *they* do or not; but whether we should live like baboons or like men, is a little uncertain. If we do not get our sleepers,[135] and forge rails, and devote days and nights to the work, but go to tinkering upon our *lives* to improve *them,* who will build railroads? And if railroads are not built, how shall we get to heaven in season? But if we stay at home and mind our business, who will want railroads? We do not ride on the railroad; it rides upon us. Did you ever think what those sleepers are that underlie the railroad? Each one is a man, an Irish-man, or a Yankee man. The rails are laid on them, and they are covered with sand, and the cars run smoothly over them. They are sound sleepers, I assure you. And every few years a new lot is laid down and run over; so that, if some have the pleasure of riding on a rail, others have the misfortune to be ridden upon. And when they run over a man that is walking in his sleep, a supernumerary sleeper in the wrong position, and wake him up, they suddenly stop the cars, and make a hue and cry about it, as if this were an exception. I am glad to know that it takes a gang of men for every five miles to keep the sleepers down and level in their beds as it is, for this is a sign that they may sometime get up again.

Why should we live with such hurry and waste of life? We are determined to be starved before we are hungry. Men say that a stitch in time saves nine, and so they take a thousand stitches to-day to save nine to-morrow. As for *work,* we haven't any of any consequence. We have the Saint Vitus' dance, and cannot possibly keep our heads still. If I should only give a few pulls at the parish bell-rope, as for a fire, that is, without setting the bell,[136] there is hardly a man on his farm in the outskirts of Concord, notwithstanding that press of engagements which was his excuse so many times this morning, nor a boy, nor a woman, I might almost say, but would forsake all and follow that sound, not mainly to save property from the flames, but, if we will confess the truth, much more to see it burn, since burn it must, and we, be it known, did not set it on fire,—or to see it put out, and have a hand in it, if that is done as handsomely; yes, even if it were the parish church itself. Hardly a man takes a half hour's nap after dinner, but when he wakes he holds up his head and asks, "What's the news?" as if the rest of mankind had stood his sentinels. Some give directions to be waked every half hour, doubtless for no other purpose; and then, to pay for it, they tell what they have dreamed. After a night's sleep the news is as indispensable as the breakfast. "Pray tell me any thing new that has happened to a man any where on this globe,"—and he reads it over his coffee and rolls, that a man has had his eyes gouged out this morning on the Wachito River;[137] never dreaming the while that he lives in the dark unfathomed mammoth cave of this world, and has but the rudiment of an eye himself.

For my part, I could easily do without the post-office. I think that there are very few important communications made through it. To speak critically, I never received more

---

[135] Railroad ties.
[136] Inverting the bell by pulling it too hard.
[137] Tributary of the Red River in Arkansas.

than one or two letters in my life—I wrote this some years ago—that were worth the postage. The penny-post is, commonly, an institution through which you seriously offer a man that penny for his thoughts which is so often safely offered in jest. And I am sure that I never read any memorable news in a newspaper. If we read of one man robbed, or murdered, or killed by accident, or one house burned, or one vessel wrecked, or one steamboat blown up, or one cow run over on the Western Railroad, or one mad dog killed, or one lot of grasshoppers in the winter,—we never need read of another. One is enough. If you are acquainted with the principle, what do you care for a myriad instances and applications? To a philosopher all *news*, as it is called, is gossip, and they who edit and read it are old women over their tea. Yet not a few are greedy after this gossip. There was such a rush, as I hear, the other day at one of the offices to learn the foreign news by the last arrival, that several large squares of plate glass belonging to the establishment were broken by the pressure,—news which I seriously think a ready wit might write a twelvemonth or twelve years beforehand with sufficient accuracy. As for Spain, for instance, if you know how to throw in Don Carlos and the Infanta, and Don Pedro[138] and Seville and Granada, from time to time in the right proportions,—they may have changed the names a little since I saw the papers,—and serve up a bull-fight when other entertainments fail, it will be true to the letter, and give us as good an idea of the exact state or ruin of things in Spain as the most succinct and lucid reports under this head in the newspapers: and as for England, almost the last significant scrap of news from that quarter was the revolution of 1649;[139] and if you have learned the history of her crops for an average year, you never need attend to that thing again, unless your speculations are of a merely pecuniary character. If one may judge who rarely looks into the newspapers, nothing new does ever happen in foreign parts, a French revolution not excepted.

What news! how much more important to know what that is which was never old! "Kieou-pe-yu (great dignitary of the state of Wei) sent a man to Khoung-tseu[140] to know his news. Khoung-tseu caused the messenger to be seated near him, and questioned him in these terms: What is your master doing? The messenger answered with respect: My master desires to diminish the number of his faults, but he cannot accomplish it. The messenger being gone, the philosopher remarked: What a worthy messenger! What a worthy messenger!" The preacher, instead of vexing the ears of drowsy farmers on their day of rest at the end of the week,—for Sunday is the fit conclusion of an ill-spent week, and not the fresh and brave beginning of a new one,—with this one other draggle-tail of a sermon, should shout with thundering voice,—"Pause! Avast! Why so seeming fast, but deadly slow?"

Shams and delusions are esteemed for soundest truths, while reality is fabulous. If men would steadily observe realities only, and not allow themselves to be deluded, life, to compare it with such things as we know, would be like a fairy tale and the Arabian Nights' Entertainments. If we respected only what is inevitable and has a right to be, music and poetry would resound along the streets. When we are unhurried and wise, we perceive that only great and worthy things have any permanent and absolute existence,—that petty fears and petty pleasures are but the shadow of the reality. This is al-

---

[138] Members of the Spanish nobility.
[139] The end of the British monarchy at the hands of the Puritan Commonwealth.

[140] Confucius. The incident is described in *The Analects*, XIV, 26.

ways exhilarating and sublime. By closing the eyes and slumbering, and consenting to be deceived by shows, men establish and confirm their daily life of routine and habit every where, which still is built on purely illusory foundations. Children, who play life, discern its true law and relations more clearly than men, who fail to live it worthily, but who think that they are wiser by experience, that is, by failure. I have read in a Hindoo book, that "there was a king's son, who, being expelled in infancy from his native city, was brought up by a forester, and, growing up to maturity in that state, imagined himself to belong to the barbarous race with which he lived. One of his father's ministers having discovered him, revealed to him what he was, and the misconception of his character was removed, and he knew himself to be a prince. So soul," continues the Hindoo philosopher, "from the circumstances in which it is placed, mistakes its own character, until the truth is revealed to it by some holy teacher, and then it knows itself to be *Brahme*."[141] I perceive that we inhabitants of New England live this mean life that we do because our vision does not penetrate the surface of things. We think that that is which *appears* to be. If a man should walk through this town and see only the reality, where, think you, would the "Mill-dam"[142] go to? If he should give us an account of the realities he beheld there, we should not recognize the place in his description. Look at a meeting-house, or a court-house, or a jail, or a shop, or a dwelling-house, and say what that thing really is before a true gaze, and they would all go to pieces in your account of them. Men esteem truth remote, in the outskirts of the system, behind the farthest star, before Adam and after the last man. In eternity there is indeed something true and sublime. But all these times and places and occasions are now and here. God himself culminates in the present moment, and will never be more divine in the lapse of all the ages. And we are enabled to apprehend at all what is sublime and noble only by the perpetual instilling and drenching of the reality which surrounds us. The universe constantly and obediently answers to our conceptions; whether we travel fast or slow, the track is laid for us. Let us spend our lives in conceiving then. The poet or the artist never yet had so fair and noble a design but some of his posterity at least could accomplish it.

Let us spend one day as deliberately as Nature, and not be thrown off the track by every nutshell and mosquito's wing that falls on the rails. Let us rise early and fast, or break fast, gently and without perturbation; let company come and let company go, let the bells ring and the children cry,—determined to make a day of it. Why should we knock under and go with the stream? Let us not be upset and overwhelmed in that terrible rapid and whirlpool called a dinner, situated in the meridian shallows. Weather this danger and you are safe, for the rest of the way is down hill. With unrelaxed nerves, with morning vigor, sail by it, looking another way, tied to the mast like Ulysses.[143] If the engine whistles, let it whistle till it is hoarse for its pains. If the bell rings, why should we run? We will consider what kind of music they are like. Let us settle ourselves, and work and wedge our feet downward through the mud and slush of opinion, and prejudice, and tradition, and delusion, and appearance, that alluvion which covers the globe, through Paris and London, through New York and Boston and Concord, through

---

[141] The foremost god in the Hindu hierarchy.
[142] Concord's town center, meeting place for idle chatter.
[143] i.e., be able to move past dangers in safety, like Ulysses in the *Odyssey*, who had himself bound to the ship's mast so that he could both listen to the Sirens' song and resist their fatal call.

church and state, through poetry and philosophy and religion, till we come to a hard bottom and rocks in place, which we can call *reality,* and say, This is, and no mistake; and then begin, having a *point d'appui,* below freshet and frost and fire, a place where you might found a wall or a state, or set a lamp-post safely, or perhaps a gauge, not a Nilometer, but a Realometer, that future ages might know how deep a freshet of shams and appearances had gathered from time to time. If you stand right fronting and face to face to a fact, you will see the sun glimmer on both its surfaces, as if it were a cimeter,[144] and feel its sweet edge dividing you through the heart and marrow, and so you will happily conclude your mortal career. Be it life or death, we crave only reality. If we are really dying, let us hear the rattle in our throats and feel cold in the extremities; if we are alive, let us go about our business.

Time is but the stream I go a-fishing in. I drink at it; but while I drink I see the sandy bottom and detect how shallow it is. Its thin current slides away, but eternity remains. I would drink deeper; fish in the sky, whose bottom is pebbly with stars. I cannot count one. I know not the first letter of the alphabet. I have always been regretting that I was not as wise as the day I was born. The intellect is a cleaver; it discerns and rifts its way into the secret of things. I do not wish to be any more busy with my hands than is necessary. My head is hands and feet. I feel all my best faculties concentrated in it. My instinct tells me that my head is an organ for burrowing, as some creatures use their snout and fore-paws, and with it I would mine and burrow my way through these hills. I think that the richest vein is somewhere hereabouts; so by the divining rod and thin rising vapors I judge; and here I will begin to mine.

Reading

With a little more deliberation in the choice of their pursuits, all men would perhaps become essentially students and observers, for certainly their nature and destiny are interesting to all alike. In accumulating property for ourselves or our posterity, in founding a family or a state, or acquiring fame even, we are mortal; but in dealing with truth we are immortal, and need fear no change nor accident. The oldest Egyptian or Hindoo philosopher raised a corner of the veil from the statue of the divinity; and still the trembling robe remains raised, and I gaze upon as fresh a glory as he did, since it was I in him that was then so bold, and it is he in me that now reviews the vision. No dust has settled on that robe; no time has elapsed since that divinity was revealed. That time which we really improve, or which is improvable, is neither past, present, nor future.

My residence was more favorable, not only to thought, but to serious reading, than a university; and though I was beyond the range of the ordinary circulating library, I had more than ever come within the influence of those books which circulate round the world, whose sentences were first written on bark, and are now merely copied from time to time on to linen paper. Says the poet Mir Camar Uddin Mast,[145] "Being seated to run through the region of the spiritual world; I have had this advantage in books. To be intoxicated by a single glass of wine; I have experienced this pleasure when I have drunk the liquor of the esoteric doctrines." I kept Homer's Iliad on my table through the summer, though I looked at his page only now and then. Incessant labor with my

---

144 Scimitar.
145 Prince Qamar-urddin Minnat, eighteenth-
    century Persian poet.

hands, at first, for I had my house to finish and my beans to hoe at the same time, made more study impossible. Yet I sustained myself by the prospect of such reading in future. I read one or two shallow books of travel in the intervals of my work, till that employment made me ashamed of myself, and I asked where it was then that *I* lived.

The student may read Homer or Æschylus[146] in the Greek without danger of dissipation or luxuriousness, for it implies that he in some measure emulate their heroes, and consecrate morning hours to their pages. The heroic books, even if printed in the character of our mother tongue, will always be in a language dead to degenerate times; and we must laboriously seek the meaning of each word and line, conjecturing a larger sense than common use permits out of what wisdom and valor and generosity we have. The modern cheap and fertile press, with all its translations, has done little to bring us nearer to the heroic writers of antiquity. They seem as solitary, and the letter in which they are printed as rare and curious, as ever. It is worth the expense of youthful days and costly hours, if you learn only some words of an ancient language, which are raised out of the trivialness of the street, to be perpetual suggestions and provocations. It is not in vain that the farmer remembers and repeats the few Latin words which he has heard. Men sometimes speak as if the study of the classics would at length make way for more modern and practical studies; but the adventurous student will always study classics, in whatever language they may be written and however ancient they may be. For what are the classics but the noblest recorded thoughts of man? They are the only oracles which are not decayed, and there are such answers to the most modern inquiry in them as Delphi and Dodona[147] never gave. We might as well omit to study Nature because she is old. To read well, that is, to read true books in a true spirit, is a noble exercise, and one that will task the reader more than any exercise which the customs of the day esteem. It requires a training such as the athletes underwent, the steady intention almost of the whole life to this object. Books must be read as deliberately and reservedly as they were written. It is not enough even to be able to speak the language of that nation by which they are written, for there is a memorable interval between the spoken and the written language, the language heard and the language read. The one is commonly transitory, a sound, a tongue, a dialect merely, almost brutish, and we learn it unconsciously, like the brutes, of our mothers. The other is the maturity and experience of that; if that is our mother tongue, this is our father tongue, a reserved and select expression, too significant to be heard by the ear, which we must be born again in order to speak. The crowds of men who merely *spoke* the Greek and Latin tongues in the middle ages were not entitled by the accident of birth to *read* the works of genius written in those languages; for these were not written in that Greek or Latin which they knew, but in the select language of literature. They had not learned the nobler dialects of Greece and Rome, but the very materials on which they were written were waste paper to them, and they prized instead a cheap contemporary literature. But when the several nations of Europe had acquired distinct though rude written languages of their own, sufficient for the purposes of their rising literatures, then first learning revived, and scholars were enabled to discern from that remoteness the treasures of antiquity. What the Roman and Grecian multitude could not *hear,* after the lapse of ages a few scholars *read,* and a few scholars only are still reading it.

---

[146] Greek dramatist (525–456 B.C.).
[147] Locations of shrines built to Apollo and
Zeus by the ancient Greeks.

However much we may admire the orator's occasional bursts of eloquence, the noblest written words are commonly as far behind or above the fleeting spoken language as the firmament with its stars is behind the clouds. *There* are the stars, and they who can may read them. The astronomers forever comment on and observe them. They are not exhalations like our daily colloquies and vaporous breath. What is called eloquence in the forum is commonly found to be rhetoric in the study. The orator yields to the inspiration of a transient occasion, and speaks to the mob before him, to those who can *hear* him; but the writer, whose more equable life is his occasion, and who would be distracted by the event and the crowd which inspire the orator, speaks to the intellect and heart of mankind, to all in any age who can *understand* him.

No wonder that Alexander[148] carried the Iliad with him on his expeditions in a precious casket. A written word is the choicest of relics. It is something at once more intimate with us and more universal than any other work of art. It is the work of art nearest to life itself. It may be translated into every language, and not only be read but actually breathed from all human lips;—not be represented on canvas or in marble only, but be carved out of the breath of life itself. The symbol of an ancient man's thought becomes a modern man's speech. Two thousand summers have imparted to the monuments of Grecian literature, as to her marbles, only a maturer golden and autumnal tint, for they have carried their own serene and celestial atmosphere into all lands to protect them against the corrosion of time. Books are the treasured wealth of the world and the fit inheritance of generations and nations. Books, the oldest and the best, stand naturally and rightfully on the shelves of every cottage. They have no cause of their own to plead, but while they enlighten and sustain the reader his common sense will not refuse them. Their authors are a natural and irresistible aristocracy in every society, and, more than kings or emperors, exert an influence on mankind. When the illiterate and perhaps scornful trader has earned by enterprise and industry his coveted leisure and independence, and is admitted to the circles of wealth and fashion, he turns inevitably at last to those still higher but yet inaccessible circles of intellect and genius, and is sensible only of the imperfection of his culture and the vanity and insufficiency of all his riches, and further proves his good sense by the pains which he takes to secure for his children that intellectual culture whose want he so keenly feels; and thus it is that he becomes the founder of a family.

Those who have not learned to read the ancient classics in the language in which they were written must have a very imperfect knowledge of the history of the human race; for it is remarkable that no transcript of them has ever been made into any modern tongue, unless our civilization itself may be regarded as such a transcript. Homer has never yet been printed[149] in English, nor Æschylus, nor Virgil[150] even,—works as refined, as solidly done, and as beautiful almost as the morning itself; for later writers, say what we will of their genius, have rarely, if ever, equalled the elaborate beauty and finish and the life-long and heroic literary labors of the ancients. They only talk of forgetting them who never knew them. It will be soon enough to forget them when we have the learning and the genius which will enable us to attend to and appreciate them.

---

[148] Alexander the Great (356–323 B.C.).
[149] i.e., successfully translated.
[150] Roman poet (70–19 B.C.).

That age will be rich indeed when those relics which we call Classics, and the still older and more than classic but even less known Scriptures of the nations, shall have still further accumulated, when the Vaticans shall be filled with Vedas and Zendavestas[151] and Bibles, with Homers and Dantes and Shakspeares, and all the centuries to come shall have successively deposited their trophies in the forum of the world. By such a pile we may hope to scale heaven at last.

The works of the great poets have never yet been read by mankind, for only great poets can read them. They have only been read as the multitude read the stars, at most astrologically, not astronomically. Most men have learned to read to serve a paltry convenience, as they have learned to cipher in order to keep accounts and not be cheated in trade; but of reading as a noble intellectual exercise they know little or nothing; yet this only is reading, in a high sense, not that which lulls us as a luxury and suffers the nobler faculties to sleep the while, but what we have to stand on tiptoe to read and devote our most alert and wakeful hours to.

I think that having learned our letters we should read the best that is in literature, and not be forever repeating our a b abs,[152] and words of one syllable, in the fourth or fifth classes, sitting on the lowest and foremost form all our lives. Most men are satisfied if they read or hear read, and perchance have been convicted by the wisdom of one good book, the Bible, and for the rest of their lives vegetate and dissipate their faculties in what is called easy reading. There is a work in several volumes in our Circulating Library entitled Little Reading, which I thought referred to a town of that name which I had not been to. There are those who, like cormorants and ostriches, can digest all sorts of this, even after the fullest dinner of meats and vegetables, for they suffer nothing to be wasted. If others are the machines to provide this provender, they are the machines to read it. They read the nine thousandth tale about Zebulon and Sephronia, and how they loved as none had ever loved before, and neither did the course of their true love run smooth,—at any rate, how it did run and stumble, and get up again and go on! how some poor unfortunate got up onto a steeple, who had better never have gone up as far as the belfry; and then, having needlessly got him up there, the happy novelist rings the bell for all the world to come together and hear, O dear! how he did get down again! For my part, I think that they had better metamorphose all such aspiring heroes of universal noveldom into man weathercocks, as they used to put heroes among the constellations, and let them swing round there till they are rusty, and not come down at all to bother honest men with their pranks. The next time the novelist rings the bell I will not stir though the meeting-house burn down. "The Skip of the Tip-Toe-Hop, a Romance of the Middle Ages, by the celebrated author of 'Tittle-Tol-Tan,' to appear in monthly parts; a great rush; don't all come together." All this they read with saucer eyes, and erect and primitive curiosity, and with unwearied gizzard, whose corrugations even yet need no sharpening, just as some little four-year-old bencher his two-cent gilt-covered edition of Cinderella,—without any improvement, that I can see, in the pronunciation, or accent, or emphasis, or any more skill in extracting or inserting the moral. The result is dulness of sight, a stagnation of the vital circulations, and a general deliquium[153] and

---

[151] Sacred texts of the Zoroastrians.
[152] Alphabet.
[153] Lessening.

sloughing off of all the intellectual faculties. This sort of gingerbread is baked daily and more sedulously than pure wheat or rye-and-Indian in almost every oven, and finds a surer market.

The best books are not read even by those who are called good readers. What does our Concord culture amount to? There is in this town, with a very few exceptions, no taste for the best or for very good books even in English literature, whose words all can read and spell. Even the college-bred and so called liberally educated men here and elsewhere have really little or no acquaintance with the English classics; and as for the recorded wisdom of mankind, the ancient classics and Bibles, which are accessible to all who will know of them, there are the feeblest efforts any where made to become acquainted with them. I know a woodchopper, of middle age, who takes a French paper, not for news as he says, for he is above that, but to "keep himself in practice," he being a Canadian by birth; and when I ask him what he considers the best thing he can do in this world, he says, beside this, to keep up and add to his English. This is about as much as the college bred generally do or aspire to do, and they take an English paper for the purpose. One who has just come from reading perhaps one of the best English books will find how many with whom he can converse about it? Or suppose he comes from reading a Greek or Latin classic in the original, whose praises are familiar even to the so called illiterate; he will find nobody at all to speak to, but must keep silence about it. Indeed, there is hardly the professor in our colleges, who, if he has mastered the difficulties of the language, has proportionally mastered the difficulties of the wit and poetry of a Greek poet, and has any sympathy to impart to the alert and heroic reader; and as for the sacred Scriptures, or Bibles of mankind, who in this town can tell me even their titles? Most men do not know that any nation but the Hebrews have had a scripture. A man, any man, will go considerably out of his way to pick up a silver dollar; but here are golden words, which the wisest men of antiquity have uttered, and whose worth the wise of every succeeding age have assured us of;—and yet we learn to read only as far as Easy Reading, the primers and classbooks, and when we leave school, the "Little Reading," and story books, which are for boys and beginners; and our reading, our conversation and thinking, are all on a very low level, worthy only of pygmies and manikins.

I aspire to be acquainted with wiser men than this our Concord soil has produced, whose names are hardly known here. Or shall I hear the name of Plato[154] and never read his book? As if Plato were my townsman and I never saw him,—my next neighbor and I never heard him speak or attended to the wisdom of his words. But how actually is it? His Dialogues, which contain what was immortal in him, lie on the next shelf, and yet I never read them. We are underbred and low-lived and illiterate; and in this respect I confess I do not make any very broad distinction between the illiterateness of my townsman who cannot read at all, and the illiterateness of him who has learned to read only what is for children and feeble intellects. We should be as good as the worthies of antiquity, but partly by first knowing how good they were. We are a race of tit-men,[155] and soar but little higher in our intellectual flights than the columns of the daily paper.

It is not all books that are as dull as their readers. There are probably words addressed to our condition exactly, which, if we could really hear and understand, would be more salutary than the morning or the spring to our lives, and possibly put a new as-

---

154 Greek philosopher (427?–347 B.C.).
155 i.e., undersized.

pect on the face of things for us. How many a man has dated a new era in his life from the reading of a book. The book exists for us perchance which will explain our miracles and reveal new ones. The at present unutterable things we may find somewhere uttered. These same questions that disturb and puzzle and confound us have in their turn occurred to all the wise men; not one has been omitted; and each has answered them, according to his ability, by his words and his life. Moreover, with wisdom we shall learn liberality. The solitary hired man on a farm in the outskirts of Concord, who has had his second birth and peculiar religious experience, and is driven as he believes into silent gravity and exclusiveness by his faith, may think it is not true; but Zoroaster, thousands of years ago, travelled the same road and had the same experience; but he, being wise, knew it to be universal, and treated his neighbors accordingly, and is even said to have invented and established worship among men. Let him humbly commune with Zoroaster then, and, through the liberalizing influence of all the worthies, with Jesus Christ himself, and let "our church" go by the board.

We boast that we belong to the nineteenth century and are making the most rapid strides of any nation. But consider how little this village does for its own culture. I do not wish to flatter my townsmen, nor to be flattered by them, for that will not advance either of us. We need to be provoked,—goaded like oxen, as we are, into a trot. We have a comparatively decent system of common schools, schools for infants only; but excepting the half-starved Lyceum[156] in the winter, and latterly the puny beginning of a library suggested by the state, no school for ourselves. We spend more on almost any article of bodily aliment or ailment than on our mental aliment. It is time that we had uncommon schools, that we did not leave off our education when we begin to be men and women. It is time that villages were universities, and their elder inhabitants the fellows of universities, with leisure—if they are indeed so well off—to pursue liberal studies the rest of their lives. Shall the world be confined to one Paris or one Oxford forever?[157] Cannot students be boarded here and get a liberal education under the skies of Concord? Can we not hire some Abelard[158] to lecture to us? Alas! what with foddering the cattle and tending the store, we are kept from school too long, and our education is sadly neglected. In this country, the village should in some respects take the place of the nobleman of Europe. It should be the patron of the fine arts. It is rich enough. It wants only the magnanimity and refinement. It can spend money enough on such things as farmers and traders value, but it is thought Utopian to propose spending money for things which more intelligent men know to be of far more worth. This town has spent seventeen thousand dollars on a town-house, thank fortune or politics, but probably it will not spend so much on living wit, the true meat to put into that shell, in a hundred years. The one hundred and twenty-five dollars annually subscribed for a Lyceum in the winter is better spent than any other equal sum raised in the town. If we live in the nineteenth century, why should we not enjoy the advantages which the nineteenth century offers? Why should our life be in any respect provincial? If we will read newspapers, why not skip the gossip of Boston and take the best newspaper in the world at once?— not be sucking the pap of "neutral family" papers, or browsing "Olive-Branches"[159]

---

156 Public lectures.
157 The universities located in those cities.
158 Peter Abélard (1079–1142), French teacher and theologian.

159 Methodist weekly.

here in New England. Let the reports of all the learned societies come to us, and we will see if they know any thing. Why should we leave it to Harper & Brothers and Redding & Co.[160] to select our reading? As the nobleman of cultivated taste surrounds himself with whatever conduces to his culture,—genius—learning—wit—books—paintings— statuary—music—philosophical instruments, and the like; so let the village do,—not stop short at a pedagogue, a parson, a sexton, a parish library, and three selectmen, be- cause our pilgrim forefathers got through a cold winter once on a bleak rock with these. To act collectively is according to the spirit of our institutions; and I am confident that, as our circumstances are more flourishing, our means are greater than the nobleman's. New England can hire all the wise men in the world to come and teach her, and board them round the while, and not be provincial at all. That is the *uncommon* school we want. Instead of noblemen, let us have noble villages of men. If it is necessary, omit one bridge over the river, go round a little there, and throw one arch at least over the darker gulf of ignorance which surrounds us.

The Ponds

Sometimes, having had a surfeit of human society and gossip, and worn out all my vil- lage friends, I rambled still farther westward then I habitually dwell, into yet more un- frequented parts of the town, "to fresh woods and pastures new,"[161] or, while the sun was setting, made my supper of huckleberries and blueberries on Fair Haven Hill, and laid up a store for several days. The fruits do not yield their true flavor to the purchaser of them, nor to him who raises them for the market. There is but one way to obtain it, yet few take that way. If you would know the flavor of huckleberries, ask the cow-boy or the partridge. It is a vulgar error to suppose that you have tasted huckleberries who never plucked them. A huckleberry never reaches Boston; they have not been known there since they grew on her three hills. The ambrosial and essential part of the fruit is lost with the bloom which is rubbed off in the market cart, and they become mere provender. As long as Eternal Justice reigns, not one innocent huckleberry can be trans- ported thither from the country's hills.

Occasionally, after my hoeing was done for the day, I joined some impatient com- panion who had been fishing on the pond since morning, as silent and motionless as a duck or a floating leaf, and, after practising various kinds of philosophy, had concluded commonly, by the time I arrived, that he belonged to the ancient sect of Cœnobites.[162] There was one older man, an excellent fisher and skilled in all kinds of woodcraft, who was pleased to look upon my house as a building erected for the convenience of fisher- men; and I was equally pleased when he sat in my doorway to arrange his lines. Once in a while we sat together on the pond, he at one end of the boat, and I at the other; but not many words passed between us, for he had grown deaf in his later years, but he oc- casionally hummed a psalm, which harmonized well enough with my philosophy. Our intercourse was thus altogether one of unbroken harmony, far more pleasing to re- member than if it had carried on by speech. When, as was commonly the case, I had none to commune with, I used to raise the echoes by striking with a paddle on the

---

[160] New York publisher and Boston book- seller, respectively.
[161] From the final line of "Lycidas," the poem by John Milton.

[162] Pun by Thoreau, based on a reference to members of a religious group; used here to describe fishermen who "see no bites."

side of my boat, filling the surrounding woods with circling and dilating sound, stirring them up as the keeper of a menagerie his wild beasts, until I elicited a growl from every wooded vale and hill-side.

In warm evenings I frequently sat in the boat playing the flute, and saw the perch, which I seemed to have charmed, hovering around me, and the moon travelling over the ribbed bottom, which was strewed with the wrecks of the forest. Formerly I had come to this pond adventurously, from time to time, in dark summer nights, with a companion, and making a fire close to the water's edge, which we thought attracted the fishes, we caught pouts with a bunch of worms strung on a thread; and when we had done, far in the night, threw the burning brands high into the air like skyrockets, which, coming down into the pond, were quenched with a loud hissing, and we were suddenly groping in total darkness. Through this, whistling a tune, we took our way to the haunts of men again. But now I had made my home by the shore.

Sometimes, after staying in a village parlor till the family had all retired, I have returned to the woods, and, partly with a view to the next day's dinner, spent the hours of midnight fishing from a boat by moonlight, serenaded by owls and foxes, and hearing, from time to time, the creaking note of some unknown bird close at hand. These experiences were very memorable and valuable to me,—anchored in forty feet of water, and twenty or thirty rods from the shore, surrounded sometimes by thousands of small perch and shiners, dimpling the surface with their tails in the moonlight, and communicating by a long flaxen line with mysterious nocturnal fishes which had their dwelling forty feet below, or sometimes dragging sixty feet of line about the pond as I drifted in the gentle night breeze, now and then feeling a slight vibration along it, indicative of some life prowling about its extremity, of dull uncertain blundering purpose there, and slow to make up its mind. At length you slowly raise, pulling hand over hand, some horned pout squeaking and squirming to the upper air. It was very queer, especially in dark nights, when your thoughts had wandered to vast and cosmogonal themes in other spheres, to feel this faint jerk, which came to interrupt your dreams and link you to Nature again. It seemed as if I might next cast my line upward into the air, as well as downward into this element which was scarcely more dense. Thus I caught two fishes as it were with one hook.

The scenery of Walden is on a humble scale, and, though very beautiful, does not approach to grandeur, nor can it much concern one who has not long frequented it or lived by its shore; yet this pond is so remarkable for its depth and purity as to merit a particular description. It is a clear and deep green well, half a mile long and a mile and three quarters in circumference, and contains about sixty-one and a half acres; a perennial spring in the midst of pine and oak woods, without any visible inlet or outlet except by the clouds and evaporation. The surrounding hills rise abruptly from the water to the height of forty to eighty feet, though on the south-east and east they attain to about one hundred and one hundred and fifty feet respectively, within a quarter and a third of a mile. They are exclusively woodland. All our Concord waters have two colors at least, one when viewed at a distance, and another, more proper, close at hand. The first depends more on the light, and follows the sky. In clear weather, in summer, they appear blue at a little distance, especially if agitated, and at a great distance all appear alike. In stormy weather they are sometimes of a dark slate color. The sea, however, is said to be blue one day and green another without any perceptible change in the atmosphere. I have seen our river, when, the landscape being covered with snow, both water and ice were almost as green as grass. Some consider blue "to be the color of pure water, whether liquid or solid."[163] But, looking directly down into our waters from a boat, they are seen to be of very different colors. Walden is blue at one time and green at another, even from the same point of view. Lying between the earth and the heavens, it partakes of the color of both. Viewed from a hill-top it reflects the color of the sky, but near at hand it is of a yellowish tint next the shore where you can see the sand, then a light green, which gradually deepens to a uniform dark green in the body of the pond. In some lights, viewed even from a hill-top, it is of a vivid green next the shore. Some have referred this to the reflection of the verdure; but it is equally green there against the railroad sand-bank, and in the spring, before the leaves are expanded, and it may be simply the result of the prevailing blue mixed with the yellow of the sand. Such is the color of its iris. This is that portion, also, where in the spring, the ice being warmed by the heat of the sun reflected from the bottom, and also transmitted through the earth, melts first and forms a narrow canal about the still frozen middle. Like the rest of our waters, when much agitated, in clear weather, so that the surface of the waves may reflect the sky at the right angle, or because there is more light mixed with it, it appears at a little distance of a darker blue than the sky itself; and at such a time, being on its surface, and looking with divided vision, so as to see the reflection, I have discerned a matchless and indescribable light blue, such as watered or changeable silks and sword blades suggest, more cerulean than the sky itself, alternating with the original dark green on the opposite sides of the waves, which last appeared but muddy in comparison. It is a vitreous greenish blue, as I remember it, like those patches of the winter sky seen through cloud vistas in the west before sundown. Yet a single glass of its water held up to the light is as colorless as an equal quantity of air. It is well known that a large plate of glass will have a green tint, owing, as the makers say, to its "body," but a small piece of the same will be colorless. How large a body of Walden water would be required to reflect a green tint I have never proved. The water of our river is black or a very dark brown to one looking directly down on it, and, like that of most ponds, imparts to the body of one bathing in it a yellowish tinge; but this water is of such crystalline purity that the body of the bather appears of an alabaster whiteness, still more unnatural, which, as the limbs are magnified and distorted withal, produces a monstrous effect, making fit studies for a Michael Angelo.

The water is so transparent that the bottom can easily be discerned at the depth of twenty-five or thirty feet. Paddling over it, you may see many feet beneath the surface the schools of perch and shiners, perhaps only an inch long, yet the former easily distinguished by their traverse bars, and you think that they must be ascetic fish that find a subsistence there. Once, in the winter, many years ago, when I had been cutting holes through the ice in order to catch pickerel, as I stepped ashore I tossed my axe back on to the ice, but, as if some evil genius had directed it, it slid four or five rods directly into one of the holes, where the water was twenty-five feet deep. Out of curiosity, I lay down on the ice and looked through the hole, until I saw the axe a little on one side, standing on its head, with its helve erect and gently swaying to and fro with the pulse of the

---

[163] Description of the color of glacial ice; from *Travels through the Alps of Savoy* (1843) by James D. Forbes.

pond; and there it might have stood erect and swaying till in the course of time the handle rotted off, if I had not disturbed it. Making another hole directly over it with an ice chisel which I had, and cutting down the longest birch which I could find in the neighborhood with my knife, I made a slip-noose, which I attached to its end, and letting it down carefully, passed it over the knob of the handle, and drew it by a line along the birch, and so pulled the axe out again.

The shore is composed of a belt of smooth rounded white stones like paving stones, excepting one or two short sand beaches, and is so steep that in many places a single leap will carry you into water over your head; and were it not for its remarkable transparency, that would be the last to be seen of its bottom till it rose on the opposite side. Some think it is bottomless. It is nowhere muddy, and a casual observer would say that there were no weeds at all in it; and of noticeable plants, except in the little meadows recently overflowed, which do not properly belong to it, a closer scrutiny does not detect a flag nor a bulrush, nor even a lily, yellow or white, but only a few small heart-leaves and potamogetons,[164] and perhaps a water-target[165] or two; all which however a bather might not perceive; and these plants are clean and bright like the element they grow in. The stones extend a rod or two into the water, and then the bottom is pure sand, except in the deepest parts, where there is usually a little sediment, probably from the decay of the leaves which have been wafted on to it so many successive falls, and a bright green weed is brought up on anchors even in midwinter.

We have one other pond just like this, White Pond in Nine Acre Corner, about two and a half miles westerly; but, though I am acquainted with most of the ponds within a dozen miles of this centre, I do not know a third of this pure and well-like character. Successive nations perchance have drank at, admired, and fathomed it, and passed away, and still its water is green and pellucid as ever. Not an intermitting spring! Perhaps on that spring morning when Adam and Eve were driven out of Eden Walden Pond was already in existence, and even then breaking up in a gentle spring rain accompanied with mist and a southerly wind, and covered with myriads of ducks and geese, which had not heard of the fall, when still such pure lakes sufficed them. Even then it had commenced to rise and fall, and had clarified its waters and colored them of the hue they now wear, and obtained a patent of heaven to be the only Walden Pond in the world and distiller of celestial dews. Who knows in how many unremembered nations' literatures this has been the Castalian Fountain?[166] or what nymphs presided over it in the Golden Age?[167] It is a gem of the first water which Concord wears in her coronet.

Yet perchance the first who came to this well have left some trace of their footsteps. I have been surprised to detect encircling the pond, even where a thick wood has just been cut down on the shore, a narrow shelf-like path in the steep hill-side, alternately rising and falling, approaching and receding from the water's edge, as old probably as the race of man here, worn by the feet of aboriginal hunters, and still from time to time unwittingly trodden by the present occupants of the land. This is particularly distinct to one standing on the middle of the pond in winter, just after a light snow has fallen, appearing as a clear undulating white line, unobscured by weeds and twigs, and very obvious a

---

164 Pond weeds.
165 Water plant.
166 In classical myth, the sacred spring of the
  Muses.

167 The perfect "original" state of the world.

quarter of a mile off in many places where in summer it is hardly distinguishable close at hand. The snow reprints it, as it were, in clear white type alto-relievo.[168] The ornamented grounds of villas which will one day be built here may still preserve some trace of this.

The pond rises and falls, but whether regularly or not, and within what period, nobody knows, though, as usual, many pretend to know. It is commonly higher in the winter and lower in the summer, though not corresponding to the general wet and dryness. I can remember when it was a foot or two lower, and also when it was at least five feet higher, than when I lived by it. There is a narrow sand-bar running into it, with very deep water on one side, on which I helped boil a kettle of chowder, some six rods from the main shore, about the year 1824, which it has not been possible to do for twenty-five years; and on the other hand, my friends used to listen with incredulity when I told them, that a few years later I was accustomed to fish from a boat in a secluded cove in the woods, fifteen rods from the only shore they knew, which place was long since converted into a meadow. But the pond has risen steadily for two years, and now, in the summer of '52, is just five feet higher than when I lived there, or as high as it was thirty years ago, and fishing goes on again in the meadow. This makes a difference of level, at the outside, of six or seven feet; and yet the water shed by the surrounding hills is insignificant in amount, and this overflow must be referred to causes which affect the deep springs. This same summer the pond has begun to fall again. It is remarkable that this fluctuation, whether periodical or not, appears thus to require many years for its accomplishment. I have observed one rise and a part of two falls, and I expect that a dozen or fifteen years hence the water will again be as low as I have ever known it. Flint's Pond, a mile eastward, allowing for the disturbance occasioned by its inlets and outlets, and the smaller intermediate ponds also, sympathize with Walden, and recently attained their greatest height at the same time with the latter. The same is true, as far as my observation goes, of White Pond.

This rise and fall of Walden at long intervals serves this use at least; the water standing at this great height for a year or more, though it makes it difficult to walk round it, kills the shrubs and trees which have sprung up about its edge since the last rise, pitch-pines, birches, alders, aspens, and others, and, falling again, leaves an unobstructed shore; for, unlike many ponds and all waters which are subject to a daily tide, its shore is cleanest when the water is lowest. On the side of the pond next my house, a row of pitch pines fifteen feet high has been killed and tipped over as if by a lever, and thus a stop put to their encroachments; and their size indicates how many years have elapsed since the last rise to this height. By this fluctuation the pond asserts its title to a shore, and thus the *shore* is *shorn,* and the trees cannot hold it by right of possession. These are the lips of the lake on which no beard grows. It licks its chaps from time to time. When the water is at its height, the alders, willows, and maples send forth a mass of fibrous red roots several feet long from all sides of their stems in the water, and to the height of three or four feet from the ground, in the effort to maintain themselves; and I have known the high-blueberry bushes about the shore, which commonly produce no fruit, bear an abundant crop under these circumstances.

Some have been puzzled to tell how the shore became so regularly paved. My townsmen have all heard the tradition, the oldest people tell me that they heard it in their youth, that anciently the Indians were holding a pow-wow upon a hill here, which rose

---

[168] High relief.

as high into the heavens as the pond now sinks deep into the earth, and they used much profanity, as the story goes, though this vice is one of which the Indians were never guilty, and while they were thus engaged the hill shook and suddenly sank, and only one old squaw, named Walden, escaped, and from her the pond was named. It has been conjectured that when the hill shook these stones rolled down its side and became the present shore. It is very certain, at any rate, that once there was no pond here, and now there is one; and this Indian fable does not in any respect conflict with the account of that ancient settler whom I have mentioned, who remembers so well when he first came here with his divining rod, saw a thin vapor rising from the sward, and the hazel pointed steadily downward, and he concluded to dig a well here. As for the stones, many still think that they are hardly to be accounted for by the action of the waves on these hills; but I observe that the surrounding hills are remarkably full of the same kind of stones, so that they have been obliged to pile them up in walls on both sides of the railroad cut nearest the pond; and, moreover, there are most stones where the shore is most abrupt; so that, unfortunately, it is no longer a mystery to me. I detect the paver.[169] If the name was not derived from that of some English locality,—Saffron Walden,[170] for instance,—one might suppose that it was called, originally, *Walled-in* Pond.

The pond was my well ready dug. For four months in the year its water is as cold as it is pure at all times; and I think that it is then as good as any, if not the best, in the town. In the winter, all water which is exposed to the air is colder than springs and wells which are protected from it. The temperature of the pond water which had stood in the room where I sat from five o'clock in the afternoon till noon the next day, the sixth of March, 1846, the thermometer having been up to 65° or 70° some of the time, owing partly to the sun on the roof, was 42°, or one degree colder than the water of one of the coldest wells in the village just drawn. The temperature of the Boiling Spring the same day was 45°, or the warmest of any water tried, though it is the coldest that I know of in summer, when, beside, shallow and stagnant surface water is not mingled with it. Moreover, in summer, Walden never becomes so warm as most water which is exposed to the sun, on account of its depth. In the warmest weather I usually placed a pailful in my cellar, where it became cool in the night, and remained so during the day; though I also re-sorted to a spring in the neighborhood. It was as good when a week old as the day it was dipped, and had no taste of the pump. Whoever camps for a week in summer by the shore of a pond, needs only bury a pail of water a few feet deep in the shade of his camp to be independent on the luxury of ice.

There have been caught in Walden, pickerel, one weighing seven pounds, to say nothing of another which carried off a reel with great velocity, which the fisherman safely set down at eight pounds because he did not see him, perch and pouts, some of each weighing over two pounds, shiners, chivins or roach, (*Leuciscus pulchellus*,) a very few breams, (*Pomotis obesus*,) and a couple of eels, one weighing four pounds,—I am thus particular because the weight of a fish is commonly its only title to fame, and these are the only eels I have heard of here;—also, I have a faint recollection of a little fish some five inches long, with silvery sides and a greenish back, somewhat dace-like in its character, which I mention here chiefly to link my facts to fable. Nevertheless, this pond is not very fertile in fish. Its pickerel, though not abundant, are its chief boast. I have

[169] Effect of glacial force.
[170] Near London.

seen at one time lying on the ice pickerel of at least three different kinds; a long and shallow one, steel-colored, most like those caught in the river; a bright golden kind, with greenish reflections and remarkably deep, which is the most common here; and another, golden-colored, and shaped like the last, but peppered on the sides with small dark brown or black spots, intermixed with a few faint blood-red ones, very much like a trout. The specific name *reticulatus*[171] would not apply to this; it should be *guttatus*[172] rather. These are all very firm fish, and weigh more than their size promises. The shiners, pouts, and perch also, and indeed all the fishes which inhabit this pond, are much cleaner, handsomer, and firmer fleshed than those in the river and most other ponds, as the water is purer, and they can easily be distinguished from them. Probably many ichthyologists would make new varieties of some of them. There are also a clean race of frogs and tortoises, and a few muscles in it; muskrats and minks leave their traces about it, and occasionally a travelling mud-turtle visits it. Sometimes, when I pushed off my boat in the morning, I disturbed a great mud-turtle which had secreted himself under the boat in the night. Ducks and geese frequent it in the spring and fall, the white-bellied swallows (*Hirundo bicolor*) skim over it, kingfishers dart away from its coves, and the peetweets (*Totanus macularius*) "teter" along its stony shores all summer. I have sometimes disturbed a fishhawk sitting on a white-pine over the water; but I doubt if it is ever profaned by the wing of a gull, like Fair Haven. At most, it tolerates one annual loon. These are all the animals of consequence which frequent it now.

You may see from a boat, in calm weather, near the sandy eastern shore, where the water is eight or ten feet deep, and also in some other parts of the pond, some circular heaps half a dozen feet in diameter by a foot in height, consisting of small stones less than a hen's egg in size, where all around is bare sand. At first you wonder if the Indians could have formed them on the ice for any purpose, and so, when the ice melted, they sank to the bottom; but they are too regular and some of them plainly too fresh for that. They are similar to those found in rivers; but as there are no suckers nor lampreys here, I know not by what fish they could be made. Perhaps they are the nests of the chivin. These lend a pleasing mystery to the bottom.

The shore is irregular enough not to be monotonous. I have in my mind's eye the western indented with deep bays, the bolder northern, and the beautifully scalloped southern shore, where successive capes overlap each other and suggest unexplored coves between. The forest has never so good a setting, nor is so distinctly beautiful, as when seen from the middle of a small lake amid hills which rise from the water's edge; for the water in which it is reflected not only makes the best foreground in such a case, but, with its winding shore, the most natural and agreeable boundary to it. There is no rawness nor imperfection in its edge there, as where the axe has cleared a part, or a cultivated field abuts on it. The trees have ample room to expand on the water side, and each sends forth its most vigorous branch in that direction. There Nature has woven a natural selvage, and the eye rises by just gradations from the low shrubs of the shore to the highest trees. There are few traces of man's hand to be seen. The water laves the shore as it did a thousand years ago.

A lake is the landscape's most beautiful and expressive feature. It is earth's eye; looking into which the beholder measures the depth of his own nature. The fluviatile trees

---

[171] Netlike.   [172] Speckled.

next the shore are the slender eyelashes which fringe it, and the wooded hills and cliffs around are its overhanging brows.

Standing on the smooth sandy beach at the east end of the pond, in a calm September afternoon, when a slight haze makes the opposite shore line indistinct, I have seen whence came the expression, "the glassy surface of a lake." When you invert your head, it looks like a thread of finest gossamer stretched across the valley, and gleaming against the distant pine woods, separating one stratum of the atmosphere from another. You would think that you could walk dry under it to the opposite hills, and that the swallows which skim over might perch on it. Indeed, they sometimes dive below the line, as it were by mistake, and are undeceived. As you look over the pond westward you are obliged to employ both your hands to defend your eyes against the reflected as well as the true sun, for they are equally bright; and if, between the two, you survey its surface critically, it is literally as smooth as glass, except where the skater insects, at equal intervals scattered over its whole extent, by their motions in the sun produce the finest imaginable sparkle on it, or, perchance, a duck plumes itself, or, as I have said, a swallow skims so low as to touch it. It may be that in the distance a fish describes an arc of three or four feet in the air, and there is one bright flash where it emerges, and another where it strikes the water; sometimes the whole silvery arc is revealed; or here and there, perhaps, is a thistle-down floating on its surface, which the fishes dart at and so dimple it again. It is like molten glass cooled but not congealed, and the few motes in it are pure and beautiful like the imperfections in glass. You may often detect a yet smoother and darker water, separated from the rest as if by an invisible cobweb, boom of the water nymphs, resting on it. From a hill-top you can see a fish leap in almost any part; for not a pickerel or shiner picks an insect from this smooth surface but it manifestly disturbs the equilibrium of the whole lake. It is wonderful with what elaborateness this simple fact is advertised,—this piscine murder will out,—and from my distant perch I distinguish the circling undulations when they are half a dozen rods in diameter. You can even detect a water-bug (*Gyrinus*) ceaselessly progressing over the smooth surface a quarter of a mile off; for they furrow the water slightly, making a conspicuous ripple bounded by two diverging lines, but the skaters glide over it without rippling it perceptibly. When the surface is considerably agitated there are no skaters nor water-bugs on it, but apparently, in calm days, they leave their havens and adventurously glide forth from the shore by short impulses till they completely cover it. It is a soothing employment, on one of those fine days in the fall when all the warmth of the sun is fully appreciated, to sit on a stump on such a height as this, overlooking the pond, and study the dimpling circles which are incessantly inscribed on its otherwise invisible surface amid the reflected skies and trees. Over this great expanse there is no disturbance but it is thus at once gently smoothed away and assuaged, as, when a vase of water is jarred, the trembling circles seek the shore and all is smooth again. Not a fish can leap or an insect fall on the pond but it is thus reported in circling dimples, in lines of beauty, as it were the constant welling up of its fountain, the gentle pulsing of its life, the heaving of its breast. The thrills of joy and thrills of pain are undistinguishable. How peaceful the phenomena of the lake! Again the works of man shine as in the spring. Ay, every leaf and twig and stone and cobweb sparkles now at mid-afternoon as when covered with dew in a spring morning. Every motion of an oar or an insect produces a flash of light; and if an oar falls, how sweet the echo!

In such a day, in September or October, Walden is a perfect forest mirror, set round with stones as precious to my eye as if fewer or rarer. Nothing so fair, so pure, and at the same time so large, as a lake, perchance, lies on the surface of the earth. Sky water. It needs no fence. Nations come and go without defiling it. It is a mirror which no stone can crack, whose quicksilver will never wear off, whose gilding Nature continually repairs; no storms, no dust, can dim its surface ever fresh;—a mirror in which all impurity presented to it sinks, swept and dusted by the sun's hazy brush,—this the light dust-cloth,—which retains no breath that is breathed on it, but sends its own to float as clouds high above its surface, and be reflected in its bosom still.

A field of water betrays the spirit that is in the air. It is continually receiving new life and motion from above. It is intermediate in its nature between land and sky. On land only the grass and trees wave, but the water itself is rippled by the wind. I see where the breeze dashes across it by the streaks or flakes of light. It is remarkable that we can look down on its surface. We shall, perhaps, look down thus on the surface of air at length, and mark where a still subtler spirit sweeps over it.

The skaters and water-bugs finally disappear in the latter part of October, when the severe frosts have come; and then and in November, usually, in a calm day, there is absolutely nothing to ripple the surface. One November afternoon, in the calm at the end of a rain storm of several days' duration, when the sky was still completely overcast and the air was full of mist, I observed that the pond was remarkably smooth, so that it was difficult to distinguish its surface; though it no longer reflected the bright tints of October, but the sombre November colors of the surrounding hills. Though I passed over it as gently as possible, the slight undulations produced by my boat extended almost as far as I could see, and gave a ribbed appearance to the reflections. But, as I was looking over the surface, I saw here and there at a distance a faint glimmer, as if some skater insects which had escaped the frosts might be collected there, or, perchance, the surface, being so smooth, betrayed where a spring welled up from the bottom. Paddling gently to one of these places, I was surprised to find myself surrounded by myriads of small perch, about five inches long, of a rich bronze color in the green water, sporting there and constantly rising to the surface and dimpling it, sometimes leaving bubbles on it. In such transparent and seemingly bottomless water, reflecting the clouds, I seemed to be floating through the air as in a balloon, and their swimming impressed me as a kind of flight or hovering, as if they were a compact flock of birds passing just beneath my level on the right or left, their fins, like sails, set all around them. There were many such schools in the pond, apparently improving the short season before winter would draw an icy shutter over their broad skylight, sometimes giving to the surface an appearance as if a slight breeze struck it, or a few rain-drops fell there. When I approached carelessly and alarmed them, they made a sudden plash and rippling with their tails, as if one had struck the water with a brushy bough, and instantly took refuge in the depths. At length the wind rose, the mist increased, and the waves began to run, and the perch leaped much higher than before, half out of water, a hundred black points, three inches long, at once above the surface. Even as late as the fifth of December, one year, I saw some dimples on the surface, and thinking it was going to rain hard immediately, the air being full of mist, I made haste to take my place at the oars and row homeward; already the rain seemed rapidly increasing, though I felt none on my cheek, and I anticipated a thorough soaking. But suddenly the dimples ceased, for they were produced by the perch, which the noise of my oars had scared into the depths, and I saw their schools dimly disappearing; so I spent a dry afternoon after all.

An old man who used to frequent this pond nearly sixty years ago, when it was dark with surrounding forests, tells me that in those days he sometimes saw it all alive with ducks and other water fowl, and that there were many eagles about it. He came here a-fishing, and used an old log canoe which he found on the shore. It was made of two white-pine logs dug out and pinned together, and was cut off square at the ends. It was very clumsy, but lasted a great many years before it became water-logged and perhaps sank to the bottom. He did not know whose it was; it belonged to the pond. He used to make a cable for his anchor of strips of hickory bark tied together. An old man, a potter, who lived by the pond before the Revolution, told him once that there was an iron chest at the bottom, and that he had seen it. Sometimes it would come floating up to the shore; but when you went toward it, it would go back into deep water and disappear. I was pleased to hear of the old log canoe, which took the place of an Indian one of the same material but more graceful construction, which perchance had first been a tree on the bank, and then, as it were, fell into the water, to float there for a generation, the most proper vessel for the lake. I remember that when I first looked into these depths there were many large trunks to be seen indistinctly lying on the bottom, which had either been blown over formerly, or left on the ice at the last cutting, when wood was cheaper; but now they have mostly disappeared.

When I first paddled a boat on Walden, it was completely surrounded by thick and lofty pine and oak woods, and in some of its coves grape vines had run over the trees next the water and formed bowers under which a boat could pass. The hills which form its shores are so steep, and the woods on them were then so high, that, as you looked down from the west end, it had the appearance of an amphitheatre for some kind of sylvan spectacle. I have spent many an hour, when I was younger, floating over its surface as the zephyr willed, having paddled my boat to the middle, and lying on my back across the seats, in a summer forenoon, dreaming awake, until I was aroused by the boat touching the sand, and I arose to see what shore my fates had impelled me to; days when idleness was the most attractive and productive industry. Many a forenoon have I stolen away, preferring to spend thus the most valued part of the day; for I was rich, if not in money, in sunny hours and summer days, and spent them lavishly; nor do I regret that I did not waste more of them in the workshop or the teacher's desk. But since I left those shores the woodchoppers have still further laid them waste, and now for many a year there will be no more rambling through the aisles of the wood, with occasional vistas through which you see the water. My Muse may be excused if she is silent henceforth. How can you expect the birds to sing when their groves are cut down?

Now the trunks of trees on the bottom, and the old log canoe, and the dark surrounding woods, are gone, and the villagers, who scarcely know where it lies, instead of going to the pond to bathe or drink, are thinking to bring its water, which should be as sacred as the Ganges[173] at least, to the village in a pipe, to wash their dishes with!—to earn their Walden by the turning of a cock or drawing of a plug! That devilish Iron Horse, whose ear-rending neigh is heard throughout the town, has muddied the Boiling

---

[173] River in India.

Spring with his foot, and he it is that has browsed off all the woods on Walden shore; that Trojan horse, with a thousand men in his belly, introduced by mercenary Greeks! Where is the country's champion, the Moore of Moore Hall,[174] to meet him at the Deep Cut[175] and thrust an avenging lance between the ribs of the bloated pest?

Nevertheless, of all the characters I have known, perhaps Walden wears best, and best preserves its purity. Many men have been likened to it, but few deserve that honor. Though the woodchoppers have laid bare first this shore and then that, and the Irish have built their sties by it, and the railroad has infringed on its border, and the ice-men have skimmed it once, it is itself unchanged, the same water which my youthful eyes fell on; all the change is in me. It has not acquired one permanent wrinkle after all its ripples. It is perennially young, and I may stand and see a swallow dip apparently to pick an insect from its surface as of yore. It struck me again tonight, as if I had not seen it almost daily for more than twenty years,—Why, here is Walden, the same woodland lake that I discovered so many years ago; where a forest was cut down last winter another is springing up by its shore as lustily as ever; the same thought is welling up to its surface that was then; it is the same liquid joy and happiness to itself and its Maker, ay, and it *may* be to me. It is the work of a brave man surely, in whom there was no guile! He rounded this water with his hand, deepened and clarified it in his thought, and in his will bequeathed it to Concord. I see by its face that it is visited by the same reflection; and I can almost say, Walden, is it you?

> It is no dream of mine,
> To ornament a line;
> I cannot come nearer to God and Heaven
> Than I live to Walden even.
> I am its stony shore,
> And the breeze that passes o'er;
> In the hollow of my hand
> Are its water and its sand,
> And its deepest resort
> Lies high in my thought.[176]

The cars never pause to look at it; yet I fancy that the engineers and firemen and brakemen, and those passengers who have a season ticket and see it often, are better men for the sight. The engineer does not forget at night, or his nature does not, that he has beheld this vision of serenity and purity once at least during the day. Though seen but once, it helps to wash out State-street[177] and the engine's soot. One proposes that it be called "God's Drop."[178]

I have said that Walden has no visible inlet nor outlet, but it is on the one hand distantly and indirectly related to Flint's Pond, which is more elevated, by a chain of small ponds coming from that quarter, and on the other directly and manifestly to Concord River, which is lower, by a similar chain of ponds through which in some other geological period it may have flowed, and by a little digging, which God forbid, it can be made

---

[174] Hero in an English ballad.
[175] Where the railroad passed near the pond.
[176] Thoreau's own verses.

[177] Center of Boston's financial activities.
[178] Medicine for the eyes.

to flow thither again. If by living thus reserved and austere, like a hermit in the woods, so long, it has acquired such wonderful purity, who would not regret that the comparatively impure waters of Flint's Pond should be mingled with it, or itself should ever go to waste its sweetness in the ocean wave?

Flint's, or Sandy Pond, in Lincoln, our greatest lake and inland sea, lies about a mile east of Walden. It is much larger, being said to contain one hundred and ninety-seven acres, and is more fertile in fish; but it is comparatively shallow, and not remarkably pure. A walk through the woods thither was often my recreation. It was worth the while, if only to feel the wind blow on your cheek freely, and see the waves run, and remember the life of mariners. I went a-chestnutting there in the fall, on windy days, when the nuts were dropping into the water and were washed to my feet; and one day, as I crept along its sedgy shore, the fresh spray blowing in my face, I came upon the mouldering wreck of a boat, the sides gone, and hardly more than the impression of its flat bottom left amid the rushes; yet its model was sharply defined, as if it were a large decayed pad, with its veins. It was as impressive a wreck as one could imagine on the sea-shore, and had as good a moral. It is by this time mere vegetable mould and undistinguishable pond shore, through which rushes and flags have pushed up. I used to admire the ripple marks on the sandy bottom, at the north end of this pond, made firm and hard to the feet of the wader by the pressure of the water, and the rushes which grew in Indian file, in waving lines, corresponding to these marks, rank behind rank, as if the waves had planted them. There also I have found, in considerable quantities, curious balls, composed apparently of fine grass or roots, of pipewort perhaps, from half an inch to four inches in diameter, and perfectly spherical. These wash back and forth in shallow water on a sandy bottom, and are sometimes cast on the shore. They are either solid grass, or have a little sand in the middle. At first you would say that they were formed by the action of the waves, like a pebble; yet the smallest are made of equally coarse materials, half an inch long, and they are produced only at one season of the year. Moreover, the waves, I suspect, do not so much construct as wear down a material which has already acquired consistency. They preserve their form when dry for an indefinite period.

Flint's Pond! Such is the poverty of our nomenclature. What right had the unclean and stupid farmer, whose farm abutted on this sky water, whose shores he has ruthlessly laid bare, to give his name to it? Some skin-flint, who loved better the reflecting surface of a dollar, or a bright cent, in which he could see his own brazen face; who regarded even the wild ducks which settled in it as trespassers; his fingers grown into crooked and horny talons from the long habit of grasping harpy-like;—so it is not named for me. I go not there to see him nor to hear of him; who never *saw* it, who never bathed in it, who never loved it, who never protected it, who never spoke a good word for it, nor thanked God that he had made it. Rather let it be named from the fishes that swim in it, the wild fowl or quadrupeds which frequent it, the wild flowers which grow by its shores, or some wild man or child the thread of whose history is interwoven with its own; not from him who could show no title to it but the deed which a like-minded neighbor or legislature gave him,—him who thought only of its money value; whose presence perchance cursed all the shore; who exhausted the land around it, would fain have exhausted the waters within it; who regretted only that it was not English hay or cranberry meadow,—there was nothing to redeem it, forsooth, in his eyes,—and would have drained and sold it for the mud at its bottom. It did not turn his mill, and it was no *privilege* to him to behold it. I respect not his labors, his farm where every thing has its price; who would carry the landscape, who would carry his God, to market, if he could get any thing for him; who goes to market *for* his god as it is; on whose farm nothing grows free, whose fields bear no crops, whose meadows no flowers, whose trees no fruits, but dollars; who loves not the beauty of his fruits, whose fruits are not ripe for him till they are turned to dollars. Give me the poverty that enjoys true wealth. Farmers are respectable and interesting to me in proportion as they are poor,—poor farmers. A model farm! where the house stands like a fungus in a muck-heap, chambers for men, horses, oxen, and swine, cleansed and uncleansed, all contiguous to one another! Stocked with men! A great grease-spot, redolent of manures and buttermilk! Under a high state of cultivation, being manured with the hearts and brains of men! As if you were to raise your potatoes in the church-yard! Such is a model farm.

No, no; if the fairest features of the landscape are to be named after men, let them be the noblest and worthiest men alone. Let our lakes receive as true names at least as the Icarian Sea, where "still the shore" a "brave attempt resounds."[179]

Goose Pond, of small extent, is on my way to Flint's; Fair-Haven, an expansion of Concord River, said to contain some seventy acres, is a mile southwest; and White Pond, of about forty acres, is a mile and a half beyond Fair-Haven. This is my lake country. These, with Concord River, are my water privileges; and night and day, year in year out, they grind such grist as I carry to them.

Since the woodcutters, and the railroad, and I myself have profaned Walden, perhaps the most attractive, if not the most beautiful, of all our lakes, the gem of the woods, is White Pond;—a poor name from its commonness, whether derived from the remarkable purity of its waters or the color of its sands. In these as in other respects, however, it is a lesser twin of Walden. They are so much alike that you would say they must be connected under ground. It has the same stony shore, and its waters are of the same hue. As at Walden, in sultry dog-day weather, looking down through the woods on some of its bays which are not so deep but that the reflection from the bottom tinges them, its waters are of a misty bluish-green or glaucous color. Many years since I used to go there to collect the sand by cart-loads, to make sand-paper with, and I have continued to visit it ever since. One who frequents it proposes to call it Virid[180] Lake. Perhaps it might be called Yellow-Pine Lake, from the following circumstance. About fifteen years ago you could see the top of a pitch-pine, of the kind called yellow-pine hereabouts, though it is not a distinct species, projecting above the surface in deep water, many rods from the shore. It was even supposed by some that the pond had sunk, and this was one of the primitive forest that formerly stood there. I find that even so long ago as 1792, in a "Topographical Description of the Town of Concord," by one of its citizens, in the Collections of the Massachusetts Historical Society, the author, after speaking of Walden and White Ponds, adds: "In the middle of the latter may be seen, when the water is very low, a tree which appears as if it grew in the place where it now

---

[179] Lines from "Icarus" by William Drummond, referring to the sea where, according to classic myth, Icarus fell after attempting to soar on wings toward the sun.

[180] Green.

stands, although the roots are fifty feet below the surface of the water; the top of this tree is broken off, and at the place measures fourteen inches in diameter." In the spring of '49 I talked with the man who lives nearest the pond in Sudbury, who told me that it was he who got out this tree ten or fifteen years before. As near as he could remember, it stood twelve or fifteen rods from the shore, where the water was thirty or forty feet deep. It was in the winter, and he had been getting out ice in the forenoon, and had resolved that in the afternoon, with the aid of his neighbors, he would take out the old yellow-pine. He sawed a channel in the ice toward the shore, and hauled it over and along and out on to the ice with oxen; but, before he had gone far in his work, he was surprised to find that it was wrong end upward, with the stumps of the branches pointing down, and the small end firmly fastened in the sandy bottom. It was about a foot in diameter at the big end, and he had expected to get a good saw-log, but it was so rotten as to be fit only for fuel, if for that. He had some of it in his shed then. There were marks of an axe and of woodpeckers on the but. He thought that it might have been a dead tree on the shore, but was finally blown over into the pond, and after the top had become waterlogged, while the but-end was still dry and light, had drifted out and sunk wrong end up. His father, eighty years old, could not remember when it was not there. Several pretty large logs may still be seen lying on the bottom, where, owing to the undulation of the surface, they look like huge water snakes in motion.

This pond has rarely been profaned by a boat, for there is little in it to tempt a fisherman. Instead of the white lily, which requires mud, or the common sweet flag, the blue flag (*Iris versicolor*) grows thinly in the pure water, rising from the stony bottom all around the shore, where it is visited by humming birds in June, and the color both of its bluish blades and its flowers, and especially their reflections, are in singular harmony with the glaucous water.

White Pond and Walden are great crystals on the surface of the earth, Lakes of Light. If they were permanently congealed, and small enough to be clutched, they would, perchance, be carried off by slaves, like precious stones, to adorn the heads of emperors; but being liquid, and ample, and secured to us and our successors forever, we disregard them, and run after the diamond of Kohinoor.[181] They are too pure to have a market value; they contain no muck. How much more beautiful than our lives, how much more transparent than our characters, are they! We never learned meanness of them. How much fairer than the pool before the farmer's door, in which his ducks swim! Hither the clean wild ducks come. Nature has no human inhabitant who appreciates her. The birds with their plumage and their notes are in harmony with the flowers, but what youth or maiden conspires with the wild luxuriant beauty of Nature? She flourishes most alone, far from the towns where they reside. Talk of heaven! ye disgrace earth.

Brute Neighbors

Sometimes I had a companion[182] in my fishing, who came through the village to my house from the other side of the town, and the catching of the dinner was as much a social exercise as the eating of it.

---

[181] Famous diamond.
[182] William Ellery Channing the younger.

Hermit. I wonder what the world is doing now. I have not heard so much as a locust over the sweet-fern these three hours. The pigeons are all asleep upon their roosts,—no flutter from them. Was that a farmer's noon horn which sounded from beyond the woods just now? The hands are coming in to boiled salt beef and cider and Indian bread. Why will men worry themselves so? He that does not eat need not work. I wonder how much they have reaped. Who would live there where a body can never think for the barking of Bose?[183] And O, the housekeeping! to keep bright the devil's door-knobs, and scour his tubs this bright day! Better not keep a house. Say, some hollow tree; and then for morning calls and dinner-parties! Only a woodpecker tapping. O, they swarm; the sun is too warm there; they are born too far into life for me. I have water from the spring, and a loaf of brown bread on the shelf.—Hark! I hear a rustling of the leaves. Is it some ill-fed village hound yielding to the instinct of the chase? or the lost pig which is said to be in these woods, whose tracks I saw after the rain? It comes on apace; my sumachs and sweet-briars tremble.—Eh, Mr. Poet, is it you? How do you like the world to-day?

Poet. See those clouds; how they hang! That's the greatest thing I have seen to-day. There's nothing like it in old paintings, nothing like it in foreign lands,—unless when we were off the coast of Spain. That's a true Mediterranean sky. I thought, as I have my living to get, and have not eaten to-day, that I might go a-fishing. That's the true industry for poets. It is the only trade I have learned. Come, let's along.

Hermit. I cannot resist. My brown bread will soon be gone. I will go with you gladly soon, but I am just concluding a serious meditation. I think that I am near the end of it. Leave me alone, then, for a while. But that we may not be delayed, you shall be digging the bait meanwhile. Angle-worms are rarely to be met with in these parts, where the soil was never fattened with manure; the race is nearly extinct. The sport of digging the bait is nearly equal to that of catching the fish, when one's appetite is not too keen; and this you may have all to yourself today. I would advise you to set in the spade down yonder among the ground-nuts, where you see the johnswort waving. I think that I may warrant you one worm to every three sods you turn up, if you look well in among the roots of the grass, as if you were weeding. Or, if you choose to go farther, it will not be unwise, for I have found the increase of fair bait to be very nearly as the squares of the distances.

Hermit alone. Let me see; where was I? Methinks I was nearly in this frame of mind; the world lay about at this angle. Shall I go to heaven or a-fishing? If I should soon bring this meditation to an end, would another so sweet occasion be likely to offer? I was as near being resolved into the essence of things as ever I was in my life. I fear my thoughts will not come back to me. If it would do any good, I would whistle for them. When they make us an offer, is it wise to say, We will think of it? My thoughts have left no track, and I cannot find the path again. What was it that I was thinking of? It was a very hazy day. I will just try these three sentences of Con-fut-see;[184] they may fetch that state about again. I know not whether it was the dumps or a budding ecstasy. Mem.[185] There never is but one opportunity of a kind.

Poet. How now, Hermit, is it too soon? I have got just thirteen whole ones, beside several which are imperfect or undersized; but they will do for the smaller fry; they do not cover up the hook so much. Those village worms are quite too large; a shiner may make a meal off one without finding the skewer.

---

[183] Like Fido, a common name for a dog in
    Thoreau's time.

[184] Confucius.

[185] Memorandum.

Hermit. Well, then, let's be off. Shall we to the Concord? There's good sport there if the water be not too high.

Why do precisely these objects which we behold make a world? Why has man just these species of animals for his neighbors; as if nothing but a mouse could have filled this crevice? I suspect that Pilpay & Co.[186] have put animals to their best use, for they are all beasts of burden, in a sense, made to carry some portion of our thoughts.

The mice which haunted my house were not the common ones, which are said to have been introduced into the country, but a wild native kind (*Mus leucopus*) not found in the village. I sent one to a distinguished naturalist, and it interested him much. When I was building, one of these had its nest underneath the house, and before I had laid the second floor, and swept out the shavings, would come out regularly at lunch time and pick up the crumbs at my feet. It probably had never seen a man before; and it soon became quite familiar, and would run over my shoes and up my clothes. It could readily ascend the sides of the room by short impulses, like a squirrel, which it resembled in its motions. At length, as I leaned with my elbow on the bench one day, it ran up my clothes, and along my sleeve, and round and round the paper which held my dinner, while I kept the latter close, and dodged and played at bo-peep with it; and when at last I held still a piece of cheese between my thumb and finger, it came and nibbled it, sitting in my hand, and afterward cleaned its face and paws, like a fly, and walked away.

A phœbe soon built in my shed, and a robin for protection in a pine which grew against the house. In June the partridge, (*Tetrao umbellus*,) which is so shy a bird, led her brood past my windows, from the woods in the rear to the front of my house, clucking and calling to them like a hen, and in all her behavior proving herself the hen of the woods. The young suddenly disperse on your approach, at a signal from the mother, as if a whirlwind had swept them away, and they so exactly resemble the dried leaves and twigs that many a traveller has placed his foot in the midst of a brood, and heard the whir of the old bird as she flew off, and her anxious calls and mewing, or seen her trail her wings to attract his attention, without suspecting their neighborhood. The parent will sometimes roll and spin round before you in such a dishabille, that you cannot, for a few moments, detect what kind of creature it is. The young squat still and flat, often running their heads under a leaf, and mind only their mother's directions given from a distance, nor will your approach make them run again and betray themselves. You may even tread on them, or have your eyes on them for a minute, without discovering them. I have held them in my open hand at such a time, and still their only care, obedient to their mother and their instinct, was to squat there without fear or trembling. So perfect is this instinct, that once, when I had laid them on the leaves again, and one accidentally fell on its side, it was found with the rest in exactly the same position ten minutes afterward. They are not callow like the young of most birds, but more perfectly developed and precocious even than chickens. The remarkably adult yet innocent expression of their open and serene eyes is very memorable. All intelligence seems reflected in them. They suggest not merely the purity of infancy, but a wisdom clarified by experience. Such an eye was not born when the bird was, but is coeval with the sky it reflects. The woods do not yield another such a gem. The traveller does not often look into such a

---

[186] Makers of tales, in reference to the teller of ancient Sanskrit fables.

limpid well. The ignorant or reckless sportsman often shoots the parent at such a time, and leaves these innocents to fall a prey to some prowling beast or bird, or gradually mingle with the decaying leaves which they so much resemble. It is said that when hatched by a hen they will directly disperse on some alarm, and so are lost, for they never hear the mother's call which gathers them again. These were my hens and chickens.

It is remarkable how many creatures live wild and free though secret in the woods, and still sustain themselves in the neighborhood of towns, suspected by hunters only. How retired the otter manages to live here! He grows to be four feet long, as big as a small boy, perhaps without any human being getting a glimpse of him. I formerly saw the raccoon in the woods behind where my house is built, and probably still heard their whinnering[187] at night. Commonly I rested an hour or two in the shade at noon, after planting, and ate my lunch, and read a little by a spring which was the source of a swamp and of a brook, oozing from under Brister's Hill, half a mile from my field. The approach to this was through a succession of descending grassy hollows, full of young pitch-pines, into a larger wood about the swamp. There, in a very secluded and shaded spot, under a spreading white-pine, there was yet a clean firm sward to sit on. I had dug out the spring and made a well of clear gray water, where I could dip up a pailful without roiling it, and thither I went for this purpose almost every day in midsummer, when the pond was warmest. Thither too the wood-cock led her brood, to probe the mud for worms, flying but a foot above them down the bank, while they ran in a troop beneath; but at last, spying me, she would leave her young and circle round and round me, nearer and nearer, till within four or five feet, pretending broken wings and legs, to attract my attention and get off her young, who would already have taken up their march, with faint wiry peep, single file through the swamp, as she directed. Or I heard the peep of the young when I could not see the parent bird. There too the turtle-doves sat over the spring, or fluttered from bough to bough of the soft white-pines over my head; or the red squirrel, coursing down the nearest bough, was particularly familiar and inquisitive. You only need sit still long enough in some attractive spot in the woods that all its inhabitants may exhibit themselves to you by turns.

I was witness to events of a less peaceful character. One day when I went out to my wood-pile, or rather my pile of stumps, I observed two large ants, the one red, the other much larger, nearly half an inch long, and black, fiercely contending with one another. Having once got hold they never let go, but struggled and wrestled and rolled on the chips incessantly. Looking farther, I was surprised to find that the chips were covered with such combatants, that it was not a *duellum,* but a *bellum,*[188] a war between two races of ants, the red always pitted against the black, and frequently two red ones to one black. The legion of these Myrmidons[189] covered all the hills and vales in my wood-yard, and the ground was already strewn with the dead and dying, both red and black. It was the only battle which I have ever witnessed, the only battle-field I ever trod while the battle was raging; internecine war; the red republicans on the one hand, and the black imperialists on the other. On every side they were engaged in deadly combat, yet without any noise that I could hear, and human soldiers never fought so resolutely. I

---

[187] A sound like whining.
[188] I.e., not a duel, but a war.
[189] Since *myrmex* is the Greek word for "ant," Thoreau is able to link the battle of the ants with the fighting done by the Myrmidons, the troops of Achilles in the Trojan War, as told in the *Iliad.*

watched a couple that were fast locked in each other's embraces, in a little sunny valley amid the chips, now at noon-day prepared to fight till the sun went down, or life went out. The smaller red champion had fastened himself like a vice to his adversary's front, and through all the tumblings on that field never for an instant ceased to gnaw at one of his feelers near the root, having already caused the other to go by the board; while the stronger black one dashed him from side to side, and, as I saw on looking nearer, had already divested him of several of his members. They fought with more pertinacity than bull-dogs. Neither manifested the least disposition to retreat. It was evident that their battle-cry was Conquer or die. In the mean while there came along a single red ant on the hill-side of this valley, evidently full of excitement, who either had despatched his foe, or had not yet taken part in the battle; probably the latter, for he had lost none of his limbs; whose mother had charged him to return with his shield or upon it. Or per-chance he was some Achilles, who had nourished his wrath apart, and had now come to avenge or rescue his Patroclus.[190] He saw this unequal combat from afar,—for the blacks were nearly twice the size of the red,—he drew near with rapid pace till he stood on his guard within half an inch of the combatants; then, watching his opportunity, he sprang upon the black warrior, and commenced his operations near the root of his right fore-leg, leaving the foe to select among his own members; and so there were three united for life, as if a new kind of attraction had been invented which put all other locks and cements to shame. I should not have wondered by this time to find that they had their respective musical bands stationed on some eminent chip, and playing their na-tional airs the while, to excite the slow and cheer the dying combatants. I was myself ex-cited somewhat even as if they had been men. The more you think of it, the less the dif-ference. And certainly there is not the fight recorded in Concord history, at least, if in the history of America, that will bear a moment's comparison with this, whether for the numbers engaged in it, or for the patriotism and heroism displayed. For numbers and for carnage it was an Austerlitz or Dresden.[191] Concord Fight![192] Two killed on the pa-triots' side, and Luther Blanchard wounded! Why here every ant was a Buttrick,—"Fire! for God's sake fire!"—and thousands shared the fate of Davis and Hosmer. There was not one hireling[193] there. I have no doubt that it was a principle they fought for, as much as our ancestors, and not to avoid a three-penny tax on their tea; and the results of this battle will be as important and memorable to those whom it concerns as those of the battle of Bunker Hill, at least.

I took up the chip on which the three I have particularly described were struggling, carried it into my house, and placed it under a tumbler on my windowsill, in order to see the issue. Holding a microscope to the first-mentioned red ant, I saw that though he was assiduously gnawing at the near fore-leg of his enemy, having severed his remaining feeler, his own breast was all torn away, exposing what vitals he had there to the jaws of the black warrior, whose breast-plate was apparently too thick for him to pierce; and the dark carbuncles of the sufferer's eyes shone with ferocity such as war only could ex-cite. They struggled half an hour longer under the tumbler, and when I looked again the

---

[190] Patroclus was Achilles' friend; when he was slain, Achilles out of wrath threw himself into the war against the Trojans.
[191] Battles fought during the wars of Napoleon.

[192] Battle of April 1775, the opening engage-ment of the American Revolution. The names and remarks that follow refer to that conflict.
[193] Mercenary.

black soldier had severed the heads of his foes from their bodies, and the still living heads were hanging on either side of him like ghastly trophies at his saddle-bow, still apparently as firmly fastened as ever, and he was endeavoring with feeble struggles, being without feelers and with only the remnant of a leg, and I know not how many other wounds, to divest himself of them; which at length, after half an hour more, he accomplished. I raised the glass, and he went off over the window-sill in that crippled state. Whether he finally survived that combat, and spent the remainder of his days in some Hotel des Invalides,[194] I do not know; but I thought that his industry would not be worth much thereafter. I never learned which party was victorious, nor the cause of the war; but I felt for the rest of that day as if I had had my feelings excited and harrowed by witnessing the struggle, the ferocity and carnage, of a human battle before my door.

Kirby and Spence tell us that the battles of ants have long been celebrated and the date of them recorded, though they say that Huber[195] is the only modern author who appears to have witnessed them. "Æneas Sylvius,"[196] say they, "after giving a very circumstantial account of one contested with great obstinacy by a great and small species on the trunk of a pear tree," adds that " 'This action was fought in the pontificate of Eugenius the Fourth,[197] in the presence of Nicholas Pistoriensis, an eminent lawyer, who related the whole history of the battle with the greatest fidelity.' A similar engagement between great and small ants is recorded by Olaus Magnus,[198] in which the small ones, being victorious, are said to have buried the bodies of their own soldiers, but left those of their giant enemies a prey to the birds. This event happened previous to the expulsion of the tyrant Christiern the Second from Sweden."[199] The battle which I witnessed took place in the Presidency of Polk, five years before the passage of Webster's Fugitive-Slave Bill.[200]

Many a village Bose, fit only to course a mud-turtle in a victualling cellar, sported his heavy quarters in the woods, without the knowledge of his master, and ineffectually smelled at old fox burrows and woodchucks' holes; led perchance by some slight cur which nimbly threaded the wood, and might still inspire a natural terror in its denizens;—now far behind his guide, barking like a canine bull toward some small squirrel which had treed itself for scrutiny, then, cantering off, bending the bushes with his weight, imagining that he is on the track of some stray member of the gerbille family. Once I was surprised to see a cat walking along the stony shore of the pond, for they rarely wander so far from home. The surprise was mutual. Nevertheless the most domestic cat, which has lain on a rug all her days, appears quite at home in the woods, and, by her sly and stealthy behavior, proves herself more native there than the regular inhabitants. Once, when berrying, I met with a cat with young kittens in the woods, quite wild, and they all, like their mother, had their backs up and were fiercely spitting at me. A few years before I lived in the woods there was what was called a "winged cat" in one of the farm-houses in Lincoln nearest the pond, Mr. Gilian Baker's. When I

[194] Veterans' hospital in Paris.
[195] Kirby and Spence's book on entomology includes the description of a battle among ants, taken from Huber's study of 1810.
[196] Name used by Pope Pius II (1405–1464) for his writings.
[197] Pope between 1431 and 1447.

[198] Swedish historian and churchman (1490–1557).
[199] Sixteenth-century king.
[200] Fugitive Slave Law (1850) supported by Daniel Webster, Massachusetts senator. James K. Polk was president between 1845 and 1849.

called to see her in June, 1842, she was gone a-hunting in the woods, as was her wont. (I am not sure, whether it was a male or female, and so use the more common pronoun,) but her mistress told me that she came into the neighborhood a little more than a year before, in April, and was finally taken into their house; that she was of a dark brownish-gray color, with a white spot on her throat, and white feet, and had a large bushy tail like a fox; that in the winter the fur grew thick and flattened out along her sides, forming strips ten or twelve inches long by two and a half wide, and under her chin like a muff, the upper side loose, the under matted like felt, and in the spring these appendages dropped off. They gave me a pair of her "wings," which I keep still. There is no appearance of a membrane about them. Some thought it was part flying-squirrel or some other wild animal, which is not impossi-ble, for, according to naturalists, prolific hybrids have been produced by the union of the marten and domestic cat. This would have been the right kind of cat for me to keep, if I had kept any; for why should not a poet's cat be winged as well as his horse?[201]

In the fall the loon (*Colymbus glacialis*) came, as usual, to moult and bathe in the pond, making the woods ring with his wild laughter before I had risen. At rumor of his arrival all the Mill-dam sportsmen are on the alert, in gigs[202] and on foot, two by two and three by three, with patent rifles and conical balls and spy-glasses. They come rustling through the woods like autumn leaves, at least ten men to one loon. Some station themselves on this side of the pond, some on that, for the poor bird cannot be omnipresent; if he dive here he must come up there. But now the kind October wind rises, rustling the leaves and rippling the surface of the water, so that no loon can be heard or seen, though his foes sweep the pond with spy-glasses, and make the woods resound with their discharges. The waves generously rise and dash angrily, taking sides with all waterfowl, and our sportsmen must beat a retreat to town and shop and unfinished jobs. But they were too often successful. When I went to get a pail of water early in the morning I frequently saw this stately bird sailing out of my cove within a few rods. If I endeavored to overtake him in a boat, in order to see how he would manœuvre, he would dive and be completely lost, so that I did not discover him again, sometimes, till the latter part of the day. But I was more than a match for him on the surface. He commonly went off in a rain.

As I was paddling along the north shore one very calm October afternoon, for such days especially they settle on to the lakes, like the milkweed down, having looked in vain over the pond for a loon, suddenly one, sailing out from the shore toward the middle a few rods in front of me, set up his wild laugh and betrayed himself. I pursued with a paddle and he dived, but when he came up I was nearer than before. He dived again, but I miscalculated the direction he would take, and we were fifty rods apart when he came to the surface this time, for I had helped to widen the interval; and again he laughed long and loud, and with more reason than before. He manœuvred so cunningly that I could not get within half a dozen rods of him. Each time, when he came to the surface, turning his head this way and that, he coolly surveyed the water and the land, and apparently chose his course so that he might come up where there was the widest expanse of water and at the greatest distance from the boat. It was surprising

---

[201] Reference to Pegasus, the winged horse ridden by poets in classic myth.   [202] Light, one-horse carriages.

how quickly he made up his mind and put his resolve into execution. He led me at once to the widest part of the pond, and could not be driven from it. While he was thinking one thing in his brain, I was endeavoring to divine his thought in mine. It was a pretty game, played on the smooth surface of the pond, a man against a loon. Suddenly your adversary's checker disappears beneath the board, and the problem is to place yours nearest to where his will appear again. Sometimes he would come up unexpectedly on the opposite side of me, having apparently passed directly under the boat. So long-winded was he and so unwearieable, that when he had swum farthest he would immediately plunge again, nevertheless; and then no wit could divine where in the deep pond, beneath the smooth surface, he might be speeding his way like a fish, for he had time and ability to visit the bottom of the pond in its deepest part. It is said that loons have been caught in the New York lakes eighty feet beneath the surface, with hooks set for trout,—though Walden is deeper than that. How surprised must the fishes be to see this ungainly visitor from another sphere speeding his way amid their schools! Yet he appeared to know his course as surely under water as on the surface, and swam much faster there. Once or twice I saw a ripple where he approached the surface, just put his head out to reconnoitre, and instantly dived again. I found that it was as well for me to rest on my oars and wait his reappearing as to endeavor to calculate where he would rise; for again and again, when I was straining my eyes over the surface one way, I would suddenly be startled by his unearthly laugh behind me. But why, after displaying so much cunning, did he invariably betray himself the moment he came up by that loud laugh? Did not his white breast enough betray him? He was indeed a silly loon, I thought. I could commonly hear the plash of the water when he came up, and so also detected him. But after an hour he seemed as fresh as ever, dived as willingly and swam yet farther than at first. It was surprising to see how serenely he sailed off with unruffled breast when he came to the surface, doing all the work with his webbed feet beneath. His usual note was this demoniac laughter, yet somewhat like that of a water-fowl; but occasionally, when he had balked me most successfully and come up a long way off, he uttered a long-drawn unearthly howl, probably more like that of a wolf than any bird; as when a beast puts his muzzle to the ground and deliberately howls. This was his looning,—perhaps the wildest sound that is ever heard here, making the woods ring far and wide. I concluded that he laughed in derision of my efforts, confident of his own resources. Though the sky was by this time overcast, the pond was so smooth that I could see when he broke the surface when I did not hear him. His white breast, the stillness of the air, and the smoothness of the water were all against him. At length, having come up fifty rods off, he uttered one of those prolonged howls, as if calling on the god of loons to aid him, and immediately there came a wind from the east and rippled the surface, and filled the whole air with misty rain, and I was impressed as if it were the prayer of the loon answered, and his god was angry with me; and so I left him disappearing far away on the tumultuous surface.

For hours, in fall days, I watched the ducks cunningly tack and veer and hold the middle of the pond, far from the sportsman; tricks which they will have less need to practise in Louisiana bayous. When compelled to rise they would sometimes circle round and round and over the pond at a considerable height, from which they could easily see to other ponds and the river, like black motes in the sky; and, when I thought they had gone off thither long since, they would settle down by a slanting flight of a quarter of a mile on to a distant part which was left free; but what beside safety they got by sailing in the middle of Walden I do not know, unless they love its water for the same reason that I do.

Spring

The opening of large tracts by the ice-cutters commonly causes a pond to break up earlier; for the water, agitated by the wind, even in cold weather, wears away the surrounding ice. But such was not the effect on Walden that year, for she had soon got a thick new garment to take the place of the old. This pond never breaks up so soon as the others in this neighborhood, on account both of its greater depth and its having no stream passing through it to melt or wear away the ice. I never knew it to open in the course of a winter, not excepting that of '52–3, which gave the ponds so severe a trial. It commonly opens about the first of April, a week or ten days later than Flint's Pond and Fair-Haven, beginning to melt on the north side and in the shallower parts where it began to freeze. It indicates better than any water hereabouts the absolute progress of the season, being least affected by transient changes of temperature. A severe cold of a few days' duration in March may very much retard the opening of the former ponds, while the temperature of Walden increases almost uninterruptedly. A thermometer thrust into the middle of Walden on the 6th of March, 1847, stood at 32°, or freezing point; near the shore at 33°; in the middle of Flint's Pond, the same day, at 32 1/2°; at a dozen rods from the shore, in shallow water, under ice a foot thick, at 36°. This difference of three and a half degrees between the temperature of the deep water and the shallow in the latter pond, and the fact that a great proportion of it is comparatively shallow, show why it should break up so much sooner than Walden. The ice in the shallowest part was at this time several inches thinner than in the middle. In mid-winter the middle had been the warmest and the ice thinnest there. So, also, every one who has waded about the shores of a pond in summer must have perceived how much warmer the water is close to the shore, where only three or four inches deep, than a little distance out, and on the surface where it is deep, than near the bottom. In spring the sun not only exerts an influence through the increased temperature of the air and earth, but its heat passes through ice a foot or more thick, and is reflected from the bottom in shallow water, and so also warms the water and melts the under side of the ice, at the same time that it is melting it more directly above, making it uneven, and causing the air bubbles which it contains to extend themselves upward and downward until it is completely honey-combed, and at last disappears suddenly in a single spring rain. Ice has its grain as well as wood, and when a cake begins to rot or "comb," that is, assume the appearance of honey-comb, whatever may be its position, the air cells are at right angles with what was the water surface. Where there is a rock or a log rising near to the surface the ice over it is much thinner, and is frequently quite dissolved by this reflected heat; and I have been told that in the experiment at Cambridge to freeze water in a shallow wooden pond, though the cold air circulated underneath, and so had access to both sides, the reflection of the sun from the bottom more than counterbalanced this advantage. When a warm rain in the middle of the winter melts off the snow-ice from Walden, and leaves a hard dark or transparent ice on the middle, there will be a strip of rotten though thicker white ice, a rod or more wide, about the shores, created by this reflected heat. Also, as I have said, the bubbles themselves within the ice operate as burning glasses to melt the ice beneath.

The phenomena of the year take place every day in a pond on a small scale. Every morning, generally speaking, the shallow water is being warmed more rapidly than the deep, though it may not be made so warm after all, and every evening it is being cooled more rapidly until the morning. The day is an epitome of the year. The night is the winter, the morning and evening are the spring and fall, and the noon is the summer. The cracking and booming of the ice indicate a change of temperature. One pleasant morning after a cold night, February 24th, 1850, having gone to Flint's Pond to spend the day, I noticed with surprise, that when I struck the ice with the head of my axe, it resounded like a gong for many rods around, or as if I had struck on a tight drum-head. The pond began to boom about an hour after sunrise, when it felt the influence of the sun's rays slanted upon it from over the hills; it stretched itself and yawned like a waking man with a gradually increasing tumult, which was kept up three or four hours. It took a short siesta at noon, and boomed once more toward night, as the sun was withdrawing his influence. In the right state of the weather a pond fires its evening gun with great regularity. But in the middle of the day, being full of cracks, and the air also being less elastic, it had completely lost its resonance, and probably fishes and muskrats could not then have been stunned by a blow on it. The fishermen say that the "thundering of the pond" scares the fishes and prevents their biting. The pond does not thunder every evening, and I cannot tell surely when to expect its thundering; but though I may perceive no difference in the weather, it does. Who would have suspected so large and cold and thick-skinned a thing to be so sensitive? Yet it has its law to which it thunders obedience when it should as surely as the buds expand in the spring. The earth is all alive and covered with papillæ. The largest pond is as sensitive to atmospheric changes as the globule of mercury in its tube.

One attraction in coming to the woods to live was that I should have leisure and opportunity to see the spring come in. The ice in the pond at length begins to be honeycombed, and I can set my heel in it as I walk. Fogs and rains and warmer suns are gradually melting the snow; the days have grown sensibly longer; and I see how I shall get through the winter without adding to my wood-pile, for large fires are no longer necessary. I am on the alert for the first signs of spring, to hear the chance note of some arriving bird, or the striped squirrel's chirp, for his stores must be now nearly exhausted, or see the woodchuck venture out of his winter quarters. On the 13th of March, after I had heard the bluebird, song-sparrow, and red-wing, the ice was still nearly a foot thick. As the weather grew warmer, it was not sensibly worn away by the water, nor broken up and floated off as in rivers, but, though it was completely melted for half a rod in width about the shore, the middle was merely honey-combed and saturated with water, so that you could put your foot through it when six inches thick; but by the next day evening, perhaps, after a warm rain followed by fog, it would have wholly disappeared, all gone off with the fog, spirited away. One year I went across the middle only five days before it disappeared entirely. In 1845 Walden was first completely open on the 1st of April; in '46, the 25th of March; in '47, the 8th of April; in '51, the 28th of March; in '52, the 18th of April, in '53, the 23d of March; in '54, about the 7th of April.

Every incident connected with the breaking up of the rivers and ponds and the settling of the weather is particularly interesting to us who live in a climate of so great extremes. When the warmer days come, they who dwell near the river hear the ice crack at night with a startling whoop as loud as artillery, as if its icy fetters were rent from end to end, and within a few days see it rapidly going out. So the alligator comes out of the mud with quakings of the earth. One old man, who has been a close observer of Nature, and seems as thoroughly wise in regard to all her operations as if she had been put upon the stocks when he was a boy, and he had helped to lay her keel,—who has come to his growth, and can hardly acquire more of natural lore if he should live to the age of Methuselah,[203]—told me, and I was surprised to hear him express wonder at any of Nature's operations, for I thought that there were no secrets between them, that one spring day he took his gun and boat, and thought that he would have a little sport with the ducks. There was ice still on the meadows, but it was all gone out of the river, and he dropped down without obstruction from Sudbury, where he lived, to Fair-Haven Pond, which he found, unexpectedly, covered for the most part with a firm field of ice. It was a warm day, and he was surprised to see so great a body of ice remaining. Not seeing any ducks, he hid his boat on the north or back side of an island in the pond, and then concealed himself in the bushes on the south side, to await them. The ice was melted for three or four rods from the shore, and there was a smooth and warm sheet of water, with a muddy bottom, such as the ducks love, within, and he thought it likely that some would be along pretty soon. After he had lain still there about an hour he heard a low and seemingly very distant sound, but singularly grand and impressive, unlike any thing he had ever heard, gradually swelling and increasing as if it would have a universal and memorable ending, a sullen rush and roar, which seemed to him all at once like the sound of a vast body of fowl coming in to settle there, and, seizing his gun, he started up in haste and excited; but he found, to his surprise, that the whole body of the ice had started while he lay there, and drifted in to the shore, and the sound he had heard was made by its edge grating on the shore,—at first gently nibbled and crumbled off, but at length heaving up and scattering its wrecks along the island to a considerable height before it came to a stand still.

At length the sun's rays have attained the right angle, and warm winds blow up mist and rain and melt the snow banks, and the sun dispersing the mist smiles on a checkered landscape of russet and white smoking with incense, through which the traveller picks his way from islet to islet, cheered by the music of a thousand tinkling rills and rivulets whose veins are filled with the blood of winter which they are bearing off.

Few phenomena gave me more delight than to observe the forms which thawing sand and clay assume in flowing down the sides of a deep cut on the railroad through which I passed on my way to the village, a phenomenon not very common on so large a scale, though the number of freshly exposed banks of the right material must have been greatly multiplied since railroads were invented. The material was sand of every degree of fineness and of various rich colors, commonly mixed with a little clay. When the frost comes out in the spring, and even in a thawing day in the winter, the sand begins to flow down the slopes like lava, sometimes bursting out through the snow and overflowing it where no sand was to be seen before. Innumerable little streams overlap and interlace one with another, exhibiting a sort of hybrid product, which obeys half way the law of currents, and half way that of vegetation. As it flows it takes the forms of sappy leaves or vines, making heaps of pulpy sprays a foot or more in depth, and resembling, as you look down on them, the laciniated lobed and imbricated thalluses of some

---

[203] He lived 969 years (Genesis 5:27).

lichens; or you are reminded of coral, of leopards' paws or birds' feet, of brains or lungs or bowels, and excrements of all kinds. It is a truly *grotesque* vegetation, whose forms and color we see imitated in bronze, a sort of architectural foliage more ancient and typical than acanthus, chiccory, ivy, vine, or any vegetable leaves; destined perhaps, under some circumstances, to become a puzzle to future geologists. The whole cut impressed me as if it were a cave with its stalactites laid open to the light. The various shades of the sand are singularly rich and agreeable, embracing the different iron colors, brown, gray, yellowish, and reddish. When the flowing mass reaches the drain at the foot of the bank it spreads out flatter into *strands,* the separate streams losing their semi-cylindrical form and gradually becoming more flat and broad, running together as they are more moist, till they form an almost flat *sand,* still variously and beautifully shaded, but in which you can trace the original forms of vegetation; till at length, in the water itself, they are converted into *banks,* like those formed off the mouths of rivers, and the forms of vegetation are lost in the ripple marks on the bottom.

The whole bank, which is from twenty to forty feet high, is sometimes overlaid with a mass of this kind of foliage, or sandy rupture, for a quarter of a mile on one or both sides, the produce of one spring day. What makes this sand foliage remarkable is its springing into existence thus suddenly. When I see on the one side the inert bank,—for the sun acts on one side first,—and on the other this luxuriant foliage, the creation of an hour, I am affected as if in a peculiar sense I stood in the laboratory of the Artist who made the world and me,—had come to where he was still at work, sporting on this bank, and with excess of energy strewing his fresh designs about. I feel as if I were nearer to the vitals of the globe, for this sandy overflow is something such a foliaceous mass as the vitals of the animal body. You find thus in the very sands an anticipation of the vegetable leaf. No wonder that the earth expresses itself outwardly in leaves, it so labors with the idea inwardly. The atoms have already learned this law, and are pregnant by it. The overhanging leaf sees here its prototype. *Internally,* whether in the globe or animal body, it is a moist thick *lobe,* a word especially applicable to the liver and lungs and the *leaves* of fat, (λείβω, *labor, lapsus,* to flow or slip downward, a lapsing; λοβος, *globus,* lobe, globe; also lap, flap, and many other words,) *externally* a dry thin *leaf,* even as the *f* and *v* are a pressed and dried *b.* The radicals of lobe are *lb,* the soft mass of the *b* (single lobed, or B, double lobed,) with a liquid *l* behind it pressing it forward. In globe, *glb,* the guttural *g* adds to the meaning the capacity of the throat. The feathers and wings of birds are still drier and thinner leaves. Thus, also, you pass from the lumpish grub in the earth to the airy and fluttering butterfly. The very globe continually transcends and translates itself, and becomes winged in its orbit. Even ice begins with delicate crystal leaves, as if it had flowed into moulds which the fronds of water plants have impressed on the watery mirror. The whole tree itself is but one leaf, and rivers are still vaster leaves whose pulp is intervening earth, and towns and cities are the ova of insects in their axils.

When the sun withdraws the sand ceases to flow, but in the morning the streams will start once more and branch and branch again into a myriad of others. You here see perchance how blood vessels are formed. If you look closely you observe that first there pushes forward from the thawing mass a stream of softened sand with a drop-like point, like the ball of the finger, feeling its way slowly and blindly downward, until at last with more heat and moisture, as the sun gets higher, the most fluid portion, in its effort to obey the law to which the most inert also yields, separates from the latter and forms for itself a meandering channel or artery within that, in which is seen a little silvery stream glancing like lightning from one stage of pulpy leaves or branches to another, and ever and anon swallowed up in the sand. It is wonderful how rapidly yet perfectly the sand organizes itself as it flows, using the best material its mass affords to form the sharp edges of its channel. Such are the sources of rivers. In the silicious matter which the water deposits is perhaps the bony system, and in the still finer soil and organic matter the fleshy fibre or cellular tissue. What is man but a mass of thawing clay? The ball of the human finger is but a drop congealed. The fingers and toes flow to their extent from the thawing mass of the body. Who knows what the human body would expand and flow out to under a more genial heaven? Is not the hand a spreading *palm* leaf with its lobes and veins? The ear may be regarded, fancifully, as a lichen, *umbilicaria*, on the side of the head, with its lobe or drop. The lip (*labium* from *labor* (?)) laps or lapses from the sides of the cavernous mouth. The nose is a manifest congealed drop or stalactite. The chin is a still larger drop, the confluent dripping of the face. The cheeks are a slide from the brows into the valley of the face, opposed and diffused by the cheek bones. Each rounded lobe of the vegetable leaf, too, is a thick and now loitering drop, larger or smaller; the lobes are the fingers of the leaf; and as many lobes as it has, in so many directions it tends to flow, and more heat or other genial influences would have caused it to flow yet farther.

Thus it seemed that this one hillside illustrated the principle of all the operations of Nature. The Maker of this earth but patented a leaf. What Champollion[204] will decipher this hieroglyphic for us, that we may turn over a new leaf at last? This phenomenon is more exhilarating to me than the luxuriance and fertility of vineyards. True, it is somewhat excrementitious in its character, and there is no end to the heaps of liver lights and bowels, as if the globe were turned wrong side outward; but this suggests at least that Nature has some bowels, and there again is mother of humanity. This is the frost coming out of the ground; this is Spring. It precedes the green and flowery spring, as mythology precedes regular poetry. I know of nothing more purgative of winter fumes and indigestions. It convinces me that Earth is still in her swaddling clothes, and stretches forth baby fingers on every side. Fresh curls spring from the baldest brow. There is nothing inorganic. These foliaceous heaps lie along the bank like the slag of a furnace, showing that Nature is "in full blast" within. The earth is not a mere fragment of dead history, stratum upon stratum like the leaves of a book, to be studied by geologists and antiquaries chiefly, but living poetry like the leaves of a tree, which precede flowers and fruit,—not a fossil earth, but a living earth; compared with whose great central life all animal and vegetable life is merely parasitic. Its throes will heave our exuviæ from their graves. You may melt your metals and cast them into the most beautiful moulds you can; they will never excite me like the forms which this molten earth flows out into. And not only it, but the institutions upon it, are plastic like clay in the hands of the potter.

Ere long, not only on these banks, but on every hill and plain and in every hollow, the frost comes out of the ground like a dormant quadruped from its burrow, and seeks the

---

[204] Jean François Champollion (1790–1832), Frenchman who deciphered the hieroglyphics inscribed on the Rosetta Stone and thus opened up ancient Egyptian culture to contemporary knowledge.

sea with music, or migrates to other climes in clouds. Thaw with his gentle persuasion is more powerful than Thor[205] with his hammer.

When the ground was partially bare of snow, and a few warm days had dried its surface somewhat, it was pleasant to compare the first tender signs of the infant year just peeping forth with stately beauty of the withered vegetation which had withstood the winter,—life-everlasting, golden-rods, pinweeds, and graceful wild grasses, more obvious and interesting frequently than in summer even, as if their beauty was not ripe till then; even cotton-grass, cat-tails, mulleins, johnswort, hard-hack, meadow-sweet, and other strong stemmed plants, those unexhausted granaries which entertain the earliest birds,—decent weeds, at least, which widowed Nature wears. I am particularly attracted by the arching and sheaf-like top of the wool-grass; it brings back the summer to our winter memories, and is among the forms which art loves to copy, and which, in the vegetable kingdom, have the same relation to types already in the mind of man that astronomy has. It is an antique style older than Greek or Egyptian. Many of the phenomena of Winter are suggestive of an inexpressible tenderness and fragile delicacy. We are accustomed to hear this king described as a rude and boisterous tyrant; but with the gentleness of a lover he adorns the tresses of Summer.

At the approach of spring the red-squirrels got under my house, two at a time, directly under my feet as I sat reading or writing, and kept up the queerest chuckling and chirruping and vocal pirouetting and gurgling sounds that ever were heard; and when I stamped they only chirruped the louder, as if past all fear and respect in their mad pranks, defying humanity to stop them. No you don't—chickaree—chickaree. They were wholly deaf to my arguments, or failed to perceive their force, and fell into a strain of invective that was irresistible.

The first sparrow of spring! The year beginning with younger hope than ever! The faint silvery warblings heard over the partially bare and moist fields from the blue-bird, the song-sparrow, and the red-wing, as if the last flakes of winter tinkled as they fell! What at such a time are histories, chronologies, traditions, and all written revelations? The brooks sing carols and glees to the spring. The marsh-hawk sailing low over the meadow is already seeking the first slimy life that awakes. The sinking sound of melting snow is heard in all dells, and the ice dissolves apace in the ponds. The grass flames up on the hillsides like a spring fire,—"et primitus oritur herba imbribus primoribus evocata,"[206]—as if the earth sent forth an inward heat to greet the returning sun; not yellow but green is the color of its flame;—the symbol of perpetual youth, the grass-blade, like a long green ribbon, streams from the sod into the summer, checked indeed by the frost, but anon pushing on again, lifting its spear of last year's hay with the fresh life below. It grows as steadily as the rill oozes out of the ground. It is almost identical with that, for in the growing days of June, when the rills are dry, the grass blades are their channels, and from year to year the herds drink at this perennial green stream, and the mower draws from it betimes their winter supply. So our human life but dies down to its root, and still puts forth its green blade to eternity.

Walden is melting apace. There is a canal two rods wide along the northerly and westerly sides, and wider still at the east end. A great field of ice has cracked off from the

[205] Norse god of thunder, whose name Thoreau liked to associate with his own. The one melts, the other but breaks in pieces.

[206] Latin: "and summoned by the early rains, the grass starts to grow." From *De Re Rustica* by Varro (116–27 B.C.).

main body. I hear a song-sparrow singing from the bushes on the shore,—*olit, olit, olit,*—*chip, chip, chip, che char,*—*che wiss, wiss, wiss.* He too is helping to crack it. How handsome the great sweeping curves in the edge of the ice, answering somewhat to those of the shore, but more regular! It is unusually hard, owing to the recent severe but transient cold, and all watered or waved like a palace floor. But the wind slides eastward over its opaque surface in vain, till it reaches the living surface beyond. It is glorious to behold this ribbon of water sparkling in the sun, the bare face of the pond full of glee and youth, as if it spoke the joy of the fishes within it, and of the sands on its shore,—a silvery sheen as from the scales of a *leuciscus,*[207] as it were all one active fish. Such is the contrast between winter and spring. Walden was dead and is alive again.[208] But this spring it broke up more steadily, as I have said.

The change from storm and winter to serene and mild weather, from dark and sluggish hours to bright and elastic ones, is a memorable crisis which all things proclaim. It is seemingly instantaneous at last. Suddenly an influx of light filled my house, though the evening was at hand, and the clouds of winter still overhung it, and the eaves were dripping with sleety rain. I looked out the window, and lo! where yesterday was cold gray ice there lay the transparent pond already calm and full of hope as on a summer evening, reflecting a summer evening sky in its bosom, though none was visible overhead, as if it had intelligence with some remote horizon. I heard a robin in the distance, the first I had heard for many a thousand years, methought, whose note I shall not forget for many a thousand more,—the same sweet and powerful song of yore. O the evening robin, at the end of a New England summer day! If I could ever find the twig he sits upon! I mean *he;* I mean *the twig.* This at least is not the *Turdus migratorius.*[209] The pitch-pines and shrub-oaks about my house, which had so long drooped, suddenly resumed their several characters, looked brighter, greener, and more erect and alive, as if effectually cleansed and restored by the rain. I knew that it would not rain any more. You may tell by looking at any twig of the forest, ay, at your very wood-pile, whether its winter is past or not. As it grew darker, I was startled by the *honking* of geese flying low over the woods, like weary travellers getting in late from southern lakes, and indulging at last in unrestrained complaint and mutual consolation. Standing at my door, I could hear the rush of their wings; when, driving toward my house, they suddenly spied my light, and with hushed clamor wheeled and settled in the pond. So I came in, and shut the door, and passed my first spring night in the woods.

In the morning I watched the geese from the door through the mist, sailing in the middle of the pond, fifty rods off, so large and tumultuous that Walden appeared like an artificial pond for their amusement. But when I stood on the shore they at once rose up with a great flapping of wings at the signal of their commander, and when they had got into rank circled about over my head, twenty-nine of them, and then steered straight to Canada, with a regular *honk* from the leader at intervals, trusting to break their fast in muddier pools. A "plump"[210] of ducks rose at the same time and took the route to the north in the wake of their noisier cousins.

[207] Freshwater fish.
[208] Here Thoreau echoes the language of the New Testament in the parable of the Prodigal Son, with perhaps also an allusion to Christ's resurrection.

[209] American robin.
[210] Flock.

For a week I heard the circling groping clangor of some solitary goose in the foggy mornings, seeking its companion, and still peopling the woods with the sound of a larger life than they could sustain. In April the pigeons were seen again flying express in small flocks, and in due time I heard the martins twittering over my clearing, though it had not seemed that the township contained so many that it could afford me any, and I fancied that they were peculiarly of the ancient race that dwelt in hollow trees ere white men came. In almost all climes the tortoise and the frog are among the precursors and heralds of this season, and birds fly with song and glancing plumage, and plants spring and bloom, and winds blow, to correct this slight oscillation of the poles and preserve the equilibrium of Nature.

As every season seems best to us in its turn, so the coming in of spring is like the creation of Cosmos out of Chaos and the realization of the Golden Age.—

> "Eurus ad Auroram, Nabathæaque regna recessit,
>   Persidaque, et radiis juga subdita matutinis."
> "The East-Wind withdrew to Aurora and the
>   Nabathæan kingdom,
> And the Persian, and the ridges placed under
>   the morning rays.
>
>   *   *   *
>
> Man was born. Whether that Artificer of things,
> The origin of a better world, made him from
>   the divine seed;
> Or the earth being recent and lately sundered
>   from the high
> Ether, retained some seeds of cognate heaven."[211]

A single gentle rain makes the grass many shades greener. So our prospects brighten on the influx of better thoughts. We should be blessed if we lived in the present always, and took advantage of every accident that befell us, like the grass which confesses the influence of the slightest dew that falls on it; and did not spend our time in atoning for the neglect of past opportunities, which we call doing our duty. We loiter in winter while it is already spring. In a pleasant spring morning all men's sins are forgiven. Such a day is a truce to vice. While such a sun holds out to burn, the vilest sinner may return. Through our own recovered innocence we discern the innocence of our neighbors. You may have known your neighbor yesterday for a thief, a drunkard, or a sensualist, and merely pitied or despised him, and despaired of the world; but the sun shines bright and warm this first spring morning, re-creating the world, and you meet him at some serene work, and see how his exhausted and debauched veins expand with still joy and bless the new day, feel the spring influence with the innocence of infancy, and all his faults are forgotten. There is not only an atmosphere of good will about him, but even a savor of holiness groping for expression, blindly and ineffectually perhaps, like a new-born instinct, and for a short hour the south hill-side echoes to no vulgar jest. You see some innocent fair shoots preparing to burst from his gnarled rind and try another year's life, tender and fresh as the youngest plant. Even he has entered into the joy of his Lord. Why the jailer

211 From Ovid's *Metamorphoses*, Book I.

does not leave open his prison doors,—why the judge does not dismiss his case,—why the preacher does not dismiss his congregation! It is because they do not obey the hint which God gives them, nor accept the pardon which he freely offers to all.

"A return to goodness produced each day in the tranquil and beneficent breath of the morning, causes that in respect to the love of virtue and the hatred of vice, one approaches a little the primitive nature of man, as the sprouts of the forest which has been felled. In like manner the evil which one does in the interval of a day prevents the germs of virtues which began to spring up again from developing themselves and destroys them.

"After the germs of virtue have thus been prevented many times from developing themselves, then the beneficent breath of evening does not suffice to preserve them. As soon as the breath of evening does not suffice longer to preserve them, then the nature of man does not differ much from that of the brute. Men seeing the nature of this man like that of the brute, think that he has never possessed the innate faculty of reason. Are those the true and natural sentiments of man?"[212]

"The Golden Age was first created, which without
    any avenger
Spontaneously without law cherished fidelity and
    rectitude.
Punishment and fear were not; nor were threaten-
    ing words read
On suspended brass; nor did the suppliant crowd
    fear
The words of their judge; but were safe without
    an avenger.
Not yet the pine felled on its mountains had de-
    scended
To the liquid waves that it might see a foreign
    world,
And mortals knew no shores but their own.

         *   *   *

There was eternal spring, and placid zephyrs with
    warm
Blasts soothed the flowers born without seed."

On the 29th of April, as I was fishing from the bank of the river near the Nine-Acre-Corner bridge, standing on the quaking grass and willow roots, where the muskrats lurk, I heard a singular rattling sound, somewhat like that of the sticks which boys play with their fingers, when, looking up, I observed a very slight and graceful hawk, like a night-hawk, alternately soaring like a ripple and tumbling a rod or two over and over, showing the underside of its wings, which gleamed like a satin ribbon in the sun, or like the pearly inside of a shell. This sight reminded me of falconry and what nobleness and poetry are associated with that sport. The Merlin it seemed to me it might be called: but I care not for its name. It was the most ethereal flight I had ever witnessed. It did not

[212] From *The Book of Mencius.* The lines that
follow are again from *Metamorphoses,*
Book I.

simply flutter like a butterfly, nor soar like the larger hawks, but it sported with proud reliance in the fields of air; mounting again and again with its strange chuckle, it repeated its free and beautiful fall, turning over and over like a kite, and then recovering from its lofty tumbling, as if it had never set its foot on *terra firma*. It appeared to have no companion in the universe,—sporting there alone,—and to need none but the morning and the ether with which it played. It was not lonely, but made all the earth lonely beneath it. Where was the parent which hatched it, its kindred, and its father in the heavens? The tenant of the air, it seemed related to the earth but by an egg hatched some time in the crevice of a crag;—or was its native nest made in the angle of a cloud, woven of the rainbow's trimmings and the sunset sky, and lined with some soft midsummer haze caught up from earth? Its eyry[213] now some cliffy cloud.

Beside this I got a rare mess of golden and silver and bright cupreous fishes, which looked like a string of jewels. Ah! I have penetrated to those meadows on the morning of many a first spring day, jumping from hummock to hummock, from willow root to willow root, when the wild river valley and the woods were bathed in so pure and bright a light as would have waked the dead, if they had been slumbering in their graves, as some suppose. There needs no stronger proof of immortality. All things must live in such a light. O Death, where was thy sting? O Grave, where was thy victory, then?[214]

Our village life would stagnate if it were not for the unexplored forests and meadows which surround it. We need the tonic of wildness,—to wade sometimes in marshes where the bittern and the meadow-hen lurk, and hear the booming of the snipe; to smell the whispering sedge where only some wilder and more solitary fowl builds her nest, and the mink crawls with its belly close to the ground. At the same time that we are earnest to explore and learn all things, we require that all things be mysterious and unexplorable, that land and sea be infinitely wild, unsurveyed and unfathomed by us because unfathomable. We can never have enough of Nature. We must be refreshed by the sight of inexhaustible vigor, vast and Titanic features, the sea-coast with its wrecks, the wilderness with its living and its decaying trees, the thunder cloud, and the rain which lasts three weeks and produces freshets. We need to witness our own limits transgressed, and some life pasturing freely where we never wander. We are cheered when we observe the vulture feeding on the carrion which disgusts and disheartens us and deriving health and strength from the repast. There was a dead horse in the hollow by the path to my house, which compelled me sometimes to go out of my way, especially in the night when the air was heavy, but the assurance it gave me of the strong appetite and inviolable health of Nature was my compensation for this. I love to see that Nature is so rife with life that myriads can be afforded to be sacrificed and suffered to prey on one another; that tender organizations can be so serenely squashed out of existence like pulp,—tadpoles which herons gobble up, and tortoises and toads run over in the road; and that sometimes it has rained flesh and blood! With the liability to accident, we must see how little account is to be made of it. The impression made on a wise man is that of universal innocence. Poison is not poisonous after all, nor are any wounds fatal. Compassion is a very untenable ground. It must be expeditious. Its pleadings will not bear to be stereotyped.

---

213 Bird's nest.
214 Allusion to 1 Corinthians 15:55.

Early in May, the oaks, hickories, maples, and other trees, just putting out amidst the pine woods around the pond, imparted a brightness like sunshine to the landscape, especially in cloudy days, as if the sun were breaking through mists and shining faintly on the hill-sides here and there. On the third or fourth of May I saw a loon in the pond, and during the first week of the month I heard the whippoorwill, the brown-thrasher, the veery, the wood-pewee, the chewink, and other birds. I had heard the wood-thrush long before. The phoebe had already come once more and looked in at my door and window, to see if my house was cavern-like enough for her, sustaining herself on humming wings with clinched talons, as if she held by the air, while she surveyed the premises. The sulphur-like pollen of the pitch-pine soon covered the pond and the stones and rotten wood along the shore, so that you could have collected a barrel-ful. This is the "sulphur showers" we hear of. Even in Calidas' drama of Sacontala,[215] we read of "rills dyed yellow with the golden dust of the lotus." And so the seasons went rolling on into summer, as one rambles into higher and higher grass.

Thus was my first year's life in the woods completed; and the second year was similar to it. I finally left Walden September 6th, 1847.

Conclusion

To the sick the doctors wisely recommend a change of air and scenery. Thank Heaven, here is not all the world. The buck-eye does not grow in New England, and the mocking-bird is rarely heard here. The wild-goose is more of a cosmopolite than we; he breaks his fast in Canada, takes a luncheon in the Ohio, and plumes himself for the night in a southern bayou. Even the bison, to some extent, keeps pace with the seasons, cropping the pastures of the Colorado only till a greener and sweeter grass awaits him by the Yellowstone. Yet we think that if rail-fences are pulled down, and stone-walls piled up on our farms, bounds are henceforth set to our lives and our fates decided. If you are chosen town-clerk, forsooth, you cannot go to Tierra del Fuego this summer: but you may go to the land of infernal fire nevertheless. The universe is wider than our views of it.

Yet we should oftener look over the tafferel[216] of our craft, like curious passengers, and not make the voyage like stupid sailors picking oakum. The other side of the globe is but the home of our correspondent. Our voyaging is only great-circle sailing,[217] and the doctors prescribe for diseases of the skin merely. One hastens to Southern Africa to chase the giraffe; but surely that is not the game he would be after. How long, pray, would a man hunt giraffes if he could? Snipes and woodcocks also may afford rare sport; but I trust it would be nobler game to shoot one's self.—

> "Direct your eye sight inward, and you'll find
> A thousand regions in your mind
> Yet undiscovered. Travel them, and be
> Expert in home-cosmography."[218]

---

[215] The Sanskrit drama *Sakuntala* by the fifth-century Hindu poet Kalidasa.
[216] Rail at the ship's stern.
[217] Traveling by direct route.

[218] From "To My Honoured Friend, Sir Ed. P. Knight" by William Habington (1605–1654).

What does Africa,—what does the West stand for? Is not our own interior white on the chart?[219] black though it may prove, like the coast, when discovered. Is it the source of the Nile, or the Niger, or the Mississippi, or a North-West Passage around this continent, that we would find? Are these the problems which most concern mankind? Is Franklin[220] the only man who is lost, that his wife should be so earnest to find him? Does Mr. Grinnell[221] know where he himself is? Be rather the Mungo Park, the Lewis and Clarke and Frobisher,[222] of your own streams and oceans; explore your own higher latitudes,—with shiploads of preserved meats to support you, if they be necessary; and pile the empty cans sky-high for a sign.[223] Were preserved meats invented to preserve meat merely? Nay, be a Columbus to whole new continents and worlds within you, opening new channels, not of trade, but of thought. Every man is the lord of a realm beside which the earthly empire of the Czar[224] is but a petty state, a hummock left by the ice. Yet some can be patriotic who have no self-respect, and sacrifice the greater to the less. They love the soil which makes their graves, but have no sympathy with the spirit which may still animate their clay. Patriotism is a maggot in their heads. What was the meaning of that South-Sea Exploring Expedition,[225] with all its parade and expense, but an indirect recognition of the fact, that there are continents and seas in the moral world, to which every man is an isthmus or an inlet, yet unexplored by him, but that it is easier to sail many thousand miles through cold and storm and cannibals, in a government ship, with five hundred men and boys to assist one, than it is to explore the private sea, the Atlantic and Pacific Ocean of one's being alone.—

> "Erret, et extremos alter scrutetur Iberos.
> Plus habet hic vitæ, plus habet ille viæ."

Let them wander and scrutinize the outlandish
   Australians.
I have more of God, they more of the road.[226]

It is not worth the while to go round the world to count the cats in Zanzibar. Yet do this even till you can do better, and you may perhaps find some "Symmes' Hole"[227] by which to get at the inside at last. England and France, Spain and Portugal, Gold Coast and Slave Coast, all front on this private sea; but no bark from them has ventured out of sight of land, though it is without doubt the direct way to India. If you would learn to

---

[219] Not yet mapped, because unexplored.

[220] Sir John Franklin (1786–1847), British explorer lost on expedition to discover open route between the Atlantic and the Pacific.

[221] Henry Grinnell (1799–1874), American who sponsored a rescue mission to find Franklin.

[222] Leaders of various explorations: Africa (Park), the American Northwest (Lewis and Clark), and Canada (Sir Martin Frobisher).

[223] A stack of cans marked one of the camps deserted by the Franklin expedition.

[224] During Thoreau's lifetime Czarist Russia was the largest country.

[225] Antarctic expedition (1838–1842) led by the American Charles Wilkes.

[226] From lines by the Roman poet Claudian, with "Australians" and "of God" replacing the original words.

[227] John Symmes (1780–1829) fostered a theory that the globe was hollow, habitable, and open at either end.

speak all tongues and conform to the customs of all nations, if you would travel farther than all travellers, be naturalized in all climes, and cause the Sphinx to dash her head against a stone,[228] even obey the precept of the old philosopher, and Explore thyself. Herein are demanded the eye and the nerve. Only the defeated and deserters go to the wars, cowards that run away and enlist. Start now on that farthest western way, which does not pause at the Mississippi or the Pacific, nor conduct toward a worn-out China or Japan, but leads on direct a tangent to this sphere, summer and winter, day and night, sun down, moon down, and at last earth down too.

It is said that Mirabeau[229] took to highway robbery "to ascertain what degree of resolution was necessary in order to place one's self in formal opposition to the most sacred laws of society." He declared that "a soldier who fights in the ranks does not require half so much courage as a foot-pad,"—"that honor and religion have never stood in the way of a well-considered and a firm resolve." This was manly, as the world goes; and yet it was idle, if not desperate. A saner man would have found himself often enough "in formal opposition" to what are deemed "the most sacred laws of society," through obedience to yet more sacred laws, and so have tested his resolution without going out of his way. It is not for a man to put himself in such an attitude to society, but to maintain himself in whatever attitude he find himself through obedience to the laws of his being, which will never be one of opposition to a just government, if he should chance to meet with such.

I left the woods for as good a reason as I went there. Perhaps it seemed to me that I had several more lives to live, and could not spare any more time for that one. It is remarkable how easily and insensibly we fall into a particular route, and make a beaten track for ourselves. I had not lived there a week before my feet wore a path from my door to the pond-side; and though it is five or six years since I trod it, it is still quite distinct. It is true, I fear that others may have fallen into it, and so helped to keep it open. The surface of the earth is soft and impressible by the feet of men; and so with the paths which the mind travels. How worn and dusty, then, must be the highways of the world, how deep the ruts of tradition and conformity! I did not wish to take a cabin passage, but rather to go before the mast and on the deck of the world, for there I could best see the moonlight amid the mountains. I do not wish to go below now.

I learned this, at least, by my experiment; that if one advances confidently in the direction of his dreams, and endeavors to live the life which he has imagined, he will meet with a success unexpected in common hours. He will put some things behind, will pass an invisible boundary; new, universal, and more liberal laws will begin to establish themselves around and within him; or the old laws be expanded, and interpreted in his favor in a more liberal sense, and he will live with the license of a higher order of beings. In proportion as he simplifies his life, the laws of the universe will appear less complex, and solitude will not be solitude, nor poverty poverty, nor weakness weakness. If you have built castles in the air, your work need not be lost; that is where they should be. Now put the foundations under them.

It is a ridiculous demand which England and America make, that you shall speak so that they can understand you. Neither men nor toad-stools grow so. As if that were im-

---

[228] In frustration over Oedipus' solving the riddle she posed to him, the Sphinx killed herself.

[229] Count de Mirabeau (1749–1791), French diplomat.

portant, and there were not enough to understand you without them. As if Nature could support but one order of understandings, could not sustain birds as well as quadrupeds, flying as well as creeping things, and *hush* and *who*,[230] which Bright can understand, were the best English. As if there were safety in stupidity alone. I fear chiefly lest my expression may not be *extra-vagant* enough, may not wander far enough beyond the narrow limits of my daily experience, so as to be adequate to the truth of which I have been convinced. *Extra vagance!* it depends on how you are yarded. The migrating buffalo, which seeks new pastures in another latitude, is not extravagant like the cow which kicks over the pail, leaps the cow-yard fence, and runs after her calf, in milking time. I desire to speak somewhere *without* bounds; like a man in a waking moment, to men in their waking moments; for I am convinced that I cannot exaggerate enough even to lay the foundation of a true expression. Who that has heard a strain of music feared then lest he should speak extravagantly any more forever? In view of the future or possible, we should live quite laxly and undefined in front, our outlines dim and misty on that side; as our shadows reveal an insensible perspiration toward the sun. The volatile truth of our words should continually betray the inadequacy of the residual statement. Their truth is instantly *translated;* its literal monument alone remains. The words which express our faith and piety are not definite; yet they are significant and fragrant like frankincense to superior natures.

Why level downward to our dullest perception always, and praise that as common sense? The commonest sense is the sense of men asleep, which they express by snoring. Sometimes we are inclined to class those who are once-and-a-half witted with the half-witted, because we appreciate only a third part of their wit. Some would find fault with the morning-red, if they ever got up early enough. "They pretend," as I hear, "that the verses of Kabir[231] have four different senses; illusion, spirit, intellect, and the exoteric doctrine of the Vedas;" but in this part of the world it is considered a ground for complaint if a man's writings admit of more than one interpretation. While England endeavors to cure the potato-rot, will not any endeavor to cure the brain-rot, which prevails so much more widely and fatally?

I do not suppose that I have attained to obscurity, but I should be proud if no more fatal fault were found with my pages on this score than was found with the Walden ice. Southern customers objected to its blue color, which is the evidence of its purity, as if it were muddy, and preferred the Cambridge ice, which is white, but tastes of weeds. The purity men love is like the mists which envelop the earth, and not like the azure ether beyond.

Some are dinning in our ears that we Americans, and moderns generally, are intellectual dwarfs compared with the ancients, or even the Elizabethan men. But what is that to the purpose? A living dog is better than a dead lion. Shall a man go and hang himself because he belongs to the race of pygmies, and not be the biggest pygmy that he can? Let every one mind his own business, and endeavor to be what he was made.

Why should we be in such desperate haste to succeed, and in such desperate enterprises? If a man does not keep pace with his companions, perhaps it is because he hears a different drummer. Let him step to the music which he hears, however measured or far away. It is not important that he should mature as soon as an apple-tree or an oak.

---

230 *Hush* and *who*: commands to an ox ("Bright") for "go" and "stop," respectively.

231 Hindu mystic.

Shall he turn his spring into summer? If the condition of things which we were made for is not yet, what were any reality which we can substitute? We will not be shipwrecked on a vain reality. Shall we with pains erect a heaven of blue glass over ourselves, though when it is done we shall be sure to gaze still at the true ethereal heaven far above, as if the former were not?

There was an artist in the city of Kouroo[232] who was disposed to strive after perfection. One day it came into his mind to make a staff. Having considered that in an imperfect work time is an ingredient, but into a perfect work time does not enter, he said to himself, It shall be perfect in all respects, though I should do nothing else in my life. He proceeded instantly to the forest for wood, being resolved that it should not be made of unsuitable material; and as he searched for and rejected stick after stick, his friends gradually deserted him, for they grew old in their works and died, but he grew not older by a moment. His singleness of purpose and resolution, and his elevated piety, endowed him, without his knowledge, with perennial youth. As he made no compromise with Time, Time kept out of his way, and only sighed at a distance because he could not overcome him. Before he had found a stock in all respects suitable the city of Kouroo was a hoary ruin, and he sat on one of its mounds to peel the stick. Before he had given it the proper shape the dynasty of the Candahars was at an end, and with the point of the stick he wrote the name of the last of that race in the sand, and then resumed his work. By the time he had smoothed and polished the staff Kalpa was no longer the pole-star; and ere he had put on the ferrule and the head adorned with precious stones, Brahma had awoke and slumbered many times. But why do I stay to mention these things? When the finishing stroke was put to his work, it suddenly expanded before the eyes of the astonished artist into the fairest of all the creations of Brahma. He had made a new system in making a staff, a world with full and fair proportions; in which, though the old cities and dynasties had passed away, fairer and more glorious ones had taken their places. And now he saw by the heap of shavings still fresh at his feet, that, for him and his work, the former lapse of time had been an illusion, and that no more time had elapsed than is required for a single scintillation from the brain of Brahma to fall on and inflame the tinder of a mortal brain. The material was pure, and his art was pure; how could the result be other than wonderful?

No face which we can give to a matter will stead us so well at last as the truth. This alone wears well. For the most part, we are not where we are, but in a false position. Through an infirmity of our natures, we suppose a case, and put ourselves into it, and hence are in two cases at the same time, and it is doubly difficult to get out. In sane moments we regard only the facts, the case that is. Say what you have to say, not what you ought. Any truth is better than make-believe. Tom Hyde, the tinker, standing on the gallows, was asked if he had any thing to say. "Tell the tailors," said he, "to remember to make a knot in their thread before they take the first stitch." His companion's prayer is forgotten.

However mean your life is, meet it and live it; do not shun it and call it hard names. It is not so bad as you are. It looks poorest when you are richest. The fault-finder will find faults even in paradise. Love your life, poor as it is. You may perhaps have some pleasant, thrilling, glorious hours, even in a poorhouse. The setting sun is reflected from the windows of the alms-house as brightly as from the rich man's abode; the snow

---

[232] This fable is most likely Thoreau's fabrication.

melts before its door as early in the spring. I do not see but a quiet mind may live as contentedly there, and have as cheering thoughts, as in a palace. The town's poor seem to me often to live the most independent lives of any. May be they are simply great enough to receive without misgiving. Most think that they are above being supported by the town; but it oftener happens that they are not above supporting themselves by dishonest means, which should be more disreputable. Cultivate poverty like a garden herb, like sage. Do not trouble yourself much to get new things, whether clothes or friends. Turn the old; return to them. Things do not change; we change. Sell your clothes and keep your thoughts. God will see that you do not want society. If I were confined to a corner of a garret all my days, like a spider, the world would be just as large to me while I had my thoughts about me. The philosopher said: "From an army of three divisions one can take away its general, and put it in disorder; from the man the most abject and vulgar one cannot take away his thought." Do not seek so anxiously to be developed, to subject yourself to many influences to be played on; it is all dissipation. Humility like darkness reveals the heavenly lights. The shadows of poverty and mean- ness gather around us, "and lo! creation widens to our view." We are often reminded that if there were bestowed on us the wealth of Crœsus,[233] our aims must still be the same, and our means essentially the same. Moreover, if you are restricted in your range by poverty, if you cannot buy books and newspapers, for instance, you are but confined to the most significant and vital experiences; you are compelled to deal with the mate- rial which yields the most sugar and the most starch. It is life near the bone where it is sweetest. You are defended from being a trifler. No man loses ever on a lower level by magnanimity on a higher. Superfluous wealth can buy superfluities only. Money is not required to buy one necessary of the soul.

I live in the angle of a leaden wall, into whose composition was poured a little alloy of bell metal. Often, in the repose of my mid-day, there reaches my ears a confused *tintinnabulum* from without. It is the noise of my contemporaries. My neighbors tell me of their adventures with famous gentlemen and ladies, what notabilities they met at the dinner-table; but I am no more interested in such things than in the contents of the Daily Times. The interest and the conversation are about costume and manners chiefly; but a goose is a goose still, dress it as you will. They tell me of California and Texas, of England and the Indies, of the Hon. Mr. ――― of Georgia or of Massachusetts, all transient and fleeting phenomena, till I am ready to leap from their court-yard like the Mameluke bey.[234] I delight to come to my bearings,—not walk in procession with pomp and parade, in a conspicuous place, but to walk even with the Builder of the uni- verse, if I may,—not to live in this restless, nervous, bustling, trivial Nineteenth Cen- tury, but stand or sit thoughtfully while it goes by. What are men celebrating? They are all on a committee of arrangements, and hourly expect a speech from somebody. God is only the president of the day, and Webster is his orator.[235] I love to weigh, to settle, to gravitate toward that which most strongly and rightfully attracts me;—not hang by the beam of the scale and try to weigh less,—not suppose a case, but take the case that is; to

[233] Legendary king who was accounted the wealthiest man of all time.
[234] The way one of the Mamelukes, a member of the Egyptian army clique, escaped being massacred in Cairo in 1811.

[235] Daniel Webster, a contemporary of Thoreau, was considered the foremost speaker on the American political scene.

travel the only path I can, and that on which no power can resist me. It affords me no satisfaction to commence to spring an arch before I have got a solid foundation. Let us not play at kittly-benders.[236] There is a solid bottom every where. We read that the traveller asked the boy if the swamp before him had a hard bottom. The boy replied that it had. But presently the traveller's horse sank in up to the girths, and he observed to the boy, "I thought you said that this bog had a hard bottom." "So it has," answered the latter, "but you have not got half way to it yet." So it is with the bogs and quicksands of society; but he is an old boy that knows it. Only what is thought said or done at a certain rare coincidence is good. I would not be one of those who will foolishly drive a nail into mere lath and plastering; such a deed would keep me awake nights. Give me a hammer, and let me feel for the furring.[237] Do not depend on the putty. Drive a nail home and clinch it so faithfully that you can wake up in the night and think of your work with satisfaction,—a work at which you would not be ashamed to invoke the Muse. So will help you God, and so only. Every nail driven should be as another rivet in the machine of the universe, you carrying on the work.

Rather than love, than money, than fame, give me truth. I sat at a table where were rich food and wine in abundance, and obsequious attendance, but sincerity and truth were not; and I went away hungry from the inhospitable board. The hospitality was as cold as the ices. I thought that there was no need of ice to freeze them. They talked to me of the age of the wine and the fame of the vintage; but I thought of an older, a newer, and purer wine, of a more glorious vintage, which they had not got, and could not buy. The style, the house and grounds and "entertainment" pass for nothing with me. I called on the king, but he made me wait in his hall, and conducted like a man incapacitated for hospitality. There was a man in my neighborhood who lived in a hollow tree. His manners were truly regal. I should have done better had I called on him.

How long shall we sit in our porticoes practising idle and musty virtues, which any work would make impertinent? As if one were to begin the day with long-suffering, and hire a man to hoe his potatoes; and in the afternoon go forth to practise Christian meekness and charity with goodness aforethought! Consider the China pride and stagnant self-complacency of mankind. This generation reclines a little to congratulate itself on being the last of an illustrious line; and in Boston and London and Paris and Rome, thinking of its long descent, it speaks of its progress in art and science and literature with satisfaction. There are the Records of the Philosophical Societies, and the public Eulogies of *Great Men!* It is the good Adam contemplating his own virtue. "Yes, we have done great deeds, and sung divine songs, which shall never die,"—that is, as long as *we* can remember them. The learned societies and great men of Assyria,—where are they? What youthful philosophers and experimentalists we are! There is not one of my readers who has yet lived a whole human life. These may be but the spring months in the life of the race. If we have had the seven-years' itch, we have not seen the seventeen-year locust yet in Concord. We are acquainted with a mere pellicle of the globe on which we live. Most have not delved six feet beneath the surface, nor leaped as many above it. We know not where we are. Beside, we are sound asleep nearly half our time. Yet we esteem ourselves wise, and have an established order on the surface. Truly, we are deep thinkers, we are ambitious spirits! As I stand over the insect crawling amid the pine nee-

---

[236] Running across thin ice.
[237] Wall studs.

dles on the forest floor, and endeavoring to conceal itself from my sight, and ask myself why it will cherish those humble thoughts, and hide its head from me who might perhaps be its benefactor, and impart to its race some cheering information, I am reminded of the greater Benefactor and Intelligence that stands over me the human insect.

There is an incessant influx of novelty into the world, and yet we tolerate incredible dulness. I need only suggest what kind of sermons are still listened to in the most enlightened countries. There are such words as joy and sorrow, but they are only the burden of a psalm, sung with a nasal twang, while we believe in the ordinary and mean. We think that we can change our clothes only. It is said that the British Empire is very large and respectable, and that the United States are a first-rate power. We do not believe that a tide rises and falls behind every man which can float the British Empire like a chip, if he should ever harbor it in his mind. Who knows what sort of seventeen-year locust will next come out of the ground? The government of the world I live in was not framed, like that of Britain, in after-dinner conversations over the wine.

The life in us is like the water in the river. It may rise this year higher than man has ever known it, and flood the parched uplands; even this may be the eventful year, which will drown out all our muskrats. It was not always dry land where we dwell. I see far inland the banks which the stream anciently washed, before science began to record its freshets. Every one has heard the story which has gone the rounds of New England, of a strong and beautiful bug which came out of the dry leaf of an old table of apple-tree wood, which had stood in a farmer's kitchen for sixty years, first in Connecticut, and afterward in Massachusetts,—from an egg deposited in the living tree many years earlier still, as appeared by counting the annual layers beyond it; which was heard gnawing out for several weeks, hatched perchance by the heat of an urn. Who does not feel his faith in a resurrection and immortality strengthened by hearing of this? Who knows what beautiful and winged life, whose egg has been buried for ages under many concentric layers of woodenness in the dead dry life of society, deposited at first in the alburnum of the green and living tree, which has been gradually converted into the semblance of its well-seasoned tomb,—heard perchance gnawing out now for years by the astonished family of man, as they sat round the festive board,—may unexpectedly come forth from amidst society's most trivial and handselled furniture, to enjoy its perfect summer life at last!

I do not say that John or Jonathan[238] will realize all this; but such is the character of that morrow which mere lapse of time can never make to dawn. The light which puts out our eyes is darkness to us. Only that day dawns to which we are awake. There is more day to dawn. The sun is but a morning star.

1846/1854

---

[238] Common terms for a Britisher ("John Bull") and an American ("Brother Jonathan"), respectively.

Resistance to Civil Government

I heartily accept the motto,—"That government is best which governs least;"[1] and I should like to see it acted up to more rapidly and systematically. Carried out, it finally amounts to this, which also I believe,—"That government is best which governs not at all;" and when men are prepared for it, that will be the kind of government which they will have. Government is at best but an expedient; but most governments are usually, and all governments are sometimes, inexpedient. The objections which have been brought against a standing army, and they are many and weighty, and deserve to prevail, may also at last be brought against a standing government. The standing army is only an arm of the standing government. The government itself, which is only the mode which the people have chosen to execute their will, is equally liable to be abused and perverted before the people can act through it. Witness the present Mexican war,[2] the work of comparatively a few individuals using the standing government as their tool; for, in the outset, the people would not have consented to this measure.

This American government,—what is it but a tradition, though a recent one, endeavoring to transmit itself unimpaired to posterity, but each instant losing some of its integrity? It has not the vitality and force of a single living man; for a single man can bend it to his will. It is a sort of wooden gun to the people themselves; and, if ever they should use it in earnest as a real one against each other, it will surely split. But it is not the less necessary for this; for the people must have some complicated machinery or other, and hear its din, to satisfy that idea of government which they have. Governments show thus how successfully men can be imposed on, even impose on themselves, for their own advantage. It is excellent, we must all allow; yet this government never of itself furthered any enterprise, but by the alacrity with which it got out of its way. *It* does not keep the country free. *It* does not settle the West. *It* does not educate. The character inherent in the American people has done all that has been accomplished; and it would have done somewhat more, if the government had not sometimes got in its way. For government is an expedient by which men would fain succeed in letting one another alone; and, as has been said, when it is most expedient, the governed are most let alone by it. Trade and commerce, if they were not made of India rubber, would never manage to bounce over the obstacles which legislators are continually putting in their way; and, if one were to judge these men wholly by the effects of their actions, and not partly by their intentions, they would deserve to be classed and punished with those mischievous persons who put obstructions on the railroads.

But, to speak practically and as a citizen, unlike those who call themselves no-government men, I ask for, not at once no government, but at *once* a better government. Let every man make known what kind of government would command his respect, and that will be one step toward obtaining it.

---

[1] Motto displayed on the masthead of the *Democratic Review,* a New York journal which, with these words, continued to support a sentiment widely upheld from the time of Thomas Jefferson.

[2] Thoreau first delivered this essay in the form of a lecture on January 26, 1848, during the height of the controversy over the Mexican War (1846–1848), which was seen by many in the North as a plan by southern slave owners to extend the slavery system to the West.

After all, the practical reason why, when the power is once in the hands of the people, a majority are permitted, and for a long period continue, to rule, is not because they are most likely to be in the right, nor because this seems fairest to the minority, but because they are physically the strongest. But a government in which the majority rule in all cases cannot be based on justice, even as far as men understand it. Can there not be a government in which majorities do not virtually decide right and wrong, but conscience?—in which majorities decide only those questions to which the rule of expediency is applicable? Must the citizen ever for a moment, or in the least degree, resign his conscience to the legislator? Why has every man a conscience, then? I think that we should be men first, and subjects afterward. It is not desirable to cultivate a respect for the law, so much as for the right. The only obligation which I have a right to assume, is to do at any time what I think right. It is truly enough said, that a corporation has no conscience; but a corporation of conscientious men is a corporation *with* a conscience. Law never made men a whit more just; and, by means of their respect for it, even the well-disposed are daily made the agents of injustice. A common and natural result of an undue respect for law is, that you may see a file of soldiers, colonel, captain, corporal, privates, powder-monkeys and all, marching in admirable order over hill and dale to the wars, against their wills, aye, against their common sense and consciences, which makes it very steep marching indeed, and produces a palpitation of the heart. They have no doubt that it is a damnable business in which they are concerned; they are all peaceably inclined. Now, what are they? Men at all? or small moveable forts and magazines, at the service of some unscrupulous man in power? Visit the Navy Yard, and behold a marine, such a man as an American government can make, or such as it can make a man with its black arts, a mere shadow and reminiscence of humanity, a man laid out alive and standing, and already, as one may say, buried under arms with funeral accompaniments, though it may be

> "Not a drum was heard, not a funeral note,
>   As his corse to the rampart we hurried;
> Not a soldier discharged his farewell shot
>   O'er the grave where our hero we buried."[3]

The mass of men serve the State thus, not as men mainly, but as machines, with their bodies. They are the standing army, and the militia, jailers, constables, *posse comitatus*,[4] &c. In most cases there is no free exercise whatever of the judgment or of the moral sense; but they put themselves on a level with wood and earth and stones, and wooden men can perhaps be manufactured that will serve the purpose as well. Such command no more respect than men of straw, or a lump of dirt. They have the same sort of worth only as horses and dogs. Yet such as these even are commonly esteemed good citizens. Others, as most legislators, politicians, lawyers, ministers, and officeholders, serve the State chiefly with their heads; and, as they rarely make any moral distinctions, they are as likely to serve the devil, without intending it, as God. A very few, as heroes, patriots,

---

[3] Song based on "The Burial of Sir John Moore at Corunna" (1817) by Charles Wolfe (1791–1823).

[4] The Latin phrase from which the term "sheriff's posse" is derived.

martyrs, reformers in the great sense, and *men,* serve the State with their consciences also, and so necessarily resist it for the most part; and they are commonly treated by it as enemies. A wise man will only be useful as a man, and will not submit to be "clay," and "stop a hole to keep the wind away,"[5] but leave that office to his dust at least:—

> "I am too high-born to be propertied,
>   To be a secondary at control,
>   Or useful serving-man and instrument
>   To any sovereign state throughout the world."[6]

He who gives himself entirely to his fellow-men appears to them useless and selfish; but he who gives himself partially to them is pronounced a benefactor and philanthropist.

How does it become a man to behave toward this American government to-day? I answer that he cannot without disgrace be associated with it. I cannot for an instant recognize that political organization as *my* government which is the *slave's* government also.

All men recognize the right of revolution; that is, the right to refuse allegiance to and to resist the government, when its tyranny or its inefficiency are great and unendurable. But almost all say that such is not the case now. But such was the case, they think, in the Revolution of '75.[7] If one were to tell me that this was a bad government because it taxed certain foreign commodities brought to its ports, it is most probable that I should not make an ado about it, for I can do without them: all machines have their friction; and possibly this does enough good to counterbalance the evil. At any rate, it is a great evil to make a stir about it. But when the friction comes to have its machine, and oppression and robbery are organized, I say, let us not have such a machine any longer. In other words, when a sixth of the population of a nation which has undertaken to be the refuge of liberty are slaves, and a whole country is unjustly overrun and conquered by a foreign army, and subjected to military law, I think that it is not too soon for honest men to rebel and revolutionize. What makes this duty the more urgent is the fact, that the country so overrun is not our own, but ours is the invading army.

Paley, a common authority with many on moral questions, in his chapter on the "Duty of Submission to Civil Government,"[8] resolves all civil obligation into expediency; and he proceeds to say, "that so long as the interest of the whole society requires it, that is, so long as the established government cannot be resisted or changed without public inconveniency, it is the will of God that the established government be obeyed, and no longer." . . . "This principle being admitted, the justice of every particular case of resistance is reduced to a computation of the quantity of the danger and grievance on the one side, and of the probability and expense of redressing it on the other." Of this, he says, every man shall judge for himself. But Paley appears never to have contemplated those cases to which the rule of expediency does not apply, in which a people, as well as an individual, must do justice, cost what it may. If I have unjustly wrested a

---

[5] *Hamlet,* Act V, Sc. i, ll. 236–237.
[6] *King John,* Act V, Sc. ii, ll. 79–82.
[7] The American Revolution (1775–1783).

[8] From *Principles of Moral and Political Philosophy* (1785) by William Paley (1743–1805), English theologian.

plank from a drowning man, I must restore it to him though I drown myself. This, according to Paley, would be inconvenient. But he that would save his life, in such a case, shall lose it.[9] This people must cease to hold slaves, and to make war on Mexico, though it cost them their existence as a people.

In their practice, nations agree with Paley; but does any one think that Massachusetts does exactly what is right at the present crisis?

> "A drab of state, a cloth-o'-silver slut,
>   To have her train borne up, and her soul trail in the dirt."[10]

Practically speaking, the opponents to a reform in Massachusetts are not a hundred thousand politicians at the South, but a hundred thousand merchants and farmers here, who are more interested in commerce and agriculture than they are in humanity, and are not prepared to do justice to the slave and to Mexico, *cost what it may.* I quarrel not with far-off foes, but with those who, near at home, co-operate with, and do the bidding of those far away, and without whom the latter would be harmless. We are accustomed to say, that the mass of men are unprepared; but improvement is slow, because the few are not materially wiser or better than the many. It is not so important that many should be as good as you, as that there be some absolute goodness somewhere; for that will leaven the whole lump.[11] There are thousands who are *in opinion* opposed to slavery and to the war, who yet in effect do nothing to put an end to them; who, esteeming themselves children of Washington and Franklin, sit down with their hands in their pockets, and say that they know not what to do, and do nothing; who even postpone the question of freedom to the question of free-trade, and quietly read the prices-current along with the latest advices[12] from Mexico, after dinner, and, it may be, fall asleep over them both. What is the price-current of an honest man and patriot to-day? They hesitate, and they regret, and sometimes they petition; but they do nothing in earnest and with effect. They will wait, well-disposed, for others to remedy the evil, that they may no longer have it to regret. At most, they give only a cheap vote, and a feeble countenance and God-speed, to the right, as it goes by them. There are nine hundred and ninety-nine patrons of virtue to one virtuous man; but it is easier to deal with the real possessor of a thing than with the temporary guardian of it.

All voting is a sort of gaming, like chequers or backgammon, with a slight moral tinge to it, a playing with right and wrong, with moral questions; and betting naturally accompanies it. The character of the voters is not staked. I cast my vote, perchance, as I think right; but I am not vitally concerned that that right should prevail. I am willing to leave it to the majority. Its obligation, therefore, never exceeds that of expediency. Even voting *for the right* is *doing* nothing for it. It is only expressing to men feebly your desire that it should prevail. A wise man will not leave the right to the mercy of chance, nor wish it to prevail through the power of the majority. There is but little virtue in the ac-

---

[9] Example of Thoreau's constant use of scriptural references; here, from Luke 9:24.

[10] *The Revenger's Tragedy* (1607), Act IV, Sc. iv, ll. 70–72, attributed to Cyril Tourneur (1575?–1629).

[11] Paraphrase of 1 Corinthians 5:6.

[12] News dispatches.

tion of masses of men. When the majority shall at length vote for the abolition of slavery, it will be because they are indifferent to slavery, or because there is but little slavery left to be abolished by their vote. *They* will then be the only slaves. Only *his* vote can hasten the abolition of slavery who asserts his own freedom by his vote.

I hear of a convention to be held at Baltimore, or elsewhere, for the selection of a candidate for the Presidency, made up chiefly of editors, and men who are politicians by profession; but I think, what is it to any independent, intelligent, and respectable man what decision they may come to, shall we not have the advantage of his wisdom and honesty, nevertheless? Can we not count upon some independent votes? Are there not many individuals in the country who do not attend conventions? But no: I find that the respectable man, so called, has immediately drifted from his position, and despairs of his country, when his country has more reason to despair of him. He forthwith adopts one of the candidates thus selected as the only *available* one, thus proving that he is himself *available* for any purposes of the demagogue. His vote is of no more worth than that of any unprincipled foreigner or hireling native, who may have been bought. Oh for a man who is a *man*, and, as my neighbor says, has a bone in his back which you cannot pass your hand through! Our statistics are at fault: the population has been returned too large. How many *men* are there to a square thousand miles in this country? Hardly one. Does not America offer any inducement for men to settle here? The American has dwindled into an Odd Fellow,[13]—one who may be known by the development of his organ of gregariousness,[14] and a manifest lack of intellect and cheerful self-reliance; whose first and chief concern, on coming into the world, is to see that the alms-houses are in good repair; and, before yet he has lawfully donned the virile garb,[15] to collect a fund for the support of the widows and orphans that may be; who, in short, ventures to live only by the aid of the mutual insurance company, which has promised to bury him decently.

It is not a man's duty, as a matter of course, to devote himself to the eradication of any, even the most enormous wrong; he may still properly have other concerns to engage him; but it is his duty, at least, to wash his hands of it, and, if he gives it no thought longer, not to give it practically his support. If I devote myself to other pursuits and contemplations, I must first see, at least, that I do not pursue them sitting upon another man's shoulders. I must get off him first, that he may pursue his contemplations too. See what gross inconsistency is tolerated. I have heard some of my townsmen say, "I should like to have them order me out to help put down an insurrection of the slaves, or to march to Mexico,—see if I would go;" and yet these very men have each, directly by their allegiance, and so indirectly, at least, by their money, furnished a substitute. The soldier is applauded who refuses to serve in an unjust war by those who do not refuse to sustain the unjust government which makes the war; is applauded by those whose own act and authority he disregards and sets at nought; as if the State were penitent to that degree that it hired one to scourge it while it sinned, but not to that degree

---

[13] Satiric reference to members of a secret fraternal society, the Independent Order of Odd Fellows, as part of Thoreau's argument that most Americans had fallen away from independent self-sufficiency into conformism.

[14] Phrenological term applied to persons who prefer belonging to the group.

[15] Attire that acknowledged that a Roman boy had attained adulthood.

that it left off sinning for a moment. Thus, under the name of order and civil government, we are all made at last to pay homage to and support our own meanness. After
the first blush of sin, comes its indifference and from immoral it becomes, as it were,
*un*moral, and not quite unnecessary to that life which we have made.

The broadest and most prevalent error requires the most disinterested virtue to sustain it. The slight reproach to which the virtue of patriotism is commonly liable, the noble are most likely to incur. Those who, while they disapprove of the character and
measures of a government, yield to it their allegiance and support, are undoubtedly its
most conscientious supporters, and so frequently the most serious obstacles to reform.
Some are petitioning the State to dissolve the Union, to disregard the requisitions of the
President.[16] Why do they not dissolve it themselves,—the union between themselves
and the State,—and refuse to pay their quota into its treasury? Do not they stand in the
same relation to the State, that the State does to the Union? And have not the same reasons prevented the State from resisting the Union, which have prevented them from resisting the State?

How can a man be satisfied to entertain an opinion merely, and enjoy *it*? Is there any
enjoyment in it, if his opinion is that he is aggrieved? If you are cheated out of a single
dollar by your neighbor, you do not rest satisfied with knowing that you are cheated, or
with saying that you are cheated, or even with petitioning him to pay you your due; but
you take effectual steps at once to obtain the full amount, and see that you are never
cheated again. Action from principle,—the perception and the performance of right,—
changes things and relations; it is essentially revolutionary, and does not consist wholly
with any thing which was. It not only divides states and churches, it divides families;
aye, it divides the *individual,* separating the diabolical in him from the divine.

Unjust laws exist: shall we be content to obey them, or shall we endeavor to amend
them, and obey them until we have succeeded, or shall we transgress them at once? Men
generally, under such a government as this, think that they ought to wait until they have
persuaded the majority to alter them. They think that, if they should resist, the remedy
would be worse than the evil. But it is the fault of the government itself that the remedy
is worse than the evil. *It* makes it worse. Why is it not more apt to anticipate and provide
for reform? Why does it not cherish its wise minority? Why does it cry and resist before
it is hurt? Why does it not encourage its citizens to be on the alert to point out its faults,
and *do* better than it would have them? Why does it always crucify Christ, and excommunicate Copernicus and Luther,[17] and pronounce Washington and Franklin rebels?

One would think, that a deliberate and practical denial of its authority was the only
offence never contemplated by government; else, why has it not assigned its definite, its
suitable and proportionate penalty? If a man who has no property refuses but once to
earn nine shillings[18] for the State, he is put in prison for a period unlimited by any law
that I know, and determined only by the discretion of those who placed him there; but

---

[16] President James K. Polk sought money and
troops for the Mexican conflict over the objections of certain New England radicals
who proposed breaking away from the
Union in order to further their aims as abolitionists.

[17] Both the Polish astronomer Copernicus

(1473–1543) and the German head of the
Protestant reformation, Martin Luther
(1483–1546), were considered heretics by
the Roman church. The former in fact died
before he could be excommunicated.

[18] The amount of some $2, which Thoreau re-
fused to pay in taxes.

if he should steal ninety times nine shillings from the State, he is soon permitted to go at large again.

If the injustice is part of the necessary friction of the machine of government, let it go, let it go: perchance it will wear smooth,—certainly the machine will wear out. If the injustice has a spring, or a pulley, or a rope, or a crank, exclusively for itself, then perhaps you may consider whether the remedy will not be worse than the evil; but if it is of such a nature that it requires you to be the agent of injustice to another, then, I say, break the law. Let your life be a counter friction to stop the machine. What I have to do is to see, at any rate, that I do not lend myself to the wrong which I condemn.

As for adopting the ways which the State has provided for remedying the evil, I know not of such ways. They take too much time, and a man's life will be gone. I have other affairs to attend to. I came into this world, not chiefly to make this a good place to live in, but to live in it, be it good or bad. A man has not every thing to do, but something; and because he cannot do *every thing*, it is not necessary that he should do *something* wrong. It is not my business to be petitioning the governor or the legislature any more than it is theirs to petition me; and, if they should not hear my petition, what should I do then? But in this case the State has provided no way: its very Constitution is the evil. This may seem to be harsh and stubborn and unconciliatory; but it is to treat with the utmost kindness and consideration the only spirit that can appreciate or deserves it. So is all change for the better, like birth and death which convulse the body.

I do not hesitate to say, that those who call themselves abolitionists should at once effectually withdraw their support, both in person and property, from the government of Massachusetts, and not wait till they constitute a majority of one, before they suffer the right to prevail through them. I think that it is enough if they have God on their side, without waiting for that other one. Moreover, any man more right than his neighbors, constitutes a majority of one already.

I meet this American government, or its representative the State government, directly, and face to face, once a year, no more, in the person of its tax-gatherer; this is the only mode in which a man situated as I am necessarily meets it; and it then says distinctly, Recognize me; and the simplest, the most effectual, and, in the present posture of affairs, the indispensablest mode of treating with it on this head, of expressing your little satisfaction with and love for it, is to deny it then. My civil neighbor, the tax-gatherer, is the very man I have to deal with,—for it is, after all, with men and not with parchment that I quarrel,—and he has voluntarily chosen to be an agent of the government. How shall he ever know well what he is and does as an officer of the government, or as a man, until he is obliged to consider whether he shall treat me, his neighbor, for whom he has respect, as a neighbor and well-disposed man, or as a maniac and disturber of the peace, and see if he can get over this obstruction to his neighborliness without a ruder and more impetuous thought or speech corresponding with his action? I know this well, that if one thousand, if one hundred, if ten men whom I could name,—if ten *honest* men only,—aye, if *one* HONEST man, in this State of Massachusetts, *ceasing to hold slaves,* were actually to withdraw from this copartnership, and be locked up in the county jail therefor, it would be the abolition of slavery in America. For it matters not how small the beginning may seem to be: what is once well done is done for ever. But we love better to talk about it: that we say is our mission. Reform keeps many scores of newspapers in its service, but not one man. If my esteemed neighbor, the

State's ambassador,[19] who will devote his days to the settlement of the question of human rights in the Council Chamber, instead of being threatened with the prisons of Carolina, were to sit down the prisoner of Massachusetts, that State which is so anxious to foist the sin of slavery upon her sister,—though at present she can discover only an act of inhospitality to be the ground of a quarrel with her,—the Legislature would not wholly waive the subject the following winter.

Under a government which imprisons any unjustly, the true place for a just man is also a prison. The proper place to-day, the only place which Massachusetts has provided for her freer and less desponding spirits, is in her prisons, to be put out and locked out of the State by her own act, as they have already put themselves out by their principles. It is there that the fugitive slave, and the Mexican prisoner on parole, and the Indian come to plead the wrongs of his race, should find them; on that separate, but more free and honorable ground, where the State places those who are not *with* her but *against* her,—the only house in a slave-state in which a free man can abide with honor. If any think that their influence would be lost there, and their voices no longer afflict the ear of the State, that they would not be as an enemy within its walls, they do not know by how much truth is stronger than error, nor how much more eloquently and effectively he can combat injustice who has experienced a little in his own person. Cast your whole vote, not a strip of paper merely, but your whole influence. A minority is powerless while it conforms to the majority; it is not even a minority then; but it is irresistible when it clogs by its whole weight. If the alternative is to keep all just men in prison, or give up war and slavery, the State will not hesitate which to choose. If a thousand men were not to pay their tax-bills this year, that would not be a violent and bloody measure, as it would be to pay them, and enable the State to commit violence and shed innocent blood. This is, in fact, the definition of a peaceable revolution, if any such is possible. If the tax-gatherer, or any other public officer, asks me, as one has done, "But what shall I do?" my answer is, "If you really wish to do any thing, resign your office." When the subject has refused allegiance, and the officer has resigned his office, then the revolution is accomplished. But even suppose blood should flow. Is there not a sort of blood shed when the conscience is wounded? Through this wound a man's real manhood and immortality flow out, and he bleeds to an everlasting death. I see this blood flowing now.

I have contemplated the imprisonment of the offender, rather than the seizure of his goods,—though both will serve the same purpose,—because they who assert the purest right, and consequently are most dangerous to a corrupt State, commonly have not spent much time in accumulating property. To such the State renders comparatively small service, and a slight tax is wont to appear exorbitant, particularly if they are obliged to earn it by special labor with their hands. If there were one who lived wholly without the use of money, the State itself would hesitate to demand it of him. But the rich man—not to make any invidious comparison—is always sold to the institution which makes him rich. Absolutely speaking, the more money, the less virtue; for money comes between a man and his objects, and obtains them for him; and it was certainly no great virtue to obtain it. It puts to rest many questions which he would otherwise be

---

[19] Samuel Hoar (1778–1856) of Concord was sent by the state of Massachusetts (which he represented as senator) to South Carolina in an attempt to aid black sailors who had been taken from Massachusetts ships in southern ports. His efforts were frustrated when he was expelled from Charleston by legal action.

taxed to answer; while the only new question which it puts is the hard but superfluous one, how to spend it. Thus his moral ground is taken from under his feet. The opportunities of living are diminished in proportion as what are called the "means" are increased. The best thing a man can do for his culture when he is rich is to endeavour to carry out those schemes which he entertained when he was poor. Christ answered the Herodians according to their condition. "Show me the tribute-money," said he;—and one took a penny out of his pocket;—If you use money which has the image of Cæsar on it, and which he has made current and valuable, that is, *if you are men of the State,* and gladly enjoy the advantages of Cæsar's government, then pay him back some of his own when he demands it; "Render therefore to Cæsar that which is Cæsar's, and to God those things which are God's,"[20]—leaving them no wiser than before as to which was which; for they did not wish to know.

When I converse with the freest of my neighbors, I perceive that, whatever they may say about the magnitude and seriousness of the question, and their regard for the public tranquillity, the long and the short of the matter is, that they cannot spare the protection of the existing government, and they dread the consequences of disobedience to it to their property and families. For my own part, I should not like to think that I ever rely on the protection of the State. But, if I deny the authority of the State when it presents its tax-bill, it will soon take and waste all my property, and so harass me and my children without end. This is hard. This makes it impossible for a man to live honestly and at the same time comfortably in outward respects. It will not be worth the while to accumulate property; that would be sure to go again. You must hire or squat somewhere, and raise but a small crop, and eat that soon. You must live within yourself, and depend upon yourself, always tucked up and ready for a start, and not have many affairs. A man may grow rich in Turkey even, if he will be in all respects a good subject of the Turkish government. Confucius said.—"If a State is governed by the principles of reason, poverty and misery are subjects of shame; if a State is not governed by the principles of reason, riches and honors are the subjects of shame."[21] No: until I want the protection of Massachusetts to be extended to me in some distant southern port, where my liberty is endangered, or until I am bent solely on building up an estate at home by peaceful enterprise, I can afford to refuse allegiance to Massachusetts, and her right to my property and life. It costs me less in every sense to incur the penalty of disobedience to the State, than it would to obey. I should feel as if I were worth less in that case.

Some years ago, the State met me in behalf of the church, and commanded me to pay a certain sum toward the support of a clergyman whose preaching my father attended, but never I myself. "Pay it," it said, "or be locked up in the jail." I declined to pay. But, unfortunately, another man saw fit to pay it. I did not see why the schoolmaster should be taxed to support the priest, and not the priest the schoolmaster; for I was not the State's schoolmaster, but I supported myself by voluntary subscription. I did not see why the lyceum should not present its tax-bill, and have the State to back its demand, as well as the church. However, at the request of the selectmen, I condescended to make some such statement as this in writing:—"Know all men by these presents, that I, Henry Thoreau, do not wish to be regarded as a member of any incorporated society

[20] See Matthew 22:16–22.
[21] From *The Analects* by the Chinese philosopher Confucius (ca. 551–479 B.C.).

which I have not joined." This I gave to the town-clerk; and he has it. The State, having thus learned that I did not wish to be regarded as a member of that church, has never made a like demand on me since; though it said that it must adhere to its original presumption that time. If I had known how to name them, I should then have signed off in detail from all the societies which I never signed on to; but I did not know where to find a complete list.

I have paid no poll-tax for six years. I was put into a jail once on this account, for one night;[22] and, as I stood considering the walls of solid stone, two or three feet thick, the door of wood and iron, a foot thick, and the iron grating which strained the light, I could not help being struck with the foolishness of that institution which treated me as if I were mere flesh and blood and bones, to be locked up. I wondered that it should have concluded at length that this was the best use it could put me to, and had never thought to avail itself of my services in some way. I saw that, if there was a wall of stone between me and my townsmen, there was a still more difficult one to climb or break through, before they could get to be as free as I was. I did not for a moment feel confined, and the walls seemed a great waste of stone and mortar. I felt as if I alone of all my townsmen had paid my tax. They plainly did not know how to treat me, but behaved like persons who are underbred. In every threat and in every compliment there was a blunder; for they thought that my chief desire was to stand the other side of that stone wall. I could not but smile to see how industriously they locked the door on my meditations, which followed them out again without let or hinderance, and *they* were really all that was dangerous. As they could not reach me, they had resolved to punish my body; just as boys, if they cannot come at some person against whom they have a spite, will abuse his dog. I saw that the State was half-witted, that it was timid as a lone woman with her silver spoons, and that it did not know its friends from its foes, and I lost all my remaining respect for it, and pitied it.

Thus the State never intentionally confronts a man's sense, intellectual or moral, but only his body, his senses. It is not armed with superior wit or honesty, but with superior physical strength. I was not born to be forced. I will breathe after my own fashion. Let us see who is the strongest. What force has a multitude? They only can force me who obey a higher law than I. They force me to become like themselves. I do not hear of *men* being *forced* to live this way or that by masses of men. What sort of life were that to live? When I meet a government which says to me, "Your money or your life," why should I be in haste to give it my money? It may be in a great strait, and not know what to do: I cannot help that. It must help itself; do as I do. It is not worth the while to snivel about it. I am not responsible for the successful working of the machinery of society. I am not the son of the engineer. I perceive that, when an acorn and a chestnut fall side by side, the one does not remain inert to make way for the other, but both obey their own laws, and spring and grow and flourish as best they can, till one, perchance, overshadows and destroys the other. If a plant cannot live according to its nature, it dies; and so a man.

The night in prison was novel and interesting enough. The prisoners in their shirt-sleeves were enjoying a chat and the evening air in the door-way, when I entered. But the jailer said, "Come, boys, it is time to lock up;" and so they dispersed, and I heard the sound of their steps returning into the hollow apartments. My roommate was intro-

---

[22] July 23 or 24, 1846.

duced to me by the jailer, as "a first-rate fellow and a clever[23] man." When the door was locked, he showed me where to hang my hat, and how he managed matters there. The rooms were whitewashed once a month; and this one, at least, was the whitest, most simply furnished, and probably the neatest apartment in the town. He naturally wanted to know where I came from, and what brought me there; and, when I had told him, I asked him in my turn how he came there, presuming him to be an honest man, of course; and, as the world goes, I believe he was. "Why," said he, "they accuse me of burning a barn; but I never did it." As near as I could discover, he had probably gone to bed in a barn when drunk, and smoked his pipe there; and so a barn was burnt. He had the reputation of being a clever man, had been there some three months waiting for his trial to come on, and would have to wait as much longer; but he was quite domesticated and contented, since he got his board for nothing, and thought that he was well treated.

He occupied one window, and I the other; and I saw, that, if one stayed there long, his principal business would be to look out the window. I had soon read all the tracts that were left there, and examined where former prisoners had broken out, and where a grate had been sawed off, and heard the history of the various occupants of that room; for I found that even here there was a history and a gossip which never circulated beyond the walls of the jail. Probably this is the only house in the town where verses are composed, which are afterward printed in a circular form, but not published. I was shown quite a long list of verses which were composed by some young men who had been detected in an attempt to escape, who avenged themselves by singing them.

I pumped my fellow-prisoner as dry as I could, for fear I should never see him again; but at length he showed me which was my bed, and left me to blow out the lamp.

It was like travelling into a far country, such as I had never expected to behold, to lie there for one night. It seemed to me that I never had heard the town-clock strike before, nor the evening sounds of the village; for we slept with the windows open, which were inside the grating. It was to see my native village in the light of the middle ages, and our Concord was turned into a Rhine stream, and visions of knights and castles passed before me. They were the voices of old burghers that I heard in the streets. I was an involuntary spectator and auditor of whatever was done and said in the kitchen of the adjacent village-inn,—a wholly new and rare experience to me. It was a closer view of my native town. I was fairly inside of it. I never had seen its institutions before. This is one of its peculiar institutions; for it is a shire town.[24] I began to comprehend what its inhabitants were about.

In the morning, our breakfasts were put through the hole in the door, in small oblong-square tin pans, made to fit, and holding a pint of chocolate, with brown bread, and an iron spoon. When they called for the vessels again, I was green enough to return what bread I had left; but my comrade seized it, and said that I should lay that up for lunch or dinner. Soon after, he was let out to work at haying in a neighboring field, whither he went every day, and would not be back till noon; so he bade me good-day, saying that he doubted if he should see me again.

When I came out of prison,—for some one interfered, and paid the tax,—I did not perceive that great changes had taken place on the common, such as he observed who

[23] Honest.
[24] County seat.

went in a youth, and emerged a tottering and grayheaded man; and yet a change had to my eyes come over the scene,—the town, and State, and country,—greater than any that mere time could effect. I saw yet more distinctly the State in which I lived. I saw to what extent the people among whom I lived could be trusted as good neighbors and friends; that their friendship was for summer weather only; that they did not greatly purpose to do right; that they were a distinct race from me by their prejudices and superstitions, as the Chinamen and Malays are; that, in their sacrifices to humanity, they ran no risks, not even to their property; that, after all, they were not so noble but they treated the thief as he had treated them, and hoped, by a certain outward observance and a few prayers, and by walking in a particular straight though useless path from time to time, to save their souls. This may be to judge my neighbors harshly; for I believe that most of them are not aware that they have such an institution as the jail in their village.

It was formerly the custom in our village, when a poor debtor came out of jail, for his acquaintances to salute him, looking through their fingers, which were crossed to represent the grating of a jail window, "How do ye do?" My neighbors did not thus salute me, but first looked at me, and then at one another, as if I had returned from a long journey. I was put into jail as I was going to the shoemaker's to get a shoe which was mended. When I was let out the next morning, I proceeded to finish my errand, and, having put on my mended shoe, joined a huckleberry party, who were impatient to put themselves under my conduct; and in half an hour,—for the horse was soon tackled,—was in the midst of a huckleberry field, on one of our highest hills, two miles off; and then the State was nowhere to be seen.

This is the whole history of "My Prisons."[25]

I have never declined paying the highway tax, because I am as desirous of being a good neighbor as I am of being a bad subject; and, as for supporting schools, I am doing my part to educate my fellow-countrymen now. It is for no particular item in the tax-bill that I refuse to pay it. I simply wish to refuse allegiance to the State, to withdraw and stand aloof from it effectually. I do not care to trace the course of my dollar, if I could, till it buys a man, or a musket to shoot one with,—the dollar is innocent,—but I am concerned to trace the effects of my allegiance. In fact, I quietly declare war with the State, after my fashion, though I will still make what use and get what advantage of her I can, as is usual in such cases.

If others pay the tax which is demanded of me, from a sympathy with the State, they do but what they have already done in their own case, or rather they abet injustice to a greater extent than the State requires. If they pay the tax from a mistaken interest in the individual taxed, to save his property or prevent his going to jail, it is because they have not considered wisely how far they let their private feelings interfere with the public good.

This, then, is my position at present. But one cannot be too much on his guard in such a case, lest his action be biassed by obstinacy, or an undue regard for the opinions of men. Let him see that he does only what belongs to himself and to the hour.

I think sometimes, Why, this people mean well; they are only ignorant; they would do better if they knew how: why give your neighbors this pain to treat you as they are not in-

---

[25] Reference to a book of that title published in 1832 by Silvio Pellico, an Italian poet imprisoned by the Austrians for his revolutionary activities against their occupation of Italy.

clined to? But I think, again, this is no reason why I should do as they do, or permit others to suffer much greater pain of a different kind. Again, I sometimes say to myself, When many millions of men, without heat, without ill-will, without personal feeling of any kind, demand of you a few shillings only, without the possibility, such is their constitution, of retracting or altering their present demand, and without the possibility, on your side, of appeal to any other millions, why expose yourself to this overwhelming brute force? You do not resist cold and hunger, the winds and the waves, thus obstinately; you quietly submit to a thousand similar necessities. You do not put your head into the fire. But just in proportion as I regard this as not wholly a brute force, but partly a human force, and consider that I have relations to those millions as to so many millions of men, and not of mere brute or inanimate things, I see that appeal is possible, first and instantaneously, from them to the Maker of them, and, secondly, from them to themselves. But, if I put my head deliberately into the fire, there is no appeal to fire or to the Maker of fire, and I have only myself to blame. If I could convince myself that I have any right to be satisfied with men as they are, and to treat them accordingly, and not according, in some respects, to my requisitions and expectations of what they and I ought to be, then, like a good Mussulman[26] and fatalist, I should endeavor to be satisfied with things as they are, and say it is the will of God. And, above all, there is this difference between resisting this and a purely brute or natural force, that I can resist this with some effect; but I cannot expect, like Orpheus,[27] to change the nature of the rocks and trees and beasts.

I do not wish to quarrel with any man or nation. I do not wish to split hairs, to make fine distinctions, or set myself up as better than my neighbors. I seek rather, I may say, even an excuse for conforming to the laws of the land. I am but too ready to conform to them. Indeed I have reason to suspect myself on this head; and each year, as the tax-gatherer comes round, I find myself disposed to review the acts and position of the general and state governments, and the spirit of the people, to discover a pretext for conformity. I believe that the State will soon be able to take all my work of this sort out of my hands, and then I shall be no better a patriot than my fellow-countrymen. Seen from a lower point of view, the Constitution, with all its faults, is very good; the law and the courts are very respectable; even this State and this American government are, in many respects, very admirable and rare things, to be thankful for, such as a great many have described them; but seen from a point of view a little higher, they are what I have described them; seen from a higher still, and the highest, who shall say what they are, or that they are worth looking at or thinking of at all?

However, the government does not concern me much, and I shall bestow the fewest possible thoughts on it. It is not many moments that I live under a government, even in this world. If a man is thought-free, fancy-free, imagination-free, that which is *not* never for a long time appearing *to be* to him, unwise rulers or reformers cannot fatally interrupt him.

I know that most men think differently from myself; but those whose lives are by profession devoted to the study of these or kindred subjects, content me as little as any. Statesmen and legislators, standing so completely within the institution, never distinctly and nakedly behold it. They speak of moving society; but have no resting-place

---

26 Mohammedan.

27 The poet-musician of classic myth whose powers of song were so great that he could throw a spell over beasts and natural objects.

without it. They may be men of a certain experience and discrimination, and have no doubt invented ingenious and even useful systems, for which we sincerely thank them; but all their wit and usefulness lie within certain not very wide limits. They are wont to forget that the world is not governed by policy and expediency. Webster[28] never goes behind government, and so cannot speak with authority about it. His words are wisdom to those legislators who contemplate no essential reform in the existing government; but for thinkers, and those who legislate for all time, he never once glances at the subject. I know of those whose serene and wise speculations on this theme would soon reveal the limits of his mind's range and hospitality. Yet, compared with the cheap professions of most reformers, and the still cheaper wisdom and eloquence of politicians in general, his are almost the only sensible and valuable words, and we thank Heaven for him. Comparatively, he is always strong, original, and, above all, practical. Still his quality is not wisdom, but prudence. The lawyer's truth is not Truth, but consistency, or a consistent expediency. Truth is always in harmony with herself, and is not concerned chiefly to reveal the justice that may consist with wrong-doing. He well deserves to be called, as he has been called, the Defender of the Constitution. There are really no blows to be given by him but defensive ones. He is not a leader, but a follower. His leaders are the men of '87.[29] "I have never made an effort," he says, "and never propose to make an effort; I have never countenanced an effort, and never mean to countenance an effort, to disturb the arrangement as originally made, by which the various States came into the Union."[30] Still thinking of the sanction which the Constitution gives to slavery, he says, "Because it was a part of the original compact,—let it stand." Notwithstanding his special acuteness and ability, he is unable to take a fact out of its merely political relations, and behold it as it lies absolutely to be disposed of by the intellect,—what, for instance, it behoves a man to do here in America to-day with regard to slavery,—but ventures, or is driven, to make some such desperate answer as the following, while professing to speak absolutely, and as a private man,—from which what new and singular code of social duties might be inferred?—"The manner," says he, "in which the governments of those States where slavery exists are to regulate it, is for their own consideration, under their responsibility to their constituents, to the general laws of propriety, humanity, and justice, and to God. Associations formed elsewhere, springing from a feeling of humanity, or any other cause, have nothing whatever to do with it. They have never received any encouragement from me, and they never will."

They who know of no purer sources of truth, who have traced up its stream no higher, stand, and wisely stand, by the Bible and the Constitution, and drink at it there with reverence and humility; but they who behold where it comes trickling into this lake or that pool, gird up their loins once more, and continue their pilgrimage toward its fountain-head.

No man with a genius for legislation has appeared in America. They are rare in the history of the world. There are orators, politicians, and eloquent men, by the thousand;

---

[28] Daniel Webster (1782–1852), influential senator from Massachusetts who was felt by the abolitionists to be a betrayer of their principles when he supported the Fugitive Slave Law, which made it possible to return slaves who had escaped to the North to their southern masters.

[29] Drafters of the Constitution in 1787.

[30] Both here and below, lines quoted from speeches delivered by Webster in 1845 and 1848. These extracts were added by Thoreau after he gave his lecture, a fact he noted when preparing the printed text of his essay.

but the speaker has not yet opened his mouth to speak, who is capable of settling the much-vexed questions of the day. We love eloquence for its own sake, and not for any truth which it may utter, or any heroism it may inspire. Our legislators have not yet learned the comparative value of free-trade and of freedom, of union, and of rectitude, to a nation. They have no genius or talent for comparatively humble questions of taxation and finance, commerce and manufactures and agriculture. If we were left solely to the wordy wit of legislators in Congress for our guidance, uncorrected by the seasonable experience and the effectual complaints of the people, America would not long retain her rank among the nations. For eighteen hundred years, though perchance I have no right to say it, the New Testament has been written; yet where is the legislator who has wisdom and practical talent enough to avail himself of the light which it sheds on the science of legislation?

The authority of government, even such as I am willing to submit to,—for I will cheerfully obey those who know and can do better than I, and in many things even those who neither know nor can do so well,—is still an impure one: to be strictly just, it must have the sanction and consent of the governed. It can have no pure right over my person and property but what I concede to it. The progress from an absolute to a limited monarchy, from a limited monarchy to a democracy, is a progress toward a true respect for the individual. Is a democracy, such as we know it, the last improvement possible in government? Is it not possible to take a step further towards recognizing and organizing the rights of man? There will never be a really free and enlightened State, until the State comes to recognize the individual as a higher and independent power, from which all its own power and authority are derived, and treats him accordingly. I please myself with imagining a State at last which can afford to be just to all men, and to treat the individual with respect as a neighbor; which even would not think it inconsistent with its own repose, if a few were to live aloof from it, not meddling with it, nor embraced by it, who fulfilled all the duties of neighbors and fellow-men. A State which bore this kind of fruit, and suffered it to drop off as fast as it ripened, would prepare the way for a still more perfect and glorious State, which also I have imagined, but not yet anywhere seen.

1849

Margaret Fuller
1810–1850

Margaret Fuller's life and work transcended virtually every stereotype American women had to endure in the first half of the nineteenth century. She matured intellectually at a very early age yet married very late. She was a feminist pioneer in East Coast literary circles at a time when women pioneers were more apt to be leading wagon trains to the West Coast. She wrote first-rate—and controversial—journalism as well as social and literary criticism when women were expected to be preoccupied with ensuring domestic tranquillity. An accomplished teacher, translator, editor, columnist, poet, critic, and feminist theorist and advocate, as well as a social and political activist, Fuller became an articulate and influential voice in America's struggle to come to terms with its literary identity and social conscience.

Sarah Margaret Fuller was born in Cambridgeport, Massachusetts, on May 23, 1810, the first of Margaret and Timothy Fuller's five children. Her father, a Harvard-trained lawyer and member of Congress, compensated for his wife's poor health by dominating the children's lives with an almost ruthless passion that apparently he alone considered affection. A stern disciplinarian and a dogmatic educational theorist, Timothy Fuller trained his daughter to read the classics by age six, Shakespeare by eight. Thereafter, he schooled her in modern languages, especially German, as well as in ancient and modern history, biblical scholarship, and English literature. Her father's intense and deliberate tutelage resulted, as she later noted, in a "premature development of the brain, that made me a 'youthful prodigy' by day, and by night a victim of spectral illusions," the most recurrent of which was a nightmare in which horses galloped across her head.

After an unsettling year attending the Misses Prescott's school in rural Groton, Massachusetts (where for a time she sat next to Oliver Wendell Holmes), Margaret Fuller returned home in 1824 and resumed the course of study her father had so carefully laid out for her. Only occasionally did she venture out into the elite, male conversational world to which her father introduced her. Of the daring young liberal clergymen and writers she met during the late 1820s and early 1830s, Margaret Fuller developed lasting friendships with but a few, most notably James Freeman Clarke and W. H. Channing, who, along with Ralph Waldo Emerson, would prepare her *Memoirs* after her death.

When Margaret Fuller's father died unexpectedly in 1835, responsibility for supporting the family fell to her. She did this principally through teaching at various schools for several years, including Boston's experimental Temple School, directed by the Transcendentalist Bronson Alcott. During this same period she intensified her study of German with the assistance of Dr. William Ellery Channing, the longtime minister at Boston's Federal Street Church. Reading Goethe would influence the course of both her thinking and teaching and prepare her for her first two book-length publications, translations titled *Eckermann's Conversations with Goethe* (1839) and *Correspondence of Franklin Günderode with Bettina von Arnim* (1842). Within a few years after her father's death, Margaret Fuller had expanded her once meager conversational network to include such soon-to-be celebrated cultural figures as Ralph Waldo Emerson (whom she first had visited in Concord in 1836), Henry David Thoreau, Frederic Henry Hedge, and most of the other liberal thinkers who came to be known as the Transcendentalists. In the years to come, her "active mind" would indeed be "busy with large topics," both in her participation in the occasional meetings of the Transcendentalist Club and in her more frequent gatherings of Boston's most distinguished women.

Margaret Fuller assembled Boston's most intellectually powerful women at weekly "Conversations" at the home of the eminent teacher Elizabeth Peabody. Fuller orchestrated discussions of topics in such wide-ranging fields as mythology, education, philosophy, theology, and the fine arts, and she encouraged the group to consider contemporary social and ethical issues. Her intellectual leadership at these meetings was rarely challenged; her prominence in Boston's intellectual life seemed assured, if rather flamboyant.

In 1840 Fuller agreed to serve as the unsalaried editor of *The Dial,* the principal journal of Transcendentalist thought, and in July of that year she saw the first issue into print. For the next two years, she energetically tried to fulfill her hopes for this quarterly publication, "[T]hat this periodical will not aim at leading public opinion, but at stimulating each man to think for himself, to think more deeply and nobly by letting them see how some minds are kept alive by wise self-trust." In addition to her literary reviews, which helped promote European romanticism among America's young intellectuals, Fuller contributed several essays to *The Dial,* the most important of which was her important statement on women's rights, "The Great Lawsuit: Man Versus Men. Woman Versus Women," later expanded to book-length form and published in 1845 under the title *Woman in the Nineteenth Century.* The original *Dial* essay, reprinted here, is a more tightly argued and powerful version of her hortatory invocation to free men and women from the social roles in which they have been trapped, although it lacks many of the book's scholarly allusions to women in history, mythology, and poetry. In both versions, however, Fuller uses what was even then the conventional analogy between the woman and the slave. At a time when the moral fervor surrounding abolition had increased dramatically, such rhetorical strategies proved particularly effective, if also controversial. Fuller's writing on women's issues helped inspire the reforms and clarify the agenda for political action proposed at the Seneca Falls conference on that subject in 1848.

Fuller resigned as the sole editor of *The Dial* after the July 1842 issue, but she continued to help Emerson edit the journal until it ceased publication in April 1844. Fuller's increasingly ambivalent attitude toward what she regarded as the inconsistent positions of the Transcendentalists was reflected in her changing attitude toward Emerson. Despite her considerable affection for him, she came to realize, for example, that his commitment to developing the self should have led him to be more interested in current social and political issues. And while she praised Emerson's "high tendency, absolute purity," she also recognized the limitations of their relationship. "I was, indeed, always called on to be worthy," she said. "He absolutely distrusted me in every region of my life with which he was unacquainted. The same trait I detected in his relations with others. He had faith in the Universal, but not in the Individual Man; he met men, not as a brother, but as a critic."

Emerson's view of their relationship was equally ambivalent. Her contemporaries contemptuously referred to her as "mountainous me," a phrase derived from Emerson's well-circulated (and perhaps apocryphal) account of her own self-estimate: "I now know all the people worth knowing in America, and I find no intellect comparable to my own." Emerson, like many of his contemporaries, failed to remember that Margaret Fuller was a brilliant, feisty woman struggling for intellectual recognition in the male-dominated literary world of mid-nineteenth-century America. At a time when women were hardly encouraged to develop an active role in the new nation's culture, she was repeatedly made to think that the problem was hers and not the culture's.

Margaret Fuller's perspective on American culture broadened considerably when she accompanied her friend James Freeman Clarke and his wife, Sarah, on a trip to the Midwest in 1843. Her journal entries during that excursion form the basis for *Summer on the Lakes* (1844). The book is an intellectual miscellany, consisting of sketches, poetry, and brief translations, as well as excerpts from the books she had been reading, along with a critical commentary on each. The newspaper publisher and editor Horace Greeley called it "one of the best works in the department ever issued from the American press." It also provided Henry David Thoreau with a convenient model for a similar compilation, *A Week on the Concord and Merrimack Rivers* (1849).

Horace Greeley's appreciation of *Summer on the Lakes* prompted him to offer Fuller a job as the literary critic for his newspaper, the *New York Tribune*. In December 1844 Fuller moved to New York to work as the first female writer on that prominent newspaper's staff. The reflective pace of editing *The Dial* quickly yielded to daily deadlines, yet Fuller took great pleasure in her work; it provided her, she noted, with "a more various view of life than any I ever before was in."

Fuller wrote literary criticism distinguished by her breadth of learning and her uncompromising standards. Her unfavorable reviews of such figures as James Russell Lowell and Henry Wadsworth Longfellow offended Boston's literary Brahmins and caused Lowell to satirize her severely in "A Fable for Critics." Yet her essays on the most durable features of the literature of that time gained her the respect of most other writers and readers, including Edgar Allan Poe, who praised her intellectual rigor and freedom from partisanship, although he, like many others, criticized her syntactic and stylistic faults.

The focus of her work gradually shifted from literary reviews to social criticism. Fuller tackled controversial public issues with great verve, exposing, for example, official neglect of such mid-nineteenth-century misfits as the blind and the insane; she also called attention to the abuses of female prisoners in New York. In 1846 she published *Papers on Literature and Art,* a collection of essays hastily assembled in the weeks preceding her eagerly anticipated departure for Europe, where she would serve as a foreign correspondent for Greeley's *Tribune.*

Soon after her arrival in Europe, Fuller met Thomas Carlyle, the renowned English writer; before leaving London, Fuller also met Giuseppe Mazzini, the Italian patriot and republican revolutionary, who sparked her interest in political action. In Paris she met the novelist George Sand and Adam Mickiewicz, a Polish émigré writer who espoused revolutionary causes. Attracted to the revolutionary ferment sweeping across Europe, Fuller traveled in 1847 to Italy, then a very unsteady alignment of independent as well as papal and Austrian-controlled states. She regularly dispatched reports to the *Tribune* on the unification efforts of Mazzini and Giuseppe Garibaldi.

In the midst of this fast-paced period in Italy, Margaret Fuller met—and eventually married—Giovanni Angelo Ossoli, an aristocratic Italian (a marquis) sympathetic to the revolutionary effort. She gave birth to a son, Angelo, in September 1848, but her writing and political action continued unabated.

By her own account, Fuller's stay in Europe helped her recognize the limitations of her liberal social conscience. At the same time that the *Communist Manifesto* was being published in London, Fuller was acting on her newly articulated belief that socialism would change the world and fulfill the promise of American democracy. Within a few months of Garibaldi's arrival in Rome and his declaration of the Roman Republic, France lay siege to the city on behalf of papal interests. Fuller served as the director of a hospital on an island in the Tiber River. When Rome fell to the French on July 4, 1849, she led her family to Florence, where, with the encouragement of Robert and Elizabeth Barrett Browning, Fuller began gathering information and anecdotes and drafting a history of the Italian revolution. That work was never completed. In dire need of money, Margaret Fuller, her husband, and son boarded a ship bound for the United States. On July 19, 1850, that ship sank off the Long Island coast at Fire Island, and all three perished.

Margaret Fuller's life and work offer ample evidence of the "cost," to use Thoreau's term, of being a productive woman in mid-nineteenth-century America. Unable to control what Hawthorne had described as her "unpliable" nature when she was among them, Fuller's friends reinterpreted her life in her *Memoirs*. The highly bowdlerized life recreated by James Freeman Clarke, W. H. Channing, and Ralph Waldo Emerson buried the aspects of her past that they regarded as radical.

Only recently has scholarship begun to recover the complexities of her identity and work. She talked of the anguish of being regarded as "either a genius or a character. . . . I love but to be a woman; but womanhood is at present too strait-bounded to give me scope. At hours, I live truly as a woman; at others, I should stifle; as, on the other hand, I should palsy, when I would play the artist." Her work expresses one of the nation's most articulate early views of women's rights, and her literary criticism helped identify and clarify the strengths and weaknesses of American writing of her time. Hers was an original and influential voice in American literature. Soon after her death, Emerson confided to his journal that "I have lost in her my audience." Henry James acknowledged in his later years that Margaret Fuller "still unmistakably walks the passages" of his novels. And, given the recent interest in her prose, the real extent of her influence may well surface in the next generations of writers who read her work.

Further Reading:

W. H. Channing, J. F. Clarke, and R. W. Emerson, *Memoirs of Margaret Fuller Ossoli,* 1852.
M. Wade, *Margaret Fuller, Whetstone of Genius,* 1940.
J. J. Deiss, *The Roman Years of Margaret Fuller,* 1969.
B. G. Chevigny, *The Woman and the Myth: Margaret Fuller's Life and Writings,* 1976.
J. Myerson, *Margaret Fuller: An Annotated Bibliography,* 1977.
M. V. Allen, *The Achievement of Margaret Fuller,* 1979.
M. O. Urbanski, *Margaret Fuller's* Woman of the Nineteenth Century: *A Literary Study of Form and Content, of Sources and Influences,* 1980.
J. Myerson, *Critical Essays on Margaret Fuller,* 1980.

D. Watson, *Margaret Fuller: An American Romantic,* 1988.
C. Balducci, *Margaret Fuller: A Life of Passion and Defiance,* 1991.
L. J. Reynolds and S. B. Smith, eds., *"These Sad But Glorious Days": Dispatches from Europe, 1846–1850,* 1991.
M. B. Stern, *The Life of Margaret Fuller,* rev. 2nd ed., 1991.
C. Capper, *Margaret Fuller: An American Romantic Life,* 1992.
D. Dickenson, *Margaret Fuller: Writing a Woman's Life,* 1993.

Texts:

"American Literature: Its Position in the Present Time, and Prospects for the Future" from *Papers on Literature and Art,* 1846.

See also *Letters of Margaret Fuller,* ed. R. N. Hudspeth, 6 vols., 1983–1995.

American Literature

Its Position in the Present Time, and Prospects for the Future

Some thinkers may object to this essay, that we are about to write of that which has as yet no existence.

For it does not follow because many books are written by persons born in America that there exists an American literature. Books which imitate or represent the thoughts and life of Europe do not constitute an American literature. Before such can exist, an original idea must animate this nation and fresh currents of life must call into life fresh thoughts along its shores.

We have no sympathy with national vanity. We are not anxious to prove that there is as yet much American literature. Of those who think and write among us in the methods and of the thoughts of Europe, we are not impatient; if their minds are still best adapted to such food and such action. If their books express life of mind and character in graceful forms, they are good and we like them. We consider them as colonists and useful schoolmasters to our people in a transition state; which lasts rather longer than is occupied in passing bodily the ocean which separates the New from the Old World.

We have been accused of an undue attachment to foreign continental literature, and it is true that in childhood we had well nigh "forgotten our English" while constantly reading in other languages. Still what we loved in the literature of continental Europe was the range and force of ideal manifestation in forms of national and individual greatness. A model was before us in the great Latins of simple masculine minds seizing upon life with unbroken power. The stamp both of nationality and individuality was very strong upon them; their lives and thoughts stood out in clear and bold relief. The English character has the iron force of the Latins, but not the frankness and expansion. Like their fruits, they need a summer sky to give them more sweetness and a richer flavor. This does not apply to Shakespeare, who has all the fine side of English genius, with the rich coloring and more fluent life of the Catholic countries. Other poets of England also are expansive more or less, and soar freely to seek the blue sky, but take it as a whole, there is in English literature, as in English character, a reminiscence of walls and ceilings, a tendency to the arbitrary and conventional that repels a mind trained in admiration of the antique spirit. It is only in later days that we are learning to prize the peculiar greatness which a thousand times outweighs this fault, and which has enabled English genius to go forth from its insular position and conquer such vast dominion in the realms both of matter and of mind.

Yet there is often between child and parent a reaction from excessive influence having been exerted, and such a one we have experienced in behalf of our country against England. We use her language and receive in torrents the influence of her thought, yet it is in many respects uncongenial and injurious to our constitution. What suits Great Britain, with her insular position and consequent need to concentrate and intensify her life, her limited monarchy and spirit of trade, does not suit a mixed race continually enriched with new blood from other stocks the most unlike that of our first descent, with ample field and verge enough to range in and leave every impulse free, and abundant opportunity to develop a genius wide and full as our rivers, flowery, luxuriant, and impassioned as our vast prairies, rooted in strength as the rocks on which the Puritan fathers landed.

That such a genius is to rise and work in this hemisphere we are confident; equally so that scarce the first faint streaks of that day's dawn are yet visible. It is sad for those that foresee, to know they may not live to share its glories, yet it is sweet, too, to know that every act and word uttered in the light of that foresight may tend to hasten or ennoble its fulfillment.

That day will not rise till the fusion of races among us is more complete. It will not rise till this nation shall attain sufficient moral and intellectual dignity to prize moral and intellectual no less highly than political freedom, not till the physical resources of the country being explored, all its regions studded with towns, broken by the plow, netted together by railways and telegraph lines, talent shall be left at leisure to turn its energies upon the higher department of man's existence. Nor then shall it be seen till from the leisurely and yearning soul of that riper time national ideas shall take birth, ideas craving to be clothed in a thousand fresh and original forms.

Without such ideas all attempts to construct a national literature must end in abortions like the monster of Frankenstein, things with forms and the instincts of forms, but soulless and therefore revolting. We cannot have expression till there is something to be expressed.

The symptoms of such a birth may be seen in a longing felt here and there for the sustenance of such ideas. At present it shows itself, where felt, in sympathy with the prevalent tone of society by attempts at external action, such as are classed under the head of social reform. But it needs to go deeper before we can have poets, needs to penetrate beneath the springs of action, to stir and remake the soil as by the action of fire.

Another symptom is the need felt by individuals of being even sternly sincere. This is the one great means by which alone progress can be essentially furthered. Truth is the nursing mother of genius. No man can be absolutely true to himself, eschewing cant, compromise, servile imitation, and complaisance, without becoming original, for there is in every creature a fountain of life which, if not choked back by stones and other dead rubbish, will create a fresh atmosphere and bring to life fresh beauty. And it is the same with the nation as with the individual man.

The best work we do for the future is by such truth. By use of that in what-ever way, we harrow the soil and lay it open to the sun and air. The winds from all quarters of the globe bring seed enough, and there is nothing wanting but preparation of the soil and freedom in the atmosphere, for ripening of a new and golden harvest.

We are sad that we cannot be present at the gathering-in of this harvest. And yet we are joyous too, when we think that though our name may not be writ on the pillar of our country's fame, we can really do far more towards rearing it than those who come at a later period and to a seemingly fairer task. *Now*, the humblest effort, made in a noble spirit and with religious hope, cannot fail to be even infinitely useful. Whether we introduce some noble model from another time and clime to encourage aspiration in our own, or cheer into blossom the simplest wood-flower that ever rose from the earth, moved by the genuine impulse to grow, independent of the lures of money or celebrity; whether we speak boldly when fear or doubt keep others silent, or refuse to swell the popular cry upon an unworthy occasion, the spirit of truth, purely worshiped, shall turn our acts and forbearances alike to profit, informing them with oracles which the latest time shall bless.

Under present circumstances the amount of talent and labor given to writing ought to surprise us. Literature is in this dim and struggling state, and its pecuniary results exceedingly pitiful. From many well-known causes it is impossible for ninety-nine out of the hundred who wish to use the pen to ransom by its use the time they need. This state of things will have to be changed in some way. No man of genius writes for money; but it is essential to the free use of his powers that he should be able to disembarrass his life from care and perplexity. This is very difficult here; and the state of things gets worse and worse, as less and less is offered in pecuniary meed for works demanding great devotion of time and labor (to say nothing of the ether engaged) and the publisher, obliged to regard the transaction as a matter of business, demands of the author to give him only what will find an immediate market, for he cannot afford to take anything else. This will not do! When an immortal poet was secure only of a few copyists to circulate his works, there were princes and nobles to patronize literature and the arts. Here is only the public, and the public must learn how to cherish the nobler and rarer plants, and to plant the aloe, able to wait a hundred years for its bloom, or its garden will contain presently nothing but potatoes and pot-herbs. We shall have in the course of the next two or three years a convention of authors to inquire into the causes of this state of things and propose measures for its remedy. Some have already been thought of that look promising, but we shall not announce them till the time be ripe; that date is not distant, for the difficulties increase from day to day in consequence of the system of cheap publication on a great scale.

The ranks that led the way in the first half century of this republic were far better situated than we, in this respect. The country was not so deluged with the dingy page reprinted from Europe, and patriotic vanity was on the alert to answer the question, "Who reads an American book?" And many were the books written as worthy to be read as any out of the first class in England. They were, most of them, except in their subject matter, English books.

The list is large, and in making some cursory comments we do not wish to be understood as designating *all* who are worthy of notice, but only those who present themselves to our minds with some special claims.

In the department of ethics and philosophy we may inscribe two names as likely to live and be blessed and honored in the later time. These are the names of Channing[1] and of Emerson.

Dr. Channing had several leading thoughts which corresponded with the wants of his time, and have made him in it a father of thought. His leading idea of the "dignity of human nature" is one of vast results, and the peculiar form in which he advocated it had a great work to do in this new world. The spiritual beauty of his writings is very great; they are all distinguished for sweetness, elevation, candor, and a severe devotion to truth. On great questions he took middle ground and sought a panoramic view; he wished also to stand high, yet never forgot what was above more than what was around and beneath him. He was not well acquainted with man on the impulsive and passionate side of his nature, so that his view of character was sometimes narrow, but it was always noble. He exercised an expansive and purifying power on the atmosphere, and stands a godfather at the baptism of this country.

[1] William Ellery Channing (1780–1842), clergyman and founder of Unitarianism.

The Sage of Concord[2] has a very different mind, in everything except that he has the same disinterestedness and dignity of purpose, the same purity of spirit. He is a profound thinker. He is a man of ideas, and deals with causes rather than effects. His ideas are illustrated from a wide range of literary culture and refined observation, and embodied in a style whose melody and subtle fragrance enchant those who stand stupefied before the thoughts themselves, because their utmost depths do not enable them to sound his shallows. His influence does not yet extend over a wide space; he is too far beyond his place and his time to be felt at once or in full, but it searches deep, and yearly widens its circles. He is a harbinger of the better day. His beautiful elocution has been a great aid to him in opening the way for the reception of his written word.

In that large department of literature which includes descriptive sketches, whether of character or scenery, we are already rich. Irving,[3] a genial and fair nature, just what he ought to be and would have been at any time of the world, has drawn the scenes amid which his youth was spent in their primitive lineaments, with all the charms of his graceful jocund humor. He has his niche and need never be deposed; it is not one that another could occupy.

The first enthusiasm about Cooper[4] having subsided, we remember more his faults than his merits. His ready resentment and way of showing it in cases which it is the wont of gentlemen to pass by in silence or meet with a good-humored smile have caused unpleasant associations with his name, and his fellow-citizens, in danger of being tormented by suits for libel if they spoke freely of him, have ceased to speak of him at all. But neither these causes, nor the baldness of his plots, shallowness of thought, and poverty in the presentation of character, should make us forget the grandeur and originality of his sea-sketches, nor the redemption from oblivion of our forest-scenery, and the noble romance of the hunter-pioneer's life. Already, but for him, this fine page of life's romance would be almost forgotten. He has done much to redeem these irrevocable beauties from the corrosive acid of a semi-civilized invasion.

[2] Title bestowed on Ralph Waldo Emerson as a resident of Concord, Massachusetts.

[3] Washington Irving (1783–1859), American writer.

[4] James Fenimore Cooper (1789–1851). The following is Fuller's note: "Since writing the above we have read some excellent remarks by Mr. W. G. Simms on the writings of Cooper. We think the reasons are given for the powerful interest excited by Hawkeye and the Pilot, with great discrimination and force. 'They both think and feel, with a highly individual nature, that has been taught, by constant contemplation, in scenes of solitude. The vast unbroken ranges of forest to its one lonely occupant press upon the mind with the same sort of solemnity which one feels condemned to a life of partial isolation upon the ocean. Both are permitted that degree of commerce with their fellow beings, which suffices to maintain in strength the sweet and sacred sources of their humanity. . . . The very isolation to which, in the most successful of his stories, Mr. Cooper subjects his favorite personages, is, alone, a proof of his strength and genius. While the ordinary writer, the man of mere talent, is compelled to look around him among masses for his material, he contents himself with one man, and flings him upon the wilderness. The picture, then, which follows, must be one of intense individuality. Out of this one man's nature, his moods and fortunes, he spins his story. The agencie and dependencies are few. With self-reliance which is only found in true genius, he goes forward into the wilderness, whether of land or ocean; and the vicissitudes of either region, acting upon the natural resources of one man's mind, furnish the whole material of his work-shop. This mode of performance is highly dramatic, and thus it is that his scout, his trapper, his hunter, his pilot, all live to our eyes and thoughts, the perfect ideals of moral individuality.' "

What shall we say of the poets? The list is scanty; amazingly so, for there is nothing in the causes that paralyze other kinds of literature that could affect lyrical and narrative poetry. Men's hearts beat, hope, and suffer always, and they must crave such means to vent them; yet of the myriad leaves garnished with smooth, stereotyped rhymes that issue yearly from our press, you will not find, one time in a million, a little piece written from any such impulse or with the least sincerity or sweetness of tone. They are written for the press in the spirit of imitation or vanity, the paltriest offspring of the human brain, for the heart disclaims, as the ear is shut against them. This is the kind of verse which is cherished by the magazines as a correspondent to the tawdry pictures of smiling milliners' dolls in the frontispiece. Like these they are only a fashion, a fashion based on no reality of love or beauty. The inducement to write them consists in a little money, or more frequently the charm of seeing an anonymous name printed at the top in capitals.

At their head Mr. Bryant[5] stands alone. His range is not great, nor his genius fertile. But his poetry is purely the language of his inmost nature, and the simple lovely garb in which his thoughts are arranged, a direct gift from the Muse. He has written nothing that is not excellent, and the atmosphere of his verse refreshes and composes the mind, like leaving the highway to enter some green lovely fragrant wood.

Longfellow[6] is artificial and imitative. He borrows incessantly, and mixes what he borrows, so that it does not appear to the best advantage. He is very faulty in using broken or mixed metaphors. The ethical part of his writing has a hollow, secondhand sound. He has, however, elegance, a love of the beautiful, and a fancy for what is large and manly, if not a full sympathy with it. His verse breathes at times much sweetness; and if not allowed to supersede what is better, may promote a taste for good poetry. Though imitative, he is not mechanical.

We cannot say as much for Lowell,[7] who, we must declare it, though to the grief of some friends and the disgust of more, is absolutely wanting in the true spirit and tone of poesy. His interest in the moral questions of the day has supplied the want of vitality in himself; his great facility at versification has enabled him to fill the ear with a copious stream of pleasant sound. But his verse is stereotyped; his thought sounds no depth; and posterity will not remember him.

R. W. Emerson, in melody, in subtle beauty of thought and expression, takes the highest rank upon this list. But his poems are mostly philosophical, which is not the truest kind of poetry. They want the simple force of nature and passion, and while they charm the ear and interest the mind, fail to wake far-off echoes in the heart. The imagery wears a symbolical air, and serves rather as illustration than to delight us by fresh and glowing forms of life.

Meanwhile the most important part of our literature, while the work of diffusion is still going on, lies in the journals which monthly, weekly, daily send their messages to every corner of this great land, and form at present the only efficient instrument for the general education of the people.

Among these, the magazines take the lowest rank. Their object is principally to cater for the amusement of vacant hours, and as there is not a great deal of wit and light talent in this country, they do not even this to much advantage. More wit, grace, and elegant trifling embellish the annals of literature in one day of France than in a year of America.

---

[5] William Cullen Bryant (1794–1878).   [7] James Russell Lowell (1819–1891).
[6] Henry Wadsworth Longfellow (1807–1882).

The reviews are more able. If they cannot compare on equal terms with those of France, England, and Germany, where if genius be rare, at least a vast amount of talent and culture is brought to bear upon all the departments of knowledge, they are yet very creditable to a new country where so large a portion of manly ability must be bent on making laws, making speeches, making railroads and canals. They are, however, much injured by a partisan spirit and the fear of censure from their own public. This last is always slow death to a journal; its natural and only safe position is to *lead;* if instead it bows to the will of the multitude, it will find the ostracism of democracy far more dangerous than the worst censure of a tyranny could be. It is not half so dangerous to a man to be immured in a dungeon alone with God and his own clear conscience as to walk the streets fearing the scrutiny of a thousand eyes, ready to veil with anxious care whatever may not suit the many-headed monster in its momentary mood. Gentleness is dignified but caution is debasing; only a noble fearlessness can give wings to the mind, with which to soar beyond the common ken and learn what may be of use to the crowd below. Writers have nothing to do but to love truth fervently, seek justice according to their ability, and then express what is in the mind; they have nothing to do with consequences, God will take care of those. The want of such noble courage, such faith in the power of truth and good desire, paralyzes mind greatly in this country. Publishers are afraid; authors are afraid; and if a worthy resistance is not made by religious souls, there is danger that all the light will soon be put under bushels, lest some wind should waft from it a spark that may kindle dangerous fire.

For want of such faith, and the catholic spirit that flows from it, we have no great leading review. The *North American* was once the best. While under the care of Edward Everett,[8] himself a host in extensive knowledge, grace and adroitness in applying it, and the power of enforcing grave meanings by a light and flexible satire that tickled while it wounded, it boasted more force, more life, a finer scope of power. But now though still exhibiting ability and information upon special points, it is entirely deficient in great leadings and the *vivida vis,*[9] but ambles and jogs at an old gentlemanly pace along a beaten path that leads to no important goal.

Several other journals have more life, energy, and directness than this, but there is none which occupies a truly great and commanding position, a beacon-light to all who sail that way. In order to do this, a journal must know how to cast aside all local and temporary considerations when new convictions command, and allow free range in its columns to all kinds of ability and all ways of viewing subjects. That would give it a life rich, bold, various.

The life of intellect is becoming more and more determined to the weekly and daily papers, whose light leaves fly so rapidly and profusely over the land. Speculations are afloat as to the influence of the electric telegraph upon their destiny, and it seems obvious that it should raise their character by taking from them in some measure the office of gathering and dispersing the news, and requiring of them rather to arrange and interpret it.

This mode of communication is susceptible of great excellence in the way of condensed essay, narrative, criticism, and is the natural receptacle for the lyrics of the day. That so few good ones deck the poet's corner, is because the indifference or unfitness of

---

[8] Everett (1794–1865) was editor of *The North American Review* (1815–1821).   [9] Latin: "living force."

editors as to choosing and refusing makes this place at present undesirable to the poet. It might be otherwise.

The means which this organ affords of diffusing knowledge and sowing the seeds of thought where they may hardly fail of an infinite harvest, cannot be too highly prized by the discerning and benevolent. Minds of the first class are generally indisposed to this kind of writing; what must be done on the spur of the occasion and cast into the world so incomplete, as the hurried offspring of a day or hour's labor must generally be, cannot satisfy their judgment or do justice to their powers. But he who looks to the benefit of others and sees with what rapidity and ease instruction and thought are assimilated by men, when they come thus as it were on the wings of the wind, may be content, as an unhonored servant to the grand purposes of Destiny, to work in such a way at the Pantheon[10] which the ages shall complete, on which his name may not be inscribed but which will breathe the life of his soul.

The confidence in uprightness of intent and the safety of truth is still more needed here than in the more elaborate kinds of writing, as meanings cannot be fully explained nor expressions revised. Newspaper-writing is next door to conversation, and should be conducted on the same principles. It has this advantage: we address not our neighbor, who forces us to remember his limitations and prejudices, but the ideal presence of human nature as we feel it ought to be and trust it will be. We address America rather than Americans.

We see we have omitted honored names in this essay. We have not spoken of Brown,[11] as a novelist by far our first in point of genius and instruction as to the soul of things. Yet his works have fallen almost out of print. It is their dark deep gloom that prevents their being popular, for their very beauties are grave and sad. But we see that *Ormond* is being republished at this moment. The picture of Roman character, of the life and resources of a single noble creature, of Constantia alone, should make that book an object of reverence. All these novels should be republished; if not favorites, they should at least not be lost sight of, for there will always be some who find in such powers of mental analysis the only response to their desires.

We have not spoken of Hawthorne,[12] the best writer of the day, in a similar range with Irving, only touching many more points and discerning far more deeply. But we have omitted many things in this slight sketch, for the subject even in this stage lies as a volume in our mind, and cannot be unrolled in completeness unless time and space were more abundant. Our object was to show that although by a thousand signs the existence is foreshown of those forces which are to animate an American literature, that faith, those hopes are not yet alive which shall usher it into a homogeneous or fully organized state of being. The future is glorious with certainties for those who do their duty in the present, and larklike, seeking the sun, challenge its eagles to an earthward flight, where their nests may be built in our mountains, and their young raise their cry of triumph unchecked by dullness in the echoes.

1846

---

[10] Greek or Roman temple of the gods.

[11] Charles Brockden Brown (1771–1810), American novelist.

[12] Nathaniel Hawthorne (1804–1864).

Edgar Allan Poe
1809–1849

There seems to be enough of Edgar Allan Poe to go around to please, or to exasperate, almost everyone. The title of Daniel Hoffman's famous study of the writer visually represents this fact: *Poe, Poe, Poe, Poe, Poe, Poe, Poe.* As Hoffman observes, there emerges from the writings "a surrogate for all of Poe's readers"—the private "I" that each of us adds to, and discovers in, the shadows cast by the tales and the poems. There is the Poe whose horror stories scared us when we were fourteen and whom we are supposed to grow away from in our maturity; but there is also the Poe whose thoughts on personal epistemologies (what we know) and cosmic ontologies (what is real) awe us with their seeming profundity. There is the dissolute wastrel portrayed by Poe's first biographers—and in part by Poe himself, in the stories he spread. There is also the helpless genius who needed lots of mothering, as put forward in the swooning remembrances of the various maternal figures with which he filled his life. There is the truth sayer on the absolutes of poetry and beauty, and the diddler who took his revenge on the stupidity of his contemporaries by making fools of them for falling for his cunningly wrought hoaxes. There is the creator of the detective Dupin, whom American mystery buffs claim as the originator of "their kind" of story, the poet whom the French appropriate as the true representative of Gallic culture, and the Gothicist whom the South likes to have share its own exile from mainstream Yankee literature. Poe comes to us as drug-sodden madman or as the cool possessor of a computerlike brain that would today move him into the executive suites of IBM. He is the anarchist self we flaunt, to the extent of welcoming death when wanting to rebel against the boring routines that limit the soul. But he is also the person who sits in his dull little office as dutiful editor and reviewer, moving all his papers into the out basket. He is Poe the incomplete poet, or the precursor of the French Symbolists. He is the cheap comedown from "good" writing, or the St. John the Baptist who announces the arrival of the modern short story and short poem.

Perhaps only two warnings are in order when we approach Poe's writings, which we tend to turn into litmus tests for our own multiple selves: not to make Poe too dull (coming to him through pedantry) and not to make him too exciting (getting at him through pathology, since even the act of sensationalizing his life and writings makes them collapse boringly in on themselves).

Neat little résumés are difficult to produce when it comes to the facts of Poe's life and the development of his career as poet, writer of tales, editor, and literary critic. Too many biographers have intervened since he was found near death in a Baltimore street on an October night in 1849. But certain details have been sorted out from the slanders that attack and the legends that extol. Even so, every "normal" fact—such as his birth in Boston on January 19, 1809—is matched by something unsettling. His parents were wandering actors, members of a disreputable profession; his drunkard father decamped and his mother died by the time the child was two. Elizabeth Arnold Poe happened to die while on tour in Richmond, and when the infant Edgar and an older brother were placed with whoever would agree to care for them, a well-to-do merchant of the city, John Allan, took charge of Edgar Poe. All went well enough for the first twenty years. Although never legally adopted by the Allans, their young ward accompanied them on their travels to England (where Poe attended school) and back again to the upper-class education and social expectations of a well-bred Richmond family. But Poe's status in the Allan household was an uncertain one. He was unable to forget how shameful his antecedents were. Friction developed between Poe and John Allan—perhaps as the result of Allan's jealousy over his wife's fondness for the boy or of Poe's reluctance to go into Allan's tobacco export business. Then again, it could have been his precociously romantic involvements with several young women of his set or the gambling debts he accumulated during his year at the University of Virginia that set him at odds with his guardian.

By 1827 the tensions were too great to bear. Poe left Richmond and went to Boston, where he published with his own funds his first collection, *Tamerlane and Other Poems,* signed simply "A Bostonian." Then he vanished for a short period into the army under the pseudonym Edgar A. Perry. A brief truce between Poe and John Allan led to his discharge from the regulars and an appointment to West Point in July 1830, less than a year after the appearance of his second volume, *Al Aaraaf, Tamerlane, and Minor Poems.* Poe did not stay at West Point long. He found that he disliked the regimen and lacked the necessary allowance from John Allan that would let him live like both an officer and a gentleman. Deliberately flaunting rules about class attendance, he encouraged his own dismissal.

Meanwhile matters had again become ugly at home. The young man wished to have his position as a "son" clarified, and John Allan refused to give him that satisfaction. Allan's first wife died, and he remarried. The new wife bore him twin sons, then became pregnant again almost immediately. By the time Poe left West Point after seven months at the Academy, he realized there was no chance for him ever to be named the Allan heir; the break was complete. He was totally on his own at the age of twenty-two.

In May 1831, Poe's friends at West Point provided him with the money he needed to publish *Poems,* dedicated to "the U.S. Corps of Cadets." This collection included revisions of earlier poems and the addition of the first and best versions of "To Helen" and "Israfel." Poe decided that writing would obviously have to be the way he would earn his living and to make a "name" for himself, now that he had been denied the name Allan and the social identity of a Virginia gentleman and West Point officer. But writing poems that appeared in "little collections" was an avocation for men of independent means, not the way to lift a poor man set adrift in the shark-rich seas of an American society more interested in rewarding tobacco merchants than brilliant young poets.

Poe launched himself as an editor, a career that would sustain him, but not very well, until his death eighteen years later. He first went to Baltimore, where he lived between 1831 and 1835 with relatives from his father's side of the family. Foremost among these were his aunt, who became one of a series of "mothers" he needed to offset his lack of true "fathers," and his aunt's young daughter Virginia, whom Poe married by 1836, when she was fourteen. This threesome lived together in poverty, with Poe working with exceptional vigor.

Five of his first stories appeared in a Philadelphia newspaper during 1832. In 1833 "MS Found in a Bottle" won first prize in a story contest run by a Baltimore paper. Tales written for publication in the popular press in those days were governed by the particular demands of newspaper space and the need to achieve immediate impact; these were formulas Poe mastered quickly. By 1835, at twenty-six, he had sufficient reputation as a writer of popular fiction to win the assistant editorship of the *Southern Literary Messenger* in Richmond, but he did not keep the job long. He performed his editorial duties brilliantly, but emotionally he could not stay the course or keep his peace with the owners. The same sarcasm that gained welcome notoriety for the magazine from the reviews he wrote did not endear him to his associates. Bouts of drinking recommenced. He was fired. He had to move quickly.

He spent a few months in New York, where Harper's published his novel *The Narrative of Arthur Gordon Pym* in 1838, to no financial or critical advantage. He moved to Philadelphia in 1839. Living for a time on a diet of bread and molasses and constantly on the edge of total discouragement, Poe worked on. "Ligeia" was only the first of the major stories he wrote in 1839. In 1842 Virginia sickened with tuberculosis (she would die at twenty-five), and Poe tried—unsuccessfully—to start a magazine of his own. But his reputation was advancing. Few readers could overlook the quality—or quantity—of his editorial writing, his critical reviews, his poems, and his stories of great impact. *Tales of the Grotesque and Arabesque* were collected in two volumes in 1840, and "The Gold Bug" won fame and the top prize of one hundred dollars in a contest sponsored by a Philadelphia newspaper.

In 1844 Poe took Virginia and his faithful aunt with him to New York, where they subsisted on the fees he earned from work on various papers and magazines. His drinking increased, gossip circulated about his eccentric behavior with various sentimental ladies who encouraged his attentions, and his sniping attacks on the literary follies he found everywhere in American letters made him the target of further vilification. Yet 1845 was a vintage year for Poe's literary career. "The Raven" appeared, and the stir it caused resulted in his giving lectures on poetry, being named the lead reviewer for the *Broadway Journal,* and being mentioned favorably by James Russell Lowell, the foremost critic of the period. Poe said proudly of "The Raven" (referring to the prize "The Gold Bug" had won him), "The bird beat the bug . . . all hollow." He made influential literary friends, and this led to the publication of *The Raven and Other Poems* by the prestigious publishing house of Wiley and Putnam. He purchased the *Broadway Journal* on credit, with the hope that the lift brought by his recent fame would bring financial success. However, by early 1846 the *Journal* had gone under, and by January 1847 Virginia was dead. What had never been a steady life now became an accelerating series of personal crises and professional disappointments.

Writing still, as ever under the compulsion to get down everything that filled his brain, Poe overextended himself even more. Despair over the loss of one's beloved, revenge on one's enemies, and exaltation over the final unification of consciousness with the cosmos—these were the themes Poe worked over in these final pieces. By now his activities were frenetic. He told tales of attempted suicides and of murder plots against his life; he gave lectures and readings of his work; he signed into a temperance group; he revisited the Richmond of his childhood. Suddenly it was over in October of 1849. On his way to Philadelphia for an editing job, he got off the train in Baltimore. He was found unconscious a few days later in the street. He died in a hospital on October 7 and was buried in Baltimore.

Poe was hardly in his grave before his biographers began to "create" a life for him. (That grave, incidently, remained unmarked for twenty-six years; when in 1875 a tombstone was placed there, the only literary representative present was Walt Whitman.) From then on, critics, editors, and biographers have continued re-creating Poe after the images that most satisfied their own imaginations. But whether Poe was seen as a demon or as a misunderstood genius, the effect was to serve up one version or other of the Byronic hero—the most serviceable romantic image of the poet that lay at hand.

Critics and poets as sophisticated as Baudelaire, Mallarmé, and Valéry transformed Poe into an "honorary" Frenchman and Symbolist poet, thereby accomplishing a double task: an attack on the bourgeois mentality of their own countrymen for its insensitivity to the poetic soul and an excoriation of the philistine qualities they associated with the American democratic system. In his own country, Poe was as much chastised for his literary failings as for his personal life. Emerson emerged long enough from the mental fog of his later years to characterize Poe as "the jingle man." In his memoirs, Henry James vividly recalled the excitement he and his brother William felt as boys waiting to snatch from the postman the latest issues of the magazines that contained Poe's horror tales. But James also registered his disapproval of adults who continued to take pleasure in a man whose writings were not sufficiently "about something." Mark Twain, D. H. Lawrence, and T. S. Eliot were also less than charitable about Poe's literary achievements. Yet through it all, Poe has been read and absorbed by almost everyone in this country, on the Continent, and in England. The roster of well-known poets and writers of fiction who have admitted the ways in which Poe's writing has colored their own imaginations is impressive. Critics of every literary persuasion find his works an inexhaustible field for cultivation. Most of all, people read Poe and respond to him with an enthusiasm that has little to do with the rise and fall of his critical status. What seems clearer these days is the nature of Poe's literary contributions. With a total of only forty-eight poems (many of them turned out at the jingle level that Emerson referred to), Poe pointed the way toward a new kind of Symbolist poetry, verses that evoke mood rather than meaning, that call attention to their own technique, and that celebrate experimentation for its own sake.

With his horror tales, Poe took over—and, in some of his best examples, transcended—the Gothic formula that had been supplying thrills to readers of popular literature for some time. Poe is credited with inventing the detective story, a form that juxtaposes the threat of anarchy (outrageous crimes whose violence and unfathomable causes upset the stability of society) with a mix of the rational (mental coolness and the application of mathematical logic) and the intuitive (emotional reactions to the illogicality of events). Poe's stories of trips to the moon, as well as his musings about the evolution and consummation of the cosmos (whether taken straight or as hoax), extended the possibilities of science fiction. Psychological literature got a boost by his tales of alter egos and outlawed urges that stalk his characters' minds. He had inherited the tradition of the romance that located terror in outward places; he relocated it, as he announced, in the soul but Poe gave the American short story form the base from which it moved toward true accomplishment.

Difficulties abound, however, in the interpretation given both to the meaning of Poe's individual works and to his literary intentions. It is difficult to know whether a particular poem or story originated from an excess of feverish emotion or from calculated designs on the reader's imagination, whether it was done as a hoax or offered in sober earnestness. Much of Poe's work exists teasingly between two poles. Critics who like to tidy things up are frustrated when they find it impossible to say whether "The Fall of the House of Usher" is a bona fide tale of horror or the parody of one, or whether the decor in the tower room in "Ligeia" is intentionally vulgar or the result of the innate verbal kitsch of a man whose own tastes were deplorably déclassé. We know that Poe could work with extreme calculation to arouse his readers' feelings. His essay "The Philosophy of Composition" reveals the clever means by which the writer can manipulate responses. But then, perhaps this essay is at the same time an exercise in leg-pulling, a way of disguising the urgency Poe felt to express his strongest passions about his literary craft.

What we finally retain from an immersion in the often nightmarish world of Poe's writings is the sense that our secret fears and desires have been touched upon: the fear of being buried alive, of being destroyed by perverse instincts that overturn the rational measures by which we protect ourselves; desires imaged in acts of revenge, cannibalism, incest, and the quest for death. It was Poe's greatest discovery that we want and yet avoid self-examination and self-knowledge. To know the secrets of the universe would be to possess will, to have power and control over our fates. Knowledge, will, power— these appear to be at the heart of Poe's authority over our imaginations. He affects us by force, not clarity. It is a lesson taken to heart by masters of the Gothic romance and of the modern literary work. The example of Poe is apparent in both.

Further Reading:

G. Woodberry, *The Life of Edgar Allan Poe.* 2 vols., 1885, 1909.

E. Davidson, *Poe: A Critical Study,* 1957.

S. Moss, *Poe's Literary Battles,* 1963.

D. Hoffman, *Poe, Poe, Poe, Poe, Poe, Poe, Poe,* 1972.

D. Reynolds, *Beneath the American Renaissance,* 1988.

D. Pease, *Visionary Compacts,* 1988.

G. Thompson, "Poe and the Writers of the Old South," *Columbia Literary History of the United States,* 1988. *Poe and His Times,* ed. B. Fisher, 1990.

K. Silverman, *Edgar Allan Poe: Mournful and Never-Ending Remembrances,* 1991.

J. Irwin, *American Hieroglyphics,* 1980.

———, "Reading Poe's Mind: Politics, Mathematics, and the Association of Ideas in 'The Murders of the Rue Morgue,' " *American Literary History* 4 (1992), 187–206.

Texts:

"Ligeia," "The Fall of the House of Usher," and "The Philosophy of Composition," and from *The Complete Works of Edgar Allan Poe,* 17 vols., 1902.

"The Purloined Letter," "The Cask of Amontillado," and poems from *Collected Works of Edgar Allan Poe,* 3 vols., 1969–1978.

Ligeia

And the will therein lieth, which dieth not. Who knoweth the mysteries of the will, with its vigor? For God is but a great will pervading all things by nature of its intentness. Man doth not yield himself to the angels, nor unto death utterly, save only through the weakness of his feeble will.

Joseph Glanville[1]

---

[1] Joseph Glanville (1636–1680), one of the Cambridge Platonists who attempted to reconcile seventeenth-century scientific thought with Christian teachings. This quotation is apparently a fabrication by Poe to suit the purposes of the narrative.

I cannot, for my soul, remember how, when, or even precisely where, I first became acquainted with the lady Ligeia. Long years have since elapsed, and my memory is feeble through much suffering. Or, perhaps, I cannot *now* bring these points to mind, because, in truth, the character of my beloved, her rare learning, her singular yet placid cast of beauty, and the thrilling and enthralling eloquence of her low musical language, made their way into my heart by paces so steadily and stealthily progressive that they have been unnoticed and unknown. Yet I believe that I met her first and most frequently in some large, old, decaying city near the Rhine. Of her family—I have surely heard her speak. That it is of a remotely ancient date cannot be doubted. Ligeia! Ligeia! Buried in studies of a nature more than all else adapted to deaden impressions of the outward world, it is by that sweet word alone—by Ligeia—that I bring before mine eyes in fancy the image of her who is no more. And now, while I write, a recollection flashes upon me that I have *never known* the paternal name of her who was my friend and my betrothed, and who became the partner of my studies, and finally the wife of my bosom. Was it a playful charge on the part of my Ligeia? or was it a test of my strength of affection, that I should institute no inquiries upon this point? or was it rather a caprice of my own—a wildly romantic offering on the shrine of the most passionate devotion? I but indistinctly recall the fact itself—what wonder that I have utterly forgotten the circumstances which originated or attended it? And, indeed, if ever that spirit which is entitled *Romance*—if ever she, the wan and the misty-winged *Ashtophet*[2] of idolatrous Egypt, presided, as they tell, over marriages ill-omened, then most surely she presided over mine.

There is one dear topic, however, on which my memory fails me not. It is the *person* of Ligeia. In stature she was tall, somewhat slender, and, in her latter days, even emaciated. I would in vain attempt to portray the majesty, the quiet ease, of her demeanor, or the incomprehensible lightness and elasticity of her footfall. She came and departed as a shadow. I was never made aware of her entrance into my closed study save by the dear music of her low sweet voice, as she placed her marble hand upon my shoulder. In beauty of face no maiden ever equalled her. It was the radiance of an opium-dream—an airy and spirit-lifting vision more wildly divine than the phantasies which hovered about the slumbering souls of the daughters of Delos.[3] Yet her features were not of that regular mould which we have been falsely taught to worship in the classical labors of the heathen. "There is no exquisite[4] beauty," says Bacon, Lord Verulam, speaking truly of all the forms and *genera* of beauty, "without some *strangeness* in the proportion." Yet, although I saw that the features of Ligeia were not of a classic regularity—although I perceived that her loveliness was indeed "exquisite," and felt that there was much of "strangeness" pervading it, yet I have tried in vain to detect the irregularity and to trace home my own perception of "the strange." I examined the contour of the lofty and pale forehead—it was faultless—how cold indeed that word when applied to a majesty so divine!—the skin rivalling the purest ivory, the commanding extent and repose, the gentle

---

[2] Fertility goddess.
[3] Aegean island frequently mentioned in classic myth.
[4] In his essay "Of Beauty" (1625), Francis Bacon, baron Verulam (1561–1626), used the word "excellent"; Poe substituted "exquisite." In the next line, *genera* is the Latin word for "races" or "kinds"; here it is used broadly for "species" (plural).

prominence of the regions above the temples; and then the raven-black, the glossy, the luxuriant and naturally-curling tresses, setting forth the full force of the Homeric epithet, "hyacinthine!"[5] I looked at the delicate outlines of the nose—and nowhere but in the graceful medallions of the Hebrews had I beheld a similar perfection. There were the same luxurious smoothness of surface, the same scarcely perceptible tendency to the aquiline, the same harmoniously curved nostrils speaking the free spirit. I regarded the sweet mouth. Here was indeed the triumph of all things heavenly—the magnificent turn of the short upper lip—the soft, voluptuous slumber of the under—the dimples which sported, and the color which spoke—the teeth glancing back, with a brilliancy almost startling, every ray of the holy light which fell upon them in her serene and placid, yet most exultingly radiant of all smiles. I scrutinized the formation of the chin—and here, too, I found the gentleness of breadth, the softness and the majesty, the fullness and the spirituality, of the Greek—the contour which the god Apollo revealed but in a dream, to Cleomenes,[6] the son of the Athenian. And then I peered into the large eyes of Ligeia.

For eyes we have no models in the remotely antique. It might have been, too, that in these eyes of my beloved lay the secret to which Lord Verulam alludes. They were, I must believe, far larger than the ordinary eyes of our own race. They were even fuller than the fullest of the gazelle eyes of the tribe of the valley of Nourjahad.[7] Yet it was only at intervals—in moments of intense excitement—that this peculiarity became more than slightly noticeable in Ligeia. And at such moments was her beauty—in my heated fancy thus it appeared perhaps—the beauty of beings either above or apart from the earth—the beauty of the fabulous Houri[8] of the Turk. The hue of the orbs was the most brilliant of black, and, far over them, hung jetty lashes of great length. The brows, slightly irregular in outline, had the same tint. The "strangeness," however, which I found in the eyes, was of a nature distinct from the formation, or the color, or the brilliancy of the features, and must, after all, be referred to the *expression*. Ah, word of no meaning! behind whose vast latitude of mere sound we intrench our ignorance of so much of the spiritual. The expression of the eyes of Ligeia! How for long hours have I pondered upon it! How have I, through the whole of a midsummer night, struggled to fathom it! What *was* it—that something more profound than the well of Democritus[9]—which lay far within the pupils of my beloved? What was it? I was possessed with a passion to discover. Those eyes! those large, those shining, those divine orbs! they became to me twin stars of Leda,[10] and I to them devoutest of astrologers.

There is no point, among the many incomprehensible anomalies of the science of mind, more thrillingly exciting than the fact—never, I believe, noticed in the schools—

5 Homer's epic poem the *Odyssey* likens the curly hair of its hero to the hyacinth.
6 Athenian sculptor said to have created the original version of the famous statue known as the Medici Venus, inspired by Apollo, god of the arts.
7 Virgins who await the faithful in the Mohammedan paradise, as described in *The History of Nourjahad* (1767) by Frances Sheridan.
8 Another reference to the beauteous women of the Moslem paradise.
9 Greek philosopher (fifth century B.C.) who observed that truth is to be found at the bottom of a well.
10 In the constellation Gemini; named after the twin sons of Leda, who were born of her rape by Zeus.

that, in our endeavors to recall to memory something long forgotten, we often find ourselves *upon the very verge* of remembrance, without being able, in the end, to remember. And thus how frequently, in my intense scrutiny of Ligeia's eyes, have I felt approaching the full knowledge of their expression—felt it approaching—yet not quite be mine—and so at length entirely depart! And (strange, oh strangest mystery of all!) I found, in the commonest objects of the universe, a circle of analogies to that expression. I mean to say that, subsequently to the period when Ligeia's beauty passed into my spirit, there dwelling as in a shrine, I derived, from many existences in the material world, a sentiment such as I felt always aroused within me by her large and luminous orbs. Yet not the more could I define that sentiment, or analyze, or even steadily view it. I recognized it, let me repeat, sometimes in the survey of a rapidly-growing vine—in the contemplation of a moth, a butterfly, a chrysalis, a stream of running water. I have felt it in the ocean; in the falling of a meteor. I have felt it in the glances of unusually aged people. And there are one or two stars in heaven—(one especially, a star of the sixth magnitude, double and changeable, to be found near the large star in Lyra[11]) in a telescopic scrutiny of which I have been made aware of the feeling. I have been filled with it by certain sounds from stringed instruments, and not unfrequently by passages from books. Among innumerable other instances, I well remember something in a volume of Joseph Glanvill, which (perhaps merely from its quaintness—who shall say?) never failed to inspire me with the sentiment;—"And the will therein lieth, which dieth not. Who knoweth the mysteries of the will, with its vigor? For God is but a great will pervading all things by nature of its intentness. Man doth not yield him to the angels, nor unto death utterly, save only through the weakness of his feeble will."

Length of years, and subsequent reflection, have enabled me to trace, indeed, some remote connection between this passage in the English moralist and a portion of the character of Ligeia. An *intensity* in thought, action, or speech, was possibly, in her, a result, or at least an index, of that gigantic volition which, during our long intercourse, failed to give other and more immediate evidence of its existence. Of all the women whom I have ever known, she, the outwardly calm, the ever-placid Ligeia, was the most violently a prey to the tumultuous vultures of stern passion. And of such passion I could form no estimate, save by the miraculous expansion of those eyes which at once so delighted and appalled me—by the almost magical melody, modulation, distinctness and placidity of her very low voice—and by the fierce energy (rendered doubly effective by contrast with her manner of utterance) of the wild words which she habitually uttered.

I have spoken of the learning of Ligeia: it was immense—such as I have never known in woman. In the classical tongues was she deeply proficient, and as far as my own acquaintance extended in regard to the modern dialects of Europe, I have never known her at fault. Indeed upon any theme of the most admired, because simply the most abstruse of the boasted erudition of the academy, have I *ever* found Ligeia at fault? How singularly—how thrillingly, this one point in the nature of my wife has forced itself, at this late period only, upon my attention! I said her knowledge was such as I have never known in woman—but where breathes the man who has traversed, and successfully, *all* the wide areas of moral, physical, and mathematical science? I saw not then what I now clearly perceive, that the acquisitions of Ligeia were gigantic, were astounding; yet I was sufficiently aware of her infinite supremacy to resign myself, with a child-like confidence, to her guid-

[11] Constellation with the brilliant star Vega.

ance through the chaotic world of metaphysical investigation at which I was most busily occupied during the earlier years of our marriage. With how vast a triumph—with how vivid a delight—with how much of all that is ethereal in hope—did I *feel,* as she bent over me in studies but little sought—but less known—that delicious vista by slow degrees expanding before me, down whose long, gorgeous, and all untrodden path, I might at length pass onward to the goal of a wisdom too divinely precious not to be forbidden!

How poignant, then, must have been the grief with which, after some years, I beheld my well-grounded expectations take wings to themselves and fly away! Without Ligeia I was but as a child groping benighted. Her presence, her readings alone, rendered vividly luminous the many mysteries of the transcendentalism in which we were immersed. Wanting the radiant lustre of her eyes, letters, lambent and golden, grew duller than Saturnian lead[12] And now those eyes shone less and less frequently upon the pages over which I pored. Ligeia grew ill. The wild eyes blazed with a too—too glorious effulgence; the pale fingers became of the transparent waxen hue of the grave, and the blue veins upon the lofty forehead swelled and sank impetuously with the tides of the most gentle emotion. I saw that she must die—and I struggled desperately in spirit with the grim Azrael.[13] And the struggles of the passionate wife were, to my astonishment, even more energetic than my own. There had been much in her stern nature to impress me with the belief that, to her, death would have come without its terrors;—but not so. Words are impotent to convey any just idea of the fierceness of resistance with which she wrestled with the Shadow. I groaned in anguish at the pitiable spectacle. I would have soothed—I would have reasoned; but, in the intensity of her wild desire for life,—for life—*but* for life—solace and reason were alike the uttermost of folly. Yet not until the last instance, amid the most convulsive writhings of her fierce spirit, was shaken the external placidity of her demeanor. Her voice grew more gentle—grew more low—yet I would not wish to dwell upon the wild meaning of the quietly uttered words. My brain reeled as I hearkened entranced, to a melody more than mortal—to assumptions and aspirations which mortality had never before known.

That she loved me I should not have doubted; and I might have been easily aware that, in a bosom such as hers, love would have reigned no ordinary passion. But in death only, was I fully impressed with the strength of her affection. For long hours, detaining my hand, would she pour out before me the overflowing of a heart whose more than passionate devotion amounted to idolatry. How had I deserved to be so blessed by such confessions?—how had I deserved to be so cursed with the removal of my beloved in the hour of her making them? But upon this subject I cannot bear to dilate. Let me say only, that in Ligeia's more than womanly abandonment to a love, alas! all unmerited, all unworthily bestowed, I at length recognized the principle of her longing with so wildly earnest a desire for the life which was now fleeing so rapidly away. It is this wild longing—it is this eager vehemence of desire for life—*but* for life—that I have no power to portray—no utterance capable of expressing.

At high noon of the night in which she departed, beckoning me, peremptorily, to her side, she bade me repeat certain verses composed by herself not many days before. I obeyed her.—They were these:

---

12 According to astrological lore the influence of Saturn (the alchemical term for lead) turns one gloomy and listless.

13 In both Jewish and Moslem legend, the Angel of Death.

Lo! 't is a gala night
　Within the lonesome latter years!
An angel throng, bewinged, bedight
　In veils, and drowned in tears,
Sit in a theatre, to see
　A play of hopes and fears,
While the orchestra breathes fitfully
　The music of the spheres.

Mimes, in the form of God on high,
　Mutter and mumble low,
And hither and thither fly—
　Mere puppets they, who come and go
At bidding of vast formless things
　That shift the scenery to and fro,
Flapping from out their Condor wings
　Invisible Wo!

That motley drama!—oh, be sure
　It shall not be forgot!
With its Phantom chased forever more,
　By a crowd that seize it not,
Through a circle that ever returneth in
　To the self-same spot,
And much of Madness and more of Sin
　And Horror the soul of the plot.

But see, amid the mimic rout,
　A crawling shape intrude!
A blood-red thing that writhes from out
　The scenic solitude!
It writhes!—it writhes!—with mortal pangs
　The mimes become its food,
And the seraphs sob at vermin fangs
　In human gore imbued.

Out—out are the lights—out all!
　And over each quivering form,
The curtain, a funeral pall,
　Comes down with the rush of a storm,
And the angels, all pallid and wan,
　Uprising, unveiling, affirm
That the play is the tragedy, "Man,"
　And its hero the Conqueror Worm.

"Oh God!" half shrieked Ligeia, leaping to her feet and extending her arms aloft with a spasmodic movement, as I made an end of these lines—"O God! O Divine Father!—

shall these things be undeviatingly so?—shall this Conqueror be not once conquered? Are we not part and parcel in Thee? Who—who knoweth the mysteries of the will with its vigor? Man doth not yield him to the angels, *nor unto death utterly,* save only through the weakness of his feeble will."

And now, as if exhausted with emotion, she suffered her white arms to fall, and returned solemnly to her bed of death. And as she breathed her last sighs, there came mingled with them a low murmur from her lips. I bent to them my ear and distinguished, again, the concluding words of the passage in Glanvill—*"Man doth not yield him to the angels, nor unto death utterly, save only through the weakness of his feeble will."*

She died;—and I, crushed into the very dust with sorrow, could no longer endure the lonely desolation of my dwelling in the dim and decaying city by the Rhine. I had no lack of what the world calls wealth. Ligeia had brought me far more, very far more than ordinarily falls to the lot of mortals. After a few months, therefore, of weary and aimless wandering, I purchased, and put in some repair, an abbey, which I shall not name, in one of the wildest and least frequented portions of fair England. The gloomy and dreary grandeur of the building, the almost savage aspect of the domain, the many melancholy and time-honored memories connected with both, had much in unison with the feelings of utter abandonment which had driven me into that remote and unsocial region of the country. Yet although the external abbey, with its verdant decay hanging about it, suffered but little alteration, I gave way, with a child-like perversity, and perchance with a faint hope of alleviating my sorrows, to a display of more than regal magnificence within.—For such follies, even in childhood, I had imbibed a taste and now they came back to me as if in the dotage of grief. Alas, I feel how much even of incipient madness might have been discovered in the gorgeous and fantastic draperies, in the solemn carvings of Egypt, in the wild cornices and furniture, in the Bedlam[14] patterns of the carpets of tufted gold! I had become a bounden slave in the trammels of opium, and my labors and my orders had taken a coloring from my dreams. But these absurdities I must not pause to detail. Let me speak only of that one chamber, ever accursed, whither in a moment of mental alienation, I led from the altar as my bride—as the successor of the unforgotten Ligeia—the fair-haired and blue-eyed Lady Rowena Trevanion, of Tremaine.

There is no individual portion of the architecture and decoration of that bridal chamber which is not now visibly before me. Where were the souls of the haughty family of the bride, when, through thirst of gold, they permitted to pass the threshold of an apartment *so* bedecked, a maiden and a daughter so beloved? I have said that I minutely remember the details of the chamber—yet I am sadly forgetful on topics of deep moment—and here there was no system, no keeping, in the fantastic display, to take hold upon the memory. The room lay in a high turret of the castellated abbey, was pentagonal in shape, and of capacious size. Occupying the whole southern face of the pentagon was the sole window—an immense sheet of unbroken glass from Venice—a single pane, and tinted of a leaden hue, so that the rays of either the sun or moon, passing through it, fell with a ghastly lustre on the objects within. Over the upper portion of this huge window, extended the trellice-work of an aged vine, which clambered up the massy walls of the turret. The ceiling, of gloomy-looking oak, was excessively lofty,

---

[14] Crazed. The London lunatic asylum Bethlehem Hospital was known as "Bedlam," a contraction of the name.

vaulted, and elaborately fretted with the wildest and most grotesque specimens of a semi-Gothic, semi-Druidical[15] device. From out the most central recess of this melancholy vaulting, depended, by a single chain of gold with long links, a huge censer of the same metal, Saracenic[16] in pattern, and with many perforations so contrived that there writhed in and out of them, as if endued with a serpent vitality, a continual succession of parti-colored fires.

Some few ottomans and golden candelabra, of Eastern figure, were in various stations about—and there was the couch, too—the bridal couch—of an Indian model, and low, and sculptured of solid ebony, with a pall-like canopy above. In each of the angles of the chamber stood on end a gigantic sarcophagus of black granite, from the tombs of the kings over against Luxor,[17] with their aged lids full of immemorial sculpture. But in the draping of the apartment lay, alas! the chief phantasy of all. The lofty walls, gigantic in height—even unproportionably so—were hung from summit to foot, in vast folds, with a heavy and massive-looking tapestry—tapestry of a material which was found alike as a carpet on the floor, as a covering for the ottomans and the ebony bed, as a canopy for the bed, and as the gorgeous volutes of the curtains which partially shaded the window. The material was the richest cloth of gold. It was spotted all over, at irregular intervals, with arabesque figures, about a foot in diameter, and wrought upon the cloth in patterns of the most jetty black. But these figures partook of the true character of the arabesque only when regarded from a single point of view. By a contrivance now common, and indeed traceable to a very remote period of antiquity, they were made changeable in aspect. To one entering the room, they bore the appearance of simple monstrosities; but upon a farther advance, this appearance gradually departed; and step by step, as the visitor moved his station in the chamber, he saw himself surrounded by an endless succession of the ghastly forms which belong to the superstition of the Norman,[18] or arise in the guilty slumbers of the monk. The phantasmagoric effect was vastly heightened by the artificial introduction of a strong continual current of wind behind the draperies—giving a hideous and uneasy animation to the whole.

In halls such as these—in a bridal chamber such as this—I passed, with the Lady of Tremaine, the unhallowed hours of the first month of our marriage—passed them with but little disquietude. That my wife dreaded the fierce moodiness of my temper—that she shunned me and loved me but little—I could not help perceiving; but it gave me rather pleasure than otherwise. I loathed her with a hatred belonging more to demon than to man. My memory flew back, (oh, with what intensity of regret!) to Ligeia, the beloved, the august, the beautiful, the entombed. I revelled in recollections of her purity, of her wisdom, of her lofty, her ethereal nature, of her passionate, her idolatrous love. Now, then, did my spirit fully and freely burn with more than all the fires of her own. In the excitement of my opium dreams (for I was habitually fettered in the shackles of the drug) I would call aloud upon her name, during the silence of the night, or among the sheltered recesses of the glens by day, as if, through the wild eagerness, the

---

[15] In the style of the Druids, the priestly class of Celtic Britain.

[16] Arabic.

[17] City in ancient Egypt.

[18] The Vikings who came from the North in conquest of that area of the European continent later known as French Normandy. Their crafts are noted for their intricate designs.

solemn passion, the consuming ardor of my longing for the departed, I could restore her to the pathway she had abandoned—ah, *could* it be forever?—upon the earth.

About the commencement of the second month of the marriage, the Lady Rowena was attacked with sudden illness, from which her recovery was slow. The fever which consumed her rendered her nights uneasy; and in her perturbed state of half-slumber, she spoke of sounds, and of motions, in and about the chamber of the turret, which I concluded had no origin save in the distemper of her fancy, or perhaps in the phantasmagoric influences of the chamber itself. She became at length convalescent—finally well. Yet but a brief period elapsed, ere a second more violent disorder again threw her upon a bed of suffering; and from this attack her frame, at all times feeble, never altogether recovered. Her illnesses were, after this epoch, of alarming character, and of more alarming recurrence, defying alike the knowledge and the great exertions of her physicians. With the increase of the chronic disease which had thus, apparently, taken too sure hold upon her constitution to be eradicated by human means, I could not fail to observe a similar increase in the nervous irritation of her temperament, and in her excitability by trivial causes of fear. She spoke again, and now more frequently and pertinaciously, of the sounds—of the slight sounds—and of the unusual motions among the tapestries, to which she had formerly alluded.

One night, near the closing in of September, she pressed this distressing subject with more than usual emphasis upon my attention. She had just awakened from an unquiet slumber, and I had been watching, with feelings half of anxiety, half of vague terror, the workings of her emaciated countenance. I sat by the side of her ebony bed, upon one of the ottomans of India. She partly arose, and spoke, in an earnest low whisper, of sounds which she *then* heard, but which I could not hear—of motions which she *then* saw, but which I could not perceive. The wind was rushing hurriedly behind the tapestries, and I wished to show her (what, let me confess it, I could not *all* believe) that those almost inarticulate breathings, and those very gentle variations of the figures upon the wall, were but the natural effects of that customary rushing of the wind. But a deadly pallor, overspreading her face, had proved to me that my exertions to reassure her would be fruitless. She appeared to be fainting, and no attendants were within call. I remembered where was deposited a decanter of light wine which had been ordered by her physicians, and hastened across the chamber to procure it. But, as I stepped beneath the light of the censer, two circumstances of a startling nature attracted my attention. I had felt that some palpable although invisible object had passed lightly by my person; and I saw that there lay upon the golden carpet, in the very middle of the rich lustre thrown from the censer, a shadow—a faint, indefinite shadow of angelic aspect—such as might be fancied for the shadow of a shade. But I was wild with the excitement of an immoderate dose of opium, and heeded these things but little, nor spoke of them to Rowena. Having found the wine, I recrossed the chamber, and poured out a goblet-ful, which I held to the lips of the fainting lady. She had now partially recovered, however, and took the vessel herself, while I sank upon an ottoman near me, with my eyes fastened upon her person. It was then that I became distinctly aware of a gentle foot-fall upon the carpet, and near the couch; and in a second thereafter, as Rowena was in the act of raising the wine to her lips, I saw, or may have dreamed that I saw, fall within the goblet, as if from some invisible spring in the atmosphere of the room, three or four large drops of a brilliant and ruby colored fluid. If this I saw—not so Rowena. She swallowed the wine unhesitatingly, and I forbore to speak to her of a circumstance which must, after all, I considered, have been but the suggestion of a vivid imagination, rendered morbidly active by the terror of the lady, by the opium, and by the hour.

Yet I cannot conceal it from my own perception that, immediately subsequent to the fall of the ruby-drops, a rapid change for the worse took place in the disorder of my wife; so that, on the third subsequent night, the hands of her menials prepared her for the tomb, and on the fourth, I sat alone, with her shrouded body, in that fantastic chamber which had received her as my bride.—Wild visions, opium-engendered, flitted, shadowlike, before me. I gazed with unquiet eye upon the sarcophagi in the angles of the room, upon the varying figures of the drapery, and upon the writhing of the parti-colored fires in the censer overhead. My eyes then fell, as I called to mind the circumstances of a former night, to the spot beneath the glare of the censer where I had seen the faint traces of the shadow. It was there, however, no longer; and breathing with greater freedom, I turned my glances to the pallid and rigid figure upon the bed. Then rushed upon me a thousand memories of Ligeia—and then came back upon my heart, with the turbulent violence of a flood, the whole of that unutterable wo with which I had regarded *her* thus enshrouded. The night waned; and still, with a bosom full of bitter thoughts of the one only and supremely beloved, I remained gazing upon the body of Rowena.

It might have been midnight, or perhaps earlier, or later, for I had taken no note of time, when a sob, low, gentle, but very distinct, startled me from my revery.—I *felt* that it came from the bed of ebony—the bed of death. I listened in an agony of superstitious terror—but there was no repetition of the sound. I strained my vision to detect any motion in the corpse—but there was not the slightest perceptible. Yet I could not have been deceived. I *had* heard the noise, however faint, and my soul was awakened within me. I resolutely and perseveringly kept my attention riveted upon the body. Many minutes elapsed before any circumstance occurred tending to throw light upon the mystery. At length it became evident that a slight, a very feeble, and barely noticeable tinge of color had flushed up within the cheeks, and along the sunken small veins of the eyelids. Through a species of unutterable horror and awe, for which the language of mortality has no sufficiently energetic expression, I felt my heart cease to beat, my limbs grow rigid where I sat. Yet a sense of duty finally operated to restore my self-possession. I could no longer doubt that we had been precipitate in our preparations—that Rowena still lived. It was necessary that some immediate exertion be made; yet the turret was altogether apart from the portion of the abbey tenanted by the servants—there were none within call—I had no means of summoning them to my aid without leaving the room for many minutes—and this I could not venture to do. I therefore struggled alone in my endeavors to call back the spirit still hovering. In a short period it was certain, however, that a relapse had taken place; the color disappeared from both eyelid and cheek, leaving a wanness even more than that of marble; the lips became doubly shrivelled and pinched up in the ghastly expression of death; a repulsive clamminess and coldness overspread rapidly the surface of the body; and all the usual rigorous stiffness immediately supervened. I fell back with a shudder upon the couch from which I had been so startlingly aroused, and again gave myself up to passionate waking visions of Ligeia.

An hour thus elapsed when (could it be possible?) I was a second time aware of some vague sound issuing from the region of the bed. I listened—in extremity of horror. The sound came again—it was a sigh. Rushing to the corpse, I saw—distinctly saw—a tremor upon the lips. In a minute afterward they relaxed, disclosing a bright line of the pearly teeth. Amazement now struggled in my bosom with the profound awe which had hitherto reigned there alone. I felt that my vision grew dim, that my reason wandered; and it was only by a violent effort that I at length succeeded in nerving myself to the task which duty thus once more had pointed out. There was now a partial glow upon the forehead and upon the cheek and throat; a perceptible warmth pervaded the whole frame; there was even a slight pulsation at the heart. The lady *lived;* and with redoubled ardor I betook myself to the task of restoration. I chafed and bathed the temples and the hands, and used every exertion which experience, and no little medical reading, could suggest. But in vain. Suddenly, the color fled, the pulsation ceased, the lips resumed the expression of the dead, and, in an instant afterward, the whole body took upon itself the icy chilliness, the livid hue, the intense rigidity, the sunken outline, and all the loathsome peculiarities of that which has been, for many days, a tenant of the tomb.

And again I sunk into visions of Ligeia—and again, (what marvel that I shudder while I write?) *again* there reached my ears a low sob from the region of the ebony bed. But why shall I minutely detail the unspeakable horrors of that night? Why shall I pause to relate how, time after time, until near the period of the gray dawn, this hideous drama of revivification was repeated; how each terrific relapse was only into a sterner and apparently more irredeemable death; how each agony wore the aspect of a struggle with some invisible foe; and how each struggle was succeeded by I know not what of wild change in the personal appearance of the corpse? Let me hurry to a conclusion.

The greater part of the fearful night had worn away, and she who had been dead, once again stirred—and now more vigorously than hitherto, although arousing from a dissolution more appalling in its utter hopelessness than any. I had long ceased to struggle or to move, and remained sitting rigidly upon the ottoman, a helpless prey to a whirl of violent emotions, of which extreme awe was perhaps the least terrible, the least consuming. The corpse, I repeat, stirred, and now more vigorously than before. The hues of life flushed up with unwonted energy into the countenance—the limbs relaxed—and, save that the eyelids were yet pressed heavily together, and that the bandages and draperies of the grave still imparted their charnel character to the figure, I might have dreamed that Rowena had indeed shaken off, utterly, the fetters of Death. But if this idea was not, even then, altogether adopted, I could at least doubt no longer, when, arising from the bed, tottering, with feeble steps, with closed eyes, and with the manner of one bewildered in a dream, the thing that was enshrouded advanced boldly and palpably into the middle of the apartment.

I trembled not—I stirred not—for a crowd of unutterable fancies connected with the air, the stature, the demeanor of the figure, rushing hurriedly through my brain, had paralyzed—had chilled me into stone. I stirred not—but gazed upon the apparition. There was a mad disorder in my thoughts—a tumult unappeasable. Could it, indeed, be the *living* Rowena who confronted me? Could it indeed be Rowena *at all*—the fair-haired, the blue-eyed Lady Rowena Trevanion of Tremaine? Why, *why* should I doubt it? The bandage lay heavily about the mouth—but then might it not be the mouth of the breathing Lady of Tremaine? And the cheeks—there were the roses as in her noon of life—yes, these might indeed be the fair cheeks of the living Lady of Tremaine. And the chin, with its dimples, as in health, might it not be hers?—but *had she then grown taller since her malady?* What inexpressible madness seized me with that thought? One bound, and I had reached her feet! Shrinking from my touch, she let fall from her head, unloosened, the ghastly cerements which had confined it, and there

streamed forth, into the rushing atmosphere of the chamber, huge masses of long and dishevelled hair; *it was blacker than the raven wings of the midnight!* And now slowly opened *the eyes* of the figure which stood before me. "Here, then, at least," I shrieked aloud, "can I never—can I never be mistaken—these are the full, and the black, and the wild eyes—of my lost love—of the lady—of the LADY LIGEIA."
1838

The Fall of the House of Usher

Son cœur est un luth suspendu;
Sitôt qu'on le touche il résonne.
De Béranger[1]

During the whole of a dull, dark, and soundless day in the autumn of the year, when the clouds hung oppressively low in the heavens, I had been passing alone, on horseback, through a singularly dreary tract of country; and at length found myself, as the shades of the evening drew on, within view of the melancholy House of Usher. I know not how it was—but, with the first glimpse of the building, a sense of insufferable gloom pervaded my spirit. I say insufferable; for the feeling was unrelieved by any of that half-pleasurable, because poetic, sentiment, with which the mind usually receives even the sternest natural images of the desolate or terrible. I looked upon the scene before me—upon the mere house, and the simple landscape features of the domain—upon the bleak walls—upon the vacant eye-like windows—upon a few rank sedges—and upon a few white trunks of decayed trees—with an utter depression of soul which I can compare to no earthly sensation more properly than to the after-dream of the reveller upon opium—the bitter lapse into every-day life—the hideous dropping off of the veil. There was an iciness, a sinking, a sickening of the heart—an unredeemed dreariness of thought which no goading of the imagination could torture into aught of the sublime. What was it—I paused to think—what was it that so unnerved me in the contemplation of the House of Usher? It was a mystery all insoluble; nor could I grapple with the shadowy fancies that crowded upon me as I pondered. I was forced to fall back upon the unsatisfactory conclusion, that while, beyond doubt, there *are* combinations of very simple natural objects which have the power of thus affecting us, still the analysis of this power lies among considerations beyond our depth. It was possible, I reflected, that a mere different arrangement of the particulars of the scene, of the details of the picture, would be sufficient to modify, or perhaps to annihilate its capacity for sorrowful impression; and, acting upon this idea, I reined my horse to the precipitous brink of a black and lurid tarn[2] that lay in unruffled lustre by the dwelling, and gazed down—but with a shudder even more thrilling than before—upon the remodelled and inverted images of the gray sedge, and the ghastly tree-stems, and the vacant and eye-like windows.

---

[1] From "Le Refus" (1831) by the French poet Pierre-Jean de Béranger (1780–1857). The lines, which Poe partly altered to read "his heart" rather than "my heart," translate as "His heart is a lute, tightly strung; / The instant one touches it, it resounds."
[2] Small mountain lake.

Nevertheless, in this mansion of gloom I now proposed to myself a sojourn of some weeks. Its proprietor, Roderick Usher, had been one of my boon companions in boyhood; but many years had elapsed since our last meeting. A letter, however, had lately reached me in a distant part of the country—a letter from him—which, in its wildly importunate nature, had admitted of no other than a personal reply. The MS. gave evidence of nervous agitation. The writer spoke of acute bodily illness—of a mental disorder which oppressed him—and of an earnest desire to see me, as his best, and indeed his only personal friend, with a view of attempting, by the cheerfulness of my society, some alleviation of his malady. It was the manner in which all this, and much more, was said—it was the apparent *heart* that went with his request—which allowed me no room for hesitation; and I accordingly obeyed forthwith what I still considered a very singular summons.

Although, as boys, we had been even intimate associates, yet I really knew little of my friend. His reserve had been always excessive and habitual. I was aware, however, that his very ancient family had been noted, time out of mind, for a peculiar sensibility of temperament, displaying itself, through long ages, in many works of exalted art, and manifested, of late, in repeated deeds of munificent yet unobtrusive charity, as well as in a passionate devotion to the intricacies, perhaps even more than to the orthodox and easily recognisable beauties, of musical science. I had learned, too, the very remarkable fact, that the stem of the Usher race, all time-honoured as it was, had put forth, at no period, any enduring branch; in other words, that the entire family lay in the direct line of descent, and had always, with very trifling and very temporary variation, so lain. It was this deficiency, I considered, while running over in thought the perfect keeping of the character of the premises with the accredited character of the people, and while speculating upon the possible influence which the one, in the long lapse of centuries, might have exercised upon the other—it was this deficiency, perhaps, of collateral issue, and the consequent undeviating transmission, from sire to son, of the patrimony with the name, which had, at length, so identified the two as to merge the original title of the estate in the quaint and equivocal appellation of the "House of Usher"—an appellation which seemed to include, in the minds of the peasantry who used it, both the family and the family mansion.

I have said that the sole effect of my somewhat childish experiment—that of looking down within the tarn—had been to deepen the first singular impression. There can be no doubt that the consciousness of the rapid increase of my superstition—for why should I not so term it?—served mainly to accelerate the increase itself. Such, I have long known, is the paradoxical law of all sentiments having terror as a basis. And it might have been for this reason only, that, when I again uplifted my eyes to the house itself, from its image in the pool, there grew in my mind a strange fancy—a fancy so ridiculous, indeed, that I but mention it to show the vivid force of the sensations which oppressed me. I had so worked upon my imagination as really to believe that about the whole mansion and domain there hung an atmosphere peculiar to themselves and their immediate vicinity—an atmosphere which had no affinity with the air of heaven, but which had reeked up from the decayed trees, and the gray wall, and the silent tarn—a pestilent and mystic vapour, dull, sluggish, faintly discernible, and leaden-hued.

Shaking off from my spirit what *must* have been a dream, I scanned more narrowly the real aspect of the building. Its principal feature seemed to be that of an excessive antiquity. The discoloration of ages had been great. Minute fungi overspread the whole exterior, hanging in a fine tangled web-work from the eaves. Yet all this was apart from any extraordinary dilapidation. No portion of the masonry had fallen; and there appeared to be a wild inconsistency between its still perfect adaptation of parts, and the crumbling condition of the individual stones. In this there was much that reminded me of the specious totality of old wood-work which has rotted for long years in some neglected vault, with no disturbance from the breath of the external air. Beyond this indication of extensive decay, however, the fabric gave little token of instability. Perhaps the eye of a scrutinising observer might have discovered a barely perceptible fissure, which, extending from the roof of the building in front, made its way down the wall in a zigzag direction, until it became lost in the sullen waters of the tarn.

Noticing these things, I rode over a short causeway to the house. A servant in waiting took my horse, and I entered the Gothic archway of the hall. A valet, of stealthy step, thence conducted me, in silence, through many dark and intricate passages in my progress to the *studio* of his master. Much that I encountered on the way contributed, I know not how, to heighten the vague sentiments of which I have already spoken. While the objects around me—while the carvings of the ceilings, the sombre tapestries of the walls, the ebon blackness of the floors, and the phantasmagoric armorial trophies which rattled as I strode, were but matters to which, or to such as which, I had been accustomed from my infancy—while I hesitated not to acknowledge how familiar was all this—I still wondered to find how unfamiliar were the fancies which ordinary images were stirring up. On one of the staircases, I met the physician of the family. His countenance, I thought, wore a mingled expression of low cunning and perplexity. He accosted me with trepidation and passed on. The valet now threw open a door and ushered me into the presence of his master.

 The room in which I found myself was very large and lofty. The windows were long, narrow, and pointed, and at so vast a distance from the black oaken floor as to be altogether inaccessible from within. Feeble gleams of encrimsoned light made their way through the trellised panes, and served to render sufficiently distinct the more prominent objects around; the eye, however, struggled in vain to reach the remoter angles of the chamber, or the recesses of the vaulted and fretted ceiling. Dark draperies hung upon the walls. The general furniture was profuse, comfortless, antique, and tattered. Many books and musical instruments lay scattered about, but failed to give any vitality to the scene. I felt that I breathed an atmosphere of sorrow. An air of stern, deep, and irredeemable gloom hung over and pervaded all.

Upon my entrance, Usher arose from a sofa on which he had been lying at full length, and greeted me with a vivacious warmth which had much in it, I at first thought, of an overdone cordiality—of the constrained effort of the *ennuyé*[3] man of the world. A glance, however, at his countenance, convinced me of his perfect sincerity. We sat down; and for some moments, while he spoke not, I gazed upon him with a feeling half of pity, half of awe. Surely, man had never before so terribly altered, in so brief a period, as had Roderick Usher! It was with difficulty that I could bring myself to admit the identity of the wan being before me with the companion of my early boyhood. Yet the character of his face had been at all times remarkable. A cadaverousness of complexion; an eye large, liquid, and luminous beyond comparison; lips somewhat thin and very pallid, but of a surpassingly beautiful curve; a nose of a delicate Hebrew model, but with a breadth of nostril unusual in similar formations; a finely moulded chin, speaking, in

---

[3] French: "bored."

its want of prominence, of a want of moral energy; hair of a more than web-like softness and tenuity; these features, with an inordinate expansion above the regions of the temple, made up altogether a countenance not easily to be forgotten. And now in the mere exaggeration of the prevailing character of these features, and of the expression they were wont to convey, lay so much of change that I doubted to whom I spoke. The now ghastly pallor of the skin, and the now miraculous lustre of the eye, above all things startled and even awed me. The silken hair, too, had been suffered to grow all unheeded, and as, in its wild gossamer texture, it floated rather than fell about the face, I could not, even with effort, connect its Arabesque[4] expression with any idea of simple humanity.

In the manner of my friend I was at once struck with an incoherence—an inconsistency; and I soon found this to arise from a series of feeble and futile struggles to overcome an habitual trepidancy—an excessive nervous agitation. For something of this nature I had indeed been prepared, no less by his letter, than by reminiscences of certain boyish traits, and by conclusions deduced from his peculiar physical conformation and temperament. His action was alternately vivacious and sullen. His voice varied rapidly from a tremulous indecision (when the animal spirits seemed utterly in abeyance) to that species of energetic concision—that abrupt, weighty, unhurried, and hollow-sounding enunciation—that leaden, self-balanced and perfectly modulated guttural utterance, which may be observed in the lost drunkard, or the irreclaimable eater of opium, during the periods of his most intense excitement.

It was thus that he spoke of the object of my visit, of his earnest desire to see me, and of the solace he expected me to afford him. He entered, at some length, into what he conceived to be the nature of his malady. It was, he said, a constitutional and a family evil, and one for which he despaired to find a remedy—a mere nervous affection, he immediately added, which would undoubtedly soon pass off. It displayed itself in a host of unnatural sensations. Some of these, as he detailed them, interested and bewildered me; although, perhaps, the terms and the general manner of the narration had their weight. He suffered much from a morbid acuteness of the senses; the most insipid food was alone endurable; he could wear only garments of certain texture; the odours of all flowers were oppressive; his eyes were tortured by even a faint light; and there were but peculiar sounds, and these from stringed instruments, which did not inspire him with horror.

To an anomalous species of terror I found him a bounden slave. "I shall perish," said he, "I *must* perish in this deplorable folly. Thus, thus, and not otherwise, shall I be lost. I dread the events of the future, not in themselves, but in their results. I shudder at the thought of any, even the most trivial, incident, which may operate upon this intolerable agitation of soul. I have, indeed, no abhorrence of danger, except in its absolute effect—in terror. In this unnerved—in this pitiable condition—I feel that the period will sooner or later arrive when I must abandon life and reason together, in some struggle with the grim phantasm, FEAR."

I learned, moreover, at intervals, and through broken and equivocal hints, another singular feature of his mental condition. He was enchained by certain superstitious impressions in regard to the dwelling which he tenanted, and whence, for many years, he had never ventured forth—in regard to an influence whose suppositious force was conveyed in terms too shadowy here to be re-stated—an influence which some peculiarities

---

[4] Fantastic, complex.

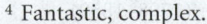

in the mere form and substance of his family mansion, had, by dint of long sufferance, he said, obtained over his spirit—an effect which the *physique* of the gray walls and turrets, and of the dim tarn into which they all looked down, had, at length, brought about upon the *morale* of his existence.

He admitted, however, although with hesitation, that much of the peculiar gloom which thus afflicted him could be traced to a more natural and far more palpable origin—to the severe and long-continued illness—indeed to the evidently approaching dissolution—of a tenderly beloved sister—his sole companion for long years—his last and only relative on earth. "Her decease," he said, with a bitterness which I can never forget, "would leave him (him the hopeless and the frail) the last of the ancient race of the Ushers." While he spoke, the lady Madeline (for so was she called) passed slowly through a remote portion of the apartment, and, without having noticed my presence, disappeared. I regarded her with an utter astonishment not unmingled with dread—and yet I found it impossible to account for such feelings. A sensation of stupor oppressed me, as my eyes followed her retreating steps. When a door, at length, closed upon her, my glance sought instinctively and eagerly the countenance of the brother—but he had buried his face in his hands, and I could only perceive that a far more than ordinary wanness had overspread the emaciated fingers through which trickled many passionate tears.

The disease of the lady Madeline had long baffled the skill of her physicians. A settled apathy, a gradual wasting away of the person, and frequent although transient affections of a partially cataleptical character, were the unusual diagnosis. Hitherto she had steadily borne up against the pressure of her malady, and had not betaken herself finally to bed; but, on the closing in of the evening of my arrival at the house, she succumbed (as her brother told me at night with inexpressible agitation) to the prostrating power of the destroyer; and I learned that the glimpse I had obtained of her person would thus probably be the last I should obtain—that the lady, at least while living, would be seen by me no more.

For several days ensuing, her name was unmentioned by either Usher or myself: and during this period I was busied in earnest endeavours to alleviate the melancholy of my friend. We painted and read together; or I listened, as if in a dream, to the wild improvisations of his speaking guitar. And thus, as a closer and still closer intimacy admitted me more unreservedly into the recesses of his spirit, the more bitterly did I perceive the futility of all attempt at cheering a mind from which darkness, as if an inherent positive quality, poured forth upon all objects of the moral and physical universe, in one unceasing radiation of gloom.

I shall ever bear about me a memory of the many solemn hours I thus spent alone with the master of the House of Usher. Yet I should fail in any attempt to convey an idea of the exact character of the studies, or of the occupations, in which he involved me, or led me the way. An excited and highly distempered ideality threw a sulphureous lustre over all. His long improvised dirges will ring forever in my ears. Among other things, I hold painfully in mind a certain singular perversion and amplification of the wild air of the last waltz of Von Weber.[5] From the paintings over which his elaborate

[5] Karl Maria von Weber (1786–1826), German Romantic composer, who was honored by "The Last Waltz of Von Weber," written by Karl Gottlieb Reissiger (1798–1859).

fancy brooded, and which grew, touch by touch, into vaguenesses at which I shuddered the more thrillingly, because I shuddered knowing not why;—from these paintings (vivid as their images now are before me) I would in vain endeavour to educe more than a small portion which should lie within the compass of merely written words. By the utter simplicity, by the nakedness of his designs, he arrested and overawed attention. If ever mortal painted an idea, that mortal was Roderick Usher. For me at least— in the circumstances then surrounding me—these arose out of the pure abstractions which the hypochondriac contrived to throw upon his canvas, an intensity of intolerable awe, no shadow of which felt I ever yet in the contemplation of the certainly glowing yet too concrete reveries of Fuseli.[6]

One of the phantasmagoric conceptions of my friend, partaking not so rigidly of the spirit of abstraction, may be shadowed forth, although feebly, in words. A small picture presented the interior of an immensely long and rectangular vault or tunnel, with low walls, smooth, white, and without interruption or device. Certain accessory points of the design served well to convey the idea that this excavation lay at an exceeding depth below the surface of the earth. No outlet was observed in any portion of its vast extent, and no torch, or other artificial source of light was discernible; yet a flood of intense rays rolled throughout, and bathed the whole in a ghastly and inappropriate splendour.

I have just spoken of that morbid condition of the auditory nerve which rendered all music intolerable to the sufferer, with the exception of certain effects of stringed instruments. It was, perhaps, the narrow limits to which he thus confined himself upon the guitar, which gave birth, in great measure, to the fantastic character of his performances. But the fervid *facility* of his *impromptus* could not be so accounted for. They must have been, and were, in the notes, as well as in the words of his wild fantasias (for he not unfrequently accompanied himself with rhymed verbal improvisations), the result of that intense mental collectedness and concentration to which I have previously alluded as observable only in particular moments of the highest artificial excitement. The words of one of these rhapsodies I have easily remembered. I was, perhaps, the more forcibly impressed with it, as he gave it, because in the under or mystic current of its meaning, I fancied that I perceived, and for the first time, a full consciousness on the part of Usher, of the tottering of his lofty reason upon her throne. The verses, which were entitled "The Haunted Palace," ran very nearly, if not accurately, thus:

I.

In the greenest of our valleys,
   By good angels tenanted,
Once a fair and stately palace—
   Radiant palace—reared its head.
In the monarch Thought's dominion—
   It stood there!
Never seraph spread a pinion
   Over fabric half so fair.

[6] Henry Fuseli (1742–1825), Swiss-born artist with a long career in England, whose paintings manifest the more nightmarish side of Romanticism.

II.

> Banners yellow, glorious, golden,
>   On its roof did float and flow;
> (This—all this—was in the olden
>   Time long ago)
> And every gentle air that dallied,
>   In that sweet day,
> Along the ramparts plumed and pallid,
>   A wingèd odour went away.

III.

> Wanderers in that happy valley
>   Through two luminous windows saw
> Spirits moving musically
>   To a lute's well-tunèd law,
> Round about a throne, where sitting
>   (Porphyrogene!)[7]
> In state his glory well befitting,
>   The ruler of the realm was seen.

IV.

> And all with pearl and ruby glowing
>   Was the fair palace door,
> Through which came flowing, flowing, flowing
>   And sparkling evermore,
> A troop of Echoes whose sweet duty
>   Was but to sing,
> In voices of surpassing beauty,
>   The wit and wisdom of their king.

V.

> But evil things, in robes of sorrow,
>   Assailed the monarch's high estate;
> (Ah, let us mourn, for never morrow
>   Shall dawn upon him, desolate!)
> And, round about his home, the glory
>   That blushed and bloomed
> Is but a dim-remembered story
>   Of the old time entombed.

7 "Born to the purple"; that is, of royal lineage.

VI.

    And travellers now within that valley,
        Through the red-litten windows, see
    Vast forms that move fantastically
        To a discordant melody;
    While, like a rapid ghastly river,
        Through the pale door,
    A hideous throng rush out forever,
        And laugh—but smile no more.

I well remember that suggestions arising from this ballad, led us into a train of thought wherein there became manifest an opinion of Usher's which I mention not so much on account of its novelty, (for other men[8] have thought thus,) as on account of the pertinacity with which he maintained it. This opinion, in its general form, was that of the sentience of all vegetable things. But, in his disordered fancy, the idea had assumed a more daring character, and trespassed, under certain conditions, upon the kingdom of inorganization. I lack words to express the full extent, or the earnest *abandon* of his persuasion. The belief, however, was connected (as I have previously hinted) with the gray stones of the home of his forefathers. The conditions of the sentience had been here, he imagined, fulfilled in the method of collocation of these stones—in the order of their arrangement, as well as in that of the many *fungi* which overspread them, and of the decayed trees which stood around—above all, in the long undisturbed endurance of this arrangement, and in its reduplication in the still waters of the tarn. Its evidence—the evidence of the sentience—was to be seen, he said, (and I here started as he spoke,) in the gradual yet certain condensation of an atmosphere of their own about the waters and the walls. The result was discoverable, he added, in that silent, yet importunate and terrible influence which for centuries had moulded the destinies of his family, and which made *him* what I now saw him—what he was. Such opinions need no comment, and I will make none.

Our books—the books which, for years, had formed no small portion of the mental existence of the invalid—were, as might be supposed, in strict keeping with this character of phantasm. We poured together over such works as the Ververt et Chartreuse of Gresset; the Belphegor of Machiavelli; the Heaven and Hell of Swedenborg; the Subterranean Voyage of Nicholas Klimm by Holberg; the Chiromancy of Robert Flud, of Jean D'Indaginé, and of De la Chambre; the Journey into the Blue Distance of Tieck; and the City of the Sun of Campanella.[9] One favourite volume was a small octavo edition of the

---

[8] Poe's note: "Watson, Dr. Percival, Spallanzani, and especially the Bishop of Landaff.— See 'Chemical Essays,' vol. v." That is, Richard Watson (1737–1816), bishop of Llandaff, English theologian, chemist, and author of *Chemical Essays*; Robert Percival (1756–1839), English physician and student of chemistry; Lazzaro Spallanzani (1739–1799), Italian physiologist.

[9] Usher's collection of occult lore contains actual works by a number of European and British authors spanning centuries of interest in the supernatural. His holdings include titles by Louis Gresset (1709–1777); Niccolò Machiavelli (1469–1527); Emanuel Swedenborg (1688–1772); Ludwig Holberg (1684–1754); Robert Fludd (1574–1637); Joannes Indaginé (early sixteenth century); Martin Cureau de la Chambre (1594–1669); Ludwig Tieck (1773–1853); Tommaso Campanella (1568–1639).

Directorium Inquisitorum, by the Dominican Eymeric de Gironne;[10] and there were passages in Pomponius Mela,[11] about the old African Satyrs and Ægipans, over which Usher would sit dreaming for hours. His chief delight, however, was found in the perusal of an exceedingly rare and curious book in quarto Gothic—the manual of a forgotten church—the *Vigiliæ Mortuorum secundum Chorum Ecclesiæ Maguntinæ.*[12]

I could not help thinking of the wild ritual of this work, and of its probable influence upon the hypochondriac, when, one evening, having informed me abruptly that the lady Madeline was no more, he stated his intention of preserving her corpse for a fortnight, (previously to its final interment,) in one of the numerous vaults within the main walls of the building. The worldly reason, however, assigned for this singular proceeding, was one which I did not feel at liberty to dispute. The brother had been led to his resolution (so he told me) by consideration of the unusual character of the malady of the deceased, of certain obtrusive and eager inquiries on the part of her medical men, and of the remote and exposed situation of the burial-ground of the family. I will not deny that when I called to mind the sinister countenance of the person whom I met upon the staircase, on the day of my arrival at the house, I had no desire to oppose what I regarded as at best but a harmless, and by no means an unnatural, precaution.[13]

At the request of Usher, I personally aided him in the arrangements for the temporary entombment. The body having been encoffined, we two alone bore it to its rest. The vault in which we placed it (and which had been so long unopened that our torches, half smothered in its oppressive atmosphere, gave us little opportunity for investigation) was small, damp, and entirely without means of admission for light; lying, at great depth, immediately beneath that portion of the building in which was my own sleeping apartment. It had been used, apparently, in remote feudal times, for the worst purposes of a donjon-keep, and, in later days, as a place of deposit for powder, or some other highly combustible substance, as a portion of its floor, and the whole interior of a long archway through which we reached it, were carefully sheathed with copper. The door, of massive iron, had been, also, similarly protected. Its immense weight caused an unusually sharp grating sound, as it moved upon its hinges.

Having deposited our mournful burden upon tressels within this region of horror, we partially turned aside the yet unscrewed lid of the coffin, and looked upon the face of the tenant. A striking similitude between the brother and sister now first arrested my attention; and Usher, divining, perhaps, my thoughts, murmured out some few words from which I learned that the deceased and himself had been twins, and that sympathies of a scarcely intelligible nature had always existed between them. Our glances, however, rested not long upon the dead—for we could not regard her unawed. The disease which had thus entombed the lady in the maturity of youth, had left, as usual in all maladies of a strictly cataleptical character, the mockery of a faint blush upon the bosom and the face, and that suspiciously lingering smile upon the lip which is so terrible

---

[10] Nicholas Eymeric de Gironne (1320?–1399), the Dominican who wrote on the tortures of the Inquisition.

[11] The Roman author, Pomponious Mela, who peopled his geography of the ancient world with fabulous beasts, including tales of satyrs and the goat-god Pan (the "Aegipan").

[12] Book written around 1500, known as *Vigils for the Dead, according to the Choir of the Church of Mayence.*

[13] To prevent Madeline's body from being stolen from its grave and sold for medical experiments, a real possibility in those days of illicit traffic in corpses.

in death. We replaced and screwed down the lid, and, having secured the door of iron, made our way, with toil, into the scarcely less gloomy apartments of the upper portion of the house.

And now, some days of bitter grief having elapsed, an observable change came over the features of the mental disorder of my friend. His ordinary manner had vanished. His ordinary occupations were neglected or forgotten. He roamed from chamber to chamber with hurried, unequal, and objectless step. The pallor of his countenance had assumed, if possible, a more ghastly hue—but the luminousness of his eye had utterly gone out. The once occasional huskiness of his tone was heard no more; and a tremulous quaver, as if of extreme terror, habitually characterized his utterance. There were times, indeed, when I thought his unceasingly agitated mind was labouring with some oppressive secret, to divulge which he struggled for the necessary courage. At times, again, I was obliged to resolve all into the mere inexplicable vagaries of madness, for I beheld him gazing upon vacancy for long hours, in an attitude of the profoundest attention as if listening to some imaginary sound. It was no wonder that his condition terrified—that it infected me. I felt creeping upon me, by slow yet certain degrees, the wild influences of his own fantastic yet impressive superstitions.

It was, especially, upon retiring to bed late in the night of the seventh or eighth day after the placing of the lady Madeline within the donjon, that I experienced the full power of such feelings. Sleep came not near my couch—while the hours waned and waned away. I struggled to reason off the nervousness which had dominion over me. I endeavoured to believe that much, if not all of what I felt, was due to the bewildering influence of the gloomy furniture of the room—of the dark and tattered draperies, which, tortured into motion by the breath of a rising tempest, swayed fitfully to and fro upon the walls, and rustled uneasily about the decorations of the bed. But my efforts were fruitless. An irrepressible tremour gradually pervaded my frame; and, at length, there sat upon my very heart an incubus of utterly causeless alarm. Shaking this off with a gasp and a struggle, I uplifted myself upon the pillows, and, peering earnestly within the intense darkness of the chamber, hearkened—I know not why, except that an instinctive spirit prompted me—to certain low and indefinite sounds which came, through the pauses of the storm, at long intervals, I knew not whence. Overpowered by an intense sentiment of horror, unaccountable yet unendurable, I threw on my clothes with haste (for I felt that I should sleep no more during the night), and endeavoured to arouse myself from the pitiable condition into which I had fallen, by pacing rapidly to and fro through the apartment.

I had taken but few turns in this manner, when a light step on an adjoining staircase arrested my attention. I presently recognised it as that of Usher. In an instant afterward he rapped, with a gentle touch, at my door, and entered, bearing a lamp. His countenance was, as usual, cadaverously wan—but, moreover, there was a species of mad hilarity in his eyes—an evidently restrained *hysteria* in his whole demeanour. His air appalled me—but anything was preferable to the solitude which I had so long endured, and I even welcomed his presence as a relief.

"And you have not seen it?" he said abruptly, after having stared about him for some moments in silence—"you have not then seen it?—but, stay! you shall." Thus speaking, and having carefully shaded his lamp, he hurried to one of the casements, and threw it freely open to the storm.

The impetuous fury of the entering gust nearly lifted us from our feet. It was, indeed, a tempestuous yet sternly beautiful night, and one wildly singular in its terror and its beauty. A whirlwind had apparently collected its force in our vicinity; for there were frequent and violent alterations in the direction of the wind; and the exceeding density of the clouds (which hung so low as to press upon the turrets of the house) did not prevent our perceiving the life-like velocity with which they flew careering from all points against each other, without passing away into the distance. I say that even their exceeding density did not prevent our perceiving this—yet we had no glimpse of the moon or stars—nor was there any flashing forth of the lightning. But the under surfaces of the huge masses of agitated vapour, as well as all terrestrial objects immediately around us, were glowing in the unnatural light of a faintly luminous and distinctly visible gaseous exhalation which hung about and enshrouded the mansion.

"You must not—you shall not behold this!" said I, shudderingly, to Usher, as I led him, with a gentle violence, from the window to a seat. "These appearances, which bewilder you, are merely electrical phenomena not uncommon—or it may be that they have their ghastly origin in the rank miasma of the tarn. Let us close this casement;—the air is chilling and dangerous to your frame. Here is one of your favourite romances. I will read, and you shall listen;—and so we will pass away this terrible night together."

The antique volume which I had taken up was the "Mad Trist"[14] of Sir Launcelot Canning; but I had called it a favourite of Usher's more in sad jest than in earnest; for, in truth, there is little in its uncouth and unimaginative prolixity which could have had interest for the lofty and spiritual ideality of my friend. It was, however, the only book immediately at hand; and I indulged a vague hope that the excitement which now agitated the hypochondriac, might find relief (for the history of mental disorder is full of similar anomalies) even in the extremeness of the folly which I should read. Could I have judged, indeed, by the wild over-strained air of vivacity with which he hearkened, or apparently hearkened, to the words of the tale, I might well have congratulated myself upon the success of my design.

I had arrived at that well-known portion of the story where Ethelred, the hero of the Trist, having sought in vain for peaceable admission into the dwelling of the hermit, proceeds to make good an entrance by force. Here, it will be remembered, the words of the narrative run thus:

"And Ethelred, who was by nature of a doughty heart, and who was now mighty withal, on account of the powerfulness of the wine which he had drunken, waited no longer to hold parley with the hermit, who, in sooth, was of an obstinate and maliceful turn, but, feeling the rain upon his shoulders, and fearing the rising of the tempest, uplifted his mace outright, and, with blows, made quickly room in the plankings of the door for his gauntleted hand; and now pulling therewith sturdily, he so cracked, and ripped, and tore all asunder, that the noise of the dry and hollow-sounding wood alarumed and reverberated throughout the forest."

At the termination of this sentence I started, and for a moment, paused; for it appeared to me (although I at once concluded that my excited fancy had deceived me)—it

[14] A title and narrative fabricated by Poe.
"Trist" (for *tryst*) is used in the sense of an appointed meeting.

appeared to me that, from some very remote portion of the mansion, there came, indistinctly, to my ears, what might have been, in its exact similarity of character, the echo (but a stifled and dull one certainly) of the very cracking and ripping sound which Sir Launcelot had so particularly described. It was, beyond doubt, the coincidence alone which had arrested my attention; for, amid the rattling of the sashes of the casements, and the ordinary commingled noises of the still increasing storm, the sound, in itself, had nothing, surely, which should have interested or disturbed me. I continued the story:

"But the good champion Ethelred, now entering within the door, was sore enraged and amazed to perceive no signal of the maliceful hermit; but, in the stead thereof, a dragon of a scaly and prodigious demeanour, and of a fiery tongue, which sate in guard before a palace of gold, with a floor of silver; and upon the wall there hung a shield of shining brass with this legend enwritten—

> Who entereth herein, a conqueror hath bin;
> Who slayeth the dragon, the shield he shall win;

And Ethelred uplifted his mace, and struck upon the head of the dragon, which fell before him, and gave up his pesty breath, with a shriek so horrid and harsh, and withal so piercing, that Ethelred had fain to close his ears with his hands against the dreadful noise of it, the like whereof was never before heard."

Here again I paused abruptly, and now with a feeling of wild amazement—for there could be no doubt whatever that, in this instance, I did actually hear (although from what direction it proceeded I found it impossible to say) a low and apparently distant, but harsh, protracted, and most unusual screaming or grating sound—the exact counterpart of what my fancy had already conjured up for the dragon's unnatural shriek as described by the romancer.

Oppressed, as I certainly was, upon the occurrence of the second and most extraordinary coincidence, by a thousand conflicting sensations, in which wonder and extreme terror were predominant, I still retained sufficient presence of mind to avoid exciting, by any observation, the sensitive nervousness of my companion. I was by no means certain that he had noticed the sounds in question; although, assuredly, a strange alteration had, during the last few minutes, taken place in his demeanour. From a position fronting my own, he had gradually brought round his chair, so as to sit with his face to the door of the chamber; and thus I could but partially perceive his features, although I saw that his lips trembled as if he were murmuring inaudibly. His head had dropped upon his breast—yet I knew that he was not asleep, from the wide and rigid opening of the eye as I caught a glance of it in profile. The motion of his body, too, was at variance with this idea—for he rocked from side to side with a gentle yet constant and uniform sway. Having rapidly taken notice of all this, I resumed the narrative of Sir Launcelot, which thus proceeded:

"And now, the champion, having escaped from the terrible fury of the dragon, bethinking himself of the brazen shield, and of the breaking up of the enchantment which was upon it, removed the carcass from out of the way before him, and approached valorously over the silver pavement of the castle to where the shield was upon the wall; which in sooth tarried not for his full coming, but fell down at his feet upon the silver floor, with a mighty great and terrible ringing sound."

No sooner had these syllables passed my lips, than—as if a shield of brass had indeed, at the moment, fallen heavily upon a floor of silver—I became aware of a distinct, hollow, metallic, and clangorous, yet apparently muffled reverberation. Completely unnerved, I leaped to my feet; but the measured rocking movement of Usher was undisturbed. I rushed to the chair in which he sat. His eyes were bent fixedly before him, and throughout his whole countenance there reigned a stony rigidity. But, as I placed my hand upon his shoulder, there came a strong shudder over his whole person; a sickly smile quivered about his lips; and I saw that he spoke in a low, hurried, and gibbering murmur, as if unconscious of my presence. Bending closely over him, I at length drank in the hideous import of his words.

"Not hear it?—yes, I hear it, and *have* heard it. Long—long—long—many minutes, many hours, many days, have I heard it—yet I dared not—oh, pity me, miserable wretch that I am!—I dared not—I *dared* not speak! *We have put her living in the tomb!* Said I not that my senses were acute? I *now* tell you that I heard her first feeble movements in the hollow coffin. I heard them—many, many days ago—yet I dared not—*I dared not speak!* And now—to-night—Ethelred—ha! ha!—the breaking of the hermit's door, and the death-cry of the dragon, and the clangour of the shield! say, rather, the rending of her coffin, and the grating of the iron hinges of her prison, and her struggles within the coppered archway of the vault! Oh whither shall I fly? Will she not be here anon? Is she not hurrying to upbraid me for my haste? Have I not heard her footstep on the stair? Do I not distinguish that heavy and horrible beating of her heart? MADMAN!" here he sprang furiously to his feet, and shrieked out his syllables, as if in the effort he were giving up his soul—"MADMAN! I TELL YOU THAT SHE NOW STANDS WITHOUT THE DOOR!"

As if in the superhuman energy of his utterance there had been found the potency of a spell—the huge antique panels to which the speaker pointed, threw slowly back, upon the instant, their ponderous and ebony jaws. It was the work of the rushing gust—but then without those doors there did stand the lofty and enshrouded figure of the lady Madeline of Usher. There was blood upon her white robes, and the evidence of some bitter struggle upon every portion of her emaciated frame. For a moment she remained trembling and reeling to and fro upon the threshold, then, with a low moaning cry, fell heavily inward upon the person of her brother, and in her violent and now final death-agonies, bore him to the floor a corpse, and a victim to the terrors he had anticipated.

From that chamber, and from that mansion, I fled aghast. The storm was still abroad in all its wrath as I found myself crossing the old causeway. Suddenly there shot along the path a wild light, and I turned to see whence a gleam so unusual could have issued; for the vast house and its shadows were alone behind me. The radiance was that of the full, setting, and blood-red moon which now shone vividly through that once barely-discernible fissure of which I have before spoken as extending from the roof of the building, in a zigzag direction, to the base. While I gazed, this fissure rapidly widened—there came a fierce breath of the whirlwind—the entire orb of the satellite burst at once upon my sight—my brain reeled as I saw the mighty walls rushing asunder—there was a long tumultuous shouting sound like the voice of a thousand waters—and the deep and dank tarn at my feet closed sullenly and silently over the fragments of the "HOUSE OF USHER."

1839

The Purloined Letter

At Paris, just after dark one gusty evening in the autumn of 18——, I was enjoying the twofold luxury of meditation and a meerschaum, in company with my friend C. Auguste Dupin, in his little back library, or book-closet, *au troisième,*[1] *No. 33, Rue Dunôt, Faubourg St. Germain.* For one hour at least we had maintained a profound silence; while each, to any casual observer, might have seemed intently and exclusively occupied with the curling eddies of smoke that oppressed the atmosphere of the chamber. For myself, however, I was mentally discussing certain topics which had formed matter for conversation between us at an earlier period of the evening; I mean the affair of the Rue Morgue, and the mystery attending the murder of Marie Rogêt.[2] I looked upon it, therefore, as something of a coincidence, when the door of our apartment was thrown open and admitted our old acquaintance, Monsieur G——, the Prefect of the Parisian police.

We gave him a hearty welcome; for there was nearly half as much of the entertaining as of the contemptible about the man, and we had not seen him for several years. We had been sitting in the dark, and Dupin now arose for the purpose of lighting a lamp, but sat down again, without doing so, upon G.'s saying that he had called to consult us, or rather to ask the opinion of my friend, about some official business which had occasioned a great deal of trouble.

"If it is any point requiring reflection," observed Dupin, as he forebore to enkindle the wick, "we shall examine it to better purpose in the dark."

"That is another of your odd notions," said the Prefect, who had a fashion of calling every thing "odd" that was beyond his comprehension, and thus lived amid an absolute legion of "oddities."

"Very true," said Dupin, as he supplied his visiter with a pipe, and rolled towards him a comfortable chair.

"And what is the difficulty now?" I asked. "Nothing more in the assassination way, I hope?"

"Oh no; nothing of that nature. The fact is, the business is *very* simple indeed, and I make no doubt that we can manage it sufficiently well ourselves; but then I thought Dupin would like to hear the details of it, because it is so excessively *odd.*"

"Simple and odd," said Dupin.

"Why, yes; and not exactly that, either. The fact is, we have all been a good deal puzzled because the affair is so simple, and yet baffles us altogether."

"Perhaps it is the very simplicity of the thing which puts you at fault," said my friend.

"What nonsense you *do* talk!" replied the Prefect, laughing heartily.

"Perhaps the mystery is a little *too* plain," said Dupin.

"Oh, good heavens! who ever heard of such an idea?"

"A little *too* self-evident."

"Ha! ha! ha!—ha! ha! ha!—ho! ho! ho!" roared our visiter, profoundly amused, "oh, Dupin, you will be the death of me yet!"

---

[1] "On the third floor" (not counting the ground floor) in French; thus, on what we call the fourth floor.

[2] Two earlier cases solved by Dupin.

"And what, after all, *is* the matter on hand?" I asked.

"Why, I will tell you," replied the Prefect, as he gave a long, steady, and contemplative puff, and settled himself in his chair. "I will tell you in a few words; but, before I begin, let me caution you that this is an affair demanding the greatest secrecy, and that I should most probably lose the position I now hold, were it known that I confided it to any one."

"Proceed," said I.

"Or not," said Dupin.

"Well, then; I have received personal information, from a very high quarter, that a certain document of the last importance, has been purloined from the royal apartments. The individual who purloined it is known; this beyond a doubt; he was seen to take it. It is known, also, that it still remains in his possession."

"How is this known?" asked Dupin.

"It is clearly inferred," replied the Prefect, "from the nature of the document, and from the non-appearance of certain results which would at once arise from its passing *out* of the robber's possession;—that is to say, from his employing it as he must design in the end to employ it."

"Be a little more explicit," I said.

"Well, I may venture so far as to say that the paper gives its holder a certain power in a certain quarter where such power is immensely valuable." The Prefect was fond of the cant of diplomacy.

"Still I do not quite understand," said Dupin.

"No? Well; the disclosure of the document to a third person, who shall be nameless, would bring in question the honor of a personage of most exalted station; and this fact gives the holder of the document an ascendancy over the illustrious personage whose honor and peace are so jeopardized."

"But this ascendancy," I interposed, "would depend upon the robber's knowledge of the loser's knowledge of the robber. Who would dare—"

"The thief," said G., "is the Minister D——, who dares all things, those unbecoming as well as those becoming a man. The method of the theft was not less ingenious than bold. The document in question—a letter, to be frank—had been received by the personage robbed while alone in the royal *boudoir*. During its perusal she was suddenly interrupted by the entrance of the other exalted personage from whom especially it was her wish to conceal it. After a hurried and vain endeavor to thrust it in a drawer, she was forced to place it, open as it was, upon a table. The address, however, was uppermost, and, the contents thus unexposed, the letter escaped notice. At this juncture enters the Minister D——. His lynx eye immediately perceives the paper, recognises the handwriting of the address, observes the confusion of the personage addressed, and fathoms her secret. After some business transactions, hurried through in his ordinary manner, he produces a letter somewhat similar to the one in question, opens it, pretends to read it, and then places it in close juxtaposition to the other. Again he converses, for some fifteen minutes, upon the public affairs. At length, in taking leave, he takes also from the table the letter to which he had no claim. Its rightful owner saw, but, of course, dared not call attention to the act, in the presence of the third personage who stood at her elbow. The minister decamped; leaving his own letter—one of no importance—upon the table."

"Here, then," said Dupin to me, "you have precisely what you demand to make the ascendancy complete—the robber's knowledge of the loser's knowledge of the robber."

"Yes," replied the Prefect; "and the power thus attained has, for some months past, been wielded, for political purposes, to a very dangerous extent. The personage robbed is more thoroughly convinced, every day, of the necessity of reclaiming her letter. But this, of course, cannot be done openly. In fine, driven to despair, she has committed the matter to me."

"Than whom," said Dupin, amid a perfect whirlwind of smoke, "no more sagacious agent could, I suppose, be desired, or even imagined."

"You flatter me," replied the Prefect; "but it is possible that some such opinion may have been entertained."

"It is clear," said I, "as you observe, that the letter is still in possession of the minister; since it is this possession, and not any employment of the letter, which bestows the power. With the employment the power departs."

"True," said G.; "and upon this conviction I proceeded. My first care was to make thorough search of the minister's hotel;[3] and here my chief embarrassment lay in the necessity of searching without his knowledge. Beyond all things, I have been warned of the danger which would result from giving him reason to suspect our design."

"But," said I, "you are quite *au fait*[4] in these investigations. The Parisian police have done this thing often before."

"O yes; and for this reason I did not despair. The habits of the minister gave me, too, a great advantage. He is frequently absent from home all night. His servants are by no means numerous. They sleep at a distance from their master's apartment, and, being chiefly Neapolitans, are readily made drunk. I have keys, as you know, with which I can open any chamber or cabinet in Paris. For three months a night has not passed, during the greater part of which I have not been engaged, personally, in ransacking the D—— Hotel. My honor is interested, and, to mention a great secret, the reward is enormous. So I did not abandon the search until I had become fully satisfied that the thief is a more astute man than myself. I fancy that I have investigated every nook and corner of the premises in which it is possible that the paper can be concealed."

"But is it not possible," I suggested, "that although the letter may be in possession of the minister, as it unquestionably is, he may have concealed it elsewhere than upon his own premises?"

"This is barely possible," said Dupin. "The present peculiar condition of affairs at court, and especially of those intrigues in which D—— is known to be involved, would render the instant availability of the document—its susceptibility of being produced at a moment's notice—a point of nearly equal importance with its possession."

"Its susceptibility of being produced?" said I.

"That is to say, of being *destroyed*," said Dupin.

"True," I observed; "the paper is clearly then upon the premises. As for its being upon the person of the minister, we may consider that as out of the question."

"Entirely," said the Prefect. "He has been twice waylaid, as if by footpads, and his person rigorously searched under my own inspection."

"You might have spared yourself this trouble," said Dupin. "D——, I presume, is not altogether a fool, and, if not, must have anticipated these waylayings, as a matter of course."

[3] Large private residence.
[4] French: "accomplished."

"Not *altogether* a fool," said G., "but then he's a poet, which I take to be only one remove from a fool."

"True," said Dupin, after a long and thoughtful whiff from his meerschaum, "although I have been guilty of certain doggrel myself."

"Suppose you detail," said I, "the particulars of your search."

"Why the fact is, we took our time, and we searched *every where*. I have had long experience in these affairs. I took the entire building, room by room; devoting the nights of a whole week to each. We examined, first, the furniture of each apartment. We opened every possible drawer; and I presume you know that, to a properly trained police agent, such a thing as a *secret* drawer is impossible. Any man is a dolt who permits a 'secret' drawer to escape him in a search of this kind. The thing is *so* plain. There is a certain amount of bulk—of space—to be accounted for in every cabinet. Then we have accurate rules. The fiftieth part of a line could not escape us. After the cabinets we took the chairs. The cushions we probed with fine long needles you have seen me employ. From the tables we removed the tops."

"Why so?"

"Sometimes the top of a table, or other similarly arranged piece of furniture, is removed by the person wishing to conceal an article; then the leg is excavated, the article deposited within the cavity, and the top replaced. The bottoms and tops of bedposts are employed in the same way."

"But could not the cavity be detected by sounding?" I asked.

"By no means, if, when the article is deposited, a sufficient wadding of cotton be placed around it. Besides, in our case, we were obliged to proceed without noise."

"But you could not have removed—you could not have taken to pieces *all* articles of furniture in which it would have been possible to make a deposit in the manner you mention. A letter may be compressed into a thin spiral roll, not differing much in shape or bulk from a large knitting-needle, and in this form it might be inserted into the rung of a chair, for example, You did not take to pieces all the chairs?"

"Certainly not; but we did better—we examined the rungs of every chair in the hotel, and, indeed, the jointings of every description of furniture, by the aid of a most powerful microscope.[5] Had there been any traces of recent disturbance we should not have failed to detect it instantly. A single grain of gimlet-dust, for example, would have been as obvious as an apple. Any disorder in the glueing—any unusual gaping in the joints—would have sufficed to insure detection."

"I presume you looked to the mirrors, between the boards and the plates, and you probed the beds and the bed-clothes, as well as the curtains and carpets."

"That of course; and when we had absolutely completed every particle of the furniture in this way, then we examined the house itself. We divided its entire surface into compartments, which we numbered, so that none might be missed; then we scrutinized each individual square inch throughout the premises, including the two houses immediately adjoining, with the microscope, as before."

"The two houses adjoining!" I exclaimed; "you must have had a great deal of trouble."

"We had; but the reward offered is prodigious."

[5] Magnifying glass.

"You include the *grounds* about the houses?"

"All the grounds are paved with brick. They gave us comparatively little trouble. We examined the moss between the bricks, and found it undisturbed."

"You looked among D——'s papers, of course, and into the books of the library?"

"Certainly; we opened every package and parcel; we not only opened every book, but we turned over every leaf in each volume, not contenting ourselves with a mere shake, according to the fashion of some of our police officers. We also measured the thickness of every book-*cover,* with the most accurate admeasurement, and applied to each the most jealous scrutiny of the microscope. Had any of the bindings been recently meddled with, it would have been utterly impossible that the fact should have escaped observation. Some five or six volumes, just from the hand of the binder, we carefully probed, longitudinally, with the needles."

"You explored the floors beneath the carpets?"

"Beyond doubt. We removed every carpet, and examined the boards with the microscope."

"And the paper on the walls?"

"Yes."

"You looked into the cellars?"

"We did."

"Then," I said, "you have been making a miscalculation, and the letter is *not* upon the premises, as you suppose."

"I fear you are right there," said the Prefect. "And now, Dupin, what would you advise me to do?"

"To make a thorough re-search of the premises."

"That is absolutely needless," replied G——. "I am not more sure that I breathe than I am that the letter is not at the Hotel."

"I have no better advice to give you," said Dupin. "You have, of course, an accurate description of the letter?"

"Oh yes!"—And here the Prefect, producing a memorandum-book, proceeded to read aloud a minute account of the internal, and especially of the external appearance of the missing document. Soon after finishing the perusal of this description, he took his departure, more entirely depressed in spirits than I had ever known the good gentleman before.

In about a month afterwards he paid us another visit, and found us occupied very nearly as before. He took a pipe and a chair and entered into some ordinary conversation. At length I said,—

"Well, but G——, what of the purloined letter? I presume you have at last made up your mind that there is no such thing as overreaching the Minister?"

"Confound him, say I—yes; I made the re-examination, however, as Dupin suggested—but it was all labor lost, as I knew it would be."

"How much was the reward offered, did you say?" asked Dupin.

"Why a very great deal—a *very* liberal reward—I don't like to say how much, precisely; but one thing I *will* say, that I wouldn't mind giving my individual check for fifty thousand francs to any one who could obtain me that letter. The fact is, it is becoming of more and more importance every day; and the reward has been lately doubled. If it were trebled, however, I could do no more than I have done."

"Why, yes," said Dupin, drawlingly, between the whiffs of his meerschaum, "I really—think, G——, you have not exerted yourself—to the utmost in this matter. You might—do a little more, I think, eh?"

"How?—in what way?"

"Why—puff, puff—you might—puff, puff—employ counsel in the matter, eh?— puff, puff, puff. Do you remember the story they tell of Abernethy?"[6]

"No; hang Abernethy!"

"To be sure! hang him and welcome. But, once upon a time, a certain rich miser conceived the design of spunging upon this Abernethy for a medical opinion. Getting up, for this purpose, an ordinary conversation in a private company, he insinuated his case to the physician, as that of an imaginary individual.

" 'We will suppose,' said the miser, 'that his symptoms are such and such; now, doctor, what would *you* have directed him to take?'

" 'Take!' said Abernethy, 'why, take *advice*, to be sure.' "

"But," said the Prefect, a little discomposed, "I am *perfectly* willing to take advice, and to pay for it. I would *really* give fifty thousand francs to any one who would aid me in the matter."

"In that case," replied Dupin, opening a drawer, and producing a check-book, "you may as well fill me up a check for the amount mentioned. When you have signed it, I will hand you the letter."

I was astounded. The Prefect appeared absolutely thunder-stricken. For some minutes he remained speechless and motionless, looking incredulously at my friend with open mouth, and eyes that seemed starting from their sockets; then, apparently recovering himself in some measure, he seized a pen, and after several pauses and vacant stares, finally filled up and signed a check for fifty thousand francs, and handed it across the table to Dupin. The latter examined it carefully and deposited it in his pocketbook; then, unlocking an *escritoire*,[7] took thence a letter and gave it to the Prefect. This functionary grasped it in a perfect agony of joy, opened it with a trembling hand, cast a rapid glance at its contents, and then, scrambling and struggling to the door, rushed at length unceremoniously from the room and from the house, without having uttered a syllable since Dupin had requested him to fill up the check.

When he had gone, my friend entered into some explanations.

"The Parisian police," he said, "are exceedingly able in their way. They are persevering, ingenious, cunning, and thoroughly versed in the knowledge which their duties seem chiefly to demand. Thus, when G—— detailed to us his mode of searching the premises at the Hotel D——, I felt entire confidence in his having made a satisfactory investigation—so far as his labors extended."

"So far as his labors extended?" said I.

"Yes," said Dupin. "The measures adopted were not only the best of their kind, but carried out to absolute perfection. Had the letter been deposited within the range of their search, these fellows would, beyond a question, have found it."

I merely laughed—but he seemed quite serious in all that he said.

"The measures, then," he continued, "were good in their kind, and well executed; their defect lay in their being inapplicable to the case, and to the man. A certain set of

[6]John Abernethy, English surgeon (1764–1831).

[7] French: "writing desk."

highly ingenious resources are, with the Prefect, a sort of Procrustean bed,[8] to which he forcibly adapts his designs. But he perpetually errs by being too deep or too shallow, for the matter in hand; and many a school-boy is a better reasoner than he. I knew one about eight years of age, whose success at guessing in the game of 'even and odd' attracted universal admiration. This game is simple, and is played with marbles. One player holds in his hand a number of these toys, and demands of another whether that number is even or odd. If the guess is right, the guesser wins one; if wrong, he loses one. The boy to whom I allude won all the marbles of the school. Of course he had some principle of guessing; and this lay in mere observation and admeasurement of the astuteness of his opponents. For example, an arrant simpleton is his opponent, and, holding up his closed hand, asks, 'are they even or odd?' Our schoolboy replies, 'odd,' and loses; but upon the second trial he wins, for he then says to himself, "the simpleton had them even upon the first trial, and his amount of cunning is just sufficient to make him have them odd upon the second; I will therefore guess odd;—he guesses odd, and wins. Now, with a simpleton a degree above the first, he would have reasoned thus: 'This fellow finds that in the first instance I guessed odd, and, in the second, he will propose to himself, upon the first impulse, a simple variation from even to odd, as did the first simpleton; but then a second thought will suggest that this is too simple a variation, and finally he will decide upon putting it even as before. I will therefore guess even;'—he guesses even, and wins. Now this mode of reasoning in the schoolboy, whom his fellows termed 'lucky,'—what, in its last analysis, is it?"

"It is merely," I said, "an identification of the reasoner's intellect with that of his opponent."

"It is," said Dupin; "and, upon inquiring of the boy by what means he effected the *thorough* identification in which his success consisted, I received answer as follows: 'When I wish to find out how wise, or how stupid, or how good, or how wicked is any one, or what are his thoughts at the moment, I fashion the expression of my face, as accurately as possible, in accordance with the expression of his, and then wait to see what thoughts or sentiments arise in my mind or heart, as if to match or correspond with the expression.' This response of the schoolboy lies at the bottom of all the spurious profundity which has been attributed to Rochefoucault, to La Bruyère, to Machiavelli, and to Campanella."[9]

"And the identification," I said, "of the reasoner's intellect with that of his opponent, depends, if I understand you aright, upon the accuracy with which the opponent's intellect is admeasured."

"For its practical value it depends upon this," replied Dupin; "and the Prefect and his cohort fail so frequently, first, by default of this identification, and, secondly, by ill-admeasurement, or rather through non-admeasurement, of the intellect with which they are engaged. They consider only their *own* ideas of ingenuity; and, in searching for anything hidden, advert only to the modes in which *they* would have hidden it. They are right in this much—that their own ingenuity is a faithful representative of that of *the mass;* but when the cunning of the individual felon is diverse in character from their own, the felon foils them, of course. This always happens when it is above their own,

---

[8] i.e., an unyielding system. Procrustes, robber in classic myth, forced his victims to fit the bed to which he tied them by cutting off their legs if they were too long or by stretching them if too short.

[9] French and Italian moralists and philosophers of the fifteenth to seventeenth centuries.

and very usually when it is below. They have no variation of principle in their investigations; at best, when urged by some unusual emergency—by some extraordinary reward—they extend or exaggerate their old modes of *practice,* without touching their principles. What, for example, in this case of D——, has been done to vary the principle of action? What is all this boring, and probing, and sounding, and scrutinizing with the microscope, and dividing the surface of the building into registered square inches—what is it all but an exaggeration *of the application* of the one principle or set of principles of search, which are based upon the one set of notions regarding human ingenuity, to which the Prefect, in the long routine of his duty, has been accustomed? Do you not see he has taken it for granted that *all* men proceed to conceal a letter,—not exactly in a gimlet-hole bored in a chair-leg—but, at least, in *some* out-of-the-way hole or corner suggested by the same tenor of thought which would urge a man to secrete a letter in a gimlet-hole bored in a chair-leg? And do you not see also, that such *recherchés*[10] nooks for concealment are adapted only for ordinary occasions, and would be adopted only by ordinary intellects; for, in all cases of concealment, a disposal of the article concealed—a disposal of it in this *recherché* manner,—is, in the very first instance, presumable and presumed; and thus its discovery depends, not at all upon the acumen, but altogether upon the mere care, patience, and determination of the seekers; and where the case is of importance—or, what amounts to the same thing in the policial eyes, when the reward is of magnitude,—the qualities in question have *never* been known to fail. You will now understand what I meant in suggesting that, had the purloined letter been hidden any where within the limits of the Prefect's examination—in other words, had the principle of its concealment been comprehended within the principles of the Prefect—its discovery would have been a matter altogether beyond question. This functionary, however, has been thoroughly mystified; and the remote source of his defeat lies in the supposition that the Minister is a fool, because he has acquired renown as a poet. All fools are poets; this the Prefect *feels;* and he is merely guilty of a *non distributio medii*[11] in thence inferring that all poets are fools."

"But is this really the poet?" I asked. "There are two brothers, I know; and both have attained reputation in letters. The Minister I believe has written learnedly on the Differential Calculus. He is a mathematician, and no poet."

"You are mistaken; I know him well; he is both. As poet *and* mathematician, he would reason well; as mere mathematician, he could not have reasoned at all, and thus would have been at the mercy of the Prefect."

"You surprise me," I said, "by these opinions, which have been contradicted by the voice of the world. You do not mean to set at naught the well-digested idea of centuries. The mathematical reason has long been regarded as *the* reason *par excel-lence.*"[12]

" '*Il y a à parier,*' " replied Dupin, quoting from Chamfort, " '*que toute idée publique, toute convention reçue, est une sottise, car elle a convenu au plus grand nombre.*'[13] The mathematicians, I grant you, have done their best to promulgate the popular error to which you allude, and which is none the less an error for its promulgation as truth.

---

[10] French: "unusual."
[11] Latin: "undistributed middle." A term in logic that indicates faulty reasoning.
[12] French: "the very best."
[13] A maxim from the eighteenth-century

French moralist Sebastien Chamfort: "There's a good chance that every generally accepted notion, every commonly received convention, is nonsense, exactly because it pleased the majority view."

With an art worthy a better cause, for example, they have insinuated the term 'analysis' into application to algebra. The French are the originators of this particular deception; but if a term is of any importance—if words derive any value from applicability—then 'analysis' conveys 'algebra' about as much as, in Latin, *'ambitus'* implies 'ambition,' *'religio'* 'religion,' or *'homines honesti,'* a set of *honorable* men."

"You have a quarrel on hand, I see," said I, "with some of the algebraists of Paris; but proceed."

"I dispute the availability, and thus the value, of that reason which is cultivated in any especial form other than the abstractly logical. I dispute, in particular, the reason educed by mathematical study. The mathematics are the science of form and quantity; mathematical reasoning is merely logic applied to observation upon form and quantity. The great error lies in supposing that even the truths of what is called *pure* algebra, are abstract or general truths. And this error is so egregious that I am confounded at the universality with which it has been received. Mathematical axioms are *not* axioms of general truth. What is true of *relation*—of form and quantity—is often grossly false in regard to morals, for example. In this latter science it is very usually *untrue* that the aggregated parts are equal to the whole. In chemistry also the axiom fails. In the consideration of motive it fails; for two motives, each of a given value, have not, necessarily, a value when united, equal to the sum of their values apart. There are numerous other mathematical truths which are only truths within the limits of *relation*. But the mathematician argues, from his *finite truths*, through habit, as if they were of an absolutely general applicability—as the world indeed imagines them to be. Bryant,[14] in his very learned 'Mythology,' mentions an analogous source of error, when he says that 'although the Pagan fables are not believed, yet we forget ourselves continually, and make inferences from them as existing realities.' With the algebraists, however, who are Pagans themselves, the 'Pagan fables' *are* believed, and the inferences are made, not so much through lapse of memory, as through an unaccountable addling of the brains. In short, I never yet encountered the mere mathematician who could be trusted out of equal roots, or one who did not clandestinely hold it as a point of his faith that x^2+px was absolutely and unconditionally equal to q. Say to one of these gentlemen, by way of experiment, if you please, that you believe occasions may occur where x^2+px is *not* altogether equal to q, and, having made him understand what you mean, get out of his reach as speedily as convenient, for, beyond doubt, he will endeavor to knock you down.

"I mean to say," continued Dupin, while I merely laughed at his last observations, "that if the Minister had been no more than a mathematician, the Prefect would have been under no necessity of giving me this check. I knew him, however, as both mathematician and poet, and my measures were adapted to his capacity, with reference to the circumstances by which he was surrounded. I knew him as a courtier, too, and as a bold *intriguant*.[15] Such a man, I considered, could not fail to be aware of the ordinary policial modes of action. He could not have failed to anticipate—and events have proved that he did not fail to anticipate—the waylayings to which he was subjected. He must have foreseen, I reflected, the secret investigations of his premises. His frequent absences from home at night, which were hailed by the Prefect as certain aids to his success, I

---

[14] Jacob Bryant (1715–1804), whose *A New System, or an Analysis of Ancient Mythology* was published between 1774 and 1776.

[15] French: "conniver."

regarded only as *ruses,* to afford opportunity for thorough search to the police, and thus the sooner to impress them with the conviction to which G——, in fact, did finally arrive—the conviction that the letter was not upon the premises. I felt, also, that the whole train of thought, which I was at some pains in detailing to you just now, concerning the invariable principle of policial action in searches for articles concealed—I felt that this whole train of thought would necessarily pass through the mind of the Minister. It would imperatively lead him to despise all the ordinary *nooks* of concealment. *He* could not, I reflected, be so weak as not to see that the most intricate and remote recess of his hotel would be as open as his commonest closets to the eyes, to the probes, to the gimlets, and to the microscopes of the Prefect. I saw, in fine, that he would be driven, as a matter of course, to *simplicity,* if not deliberately induced to it as a matter of choice. You will remember, perhaps, how desperately the Prefect laughed when I suggested, upon our first interview, that it was just possible this mystery troubled him so much on account of its being so *very* self-evident.”

“Yes,” said I, “I remember his merriment well. I really thought he would have fallen into convulsions.”

“The material world,” continued Dupin, “abounds with very strict analogies to the immaterial; and thus some color of truth has been given to the rhetorical dogma, that metaphor, or simile, may be made to strengthen an argument, as well as to embellish a description. The principle of the *vis inertiæ,*[16] for example, seems to be identical in physics and metaphysics. It is not more true in the former, that a large body is with more difficulty set in motion than a smaller one, and that its subsequent *momentum* is commensurate with this difficulty, than it is, in the latter, that intellects of the vaster capacity, while more forcible, more constant, and more eventful in their movements than those of inferior grade, are yet the less readily moved, and more embarrassed and full of hesitation in the first few steps of their progress. Again: have you ever noticed which of the street signs, over the shop-doors, are the most attractive of attention?”

“I have never given the matter a thought,” I said.

“There is a game of puzzles,” he resumed, “which is played upon a map. One party playing requires another to find a given word—the name of town, river, state or empire—any word, in short, upon the motley and perplexed surface of the chart. A novice in the game generally seeks to embarrass his opponents by giving them the most minutely lettered names; but the adept selects such words as stretch, in large characters, from one end of the chart to the other. These, like the over-largely lettered signs and placards of the street, escape observation by dint of being excessively obvious; and here the physical oversight is precisely analogous with the moral inapprehension by which the intellect suffers to pass unnoticed those considerations which are too obtrusively and too palpably self-evident. But this is a point, it appears, somewhat above or beneath the understanding of the Prefect. He never once thought it probable, or possible, that the Minister had deposited the letter immediately beneath the nose of the whole world, by way of best preventing any portion of that world from perceiving it.

“But the more I reflected upon the daring, dashing, and discriminating ingenuity of D——; upon the fact that the document must always have been *at hand,* if he intended to use it to good purpose; and upon the decisive evidence, obtained by the Prefect, that it was not hidden within the limits of that dignitary’s ordinary search—the more satis-

[16] Latin: “power of inertia.”

fied I became that, to conceal this letter, the Minister had resorted to the comprehensive and sagacious expedient of not attempting to conceal it at all.

"Full of these ideas, I prepared myself with a pair of green spectacles, and called one fine morning, quite by accident, at the Ministerial hotel. I found D—— at home, yawning, lounging, and dawdling, as usual, and pretending to be in the last extremity of *ennui*. He is, perhaps, the most really energetic human being now alive—but that is only when nobody sees him.

"To be even with him, I complained of my weak eyes, and lamented the necessity of the spectacles, under cover of which I cautiously and thoroughly surveyed the apartment, while seemingly intent only upon the conversation of my host.

"I paid especial attention to a large writing-table near which he sat, and upon which lay confusedly, some miscellaneous letters and other papers, with one or two musical instruments and a few books. Here, however, after a long and very deliberate scrutiny, I saw nothing to excite particular suspicion.

"At length my eyes, in going the circuit of the room, fell upon a trumpery fillagree card-rack of pasteboard, that hung dangling by a dirty blue ribbon from a little brass knob just beneath the middle of the mantel-piece. In this rack, which had three or four compartments, were five or six visiting cards and a solitary letter. This last was much soiled and crumpled. It was torn nearly in two, across the middle—as if a design, in the first instance, to tear it entirely up as worthless, had been altered, or stayed, in the second. It had a large black seal, bearing the D—— cipher *very* conspicuously, and was addressed, in a diminutive female hand, to D——, the minister, himself. It was thrust carelessly, and even, as it seemed, contemptuously, into one of the upper divisions of the rack.

"No sooner had I glanced at this letter, than I concluded it to be that of which I was in search. To be sure, it was, to all appearance, radically different from the one of which the Prefect had read us so minute a description Here the seal was large and black, with the D—— cipher; there it was small and red, with the ducal arms of the S—— family. Here, the address, to the Minister, was diminutive and feminine; there the superscription, to a certain royal personage, was markedly bold and decided; the size alone formed a point of correspondence. But, then, the *radicalness* of these differences, which was excessive; the dirt; the soiled and torn condition of the paper, so inconsistent with the *true* methodical habits of D——, and so suggestive of a design to delude the beholder into an idea of the worthlessness of the document; these things, together with the hyperobtrusive situation of this document, full in the view of every visiter, and thus exactly in accordance with the conclusions to which I had previously arrived; these things, I say, were strongly corroborative of suspicion, in one who came with the intention to suspect.

"I protracted my visit as long as possible, and, while I maintained a most animated discussion with the Minister, on a topic which I knew well had never failed to interest and excite him, I kept my attention really riveted upon the letter. In this examination, I committed to memory its external appearance and arrangement in the rack; and also fell, at length, upon a discovery which set at rest whatever trivial doubt I might have entertained. In scrutinizing the edges of the paper, I observed them to be more *chafed* than seemed necessary. They presented the *broken* appearance which is manifested when a stiff paper, having been once folded and pressed with a folder, is refolded in a reversed direction, in the same creases or edges which had formed the original fold.

This discovery was sufficient. It was clear to me that the letter had been turned, as a glove, inside out, re-directed, and re-sealed. I bade the Minister good morning, and took my departure at once, leaving a gold snuff-box upon the table.

"The next morning I called for the snuff-box, when we resumed, quite eagerly, the conversation of the preceding day. While thus engaged, however, a loud report, as if of a pistol, was heard immediately beneath the windows of the hotel, and was succeeded by a series of fearful screams, and the shoutings of a mob. D—— rushed to a casement, threw it open, and looked out. In the meantime, I stepped to the card-rack, took the letter, put it in my pocket, and replaced it by a *fac-simile*, (so far as regards externals,) which I had carefully prepared at my lodgings; imitating the D—— cipher, very readily, by means of a seal formed of bread.

"The disturbance in the street had been occasioned by the frantic behavior of a man with a musket. He had fired it among a crowd of women and children. It proved, however, to have been without ball, and the fellow was suffered to go his way as a lunatic or a drunkard. When he had gone, D—— came from the window, whither I had followed him immediately upon securing the object in view. Soon afterwards I bade him farewell. The pretended lunatic was a man in my own pay."

"But what purpose had you," I asked, "in replacing the letter by a *fac-simile?* Would it not have been better, at the first visit, to have seized it openly, and departed?"

"D——," replied Dupin, "is a desperate man, and a man of nerve. His hotel, too, is not without attendants devoted to his interests. Had I made the wild attempt you suggest, I might never have left the Ministerial presence alive. The good people of Paris might have heard of me no more. But I had an object apart from these considerations. You know my political prepossessions. In this matter, I act as a partisan of the lady concerned. For eighteen months the Minister has had her in his power. She has now him in hers; since, being unaware that the letter is not in his possession, he will proceed with his exactions as if it was. Thus will he inevitably commit himself, at once, to his political destruction. His downfall, too, will not be more precipitate than awkward. It is all very well to talk about the *facilis descensus Averni;*[17] but in all kinds of climbing, as Catalani[18] said of singing, it is far more easy to get up than to come down. In the present instance I have no sympathy—at least no pity—for him who descends. He is that *monstrum horrendum,*[19] an unprincipled man of genius. I confess, however, that I should like very well to know the precise character of his thoughts, when, being defied by her whom the Prefect terms 'a certain personage,' he is reduced to opening the letter which I left for him in the card-rack."

"How? did you put any thing particular in it?"

"Why—it did not seem altogether right to leave the interior blank—that would have been insulting. D——, at Vienna once, did me an evil turn, which I told him, quite good-humoredly, that I should remember. So, as I knew he would feel some curiosity in regard to the identity of the person who had outwitted him, I thought it a pity not to

---

[17] Paraphrase from Virgil's *Aeneid:* "The way down to Hell is easy."

[18] Angelica Catalani (1780–1849), Italian soprano.

[19] Latin: "hideous monstrosity."

give him a clue. He is well acquainted with my MS., and I just copied into the middle of the blank sheet the words—

> —Un dessein si funeste,
> S'il n'est digne d'Atrée, est digne de Thyeste.

They are to be found in Crébillon's 'Atrée.' "[20]
1844

The Cask of Amontillado

The thousand injuries of Fortunato I had borne as I best could; but when he ventured upon insult, I vowed revenge. You, who so well know the nature of my soul, will not suppose, however, that I gave utterance to a threat. *At length* I would be avenged; this was a point definitively settled—but the very definitiveness with which it was resolved precluded the idea of risk. I must not only punish, but punish with impunity. A wrong is unredressed when retribution overtakes its redresser. It is equally unredressed when the avenger fails to make himself felt such to him who has done the wrong.

It must be understood that neither by word nor deed had I given Fortunato cause to doubt my good will. I continued, as was my wont, to smile in his face, and he did not perceive that my smile *now* was at the thought of his immolation.

He had a weak point—this Fortunato—although in other regards he was a man to be respected and even feared. He prided himself on his connoisseurship in wine. Few Italians have the true virtuoso spirit. For the most part their enthusiasm is adopted to suit the time and opportunity—to practice imposture upon the British and Austrian *millionaires*. In painting and gemmary[1] Fortunato, like his countrymen, was a quack—but in the matter of old wines he was sincere. In this respect I did not differ from him materially; I was skilful in the Italian vintages myself, and bought largely whenever I could.

It was about dusk, one evening during the supreme madness of the carnival season, that I encountered my friend. He accosted me with excessive warmth, for he had been drinking much. The man wore motley. He had on a tight-fitting parti-striped dress, and his head was surmounted by the conical cap and bells. I was so pleased to see him that I thought I should never have done wringing his hand.

I said to him—"My dear Fortunato, you are luckily met. How remarkably well you are looking to-day! But I have received a pipe of what passes for Amontillado, and I have my doubts."

"How?" said he. "Amontillado? A pipe? Impossible! And in the middle of the carnival!"

---

[20] The drama *Atrée et Thyeste* (1770) by Prosper de Crébillon (1674–1762), based on the classic myth of the revenge of Atreus. Having seduced Atreus' wife, Thyestes is served a feast prepared from the bodies of his sons, whom Atreus has murdered. The quotation states: "So dire a scheme, / Though unworthy of Atreus, is worthy of Thyestes."
[1] Knowledge of precious gems.

"I have my doubts," I replied; "and I was silly enough to pay the full Amontillado price without consulting you in the matter. You were not to be found, and I was fearful of losing a bargain."

"Amontillado!"

"I have my doubts."

"Amontillado!"

"And I must satisfy them."

"Amontillado!"

"As you are engaged, I am on my way to Luchesi. If any one has a critical turn, it is he. He will tell me—"

"Luchesi cannot tell Amontillado from Sherry."

"And yet some fools will have it that his taste is a match for your own."

"Come, let us go."

"Whither?"

"To your vaults."

"My friend, no; I will not impose upon your good nature. I perceive you have an engagement. Luchesi—"

"I have no engagement;—come."

"My friend, no. It is not the engagement, but the severe cold with which I perceive you are afflicted. The vaults are insufferably damp. They are encrusted with nitre."

"Let us go, nevertheless. The cold is merely nothing. Amontillado! You have been imposed upon. And as for Luchesi, he cannot distinguish Sherry from Amontillado."

Thus speaking, Fortunato possessed himself of my arm. Putting on a mask of black silk, and drawing a *roquelaire* closely about my person, I suffered him to hurry me to my palazzo.[2]

There were no attendants at home; they had absconded to make merry in honor of the time. I had told them that I should not return until the morning, and had given them explicit orders not to stir from the house. These orders were sufficient, I well knew, to insure their immediate disappearance, one and all, as soon as my back was turned.

I took from their sconces two flambeaux, and giving one to Fortunato, bowed him through several suites of rooms to the archway that led into the vaults. I passed down a long and winding staircase, requesting him to be cautious as he followed. We came at length to the foot of the descent, and stood together on the damp ground of the catacombs of the Montresors.

The gait of my friend was unsteady, and the bells upon his cap jingled as he strode.

"The pipe," said he.

"It is farther on," said I; "but observe the white web-work which gleams from these cavern walls."

He turned towards me, and looked into my eyes with two filmy orbs that distilled the rheum of intoxication.

"Nitre?" he asked, at length.

"Nitre," I replied. "How long have you had that cough?"

"Ugh! ugh! ugh!—ugh! ugh! ugh!—ugh! ugh! ugh!—ugh! ugh! ugh!—ugh! ugh! ugh!"

My poor friend found it impossible to reply for many minutes.

---

2 Large residence.

"It is nothing," he said, at last.

"Come," I said, with decision, "we will go back; your health is precious. You are rich, respected, admired, beloved; you are happy, as once I was. You are a man to be missed. For me it is no matter. We will go back; you will be ill, and I cannot be responsible. Besides, there is Luchesi—"

"Enough," he said; "the cough is a mere nothing; it will not kill me. I shall not die of a cough."

"True—true," I replied; "and, indeed, I had no intention of alarming you unnecessarily—but you should use all proper caution. A draught of this Medoc will defend us from the damps."

Here I knocked off the neck of a bottle which I drew from a long row of its fellows that lay upon the mould.

"Drink" I said, presenting him the wine.

He raised it to his lips with a leer. He paused and nodded to me familiarly, while his bells jingled.

"I drink," he said, "to the buried that repose around us."

"And I to your long life."

He again took my arm, and we proceeded.

"These vaults," he said, "are extensive."

"The Montresors," I replied, "were a great and numerous family."

"I forget your arms."

"A huge human foot d'or, in a field azure;[3] the foot crushes a serpent rampant whose fangs are imbedded in the heel."

"And the motto?"

"*Nemo me impune lacessit.*"[4]

"Good!" he said.

The wine sparkled in his eyes and the bells jingled. My own fancy grew warm with the Medoc. We had passed through walls of piled bones, with casks and puncheons intermingling, into the inmost recesses of the catacombs. I paused again, and this time I made bold to seize Fortunato by an arm above the elbow.

"The nitre!" I said; "see, it increases. It hangs like moss upon the vaults. We are below the river's bed. The drops of moisture trickle among the bones. Come, we will go back ere it is too late. Your cough—"

"It is nothing," he said; "let us go on. But first, another draught of the Medoc."

I broke and reached him a flaçon of De Grâve.[5] He emptied it at a breath. His eyes flashed with a fierce light. He laughed and threw the bottle upwards with a gesticulation I did not understand.

I looked at him in surprise. He repeated the movement—a grotesque one.

"You do not comprehend?" he said.

"Not I," I replied.

"Then you are not of the brotherhood."

---

[3] Heraldic terms describing a golden foot laid upon a blue background.

[4] "No one may insult me without fearing punishment."

[5] White wine from Bordeaux.

"How?"

"You are not of the masons."

"Yes, yes," I said, "yes, yes."

"You? Impossible! A mason?"

"A mason," I replied.

"A sign," he said.

"It is this," I answered, producing a trowel from beneath the folds of my *roquelaire.*

"You jest," he exclaimed, recoiling a few paces. "But let us proceed to the Amontillado."

"Be it so," I said, replacing the tool beneath the cloak, and again offering him my arm. He leaned upon it heavily. We continued our route in search of the Amontillado. We passed through a range of low arches, descended, passed on, and descending again, arrived at a deep crypt, in which the foulness of the air caused our flambeaux rather to glow than flame.

At the most remote end of the crypt there appeared another less spacious. Its walls had been lined with human remains, piled to the vault overhead, in the fashion of the great catacombs of Paris. Three sides of this interior crypt were still ornamented in this manner. From the fourth the bones had been thrown down, and lay promiscuously upon the earth, forming at one point a mound of some size. Within the wall thus exposed by the displacing of the bones, we perceived a still interior recess, in depth about four feet, in width three, in height six or seven. It seemed to have been constructed for no especial use within itself, but formed merely the interval between two of the colossal supports of the roof of the catacombs, and was backed by one of their circumscribing walls of solid granite.

It was in vain that Fortunato, uplifting his dull torch, endeavored to pry into the depth of the recess. Its termination the feeble light did not enable us to see.

"Proceed," I said; "herein is the Amontillado. As for Luchesi—"

"He is an ignoramus," interrupted my friend, as he stepped unsteadily forward, while I followed immediately at his heels. In an instant he had reached the extremity of the niche, and finding his progress arrested by the rock, stood stupidly bewildered. A moment more and I had fettered him to the granite. In its surface were two iron staples, distant from each other about two feet, horizontally. From one of these depended a short chain, from the other a padlock. Throwing the links about his waist, it was but the work of a few seconds to secure it. He was too much astounded to resist. Withdrawing the key I stepped back from the recess.

"Pass your hand," I said, "over the wall; you cannot help feeling the nitre. Indeed it is *very* damp. Once more let me *implore* you to return. No? Then I must positively leave you. But I must first render you all the little attentions in my power."

"The Amontillado!" ejaculated my friend, not yet recovered from his astonishment.

"True," I replied; "the Amontillado."

As I said these words I busied myself among the pile of bones of which I have before spoken. Throwing them aside, I soon uncovered a quantity of building stone and mortar. With these materials and with the aid of my trowel, I began vigorously to wall up the entrance of the niche.

I had scarcely laid the first tier of the masonry when I discovered that the intoxication of Fortunato had in a great measure worn off. The earliest indication I had of this was a low moaning cry from the depth of the recess. It was *not* the cry of a drunken man.

There was then a long and obstinate silence. I laid the second tier, and the third, and the fourth; and then I heard the furious vibrations of the chain. The noise lasted for several minutes, during which, that I might hearken to it with the more satisfaction, I ceased my labors and sat down upon the bones. When at last the clanking subsided, I resumed the trowel, and finished without interruption the fifth, the sixth, and the seventh tier. The wall was now nearly upon a level with my breast. I again paused, and holding the flambeaux over the mason-work, threw a few feeble rays upon the figure within.

A succession of loud and shrill screams, bursting suddenly from the throat of the chained form, seemed to thrust me violently back. For a brief moment I hesitated—I trembled. Unsheathing my rapier, I began to grope with it about the recess: but the thought of an instant reassured me. I placed my hand upon the solid fabric of the catacombs, and felt satisfied. I reapproached the wall. I replied to the yells of him who clamored. I re-echoed—I aided—I surpassed them in volume and in strength. I did this, and the clamorer grew still.

It was now midnight, and my task was drawing to a close. I had completed the eighth, the ninth, and the tenth tier. I had finished a portion of the last and the eleventh; there remained but a single stone to be fitted and plastered in. I struggled with its weight; I placed it partially in its destined position. But now there came from out the niche a low laugh that erected the hairs upon my head. It was succeeded by a sad voice, which I had difficulty in recognising as that of the noble Fortunato. The voice said—

"Ha! ha! ha?—he! he!—a very good joke indeed—an excellent jest. We will have many a rich laugh about it at the palazzo—he! he! he!—over our wine—he! he! he!"

"The Amontillado!" I said.

"He! he! he!—he! he! he!—yes, the Amontillado. But is it not getting late? Will not they be awaiting us at the palazzo, the Lady Fortunato and the rest? Let us be gone."

"Yes," I said, "let us be gone."

"For the love of God, Montresor!"

"Yes," I said, "for the love of God!"

But to these words I hearkened in vain for a reply. I grew impatient. I called aloud—

"Fortunato!"

No answer. I called again—

"Fortunato!"

No answer still. I thrust a torch through the remaining aperture and let it fall within. There came forth in return only a jingling of the bells. My heart grew sick—on account of the dampness of the catacombs. I hastened to make an end of my labor. I forced the last stone into its position; I plastered it up. Against the new masonry I re-erected the old rampart of bones. For the half of a century no mortal has disturbed them. *In pa'ce requiescat!*[6]

1846

6 "Rest in peace!"

The Philosophy of Composition

Charles Dickens, in a note now lying before me, alluding to an examination I once made of the mechanism of "Barnaby Rudge,"[1] says—"By the way, are you aware that Godwin wrote his 'Caleb Williams' backwards?[2] He first involved his hero in a web of difficulties, forming the second volume and then, for the first, cast about him for some mode of accounting for what had been done."

I cannot think this the *precise* mode of procedure on the part of Godwin—and indeed what he himself acknowledges, is not altogether in accordance with Mr. Dickens' idea—but the author of "Caleb Williams" was too good an artist not to perceive the advantage derivable from at least a somewhat similar process. Nothing is more clear than that every plot, worth the name, must be elaborated to its *dénouement* before anything be attempted with the pen. It is only with the *dénouement* constantly in view that we can give a plot its indispensable air of consequence, or causation, by making the incidents, and especially the tone at all points, tend to the development of the intention.

There is a radical error, I think, in the usual mode of constructing a story. Either history affords a thesis—or one is suggested by an incident of the day—or, at best, the author sets himself to work in the combination of striking events to form merely the basis of his narrative—designing, generally, to fill in with description, dialogue, or autorial comment, whatever crevices of fact, or action, may, from page to page, render themselves apparent.

I prefer commencing with the consideration of an *effect*. Keeping originality *always* in view—for he is false to himself who ventures to dispense with so obvious and so easily attainable a source of interest—I say to myself, in the first place, "Of the innumerable effects, or impressions, of which the heart, the intellect, or (more generally) the soul is susceptible, what one shall I, on the present occasion, select?" Having chosen a novel, first, and secondly a vivid effect, I consider whether it can be best wrought by incident or tone—whether by ordinary incidents and peculiar tone, or the converse, or by peculiarity both of incident and tone—afterward looking about me (or rather within) for such combinations of event, or tone, as shall best aid me in the construction of the effect.

I have often thought how interesting a magazine paper might be written by any author who would—that is to say who could—detail, step by step, the processes by which any one of his compositions attained its ultimate point of completion. Why such a paper has never been given to the world, I am much at a loss to say—but, perhaps, the autorial vanity has had more to do with the omission that any one other cause. Most writers—poets in especial—prefer having it understood that they compose by a species of fine frenzy—an ecstatic intuition—and would positively shudder at letting the public take a peep behind the scenes, at the elaborate and vacillating crudities of thought—at the true purposes seized only at the last moment—at the innumerable glimpses of idea that arrived not at the maturity of full view—at the fully matured fancies discarded in

---

[1] While the opening chapters of Dickens's novel were appearing in serialized form during 1841, Poe wrote an essay in which he conjectured about the conclusion to the extent of correctly naming the murderer.

[2] The 1832 preface which William Godwin wrote for his novel, first published in 1794, makes the assertion that he wrote it from end to beginning.

despair as unmanageable—at the cautious selections and rejections—at the painful erasures and interpolations—in a word, at the wheels and pinions—the tackle for scene-shifting—the step-ladders and demon-traps—the cock's feathers, the red paint and the black patches, which, in ninety-nine cases out of the hundred, constitute the properties of the literary *histrio*.[3]

I am aware, on the other hand, that the case is by no means common, in which an author is at all in condition to retrace the steps by which his conclusions have been attained. In general, suggestions, having arisen pell-mell, are pursued and forgotten in a similar manner.

For my own part, I have neither sympathy with the repugnance alluded to, nor, at any time the least difficulty in recalling to mind the progressive steps of any of my compositions; and, since the interest of an analysis, or reconstruction, such as I have considered a *desideratum,* is quite independent of any real or fancied interest in the thing analyzed, it will not be regarded as a breach of decorum on my part to show the *modus operandi* by which some one of my own works was put together. I select "The Raven," as most generally known. It is my design to render it manifest that no one point in its composition is referrible either to accident or intuition—that the work proceeded, step by step, to its completion with the precision and rigid consequence of a mathematical problem.

Let us dismiss, as irrelevant to the poem, *per se,* the circumstance—or say the necessity—which, in the first place, gave rise to the intention of composing a poem that should suit at once the popular and the critical taste.

We commence, then, with this intention.

The initial consideration was that of extent. If any literary work is too long to be read at one sitting, we must be content to dispense with the immensely important effect derivable from unity of impression—for, if two sittings be required, the affairs of the world interfere, and every thing like totality is at once destroyed. But since, *ceteris paribus,*[4] no poet can afford to dispense with *any thing* that may advance his design, it but remains to be seen whether there is, in extent, any advantage to counterbalance the loss of unity which attends it. Here I say no, at once. What we term a long poem is, in fact, merely a succession of brief ones—that is to say, of brief poetical effects. It is needless to demonstrate that a poem is such, only inasmuch as it intensely excites, by elevating, the soul; and all intense excitements are, through a psychal[5] necessity, brief. For this reason, at least one half of the "Paradise Lost"[6] is essentially prose—a succession of poetical excitements interspersed, *inevitably,* with corresponding depressions—the whole being deprived, through the extremeness of its length, of the vastly important artistic element, totality, or unity, of effect.

It appears evident, then, that there is a distinct limit, as regards length, to all works of literary art—the limit of a single sitting—and that, although in certain classes of prose composition, such as "Robinson Crusoe,"[7] (demanding no unity,) this limit may be advantageously overpassed, it can never properly be overpassed in a poem. Within this limit, the extent of a poem may be made to bear mathematical relation to its merit—in

[3] Performer.
[4] Latin: "other things being equal."
[5] Emotional or spiritual.
[6] This epic poem by John Milton is an exam-

ple of the extreme length Poe sought to reject.
[7] Lengthy novel by Daniel Defoe, published in 1719.

other words, to the excitement or elevation—again in other words, to the degree of the true poetical effect which it is capable of inducing; for it is clear that the brevity must be in direct ratio of the intensity of the intended effect:—this, with one proviso—that a certain degree of duration is absolutely requisite for the production of any effect at all.

Holding in view these considerations, as well as that degree of excitement which I deemed not above the popular, while not below the critical, taste, I reached at once what I conceived the proper *length* for my intended poem—a length of about one hundred lines. It is, in fact, a hundred and eight.

My next thought concerned the choice of an impression, or effect, to be conveyed: and here I may as well observe that, throughout the construction, I kept steadily in view the design of rendering the work *universally* appreciable. I should be carried too far out of my immediate topic were I to demonstrate a point upon which I have repeatedly insisted, and which, with the poetical, stands not in the slightest need of demonstration—the point, I mean, that Beauty is the sole legitimate province of the poem. A few words, however, in elucidation of my real meaning, which some of my friends have evinced a disposition to misrepresent. That pleasure which is at once the most intense, the most elevating, and the most pure, is, I believe, found in the contemplation of the beautiful. When, indeed, men speak of Beauty, they mean, precisely, not a quality, as is supposed, but an effect—they refer, in short, just to that intense and pure elevation of *soul*—*not* of intellect, or of heart—upon which I have commented, and which is experienced in consequence of contemplating "the beautiful." Now I designate Beauty as the province of the poem, merely because it is an obvious rule of Art that effects should be made to spring from direct causes—that objects should be attained through means best adapted for their attainment—no one as yet having been weak enough to deny that the peculiar elevation alluded to is *most readily* attained in the poem. Now the object, Truth, or the satisfaction of the intellect, and the object Passion, or the excitement of the heart, are, although attainable, to a certain extent, in poetry, far more readily attainable in prose. Truth, in fact, demands a precision, and Passion a *homeliness* (the truly passionate will comprehend me) which are absolutely antagonistic to that Beauty which, I maintain, is the excitement, or pleasurable elevation, of the soul. It by no means follows from any thing here said, that passion, or even truth, may not be introduced, and even profitably introduced, into a poem—for they may serve in elucidation, or aid the general effect, as do discords in music, by contrast—but the true artist will always contrive, first, to tone them into proper subservience to the predominant aim, and, secondly, to enveil them, as far as possible, in that Beauty which is the atmosphere and the essence of the poem.

Regarding, then, Beauty as my province, my next question referred to the *tone* of its highest manifestation—and all experience has shown that this tone is one of *sadness.* Beauty of whatever kind, in its supreme development, invariably excites the sensitive soul to tears. Melancholy is thus the most legitimate of all the poetical tones.

The length, the province, and the tone, being thus determined, I betook myself to ordinary induction, with the view of obtaining some artistic piquancy which might serve me as a key-note in the construction of the poem—some pivot upon which the whole structure might turn. In carefully thinking over all the usual artistic effects—or more properly *points,* in the theatrical sense—I did not fail to perceive immediately that no one had been so universally employed as that of the *refrain.* The universality of its employment sufficed to assure me of its intrinsic value, and spared me the necessity of submitting it to analysis. I considered it, however, with regard to its susceptibility of improvement, and soon saw it to be in a primitive condition. As commonly used, the *refrain,* or burden, not only is limited to lyric verse, but depends for its impression upon the force of monotone—both in sound and thought. The pleasure is deduced solely from the sense of identity—of repetition. I resolved to diversify, and so heighten, the effect, by adhering, in general, to the monotone of sound, while I continually varied that of thought: that is to say, I determined to produce continuously novel effects, by the variation *of the application* of the *refrain*—the *refrain* itself remaining, for the most part, unvaried.

These points being settled, I next bethought me of the *nature* of my *refrain.* Since its application was to be repeatedly varied, it was clear that the *refrain* itself must be brief, for there would have been an insurmountable difficulty in frequent variations of application in any sentence of length. In proportion to the brevity of the sentence, would, of course, be the facility of the variation. This led me at once to a single word as the best *refrain.*

The question now arose as to the *character* of the word. Having made up my mind to a *refrain,* the division of the poem into stanzas was, of course, a corollary: the *refrain* forming the close of each stanza. That such a close, to have force, must be sonorous and susceptible of protracted emphasis, admitted no doubt: and these considerations inevitably led me to the long *o* as the most sonorous vowel, in connection with *r* as the most producible consonant.

The sound of the *refrain* being thus determined, it became necessary to select a word embodying this sound, and at the same time in the fullest possible keeping with that melancholy which I had predetermined as the tone of the poem. In such a search it would have been absolutely impossible to overlook the word "Nevermore." In fact, it was the very first which presented itself.

The next *desideratum* was a pretext for the continuous use of the word "nevermore." In observing the difficulty which I at once found in inventing a sufficiently plausible reason for its continuous repetition, I did not fail to perceive that this difficulty arose solely from the pre-assumption that the word was to be so continuously or monotonously spoken by a *human* being—I did not fail to perceive, in short, that the difficulty lay in the reconciliation of this monotony with the exercise of reason on the part of the creature repeating the word. Here, then, immediately arose the idea of a *non*-reasoning creature capable of speech; and, very naturally, a parrot, in the first instance, suggested itself, but was superseded forthwith by a Raven, as equally capable of speech, and infinitely more in keeping with the intended *tone.*

I had now gone so far as the conception of a Raven—the bird of ill omen—monotonously repeating the one word, "Nevermore," at the conclusion of each stanza, in a poem of melancholy tone, and in length about one hundred lines. Now, never losing sight of the object *supremeness,* or perfection, at all points, I asked myself—"Of all melancholy topics, what, according to the *universal* understanding of mankind, is the *most* melancholy?" Death—was the obvious reply. "And when," I said, "is this most melancholy of topics most poetical?" From what I have already explained at some length, the answer, here also, is obvious—"When it most closely allies itself to *Beauty:* the death, then, of a beautiful woman is, unquestionably, the most poetical topic in the world—and equally is it beyond doubt that the lips best suited for such topic are those of a bereaved lover."

I had now to combine the two ideas, of a lover lamenting his deceased mistress and a Raven continuously repeating the word "Nevermore."—I had to combine these, bearing in mind my design of varying, at every turn, the *application* of the word repeated; but the only intelligible mode of such combination is that of imagining the Raven employing the word in answer to the queries of the lover. And here it was that I saw at once the opportunity afforded for the effect on which I had been depending—that is to say, the effect of the *variation of application.* I saw that I could make the first query propounded by the lover—the first query to which the Raven should reply "Nevermore"—that I could make this first query a commonplace one—the second less so—the third still less, and so on—until at length the lover, startled from his original *nonchalance* by the melancholy character of the word itself—by its frequent repetition—and by a consideration of the ominous reputation of the fowl that uttered it—is at length excited to superstition, and wildly propounds queries of a far different character—queries whose solution he has passionately at heart—propounds them half in superstition and half in that species of despair which delights in self-torture—propounds them not altogether because he believes in the prophetic or demoniac character of the bird (which, reason assures him, is merely repeating a lesson learned by rote) but because he experiences a phrenzied pleasure in so modeling his questions as to receive from the *expected* "Nevermore" the most delicious because the most intolerable of sorrow. Perceiving the opportunity thus afforded me—or, more strictly, thus forced upon me in the progress of the construction—I first established in mind the climax, or concluding query—that query to which "Nevermore" should be in the last place an answer—that in reply to which this word "Nevermore" should involve the utmost conceivable amount of sorrow and despair.

Here then the poem may be said to have its beginning—at the end, where all works of art should begin—for it was here, at this point of my preconsiderations, that I first put pen to paper in the composition of the stanza:

> "Prophet," said I, "thing of evil! prophet still if bird or devil!
> By that heaven that bends above us—by that God we both adore,
> Tell this soul with sorrow laden, if within the distant Aidenn,
> It shall clasp a sainted maiden whom the angels name Lenore–
> Clasp a rare and radiant maiden whom the angels name Lenore."
> Quoth the raven "Nevermore."

I composed this stanza, at this point, first that, by establishing the climax, I might the better vary and graduate, as regards seriousness and importance, the preceding queries of the lover—and, secondly, that I might definitely settle the rhythm, the metre, and the length and general arrangement of the stanza—as well as graduate the stanzas which were to precede, so that none of them might surpass this in rhythmical effect. Had I been able, in the subsequent composition, to construct more vigorous stanzas, I should, without scruple, have purposely enfeebled them, so as not to interfere with the climacteric effect.

And here I may as well say a few words of the versification. My first object (as usual) was originality. The extent to which this has been neglected, in versification, is one of the most unaccountable things in the world. Admitting that there is little possibility of variety in mere *rhythm*, it is still clear that the possible varieties of metre and stanza are absolutely infinite—and yet, *for centuries, no man, in verse, has ever done, or ever seemed to think of doing, an original thing.* The fact is, that originality (unless in minds of very unusual force) is by no means a matter, as some suppose, of impulse or intuition. In general, to be found, it must be elaborately sought, and although a positive merit of the highest class, demands in its attainment less of invention than negation.

Of course, I pretend to no originality in either the rhythm or metre of the "Raven." The former is trochaic—the latter is octameter acatalectic, alternating with heptameter catalectic repeated in the *refrain* of the fifth verse, and terminating with tetrameter catalectic. Less pedantically—the feet employed throughout (trochees) consist of a long syllable followed by a short: the first line of the stanza consists of eight of these feet—the second of seven and a half (in effect two-thirds)—the third of eight—the fourth of seven and a half—the fifth the same—the sixth three and a half. Now, each of these lines, taken individually, has been employed before, and what originality the "Raven" has, is in their *combination into stanza;* nothing even remotely approaching this combination has ever been attempted. The effect of this originality of combination is aided by other unusual, and some altogether novel effects, arising from an extension of the application of the principles of rhyme and alliteration.

The next point to be considered was the mode of bringing together the lover and the Raven—and the first branch of this consideration was the *locale.* For this the most natural suggestion might seem to be a forest, or the fields—but it has always appeared to me that a close *circumscription of space* is absolutely necessary to the effect of insulated incident:— it has the force of a frame to a picture. It has an indisputable moral power in keeping concentrated the attention, and, of course, must not be confounded with mere unity of place.

I determined, then, to place the lover in his chamber—in a chamber rendered sacred to him by memories of her who had frequented it. The room is represented as richly furnished—this in mere pursuance of the ideas I have already explained on the subject of Beauty, as the sole true poetical thesis.

The *locale* being thus determined, I had now to introduce the bird—and the thought of introducing him through the window, was inevitable. The idea of making the lover suppose, in the first instance, that the flapping of the wings of the bird against the shutter, is a "tapping" at the door, originated in a wish to increase, by prolonging, the reader's curiosity, and in a desire to admit the incidental effect arising from the lover's throwing open the door, finding all dark, and thence adopting the half-fancy that it was the spirit of his mistress that knocked.

I made the night tempestuous, first, to account for the Raven's seeking admission, and secondly, for the effect of contrast with the (physical) serenity within the chamber.

I made the bird alight on the bust of Pallas,[8] also for the effect of contrast between the marble and the plumage—it being understood that the bust was absolutely *suggested* by the bird—the bust of *Pallas* being chosen, first, as most in keeping with the scholarship of the lover, and, secondly, for the sonorousness of the word, Pallas, itself.

About the middle of the poem, also, I have availed myself of the force of contrast, with a view of deepening the ultimate impression. For example, an air of the fantastic— approaching as nearly to the ludicrous as was admissible—is given to the Raven's entrance. He comes in "with many a flirt and flutter."

> Not the *least obeisance made he*—not a moment stopped or stayed he,
> But with *mien of lord or lady,* perched above my chamber door.

---

[8] Marble bust of Pallas Athena, goddess of wisdom in classic myth.

In the two stanzas which follow, the design is more obviously carried out:—

> Then this ebony bird beguiling my sad fancy into smiling
> By the *grave and stern decorum of the countenance it wore*,
> "Though thy *crest be shorn and shaven* thou," I said, "art sure no craven,
> Ghastly grim and ancient Raven wandering from the nightly shore—
> Tell me what thy lordly name is on the Night's Plutonian shore?"
> > Quoth the Raven "Nevermore."

> Much I marvelled *this ungainly fowl* to hear discourse so plainly
> Though its answer little meaning—little relevancy bore;
> For we cannot help agreeing that no living human being
> *Ever yet was blessed with seeing bird above his chamber door—*
> *Bird or beast upon the sculptured bust above his chamber door,*
> > With such name as "Nevermore."

The effect of the *dénouement* being thus provided for, I immediately drop the fantastic for a tone of the most profound seriousness:—this tone commencing in the stanza directly following the one last quoted, with the line,

> But the Raven, sitting lonely on that placid bust, spoke only, etc.

From this epoch the lover no longer jests—no longer sees any thing even of the fantastic in the Raven's demeanor. He speaks of him as a "grim, ungainly, ghastly, gaunt, and ominous bird of yore," and feels the "fiery eyes" burning into his "bosom's core." This revolution of thought, or fancy, on the lover's part, is intended to induce a similar one on the part of the reader—to bring the mind into a proper frame for the *dénouement*—which is now brought about as rapidly and as *directly* as possible.

With the *dénouement* proper—with the Raven's reply, "Nevermore," to the lover's final demand if he shall meet his mistress in another world—the poem, in its obvious phase, that of a simple narrative, may be said to have its completion. So far, every thing is within the limits of the accountable—of the real. A raven, having learned by rote the single word "Nevermore," and having escaped from the custody of its owner, is driven at midnight, through the violence of a storm, to seek admission at a window from which a light still gleams—the chamber-window of a student, occupied half in pouring over a volume, half in dreaming of a beloved mistress deceased. The casement being thrown open at the fluttering of the bird's wings, the bird itself perches on the most convenient seat out of the immediate reach of the student, who, amused by the incident and the oddity of the visitor's demeanor, demands of it, in jest and without looking for a reply, its name. The raven addressed, answers with its customary word, "Nevermore"—a word which finds immediate echo in the melancholy heart of the student, who, giving utterance aloud to certain thoughts suggested by the occasion, is again startled by the fowl's repetition of "Nevermore." The student now guesses the state of the case, but is impelled, as I have before explained, by the human thirst for self-torture, and in part by superstition, to propound such queries to the bird as will bring him, the lover, the most of the luxury of sorrow, through the anticipated answer "Nevermore."

With the indulgence, to the extreme, of this self-torture, the narration, in what I have termed its first or obvious phase, has a natural termination, and so far there has been no overstepping of the limits of the real.

But in subjects so handled, however skilfully, or with however vivid an array of incident, there is always a certain hardness or nakedness, which repels the artistical eye. Two things are invariably required—first, some amount of complexity, or more properly, adaptation; and, secondly, some amount of suggestiveness—some under-current, however indefinite, of meaning. It is this latter, in especial, which imparts to a work of art so much of that *richness* (to borrow from colloquy a forcible term) which we are too fond of confounding with *the ideal.* It is the *excess* of the suggested meaning—it is the rendering this the upper instead of the under current of the theme—which turns into prose (and that of the very flattest kind) the so called poetry of the so called transcendentalists.

Holding these opinions, I have added the two concluding stanzas of the poem—their suggestiveness being thus made to pervade all the narrative which has preceded them. The under-current of meaning is rendered first apparent in the lines—

> "Take thy beak from out *my heart,* and take thy form from off
>   my door!"
>   Quoth the Raven "Nevermore!"

It will be observed that the words, "from out my heart," involve the first metaphorical expression in the poem. They, with the answer, "Nevermore," dispose the mind to seek a moral in all that has been previously narrated. The reader begins now to regard the Raven as emblematical—but it is not until the very last line of the very last stanza, that the intention of making him emblematical of *Mournful and Never-ending Remembrance* is permitted distinctly to be seen:

> And the Raven, never flitting, still is sitting, still is sitting,
> On the pallid bust of Pallas, just above my chamber door;
> And his eyes have all the seeming of a demon's that is dreaming,
> And the lamplight o'er him streaming throws his shadow on the floor;
> And my soul *from out that shadow* that lies floating on the floor
>   Shall be lifted—nevermore.

1846

Sonnet—to Science

> Science! true daughter of Old Time thou art!
>   Who alterest all things with thy peering eyes.
> Why preyest thou thus upon the poet's heart,
>   Vulture, whose wings are dull realities?

How should he love thee? or how deem thee wise,   5
   Who wouldst not leave him in his wandering
To seek for treasure in the jewelled skies,
   Albeit he soared with an undaunted wing?
Hast thou not dragged Diana from her car?
   And driven the Hamadryad from the wood   10
To seek a shelter in some happier star?
   Hast thou not torn the Naiad from her flood,
The Elfin from the green grass, and from me
The summer dream beneath the tamarind tree?

1829

To Helen*

Helen,[1] thy beauty is to me
   Like those Nicéan[2] barks of yore,
That gently, o'er a perfumed sea,
   The weary, way-worn wanderer bore
To his own native shore.   5

On desperate seas long wont to roam,
   Thy hyacinth[3] hair, thy classic face,
Thy Naiad[4] airs have brought me home
   To the glory that was Greece,
And the grandeur that was Rome.   10

Lo! in yon brilliant window-niche
   How statue-like I see thee stand,
The agate lamp within thy hand!
   Ah, Psyche,[5] from the regions which
Are Holy-Land![6]   15

1831–1843

---

* This poem first appeared in 1831 but was rewritten over the next 12 years. This version was included in the 1845 edition of *The Raven and Other Poems*.

[1] Helen of Troy, considered the most beautiful woman of ancient times, was celebrated in the Homeric epic the *Iliad*. She was considered the cause of the Trojan War.

[2] Probably derived from Nike, the Greek goddess of Victory; thus, "victorious."

[3] Lustrous, curling hair.

[4] Water nymph.

[5] Greek word for soul.

[6] If Palestine is a religious holy land, Greece is the sacred place of art.

The Raven*

Once upon a midnight dreary, while I pondered, weak and weary,
Over many a quaint and curious volume of forgotten lore—
While I nodded, nearly napping, suddenly there came a tapping,
As of some one gently rapping, rapping at my chamber door—
" 'Tis some visiter," I muttered, "tapping at my chamber door—   5
    Only this and nothing more."

Ah, distinctly I remember it was in the bleak December;
And each separate dying ember wrought its ghost upon the floor.
Eagerly I wished the morrow;—vainly I had sought to borrow
From my books surcease of sorrow—sorrow for the lost Lenore—   10
For the rare and radiant maiden whom the angels name Lenore—
    Nameless *here* for evermore.

And the silken, sad, uncertain rustling of each purple curtain
Thrilled me—filled me with fantastic terrors never felt before;
So that now, to still the beating of my heart, I stood repeating   15
" 'Tis some visiter entreating entrance at my chamber door—
Some late visiter entreating entrance at my chamber door;—
    This it is and nothing more."

Presently my soul grew stronger; hesitating then no longer,
"Sir," said I, "or Madam, truly your forgiveness I implore;   20
But the fact is I was napping, and so gently you came rapping,
And so faintly you came tapping, tapping at my chamber door,
That I scarce was sure I heard you"—here I opened wide the door;——
    Darkness there and nothing more.

Deep into that darkness peering, long I stood there wondering, fearing,   25
Doubting, dreaming dreams no mortal ever dared to dream before;
But the silence was unbroken, and the stillness gave no token,
And the only word there spoken was the whispered word, "Lenore?"
This I whispered, and an echo murmured back the word, "Lenore!"
    Merely this and nothing more.   30

Back into the chamber turning, all my soul within me burning,
Soon again I heard a tapping somewhat louder than before.
"Surely," said I, "surely that is something at my window lattice;
Let me see, then, what thereat is, and this mystery explore—
Let my heart be still a moment and this mystery explore;—   35
    'Tis the wind and nothing more!"

* This poem was probably written during 1844. It was first published in January 1845. This version was published in September 1849.

Open here I flung the shutter, when with many a flirt and flutter,
In there stepped a stately Raven of the saintly days of yore;
Not the least obeisance made he; not a minute stopped or stayed he;
But, with mien of lord or lady, perched above my chamber door—   40
Perched upon a bust of Pallas[1] just above my chamber door—
     Perched, and sat, and nothing more.

Then this ebony bird beguiling my sad fancy into smiling,
By the grave and stern decorum of the countenance it wore,
"Though thy crest be shorn and shaven, thou," I said, "art sure no craven,   45
Ghastly grim and ancient Raven wandering from the Nightly shore—
Tell me what thy lordly name is on the Night's Plutonian[2] shore!"
     Quoth the Raven "Nevermore."

Much I marvelled this ungainly fowl to hear discourse so plainly,
Though its answer little meaning—little relevancy bore;   50
For we cannot help agreeing that no living human being
Ever yet was blessed with seeing bird above his chamber door—
Bird or beast upon the sculptured bust above his chamber door,
     With such name as "Nevermore."

But the Raven, sitting lonely on the placid bust, spoke only   55
That one word, as if his soul in that one word he did outpour.
Nothing farther then he uttered—not a feather then he fluttered—
Till I scarcely more than muttered "Other friends have flown before—
On the morrow *he* will leave me, as my Hopes have flown before."
     Then the bird said "Nevermore."   60

Startled at the stillness broken by reply so aptly spoken,
"Doubtless," said I, "what it utters is its only stock and store
Caught from some unhappy master whom unmerciful Disaster
Followed fast and followed faster till his songs one burden bore—
Till the dirges of his Hope that melancholy burden bore   65
     Of 'Never—nevermore.' "

But the Raven still beguiling my sad fancy into smiling,
Straight I wheeled a cushioned seat in front of bird, and bust and door;
Then, upon the velvet sinking, I betook myself to linking
Fancy unto fancy, thinking what this ominous bird of yore—   70
What this grim, ungainly, ghastly, gaunt, and ominous bird of yore
     Meant in croaking "Nevermore."

This I sat engaged in guessing, but no syllable expressing
To the fowl whose fiery eyes now burned into my bosom's core;

[1] Athena, in classic myth the goddess of wisdom.

[2] i.e., as black as the region of the underworld ruled over by Pluto in mythology.

This and more I sat divining, with my head at ease reclining   75
On the cushion's velvet lining that the lamp-light gloated[3] o'er,
But whose velvet-violet lining with the lamp-light gloating o'er,
     She shall press, ah, nevermore!

Then, methought, the air grew denser, perfumed from an unseen censer
Swung by seraphim whose foot-falls tinkled on the tufted floor.   80
"Wretch," I cried, "thy God hath lent thee—by these angels he hath sent
   thee
Respite—respite and nepenthe from thy memories of Lenore;
Quaff, oh quaff this kind nepenthe and forget this lost Lenore!"
     Quoth the Raven "Nevermore."

"Prophet!" said I, "thing of evil!—prophet still, if bird, or devil!—   85
Whether Tempter sent, or whether tempest tossed thee here ashore,
Desolate yet all undaunted, on this desert land enchanted—
On this home by Horror haunted—tell me truly, I implore—
Is there—*is* there balm in Gilead?[4]—tell me—tell me, I implore!"
     Quoth the Raven "Nevermore."   90

"Prophet!" said I, "thing of evil!—prophet still, if bird or devil!
By that Heaven that bends above us—by that God we both adore—
Tell this soul with sorrow laden if, within the distant Aidenn,[5]
It shall clasp a sainted maiden whom the angels name Lenore—
Clasp a rare and radiant maiden whom the angels name Lenore."   95
     Quoth the Raven "Nevermore."

"Be that word our sign of parting, bird or fiend!" I shrieked, upstarting—
"Get thee back into the tempest and the Night's Plutonian shore!
Leave no black plume as a token of that lie thy soul hath spoken!
Leave my loneliness unbroken!—quit the bust above my door!   100
Take thy beak from out my heart, and take thy form from off my door!"
     Quoth the Raven "Nevermore."

And the Raven, never flitting, still is sitting, *still* is sitting
On the pallid bust of Pallas just above my chamber door;
And his eyes have all the seeming of a demon's that is dreaming,   105
And the lamp-light o'er him streaming throws his shadow on the floor;
And my soul from out that shadow that lies floating on the floor
     Shall be lifted—nevermore!

1844–1849

---

[3] Here meaning both glowed and relished with malicious pleasure.

[4] Reference to lines from Jeremiah 8:22, which speak ironically of the healing medicinal resin taken from evergreen trees in the region of Gilead in Jordan.

[5] Of Arabic derivation, suggesting Eden.

Ulalume—a Ballad*

The skies they were ashen and sober;
    The leaves they were crispéd and sere—
    The leaves they were withering and sere:
It was night, in the lonesome October
    Of my most immemorial[1] year: 5
It was hard by the dim lake of Auber,
    In the misty mid region of Weir:—
It was down by the dank tarn[2] of Auber,
    In the ghoul-haunted woodland of Weir.

Here once, through an alley Titanic,   10
    Of cypress, I roamed with my Soul—
    Of cypress, with Psyche, my Soul.
These were days when my heart was volcanic
    As the scoriac[3] rivers that roll—
    As the lavas that restlessly roll   15
Their sulphurous currents down Yaanek,
    In the ultimate climes of the Pole[4]—
That groan as they roll down Mount Yaanek,
    In the realms of the Boreal[5] Pole.

Our talk had been serious and sober.   20
    By our thoughts they were palsied and sere—
    Our memories were treacherous and sere;
For we knew not the month was October,
    And we marked not the night of the year—
    (Ah, night of all nights in the year!)[6]   25
We noted not the dim lake of Auber,
    (Though once we had journeyed down here)
We remembered not the dank tarn of Auber,
    Nor the ghoul-haunted woodland of Weir.

And now, as the night was senescent,   30
    And star-dials pointed to morn—
    As the star-dials hinted of morn—
At the end of our path a liquescent
    And nebulous lustre was born,

---

* This poem was first written and published in 1847. This version is from a revision written in 1849.
[1] Memorable.
[2] Mountain lake.
[3] Lavalike.
[4] The South Pole.
[5] Here, the direction of the south magnetic pole.
[6] All Saints' Eve.

Out of which a miraculous crescent   35
  Arose with a duplicate horn—
Astarte's[7] bediamonded crescent,
  Distinct with its duplicate horn.

And I said—"She is warmer than Dian;[8]
  She rolls through an ether of sighs—   40
  She revels in a region of sighs.
She has seen that the tears are not dry on
  These cheeks where the worm never dies,
And has come past the stars of the Lion,[9]
  To point us the path to the skies—   45
  To the Lethean[10] peace of the skies—
Come up, in despite of the Lion,
  To shine on us with her bright eyes—
Come up, through the lair of the Lion,
  With love in her luminous eyes."   50

But Psyche, uplifting her finger,
  Said—"Sadly this star I mistrust—
  Her pallor I strangely mistrust—
Ah, hasten!—ah, let us not linger!
  Ah, fly!—let us fly!—for we must."   55
In terror she spoke; letting sink her
  Wings till they trailed in the dust—
In agony sobbed; letting sink her
  Plumes till they trailed in the dust—
  Till they sorrowfully trailed in the dust.   60

I replied—"This is nothing but dreaming.
  Let us on, by this tremulous light!
  Let us bathe in this crystalline light!
Its Sibyllic[11] splendor is beaming
  With Hope and in Beauty to-night—   65
  See!—it flickers up the sky through the night!
Ah, we safely may trust to its gleaming
  And be sure it will lead us aright—
We surely may trust to a gleaming
  That cannot but guide us aright   70
Since it flickers up to Heaven through the night."

---

[7] Astarte: Phoenician fertility goddess, patroness of carnal love.
[8] Diana, virgin goddess of the moon.
[9] The constellation Leo, sign of uneasy love.
[10] Forgetfulness, caused by drinking from the river Lethe in Hades.
[11] In classic myth, the Sibyls prophesied the future.

Thus I pacified Psyche and kissed her,
　　And tempted her out of her gloom—
　　And conquered her scruples and gloom;
And we passed to the end of the vista—　　　　75
　　But were stopped by the door of a tomb—
　　By the door of a legended tomb:—
And I said—"What is written, sweet sister.
　　On the door of this legended tomb?"
She replied—"Ulalume—Ulalume!—　　　　　80
　　'Tis the vault of thy lost Ulalume!"

Then my heart it grew ashen and sober
　　As the leaves that were crispéd and sere—
　　As the leaves that were withering and sere—
And I cried—"It was surely October,　　　　　85
　　On *this* very night of last year,
　　That I journeyed—I journeyed down here!—
　　That I brought a dread burden down here—
　　On this night, of all nights in the year,
　　Ah, what demon hath tempted me here?　　90
Well I know, now, this dim lake of Auber—
　　This misty mid region of Weir:—
Well I know, now, this dank tarn of Auber—
　　This ghoul-haunted woodland of Weir."

Said we, then—the two, then—"Ah, can it　　　95
　　Have been that the woodlandish ghouls—
　　The pitiful, the merciful ghouls,
To bar up our way and to ban it
　　From the secret that lies in these wolds—
　　From the thing that lies hidden in these wolds—　100
Have drawn up the spectre of a planet
　　From the limbo[12] of lunary souls—

This sinfully scintillant planet
　　From the Hell of the planetary souls?"
1847–1849

---

[12] The resting place of the unbaptized on the
fringes of hell.

Annabel Lee

It was many and many a year ago,
   In a kingdom by the sea,
That a maiden there lived whom you may know
   By the name of Annabel Lee;—
And this maiden she lived with no other thought   5
   Than to love and be loved by me.

I was a child and *she* was a child,
   In this kingdom by the sea;
But we loved with a love that was more than love—
   I and my Annabel Lee—   10
With a love that the wingéd seraphs in Heaven
   Coveted her and me.

And this was the reason that, long ago,
   In this kingdom by the sea,
A wind blew out of a cloud, chilling   15
   My beautiful Annabel Lee;
So that her high-born kinsmen came
   And bore her away from me,
To shut her up in a sepulchre,
   In this kingdom by the sea.   20

The angels, not half so happy in Heaven,
   Went envying her and me—
Yes!—that was the reason (as all men know,
   In this kingdom by the sea)
That the wind came out of the cloud by night,   25
   Chilling and killing my Annabel Lee.

But our love it was stronger by far than the love
   Of those who were older than we—
   Of many far wiser than we—
And neither the angels in Heaven above,   30
   Nor the demons down under the sea,
Can ever dissever my soul from the soul
   Of the beautiful Annabel Lee:—

For the moon never beams, without bringing me dreams
   Of the beautiful Annabel Lee;   35
And the stars never rise, but I feel the bright eyes
   Of the beautiful Annabel Lee:—
And so, all the night-tide, I lie down by the side

Of my darling—my darling—my life and my bride,
   In her sepulchre there by the sea—   40
   In her tomb by the sounding sea.

1849

The Bells

I

     Hear the sledges with the bells—
        Silver bells!
What a world of merriment their melody foretells!
     How they tinkle, tinkle, tinkle,
       In the icy air of night!   5
While the stars that oversprinkle
All the heavens, seem to twinkle
     With a crystalline delight;
       Keeping time, time, time,
       In a sort of Runic rhyme,   10
To the tintinnabulation that so musically wells
     From the bells, bells, bells, bells.
       Bells, bells, bells—
From the jingling and the tinkling of the bells.

II

     Hear the mellow wedding bells—   15
        Gold bells!
What a world of happiness their harmony foretells!
     Through the balmy air of night
     How they ring out their delight!—
       From the molten-golden notes,   20
       And all in tune,
     What a liquid ditty floats
To the turtle-dove that listens, while she gloats
       On the moon!
     Oh, from out the sounding cells,   25
What a gush of euphony voluminously wells!
       How it swells!
       How it dwells
     On the Future!—how it tells
     Of the rapture that impels   30
       To the swinging and the ringing
       Of the bells, bells, bells—
Of the bells, bells, bells, bells,
       Bells, bells, bells—
To the rhyming and the chiming of the bells!   35

III

Hear the loud alarum bells—
        Brazen bells!
What a tale of terror, now, their turbulency tells!
        In the startled ear of night
        How they scream out their affright!   40
            Too much horrified to speak,
            They can only shriek, shriek,
                Out of tune,
In a clamorous appealing to the mercy of the fire,
In a mad expostulation with the deaf and frantic fire,   45
            Leaping higher, higher, higher,
            With a desperate desire,
            And a resolute endeavor
            Now—now to sit, or never,
        By the side of the pale-faced moon,   50
            Oh, the bells, bells, bells!
            What a tale their terror tells
                Of Despair!
        How they clang, and clash, and roar!
        What a horror they outpour   55
On the bosom of the palpitating air!
            Yet the ear, it fully knows,
                By the twanging
                And the clanging,
            How the danger ebbs and flows;   60
        Yet the ear distinctly tells,
                In the jangling
                And the wrangling,
        How the danger sinks and swells,
By the sinking or the swelling in the anger of the bells—   65
            Of the bells,—
        Of the bells, bells, bells, bells,
            Bells, bells, bells—
In the clamor and the clangor of the bells!

                IV
Hear the tolling of the bells—   70
        Iron bells!
What a world of solemn thought their monody compels!
        In the silence of the night,
        How we shiver with affright
At the melancholy menace of their tone!   75
        For every sound that floats
        From the rust within their throats
                Is a groan.
            And the people—ah, the people—

They that dwell up in the steeple,   80
   All alone,
And who tolling, tolling, tolling,
   In that muffled monotone,
Feel a glory in so rolling
   On the human heart a stone—   85
They are neither man nor woman—
They are neither brute nor human—
   They are Ghouls:—
  And their king it is who tolls:—
  And he rolls, rolls, rolls,   90
   Rolls
  A paean from the bells!
And his merry bosom swells
  With the paean of the bells!
And he dances, and he yells;   95
Keeping time, time, time,
In a sort of Runic rhyme,
   To the paean of the bells—
   Of the bells:
Keeping time, time, time,   100
In a sort of Runich rhyme,
   To the throbbing of the bells—
  Of the bells, bells, bells—
   To the sobbing of the bells—
Keeping time, time, time,   105
  As he knells, knells, knells,
In a happy Runic rhyme,
   To the rolling of the bells—
  Of the bells, bells, bells:—
   To the tolling of the bells—   110
Of the bells, bells, bells, bells,
   Bells, bells, bells—
To the moaning and groaning of the bells.
1849

Nathaniel Hawthorne
1804–1864

Nathaniel Hawthorne rarely seemed at ease with himself, his work, or his place in American literary history. The author of America's most famous novel of religious conscience, he nevertheless characterized his regularly enforced attendance at the services at Salem's Meeting House, where his ancestors had worshiped for nearly two centuries, as "the frozen purgatory of my childhood." A writer who spent twelve years in self-imposed retirement from the world, ensconced in the literary solitude of a small room tucked under the eaves of the family house in Salem, he nevertheless yearned to participate in what he called "the opaque substance of today." He seemed interested in creating a literary world abstracted from reality, yet he also noted that "the most desirable mode of existence might be that of a spiritualized Paul Pry, hovering invisible round men and women, witnessing their deeds, searching their hearts, borrowing brightness from their felicity and shade from their sorrow, and retaining no emotion peculiar to himself." Henry James, in his celebrated study of the writer, perceptively identified this as Hawthorne's paradoxical mixture of "evasive and inquisitive tendencies." And while the circumstances of his life may appear uneventful, the drama in his life—much like the conflict in his fiction—took place in the private moral and psychic recesses of this complex individual.

Nathaniel Hawthorne was born on July 4, 1804, in Salem, Massachusetts. His Puritan ancestors were among the first settlers in the state and included two prominent judges, one active in the persecution of the Quakers in the 1650s, the other in the witch trials of the 1690s. By Hawthorne's time, however, the family had receded from public eminence. Both his father and his grandfather were captains of merchant ships. In 1808 his father died of yellow fever in Dutch Guiana (now Surinam), leaving his widow with three children. Taking the customs of Puritan bereavement to an unusual extreme, the mother moved with her children back into the household of her parents and rarely left her room for the forty remaining years of her life, eating nearly all her meals alone. Her grief, Hawthorne later noted, "outlasted its vitality, and grew to be merely a torpid habit."

Hawthorne attended school in Salem but at the age of nine was hurt playing ball. Partially lame for three years, he was tutored at home, where his devotion to reading Spenser, Shakespeare, Milton, Thomson, and Bunyan's *The Pilgrim's Progress* first showed itself. (The first book he bought with his own money was *The Faerie Queene*.) He did not remain entirely inactive, however. His mother's family owned some land and houses in Raymond, Maine, and Hawthorne made several lengthy visits there, one lasting a year. "I lived in Maine like a bird of the air, so perfect was the freedom I enjoyed. But it was there I first got my cursed habits of solitude."

In 1821 he entered Bowdoin College in Maine; his career there suggests that his habits of solitude were temporarily modified. He joined, for example, a literary society, a card-playing club, and a student militia led by his friend Franklin Pierce, who was to become the fourteenth president of the United States. Hawthorne described himself during this period as an "idle student," one who was "negligent of college rules and the Procrustean details of academic life, rather choosing to nurse my own fancies than to dig into Greek roots." An unusually handsome and charming young man, he participated in social activities; yet full of self-effacement and reserve, he avoided drawing attention to himself. His classmates described him as aloof when in company, and one remarked at the time: "He lives in a mysterious world of thought and imagination which he never permits me to enter." Hawthorne graduated in 1825, an undistinguished eighteenth in a class of thirty-eight.

Returning to Salem, he lived with his mother and sisters and settled once again into a solitary way of life. With no immediate need to work for pay, he was able to read widely, showing a special interest in the history of Puritan New England, in Gothic romances, and in the great novelists of the eighteenth century, especially Fielding, Smollett, and Richardson. He also took long walks along the seashore and, after dark, through town. But he was also at work writing. In 1828 his first novel, *Fanshawe,* was published anonymously. Though generally regarded as a minor work, *Fanshawe* is an accomplished performance for a twenty-four-year-old author, one that reflected the styles of Fielding and Scott. However, the novel did not sell many copies, and Hawthorne soon became dissatisfied with it himself. He never later acknowledged it as his work.

Hawthorne's first short stories were published in the early 1830s. They appeared in "gift-books," a kind of magazine published annually that printed poems, stories, and essays, usually with no attribution to the author. During this period, he also worked for six months in Boston as the editor of *The American Magazine of Useful and Entertaining Knowledge,* for which he and his sister Elizabeth wrote nearly all the material. When a fire pushed the magazine to the brink of bankruptcy, Hawthorne resigned and wrote a history of the world for children. The volume sold well over a million copies, yet Hawthorne had signed a contract that earned him only a $100 fee.

In 1837 *Twice-Told Tales,* his first acknowledged book, was published. Of it, Hawthorne reported in a letter to Henry Wadsworth Longfellow, a former fellow student at Bowdoin, "I have . . . great difficulty in the lack of materials, for I have seen so little of the world that I have nothing but thin air to concoct my stories of, and it is not easy to give a life-like semblance to such shadowy stuff." Hawthorne began to address this problem in one way by keeping a notebook and filling it with telling observations of daily life—many of which were incorporated into his fiction. The collection received favorable reviews and sold steadily for many months, gradually earning him a considerable reputation.

At the same time, Hawthorne began to mix in the society of Salem, most notably with the Peabody family. Sophia Peabody, seven years younger, was a well-educated, talented artist and a near invalid; by the end of 1838 they were secretly engaged. In 1839, through the political influence of old friends, he obtained a position as an inspector at the Boston Custom House. He composed some short tales for children in these years, but he was distracted from doing any more substantial literary work. Increasingly displeased by the working conditions at the port, Hawthorne was glad to be relieved of the job when the political administration changed in 1841.

He moved almost immediately to the Brook Farm Institute of Agriculture and Education, a communal experiment founded by a group of writers and thinkers associated with Transcendentalism. There he intended to "establish a mode of life which shall combine the enchantments of poetry with the facts of daily experience." He worked conscientiously on the farm but gradually judged the chores disagreeable and his fellow workers troublesome and intrusive. He left after eight months. "I can best attain the higher ends of my life by retaining the ordinary relation to society," he announced in a letter at the time.

He married Sophia Peabody in 1842, and soon afterward they took up residence at Concord in the Old Manse, a house built by Ralph Waldo Emerson's grandfather. He mixed, sometimes, with such illustrious neighbors as Emerson, Margaret Fuller, Ellery Channing, Amos Bronson Alcott, and Henry David Thoreau. His conversations with Emerson and Fuller were awkward at best. Emerson, Hawthorne noted, was "a great searcher for facts; but they seem to melt away and become unsubstantial in his grasp." (Henry James explained the incompatibility from a more distant and generous perspective: "Emerson, as a spiritual sun-worshipper, could have attached but a moderate value to Hawthorne's catlike faculty of seeing in the dark.") Hawthorne seemed unable—perhaps finally unwilling—to share Emerson's cosmic optimism and his Transcendentalist belief in the salvific qualities of experience. The young Herman Melville, in reviewing *Mosses from an Old Manse,* had also recognized Hawthorne's "Calvinistic sense of Innate Depravity and Original Sin, from whose visitations . . . no deeply thinking mind is always and wholly free."

In 1846 Hawthorne moved his family back into his mother's house and began a three-year stint as surveyor of customs, under conditions he described fully in the essay "The Custom-House," printed as a preface to *The Scarlet Letter;* an extraordinary period of creative work was to follow. As before, Hawthorne's job had been a political appointment, and he lost it when the presidential administration changed in 1849. Soon after, his mother died. Through the summer and autumn of that year, his family living on money Sophia had saved and from unsolicited loans from friends, Hawthorne composed *The Scarlet Letter,* generally considered his greatest work.

The central idea of the novel—a woman sentenced to wear a lettered badge as punishment for adultery—had been conceived by Hawthorne more than a decade earlier in his short story "Endicott and the Red Cross" (1838). Usually rather desultory in his writing habits, Hawthorne threw himself into drafting *The Scarlet Letter,* writing "immensely," as his wife said—up to nine hours a day, completing it in February 1850.

Hawthorne judged the book to be "positively a hell-fired story, into which I found it almost impossible to throw a cheering light," and he feared it would not be well received. His anxiety was short lived. The first edition sold out in ten days, and reviewers variously classed him with Alexander Pope, Sir Walter Scott, Charles Lamb, and Charles Dickens.

In the spring of 1850, Hawthorne moved with his wife and children (a son, Julian, had been born in 1846) to Lenox, Massachussetts, at the time a rural community where many literary people spent the summer. Characteristically, Hawthorne was found by many to be an aloof, even reluctant member of the community. During this time, he and Melville saw each other often, usually at Melville's suggestion. With the success of *The Scarlet Letter,* Hawthorne began work on a new romance, *The House of the Seven Gables,* which he intended to be more varied in tone and less uniformly somber than *The Scarlet Letter;* it proved to be as popular as its predecessor. Other new work included another volume of stories for children, *Tanglewood Tales for Boys and Girls* (1851), a new edition of *Twice-Told Tales* (1851), and another collection of stories, *The Snow-Image, and Other Twice-Told Tales* (1851). For the first time Hawthorne was earning enough from his writing to support his family. (A daughter, Rose, was born in 1852.) Looking for a less rustic environment than Lenox, the family moved to West Newton, a suburb of Boston. Here Hawthorne began *The Blithedale Romance* (1852), a book satirizing the pretensions and delusions of social reformers.

Acclaimed in both America and Britain as one of the preeminent writers of the day, Hawthorne could finally afford to buy a permanent home for his family. In 1852 he bought The Wayside, the former house of Bronson Alcott in Concord, and once again entered the neighborhood of Emerson, Fuller, Channing, and Thoreau. Here he worked on a final volume of children's stories as well as on a campaign biography of his college friend Franklin Pierce, who had been unexpectedly chosen the Democratic candidate for president. Soon after Pierce's election, he appointed Hawthorne American consul at Liverpool, England.

Hawthorne served as consul from 1853 to 1857, but soon grew to dislike the job. Once again he composed no fiction while employed, but he wrote copiously in his notebooks. And though he traveled widely through the English countryside, he did not seek out the company of literary people. As the title of his published recollections of this time, *Our Old Home,* suggests, he felt a certain hereditary connection to the culture of England, yet as an American he felt a more immediate link to the increasingly distinct culture of America. Hawthorne's relation to America in the years immediately preceding the Civil War was, however, still uneasy. "It sickens me to look back at America," he wrote in a letter from England. "I am sick to death of the continual fuss and tumult and excitement and bad blood which we keep up about political topics."

When Hawthorne left the consulate in 1857, he moved his family to Italy. They settled eventually in the countryside near Florence, not far from Robert and Elizabeth Barrett Browning, with whom they had become friendly. Here Hawthorne began work, slowly, on his last completed romance, *The Marble Faun,* which treats the conflict between American and Old World values. He returned to The Wayside in June 1860.

Though he supported the Union during the Civil War, Hawthorne shared little of the abolitionist zeal of many of his neighbors in New England. During this period, he felt increasingly out of touch with the nation that had gone to war with itself. Henry James, Sr., the novelist's father, described Hawthorne at the time as having the look "of a rogue who suddenly finds himself in the company of detectives." Hawthorne continued to work, revising his English notebooks for publication and sketching new romances, but he found it difficult to complete these drafts, and finally he abandoned them.

By the spring of 1864, Hawthorne's health had mysteriously and rapidly declined; he could hardly hold the pen as he wrote. Oliver Wendell Holmes, visiting him at the time, inferred that he had a brain tumor. Pierce proposed to take him on a trip to the seacoast of Maine, hoping this might revive his health and spirit. But on May 19, soon after they reached Plymouth, New Hampshire, Hawthorne died quietly in his sleep. His body was returned to Concord, where he was buried at Sleepy Hollow cemetery.

At a time when, as Emerson said, "things are in the saddle," Hawthorne devoted himself to a more aesthetic purpose—to explore the territory "where the Actual and the Imaginary might meet." And the setting Hawthorne most often chose for this encounter was Puritan New England, a place of "dark necessity," as he called it, an overbearing, threatening world where the responsibility for moral order remained with individuals who were themselves seriously flawed. He drew on Puritan orthodoxy not to study theology but to examine individual and collective consciousness under the pressures of anguish and suffering. He sought to dramatize the relation between society and powerful individuals; to probe such themes as the individual's relation to sin, guilt, and retribution; to explore the mysteries of the human heart; to examine characters caught in the grip of the past or in the need for greater experience and knowledge. His writing is marked by its introspective depth, by its urge to get inside the characters he created. In this respect, Hawthorne is one of the first major American writers of fiction to focus on the interior lives of his characters, to explore what Henry James would later call "the deeper psychology of art." He leaves us with a fictional world in which, as in reality, the consequences of trying to transcend the mortal and the moral remain all too painfully apparent.

   Hawthorne never stopped studying his own techniques as a writer. Perhaps this is one reason so many other major writers were so attracted to his work. Poe admired him, as did Henry James, Thomas Hardy, and D. H. Lawrence. And Herman Melville dedicated *Moby-Dick* to Hawthorne "in token of my admiration for his genius." And yet it may be most fitting to turn to one of Hawthorne's own early sketches for a projection of his contribution to an indigenous American literature. In "A Select Party," Hawthorne creates a character, not unlike himself in appearance, manner, and aspiration, who is "as yet unhonored" by those around him but "for whom our country is looking anxiously into the mist of Time, as destined to fulfill the great mission of creating an American literature, as it were, out of our intellectual quarries." The enduring strength of Hawthorne's writing suggests that he accomplished that mission.

Further Reading:

H. James, *Hawthorne*, 1879.

J. Hawthorne, *Nathaniel Hawthorne and His Wife*, 2 vols., 1884; rpt. 1968.

G. Woodberry, *Nathaniel Hawthorne*, 1902.

D. H. Lawrence, *Studies in Classic American Literature*, 1923.

F. O. Matthiessen, *The American Renaissance*, 1941.

H. Levin, *The Power of Blackness*, 1958; rpt. 1980.

A. Turner, *Nathaniel Hawthorne: An Introduction and Interpretation*, 1961.

R. H. Pearce, ed., *Hawthorne Centenary Essays*, 1964.

F. Crews, *The Sins of the Fathers: Hawthorne's Psychological Themes*, 1966.

A. Kaul, ed., *Hawthorne: A Collection of Critical Essays*, 1966.

K. Cameron, ed., *Hawthorne Among His Contemporaries*, 1968.

J. C. Stubbs, *The Pursuit of Form: A Study of Hawthorne and the Romance*, 1970.

N. F. Doubleday, *Hawthorne's Early Tales: A Critical Study*, 1972.

R. H. Brodhead, *Hawthorne, Melville, and the Novel*, 1976.

A. Turner, *Nathaniel Hawthorne: A Biography*, 1980.

J. Mellows, *Nathaniel Hawthorne in His Times*, 1980.

T. Martin, *Nathaniel Hawthorne*, 1983.

M. Colacurcio, *The Province of Piety: Moral History in Hawthorne's Early Tales*, 1984.

M. Colacurcio, ed., *New Essays on The Scarlet Letter*, 1985.

H. Bloom, ed., *Nathaniel Hawthorne*, 1986.

R. Brodhead, *The School of Hawthorne*, 1987.

E. Greenwald, *Realism and Romance: Nathaniel Hawthorne, Henry James, and American Fiction*, 1989.

R. S. Levine, *Conspiracy and Romance: Studies in Brockden Brown, Cooper, Hawthorne, and Melville*, 1989.

L. S. Luedtke, *Nathaniel Hawthorne and the Romance of the Orient*, 1989.

G. Brown, *Domestic Individualism: Imagining Self in Nineteenth-Century America*, 1990.

E. H. Cady and L. J. Budd, eds., *On Hawthorne*, 1990.

S. Bercovitch, *The Office of The Scarlet Letter*, 1991.

S. Cameron, *The Corporeal Self: Allegories of the Body in Melville and Hawthorne*, 1991.

K. P. Hansen, *Sin and Sympathy: Nathaniel Hawthorne's Sentimental Religion*, 1991.

E. H. Miller, *Salem Is My Dwelling Place: A Life of Nathaniel Hawthorne*, 1991.

J. H. Miller, *Hawthorne and History: Defacing It*, 1991.

C. Swann, *Nathaniel Hawthorne, Tradition and Revolution*, 1991.

R. H. Millington, *Practicing Romance: Narrative Form and Cultural Engagement in Hawthorne's Fiction*, 1992.

G. Scharnhorst, ed., *The Critical Response to Nathaniel Hawthorne's The Scarlet Letter*, 1992.

T. W. Herbert, *Dearest Beloved: The Hawthornes and the Making of the Middle-Class Family*, 1993.

Texts:

Stories and novels from *The Complete Works of Nathaniel Hawthorne*, 12 vols., 1883.

See also *The American Notebooks*, ed. R. Stewart, 1932.

The English Notebooks, ed. R. Stewart, 1941.

Nathaniel Hawthorne: Tales and Sketches, ed. R. H. Pearce, 1982.

Nathaniel Hawthorne: Novels, ed. M. Bell, 1983.

T. Woodson, L. Neal Smith, and N. H. Pearson, eds., *The Letters/Nathaniel Hawthorne*, 1984–1987.

My Kinsman, Major Molineux

After the kings of Great Britain had assumed the right of appointing the colonial governors,[1] the measures of the latter seldom met with the ready and general approbation which had been paid to those of their predecessors, under the original charters. The people looked with most jealous scrutiny to the exercise of power which did not emanate from themselves, and they usually rewarded their rulers with slender gratitude for the compliances by which, in softening their instructions from beyond the sea, they had incurred the reprehension of those who gave them. The annals of Massachusetts Bay will inform us, that of six governors in the space of about forty years from the surrender of the old charter, under James II., two were imprisoned by a popular insurrection; a third, as Hutchinson[2] inclines to believe, was driven from the province by the whizzing of a musket-ball; a fourth, in the opinion of the same historian, was hastened to his grave by continual bickerings with the House of Representatives; and the remaining two, as well as their successors, till the Revolution, were favored with few and brief intervals of peaceful sway. The inferior members of the court party,[3] in times of high political excitement, led scarcely a more desirable life. These remarks may serve as a preface to the following adventures, which chanced upon a summer night, not far from a hundred years ago. The reader, in order to avoid a long and dry detail of colonial affairs, is requested to dispense with an account of the train of circumstances that had caused much temporary inflammation of the popular mind.

It was near nine o'clock of a moonlight evening, when a boat crossed the ferry with a single passenger, who had obtained his conveyance at that unusual hour by the promise of an extra fare. While he stood on the landing-place, searching in either pocket for the means of fulfilling his agreement, the ferryman lifted a lantern, by the aid of which, and the newly risen moon, he took a very accurate survey of the stranger's figure. He was a youth of barely eighteen years, evidently country-bred, and now, as it should seem, upon his first visit to town. He was clad in a coarse gray coat, well worn, but in excellent repair; his under garments were durably constructed of leather, and fitted tight to a pair of serviceable and well-shaped limbs; his stockings of blue yarn were the incontrovertible work of a mother or a sister; and on his head was a three-cornered hat, which in its better days had perhaps sheltered the graver brow of the lad's father. Under his left arm was a heavy cudgel formed of an oak sapling, and retaining a part of the hardened root; and his equipment was completed by a wallet,[4] not so abundantly stocked as to incommode the vigorous shoulders on which it hung. Brown, curly hair, well-shaped features, and bright, cheerful eyes were nature's gifts, and worth all that art could have done for his adornment.

The youth, one of whose names was Robin, finally drew from his pocket the half of a little province bill[5] of five shillings, which, in the depreciation in that sort of currency,

---

[1] The first royal governor of Massachusetts was appointed in 1685 by James II, after the Massachusetts Charter had been annulled.
[2] Thomas Hutchinson (1711–1780), the last royal governor of Massachusetts, was also a historian and author of *The History of the*

Colony and Province of Massachusetts-Bay (1764, 1767).
[3] The pro-royal party.
[4] Knapsack.
[5] Colonial paper money.

did but satisfy the ferryman's demand, with the surplus of a sexangular piece of parchment, valued at three pence. He then walked forward into the town, with as light a step as if his day's journey had not already exceeded thirty miles, and with as eager an eye as if he were entering London city, instead of the little metropolis of a New England colony. Before Robin had proceeded far, however, it occurred to him that he knew not whither to direct his steps; so he paused, and looked up and down the narrow street, scrutinizing the small and mean wooden buildings that were scattered on either side.

"This low hovel cannot be my kinsman's dwelling," thought he, "nor yonder old house, where the moonlight enters at the broken casement; and truly I see none hereabouts that might be worthy of him. It would have been wise to inquire my way of the ferryman, and doubtless he would have gone with me, and earned a shilling from the Major for his pains. But the next man I meet will do as well."

He resumed his walk, and was glad to perceive that the street now became wider, and the houses more respectable in their appearance. He soon discerned a figure moving on moderately in advance, and hastened his steps to overtake it. As Robin drew nigh, he saw that the passenger was a man in years, with a full periwig of gray hair, a wide-skirted coat of dark cloth, and silk stockings rolled above his knees. He carried a long and polished cane, which he struck down perpendicularly before him at every step; and at regular intervals he uttered two successive hems, of a peculiarly solemn and sepulchral intonation. Having made these observations, Robin laid hold of the skirt of the old man's coat, just when the light from the open door and windows of a barber's shop fell upon both their figures.

"Good evening to you, honored sir," said he, making a low bow, and still retaining his hold of the skirt. "I pray you tell me whereabouts is the dwelling of my kinsman, Major Molineux."

The youth's question was uttered very loudly; and one of the barbers, whose razor was descending on a well-soaped chin, and another who was dressing a Ramillies wig,[6] left their occupations, and came to the door. The citizen, in the mean time, turned a long-favored countenance upon Robin, and answered him in a tone of excessive anger and annoyance. His two sepulchral hems, however, broke into the very centre of his rebuke, with most singular effect, like a thought of the cold grave obtruding among wrathful passions.

"Let go my garment, fellow! I tell you, I know not the man you speak of. What! I have authority, I have—hem, hem—authority; and if this be the respect you show for your betters, your feet shall be brought acquainted with the stocks[7] by daylight, tomorrow morning!"

Robin released the old man's skirt, and hastened away, pursued by an ill-mannered roar of laughter from the barber's shop. He was at first considerably surprised by the result of his question, but, being a shrewd youth, soon thought himself able to account for the mystery.

"This is some country representative," was his conclusion, "who has never seen the inside of my kinsman's door, and lacks the breeding to answer a stranger civilly. The man is old, or verily—I might be tempted to turn back and smite him on the nose. Ah,

---

[6] Elaborately braided wig named for a British victory at Ramillies, Belgium.

[7] Heavy wooden instruments, used for public punishment, that lock around the ankles and sometimes the wrists.

Robin, Robin! even the barber's boys laugh at you for choosing such a guide! You will be wiser in time, friend Robin."

He now became entangled in a succession of crooked and narrow streets, which crossed each other, and meandered at no great distance from the water-side. The smell of tar was obvious to his nostrils, the masts of vessels pierced the moonlight above the tops of the buildings, and the numerous signs, which Robin paused to read, informed him that he was near the centre of business. But the streets were empty, the shops were closed, and lights were visible only in the second stories of a few dwelling-houses. At length, on the corner of a narrow lane, through which he was passing, he beheld the broad countenance of a British hero swinging before the door[8] of an inn, whence proceeded the voices of many guests. The casement of one of the lower windows was thrown back, and a very thin curtain permitted Robin to distinguish a party at supper, round a well-furnished table. The fragrance of the good cheer steamed forth into the outer air, and the youth could not fail to recollect that the last remnant of his travelling stock of provision had yielded to his morning appetite, and that noon had found and left him dinnerless.

"Oh, that a parchment three-penny might give me a right to sit down at yonder table!" said Robin, with a sigh. "But the Major will make me welcome to the best of his victuals; so I will even step boldly in, and inquire my way to his dwelling."

He entered the tavern, and was guided by the murmur of voices and the fumes of tobacco to the public-room. It was a long and low apartment, with oaken walls, grown dark in the continual smoke, and a floor which was thickly sanded, but of no immaculate purity. A number of persons—the larger part of whom appeared to be mariners, or in some way connected with the sea—occupied the wooden benches, or leather-bottomed chairs, conversing on various matters, and occasionally lending their attention to some topic of general interest. Three or four little groups were draining as many bowls of punch, which the West India trade had long since made a familiar drink in the colony. Others, who had the appearance of men who lived by regular and laborious handicraft, preferred the insulated bliss of an unshared potation, and became more taciturn under its influence. Nearly all, in short, evinced a predilection for the Good Creature[9] in some of its various shapes, for this is a vice to which, as Fast Day[10] sermons of a hundred years ago will testify, we have a long hereditary claim. The only guests to whom Robin's sympathies inclined him were two or three sheepish countrymen, who were using the inn somewhat after the fashion of a Turkish caravansary,[11] they had gotten themselves into the darkest corner of the room, and heedless of the Nicotian[12] atmosphere, were supping on the bread of their own ovens, and the bacon cured in their own chimney-smoke. But though Robin felt a sort of brotherhood with these strangers, his eyes were attracted from them to a person who stood near the door, holding whispered conversation with a group of ill-dressed associates. His features were separately striking almost to grotesqueness, and the whole face left a deep impression on the memory. The forehead bulged out into a double prominence, with a vale between; the

---

[8] i.e., on a signboard.
[9] See 1 Timothy 4:4: "For every creature of God is good and nothing to be refused, if it be received with Thanksgiving."
[10] A day for public penitence.

[11] Inn built to accommodate caravans.
[12] Smoke-filled from tobacco. Jean Nicot (hence "nicotine") brought the first tobacco to France from Lisbon.

nose came boldly forth in an irregular curve, and its bridge was of more than a finger's breadth; the eyebrows were deep and shaggy, and the eyes glowed beneath them like fire in a cave.

While Robin deliberated of whom to inquire respecting his kinsman's dwelling, he was accosted by the innkeeper, a little man in a stained white apron, who had come to pay his professional welcome to the stranger. Being in the second generation from a French Protestant, he seemed to have inherited the courtesy of his parent nation; but no variety of circumstances was ever known to change his voice from the one shrill note in which he now addressed Robin.

"From the country, I presume, sir?" said he, with a profound bow. "Beg leave to congratulate you on your arrival, and trust you intend a long stay with us. Fine town here, sir, beautiful buildings, and much that may interest a stranger. May I hope for the honor of your commands in respect to supper?"

"The man sees a family likeness! the rogue has guessed that I am related to the Major!" thought Robin, who had hitherto experienced little superfluous civility.

All eyes were now turned on the country lad, standing at the door, in his worn three-cornered hat, gray coat, leather breeches, and blue yarn stockings, leaning on an oaken cudgel, and bearing a wallet on his back.

Robin replied to the courteous innkeeper, with such an assumption of confidence as befitted the Major's relative. "My honest friend," he said, "I shall make it a point to patronize your house on some occasion, when"—here he could not help lowering his voice—"when I may have more than a parchment three-pence in my pocket. My present business," continued he, speaking with lofty confidence, "is merely to inquire my way to the dwelling of my kinsman, Major Molineux."

There was a sudden and general movement in the room, which Robin interpreted as expressing the eagerness of each individual to become his guide. But the innkeeper turned his eyes to a written paper on the wall, which he read, or seemed to read, with occasional recurrences to the young man's figure.

"What have we here?" said he, breaking his speech into little dry fragments. " 'Left the house of the subscriber, bounden servant,[13] Hezekiah Mudge,—had on, when he went away, gray coat, leather breeches, master's third-best hat. One pound currency reward to whosoever shall lodge him in any jail of the province.' Better trudge, boy; better trudge!"

Robin had begun to draw his hand towards the lighter end of the oak cudgel, but a strange hostility in every countenance induced him to relinquish his purpose of breaking the courteous innkeeper's head. As he turned to leave the room, he encountered a sneering glance from the bold-featured personage whom he had before noticed; and no sooner was he beyond the door, than he heard a general laugh, in which the innkeeper's voice might be distinguished, like the dropping of small stones into a kettle.

"Now, is it not strange," thought Robin, with his usual shrewdness,—"is it not strange that the confession of an empty pocket should outweigh the name of my kinsman, Major Molineux? Oh, if I had one of those grinning rascals in the woods, where I and my oak sapling grew up together, I would teach him that my arm is heavy though my purse be light!"

---

[13] Person bound to servitude (indentured) for a specific period, usually in exchange for transportation to the colonies.

On turning the corner of the narrow lane, Robin found himself in a spacious street, with an unbroken line of lofty houses on each side, and a steepled building at the upper end, whence the ringing of a bell announced the hour of nine. The light of the moon, and the lamps from the numerous shop-windows, discovered people promenading on the pavement, and amongst them Robin hoped to recognize his hitherto inscrutable relative. The result of his former inquiries made him unwilling to hazard another, in a scene of such publicity, and he determined to walk slowly and silently up the street, thrusting his face close to that of every elderly gentleman, in search of the Major's lineaments. In his progress, Robin encountered many gay and gallant figures. Embroidered garments of showy colors, enormous periwigs, gold-laced hats, and silver-hilted swords glided past him and dazzled his optics. Travelled youths, imitators of the European fine gentlemen of the period, trod jauntily along, half dancing to the fashionable tunes which they hummed, and making poor Robin ashamed of his quiet and natural gait. At length, after many pauses to examine the gorgeous display of goods in the shop-windows, and after suffering some rebukes for the impertinence of his scrutiny into people's faces, the Major's kinsman found himself near the steepled building, still unsuccessful in his search. As yet, however, he had seen only one side of the thronged street; so Robin crossed, and continued the same sort of inquisition down the opposite pavement, with stronger hopes than the philosopher seeking an honest man,[14] but with no better fortune. He had arrived about midway towards the lower end, from which his course began, when he overheard the approach of some one who struck down a cane on the flag-stones at every step, uttering, at regular intervals, two sepulchral hems.

"Mercy on us!" quoth Robin, recognizing the sound.

Turning a corner, which chanced to be close at his right hand, he hastened to pursue his researches in some other part of the town. His patience now was wearing low, and he seemed to feel more fatigue from his rambles since he crossed the ferry, than from his journey of several days on the other side. Hunger also pleaded loudly within him, and Robin began to balance the propriety of demanding, violently, and with lifted cudgel, the necessary guidance from the first solitary passenger whom he should meet. While a resolution to this effect was gaining strength, he entered a street of mean appearance, on either side of which a row of ill-built houses was straggling towards the harbor. The moonlight fell upon no passenger along the whole extent, but in the third domicile which Robin passed there was a half-opened door, and his keen glance detected a woman's garment within.

"My luck may be better here," said he to himself.

Accordingly, he approached the door, and beheld it shut closer as he did so; yet an open space remained, sufficing for the fair occupant to observe the stranger, without a corresponding display on her part. All that Robin could discern was a strip of scarlet petticoat, and the occasional sparkle of an eye, as if the moon-beams were trembling on some bright thing.

"Pretty mistress," for I may call her so with a good conscience, thought the shrewd youth, since I know nothing to the contrary,—"my sweet pretty mistress, will you be kind enough to tell me whereabouts I must seek the dwelling of my kinsman, Major Molineux?"

---

[14] Diogenes, Greek Cynic philosopher (412?–323 B.C.), supposedly roamed the world in search of an honest man.

Robin's voice was plaintive and winning, and the female, seeing nothing to be shunned in the handsome country youth, thrust open the door, and came forth into the moonlight. She was a dainty little figure, with a white neck, round arms, and a slender waist, at the extremity of which her scarlet petticoat jutted out over a hoop, as if she were standing in a balloon. Moreover, her face was oval and pretty, her hair dark beneath the little cap, and her bright eyes possessed a sly freedom, which triumphed over those of Robin.

"Major Molineux dwells here," said this fair woman.

Now, her voice was the sweetest Robin had heard that night, the airy counterpart of a stream of melted silver; yet he could not help doubting whether that sweet voice spoke Gospel truth. He looked up and down the mean street, and then surveyed the house before which they stood. It was a small, dark edifice of two stories, the second of which projected over the lower floor, and the front apartment had the aspect of a shop for petty commodities.

"Now, truly, I am in luck," replied Robin, cunningly, "and so indeed is my kinsman, the Major, in having so pretty a housekeeper. But I prithee trouble him to step to the door; I will deliver him a message from his friends in the country, and then go back to my lodgings at the inn."

"Nay, the Major has been abed this hour or more," said the lady of the scarlet petticoat; "and it would be to little purpose to disturb him to-night, seeing his evening draught was of the strongest. But he is a kind-hearted man, and it would be as much as my life's worth to let a kinsman of his turn away from the door. You are the good old gentleman's very picture, and I could swear that was his rainy-weather hat. Also he has garments very much resembling those leather small-clothes. But come in, I pray, for I bid you hearty welcome in his name."

So saying, the fair and hospitable dame took our hero by the hand; and the touch was light, and the force was gentleness, and though Robin read in her eyes what he did not hear in her words, yet the slender-waisted woman in the scarlet petticoat proved stronger than the athletic country youth. She had drawn his half-willing footsteps nearly to the threshold, when the opening of a door in the neighborhood startled the Major's housekeeper, and, leaving the Major's kinsman, she vanished speedily into her own domicile. A heavy yawn preceded the appearance of a man, who, like the Moonshine of Pyramus and Thisbe,[15] carried a lantern, needlessly aiding his sister luminary in the heavens. As he walked sleepily up the street, he turned his broad, dull face on Robin, and displayed a long staff, spiked at the end.

"Home, vagabond, home!" said the watchman, in accents that seemed to fall asleep as soon as they were uttered. "Home, or we'll set you in the stocks by peep of day!"

"This is the second hint of the kind," thought Robin. "I wish they would end my difficulties, by setting me there to-night."

Nevertheless, the youth felt an instinctive antipathy towards the guardian of midnight order, which at first prevented him from asking his usual question. But just when the man was about to vanish behind the corner, Robin resolved not to lose the opportunity, and shouted lustily after him,—

"I say, friend! will you guide me to the house of my kinsman, Major Molineux?"

[15] Moonshine appears in a bumbling enactment of the story of Pyramus and Thisbe by characters in Shakespeare's play *A Midsummer Night's Dream*.

The watchman made no reply, but turned the corner and was gone; yet Robin seemed to hear the sound of drowsy laughter stealing along the solitary street. At that moment, also, a pleasant titter saluted him from the open window above his head; he looked up, and caught the sparkle of a saucy eye; a round arm beckoned to him, and next he heard light footsteps descending the staircase within. But Robin, being of the household of a New England clergyman, was a good youth, as well as a shrewd one; so he resisted temptation, and fled away.

He now roamed desperately, and at random, through the town, almost ready to believe that a spell was on him, like that by which a wizard of his country had once kept three pursuers wandering, a whole winter night, within twenty paces of the cottage which they sought. The streets lay before him, strange and desolate, and the lights were extinguished in almost every house. Twice, however, little parties of men, among whom Robin distinguished individuals in outlandish attire, came hurrying along; but, though on both occasions they paused to address him, such intercourse did not at all enlighten his perplexity. They did but utter a few words in some language of which Robin knew nothing, and perceiving his inability to answer, bestowed a curse upon him in plain English and hastened away. Finally, the lad determined to knock at the door of every mansion that might appear worthy to be occupied by his kinsman, trusting that perseverance would overcome the fatality that had hitherto thwarted him. Firm in this resolve, he was passing beneath the walls of a church, which formed the corner of two streets, when, as he turned into the shade of its steeple, he encountered a bulky stranger, muffled in a cloak. The man was proceeding with the speed of earnest business, but Robin planted himself full before him, holding the oak cudgel with both hands across his body as a bar to further passage.

"Halt, honest man, and answer me a question," said he, very resolutely. "Tell me, this instant, whereabouts is the dwelling of my kinsman, Major Molineux!"

"Keep your tongue between your teeth, fool, and let me pass!" said a deep, gruff voice, which Robin partly remembered. "Let me pass, I say, or I'll strike you to the earth!"

"No, no, neighbor!" cried Robin, flourishing his cudgel, and then thrusting its larger end close to the man's muffled face. "No, no, I'm not the fool you take me for, nor do you pass till I have an answer to my question. Whereabouts is the dwelling of my kinsman, Major Molineux?"

The stranger, instead of attempting to force his passage, stepped back into the moonlight, unmuffled his face, and stared full into that of Robin.

"Watch here an hour, and Major Molineux will pass by," said he.

Robin gazed with dismay and astonishment on the unprecedented physiognomy of the speaker. The forehead with its double prominence, the broad hooked nose, the shaggy eyebrows, and fiery eyes were those which he had noticed at the inn, but the man's complexion had undergone a singular, or, more properly, a twofold change. One side of the face blazed an intense red, while the other was black as midnight, the division line being in the broad bridge of the nose; and a mouth which seemed to extend from ear to ear was black or red, in contrast to the color of the cheek. The effect was as if two individual devils, a fiend of fire and a fiend of darkness, had united themselves to form this infernal visage. The stranger grinned in Robin's face, muffled his party-colored features, and was out of sight in a moment.

"Strange things we travellers see!" ejaculated Robin.

He seated himself, however, upon the steps of the church-door, resolving to wait the appointed time for his kinsman. A few moments were consumed in philosophical speculations upon the species of man who had just left him; but having settled this point shrewdly, rationally, and satisfactorily, he was compelled to look elsewhere for his amusement. And first he threw his eyes along the street. It was of more respectable appearance than most of those into which he had wandered; and the moon, creating, like the imaginative power, a beautiful strangeness in familiar objects, gave something of romance to a scene that might not have possessed it in the light of day. The irregular and often quaint architecture of the houses, some of whose roofs were broken into numerous little peaks, while others ascended, steep and narrow, into a single point, and others again were square; the pure snow-white of some of their complexions, the aged darkness of others, and the thousand sparklings, reflected from bright substances in the walls of many; these matters engaged Robin's attention for a while, and then began to grow wearisome. Next he endeavored to define the forms of distant objects, starting away, with almost ghostly indistinctness, just as his eye appeared to grasp them; and finally he took a minute survey of an edifice which stood on the opposite side of the street, directly in front of the church-door, where he was stationed. It was a large, square mansion, distinguished from its neighbors by a balcony, which rested on tall pillars, and by an elaborate Gothic window, communicating therewith.

"Perhaps this is the very house I have been seeking," thought Robin.

Then he strove to speed away the time, by listening to a murmur which swept continually along the street, yet was scarcely audible, except to an unaccustomed ear like his; it was a low, dull, dreamy sound, compounded of many noises, each of which was at too great a distance to be separately heard. Robin marvelled at this snore of a sleeping town, and marvelled more whenever its continuity was broken by now and then a distant shout, apparently loud where it originated. But altogether it was a sleep-inspiring sound, and, to shake off its drowsy influence, Robin arose, and climbed a window-frame, that he might view the interior of the church. There the moonbeams came trembling in, and fell down upon the deserted pews, and extended along the quiet aisles. A fainter yet more awful radiance was hovering around the pulpit, and one solitary ray had dared to rest upon the open page of the great Bible. Had nature, in that deep hour, become a worshipper in the house which man had builded? Or was that heavenly light the visible sanctity of the place,—visible because no earthly and impure feet were within the walls? The scene made Robin's heart shiver with a sensation of loneliness stronger than he had ever felt in the remotest depths of his native woods; so he turned away and sat down again before the door. There were graves around the church, and now an uneasy thought obtruded into Robin's breast. What if the object of his search, which had been so often and so strangely thwarted, were all the time mouldering in his shroud? What if his kinsman should glide through yonder gate, and nod and smile to him in dimly passing by?

"Oh that any breathing thing were here with me!" said Robin.

Recalling his thoughts from this uncomfortable track, he sent them over forest, hill, and stream, and attempted to imagine how that evening of ambiguity and weariness had been spent by his father's household. He pictured them assembled at the door, beneath the tree, the great old tree, which had been spared for its huge twisted trunk and venerable shade, when a thousand leafy brethren fell. There, at the going down of the summer sun, it was his father's custom to perform domestic worship, that the neighbors might come and join with him like brothers of the family, and that the wayfaring man might pause to drink at that fountain, and keep his heart pure by freshening the memory of home. Robin distinguished the seat of every individual of the little audience; he saw the good man in the midst, holding the Scriptures in the golden light that fell from the western clouds; he beheld him close the book and all rise up to pray. He heard the old thanksgivings for daily mercies, the old supplications for their continuance, to which he had so often listened in weariness, but which were now among his dear remembrances. He perceived the slight inequality of his father's voice when he came to speak of the absent one; he noted how his mother turned her face to the broad and knotted trunk; how his elder brother scorned, because the beard was rough upon his upper lip, to permit his features to be moved; how the younger sister drew down a low hanging branch before her eyes; and how the little one of all, whose sports had hitherto broken the decorum of the scene, understood the prayer for her playmate, and burst into clamorous grief. Then he saw them go in at the door; and when Robin would have entered also, the latch tinkled into its place, and he was excluded from his home.

"Am I here, or there?" cried Robin, starting; for all at once, when his thoughts had become visible and audible in a dream, the long, wide, solitary street shone out before him.

He aroused himself, and endeavored to fix his attention steadily upon the large edifice which he had surveyed before. But still his mind kept vibrating between fancy and reality; by turns, the pillars of the balcony lengthened into the tall, bare stems of pines, dwindled down to human figures, settled again into their true shape and size, and then commenced a new succession of changes. For a single moment, when he deemed himself awake, he could have sworn that a visage—one which he seemed to remember, yet could not absolutely name as his kinsman's—was looking towards him from the Gothic window. A deeper sleep wrestled with and nearly overcame him, but fled at the sound of footsteps along the opposite pavement. Robin rubbed his eyes, discerned a man passing at the foot of the balcony, and addressed him in a loud, peevish, and lamentable cry.

"Hallo, friend! must I wait here all night for my kinsman, Major Molineux?"

The sleeping echoes awoke, and answered the voice; and the passenger, barely able to discern a figure sitting in the oblique shade of the steeple, traversed the street to obtain a nearer view. He was himself a gentleman in his prime, of open, intelligent, cheerful, and altogether prepossessing countenance. Perceiving a country youth, apparently homeless and without friends, he accosted him in a tone of real kindness, which had become strange to Robin's ears.

"Well, my good lad, who are you sitting here?" inquired he. "Can I be of service to you in any way?"

"I am afraid not, sir," replied Robin, despondingly; "yet I shall take it kindly, if you'll answer me a single question. I've been searching, half the night, for one Major Molineux; now, sir, is there really such a person in these parts, or am I dreaming?"

"Major Molineux! The name is not altogether strange to me," said the gentleman, smiling. "Have you any objection to telling me the nature of your business with him?"

Then Robin briefly related that his father was a clergyman, settled on a small salary, at a long distance back in the country, and that he and Major Molineux were brothers' children. The Major, having inherited riches, and acquired civil and military rank, had visited his cousin, in great pomp, a year or two before; had manifested much interest in

Robin and an elder brother, and, being childless himself, had thrown out hints respecting the future establishment of one of them in life. The elder brother was destined to succeed to the farm which his father cultivated in the interval of sacred duties; it was therefore determined that Robin should profit by his kinsman's generous intentions, especially as he seemed to be rather the favorite, and was thought to possess other necessary endowments.

"For I have the name of being a shrewd youth," observed Robin, in this part of his story.

"I doubt not you deserve it," replied his new friend, good-naturedly; "but pray proceed."

"Well, sir, being nearly eighteen years old, and well grown, as you see," continued Robin, drawing himself up to his full height, "I thought it high time to begin the world. So my mother and sister put me in handsome trim, and my father gave me half the remnant of his last year's salary, and five days ago I started for this place, to pay the Major a visit. But, would you believe it, sir! I crossed the ferry a little after dark, and have yet found nobody that would show me the way to his dwelling; only, an hour or two since, I was told to wait here, and Major Molineux would pass by."

"Can you describe the man who told you this?" inquired the gentleman.

"Oh, he was a very ill-favored fellow, sir," replied Robin, "with two great bumps on his forehead, a hook nose, fiery eyes; and, what struck me as the strangest, his face was of two different colors. Do you happen to know such a man, sir?"

"Not intimately," answered the stranger, "but I chanced to meet him a little time previous to your stopping me. I believe you may trust his word, and that the Major will very shortly pass through this street. In the mean time, as I have a singular curiosity to witness your meeting, I will sit down here upon the steps and bear you company."

He seated himself accordingly, and soon engaged his companion in animated discourse. It was but of brief continuance, however, for a noise of shouting, which had long been remotely audible, drew so much nearer that Robin inquired its cause.

"What may be the meaning of this uproar?" asked he. "Truly, if your town be always as noisy, I shall find little sleep while I am an inhabitant."

"Why, indeed, friend Robin, there do appear to be three or four riotous fellows abroad to-night," replied the gentleman. "You must not expect all the stillness of your native woods here in our streets. But the watch will shortly be at the heels of these lads and"—

"Ay, and set them in the stocks by peep of day," interrupted Robin, recollecting his own encounter with the drowsy lantern-bearer. "But, dear sir, if I may trust my ears, an army of watchmen would never make head against such a multitude of rioters. There were at least a thousand voices went up to make that one shout."

"May not a man have several voices, Robin, as well as two complexions?" said his friend.

"Perhaps a man may; but Heaven forbid that a woman should!" responded the shrewd youth, thinking of the seductive tones of the Major's housekeeper.

The sounds of a trumpet in some neighboring street now became so evident and continual, that Robin's curiosity was strongly excited. In addition to the shouts, he heard frequent bursts from many instruments of discord, and a wild and confused laughter filled up the intervals. Robin rose from the steps, and looked wistfully towards a point whither people seemed to be hastening.

"Surely some prodigious merry-making is going on," exclaimed he. "I have laughed very little since I left home, sir, and should be sorry to lose an opportunity. Shall we step round the corner by that darkish house, and take our share of the fun?"

"Sit down again, sit down, good Robin," replied the gentleman, laying his hand on the skirt of the gray coat. "You forget that we must wait here for your kinsman; and there is reason to believe that he will pass by, in the course of a very few moments."

The near approach of the uproar had now disturbed the neighborhood; windows flew open on all sides: and many heads, in the attire of the pillow, and confused by sleep suddenly broken, were protruded to the gaze of whoever had leisure to observe them. Eager voices hailed each other from house to house, all demanding the explanation, which not a soul could give. Half-dressed men hurried towards the unknown commotion, stumbling as they went over the stone steps that thrust themselves into the narrow foot-walk. The shouts, the laughter, and the tuneless bray, the antipodes of music, came onwards with increasing din, till scattered individuals, and then denser bodies, began to appear round a corner at the distance of a hundred yards.

"Will you recognize your kinsman, if he passes in this crowd?" inquired the gentleman.

"Indeed, I can't warrant it, sir; but I'll take my stand here, and keep a bright lookout," answered Robin, descending to the outer edge of the pavement.

A mighty stream of people now emptied into the street, and came rolling slowly towards the church. A single horseman wheeled the corner in the midst of them, and close behind him came a band of fearful wind-instruments, sending forth a fresher discord now that no intervening buildings kept it from the ear. Then a redder light disturbed the moonbeams, and a dense multitude of torches shone along the street, concealing, by their glare, whatever object they illuminated. The single horseman, clad in a military dress, and bearing a drawn sword, rode onward as the leader, and, by his fierce and variegated countenance, appeared like war personified; the red of one cheek was an emblem of fire and sword; the blackness of the other betokened the mourning that attends them. In his train were wild figures in the Indian dress, and many fantastic shapes without a model, giving the whole march a visionary air, as if a dream had broken forth from some feverish brain, and were sweeping visibly through the midnight streets. A mass of people, inactive, except as applauding spectators, hemmed the procession in; and several women ran along the sidewalk, piercing the confusion of heavier sounds with their shrill voices of mirth or terror.

"The double-faced fellow has his eye upon me," muttered Robin, with an indefinite but an uncomfortable idea that he was himself to bear a part in the pageantry.

The leader turned himself in the saddle, and fixed his glance full upon the country youth, as the steed went slowly by. When Robin had freed his eyes from those fiery ones, the musicians were passing before him, and the torches were close at hand; but the unsteady brightness of the latter formed a veil which he could not penetrate. The rattling of wheels over the stones sometimes found its way to his ear, and confused traces of a human form appeared at intervals, and then melted into the vivid light. A moment more, and the leader thundered a command to halt: the trumpets vomited a horrid breath, and then held their peace; the shouts and laughter of the people died away, and there remained only a universal hum, allied to silence. Right before Robin's eyes was an uncovered cart. There the torches blazed the brightest, there the moon shone out like day, and there, in tar-and-feathery dignity, sat his kinsman, Major Molineux!

He was an elderly man, of large and majestic person, and strong, square features, betokening a steady soul; but steady as it was, his enemies had found means to shake it. His face was pale as death, and far more ghastly; the broad forehead was contracted in his agony, so that his eyebrows formed one grizzled line; his eyes were red and wild, and the foam hung white upon his quivering lip. His whole frame was agitated by a quick and continual tremor, which his pride strove to quell, even in those circumstances of overwhelming humiliation. But perhaps the bitterest pang of all was when his eyes met those of Robin; for he evidently knew him on the instant, as the youth stood witnessing the foul disgrace of a head grown gray in honor. They stared at each other in silence, and Robin's knees shook, and his hair bristled, with a mixture of pity and terror. Soon, however, a bewildering excitement began to seize upon his mind; the preceding adventures of the night, the unexpected appearance of the crowd, the torches, the confused din and the hush that followed, the spectre of his kinsman reviled by that great multitude,—all this, and, more than all, a perception of tremendous ridicule in the whole scene, affected him with a sort of mental inebrity. At that moment a voice of sluggish merriment saluted Robin's ears; he turned instinctively, and just behind the corner of the church stood the lantern-bearer, rubbing his eyes, and drowsily enjoying the lad's amazement. Then he heard a peal of laughter like the ringing of silvery bells; a woman twitched his arm, a saucy eye met his, and he saw the lady of the scarlet petticoat. A sharp, dry cachinnation[16] appealed to his memory, and, standing on tiptoe in the crowd, with his white apron over his head, he beheld the courteous little innkeeper. And lastly, there sailed over the heads of the multitude a great, broad laugh, broken in the midst by two sepulchral hems; thus, "Haw, haw, haw,—hem, hem,—haw, haw, haw, haw!"

The sound proceeded from the balcony of the opposite edifice, and thither Robin turned his eyes. In front of the Gothic window stood the old citizen, wrapped in a wide gown, his gray periwig exchanged for a nightcap, which was thrust back from his forehead, and his silk stockings hanging about his legs. He supported himself on his polished cane in a fit of convulsive merriment, which manifested itself on his solemn old features like a funny inscription on a tomb-stone. Then Robin seemed to hear the voices of the barbers, of the guests of the inn, and of all who had made sport of him that night. The contagion was spreading among the multitude, when all at once, it seized upon Robin, and he sent forth a shout of laughter that echoed through the street,—every man shook his sides, every man emptied his lungs, but Robin's shout was the loudest there. The cloud-spirits peeped from their silvery islands, as the congregated mirth went roaring up the sky! The Man in the Moon heard the far bellow. "Oho," quoth he, "the old earth is frolicsome to-night!"

When there was a momentary calm in that tempestuous sea of sound, the leader gave the sign, the procession resumed its march. On they went, like fiends that throng in mockery around some dead potentate, mighty no more, but majestic still in his agony. On they went, in counterfeited pomp, in senseless uproar, in frenzied merriment, trampling all on an old man's heart. On swept the tumult, and left a silent street behind. . . .

"Well, Robin, are you dreaming?" inquired the gentleman, laying his hand on the youth's shoulder.

---

[16] Laugh.

Robin started, and withdrew his arm from the stone post to which he had instinctively clung, as the living stream rolled by him. His cheek was somewhat pale, and his eye not quite as lively as in the earlier part of the evening.

"Will you be kind enough to show me the way to the ferry?" said he, after a moment's pause.

"You have, then, adopted a new subject of inquiry?" observed his companion, with a smile.

"Why, yes, sir," replied Robin, rather dryly. "Thanks to you, and to my other friends, I have at last met my kinsman, and he will scarce desire to see my face again. I begin to grow weary of a town life, sir. Will you show me the way to the ferry?"

"No, my good friend Robin,—not to-night, at least," said the gentleman. "Some few days hence, if you wish it, I will speed you on your journey. Or, if you prefer to remain with us, perhaps, as you are a shrewd youth, you may rise in the world without the help of your kinsman, Major Molineux."

1832

Young Goodman Brown

Young Goodman[1] Brown came forth at sunset into the street at Salem village; but put his head back, after crossing the threshold, to exchange a parting kiss with his young wife. And Faith, as the wife was aptly named, thrust her own pretty head into the street, letting the wind play with the pink ribbons of her cap while she called to Goodman Brown.

"Dearest heart," whispered she, softly and rather sadly, when her lips were close to his ear, "prithee put off your journey until sunrise and sleep in your own bed to-night. A lone woman is troubled with such dreams and such thoughts that she's afeard of herself sometimes. Pray tarry with me this night, dear husband, of all nights in the year."

"My love and my Faith," replied young Goodman Brown, "of all nights in the year, this one night must I tarry away from thee. My journey, as thou callest it, forth and back again, must needs be done 'twixt now and sunrise. What, my sweet, pretty wife, dost thou doubt me already, and we but three months married?"

"Then God bless you!" said Faith, with the pink ribbons; "and may you find all well when you come back."

"Amen!" cried Goodman Brown. "Say thy prayers, dear Faith, and go to bed at dusk, and no harm will come to thee."

So they parted; and the young man pursued his way until, being about to turn the corner by the meeting-house, he looked back and saw the head of Faith still peeping after him with a melancholy air, in spite of her pink ribbons.

"Poor little Faith!" thought he, for his heart smote him. "What a wretch am I to leave her on such an errand! She talks of dreams, too. Methought as she spoke there was

---

[1] Polite term of address for a man of humble standing.

trouble in her face, as if a dream had warned her what work is to be done tonight. But no, no; 't would kill her to think it. Well, she's a blessed angel on earth; and after this one night I'll cling to her skirts and follow her to heaven."

With this excellent resolve for the future, Goodman Brown felt himself justified in making more haste on his present evil purpose. He had taken a dreary road, darkened by all the gloomiest trees of the forest, which barely stood aside to let the narrow path creep through, and closed immediately behind. It was all as lonely as could be; and there is this peculiarity in such a solitude, that the traveller knows not who may be concealed by the innumerable trunks and the thick boughs over-head; so that with lonely footsteps he may yet be passing through an unseen multitude.

"There may be a devilish Indian behind every tree," said Goodman Brown to himself; and he glanced fearfully behind him as he added, "What if the devil himself should be at my very elbow!"

His head being turned back, he passed a crook of the road, and, looking forward again, beheld the figure of a man, in grave and decent attire, seated at the foot of an old tree. He arose at Goodman Brown's approach and walked onward side by side with him.

"You are late, Goodman Brown," said he. "The clock of the Old South[2] was striking as I came through Boston, and that is full fifteen minutes agone."

"Faith kept me back a while," replied the young man, with a tremor in his voice, caused by the sudden appearance of his companion, though not wholly unexpected.

It was now deep dusk in the forest, and deepest in that part of it where these two were journeying. As nearly as could be discerned, the second traveller was about fifty years old, apparently in the same rank of life as Goodman Brown, and bearing a considerable resemblance to him, though perhaps more in expression than features. Still they might have been taken for father and son. And yet, though the elder person was as simply clad as the younger, and as simple in manner too, he had an indescribable air of one who knew the world, and who would not have felt abashed at the governor's dinner table or in King William's[3] court, were it possible that his affairs should call him thither. But the only thing about him that could be fixed upon as remarkable was his staff, which bore the likeness of a great black snake, so curiously wrought that it might almost be seen to twist and wriggle itself like a living serpent. This, of course, must have been an ocular deception, assisted by the uncertain light.

"Come, Goodman Brown," cried his fellow-traveller, "this is a dull pace for the beginning of a journey. Take my staff, if you are so soon weary."

"Friend," said the other, exchanging his slow pace for a full stop, "having kept covenant by meeting thee here, it is my purpose now to return whence I came. I have scruples touching the matter thou wot'st[4] of."

"Sayest thou so?" replied he of the serpent, smiling apart. "Let us walk on, nevertheless, reasoning as we go; and if I convince thee not thou shalt turn back. We are but a little way in the forest yet."

"Too far! too far!" exclaimed the goodman, unconsciously resuming his walk. "My father never went into the woods on such an errand, nor his father before him. We have

[2] Famous church in Boston.
[3] William III ruled England jointly with Queen Mary II from 1689 to 1702.

[4] Knowest.

been a race of honest men and good Christians since the days of the martyrs;[5] and shall I be the first of the name of Brown that ever took this path and kept"—

"Such company, thou wouldst say," observed the elder person, interpreting his pause. "Well said, Goodman Brown! I have been as well acquainted with your family as with ever a one among the Puritans; and that's no trifle to say. I helped your grandfather, the constable, when he lashed the Quaker woman so smartly through the streets of Salem; and it was I that brought your father a pitch-pine knot, kindled at my own hearth, to set fire to an Indian village, in King Philip's war.[6] They were my good friends, both; and many a pleasant walk have we had along this path, and returned merrily after midnight. I would fain be friends with you for their sake."

"If it be as thou sayest," replied Goodman Brown, "I marvel they never spoke of these matters; or, verily, I marvel not, seeing that the least rumor of the sort would have driven them from New England. We are a people of prayer, and good works to boot, and abide no such wickedness."

"Wickedness or not," said the traveller with the twisted staff, "I have a very general acquaintance here in New England. The deacons of many a church have drunk the communion wine with me; the selectmen of divers towns make me their chairman; and a majority of the Great and General Court[7] are firm supporters of my interest. The governor and I, too—But these are state secrets."

"Can this be so?" cried Goodman Brown, with a stare of amazement at his undisturbed companion. "Howbeit, I have nothing to do with the governor and council; they have their own ways, and are no rule for a simple husbandman[8] like me. But, were I to go on with thee, how should I meet the eye of that good old man, our minister, at Salem village? Oh, his voice would make me tremble both Sabbath day and lecture day."[9]

Thus far the elder traveller had listened with due gravity; but now burst into a fit of irrepressible mirth, shaking himself so violently that his snake-like staff actually seemed to wriggle in sympathy.

"Ha! ha! ha!" shouted he again and again; then composing himself, "Well, go on, Goodman Brown, go on; but, prithee, don't kill me with laughing."

"Well, then, to end the matter at once," said Goodman Brown, considerably nettled, "there is my wife, Faith. It would break her dear little heart; and I'd rather break my own."

"Nay, if that be the case," answered the other, "e'en go thy ways, Goodman Brown. I would not for twenty old women like the one hobbling before us that Faith should come to any harm."

As he spoke he pointed his staff at a female figure on the path, in whom Goodman Brown recognized a very pious and exemplary dame, who had taught him his catechism in youth, and was still his moral and spiritual adviser, jointly with the minister and Deacon Gookin.

[5] Allusion to the treatment of Protestants in England under the Catholic monarch Mary Tudor (1553–1558).

[6] War waged (1675–1676) against the New England colonists by the Indian leader Metacomset, also known as "King Philip."

[7] Legislature of the Puritan colony.

[8] Most often a farmer, but here a man of ordinary standing.

[9] Midweek sermon day, either Wednesday or Thursday.

"A marvel, truly, that Goody[10] Cloyse[11] should be so far in the wilderness at night-fall," said he. "But with your leave, friend, I shall take a cut through the woods until we have left this Christian woman behind. Being a stranger to you, she might ask whom I was consorting with and whither I was going."

"Be it so," said his fellow-traveller. "Betake you to the woods, and let me keep the path."

Accordingly the young man turned aside, but took care to watch his companion, who advanced softly along the road until he had come within a staff's length of the old dame. She, meanwhile, was making the best of her way, with singular speed for so aged a woman, and mumbling some indistinct words—a prayer, doubtless—as she went. The traveller put forth his staff and touched her withered neck with what seemed the serpent's tail.

"The devil!" screamed the pious old lady.

"Then Goody Cloyse knows her old friend?" observed the traveller, confronting her and leaning on his writhing stick.

"Ah, forsooth, and is it your worship indeed?" cried the good dame. "Yea, truly is it, and in the very image of my old gossip, Goodman Brown, the grandfather of the silly fellow that now is. But—would your worship believe it?—my broomstick hath strangely disappeared, stolen, as I suspect, by that unhanged witch, Goody Cory, and that, too, when I was all anointed with the juice of smallage, and cinquefoil, and wolf's bane"[12]—

"Mingled with fine wheat and the fat of a new-born babe," said the shape of old Goodman Brown.

"Ah, your worship knows the recipe," cried the old lady, cackling aloud. "So, as I was saying, being all ready for the meeting, and no horse to ride on, I made up my mind to foot it; for they tell me there is a nice young man to be taken into communion to-night. But now your good worship will lend me your arm, and we shall be there in a twinkling."

"That can hardly be," answered her friend. "I may not spare you my arm, Goody Cloyse; but here is my staff, if you will."

So saying, he threw it down at her feet, where, perhaps, it assumed life, being one of the rods which its owner had formerly lent to the Egyptian magi.[13] Of this fact, however, Goodman Brown could not take cognizance. He had cast up his eyes in astonishment, and, looking down again, beheld neither Goody Cloyse nor the serpentine staff, but his fellow-traveller alone, who waited for him as calmly as if nothing had happened.

"That old woman taught me my catechism," said the young man; and there was a world of meaning in this simple comment.

They continued to walk onward, while the elder traveller exhorted his companion to make good speed and persevere in the path, discoursing so aptly that his arguments seemed rather to spring up in the bosom of his auditor than to be suggested by himself. As they went, he plucked a branch of maple to serve for a walking stick, and began to strip it of the twigs and little boughs, which were wet with evening dew. The moment

---

[10] Contraction of "goodwife" and a polite term for a married woman of humble standing.

[11] Hawthorne uses given names (such as Cloyse and Cory) of people involved in the Salem witch trials.

[12] The plants mentioned here were associated with magic and witchcraft.

[13] See Exodus 7 for a description of the Egyptian magicians who turned their rods into serpents.

his fingers touched them they became strangely withered and dried up as with a week's sunshine. Thus the pair proceeded, at a good free pace, until suddenly, in a gloomy hollow of the road, Goodman Brown sat himself down on the stump of a tree and refused to go any farther.

"Friend," said he, stubbornly, "my mind is made up. Not another step will I budge on this errand. What if a wretched old woman do choose to go to the devil when I thought she was going to heaven: is that any reason why I should quit my dear Faith and go after her?"

"You will think better of this by and by," said his acquaintance, composedly. "Sit here and rest yourself a while; and when you feel like moving again, there is my staff to help you along."

Without more words, he threw his companion the maple stick, and was as speedily out of sight as if he had vanished into the deepening gloom. The young man sat a few moments by the roadside, applauding himself greatly, and thinking with how clear a conscience he should meet the minister in his morning walk, nor shrink from the eye of good old Deacon Gookin. And what calm sleep would be his that very night, which was to have been spent so wickedly, but so purely and sweetly now, in the arms of Faith! Amidst these pleasant and praiseworthy meditations, Goodman Brown heard the tramp of horses along the road, and deemed it advisable to conceal himself within the verge of the forest, conscious of the guilty purpose that had brought him thither, though now so happily turned from it.

On came the hoof tramps and the voices of the riders, two grave old voices, conversing soberly as they drew near. These mingled sounds appeared to pass along the road, within a few yards of the young man's hiding-place; but, owing doubtless to the depth of the gloom at that particular spot, neither the travellers nor their steeds were visible. Though their figures brushed the small boughs by the wayside, it could not be seen that they intercepted, even for a moment, the faint gleam from the strip of bright sky athwart which they must have passed. Goodman Brown alternately crouched and stood on tiptoe, pulling aside the branches and thrusting forth his head as far as he durst without discerning so much as a shadow. It vexed him the more, because he could have sworn, were such a thing possible, that he recognized the voices of the minister and Deacon Gookin, jogging along quietly, as they were wont to do, when bound to some ordination or ecclesiastical council. While yet within hearing, one of the riders stopped to pluck a switch.

"Of the two, reverend sir," said the voice like the deacon's, "I had rather miss an ordination dinner than to-night's meeting. They tell me that some of our community are to be here from Falmouth[14] and beyond, and others from Connecticut and Rhode Island, besides several of the Indian powwows,[15] who, after their fashion, know almost as much deviltry as the best of us. Moreover, there is a goodly young woman to be taken into communion."

"Mighty well, Deacon Gookin!" replied the solemn old tones of the minister. "Spur up, or we shall be late. Nothing can be done, you know, until I get on the ground."

The hoofs clattered again; and the voices, talking so strangely in the empty air, passed on through the forest, where no church had ever been gathered or solitary Christian prayed. Whither, then, could these holy men be journeying so deep into the hea-

---

[14] Town on Cape Cod, seventy miles from Salem, Massachusetts.

[15] Medicine men.

then wilderness? Young Goodman Brown caught hold of a tree for support, being ready to sink down on the ground, faint and overburdened with the heavy sickness of his heart. He looked up to the sky, doubting whether there really was a heaven above him. Yet there was the blue arch, and the stars brightening in it.

"With heaven above and Faith below, I will yet stand firm against the devil!" cried Goodman Brown.

While he still gazed upward into the deep arch of the firmament and had lifted his hands to pray, a cloud, though no wind was stirring, hurried across the zenith and hid the brightening stars. The blue sky was still visible, except directly overhead, where this black mass of cloud was sweeping swiftly northward. Aloft in the air, as if from the depths of the cloud, came a confused and doubtful sound of voices. Once the listener fancied that he could distinguish the accents of towns-people of his own, men and women, both pious and ungodly, many of whom he had met at the communion table, and had seen others rioting at the tavern. The next moment, so indistinct were the sounds, he doubted whether he had heard aught but the murmur of the old forest, whispering without a wind. Then came a stronger swell of those familiar tones, heard daily in the sunshine at Salem village, but never until now from a cloud of night. There was one voice, of a young woman, uttering lamentations, yet with an uncertain sorrow, and entreating for some favor, which, perhaps, it would grieve her to obtain; and all the unseen multitude, both saints and sinners, seemed to encourage her onward.

"Faith!" shouted Goodman Brown, in a voice of agony and desperation; and the echoes of the forest mocked him, crying, "Faith! Faith!" as if bewildered wretches were seeking her all through the wilderness.

The cry of grief, rage, and terror was yet piercing the night, when the unhappy husband held his breath for a response. There was a scream, drowned immediately in a louder murmur of voices, fading into far-off laughter, as the dark cloud swept away, leaving the clear and silent sky above Goodman Brown. But something fluttered lightly down through the air and caught on the branch of a tree. The young man seized it, and beheld a pink ribbon.

"My Faith is gone!" cried he, after one stupefied moment. "There is no good on earth; and sin is but a name. Come, devil; for to thee is this world given."

And, maddened with despair, so that he laughed loud and long, did Goodman Brown grasp his staff and set forth again, at such a rate that he seemed to fly along the forest path rather than to walk or run. The road grew wilder and drearier and more faintly traced, and vanished at length, leaving him in the heart of the dark wilderness, still rushing onward with the instinct that guides mortal man to evil. The whole forest was peopled with frightful sounds—the creaking of the trees, the howling of wild beasts, and the yell of Indians; while sometimes the wind tolled like a distant church bell, and sometimes gave a broad roar around the traveller, as if all Nature were laughing him to scorn. But he was himself the chief horror of the scene, and shrank not from its other horrors.

"Ha! ha! ha!" roared Goodman Brown when the wind laughed at him. "Let us hear which will laugh loudest. Think not to frighten me with your deviltry. Come witch, come wizard, come Indian powwow, come devil himself, and here comes Goodman Brown. You may as well fear him as he fear you."

In truth, all through the haunted forest there could be nothing more frightful than the figure of Goodman Brown. On he flew among the black pines, brandishing his staff with frenzied gestures, now giving vent to an inspiration of horrid blasphemy, and now shouting forth such laughter as set all the echoes of the forest laughing like demons around him. The fiend in his own shape is less hideous than when he rages in the breast of man. Thus sped the demoniac on his course, until, quivering among the trees, he saw a red light before him, as when the felled trunks and branches of a clearing have been set on fire, and throw up their lurid blaze against the sky, at the hour of midnight. He paused, in a lull of the tempest that had driven him onward, and heard the swell of what seemed a hymn, rolling solemnly from a distance with the weight of many voices. He knew the tune; it was a familiar one in the choir of the village meeting-house. The verse died heavily away, and was lengthened by a chorus, not of human voices, but of all the sounds of the benighted wilderness pealing in awful harmony together. Goodman Brown cried out, and his cry was lost to his own ear by its unison with the cry of the desert.

In the interval of silence he stole forward until the light glared full upon his eyes. At one extremity of an open space, hemmed in by the dark wall of the forest, arose a rock, bearing some rude, natural resemblance either to an altar or a pulpit, and surrounded by four blazing pines, their tops aflame, their stems untouched, like candles at an evening meeting. The mass of foliage that had overgrown the summit of the rock was all on fire, blazing high into the night and fitfully illuminating the whole field. Each pendent twig and leafy festoon was in a blaze. As the red light arose and fell, a numerous congregation alternately shone forth, then disappeared in shadow, and again grew, as it were, out of the darkness, peopling the heart of the solitary woods at once.

"A grave and dark-clad company," quoth Goodman Brown.

In truth they were such. Among them, quivering to and fro between gloom and splendor, appeared faces that would be seen next day at the council board of the province, and others which, Sabbath after Sabbath, looked devoutly heavenward, and benignantly over the crowded pews, from the holiest pulpits in the land. Some affirm that the lady of the governor was there. At least there were high dames well known to her, and wives of honored husbands, and widows, a great multitude, and ancient maidens, all of excellent repute, and fair young girls, who trembled lest their mothers should espy them. Either the sudden gleams of light flashing over the obscure field bedazzled Goodman Brown, or he recognized a score of the church members of Salem village famous for their especial sanctity. Good old Deacon Gookin had arrived, and waited at the skirts of that venerable saint, his revered pastor. But, irreverently consorting with these grave, reputable, and pious people, these elders of the church, these chaste dames and dewy virgins, there were men of dissolute lives and women of spotted fame, wretches given over to all mean and filthy vice, and suspected even of horrid crimes. It was strange to see that the good shrank not from the wicked, nor were the sinners abashed by the saints. Scattered also among their pale-faced enemies were the Indian priests, or powwows, who had often scared their native forest with more hideous incantations than any known to English witchcraft.

"But where is Faith?" thought Goodman Brown; and, as hope came into his heart, he trembled.

Another verse of the hymn arose, a slow and mournful strain, such as the pious love, but joined to words which expressed all that our nature can conceive of sin, and darkly hinted at far more. Unfathomable to mere mortals is the lore of fiends. Verse after verse was sung; and still the chorus of the desert swelled between like the deepest tone of a mighty organ; and with the final peal of that dreadful anthem there came a sound, as if the roaring wind, the rushing streams, the howling beasts, and every other voice of the unconcerted wilderness were mingling and according with the voice of guilty man in homage to the prince of all. The four blazing pines threw up a loftier flame, and obscurely discovered shapes and visages of horror on the smoke wreaths above the impious assembly. At the same moment the fire on the rock shot redly forth and formed a glowing arch above its base, where now appeared a figure. With reverence be it spoken, the figure bore no slight similitude, both in garb and manner, to some grave divine of the New England churches.

"Bring forth the converts!" cried a voice that echoed through the field and rolled into the forest.

At the word, Goodman Brown stepped forth from the shadow of the trees and approached the congregation, with whom he felt a loathful brotherhood by the sympathy of all that was wicked in his heart. He could have well-nigh sworn that the shape of his own dead father beckoned him to advance, looking downward from a smoke wreath, while a woman, with dim features of despair, threw out her hand to warn him back. Was it his mother? But he had no power to retreat one step, nor to resist, even in thought, when the minister and good old Deacon Gookin seized his arms and led him to the blazing rock. Thither came also the slender form of a veiled female, led between Goody Cloyse, that pious teacher of the catechism, and Martha Carrier,[16] who had received the devil's promise to be queen of hell. A rampant hag was she. And there stood the proselytes beneath the canopy of fire.

"Welcome, my children," said the dark figure, "to the communion of your race. You have found thus young your nature and your destiny. My children, look behind you!"

They turned; and flashing forth, as it were, in a sheet of flame, the fiend worshippers were seen; the smile of welcome gleamed darkly on every visage.

"There," resumed the sable form, "are all whom ye have reverenced from youth. Ye deemed them holier than yourselves, and shrank from your own sin, contrasting it with their lives of righteousness and prayerful aspirations heavenward. Yet here are they all in my worshipping assembly. This night it shall be granted you to know their secret deeds: how hoary-bearded elders of the church have whispered wanton words to the young maids of their households; how many a woman, eager for widows' weeds, has given her husband a drink at bedtime and let him sleep his last sleep in her bosom; how beardless youths have made haste to inherit their fathers' wealth; and how fair damsels—blush not, sweet ones—have dug little graves in the garden, and bidden me, the sole guest, to an infant's funeral. By the sympathy of your human hearts for sin ye shall scent out all the places—whether in church, bed-chamber, street, field, or forest—where crime has been committed, and shall exult to behold the whole earth one stain of guilt, one mighty blood spot. Far more than this. It shall be yours to penetrate, in every bosom, the deep mystery of sin, the fountain of all wicked arts, and which inexhaustibly supplies more evil impulses than human power—than my power at its utmost—can make manifest in deeds. And now, my children, look upon each other."

They did so; and, by the blaze of the hell-kindled torches, the wretched man beheld his Faith, and the wife her husband, trembling before that unhallowed altar.

---

[16] Woman hanged in Salem in 1697 for claiming the devil had appointed her queen of hell.

"Lo, there ye stand, my children," said the figure, in a deep and solemn tone, almost sad with its despairing awfulness, as if his once angelic nature could yet mourn for our miserable race. "Depending upon one another's hearts, ye had still hoped that virtue were not all a dream. Now are ye undeceived. Evil is the nature of mankind. Evil must be your only happiness. Welcome again, my children, to the communion of your race."

"Welcome," repeated the fiend worshippers, in one cry of despair and triumph.

And there they stood, the only pair, as it seemed, who were yet hesitating on the verge of wickedness in this dark world. A basin was hollowed, naturally, in the rock. Did it contain water, reddened by the lurid light? or was it blood? or, perchance, a liquid flame? Herein did the shape of evil dip his hand and prepare to lay the mark of baptism upon their foreheads, that they might be partakers of the mystery of sin, more conscious of the secret guilt of others, both in deed and thought, than they could now be of their own. The husband cast one look at his pale wife, and Faith at him. What polluted wretches would the next glance show them to each other, shuddering alike at what they disclosed and what they saw!

"Faith! Faith!" cried the husband, "look up to heaven, and resist the wicked one."

Whether Faith obeyed he knew not. Hardly had he spoken when he found himself amid calm night and solitude, listening to a roar of the wind which died heavily away through the forest. He staggered against the rock, and felt it chill and damp; while a hanging twig, that had been all on fire, besprinkled his cheek with the coldest dew.

The next morning young Goodman Brown came slowly into the street of Salem village, staring around him like a bewildered man. The good old minister was taking a walk along the graveyard to get an appetite for breakfast and meditate his sermon, and bestowed a blessing, as he passed, on Goodman Brown. He shrank from the venerable saint as if to avoid an anathema. Old Deacon Gookin was at domestic worship, and the holy words of his prayer were heard through the open window. "What God doth the wizard pray to?" quoth Goodman Brown. Goody Cloyse, that excellent old Christian, stood in the early sunshine at her own lattice, catechizing a little girl who had brought her a pint of morning's milk. Goodman Brown snatched away the child as from the grasp of the fiend himself. Turning the corner by the meeting-house, he spied the head of Faith, with the pink ribbons, gazing anxiously forth, and bursting into such joy at sight of him that she skipped along the street and almost kissed her husband before the whole village. But Goodman Brown looked sternly and sadly into her face, and passed on without a greeting.

Had Goodman Brown fallen asleep in the forest and only dreamed a wild dream of a witch-meeting?

Be it so if you will; but, alas! it was a dream of evil omen for young Goodman Brown. A stern, a sad, a darkly meditative, a distrustful, if not a desperate man did he become from the night of that fearful dream. On the Sabbath day, when the congregation were singing a holy psalm, he could not listen because an anthem of sin rushed loudly upon his ear and drowned all the blessed strain. When the minister spoke from the pulpit with power and fervid eloquence, and, with his hand on the open Bible, of the sacred truths of our religion, and of saint-like lives and triumphant deaths, and of future bliss or misery unutterable, then did Goodman Brown turn pale, dreading lest the roof should thunder down upon the gray blasphemer and his hearers. Often, awaking suddenly at midnight, he shrank from the bosom of Faith; and at morning or eventide, when the family knelt down at prayer, he scowled and muttered to himself, and gazed sternly at his wife, and turned away. And when he had lived long, and was borne to his grave a hoary corpse, followed by Faith, an aged woman, and children and grandchildren, a goodly procession, besides neighbors not a few, they carved no hopeful verse upon his tombstone, for his dying hour was gloom.

1835

Wakefield

In some old magazine or newspaper I recollect a story, told as truth, of a man—let us call him Wakefield—who absented himself for a long time from his wife. The fact, thus abstractedly stated, is not very uncommon, nor—without a proper distinction of circumstances—to be condemned either as naughty or nonsensical. Howbeit, this, though far from the most aggravated, is perhaps the strangest, instance on record, of marital delinquency; and, moreover, as remarkable a freak as may be found in the whole list of human oddities. The wedded couple lived in London. The man, under pretence of going a journey, took lodgings in the next street to his own house, and there, unheard of by his wife or friends, and without the shadow of a reason for such self-banishment, dwelt upwards of twenty years. During that period, he beheld his home every day, and frequently the forlorn Mrs. Wakefield. And after so great a gap in his matrimonial felicity—when his death was reckoned certain, his estate settled, his name dismissed from memory, and his wife, long, long ago, resigned to her autumnal widowhood—he entered the door one evening, quietly, as from a day's absence, and became a loving spouse till death.

This outline is all that I remember. But the incident, though of the purest originality, unexampled, and probably never to be repeated, is one, I think, which appeals to the generous sympathies of mankind. We know, each for himself, that none of us would perpetrate such a folly, yet feel as if some other might. To my own contemplations, at least, it has often recurred, always exciting wonder, but with a sense that the story must be true, and a conception of its hero's character. Whenever any subject so forcibly affects the mind, time is well spent in thinking of it. If the reader choose, let him do his own meditation; or if he prefer to ramble with me through the twenty years of Wakefield's vagary, I bid him welcome; trusting that there will be a pervading spirit and a moral, even should we fail to find them, done up neatly, and condensed into the final sentence. Thought has always its efficacy, and every striking incident its moral.

What sort of a man was Wakefield? We are free to shape out our own idea, and call it by his name. He was now in the meridian of life; his matrimonial affections, never violent, were sobered into a calm, habitual sentiment; of all husbands, he was likely to be the most constant, because a certain sluggishness would keep his heart at rest, wherever it might be placed. He was intellectual, but not actively so; his mind occupied itself in long and lazy musings, that ended to no purpose, or had not vigor to attain it; his thoughts were seldom so energetic as to seize hold of words. Imagination, in the proper meaning of the term, made no part of Wakefield's gifts. With a cold but not depraved nor wandering heart, and a mind never feverish with riotous thoughts, nor perplexed with originality, who could have anticipated that our friend would entitle himself to a foremost place among the doers of eccentric deeds? Had his acquaintances been asked, who was the man in London the surest to perform nothing to-day which should be remembered on the morrow, they would have thought of Wakefield. Only the wife of his bosom might have hesitated. She, without having analyzed his character, was partly aware of a quiet selfishness, that had rusted into his inactive mind; of a peculiar sort of vanity, the most uneasy attribute about him; of a disposition to craft, which had seldom produced more positive effects than the keeping of petty secrets, hardly worth revealing; and, lastly, of what she called a little strangeness, sometimes, in the good man. This latter quality is indefinable, and perhaps non-existent.

Let us now imagine Wakefield bidding adieu to his wife. It is the dusk of an October evening. His equipment is a drab great-coat, a hat covered with an oilcloth, top-boots, an umbrella in one hand and a small portmanteau in the other. He has informed Mrs. Wakefield that he is to take the night coach into the country. She would fain inquire the length of his journey, its object, and the probable time of his return; but, indulgent to his harmless love of mystery, interrogates him only by a look. He tells her not to expect him positively by the return coach, nor to be alarmed should he tarry three or four days; but, at all events, to look for him at supper on Friday evening. Wakefield himself, be it considered, has no suspicion of what is before him. He holds out his hand, she gives her own, and meets his parting kiss in the matter-of-course way of a ten years' matrimony; and forth goes the middle-aged Mr. Wakefield, almost resolved to perplex his good lady by a whole week's absence. After the door has closed behind him, she perceives it thrust partly open, and a vision of her husband's face, through the aperture, smiling on her, and gone in a moment. For the time, this little incident is dismissed without a thought. But, long afterwards, when she has been more years a widow than a wife, that smile recurs, and flickers across all her reminiscences of Wakefield's visage. In her many musings, she surrounds the original smile with a multitude of fantasies, which make it strange and awful: as, for instance, if she imagines him in a coffin, that parting look is frozen on his pale features; or, if she dreams of him in heaven, still his blessed spirit wears a quiet and crafty smile. Yet, for its sake, when all others have given him up for dead, she sometimes doubts whether she is a widow.

But our business is with the husband. We must hurry after him along the street, ere he lose his individuality, and melt into the great mass of London life. It would be vain searching for him there. Let us follow close at his heels, therefore, until, after several superfluous turns and doublings, we find him comfortably established by the fireside of a small apartment, previously bespoken. He is in the next street to his own, and at his journey's end. He can scarcely trust his good fortune, in having got thither unperceived—recollecting that, at one time, he was delayed by the throng, in the very focus of a lighted lantern; and, again, there were footsteps that seemed to tread behind his own, distinct from the multitudinous tramp around him; and, anon, he heard a voice shouting afar, and fancied that it called his name. Doubtless, a dozen busybodies had been watching him, and told his wife the whole affair. Poor Wakefield! Little knowest thou thine own insignificance in this great world! No mortal eye but mine has traced thee. Go quietly to thy bed, foolish man; and, on the morrow, if thou wilt be wise, get thee home to good Mrs. Wakefield, and tell her the truth. Remove not thyself, even for a little week, from thy place in her chaste bosom. Were she, for a single moment, to deem thee dead, or lost, or lastingly divided from her, thou wouldst be wofully conscious of a change in thy true wife forever after. It is perilous to make a chasm in human affections; not that they gape so long and wide—but so quickly close again!

Almost repenting of his frolic, or whatever it may be termed, Wakefield lies down betimes, and starting from his first nap, spreads forth his arms into the wide and solitary waste of the unaccustomed bed. "No,"—thinks he, gathering the bedclothes about him,—"I will not sleep alone another night."

In the morning he rises earlier than usual, and sets himself to consider what he really means to do. Such are his loose and rambling modes of thought that he has taken this very singular step with the consciousness of a purpose, indeed, but without being able to define it sufficiently for his own contemplation. The vagueness of the project, and the convulsive effort with which he plunges into the execution of it, are equally characteristic of a feeble-minded man. Wakefield sifts his ideas, however, as minutely as he may, and finds himself curious to know the progress of matters at home—how his exemplary wife will endure her widowhood of a week; and, briefly, how the little sphere of creatures and circumstances, in which he was a central object, will be affected by his removal. A morbid vanity, therefore, lies nearest the bottom of the affair. But, how is he to attain his ends? Not, certainly, by keeping close in this comfortable lodging, where, though he slept and awoke in the next street to his home, he is as effectually abroad as if the stage-coach had been whirling him away all night. Yet, should he reappear, the whole project is knocked in the head. His poor brains being hopelessly puzzled with this dilemma, he at length ventures out, partly resolving to cross the head of the street, and send one hasty glance towards his forsaken domicile. Habit—for he is a man of habits—takes him by the hand, and guides him, wholly unaware, to his own door, where, just at the critical moment, he is aroused by the scraping of his foot upon the step. Wakefield! whither are you going?

At that instant his fate was turning on the pivot. Little dreaming of the doom to which his first backward step devotes him, he hurries away, breathless with agitation hitherto unfelt, and hardly dares turn his head at the distant corner. Can it be that nobody caught sight of him? Will not the whole household—the decent Mrs. Wakefield, the smart maid servant, and the dirty little footboy—raise a hue and cry, through London streets, in pursuit of their fugitive lord and master? Wonderful escape! He gathers courage to pause and look homeward, but is perplexed with a sense of change about the familiar edifice, such as affects us all, when, after a separation of months or years, we again see some hill or lake, or work of art, with which we were friends of old. In ordinary cases, this indescribable impression is caused by the comparison and contrast between our imperfect reminiscences and the reality. In Wakefield, the magic of a single night has wrought a similar transformation, because, in that brief period, a great moral change has been effected. But this is a secret from himself. Before leaving the spot, he catches a far and momentary glimpse of his wife, passing athwart the front window, with her face turned towards the head of the street. The crafty nincompoop takes to his heels, scared with the idea that, among a thousand such atoms of mortality, her eye must have detected him. Right glad is his heart, though his brain be somewhat dizzy, when he finds himself by the coal fire of his lodgings.

So much for the commencement of this long whim-wham. After the initial conception, and the stirring up of the man's sluggish temperament to put it in practice, the whole matter evolves itself in a natural train. We may suppose him, as the result of deep deliberation, buying a new wig, of reddish hair, and selecting sundry garments, in a fashion unlike his customary suit of brown, from a Jew's old-clothes bag. It is accomplished. Wakefield is another man. The new system being now established, a retrograde movement to the old would be almost as difficult as the step that placed him in his unparalleled position. Furthermore, he is rendered obstinate by a sulkiness occasionally incident to his temper, and brought on at present by the inadequate sensation which he conceives to have been produced in the bosom of Mrs. Wakefield. He will not go back until she be frightened half to death. Well; twice or thrice has she passed before his sight, each time with a heavier step, a paler cheek, and more anxious brow; and in the third week of his non-appearance he detects a portent of evil entering the house, in the guise of an apothecary. Next day the knocker is muffled. Towards nightfall comes the chariot of a physician, and deposits its big-wigged and solemn burden at Wakefield's door, whence, after a quarter of an hour's visit, he emerges, perchance the herald of a funeral. Dear woman! Will she die? By this time, Wakefield is excited to something like energy of feeling, but still lingers away from his wife's bedside, pleading with his conscience that she must not be disturbed at such a juncture. If aught else restrains him, he does not know it. In the course of a few weeks she gradually recovers; the crisis is over; her heart is sad, perhaps, but quiet; and, let him return soon or late, it will never be feverish for him again. Such ideas glimmer through the mist of Wakefield's mind, and render him indistinctly conscious that an almost impassable gulf divides his hired apartment from his former home. "It is but in the next street!" he sometimes says. Fool! it is in another world. Hitherto, he has put off his return from one particular day to another; henceforward, he leaves the precise time undetermined. Not to-morrow—probably next week—pretty soon. Poor man! The dead have nearly as much chance of revisiting their earthly homes as the self-banished Wakefield.

Would that I had a folio to write, instead of an article of a dozen pages! Then might I exemplify how an influence beyond our control lays its strong hand on every deed which we do, and weaves its consequences into an iron tissue of necessity. Wakefield is spell-bound. We must leave him, for ten years or so, to haunt around his house, without once crossing the threshold, and to be faithful to his wife, with all the affection of which his heart is capable, while he is slowly fading out of hers. Long since, it must be remarked, he had lost the perception of singularity in his conduct.

Now for a scene! Amid the throng of a London street we distinguish a man, now waxing elderly, with few characteristics to attract careless observers, yet bearing, in his whole aspect, the handwriting of no common fate, for such as have the skill to read it. He is meagre; his low and narrow forehead is deeply wrinkled; his eyes, small and lustreless, sometimes wander apprehensively about him, but oftener seem to look inward. He bends his head, and moves with an indescribable obliquity of gait, as if unwilling to display his full front to the world. Watch him long enough to see what we have described, and you will allow that circumstances—which often produce remarkable men from nature's ordinary handiwork—have produced one such here. Next, leaving him to sidle along the footwalk, cast your eyes in the opposite direction, where a portly female, considerably in the wane of life, with a prayer-book in her hand, is proceeding to yonder church. She has the placid mien of settled widowhood. Her regrets have either died away, or have become so essential to her heart, that they would be poorly exchanged for joy. Just as the lean man and well-conditioned woman are passing, a slight obstruction occurs, and brings these two figures directly in contact. Their hands touch; the pressure of the crowd forces her bosom against his shoulder; they stand, face to face, staring into each other's eyes. After a ten years' separation, thus Wakefield meets his wife!

The throng eddies away, and carries them asunder. The sober widow, resuming her former pace, proceeds to church, but pauses in the portal, and throws a perplexed glance along the street. She passes in, however, opening her prayer-book as she goes. And the man! with so wild a face that busy and selfish London stands to gaze after him, he hurries to his lodgings, bolts the door, and throws himself upon the bed. The latent feelings of years break out; his feeble mind acquires a brief energy from their strength; all the miserable strangeness of his life is revealed to him at a glance: and he cries out, passionately, "Wakefield! Wakefield! You are mad!"

Perhaps he was so. The singularity of his situation must have so moulded him to himself, that, considered in regard to his fellow-creatures and the business of life, he could not be said to possess his right mind. He had contrived, or rather he had happened, to dissever himself from the world—to vanish—to give up his place and privileges with living men, without being admitted among the dead. The life of a hermit is nowise parallel to his. He was in the bustle of the city, as of old; but the crowd swept by and saw him not; he was, we may figuratively say, always beside his wife and at his hearth, yet must never feel the warmth of the one nor the affection of the other. It was Wakefield's unprecedented fate to retain his original share of human sympathies, and to be still involved in human interests, while he had lost his reciprocal influence on them. It would be a most curious speculation to trace out the effect of such circumstances on his heart and intellect, separately, and in unison. Yet, changed as he was, he would seldom be conscious of it, but deem himself the same man as ever; glimpses of the truth, indeed, would come, but only for the moment; and still he would keep saying, "I shall soon go back!"—nor reflect that he had been saying so for twenty years.

I conceive, also, that these twenty years would appear, in the retrospect, scarcely longer than the week to which Wakefield had at first limited his absence. He would look on the affair as no more than an interlude in the main business of his life. When, after a little while more, he should deem it time to reënter his parlor, his wife would clap her hands for joy, on beholding the middle-aged Mr. Wakefield. Alas, what a mistake! Would Time but await the close of our favorite follies, we should be young men, all of us, and till Doomsday.

One evening, in the twentieth year since he vanished, Wakefield is taking his customary walk towards the dwelling which he still calls his own. It is a gusty night of autumn, with frequent showers that patter down upon the pavement, and are gone before a man can put up his umbrella. Pausing near the house, Wakefield discerns, through the parlor windows of the second floor, the red glow and the glimmer and fitful flash of a comfortable fire. On the ceiling appears a grotesque shadow of good Mrs. Wakefield. The cap, the nose and chin, and the broad waist, form an admirable caricature, which dances, moreover, with the up-flickering and down-sinking blaze, almost too merrily for the shade of an elderly widow. At this instant a shower chances to fall, and is driven, by the unmannerly gust, full into Wakefield's face and bosom. He is quite penetrated with its autumnal chill. Shall he stand, wet and shivering here, when his own hearth has a good fire to warm him, and his own wife will run to fetch the gray coat and small-clothes, which, doubtless, she has kept carefully in the closet of their bed chamber? No! Wakefield is no such fool. He ascends the steps—heavily!—for twenty years have stiffened his legs since he came down—but he knows it not. Stay, Wakefield! Would you go to the sole home that is left you? Then step into your grave! The door opens. As he passes in, we have a parting glimpse of his visage, and recognize the crafty smile, which was the precursor of the little joke that he has ever since been playing off at his wife's expense. How unmercifully has he quizzed the poor woman! Well, a good night's rest to Wakefield!

This happy event—supposing it to be such—could only have occurred at an unpremeditated moment. We will not follow our friend across the threshold. He has left us much food for thought, a portion of which shall lend its wisdom to a moral, and be shaped into a figure. Amid the seeming confusion of our mysterious world, individuals are so nicely adjusted to a system, and systems to one another and to a whole, that, by stepping aside for a moment, a man exposes himself to a fearful risk of losing his place forever. Like Wakefield, he may become, as it were, the Outcast of the Universe.

1835

The Maypole of Merry Mount*

There is an admirable foundation for a philosophic romance in the curious history of the early settlement of Mount Wollaston, or Merry Mount. In the slight sketch here attempted, the facts, recorded on the grave pages of our New England annalists, have wrought themselves, almost spontaneously, into a sort of allegory. The masques, mummeries, and festive customs, described in the text, are in accordance with the manners of the age. Authority on these points may be found in Strutt's Book of English Sports and Pastimes.[1]

Bright were the days at Merry Mount, when the Maypole[2] was the banner staff of that gay colony! They who reared it, should their banner be triumphant, were to pour sunshine over New England's rugged hills, and scatter flower seeds throughout the soil. Jollity and gloom were contending for an empire. Midsummer eve[3] had come, bringing deep verdure to the forest, and roses in her lap, of a more vivid hue than the tender buds of Spring. But May, or her mirthful spirit, dwelt all the year round at Merry Mount, sporting with the Summer months, and revelling with Autumn, and basking in the glow of Winter's fireside. Through a world of toil and care she flitted with a dreamlike smile, and came hither to find a home among the lightsome hearts of Merry Mount.

Never had the Maypole been so gayly decked as at sunset on midsummer eve. This venerated emblem was a pine-tree, which had preserved the slender grace of youth, while it equalled the loftiest height of the old wood monarchs. From its top streamed a

---

* For additional information on the colony of Merry Mount, see William Bradford's *Of Plymouth Plantation*.

[1] Joseph Strutt, *The Sports and Pastimes of the People of England* (1801).

[2] The tall, flower-wreathed pole that is the chief symbol of May Day. Participants in May Day celebrations dressed in outlandish paganlike costumes and wore animal masks; the Puritans condemned these activities as licentious.

[3] The evening before Midsummer Day (June 24), which is the celebration of the nativity of John the Baptist.

silken banner, colored like the rainbow. Down nearly to the ground the pole was dressed with birchen boughs, and others of the liveliest green, and some with silvery leaves, fastened by ribbons that fluttered in fantastic knots of twenty different colors, but no sad ones. Garden flowers, and blossoms of the wilderness, laughed gladly forth amid the verdure, so fresh and dewy that they must have grown by magic on that happy pinetree. Where this green and flowery splendor terminated, the shaft of the Maypole was stained with the seven brilliant hues of the banner at its top. On the lowest green bough hung an abundant wreath of roses, some that had been gathered in the sunniest spots of the forest, and others, of still richer blush, which the colonists had reared from English seed. O, people of the Golden Age, the chief of your husbandry was to raise flowers!

But what was the wild throng that stood hand in hand about the Maypole? It could not be that the fauns and nymphs, when driven from their classic groves and homes of ancient fable, had sought refuge, as all the persecuted did, in the fresh woods of the West. These were Gothic monsters, though perhaps of Grecian ancestry. On the shoulders of a comely youth uprose the head and branching antlers of a stag; a second, human in all other points, had the grim visage of a wolf; a third, still with the trunk and limbs of a mortal man, showed the beard and horns of a venerable he-goat. There was the likeness of a bear erect, brute in all but his hind legs, which were adorned with pink silk stockings. And here again, almost as wondrous, stood a real bear of the dark forest, lending each of his fore paws to the grasp of a human hand, and as ready for the dance as any in that circle. His inferior nature rose half way, to meet his companions as they stooped. Other faces wore the similitude of man or woman, but distorted or extravagant, with red noses pendulous before their mouths, which seemed of awful depth, and stretched from ear to ear in an eternal fit of laughter. Here might be seen the Salvage Man,[4] well known in heraldry, hairy as a baboon, and girdled with green leaves. By his side, a noble figure, but still a counterfeit, appeared an Indian hunter, with feathery crest and wampum belt. Many of this strange company wore foolscaps, and had little bells appended to their garments, tinkling with a silvery sound, responsive to the inaudible music of their gleesome spirits. Some youths and maidens were of soberer garb, yet well maintained their places in the irregular throng by the expression of wild revelry upon their features. Such were the colonists of Merry Mount, as they stood in the broad smile of sunset round their venerated Maypole.

Had a wanderer, bewildered in the melancholy forest, heard their mirth, and stolen a half-affrighted glance, he might have fancied them the crew of Comus,[5] some already transformed to brutes, some midway between man and beast, and the others rioting in the flow of tipsy jollity that foreran the change. But a band of Puritans, who watched the scene, invisible themselves, compared the masques to those devils and ruined souls with whom their superstition peopled the black wilderness.

Within the ring of monsters appeared the two airiest forms that had ever trodden on any more solid footing than a purple and golden cloud. One was a youth in glistening apparel, with a scarf of the rainbow pattern crosswise on his breast. His right hand held a gilded staff, the ensign[6] of high dignity among the revellers, and his left grasped the

[4] Someone dressed in foliage to represent a savage.
[5] The classical god of merrymaking, here associated with John Milton's poem "Comus."
[6] Symbolic emblem or flag.

slender fingers of a fair maiden, not less gayly decorated than himself. Bright roses glowed in contrast with the dark and glossy curls of each, and were scattered round their feet, or had sprung up spontaneously there. Behind this lightsome couple, so close to the Maypole that its boughs shaded his jovial face, stood the figure of an English priest, canonically dressed, yet decked with flowers, in heathen fashion, and wearing a chaplet[7] of the native vine leaves. By the riot of his rolling eye, and the pagan decorations of his holy garb, he seemed the wildest monster there, and the very Comus of the crew.

"Votaries[8] of the Maypole," cried the flower-decked priest, "merrily, all day long, have the woods echoed to your mirth. But be this your merriest hour, my hearts! Lo, here stand the Lord and Lady of the May, whom I, a clerk[9] of Oxford, and high priest of Merry Mount, am presently to join in holy matrimony. Up with your nimble spirits, ye morris-dancers, green men, and glee maidens,[10] bears and wolves, and horned gentlemen! Come; a chorus now, rich with the old mirth of Merry England, and the wilder glee of this fresh forest; and then a dance, to show the youthful pair what life is made of, and how airily they should go through it! All ye that love the Maypole, lend your voices to the nuptial song of the Lord and Lady of the May!"

This wedlock was more serious than most affairs of Merry Mount, where jest and delusion, trick and fantasy, kept up a continual carnival. The Lord and Lady of the May, though their titles must be laid down at sunset, were really and truly to be partners for the dance of life, beginning the measure that same bright eve. The wreath of roses, that hung from the lowest green bough of the Maypole, had been twined for them, and would be thrown over both their heads, in symbol of their flowery union. When the priest had spoken, therefore, a riotous uproar burst from the rout of monstrous figures.

"Begin you the stave,[11] reverend Sir," cried they all; "and never did the woods ring to such a merry peal as we of the Maypole shall send up!"

Immediately a prelude of pipe, cithern,[12] and viol, touched with practised minstrelsy, began to play from a neighboring thicket, in such a mirthful cadence that the boughs of the Maypole quivered to the sound. But the May Lord, he of the gilded staff, chancing to look into his Lady's eyes, was wonder struck at the almost pensive glance that met his own.

"Edith, sweet Lady of the May," whispered he reproachfully, "is yon wreath of roses a garland to hang above our graves, that you look so sad? O, Edith, this is our golden time! Tarnish it not by any pensive shadow of the mind; for it may be that nothing of futurity will be brighter than the mere remembrance of what is now passing."

"That was the very thought that saddened me! How came it in your mind too?" said Edith, in a still lower tone than he, for it was high treason to be sad at Merry Mount. "Therefore do I sigh amid this festive music. And besides, dear Edgar, I struggle as with a dream, and fancy that these shapes of our jovial friends are visionary, and their mirth unreal, and that we are no true Lord and Lady of the May. What is the mystery in my heart?"

---

[7] Wreath.

[8] Devotees.

[9] One who assists the clergyman.

[10] Morris dancers, green men, and glee maidens were all part of the traditional May Day celebrations.

[11] Stanza.

[12] Cittern or lute.

Just then, as if a spell had loosened them, down came a little shower of withering rose leaves from the Maypole. Alas, for the young lovers! No sooner had their hearts glowed with real passion than they were sensible of something vague and unsubstantial in their former pleasures, and felt a dreary presentiment of inevitable change. From the moment that they truly loved, they had subjected themselves to earth's doom of care and sorrow, and troubled joy, and had no more a home at Merry Mount. That was Edith's mystery. Now leave we the priest to marry them, and the masquers to sport round the Maypole, till the last sunbeam be withdrawn from its summit, and the shadows of the forest mingle gloomily in the dance. Meanwhile, we may discover who these gay people were.

Two hundred years ago, and more, the old world and its inhabitants became mutually weary of each other. Men voyaged by thousands to the West: some to barter glass beads, and such like jewels, for the furs of the Indian hunter; some to conquer virgin empires; and one stern band to pray. But none of these motives had much weight with the colonists of Merry Mount. Their leaders were men who had sported so long with life, that when Thought and Wisdom came, even these unwelcome guests were led astray by the crowd of vanities which they should have put to flight. Erring Thought and perverted Wisdom were made to put on masques, and play the fool. The men of whom we speak, after losing the heart's fresh gayety, imagined a wild philosophy of pleasure, and came hither to act out their latest day-dream. They gathered followers from all that giddy tribe whose whole life is like the festal[13] days of soberer men. In their train were minstrels, not unknown in London streets: wandering players, whose theatres had been the halls of noblemen; mummers,[14] rope-dancers, and mountebanks,[15] who would long be missed at wakes, church ales, and fairs; in a word, mirth makers of every sort, such as abounded in that age, but now began to be discountenanced by the rapid growth of Puritanism. Light had their footsteps been on land, and as lightly they came across the sea. Many had been maddened by their previous troubles into a gay despair; others were as madly gay in the flush of youth, like the May Lord and his Lady; but whatever might be the quality of their mirth, old and young were gay at Merry Mount. The young deemed themselves happy. The elder spirits, if they knew that mirth was but the counterfeit of happiness, yet followed the false shadow wilfully, because at least her garments glittered brightest. Sworn triflers of a lifetime, they would not venture among the sober truths of life not even to be truly blest.

All the hereditary pastimes of Old England were transplanted hither. The King of Christmas was duly crowned, and the Lord of Misrule[16] bore potent sway. On the Eve of St. John,[17] they felled whole acres of the forest to make bonfires, and danced by the blaze all night, crowned with garlands, and throwing flowers into the flame. At harvest time, though their crop was of the smallest, they made an image with the sheaves of Indian corn, and wreathed it with autumnal garlands, and bore it home triumphantly. But what chiefly characterized the colonists of Merry Mount was their veneration for the Maypole. It has made their true history a poet's tale. Spring decked the hallowed

---

[13] Festive.
[14] Costumed revelers.
[15] Street venders who peddle quack medicines.

[16] Leader of Christmas revelry.
[17] June 23, Midsummer's Eve.

emblem with young blossoms and fresh green boughs; Summer brought roses of the deepest blush, and the perfected foliage of the forest; Autumn enriched it with that red and yellow gorgeousness which converts each wildwood leaf into a painted flower; and Winter silvered it with sleet, and hung it round with icicles, till it flashed in the cold sunshine, itself a frozen sunbeam. Thus each alternate season did homage to the May-pole, and paid it a tribute of its own richest splendor. Its votaries danced round it, once, at least, in every month; sometimes they called it their religion, or their altar; but always, it was the banner staff of Merry Mount.

Unfortunately, there were men in the new world of a sterner faith than these May-pole worshippers. Not far from Merry Mount was a settlement of Puritans, most dismal wretches, who said their prayers before daylight, and then wrought in the forest or the cornfield till evening made it prayer time again. Their weapons were always at hand to shoot down the straggling savage. When they met in conclave, it was never to keep up the old English mirth, but to hear sermons three hours long, or to proclaim bounties on the heads of wolves and the scalps of Indians. Their festivals were fast days, and their chief pastime the singing of psalms. Woe to the youth or maiden who did but dream of a dance! The selectman nodded to the constable; and there sat the light-heeled repro-bate in the stocks; or if he danced, it was round the whipping-post, which might be termed the Puritan Maypole.

A party of these grim Puritans, toiling through the difficult woods, each with a horseload of iron armor to burden his footsteps, would sometimes draw near the sunny precincts of Merry Mount. There were the silken colonists, sporting round their May-pole; perhaps teaching a bear to dance, or striving to communicate their mirth to the grave Indian; or masquerading in the skins of deer and wolves, which they had hunted for that especial purpose. Often, the whole colony were playing at blindman's buff, magistrates and all, with their eyes bandaged, except a single scapegoat, whom the blinded sinners pursued by the tinkling of the bells at his garments. Once, it is said, they were seen following a flower-decked corpse, with merriment and festive music, to his grave. But did the dead man laugh? In their quietest times, they sang ballads and told tales, for the edification of their pious visitors; or perplexed them with juggling tricks; or grinned at them through horse collars; and when sport itself grew wearisome, they made game of their own stupidity, and began a yawning match. At the very least of these enormities, the men of iron shook their heads and frowned so darkly that the rev-ellers looked up, imagining that a momentary cloud had overcast the sunshine, which was to be perpetual there. On the other hand, the Puritans affirmed that, when a psalm was pealing from their place of worship, the echo which the forest sent them back seemed often like the chorus of a jolly catch, closing with a roar of laughter. Who but the fiend, and his bond slaves, the crew of Merry Mount, had thus disturbed them? In due time, a feud arose, stern and bitter on one side, and as serious on the other as any-thing could be among such light spirits as had sworn allegiance to the Maypole. The fu-ture complexion of New England was involved in this important quarrel. Should the grizzly saints establish their jurisdiction over the gay sinners, then would their spirits darken all the clime, and make it a land of clouded visages, of hard toil, of sermon and psalm forever. But should the banner staff of Merry Mount be fortunate, sunshine would break upon the hills, and flowers would beautify the forest, and late posterity do homage to the Maypole.

After these authentic passages from history, we return to the nuptials of the Lord and Lady of the May. Alas! we have delayed too long, and must darken our tale too suddenly. As we glance again at the Maypole, a solitary sunbeam is fading from the summit, and leaves only a faint, golden tinge blended with the hues of the rainbow banner. Even that dim light is now withdrawn, relinquishing the whole domain of Merry Mount to the evening gloom, which has rushed so instantaneously from the black surrounding woods. But some of these black shadows have rushed forth in human shape.

Yes, with the setting sun, the last day of mirth had passed from Merry Mount. The ring of gay masquers was disordered and broken; the stag lowered his antlers in dismay; the wolf grew weaker than a lamb; the bells of the morris-dancers tinkled with tremulous affright. The Puritans had played a characteristic part in the Maypole mummeries. Their darksome figures were intermixed with the wild shapes of their foes, and made the scene a picture of the moment, when waking thoughts start up amid the scattered fantasies of a dream. The leader of the hostile party stood in the centre of the circle, while the route of monsters cowered around him, like evil spirits in the presence of a dread magician. No fantastic foolery could look him in the face. So stern was the energy of his aspect, that the whole man, visage, frame, and soul, seemed wrought of iron, gifted with life and thought, yet all of one substance with his headpiece and breastplate. It was the Puritan of Puritans; it was Endicott[18] himself!

"Stand off, priest of Baal!"[19] said he, with a grim frown, and laying no reverent hand upon the surplice. "I know thee, Blackstone![20] Thou art the man who couldst not abide the rule even of thine own corrupted church,[21] and hast come hither to preach iniquity, and to give example of it in thy life. But now shall it be seen that the Lord hath sanctified this wilderness for his peculiar people. Woe unto them that would defile it! And first, for this flower-decked abomination, the altar of thy worship!"

And with his keen sword Endicott assaulted the hallowed Maypole. Nor long did it resist his arm. It groaned with a dismal sound; it showered leaves and rosebuds upon the remorseless enthusiast; and finally, with all its green boughs and ribbons and flowers, symbolic of departed pleasures, down fell the banner staff of Merry Mount. As it sank, tradition says, the evening sky grew darker, and the woods threw forth a more sombre shadow.

"There," cried Endicott, looking triumphantly on his work, "there lies the only Maypole in New England! The thought is strong within me that, by its fall, is shadowed forth the fate of light and idle mirth makers, amongst us and our posterity. Amen, saith John Endicott."

"Amen!" echoed his followers.

But the votaries of the Maypole gave one groan for their idol. At the sound, the Puritan leader glanced at the crew of Comus, each a figure of broad mirth, yet, at this moment, strangely expressive of sorrow and dismay.

---

[18] John Endicott (1589–1665), governor of the colony of Massachusetts.

[19] Fertility god (see 1 Kings 18).

[20] Hawthorne's note: "Did Governor Endicott speak less positively, we should suspect a mistake here. The Reverend Blackstone, though an eccentric, is not known to have been an immoral man. We rather doubt his identity with the priest of Merry Mount."

[21] i.e., the Church of England.

"Valiant captain," quoth Peter Palfrey, the Ancient[22] of the band, "what order shall be taken with the prisoners?"

"I thought not to repent me of cutting down a Maypole," replied Endicott, "yet now I could find in my heart to plant it again, and give each of these bestial pagans one other dance round their idol. It would have served rarely for a whipping-post!"

"But there are pine-trees enow," suggested the lieutenant.

"True, good Ancient," said the leader. "Wherefore, bind the heathen crew, and bestow on them a small matter of stripes apiece, as earnest of our future justice. Set some of the rogues in the stocks to rest themselves, so soon as Providence shall bring us to one of our own well-ordered settlements, where such accommodations may be found. Further penalties, such as branding and cropping of ears, shall be thought of hereafter."

"How many stripes for the priest?" inquired Ancient Palfrey.

"None as yet," answered Endicott, bending his iron frown upon the culprit. "It must be for the Great and General Court to determine, whether stripes and long imprisonment, and other grievous penalty, may atone for his transgressions. Let him look to himself! For such as violate our civil order, it may be permitted us to show mercy. But woe to the wretch that troubleth our religion!"

"And this dancing bear," resumed the officer. "Must he share the stripes of his fellows?"

"Shoot him through the head!" said the energetic Puritan. "I suspect witchcraft in the beast."

"Here be a couple of shining ones," continued Peter Palfrey, pointing his weapon at the Lord and Lady of the May. "They seem to be of high station among these misdoers. Methinks their dignity will not be fitted with less than a double share of stripes."

Endicott rested on his sword, and closely surveyed the dress and aspect of the hapless pair. There they stood, pale, downcast, and apprehensive. Yet there was an air of mutual support, and of pure affection, seeking aid and giving it, that showed them to be man and wife, with the sanction of a priest upon their love. The youth, in the peril of the moment, had dropped his gilded staff, and thrown his arm about the Lady of the May, who leaned against his breast, too lightly to burden him, but with weight enough to express that their destinies were linked together, for good or evil. They looked first at each other, and then into the grim captain's face. There they stood, in the first hour of wedlock, while the idle pleasures, of which their companions were the emblems, had given place to the sternest cares of life, personified by the dark Puritans. But never had their youthful beauty seemed so pure and high as when its glow was chastened by adversity.

"Youth," said Endicott, "ye stand in an evil case thou and thy maiden wife. Make ready presently, for I am minded that ye shall both have a token to remember your wedding day!"

"Stern man," cried the May Lord, "how can I move thee? Were the means at hand, I would resist to the death. Being powerless, I entreat! Do with me as thou wilt, but let Edith go untouched!"

"Not so," replied the immitigable zealot. "We are not wont to show an idle courtesy to that sex, which requireth the stricter discipline. What sayest thou, maid? Shall thy silken bridegroom suffer thy share of the penalty, besides his own?"

"Be it death," said Edith, "and lay it all on me!"

---

22 Bearer of an emblem or flag.

Truly, as Endicott had said, the poor lovers stood in a woful case. Their foes were triumphant, their friends captive and abased, their home desolate, the benighted wilderness around them, and a rigorous destiny, in the shape of the Puritan leader, their only guide. Yet the deepening twilight could not altogether conceal that the iron man was softened; he smiled at the fair spectacle of early love; he almost sighed for the inevitable blight of early hopes.

"The troubles of life have come hastily on this young couple," observed Endicott. "We will see how they comport themselves under their present trials ere we burden them with greater. If, among the spoil, there be any garments of a more decent fashion, let them be put upon this May Lord and his Lady, instead of their glistening vanities. Look to it, some of you."

"And shall not the youth's hair be cut?" asked Peter Palfrey, looking with abhorrence at the lovelock and long glossy curls of the young man.

"Crop it forthwith, and that in the true pumpkin-shell[23] fashion," answered the captain. "Then bring them along with us, but more gently than their fellows. There be qualities in the youth, which may make him valiant to fight, and sober to toil, and pious to pray; and in the maiden, that may fit her to become a mother in our Israel,[24] bringing up babes in better nurture than her own hath been. Nor think ye, young ones, that they are the happiest, even in our lifetime of a moment, who misspend it in dancing round a Maypole!"

And Endicott, the severest Puritan of all who laid the rock foundation of New England, lifted the wreath of roses from the ruin of the Maypole, and threw it, with his own gauntleted hand, over the heads of the Lord and Lady of the May. It was a deed of prophecy. As the moral gloom of the world overpowers all systematic gayety, even so was their home of wild mirth made desolate amid the sad forest. They returned to it no more. But as their flowery garland was wreathed of the brightest roses that had grown there, so, in the tie that united them, were intertwined all the purest and best of their early joys. They went heavenward, supporting each other along the difficult path which it was their lot to tread, and never wasted one regretful thought on the vanities of Merry Mount.

1836

The Minister's Black Veil

A Parable[1]

The sexton stood in the porch of Milford meeting house, pulling busily at the bell-rope. The old people of the village came stooping along the street. Children, with bright faces,

---

23 The Puritan style of closely cropped hair.
24 Puritan name for the promised land, envisioned as America.
1 Hawthorne's note: "Another clergyman in New England, Mr. Joseph Moody, of York, Maine, who died about eighty years since made himself remarkable by the same ec-

centricity that is here related of the Reverend Mr. Hooper. In this case, however, the symbol had a different import. In early life he had accidentally killed a beloved friend; and from that day till the hour of his own death, he hid his face from men."

tripped merrily beside their parents, or mimicked a graver gait, in the conscious dignity of their Sunday clothes. Spruce bachelors looked sidelong at the pretty maidens, and fancied that the Sabbath sunshine made them prettier than on week days. When the throng had mostly streamed into the porch, the sexton began to toll the bell, keeping his eye on the Reverend Mr. Hooper's door. The first glimpse of the clergyman's figure was the signal for the bell to cease its summons.

"But what has good Parson Hooper got upon his face?" cried the sexton in astonishment.

All within hearing immediately turned about, and beheld the semblance of Mr. Hooper, pacing slowly his meditative way towards the meeting-house. With one accord they started, expressing more wonder than if some strange minister were coming to dust the cushions of Mr. Hooper's pulpit.

"Are you sure it is our parson?" inquired Goodman Gray of the sexton.

"Of a certainty it is good Mr. Hooper," replied the sexton. "He was to have exchanged pulpits with Parson Shute, of Westbury; but Parson Shute sent to excuse himself yesterday, being to preach a funeral sermon."

The cause of so much amazement may appear sufficiently slight. Mr. Hooper, a gentlemanly person, of about thirty, though still a bachelor, was dressed with due clerical neatness, as if a careful wife had starched his band, and brushed the weekly dust from his Sunday's garb. There was but one thing remarkable in his appearance. Swathed about his forehead, and hanging down over his face, so low as to be shaken by his breath, Mr. Hooper had on a black veil. On a nearer view it seemed to consist of two folds of crape, which entirely concealed his features, except the mouth and chin, but probably did not intercept his sight, further than to give a darkened aspect to all living and inanimate things. With this gloomy shade before him, good Mr. Hooper walked onward, at a slow and quiet pace, stooping somewhat, and looking on the ground, as is customary with abstracted men, yet nodding kindly to those of his parishioners who still waited on the meeting-house steps. But so wonder-struck were they that his greeting hardly met with a return.

"I can't really feel as if good Mr. Hooper's face was behind that piece of crape," said the sexton.

"I don't like it," muttered an old woman, as she hobbled into the meeting-house. "He has changed himself into something awful, only by hiding his face."

"Our parson has gone mad!" cried Goodman Gray, following him across the threshold.

A rumor of some unaccountable phenomenon had preceded Mr. Hooper into the meeting-house, and set all the congregation astir. Few could refrain from twisting their heads towards the door; many stood upright, and turned directly about; while several little boys clambered upon the seats, and came down again with a terrible racket. There was a general bustle, a rustling of the women's gowns and shuffling of the men's feet, greatly at variance with that hushed repose which should attend the entrance of the minister. But Mr. Hooper appeared not to notice the perturbation of his people. He entered with an almost noiseless step, bent his head mildly to the pews on each side, and bowed as he passed his oldest parishioner, a white-haired great-grandsire, who occupied an arm-chair in the centre of the aisle. It was strange to observe how slowly this venerable man became conscious of something singular in the appearance of his pastor. He seemed not fully to partake of the prevailing wonder, till Mr. Hooper had ascended the stairs, and showed himself in the pulpit, face to face with his congregation, except for the black veil. That mysterious emblem was never once withdrawn. It shook with his measured breath, as he gave out the psalm; it threw its obscurity between him and the holy page, as he read the Scriptures; and while he prayed, the veil lay heavily on his uplifted countenance. Did he seek to hide it from the dread Being whom he was addressing?

Such was the effect of this simple piece of crape, that more than one woman of delicate nerves was forced to leave the meeting-house. Yet perhaps the pale-faced congregation was almost as fearful a sight to the minister, as his black veil to them.

Mr. Hooper had the reputation of a good preacher, but not an energetic one: he strove to win his people heavenward by mild, persuasive influences, rather than to drive them thither by the thunders of the Word. The sermon which he now delivered was marked by the same characteristics of style and manner as the general series of his pulpit oratory. But there was something, either in the sentiment of the discourse itself, or in the imagination of the auditors, which made it greatly the most powerful effort that they had ever heard from their pastor's lips. It was tinged, rather more darkly than usual, with the gentle gloom of Mr. Hooper's temperament. The subject had reference to secret sin, and those sad mysteries which we hide from our nearest and dearest, and would fain conceal from our own consciousness, even forgetting that the Omniscient can detect them. A subtle power was breathed into his words. Each member of the congregation, the most innocent girl, and the man of hardened breast, felt as if the preacher had crept upon them, behind his awful veil, and discovered their hoarded iniquity of deed or thought. Many spread their clasped hands on their bosoms. There was nothing terrible in what Mr. Hooper said, at least, no violence; and yet, with every tremor of his melancholy voice, the hearers quaked. An unsought pathos came hand in hand with awe. So sensible were the audience of some unwonted attribute in their minister, that they longed for a breath of wind to blow aside the veil, almost believing that a stranger's visage would be discovered, though the form, gesture, and voice were those of Mr. Hooper.

At the close of the services, the people hurried out with indecorous confusion, eager to communicate their pent-up amazement, and conscious of lighter spirits the moment they lost sight of the black veil. Some gathered in little circles, huddled closely together, with their mouths all whispering in the centre; some went homeward alone, wrapt in silent meditation; some talked loudly, and profaned the Sabbath day with ostentatious laughter. A few shook their sagacious heads, intimating that they could penetrate the mystery; while one or two affirmed that there was no mystery at all, but only that Mr. Hooper's eyes were so weakened by the midnight lamp, as to require a shade. After a brief interval, forth came good Mr. Hooper also, in the rear of his flock. Turning his veiled face from one group to another, he paid due reverence to the hoary heads, saluted the middle aged with kind dignity as their friend and spiritual guide, greeted the young with mingled authority and love, and laid his hands on the little children's heads to bless them. Such was always his custom on the Sabbath day. Strange and bewildered looks repaid him for his courtesy. None, as on former occasions, aspired to the honor of walking by their pastor's side. Old Squire Saunders, doubtless by an accidental lapse of memory, neglected to invite Mr. Hooper to his table, where the good clergyman had been wont to bless the food, almost every Sunday since his settlement. He returned, therefore, to the parsonage, and, at the moment of closing the door, was observed to look back upon the people, all of whom had their eyes fixed upon the minister. A sad smile gleamed faintly from beneath the black veil, and flickered about his mouth, glimmering as he disappeared.

"How strange," said a lady, "that a simple black veil, such as any woman might wear on her bonnet, should become such a terrible thing on Mr. Hooper's face!"

"Something must surely be amiss with Mr. Hooper's intellects," observed her husband, the physician of the village. "But the strangest part of the affair is the effect of this vagary, even on a sober-minded man like myself. The black veil, though it covers only our pastor's face, throws its influence over his whole person, and makes him ghostlike from head to foot. Do you not feel it so?"

"Truly do I," replied the lady; "and I would not be alone with him for the world. I wonder he is not afraid to be alone with himself!"

"Men sometimes are so," said her husband.

The afternoon service was attended with similar circumstances. At its conclusion, the bell tolled for the funeral of a young lady. The relatives and friends were assembled in the house, and the more distant acquaintances stood about the door, speaking of the good qualities of the deceased, when their talk was interrupted by the appearance of Mr. Hooper, still covered with his black veil. It was now an appropriate emblem. The clergyman stepped into the room where the corpse was laid, and bent over the coffin, to take a last farewell of his deceased parishioner. As he stooped, the veil hung straight down from his forehead, so that, if her eyelids had not been closed forever, the dead maiden might have seen his face. Could Mr. Hooper be fearful of her glance, that he so hastily caught back the black veil? A person who watched the interview between the dead and living, scrupled not to affirm, that, at the instant when the clergyman's features were disclosed, the corpse had slightly shuddered, rustling the shroud and muslin cap, though the countenance retained the composure of death. A superstitious old woman was the only witness of this prodigy. From the coffin Mr. Hooper passed into the chamber of the mourners, and thence to the head of the staircase, to make the funeral prayer. It was a tender and heart-dissolving prayer, full of sorrow, yet so imbued with celestial hopes, that the music of a heavenly harp, swept by the fingers of the dead, seemed faintly to be heard among the saddest accents of the minister. The people trembled, though they but darkly understood him when he prayed that they, and himself, and all of mortal race, might be ready, as he trusted this young maiden had been, for the dreadful hour that should snatch the veil from their faces. The bearers went heavily forth, and the mourners followed, saddening all the street, with the dead before them, and Mr. Hooper in his black veil behind.

"Why do you look back?" said one in the procession to his partner.

"I had a fancy," replied she, "that the minister and the maiden's spirit were walking hand in hand."

"And so had I, at the same moment," said the other.

That night, the handsomest couple in Milford village were to be joined in wedlock. Though reckoned a melancholy man, Mr. Hooper had a placid cheerfulness for such occasions, which often excited a sympathetic smile where livelier merriment would have been thrown away. There was no quality of his disposition which made him more beloved than this. The company at the wedding awaited his arrival with impatience, trusting that the strange awe, which had gathered over him throughout the day, would now be dispelled. But such was not the result. When Mr. Hooper came, the first thing that their eyes rested on was the same horrible black veil, which had added deeper gloom to the funeral, and could portend nothing but evil to the wedding. Such was its immediate effect on the guests that a cloud seemed to have rolled duskily from beneath the black crape, and dimmed the light of the candles. The bridal pair stood up before the minister. But the bride's cold fingers quivered in the tremulous hand of the bridegroom, and her deathlike paleness caused a whisper that the maiden who had been buried a few hours before was come from her grave to be married. If ever another wedding were so dismal, it was that famous one where they tolled the wedding knell. After performing the ceremony, Mr. Hooper raised a glass of wine to his lips, wishing happiness to the new-married couple in a strain of mild pleasantry that ought to have brightened the features of the guests, like a cheerful gleam from the hearth. At that instant, catching a glimpse of his figure in the looking-glass, the black veil involved his own spirit in the horror with which it overwhelmed all others. His frame shuddered, his lips grew white, he spilt the untasted wine upon the carpet, and rushed forth into the darkness. For the Earth, too, had on her Black Veil.

The next day, the whole village of Milford talked of little else than Parson Hooper's black veil. That, and the mystery concealed behind it, supplied a topic for discussion between acquaintances meeting in the street, and good women gossiping at their open windows. It was the first item of news that the tavernkeeper told to his guests. The children babbled of it on their way to school. One imitative little imp covered his face with an old black handkerchief, thereby so affrighting his playmates that the panic seized himself, and he well-nigh lost his wits by his own waggery.

It was remarkable that of all the busybodies and impertinent people in the parish, not one ventured to put the plain question to Mr. Hooper, wherefore he did this thing. Hitherto, whenever there appeared the slightest call for such interference, he had never lacked advisers, nor shown himself averse to be guided by their judgment. If he erred at all, it was by so painful a degree of self-distrust, that even the mildest censure would lead him to consider an indifferent action as a crime. Yet, though so well acquainted with this amiable weakness, no individual among his parishioners chose to make the black veil a subject of friendly remonstrance. There was a feeling of dread, neither plainly confessed nor carefully concealed, which caused each to shift the responsibility upon another, till at length it was found expedient to send a deputation of the church, in order to deal with Mr. Hooper about the mystery, before it should grow into a scandal. Never did an embassy so ill discharge its duties. The minister received them with friendly courtesy, but became silent, after they were seated, leaving to his visitors the whole burden of introducing their important business. The topic, it might be supposed, was obvious enough. There was the black veil swathed round Mr. Hooper's forehead, and concealing every feature above his placid mouth, on which, at times, they could perceive the glimmering of a melancholy smile. But that piece of crape, to their imagination, seemed to hang down before his heart, the symbol of a fearful secret between him and them. Were the veil but cast aside, they might speak freely of it, but not till then. Thus they sat a considerable time, speechless, confused, and shrinking uneasily from Mr. Hooper's eye, which they felt to be fixed upon them with an invisible glance. Finally, the deputies returned abashed to their constituents, pronouncing the matter too weighty to be handled, except by a council of the churches, if, indeed, it might not require a general synod.

But there was one person in the village unappalled by the awe with which the black veil had impressed all beside herself. When the deputies returned without an explanation, or even venturing to demand one, she, with the calm energy of her character, determined to chase away the strange cloud that appeared to be settling round Mr. Hooper, every moment more darkly than before. As his plighted wife, it should be her privilege to know what the black veil concealed. At the minister's first visit, therefore, she entered upon the subject with a direct simplicity, which made the task easier both for him and her. After he had seated himself, she fixed her eyes steadfastly upon the veil, but could discern nothing of the dreadful gloom that had so overawed the multitude: it was but a double fold of crape, hanging down from his forehead to his mouth, and slightly stirring with his breath.

"No," said she aloud, and smiling, "there is nothing terrible in this piece of crape, except that it hides a face which I am always glad to look upon. Come, good sir, let the sun shine from behind the cloud. First lay aside your black veil: then tell me why you put it on."

Mr. Hooper's smile glimmered faintly.

"There is an hour to come," said he, "when all of us shall cast aside our veils. Take it not amiss, beloved friend, if I wear this piece of crape till then."

"Your words are a mystery, too," returned the young lady. "Take away the veil from them, at least."

"Elizabeth, I will," said he, "so far as my vow may suffer me. Know, then, this veil is a type and a symbol, and I am bound to wear it ever, both in light and darkness, in solitude and before the gaze of multitudes, and as with strangers, so with my familiar friends. No mortal eye will see it withdrawn. This dismal shade must separate me from the world: even you, Elizabeth, can never come behind it!"

"What grievous affliction hath befallen you," she earnestly inquired, "that you should thus darken your eyes forever?"

"If it be a sign of mourning," replied Mr. Hooper, "I, perhaps, like most other mortals, have sorrows dark enough to be typified by a black veil."

"But what if the world will not believe that it is the type of an innocent sorrow?" urged Elizabeth. "Beloved and respected as you are, there may be whispers that you hide your face under the consciousness of secret sin. For the sake of your holy office, do away this scandal!"

The color rose into her cheeks as she intimated the nature of the rumors that were already abroad in the village. But Mr. Hooper's mildness did not forsake him. He even smiled again—that same sad smile, which always appeared like a faint glimmering of light, proceeding from the obscurity beneath the veil.

"If I hide my face for sorrow, there is cause enough," he merely replied; "and if I cover it for secret sin, what mortal might not do the same?"

And with this gentle, but unconquerable obstinacy did he resist all her entreaties. At length Elizabeth sat silent. For a few moments she appeared lost in thought, considering, probably, what new methods might be tried to withdraw her lover from so dark a fantasy, which, if it had no other meaning, was perhaps a symptom of mental disease. Though of a firmer character than his own, the tears rolled down her cheeks. But, in an instant, as it were, a new feeling took the place of sorrow: her eyes were fixed insensibly on the black veil, when, like a sudden twilight in the air, its terrors fell around her. She arose, and stood trembling before him.

"And do you feel it then, at last?" said he mournfully.

She made no reply, but covered her eyes with her hand, and turned to leave the room. He rushed forward and caught her arm.

"Have patience with me, Elizabeth!" cried he, passionately. "Do not desert me, though this veil must be between us here on earth. Be mine, and hereafter there shall be no veil over my face, no darkness between our souls! It is but a mortal veil—it is not for eternity! O! you know not how lonely I am, and how frightened, to be alone behind my black veil. Do not leave me in this miserable obscurity forever!"

"Lift the veil but once, and look me in the face," said she.

"Never! It cannot be!" replied Mr. Hooper.

"Then farewell!" said Elizabeth.

She withdrew her arm from his grasp, and slowly departed, pausing at the door, to give one long shuddering gaze, that seemed almost to penetrate the mystery of the black veil. But, even amid his grief, Mr. Hooper smiled to think that only a material emblem had separated him from happiness, though the horrors, which it shadowed forth, must be drawn darkly between the fondest of lovers.

From that time no attempts were made to remove Mr. Hooper's black veil, or, by a direct appeal, to discover the secret which it was supposed to hide. By persons who claimed a superiority to popular prejudice, it was reckoned merely an eccentric whim, such as often mingles with the sober actions of men otherwise rational, and tinges them all with its own semblance of insanity. But with the multitude, good Mr. Hooper was irreparably a bugbear. He could not walk the street with any peace of mind, so conscious was he that the gentle and timid would turn aside to avoid him, and that others would make it a point of hardihood to throw themselves in his way. The impertinence of the latter class compelled him to give up his customary walk at sunset to the burial ground; for when he leaned pensively over the gate, there would always be faces behind the gravestones, peeping at his black veil. A fable went the rounds that the stare of the dead people drove him thence. It grieved him, to the very depth of his kind heart, to observe how the children fled from his approach, breaking up their merriest sports, while his melancholy figure was yet afar off. Their instinctive dread caused him to feel more strongly than aught else, that a preternatural horror was interwoven with the threads of the black crape. In truth, his own antipathy to the veil was known to be so great, that he never willingly passed before a mirror, nor stooped to drink at a still fountain, lest, in its peaceful bosom, he should be affrighted by himself. This was what gave plausibility to the whispers, that Mr. Hooper's conscience tortured him for some great crime too horrible to be entirely concealed, or otherwise than so obscurely intimated. Thus, from beneath the black veil, there rolled a cloud into the sunshine, an ambiguity of sin or sorrow, which enveloped the poor minister, so that love or sympathy could never reach him. It was said that ghost and fiend consorted with him there. With self-shudderings and outward terrors, he walked continually in its shadow, groping darkly within his own soul, or gazing through a medium that saddened the whole world. Even the lawless wind, it was believed, respected his dreadful secret, and never blew aside the veil. But still good Mr. Hooper sadly smiled at the pale visages of the worldly throng as he passed by.

Among all its bad influences, the black veil had the one desirable effect, of making its wearer a very efficient clergyman. By the aid of his mysterious emblem—for there was no other apparent cause—he became a man of awful power over souls that were in agony for sin. His converts always regarded him with a dread peculiar to themselves, affirming, though but figuratively, that, before he brought them to celestial light, they had been with him behind the black veil. Its gloom, indeed, enabled him to sympathize with all dark affections. Dying sinners cried aloud for Mr. Hooper, and would not yield their breath till he appeared; though ever, as he stooped to whisper consolation, they shuddered at the veiled face so near their own. Such were the terrors of the black veil, even when Death had bared his visage! Strangers came long distances to attend service at his church, with the mere idle purpose of gazing at his figure, because it was forbidden them to behold his face. But many were made to quake ere they departed! Once, during Governor Belcher's administration,[2] Mr. Hooper was appointed to preach the election sermon.[3] Covered with his black veil, he stood before the chief magistrate, the council, and the representatives, and wrought so deep an impression, that the legislative measures of that year were characterized by all the gloom and piety of our earliest ancestral sway.

In this manner Mr. Hooper spent a long life, irreproachable in outward act, yet shrouded in dismal suspicions; kind and loving, though unloved, and dimly feared; a man apart from men, shunned in their health and joy, but ever summoned to their aid in mortal anguish. As years wore on, shedding their snows above his sable veil, he acquired a name throughout the New England churches, and they called him Father Hooper. Nearly all his parishioners, who were of mature age when he was settled, had been borne away by many a funeral: he had one congregation in the church, and a more crowded one in the churchyard; and having wrought so late into the evening, and done his work so well, it was now good Father Hooper's turn to rest.

Several persons were visible by the shaded candlelight, in the death chamber of the old clergyman. Natural connections he had none. But there was the decorously grave, though unmoved physician, seeking only to mitigate the last pangs of the patient whom he could not save. There were the deacons, and other eminently pious members of his church. There, also, was the Reverend Mr. Clark, of Westbury, a young and zealous divine, who had ridden in haste to pray by the bedside of the expiring minister. There was the nurse, no hired handmaiden of death, but one whose calm affection had endured thus long in secrecy, in solitude, amid the chill of age, and would not perish, even at the dying hour. Who, but Elizabeth! And there lay the hoary head of good Father Hooper upon the death pillow, with the black veil still swathed about his brow, and reaching down over his face, so that each more difficult gasp of his faint breath caused it to stir. All through life that piece of crape had hung between him and the world: it had separated him from cheerful brotherhood and woman's love, and kept him in that saddest of all prisons, his own heart; and still it lay upon his face, as if to deepen the gloom of his darksome chamber, and shade him from the sunshine of eternity.

For some time previous, his mind had been confused, wavering doubtfully between the past and the present, and hovering forward, as it were, at intervals, into the indistinctness of the world to come. There had been feverish turns, which tossed him from

---

[2] Jonathan Belcher (1682–1757) was governor of Massachusetts and New Hampshire from 1730 to 1741.

[3] It was an honor to be chosen to preach the special sermon at the inauguration of a new governor.

side to side, and wore away what little strength he had. But in his most convulsive struggles, and in the wildest vagaries of his intellect, when no other thought retained its sober influence, he still showed an awful solicitude lest the black veil should slip aside. Even if his bewildered soul could have forgotten, there was a faithful woman at his pillow, who, with averted eyes, would have covered that aged face, which she had last beheld in the comeliness of manhood. At length the death-stricken old man lay quietly in the torpor of mental and bodily exhaustion, with an imperceptible pulse, and breath that grew fainter and fainter, except when a long, deep, and irregular inspiration seemed to prelude the flight of his spirit.

The minister of Westbury approached the bedside.

"Venerable Father Hooper," said he, "the moment of your release is at hand. Are you ready for the lifting of the veil that shuts in time from eternity?"

Father Hooper at first replied merely by a feeble motion of his head; then, apprehensive, perhaps, that his meaning might be doubtful, he exerted himself to speak.

"Yea," said he, in faint accents, "my soul hath a patient weariness until that veil be lifted."

"And is it fitting," resumed the Reverend Mr. Clark, "that a man so given to prayer, of such a blameless example, holy in deed and thought, so far as mortal judgment may pronounce; is it fitting that a father in the church should leave a shadow on his memory, that may seem to blacken a life so pure? I pray you, my venerable brother, let not this thing be! Suffer us to be gladdened by your triumphant aspect as you go to your reward. Before the veil of eternity be lifted, let me cast aside this black veil from your face!"

And thus speaking, the Reverend Mr. Clark bent forward to reveal the mystery of so many years. But, exerting a sudden energy, that made all the beholders stand aghast, Father Hooper snatched both his hands from beneath the bedclothes, and pressed them strongly on the black veil, resolute to struggle, if the minister of Westbury would contend with a dying man.

"Never!" cried the veiled clergyman. "On earth, never!"

"Dark old man!" exclaimed the affrighted minister, "with what horrible crime upon your soul are you now passing to the judgment?"

Father Hooper's breath heaved; it rattled in his throat; but, with a mighty effort, grasping forward with his hands, he caught hold of life, and held it back till he should speak. He even raised himself in bed; and there he sat, shivering with the arms of death around him, while the black veil hung down, awful, at that last moment, in the gathered terrors of a lifetime. And yet the faint, sad smile, so often there, now seemed to glimmer from its obscurity, and linger on Father Hooper's lips.

"Why do you tremble at me alone?" cried he, turning his veiled face round the circle of pale spectators. "Tremble also at each other! Have men avoided me, and women shown no pity, and children screamed and fled, only for my black veil? What, but the mystery which it obscurely typifies, has made this piece of crape so awful? When the friend shows his inmost heart to his friend; the lover to his best beloved; when man does not vainly shrink from the eye of his Creator, loathsomely treasuring up the secret of his sin; then deem me a monster, for the symbol beneath which I have lived, and die! I look around me, and, lo! on every visage a Black Veil!"

While his auditors shrank from one another, in mutual affright, Father Hooper fell back upon his pillow, a veiled corpse, with a faint smile lingering on the lips. Still veiled, they laid him in his coffin, and a veiled corpse they bore him to the grave. The grass of many years has sprung up and withered on that grave, the burial stone is moss-grown, and good Mr. Hooper's face is dust; but awful is still the thought that it mouldered beneath the Black Veil!

1836

Rappaccini's Daughter

(From the writings of Aubépine.[1])

We do not remember to have seen any translated specimens of the productions of M. de l'Aubépine—a fact the less to be wondered at, as his very name is unknown to many of his own countrymen as well as to the student of foreign literature. As a writer, he seems to occupy an unfortunate position between the Transcendentalists (who, under one name or another, have their share in all the current literature of the world) and the great body of pen-and-ink men who address the intellect and sympathies of the multitude. If not too refined, at all events too remote, too shadowy, and unsubstantial in his modes of development to suit the taste of the latter class, and yet too popular to satisfy the spiritual or metaphysical requisitions of the former, he must necessarily find himself without an audience, except here and there an individual or possibly an isolated clique. His writings, to do them justice, are not altogether destitute of fancy and originality; they might have won him greater reputation but for an inveterate love of allegory, which is apt to invest his plots and characters with the aspect of scenery and people in the clouds, and to steal away the human warmth out of his conceptions. His fictions are sometimes historical, sometimes of the present day, and sometimes, so far as can be discovered, have little or no reference either to time or space. In any case, he generally contents himself with a very slight embroidery of outward manners,—the faintest possible counterfeit of real life,—and endeavors to create an interest by some less obvious peculiarity of the subject. Occasionally a breath of Nature, a raindrop of pathos and tenderness, or a gleam of humor, will find its way into the midst of his fantastic imagery, and make us feel as if, after all, we were yet within the limits of our native earth. We will only add to this very cursory notice that M. de l'Aubépine's productions, if the reader chance to take them in precisely the proper point of view, may amuse a leisure hour as well as those of a brighter man; if otherwise, they can hardly fail to look excessively like nonsense.

Our author is voluminous; he continues to write and publish with as much praiseworthy and indefatigable prolixity as if his efforts were crowned with the brilliant success that so justly attends those of Eugene Sue.[2] His first appearance was by a collection

---

[1] French: "Hawthorne."
[2] Popular French novelist (1804–1857).

of stories in a long series of volumes entitled "Contes deux fois racontées."[3] The titles of some of his more recent works (we quote from memory) are as follows: "Le Voyage Céleste à Chemin de Fer," 3 tom., 1838; "Le nouveau Père Adam et la nouvelle Mère Eve," 2 tom., 1839; "Roderic; ou le Serpent à l'estomac," 2 tom., 1840; "Le Culte du Feu," a folio volume of ponderous research into the religion and ritual of the old Persian Ghebers, published in 1841; "La Soirée du Chateau en Espagne," 1 tom., 8vo, 1842; and "L'Artiste du Beau; ou le Papillon Mécanique," 5 tom., 4to, 1843.[4] Our somewhat wearisome perusal of this startling catalogue of volumes has left behind it a certain personal affection and sympathy, though by no means admiration, for M. de l'Aubépine; and we would fain do the little in our power towards introducing him favorably to the American public. The ensuing tale is a translation of his "Beatrice; ou la Belle Empoisonneuse," recently published in "La Revue Anti-Aristocratique." This journal, edited by the Comte de Bearhaven,[5] has for some years past led the defence of liberal principles and popular rights with a faithfulness and ability worthy of all praise.

A young man, named Giovanni Guasconti, came, very long ago, from the more southern region of Italy, to pursue his studies at the University of Padua. Giovanni, who had but a scanty supply of gold ducats in his pocket, took lodgings in a high and gloomy chamber of an old edifice which looked not unworthy to have been the palace of a Paduan noble, and which, in fact, exhibited over its entrance the armorial bearings of a family long since extinct. The young stranger, who was not unstudied in the great poem of his country, recollected that one of the ancestors of this family, and perhaps an occupant of this very mansion, had been pictured by Dante as a partaker of the immortal agonies of his Inferno. These reminiscences and associations, together with the tendency to heartbreak natural to a young man for the first time out of his native sphere, caused Giovanni to sigh heavily as he looked around the desolate and ill-furnished apartment.

"Holy Virgin, signor!" cried old Dame Lisabetta, who, won by the youth's remarkable beauty of person, was kindly endeavoring to give the chamber a habitable air, "what a sigh was that to come out of a young man's heart! Do you find this old mansion gloomy? For the love of Heaven, then, put your head out of the window, and you will see as bright sunshine as you have left in Naples."

Guasconti mechanically did as the old woman advised, but could not quite agree with her that the Paduan sunshine was as cheerful as that of southern Italy. Such as it was, however, it fell upon a garden beneath the window and expended its fostering influences on a variety of plants, which seemed to have been cultivated with exceeding care.

"Does this garden belong to the house?" asked Giovanni.

"Heaven forbid, signor, unless it were fruitful of better pot herbs than any that grow there now," answered old Lisabetta. "No; that garden is cultivated by the own hands of Signor Giacomo Rappaccini, the famous doctor, who, I warrant him, has been heard of as far as Naples. It is said that he distils these plants into medicines that are as potent as

---

[3] i.e., Hawthorne's *Twice-Told Tales* (1837).

[4] Mock bibliographic references, including the supposed volume ("tom"), octavo ("8vo"), and quarto ("4to") of each work.

[5] John O'Sullivan, editor of *The Democractic Review.*

a charm. Oftentimes you may see the signor doctor at work, and perchance the signora, his daughter, too, gathering the strange flowers that grow in the garden."

The old woman had now done what she could for the aspect of the chamber; and, commending the young man to the protection of the saints, took her departure.

Giovanni still found no better occupation than to look down into the garden beneath his window. From its appearance, he judged it to be one of those botanic gardens which were of earlier date in Padua than elsewhere in Italy or in the world. Or, not improbably, it might once have been the pleasure-place of an opulent family; for there was the ruin of a marble fountain in the centre, sculptured with rare art, but so wofully shattered that it was impossible to trace the original design from the chaos of remaining fragments. The water, however, continued to gush and sparkle into the sunbeams as cheerfully as ever. A little gurgling sound ascended to the young man's window, and made him feel as if the fountain were an immortal spirit that sung its song unceasingly and without heeding the vicissitudes around it, while one century imbodied it in marble and another scattered the perishable garniture on the soil. All about the pool into which the water subsided grew various plants, that seemed to require a plentiful supply of moisture for the nourishment of gigantic leaves, and, in some instances, flowers gorgeously magnificent. There was one shrub in particular, set in a marble vase in the midst of the pool, that bore a profusion of purple blossoms, each of which had the lustre and richness of a gem; and the whole together made a show so resplendent that it seemed enough to illuminate the garden, even had there been no sunshine. Every portion of the soil was peopled with plants and herbs, which, if less beautiful, still bore tokens of assiduous care, as if all had their individual virtues, known to the scientific mind that fostered them. Some were placed in urns, rich with old carving, and others in common garden pots; some crept serpent-like along the ground or climbed on high, using whatever means of ascent was offered them. One plant had wreathed itself round a statue of Vertumnus,[6] which was thus quite veiled and shrouded in a drapery of hanging foliage, so happily arranged that it might have served a sculptor for a study.

While Giovanni stood at the window he heard a rustling behind a screen of leaves, and became aware that a person was at work in the garden. His figure soon emerged into view, and showed itself to be that of no common laborer, but a tall, emaciated, sallow, and sickly-looking man, dressed in a scholar's garb of black. He was beyond the middle term of life, with gray hair, a thin, gray beard, and a face singularly marked with intellect and cultivation, but which could never, even in his more youthful days, have expressed much warmth of heart.

Nothing could exceed the intentness with which this scientific gardener examined every shrub which grew in his path: it seemed as if he was looking into their inmost nature, making observations in regard to their creative essence, and discovering why one leaf grew in this shape and another in that, and wherefore such and such flowers differed among themselves in hue and perfume. Nevertheless, in spite of this deep intelligence on his part, there was no approach to intimacy between himself and these vegetable existences. On the contrary, he avoided their actual touch or the direct inhaling of their odors with a caution that impressed Giovanni most disagreeably; for the man's demeanor was that of one walking among malignant influences, such as savage beasts,

[6] Mythic god who controlled plant growth by
presiding over the seasons.

or deadly snakes, or evil spirits, which, should he allow them one moment of license, would wreak upon him some terrible fatality. It was strangely frightful to the young man's imagination to see this air of insecurity in a person cultivating a garden, that most simple and innocent of human toils, and which had been alike the joy and labor of the unfallen parents of the race. Was this garden, then, the Eden of the present world? And this man, with such a perception of harm in what his own hands caused to grow,— was he the Adam?

The distrustful gardener, while plucking away the dead leaves or pruning the too luxuriant growth of the shrubs, defended his hands with a pair of thick gloves. Nor were these his only armor. When, in his walk through the garden, he came to the magnificent plant that hung its purple gems beside the marble fountain, he placed a kind of mask over his mouth and nostrils, as if all this beauty did but conceal a deadlier malice; but, finding his task still too dangerous, he drew back, removed the mask, and called loudly, but in the infirm voice of a person affected with inward disease,—

"Beatrice! Beatrice!"

"Here am I, my father. What would you?" cried a rich and youthful voice from the window of the opposite house—a voice as rich as a tropical sunset, and which made Giovanni, though he knew not why, think of deep hues of purple or crimson and of perfumes heavily delectable. "Are you in the garden?"

"Yes, Beatrice," answered the gardener, "and I need your help."

Soon there emerged from under a sculptured portal the figure of a young girl, arrayed with as much richness of taste as the most splendid of the flowers, beautiful as the day, and with a bloom so deep and vivid that one shade more would have been too much. She looked redundant with life, health, and energy; all of which attributes were bound down and compressed, as it were, and girdled tensely, in their luxuriance, by her virgin zone.[7] Yet Giovanni's fancy must have grown morbid while he looked down into the garden; for the impression which the fair stranger made upon him was as if here were another flower, the human sister of those vegetable ones, as beautiful as they, more beautiful than the richest of them, but still to be touched only with a glove, nor to be approached without a mask. As Beatrice came down the garden path, it was observable that she handled and inhaled the odor of several of the plants which her father had most sedulously avoided.

"Here, Beatrice," said the latter, "see how many needful offices require to be done to our chief treasure. Yet, shattered as I am, my life might pay the penalty of approaching it so closely as circumstances demand. Henceforth, I fear, this plant must be consigned to your sole charge."

"And gladly will I undertake it," cried again the rich tones of the young lady, as she bent towards the magnificent plant and opened her arms as if to embrace it. "Yes, my sister, my splendor, it shall be Beatrice's task to nurse and serve thee; and thou shalt reward her with thy kisses and perfumed breath, which to her is as the breath of life."

Then, with all the tenderness in her manner that was so strikingly expressed in her words, she busied herself with such attentions as the plant seemed to require; and Giovanni, at his lofty window, rubbed his eyes and almost doubted whether it were a girl tending her favorite flower, or one sister performing the duties of affection to another.

---

[7] Belt or girdle customarily worn by unmarried women.

The scene soon terminated. Whether Dr. Rappaccini had finished his labors in the garden, or that his watchful eye had caught the stranger's face, he now took his daughter's arm and retired. Night was already closing in; oppressive exhalations seemed to proceed from the plants and steal upward past the open window; and Giovanni, closing the lattice, went to his couch and dreamed of a rich flower and beautiful girl. Flower and maiden were different, and yet the same, and fraught with some strange peril in either shape.

But there is an influence in the light of morning that tends to rectify whatever errors of fancy, or even of judgment, we may have incurred during the sun's decline, or among the shadows of the night, or in the less wholesome glow of moonshine. Giovanni's first movement, on starting from sleep, was to throw open the window and gaze down into the garden which his dreams had made so fertile of mysteries. He was surprised and a little ashamed to find how real and matter-of-fact an affair it proved to be, in the first rays of the sun which gilded the dew-drops that hung upon leaf and blossom, and, while giving a brighter beauty to each rare flower, brought everything within the limits of ordinary experience. The young man rejoiced that, in the heart of the barren city, he had the privilege of overlooking this spot of lovely and luxuriant vegetation. It would serve, he said to himself, as a symbolic language to keep him in communion with Nature. Neither the sickly and thought-worn Dr. Giacomo Rappaccini, it is true, nor his brilliant daughter, were now visible; so that Giovanni could not determine how much of the singularity which he attributed to both was due to their own qualities and how much to his wonder-working fancy; but he was inclined to take a most rational view of the whole matter.

In the course of the day he paid his respects to Signor Pietro Baglioni, professor of medicine in the university, a physician of eminent repute, to whom Giovanni had brought a letter of introduction. The professor was an elderly personage, apparently of genial nature, and habits that might almost be called jovial. He kept the young man to dinner, and made himself very agreeable by the freedom and liveliness of his conversation, especially when warmed by a flask or two of Tuscan wine. Giovanni, conceiving that men of science, inhabitants of the same city, must needs be on familiar terms with one another, took an opportunity to mention the name of Dr. Rappaccini. But the professor did not respond with so much cordiality as he had anticipated.

"Ill would it become a teacher of the divine art of medicine," said Professor Pietro Baglioni, in answer to a question of Giovanni, "to withhold due and well-considered praise of a physician so eminently skilled as Rappaccini; but, on the other hand, I should answer it but scantily to my conscience were I to permit a worthy youth like yourself, Signor Giovanni, the son of an ancient friend, to imbibe erroneous ideas respecting a man who might hereafter chance to hold your life and death in his hands. The truth is, our worshipful Dr. Rappaccini has as much science as any member of the faculty—with perhaps one single exception—in Padua, or all Italy; but there are certain grave objections to his professional character."

"And what are they?" asked the young man.

"Has my friend Giovanni any disease of body or heart, that he is so inquisitive about physicians?" said the professor, with a smile. "But as for Rappaccini, it is said of him—and I, who know the man well, can answer for its truth—that he cares infinitely more for science than for mankind. His patients are interesting to him only as subjects for some new experiment. He would sacrifice human life, his own among the rest, or whatever else was dearest to him, for the sake of adding so much as a grain of mustard seed to the great heap of his accumulated knowledge."

"Methinks he is an awful man indeed," remarked Guasconti, mentally recalling the cold and purely intellectual aspect of Rappaccini. "And yet, worshipful professor, is it not a noble spirit? Are there many men capable of so spiritual a love of science?"

"God forbid," answered the professor, somewhat testily; "at least, unless they take sounder views of the healing art than those adopted by Rappaccini. It is his theory that all medicinal virtues are comprised within those substances which we term vegetable poisons. These he cultivates with his own hands, and is said even to have produced new varieties of poison, more horribly deleterious than Nature, without the assistance of this learned person, would ever have plagued the world withal. That the signor doctor does less mischief than might be expected with such dangerous substances is undeniable. Now and then, it must be owned, he has effected, or seemed to effect, a marvellous cure; but, to tell you my private mind, Signor Giovanni, he should receive little credit for such instances of success,—they being probably the work of chance,—but should be held strictly accountable for his failures, which may justly be considered his own work."

The youth might have taken Baglioni's opinions with many grains of allowance had he known that there was a professional warfare of long continuance between him and Dr. Rappaccini, in which the latter was generally thought to have gained the advantage. If the reader be inclined to judge for himself, we refer him to certain black-letter tracts on both sides, preserved in the medical department of the University of Padua.

"I know not, most learned professor," returned Giovanni, after musing on what had been said of Rappaccini's exclusive zeal for science,—"I know not how dearly this physician may love his art; but surely there is one object more dear to him. He has a daughter."

"Aha!" cried the professor, with a laugh. "So now our friend Giovanni's secret is out. You have heard of this daughter, whom all the young men in Padua are wild about, though not half a dozen have ever had the good hap to see her face. I know little of the Signora Beatrice save that Rappaccini is said to have instructed her deeply in his science, and that, young and beautiful as fame reports her, she is already qualified to fill a professor's chair. Perchance her father destines her for mine! Other absurd rumors there be, not worth talking about or listening to. So now, Signor Giovanni, drink off your glass of lachryma."[8]

Guasconti returned to his lodgings somewhat heated with the wine he had quaffed, and which caused his brain to swim with strange fantasies in reference to Dr. Rappaccini and the beautiful Beatrice. On his way, happening to pass by a florist's, he bought a fresh bouquet of flowers.

Ascending to his chamber, he seated himself near the window, but within the shadow thrown by the depth of the wall, so that he could look down into the garden with little risk of being discovered. All beneath his eye was a solitude. The strange plants were basking in the sunshine, and now and then nodding gently to one another, as if in acknowledgment of sympathy and kindred. In the midst, by the shattered fountain, grew the magnificent shrub, with its purple gems clustering all over it; they glowed in the air, and gleamed back again out of the depths of the pool, which thus seemed to

[8] i.e., Lachryma Christi ("Tears of Christ"), an Italian wine produced near Vesuvius.

overflow with colored radiance from the rich reflection that was steeped in it. At first, as we have said, the garden was a solitude. Soon, however,—as Giovanni had half hoped, half feared, would be the case,—a figure appeared beneath the antique sculptured portal, and came down between the rows of plants, inhaling their various perfumes as if she were one of those beings of old classic fable that lived upon sweet odors. On again beholding Beatrice, the young man was even startled to perceive how much her beauty exceeded his recollection of it; so brilliant, so vivid, was its character, that she glowed amid the sunlight, and, as Giovanni whispered to himself, positively illuminated the more shadowy intervals of the garden path. Her face being now more revealed than on the former occasion, he was struck by its expression of simplicity and sweetness,—qualities that had not entered into his idea of her character, and which made him ask anew what manner of mortal she might be. Nor did he fail again to observe, or imagine, an analogy between the beautiful girl and the gorgeous shrub that hung its gemlike flowers over the fountain,—a resemblance which Beatrice seemed to have indulged a fantastic humor in heightening, both by the arrangement of her dress and the selection of its hues.

Approaching the shrub, she threw open her arms, as with a passionate ardor, and drew its branches into an intimate embrace—so intimate that her features were hidden in its leafy bosom and her glistening ringlets all intermingled with the flowers.

"Give me thy breath, my sister," exclaimed Beatrice; "for I am faint with common air. And give me this flower of thine, which I separate with gentlest fingers from the stem and place it close beside my heart."

With these words the beautiful daughter of Rappaccini plucked one of the richest blossoms of the shrub, and was about to fasten it in her bosom. But now, unless Giovanni's draughts of wine had bewildered his senses, a singular incident occurred. A small orange-colored reptile, of the lizard or chameleon species, chanced to be creeping along the path, just at the feet of Beatrice. It appeared to Giovanni,—but, at the distance from which he gazed, he could scarcely have seen anything so minute,—it appeared to him, however, that a drop or two of moisture from the broken stem of the flower descended upon the lizard's head. For an instant the reptile contorted itself violently, and then lay motionless in the sunshine. Beatrice observed this remarkable phenomenon, and crossed herself, sadly, but without surprise; nor did she therefore hesitate to arrange the fatal flower in her bosom. There it blushed, and almost glimmered with the dazzling effect of a precious stone, adding to her dress and aspect the one appropriate charm which nothing else in the world could have supplied. But Giovanni, out of the shadow of his window, bent forward and shrank back, and murmured and trembled.

"Am I awake? Have I my senses?" said he to himself. "What is this being? Beautiful shall I call her, or inexpressibly terrible?"

Beatrice now strayed carelessly through the garden, approaching closer beneath Giovanni's window, so that he was compelled to thrust his head quite out of its concealment in order to gratify the intense and painful curiosity which she excited. At this moment there came a beautiful insect over the garden wall; it had, perhaps, wandered through the city, and found no flowers or verdure among those antique haunts of men until the heavy perfumes of Dr. Rappaccini's shrubs had lured it from afar. Without alighting on the flowers, this winged brightness seemed to be attracted by Beatrice, and lingered in the air and fluttered about her head. Now, here it could not be but that Giovanni Guasconti's eyes deceived him. Be that as it might, he fancied that, while Beatrice was gazing at the insect with childish delight, it grew faint and fell at her feet; its bright wings shivered; it was dead—from no cause that he could discern, unless it were the atmosphere of her breath. Again Beatrice crossed herself and sighed heavily as she bent over the dead insect.

An impulsive movement of Giovanni drew her eyes to the window. There she beheld the beautiful head of the young man—rather a Grecian than an Italian head, with fair, regular features, and a glistening of gold among his ringlets—gazing down upon her like a being that hovered in mid air. Scarcely knowing what he did, Giovanni threw down the bouquet which he had hitherto held in his hand.

"Signora," said he, "there are pure and healthful flowers. Wear them for the sake of Giovanni Guasconti."

"Thanks, signor," replied Beatrice, with her rich voice, that came forth as it were like a gush of music, and with a mirthful expression half childish and half woman-like. "I accept your gift, and would fain recompense it with this precious purple flower; but if I toss it into the air it will not reach you. So Signor Guasconti must even content himself with my thanks."

She lifted the bouquet from the ground, and then, as if inwardly ashamed at having stepped aside from her maidenly reserve to respond to a stranger's greeting, passed swiftly homeward through the garden. But few as the moments were, it seemed to Giovanni, when she was on the point of vanishing beneath the sculptured portal, that his beautiful bouquet was already beginning to wither in her grasp. It was an idle thought; there could be no possibility of distinguishing a faded flower from a fresh one at so great a distance.

For many days after this incident the young man avoided the window that looked into Dr. Rappaccini's garden, as if something ugly and monstrous would have blasted his eyesight had he been betrayed into a glance. He felt conscious of having put himself, to a certain extent, within the influence of an unintelligible power by the communication which he had opened with Beatrice. The wisest course would have been, if his heart were in any real danger, to quit his lodgings and Padua itself at once; the next wiser, to have accustomed himself, as far as possible, to the familiar and daylight view of Beatrice—thus bringing her rigidly and systematically within the limits of ordinary experience. Least of all, while avoiding her sight, ought Giovanni to have remained so near this extraordinary being that the proximity and possibility even of intercourse should give a kind of substance and reality to the wild vagaries which his imagination ran riot continually in producing. Guasconti had not a deep heart—or, at all events, its depths were not sounded now; but he had a quick fancy, and an ardent southern temperament, which rose every instant to a higher fever pitch. Whether or no Beatrice possessed those terrible attributes, that fatal breath, the affinity with those so beautiful and deadly flowers which were indicated by what Giovanni had witnessed, she had at least instilled a fierce and subtle poison into his system. It was not love, although her rich beauty was a madness to him; nor horror, even while he fancied her spirit to be imbued with the same baneful essence that seemed to pervade her physical frame; but a wild offspring of both love and horror that had each parent in it, and burned like one and shivered like the other. Giovanni knew not what to dread; still less did he know what to hope; yet hope and dread kept a continual warfare in his breast, alternately vanquishing one another and starting up afresh to renew the contest. Blessed are all simple emotions, be they dark or bright! It is the lurid intermixture of the two that produces the illuminating blaze of the infernal regions.

Sometimes he endeavored to assuage the fever of his spirit by a rapid walk through the streets of Padua or beyond its gates: his footsteps kept time with the throbbings of his brain, so that the walk was apt to accelerate itself to a race. One day he found himself arrested; his arm was seized by a portly personage, who had turned back on recognizing the young man and expended much breath in overtaking him.

"Signor Giovanni! Stay, my young friend!" cried he. "Have you forgotten me? That might well be the case if I were as much altered as yourself."

It was Baglioni, whom Giovanni had avoided ever since their first meeting, from a doubt that the professor's sagacity would look too deeply into his secrets. Endeavoring to recover himself, he stared forth wildly from his inner world into the outer one and spoke like a man in a dream.

"Yes; I am Giovanni Guasconti. You are Professor Pietro Baglioni. Now let me pass!"

"Not yet, not yet, Signor Giovanni Guasconti," said the professor, smiling, but at the same time scrutinizing the youth with an earnest glance. "What! did I grow up side by side with your father? and shall his son pass me like a stranger in these old streets of Padua? Stand still, Signor Giovanni; for we must have a word or two before we part."

"Speedily, then, most worshipful professor, speedily," said Giovanni, with feverish impatience. "Does not your worship see that I am in haste?"

Now, while he was speaking there came a man in black along the street, stooping and moving feebly like a person in inferior health. His face was all overspread with a most sickly and sallow hue, but yet so pervaded with an expression of piercing and active intellect that an observer might easily have overlooked the merely physical attributes and have seen only this wonderful energy. As he passed, this person exchanged a cold and distant salutation with Baglioni, but fixed his eyes upon Giovanni with an intentness that seemed to bring out whatever was within him worthy of notice. Nevertheless, there was a peculiar quietness in the look, as if taking merely a speculative, not a human, interest in the young man.

"It is Dr. Rappaccini!" whispered the professor when the stranger had passed. "Has he ever seen your face before?"

"Not that I know," answered Giovanni, starting at the name.

"He *has* seen you! he must have seen you!" said Baglioni, hastily. "For some purpose or other, this man of science is making a study of you. I know that look of his! It is the same that coldly illuminates his face as he bends over a bird, a mouse, or a butterfly, which, in pursuance of some experiment, he has killed by the perfume of a flower; a look as deep as Nature itself, but without Nature's warmth of love. Signor Giovanni, I will stake my life upon it, you are the subject of one of Rappaccini's experiments!"

"Will you make a fool of me?" cried Giovanni, passionately. "*That,* signor professor, were an untoward experiment."

"Patience! patience!" replied the imperturbable professor. "I tell thee, my poor Giovanni, that Rappaccini has a scientific interest in thee. Thou hast fallen into fearful hands! And the Signora Beatrice,—what part does she act in this mystery?"

But Guasconti, finding Baglioni's pertinacity intolerable, here broke away, and was gone before the professor could again seize his arm. He looked after the young man intently and shook his head.

"This must not be," said Baglioni to himself. "The youth is the son of my old friend, and shall not come to any harm from which the arcana of medical science can preserve him. Besides, it is too insufferable an impertinence in Rappaccini, thus to snatch the lad out of my own hands, as I may say, and make use of him for his infernal experiments. This daughter of his! It shall be looked to. Perchance, most learned Rappaccini, I may foil you where you little dream of it!"

Meanwhile Giovanni had pursued a circuitous route, and at length found himself at the door of his lodgings. As he crossed the threshold he was met by old Lisabetta, who smirked and smiled, and was evidently desirous to attract his attention; vainly, however, as the ebullition of his feelings had momentarily subsided into a cold and dull vacuity. He turned his eyes full upon the withered face that was puckering itself into a smile, but seemed to behold it not. The old dame, therefore, laid her grasp upon his cloak.

"Signor! signor!" whispered she, still with a smile over the whole breadth of her visage, so that it looked not unlike a grotesque carving in wood, darkened by centuries. "Listen, signor! There is a private entrance into the garden!"

"What do you say?" exclaimed Giovanni, turning quickly about, as if an inanimate thing should start into feverish life. "A private entrance into Dr. Rappaccini's garden?"

"Hush! hush! not so loud!" whispered Lisabetta, putting her hand over his mouth. "Yes; into the worshipful doctor's garden, where you may see all his fine shrubbery. Many a young man in Padua would give gold to be admitted among those flowers."

Giovanni put a piece of gold into her hand.

"Show me the way," said he.

A surmise, probably excited by his conversation with Baglioni, crossed his mind, that this interposition of old Lisabetta might perchance be connected with the intrigue, whatever were its nature, in which the professor seemed to suppose that Dr. Rappaccini was involving him. But such a suspicion, though it disturbed Giovanni, was inadequate to restrain him. The instant that he was aware of the possibility of approaching Beatrice, it seemed an absolute necessity of his existence to do so. It mattered not whether she were angel or demon; he was irrevocably within her sphere, and must obey the law that whirled him onward, in ever-lessening circles, towards a result which he did not attempt to foreshadow; and yet, strange to say, there came across him a sudden doubt whether this intense interest on his part were not delusory; whether it were really of so deep and positive a nature as to justify him in now thrusting himself into an incalculable position; whether it were not merely the fantasy of a young man's brain, only slightly or not at all connected with his heart.

He paused, hesitated, turned half about, but again went on. His withered guide led him along several obscure passages, and finally undid a door, through which, as it was opened, there came the sight and sound of rustling leaves, with the broken sunshine glimmering among them. Giovanni stepped forth, and, forcing himself through the entanglement of a shrub that wreathed its tendrils over the hidden entrance, stood beneath his own window in the open area of Dr. Rappaccini's garden.

How often is it the case that, when impossibilities have come to pass and dreams have condensed their misty substance into tangible realities, we find ourselves calm, and even coldly self-possessed, amid circumstances which it would have been a delirium of joy or agony to anticipate! Fate delights to thwart us thus. Passion will choose his own time to rush upon the scene, and lingers sluggishly behind when an appropriate adjustment of events would seem to summon his appearance. So was it now with Giovanni. Day after day his pulses had throbbed with feverish blood at the improbable idea of an interview with Beatrice, and of standing with her, face to face, in this very garden, basking in the Oriental sunshine of her beauty, and snatching from her full gaze the mystery which he deemed the riddle of his own existence. But now there was a singular and untimely equanimity within his breast. He threw a glance around the garden to discover if Beatrice or her father were present, and, perceiving that he was alone, began a critical observation of the plants.

The aspect of one and all of them dissatisfied him; their gorgeousness seemed fierce, passionate, and even unnatural. There was hardly an individual shrub which a wanderer, straying by himself through a forest, would not have been startled to find growing wild, as if an unearthly face had glared at him out of the thicket. Several also would have shocked a delicate instinct by an appearance of artificialness indicating that there had been such commixture, and, as it were, adultery, of various vegetable species, that the production was no longer of God's making, but the monstrous offspring of man's depraved fancy, glowing with only an evil mockery of beauty. They were probably the result of experiment, which in one or two cases had succeeded in mingling plants individually lovely into a compound possessing the questionable and ominous character that distinguished the whole growth of the garden. In fine, Giovanni recognized but two or three plants in the collection, and those of a kind that he well knew to be poisonous. While busy with these contemplations he heard the rustling of a silken garment, and, turning, beheld Beatrice emerging from beneath the sculptured portal.

Giovanni had not considered with himself what should be his deportment; whether he should apologize for his intrusion into the garden, or assume that he was there with the privity at least, if not by the desire, of Dr. Rappaccini or his daughter; but Beatrice's manner placed him at his ease, though leaving him still in doubt by what agency he had gained admittance. She came lightly along the path and met him near the broken fountain. There was surprise in her face, but brightened by a simple and kind expression of pleasure.

"You are a connoisseur in flowers, signor," said Beatrice, with a smile, alluding to the bouquet which he had flung her from the window. "It is no marvel, therefore, if the sight of my father's rare collection has tempted you to take a nearer view. If he were here, he could tell you many strange and interesting facts as to the nature and habits of these shrubs; for he has spent a lifetime in such studies, and this garden is his world."

"And yourself, lady," observed Giovanni, "if fame says true,—you likewise are deeply skilled in the virtues indicated by these rich blossoms and these spicy perfumes. Would you deign to be my instructress, I should prove an apter scholar than if taught by Signor Rappaccini himself."

"Are there such idle rumors?" asked Beatrice, with the music of a pleasant laugh. "Do people say that I am skilled in my father's science of plants? What a jest is there! No; though I have grown up among these flowers, I know no more of them than their hues and perfume; and sometimes methinks I would fain rid myself of even that small knowledge. There are many flowers here, and those not the least brilliant, that shock and offend me when they meet my eye. But pray, signor, do not believe these stories about my science. Believe nothing of me save what you see with your own eyes."

"And must I believe all that I have seen with my own eyes?" asked Giovanni, pointedly, while the recollection of former scenes made him shrink. "No, signora; you demand too little of me. Bid me believe nothing save what comes from your own lips."

It would appear that Beatrice understood him. There came a deep flush to her cheek; but she looked full into Giovanni's eyes, and responded to his gaze of uneasy suspicion with a queenlike haughtiness.

"I do so bid you, signor," she replied. "Forget whatever you may have fancied in regard to me. If true to the outward senses, still it may be false in its essence; but the words of Beatrice Rappaccini's lips are true from the depths of the heart outward. Those you may believe."

A fervor glowed in her whole aspect and beamed upon Giovanni's consciousness like the light of truth itself; but while she spoke there was a fragrance in the atmosphere around her, rich and delightful, though evanescent, yet which the young man, from an indefinable reluctance, scarcely dared to draw into his lungs. It might be the odor of the flowers. Could it be Beatrice's breath which thus embalmed her words with a strange richness, as if by steeping them in her heart? A faintness passed like a shadow over Giovanni and flitted away; he seemed to gaze through the beautiful girl's eyes into her transparent soul, and felt no more doubt or fear.

The tinge of passion that had colored Beatrice's manner vanished; she became gay, and appeared to derive a pure delight from her communion with the youth not unlike what the maiden of a lonely island might have felt conversing with a voyager from the civilized world. Evidently her experience of life had been confined within the limits of that garden. She talked now about matters as simple as the daylight or summer clouds, and now asked questions in reference to the city, or Giovanni's distant home, his friends, his mother, and his sisters—questions indicating such seclusion, and such lack of familiarity with modes and forms, that Giovanni responded as if to an infant. Her spirit gushed out before him like a fresh rill that was just catching its first glimpse of the sunlight and wondering at the reflections of earth and sky which were flung into its bosom. There came thoughts, too, from a deep source, and fantasies of a gemlike brilliancy, as if diamonds and rubies sparkled upward among the bubbles of the fountain. Ever and anon there gleamed across the young man's mind a sense of wonder that he should be walking side by side with the being who had so wrought upon his imagination, whom he had idealized in such hues of terror, in whom he had positively witnessed such manifestations of dreadful attributes,—that he should be conversing with Beatrice like a brother, and should find her so human and so maidenlike. But such reflections were only momentary; the effect of her character was too real not to make itself familiar at once.

In this free intercourse they had strayed through the garden, and now, after many turns among its avenues, were come to the shattered fountain, beside which grew the magnificent shrub, with its treasury of glowing blossoms. A fragrance was diffused from it which Giovanni recognized as identical with that which he had attributed to Beatrice's breath, but incomparably more powerful. As her eyes fell upon it, Giovanni beheld her press her hand to her bosom as if her heart were throbbing suddenly and painfully.

"For the first time in my life," murmured she, addressing the shrub, "I had forgotten thee."

"I remember, signora," said Giovanni, "that you once promised to reward me with one of these living gems for the bouquet which I had the happy boldness to fling to your feet. Permit me now to pluck it as a memorial of this interview."

He made a step towards the shrub with extended hand; but Beatrice darted forward, uttering a shriek that went through his heart like a dagger. She caught his hand and drew it back with the whole force of her slender figure. Giovanni felt her touch thrilling through his fibers.

"Touch it not!" exclaimed she, in a voice of agony. "Not for thy life! It is fatal!"

Then, hiding her face, she fled from him and vanished beneath the sculptured portal. As Giovanni followed her with his eyes, he beheld the emaciated figure and pale intelligence of Dr. Rappaccini, who had been watching the scene, he knew not how long, within the shadow of the entrance.

No sooner was Guasconti alone in his chamber than the image of Beatrice came back to his passionate musings, invested with all the witchery that had been gathering around it ever since his first glimpse of her, and now likewise imbued with a tender warmth of girlish womanhood. She was human; her nature was endowed with all gentle and feminine qualities; she was worthiest to be worshipped; she was capable, surely, on her part, of the height and heroism of love. Those tokens which he had hitherto considered as proofs of a frightful peculiarity in her physical and moral system were now either forgotten, or, by the subtle sophistry of passion transmitted into a golden crown of enchantment, rendering Beatrice the more admirable by so much as she was the more unique. Whatever had looked ugly was now beautiful; or, if incapable of such a change, it stole away and hid itself among those shapeless half ideas which throng the dim region beyond the daylight of our perfect consciousness. Thus did he spend the night, nor fell asleep until the dawn had begun to awake the slumbering flowers in Dr. Rappaccini's garden, whither Giovanni's dreams doubtless led him. Up rose the sun in his due season, and, flinging his beams upon the young man's eyelids, awoke him to a sense of pain. When thoroughly aroused, he became sensible of a burning and tingling agony in his hand—in his right hand—the very hand which Beatrice had grasped in her own when he was on the point of plucking one of the gemlike flowers. On the back of that hand there was now a purple print like that of four small fingers, and the likeness of a slender thumb upon his wrist.

Oh, how stubbornly does love,—or even that cunning semblance of love which flourishes in the imagination, but strikes no depth of root into the heart,—how stubbornly does it hold its faith until the moment comes when it is doomed to vanish into thin mist! Giovanni wrapped a handkerchief about his hand and wondered what evil thing had stung him, and soon forgot his pain in a reverie of Beatrice.

After the first interview, a second was in the inevitable course of what we call fate. A third; a fourth; and a meeting with Beatrice in the garden was no longer an incident in Giovanni's daily life, but the whole space in which he might be said to live; for the anticipation and memory of that ecstatic hour made up the remainder. Nor was it otherwise with the daughter of Rappaccini. She watched for the youth's appearance, and flew to his side with confidence as unreserved as if they had been playmates from early infancy—as if they were such playmates still. If, by any unwonted chance, he failed to come at the appointed moment, she stood beneath the window and sent up the rich sweetness of her tones to float around him in his chamber and echo and reverberate throughout his heart: "Giovanni! Giovanni! Why tarriest thou? Come down!" And down he hastened into that Eden of poisonous flowers.

But, with all this intimate familiarity, there was still a reserve in Beatrice's demeanor, so rigidly and invariably sustained that the idea of infringing it scarcely occurred to his imagination. By all appreciable signs, they loved; they had looked love with eyes that conveyed the holy secret from the depths of one soul into the depths of the other, as if it were too sacred to be whispered by the way; they had even spoken love in those gushes of passion when their spirits darted forth in articulated breath like tongues of long-hidden flame; and yet there had been no seal of lips, no clasp of hands, nor any slightest caress such as love claims and hallows. He had never touched one of the gleaming ringlets of her hair; her garment—so marked was the physical barrier between them—had never been waved against him by a breeze. On the few occasions when Giovanni had seemed tempted to overstep the limit, Beatrice grew so sad, so stern, and withal wore such a look of desolate separation, shuddering at itself, that not a spoken word was requisite to repel him. At such times he was startled at the horrible suspicions that rose, monster-like, out of the caverns of his heart and stared him in the face; his love grew thin and faint as the morning mist, his doubts alone had substance. But, when Beatrice's face brightened again after the momentary shadow, she was transformed at once from the mysterious, questionable being whom he had watched with so much awe and horror; she was now the beautiful and unsophisticated girl whom he felt that his spirit knew with a certainty beyond all other knowledge.

A considerable time had now passed since Giovanni's last meeting with Baglioni. One morning, however, he was disagreeably surprised by a visit from the professor, whom he had scarcely thought of for whole weeks, and would willingly have forgotten still longer. Given up as he had long been to a pervading excitement, he could tolerate no companions except upon condition of their perfect sympathy with his present state of feeling. Such sympathy was not to be expected from Professor Baglioni.

The visitor chatted carelessly for a few moments about the gossip of the city and the university, and then took up another topic.

"I have been reading an old classic author lately," said he, "and met with a story[9] that strangely interested me. Possibly you may remember it. It is of an Indian prince, who sent a beautiful woman as a present to Alexander the Great. She was as lovely as the dawn and gorgeous as the sunset; but what especially distinguished her was a certain rich perfume in her breath—richer than a garden of Persian roses. Alexander, as was natural to a youthful conqueror, fell in love at first sight with this magnificent stranger; but a certain sage physician, happening to be present, discovered a terrible secret in regard to her."

"And what was that?" asked Giovanni, turning his eyes downward to avoid those of the professor.

"That this lovely woman," continued Baglioni, with emphasis, "had been nourished with poisons from her birth upward, until her whole nature was so imbued with them that she herself had become the deadliest poison in existence. Poison was her element of life. With that rich perfume of her breath she blasted the very air. Her love would have been poison—her embrace death. Is not this a marvellous tale?"

"A childish fable," answered Giovanni, nervously starting from his chair. "I marvel how your worship finds time to read such nonsense among your graver studies."

"By the by," said the professor, looking uneasily about him, "what singular fragrance is this in your apartment? Is it the perfume of your gloves? It is faint, but delicious; and yet, after all, by no means agreeable. Were I to breathe it long, methinks it would make me ill. It is like the breath of a flower; but I see no flowers in the chamber."

"Nor are there any," replied Giovanni, who had turned pale as the professor spoke; "nor, I think, is there any fragrance except in your worship's imagination. Odors, being a sort of element combined of the sensual and the spiritual, are apt to deceive us in this

[9] See *Vulgar Errors* (1646) by Sir Thomas Browne (1605–1682), English physician and author.

manner. The recollection of a perfume, the bare idea of it, may easily be mistaken for a present reality."

"Ay; but my sober imagination does not often play such tricks," said Baglioni; "and, were I to fancy any kind of odor, it would be that of some vile apothecary drug, wherewith my fingers are likely enough to be imbued. Our worshipful friend Rappaccini, as I have heard, tinctures his medicaments with odors richer than those of Araby. Doubtless, likewise, the fair and learned Signora Beatrice would minister to her patients with draughts as sweet as a maiden's breath; but woe to him that sips them!"

Giovanni's face evinced many contending emotions. The tone in which the professor alluded to the pure and lovely daughter of Rappaccini was a torture to his soul; and yet the intimation of a view of her character, opposite to his own, gave instantaneous distinctness to a thousand dim suspicions, which now grinned at him like so many demons. But he strove hard to quell them and to respond to Baglioni with a true lover's perfect faith.

"Signor professor," said he, "you were my father's friend; perchance, too, it is your purpose to act a friendly part towards his son. I would fain feel nothing towards you save respect and deference; but I pray you to observe, signor, that there is one subject on which we must not speak. You know not the Signora Beatrice. You cannot, therefore, estimate the wrong—the blasphemy, I may even say—that is offered to her character by a light or injurious word."

"Giovanni! my poor Giovanni!" answered the professor, with a calm expression of pity, "I know this wretched girl far better than yourself. You shall hear the truth in respect to the poisoner Rappaccini and his poisonous daughter; yes, poisonous as she is beautiful. Listen; for, even should you do violence to my gray hairs, it shall not silence me. That old fable of the Indian woman has become a truth by the deep and deadly science of Rappaccini and in the person of the lovely Beatrice."

Giovanni groaned and hid his face.

"Her father," continued Baglioni, "was not restrained by natural affection from offering up his child in this horrible manner as the victim of his insane zeal for science; for, let us do him justice, he is as true a man of science as ever distilled his own heart in an alembic.[10] What, then, will be your fate? Beyond a doubt you are selected as the material of some new experiment. Perhaps the result is to be death; perhaps a fate more awful still. Rappaccini, with what he calls the interest of science before his eyes, will hesitate at nothing."

"It is a dream," muttered Giovanni to himself; "surely it is a dream."

"But," resumed the professor, "be of good cheer, son of my friend. It is not yet too late for the rescue. Possibly we may even succeed in bringing back this miserable child within the limits of ordinary nature, from which her father's madness has estranged her. Behold this little silver vase! It was wrought by the hands of the renowned Benvenuto Cellini,[11] and is well worthy to be a love gift to the fairest dame in Italy. But its contents are invaluable. One little sip of this antidote would have rendered the most virulent poisons of the Borgias[12] innocuous. Doubt not that it will be as efficacious

---

[10] Laboratory device for distillation of substances.

[11] Italian artisan, artist, and writer Benvenuto Cellini (1500–1571).

[12] Aristocratic Italian family influential in Renaissance religion and politics, and notorious for its cruelty and licentiousness.

against those of Rappaccini. Bestow the vase, and the precious liquid within it, on your Beatrice, and hopefully await the result."

Baglioni laid a small, exquisitely wrought silver vial on the table and withdrew, leaving what he had said to produce its effect upon the young man's mind.

"We will thwart Rappaccini yet," thought he, chuckling to himself, as he descended the stairs; "but, let us confess the truth of him, he is a wonderful man—a wonderful man indeed; a vile empiric, however, in his practice, and therefore not to be tolerated by those who respect the good old rules of the medical profession."

Throughout Giovanni's whole acquaintance with Beatrice, he had occasionally, as we have said, been haunted by dark surmises as to her character; yet so thoroughly had she made herself felt by him as a simple, natural, most affectionate, and guileless creature, that the image now held up by Professor Baglioni looked as strange and incredible as if it were not in accordance with his own original conception. True, there were ugly recollections connected with his first glimpses of the beautiful girl; he could not quite forget the bouquet that withered in her grasp, and the insect that perished amid the sunny air, by no ostensible agency save the fragrance of her breath. These incidents, however, dissolving in the pure light of her character, had no longer the efficacy of facts, but were acknowledged as mistaken fantasies, by whatever testimony of the senses they might appear to be substantiated. There is something truer and more real than what we can see with the eyes and touch with the finger. On such better evidence had Giovanni founded his confidence in Beatrice, though rather by the necessary force of her high attributes than by any deep and generous faith on his part. But now his spirit was incapable of sustaining itself at the height to which the early enthusiasm of passion had exalted it; he fell down, grovelling among earthly doubts, and defiled therewith the pure whiteness of Beatrice's image. Not that he gave her up; he did but distrust. He resolved to institute some decisive test that should satisfy him, once for all, whether there were those dreadful peculiarities in her physical nature which could not be supposed to exist without some corresponding monstrosity of soul. His eyes, gazing down afar, might have deceived him as to the lizard, the insect, and the flowers; but if he could witness, at the distance of a few paces, the sudden blight of one fresh and healthful flower in Beatrice's hand, there would be room for no further question. With this idea he hastened to the florist's and purchased a bouquet that was still gemmed with the morning dew-drops.

It was now the customary hour of his daily interview with Beatrice. Before descending into the garden, Giovanni failed not to look at his figure in the mirror,—a vanity to be expected in a beautiful young man, yet, as displaying itself at that troubled and feverish moment, the token of a certain shallowness of feeling and insincerity of character. He did gaze, however, and said to himself that his features had never before possessed so rich a grace, nor his eyes such vivacity, nor his cheeks so warm a hue of super-abundant life.

"At least," thought he, "her poison has not yet insinuated itself into my system. I am no flower to perish in her grasp."

With that thought he turned his eyes on the bouquet, which he had never once laid aside from his hand. A thrill of indefinable horror shot through his frame on perceiving that those dewy flowers were already beginning to droop; they wore the aspect of things that had been fresh and lovely yesterday. Giovanni grew white as marble, and stood motionless before the mirror, staring at his own reflection there as at the likeness of something frightful. He remembered Baglioni's remark about the fragrance that seemed to pervade the chamber. It must have been the poison in his breath! Then he shuddered—shuddered at himself. Recovering from his stupor, he began to watch with curious eye a spider that was busily at work hanging its web from the antique cornice of the apartment, crossing and recrossing the artful system of interwoven lines—as vigorous and active a spider as ever dangled from an old ceiling. Giovanni bent towards the insect, and emitted a deep, long breath. The spider suddenly ceased its toil; the web vibrated with a tremor originating in the body of the small artisan. Again Giovanni sent forth a breath, deeper, longer, and imbued with a venomous feeling out of his heart: he knew not whether he were wicked, or only desperate. The spider made a convulsive gripe with his limbs and hung dead across the window.

"Accursed! accursed!" muttered Giovanni, addressing himself. "Hast thou grown so poisonous that this deadly insect perishes by thy breath?"

At that moment a rich, sweet voice came floating up from the garden.

"Giovanni! Giovanni! It is past the hour! Why tarriest thou? Come down!"

"Yes," muttered Giovanni again. "She is the only being whom my breath may not slay! Would that it might!"

He rushed down, and in an instant was standing before the bright and loving eyes of Beatrice. A moment ago his wrath and despair had been so fierce that he could have desired nothing so much as to wither her by a glance; but with her actual presence there came influences which had too real an existence to be at once shaken off: recollections of the delicate and benign power of her feminine nature, which had so often enveloped him in a religious calm; recollections of many a holy and passionate outgush of her heart, when the pure fountain had been unsealed from its depths and made visible in its transparency to his mental eye; recollections which, had Giovanni known how to estimate them, would have assured him that all this ugly mystery was but an earthly illusion, and that, whatever mist of evil might seem to have gathered over her, the real Beatrice was a heavenly angel. Incapable as he was of such high faith, still her presence had not utterly lost its magic. Giovanni's rage was quelled into an aspect of sullen insensibility. Beatrice, with a quick spiritual sense, immediately felt that there was a gulf of blackness between them which neither he nor she could pass. They walked on together, sad and silent, and came thus to the marble fountain and to its pool of water on the ground, in the midst of which grew the shrub that bore gem-like blossoms. Giovanni was affrighted at the eager enjoyment—the appetite, as it were—with which he found himself inhaling the fragrance of the flowers.

"Beatrice," asked he, abruptly, "whence came this shrub?"

"My father created it," answered she, with simplicity.

"Created it! created it!" repeated Giovanni. "What mean you, Beatrice?"

"He is a man fearfully acquainted with the secrets of Nature," replied Beatrice; "and, at the hour when I first drew breath, this plant sprang from the soil, the offspring of his science, of his intellect, while I was but his earthly child. Approach it not!" continued she, observing with terror that Giovanni was drawing nearer to the shrub. "It has qualities that you little dream of. But I, dearest Giovanni,—I grew up and blossomed with the plant and was nourished with its breath. It was my sister, and I loved it with a human affection; for, alas!—hast thou not suspected it?—there was an awful doom."

Here Giovanni frowned so darkly upon her that Beatrice paused and trembled. But her faith in his tenderness reassured her, and made her blush that she had doubted for an instant.

"There was an awful doom," she continued, "the effect of my father's fatal love of science, which estranged me from all society of my kind. Until Heaven sent thee, dearest Giovanni, oh, how lonely was thy poor Beatrice!"

"Was it a hard doom?" asked Giovanni, fixing his eyes upon her.

"Only of late have I known how hard it was," answered she, tenderly. "Oh, yes; but my heart was torpid, and therefore quiet."

Giovanni's rage broke forth from his sullen gloom like a lightning flash out of a dark cloud.

"Accursed one!" cried he, with venomous scorn and anger. "And, finding thy solitude wearisome, thou hast severed me likewise from all the warmth of life and enticed me into thy region of unspeakable horror!"

"Giovanni!" exclaimed Beatrice, turning her large bright eyes upon his face. The force of his words had not found its way into her mind; she was merely thunderstruck.

"Yes, poisonous thing!" repeated Giovanni, beside himself with passion. "Thou hast done it! Thou hast blasted me! Thou hast filled my veins with poison! Thou hast made me as hateful, as ugly, as loathsome and deadly a creature as thyself—a world's wonder of hideous monstrosity! Now, if our breath be happily as fatal to ourselves as to all others, let us join our lips in one kiss of unutterable hatred, and so die!"

"What has befallen me?" murmured Beatrice, with a low moan out of her heart. "Holy Virgin, pity me, a poor heart-broken child!"

"Thou,—dost thou pray?" cried Giovanni, still with the same fiendish scorn. "Thy very prayers, as they come from thy lips, taint the atmosphere with death. Yes, yes; let us pray! Let us to church and dip our fingers in the holy water at the portal! They that come after us will perish as by a pestilence! Let us sign crosses in the air! It will be scattering curses abroad in the likeness of holy symbols!"

"Giovanni," said Beatrice, calmly, for her grief was beyond passion, "why dost thou join thyself with me thus in those terrible words? I, it is true, am the horrible thing thou namest. But thou,—what hast thou to do, save with one other shudder at my hideous misery to go forth out of the garden and mingle with thy race, and forget that there ever crawled on earth such a monster as poor Beatrice?"

"Dost thou pretend ignorance?" asked Giovanni, scowling upon her. "Behold! this power have I gained from the pure daughter of Rappaccini."

There was a swarm of summer insects flitting through the air in search of the food promised by the flower odors of the fatal garden. They circled round Giovanni's head, and were evidently attracted towards him by the same influence which had drawn them for an instant within the sphere of several of the shrubs. He sent forth a breath among them, and smiled bitterly at Beatrice as at least a score of the insects fell dead upon the ground.

"I see it! I see it!" shrieked Beatrice. "It is my father's fatal science! No, no, Giovanni; it was not I! Never! never! I dreamed only to love thee and be with thee a little time, and so to let thee pass away, leaving but thine image in mine heart; for, Giovanni, believe it, though my body be nourished with poison, my spirit is God's creature, and craves love as its daily food. But my father,—he has united us in this fearful sympathy. Yes; spurn me, tread upon me, kill me! Oh, what is death after such words as thine? But it was not I. Not for a world of bliss would I have done it."

Giovanni's passion had exhausted itself in its outburst from his lips. There now came across him a sense, mournful, and not without tenderness, of the intimate and peculiar relationship between Beatrice and himself. They stood, as it were, in an utter solitude, which would be made none the less solitary by the densest throng of human life. Ought not, then, the desert of humanity around them to press this insulated pair closer together? If they should be cruel to one another, who was there to be kind to them? Besides, thought Giovanni, might there not still be a hope of his returning within the limits of ordinary nature, and leading Beatrice, the redeemed Beatrice, by the hand? O, weak, and selfish, and unworthy spirit, that could dream of an earthly union and earthly happiness as possible, after such deep love had been so bitterly wronged as was Beatrice's love by Giovanni's blighting words! No, no; there could be no such hope. She must pass heavily, with that broken heart, across the borders of Time—she must bathe her hurts in some fount of paradise, and forget her grief in the light of immortality, and *there* be well.

But Giovanni did not know it.

"Dear Beatrice," said he, approaching her, while she shrank away as always at his approach, but now with a different impulse, "dearest Beatrice, our fate is not yet so desperate. Behold! there is a medicine, potent, as a wise physician has assured me, and almost divine in its efficacy. It is composed of ingredients the most opposite to those by which thy awful father has brought this calamity upon thee and me. It is distilled of blessed herbs. Shall we not quaff it together, and thus be purified from evil?"

"Give it me!" said Beatrice, extending her hand to receive the little silver vial which Giovanni took from his bosom. She added, with a peculiar emphasis, "I will drink; but do thou await the result."

She put Baglioni's antidote to her lips; and, at the same moment, the figure of Rappaccini emerged from the portal and came slowly towards the marble fountain. As he drew near, the pale man of science seemed to gaze with a triumphant expression at the beautiful youth and maiden, as might an artist who should spend his life in achieving a picture or a group of statuary and finally be satisfied with his success. He paused; his bent form grew erect with conscious power; he spread out his hands over them in the attitude of a father imploring a blessing upon his children; but those were the same hands that had thrown poison into the stream of their lives. Giovanni trembled. Beatrice shuddered nervously, and pressed her hand upon her heart.

"My daughter," said Rappaccini, "thou art no longer lonely in the world. Pluck one of those precious gems from thy sister shrub and bid thy bridegroom wear it in his bosom. It will not harm him now. My science and the sympathy between thee and him have so wrought within his system that he now stands apart from common men, as thou dost, daughter of my pride and triumph, from ordinary women. Pass on, then, through the world, most dear to one another and dreadful to all besides!"

"My father," said Beatrice, feebly,—and still as she spoke she kept her hand upon her heart,—"wherefore didst thou inflict this miserable doom upon thy child?"

"Miserable!" exclaimed Rappaccini. "What mean you, foolish girl? Dost thou deem it misery to be endowed with marvellous gifts against which no power nor strength could avail an enemy—misery, to be able to quell the mightiest with a breath—misery, to be as terrible as thou art beautiful? Wouldst thou, then, have preferred the condition of a weak woman, exposed to all evil and capable of none?"

"I would fain have been loved, not feared," murmured Beatrice, sinking down upon the ground. "But now it matters not. I am going, father, where the evil which thou hast striven to mingle with my being will pass away like a dream—like the fragrance of these poisonous flowers, which will no longer taint my breath among the flowers of Eden. Farewell, Giovanni! Thy words of hatred are like lead within my heart; but they, too, will fall away as I ascend. Oh, was there not, from the first, more poison in thy nature than in mine?"

To Beatrice,—so radically had her earthly part been wrought upon by Rappaccini's skill,—as poison had been life, so the powerful antidote was death; and thus the poor victim of man's ingenuity and of thwarted nature, and of the fatality that attends all such efforts of perverted wisdom, perished there, at the feet of her father and Giovanni. Just at that moment Professor Pietro Baglioni looked forth from the window, and called loudly, in a tone of triumph mixed with horror, to the thunderstricken man of science,—

"Rappaccini! Rappaccini! and is *this* the upshot of your experiment!"

1844

Herman Melville
1819–1891

The twentieth century recognizes Herman Melville as a major American writer, but in his lifetime Melville was regarded only as an exciting and once-popular travel writer those strange fiction cast doubt on his sanity. Melville traced his ancestry to two Revolutionary War figures. The family took pride in its ties to American history. Typical of their educated merchant class, they enrolled Herman, the third child of eight, at the New York Male High School at the age of seven. When Allan Melville's business was sent bankrupt, however, the family moved to Albany where young Herman pursued the commercial course. But once again Allan suffered business reverses, which led to the mental and physical breakdown that preceded his death in 1832.

Melville's next years were a scramble for a career. Forced to leave school, he became successively a bank clerk, a farmhand on his uncle Thomas's western Massachusetts acreage, a store clerk and bookkeeper for his successful older brother Gansvoort, and, when Gansvoort's business failed, a country schoolmaster. Hoping in vain for work on the new Erie Canal, Melville looked downstate, toward New York City, where a packet of Liverpool had a berth for him. Melville's maritime experience continued in 1841, when he shipped out from New Bedford, Massachusetts, on the whaling ship *Acushnet*, bound for the South Pacific.

Melville's maritime adventures have been well documented. The *Acushner* killed few whales. As a result, morale sank as dissension mounted between the captain and officers. With a shipmate, Melville jumped ship in the summer of 1842 and lived with a native tribe in the Marquesas for several weeks. Picked up by an Australian whaler, he participated in a revolt that landed him in a Tahiti prison along with a physician-companion, who later helped him explore the flora and fauna of Tahiti and Eimeo, where Melville shipped aboard a Nantucket whaler. Discharged at Honolulu, Melville stayed in Hawaii for a few months as a beachcomber, then signed on to the frigate *United States*. That ship's captain of the maintop, John J. ("Jack") Chase, proved to be a Melvillian hero (Billy Budd is dedicated to him). The *United States* toured the Pacific before sailing for Boston, arriving in autumn 1844, when Melville was twenty-five years old and, after drawing his pay, an unemployed sailor.

Melville's literary career began with fictionalized versions of his South Sea adventures. *Typee* (1846) and *Omoo* (1847) were popular successes with American and English readers eager for tales of exotic places. Some close readers were offended by Melville's critique of the missionaries who "evangelized" and "civilized" the islanders into "draft horses" or "beasts of burden," but prospects were generally bright for the young author.

Largely on the strength of his prospects as a professional author, Melville married Elizabeth Shaw and settled in New York City in a house that also accommodated his younger brother Allan and Allan's new bride, Melville's mother, and his unmarried sisters. He also took his place in the New York literary life. Had he continued to write adventure stories in the mold of his early books, he might have been a financially successful "pen-and-ink man" and a footnote in literary history. Instead, Melville's third novel, *Mardi*, took a radical midway departure into philosophy, satire, fantasy, and allegory. The young writer had discovered the works of Robert Burton, Sir Thomas Browne, Francois Rabelais, and others and, encouraged by their example, broke the bounds of conventional form. He was taken aback when the public spurned his efforts and reviewers urged him to resume the style and structure of his adventure narratives.

Melville now faced the terrible problem common to American writers from the eighteenth century into the twentieth. To earn a living from the sale of his books, he needed to win the very readers who professed values and beliefs he attacked. How could he possibly find favor with a public that wished only to be entertained, when he offered probing, experimental, critical writings in the face of social complacency? The issue was especially pressing because Melville now had an infant son, Malcolm, to support. Chastened, he wrote two novels intended to satisfy popular taste, *Redburn* (1849) and *White-Jacket* (1850), based respectively on his youthful Liverpool voyage and on his South Pacific tour. Though Melville called both books the literary equivalent of "sawing wood," each sold well in the United States and Europe.

A newly confident Melville now began his whaling book. Initially he may have intended once again to write an adventure story based on his experiences on whaling ships. But Melville had been rereading Shakespeare and the works of Thomas Carlyle. He also had made the acquaintance of Nathaniel Hawthorne, whom he would soon call an American Shakespeare in a review essay titled "Hawthorne and His Mosses," a survey of the state of American writers in the English-speaking world. In *Moby-Dick,* Melville continued to unfold his psyche. Style and structure of the new work embodied the change. He was relentlessly speculative, posing challenge to the literary and social status quo, probing society's hypocrisies, its complacency, its contradictions.

Meanwhile, the crowded conditions of the New York City household made it necessary for Melville to move his family. Western Massachusetts had become a summer resort for American writers, who picnicked together in an occasional "pleasure party." Doubtlessly anticipating the seasonal literary comradeship, Melville moved his family to a 160-acre farm called Arrowhead in autumn 1850. The farm was purchased in part with a loan from the formidable Judge Lemuel Shaw, Melville's father-in-law. By winter Melville had completed his book on whaling, which he revised in the study whose window looked out upon Mt. Greylock, its peak shaped rather like the outline of a whale. Customarily Melville wrote into the afternoon, then read and gathered materials in the evening and at night. His meals were sometimes served on trays left at his study door. Beyond the door and walls he could hear all household noises.

Moby-Dick (1851) was published to a mixed reception, and sales were disappointing. This masculine, experimental novel did not appeal to a novel-reading public principally comprising women. By now Melville was financially pressed, in debt to his publisher, Harper, for advances, and responsible for a household that included his mother, his sisters, one small child, and a pregnant wife. Once again he attempted to capture a popular audience, this time with a long, deliberately sentimental Gothic novel, *Pierre,* a dark exploration of sexuality, identity, depravity, tragic, and inevitable destruction, and, covertly, the plight of the American artist. The reception of the book was hostile. Reviewers attacked Melville personally. Everette Duyckinck, a reviewer who had thought *Moby-Dick* immoral, was scandalized and concluded that Melville had gone insane.

Under severe personal and financial strain, Melville turned to short fiction (for example, "Bartleby, the Scrivener"), which he wrote for such magazines as *Harper's* and *Putnam's,* and cast in a style intended to be accessible to a large readership. "The Paradise of Bachelors and the Tartarus of Maids," a commentary on industrial conditions and on men's and women's lives is characteristic of this work.

Melville went abroad alone in 1856 for his health under the financial sponsorship of his family. In 1866, Harper published his Civil War Poems, *Battle-Pieces,* though that work, too, was soon forgotten. Melville seemed destined, as he once observed to Hawthorne, to be known as "the man who lived among the cannibals." Considered a failure by his in-laws, Melville at least obtained a political job in 1866 as deputy inspector of customs in New York City. Through the 1860s and 1870s he worked on *Clarel,* an eighteen-thousand-line poem, in which this "pondering man," as Melville called himself, explored the relation between religious faith and skepticism in the age of Darwinian theory.

Melville's last years were tragic and ironic. Several bequests left him and his wife materially comfortable, but his first child, Malcolm, had committed suicide in 1867, and his second, Stanwyx, had become a drifter; Stanwyx died in San Francisco in 1886. One of his daughters, Bessie, was severely arthritic; and the second, Frances, felt only bitterness towards her father. In the late 1880s Melville wrote *Billy Budd,* a work perhaps motivated by the suicide of his son and found nearly complete among his papers after his death. *Billy Budd* was published in 1924 and stands as a major achievement in American Literature. When Melville died, a newspaper obituary speculated that "his own generation has long thought him dead." Hawthorne had already offered a fitting epitaph: "He was a very high and noble nature, and better worth immortality than most of us."

Further Reading:
R. Chase, *Herman Melville: A Critical Study,* 1949.
N. Arvin, *Herman Melville,* 1950, 1957.
J. Leyda, *The Melville Log,* 2 vols., 1951, 1969.
L. Howard, *Herman Melville,* 1951, 1958.
M. Davis and W. Gilman, eds., *The Letters of Herman Melville,* 1960.

J. Seelye, *Melville: The Ironic Diagram,* 1970.
T. Herbert, *Marquesan Encounters,* 1981.
J. Bryant, *Melville and Repose,* 1993.
D. Robillard, *Melville and the Visual Arts,* 1997.
R. Levine, *The Cambridge Companion to Herman Melville,* 1998.

Texts:
"Bartleby" and "Benito Cerino" from *The Piazza Tales*, ed. E. Oliver, 1962.
"The Paradise of Bachelors . . . " from *Complete Stories of Herman Melville*, ed. J. Leyda, 1948.
Billy Budd, Sailor, ed. H. Hayford and M. Sealts, 1962.
Battle Pieces and Aspects of the War, 1866.
Timoleon selections from *The Collected Poems*, ed. H. P. Vincent, 1948, 1981.

See also *The Works of Herman Melville*, 16 vols., 1922–1924, 1963.
Writings of Herman Melville, 16 vols. projected, 15 published, ed. H. Hayford, 1968–.
The Portable Melville, ed. J. Leyda, 1952.
Selected Poems of Herman Melville, ed. H. Cohen, 1964.

Bartleby, the Scrivener:
A Tale of Wall Street

I am a rather elderly man. The nature of my avocations, for the last thirty years, has brought me into more than ordinary contact with what would seem an interesting and somewhat singular set of men, of whom, as yet, nothing, that I know of, has ever been written—I mean, the law-copyists, or scriveners. I have known very many of them, professionally and privately, and, if I pleased, could relate divers histories, at which good-natured gentlemen might smile, and sentimental souls might weep. But I waive the biographies of all other scriveners, for a few passages in the life of Bartleby, who was a scrivener, the strangest I ever saw, or heard of. While, of other law-copyists, I might write the complete life, of Bartleby nothing of that sort can be done. I believe that no materials exist, for a full and satisfactory biography of this man. It is an irreparable loss to literature. Bartleby was one of those beings of whom nothing is ascertainable, except from the original sources, and, in his case, those are very small. What my own astonished eyes saw of Bartleby, *that* is all I know of him, except, indeed, one vague report, which will appear in the sequel.

Ere introducing the scrivener, as he first appeared to me, it is fit I make some mention of myself, my *employés,* my business, my chambers, and general surroundings; because some such description is indispensable to an adequate understanding of the chief character about to be presented. Imprimis: I am a man who, from his youth upwards, has been filled with a profound conviction that the easiest way of life is the best. Hence, though I belong to a profession proverbially energetic and nervous, even to turbulence, at times, yet nothing of that sort have I ever suffered to invade my peace. I am one of those unambitious lawyers who never addresses a jury, or in any way draws down public applause; but, in the cool tranquillity of a snug retreat, do a snug business among rich men's bonds, and mortgages, and title-deeds. All who know me, consider me an eminently *safe* man. The late John Jacob Astor, a personage little given to poetic enthusiasm, had no hesitation in pronouncing my first grand point to be prudence; my next, method. I do not speak it in vanity, but simply record the fact, that I was not unemployed in my profession by the late John Jacob Astor; a name which, I admit, I love to repeat; for it hath a rounded and orbicular sound to it, and rings like unto bullion. I will freely add, that I was not insensible to the late John Jacob Astor's good opinion.

Some time prior to the period at which this little history begins, my avocations had been largely increased. The good old office, now extinct in the State of New York, of a

Master in Chancery, had been conferred upon me. It was not a very arduous office, but very pleasantly remunerative. I seldom lose my temper; much more seldom indulge in dangerous indignation at wrongs and outrages; but, I must be permitted to be rash here, and declare, that I consider the sudden and violent abrogation of the office of Master in Chancery, by the new Constitution, as a—premature act; inasmuch as I had counted upon a life-lease of the profits, whereas I only received those of a few short years. But this is by the way.

My chambers were up stairs, at No. ——— Wall Street. At one end, they looked upon the white wall of the interior of a spacious sky-light shaft, penetrating the building from top to bottom.

This view might have been considered rather tame than otherwise, deficient in what landscape painters call "life." But, if so, the view from the other end of my chambers offered, at least, a contrast, if nothing more. In that direction, my windows commanded an unobstructed view of a lofty brick wall, black by age and everlasting shade; which wall required no spy-glass to bring out its lurking beauties, but, for the benefit of all near-sighted spectators, was pushed up to within ten feet of my window panes. Owing to the great height of the surrounding buildings, and my chambers being on the second floor, the interval between this wall and mine not a little resembled a huge square cistern.

At the period just preceding the advent of Bartleby, I had two persons as copyists in my employment, and a promising lad as an office-boy. First, Turkey; second, Nippers; third, Ginger Nut. These may seem names, the like of which are not usually found in the Directory. In truth, they were nicknames, mutually conferred upon each other by my three clerks, and were deemed expressive of their respective persons or characters. Turkey was a short, pursy[1] Englishman, of about my own age—that is, somewhere not far from sixty. In the morning, one might say, his face was of a fine florid hue, but after twelve o'clock, meridian—his dinner hour—it blazed like a grate full of Christmas coals; and continued blazing—but, as it were, with a gradual wane—till six o'clock, P.M., or thereabouts; after which, I saw no more of the proprietor of the face, which, gaining its meridian with the sun, seemed to set with it, to rise, culminate, and decline the following day, with the like regularity and undiminished glory. There are many singular coincidences I have known in the course of my life, not the least among which was the fact, that, exactly when Turkey displayed his fullest beams from his red and radiant countenance, just then, too, at that critical moment, began the daily period when I considered his business capacities as seriously disturbed for the remainder of the twenty-four hours. Not that he was absolutely idle, or averse to business, then; far from it. The difficulty was, he was apt to be altogether too energetic. There was a strange, inflamed, flurried, flighty recklessness of activity about him. He would be incautious in dipping his pen into his inkstand. All his blots upon my documents were dropped there after twelve o'clock, meridian. Indeed, not only would he be reckless, and sadly given to making blots in the afternoon, but, some days, he went further, and was rather noisy. At such times, too, his face flamed with augmented blazonry, as if cannel coal had been heaped on anthracite. He made an unpleasant racket with his chair; spilled his sandbox; in mending his pens, impatiently split them all to pieces, and threw them on the floor in a sudden passion; stood up, and leaned over his table, boxing his papers about

[1] Short-winded, especially from fatness.

in a most indecorous manner, very sad to behold in an elderly man like him. Nevertheless, as he was in many ways a most valuable person to me, and all the time before twelve o'clock, meridian, was the quickest, steadiest creature, too, accomplishing a great deal of work in a style not easily to be matched—for these reasons, I was willing to overlook his eccentricities, though, indeed, occasionally, I remonstrated with him. I did this very gently, however, because, though the civilest, nay, the blandest and most reverential of men in the morning, yet, in the afternoon, he was disposed, upon provocation, to be slightly rash with his tongue—in fact, insolent. Now, valuing his morning services as I did, and resolved not to lose them—yet, at the same time, made uncomfortable by his inflamed ways after twelve o'clock—and being a man of peace, unwilling by my admonitions to call forth unseemly retorts from him, I took upon me, one Saturday noon (he was always worse on Saturdays) to hint to him, very kindly, that, perhaps, now that he was growing old, it might be well to abridge his labors; in short, he need not come to my chambers after twelve o'clock, but, dinner over, had best go home to his lodgings, and rest himself till tea-time. But no; he insisted upon his afternoon devotions. His countenance became intolerably fervid, as he oratorically assured me—gesticulating with a long ruler at the other end of the room—that if his services in the morning were useful, how indispensable, then, in the afternoon?

"With submission, sir," said Turkey, on this occasion, "I consider myself your right-hand man. In the morning I but marshal and deploy my columns; but in the afternoon I put myself at their head, and gallantly charge the foe, thus"—and he made a violent thrust with the ruler.

"But the blots, Turkey," intimated I.

"True; but, with submission, sir, behold these hairs! I am getting old. Surely, sir, a blot or two of a warm afternoon is not to be severely urged against gray hairs. Old age—even if it blot the page—is honorable. With submission, sir, we *both* are getting old."

This appeal to my fellow-feeling was hardly to be resisted. At all events, I saw that go he would not. So, I made up my mind to let him stay, resolving, nevertheless, to see to it that, during the afternoon, he had to do with my less important papers.

Nippers, the second on my list, was a whiskered, sallow, and, upon the whole, rather piratical-looking young man, of about five and twenty. I always deemed him the victim of two evil powers—ambition and indigestion. The ambition was evinced by a certain impatience of the duties of a mere copyist, an unwarrantable usurpation of strictly professional affairs, such as the original drawing up of legal documents. The indigestion seemed betokened in an occasional nervous testiness and grinning irritability, causing the teeth to audibly grind together over mistakes committed in copying; unnecessary maledictions, hissed, rather than spoken, in the heat of business; and especially by a continual discontent with the height of the table where he worked. Though of a very ingenious mechanical turn, Nippers could never get this table to suit him. He put chips under it, blocks of various sorts, bits of pasteboard, and at last went so far as to attempt an exquisite adjustment, by final pieces of folded blotting-paper. But no invention would answer. If, for the sake of easing his back, he brought the table lid at a sharp angle well up towards his chin, and wrote there like a man using the steep roof of a Dutch house for his desk, then he declared that it stopped the circulation in his arms. If now he lowered the table to his waistbands, and stooped over it in writing, then there was a sore aching in his back. In short, the truth of the matter was, Nippers knew not what he wanted. Or, if he wanted anything, it was to be rid of a scrivener's table altogether.

Among the manifestations of his diseased ambition was a fondness he had for receiving visits from certain ambiguous-looking fellows in seedy coats, whom he called his clients. Indeed, I was aware that not only was he, at times, considerable of a ward-politician, but he occasionally did a little business at the Justices' courts, and was not unknown on the steps of the Tombs. I have good reason to believe, however, that one individual who called upon him at my chambers, and who, with a grand air, he insisted was his client, was no other than a dun,[2] and the alleged title-deed, a bill. But, with all his failings, and the annoyances he caused me, Nippers, like his compatriot Turkey, was a very useful man to me; wrote a neat, swift hand; and, when he chose, was not deficient in a gentlemanly sort of deportment. Added to this, he always dressed in a gentlemanly sort of way; and so, incidentally, reflected credit upon my chambers. Whereas, with respect to Turkey, I had much ado to keep him from being a reproach to me. His clothes were apt to look oily, and smell of eating-houses. He wore his pantaloons very loose and baggy in summer. His coats were execrable; his hat not to be handled. But while the hat was a thing of indifference to me, inasmuch as his natural civility and deference, as a dependent Englishman, always led him to doff it the moment he entered the room, yet his coat was another matter. Concerning his coats, I reasoned with him; but with no effect. The truth was, I suppose, that a man with so small an income could not afford to sport such a lustrous face and a lustrous coat at one and the same time. As Nippers once observed, Turkey's money went chiefly for red ink. One winter day, I presented Turkey with a highly respectable-looking coat of my own—a padded gray coat, of a most comfortable warmth, and which buttoned straight up from the knee to the neck. I thought Turkey would appreciate the favor, and abate his rashness and obstreperousness of afternoons. But no; I verily believe that buttoning himself up in so downy and blanket-like a coat had a pernicious effect upon him—upon the same principle that too much oats are bad for horses. In fact, precisely as a rash, restive horse is said to feel his oats, so Turkey felt his coat. It made him insolent. He was a man whom prosperity harmed.

Though, concerning the self-indulgent habits of Turkey, I had my own private surmises, yet, touching Nippers, I was well persuaded that, whatever might be his faults in other respects, he was, at least, a temperate young man. But, indeed, nature herself seemed to have been his vintner, and, at his birth, charged him so thoroughly with an irritable, brandy-like disposition, that all subsequent potations were needless. When I consider how, amid the stillness of my chambers, Nippers would sometimes impatiently rise from his seat, and stooping over his table, spread his arms wide apart, seize the whole desk, and move it, and jerk it, with a grim, grinding motion on the floor, as if the table were a perverse voluntary agent, intent on thwarting and vexing him, I plainly perceive that, for Nippers, brandy-and-water were altogether superfluous.

It was fortunate for me that, owing to its peculiar cause—indigestion—the irritability and consequent nervousness of Nippers were mainly observable in the morning, while in the afternoon he was comparatively mild. So that, Turkey's paroxysms only coming on about twelve o'clock, I never had to do with their eccentricities at one time. Their fits relieved each other, like guards. When Nippers's was on, Turkey's was off; and *vice versa*. This was a good natural arrangement, under the circumstances.

Ginger Nut, the third on my list, was a lad, some twelve years old. His father was a car-man, ambitious of seeing his son on the bench instead of a cart, before he died. So

[2] Bill collector.

he sent him to my office, as student at law, errand-boy, cleaner and sweeper, at the rate of one dollar a week. He had a little desk to himself, but he did not use it much. Upon inspection, the drawer exhibited a great array of the shells of various sorts of nuts. Indeed, to this quick-witted youth, the whole noble science of the law was contained in a nutshell. Not the least among the employments of Ginger Nut, as well as one which he discharged with the most alacrity, was his duty as cake and apple purveyor for Turkey and Nippers. Copying law-papers being proverbially a dry, husky sort of business, my two scriveners were fain to moisten their mouths very often with Spitzenbergs,[3] to be had at the numerous stalls nigh the Custom House and Post Office. Also, they sent Ginger Nut very frequently for that peculiar cake—small, flat, round, and very spicy—after which he had been named by them. Of a cold morning, when business was but dull, Turkey would gobble up scores of these cakes, as if they were mere wafers—indeed, they sell them at the rate of six or eight for a penny—the scrape of his pen blending with the crunching of the crisp particles in his mouth. Of all the fiery afternoon blunders and flurried rashnesses of Turkey, was his once moistening a ginger-cake between his lips, and clapping it on to a mortgage, for a seal. I came within an ace of dismissing him then. But he mollified me by making an oriental bow, and saying—

"With submission, sir, it was generous of me to find you in stationery on my own account."

Now my original business—that of a conveyancer and title hunter, and drawer-up of recondite documents of all sorts[4]—was considerably increased by receiving the master's office. There was now great work for scriveners. Not only must I push the clerks already with me, but I must have additional help.

In answer to my advertisement, a motionless young man one morning stood upon my office threshold, the door being open, for it was summer. I can see that figure now—pallidly neat, pitiably respectable, incurably forlorn! It was Bartleby.

After a few words touching his qualifications, I engaged him, glad to have among my corps of copyists a man of so singularly sedate an aspect, which I thought might operate beneficially upon the flighty temper of Turkey, and the fiery one of Nippers.

I should have stated before that ground glass folding-doors divided my premises into two parts, one of which was occupied by my scriveners, the other by myself. According to my humor, I threw open these doors, or closed them. I resolved to assign Bartleby a corner by the folding-doors, but on my side of them, so as to have this quiet man within easy call, in case any trifling thing was to be done. I placed his desk close up to a small side-window in that part of the room, a window which originally had afforded a lateral view of certain grimy back-yards and bricks, but which, owing to subsequent erections, commanded at present no view at all, though it gave some light. Within three feet of the panes was a wall, and the light came down from far above, between two lofty buildings, as from a very small opening in a dome. Still further to a satisfactory arrangement, I procured a high green folding screen, which might entirely isolate Bartleby from my sight, though not remove him from my voice. And thus, in a manner, privacy and society were conjoined.

---

[3] Apples.

[4] Legal work beyond ordinary knowledge, such as drawing up deeds for property transfers or checking records to ascertain that there are no prior claims on property to be transferred.

At first, Bartleby did an extraordinary quantity of writing. As if long famishing for something to copy, he seemed to gorge himself on my documents. There was no pause for digestion. He ran a day and night line, copying by sun-light and by candle-light. I should have been quite delighted with his application, had he been cheerfully industrious. But he wrote on silently, palely, mechanically.

It is, of course, an indispensable part of a scrivener's business to verify the accuracy of his copy, word by word. Where there are two or more scriveners in an office, they assist each other in this examination, one reading from the copy, the other holding the original. It is a very dull, wearisome, and lethargic affair. I can readily imagine that, to some sanguine temperaments, it would be altogether intolerable. For example, I cannot credit that the mettlesome poet, Byron, would have contentedly sat down with Bartleby to examine a law document of, say five hundred pages, closely written in a crimpy hand.

Now and then, in the haste of business, it had been my habit to assist in comparing some brief document myself, calling Turkey or Nippers for this purpose. One object I had, in placing Bartleby so handy to me behind the screen, was, to avail myself of his services on such trivial occasions. It was on the third day, I think, of his being with me, and before any necessity had arisen for having his own writing examined, that, being much hurried to complete a small affair I had in hand, I abruptly called to Bartleby. In my haste and natural expectancy of instant compliance, I sat with my head bent over the original on my desk, and my right hand sideways, and somewhat nervously extended with the copy, so that, immediately upon emerging from his retreat, Bartleby might snatch it and proceed to business without the least delay.

In this very attitude did I sit when I called to him, rapidly stating what it was I wanted him to do—namely, to examine a small paper with me. Imagine my surprise, nay, my consternation, when, without moving from his privacy, Bartleby, in a singularly mild, firm voice, replied, "I would prefer not to."

I sat awhile in perfect silence, rallying my stunned faculties. Immediately it occurred to me that my ears had deceived me, or Bartleby had entirely misunderstood my meaning. I repeated my request in the clearest tone I could assume; but in quite as clear a one came the previous reply, "I would prefer not to."

"Prefer not to," echoed I, rising in high excitement, and crossing the room with a stride. "What do you mean? Are you moon-struck? I want you to help me compare this sheet here—take it," and I thrust it towards him.

"I would prefer not to," said he.

I looked at him steadfastly. His face was leanly composed; his gray eye dimly calm. Not a wrinkle of agitation rippled him. Had there been the least uneasiness, anger, impatience or impertinence in his manner; in other words, had there been any thing ordinarily human about him, doubtless I should have violently dismissed him from the premises. But as it was, I should have as soon thought of turning my pale plaster-of-paris bust of Cicero[5] out of doors. I stood gazing at him awhile, as he went on with his own writing, and then reseated myself at my desk. This is very strange, thought I. What had one best do? But my business hurried me. I concluded to forget the matter for the present, reserving it for my future leisure. So calling Nippers from the other room, the paper was speedily examined.

[5] Roman statesman and orator (106–42 B.C.).

A few days after this, Bartleby concluded four lengthy documents, being quadruplicates of a week's testimony taken before me in my High Court of Chancery. It became necessary to examine them. It was an important suit, and great accuracy was imperative. Having all things arranged, I called Turkey, Nippers, and Ginger Nut, from the next room, meaning to place the four copies in the hands of my four clerks, while I should read from the original. Accordingly, Turkey, Nippers, and Ginger Nut had taken their seats in a row, each with his document in his hand, when I called to Bartleby to join this interesting group.

"Bartleby! quick, I am waiting."

I heard a slow scrape of his chair legs on the uncarpeted floor, and soon he appeared standing at the entrance of his hermitage.

"What is wanted?" said he, mildly.

"The copies, the copies," said I, hurriedly. "We are going to examine them. There"— and I held towards him the fourth quadruplicate.

"I would prefer not to," he said, and gently disappeared behind the screen.

For a few moments I was turned into a pillar of salt,[6] standing at the head of my seated column of clerks. Recovering myself, I advanced towards the screen, and demanded the reason for such extraordinary conduct.

"*Why* do you refuse?"

"I would prefer not to."

With any other man I should have flown outright into a dreadful passion, scorned all further words, and thrust him ignominiously from my presence. But there was something about Bartleby that not only strangely disarmed me, but, in a wonderful manner, touched and disconcerted me. I began to reason with him.

"These are your own copies we are about to examine. It is labor saving to you, because one examination will answer for your four papers. It is common usage. Every copyist is bound to help examine his copy. Is it not so? Will you not speak? Answer!"

"I prefer not to," he replied in a flutelike tone. It seemed to me that, while I had been addressing him, he carefully revolved every statement that I made; fully comprehended the meaning; could not gainsay the irresistible conclusion; but, at the same time, some paramount consideration prevailed with him to reply as he did.

"You are decided, then, not to comply with my request—a request made according to common usage and common sense?"

He briefly gave me to understand, that on that point my judgment was sound. Yes: his decision was irreversible.

It is not seldom the case that, when a man is browbeaten in some unprecedented and violently unreasonable way, he begins to stagger in his own plainest faith. He begins, as it were, vaguely to surmise that, wonderful as it may be, all the justice and all the reason is on the other side. Accordingly, if any disinterested persons are present, he turns to them for some reinforcement of his own faltering mind.

"Turkey," said I, "what do you think of this? Am I not right?"

"With submission, sir," said Turkey, in his blandest tone, "I think that you are."

"Nippers," said I, "what do *you* think of it?"

---

[6] Like Lot's disobedient wife (Genesis 19:26).

"I think I should kick him out of the office."

(The reader, of nice perceptions, will here perceive that, it being morning, Turkey's answer is couched in polite and tranquil terms, but Nippers replies in ill-tempered ones. Or, to repeat a previous sentence, Nippers's ugly mood was on duty, and Turkey's off.)

"Ginger Nut," said I, willing to enlist the smallest suffrage in my behalf, "what do *you* think of it?"

"I think, sir, he's a little *luny*," replied Ginger Nut, with a grin.

"You hear what they say," said I, turning towards the screen, "come forth and do your duty."

But he vouchsafed no reply. I pondered a moment in sore perplexity. But once more business hurried me. I determined again to postpone the consideration of this dilemma to my future leisure. With a little trouble we made out to examine the papers without Bartleby, though at every page or two Turkey deferentially dropped his opinion, that this proceeding was quite out of the common; while Nippers, twitching in his chair with a dyspeptic nervousness, ground out, between his set teeth, occasional hissing maledictions against the stubborn oaf behind the screen. And for his (Nippers's) part, this was the first and the last time he would do another man's business without pay.

Meanwhile Bartleby sat in his hermitage, oblivious to everything but his own peculiar business there.

Some days passed, the scrivener being employed upon another lengthy work. His late remarkable conduct led me to regard his ways narrowly. I observed that he never went to dinner; indeed, that he never went anywhere. As yet I had never, of my personal knowledge, known him to be outside of my office. He was a perpetual sentry in the corner. At about eleven o'clock though, in the morning, I noticed that Ginger Nut would advance toward the opening in Bartleby's screen, as if silently beckoned thither by a gesture invisible to me where I sat. The boy would then leave the office, jingling a few pence, and reappear with a handful of ginger-nuts, which he delivered in the hermitage, receiving two of the cakes for his trouble.

He lives, then, on ginger-nuts, thought I; never eats a dinner, properly speaking; he must be a vegetarian, then; but no; he never eats even vegetables, he eats nothing but ginger-nuts. My mind then ran on in reveries concerning the probable effects upon the human constitution of living entirely on ginger-nuts. Ginger-nuts are so called, because they contain ginger as one of their peculiar constituents, and the final flavoring one. Now, what was ginger? A hot, spicy thing. Was Bartleby hot and spicy? Not at all. Ginger, then, had no effect upon Bartleby. Probably he preferred it should have none.

Nothing so aggravates an earnest person as a passive resistance. If the individual so resisted be of a not inhumane temper, and the resisting one perfectly harmless in his passivity, then, in the better moods of the former, he will endeavor charitably to construe to his imagination what proves impossible to be solved by his judgment. Even so, for the most part, I regarded Bartleby and his ways. Poor fellow! thought I, he means no mischief; it is plain he intends no insolence; his aspect sufficiently evinces that his eccentricities are involuntary. He is useful to me. I can get along with him. If I turn him away, the chances are he will fall in with some less-indulgent employer, and then he will be rudely treated, and perhaps driven forth miserably to starve. Yes. Here I can cheaply purchase a delicious self-approval. To befriend Bartleby; to humor him in his strange willfulness, will cost me little or nothing, while I lay up in my soul what will eventually prove a sweet morsel for my conscience. But this mood was not invariable with me. The passiveness of Bartleby sometimes irritated me. I felt strangely goaded on to encounter him in new opposition—to elicit some angry spark from him answerable to my own. But, indeed, I might as well have essayed to strike fire with my knuckles against a bit of Windsor soap. But one afternoon the evil impulse in me mastered me, and the following little scene ensued:

"Bartleby," said I, "when those papers are all copied, I will compare them with you."

"I would prefer not to."

"How? Surely you do not mean to persist in that mulish vagary?"

No answer.

I threw open the folding-doors near by, and, turning upon Turkey and Nippers, exclaimed:

"Bartleby a second time says, he won't examine his papers. What do you think of it, Turkey?"

It was afternoon, be it remembered. Turkey sat glowing like a brass boiler; his bald head steaming; his hands reeling among his blotted papers.

"Think of it?" roared Turkey; "I think I'll just step behind his screen, and black his eyes for him!"

So saying, Turkey rose to his feet and threw his arms into a pugilistic position. He was hurrying away to make good his promise, when I detained him, alarmed at the effect of incautiously rousing Turkey's combativeness after dinner.

"Sit down, Turkey," said I, "and hear what Nippers has to say. What do you think of it, Nippers? Would I not be justified in immediately dismissing Bartleby?"

"Excuse me, that is for you to decide, sir. I think his conduct quite unusual, and, indeed, unjust, as regards Turkey and myself. But it may only be a passing whim."

"Ah," exclaimed I, "you have strangely changed your mind, then—you speak very gently of him now."

"All beer," cried Turkey; "gentleness is effects of beer—Nippers and I dined together to-day. You see how gentle I am, sir. Shall I go and black his eyes?"

"You refer to Bartleby, I suppose. No, not to-day, Turkey," I replied; "pray, put up your fists."

I closed the doors, and again advanced towards Bartleby. I felt additional incentives tempting me to my fate. I burned to be rebelled against again. I remembered that Bartleby never left the office.

"Bartleby," said I, "Ginger Nut is away; just step around to the Post Office, won't you? (it was but a three minutes' walk), and see if there is anything for me."

"I would prefer not to."

"You will not?"

"I prefer not."

I staggered to my desk, and sat there in a deep study. My blind inveteracy returned. Was there any other thing in which I could procure myself to be ignominiously repulsed by this lean, penniless wight?—my hired clerk? What added thing is there, perfectly reasonable, that he will be sure to refuse to do?

"Bartleby!"

No answer.

"Bartleby," in a louder tone.

No answer.

"Bartleby," I roared.

Like a very ghost, agreeably to the laws of magical invocation, at the third summons, he appeared at the entrance of his hermitage.

"Go to the next room, and tell Nippers to come to me."

"I prefer not to," he respectfully and slowly said, and mildly disappeared.

"Very good, Bartleby," said I, in a quiet sort of serenely-severe self-possessed tone, intimating the unalterable purpose of some terrible retribution very close at hand. At the moment I half intended something of the kind. But upon the whole, as it was drawing towards my dinner-hour, I thought it best to put on my hat and walk home for the day, suffering much from perplexity and distress of mind.

Shall I acknowledge it? The conclusion of this whole business was, that it soon became a fixed fact of my chambers, that a pale young scrivener, by the name of Bartleby, had a desk there; that he copied for me at the usual rate of four cents a folio (one hundred words); but he was permanently exempt from examining the work done by him, that duty being transferred to Turkey and Nippers, out of compliment, doubtless, to their superior acuteness; moreover, said Bartleby was never, on any account, to be dispatched on the most trivial errand of any sort; and that even if entreated to take upon him such a matter, it was generally understood that he would "prefer not to"—in other words, that he would refuse point-blank.

As days passed on, I became considerably reconciled to Bartleby. His steadiness, his freedom from all dissipation, his incessant industry (except when he chose to throw himself into a standing revery behind his screen), his great stillness, his unalterableness of demeanor under all circumstances, made him a valuable acquisition. One prime thing was this—*he was always there*—first in the morning, continually through the day, and the last at night. I had a singular confidence in his honesty. I felt my most precious papers perfectly safe in his hands. Sometimes, to be sure, I could not, for the very soul of me, avoid falling into sudden spasmodic passions with him. For it was exceeding difficult to bear in mind all the time those strange peculiarities, privileges, and unheard of exemptions, forming the tacit stipulations on Bartleby's part under which he remained in my office. Now and then, in the eagerness of dispatching pressing business, I would inadvertently summon Bartleby, in a short, rapid tone, to put his finger, say, on the incipient tie of a bit of red tape with which I was about compressing some papers. Of course, from behind the screen the usual answer, "I prefer not to," was sure to come; and then, how could a human creature, with the common infirmities of our nature, refrain from bitterly exclaiming upon such perverseness—such unreasonableness. However, every added repulse of this sort which I received only tended to lessen the probability of my repeating the inadvertence.

Here it must be said, that according to the custom of most legal gentlemen occupying chambers in densely-populated law buildings, there were several keys to my door. One was kept by a woman residing in the attic, which person weekly scrubbed and daily swept and dusted my apartments. Another was kept by Turkey for convenience sake. The third I sometimes carried in my own pocket. The fourth I knew not who had.

Now, one Sunday morning I happened to go to Trinity Church, to hear a celebrated preacher, and finding myself rather early on the ground I thought I would walk around to my chambers for a while. Luckily I had my key with me; but upon applying it to the lock, I found it resisted by something inserted from the inside. Quite surprised, I called out; when to my consternation a key was turned from within; and thrusting his lean visage at me, and holding the door ajar, the apparition of Bartleby appeared, in his shirt sleeves, and otherwise in a strangely tattered deshabille, saying quietly that he was sorry, but he was deeply engaged just then, and—preferred not admitting me at present. In a brief word or two, he moreover added, that perhaps I had better walk around the block two or three times, and by that time he would probably have concluded his affairs.

Now, the utterly unsurmised appearance of Bartleby, tenanting my law-chambers of a Sunday morning, with his cadaverously gentlemanly *nonchalance,* yet withal firm and self-possessed, had such a strange effect upon me, that incontinently I slunk away from my own door, and did as desired. But not without sundry twinges of impotent rebellion against the mild effrontery of this unaccountable scrivener. Indeed, it was his wonderful mildness chiefly, which not only disarmed me, but unmanned me as it were. For I consider that one, for the time, is a sort of unmanned when he tranquilly permits his hired clerk to dictate to him, and order him away from his own premises. Furthermore, I was full of uneasiness as to what Bartleby could possibly be doing in my office in his shirt sleeves, and in an otherwise dismantled condition of a Sunday morning. Was anything amiss going on? Nay, that was out of the question. It was not to be thought of for a moment that Bartleby was an immoral person. But what could he be doing there?—copying? Nay again, whatever might be his eccentricities, Bartleby was an eminently decorous person. He would be the last man to sit down to his desk in any state approaching to nudity. Besides, it was Sunday; and there was something about Bartleby that forbade the supposition that he would by any secular occupation violate the proprieties of the day.

Nevertheless, my mind was not pacified; and full of a restless curiosity, at last I returned to the door. Without hindrance I inserted my key, opened it, and entered. Bartleby was not to be seen. I looked round anxiously, peeped behind his screen; but it was very plain that he was gone. Upon more closely examining the place, I surmised that for an indefinite period Bartleby must have ate, dressed, and slept in my office, and that, too without plate, mirror, or bed. The cushioned seat of a ricketty old sofa in one corner bore the faint impress of a lean, reclining form. Rolled away under his desk, I found a blanket; under the empty grate, a blacking box and brush; on a chair, a tin basin, with soap and a ragged towel; in a newspaper a few crumbs of ginger-nuts and a morsel of cheese. Yes, thought I, it is evident enough that Bartleby has been making his home here, keeping bachelor's hall all by himself. Immediately then the thought came sweeping across me, what miserable friendlessness and loneliness are here revealed! His poverty is great; but his solitude, how horrible! Think of it. Of a Sunday, Wall Street is deserted as Petra;[7] and every night of every day it is an emptiness. This building, too, which of week-days hums with industry and life, at nightfall echoes with sheer vacancy, and all through Sunday is forlorn. And here Bartleby makes his home; sole spectator of a solitude which he has seen all populous—a sort of innocent and transformed Marius brooding among the ruins of Carthage![8]

For the first time in my life a feeling of over-powering stinging melancholy seized me. Before, I had never experienced aught but a not unpleasing sadness. The bond of a

---

[7] Ruins of ancient city on Mt. Hor, Jordan.
[8] Marius: Gaius Marius (157–86 B.C.), Roman general; Carthage: commercial empire destroyed by Rome in the Third Punic War.

common humanity now drew me irresistibly to gloom. A fraternal melancholy! For both I and Bartleby were sons of Adam. I remembered the bright silks and sparkling faces I had seen that day, in gala trim, swan-like sailing down the Mississippi of Broadway; and I contrasted them with the pallid copyist, and thought to myself, Ah, happiness courts the light, so we deem the world is gay; but misery hides aloof, so we deem that misery there is none. These sad fancyings—chimeras, doubtless, of a sick and silly brain—led on to other and more special thoughts, concerning the eccentricities of Bartleby. Presentiments of strange discoveries hovered round me. The scrivener's pale form appeared to me laid out, among uncaring strangers, in its shivering winding sheet.

Suddenly I was attracted by Bartleby's closed desk, the key in open sight left in the lock.

I mean no mischief, seek the gratification of no heartless curiosity, thought I; besides, the desk is mine, and its contents, too, so I will make bold to look within. Everything was methodically arranged, the papers smoothly placed. The pigeon holes were deep, and removing the files of documents, I groped into their recesses. Presently I felt something there, and dragged it out. It was an old bandanna handkerchief, heavy and knotted. I opened it, and saw it was a savings's bank.

I now recalled all the quiet mysteries which I had noted in the man. I remembered that he never spoke but to answer; that, though at intervals he had considerable time to himself, yet I had never seen him reading—no, not even a newspaper; that for long periods he would stand looking out, at his pale window behind the screen, upon the dead brick wall; I was quite sure he never visited any refectory or eating house; while his pale face clearly indicated that he never drank beer like Turkey, or tea and coffee even, like other men; that he never went anywhere in particular that I could learn; never went out for a walk, unless, indeed, that was the case at present; that he had declined telling who he was, or whence he came, or whether he had any relatives in the world; that though so thin and pale, he never complained of ill health. And more than all, I remembered a certain unconscious air of pallid—how shall I call it?—of pallid haughtiness, say, or rather an austere reserve about him, which had positively awed me into my tame compliance with his eccentricities, when I had feared to ask him to do the slightest incidental thing for me, even though I might know, from his long-continued motionlessness, that behind his screen he must be standing in one of those dead-wall reveries of his.

Revolving all these things, and coupling them with the recently discovered fact, that he made my office his constant abiding place and home, and not forgetful of his morbid moodiness; revolving all these things, a prudential feeling began to steal over me. My first emotions had been those of pure melancholy and sincerest pity; but just in proportion as the forlornness of Bartleby grew and grew to my imagination, did that same melancholy merge into fear, that pity into repulsion. So true it is, and so terrible, took that up to a certain point the thought or sight of misery enlists our best affections; but, in certain special cases, beyond that point it does not. They err who would assert that invariably this is owing to the inherent selfishness of the human heart. It rather proceeds from a certain hopelessness of remedying excessive and organic ill. To a sensitive being, pity is not seldom pain. And when at last it is perceived that such pity cannot lead to effectual succor, common sense bids the soul be rid of it. What I saw that morning persuaded me that the scrivener was the victim of innate and incurable disorder. I might give alms to his body; but his body did not pain him; it was his soul that suffered, and his soul I could not reach.

I did not accomplish the purpose of going to Trinity Church that morning. Somehow, the things I had seen disqualified me for the time from church-going. I walked homeward, thinking what I would do with Bartleby. Finally, I resolved upon this—I would put certain calm questions to him the next morning, touching his history, etc., and if he declined to answer them openly and unreservedly (and I supposed he would prefer not), then to give him a twenty dollar bill over and above whatever I might owe him, and tell him his services were no longer required; but that if in any other way I could assist him, I would be happy to do so, especially if he desired to return to his native place, wherever that might be, I would willingly help to defray the expenses. Moreover, if, after reaching home, he found himself at any time in want of aid, a letter from him would be sure of a reply.

The next morning came.

"Bartleby," said I, gently calling to him behind his screen.

No reply.

"Bartleby," said I, in a still gentler tone, "come here; I am not going to ask you to do anything you would prefer not to do—I simply wish to speak to you."

Upon this he noiselessly slid into view.

"Will you tell me, Bartleby, where you were born?"

"I would prefer not to."

"Will you tell me *anything* about yourself?"

"I would prefer not to."

"But what reasonable objection can you have to speak to me? I feel friendly towards you."

He did not look at me while I spoke, but kept his glance fixed upon my bust of Cicero, which, as I then sat, was directly behind me, some six inches above my head.

"What is your answer, Bartleby," said I, after waiting a considerable time for a reply, during which his countenance remained immovable, only there was the faintest conceivable tremor of the white attenuated mouth.

"At present I prefer to give no answer," he said, and retired into his hermitage.

It was rather weak in me I confess, but his manner, on this occasion, nettled me. Not only did there seem to lurk in it a certain calm disdain, but his perverseness seemed ungrateful, considering the undeniable good usage and indulgence he had received from me.

Again I sat ruminating what I should do. Mortified as I was at his behavior, and resolved as I had been to dismiss him when I entered my office, nevertheless I strangely felt something superstitious knocking at my heart, and forbidding me to carry out my purpose, and denouncing me for a villain if I dared to breathe one bitter word against this forlornest of mankind. At last, familiarly drawing my chair behind his screen, I sat down and said: "Bartleby, never mind, then, about revealing your history; but let me entreat you, as a friend, to comply as far as may be with the usages of this office. Say now, you will help to examine papers to-morrow or next day: in short, say now, that in a day or two you will begin to be a little reasonable:—say so, Bartleby."

"At present I would prefer not to be a little reasonable," was his mildly cadaverous reply.

Just then the folding-doors opened, and Nippers approached. He seemed suffering from an unusually bad night's rest, induced by severer indigestion than common. He overheard those final words of Bartleby.

"*Prefer not*, eh?" gritted Nippers—"I'd *prefer* him, if I were you, sir," addressing me—"I'd *prefer* him; I'd give him preferences, the stubborn mule! What is it, sir, pray, that he *prefers* not to do now?"

Bartleby moved not a limb.

"Mr. Nippers," said I, "I'd prefer that you would withdraw for the present."

Somehow, of late, I had got into the way of involuntarily using this word "prefer" upon all sorts of not exactly suitable occasions. And I trembled to think that my contact with the scrivener had already and seriously affected me in a mental way. And what further and deeper aberration might it not yet produce? This apprehension had not been without efficacy in determining me to summary measures.

As Nippers, looking very sour and sulky, was departing, Turkey blandly and deferentially approached.

"With submission, sir," said he, "yesterday I was thinking about Bartleby here, and I think that if he would but prefer to take a quart of good ale every day, it would do much towards mending him, and enabling him to assist in examining his papers."

"So you have got the word, too," said I, slightly excited.

"With submission, what word, sir," asked Turkey, respectfully crowding himself into the contracted space behind the screen, and by so doing, making me jostle the scrivener. "What word, sir?"

"I would prefer to be left alone here," said Bartleby, as if offended at being mobbed in his privacy.

"*That's* the word, Turkey," said I—"*that's* it."

"Oh, *prefer?* oh yes—queer word. I never use it myself. But, sir, as I was saying, if he would but prefer—"

"Turkey," interrupted I, "you will please withdraw."

"Oh, certainly, sir, if you prefer that I should."

As he opened the folding-door to retire, Nippers at his desk caught a glimpse of me, and asked whether I would prefer to have a certain paper copied on blue paper or white. He did not in the least roguishly accent the word prefer. It was plain that it involuntarily rolled from his tongue. I thought to myself, surely I must get rid of a demented man, who already has in some degree turned the tongues, if not the heads of myself and clerks. But I thought it prudent not to break the dismission at once.

The next day I noticed that Bartleby did nothing but stand at his window in his dead-wall revery. Upon asking him why he did not write, he said that he had decided upon doing no more writing.

"Why, how now? what next?" exclaimed I, "do no more writing?"

"No more."

"And what is the reason?"

"Do you not see the reason for yourself," he indifferently replied.

I looked steadfastly at him, and perceived that his eyes looked dull and glazed. Instantly it occurred to me, that his unexampled diligence in copying by his dim window for the first few weeks of his stay with me might have temporarily impaired his vision.

I was touched. I said something in condolence with him. I hinted that of course he did wisely in abstaining from writing for a while; and urged him to embrace that opportunity of taking wholesome exercise in the open air. This, however, he did not do. A few days after this, my other clerks being absent, and being in a great hurry to dispatch certain letters by the mail, I thought that, having nothing else earthly to do, Bartleby would surely be less inflexible than usual, and carry these letters to the post-office. But he blankly declined. So, much to my inconvenience, I went myself.

Still added days went by. Whether Bartleby's eyes improved or not, I could not say. To all appearance, I thought they did. But when I asked him if they did, he vouchsafed no answer. At all events, he would do no copying. At last, in reply to my urgings, he informed me that he had permanently given up copying.

"What!" exclaimed I; "suppose your eyes should get entirely well—better than ever before—would you not copy then?"

"I have given up copying," he answered, and slid aside.

He remained as ever, a fixture in my chamber. Nay—if that were possible—he became still more of a fixture than before. What was to be done? He would do nothing in the office; why should he stay there? In plain fact, he had now become a millstone to me, not only useless as a necklace, but afflictive to bear. Yet I was sorry for him. I speak less than truth when I say that, on his own account, he occasioned me uneasiness. If he would but have named a single relative or friend, I would instantly have written, and urged their taking the poor fellow away to some convenient retreat. But he seemed alone, absolutely alone in the universe. A bit of wreck in the mid Atlantic. At length, necessities connected with my business tyrannized over all other considerations. Decently as I could, I told Bartleby that in six days time he must unconditionally leave the office. I warned him to take measures, in the interval, for procuring some other abode. I offered to assist him in this endeavor, if he himself would but take the first step towards a removal. "And when you finally quit me, Bartleby," added I, "I shall see that you go not away entirely unprovided. Six days from this hour, remember."

At the expiration of that period, I peeped behind the screen, and lo! Bartleby was there.

I buttoned up my coat, balanced myself; advanced slowly towards him, touched his shoulder, and said, "The time has come; you must quit this place; I am sorry for you; here is money; but you must go."

"I would prefer not," he replied, with his back still towards me.

"You *must*."

He remained silent.

Now I had an unbounded confidence in this man's common honesty. He had frequently restored to me sixpences and shillings carelessly dropped upon the floor, for I am apt to be very reckless in such shirt-button affairs. The proceeding, then, which followed will not be deemed extraordinary.

"Bartleby," said I, "I owe you twelve dollars on account; here are thirty-two; the odd twenty are yours—Will you take it?" and I handed the bills towards him.

But he made no motion.

"I will leave them here, then," putting them under a weight on the table. Then taking my hat and cane and going to the door, I tranquilly turned and added—"After you have removed your things from these offices, Bartleby, you will of course lock the door—since every one is now gone for the day but you—and if you please, slip your key underneath the mat, so that I may have it in the morning. I shall not see you again; so good-by to you. If, hereafter, in your new place of abode, I can be of any service to you, do not fail to advise me by letter. Good-by, Bartleby, and fare you well."

But he answered not a word; like the last column of some ruined temple, he remained standing mute and solitary in the middle of the otherwise deserted room.

As I walked home in a pensive mood, my vanity got the better of my pity. I could not but highly plume myself on my masterly management in getting rid of Bartleby. Masterly I call it, and such it must appear to any dispassionate thinker. The beauty of my procedure seemed to consist in its perfect quietness. There was no vulgar bullying, no bravado of any sort, no choleric hectoring, and striding to and fro across the apartment, jerking out vehement commands for Bartleby to bundle himself off with his beggarly traps. Nothing of the kind. Without loudly bidding Bartleby depart—as an inferior genius might have done—I *assumed* the ground that depart he must; and upon that assumption built all I had to say. The more I thought over my procedure, the more I was charmed with it. Nevertheless, next morning, upon awakening, I had my doubts—I had somehow slept off the fumes of vanity. One of the coolest and wisest hours a man has, is just after he awakes in the morning. My procedure seemed as sagacious as ever—but only in theory. How it would prove in practice—there was the rub. It was truly a beautiful thought to have assumed Bartleby's departure; but, after all, that assumption was simply my own, and none of Bartleby's. The great point was, not whether I had assumed that he would quit me, but whether he would prefer so to do. He was more a man of preferences than assumptions.

After breakfast, I walked down town, arguing the probabilities *pro* and *con*. One moment I thought it would prove a miserable failure, and Bartleby would be found all alive at my office as usual; the next moment it seemed certain that I should find his chair empty. And so I kept veering about. At the corner of Broadway and Canal Street, I saw quite an excited group of people standing in earnest conversation.

"I'll take odds he doesn't," said a voice as I passed.

"Doesn't go?—done!" said I, "put up your money."

I was instinctively putting my hand in my pocket to produce my own, when I remembered that this was an election day. The words I had overheard bore no reference to Bartleby, but to the success or non-success of some candidate for the mayoralty. In my intent frame of mind, I had, as it were, imagined that all Broadway shared in my excitement, and were debating the same question with me. I passed on, very thankful that the uproar of the street screened my momentary absent-mindedness.

As I had intended, I was earlier than usual at my office door. I stood listening for a moment. All was still. He must be gone. I tried the knob. The door was locked. Yes, my procedure had worked to a charm; he indeed must be vanished. Yet a certain melancholy mixed with this: I was almost sorry for my brilliant success. I was fumbling under the door mat for the key, which Bartleby was to have left there for me, when accidentally my knee knocked against a panel, producing a summoning sound, and in response a voice came to me from within—"Not yet; I am occupied."

It was Bartleby.

I was thunderstruck. For an instant I stood like the man who, pipe in mouth, was killed one cloudless afternoon long ago in Virginia, by summer lightning; at his own warm open window he was killed, and remained leaning out there upon the dreamy afternoon, till some one touched him, when he fell.

"Not gone!" I murmured at last. But again obeying that wondrous ascendancy which the inscrutable scrivener had over me, and from which ascendancy, for all my chafing, I could not completely escape, I slowly went down stairs and out into the street, and while walking round the block, considered what I should next do in this unheard-of perplexity. Turn the man out by an actual thrusting I could not; to drive him away by calling him hard names would not do; calling in the police was an unpleasant idea; and yet, permit him to enjoy his cadaverous triumph over me—this, too, I could not think of. What was to be done? or, if nothing could be done, was there anything further that I could *assume* in the matter? Yes, as before I had prospectively assumed that Bartleby would depart, so now I might retrospectively assume that departed he was. In the legitimate carrying out of this assumption, I might enter my office in a great hurry, and pretending not to see Bartleby at all, walk straight against him as if he were air. Such a proceeding would in a singular degree have the appearance of a home-thrust. It was hardly possible that Bartleby could withstand such an application of the doctrine of assumptions. But upon second thoughts the success of the plan seemed rather dubious. I resolved to argue the matter over with him again.

"Bartleby," said I, entering the office, with a quietly severe expression, "I am seriously displeased. I am pained, Bartleby. I had thought better of you. I had imagined you of such a gentlemanly organization, that in any delicate dilemma a slight hint would suffice—in short, an assumption. But it appears I am deceived. Why," I added, unaffectedly starting, "you have not even touched that money yet," pointing to it, just where I had left it the evening previous.

He answered nothing.

"Will you, or will you not, quit me?" I now demanded in a sudden passion, advancing close to him.

"I would prefer *not* to quit you," he replied, gently emphasizing the *not*.

"What earthly right have you to stay here? Do you pay any rent? Do you pay my taxes? Or is this property yours?"

He answered nothing.

"Are you ready to go on and write now? Are your eyes recovered? Could you copy a small paper for me this morning? or help examine a few lines? or step round to the post-office? In a word, will you do anything at all, to give a coloring to your refusal to depart the premises?"

He silently retired into his hermitage.

I was now in such a state of nervous resentment that I thought it but prudent to check myself at present from further demonstrations. Bartleby and I were alone. I remembered the tragedy of the unfortunate Adams and the still more unfortunate Colt in the solitary office of the latter; and how poor Colt, being dreadfully incensed by Adams, and imprudently permitting himself to get wildly excited, was at unawares hurried into his fatal act—an act which certainly no man could possibly deplore more than the actor himself.[9] Often it had occurred to me in my ponderings upon the subject, that had that altercation taken place in the public street, or at a private residence, it would not have terminated as it did. It was the circumstance of being alone in a solitary office, up stairs, of a building entirely unhallowed by humanizing domestic associations—an uncarpeted office, doubtless, of a dusty, haggard sort of appearance—this it must have been, which greatly helped to enhance the irritable desperation of the hapless Colt.

But when this old Adam of resentment rose in me and tempted me concerning Bartleby, I grappled him and threw him. How? Why, simply by recalling the divine in-

[9] In 1841 John C. Colt axe-murdered his creditor, Samuel Adams, and committed suicide following his conviction for the crime, which was widely publicized.

junction: "A new commandment give I unto you, that ye love one another." Yes, this it was that saved me. Aside from higher considerations, charity often operates as a vastly wise and prudent principle—a great safeguard to its possessor. Men have committed murder for jealousy's sake, and anger's sake, and hatred's sake, and selfishness' sake, and spiritual pride's sake; but no man, that ever I heard of, ever committed a diabolical murder for sweet charity's sake. Mere self-interest, then, if no better motive can be enlisted, should, especially with high-tempered men, prompt all beings to charity and philanthropy. At any rate, upon the occasion in question, I strove to drown my exasperated feelings towards the scrivener by benevolently construing his conduct. Poor fellow, poor fellow! thought I, he don't mean anything; and besides, he has seen hard times, and ought to be indulged.

I endeavored, also, immediately to occupy myself, and at the same time to comfort my despondency. I tried to fancy, that in the course of the morning, at such time as might prove agreeable to him, Bartleby, of his own free accord, would emerge from his hermitage and take up some decided line of march in the direction of the door. But no. Half-past twelve o'clock came; Turkey began to glow in the face, overturn his inkstand, and become generally obstreperous; Nippers abated down into quietude and courtesy; Ginger Nut munched his noon apple; and Bartleby remained standing at his window in one of his profoundest dead-wall reveries. Will it be credited? Ought I to acknowledge it? That afternoon I left the office without saying one further word to him.

Some days now passed, during which, at leisure intervals I looked a little into "Edwards on the Will," and "Priestly on Necessity."[10] Under the circumstances, those books induced a salutary feeling. Gradually I slid into the persuasion that these troubles of mine, touching the scrivener, had been all predestined from eternity, and Bartleby was billeted upon me for some mysterious purpose of an allwise Providence, which it was not for a mere mortal like me to fathom. Yes, Bartleby, stay there behind your screen, thought I; I shall persecute you no more; you are harmless and noiseless as any of these old chairs; in short, I never feel so private as when I know you are here. At last I see it, I feel it; I penetrate to the predestinated purpose of my life. I am content. Others may have loftier parts to enact; but my mission in this world, Bartleby, is to furnish you with office-room for such period as you may see fit to remain.

I believe that this wise and blessed frame of mind would have continued with me, had it not been for the unsolicited and uncharitable remarks obtruded upon me by my professional friends who visited the rooms. But thus it often is, that the constant friction of illiberal minds wears out at last the best resolves of the more generous. Though to be sure, when I reflected upon it, it was not strange that people entering my office should be struck by the peculiar aspect of the unaccountable Bartleby, and so be tempted to throw out some sinister observations concerning him. Sometimes an attorney, having business with me, and calling at my office, and finding no one but the scrivener there, would undertake to obtain some sort of precise information from him touching my whereabouts; but without heeding his idle talk, Bartleby would remain standing immovable in the middle of the room. So after contemplating him in that position for a time, the attorney would depart, no wiser than he came.

[10] Both the Puritan theologian Jonathan Edwards and the English scientist Joseph Priestly concluded that the will is not free.

Also, when a reference[11] was going on, and the room full of lawyers and witnesses, and business driving fast, some deeply-occupied legal gentleman present, seeing Bartleby wholly unemployed, would request him to run round to his (the legal gentleman's) office and fetch some papers for him. Thereupon, Bartleby would tranquilly decline, and yet remain idle as before. Then the lawyer would give a great stare, and turn to me. And what could I say? At last I was made aware that all through the circle of my professional acquaintance, a whisper of wonder was running round, having reference to the strange creature I kept at my office. This worried me very much. And as the idea came upon me of his possibly turning out a long-lived man, and keep occupying my chambers, and denying my authority; and perplexing my visitors; and scandalizing my professional reputation; and casting a general gloom over the premises; keeping soul and body together to the last upon his savings (for doubtless he spent but half a dime a day), and in the end perhaps outlive me, and claim possession of my office by right of his perpetual occupancy: as all these dark anticipations crowded upon me more and more, and my friends continually intruded their relentless remarks upon the apparition in my room; a great change was wrought in me. I resolved to gather all my faculties together, and forever rid me of this intolerable incubus.

Ere revolving any complicated project, however, adapted to this end, I first simply suggested to Bartleby the propriety of his permanent departure. In a calm and serious tone, I commended the idea to his careful and mature consideration. But, having taken three days to meditate upon it, he apprised me, that his original determination remained the same; in short, that he still preferred to abide with me.

What shall I do? I now said to myself, buttoning up my coat to the last button. What shall I do? what ought I to do? what does conscience say I *should* do with this man, or, rather, ghost. Rid myself of him, I must; go, he shall. But how? You will not thrust him, the poor, pale, passive mortal—you will not thrust such a helpless creature out of your door? you will not dishonor yourself by such cruelty? No, I will not, I cannot do that. Rather would I let him live and die here, and then mason up his remains in the wall. What, then, will you do? For all your coaxing, he will not budge. Bribes he leaves under your own paper-weight on your table; in short, it is quite plain that he prefers to cling to you.

Then something severe, something unusual must be done. What! surely you will not have him collared by a constable, and commit his innocent pallor to the common jail? And upon what ground could you procure such a thing to be done?—a vagrant, is he? What! he a vagrant, a wanderer, who refuses to budge? It is because he will *not* be a vagrant, then, that you seek to count him *as* a vagrant. That is too absurd. No visible means of support: there I have him. Wrong again: for indubitably he *does* support himself, and that is the only unanswerable proof that any man can show of his possessing the means so to do. No more, then. Since he will not quit me, I must quit him. I will change my offices; I will move elsewhere, and give him fair notice, that if I find him on my new premises I will then proceed against him as a common trespasser.

Acting accordingly, next day I thus addressed him: "I find these chambers too far from the City Hall; the air is unwholesome. In a word, I propose to remove my offices next week, and shall no longer require your services. I tell you this now, in order that you may seek another place."

---

[11] The referring of disputes to arbitrators.

He made no reply, and nothing more was said.

On the appointed day I engaged carts and men, proceeded to my chambers, and, having but little furniture, everything was removed in a few hours. Throughout, the scrivener remained standing behind the screen, which I directed to be removed the last thing. It was withdrawn; and, being folded up like a huge folio, left him the motion-less occupant of a naked room. I stood in the entry watching him a moment, while something from within me upbraided me.

I re-entered, with my hand in my pocket—and—and my heart in my mouth.

"Good-by, Bartleby; I am going—good-by, and God some way bless you; and take that," slipping something in his hand. But it dropped upon the floor, and then—strange to say—I tore myself from him whom I had so longed to be rid of.

Established in my new quarters, for a day or two I kept the door locked, and started at every footfall in the passages. When I returned to my rooms, after any little absence, I would pause at the threshold for an instant, and attentively listen, ere applying my key. But these fears were needless. Bartleby never came nigh me.

I thought all was going well, when a perturbed-looking stranger visited me, inquiring whether I was the person who had recently occupied rooms at No.——— Wall Street.

Full of forebodings, I replied that I was.

"Then, sir," said the stranger, who proved a lawyer, "you are responsible for the man you left there. He refuses to do any copying; he refuses to do anything; he says he prefers not to; and he refuses to quit the premises."

"I am very sorry, sir," said I, with assumed tranquillity, but an inward tremor, "but, really, the man you allude to is nothing to me—he is no relation or apprentice of mine, that you should hold me responsible for him."

"In mercy's name, who is he?"

"I certainly cannot inform you. I know nothing about him. Formerly I employed him as a copyist; but he has done nothing for me now for some time past."

"I shall settle him, then—good morning, sir."

Several days passed, and I heard nothing more; and, though I often felt a charitable prompting to call at the place and see poor Bartleby, yet a certain squeamishness, of I know not what, withheld me.

All is over with him, by this time, thought I, at last, when, through another week, no further intelligence reached me. But, coming to my room the day after, I found several persons waiting at my door in a high state of nervous excitement.

"That's the man—here he comes," cried the foremost one, whom I recognized as the lawyer who had previously called upon me alone.

"You must take him away, sir, at once," cried a portly person among them, advancing upon me, and whom I knew to be the landlord of No. ——— Wall Street. "These gentlemen, my tenants, cannot stand it any longer; Mr. B——," pointing to the lawyer, "has turned him out of his room, and he now persists in haunting the building generally, sitting upon the banisters of the stairs by day, and sleeping in the entry by night. Everybody is concerned; clients are leaving the offices; some fears are entertained of a mob; something you must do, and that without delay."

Aghast at this torrent, I fell back before it, and would fain have locked myself in my new quarters. In vain I persisted that Bartleby was nothing to me—no more than to any one else. In vain—I was the last person known to have anything to do with him, and they held me to the terrible account. Fearful, then, of being exposed in the papers (as one person present obscurely threatened), I considered the matter, and, at length, said, that if the lawyer would give me a confidential interview with the scrivener, in his (the lawyer's) own room, I would, that afternoon, strive my best to rid them of the nuisance they complained of.

Going up stairs to my old haunt, there was Bartleby silently sitting upon the banister at the landing.

"What are you doing here, Bartleby?" said I.

"Sitting upon the banister," he mildly replied.

I motioned him into the lawyer's room, who then left us.

"Bartleby," said I, "are you aware that you are the cause of great tribulation to me, by persisting in occupying the entry after being dismissed from the office?"

No answer.

"Now one of two things must take place. Either you must do something, or something must be done to you. Now what sort of business would you like to engage in? Would you like to re-engage in copying for some one?"

"No; I would prefer not to make any change."

"Would you like a clerkship in a dry-goods store?"

"There is too much confinement about that. No, I would not like a clerkship; but I am not particular."

"Too much confinement," I cried, "why you keep yourself confined all the time!"

"I would prefer not to take a clerkship," he rejoined, as if to settle that little item at once.

"How would a bar-tender's business suit you? There is no trying of the eye-sight in that."

"I would not like it at all; though, as I said before, I am not particular."

His unwonted wordiness inspirited me. I returned to the charge.

"Well, then, would you like to travel through the country collecting bills for the merchants? That would improve your health."

"No, I would prefer to be doing something else."

"How, then, would going as a companion to Europe, to entertain some young gentleman with your conversation—how would that suit you?"

"Not at all. It does not strike me that there is anything definite about that. I like to be stationary. But I am not particular."

"Stationary you shall be, then," I cried, now losing all patience, and, for the first time in all my exasperating connection with him, fairly flying into a passion. "If you do not go away from these premises before night, I shall feel bound—indeed, I *am* bound—to—to—to quit the premises myself!" I rather absurdly concluded, knowing not with what possible threat to try to frighten his immobility into compliance. Despairing of all further efforts, I was precipitately leaving him, when a final thought occurred to me—one which had not been wholly unindulged before.

"Bartleby," said I, in the kindest tone I could assume under such exciting circumstances, "will you go home with me now—not to my office, but my dwelling—and remain there till we can conclude upon some convenient arrangement for you at our leisure? Come, let us start now, right away."

"No: at present I would prefer not to make any change at all."

I answered nothing; but, effectually dodging every one by the suddenness and rapidity of my flight, rushed from the building, ran up Wall Street towards Broadway, and, jumping into the first omnibus, was soon removed from pursuit. As soon as tranquillity returned, I distinctly perceived that I had now done all that I possibly could, both in respect to the demands of the landlord and his tenants, and with regard to my own desire and sense of duty, to benefit Bartleby, and shield him from rude persecution. I now strove to be entirely care-free and quiescent; and my conscience justified me in the attempt; though, indeed, it was not so successful as I could have wished. So fearful was I of being again hunted out by the incensed landlord and his exasperated tenants, that, surrendering my business to Nippers, for a few days, I drove about the upper part of the town and through the suburbs, in my rockaway;[12] crossed over to Jersey City and Hoboken, and paid fugitive visits to Manhattanville and Astoria. In fact, I almost lived in my rockaway for the time.

When again I entered my office, lo, a note from the landlord lay upon the desk. I opened it with trembling hands. It informed me that the writer had sent to the police, and had Bartleby removed to the Tombs as a vagrant. Moreover, since I knew more about him than any one else, he wished me to appear at that place, and make a suitable statement of the facts. These tidings had a conflicting effect upon me. At first I was indignant; but, at last, almost approved. The landlord's energetic, summary disposition, had led him to adopt a procedure which I do not think I would have decided upon myself; and yet, as a last resort, under such peculiar circumstances, it seemed the only plan.

As I afterwards learned, the poor scrivener, when told that he must be conducted to the Tombs, offered not the slightest obstacle; but, in his pale, unmoving way, silently acquiesced.

Some of the compassionate and curious bystanders joined the party; and headed by one of the constables arm in arm with Bartleby, the silent procession filed its way through all the noise, and heat, and joy of the roaring thoroughfares at noon.

The same day I received the note, I went to the Tombs, or, to speak more properly, the Halls of Justice. Seeking the right officer, I stated the purpose of my call, and was informed that the individual I described was, indeed, within. I then assured the functionary that Bartleby was a perfectly honest man, and greatly to be compassionated, however unaccountably eccentric. I narrated all I knew, and closed by suggesting the idea of letting him remain in as indulgent confinement as possible, till something less harsh might be done—though, indeed, I hardly knew what. At all events, if nothing else could be decided upon, the alms-house must receive him. I then begged to have an interview.

Being under no disgraceful charge, and quite serene and harmless in all his ways, they had permitted him freely to wander about the prison, and, especially, in the inclosed grass-platted yards thereof. And so I found him there, standing all alone in the quietest of the yards, his face towards a high wall, while all around, from the narrow slits of the jail windows, I thought I saw peering out upon him the eyes of murderers and thieves.

"Bartleby!"

"I know you," he said, without looking around—"and I want nothing to say to you."

"It was not I that brought you here, Bartleby," said I, keenly pained at his implied suspicion. "And to you, this should not be so vile a place. Nothing reproachful attaches to you by being here. And see, it is not so sad a place as one might think. Look, there is the sky, and here is the grass."

[12] Carriage.

"I know where I am," he replied, but would say nothing more, and so I left him.

As I entered the corridor again, a broad meat-like man, in an apron, accosted me, and, jerking his thumb over his shoulder, said—"Is that your friend?"

"Yes."

"Does he want to starve? If he does, let him live on the prison fare, that's all."

"Who are you?" asked I, not knowing what to make of such an unofficially speaking person in such a place.

"I am the grub-man. Such gentlemen as have friends here, hire me to provide them with something good to eat."

"Is this so?" said I, turning to the turnkey.

He said it was.

"Well, then," said I, slipping some silver into the grub-man's hands (for so they called him), "I want you to give particular attention to my friend there; let him have the best dinner you can get. And you must be as polite to him as possible."

"Introduce me, will you?" said the grub-man, looking at me with an expression which seemed to say he was all impatience for an opportunity to give a specimen of his breeding.

Thinking it would prove of benefit to the scrivener, I acquiesced; and, asking the grub-man his name, went up with him to Bartleby.

"Bartleby, this is a friend; you will find him very useful to you."

"Your sarvant, sir, your sarvant," said the grub-man, making a low salutation behind his apron. "Hope you find it pleasant here, sir; nice grounds—cool apartments—hope you'll stay with us sometime—try to make it agreeable. What will you have for dinner to-day?"

"I prefer not to dine to-day," said Bartleby, turning away. "It would disagree with me; I am unused to dinners." So saying, he slowly moved to the other side of the inclosure, and took up a position fronting the dead-wall.

"How's this?" said the grub-man, addressing me with a stare of astonishment. "He's odd, ain't he?"

"I think he is a little deranged," said I, sadly.

"Deranged? deranged is it? Well, now, upon my word, I thought that friend of yourn was a gentleman forger; they are always pale and genteel-like, them forgers. I can't help pity 'em—can't help it, sir. Did you know Monroe Edwards?"[13] he added, touchingly, and paused. Then, laying his hand piteously on my shoulder, sighed, "he died of consumption at Sing-Sing. So you weren't acquainted with Monroe?"

"No, I was never socially acquainted with any forgers. But I cannot stop longer. Look to my friend yonder. You will not lose by it. I will see you again."

Some few days after this, I again obtained admission to the Tombs, and went through the corridors in quest of Bartleby; but without finding him.

"I saw him coming from his cell not long ago," said a turnkey, "may be he's gone to loiter in the yards."

So I went in that direction.

[13] Financier convicted in 1842 of forgery and swindle.

"Are you looking for the silent man?" said another turnkey, passing me. "Yonder he lies—sleeping in the yard there. 'Tis not twenty minutes since I saw him lie down."

The yard was entirely quiet. It was not accessible to the common prisoners. The surrounding walls, of amazing thickness, kept off all sounds behind them. The Egyptian character of the masonry weighed upon me with its gloom. But a soft imprisoned turf grew under foot. The heart of the eternal pyramids, it seemed, wherein, by some strange magic, through the clefts, grass-seed, dropped by birds, had sprung.

Strangely huddled at the base of the wall, his knees drawn up, and lying on his side, his head touching the cold stones, I saw the wasted Bartleby. But nothing stirred. I paused; then went close up to him; stooped over, and saw that his dim eyes were open; otherwise he seemed profoundly sleeping. Something prompted me to touch him. I felt his hand, when a tingling shiver ran up my arm and down my spine to my feet.

The round face of the grub-man peered upon me now. "His dinner is ready. Won't he dine to-day, either? Or does he live without dining?"

"Lives without dining," said I, and closed the eyes.

"Eh!—He's asleep, ain't he?"

"With kings and counselors,"[14] murmured I.

There would seem little need for proceeding further in this history. Imagination will readily supply the meagre recital of poor Bartleby's interment. But, ere parting with the reader, let me say, that if this little narrative has sufficiently interested him, to awaken curiosity as to who Bartleby was, and what manner of life he led prior to the present narrator's making his acquaintance, I can only reply, that in such curiosity I fully share, but am wholly unable to gratify it. Yet here I hardly know whether I should divulge one little item of rumor, which came to my ear a few months after the scrivener's decease. Upon what basis it rested, I could never ascertain; and hence, how true it is I cannot now tell. But, inasmuch as this vague report has not been without a certain suggestive interest to me, however sad, it may prove the same with some others; and so I will briefly mention it. The report was this: that Bartleby had been a subordinate clerk in the Dead Letter Office at Washington, from which he had been suddenly removed by a change in the administration. When I think over this rumor, hardly can I express the emotions which seize me. Dead letters! does it not sound like dead men? Conceive a man by nature and misfortune prone to a pallid hopelessness, can any business seem more fitted to heighten it than that of continually handling these dead letters, and assorting them for the flames? For by the cart-load they are annually burned. Sometimes from out the folded paper the pale clerk takes a ring—the finger it was meant for, perhaps, moulders in the grave; a bank-note sent in swiftest charity—he whom it would relieve, nor eats nor hungers any more; pardon for those who died despairing; hope for those who died unhoping; good tidings for those who died stifled by unrelieved calamities. On errands of life, these letters speed to death.

Ah, Bartleby! Ah, humanity!

1853/1856

---

[14] Job 3:14.

The Paradise of Bachelors
and the Tartarus of Maids

I: *The Paradise of Bachelors*

It lies not far from Temple Bar.[1]

Going to it, by the usual way, is like stealing from a heated plain into some cool, deep glen, shady among harboring hills.

Sick with the din and soiled with the mud of Fleet Street—where the Benedick[2] tradesmen are hurrying by, with ledger-lines ruled along their brows, thinking upon rise of bread and fall of babies—you adroitly turn a mystic corner—not a street—glide down a dim, monastic way, flanked by dark, sedate, and solemn piles, and still wending on, give the whole care-worn world the slip, and, disentangled, stand beneath the quiet cloisters of the Paradise of Bachelors.

Sweet are the oases in Sahara; charming the isle-groves of August prairies; delectable pure faith amidst a thousand perfidies; but sweeter, still more charming, most delectable, the dreamy Paradise of Bachelors, found in the stony heart of stunning London.

In mild meditation pace the cloisters; take your pleasure, sip your leisure, in the garden waterward; go linger in the ancient library; go worship in the sculptured chapel; but little have you seen, just nothing do you know, not the sweet kernel have you tasted, till you dine among the banded Bachelors, and see their convivial eyes and glasses sparkle. Not dine in bustling commons, during term-time, in the hall; but tranquilly, by private hint, at a private table; some fine Templar's[3] hospitably invited guest.

Templar? That's a romantic name. Let me see. Brian de Bois-Guilbert was a Templar, I believe. Do we understand you to insinuate that those famous Templars still survive in modern London? May the ring of their armed heels be heard, and the rattle of their shields, as in mailed prayer the monk-knights kneel before the consecrated Host? Surely a monk-knight were a curious sight picking his way along the Strand, his gleaming corselet[4] and snowy surcoat spattered by an omnibus. Long-bearded, too, according to his order's rule; his face fuzzy as a pard's;[5] how would the grim ghost look among the crop-haired, close-shaven citizens? We know indeed—sad history recounts it—that a moral blight tainted at last this sacred Brotherhood. Though no sworded foe might outskill them in the fence, yet the worm of luxury crawled beneath their guard, gnawing the core of knightly troth, nibbling the monastic vow, till at last the monk's austerity relaxed to wassailing, and the sworn knights-bachelors grew to be but hypocrites and rakes.

But for all this, quite unprepared were we to learn that Knights-Templars (if at all in being) were so entirely secularized as to be reduced from carving out immortal fame in glorious battling for the Holy Land, to the carving of roast-mutton at a dinner-board.

---

[1] Chambers principally of barristers or attorneys in London; also name of the gateway closing the entrance to the City of London (removed in 1878).

[2] Determined bachelor in Shakespeare's comedy *Much Ado About Nothing* (ca. 1598).

[3] Member of a military and religious order founded in 1118 for the protection of the Holy Sepulchre and of Christian pilgrims visiting the Holy Land.

[4] Suit of light armor over which an embroidered outer coat, or surcoat, was often worn.

[5] Pard: medieval word for leopard.

Like Anacreon,[6] do these degenerate Templars now think it sweeter far to fall in banquet than in war? Or, indeed, how can there be any survival of that famous order? Templars in modern London! Templars in their red-cross mantles smoking cigars at the Divan! Templars crowded in a railway train, till, stacked with steel helmet, spear, and shield, the whole train looks like one elongated locomotive!

No. The genuine Templar is long since departed. Go view the wondrous tombs in the Temple Church; see there the rigidly-haughty forms stretched out, with crossed arms upon their stilly hearts, in everlasting and undreaming rest. Like the years before the flood, the bold Knights-Templars are no more. Nevertheless, the name remains, and the nominal society, and the ancient grounds, and some of the ancient edifices. But the iron heel is changed to a boot of patent-leather; the long two-handed sword to a one-handed quill; the monk-giver of gratuitous ghostly counsel now counsels for a fee; the defender of the sarcophagus (if in good practice with his weapon) now has more than one case to defend; the vowed opener and clearer of all highways leading to the Holy Sepulchre, now has it in particular charge to check, to clog, to hinder, and embarrass all the courts and avenues of Law; the knight-combatant of the Saracen,[7] breasting spear-points at Acre, now fights law-points in Westminster Hall. The helmet is a wig. Struck by Time's enchanter's wand, the Templar is to-day a Lawyer.

But, like many others tumbled from proud glory's height—like the apple, hard on the bough but mellow on the ground—the Templar's fall has but made him all the finer fellow.

I dare say those old warrior-priests were but gruff and grouty at the best; cased in Birmingham[8] hardware, how could their crimped arms give yours or mine a hearty shake? Their proud, ambitious, monkish souls clasped shut, like horn-book missals; their very faces clapped in bomb-shells; what sort of genial men were these? But best of comrades, most affable of hosts, capital diner is the modern Templar. His wit and wine are both of sparkling brands.

The church and cloisters, courts and vaults, lanes and passages, banquet-halls, refectories, libraries, terraces, gardens, broad walks, domiciles, and dessert-rooms, covering a very large space of ground, and all grouped in central neighborhood, and quite sequestered from the old city's surrounding din; and everything about the place being kept in most bachelor-like particularity, no part of London offers to a quiet wight so agreeable a refuge.

The Temple is, indeed, a city by itself. A city with all the best appurtenances, as the above enumeration shows. A city with a park to it, and flower-beds, and a river-side— the Thames flowing by as openly, in one part, as by Eden's primal garden flowed the mild Euphrates. In what is now the Temple Garden the old Crusaders used to exercise their steeds and lances; the modern Templars now lounge on the benches beneath the trees, and, switching their patent-leather boots, in gay discourse exercise at repartee.

Long lines of stately portraits in the banquet-halls, show what great men of mark— famous nobles, judges, and Lord Chancellors—have in their time been Templars. But all Templars are not known to universal fame; though, if the having warm hearts and warmer welcomes, full minds and fuller cellars, and giving good advice and glorious

---

[6] Sixth-century Greek lyric poet of love and wine.

[7] Member of Muslim nomadic tribes on the Syrian borders of the Roman Empire.

[8] English city noted for manufacture of steel and armaments.

dinners, spiced with rare divertisements of fun and fancy, merit immortal mention, set down, ye muses, the names of R. F. C. and his imperial brother.

Though to be a Templar, in the one true sense, you must needs be a lawyer, or a student at the law, and be ceremoniously enrolled as member of the order, yet as many such, though Templars, do not reside within the Temple's precincts, though they may have their offices there, just so, on the other hand, there are many residents of the hoary old domiciles who are not admitted Templars. If being, say, a lounging gentleman and bachelor, or a quiet, unmarried, literary man, charmed with the soft seclusion of the spot, you much desire to pitch your shady tent among the rest in this serene encampment, then you must make some special friend among the order, and procure him to rent, in his name but at your charge, whatever vacant chamber you may find to suit.

Thus, I suppose, did Dr. Johnson,[9] that nominal Benedick and widower but virtual bachelor, when for a space he resided here. So, too, did that undoubted bachelor and rare good soul, Charles Lamb.[10] And hundreds more, of sterling spirits, Brethren of the Order of Celibacy, from time to time have dined, and slept, and tabernacled here. Indeed, the place is all a honey-comb of offices and domiciles. Like any cheese, it is quite perforated through and through in all directions with the snug cells of bachelors. Dear, delightful spot! Ah! when I bethink me of the sweet hours there passed, enjoying such genial hospitalities beneath those time-honored roofs, my heart only finds due utterance through poetry; and, with a sigh, I softly sing, "Carry me back to old Virginny!"

Such then, at large, is the Paradise of Bachelors. And such I found it one pleasant afternoon in the smiling month of May, when, sallying from my hotel in Trafalgar Square, I went to keep my dinner-appointment with that fine Barrister, Bachelor, and Bencher, R. F. C. (he *is* the first and second, and *should be* the third; I hereby nominate him), whose card I kept fast pinched between my gloved forefinger and thumb, and every now and then snatched still another look at the pleasant address inscribed beneath the name, "No.——, Elm Court, Temple."

At the core he was a right bluff, care-free, right comfortable, and most companionable Englishman. If on a first acquaintance he seemed reserved, quite icy in his air—patience; this Champagne will thaw. And if it never do, better frozen Champagne than liquid vinegar.

There were nine gentlemen, all bachelors, at the dinner. One was from "No.——, King's Bench Walk, Temple"; a second, third, and fourth, and fifth, from various courts or passages christened with some similarly rich resounding syllables. It was, indeed, a sort of Senate of the Bachelors, sent to this dinner from widely scattered districts, to represent the general celibacy of the Temple. Nay, it was, by representation, a Grand Parliament of the best Bachelors in universal London; several of those present being from distant quarters of the town, noted immemorial seats of lawyers and unmarried men—Lincoln's Inn, Furnival's Inn; and one gentleman, upon whom I looked with a sort of collateral awe, hailed from the spot where Lord Verulam once abode a bachelor—Grey's Inn.[11]

---

[9] Samuel Johnson (1709–1784), English writer and lexicographer.

[10] English essayist and critic (1775–1834).

[11] Lincoln's Inn, Furnival's Inn, and Grey's Inn were legal societies.

The apartment was well up toward heaven. I know not how many strange old stairs I climbed to get to it. But a good dinner, with famous company, should be well earned. No doubt our host had his dining-room so high with a view to secure the prior exercise necessary to the due relishing and digesting of it.

The furniture was wonderfully unpretending, old, and snug. No new shining mahogany, sticky with undried varnish; no uncomfortably luxurious ottomans, and sofas too fine to use, vexed you in this sedate apartment. It is a thing which every sensible American should learn from every sensible Englishman, that glare and glitter, gimcracks and gewgaws, are not indispensable to domestic solacement. The American Benedick snatches, down-town, a tough chop in a gilded show-box; the English bachelor leisurely dines at home on that incomparable South Down of his, off a plain deal board.

The ceiling of the room was low. Who wants to dine under the dome of St. Peter's? High ceilings! If that is your demand, and the higher the better, and you be so very tall, then go dine out with the topping giraffe in the open air.

In good time the nine gentlemen sat down to nine covers, and soon were fairly under way.

If I remember right, ox-tail soup inaugurated the affair. Of a rich russet hue, its agreeable flavor dissipated my first confounding of its main ingredient with teamsters' gads and the raw-hides[12] of ushers. (By way of interlude, we here drank a little claret.) Neptune's[13] was the next tribute rendered—turbot coming second; snow-white, flaky, and just gelatinous enough, not too turtleish in its unctuousness.

(At this point we refreshed ourselves with a glass of sherry.) After these light skirmishers had vanished, the heavy artillery of the feast marched in, led by that well-known English generalissimo, roast beef. For aides-de-camp we had a saddle of mutton, a fat turkey, a chicken-pie, and endless other savory things; while for avant-couriers came nine silver flagons of humming ale. This heavy ordnance having departed on the track of the light skirmishers, a picked brigade of game-fowl encamped upon the board, their camp-fires lit by the ruddiest of decanters.

Tarts and puddings followed, with innumerable niceties; then cheese and crackers. (By way of ceremony, simply, only to keep up good old fashions, we here each drank a glass of good old port.)

The cloth was now removed; and, like Blucher's[14] army coming in at the death on the field of Waterloo, in marched a fresh detachment of bottles, dusty with their hurried march.

All these manoeuvrings of the forces were superintended by a surprising old field-marshal (I can not school myself to call him by the inglorious name of waiter), with snowy hair and napkin, and a head like Socrates. Amidst all the hilarity of the feast, intent on important business, he disdained to smile. Venerable man!

I have above endeavored to give some slight schedule of the general plan of operations. But any one knows that a good, genial dinner is a sort of pell-mell, indiscriminate affair, quite baffling to detail in all particulars. Thus, I spoke of taking a glass of claret, and a glass of sherry, and a glass of port, and a mug of ale—all at certain specific periods

---

[12] Whips.
[13] i.e., for the Roman god of the sea; hence the fish, turbot.

[14] Gebhart von Blucher (1742–1819), Prussian field marshal.

and times. But those were merely the state bumpers,[15] so to speak. Innumerable impromptu glasses were drained between the periods of those grand imposing ones.

The nine bachelors seemed to have the most tender concern for each other's health. All the time, in flowing wine, they most earnestly expressed their sincerest wishes for the entire well-being and lasting hygiene of the gentleman on the right and on the left. I noticed that when one of these kind bachelors desired a little more wine (just for his stomach's sake, like Timothy,[16]) he would not help himself to it unless some other bachelor would join him. It seemed held something indelicate, selfish, and unfraternal, to be seen taking a lonely, unparticipated glass. Meantime, as the wine ran apace, the spirits of the company grew more and more to perfect genialness and unconstraint. They related all sorts of pleasant stories. Choice experiences in their private lives were now brought out, like choice brands of Moselle or Rhenish, only kept for particular company. One told us how mellowly he lived when a student at Oxford; with various spicy anecdotes of most frank-hearted noble lords, his liberal companions. Another bachelor, a gray-headed man, with a sunny face, who, by his own account, embraced every opportunity of leisure to cross over into the Low Countries, on sudden tours of inspection of the fine old Flemish architecture there—this learned, white-haired, sunny-faced old bachelor excelled in his descriptions of the elaborate splendors of those old guild-halls, town-halls, and stadthold-houses, to be seen in the land of the ancient Flemings. A third was a great frequenter of the British Museum, and knew all about scores of wonderful antiquities, of Oriental manuscripts, and costly books without a duplicate. A fourth had lately returned from a trip to Old Granada, and, of course, was full of Saracenic scenery. A fifth had a funny case in law to tell. A sixth was erudite in wines. A seventh had a strange characteristic anecdote of the private life of the Iron Duke, never printed, and never before announced in any public or private company. An eighth had lately been amusing his evenings, now and then, with translating a comic poem of Pulci's. He quoted for us the more amusing passages.

And so the evening slipped along, the hours told, not by a water-clock, like King Alfred's, but a wine-chronometer. Meantime the table seemed a sort of Epsom Heath;[17] a regular ring, where the decanters galloped round. For fear one decanter should not with sufficient speed reach his destination, another was sent express after him to hurry him; and then a third to hurry the second; and so on with a fourth and fifth. And throughout all this nothing loud, nothing unmannerly, nothing turbulent. I am quite sure, from the scrupulous gravity and austerity of his air, that had Socrates, the field-marshal, perceived aught of indecorum in the company he served, he would have forthwith departed without giving warning. I afterward learned that, during the repast, an invalid bachelor in an adjoining chamber enjoyed his first sound refreshing slumber in three long, weary weeks.

It was the very perfection of quiet absorption of good living, good drinking, good feeling, and good talk. We were a band of brothers. Comfort—fraternal, household comfort, was the grand trait of the affair. Also, you could plainly see that these easy-

---

[15] Cups or glasses filled to the brim.

[16] Disciple and companion of the Apostle
Paul, to whom Paul addressed two Epistles,
1 Timothy and 2 Timothy.

[17] Racetrack.

hearted men had no wives or children to give an anxious thought. Almost all of them were travelers, too; for bachelors alone can travel freely, and without any twinges of their consciences touching desertion of the fireside.

The thing called pain, the bugbear styled trouble—those two legends seemed preposterous to their bachelor imaginations. How could men of liberal sense, ripe scholarship in the world, and capacious philosophical and convivial understandings—how could they suffer themselves to be imposed upon by such monkish fables? Pain! Trouble! As well talk of Catholic miracles. No such thing.—Pass the sherry, sir.—Pooh, pooh! Can't be!—The port, sir, if you please. Nonsense; don't tell me so.—The decanter stops with you, sir, I believe.

And so it went.

Not long after the cloth was drawn our host glanced significantly upon Socrates, who, solemnly stepping to a stand, returned with an immense convolved horn, a regular Jericho horn,[18] mounted with polished silver, and otherwise chased and curiously enriched; not omitting two life-like goats' heads, with four more horns of solid silver, projecting from opposite sides of the mouth of the noble main horn.

Not having heard that our host was a performer on the bugle, I was surprised to see him lift this horn from the table, as if he were about to blow an inspiring blast. But I was relieved from this, and set quite right as touching the purposes of the horn, by his now inserting his thumb and forefinger into its mouth; whereupon a slight aroma was stirred up, and my nostrils were greeted with the smell of some choice Rappee. It was a mull of snuff. It went the rounds. Capital idea this, thought I, of taking snuff about this juncture. This goodly fashion must be introduced among my countrymen at home, further ruminated I.

The remarkable decorum of the nine bachelors—a decorum not to be affected by any quantity of wine—a decorum unassailable by any degree of mirthfulness—this was again set in a forcible light to me, by now observing that, though they took snuff very freely, yet not a man so far violated the proprieties, or so far molested the invalid bachelor in the adjoining room as to indulge himself in a sneeze. The snuff was snuffed silently, as if it had been some fine innoxious powder brushed off the wings of butterflies.

But fine though they be, bachelors' dinners, like bachelors' lives, can not endure forever. The time came for breaking up. One by one the bachelors took their hats, and two by two, and arm-in-arm they descended, still conversing, to the flagging of the court; some going to their neighboring chambers to turn over the *Decameron* ere retiring for the night; some to smoke a cigar, promenading in the garden on the cool river-side; some to make for the street, call a hack, and be driven snugly to their distant lodgings.

I was the last lingerer.

"Well," said my smiling host, "what do you think of the Temple here, and the sort of life we bachelors make out to live in it?"

"Sir," said I, with a burst of admiring candor—"Sir, this is the very Paradise of Bachelors!"

---

[18] Ram's horn made into a wind instrument.

II: The Tartarus[19] of Maids

It lies not far from Woedolor Mountain in New England. Turning to the East, right out from among bright farms and sunny meadows, nodding in early June with odorous grasses, you enter ascendingly among bleak hills. These gradually close in upon a dusky pass, which, from the violent Gulf Stream of air unceasingly driving between its cloven walls of haggard rock, as well as from the tradition of a crazy spinster's hut having long ago stood somewhere hereabouts, is called the Mad Maid's Bellows-pipe.

Winding along at the bottom of the gorge is a dangerously narrow wheel-road, occupying the bed of a former torrent. Following this road to its highest point, you stand as within a Dantean[20] gateway. From the steepness of the walls here, their strangely ebon hue, and the sudden contraction of the gorge, this particular point is called the Black Notch. The ravine now expandingly descends into a great, purple, hopper-shaped hollow, far sunk among many Plutonian,[21] shaggy-wooded mountains. By the country people this hollow is called the Devil's Dungeon. Sounds of torrents fall on all sides upon the ear. These rapid waters unite at last in one turbid brick-colored stream, boiling through a flume among enormous boulders. They call this strange-colored torrent Blood River. Gaining a dark precipice it wheels suddenly to the West, and makes one maniac spring of sixty feet into the arms of a stunted wood of gray-haired pines, between which it thence eddies on its further way down to the invisible low-lands.

Conspicuously crowning a rocky bluff high to one side, at the cataract's verge, is the ruin of an old saw-mill, built in those primitive times when vast pines and hemlocks superabounded throughout the neighboring region. The black-mossed bulk of those immense, rough-hewn, and spike-knotted logs, here and there tumbled all together, in long abandonment and decay, or left in solitary, perilous projection over the cataract's gloomy brink, impart to this rude wooden ruin not only much of the aspect of one of rough-quarried stone, but also a sort of feudal, Rhineland, and Thurmberg[22] look, derived from the pinnacled wildness of the neighboring scenery.

Not far from the bottom of the Dungeon stands a large whitewashed building, relieved, like some great whited sepulchre, against the sullen background of mountainside firs, and other hardy evergreens, inaccessibly rising in grim terraces for some two thousand feet.

The building is a paper-mill.

Having embarked on a large scale in the seedsman's business (so extensively and broadcast, indeed, that at length my seeds were distributed through all the Eastern and Northern States, and even fell into the far soil of Missouri and the Carolinas), the demand for paper at my place became so great, that the expenditure soon amounted to a most important item in the general account. It need hardly be hinted how paper comes into use with seedsmen, as envelopes. These are mostly made of yellowish paper, folded square; and when filled, are all but flat, and being stamped, and superscribed with the nature of the seeds contained, assume not a little the appearance of business-letters ready for the mail. Of these small envelopes I used an incredible quantity—several hun-

---

[19] In Greek myth, a sunless abyss below Hades.

[20] Dante Alighieri (1265–1321), Italian poet of whose allegorical epic poem, *Divine Comedy,* the *Inferno* is a part.

[21] In Greek myth, Pluto or Hades is the god of the underworld or region of the dead.

[22] German forest lands.

dreds of thousands in a year. For a time I had purchased my paper from the wholesale dealers in a neighboring town. For economy's sake, and partly for the adventure of the trip, I now resolved to cross the mountains, some sixty miles, and order my future paper at the Devil's Dungeon paper-mill.

The sleighing being uncommonly fine toward the end of January, and promising to hold so for no small period, in spite of the bitter cold I started one gray Friday noon in my pung,[23] well fitted with buffalo and wolf robes; and, spending one night on the road, next noon came in sight of Woedolor Mountain.

The far summit fairly smoked with frost; white vapors curled up from its white-wooded top, as from a chimney. The intense congelation made the whole country look like one petrifaction.[24] The steel shoes of my pung craunched and gritted over the vitreous, chippy snow, as if it had been broken glass. The forests here and there skirting the route, feeling the same all-stiffening influence, their inmost fibres penetrated with the cold, strangely groaned—not in the swaying branches merely, but likewise in the vertical trunk—as the fitful gusts remorselessly swept through them. Brittle with excessive frost, many colossal tough-grained maples, snapped in twin like pipestems, cumbered the unfeeling earth.

Flaked all over with frozen sweat, white as a milky ram, his nostrils at each breath sending forth two horn-shaped shoots of heated respiration, Black, my good horse, but six years old, started at a sudden turn, where, right across the track—not ten minutes fallen—an old distorted hemlock lay, darkly undulatory as an anaconda.

Gaining the Bellows-pipe, the violent blast, dead from behind, all but shoved my high-backed pung up-hill. The gust shrieked through the shivered pass, as if laden with lost spirits bound to the unhappy world. Ere gaining the summit, Black, my horse, as if exasperated by the cutting wind, slung out with his strong hind legs, tore the light pung straight up-hill, and sweeping grazingly through the narrow notch, sped downward madly past the ruined saw-mill. Into the Devil's Dungeon horse and cataract rushed together.

With might and main, quitting my seat and robes, and standing backward, with one foot braced against the dashboard, I rasped and churned the bit, and stopped him just in time to avoid collision, at a turn, with the bleak nozzle of a rock, couchant like a lion in the way—a roadside rock.

At first I could not discover the paper-mill.

The whole hollow gleamed with the white, except, here and there, where a pinnacle of granite showed one wind-swept angle bare. The mountains stood pinned in shrouds—a pass of Alpine corpses. Where stands the mill? Suddenly a whirring, humming sound broke upon my ear. I looked, and there, like an arrested avalanche, lay the large whitewashed factory. It was subordinately surrounded by a cluster of other and smaller buildings, some of which, from their cheap, blank air, great length, gregarious windows, and comfortless expression, no doubt were boarding-houses of the operatives.[25] A snow-white hamlet amidst the snows. Various rude, irregular squares and courts resulted from the somewhat picturesque clusterings of these buildings, owing to the broken, rocky nature of the ground, which forbade all method in their relative

---

[23] Boxlike sleigh on runners.
[24] i.e., in the process of petrifying.

[25] Factory workers.

arrangement. Several narrow lanes and alleys, too, partly blocked with snow fallen from the roof, cut up the hamlet in all directions.

When, turning from the traveled highway, jingling with bells of numerous farmers—who, availing themselves of the fine sleighing, were dragging their wood to market—and frequently diversified with swift cutters dashing from inn to inn of the scattered villages—when, I say, turning from that bustling main-road, I by degrees wound into the Mad Maid's Bellows-pipe, and saw the grim Black Notch beyond, then something latent, as well as something obvious in the time and scene, strangely brought back to my mind my first sight of dark and grimy Temple Bar. And when Black, my horse, went darting through the Notch, perilously grazing its rocky wall, I remembered being in a runaway London omnibus, which in much the same sort of style, though by no means at an equal rate, dashed through the ancient arch of Wren.[26] Though the two objects did by no means completely correspond, yet this partial inadequacy but served to tinge the similitude not less with the vividness than the disorder of a dream. So that, when upon reining up at the protruding rock I at last caught sight of the quaint groupings of the factory-buildings, and with the traveled highway and the Notch behind, found myself all alone, silently and privily stealing through deep-cloven passages into this sequestered spot, and saw the long, high-gabled main factory edifice, with a rude tower—for hoisting heavy boxes—at one end, standing among its crowded outbuildings and boarding-houses, as the Temple Church amidst the surrounding offices and dormitories, and when the marvelous retirement of this mysterious mountain nook fastened its whole spell upon me, then, what memory lacked, all tributary imagination furnished, and I said to myself, "This is the very counterpart of the Paradise of Bachelors, but snowed upon, and frost-painted to a sepulchre."

Dismounting and warily picking my way down the dangerous declivity—horse and man both sliding now and then upon the icy ledges—at length I drove, or the blast drove me, into the largest square, before one side of the main edifice. Piercingly and shrilly the shotted blast blew by the corner; and redly and demoniacally boiled Blood River at one side. A long wood-pile, of many scores of cords, all glittering in mail of crusted ice, stood crosswise in the square. A row of horse-posts, their north sides plastered with adhesive snow, flanked the factory wall. The bleak frost packed and paved the square as with some ringing metal.

The inverted similitude recurred—"The sweet, tranquil Temple garden, with the Thames bordering its green beds," strangely mediated I.

But where are the gay bachelors?

Then, as I and my horse stood shivering in the wind-spray, a girl ran from a neighboring dormitory door, and throwing her thin apron over her bare head, made for the opposite building.

"One moment, my girl; is there no shed hereabouts which I may drive into?"

Pausing, she turned upon me a face pale with work, and blue with cold; an eye supernatural with unrelated misery.

"Nay," faltered I, "I mistook you. Go on; I want nothing."

---

[26] Sir Christopher Wren (1632–1723), noted English architect.

Leading my horse close to the door from which she had come, I knocked. Another pale, blue girl appeared, shivering in the doorway as, to prevent the blast, she jealously held the door ajar.

"Nay, I mistake again. In God's name shut the door. But hold, is there no man about?"

That moment a dark-complexioned, well-wrapped personage passed, making for the factory door, and spying him coming, the girl rapidly closed the other one.

"Is there no horse-shed here, sir?"

"Yonder, to the wood-shed," he replied, and disappeared inside the factory.

With much ado I managed to wedge in horse and pung between the scattered piles of wood all sawn and split. Then, blanketing my horse, and piling my buffalo on the blanket's top, and tucking in its edges well around the breast-band and breeching, so that the wind might not strip him bare, I tied him fast, and ran lamely for the factory door, stiff with frost, and cumbered with my driver's dread-naught.

Immediately I found myself standing in a spacious place, intolerably lighted by long rows of windows, focusing inward the snowy scene without.

At rows of blank-looking counters sat rows of blank-looking girls, with blank, white folders in their blank hands, all blankly folding blank paper.

In one corner stood some huge frame of ponderous iron, with a vertical thing like a piston periodically rising and falling upon a heavy wooden block. Before it—its tame minister—stood a tall girl, feeding the iron animal with half-quires[27] of rose-hued note-paper which, at every downward dab of the piston-like machine, received in the corner the impress of a wreath of roses. I looked from the rosy paper to the pallid cheek, but said nothing.

Seated before a long apparatus, strung with long, slender strings like any harp, another girl was feeding it with foolscap[28] sheets which, so soon as they curiously traveled from her on the cords, were withdrawn at the opposite end of the machine by a second girl. They came to the first girl blank; they went to the second girl ruled.

I looked upon the first girl's brow, and saw it was young and fair; I looked upon the second girl's brow, and saw it was ruled and wrinkled. Then, as I still looked, the two— for some small variety to the monotony—changed places; and where had stood the young, fair brow, now stood the ruled and wrinkled one.

Perched high upon a narrow platform, and still higher upon a high stool crowning it, sat another figure serving some other iron animal; while below the platform sat her mate in some sort of reciprocal attendance.

Not a syllable was breathed. Nothing was heard but the low, steady overruling hum of the iron animals. The human voice was banished from the spot. Machinery—that vaunted slave of humanity—here stood menially served by human beings, who served mutely and cringingly as the slave serves the Sultan. The girls did not so much seem accessory wheels to the general machinery as mere cogs to the wheels.

All this scene around me was instantaneously taken in at one sweeping glance—even before I had proceeded to unwind the heavy fur tippet[29] from around my neck. But as soon as this fell from me, the dark-complexioned man, standing close by, raised a sud-

[27] Sets of uniform sheets of paper.
[28] A size (13 1/2 × 17 inches) of drawing or printing paper.

[29] Neck scarf.

den cry, and seizing my arm, dragged me out into the open air, and without pausing for a word instantly caught up some congealed snow and began rubbing both my cheeks.

"Two white spots like the whites of your eyes," he said; "man, your cheeks are frozen."

"That may well be," muttered I; " 'tis some wonder the frost of the Devil's Dungeon strikes in no deeper. Rub away."

Soon a horrible, tearing pain caught at my reviving cheeks. Two gaunt bloodhounds, one on each side, seemed mumbling them. I seemed Actaeon.[30]

Presently, when all was over, I re-entered the factory, made known my business, concluded it satisfactorily, and then begged to be conducted throughout the place to view it.

"Cupid is the boy for that," said the dark-complexioned man. "Cupid!" and by this odd fancy-name calling a dimpled, red-cheeked, spirited-looking, forward little fellow, who was rather impudently, I thought, gliding about among the passive-looking girls— like a gold-fish through hueless waves—yet doing nothing in particular that I could see, the man bade him lead the stranger through the edifice.

"Come first and see the water-wheel," said this lively lad, with the air of boyishly-brisk importance.

Quitting the folding-room, we crossed some damp, cold boards, and stood beneath a great wet shed, incessantly showering with foam, like the green barnacled bow of some East Indiaman in a gale. Round and round here went the enormous revolutions of the dark colossal water-wheel, grim with its one immutable purpose.

"This sets our whole machinery a-going, sir; in every part of all these buildings; where the girls work and all."

I looked, and saw that the turbid waters of Blood River had not changed their hue by coming under the use of man.

"You make only blank paper; no printing of any sort, I suppose? All blank paper, don't you?"

"Certainly; what else should a paper-factory make?"

The lad here looked at me as if suspicious of my commonsense.

"Oh, to be sure!" said I, confused and stammering; "it only struck me as so strange that red waters should turn out pale chee—— paper, I mean."

He took me up a wet and rickety stair to a great light room, furnished with no visible thing but rude, manger-like receptacles running all round its sides; and up to these mangers, like so many mares haltered to the rack, stood rows of girls. Before each was vertically thrust up a long, glittering scythe, immovably fixed at bottom to the manger-edge. The curve of the scythe, and its having no snath to it, made it look exactly like a sword. To and fro, across the sharp edge, the girls forever dragged long strips of rags, washed white, picked from baskets at one side; thus ripping asunder every seam, and converting the tatters almost into lint. The air swam with the fine, poisonous particles, which from all sides darted, subtilely, as motes in sunbeams, into the lungs.

"This is the rag-room," coughed the boy.

"You find it rather stifling here," coughed I, in answer; "but the girls don't cough."

"Oh, they are used to it."

---

[30] In Greek myth, hunter who was changed into a stag and torn to pieces by his own hounds.

"Where do you get such hosts of rags?" picking up a handful from a basket.

"Some from the country round about; some from far over sea—Leghorn and London."

" 'Tis not unlikely, then," murmured I, "that among these heaps of rags there may be some old shirts, gathered from the dormitories of the Paradise of Bachelors. But the buttons are all dropped off. Pray, my lad, do you ever find any bachelors' buttons hereabouts?"

"None grow in this part of the country. The Devil's Dungeon is no place for flowers."

"Oh! you mean the *flowers* so called—the Bachelor's Buttons?"

"And was not that what you asked about? Or did you mean the gold bosom-buttons of our boss, Old Bach, as our whispering girls all call him?"

"The man, then, I saw below is a bachelor, is he?"

"Oh, yes, he's a Bach."

"The edges of those swords, they are turned outward from the girls, if I see right; but their rags and fingers fly so, I can not distinctly see."

"Turned outward."

Yes, murmured I to myself; I see it now; turned outward; and each erected sword is so borne, edge-outward, before each girl. If my reading fails me not, just so, of old, condemned state-prisoners went from the hall of judgment to their doom: an officer before, bearing a sword, its edge turned outward, in significance of their fatal sentence. So, through consumptive pallors of this blank, raggy life, go these white girls to death.

"Those scythes look very sharp," again turning toward the boy.

"Yes; they have to keep them so. Look!"

That moment two of the girls, dropping their rags, plied each a whet-stone up and down the sword-blade. My unaccustomed blood curdled at the sharp shriek of the tormented steel.

Their own executioners; themselves whetting the very swords that slay them; meditated I.

"What makes those girls so sheet-white, my lad?"

"Why"—with a roguish twinkle, pure ignorant drollery, not knowing heartlessness—"I suppose the handling of such white bits of sheets all the time makes them so sheety."

"Let us leave the rag-room now, my lad."

More tragical and more inscrutably mysterious than any mystic sight, human or machine, throughout the factory, was the strange innocence of cruel-heartedness in this usage-hardened boy.

"And now," said he, cheerily, "I suppose you want to see our great machine, which cost us twelve thousand dollars only last autumn. That's the machine that makes the paper, too. This way, sir."

Following him, I crossed a large, bespattered place, with two great round vats in it, full of a white, wet, woolly-looking stuff, not unlike the albuminous part of an egg, soft-boiled.

"There," said Cupid, tapping the vats carelessly, "these are the first beginnings of the paper, this white pulp you see. Look how it swims bubbling round and round, moved by the paddle here. From hence it pours from both vats into that one common channel yonder, and so goes, mixed up and leisurely, to the great machine. And now for that."

He led me into a room, stifling with a strange, blood-like, abdominal heat, as if here, true enough, were being finally developed the germinous particles lately seen.

Before me, rolled out like some long Eastern manuscript, lay stretched one continuous length of iron frame-word—multitudinous and mystical, with all sorts of rollers, wheels, and cylinders, in slowly-measured and unceasing motion.

"Here first comes the pulp now," said Cupid, pointing to the nighest end of the machine. "See; first it pours out and spreads itself upon this wide, sloping board; and then—look—slides, thin and quivering, beneath the first roller there. Follow on now, and see it as it slides from under that to the next cylinder. There; see how it has become just a very little less pulpy now. One step more, and it grows still more to some slight consistence. Still another cylinder, and it is so knitted—though as yet mere dragon-fly wing—that it forms an air-bridge here, like a suspended cobweb, between two more separated rollers; and flowing over the last one, and under again, and doubling about there out of sight for a minute among all those mixed cylinders you indistinctly see, it reappears here, looking now at last a little less like pulp and more like paper, but still quite delicate and defective yet awhile. But—a little further onward, sir, if you please— here now, at this further point, it puts on something of a real look, as if it might turn out to be something you might possibly handle in the end. But it's not yet done, sir. Good way to travel yet, and plenty more of cylinders must roll it."

"Bless my soul!" said I, amazed at the elongation, interminable convolutions, and deliberate slowness of the machine; "it must take a long time for the pulp to pass from end to end, and come out paper."

"Oh! not so long," smiled the precocious lad, with a superior and patronizing air; "only nine minutes. But look; you may try it for yourself. Have you a bit of paper? Ah! here's a bit on the floor. Now mark that with any word you please, and let me dab it on here, and we'll see how long before it comes out at the other end."

"Well, let me see," said I, taking out my pencil; "come, I'll mark it with your name."

Bidding me take out my watch, Cupid adroitly dropped the inscribed slip on an exposed part of the incipient mass.

Instantly my eye marked the second-hand on my dial-plate.

Slowly I followed the slip, inch by inch; sometimes pausing for full half a minute as it disappeared beneath inscrutable groups of the lower cylinders, but only gradually to emerge again; and so, on, and on, and on—inch by inch; now in open sight, sliding along like a freckle on the quivering sheet; and then again wholly vanished; and so, on, and on, and on—inch by inch; all the time the main sheet growing more and more to final firmness—when, suddenly, I saw a sort of paper-fall, not wholly unlike a waterfall; a scissory sound smote my ear, as of some cord being snapped; and down dropped an unfolded sheet of perfect foolscap, with my "Cupid" half faded out of it, and still moist and warm.

My travels were at an end, for here was the end of the machine.

"Well, how long was it?" said Cupid.

"Nine minutes to a second," replied I, watch in hand.

"I told you so."

For a moment a curious emotion filled me, not wholly unlike that which one might experience at the fulfillment of some mysterious prophecy. But how absurd, thought I again; the thing is a mere machine, the essence of which is unvarying punctuality and precision.

Previously absorbed by the wheels and cylinders, my attention was now directed to a sad-looking woman standing by.

"That is rather an elderly person so silently tending the machine-end here. She would not seem wholly used to it either."

"Oh," knowingly whispered Cupid, through the din, "she only came last week. She was a nurse formerly. But the business is poor in these parts, and she's left it. But look at the paper she is piling there."

"Aye, foolscap," handling the piles of moist, warm sheets, which continually were being delivered into the woman's waiting hands. "Don't you turn out anything but foolscap at this machine?"

"Oh, sometimes, but not often, we turn out finer work—cream-laid and royal sheets, we call them. But foolscap being in chief demand, we turn out foolscap most."

It was very curious. Looking at that blank paper continually dropping, dropping, dropping, my mind ran on in wonderings of those strange uses to which those thousand sheets eventually would be put. All sorts of writings would be writ on those now vacant things—sermons, lawyers' briefs, physicians' prescriptions, love-letters, marriage certificates, bills of divorce, registers of births, death-warrants, and so on, without end. Then, recurring back to them as they here lay all blank, I could not but bethink me of that celebrated comparison of John Locke,[31] who, in demonstration of his theory that man had no innate ideas, compared the human mind at birth to a sheet of blank paper; something destined to be scribbled on, but what sort of characters no soul might tell.

Pacing slowly to and fro along the involved machine, still humming with its play, I was struck as well by the inevitability as the evolvement-power in all its motions.

"Does that thin cobweb there," said I, pointing to the sheet in its more imperfect stage, "does that never tear or break? It is marvelous fragile, and yet this machine it passes through is so mighty."

"It never is known to tear a hair's point."

"Does it never stop—get clogged?"

"No. It *must* go. The machinery makes it go just *so;* just that very way, and at that very pace you there plainly *see* it go. The pulp can't help going."

Something of awe now stole over me, as I gazed upon this inflexible iron animal. Always, more or less, machinery of this ponderous, elaborate sort strikes, in some moods, strange dread into the human heart, as some living, panting Behemoth might. But what made the thing I saw so specially terrible to me was the metallic necessity, the unbudging fatality which governed it. Though, here and there, I could not follow the thin, gauzy vail of pulp in the course of its more mysterious or entirely invisible advance, yet it was indubitable that, at those points where it eluded me, it still marched on in unvarying docility to the autocratic cunning of the machine. A fascination fastened on me. I stood spell-bound and wandering in my soul. Before my eyes—there, passing in slow procession along the wheeling cylinders, I seemed to see, glued to the pallid incipience of the pulp, the yet more pallid faces of all the pallid girls I had eyed that heavy day. Slowly, mournfully, beseechingly, yet unresistingly, they gleamed along, their agony dimly outlined on the imperfect paper, like the print of the tormented face on the handkerchief of Saint Veronica.[32]

---

[31] English philosopher (1632–1704).
[32] A woman of Jerusalem who wiped the brow
of Jesus as he carried the cross to Calvary.

"Halloa! the heat of the room is too much for you," cried Cupid, staring at me.

"No—I am rather chill, if anything."

"Come out, sir—out—out," and, with the protecting air of a careful father, the precocious lad hurried me outside.

In a few moments, feeling revived a little, I went into the folding-room—the first room I had entered, and where the desk for transacting business stood, surrounded by the blank counters and blank girls engaged at them.

"Cupid here has led me a strange tour," said I to the dark-complexioned man before mentioned, whom I had ere this discovered not only to be an old bachelor, but also the principal proprietor. "Yours is a most wonderful factory. Your great machine is a miracle of inscrutable intricacy."

"Yes, all our visitors think it so. But we don't have many. We are in a very out-of-the-way corner here. Few inhabitants, too. Most of our girls come from far-off villages."

"The girls," echoed I, glancing round at their silent forms. "Why is it, sir, that in most factories, female operatives, of whatever age, are indiscriminately called girls, never women?"

"Oh! as to that—why, I suppose, the fact of their being generally unmarried—that's the reason, I should think. But it never struck me before. For our factory here, we will not have married women; they are apt to be off-and-on too much. We want none but steady workers: twelve hours to the day, day after day, through the three hundred and sixty-five days, excepting Sundays, Thanksgiving, and Fast-days. That's our rule. And so, having no married women, what females we have are rightly enough called girls."

"Then these are all maids," said I, while some pained homage to their pale virginity made me involuntarily bow.

"All maids."

Again the strange emotion filled me.

"Your cheeks look whitish yet, sir," said the man, gazing at me narrowly. "You must be careful going home. Do they pain you at all now? It's a bad sign, if they do."

"No doubt, sir," answered I, "when once I have got out of the Devil's Dungeon, I shall feel them mending."

"Ah, yes; the winter air in valleys, or gorges, or any sunken place, is far colder and more bitter than elsewhere. You would hardly believe it now, but it is colder here than at the top of Woedolor Mountain."

"I dare say it is, sir. But time presses me; I must depart."

With that, remuffling myself in dread-naught and tippet, thrusting my hands into my huge seal-skin mittens, I sallied out into the nipping air, and found poor Black, my horse, all cringing and doubled up with the cold.

Soon, wrapped in furs and meditations, I ascended from the Devil's Dungeon.

At the Black Notch I paused, and once more bethought me of Temple Bar. Then, shooting through the pass, all alone with inscrutable nature, I exclaimed—Oh! Paradise of Bachelors! and oh! Tartarus of Maids!

1835

Billy Budd, Sailor
(An Inside Narrative)*

Dedicated
to
JACK CHASE
Englishman
Wherever that great heart may now be
Here on Earth or harbored in Paradise.
Captain of the Maintop
in the year 1843
in the U.S. Frigate
United States[1]

1

In the time before steamships, or then more frequently than now, a stroller along the docks of any considerable seaport would occasionally have his attention arrested by a group of bronzed mariners, man-of-war's men or merchant sailors in holiday attire, ashore on liberty. In certain instances they would flank, or like a bodyguard quite surround, some superior figure of their own class, moving along with them like Aldebaran[2] among the lesser lights of his constellation. That signal object was the "Handsome Sailor" of the less prosaic time alike of the military and merchant navies. With no perceptible trace of the vain-glorious about him, rather with the offhand unaffectedness of natural regality, he seemed to accept the spontaneous homage of his shipmates.

A somewhat remarkable instance recurs to me. In Liverpool, now half a century ago, I saw under the shadow of the great dingy street-wall of Prince's Dock (an obstruction long since removed) a common sailor so intensely black that he must needs have been a native African of the unadulterate blood of Ham[3]—a symmetric figure much above the average height. The two ends of a gay silk handkerchief thrown loose about the neck danced upon the displayed ebony of his chest, in his ears were big hoops of gold, and a Highland bonnet with a tartan band set off his shapely head. It was a hot noon in July; and his face, lustrous with perspiration, beamed with barbaric good humor. In jovial

---

* Melville's mysterious phrase has been interpreted in several ways. Historically *Billy Budd* is based upon a 1797 mutiny in the British Navy, yet it also is the insider's version of an 1842 mutiny on the *Somers,* an American naval ship. Psychologically, *Billy Budd* may represent Melville's private, inner life. And the narrative, which on one level is an adventure story, also yields deeper, "inside" meanings. *Billy Budd* was written in the late 1880s, then found in manuscript among Melville's belongings after his death, and finally published in 1924.

[1] Jack Chase, Melville's shipmate on the *United States,* appeared in Melville's novel *White-Jacket* (1850) as the leader of the skilled crew assigned to the top of the mainmast.

[2] The brightest star and "eye" of the constellation Taurus, the Bull.

[3] Noah's curse on his son Ham, in Genesis 9:22–25, was assumed to result in black skin in Ham's descendants.

Black & white representation

sallies right and left, his white teeth flashing into view, he rollicked along, the center of a company of his shipmates. These were made up of such an assortment of tribes and complexions as would have well fitted them to be marched up by Anacharsis Cloots[4] before the bar of the first French Assembly as Representatives of the Human Race. At each spontaneous tribute rendered by the wayfarers to this black pagod[5] of a fellow—the tribute of a pause and stare, and less frequently an exclamation—the motley retinue showed that they took that sort of pride in the evoker of it which the Assyrian priests doubtless showed for their grand sculptured Bull when the faithful prostrated themselves.

To return. If in some cases a bit of a nautical Murat[6] in setting forth his person ashore, the Handsome Sailor of the period in question evinced nothing of the dandified Billy-be-Dam, an amusing character all but extinct now, but occasionally to be encountered, and in a form yet more amusing than the original, at the tiller of the boats on the tempestuous Erie Canal or, more likely, vaporing in the groggeries along the towpath.[7] Invariably a proficient in his perilous calling, he was also more or less of a mighty boxer or wrestler. It was strength and beauty. Tales of his prowess were recited. Ashore he was the champion; afloat the spokesman; on every suitable occasion always foremost. Close-reefing topsails in a gale, there he was, astride the weather yardarm-end, foot in the Flemish horse as stirrup,[8] both hands tugging at the earing as at a bridle, in very much the attitude of young Alexander curbing the fiery Bucephalus.[9] A superb figure, tossed up as by the horns of Taurus against the thunderous sky, cheerily hallooing to the strenuous file along the spar.

The moral nature was seldom out of keeping with the physical make. Indeed, except as toned by the former, the comeliness and power, always attractive in masculine conjunction, hardly could have drawn the sort of honest homage the Handsome Sailor in some examples received from his less gifted associates.

Such a cynosure, at least in aspect, and something such too in nature, though with important variations made apparent as the story proceeds, was welkin-eyed[10] Billy Budd—or Baby Budd, as more familiarly, under circumstances hereafter to be given, he at last came to be called—aged twenty-one, a foretopman[11] of the British fleet toward the close of the last decade of the eighteenth century. It was not very long prior to the time of the narration that follows that he had entered the King's service, having been impressed on the Narrow Seas[12] from a homeward-bound English merchantman into a seventy-four[13] outward bound, H.M.S. *Bellipotent;* which ship, as was not unusual in those hurried days, having been obliged to put to sea short of her proper complement

---

[4] Revolutionary Prussian (1755–1794) who demonstrated the variety and unity of mankind by parading men of different classes and nationalities before the French National Assembly.

[5] Idol.

[6] Joachim Murat (1767–1815), a dandy and king of Naples.

[7] i.e., boasting in the saloons, the placid Erie Canal being hardly tempestuous.

[8] i.e., he was lowering sails and fastening them to a yardarm or spar while braced in the foot rope on the end of the yardarm on the windward side.

[9] Horse of Alexander the Great (356–323 B.C.).

[10] Blue-eyed.

[11] Crewman assigned to the top of the foretop mast.

[12] Forced into naval service on the channels separating England from Ireland and Europe.

[13] Battleship of an impressive 74 guns.

of men. Plump upon Billy at first sight in the gangway the boarding officer, Lieutenant Ratcliffe, pounced, even before the merchantman's crew was formally mustered on the quarter-deck for his deliberate inspection. And him only he elected. For whether it was because the other men when ranged before him showed to ill advantage after Billy, or whether he had some scruples in view of the merchantman's being rather short-handed, however it might be, the officer contented himself with his first spontaneous choice. To the surprise of the ship's company, though much to the lieutenant's satisfaction, Billy made no demur. But, indeed, any demur would have been as idle as the protest of a goldfinch popped into a cage.

Noting this uncomplaining acquiescence, all but cheerful, one might say, the shipmaster turned a surprised glance of silent reproach at the sailor. The shipmaster was one of those worthy mortals found in every vocation, even the humbler ones—the sort of person whom everybody agrees in calling "a respectable man." And—nor so strange to report as it may appear to be—though a ploughman of the troubled waters, lifelong contending with the intractable elements, there was nothing this honest soul at heart loved better than simple peace and quiet. For the rest, he was fifty or thereabouts, a little inclined to corpulence, a prepossessing face, unwhiskered, and of an agreeable color—a rather full face, humanely intelligent in expression. On a fair day with a fair wind and all going well, a certain musical chime in his voice seemed to be the veritable unobstructed outcome of the innermost man. He had much prudence, much conscientiousness, and there were occasions when these virtues were the cause of overmuch disquietude in him. On a passage, so long as his craft was in any proximity to land, no sleep for Captain Graveling. He took to heart those serious responsibilities not so heavily borne by some shipmasters.

Now while Billy Budd was down in the forecastle[14] getting his kit together, the *Bellipotent's* lieutenant, burly and bluff, nowise disconcerted by Captain Graveling's omitting to proffer the customary hospitalities on an occasion so unwelcome to him, an omission simply caused by preoccupation of thought, unceremoniously invited himself into the cabin, and also to a flask from the spirit locker, a receptacle which his experienced eye instantly discovered. In fact he was one of those sea dogs in whom all the hardship and peril of naval life in the great prolonged wars of his time never impaired the natural instinct for sensuous enjoyment. His duty he always faithfully did; but duty is sometimes a dry obligation, and he was for irrigating its aridity, whensoever possible, with a fertilizing decoction of strong waters. For the cabin's proprietor there was nothing left but to play the part of the enforced host with whatever grace and alacrity were practicable. As necessary adjuncts to the flask, he silently placed tumbler and water jug before the irrepressible guest. But excusing himself from partaking just then, he dismally watched the unembarrassed officer deliberately diluting his grog a little, then tossing it off in three swallows, pushing the empty tumbler away, yet not so far as to be beyond easy reach, at the same time settling himself in his seat and smacking his lips with high satisfaction, looking straight at the host.

These proceedings over, the master broke the silence; and there lurked a rueful reproach in the tone of his voice: "Lieutenant, you are going to take my best man from me, the jewel of 'em."

---

[14] Crew's quarters in the forward part of the ship.

"Yes, I know," rejoined the other, immediately drawing back the tumbler preliminary to a replenishing. "Yes, I know. Sorry."

"Beg pardon, but you don't understand, Lieutenant. See here, now. Before I shipped that young fellow, my forecastle was a rat-pit of quarrels. It was black times, I tell you, aboard the *Rights* here. I was worried to that degree my pipe had no comfort for me. But Billy came; and it was like a Catholic priest striking peace in an Irish shindy.[15] Not that he preached to them or said or did anything in particular; but a virtue went out of him, sugaring the sour ones. They took to him like hornets to treacle; all but the buffer[16] of the gang, the big shaggy chap with the fire-red whiskers. He indeed, out of envy, perhaps, of the newcomer, and thinking such a "sweet and pleasant fellow," as he mockingly designated him to the others, could hardly have the spirit of a gamecock, must needs bestir himself in trying to get up an ugly row with him. Billy forebore with him and reasoned with him in a pleasant way—he is something like myself, Lieutenant, to whom aught like a quarrel is hateful—but nothing served. So, in the second dog-watch one day, the Red Whiskers in presence of the others, under pretense of showing Billy just whence a sirloin steak was cut—for the fellow had once been a butcher—insultingly gave him a dig under the ribs. Quick as lightning Billy let fly his arm. I dare say he never meant to do quite as much as he did, but anyhow he gave the burly fool a terrible drubbing. It took about half a minute, I should think. And, lord bless you, the lubber was astonished at the celerity. And will you believe it, Lieutenant, the Red Whiskers now really loves Billy—loves him, or is the biggest hypocrite that ever I heard of. But they all love him. Some of 'em do his washing, darn his old trousers for him; the carpenter is at odd times making a pretty little chest of drawers for him. Anybody will do anything for Billy Budd; and it's the happy family here. But now, Lieutenant, if that young fellow goes—I know how it will be aboard the *Rights*. Not again very soon shall I, coming up from dinner, lean over the capstan smoking a quiet pipe—no, not very soon again, I think. Ay, Lieutenant, you are going to take away the jewel of 'em; you are going to take away my peacemaker!" And with that the good soul had really some ado in checking a rising sob.

"Well," said the lieutenant, who had listened with amused interest to all this and now was waxing merry with his tipple; "well, blessed are the peacemakers, especially the fighting peacemakers. And such are the seventy-four beauties some of which you see poking their noses out of the portholes of yonder warship lying to for me," pointing through the cabin window at the *Bellipotent*. "But courage! Don't look so downhearted, man. Why, I pledge you in advance the royal approbation. Rest assured that His Majesty will be delighted to know that in a time when his hardtack is not sought for by sailors with such avidity as should be, a time also when some shipmasters privily resent the borrowing from them a tar or two for the service; His Majesty, I say, will be delighted to learn that *one* shipmaster at least cheerfully surrenders to the King the flower of his flock, a sailor who with equal loyalty makes no dissent.—But where's my beauty? Ah," looking through the cabin's open door, "here he comes; and, by Jove, lugging along his chest—Apollo with his portmanteau!—My man," stepping out to him, "you can't take that big box aboard a warship. The boxes there are mostly shot boxes. Put

---

[15] Brawl.
[16] Bully.

your duds in a bag, lad. Boot and saddle for the cavalryman, bag and hammock for the man-of-war's man."

The transfer from chest to bag was made. And, after seeing his man into the cutter and then following him down, the lieutenant pushed off from the *Rights-of-Man*[17] That was the merchant ship's name, though by her master and crew abbreviated in sailor fashion into the *Rights.* The hardheaded Dundee owner[18] was a staunch admirer of Thomas Paine, whose book in rejoinder to Burke's arraignment of the French Revolution had then been published for some time and had gone everywhere. In christening his vessel after the title of Paine's volume the man of Dundee was something like his contemporary shipowner, Stephen Girard[19] of Philadelphia, whose sympathies, alike with his native land and its liberal philosophers, he evinced by naming his ships after Voltaire, Diderot, and so forth.

But now, when the boat swept under the merchantman's stern, and officer and oarsmen were noting—some bitterly and others with a grin—the name emblazoned there; just then it was that the new recruit jumped up from the bow where the coxswain[20] had directed him to sit, and waving hat to his silent shipmates sorrowfully looking over at him from the taffrail,[21] bade the lads a genial good-bye. Then, making a salutation as to the ship herself, "And good-bye to you too, old *Rights-of-Man.*"

"Down, sir!" roared the lieutenant, instantly assuming all the rigor of his rank, though with difficulty repressing a smile.

To be sure, Billy's action was a terrible breach of naval decorum. But in that decorum he had never been instructed; in consideration of which the lieutenant would hardly have been so energetic in reproof but for the concluding farewell to the ship. This he rather took as meant to convey a covert sally on the new recruit's part, a sly slur at impressment in general, and that of himself in especial. And yet, more likely, if satire it was in effect, it was hardly so by intention, for Billy, though happily endowed with the gaiety of high health, youth, and a free heart, was yet by no means of a satirical turn. The will to it and the sinister dexterity were alike wanting. To deal in double meanings and insinuations of any sort was quite foreign to his nature.

As to his enforced enlistment, that he seemed to take pretty much as he was wont to take any vicissitude of weather. Like the animals, though no philosopher, he was, without knowing it, practically a fatalist. And it may be that he rather liked this adventurous turn in his affairs, which promised an opening into novel scenes and martial excitements.

Aboard the *Bellipotent* our merchant sailor was forthwith rated as an able seaman and assigned to the starboard watch of the foretop. He was soon at home in the service, not at all disliked for his unpretentious good looks and a sort of genial happy-go-lucky air. No merrier man in his mess: in marked contrast to certain other individuals included like himself among the impressed portion of the ship's company; for these when

[17] Thomas Paine's *The Rights of Man* (1791–1792) argued for individual human rights. It was a direct response to Edmund Burke's *Reflections on the Revolution in France* (1790), which stated that human rights are best preserved through strong social and political institutions.

[18] Scotsman from the seaport of Dundee.

[19] Merchant and shipper who admired the views of the French philosophers Voltaire (1694–1778) and Denis Diderot (1713–1784).

[20] Boat steersman.

[21] Rail at ship's rear or stern.

not actively employed were sometimes, and more particularly in the last dogwatch[22] when the drawing near of twilight induced revery, apt to fall into a saddish mood which in some partook of sullenness. But they were not so young as our foretopman, and no few of them must have known a hearth of some sort, others may have had wives and children left, too probably, in uncertain circumstances, and hardly any but must have had acknowledged kith and kin, while for Billy, as will shortly be seen, his entire family was practically invested in himself.

2

Though our new-made foretopman was well received in the top and on the gun decks, hardly here was he that cynosure he had previously been among those minor ship's companies of the merchant marine, with which companies only had he hitherto consorted.

He was young; and despite his all but fully developed frame, in aspect looked even younger than he really was, owing to a lingering adolescent expression in the as yet smooth face all but feminine in purity of natural complexion but where, thanks to his seagoing, the lily was quite suppressed and the rose had some ado visibly to flush through the tan.

To one essentially such a novice in the complexities of factitious life, the abrupt transition from his former and simpler sphere to the ampler and more knowing world of a great warship; this might well have abashed him had there been any conceit or vanity in his composition. Among her miscellaneous multitude, the *Bellipotent* mustered several individuals who however inferior in grade were of no common natural stamp, sailors more signally susceptive of that air which continuous martial discipline and repeated presence in battle can in some degree impart even to the average man. As the Handsome Sailor, Billy Budd's position aboard the seventy-four was something analogous to that of a rustic beauty transplanted from the provinces and brought into competition with the highborn dames of the court. But this change of circumstances he scarce noted. As little did he observe that something about him provoked an ambiguous smile in one or two harder faces among the blue jackets. Nor less unaware was he of the peculiar favorable effect his person and demeanor had upon the more intelligent gentlemen of the quarter-deck.[23] Nor could this well have been otherwise. Cast in a mold peculiar to the finest physical examples of those Englishmen in whom the Saxon strain would seem not at all to partake of any Norman or other admixture, he showed in face that humane look of reposeful good nature which the Greek sculptor in some instances gave to his heroic strong man, Hercules. But this again was subtly modified by another and pervasive quality. The ear, small and shapely, the arch of the foot, the curve in mouth and nostril, even the indurated hand dyed to the orange-tawny of the toucan's bill, a hand telling alike of the halyards and tar bucket; but, above all, something in the mobile expression, and every chance attitude and movement, something suggestive of a mother eminently favored by Love and the Graces; all this strangely indicated a lineage in direct contradiction to his lot. The mysteriousness here became less mysterious

---

[22] A two-hour watch between 4 and 8 P.M. Billy's assignment as foretopman and rating as an able-bodied seaman indicate his skills as a sailor.

[23] Rear section of the main deck, customarily reserved for officers.

through a matter of fact elicited when Billy at the capstan was being formally mustered into the service. Asked by the officer, a small, brisk little gentleman as it chanced, among other questions, his place of birth, he replied, "Please, sir, I don't know."

"Don't know where you were born? Who was your father?"

"God knows, sir."

Struck by the straightforward simplicity of these replies, the officer next asked, "Do you know anything about your beginning?"

"No, sir. But I have heard that I was found in a pretty silk-lined basket hanging one morning from the knocker of a good man's door in Bristol."

"*Found,* say you? Well," throwing back his head and looking up and down the new recruit; "well, it turns out to have been a pretty good find. Hope they'll find some more like you, my man; the fleet sadly needs them."

Yes, Billy Budd was a foundling, a presumable by-blow,[24] and, evidently, no ignoble one. Noble descent was as evident in him as in a blood horse.

For the rest, with little or no sharpness of faculty or any trace of the wisdom of the serpent, nor yet quite a dove,[25] he possessed that kind and degree of intelligence going along with the unconventional rectitude of a sound human creature, one to whom not yet has been proffered the questionable apple of knowledge. He was illiterate; he could not read, but he could sing, and like the illiterate nightingale was sometimes the composer of his own song.

Of self-consciousness he seemed to have little or none, or about as much as we may reasonably impute to a dog of Saint Bernard's breed.

Habitually living with the elements and knowing little more of the land than as a beach, or, rather, that portion of the terraqueous globe providentially set apart for dance-houses, doxies, and tapsters, in short what sailors call a "fiddler's green,"[26] his simple nature remained unsophisticated by those moral obliquities which are not in every case incompatible with that manufacturable thing known as respectability. But are sailors, frequenters of fiddlers' greens, without vices? No; but less often than with landsmen do their vices, so called, partake of crookedness of heart, seeming less to proceed from viciousness than exuberance of vitality after long constraint: frank manifestations in accordance with natural law. By his original constitution aided by the co-operating influences of his lot, Billy in many respects was little more than a sort of upright barbarian, much such perhaps as Adam presumably might have been ere the urbane Serpent wriggled himself into his company.

And here be it submitted that apparently going to corroborate the doctrine of man's Fall,[27] a doctrine now popularly ignored, it is observable that where certain virtues pristine and unadulterate peculiarly characterize anybody in the external uniform of civilization, they will upon scrutiny seem not to be derived from custom or convention, but rather to be out of keeping with these, as if indeed exceptionally transmitted from a period prior to Cain's city[28] and citified man. The character marked by such qualities has to an unvitiated taste an untampered-with flavor like that of berries, while the man

---

[24] Bastard.

[25] Matthew 10:16: "Behold, I send you forth as sheep in the midst of wolves; be ye therefore wise as serpents and harmless as doves."

[26] Doxies: wenches; tapsters: bartenders; "fiddler's green": a sailors' pleasureground.

[27] Human downfall caused by Adam and Eve's sin.

[28] See Genesis 4:16–17. Cain killed his brother, Abel, and then "went out from the presence of the Lord. . . . And he builded a city."

thoroughly civilized, even in a fair specimen of the breed, has to the same moral palate a questionable smack as of a compounded wine. To any stray inheritor of these primitive qualities found, like Caspar Hauser,[29] wandering dazed in any Christian capital of our time, the good-natured poet's famous invocation, near two thousand years ago, of the good rustic out of his latitude in the Rome of the Caesars, still appropriately holds:

> Honest and poor, faithful in word and thought,
> What hath thee, Fabian, to the city brought?[30]

Though our Handsome Sailor had as much of masculine beauty as one can expect anywhere to see; nevertheless, like the beautiful woman in one of Hawthorne's minor tales,[31] there was just one thing amiss in him. No visible blemish indeed, as with the lady; no, but an occasional liability to a vocal defect. Though in the hour of elemental uproar or peril he was everything that a sailor should be, yet under sudden provocation of strong heart-feeling his voice, otherwise singularly musical, as if expressive of the harmony within, was apt to develop an organic hesitancy, in fact more or less of a stutter or even worse. In this particular Billy was a striking instance that the arch interferer, the envious marplot of Eden, still has more or less to do with every human consignment to this planet of Earth. In every case, one way or another he is sure to slip in his little card, as much as to remind us—I too have a hand here.

The avowal of such an imperfection in the Handsome Sailor should be evidence not alone that he is not presented as a conventional hero, but also that the story in which he is the main figure is no romance.

3

At the time of Billy Budd's arbitrary enlistment into the *Bellipotent* that ship was on her way to join the Mediterranean fleet. No long time elapsed before the junction was effected. As one of that fleet the seventy-four participated in its movements, though at times on account of her superior sailing qualities, in the absence of frigates, dispatched on separate duty as a scout and at times on less temporary service. But with all this the story has little concernment, restricted as it is to the inner life of one particular ship and the career of an individual sailor.

It was the summer of 1797. In the April of that year had occurred the commotion at Spithead followed in May by a second and yet more serious outbreak in the fleet at the Nore.[32] The latter is known, and without exaggeration in the epithet, as "the Great Mutiny." It was indeed a demonstration more menacing to England than the contemporary manifestoes and conquering and proselyting armies of the French Directory.[33] To the British Empire the Nore Mutiny was what a strike in the fire brigade would be to London threatened by general arson. In a crisis when the kingdom might well have an-

---

[29] German boy (1812?–1833) of mysterious origins, supposed to be of noble birth and to exhibit an innocent nature.
[30] Martial, *Epigrams*, I, iv.
[31] Hawthorne's "The Birthmark."

[32] Spithead and Nore were locations in which British seamen mutinied.
[33] Post-Revolutionary French governing body (1795–1799).

ticipated the famous signal[34] that some years later published along the naval line of battle what it was that upon occasion England expected of Englishmen; *that* was the time when at the mastheads of the three-deckers and seventy-fours moored in her own roadstead—a fleet the right arm of a Power then all but the sole free conservative one of the Old World—the bluejackets, to be numbered by thousands, ran up with huzzas the British colors with the union and cross wiped out; by that cancellation transmuting the flag of founded law and freedom defined, into the enemy's red meteor of unbridled and unbounded revolt. Reasonable discontent growing out of practical grievances in the fleet had been ignited into irrational combustion as by live cinders blown across the Channel from France in flames.

The event converted into irony for a time those spirited strains of Dibdin[35]—as a song-writer no mean auxiliary to the English government at that European conjuncture—strains celebrating, among other things, the patriotic devotion of the British tar: "And as for my life, 'tis the King's!"

Such an episode in the Island's grand naval story her naval historians naturally abridge, one of them (William James) candidly acknowledging that fain would he pass it over did not "impartiality forbid fastidiousness." And yet his mention is less a narration than a reference, having to do hardly at all with details. Nor are these readily to be found in the libraries. Like some other events in every age befalling states everywhere, including America, the Great Mutiny was of such character that national pride along with views of policy would fain shade it off into the historical background. Such events cannot be ignored, but there is a considerate way of historically treating them. If a well-constituted individual refrains from blazoning aught amiss or calamitous in his family, a nation in the like circumstance may without reproach be equally discreet.

Though after parleyings between government and the ringleaders, and concessions by the former as to some glaring abuses, the first uprising—that at Spithead—with difficulty was put down, or matters for the time pacified; yet at the Nore the unforeseen renewal of insurrection on a yet larger scale, and emphasized in the conferences that ensued by demands deemed by the authorities not only inadmissible but aggressively insolent, indicated—if the Red Flag[36] did not sufficiently do so—what was the spirit animating the men. Final suppression, however, there was; but only made possible perhaps by the unswerving loyalty of the marine corps[37] and a voluntary resumption of loyalty among influential sections of the crews.

To some extent the Nore Mutiny may be regarded as analogous to the distempering irruption of contagious fever in a frame constitutionally sound, and which anon throws it off.

At all events, of these thousands of mutineers were some of the tars who not so very long afterwards—whether wholly prompted thereto by patriotism, or pugnacious instinct, or by both—helped to win a coronet for Nelson at the Nile, and the naval crown of crowns for him at Trafalgar. To the mutineers, those battles and especially Trafalgar were a plenary absolution and a grand one. For all that goes to make up scenic naval

---

[34] Reference to British Admiral Nelson's famous signal, "England expects every man to do his duty," prior to the Battle of Trafalgar (1805).

[35] Charles Dibdin (1745–1815), English writer of patriotic songs.

[36] Traditional banner of revolution.

[37] Marines were stationed on men-of-war and often had an antagonistic relation to the crew.

display and heroic magnificence in arms, those battles, especially Trafalgar, stand unmatched in human annals.

4

In this matter of writing, resolve as one may to keep to the main road, some bypaths have an enticement not readily to be withstood. I am going to err into such a bypath. If the reader will keep me company I shall be glad. At the least, we can promise ourselves that pleasure which is wickedly said to be in sinning, for a literary sin the divergence will be.

Very likely it is no new remark that the inventions of our time have at last brought about a change in sea warfare in degree corresponding to the revolution in all warfare effected by the original introduction from China into Europe of gunpowder. The first European firearm, a clumsy contrivance, was, as is well known, scouted by no few of the knights as a base implement, good enough peradventure for weavers too craven to stand up crossing steel with steel in frank fight. But as ashore knightly valor, though shorn of its blazonry, did not cease with the knights, neither on the seas—though nowadays in encounters there a certain kind of displayed gallantry be fallen out of date as hardly applicable under changed circumstances—did the nobler qualities of such naval magnates as Don John of Austria, Doria, Van Tromp, Jean Bart, the long line of British admirals, and the American Decaturs of 1812 become obsolete with their wooden walls.[38]

Nevertheless, to anybody who can hold the Present at its worth without being inappreciative of the Past, it may be forgiven, if to such an one the solitary old hulk at Portsmouth, Nelson's *Victory,* seems to float there, not alone as the decaying monument of a fame incorruptible, but also as a poetic reproach, softened by its picturesqueness, to the *Monitors* and yet mightier hulls of the European ironclads.[39] And this not altogether because such craft are unsightly, unavoidably lacking the symmetry and grand lines of the old battleships, but equally for other reasons.

There are some, perhaps, who while not altogether inaccessible to that poetic reproach just alluded to, may yet on behalf of the new order be disposed to parry it; and this to the extent of iconoclasm, if need be. For example, prompted by the sight of the star inserted in the *Victory*'s quarter-deck designating the spot where the Great Sailor fell, these martial utilitarians may suggest considerations implying that Nelson's ornate publication of his person in battle was not only unnecessary, but not military, nay, savored of foolhardiness and vanity. They may add, too, that at Trafalgar it was in effect nothing less than a challenge to death; and death came; and that but for his bravado the victorious admiral might possibly have survived the battle, and so, instead of having his sagacious dying injunctions overruled by his immediate successor in command, he himself when the contest was decided might have brought his shattered fleet to anchor,

---

[38] Don Juan of Austria (1547–1578) led a fleet to defeat Turkey (1571); Andrea Doria (1466–1560) was renowned as admiral of the Genoese and French fleet; Maarten Van Tromp (1597–1653) commanded Dutch fleets against Britain and Spain; Jean Bart (1651?–1702) led French privateers against the Dutch; Stephen Decatur (1779–1820) led American naval ships against Tripoli pirates and against Britain in the War of 1812.

[39] The *Victory* was Nelson's flagship at Trafalgar, where he died; the iron-clad Union *Monitor* defeated the Confederate *Merrimac* in the American Civil War.

a proceeding which might have averted the deplorable loss of life by shipwreck in the elemental tempest that followed the martial one.

Well, should we set aside the more than disputable point whether for various reasons it was possible to anchor the fleet, then plausibly enough the Benthamites[40] of war may urge the above. But the *might-have-been* is but boggy ground to build on. And, certainly, in foresight as to the larger issue of an encounter, and anxious preparations for it—buoying the deadly way and mapping it out, as at Copenhagen[41]—few commanders have been so painstakingly circumspect as this same reckless declarer of his person in fight.

Personal prudence, even when dictated by quite other than selfish considerations, surely is no special virtue in a military man; while an excessive love of glory, impassioning a less burning impulse, the honest sense of duty, is the first. If the name *Wellington* is not so much of a trumpet to the blood as the simpler name *Nelson,* the reason for this may perhaps be inferred from the above. Alfred[42] in his funeral ode on the victor of Waterloo ventures not to call him the greatest soldier of all time, though in the same ode he invokes Nelson as "the greatest sailor since our world began."

At Trafalgar Nelson on the brink of opening the fight sat down and wrote his last brief will and testament. If under the presentiment of the most magnificent of all victories to be crowned by his own glorious death, a sort of priestly motive led him to dress his person in the jewelled vouchers of his own shining deeds; if thus to have adorned himself for the altar and the sacrifice were indeed vainglory, then affectation and fustian is each more heroic line in the great epics and dramas, since in such lines the poet but embodies in verse those exaltations of sentiment that a nature like Nelson, the opportunity being given, vitalizes into acts.

5

Yes, the outbreak at the Nore was put down. But not every grievance was redressed. If the contractors, for example, were no longer permitted to ply some practices peculiar to their tribe everywhere, such as providing shoddy cloth, rations not sound, or false in the measure; not the less impressment, for one thing, went on. By custom sanctioned for centuries, and judicially maintained by a Lord Chancellor as late as Mansfield,[43] that mode of manning the fleet, a mode now fallen into a sort of abeyance but never formally renounced, it was not practicable to give up in those years. Its abrogation would have crippled the indispensable fleet, one wholly under canvas, no steam power, its innumerable sails and thousands of cannon, everything in short, worked by muscle alone; a fleet the more insatiate in demand for men, because then multiplying its ships of all grades against contingencies present and to come of the convulsed Continent.

Discontent foreran the Two Mutinies, and more or less it lurkingly survived them. Hence it was not unreasonable to apprehend some return of trouble sporadic or general. One instance of such apprehensions: In the same year with this story, Nelson, then Rear Admiral Sir Horatio, being with the fleet off the Spanish coast, was directed by the

---

[40] Followers of Jeremy Bentham (1748–1832), English advocate of utilitarianism.

[41] Reference to Nelson's careful preparations for the Battle of Copenhagen (1801).

[42] Alfred, Lord Tennyson (1809–1892) commemorated the English victory over Napoleon at Waterloo (1815) in "Ode on the Death of the Duke of Wellington."

[43] William Murray, the earl of Mansfield (1705–1793), authorized impressment, virtual kidnapping, to secure sailors for the naval fleet.

admiral in command to shift his pennant from the *Captain* to the *Theseus;* and for this reason: that the latter ship having newly arrived on the station from home, where it had taken part in the Great Mutiny, danger was apprehended from the temper of the men; and it was thought that an officer like Nelson was the one, not indeed to terrorize the crew into base subjection, but to win them, by force of his mere presence and heroic personality, back to an allegiance if not as enthusiastic as his own yet as true.

So it was that for a time, on more than one quarter-deck, anxiety did exist. At sea, precautionary vigilance was strained against relapse. At short notice an engagement might come on. When it did, the lieutenants assigned to batteries felt it incumbent on them, in some instances, to stand with drawn swords behind the men working the guns.

6

But on board the seventy-four in which Billy now swung his hammock, very little in the manner of the men and nothing obvious in the demeanor of the officers would have suggested to an ordinary observer that the Great Mutiny was a recent event. In their general bearing and conduct the commissioned officers of a warship naturally take their tone from the commander, that is if he have that ascendancy of character that ought to be his.

Captain the Honorable Edward Fairfax Vere, to give his full title, was a bachelor of forty or thereabouts, a sailor of distinction even in a time prolific of renowned seamen. Though allied to the higher nobility, his advancement had not been altogether owing to influences connected with that circumstance. He had seen much service, been in various engagements, always acquitting himself as an officer mindful of the welfare of his men, but never tolerating an infraction of discipline; thoroughly versed in the science of his profession, and intrepid to the verge of temerity, though never injudiciously so. For his gallantry in the West Indian waters as flag lieutenant under Rodney in that admiral's crowning victory over De Grasse,[44] he was made a post captain.

Ashore, in the garb of a civilian, scarce anyone would have taken him for a sailor, more especially that he never garnished unprofessional talk with nautical terms, and grave in his bearing, evinced little appreciation of mere humor. It was not out of keeping with these traits that on a passage when nothing demanded his paramount action, he was the most undemonstrative of men. Any landsman observing this gentleman not conspicuous by his stature and wearing no pronounced insignia, emerging from his cabin to the open deck, and noting the silent deference of the officers retiring to leeward, might have taken him for the King's guest, a civilian aboard the King's ship, some highly honorable discreet envoy on his way to an important post. But in fact this unobtrusiveness of demeanor may have proceeded from a certain unaffected modesty of manhood sometimes accompanying a resolute nature, a modesty evinced at all times not calling for pronounced action, which shown in any rank of life suggests a virtue aristocratic in kind. As with some others engaged in various departments of the world's more heroic activities, Captain Vere though practical enough upon occasion would at times betray a certain dreaminess of mood. Standing alone on the weather side of the quarter-deck, one hand holding by the rigging, he would absently gaze off at the black

---

[44] British Admiral George Rodney (1719–1792) defeated French admiral   François Paul DeGrasse (1722–1788) in the West Indies in 1782.

sea. At the presentation to him then of some minor matter interrupting the current of his thoughts, he would show more or less irascibility; but instantly he would control it.

In the navy he was popularly known by the appellation "Starry Vere." How such a designation happened to fall upon one who whatever his sterling qualities was without any brilliant ones, was in this wise: A favorite kinsman, Lord Denton, a freehearted fellow, had been the first to meet and congratulate him upon his return to England from his West Indian cruise; and but the day previous turning over a copy of Andrew Marvell's poems had lighted, not for the first time, however, upon the lines entitled "Appleton House," the name of one of the seats of their common ancestor, a hero in the German wars of the seventeenth century, in which poem occur the lines:

> This 'tis to have been from the first
> In a domestic heaven nursed,
> Under the discipline severe
> Of Fairfax and the starry Vere.[45]

And so, upon embracing his cousin fresh from Rodney's great victory wherein he had played so gallant a part, brimming over with just family pride in the sailor of their house, he exuberantly exclaimed, "Give ye joy, Ed; give ye joy, my starry Vere!" This got currency, and the novel prefix serving in familiar parlance readily to distinguish the *Bellipotent*'s captain from another Vere his senior, a distant relative, an officer of like rank in the navy, it remained permanently attached to the surname.

7

In view of the part that the commander of the *Bellipotent* plays in scenes shortly to follow, it may be well to fill out that sketch of him outlined in the previous chapter.

Aside from his qualities as a sea officer Captain Vere was an exceptional character. Unlike no few of England's renowned sailors, long and arduous service with signal devotion to it had not resulted in absorbing and *salting* the entire man. He had a marked leaning toward everything intellectual. He loved books, never going to sea without a newly replenished library, compact but of the best. The isolated leisure, in some cases so wearisome, falling at intervals to commanders even during a war cruise, never was tedious to Captain Vere. With nothing of that literary taste which less heeds the thing conveyed than the vehicle, his bias was toward those books to which every serious mind of superior order occupying any active post of authority in the world naturally inclines: books treating of actual men and events no matter of what era—history, biography, and unconventional writers like Montaigne, who, free from cant and convention, honestly and in the spirit of common sense philosophize upon realities. In this line of reading he found confirmation of his own more reserved thoughts—confirmation which he had vainly sought in social converse, so that as touching most fundamental topics, there had got to be established in him some positive convictions which he forefelt would abide in him essentially unmodified so long as his intelligent part remained unimpaired. In view

[45] The poet Andrew Marvell's lines refer to Ann Vere, wife of Lord Fairfax (1612–1671); Melville adapts the material to his own fictional uses here.

of the troubled period in which his lot was cast, this was well for him. His settled convictions were as a dike against those invading waters of novel opinion social, political, and otherwise, which carried away as in a torrent no few minds in those days, minds by nature not inferior to his own. While other members of that aristocracy to which by birth he belonged were incensed at the innovators mainly because their theories were inimical to the privileged classes, Captain Vere disinterestedly opposed them not alone because they seemed to him insusceptible of embodiment in lasting institutions, but at war with the peace of the world and the true welfare of mankind.

With minds less stored than his and less earnest, some officers of his rank, with whom at times he would necessarily consort, found him lacking in the companionable quality, a dry and bookish gentleman, as they deemed. Upon any chance withdrawal from their company one would be apt to say to another something like this: "Vere is a noble fellow, Starry Vere. 'Spite the gazettes,[46] Sir Horatio" (meaning him who became Lord Nelson) "is at bottom scarce a better seaman or fighter. But between you and me now, don't you think there is a queer streak of the pedantic running through him? Yes, like the King's yarn[47] in a coil of navy rope?"

Some apparent ground there was for this sort of confidential criticism; since not only did the captain's discourse never fall into the jocosely familiar, but in illustrating of any point touching the stirring personages and events of the time he would be as apt to cite some historic character or incident of antiquity as he would be to cite from the moderns. He seemed unmindful of the circumstance that to his bluff company such remote allusions, however pertinent they might really be, were altogether alien to men whose reading was mainly confined to the journals. But considerateness in such matters is not easy to natures constituted like Captain Vere's. Their honesty prescribes to them directness, sometimes far-reaching like that of a migratory fowl that in its flight never heeds when it crosses a frontier.

8

The lieutenants and other commissioned gentlemen forming Captain Vere's staff it is not necessary here to particularize, nor needs it to make any mention of any of the warrant officers. But among the petty officers was one who, having much to do with the story, may as well be forthwith introduced. His portrait I essay, but shall never hit it. This was John Claggart, the master-at-arms. But that sea title may to landsmen seem somewhat equivocal. Originally, doubtless, that petty officer's function was the instruction of the men in the use of arms, sword or cutlass. But very long ago, owing to the advance in gunnery making hand-to-hand encounters less frequent and giving to niter and sulphur the pre-eminence over steel,[48] that function ceased; the master-at-arms of a great warship becoming a sort of chief of police charged among other matters with the duty of preserving order on the populous lower gun decks.

Claggart was a man about five-and-thirty, somewhat spare and tall, yet of no ill figure upon the whole. His hand was too small and shapely to have been accustomed to hard toil. The face was a notable one, the features all except the chin cleanly cut as those

---

[46] Despite newspaper reports.
[47] Noticeable thread in a length of rope.

[48] Gunpowder formed by mixture of charcoal, sulphur, and potassium nitrate.

on a Greek medallion; yet the chin, beardless as Tecumseh's,[49] had something of strange protuberant broadness in its make that recalled the prints of the Reverend Dr. Titus Oates, the historic deponent with the clerical drawl in the time of Charles II and the fraud of the alleged Popish Plot.[50] It served Claggart in his office that his eye could cast a tutoring glance. His brow was of the sort phrenologically associated with more than average intellect; silken jet curls partly clustering over it, making a foil to the pallor below, a pallor tinged with a faint shade of amber akin to the hue of time-tinted marbles of old. This complexion, singularly contrasting with the red or deeply bronzed visages of the sailors, and in part the result of his official seclusion from the sunlight, though it was not exactly displeasing, nevertheless seemed to hint of something defective or abnormal in the constitution and blood. But his general aspect and manner were so suggestive of an education and career incongruous with his naval function that when not actively engaged in it he looked like a man of high quality, social and moral, who for reasons of his own was keeping incog.[51] Nothing was known of his former life. It might be that he was an Englishman; and yet there lurked a bit of accent in his speech suggesting that possibly he was not such by birth, but through naturalization in early childhood. Among certain grizzled sea gossips of the gun decks and forecastle went a rumor perdue that the master-at-arms was a *chevalier*[52] who had volunteered into the King's navy by way of compounding for some mysterious swindle whereof he had been arraigned at the King's Bench.[53] The fact that nobody could substantiate this report was, of course, nothing against its secret currency. Such a rumor once started on the gun decks in reference to almost anyone below the rank of a commissioned officer would, during the period assigned to this narrative, have seemed not altogether wanting in credibility to the tarry old wiseacres of a man-of-war crew. And indeed a man of Claggart's accomplishments, without prior nautical experience entering the navy at mature life, as he did, and necessarily allotted at the start to the lowest grade in it; a man too who never made allusion to his previous life ashore; these were circumstances which in the dearth of exact knowledge as to his true antecedents opened to the invidious a vague field for unfavorable surmise.

But the sailors' dogwatch gossip concerning him derived a vague plausibility from the fact that now for some period the British navy could so little afford to be squeamish in the matter of keeping up the muster rolls, that not only were press gangs notoriously abroad both afloat and ashore, but there was little or no secret about another matter, namely, that the London police were at liberty to capture any able-bodied suspect, any questionable fellow at large, and summarily ship him to the dockyard or fleet. Furthermore, even among voluntary enlistments there were instances where the motive thereto partook neither of patriotic impulse nor yet of a random desire to experience a bit of sea life and martial adventure. Insolvent debtors of minor grade, together with the promiscuous lame ducks of morality, found in the navy a convenient and secure refuge, secure because, once enlisted aboard a King's ship, they were as much in sanctuary as the transgressor of the Middle Ages harboring himself under the shadow of the altar.

---

[49] Tecumseh: Shawnee Indian chief (1768?–1813).

[50] The perjurer Oates (1649–1705) accused Catholics of plotting to murder English Protestants and King Charles II, and to burn London.

[51] Incognito.

[52] Adventurer.

[53] Court of law.

Such sanctioned irregularities, which for obvious reasons the government would hardly think to parade at the time and which consequently, and as affecting the least influential class of mankind, have all but dropped into oblivion, lend color to something for the truth whereof I do not vouch, and hence have some scruple in stating; something I remember having seen in print though the book I cannot recall; but the same thing was personally communicated to me now more than forty years ago by an old pensioner in a cocked hat with whom I had a most interesting talk on the terrace at Greenwich, a Baltimore Negro, a Trafalgar man. It was to this effect: In the case of a warship short of hands whose speedy sailing was imperative, the deficient quota, in lack of any other way of making it good, would be eked out by drafts culled direct from the jails. For reasons previously suggested it would not perhaps be easy at the present day directly to prove or disprove the allegation. But allowed as a verity, how significant would it be of England's straits at the time confronted by those wars[54] which like a flight of harpies rose shrieking from the din and dust of the fallen Bastille. That era appears measurably clear to us who look back at it, and but read of it. But to the grandfathers of us graybeards, the more thoughtful of them, the genius of it presented an aspect like that of Camoëns'[55] Spirit of the Cape, an eclipsing menace mysterious and prodigious. Not America was exempt from apprehension. At the height of Napoleon's unexampled conquests, there were Americans who had fought at Bunker Hill who looked forward to the possibility that the Atlantic might prove no barrier against the ultimate schemes of this French portentous upstart from the revolutionary chaos who seemed in act of fulfilling judgment prefigured in the Apocalypse.

But the less credence was to be given to the gun-deck talk touching Claggart, seeing that no man holding his office in a man-of-war can ever hope to be popular with the crew. Besides, in derogatory comments upon anyone against whom they have a grudge, or for any reason or no reason mislike, sailors are much like landsmen: they are apt to exaggerate or romance it.

About as much was really known to the *Bellipotent*'s tars of the master-at-arms' career before entering the service as an astronomer knows about a comet's travels prior to its first observable appearance in the sky. The verdict of the sea quidnuncs[56] has been cited only by way of showing what sort of moral impression the man made upon rude uncultivated natures whose conceptions of human wickedness were necessarily of the narrowest, limited to ideas of vulgar rascality—a thief among the swinging hammocks during a night watch, or the man-brokers and land-sharks of the seaports.

It was no gossip, however, but fact that though, as before hinted, Claggart upon his entrance into the navy was, as a novice, assigned to the least honorable section of a man-of-war's crew, embracing the drudgery, he did not long remain there. The superior capacity he immediately evinced, his constitutional sobriety, an ingratiating deference to superiors, together with a peculiar ferreting genius manifested on a singular occasion; all this, capped by a certain austere patriotism, abruptly advanced him to the position of master-at-arms.

Of this maritime chief of police the ship's corporals, so called, were the immediate subordinates, and compliant ones; and this, as is to be noted in some business depart-

---

[54] i.e., the Napoleonic wars (1796–1815).
[55] Luis de Camoëns (1524–1580), Portuguese epic poet of Vasco da Gama's voyage to India via the treacherous Cape of Good Hope.
[56] Gossips.

ments ashore, almost to a degree inconsistent with entire moral volition. His place put various converging wires of underground influence under the chief's control, capable when astutely worked through his understrappers of operating to the mysterious discomfort, if nothing worse, of any of the sea commonalty.

9

Life in the foretop well agreed with Billy Budd. There, when not actually engaged on the yards yet higher aloft, the topmen, who as such had been picked out for youth and activity, constituted an aerial club lounging at ease against the smaller stun'sails rolled up into cushions, spinning yarns like the lazy gods, and frequently amused with what was going on in the busy world of the decks below. No wonder then that a young fellow of Billy's disposition was well content in such society. Giving no cause of offense to anybody, he was always alert at a call. So in the merchant service it had been with him. But now such a punctiliousness in duty was shown that his topmates would sometimes good-naturedly laugh at him for it. This heightened alacrity had its cause, namely, the impression made upon him by the first formal gangway-punishment he had ever witnessed, which befell the day following his impressment. It had been incurred by a little fellow, young, a novice afterguardsman absent from his assigned post when the ship was being put about; a dereliction resulting in a rather serious hitch to that maneuver, one demanding instantaneous promptitude in letting go and making fast. When Billy saw the culprit's naked back under the scourge, gridironed with red welts and worse, when he marked the dire expression in the liberated man's face as with his woolen shirt flung over him by the executioner he rushed forward from the spot to bury himself in the crowd, Billy was horrified. He resolved that never through remissness would he make himself liable to such a visitation or do or omit aught that might merit even verbal reproof. What then was his surprise and concern when ultimately he found himself getting into petty trouble occasionally about such matters as the stowage of his bag or something amiss in his hammock, matters under the police oversight of the ship's corporals of the lower decks, and which brought down on him a vague threat from one of them.

So heedful in all things as he was, how could this be? He could not understand it, and it more than vexed him. When he spoke to his young topmates about it they were either lightly incredulous or found something comical in his unconcealed anxiety. "Is it your bag, Billy?" said one. "Well, sew yourself up in it, bully boy, and then you'll be sure to know if anybody meddles with it."

Now there was a veteran aboard who because his years began to disqualify him for more active work had been recently assigned duty as mainmastman in his watch, looking to the gear belayed at the rail roundabout that great spar near the deck. At off-times the foretopman had picked up some acquaintance with him, and now in his trouble it occurred to him that he might be the sort of person to go to for wise counsel. He was an old Dansker[57] long anglicized in the service, of few words, many wrinkles, and some honorable scars. His wizened face, time-tinted and weather-stained to the complexion of an antique parchment, was here and there peppered blue by the chance explosion of a gun cartridge in action.

He was an *Agamemnon* man, some two years prior to the time of this story having served under Nelson when still captain in that ship immortal in naval memory, which

[57] Dane.

dismantled and in part broken up to her bare ribs is seen a grand skeleton in Haden's etching.[58] As one of a boarding party from the *Agamemnon* he had received a cut slantwise along one temple and cheek leaving a long pale scar like a streak of dawn's light falling athwart the dark visage. It was on account of that scar and the affair in which it was known that he had received it, as well as from his blue-peppered complexion, that the Dansker went among the *Bellipotent*'s crew by the name of "Board-Her-in-the-Smoke."

Now the first time that his small weasel eyes happened to light on Billy Budd, a certain grim internal merriment set all his ancient wrinkles into antic play. Was it that his eccentric unsentimental old sapience, primitive in its kind, saw or thought it saw something which in contrast with the warship's environment looked oddly incongruous in the Handsome Sailor? But after slyly studying him at intervals, the old Merlin's[59] equivocal merriment was modified; for now when the twain would meet, it would start in his face a quizzing sort of look, but it would be but momentary and sometimes replaced by an expression of speculative query as to what might eventually befall a nature like that, dropped into a world not without some mantraps and against whose subtleties simple courage lacking experience and address, and without any touch of defensive ugliness, is of little avail; and where such innocence as man is capable of does yet in a moral emergency not always sharpen the faculties or enlighten the will.

However it was, the Dansker in his ascetic way rather took to Billy. Nor was this only because of a certain philosophic interest in such a character. There was another cause. While the old man's eccentricities, sometimes bordering on the ursine, repelled the juniors, Billy, undeterred thereby, revering him as a salt hero, would make advances, never passing the old *Agamemnon* man without a salutation marked by that respect which is seldom lost on the aged, however crabbed at times or whatever their station in life.

There was a vein of dry humor, or what not, in the mastman; and, whether in freak of patriarchal irony touching Billy's youth and athletic frame, or for some other and more recondite reason, from the first in addressing him he always substituted *Baby* for Billy, the Dansker in fact being the originator of the name by which the foretopman eventually became known aboard ship.

Well then, in his mysterious little difficulty going in quest of the wrinkled one, Billy found him off duty in a dogwatch ruminating by himself, seated on a shot box of the upper gun deck, now and then surveying with a somewhat cynical regard certain of the more swaggering promenaders there. Billy recounted his trouble, again wondering how it all happened. The salt seer attentively listened, accompanying the foretopman's recital with queer twitchings of his wrinkles and problematical little sparkles of his small ferret eyes. Making an end of his story, the foretopman asked, "And now, Dansker, do tell me what you think of it."

The old man, shoving up the front of his tarpaulin[60] and deliberately rubbing the long slant scar at the point where it entered the thin hair, laconically said, "Baby Budd, *Jemmy Legs*" (meaning the master-at-arms) "is down on you."

"*Jemmy Legs!*" ejaculated Billy, his welkin eyes expanding. "What for? Why, he calls me 'the sweet and pleasant young fellow,' they tell me."

---

[58] Francis Seymour Haden's (1818–1910) popular etching *The Breaking Up of Ole Agamemnon* (1870).

[59] Merlin: Magician in the legends of King Arthur.

[60] Waterproof hat.

"Does he so?" grinned the grizzled one; then said, "Ay, Baby had, a sweet voice has Jemmy Legs."

"No, not always. But to me he has. I seldom pass him but there comes a pleasant word."

"And that's because he's down upon you, Baby Budd."

Such reiteration, along with the manner of it, incomprehensible to a novice, disturbed Billy almost as much as the mystery for which he had sought explanation. Something less unpleasingly oracular he tried to extract; but the old sea Chiron,[61] thinking perhaps that for the nonce he had sufficiently instructed his young Achilles, pursed his lips, gathered all his wrinkles together, and would commit himself to nothing further.

Years, and those experiences which befall certain shrewder men subordinated lifelong to the will of superiors, all this had developed in the Dansker the pithy guarded cynicism that was his leading characteristic.

10

The next day an incident served to confirm Billy Budd in his incredulity as to the Dansker's strange summing up of the case submitted. The ship at noon, going large before the wind, was rolling on her course, and he below at dinner and engaged in some sportful talk with the members of his mess, chanced in a sudden lurch to spill the entire contents of his soup pan upon the new-scrubbed deck. Claggart, the master-at-arms, official rattan[62] in hand, happened to be passing along the battery in a bay of which the mess was lodged, and the greasy liquid streamed just across his path. Stepping over it, he was proceeding on his way without comment, since the matter was nothing to take notice of under the circumstances, when he happened to observe who it was that had done the spilling. His countenance changed. Pausing, he was about to ejaculate something hasty at the sailor, but checked himself, and pointing down to the streaming soup, playfully tapped him from behind with his rattan, saying in a low musical voice peculiar to him at times, "Handsomely done, my lad! And handsome is as handsome did it, too!" And with that passed on. Not noted by Billy as not coming within his view was the involuntary smile, or rather grimace, that accompanied Claggart's equivocal words. Aridly it drew down the thin corners of his shapely mouth. But everybody taking his remark as meant for humorous, and at which therefore as coming from a superior they were bound to laugh "with counterfeited glee,"[63] acted accordingly; and Billy, tickled, it may be, by the allusion to his being the Handsome Sailor, merrily joined in; then addressing his messmates exclaimed, "There now, who says that Jemmy Legs is down on me!"

"And who said he was, Beauty?" demanded one Donald with some surprise. Whereat the foretopman looked a little foolish, recalling that it was only one person, Board-Her-in-the-Smoke, who had suggested what to him was the smoky idea that this master-at-arms was in any peculiar way hostile to him. Meantime that functionary, resuming his path, must have momentarily worn some expression less guarded than that of the bitter smile, usurping the face from the heart—some distorting expression perhaps, for a drummer-boy heedlessly frolicking along from the opposite direction and

---

[61] Teacher of Achilles in Greek myth.
[62] Cane.
[63] In Oliver Goldsmith's poem "The Deserted Village" (1770), the schoolchildren laugh "with counterfeited glee" at the jokes of the tyrannical schoolmaster.

chancing to come into light collision with his person was strangely disconcerted by his aspect. Nor was the impression lessened when the official, impetuously giving him a sharp cut with the rattan, vehemently exclaimed, "Look where you go!"

11

What was the matter with the master-at-arms? And, be the matter what it might, how could it have direct relation to Billy Budd, with whom prior to the affair of the spilled soup he had never come into any special contact official or otherwise? What indeed could the trouble have to do with one so little inclined to give offense as the merchant-ship's "peacemaker," even him who in Claggart's own phrase was "the sweet and pleasant young fellow"? Yes, why should Jemmy Legs, to borrow the Dansker's expression, be "down" on the Handsome Sailor? But, at heart and not for nothing, as the late chance encounter may indicate to the discerning, down on him, secretly down on him, he assuredly was.

Now to invent something touching the more private career of Claggart, something involving Billy Budd, of which something the latter should be wholly ignorant, some romantic incident implying that Claggart's knowledge of the young blue-jacket began at some period anterior to catching sight of him on board the seventy-four—all this, not so difficult to do, might avail in a way more or less interesting to account for whatever of enigma may appear to lurk in the case. But in fact there was nothing of the sort. And yet the cause necessarily to be assumed as the sole one assignable is in its very realism as much charged with that prime element of Radcliffian romance, the mysterious, as any that the ingenuity of the author of *The Mysteries of Udolpho* could devise.[64] For what can more partake of the mysterious than an antipathy spontaneous and profound such as is evoked in certain exceptional mortals by the mere aspect of some other mortal, however harmless he may be, if not called forth by this very harmlessness itself?

Now there can exist no irritating juxtaposition of dissimilar personalities comparable to that which is possible aboard a great warship fully manned and at sea. There, every day among all ranks, almost every man comes into more or less of contact with almost every other man. Wholly there to avoid even the sight of an aggravating object one must needs give it Jonah's toss[65] or jump overboard himself. Imagine how all this might eventually operate on some peculiar human creature the direct reverse of a saint!

But for the adequate comprehending of Claggart by a normal nature these hints are insufficient. To pass from a normal nature to him one must cross "the deadly space between." And this is best done by indirection.

Long ago an honest scholar, my senior, said to me in reference to one who like himself is now no more, a man so unimpeachably respectable that against him nothing was ever openly said though among the few something was whispered, "Yes, X—— is a nut not to be cracked by the tap of a lady's fan. You are aware that I am the adherent of no organized religion, much less of any philosophy built into a system. Well, for all that, I think that to try and get into X——, enter his labyrinth and get out again, without a

---

[64] Ann Radcliffe (1764–1823) wrote *The Mysteries of Udolpho* (1794) and other gothic novels.

[65] Jonah 1:15: "So they took up Jonah, and cast him forth into the sea" (i.e., threw him overboard).

clue derived from some source other than what is known as 'knowledge of the world'—that were hardly possible, at least for me."

"Why," said I, "X——, however singular a study to some, is yet human, and knowledge of the world assuredly implies the knowledge of human nature, and in most of its varieties."

"Yes, but a superficial knowledge of it, serving ordinary purposes. But for anything deeper, I am not certain whether to know the world and to know human nature be not two distinct branches of knowledge, which while they may coexist in the same heart, yet either may exist with little or nothing of the other. Nay, in an average man of the world, his constant rubbing with it blunts that finer spiritual insight indispensable to the understanding of the essential in certain exceptional characters, whether evil ones or good. In a matter of some importance I have seen a girl wind an old lawyer about her little finger. Nor was it the dotage of senile love. Nothing of the sort. But he knew law better than he knew the girl's heart. Coke and Blackstone[66] hardly shed so much light into obscure spiritual places as the Hebrew prophets. And who were they? Mostly recluses."

At the time, my inexperience was such that I did not quite see the drift of all this. It may be that I see it now. And, indeed, if that lexicon which is based on Holy Writ were any longer popular, one might with less difficulty define and denominate certain phenomenal men. As it is, one must turn to some authority not liable to the charge of being tinctured with the biblical element.

In a list of definitions included in the authentic translation of Plato, a list attributed to him, occurs this: "Natural Depravity: a depravity according to nature," a definition which, though savoring of Calvinism, by no means involves Calvin's dogma as to total mankind.[67] Evidently its intent makes it applicable but to individuals. Not many are the examples of this depravity which the gallows and jail supply. At any rate, for notable instances, since these have no vulgar alloy of the brute in them, but invariably are dominated by intellectuality, one must go elsewhere. Civilization, especially if of the austerer sort, is suspicious to it. It folds itself in the mantle of respectability. It has its certain negative virtues serving as silent auxiliaries. It never allows wine to get within its guard. It is not going too far to say that it is without vices or small sins. There is a phenomenal pride in it that excludes them. It is never mercenary or avaricious. In short, the depravity here meant partakes nothing of the sordid or sensual. It is serious, but free from acerbity. Though no flatterer of mankind it never speaks ill of it.

But the thing which in eminent instances signalizes so exceptional a nature is this: Though the man's even temper and discreet bearing would seem to intimate a mind peculiarly subject to the law of reason, not the less in heart he would seem to riot in complete exemption from that law, having apparently little to do with reason further than to employ it as an ambidexter implement for effecting the irrational. That is to say: Toward the accomplishment of an aim which in wantonness of atrocity would seem to partake of the insane, he will direct a cool judgment sagacious and sound. These men are madmen, and of the most dangerous sort, for their lunacy is not continuous, but occasional, evoked by some special object; it is protectively secretive, which is as much

---

66 Sir Edward Coke (1552–1634) and Sir William Blackstone (1723–1780) were renowned British jurists.

67 The theologian John Calvin (1509–1564) emphasized that all mankind is born depraved as a consequence of the sin of Adam and Eve.

as to say it is self-contained, so that when, moreover, most active it is to the average mind not distinguishable from sanity, and for the reason above suggested: that whatever its aims may be—and the aim is never declared—the method and the outward proceeding are always perfectly rational.

Now something such an one was Claggart, in whom was the mania of an evil nature, not engendered by vicious training or corrupting books or licentious living, but born with him and innate, in short "a depravity according to nature."

Dark sayings are these, some will say. But why? Is it because they somewhat savor of Holy Writ in its phrase "mystery of iniquity?"[68] If they do, such savor was far enough from being intended, for little will it commend these pages to many a reader of today.

The point of the present story turning on the hidden nature of the master-at-arms has necessitated this chapter. With an added hint or two in connection with the incident at the mess, the resumed narrative must be left to vindicate, as it may, its own credibility.

12

That Claggart's figure was not amiss, and his face, save the chin, well molded, has already been said. Of these favorable points he seemed not insensible, for he was not only neat but careful in his dress. But the form of Billy Budd was heroic; and if his face was without the intellectual look of the pallid Claggart's, not the less was it lit, like his, from within, though from a different source. The bonfire in his heart made luminous the rose-tan in his cheek.

In view of the marked contrast between the persons of the twain, it is more than probable that when the master-at-arms in the scene last given applied to the sailor the proverb "Handsome is as handsome does," he there let escape an ironic inkling, not caught by the young sailors who heard it, as to what it was that had first moved him against Billy, namely, his significant personal beauty.

Now envy and antipathy, passions irreconcilable in reason, nevertheless in fact may spring conjoined like Chang and Eng[69] in one birth. Is Envy then such a monster? Well, though many an arraigned mortal has in hopes of mitigated penalty pleaded guilty to horrible actions, did ever anybody seriously confess to envy? Something there is in it universally felt to be more shameful than even felonious crime. And not only does everybody disown it, but the better sort are inclined to incredulity when it is in earnest imputed to an intelligent man. But since its lodgment is in the heart not the brain, no degree of intellect supplies a guarantee against it. But Claggart's was no vulgar form of the passion. Nor, as directed toward Billy Budd, did it partake of that streak of apprehensive jealousy that marred Saul's visage perturbedly brooding on the comely young David.[70] Claggart's envy struck deeper. If askance he eyed the good looks, cheery health, and frank enjoyment of young life in Billy Budd, it was because these went along with a nature that, as Claggart magnetically felt, had in its simplicity never willed malice or experienced the reactionary bite of that serpent. To him, the spirit lodged within Billy, and looking out from his welkin eyes as from windows, that ineffability it was which made the dimple in his dyed cheek, suppled his joints, and dancing in his yellow curls

---

[68] See 2 Thessalonians 2:7: ". . . the mystery of iniquity doth already work."

[69] Famous Siamese twins displayed by P. T. Barnum in the United States.

[70] Saul's jealousy of David, recounted in 1 Samuel 16, 18.

made him pre-eminently the Handsome Sailor. One person excepted, the master-at-arms was perhaps the only man in the ship intellectually capable of adequately appreciating the moral phenomenon presented in Billy Budd. And the insight but intensified his passion, which assuming various secret forms within him, at times assumed that of cynic disdain, disdain of innocence—to be nothing more than innocent! Yet in an aesthetic way he saw the charm of it, the courageous free-and-easy temper of it, and fain would have shared it, but he despaired of it.

With no power to annul the elemental evil in him, though readily enough he could hide it; apprehending the good, but powerless to be it; a nature like Claggart's, surcharged with energy as such natures almost invariably are, what recourse is left to it but to recoil upon itself and, like the scorpion for which the Creator alone is responsible, act out to the end the part allotted it.

13

Passion, and passion in its profoundest, is not a thing demanding a palatial stage whereon to play its part. Down among the groundlings, among the beggars and rakers of the garbage, profound passion is enacted. And the circumstances that provoke it, however trivial or mean, are no measure of its power. In the present instance the stage is a scrubbed gun deck, and one of the external provocations a man-of-war's man's spilled soup.

Now when the master-at-arms noticed whence came that greasy fluid streaming before his feet, he must have taken it—to some extent wilfully, perhaps—not for the mere accident it assuredly was, but for the sly escape of a spontaneous feeling on Billy's part more or less answering to the antipathy on his own. In effect a foolish demonstration, he must have thought, and very harmless, like the futile kick of a heifer, which yet were the heifer a shod stallion would not be so harmless. Even so was it that into the gall of Claggart's envy he infused the vitriol of his contempt. But the incident confirmed to him certain telltale reports purveyed to his ear by "Squeak," one of his more cunning corporals, a grizzled little man, so nicknamed by the sailors on account of his squeaky voice and sharp visage ferreting about the dark corners of the lower decks after interlopers, satirically suggesting to them the idea of a rat in a cellar.

From his chief's employing him as an implicit tool in laying little traps for the worriment of the foretopman—for it was from the master-at-arms that the petty persecutions heretofore adverted to had proceeded—the corporal, having naturally enough concluded that his master could have no love for the sailor, made it his business, faithful understrapper that he was, to foment the ill blood by perverting to his chief certain innocent frolics of the good-natured foretopman, besides inventing for his mouth sundry contumelious epithets he claimed to have overheard him let fall. The master-at-arms never suspected the veracity of these reports, more especially as to the epithets, for he well knew how secretly unpopular may become a master-at-arms, at least a master-at-arms of those days, zealous in his function, and how the bluejackets shoot at him in private their raillery and wit; the nickname by which he goes among them (Jemmy Legs) implying under the form of merriment their cherished disrespect and dislike. But in view of the greediness of hate for pabulum[71] it hardly needed a purveyor to feed Claggart's passion.

---

[71] Food.

An uncommon prudence is habitual with the subtler depravity, for it has everything to hide. And in case of an injury but suspected, its secretiveness voluntarily cuts it off from enlightenment or disillusion; and, not unreluctantly, action is taken upon surmise as upon certainty. And the retaliation is apt to be in monstrous disproportion to the supposed offense; for when in anybody was revenge in its exactions aught else but an inordinate usurer? But how with Claggart's conscience? For though consciences are unlike as foreheads, every intelligence, not excluding the scriptural devils who "believe and tremble,"[72] has one. But Claggart's conscience being but the lawyer to his will, made ogres of trifles, probably arguing that the motive imputed to Billy in spilling the soup just when he did, together with the epithets alleged, these, if nothing more, made a strong case against him; nay, justified animosity into a sort of retributive righteousness. The Pharisee is the Guy Fawkes[73] prowling in the hid chambers underlying some natures like Claggart's. And they can really form no conception of an unreciprocated malice. Probably the master-at-arms' clandestine persecution of Billy was started to try the temper of the man; but it had not developed any quality in him that enmity could make official use of or even pervert into plausible self-justification; so that the occurrence at the mess, petty if it were, was a welcome one to that peculiar conscience assigned to be the private mentor of Claggart; and, for the rest, not improbably it put him upon new experiments.

14

Not many days after the last incident narrated, something befell Billy Budd that more graveled him than aught that had previously occurred.

It was a warm night for the latitude; and the foretopman, whose watch at the time was properly below, was dozing on the uppermost deck whither he had ascended from his hot hammock, one of hundreds suspended so closely wedged together over a lower gun deck that there was little or no swing to them. He lay as in the shadow of a hillside, stretched under the lee of the booms, a piled ridge of spare spars amidships between foremast and mainmast among which the ship's largest boat, the launch, was stowed. Alongside of three other slumberers from below, he lay near that end of the booms which approaches the foremast; his station aloft on duty as a foretopman being just over the deck-station of the forecastlemen, entitling him according to usage to make himself more or less at home in that neighborhood.

Presently he was stirred into semiconsciousness by somebody, who must have previously sounded the sleep of the others, touching his shoulder, and then, as the foretopman raised his head, breathing into his ear in a quick whisper, "Slip into the lee forechains, Billy; there is something in the wind. Don't speak. Quick, I will meet you there," and disappearing.

Now Billy, like sundry other essentially good-natured ones, had some of the weaknesses inseparable from essential good nature; and among these was a reluctance, almost an incapacity of plumply saying *no* to an abrupt proposition not obviously absurd on the face of it, nor obviously unfriendly, nor iniquitous. And being of warm blood, he had not the phlegm[74] tacitly to negative any proposition by unresponsive inaction. Like his sense of fear, his apprehension as to aught outside of the honest and natural was sel-

---

[72] James 2:19.
[73] Conspirator in the Gunpowder Plot to blow up Parliament.

[74] Cool self-control.

dom very quick. Besides, upon the present occasion, the drowse from his sleep still hung upon him.

However it was, he mechanically rose and, sleepily wondering what could be in the wind, betook himself to the designated place, a narrow platform, one of six, outside of the high bulwarks and screened by the great deadeyes and multiple columned lanyards of the shrouds and backstays; and, in a great warship of that time, of dimensions commensurate to the hull's magnitude; a tarry balcony in short, overhanging the sea, and so secluded that one mariner of the *Bellipotent,* a Nonconformist old tar of a serious turn, made it even in daytime his private oratory.[75]

In this retired nook the stranger soon joined Billy Budd. There was no moon as yet; a haze obscured the starlight. He could not distinctly see the stranger's face. Yet from something in the outline and carriage, Billy took him, and correctly, for one of the afterguard.

"Hist! Billy," said the man, in the same quick cautionary whisper as before. "You were impressed, weren't you? Well, so was I"; and he paused, as to mark the effect. But Billy, not knowing exactly what to make of this, said nothing. Then the other: "We are not the only impressed ones, Billy. There's a gang of us.—Couldn't you—help—at a pinch?"

"What do you mean?" demanded Billy, here thoroughly shaking off his drowse.

"Hist, hist!" the hurried whisper now growing husky. "See here," and the man held up two small objects faintly twinkling in the night-light; "see, they are yours, Billy, if you'll only—"

But Billy broke in, and in his resentful eagerness to deliver himself his vocal infirmity somewhat intruded. "D—d—damme, I don't know what you are d—d—driving at, or what you mean, but you had better g—g—go where you belong!" For the moment the fellow, as confounded, did not stir; and Billy, springing to his feet, said, "If you d— don't start, I'll t—t—toss you back over the r—rail!" There was no mistaking this, and the mysterious emissary decamped, disappearing in the direction of the mainmast in the shadow of the booms.[76]

"Hallo, what's the matter?" here came growling from a forecastleman awakened from his deck-doze by Billy's raised voice. And as the foretopman reappeared and was recognized by him: "Ah, Beauty, is it you? Well, something must have been the matter, for you st—st—stuttered."

"Oh," rejoined Billy, now mastering the impediment, "I found an afterguardsman in our part of the ship here, and I bid him be off where he belongs."

"And is that all you did about it, Foretopman?" gruffly demanded another, an irascible old fellow of brick-colored visage and hair who was known to his associate forecastlemen as "Red Pepper." "Such sneaks I should like to marry to the gunner's daughter!"—by that expression meaning that he would like to subject them to disciplinary castigation over a gun.

However, Billy's rendering of the matter satisfactorily accounted to these inquirers for the brief commotion, since of all the sections of a ship's company the forecastlemen, veterans for the most part and bigoted in their sea prejudices, are the most jealous in resenting territorial encroachments, especially on the part of any of the afterguard, of

---

[75] Place for prayer.
[76] Horizontal poles for extending the feet or
bottoms of sails.

whom they have but a sorry opinion—chiefly landsmen, never going aloft except to reef or furl the mainsail, and in no wise competent to handle a marlinspike or turn in a deadeye,[77] say.

15

This incident sorely puzzled Billy Budd. It was an entirely new experience, the first time in his life that he had ever been personally approached in underhand intriguing fashion. Prior to this encounter he had known nothing of the afterguardsman, the two men being stationed wide apart, one forward and aloft during his watch, the other on deck and aft.

What could it mean? And could they really be guineas, those two glittering objects the interloper had held up to his (Billy's) eyes? Where could the fellow get guineas? Why, even spare buttons are not so plentiful at sea. The more he turned the matter over, the more he was nonplussed, and made uneasy and discomfited. In his disgustful recoil from an overture which, though he but ill comprehended, he instinctively knew must involve evil of some sort, Billy Budd was like a young horse fresh from the pasture suddenly inhaling a vile whiff from some chemical factory, and by repeated snortings trying to get it of his nostrils and lungs. This frame of mind barred all desire of holding further parley with the fellow, even were it but for the purpose of gaining some enlightenment as to his design in approaching him. And yet he was not without natural curiosity to see how such a visitor in the dark would look in broad day.

He espied him the following afternoon in his first dogwatch below, one of the smokers on that forward part of the upper gun deck allotted to the pipe. He recognized him by his general cut and build more than by his round freckled face and glassy eyes of pale blue, veiled with lashes all but white. And yet Billy was a bit uncertain whether indeed it were he—yonder chap about his own age chatting and laughing in freehearted way, leaning against a gun; a genial young fellow enough to look at, and something of a rattlebrain, to all appearance. Rather chubby too for a sailor, even an afterguardsman. In short, the last man in the world, one would think, to be overburdened with thoughts, especially those perilous thoughts that must needs belong to a conspirator in any serious project, or even to the underling of such a conspirator.

Although Billy was not aware of it, the fellow, with a sidelong watchful glance, had perceived Billy first, and then noting that Billy was looking at him, thereupon nodded a familiar sort of friendly recognition as to an old acquaintance, without interrupting the talk he was engaged in with the group of smokers. A day or two afterwards, chancing in the evening promenade on a gun deck to pass Billy, he offered a flying word of good-fellowship, as it were, which by its unexpectedness, and equivocalness under the circumstances, so embarrassed Billy that he knew not how to respond to it, and let it go unnoticed.

Billy was now left more at a loss than before. The ineffectual speculations into which he was led were so disturbingly alien to him that he did his best to smother them. It never entered his mind that here was a matter which, from its extreme questionableness, it was his duty as a loyal bluejacket to report in the proper quarter. And, probably, had such a step been suggested to him, he would have been deterred from taking it by the thought, one of novice magnanimity, that it would savor overmuch of the dirty work of a telltale. He kept the thing to himself. Yet upon one occasion he could not for-

---

[77] i.e., to use a rope-splicing tool or a rope-threaded wood block as a pulley.

bear a little disburdening himself to the old Dansker, tempted thereto perhaps by the influence of a balmy night when the ship lay becalmed; the twain, silent for the most part, sitting together on deck, their heads propped against the bulwarks. But it was only a partial and anonymous account that Billy gave, the unfounded scruples above referred to preventing full disclosure to anybody. Upon hearing Billy's version, the sage Dansker seemed to divine more than he was told; and after a little meditation, during which his wrinkles were pursed as into a point, quite effacing for the time that quizzing expression his face sometimes wore: "Didn't I say so, Baby Budd?"

"Say what?" demanded Billy.

"Why, *Jemmy Legs* is *down* on you."

"And what," rejoined Billy in amazement, "has *Jemmy Legs* to do with that cracked afterguardsman?"

"Ho, it was an afterguardsman, then. A cat's-paw, a cat's-paw!" And with that exclamation, whether it had reference to a light puff of air just then coming over the calm sea, or a subtler relation to the afterguardsman, there is no telling, the old Merlin gave a twisting wrench with his black teeth at his plug of tobacco, vouchsafing no reply to Billy's impetuous question, though now repeated, for it was his wont to relapse into grim silence when interrogated in skeptical sort as to any of his sententious oracles, not always very clear ones, rather partaking of that obscurity which invests most Delphic deliverances[78] from any quarter.

Long experience had very likely brought this old man to that bitter prudence which never interferes in aught and never gives advice.

16

Yes, despite the Dansker's pithy insistence as to the master-at-arms being at the bottom of these strange experiences of Billy on board the *Bellipotent,* the young sailor was ready to ascribe them to almost anybody but the man who, to use Billy's own expression, "always had a pleasant word for him." This is to be wondered at. Yet not so much to be wondered at. In certain matters, some sailors even in mature life remain unsophisticated enough. But a young seafarer of the disposition of our athletic foretopman is much of a child-man. And yet a child's utter innocence is but its blank ignorance, and the innocence more or less wanes as intelligence waxes. But in Billy Budd intelligence, such as it was, had advanced while yet his simple-mindedness remained for the most part unaffected. Experience is a teacher indeed; yet did Billy's years make his experience small. Besides, he had none of that intuitive knowledge of the bad which in natures not good or incompletely so foreruns experience, and therefore may pertain, as in some instances it too clearly does pertain, even to youth.

And what could Billy know of man except of man as a mere sailor? And the old-fashioned sailor, the veritable man before the mast, the sailor from boyhood up, he, though indeed of the same species as a landsman, is in some respects singularly distinct from him. The sailor is frankness, the landsman is finesse. Life is not a game with the sailor, demanding the long head—no intricate game of chess where few moves are made in straightforwardness and ends are attained by indirection, an oblique, tedious, barren game hardly worth that poor candle burnt out in playing it.

[78] Prophesies of the priests at the shrine of
    Apollo at Delphi in Greece.

Yes, as a class, sailors are in character a juvenile race. Even their deviations are marked by juvenility, this more especially holding true with the sailors of Billy's time. Then too, certain things which apply to all sailors do more pointedly operate here and there upon the junior one. Every sailor, too, is accustomed to obey orders without debating them; his life afloat is externally ruled for him; he is not brought into that promiscuous commerce with mankind where unobstructed free agency on equal terms—equal superficially, at least—soon teaches one that unless upon occasion he exercise a distrust keen in proportion to the fairness of the appearance, some foul turn may be served him. A ruled undemonstrative distrustfulness is so habitual, not with businessmen so much as with men who know their kind in less shallow relations than business, namely, certain men of the world, that they come at last to employ it all but unconsciously; and some of them would very likely feel real surprise at being charged with it as one of their general characteristics.

17

But after the little matter at the mess Billy Budd no more found himself in strange trouble at times about his hammock or his clothes bag or what not. As to that smile that occasionally sunned him, and the pleasant passing word, these were, if not more frequent, yet if anything more pronounced than before.

But for all that, there were certain other demonstrations now. When Claggart's unobserved glance happened to light on belted Billy rolling along the upper gun deck in the leisure of the second dogwatch, exchanging passing broadsides of fun with other young promenaders in the crowd, that glance would follow the cheerful sea Hyperion[79] with a settled meditative and melancholy expression, his eyes strangely suffused with incipient feverish tears. Then would Claggart look like the man of sorrows.[80] Yes, and sometimes the melancholy expression would have in it a touch of soft yearning, as if Claggart could even have loved Billy but for fate and ban. But this was an evanescence, and quickly repented of, as it were, by an immitigable look, pinching and shriveling the visage into the momentary semblance of a wrinkled walnut. But sometimes catching sight in advance of the foretopman coming in his direction, he would, upon their nearing, step aside a little to let him pass, dwelling upon Billy for the moment with the glittering dental satire of a Guise.[81] But upon any abrupt unforeseen encounter a red light would flash forth from his eye like a spark from an anvil in a dusk smithy. That quick, fierce light was a strange one, darted from orbs which in repose were of a color nearest approaching a deeper violet, the softest of shades.

Though some of these caprices of the pit could not but be observed by their object, yet were they beyond the construing of such a nature. And the thews of Billy were hardly compatible with that sort of sensitive spiritual organization which in some cases instinctively conveys to ignorant innocence an admonition of the proximity of the malign. He thought the master-at-arms acted in a manner rather queer at times. That was all. But the occasional frank air and pleasant word went for what they purported to be, the young sailor never having heard as yet of the "too fair-spoken man."

---

[79] Titan in Greek myth.
[80] See Isaiah 53:3.

[81] French family known for villainies masked by smiles.

Had the foretopman been conscious of having done or said anything to provoke the ill will of the official, it would have been different with him, and his sight might have been purged if not sharpened. As it was, innocence was his blinder.

So was it with him in yet another matter. Two minor officers, the armorer and captain of the hold, with whom he had never exchanged a word, his position in the ship not bringing him into contact with them, these men now for the first began to cast upon Billy, when they chanced to encounter him, that peculiar glance which evidences that the man from whom it comes has been some way tampered with, and to the prejudice of him upon whom the glance lights. Never did it occur to Billy as a thing to be noted or a thing suspicious, though he well knew the fact, that the armorer and captain of the hold, with the ship's yeoman, apothecary, and others of that grade, were by naval usage messmates of the master-at-arms, men with ears convenient to his confidential tongue.

But the general popularity that came from our Handsome Sailor's manly forwardness upon occasion and irresistible good nature, indicating no mental superiority tending to excite an invidious feeling, this good will on the part of most of his shipmates made him the less to concern himself about such mute aspects toward him as those whereto allusion has just been made, aspects he could not so fathom as to infer their whole import.

As to the afterguardsman, though Billy for reasons already given necessarily saw little of him, yet when the two did happen to meet, invariably came the fellow's offhand cheerful recognition, sometimes accompanied by a passing pleasant word or two. Whatever that equivocal young person's original design may really have been, or the design of which he might have been the deputy, certain it was from his manner upon these occasions that he had wholly dropped it.

It was as if his precocity of crookedness (and every vulgar villain is precocious) had for once deceived him, and the man he had sought to entrap as a simpleton had through his very simplicity ignominiously baffled him.

But shrewd ones may opine that it was hardly possible for Billy to refrain from going up to the afterguardsman and bluntly demanding to know his purpose in the initial interview so abruptly closed in the forechains. Shrewd ones may also think it but natural in Billy to set about sounding some of the other impressed men of the ship in order to discover what basis, if any, there was for the emissary's obscure suggestions as to plotting disaffection abroad. Yes, shrewd ones may so think. But something more, or rather something else than mere shrewdness is perhaps needful for the due understanding of such a character as Billy Budd's.

As to Claggart, the monomania in the man—if that indeed it were—as involuntarily disclosed by starts in the manifestations detailed, yet in general covered over by his self-contained and rational demeanor; this, like a subterranean fire, was eating its way deeper and deeper in him. Something decisive must come of it.

18

After the mysterious interview in the forechains, the one so abruptly ended there by Billy, nothing especially germane to the story occurred until the events now about to be narrated.

Elsewhere it has been said that in the lack of frigates (of course better sailers than line-of-battleships) in the English squadron up the Straits at that period, the *Bellipotent*

74 was occasionally employed not only as an available substitute for a scout, but at times on detached service of more important kind. This was not alone because of her sailing qualities, not common in a ship of her rate, but quite as much, probably, that the character of her commander, it was thought, specially adapted him for any duty where under unforeseen difficulties a prompt initiative might have to be taken in some matter demanding knowledge and ability in addition to those qualities implied in good seamanship. It was on an expedition of the latter sort, a somewhat distant one, and when the *Bellipotent* was almost at her furthest remove from the fleet, that in the latter part of an afternoon watch she unexpectedly came in sight of a ship of the enemy. It proved to be a frigate. The latter, perceiving through the glass that the weight of men and metal would be heavily against her, invoking her light heels crowded sail to get away. After a chase urged almost against hope and lasting until about the middle of the first dogwatch, she signally succeeded in effecting her escape.

Not long after the pursuit had been given up, and ere the excitement incident thereto had altogether waned away, the master-at-arms, ascending from his cavernous sphere, made his appearance cap in hand by the mainmast respectfully waiting the notice of Captain Vere, then solitary walking the weather side of the quarter-deck, doubtless somewhat chafed at the failure of the pursuit. The spot where Claggart stood was the place allotted to men of lesser grades seeking some more particular interview either with the officer of the deck or the captain himself. But from the latter it was not often that a sailor or petty officer of those days would seek a hearing; only some exceptional cause would, according to established custom, have warranted that.

Presently, just as the commander, absorbed in his reflections, was on the point of turning aft in his promenade, he became sensible of Claggart's presence, and saw the doffed cap held in deferential expectancy. Here be it said that Captain Vere's personal knowledge of this petty officer had only begun at the time of the ship's last sailing from home, Claggart then for the first, in transfer from a ship detained for repairs, supplying on board the *Bellipotent* the place of a previous master-at-arms disabled and ashore.

No sooner did the commander observe who it was that now deferentially stood awaiting his notice than a peculiar expression came over him. It was not unlike that which uncontrollably will flit across the countenance of one at unawares encountering a person who, though known to him indeed, has hardly been long enough known for thorough knowledge, but something in whose aspect nevertheless now for the first provokes a vaguely repellent distaste. But coming to a stand and resuming much of his wonted official manner, save that a sort of impatience lurked in the intonation of the opening word, he said "Well? What is it, Master-at-arms?"

With the air of a subordinate grieved at the necessity of being a messenger of ill tidings, and while conscientiously determined to be frank yet equally resolved upon shunning overstatement, Claggart at this invitation, or rather summons to disburden, spoke up. What he said, conveyed in the language of no uneducated man, was to the effect following, if not altogether in these words, namely, that during the chase and preparations for the possible encounter he had seen enough to convince him that at least one sailor aboard was a dangerous character in a ship mustering some who not only had taken a guilty part in the late serious troubles, but others also who, like the man in question, had entered His Majesty's service under another form than enlistment.

At this point Captain Vere with some impatience interrupted him: "Be direct, man; say *impressed men*."

Claggart made a gesture of subservience, and proceeded. Quite lately he (Claggart) had begun to suspect that on the gun decks some sort of movement prompted by the sailor in question was covertly going on, but he had not thought himself warranted in reporting the suspicion so long as it remained indistinct. But from what he had that afternoon observed in the man referred to, the suspicion of something clandestine going on had advanced to a point less removed from certainty. He deeply felt, he added, the serious responsibility assumed in making a report involving such possible consequences to the individual mainly concerned, besides tending to augment those natural anxieties which every naval commander must feel in view of extraordinary outbreaks so recent as those which, he sorrowfully said it, it needed not to name.

Now at the first broaching of the matter Captain Vere, taken by surprise, could not wholly dissemble his disquietude. But as Claggart went on, the former's aspect changed into restiveness under something in the testifier's manner in giving his testimony. However, he refrained from interrupting him. And Claggart, continuing, concluded with this: "God forbid, your honor, that the *Bellipotent*'s should be the experience of the—"

"Never mind that!" here peremptorily broke in the superior, his face altering with anger, instinctively divining the ship that the other was about to name, one in which the Nore Mutiny had assumed a singularly tragical character that for a time jeopardized the life of its commander. Under the circumstances he was indignant at the purposed allusion. When the commissioned officers themselves were on all occasions very heedful how they referred to the recent events in the fleet, for a petty officer unnecessarily to allude to them in the presence of his captain, this struck him as a most immodest presumption. Besides, to his quick sense of self-respect it even looked under the circumstances something like an attempt to alarm him. Nor at first was he without some surprise that one who so far as he had hitherto come under his notice had shown considerable tact in his function should in this particular evince such lack of it.

But these thoughts and kindred dubious ones flitting across his mind were suddenly replaced by an intuitional surmise which, though as yet obscure in form, served practically to affect his reception of the ill tidings. Certain it is that, long versed in everything pertaining to the complicated gun-deck life, which like every other form of life has its secret mines and dubious side, the side popularly disclaimed, Captain Vere did not permit himself to be unduly disturbed by the general tenor of his subordinate's report.

Furthermore, if in view of recent events prompt action should be taken at the first palpable sign of recurring insubordination, for all that, not judicious would it be, he thought, to keep the idea of lingering disaffection alive by undue forwardness in crediting an informer, even if his own subordinate and charged among other things with police surveillance of the crew. This feeling would not perhaps have so prevailed with him were it not that upon a prior occasion that patriotic zeal officially evinced by Claggart had somewhat irritated him as appearing rather supersensible and strained. Furthermore, something even in the official's self-possessed and somewhat ostentatious manner in making his specifications strangely reminded him of a bandsman, a perjurous witness in a capital case before a court-martial ashore of which when a lieutenant he (Captain Vere) had been a member.

Now the peremptory check given to Claggart in the matter of the arrested allusion was quickly followed up by this: "You say that there is at least one dangerous man aboard. Name him."

"William Budd, a foretopman, your honor."

"William Budd!" repeated Captain Vere with unfeigned astonishment. "And mean you the man that Lieutenant Ratcliffe took from the merchantman not very long ago, the young fellow who seems to be so popular with the men—Billy, the Handsome Sailor, as they call him?"

"The same, your honor; but for all his youth and good looks, a deep one. Not for nothing does he insinuate himself into the good will of his shipmates, since at the least they will at a pinch say—all hands will—a good word for him, and at all hazards. Did Lieutenant Ratcliffe happen to tell your honor of that adroit fling of Budd's, jumping up in the cutter's bow under the merchantman's stern when he was being taken off? It is even masked by that sort of good-humored air that at heart he resents his impressment. You have but noted his fair cheek. A mantrap may be under the ruddy-tipped daisies."

Now the Handsome Sailor as a signal figure among the crew had naturally enough attracted the captain's attention from the first. Though in general not very demonstrative to his officers, he had congratulated Lieutenant Ratcliffe upon his good fortune in lighting on such a fine specimen of the *genus homo,* who in the nude might have posed for a statue of young Adam before the Fall. As to Billy's adieu to the ship *Rights-of-Man,* which the boarding lieutenant had indeed reported to him, but, in a deferential way, more as a good story than aught else, Captain Vere, though mistakenly understanding it as a satiric sally, had but thought so much the better of the impressed man for it; as a military sailor, admiring the spirit that could take an arbitrary enlistment so merrily and sensibly. The foretopman's conduct, too, so far as it had fallen under the captain's notice, had confirmed the first happy augury, while the new recruit's qualities as a "sailor-man" seemed to be such that he had thought of recommending him to the executive officer for promotion to a place that would more frequently bring him under his own observation, namely, the captaincy of the mizzentop, replacing there in the starboard watch a man not so young whom partly for that reason he deemed less fitted for the post. Be it parenthesized here that since the mizzentopmen have not to handle such breadths of heavy canvas as the lower sails on the mainmast and foremast, a young man if of the right stuff not only seems best adapted to duty there, but in fact is generally selected for the captaincy of that top, and the company under him are light hands and often but striplings. In sum, Captain Vere had from the beginning deemed Billy Budd to be what in the naval parlance of the time was called a "King's bargain": that is to say, for His Britannic Majesty's navy a capital investment at small outlay or none at all.

After a brief pause, during which the reminiscences above mentioned passed vividly through his mind and he weighed the import of Claggart's last suggestion conveyed in the phrase "mantrap under the daisies," and the more he weighed it the less reliance he felt in the informer's good faith, suddenly he turned upon him and in a low voice demanded: "Do you come to me, Master-at-arms, with so foggy a tale? As to Budd, cite me an act or spoken word of his confirmatory of what you in general charge against him. Stay," drawing nearer to him; "heed what you speak. Just now, and in a case like this, there is a yardarm-end[82] for the false witness."

"Ah, your honor!" sighed Claggart, mildly shaking his shapely head as in sad depreciation of such unmerited severity of tone. Then, bridling—erecting himself as in virtuous self-assertion—he circumstantially alleged certain words and acts which collec-

[82] i.e., hanging.

tively, if credited, led to presumptions mortally inculpating Budd. And for some of these averments, he added, substantiating proof was not far.

With gray eyes impatient and distrustful essaying to fathom to the bottom Claggart's calm violet ones, Captain Vere again heard him out; then for the moment stood ruminating. The mood he evinced, Claggart—himself for the time liberated from the other's scrutiny—steadily regarded with a look difficult to render: a look curious of the operation of his tactics, a look such as might have been that of the spokesman of the envious children of Jacob deceptively imposing upon the troubled patriarch the blood-dyed coat of young Joseph.[83]

Though something exceptional in the moral quality of Captain Vere made him, in earnest encounter with a fellow man, a veritable touchstone of that man's essential nature, yet now as to Claggart and what was really going on in him his feeling partook less of intuitional conviction than of strong suspicion clogged by strange dubieties. The perplexity he evinced proceeded less from aught touching the man informed against—as Claggart doubtless opined—than from considerations how best to act in regard to the informer. At first, indeed, he was naturally for summoning that substantiation of his allegations which Claggart said was at hand. But such a proceeding would result in the matter at once getting abroad, which in the present stage of it, he thought, might undesirably affect the ship's company. If Claggart was a false witness—that closed the affair. And therefore, before trying the accusation, he would first practically test the accuser; and he thought this could be done in a quiet, undemonstrative way.

The measure he determined upon involved a shifting of the scene, a transfer to a place less exposed to observation than the broad quarter-deck. For although the few gun-room officers there at the time had, in due observance of naval etiquette, withdrawn to leeward the moment Captain Vere had begun his promenade on the deck's weather side; and though during the colloquy with Claggart they of course ventured not to diminish the distance; and though throughout the interview Captain Vere's voice was far from high, and Claggart's silvery and low; and the wind in the cordage and the wash of the sea helped the more to put them beyond earshot; nevertheless, the interview's continuance already had attracted observation from some topmen aloft and other sailors in the waist or further forward.

Having determined upon his measures, Captain Vere forthwith took action. Abruptly turning to Claggart, he asked, "Master-at-arms, is it now Budd's watch aloft?"

"No, your honor."

Whereupon, "Mr. Wilkes!" summoning the nearest midshipman. "Tell Albert to come to me." Albert was the captain's hammock-boy, a sort of sea valet in whose discretion and fidelity his master had much confidence. The lad appeared.

"You know Budd, the foretopman?"

"I do, sir."

"Go find him. It is his watch off. Manage to tell him out of earshot that he is wanted aft. Contrive it that he speaks to nobody. Keep him in talk yourself. And not till you get well aft here, not till then let him know that the place where he is wanted is my cabin. You understand. Go.—Master-at-arms, show yourself on the decks below, and when

---

[83] In Genesis 37:31–32, Joseph's brothers use the coat, stained with a goat's blood, to convince their father, Jacob, that Joseph is dead.

you think it time for Albert to be coming with his man, stand by quietly to follow the sailor in."

19

Now when the foretopman found himself in the cabin, closeted there, as it were, with the captain and Claggart, he was surprised enough. But it was a surprise unaccompanied by apprehension or distrust. To an immature nature essentially honest and humane, forewarning intimations of subtler danger from one's kind come tardily if at all. The only thing that took shape in the young sailor's mind was this: Yes, the captain, I have always thought, looks kindly upon me. Wonder if he's going to make me his coxswain.[84] I should like that. And may be now he is going to ask the master-at-arms about me.

"Shut the door there, sentry," said the commander; "stand without, and let nobody come in.—Now, Master-at-arms, tell this man to his face what you told of him to me," and stood prepared to scrutinize the mutually confronting visages.

With the measured step and calm collected air of an asylum physician approaching in the public hall some patient beginning to show indications of a coming paroxysm, Claggart deliberately advanced within short range of Billy and, mesmerically looking him in the eye, briefly recapitulated the accusation.

Not at first did Billy take it in. When he did, the rose-tan of his cheek looked struck as by white leprosy. He stood like one impaled and gagged. Meanwhile the accuser's eyes, removing not as yet from the blue dilated ones, underwent a phenomenal change, their wonted rich violet color blurring into a muddy purple. Those lights of human intelligence, losing human expression, were gelidly protruding like the alien eyes of certain uncatalogued creatures of the deep. The first mesmeristic glance was one of serpent fascination; the last was as the paralyzing lurch of the torpedo fish.[85]

"Speak, man!" said Captain Vere to the transfixed one, struck by his aspect even more than by Claggart's. "Speak! Defend yourself!" Which appeal caused but a strange dumb gesturing and gurgling in Billy; amazement at such an accusation so suddenly sprung on inexperienced nonage; this, and, it may be, horror of the accuser's eyes, serving to bring out his lurking defect and in this instance for the time intensifying it into a convulsed tongue-tie; while the intent head and entire form straining forward in an agony of ineffectual eagerness to obey the injunction to speak and defend himself, gave an expression to the face like that of a condemned vestal priestess in the moment of being buried alive, and in the first struggle against suffocation.

Though at the time Captain Vere was quite ignorant of Billy's liability to vocal impediment, he now immediately divined it, since vividly Billy's aspect recalled to him that of a bright young schoolmate of his whom he had once seen struck by much the same startling impotence in the act of eagerly rising in the class to be foremost in response to a testing question put to it by the master. Going close up to the young sailor, and laying a soothing hand on his shoulder, he said, "There is no hurry, my boy. Take your time, take your time." Contrary to the effect intended, these words so fatherly in tone, doubtless touching Billy's heart to the quick, prompted yet more violent efforts at utterance—efforts soon ending for the time in confirming the paralysis, and bringing to

---

[84] Steerer and crew leader of the captain's own boat.

[85] Fish that stuns its prey with electrical shocks.

his face an expression which was as a crucifixion to behold. The next instant, quick as the flame from a discharged cannon at night, his right arm shot out, and Claggart dropped to the deck. Whether intentionally or but owing to the young athlete's superior height, the blow had taken effect full upon the forehead, so shapely and intellectual-looking a feature in the master-at-arms; so that the body fell over lengthwise, like a heavy plank tilted from erectness. A gasp or two, and he lay motionless.

"Fated boy," breathed Captain Vere in tone so low as to be almost a whisper, "what have you done! But here, help me."

The twain raised the felled one from the loins up into a sitting position. The spare form flexibly acquiesced, but inertly. It was like handling a dead snake. They lowered it back. Regaining erectness, Captain Vere with one hand covering his face stood to all appearance as impassive as the object at his feet. Was he absorbed in taking in all the bearings of the event and what was best not only now at once to be done, but also in the sequel? Slowly he uncovered his face; and the effect was as if the moon emerging from eclipse should reappear with quite another aspect than that which had gone into hiding. The father in him, manifested towards Billy thus far in the scene, was replaced by the military disciplinarian. In his official tone he bade the foretopman retire to a stateroom aft (pointing it out), and there remain till thence summoned. This order Billy in silence mechanically obeyed. Then going to the cabin door where it opened on the quarter-deck, Captain Vere said to the sentry without, "Tell somebody to send Albert here." When the lad appeared, his master so contrived it that he should not catch sight of the prone one. "Albert," he said to him, "tell the surgeon I wish to see him. You need not come back till called."

When the surgeon entered—a self-poised character of that grave sense and experience that hardly anything could take him aback—Captain Vere advanced to meet him, thus unconsciously intercepting his view of Claggart, and, interrupting the other's wonted ceremonious salutation, said, "Nay. Tell me how it is with yonder man," directing his attention to the prostrate one.

The surgeon looked, and for all his self-command somewhat started at the abrupt revelation. On Claggart's always pallid complexion, thick black blood was now oozing from nostril and ear. To the gazer's professional eye it was unmistakably no living man that he saw.

"Is it so, then?" said Captain Vere, intently watching him. "I thought it. But verify it." Whereupon the customary tests confirmed the surgeon's first glance, who now, looking up in unfeigned concern, cast a look of intense inquisitiveness upon his superior. But Captain Vere, with one hand to his brow, was standing motionless. Suddenly, catching the surgeon's arm convulsively, he exclaimed, pointing down to the body, "It is the divine judgment on Ananias![86] Look!"

Disturbed by the excited manner he had never before observed in the *Bellipotent*'s captain, and as yet wholly ignorant of the affair, the prudent surgeon nevertheless held his peace, only again looking an earnest interrogatory as to what it was that had resulted in such a tragedy.

But Captain Vere was now again motionless, standing absorbed in thought. Again starting, he vehemently exclaimed, "Struck dead by an angel of God! Yet the angel must hang!"

[86] According to Acts 5:3–5, Ananias dropped
   dead when told he had lied to God.

At these passionate interjections, mere incoherences to the listener as yet unapprised of the antecedents, the surgeon was profoundly discomposed. But now, as recollecting himself, Captain Vere in less passionate tone briefly related the circumstances leading up to the event. "But come; we must dispatch," he added. "Help me to remove him" (meaning the body) "to yonder compartment," designating one opposite that where the foretopman remained immured. Anew disturbed by a request that, as implying a desire for secrecy, seemed unaccountably strange to him, there was nothing for the subordinate to do but comply.

"Go now," said Captain Vere with something of his wonted manner. "Go now. I presently shall call a drumhead court.[87] Tell the lieutenants what has happened, and tell Mr. Mordant" (meaning the captain of marines), "and charge them to keep the matter to themselves."

20

Full of disquietude and misgiving, the surgeon left the cabin. Was Captain Vere suddenly affected in his mind, or was it but a transient excitement, brought about by so strange and extraordinary a tragedy? As to the drumhead court, it struck the surgeon as impolitic, if nothing more. The thing to do, he thought, was to place Billy Budd in confinement, and in a way dictated by usage, and postpone further action in so extraordinary a case to such time as they should rejoin the squadron, and then refer it to the admiral. He recalled the unwonted agitation of Captain Vere and his excited exclamations, so at variance with his normal manner. Was he unhinged?

But assuming that he is, it is not so susceptible of proof. What then can the surgeon do? No more trying situation is conceivable than that of an officer subordinate under a captain whom he suspects to be not mad, indeed, but yet not quite unaffected in his intellects. To argue his order to him would be insolence. To resist him would be mutiny.

In obedience to Captain Vere, he communicated what had happened to the lieutenants and captain of marines, saying nothing as to the captain's state. They fully shared his own surprise and concern. Like him too, they seemed to think that such a matter should be referred to the admiral.

21

Who in the rainbow can draw the line where the violet tint ends and the orange tint begins? Distinctly we see the difference of the colors, but where exactly does the one first blendingly enter into the other? So with sanity and insanity. In pronounced cases there is no question about them. But in some supposed cases, in various degrees supposedly less pronounced, to draw the exact line of demarcation few will undertake, though for a fee becoming considerate some professional experts will. There is nothing namable but that some men will, or undertake to, do it for pay.

Whether Captain Vere, as the surgeon professionally and privately surmised, was really the sudden victim of any degree of aberration, every one must determine for himself by such light as this narrative may afford.

That the unhappy event which has been narrated could not have happened at a worse juncture was but too true. For it was close on the heel of the suppressed insurrec-

[87] Court-martial.

tions, an aftertime very critical to naval authority, demanding from every English sea commander two qualities not readily interfusable—prudence and rigor. Moreover, there was something crucial in the case.

In the jugglery of circumstances preceding and attending the event on board the *Bellipotent,* and in the light of that martial code whereby it was formally to be judged, innocence and guilt personified in Claggart and Budd in effect changed places. In a legal view the apparent victim of the tragedy was he who had sought to victimize a man blameless; and the indisputable deed of the latter, navally regarded, constituted the most heinous of military crimes. Yet more. The essential right and wrong involved in the matter, the clearer that might be, so much the worse for the responsibility of a loyal sea commander, inasmuch as he was not authorized to determine the matter on that primitive basis.

Small wonder then that the *Bellipotent*'s captain, though in general a man of rapid decision, felt that circumspectness not less than promptitude was necessary. Until he could decide upon his course, and in each detail; and not only so, but until the concluding measure was upon the point of being enacted, he deemed it advisable, in view of all the circumstances, to guard as much as possible against publicity. Here he may or may not have erred. Certain it is, however, that subsequently in the confidential talk of more than one or two gun rooms and cabins he was not a little criticized by some officers, a fact imputed by his friends and vehemently by his cousin Jack Denton to professional jealousy of Starry Vere. Some imaginative ground for invidious comment there was. The maintenance of secrecy in the matter, the confining all knowledge of it for a time to the place where the homicide occurred, the quarter-deck cabin; in these particulars lurked some resemblance to the policy adopted in those tragedies of the palace which have occurred more than once in the capital founded by Peter the Barbarian.[88]

The case indeed was such that fain would the *Bellipotent*'s captain have deferred taking any action whatever respecting it further than to keep the foretopman a close prisoner till the ship rejoined the squadron and then submitting the matter to the judgment of his admiral.

But a true military officer is in one particular like a true monk. Not with more of self-abnegation will the latter keep his vows of monastic obedience than the former his vows of allegiance to martial duty.

Feeling that unless quick action was taken on it, the deed of the foretopman, so soon as it should be known on the gun decks, would tend to awaken any slumbering embers of the Nore among the crew, a sense of the urgency of the case overruled in Captain Vere every other consideration. But though a conscientious disciplinarian, he was no lover of authority for mere authority's sake. Very far was he from embracing opportunities for monopolizing to himself the perils of moral responsibility, none at least that could properly be referred to an official superior or shared with him by his official equals or even subordinates. So thinking, he was glad it would not be at variance with usage to turn the matter over to a summary court of his own officers, reserving to himself, as the one on whom the ultimate accountability would rest, the right of maintaining a supervision of it, or formally or informally interposing at need. Accordingly a drumhead court was summarily convened, he electing the individuals composing it: the first lieutenant, the captain of marines, and the sailing master.

[88] Peter the Great of Russia (1672–1725),
   founder of St. Petersburg (now Leningrad).

In associating an officer of marines with the sea lieutenant and the sailing master in a case having to do with a sailor, the commander perhaps deviated from general custom. He was prompted thereto by the circumstance that he took that soldier to be a judicious person, thoughtful, and not altogether incapable of grappling with a difficult case unprecedented in his prior experience. Yet even as to him he was not without some latent misgiving, for withal he was an extremely good-natured man, an enjoyer of his dinner, a sound sleeper, and inclined to obesity—a man who though he would always maintain his manhood in battle might not prove altogether reliable in a moral dilemma involving aught of the tragic. As to the first lieutenant and the sailing master, Captain Vere could not but be aware that though honest natures, of approved gallantry upon occasion, their intelligence was mostly confined to the matter of active seamanship and the fighting demands of their profession.

The court was held in the same cabin where the unfortunate affair had taken place. This cabin, the commander's, embraced the entire area under the poop deck. Aft, and on either side, was a small stateroom, the one now temporarily a jail and the other a dead-house, and a yet smaller compartment, leaving a space between expanding forward into a goodly oblong of length coinciding with the ship's beam. A skylight of moderate dimension was overhead, and at each end of the oblong space were two sashed porthole windows easily convertible back into embrasures for short carronades.[89]

All being quickly in readiness, Billy Budd was arraigned, Captain Vere necessarily appearing as the sole witness in the case, and as such temporarily sinking his rank, though singularly maintaining it in a matter apparently trivial, namely, that he testified from the ship's weather side, with that object having caused the court to sit on the lee side. Concisely he narrated all that had led up to the catastrophe, omitting nothing in Claggart's accusation and deposing as to the manner in which the prisoner had received it. At this testimony the three officers glanced with no little surprise at Billy Budd, the last man they would have suspected either of the mutinous design alleged by Claggart or the undeniable deed he himself had done. The first lieutenant, taking judicial primacy and turning toward the prisoner, said, "Captain Vere has spoken. Is it or is it not as Captain Vere says?"

In response came syllables not so much impeded in the utterance as might have been anticipated. They were these: "Captain Vere tells the truth. It is just as Captain Vere says, but it is not as the master-at-arms said. I have eaten the King's bread and I am true to the King."

"I believe you, my man," said the witness, his voice indicating a suppressed emotion not otherwise betrayed.

"God will bless you for that, your honor!" not without stammering said Billy, and all but broke down. But immediately he was recalled to self-control by another question, to which with the same emotional difficulty of utterance he said, "No, there was no malice between us. I never bore malice against the master-at-arms. I am sorry that he is dead. I did not mean to kill him. Could I have used my tongue I would not have struck him. But he foully lied to my face and in presence of my captain, and I had to say something, and I could only say it with a blow, God help me!"

In the impulsive aboveboard manner of the frank one the court saw confirmed all that was implied in words that just previously had perplexed them, coming as they did from the testifier to the tragedy and promptly following Billy's impassioned disclaimer of mutinous intent—Captain Vere's words, "I believe you, my man."

Next it was asked of him whether he knew of or suspected aught savoring of incipient trouble (meaning mutiny, though the explicit term was avoided) going on in any section of the ship's company.

The reply lingered. This was naturally imputed by the court to the same vocal embarrassment which had retarded or obstructed previous answers. But in main it was otherwise here, the question immediately recalling to Billy's mind the interview with the afterguardsman in the forechains. But an innate repugnance to playing a part at all approaching that of an informer against one's own shipmates—the same erring sense of uninstructed honor which had stood in the way of his reporting the matter at the time, though as a loyal man-of-war's man it was incumbent on him, and failure so to do, if charged against him and proven, would have subjected him to the heaviest of penalties; this, with the blind feeling now his that nothing really was being hatched, prevailed with him. When the answer came it was a negative.

"One question more," said the officer of marines, now first speaking and with a troubled earnestness. "You tell us that what the master-at-arms said against you was a lie. Now why should he have so lied, so maliciously lied, since you declare there was no malice between you?"

At that question, unintentionally touching on a spiritual sphere wholly obscure to Billy's thoughts, he was nonplussed, evincing a confusion indeed that some observers, such as can readily be imagined, would have construed into involuntary evidence of hidden guilt. Nevertheless, he strove some way to answer, but all at once relinquished the vain endeavor, at the same time turning an appealing glance towards Captain Vere as deeming him his best helper and friend. Captain Vere, who had been seated for a time, rose to his feet, addressing the interrogator. "The question you put to him comes naturally enough. But how can he rightly answer it?—or anybody else, unless indeed it be he who lies within there," designating the compartment where lay the corpse. "But the prone one there will not rise to our summons. In effect, though, as it seems to me, the point you make is hardly material. Quite aside from any conceivable motive actuating the master-at-arms, and irrespective of the provocation to the blow, a martial court must needs in the present case confine its attention to the blow's consequence, which consequence justly is to be deemed not otherwise than as the striker's deed."

This utterance, the full significance of which it was not at all likely that Billy took in, nevertheless caused him to turn a wistful interrogative look toward the speaker, a look in its dumb expressiveness not unlike that which a dog of generous breed might turn upon his master, seeking in his face some elucidation of a previous gesture ambiguous to the canine intelligence. Nor was the same utterance without marked effect upon the three officers, more especially the soldier. Couched in it seemed to them a meaning unanticipated, involving a prejudgment on the speaker's part. It served to augment a mental disturbance previously evident enough.

The soldier once more spoke, in a tone of suggestive dubiety addressing at once his associates and Captain Vere: "Nobody is present—none of the ship's company, I mean—who might shed lateral light, if any is to be had, upon what remains mysterious in this matter."

"That is thoughtfully put," said Captain Vere; "I see your drift. Ay, there is a mystery; but, to use a scriptural phrase, it is a 'mystery of iniquity,' a matter for psychologic theologians to discuss. But what has a military court to do with it? Not to add that for us any possible investigation of it is cut off by the lasting tongue-tie of—him—in yonder," again designating the mortuary sateroom. "The prisoner's deed—with that alone we have to do."

To this, and particularly the closing reiteration, the marine soldier, knowing not how aptly to reply, sadly abstained from saying aught. The first lieutenant, who at the outset had not unnaturally assumed primacy in the court, now overrulingly instructed by a glance from Captain Vere, a glance more effective than words, resumed that primacy. Turning to the prisoner, "Budd," he said, and scarce in equable tones, "Budd, if you have aught further to say for yourself, say it now."

Upon this the young sailor turned another quick glance toward Captain Vere; then, as taking a hint from that aspect, a hint confirming his own instinct that silence was now best, replied to the lieutenant, "I have said all, sir."

The marine—the same who had been the sentinel without the cabin door at the time that the foretopman, followed by the master-at-arms, entered it—he, standing by the sailor throughout these judicial proceedings, was now directed to take him back to the after compartment originally assigned to the prisoner and his custodian. As the twain disappeared from view, the three officers, as partially liberated from some inward constraint associated with Billy's mere presence, simultaneously stirred in their seats. They exchanged looks of troubled indecision, yet feeling that decide they must and without long delay. For Captain Vere, he for the time stood—unconsciously with his back toward them, apparently in one of his absent fits—gazing out from a sashed porthole to windward upon the monotonous blank of the twilight sea. But the court's silence continuing, broken only at moments by brief consultations, in low earnest tones, this served to arouse him and energize him. Turning, he to-and-fro paced the cabin athwart; in the returning ascent to windward climbing the slant deck in the ship's lee roll, without knowing it symbolizing thus in his action a mind resolute to surmount difficulties even if against primitive instincts strong as the wind and the sea. Presently he came to a stand before the three. After scanning their faces he stood less as mustering his thoughts for expression than as one inly deliberating how best to put them to well-meaning men not intellectually mature, men with whom it was necessary to demonstrate certain principles that were axioms to himself. Similar impatience as to talking is perhaps one reason that deters some minds from addressing any popular assemblies.

When speak he did, something, both in the substance of what he said and his manner of saying it, showed the influence of unshared studies modifying and tempering the practical training of an active career. This, along with his phraseology, now and then was suggestive of the grounds whereon rested that imputation of a certain pedantry socially alleged against him by certain naval men of wholly practical cast, captains who nevertheless would frankly concede that His Majesty's navy mustered no more efficient officer of their grade than Starry Vere.

What he said was to this effect: "Hitherto I have been but the witness, little more; and I should hardly think now to take another tone, that of your coadjutor for the time, did I not perceive in you—at the crisis too—a troubled hesitancy, proceeding, I doubt not, from the clash of military duty with moral scruple—scruple vitalized by compassion. For the compassion, how can I otherwise than share it? But, mindful of paramount obligations, I strive against scruples that may tend to enervate decision. Not, gentlemen, that I hide from myself that the case is an exceptional one. Speculatively regarded, it well might be referred to a jury of casuists. But for us here, acting not as casuists or moralists, it is a case practical, and under martial law practically to be dealt with.

"But your scruples: do they move as in a dusk? Challenge them. Make them advance and declare themselves. Come now; do they import something like this: If, mindless of palliating circumstances, we are bound to regard the death of the master-at-arms as the prisoner's deed, then does that deed constitute a capital crime whereof the penalty is a mortal one. But in natural justice is nothing but the prisoner's overt act to be considered? How can we adjudge to summary and shameful death a fellow creature innocent before God, and whom we feel to be so?—Does that state it aright? You sign sad assent. Well, I too feel that, the full force of that. It is Nature. But do these buttons that we wear attest that our allegiance is to Nature? No, to the King. Though the ocean, which is inviolate Nature primeval, though this be the element where we move and have our being as sailors, yet as the King's officers lies our duty in a sphere correspondingly natural? So little is that true, that in receiving our commissions we in the most important regards ceased to be natural free agents. When war is declared are we the commissioned fighters previously consulted? We fight at command. If our judgments approve the war, that is but coincidence. So in other particulars. So now. For suppose condemnation to follow these present proceedings. Would it be so much we ourselves that would condemn as it would be martial law operating through us? For that law and the rigor of it, we are not responsible. Our vowed responsibility is in this: That however pitilessly that law may operate in any instances, we nevertheless adhere to it and administer it.

"But the exceptional in the matter moves the hearts within you. Even so too is mine moved. But let not warm hearts betray heads that should be cool. Ashore in a criminal case, will an upright judge allow himself off the bench to be waylaid by some tender kinswoman of the accused seeking to touch him with her tearful plea? Well, the heart here, sometimes the feminine in man, is as that piteous woman, and hard though it be, she must here be ruled out."

He paused, earnestly studying them for a moment; then resumed.

"But something in your aspect seems to urge that it is not solely the heart that moves in you, but also the conscience, the private conscience. But tell me whether or not, occupying the position we do, private conscience should not yield to that imperial one formulated in the code under which alone we officially proceed?"

Here the three men moved in their seats, less convinced than agitated by the course of an argument troubling but the more the spontaneous conflict within.

Perceiving which, the speaker paused for a moment; then abruptly changing his tone, went on.

"To steady us a bit, let us recur to the facts.—In wartime at sea a man-of-war's man strikes his superior in grade, and the blow kills. Apart from its effect the blow itself is, according to the Articles of War, a capital crime. Furthermore—"

"Ay, sir," emotionally broke in the officer of marines, "in one sense it was. But surely Budd purposed neither mutiny nor homicide."

"Surely not, my good man. And before a court less arbitrary and more merciful than a martial one, that plea would largely extenuate. At the Last Assizes[90] it shall acquit. But how here? We proceed under the law of the Mutiny Act. In feature no child can resemble his father more than that Act resembles in spirit the thing from which it derives—

[90] On Judgment Day.

War. In His Majesty's service—in this ship, indeed—there are Englishmen forced to fight for the King against their will. Against their conscience, for aught we know. Though as their fellow creatures some of us may appreciate their position, yet as navy officers what reck we of it? Still less recks the enemy. Our impressed men he would fain cut down in the same swath with our volunteers. As regards the enemy's naval conscripts, some of whom may even share our own abhorrence of the regicidal French Directory, it is the same on our side. War looks but to the frontage, the appearance. And the Mutiny Act, War's child, takes after the father. Budd's intent or non-intent is nothing to the purpose.

"But while, put to it by those anxieties in you which I cannot but respect, I only repeat myself—while thus strangely we prolong proceedings that should be summary—the enemy may be sighted and an engagement result. We must do; and one of two things must we do—condemn or let go."

"Can we not convict and yet mitigate the penalty?" asked the sailing master, here speaking, and falteringly, for the first.

"Gentlemen, were that clearly lawful for us under the circumstances, consider the consequences of such clemency. The people" (meaning the ship's company) "have native sense; most of them are familiar with our naval usage and tradition; and how would they take it? Even could you explain to them—which our official position forbids—they, long molded by arbitrary discipline, have not that kind of intelligent responsiveness that might qualify them to comprehend and discriminate. No, to the people the foretopman's deed, however it be worded in the announcement, will be plain homicide committed in a flagrant act of mutiny. What penalty for that should follow, they know. But it does not follow. *Why?* they will ruminate. You know what sailors are. Will they not revert to the recent outbreak at the Nore? Ay. They know the well-founded alarm—the panic it struck throughout England. Your clement sentence they would account pusillanimous. They would think that we flinch, that we are afraid of them—afraid of practicing a lawful rigor singularly demanded at this juncture, lest it should provoke new troubles. What shame to us such a conjecture on their part, and how deadly to discipline. You see then, whither, prompted by duty and the law, I steadfastly drive. But I beseech you, my friends, do not take me amiss. I feel as you do for this unfortunate boy. But did he know our hearts, I take him to be of that generous nature that he would feel even for us on whom in this military necessity so heavy a compulsion is laid."

With that, crossing the deck he resumed his place by the sashed porthole, tacitly leaving the three to come to a decision. On the cabin's opposite side the troubled court sat silent. Loyal lieges, plain and practical, though at bottom they dissented from some points Captain Vere had put to them, they were without the faculty, hardly had the inclination, to gainsay one whom they felt to be an earnest man, one too not less their superior in mind than in naval rank. But it is not improbable that even such of his words as were not without influence over them, less came home to them than his closing appeal to their instinct as sea officers: in the forethought he threw out as to the practical consequences to discipline, considering the unconfirmed tone of the fleet at the time, should a man-of-war's man's violent killing at sea of a superior in grade be allowed to pass for aught else than a capital crime demanding prompt infliction of the penalty.

Not unlikely they were brought to something more or less akin to that harassed frame of mind which in the year 1842 actuated the commander of the U.S. brig-of-war *Somers* to resolve, under the so-called Articles of War, Articles modeled upon the English Mutiny Act, to resolve upon the execution at sea of a midshipman and two sailors as mutineers designing the seizure of the brig. Which resolution was carried out though in a time of peace and within not many days' sail of home. An act vindicated by a naval court of inquiry subsequently convened ashore. History, and here cited without comment. True, the circumstances on board the *Somers* were different from those on board the *Bellipotent*. But the urgency felt, well-warranted or otherwise, was much the same.

Says a writer whom few know,[91] "Forty years after a battle it is easy for a noncombatant to reason about how it ought to have been fought. It is another thing personally and under fire to have to direct the fighting while involved in the obscuring smoke of it. Much so with respect to other emergencies involving considerations both practical and moral, and when it is imperative promptly to act. The greater the fog the more it imperils the steamer, and speed is put on though at the hazard of running somebody down. Little ween[92] the snug card players in the cabin of the responsibilities of the sleepless man on the bridge."

In brief, Billy Budd was formally convicted and sentenced to be hung at the yardarm in the early morning watch, it being now night. Otherwise, as is customary in such cases, the sentence would forthwith have been carried out. In wartime on the field or in the fleet, a mortal punishment decreed by a drumhead court—on the field sometimes decreed by but a nod from the general—follows without delay on the heel of conviction, without appeal.

22

It was Captain Vere himself who of his own motion communicated the finding of the court to the prisoner, for that purpose going to the compartment where he was in custody and bidding the marine there to withdraw for the time.

Beyond the communication of the sentence, what took place at this interview was never known. But in view of the character of the twain briefly closeted in that stateroom, each radically sharing in the rarer qualities of our nature—so rare indeed as to be all but incredible to average minds however much cultivated—some conjectures may be ventured.

It would have been in consonance with the spirit of Captain Vere should he on this occasion have concealed nothing from the condemned one—should he indeed have frankly disclosed to him the part he himself had played in bringing about the decision, at the same time revealing his actuating motives. On Billy's side it is not improbable that such a confession would have been received in much the same spirit that prompted it. Not without a sort of joy, indeed, he might have appreciated the brave opinion of him implied in his captain's making such a confidant of him. Nor, as to the sentence itself, could he have been insensible that it was imparted to him as to one not afraid to die. Even more may have been. Captain Vere in end may have developed the passion sometimes latent under an exterior stoical or indifferent. He was old enough to have been Billy's father. The austere devotee of military duty, letting himself melt back into what remains primeval in our formalized humanity, may in end have caught Billy to his heart, even as Abraham may have caught young Isaac on the brink of resolutely offering

[91] Melville is perhaps referring to himself.
[92] Think.

him up in obedience to the exacting behest.[93] But there is no telling the sacrament, seldom if in any case revealed to the gadding world, wherever under circumstances at all akin to those here attempted to be set forth two of great Nature's nobler order embrace. There is privacy at the time, inviolable to the survivor; and holy oblivion, the sequel to each diviner magnanimity, providentially covers all at last.

The first to encounter Captain Vere in act of leaving the compartment was the senior lieutenant. The face he beheld, for the moment one expressive of the agony of the strong, was to that officer, though a man of fifty, a startling revelation. That the condemned one suffered less than he who mainly had effected the condemnation was apparently indicated by the former's exclamation in the scene soon perforce to be touched upon.

23

Of a series of incidents within a brief term rapidly following each other, the adequate narration may take up a term less brief, especially if explanation or comment here and there seem requisite to the better understanding of such incidents. Between the entrance into the cabin of him who never left it alive, and him who when he did leave it left it as one condemned to die; between this and the closeted interview just given, less than an hour and a half had elapsed. It was an interval long enough, however, to awaken speculations among no few of the ship's company as to what it was that could be detaining in the cabin the master-at-arms and the sailor; for a rumor that both of them had been seen to enter it and neither of them had been seen to emerge, this rumor had got abroad upon the gun decks and in the tops, the people of a great warship being in one respect like villagers, taking microscopic note of every outward movement or non-movement going on. When therefore, in weather not at all tempestuous, all hands were called in the second dogwatch, a summons under such circumstances not usual in those hours, the crew were not wholly unprepared for some announcement extraordinary, one having connection too with the continued absence of the two men from their wonted haunts.

There was a moderate sea at the time; and the moon, newly risen and near to being at its full, silvered the white spar deck wherever not blotted by the clear-cut shadows horizontally thrown of fixtures and moving men. On either side the quarterdeck the marine guard under arms was drawn up; and Captain Vere, standing in his place surrounded by all the wardroom officers, addressed his men. In so doing, his manner showed neither more nor less than that properly pertaining to his supreme position aboard his own ship. In clear terms and concise he told them what had taken place in the cabin: that the master-at-arms was dead, that he who had killed him had been already tried by a summary court and condemned to death, and that the execution would take place in the early morning watch. The word *mutiny* was not named in what he said. He refrained too from making the occasion an opportunity for any preachment as to the maintenance of discipline, thinking perhaps that under existing circumstances in the navy the consequence of violating discipline should be made to speak for itself.

---

[93] See Genesis 22:1–18. God tested Abraham by commanding him to sacrifice his son Isaac. At the moment of sacrifice, God withdrew the command.

Their captain's announcement was listened to by the throng of standing sailors in a dumbness like that of a seated congregation of believers in hell listening to the clergyman's announcement of his Calvinistic text.

At the close, however, a confused murmur went up. It began to wax. All but instantly, then, at a sign, it was pierced and suppressed by shrill whistles of the boatswain and his mates. The word was given to about ship.

To be prepared for burial Claggart's body was delivered to certain petty officers of his mess. And here, not to clog the sequel with lateral matters, it may be added that at a suitable hour, the master-at-arms was committed to the sea with every funeral honor properly belonging to his naval grade.

In this proceeding as in every public one growing out of the tragedy strict adherence to usage was observed. Nor in any point could it have been at all deviated from, either with respect to Claggart or Billy Budd, without begetting undesirable speculations in the ship's company, sailors, and more particularly men-of-war's men, being of all men the greatest sticklers for usage. For similar cause, all communication between Captain Vere and the condemned one ended with the closeted interview already given, the latter being now surrendered to the ordinary routine preliminary to the end. His transfer under guard from the captain's quarters was effected without unusual precautions—at least no visible ones. If possible, not to let the men so much as surmise that their officers anticipate aught amiss from them is the tacit rule in a military ship. And the more that some sort of trouble should really be apprehended, the more do the officers keep that apprehension to themselves, though not the less unostentatious vigilance may be augmented. In the present instance, the sentry placed over the prisoner had strict orders to let no one have communication with him but the chaplain. And certain unobtrusive measures were taken absolutely to insure this point.

24

In a seventy-four of the old order the deck known as the upper gun deck was the one covered over by the spar deck, which last, though not without its armament, was for the most part exposed to the weather. In general it was at all hours free from hammocks; those of the crew swinging on the lower gun deck and berth deck, the latter being not only a dormitory but also the place for the stowing of the sailors' bags, and on both sides lined with the large chests or movable pantries of the many messes of the men.

On the starboard side of the *Bellipotent*'s upper gun deck, behold Billy Budd under sentry lying prone in irons in one of the bays formed by the regular spacing of the guns comprising the batteries on either side. All these pieces were of the heavier caliber of that period. Mounted on lumbering wooden carriages, they were hampered with cumbersome harness of breeching and strong side-tackles for running them out. Guns and carriages, together with the long rammers and shorter linstocks[94] lodged in loops overhead—all these, as customary, were painted black; and the heavy hempen breechings, tarred to the same tint, wore the like livery of the undertakers. In contrast with the funereal hue of these surroundings, the prone sailor's exterior apparel, white jumper and white duck trousers, each more or less soiled, dimly glimmered in the obscure light of

[94] Sticks that hold the match used to fire cannon.

the bay like a patch of discolored snow in early April lingering at some upland cave's black mouth. In effect he is already in his shroud, or the garments that shall serve him in lieu of one. Over him but scarce illuminating him, two battle lanterns swing from two massive beams of the deck above. Fed with the oil supplied by the war contractors (whose gains, honest or otherwise, are in every land an anticipated portion of the harvest of death), with flickering splashes of dirty yellow light they pollute the pale moonshine all but ineffectually struggling in obstructed flecks through the open ports from which the tampioned[95] cannon protrude. Other lanterns at intervals serve but to bring out somewhat the obscurer bays which, like small confessionals or side-chapels in a cathedral, branch from the long dim-vistaed broad aisle between the two batteries of that covered tier.

Such was the deck where now lay the Handsome Sailor. Through the rose-tan of his complexion no pallor could have shown. It would have taken days of sequestration from the winds and the sun to have brought about the effacement of that. But the skeleton in the cheekbone at the point of its angle was just beginning delicately to be defined under the warm-tinted skin. In fervid hearts self-contained, some brief experiences devour our human tissue as secret fire in a ship's hold consumes cotton in the bale.

But now lying between the two guns, as nipped in the vice of fate, Billy's agony, mainly proceeding from a generous young heart's virgin experience of the diabolical incarnate and effective in some men—the tension of that agony was over now. It survived not the something healing in the closeted interview with Captain Vere. Without movement, he lay as in a trance, that adolescent expression previously noted as his taking on something akin to the look of a slumbering child in the cradle when the warm hearthglow of the still chamber at night plays on the dimples that at whiles mysteriously form in the cheek, silently coming and going there. For now and then in the gyved[96] one's trance a serene happy light born of some wandering reminiscence or dream would diffuse itself over his face, and then wane away only anew to return.

The chaplain, coming to see him and finding him thus, and perceiving no sign that he was conscious of his presence, attentively regarded him for a space, then slipping aside, withdrew for the time, peradventure feeling that even he, the minister of Christ though receiving his stipend from Mars, had no consolation to proffer which could result in a peace transcending that which he beheld. But in the small hours he came again. And the prisoner, now awake to his surroundings, noticed his approach, and civilly, all but cheerfully, welcomed him. But it was to little purpose that in the interview following, the good man sought to bring Billy Budd to some godly understanding that he must die, and at dawn. True, Billy himself freely referred to his death as a thing close at hand; but it was something in the way that children will refer to death in general, who yet among their other sports will play a funeral with hearse and mourners.

Not that like children Billy was incapable of conceiving what death really is. No, but he was wholly without irrational fear of it, a fear more prevalent in highly civilized communities than those so-called barbarous ones which in all respects stand nearer to unadulterate Nature. And, as elsewhere said, a barbarian Billy radically was—as much

[95] Plugged.
[96] Shackled.

so, for all the costume, as his countrymen the British captives, living trophies, made to march in the Roman triumph of Germanicus.[97] Quite as much so as those later barbarians, young men probably, and picked specimens among the earlier British converts to Christianity, at least nominally such, taken to Rome (as today converts from lesser isles of the sea may be taken to London), of whom the Pope[98] of that time, admiring the strangeness of their personal beauty so unlike the Italian stamp, their clear ruddy complexion and curled flaxen locks, exclaimed, "Angles" (meaning *English,* the modern derivative), "Angels, do you call them? And is it because they look so like angels?" Had it been later in time, one would think that the Pope had in mind Fra Angelico's[99] seraphs, some of whom, plucking apples in gardens of the Hesperides,[100] have the faint rosebud complexion of the more beautiful English girls.

If in vain the good chaplain sought to impress the young barbarian with ideas of death akin to those conveyed in the skull, dial, and crossbones on old tombstones, equally futile to all appearance were his efforts to bring home to him the thought of salvation and a Savior. Billy listened, but less out of awe or reverence, perhaps, than from a certain natural politeness, doubtless at bottom regarding all that in much the same way that most mariners of his class take any discourse abstract or out of the common tone of the workaday world. And this sailor way of taking clerical discourse is not wholly unlike the way in which the primer of Christianity, full of transcendent miracles, was received long ago on tropic isles by any superior *savage,* so called—a Tahitian, say, of Captain Cook's[101] time or shortly after that time. Out of natural courtesy he received, but did not appropriate. It was like a gift placed in the palm of an outreached hand upon which the fingers do not close.

But the *Bellipotent*'s chaplain was a discreet man possessing the good sense of a good heart. So he insisted not in his vocation here. At the instance of Captain Vere, a lieutenant had apprised him of pretty much everything as to Billy; and since he felt that innocence was even a better thing than religion wherewith to go to Judgment, he reluctantly withdrew; but in his emotion not without first performing an act strange enough in an Englishman, and under the circumstances yet more so in any regular priest. Stooping over, he kissed on the fair cheek his fellow man, a felon in martial law, one whom though on the confines of death he felt he could never convert to a dogma; nor for all that did he fear for his future.

Marvel not that having been made acquainted with the young sailor's essential innocence the worthy man lifted not a finger to avert the doom of such a martyr to martial discipline. So to do would not only have been as idle as invoking the desert, but would also have been an audacious transgression of the bounds of his function, one as exactly prescribed to him by military law as that of the boatswain or any other naval officer. Bluntly put, a chaplain is the minister of the Prince of Peace serving in the host of the God of War—Mars. As such, he is as incongruous as a musket would be on the altar at Christmas. Why, then, is he there? Because he indirectly subserves the purpose attested

---

[97] Germanicus Caesar (15 B.C.–A.D. 19), whose military victories were celebrated in Rome.

[98] Gregory the Great (540–604).

[99] Fra Angelico: Italian painter (1387–1455).

[100] In Greek myth, gardens in which golden apples grow.

[101] James Cook (1728–1779), English explorer of the Pacific.

by the cannon; because too he lends the sanction of the religion of the meek to that which practically is the abrogation of everything but brute Force.

25

The night so luminous on the spar deck, but otherwise on the cavernous ones below, levels so like the tiered galleries in a coal mine—the luminous night passed away. But like the prophet in the chariot disappearing in heaven and dropping his mantle to Elisha,[102] the withdrawing night transferred its pale robe to the breaking day. A meek, shy light appeared in the East, where stretched a diaphanous fleece of white furrowed vapor. That light slowly waxed. Suddenly *eight bells* was struck aft, responded to by one louder metallic stroke from forward. It was four o'clock in the morning. Instantly the silver whistles were heard summoning all hands to witness punishment. Up through the great hatchways rimmed with racks of heavy shot the watch below came pouring, overspreading with the watch already on deck the space between the mainmast and foremast including that occupied by the capacious launch and the black booms tiered on either side of it, boat and booms making a summit of observation for the powder-boys and younger tars. A different group comprising one watch of topmen leaned over the rail of that sea balcony, no small one in a seventy-four, looking down on the crowd below. Man or boy, none spake but in whisper, and few spake at all. Captain Vere—as before, the central figure among the assembled commissioned officers—stood nigh the break of the poop deck[103] facing forward. Just below him on the quarter-deck the marines in full equipment were drawn up much as at the scene of the promulgated sentence.

At sea in the old time, the execution by halter of a military sailor was generally from the foreyard. In the present instance, for special reasons the mainyard was assigned. Under an arm of that yard the prisoner was presently brought up, the chaplain attending him. It was noted at the time, and remarked upon afterwards, that in this final scene the good man evinced little or nothing of the perfunctory. Brief speech indeed he had with the condemned one, but the genuine Gospel was less on his tongue than in his aspect and manner towards him. The final preparations personal to the latter being speedily brought to an end by two boatswain's mates, the consummation impended. Billy stood facing aft. At the penultimate moment, his words, his only ones, words wholly unobstructed in the utterance, were these: "God bless Captain Vere!" Syllables so unanticipated coming from one with the ignominious hemp about his neck—a conventional felon's benediction directed aft towards the quarters of honor; syllables too delivered in the clear melody of a singing bird on the point of launching from the twig—had a phenomenal effect, not unenhanced by the rare personal beauty of the young sailor, spiritualized now through late experiences so poignantly profound.

Without volition, as it were, as if indeed the ship's populace were but the vehicles of some vocal current electric, with one voice from alow and aloft came a resonant sympathetic echo: "God bless Captain Vere!" And yet at that instant Billy alone must have been in their hearts, even as in their eyes.

---

[102] In 2 Kings 2:11–13, the prophet Elijah, ascending to heaven, drops his mantle, which Elisha then takes up.

[103] Raised deck at ship's stern.

At the pronounced words and the spontaneous echo that voluminously rebounded them, Captain Vere, either through stoic self-control or a sort of momentary paralysis induced by emotional shock, stood erectly rigid as a musket in the ship-armorer's rack.

The hull, deliberately recovering from the periodic roll to leeward, was just regaining an even keel when the last signal, a preconcerted dumb one, was given. At the same moment it chanced that the vapory fleece hanging low in the East was shot through with a soft glory as of the fleece of the Lamb of God seen in mystical vision, and simultaneously therewith, watched by the wedged mass of upturned faces, Billy ascended; and, ascending, took the full rose of the dawn.

In the pinioned figure arrived at the yard-end, to the wonder of all no motion was apparent, none save that created by the slow roll of the hull in moderate weather, so majestic in a great ship ponderously cannoned.

26

When some days afterwards, in reference to the singularity just mentioned, the purser,[104] a rather ruddy, rotund person more accurate as an accountant than profound as a philosopher, said at mess to the surgeon, "What testimony to the force lodged in will power," the latter, saturnine, spare, and tall, one in whom a discreet causticity went along with a manner less genial than polite, replied, "Your pardon, Mr. Purser. In a hanging scientifically conducted—and under special orders I myself directed how Budd's was to be effected—any movement following the completed suspension and originating in the body suspended, such movement indicates mechanical spasm in the muscular system. Hence the absence of that is no more attributable to will power, as you call it, than to horsepower—begging your pardon."

"But this muscular spasm you speak of, is not that in a degree more or less invariable in these cases?"

"Assuredly so, Mr. Purser."

"How then, my good sir, do you account for its absence in this instance?"

"Mr. Purser, it is clear that your sense of the singularity in this matter equals not mine. You account for it by what you call will power—a term not yet included in the lexicon of science. For me, I do not, with my present knowledge, pretend to account for it at all. Even should we assume the hypothesis that at the first touch of the halyards the action of Budd's heart, intensified by extraordinary emotion at its climax, abruptly stopped—much like a watch when in carelessly winding it up you strain at the finish, thus snapping the chain—even under that hypothesis how account for the phenomenon that followed?"

"You admit, then, that the absence of spasmodic movement was phenomenal."

"It was phenomenal, Mr. Purser, in the sense that it was an appearance the cause of which is not immediately to be assigned."

"But tell me, my dear sir," pertinaciously continued the other, "was the man's death effected by the halter, or was it a species of euthanasia?"[105]

---

[104] Ship's financial officer.
[105] Mercy killing.

"*Euthanasia*, Mr. Purser, is something like your *will power:* I doubt its authenticity as a scientific term—begging your pardon again. It is at once imaginative and metaphysical—in short, Greek.—But," abruptly changing his tone, "there is a case in the sick bay that I do not care to leave to my assistants. Beg your pardon, but excuse me." And rising from the mess he formally withdrew.

27

The silence at the moment of execution and for a moment or two continuing thereafter, a silence but emphasized by the regular wash of the sea against the hull or the flutter of a sail caused by the helmsman's eyes being tempted astray, this emphasized silence was gradually disturbed by a sound not easily to be verbally rendered. Whoever has heard the freshet-wave of a torrent suddenly swelled by pouring showers in tropical mountains, showers not shared by the plain; whoever has heard the first muffled murmur of its sloping advance through precipitous woods may form some conception of the sound now heard. The seeming remoteness of its source was because of its murmurous indistinctness, since it came from close by, even from the men massed on the ship's open deck. Being inarticulate, it was dubious in significance further than it seemed to indicate some capricious revulsion of thought or feeling such as mobs ashore are liable to, in the present instance possibly implying a sullen revocation on the men's part of their involuntary echoing of Billy's benediction. But ere the murmur had time to wax into clamor it was met by a strategic command, the more telling that it came with abrupt unexpectedness: "Pipe down the starboard watch, Boatswain, and see that they go."

Shrill as the shriek of the sea hawk, the silver whistles of the boatswain and his mates pierced that ominous low sound, dissipating it; and yielding to the mechanism of discipline the throng was thinned by one-half. For the remainder, most of them were set to temporary employments connected with trimming the yards and so forth, business readily to be got up to serve occasion by any officer of the deck.

Now each proceeding that follows a mortal sentence pronounced at sea by a drum-head court is characterized by promptitude not perceptibly merging into hurry, though bordering that. The hammock, the one which had been Billy's bed when alive, having already been ballasted with shot and otherwise prepared to serve for his canvas coffin, the last offices of the sea undertakers, the sailmaker's mates, were now speedily completed. When everything was in readiness a second call for all hands, made necessary by the strategic movement before mentioned, was sounded, now to witness burial.

The details of this closing formality it needs not to give. But when the tilted plank let slide its freight into the sea, a second strange human murmur was heard, blended now with another inarticulate sound proceeding from certain larger seafowl who, their attention having been attracted by the peculiar commotion in the water resulting from the heavy sloped dive of the shotted hammock into the sea, flew screaming to the spot. So near the hull did they come, that the stridor or bony creak of their gaunt double-jointed pinions was audible. As the ship under light airs passed on, leaving the burial spot astern, they still kept circling it low down with the moving shadow of their out-stretched wings and the croaked requiem of their cries.

Upon sailors as superstitious as those of the age preceding ours, men-of-war's men too who had just beheld the prodigy of repose in the form suspended in air, and now foundering in the deeps; to such mariners the action of the seafowl, though dictated by mere animal greed for prey, was big with no prosaic significance. An uncertain movement began among them, in which some encroachment was made. It was tolerated but for a moment. For suddenly the drum beat to quarters, which familiar sound happening at least twice every day, had upon the present occasion a signal peremptoriness in it. True martial discipline long continued superinduces in average man a sort of impulse whose operation at the official word of command much resembles in its promptitude the effect of an instinct.

The drumbeat dissolved the multitude, distributing most of them along the batteries of the two covered gun decks. There, as wonted, the guns' crews stood by their respective cannon erect and silent. In due course the first officer, sword under arm and standing in his place on the quarter-deck, formally received the successive reports of the sworded lieutenants commanding the sections of batteries below; the last of which reports being made, the summed report he delivered with the customary salute to the commander. All this occupied time, which in the present case was the object in beating to quarters at an hour prior to the customary one. That such variance from usage was authorized by an officer like Captain Vere, a martinet as some deemed him, was evidence of the necessity for unusual action implied in what he deemed to be temporarily the mood of his men. "With mankind," he would say, "forms, measured forms, are everything; and that is the import couched in the story of Orpheus[106] with his lyre spellbinding the wild denizens of the wood." And this he once applied to the disruption of forms going on across the Channel and the consequences thereof.

At this unwonted muster at quarters, all proceeded as at the regular hour. The band on the quarter-deck played a sacred air, after which the chaplain went through the customary morning service. That done, the drum beat the retreat; and toned by music and religious rites subserving the discipline and purposes of war, the men in their wonted orderly manner dispersed to the places allotted them when not at the guns.

And now it was full day. The fleece of low-hanging vapor had vanished, licked up by the sun that late had so glorified it. And the circumambient air in the clearness of its serenity was like smooth white marble in the polished block not yet removed from the marble-dealer's yard.

28

The symmetry of form attainable in pure fiction cannot so readily be achieved in a narration essentially having less to do with fable than with fact. Truth uncompromisingly told will always have its ragged edges; hence the conclusion of such a narration is apt to be less finished than an architectural finial.

How it fared with the Handsome Sailor during the year of the Great Mutiny has been faithfully given. But though properly the story ends with his life, something in way of sequel will not be amiss. Three brief chapters will suffice.

In the general rechristening under the Directory of the craft originally forming the navy of the French monarchy, the *St. Louis* line-of-battle ship was named the *Athée* (the *Atheist*). Such a name, like some other substituted ones in the Revolutionary fleet, while proclaiming the infidel audacity of the ruling power, was yet, though not so intended to

---

[106] In Greek myth, the poet whose music charmed wild beasts.

be, the aptest name, if one consider it, ever given to a warship; far more so indeed than the *Devastation,* the *Erebus* (the *Hell*), and similar names bestowed upon fighting ships.

On the return passage to the English fleet from the detached cruise during which occurred the events already recorded, the *Bellipotent* fell in with the *Athée.* An engagement ensued, during which Captain Vere, in the act of putting his ship alongside the enemy with a view of throwing his boarders across her bulwarks, was hit by a musket ball from a porthole of the enemy's main cabin. More than disabled, he dropped to the deck and was carried below to the same cockpit where some of his men already lay. The senior lieutenant took command. Under him the enemy was finally captured, and though much crippled was by rare good fortune successfully taken into Gibraltar, an English port not very distant from the scene of the fight. There, Captain Vere with the rest of the wounded was put ashore. He lingered for some days, but the end came. Unhappily he was cut off too early for the Nile and Trafalgar.[107] The spirit that 'spite its philosophic austerity may yet have indulged in the most secret of all passions, ambition, never attained to the fulness of fame.

Not long before death, while lying under the influence of that magical drug which, soothing the physical frame, mysteriously operates on the subtler element in man, he was heard to murmur words inexplicable to his attendant: "Billy Budd, Billy Budd." That these were not the accents of remorse would seem clear from what the attendant said to the *Bellipotent*'s senior officer of marines, who, as the most reluctant to condemn of the members of the drumhead court, too well knew, though here he kept the knowledge to himself, who Billy Budd was.

29

Some few weeks after the execution, among other matters under the head of "News from the Mediterranean," there appeared in a naval chronicle of the time, an authorized weekly publication, an account of the affair. It was doubtless for the most part written in good faith, though the medium, partly rumor, through which the facts must have reached the writer served to deflect and in part falsify them. The account was as follows:

"On the tenth of the last month a deplorable occurrence took place on board H.M.S. *Bellipotent.* John Claggart, the ship's master-at-arms, discovering that some sort of plot was incipient among an inferior section of the ship's company, and that the ringleader was one William Budd; he, Claggart, in the act of arraigning the man before the captain, was vindictively stabbed to the heart by the suddenly drawn sheath knife of Budd.

"The deed and the implement employed sufficiently suggest that though mustered into the service under an English name the assassin was no Englishman, but one of those aliens adopting English cognomens whom the present extraordinary necessities of the service have caused to be admitted into it in considerable numbers.

"The enormity of the crime and the extreme depravity of the criminal appear the greater in view of the character of the victim, a middle-aged man respectable and discreet, belonging to that minor official grade, the petty officers, upon whom, as none know better than the commissioned gentlemen, the efficiency of His Majesty's navy so largely depends. His function was a responsible one, at once onerous and thankless; and his fidelity in it the greater because of his strong patriotic impulse. In this instance as in

[107] Subsequent battles (Nile, 1798; Trafalgar, 1805).

so many other instances in these days, the character of this unfortunate man signally refutes, if refutation were needed, that peevish saying attributed to the late Dr. Johnson,[108] that patriotism is the last refuge of a scoundrel.

"The criminal paid the penalty of his crime. The promptitude of the punishment has proved salutary. Nothing amiss is now apprehended aboard H.M.S. *Bellipotent*."

The above, appearing in a publication now long ago superannuated and forgotten, is all that hitherto has stood in human record to attest what manner of men respectively were John Claggart and Billy Budd.

30

Everything is for a term venerated in navies. Any tangible object associated with some striking incident of the service is converted into a monument. The spar from which the foretopman was suspended was for some few years kept trace of by the bluejackets. Their knowledges followed it from ship to dockyard and again from dockyard to ship, still pursuing it even when at last reduced to a mere dockyard boom. To them a chip of it was as a piece of the Cross. Ignorant though they were of the secret facts of the tragedy, and not thinking but that the penalty was somehow unavoidably inflicted from the naval point of view, for all that, they instinctively felt that Billy was a sort of man as incapable of mutiny as of wilful murder. They recalled the fresh young image of the Handsome Sailor, that face never deformed by a sneer or subtler vile freak of the heart within. This impression of him was doubtless deepened by the fact that he was gone, and in a measure mysteriously gone. On the gun decks of the *Bellipotent* the general estimate of his nature and its unconscious simplicity eventually found rude utterance from another foretopman, one of his own watch, gifted, as some sailors are, with an artless *poetic* temperament. The tarry hand made some lines which, after circulating among the shipboard crews for a while, finally got rudely printed at Portsmouth as a ballad. The title given to it was the sailor's.

BILLY IN THE DARBIES[109]

> Good of the chaplain to enter Lone Bay
> And down on his marrowbones here and pray
> For the likes just o' me, Billy Budd.—But, look:
> Through the port comes the moonshine astray!
> It tips the guard's cutlass and silvers this nook;
> But 'twill die in the dawning of Billy's last day.
> A jewel-block they'll make of me tomorrow,
> Pendant pearl from the yardarm-end
> Like the eardrop I gave to Bristol Molly—
> O, 'tis me, not the sentence they'll suspend.
> Ay, ay, all is up; and I must up too,
> Early in the morning, aloft from alow.
> On an empty stomach now never it would do.

---

[108] The lexicographer Samuel Johnson
   (1709–1784).
[109] Handcuffs.

They'll give me a nibble—bit o' biscuit ere I go.
Sure, a messmate will reach me the last parting cup;
But, turning heads away from the hoist and the belay.
Heaven knows who will have the running of me up!
No pipe to those halyards.—But aren't it all sham?
A blur's in my eyes; it is dreaming that I am.
A hatchet to my hawser? All adrift to go?
The drum roll to grog, and Billy never know?
But Donald he has promised to stand by the plank;
So I'll shake a friendly hand ere I sink.
But—no! It is dead then I'll be, come to think.
I remember Taff the Welshman when he sank.
And his cheek it was like the budding pink.
But me they'll lash in hammock, drop me deep.
Fathoms down, fathoms down, how I'll dream fast asleep.
I feel it stealing now. Sentry, are you there?
Just ease these darbies at the wrist,
And roll me over fair!
I am sleepy, and the oozy weeds about me twist.

1924

---

from # Battle Pieces and Aspects
of the War

The Portent

(1859)

Hanging from the beam,
  Slowly swaying (such the law),
Gaunt the shadow on your green,
  Shenandoah!

The cut is on the crown   5
  (Lo, John Brown),[1]
And the stabs shall heal no more.

Hidden in the cap[2]
  Is the anguish none can draw;

---

[1] In 1859 the bearded abolitionist John Brown
was hanged for treason after he had incited a
slave rebellion and led an attack on a federal
arsenal at Harper's Ferry, Virginia. He had
received a scalp wound when captured.

[2] Hood placed over the head of the condemned man.

So your future veils its face,   10
    Shenandoah!
But the streaming beard is shown
    (Weird John Brown),
The meteor of the war.
1866

A Utilitarian View of the Monitor's Fight[3]

Plain be the phrase, yet apt the verse,
    More ponderous than nimble;
For since grimed War here laid aside
His Orient pomp, 'twould ill befit
        Overmuch to ply   5
    The rhyme's barbaric cymbal.

Hail to victory without the gaud
    Of glory; zeal that needs no fans
Of banners; plain mechanic power
Plied cogently in War now placed—   10
    Where War belongs—
    Among the trades and artisans.

Yet this was battle, and intense—
    Beyond the strife of fleets heroic;
Deadlier, closer, calm 'mid storm;   15
No passion; all went on by crank,
        Pivot, and screw,
    And calculations of caloric.

Needless to dwell; the story's known.
    The ringing of those plates on plates   20
Still ringeth round the world—
The clangor of that blacksmiths' fray.
        The anvil-din
    Resounds this message from the Fates:

War yet shall be, and to the end;   25
    But war-paint shows the streaks of weather;
War yet shall be, but warriors
Are now but operatives;[4] War's made
        Less grand than Peace,
    And a singe runs through lace and feather.   30
1866

---

[3] One of the two ironclad vessels that battled in May 1862, at Hampton Roads, Virginia. The *Monitor* belonged to the Union navy, and its adversary was the Confederate *Merrimack*.
[4] Factory workers.

Shiloh[5]

A Requiem

(April, 1862)

Skimming lightly, wheeling still,
 The swallows fly low
Over the field in clouded days,
 The forest-field of Shiloh—
Over the field where April rain   5
Solaced the parched ones stretched in pain
Through the pause of night
That followed the Sunday fight
 Around the church of Shiloh—
The church so lone, the log-built one,   10
That echoed to many a parting groan
  And natural prayer
 Of dying foemen mingled there—
Foemen at morn, but friends at eve—
 Fame or country least their care: 15
(What like a bullet can undeceive!)
 But now they lie low,
While over them the swallows skim,
And all is hushed at Shiloh.

1866

---

from Timoleon, Etc.

Monody[1]

To have known him, to have loved him
 After loneness long;
And then to be estranged in life,
 And neither in the wrong;
And now for death to set his seal—   5
 Ease me, a little ease, my song!

---

[5] Site of battle and Confederate victory over Union forces in western Tennessee, April 1862.

[1] Ode, elegy, or dirge sung by one voice. "Monody" is thought to be a lament for Melville's fellow writer, Nathaniel Hawthorne.

By wintry hills his hermit-mound
    The sheeted snow-drifts drape,
And houseless there the snow-bird flits
    Beneath the fir-trees' crape: 10
Glazed now with ice the cloistral vine
    That hid the shyest grape.

1891

Art

In placid hours well-pleased we dream
Of many a brave unbodied scheme.
But form to lend, pulsed life create,
What unlike things must meet and mate:
A flame to melt—a wind to freeze;   5
Sad patience—joyous energies;
Humility—yet pride and scorn;
Instinct and study; love and hate;
Audacity—reverence. These must mate,
And fuse with Jacob's[2] mystic heart,   10
To wrestle with the angel—Art.

1891

John Greenleaf Whittier
1807–1892

A century-old, hand-hewn oak cabin north of Boston, near the seacoast town of Haverhill, Massachusetts, provided the unassuming setting for John Greenleaf Whittier's birth in 1807. The son of devout and industrious Quaker farmers, Whittier was limited by his daily chores and frail health to irregular attendance at the local country school. There he was introduced to the works of Robert Burns, which he described as "about the first poetry I had ever read" and which "had a lasting influence upon me." Reflecting on the modest circumstances of his childhood, Whittier noted somewhat wistfully, "I had at that time a great thirst for knowledge and little means to gratify it."

Whittier nourished his youthful "thirst for knowledge" both by reading the "few books within my reach," most notably such staples of the Quaker tradition as the Bible and Bunyan's *Pilgrim's Progress,* as well as by writing what he later called "wood hymns" devoted to nature and country folklore. His older sister, confident of his ability, sent several of these poems to local newspapers, one of which, the Newburyport

---

[2] According to Genesis 32:24–30, Jacob
  wrestled with an angel.

Free Press, was edited by the youthful abolitionist William Lloyd Garrison. Delighted with what he read, Garrison published the first of many of Whittier's poems in 1826 and soon traveled to the Whittier farm to encourage this young poet and to urge his father to provide his son with "every facility for the development of his remarkable genius"—to which the senior Whittier quickly replied, "Sir, poetry will not give him bread." An "over-wearied child," too slender for the heavy work required of him, Whittier enrolled, with his father's reluctant permission, at nearby Haverhill Academy and supported himself through two terms with odd jobs, including service as a cobbler. Unable to afford a college education, Whittier worked as a country journalist and editorial assistant at several minor newspapers in Boston and Hartford while continuing to circulate his verse. In the years that followed, the public recognition his poetry earned him was invariably offset by his poor health, which often forced him to resign his newspaper work and return to the family farm to recuperate.

As a young adult, Whittier suffered through several years of personal turmoil filled with depression, self-pity, and insomnia and marked by a series of unrequited loves. (He was to remain a lifelong bachelor.) During this period he began to gain considerable attention as his poetry reached a wider audience. Conscious of both what he called his own "slumbering powers" and of his neighbors' confidence in him, Whittier began to speak out on public issues and to participate in local politics. At the age of thirty, he was elected to the Massachusetts state legislature and reelected the following year. He declined another term, responding instead to Garrison's call that he devote his energies to the abolition of slavery.

Resolving to knock "Pegasus on the head," Whittier began what would be a distinguished three-decade career as an abolitionist poet and editorialist when he published at his own expense a pamphlet entitled *Justice and Expediency* (1833). In that same year, he represented the state of Massachusetts at the first meeting of the American Anti-Slavery Society. He later declared that having drafted and then signed the resolutions of that convention meant to him than having his name on any book he had written. Throughout these years, Whittier sustained himself as a full-time political activist and a part-time editor of several abolitionist newspapers, including the *Pennsylvania Freeman* and *The National Era,* which would later publish Harriet Beecher Stowe's *Uncle Tom's Cabin* as a serial.

Whittier quickly became the most eloquent voice in the abolitionist movement by publishing in virtually every major newspaper and periodical sympathetic to the cause. He first gathered the work of this period in a volume entitled *Poems Written During the Progress of the Abolition Question* (1837). Subsequent volumes included *Lays of My Home* (1843), *Voices of Freedom* (1846), *Songs of Labor and Other Poems* (1850), *The Chapel of the Hermits and Other Poems* (1853), and *The Panorama and Other Poems* (1856). Describing himself as a "silent, shy, peace-loving man," Whittier was an early advocate of organized nonviolence and always hoped that reform rather than war could resolve the slavery issue. Yet Whittier eventually aligned himself, as did such writers as James Russell Lowell, with several of the more extreme positions of the abolitionists, including their willingness to see the Union dissolve if that were necessary to end the injustice of slavery.

Whittier's prominence during his three-decade struggle to defeat slavery did not prevent him from quietly continuing to write reflective verse focusing on New England's rustic life. Like Cooper, Longfellow, and Hawthorne, Whittier frequently turned to the New England past, an interest reflected in such volumes as *Moll Pitcher* (1832), *Mogg Megone* (1836), and a historical novel, *Leaves from Margaret Smith's Journal* (1849), a richly textured tale of Quaker life in colonial New England told in the form of a young girl's diary. But he did not enjoy some measure of financial security until 1857, when James Russell Lowell, the editor of the newly founded *Atlantic Monthly,* invited Whittier to be a regular contributor to the magazine.

Widespread recognition for the quality of Whittier's verse came late—when, after the Emancipation Proclamation, he could turn from engaging in polemic battles over slavery to devoting more time to cultivating his literary talents. In 1866, the same year that Herman Melville published *Battle-Pieces* in relative obscurity, Whittier published "Snow-Bound" to critical acclaim. "Snow-Bound" remains universally regarded as his most significant work. The poem offers in direct, simple, concrete, and sincere terms an idyllic vision of American life that the war-torn nation could take great comfort in. And as the nation became increasingly swept up in the rush toward industrialization in the decades that followed, new generations continued to find Whittier's Edenic view of village and farm life singularly appealing.

In the post-Civil War years, Whittier published several more volumes, including *Among the Hills and Other Poems* (1869) and *Ballads of New England* (1870), each replete with charming poetic renditions of local folklore and superstition. In his later years, his poetic interests broadened to include religious humanism; he became preoccupied as much with the possibility of moral perfection as with the prospect of political and social reform. His poems quickly became schoolroom classics. Venerated as a public figure, he celebrated his seventieth birthday at a public reception in the company of nearly every major American writer, from the elderly William Cullen Bryant to the feisty Mark Twain. Each came to sing his praises.

Whittier delighted in the public adulation. Like Walt Whitman, he began to manage his public image. He interviewed himself for publication; he wrote a flattering entry for himself in an encyclopedia of biography; he provided photographers with numerous opportunities to portray him in his favorite rural settings. Whittier's final volume, *At Sundown,* was published shortly before his death in 1892, the same year as Whitman's.

In the prelude to his volume *The Tent on the Beach and Other Poems* (1867), Whittier described himself as a "dreamer" who had "a mission to fulfill," a writer who had "left the Muses' haunts to turn / The crank of an opinion-mill, / Making his rustic reed of song / A weapon in the war with wrong." He readily recognized his own limitations as a poet. In a letter to Francis H. Underwood, who had begun work on Whittier's biography, the old poet endorsed James Russell Lowell's assessment of him in "A Fable for Critics": Whittier's was "a fervor of mind which knows no separation / 'Twixt simple excitement and pure inspiration." Yet the best of Whittier's poetry focuses on the place he knew best—rural New England. His lifelong interest in rendering the universal qualities of the everyday experiences of commonplace people remains an eloquent response to Ralph Waldo Emerson's plea in "The American Scholar" that American writers embrace "the near, the low, the common."

Further Reading:

S. T. Pickard, *The Life and Letters of John Greenleaf Whittier,* 2 vols., 1894, 1907.

A. Mordell, *Quaker Militant: John Greenleaf Whittier,* 1933.

W. T. Scott, "Poetry in America: A New Consideration of Whittier's Verse," *New England Quarterly* 7, 1934.

T. F. Currier, *A Bibliography of John Greenleaf Whittier*, 1937.

W. Bennett, *Whittier, Bard of Freedom*, 1941.

E. H. Cady and H. H. Clark, eds., *Whittier on Writers and Writing*, 1950.

G. Arms, *The Fields Were Green*, 1953.

J. B. Pickard, *John Greenleaf Whittier: An Introduction and Interpretation*, 1961.

L. Leary, *John Greenleaf Whittier*, 1961.

E. Wagenknecht, *John Greenleaf Whittier: A Portrait in Paradox*, 1967.

R. P. Warren, *John Greenleaf Whittier's Poetry: An Appraisal and a Selection*, 1971.

W. J. Linton, *Life of Whittier*, 1972.

D. C. Freeman, J. B. Pickard, and R. C. Woodwell, *Whittier and Whittierland: Portrait of a Poet and His World*, 1976.

J. K. Kribbs, ed., *Critical Essays on John Greenleaf Whittier*, 1980.

R. H. Woodwell, *John Greenleaf Whittier: A Biography*, 1985.

Text:

The Complete Poetical Works of John Greenleaf Whittier, ed. H. E. Scudder, 1892.

Massachusetts to Virginia*

The blast from Freedom's Northern hills, upon its Southern way,
Bears greeting to Virginia from Massachusetts Bay:
No word of haughty challenging, nor battle bugle's peal,
Nor steady tread of marching files, nor clang of horsemen's steel.

No trains of deep-mouthed cannon along our highways go;   5
Around our silent arsenals untrodden lies the snow;
And to the land-breeze of our ports, upon their errands far,
A thousand sails of commerce swell, but none are spread for war.

We hear thy threats, Virginia! thy stormy words and high
Swell harshly on the Southern winds which melt along our sky;   10
Yet, not one brown, hard hand foregoes its honest labor here,
No hewer of our mountain oaks suspends his axe in fear.

Wild are the waves which lash the reefs along St. George's bank;[1]
Cold on the shores of Labrador the fog lies white and dank;

---

* Whittier's note: "Written on reading an account of the proceedings of the citizens of Norfolk, Va., in reference to George Latimer, the alleged fugitive slave, who was seized in Boston without warrant at the request of James B. Grey, of Norfolk, claiming to be his master. The case caused great excitement North and South, and led to the presentation of a petition to Congress, signed by more than fifty thousand citizens of Massachusetts, calling for such laws and proposed amendments to the Constitution as should relieve the Commonwealth from all further participation in the crime of oppression. George Latimer himself was finally given free papers for the sum of four hundred dollars."

[1] Off Newfoundland.

Through storm, and wave, and blinding mist, stout are the hearts which man 15
The fishing-smacks of Marblehead, the seaboats of Cape Ann.[2]

The cold north light and wintry sun glare on their icy forms,
Bent grimly o'er their straining lines or wrestling with the storms;
Free as the winds they drive before, rough as the waves they roam,
They laugh to scorn the slaver's threat against their rocky home. 20

What means the Old Dominion?[3] Hath she forgot the day
When o'er her conquered valleys swept the Briton's steel array?
How side by side, with sons of hers, the Massachusetts men
Encountered Tarleton's charge of fire, and stout Cornwallis,[4] then?

Forgets she how the Bay State,[5] in answer to the call 25
Of her old House of Burgesses,[6] spoke out from Faneuil Hall?[7]
When, echoing back her Henry's cry,[8] came pulsing on each breath
Of Northern winds the thrilling sounds of "Liberty or Death!"

What asks the Old Dominion? If now her sons have proved
False to their fathers' memory, false to the faith they loved; 30
If she can scoff at Freedom, and its great charter[9] spurn,
Must we of Massachusetts from truth and duty turn?

We hunt your bondmen,[10] flying from Slavery's hateful hell;
Our voices, at your bidding, take up the bloodhound's yell;
We gather, at your summons, above our fathers' graves, 35
From Freedom's holy altar-horns[11] to tear your wretched slaves!

Thank God! not yet so vilely can Massachusetts bow;
The spirit of her early time is with her even now;
Dream not because her Pilgrim blood moves slow and calm and cool,
She thus can stoop her chainless neck, a sister's slave and tool! 40

---

[2] On the Massachusetts coast.
[3] Nickname for the state of Virginia.
[4] General Charles Cornwallis (1738–1805), commander of British forces in Virginia during the American Revolution.
[5] Massachusetts.
[6] Lower house of Virginia's colonial legislature.
[7] Boston meeting hall.

[8] Reference to Patrick Henry's speech at the Virginia convention.
[9] i.e., the Declaration of Independence.
[10] The Northern states were required by the fugitive slave laws to capture and return escaped slaves to the South.
[11] Horns projecting from the corners of Hebrew altars offered sanctuary to fugitives. (See 1 Kings 1:50–53 and 2:28.)

All that a sister State should do, all that a free State may,
Heart, hand, and purse we proffer, as in our early day;
But that one dark loathsome burden ye must stagger with alone,
And reap the bitter harvest which ye yourselves have sown!

Hold, while ye may, your struggling slaves, and burden God's free air   45
With woman's shriek beneath the lash, and manhood's wild despair;
Cling closer to the "cleaving curse"[12] that writes upon your plains
The blasting of Almighty wrath against a land of chains.

Still shame your gallant ancestry, the cavaliers of old,
By watching round the shambles[13] where human flesh is sold;   50
Gloat o'er the new-born child, and count his market value, when
The maddened mother's cry of woe shall pierce the slaver's den!

Lower than plummet[14] soundeth, sink the Virginia name;
Plant, if ye will, your fathers' graves with rankest weeds of shame;
Be, if ye will, the scandal of God's fair universe;   55
We wash our hands forever of your sin and shame and curse.

A voice from lips whereon the coal from Freedom's shrine hath been,[15]
Thrilled, as but yesterday, the hearts of Berkshire's[16] mountain men:
The echoes of that solemn voice are sadly lingering still
In all our sunny valleys, on every windswept hill.   60

And when the prowling man-thief[17] came hunting for his prey
Beneath the very shadow of Bunker's shaft[18] of gray,
How, through the free lips of the son, the father's warning spoke;
How, from its bonds of trade and sect, the Pilgrim city broke!

A hundred thousand right arms were lifted up on high,   65
A hundred thousand voices sent back their loud reply;

[12] Some slavery advocates asserted that as Cain's descendants African Americans bore a curse "cleaving" them from the human race. (See Genesis 4:11–12.)
[13] Meat market and slaughterhouse.
[14] Lead weight for measuring depths (as in Shakespeare's *The Tempest*, Act III, Sc. iii, ll. 101–102: "I'll seek him deeper than the plummet soundeth / and with him there lie mudded").
[15] Isaiah 6:6–7: "Then flew one of the seraphims unto me, having a live coal in his hand, which he had taken with tongs from off the altar: And he laid it upon my mouth, and said, Lo, this hath touched thy lips; and thine iniquity is taken away, and thy sin purged."
[16] Berkshire: a county in Massachusetts, along with Essex, Middlesex, Norfolk, Plymouth, Worcester, Barnstable, Bristol, Hampden, and Hampshire in the lines that follow.
[17] Slave catcher.
[18] Monument commemorating the Battle of Bunker Hill in the American Revolution.

Through the thronged towns of Essex the startling summons rang,
And up from bench and loom and wheel her young mechanics sprang!

The voice of free, broad Middlesex, of thousands as of one,
The shaft of Bunker calling to that of Lexington;   70
From Norfolk's ancient villages, from Plymouth's rocky bound
To where Nantucket[19] feels the arms of ocean close her round;

From rich and rural Worcester, where through the calm repose
Of cultured vales and fringing woods the gentle Nashua flows,[20]
To where Wachuset's[21] wintry blasts the mountain larches stir,   75
Swelled up to Heaven the thrilling cry of "God save Latimer!"

And sandy Barnstable rose up, wet with the salt sea spray;
And Bristol sent her answering shout down Narragansett Bay!
Along the broad Connecticut[22] old Hampden felt the thrill,
And the cheer of Hampshire's woodmen swept down from Holyoke Hill.   80

The voice of Massachusetts! Of her free sons and daughters,
Deep calling unto deep aloud, the sound of many waters![23]
Against the burden of that voice what tyrant power shall stand?
No fetters in the Bay State! No slave upon her land!

Look to it well, Virginians! In calmness, we have borne,   85
In answer to our faith and trust, your insult and your scorn;
You've spurned our kindest counsels; you've hunted for our lives;
And shaken round our hearths and homes your manacles and gyves!

We wage no war, we lift no arm, we fling no torch within
The fire-damps[24] of the quaking mine beneath your soil of sin;   90
We leave ye with your bondmen, to wrestle, while ye can,
With the strong upward tendencies and godlike soul of man!

But for us and for our children, the vow which we have given
For freedom and humanity is registered in heaven;
No slave-hunt in our borders,—no pirate on our strand!   95
No fetters in the Bay State,—no slave upon our land!

1843

---

[19] Island off the coast of Massachusetts.
[20] River in Massachusetts.
[21] Mountain in Massachusetts.
[22] River flowing through Massachusetts.

[23] Psalms 42:7: "Deep calleth unto deep at the noise of thy water spouts"; Ezekiel 43:2: "His voice was like a noise of many waters."
[24] Explosive gases formed in mines.

Ichabod*

So fallen! so lost! the light withdrawn
    Which once he wore!
The glory from his gray hairs gone
    Forevermore!

Revile him not, the Tempter hath   5
    A snare for all;
And pitying tears, not scorn and wrath,
    Befit his fall!

Oh, dumb be passion's stormy rage,
    When he who might   10
Have lighted up and led his age,
    Falls back in night.

Scorn! would the angels laugh, to mark
    A bright soul driven,
Fiend-goaded, down the endless dark,   15
    From hope and heaven!

Let not the land once proud of him
    Insult him now,
Nor brand with deeper shame his dim,
    Dishonored brow.   20

But let its humbled sons, instead,
    From sea to lake,

---

* The title is from 1 Samuel 4:21: "And she named the child Ichabod, saying the glory is departed from Israel." Whittier's note: "This poem was the outcome of the surprise and grief and forecast of evil consequences which I felt on reading the seventh of March speech of Daniel Webster in support of the 'compromise,' and the Fugitive Slave Law. No partisan or personal enmity dictated it. On the contrary my admiration of the splendid personality and intellectual power of the great Senator was never stronger than when I laid down his speech, and, in one of the saddest moments of my life, penned my protest. I saw, as I wrote, with painful clearness its sure results,—the Slave Power arrogant and defiant, strengthened and encouraged to carry out its scheme for the extension of its baleful system, or the dissolution of the Union, the guaranties of personal liberty in the free States broken down, and the whole country made the hunting-ground of slave-catchers. In the horror of such a vision, so soon fearfully fulfilled, if one spoke at all, he could only speak in tones of stern and sorrowful rebuke.

But death softens all resentments, and the consciousness of a common inheritance of frailty and weakness modifies the severity of judgment. Years after, in *The Lost Occasion*, I gave utterance to an almost universal regret that the great statesman did not live to see the flag which he loved trampled under the feet of Slavery, and, in view of this desecration, make his last days glorious in defence of 'Liberty and Union, one and inseparable.'"

A long lament, as for the dead,
  In sadness make.

Of all we loved and honored, naught   25
  Save power remains;
A fallen angel's pride of thought,
  Still strong in chains.

All else is gone; from those great eyes
  The soul has fled: 30
When faith is lost, when honor dies,
  The man is dead!

Then, pay the reverence of old days
  To his dead fame;
Walk backward, with averted gaze,   35
  And hide the shame!
1850

Skipper Ireson's Ride*

Of all the rides since the birth of time,
Told in story or sung in rhyme,—
On Apuleius's Golden Ass,[1]
Or one-eyed Calender's horse of brass,[2]
Witch astride of a human back,   5
Islam's prophet on Al-Borák,[3]—
The strangest ride that ever was sped
Was Ireson's, out from Marblehead![4]
  Old Floyd Ireson, for his hard heart,
  Tarred and feathered and carried in a cart   10
  By the women of Marblehead!

* Whittier claims that this ballad "was founded solely on a fragment of rhyme which I heard from one of my early schoolmates, a native of Marblehead." The fragment is presumably the refrain sung by either the women escorting Captain Ireson in his cart or by the skipper himself. This record of events is "pure fancy," as Whittier declared in his note for the 1888 edition, and not according to the facts about the case presented in *History of Marblehead* (1879) by Samuel Roads.

[1] Roman satirist Lucius Apuleius (second century B.C.) tells of the metamorphosis of Aman into an "excellent" ass in *The Golden Ass.*

[2] In the *Arabian Nights* tale, "the story of the third royal mendicant," a calender (or dervish) slew the owner of a horse of brass and later lost an eye.

[3] In one legend, Mohammed was carried to highest heaven by a supernatural winged animal.

[4] Massachusetts seaport.

Body of turkey, head of owl,
Wings a-droop like a rained-on fowl,
Feathered and ruffled in every part,
Skipper Ireson stood in the cart.   15
Scores of women, old and young,
Strong of muscle, and glib of tongue,
Pushed and pulled up the rocky lane,
Shouting and singing the shrill refrain:
    "Here's Flud Oirson, fur his horrd horrt,   20
    Torr'd an' futherr'd an' corr'd in a corrt
    By the women o' Morble'ead!"[5]

Wrinkled scolds with hands on hips,
Girls in bloom of cheek and lips,
Wild-eyed, free-limbed, such as chase   25
Bacchus[6] round some antique vase,
Brief of skirt, with ankles bare,
Loose of kerchief and loose of hair,
With conch-shells blowing and fish-horns'[7] twang,
Over and over the Mænads sang: 30
    "Here's Flud Oirson, fur his horrd horrt,
    Torr'd an' futherr'd an' corr'd in a corrt
    By the women o' Morble'ead!"

Small pity for him!—He sailed away
From a leaking ship in Chaleur Bay,[8]—   35
Sailed away from a sinking wreck,
With his own town's-people on her deck!
"Lay by! lay by!" they called to him.
Back he answered, "Sink or swim!
Brag of your catch of fish again!"   40
And off he sailed through the fog and rain!
    Old Floyd Ireson, for his hard heart,
    Tarred and feathered and carried in a cart
    By the women of Marblehead!

Fathoms deep in dark Chaleur   45
That wreck shall lie forevermore.
Mother and sister, wife and maid,
Looked from the rocks of Marblehead
Over the moaning and rainy sea,—
Looked for the coming that might not be!   50

---

5 James Russell Lowell, Whittier's editor, suggested that the Marblehead dialect be used
for the refrain in stanzas 2, 3, 6, and 7 in
contrast to the standard English used in the
refrain in stanzas 1, 4, 5, 8, and 9.

6 Roman god of wine, usually depicted as surrounded by frenetic women known as
maenads.
7 Fish peddler's horns.
8 In the Gulf of St. Lawrence.

What did the winds and the sea-birds say
Of the cruel captain who sailed away?—
Old Floyd Ireson, for his hard heart,
Tarred and feathered and carried in a cart
   By the women of Marblehead!   55

Through the street, on either side,
Up flew windows, doors swung wide;
Sharp-tongued spinsters, old wives gray,
Treble lent the fish-horn's bray.
Sea-worn grandsires, cripple-bound,   60
Hulks of old sailors run aground,
Shook head, and fist, and hat, and cane,
And cracked with curses the hoarse refrain:
   "Here's Flud Oirson, fur his horrd horrt,
   Torr'd an' futherr'd an' corr'd in a corrt   65
   By the women o' Morble'ead!"

Sweetly along the Salem road
Bloom of orchard and lilac showed.
Little the wicked skipper knew
Of the fields so green and the sky so blue.   70
Riding there in his sorry trim,
Like an Indian idol glum and grim,
Scarcely he seemed the sound to hear
Of voices shouting, far and near:
   "Here's Flud Oirson, fur his horrd horrt,   75
   Torr'd an' futherr'd an' corr'd in a corrt
   By the women o' Morble'ead!"

"Hear me, neighbors!" at last he cried,—
"What to me is this noisy ride?
What is the shame that clothes the skin   80
To the nameless horror that lives within?
Waking or sleeping, I see a wreck,
And hear a cry from a reeling deck!
Hate me and curse me,—I only dread
The hand of God and the face of the dead!"   85
   Said old Floyd Ireson, for his hard heart,
   Tarred and feathered and carried in a cart
   By the women of Marblehead!

Then the wife of the skipper lost at sea
Said, "God has touched him! why should we!"   90
Said an old wife mourning her only son,
"Cut the rogue's tether and let him run!"
So with soft relentings and rude excuse,
Half scorn, half pity, they cut him loose,

And gave him a cloak to hide him in,   95
    And left him alone with his shame and sin.
    Poor Floyd Ireson, for his hard heart,
    Tarred and feathered and carried in a cart
    By the women of Marblehead!
1857

Telling the Bees*

Here is the place; right over the hill
    Runs the path I took;
You can see the gap in the old wall still,
    And the stepping-stones in the shallow brook.

There is the house, with the gate red-barred,   5
    And the poplars tall;
And the barn's brown length, and the cattle-yard,
    And the white horns tossing above the wall.

There are the beehives ranged in the sun;
    And down by the brink   10
Of the brook are her poor flowers, weed-o'errun,
    Pansy and daffodil, rose and pink.

A year has gone, as the tortoise goes,
    Heavy and slow;
And the same rose blows, and the same sun glows,   15
    And the same brook sings of a year ago.

There's the same sweet clover-smell in the breeze;
    And the June sun warm
Tangles his wings of fire in the trees,
    Setting, as then, over Fernside farm.   20

I mind me how with a lover's care
    From my Sunday coat

* Whittier's note: "A remarkable custom, brought from the Old Country, formerly prevailed in the rural districts of New England. On the death of a member of the family, the bees were at once informed of the event, and their hives dressed in mourning. This ceremonial was supposed to be necessary to prevent the swarms from leaving their hives and seeking a new home."

I brushed off the burrs, and smoothed my hair,
 And cooled at the brookside my brow and throat.

Since we parted, a month had passed,—   25
 To love, a year;
Down through the beeches I looked at last
 On the little red gate and the well-sweep near.

I can see it all now,—the slantwise rain
 Of light through the leaves,   30
The sundown's blaze on her window-pane,
 The bloom of her roses under the eaves.

Just the same as a month before,—
 The house and the trees,
The barn's brown gable, the vine by the door,—   35
 Nothing changed but the hives of bees.

Before them, under the garden wall,
 Forward and back,
Went drearily singing the chore-girl small,
 Draping each hive with a shred of black.   40

Trembling, I listened: the summer sun
 Had the chill of snow;
For I knew she was telling the bees of one
 Gone on the journey we all must go!

Then I said to myself, "My Mary weeps   45
 For the dead to-day:
Haply her blind old grandsire sleeps
 The fret and the pain of his age away."

But her dog whined low; on the doorway sill,
 With his cane to his chin,   50
The old man sat; and the chore-girl still
 Sung to the bees stealing out and in.

And the song she was singing ever since
 In my ear sounds on:—
"Stay at home, pretty bees, fly not hence!   55
 Mistress Mary is dead and gone!"
1858

Harriet Beecher Stowe
1811–1896

Harriet Beecher Stowe was the daughter of a New England Congregational preacher, the sister of five preachers, and the wife of another. Born in Litchfield, Connecticut, on June 14, 1811, she was raised in a family whose members had devoted themselves to Christian purpose, self-abnegation, and spiritual rebirth, "a kind of moral heaven, replete with moral oxygen—fully charged with intellectual electricity." She was educated at a local school for girls and in 1824 graduated from—and then taught at— the Hartford Female Seminary, founded by her famous sister Catherine, a pioneer in women's education. When her father accepted an appointment to head the Lane Theological Seminary in 1832, she moved with her family to Cincinnati, a town at the border of North and South, East and West and at the center of increasing antislavery sentiment. While working at Catherine's newly founded Western Female Institute, Harriet Beecher began writing sketches and stories for literary and evangelical periodicals. In 1836, she married the Reverend Calvin Ellis Stowe, a preacher and a professor of biblical literature at Lane Theological Seminary. The demands of raising their seven children forced Mrs. Stowe to set aside the idea of a literary career. Yet during what would amount to nearly fifteen years, she wrote, when she could find the time, mostly to help support their large family. And she came to realize that she was a woman writer drawn to a provocative subject: the moral, political, and ethical issues surrounding the slavery question.

The moral principles that guided her life infused her thinking and writing. Her views on slavery derived from reading both slave narratives and abolitionist tracts, visiting slaveholding plantations in Kentucky, and feeling moral revulsion at the passage of the Fugitive Slave Law (1850), which legally obligated residents of free states to return fugitives to their "rightful owners." Her plans to write a moral "epic of negro bondage" crystallized in a vision of a slave's suffering and death she had in a church in Brunswick, Maine, where the family had moved in 1850. Eventually, she came to believe that she was simply God's instrument for writing *Uncle Tom's Cabin,* a book she hoped would "make this whole nation feel what an accursed thing slavery is."

With an incomplete draft in hand, Stowe approached *The National Era,* a Washington, D.C., antislavery weekly, with plans to publish her novel in three or four installments. The success of this serial led in 1852 to the publication in two volumes of what was originally entitled *Uncle Tom's Cabin, or The Man That Was a Thing.* It was a historic event in publishing: Ten thousand copies were sold in the first week, over three hundred thousand in the first year. By the outbreak of the Civil War that number had soared beyond three million. The book was translated into thirty-seven languages. Praise poured in from all over the world. Ralph Waldo Emerson spoke for many when he hailed Stowe's ability to create a book that at once could enjoy popular success, speak "to the universal heart," and be "read with equal interest to three audiences, namely, in the parlor, in the kitchen, and in the nursery of every house." Suddenly, Harriet Beecher Stowe found herself the most famous literary figure in America and an international celebrity. She toured England and met many of the leading literary figures there and on the Continent. Several years later, when the diminutive Stowe met the towering president, Lincoln is reported to have said, "So this is the little lady who made this big war!"

A powerful but controversial instrument of reform, *Uncle Tom's Cabin* had an extraordinary impact on the culture and politics of its time. Its publication helped change public opinion and sway political action. Its message—that the slave, the master, and their respective families are all destroyed by slavery—stirred the nation. And its principal characters—Simon Legree, Eliza, Little Eva, and Uncle Tom—became archetypes in the national literary consciousness.

In 1853, Stowe published *A Key to Uncle Tom's Cabin,* in which she defended herself against widespread charges that she had distorted the reality of slave life. Stowe's reliance on slave narratives as her primary sources and her correspondence with Frederick Douglass to verify the accuracy of her presentation of Tom made *Uncle Tom's Cabin* a significant early example of African American literature's influence on a mainstream American novel. In a similar manner, Stowe's second novel on slavery, *Dred* (1856), drew heavily on the widely circulated slave narrative *Confessions of Nat Turner* (1831) but enjoyed no comparable popular success.

Harriet Beecher Stowe applied her considerable literary skills to subjects other than the moral and social reform advocated in her novels about slavery. She had an excellent ear for local idiom and a practiced eye for telling details. She wrote at least one book in each of the years between 1862 and 1884, and many—including *The Minister's Wooing* (1859), *The Pearl of Orr's Island* (1862), and *Oldtown Fireside Stories* (1872)—captured domestic life and local color and vividness. Stowe called *Oldtown Folks* (1869) "my résumé of the whole spirit and body of New England" and her novels anticipate much of the local-color realism of Mary Wilkins Freeman and especially Sarah Orne Jewett, who acknowledged her indebtedness to Stowe.

Within Stowe's lifetime, the characters over whom half the world had anguished were gradually refashioned into stereotypes and burlesqued on stage and in literature. Aunt Chloe was transformed into Aunt Jemima, and Uncle Tom, once the focus of compassion, became an object of derision, a symbol of the foot-shuffling, servile African American. There was little in Stowe's later years that turned out the way she would have preferred. One of her children died from alcoholism, another from drug addiction, a third from drowning, a fourth from cholera. Most of what she received in royalties from *Uncle Tom's Cabin* was lost in mismanaged real estate investments. The adultery trial of her brother Henry Ward Beecher, one of the most famous preachers in the nineteenth century, greatly affected her. And her friendship with Lady Byron—and her exposé in the *Atlantic Monthly* of the Lord Byron-Augusta Leigh incest episode—cost the magazine nearly fifteen thousand subscribers and caused many readers of her fiction to regard her as a spiteful gossip. She died in 1896, several years after senility had taken its toll. At her funeral her coffin was draped with a wreath from a group of Boston African Americans. The note read, "The Children of Uncle Tom."

Further Reading:

C. E. Stowe, ed., *The Life of Harriet Beecher Stowe from Her Letters and Journals,* 1889.

F. Wilson, *Crusader in Crinoline: The Life of Harriet Beecher Stowe,* 1941.

J. Baldwin, "Everybody's Protest Novel," *Partisan Review* 16, 1949.

C. H. Foster, *The Rungless Ladder: Harriet Beecher Stowe and New England Puritanism,* 1954.

E. Wilson, *Patriotic Gore,* 1962.

J. R. Adams, *Harriet Beecher Stowe,* 1963.

E. Wagenknecht, *Harriet Beecher Stowe: The Known and the Unknown,* 1965.

A. Crozier, *The Novels of Harriet Beecher Stowe*, 1970.

E. B. Kirkham, *The Building of "Uncle Tom's Cabin*," 1977.

T. F. Gossett, Uncle Tom's Cabin *and American Culture*, 1985.

J. Tompkins, *Sensational Designs: The Cultural Work of American Fiction*, 1985.

E. Sundquist, ed., *New Essays on* Uncle Tom's Cabin, 1986.

J. Boydston, *The Limits of Sisterhood: The Beecher Sisters on Women's Rights and Woman's Sphere*, 1988.

T. R. Hovet, *The Master Narrative: Harriet Beecher Stowe's Subversive Story of Master and Slave in* Uncle Tom's Cabin *and* Dred, 1989.

G. Brown, *Domestic Individualism: Imagining Self in Nineteenth-Century America*, 1990.

J. Hedrick, *Harriet Beecher Stowe*, 1994.

Text:
The Writings of Harriet Beecher Stowe, 16 vols., 1896.

Uncle Tom's Cabin;
Or, Life Among the Lowly

Chapter V: Showing the Feelings of Living Property on Changing Owners

Mr. and Mrs. Shelby had retired to their apartment for the night. He was lounging in a large easy-chair, looking over some letters that had come in the afternoon mail, and she was standing before her mirror, brushing out the complicated braids and curls in which Eliza had arranged her hair; for, noticing her pale cheeks and haggard eyes, she had excused her attendance that night, and ordered her to bed. The employment, naturally enough, suggested her conversation with the girl in the morning; and, turning to her husband, she said carelessly,—

"By the bye, Arthur, who was that low-bred fellow that you lugged in to our dinner-table to-day?"

"Haley is his name," said Shelby, turning himself rather uneasily in his chair, and continuing with his eyes fixed on a letter.

"Haley! Who is he, and what may be his business here, pray?"

"Well, he's a man that I transacted some business with, last time I was at Natchez," said Mr. Shelby.

"And he presumed on it to make himself quite at home, and call and dine here, ay?"

"Why, I invited him; I had some accounts with him," said Shelby.

"Is he a negro-trader?" said Mrs. Shelby, noticing a certain embarrassment in her husband's manner.

"Why, my dear, what put that into your head?" said Shelby, looking up.

"Nothing,—only Eliza came in here, after dinner, in a great worry, crying and taking on, and said you were talking with a trader, and that she heard him make an offer for her boy,—the ridiculous little goose!"

"She did, hey?" said Mr. Shelby, returning to his paper, which he seemed for a few moments quite intent upon, not perceiving that he was holding it bottom upwards.

"It will have to come out," said he mentally; "as well now as ever."

"I told Eliza," said Mrs. Shelby, as she continued brushing her hair, "that she was a little fool for her pains, and that you never had anything to do with that sort of persons. Of course, I knew you never meant to sell any of our people,—least of all, to such a fellow."

135,000 SETS, 270,000 VOLUMES SOLD.

UNCLE TOM'S CABIN

FOR SALE HERE.

AN EDITION FOR THE MILLION, COMPLETE IN 1 Vol., PRICE 37 1-2 CENTS.

"   "   IN GERMAN, IN 1 Vol., PRICE 50 CENTS.

"   "   IN 2 Vols,. CLOTH, 6 PLATES, PRICE $1.50.

SUPERB ILLUSTRATED EDITION, IN 1 Vol., WITH 153 ENGRAVINGS,
PRICES FROM $2.50 TO $5.00.

The Greatest Book of the Age.

Unidentified Artist
*More than 300,000 copies of Uncle Tom's Cabin
were sold in the first year of publication.*
1852
(Collection of the New York Historical Society)

Robert S. Duncanson
Uncle Tom and Little Eva
oil on canvas, 1853
(The Detroit Institute of Arts, 1994)

"Well, Emily," said her husband, "so I have always felt and said; but the fact is that my business lies so that I cannot get on without. I shall have to sell some of my hands."

"To that creature? Impossible! Mr. Shelby, you cannot be serious."

"I'm sorry to say that I am," said Mr. Shelby. "I've agreed to sell Tom."

"What! our Tom?—that good, faithful creature!—been your faithful servant from a boy! Oh, Mr. Shelby!—and you have promised him his freedom, too,—you and I have spoken to him a hundred times of it. Well, I can believe anything now,—I can believe *now* that you could sell little Harry, poor Eliza's only child!" said Mrs. Shelby, in a tone between grief and indignation.

"Well, since you must know all, it is so. I have agreed to sell Tom and Harry both; and I don't know why I am to be rated, as if I were a monster, for doing what every one does every day."

"But why, of all others, choose these?" said Mrs. Shelby. "Why sell them, of all on the place, if you must sell at all?"

"Because they will bring the highest sum of any,—that's why. I could choose another, if you say so. The fellow made me a high bid on Eliza, if that would suit you any better," said Mr. Shelby.

"The wretch!" said Mrs. Shelby vehemently.

"Well, I didn't listen to it, a moment,—out of regard to your feelings, I wouldn't; —so give me some credit."

"My dear," said Mrs. Shelby, recollecting herself, "forgive me; I have been hasty. I was surprised, and entirely unprepared for this;—but surely you will allow me to intercede for these poor creatures. Tom is a noble-hearted, faithful fellow, if he is black. I do believe, Mr. Shelby, that if he were put to it, he would lay down his life for you."

"I know it,—I dare say;—but what's the use of all this?—I can't help myself."

"Why not make a pecuniary sacrifice? I'm willing to bear my part of the inconvenience. Oh, Mr. Shelby, I have tried—tried most faithfully, as a Christian woman should—to do my duty to these poor, simple, dependent creatures. I have cared for them, instructed them, watched over them, and known all their little cares and joys, for years; and how can I ever hold up my head again among them if, for the sake of a little paltry gain, we sell such a faithful, excellent, confiding creature as poor Tom, and tear from him in a moment all we have taught him to love and value? I have taught them the duties of the family, of parent and child, and husband and wife; and how can I bear to have this open acknowledgment that we care for no tie, no duty, no relation, however sacred, compared with money? I have talked with Eliza about her boy,—her duty to him as a Christian mother, to watch over him, pray for him, and bring him up in a Christian way; and now what can I say, if you tear him away, and sell him, soul and body, to a profane, unprincipled man, just to save a little money? I have told her that one soul is worth more than all the money in the world; and how will she believe me when she sees us turn round and sell her child?—sell him, perhaps, to certain ruin of body and soul!"

"I'm sorry you feel so about it, Emily,—indeed I am," said Mr. Shelby; "and I respect your feelings, too, though I don't pretend to share them to their full extent; but I tell you now, solemnly, it's of no use,—I can't help myself. I didn't mean to tell you this, Emily; but in plain words, there is no choice between selling these two and selling everything. Either they must go, or *all* must. Haley has come into possession of a mortgage which, if I don't clear off with him directly, will take everything before it. I've raked, and scraped, and borrowed, and all but begged,—and the price of these two was needed to make up the balance, and I had to give them up. Haley fancied the child; he agreed to settle the matter that way and no other. I was in his power, and *had* to do it. If you feel so to have them sold, would it be any better to have *all* sold?"

Mrs. Shelby stood like one stricken. Finally, turning to her toilet, she rested her face in her hands, and gave a sort of groan.

"This is God's curse on slavery!—a bitter, bitter, most accursed thing!—a curse to the master and a curse to the slave! I was a fool to think I could make anything good out of such a deadly evil. It is a sin to hold a slave under laws like ours,—I always felt it was,—I always thought so when I was a girl,—I thought so still more after I joined the church; but I thought I could gild it over,—I thought, by kindness, and care, and instruction, I could make the condition of mine better than freedom,—fool that I was!"

"Why, wife, you are getting to be an abolitionist, quite."

"Abolitionist! if they knew all I know about slavery they *might* talk! We don't need them to tell us; you know I never thought that slavery was right,—never felt willing to own slaves."

"Well, therein you differ from many wise and pious men," said Mr. Shelby. "You remember Mr. B.'s sermon, the other day?"

"I don't want to hear such sermons; I never wish to hear Mr. B. in our church again. Ministers can't help the evil, perhaps,—can't cure it, any more than we can,— but defend it!—it always went against my common sense. And I think you did n't think much of that sermon, either."

"Well," said Shelby, "I must say these ministers sometimes carry matters further than we poor sinners would exactly dare to do. We men of the world must wink pretty hard at various things, and get used to a deal that is n't the exact thing. But we don't quite fancy, when women and ministers come out broad and square, and go beyond us in matters of either modesty or morals, that's a fact. But now, my dear, I trust you see the necessity of the thing, and you see that I have done the very best that circumstances would allow."

"Oh, yes, yes!" said Mrs. Shelby, hurriedly and abstractedly fingering her gold watch,—"I have n't any jewelry of any amount," she added thoughtfully; "but would not this watch do something?—it was an expensive one when it was bought. If I could only at least save Eliza's child, I would sacrifice anything I have."

"I'm sorry, very sorry, Emily," said Mr. Shelby. "I'm sorry this takes hold of you so; but it will do no good. The fact is, Emily, the thing's done; the bills of sale are already signed, and in Haley's hands; and you must be thankful it is no worse. That man has had it in his power to ruin us all,—and now he is fairly off. If you knew the man as I do, you'd think that we had had a narrow escape."

"Is he so hard, then?"

"Why, not a cruel man, exactly, but a man of leather,— a man alive to nothing but trade and profit,—cool, and unhesitating, and unrelenting, as death and the grave. He'd sell his own mother at a good percentage,—not wishing the old woman any harm, either."

"And this wretch owns that good, faithful Tom and Eliza's child!"

"Well, my dear, the fact is that this goes rather hard with me; it's a thing I hate to think of. Haley wants to drive matters, and take possession to-morrow. I'm going to get out my horse bright and early, and be off. I can't see Tom, that's a fact; and you had better arrange a drive somewhere, and carry Eliza off. Let the thing be done when she is out of sight."

"No, no," said Mrs. Shelby; "I'll be in no sense accomplice or help in this cruel business. I'll go and see poor old Tom, God help him, in his distress! They shall see, at any rate, that their mistress can feel for and with them. As to Eliza, I dare not think about it. The Lord forgive us! What have we done, that this cruel necessity should come on us?"

There was one listener to this conversation whom Mr. and Mrs. Shelby little suspected.

Communicating with their apartment was a large closet, opening by a door into the outer passage. When Mrs. Shelby had dismissed Eliza for the night, her feverish and excited mind had suggested the idea of this closet; and she had hidden herself there, and, with her ear pressed close against the crack of the door, had lost not a word of the conversation.

When the voices died into silence, she rose and crept stealthily away. Pale, shivering, with rigid features and compressed lips, she looked an entirely altered being from the soft and timid creature she had been hitherto. She moved cautiously along the entry, paused one moment at her mistress's door and raised her hands in mute appeal to

Heaven, and then turned and glided into her own room. It was a quiet, neat apartment, on the same floor with her mistress. There was the pleasant sunny window, where she had often sat singing at her sewing; there, a little case of books, and various little fancy articles, ranged by them, the gifts of Christmas holidays; there was her simple wardrobe in the closet and in the drawers:—here was, in short, her home; and, on the whole, a happy one it had been to her. But there, on the bed, lay her slumbering boy, his long curls falling negligently around his unconscious face, his rosy mouth half open, his little fat hands thrown out over the bedclothes, and a smile spread like a sunbeam over his whole face.

"Poor boy! poor fellow!" said Eliza; "they have sold you! but your mother will save you yet!"

No tear dropped over that pillow; in such straits as these the heart has no tears to give,—it drops only blood, bleeding itself away in silence. She took a piece of paper and a pencil, and wrote hastily,—

"Oh, Missis! dear Missis! don't think me ungrateful,—don't think hard of me, any-way,—I heard all you and Master said to-night. I am going to try to save my boy,—you will not blame me! God bless and reward you for all your kindness!"

Hastily folding and directing this, she went to a drawer and made up a little package of clothing for her boy, which she tied with a handkerchief firmly round her waist; and, so fond is a mother's remembrance that, even in the terrors of that hour, she did not forget to put in the little package one or two of his favorite toys, reserving a gayly painted parrot to amuse him, when she should be called on to awaken him. It was some trouble to arouse the little sleeper; but, after some effort, he sat up, and was playing with his bird, while his mother was putting on her bonnet and shawl.

"Where are you going, mother?" said he, as she drew near the bed, with his little coat and cap.

His mother drew near, and looked so earnestly into his eyes that he at once divined that something unusual was the matter.

"Hush, Harry," she said; "mustn't speak loud, or they will hear us. A wicked man was coming to take little Harry away from his mother, and carry him 'way off in the dark; but mother won't let him,—she's going to put on her little boy's cap and coat, and run off with him, so the ugly man can't catch him."

Saying these words, she had tied and buttoned on the child's simple outfit, and, taking him in her arms, she whispered to him to be very still; and, opening a door in her room which led into the outer veranda, she glided noiselessly out.

It was a sparkling, frosty, starlight night, and the mother wrapped the shawl close round her child, as, perfectly quiet with vague terror, he clung round her neck.

Old Bruno, a great Newfoundland, who slept at the end of the porch, rose, with a low growl, as she came near. She gently spoke his name, and the animal, an old pet and playmate of hers, instantly, wagging his tail, prepared to follow her, though apparently revolving much, in his simple dog's head, what such an indiscreet midnight promenade might mean. Some dim ideas of imprudence or impropriety in the measure seemed to embarrass him considerably; for he often stopped, as Eliza glided forward, and looked wistfully, first at her and then at the house, and then, as if reassured by reflection, he pattered along after her again. A few minutes brought them to the window of Uncle Tom's cottage, and Eliza, stopping, tapped lightly on the window-pane.

The prayer-meeting at Uncle Tom's had, in the order of hymn-singing, been pro-tracted to a very late hour; and, as Uncle Tom had indulged himself in a few lengthy so-los afterwards, the consequence was that, although it was now between twelve and one o'clock, he and his worthy helpmeet were not yet asleep.

"Good Lord! what's that?" said Aunt Chloe, starting up and hastily drawing the cur-tain. "My sakes alive, if it ain't Lizy! Get on your clothes, old man, quick!—there's old Bruno, too, a-pawin' round. What on airth—I'm gwine to open the door."

And, suiting the action to the word, the door flew open, and the light of the tallow candle, which Tom had hastily lighted, fell on the haggard face and dark, wild eyes of the fugitive.

"Lord bless you!—I'm skeered to look at ye, Lizy! Are ye tuck sick, or what's come over ye?"

"I'm running away,—Uncle Tom and Aunt Chloe,—carrying off my child,—Master sold him!"

"Sold him?" echoed both, lifting up their hands in dismay.

"Yes, sold him!" said Eliza firmly. "I crept into the closet by Mistress's door to-night, and I heard Master tell Missis that he had sold my Harry, and you, Uncle Tom, both to a trader; and that he was going off this morning on his horse, and that the man was to take possession to-day."

Tom had stood, during the speech, with his hands raised, and his eyes dilated, like a man in a dream. Slowly and gradually, as its meaning came over him, he collapsed, rather than seated himself, on his old chair, and sunk his head down upon his knees.

"The good Lord have pity on us!" said Aunt Chloe. "Oh, it don't seem as if it was true! What has he done, that Mas'r should sell *him*?"

"He hasn't done anything,—it isn't for that. Master don't want to sell; and Missis,—she's always good. I heard her plead and beg for us; but he told her 't was no use; that he was in this man's debt, and that this man had got the power over him; and that if he didn't pay him off clear, it would end in his having to sell the place and all the people, and move off. Yes, I heard him say there was no choice between selling these two and selling all, the man was driving him so hard. Master said he was sorry; but oh, Missis,—you ought to have heard her talk! If she ain't a Christian and an angel, there never was one. I'm a wicked girl to leave her so; but, then, I can't help it. She said, herself, one soul was worth more than the world; and this boy has a soul, and if I let him be carried off, who knows what'll become of it? It must be right; but, if it ain't right, the Lord forgive me, for I can't help doing it!"

"Well, old man!" said Aunt Chloe, "why don't you go, too? Will you wait to be toted down river, where they kill niggers with hard work and starving? I'd a heap rather die than go there, any day! There's time for ye,—be off with Lizy,—you've got a pass to come and go any time. Come, bustle up, and I'll get your things together."

Tom slowly raised his head, and looked sorrowfully but quietly around, and said,—

"No, no,—I ain't going. Let Eliza go,—it's her right! I wouldn't be the one to say no,—'t ain't in *natur* for her to stay; but you heard what she said! If I must be sold, or all the people on the place, and everything go to rack, why, let me be sold. I s'pose I can b'ar it as well as any on 'em," he added, while something like a sob and a sigh shook his broad, rough chest convulsively. "Mas'r always found me on the spot,—he always will. I never have broke trust, nor used my pass noways contrary to my word, and I never will.

It's better for me alone to go, than to break up the place and sell all. Mas'r ain't to blame, Chloe, and he'll take care of you and the poor"—

Here he turned to the rough trundle-bed full of little woolly heads, and broke fairly down. He leaned over the back of the chair, and covered his face with his large hands. Sobs, heavy, hoarse, and loud, shook the chair, and great tears fell through his fingers on the floor: just such tears, sir, as you dropped into the coffin where lay your firstborn son; such tears, woman, as you shed when you heard the cries of your dying babe. For, sir, he was a man,—and you are but another man. And, woman, though dressed in silk and jewels, you are but a woman, and, in life's great straits and mighty griefs, ye feel but one sorrow!

"And now," said Eliza, as she stood in the door, "I saw my husband only this afternoon, and I little knew then what was to come. They have pushed him to the very last standing-place, and he told me, to-day, that he was going to run away. Do try, if you can, to get word to him. Tell him how I went, and why I went; and tell him I'm going to try and find Canada. You must give my love to him, and tell him, if I never see him again,"—she turned away, and stood with her back to them for a moment, and then added, in a husky voice,—"tell him to be as good as he can, and try and meet me in the kingdom of heaven."

"Call Bruno in there," she added. "Shut the door on him, poor beast! He must n't go with me!"

A few last words and tears, a few simple adieus and blessings, and, clasping her wondering and affrighted child in her arms, she glided noiselessly away.

Chapter VII: The Mother's Struggle

It is impossible to conceive of a human creature more wholly desolate and forlorn than Eliza, when she turned for footsteps from Uncle Tom's cabin.

Her husband's suffering and dangers, and the danger of her child, all blended in her mind, with a confused and stunning sense of the risk she was running, in leaving the only home she had ever known, and cutting loose from the protection of a friend whom she loved and revered. Then there was the parting from every familiar object,—the place where she had grown up, the trees under which she had played, the groves where she had walked many an evening in happier days, by the side of her young husband,—everything, as it lay in the clear, frosty starlight, seemed to speak reproachfully to her, and ask her whither could she go from a home like that?

But stronger than all was maternal love, wrought into a paroxysm of frenzy by the near approach of a fearful danger. Her boy was old enough to have walked by her side, and, in an indifferent case, she would only have led him by the hand; but now the bare thought of putting him out of her arms made her shudder, and she strained him to her bosom with a convulsive grasp, as she went rapidly forward.

The frosty ground creaked beneath her feet, and she trembled at the sound; every quaking leaf and fluttering shadow sent the blood backward to her heart, and quickened her footsteps. She wondered within herself at the strength that seemed to become upon her; for she felt the weight of her boy as if it had been a feather, and every flutter of fear seemed to increase the supernatural power that bore her on, while from her pale lips burst forth, in frequent ejaculations, the prayer to a Friend above—"Lord, help! Lord, save me!"

If it were *your* Harry, mother, or your Willie, that were going to be torn from you by a brutal trader, to-morrow,—if you had seen the man, and heard that the papers were signed and delivered, and you had only from twelve o'clock till morning to make good your escape,—how fast could *you* walk? How many miles could you make in those few brief hours, with the darling at your bosom,—the little sleepy head on your shoulder,—the small, soft arms trustingly holding on to your neck?

For the child slept. At first, the novelty and alarm kept him waking; but his mother so hurriedly repressed every breath or sound, and so assured him that if he were only still she would certainly save him, that he clung quietly round her neck, only asking, as he found himself sinking to sleep.

"Mother, I don't need to keep awake, do I?"

"No, my darling; sleep, if you want to."

"But, mother, if I do get asleep, you won't let him get me?"

"No! so may God help me!" said his mother, with a paler cheek, and a brighter light in her large, dark eyes.

"You're *sure*, an't you, mother?"

"Yes, *sure!*" said the mother, in a voice that startled herself; for it seemed to her to come from a spirit within, that was no part of her; and the boy dropped his little, weary head on her shoulder, and was soon asleep. How the touch of those warm arms, the gentle breathings that came in her neck, seemed to add fire and spirit to her movements! It seemed to her as if strength poured into her in electric streams, from every gentle touch and movement of the sleeping, confiding child. Sublime is the dominion of the mind over the body, that, for a time, can make flesh and nerve impregnable, and string the sinews like steel, so that the weak become so mighty.

The boundaries of the farm, the grove, the wood-lot, passed by her dizzily, as she walked on; and still she went, leaving one familiar object after another, slacking not, pausing not, till reddening daylight found her many a long mile from all traces of any familiar objects upon the open highway.

She had often been, with her mistress, to visit some connections, in the little village of T———, not far from the Ohio River, and knew the road well. To go thither, to escape across the Ohio River, were the first hurried outlines of her plan of escape; beyond that, she could only hope in God.

When horses and vehicles began to move along the highway, with that alert perception peculiar to a state of excitement, and which seems to be a sort of inspiration, she became aware that her headlong pace and distracted air might bring on her remark and suspicion. She therefore put the boy on the ground, and adjusting her dress and bonnet, she walked on at as rapid a pace as she thought consistent with the preservation of appearances. In her little bundle she had provided a store of cakes and apples, which she used as expedients for quickening the speed of the child, rolling the apple some yards before them, when the boy would run with all his might after it; and this ruse, often repeated, carried them over many a half-mile.

After a while they came to a thick patch of woodland, through which murmured a clear brook. As the child complained of hunger and thirst, she climbed over the fence with him; and, sitting down behind a large rock which concealed them from the road, she gave him a breakfast out of her little package. The boy wondered and grieved that she could not eat; and when, putting his arms round her neck, he tried to wedge some of his cake into her mouth, it seemed to her that the rising in her throat would choke her.

"No, no, Harry darling! mother can't eat till you are safe! We must go on—on—till we come to the river!" And she hurried again into the road, and again constrained herself to walk regularly and composedly forward.

She was many miles past any neighborhood where she was personally known. If she should chance to meet any who knew her, she reflected that the well-known kindness of the family would be of itself a blind to suspicion, as making it an unlikely supposition that she could be a fugitive. As she was also so white as not to be known as of colored lineage, without a critical survey, and her child was white also, it was much easier for her to pass on unsuspected.

On this presumption, she stopped at noon at a neat farm-house, to rest herself, and buy some dinner for her child and self; for, as the danger decreased with the distance, the supernatural tension of the nervous system lessened, and she found herself both weary and hungry.

The good woman, kindly and gossiping, seemed rather pleased than otherwise with having somebody come in to talk with; and accepted, without examination, Eliza's statement, that she "was going on a little piece, to spend with her friends,"—all which she hoped in her heart might prove strictly true.

An hour before sunset, she entered the village of T———, by the Ohio River, weary and foot-sore, but still strong in heart. Her first glance was at the river, which lay, like Jordan, between her and the Canaan of liberty on the other side.

It was now early spring, and the river was swollen and turbulent: great cakes of floating ice were swinging heavily to and fro in the turbid waters. Owing to the peculiar form of the shore on the Kentucky side, the land bending far out into the water, the ice had been lodged and detained in great quantities, and the narrow channel which swept round the bend was full of ice, piled one cake over another, thus forming a temporary barrier to the descending ice, which lodged, and formed a great, undulating raft, filling up the whole river, and extending almost to the Kentucky shore.

Eliza stood, for a moment, contemplating this unfavorable aspect of things, which she saw at once must prevent the usual ferry-boat from running, and then turned into a small public house on the bank, to make a few inquiries.

The hostess, who was busy in various fizzing and stewing operations over the fire, preparatory to the evening meal, stopped, with a fork in her hand, as Eliza's sweet and plaintive voice arrested her.

"What is it?" she said.

"Isn't there any ferry or boat, that takes people over to B———, now?" she said.

"No, indeed!" said the woman; "the boats has stopped running."

Eliza's look of dismay and disappointment struck the woman, and she said, inquiringly.

"May be your're wanting to get over?—anybody sick? Ye seem mighty anxious?"

"I've got a child that's very dangerous," said Eliza. "I never heard of it till last night, and I've walked quite a piece to-day, in hopes to get to the ferry."

"Well, now, that's onlucky," said the woman, whose motherly sympathies were much aroused; "I'm re'lly consarned for ye. Solomon!" she called, from the window, towards a small back building. A man, in leather apron and very dirty hands, appeared at the door.

"I say, Sol," said the woman, "is that ar man going to tote them bar'ls over to-night?"

"He said he should try, if 'twas any way prudent," said the man.

"There's a man a piece down here, that's going over with some truck this evening, if he dur's to; he'll be in here to supper to-night, so you'd better set down and wait. That's a sweet little fellow," added the woman, offering him a cake.

But the child, wholly exhausted, cried with weariness.

"Poor fellow! he isn't used to walking, and I've hurried him on so," said Eliza.

"Well, take him into this room," said the woman, opening into a small bedroom, where stood a comfortable bed, Eliza laid the weary boy upon it, and held his hands in hers till he was fast asleep. For her there was no rest. As a fire in her bones, the thought of the pursuer urged her on; and she gazed with longing eyes on the sullen, surging waters that lay between her and liberty.

Here we must take our leave of her for the present, to follow the course of her pursuers.

Though Mrs. Shelby had promised that the dinner should be hurried on the table, yet it was soon seen, as the thing has often been seen before, that it required more than one to make a bargain. So although the order was fairly given out in Haley's hearing, and carried to Aunt Chloe by at least half a dozen juvenile messengers, that dignitary only gave certain very gruff snorts, and tosses of her head, and went on with every operation in an unusually leisurely and circumstantial manner.

For some singular reason, an impression seemed to reign among the servants generally that Missis would not be particularly disobliged by delay; and it was wonderful what a number of counter accidents occurred constantly, to retard the course of things. One luckless wight contrived to upset the gravy; and then gravy had to be got up *de novo*, with due care and formality, Aunt Chloe watching and stirring with dogged precision, answering shortly, to all suggestions of haste, that she "warn't a-going to have raw gravy on the table, to help nobody's catchings." One tumbled down with the water, and had to go to the spring for more; and another precipitated the butter into the path of events; and there was from time to time giggling news brought into the kitchen that "Mas'r Haley was mighty oneasy, and that he couldn't sit in his cheer no ways, but was a-walkin' and stalkin' to the winders and through the porch."

"Sarves him right!" said Aunt Chloe, indignantly. "He'll get wus nor oneasy, one of these days, if he don't mend his ways. *His* master'll be sending for him, and then see how he'll look!"

"He'll go to torment, and no mistake," said little Jake.

"He desarves it!" said Aunt Chloe, grimly, "he's broke many, many, many hearts,—I tell ye all!" she said, stopping, with a fork uplifted in her hands; "it's like what Mas'r George reads in Revelations,—souls a-callin' under the altar! and a-callin' on the Lord for vengeance on sich!—and by and by the Lord he'll hear 'em—so he will!"

Aunt Chloe, who was much revered in the kitchen, was listened to with open mouth; and, the dinner being now fairly sent in, the whole kitchen was at leisure to gossip with her, and to listen to her remarks.

"Sich'll be burnt up forever, and no mistake; won't they" said Andy.

"I'd be glad to see it, I'll be boun'," said little Jake.

"Chil'en!" said a voice, that made them all start. It was Uncle Tom, who had come in, and stood listening to the conversation at the door.

"Chil'en," he said, "I'm afeared you don't know what ye're sayin'. Forever is a *dre'ful* word, chil'en; it's awful to think on't. You oughtenter wish that ar to any human crittur."

"We wouldn't to anybody but the soul-drivers," said Andy; "nobody can help wishing it to them, they's so awful wicked."

"Don't natur herself kinder cry out on 'em?" said Aunt Chloe. "Don't dey tear der suckin' baby right off his mother's breast, and sell him, and der little children as is crying and holding on by her clothes,—don't dey pull 'em off and sells 'em? Don't dey tear wife and husband apart?" said Aunt Chloe, beginning to cry, "when it's jest takin' the very life on 'em?—and all the while does they feel one bit,—don't dey drink and smoke, and take it oncommon easy? Lor, if the devil don't get them, what's he good for?" And Aunt Chloe covered her face with her checked apron, and began to sob in good earnest.

"Pray for them that 'spitefully use you, the good book says," says Tom.

"Pray for 'em?" said Aunt Chloe; "Lor, it's too tough? I can't pray for 'em."

"It's natur, Chloe, and natur's strong," said Tom, "but the Lord's grace is stronger; besides, you oughter think what an awful state a poor crittur's soul's in that'll do them ar things,—you oughter thank God that you an't *like* him, Chloe. I'm sure I'd rather be sold, ten thousand times over, than to have all that ar poor crittur's got to answer for."

"So'd I, a heap," said Jake. "Lor, *shouldn't* we cotch it, Andy?"

Andy shrugged his shoulders, and gave an acquiescent whistle.

"I'm glad Mas'r didn't go off this morning, as he looked to," said Tom; "that ar hurt me more than sellin', it did. Mebbe it might have been natural for him, but 'twould have come desp't hard on me, as has known him from a baby; but I've seen Mas'r, and I begin ter feel sort o' reconciled to the Lord's will now. Mas'r couldn't help hisself; he did right, but I'm feared things will be kinder goin' to rack, when I'm gone. Mas'r can't be spected to be a-pryin' round everywhar, as I've done, a-keepin' up all the ends. The boys all means well, but they's powerful car'less. That ar troubles me."

The bell here rang, and Tom was summoned to the parlor.

"Tom," said his master, kindly, "I want you to notice that I give this gentleman bonds to forfeit a thousand dollars if you are not on the spot when he wants you; he's going to-day to look after his other business, and you can have the day to yourself. Go anywhere you like, boy."

"Thank you, Mas'r," said Tom.

"And mind yerself," said the trader, "and don't come it over your master with any o' yer nigger tricks; for I'll take every cent out of him, if you an't thar. If he'd hear to me, he wouldn't trust any on ye—slippery as eels!"

"Mas'r," said Tom,—and he stood very straight,—"I was jist eight years old when ole Missis put you into my arms, and you wasn't a year old. 'Thar,' say she, 'Tom,' that's to be *your* young Mas'r; take good care on him,' says she. And now I jist ask you, Mas'r, have I ever broke word to you, or gone contrary to you, 'specially since I was a Christian?"

Mr. Shelby was fairly overcome, and the tears rose to his eyes.

"My good boy," said he, "the Lord knows you say the truth; and if I was able to help it, all the world shouldn't buy you."

"And sure as I am a Christian woman," said Mrs. Shelby, "you shall be redeemed as soon as I can any way bring together means. Sir," she said to Haley, "take good account of who you sell him to, and let me know."

"Lor, yes, for that matter," said the trader, "I may bring him up in a year, not much the wuss for wear, and trade him back."

"I'll trade with you then, and make it for your advantage," said Mrs. Shelby.

"Of course," said the trader, "all's equal with me; li'ves trade 'em up as down, so I does a good business. All I want is a livin', you know, ma'am; that's all any on us want, I s'pose."

Mr. and Mrs. Shelby both felt annoyed and degraded by the familiar impudence of the trader, and yet both saw the absolute necessity of putting a constraint on their feelings. The more hopelessly sordid and insensible he appeared, the greater became Mrs. Shelby's dread of his succeeding in recapturing Eliza and her child, and of course the greater her motive for detaining him by every female artifice. She therefore graciously smiled, assented, chatted familarly, and did all she could to make time pass imperceptibly.

At two o'clock Sam and Andy brought the horses up to the posts, apparently greatly refreshed and invigorated by the scamper of the morning.

Sam was there new oiled from dinner, with an abundance of zealous and ready officiousness. As Haley approached, he was boasting, in a flourishing style, to Andy, of the evident and eminent success of the operation, now that he had "fairly come to it."

"Your master, I s'pose, don't keep no dogs," said Haley, thoughtfully, as he prepared to mount.

"Heaps on 'em," said Sam, triumphantly; "thar's Bruno—he's a roarer! and, besides that, 'bout every nigger of us keeps a pup of some natur' or uther."

"Poh!" said Haley,—and he said something else too, with regard to the said dogs, at which Sam muttered,

"I don't see no use cussin' on 'em, no way."

"But your master don't keep no dogs (I pretty much know he don't) for trackin' out niggers."

Sam knew exactly what he meant, but he kept on a look of earnest and desperate simplicity.

"Our dogs all smells round consid'able sharp. I spect they's the kind, though they han't never had no practice. They's *far* dogs, though, at most anything, if you'd get 'em started. Here, Bruno," he called, whistling to the lumbering Newfoundland, who came pitching tumultuously towards them.

"You go hang!" said Haley, getting up. "Come, tumble up now."

Sam tumbled up accordingly, dexterously contriving to tickle Andy as he did so, which occasioned Andy to split out into a laugh, greatly to Haley's indignation, who made a cut at him with his riding-whip.

"I's 'stonished at yer, Andy," said Sam, with awful gravity, "This yer's a seris business, Andy. Yer mustn't be a-makin' game. This yer an't no way to help Mas'r."

"I shall take the straight road to the river," said Haley, decidedly, after they had come to the boundaries of the estate. "I know the way of all of 'em,—they makes tracks for the underground."

"Sartin," said Sam, "dat's de idee. Mas'r Haley hits de thing right in de middle. Now, der's two roads to de river,—de dirt road and der pike,—which Mas'r mean to take?"

Andy looked up innocently at Sam, surprised at hearing this new geographical fact, but instantly confirmed what he said by a vehement reiteration.

" 'Cause," said Sam, "I'd rather be 'clined to 'magine that 'Lizy'd take de dirt road, bein' it's the least travelled."

Haley, notwithstanding that he was a very old bird, and naturally inclined to be suspicious of chaff, was rather brought up by this view of the case.

"If yer warn't both on yer such cussed liars, now!" he said, contemplatively, as he pondered a moment.

The pensive, reflective tone in which this was spoken appeared to amuse Andy prodigiously, and he drew a little behind, and shook so as apparently to run a great risk of falling off his horse, while Sam's face was immovably composed into the most doleful gravity.

"Course," said Sam. "Mas'r can do as he'd ruther; go de straight road, if Mas'r thinks best,—it's all one to us. Now, when I study 'pon it. I think de straight road de best, *deridedly.*"

"She would naturally go a lonesome way," said Haley, thinking aloud, and not minding Sam's remark.

"Dar an't no sayin'," said Sam: "gals is pecular; they never does nothin' ye thinks they will; mose gen'lly the contrar. Gals is nat'lly made contrary and so, if you thinks they've gone one road, it is sartin you'd better go t'other, and then you'll be sure to find 'em. Now, my private 'pinion is, 'Lizy took der dirt road; so I think we'd better take de straight one."

This profound generic view of the female sex did not seem to dispose Haley particularly to the straight road, and he announced decidedly that he should go the other and asked Sam when they should come to it.

"A little piece ahead," said Sam, giving a wink to Andy with the eye which was on Andy's side of the head; and he added, gravely, "but I've studded on de matter, and I'm quite clar we ought not to go dat ar way. I nebber been over it no way. It's despite lonesome, and we might lose our way,—whar we'd come to, de Lord only knows."

"Nevertheless," said Haley, "I shall go that way."

"Now I think on't, I think I hearn 'em tell that dat ar road was all fenced up and down by der creek, and thar, an't it, Andy?"

Andy wasn't certain, he'd only "hearn tell," about the road, but never been over it. In short, he was strictly non-committal.

Haley, accustomed to strike the balance of probabilities between lies of greater or lesser magnitude, thought that it lay in favor of the dirt road aforesaid. The mention of the thing he thought he perceived was involuntary on Sam's part at first, and his confused attempts to dissuade him he set down to a desperate lying on second thoughts, as being unwilling to implicate Eliza.

When, therefore, Sam indicated the road, Haley plunged briskly into it, followed by Sam and Andy.

Now, the road, in fact, was an old one, that had formerly been a thoroughfare to the river, but abandoned for many years after the laying of the new pike. It was open for about an hour's ride, and after that it was cut across by various farms and fences. Sam knew this fact perfectly well,—indeed, the road had been so long closed up, that Andy had never heard of it. He therefore rode along with an air of dutiful submission, only groaning and vociferating occasionally that 'twas "desp't rough, and bad for Jerry's foot."

"Now, I jest give yer warning," said Haley, "I know yer; yer won't get me to turn off this road, with all yer fussin'—so you shet up!"

"Mas'r will go his own way!" said Sam, with rueful submission, at the same time winking most portentously to Andy, whose delight was now very near the explosive point.

Sam was in wonderful spirits,—professed to keep a very brisk look-out,—at one time exclaiming that he saw "a gal's bonnet," on the top of some distant eminence, or calling to Andy "if that thar wasn't "Lizy' down in the hollow;" always making these exclamations in some rough or craggy part of the road, where the sudden quickening of speed was a special inconvenience to all parties concerned, and thus keeping Haley in a state of constant commotion.

After riding about an hour in this way, the whole party made a precipitate and tumultous descent into a barn-yard belonging to a large farming establishment. Not a soul was in sight, all the hands being employed in the fields; but, as the barn stood conspicuously and plainly square across the road, it was evident that their journey in that direction had reached a decided finale.

"Wan't dat ar what I telled mas'r?" said Sam, with an air of injured innocence. "How does strange gentlemen spect to know more about a country dan de natives born and raised?"

"You rascal!" said Haley, "you knew all about this."

"Didn't I tell yer I *know'd*, and yer wouldn't believe me? I telled Mas'r 'twas all shet up, and fenced up, and I didn't spect we could get through,—Andy heard me."

It was all too true to be disputed, and the unlucky man had to pocket his wrath with the best grace he was able, and all three faced to the right-about, and took up their line of march for the highway.

In consequence of all the various delays, it was about three-quarters of an hour after Eliza had laid her child to sleep in the village tavern that the party came riding into the same place. Eliza was standing by the window, looking out in another direction, when Sam's quick eye caught a glimpse of her. Haley and Andy were two yards behind. At this crisis, Sam contrived to have his hat blown off, and uttered a loud and characteristic ejaculation, which startled her at once; she drew suddenly back; the whole train swept by the window, round to the front door.

A thousand lives seemed to be concentrated in that one moment to Eliza. Her room opened by a side door to the river. She caught her child, and sprang down the steps towards it. The trader caught a full glimpse of her, just as she was disappearing down the bank; and throwing himself from his horse, calling loudly on Sam and Andy, he was after her like a hound after a deer. In that dizzy moment her feet to her scarce seemed to touch the ground, and a moment brought her to the water's edge. Right on behind they came; and, nerved with strength such as God gives only to the desperate, with one wild cry and flying leap, she vaulted sheer over the turbid current by the shore, on to the raft of ice beyond. It was a desperate leap—impossible to anything but madness and despair; and Haley, Sam, and Andy, instinctively cried out, and lifted up their hands, as she did it.

The huge green fragment of ice on which she alighted pitched and creaked as her weight came on it, but she stayed there not a moment. With wild cries and desperate energy she leaped to another and still another cake;—stumbling—leaping—slipping—springing upwards again! Her shoes are gone—her stockings cut from her feet—while blood marked every step; but she saw nothing, felt nothing, till dimly, as in a dream, she saw the Ohio side, and a man helping her up the bank.

"Yer a brave gal, now, whoever ye ar!" said the man, with an oath.

Eliza recognized the voice and face of a man who owned a farm not far from her old home.

"O Mr. Symmes!—save me—do save me—do hide me!" said Eliza.

"Why, what's this?" said the man. "Why, if 'tan't Shelby's gal!"

"My child!—this boy!—he'd sold him! There is his Mas'r," said she, pointing to the Kentucky shore. "O Mr. Symmes, you've got a little boy!"

"So I have," said the man, as he roughly, but kindly drew her up the steep bank. "Besides, you're a right brave gal. I like grit, wherever I see it."

When they had gained the top of the bank the man paused.

"I'd be glad to do something for ye," said he; "but then thar's nowhar I could take ye. The best I can do is to tell ye to go *thar*," said he, pointing to a large white house which stood by itself, off the main street of the village. "Go thar; they're kind folks. Thar's no kind o' danger but they'll help you,—they're up to all that sort o' thing."

"The Lord bless you!" said Eliza earnestly.

"No 'casion, no 'casion in the world," said the man. "What I've done's of no 'count."

"And, oh, surely, sir, you won't tell any one!"

"Go to thunder, gal! What do you take a feller for? In course not," said the man. "Come, now, go along like a likely, sensible gal, as you are. You've arnt your liberty, and you shall have it, for all me."

The woman folded her child to her bosom, and walked firmly and swiftly away. The man stood and looked after her.

"Shelby, now, mebbe won't think this yer the most neighborly thing in the world; but what's a feller to do? If he catches one of my gals in the same fix, he's welcome to pay back. Somehow I never could see no kind o' critter a-strivin' and pantin', and trying to clar theirselves, with the dogs arter 'em, and go agin 'em. Besides, I don't see no kind of 'casion for me to be hunter and catcher for other folks, neither."

So spoke this poor, heathenish Kentuckian, who had not been instructed in his constitutional relations, and consequently was betrayed into acting in a sort of Christianized manner, which, if he had been better situated and more enlightened, he would not have been left to do.

Haley had stood a perfectly amazed spectator of the scene, till Eliza had disappeared up the bank, when he turned a blank, inquiring look on Sam and Andy.

"That ar was a tol'able fair stroke of business," said Sam.

"The gal's got seven devils in her, I believe!" said Haley. "How like a wildcat she jumped!"

"Wal, now," said Sam, scratching his head, "I hope Mas'r'll 'scuse us tryin' dat ar road. Don't think I feel spry enough for dat ar, no way!" and Sam gave a hoarse chuckle.

"*You* laugh!" said the trader with a growl.

"Lord bless you, Mas'r, I couldn't help it, now," said Sam, giving way to the long pent-up delight of his soul. "She looked so curi's, a leapin' and springin'—ice a crackin'—and only to hear her,—plump! ker chunk! ker splash! Spring! Lord! how she goes it!" and Sam and Andy laughed till the tears rolled down their cheeks.

"I'll make ye laugh t'other side yer mouths!" said the trader, laying about their heads with his riding-whip.

Both ducked, and ran shouting up the bank, and were on their horses before he was up.

"Good-evening, Mas'r!" said Sam, with much gravity. "I berry much 'spect Missis be anxious 'bout Jerry. Mas'r Haley won't want us no longer. Missis wouldn't hear of our ridin' the critters over 'Lizy's bridge to-night;" and, with a facetious poke into Andy's ribs, he started off, followed by the latter, at full speed,—their shouts of laughter coming faintly on the wind.

1851–1852

Harriet Ann Jacobs
(1813–1897)

Harriet Ann Jacobs took great risks in publishing *Incidents in the Life of a Slave Girl: Written by Herself,* an account of her experiences as a slave. While the narrative of the suffering of this "poor Slave Mother" (including her efforts to elude her master's sexual advances, her years hiding in a cramped garret, her escape to the North, and her separation from her family) could win converts to the abolition movement, her failure to observe nineteenth-century sexual standards when she had children out of wedlock might prompt the Victorian women who would constitute her readership to condemn her. Jacobs resolved this tension in her narrative by drawing on the popular language of sentimentalism and melodrama to dramatize her experiences, frequently stepping back from the actual storytelling to analyze, explain, and criticize the corrupt system of slavery that created the circumstances of her life—although she is careful always to exonerate northern women from guilt.

In effect, Jacobs skillfully controls the meaning of the experiences she relates and leads her readers toward emphatic social activism. In the following passage, Jacobs speaks directly to her readers, showing that the protagonist's sin is the result of a corrupt, evil system—that her fall, her lost chastity, could have been their own loss:

> O, ye happy women, whose purity has been sheltered from childhood, who have been free to choose the objects of your affection, whose homes are protected by law, do not judge the poor desolate slave girl too severely! If slavery had been abolished, I, also, could have married the man of my choice; I could have had a home shielded by the laws; and I should have been spared the painful task of confessing what I am now about to relate; but all my prospects had been blighted by slavery. I wanted to keep myself pure; and under the most adverse circumstances, I tried hard to preserve my self-respect; but I was struggling alone in the powerful grasp of the demon Slavery; and the monster proved too strong for me. I felt as if I was forsaken by God and man; as if all my efforts must be frustrated; and I became reckless in my despair.

Her experience becomes that of a representative female protagonist—virtuous, delicate, innocent, and forsaken. As such, Jacobs' narrative operates on multiple levels: her account of her own slavery is not only a moving autobiography but also a powerful political document that skillfully manipulates the reader's emotions through sentimental rhetoric and narrative pace.

Harriet Jacobs was born in the autumn of 1813 in Edenton, North Carolina, the daughter of slaves Molly Horniblow and Daniel Jacobs. Young Harriet was unaware of her identity as a slave for the first six years of her life—until the death of her mother. Soon after, Harriet began to live with her mistress, Margaret Horniblow, her mother's foster sister. (Horniblow's mother was the mistress of Jacobs's grandmother; their daughters were raised together from infancy.) Margaret Horniblow imposed no "toilsome or disagreeable duties" on Harriet and taught her to read, spell, and sew.

With the death of Margaret Horniblow in 1825, Jacobs' circumstances changed radically. She had been willed to her mistress's three-year-old niece, Mary Matilda Norcom, and within a short period Harriet and her brother John had moved into the home of Dr. James Norcom. By the time she was fifteen, "a sad epoch in the life of a slave girl," Jacobs had become the target of Dr. Norcom's campaign of seduction— alternately threatening and wheedling Jacobs in an attempt to make her his concubine. Jacobs refused him, and the misery she experienced in his household was compounded by the fact that she had fallen in love with a free African American whom she was forbidden to marry. As a secret revenge on her master, Jacobs began a sexual relationship with Samuel Treadwell Sawyer, a "white unmarried gentleman" who lived near the Norcoms. Sawyer fathered her two children, Joseph, born in 1829, and Louisa Matilda, born in 1833.

In 1835, after repeatedly rebuffing Norcom, Jacobs became a fugitive, fleeing Norcom's plantation outside Edenton. In retaliation, Norcom had Jacobs' brother and her two children imprisoned, but Sawyer managed to purchase them through a slave trader. The children were sent to live with their great-grandmother, who, by the end of the year, was also providing a safe haven for Harriet Jacobs. She spent the next seven years in hiding, in a tiny crawl space above her grandmother's storeroom.

In 1837, while Jacobs was still in hiding, Sawyer was elected to Congress and left for Washington, D.C. without his children. Within a year, Sawyer married Lavinia Peyton, who, upon discovering her husband's "parental relation" to Jacobs' children, decided that seven-year-old Louisa Matilda should come to live with them in Washington. After five months, the youngster was sent to live with her father's cousins in Brooklyn, New York, where she began to learn to read and write.

After seven years in hiding, Jacobs escaped to the North, and quickly found work as a nurse caring for Imogen Willis, the infant daughter of Mary Stace Willis. However, as a fugitive slave, Jacobs constantly faced the threat of being discovered and returned to the South. By 1843, she and her son were reunited in Boston, and in 1844 she retrieved her daughter from New York. She supported her children by working as a seamstress, and in 1845 she traveled to England as the nurse for the now three-year-old Imogen Willis.

In 1846, Jacobs returned to New York, only to be harassed by Mary Matilda Norcom, who attempted to re-enslave her. In 1849, Jacobs sent her daughter to school in Clinton, New York. Later that year, Jacobs moved to Rochester, New York and began working at the Anti-Slavery Office and Reading Room, directed by her brother, John S. Jacobs, who had escaped to the North years earlier. Here she met Amy Post and a number of antislavery feminists, who would be instrumental in helping to secure a publisher for *Incidents in the Life of a Slave Girl*.

After the Fugitive Slave Law was passed in 1850 (authorizing the punishment of any citizen aiding a fugitive slave), Jacobs returned to New York City, working once again for the Willis family. Her brother and son followed the Gold Rush to California and later traveled to Australia, where they lived beyond the reach of Dr. Norcom's pursuit. When Norcom died in 1850, the search for Harriet Jacobs was taken up by Mary

Matilda Norcom's husband. In 1852, Jacobs secured her status as a free woman through the generosity of her employer, Cornelia Grinnell Willis, who paid for Jacobs' freedom.

At the urging of her friend Amy Post, Jacobs began writing *Incidents in the Life of a Slave Girl* in 1853. Originally, Harriet Beecher Stowe had proposed including Jacobs' life in *Uncle Tom's Cabin,* but Jacobs declined, preferring to maintain control of her own story. In the summer of 1853, Jacobs published several letters in the *New York Tribune,* and she moved with the Willis family to Cornwall, New York. She developed her interest in political causes and over the next five years, Jacobs maintained close contact with her feminist and abolitionist friends. In 1858, Jacobs completed the manuscript, for which the celebrated abolitionist Lydia Maria Child wrote the "Introduction." Jacobs tried unsuccessfully to sell her book in England, but she did find a publisher in Boston, Phillips and Sampson, a company which soon after filed for bankruptcy. Her second publisher, Thayer and Eldridge, also went bankrupt. After purchasing the plates of the book, Jacobs had *Incidents* printed privately in Boston in 1861. (A British version, *The Deeper Wrong,* was published in 1862.)

Harriet Jacobs devoted the war years to relief work in the South—under the sponsorship of both the newly established Freedman's Relief Association and various Quakers in Philadelphia and New York. In 1868, she and her daughter traveled to London to raise money for an orphanage and home for the elderly in Savannah, Georgia, which, because of the "unsettled state of affairs" that followed the Reconstruction Act, was never built. By 1870, Jacobs and her daughter had returned to Massachusetts and operated a boardinghouse in Cambridge. In 1885, she and her daughter moved to Washington, D.C. She died there on March 7, 1897, and is buried in Cambridge, Massachusetts.

Although *Incidents in the Life of a Slave Girl: Written by Herself* is an autobiography, Jacobs masked her identity by renaming her characters and by changing many identifying features of her story. Jacobs called herself, for example, "Linda Brent," and her children "Benny" and "Ellen." Her grandmother Molly Horniblow was rechristened "Aunt Martha," and her Uncle Mark and Aunt Betty were renamed "Phillip" and "Nancy." Her brother was called "William"; the Norcoms became the "Flints," and the Willises, the "Bruces." Samuel Treadwell Sawyer became "Mr. Sands," and the location of her childhood home was moved to South Carolina.

Further Reading:

D. Sterling, *We Are Your Sisters: Black Women of the 19th Century,* 1984.

J. Fagan Yellin, "Text and Contexts of Harriet Jacobs'," *Incidents in the Life of a Slave Girl: Written by Herself,* in C. T. Davis and H. L. Gates, eds., *The Slave's Narrative,* 1985.

W. Andrews, *To Tell a Free Story: The First Century of Afro-American Autobiography, 1760–1865,* 1986.

J. Fagan Yellin, "Introduction," *Incidents in the Life of a Slave Girl: Written by Herself,* 1987.

H. Carby, *Reconstructing Womanhood,* 1987.

M. H. Washington, "Meditations on History: The Slave Narrative of Linda Brent," in *Invented Lives: Narratives of Black Women, 1860–1960,* 1987.

V. Smith, *Discovery and Authority in Afro-American Narrative,* 1988.

J. Fagan Yellin, *Women and Sisters: The Anti-Slavery Feminists in American Culture,* 1989.

T. Goddu, *Gothic America,* 1997.

Text:

Incidents in the Life of a Slave Girl: Written by Herself, J. Fagan Yellin, ed., 1987.

Incidents in the Life of a Slave Girl

Chapter 1: Childhood

I was born a slave; but I never knew it till six years of happy childhood had passed away. My father was a carpenter, and considered so intelligent and skilful in his trade, that, when buildings out of the common line were to be erected, he was sent for from long distances, to be head workman. On condition of paying his mistress two hundred dollars a year, and supporting himself, he was allowed to work at his trade, and manage his own affairs. His strongest wish was to purchase his children; but, though he several times offered his hard earnings for that purpose, he never succeeded. In complexion my parents were a light shade of brownish yellow, and were termed mulattoes. They lived together in a comfortable home; and, though we were all slaves, I was so fondly shielded that I never dreamed I was a piece of merchandise, trusted to them for safe keeping, and liable to be demanded of them at any moment. I had one brother, William, who was two years younger than myself—a bright, affectionate child. I had also a great treasure in my maternal grandmother, who was a remarkable woman in many respects. She was the daughter of a planter in South Carolina, who, at his death, left her mother and his three children free,[1] with money to go to St. Augustine, where they had relatives. It was during the Revolutionary War; and they were captured on their passage, carried back, and sold to different purchasers. Such was the story my grandmother used to tell me; but I do not remember all the particulars. She was a little girl when she was captured and sold to the keeper of a large hotel. I have often heard her tell how hard she fared during childhood. But as she grew older she evinced so much intelligence, and was so faithful, that her master and mistress could not help seeing it was for their interest to take care of such a valuable piece of property. She became an indispensable personage in the household, officiating in all capacities, from cook and wet nurse to seamstress. She was much praised for her cooking; and her nice crackers became so famous in the neighborhood that many people were desirous of obtaining them. In consequence of numerous requests of this kind, she asked permission of her mistress to bake crackers at night, after all the household work was done; and she obtained leave to do it, provided she would clothe herself and her children from the profits. Upon these terms, after working hard all day for her mistress, she began her midnight bakings, assisted by her two oldest children. The business proved profitable; and each year she laid by a little, which was saved for a fund to purchase her children. Her master died, and the property was divided among his heirs. The widow had her dower in the hotel, which she continued to keep open. My grandmother remained in her service as a slave; but her children

---

[1] The accumulation of detail about the sexual freedoms white masters took with their female slaves is one of the more striking features of Jacobs' memoir. As Hazel Carby notes in *Reconstructing Womanhood*, p. 35, this feature distinguishes Jacobs' narrative not only from traditional histories, but from the slave narratives of men. "Slave women, figures of secondary importance within male-authored narratives, are representative in these contexts as victims of sexual abuse. Rare are glimpses of the interior lives or survival strategies of women so victimized." Jacobs offers that glimpse.

Jacobs' emancipated great grandmother and her grandmother (called Yellow Molly for her fair complexion) were apparently sailing under the British flag when they were captured between Charleston and St. Augustine in the early 1780s.

were divided among her master's children. As she had five, Benjamin, the youngest one, was sold, in order that each heir might have an equal portion of dollars and cents. There was so little difference in our ages that he seemed more like my brother than my uncle. He was a bright, handsome lad, nearly white; for he inherited the complexion my grandmother had derived from Anglo-Saxon ancestors. Though only ten years old, seven hundred and twenty dollars were paid for him. His sale was a terrible blow to my grandmother; but she was naturally hopeful, and she went to work with renewed energy, trusting in time to be able to purchase some of her children. She had laid up three hundred dollars, which her mistress one day begged as a loan, promising to pay her soon. The reader probably knows that no promise or writing given to a slave is legally binding; for, according to Southern laws, a slave, *being* property, can *hold* no property. When my grandmother lent her hard earnings to her mistress, she trusted solely to her honor. The honor of a slaveholder to a slave!

To this good grandmother I was indebted for many comforts. My brother Willie and I often received portions of the crackers, cakes, and preserves, she made to sell; and after we ceased to be children we were indebted to her for many more important services.

Such were the unusually fortunate circumstances of my early childhood. When I was six years old, my mother died; and then, for the first time, I learned, by the talk around me, that I was a slave. My mother's mistress was the daughter of my grandmother's mistress. She was the foster sister of my mother; they were both nourished at my grandmother's breast. In fact, my mother had been weaned at three months old, that the babe of the mistress might obtain sufficient food. They played together as children; and, when they became women, my mother was a most faithful servant to her whiter foster sister. On her death-bed her mistress promised that her children should never suffer for any thing; and during her lifetime she kept her word. They all spoke kindly of my dead mother, who had been a slave merely in name, but in nature was noble and womanly. I grieved for her, and my young mind was troubled with the thought who would now take care of me and my little brother. I was told that my home was now to be with her mistress; and I found it a happy one. No toilsome or disagreeable duties were imposed upon me. My mistress was so kind to me that I was always glad to do her bidding, and proud to labor for her as much as my young years would permit. I would sit by her side for hours, sewing diligently, with a heart as free from care as that of any free-born white child. When she thought I was tired, she would send me out to run and jump; and away I bounded, to gather berries or flowers to decorate her room. Those were happy days— too happy to last. The slave child had no thought for the morrow; but there came that blight, which too surely waits on every human being born to be a chattel.

When I was nearly twelve years old, my kind mistress sickened and died.[2] As I saw the cheek grow paler, and the eye more glassy, how earnestly I prayed in my heart that she might live! I loved her; for she had been almost like a mother to me. My prayers were not answered. She died, and they buried her in the little churchyard, where, day after day, my tears fell upon her grave.

I was sent to spend a week with my grandmother. I was now old enough to begin to think of the future; and again and again I asked myself what they would do with me. I felt sure I should never find another mistress so kind as the one who was gone. She had

[2] Margaret Horniblow died at Edenton on July 3, 1825.

promised my dying mother that her children should never suffer for any thing; and when I remembered that, and recalled her many proofs of attachment to me, I could not help having some hopes that she had left me free. My friends were almost certain it would be so. They thought she would be sure to do it, on account of my mother's love and faithful service. But, alas! we all know that the memory of a faithful slave does not avail much to save her children from the auction block.

After a brief period of suspense, the will of my mistress was read, and we learned that she had bequeathed me to her sister's daughter, a child of five years old. So vanished our hopes. My mistress had taught me the precepts of God's Word: "Thou shalt love thy neighbor as thyself." "Whatsoever ye would that men should do unto you, do ye even so unto them." But I was her slave, and I suppose she did not recognize me as her neighbor. I would give much to blot out from my memory that one great wrong. As a child, I loved my mistress; and, looking back on the happy days I spent with her, I try to think with less bitterness of this act of injustice. While I was with her, she taught me to read and spell; and for this privilege, which so rarely falls to the lot of a slave, I bless her memory.

She possessed but few slaves; and at her death those were all distributed among her relatives. Five of them were my grandmother's children, and had shared the same milk that nourished her mother's children. Notwithstanding my grandmother's long and faithful service to her owners, not one of her children escaped the auction block. These God-breathing machines are no more, in the sight of their masters, than the cotton they plant, or the horses they tend.[3]

Chapter 6: The Jealous Mistress

I would ten thousand times rather that my children should be the half-starved paupers of Ireland than to be the most pampered among the slaves of America. I would rather drudge out my life on a cotton plantation, till the grave opened to give me rest, than to live with an unprincipled master and a jealous mistress. The felon's home in a penitentiary is preferable. He may repent, and turn from the error of his ways, and so find peace; but it is not so with a favorite slave. She is not allowed to have any pride of character. It is deemed a crime in her to wish to be virtuous.[4]

Mrs. Flint possessed the key to her husband's character before I was born. She might have used this knowledge to counsel and to screen the young and the innocent among her slaves; but for them she had no sympathy. They were the objects of her constant suspicion and malevolence. She watched her husband with unceasing vigilance; but he was well practised in means to evade it. What he could not find opportunity to say in words he manifested in signs. He invented more than were ever thought of in a deaf and dumb asylum. I let them pass, as if I did not understand what he meant; and many were the curses and threats bestowed on me for my stupidity. One day he caught me teaching myself to write. He frowned, as if he was not well pleased; but I suppose he came to the conclusion that such an accomplishment might help to advance his favorite scheme.

---

[3] The theme of slaves as merchandise becomes important in the later narrative when Jacobs' new master conflates property rights and sexual relationships.

[4] "Slavery converted into liabilities the very qualities elite white women were taught to cultivate," Valerie Smith, introduction to Jacobs' *Incidents in the Life of a Slave Girl* (New York: Oxford University Press, 1988), p. 12.

Before long, notes were often slipped into my hand. I would return them, saying, "I can't read them, sir." "Can't you?" he replied; "then I must read them to you." He always finished the reading by asking, "Do you understand?" Sometimes he would complain of the heat of the tea room, and order his supper to be placed on a small table in the piazza. He would seat himself there with a well-satisfied smile, and tell me to stand by and brush away the flies. He would eat very slowly, pausing between the mouthfuls. These intervals were employed in describing the happiness I was so foolishly throwing away, and in threatening me with the penalty that finally awaited my stubborn disobedience. He boasted much of the forbearance he had exercised towards me, and reminded me that there was a limit to his patience. When I succeeded in avoiding opportunities for him to talk to me at home, I was ordered to come to his office, to do some errand. When there, I was obliged to stand and listen to such language as he saw fit to address to me. Sometimes I so openly expressed my contempt for him that he would become violently enraged, and I wondered why he did not strike me. Circumstanced as he was, he probably thought it was better policy to be forbearing. But the state of things grew worse and worse daily. In desperation I told him that I must and would apply to my grandmother for protection. He threatened me with death, and worse than death, if I made any complaint to her. Strange to say, I did not despair. I was naturally of a buoyant disposition, and always I had a hope of somehow getting out of his clutches. Like many a poor, simple slave before me, I trusted that some threads of joy would yet be woven into my dark destiny.

I had entered my sixteenth year, and every day it became more apparent that my presence was intolerable to Mrs. Flint. Angry words frequently passed between her and her husband. He had never punished me himself, and he would not allow any body else to punish me. In that respect, she was never satisfied; but, in her angry moods, no terms were too vile for her to bestow upon me. Yet I, whom she detested so bitterly, had far more pity for her than he had, whose duty it was to make her life happy. I never wronged her, or wished to wrong her; and one word of kindness from her would have brought me to her feet.

After repeated quarrels between the doctor and his wife, he announced his intention to take his youngest daughter, then four years old, to sleep in his apartment. It was necessary that a servant should sleep in the same room, to be on hand if the child stirred. I was selected for that office, and informed for what purpose that arrangement had been made. By managing to keep within sight of people, as much as possible, during the day time, I had hitherto succeeded in eluding my master, though a razor was often held to my throat to force me to change this line of policy. At night I slept by the side of my great aunt, where I felt safe. He was too prudent to come into her room. She was an old woman, and had been in the family many years. Moreover, as a married man, and a professional man, he deemed it necessary to save appearances in some degree. But he resolved to remove the obstacle in the way of his scheme; and he thought he had planned it so that he should evade suspicion. He was well aware how much I prized my refuge by the side of my old aunt, and he determined to dispossess me of it. The first night the doctor had the little child in his room alone. The next morning, I was ordered to take my station as nurse the following night. A kind Providence interposed in my favor. During the day Mrs. Flint heard of this new arrangement, and a storm followed. I rejoiced to hear it rage.

After a while my mistress sent for me to come to her room. Her first question was, "Did you know you were to sleep in the doctor's room?"

"Yes, ma'am."

"Who told you?"

"My master."

"Will you answer truly all the questions I ask?"

"Yes, ma'am."

"Tell me, then, as you hope to be forgiven, are you innocent of what I have accused you?"

"I am."

She handed me a Bible, and said, "Lay your hand on your heart, kiss this holy book, and swear before God that you tell me the truth."

I took the oath she required, and I did it with a clear conscience.

"You have taken God's holy word to testify your innocence," said she. "If you have deceived me, beware! Now take this stool, sit down, look me directly in the face, and tell me all that has passed between your master and you."

I did as she ordered. As I went on with my account her color changed frequently, she wept, and sometimes groaned. She spoke in tones so sad, that I was touched by her grief. The tears came to my eyes; but I was soon convinced that her emotions arose from anger and wounded pride. She felt that her marriage vows were desecrated, her dignity insulted; but she had no compassion for the poor victim of her husband's perfidy. She pitied herself as a martyr; but she was incapable of feeling for the condition of shame and misery in which her unfortunate, helpless slave was placed.

Yet perhaps she had some touch of feeling for me; for when the conference was ended, she spoke kindly, and promised to protect me. I should have been much comforted by this assurance if I could have had confidence in it; but my experiences in slavery had filled me with distrust. She was not a very refined woman, and had not much control over her passions. I was an object of her jealousy, and, consequently, of her hatred; and I knew I could not expect kindness or confidence from her under the circumstances in which I was placed. I could not blame her. Slaveholders' wives feel as other women would under similar circumstances. The fire of her temper kindled from small sparks, and now the flame became so intense that the doctor was obliged to give up his intended arrangement.

I knew I had ignited the torch, and I expected to suffer for it afterwards; but I felt too thankful to my mistress for the timely aid she rendered me to care much about that. She now took me to sleep in a room adjoining her own. There I was an object of her especial care, though not of her especial comfort, for she spent many a sleepless night to watch over me. Sometimes I woke up, and found her bending over me. At other times she whispered in my ear, as though it was her husband who was speaking to me, and listened to hear what I would answer. If she startled me, on such occasions, she would glide stealthily away; and the next morning she would tell me I had been talking in my sleep, and ask who I was talking to. At last, I began to be fearful for my life. It had been often threatened; and you can imagine, better than I can describe, what an unpleasant sensation it must produce to wake up in the dead of night and find a jealous woman bending over you. Terrible as this experience was, I had fears that it would give place to one more terrible.

My mistress grew weary of her vigils; they did not prove satisfactory. She changed her tactics. She now tried the trick of accusing my master of crime, in my presence, and gave my name as the author of the accusation. To my utter astonishment, he replied, "I don't believe it: but if she did acknowledge it, you tortured her into exposing me." Tortured into exposing him! Truly, Satan had no difficulty in distinguishing the color of his soul! I understood his object in making this false representation. It was to show me that I gained nothing by seeking the protection of my mistress; that the power was still all in his own hands. I pitied Mrs. Flint. She was a second wife, many years the junior of her husband; and the hoary-headed miscreant was enough to try the patience of a wiser and better woman. She was completely foiled, and knew not how to proceed. She would gladly have had me flogged for my supposed false oath; but, as I have already stated, the doctor never allowed any one to whip me. The old sinner was politic. The application of the lash might have led to remarks that would have exposed him in the eyes of his children and grandchildren. How often did I rejoice that I lived in a town where all the inhabitants knew each other! If I had been on a remote plantation, or lost among the multitude of a crowded city, I should not be a living woman at this day.

The secrets of slavery are concealed like those of the Inquisition.[5] My master was, to my knowledge, the father of eleven slaves. But did the mothers dare to tell who was the father of their children? Did the other slaves dare to allude to it, except in whispers among themselves? No, indeed! They knew too well the terrible consequences.

My grandmother could not avoid seeing things which excited her suspicions. She was uneasy about me, and tried various ways to buy me; but the neverchanging answer was always repeated: "Linda[6] does not belong to *me*. She is my daughter's property, and I have no legal right to sell her." The conscientious man! He was too scrupulous to *sell* me; but he had no scruples whatever about committing a much greater wrong against the helpless young girl placed under his guardianship, as his daughter's property. Sometimes my persecutor would ask me whether I would like to be sold. I told him I would rather be sold to any body than to lead such a life as I did. On such occasions he would assume the air of a very injured individual, and reproach me for my ingratitude. "Did I not take you into the house, and make you the companion of my own children?" he would say. "Have I ever treated you like a negro? I have never allowed you to be punished, not even to please your mistress. And this is the recompense I get, you ungrateful girl!" I answered that he had reasons of his own for screening me from punishment, and that the course he pursued made my mistress hate me and persecute me. If I wept, he would say, "Poor child! Don't cry! don't cry! I will make peace for you with your mistress. Only let me arrange matters in my own way. Poor, foolish girl! you don't know what is for your own good. I would cherish you. I would make a lady of you. Now go, and think of all I have promised you."

---

[5] "Some conscientious slave holders applied the Victorian moral code to the quarters as well as to the big house, but most—their sons, neighbors and overseers—held a double standard, veneration for white women, disrespect for black. House slaves were particularly vulnerable to sexual exploitation." See Sterling, *We Are Your Sisters* (New York: W. W. Norton, 1984), pp. 18–31 for a thorough description of seduction, rape and concubinage as tools of the white male slaveholder's control.

[6] At the urging of her later abolitionist friends from Boston, Jacobs disguised her identity as Linda Brent.

I did think of it.

Reader, I draw no imaginary pictures of southern homes. I am telling you the plain truth. Yet when victims make their escape from this wild beast of Slavery, northerners consent to act the part of bloodhounds, and hunt the poor fugitive back into his den, "full of dead men's bones, and all uncleanness."[7] Nay, more, they are not only willing, but proud, to give their daughters in marriage to slaveholders. The poor girls have romantic notions of a sunny clime, and of the flowering vines that all the year round shade a happy home. To what disappointments are they destined! The young wife soon learns that the husband in whose hands she has placed her happiness pays no regard to his marriage vows. Children of every shade of complexion play with her own fair babies, and too well she knows that they are born unto him of his own household. Jealousy and hatred enter the flowery home, and it is ravaged of its loveliness.

Southern women often marry a man knowing that he is the father of many little slaves. They do not trouble themselves about it. They regard such children as property, as marketable as the pigs on the plantation; and it is seldom that they do not make them aware of this by passing them into the slavetrader's hands as soon as possible, and thus getting them out of their sight. I am glad to say there are some honorable exceptions.

I have myself known two southern wives who exhorted their husbands to free those slaves towards whom they stood in a "parental relation;" and their request was granted. These husbands blushed before the superior nobleness of their wives' natures. Though they had only counselled them to do that which it was their duty to do, it commanded their respect, and rendered their conduct more exemplary. Concealment was at an end, and confidence took the place of distrust.

Though this bad institution deadens the moral sense, even in white women, to a fearful extent, it is not altogether extinct. I have heard southern ladies say of Mr. Such a one, "He not only thinks it no disgrace to be the father of those little niggers, but he is not ashamed to call himself their master. I declare, such things ought not to be tolerated in any decent society!"

Chapter 10: A Perilous Passage *in the Slave Girl's Life*

After my lover went away,[8] Dr. Flint contrived a new plan. He seemed to have an idea that my fear of my mistress was his greatest obstacle. In the blandest tones, he told me that he was going to build a small house for me, in a secluded place, four miles away from the town. I shuddered; but I was constrained to listen, while he talked of his intention to give me a home of my own, and to make a lady of me. Hitherto, I had escaped my dreaded fate, by being in the midst of people. My grandmother had already had high words with my master about me. She had told him pretty plainly what she thought of his character, and there was considerable gossip in the neighborhood about our affairs, to which the open-mouthed jealousy of Mrs. Flint contributed not a little. When

---

[7] Matthew 23:37. Here Jacobs begins her feminist exhortation to the reader's moral sense, mentioning the "good" white wives repulsed by their husbands' irresponsibility toward their mixed-race, slave-born children.

[8] As a teenager, Linda (Jacobs) fell in love with a free Black man, a carpenter like her father. He wanted to marry her and buy her freedom. Flint, who wanted to have her himself, forbade the match and punished Jacobs.

my master said he was going to build a house for me,[9] and that he could do it with little trouble and expense, I was in hopes something would happen to frustrate his scheme; but I soon heard that the house was actually begun. I vowed before my Maker that I would never enter it. I had rather toil on the plantation from dawn till dark; I had rather live and die in jail, than drag on, from day to day, through such a living death. I was determined that the master, whom I so hated and loathed, who had blighted the prospects of my youth, and made my life a desert, should not, after my long struggle with him, succeed at last in trampling his victim under his feet. I would do any thing, every thing, for the sake of defeating him. What *could* I do? I thought and thought, till I became desperate, and made a plunge into the abyss.

And now, reader, I come to a period in my unhappy life, which I would gladly forget if I could. The remembrance fills me with sorrow and shame. It pains me to tell you of it; but I have promised to tell you the truth, and I will do it honestly, let it cost me what it may. I will not try to screen myself behind the plea of compulsion from a master; for it was not so. Neither can I plead ignorance or thoughtlessness. For years, my master had done his utmost to pollute my mind with foul images, and to destroy the pure principles inculcated by my grandmother, and the good mistress of my childhood. The influences of slavery had had the same effect on me that they had on other young girls; they had made me prematurely knowing, concerning the evil ways of the world. I knew what I did, and I did it with deliberate calculation.[10]

But, O, ye happy women, whose purity has been sheltered from childhood, who have been free to choose the objects of your affection, whose homes are protected by law, do not judge the poor desolate slave girl too severely! If slavery had been abolished, I, also, could have married the man of my choice; I could have had a home shielded by the laws; and I should have been spared the painful task of confessing what I am now about to relate; but all my prospects had been blighted by slavery. I wanted to keep myself pure; and, under the most adverse circumstances, I tried hard to preserve my self-respect; but I was struggling alone in the powerful grasp of the demon Slavery; and the monster proved too strong for me. I felt as if I was forsaken by God and man; as if all my efforts must be frustrated; and I became reckless in my despair.

I have told you that Dr. Flint's persecutions and his wife's jealousy had given rise to some gossip in the neighborhood. Among others, it chanced that a white unmarried gentleman[11] had obtained some knowledge of the circumstances in which I was placed. He knew my grandmother, and often spoke to me in the street. He became interested for me, and asked questions about my master, which I answered in part. He expressed a

---

[9] Dr. Flint (Norcum) offered Linda the bargain many slaveholders found congenial—a "favored" state of concubinage. See Sterling, pp. 22–25.

[10] Jacobs gives many such examples of her family's independence of mind and spirit, so incompatible with slavery. She inherited these survival strategies, it seems, from her grandmother.

[11] This was Samuel Tredwell Sawyer who lived in the same block on King Street as Molly Horniblow. He studied law at the University of North Carolina at Chapel Hill and practiced in Edenton. He later was elected to Congress and married. His wife acknowledged his children by Jacobs and, for a time, had their daughter Louisa Matilda (here called Ellen) living with the Sawyer family in Washington, D.C.

great deal of sympathy, and a wish to aid me. He constantly sought opportunities to see me, and wrote to me frequently. I was a poor slave girl, only fifteen years old.

So much attention from a superior person was, of course, flattering; for human nature is the same in all. I also felt grateful for his sympathy, and encouraged by his kind words. It seemed to me a great thing to have such a friend. By degrees, a more tender feeling crept into my heart. He was an educated and eloquent gentleman; too eloquent, alas, for the poor slave girl who trusted in him. Of course I saw whither all this was tending. I knew the impassable gulf between us; but to be an object of interest to a man who is not married, and who is not her master, is agreeable to the pride and feelings of a slave, if her miserable situation has left her any pride or sentiment. It seems less degrading to give one's self, than to submit to compulsion. There is something akin to freedom in having a lover who has no control over you, except that which he gains by kindness and attachment. A master may treat you as rudely as he pleases, and you dare not speak; moreover, the wrong does not seem so great with an unmarried man, as with one who has a wife to be made unhappy. There may be sophistry in all this; but the condition of a slave confuses all principles of morality, and, in fact, renders the practice of them impossible.

When I found that my master had actually begun to build the lonely cottage, other feelings mixed with those I have described. Revenge, and calculations of interest, were added to flattered vanity and sincere gratitude for kindness. I knew nothing would enrage Dr. Flint so much as to know that I favored another; and it was something to triumph over my tyrant even in that small way. I thought he would revenge himself by selling me, and I was sure my friend, Mr. Sands, would buy me. He was a man of more generosity and feeling than my master, and I thought my freedom could be easily obtained from him. The crisis of my fate now came so near that I was desperate. I shuddered to think of being the mother of children that should be owned by my old tyrant. I knew that as soon as a new fancy took him, his victims were sold far off to get rid of them; especially if they had children. I had seen several women sold, with his babies at the breast. He never allowed his offspring by slaves to remain long in sight of himself and his wife. Of a man who was not my master I could ask to have my children well supported; and in this case, I felt confident I should obtain the boon. I also felt quite sure that they would be made free. With all these thoughts revolving in my mind, and seeing no other way of escaping the doom I so much dreaded, I made a headlong plunge. Pity me, and pardon me, O virtuous reader! You never knew what it is to be a slave; to be entirely unprotected by law or custom; to have the laws reduce you to the condition of a chattel, entirely subject to the will of another. You never exhausted your ingenuity in avoiding the snares, and eluding the power of a hated tyrant; you never shuddered at the sound of his footsteps, and trembled within hearing of his voice. I know I did wrong. No one can feel it more sensibly than I do. The painful and humiliating memory will haunt me to my dying day. Still, in looking back, calmly, on the events of my life, I feel that the slave woman ought not to be judged by the same standard as others.

The months passed on. I had many unhappy hours. I secretly mourned over the sorrow I was bringing on my grandmother, who had so tried to shield me from harm. I knew that I was the greatest comfort of her old age, and that it was a source of pride to her that I had not degraded myself, like most of the slaves. I wanted to confess to her that I was no longer worthy of her love; but I could not utter the dreaded words.

As for Dr. Flint, I had a feeling of satisfaction and triumph in the thought of telling *him*. From time to time he told me of his intended arrangements, and I was silent. At last, he came and told me the cottage was completed, and ordered me to go to it. I told him I would never enter it. He said, "I have heard enough of such talk as that. You shall go, if you are carried by force; and you shall remain there."

I replied, "I will never go there. In a few months I shall be a mother."

He stood and looked at me in dumb amazement, and left the house without a word. I thought I should be happy in my triumph over him. But now that the truth was out, and my relatives would hear of it, I felt wretched. Humble as were their circumstances, they had pride in my good character. Now, how could I look them in the face? My self-respect was gone! I had resolved that I would be virtuous, though I was a slave. I had said, "Let the storm beat! I will brave it till I die." And now, how humiliated I felt!

I went to my grandmother. My lips moved to make confession, but the words stuck in my throat. I sat down in the shade of a tree at her door and began to sew. I think she saw something unusual was the matter with me. The mother of slaves is very watchful. She knows there is no security for her children. After they have entered their teens she lives in daily expectation of trouble. This leads to many questions. If the girl is of a sensitive nature, timidity keeps her from answering truthfully, and this well-meant course has a tendency to drive her from maternal counsels. Presently, in came my mistress, like a mad woman, and accused me concerning her husband. My grandmother, whose suspicions had been previously awakened, believed what she said. She exclaimed, "O Linda! Has it come to this? I had rather see you dead than to see you as you now are. You are a disgrace to your dead mother." She tore from my fingers my mother's wedding ring and her silver thimble. "Go away!" she exclaimed, "and never come to my house, again." Her reproaches fell so hot and heavy, that they left me no chance to answer. Bitter tears, such as the eyes never shed but once, were my only answer. I rose from my seat, but fell back again, sobbing. She did not speak to me; but the tears were running down her furrowed cheeks, and they scorched me like fire. She had always been so kind to me! *So* kind! How I longed to throw myself at her feet, and tell her all the truth! But she had ordered me to go, and never to come there again. After a few minutes, I mustered strength, and started to obey her. With what feelings did I now close that little gate, which I used to open with such an eager hand in my childhood! It closed upon me with a sound I never heard before.

Where could I go? I was afraid to return to my master's. I walked on recklessly, not caring where I went, or what would become of me. When I had gone four or five miles, fatigue compelled me to stop. I sat down on the stump of an old tree. The stars were shining through the boughs above me. How they mocked me, with their bright, calm light! The hours passed by, and as I sat there alone a chil-iness and deadly sickness came over me. I sank on the ground. My mind was full of horrid thoughts. I prayed to die; but the prayer was not answered. At last, with great effort I roused myself, and walked some distance further, to the house of a woman who had been a friend of my mother. When I told her why I was there, she spoke soothingly to me; but I could not be comforted. I thought I could bear my shame if I could only be reconciled to my grandmother. I longed to open my heart to her. I thought if she could know the real state of the case, and all I had been bearing for years, she would perhaps judge me less harshly. My friend advised me to send for her. I did so; but days of agonizing suspense passed before she came. Had she utterly forsaken me? No. She came at last. I knelt before her, and told her the things that had poisoned my life; how long I had been persecuted; that I saw no way of escape; and in an hour of extremity I had become desperate. She listened in silence. I told her I would bear any thing and do any thing, if in time I had hopes of obtaining her forgiveness. I begged of her to pity me, for my dead mother's sake. And she did pity me. She did not say, "I forgive you;" but she looked at me lovingly, with her eyes full of tears. She laid her old hand gently on my head, and murmured, "Poor child! Poor child!"

Chapter 16: Scenes at the Plantation

Early the next morning I left my grandmother's with my youngest child.[12] My boy was ill, and I left him behind. I had many sad thoughts as the old wagon jolted on. Hitherto, I had suffered alone; now, my little one was to be treated as a slave. As we drew near the great house, I thought of the time when I was formerly sent there out of revenge. I wondered for what purpose I was now sent. I could not tell. I resolved to obey orders so far as duty required; but within myself, I determined to make my stay as short as possible. Mr. Flint was waiting to receive us, and told me to follow him up stairs to receive orders for the day. My little Ellen was left below in the kitchen. It was a change for her, who had always been so carefully tended. My young master said she might amuse herself in the yard. This was kind of him, since the child was hateful to his sight. My task was to fit up the house for the reception of the bride. In the midst of sheets, tablecloths, towels, drapery, and carpeting, my head was as busy planning, as were my fingers with the needle. At noon I was allowed to go to Ellen. She had sobbed herself to sleep. I heard Mr. Flint say to a neighbor, "I've got her down here, and I'll soon take the town notions out of her head. My father is partly to blame for her nonsense. He ought to have broke her in long ago." The remark was made within my hearing, and it would have been quite as manly to have made it to my face. He *had* said things to my face which might, or might not, have surprised his neighbor if he had known of them. He was "a chip of the old block."

I resolved to give him no cause to accuse me of being too much of a lady, so far as work was concerned. I worked day and night, with wretchedness before me. When I lay down beside my child, I felt how much easier it would be to see her die than to see her master beat her about, as I daily saw him beat other little ones.[13] The spirit of the mothers was so crushed by the lash, that they stood by, without courage to remonstrate. How much more must I suffer, before I should be "broke in" to that degree?

I wished to appear as contented as possible. Sometimes I had an opportunity to send a few lines home; and this brought up recollections that made it difficult, for a time, to seem calm and indifferent to my lot. Notwithstanding my efforts, I saw that Mr. Flint regarded me with a suspicious eye. Ellen broke down under the trials of her new life.

---

[12] When Linda became pregnant, Mrs. Flint expelled her from the house. She went to her grandmother's where her son and daughter were born. Later, Dr. Flint resumed his suit and attempted to make her his concubine. When she refused he sent her to work on his plantation. Sensing that he would bring her children there to "break them in" to slavery, she determined to escape to freedom. The chapter begins with Linda's arrival at the plantation.

[13] In her epic fiction *Beloved,* Nobel Prize-winning African American novelist Toni Morrison develops this theme. A mother chooses death for her children rather than the slave girl's life of harassment, rape, and sexual humiliation.

Separated from me, with no one to look after her, she wandered about, and in a few days cried herself sick. One day, she sat under the window where I was at work, crying that weary cry which makes a mother's heart bleed. I was obliged to steel myself to bear it. After a while it ceased. I looked out, and she was gone. As it was near noon, I ventured to go down in search of her. The great house was raised two feet above the ground. I looked under it, and saw her about midway, fast asleep. I crept under and drew her out. As I held her in my arms, I thought how well it would be for her if she never waked up; and I uttered my thought aloud. I was startled to hear some one say, "Did you speak to me?" I looked up, and saw Mr. Flint standing beside me. He said nothing further, but turned, frowning, away. That night he sent Ellen a biscuit and a cup of sweetened milk. This generosity surprised me. I learned afterwards, that in the afternoon he had killed a large snake, which crept from under the house; and I supposed that incident had prompted his unusual kindness.

The next morning the old cart was loaded with shingles for town. I put Ellen into it, and sent her to her grandmother. Mr. Flint said I ought to have asked his permission. I told him the child was sick, and required attention which I had no time to give. He let it pass; for he was aware that I had accomplished much work in a little time.

I had been three weeks on the plantation, when I planned a visit home. It must be at night, after every body was in bed. I was six miles from town, and the road was very dreary. I was to go with a young man, who, I knew, often stole to town to see his mother. One night, when all was quiet, we started. Fear gave speed to our steps, and we were not long in performing the journey. I arrived at my grandmother's. Her bed room was on the first floor, and the window was open, the weather being warm. I spoke to her and she awoke. She let me in and closed the window, lest some late passerby should see me. A light was brought, and the whole household gathered round me, some smiling and some crying. I went to look at my children, and thanked God for their happy sleep. The tears fell as I leaned over them. As I moved to leave, Benny stirred. I turned back, and whispered, "Mother is here." After digging at his eyes with his little fist, they opened, and he sat up in bed, looking at me curiously. Having satisfied himself that it was I, he exclaimed, "O mother! you ain't dead, are you? They didn't cut off your head at the plantation, did they?"

My time was up too soon, and my guide was waiting for me. I laid Benny back in his bed, and dried his tears by a promise to come again soon. Rapidly we retraced our steps back to the plantation. About half way we were met by a company of four patrols. Luckily we heard their horses' hoofs before they came in sight, and we had time to hide behind a large tree. They passed, hallooing and shouting in a manner that indicated a recent carousal. How thankful we were that they had not their dogs with them! We hastened our footsteps, and when we arrived on the plantation we heard the sound of the hand-mill. The slaves were grinding their corn. We were safely in the house before the horn summoned them to their labor. I divided my little parcel of food with my guide, knowing that he had lost the chance of grinding his corn, and must toil all day in the field.

Mr. Flint often took an inspection of the house, to see that no one was idle. The entire management of the work was trusted to me, because he knew nothing about it; and rather than hire a superintendent he contented himself with my arrangements. He had often urged upon his father the necessity of having me at the plantation to take charge of his affairs, and make clothes for the slaves; but the old man knew him too well to consent to that arrangement.

When I had been working a month at the plantation, the great aunt of Mr. Flint came to make him a visit. This was the good old lady who paid fifty dollars for my grandmother, for the purpose of making her free, when she stood on the auction block. My grandmother loved this old lady, whom we all called Miss Fanny. She often came to take tea with us. On such occasions the table was spread with a snow-white cloth, and the china cups and silver spoons were taken from the old-fashioned buffet. There were hot muffins, tea rusks, and delicious sweetmeats. My grandmother kept two cows, and the fresh cream was Miss Fanny's delight. She invariably declared that it was the best in town. The old ladies had cosey times together. They would work and chat, and sometimes, while talking over old times, their spectacles would get dim with tears, and would have to be taken off and wiped. When Miss Fanny bade us good by, her bag was filled with grandmother's best cakes, and she was urged to come again soon.

There had been a time when Dr. Flint's wife came to take tea with us, and when her children were also sent to have a feast of "Aunt Marthy's" nice cooking. But after I became an object of her jealousy and spite, she was angry with grandmother for giving a shelter to me and my children. She would not even speak to her in the street. This wounded my grandmother's feelings, for she could not retain ill will against the woman whom she had nourished with her milk when a babe. The doctor's wife would gladly have prevented our intercourse with Miss Fanny if she could have done it, but fortunately she was not dependent on the bounty of the Flints. She had enough to be independent; and that is more than can ever be gained from charity, however lavish it may be.

Miss Fanny was endeared to me by many recollections, and I was rejoiced to see her at the plantation. The warmth of her large, loyal heart made the house seem pleasanter while she was in it. She staid a week, and I had many talks with her. She said her principal object in coming was to see how I was treated, and whether any thing could be done for me. She inquired whether she could help me in any way. I told her I believed not. She condoled with me in her own peculiar way; saying she wished that I and all my grandmother's family were at rest in our graves, for not until then should she feel any peace about us. The good old soul did not dream that I was planning to bestow peace upon her, with regard to myself and my children; not by death, but by securing our freedom.

Again and again I had traversed those dreary twelve miles, to and from the town; and all the way, I was meditating upon some means of escape for myself and my children. My friends had made every effort that ingenuity could devise to effect our purchase, but all their plans had proved abortive. Dr. Flint was suspicious, and determined not to loosen his grasp upon us. I could have made my escape alone; but it was more for my helpless children than for myself that I longed for freedom. Though the boon would have been precious to me, above all price, I would not have taken it at the expense of leaving them in slavery. Every trial I endured, every sacrifice I made for their sakes, drew them closer to my heart, and gave me fresh courage to beat back the dark waves that rolled and rolled over me in a seemingly endless night of storms.

The six weeks were nearly completed, when Mr. Flint's bride was expected to take possession of her new home. The arrangements were all completed, and Mr. Flint said I had done well. He expected to leave home on Saturday, and return with his bride the following Wednesday. After receiving various orders from him, I ventured to ask permission to spend Sunday in town. It was granted; for which favor I was thankful. It was the first I had ever asked of him, and I intended it should be the last. It needed more than one night to accomplish the project I had in view; but the whole of Sunday would give me an opportunity. I spent the Sabbath with my grandmother. A calmer, more beautiful day never came down out of heaven. To me it was a day of conflicting emotions. Perhaps it was the last day I should ever spend under that dear, old sheltering roof! Perhaps these were the last talks I should ever have with the faithful old friend of my whole life! Perhaps it was the last time I and my children should be together! Well, better so, I thought, than that they should be slaves. I knew the doom that awaited my fair baby in slavery, and I determined to save her from it, or perish in the attempt. I went to make this vow at the graves of my poor parents, in the burying-ground of the slaves. "There the wicked cease from troubling, and there the weary be at rest. There the prisoners rest together; they hear not the voice of the oppressor; the servant is free from his master."[14] I knelt by the graves of my parents, and thanked God, as I had often done before, that they had not lived to witness my trials, or to mourn over my sins. I had received my mother's blessing when she died; and in many an hour of tribulation I had seemed to hear her voice, sometimes chiding me, sometimes whispering loving words into my wounded heart. I have shed many and bitter tears, to think that when I am gone from my children they cannot remember me with such entire satisfaction as I remembered my mother.

The graveyard was in the woods, and twilight was coming on. Nothing broke the death-like stillness except the occasional twitter of a bird. My spirit was overawed by the solemnity of the scene. For more than ten years I had frequented this spot, but never had it seemed to me so sacred as now. A black stump, at the head of my mother's grave, was all that remained of a tree my father had planted. His grave was marked by a small wooden board, bearing his name, the letters of which were nearly obliterated. I knelt down and kissed them, and poured forth a prayer to God for guidance and support in the perilous step I was about to take. As I passed the wreck of the old meeting house, where, before Nat Turner's time, the slaves had been allowed to meet for worship, I seemed to hear my father's voice come from it, bidding me not to tarry till I reached freedom or the grave. I rushed on with renovated hopes. My trust in God had been strengthened by that prayer among the graves.

My plan was to conceal myself at the house of a friend, and remain there a few weeks till the search was over. My hope was that the doctor would get discouraged, and, for fear of losing my value, and also of subsequently finding my children among the missing, he would consent to sell us; and I knew somebody would buy us. I had done all in my power to make my children comfortable during the time I expected to be separated from them. I was packing my things, when grandmother came into the room, and asked what I was doing. "I am putting my things in order," I replied. I tried to look and speak cheerfully; but her watchful eye detected something beneath the surface. She drew me towards her, and asked me to sit down. She looked earnestly at me, and said, "Linda, do you want to kill your old grandmother? Do you mean to leave your little, helpless children? I am old now, and cannot do for your babies as I once did for you."

I replied, that if I went away, perhaps their father would be able to secure their freedom.

"Ah, my child," said she, "don't trust too much to him. Stand by your own children, and suffer with them till death. Nobody respects a mother who forsakes her children; and if you leave them, you will never have a happy moment. If you go, you will make

14 Job 3:17–19.

me miserable the short time I have to live. You would be taken and brought back, and your sufferings would be dreadful. Remember poor Benjamin. Do give it up, Linda. Try to bear a little longer. Things may turn out better than we expect."

My courage failed me, in view of the sorrow I should bring on that faithful, loving old heart. I promised that I would try longer, and that I would take nothing out of her house without her knowledge.

Whenever the children climbed on my knee, or laid their heads on my lap, she would say, "Poor little souls! what would you do without a mother? She don't love you as I do." And she would hug them to her own bosom, as if to reproach me for my want of affection; but she knew all the while that I loved them better than my life. I slept with her that night, and it was the last time. The memory of it haunted me for many a year.

On Monday I returned to the plantation, and busied myself with preparations for the important day. Wednesday came. It was a beautiful day, and the faces of the slaves were as bright as the sunshine. The poor creatures were merry. They were expecting little presents from the bride, and hoping for better times under her administration. I had no such hopes for them. I knew that the young wives of slaveholders often thought their authority and importance would be best established and maintained by cruelty; and what I had heard of young Mrs. Flint gave me no reason to expect that her rule over them would be less severe than that of the master and overseer. Truly, the colored race are the most cheerful and forgiving people on the face of the earth. That their masters sleep in safety is owing to their superabundance of heart; and yet they look upon their sufferings with less pity than they would bestow on those of a horse or a dog.

I stood at the door with others to receive the bridegroom and bride. She was a handsome, delicate-looking girl, and her face flushed with emotion at sight of her new home. I thought it likely that visions of a happy future were rising before her. It made me sad; for I knew how soon clouds would come over her sunshine. She examined every part of the house, and told me she was delighted with the arrangements I had made. I was afraid old Mrs. Flint had tried to prejudice her against me, and I did my best to please her.

All passed off smoothly for me until dinner time arrived. I did not mind the embarrassment of waiting on a dinner party, for the first time in my life, half so much as I did the meeting with Dr. Flint and his wife, who would be among the guests. It was a mystery to me why Mrs. Flint had not made her appearance at the plantation during all the time I was putting the house in order. I had not met her, face to face, for five years, and I had no wish to see her now. She was a praying woman, and, doubtless, considered my present position a special answer to her prayers. Nothing could please her better than to see me humbled and trampled upon. I was just where she would have me—in the power of a hard, unprincipled master. She did not speak to me when she took her seat at table; but her satisfied, triumphant smile, when I handed her plate, was more eloquent than words. The old doctor was not so quiet in his demonstrations. He ordered me here and there, and spoke with peculiar emphasis when he said "your *mistress*." I was drilled like a disgraced soldier. When all was over, and the last key turned, I sought my pillow, thankful that God had appointed a season of rest for the weary.

The next day my new mistress began her housekeeping. I was not exactly appointed maid of all work; but I was to do whatever I was told. Monday evening came. It was always a busy time. On that night the slaves received their weekly allowance of food. Three pounds of meat, a peck of corn, and perhaps a dozen herring were allowed to each man. Women received a pound and a half of meat, a peck of corn, and the same number of herring. Children over twelve years old had half the allowance of the women. The meat was cut and weighed by the foreman of the field hands, and piled on planks before the meat house. Then the second foreman went behind the building, and when the first foreman called out, "Who takes this piece of meat?" he answered by calling somebody's name. This method was resorted to as means of preventing partiality in distributing the meat. The young mistress came out to see how things were done on her plantation, and she soon gave a specimen of her character. Among those in waiting for their allowance was a very old slave, who had faithfully served the Flint family through three generations. When he hobbled up to get his bit of meat, the mistress said he was too old to have any allowance; that when niggers were too old to work, they ought to be fed on grass. Poor old man! He suffered much before he found rest in the grave.

My mistress and I got along very well together. At the end of a week, old Mrs. Flint made us another visit, and was closeted a long time with her daughter-in-law. I had my suspicions what was the subject of the conference. The old doctor's wife had been informed that I could leave the plantation on one condition, and she was very desirous to keep me there. If she had trusted me, as I deserved to be trusted by her, she would have had no fears of my accepting that condition. When she entered her carriage to return home, she said to young Mrs. Flint, "Don't neglect to send for them as quick as possible." My heart was on the watch all the time, and I at once concluded that she spoke of my children. The doctor came the next day, and as I entered the room to spread the tea table, I heard him say, "Don't wait any longer. Send for them to-morrow." I saw through the plan. They thought my children's being there would fetter me to the spot, and that it was a good place to break us all in to abject submission to our lot as slaves. After the doctor left, a gentleman called, who had always manifested friendly feelings towards my grandmother and her family. Mr. Flint carried him over the plantation to show him the results of labor performed by men and women who were unpaid, miserably clothed, and half famished. The cotton crop was all they thought of. It was duly admired, and the gentleman returned with specimens to show his friends. I was ordered to carry water to wash his hands. As I did so, he said, "Linda, how do you like your new home?" I told him I liked it as well as I expected. He replied, "They don't think you are contented, and to-morrow they are going to bring your children to be with you. I am sorry for you, Linda. I hope they will treat you kindly." I hurried from the room, unable to thank him. My suspicions were correct. My children were to be brought to the plantation to be "broke in."

To this day I feel grateful to the gentleman who gave me this timely information. It nerved me to immediate action.

Chapter 21: The Loophole of Retreat[15]

A small shed had been added to my grandmother's house years ago. Some boards were laid across the joists at the top, and between these boards and the roof was a very small garret, never occupied by any thing but rats and mice. It was a pent roof, covered with nothing but shingles, according to the southern custom for such buildings. The garret

---

[15] The title is a quotation from the English poet William Cowper's "The Task," IV, 88–90: "'Tis pleasant, through the loopholes of retreat, To peep at such a world,—to see the stir Of the great Babel, and not feel the crowd. The loophole faced West King Street with Dr. Flint's office about a block away."

was only nine feet long and seven wide. The highest part was three feet high, and sloped down abruptly to the loose board floor. There was no admission for either light or air. My uncle Phillip, who was a carpenter, had very skilfully made a concealed trap-door, which communicated with the storeroom. He had been doing this while I was waiting in the swamp. The storeroom opened upon a piazza. To this hole I was conveyed as soon as I entered the house. The air was stifling; the darkness total. A bed had been spread on the floor. I could sleep quite comfortably on one side; but the slope was so sudden that I could not turn on the other without hitting the roof. The rats and mice ran over my bed; but I was weary, and I slept such sleep as the wretched may, when a tempest has passed over them. Morning came. I knew it only by the noises I heard; for in my small den day and night were all the same. I suffered for air even more than for light. But I was not comfortless. I heard the voices of my children. There was joy and there was sadness in the sound. It made my tears flow. How I longed to speak to them! I was eager to look on their faces; but there was no hole, no crack, through which I could peep. This continued darkness was oppressive. It seemed horrible to sit or lie in a cramped position day after day, without one gleam of light. Yet I would have chosen this, rather than my lot as a slave, though white people considered it an easy one; and it was so compared with the fate of others. I was never cruelly over-worked; I was never lacerated with the whip from head to foot; I was never so beaten and bruised that I could not turn from one side to the other; I never had my heel-strings cut to prevent my running away; I was never chained to a log and forced to drag it about, while I toiled in the fields from morning till night; I was never branded with hot iron, or torn by blood-hounds. On the contrary, I had always been kindly treated, and tenderly cared for, until I came into the hands of Dr. Flint. I had never wished for freedom till then. But though my life in slavery was comparatively devoid of hardships, God pity the woman who is compelled to lead such a life!

My food was passed up to me through the trap-door my uncle had contrived; and my grandmother, my uncle Phillip, and aunt Nancy would seize such opportunities as they could, to mount up there and chat with me at the opening. But of course this was not safe in the daytime. It must all be done in darkness. It was impossible for me to move in an erect position, but I crawled about my den for exercise. One day I hit my head against something, and found it was a gimlet. My uncle had left it sticking there when he made the trap-door. I was as rejoiced as Robinson Crusoe could have been at finding such a treasure. It put a lucky thought into my head. I said to myself, "Now I will have some light. Now I will see my children." I did not dare to begin my work during the daytime, for fear of attracting attention. But I groped round; and having found the side next the street, where I could frequently see my children, I stuck the gimlet in and waited for evening. I bored three rows of holes, one above another; then I bored out the interstices between. I thus succeeded in making one hole about an inch long and an inch broad. I sat by it till late into the night, to enjoy the little whiff of air that floated in. In the morning I watched for my children. The first person I saw in the street was Dr. Flint. I had a shuddering, superstitious feeling that it was a bad omen. Several familiar faces passed by. At last I heard the merry laugh of children, and presently two sweet little faces were looking up at me, as though they knew I was there, and were conscious of the joy they imparted. How I longed to *tell* them I was there!

My condition was now a little improved. But for weeks I was tormented by hundreds of little red insects, fine as a needle's point, that pierced through my skin, and produced an intolerable burning. The good grandmother gave me herb teas and cooling medicines, and finally I got rid of them. The heat of my den was intense, for nothing but thin shingles protected me from the scorching summer's sun. But I had my consolations. Through my peeping-hole I could watch the children, and when they were near enough, I could hear their talk. Aunt Nancy brought me all the news she could hear at Dr. Flint's. From her I learned that the doctor had written to New York to a colored woman, who had been born and raised in our neighborhood, and had breathed his contaminating atmosphere. He offered her a reward if she could find out any thing about me. I know not what was the nature of her reply; but he soon after started for New York in haste, saying to his family that he had business of importance to transact. I peeped at him as he passed on his way to the steamboat. It was a satisfaction to have miles of land and water between us, even for a little while; and it was a still greater satisfaction to know that he believed me to be in the Free States. My little den seemed less dreary than it had done. He returned, as he did from his former journey to New York, without obtaining any satisfactory information. When he passed our house next morning, Benny was standing at the gate. He had heard them say that he had gone to find me, and he called out, "Dr. Flint, did you bring my mother home? I want to see her." The doctor stamped his foot at him in a rage, and exclaimed, "Get out of the way, you little damned rascal! If you don't, I'll cut off your head."

Benny ran terrified into the house, saying, "You can't put me in jail again. I don't belong to you now." It was well that the wind carried the words away from the doctor's ear. I told my grandmother of it, when we had our next conference at the trap-door; and begged of her not to allow the children to be impertinent to the irascible old man.

Autumn came, with a pleasant abatement of heat. My eyes had become accustomed to the dim light, and by holding my book or work in a certain position near the aperture I contrived to read and sew. That was a great relief to the tedious monotony of my life. But when winter came, the cold penetrated through the thin shingle roof, and I was dreadfully chilled. The winters there are not so long, or so severe, as in northern latitudes; but the houses are not built to shelter from cold, and my little den was peculiarly comfortless. The kind grandmother brought me bed-clothes and warm drinks. Often I was obliged to lie in bed all day to keep comfortable; but with all my precautions, my shoulders and feet were frostbitten. O, those long, gloomy days, with no object for my eye to rest upon, and no thoughts to occupy my mind, except the dreary past and the uncertain future! I was thankful when there came a day sufficiently mild for me to wrap myself up and sit at the loophole to watch the passers by. Southerners have the habit of stopping and talking in the streets, and I heard many conversations not intended to meet my ears. I heard slave-hunters planning how to catch some poor fugitive. Several times I heard allusions to Dr. Flint, myself, and the history of my children, who, perhaps, were playing near the gate. One would say, "I wouldn't move my little finger to catch her, as old Flint's property." Another would say, "I'll catch *any* nigger for the reward. A man ought to have what belongs to him, if he *is* a damned brute." The opinion was often expressed that I was in the Free States. Very rarely did any one suggest that I might be in the vicinity. Had the least suspicion rested on my grandmother's house, it would have been burned to the ground. But it was the last place they thought of. Yet there was no place, where slavery existed, that could have afforded me so good a place of concealment.

Dr. Flint and his family repeatedly tried to coax and bribe my children to tell something they had heard said about me. One day the doctor took them into a shop, and offered them some bright little silver pieces and gay handkerchiefs if they would tell where their mother was. Ellen shrank away from him, and would not speak; but Benny spoke up, and said, "Dr. Flint, I don't know where my mother is. I guess she's in New York; and when you go there again, I wish you'd ask her to come home, for I want to see her; but if you put her in jail, or tell her you'll cut her head off, I'll tell her to go right back."

Chapter 41: Free at Last[16]

Mrs. Bruce, and every member of her family, were exceedingly kind to me. I was thankful for the blessings of my lot, yet I could not always wear a cheerful countenance. I was doing harm to no one; on the contrary, I was doing all the good I could in my small way; yet I could never go out to breathe God's free air without trepidation at my heart. This seemed hard; and I could not think it was a right state of things in any civilized country.

From time to time I received news from my good old grandmother. She could not write; but she employed others to write for her. The following is an extract from one of her last letters:—

"Dear Daughter: I cannot hope to see you again on earth; but I pray to God to unite us above, where pain will no more rack this feeble body of mine; where sorrow and parting from my children will be no more.[17] God has promised these things if we are faithful unto the end. My age and feeble health deprive me of going to church now; but God is with me here at home. Thank your brother for his kindness. Give much love to him, and tell him to remember the Creator in the days of his youth, and strive to meet me in the Father's kingdom.[18] Love to Ellen and Benjamin. Don't neglect him. Tell him for me, to be a good boy. Strive, my child, to train them for God's children. May he protect and provide for you, is the prayer of your loving old mother."

These letters both cheered and saddened me. I was always glad to have tidings from the kind, faithful old friend of my unhappy youth; but her messages of love made my heart yearn to see her before she died, and I mourned over the fact that it was impossible. Some months after I returned from my flight to New England, I received a letter from her, in which she wrote, "Dr. Flint is dead. He has left a distressed family. Poor old man! I hope he made his peace with God."

I remembered how he had defrauded my grandmother of the hard earnings she had loaned; how he had tried to cheat her out of the freedom her mistress had promised her, and how he had persecuted her children; and I thought to myself that she was a better Christian than I was, if she could entirely forgive him. I cannot say, with truth, that the news of my old master's death softened my feelings towards him. There are wrongs which even the grave does not bury. The man was odious to me while he lived, and his memory is odious now.

His departure from this world did not diminish my danger. He had threatened my grandmother that his heirs should hold me in slavery after he was gone; that I never

[16] The chapter title, spoken at the close of Martin Luther King's "I Have a Dream Speech" at the Lincoln Memorial, comes from an anonymous spiritual. It is one of many collected by John W. Work in his *Folk Song of the American Negro*, Nashville, 1915.
[17] Revelations 21:4.
[18] Ecclesiastes 12:1.

should be free so long as a child of his survived. As for Mrs. Flint, I had seen her in deeper afflictions than I supposed the loss of her husband would be, for she had buried several children; yet I never saw any signs of softening in her heart. The doctor had died in embarrassed circumstances, and had little to will to his heirs, except such property as he was unable to grasp. I was well aware what I had to expect from the family of Flints; and my fears were confirmed by a letter from the south, warning me to be on my guard, because Mrs. Flint openly declared that her daughter could not afford to lose so valuable a slave as I was.

I kept close watch of the newspapers for arrivals; but one Saturday night, being much occupied, I forgot to examine the Evening Express as usual. I went down into the parlor for it, early in the morning, and found the boy about to kindle a fire with it. I took it from him and examined the list of arrivals. Reader, if you have never been a slave, you cannot imagine the acute sensation of suffering at my heart, when I read the names of Mr. and Mrs. Dodge, at a hotel in Courtland Street. It was a third-rate hotel, and that circumstance convinced me of the truth of what I had heard, that they were short of funds and had need of my value, as *they* valued me; and that was by dollars and cents. I hastened with the paper to Mrs. Bruce. Her heart and hand were always open to every one in distress, and she always warmly sympathized with mine. It was impossible to tell how near the enemy was. He might have passed and repassed the house while we were sleeping. He might at that moment be waiting to pounce upon me if I ventured out of doors. I had never seen the husband of my young mistress, and therefore I could not distinguish him from any other stranger. A carriage was hastily ordered; and, closely veiled, I followed Mrs. Bruce, taking the baby again with me into exile. After various turnings and crossings, and returnings, the carriage stopped at the house of one of Mrs. Bruce's friends, where I was kindly received. Mrs. Bruce returned immediately, to instruct the domestics what to say if any one came to inquire for me.

It was lucky for me that the evening paper was not burned up before I had a chance to examine the list of arrivals. It was not long after Mrs. Bruce's return to her house, before several people came to inquire for me. One inquired for me, another asked for my daughter Ellen, and another said he had a letter from my grandmother, which he was requested to deliver in person.

They were told, "She *has* lived here, but she has left."

"How long ago?"

"I don't know, sir."

"Do you know where she went?"

"I do not, sir." And the door was closed.

This Mr. Dodge, who claimed me as his property, was originally a Yankee pedler in the south; then he became a merchant, and finally a slaveholder. He managed to get introduced into what was called the first society, and married Miss Emily Flint. A quarrel arose between him and her brother, and the brother cowhided him. This led to a family feud, and he proposed to remove to Virginia. Dr. Flint left him no property, and his own means had become circumscribed, while a wife and children depended upon him for support. Under these circumstances, it was very natural that he should make an effort to put me into his pocket.

I had a colored friend, a man from my native place, in whom I had the most implicit confidence. I sent for him, and told him that Mr. and Mrs. Dodge had arrived in New York. I proposed that he should call upon them to make inquiries about his friends at the south, with whom Dr. Flint's family were well acquainted. He thought there was no impropriety in his doing so, and he consented. He went to the hotel, and knocked at the door of Mr. Dodge's room, which was opened by the gentleman himself, who gruffly inquired, "What brought you here? How came you to know I was in the city?"

"Your arrival was published in the evening papers, sir; and I called to ask Mrs. Dodge about my friends at home. I didn't suppose it would give any offence."

"Where's that negro girl, that belongs to my wife?"

"What girl, sir?"

"You know well enough. I mean Linda, that ran away from Dr. Flint's plantation, some years ago. I dare say you've seen her, and know where she is."

"Yes, sir, I've seen her, and know where she is. She is out of your reach, sir."

"Tell me where she is, or bring her to me, and I will give her a chance to buy her freedom."

"I don't think it would be of any use, sir. I have heard her say she would go to the ends of the earth, rather than pay any man or woman for her freedom, because she thinks she has a right to it. Besides, she couldn't do it, if she would, for she has spent her earnings to educate her children."

This made Mr. Dodge very angry, and some high words passed between them. My friend was afraid to come where I was; but in the course of the day I received a note from him. I supposed they had not come from the south, in the winter, for a pleasure excursion; and now the nature of their business was very plain.

Mrs. Bruce came to me and entreated me to leave the city the next morning. She said her house was watched, and it was possible that some clew to me might be obtained. I refused to take her advice. She pleaded with an earnest tenderness, that ought to have moved me; but I was in a bitter, disheartened mood. I was weary of flying from pillar to post. I had been chased during half my life, and it seemed as if the chase was never to end. There I sat, in that great city, guiltless of crime, yet not daring to worship God in any of the churches. I heard the bells ringing for afternoon service, and, with contemptuous sarcasm, I said, "Will the preachers take for their text, 'Proclaim liberty to the captive, and the opening of prison doors to them that are bound'? or will they preach from the text, 'Do unto others as ye would they should do unto you'?"[19] Oppressed Poles and Hungarians could find a safe refuge in that city; John Mitchell was free to proclaim in the City Hall his desire for "a plantation well stocked with slaves;" but there I sat, an oppressed American, not daring to show my face.[20] God forgive the black and bitter thoughts I indulged on that Sabbath day! The Scripture says, "Oppression makes even a wise man mad;"[21] and I was not wise.

I had been told that Mr. Dodge said his wife had never signed away her right to my children, and if he could not get me, he would take them. This it was, more than any thing else, that roused such a tempest in my soul. Benjamin was with his uncle William in California, but my innocent young daughter had come to spend a vacation with me. I thought of what I had suffered in slavery at her age, and my heart was like a tiger's when a hunter tries to seize her young.

[19] Matthew 7:12.
[20] Mitchell was an Irish nationalist and founder of the pro-slavery newspaper *The Citizen*.

[21] Ecclesiastes 7:17.

Dear Mrs. Bruce! I seem to see the expression of her face, as she turned away discouraged by my obstinate mood. Finding her expostulations unavailing, she sent Ellen to entreat me. When ten o'clock in the evening arrived and Ellen had not returned, this watchful and unwearied friend became anxious. She came to us in a carriage, bringing a well-filled trunk for my journey—trusting that by this time I would listen to reason. I yielded to her, as I ought to have done before.

The next day, baby and I set out in a heavy snow storm, bound for New England again. I received letters from the City of Iniquity, addressed to me under an assumed name. In a few days one came from Mrs. Bruce, informing me that my new master was still searching for me, and that she intended to put an end to this persecution by buying my freedom. I felt grateful for the kindness that prompted this offer, but the idea was not so pleasant to me as might have been expected. The more my mind had become enlightened, the more difficult it was for me to consider myself an article of property; and to pay money to those who had so grievously oppressed me seemed like taking from my sufferings the glory of triumph.[22] I wrote to Mrs. Bruce, thanking her, but saying that being sold from one owner to another seemed too much like slavery; that such a great obligation could not be easily cancelled; and that I preferred to go to my brother in California.

Without my knowledge, Mrs. Bruce employed a gentleman in New York to enter into negotiations with Mr. Dodge. He proposed to pay three hundred dollars down, if Mr. Dodge would sell me, and enter into obligations to relinquish all claim to me or my children forever after. He who called himself my master said he scorned so small an offer for such a valuable servant. The gentleman replied, "You can do as you choose, sir. If you reject this offer you will never get any thing; for the woman has friends who will convey her and her children out of the country."

Mr. Dodge concluded that "half a loaf was better than no bread," and he agreed to the proffered terms. By the next mail I received this brief letter from Mrs. Bruce: "I am rejoiced to tell you that the money for your freedom has been paid to Mr. Dodge. Come home to-morrow. I long to see you and my sweet babe."

My brain reeled as I read these lines. A gentleman near me said, "It's true; I have seen the bill of sale." "The bill of sale!" Those words struck me like a blow. So I was *sold* at last! A human being *sold* in the free city of New York! The bill of sale is on record, and future generations will learn from it that women were articles of traffic in New York, late in the nineteenth century of the Christian religion. It may hereafter prove a useful document to antiquaries, who are seeking to measure the progress of civilization in the United States. I well know the value of that bit of paper; but much as I love freedom, I do not like to look upon it. I am deeply grateful to the generous friend who procured it, but I despise the miscreant who demanded payment for what never rightfully belonged to him or his.

I had objected to having my freedom bought, yet I must confess that when it was done I felt as if a heavy load had been lifted from my weary shoulders. When I rode home in the cars I was no longer afraid to unveil my face and look at people as they passed. I should have been glad to have met Daniel Dodge himself; to have had him seen me and known me, that he might have mourned over the untoward circumstances which compelled him to sell me for three hundred dollars.

22 Job 19:9.

When I reached home, the arms of my benefactress were thrown round me, and our tears mingled. As soon as she could speak, she said, "O Linda, I'm *so* glad it's all over! You wrote to me as if you thought you were going to be transferred from one owner to another. But I did not buy you for your services. I should have done just the same, if you had been going to sail for California tomorrow. I should, at least, have the satisfaction of knowing that you left me a free woman."

My heart was exceedingly full. I remembered how my poor father had tried to buy me, when I was a small child, and how he had been disappointed. I hoped his spirit was rejoicing over me now. I remembered how my good old grandmother had laid up her earnings to purchase me in later years, and how often her plans had been frustrated. How that faithful, loving old heart would leap for joy, if she could look on me and my children now that we were free! My relatives had been foiled in all their efforts, but God had raised me up a friend among strangers, who had bestowed on me the precious, long-desired boon. Friend! It is a common word, often lightly used. Like other good and beautiful things, it may be tarnished by careless handling; but when I speak of Mrs. Bruce as my friend, the word is sacred.

My grandmother lived to rejoice in my freedom; but not long after, a letter came with a black seal. She had gone "where the wicked cease from troubling, and the weary are at rest."[23]

Time passed on, and a paper came to me from the south, containing an obituary notice of my uncle Phillip. It was the only case I ever knew of such an honor conferred upon a colored person. It was written by one of his friends, and contained these words: "Now that death has laid him low, they call him a good man and a useful citizen; but what are eulogies to the black man, when the world has faded from his vision? It does not require man's praise to obtain rest in God's kingdom." So they called a colored man a *citizen!* Strange words to be uttered in that region!

Reader, my story ends with freedom; not in the usual way, with marriage.[24] I and my children are now free! We are as free from the power of slaveholders as are the white people of the north; and though that, according to my ideas, is not saying a great deal, it is a vast improvement in *my* condition. The dream of my life is not yet realized. I do not sit with my children in a home of my own. I still long for a hearthstone of my own, however humble. I wish it for my children's sake far more than for my own. But God so orders circumstances as to keep me with my friend Mrs. Bruce. Love, duty, gratitude, also bind me to her side. It is a privilege to serve her who pities my oppressed people, and who has bestowed the inestimable boon of freedom on me and my children.

It has been painful to me, in many ways, to recall the dreary years I passed in bondage. I would gladly forget them if I could. Yet the retrospection is not altogether without solace; for with those gloomy recollections come tender memories of my good old grandmother, like light, fleecy clouds floating over a dark and troubled sea.

1861

[23] Job 3:17. Molly Horniblow was buried at Edenton in September, 1853.

[24] A reference to the usual ending of romantic or sentimental fiction in which the heroine marries, with the implication "happily ever after." Jacobs here resolves the narrative tension between the conventional language of sentimental fiction and her tough, political purpose.

Thomas Bangs Thorpe
1815–1878

"Our eyes will be turned westward," Emerson wrote in 1843, "and a new and stronger tone in literature will be the result." Emerson was not thinking here of James Fenimore Cooper and Washington Irving, writers who had helped launch American literature's western movement yet who clearly felt more at home in European capitals than in frontier towns. Instead, Emerson envisioned a western American literature arising from a new generation of frontier writers whose work was steeped in an authentic idiom. Daniel Boone's legendary adventures first appeared in print in 1784, and Davy Crockett's distinctive blend of backwoods humor and self-promotion made for exciting reading throughout the 1830s. By the next decade, a sizable body of writing from the Midwest and Old Southwest had begun to attract the attention of eastern writers and editors.

One of these editors was William T. Porter, a Vermonter who had moved to New York City and in 1831 founded *Spirit of the Times,* a racy "Chronicle of the Turf, Agriculture, Field Sports, Literature, and the Stage." With a nationwide circulation of over forty thousand, *Spirit of the Times* soon grew to be a leading organ of southwestern humor, printing such classics as the Sut Lovingood tales of George Washington Harris. In 1841, Porter published what would become one of the most famous tall tales of American frontier literature, Thomas Bangs Thorpe's "The Big Bear of Arkansas." Arkansas (known as the "Bear State" until 1923) had been admitted into the Union as the twenty-fifth state in 1836. Thorpe's tale is as much a piece of self-conscious regional boosterism for "the creation state, the finishing-up country" as it is an enduring frontier myth about an "unhuntable bar."

Thomas Bangs Thorpe was born in Westfield, Massachusetts, on March 1, 1815. He grew up in New York City, where he studied painting with John Quidon, a fine early American historical and figure painter who derived many of his themes from the work of Washington Irving. Thorpe attended Wesleyan University in Middletown, Connecticut, from 1834 to 1836 but because of ill health moved to Louisiana, painting portraits and landscapes as well as contributing tales and hunting sketches to Porter's *Spirit of the Times.* In 1846, Thorpe published a collection of his stories, *The Mysteries of the Backwoods,* and in the same year wrote and illustrated a book on the Mexican War, *Our Army on the Rio Grande.* Thorpe returned to New York City in 1854; he published a second collection of backwoods tales, *The Hive of "The Bee-Hunter"* (1854), and after Porter's death in 1858 took over *Spirit of the Times* until it folded in 1861. As a colonel in the Union army, Thorpe served as city administrator of New Orleans during the occupation. From 1869 until his death in 1878, he worked at the customs house in New York City and continued to write for various magazines. But never again did he capture the American literary imagination as he did with that one short sketch of Jim Doggett and his pursuit of the fabulous bear.

Further Reading:

W. Blair, "The Technique of 'The Big Bear of Arkansas,' " *Southwest Review*, Summer 1943.

M. Rickels, *Thomas Bangs Thorpe: Humorist of the Old Southwest*, 1962.

Text:

The Big Bear of Arkansas, and Other Sketches Illustrative of Characters and Incidents in the South and South-West, ed. W. T. Porter, 1845.

The Big Bear of Arkansas

As the author of "Tom Owen the Bee Hunter," and other tales and sketches, Mr. THORPE has acquired a distinguished reputation on both sides of the Atlantic. Though by profession a painter, his time for several years past has been about equally divided between the brush and the pen. He is now engaged in the publication of the "Concordia Intelligencer," a journal of unusual ability, issued weekly in the pleasant little village situated directly opposite the city of Natchez. The New York "Spirit of the Times" was the medium through which Mr. T. first appeared before the world of letters; and his inimitable delineations of South-western characters, incidents, and scenery, soon attracted attention. Now, wherever the language is spoken, he is deemed
—"Great in mouths of wisest censure."

It is understood to be his intention to publish, at an early day, a collection of his writings, original and selected, to be illustrated by himself. As he is alike felicitous in the use of crayon, brush, or pen, we anticipate a brace or two of volumes of the highest pictorial and literary interest. The story annexed will give the reader an idea of his peculiar style in hitting off the original "characters" frequently met with in the great valley of the Mississippi.

A steamboat on the Mississippi frequently, in making her regular trips, carries between places varying from one to two thousand miles apart; and as these boats advertise to land passengers and freight at "all intermediate landings," the heterogeneous character of the passengers of one of these up-country boats can scarcely be imagined by one who has never seen it with his own eyes. Starting from New Orleans in one of these boats, you will find yourself associated with men from every state in the Union, and from every portion of the globe; and a man of observation need not lack for amusement or instruction in such a crowd, if he will take the trouble to read the great book of character so favourably opened before him. Here may be seen jostling together the wealthy Southern planter, and the pedler of tin-ware from New England—the Northern merchant, and the Southern jockey—a venerable bishop, and a desperate gambler—the land speculator, and the honest farmer—professional men of all creeds and characters—Wolvereens, Suckers, Hoosiers, Buckeyes, and Corncrackers,[1] beside a "plentiful sprinkling" of the half-horse

[1] Nicknames for the inhabitants of Michigan, Illinois, Indiana, Ohio, and Kentucky, respectively.

and half-alligator species of men,[2] who are peculiar to "old Mississippi," and who appear to gain a livelihood simply by going up and down the river. In the pursuit of pleasure or business, I have frequently found myself in such a crowd.

On one occasion, when in New Orleans, I had occasion to take a trip of a few miles up the Mississippi, and I hurried on board the well-known "high-pressure-and-beat-every-thing" steamboat "Invincible," just as the last note of the last bell was sounding; and when the confusion and bustle that is natural to a boat's getting under way had subsided, I discovered that I was associated in as heterogeneous a crowd as was ever got together. As my trip was to be of a few hours' duration only, I made no endeavours to become acquainted with my fellow passengers, most of whom would be together many days. Instead of this, I took out of my pocket the "latest paper," and more critically than usual examined its contents; my fellow passengers at the same time disposed of themselves in little groups. While I was thus busily employed in reading, and my companions were more busily still employed in discussing such subjects as suited their humours best, we were startled most unexpectedly by a loud Indian whoop, uttered in the "social hall," that part of the cabin fitted off for a bar; then was to be heard a loud crowing, which would not have continued to have interested us—such sounds being quite common in that *place of spirits*—had not the hero of these windy accomplishments stuck his head into the cabin and hallooed out, "Hurra for the Big Bar of Arkansaw!" and then might be heard a confused hum of voices, unintelligible, save in such broken sentences as "horse," "screamer,"[3] "lightning is slow," &c. As might have been expected, this continued interruption attracted the attention of every one in the cabin; all conversation dropped, and in the midst of this surprise the "Big Bar" walked into the cabin, took a chair, put his feet on the stove, and looking back over his shoulder, passed the general and familiar salute of "Strangers, how are you?" He then expressed himself as much at home as if he had been at "the Forks of Cypress," and "prehaps a little more so." Some of the company at this familiarity looked a little angry, and some astonished; but in a moment every face was wreathed in a smile. There was something about the intruder that won the heart on sight. He appeared to be a man enjoying perfect health and contentment: his eyes were as sparkling as diamonds, and good-natured to simplicity. Then his perfect confidence in himself was irresistibly droll. "Prehaps," said he, "gentlemen," running on without a person speaking, "prehaps you have been to New Orleans often; I never made *the first visit before,* and I don't intend to make another in a crow's life. I am thrown away in that ar place, and useless, that ar a fact. Some of the gentlemen thar called me *green*—well, prehaps I am, said I, *but I arn't so at home;* and if I aint off my trail much, the heads of them perlite chaps themselves wern't much the hardest; for according to my notion, they were *real know-nothings,* green as a pumpkin-vine—could'nt, in farming, I'll bet, raise a crop of turnips: and as for shooting, they'd miss a barn if the door was swinging, and that, too, with the best rifle in the country. And then

---

[2] Popular expression for the breed of noisy, boasting Mississippi River raftsmen and backwoodsmen. Washington Irving: "It is an old remark that persons of Indian mixture are half civilized, half savage, and half devil—a third half being provided for their particular convenience. It is for similar reasons, and probably with equal truth, that the backwoodsmen of Kentucky are styled half man, half horse, and half alligator, by the settlers on the Mississippi, and held accordingly in great respect and abhorrence."

[3] Slang expression for a burly, noisy, bragging backwoodsman; i.e., a "Kentucky Screamer."

they talked to me 'bout hunting, and laughed at my calling the principal game in Arkansaw poker, and high-low-jack. 'Prehaps,' said I, 'you prefer, chickens and ro-lette;'[4] at this they laughed harder than ever, and asked me if I lived in the woods, and didn't know what *game* was? At this I rather think I laughed. 'Yes,' I roared, and says, 'Strangers, if you'd asked me *how we got our meat* in Arkansaw, I'd a told you at once, and given you a list of varmints that would make a caravan, beginning with the bar, and ending off with the cat; that's *meat* though, not game.' Game, indeed, that's what city folks call it; and with them it means chippen-birds and shite-pokes;[5] maybe such trash live in my diggins, but I arn't noticed them yet: a bird any way is too trifling. I never did shoot at but one, and I'd never forgiven myself for that, had it weighed less than forty pounds. I wouldn't draw a rifle on any thing less than that; and when I meet with an-other wild turkey of the same weight I will drap him."

"A wild turkey weighing forty pounds!" exclaimed twenty voices in the cabin at once.

"Yes, strangers, and wasn't it a whopper? You see, the thing was so fat that it couldn't fly far; and when he fell out of the tree, after I shot him, on striking the ground he bust open behind, and the way the pound gobs of tallow rolled out of the opening was per-fectly beautiful."

"Where did all that happen?" asked a cynical-looking Hoosier.

"Happen! happened in Arkansaw: where else could it have happened, but in the cre-ation state, the finishing-up country—a state where the *sile* runs down to the centre of the 'arth, and government gives you a title to every inch of it? Then its airs—just breathe them, and they will make you snort like a horse. It's a state without a fault, it is."

"Excepting mosquitoes," cried the Hoosier.

"Well, stranger, except them; for it ar a fact that they are rather *enormous,* and do push themselves in somewhat troublesome. But, stranger, they never stick twice in the same place; and give them a fair chance for a few months, and you will get as much above noticing them as an alligator. They can't hurt my feelings, for they lay under the skin; and I never knew but one case of injury resulting from them, and that was to a Yankee: and they take worse to foreigners, any how, than they do to natives. But the way they used that fellow up! first they punched him until he swelled up and busted; then he sup-per-a-ted, as the doctor called it, until he was as raw as beef; then he took the ager,[6] owing to the warm weather, and finally he took a steamboat and left the country. He was the only man that ever took mosquitoes at heart that I know of. But mosquitoes is natur, and I never find fault with her. If they ar large, Arkansaw is large, her varmints ar large, her trees ar large, her rivers ar large, and a small mosquitoe would be of no more use in Arkansaw than preaching in a cane-brake."

This knock-down argument in favour of big mosquitoes used the Hoosier up, and the logician started on a new track, to explain how numerous bear were in his "diggins," where he represented them to be "about as plenty as blackberries, and a little plentifuler."

Upon the utterance of this assertion, a timid little man near me inquired if the bear in Arkansaw ever attacked the settlers in numbers.

"No," said our hero, warming with the subject, "no, stranger, for you see it ain't the natur of bar to go in droves; but the way they squander about in pairs and single ones is edifying. And then the way I hunt them—the old black rascals know the crack of my

---

[4] "Chickens" is probably a misprint for "checkers"; "rolette": roulette.

[5] Chirping sparrows and herons, respectively.

[6] Fever and chills; ague.

gun as well as they know a pig's squealing. They grow thin in our parts, it frightens them so, and they do take the noise dreadfully, poor things. That gun of mine is a perfect *epidemic among bar:* if not watched closely, it will go off as quick on a warm scent as my dog Bowie-knife[7] will: and then that dog—whew! why the fellow thinks that the world is full of bar, he finds them so easy. It's lucky he don't talk as well as think; for with his natural modesty, if he should suddenly learn how much he is acknowledged to be ahead of all other dogs in the universe, he would be astonished to death in two minutes. Strangers, that dog knows a bar's way as well as a horse-jockey knows a woman's: he always barks at the right time, bites at the exact place, and whips without getting a scratch. I never could tell whether he was made expressly to hunt bar, or whether bar was made expressly for him to hunt: any way, I believe they were ordained to go together as naturally as Squire Jones says a man and woman is, when he moralizes in marrying a couple. In fact, Jones once said, said he, 'Marriage according to law is a civil contract of divine origin; it's common to all countries as well as Arkansaw, and people take to it as naturally as Jim Doggett's Bowie-knife takes to bar.' "

"What season of the year do your hunts take place?" inquired a gentlemanly foreigner, who, from some peculiarities of his baggage, I suspected to be an Englishman, on some hunting expedition, probably at the foot of the Rocky mountains.

"The season for bar hunting, stranger," said the man of Arkansaw, "is generally all the year round, and the hunts take place about as regular. I read in history that varmints have their fat season, and their lean season. That is not the case in Arkansaw, feeding as they do upon the *spontenacious* productions of the sile, they have one continued fat season the year round: though in winter things in this way is rather more greasy than in summer, I must admit. For that reason bar with us run in warm weather, but in winter they only waddle. Fat, fat! it's an enemy to speed; it tames every thing that has plenty of it. I have seen wild turkeys, from its influence, as gentle as chickens. Run a bar in this fat condition, and the way it improves the critter for eating is amazing; it sort of mixes the ile up with the meat, until you can't tell t'other from which. I've done this often. I recollect one perty morning in particular, of putting an old he fellow on the stretch, and considering the weight he carried, he run well. But the dogs soon tired him down, and when I came up with him wasn't he in a beautiful sweat—I might say fever; and then to see his tongue sticking out of his mouth a feet,[8] and his sides sinking and opening like a bellows, and his cheeks so fat he couldn't look cross. In this fix I blazed at him, and pitch me naked into a briar patch if the steam didn't come out of the bullet-hole ten foot in a straight line. The fellow, I reckon, was made on the high-pressure system, and the lead sort of bust his biler."

"That column of steam was rather curious, or else the bear must have been warm," observed the foreigner, with a laugh.

"Stranger, as you observe, that bar was WARM, and the blowing off of the steam show'd it, and also how hard the varmint had been run. I have no doubt if he had kept on two miles farther his insides would have been stewed; and I expect to meet with a varmint yet of extra bottom, who will run himself into a skinfull of bar's grease: it is possible; much onlikelier things have happened."

---

[7] Famous knife named for the frontiersman and soldier James Bowie (1799–1836).

[8] Probably misprint for "foot."

"Whereabouts are these bears so abundant?" inquired the foreigner, with increasing interest.

"Why, stranger, they inhabit the neighbourhood of my settlement, one of the prettiest places on old Mississippi—a perfect location, and no mistake; a place that had some defects until the river made the 'cut-off' at 'Shirt-tail bend,' and that remedied the evil, as it brought my cabin on the edge of the river—a great advantage in wet weather, I assure you, as you can now roll a barrel of whiskey into my yard in high water from a boat, as easy as falling off a log. It's a great improvement, as toting it by land in a jug, as I used to do, *evaporated* it too fast, and it became expensive. Just stop with me, stranger, a month or two, or a year if you like, and you will appreciate my place. I can give you plenty to eat; for beside hog and hominy, you can have bar-ham, and bar-sausages, and a mattrass of bar-skins to sleep on, and a wildcat-skin, pulled off hull, stuffed with corn-shucks, for a pillow. That bed would put you to sleep if you had the rheumatics in every joint in your body. I call that ar bed a *quietus.*[9] Then look at my land—the government ain't got another such a piece to dispose of. Such timber, and such bottom land, why you can't preserve any thing natural you plant in it unless you pick it young, things thar will grow out of shape so quick. I once planted in those diggins a few potatoes and beets: they took a fine start, and after that an ox team couldn't have kept them from growing. About that time I went off to old Kentuck on bisiness, and did not hear from them things in three months, when I accidentally stumbled on a fellow who had stopped at my place, with an idea of buying me out. 'How did you like things?' said I. 'Pretty well,' said he; 'the cabin is convenient, and the timber land is good; but that bottom land ain't worth the first red cent.' 'Why?' said I. ' 'Cause,' said he. ' 'Cause what?' said I. ' 'Cause it's full of cedar stumps and Indian mounds,' said he, 'and *it can't be cleared.*' 'Lord,' said I, 'them ar "cedar stumps" is beets, and them ar "Indian mounds" ar tater hills.' As I expected, the crop was overgrown and useless: the sile is too rich, *and planting in Arkansaw is dangerous.* I had a good-sized sow killed in that same bottom land. The old thief stole an ear of corn, and took it down where she slept at night to eat. Well, she left a grain or two on the ground, and lay down on them: before morning the corn shot up, and the percussion killed her dead. I don't plant any more: natur intended Arkansaw for a hunting ground, and I go according to natur."

The questioner who thus elicited the description of our hero's settlement, seemed to be perfectly satisfied, and said no more; but the "Big Bar of Arkansaw" rambled on from one thing to another with a volubility perfectly astonishing, occasionally disputing with those around him, particularly with a "live Sucker" from Illinois, who had the daring to say that our Arkansaw friend's stories "smelt rather tall."

In this manner the evening was spent; but conscious that my own association with so singular a personage would probably end before morning, I asked him if he would not give me a description of some particular bear hunt; adding, that I took great interest in such things, though I was no sportsman. The desire seemed to please him, and he squared himself round towards me, saying, that he could give me an idea of a bar hunt that was never beat in this world, or in any other. His manner was so singular, that half of his story consisted in his excellent way of telling it, the great peculiarity of which was, the happy manner he had of emphasizing the prominent parts of his conversation. As near as I can recollect, I have italicized them, and given the story in his own words.

[9] Final release from all cares; i.e., death.

"Stranger," said he, "in bar hunts *I am numerous,* and which particular one, as you say, I shall tell, puzzles me. There was the old she devil I shot at the Hurricane last fall— then there was the old hog thief I popped over at the Bloody Crossing, and then—Yes, I have it! I will give you an idea of a hunt, in which the greatest bar was killed that ever lived, *none excepted;* about an old fellow that I hunted, more or less, for two or three years; and if that ain't a *particular bar hunt,* I ain't got one to tell. But in the first place, stranger, let me say, I am pleased with you, because you ain't ashamed to gain information by asking, and listening; and that's what I say to Countess's pups every day when I'm home; and I have got great hopes of them ar pups, because they are continually *nosing* about; and though they stick it sometimes in the wrong place, they gain experience any how, and may learn something useful to boot. Well, as I was saying about this big bar, you see when I and some more first settled in our region, we were drivin to hunting naturally; we soon liked it, and after that we found it an easy matter to make the thing our business. One old chap who had pioneered 'afore us, gave us to understand that we had settled in the right place. He dwelt upon its merits until it was affecting, and showed us, to prove his assertions, more marks on the sassafras trees than I ever saw on a tavern door 'lection time.[10] 'Who keeps that ar reckoning?' said I. 'The bar,' said he. 'What for?' said I. 'Can't tell,' said he; 'but so it is: the bar bite the bark and wood too, at the highest point from the ground they can reach, and you can tell, by the marks,' said he, 'the length of the bar to an inch.' 'Enough,' said I; 'I've learned something here a'ready, and I'll put it in practice.'

"Well, stranger, just one month from that time I killed a bar, and told its exact length before I measured it, by those very marks; and when I did that, I swelled up considerable—I've been a prouder man ever since. So I went on, larning something every day, until I was reckoned a buster,[11] and allowed to be decidedly the best bar hunter in my district; and that is a reputation as much harder to earn than to be reckoned first man in Congress, as an iron ramrod is harder than a toad-stool. Did the varmints grow overcunning by being fooled with by green-horn hunters, and by this means get troublesome, they send for me as a matter of course; and thus I do my own hunting, and most of my neighbours'. I walk into the varmints though, and it has become about as much the same to me as drinking. It is told in two sentences—a bar is started, and he is killed. The thing is somewhat monotonous now—I know just how much they will run, where they will tire, how much they will growl, and what a thundering time I will have in getting them home. I could give you this history of the chase with all the particulars at the commencement, I know the signs so well—*Stranger, I'm certain.* Once I met with a match though, and I will tell you about it; for a common hunt would not be worth relating.

"On a fine fall day, long time ago, I was trailing about for bar, and what should I see but fresh marks on the sassafras trees, about eight inches above any in the forests that I knew of. Says I, 'them marks is a hoax, or it indicates the d——t bar that was ever grown.' In fact, stranger, I couldn't believe it was real, and I went on. Again I saw the same marks, at the same height, and *I knew the thing lived.* That conviction came home to my soul like an earthquake. Says I, 'here is something a-purpose for me: that bar is mine, or I give up the hunting business.' The very next morning what should I see but a number of buzzards hovering over my corn-field. 'The rascal has been there,' said I, 'for

---

[10] Drinking was notoriously heavy at election time, and the reckonings of bills were marked on the doors of taverns.

[11] Slang for a big, roaring fellow.

that sign is certain:' and, sure enough, on examining, I found the bones of what had been as beautiful a hog the day before, as was ever raised by a Buckeye. Then I tracked the critter out of the field to the woods, and all the marks he left behind, showed me that he was *the bar*.

"Well, stranger, the first fair chase I ever had with that big critter, I saw him no less than three distinct times at a distance: the dogs run him over eighteen miles and broke down, my horse gave out, and I was as nearly used up as a man can be, made on *my* principle, *which is patent*. Before this adventure, such things were unknown to me as possible; but, strange as it was, that bar got me used to it before I was done with him; for he got so at last, that he would leave me on a long chase *quite easy*. How he did it, I never could understand. That a bar runs at all, is puzzling; but how this one could tire down and bust up a pack of hounds and a horse, that were used to overhauling every-thing they started after in no time, was past my understanding. Well, stranger, that bar finally got so sassy, that he used to help himself to a hog off my premises whenever he wanted one; the buzzards followed after what he left, and so, between *bar and buzzard*, I rather think I was *out of pork*.

"Well, missing that bar so often took hold of my vitals, and I wasted away. The thing had been carried too far, and it reduced me in flesh faster than an ager. I would see that bar in every thing I did: *he hunted me,* and that, too, like a devil, which I began to think he was. While in this fix, I made preparations to give him a last brush, and be done with it. Having completed every thing to my satisfaction, I started at sunrise, and to my great joy, I discovered from the way the dogs run, that they were near him; finding his trail was nothing, for that had become as plain to the pack as a turnpike road. On we went, and coming to an open country, what should I see but the bar very leisurely ascending a hill, and the dogs close at his heels, either a match for him this time in speed, or else he did not care to get out of their way—I don't know which. But wasn't he a beauty, though? I loved him like a brother.

"On he went, until he came to a tree, the limbs of which formed a crotch about six feet from the ground. Into this crotch he got and seated himself, the dogs yelling all around it; and there he sat eyeing them as quiet as a pond in low water. A green-horn friend of mine, in company, reached shooting distance before me, and blazed away, hit-ting the critter in the centre of his forehead. The bar shook his head as the ball struck it, and then walked down from that tree as gently as a lady would from a carriage. 'Twas a beautiful sight to see him do that—he was in such a rage that he seemed to be as little afraid of the dogs as if they had been sucking pigs; and the dogs warn't slow in making a ring around him at a respectful distance, I tell you; even Bowie-knife, himself, stood off. Then the way his eyes flashed—why the fire of them would have singed a cat's hair; in fact that bar was in a *wrath all over*. Only one pup came near him, and he was brushed out so totally with the bar's left paw, that he entirely disappeared; and that made the old dogs more cautious still. In the mean time, I came up, and taking deliberate aim as a man should do, at his side, just back of his foreleg, if *my gun did not snap,*[12] call me a coward, and I won't take it personal. Yes, stranger, *it snapped,* and I could not find a cap[13] about my person. While in this predicament, I turned round to my fool friend— says I, 'Bill,' says I, 'you're an ass—you're a fool—you might as well have tried to kill

---

[12] Misfire.
[13] Percussion cap.

that bar by barking the tree under his belly, as to have done it by hitting him in the head. Your shot has made a tiger of him, and blast me, if a dog gets killed or wounded when they come to blows, I will stick my knife into your liver, I will ————, my wrath was up. I had lost my caps, my gun had snapped, the fellow with me had fired at the bar's head, and I expected every moment to see him close in with the dogs, and kill a dozen of them at least. In this thing I was mistaken, for the bar leaped over the ring formed by the dogs, and giving a fierce growl, was off—the pack, of course, in full cry after him. The run this time was short, for coming to the edge of a lake the varmint jumped in, and swam to a little island in the lake, which it reached just a moment before the dogs. 'I'll have him now,' said I, for I had found my caps in the *lining of my coat*—so, rolling a log into the lake, I paddled myself across to the island, just as the dogs had cornered the bar in a thicket. I rushed up and fired—at the same time the critter leaped over the dogs and came within three feet of me, running like mad; he jumped into the lake, and tried to mount the log I had just deserted, but every time he got half his body on it, it would roll over and send him under; the dogs, too, got around him, and pulled him about, and finally Bowie-knife clenched with him, and they sunk into the lake together. Stranger, about this time I was excited, and I stripped off my coat, drew my knife, and intended to have taken a part with Bowie-knife myself, when the bar rose to the surface. But the varmint staid under—Bowie-knife came up alone, more dead than alive, and with the pack came ashore. 'Thank God,' said I, 'the old villain has got his deserts at last.' Determined to have the body, I cut a grape-vine for a rope, and dove down where I could see the bar in the water, fastened my queer rope to his leg, and fished him, with great difficulty, ashore. Stranger, may I be chawed to death by young alligators, if the thing I looked at wasn't a *she bar, and not the old critter after all.* The way matters got mixed on that island was onaccountably curious, and thinking of it made me more than ever convinced that I was hunting the devil himself. I went home that night and took to my bed—the thing was killing me. The entire team of Arkansaw in bar-hunting, acknowledged himself used up, and the fact sunk into my feelings like a snagged boat will in the Mississippi. I grew as cross as a bar with two cubs and a sore tail. The thing got out 'mong my neighbours, and I was asked how come on that individ-u-al that never lost a bar when once started? and if that same individ-u-al didn't wear telescopes when he turned a she bar, of ordinary size, into an old he one, a little larger than a horse? 'Prehaps,' said I, 'friends'—getting wrathy—'prehaps you want to call somebody a liar.' 'Oh, no,' said they, 'we only heard such things as being *rather common* of late, but we don't believe one word of it; oh, no,'—and then they would ride off and laugh like so many hyenas over a dead nigger. It was too much, and I determined to catch that bar, go to Texas, or die,—and I made my preparations accordin'. I had the pack shut up and rested. I took my rifle to pieces, and iled it. I put caps in every pocket about my person, *for fear of the lining*. I then told my neighbours, that on Monday morning—naming the day—I would start THAT BAR, and bring him home with me, or they might divide my settlement among them, the owner having disappeared. Well, stranger, on the morning previous to the great day of my hunting expedition, I went into the woods near my house, taking my gun and Bowie-knife along, just *from habit*, and there sitting down also from habit,[14] what should I see, getting over my fence, but *the bar!* Yes, the old varmint was within a hundred yards of me, and the way he walked

[14] i.e., habitual morning bowel movement.

over that fence—stranger, he loomed up like a *black mist,* he seemed so large, and he walked right towards me. I raised myself, took deliberate aim, and fired. Instantly the varmint wheeled, gave a yell, and *walked through the fence* like a falling tree would through a cobweb. I started after, but was tripped up by my inexpressibles,[15] which either from habit, or the excitement of the moment, were about my heels, and before I had really gathered myself up, I heard the old varmint groaning in a thicket near by, like a thousand sinners, and by the time I reached him he was a corpse. Stranger, it took five niggers and myself to put that carcase on a mule's back, and old long-ears waddled under his load, as if he was foundered in every leg of his body, and with a common whopper of a bar, he would have trotted off, and enjoyed himself. 'Twould astonish you to know how big he was: I made a *bed-spread of his skin,* and the way it used to cover my bar mattress, and leave several feet on each side to tuck up, would have delighted you. It was in fact a creation bar, and if it had lived in Samson's[16] time, and had met him, in a fair fight, it would have licked him in the twinkling of a dice-box. But, stranger, I never liked the way I hunted him, *and missed him.* There is something curious about it, I could never understand,—and I never was satisfied at his giving in so *easy at last.* Prehaps, he had heard of my preparations to hunt him the next day, so he jist come in, like Capt. Scott's coon,[17] to save his wind to grunt with in dying; but that ain't likely. My private opinion is, that that bar was an *unhuntable bar, and died when his time come.*"

When the story was ended, our hero sat some minutes with his auditors in a grave silence; I saw there was a mystery to him connected with the bear whose death he had just related, that had evidently made a strong impression on his mind. It was also evident that there was some superstitious awe connected with the affair,—a feeling common with all "children of the wood," when they meet with any thing out of their everyday experience. He was the first one, however, to break the silence, and jumping up, he asked all present to "liquor" before going to bed,—a thing which he did, with a number of companions, evidently to his heart's content.

Long before day, I was put ashore at my place of destination, and I can only follow with the reader, in imagination, our Arkansas friend, in his adventures at the "Forks of Cypress" on the Mississippi.

1841

Frederick Douglass
(1818–1895)

This African American, who did not know his father, who rarely saw his mother after he was taken from her as a child, and who had to employ guile to become literate in

---

[15] Euphemism for trousers. Doggett had lowered them from "habit."

[16] Samson: Biblical hero famous for his great strength (Judges 13–16).

[17] Allusion to a popular anecdote in which a raccoon, seeing that it is about to be shot, wisely gives up.

defiance of laws that prohibited slaves from learning to read or write, created a life for himself out of the nothingness his slave status conferred upon him and his race. At twenty-one, the year that symbolizes the moment most men come into their inheritance, Frederick Bailey escaped to the North from Maryland. There he changed his name to Douglass, ostensibly to throw his pursuers off his trail but also as the first step in forging an identity for himself as a free man.

What weapons had his experiences as a slave given to him? What incidents could he convert into symbolic stories that stirred members of the abolitionist cause, setting him on his way to become a towering figure in this nation's history?

Douglass's mother was Harriet Bailey. The exact identity of his white father is unknown, but it is likely that it was Aaron Anthony, the overseer of the large Lloyd plantation in Maryland where the child was born who would be called Frederick Augustus Washington Bailey. Neither mother nor child had any say in his "use" as a piece of owned property, and at age eight Douglass was sent along to Baltimore to work for the Auld family as a house servant. At sixteen Douglass was rudely introduced to yet another aspect of slave existence when he was farmed out as a field hand to Edward Covey, whose brutal treatment left upon Douglass's back the literal scars of the whip which he later likened to the "words" of slavery bitten into his flesh. Douglass's resistance to Covey's efforts to break his will and the blows he directed in his self-defense mark that point when Douglass stopped being a slave in his soul. Four years later he fled the site of his servitude, first for New York City, then for New Bedford, Massachusetts, although it was almost a decade before he was able to purchase his freedom and end the anxious years of being a fugitive on the run.

It was not in Douglass's character to rest content with having a new name, a new wife, and a new life in the North. Within a year of his escape to the North he was avidly reading the *Liberator,* the inflammatory abolitionist paper published by Boston's William Lloyd Garrison. By 1841 he began to speak out in New Bedford against slavery. The moment of true commitment to his lifetime cause came, however, later that year. Persuaded to speak before a Nantucket antislavery rally, he soon after decided to devote himself full-time as a featured lecturer on behalf of the Massachusetts Anti-Slavery Society.

With the Boston publication in 1845 of the *Narrative of the Life of Frederick Douglass, an American Slave* Douglass became both famous and at further risk as a fugitive slave. He found it necessary to leave the United States for England where he lectured extensively throughout 1845–1847. Upon securing his freedom by "buying" himself back for his own use, he returned to America. He soon broke with Garrison over the strategies each man proposed for destroying the slavery system, as over the issue of nonresistance which Garrison supported and the activist stance Douglass now assumed.

It was time for Douglass to take charge of his own voice. He had become increasingly incensed over the way white abolitionists coached him on how to speak (use dialect, they urged) and how they identified him to the public ("a piece of southern 'property' " and "chattel" who was dangerously close to becoming only a "thing" in the eyes of his new masters). Setting himself up in Rochester, New York, as editor of his own newspaper, *The North Star* (in reference to the sign in the night sky that inspired slaves to head to the North toward freedom), Douglass gained control over his own message—one which now widened to include not only the rights of people of color but also of all women.

With the start of the Civil War Douglass kept himself at the eye of the storm. He helped make certain that the North would not forget its commitment to the emancipation of slaves and he urged Lincoln to bring African American soldiers into the Union Army. After the war Douglass continued his tireless strivings for the elevation of his race. A leader in the Republican Party, he held a number of appointments, including U.S. Marshall for the District of Columbia and Minister to Haiti. More important, throughout the thirty years between the war's end and his death in 1895 Douglass continued to speak and to write with great eloquence. Now his message was that although the sins of the slavery system were officially ended, they continued in the explicit expressions of racism that increased in ugliness throughout the Reconstruction and post-Reconstruction years. Douglass also added vigorous support for women's suffrage, antilynching laws, and the betterment of conditions for poor tenant farmers to the list of the imperatives pursued by this indefatigable essayist, speaker, editor, and political leader.

Douglass was granted many honors during his lifetime, but he also suffered revilement, as when he married a white woman and when he voiced his support of John Brown's activism. But whatever opinions his white champions or detractors held toward him, he acted as his own man. Nowhere is this more apparent than in the intriguing history of the development of the various versions of the narrative he created about his life as a slave.

The first version of Douglass's memoirs appearing in 1845 under the title *Narrative of the Life of Frederick Douglass* was followed by the second version, published in 1855 as *My Bondage and My Freedom.* Two later revisions resulted in the *Life and Times of Frederick Douglass,* brought out in 1881 and 1892. Scholars and critics of American life and letters are currently at work exploring what makes each of these retellings a distinctive phase in an autobiographical project lasting almost fifty years.

The literary autobiography has long been considered a particularly appropriate "American" mode. From the time of the Puritans, there has been the pressing need to tell one's story in terms of New World conditions, in order to test whether one has indeed become a new person, redeemed into a new and better life. The model life of Benjamin Franklin provided the formula for young men mounting toward fame and fortune, a model that received endless revisions (ironic and otherwise) at the hands of free white males such as Thoreau and Henry Adams. But what were the possibilities for "autobiography" by men of color born into slavery?

Gustavus Vassa's *The Life of Olaudah Equiano* in 1789 pointed the way, but Douglass had to find his own means for narrating himself into the identity of a free man; just as the autobiographies of slave *women* have had to go in still other directions, as evidenced by Harriet Jacobs's *Incidents in the Life of a Slave Girl.* But it is important to realize that all slave narratives begin with the terrible fact of the oppression of a people not considered human enough to have access to the rights of autobiography.

Between 1845 and 1892 Douglass, for one, finally arrived at that title—*Life and Times of Frederick Douglass*—that suggests the forces that acted to make him and the force he applied to make himself. His autobiography now stands as one of the most memorable of exemplary lives written by self-created Americans.

Further Reading:

C. Chesnutt, *Frederick Douglass* 1899; rpt. 1970.

B. Washington, *Frederick Douglass*, 1906; rpt. 1969.

P. Foner, *Frederick Douglass*, 1964; rpt. 1969.

J. Gregory, *Frederick Douglass, The Orator*, 1969.

C. Hoexter, *Black Crusader: Frederick Douglass*, 1970.

A. Bontemps, *Free at Last: The Life of Frederick Douglass*, 1971.

P. Foner, ed., *Frederick Douglass on Women's Rights*, 1976.

J. Blessingame, *Frederick Douglass, Clarion Voice*, 1976.

J. Blassingame, ed., *The Frederick Douglass Papers*, 2 vols., 1979.

N. Huggins, *Slave and Citizen: Life of Frederick Douglass*, 1980.

D. Preston, *Young Frederick Douglass: The Maryland Years*, 1980; rpt. 1985.

W. Martin, *The Mind of Frederick Douglass*, 1984.

E. Sundquist, ed., *Frederick Douglass: New Literary and Historical Essays*, 1990.

G. Jay, "American Literature and the New Historicism: Example of Frederick Douglass," *Boundary*, 1990.

A. Levy, "Douglass, Franklin, and the Trickster Reader," *College English* 1990.

H. Baker, *Blues, Ideology, and Afro-American Literature*, 1984.

C. Ripley, "Autobiographical Writings of Douglass," *Southern Studies*, 1985.

J. Sekora, "Comprehending Slavery: Language and Personal History in Douglass's Narrative of 1845," *College Language Association Journal* 1985.

D. Gibson, "Reconciling Public and Private in Douglass's *Narrative*," *American Literature*, 1985.

W. McFeely, *Frederick Douglass*, 1991.

Texts:

Narrative of the Life of Frederick Douglass, an American Slave Written by Himself, 1847.

See also *The Life and Writings of Frederick Douglass*, 4 vols., ed. P. Foner, 1950–1953.

Narrative of the Life of Frederick Douglass, an American Slave Written by Himself *

Preface[1]

In the month of August, 1841, I attended an anti-slavery convention in Nantucket, at which it was my happiness to become acquainted with FREDERICK DOUGLASS, the writer of the following Narrative. He was a stranger to nearly every member of that body; but, having recently made his escape from the southern prisonhouse of bondage, and feeling his curiosity excited to ascertain the principles and measures of the abolitionists,—of whom he had heard a somewhat vague description while he was a slave,—he was induced to give his attendance, on the occasion alluded to, though at that time a resident in New Bedford.

Fortunate, most fortunate occurrence!—fortunate for the millions of his manacled brethren, yet panting for deliverance from their awful thraldom!—fortunate for the cause of negro emancipation, and of universal liberty!—fortunate for the land of his birth, which he has already done so much to save and bless!—fortunate for a large circle of friends and acquaintances, whose sympathy and affection he has strongly secured by the many sufferings he has endured, by his virtuous traits of character, by his ever-abiding remembrance of those who are in bonds, as being bound with them!—fortunate for the multitudes, in various parts of our republic, whose minds he has enlightened on the

---

* Boston's Anti-Slavery Office first printed Douglass's "Narrative" in 1845; this text is based upon the edition of 1847.

[1] Provided by William Lloyd Garrison, leading Boston abolitionist.

subject of slavery, and who have been melted to tears by his pathos, or roused to virtuous indignation by his stirring eloquence against the enslavers of men!—fortunate for himself, as it at once brought him into the field of public usefulness, "gave the world assurance of a MAN," quickened the slumbering energies of his soul, and consecrated him to the great work of breaking the rod of the oppressor, and letting the oppressed go free!

I shall never forget his first speech at the convention—the extraordinary emotion it excited in my own mind—the powerful impression it created upon a crowded auditory, completely taken by surprise—the applause which followed from the beginning to the end of his felicitous remarks. I think I never hated slavery so intensely as at that moment; certainly, my perception of the enormous outrage which is inflicted by it, on the godlike nature of its victims, was rendered far more clear than ever. There stood one, in physical proportion and stature commanding and exact—in intellect richly endowed—in natural eloquence a prodigy—in soul manifestly "created but a little lower than the angels"—yet a slave, ay, a fugitive slave,—trembling for his safety, hardly daring to believe that on the American soil, a single white person could be found who would befriend him at all hazards, for the love of God and humanity! Capable of high attainments as an intellectual and moral being—needing nothing but a comparatively small amount of cultivation to make him an ornament to society and a blessing to his race—by the law of the land, by the voice of the people, by the terms of the slave code, he was only a piece of property, a beast of burden, a chattel personal, nevertheless!

A beloved friend from New Bedford prevailed on Mr. DOUGLASS to address the convention: He came forward to the platform with a hesitancy and embarrassment, necessarily the attendants of a sensitive mind in such a novel position. After apologizing for his ignorance, and reminding the audience that slavery was a poor school for the human intellect and heart, he proceeded to narrate some of the facts in his own history as a slave, and in the course of his speech gave utterance to many noble thoughts and thrilling reflections. As soon as he had taken his seat, filled with hope and admiration, I rose, and declared that PATRICK HENRY,[2] of revolutionary fame, never made a speech more eloquent in the cause of liberty, than the one we had just listened to from the lips of that hunted fugitive. So I believed at that time—such is my belief now. I reminded the audience of the peril which surrounded this self-emancipated young man at the North,—even in Massachusetts, on the soil of the Pilgrim Fathers, among the descendants of revolutionary sires; and I appealed to them, whether they would ever allow him to be carried back into slavery,—law or no law, constitution or no constitution. The response was unanimous and in thunder-tones—"NO!" "Will you succor and protect him as a brother-man—a resident of the old Bay State."[3] "YES!" shouted the whole mass, with an energy so startling, that the ruthless tyrants south of Mason and Dixon's line might almost have heard the mighty burst of feeling, and recognized it as the pledge of an invincible determination, on the part of those who gave it, never to betray him that wanders, but to hide the outcast, and firmly to abide the consequences.

It was at once deeply impressed upon my mind, that, if Mr. DOUGLASS could be persuaded to consecrate his time and talents to the promotion of the anti-slavery enterprise, a powerful impetus would be given to it, and a stunning blow at the same time inflicted on northern prejudice against a colored complexion. I therefore endeavored to instill

[2] Virginia statesman (1736–1799) who delivered speech to fellow delegates in defiance of British rule containing the famous phrase, "I know not what course others may take; but as for me, give me liberty, or give me death!"

[3] Massachusetts.

hope and courage into his mind, in order that he might dare to engage in a vocation so anomalous and responsible for a person in his situation; and I was seconded in this effort by warm-hearted friends, especially by the late General Agent of the Massachusetts Anti-Slavery Society, Mr. JOHN A. COLLINS, whose judgment in this instance entirely coincided with my own. At first, he could give no encouragement; with unfeigned diffidence, he expressed his conviction that he was not adequate to the performance of so great a task; the path marked out was wholly an untrodden one; he was sincerely apprehensive that he should do more harm than good. After much deliberation, however, he consented to make a trial; and ever since that period, he has acted as a lecturing agent, under the auspices either of the American or the Massachusetts Anti-Slavery Society. In labors he has been most abundant; and his success in combating prejudice, in gaining proselytes, in agitating the public mind, has far surpassed the most sanguine expectations that were raised at the commencement of his brilliant career. He has borne himself with gentleness and meekness, yet with true manliness of character. As a public speaker, he excels in pathos, wit, comparison, imitation, strength of reasoning, and fluency of language. There is in him that union of head and heart, which is indispensable to an enlightenment of the heads and a winning of the hearts of others. May his strength continue to be equal to his day! May he continue to "grow in grace, and in the knowledge of God," that he may be increasingly serviceable in the cause of bleeding humanity, whether at home or abroad!

It is certainly a very remarkable fact, that one of the most efficient advocates of the slave population, now before the public, is a fugitive slave, in the person of FREDERICK DOUGLASS; and that the free colored population of the United States are as ably represented by one of their own number, in the person of CHARLES LENOX REMOND,[4] whose eloquent appeals have extorted the highest applause of multitudes on both sides of the Atlantic. Let the calumniators of the colored race despise themselves for their baseness and illiberality of spirit, and henceforth cease to talk of the natural inferiority of those who require nothing but time and opportunity to attain to the highest point of human excellence.

It may, perhaps, be fairly questioned, whether any other portion of the population of the earth could have endured the privations, sufferings and horrors of slavery, without having become more degraded in the scale of humanity than the slaves of African descent. Nothing has been left undone to cripple their intellects, darken their minds, debase their moral nature, obliterate all traces of their relationship to mankind; and yet how wonderfully they have sustained the mighty load of a most frightful bondage, under which they have been groaning for centuries! To illustrate the effect of slavery on the white man,—to show that he has no powers of endurance, in such a condition, superior to those of his black brother,—DANIEL O'CONNELL,[5] the distinguished advocate of universal emancipation, and the mightiest champion of prostrate but not conquered Ireland, relates the following anecdote in a speech delivered by him in the Conciliation Hall, Dublin, before the Loyal National Repeal Association, March 31, 1845. "No matter," said Mr. O'CONNELL, "under what specious term it may disguise itself, slavery is still hideous. *It has a natural, an inevitable tendency to brutalize every noble faculty of man.* An American sailor, who was cast away on the shore of Africa, where he was kept

---

[4] African American orator (1810–1873) who often joined Douglass in delivering abolitionist speeches.

[5] Irish statesman (1775–1847) who agitated for freedom from British rule.

in slavery for three years, was at the expiration of that period, found to be imbruted and stultified—he had lost all reasoning power; and having forgotten his native language, could only utter some savage gibberish between Arabic and English, which nobody could understand, and which even he himself found difficulty in pronouncing. So much for the humanizing influence of THE DOMESTIC INSTITUTION!" Admitting this to have been an extraordinary case of mental deterioration, it proves at least that the white slave can sink as low in the scale of humanity as the black one.

Mr. DOUGLASS has very properly chosen to write his own Narrative, in his own style, and according to the best of his ability, rather than to employ some one else. It is, therefore, entirely his own production; and, considering how long and dark was the career he had to run as a slave,—how few have been his opportunities to improve his mind since he broke his iron fetters,—it is, in my judgment, highly creditable to his head and heart. He who can peruse it without a tearful eye, a heaving breast, an afflicted spirit,—without being filled with an unutterable abhorrence of slavery and all its abettors, and animated with a determination to seek the the immediate overthrow of that execrable system,—without trembling for the fate of this country in the hands of a righteous God, who is ever on the side of the oppressed, and whose arm is not shortened that it cannot save,—must have a flinty heart, and be qualified to act the part of a trafficker "in slaves and the souls of men." I am confident that it is essentially true in all its statements; that nothing has been set down in malice, nothing exaggerated, nothing drawn from the imagination; that it comes short of the reality, rather than overstates a single fact in regard to SLAVERY AS IT IS.[6] The experience of FREDERICK DOUGLASS, as a slave, was not a peculiar one; his lot was not especially a hard one; his case may be regarded as a very fair specimen of the treatment of slaves in Maryland, in which State it is conceded that they are better fed and less cruelly treated than in Georgia, Alabama, or Louisiana. Many have suffered incomparably more, while very few on the plantations have suffered less, than himself. Yet how deplorable was his situation! what terrible chastisements were inflicted upon his person! what still more shocking outrages were perpetrated upon his mind! with all his noble powers and sublime aspirations, how like a brute was he treated, even by those professing to have the same mind in them that was in Christ Jesus! to what dreadful liabilities was he continually subjected! how destitute of friendly counsel and aid, even in his greatest extremities! how heavy was the midnight of woe which shrouded in blackness the last ray of hope, and filled the future with terror and gloom! what longings after freedom took possession of his breast, and how his misery augmented, in proportion as he grew reflective and intelligent,—thus demonstrating that a happy slave is an extinct man! how he thought, reasoned, felt, under the lash of the driver, with the chains upon his limbs! what perils he encountered in his endeavors to escape from his horrible doom! and how signal have been his deliverance and preservation in the midst of a nation of pitiless enemies!

This Narrative contains many affecting incidents, many passages of great eloquence and power; but I think the most thrilling one of them all is the description DOUGLASS gives of his feelings, as he stood soliloquizing respecting his fate, and the chances of his one day being a freeman, on the banks of the Chesapeake Bay—viewing the receding vessels as they flew with their white wings before the breeze, and apostrophizing them

[6] Title of 1839 antislavery pamphlet by
   Theodore Weld.

as animated by the living spirit of freedom. Who can read that passage, and be insensible to its pathos and sublimity? Compressed into it is a whole Alexandrian library[7] of thought, feeling, and sentiment—all that can, all that need be urged, in the form of expostulation, entreaty, rebuke, against that crime of crimes,—making man the property of his fellow-man! O, how accursed is that system, which entombs the godlike mind of man, defaces the divine image, reduces those who by creation were crowned with glory and honor to a level with four-footed beasts, and exalts the dealer in human flesh above all that is called God! Why should its existence be prolonged one hour? Is it not evil, only evil, and that continually? What does its presence imply but the absence of all fear of God, all regard for man, on the part of the people of the United States? Heaven speed its eternal overthrow!

So profoundly ignorant of the nature of slavery are many persons, that they are stubbornly incredulous whenever they read or listen to any recital of the cruelties which are daily inflicted on its victims. They do not deny that the slaves are held as property; but that terrible fact seems to convey to their minds no idea of injustice, exposure to outrage, or savage barbarity. Tell them of cruel scourgings, of mutilations and brandings, of scenes of pollution and blood, of the banishment of all light and knowledge, and they affect to be greatly indignant at such enormous exaggerations, such wholesale misstatements, such abominable libels on the character of the southern planters! As if all these direful outrages were not the natural results of slavery! As if it were less cruel to reduce a human being to the condition of a thing, than to give him a severe flagellation, or to deprive him of necessary food and clothing! As if whips, chains, thumb-screws, paddles, bloodhounds, overseers, drivers, patrols, were not all indispensable to keep the slaves down, and to give protection to their ruthless oppressors! As if, when the marriage institution is abolished, concubinage, adultery, and incest, must not necessarily abound; when all the rights of humanity are annihilated, any barrier remains to protect the victim from the fury of the spoiler; when absolute power is assumed over life and liberty, it will not be wielded with destructive sway! Skeptics of this character abound in society. In some few instances, their incredulity arises from a want of reflection; but, generally, it indicates a hatred of the light, a desire to shield slavery from the assaults of its foes, a contempt of the colored race, whether bond or free. Such will try to discredit the shocking tales of slaveholding cruelty which are recorded in this truthful Narrative; but they will labor in vain. Mr. Douglass has frankly disclosed the place of his birth, the names of those who claimed ownership in his body and soul, and the names also of those who committed the crimes which he has alleged against them. His statements, therefore, may easily be disproved, if they are untrue.

In the course of his Narrative, he relates two instances of murderous cruelty,—in one of which a planter deliberately shot a slave belonging to a neighboring plantation, who had unintentionally gotten within his lordly domain in quest of fish; and in the other, an overseer blew out the brains of a slave who had fled to a stream of water to escape a bloody scourging. Mr. Douglass states that in neither of these instances was any thing done by way of legal arrest or judicial investigation. The Baltimore American, of March 17, 1845, relates a similar case of atrocity, perpetrated with similar impunity—as follows:—"*Shooting a Slave.*—We learn, upon the authority of a letter from Charles

---

[7] Located in Alexandria, Egypt, and destroyed
by fire; said to have contained all the wealth
of ancient knowledge.

county, Maryland, received by a gentleman of this city, that a young man, named Matthews, a nephew of General Matthews, and whose father, it is believed, holds an office at Washington, killed one of the slaves upon his father's farm by shooting him. The letter states that young Matthews had been left in charge of the farm; that he gave an order to the servant, which was disobeyed, when he proceeded to the house, *obtained a gun, and, returning, shot the servant.* He immediately, the letter continues, fled to his father's residence, where he still remains unmolested."—Let it never be forgotten, that no slaveholder or overseer can be convicted of any outrage perpetrated on the person of a slave, however diabolical it may be, on the testimony of colored witnesses, whether bond or free. By the slave code, they are adjudged to be as incompetent to testify against a white man, as though they were indeed a part of the brute creation. Hence, there is no legal protection in fact, whatever there may be inform, for the slave population; and any amount of cruelty may be inflicted on them with impunity. Is it possible for the human mind to conceive of a more horrible state of society?

The effect of a religious profession on the conduct of southern masters is vividly described in the following Narrative, and shown to be any thing but salutary. In the nature of the case, it must be in the highest degree pernicious. The testimony of Mr. DOUGLASS, on this point, is sustained by a cloud of witnesses, whose veracity is unimpeachable. "A slaveholder's profession of Christianity is a palpable imposture. He is a felon of the highest grade. He is a man-stealer. It is of no importance what you put in the other scale."

Reader! are you with the man-stealers in sympathy and purpose, or on the side of their down-trodden victims? If with the former, then are you the foe of God and man. If with the latter, what are you prepared to do and dare in their behalf? Be faithful, be vigilant, be untiring in your efforts to break every yoke, and let the oppressed go free. Come what may—cost what it may—inscribe on the banner which you unfurl to the breeze, as your religious and political motto—"NO COMPROMISE WITH SLAVERY! NO UNION WITH SLAVEHOLDERS!"

WM. LLOYD GARRISON

Boston, May 1, 1845.

Letter from Wendell Phillips, Esq.[8]

BOSTON, *April 22, 1845.*

My Dear Friend:

You remember the old fable of "The Man and the Lion," where the lion complained that he should not be so misrepresented "when the lions wrote history."

I am glad the time has come when the "lions write history." We have been left long enough to gather the character of slavery from the involuntary evidence of the masters. One might, indeed, rest sufficiently satisfied with what, it is evident, must be, in general, the results of such a relation, without seeking farther to find whether they have followed in every instance. Indeed, those who stare at the half-peck of corn a week, and love to count the lashes on the slave's back, are seldom the "stuff" out of which reformers and

[8] Well-known Boston abolitionist lecturer (1811–1884).

abolitionists are to be made. I remember that, in 1838, many were waiting for the results of the West India experiment,[9] before they could come into our ranks. Those "results" have come long ago; but, alas! few of that number have come with them, as converts. A man must be disposed to judge of emancipation by other tests than whether it
has increased the produce of sugar,—and to hate slavery for other reasons than because
it starves men and whips womens,—before he is ready to lay the first stone of his anti-
slavery life.

I was glad to learn, in your story, how early the most neglected of God's children
waken to a sense of their rights, and of the injustice done them. Experience is a keen
teacher; and long before you had mastered your A B C, or knew where the "white sails"
of the Chesapeake were bound, you began, I see, to gauge the wretchedness of the slave,
not by his hunger and want, not by his lashes and toil, but by the cruel and blighting
death which gathers over his soul.

In connection with this, there is one circumstance which makes your recollections
peculiarly valuable, and renders your early insight the more remarkable. You come
from that part of the country where we are told slavery appears with its fairest features.
Let us hear, then, what it is at its best estate—gaze on its bright side, if it has one; and
then imagination may task her powers to add dark lines to the picture, as she travels
southward to that (for the colored man) Valley of the Shadow of Death, where the Mississippi sweeps along.

Again, we have known you long, and can put the most entire confidence in your
truth, candor, and sincerity. Every one who has heard you speak has felt, and, I am confident, every one who reads your book will feel, persuaded that you give them a fair
specimen of the whole truth. No one-sided portrait,—no wholesale complaints,—but
strict justice done, whenever individual kindliness has neutralized, for a moment, the
deadly system with which it was strangely allied. You have been with us, too, some
years, and can fairly compare the twilight of rights, which your race enjoy at the North,
with that "noon of night" under which they labor south of Mason and Dixon's line. Tell
us whether, after all, the half-free colored man of Massachusetts is worse off than the
pampered slave of the rice swamps!

In reading your life, no one can say that we have unfairly picked out some rare specimens of cruelty. We know that the bitter drops, which even you have drained from the
cup, are no incidental aggravations, no individual ills, but such as must mingle always
and necessarily in the lot of every slave. They are the essential ingredients, not the occasional results, of the system.

After all, I shall read your book with trembling for you. Some years ago, when you
were beginning to tell me your real name and birthplace, you may remember I stopped
you, and preferred to remain ignorant of all. With the exception of a vague description,
so I continued, till the other day, when you read me your memoirs. I hardly knew, at
the time, whether to thank you or not for the sight of them, when I reflected that it was
still dangerous, in Massachusetts, for honest men to tell their names! They say the fathers, in 1776, signed the Declaration of Independence with the halter about their
necks. You, too, publish your declaration of freedom with danger compassing you
around. In all the broad lands which the Constitution of the United States overshad-

[9] In 1834 Great Britain ended slavery in the
British West Indies.

ows, there is no single spot,—however narrow or desolate,—where a fugitive slave can plant himself and say, "I am safe." The whole armory of Northern Law has no shield for you. I am free to say that, in your place, I should throw the MS. into the fire.

You, perhaps, may tell your story in safety, endeared as you are to so many warm hearts by rare gifts, and a still rare devotion of them to the service of others. But it will be owing only to your labors, and the fearless efforts of those who, trampling the laws and Constitution of the country under their feet, are determined that they will "hide the outcast," and that their hearths shall be, spite of the law, an asylum for the oppressed, if, some time or other, the humblest may stand in our streets, and bear witness in safety against the cruelties of which he has been the victim.

Yet it is sad to think, that these very throbbing hearts which welcome your story, and form your best safeguard in telling it, are all beating contrary to the "statute in such case made and provided." Go on, my dear friend, till you, and those who, like you, have been saved, so as by fire, from the dark prisonhouse, shall stereotype these free, illegal pulses into statutes; and New England, cutting loose from a blood-stained Union, shall glory in being the house of refuge for the oppressed;—till we no longer merely "*hide* the outcast," or make a merit of standing idly by while he is hunted in our midst; but, con- secrating anew the soil of the Pilgrims as an asylum for the oppressed, proclaim our *welcome* to the slave so loudly, that the tones shall reach every hut in the Carolinas, and make the broken-hearted bondman leap up at the thought of old Massachusetts.

God speed the day!

Till then, and ever,
Yours truly,
WENDELL PHILLIPS

Chapter I

I was born in Tuckahoe, near Hillsborough, and about twelve miles from Easton, in Talbot county, Maryland. I have no accurate knowledge of my age, never having seen any authentic record containing it. By far the larger part of the slaves know as little of their ages as horses know of theirs, and it is the wish of most masters within my knowl- edge to keep their slaves thus ignorant. I do not remember to have ever met a slave who could tell of his birthday. They seldom come nearer to it than planting-time, harvest- time, cherry-time, spring-time, or fall-time. A want of information concerning my own was a source of unhappiness to me even during childhood. The white children could tell their ages. I could not tell why I ought to be deprived of the same privilege. I was not allowed to make any inquiries of my master concerning it. He deemed all such inquiries on the part of a slave improper and impertinent, and evidence of a restless spirit. The nearest estimate I can give makes me now between twenty-seven and twenty-eight years of age. I come to this, from hearing my master say, some time during 1835, I was about seventeen years old.

My mother was named Harriet Bailey. She was the daughter of Isaac and Betsey Bai- ley, both colored, and quite dark. My mother was of a darker complexion than either my grandmother or grandfather.

My father was a white man. He was admitted to be such by all I ever heard speak of my parentage. The opinion was also whispered that my master was my father; but of the correctness of this opinion, I know nothing; the means of knowing was withheld from me. My mother and I were separated when I was but an infant—before I knew her as my mother. It is a common custom, in the part of Maryland from which I ran away, to part children from their mothers at a very early age. Frequently, before the child has reached its twelfth month, its mother is taken from it, and hired out on some farm a considerable distance off, and the child is placed under the care of an old woman, too old for field labor. For what this separation is done, I do not know, unless it be to hinder the development of the child's affection toward its mother, and to blunt and destroy the natural affection of the mother for the child. This is the inevitable result.

I never saw my mother, to know her as such, more than four or five times in my life; and each of these times was very short in duration, and at night. She was hired by a Mr. Stewart, who lived about twelve miles from my home. She made her journeys to see me in the night, travelling the whole distance on foot, after the performance of her day's work. She was a field hand, and a whipping is the penalty of not being in the field at sunrise, unless a slave has special permission from his or her master to the contrary—a permission which they seldom get, and one that gives to him that gives it the proud name of being a kind master. I do not recollect of ever seeing my mother by the light of day. She was with me in the night. She would lie down with me, and get me to sleep, but long before I waked she was gone. Very little communication ever took place between us. Death soon ended what little we could have while she lived, and with it her hardships and suffering. She died when I was about seven years old, on one of my master's farms, near Lee's Mill. I was not allowed to be present during her illness, at her death, or burial. She was gone long before I knew anything about it. Never having enjoyed, to any considerable extent, her soothing presence, her tender and watchful care, I received the tidings of her death with much the same emotions I should have probably felt at the death of a stranger.

Called thus suddenly away, she left me without the slightest intimation of who my father was. The whisper that my master was my father, may or may not be true; and, true or false, it is of but little consequence to my purpose whilst the fact remains, in all its glaring odiousness, that slaveholders have ordained, and by law established, that the children of slave women shall in all cases follow the condition of their mothers; and this is done too obviously to administer to their own lusts, and make a gratification of their wicked desires profitable as well as pleasurable; for by this cunning arrangement, the slaveholder, in cases not a few, sustains to his slaves the double relation of master and father.

I know of such cases; and it is worthy of remark that such slaves invariably suffer greater hardships, and have more to contend with, than others. They are, in the first place, a constant offence to their mistress. She is ever disposed to find fault with them; they can seldom do any thing to please her; she is never better pleased than when she sees them under the lash, especially when she suspects her husband of showing to his mulatto children favors which he withholds from his black slaves. The master is frequently compelled to sell this class of his slaves, out of deference to the feelings of his white wife; and, cruel as the deed may strike any one to be, for a man to sell his own children to human flesh-mongers, it is often the dictate of humanity for him to do so; for, unless he does this, he must not only whip them himself, but must stand by and see one white son tie up his brother, of but few shades darker complexion than himself, and ply the gory lash to his naked back; and if he lisp one word of disapproval, it is set down to his parental partiality, and only makes a bad matter worse, both for himself and the slave whom he would protect and defend.

Every year brings with it multitudes of this class of slaves. It was doubtless in consequence of a knowledge of this fact, that one great statesman of the south predicted the downfall of slavery by the inevitable laws of population. Whether this prophecy is ever fulfilled or not, it is nevertheless plain that a very different-looking class of people are springing up at the south, and are now held in slavery, from those originally brought to this country from Africa; and if their increase will do no other good, it will do away the force of the argument, that God cursed Ham, and therefore American slavery is right.[10] If the lineal descendants of Ham are alone to be scripturally enslaved, it is certain that slavery at the south must soon become unscriptural; for thousands are ushered into the world, annually, who, like myself, owe their existence to white fathers, and those fathers most frequently their own masters.

I have had two masters. My first master's name was Anthony. I do not remember his first name. He was generally called Captain Anthony—a title which, I presume, he acquired by sailing a craft on the Chesapeake Bay. He was not considered a rich slaveholder. He owned two or three farms, and about thirty slaves. His farms and slaves were under the care of an overseer. The overseer's name was Plummer. Mr. Plummer was a miserable drunkard, a profane swearer, and a savage monster. He always went armed with a cowskin[11] and a heavy cudgel. I have known him to cut and slash the women's heads so horribly, that even master would be enraged at his cruelty, and would threaten to whip him if he did not mind himself. Master, however, was not a humane slaveholder. It required extraordinary barbarity on the part of an overseer to affect him. He was a cruel man, hardened by a long life of slaveholding. He would at times seem to take great pleasure in whipping a slave. I have often been awakened at the dawn of day by the most heartrending shrieks of an own aunt of mine, whom he used to tie up to a joist, and whip upon her naked back till she was literally covered with blood. No words, no tears, no prayers, from his gory victim, seemed to move his iron heart from its bloody purpose. The louder she screamed, the harder he whipped; and where the blood ran fastest, there he whipped longest. He would whip her to make her scream, and whip her to make her hush; and not until overcome by fatigue, would he cease to swing the blood-clotted cowskin. I remember the first time I ever witnessed this horrible exhibition. I was quite a child, but I well remember it. I never shall forget it whilst I remember any thing. It was the first of a long series of such outrages, of which I was doomed to be a witness and a participant. It struck me with awful force. It was the blood-stained gate, the entrance to the hell of slavery, through which I was about to pass. It was a most terrible spectacle. I wish I could commit to paper the feelings with which I beheld it.

This occurrence took place very soon after I went to live with my old master, and under the following circumstances. Aunt Hester went out one night,—where or for what I do not know,—and happened to be absent when my master desired her presence. He had ordered her not to go out evenings, and warned her that she must never let him

---

[10] Reference to Scripture (Genesis 9) telling of Noah's curse upon his son Ham that gave him over to slavery; used by Southern slave-holders as justification for keeping African Americans in bondage.

[11] Whip.

catch her in company with a young man, who was paying attention to her belonging to Colonel Lloyd. The young man's named was Ned Roberts, generally called Lloyd's Ned. Why master was so careful of her, may be safely left to conjecture. She was a woman of noble form, and of graceful proportions, having very few equals, and fewer superiors, in personal appearance, among the colored or white women of our neighborhood.

Aunt Hester had not only disobeyed his orders in going out, but had been found in company with Lloyd's Ned; which circumstance, I found, from what he said while whipping her, was the chief offence. Had he been a man of pure morals himself, he might have been thought interested in protecting the innocence of my aunt; but those who knew him will not suspect him of any such virtue. Before he commenced whipping Aunt Hester, he took her into the kitchen, and stripped her from neck to waist, leaving her neck, shoulders, and back, entirely naked. He then told her to cross her hands, calling her at the same time a d—d b—h. After crossing her hands, he tied them with a strong rope, and led her to a stool under a large hook in the joist, put in for the purpose. He made her get upon the stool, and tied her hands to the hook. She now stood fair for his infernal purpose. Her arms were stretched up at their full length, so that she stood upon the ends of her toes. He then said to her, "Now, you d—d b—h, I'll learn you how to disobey my orders!" and after rolling up his sleeves, he commenced to lay on the heavy cowskin, and soon the warm, red blood (amid heart-rending shrieks from her, and horrid oaths from him) came dripping to the floor. I was so terrified and horror-stricken at the sight, that I hid myself in a closet, and dared not venture out till long after the bloody transaction was over. I expected it would be my turn next. It was all new to me. I had never seen any thing like it before. I had always lived with my grandmother on the outskirts of the plantation, where she was put to raise the children of the younger women. I had therefore been, until now, out of the way of the bloody scenes that often occurred on the plantation.

Chapter II

My master's family consisted of two sons, Andrew and Richard; one daughter, Lucretia, and her husband, Captain Thomas Auld. They lived in one house, upon the home plantation of Colonel Edward Lloyd. My master was Colonel Lloyd's clerk and superintendent. He was what might be called the overseer of the overseers. I spent two years of childhood on this plantation in my old master's family. It was here that I witnessed the bloody transaction recorded in the first chapter; and as I received my first impressions of slavery on this plantation, I will give some description of it, and of slavery as it there existed. The plantation is about twelve miles north of Easton, in Talbot county, and is situated on the border of Miles River. The principal products raised upon it were tobacco, corn, and wheat. These were raised in great abundance; so that, with the products of this and the other farms belonging to him, he was able to keep in almost constant employment a large sloop, in carrying them to market at Baltimore. This sloop was named Sally Lloyd, in honor of one of the colonel's daughters. My master's son-in-law, Captain Auld, was master of the vessel; she was otherwise manned by the colonel's own slaves. Their names were Peter, Isaac, Rich, and Jake. These were esteemed very highly by the other slaves, and looked upon as the privileged ones of the plantation; for it was no small affair, in the eyes of the slaves, to be allowed to see Baltimore.

Colonel Lloyd kept from three to four hundred slaves on his home plantation, and owned a large number more on the neighboring farms belonging to him. The names of the farms nearest to the home plantation were Wye Town and New Design. "Wye Town" was under the overseership of a man named Noah Willis. New Design was under the overseership of a Mr. Townsend. The overseers of these, and all the rest of the farms, numbering over twenty, received advice and direction from the managers of the home plantation. This was the great business place. It was the seat of government for the whole twenty farms. All disputes among the overseers were settled here. If a slave was convicted of any high misdemeanor, became unmanageable, or evinced a determination to run away, he was brought immediately here, severely whipped, put on board the sloop, carried to Baltimore, and sold to Austin Woolfolk, or some other slave-trader, as a warning to the slaves remaining.

Here, too, the slaves of all the other farms received their monthly allowance of food, and their yearly clothing. The men and women slaves received, as their monthly allowance of food, eight pounds of pork, or its equivalent in fish, and one bushel of corn meal. Their yearly clothing consisted of two coarse linen shirts, one pair of linen trousers, like the shirts, one jacket, one pair of trousers for winter, made of coarse negro cloth, one pair of stockings, and one pair of shoes; the whole of which could not have cost more than seven dollars. The allowance of the slave children was given to their mothers, or the old women having the care of them. The children unable to work in the field had neither shoes, stockings, jackets, nor trousers, given to them; their clothing consisted of two coarse linen shirts per year. When these failed them, they went naked until the next allowance-day. Children from seven to ten years old, of both sexes, almost naked, might be seen at all seasons of the year.

There were no beds given the slaves, unless one coarse blanket be considered such, and none but the men and women had these. This, however, is not considered a very great privation. They find less difficulty from the want of beds, than from the want of time to sleep; for when their day's work in the field is done, the most of them having their washing, mending, and cooking to do, and having few or none of the ordinary facilities for doing either of these, very many of their sleeping hours are consumed in preparing for the field the coming day; and when this is done, old and young, male and female, married and single, drop down side by side, on one common bed,—the cold, damp floor,—each covering himself or herself with their miserable blankets; and here they sleep till they are summoned to the field by the driver's horn. At the sound of this, all must rise, and be off to the field. There must be no halting; every one must be at his or her post; and woe betides them who hear not this morning summons to the field; for if they are not awakened by the sense of hearing, they are by the sense of feeling: no age nor sex finds any favor. Mr. Severe, the overseer, used to stand by the door of the quarter, armed with a large hickory stick and heavy cowskin, ready to whip any one who was so unfortunate as not to hear, or, from any other cause, was prevented from being ready to start for the field at the sound of the horn.

Mr. Severe was rightly named: he was a cruel man. I have seen him whip a woman, causing the blood to run half an hour at the time; and this, too, in the midst of her crying children, pleading for their mother's release. He seemed to take pleasure in manifesting his fiendish barbarity. Added to his cruelty, he was a profane swearer. It was enough to chill the blood and stiffen the hair of an ordinary man to hear him talk.

Scarce a sentence escaped him but that was commenced or concluded by some horrid oath. The field was the place to witness his cruelty and profanity. His presence made it both the field of blood and of blasphemy. From the rising till the going down of the sun, he was cursing, raving, cutting, and slashing among the slaves of the field, in the most frightful manner. His career was short. He died very soon after I went to Colonel Lloyd's; and he died as he lived, uttering, with his dying groans, bitter curses and horrid oaths. His death was regarded by the slaves as the result of a merciful providence.

Mr. Severe's place was filled by a Mr. Hopkins. He was a very different man. He was less cruel, less profane, and made less noise, than Mr. Severe. His course was character- ized by no extraordinary demonstrations of cruelty. He whipped, but seemed to take no pleasure in it. He was called by the slaves a good overseer.

The home plantation of Colonel Lloyd wore the appearance of a country village. All the mechanical operations for all the farms were performed here. The shoemaking and mending, the black-smithing, cartwrighting, coopering, weaving, and grain-grinding, were all performed by the slaves on the home plantation. The whole place wore a busi- ness-like aspect very unlike the neighboring farms. The number of houses, too, con- spired to give it advantage over the neighboring farms. It was called by the slaves the *Great House Farm.* Few privileges were esteemed higher, by the slaves of the out-farms, than that of being selected to do errands at the Great House Farm. It was associated in their minds with greatness. A representative could not be prouder of his election to a seat in the American Congress, than a slave on one of the out-farms would be of his election to do errands at the Great House Farm. They regarded it as evidence of great confidence reposed in them by their overseers; and it was on this account, as well as a constant desire to be out of the field from under the driver's lash, that they esteemed it a high privilege, one worth careful living for. He was called the smartest and most trusty fellow, who had this honor conferred upon him the most frequently. The competitors for this office sought as diligently to please their overseers, as the office-seekers in the political parties seek to please and deceive the people. The same traits of character might be seen in Colonel Lloyd's slaves, as are seen in the slaves of the political parties.

The slaves selected to go to the Great House Farm, for the monthly allowance for themselves and their fellow-slaves, were peculiarly enthusiastic. While on their way, they would make the dense old woods, for miles around, reverberate with their wild songs, revealing at once the highest joy and the deepest sadness. They would compose and sing as they went along, consulting neither time nor tune. The thought that came up, came out—if not in the word, in the sound;—and as frequently in the one as in the other. They would sometimes sing the most pathetic sentiment in the most rapturous tone, and the most rapturous sentiment in the most pathetic tone. Into all of their songs they would manage to weave something of the Great House Farm. Especially would they do this, when leaving home. They would then sing most exultingly the following words:

> "I am going away to the Great House Farm!
> O, yea! O, yea! O!"

This they would sing, as a chorus, to words which to many would seem unmeaning jar- gon, but which, nevertheless, were full of meaning to themselves. I have sometimes thought that the mere hearing of those songs would do more to impress some minds with the horrible character of slavery, than the reading of whole volumes of philosophy on the subject could do.

I did not, when a slave, understand the deep meaning of those rude and apparently incoherent songs. I was myself within the circle; so that I neither saw nor heard as those without might see and hear. They told a tale of woe which was then altogether beyond my feeble comprehension; they were tones loud, long, and deep; they breathed the prayer and complaint of souls boiling over with the bitterest anguish. Every tone was a testimony against slavery, and a prayer to God for deliverance from chains. The hearing of those wild notes always depressed my spirit, and filled me with ineffable sadness. I have frequently found myself in tears while hearing them. The mere recurrence to those songs, even now, afflicts me; and while I am writing these lines, an expression of feeling has already found its way down my cheek. To those songs I trace my first glimmering conception of the dehumanizing character of slavery. I can never get rid of that conception. Those songs still follow me, to deepen my hatred of slavery, and quicken my sympathies for my brethren in bonds. If any one wishes to be impressed with the soul-killing effects of slavery, let him go to Colonel Lloyd's plantation, and, on allowance-day, place himself in the deep pine woods, and there let him, in silence analyze the sounds that shall pass through the chambers of his soul,—and if he is not thus impressed, it will only be because "there is no flesh in his obdurate heart."

I have often been utterly astonished, since I came to the north, to find persons who could speak of the singing, among slaves, as evidence of their contentment and happiness. It is impossible to conceive of a greater mistake. Slaves sing most when they are most unhappy. The songs of the slave represent the sorrows of his heart; and he is relieved by them, only as an aching heart is relieved by its tears. At least, such is my experience. I have often sung to drown my sorrow, but seldom to express my happiness. Crying for joy, and singing for joy, were alike uncommon to me while in the jaws of slavery. The singing of a man cast away upon a desolate island might be as appropriately considered as evidence of contentment and happiness, as the singing of a slave; the songs of the one and of the other are prompted by the same emotion.

Chapter III

Colonel Lloyd kept a large and finely cultivated garden, which afforded almost constant employment for four men, besides the chief gardener, (Mr. M'Durmond.) This garden was probably the greatest attraction of the place. During the summer months, people came from far and near—from Baltimore, Easton, and Annapolis—to see it. It abounded in fruits of almost every description, from the hardy apple of the north to the delicate orange of the south. This garden was not the least source of trouble on the plantation. Its excellent fruit was quite a temptation to the hungry swarms of boys, as well as the older slaves, belonging to the colonel, few of whom had the virtue or the vice to resist it. Scarcely a day passed, during the summer, but that some slave had to take the lash for stealing fruit. The colonel had to resort to all kinds of stratagems to keep his slaves out of the garden. The last and most successful one was that of tarring his fence all around, after which, if a slave was caught with any tar upon his person, it was deemed sufficient proof that he had either been into the garden, or had tried to get in.

In either case, he was severely whipped by the chief gardener. This plan worked well; the slaves became as fearful of tar as of the lash. They seemed to realize the impossibility of touching *tar* without being defiled.

The colonel also kept a splendid riding equipage. His stable and carriage-house presented the appearance of some of our large city livery establishments. His horses were of the finest form and noblest blood. His carriage-house contained three splendid coaches, three or four gigs, besides dearborns and barouches of the most fashionable style.[12]

This establishment was under the care of two slaves—old Barney and young Barney—father and son. To attend to this establishment was their sole work. But it was by no means an easy employment; for in nothing was Colonel Lloyd more particular than in the management of his horses. The slightest inattention to these was unpardonable, and was visited upon those, under whose care they were placed, with the severest punishment; no excuse could shield them, if the colonel only suspected any want of attention to his horses—a supposition which he frequently indulged, and one which, of course, made the office of old and young Barney a very trying one. They never knew when they were safe from punishment. They were frequently whipped when least deserving, and escaped whipping when most deserving it. Every thing depended upon the looks of the horses, and the state of Colonel Lloyd's own mind when his horses were brought to him for use. If a horse did not move fast enough, or hold his head high enough, it was owing to some fault of his keepers. It was painful to stand near the stable-door, and hear the various complaints against the keepers when a horse was taken out for use. "This horse has not had proper attention. He has not been sufficiently rubbed and curried, or he has not been properly fed; his food was too wet or too dry; he got it too soon or too late; he was too hot or too cold; he had too much hay, and not enough of grain; or he had too much grain, and not enough of hay; instead of old Barney's attending to the horse, he had very improperly left it to his son." To all these complaints, no matter how unjust, the slave must answer never a word. Colonel Lloyd could not brook any contradiction from a slave. When he spoke, a slave must stand, listen, and tremble; and such was literally the case. I have seen Colonel Lloyd make old Barney, a man between fifty and sixty years of age, uncover his bald head, kneel down upon the cold, damp ground, and receive upon his naked and toil-worn shoulders more than thirty lashes at the time. Colonel Lloyd had three sons—Edward, Murray, and Daniel,—and three sons-in-law, Mr. Winder, Mr. Nicholson, and Mr. Lowndes. All of these lived at the Great House Farm, and enjoyed the luxury of whipping the servants when they pleased, from old Barney down to William Wilkes, the coach-driver. I have seen Winder make one of the house-servants stand off from him a suitable distance to be touched with the end of his whip, and at every stroke raise great ridges upon his back.

To describe the wealth of Colonel Lloyd would be almost equal to describing the riches of Job.[13] He kept from ten to fifteen house-servants. He was said to own a thousand slaves, and I think this estimate quite within the truth. Colonel Lloyd owned so many that he did not know them when he saw them; nor did all the slaves of the out-farms know him. It is reported of him, that, while riding along the road one day, he met a colored man, and addressed him in the usual manner of speaking to colored people

---

12 Coaches, gigs, dearborns, and barouches are horse-drawn conveyances.
13 Biblical figure of great wealth whose faith in

God is later tested when stripped of his possessions.

on the public highways of the south: "Well, boy, whom do you belong to?" "To Colonel Lloyd," replied the slave. "Well, does the colonel treat you well?" "No, sir," was the ready reply. "What, does he work you too hard?" "Yes, sir." "Well, don't he give you enough to eat?" "Yes, sir, he gives me enough, such as it is."

The colonel, after ascertaining where the slave belonged, rode on; the man also went on about his business, not dreaming that he had been conversing with his master. He thought, said, and heard nothing more of the matter, until two or three weeks afterwards. The poor man was then informed by his overseer that, for having found fault with his master, he was now to be sold to a Georgia trader. He was immediately chained and handcuffed; and thus, without a moment's warning, he was snatched away, and forever sundered, from his family and friends, by a hand more unrelenting than death. This is the penalty of telling the truth, of telling the simple truth, in answer to a series of plain questions.

It is partly in consequence of such facts, that slaves, when inquired of as to their condition and the character of their masters, almost universally say they are contented, and that their masters are kind. The slaveholders have been known to send in spies among their slaves, to ascertain their views and feelings in regard to their condition. The frequency of this has had the effect to establish among the slaves the maxim, that a still tongue makes a wise head. They suppress the truth rather than take the consequences of telling it, and in so doing prove themselves a part of the human family. If they have any thing to say of their masters, it is generally in their masters' favor, especially when speaking to an untried man. I have been frequently asked, when a slave, if I had a kind master, and do not remember ever to have given a negative answer; nor did I, in pursuing this course, consider myself as uttering what was absolutely false; for I always measured the kindness of my master by the standard of kindness set up among slaveholders around us. Moreover, slaves are like other people, and imbibe prejudices quite common to others. They think their own better than that of others. Many, under the influence of this prejudice, think their own masters are better than the masters of other slaves; and this, too, in some cases, when the very reverse is true. Indeed, it is not uncommon for slaves even to fall out and quarrel among themselves about the relative goodness of their masters, each contending for the superior goodness of his own over that of the others. At the very same time, they mutually execrate their masters when viewed separately. It was so on our plantation. When Colonel Lloyd's slaves met the slaves of Jacob Jepson, they seldom parted without a quarrel about their masters; Colonel Lloyd's slaves contending that he was the richest, and Mr. Jepson's slaves that he was the smartest, and most of a man. Colonel Lloyd's slaves would boast his ability to buy and sell Jacob Jepson. Mr. Jepson's slaves would boast his ability to whip Colonel Lloyd. These quarrels would almost always end in a fight between the parties, and those that whipped were supposed to have gained the point at issue. They seemed to think that the greatness of their masters was transferable to themselves. It was considered as being bad enough to be a slave; but to be a poor man's slave was deemed a disgrace indeed!

Chapter IV

Mr. Hopkins remained but a short time in the office of overseer. Why his career was so short, I do not know, but suppose he lacked the necessary severity to suit Colonel Lloyd. Mr. Hopkins was succeeded by Mr. Austin Gore, a man possessing, in an eminent degree, all those traits of character indispensable to what is called a first-rate overseer. Mr. Gore had served Colonel Lloyd, in the capacity of overseer, upon one of the out-farms, and had shown himself worthy of the high station of overseer upon the home or Great House Farm.

Mr. Gore was proud, ambitious, and persevering. He was artful, cruel, and obdurate. He was just the man for such a place, and it was just the place for such a man. It afforded scope for the full exercise of all his powers, and he seemed to be perfectly at home in it. He was one of those who could torture the slightest look, word, or gesture, on the part of the slave, into impudence, and would treat it accordingly. There must be no answering back to him; no explanation was allowed a slave, showing himself to have been wrongfully accused. Mr. Gore acted fully up to the maxim laid down by slaveholders,—"It is better that a dozen slaves suffer under the lash, than that the overseer should be convicted, in the presence of the slaves, of having been at fault." No matter how innocent a slave might be—it availed him nothing, when accused by Mr. Gore of any misdemeanor. To be accused was to be convicted, and to be convicted was to be punished; the one always following the other with immutable certainty. To escape punishment was to escape accusation; and few slaves had the fortune to do either, under the overseership of Mr. Gore. He was just proud enough to demand the most debasing homage of the slave, and quite servile enough to crouch, himself, at the feet of the master. He was ambitious enough to be contented with nothing short of the highest rank of overseers, and persevering enough to reach the height of his ambition. He was cruel enough to inflict the severest punishment, artful enough to descend to the lowest trickery, and obdurate enough to be insensible to the voice of a reproving conscience. He was, of all the overseers, the most dreaded by the slaves. His presence was painful; his eye flashed confusion; and seldom was his sharp, shrill voice heard, without producing horror and trembling in their ranks.

Mr. Gore was a grave man, and, though a young man, he indulged in no jokes, said no funny words, seldom smiled. His words were in perfect keeping with his looks, and his looks were in perfect keeping with his words. Overseers will sometimes indulge in a witty word, even with the slaves; not so with Mr. Gore. He spoke but to command, and commanded but to be obeyed; he dealt sparingly with his words, and bountifully with his whip, never using the former where the latter would answer as well. When he whipped, he seemed to do so from a sense of duty, and feared no consequences. He did nothing reluctantly, no matter how disagreeable; always at his post, never inconsistent. He never promised but to fulfil. He was, in a word, a man of the most inflexible firmness and stone-like coolness.

His savage barbarity was equalled only by the consummate coolness with which he committed the grossest and most savage deeds upon the slaves under his charge. Mr. Gore once undertook to whip one of Colonel Lloyd's slaves, by the name of Demby. He had given Demby but few stripes, when, to get rid of the scourging, he ran and plunged himself into a creek, and stood there at the depth of his shoulders, refusing to come out. Mr. Gore told him that he would give him three calls, and that, if he did not come out at the third call, he would shoot him. The first call was given. Demby made no response, but stood his ground. The second and third calls were given with the same result. Mr. Gore then, without consultation or deliberation with any one, not even giving Demby an additional call, raised his musket to his face, taking deadly aim at his standing victim, and in an instant poor Demby was no more. His mangled body sank out of sight, and blood and brains marked the water where he had stood.

A thrill of horror flashed through every soul upon the plantation, excepting Mr. Gore. He alone seemed cool and collected. He was asked by Colonel Lloyd and my old master, why he resorted to this extraordinary expedient. His reply was, (as well as I can remember,) that Demby had become unmanageable. He was setting a dangerous example to the other slaves,—one which, if suffered to pass without some such demonstration on his part, would finally lead to the total subversion of all rule and order upon the plantation. He argued that if one slave refused to be corrected, and escaped with his life, the other slaves would soon copy the example; the result of which would be, the freedom of the slaves, and the enslavement of the whites. Mr. Gore's defence was satisfactory. He was continued in his station as overseer upon the home plantation. His fame as an overseer went abroad. His horrid crime was not even submitted to judicial investigation. It was committed in the presence of slaves, and they of course could neither institute a suit, nor testify against him; and thus the guilty perpetrator of one of the bloodiest and most foul murders goes unwhipped of justice, and uncensured by the community in which he lives. Mr. Gore lived in St. Michael's, Talbot county, Maryland, when I left there; and if he is still alive, he very probably lives there now; and if so, he is now, as he was then, as highly esteemed and as much respected as though his guilty soul had not been stained with his brother's blood.

I speak advisedly when I say this,—that killing a slave, or any colored person, in Talbot county, Maryland, is not treated as a crime, either by the courts or the community. Mr. Thomas Lanman, of St Michael's, killed two slaves, one of whom he killed with a hatchet, by knocking his brains out. He used to boast of the commission of the awful and bloody deed. I have heard him do so laughingly, saying, among other things, that he was the only benefactor of his country in the company, and that when others would do as much as he had done, we should be relieved of "the d——d niggers."

The wife of Mr. Giles Hicks, living but a short distance from where I used to live, murdered my wife's cousin, a young girl between fifteen and sixteen years of age, mangling her person in the most horrible manner, breaking her nose and breastbone with a stick, so that the poor girl expired in a few hours afterward. She was immediately buried, but had not been in her untimely grave but a few hours before she was taken up and examined by the coroner, who decided that she had come to her death by severe beating. The offence for which this girl was thus murdered was this:—She had been set that night to mind Mrs. Hicks's baby, and during the night she fell asleep, and the baby cried. She, having lost her rest for several night previous, did not hear the crying. They were both in the room with Mrs. Hicks. Mrs. Hicks, finding the girl slow to move, jumped from her bed, seized an oak stick of wood by the fireplace, and with it broke the girl's nose and breastbone, and thus ended her life. I will not say that this most horrid murder produced no sensation in the community. It did produce sensation, but not enough to bring the murderess to punishment. There was a warrant issued for her arrest, but it was never served. Thus she escaped not only punishment, but even the pain of being arraigned before a court for her horrid crime.

Whilst I am detailing bloody deeds which took place during my stay on Colonel Lloyd's plantation, I will briefly narrate another, which occurred about the same time as the murder of Demby by Mr. Gore.

Colonel Lloyd's slaves were in the habit of spending a part of their nights and Sundays in fishing for oysters, and in this way made up the deficiency of their scanty allowance. An old man belonging to Colonel Lloyd, while thus engaged, happened to get beyond the limits of Colonel Lloyd's, and on the premises of Mr. Beal Bondly. At this trespass, Mr. Bondly took offence, and with his musket came down to the shore, and blew its deadly contents into the poor old man.

Mr. Bondly came over to see Colonel Lloyd the next day, whether to pay him for his property, or to justify himself in what he had done, I know not. At any rate, this whole fiendish transaction was soon hushed up. There was very little said about it at all, and nothing done. It was a common saying, even among little white boys, that it was worth a half-cent to kill a "nigger," and a half-cent to bury one.

Chapter V

As to my own treatment while I lived on Colonel Lloyd's plantation, it was very similar to that of the other slave children. I was not old enough to work in the field, and there being little else than field work to do, I had a great deal of leisure time. The most I had to do was to drive up the cows at evening, keep the fowls out of the garden, keep the front yard clean, and run of errands for my old master's daughter, Mrs. Lucretia Auld. The most of my leisure time I spent in helping Master Daniel Lloyd in finding his birds, after he had shot them. My connection with Master Daniel was of some advantage to me. He became quite attached to me, and was a sort of protector of me. He would not allow the older boys to impose upon me, and would divide his cakes with me.

I was seldom whipped by my old master, and suffered little from any thing else than hunger and cold. I suffered much from hunger, but much more from cold. In hottest summer and coldest winter, I was kept almost naked—no shoes, no stockings, no jacket, no trousers, nothing on but a coarse tow linen shirt, reaching only to my knees. I had no bed. I must have perished with cold, but that, the coldest nights, I used to steal a bag which was used for carrying corn to the mill. I would crawl into this bag, and there sleep on the cold, damp, clay floor, with my head in and feet out. My feet have been so cracked with the frost, that the pen with which I am writing might be laid in the gashes.

We were not regularly allowanced. Our food was coarse corn meal boiled. This was called *mush*. It was put into a large wooden tray or trough, and set down upon the ground. The children were then called, like so many pigs, and like so many pigs they would come and devour the mush; some with oyster-shells, others with pieces of shingle, some with naked hands, and none with spoons. He that ate fastest got most; he that was strongest secured the best place; and few left the trough satisfied.

I was probably between seven and eight years old when I left Colonel Lloyd's plantation. I left it with joy. I shall never forget the ecstasy with which I received the intelligence that my old master (Anthony) had determined to let me go to Baltimore, to live with Mr. Hugh Auld, brother to my old master's son-in-law, Captain Thomas Auld. I received this information about three days before my departure. They were three of the happiest days I ever enjoyed. I spent the most part of all these three days in the creek, washing off the plantation scurf, and preparing myself for my departure.

The pride of appearance which this would indicate was not my own. I spent the time in washing, not so much because I wished to, but because Mrs. Lucretia had told me I must get all the dead skin off my feet and knees before I could go to Baltimore; for the people in Baltimore were very cleanly, and would laugh at me if I looked dirty. Besides, she was going to give me a pair of trousers, which I should not put on unless I got all the dirt off me. The thought of owning a pair of trousers was great indeed! It was almost a sufficient motive, not only to make me take off what would be called by pigdrovers the mange, but the skin itself. I went at it in good earnest, working for the first time with the hope of reward.

The ties that ordinarily bind children to their homes were all suspended in my case. I found no severe trial in my departure. My home was charmless; it was not home to me; on parting from it, I could not feel that I was leaving any thing which I could have enjoyed by staying. My mother was dead, my grandmother lived far off, so that I seldom saw her. I had two sisters and one brother, that lived in the same house with me; but the early separation of us from our mother had well nigh blotted the fact of our relationship from our memories. I looked for home elsewhere, and was confident of finding none which I should relish less than the one which I was leaving. If, however, I found in my new home hardship, hunger, whipping, and nakedness, I had the consolation that I should not have escaped any one of them by staying. Having already had more than a taste of them in the house of my old master, and having endured them there, I very naturally inferred my ability to endure them elsewhere, and especially at Baltimore; for I had something of the feeling about Baltimore that is expressed in the proverb, that "being hanged in England is preferable to dying a natural death in Ireland." I had the strongest desire to see Baltimore. Cousin Tom, though not fluent in speech, had inspired me with that desire by his eloquent description of the place. I could never point out any thing at the Great House, no matter how beautiful or powerful, but that he had seen something at Baltimore far exceeding, both in beauty and strength, the object which I pointed out to him. Even the Great House itself, with all its pictures, was far inferior to many buildings in Baltimore. So strong was my desire, that I thought a gratification of it would fully compensate for whatever loss of comforts I should sustain by the exchange. I left without a regret, and with the highest hopes of future happiness.

We sailed out of Miles River for Baltimore on a Saturday morning. I remember only the day of the week, for at that time I had no knowledge of the days of the month, nor the months of the year. On setting sail, I walked aft, and gave to Colonel Lloyd's plantation what I hoped would be the last look. I then placed myself in the bows of the sloop, and there spent the remainder of the day in looking ahead, interesting myself in what was in the distance rather than in things near by or behind.

In the afternoon of that day, we reached Annapolis, the capital of the State. We stopped but a few moments, so that I had no time to go on shore. It was the first large town that I had ever seen, and though it would look small compared with some of our New England factory villages, I thought it a wonderful place for its size—more imposing even than the Great House Farm!

We arrived at Baltimore early on Sunday morning, landing at Smith's Wharf, not far from Bowley's Wharf. We had on board the sloop a large flock of sheep; and after aiding in driving them to the slaughterhouse of Mr. Curtis on Louden Slater's Hill, I was conducted by Rich, one of the hands belonging on board of the sloop to my new home in Alliciana Street, near Mr. Gardner's ship-yard, on Fells Point.

Mr. and Mrs. Auld were both at home, and met me at the door with their little son Thomas, to take care of whom I had been given. And here I saw what I had never seen before; it was a white face beaming with the most kindly emotions; it was the face of my new mistress, Sophia Auld. I wish I could describe the rapture that flashed through my soul as I beheld it. It was a new and strange sight to me, brightening up my pathway with the light of happiness. Little Thomas was told, there was his Freddy,—and I was told to take care of little Thomas; and thus I entered upon the duties of my new home with the most cheering prospect ahead.

I looked upon my departure from Colonel Lloyd's plantation as one of the most interesting events of my life. It is possible, and even quite probable, that but for the mere circumstance of being removed from that plantation to Baltimore, I should have to-day, instead of being here seated by my own table, in the enjoyment of freedom and the happiness of home, writing this Narrative, been confined in the galling chains of slavery. Going to live at Baltimore laid the foundation, and opened the gateway, to all my subsequent prosperity. I have ever regarded it as the first plain manifestation of that kind providence which has ever since attended me, and marked my life with so many favors. I regarded the selection of myself as being somewhat remarkable. There were a number of slave children that might have been sent from the plantation to Baltimore. There were those younger, those older, and those of the same age. I was chosen from among them all, and was the first, last, and only choice.

I may be deemed superstitious, and even egotistical, in regarding this event as a special interposition of divine Providence in my favor. But I should be false to the earliest sentiments of my soul, if I suppressed the opinion. I prefer to be true to myself, even at the hazard of incurring the ridicule of others, rather than to be false, and incur my own abhorrence. From my earliest recollection, I date the entertainment of a deep conviction that slavery would not always be able to hold me within its foul embrace; and in the darkest hours of my career in slavery, this living word of faith and spirit of hope departed [not] from me, but remained like ministering angels to cheer me through the gloom. This good spirit was from God, and to him I offer thanksgiving and praise.

Chapter VI

My new mistress proved to be all she appeared when I first met her at the door,—a woman of the kindest heart and finest feelings. She had never had a slave under her control previously to myself, and prior to her marriage she had been dependent upon her own industry for a living. She was by trade a weaver; and by constant application to her business, she had been in a good degree preserved from the blighting and dehumanizing effects of slavery. I was utterly astonished at her goodness. I scarcely knew how to behave towards her. She was entirely unlike any other white woman I had ever seen. I could not approach her as I was accustomed to approach other white ladies. My early instruction was all out of place. The crouching servility, usually so acceptable a quality in a slave, did not answer when manifested toward her. Her favor was not gained by it; she seemed to be disturbed by it. She did not deem it impudent or unmannerly for a slave to look her in the face. The meanest slave was put fully at ease in her presence, and none left without feeling better for having seen her. Her face was made of heavenly smiles, and her voice of tranquil music.

But, alas! this kind heart had but a short time to remain such. The fatal poison of irresponsible power was already in her hands, and soon commenced its infernal work. That cheerful eye, under the influence of slavery, soon became red with rage; that voice, made all of sweet accord, changed to one of harsh and horrid discord; and that angelic face gave place to that of a demon.

Very soon after I went to live with Mr. and Mrs. Auld, she was kindly commenced to teach me the A, B, C. After I had learned this, she assisted me in learning to spell words of three or four letters. Just at this point of my progress, Mr. Auld found out what was going on, and at once forbade Mrs. Auld to instruct me further, telling her, among other things, that it was unlawful,[14] as well as unsafe, to teach a slave to read. To use his own words further, he said, "If you give a nigger an inch, he will take an ell. A nigger should know nothing but to obey his master—to do as he is told to do. Learning would *spoil* the best nigger in the world. Now," said he, "if you teach that nigger (speaking of myself) how to read, there would be no keeping him. It would forever unfit him to be a slave. He would at once become unmanageable, and of no value to his master. As to himself, it could do him no good, but a great deal of harm. It would make him discontented and unhappy." These words sank deep into my heart, stirred up sentiments within that lay slumbering, and called into existence an entirely new train of thought. It was a new and special revelation, explaining dark and mysterious things, with which my youthful understanding had struggled, but struggled in vain. I now understood what had been to me a most perplexing difficulty—to wit, the white man's power to enslave the black man. It was a grand achievement, and I prized it highly. From that moment, I understood the pathway from slavery to freedom. It was just what I wanted, and I got it at a time when I the least expected it. Whilst I was saddened by the thought of losing the aid of my kind mistress, I was gladdened by the invaluable instruction which, by the merest accident, I had gained from my master. Though conscious of the difficulty of learning without a teacher, I set out with high hope, and a fixed purpose, at whatever cost of trouble, to learn how to read. The very decided manner with which he spoke, and strove to impress his wife with the evil consequences of giving me instruction, served to convince me that he was deeply sensible of the truths he was uttering. It gave me the best assurance that I might rely with the utmost confidence on the results which, he said, would flow from teaching me to read. What he most dreaded, that I most desired. What he most loved, that I most hated. That which to him was a great evil, to be carefully shunned, was to me a great good, to be diligently sought; and the argument which he so warmly urged, against my learning to read, only served to inspire me with a desire and determination to learn. In learning to read, I owe almost as much to the bitter opposition of my master, as to the kindly aid of my mistress. I acknowledge the benefit of both.

I had resided but a short time in Baltimore before I observed a marked difference, in the treatment of slaves, from that which I had witnessed in the country. A city slave is almost a freeman, compared with a slave on the plantation. He is much better fed and clothed, and enjoys privileges altogether unknown to the slave on the plantation. There is a vestige of decency, a sense of shame, that does much to curb and check those outbreaks of atrocious cruelty so commonly enacted upon the plantation. He is a desperate slaveholder, who will shock the humanity of his nonslaveholding neighbors with the cries of his lacerated slave. Few are willing to incur the odium attaching to the reputation of being a cruel master; and above all things, they would not be known as not giving a slave enough to eat. Every city slaveholder is anxious to have it known of him, that he feeds his slaves well; and it is due to them to say, that most of them do give their slaves enough to eat. There are, however, some painful exceptions to this rule. Directly

---

[14] The reading instruction of slaves was considered an illegal act in many southern states.

opposite to us, on Philpot Street, lived Mr. Thomas Hamilton. He owned two slaves. Their names were Henrietta and Mary. Henrietta was about twenty-two years of age, Mary was about fourteen; and of all the mangled and emaciated creatures I ever looked upon, these two were the most so. His heart must be harder than stone, that could look upon these unmoved. The head, neck, and shoulders of Mary were literally cut to pieces. I have frequently felt her head, and found it nearly covered with festering sores, caused by the lash of her cruel mistress. I do not know that her master ever whipped her, but I have been an eye-witness to the cruelty of Mrs. Hamilton. I used to be in Mr. Hamilton's house nearly every day. Mrs. Hamilton used to sit in a large chair in the middle of the room, with a heavy cowskin always by her side, and scarce an hour passed during the day but was marked by the blood of one of these slaves. The girls seldom passed her without her saying, "Move faster, you *black gip!*" at the same time giving them a blow with the cowskin over the head or shoulders, often drawing the blood. She would then say, "Take that, you *black gip!*"—continuing, "If you don't move faster, I'll move you!" Added to the cruel lashings to which these slaves were subjected, they were kept nearly half-starved. They seldom knew what it was to eat a full meal. I have seen Mary contending with the pigs for the offal thrown into the street. So much was Mary kicked and cut to pieces, that she was oftener called *"pecked"* than by her name.

Chapter VII

I lived in Master Hugh's family about seven years. During this time, I succeeded in learning to read and write. In accomplishing this, I was compelled to resort to various stratagems. I had no regular teacher. My mistress, who had kindly commenced to instruct me, had, in compliance with the advice and direction of her husband, not only ceased to instruct, but had set her face against my being instructed by any one else. It is due, however, to my mistress to say of her, that she did not adopt this course of treatment immediately. She at first lacked the depravity indispensable to shutting me up in mental darkness. It was at least necessary for her to have some training in the exercise of irresponsible power, to make her equal to the task of treating me as though I were a brute.

My mistress was, as I have said, a kind and tender-hearted woman; and in the simplicity of her soul she commenced, when I first went to live with her, to treat me as she supposed one human being ought to treat another. In entering upon the duties of a slaveholder, she did not seem to perceive that I sustained to her the relation of a mere chattel, and that for her to treat me as a human being was not only wrong, but dangerously so. Slavery proved as injurious to her as it did to me. When I went there, she was a pious, warm, and tender-hearted woman. There was no sorrow or suffering for which she had not a tear. She had bread for the hungry, clothes for the naked, and comfort for every mourner that came within her reach. Slavery soon proved its ability to divest her of these heavenly qualities. Under its influence, the tender heart became stone, and the lamblike disposition gave way to one of tigerlike fierceness. The first step in her downward course was in her ceasing to instruct me. She now commenced to practise her husband's precepts. She finally became even more violent in her opposition than her husband himself. She was not satisfied with simply doing as well as he had commanded; she seemed anxious to do better. Nothing seemed to make her more angry than to see me with a newspaper. She seemed to think that here lay the danger. I have had her rush at me with a face made all up of fury, and snatch from me a newspaper, in a manner that fully revealed her apprehension. She was an apt woman; and a little experience soon demonstrated, to her satisfaction, that education and slavery were incompatible with each other.

From this time I was most narrowly watched. If I was in a separate room any considerable length of time, I was sure to be suspected of having a book, and was at once called to give an account of myself. All this, however, was too late. The first step had been taken. Mistress, in teaching me the alphabet, had given me the *inch,* and no precaution could prevent me from taking the *ell.*

The plan which I adopted, and the one by which I was most successful, was that of making friends of all the little white boys whom I met in the street. As many of these as I could, I converted into teachers. With their kindly aid, obtained at different times and in different places, I finally succeeded in learning to read. When I was sent of errands, I always took my book with me, and by going one part of my errand quickly, I found time to get a lesson before my return. I used also to carry bread with me, enough of which was always in the house, and to which I was always welcome; for I was much better off in this regard than many of the poor white children in our neighborhood. This bread I used to bestow upon the hungry little urchins, who, in return, would give me that more valuable bread of knowledge. I am strongly tempted to give the names of two or three of those little boys, as a testimonial of the gratitude and affection I bear them; but prudence forbids;—not that it would injure me, but it might embarrass them; for it is almost an unpardonable offence to teach slaves to read in this Christian country. It is enough to say of the dear little fellows, that they lived on Philpot Street, very near Durgin and Bailey's ship-yard. I used to talk this matter of slavery over with them. I would sometimes say to them, I wished I could be as free as they would be when they got to be men. "You will be free as soon as you are twenty-one, *but I am a slave for life!* Have not I as good a right to be free as you have?" These words used to trouble them; they would express for me the liveliest sympathy, and console me with the hope that something would occur by which I might be free.

I was now about twelve years old, and the thought of being *a slave for life* began to bear heavily upon my heart. Just about this time, I got hold of a book entitled "The Columbian Orator."[15] Every opportunity I got, I used to read this book. Among much of other interesting matter, I found in it a dialogue between a master and his slave. The slave was represented as having run away from his master three times. The dialogue represented the conversation which took place between them, when the slave was retaken the third time. In this dialogue, the whole argument in behalf of slavery was brought forward by the master, all of which was disposed of by the slave. The slave was made to say some very smart as well as impressive things in reply to his master—things which had the desired though unexpected effect; for the conversation resulted in the voluntary emancipation of the slave on the part of the master.

In the same book, I met with one of Sheridan's[16] mighty speeches on and in behalf of Catholic emancipation. These were choice documents to me. I read them over and over again with unabated interest. They gave tongue to interesting thoughts of my own soul, which had frequently flashed through my mind, and died away for want of utterance.

---

[15] Collection of literary pieces.
[16] Richard Brinsley Sheridan (1751–1816):   Irish playwright and champion of the Catholic Emancipation.

The moral which I gained from the dialogue was the power of truth over the conscience of even a slaveholder. What I got from Sheridan was a bold denunciation of slavery, and a powerful vindication of human rights. The reading of these documents enabled me to utter my thoughts, and to meet the arguments brought forward to sustain slavery; but while they relieved me of one difficulty, they brought on another even more painful than the one of which I was relieved. The more I read, the more I was led to abhor and detest my enslavers. I could regard them in no other light than a band of successful robbers, who had left their homes, and gone to Africa, and stolen us from our homes, and in a strange land reduced us to slavery. I loathed them as being the meanest as well as the most wicked of men. As I read and contemplated the subject, behold! that very discontentment which Master Hugh had predicted would follow my learning to read had already come, to torment and sting my soul to unutterable anguish. As I writhed under it, I would at times feel that learning to read had been a curse rather than a blessing. It had given me a view of my wretched condition, without the remedy. It opened my eyes to the horrible pit, but to no ladder upon which to get out. In moments of agony, I envied my fellow-slaves for their stupidity. I have often wished myself a beast. I preferred the condition of the meanest reptile to my own. Any thing, no matter what, to get rid of thinking! It was this everlasting thinking of my condition that tormented me. There was no getting rid of it. It was pressed upon me by every object within sight or hearing, animate or inanimate. The silver trump of freedom had roused my soul to eternal wakefulness. Freedom now appeared, to disappear no more forever. It was heard in every sound, and seen in every thing. It was ever present to torment me with a sense of my wretched condition. I saw nothing without seeing it, I heard nothing without hearing it, and felt nothing without feeling it. It looked from every star, it smiled in every calm, breathed in every wind, and moved in every storm.

I often found myself regretting my own existence, and wishing myself dead; and but for the hope of being free, I have no doubt but that I should have killed myself, or done something for which I should have been killed. While in this state of mind, I was eager to hear any one speak of slavery. I was a ready listener. Every little while, I could hear something about the abolitionists. It was some time before I found what the word meant. It was always used in such connections as to make it an interesting word to me. If a slave ran away and succeeded in getting clear, or if a slave killed his master, set fire to a barn, or did any thing very wrong in the mind of a slaveholder, it was spoken of as the fruit of *abolition.* Hearing the word in this connection very often, I set about learning what it meant. The dictionary afforded me little or no help. I found it was "the act of abolishing;" but then I did not know what was to be abolished. Here I was perplexed. I did not dare to ask any one about its meaning, for I was satisfied that it was something they wanted me to know very little about. After a patient waiting, I got one of our city papers, containing an account of the number of petitions from the north, praying for the abolition of slavery in the District of Columbia, and of the slave trade between the States. From this time I understood the words *abolition* and *abolitionist,* and always drew near when that word was spoken, expecting to hear something of importance to myself and fellow-slaves. The light broke in upon me by degrees. I went one day down on the wharf of Mr. Waters; and seeing two Irishmen unloading a scow of stone, I went, unasked, and helped them. When we had finished, one of them came to me and asked me if I were a slave. I told him I was. He asked, "Are ye a slave for life?" I told him that I was. The good Irishman seemed to be deeply affected by the statement. He said to the other that it was a pity so fine a little fellow as myself should be a slave for life. He said it was a shame to hold me. They both advised me to run away to the north; that I should find friends there, and that I should be free. I pretended not to be interested in what they said, and treated them as if I did not understand them; for I feared they might be treacherous. White men have been known to encourage slaves to escape, and then, to get the reward, catch them and return them to their masters. I was afraid that these seemingly good men might use me so; but I nevertheless remembered their advice, and from that time I resolved to run away. I looked forward to a time at which it would be safe for me to escape. I was too young to think of doing so immediately; besides, I wished to learn how to write, as I might have occasion to write my own pass. I consoled myself with the hope that I should one day find a good chance. Meanwhile, I would learn to write.

The idea as to how I might learn to write was suggested to me by being in Durgin and Bailey's ship-yard, and frequently seeing the ship carpenters, after hewing, and getting a piece of timber ready for use, write on the timber the name of that part of the ship for which it was intended. When a piece of timber was intended for the larboard side, it would be marked—"L." When a piece was for the starboard side, it would be marked thus—"S." A piece for the larboard side forward, would be marked thus—"L. F." When a piece was for starboard side forward, it would be marked thus—"S. F." For larboard aft, it would be marked thus—"L. A." For starboard aft, it would be marked thus— "S. A." I soon learned the names of these letters, and for what they were intended when placed upon a piece of timber in the ship-yard. I immediately commenced copying them, and in a short time was able to make the four letters named. After that, when I met with any boy who I knew could write, I would tell him I could write as well as he. The next word would be, "I don't believe you. Let me see you try it." I would then make the letters which I had been so fortunate as to learn, and ask him to beat that. In this way I got a good many lessons in writing, which it is quite possible I should never have gotten in any other way. During this time, my copy-book was the board fence, brick way, and pavement; my pen and ink was a lump of chalk. With these, I learned mainly how to write. I then commenced and continued copying the Italics in Webster's Spelling Book,[17] until I could make them all without looking on the book. By this time, my little Master Thomas had gone to school, and learned how to write, and had written over a number of copy-books. These had been brought home, and shown to some of our near neighbors, and then laid aside. My mistress used to go to class meeting at the Wilk Street meetinghouse every Monday afternoon, and leave me to take care of the house. When left thus, I used to spend the time in writing in the spaces left in Master Thomas's copy-book, copying what he had written. I continued to do this until I could write a hand very similar to that of Master Thomas. Thus, after a long, tedious effort for years, I finally succeeded in learning how to write.

Chapter VIII

In a very short time after I went to live at Baltimore, my old master's youngest son Richard died; and in about three years and six months after his death, my old master, Captain Anthony, died, leaving only his son, Andrew, and daughter, Lucretia, to share

[17] Popular school text compiled by Noah Webster (1758–1843).

his estate. He died while on a visit to see his daughter at Hillsborough. Cut off thus unexpectedly, he left no will as to the disposal of his property. It was therefore necessary to have a valuation of the property, that it might be equally divided between Mrs. Lucretia and Master Andrew. I was immediately sent for, to be valued with the other property. Here again my feelings rose up in detestation of slavery. I had now a new conception of my degraded condition. Prior to this, I had become, if not insensible to my lot, at least partly so. I left Baltimore with a young heart overborne with sadness, and a soul full of apprehension. I took passage with Captain Rowe, in the schooner Wild Cat, and, after a sail of about twenty-four hours, I found myself near the place of my birth. I had now been absent from it almost, if not quite, five years. I, however, remembered the place very well. I was only about five years old when I left it, to go and live with my old master on Colonel Lloyd's plantation; so that I was now between ten and eleven years old.

We were all ranked together at the valuation. Men and women, old and young, married and single, were ranked with horses, sheep and swine. There were horses and men, cattle and women, pigs and children, all holding the same rank in the scale of being, and were all subjected to the same narrow examination. Silvery-headed age and sprightly youth, maids and matrons, had to undergo the same indelicate inspection. At this moment, I saw more clearly than ever the brutalizing effects of slavery upon both slave and slaveholder.

After the valuation, then came the division. I have no language to express the high excitement and deep anxiety which were felt among us poor slaves during this time. Our fate for life was now to be decided. We had no more voice in that decision than the brutes among whom we were ranked. A single word from the white men was enough—against all our wishes, prayers, and entreaties—to sunder forever the dearest friends, dearest kindred, and strongest ties known to human beings. In addition to the pain of separation, there was the horrid dread of falling into the hands of Master Andrew. He was known to us all as being a most cruel wretch,—a common drunkard, who had, by his reckless mismanagement and profligate dissipation, already wasted a large portion of his father's property. We all felt that we might as well be sold at once to the Georgia traders, as to pass into his hands; for we knew that that would be our inevitable condition,—a condition held by us all in the utmost horror and dread.

I suffered more anxiety than most of my fellowslaves. I had known what it was to be kindly treated; they had known nothing of the kind. They had seen little or nothing of the world. They were in very deed men and women of sorrow, and acquainted with grief. Their back had been made familiar with the bloody lash, so that they had become callous; mine was yet tender; for while at Baltimore I got few whippings, and few slaves could boast of a kinder master and mistress than myself; and the thought of passing out of their hands into those of Master Andrew—a man who, but a few days before, to give me a sample of his bloody disposition, took my little brother by the throat, threw him on the ground, and with the heel of his boot stamped upon his head till the blood gushed from his nose and ears—was well calculated to make me anxious as to my fate. After he had committed this savage outrage upon my brother, he turned to me, and said that was the way he meant to serve me one of these days,—meaning, I suppose, when I came into his possession.

Thanks to a kind Providence, I fell to the portion of Mrs. Lucretia, and was sent immediately back to Baltimore, to live again in the family of Master Hugh. Their joy at my return equalled their sorrow at my departure. It was a glad day to me. I had escaped a

[fate] worse than lion's jaws. I was absent from Baltimore, for the purpose of valuation and division, just about one month, and it seemed to have been six.

Very soon after my return to Baltimore, my mistress, Lucretia, died, leaving her husband and one child, Amanda; and in a very short time after her death, Master Andrew died. Now all the property of my old master, slaves included, was in the hands of strangers,—strangers who had had nothing to do with accumulating it. Not a slave was left free. All remained slaves, from the youngest to the oldest. If any one thing in my experience, more than another, served to deepen my conviction of the infernal character of slavery, and to fill me with unutterable loathing of slaveholders, it was their base ingratitude to my poor old grandmother. She had served my old master faithfully from youth to old age. She had been the source of all his wealth; she had peopled his plantation with slaves; she had become a great grandmother in his service. She had rocked him in infancy, attended him in childhood, served him through life, and at his death wiped from his icy brow the cold death-sweat, and closed his eyes forever. She was nevertheless left a slave—a slave for life—a slave in the hands of strangers; and in their hands she saw her children, her grandchildren, and her great-grandchildren, divided, like so many sheep, without being gratified with the small privilege of a single word, as to their or her own destiny. And, to cap the climax of their base ingratitude and fiendish barbarity, my grandmother, who was now very old, having outlived my old master and all his children, having seen the beginning and end of all of them, and her present owners finding she was of but little value, her frame already racked with the pains of old age, and complete helplessness fast stealing over her once active limbs, they took her to the woods, built her a little hut, put up a little mud-chimney, and then made her welcome to the privilege of supporting herself there in perfect loneliness; thus virtually turning her out to die! If my poor old grandmother now lives, she lives to suffer in utter loneliness; she lives to remember and mourn over the loss of children, the loss of grandchildren, and the loss of great-grandchildren. They are, in the language of the slave's poet, Whittier,—

> "Gone, gone, sold and gone
> To the rice swamp dank and lone,
> Where the slave-whip ceaseless swings,
> Where the noisome insect stings,
> Where the fever-demon strews
> Poison with the falling dews,
> Where the sickly sunbeams glare
> Through the hot and misty air:—
>   Gone, gone, sold and gone
> To the rice swamp dank and lone,
> From Virginia hills and waters—
> Woe is me, my stolen daughters!"[18]

The hearth is desolate. The children, the unconscious children, who once sang and danced in her presence, are gone. She gropes her way, in the darkness of age, for a drink

---

[18] Lines from "The Farewell: Of a Virginia Slave Mother to Her Daughter Sold Into Southern Bondage" (1838).

of water. Instead of the voices of her children, she hears by day the moans of the dove, and by night the screams of the hideous owl. All is gloom. The grave is at the door. And now, when weighed down by the pains and aches of old age, when the head inclines to the feet, when the beginning and ending of human existence meet, and helpless infancy and painful old age combine together—at this time, this most needful time, the time for the exercise of that tenderness and affection which children only can exercise toward a declining parent—my poor old grandmother, the devoted mother of twelve children, is left all alone, in yonder little hut, before a few dim embers. She stands—she sits—she staggers—she falls—she groans—she dies—and there are none of her children or grandchildren present, to wipe from her wrinkled brow the cold sweat of death, or to place beneath the sod her fallen remains. Will not a righteous God visit for these things?

In about two years after the death of Mrs. Lucretia, Master Thomas married his second wife. Her name was Rowena Hamilton. She was the eldest daughter of Mr. William Hamilton. Master now lived in St. Michael's. Not long after his marriage, a misunderstanding took place between himself and Master Hugh; and as a means of punishing his brother, he took me from him to live with himself at St. Michael's. Here I underwent another most painful separation. It, however, was not so severe as the one I dreaded at the division of property; for, during this interval, a great change had taken place in Master Hugh and his once kind and affectionate wife. The influence of brandy upon him, and of slavery upon her, had effected a disastrous change in the characters of both; so that, as far as they were concerned, I thought I had little to lose by the change. But it was not to them that I was attached. It was to those little Baltimore boys that I felt the strongest attachment. I had received many good lessons from them, and was still receiving them, and the thought of leaving them was painful indeed. I was leaving, too, without the hope of ever being allowed to return. Master Thomas had said he would never let me return again. The barrier betwixt himself and brother he considered impassable.

I then had to regret that I did not at least make the attempt to carry out my resolution to run away; for the chances of success are tenfold greater from the city than from the country.

I sailed from Baltimore for St. Michael's in the sloop Amanda, Captain Edward Dodson. On my passage, I paid particular attention to the direction which the steamboats took to go to Philadelphia. I found, instead of going down, on reaching North Point they went up the bay, in a north-easterly direction. I deemed this knowledge of the utmost importance. My determination to run away was again revived. I resolved to wait only so long as the offering of a favorable opportunity. When that came, I was determined to be off.

Chapter IX

I have now reached a period of my life when I can give dates. I left Baltimore, and went to live with Master Thomas Auld, at St. Michael's, in March, 1832. It was now more than seven years since I lived with him in the family of my old master, on Colonel Lloyd's plantation. We of course were now almost entire strangers to each other. He was to me a new master, and I to him a new slave. I was ignorant of his temper and disposition; he was equally so of mine. A very short time, however, brought us into full acquaintance with each other. I was made acquainted with his wife not less than with himself. They were well matched, being equally mean and cruel. I was now, for the first time during a space of more than seven years, made to feel the painful gnawings of hunger—a something which I had not experienced before since I left Colonel Lloyd's plantation. It went hard enough with me then, when I could look back at no period at which I had enjoyed a sufficiency. It was tenfold harder after living in Master Hugh's family, where I had always had enough to eat, and of that which was good. I have said Master Thomas was a mean man. He was so. Not to give a slave enough to eat, is regarded as the most aggravated development of meanness even among slaveholders. The rule is, no matter how coarse the food, only let there be enough of it. This is the theory; and in the part of Maryland from which I came, it is the general practice,—though there are many exceptions. Master Thomas gave us enough of neither coarse nor fine food. There were four slaves of us in the kitchen—my sister Eliza, my aunt Priscilla, Henny, and myself; and we were allowed less than half of a bushel of cornmeal per week, and very little else, either in the shape of meat or vegetables. It was not enough for us to subsist upon. We were therefore reduced to the wretched necessity of living at the expense of our neighbors. This we did by begging and stealing, whichever came handy in the time of need, the one being considered as legitimate as the other. A great many times have we poor creatures been nearly perishing with hunger, when food in abundance lay mouldering in the safe and smoke-house, and our pious mistress was aware of the fact; and yet that mistress and her husband would kneel every morning, and pray that God would bless them in basket and store!

Bad as all slaveholders are, we seldom meet one destitute of every element of character commanding respect. My master was one of this rare sort. I do not know of one single noble act ever performed by him. The leading trait in his character was meanness; and if there were any other element in his nature, it was made subject to this. He was mean; and, like most other mean men, he lacked the ability to conceal his meanness. Captain Auld was not born a slaveholder. He had been a poor man, master only of a Bay craft. He came into possession of all his slaves by marriage; and of all men, adopted slaveholders are the worst. He was cruel, but cowardly. He commanded without firmness. In the enforcement of his rules, he was at times rigid, and at times lax. At times, he spoke to his slaves with the firmness of Napoleon and the fury of a demon; at other times, he might well be mistaken for an inquirer who had lost his way. He did nothing of himself. He might have passed for a lion, but for his ears. In all things noble which he attempted, his own meanness shone most conspicuous. His airs, words, and actions, were the airs, words, and actions of born slaveholders, and, being assumed, were awkward enough. He was not even a good imitator. He possessed all the disposition to deceive, but wanted the power. Having no resources within himself, he was compelled to be the copyist of many, and being such, he was forever the victim of inconsistency; and of consequence he was an object of contempt, and was held as such even by his slaves. The luxury of having slaves of his own to wait upon him was something new and unprepared for. He was a slaveholder without the ability to hold slaves. He found himself incapable of managing his slaves either by force, fear, or fraud. We seldom called him "master," we generally called him "Captain Auld," and were hardly disposed to title him at all. I doubt not that our conduct had much to do with making him appear awkward, and of consequence fretful. Our want of reverence for him must have perplexed him greatly. He wished to have us call him master, but lacked the firmness necessary to command us to do so. His wife used to insist upon our calling him so, but to no purpose. In August, 1832, my master attended a Methodist camp-meeting held in the Bayside, Talbot county, and there experienced religion. I indulged a faint hope that his conversion would lead him to emancipate his slaves, and that, if he did not do this, it would at any rate, make him more kind and humane. I was disappointed in both these respects. It neither made him to be humane to his slaves, nor to emancipate them. If it had any effect on his character, it made him more cruel and hateful in all his ways; for I believe him to have been a much worse man after his conversion than before. Prior to his conversion, he relied upon his own depravity to shield and sustain him in his savage barbarity; but after his conversion, he found religious sanction and support for his slaveholding cruelty. He made the greatest pretensions to piety. His house was the house of prayer. He prayed morning, noon, and night. He very soon distinguished himself among his brethren, and was soon made a class-leader and exhorter. His activity in revivals was great, and he proved himself an instrument in the hands of the church in converting many souls. His house was the preachers' home. They used to take great pleasure in coming there to put up; for while he starved us, he stuffed them. We have had three or four preachers there at a time. The names of those who used to come most frequently while I lived there, were Mr. Storks, Mr. Ewery, Mr. Humphry, and Mr. Hickey. I have also seen Mr. George Cookman at our house. We slaves loved Mr. Cookman. We believed him to be a good man. We thought him instrumental in getting Mr. Samuel Harrison, a very rich slaveholder, to emancipate his slaves; and by some means got the impression that he was laboring to effect the emancipation of all the slaves. When he was at our house, we were sure to be called in to prayers. When the others were there, we were sometimes called in and sometimes not. Mr. Cookman took more notice of us than either of the other ministers. He could not come among us without betraying his sympathy for us, and, stupid as we were, we had the sagacity to see it.

While I lived with my master in St. Michael's, there was a white young man, a Mr. Wilson, who proposed to keep a Sabbath school for the instruction of such slaves as might be disposed to learn to read the New Testament. We met but three times, when Mr. West and Mr. Fairbanks, both class-leaders, with many others, came upon with us with sticks and other missiles, drove us off, and forbade us to meet again. Thus ended our little Sabbath school in the pious town of St. Michael's.

I have said my master found religious sanction for his cruelty. As an example, I will state one of many facts going to prove the charge. I have seen him tie up a lame young woman, and whip her with a heavy cowskin upon her naked shoulders, causing the warm red blood to drip; and, in justification of the bloody deed, he would quote this passage of Scripture—"He that knoweth his master's will, and doeth it not, shall be beaten with many stripes."

Master would keep this lacerated young woman tied up in this horrid situation four or five hours at a time. I have known him to tie her up early in the morning, and whip her before breakfast; leave her, go to his store, return at dinner, and whip her again, cutting her in the places already made raw with his cruel lash. The secret of master's cruelty toward "Henny" is found in the fact of her being almost helpless. When quite a child, she fell into the fire, and burned herself horribly. Her hands were so burnt that she never got the use of them. She could do very little but bear heavy burdens. She was to master a bill of expense; and as he was a mean man, she was a constant offence to him. He seemed desirous of getting the poor girl out of existence. He gave her away once to his sister; but, being a poor gift, she was not disposed to keep her. Finally, my benevolent master, to use his own words, "set her adrift to take care of herself." Here was a recently-converted man, holding on upon the mother, and at the same time turning out her helpless child, to starve and die! Master Thomas was one of the many pious slaveholders who hold slaves for the very charitable purpose of taking care of them.

My master and myself had quite a number of differences. He found me unsuitable to his purpose. My city life, he said, had had a very pernicious effect upon me. It had almost ruined me for every good purpose, and fitted me for every thing which was bad. One of my greatest faults was that of letting his horse run away, and go down to his father-in-law's farm, which was about five miles from St. Michael's. I would then have to go after it. My reason for this kind of carelessness, or carefulness, was, that I could always get something to eat when I went there. Master William Hamilton, my master's father-in-law, always gave his slaves enough to eat. I never left there hungry, no matter how great the need of my speedy return. Master Thomas at length said he would stand it no longer. I had lived with him nine months, during which time he had given me a number of severe whippings, all to no good purpose. He resolved to put me out, as he said, to be broken; and, for this purpose, he let me for one year to a man named Edward Covey. Mr. Covey was a poor man, a farm-renter. He rented the place upon which he lived, as also the hands with which he tilled it. Mr. Covey had acquired a very high reputation for breaking young slaves, and this reputation was of immense value to him. It enabled him to get his farm tilled with much less expense to himself than he could have had it done without such a reputation. Some slaveholders thought it not much loss to allow Mr. Covey to have their slaves one year, for the sake of the training to which they were subjected, without any other compensation. He could hire young help with great ease, in consequence of this reputation. Added to the natural good qualities of Mr. Covey, he was a professor of religion—a pious soul—a member and a class-leader in the Methodist church. All of this added weight to his reputation as a "nigger-breaker." I was aware of all the facts, having been made acquainted with them by a young man who had lived there. I nevertheless made the change gladly; for I was sure of getting enough to eat, which is not the smallest consideration to a hungry man.

Chapter X

I left Master Thomas's house, and went to live with Mr. Covey, on the 1st of January, 1833. I was now, for the first time in my life, a field hand. In my new employment, I found myself even more awkward than a country boy appeared to be in a large city. I had been at my new home but one week before Mr. Covey gave me a very severe whipping, cutting my back, causing the blood to run, and raising ridges on my flesh as large as my little finger. The details of this affair are as follows: Mr. Covey sent me, very early in the morning of one of our coldest days in the month of January, to the woods, to get a load of wood. He gave me a team of unbroken oxen. He told me which was the in-hand ox, and which the off-hand one. He then tied the end of a large rope around the horns of the in-hand ox, and gave me the other end of it, and told me, if the oxen started to run, that I must hold on upon the rope. I had never driven oxen before, and of course I was very awkward. I, however, succeeded in getting to the edge of the woods with little difficulty; but I had got a very few rods into the woods, when the oxen took fright, and started full tilt, carrying the cart against trees, and over stumps, in the most frightful manner. I expected every moment that my brains would be dashed out against the trees. After running thus for a considerable distance, they finally upset the cart, dashing it with great force against a tree, and threw themselves into a dense thicket. How I escaped death, I do not know. There I was, entirely alone, in a thick wood, in a place new to me. My cart was upset and shattered, my oxen were entangled among the young trees, and there was none to help me. After a long spell of effort, I succeeded in getting my cart righted, my oxen disentangled and again yoked to the cart. I now proceeded with my team to the place where I had, the day before, been chopping wood, and loaded my cart pretty heavily, thinking in this way to tame my oxen. I then proceeded on my way home. I had now consumed one half of the day. I got out of the woods safely, and now felt out of danger. I stopped my oxen to open the woods gate; and just as I did so, before I could get hold of my ox-rope, the oxen again started, rushed through the gate, catching it between the wheel and the body of the cart, tearing it to pieces, and coming within a few inches of crushing me against the gate-post. Thus twice, in one short day, I escaped death by the merest chance. On my return, I told Mr. Covey what had happened, and how it happened. He ordered me to return to the woods again immediately. I did so, and he followed on after me. Just as I got into the woods, he came up and told me to stop my cart, and that he would teach me how to trifle away my time, and break gates. He then went to a large gum-tree, and with his axe cut three large switches, and, after trimming them up neatly with his pocketknife, he ordered me to take off my clothes. I made him no answer, but stood with my clothes on. He repeated his order. I still made him no answer, nor did I move to strip myself. Upon this he rushed at me with the fierceness of a tiger, tore off my clothes, and lashed me till he had worn out his switches, cutting me so savagely as to leave the marks visible for a long time after. This whipping was the first of a number just like it, and for similar offences.

I lived with Mr. Covey one year. During the first six months, of that year, scarce a week passed without his whipping me. I was seldom free from a sore back. My awkwardness was almost always his excuse for whipping me. We were worked fully up to the point of endurance. Long before day we were up, our horses fed, and by the first approach of day we were off to the field with our hoes and ploughing teams. Mr. Covey gave us enough to eat, but scarce time to eat it. We were often less than five minutes taking our meals. We were often in the field from the first approach of day till its last lingering ray had left us; and at saving-fodder time, midnight often caught us in the field binding blades.[19]

Covey would be out with us. The way he used to stand it, was this. He would spend the most of his afternoons in bed. He would then come out fresh in the evening, ready to urge us on with his words, example, and frequently with the whip. Mr. Covey was one of the few slaveholders who could and did work with his hands. He was a hardworking man. He knew by himself just what a man or a boy could do. There was no deceiving him. His work went on in his absence almost as well as in his presence; and he had the faculty of making us feel that he was ever present with us. This he did by surprising us. He seldom approached the spot where we were at work openly, if he could do it secretly. He always aimed at taking us by surprise. Such was his cunning, that we used to call him, among ourselves, "the snake." When we were at work in the cornfield, he would sometimes crawl on his hands and knees to avoid detection, and all at once he

---

[19] Sheaves of grain.

would rise nearly in our midst, and scream out, "Ha, ha! Come, come! Dash on, dash on!" This being his mode of attack, it was never safe to stop a single minute. His comings were like a thief in the night. He appeared to us as being ever at hand. He was under every tree, behind every stump, in every bush, and at every window, on the plantation. He would sometimes mount his horse, as if bound to St. Michael's, a distance of seven miles, and in half an hour afterwards you would see him coiled up in the corner of the wood-fence, watching every motion of the slaves. He would, for this purpose, leave his horse tied up in the woods. Again, he would sometimes walk up to us, and give us orders as though he was upon the point of starting on a long journey, turn his back upon us, and make as though he was going to the house to get ready; and, before he would get half way thither, he would turn short and crawl into a fence-corner, or behind some tree, and there watch us till the going down of the sun.

   Mr. Covey's *forte* consisted in his power to deceive. His life was devoted to planning and perpetrating the grossest deceptions. Every thing he possessed in the shape of learning or religion, he made conform to his disposition to deceive. He seemed to think himself equal to deceiving the Almighty. He would make a short prayer in the morning, and a long prayer at night; and, strange as it may seem, few men would at times appear more devotional than he. The exercises of his family devotions were always commenced with singing; and, as he was a very poor singer himself, the duty of raising the hymn generally came upon me. He would read his hymn, and nod at me to commence. I would at times do so; at others, I would not. My non-compliance would almost always produce much confusion. To show himself independent of me, he would start and stagger through with his hymn in the most discordant manner. In this state of mind, he prayed with more than ordinary spirit. Poor man! such was his disposition, and success at deceiving, I do verily believe that he sometimes deceived himself into the solemn belief, that he was a sincere worshipper of the most high God; and this, too, at a time when he may be said to have been guilty of compelling his woman slave to commit the sin of adultery. The facts in the case are these: Mr. Covey was a poor man; he was just commencing in life; he was only able to buy one slave; and, shocking as is the fact, he bought her, as he said, for a *breeder*. This woman was named Caroline. Mr. Covey bought her from Mr. Thomas Lowe, about six miles from St. Michael's. She was a large, able-bodied woman, about twenty years old. She had already given birth to one child, which proved her to be just what he wanted. After buying her, he hired a married man of Mr. Samuel Harrison, to live with him one year; and him he used to fasten up with her every night! The result was, that, at the end of the year, the miserable woman gave birth to twins. At this result Mr. Covey seemed to be highly pleased, both with the man and the wretched woman. Such was his joy, and that of his wife, that nothing they could do for Caroline during her confinement was too good, or too hard to be done. The children were regarded as being quite an addition to his wealth.

   If at any one time of my life more than another, I was made to drink the bitterest dregs of slavery, that time was during the first six months of my stay with Mr. Covey. We were worked in all weathers. It was never too hot or too cold; it could never rain, blow, hail, or snow, too hard for us to work in the field. Work, work, work, was scarcely more the order of the day than of the night. The longest days were too short for him, and the shortest nights too long for him. I was somewhat unmanageable when I first went there, but a few months of this discipline tamed me. Mr. Covey succeeded in breaking me. I was broken in body, soul, and spirit. My natural elasticity was crushed, my intellect languished, the disposition to read departed, the cheerful spark that lingered about my eye died; the dark night of slavery closed in upon me, and behold a man transformed into a brute!

Sunday was my only leisure time. I spent this in a sort of beastlike stupor, between sleep and wake, under some large tree. At times I would rise up, a flash of energetic freedom would dart through my soul, accompanied with a faint beam of hope, that flickered for a moment, and then vanished. I sank down again, mourning over my wretched condition. I was sometimes prompted to take my life, and that of Covey, but was prevented by a combination of hope and fear. My sufferings on this plantation seem now like a dream rather than a stern reality.

Our house stood within a few rods of the Chesapeake Bay, whose broad bosom was ever white with sails from every quarter of the habitable globe. Those beautiful vessels, robed in purest white, so delightful to the eye of freemen, were to me so many shrouded ghosts, to terrify and torment me with thoughts of my wretched condition. I have often, in the deep stillness of a summer's Sabbath, stood all alone upon the lofty banks of that noble bay, and traced, with saddened heart and tearful eye, the countless number of sails moving off to the mighty ocean. The sight of these always affected me powerfully. My thoughts would compel utterance; and there, with no audience but the Almighty, I would pour out my soul's complaint, in my rude way, with an apostrophe to the moving multitude of ships:—

"You are loosed from your moorings, and are free; I am fast in my chains, and am a slave! You move merrily before the gentle gale, and I sadly before the bloody whip! You are freedom's swiftwinged angels, that fly round the world; I am confined in bands of iron! O that I were free! Oh, that I were on one of your gallant decks, and under your protecting wing! Alas! betwixt me and you, the turbid waters roll. Go on, go on. O that I could also go! Could I but swim! If I could fly! Oh, why was I born a man, of whom to make a brute! The glad ship is gone; she hides in the dim distance. I am left in the hottest hell of unending slavery. O God, save me! God, deliver me! Let me be free! Is there any God? Why am I a slave? I will run away. I will not stand it. Get caught, or get clear, I'll try it. I had as well die with ague as the fever. I have only one life to lose. I had as well be killed running as die standing. Only think of it; one hundred miles straight north, and I am free! Try it? Yes! God helping me, I will. It cannot be that I shall live and die a slave. I will take to the water. This very bay shall yet bear me into freedom. The steamboats steered in a north-east course from North Point. I will do the same; and when I get to the head of the bay, I will turn my canoe adrift, and walk straight through Delaware into Pennsylvania. When I get there, I shall not be required to have a pass; I can travel without being disturbed. Let but the first opportunity offer, and, come what will, I am off. Meanwhile, I will try to bear up under the yoke. I am not the only slave in the world. Why should I fret? I can bear as much as any of them. Besides, I am but a boy, and all boys are bound to some one. It may be that my misery in slavery will only increase my happiness when I get free. There is a better day coming."

Thus I used to think, and thus I used to speak to myself; goaded almost to madness at one moment, and at the next reconciling myself to my wretched lot.

I have already intimated that my condition was much worse, during the first six months of my stay at Mr. Covey's, than in the last six. The circumstances leading to the change in Mr. Covey's course toward me form an epoch in my humble history. You have seen how a man was made a slave; you shall see how a slave was made a man. On one of the hottest days of the month of August, 1833, Bill Smith, William Hughes, a slave named Eli, and myself, were engaged in fanning wheat.[20] Hughes was clearing the fanned wheat from before the fan. Eli was turning, Smith was feeding, and I was carrying wheat to the fan. The work was simple, requiring strength rather than intellect; yet, to one entirely unused to such work, it came very hard. About three o'clock of that day, I broke down; my strength failed me; I was seized with a violent aching of the head, attended with extreme dizziness; I trembled in every limb. Finding what was coming, I nerved myself up, feeling it would never do to stop work. I stood as long as I could stagger to the hopper with grain. When I could stand no longer, I fell, and felt as if held down by an immense weight. The fan of course stopped; every one had his own work to do; and no one could do the work of the other, and have his own go on at the same time.

Mr. Covey was at the house, about one hundred yards from the treading-yard where we were fanning. On hearing the fan stop, he left immediately, and came to the spot where we were. He hastily inquired what the matter was. Bill answered that I was sick, and there was no one to bring wheat to the fan. I had by this time crawled away under the side of the post and rail-fence by which the yard was enclosed, hoping to find relief by getting out of the sun. He then asked where I was. He was told by one of the hands. He came to the spot, and, after looking at me awhile, asked me what was the matter. I told him as well as I could, for I scarce had strength to speak. He then gave me a savage kick in the side, and told me to get up. I tried to do so, but fell back in the attempt. He gave me another kick, and again told me to rise. I again tried, and succeeded in gaining my feet; but, stooping to get the tub with which I was feeding the fan, I again staggered and fell. While down in this situation, Mr. Covey took up the hickory slat with which Hughes had been striking off the half-bushel measure, and with it gave me a heavy blow upon the head, making a large wound, and the blood ran freely; and with this again told me to get up. I made no effort to comply, having now made up my mind to let him do his worst. In a short time after receiving this blow, my head grew better. Mr. Covey had now left me to my fate. At this moment I resolved, for the first time, to go to my master, enter a complaint, and ask his protection. In order to do this, I must that afternoon walk seven miles; and this, under the circumstances, was truly a severe undertaking. I was exceedingly feeble; made so as much by the kicks and blows which I received, as by the severe fit of sickness to which I had been subjected. I, however, watched my chance, while Covey was looking in an opposite direction, and started for St. Michael's. I succeeded in getting a considerable distance on my way to the woods, when Covey discovered me, and called after me to come back, threatening what he would do if I did not come. I disregarded both his calls and his threats, and made my way to the woods as fast as my feeble state would allow; and thinking I might be overhauled by him if I kept the road, I walked through the woods, keeping far enough from the road to avoid detection, and near enough to prevent losing my way. I had not gone far before my little strength again failed me. I could go no farther. I fell down, and lay for a considerable time. The blood was yet oozing from the wound on my head. For a time I thought I should bleed to death; and think now that I should have done so, but that the blood so matted my hair as to stop the wound. After lying there about three quarters of an hour, I nerved myself up again, and started on my way, through bogs and briers, barefooted and bareheaded, tearing my feet

---

[20] Method of sifting grains of wheat from unwanted chaff.

sometimes at nearly every step; and after a journey of about seven miles, occupying some five hours to perform it, I arrived at master's store. I then presented an appearance enough to affect any but a heart of iron. From the crown of my head to my feet, I was covered with blood. My hair was all clotted with dust and blood; my shirt was stiff with blood. My legs and feet were torn in sundry places with briers and thorns, and were also covered with blood. I suppose I looked like a man who had escaped a den of wild beasts, and barely escaped them. In this state I appeared before my master, humbly entreating him to interpose his authority for my protection. I told him all the circumstances as well as I could, and it seemed, as I spoke, at times to affect him. He would then walk the floor, and seek to justify Covey by saying he expected I deserved it. He asked me what I wanted. I told him, to let me get a new home; that as sure as I lived with Mr. Covey again, I should live with but to die with him; that Covey would surely kill me; he was in a fair way for it. Master Thomas ridiculed the idea that there was any danger of Mr. Covey's killing me, and said that he knew Mr. Covey; that he was a good man, and that he could not think of taking me from him; that, should he do so, he would lose the whole year's wages; that I belonged to Mr. Covey for one year, and that I must go back to him, come what might; and that I must not trouble him with any more stories, or that he would himself *get hold of me*. After threatening me thus, he gave me a very large dose of salts, telling me that I might remain in St. Michael's that night, (it being quite late,) but that I must be off back to Mr. Covey's early in the morning; and that if I did not, he would *get hold of me*, which meant that he would whip me.

I remained all night, and, according to his orders, I started off to Covey's in the morning, (Saturday morning), wearied in body and broken in spirit. I got no supper that night, or breakfast that morning. I reached Covey's about nine o'clock; and just as I was getting over the fence that divided Mrs. Kemp's fields from ours, out ran Covey with his cowskin, to give me another whipping. Before he could reach me, I succeeded in getting to the cornfield; and as the corn was very high, it afforded me the means of hiding. He seemed very angry, and searched for me a long time. My behavior was altogether unaccountable. He finally gave up the chase, thinking, I suppose, that I must come home for something to eat; he would give himself no further trouble in looking for me. I spent that day mostly in the woods, having the alternative before me,—to go home and be whipped to death, or stay in the woods and be starved to death. That night, I fell in with Sandy Jenkins, a slave with whom I was somewhat acquainted. Sandy had a free wife who lived about four miles from Mr. Covey's; and it being Saturday, he was on his way to see her. I told him my circumstances, and he very kindly invited me to go home with him. I went home with him, and talked this whole matter over, and got his advice as to what course it was best for me to pursue. I found Sandy an old adviser. He told me, with great solemnity, I must go back to Covey; but that before I went, I must go with him into another part of the woods, where there was a certain *root*, which, if I would take some of it with me, carrying it *always on my right side*, would render it impossible for Mr. Covey, or any other white man, to whip me. He said he had carried it for years; and since he had done so, he had never received a blow, and never expected to while he carried it. I at first rejected the idea, that the simple carrying of a root in my pocket would have any such effect as he had said, and was not disposed to take it; but Sandy impressed the necessity with much earnestness, telling me it could do no harm, if it did no good. To please him, I at length took the root, and, according to his direction, carried it upon my right side. This was Sunday morning. I immediately started for home; and upon entering the yard gate, out came Mr. Covey on his way to meeting. He spoke to me very kindly, bade me drive the pigs from a lot near by, and passed on towards the church. Now, this singular conduct of Mr. Covey really made me begin to think that there was something in the *root* which Sandy had given me; and had it been on any other day than Sunday, I could have attributed the conduct to no other cause then the influence of that root; and as it was, I was half inclined to think the *root* to be something more than I at first had taken it to be. All went well till Monday morning. On this morning, the virtue of the *root* was fully tested. Long before daylight, I was called to go and rub, curry, and feed, the horses. I obeyed, and was glad to obey. But whilst thus engaged, whilst in the act of throwing down some blades from the loft, Mr. Covey entered the stable with a long rope; and just as I was half out of the loft, he caught hold of my legs, and was about tying me. As soon as I found what he was up to, I gave a sudden spring, and as I did so, he holding to my legs, I was brought sprawling on the stable floor. Mr. Covey seemed now to think he had me, and could do what he pleased; but at this moment—from whence came the spirit I don't know—I resolved to fight; and, suiting my action to the resolution, I seized Covey hard by the throat; and as I did so, I rose. He held on to me, and I to him. My resistance was so entirely unexpected, that Covey seemed taken all aback. He trembled like a leaf. This gave me assurance, and I held him uneasy, causing the blood to run where I touched him with the ends of my fingers. Mr. Covey soon called out to Hughes for help. Hughes came, and, while Covey held me, attempted to tie my right hand. While he was in the act of doing so, I watched my chance, and gave him a heavy kick close under the ribs. This kick fairly sickened Hughes, so that he left me in the hands of Mr. Covey. This kick had the effect of not only weakening Hughes, but Covey also. When he saw Hughes bending over with pain, his courage quailed. He asked me if I meant to persist in my resistance. I told him I did, come what might; that he had used me like a brute for six months, and that I was determined to be used so no longer. With that, he strove to drag me to a stick that was lying just out of the stable door. He meant to knock me down. But just as he was leaning over to get the stick, I seized him with both hands by his collar, and brought him by a sudden snatch to the ground. By this time, Bill came. Covey called upon him for assistance. Bill wanted to know what he could do. Covey said, "Take hold of him, take hold of him!" Bill said his master hired him out to work, and not to help to whip me; so he left Covey and myself to fight our own battle out. We were at it for nearly two hours. Covey at length let me go, puffing and blowing at a great rate, saying that if I had not resisted, he would not have whipped me half so much. The truth was, that he had not whipped me at all. I considered him as getting entirely the worst end of the bargain; for he had drawn no blood from me, but I had from him. The whole six months afterwards, that I spent with Mr. Covey, he never laid the weight of his finger upon me in anger. He would occasionally say, he didn't want to get hold of me again. "No," thought I, "you need not; for you will come off worse than you did before."

This battle with Mr. Covey was the turning-point in my career as a slave. It rekindled the few expiring embers of freedom, and revived within me a sense of my own manhood. It recalled the departed self-confidence, and inspired me again with a determination to be free. The gratification afforded by the triumph was a full compensation for whatever else might follow, even death itself. He only can understand the deep satisfaction which I experienced, who has himself repelled by force the bloody arm of slavery. I felt as I never felt before. It was a glorious resurrection, from the tomb of slavery, to the heaven of freedom. My long-crushed spirit rose, cowardice departed, bold defiance took its place; and I now resolved that, however long I might remain a slave in form, the day had passed forever when I could be a slave in fact. I did not hesitate to let it be known of me, that the white man who expected to succeed in whipping, must also succeed in killing me.

From this time I was never again what might be called fairly whipped, though I remained a slave four years afterwards. I had several fights, but was never whipped.

It was for a long time a matter of surprise to me why Mr. Covey did not immediately have me taken by the constable to the whipping-post, and there regularly whipped for the crime of raising my hand against a white man in defence of myself. And the only explanation I can now think of does not entirely satisfy me; but such as it is, I will give it. Mr. Covey enjoyed the most unbounded reputation for being a first-rate overseer and negro-breaker. It was of considerable importance to him. That reputation was at stake; and had he sent me—a boy about sixteen years old—to the public whipping-post, his reputation would have been lost; so, to save his reputation, he suffered me to go unpunished.

My term of actual service to Mr. Edward Covey ended on Christmas day, 1833. The days between Christmas and New Year's day are allowed as holidays; and, accordingly, we were not required to perform any labor, more than to feed and take care of the stock. This time we regarded as our own, by the grace of our masters; and we therefore used or abused it nearly as we pleased. Those of us who had families at a distance, were generally allowed to spend the whole six days in their society. This time, however, was spent in various ways. The staid, sober, thinking and industrious ones of our number would employ themselves in making cornbrooms, mats, horse-collars, and baskets; and another class of us would spend the time hunting opossums, hares, and coons. But by far the larger part engaged in such sports and merriments as playing ball, wrestling, running foot-races, fiddling, dancing, and drinking whisky; and this latter mode of spending the time was by far the most agreeable to the feelings of our master. A slave who would work during the holidays was considered by our masters as scarcely deserving them. He was regarded as one who rejected the favor of his master. It was deemed a disgrace not to get drunk at Christmas; and he was regarded as lazy indeed, who had not provided himself with the necessary means, during the year, to get whisky enough to last him through Christmas.

From what I know of the effect of these holidays upon the slave, I believe them to be among the most effective means in the hands of the slaveholder in keeping down the spirit of insurrection. Were the slaveholders at once to abandon this practice, I have not the slightest doubt it would lead to an immediate insurrection among the slaves. These holidays serve as conductors, or safety-valves, to carry off the rebellious spirit of enslaved humanity. But for these, the slave would be forced up to the wildest desperation; and woe betide the slaveholder, the day he ventures to remove or hinder the operation of those conductors! I warn him that, in such an event, a spirit will go forth in their midst, more to be dreaded than the most appalling earthquake.

The holidays are part and parcel of the gross fraud, wrong, and inhumanity of slavery. They are professedly a custom established by the benevolence of the slaveholders; but I undertake to say, it is the result of selfishness, and one of the grossest frauds committed upon the down-trodden slave. They do not give the slaves this time because they would not like to have their work during its continuance, but because they know it would be unsafe to deprive them of it. This will be seen by the fact, that the slaveholders like to have their slaves spend those days just in such a manner as to make them as glad of their ending as of their beginning. Their object seems to be, to disgust their slaves with freedom, by plunging them into the lowest depths of dissipation. For instance, the slaveholders not only like to see the slave drink of his own accord, but will adopt various plans to make him drunk. One plan is, to make bets on their slaves, as to who can drink the most whisky without getting drunk; and in this way they succeed in getting whole multitudes to drink to excess. Thus, when the slave asks for virtuous freedom, the cunning slaveholder, knowing his ignorance, cheats him with a dose of vicious dissipation, artfully labelled with the name of liberty. The most of us used to drink it down, and the result was just what might be supposed: many of us were led to think that there was little to choose between liberty and slavery. We felt, and very properly too, that we had almost as well be slaves to man as to rum. So, when the holidays ended, we staggered up from the filth of our wallowing, took a long breath, and marched to the field,—feeling, upon the whole, rather glad to go, from what our master had deceived us into a belief was freedom, back to the arms of slavery.

I have said that this mode of treatment is a part of the whole system of fraud and inhumanity of slavery. It is so. The mode here adopted to disgust the slave with freedom, by allowing him to see only the abuse of it, is carried out in other things. For instance, a slave loves molasses; he steals some. His master, in many cases, goes off to town, and buys a large quantity; he returns, takes his whip, and commands the slave to eat the molasses, until the poor fellow is made sick at the very mention of it. The same mode is sometimes adopted to make the slaves refrain from asking for more food than their regular allowance. A slave runs through his allowance, and applies for more. His master is enraged at him; but, not willing to send him off without food, gives him more than is necessary, and compels him to eat it within a given time. Then, if he complains that he cannot eat it, he is said to be satisfied neither full nor fasting, and is whipped for being hard to please! I have an abundance of such illustrations of the same principle, drawn from my own observation, but think the cases I have cited sufficient. The practice is a very common one.

On the first of January, 1834, I left Mr. Covey, and went to live with Mr. William Freeland, who lived about three miles from St. Michael's. I soon found Mr. Freeland a very different man from Mr. Covey. Though not rich, he was what would be called an educated southern gentleman. Mr. Covey, as I have shown, was a well-trained negro-breaker and slave-driver. The former (slaveholder though he was) seemed to possess some regard for honor, some reverence for justice, and some respect for humanity. The latter seemed totally insensible to all such sentiments. Mr. Freeland had many of the faults peculiar to slaveholders, such as being very passionate and fretful; but I must do him the justice to say, that he was exceedingly free from those degrading vices to which Mr. Covey was constantly addicted. The one was open and frank, and we always knew where to find him. The other was a most artful deceiver, and could be understood only by such as were skilful enough to detect his cunningly-devised frauds. Another advantage I gained in my new master was, he made no pretensions to, or profession of, religion; and this, in my opinion, was truly a great advantage. I assert most unhesitatingly, that the religion of the south is a mere covering for the most horrid crimes,—a justifier of the most appalling barbarity,—a sanctifier of the most hateful frauds,—and a dark shelter under, which the darkest, foulest, grossest, and most infernal deeds of slaveholders find the strongest protection. Were I to be again reduced to the chains of slavery, next to that enslavement, I should regard being the slave of a religious master the greatest calamity that could befall me. For of all slaveholders with whom I have ever met, religious slaveholders are the worst. I have ever found them the meanest and basest, the most cruel and cowardly, of all others. It was my unhappy lot not only to belong to a religious slaveholder, but to live in a community of such religionists. Very near Mr. Freeland lived the Rev. Daniel Weeden, and in the same neighborhood lived the Rev. Rigby Hopkins. These were members and ministers in the Reformed Methodist Church. Mr. Weeden owned, among others, a woman slave, whose name I have forgotten. This woman's back, for weeks, was kept literally raw, made so by the lash of this merciless, *religious* wretch. He used to hire hands. His maxim was, Behave well or behave ill, it is the duty of a master occasionally to whip a slave, to remind him of his master's authority. Such was his theory, and such his practice.

Mr. Hopkins was even worse than Mr. Weeden. His chief boast was his ability to manage slaves. The peculiar feature of his government was that of whipping slaves in advance of deserving it. He always managed to have one or more of his slaves to whip every Monday morning. He did this to alarm their fears, and strike terror into those who escaped. His plan was to whip for the smallest offences, to prevent the commission of large ones. Mr. Hopkins could always find some excuse for whipping a slave. It would astonish one, unaccustomed to a slave-holding life, to see with what wonderful ease a slave-holder can find things, of which to make occasion to whip a slave. A mere look, word, or motion,—a mistake, accident, or want of power,—are all matters for which a slave may be whipped at any time. Does a slave look dissatisfied? It is said, he has the devil in him, and it must be whipped out. Does he speak loudly when spoken to by his master? Then he is wanting in reverence, and should be whipped for it. Does he ever venture to vindicate his conduct, when censured for it? Then he is guilty of impudence,—one of the greatest crimes of which a slave can be guilty. Does he ever venture to suggest a different mode of doing things from that pointed out by his master? He is indeed presumptuous, and getting above himself; and nothing less than a flogging will do for him. Does he, while ploughing, break a plough,—or, while hoeing, break a hoe? It is owing to his carelessness, and for it a slave must always be whipped. Mr. Hopkins could always find something of this sort to justify the use of the lash, and he seldom failed to embrace such opportunities. There was not a man in the whole county, with whom the slaves who had the getting their own home, would not prefer to live, rather than with this Rev. Mr. Hopkins. And yet there was not a man any where round, who made higher professions of religion, or was more active in revivals,—more attentive to the class, love-feast, prayer and preaching meetings, or more devotional in his family,— that prayed earlier, later, louder, and longer,—than this same reverend slave-driver, Rigby Hopkins.

But to return to Mr. Freeland, and to my experience while in his employment. He, like Mr. Covey, gave us enough to eat; but, unlike Mr. Covey, he also gave us sufficient time to take our meals. He worked us hard, but always between sunrise and sunset. He required a good deal of work to be done, but gave us good tools with which to work. His farm was large, but he employed hands enough to work it, and with ease, compared with many of his neighbors. My treatment, while in his employment, was heavenly, compared with what I experienced at the hands of Mr. Edward Covey.

Mr. Freeland was himself the owner of but two slaves. Their names were Henry Harris and John Harris. The rest of his hands he hired. These consisted of myself, Sandy

Jenkins,[21] and Handy Caldwell. Henry and John were quite intelligent, and in a very little while after I went there, I succeeded in creating in them a strong desire to learn how to read. This desire soon sprang up in the others also. They very soon mustered up some old spelling-books, and nothing would do but that I must keep a Sabbath school. I agreed to do so, and accordingly devoted my Sundays to teaching these my loved fellow-slaves how to read. Neither of them knew his letters when I went there. Some of the slaves of the neighboring farms found what was going on, and also availed themselves of this little opportunity to learn to read. It was understood, among all who came, that there must be as little display about it as possible. It was necessary to keep our religious masters at St. Michael's unacquainted with the fact, that, instead of spending the Sabbath in wrestling, boxing, and drinking whisky, we were trying to learn how to read the will of God; for they had much rather see us engaged in those degrading sports, than to see us behaving like intellectual, moral, and accountable beings. My blood boils as I think of the bloody manner in which Messrs. Wright Fairbanks and Garrison West, both classleaders, in connection with many others, rushed in upon us with sticks and stones, and broke up our virtuous little Sabbath school, at St. Michael's—all calling themselves Christians! humble followers of the Lord Jesus Christ! But I am again digressing.

I held my Sabbath school at the house of a free colored man, whose name I deem it imprudent to mention; for should it be known, it might embarrass him greatly, though the crime of holding the school was committed ten years ago. I had at one time over forty scholars, and those of the right sort, ardently desiring to learn. They were of all ages, though mostly men and women. I look back to those Sundays with an amount of pleasure not to be expressed. They were great days to my soul. The work of instructing my dear fellow-slaves was the sweetest engagement with which I was ever blessed. We loved each other, and to leave them at the close of the Sabbath was a severe cross indeed. When I think that these precious souls are to-day shut up in the prison-house of slavery, my feelings overcome me, and I am almost ready to ask, "Does a righteous God govern the universe? and for what does he hold the thunders in his right hand, if not to smite the oppressor, and deliver the spoiled out of the hand of the spoiler?" These dear souls came not to Sabbath school because it was popular to do so, nor did I teach them because it was reputable to be thus engaged. Every moment they spent in that school, they were liable to be taken up, and given thirty-nine lashes. They came because they wished to learn. Their minds had been starved by their cruel masters. They had been shut up in mental darkness. I taught them, because it was the delight of my soul to be doing something that looked like bettering the condition of my race. I kept up my school nearly the whole year I lived with Mr. Freeland; and, beside my Sabbath school, I devoted three evenings in the week, during the winter, to teaching the slaves at home. And I have the happiness to know, that several of those who came to Sabbath school learned how to read; and that one, at least, is now free through my agency.

The year passed off smoothly. It seemed only about half as long as the year which preceded it. I went through it without receiving a single blow. I will give Mr. Freeland

---

[21] Douglass's note: "This was the same man who gave the roots to prevent my being whipped by Mr. Covey. He was a 'clever soul.' We used frequently to talk about the fight with Covey, and as often as we did so, he would claim my success as the result of the roots which he gave me. This superstition is very common among the more ignorant slaves. A slave seldom dies but that his death is attributed to trickery."

the credit of being the best master I ever had, *till I became my own master*. For the ease with which I passed the year, I was, however, somewhat indebted to the society of my fellow-slaves. They were noble souls; they not only possessed loving hearts, but brave ones. We were linked and interlinked with each other. I loved them with a love stronger than any thing I have experienced since. It is sometimes said that we slaves do not love and confide in each other. In answer to this assertion, I can say, I never loved any or confided in any people more than my fellow-slaves, and especially those with whom I lived at Mr. Freeland's. I believe we would have died for each other. We never undertook to do any thing, of any importance, without a mutual consultation. We never moved separately. We were one; and as much so by our tempers and dispositions, as by the mutual hardships to which we were necessarily subjected by our condition as slaves.

At the close of the year 1834, Mr. Freeland again hired me of my master, for the year 1835. But, by this time, I began to want to live *upon free land* as well as *with Freeland;* and I was no longer content, therefore, to live with him or any other slaveholder. I began, with the commencement of the year, to prepare myself for a final struggle, which should decide my fate one way or the other. My tendency was upward. I was fast approaching manhood, and year after year had passed, and I was still a slave. These thoughts roused me—I must do something. I therefore resolved that 1835 should not pass without witnessing an attempt, on my part, to secure my liberty. But I was not willing to cherish this determination alone. My fellow-slaves were dear to me. I was anxious to have them participate with me in this, my life-giving determination. I therefore, though with great prudence, commenced early to ascertain their views and feelings in regard to their condition, and to imbue their minds with thoughts of freedom. I bent myself to devising ways and means for our escape, and meanwhile strove, on all fitting occasions, to impress them with the gross fraud and inhumanity of slavery. I went first to Henry, next to John, then to the others. I found, in them all, warm hearts and noble spirits. They were ready to hear, and ready to act when a feasible plan should be proposed. This was what I wanted. I talked to them of our want of manhood, if we submitted to our enslavement without at least one noble effort to be free. We met often, and consulted frequently, and told our hopes and fears, recounted the difficulties, real and imagined, which we should be called on to meet. At times we were almost disposed to give up and try to content ourselves with our wretched lot; at others, we were firm and unbending in our determination to go. Whenever we suggested any plan, there was shrinking—the odds were fearful. Our path was beset with the greatest obstacles; and if we succeeded in gaining the end of it, our right to be free was yet questionable—we were yet liable to be returned to bondage. We could see no spot, this side of the ocean, where we could be free. We knew nothing about Canada. Our knowledge of the north did not extend farther than New York; and to go there, and be forever harassed with the frightful liability of being returned to slavery—with the certainty of being treated tenfold worse than before—the thought was truly a horrible one, and one which it was not easy to overcome. The case sometimes stood thus: At every gate through which we were to pass, we saw a watchman—at every ferry a guard—on every bridge a sentinel—and in every wood a patrol. We were hemmed in upon every side. Here were the difficulties, real or imagined—the good to be sought, and the evil to be shunned. On the one hand, there stood slavery, a stern reality, glaring frightfully upon us,—its robes already crimsoned with the blood of millions, and even now feasting itself greedily upon our own flesh. On the other hand, away back in the dim distance, under the flickering light of the

north star, behind some craggy hill or snow-covered mountain, stood a doubtful freedom—half frozen—beckoning us to come and share its hospitality. This in itself was
sometimes enough to stagger us; but when we permitted ourselves to survey the road,
we were frequently appalled. Upon either side we saw grim death, assuming the most
horrid shapes. Now it was starvation, causing us to eat our own flesh;—now we were
contending with the waves, and were drowned;—now we were overtaken, and torn to
pieces by the fangs of the terrible bloodhound. We were stung by scorpions, chased by
wild beasts, bitten by snakes, and finally, after having nearly reached the desired spot,—
after swimming rivers, encountering wild beasts, sleeping in the woods, suffering
hunger and nakedness,—we were overtaken by our pursuers, and in our resistance, we
were shot dead upon the spot! I say, this picture sometimes appalled us, and made us

> "rather bear those ills we had,
> Than fly to others, that we knew not of."[22]

In coming to a fixed determination to run away, we did more than Patrick Henry,
when he resolved upon liberty or death. With us it was a doubtful liberty at most, and
almost certain death if we failed. For my part, I should prefer death to hopeless bondage.

Sandy, one of our number, gave up the notion, but still encouraged us. Our company then consisted of Henry Harris, John Harris, Henry Bailey, Charles Roberts, and
myself. Henry Bailey was my uncle, and belonged to my master. Charles married my
aunt: he belonged to my master's father-in-law, Mr. William Hamilton.

The plan we finally concluded upon was, to get a large canoe belonging to Mr.
Hamilton, and upon the Saturday night previous to Easter holidays, paddle directly up
the Chesapeake Bay. On our arrival at the head of the bay, a distance of seventy or
eighty miles from where we lived, it was our purpose to turn our canoe adrift, and follow the guidance of the north star till we got beyond the limits of Maryland. Our reason
for taking the water route was, that we were less liable to be suspected as runaways; we
hoped to be regarded as fishermen; whereas, if we should take the land route, we should
be subjected to interruptions of almost every kind. Any one having a white face, and being so disposed, could stop us, and subject us to examination.

The week before our intended start, I wrote several protections, one for each of us.
As well as I can remember they were in the following words, to wit:—

"This is to certify that I, the undersigned, have given the bearer, my servant, full liberty to go to Baltimore, and spend the Easter holidays. Written with mine own hand
&c., 1835.

"William Hamilton,
"Near St. Michael's, in Talbot county, Maryland."

We were not going to Baltimore; but, in going up the bay, we went toward Baltimore, and these protections were only intended to protect us while on the bay.

As the time drew near for our departure, our anxiety became more and more intense. It was truly a matter of life and death with us. The strength of our determination
was about to be fully tested. At this time, I was very active in explaining every difficulty,

[22] From *Hamlet*, Act III, Sc. i, 11.81–82.

removing every doubt, dispelling every fear, and inspiring all with the firmness indispensable to success in our undertaking; assuring them that half was gained the instant we made the move; we had talked long enough; we were now ready to move; if not now, we never should be; and if we did not intend to move now, we had as well fold our arms, sit down, and acknowledge ourselves fit only to be slaves. This, none of us were prepared to acknowledge. Every man stood firm; and at our last meeting, we pledged ourselves afresh, in the most solemn manner, that at the time appointed, we would certainly start in pursuit of freedom. This was in the middle of the week, at the end of which we were to be off. We went, as usual, to our several fields of labor, but with bosoms highly agitated with thoughts of our truly hazardous undertaking. We tried to conceal our feelings as much as possible; and I think we succeeded very well.

After a painful waiting, the Saturday morning, whose night was to witness our departure, came. I hailed it with joy, bring what of sadness it might. Friday night was a sleepless one for me. I probably felt more anxious than the rest, because I was, by common consent, at the head of the whole affair. The responsibility of success or failure lay heavily upon me. The glory of the one, and the confusion of the other, were alike mine. The first two hours of that morning were such as I never experienced before, and hope never to again. Early in the morning, we went, as usual, to the field. We were spreading manure; and all at once, while thus engaged, I was overwhelmed with an indescribable feeling, in the fulness of which I turned to Sandy, who was near by, and said, "We are betrayed!" "Well," said he, "that thought has this moment struck me." We said no more. I was never more certain of any thing.

The horn was blown as usual, and we went up from the field to the house for breakfast. I went for the form, more than for want of any thing to eat that morning. Just as I got to the house, in looking out at the lane gate, I saw four white men, with two colored men. The white men were on horseback, and the colored ones were walking behind, as if tied. I watched them a few moments till they got up to our lane gate. Here they halted, and tied the colored men to the gate-post. I was not yet certain as to what the matter was. In a few moments, in rode Mr. Hamilton, with a speed betokening great excitement. He came to the door, and inquired if Master William was in. He was told he was at the barn. Mr. Hamilton, without dismounting, rode up to the barn with extraordinary speed. In a few moments, he and Mr. Freeland returned to the house. By this time, the three constables rode up, and in great haste dismounted, tied their horses, and met Master William and Mr. Hamilton returning from the barn; and after talking awhile, they all walked up to the kitchen door. There was no one in the kitchen but myself and John. Henry and Sandy were up at the barn. Mr. Freeland put his head in at the door, and called me by name, saying, there were some gentlemen at the door who wished to see me. I stepped to the door, and inquired what they wanted. They at once seized me, and, without giving me any satisfaction, tied me—lashing my hands closely together. I insisted upon knowing what the matter was. They at length said, that they had learned I had been in a "scrape," and that I was to be examined before my master; and if their information proved false, I should not be hurt.

In a few moments, they succeeded in tying John. They then turned to Henry, who had by this time returned, and commanded him to cross his hands. "I won't!" said Henry, in a firm tone, indicating his readiness to meet the consequences of his refusal. "Won't you?" said Tom Graham, the constable. "No, I won't!" said Henry, in a still stronger tone. With this, two of the constables pulled out their shining pistols, and swore, by their Creator, that they would make him cross his hands or kill him. Each cocked his pistol, and, with fingers on the trigger, walked up to Henry, saying, at the same time, if he did not cross his hands, they would blow his damned heart out. "Shoot me, shoot me!" said Henry; "you can't kill me but once. Shoot, shoot,—and be damned! *I won't be tied!*" This he said in a tone of loud defiance; and at the same time, with a motion as quick as lightning, he with one single stroke dashed the pistols from the hand of each constable. As he did this, all hands fell upon him, and, after beating him some time, they finally overpowered him, and got him tied.

During the scuffle, I managed, I know not how, to get my pass out, and, without being discovered, put it into the fire. We were all now tied; and just as we were to leave for Easton jail, Betsy Freeland, mother of William Freeland, came to the door with her hands full of biscuits, and divided them between Henry and John. She then delivered herself of a speech, to the following effect:—addressing herself to me, she said, "*You devil! You yellow devil!* it was you that put it into the heads of Henry and John to run away. But for you, you long-legged mulatto devil! Henry nor John would never have thought of such a thing." I made no reply, and was immediately hurried off towards St. Michael's. Just a moment previous to the scuffle with Henry, Mr. Hamilton suggested the propriety of making a search for the protections which he had understood Frederick had written for himself and the rest. But, just at the moment he was about carrying his proposal into effect, his aid was needed in helping to tie Henry; and the excitement attending the scuffle caused them either to forget, or to deem it unsafe, under the circumstances, to search. So we were not yet convicted of the intention to run away.

When we got about half way to St. Michael's, while the constables having us in charge were looking ahead, Henry inquired of me what he should do with his pass. I told him to eat it with his biscuit, and own nothing; and we passed the word around, "*Own nothing;*" and "*Own nothing!*" said we all. Our confidence in each other was unshaken. We were resolved to succeed or fail together, after the calamity had befallen us as much as before. We were now prepared for any thing. We were to be dragged that morning fifteen miles behind horses, and then to be placed in the Easton jail. When we reached St. Michael's, we underwent a sort of examination. We all denied that we ever intended to run away. We did this more to bring out the evidence against us, than from any hope of getting clear of being sold; for, as I have said, we were ready for that. The fact was, we cared but little where we went, so we went together. Our greatest concern was about separation. We dreaded that more than any thing this side of death. We found the evidence against us to be the testimony of one person; our master would not tell who it was; but we came to a unanimous decision among ourselves as to who their informant was. We were sent off to the jail at Easton. When we got there, we were delivered up to the sheriff, Mr. Joseph Graham, and by him placed in jail. Henry, John, and myself, were placed in one room together—Charles, and Henry Bailey, in another. Their object in separating us was to hinder concert.

We had been in jail scarcely twenty minutes, when a swarm of slave traders, and agents for slave traders, flocked into jail to look at us, and to ascertain if we were for sale. Such a set of beings I never saw before! I felt myself surrounded by so many fiends from perdition. A band of pirates never looked more like their father, the devil. They laughed and grinned over us, saying, "Ah, my boys! we have got you, haven't we?" And after taunting us in various ways, they one by one went into an examination of us, with intent to ascertain our value. They would impudently ask us if we would not like to have them for our masters. We would make them no answer, and leave them to find out as best they could. Then they would curse and swear at us, telling us that they could take the devil out of us in a very little while, if we were only in their hands.

While in jail, we found ourselves in much more comfortable quarters than we expected when we went there. We did not get much to eat, nor that which was very good; but we had a good clean room, from the windows of which we could see what was going on in the street, which was very much better than though we had been placed in one of the dark, damp cells. Upon the whole, we got along very well, so far as the jail and its keeper were concerned. Immediately after the holidays were over, contrary to all our expectations, Mr. Hamilton and Mr. Freeland came up to Easton, and took Charles, the two Henrys, and John, out of jail, and carried them home, leaving me alone. I regarded this separation as a final one. It caused me more pain than any thing else in the whole transaction. I was ready for any thing rather than separation. I supposed that they had consulted together, and had decided that, as I was the whole cause of the intention of the others to run away, it was hard to make the innocent suffer with the guilty; and that they had, therefore, concluded to take the others home, and sell me, as a warning to the others that remained. It is due to the noble Henry to say, he seemed almost as reluctant at leaving the prison as at leaving home to come to the prison. But we knew we should, in all probability, be separated, if we were sold; and since he was in their hands, he concluded to go peaceably home.

I was now left to my fate. I was all alone, and within the walls of a stone prison. But a few days before, and I was full of hope. I expected to have been safe in a land of freedom; but now I was covered with gloom, sunk down to the utmost despair. I thought the possibility of freedom was gone. I was kept in this way about one week, at the end of which, Captain Auld, my master, to my surprise and utter astonishment, came up, and took me out, with the intention of sending me, with a gentleman of his acquaintance, into Alabama. But, from some cause or other, he did not send me to Alabama, but concluded to send me back to Baltimore, to live again with his brother Hugh, and to learn a trade.

Thus, after an absence of three years and one month, I was once more permitted to return to my old home at Baltimore. My master sent me away, because there existed against me a very great prejudice in the community, and he feared I might be killed.

In a few weeks after I went to Baltimore, Master Hugh hired me to Mr. William Gardner, an extensive ship-builder, on Fell's Point. I was put there to learn how to calk. It, however, proved a very unfavorable place for the accomplishment of this object. Mr. Gardner was engaged that spring in building two large man-of-war brigs, professedly for the Mexican government. The vessels were to be launched in the July of that year, and in failure thereof, Mr. Gardner was to lose a considerable sum; so that when I entered, all was hurry. There was no time to learn any thing. Every man had to do that which he knew how to do. In entering the shipyard, my orders from Mr. Gardner were, to do whatever the carpenters commanded me to do. This was placing me at the beck and call of about seventy-five men. I was to regard all these as masters. Their word was to be my law. My situation was a most trying one. At times I needed a dozen pair of hands. I was called a dozen ways in the space of a single minute. Three or four voices would strike my ear at the same moment. It was—"Fred., come help me to cant this timber here."—"Fred., come carry this timber yonder."—"Fred., bring that roller here."—"Fred., go get a fresh can of water."—"Fred., come help saw off the end of this timber."—"Fred., go quick, and get the crowbar."—"Fred., hold on the end of this fall."[23]—"Fred., go to the blacksmith's shop, and get a new punch."—"Hurra, Fred.! run and bring me a cold chisel."—"I say, Fred., bear a hand, and get up a fire as quick as lightning under that steam-box."—"Halloo, nigger! come, turn this grindstone."—"Come, come! move, move! and *bowse*[24] this timber forward."—"I say, darky, blast your eyes, why don't you heat up some pitch?"—"Halloo! halloo! halloo!" (Three voices at the same time.) "Come here!—Go there!—Hold on where you are! Damn you, if you move, I'll knock your brains out!"

This was my school for eight months; and I might have remained there longer, but for a most horrid fight I had with four of the white apprentices, in which my left eye was nearly knocked out and I was horribly mangled in other respects. The facts in the case were these: Until a very little while after I went there, white and black ship-carpenters worked side by side, and no one seemed to see any impropriety in it. All hands seemed to be very well satisfied. Many of the black carpenters were freemen. Things seemed to be going on very well. All at once, the white carpenters knocked off, and said they would not work with free colored workmen. Their reason for this, as alleged, was, that if free colored carpenters were encouraged, they would soon take the trade into their own hands, and poor white men would be thrown out of employment. They therefore felt called upon at once to put a stop to it. And, taking advantage of Mr. Gardner's necessities, they broke off, swearing they would work no longer, unless he would discharge his black carpenters. Now, though this did not extend to me in form, it did reach me in fact. My fellow-apprentices very soon began to feel it degrading to them to work with me. They began to put on airs, and talk about the "niggers" taking the country, saying we all ought to be killed; and, being encouraged by the journeymen, they commenced making my condition as hard as they could, by hectoring me around, and sometimes striking me. I, of course, kept the vow I made after the fight with Mr. Covey, and struck back again, regardless of consequences; and while I kept them from combining, I succeeded very well; for I could whip the whole of them, taking them separately. They, however, at length combined, and came upon me, armed with sticks, stones, and heavy handspikes. One came in front with a half brick. There was one at each side of me, and one behind me. While I was attending to those in front, and on either side, the one behind ran up with the handspike, and struck me a heavy blow upon the head. It stunned me. I fell, and with this they all ran upon me, and fell to beating me with their fists. I let them lay on for a while, gathering strength. In an instant, I gave a sudden surge, and rose to my hands and knees. Just as I did that, one of their number gave me, with his heavy boot, a powerful kick in the left eye. My eyeball seemed to have burst. When they saw my eye closed, and badly swollen, they left me. With this I seized the handspike, and for a time pursued them. But here the carpenters interfered, and I thought I might as well give it up. It was impossible to stand my hand against so many. All this took place in sight of not less than fifty white ship-carpenters, and not one interposed a friendly word; but some cried, "Kill the damned nigger! Kill him! kill him! He struck a white person." I found my only chance for life was in flight. I succeeded in getting away without an additional blow, and barely so, for to strike a white man is death by Lynch law,—and that was the law in Mr. Gardner's ship-yard; nor is there much of any other out of Mr. Gardner's ship-yard.

[23] Tackle.
[24] Heft.

I went directly home, and told the story of my wrongs to Master Hugh; and I am happy to say of him, irreligious as he was, his conduct was heavenly, compared with that of his brother Thomas under similar circumstances. He listened attentively to my narration of the circumstances leading to the savage outrage, and gave many proofs of his strong indignation at it. The heart of my once overkind mistress was again melted into pity. My puffed-out eye and blood-covered face moved her to tears. She took a chair by me, washed the blood from my face, and, with a mother's tenderness, bound up my head, covering the wounded eye with a lean piece of fresh beef. It was almost compensation for my suffering to witness, once more, a manifestation of kindness from this, my once affectionate old mistress. Master Hugh was very much enraged. He gave expression to his feelings by pouring out curses upon the heads of those who did the deed. As soon as I got a little the better of my bruises, he took me with him to Esquire Watson's, on Bond Street, to see what could be done about the matter. Mr. Watson inquired who saw the assault committed. Master Hugh told him it was done in Mr. Gardner's ship-yard, at midday, where there were a large company of men at work. "As to that," he said, "the deed was done, and there was no question as to who did it." His answer was, he could do nothing in the case, unless some white man would come forward and testify. He could issue no warrant on my word. If I had been killed in the presence of a thousand colored people, their testimony combined would have been insufficient to have arrested one of the murderers. Master Hugh, for once, was compelled to say this state of things was too bad. Of course, it was impossible to get any white man to volunteer his testimony in my behalf, and against the white young men. Even those who may have sympathized with me were not prepared to do this. It required a degree of courage unknown to them to do so; for just at that time, the slightest manifestation of humanity toward a colored person was denounced as abolitionism, and that name subjected its bearer to frightful liabilities. The watchwords of the bloody-minded in that region, and in those days, were, "Damn the abolitionists!" and "Damn the niggers!" There was nothing done, and probably nothing would have been done if I had been killed. Such was, and such remains, the state of things in the Christian city of Baltimore.

Master Hugh, finding he could get no redress, refused to let me go back again to Mr. Gardner. He kept me himself, and his wife dressed my wound till I was again restored to health. He then took me into the ship-yard of which he was foreman, in the employment of Mr. Walter Price. There I was immediately set to calking, and very soon learned the art of using my mallet and irons. In the course of one year from the time I left Mr. Gardner's, I was able to command the highest wages given to the most experienced calkers. I was now of some importance to my master. I was bringing him from six to seven dollars per week. I sometimes brought him nine dollars per week: my wages were a dollar and a half a day. After learning how to calk, I sought my own employment, made my own contracts, and collected the money which I earned. My pathway became much more smooth than before; my condition was now much more comfortable. When I could get no calking to do, I did nothing. During these leisure times, those old notions about freedom would steal over me again. When in Mr. Gardner's employment, I was kept in such a perpetual whirl of excitement, I could think of nothing, scarcely, but my life; and in thinking of my life, I almost forgot my liberty. I have observed this in my experience of slavery,—that whenever my condition was improved, instead of its increasing my contentment, it only increased my desire to be free, and set me to thinking of plans to gain my freedom. I have found that, to make a contented slave, it is necessary to make a thoughtless one. It is necessary to darken his moral and mental vision, and, as far as possible, to annihilate the power of reason. He must be able to detect no inconsistencies in slavery; he must be made to feel that slavery is right; and he can be brought to that only when he ceases to be a man.

I was now getting, as I have said, one dollar and fifty cents per day. I contracted for it; I earned it; it was paid to me; it was rightfully my own; yet, upon each returning Saturday night, I was compelled to deliver every cent of that money to Master Hugh. And why? Not because he earned it,—not because he had any hand in earning it,—not because I owed it to him,—nor because he possessed the slightest shadow of a right to it; but solely because he had the power to compel me to give it up. The right of the grim-visaged pirate upon the high seas is exactly the same.

Chapter XI

I now come to that part of my life during which I planned, and finally succeeded in making, my escape from slavery. But before narrating any of the peculiar circumstances, I deem it proper to make known my intention not to state all the facts connected with the transaction. My reasons for pursuing this course may be understood from the following: First, were I to give a minute statement of all the facts, it is not only possible but quite probable, that others would thereby be involved in the most embarrassing difficulties. Secondly, such a statement would most undoubtedly induce greater vigilance on the part of slaveholders than has existed heretofore among them; which would, of course, be the means of guarding a door whereby some dear brother bondman might escape his galling chains. I deeply regret the necessity that impels me to suppress any thing of importance connected with my experience in slavery. It would afford me great pleasure indeed, as well as materially add to the interest of my narrative, were I at liberty to gratify a curiosity, which I know exists in the minds of many, by an accurate statement of all the facts pertaining to my most fortunate escape. But I must deprive myself of this pleasure, and the curious of the gratification which such a statement would afford. I would allow myself to suffer under the greatest imputations which evil-minded men might suggest, rather than exculpate myself, and thereby run the hazard of closing the slightest avenue by which a brother slave might clear himself of the chains and fetters of slavery.

I have never approved of the very public manner in which some of our western friends have conducted what they call the *underground railroad*,[25] but which I think by their open declarations, has been made most emphatically the *upperground railroad*. I honor those good men and women for their noble daring, and applaud them for willingly subjecting themselves to bloody persecution, by openly avowing their participation in the escape of slaves. I, however, can see very little good resulting from such a course, either to themselves or the slaves escaping; while, upon the other hand, I see and feel assured that those open declarations are a positive evil to the slaves remaining, who are seeking to escape. They do nothing towards enlightening the slave, whilst they do much towards enlightening the master. They stimulate him to greater watchfulness, and enhance his power to capture his slave. We owe something to the slave south of the line as well as to those north of it; and in aiding the latter on their way to freedom, we

[25] Network of surreptitious aids by which slaves were helped in their escape to the North.

should be careful to do nothing which would be likely to hinder the former from escaping from slavery. I would keep the merciless slaveholder profoundly ignorant of the means of flight adopted by the slave. I would leave him to imagine himself surrounded by myriads of invisible tormentors, ever ready to snatch from his infernal grasp his trembling prey. Let him be left to feel his way in the dark; let darkness commensurate with his crime hover over him; and let him feel that at every step he takes, in pursuit of the flying bondman, he is running the frightful risk of having his hot brains dashed out by an invisible agency. Let us render the tyrant no aid; let us not hold the light by which he can trace the footprints of our flying brother. But enough of this. I will now proceed to the statement of those facts, connected with my escape, for which I am alone responsible, and for which no one can be made to suffer but myself.

In the early part of the year 1838, I became quite restless. I could see no reason why I should, at the end of each week, pour the reward of my toil into the purse of my master. When I carried to him my weekly wages, he would, after counting the money, look me in the face with a robber-like fierceness, and say, "Is this all?" He was satisfied with nothing less than the last cent. He would, however, when I made him six dollars, sometimes give me six cents, to encourage me. It had the opposite effect. I regarded it as a sort of admission of my right to the whole. The fact that he gave me any part of my wages was proof, to my mind, that he believed me entitled to the whole of them. I always felt worse for having received any thing; for I feared that the giving me a few cents would ease his conscience, and make him feel himself to be a pretty honorable sort of robber. My discontent grew upon me. I was ever on the look-out for means of escape; and, finding no direct means, I determined to try to hire my time, with a view of getting money with which to make my escape. In the spring of 1838, when Master Thomas came to Baltimore to purchase his spring goods, I got an opportunity, and applied to him to allow me to hire my time. He unhesitatingly refused my request, and told me this was another stratagem by which to escape. He told me I could go nowhere but that he could get me; and that, in the event of my running away, he should spare no pains in his efforts to catch me. He exhorted me to content myself, and be obedient. He told me, if I would be happy, I must lay out no plans for the future. He said, if I behaved myself properly, he would take care of me. Indeed, he advised me to complete thoughtlessness of the future, and taught me to depend solely upon him for happiness. He seemed to see fully the pressing necessity of setting aside my intellectual nature, in order to [insure] contentment in slavery. But in spite of him, and even in spite of myself, I continued to think, and to think about the injustice of my enslavement, and the means of escape.

About two months after this, I applied to Master Hugh for the privilege of hiring my time. He was not acquainted with the fact that I had applied to Master Thomas, and had been refused. He too, at first, seemed disposed to refuse; but, after some reflection, he granted me the privilege, and proposed the following terms: I was to be allowed all my time, make all contracts with those for whom I worked, and find my own employment; and, in return for this liberty, I was to pay him three dollars at the end of each week; find myself in calking tools, and in board and clothing. My board was two dollars and a half per week. This, with the wear and tear of clothing and calking tools, made my regular expenses about six dollars per week. This amount I was compelled to make up, or relinquish the privilege of hiring my time. Rain or shine, work or no work, at the end of each week the money must be forthcoming, or I must give up my privilege. This arrangement, it will be perceived, was decidedly in my master's favor. It relieved him of all need of looking after me. His money was sure. He received all the benefits of slave-holding without its evils; while I endured all the evils of a slave, and suffered all the care and anxiety of a freeman. I found it a hard bargain. But, hard as it was I thought it better than the old mode of getting along. It was a step towards freedom to be allowed to bear the responsibilities of a freeman, and I was determined to hold on upon it. I bent myself to the work of making money. I was ready to work at night as well as day, and by the most untiring perservance and industry, I made enough to meet my expenses, and lay up a little money every week. I went on thus from May till August. Master Hugh then refused to allow me to hire my time longer. The ground for his refusal was a failure on my part, one Saturday night, to pay him for my week's time. This failure was occasioned by my attending a camp meeting about ten miles from Baltimore. During the week, I had entered into an engagement with a number of young friends to start from Baltimore to the camp ground early Saturday evening: and being detained by my employer, I was unable to get down to Master Hugh's without disappointing the company. I knew that Master Hugh was in no special need of the money that night. I therefore decided to go to the camp meeting, and upon my return pay him the three dollars. I staid at the camp meeting one day longer than I intended when I left. But as soon as I returned, I called upon him to pay him what he considered his due. I found him very angry; he could scarce restrain his wrath. He said he had a great mind to give me a severe whipping. He wished to know how I dared go out of the city without asking his permission. I told him I hired my time, and while I paid him the price which he asked for it, I did not know that I was bound to ask him when and where I should go. This reply troubled him; and, after reflecting a few moments, he turned to me, and said I should hire my time no longer; that the next thing he should know of, I would be running away. Upon the same plea, he told me to bring my tools and clothing home forthwith. I did so; but instead of seeking work, as I had been accustomed to do previously to hiring my time, I spent the whole week without the performance of a single stroke of work. I did this in retaliation. Saturday night, he called upon me as usual for my week's wages. I told him I had no wages; I had done no work that week. Here we were upon the point of coming to blows. He raved, and swore his determination to get hold of me. I did not allow myself a single word; but was resolved, if he laid the weight of his hand upon me, it should be blow for blow. He did not strike me, but told me that he would find me in constant employment in future. I thought the matter over during the next day, Sunday, and finally resolved upon the third day of September, as the day upon which I would make a second attempt to secure my freedom. I now had three weeks during which to prepare for my journey. Early on Monday morning, before Master Hugh had time to make any engagement for me, I went out and got employment of Mr. Butler, at his ship-yard near the drawbridge, upon what is called the City Block, thus making it unnecessary for him to seek employment for me. At the end of the week, I brought him between eight and nine dollars. He seemed very well pleased, and asked why I did not do the same the week before. He little knew what my plans were. My object in working steadily was to remove any suspicion he might entertain of my intent to run away; and in this I succeeded admirably. I suppose he thought I was never better satisfied with my condition than at the very time during which I was planning my escape. The second week passed, and again I carried him my full wages; and so well pleased was he, that he gave me twenty-five cents, (quite a large sum for a slaveholder to give a slave), and bade me to make a good use of it. I told him I would.

Things went on without very smoothly indeed, but within there was trouble. It is impossible for me to describe my feelings as the time of my contemplated start drew near. I had a number of warm-hearted friends in Baltimore,—friends that I loved almost as I did my life,—and the thought of being separated from them forever was painful beyond expression. It is my opinion that thousands would escape from slavery, who now remain, but for the strong cords of affection that bind them to their friends. The thought of leaving my friends was decidedly the most painful thought with which I had to contend. The love of them was my tender point, and shook my decision more than all things else. Besides the pain of separation, the dread and apprehension of a failure exceeded what I had experienced at my first attempt. The appalling defeat I then sustained returned to torment me. I felt assured that, if I failed in this attempt, my case would be hopeless one—it would seal my fate as a slave forever. I could not hope to get off with any thing less than the severest punishment, and being placed beyond the means of escape. It required no very vivid imagination to depict the most frightful scenes through which I should have to pass, in case I failed. The wretchedness of slavery, and the blessedness of freedom, were perpetually before me. It was life and death with me. But I remained firm, and, according to my resolution, on the third day of September, 1838, I left my chains, and succeeded in reaching New York without the slightest interruption of any kind. How I did so,—what means I adopted,—what direction I travelled, and by what mode of conveyance,—I must leave unexplained, for the reasons before mentioned.

I have been frequently asked how I felt when I found myself in a free State. I have never been able to answer the question with any satisfaction to myself. It was a moment of the highest excitement I ever experienced. I suppose I felt as one may imagine the unarmed mariner to feel when he is rescued by a friendly man-of-war from the pursuit of a pirate. In writing to a dear friend, immediately after my arrival at New York, I said I felt like one who had escaped a den of hungry lions. This state of mind, however, very soon subsided; and I was again seized with a feeling of great insecurity and loneliness. I was yet liable to be taken back, and subjected to all the tortures of slavery. This in itself was enough to damp the ardor of my enthusiasm. But the loneliness overcame me. There I was in the midst of thousands, and yet a perfect stranger; without home and without friends, in the midst of thousands of my own brethren—children of a common Father, and yet I dared not to unfold to any one of them my sad condition. I was afraid to speak to any one for fear of speaking to the wrong one, and thereby falling into the hands of money-loving kidnappers, whose business it was to lie in wait for the panting fugitive, as the ferocious beasts of the forest lie in wait for their prey. The motto which I adopted when I started from slavery was this—"Trust no man!" I saw in every white man an enemy, and in almost every colored man cause for distrust. It was a most painful situation; and, to understand it, one must needs experience it, or imagine himself in similar circumstances. Let him be a fugitive slave in a strange land—a land given up to be the hunting-ground for slaveholders—whose inhabitants are legalized kidnappers—where he is every moment subjected to the terrible liability of being seized upon by his fellowmen, as the hideous crocodile seizes upon his prey!—I say, let him place himself in my situation—without home or friends—without money or credit—wanting shelter, and no one to give it—wanting bread, and no money to buy it,—and at the same time let him feel that he is pursued by merciless men-hunters, and in total darkness as to what to do, where to go, or where to stay,—perfectly helpless both as to the means of defence and means of escape,—in the midst of plenty, yet suffering the terrible gnawings of hunger,—in the midst of houses, yet having no home,—among fellow-men, yet feeling as if in the midst of wild beasts, whose greediness to swallow up the trembling and half-famished fugitive is only equalled by that with which the monsters of the deep swallow up the helpless fish upon which they subsist,—I say, let him be placed in this most trying situation,—the situation in which I was placed,—then, and not till then, will he fully appreciate the hardships of, and know how to sympathize with, the toil-worn and whip-scarred fugitive slave.

Thank Heaven, I remained but a short time in this distressed situation. I was relieved from it by the humane hand of Mr. DAVID RUGGLES,[26] whose vigilance, kindness, and perseverance, I shall never forget. I am glad of an opportunity to express, as far as words can, the love and gratitude I bear him. Mr. Ruggles is now afflicted with blindness, and is himself in need of the same kind offices which he was once so forward in the performance of toward others. I had been in New York but a few days, when Mr. Ruggles sought me out, and very kindly took me to his boarding-house at the corner of Church and Lespenard Streets. Mr. Ruggles was then very deeply engaged in the memorable *Darg* case, as well as attending to a number of other fugitive slaves; devising ways and means for their successful escape; and, though watched and hemmed in on almost every side, he seemed to be more than a match for his enemies.

Very soon after I went to Mr. Ruggles, he wished to know of me where I wanted to go; as he deemed it unsafe for me to remain in New York. I told him I was a calker, and should like to go where I could get work. I thought of going to Canada; but he decided against it, and in favor of my going to New Bedford, thinking I should be able to get work there at my trade. At this time, Anna,[27] my intended wife, came on; for I wrote to her immediately after my arrival at New York, (notwithstanding my homeless, house-less, and helpless condition,) informing her of my successful flight, and wishing her to come on forthwith. In a few days after her arrival, Mr. Ruggles called in the Rev. J.W.C. Pennington, who, in the presence of Mr. Ruggles, Mrs. Michaels, and two or three others, performed the marriage ceremony, and gave us a certificate, of which the following is an exact copy:—

> "This may certify, that I joined together in holy matrimony Frederick Johnson[28] and Anna Murray, as man and wife, in the presence of Mr. David Ruggles and Mrs. Michaels.
>
> "James W.C. Pennington
> "New York, Sept. 15, 1838."

Upon receiving this certificate, and a five-dollar bill from Mr. Ruggles, I shouldered one part of our baggage, and Anna took up the other, and we set out forthwith to take passage on board of the steamboat John W. Richmond for Newport, on our way to New Bedford. Mr. Ruggles gave me a letter to a Mr. Shaw in Newport, and told me, in case my money did not serve me to New Bedford, to stop in Newport and obtain further assistance; but upon our arrival at Newport, we were so anxious to get to a place of safety, that, notwithstanding we lacked the necessary money to pay our fare, we decided to take

---

[26] African American activist (1810–1849) who counted Douglass among the many fugitives he aided; he was also instrumental in arranging Douglass's marriage.

[27] Douglass's note—"She was free."

[28] Douglass's note—"I had changed my name from Frederick *Bailey* to that of *Johnson*."

seats in the stage, and promise to pay when we got to New Bedford. We were encouraged to do this by two excellent gentlemen, residents of New Bedford, whose names I afterward ascertained to be Joseph Ricketson and William C. Taber. They seemed at once to understand our circumstances, and gave us such assurance of their friendliness as put us fully at ease in their presence. It was good indeed to meet with such friends, at such a time. Upon reaching New Bedford, we were directed to the house of Mr. Nathan Johnson, by whom we were kindly received, and hospitably provided for. Both Mr. and Mrs. Johnson took a deep and lively interest in our welfare. They proved themselves quite worthy of the name of abolitionists. When the stage-driver found us unable to pay our fare, he held on upon our baggage as security for the debt. I had but to mention the fact to Mr. Johnson, and he forthwith advanced the money.

We now began to feel a degree of safety, and to prepare ourselves for the duties and responsibilities of a life of freedom. On the morning after our arrival at New Bedford, while at the breakfast-table, the question arose as to what name I should be called by. The name given me by my mother was, "Frederick Augustus Washington Bailey." I, however, had dispensed with the two middle names long before I left Maryland so that I was generally known by the name of "Frederick Bailey." I started from Baltimore bearing the name of "Stanley." When I got to New York I again changed my name to "Frederick Johnson," and thought that would be the last change. But when I got to New Bedford, I found it necessary again to change my name. The reason of this necessity was, that there were so many Johnsons in New Bedford, it was already quite difficult to distinguish between them. I gave Mr. Johnson the privilege of choosing me a name, but told him he must not take from me the name of "Frederick." I must hold on to that, to preserve a sense of my identity. Mr. Johnson had just been reading the "Lady of the Lake," and at once suggested that my name be "Douglass."[29] From that time until now I have been called "Frederick Douglass"; and as I am more widely known by that name than by either of the others, I shall continue to use it as my own.

I was quite disappointed at the general appearance of things in New Bedford. The impression which I had received respecting the character and condition of the people of the north, I found to be singularly erroneous. I had very strangely supposed, while in slavery, that few of the comforts, and scarcely any of the luxuries, of life were enjoyed at the north, compared with what were enjoyed by the slaveholders of the south. I probably came to this conclusion from the fact that northern people owned no slaves. I supposed that they were about upon a level with the non-slaveholding population of the south. I knew *they* were exceedingly poor, and I had been accustomed to regard their poverty as the necessary consequence of their being non-slaveholders. I had somehow imbibed the opinion that, in the absence of slaves, there could be no wealth, and very little refinement. And upon coming to the north, I expected to meet with a rough, hard-handed, and uncultivated population, living in the most Spartanlike simplicity, knowing nothing of the ease, luxury, pomp, and grandeur of southern slaveholders. Such being my conjectures, any one acquainted with the appearance of New Bedford may very readily infer how palpably I must have seen my mistake.

In the afternoon of the day when I reached New Bedford, I visited the wharves, to take a view of the shipping. Here I found myself surrounded with the strongest proofs

[29] For the last of his name-changes, Douglass selected that of an important figure from "Lady of the Lake," a long narrative poem by Sir Walter Scott.

of wealth. Lying at the wharves, and riding in the stream, I saw many ships of the finest model, in the best order, and of the largest size. Upon the right and left, I was walled in by granite warehouses of the widest dimensions, stowed to their utmost capacity with the necessaries and comforts of life. Added to this, almost every body seemed to be at work, but noiselessly so, compared with what I had been accustomed to in Baltimore. There were no loud songs heard from those engaged in loading and unloading ships. I heard no deep oaths or horrid curses on the laborer. I saw no whipping of men; but all seemed to go smoothly on. Every man appeared to understand his work, and went at it with a sober, yet cheerful earnestness, which betokened the deep interest which he felt in what he was doing, as well as a sense of his own dignity as man. To me this looked exceedingly strange. From the wharves I strolled around and over the town, gazing with wonder and admiration at the splendid churches, beautiful dwellings, and finely-cultivated gardens; evincing an amount of wealth, comfort, taste, and refinement, such as I had never seen in any part of slaveholding Maryland.

Every thing looked clean, new, and beautiful. I saw few or no dilapidated houses, with poverty-stricken inmates; no half-naked children and barefooted women, such as I had been accustomed to see in Hillsborough, Easton, St. Michael's, and Baltimore. The people looked more able, stronger, healthier, and happier, than those of Maryland. I was for once made glad by a view of extreme wealth, without being saddened by seeing extreme poverty. But the most astonishing as well as the most interesting thing to me was the condition of the colored people, a great many of whom, like myself, had escaped thither as a refuge from the hunters of men. I found many, who had not been seven years out of their chains, living in finer houses, and evidently enjoying more of the comforts of life, than the average of slaveholders in Maryland. I will venture to assert, that my friend Mr. Nathan Johnson (of whom I can say with a grateful heart, "I was hungry, and he gave me meat; I was thirsty, and he gave me drink; I was a stranger, and he took me in")[30] lived in a neater house; dined at a better table; took, paid for, and read, more newspapers; better understood the moral, religious, and political character of the nation,—than nine tenths of the slaveholders in Talbot county Maryland. Yet Mr. Johnson was a working man. His hands were hardened by toil, and not his alone, but those also of Mrs. Johnson. I found the colored people much more spirited than I had supposed they would be. I found among them a determination to protect each other from the blood-thirsty kidnapper, at all hazards. Soon after my arrival, I was told a circumstance which illustrated their spirit. A colored man and a fugitive slave were on unfriendly terms. The former was heard to threaten the latter with informing his master of his whereabouts. Straightway a meeting was called among the colored people, under the stereotyped notice, "Business of importance!" The betrayer was invited to attend. The people came at the appointed hour, and organized the meeting by appointing a very religious old gentleman as president, who, I believe, made a prayer, after which he addressed the meeting as follows: *Friends, we have got him here, and I would recommend that you young men just take him outside the door, and kill him!*" With this, a number of them bolted at him; but they were intercepted by some more timid than themselves, and the betrayer escaped their vengeance, and has not been seen in New Bedford since. I believe there have been no more such threats, and should there be hereafter, I doubt not that death would be the consequence.

[30] Matthew 25:35.

I found employment, the third day after my arrival, in stowing a sloop with a load of oil. It was new, dirty, and hard work for me; but I went at it with a glad heart and a willing hand. I was now my own master. It was a happy moment, the rapture of which can be understood only by those who have been slaves. It was the first work, the reward of which was to be entirely my own. There was no Master Hugh standing ready, the moment I earned the money, to rob me of it. I worked that day with a pleasure I had never before experienced. I was at work for myself and newly-married wife. It was to me the starting-point of a new existence. When I got through with that job, I went in pursuit of a job of calking; but such was the strength of prejudice against color, among the white calkers, that they refused to work with me, and of course I could get no employment.[31] Finding my trade of no immediate benefit, I threw off my calking habiliments, and prepared myself to do any kind of work I could get to do. Mr. Johnson kindly let me have his wood-horse and saw, and I very soon found myself, a plenty of work. There was no work too hard—none too dirty. I was ready to saw wood, shovel coal, carry wood, sweep the chimney, or roll oil casks,—all of which I did for nearly three years in New Bedford, before I became known to the anti-slavery world.

In about four months after I went to New Bedford, there came a young man to me, and inquired if I did not wish to take the "Liberator."[32] I told him I did; but, just having made my escape from slavery, I remarked that I was unable to pay for it then. I, however, finally became a subscriber to it. The paper came, and I read it from week to week with such feelings as it would be quite idle for me to attempt to describe. The paper became my meat and my drink. My soul was set all on fire. Its sympathy for my brethren in bonds—its scathing denunciations of slaveholders—its faithful exposures of slavery—and its powerful attacks upon the upholders of the institution—sent a thrill of joy through my soul, such as I had never felt before!

I had not long been a reader of the "Liberator," before I got a pretty correct idea of the principles, measures and spirit of the anti-slavery reform. I took right hold of the cause. I could do but little; but what I could, I did with a joyful heart, and never felt happier than when in an anti-slavery meeting. I seldom had much to say at the meetings, because what I wanted to say was said so much better by others. But, while attending an anti-slavery convention at Nantucket, on the 11th of August, 1841, I felt strongly moved to speak, and was at the same time much urged to do so by Mr. William C. Coffin, a gentleman who had heard me speak in the colored people's meeting at New Bedford. It was a severe cross, and I took it up reluctantly. The truth was, I felt myself a slave, and the idea of speaking to white people weighed me down. I spoke but a few moments, when I felt a degree of freedom, and said what I desired with considerable ease. From that time until now, I have been engaged in pleading the cause of my brethren—with what success, and with what devotion, I leave those acquainted with my labors to decide.

Appendix

I find, since reading over the foregoing Narrative, that I have, in several instances, spoken in such a tone and manner, respecting religion, as may possibly lead those unacquainted with my religious views to suppose me an opponent of all religion. To remove

---

[31] Douglass's note—"I am told that colored persons can now get employment at calking in New Bedford—a result of anti-slavery effort."

[32] Antislavery Boston newspaper established in 1831 by William Lloyd Garrison.

the liability of such misapprehension, I deem it proper to append the following brief explanation. What I have said respecting and against religion, I mean strictly to apply to the *slaveholding religion* of this land, and with no possible reference to Christianity proper; for, between the Christianity of this land, and the Christianity of Christ, I recognize the widest possible difference—so wide, that to receive the one as good, pure, and holy, is of necessity to reject the other as bad, corrupt, and wicked. To be the friend of the one, is of necessity to be the enemy of the other. I love the pure, peaceable, and impartial Christianity of Christ: I therefore hate the corrupt, slaveholding, women-whipping, cradle-plundering, partial and hypocritical Christianity of this land. Indeed, I can see no reason, but the most deceitful one, for calling the religion of this land Christianity. I look upon it as the climax of all misnomers, the boldest of all frauds, and the grossest of all libels. Never was there a clearer case of "stealing the livery of the court of heaven to serve the devil in." I am filled with unutterable loathing when I contemplate the religious pomp and show, together with the horrible inconsistencies, which every where surrounded me. We have men-stealers for ministers, women-whippers for missionaries, and cradle-plunderers for church members. The man who wields the blood-clotted cowskin during the week fills the pulpit on Sunday, and claims to be a minister of the meek and lowly Jesus. The man who robs me of my earnings at the end of each week meets me as a class-leader on Sunday morning, to show me the way of life, and the path of salvation. He who sells my sister, for purposes of prostitution, stands forth as the pious advocate of purity. He who proclaims it a religious duty to read the Bible denies me the right of learning to read the name of the God who made me. He who is the religious advocate of marriage robs whole millions of its sacred influence, and leaves them to the ravages of wholesale pollution. The warm defender of the sacredness of the family relation is the same that scatters whole families,—sundering husbands and wives, parents and children, sisters and brothers,—leaving the hut vacant, and the hearth desolate. We see the thief preaching against theft, and the adulterer against adultery. We have men sold to build churches, women sold to support the gospel, and babes sold to purchase Bibles for the *poor heathen! all for the glory of God and the good of souls!* The slave auctioneer's bell and the church-going bell chime in with each other, and the bitter cries of the heart-broken slave are drowned in the religious shouts of his pious master. Revivals of religion and revivals in the slave-trade go hand in hand together. The slave prison and the church stand near each other. The clanking of fetters and the rattling of chains in the prison, and the pious psalm and solemn prayer in the church, may be heard at the same time. The dealers in the bodies and souls of men erect their stand in the presence of the pulpit, and they mutually help each other. The dealer gives his blood-stained gold to support the pulpit, and the pulpit, in return, covers his infernal business with the garb of Christianity. Here we have religion and robbery the allies of each other—devils dressed in angels' robes, and hell presenting the semblance of paradise.

> "Just God! and these are they,
>   Who minister at thine altar, God of right!
> Men who their hands, with prayer and blessing, lay
>   On Israel's ark of light.[33]

[33] The Torah, the Hebrew holy writings, are
   contained within the Ark of the Covenant
   in every synagogue.

"What! preach, and kidnap men?
    Give thanks, and rob thy own afflicted poor?
Talk of thy glorious liberty, and then
    Bolt hard the captive's door?

"What! servants of thy own
    Merciful Son, who came to seek and save
The homeless and the outcast, fettering down
    The tasked and plundered slave!

"Pilate and Herod friends![34]
    Chief priests and rulers, as of old, combine!
Just God and holy! is that church which lends
    Strength to the spoiler thine?"

The Christianity of America is a Christianity, of whose votaries it may be as truly said, as it was of the ancient scribes and Pharisees,[35] "They bind heavy burdens, and grievous to be borne, and lay them on men's shoulders, but they themselves will not move them with one of their fingers. All their works they do for to be seen of men.— They love the uppermost rooms at feasts, and the chief seats in the synagogues, ... and to be called of men, Rabbi, Rabbi.—But woe unto you, scribes and Pharisees, hypocrites! for ye shut up the kingdom of heaven against men; for ye neither go in yourselves, neither suffer ye them that are entering to go in. Ye devour widows' houses, and for a pretence make long prayers; therefore ye shall receive the greater damnation. Ye compass sea and land to make one proselyte, and when he is made, ye make him twofold more the child of hell than yourselves.—Woe unto you, scribes and Pharisees, hypocrites! for ye pay tithe of mint, and anise, and cumin, and have omitted the weightier matters of the law, judgment, mercy, and faith; these ought ye to have done, and not to leave the other undone. Ye blind guides! which strain at a gnat, and swallow a camel. Woe unto you, scribes and Pharisees, hypocrites! for ye make clean the outside of the cup and of the platter; but within, they are full of extortion and excess.—Woe unto you, scribes and Pharisees, hypocrites! for ye are like unto whited sepulchres, which indeed appear beautiful outward, but are within full of dead men's bones, and of all uncleanness. Even so ye also outwardly appear righteous unto men, but within ye are full of hypocrisy and iniquity."[36]

Dark and terrible as is this picture, I hold it to be strictly true of the overwhelming mass of professed Christians in America. They strain at a gnat, and swallow a camel. Could any thing be more true of our churches? They would be shocked at the proposition of fellowshipping, a *sheep*-stealer; and at the same time they hug to their communion a *man*-stealer, and brand me with being an infidel, if I find fault with them for it.

---

[34] Pontius Pilate, Roman leader in Jerusalem who handed Jesus over to the people for crucifixion; Herod Antipas, another personage of high rank to hand over an innocent prisoner to death, in this instance, John the Baptist, whose head had been requested by Herod's stepdaughter Salome.

[35] Self-proclaimed enemies of Jesus whom they felt threatened their authority and their sense of piety.

[36] Matthew 23.

They attend with Pharisaical strictness to the outward forms of religion, and at the same time neglect the weightier matters of the law, judgment, mercy, and faith. They are always ready to sacrifice, but seldom to show mercy. They are they who are represented as professing to love God whom they have not seen, whilst they hate their brother whom they have seen. They love the heathen on the other side of the globe. They can pray for him, pay money to have the Bible put into his hand, and missionaries to instruct him; while they despise and totally neglect the heathen at their own doors.

Such is, very briefly, my view of the religion of this land; and to avoid any misunderstanding, growing out of the use of general terms, I mean, by the religion of this land, that which is revealed in the words, deeds, and actions, of those bodies, north and south, calling themselves Christian churches, and yet in union with slaveholders. It is against religion, as presented by these bodies, that I have felt it my duty to testify.

I conclude these remarks by copying the following portrait of the religion of the south, (which is, by communion and fellowship, the religion of the north,) which I soberly affirm is "true to the life," and without caricature or the slightest exaggeration. It is said to have been drawn, several years before the present anti-slavery agitation began, by a northern Methodist preacher, who, while residing at the south, had an opportunity to see slaveholding morals, manners, and piety, with his own eyes. "Shall I not visit for these things? saith the Lord. Shall not my soul be avenged on such a nation as this?"[37]

A Parody[38]

"Come, saints and sinners, hear me tell
How pious priests whip Jack and Nell,
And women buy and children sell,
And preach all sinners down to hell,
   And sing of heavenly union.

"They'll bleat and baa, dona like goats,
Gorge down black sheep, and strain at motes,
Array their backs in fine black coats,
Then seize their negroes by their throats,
   And choke, for heavenly union.

"They'll church you if you sip a dram,
And damn you if you steal a lamb;
Yet rob old Tony, Doll, and Sam,
Of human rights, and bread and ham;
   Kidnapper's heavenly union.

"They'll loudly talk of Christ's reward,
And bind his image with a cord
And scold, and swing the lash abhorred,

---

[37] Jeremiah 5:9.
[38] Based on a popular southern hymn.

And sell their brother in the Lord
  To handcuffed heavenly union.

"They'll read and sing a sacred song,
And make a prayer both loud and long,
And teach the right and do the wrong,
Hailing the brother, sister throng,
  With words of heavenly union.

"We wonder how such saints can sing,
Or praise the Lord upon the wing,
Who roar, and scold, and whip, and sting,
And to their slaves and mammon cling,
  In guilty conscience union.

"They'll raise tobacco, corn, and rye,
And drive, and thieve, and cheat, and lie,
And lay up treasures in the sky,
By making switch and cowskin fly,
  In hope of heavenly union.

"They'll crack old Tony on the skull,
And preach and roar like Bashan bull,
Or braying ass, of mischief full,
Then seize old Jacob by the wool,
  And pull for heavenly union.

"A roaring, ranting, sleek man-thief,
Who lived on mutton, veal, and beef,
Yet never would afford relief
To needy, sable sons of grief,
  Was big with heavenly union.

" 'Love not the world,' the preacher said,
And winked his eye, and shook his head;
He seized on Tom, and Dick, and Ned,
Cut short their meat, and clothes, and bread,
  Yet still loved heavenly union.

"Another preacher whining spoke
Of One whose heart for sinners broke:
He tied old Nanny to an oak,
And drew the blood at every stroke,
  And prayed for heavenly union.

"Two others oped their iron jaws,
And waved their children-stealing paws;
There sat their children in gewgaws;
By stinting negroes' backs and maws,
    They kept up heavenly union.

"All good from Jack another takes,
And entertains their flirts and rakes,
Who dress as sleek as glossy snakes,
And cram their mouths with sweetened cakes;
    And this goes down for union."

Sincerely and earnestly hoping that this little book may do something toward throwing light on the American slave system, and hastening the glad day of deliverance to the millions of my brethren in bonds—faithfully relying upon the power of truth, love, and justice, for success in my humble efforts—and solemnly pledging my self anew to the sacred cause,—I subscribe myself,

FREDERICK DOUGLASS
Lynn, *Mass., April 28, 1845.*

1845, 1847

Mary Boykin Miller Chesnut
(1823–1886)

The diary of Mary Boykin Miller Chesnut presents an important aspect of U.S. history, for in her writing is seen a different South—and southern woman—than ever before. Mary Chesnut's work is an excellent social and historical source, for she was extremely well educated, informed as to current events, and prolific. She reveals a South in which the bawdy, the risque, and the scandalous were relished and laughed over; her characters are infinitely more human and believable than many of those that people other works of southern literature. Chesnut does not shy away from discussing taboo subjects (such as the rampant miscegenation occurring in many slave-owning households) and is unafraid of addressing the most horrific. She writes with bluntness and clarity, giving a thorough portrait of the people of her time.

Hers is the wealthy white southern woman's response to slavery. She sees negroes as "dirty, slatternly, idle, ill-smelling by nature" and believes that they prefer slavery, and its dependence, to any freedom which might require more effort and civilization on their part. Chesnut agrees that "slavery has to go, of course," but because "all that has been gained by it [slavery] goes to the North and to Negroes," and not because of any deep Christian feeling on her part. She does not trust negro women at all, for she believes they possess low morals by nature, and she would prefer to have them far away from white southern men, who are "degraded" by their low mistresses. She claims that "bad women, if they are not white and serve in a menial capacity, may swarm the house unmolested" while their white mistresses refuse to acknowledge the behavior occurring under their own roofs.

Born on May 31, 1823, in Statesboro, South Carolina, Mary Miller Chesnut was "a rebel born," inextricably caught up in the political currents of the age. Her father, Stephen Decatur Miller, was a U.S. senator, and in 1826 was elected governor of South Carolina as a proponent of nullification. In 1840, at the age of seventeen, Mary Miller married James Chesnut who, according to his wife, was a gentle man, becoming "the more polite" "the more raggeder and more squalid the creature" he addressed. Like her father, Chesnut's husband was also a politician, serving as a member of the South Carolina senate from 1852–1858. James Chesnut was proslavery and was the leader of the state's secession party; he participated in the Nashville secession convention in 1850. Elected to the U.S. Senate in 1858, James Chesnut resigned after Abraham Lincoln's election in 1860 and helped to draft the Confederate ordinance of secession and permanent constitution. During the Civil War, James Chesnut served in the Provisional Congress of the Confederate States of America, and later was an aide to General P. G. T. Beauregard and to Confederate President Jefferson Davis; in 1864, he became brigadier general in command of South Carolina's reserve forces. With the exception of her stand on slavery, Chesnut was a loyal Confederate, accompanying her husband to Washington in 1858 and traveling with him during the war to Charleston, Montgomery, Columbia, and Richmond. She was unhappy with any dissension within the party, and spoke of it in terms of an "unbrotherly love" which could wreck the Confederacy. She always backed Jefferson Davis against other Confederate statesmen, and was a close friend of Mrs. Jefferson Davis and of many other politically and socially high-ranking Confederates, whom she mentions at length in her diary.

In addition to her diaries, Mary Chesnut wrote some fiction. She finished but never published three novels, and in the early 1880s expanded and revised her diaries into a full-scale book. Chesnut died in Camden, South Carolina, on November 22, 1886.

Further Reading:

E. Muhlenfeld, *Mary Boykin Chesnut: A Biography*, 1981.

B. I. Wiley, *Confederate Women*, 1975.

C. V. Woodward and E. Muhlenfeld, eds., *The Private Mary Chesnut: The Unpublished Civil War Diaries*, 1984.

Texts:

A Diary from Dixie, ed. Ben Ames Williams, 1980.

---

from A Diary from Dixie

February 15, 1861

My father was a South Carolina nullifier, Governor of the state at the time of the nullification now, and then United States Senator; so I was of necessity a rebel born. My husband's family being equally pledged to the Union party rather exasperated my zeal. Yet I felt a nervous dread and horror of this break with so great a power as the United States, but I was ready and willing. South Carolina had been rampant for years. She was the torment of herself and everybody else. Nobody could live in this state unless he were a fire-eater. Come what would, I wanted them to fight and stop talking. South Carolinians had exasperated and heated themselves into a fever that only blood-letting could ever cure. It was the inevitable remedy. So I was a seceder.

March 4, 1861

I have seen a Negro woman sold upon the block at auction. I was walking. The woman on the block overtopped the crowd. I felt faint, seasick. The creature looked so like my good little Nancy. She was a bright mulatto, with a pleasant face. She was magnificently gotten up in silks and satins. She seemed delighted with it all, sometimes ogling the bidders, sometimes looking quite coy and modest; but her mouth never relaxed from its expanded grin of excitement. I dare say the poor thing knew who would buy her. My very soul sickened. It was too dreadful. I tried to reason. "You know how women sell themselves and are sold in marriage, from queens downwards, eh? You know what the Bible says about slavery, and marriage. Poor women, poor slaves."

We separated from the North because of incompatibility of temper. We are divorced, North from South, because we have hated each other so. If we could only separate politely, and not have a horrid fight for divorce. . . .

I met a recent bride, Mrs. Elsbury. She was so very large and handsome and strong; so calm, so covered with a tangle and frizzle frazzle of finery. Silent and grave, she found it all she could do to take care of her cloud of drapery in the crowd. She guarded her dress with her hands, and as it was caught by the passersby, with quiet dignity she unhooked herself. On every side, the tag end of her costume required to be detached from man or woman. Her occupation being to take care of her clothes, like the unkind Jew in the parable, I passed by on the other side.

I wonder if it be a sin to think slavery a curse to any land. Men and women are punished when their masters and mistresses are brutes, not when they do wrong. Under slavery, we live surrounded by prostitutes, yet an abandoned woman is sent out of any decent house. Who thinks any worse of a Negro or mulatto woman for being a thing we can't name? God forgive us, but ours is a monstrous system, a wrong and an iniquity! Like the patriarchs of old, our men live all in one house with their wives and their concubines; and the mulattoes one sees in every family partly resemble the white children. Any lady is ready to tell you who is the father of all the mulatto children in everybody's household but her own. Those, she seems to think, drop from the clouds. My disgust sometimes is boiling over. Thank God for my country women, but alas for the men! They are probably no worse than men everywhere, but the lower their mistresses, the more degraded they must be.

April 13, 1861

Fort Sumter has been on fire. He has not yet silenced any of our guns, or so the aids—still with swords and red sashes by way of uniform—tell us. But the sound of those guns makes regular meals impossible. None of us go to table, but tea trays pervade the corridors going everywhere. Some of the anxious hearts lie on their beds and moan in solitary misery. Mrs. Wigfall and I solace ourselves with tea in my room. These women have all a satisfying faith. "God is on our side," they cry. When we are shut in, we, Mrs. Wigfall and I, ask: "Why?" Answer: "Of course, He hates the Yankees! You'll think that well of Him."

Not by one word or look can we detect any change in the demeanor of these Negro servants. Lawrence sits at our door, as sleepy and as respectful and as profoundly indifferent. So are they all. They carry it too far. You could not tell that they even hear the awful noise that is going on in the bay, though it is dinning in their ears night and day. And people talk before them as if they were chairs and tables, and they make no sign. Are they stolidly stupid, or wiser than we are, silent and strong, biding their time.

April 20, 1861

Note the glaring inconsistencies of life. Our Chatelaine locked up Eugène Sue, and returned even Washington Allston's novel with thanks and a decided hint that it should be burned; at least it should not remain in her house. Bad books are not allowed house room except in the library and under lock and key, the key in the Master's pocket; but bad women, if they are not white and serve in a menial capacity, may swarm the house unmolested. The ostrich game is thought a Christian act. These women are no more regarded as a dangerous contingent than canary birds would be.

If you show by a chance remark that you see that some particular creature more shameless than the rest has no end of children and no beginning of a husband, you are frowned down. You are talking on improper subjects. There are certain subjects pure-minded ladies never touch upon, even in their thoughts. It does not do to be so hard and cruel to the poor things. It is best to let them alone, if they are good servants otherwise. Do not dismiss them. All that will come straight as they grow older. And it does. They are frantic, one and all, to be members of the church, and the Methodist Church is not so pure-minded as to shut its eyes. And it has them up and turns them out with a high hand if they are found going astray as to any of the Ten Commandments.

September 19, 1861

The high and disinterested conduct our enemies seem to expect of us is involuntary and unconscious praise. They pay us the compliment to look for from us—and execrate us for the want of it—a degree of virtue they were never able to practice themselves. They say our crowning misdemeanour is to hold in slavery still those Africans they brought over here from Africa, or sold to us when they found to own them did not pay. They gradually slid them off down here, giving themselves years to get rid of them in a remunerative way. We want to spread them too, west and south, or northwest, where the climate would free them or kill them; would improve them out of the world as the Yankees do Indians. If they had been forced to keep them in New England, I dare say they would have shared the Indians' fate; for they are wise in their generation, these Yankee children of light. Those pernicious Africans!

October 1, 1861

One begins to understand the power which the ability to vote gives the meanest citizen. We went to one of Uncle Hamilton's splendid dinners, plate, glass, china, and everything that was nice to eat. In the piazza, when the gentlemen were smoking after dinner, in the midst of them sat Squire MacDonald, the well-digger. He was officiating in that capacity at Plain Hill, and apparently he was most at his ease of all. He had his clay pipe in his mouth, he was cooler than the rest, being in his shirt sleeves, and he leaned back luxuriously in his chair tilted on its two hind legs, with his naked feet up on the bannister. Said Louisa—"Look, the mud from the well is sticking through his toes! See how solemnly polite and attentive Mr. Chesnut is to him!" "Oh, that's his way. The raggeder and more squalid the creature, the more polite and the softer Mr. Chesnut grows."

November 28, 1861

On one side Mrs. Stowe, Greeley, Thoreau, Emerson, Sumner.[1] They live in nice New England homes, clean, sweet-smelling, shut up in libraries, writing books which ease their hearts of their bitterness against us. What self-denial they do practice is to tell John Brown to come down here and cut our throats in Christ's name. Now consider what I have seen of my mother's life, my grandmother's, my mother-in-law's. These people were educated at Northern schools, they read the same books as their Northern contemporaries, the same daily papers, the same Bible. They have the same ideas of right and wrong, are high-bred, lovely, good, pious, doing their duty as they conceive it. They live in Negro villages. They do not preach and teach hate as a gospel, and the sacred duty of murder and insurrection; but they strive to ameliorate the condition of these Africans in every particular. They set them the example of a perfect life, a life of utter self-abnegation. Think of these holy New Englanders forced to have a Negro village walk through their houses whenever they see fit, dirty, slatternly, idle, ill-smelling by nature. These women I love have less chance to live their own lives in peace than if they were African missionaries. They have a swarm of blacks about them like children under their care, not as Mrs. Stowe's fancy painted them, and they hate slavery worse than Mrs. Stowe does. Book-making which leads you to a round of visits among crowned heads is an easier way to be a saint than martyrdom down here, doing unpleasant duty among the Negroes with no reward but the threat of John Brown hanging like a drawn sword over your head in this world, and threats of what is to come to you from blacker devils in the next.

The Mrs. Stowes have the plaudits of crowned heads; we take our chances, doing our duty as best we may among the woolly heads. My husband supported his plantation by his law practice. Now it is running him in debt. Our people have never earned their own bread. Take this estate, what does it do, actually? It all goes back in some shape to what are called slaves here, called operatives, or tenants, or peasantry elsewhere. I doubt if ten thousand in money ever comes to this old gentleman's hands. When Mrs. Chesnut married South, her husband was as wealthy as her brothers-in-law. How is it now? Their money has accumulated for their children. This old man's goes to support a horde of idle dirty Africans, while he is abused as a cruel slave owner. I say we are no better than our judges in the North, and no worse. We are human beings of the nineteenth century and slavery has to go, of course. All that has been gained by it goes to the North and to Negroes. The slave owners, when they are good men and women, are the martyrs. I hate slavery. I even hate the harsh authority I see parents think it their duty to exercise toward their children.

[1] Writers, a journalist (Horace Greeley), and a U.S. senator (Charles Sumner), all New Englanders opposed to slavery.

November 30, 1861

Yes, how I envy those saintly Yankee women, in their clean cool New England homes, writing books to make their fortunes and to shame us. The money they earn goes to them. Here every cent goes to pay the factor[2] who supplies the plantation.

April 27, 1862

—New Orleans is gone, and with it the Confederacy! Are we not cut in two? The Mississippi ruins us if it is lost. The Confederacy is done to death by the politicians. Those wretched creatures, the Congress, could never rise to the greatness of the occasion. They seem to think they were in a neighborhood squabble about precedence. The soldiers have done their duty. All honor to the army. But statesmen, busy bees about their own places or their personal honor, are too busy to see the enemy at a distance. With a microscope they are examining their own interest or their own wrongs, forgetting the interest of the people they represented.

CHARLESTON

MERCURY

EXTRA:

Passed unanimously at 1.15 o'clock, P. M. December 20th, 1860.

AN ORDINANCE

To dissolve the Union between the State of South Carolina and other States united with her under the compact entitled "The Constitution of the United States of America."

We, the People of the State of South Carolina, in Convention assembled, do declare and ordain, and it is hereby declared and ordained,

That the Ordinance adopted by us in Convention, on the twenty-third day of May, in the year of our Lord one thousand seven hundred and eighty-eight, whereby the Constitution of the United States of America was ratified, and also, all Acts and parts of Acts of the General Assembly of this State, ratifying amendments of the said Constitution, are hereby repealed; and that the union now subsisting between South Carolina and other States, under the name of "The United States of America," is hereby dissolved.

THE

UNION

IS

DISSOLVED!

This 1860 broadside was one of the earliest announcements that South Carolina had voted to become the first state to separate from the Union. "The state of South Carolina has resumed her place among the nations of the world," the delegates announced. (Reproduced from the collections of the Library of Congress)

2 Merchant-salesman.

Abraham Lincoln
1809–1865

Abraham Lincoln came to the presidency from a successful law practice and exercised unprecedented executive authority during a civil war far bloodier and longer than anyone had foreseen. Midway through the war, Whitman described Lincoln:

> He has a face like a hoosier Michael Angelo, so awful ugly it becomes beautiful, with its strange mouth, its deep cut, cris-cross lines, and its doughnut complexion. . . . He has shown, I sometimes think, an almost supernatural tack in keeping the ship afloat at all, with head steady, not only not going down, and now certain not to, but with proud and resolute spirit, and flag flying in sight of the world, menacing and high as ever.

Lincoln's "idiomatic western genius," as Whitman called it, was above all conspicuous in his spoken and written prose, a supple middle style that was lofty and colloquial, beautiful and homely, and always got to the point. Lincoln's prose showed that the basic forms of American humor, including the tall tale and the anecdote, were appropriate in statecraft as well as literature. For the thirty-year-old Mark Twain, Lincoln's "With malice toward none" address proved that simplicity was one of the secrets of eloquence.

Only Andrew Jackson among the presidents was as true a child of the frontier as Lincoln, though many others claimed birth in a log cabin. Born in a clearing in Hardin County, Kentucky, to illiterate parents, Lincoln had a harsh father and a loving mother whom he lost when he was nine. Largely self-educated, Lincoln was deeply read in the few books he could find, including the Bible and Shakespeare, two major sources he drew on in preparing his public addresses.

It was Lincoln's destiny to lead the disunited states through the fire of a civil war that established the Union as we know it. His addresses have passed beyond literature into the heritage, character, and soul of the nation. The style was the man, a powerful genius of a politician joined to the mystical sensitivity of a poet.

Further Reading:

C. B. Strozier, *Lincoln's Quest for Union*, 1982.
S. B. Oates, *Abraham Lincoln: The Man Behind the Myths*, 1984.

G. Vidal, *Lincoln*, 1984.
G. Wills, *Lincoln at Gettysburg*, 1992.

Text:

The Collected Works of Abraham Lincoln, 9 vols., ed., R. P. Basler, *et al.*, 1953.

Address Delivered at the Dedication of the Cemetery at Gettysburg*

November 19, 1863

Four score and seven years ago our fathers brought forth on this continent, a new nation, conceived in Liberty, and dedicated to the proposition that all men are created equal.

Now we are engaged in a great civil war, testing whether that nation, or any nation so conceived and so dedicated, can long endure. We are met on a great battle-field of that war. We have come to dedicate a portion of that field, as a final resting place for those who here gave their lives that that nation might live. It is altogether fitting and proper that we should do this.

But, in a larger sense, we can not dedicate—we can not consecrate—we can not hallow—this ground. The brave men, living and dead, who struggled here, have consecrated it, far above our poor power to add or detract. The world will little note, nor long remember what we say here, but it can never forget what they did here. It is for us the living, rather, to be dedicated here to the unfinished work which they who fought here have thus far so nobly advanced. It is rather for us to be here dedicated to the great task remaining before us—that from these honored dead we take increased devotion to that cause for which they gave the last full measure of devotion—that we here highly resolve that these dead shall not have died in vain—that this nation, under God, shall have a new birth of freedom—and that government of the people, by the people, for the people, shall not perish from the earth.

Abraham Lincoln.

November 19, 1863.

1863

---

* Only four months before Lincoln's address, Robert E. Lee, with 70,000 southern troops, had engaged George Gordon Meade, with an army of 90,000, in a three-day battle resulting in over 6,000 deaths and many thousands of injuries. (Meade, to Lincoln's private disgust, failed to pursue the retreating Lee, who led his army safely back to Virginia.) The Union dead were buried on Cemetery Hill, where Lincoln spoke. Lee's defeat at Gettysburg, Pennsylvania, coming on the same day Ulysses Grant took Vicksburg, one thousand miles to the southwest (and thus cutting the Confederacy in two), spelled the end of the South's realistic chances for world recognition as an independent country, ensured the preservation of the Union, and guaranteed the final abolition of slavery. These prospects notwithstanding, the war was to continue for nearly another two years.

Second Inaugural Address*

March 4, 1865

At this second appearing to take the oath of the presidential office, there is less occasion for an extended address than there was at the first. Then a statement, somewhat in detail, of a course to be pursued, seemed fitting and proper. Now, at the expiration of four years, during which public declarations have been constantly called forth on every point and phase of the great contest which still absorbs the attention, and engrosses the energies of the nation, little that is new could be presented. The progress of our arms, upon which all else chiefly depends, is as well known to the public as to myself; and it is, I trust, reasonably satisfactory and encouraging to all. With high hope for the future, no prediction in regard to it is ventured.

On the occasion corresponding to this four years ago, all thoughts were anxiously directed to an impending civil war. All dreaded it—all sought to avert it. While the inaugural address was being delivered from this place, devoted altogether to *saving* the Union without war, insurgent agents were in the city seeking to *destroy* it without war—seeking to dissolve the Union, and divide effects, by negotiation. Both parties deprecated war; but one of them would *make* war rather than let the nation survive; and the other would *accept* war rather than let it perish. And the war came.

One eighth of the whole population were colored slaves, not distributed generally over the Union, but localized in the Southern part of it. These slaves constituted a peculiar and powerful interest. All knew that this interest was, somehow, the cause of the war. To strengthen, perpetuate, and extend this interest was the object for which the insurgents would rend the Union, even by war; while the government claimed no right to do more than to restrict the territorial enlargement of it. Neither party expected for the war, the magnitude, or the duration, which it has already attained. Neither anticipated that the *cause* of the conflict might cease with, or even before, the conflict itself should cease. Each looked for an easier triumph, and a result less fundamental and astounding. Both read the same Bible, and pray to the same God and each invokes His aid against the other. It may seem strange that any men should dare to ask a just God's assistance in wringing their bread from the sweat of other men's faces; but let us judge not that we be not judged. The prayers of both could not be answered; that of neither has been answered fully. The Almighty has his own purposes. "Woe unto the world because of offences! for it must needs be that offences come; but woe to that man by whom the offence cometh!"[1] If we shall suppose that American Slavery is one of those offences which, in the providence of God, must needs come, but which, having continued

---

* Delivered a month before the Union victories at Petersburg and Richmond (Virginia) and thirty-five days before the decisive surrender of General Robert E. Lee to the Union commander, Ulysses S. Grant, at Appomattox. On April 14, only days after the war officially ended, Lincoln was fatally shot; he died the following day. In its reason and compassion the Second Inaugural Address is considered to rank in world literature with Pericles' funeral oration to the Athenians.

[1] Matthew 18:7.

Mathew Brady
Wounded soldiers outside hopital, Fredericksburg, VA
(Reproduced from the collections of the Library of Congress)

through His appointed time, He now wills to remove, and that He gives to both North and South, this terrible war, as the woe due to those by whom the offence came, shall we discern therein any departure from those divine attributes which the believers in a Living God always ascribe to Him? Fondly do we hope—fervently do we pray—that this mighty scourge of war may speedily pass away. Yet, if God wills that it continue, until all the wealth piled by the bond-man's two hundred and fifty years of unrequited toil shall be sunk, and until every drop of blood drawn with the lash, shall be paid by an-other drawn with the sword, as was said three thousand years ago, so still it must be said "the judgments of the Lord, are true and righteous altogether."[2]

   With malice toward none; with charity for all; with firmness in the right, as God gives us to see the right, let us strive on to finish the work we are in; to bind up the na-tion's wounds; to care for him who shall have borne the battle, and for his widow, and his orphan—to do all which may achieve and cherish a just and lasting peace, among ourselves, and with all nations.

1865

---

[2] Psalm 19:9.

As the bloodiest war in U.S. history raged on, a Northern cartoonist parodied the Confederacy and its leader. The skeletal Southern citizens are reading a proclamation requiring fasting and prayer while its author, the develish Jefferson Davis, looks on.
(Harper's Weekly)

My Paramount Object in This Struggle

I would save the Union. I would save it the shortest way under the Constitution. The sooner the national authority can be restored; the nearer the Union will be "the Union as it was." If there be those who would not save the Union, unless they could at the same time *save* slavery, I do not agree with them. If there be those who would not save the Union unless they could at the same time *destroy* slavery, I do not agree with them. My paramount object in this struggle *is* to save the Union, and is *not* either to save or destroy slavery.

Abraham Lincoln, letter to Horace Greeley, August 22, 1862

Louisa May Alcott
(1832–1888)

Louisa May Alcott is one of the nineteenth century's best-known authors. Her successful and popular novel *Little Women* has been continually in print since its 1868 publication. Alcott was much more than a children's author, however; an outspoken abolitionist and feminist, Alcott created women characters who refused to submit to stereotypical representations of women. She herself remained unmarried—claiming, "I'd rather be a free spinster and paddle my own canoe"—and she used her eventually quite profitable writing to support her family.

Little Women is often remembered for the warm picture of family life it portrays. The March family is based on the Alcotts. The Marches are poor, as the Alcott family was, and the Marches' well-meaning but financially unsuccessful father was modeled on Alcott's own father, the radical Transcendentalist Bronson Alcott. The novel presents a range of positive female characters, from the wise and compassionate mother, Marmee, to the four sisters—Meg, Jo, Beth, and Amy.

The most memorable woman in *Little Women* is certainly Jo, a character modeled after Alcott herself. Jo is a forceful, adventurous character who rebels against the constraints of true womanhood, attempting to experience as much of life as she can. One way in which she claims control of her life is through her writing. In the following excerpts from the novel, Jo puts herself forth as a professional author, moving from short, romantic magazine sketches to gothic stories and a gothic novel. Jo experiences the difficulties attendant on women's publication; when the Marches' neighbor, Laurie, sees Jo enter and exit the publisher's office, he thinks she has been to the dentist. In addition, Jo experiences the satisfaction of succeeding in this profession which may allow her "to support myself and help the girls."

Alcott herself wrote romantic and gothic stories under various pseudonyms before the successful publication of *Hospital Sketches* in 1863 and later *Little Women.* She told a friend, "I think my natural ambition is for the lurid style." *Behind a Mask: or, a Woman's Power* was a novella in this "lurid style" published under the pseudonym A. M. Barnard in *The Flag of Our Union* in 1866. In this story, Jean Muir, a world-weary actress, preys on the wealthy Coventry family, pretending to be a young, innocent governess, in an attempt to win a husband and life-long security. Muir is a devious, deceitful character, and, significantly, she succeeds in her plan, eventually marrying the wealthy patriarch Sir Coventry. In gothic stories like this one, Alcott expressed subversive sentiments, allowing independent, transgressive women like Muir to achieve goals that would have been unthinkable within the world of the March family and within what Alcott characterized as "the proper grayness of old Concord." Muir is an example of a woman using stereotypical nineteenth-century ideals of womanhood as a "mask" for her real motives, an attempt to gain economic security.

Nineteenth-century women's need for economic security and independence is a theme that reappears in Alcott's autobiographical essay, "How I Went Out to Service," published in 1874. In this comical essay, Alcott describes her experiences working as a companion for an invalid woman. This essay discusses the scarcity of options available for women like Alcott who were "ready to work, eager to be independent, and too proud to endure patronage." When Alcott does secure employment, she finds that she is expected to do whatever the family wants—from listening to Josephus's "sentimental rubbish" to hauling firewood. At the end of seven weeks of intensive labor, Alcott receives four dollars—a sum almost as ridiculously small then as it would be now. This essay demonstrates Alcott at her most confident and satirical as a writer.

Further Reading:

M. Bedell, *The Alcotts*, 1980.
S. Elbert, *A Hunger for Home*, 1984.

J. Meyerson, *et. al., Journals of Louisa May Alcott*, 1984.

Texts:

Little Women, 1868.
Alternate Alcott, ed., E. Showalter, 1988.

Little Women

from **Chapter 14: Secrets**

Jo was very busy up in the garret, for the October days began to grow chilly, and the afternoons were short. For two or three hours the sun lay warmly in at the high window, showing Jo seated on the old sofa writing busily, with her papers spread out upon a trunk before her, while Scrabble, the pet rat, promenaded the beams overhead, accompanied by his oldest son, a fine young fellow, who was evidently very proud of his whiskers. Quite absorbed in her work, Jo scribbled away till the last page was filled, when she signed her name with a flourish, and threw down her pen, exclaiming,—

"There, I've done my best! If this don't suit I shall have to wait till I can do better."

Lying back on the sofa, she read the manuscript carefully through, making dashes here and there, and putting in many exclamation points, which looked like little balloons; then she tied it up with a smart red ribbon, and sat a minute looking at it with a sober, wistful expression, which plainly showed how earnest her work had been. Jo's desk up here was an old tin kitchen, which hung against the wall. In it she kept her papers, and a few books safely shut away from Scrabble, who, being likewise of a literary turn, was fond of making a circulating library of such books as were left in his way, by eating the leaves. From this tin receptacle Jo produced another manuscript; and, putting both in her pocket, crept quietly down stairs, leaving her friends to nibble her pens and taste her ink.

She put on her hat and jacket as noiselessly as possible, and, going to the back entry window, got out upon the roof of a low porch, swung herself down to the grassy bank, and took a round-about way to the road. Once there she composed herself, hailed a passing omnibus, and rolled away to town, looking very merry and mysterious.

If any one had been watching her, he would have thought her movements decidedly peculiar; for, on alighting, she went off at a great pace till she reached a certain number in a certain busy street; having found the place with some difficulty, she went into the door-way, looked up the dirty stairs, and, after standing stock still a minute, suddenly dived into the street, and walked away as rapidly as she came. This manoeuvre she repeated several times, to the great amusement of a black-eyed young gentleman lounging in the window of a building opposite. On returning for the third time, Jo gave herself a shake, pulled her hat over her eyes, and walked up the stairs, looking as if she was going to have all her teeth out.

There was a dentist's sign, among others, which adorned the entrance, and, after staring a moment at the pair of artificial jaws which slowly opened and shut to draw attention to a fine set of teeth, the young gentleman put on his coat, took his hat, and went down to post himself in the opposite door-way, saying, with a smile and a shiver,—

"It's like her to come alone, but if she has a bad time she'll need some one to help her home."

In ten minutes Jo came running down stairs with a very red face, and the general appearance of a person who had just passed through a trying ordeal of some sort. When she saw the young gentleman she looked anything but pleased, and passed him with a nod; but he followed, asking with an air of sympathy,—

"Did you have a bad time?"

"Not very."

"You got through quick."

"Yes, thank goodness!"

"Why did you go alone?"

"Didn't want any one to know."

"You're the oddest fellow I ever saw. How many did you have out?"

Jo looked at her friend as if she did not understand him; then began to laugh, as if mightily amused at something.

"There are two which I want to come out, but I must wait a week."

"What are you laughing at? You are up to some mischief, Jo," said Laurie, looking mystified. . . .

"Well, I've left two stories with a newspaper man, and he's to give his answer next week," whispered Jo, in her confidant's ear.

"Hurrah for Miss March, the celebrated American authoress!" cried Laurie, throwing up his hat and catching it again, to the great delight of two ducks, four cats, five hens, and half a dozen Irish children; for they were out of the city now.

"Hush! it won't come to anything, I dare say; but I couldn't rest till I had tried, and I said nothing about it, because I don't want any one else to be disappointed."

"It won't fail! Why, Jo, your stories are works of Shakespeare compared to half the rubbish that's published every day. Won't it be fun to see them in print; and shan't we feel proud of our authoress?"

Jo's eyes sparkled, for it's always pleasant to be believed in; and a friend's praise is always sweeter than a dozen newspaper puffs. . . .

For a week or two Jo behaved so queerly, that her sisters got quite bewildered. She rushed to the door when the postman rang; . . . Laurie and she were always making signs to one another, and talking about "Spread Eagles," till the girls declared they had both lost their wits. On the second Saturday after Jo got out of the window, Meg, as she sat sewing at her window, was scandalized by the sight of Laurie chasing Jo all over the garden, and finally capturing her in Amy's bower. What went on there, Meg could not see, but shrieks of laughter were heard, followed by the murmur of voices, and a great flapping of newspapers.

"What shall we do with that girl? She never *will* behave like a young lady," sighed Meg, as she watched the race with a disapproving face.

"I hope she won't; she is so funny and dear as she is," said Beth, who had never betrayed that she was a little hurt at Jo's having secrets with any one but her.

"It's very trying, but we never can make her *comme la fo*," added Amy, who sat making some new frills for herself, with her curls tied up in a very becoming way,—two agreeable things, which made her feel unusually elegant and lady-like.

In a few minutes Jo bounced in, laid herself on the sofa, and affected to read.

"Have you anything interesting there?" asked Meg, with condescension.

"Nothing but a story; don't amount to much, I guess," returned Jo, carefully keeping the name of the paper out of sight.

"You'd better read it loud; that will amuse us, and keep you out of mischief," said Amy, in her most grown-up tone.

"What's the name?" asked Beth, wondering why Jo kept her face behind the sheet.

"The Rival Painters."

"That sounds well; read it," said Meg.

With a loud "hem!" and a long breath, Jo began to read very fast. The girls listened with interest, for the tale was romantic, and somewhat pathetic, as most of the characters died in the end.

"I like that about the splendid picture," was Amy's approving remark, as Jo paused.

"I prefer the lovering part. Viola and Angelo are two of our favorite names; isn't that queer?" said Meg, wiping her eyes, for the "lovering part" was tragical.

"Who wrote it?" asked Beth, who had caught a glimpse of Jo's face.

The reader suddenly sat up, cast away the paper, displayed a flushed countenance, and, with a funny mixture of solemnity and excitement, replied in a loud voice, "Your sister!"

"You?" cried Meg, dropping her work.

"It's very good," said Amy, critically.

"I knew it! I knew it! oh, my Jo, I *am* so proud!" and Beth ran to hug her sister and exult over this splendid success.

Dear me, how delighted they all were, to be sure; how Meg wouldn't believe it till she saw the words, "Miss Josephine March," actually printed in the paper; how graciously Amy criticised the artistic parts of the story, and offered hints for a sequel, which unfortunately couldn't be carried out, as the hero and heroine were dead; how Beth got excited, and skipped and sung with joy; how Hannah came in to exclaim, "Sakes alive, well I never!" in great astonishment at "that Jo's doin's;" how proud Mrs. March was when she knew it; how Jo laughed, with tears in her eyes, as she declared she might as well be a peacock and done with it; and how the "Spread Eagle" might be said to flap his wings triumphantly over the house of March, as the paper passed from hand to hand.

"Tell us about it." "When did it come?" "How much did you get for it?" "What *will* father say?" "Won't Laurie laugh?" cried the family, all in one breath, as they clustered about Jo; for these foolish, affectionate people made a jubilee of every little household joy.

"Stop jabbering, girls, and I'll tell you everything," said Jo, wondering if Miss Burney felt any grander over her "Evelina" than she did over her "Rival Painters." Having told how she disposed of her tales, Jo added,—"And when I went to get my answer the man said he liked them both, but didn't pay beginners, only let them print in his paper, and noticed the stories. It was good practice, he said; and, when the beginners improved, any one would pay. So I let him have the two stories, and today this was sent to me, and Laurie caught me with it, and insisted on seeing it, so I let him; and he said it was good, and I shall write more, and he's going to get the next paid for, and oh—I *am* so happy, for in time I may be able to support myself and help the girls."

Jo's breath gave out here; and, wrapping her head in the paper, she bedewed her little story with a few natural tears; for to be independent, and earn the praise of those she loved, were the dearest wishes of her heart, and this seemed to be the first step toward that happy end.

Chapter 27: Literary Lessons

Fortune suddenly smiled upon Jo, and dropped a good-luck penny in her path. Not a golden penny, exactly, but I doubt if half a million would have given more real happiness than did the little sum that came to her in this wise.

Every few weeks she would shut herself up in her room, put on her scribbling suit, and "fall into a vortex," as she expressed it, writing away at her novel with all her heart and soul, for till that was finished she could find no peace. Her "scribbling suit" consisted of a black pinafore on which she could wipe her pen at will, and a cap of the same material, adorned with a cheerful red bow, into which she bundled her hair when the decks were cleared for action. This cap was a beacon to the inquiring eyes of her family, who, during these periods, kept their distance, merely popping in their heads semi-occasionally, to ask, with interest, "Does genius burn, Jo?" They did not always venture even to ask this question, but took an observation of the cap, and judged accordingly. If this expressive article of dress was drawn low upon the forehead, it was a sign that hard work was going on; in exciting moments it was pushed rakishly askew, and when despair seized the author it was plucked wholly off, and cast upon the floor. At such times the intruder silently withdrew; and not until the red bow was seen gaily erect upon the gifted brow, did any one dare address Jo.

She did not think herself a genius by any means; but when the writing fit came on, she gave herself up to it with entire abandon, and led a blissful life, unconscious of want, care, or bad weather, while she sat safe and happy in an imaginary world, full of friends almost as real and dear to her as any in the flesh. Sleep forsook her eyes, meals stood untasted, day and night were all too short to enjoy the happiness which blessed her only at such times, and made these hours worth living, even if they bore no other fruit. The divine afflatus usually lasted a week or two, and then she emerged from her "vortex" hungry, sleepy, cross, or despondent.

She was just recovering from one of these attacks when she was prevailed upon to escort Miss Crocker to a lecture, and in return for her virtue was rewarded with a new idea. It was a People's Course,—the lecture on the Pyramids,—and Jo rather wondered at the choice of such a subject for such an audience, but took it for granted that some great social evil would be remedied, or some great want supplied by unfolding the glories of the Pharaohs, to an audience whose thoughts were busy with the price of coal and flour, and whose lives were spent in trying to solve harder riddles than that of the Sphinx.

They were early; and while Miss Crocker set the heel of her stocking, Jo amused herself by examining the faces of the people who occupied the seat with them. On her left were two matrons with massive foreheads, and bonnets to match, discussing Woman's Rights and making tatting. Beyond sat a pair of humble lovers artlessly holding each other by the hand, a sombre spinster eating peppermints out of a paper bag, and an old gentleman taking his preparatory nap behind a yellow bandanna. On her right, her only neighbor was a studious-looking lad absorbed in a newspaper.

It was a pictorial sheet, and Jo examined the work of art nearest her, idly wondering what unfortuitous concatenation of circumstances needed the melodramatic illustration of an Indian in full war costume, tumbling over a precipice with a wolf at his throat, while two infuriated young gentlemen, with unnaturally small feet and big eyes, were stabbing each other close by, and a dishevelled female was flying away in the background, with her mouth wide open. Pausing to turn a page, the lad saw her looking, and with boyish good-nature, offered half his paper, saying, bluntly, "Want to read it? That's a first-rate story."

Jo accepted it with a smile, for she had never outgrown her liking for lads, and soon found herself involved in the usual labyrinth of love, mystery, and murder,—for the story belonged to that class of light literature in which the passions have a holiday, and when the author's invention fails, a grand catastrophe clears the stage of one-half the *dramatis personæ*, leaving the other half to exult over their downfall.

"Prime, isn't it?" asked the boy, as her eye went down the last paragraph of her portion.

"I guess you and I could do most as well as that if we tried," returned Jo, amused at his admiration of the trash.

"I should think I was a pretty lucky chap if I could. She makes a good living out of such stories, they say;" and he pointed to the name of Mrs. S. L. A. N. G. Northbury, under the title of the tale.

"Do you know her?" asked Jo, with sudden interest.

"No; but I read all her pieces, and I know a fellow that works in the office where this paper is printed."

"Do you say she makes a good living out of stories like this?" and Jo looked more respectfully at the agitated group and thickly-sprinkled exclamation points that adorned the page.

"Guess she does! she knows just what folks like, and gets paid well for writing it."

Here the lecture began, but Jo heard very little of it, for while Professor Sands was prosing away about Belzoni, Cheops, scarabei, and hieroglyphics, she was covertly taking down the address of the paper, and boldly resolving to try for the hundred dollar prize offered in its columns for a sensational story. By the time the lecture ended, and the audience awoke, she had built up a splendid fortune for herself (not the first founded upon paper), and was already deep in the concoction of her story, being unable to decide whether the duel should come before the elopement or after the murder.

She said nothing of her plan at home, but fell to work next day, much to the disquiet of her mother, who always looked a little anxious when "genius took to burning." Jo had never tried this style before, contenting herself with very mild romances for the "Spread Eagle." Her theatrical experience and miscellaneous reading were of service now, for they gave her some idea of dramatic effect, and supplied plot, language, and costumes. Her story was as full of desperation and despair as her limited acquaintance with those uncomfortable emotions enabled her to make it, and, having located it in Lisbon, she wound up with an earthquake, as a striking and appropriate *dénouement*. The manuscript was privately despatched, accompanied by a note, modestly saying that if the tale didn't get the prize, which the writer hardly dared expect, she would be very glad to receive any sum it might be considered worth.

Six weeks is a long time to wait, and a still longer time for a girl to keep a secret; but

Jo did both, and was just beginning to give up all hope of ever seeing her manuscript again, when a letter arrived which almost took her breath away; for, on opening it, a check for a hundred dollars fell into her lap. For a minute she stared at it as if it had been a snake, then she read the letter, and began to cry. If the amiable gentleman who wrote that kindly note could have known what intense happiness he was giving a fellow-creature, I think he would devote his leisure hours, if he has any, to that amusement; for Jo valued the letter more than the money, because it was encouraging; and after years of effort it was so pleasant to find that she had learned to do *something*, though it was only to write a sensation story.

A prouder young woman was seldom seen than she, when, having composed herself, she electrified the family by appearing before them with the letter in one hand, the check in the other, announcing that she had won the prize! Of course there was a great jubilee, and when the story came every one read and praised it; though after her father had told her that the language was good, the romance fresh and hearty, and the tragedy quite thrilling, he shook his head, and said in his unworldly way,—

"You can do better than this, Jo. Aim at the highest, and never mind the money."

"*I* think the money is the best part of it. What *will* you do with such a fortune?" asked Amy, regarding the magic slip of paper with a reverential eye.

"Send Beth and mother to the sea-side for a month or two," answered Jo promptly.

"Oh, how splendid! No, I can't do it, dear, it would be so selfish," cried Beth, who had clapped her thin hands, and taken a long breath, as if pining for fresh ocean breezes; then stopped herself, and motioned away the check which her sister waved before her.

"Ah, but you shall go, I've set my heart on it; that's what I tried for, and what's why I succeeded. I never get on when I think of myself alone, so it will help me to work for you, don't you see. Besides, Marmee needs the change, and she won't leave you, so you *must* go. Won't it be fun to see you come home plump and rosy again? Hurrah for Dr. Jo, who always cures her patients!"

To the sea-side they went, after much discussion; and though Beth didn't come home as plump and rosy as could be desired, she was much better, while Mrs. March declared she felt ten years younger; so Jo was satisfied with the investment of her prizemoney, and fell to work with a cheery spirit, bent on earning more of those delightful checks. She did earn several that year, and began to feel herself a power in the house; for by the magic of a pen, her "rubbish" turned into comforts for them all. "The Duke's Daughter" paid the butcher's bill, "A Phantom Hand" put down a new carpet, and "The Curse of the Coventrys" proved the blessing of the Marches in the way of groceries and gowns.

Wealth is certainly a most desirable thing, but poverty has its sunny side, and one of the sweet uses of adversity, is the genuine satisfaction which comes from hearty work of head or hand; and to the inspiration of necessity, we owe half the wise, beautiful, and useful blessings of the world. Jo enjoyed a taste of this satisfaction, and ceased to envy richer girls, taking great comfort in the knowledge that she could supply her own wants, and need ask no one for a penny.

Little notice was taken of her stories, but they found a market; and, encouraged by this fact, she resolved to make a bold stroke for fame and fortune. Having copied her novel for the fourth time, read it to all her confidential friends, and submitted it with fear and trembling to three publishers, she at last disposed of it, on condition that she would cut it down one-third, and omit all the parts which she particularly admired.

"Now I must either bundle it back into my tin-kitchen, to mould, pay for printing it myself, or chop it up to suit purchasers, and get what I can for it. Fame is a very good thing to have in the house, but cash is more convenient; so I wish to take the sense of the meeting on this important subject," said Jo, calling a family council.

"Don't spoil your book, my girl, for there is more in it than you know, and the idea is well worked out. Let it wait and ripen," was her father's advice; and he practised as he preached, having waited patiently thirty years for fruit of his own to ripen, and being in no haste to gather it, even now, when it was sweet and mellow.

"It seems to me that Jo will profit more by making the trial than by waiting," said Mrs. March. "Criticism is the best test of such work, for it will show her both unsuspected merits and faults, and help her to do better next time. We are too partial; but the praise and blame of outsiders will prove useful, even if she gets but little money."

"Yes," said Jo, knitting her brows, "that's just it; I've been fussing over the thing so long, I really don't know whether it's good, bad, or indifferent. It will be a great help to have cool, impartial persons take a look at it, and tell me what they think of it."

"I wouldn't leave out a word of it; you'll spoil it if you do, for the interest of the story is more in the minds than in the actions of the people, and it will be all a muddle if you don't explain as you go on," said Meg, who firmly believed that this book was the most remarkable novel ever written.

"But Mr. Allen says, 'Leave out the explanations, make it brief and dramatic, and let the characters tell the story,'" interrupted Jo, turning to the publisher's note.

"Do as he tells you; he knows what will sell, and we don't. Make a good, popular book, and get as much money as you can. By and by, when you've got a name, you can afford to digress, and have philosophical and metaphysical people in your novels," said Amy, who took a strictly practical view of the subject.

"Well," said Jo, laughing, "if my people *are* 'philosophical and metaphysical,' it isn't my fault, for I know nothing about such things, except what I hear father say, sometimes. If I've got some of his wise ideas jumbled up with my romance, so much the better for me. Now, Beth, what do you say?"

"I should so like to see it printed *soon*," was all Beth said, and smiled in saying it; but there was an unconscious emphasis on the last word, and a wistful look in the eyes that never lost their childlike candor, which chilled Jo's heart, for a minute, with a foreboding fear, and decided her to make her little venture "soon."

So, with Spartan firmness, the young authoress laid her first-born on her table, and chopped it up as ruthlessly as any ogre. In the hope of pleasing every one, she took every one's advice; and like the old man and his donkey in the fable, suited nobody.

Her father liked the metaphysical streak which had unconsciously got into it, so that was allowed to remain, though she had her doubts about it. Her mother thought that there *was* a trifle too much description; out, therefore, it nearly all came, and with it many necessary links in the story. Meg admired the tragedy; so Jo piled up the agony to suit her, while Amy objected to the fun, and, with the best intentions in life, Jo quenched the sprightly scenes which relieved the sombre character of the story. Then, to complete the ruin, she cut it down one-third, and confidingly sent the poor little romance, like a picked robin, out into the big, busy world, to try its fate.

Well, it was printed, and she got three hundred dollars for it; likewise plenty of praise and blame, both so much greater than she expected, that she was thrown into a state of bewilderment, from which it took some time to recover.

"You said, mother, that criticism would help me; but how can it, when it's so contradictory that I don't know whether I have written a promising book, or broken all the ten commandments," cried poor Jo, turning over a heap of notices, the perusal of which filled her with pride and joy one minute—wrath and dire dismay the next. "This man says 'An exquisite book, full of truth, beauty, and earnestness; all is sweet, pure, and healthy,'" continued the perplexed authoress. "The next, 'The theory of the book is bad,—full or morbid fancies, spiritualistic ideas, and unnatural characters.' Now, as I had no theory of any kind, don't believe in spiritualism, and copied my characters from life, I don't see how this critic *can* be right. Another says, 'It's one of the best American novels which has appeared for years'" (I know better than that); "and the next asserts that 'though it is original, and written with great force and feeling, it is a dangerous book.' 'Tisn't! Some make fun of it, some over-praise, and nearly all insist that I had a deep theory to expound, when I only wrote it for the pleasure and the money. I wish I'd printed it whole, or not at all, for I do hate to be so horridly misjudged."

Her family and friends administered comfort and commendation liberally; yet it was a hard time for sensitive, high-spirited Jo, who meant so well, and had apparently done so ill. But it did her good, for those whose opinion had real value, gave her the criticism which is an author's best education; and when the first soreness was over, she could laugh at her poor little book, yet believe in it still, and feel herself the wiser and stronger for the buffeting she had received.

"Not being a genius, like Keats, it won't kill me," she said stoutly; "and I've got the joke on my side, after all; for the parts that were taken straight out of real life, are denounced as impossible and absurd, and the scenes that I made up out of my own silly head, are pronounced 'charmingly natural, tender, and true.' So I'll comfort myself with that; and, when I'm ready, I'll up again and take another."

Jean Muir

"Has she come?"

"No, Mamma, not yet."

"I wish it were well over. The thought of it worries and excites me. A cushion for my back, Bella."

And poor, peevish Mrs. Coventry sank into an easy chair with a nervous sigh and the air of a martyr, while her pretty daughter hovered about her with affectionate solicitude.

"Who are they talking of, Lucia?" asked the languid young man lounging on a couch near his cousin, who bent over her tapestry work with a happy smile on her usually haughty face.

"The new governess, Miss Muir. Shall I tell you about her?"

"No, thank you. I have an inveterate aversion to the whole tribe. I've often thanked heaven that I had but one sister, and she a spoiled child, so that I have escaped the infliction of a governess so long."

"How will you bear it now?" asked Lucia.

"Leave the house while she is in it."

"No, you won't. You're too lazy, Gerald," called out a younger and more energetic man, from the recess where he stood teasing his dogs.

"I'll give her a three days' trial; if she proves endurable I shall not disturb myself; if, as I am sure, she is a bore, I'm off anywhere, anywhere out of her way."

"I beg you won't talk in that depressing manner, boys. I dread the coming of a stranger more than you possibly can, but Bella *must* not be neglected; so I have nerved myself to endure this woman, and Lucia is good enough to say she will attend to her after tonight."

"Don't be troubled, Mamma. She is a nice person, I dare say, and when once we are used to her, I've no doubt we shall be glad to have her, it's so dull here just now. Lady Sydney said she was a quiet, accomplished, amiable girl, who needed a home, and would be a help to poor stupid me, so try to like her for my sake."

"I will, dear, but isn't it getting late? I do hope nothing has happened. Did you tell them to send a carriage to the station for her, Gerald?

"I forgot it. But it's not far, it won't hurt her to walk" was the languid reply.

"It was indolence, not forgetfulness, I know. I'm very sorry; she will think it so rude to leave her to find her way so late. Do go and see to it, Ned."

"Too late, Bella, the train was in some time ago. Give your orders to me next time, Mother, and I'll see that they are obeyed," said Edward.

"Ned is just at an age to make a fool of himself for any girl who comes in his way. Have a care of the governess, Lucia, or she will bewitch him."

Gerald spoke in a satirical whisper, but his brother heard him and answered with a good-humored laugh.

"I wish there was any hope of your making a fool of yourself in that way, old fellow. Set me a good example, and I promise to follow it. As for the governess, she is a woman, and should be treated with common civility. I should say a little extra kindness wouldn't be amiss, either, because she is poor, and a stranger."

"That is my dear, good-hearted Ned! We'll stand by poor little Muir, won't we?" And running to her brother, Bella stood on tiptoe to offer him a kiss which he could not refuse, for the rosy lips were pursed up invitingly, and the bright eyes full of sisterly affection.

"I do hope she has come, for, when I make an effort to see anyone, I hate to make it in vain. Punctuality is *such* a virtue, and I know this woman hasn't got it, for she promised to be here at seven, and now it is long after," began Mrs. Coventry, in an injured tone.

Before she could get breath for another complaint, the clock struck seven and the doorbell rang.

"There she is!" cried Bella, and turned toward the door as if to go and meet the newcomer.

But Lucia arrested her, saying authoritatively, "Stay here, child. It is her place to come to you, not yours to go to her."

"Miss Muir," announced a servant, and a little black-robed figure stood in the doorway. For an instant no one stirred, and the governess had time to see and be seen before a word was uttered. All looked at her, and she cast on the household group a keen glance that impressed them curiously; then her eyes fell, and bowing slightly she walked in. Edward came forward and received her with the frank cordiality which nothing could daunt or chill.

"Mother, this is the lady whom you expected. Miss Muir, allow me to apologize for our apparent neglect in not sending for you. There was a mistake about the carriage, or, rather, the lazy fellow to whom the order was given forgot it. Bella, come here."

"Thank you, no apology is needed. I did not expect to be sent for." And the governess meekly sat down without lifting her eyes.

"I am glad to see you. Let me take your things," said Bella, rather shyly, for Gerald, still lounging, watched the fireside group with languid interest, and Lucia never stirred. Mrs. Coventry took a second survey and began:

"You were punctual, Miss Muir, which pleases me. I'm a sad invalid, as Lady Sydney told you, I hope; so that Miss Coventry's lessons will be directed by my niece, and you will go to her for directions, as she knows what I wish. You will excuse me if I ask you a few questions, for Lady Sydney's note was very brief, and I left everything to her judgment."

"Ask anything you like, madam," answered the soft, sad voice.

"You are Scotch, I believe."

'Yes, madam.'

"Are your parents living?"

"I have not a relation in the world."

"Dear me, how sad! Do you mind telling me your age?"

"Nineteen." And a smile passed over Miss Muir's lips, as she folded her hands with an air of resignation, for the catechism was evidently to be a long one.

"So young! Lady Sydney mentioned five-and-twenty, I think, didn't she, Bella?"

"No, Mamma, she only said she thought so. Don't ask such questions. It's not pleasant before us all," whispered Bella.

A quick, grateful glance shone on her from the suddenly lifted eyes of Miss Muir, as she said quietly, "I wish I was thirty, but, as I am not, I do my best to look and seem old."

Of course, every one looked at her then, and all felt a touch of pity at the sight of the pale-faced girl in her plain black dress, with no ornament but a little silver cross at her throat. Small, thin, and colorless she was, with yellow hair, gray eyes, and sharply cut, irregular, but very expressive features. Poverty seemed to have set its bond stamp upon her, and life to have had for her more frost than sunshine. But something in the lines of the mouth betrayed strength, and the clear, low voice had a curious mixture of command and entreaty in its varying tones. Not an attractive woman, yet not an ordinary one; and, as she sat there with her delicate hands lying in her lap, her head bent, and a bitter look on her thin face, she was more interesting than many a blithe and blooming girl. Bella's heart warmed to her at once, and she drew her seat nearer, while Edward went back to his dogs that his presence might not embarrass her.

"You have been ill, I think," continued Mrs. Coventry, who considered this fact the most interesting of all she had heard concerning the governess.

"Yes, madam, I left the hospital only a week ago."

"Are you quite sure it is safe to begin teaching so soon?"

"I have no time to lose, and shall soon gain strength here in the country, if you care to keep me."

"And you are fitted to teach music, French, and drawing?"

"I shall endeavor to prove that I am."

"Be kind enough to go and play an air or two. I can judge by your touch; I used to play finely when a girl."

Miss Muir rose, looked about her for the instrument, and seeing it at the other end of the room went toward it, passing Gerald and Lucia as if she did not see them. Bella followed, and in a moment forgot everything in admiration. Miss Muir played like one who loved music and was perfect mistress of her art. She charmed them all by the magic of this spell; even indolent Gerald sat up to listen, and Lucia put down her needle, while Ned watched the slender white fingers as they flew, and wondered at the strength and skill which they possessed.

"Please sing," pleaded Bella, as a brilliant overture ended.

With the same meek obedience Miss Muir complied, and began a little Scotch melody, so sweet, so sad, that the girl's eyes filled, and Mrs. Coventry looked for one of her many pocket-hankerchiefs. But suddenly the music ceased, for, with a vain attempt to support herself, the singer slid from her seat and lay before the startled listeners, as white and rigid as if stuck with death. Edward caught her up, and, ordering his brother off the couch, laid her there, while Bella chafed her hands, and her mother rang for her maid. Lucia bathed the poor girl's temples, and Gerald, with unwonted energy, brought a glass of wine. Soon Miss Muir's lips trembled, she sighed, then murmured, tenderly, with a pretty Scotch accent, as if wandering in the past, "Bide wi' me, Mither, I'm sae sick an sad here all alone."

"Take a sip of this, and it will do you good, my dear," said Mrs. Coventry, quite touched by the plaintive words.

The strange voice seemed to recall her. She sat up, looked about her, a little wildly, for a moment, then collected herself and said, with a pathetic look and tone, "Pardon me. I have been on my feet all day, and, in my eagerness to keep my appointment, I forgot to eat since morning. I'm better now; shall I finish the song?"

"By no means. Come and have some tea," said Bella, full of pity and remorse.

"Scene first, very well done," whispered Gerald to his cousin.

Miss Muir was just before them, apparently listening to Mrs. Coventry's remarks upon fainting fits; but she heard, and looked over her shoulders with a gesture like Rachel. Her eyes were gray, but at that instant they seemed black with some strong emotion of anger, pride, or defiance. A curious smile passed over her face as she bowed, and said in her penetrating voice, "Thanks. The last scene shall be still better."

Young Coventry was a cool, indolent man, seldom conscious of any emotion, any passion, pleasurable or otherwise; but at the look, the tone of the governess, he experienced a new sensation, indefinable, yet strong. He colored and, for the first time in his life, looked abashed. Lucia saw it, and hated Miss Muir with a sudden hatred; for, in all the years she had passed with her cousin, no look or word of hers had possessed such power. Coventry was himself again in an instant, with no trace of that passing change, but a look of interest in his usually dreamy eyes, and a touch of anger in his sarcastic voice.

"What a melodramatic young lady! I shall go tomorrow."

Lucia laughed, and was well pleased when he sauntered away to bring her a cup of tea from the table where a little scene was just taking place. Mrs. Coventry had sunk into her chair again, exhausted by the flurry of the fainting fit. Bella was busied about her; and Edward, eager to feed the pale governess, was awkwardly trying to make the tea, after a beseeching glance at his cousin which she did not choose to answer. As he upset the caddy and uttered a despairing exclamation, Miss Muir quietly took her place behind the urn, saying with a smile, and a shy glance at the young man, "Allow me to assume my duty at once, and serve you all. I understand the art of making people comfortable in this way. The scoop, please. I can gather this up quite well alone, if you will tell me how your mother likes her tea."

Edward pulled a chair to the table and made merry over his mishaps, while Miss Muir performed her little task with a skill and grace that made it pleasant to watch her. Coventry lingered a moment after she had given him a steaming cup, to observe her more nearly, while he asked a question or two of his brother. She took no more notice of him than if he had been a statue, and in the middle of the one remark he addressed to her, she rose to take the sugar basin to Mrs. Coventry, who was quite won by the modest, domestic graces of the new governess.

"Really, my dear, you are a treasure; I haven't tasted such tea since my poor maid Ellis died. Bella never makes it good, and Miss Lucia always forgets the cream. Whatever you do you seem to do well, and that is *such* a comfort."

"Let me always do this for you, then. It will be a pleasure, madam." And Miss Muir came back to her seat with a faint color in her cheek which improved her much.

"My brother asked if young Sydney was at home when you left," said Edward, for Gerald would not take the trouble to repeat the question.

Miss Muir fixed her eyes on Coventry, and answered with a slight tremor of the lips, "No, he left home some weeks ago."

The young man went back to his cousin, saying, as he threw himself down beside her, "I shall not go tomorrow, but wait till the three days are out."

"Why?" demanded Lucia.

Lowering his voice he said, with a significant nod toward the governess, "Because I have a fancy that she is at the bottom of Sydney's mystery. He's not been himself lately, and now he is gone without a word. I rather like romances in real life, if they are not too long, or difficult to read."

"Do you think her pretty?"

"Far from it, a most uncanny little specimen."

"Then why fancy Sydney loves her?"

"He is an oddity, and likes sensations and things of that sort."

"What do you mean, Gerald?"

"Get the Muir to look at you, as she did at me, and you will understand. Will you have another cup, Juno?"

"Yes, please." She liked to have him wait upon her, for he did it to no other woman except his mother.

Before he could slowly rise, Miss Muir glided to them with another cup on the salver; and, as Lucia took it with a cold nod, the girl said under her breath, "I think it honest to tell you that I possess a quick ear, and cannot help hearing what is said anywhere in the room. What you say of me is of no consequence, but you may speak of things which you prefer I should not hear; therefore, allow me to warn you." And she was gone again as noiselessly as she came.

"How do you like that?" whispered Coventry, as his cousin sat looking after the girl, with a disturbed expression.

"What an uncomfortable creature to have in the house! I am very sorry I urged her coming, for your mother had taken a fancy to her, and it will be hard to get rid of her." said Lucia, half angry, half amused.

"Hush, she hears every word you say. I know it by the expression of her face, for Ned is talking about horses, and she looks as haughty as ever you did, and that is saying much. Faith, this is getting interesting."

"Hark, she is speaking; I want to hear," and Lucia laid her hand on her cousin's lips. He kissed it, and then idly amused himself with turning the rings to and fro on the slender fingers.

"I have been in France several years, madam, but my friends died and I came back to be with Lady Sydney, till—" Muir paused an instant, then added, slowly, "till I fell ill. It was a contagious fever, so I went of my own accord to the hospital, not wishing to endanger her."

"Very right, but are you sure there is no danger of infection now?" asked Mrs. Coventry anxiously.

"None, I assure you. I have been well for some time, but did not leave because I preferred to stay there, than to return to Lady Sydney."

"No quarrel, I hope? No trouble of any kind?"

"No quarrel, but—well, why not? You have a right to know, and I will not make a foolish mystery out of a very simple thing. As your family, only, is present, I may tell the truth. I did not go back on the young gentleman's account. Please ask no more."

"Ah, I see. Quite prudent and proper, Miss Muir. I shall never allude to it again. Thank you for your frankness. Bella, you will be careful not to mention this to your young friends; girls gossip sadly, and it would annoy Lady Sydney beyond everything to have this talked of."

"Very neighborly of Lady S. to send the dangerous young lady here, where there are *two* young gentlemen to be captivated. I wonder why she didn't keep Sydney after she had caught him," murmured Coventry to his cousin.

"Because she had the utmost contempt for a titled fool." Miss Muir dropped the words almost into his ear, as she bent to take her shawl from the sofa corner.

"How the deuce did she get there?" ejaculated Coventry, looking as if he had received another sensation. "She has spirit, though, and upon my word I pity Sydney, if he did try to dazzle her, for he must have got a splendid dismissal."

"Come and play billiards. You promised, and I hold you to your word," said Lucia, rising with decision, for Gerald was showing too much interest in another to suit Miss Beaufort.

"I am, as ever, your most devoted. My mother is a charming woman, but I find our evening parties slightly dull, when only my own family are present. Good night, Mamma." He shook hands with his mother, whose pride and idol he was, and, with a comprehensive nod to the others, strolled after his cousin.

"Now they are gone we can be quite cozy, and talk over things, for I don't mind Ned any more than I do his dogs," said Bella, settling herself on her mother's footstool.

"I merely wish to say, Miss Muir, that my daughter has never had a governess and is sadly backward for a girl of sixteen. I want you to pass the mornings with her, and get her on as rapidly as possible. In the afternoon you will walk or drive with her, and in the evening sit with us here, if you like, or amuse yourself as you please. While in the country we are very quiet, for I cannot bear much company, and when my sons want gaiety, they go away for it. Miss Beaufort oversees the servants, and takes my place as far as possible. I am very delicate and keep my room till evening, except for an airing at noon. We will try each other for a month, and I hope we shall get on quite comfortably together."

"I shall do my best, madam."

One would not have believed that the meek spiritless voice which uttered these words was the same that had startled Conventry a few minutes before, nor that the pale, patient face could ever have kindled with such sudden fire as that which looked over Miss Muir's shoulder when she answered her young host's speech.

Edward thought within himself, Poor little woman! She has had a hard life. We will try and make it easier while she is here; and began his charitable work by suggesting that she might be tired. She acknowledged she was, and Bella led her away to a bright, cozy room, where with a pretty little speech and a good-night kiss she left her.

When alone Miss Muir's conduct was decidedly peculiar. Her first act was to clench her hands and mutter between her teeth, with passionate force, "I'll not fail again if there is a power in a woman's wit and will!" She stood a moment motionless, with an expression of almost fierce disdain on her face, then shook her clenched hand as if menacing some unseen enemy. Next she laughed, and shrugged her shoulders with a true French shrug, saying low to herself, "Yes, the last scene shall be better than the first. *Mon dieu,* how tired and hungry I am!"

Kneeling before the one small trunk which held her worldly possessions, she opened it, drew out a flask, and mixed a glass of some ardent cordial, which she seemed to enjoy extremely as she sat on the carpet, musing, while her quick eyes examined every corner of the room.

"Not bad! It will be a good field for me to work in, and the harder the task the better I shall like it. *Merci,* old friend. You put heart and courage into me when nothing else will. Come, the curtain is down, so I may be myself for a few hours, if actresses ever are themselves."

Still sitting on the floor she unbound and removed the long abundant braids from her head, wiped the pink from her face, took out several pearly teeth, and slipping off her dress appeared herself indeed, a haggard, worn, and moody woman of thirty at least. The metamorphosis was wonderful, but the disguise was more in the expression she assumed than in any art of costume or false adornment. Now she was alone, and her mobile features settled into their natural expression, weary, hard, bitter. She had been lovely once, happy, innocent, and tender; but nothing of all this remained to the gloomy woman who leaned there brooding over some wrong, or loss, or disappointment which had darkened all her life. For an hour she sat so, sometimes playing absently with the scanty locks that hung about her face, sometimes lifting the glass to her lips as if the fiery draught warmed her cold blood; and once she half uncovered her breast to eye with a terrible glance the scar of a newly healed wound. At last she rose and crept to bed, like one worn out with weariness and mental pain.

1866

How I Went Out to Service

When I was eighteen I wanted something to do. I had tried teaching for two years, and hated it; I had tried sewing, and could not earn my bread in that way, at the cost of health; I tried story-writing and got five dollars for stories which now bring a hundred; I had thought seriously of going upon the stage, but certain highly respectable relatives were so shocked at the mere idea that I relinquished my dramatic aspirations.

"What *shall* I do?" was still the question that perplexed me. I was ready to work, eager to be independent, and too proud to endure patronage. But the right task seemed hard to find, and my bottled energies were fermenting in a way that threatened an explosion before long.

My honored mother was a city missionary that winter, and not only served the clamorous poor, but often found it in her power to help decayed gentlefolk by quietly placing them where they could earn their bread without the entire sacrifice of taste and talent which makes poverty so hard for such to bear. Knowing her tact and skill, people often came to her for companions, housekeepers, and that class of the needy who do not make their wants known through an intelligence office.

One day, as I sat dreaming splendid dreams, while I made a series of little petticoats out of the odds and ends sent in for the poor, a tall, ministerial gentleman appeared, in search of a companion for his sister. He possessed an impressive nose, a fine flow of language, and a pair of large hands, encased in black kid gloves. With much waving of these somber members, Mr. R. set forth the delights awaiting the happy soul who should secure this home. He described it as a sort of heaven on earth. "There are books, pictures, flowers, a piano, and the best of society," he said. "This person will be one of the family in all respects, and only required to help about the lighter work, which my sister has done herself hitherto, but is now a martyr to neuralgia and needs a gentle friend to assist her."

My mother, who never lost her faith in human nature, in spite of many impostures, believed every word, and quite beamed with benevolent interest as she listened and tried to recall some needy young woman to whom this charming home would be a blessing. I also innocently thought:

"That sounds inviting. I like housework and can do it well. I should have time to enjoy the books and things I love, and D—is not far away from home. Suppose I try it."

So, when my mother turned to me, asking if I could suggest any one, I became as red as a poppy and said abruptly:

"Only myself."

"Do you really mean it?" cried my astonished parent.

"I really do if Mr. R. thinks I should suit," was my steady reply, as I partially obscured my crimson countenance behind a little flannel skirt, still redder.

The Reverend Josephus gazed upon me with the benign regard which a bachelor of five and thirty may accord a bashful damsel of eighteen. A smile dawned upon his countenance, "sicklied o'er with the pale cast of thought," or dyspepsia; and he softly folded the black gloves, as if about to bestow a blessing as he replied, with emphasis:

"I am sure you would, and we should think ourselves most fortunate if we could secure your society, and—ahem—services for my poor sister."

"Then I'll try it," responded the impetuous maid.

"We will talk it over a little first, and let you know to-morrow, sir," put in my prudent parent, adding, as Mr. R. arose: "What wages do you pay?"

"My dear madam, in a case like this let me not use such words as those. Anything you may think proper we shall gladly give. The labor is very light, for there are but three of us and our habits are of the simplest sort. I am a frail reed and may break at any moment; so is my sister, and my aged father cannot long remain; therefore, money is little to us, and any one who comes to lend her youth and strength to our feeble household will not be forgotten in the end, I assure you." And, with another pensive smile, a farewell wave of the impressive gloves, the Reverend Josephus bowed like a well-sweep and departed.

"My dear, are you in earnest?" asked my mother.

"Of course, I am. Why not try this experiment? It can but fail, like all the others."

"I have no objection; only I fancied you were rather too proud for this sort of thing."

"I am too proud to be idle and dependent, ma'am. I'll scrub floors and take in washing first. I do housework at home for love; why not do it abroad for money? I like it better than teaching. It is healthier than sewing and surer than writing. So why not try it?"

"It is going out to service, you know, though you are called a companion. How does that suit?"

"I don't care. Every sort of work that is paid for is service; and I don't mind being a companion, if I can do it well. I may find it is my mission to take care of neuralgic old ladies and lackadaisical clergymen. It does not sound exciting, but it's better than nothing," I answered, with a sigh; for it *was* rather a sudden downfall to give up being a Siddons and become a Betcinder.

How my sisters laughed when they heard the new plan! But they soon resigned themselves, sure of fun, for Lu's adventures were the standing joke of the family. Of course, the highly respectable relatives held up their hands in holy horror at the idea of one of the clan degrading herself by going out to service. Teaching a private school was the proper thing for an indigent gentlewoman. Sewing even, if done in the seclusion of home and not mentioned in public, could be tolerated. Story-writing was a genteel accomplishment and reflected credit upon the name. But leaving the paternal roof to wash other people's teacups, nurse other people's ails, and obey other people's orders for hire—this, this was degradation; and headstrong Louisa would disgrace her name forever if she did it.

Opposition only fired the revolutionary blood in my veins, and I crowned my iniquity by the rebellious declaration:

"If doing this work hurts my respectability, I wouldn't give much for it. My aristocratic ancestors don't feed or clothe me and my democratic ideas of honesty and honor won't let me be idle or dependent. You need not know me if you are ashamed of me, and I won't ask you for a penny; so, if I never do succeed in anything, I shall have the immense satisfaction of knowing I am under no obligation to any one."

In spite of the laughter and the lamentation, I got ready my small wardrobe, consisting of two calico dresses and one delaine, made by myself, also several large and uncompromising blue aprons and three tidy little sweeping-caps; for I had some English notions about housework and felt that my muslin hair-protectors would be useful in some of the "light labors" I was to undertake. It is needless to say they were very becoming. Then, firmly embracing my family, I set forth, one cold January day, with my little trunk, a stout heart, and a five-dollar bill for my fortune.

"She will be back in a week," was my sister's prophecy as she wiped her weeping eye.

"No, she won't, for she has promised to say the month out and she will keep her word," answered my mother, who always defended the black sheep of her flock.

I heard both speeches, and registered a tremendous vow to keep that promise, if I died in the attempt—little dreaming, poor innocent, what lay before me.

Josephus meantime had written me several remarkable letters, describing the different members of the family I was about to enter. His account was peculiar, but I believed every word of it and my romantic fancy was much excited by the details he gave. The principal ones are as follows, condensed from the voluminous epistles which he evidently enjoyed writing:

"You will find a stately mansion, fast falling to decay, for my father will have nothing repaired, preferring that the old house and its master should crumble away together. I have, however, been permitted to rescue a few rooms from ruin; and here I pass my recluse life, surrounded by the things I love. This will naturally be more attractive to you than the gloomy apartments my father inhabits, and I hope you will here allow me to minister to your young and cheerful nature when your daily cares are over. I need such companionship and shall always welcome you to my abode.

"Eliza, my sister, is a child at forty, for she has lived alone with my father and an old servant all her life. She is a good creature, but not lively, and needs stirring up, as you will soon see. Also I hope by your means to rescue her from the evil influence of Puah, who, in my estimation, is a *wretch*. She has gained entire control over Eliza, and warps her mind with great skill, prejudicing her against *me* and thereby desolating my home. Puah hates *me* and always has. Why I know not, except that I will not yield to her control. She ruled here for years while I was away, and my return upset all her nefarious plans. It will always be my firm opinion that she has tried to *poison me*, and may again. But even this dark suspicion will not deter me from my duty. I cannot send her away, for both my deluded father and my sister have entire faith in her, and I cannot shake it. She is faithful and kind to them, so I submit and remain to guard them, even at the risk of my life.

"I tell you these things because I wish you to know all and be warned, for this old hag has a specious tongue, and I should grieve to see you deceived by her lies. Say nothing, but watch her silently, and help me to thwart her evil plots; but do not trust her, or beware."

Now this was altogether romantic and sensational, and I felt as if about to enter one of those delightfully dangerous houses we read of in novels, where perils, mysteries, and sins freely disport themselves, till the newcomer sets all to rights, after unheard of trials and escapes.

I arrived at twilight, just the proper time for the heroine to appear; and, as no one answered my modest solo on the rusty knocker, I walked in and looked about me. Yes, here was the long, shadowy hall, where the ghosts doubtless walked at midnight. Peering in at an open door on the right, I saw a parlor full of ancient furniture, faded, dusty, and dilapidated. Old portraits stared at me from the walls and a damp child froze the marrow of my bones in the most approved style.

"The romance opens well," I thought, and, peeping in at an opposite door, beheld a luxurious apartment, full of the warm glow of firelight, the balmy breath of hyacinths and roses, the white glimmer of piano keys, and tempting rows of books along the walls.

The contrast between the two rooms was striking, and, after an admiring survey, I continued my explorations, thinking that I should not mind being "ministered to" in that inviting place when my work was done.

A third door showed me a plain, dull sitting room, with an old man napping in his easy-chair. I heard voices in the kitchen beyond, and entering there, beheld Puah the fiend. Unfortunately, for the dramatic effect of the tableaux, all I saw was a mild-faced old woman, buttering toast, while she conversed with her familiar, a comfortable gray cat.

The old lady greeted me kindly, but I fancied her faded blue eye had a weird expression and her amiable words were all a snare, though I own I was rather disappointed at the commonplace appearance of this humble Borgia.

She showed me to a tiny room, where I felt more like a young giantess than ever, and was obliged to stow away my possessions as snugly as in a ship's cabin. When I presently descended, armed with a blue apron and "a heart for any fate," I found the old man awake and received from him a welcome full of ancient courtesy and kindliness. Miss Eliza crept in like a timid mouse, looking so afraid of her buxom companion that I forgot my own shyness in trying to relieve hers. She was so enveloped in shawls that all I could discover was that my mistress was a very nervous little woman, with a small button of pale hair on the outside of her head and the vaguest notions of work inside. A few spasmodic remarks and many awkward pauses brought me to teatime, when Josephus appeared, as tall, thin, and cadaverous as ever. After his arrival there was no more silence, for he preached all suppertime something in this agreeable style.

"My young friend, our habits, as you see, are of the simplest. We eat in the kitchen, and all together, in the primitive fashion; for it suits my father and saves labor. I could wish more order and elegance; but *my* wishes are not consulted and I submit. I live above these petty crosses, and, though my health suffers from bad cookery, I do not murmur. Only, I must say, in passing, that if you *will* make your battercakes green with saleratus, Puah, I shall feel it my duty to throw them out of the window. *I* am used to poison; but I cannot see the coals of this blooming girl's stomach destroyed, as mine have been. And, speaking of duties, I may as well mention to you, Louisa (I call you so in a truly fraternal spirit), that I like to find my study in order when I come down in the morning; for I often need a few moments of solitude before I face the daily annoyances of my life. I shall permit *you* to perform this light task, for *you* have some idea of order (I see it in the formation of your brow), and feel sure that *you* will respect the sanctuary of thought. Eliza is so blind she does not see dust, and Puah enjoys devastating the one poor refuge I can call my own this side the grave. We are all waiting for you, sir. My father keeps up the old formalities, you observe; and I endure them, though *my* views are more advanced."

The old gentleman hastily finished his tea and returned thanks, when his son stalked gloomily away, evidently oppressed with the burden of his wrongs, also, as I irreverently fancied, with the seven "green" flapjacks he had devoured during the sermon.

I helped wash up the cups, and during that domestic rite Puah chatted in what I should have considered a cherry, social way had I not been darkly warned against her wiles.

"You needn't mind half Josephus says, my dear. He likes to hear himself talk and always goes on so before folks. I sometimes thinks his books and new ideas have sort of muddled his wits, for he is as full of notions as a paper is of pins; and he gets dreadfully put out if we don't give in to 'em. But, gracious me! they are so redicklus sometimes and so selfish I can't allow him to make a fool of himself or plague Lizy. She don't dare to say her soul is her own; so I have to stand up for her. His pa don't know half his odd doings; for I try to keep the old gentleman comfortable and have to manage 'em all, which is not an easy job I do assure you."

I had a secret conviction that she was right, but did not commit myself in any way, and we joined the social circle in the sitting room. The prospect was not a lively one, for the old gentleman nodded behind his newspaper; Eliza, with her head pinned up in a little blanket, slumbered on the sofa, Puah fell to knitting silently; and the plump cat dozed under the stove. Josephus was visible, artistically posed in the luxurious recesses of his cell, with the light beaming on his thoughtful brow, as he pored over a large volume or mused with upturned eye.

Having nothing else to do, I sat and stared at him, till, emerging from a deep reverie, with an effective start, he became conscious of my existence and beckoned me to approach the "sanctuary of thought" with a dramatic waft of his large hand.

I went, took possession of an easy chair, and prepared myself for elegant conversation. I was disappointed, however; for Josephus showed me a list of his favorite dishes, sole fruit of all that absorbing thought, and, with an earnestness that flushed his saffron countenance, gave me hints as to the proper preparation of these delicacies.

I mildly mentioned that I was not a cook; but was effectually silenced by being reminded that I came to be generally useful, to take his sister's place, and see that the flame of life which burned so feebly in this earthly tabernacle was fed with proper fuel. Mince pies, Welsh rarebits, sausages, and strong coffee did not strike me as strictly spiritual fare; but I listened meekly and privately resolved to shift this awful responsibility to Puah's shoulders.

Detecting me in gape, after an hour of this high converse, he presented me with an overblown rose, which fell to pieces before I got out of the room, pressed my hand, and dismissed me with a fervent "God bless you, child. Don't forget the dropped eggs for breakfast."

I was up betimes next morning and had the study in perfect order before the recluse appeared, enjoying a good prowl among the books as I worked and becoming so absorbed that I forgot the eggs, till a gusty sigh startled me, and I beheld Josephus, in dressing gown and slippers, languidly surveying the scene.

"Nay, do not fly," he said, as I grasped my duster in guilty haste. "It pleases me to see you here and lends a sweet, domestic charm to my solitary room. I like that graceful cap, the housewifely apron, and I beg you to wear them often; for it refreshes my eye to see something tasteful, young, and womanly about me. Eliza makes a bundle of herself and Puah is simply detestable."

He sank languidly into a chair and closed his eyes, as if the mere thought of his enemy was to much for him. I took advantage of this momentary prostration to slip away, convulsed with laughter at the looks and words of this bald-headed sentimentalist.

After breakfast I fell to work with a will, eager to show my powers and glad to put things to rights, for many hard jobs had evidently been waiting for a stronger arm than Puah's and a more methodical head than Eliza's.

Everything was dusty, moldy, shiftless, and neglected, except the domain of Josephus. Up-stairs the paper was dropping from the walls, the ancient furniture was all more or less dilapidated, and every hold and corner was full of relics tucked away by Puah, who was a regular old magpie. Rats and mice revealed in the empty rooms and spiders wove their tapestry undisturbed, for the old man would have nothing altered or repaired and his part of the house was fast going to ruin.

I longed to have a grand "clearing up"; but was forbidden to do more than to keep things in livable order. On the whole, it was fortunate, for I soon found that my hands would be kept busy with the realms of Josephus whose ethereal being shrank from dust, shivered at a cold breath, and needed much cosseting with dainty food, hot fires, soft beds, and endless service, else, as he expressed it, the frail reed would break.

I regret to say that a time soon came when I felt supremely indifferent as to the breakage, and very skeptical as to the fragility of a reed that ate, slept, dawdled, and scolded so energetically. The rose that fell to pieces so suddenly was a good symbol of the rapid disappearance of all the romantic delusions I had indulged in for a time. A week's acquaintance with the inmates of this old house quite settled my opinion, and further developments only confirmed it.

Miss Eliza was a nonentity and made no more impression on me than a fly. The old gentleman passed his days in a placid sort of doze and took no notice of what went on about him. Puah had been a faithful drudge for years, and, instead of being a "wretch," was, as I soon satisfied myself, a motherly old soul, with no malice in her. The secret of Josephus's dislike was that the reverend tyrant ruled the house, and all obeyed him but Puah, who had nursed him as a baby, boxed his ears as a boy, and was not afraid of him even when he became a man and a minister. I soon repented of my first suspicions, and grew fond of her, for without my old gossip I should have fared ill when my day of tribulations came.

At first I innocently accepted the fraternal invitations to visit the study, feeling that when my day's work was done I earned a right to rest and read. But I soon found that this was not the idea. I was not to read; but to be read to. I was not to enjoy the flowers, pictures, fire, and books; but to keep them in order for my lord to enjoy. I was also to be a passive bucket, into which he was to pour all manner of philosophic, metaphysical, and sentimental rubbish. I was to serve his needs, soothe his sufferings, and sympathize with all his sorrows—be a galley slave, in fact.

As soon as I clearly understood this, I tried to put an end to it by shunning the study and never lingering there an instant after my work was done. But it availed little, for Josephus demanded much sympathy and was bound to have it. So he came and read poems while I washed dishes, discussed his pet problems all meal-times, and put reproachful notes under my door, in which were comically mingled complaints of neglect and orders for dinner.

I bore it as long as I could, and then freed my mind in a declaration of independence, delivered in the kitchen, where he found me scrubbing the hearth. It was not an impressive attitude for an orator, nor was the occupation one a girl would choose when receiving calls; but I have always felt grateful for the intense discomfort of that moment, since it gave me the courage to rebel outright. Stranded on a small island of mat, in a sea of soapsuds, I brandished a scrubbing brush, as I indignantly informed him that I came to be a companion to his sister, not to him, and I should keep that post or none. This I followed up by reproaching him with the delusive reports he had given me of the place and its duties, and assuring him that I should not stay long unless matters mended.

"But I offer you lighter tasks, and you refuse them," he began, still hovering in the doorway, whither he had hastily retired when I opened my batteries.

"But I don't like the tasks, and consider them much worse than hard work," was my ungrateful answer, as I sat upon my island, with the softsoap conveniently near.

"Do you mean to say you prefer to scrub the hearth to sitting in my charming room while I read Hegel to you?" he demanded, glaring down upon me.

"Infinitely," I responded promptly, and emphasized my words by beginning to scrub with a zeal that made the bricks white with foam.

"Is it possible!" and, with a groan at my depravity, Josephus retired, full of ungodly wrath.

I remember that I immediately burst into jocund song, so that no doubt might remain in his mind, and continued to warble cheerfully till my task was done. I also remember that I cried heartily [?] when I got to my room, I was so vexed, disappointed, and tired. But my bower was so small I should soon have swamped the furniture if I had indulged copiously in tears; therefore I speedily dried them up, wrote a comic letter home, and waited with interest to see what would happen next.

Far be it from me to accuse one of the nobler sex of spite or the small revenge of underhand annoyances and slights to one who could not escape and would not retaliate; but after that day a curious change came over the spirit of that very unpleasant dream. Gradually all the work of the house had been slipping into my hands; for Eliza was too poorly to help and direct, and Puah too old to do much besides the cooking. About this time I found that even the roughest work was added to my share, for Josephus was unusually feeble and no one was hired to do his chores. Having made up my mind to go when the month was out, I said nothing, but dug paths, brought water from the well, split kindlings, made fires, and sifted ashes, like a true Cinderella.

There never had been any pretense of companionship with Eliza, who spent her days mulling over the fire, and seldom exerted herself except to find odd jobs for me to do— rusty knives to clean, sheets to turn, old stockings to mend, and, when all else failed, some paradise of moths and mice to be cleared up; for the house was full of such "glory holds."

If I remonstrated, Eliza at once dissolved into tears and said she must do as she was told; Puah begged me to hold on till spring, when things would be much better; and pity pleaded for the two poor souls. But I don't think I could have stood it if my promise had not bound me, for when the fiend said "Budge" honor said "Budge not" and I stayed.

But, being a mortal worm, I turned now and then when ireful Josephus trod upon me too hard, especially in the matter of boot-blacking. I really don't know why that is considered such humiliating work for a woman; but so it is, and there I drew the line. I would have cleaned the old man's shoes without a murmur; but he preferred to keep their native rustiness intact. Eliza never went out, and Puah affected carpet-slippers of the Chinese-junk pattern. Josephus, however, plumed himself upon his feet, which, like his nose, were large, and never took his walks abroad without having his boots in a high state of polish. He had brushed them himself at first; but soon after the explosion I discovered a pair of muddy boots in the shed, set suggestively near the blacking-box. I did not take the hint; feeling instinctively that this amiable being was trying how much I would bear for the sake of peace.

The boots remained untouched; and another pair soon came to keep them company, whereat I smiled wickedly as I chopped just kindlings enough for my own use. Day after day the collection grew, and neither party gave in. Boots were succeeded by shoes, then rubbers gave a pleasing variety to the long line, and then I knew the end was near.

"Why are not my boots attended to?" demanded Josephus, one evening, when obliged to go out.

"I'm sure I don't know," was Eliza's helpless answer.

"I told Louizy I guessed you'd want some of 'em before long," observed Puah with an exasperating twinkle in her old eye.

"And what did she say?" asked my lord with an ireful whack of his velvet slippers as he cast them down.

"Oh! she said she was so busy doing your other work you'd have to do that yourself; and I thought she was about right."

"Louizy" heard it all through the slide, and could have embraced the old woman for her words, but kept still till Josephus had resumed his slippers with a growl and retired to the shed, leaving Eliza in tears, Puah chuckling, and the rebellious handmaid exulting in the china-closet.

Alas! for romance and the Christian virtues, several pairs of boots were cleaned that night, and my sinful soul enjoyed the spectacle of the reverend bootblack at his task. I even found my "fancy work," as I called the evening job of pairing a bucketful of hard russets with a dull knife, much cheered by the shoe-brush accompaniment played in the shed.

Thunder-clouds rested upon the martyr's brow at breakfast, and I was as much ignored as the cat. And what a relief that was! The piano was locked up, so were the book-cases, the newspapers mysteriously disappeared, and a solemn silence reigned at table, for no one dared to talk when that gifted tongue was mute. Eliza fled from the gathering storm and had a comfortable fit of neuralgia in her own room, where Puah nursed her, leaving me to skirmish with the enemy.

It was not a fair fight, and that experience lessened my respect for mankind immensely. I did my best, however—grubbed about all day and amused my dreary evenings as well as I could; too proud even to borrow a book, lest it should seem like a surrender. What a long month it was, and how eagerly I counted the hours of that last week, for my time was up Saturday and I hoped to be off at once. But when I announced my intention such dismay fell upon Eliza that my heart was touched, and Puah so urgently begged me to stay till they could get some one that I consented to remain a few days longer, and wrote posthaste to my mother, telling her to send a substitute quickly or I should do something desperate.

That blessed woman, little dreaming of all the woes I had endured, advised me to be patient, to do the generous thing, and be sure I should not regret it in the end. I groaned, submitted, and did regret it all the days of my life.

Three mortal weeks I waited; for, though two other victims came, I was implored to set them going, and tried to do it. But both fled after a day or two, condemning the place as a very hard one and calling me a fool to stand it another hour. I entirely agreed with them on both points, and, when I had cleared up after the second incapable lady, I tarried not for the coming of a third, but clutched my property and announced my departure by the next train.

Of course, Eliza wept, Puah moaned, the old man politely regretted, and the younger one washed his hands of the whole affair by shutting himself up in his room and forbidding me to say farewell because "he could not bear it." I laughed, and fancied it done for effect then; but I soon understood it better and did not laugh.

At the last moment, Eliza nervously tucked a sixpenny pocketbook into my hand and shrouded herself in the little blanket with a sob. But Puah kissed me kindly and whispered, with an odd look: "Don't blame us for anything. Some folks is liberal and some ain't." I thanked the poor old soul for her kindness to me and trudged gayly away to the station, whither my property had proceded me on a wheelbarrow, hired at my own expense.

I never shall forget that day. A bleak March afternoon, a sloppy, lonely road, and one hoarse crow stalking about a field, so like Josephus that I could not resist throwing a snowball at him. Behind me stood the dull old house, no longer either mysterious or romantic in my disenchanted eyes; before me rumbled the barrow, bearing my dilapidated wardrobe; and in my pocket reposed what I fondly hoped was, if not a liberal, at least an honest return for seven weeks of the hardest work I ever did.

Unable to resist the desire to see what my earnings were, I opened the purse and beheld *four dollars.*

I have had a good many bitter minutes in my life; but one of the bitterest came to me as I stood there in the windy road, with the sixpenny pocket-book open before me, and looked from my poor chapped, grimy, chill-blained hands to the paltry sum that was considered reward enough for all the hard and humble labor they had done.

A girl's heart is a sensitive thing. And mine had been very full lately; for it had suffered many of the trials that wound deeply yet cannot be told; so I think it as but natural that my first impulse was to go straight back to that sacred study and fling this insulting money at the feet of him who sent it. But I was so boiling over with indignation that I could not trust myself in his presence, lest I should be unable to resist the temptation to shake him, in spite of his cloth.

No, I would go home, show my honorable wounds, tell my pathetic tale, and leave my parents to avenge my wrongs. I did so; but over that harrowing scene I drop a veil, for my feeble pen refuses to depict the emotions of my outraged family. I will merely mention that the four dollars went back and the reverend Josephus never heard the last of it in that neighborhood.

My experiment seemed a dire failure and I mourned it as such for years; but more than once in my life I have been grateful for the serio-comico experience, since it has taught me many lessons. One of the most useful of these has been the power of successfully making a companion, not a servant, of those whose aid I need, and helping to gild their honest wages with the sympathy and justice which can sweeten the humblest and lighten the hardest task.

1874

Rebecca Harding Davis
(1831–1910)

To have a son's literary fame eclipse the mother's own contributions is indeed a sad fate. Yet this is the fate that befell Rebecca Harding Davis during what were called "the Richard Harding Davis Years"—the title of the book that subsumes her biography within that of the son whose dashing good looks, highly publicized exploits as war correspondent, and facility as a writer of popular stories and novels captivated turn-of-the-century America. Rebecca Harding Davis's own autobiography bears the self-deprecatory title *Bits of Gossip,* but we know better than she that her literary contributions may no longer be overlooked, nor the fact that very early on she introduced telling insights into the lives of working women, soldiers at war, and the victims of racial injustice and political chicanery.

Born in 1831, the eldest of five children and the daughter of a successful businessman and civic leader, Davis grew up in Wheeling, West Virginia, and attended the Female Seminary in Washington, Pennsylvania—the product of a conventional upper-middle-class culture. But during those formative years in Wheeling, Davis had been watching and listening to the mill workers of the community; those whom she later named "the dumb" whose terrible needs are ignored by "the deaf" in power over them.

Davis's first story, "Life in the Iron-Mills," appeared in the *Atlantic Monthly* in 1861. In its grimness and unrelenting exposure of the effects of industrialization upon the working class, her narrative seemed not to have emerged from the sentimentalized culture in which most Americans of her class chose to envelop themselves. As Leo Marx's famous study of the clash of the pastoral ideal against the brute facts of the industrial age makes clear, the Machine *was* in the Garden by 1861, but only a few writers like Davis were willing to force notice of its presence upon their readers. Davis was writing well ahead of her times. It was as if neither Emerson nor Bronson Alcott were her true contemporaries, but that Emilé Zola, Theodore Dreiser, and Upton Sinclair were.

"A Story of To-day," Davis's second intensely realistic portrayal of working-class life, was also published originally in the *Atlantic,* but in 1862 was printed as a book entitled *Margret Howth.* While the Civil War was underway, Davis contributed "John Lamar" and "David Gaunt" to the *Atlantic* as stories that refused to romanticize battle agonies or to ignore underlying race tensions. (In regard to their attitudes toward war and race, Rebecca Harding Davis and her son Richard could hardly have been more unlike, although Richard's views were the acceptable ones at the time of *his* wars—in Cuba, the Philippines, and Latin America.)

Davis's marriage to Lemuel Clarke Davis in 1863 (first a struggling lawyer, later a successful Philadelphia newspaper editor) brought her three children, intense devotion to home and family, and continued years of writing. It is generally acknowledged, however, that her postmarriage writings (essays, reviews, children's stories, romances) slipped well below the level of her early fiction. The issues around which she centered her writings indicate that she never lost sight of the importance of the mulatto's plight, as in *Waiting for the Verdict* (1868), of political corruption, as in *John Andross* (1874), or of the struggles of villagers isolated in regions passed over by the currents of urbanization and industrialization, as in "Out of the Sea" (1865) and "Life-Saving Stations" (1876). But her former ability to resist sentimentalization by the assertion of unflinching realism was blunted.

Later, journalists of the "muck-raking" persuasion found ways to make sentimentality and melodrama *work for*, not against, the realist's exposure of social inequities, but Davis remained caught within the either/or situation that crippled the literary forcefulness of many members of her generation: either write "hard" like a man or write "soft" like a woman. That her famous son became a popular idol because he epitomized turn-of-the-century masculinity, which often went "soft" when writing about war, race, and social ills, is just one of the ironies that mark the fascinating, frustrating, but lastingly important career of Rebecca Harding Davis.

Further Reading:

G. Langford, *The Richard Harding Davis Years: A Biography of a Mother and a Son,* 1961.

J. Austin, "Success and Failure of Rebecca Harding Davis," *Midcontinent American Studies Journal* 1962.

W. Hesford, "Literary Context of *Life in the Iron Mills,*" *American Literature* 1977.

J. Pfaelzer, "Rebecca Harding Davis: Domesticity, Social Order and the Industrial Novel," *International Journal of Women's Studies* 1981.

J. Fetterley, Introduction, "Life in the Iron Mills," *Provisions: A Reader from 19th-Century American Women,* ed. J. Fetterley, 1985.

F. Malpezzi, "Sisters in Protest: Rebecca Harding Davis and Tillie Olsen," *Re Artes Liberales* Spring 1988.

J. Yellin, "The 'Feminization' of Rebecca Harding Davis," *American Literature* 1990.

J. Pfaelzer, "Rebecca Harding Davis," *Legacy,* Fall 1990.

M. Molyneaux, "Sculpture in the Iron Mills: Davis's Korl Woman," *Women's Studies* 1900.

S. Harris, *Rebecca Harding Davis and American Realism,* 1991.

Text:

"Life in the Iron-Mills," *Atlantic Monthly,* 1861.

Two Ways of Looking at War

That was the first peculiarity which struck an outsider in Emerson, Hawthorne, and the other members of the "Atlantic" coterie; that while they thought they were guiding the real world, they stood quite outside of it, and never would see it as it was.

. . . . I remember listening during one long summer morning to Louise Alcott's father as he chanted paeans to the war, the "armed angel which was wakening the nation to a lofty life unknown before." . . . .

I had just come from the border where I had seen the actual war; the filthy spewings of it; the political jobbery in Union and Confederate camps; the malignant personal hatreds wearing patriotic masks, and glutted by burning homes and outraged women; the chances in it, well improved on both sides, for brutish men to grow more brutish, and for honorable gentlemen to degenerate into thieves and sots. War may be an armed angel with a mission, but she has the personal habits of the slums.

Rebecca Harding Davis (1904)

Life in the Iron-Mills

"Is this the end?
O Life, as futile, then, as frail!
What hope of answer or redress?"

A CLOUDY day: do you know what that is in a town of iron-works? The sky sank down before dawn, muddy, flat, immovable. The air is thick, clammy with the breath of crowded human beings. It stifles me. I open the window, and, looking out, can scarcely see through the rain the grocer's shop opposite, where a crowd of drunken Irishmen are puffing Lynchburg tobacco in their pipes. I can detect the scent through all the foul smells ranging loose in the air.

The idiosyncrasy of this town is smoke. It rolls sullenly in slow folds from the great chimneys of the iron-foundries, and settles down in black, slimy pools on the muddy streets. Smoke on the wharves, smoke on the dingy boats, on the yellow river,—clinging in a coating of greasy soot to the house-front, the two faded poplars, the faces of the passers-by. The long train of mules, dragging masses of pig-iron through the narrow street, have a foul vapor hanging to their reeking sides. Here, inside, is a little broken figure of an angel pointing upward from the mantel-shelf; but even its wings are covered with smoke, clotted and black. Smoke everywhere! A dirty canary chirps desolately in a cage beside me. Its dream of green fields and sunshine is a very old dream,—almost worn out, I think.

From the back-window I can see a narrow brick-yard sloping down to the river-side, strewed with rain-butts and tubs. The river, dull and tawny-colored, *(la belle rivière!)*[1] drags itself sluggishly along, tired of the heavy weight of boats and coal-barges. What wonder? When I was a child, I used to fancy a look of weary, dumb appeal upon the face of the negro-like river slavishly bearing its burden day after day. Something of the same idle notion comes to me to-day, when from the street-window I look on the slow stream of human life creeping past night and morning, to the great mills. Masses of men, with dull, besotted faces bent to the ground, sharpened here and there by pain or cunning; skin and muscle and flesh begrimed with sacks and ashes; stooping all night over boiling caldrons of metal, laired by day in dens of drunkenness and infamy; breathing from infancy to death an air saturated with fog and grease and soot, vileness for soul and body. What do you make of a case like that, amateur psychologist? You call it an altogether serious thing to be alive: to these men it is a drunken jest, a joke,—horrible to angels perhaps, to them commonplace enough. My fancy about the river was an idle one: it is no type of such a life. What if it be stagnant and slimy here? It knows that beyond there waits for it odorous sunlight,—quaint old gardens, dusky with soft, green foliage of apple-trees, and flushing crimson with roses,—air, and fields, and mountains. The future of the Welsh puddler[2] passing just now is not so pleasant. To be stowed away, after his grimy work is done, in a hole in the muddy graveyard, and after that,—*not* air, nor green fields, nor curious roses.

---

[1] Beautiful stream.
[2] Puddler: assigned to work with malleable
iron bars.

Can you see how foggy the day is? As I stand here, idly tapping the window-pane, and looking out through the rain at the dirty back-yard and the coal-boats below, fragments of an old story float up before me,—a story of this old house into which I happened to come today. You may think it a tiresome story enough, as foggy as the day, sharpened by no sudden flashes of pain or pleasure.—I know: only the outline of a dull life, that long since, with thousands of dull lives like its own, was vainly lived and lost: thousands of them,—massed, vile, slimy lives, like those of the torpid lizards in yonder stagnant water-butt.—Lost? There is a curious point for you to settle, my friend, who study psychology in a lazy, *dilettante*[3] way. Stop a moment. I am going to be honest. This is what I want you to do. I want you to hide your disgust, take no heed to your clean clothes, and come right down with me,—here, into the thickest of the fog and mud and foul effluvia. I want you to hear this story. There is a secret down here, in this nightmare fog, that has lain dumb for centuries: I want to make it a real thing to you. You, Egoist, or Pantheist, or Arminian,[4] busy in making straight paths for your feet on the hills, do not see it clearly,—this terrible question which men here have gone mad and died trying to answer. I dare not put this secret into words. I told you it was dumb. These men, going by with drunken faces and brains full of unawakened power, do not ask it of Society or of God. Their lives ask it; their deaths ask it. There is no reply. I will tell you plainly that I have a great hope; and I bring it to you to be tested. It is this: that this terrible dumb question is its own reply; that it is not the sentence of death we think it, but, from the very extremity of its darkness, the most solemn prophecy which the world has known of the Hope to come. I dare make my meaning no clearer, but will only tell my story. It will, perhaps, seem to you as foul and dark as this thick vapor about us, and as pregnant with death; but if your eyes are free as mine are to look deeper, no perfume-tinted dawn will be so fair with promise of the day that shall surely come.

My story is very simple,—only what I remember of the life of one of these men,—a furnace-tender in one of Kirby & John's rolling-mills,—Hugh Wolfe. You know the mills? They took the great order for the Lower Virginia railroad there last winter; run usually with about a thousand men. I cannot tell why I choose the half-forgotten story of this Wolfe more than that of myriads of other furnace-hands. Perhaps because there is a secret underlying sympathy between that story and this day with its impure fog and thwarted sunshine,—or perhaps simply for the reason that this house is the one where the Wolfes lived. There were the father and son,—both hands, as I said, in one of Kirby & John's mills for making railroad-iron,—and Deborah, their cousin, a picker in some of the cotton-mills. The house was rented then to half a dozen families. The Wolfes had two of the cellar-rooms. The old man, like many of the puddlers and feeders of the mills, was Welsh,—had spent half of his life in the Cornish tin-mines.[5] You may pick the Welsh emigrants, Cornish miners, out of the throng passing the windows, any day. They are a trifle more filthy; their muscles are not so brawny; they stoop more. When they are drunk, they neither yell, nor shout, nor stagger, but skulk along like beaten hounds. A pure, unmixed blood, I fancy: shows itself in the slight angular bodies and

---

[3] Amateur.
[4] Egoist: one who centers belief in one's self; pantheist: one who locates power in the spirit flowing through the universe; Arminian: one who has faith in power of Jesus' sac-rifice to redeem all humankind—each finds clear answers to difficult problems.
[5] Immigrants who had previously worked as miners in Cornwall, westernmost area of England.

sharply-cut facial lines. It is nearly thirty years since the Wolfes lived here. Their lives were like those of their class: incessant labor, sleeping in kennel-like rooms, eating rank pork and molasses, drinking—God and the distillers only know what; with an occasional night in jail, to atone for some drunken excess. Is that all of their lives?—of the portion given to them and these their duplicates swarming the streets to-day?—nothing beneath?—all? So many a political reformer will tell you,—and many a private reformer, too, who has gone among them with a heart tender with Christ's charity, and come out outraged, hardened.

One rainy night, about eleven o'clock, a crowd of half-clothed women stopped outside of the cellar-door. They were going home from the cotton-mill.

"Good-night, Deb," said one, a mulatto, steadying herself against the gas-post. She needed the post to steady her. So did more than one of them.

"Dah 's a ball to Miss Potts' to-night. Ye 'd best come."

"Inteet, Deb, if hur 'll come, hur 'll hef fun," said a shrill Welsh voice in the crowd.

Two or three dirty hands were thrust out to catch the gown of the woman, who was groping for the latch of the door.

"No."

"No? Where 's Kit Small, then?"

"Begorra![6] on the spools. Alleys behint, though we helped her, we dud. An wid ye! Let Deb alone! It's ondacent frettin' a quite body. Be the powers, an' we 'll have a night of it! there 'll be lashin's o' drink,—the Vargent be blessed and praised for 't!"

They went on, the mulatto inclining for a moment to show fight, and drag the woman Wolfe off with them; but, being pacified, she staggered away.

Deborah groped her way into the cellar, and, after considerable stumbling, kindled a match, and lighted a tallow dip, that sent a yellow glimmer over the room. It was low, damp,—the earthen floor covered with a green, slimy moss,—a fetid air smothering the breath. Old Wolfe lay asleep on a heap of straw, wrapped in a torn horse-blanket. He was a pale, meek little man, with a white face and red rabbit-eyes. The woman Deborah was like him; only her face was even more ghastly, her lips bluer, her eyes more watery. She wore a faded cotton gown and a slouching bonnet. When she walked, one could see that she was deformed, almost a hunchback. She trod softly, so as not to waken him, and went through into the room beyond. There she found by the half-extinguished fire an iron saucepan filled with cold boiled potatoes, which she put upon a broken chair with a pint-cup of ale. Placing the old candlestick beside this dainty repast, she untied her bonnet, which hung limp and wet over her face, and prepared to eat her supper. It was the first food that had touched her lips since morning. There was enough of it, however: there is not always. She was hungry,—one could see that easily enough,—and not drunk, as most of her companions would have been found at this hour. She did not drink, this woman,—her face told that, too,—nothing stronger than ale. Perhaps the weak, flaccid wretch had some stimulant in her pale life to keep her up,—some love or hope, it might be, or urgent need. When that stimulant was gone, she would take to whiskey. Man cannot live by work alone.[7] While she was skinning the potatoes, and munching them, a noise behind her made her stop.

---

[6] Irish euphemism for "By God!"
[7] Bitter parody of Jesus' teaching that men

cannot live only for the sake of earning bread.

"Janey!" she called, lifting the candle and peering into the darkness. "Janey, are you there?"

A heap of ragged coats was heaved up, and the face of a young girl emerged, staring sleepily at the woman.

"Deborah," she said, at last, "I'm here the night."

"Yes, child. Hur's welcome," she said, quietly eating on.

The girl's face was haggard and sickly; her eyes were heavy with sleep and hunger: real Milesian eyes they were, dark, delicate blue, glooming out from black shadows with a pitiful fright.

"I was alone," she said, timidly.

"Where's the father?" asked Deborah, holding out a potato, which the girl greedily seized.

"He's beyant,—wid Haley,—in the stone house." (Did you ever hear the word *jail* from an Irish mouth?) "I came here. Hugh told me never to stay me-lone."

"Hugh?"

"Yes."

A vexed frown crossed her face. The girl saw it, and added quickly,—

"I have not seen Hugh the day, Deb. The old man says his watch lasts till the mornin'."

The woman sprang up, and hastily began to arrange some bread and flitch in a tin pail, and to pour her own measure of ale into a bottle. Tying on her bonnet, she blew out the candle.

"Lay ye down, Janey dear," she said, gently, covering her with the old rags. "Hur can eat the potatoes, if hur 's hungry."

"Where are ye goin', Deb? The rain's sharp."

"To the mill, with Hugh's supper."

"Let him bide till th' morn. Sit ye down."

"No, no,"—sharply pushing her off. "The boy 'll starve."

She hurried from the cellar, while the child wearily coiled herself up for sleep. The rain was falling heavily, as the woman, pail in hand, emerged from the mouth of the alley, and turned down the narrow street, that stretched out, long and black, miles before her. Here and there a flicker of gas lighted an uncertain space of muddy footwalk and gutter; the long rows of houses, except an occasional lager-bier shop, were closed; now and then she met a band of mill-hands skulking to or from their work.

Not many even of the inhabitants of a manufacturing town know the vast machinery of system by which the bodies of workmen are governed, that goes on unceasingly from year to year. The hands of each mill are divided into watches that relieve each other as regularly as the sentinels of an army. By night and day the work goes on, the unsleeping engines groan and shriek, the fiery pools of metal boil and surge. Only for a day in the week, in half-courtesy to public censure, the fires are partially veiled; but as soon as the clock strikes midnight, the great furnaces break forth with renewed fury, the clamor begins with fresh, breathless vigor, the engines sob and shriek like "gods in pain."

As Deborah hurried down through the heavy rain, the noise of these thousand engines sounded through the sleep and shadow of the city like far-off thunder. The mill to which she was going lay on the river, a mile below the city-limits. It was far, and she was weak, aching from standing twelve hours at the spools. Yet it was her almost nightly walk to take this man his supper, though at every square she sat down to rest, and she knew she should receive small word of thanks.

Perhaps, if she had possessed an artist's eye, the picturesque oddity of the scene might have made her step stagger less, and the path seem shorter; but to her the mills were only "summat deilish to look at by night."

The road leading to the mills had been quarried from the solid rock, which rose abrupt and bare on one side of the cinder-covered road, while the river, sluggish and black, crept past on the other. The mills for rolling iron are simply immense tent-like roofs, covering acres of ground, open on every side. Beneath these roofs Deborah looked in on a city of fires, that burned hot and fiercely in the night. Fire in every horrible form: pits of flame waving in the wind; liquid metal-flames writhing in tortuous streams through the sand; wide caldrons filled with boiling fire, over which bent ghastly wretches stirring the strange brewing; and through all, crowds of half-clad men, looking like revengeful ghosts in the red light, hurried, throwing masses of glittering fire. It was like a street in Hell. Even Deborah muttered, as she crept through, " 'T looks like t' Devil's place!" It did,—in more ways than one.

She found the man she was looking for, at last, heaping coal on a furnace. He had not time to eat his supper; so she went behind the furnace, and waited. Only a few men were with him, and they noticed her only by a "Hyur comes t' hunchback, Wolfe."

Deborah was stupid with sleep; her back pained her sharply; and her teeth chattered with cold, with the rain that soaked her clothes and dripped from her at every step. She stood, however, patiently holding the pail, and waiting.

"Hout, woman! ye look like a drowned cat. Come near to the fire,"—said one of the men, approaching to scrape away the ashes.

She shook her head. Wolfe had forgotten her. He turned, hearing the man, and came closer.

"I did no' think; gi' me my supper, woman."

She watched him eat with a painful eagerness. With a woman's quick instinct, she saw that he was not hungry,—was eating to please her. Her pale, watery eyes began to gather a strange light.

"Is 't good, Hugh? T' ale was a bit sour, I feared."

"No, good enough." He hesitated a moment. "Ye 're tired, poor lass! Bide here till I go. Lay down there on that heap of ash, and go to sleep."

He threw her an old coat for a pillow, and turned to his work. The heap was the refuse of the burnt iron, and was not a hard bed; the half-smothered warmth, too, penetrated her limbs, dulling their pain and cold shiver.

Miserable enough she looked, lying there on the ashes like a limp, dirty rag,—yet not an unfitting figure to crown the scene of hopeless discomfort and veiled crime: more fitting, if one looked deeper into the heart of things,—at her thwarted woman's form, her colorless life, her waking stupor that smothered pain and hunger,—even more fit to be a type of her class. Deeper yet if one could look, was there nothing worth reading in this wet, faded thing, half-covered with ashes? no story of a soul filled with groping passionate love, heroic unselfishness, fierce jealousy? of years of weary trying to please the one human being whom she loved, to gain one look of real heart-kindness from him? If anything like this were hidden beneath the pale, bleared eyes, and dull, washed-out-looking face, no one had ever taken the trouble to read its faint signs: not the half-clothed furnace-tender, Wolfe, certainly. Yet he was kind to her: it was his nature to be kind, even to the very rats that swarmed in the cellar: kind to her in just the same way. She knew that. And it might be that very knowledge had given to her face its apathy and vacancy more than her low, torpid life. One sees that dead, vacant look steal sometimes over the rarest, finest of women's faces,—in the very midst, it may be, of their warmest summer's day; and then one can guess at the secret of intolerable solitude that lies hid beneath the delicate laces and brilliant smile. There was no warmth, no brilliancy, no summer for this woman; so the stupor and vacancy had time to gnaw into her face perpetually. She was young, too, though no one guessed it; so the gnawing was the fiercer.

She lay quiet in the dark corner. Intening, through the monotonous din and uncertain glare of the works, to the dull plash of the rain in the far distance,—shrinking back whenever the man Wolfe happened to look towards her. She knew, in spite of all his kindness, that there was that in her face and form which made him loathe the sight of her. She felt by instinct, although she could not comprehend it, the finer nature of the man, which made him among his fellow-workmen something unique, set apart. She knew, that, down under all the vileness and coarseness of his life, there was a groping passion for whatever was beautiful and pure,—that his soul sickened with disgust at her deformity, even when his words were kindest. Through this dull consciousness, which never left her, came, like a sting, the recollection of the dark blue eyes and lithe figure of the little Irish girl she had left in the cellar. The recollection struck through even her stupid intellect with a vivid glow of beauty and of grace. Little Janey, timid, helpless, clinging to Hugh as her only friend: that was the sharp thought, the bitter thought, that drove into the glazed eyes a fierce light of pain. You laugh at it? Are pain and jealousy less savage realities down here in this place I am taking you to than in your own house or your own heart,—your heart, which they clutch at sometimes? The note is the same, I fancy, be the octave high or low.

If you could go into this mill where Deborah lay, and drag out from the hearts of these men the terrible tragedy of their lives, taking it as a symptom of the disease of their class, no ghost Horror would terrify you more. A reality of soul-starvation, of living death, that meets you every day under the besotted faces on the street,—I can paint nothing of this, only give you the outside outlines of a night, a crisis in the life of one man: whatever muddy depth of soul-history lies beneath you can read according to the eyes God has given you.

Wolfe, while Deborah watched him as a spaniel its master, bent over the furnace with his iron pole, unconscious of her scrutiny, only stopping to receive orders. Physically, Nature had promised the man but little. He had already lost the strength and instinct vigor of a man, his muscles were thin, his nerves weak, his face (a meek, woman's face) haggard, yellow with consumption. In the mill he was known as one of the girl-men: "Molly Wolfe" was his *sobriquet*.[8] He was never seen in the cockpit, did not own a terrier, drank but seldom; when he did, desperately. He fought sometimes, but was always thrashed, pommelled to a jelly. The man was game enough, when his blood was up: but he was no favorite in the mill; he had the taint of school-learning on him,—not to a dangerous extent, only a quarter or so in the free-school in fact, but enough to ruin him as a good hand in a fight.

For other reasons, too, he was not popular. Not one of themselves, they felt that, though outwardly as filthy and ash-covered; silent, with foreign thoughts and longings

---

[8] Nickname.

breaking out through his quietness in innumerable curious ways: this one, for instance. In the neighboring furnace-buildings lay great heaps of the refuse from the ore after the pig-metal is run. *Korl* we call it here: a light, porous substance, of a delicate, waxen, flesh-colored tinge. Out of the blocks of this korl, Wolfe, in his off-hours from the furnace, had a habit of chipping and moulding figures,—hideous, fantastic enough, but sometimes strangely beautiful: even the mill-men saw that, while they jeered at him. It was a curious fancy in the man, almost a passion. The few hours for rest he spent hewing and hacking with his blunt knife, never speaking, until his watch came again,—working at one figure for months, and when it was finished, breaking it to pieces perhaps, in a fit of disappointment. A morbid, gloomy man, untaught, unled, left to feed his soul in grossness and crime, and hard, grinding labor.

I want you to come down and look at this Wolfe, standing there among the lowest of his kind, and see him just as he is, that you may judge him justly when you hear the story of this night. I want you to look back, as he does every day, at his birth in vice, his starved infancy; to remember the heavy years he has groped through as boy and man,—the slow, heavy years of constant, hot work. So long ago he began, that he thinks sometimes he has worked there for ages. There is no hope that it will ever end. Think that God put into this man's soul a fierce thirst for beauty,—to know it, to create it; to *be*—something, he knows not what,—other than he is. There are moments when a passing cloud, the sun glinting on the purple thistles, a kindly smile, a child's face, will rouse him to a passion of pain,—when his nature starts up with a mad cry of rage against God, man, whoever it is that has forced this vile, slimy life upon him. With all this groping, this mad desire, a great blind intellect stumbling through wrong, a loving poet's heart, the man was by habit only a coarse, vulgar laborer, familiar with sights and words you would blush to name. Be just: when I tell you about this night, see him as he is. Be just,—not like man's law, which seizes on one isolated fact, but like God's judging angel, whose clear, sad eye saw all the countless cankering days of this man's life, all the countless nights, when, sick with starving, his soul fainted in him, before it judged him for this night, the saddest of all.

I called this night the crisis of his life. If it was, it stole on him unawares. These great turning-days of life cast no shadow before, slip by unconsciously. Only a trifle, a little turn of the rudder, and the ship goes to heaven or hell.

Wolfe, while Deborah watched him, dug into the furnace of melting iron with his pole, dully thinking only how many rails the lump would yield. It was late,—nearly Sunday morning; another hour, and the heavy work would be done,—only the furnaces to replenish and cover for the next day. The workmen were growing more noisy, shouting, as they had to do, to be heard over the deep clamor of the mills. Suddenly they grew less boisterous,—at the far end, entirely silent. Something unusual had happened. After a moment, the silence came nearer; the men stopped their jeers and drunken choruses. Deborah, stupidly lifting up her head, saw the cause of the quiet. A group of five or six men were slowly approaching, stopping to examine each furnace as they came. Visitors often came to see the mills after night: except by growing less noisy, the men took no notice of them. The furnace where Wolfe worked was near the bounds of the works; they halted there hot and tired: a walk over one of these great foundries is no trifling task. The woman, drawing out of sight, turned over to sleep. Wolfe, seeing them stop, suddenly roused from his indifferent stupor, and watched them keenly. He knew some of them: the overseer, Clarke,—a son of Kirby, one of the mill-owners,—and a Doctor May, one of the town-physicians. The other two were strangers. Wolfe came closer. He seized eagerly every chance that brought him into contact with this mysterious class that shone down on him perpetually with the glamour of another order of being. What made the difference between them? That was the mystery of his life. He had a vague notion that perhaps to-night he could find it out. One of the strangers sat down on a pile of bricks, and beckoned young Kirby to his side.

"This *is* hot, with a vengeance. A match, please?"—lighting his cigar. "But the walk is worth the trouble. If it were not that you must have heard it so often, Kirby, I would tell you that your works look like Dante's Inferno."

Kirby laughed.

"Yes. Yonder is Farinata himself in the burning tomb,"[9]—pointing to some figure in the shimmering shadows.

"Judging from some of the faces of your men," said the other, "they bid fair to try the reality of Dante's vision, some day."

Young Kirby looked curiously around, as if seeing the faces of his hands for the first time.

"They 're bad enough, that 's true. A desperate set, I fancy. Eh, Clarke?"

The overseer did not hear him. He was talking of net profits just then,—giving, in fact, a schedule of the annual business of the firm to a sharp peering little Yankee, who jotted down notes on a paper laid on the crown of his hat: a reporter for one of the city-papers, getting up a series of reviews of the leading manufactories. The other gentlemen had accompanied them merely for amusement. They were silent until the notes were finished, drying their feet at the furnaces, and sheltering their faces from the intolerable heat. At last the overseer concluded with—

"I believe that is a pretty fair estimate, Captain."

"Here, some of you men!" said Kirby, "bring up those boards. We may as well sit down, gentlemen, until the rain is over. It cannot last much longer at this rate."

"Pig-metal,"—mumbled the reporter,—"um!—coal facilities,—um!—hands employed, twelve hundred,—bitumen,—um!—all right, I believe, Mr. Clarke;—sinking-fund,—what did you say was your sinking-fund?"

"Twelve hundred hands?" said the stranger, the young man who had first spoken. "Do you control their votes, Kirby?"

"Control? No." The young man smiled complacently. "But my father brought seven hundred votes to the polls for his candidate last November. No force-work, you understand,—only a speech or two, a hint to form themselves into a society, and a bit of red and blue bunting to make them a flag. The Invincible Roughs,—I believe that is their name. I forget the motto: 'Our country's hope,' I think."

There was a laugh. The young man talking to Kirby sat with an amused light in his cool gray eye, surveying critically the half-clothed figures of the puddlers, and the slow swing of their brawny muscles. He was a stranger in the city,—spending a couple of months in the borders of a Slave State, to study the institutions of the South,—a brother-in-law of Kirby's,—Mitchell. He was an amateur gymnast,—hence his anatomical eye; a patron, in a *blasé*[10] way, of the prize-ring; a man who sucked the essence out of a science or philosophy in an indifferent, gentlemanly way; who took Kant, Novalis,

---

[9] Farinata: reference to the Sixth Circle of the Inferno in *The Divine Comedy* where Dante finds the leader of a rival Florentine political faction in torment together with other heretics.

[10] Jaded, indifferent.

Humboldt,[11] for what they were worth in his own scales; accepting all, despising nothing, in heaven, earth, or hell, but one-idead men; with a temper yielding and brilliant as summer water, until his Self was touched, when it was ice, though brilliant still. Such men are not rare in the States.

As he knocked the ashes from his cigar, Wolfe caught with a quick pleasure the contour of the white hand, the blood-glow of a red ring he wore. His voice, too, and that of Kirby's, touched him like music,—low, even, with chording cadences. About this man Mitchell hung the impalpable atmosphere belonging to the thorough-bred gentleman. Wolfe, scraping away the ashes beside him, was conscious of it, did obeisance to it with his artist sense, unconscious that he did so.

The rain did not cease. Clarke and the reporter left the mills; the others, comfortably seated near the furnace, lingered, smoking and talking in a desultory way. Greek would not have been more unintelligible to the furnace-tenders, whose presence they soon forgot entirely. Kirby drew out a newspaper from his pocket and read aloud some article, which they discussed eagerly. At every sentence, Wolfe listened more and more like a dumb, hopeless animal, with a duller, more stolid look creeping over his face, glancing now and then at Mitchell, marking acutely every smallest sign of refinement, then back to himself, seeing as in a mirror his filthy body, his more stained soul.

Never! He had no words for such a thought, but he knew now, in all the sharpness of the bitter certainty, that between them there was a great gulf never to be passed. Never!

The bell of the mills rang for midnight. Sunday morning had dawned. Whatever hidden message lay in the tolling bells floated past these men unknown. Yet it was there. Veiled in the solemn music ushering the risen Saviour was a key-note to solve the darkest secrets of a world gone wrong,—even this social riddle which the brain of the grimy puddler grappled with madly to-night.

The men began to withdraw the metal from the caldrons. The mills were deserted on Sundays, except by the hands who fed the fires, and those who had no lodgings and slept usually on the ash-heaps. The three strangers sat still during the next hour, watching the men cover the furnaces, laughing now and then at some jest of Kirby's.

"Do you know," said Mitchell, "I like this view of the works better than when the glare was fiercest? These heavy shadows and the amphitheatre of smothered fires are ghostly, unreal. One could fancy these red smouldering lights to be the half-shut eyes of wild beasts, and the spectral figures their victims in the den."

Kirby laughed. "You are fanciful. Come, let us get out of the den. The spectral figures, as you call them, are a little too real for me to fancy a close proximity in the darkness,—unarmed, too."

The others rose, buttoning their overcoats, and lighting cigars.

"Raining, still," said Doctor May, "and hard. Where did we leave the coach, Mitchell?"

"At the other side of the works.—Kirby, what 's that?"

Mitchell started back, half-frightened, as, suddenly turning a corner, the white figure of a woman faced him in the darkness,—a woman, white, of giant proportions, crouching on the ground, her arms flung out in some wild gesture of warning.

---

[11] Immanuel Kant (1724–1804), German philosopher; Novalis (1772–1801), pseudonym for German poet and novelist, Friedrich von Hardenberg; Friedrich von Humboldt (1769–1859), German naturalist and explorer.

"Stop! Make that fire burn there!" cried Kirby, stopping short.

The flame burst out, flashing the gaunt figure into bold relief.

Mitchell drew a long breath.

"I thought it was alive," he said, going up curiously.

The others followed.

"Not marble, eh?" asked Kirby, touching it.

One of the lower overseers stopped.

"Korl, Sir."

"Who did it?"

"Can't say. Some of the hands; chipped it out in off-hours."

"Chipped to some purpose, I should say. What a flesh-tint the stuff has! Do you see, Mitchell?"

"I see."

He had stepped aside where the light fell boldest on the figure, looking at it in silence. There was not one line of beauty or grace in it: a nude woman's form, muscular, grown coarse with labor, the powerful limbs instinct with some one poignant longing. One idea: there it was in the tense, rigid muscles, the clutching hands, the wild, eager face, like that of a starving wolf's. Kirby and Doctor May walked around it, critical, curious. Mitchell stood aloof, silent. The figure touched him strangely.

"Not badly done," said Doctor May. "Where did the fellow learn that sweep of the muscles in the arm and hand? Look at them! They are groping,—do you see?—clutching: the peculiar action of a man dying of thirst."

"They have ample facilities for studying anatomy," sneered Kirby, glancing at the half-naked figures.

"Look," continued the Doctor, "at this bony wrist, and the strained sinews of the instep! A working-woman,—the very type of her class."

"God forbid!" muttered Mitchell.

"Why?" demanded May. "What does the fellow intend by the figure? I cannot catch the meaning."

"Ask him," said the other, dryly. "There he stands,"—pointing to Wolfe, who stood with a group of men, leaning on his ash-rake.

The Doctor beckoned him with the affable smile which kind-hearted men put on, when talking to these people.

"Mr. Mitchell has picked you out as the man who did this,—I'm sure I don't know why. But what did you mean by it?"

"She be hungry."

Wolfe's eyes answered Mitchell, not the Doctor.

"Oh-h! But what a mistake you have made, my fine fellow! You have given no sign of starvation to the body. It is strong,—terribly strong. It has the mad, half-despairing gesture of drowning."

Wolfe stammered, glanced appealingly at Mitchell, who saw the soul of the thing, he knew. But the cool, probing eyes were turned on himself now,—mocking, cruel, relentless.

"Not hungry for meat," the furnace-tender said at last.

"What then? Whiskey?" jeered Kirby, with a coarse laugh.

Wolfe was silent a moment, thinking.

"I dunno," he said, with a bewildered look. "It mebbe. Summat to make her live, I think,—like you. Whiskey ull do it, in a way."

The young man laughed again. Mitchell flashed a look of disgust somewhere,—not at Wolfe.

"May," he broke out impatiently, "are you blind? Look at that woman's face! It asks questions of God, and says, 'I have a right to know.' Good God, how hungry it is!"

They looked a moment; then May turned to the mill-owner:—

"Have you many such hands as this? What are you going to do with them? Keep them at puddling iron?"

Kirby shrugged his shoulders. Mitchell's look had irritated him.

"*Ce n'est pas mon affaire.*[12] I have no fancy for nursing infant geniuses. I suppose there are some stray gleams of mind and soul among these wretches. The Lord will take care of his own; or else they can work out their own salvation. I have heard you call our American system a ladder which any man can scale. Do you doubt it? Or perhaps you want to banish all social ladders, and put us all on a flat table-land,—eh, May?"

The Doctor looked vexed, puzzled. Some terrible problem lay hid in this woman's face, and troubled these men. Kirby waited for an answer, and, receiving none, went on, warming with his subject.

"I tell you, there 's something wrong that no talk of '*Liberté*' or '*Égalité*'[13] will do away. If I had the making of men, these men who do the lowest part of the world's work should be machines,—nothing more,—hands. It would be kindness. God help them! What are taste, reason, to creatures who must live such lives as that?" He pointed to Deborah, sleeping on the ash-heap. "So many nerves to sting them to pain. What if God had put your brain, with all its agony of touch, into your fingers, and bid you work and strike with that?"

"You think you could govern the world better?" laughed the Doctor.

"I do not think at all."

"That is true philosophy. Drift with the stream, because you cannot dive deep enough to find bottom, eh?"

"Exactly," rejoined Kirby. "I do not think. I wash my hands of all social problems,— slavery, caste, white or black. My duty to my operatives has a narrow limit,—the pay-hour on Saturday night. Outside of that, if they cut korl, or cut each other's throats, (the more popular amusement of the two,) I am not responsible."

The Doctor sighed,—a good honest sigh, from the depths of his stomach.

"God help us! Who is responsible?"

"Not I, I tell you," said Kirby, testily. "What has the man who pays them money to do with their souls' concerns, more than the grocer or butcher who takes it?"

"And yet," said Mitchell's cynical voice, "look at her! How hungry she is!"

Kirby tapped his boot with his cane. No one spoke. Only the dumb face of the rough image looking into their faces with the awful question, "What shall we do to be saved?" Only Wolfe's face, with its heavy weight of brain, its weak, uncertain mouth, its desperate eyes, out of which looked the soul of his class,—only Wolfe's face turned towards Kirby's. Mitchell laughed,—a cool, musical laugh.

12 It's not my business.
13 Slogans from the French Revolution which

promised that citizens would possess both liberty and equality.

"Money has spoken!" he said, seating himself lightly on a stone with the air of an amused spectator at a play. "Are you answered?"—turning to Wolfe his clear, magnetic face.

Bright and deep and cold as Arctic air, the soul of the man lay tranquil beneath. He looked at the furnace-tender as he had looked at a rare mosaic in the morning; only the man was the more amusing study of the two.

"Are you answered? Why, May, look at him! *'De profundis clamavi.'* Or, to quote in English, 'Hungry and thirsty, his soul faints in him.' And so Money sends back its answer into the depths through you, Kirby! Very clear the answer, too!—I think I remember reading the same words somewhere:—washing your hands in Eau de Cologne, and saying, 'I am innocent of the blood of this man. See ye to it!' "

Kirby flushed angrily.

"You quote Scripture freely."

"Do I not quote correctly? I think I remember another line, which may amend my meaning: 'Inasmuch as ye did it unto one of the least of these, ye did it unto me.' Deist?[14] Bless you, man, I was raised on the milk of the Word. Now, Doctor, the pocket of the world having uttered its voice, what has the heart to say? You are a philanthropist, in a small way,—*n'est ce pas?*[15] Here, boy, this gentleman can show you how to cut korl better,—or your destiny. Go on, May!"

"I think a mocking devil possesses you to-night," rejoined the Doctor, seriously.

He went to Wolfe and put his hand kindly on his arm. Something of a vague idea possessed the Doctor's brain that much good was to be done here by a friendly word or two: a latent genius to be warmed into life by a waited-for sunbeam. Here it was: he had brought it. So he went on complacently:—

"Do you know, boy, you have it in you to be a great sculptor, a great man?—do you understand?" (talking down to the capacity of his hearer: it is a way people have with children, and men like Wolfe,)—"to live a better, stronger life than I, or Mr. Kirby here? A man may make himself anything he chooses. God has given you stronger powers than many men,—me, for instance."

May stopped, heated, glowing with his own magnanimity. And it was magnanimous. The puddler had drunk in every word, looking through the Doctor's flurry, and generous heat, and self-approval, into his will, with those slow, absorbing eyes of his.

"Make yourself what you will. It is your right."

"I know," quietly. "Will you help me?"

Mitchell laughed again. The Doctor turned now, in a passion,—

"You know, Mitchell, I have not the means. You know, if I had, it is in my heart to take this boy and educate him for"—

"The glory of God, and the glory of John May."

May did not speak for a moment; then, controlled, he said,—

"Why should one be raised, when myriads are left?—I have not the money, boy," to Wolfe, shortly.

"Money?" He said it over slowly, as one repeats the guessed answer to a riddle, doubtfully. "That is it? Money?"

---

[14] A person who does not believe in the teachings of Jesus exemplified by the quoted scriptural admonition to care for one another.

[15] Isn't that so?

"Yes, money,—that is it," said Mitchell, rising, and drawing his furred coat about him. "You've found the cure for all the world's diseases.—Come, May, find your good-humor, and come home. This damp wind chills my very bones. Come and preach your Saint-Simonian doctrines[16] to-morrow to Kirby's hands. Let them have a clear idea of the rights of the soul, and I'll venture next week they'll strike for higher wages. That will be the end of it."

"Will you send the coach-driver to this side of the mills?" asked Kirby, turning to Wolfe.

He spoke kindly: it was his habit to do so. Deborah, seeing the puddler go, crept after him. The three men waited outside. Doctor May walked up and down, chafed. Suddenly he stopped.

"Go back, Mitchell! You say the pocket and the heart of the world speak without meaning to these people. What has its head to say? Taste, culture, refinement? Go!"

Mitchell was leaning against a brick wall. He turned his head indolently, and looked into the mills. There hung about the place a thick, unclean odor. The slightest motion of his hand marked that he perceived it, and his insufferable disgust. That was all. May said nothing, only quickened his angry tramp.

"Besides," added Mitchell, giving a corollary to his answer, "it would be of no use. I am not one of them."

"You do not mean"——said May, facing him.

"Yes, I mean just that. Reform is born of need, not pity. No vital movement of the people's has worked down, for good or evil; fermented, instead, carried up the heaving, cloggy mass. Think back through history, and you will know it. What will this lowest deep—thieves, Magdalens, negroes—do with the light filtered through ponderous Church creeds, Baconian theories, Goethe schemes?[17] Some day, out of their bitter need will be thrown up their own light-bringer,—their Jean Paul, their Cromwell, their Messiah."[18]

"Bah!" was the Doctor's inward criticism. However, in practice, he adopted the theory; for, when, night and morning, afterwards, he prayed that power might be given these degraded souls to rise, he glowed at heart, recognizing an accomplished duty.

Wolfe and the woman had stood in the shadow of the works as the coach drove off. The Doctor had held out his hand in a frank, generous way, telling him to "take care of himself, and to remember it was his right to rise." Mitchell had simply touched his hat, as to an equal, with a quiet look of thorough recognition. Kirby had thrown Deborah some money, which she found, and clutched eagerly enough. They were gone now, all of them. The man sat down on the cinderroad, looking up into the murky sky.

" 'T be late, Hugh. Wunnot hur come?"

He shook his head doggedly, and the woman crouched out of his sight against the wall. Do you remember rare moments when a sudden light flashed over yourself, your world, God? when you stood on a mountain-peak, seeing your life as it might have

---

[16] Teachings of the French socialist Comte Claude de Saint-Simeon (1760–1825).

[17] Orthodox Christian beliefs; theories offered by Francis Bacon (1561–1626), English philosopher who perfected methods of scientific classification; vast array of ideas devised by Johann Wolfgang von Goethe (1749–1832), polymath in the fields of science, literature, the visual arts, and government; respectively.

[18] Visionary activists who break away from established doctrines in order to lead the people toward a better society.

been, as it is? one quick instant, when custom lost its force and every-day usage? when your friend, wife, brother, stood in a new light? your soul was bared, and the grave,—a foretaste of the nakedness of the Judgment-Day? So it came before him, his life, that night. The slow tides of pain he had borne gathered themselves up and surged against his soul. His squalid daily life, the brutal coarseness eating into his brain, as the ashes into his skin: before, these things had been a dull aching into his consciousness; to-night, they were reality. He griped the filthy red shirt that clung, stiff with soot, about him, and tore it savagely from his arm. The flesh beneath was muddy with grease and ashes,—and the heart beneath that! And the soul? God knows.

Then flashed before his vivid poetic sense the man who had left him,—the pure face, the delicate, sinewy limbs, in harmony with all he knew of beauty or truth. In his cloudy fancy he had pictured a Something like this. He had found it in this Mitchell, even when he idly scoffed at his pain: a Man all-knowing, all-seeing, crowned by Nature, reigning,—the keen glance of his eye falling like a sceptre on other men. And yet his instinct taught him that he too——He! He looked at himself with sudden loathing, sick, wrung his hands with a cry, and then was silent. With all the phantoms of his heated, ignorant fancy, Wolfe had not been vague in his ambitions. They were practical, slowly built up before him out of his knowledge of what he could do. Through years he had day by day made this hope a real thing to himself,—a clear, projected figure of himself, as he might become.

Able to speak, to know what was best, to raise these men and women working at his side up with him: sometimes he forgot this defined hope in the frantic anguish to escape,—only to escape,—out of the wet, the pain, the ashes, somewhere, anywhere,— only for one moment of free air on a hill-side, to lie down and let his sick soul throb itself out in the sunshine. But to-night he panted for life. The savage strength of his nature was roused; his cry was fierce to God for justice.

"Look at me!" he said to Deborah, with a low, bitter laugh, striking his puny chest savagely. "What am I worth, Deb? Is it my fault that I am no better? My fault? My fault?"

He stopped, stung with a sudden remorse, seeing her hunchback shape writhing with sobs. For Deborah was crying thankless tears, according to the fashion of women.

"God forgi' me, woman! Things go harder wi' you nor me. It 's a worse share."

He got up and helped her to rise; and they went doggedly down the muddy street, side by side.

"It's all wrong," he muttered, slowly,—"all wrong! I dunnot understan'. But it 'll end some day."

"Come home, Hugh!" she said, coaxingly; for he had stopped, looking around bewildered.

"Home,—and back to the mill!" He went on saying this over to himself, as if he would mutter down every pain in this dull despair.

She followed him through the fog, her blue lips chattering with cold. They reached the cellar at last. Old Wolfe had been drinking since she went out, and had crept nearer the door. The girl Janey slept heavily in the corner. He went up to her, touching softly the worn white arm with his fingers. Some bitterer thought stung him, as he stood there. He wiped the drops from his forehead, and went into the room beyond, livid, trembling. A hope, trifling, perhaps, but very dear, had died just then out of the poor puddler's life, as he looked at the sleeping, innocent girl,—some plan for the future, in which she had borne a part. He gave it up that moment, then and forever. Only a trifle, perhaps, to us: his face grew a shade paler,—that was all. But, somehow, the man's soul, as God and the angels looked down on it, never was the same afterwards.

Deborah followed him into the inner room. She carried a candle, which she placed on the floor, closing the door after her. She had seen the look on his face, as he turned away: her own grew deadly. Yet, as she came up to him, her eyes glowed. He was seated on an old chest, quiet, holding his face in his hands.

"Hugh!" she said, softly.

He did not speak.

"Hugh, did hur hear what the man said,—him with the clear voice? Did hur hear? Money, money,—that it wud do all?"

He pushed her away,—gently, but he was worn out; her rasping tone fretted him.

"Hugh!"

The candle flared a pale yellow light over the cobwebbed brick walls, and the woman standing there. He looked at her. She was young, in deadly earnest; her faded eyes, and wet, ragged figure caught from their frantic eagerness a power akin to beauty.

"Hugh, it is true! Money ull do it! Oh, Hugh, boy, listen till me! He said it true! It is money!"

"I know. Go back! I do not want you here."

"Hugh, it is t' last time. I 'll never worrit hur again."

There were tears in her voice now, but she choked them back.

"Hear till me only to-night! If one of t' witch people wud come, them we heard of t' home, and gif hur all hur wants, what then? Say, Hugh!"

"What do you mean?"

"I mean money."

Her whisper shrilled through his brain.

"If one of t' witch dwarfs wud come from t' lane moors to-night, and gif hur money, to go out,—out, I say,—out, lad, where t' sun shines, and t' heath grows, and t' ladies walk in silken gownds, and God stays all t' time,—where t' man lives that talked to us to-night,—Hugh knows,—Hugh could walk there like a king!"

He thought the woman mad, tried to check her, but she went on, fierce in her eager haste.

"If *I* were t' witch dwarf, if I had t' money, wud hur thank me? Wud hur take me out o' this place wid hur and Janey? I wud not come into the gran' house hur wud build, to vex hur wid t' hunch,—only at night, when t' shadows were dark, stand far off to see hur."

Mad? Yes! Are many of us mad in this way?

"Poor Deb! poor Deb!" he said, soothingly.

"It is here," she said, suddenly jerking into his hand a small roll. "I took it! I did it! Me, me!—not hur! I shall be hanged, I shall be burnt in hell, if anybody knows I took it! Out of his pocket, as he leaned against t' bricks. Hur knows?"

She thrust it into his hand, and then, her errand done, began to gather chips together to make a fire, choking down hysteric sobs.

"Has it come to this?"

That was all he said. The Welsh Wolfe blood was honest. The roll was a small green pocket-book containing one or two gold pieces, and a check for an incredible amount, as it seemed to the poor puddler. He laid it down, hiding his face again in his hands.

"Hugh, don't be angry wud me! It 's only poor Deb,—hur knows?"

He took the long skinny fingers kindly in his.

"Angry? God help me, no! Let me sleep. I am tired."

He threw himself heavily down on the wooden bench, stunned with pain and weariness. She brought some old rags to cover him.

It was late on Sunday evening before he awoke. I tell God's truth, when I say he had then no thought of keeping this money. Deborah had hid it in his pocket. He found it there. She watched him eagerly, as he took it out.

"I must gif it to him," he said, reading her face.

"Hur knows," she said with a bitter sigh of disappointment. "But it is hur right to keep it."

His right! The word struck him. Doctor May had used the same. He washed himself, and went out to find this man Mitchell. His right! Why did this chance word cling to him so obstinately? Do you hear the fierce devils whisper in his ear, as he went slowly down the darkening street?

The evening came on, slow and calm. He seated himself at the end of an alley leading into one of the larger streets. His brain was clear to-night, keen, intent, mastering. It would not start back, cowardly, from any hellish temptation, but meet it face to face. Therefore the great temptation of his life came to him veiled by no sophistry, but bold, defiant, owning its own vile name, trusting to one bold blow for victory.

He did not deceive himself. Theft! That was it. At first the word sickened him; then he grappled with it. Sitting there on a broken cart-wheel, the fading day, the noisy groups, the church-bells' tolling passed before him like a panorama, while the sharp struggle went on within. This money! He took it out, and looked at it. If he gave it back, what then? He was going to be cool about it.

People going by to church saw only a sickly mill-boy watching them quietly at the alley's mouth. They did not know that he was mad, or they would not have gone by so quietly: mad with hunger; stretching out his hands to the world, that had given so much to them, for leave to live the life God meant him to live. His soul within him was smothering to death; he wanted so much, thought so much, and *knew*—nothing. There was nothing of which he was certain, except the mill and things there. Of God and heaven he had heard so little, that they were to him what fairy-land is to a child: something real, but not here; very far off. His brain, greedy, dwarfed, full of thwarted energy and unused powers, questioned these men and women going by, coldly, bitterly, that night. Was it not his right to live as they,—a pure life, a good, true-hearted life, full of beauty and kind words? He only wanted to know how to use the strength within him. His heart warmed, as he thought of it. He suffered himself to think of it longer. If he took the money?

Then he saw himself as he might be, strong, helpful, kindly. The night crept on, as this one image slowly evolved itself from the crowd of other thoughts and stood triumphant. He looked at it. As he might be! What wonder, if it blinded him to delirium,—the madness that underlies all revolution, all progress, and all fall?

You laugh at the shallow temptation? You see the error underlying its argument so clearly,—that to him a true life was one of full development rather than self-restraint? that he was deaf to the higher tone in a cry of voluntary suffering for truth's sake than in the fullest flow of spontaneous harmony? I do not plead his cause. I only want to show you the mote in my brother's eye: then you can see clearly to take it out.

The money,—there it lay on his knee, a little blotted slip of paper, nothing in itself; used to raise him out of the pit; something straight from God's hand. A thief! Well, what was it to be a thief? He met the question at last, face to face, wiping the clammy drops of sweat from his forehead. God made this money—the fresh air, too—for his children's use. He never made the difference between poor and rich. The Something who looked down on him that moment through the cool gray sky had a kindly face, he knew,—loved his children alike. Oh, he knew that!

There were times when the soft floods of color in the crimson and purple flames, or the clear depth of amber in the water below the bridge, had somehow given him a glimpse of another world than this,—of an infinite depth of beauty and of quiet some-where,—somewhere,—a depth of quiet and rest and love. Looking up now, it became strangely real. The sun had sunk quite below the hills, but his last rays struck upward, touching the zenith. The fog had risen, and the town and river were steeped in its thick, gray damp; but overhead, the sun-touched smoke-clouds opened like a cleft ocean,— shifting, rolling seas of crimson mist, waves of billowy silver veined with blood-scarlet, inner depths unfathomable of glancing light. Wolfe's artist-eye grew drunk with color. The gates of that other world! Fading, flashing before him now! What, in that world of Beauty, Content, and Right, were the petty laws, the mine and thine, of mill-owners and mill-hands?

A consciousness of power stirred within him. He stood up. A man,—he thought, stretching out his hands,—free to work, to live, to love! Free! His right! He folded the scrap of paper in his hand. As his nervous fingers took it in, limp and blotted, so his soul took in the mean temptation, lapped it in fancied rights, in dreams of improved existences, drifting and endless as the cloud-seas of color. Clutching it, as if the tight-ness of his hold would strengthen his sense of possession, he went aimlessly down the street. It was his watch at the mill. He need not go, need never go again, thank God!— shaking off the thought with unspeakable loathing.

Shall I go over the history of the hours of that night? how the man wandered from one to another of his old haunts, with a half-consciousness of bidding them farewell,— lanes and alleys and back-yards where the mill-hands lodged,—noting, with a new ea-gerness, the filth and drunkenness, the pig-pens, the ash-heaps covered with potato-skins, the bloated, pimpled women at the doors,—with a new disgust, a new sense of sudden triumph, and, under all, a new, vague dread, unknown before, smothered down, kept under, but still there? It left him but once during the night, when, for the second time in his life, he entered a church. It was a sombre Gothic pile, where the stained light lost itself in far-retreating arches; built to meet the requirements and sym-pathies of a far other class than Wolfe's. Yet it touched, moved him uncontrollably. The distances, the shadows, the still, marble figures, the mass of silent kneeling worshippers, the mysterious music, thrilled, lifted his soul with a wonderful pain. Wolfe forgot him-self, forgot the new life he was going to live, the mean terror gnawing underneath. The voice of the speaker strengthened the charm; it was clear, feeling, full, strong. An old man, who had lived much, suffered much; whose brain was keenly alive, dominant; whose heart was summer-warm with charity. He taught it to-night. He held up Hu-manity in its grand total; showed the great world-cancer to his people. Who could show it better? He was a Christian reformer; he had studied the age thoroughly; his outlook at man had been free, world-wide, over all time. His faith stood sublime upon the Rock of Ages; his fiery zeal guided vast schemes by which the gospel was to be preached to all nations. How did he preach it to-night? In burning, light-laden words he painted the incarnate Life, Love, the universal Man: words that became reality in the lives of these people,—that lived again in beautiful words and actions, trifling, but heroic. Sin, as he defied it, was a real foe to them; their trials, temptations, were his. His words passed far over the furnace-tender's grasp, toned to suit another class of culture; they sounded in his ears a very pleasant song in an unknown tongue. He meant to cure this world-cancer with a steady eye that had never glared with hunger, and a hand that neither poverty nor strychnine-whiskey had taught to shake. In this morbid, distorted heart of the Welsh puddler he had failed.

Wolfe rose at last, and turned from the church down the street. He looked up; the night had come on foggy, damp; the golden mists had vanished, and the sky lay dull and ash-colored. He wandered again aimlessly down the street, idly wondering what had become of the cloud-sea of crimson and scarlet. The trial-day of this man's life was over, and he had lost the victory. What followed was mere drifting circumstance,—a quicker walking over the path,—that was all. Do you want to hear the end of it? You wish me to make a tragic story out of it? Why, in the police-reports of the morning paper you can find a dozen such tragedies: hints of shipwrecks unlike any that ever befell on the high seas; hints that here a power was lost to heaven,—that there a soul went down where no tide can ebb or flow. Commonplace enough the hints are,—jocose sometimes, done up in rhyme.

Doctor May, a month after the night I have told you of, was reading to his wife at breakfast from this fourth column of the morning-paper: an unusual thing,—these police-reports not being, in general, choice reading for ladies; but it was only one item he read.

"Oh, my dear! You remember that man I told you of, that we saw at Kirby's mill?— that was arrested for robbing Mitchell? Here he is; just listen:—'Circuit Court. Judge Day. Hugh Wolfe, operative in Kirby & John's Loudon Mills. Charge, grand larceny. Sentence, nineteen years hard labor in penitentiary.'—Scoundrel! Serves him right! After all our kindness that night! Picking Mitchell's pocket at the very time!"

His wife said something about the ingratitude of that kind of people, and then they began to talk of something else.

Nineteen years! How easy that was to read! What a simple word for Judge Day to utter! Nineteen years! Half a lifetime!

Hugh Wolfe sat on the window-ledge of his cell, looking out. His ankles were ironed. Not usual in such cases; but he had made two desperate efforts to escape. "Well," as Haley, the jailer, said, "small blame to him! Nineteen years' imprisonment was not a pleasant thing to look forward to." Haley was very good-natured about it, though Wolfe had fought him savagely.

"When he was first caught," the jailer said afterwards, in telling the story, "before the trial, the fellow was cut down at once,—laid there on that pallet like a dead man, with his hands over his eyes. Never saw a man so cut down in my life. Time of the trial, too, came the queerest dodge of any customer I ever had. Would choose no lawyer. Judge gave him one, of course. Gibson it was. He tried to prove the fellow crazy; but it wouldn't go. Thing was plain as daylight: money found on him. 'Twas a hard sentence,—all the law allows; but it was for 'xample's sake. These millhands are gettin' onbearable. When the sentence was read, he just looked up, and said the money was his by rights, and that all the world had gone wrong. That night, after the trial, a gentleman came to see him here, name of Mitchell,—him as he stole from. Talked to him for an hour. Thought he came for curiosity, like. After he was gone, thought Wolfe was remarkable quiet, and went into his cell. Found him very low; bed all bloody. Doctor said he had been bleeding at the lungs. He was as weak as a cat; yet, if ye 'll b'lieve me, he tried to get a-past me and get out. I just carried him like a baby, and threw him on the pallet. Three days after, he tried it again: that time reached the wall. Lord help you! he fought like a tiger,—giv' some terrible blows. Fightin' for life, you see; for he can't live long, shut up in the stone crib down yonder. Got a death-cough now. 'T took two of us to bring him down that day; so I just put the irons on his feet. There he sits, in there. Goin' to-morrow, with a batch more of 'em. That woman, hunchback, tried with him,—you remember?—she's only got three years. 'Complice. But *she's* a woman, you know. He's been quiet ever since I put on irons: giv' up, I suppose. Looks white, sick-lookin'. It acts different on 'em, bein' sentenced. Most of 'em gets reckless, devilish-like. Some prays awful, and sings them vile songs of the mills, all in a breath. That woman, now, she 's desper't'. Been beggin' to see Hugh, as she calls him, for three days. I'm a-goin' to let her in. She don't go with him. Here she is in this next cell. I'm a-goin' now to let her in."

He let her in. Wolfe did not see her. She crept into a corner of the cell, and stood watching him. He was scratching the iron bars of the window with a piece of tin which he had picked up, with an idle, uncertain, vacant stare, just as a child or idiot would do.

"Tryin' to get out, old boy?" laughed Haley. "Them irons will need a crowbar beside your tin, before you can open 'em."

Wolfe laughed, too, in a senseless way.

"I think I'll get out," he said.

"I believe his brain's touched," said Haley, when he came out.

The puddler scraped away with the tin for half an hour. Still Deborah did not speak. At last she ventured nearer, and touched his arm.

"Blood?" she said, looking at some spots on his coat with a shudder.

He looked up at her. "Why, Deb!" he said, smiling,—such a bright, boyish smile, that it went to poor Deborah's heart directly, and she sobbed and cried out loud.

"Oh, Hugh, lad! Hugh! dunnot look at me, when it wur my fault! To think I brought hur to it! And I loved hur so! Oh, lad, I dud!"

The confession, even in this wretch, came with the woman's blush through the sharp cry.

He did not seem to hear her,—scraping away diligently at the bars with the bit of tin.

Was he going mad? She peered closely into his face. Something she saw there made her draw suddenly back,—something which Haley had not seen, that lay beneath the pinched, vacant look it had caught since the trial, or the curious gray shadow that rested on it. That gray shadow,—yes, she knew what that meant. She had often seen it creeping over women's faces for months, who died at last of slow hunger or consumption. That meant death, distant, lingering: but this——Whatever it was the woman saw, or thought she saw, used as she was to crime and misery, seemed to make her sick with a new horror. Forgetting her fear of him, she caught his shoulders, and looked keenly, steadily, into his eyes.

"Hugh!" she cried, in a desperate whisper,—"oh, boy, not that! for God's sake, not *that!*"

The vacant laugh went off his face, and he answered her in a muttered word or two that drove her away. Yet the words were kindly enough. Sitting there on his pallet, she cried silently a hopeless sort of tears, but did not speak again. The man looked up furtively at her now and then. Whatever his own trouble was, her distress vexed him with a momentary sting.

It was market-day. The narrow window of the jail looked down directly on the carts and wagons drawn up in a long line, where they had unloaded. He could see, too, and hear distinctly the clink of money as it changed hands, the busy crowd of whites and blacks shoving, pushing one another, and the chaffering and swearing at the stalls. Somehow, the sound, more than anything else had done, wakened him up,—made the whole real to him. He was done with the world and the business of it. He let the tin fall, and looked out, pressing his face close to the rusty bars. How they crowded and pushed! And he,—he should never walk that pavement again! There came Neff Sanders, one of the feeders at the mill, with a basket on his arm. Sure enough, Neff was married the other week. He whistled, hoping he would look up; but he did not. He wondered if Neff remembered he was there,—if any of the boys thought of him up there, and thought that he never was to go down that old cinder-road again. Never again! He had not quite understood it before; but now he did. Not for days or years, but never!—that was it.

How clear the light fell on that stall in front of the market! and how like a picture it was, the dark-green heaps of corn, and the crimson beets, and golden melons! There was another with game: how the light flickered on that pheasant's breast, with the purplish blood dripping over the brown feathers! He could see the red shining of the drops, it was so near. In one minute he could be down there. It was just a step. So easy, as it seemed, so natural to go! Yet it could never be—not in all the thousands of years to come—that he should put his foot on that street again! He thought of himself with a sorrowful pity, as of some one else. There was a dog down in the market, walking after his master with such a stately, grave look!—only a dog, yet he could go backwards and forwards just as he pleased: he had good luck! Why, the very vilest cur, yelping there in the gutter, had not lived his life, had been free to act out whatever thought God had put into his brain; while he——No, he would not think of that! He tried to put the thought away, and to listen to a dispute between a countryman and a woman about some meat; but it would come back. He, what had he done to bear this?

Then came the sudden picture of what might have been, and now. He knew what it was to be in the penitentiary,—how it went with men there. He knew how in these long years he should slowly die, but not until soul and body had become corrupt and rotten,—how, when he came out, if he lived to come, even the lowest of the mill-hands would jeer him,—how his hands would be weak, and his brain senseless and stupid. He believed he was almost that now. He put his hand to his head, with a puzzled, weary look. It ached, his head, with thinking. He tried to quiet himself. It was only right, perhaps; he had done wrong. But was there right or wrong for such as he? What was right? And who had ever taught him? He thrust the whole matter away. A dark, cold quiet crept through his brain. It was all wrong; but let it be! It was nothing to him more than the others. Let it be!

The door grated, as Haley opened it.

"Come, my woman! Must lock up for t' night. Come, stir yerself!"

She went up and took Hugh's hand.

"Good-night, Deb," he said, carelessly.

She had not hoped he would say more; but the tired pain on her mouth just then was bitterer than death. She took his passive hand and kissed it.

"Hur 'll never see Deb again!" she ventured, her lips growing colder and more bloodless.

What did she say that for? Did he not know it? Yet he would not be impatient with poor old Deb. She had trouble of her own, as well as he.

"No, never again," he said, trying to be cheerful.

She stood just a moment, looking at him. Do you laugh at her, standing there, with her hunchback, her rags, her bleared, withered face, and the great despised love tugging at her heart?

"Come, you!" called Haley, impatiently.

She did not move.

"Hugh!" she whispered.

It was to be her last word. What was it?

"Hugh, boy, not THAT!"

He did not answer. She wrung her hands, trying to be silent, looking in his face in an agony of entreaty. He smiled again, kindly.

"It is best, Deb. I cannot bear to be hurted any more."

"Hur knows," she said, humbly.

"Tell my father good-bye; and—and kiss little Janey."

She nodded, saying nothing, looked in his face again, and went out of the door. As she went, she staggered.

"Drinkin' to-day?" broke out Haley, pushing her before him. "Where the Devil did you get it? Here, in with ye!" and he shoved her into her cell, next to Wolfe's, and shut the door.

Along the wall of her cell there was a crack low down by the floor, through which she could see the light from Wolfe's. She had discovered it days before. She hurried in now, and, kneeling down by it, listened, hoping to hear some sound. Nothing but the rasping of the tin on the bars. He was at his old amusement again. Something in the noise jarred on her ear, for she shivered as she heard it. Hugh rasped away at the bars. A dull old bit of tin, not fit to cut korl with.

He looked out of the window again. People were leaving the market now. A tall mulatto girl, following her mistress, her basket on her head, crossed the street just below, and looked up. She was laughing; but, when she caught sight of the haggard face peering out through the bars, suddenly grew grave, and hurried by. A free, firm step, a clear-cut olive face, with a scarlet turban tied on one side, dark, shining eyes, and on the head the basket poised, filled with fruit and flowers, under which the scarlet turban and bright eyes looked out half-shadowed. The picture caught his eye. It was good to see a face like that. He would try to-morrow, and cut one like it. *To-morrow!* He threw down the tin, trembling, and covered his face with his hands. When he looked up again, the daylight was gone.

Deborah, crouching near by on the other side of the wall, heard no noise. He sat on the side of the low pallet, thinking. Whatever was the mystery which the woman had seen on his face, it came out now slowly, in the dark there, and became fixed,—a something never seen on his face before. The evening was darkening fast. The market had been over for an hour; the rumbling of the carts over the pavement grew more infrequent: he listened to each, as it passed, because he thought it was to be for the last time. For the same reason, it was, I suppose, that he strained his eyes to catch a glimpse of each passer-by, wondering who they were, what kind of homes they were going to, if they had children,—listening eagerly to every chance word in the street, as if—(God be merciful to the man! what strange fancy was this?)—as if he never should hear human voices again.

It was quite dark at last. The street was a lonely one. The last passenger, he thought, was gone. No,—there was a quick step: Joe Hill, lighting the lamps. Joe was a good old chap; never passed a fellow without some joke or other. He remembered once seeing the place where he lived with his wife. "Granny Hill" the boys called her. Bedridden she was; but so kind as Joe was to her! kept the room so clean!—and the old woman, when he was there, was laughing at "some of t' lad's foolishness." The step was far down the street; but he could see him place the ladder, run up, and light the gas. A longing seized him to be spoken to once more.

"Joe!" he called, out of the grating. "Good-bye, Joe!"

The old man stopped a moment, listening uncertainly; then hurried on. The prisoner thrust his hand out of the window, and called again, louder; but Joe was too far down the street. It was a little thing; but it hurt him,—this disappointment.

"Good-bye, Joe!" he called, sorrowfully enough.

"Be quiet!" said one of the jailers, passing the door, striking on it with his club.

Oh, that was the last, was it?

There was an inexpressible bitterness on his face, as he lay down on the bed, taking the bit of tin, which he had rasped to a tolerable degree of sharpness, in his hand,—to play with, it may be. He bared his arms, looking intently at their corded veins and sinews. Deborah, listening in the next cell, heard a slight clicking sound, often repeated. She shut her lips tightly, that she might not scream; the cold drops of sweat broke over her, in her dumb agony.

"Hur knows best," she muttered at last, fiercely clutching the boards where she lay.

If she could have seen Wolfe, there was nothing about him to frighten her. He lay quite still, his arms outstretched, looking at the pearly stream of moonlight coming into the window. I think in that one hour that came then he lived back over all the years that had gone before. I think that all the low, vile life, all his wrongs, all his starved hopes, came then, and stung him with a farewell poison that made him sick unto death. He made neither moan nor cry, only turned his worn face now and then to the pure light, that seemed so far off, as one that said, "How long, O Lord? how long?"

The hour was over at last. The moon, passing over her nightly path, slowly came nearer, and threw the light across his bed on his feet. He watched it steadily, as it crept up, inch by inch, slowly. It seemed to him to carry with it a great silence. He had been so hot and tired there always in the mills! The years had been so fierce and cruel! There was coming now quiet and coolness and sleep. His tense limbs relaxed, and settled in a calm languor. The blood ran fainter and slow from his heart. He did not think now with a savage anger of what might be and was not; he was conscious only of deep stillness creeping over him. At first he saw a sea of faces: the mill-men,—women he had known, drunken and bloated,—Janeys timid and pitiful,—poor old Debs: then they floated together like a mist, and faded away, leaving only the clear, pearly moonlight.

Whether, as the pure light crept up the stretched-out figure, it brought with it calm and peace, who shall say? His dumb soul was alone with God in judgment. A Voice may have spoken for it from far-off Calvary, "Father, forgive them, for they know not what they do!" Who dare say? Fainter and fainter the heart rose and fell, slower and slower the moon floated from behind a cloud, until, when at last its full tide of white splendor swept over the cell, it seemed to wrap and fold into a deeper stillness the dead figure that never should move again. Silence deeper than the Night! Nothing that moved, save the black, nauseous stream of blood dripping slowly from the pallet to the floor!

There was outcry and crowd enough in the cell the next day. The coroner and his jury, the local editors, Kirby himself, and boys with their hands thrust knowingly into their pockets and heads on one side, jammed into the corners. Coming and going all day. Only one woman. She came late, and outstayed them all. A Quaker, or Friend, as they call themselves. I think this woman was known by that name in heaven. A homely body, coarsely dressed in gray and white. Deborah (for Haley had let her in) took notice of her. She watched them all—sitting on the end of the pallet, holding his head in her arms—with the ferocity of a watch-dog, if any of them touched the body. There was no meekness, no sorrow, in her face; the stuff out of which murderers are made, instead. All the time Haley and the woman were laying straight the limbs and cleaning the cell, Deborah sat still, keenly watching the Quaker's face. Of all the crowd there that day, this woman alone had not spoken to her,—only once or twice had put some cordial to her lips. After they all were gone, the woman, in the same still, gentle way, brought a vase of wood-leaves and berries, and placed it by the pallet, then opened the narrow window. The fresh air blew in, and swept the woody fragrance over the dead face. Deborah looked up with a quick wonder.

"Did hur know my boy wud like it? Did hur know Hugh?"

"I know Hugh now."

The white fingers passed in a slow, pitiful way over the dead, worn face. There was a heavy shadow in the quiet eyes.

"Did hur know where they'll bury Hugh?" said Deborah in a shrill tone, catching her arm.

This had been the question hanging on her lips all day.

"In t' town-yard? Under t' mud and ash? T' lad 'll smother, woman! He wur born on t' lane moor, where t' air is frick and strong. Take hur out, for God's sake, take hur out where t' air blows!"

The Quaker hesitated, but only for a moment. She put her strong arm around Deborah and led her to the window.

"Thee sees the hills, friend, over the river? Thee sees how the light lies warm there, and the winds of God blow all the day? I live there,—where the blue smoke is, by the trees. Look at me." She turned Deborah's face to her own, clear and earnest. "Thee will believe me? I will take Hugh and bury him there to-morrow."

Deborah did not doubt her. As the evening wore on, she leaned against the iron bars, looking at the hills that rose far off, through the thick sodden clouds, like a bright, unattainable calm. As she looked, a shadow of their solemn repose fell on her face: its fierce discontent faded into a pitiful, humble quiet. Slow, solemn tears gathered in her eyes: the poor weak eyes turned so hopelessly to the place where Hugh was to rest, the grave heights looking higher and brighter and more solemn than ever before. The Quaker watched her keenly. She came to her at last, and touched her arm.

"When thee comes back," she said, in a low, sorrowful tone, like one who speaks from a strong heart deeply moved with remorse or pity, "thee shall begin thy life again,—there on the hills. I came too late; but not for thee,—by God's help, it may be."

Not too late. Three years after, the Quaker began her work. I end my story here. At evening-time it was light. There is no need to tire you with the long years of sunshine, and fresh air, and slow, patient Christ-love, needed to make healthy and hopeful this impure body and soul. There is a homely pine house, on one of these hills, whose windows overlook broad, wooded slopes and clover-crimsoned meadows,—niched into the very place where the light is warmest, the air freest. It is the Friends' meeting-house. Once a week they sit there, in their grave, earnest way, waiting for the Spirit of Love to speak, opening their simple hearts to receive His words. There is a woman, old, deformed, who takes a humble place among them: waiting like them: in her gray dress, her worn face, pure and meek, turned now and then to the sky. A woman much loved by these silent, restful people; more silent than they, more humble, more loving. Waiting: with her eyes turned to hills higher and purer than these on which she lives,—dim and far off now, but to be reached some day. There may be in her heart some latent hope to meet there the love denied her here,—that she shall find him whom she lost, and that then she will not be all-unworthy. Who blames her? Something is lost in the passage of every soul from one eternity to the other,—something pure and beautiful, which might have been and was not: a hope, a talent, a love, over which the soul mourns, like Esau deprived of his birthright. What blame to the meek Quaker, if she took her lost hope to make the hills of heaven more fair?

Nothing remains to tell that the poor Welsh puddler once lived, but this figure of the mill-woman cut in korl. I have it here in a corner of my library. I keep it hid behind a curtain,—it is such a rough, ungainly thing. Yet there are about it touches, grand sweeps of outline, that show a master's hand. Sometimes,—tonight, for instance,—the curtain is accidentally drawn back, and I see a bare arm stretched out imploringly in the darkness, and an eager, wolfish face watching mine: a wan, woful face, through which the spirit of the dead korl-cutter looks out, with its thwarted life, its mighty hunger, its unfinished work. Its pale, vague lips seem to tremble with a terrible question. "Is this the End?" they say,—"nothing beyond?—no more?" Why, you tell me you have seen that look in the eyes of dumb brutes,—horses dying under the lash. I know.

The deep of the night is passing while I write. The gas-light wakens from the shadows here and there the objects which lie scattered through the room: only faintly, though; for they belong to the open sunlight. As I glance at them, they each recall some task or pleasure of the coming day. A half-moulded child's head; Aphrodite[19] a bough of forest-leaves; music; work; homely fragments, in which lie the secrets of all eternal truth and beauty. Prophetic all! Only this dumb, woful face seems to belong to and end with the night. I turn to look at it. Has the power of its desperate need commanded the darkness away? While the room is yet steeped in heavy shadow, a cool, gray light suddenly touches its head like a blessing hand, and its groping arm points through the broken cloud to the far East, where, in the flickering, nebulous crimson, God has set the promise of the Dawn.

1861

---

[19] Goddess of love and beauty.

RELATED VOICES

Iron Interests of Wheeling

Wheeling is chiefly known as the centre of a large iron industry. . . . The growth of this business, as indeed of all the manufactures of Wheeling, is due to the abundance of cheap fuel (stone coal) in the hills around the city, and to the facilities for reaching all the markets of the country, either by rail or water, at low rates for freight.

The iron . . . is produced on the spot, mostly from mixtures of Missouri and Lake Superior ores, and when made is immediately in market, without cost for transportation. There are now, at Wheeling and Steubenville, nine blast furnaces for the manufacture of iron, as follows: On the Wheeling side of the river, the "Top Mill" furnace, the "Belmont," and the "Riverside." On the Ohio side, the "Bellaire" furnace, the "Benwood," the "Mingo," the two "Jefferson" furnaces, and the "Stony Hollow." These furnaces have mostly 16 feet boshes and 60 feet stacks. The "Top Mill" has an 18 foot bosh,[1] and the Benwood a 13 foot. They produce mostly "Red Short" irons, such as are used for Nails. At this time iron is made as low as $19 per ton, worth in the market say $22, on four months' time. The connection now being made, via the Hempfield Short-line, between Wheeling and Connellsville, will so reduce the price of coke as to give Wheeling a further margin in its manufacture of iron.

The Nail mills at Wheeling and vicinity are as follows: The "Riverside" works, running 126 machines, including, also, a separate Bar and Rail mill belonging to the same company. Their blast furnace is three miles below their mills, with which they connect by rail and water.

The "Top Mill," running 106 machines, situated in the north part of the city, on the line of the Pittsburgh, Wheeling and Kentucky railroad—a new road not yet completed. Their blast furnace immediately adjoins their mill, and iron can be handled at a minimum cost through all its processes. . . .

The other principal iron manufactories of Wheeling and vicinity, are as follows:

The Wheeling Hinge Company, now in the 12th year of its existence, has steadily grown from a small affair to be a large concern. It owns the patent for the Dunning hinge—an article intended to supersede, to a certain extent, the old screw and strap hinge.

The Superior Machine Works, a large concern organized for the manufacture of the Superior Reaping and Mowing Machines, and where also engines and other machinery are built.

The Centripetal Power Company Works, organized for the manufacture of portable machinery for the use (principally) of farmers, whereby important advantages are claimed in overcoming friction, and in the relation of speed and momentum.

The Crescent Rail and Sheet Mills—situated on the south bank of Wheeling creek—connected by a bridge across said creek with the 4th ward of the city, and directly opposite the works of the Wheeling Hinge Co. A large concern, owned by the Whitakers, well known iron men. Is principally run now on sheet iron.

---

[1] Bosh: Section of blast furnace between the hearth and the stack.

The Ætna Iron Works, situated in the suburb of Ætnaville, a new village just growing up opposite the city, midway between Bridgeport and Martin's Ferry. Manufactures bar and sheet iron, and also small rails, for coal banks and light roads.

The Norway Tack Factory, situated in the 4th ward of the city; started in 1865—owned by Jones, Heald & Phinney—manufactures all varieties of tacks and a fine three-penny nail.

The Arlington Stove Works and Foundry of Joseph Bell & Co.; the Star Stove Works and Foundry of Benjamin Fisher; the Boiler Works of Moorehead & Son; the Foundry, Machine and Repair Works of A. J. Sweeney & Son; the Foundry, Machine and Repair Works of Cecil, Hobbs & Co.; the Bellaire Implement Factory; the Stove Works and Foundry of Spence, Baggs & Co., at Martin's Ferry; the Ohio Valley Machine Works of L. Spence & Co., (same place,) whereat were built the engines of the Belmont Blast Furnace, and where also are made Threshers and Cleaners, and other machinery; the large Foundry of Culbertson, Wiley & Co., (same place,) where was cast the heavy iron work of the Ætna Mill.

The foregoing are the principal iron establishments in and around Wheeling. Quite a number of them are of recent origin, either in whole or part. Just previous to the panic of 1873, an important impetus had been given to the development of the iron business of this vicinity, growing out, as we have said, of the abundance of cheap fuel and the facilities for shipment. It is hoped that these advantages will, at an early day, re-assert themselves, and go on, as in the years '72 and '73, increasing the number of our manufactories.

A. W. Campbell, Resources of West Virginia, 1876

The Gospel of Wealth

. . . You know how people moan about poverty as being a great evil, and it seems to be accepted that if people had only plenty of money and were rich, they would be happy and more useful, and get more out of life.

As a rule, there is more genuine satisfaction, a truer life, and more obtained from life in the humble cottages of the poor than in the places of the rich. I always pity the sons and daughters of rich men, who are attended by servants, and have governesses at a later age, but am glad to remember that they do not know what they have missed.

They have kind fathers and mothers, too, and think that they enjoy the sweetness of these blessings to the fullest: but this they cannot do; for the poor boy who has in his father his constant companion, tutor, and model, and in his mother—holy name!—his nurse, teacher, guardian angel, saint, all in one, has a richer, more precious fortune in life than any rich man's son who is not so favored can possibly know, and compared with which all other fortunes count for little.

It is because I know how sweet and happy and pure the home of honest poverty is, how free from perplexing care, from social envies and emulations, how loving and how united its members may be in the common interest of supporting the family, that I sympathize with the rich man's boy and congratulate the poor man's boy; and it is for these reasons that from the ranks of the poor so many strong, eminent, self-reliant men have always sprung and always must spring.

If you will read the list of the immortals who "were not born to die," you will find that most of them have been born to the precious heritage of poverty.

It seems, nowadays, a matter of universal desire that poverty should be abolished. We should be quite willing to abolish luxury, but to abolish honest, industrious, self-denying poverty would be to destroy the soil upon which mankind produces the virtues which enable our race to reach a still higher civilization than it now possesses. . . .

Andrew Carnegie, The Gospel of Wealth, 1900

Iron Foundry Proprietor, Before the United States Senate Committee on Labor and Education, 1883

There [is] no man, however humble he might be, who could not own his own house, his own farm, or his own workshop. It is only necessary for a man to aim at that object when he starts out in life. He should begin to think of it at least when he is eighteen, and if he strikes out in that way with a definite object in view, remembering he is probably going to have a family of children who will be as dear to him as his own life, and that old age will come on in due time—if a man strikes out with that object in view from the beginning, and pursues it in a straightforward and industrious and prudent manner, he cannot fail. I have never known such a man to fail, and I can cite thousands of instances where such men have succeeded in the highest degree.

But a new theory has been spreading among the working people. Two men start out in life together at the same time and with equal chances, both depending upon their labor for success; one of them after awhile becomes discontented, begins to think that he ought to enjoy life as he goes along and to have more days for excursions and for enjoyments; that he ought to have more cigars and other luxuries and indulgences, and he lags and lingers on the way. The other man is thoughtful, prudent, industrious; he has a definite object in life, and he keeps that object always in view and works towards it constantly, and he succeeds. Now there is no mystery in the failure of one of these men or in the success of the other. It is all nonsense for any man to think of ever accomplishing anything in this world, no matter how trifling it may be, if he has not a definite object and motive, and is not *determined* to do it. The first of these men lagged and stumbled on the way through his own fault entirely. He took his choice. He preferred to smoke his cigars, to go on excursions, to frequent the liquor saloons, or to go gunning (for I have seen men go out of my shop and spend a week at a time gunning when they had not enough to keep them out of the poorhouse for six months), and then when he finds that he is not succeeding, and that other men of more energy and industry are getting ahead of him in life, he comes out and says, "I am injured: I am suffering from injustice; I want legislation to compel this other man to divide with me that which he has acquired by his own diligence and thrift." Very often you will hear men of the character I have described taking that view and claiming that some remedy for the evils they suffer under ought to be provided by legislation, when the difficulty is all in themselves.

Testimony of John Roach, U.S. Senate, 1885

Lectures to Young Men

It is not a small thing for a man to be able to make his hands light by supplementing them with his head. The advantage which intelligence gives a man is very great. It oftentimes increases one's mere physical ability full one half. Active thought, or quickness in the use of the mind, is very important in teaching us how to use our hands rightly in every possible relation and situation in life. The use of the head abridges the labor of the hands. There is no drudgery, there is no mechanical routine, there is no minuteness of function, that is not advantaged by education. If a man has nothing to do but to turn a grindstone, he had better be educated; if a man has nothing to do but to stick pins on a paper, he had better be educated; if he has to sweep the streets, he had better be educated. It makes no difference what you do, you do it better if you are educated. An intelligent man knows how to bring knowledge to bear upon whatever he has to do. It is a mistake to suppose that a stupid man makes a better laborer than one who is intelligent. If I wanted a man to drain my farm, or merely to throw the dirt out from a ditch, I would not get a stupid drudge if I could help it. In times when armies have to pass through great hardships, it is the stupid soldiers that break down quickest; while the men of intelligence, who have mental resources, hold out longest. It is a common saying that blood will always tell in horses: I know that intelligence will tell in men.

Whatever your occupation may be, it is worth your while to be a man of thought and intellectual resources. It is worth your while to be educated thoroughly for any business. If you are a mechanic or tradesman, education is good enough for you, and you are good enough for it. Sometimes wonder is expressed that a man who has been through college, and who is therefore supposed to be educated, should bury himself in business. But why should he not? Has not a merchant a right to be an educated man? Do you suppose a man has no right to an education unless he is going to be a doctor, a minister, a lawyer, or some kind of a public man? I affirm the right of every man in the community to an education. A man should educate himself for his own sake, even if his education should benefit no one else in the world. Every man's education does, however, benefit others besides himself. There is no calling, except that of slave-catching, for Christian governments, that is not made better by brains. No matter what a man's work is, he is a better man for having had a thorough mind-drilling. If you are to be a farmer, go to college or to the academy, first. If you are to be a mechanic, and you have an opportunity of getting an education, get that first. If you mean to follow the lowest calling,—one of those callings termed "menial,"—do not be ignorant; have knowledge. A man can do without luxuries and wealth and public honors, but not without knowledge. Poverty is not disreputable, but ignorance is.

One of the things which our age and which this land has to develop, is the compatibility of manual labor with real refinement and education. This is to be one of the problems of the age. We must show that knowledge is not the monopoly of professions, not the privilege of wealth, not the prerogative of leisure, but that knowledge and refinement belong to hard-working men as much as to any other class of men. And I hope to see the day when there will be educated day-laborers, educated mechanics, refined and educated farmers and ship-masters;

for we must carry out into practice our theory of men's equality, and of common worth in matters of education. We must endeavor to inspire every calling in life with an honest ambition for intelligence. There is no calling that will not be lifted up by it. Whatever may be your business, then, make it a point to get from it, or in spite of it, a good education.

Never whine over what you may suppose to be the loss of early opportunities. A great many men have good early opportunities who never improve them; and many have lost their early opportunities without losing much. Every man may educate himself that wishes to. It is the will that makes the way. Many a slave that wanted knowledge has listened while his master's children were saying their letters and putting them together to form easy words, and thus caught the first elements of spelling; and then, lying flat on his belly before the raked-up coals and embers, with a stolen book, has learned to read and write. If a man has such a thirst for knowledge as that, I do not care where you put him, he will become an educated man. . . .

You can educate yourself. Where there is a will there is a way.

Henry Ward Beecher, Lectures to Young Men, 1873

Art, Beauty, Ugliness

It was the artist's opinion that there is no essential difference between beauty and ugliness; that they overlap and intermingle in a quite inextricable manner; that there is no saying where one begins and the other ends; that hideousness grimaces at you suddenly from out of the very bosom of loveliness, and beauty blooms before your eyes in the lap of vileness; that it is a waste of wit to nurse metaphysical distinctions, and a sadly meagre entertainment to caress imaginary lines; that the thing to aim at is the expressive, and the way to reach it is by ingenuity; that for this purpose everything may serve, and that a consummate work is a sort of hotch-potch of the pure and the impure, the graceful and the grotesque.

Henry James, "Roderick Hudson," The Atlantic Monthly, 1875

Walt Whitman
1819–1892

Whitman is the great bridge figure of nineteenth-century American literature. He links the era of Hawthorne and Thoreau to that of Mark Twain and Henry James. He fulfilled the promise of romanticism while pointing to the open road of modernist form, vision, and experiment. His powerful, imperial presence asserts itself in the work of Wallace Stevens, William Carlos Williams, Ezra Pound, Hart Crane, and the generation of Allen Ginsberg. He worshiped boldness, contradiction, and change, shocked contemporaries with his candor about sexuality, and created a radical poetry voicing a radical consciousness: "For I confront peace, security, and all the settled laws, to unsettle them." He was the most ardent of nationalists and said that *Leaves of Grass* "could not possibly have emerged or been fashion'd or completed, from any other era than the latter half of the Nineteenth Century, nor from any other land than democratic America." Yet he was also America's chief poet of international standing, with followers in the British Isles, Europe, and Scandinavia. Today his work is read in Chinese, Japanese, Russian, and every other major tongue.

When Whitman was born in 1819, in a farmhouse on eastern Long Island, New York, the United States was rural and relatively isolated. The President, James Monroe, had fought in the Revolution and still wore knee breeches. When Whitman died in 1892, in a working-class neighborhood of Camden, New Jersey, a corporation lawyer, Benjamin Harrison, occupied the White House and the United States was a world power.

During the poet's early years, the Whitmans, descendants of early Dutch and English settlers, fell on hard times and moved from the country districts to Brooklyn, then a thriving, independent city. They were in psychic as well as economic disarray. A failure at farming and business, Walter Whitman, Sr., was "addicted to alcohol," according to his son, and frequently depressed. Of the eight children who survived infancy, four were disturbed or incompetent, but one went on to celebrate "physiology from top to toe . . . Life immense in passion, pulse, and power."

Walt Whitman's dependent childhood, along with all the formal schooling he was ever to have, came to an end when he was about twelve. Like Benjamin Franklin, Mark Twain, and William Dean Howells, he learned the printing trade and in the printing office, the poor-boy's college for many Americans, began to acquire a miscellaneous literary and intellectual culture. He worked in Brooklyn and New York and on Long Island as a typesetter, schoolteacher, newspaper editor, free-lance journalist, storekeeper, and housebuilder. During the 1840s he published a novel, *Franklin Evans,*

Frontispiece and title page to the 1855 edition of Leaves of Grass.
(Reproduced from the Collections of the Library of Congress)

about the evils of drink, at least sixteen conventional poems, and about two dozen stories and sketches, most of them imitative or hackwork, that nevertheless anticipate many of the themes and images of his mature work.

The poet, Whitman was to say, "must flood himself with the immediate age as with vast oceanic tides." He absorbed the Emersonian gospel of self-trust and the infinitude of the private man; oratory; the writings of George Sand and Thomas Carlyle; science, art, and philosophy; the Free-Soil movement; the vibrant life of Broadway and "million-footed Manhattan." He studied linguistics and the American vernacular, believing that "a perfect writer would make words sing, dance, kiss, do the male and female act, bear children . . . or do any thing that man or woman or the natural powers can do." Whitman's discovery of grand opera, then enjoying its first vogue in the United States, released his emotions, suggested poetic equivalents for recitative and aria, and helped free him from conventional forms and meters. Although he may have reasoned his way to the right conclusions by using the wrong data, phrenology and other pseudosciences and improving regimens revealed a creative potential within himself that he believed was as large as the American continent. He saw the continent itself and democratic vistas of city and wilderness in a five-thousand-mile journey he took in 1848 from New York to New Orleans and back. Egyptology and Eastern wisdom-writing opened up other vistas of time and space.

"I was simmering, simmering, simmering." In his early thirties Whitman at last found a supreme purpose, to be "a master after my own kind, making the poems of emotions, as they pass or stay, the poems of freedom, and the exposé of personality— singing in high tones democracy and the New World of it through These States." He intended *Leaves of Grass* to be nothing less than a "new Bible" for the new age of democracy and science.

In July 1855, "after many MS. doings and undoings—(I had great trouble in leaving out the stock 'poetical' touches—but succeeded at last)," Whitman issued the first edition of *Leaves of Grass*. A slim volume, with its title stamped on the cloth cover in tendriled letters, Whitman's ninety-six-page book opened with an uncaptioned frontispiece portrait of a bearded man wearing a broad-brimmed hat and an open-necked shirt. The facing title page did not give the author's name. An eccentrically punctuated prose preface, the most decisive of Whitman's critical manifestos, introduced twelve as yet untitled poems, at first glance clusters of prose sentences set up like Bible verses. Not until page twenty-nine did the author declare his identity: "Walt Whitman, An American, one of the roughs, a kosmos, / Disorderly, fleshy and sensual."

Leaves of Grass came into a largely indifferent world in 1855 not as a trial venture, not as a greatly "promising" book, but as a stylistically and substantively achieved masterpiece. "I find it the most extraordinary piece of wit and wisdom that America has yet contributed," Emerson wrote to the new poet that July, "I give you joy of your free and brave thought. I have great joy in it. I find incomparable things said incomparably well, as they must be. I find the courage of treatment which so delights us, and which large perception only can inspire. I greet you at the beginning of a great career, which yet must have had a long foreground somewhere, for such a start." Emerson's celebrated letter remains unequaled for the generosity, force, and simple justice of its understanding.

Walt Whitman
daguerreotype, 1854
(New York Public Library)

Leaves of Grass changed and grew over the next four decades. Whitman wished to endow it with the scope and structure of something monumental, a great tree with many growth rings, a cathedral, a modern city like his million-footed Manhattan. His second edition (1856) added twenty new poems, among them "Crossing Brooklyn Ferry"; his third (1860) added 146, including "Out of the Cradle Endlessly Rocking" and two cycles, or "clusters," "Calamus" (treating "manly love," or "the love of comrades") and "Children of Adam" (treating heterosexual love); his fourth (1867) added the Civil War cycle "Drum-Taps" and the majestic poem of mourning for Abraham Lincoln, "When Lilacs Last in the Dooryard Bloom'd." By the time Whitman issued his final ("deathbed") edition of 1891–1892, the original ninety-six printed pages of 1855 had grown to 438. After the late 1850s, a markedly tragic element tempered his early, lyric celebrations. Still later, his diction, once assertively American and vernacular, tended to become somewhat denatured, even transatlantic, and he vacillated between a poetry of precise observation and a poetry of ideas and large declarations.

"The proof of a poet," Whitman declared in his preface, "is that his country absorbs him as affectionately as he has absorbed it." Years later he was to concede, "I have not gain'd the acceptance of my time." While he lived, his most fervent readers as a group

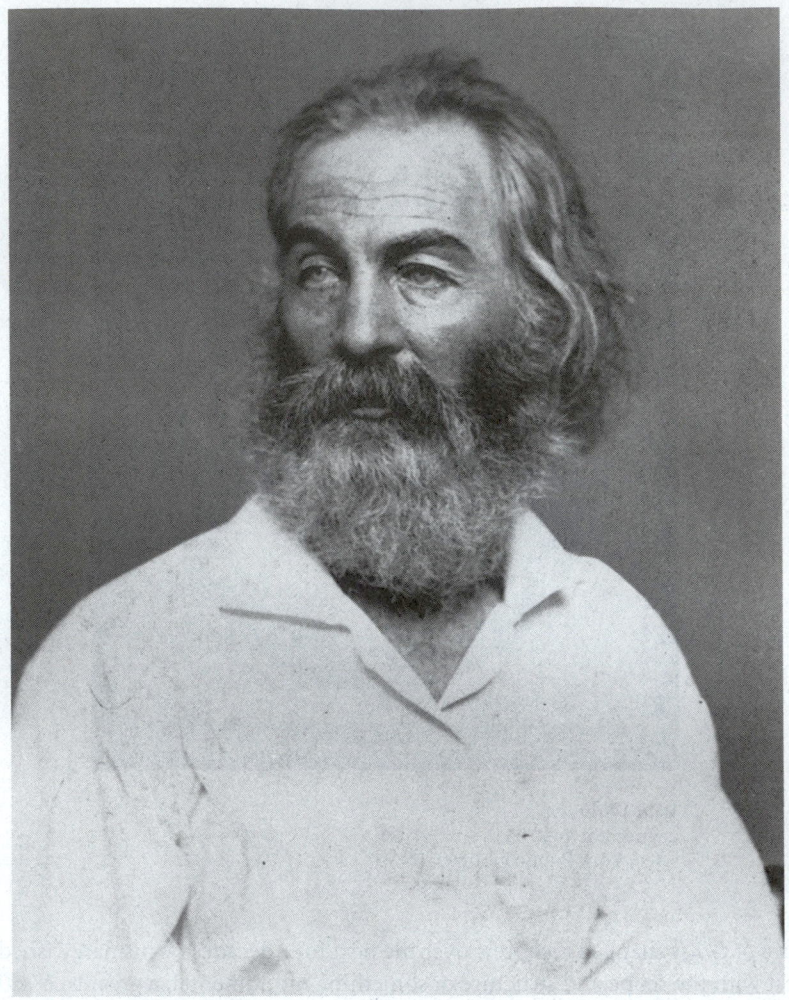

Mathew Brady
Walt Whitman
photograph, 1862
(National Archives)

turned out to be not the working-class American men and women—the democratic leaven—he had hoped to reach but another class altogether, even another nationality: highly cultivated foreign writers and intellectuals like William Michael Rossetti, Oscar Wilde, Algernon Charles Swinburne, Robert Louis Stevenson, Gerard Manley Hopkins, poet laureate Alfred Tennyson, John Addington Symonds, and Professor Edward Dowden of Trinity College, Dublin. One English admirer, Anne Gilchrist, wrote an important appreciation, fell in love with Whitman, and came to America with the hope of marrying him. But aside from his attachments to semiliterate younger men, it was Whitman's book that remained his sole heart's companion, the center of his life. He was willing to go to any length to preserve, protect, and defend it.

Whitman's effective exploitation of Emerson's private letter (he circulated it without permission and used it as promotional material) distressed the Concord sage and his friends. But this episode only marked the beginning of Whitman's unremitting campaign to assure *Leaves of Grass* a breathing space in the world. Like Mark Twain a brilliant publicist, he reviewed his own book on several occasions, planted newspaper stories about his doings and whereabouts, interviewed himself, collaborated with the authors of biographies, polemics, and encomiums, and eagerly sat for hundreds of photographs and portraits that called attention to his trademark flowing beard and open-necked shirts.

For a few years after 1855, Whitman made a living as a newspaper editor and free-lance journalist. During the Civil War, having vowed to live a "purged" and "cleansed" life, he turned his back on New York's literary and artistic bohemia and moved to beleaguered Washington. There, supporting himself by part-time clerking in the army paymaster's office, he served as volunteer nurse and comforter—"wound-dresser"—in the military hospitals. This caring for the sick, wounded, and dying may have been the most intense emotional experience of his middle and later years. In 1865 he was appointed to a full-time government clerkship, a job that paid him about $1,600 a year until 1874. By then he was an invalid, having suffered a paralytic stroke the year before, and had moved, permanently, from Washington to Camden. With the major exceptions of trips to Colorado and Canada in 1879 and 1880, he spent the rest of his life in Camden, first as a paying guest in his brother's house and finally as the owner of 328 Mickle Street, "a little old shanty of my own" that he bought for $1,750. Whitman managed to live in frugal comfort, and even build an imposing tomb, on money derived from royalties, direct sales of books, fees and honoraria, and gifts from admirers. His average annual income from 1876 to 1892 was $1,270. During those years, as for most of his career, he mainly isolated himself from professional literary people in New York, Philadelphia, and Boston, preferring the company of the small band of disciples that had formed around him and celebrated his birthdays with eucharistic feasts.

An important prose writer as well as a poet, Whitman published *Democratic Vistas* (1871), a searching essay on American society and ideals, and *Specimen Days* (1882), a loosely structured autobiography focusing on the Civil War period. His history after 1855, however, is largely the history of *Leaves of Grass* in its successive editions and collisions with guardians of public taste and morals. Despite Emerson's endorsement, early reviewers called Whitman's poetry "a mass of stupid filth" and its author a pig rooting "among a rotten garbage of licentious thoughts." In 1865 the secretary of the Interior fired Whitman from his clerkship on the grounds that *Leaves of Grass* violated "the rules of decorum and propriety prescribed by a Christian Civilization." Whitman was quickly transferred to an equivalent post in the attorney general's office, but in the hands of supporters like William Douglas O'Connor, Whitman's dismissal became a cause célèbre and served an important purpose in his developing reputation: No longer "one of the roughs," he was now, in O'Connor's words, "The Good Gray Poet," sage, martyr, and redeemer. Fifteen years later a district attorney in Boston found *Leaves of Grass* actionable under "the Public Statutes respecting obscene literature" and in effect forced Whitman's publishers there to withdraw the book. *Leaves of Grass* moved to Philadelphia for its final editions. Such "bruises" and "buffetings" did not discourage its author. Whitman believed that his book was "a candidate for the future" and that its value would be "decided by time."

Further Reading:

H. Traubel, *With Walt Whitman in Camden*, 7 vols., 1906–1992.

N. Arvin, *Whitman*, 1938.

H. S. Canby, *Walt Whitman, An American*, 1943.

R. D. Faner, *Walt Whitman and Opera*, 1951.

R. Chase, *Walt Whitman Reconsidered*, 1955.

Leaves of Grass One Hundred Years After, ed. M. Hindus, 1955.

J. E. Miller, Jr., *A Critical Guide to Leaves of Grass*, 1957.

R. Asselineau, *The Evolution of Walt Whitman*, 2 vols., 1960, 1962.

Whitman: A Collection of Critical Essays, ed. R. H. Pierce, 1962.

G. W. Allen, *The Solitary Singer*, 1967.

G. W. Allen, *The New Walt Whitman Handbook*, 1975.

S. Black, *Whitman's Journey into Chaos*, 1975.

J. Kaplan, *Walt Whitman: A Life*, 1980.

P. Zweig, *Walt Whitman: The Making of the Poet*, 1984.

M. W. Thomas, *The Lunar Light of Whitman's Poetry*, 1987.

D. S. Reynolds, *Walt Whitman's America: A Cultural Biography*, 1995.

Texts:

Leaves of Grass, 1891–1892.
Collected Prose Works, 1892.

See also *The Collected Writings of Walt Whitman*, ed. G. W. Allen and S. Bradley, 1963–1984.

Preface to the 1855 Edition of Leaves of Grass*

America does not repel the past or what it has produced under its forms or amid other politics or the idea of castes or the old religions . . . . accepts the lesson with calmness . . . is not so impatient as has been supposed that the slough still sticks to opinions and manners and literature while the life which served its requirements has passed into the new life of the new forms . . . perceives that the corpse is slowly borne from the eating and sleeping rooms of the house . . . perceives that it waits a little while in the door . . . that it was fittest for its days . . . that its action has descended to the stalwart and well-shaped heir who approaches . . . and that he shall be fittest for his days.

The Americans of all nations at any time upon the earth have probably the fullest poetical nature. The United States themselves are essentially the greatest poem. In the history of the earth hitherto the largest and most stirring appear tame and orderly to their ampler largeness and stir. Here at last is something in the doings of man that corresponds with the broadcast doings of the day and night. Here is not merely a nation but a teeming nation of nations. Here is action untied from strings necessarily blind to particulars and details magnificently moving in vast masses. Here is the hospitality which forever indicates heroes. . . . Here are the roughs and beards and space and ruggedness and nonchalance that the soul loves. Here the performance disdaining the trivial unapproached in the tremendous audacity of its crowds and groupings and the

---

* Untitled in 1855 and omitted from subsequent editions.

push of its perspective spreads with crampless and flowing breadth and showers its prolific and splendid extravagance. One sees it must indeed own the riches of the summer
and winter, and need never be bankrupt while corn grows from the ground or the orchards drop apples or the bays contain fish or men beget children upon women.

Other states indicate themselves in their deputies. . . . but the genius of the United
States is not best or most in its executives or legislatures, nor in its ambassadors or authors or colleges or churches or parlors, nor even in its newspapers or inventors . . . but
always most in the common people. Their manners speech dress friendships—the
freshness and candor of their physiognomy—the picturesque looseness of their carriage
. . . their deathless attachment to freedom—their aversion to anything indecorous or
soft or mean—the practical acknowledgment of the citizens of one state by the citizens
of all other states—the fierceness of their roused resentment—their curiosity and welcome of novelty—their self-esteem and wonderful sympathy—their susceptibility to a
slight—the air they have of persons who never knew how it felt to stand in the presence
of superiors—the fluency of their speech—their delight in music, the sure symptom of
manly tenderness and native elegance of soul . . . their good temper and open-handed-
ness—the terrible significance of their elections—the President's taking off his hat to
them not they to him—these too are unrhymed poetry. It awaits the gigantic and generous treatment worthy of it.

The largeness of nature or the nation were monstrous without a corresponding
largeness and generosity of the spirit of the citizen. Not nature nor swarming states nor
streets and steamships nor prosperous business nor farms nor capital nor learning may
suffice for the ideal of man . . . nor suffice the poet. No reminiscences may suffice either.
A live nation can always cut a deep mark and can have the best authority the cheapest . . .
namely from its own soul. This is the sum of the profitable uses of individuals or states
and of present action and grandeur and of the subjects of poets.—As if it were necessary
to trot back generation after generation to the eastern records! As if the beauty and sacredness of the demonstrable must fall behind that of the mythical! As if men do not
make their mark out of any times! As if the opening of the western continent by discovery and what has transpired since in North and South America were less than the small
theatre of the antique or the aimless sleepwalking of the middle ages! The pride of the
United States leaves the wealth and finesse of the cities and all returns of commerce and
agriculture and all the magnitude of geography or shows of exterior victory to enjoy the
breed of fullsized men or one fullsized man unconquerable and simple.

The American poets are to enclose old and new for America is the race of races. Of
them a bard is to be commensurate with a people. To him the other continents arrive as
contributions . . . he gives them reception for their sake and his own sake. His spirit responds to his country's spirit . . . . he incarnates its geography and natural life and rivers
and lakes. Mississippi with annual freshets and changing chutes, Missouri and Columbia and Ohio and Saint Lawrence with the falls and beautiful masculine Hudson, do not
embouchure where they spend themselves more than they embouchure into him. The
blue breadth over the inland sea of Virginia and Maryland and the sea off Massachusetts and Maine and over Manhattan bay and over Champlain and Erie and over Ontario and Huron and Michigan and Superior, and over the Texan and Mexican and
Floridian and Cuban seas and over the seas off California and Oregon, is not tallied by
the blue breadth of the waters below more than the breadth of above and below is tallied by him. When the long Atlantic coast stretches longer and the Pacific coast

stretches longer he easily stretches with them north or south. He spans between them also from east to west and reflects what is between them. On him rise solid growths that offset the growths of pine and cedar and hemlock and liveoak and locust and chestnut and cypress and hickory and limetree and cottonwood and tuliptree and cactus and wildvine and tamarind and persimmon . . . . and tangles as tangled as any canebrake or swamp . . . . and forests coated with transparent ice and icicles hanging from the boughs and crackling in the wind . . . . and sides and peaks of mountains . . . . and pasturage sweet and free as savannah or upland or prairie . . . . with flights and songs and screams that answer those of the wildpigeon and highhold and orchard-oriole and coot and surf-duck and redshouldered-hawk and fish-hawk and white-ibis and indian-hen and cat-owl and water-pheasant and qua-bird and piedsheldrake and blackbird and mockingbird and buzzard and condor and night-heron and eagle. To him the hereditary countenance descends both mother's and father's. To him enter the essences of the real things and past and present events—of the enormous diversity of temperature and agriculture and mines—the tribes of red aborigines—the weatherbeaten vessels entering new ports or making landings on rocky coasts—the first settlements north or south—the rapid stature and muscle—the haughty defiance of '76, and the war and peace and formation of the constitution . . . . the union always surrounded by blatherers and always calm and impregnable—the perpetual coming of immigrants—the wharfhem'd cities and superior marine—the unsurveyed interior—the loghouses and clearings and wild animals and hunters and trappers . . . . the free commerce—the fisheries and whaling and gold-digging—the endless gestation of new states—the convening of Congress every December, the members duly coming up from all climates and the uttermost parts . . . . the noble character of the young mechanics and of all free American workmen and workwomen . . . . the general ardor and friendliness and enterprise—the perfect equality of the female with the male . . . . the large amativeness—the fluid movement of the population—the factories and mercantile life and laborsaving machinery—the Yankee swap—the New-York firemen and the target excursion—the southern plantation life—the character of the northeast and of the northwest and southwest—slavery and the tremulous spreading of hands to protect it, and the stern opposition to it which shall never cease till it ceases or the speaking of tongues and the moving of lips cease. For such the expression of the American poet is to be transcendant and new. It is to be indirect and not direct or descriptive or epic. Its quality goes through these to much more. Let the age and wars of other nations be chanted and their eras and characters be illustrated and that finish the verse. Not so the great psalm of the republic. Here the theme is creative and has vista. Here comes one among the wellbeloved stonecutters and plans with decision and science and sees the solid and beautiful forms of the future where there are now no solid forms.

Of all nations the United States with veins full of poetical stuff most need poets and will doubtless have the greatest and use them the greatest. Their Presidents shall not be their common referee so much as their poets shall. Of all mankind the great poet is the equable man. Not in him but off from him things are grotesque or eccentric or fail of their sanity. Nothing out of its place is good and nothing in its place is bad. He bestows on every object or quality its fit proportions neither more nor less. He is the arbiter of the diverse and he is the key. He is the equalizer of his age and land . . . . he supplies what wants supplying and checks what wants checking. If peace is the routine out of him speaks the spirit of peace, large, rich, thrifty, building vast and populous cities, encouraging agriculture and the arts and commerce—lighting the study of man, the soul, immortality—federal, state or municipal government, marriage, health, freetrade, intertravel by land and sea . . . . nothing too close, nothing too far off . . . the stars not too far off. In war he is the most deadly force of the war. Who recruits him recruits horse and foot . . . he fetches parks of artillery the best that engineer ever knew. If the time becomes slothful and heavy he knows how to arouse it . . . he can make every word he speaks draw blood. Whatever stagnates in the flat of custom or obedience or legislation he never stagnates. Obedience does not master him, he masters it. High up out of reach he stands turning a concentrated light . . . he turns the pivot with his finger . . . he baffles the swiftest runners as he stands and easily overtakes and envelops them. The time straying toward infidelity and confections and persiflage he withholds by his steady faith . . . he spreads out his dishes . . . he offers the sweet firmfibred meat that grows men and women. His brain is the ultimate brain. He is no arguer . . . he is judgment. He judges not as the judge judges but as the sun falling around a helpless thing. As he sees the farthest he has the most faith. His thoughts are the hymns of the praise of things. In the talk on the soul and eternity and God off of his equal plane he is silent. He sees eternity less like a play with a prologue and denouement . . . . he sees eternity in men and women . . . he does not see men and women as dreams or dots. Faith is the antiseptic of the soul . . . it pervades the common people and preserves them . . . they never give up believing and expecting and trusting. There is that indescribable freshness and unconsciousness about an illiterate person that humbles and mocks the power of the noblest expressive genius. The poet sees for a certainty how one not a great artist may be just as sacred and perfect as the greatest artist. . . . . . The power to destroy or remould is freely used by him but never the power of attack. What is past is past. If he does not expose superior models and prove himself by every step he takes he is not what is wanted. The presence of the greatest poet conquers . . . not parleying or struggling or any prepared attempts. Now he has passed that way see after him! there is not left any vestige of despair or misanthropy or cunning or exclusiveness or the ignominy of a nativity or color or delusion of hell or the necessity of hell . . . . . and no man thenceforward shall be degraded for ignorance or weakness or sin.

The greatest poet hardly knows pettiness or triviality. If he breathes into any thing that was before thought small it dilates with the grandeur and life of the universe. He is a seer . . . . he is individual . . . he is complete in himself . . . . the others are as good as he, only he sees it and they do not. He is not one of the chorus . . . . he does not stop for any regulation . . . he is the president of regulation. What the eyesight does to the rest he does to the rest. Who knows the curious mystery of the eyesight? The other senses corroborate themselves, but this is removed from any proof but its own and foreruns the identities of the spiritual world. A single glance of it mocks all the investigations of man and all the instruments and books of the earth and all reasoning. What is marvellous? what is unlikely? what is impossible or baseless or vague? after you have once just opened the space of a peachpit and given audience to far and near and to the sunset and had all things enter with electric swiftness softly and duly without confusion or jostling or jam.

The land and sea, the animals fishes and birds, the sky of heaven and the orbs, the forests mountains and rivers, are not small themes . . . but folks expect of the poet to indicate more than the beauty and dignity which always attach to dumb real objects . . . . they expect him to indicate the path between reality and their souls. Men and women perceive the beauty well enough . . . probably as well as he. The passionate tenacity of hunters, woodmen, early risers, cultivators of gardens and orchards and fields, the love of healthy women for the manly form, seafaring persons, drivers of horses, the passion for light and the open air, all is an old varied sign of the unfailing perception of beauty and of a residence of the poetic in outdoor people. They can never be assisted by poets to perceive . . . some may but they never can. The poetic quality is not marshalled in rhyme or uniformity or abstract addresses to things nor in melancholy complaints or good precepts, but is the life of these and much else and is in the soul. The profit of rhyme is that it drops seeds of a sweeter and more luxuriant rhyme, and of uniformity that it conveys itself into its own roots in the ground out of sight. The rhyme and uniformity of perfect poems show the free growth of metrical laws and bud from them as unerringly and loosely as lilacs or roses on a bush, and take shapes as compact as the shapes of chestnuts and oranges and melons and pears, and shed the perfume impalpable to form. The fluency and ornaments of the finest poems or music or orations or recitations are not independent but dependent. All beauty comes from beautiful blood and a beautiful brain. If the greatnesses are in conjunction in a man or woman it is enough . . . . the fact will prevail through the universe . . . . but the gaggery and gilt of a million years will not prevail. Who troubles himself about his ornaments or fluency is lost. This is what you shall do: Love the earth and sun and the animals, despise riches, give alms to every one that asks, stand up for the stupid and crazy, devote your income and labor to others, hate tyrants, argue not concerning God, have patience and indulgence toward the people, take off your hat to nothing known or unknown or to any man or number of men, go freely with powerful uneducated persons and with the young and with the mothers of families, read these leaves in the open air every season of every year of your life, re-examine all you have been told at school or church or in any book, dismiss whatever insults your own soul, and your very flesh shall be a great poem and have the richest fluency not only in its words but in the silent lines of its lips and face and between the lashes of your eyes and in every motion and joint of your body . . . . The poet shall not spend his time in unneeded work. He shall know that the ground is always ready ploughed and manured . . . . others may not know it but he shall. He shall go directly to the creation. His trust shall master the trust of everything he touches . . . . and shall master all attachment.

The known universe has one complete lover and that is the greatest poet. He consumes an eternal passion and is indifferent which chance happens and which possible contingency of fortune or misfortune and persuades daily and hourly his delicious pay. What balks or breaks others is fuel for his burning progress to contact and amorous joy. Other proportions of the reception of pleasure dwindle to nothing to his proportions. All expected from heaven or from the highest he is rapport with in the sight of the daybreak or a scene of the winter woods or the presence of children playing or with his arm round the neck of a man or woman. His love above all love has leisure and expanse . . . . he leaves room ahead of himself. He is no irresolute or suspicious lover . . . he is sure . . . he scorns intervals. His experience and the showers and thrills are not for nothing. Nothing can jar him . . . . suffering and darkness cannot—death and fear cannot. To him complaint and jealousy and envy are corpses buried and rotten in the earth . . . . . he saw them buried. The sea is not surer of the shore or the shore of the sea than he is of the fruition of his love and of all perfection and beauty.

The fruition of beauty is no chance of hit or miss . . . it is inevitable as life . . . . it is exact and plumb as gravitation. From the eyesight proceeds another eyesight and from the hearing proceeds another hearing and from the voice proceeds another voice eternally curious of the harmony of things with man. To these respond perfections not only in the committees that were supposed to stand for the rest but in the rest themselves just the same. These understand the law of perfection in masses and floods . . . that its finish is to each for itself and onward from itself . . . that it is profuse and impartial . . . that there is not a minute of the light or dark nor an acre of the earth or sea without it— nor any direction of the sky nor any trade or employment nor any turn of events. This is the reason that about the proper expression of beauty there is precision and balance . . . one part does not need to be thrust above another. The best singer is not the one who has the most lithe and powerful organ . . . the pleasure of poems is not in them that take the handsomest measure and similes and sound.

Without effort and without exposing in the least how it is done the greatest poet brings the spirit of any or all events and passions and scenes and persons some more and some less to bear on your individual character as you hear or read. To do this well is to compete with the laws that pursue and follow time. What is the purpose must surely be there and the clue of it must be there . . . . and the faintest indication is the indication of the best and then becomes the clearest indication. Past and present and future are not disjoined but joined. The greatest poet forms the consistence of what is to be from what has been and is. He drags the dead out of their coffins and stands them again on their feet . . . . he says to the past, Rise and walk before me that I may realize you. He learns the lesson . . . . he places himself where the future becomes present. The greatest poet does not only dazzle his rays over character and scenes and passions . . . he finally ascends and finishes all . . . he exhibits the pinnacles that no man can tell what they are for or what is beyond . . . . he glows a moment on the extremest verge. He is most wonderful in his last half-hidden smile or frown . . . by that flash of the moment of parting the one that sees it shall be encouraged or terrified afterward for many years. The greatest poet does not moralize or make applications of morals . . . he knows the soul. The soul has that measureless pride which consists in never acknowledging any lessons but its own. But it has sympathy as measureless as its pride and the one balances the other and neither can stretch too far while it stretches in company with the other. The inmost secrets of art sleep with the twain. The greatest poet has lain close betwixt both and they are vital in his style and thoughts.

The art of art, the glory of expression and the sunshine of the light of letters is simplicity. Nothing is better than simplicity . . . . nothing can make up for excess or for the lack of definiteness. To carry on the heave of impulse and pierce intellectual depths and give all subjects their articulations are powers neither common nor very uncommon. But to speak in literature with the perfect rectitude and insousiance of the movements of animals and the unimpeachableness of the sentiment of trees in the woods and grass by the roadside is the flawless triumph of art. If you have looked on him who has achieved it you have looked on one of the masters of the artists of all nations and times. You shall not contemplate the flight of the graygull over the bay or the mettlesome action of the blood horse or the tall leaning of sunflowers on their stalk or the appearance of the sun journeying through heaven or the appearance of the moon afterward with any more satisfaction than you shall contemplate him. The greatest poet has less a marked style and is more the channel of thoughts and things without increase or diminution, and is the free channel of himself. He swears to his art, I will not be meddlesome, I will not have in my writing any elegance or effect or originality to hang in the way between me and the rest like curtains. I will have nothing hang in the way, not the richest curtains. What I tell I tell for precisely what it is. Let who may exalt or startle or fascinate or soothe I will have purposes as health or heat or snow has and be as regardless of observation. What I experience or portray shall go from my composition without a shred of my composition. You shall stand by my side and look in the mirror with me.

The old red blood and stainless gentility of great poets will be proved by their unconstraint. A heroic person walks at his ease through and out of that custom or precedent or authority that suits him not. Of the traits of the brotherhood of writers savans musicians inventors and artists nothing is finer than silent defiance advancing from new free forms. In the need of poems philosophy politics mechanism science behaviour, the craft of art, an appropriate native grand-opera, shipcraft, or any craft, he is greatest forever and forever who contributes the greatest original practical example. The cleanest expression is that which finds no sphere worthy of itself and makes one.

The messages of great poets to each man and woman are, Come to us on equal terms, Only then can you understand us, We are no better than you, What we enclose you enclose, What we enjoy you may enjoy. Did you suppose there could be only one Supreme? We affirm there can be unnumbered Supremes, and that one does not countervail another any more than one eyesight countervails another . . and that men can be good or grand only of the consciousness of their supremacy within them. What do you think is the grandeur of storms and dismemberments and the deadliest battles and wrecks and the wildest fury of the elements and the power of the sea and the motion of nature and of the throes of human desires and dignity and hate and love? It is that something in the soul which says, Rage on, Whirl on, I tread master here and everywhere, Master of the spasms of the sky and of the shatter of the sea, Master of nature and passion and death, And of all terror and all pain.

The American bards shall be marked for generosity and affection and for encouraging competitors . . They shall be kosmos . . without monopoly or secrecy . . glad to pass any thing to any one . . hungry for equals night and day. They shall not be careful of riches and privilege . . . . they shall be riches and privilege . . . . they shall perceive who the most affluent man is. The most affluent man is he that confronts all the shows he sees by equivalents out of the stronger wealth of himself. The American bard shall delineate no class of persons nor one or two out of the strata of interests nor love most nor truth most nor the soul most nor the body most . . . . and not be for the eastern states more than the western or the northern states more than the southern.

Exact science and its practical movements are no checks on the greatest poet but always his encouragement and support. The outset and remembrance are there . . there the arms that lifted him first and brace him best . . . . there he returns after all his goings and comings. The sailor and traveler . . the anatomist chemist astronomer geologist phrenologist spiritualist mathematician historian and lexicographer are not poets, but they are the lawgivers of poets and their construction underlies the structure of every perfect poem. No matter what rises or is uttered they sent the seed of the conception of it . . . of them and by them stand the visible proofs of souls . . . . . always of their father-stuff must be begotten the sinewy races of bards. If there shall be love and content between the father and the son and if the greatness of the son is the exuding of the greatness of the father there shall be love between the poet and the man of demonstrable science. In the beauty of poems are the tuft and final applause of science.

Great is the faith of the flush of knowledge and of the investigation of the depths of qualities and things. Cleaving and circling here swells the soul of the poet yet is president of itself always. The depths are fathomless and therefore calm. The innocence and nakedness are resumed . . . they are neither modest nor immodest. The whole theory of the special and supernatural and all that was twined with it or educed out of it departs as a dream. What has ever happened . . . . what happens and whatever may or shall happen, the vital laws enclose all . . . . they are sufficient for any case and for all cases . . . none to be hurried or retarded . . . . any miracle of affairs or persons inadmissible in the vast clear scheme where every motion and every spear of grass and the frames and spirits of men and women and all that concerns them are unspeakably perfect miracles all referring to all and each distinct and in its place. It is also not consistent with the reality of the soul to admit that there is anything in the known universe more divine than men and women.

Men and women and the earth and all upon it are simply to be taken as they are, and the investigation of their past and present and future shall be unintermitted and shall be done with perfect candor. Upon this basis philosophy speculates ever looking toward the poet, ever regarding the eternal tendencies of all toward happiness never inconsistent with what is clear to the senses and to the soul. For the eternal tendencies of all toward happiness make the only point of sane philosophy. Whatever comprehends less than that . . . whatever is less than the laws of light and of astronomical motion . . . or less than the laws that follow the thief the liar the glutton and the drunkard through this life and doubtless afterward . . . . . . or less than vast stretches of time or the slow formation of density or the patient upheaving of strata—is of no account. Whatever would put God in a poem or system of philosophy as contending against some being or influence is also of no account. Sanity and ensemble characterise the great master . . . spoilt in one principle all is spoilt. The great master has nothing to do with miracles. He sees health for himself in being one of the mass . . . . he sees the hiatus in singular eminence. To the perfect shape comes common ground. To be under the general law is great for that is to correspond with it. The master knows that he is unspeakably great and that all are unspeakably great . . . . that nothing for instance is greater than to conceive children and bring them up well . . . that to be is just as great as to perceive or tell.

In the make of the great masters the idea of political liberty is indispensable. Liberty takes the adherence of heroes wherever men and women exist . . . . but never takes any adherence or welcome from the rest more than from poets. They are the voice and exposition of liberty. They out of ages are worthy the grand idea . . . . to them it is confided and they must sustain it. Nothing has precedence of it and nothing can warp or degrade it. The attitude of great poets is to cheer up slaves and horrify despots. The turn of their necks, the sound of their feet, the motions of their wrists, are full of hazard to the one and hope to the other. Come nigh them awhile and though they neither speak or advise you shall learn the faithful American lesson. Liberty is poorly served by men whose good intent is quelled from one failure or two failures or any number of failures, or from the casual indifference or ingratitude of the people, or from the sharp show of the tushes of power, or the bringing to bear soldiers and cannon or any penal statutes. Liberty relies upon itself, invites no one, promises nothing, sits in calmness and light, is positive and composed, and knows no discouragement. The battle rages with many a loud alarm and frequent advance and retreat . . . . the enemy triumphs . . . . the prison, the handcuffs, the iron necklace and anklet, the scaffold, garrote and leadballs do their work . . . . the cause is asleep . . . . the strong throats are choked with their own blood . . . . the young men drop their eyelashes toward the ground when they pass each other . . . . and is liberty gone out of that place? No never. When liberty goes it is not the first to go nor the second or third to go . . it waits for all the rest to go . . it is the last . . . When the memories of the old martyrs are faded utterly away . . . . when the large names of patriots are laughed at in the public halls from the lips of the orators . . . . when the boys are no more christened after the same but christened after tyrants and traitors instead . . . . when the laws of the free are grudgingly permitted and laws for informers and blood-money are sweet to the taste of the people . . . . when I and you walk abroad upon the earth stung with compassion at the sight of numberless brothers answering our equal friendship and calling no man master—and when we are elated with noble joy at the sight of slaves . . . . when the soul retires in the cool communion of the night and surveys its experience and has much extasy over the word and deed that put back a helpless innocent person into the gripe of the gripers or into any cruel inferiority . . . . when those in all parts of these states who could easier realize the true American character but do not yet—when the swarms of cringers, suckers, doughfaces, lice of politics, planners of sly involutions for their own preferment to city offices or state legislatures or the judiciary or congress or the presidency, obtain a response of love and natural deference from the people whether they get the offices or no . . . . when it is better to be a bound booby and rogue in office at a high salary than the poorest free mechanic or farmer with his hat unmoved from his head and firm eyes and a candid and generous heart . . . . and when servility by town or state or the federal government or any oppression on a large scale or small scale can be tried on without its own punishment following duly after in exact proportion against the smallest chance of escape . . . . or rather when all life and all the souls of men and women are discharged from any part of the earth—then only shall the instinct of liberty be discharged from that part of the earth.

As the attributes of the poets of the kosmos concentre in the real body and soul and in the pleasure of things they possess the superiority of genuineness over all fiction and romance. As they emit themselves facts are showered over with light . . . . the daylight is lit with more volatile light . . . . also the deep between the setting and rising sun goes deeper many fold. Each precise object or condition or combination or process exhibits a beauty . . . . the multiplication table its—old age its—the carpenter's trade its—the grand-opera its . . . . the hugehulled cleanshaped New-York clipper at sea under steam or full sail gleams with unmatched beauty . . . . the American circles and large harmonies of government gleam with theirs . . . . and the commonest definite intentions and actions with theirs. The poets of the kosmos advance through all interpositions and coverings and turmoils and stratagems to first principles. They are of use . . . . they dissolve poverty from its need and riches from its conceit. You large proprietor they say shall not realize or perceive more than any one else. The owner of the library is not he who holds a legal title to it having bought and paid for it. Any one and every one is owner of the library who can read the same through all the varieties of tongues and subjects and styles, and in whom they enter with ease and take residence and force toward paternity and maternity, and make supple and powerful and rich and large . . . . These American states strong and healthy and accomplished shall receive no pleasure from violations of natural models and must not permit them. In paintings or mouldings or carvings in mineral or wood, or in the illustrations of books or newspapers, or in any comic or tragic prints, or in the patterns of woven stuffs or any thing to beautify rooms or furniture or costumes, or to put upon cornices or monuments or on the prows or sterns of ships, or to put anywhere before the human eye indoors or out, that which distorts honest shapes or which creates unearthly beings or places or contingencies is a nuisance and revolt. Of the human form especially it is so great it must never be made ridiculous. Of ornaments to a work nothing outre can be allowed . . but those ornaments can be allowed that conform to the perfect facts of the open air and that flow out of the nature of the work and come irrepressibly from it and are necessary to the completion of the work. Most works are most beautiful without ornament. . . Exaggerations will be revenged in human physiology. Clean and vigorous children are jetted and conceived only in those communities where the models of natural forms are public every day. . . . . Great genius and the people of these states must never be demeaned to romances. As soon as histories are properly told there is no more need of romances.

The great poets are also to be known by the absence in them of tricks and by the justification of perfect personal candor. Then folks echo a new cheap joy and a divine voice leaping from their brains: How beautiful is candor! All faults may be forgiven of him who has perfect candor. Henceforth let no man of us lie, for we have seen that openness wins the inner and outer world and that there is no single exception, and that never since our earth gathered itself in a mass have deceit or subterfuge or prevarication attracted its smallest particle or the faintest tinge of a shade—and that through the enveloping wealth and rank of a state or the whole republic of states a sneak or sly person shall be discovered and despised . . . . and that the soul has never been once fooled and never can be fooled . . . . and thrift without the loving nod of the soul is only a fœtid puff . . . . and there never grew up in any of the continents of the globe nor upon any planet or satellite or star, nor upon the asteroids, nor in any part of ethereal space, nor in the midst of density, nor under the fluid wet of the sea, nor in that condition which precedes the birth of babes, nor at any time during the changes of life, nor in that condition that follows what we term death, nor in any stretch of abeyance or action afterward of vitality, nor in any process of formation or reformation anywhere, a being whose instinct hated the truth.

Extreme caution or prudence, the soundest organic health, large hope and comparison and fondness for women and children, large alimentiveness and destructiveness and causality, with a perfect sense of the oneness of nature and the propriety of the same spirit applied to human affairs . . these are called up of the float of the brain of the world to be parts of the greatest poet from his birth out of his mother's womb and from her birth out of her mother's. Caution seldom goes far enough. It has been thought that the prudent citizen was the citizen who applied himself to solid gains and did well for himself and his family and completed a lawful life without debt or crime. The greatest poet sees and admits these economies as he sees the economies of food and sleep, but has higher notions of prudence than to think he gives much when he gives a few slight attentions at the latch of the gate. The premises of the prudence of life are not the hospitality of it or the ripeness and harvest of it. Beyond the independence of a little sum laid aside for burial-money, and of a few clapboards around and shingles overhead on a lot of American soil owned, and the easy dollars that supply the year's plain clothing and meals, the melancholy prudence of the abandonment of such a great being as a man is to the toss and pallor of years of moneymaking with all their scorching days and icy nights and all their stifling deceits and underhanded dodgings, or infinitessimals of parlors, or shameless stuffing while others starve . . and all the loss of the bloom and odor of the earth and of the flowers and atmosphere and of the sea and of the true taste of the women and men you pass or have to do with in youth or middle age, and the issuing sickness and desperate revolt at the close of a life without elevation or naivete, and the ghastly chatter of a death without serenity or majesty, is the great fraud upon modern civilization and forethought, blotching the surface and system which civilization undeniably drafts, and moistening with tears the immense features it spreads and spreads with such velocity before the reached kisses of the soul. . . Still the right explanation remains to be made about prudence. The prudence of the mere wealth and respectability of the most esteemed life appears too faint for the eye to observe at all when little and large alike drop quietly aside at the thought of the prudence suitable for immortality. What is wisdom that fills the thinness of a year or seventy or eighty years to wisdom spaced out by ages and coming back at a certain time with strong reinforcements and rich presents and the clear faces of wedding-guests as far as you can look in every direction running gaily toward you? Only the soul is of itself . . . . all else has reference to what ensues. All that a person does or thinks is of consequence. Not a move can a man or woman make that affects him or her in a day or a month or any part of the direct lifetime or the hour of death but the same affects him or her onward afterward through the indirect lifetime. The indirect is always as great and real as the direct. The spirit receives from the body just as much as it gives to the body. Not one name of word or deed . . not of venereal sores or discolorations . . not the privacy of the onanist . . not of the putrid veins of gluttons or rumdrinkers . . . not peculation or cunning or betrayal or murder . . no serpentine poison of those that seduce women . . not the foolish yielding of women . . not prostitution . . not of any depravity of young men . . not of the attainment of gain by discreditable means . . not any nastiness of appetite . . not any harshness of officers to men or judges to prisoners or fathers to sons or sons to fathers or of husbands to wives or bosses to their boys . . not of greedy looks or malignant wishes . . . nor any of the wiles practised by people upon themselves . . . ever is or ever can be stamped on the programme but it is duly realized and returned, and that returned in further performances . . . and they returned again. Nor can the push of charity or personal force ever be any thing else than the profoundest reason, whether it brings arguments to hand or no. No specification is necessary . . to add or subtract or divide is in vain. Little or big, learned or unlearned, white or black, legal or illegal, sick or well, from the first inspiration down the windpipe to the last expiration out of it, all that a male or female does that is vigorous and benevolent and clean is so much sure profit to him or her in the unshakable order of the universe and through the whole scope of it forever. If the savage or felon is wise it is well . . . . if the greatest poet or savan is wise it is simply the same . . if the President or chief justice is wise it is the same . . . if the young mechanic or farmer is wise it is no more or less . . if the prostitute is wise it is no more nor less.

The interest will come round . . all will come round. All the best actions of war and peace . . . all help given to relatives and strangers and the poor and old and sorrowful and young children and widows and the sick, and to all shunned persons . . all furtherance of fugitives and of the escape of slaves . . all the self-denial that stood steady and aloof on wrecks and saw others take the seats of the boats . . . all offering of substance or life for the good old cause, or for a friend's sake or opinion's sake . . . all pains of enthusiasts scoffed at by their neighbors . . all the vast sweet love and precious suffering of mothers .

. . all honest men baffled in strifes recorded or unrecorded . . . . all the grandeur and good of the few ancient nations whose fragments of annals we inherit . . and all the good of the hundreds of far mightier and more ancient nations unknown to us by name or date or location . . . . all that was ever manfully begun, whether it succeeded or no . . . . all that has at any time been well suggested out of the divine heart of man or by the divinity of his mouth or by the shaping of his great hands . . and all that is well thought or done this day on any part of the surface of the globe . . or on any of the wandering stars or fixed stars by those there as we are here . . or that is henceforth to be well thought or done by you whoever you are, or by any one—these singly and wholly inured at their time and inure now and will inure always to the identities from which they sprung or shall spring. . . Did you guess any of them lived only its moment? The world does not so exist . . no parts palpable or impalpable so exist . . . no result exists now without being from its long antecedent result, and that from its antecedent, and so backward without the farthest mentionable spot coming a bit nearer the beginning than any other spot. . . . . Whatever satisfies the soul is truth. The prudence of the greatest poet answers at last the craving and glut of the soul, is not contemptuous of less ways of prudence if they conform to its ways, puts off nothing, permits no let-up for its own case or any case, has no particular sabbath or judgment-day, divides not the living from the dead or the righteous from the unrighteous, is satisfied with the present, matches every thought or act by its correlative, knows no possible forgiveness or deputed atonement . . knows that the young man who composedly periled his life and lost it has done exceeding well for himself, while the man who has not periled his life and retains it to old age in riches and ease has perhaps achieved nothing for himself worth mentioning . . and that only that person has no great prudence to learn who has learnt to prefer real longlived things, and favors body and soul the same, and perceives the indirect assuredly following the direct, and what evil or good he does leaping onward and waiting to meet him again—and who in his spirit in any emergency whatever neither hurries or avoids death.

The direct trial of him who would be the greatest poet is today. If he does not flood himself with the immediate age as with vast oceanic tides . . . . . and if he does not attract his own land body and soul to himself and hang on its neck with incomparable love and plunge his semitic muscle into its merits and demerits . . . and if he be not himself the age transfigured . . . . and if to him is not opened the eternity which gives similitude to all periods and locations and processes and animate and inanimate forms, and which is the bond of time, and rises up from its inconceivable vagueness and infiniteness in the swimming shape of today, and is held by the ductile anchors of life, and makes the present spot the passage from what was to what shall be, and commits itself to the representation of this wave of an hour and this one of the sixty beautiful children of the wave— let him merge in the general run and wait his development. . . . . Still the final test of poems or any character or work remains. The prescient poet projects himself centuries ahead and judges performer or perfor-mance after the changes of time. Does it live through them? Does it still hold on untired? Will the same style and the direction of genius to similar points be satisfactory now? Has no new discovery in science or arrival at superior planes of thought and judgment and behaviour fixed him or his so that either can be looked down upon? Have the marches of tens and hundreds and thousands of years made willing detours to the right hand and the left hand for his sake? Is he beloved long and long after he is buried? Does the young man think often of him? and the young woman think often of him? and do the middleaged and the old think of him?

A great poem is for ages and ages in common and for all degrees and complexions and all departments and sects and for a woman as much as a man and a man as much as a woman. A great poem is no finish to a man or woman but rather a beginning. Has any one fancied he could sit at last under some due authority and rest satisfied with explanations and realize and be content and full? To no such terminus does the greatest poet bring . . . he brings neither cessation or sheltered fatness and ease. The touch of him tells in action. Whom he takes he takes with firm sure grasp into live regions previously unattained . . . . thenceforward is no rest . . . . they see the space and ineffable sheen that turn the old spots and lights into dead vacuums. The companion of him beholds the birth and progress of stars and learns one of the meanings. Now there shall be a man cohered out of tumult and chaos . . . . the elder encourages the younger and shows him how . . . they two shall launch off fearlessly together till the new world fits an orbit for itself and looks unabashed on the lesser orbits of the stars and sweeps through the ceaseless rings and shall never be quiet again.

There will soon be no more priests. Their work is done. They may wait awhile . . per-haps a generation or two . . dropping off by degrees. A superior breed shall take their place . . . . the gangs of kosmos and prophets en masse shall take their place. A new order shall arise and they shall be the priests of man, and every man shall be his own priest. The churches built under their umbrage shall be the churches of men and women. Through the divinity of themselves shall the kosmos and the new breed of poets be interpreters of men and women and of all events and things. They shall find their inspiration in real objects today, symptoms of the past and future . . . . They shall not deign to defend immortality or God or the perfection of things or liberty or the exquisite beauty and reality of the soul. They shall arise in America and be responded to from the remainder of the earth.

The English language befriends the grand American expression . . . . it is brawny enough and limber and full enough. On the tough stock of a race who through all change of circumstance was never without the idea of political liberty, which is the animus of all liberty, it has attracted the terms of daintier and gayer and subtler and more elegant tongues. It is the powerful language of resistance . . . it is the dialect of common sense. It is the speech of the proud and melancholy races and of all who aspire. It is the chosen tongue to express growth faith self-esteem freedom justice equality friendliness amplitude prudence decision and courage. It is the medium that shall well nigh express the inexpressible.

No great literature nor any like style of behaviour or oratory or social intercourse or household arrangements or public institutions or the treatment by bosses of employed people, nor executive detail or detail of the army or navy, nor spirit of legislation or courts or police or tuition or architecture or songs or amusements or the costumes of young men, can long elude the jealous and passionate instinct of American standards. Whether or no the sign appears from the mouths of the people, it throbs a live interrogation in every freeman's and freewoman's heart after that which passes by or this built to remain. Is it uniform with my country? Are its disposals without ignominious distinctions? Is it for the evergrowing communes of brothers and lovers, large, well-united, proud beyond the old models, generous beyond all models? Is it something grown fresh out of the fields or drawn from the sea for use to me today here? I know that what answers for me an American must answer for any individual or nation that serves for a part of my materials. Does this answer? or is it without reference to universal needs? or sprung of the needs of the less developed society of special ranks? or old needs of pleasure overlaid by modern science and forms? Does this acknowledge liberty with audible and absolute acknowledgement, and set slavery at nought for life and death? Will it help breed one goodshaped and wellhung man, and a woman to be his perfect and independent mate? Does it improve manners? Is it for the nursing of the young of the republic? Does it solve readily with the sweet milk of the nipples of the breasts of the mother of many children? Has it too the old ever-fresh forbearance and impartiality? Does it look with the same love on the last born and on those hardening toward stature, and on the errant, and on those who disdain all strength of assault outside of their own?

The poems distilled from other poems will probably pass away. The coward will surely pass away. The expectation of the vital and great can only be satisfied by the demeanor of the vital and great. The swarms of the polished deprecating and reflectors and the polite float off and leave no remembrance. America prepares with composure and goodwill for the visitors that have sent word. It is not intellect that is to be their warrant and welcome. The talented, the artist, the ingenious, the editor, the statesman, the erudite . . they are not unappreciated . . they fall in their place and do their work. The soul of the nation also does its work. No disguise can pass on it . . no disguise can conceal from it. It rejects none, it permits all. Only toward as good as itself and toward the like of itself will it advance half-way. An individual is as superb as a nation when he has the qualities which make a superb nation. The soul of the largest and wealthiest and proudest nation may well go half-way to meet that of its poets. The signs are effectual. There is no fear of mistake. If the one is true the other is true. The proof of a poet is that his country absorbs him as affectionately as he has absorbed it.

---

from Leaves of Grass [1891–1892]

from Inscriptions

One's-Self I Sing

One's-Self I sing, a simple separate person,
Yet utter the word Democratic, the word En-Masse.

Of physiology from top to toe I sing,
Not physiognomy alone nor brain alone is worthy for the
    Muse, I say the Form complete is worthier far,   5
The Female equally with the Male I sing.

Of Life immense in passion, pulse, and power,
Cheerful, for freest action form'd under the laws divine,
The Modern Man I sing.
1867

I Hear America Singing

I hear America singing, the varied carols I hear,
Those of mechanics, each one singing his as it should be blithe and strong,
The carpenter singing his as he measures his plank or beam,
The mason singing his as he makes ready for work, or leaves off work,
The boatman singing what belongs to him in his boat, the deckhand singing on the
    steamboat deck,   5
The shoemaker singing as he sits on his bench, the hatter singing as he stands,
The wood-cutter's song, the ploughboy's on his way in the morning, or at noon
    intermission or at sundown,
The delicious singing of the mother, or of the young wife at work, or of the
    girl sewing or washing,
Each singing what belongs to him or her and to none else,
The day what belongs to the day—at night the party of young fellows, robust,
    friendly,   10
Singing with open mouths their strong melodious songs.
1860

Song of Myself *

1

I celebrate myself, and sing myself,
And what I assume you shall assume,
For every atom belonging to me as good belongs to you.

I loafe and invite my soul,
I lean and loafe at my ease observing a spear of summer grass.   5

My tongue, every atom of my blood, form'd from this soil, this air,
Born here of parents born here from parents the same, and their parents the same,
I, now thirty-seven years old in perfect health begin,
Hoping to cease not till death.

Creeds and schools in abeyance,   10
Retiring back a while sufficed at what they are, but never forgotten,
I harbor for good or bad, I permit to speak at every hazard,
Nature without check with original energy.

2

Houses and rooms are full of perfumes, the shelves are crowded with perfumes,
I breathe the fragrance myself and know it and like it,   15

---

* Untitled when first published in the 1855
edition of *Leaves of Grass,* "Song of Myself"
became "Poem of Walt Whitman, an
American" and then "Walt Whitman" before being given its final title in 1881.

The distillation would intoxicate me also, but I shall not let it.
The atmosphere is not a perfume, it has no taste of the distillation, it is odorless,
It is for my mouth forever, I am in love with it,
I will go to the bank by the wood and become undisguised and naked,
I am mad for it to be in contact with me.   20

The smoke of my own breath,
Echoes, ripples, buzz'd whispers, love-root, silk-thread, crotch and vine,
My respiration and inspiration, the beating of my heart, the passing of blood
   and air through my lungs,
The sniff of green leaves and dry leaves, and of the shore and dark-color'd sea-rocks,
   and of hay in the barn,
The sound of the belch'd words of my voice loos'd to the eddies of the wind,   25
A few light kisses, a few embraces, a reaching around of arms,
The play of shine and shade on the trees as the supple boughs wag,
The delight alone or in the rush of the streets, or along the fields and hill-sides,
The feeling of health, the full-noon trill, the song of me rising from bed and
   meeting the sun.

Have you reckon'd a thousand acres much? have you reckon'd the earth much?   30
Have you practis'd so long to learn to read?
Have you felt so proud to get at the meaning of poems?

Stop this day and night with me and you shall possess the origin of all poems,
You shall possess the good of the earth and sun, (there are millions of suns left,)
You shall no longer take things at second or third hand, nor look through the
   eyes of the dead, nor feed on the spectres in books,   35
You shall not look through my eyes either, nor take things from me,
You shall listen to all sides and filter them from your self.

3

I have heard what the talkers were talking, the talk of the beginning and the end,
But I do not talk of the beginning or the end.

There was never any more inception than there is now,   40
Nor any more youth or age than there is now,
And will never be any more perfection than there is now,
Nor any more heaven or hell than there is now.

Urge and urge and urge,
Always the procreant urge of the world.   45

Out of the dimness opposite equals advance, always substance and increase,
   always sex,
Always a knit of identity, always distinction, always a breed of life.

To elaborate is no avail, learn'd and unlearn'd feeling that it is so.

Sure as the most certain sure, plumb in the uprights, well entretied,[1] braced in
    the beams,
Stout as a horse, affectionate, haughty, electrical,
I and this mystery here we stand.

Clear and sweet is my soul, and clear and sweet is all that is not my soul.

Lack one lacks both, and the unseen is proved by the seen,
Till that becomes unseen and receives proof in its turn.

Showing the best and dividing it from the worst age vexes age,
Knowing the perfect fitness and equanimity of things, while they discuss I am
    silent, and go bathe and admire myself.

Welcome is every organ and attribute of me, and of any man hearty and clean,
Not an inch nor a particle of an inch is vile, and none shall be less familiar than
    the rest.

I am satisfied—I see, dance, laugh, sing;
As the hugging and loving bed-fellow sleeps at my side through the night, and
    withdraws at the peep of the day with stealthy tread,
Leaving me baskets cover'd with white towels swelling the house with their plenty,
Shall I postpone my acceptation and realization and scream at my eyes,
That they turn from gazing after and down the road,
And forthwith cipher and show me to a cent,
Exactly the value of one and exactly the value of two, and which is ahead?

50

55

60

65

4

Trippers and askers surround me,
People I meet, the effect upon me of my early life or the ward and city I live
    in, or the nation,
The latest dates, discoveries, inventions, societies, authors old and new,
My dinner, dress, associates, looks, compliments, dues,
The real or fancied indifference of some man or woman I love,
The sickness of one of my folks or of myself, or ill-doing or loss or lack of
    money, or depressions or exaltations,
Battles, the horrors of fratricidal war, the fever of doubtful news, the fitful
    events;
These come to me days and nights and go from me again,
But they are not the Me myself.

70

[1] Cross-braced.

Apart from the pulling and hauling stands what I am,   75
Stands amused, complacent, compassionating, idle, unitary,
Looks down, is erect, or bends an arm on an impalpable certain rest,
Looking with side-curved head curious what will come next,
Both in and out of the game and watching and wondering at it.

Backward I see in my own days where I sweated through fog with linguists
    and contenders,   80
I have no mockings or arguments, I witness and wait.

5   *Identity*

I believe in you my soul, the other I am must not abase itself to you,
And you must not be abased to the other.

Loafe with me on the grass, loose the stop from your throat,
Not words, not music or rhyme I want, not custom or lecture, not even the
    best,   85
Only the lull I like, the hum of your valvèd voice.

I mind how once we lay such a transparent summer morning,
How you settled your head athwart my hips and gently turn'd over upon me,
And parted the shirt from my bosom-bone, and plunged your tongue to my
    bare-stript heart,
And reach'd till you felt my beard, and reach'd till you held my feet.   90

Swiftly arose and spread around me the peace and knowledge that pass all the
    argument of the earth,
And I know that the hand of God is the promise of my own,
And I know that the spirit of God is the brother of my own,
And that all the men ever born are also my brothers, and the women my sisters and
    lovers,
And that a kelson[2] of the creation is love,   95
And limitless are leaves stiff or drooping in the fields,
And brown ants in the little wells beneath them,
And mossy scabs of the worm fence, heap'd stones, elder, mullein and
    poke-weed.

6

A child said *What is the grass?* fetching it to me with full hands;
How could I answer the child? I do not know what it is any more than he.   100

I guess it must be the flag of my disposition, out of hopeful green stuff woven.

---

2 Superstructure of a ship's keel.

Or I guess it is the handkerchief of the Lord,
A scented gift and remembrancer designedly dropt,
Bearing the owner's name someway in the corners, that we may see and remark,
    and say *Whose?*

Or I guess the grass is itself a child, the produced babe of the vegetation.   105

Or I guess it is a uniform hieroglyphic,
And it means, Sprouting alike in broad zones and narrow zones,
Growing among black folks as among white,
Kanuck,[3] Tuckahoe,[4] Congressman, Cuff,[5] I give them the same, I receive them
    the same.

And now it seems to me the beautiful uncut hair of graves.   110

Tenderly will I use you curling grass,
It may be you transpire from the breasts of young men,
It may be if I had known them I would have loved them,
It may be you are from old people, or from offspring taken soon out of
    their mothers' laps,
And here you are the mothers' laps.   115

This grass is very dark to be from the white heads of old mothers,
Darker than the colorless beards of old men,
Dark to come from under the faint red roofs of mouths.

O I perceive after all so many uttering tongues,
And I perceive they do not come from the roofs of mouths for nothing.   120

I wish I could translate the hints about the dead young men and women,
And the hints about old men and mothers, and the offspring taken soon out
    of their laps.

What do you think has become of the young and old men?
And what do you think has become of the women and children?

They are alive and well somewhere,   125
The smallest sprout shows there is really no death,
And if ever there was it led forward life, and does not wait at the end to arrest
    it,
And ceas'd the moment life appear'd.

All goes onward and outward, nothing collapses,
And to die is different from what any one supposed, and luckier.   130

---

[3] French Canadian.
[4] Native of tidewater Virginia.
[5] Black.

7

[handwritten annotation: a sense of unity with all things]

Has any one supposed it lucky to be born?
I hasten to inform him or her it is just as lucky to die, and I know it.

I pass death with the dying and birth with the new-wash'd babe, and am not
    contain'd between my hat and boots,
And peruse manifold objects, no two alike and every one good,
The earth good and the stars good, and their adjuncts all good.   135

I am not an earth nor an adjunct of an earth,
I am the mate and companion of people, all just as immortal and fathomless as
    myself,
(They do not know how immortal, but I know.)

Every kind for itself and its own, for me mine male and female,
For me those that have been boys and that love women,   140
For me the man that is proud and feels how it stings to be slighted,
For me the sweet-heart and the old maid, for me mothers and the mothers of
    mothers,
For me lips that have smiled, eyes that have shed tears,
For me children and the begetters of children.

Undrape! you are not guilty to me, nor stale nor discarded,   145
I see through the broadcloth and gingham whether or no,
And am around, tenacious, acquisitive, tireless, and cannot be shaken away.

8

[handwritten annotation: negative image]

The little one sleeps in its cradle,
I lift the gauze and look a long time, and silently brush away flies with my hand.

The youngster and the red-faced girl turn aside up the bushy hill,   150
I peeringly view them from the top.

The suicide sprawls on the bloody floor of the bedroom,
I witness the corpse with its dabbled hair, I note where the pistol has fallen.

The blab of the pave, tires of carts, sluff of boot-soles, talk of the promenaders,
The heavy omnibus, the driver with his interrogating thumb, the clank of the
    shod horses on the granite floor,   155
The snow-sleighs, clinking, shouted jokes, pelts of snow-balls,
The hurrahs for popular favorites, the fury of rous'd mobs,
The flap of the curtain'd litter, a sick man inside borne to the hospital,
The meeting of enemies, the sudden oath, the blows and fall,
The excited crowd, the policeman with his star quickly working his passage to
    the centre of the crowd,   160
The impassive stones that receive and return so many echoes,
What groans of over-fed or half-starv'd who fall sunstruck or in fits,

What exclamations of women taken suddenly who hurry home and give
    birth to babes,
What living and buried speech is always vibrating here, what howls restrain'd
    by decorum,
Arrests of criminals, slights, adulterous offers made, acceptances, rejections
    with convex lips,   165
I mind them or the show or resonance of them—I come and I depart.

9

The big doors of the country barn stand open and ready,
The dried grass of the harvest-time loads the slow-drawn wagon,
The clear light plays on the brown gray and green intertinged,
The armfuls are pack'd to the sagging mow.   170

I am there, I help, I came stretch'd atop of the load,
I felt its soft jolts, one leg reclined on the other,
I jump from the cross-beams and seize the clover and timothy,
And roll head over heels and tangle my hair full of wisps.

10

Alone far in the wilds and mountains I hunt,   175
Wandering amazed at my own lightness and glee,
In the late afternoon choosing a safe spot to pass the night,
Kindling a fire and broiling the fresh-kill'd game,
Falling asleep on the gather'd leaves with my dog and gun by my side.

The Yankee clipper is under her sky-sails, she cuts the sparkle and scud,   180
My eyes settle the land, I bend at her prow or shout joyously from the deck.

The boatmen and clam-diggers arose early and stopt for me,
I tuck'd my trowser-ends in my boots and went and had a good time;
You should have been with us that day round the chowder-kettle.

I saw the marriage of the trapper in the open air in the far west, the bride was
    a red girl,   185
Her father and his friends sat near cross-legged and dumbly smoking, they had
    moccasins to their feet and large thick blankets hanging from their shoulders,
On a bank lounged the trapper, he was drest mostly in skins, his luxuriant beard
    and curls protected his neck, he held his bride by the hand,
She had long eyelashes, her head was bare, her coarse straight locks descended
    upon her voluptuous limbs and reach'd to her feet.

The runaway slave came to my house and stopt outside,
I heard his motions crackling the twigs of the woodpile,   190
Through the swung half-door of the kitchen I saw him limpsy and weak,
And went where he sat on a log and led him in and assured him,

And brought water and fill'd a tub for his sweated body and bruis'd feet,
And gave him a room that enter'd from my own, and gave him some coarse
  clean clothes,
And remember perfectly well his revolving eyes and his awkwardness,   195
And remember putting plasters on the galls of his neck and ankles;
He staid with me a week before he was recuperated and pass'd north,
I had him sit next me at table, my fire-lock lean'd in the corner.

11

Twenty-eight young men bathe by the shore,
Twenty-eight young men and all so friendly;   200
Twenty-eight years of womanly life and all so lonesome.

She owns the fine house by the rise of the bank,
She hides handsome and richly drest aft the blinds of the window.

Which of the young men does she like the best?
Ah the homeliest of them is beautiful to her.   205

Where are you off to, lady? for I see you,
You splash in the water there, yet stay stock still in your room.

Dancing and laughing along the beach came the twenty-ninth bather,
The rest did not see her, but she saw them and loved them.

The beards of the young men glisten'd with wet, it ran from their long hair,   210
Little streams pass'd all over their bodies.

An unseen hand also pass'd over their bodies,
It descended tremblingly from their temples and ribs.

The young men float on their backs, their white bellies bulge to the sun, they
  do not ask who seizes fast to them,
They do not know who puffs and declines with pendant and bending arch,   215
They do not think whom they souse with spray.

12

The butcher-boy puts off his killing-clothes, or sharpens his knife at the stall in the
  market,
I loiter enjoying his repartee and his shuffle[6] and break-down.[7]

Blacksmiths with grimed and hairy chests environ the anvil,
Each has his main-sledge, they are all out, there is a great heat in the fire.   220

---

6 Slow dance.
7 Rollicking dance.

From the cinder-strew'd threshold I follow their movements,
The lithe sheer of their waists plays even with their massive arms,
Overhand the hammers swing, overhand so slow, overhand so sure,
They do not hasten, each man hits in his place.

13

The negro holds firmly the reins of his four horses, the block swags underneath
    on its tied-over chain,   225
The negro that drives the long dray of the stone-yard, steady and tall he stands
    pois'd on one leg on the string-piece,[8]
His blue shirt exposes his ample neck and breast and loosens over his hip-band,
His glance is calm and commanding, he tosses the slouch of his hat away from
    his forehead,
The sun falls on his crispy hair and mustache, falls on the black of his polish'd
    and perfect limbs.

I behold the picturesque giant and love him, and I do not stop there,   230
I go with the team also.

In me the caresser of life wherever moving, backward as well as forward sluing,
To niches aside and junior bending, not a person or object missing,
Absorbing all to myself and for this song.

Oxen that rattle the yoke and chain or halt in the leafy shade, what is that you
    express in your eyes?   235
It seems to me more than all the print I have read in my life.

My tread scares the wood-drake and wood-duck on my distant and day-long
    ramble,
They rise together, they slowly circle around.

I believe in those wing'd purposes,
And acknowledge red, yellow, white, playing within me,   240
And consider green and violet and the tufted crown intentional,
And do not call the tortoise unworthy because she is not something else,
And the jay in the woods never studied the gamut, yet trills pretty well to me,
And the look of the bay mare shames silliness out of me.

14

The wild gander leads his flock through the cool night,   245
Ya-honk he says, and sounds it down to me like an invitation,
The pert may suppose it meaningless, but I listening close,
Find its purpose and place up there toward the wintry sky.

---

[8] Connective or supporting timber.

The sharp-hoof'd moose of the north, the cat on the house-sill, the chickadee,
    the prairie-dog,
The litter of the grunting sow as they tug at her teats,   250
The brood of the turkey-hen and she with her half-spread wings,
I see in them and myself the same old law.

The press of my foot to the earth springs a hundred affections,
They scorn the best I can do to relate them.

I am enamour'd of growing out-doors,   255
Of men that live among cattle or taste of the ocean or woods,
Of the builders and steerers of ships and the wielders of axes and mauls, and the
    drivers of horses,
I can eat and sleep with them week in and week out.

What is commonest, cheapest, nearest, easiest, is Me,
Me going in for my chances, spending for vast returns,   260
Adorning myself to bestow myself on the first that will take me,
Not asking the sky to come down to my good will,
Scattering it freely forever.

15

The pure contralto sings in the organ loft,
The carpenter dresses his plank, the tongue of his foreplane whistles its wild
    ascending lisp,   265
The married and unmarried children ride home to their Thanksgiving dinner,
The pilot seizes the king-pin, he heaves down with a strong arm,
The mate stands braced in the whale-boat, lance and harpoon are ready,
The duck-shooter walks by silent and cautious stretches,
The deacons are ordain'd with cross'd hands at the altar,   270
The spinning-girl retreats and advances to the hum of the big wheel,
The farmer stops by the bars as he walks on a First-day loafe and looks at the
    oats and rye,
The lunatic is carried at last to the asylum a confirm'd case,
(He will never sleep any more as he did in the cot in his mother's bed-room;)
The jour printer[9] with gray head and gaunt jaws works at his case,   275
He turns his quid of tobacco while his eyes blurr with the manuscript;
The malform'd limbs are tied to the surgeon's table,
What is removed drops horribly in a pail;
The quadroon girl is sold at the auction-stand, the drunkard nods by the
    bar-room stove,
The machinist rolls up his sleeves, the policeman travels his beat, the gate-keeper
    marks who pass,   280
The young fellow drives the express-wagon, (I love him, though I do not
    know him;)

[handwritten annotation: stanza of diversity of the different types of people in America]

---

[9] Journeyman or working printer (from
  French *jour:* "day").

The half-breed straps on his light boots to compete in the race,
The western turkey-shooting draws old and young, some lean on their rifles,
    some sit on logs,
Out from the crowd steps the marksman, takes his position, levels his piece;
The groups of newly-come immigrants cover the wharf or levee,   285
As the woolly-pates hoe in the sugar-field, the overseer views them from his
    saddle,
The bugle calls in the ball-room, the gentlemen run for their partners, the
    dancers bow to each other,
The youth lies awake in the cedar-roof'd garret and harks to the musical rain,
The Wolverine[10] sets traps on the creek that helps fill the Huron,
The squaw wrapt in her yellow-hemm'd cloth is offering moccasins and
    bead-bags for sale,   290
The connoisseur peers along the exhibition-gallery with half-shut eyes bent
    sideways,
As the deck-hands make fast the steamboat the plank is thrown for the
    shore-going passengers,
The young sister holds out the skein while the elder sister winds it off in a ball,
    and stops now and then for the knots,
The one-year wife is recovering and happy having a week ago borne her first
    child,
The clean-hair'd Yankee girl works with her sewing-machine or in the factory
    or mill,   295
The paving-man leans on his two-handed rammer, the reporter's lead flies
    swiftly over the note-book, the sign-painter is lettering with blue and gold,
The canal boy trots on the tow-path, the book-keeper counts at his desk,
    the shoemaker waxes his thread,
The conductor beats time for the band and all the performers follow him,
The child is baptized, the convert is making his first professions,
The regatta is spread on the bay, the race is begun, (how the white sails
    sparkle!)   300
The drover watching his drove sings out to them that would stray,
The pedler sweats with his pack on his back, (the purchaser higgling about the
    odd cent;)
The bride unrumples her white dress, the minute-hand of the clock moves
    slowly,
The opium-eater reclines with rigid head and just-open'd lips,
The prostitute draggles her shawl, her bonnet bobs on her tipsy and pimpled
    neck,   305
The crowd laugh at her blackguard oaths, the men jeer and wink to each other,
(Miserable! I do not laugh at your oaths nor jeer you;)
The President holding a cabinet council is surrounded by the great Secretaries,
On the piazza walk three matrons stately and friendly with twined arms,
The crew of the fish-smack pack repeated layers of halibut in the hold,   310
The Missourian crosses the plains toting his wares and his cattle,

[10] Native of Michigan.

As the fare-collector goes through the train he gives notice by the jingling of
  loose change,
The floor-men are laying the floor, the tinners are tinning the roof, the masons are
  calling for mortar,
In single file each shouldering his hod pass onward the laborers;
Seasons pursuing each other the indescribable crowd is gather'd, it is the fourth
  of Seventh-month, (what salutes of cannon and small arms!)   315
Seasons pursuing each other the plougher ploughs, the mower mows, and the
  winter-grain falls in the ground;
Off on the lakes the pike-fisher watches and waits by the hole in the frozen
  surface,
The stumps stand thick round the clearing, the squatter strikes deep with his axe,
Flatboatmen make fast towards dusk near the cotton-wood or pecan-trees,
Coon-seekers go through the regions of the Red river or through those drain'd
  by the Tennessee, or through those of the Arkansas,   320
Torches shine in the dark that hangs on the Chattahooche or Altamahaw,
Patriarchs sit at supper with sons and grandsons and great-grandsons around
  them,
In walls of adobie, in canvas tents, rest hunters and trappers after their day's
  sport,
The city sleeps and the country sleeps,
The living sleep for their time, the dead sleep for their time,   325
The old husband sleeps by his wife and the young husband sleeps by his wife;
And these tend inward to me, and I tend outward to them,
And such as it is to be of these more or less I am,
And of these one and all I weave the song of myself.

[handwritten marginal note: *Concept of reaching for each other to become 1 / diversity → unity*]

16

I am of old and young, of the foolish as much as the wise,   330
Regardless of others, ever regardful of others,
Maternal as well as paternal, a child as well as a man,
Stuff'd with the stuff that is coarse and stuff'd with the stuff that is fine,
One of the Nation of many nations, the smallest the same and the largest the
  same,
A Southerner soon as a Northerner, a planter nonchalant and hospitable down
  by the Oconee I live,   335
A Yankee bound my own way ready for trade, my joints the limberest joints
  on earth and the sternest joints on earth,
A Kentuckian walking the vale of the Elkhorn in my deerskin leggings, a
  Louisianian or Georgian,
A boatman over lakes or bays or along coasts, a Hoosier, Badger, Buckeye;[11]
At home on Kanadian snow-shoes or up in the bush, or with fishermen off
  Newfoundland,

[11] Hoosier; Badger; Buckeye: natives, respectively, of Indiana, Wisconsin, and Ohio.

At home in the fleet of ice-boats, sailing with the rest and tacking,   340
At home on the hills of Vermont or in the woods of Maine, or the Texan ranch,
Comrade of Californians, comrade of free North-Westerners, (loving their big
    proportions,)
Comrade of raftsmen and coalmen, comrade of all who shake hands and
    welcome to drink and meat,
A learner with the simplest, a teacher of the thoughtfullest,
A novice beginning yet experient of myriads of seasons,   345
Of every hue and caste am I, of every rank and religion,
A farmer, mechanic, artist, gentleman, sailor, quaker,
Prisoner, fancy-man, rowdy, lawyer, physician, priest.

I resist any thing better than my own diversity,
Breathe the air but leave plenty after me,   350
And am not stuck up, and am in my place.

(The moth and the fish-eggs are in their place,
The bright suns I see and the dark suns I cannot see are in their place,
The palpable is in its place and the impalpable is in its place.)

17

These are really the thoughts of all men in all ages and lands, they are not
    original with me,   355
If they are not yours as much as mine they are nothing, or next to nothing,
If they are not the riddle and the untying of the riddle they are nothing,
If they are not just as close as they are distant they are nothing.

This is the grass that grows wherever the land is and the water is,
This the common air that bathes the globe.   360

18

With music strong I come, with my cornets and my drums,
I play not marches for accepted victors only, I play marches for conquer'd and
    slain persons.

Have you heard that it was good to gain the day?
I also say it is good to fall, battles are lost in the same spirit in which they are won.

I beat and pound for the dead,   365
I blow through my embouchures[12] my loudest and gayest for them.

Vivas to those who have fail'd!
And to those whose war-vessels sank in the sea!
And to those themselves who sank in the sea!
And to all generals that lost engagements, and all overcome heroes!   370
And the numberless unknown heroes equal to the greatest heroes known!

[12] Mouthpieces of wind instruments.

19

This is the meal equally set, this the meat for natural hunger,
It is for the wicked just the same as the righteous, I make appointments with all,
I will not have a single person slighted or left away,
The kept-woman, sponger, thief, are hereby invited,   375
The heavy-lipp'd slave is invited, the venerealee is invited;
There shall be no difference between them and the rest.

This is the press of a bashful hand, this the float and odor of hair,
This the touch of my lips to yours, this the murmur of yearning,
This the far-off depth and height reflecting my own face,   380
This the thoughtful merge of myself, and the outlet again.

Do you guess I have some intricate purpose?
Well I have, for the Fourth-month showers have, and the mica on the side of a
    rock has.
Do you take it I would astonish?
Does the daylight astonish? does the early redstart twittering through the
    woods?   385
Do I astonish more than they?

This hour I tell things in confidence,
I might not tell everybody, but I will tell you.

20

— desiring
— Physical
— Spiritual
— in the end we are all nude

Who goes there? hankering, gross, mystical, nude;
How is it I extract strength from the beef I eat?   390

What is a man anyhow? what am I? what are you?

All I mark as my own you shall offset it with your own,
Else it were time lost listening to me.

I do not snivel that snivel the world over,
That months are vacuums and the ground but wallow and filth.   395

Whimpering and truckling fold with powders for invalids, conformity goes to
    the fourth-remov'd,
I wear my hat as I please indoors or out.

Why should I pray? why should I venerate and be ceremonious?

Having pried through the strata, analyzed to a hair, counsel'd with doctors and
    calculated close,
I find no sweeter fat than sticks to my own bones.   400

In all people I see myself, none more and not one a barley-corn less,
And the good or bad I say of myself I say of them.

I know I am solid and sound,
To me the converging objects of the universe perpetually flow,
All are written to me, and I must get what the writing means.   405

I know I am deathless,
I know this orbit of mine cannot be swept by a carpenter's compass,
I know I shall not pass like a child's carlacue[13] cut with a burnt stick at night.

I know I am august, — *supreme*
I do not trouble my spirit to vindicate itself or be understood,   410
I see that the elementary laws never apologize,
(I reckon I behave no prouder than the level I plant my house by, after all.)

— I don't have to explain myself to you

I exist as I am, that is enough,
If no other in the world be aware I sit content,
And if each and all be aware I sit content.   415

One world is aware and by far the largest to me, and that is myself,
And whether I come to my own to-day or in ten thousand or ten million years,
I can cheerfully take it now, or with equal cheerfulness I can wait.

My foothold is tenon'd and mortis'd in granite,
I laugh at what you call dissolution,   420
And I know the amplitude of time.

21

I am the poet of the Body and I am the poet of the Soul,
The pleasures of heaven are with me and the pains of hell are with me,
The first I graft and increase upon myself, the latter I translate into a new
      tongue.

I am the poet of the woman the same as the man,   425
And I say it is as great to be a woman as to be a man,
And I say there is nothing greater than the mother of men.

I chant the chant of dilation or pride,
We have had ducking and deprecating about enough,
I show that size is only development.   430

Have you outstript the rest? are you the President?
It is a trifle, they will more than arrive there every one, and still pass on.

I am he that walks with the tender and growing night,
I call to the earth and sea half-held by the night.

Press close bare-bosom'd night—press close magnetic nourishing night! 435
Night of south winds—night of the large few stars!
Still nodding night—mad naked summer night.

[13] Curlicue.

Smile O voluptuous cool-breath'd earth!
Earth of the slumbering and liquid trees!
Earth of departed sunset—earth of the mountains misty-topt!   440
Earth of the vitreous pour of the full moon just tinged with blue!
Earth of shine and dark mottling the tide of the river!
Earth of the limpid gray of clouds brighter and clearer for my sake!
Far-swooping elbow'd earth—rich apple-blossom'd earth!
Smile, for your lover comes.   445

Prodigal, you have given me love—therefore I to you give love!
O unspeakable passionate love.

22

You sea! I resign myself to you also—I guess what you mean,
I behold from the beach your crooked inviting fingers,
I believe you refuse to go back without feeling of me,   450
We must have a turn together, I undress, hurry me out of sight of the land,
Cushion me soft, rock me in billowy drowse,
Dash me with amorous wet, I can repay you.

Sea of stretch'd ground-swells,
Sea breathing broad and convulsive breaths,   455
Sea of the brine of life and of unshovell'd yet always-ready graves,
Howler and scooper of storms, capricious and dainty sea,
I am integral with you, I too am of one phase and of all phases.

Partaker of influx and efflux I, extoller of hate and conciliation,
Extoller of amies and those that sleep in each others' arms.   460

I am he attesting sympathy,
(Shall I make my list of things in the house and skip the house that supports
    them?)

I am not the poet of goodness only, I do not decline to be the poet of
    wickedness also.

What blurt is this about virtue and about vice?
Evil propels me and reform of evil propels me, I stand indifferent,   465
My gait is no fault-finder's or rejecter's gait,
I moisten the roots of all that has grown.

Did you fear some scrofula out of the unflagging pregnancy?
Did you guess the celestial laws are yet to be work'd over and rectified?

I find one side a balance and the antipodal side a balance,   470
Soft doctrine as steady help as stable doctrine,
Thoughts and deeds of the present our rouse and early start.

This minute that comes to me over the past decillions,
There is no better than it and now.

What behaved well in the past or behaves well to-day is not such a wonder,   475
The wonder is always and always how there can be a mean man or an infidel.

23

Endless unfolding of words of ages!
And mine a word of the modern, the word En-Masse.

A word of the faith that never balks,
Here or henceforward it is all the same to me, I accept Time absolutely.   480

It alone is without flaw, it alone rounds and completes all,
That mystic baffling wonder alone completes all.

I accept Reality and dare not question it,
Materialism first and last imbuing.

Hurrah for positive science! long live exact demonstration!   485
Fetch stonecrop mixt with cedar and branches of lilac,
This is the lexicographer, this the chemist, this made a grammar of the old
    cartouches,
These mariners put the ship through dangerous unknown seas.
This is the geologist, this works with the scalpel, and this is a mathematician.

Gentlemen, to you the first honors always!   490
Your facts are useful, and yet they are not my dwelling,
I but enter by them to an area of my dwelling.

Less the reminders of properties told my words,
And more the reminders they of life untold, and of freedom and extrication,
And make short account of neuters and geldings, and favor men and women fully
    equipt,   495
And beat the gong of revolt, and stop with fugitives and them that plot and
    conspire.

24

Walt Whitman, a kosmos, of Manhattan the son,
Turbulent, fleshy, sensual, eating, drinking and breeding,
No sentimentalist, no stander above men and women or apart from them,
No more modest than immodest.   500

Unscrew the locks from the doors!
Unscrew the doors themselves from their jambs!

Whoever degrades another degrades me,
And whatever is done or said returns at last to me.

Through me the afflatus surging and surging, through me the current and index.   505
I speak the pass-word primeval, I give the sign of democracy,
By God! I will accept nothing which all cannot have their counterpart of on the
    same terms.

Through me many long dumb voices,
Voices of the interminable generations of prisoners and slaves,
Voices of the diseas'd and despairing and of thieves and dwarfs,   510
Voices of cycles of preparation and accretion,
And of the threads that connect the stars, and of wombs and of the father-stuff,
And of the rights of them the others are down upon,
Of the deform'd, trivial, flat, foolish, despised,
Fog in the air, beetles rolling balls of dung.   515

Through me forbidden voices,
Voices of sexes and lusts, voices veil'd and I remove the veil,
Voices indecent by me clarified and transfigur'd.

I do not press my fingers across my mouth,
I keep as delicate around the bowels as around the head and heart,   520
Copulation is no more rank to me than death is.

I believe in the flesh and the appetites,
Seeing, hearing, feeling, are miracles, and each part and tag of me is a miracle.

Divine am I inside and out, and I make holy whatever I touch or am touch'd
    from,
The scent of these arm-pits aroma finer than prayer,   525
This head more than churches, bibles, and all the creeds.

If I worship one thing more than another it shall be the spread of my own
    body, or any part of it,
Translucent mould of me it shall be you!
Shaded ledges and rests it shall be you!
Firm masculine colter it shall be you!   530
Whatever goes to the tilth of me it shall be you!
You my rich blood! your milky stream pale strippings of my life!
Breast that presses against other breasts it shall be you!
My brain it shall be your occult convolutions!
Root of wash'd sweet-flag! timorous pond-snipe! nest of guarded duplicate
    eggs! it shall be you!   535
Mix'd tussled hay of head, beard, brawn, it shall be you!
Trickling sap of maple, fibre of manly wheat, it shall be you!
Sun so generous it shall be you!
Vapors lighting and shading my face it shall be you!

You sweaty brooks and dews it shall be you!   540
Winds whose soft-tickling genitals rub against me it shall be you!

Broad muscular fields, branches of live oak, loving lounger in my winding paths,
    it shall be you!
Hands I have taken, face I have kiss'd, mortal I have ever touch'd, it shall be you.

I dote on myself, there is that lot of me and all so luscious,
Each moment and whatever happens thrills me with joy,   545
I cannot tell how my ankles bend, nor whence the cause of my faintest wish,
Nor the cause of the friendship I emit, nor the cause of the friendship I take
    again.

That I walk up my stoop, I pause to consider if it really be,
A morning-glory at my window satisfies me more than the metaphysics of books.

To behold the day-break!   550
The little light fades the immense and diaphanous shadows,
The air tastes good to my palate.

Hefts of the moving world at innocent gambols silently rising freshly exuding,
Scooting obliquely high and low.

Something I cannot see puts upward libidinous prongs,   555
Seas of bright juice suffuse heaven.

The earth by the sky staid with, the daily close of their junction,
The heav'd challenge from the east that moment over my head,
The mocking taunt. See then whether you shall be master!

25

Dazzling and tremendous how quick the sun-rise would kill me,   560
If I could not now and always send sun-rise out of me.

We also ascend dazzling and tremendous as the sun,
We found our own O my soul in the calm and cool of the day-break.

My voice goes after what my eyes cannot reach,
With the twirl of my tongue I encompass worlds and volumes of worlds.   565

Speech is the twin of my vision, it is unequal to measure itself,
It provokes me forever, it says sarcastically,
Walt you contain enough, why don't you let it out then?

Come now I will not be tantalized, you conceive too much of articulation,
Do you not know O speech how the buds beneath you are folded?   570
Waiting in gloom, protected by frost,
The dirt receding before my prophetical screams,

I underlying causes to balance them at last,
My knowledge my live parts, it keeping tally with the meaning of all things,
Happiness, (which whoever hears me let him or her set out in search of this day.)   575

My final merit I refuse you, I refuse putting from me what I really am,
Encompass worlds, but never try to encompass me,
I crowd your sleekest and best by simply looking toward you.

Writing and talk do not prove me,
I carry the plenum of proof and every thing else in my face,   580
With the hush of my lips I wholly confound the skeptic.

26

Now I will do nothing but listen,
To accrue what I hear into this song, to let sounds contribute toward it.

I hear bravuras of birds, bustle of growing wheat, gossip of flames, clack of sticks
   cooking my meals,
I hear the sound I love, the sound of the human voice,   585
I hear all sounds running together, combined, fused or following,
Sounds of the city and sounds out of the city, sounds of the day and night,
Talkative young ones to those that like them, the loud laugh of work-people at their
   meals,
The angry base of disjointed friendship, the faint tones of the sick,
The judge with hands tight to the desk, his pallid lips pronouncing a
   death-sentence,   590
The heave'e'yo of stevedores unlading ships by the wharves, the refrain of the
   anchor-lifters,
The ring of alarm-bells, the cry of fire, the whirr of swift-streaking engines and
   hose-carts with premonitory tinkles and color'd lights,
The steam-whistle, the solid roll of the train of approaching cars,
The slow march play'd at the head of the association marching two and two,
(They go to guard some corpse, the flag-tops are draped with black muslin.)   595

I hear the violoncello, ('tis the young man's heart's complaint,)
I hear the key'd cornet, it glides quickly in through my ears,
It shakes mad-sweet pangs through my belly and breast.

I hear the chorus, it is a grand opera,
Ah this indeed is music—this suits me.   600

A tenor large and fresh as the creation fills me,
The orbic flex of his mouth is pouring and filling me full.

I hear the train'd soprano (what work with hers is this?)
The orchestra whirls me wider than Uranus flies,
It wrenches such ardors from me I did not know I possess'd them,   605

It sails me, I dab with bare feet, they are lick'd by the indolent waves,
I am cut by bitter and angry hail, I lose my breath,
Steep'd amid honey'd morphine, my windpipe throttled in fakes of death,
At length let up again to feel the puzzle of puzzles,
And that we call Being.   610

27

To be in any form, what is that?
(Round and round we go, all of us, and ever come back thither,)
If nothing lay more develop'd the quahaug in its callous shell were enough.

Mine is no callous shell,
I have instant conductors all over me whether I pass or stop,   615
They seize every object and lead it harmlessly through me.

I merely stir, press, feel with my fingers, and am happy,
To touch my person to some one else's is about as much as I can stand.

28

Is this then a touch? quivering me to a new identity,
Flames and ether making a rush for my veins,   620
Treacherous tip of me reaching and crowding to help them,
My flesh and blood playing out lightning to strike what is hardly different
    from myself,
On all sides prurient provokers stiffening my limbs,
Straining the udder of my heart for its withheld drip,
Behaving licentious toward me, taking no denial,   625
Depriving me of my best as for a purpose,
Unbuttoning my clothes, holding me by the bare waist,
Deluding my confusion with the calm of the sunlight and pasture-fields,
Immodestly sliding the fellow-senses away,
They bribed to swap off with touch and go and graze at the edges of me,   630
No consideration, no regard for my draining strength or my anger,
Fetching the rest of the herd around to enjoy them a while,
Then all uniting to stand on a headland and worry me.

The sentries desert every other part of me,
They have left me helpless to a red marauder,   635
They all come to the headland to witness and assist against me.
I am given up by traitors,
I talk wildly, I have lost my wits, I and nobody else am the greatest traitor,
I went myself first to the headland, my own hands carried me there.

You villain touch! what are you doing? my breath is tight in its throat,   640
Unclench your floodgates, you are too much for me.

29

Blind loving wrestling touch, sheath'd hooded sharp-tooth'd touch!
Did it make you ache so, leaving me?

Parting track'd by arriving, perpetual payment of perpetual loan,
Rich showering rain, and recompense richer afterward.   645

Sprouts take and accumulate, stand by the curb prolific and vital,
Landscapes projected masculine, full-sized and golden.

30

All truths wait in all things,
They neither hasten their own delivery nor resist it,
They do not need the obstetric forceps of the surgeon,   650
The insignificant is as big to me as any,
(What is less or more than a touch?)

Logic and sermons never convince,
The damp of the night drives deeper into my soul.

(Only what proves itself to every man and woman is so,   655
Only what nobody denies is so.)

A minute and a drop of me settle my brain,
I believe the soggy clods shall become lovers and lamps,
And a compend of compends is the meat of a man or woman,
And a summit and flower there is the feeling they have for each other,   660
And they are to branch boundlessly out of that lesson until it becomes omnific,
And until one and all shall delight us, and we them.

31

I believe a leaf of grass is no less than the journey-work of the stars,
And the pismire is equally perfect, and a grain of sand, and the egg of the wren,
And the tree-toad is a chef-d'œuvre for the highest,
And the running blackberry would adorn the parlors of heaven,
And the narrowest hinge in my hand puts to scorn all machinery,   665
And the cow crunching with depress'd head surpasses any statue,
And a mouse is miracle enough to stagger sextillions of infidels.

I find I incorporate gneiss, coal, long-threaded moss, fruits, grains, esculent
   roots,   670
And am stucco'd with quadrupeds and birds all over,
And have distanced what is behind me for good reasons,
But call any thing back again when I desire it.
In vain the speeding or shyness,

In vain the plutonic rocks send their old heat against my approach,   675
In vain the mastodon retreats beneath its own powder'd bones,
In vain objects stand leagues off and assume manifold shapes,
In vain the ocean settling in hollows and the great monsters lying low,
In vain the buzzard houses herself with the sky,
In vain the snake slides through the creepers and logs,   680
In vain the elk takes to the inner passes of the woods,
In vain the razor-bill'd auk sails far north to Labrador,
I follow quickly, I ascend to the nest in the fissure of the cliff.

32

I think I could turn and live with animals, they are so placid and self-contain'd,
I stand and look at them long and long.   685

They do not sweat and whine about their condition,
They do not lie awake in the dark and weep for their sins,
They do not make me sick discussing their duty to God,
Not one is dissatisfied, not one is demented with the mania of owning things,
Not one kneels to another, nor to his kind that lived thousands of years ago,   690
Not one is respectable or unhappy over the whole earth.

So they show their relations to me and I accept them,
They bring me tokens of myself, they evince them plainly in their possession.

I wonder where they get those tokens,
Did I pass that way huge times ago and negligently drop them?   695

Myself moving forward then and now and forever,
Gathering and showing more always and with velocity,
Infinite and omnigenous,[14] and the like of these among them,
Not too exclusive toward the reachers of my remembrancers,
Picking out here one that I love, and now go with him on brotherly terms.   700

A gigantic beauty of a stallion, fresh and responsive to my caresses,
Head high in the forehead, wide between the ears,
Limbs glossy and supple, tail dusting the ground,
Eyes full of sparkling wickedness, ears finely cut, flexibly moving.

His nostrils dilate as my heels embrace him,   705
His well-built limbs tremble with pleasure as we race around and return.

I but use you a minute, then I resign you, stallion,
Why do I need your paces when I myself out-gallop them?
Even as I stand or sit passing faster than you.

[14] Of all kinds.

33

Space and Time! now I see it is true, what I guess'd at,   710
What I guess'd when I loaf'd on the grass,
What I guess'd while I lay alone in my bed,
And again as I walk'd the beach under the paling stars of the morning.

the structure of entire poem
the vision of America

My ties and ballasts leave me, my elbows rest in sea-gaps,
I skirt sierras, my palms cover continents,   715
I am afoot with my vision.

By the city's quadrangular houses—in log huts, camping with lumbermen,
Along the ruts of the turnpike, along the dry gulch and rivulet bed,
Weeding my onion-patch or hoeing rows of carrots and parsnips, crossing
    savannas, trailing in forests,
Prospecting, gold-digging, girdling the trees of a new purchase,   720
Scorch'd ankle-deep by the hot sand, hauling my boat down the shallow river,
Where the panther walks to and fro on a limb overhead, where the buck turns
    furiously at the hunter,
Where the rattlesnake suns his flabby length on a rock, where the otter is feeding
    on fish,
Where the alligator in his tough pimples sleeps by the bayou,
Where the black bear is searching for roots or honey, where the beaver pats the
    mud with his paddle-shaped tail;   725
Over the growing sugar, over the yellow-flower'd cotton plant, over the rice in
    its low moist field,
Over the sharp-peak'd farm house, with its scallop'd scum and slender shoots
    from the gutters,
Over the western persimmon, over the long-leav'd corn, over the delicate
    blue-flower flax,
Over the white and brown buckwheat, a hummer and buzzer there with the rest,
Over the dusky green of the rye as it ripples and shades in the breeze;   730
Scaling mountains, pulling myself cautiously up, holding on by low scragged
    limbs,
Walking the path worn in the grass and beat through the leaves of the brush,
Where the quail is whistling betwixt the woods and the wheat-lot,
Where the bat flies in the Seventh-month eve, where the great goldbug drops
    through the dark,
Where the brook puts out of the roots of the old tree and flows to the
    meadow,   735
Where cattle stand and shake away flies with the tremulous shuddering of their
    hides,
Where the cheese-cloth hangs in the kitchen, where andirons straddle the hearth-slab,
    where cobwebs fall in festoons from the rafters;
Where trip-hammers crash, where the press is whirling its cylinders,
Wherever the human heart beats with terrible throes under its ribs,
Where the pear-shaped balloon is floating aloft, (floating in it myself and
    looking composedly down,)   740

Where the life-car is drawn on the slip-noose, where the heat hatches pale-green
    eggs in the dented sand,
Where the she-whale swims with her calf and never forsakes it,
Where the steam-ship trails hind-ways its long pennant of smoke,
Where the fin of the shark cuts like a black chip out of the water,
Where the half-burn'd brig is riding on unknown currents,   745
Where shells grow to her slimy deck, where the dead are corrupting below;
Where the dense-starr'd flag is borne at the head of the regiments,
Approaching Manhattan up by the long-stretching island,
Under Niagara, the cataract falling like a veil over my countenance,
Upon a door-step, upon the horse-block of hard wood outside,   750
Upon the race-course, or enjoying picnics or jigs or a good game of base-ball,
At he-festivals, with blackguard gibes, ironical license, bull-dances, drinking,
    laughter,
At the cider-mill tasting the sweets of the brown mash, sucking the juice
    through a straw,
At apple-peelings wanting kisses for all the red fruit I find,
At musters, beach-parties, friendly bees, huskings, house-raisings;   755
Where the mocking-bird sounds his delicious gurgles, cackles, screams, weeps,
Where the hay-rick stands in the barn-yard, where the dry-stalks are scatter'd,
    where the brood-cow waits in the hovel,
Where the bull advances to do his masculine work, where the stud to the mare,
    where the cock is treading the hen,
Where the heifers browse, where geese nip their food with short jerks,
Where sun-down shadows lengthen over the limitless and lonesome prairie,   760
Where herds of buffalo make a crawling spread of the square miles far and near,
Where the humming-bird shimmers, where the neck of the long-lived swan is
    curving and winding,
Where the laughing-gull scoots by the shore, where she laughs her near-human
    laugh,
Where bee-hives range on a gray bench in the garden half hid by the high
    weeds,
Where band-neck'd partridges roost in a ring on the ground with their heads
    out,   765
Where burial coaches enter the arch'd gates of a cemetery,
Where winter wolves bark amid wastes of snow and icicled trees,
Where the yellow-crown'd heron comes to the edge of the marsh at night and
    feeds upon small crabs,
Where the splash of swimmers and divers cools the warm noon,
Where the katy-did works her chromatic reed on the walnut-tree over the
    well,   770
Through patches of citrons and cucumbers with silver-wired leaves,
Through the salt-lick or orange glade, or under conical firs,
Through the gymnasium, through the curtain'd saloon, through the office or
    public hall;
Pleas'd with the native and pleas'd with the foreign, pleas'd with the new and
    old,

Pleas'd with the homely woman as well as the handsome,   775
Pleas'd with the quakeress as she puts off her bonnet and talks melodiously,
Pleas'd with the tune of the choir of the whitewash'd church,
Pleas'd with the earnest words of the sweating Methodist preacher, impress'd
    seriously at the camp-meeting;
Looking in at the shop-windows of Broadway the whole forenoon, flatting the
    flesh of my nose on the thick plate glass,
Wandering the same afternoon with my face turn'd up to the clouds, or down
    a lane or along the beach,   780
My right and left arms round the sides of two friends, and I in the middle;
Coming home with the silent and dark-cheek'd bush-boy, (behind me he rides
    at the drape of the day,)
Far from the settlements studying the print of animals' feet, or the moccasin
    print,
By the cot in the hospital reaching lemonade to a feverish patient,
Nigh the coffin'd corpse when all is still, examining with a candle;   785
Voyaging to every port to dicker and adventure,
Hurrying with the modern crowd as eager and fickle as any,
Hot toward one I hate, ready in my madness to knife him,
Solitary at midnight in my back yard, my thoughts gone from me a long while,
Walking the old hills of Judæa with the beautiful gentle God by my side,   790
Speeding through space, speeding through heaven and the stars,
Speeding amid the seven satellites and the broad ring, and the diameter of
    eighty thousand miles,
Speeding with tail'd meteors, throwing fire-balls like the rest,
Carrying the crescent child that carries its own full mother in its belly,
Storming, enjoying, planning, loving, cautioning,   795
Backing and filling, appearing and disappearing,
I tread day and night such roads.

I visit the orchards of spheres and look at the product,
And look at quintillions ripen'd and look at quintillions green.

I fly those flights of a fluid and swallowing soul,   800
My course runs below the soundings of plummets.

I help myself to material and immaterial,
No guard can shut me off, no law prevent me.

I anchor my ship for a little while only,
My messengers continually cruise away or bring their returns to me.   805

I go hunting polar furs and the seal, leaping chasms with a pike-pointed staff,
    clinging to topples of brittle and blue.

I ascend to the foretruck,
I take my place late at night in the crow's-nest,

We sail the arctic sea, it is plenty light enough,
Through the clear atmosphere I stretch around on the wonderful beauty,   810
The enormous masses of ice pass me and I pass them, the scenery is plain in all
    directions,
The white-topt mountains show in the distance, I fling out my fancies toward
    them,
We are approaching some great battle-field in which we are soon to be
    engaged,
We pass the colossal outposts of the encampment, we pass with still feet and
    caution,
Or we are entering by the suburbs some vast and ruin'd city,   815
The blocks and fallen architecture more than all the living cities of the globe.

I am a free companion, I bivouac by invading watchfires,
I turn the bridegroom out of bed and stay with the bride myself,
I tighten her all night to my thighs and lips.

My voice is the wife's voice, the screech by the rail of the stairs,   820
They fetch my man's body up dripping and drown'd.

I understand the large hearts of heroes,
The courage of present times and all times,
How the skipper saw the crowded and rudderless wreck of the steam-ship, and
    Death chasing it up and down the storm,
How he knuckled tight and gave not back an inch, and was faithful of days
    and faithful of nights,   825
And chalk'd in large letters on a board, *Be of good cheer, we will not desert you;*
How he follow'd with them and tack'd with them three days and would not
    give it up,
How he saved the drifting company at last,
How the lank loose-gown'd women look'd when boated from the side of their
    prepared graves,
How the silent old-faced infants and the lifted sick, and the sharp-lipp'd
    unshaved men;   830
All this I swallow, it tastes good, I like it well, it becomes mine,
I am the man, I suffer'd, I was there.

The disdain and calmness of martyrs,
The mother of old, condemn'd for a witch, burnt with dry wood, her children
    gazing on,
The hounded slave that flags in the race, leans by the fence, blowing, cover'd
    with sweat,   835
The twinges that sting like needles his legs and neck, the murderous buckshot
    and the bullets,
All these I feel or am.

I am the hounded slave, I wince at the bite of the dogs,
Hell and despair are upon me, crack and again crack the marksmen,

I clutch the rails of the fence, my gore dribs, thinn'd with the ooze of my skin,   840
I fall on the weeds and stones,
The riders spur their unwilling horses, haul close,
Taunt my dizzy ears and beat me violently over the head with whip-stocks.

Agonies are one of my changes of garments,
I do not ask the wounded person how he feels, I myself become the wounded
    person,   845
My hurts turn livid upon me as I lean on a cane and observe.

I am the mash'd fireman with breast-bone broken,
Tumbling walls buried me in their debris,
Heat and smoke I inspired, I heard the yelling shouts of my comrades,
I heard the distant click of their picks and shovels,   850
They have clear'd the beams away, they tenderly lift me forth.

I lie in the night air in my red shirt, the pervading hush is for my sake,
Painless after all I lie exhausted but not so unhappy,
White and beautiful are the faces around me, the heads are bared of their
    fire-caps,
The kneeling crowd fades with the light of the torches.   855

Distant and dead resuscitate,
They show as the dial or move as the hands of me, I am the clock myself.

I am an old artillerist, I tell of my fort's bombardment,
I am there again.

Again the long roll of the drummers,   860
Again the attacking cannon, mortars,
Again to my listening ears the cannon responsive.

I take part, I see and hear the whole,
The cries, curses, roar, the plaudits for well-aim'd shots,
The ambulanza[15] slowly passing trailing its red drip,   865
Workmen searching after damages, making indispensable repairs,
The fall of grenades through the rent roof, the fan-shaped explosion,
The whizz of limbs, heads, stone, wood, iron, high in the air.

Again gurgles the mouth of my dying general, he furiously waves with his hand,
He gasps through the clot *Mind not me—mind—the entrenchments.*   870

34

Now I tell what I knew in Texas in my early youth,
(I tell not the fall of Alamo,

---

[15] Italian: "ambulance."

Not one escaped to tell the fall of Alamo,
The hundred and fifty are dumb yet at Alamo,)
'Tis the tale of the murder in cold blood of four hundred and twelve young men.   875

Retreating they had form'd in a hollow square with their baggage for breastworks,
Nine hundred lives out of the surrounding enemy's, nine times their number,
 was the price they took in advance,
Their colonel was wounded and their ammunition gone,
They treated for an honorable capitulation, receiv'd writing and seal, gave up their
 arms and march'd back prisoners of war.

They were the glory of the race of rangers,   880
Matchless with horse, rifle, song, supper, courtship,
Large, turbulent, generous, handsome, proud, and affectionate,
Bearded, sunburnt, drest in the free costume of hunters,
Not a single one over thirty years of age.

The second First-day morning they were brought out in squads and massacred,
 it was beautiful early summer,   885
The work commenced about five o'clock and was over by eight.

None obey'd the command to kneel,
Some made a mad and helpless rush, some stood stark and straight,
A few fell at once, shot in the temple or heart, the living and dead lay together,
The maim'd and mangled dug in the dirt, the new-comers saw them there,   890
Some half-kill'd attempted to crawl away,
These were despatch'd with bayonets or batter'd with the blunts of muskets,
A youth not seventeen years old seiz'd his assassin till two more came to release
 him,
The three were all torn and cover'd with the boy's blood.

At eleven o'clock began the burning of the bodies;   895
That is the tale of the murder of the four hundred and twelve young men.

35

Would you hear of an old-time sea-fight?
Would you learn who won by the light of the moon and stars?
List to the yarn, as my grandmother's father the sailor told it to me.

Our foe was no skulk in his ship I tell you, (said he,)   900
His was the surly English pluck, and there is no tougher or truer, and never was,
 and never will be;
Along the lower'd eve he came horribly raking us.

We closed with him, the yards entangled, the cannon touch'd,
My captain lash'd fast with his own hands.

We had receiv'd some eighteen pound shots under the water,   905
On our lower-gun-deck two large pieces had burst at the first fire, killing all
    around and blowing up overhead.

Fighting at sun-down, fighting at dark,
Ten o'clock at night, the full moon well up, our leaks on the gain, and five feet
    of water reported,
The master-at-arms loosing the prisoners confined in the after-hold to give them
    a chance for themselves.

The transit to and from the magazine is now stopt by the sentinels,   910
They see so many strange faces they do not know whom to trust.

Our frigate takes fire,
The other asks if we demand quarter?
If our colors are struck and the fighting done?

Now I laugh content, for I hear the voice of my little captain,   915
We have not struck, he composedly cries, *we have just begun our part of the*
    fighting.

Only three guns are in use,
One is directed by the captain himself against the enemy's mainmast,
Two well serv'd with grape and canister silence his musketry and clear his decks.

The tops alone second the fire of this little battery, especially the main-top,   920
They hold out bravely during the whole of the action.

Not a moment's cease,
The leaks gain fast on the pumps, the fire eats toward the powder-magazine.

One of the pumps has been shot away, it is generally thought we are sinking.

Serene stands the little captain,   925
He is not hurried, his voice is neither high nor low,
His eyes give more light to us than our battle-lanterns.

Toward twelve there in the beams of the moon they surrender to us.

36

Stretch'd and still lies the midnight,
Two great hulls motionless on the breast of the darkness,   930
Our vessel riddled and slowly sinking, preparations to pass to the one we have
    conquer'd,
The captain on the quarter-deck coldly giving his orders through a countenance
    white as a sheet,
Near by the corpse of the child that serv'd in the cabin,
The dead face of an old salt with long white hair and carefully curl'd whiskers,

The flames spite of all that can be done flickering aloft and below,   935
The husky voices of the two or three officers yet fit for duty,
Formless stacks of bodies and bodies by themselves, dabs of flesh upon the masts
    and spars,
Cut of cordage, dangle of rigging, slight shock of the soothe of waves,
Black and impassive guns, litter of powder-parcels, strong scent,
A few large stars overhead, silent and mournful shining,   940
Delicate sniffs of sea-breeze, smells of sedgy grass and fields by the shore,
    death-messages given in charge to survivors,
The hiss of the surgeon's knife, the gnawing teeth of his saw,
Wheeze, cluck, swash of falling blood, short wild scream, and long, dull,
    tapering groan,
These so, these irretrievable.

37

You laggards there on guard! look to your arms!   945
In at the conquer'd doors they crowd! I am possess'd!
Embody all presences outlaw'd or suffering,
See myself in prison shaped like another man,
And feel the dull unintermitted pain.

For me the keepers of convicts shoulder their carbines and keep watch,   950
It is I let out in the morning and barr'd at night.

Not a mutineer walks handcuff'd to jail but I am handcuff'd to him and walk
    by his side,
(I am less the jolly one there, and more the silent one with sweat on my
    twitching lips.)

Not a youngster is taken for larceny but I go up too, and am tried and
    sentenced.

Not a cholera patient lies at the last gasp but I also lie at the last gasp,   955
My face is ash-color'd, my sinews gnarl, away from me people retreat.

Askers embody themselves in me and I am embodied in them,
I project my hat, sit shame-faced, and beg.

38

Enough! enough! enough!
Somehow I have been stunn'd. Stand back!   960
Give me a little time beyond my cuff'd head, slumbers, dreams, gaping,
I discover myself on the verge of a usual mistake.

That I could forget the mockers and insults!
That I could forget the trickling tears and the blows of the bludgeons and
    hammers!

That I could look with a separate look on my own crucifixion and bloody
　　crowning.　　　　　　　　　　　　　　　　　　　　　　　　　　　　965

I remember now,
I resume the overstaid fraction,
The grave of rock multiplies what has been confided to it, or to any graves,
Corpses rise, gashes heal, fastenings roll from me.

I troop forth replenish'd with supreme power, one of an average unending
　　procession,　　　　　　　　　　　　　　　　　　　　　　　　　　970
Inland and sea-coast we go, and pass all boundary lines,
Our swift ordinances on their way over the whole earth,
The blossoms we wear in our hats the growth of thousands of years.

Eleves,[16] I salute you! come forward!
Continue your annotations, continue your questionings.　　　　　　　975

39

The friendly and flowing savage, who is he?
Is he waiting for civilization, or past it and mastering it?

Is he some Southwesterner rais'd out-doors? is he Kanadian?
Is he from the Mississippi country? Iowa, Oregon, California?
The mountains? prairie-life, bush-life? or sailor from the sea?　　　980

Wherever he goes men and women accept and desire him,
They desire he should like them, touch them, speak to them, stay with them.

Behavior lawless as snow-flakes, words simple as grass, uncomb'd head, laughter,
　　and naivetè,
Slow-stepping feet, common features, common modes and emanations,
They descend in new forms from the tips of his fingers,　　　　　　985
They are wafted with the odor of his body or breath, they fly out of the glance
　　of his eyes.

40

Flaunt of the sunshine I need not your bask—lie over!
You light surfaces only, I force surfaces and depths also.

Earth! you seem to look for something at my hands,
Say, old top-knot,[17] what do you want?　　　　　　　　　　　　　990

Man or woman, I might tell how I like you, but cannot,
And might tell what it is in me and what it is in you, but cannot,

---

[16] Pupils or disciples (from French *élève*:
　"student").

[17] An Indian.

And might tell that pining I have, that pulse of my nights and days.

Behold, I do not give lectures or a little charity,
When I give I give myself.   995

You there, impotent, loose in the knees,
Open your scarf'd chops till I blow grit within you,
Spread your palms and lift the flaps of your pockets,
I am not to be denied, I compel, I have stores plenty and to spare,
And any thing I have I bestow.   1000

I do not ask who you are, that is not important to me,
You can do nothing and be nothing but what I will infold you.

To cotton-field drudge or cleaner of privies I lean,
On his right cheek I put the family kiss,
And in my soul I swear I never will deny him.   1005

On women fit for conception I start bigger and nimbler babes,
(This day I am jetting the stuff of far more arrogant republics.)

To any one dying, thither I speed and twist the knob of the door,
Turn the bed-clothes toward the foot of the bed,
Let the physician and the priest go home.   1010

I seize the descending man and raise him with resistless will,
O despairer, here is my neck,
By God, you shall not go down! hang your whole weight upon me.

I dilate you with tremendous breath, I buoy you up,
Every room of the house do I fill with an arm'd force,   1015
Lovers of me, bafflers of graves.

Sleep—I and they keep guard all night,
Not doubt, not decease shall dare to lay finger upon you,
I have embraced you, and henceforth possess you to myself,
And when you rise in the morning you will find what I tell you is so.   1020

41

I am he bringing help for the sick as they pant on their backs,
And for strong upright men I bring yet more needed help.
I heard what was said of the universe,
Heard it and heard it of several thousand years;
It is middling well as far as it goes—but is that all?   1025

Magnifying and applying come I,
Outbidding at the start the old cautious hucksters,
Taking myself the exact dimensions of Jehovah,

Lithographing Kronos, Zeus his son, and Hercules[18] his grandson,
Buying drafts of Osiris, Isis,[19] Belus, Brahma,[20] Buddha,[21]   1030
In my portfolio placing Manito[22] loose, Allah[23] on a leaf, the crucifix engraved,
With Odin[24] and the hideous-faced Mexitli[25] and every idol and image,
Taking them all for what they are worth and not a cent more,
Admitting they were alive and did the work of their days,
(They bore mites as for unfledg'd birds who have now to rise and fly and sing
　　for themselves,)   1035
Accepting the rough deific sketches to fill out better in myself, bestowing them
　　freely on each man and woman I see,
Discovering as much or more in a framer framing a house,
Putting higher claims for him there with his roll'd-up sleeves driving the mallet
　　and chisel,
Not objecting to special revelations, considering a curl of smoke or a hair on
　　the back of my hand just as curious as any revelation,
Lads ahold of fire-engines and hook-and-ladder ropes no less to me than the
　　gods of the antique wars,   1040
Minding their voices peal through the crash of destruction,
Their brawny limbs passing safe over charr'd laths, their white foreheads whole
　　and unhurt out of the flames;
By the mechanic's wife with her babe at her nipple interceding for every person
　　born,
Three scythes at harvest whizzing in a row from three lusty angels with shirts
　　bagg'd out at their waists,
The snag-tooth'd hostler with red hair redeeming sins past and to come,   1045
Selling all he possesses, traveling on foot to fee lawyers for his brother and sit
　　by him while he is tried for forgery;
What was strewn in the amplest strewing the square rod about me, and not
　　filling the square rod then,
The bull and the bug never worshipp'd half enough,
Dung and dirt more admirable than was dream'd,
The supernatural of no account, myself waiting my time to be one of the
　　supremes,   1050
The day getting ready for me when I shall do as much good as the best, and
　　be as prodigious;
By my life-lumps! becoming already a creator,
Putting myself here and now to the ambush'd womb of the shadows.

42

A call in the midst of the crowd,
My own voice, orotund sweeping and final.   1055

---

[18] Kronos; Zeus; Hercules: divinities in Greek
　　mythology.
[19] Osiris; Isis: Egyptian deities.
[20] Belus; Brahma: Hindu gods.
[21] Indian religious leader ("the Enlightened
　　One").

[22] Algonquin Indian nature spirit.
[23] Moslem supreme being.
[24] Norse god of war.
[25] Aztec god of war.

Come my children,
Come my boys and girls, my women, household and intimates,
Now the performer launches his nerve, he has pass'd his prelude on the reeds |
    within.

Easily written loose-finger'd chords—I feel the thrum of your climax and close.

My head slues round on my neck,   1060
Music rolls, but not from the organ,
Folks are around me, but they are no household of mine.

Ever the hard unsunk ground,
Ever the eaters and drinkers, ever the upward and downward sun, ever the air
    and the ceaseless tides,
Ever myself and my neighbors, refreshing, wicked, real,   1065
Ever the old inexplicable query, ever that thorn'd thumb, that breath of itches
    and thirsts,
Ever the vexer's *hoot! hoot!* till we find where the sly one hides and bring him
    forth,
Ever love, ever the sobbing liquid of life,
Ever the bandage under the chin, ever the trestles of death.

Here and there with dimes on the eyes walking,   1070
To feed the greed of the belly the brains liberally spooning,
Tickets buying, taking, selling, but in to the feast never once going.
Many sweating, ploughing, thrashing, and then the chaff for payment receiving,
A few idly owning, and they the wheat continually claiming.

This is the city and I am one of the citizens,   1075
Whatever interests the rest interests me, politics, wars, markets, newspapers,
    schools,
The mayor and councils, banks, tariffs, steamships, factories, stocks, stores,
    real estate and personal estate.

The little plentiful manikins skipping around in collars and tail'd coats,

I am aware who they are, (they are positively not worms or fleas,)
I acknowledge the duplicates of myself, the weakest and shallowest is deathless
    with me,   1080
What I do and say the same waits for them,
Every thought that flounders in me the same flounders in them.

I know perfectly well my own egotism,
Know my omnivorous lines and must not write any less,
And would fetch you whoever you are flush with myself.   1085

Not words of routine this song of mine,
But abruptly to question, to leap beyond yet nearer bring;
This printed and bound book—but the printer and the printing-office boy?

The well-taken photographs—but your wife or friend close and solid in your
    arms?
The black ship mail'd with iron, her mighty guns in her turrets—but the pluck
    of the captain and engineers?   1090
In the houses the dishes and fare and furniture—but the host and hostess, and
    the look out of their eyes?
The sky up there—yet here or next door, or across the way?
The saints and sages in history—but you yourself?
Sermons, creeds, theology—but the fathomless human brain,
And what is reason? and what is love? and what is life?   1095

43

I do not despise you priests, all time, the world over,
My faith is the greatest of faiths and the least of faiths,
Enclosing worship ancient and modern and all between ancient and modern,
Believing I shall come again upon the earth after five thousand years,
Waiting responses from oracles, honoring the gods, saluting the sun,   1100
Making a fetich of the first rock or stump, powowing with sticks in the circle
    of obis,[26]
Helping the llama[27] or brahmin as he trims the lamps of the idols,
Dancing yet through the streets in a phallic procession, rapt and austere in the
    woods a gymnosophist,[28]
Drinking mead from the skull-cup, to Shastas[29] and Vedas admirant,
    minding the Koran,
Walking the teokallis,[30] spotted with gore from the stone and knife,
    beating the serpent-skin drum,   1105
Accepting the Gospels, accepting him that was crucified, knowing assuredly that
    he is divine,
To the mass kneeling or the puritan's prayer rising, or sitting patiently in a pew,
Ranting and frothing in my insane crisis, or waiting deadlike till my spirit
    arouses me,
Looking forth on pavement and land, or outside of pavement and land,
Belonging to the winders of the circuit of circuits.   1110

One of that centripetal and centrifugal gang I turn and talk like a man leaving
    charges before a journey.

Down-hearted doubters dull and excluded,
Frivolous, sullen, moping, angry, affected, dishearten'd, atheistical,
I know every one of you, I know the sea of torment, doubt, despair and unbelief.

How the flukes splash!   1115
How they contort rapid as lightning, with spasms and spouts of blood!

---

[26] i.e., obeah, referring to West African witch-
    craft and sorcery.
[27] i.e., lama, a Buddhist monk.
[28] Hindu ascetic.

[29] i.e., Shastras, Hindu sacred writings (cf. the
    Vedas).
[30] Aztec temples.

Be at peace bloody flukes of doubters and sullen mopers,
I take my place among you as much as among any,
The past is the push of you, me, all, precisely the same,
And what is yet untried and afterward is for you, me, all, precisely the same.   1120

I do not know what is untried and afterward,
But I know it will in its turn prove sufficient, and cannot fail.

Each who passes is consider'd, each who stops is consider'd, not a single one
    can it fail.

It cannot fail the young man who died and was buried,
Nor the young woman who died and was put by his side,   1125
Nor the little child that peep'd in at the door, and then drew back and was
    never seen again,
Nor the old man who has lived without purpose, and feels it with bitterness
    worse than gall,
Nor him in the poor house tubercled by rum and the bad disorder,
Nor the numberless slaughter'd and wreck'd, nor the brutish koboo[31] call'd
    the ordure of humanity,
Nor the sacs merely floating with open mouths for food to slip in,   1130
Nor any thing in the earth, or down in the oldest graves of the earth,
Nor any thing in the myriads of spheres, nor the myriads of myriads that
    inhabit them,
Nor the present, nor the least wisp that is known.

44

It is time to explain myself—let us stand up.

What is known I strip away,   1135
I launch all men and women forward with me into the Unknown.

The clock indicates the moment—but what does eternity indicate?

We have thus far exhausted trillions of winters and summers,
There are trillions ahead, and trillions ahead of them.

Births have brought us richness and variety,   1140
And other births will bring us richness and variety.

I do not call one greater and one smaller,
That which fills its period and place is equal to any.

Were mankind murderous or jealous upon you, my brother, my sister?

I am sorry for you, they are not murderous or jealous upon me,   1145

---

[31] Sumatran savage.

All has been gentle with me, I keep no account with lamentation,
(What have I to do with lamentation?)

I am an acme of things accomplish'd, and I an encloser of things to be.
My feet strike an apex of the apices of the stairs,
On every step bunches of ages, and larger bunches between the steps,   1150
All below duly travel'd, and still I mount and mount.

Rise after rise bow the phantoms behind me,
Afar down I see the huge first Nothing, I know I was even there,
I waited unseen and always, and slept through the lethargic mist,
And took my time, and took no hurt from the fetid carbon.   1155

Long I was hugg'd close—long and long.

Immense have been the preparations for me,
Faithful and friendly the arms that have help'd me.

Cycles ferried my cradle, rowing and rowing like cheerful boatmen,
For room to me stars kept aside in their own rings,   1160
They sent influences to look after what was to hold me.

Before I was born out of my mother generations guided me,
My embryo has never been torpid, nothing could overlay it.

For it the nebula cohered to an orb,
The long slow strata piled to rest it on,   1165
Vast vegetables gave it sustenance,
Monstrous sauroids[32] transported it in their mouths and deposited it
    with care.

All forces have been steadily employ'd to complete and delight me,
Now on this spot I stand with my robust soul.

45

O span of youth! ever-push'd elasticity!   1170
O manhood, balanced, florid and full.

My lovers suffocate me,
Crowding my lips, thick in the pores of my skin,
Jostling me through streets and public halls, coming naked to me at night,
Crying by day *Ahoy!* from the rocks of the river, swinging and chirping over
    my head,   1175

---

[32] Prehistoric reptiles.

Calling my name from flower-beds, vines, tangled underbrush.
Lighting on every moment of my life,
Bussing my body with soft balsamic busses,
Noiselessly passing handfuls out of their hearts and giving them to be mine.

Old age superbly rising! O welcome, ineffable grace of dying days!   1180

Every condition promulges not only itself, it promulges[33] what grows after
    and out of itself,
And the dark hush promulges as much as any.

I open my scuttle at night and see the far-sprinkled systems,
And all I see multiplied as high as I can cipher edge but the rim of the farther
    systems.

Wider and wider they spread, expanding, always expanding,   1185
Outward and outward and forever outward.

My sun has his sun and round him obediently wheels,
He joins with his partners a group of superior circuit,
And greater sets follow, making specks of the greatest inside them.

There is no stoppage and never can be stoppage,   1190
If I, you, and the worlds, and all beneath or upon their surfaces, were this
    moment reduced back to a pallid float, it would not avail in the long run,
We should surely bring up again where we now stand,
And surely go as much farther, and then farther and farther.

A few quadrillions of eras, a few octillions of cubic leagues, do not hazard the
    span or make it impatient,   1195
They are but parts, any thing is but a part.

See ever so far, there is limitless space outside of that,
Count ever so much, there is limitless time around that.

My rendezvous is appointed, it is certain,
The Lord will be there and wait till I come on perfect terms,   1200
The great Camerado, the lover true for whom I pine will be there.

46

I know I have the best of time and space, and was never measured and never
    will be measured.

I tramp a perpetual journey, (come listen all!)
My signs are a rain-proof coat, good shoes, and a staff cut from the woods,

---

[33] Promulgates.

No friend of mine takes his ease in my chair,   1205
I have no chair, no church, no philosophy,
I lead no man to a dinner-table, library, exchange,
But each man and each woman of you I lead upon a knoll,
My left hand hooking you round the waist,
My right hand pointing to landscapes of continents and the public road.   1210

Not I, not any one else can travel that road for you,
You must travel it for yourself.

It is not far, it is within reach,
Perhaps you have been on it since you were born and did not know,
Perhaps it is everywhere on water and on land.   1215

Shoulder your duds dear son, and I will mine, and let us hasten forth,
Wonderful cities and free nations we shall fetch as we go.

If you tire, give me both burdens, and rest the chuff[34] of your hand on my hip,
And in due time you shall repay the same service to me,
For after we start we never lie by again.   1220

This day before dawn I ascended a hill and look'd at the crowded heaven,
And I said to my spirit *When we become the enfolders of those orbs, and the*
     pleasure and knowledge of every thing in them, shall we be fill'd and satisfied then?
And my spirit said *No, we but level that lift to pass and continue beyond.*

You are also asking me questions and I hear you,
I answer that I cannot answer, you must find out for yourself.   1225

Sit a while dear son,
Here are biscuits to eat and here is milk to drink,
But as soon as you sleep and renew yourself in sweet clothes, I kiss you with
     a good-by kiss and open the gate for your egress hence.

Long enough have you dream'd contemptible dreams,
Now I wash the gum from your eyes,   1230
You must habit yourself to the dazzle of the light and of every moment of
     your life.

Long have you timidly waded holding a plank by the shore,
Now I will you to be a bold swimmer,
To jump off in the midst of the sea, rise again, nod to me, shout, and laughingly dash
     with your hair.

---

[34] Heel.

47

I am the teacher of athletes,   1235
He that by me spreads a wider breast than my own proves the width of my
    own,
He most honors my style who learns under it to destroy the teacher.

The boy I love, the same becomes a man not through derived power, but in
    his own right,
Wicked rather than virtuous out of conformity or fear,
Fond of his sweetheart, relishing well his steak,   1240
Unrequited love or a slight cutting him worse than sharp steel cuts,
First-rate to ride, to fight, to hit the bull's eye, to sail a skiff, to sing a song or
    play on the banjo,
Preferring scars and the beard and faces pitted with smallpox over all latherers,
And those well-tann'd to those that keep out of the sun.

I teach straying from me, yet who can stray from me?   1245
I follow you whoever you are from the present hour
My words itch at your ears till you understand them.

I do not say these things for a dollar or to fill up the time while I wait for a
    boat,
(It is you talking just as much as myself, I act as the tongue of you,
Tied in your mouth, in mine it begins to be loosen'd.)   1250

I swear I will never again mention love or death inside a house,
And I swear I will never translate myself at all, only to him or her who privately
    stays with me in the open air.

If you would understand me go to the heights or water-shore,
The nearest gnat is an explanation, and a drop or motion of waves a key,
The maul, the oar, the hand-saw, second my words.   1255

No shutter'd room or school can commune with me,
But roughs and little children better than they.

The young mechanic is closest to me, he knows me well,
The woodman that takes his axe and jug with him shall take me with him all
    day,
The farm-boy ploughing in the field feels good at the sound of my voice,   1260
In vessels that sail my words sail, I go with fishermen and seamen and love them.

The soldier camp'd or upon the march is mine,
On the night ere the pending battle many seek me, and I do not fail them,
On that solemn night (it may be their last) those that know me seek me.

My face rubs to the hunter's face when he lies down alone in his blanket,   1265
The driver thinking of me does not mind the jolt of his wagon,
The young mother and old mother comprehend me,

The girl and the wife rest the needle a moment and forget where they are,
They and all would resume what I have told them.

48

I have said that the soul is not more than the body,   1270
And I have said that the body is not more than the soul,
And nothing, not God, is greater to one than one's self is,
And whoever walks a furlong without sympathy walks to his own funeral drest
    in his shroud,
And I or you pocketless of a dime may purchase the pick of the earth,
And to glance with an eye or show a bean in its pod confounds the learning of
    all times,   1275
And there is no trade or employment but the young man following it may
    become a hero,
And there is no object so soft but it makes a hub for the wheel'd universe,
And I say to any man or woman, Let your soul stand cool and composed before
    a million universes.

And I say to mankind, Be not curious about God,
For I who am curious about each am not curious about God,   1280
(No array of terms can say how much I am at peace about God and about
    death.)

I hear and behold God in every object, yet understand God not in the least,
Nor do I understand who there can be more wonderful than myself.

Why should I wish to see God better than this day?
I see something of God each hour of the twenty-four, and each moment then,   1285
In the faces of men and women I see God, and in my own face in the glass,
I find letters from God dropt in the street, and every one is sign'd by God's
    name,
And I leave them where they are, for I know that wheresoe'er I go,
Others will punctually come for ever and ever.

49   *Death*

And as to you Death, and you bitter hug of mortality, it is idle to try to alarm
    me.   1290

To his work without flinching the accoucheur[35] comes,
I see the elder-hand pressing receiving supporting,
I recline by the sills of the exquisite flexible doors,
And mark the outlet, and mark the relief and escape.   *• reincarnation / natural way*

And as to you Corpse I think you are good manure, but that does not offend
    me,   1295

---

[35] Midwife.

I smell the white roses sweet-scented and growing,
I reach to the leafy lips, I reach to the polish'd breasts of melons.

And as to you Life I reckon you are the leavings of many deaths,
(No doubt I have died myself ten thousand times before.)

I hear you whispering there O stars of heaven,   1300
O suns—O grass of graves—O perpetual transfers and promotions,
If you do not say any thing how can I say any thing?

Of the turbid pool that lies in the autumn forest,
Of the moon that descends the steeps of the soughing twilight,
Toss, sparkles of day and dusk—toss on the black stems that decay in the muck,   1305
Toss to the moaning gibberish of the dry limbs.

I ascend from the moon, I ascend from the night,
I perceive that the ghastly glimmer is noonday sunbeams reflected,
And debouch to the steady and central from the offspring great or small.

descending - death

50

There is that in me—I do not know what it is—but I know it is in me.   1310

Wrench'd and sweaty—calm and cool then my body becomes,
I sleep—I sleep long.

I do not know it—it is without name—it is a word unsaid,
It is not in any dictionary, utterance, symbol.

Something it swings on more than the earth I swing on,   1315
To it the creation is the friend whose embracing awakes me.

Perhaps I might tell more. Outlines! I plead for my brothers and sisters.

Do you see O my brothers and sisters?
It is not chaos or death—it is form, union, plan—it is eternal life—it is Happiness.

fine

(51)

The past and present wilt—I have fill'd them, emptied them,   1320
And proceed to fill my next fold of the future.

Listener up there! what have you to confide to me?
Look in my face while I snuff the sidle of evening,
(Talk honestly, no one else hears you, and I stay only a minute longer.)

Do I contradict myself?   1325
Very well then I contradict myself,

(I am large, I contain multitudes.)
I concentrate toward them that are night, I wait on the door-slab.

Who has done his day's work? who will soonest be through with his supper?
Who wishes to walk with me?   1330

Will you speak before I am gone? will you prove already too late?

52

The spotted hawk swoops by and accuses me, he complains of my gab and my
   loitering.

I too am not a bit tamed, I too am untranslatable,
I sound my barbaric yawp over the roofs of the world.

The last scud of day holds back for me,   1335
It flings my likeness after the rest and true as any on the shadow'd wilds,
It coaxes me to the vapor and the dusk.

I depart as air, I shake my white locks at the runaway sun,
I effuse my flesh in eddies, and drift it in lacy jags.

I bequeath myself to the dirt to grow from the grass I love,   1340
If you want me again look for me under your boot-soles.

You will hardly know who I am or what I mean,
But I shall be good health to you nevertheless,
And filter and fibre your blood.

Failing to fetch me at first keep encouraged,   1345
Missing me one place search another,
I stop somewhere waiting for you.
1855

from **Children of Adam**

*I Sing the Body Electric**

1

I sing the body electric,
The armies of those I love engirth me and I engirth them,
They will not let me off till I go with them, respond to them,
And discorrupt them, and charge them full with the charge of the soul.

* Untitled when first published in the 1855
   edition of *Leaves of Grass*.

Was it doubted that those who corrupt their own bodies conceal themselves?   5
And if those who defile the living are as bad as they who defile the dead?
And if the body does not do fully as much as the soul?
And if the body were not the soul, what is the soul?

2

The love of the body of man or woman balks account, the body itself balks
    account,
That of the male is perfect, and that of the female is perfect.   10

The expression of the face balks account,
But the expression of a well-made man appears not only in his face,
It is in his limbs and joints also, it is curiously in the joints of his hips and wrists,
It is in his walk, the carriage of his neck, the flex of his waist and knees, dress
    does not hide him,
The strong sweet quality he has strikes through the cotton and broadcloth,   15
To see him pass conveys as much as the best poem, perhaps more,
You linger to see his back, and the back of his neck and shoulder-side.

The sprawl and fulness of babes, the bosoms and heads of women, the folds
    of their dress, their style as we pass in the street, the contour of their shape
    downwards,
The swimmer naked in the swimming-bath, seen as he swims through the
    transparent green-shine, or lies with his face up and rolls silently to and fro
    in the heave of the water,
The bending forward and backward of rowers in row-boats, the horseman in
    his saddle,   20
Girls, mothers, house-keepers, in all their performances,
The group of laborers seated at noon-time with their open dinner-kettles, and
    their wives waiting,
The female soothing a child, the farmer's daughter in the garden or cow-yard,
The young fellow hoeing corn, the sleigh-driver driving his six horses through
    the crowd,
The wrestle of wrestlers, two apprentice-boys, quite grown, lusty, good-natured,
    native-born, out on the vacant lot at sundown after work,   25
The coats and caps thrown down, the embrace of love and resistance,
The upper-hold and under-hold, the hair rumpled over and blinding the eyes;
The march of firemen in their own costumes, the play of masculine muscle
    through clean-setting trowsers and waist-straps,
The slow return from the fire, the pause when the bell strikes suddenly again,
    and the listening on the alert,
The natural, perfect, varied attitudes, the bent head, the curv'd neck and the
    counting;   30
Such-like I love—I loosen myself, pass freely, am at the mother's breast with
    the little child,

Swim with the swimmers, wrestle with wrestlers, march in line with the firemen,
    and pause, listen, count.

3

I knew a man, a common farmer, the father of five sons,
And in them the fathers of sons, and in them the fathers of sons.

This man was of wonderful vigor, calmness, beauty of person,   35
The shape of his head, the pale yellow and white of his hair and beard, the
    immeasurable meaning of his black eyes, the richness and breadth of his
    manners,
These I used to go and visit him to see, he was wise also,
He was six feet tall, he was over eighty years old, his sons were massive, clean,
    bearded, tan-faced, handsome,
They and his daughters loved him, all who saw him loved him,
They did not love him by allowance, they loved him with personal love,   40
He drank water only, the blood show'd like scarlet through the clear-brown
    skin of his face,
He was a frequent gunner and fisher, he sail'd his boat himself, he had a fine
    one presented to him by a ship-joiner, he had fowling-pieces presented to
    him by men that loved him,
When he went with his five sons and many grand-sons to hunt or fish, you
    would pick him out as the most beautiful and vigorous of the gang,
You would wish long and long to be with him, you would wish to sit by him
    in the boat that you and he might touch each other.

4

I have perceiv'd that to be with those I like is enough,   45
To stop in company with the rest at evening is enough,
To be surrounded by beautiful, curious, breathing, laughing flesh is enough,
To pass among them or touch any one, or rest my arm ever so lightly round
    his or her neck for a moment, what is this then?
I do not ask any more delight, I swim in it as in a sea.

There is something in staying close to men and women and looking on them,
    and in the contact and odor of them, that pleases the soul well,   50
All things please the soul, but these please the soul well.

5

This is the female form,
A divine nimbus exhales from it from head to foot,
It attracts with fierce undeniable attraction,
I am drawn by its breath as if I were no more than a helpless vapor, all falls
    aside but myself and it,   55

Books, art, religion, time, the visible and solid earth, and what was expected
 of heaven or fear'd of hell, are now consumed,
Mad filaments, ungovernable shoots play out of it, the response likewise
 ungovernable,
Hair, bosom, hips, bend of legs, negligent falling hands all diffused, mine too
 diffused,
Ebb stung by the flow and flow stung by the ebb, love-flesh swelling and
 deliciously aching,
Limitless limpid jets of love hot and enormous, quivering jelly of love,
 white-blow and delirious juice,   60
Bridegroom night of love working surely and softly into the prostrate dawn,
Undulating into the willing and yielding day,
Lost in the cleave of the clasping and sweet-flesh'd day.
This the nucleus—after the child is born of woman, man is born of woman,
This the bath of birth, this the merge of small and large, and the outlet again.   65

Be not ashamed women, your privilege encloses the rest, and is the exit of the
 rest,
You are the gates of the body, and you are the gates of the soul.

The female contains all qualities and tempers them,
She is in her place and moves with perfect balance,
She is all things duly veil'd, she is both passive and active,   70
She is to conceive daughters as well as sons, and sons as well as daughters.

As I see my soul reflected in Nature,
As I see through a mist, One with inexpressible completeness, sanity, beauty,
See the bent head and arms folded over the breast, the Female I see.

6

The male is not less the soul nor more, he too is in his place,   75
He too is all qualities, he is action and power,
The flush of the known universe is in him,
Scorn becomes him well, and appetite and defiance become him well,
The wildest largest passions, bliss that is utmost, sorrow that is utmost become
 him well, pride is for him,
The full-spread pride of man is calming and excellent to the soul,   80
Knowledge becomes him, he likes it always, he brings every thing to the test of
 himself,
Whatever the survey, whatever the sea and the sail he strikes soundings at last
 only here,
(Where else does he strike soundings except here?)

The man's body is sacred and the woman's body is sacred,
No matter who it is, it is sacred—is it the meanest one in the laborers' gang?   85
Is it one of the dull-faced immigrants just landed on the wharf?
Each belongs here or anywhere just as much as the well-off, just as much as you,
Each has his or her place in the procession.

(All is a procession,
The universe is a procession with measured and perfect motion.)   90

Do you know so much yourself that you call the meanest ignorant?
Do you suppose you have a right to a good sight, and he or she has no right
    to a sight?
Do you think matter has cohered together from its diffuse float, and the soil is
    on the surface, and water runs and vegetation sprouts,
For you only, and not for him and her?

7

A man's body at auction,   95
(For before the war I often go to the slave-mart and watch the sale,)
I help the auctioneer, the sloven does not half know his business.

Gentlemen look on this wonder,
Whatever the bids of the bidders they cannot be high enough for it,
For it the globe lay preparing quintillions of years without one animal or plant,   100
For it the revolving cycles truly and steadily roll'd.

In this head the all-baffling brain,
In it and below it the makings of heroes.

Examine these limbs, red, black, or white, they are cunning in tendon and
    nerve,
They shall be stript that you may see them.   105

Exquisite senses, life-lit eyes, pluck, volition,
Flakes of breast-muscle, pliant backbone and neck, flesh not flabby, good-sized
    arms and legs,
And wonders within there yet.

Within there runs blood,
The same old blood! the same red-running blood!   110
There swells and jets a heart, there all passions, desires, reachings, aspirations,
(Do you think they are not there because they are not express'd in parlors
    and lecture-rooms?)

This is not only one man, this the father of those who shall be fathers in their
    turns,
In him the start of populous states and rich republics,
Of him countless immortal lives with countless embodiments and enjoyments.   115

How do you know who shall come from the offspring of his offspring through
    the centuries?
(Who might you find you have come from yourself, if you could trace back
    through the centuries?)

8

A woman's body at auction,
She too is not only herself, she is the teeming mother of mothers,
She is the bearer of them that shall grow and be mates to the mothers.   120

Have you ever loved the body of a woman?
Have you ever loved the body of a man?
Do you not see that these are exactly the same to all in all nations and times
    all over the earth?

If any thing is sacred the human body is sacred,
And the glory and sweet of a man is the token of manhood untainted,   125
And in man or woman a clean, strong, firm-fibred body, is more beautiful than
    the most beautiful face.

Have you seen the fool that corrupted his own live body? or the fool that
    corrupted her own live body?
For they do not conceal themselves, and cannot conceal themselves.

9

O my body! I dare not desert the likes of you in other men and women, nor
    the likes of the parts of you,
I believe the likes of you are to stand or fall with the likes of the soul, (and
    that they are the soul,)   130
I believe the likes of you shall stand or fall with my poems, and that they are
    my poems,
Man's, woman's, child's, youth's, wife's, husband's, mother's, father's, young
    man's, young woman's poems,
Head, neck, hair, ears, drop and tympan of the ears,
Eyes, eye-fringes, iris of the eye, eyebrows, and the waking or sleeping of the
    lids,
Mouth, tongue, lips, teeth, roof of the mouth, jaws, and the jaw-hinges,   135
Nose, nostrils of the nose, and the partition,
Cheeks, temples, forehead, chin, throat, back of the neck, neck-slue,
Strong shoulders, manly beard, scapula, hind-shoulders, and the ample
    side-round of the chest,
Upper-arm, armpit, elbow-socket, lower-arm, arm-sinews, arm-bones,
Wrist and wrist-joints, hand, palm, knuckles, thumb, forefinger, finger-joints,
    finger-nails,   140
Broad breast-front, curling hair of the breast, breast-bone, breast-side,
Ribs, belly, backbone, joints of the backbone,
Hips, hip-sockets, hip-strength, inward and outward round, man-balls,
    man-root,
Strong set of thighs, well carrying the trunk above,
Leg-fibres, knee, knee-pan, upper-leg, under-leg,   145

Ankles, instep, foot-ball, toes, toe-joints, the heel;
All attitudes, all the shapeliness, all the belongings of my or your body or of
    any one's body, male or female,
The lung-sponges, the stomach-sac, the bowels sweet and clean,
The brain in its folds inside the skull-frame,
Sympathies, heart-valves, palate-valves, sexuality, maternity,   150
Womanhood, and all that is a woman, and the man that comes from woman,
The womb, the teats, nipples, breast-milk, tears, laughter, weeping, love-looks,
    love-perturbations and risings,
The voice, articulation, language, whispering, shouting aloud,
Food, drink, pulse, digestion, sweat, sleep, walking, swimming,
Poise on the hips, leaping, reclining, embracing, arm-curving and tightening,   155
The continual changes of the flex of the mouth, and around the eyes,
The skin, the sunburnt shade, freckles, hair,
The curious sympathy one feels when feeling with the hand the naked meat of
    the body,
The circling rivers the breath, and breathing it in and out,
The beauty of the waist, and thence of the hips, and thence downward toward
    the knees,   160
The thin red jellies within you or within me, the bones and the marrow in
    the bones,
The exquisite realization of health;
O I say these are not the parts and poems of the body only, but of the soul,
O I say now these are the soul!
1855

Once I Pass'd Through a Populous City

Once I pass'd through a populous city imprinting my brain for future use with
    its shows, architecture, customs, traditions,
Yet now of all that city I remember only a woman I casually met there who
    detain'd me for love of me,
Day by day and night by night we were together—all else has long been forgotten
    by me,
I remember I say only that woman who passionately clung to me,
Again we wander, we love, we separate again,   5
Again she holds me by the hand, I must not go,
I see her close beside me with silent lips sad and tremulous.
1860

Facing West from California's Shores

Facing west from California's shores,
Inquiring, tireless, seeking what is yet unfound,
I, a child, very old, over waves, towards the house of maternity, the land of
    migrations, look afar,
Look off the shores of my Western sea, the circle almost circled;

For starting westward from Hindustan, from the vales of Kashmere,   5
From Asia, from the north, from the God, the sage, and the hero,
From the south, from the flowery peninsulas and the spice islands,
Long having wander'd since, round the earth having wander'd,
Now I face home again, very pleas'd and joyous,
(But where is what I started for so long ago?   10
And why is it yet unfound?)
1860

As Adam Early in the Morning

As Adam early in the morning,
Walking forth from the bower refresh'd with sleep,
Behold me where I pass, hear my voice, approach,
Touch me, touch the palm of your hand to my body as I pass,
Be not afraid of my body.   5
1861

from Calamus

I Saw in Louisiana a Live-Oak Growing

I saw in Louisiana a live-oak growing,
All alone stood it and the moss hung down from the branches,
Without any companion it grew there uttering joyous leaves of dark green,
And its look, rude, unbending, lusty, made me think of myself,
But I wonder'd how it could utter joyous leaves standing alone there without
    its friend near, for I knew I could not,   5
And I broke off a twig with a certain number of leaves upon it, and twined
    around it a little moss,
And brought it away, and I have placed it in sight in my room,
It is not needed to remind me as of my own dear friends,
(For I believe lately I think of little else than of them,)
Yet it remains to me a curious token, it makes me think of manly love;   10
For all that, and though the live-oak glistens there in Louisiana solitary in a
    wide flat space,
Uttering joyous leaves all its life without a friend a lover near,
I know very well I could not.
1860

Here the Frailest Leaves of Me

Here the frailest leaves of me and yet my strongest lasting,
Here I shade and expose my thoughts, I myself do not expose them,
And yet they expose me more than all my other poems.
1860

Crossing Brooklyn Ferry*

1

Flood-tide below me! I see you face to face!
Clouds of the west—sun there half an hour high—I see you also face to face.

Crowds of men and women attired in the usual costumes, how curious you are to me!
On the ferry-boats the hundreds and hundreds that cross, returning home, are more
    curious to me than you suppose,
And you that shall cross from shore to shore years hence are more to me, and more in
    my meditations, than you might suppose.   5

2

The impalpable sustenance of me from all things at all hours of the day,
The simple, compact, well-join'd scheme, myself disintegrated, every one
    disintegrated yet part of the scheme,
The similitudes of the past and those of the future,
The glories strung like beads on my smallest sights and hearings, on the walk in the
    street and the passage over the river,
The current rushing so swiftly and swimming with me far away,   10
The others that are to follow me, the ties between me and them,
The certainty of others, the life, love, sight, hearing of others.

Others will enter the gates of the ferry and cross from shore to shore,
Others will watch the run of the flood-tide,
Others will see the shipping of Manhattan north and west, and the heights
    of Brooklyn to the south and east,   15
Others will see the islands large and small;
Fifty years hence, others will see them as they cross, the sun half an hour high,
A hundred years hence, or ever so many hundred years hence, others will see
    them,
Will enjoy the sunset, the pouring-in of the flood-tide, the falling-back to the sea
    of the ebb-tide.

3

It avails not, time nor place—distance avails not,   20
I am with you, you men and women of a generation, or ever so many
    generations hence,
Just as you feel when you look on the river and sky, so I felt,
Just as any of you is one of a living crowd, I was one of a crowd,
Just as you are refresh'd by the gladness of the river and the bright flow, I was
    refresh'd,

* Titled "Sun-Down Poem" when first published in 1856.

Just as you stand and lean on the rail, yet hurry with the swift current, I stood
    yet was hurried,   25
Just as you look on the numberless masts of ships and the thick-stemm'd pipes
    of steamboats, I look'd.

I too many and many a time cross'd the river of old,
Watched the Twelfth-month[36] sea-gulls, saw them high in the air
    floating with motionless wings, oscillating their bodies,
Saw how the glistening yellow lit up parts of their bodies and left the rest in
    strong shadow,
Saw the slow-wheeling circles and the gradual edging toward the south,   30
Saw the reflection of the summer sky in the water,
Had my eyes dazzled by the shimmering track of beams,
Look'd at the fine centrifugal spokes of light round the shape of my head in the
    sunlit water,
Look'd on the haze on the hills southward and southwestward,
Look'd on the vapor as it flew in fleeces tinged with violet,   35
Look'd toward the lower bay to notice the vessels arriving,
Saw their approach, saw aboard those that were near me,
Saw the white sails of schooners and sloops, saw the ships at anchor,
The sailors at work in the rigging or out astride the spars,
The round masts, the swinging motion of the hulls, the slender serpentine
    pennants,   40
The large and small steamers in motion, the pilots in their pilot-houses,
The white wake left by the passage, the quick tremulous whirl of the wheels,
The flags of all nations, the falling of them at sunset,
The scallop-edged waves in the twilight, the ladled cups, the frolicsome crests
    and glistening,
The stretch afar growing dimmer and dimmer, the gray walls of the granite
    storehouses by the docks,   45
On the river the shadowy group, the big steam-tug closely flank'd on each side
    by the barges, the hay-boat, the belated lighter,
On the neighboring shore the fires from the foundry chimneys burning high
    and glaringly into the night,
Casting their flicker of black contrasted with wild red and yellow light over the
    tops of houses, and down into the clefts of streets.

4

These and all else were to me the same as they are to you,
I loved well those cities, loved well the stately and rapid river,   50
The men and women I saw were all near to me,

---

[36] December (Quaker style).

Others the same—others who look back on me because I look'd forward to them,
(The time will come, though I stop here to-day and to-night.)

5

What is it then between us?
What is the count of the scores or hundreds of years between us?   55

Whatever it is, it avails not—distance avails not, and place avails not,
I too lived, Brooklyn of ample hills was mine,
I too walk'd the streets of Manhattan island, and bathed in the waters around it,
I too felt the curious abrupt questionings stir within me,
In the day among crowds of people sometimes they came upon me,   60
In my walks home late at night or as I lay in my bed they came upon me,
I too had been struck from the float forever held in solution,
I too had receiv'd identity by my body,
That I was I knew was of my body, and what I should be I knew I should be
     of my body.

6

It is not upon you alone the dark patches fall,   65
The dark threw its patches down upon me also,
The best I had done seem'd to me blank and suspicious,
My great thoughts as I supposed them, were they not in reality meagre?
Nor is it you alone who know what it is to be evil,
I am he who knew what it was to be evil,   70
I too knotted the old knot of contrariety,
Blabb'd, blush'd, resented, lied, stole, grudg'd,
Had guile, anger, lust, hot wishes I dared not speak,
Was wayward, vain, greedy, shallow, sly, cowardly, malignant,
The wolf, the snake, the hog, not wanting in me,   75
The cheating look, the frivolous word, the adulterous wish, not wanting,
Refusals, hates, postponements, meanness, laziness, none of these wanting,
Was one with the rest, the days and haps of the rest,
Was call'd by my nighest name by clear loud voices of young men as they saw
     me approaching or passing,
Felt their arms on my neck as I stood, or the negligent leaning of their flesh
     against me as I sat,   80
Saw many I loved in the street or ferry-boat or public assembly, yet never told
     them a word,
Lived the same life with the rest, the same old laughing, gnawing, sleeping,
Play'd the part that still looks back on the actor or actress,
The same old role, the role that is what we make it, as great as we like,
Or as small as we like, or both great and small.   85

7

Closer yet I approach you,
What thought you have of me now, I had as much of you—I laid in my stores
    in advance,
I consider'd long and seriously of you before you were born.
Who was to know what should come home to me?
Who knows but I am enjoying this?   90
Who knows, for all the distance, but I am as good as looking at you now, for
    all you cannot see me?

8

Ah, what can ever be more stately and admirable to me than mast-hemm'd
    Manhattan?
River and sunset and scallop-edg'd waves of flood-tide?
The sea-gulls oscillating their bodies, the hat-boat in the twilight, and the
    belated lighter?
What gods can exceed these that clasp me by the hand, and with voices I love
    call me promptly and loudly by my nighest name as I approach?   95
What is more subtle than this which ties me to the woman or man that looks
    in my face?
Which fuses me into you now, and pours my meaning into you?

We understand then do we not?
What I promis'd without mentioning it, have you not accepted?
What the study could not teach—what the preaching could not accomplish is
    accomplish'd, is it not?   100

9

Flow on, river! flow with the flood-tide, and ebb with the ebb-tide!
Frolic on, crested and scallop-edg'd waves!
Gorgeous clouds of the sunset! drench with your splendor me, or the men and
    women generations after me!
Cross from shore to shore, countless crowds of passengers!
Stand up, tall masts of Mannahatta! stand up, beautiful hills of Brooklyn!   105
Throb, baffled and curious brain! throw out questions and answers!
Suspend here and everywhere, eternal float of solution!
Gaze, loving and thirsting eyes, in the house or street or public assembly!
Sound out, voices of young men! loudly and musically call me by my nighest
    name!
Live, old life! play the part that looks back on the actor or actress!   110
Play the old role, the role that is great or small according as one makes it!
Consider, you who peruse me, whether I may not in unknown ways be looking
    upon you;
Be firm, rail over the river, to support those who lean idly, yet haste with the
    hasting current;

Fly on, sea-birds! fly sideways, or wheel in large circles high in the air;
Receive the summer sky, you water, and faithfully hold it till all downcast eyes
    have time to take it from you!   115
Diverge, fine spokes of light, from the shape of my head, or any one's head, in
    the sunlit water!
Come on, ships from the lower bay! pass up or down, white-sail'd schooners,
    sloops, lighters!
Flaunt away, flags of all nations! be duly lower'd at sunset!
Burn high your fires, foundry chimneys! cast black shadows at nightfall! cast red
    and yellow light over the tops of the houses!
Appearances, now or henceforth, indicate what you are,   120
You necessary film, continue to envelop the soul,
About my body for me, and your body for you, be hung out divinest aromas,
Thrive, cities—bring your freight, bring your shows, ample and sufficient rivers,
Expand, being than which none else is perhaps more spiritual,
Keep your places, objects than which none else is more lasting.   125
You have waited, you always wait, you dumb, beautiful ministers,
We receive you with free sense at last, and are insatiate henceforward,
Not you any more shall be able to foil us, or withhold yourselves from us,
We use you, and do not cast you aside—we plant you permanently within us,
We fathom you not—we love you—there is perfection in you also,   130
You furnish your parts toward eternity,
Great or small, you furnish your parts toward the soul.
1856

from **Sea-Drift**

*Out of the Cradle Endlessly Rocking**

Out of the cradle endlessly rocking,
Out of the mocking-bird's throat, the musical shuttle,
Out of the Ninth-month[37] midnight,
Over the sterile sands and the fields beyond, where the child leaving his bed wander'd
    alone, bareheaded, barefoot,
Down from the shower'd halo,   5
Up from the mystic play of shadows twining and twisting as if they were alive,
Out from the patches of briers and blackberries,
From the memories of the bird that chanted to me,
From your memories sad brother, from the fitful risings and fallings I heard,
From under that yellow half-moon late-risen and swollen as if with tears,   10
From those beginning notes of yearning and love there in the mist,
From the thousand responses of my heart never to cease,
From the myriad thence-arous'd words,
From the word stronger and more delicious than any,

---

* Titled "A Child's Reminiscence" when first   [37] September (Quaker style).
  published in *Saturday Press* (New York),
  December 24, 1859.

From such as now they start the scene revisiting,   15
As a flock, twittering, rising, or overhead passing,
Borne hither, ere all eludes me, hurriedly,
A man, yet by these tears a little boy again,
Throwing myself on the sand, confronting the waves,
I, chanter of pains and joys, uniter of here and hereafter,   20
Taking all hints to use them, but swiftly leaping beyond them,
A reminiscence sing.

Once Paumanok,[38]
When the lilac-scent was in the air and Fifth-month[39] grass was growing,
Up this seashore in some briers,   25
Two feather'd guests from Alabama, two together,
And their nest, and four light-green eggs spotted with brown,
And every day the he-bird to and fro near at hand,
And every day the she-bird crouch'd on her nest, silent, with bright eyes,
And every day I, a curious boy, never too close, never disturbing them,   30
Cautiously peering, absorbing, translating.

Shine! shine! shine!
Pour down your warmth, great sun!
While we bask, we two together.

Two together!   35
Winds blow south, or winds blow north,
Day come white, or night come black,
Home, or rivers and mountains from home,
Singing all time, minding no time,
While we two keep together.   40

Till of a sudden,
May-be kill'd, unknown to her mate,
One forenoon the she-bird crouch'd not on the nest,
Nor return'd that afternoon, nor the next,
Nor ever appear'd again.   45

And thenceforward all summer in the sound of the sea,
And at night under the full of the moon in calmer weather,
Over the hoarse surging of the sea,
Or flitting from brier to brier by day,
I saw, I heard at intervals the remaining one, the he-bird,   50
The solitary guest from Alabama.

Blow! blow! blow!
Blow up sea-winds along Paumanok's shore;
I wait and I wait till you blow my mate to me.

[38] Algonquian Indian name for Long Island.   [39] May (Quaker style).

Yes, when the stars glisten'd,   55
All night long on the prong of a moss-scallop'd stake,
Down almost amid the slapping waves,
Sat the lone singer wonderful causing tears.

He call'd on his mate,
He pour'd forth the meanings which I of all men know.   60

Yes my brother I know,
The rest might not, but I have treasur'd every note,
For more than once dimly down to the beach gliding,
Silent, avoiding the moonbeams, blending myself with the shadows,
Recalling now the obscure shapes, the echoes, the sounds and sights after
      their sorts,   65
The white arms out in the breakers tirelessly tossing,
I, with bare feet, a child, the wind wafting my hair,
Listen'd long and long.

Listen'd to keep, to sing, now translating the notes,
Following you my brother.   70

Soothe! soothe! soothe!
Close on its wave soothes the wave behind,
And again another behind embracing and lapping, every one close,
But my love soothes not me, not me.

Low hangs the moon, it rose late,   75
It is lagging—O I think it is heavy with love, with love.

O madly the sea pushes upon the land,
With love, with love.

O night! do I not see my love fluttering out among the breakers?
What is that little black thing I see there in the white?   80

Loud! loud! loud!
Loud I call to you, my love!
High and clear I shoot my voice over the waves,
Surely you must know who is here, is here,
You must know who I am, my love.   85

Low-hanging moon!
What is that dusky spot in your brown yellow?
O it is the shape, the shape of my mate!
O moon do not keep her from me any longer.

Land! land! O land!   90
Whichever way I turn, O I think you could give me my mate back again if you
    only would,
For I am almost sure I see her dimly whichever way I look.

O rising stars!
Perhaps the one I want so much will rise, will rise with some of you.

O throat! O trembling throat!   95
Sound clearer through the atmosphere!
Pierce the woods, the earth,
Somewhere listening to catch you must be the one I want.

Shake out carols!
Solitary here, the night's carols!   100
Carols of lonesome love! death's carols!
Carols under that lagging, yellow, waning moon!
O under that moon where she droops almost down into the sea!
O reckless despairing carols.

But soft! sink low!   105
Soft! let me just murmur,
And do you wait a moment you husky-nois'd sea,
For somewhere I believe I heard my mate responding to me,
So faint, I must be still, be still to listen,
But not altogether still, for then she might not come immediately to me.   110

Hither my love!
Here I am! here!
With this just-sustain'd note I announce myself to you,
This gentle call is for you my love, for you.

Do not be decoy'd elsewhere,   115
That is the whistle of the wind, it is not my voice,
That is the fluttering, the fluttering of the spray,
Those are the shadows of leaves.

O darkness! O in vain!
O I am very sick and sorrowful.   120

O brown halo in the sky near the moon, drooping upon the sea!
O troubled reflection in the sea!
O throat! O throbbing heart!
And I singing uselessly, uselessly all the night.

O past! O happy life! O songs of joy!   125
In the air, in the woods, over fields,
Loved! loved! loved! loved! loved!

But my mate no more, no more with me!
We two together no more.

The aria sinking,   130
All else continuing, the stars shining,
The winds blowing, the notes of the bird continuous echoing,
With angry moans the fierce old mother incessantly moaning,
On the sands of Paumanok's shore gray and rustling,
The yellow half-moon enlarged, sagging down, drooping, the face of the sea
    almost touching,   135
The boy ecstatic, with his bare feet the waves, with his hair the atmosphere
    dallying,
The love in the heart long pent, now loose, now at last tumultuously bursting,
The aria's meaning, the ears, the soul, swiftly depositing,
The strange tears down the cheeks coursing,
The colloquy there, the trio, each uttering,   140
The undertone, the savage old mother incessantly crying,
To the boy's soul's questions sullenly timing, some drown'd secret hissing,
To the outsetting bard.

Demon or bird! (said the boy's soul,)
Is it indeed toward your mate you sing? or is it really to me?   145
For I, that was a child, my tongue's use sleeping, now I have heard you,
Now in a moment I know what I am for, I awake,
And already a thousand singers, a thousand songs, clearer, louder and more
    sorrowful than yours,
A thousand warbling echoes have started to life within me, never to die.

O you singer solitary, singing by yourself, projecting me,   150
O solitary me listening, never more shall I cease perpetuating you,
Never more shall I escape, never more the reverberations,
Never more the cries of unsatisfied love be absent from me,
Never again leave me to be the peaceful child I was before what there in the
    night,
By the sea under the yellow and sagging moon,   155
The messenger there arous'd, the fire, the sweet hell within,
The unknown want, the destiny of me.

O give me the clew! (it lurks in the night here somewhere,)
O if I am to have so much, let me have more!

A word then, (for I will conquer it,)   160
The word final, superior to all,
Subtle, sent up—what is it?—I listen;
Are you whispering it, and have been all the time, you seawaves?
Is that it from your liquid rims and wet sands?

Whereto answering, the sea,   165
Delaying not, hurrying not,

Whisper'd me through the night, and very plainly before daybreak,
Lisp'd to me the low and delicious word death,
And again death, death, death, death,
Hissing melodious, neither like the bird nor like my arous'd child's heart,   170
But edging near as privately for me rustling at my feet,
Creeping thence steadily up to my ears and laving me softly all over,
Death, death, death, death, death.

Which I do not forget,
But fuse the song of my dusky demon and brother,   175
That he sang to me in the moonlight on Paumanok's gray beach,
With the thousand responsive songs at random,
My own songs awaked from that hour,
And with them the key, the word up from the waves,
The word of the sweetest song and all songs,   180
That strong and delicious word which, creeping to my feet,
(Or like some old crone rocking the cradle, swathed in sweet garments, bending
    aside,)
The sea whisper'd me.
1859

As I Ebb'd with the Ocean of Life*

1

As I ebb'd with the ocean of life,
As I wended the shores I know,
As I walk'd where the ripples continually wash you Paumanok,
Where they rustle up hoarse and sibilant,
Where the fierce old mother endlessly cries for her castaways,   5
I musing late in the autumn day, gazing off southward,
Held by this electric self out of the pride of which I utter poems,
Was seiz'd by the spirit that trails in the lines underfoot,
The rim, the sediment that stands for all the water and all the land of the globe.

Fascinated, my eyes reverting from the south, dropt, to follow those slender
    windrows,   10
Chaff, straw, splinters of wood, weeds, and the sea-gluten,
Scum, scales from shining rocks, leaves of salt-lettuce, left by the tide,
Miles walking, the sound of breaking waves the other side of me,
Paumanok there and then as I thought the old thought of likenesses,
These you presented to me you fish-shaped island,   15
As I wended the shores I know,
As I walk'd with that electric self seeking types.

---

* First published with the title "Bardic Symbols" in the *Atlantic Monthly*, April 1860.

2

As I wend to the shores I know not,
As I list to the dirge, the voices of men and women wreck'd,
As I inhale the impalpable breezes that set in upon me,   20
As the ocean so mysterious rolls toward me closer and closer,
I too but signify at the utmost a little wash'd-up drift,
A few sands and dead leaves to gather,
Gather, and merge myself as part of the sands and drift.

O baffled, balk'd, bent to the very earth,   25
Oppress'd with myself that I have dared to open my mouth,
Aware now that amid all that blab whose echoes recoil upon me I have not once
    had the least idea who or what I am,
But that before all my arrogant poems the real Me stands yet untouch'd, untold,
    altogether unreach'd,
Withdrawn far, mocking me with mock-congratulatory signs and bows,
With peals of distant ironical laughter at every word I have written,   30
Pointing in silence to these songs, and then to the sand beneath.

I perceive I have not really understood any thing, not a single object, and that
    no man ever can,
Nature here in sight of the sea taking advantage of me to dart upon me and
    sting me,
Because I have dared to open my mouth to sing at all.

3

You oceans both, I close with you,   35
We murmur alike reproachfully rolling sands and drift, knowing not why,
These little shreds indeed standing for you and me and all.

You friable shore with trails of debris,
You fish-shaped island, I take what is underfoot,
What is yours is mine my father.   40

I too Paumanok,
I too have bubbled up, floated the measureless float, and been wash'd on your
    shores,
I too am but a trail of drift and debris,
I too leave little wrecks upon you, you fish-shaped island.

I throw myself upon your breast my father,   45
I cling to you so that you cannot unloose me,
I hold you so firm till you answer me something.

Kiss me my father,
Touch me with your lips as I touch those I love,
Breathe to me while I hold you close the secret of the murmuring I envy.   50

4

Ebb, ocean of life, (the flow will return,)
Cease not your moaning you fierce old mother,
Endlessly cry for your castaways, but fear not, deny not me,
Rustle not up so hoarse and angry against my feet as I touch you or gather
    from you.

I mean tenderly by you and all,   55
I gather for myself and for this phantom looking down where we lead, and
    following me and mine.

Me and mine, loose windrows, little corpses,
Froth, snowy white, and bubbles,
(See, from my dead lips the ooze exuding at last,   60
See, the prismatic colors glistening and rolling,)
Tufts of straw, sands, fragments,
Buoy'd hither from many moods, one contradicting another,
From the storm, the long calm, the darkness, the swell,
Musing, pondering, a breath, a briny tear, a dab of liquid or soil,   65
Up just as much out of fathomless workings fermented and thrown,
A limp blossom or two, torn, just as much over waves floating, drifted at random,
Just as much for us that sobbing dirge of Nature,
Just as much whence we come that blare of the cloud-trumpets,
We, capricious, brought hither we know not whence, spread out before you,
You up there walking or sitting,   70
Whoever you are, we too lie in drifts at your feet.
1860

from By the Roadside

When I Heard the Learn'd Astronomer

When I Heard the Learn'd Astronomer
When I heard the learn'd astronomer,
When the proofs, the figures, were ranged in columns before me,
When I was shown the charts and diagrams, to add, divide, and measure them,
When I sitting heard the astronomer where he lectured with much applause
    in the lecture-room,
How soon unaccountable I became tired and sick,   5
Till rising and gliding out I wander'd off by myself,
In the mystical moist night-air, and from time to time,
Look'd up in perfect silence at the stars.
1865

from **Drum-Taps**

Cavalry Crossing a Ford

A line in long array where they wind betwixt green islands,
They take a serpentine course, their arms flash in the sun—hark to the musical
    clank,
Behold the silvery river, in it the splashing horses loitering stop to drink,
Behold the brown-faced men, each group, each person a picture, the negligent
    rest on the saddles,
Some emerge on the opposite bank, others are just entering the ford—while,   5
Scarlet and blue and snowy white,
The guidon flags flutter gayly in the wind.
1865

A March in the Ranks Hard-Prest, and the Road Unknown

A march in the ranks hard-prest, and the road unknown,
A route through a heavy wood with muffled steps in the darkness,
Our army foil'd with loss severe, and the sullen remnant retreating,
Till after midnight glimmer upon us the lights of a dim-lighted building,
We come to an open space in the woods, and halt by the dim-lighted building,   5
'Tis a large old church at the crossing roads, now an impromptu hospital,
Entering but for a minute I see a sight beyond all the pictures and poems ever
    made,
Shadows of deepest, deepest black, just lit by moving candles and lamps,
And by one great pitchy torch stationary with wild red flame and clouds of
    smoke,
By these, crowds, groups of forms vaguely I see on the floor, some in the pews
    laid down,   10
At my feet more distinctly a soldier, a mere lad, in danger of bleeding to death,
    (he is shot in the abdomen,)
I stanch the blood temporarily, (the youngster's face is white as a lily,)
Then before I depart I sweep my eyes o'er the scene fain to absorb it all,
Faces, varieties, postures beyond description, most in obscurity, some of them
    dead,
Surgeons operating, attendants holding lights, the smell of ether, the odor
    of blood,   15
The crowd, O the crowd of the bloody forms, the yard outside also fill'd,
Some on the bare ground, some on planks or stretchers, some in the
    death-spasm sweating,
An occasional scream or cry, the doctor's shouted orders or calls,
The glisten of the little steel instruments catching the glint of the torches,
These I resume as I chant, I see again the forms, I smell the odor,   20
Then hear outside the orders given, *Fall in, my men, fall in;*
But first I bend to the dying lad, his eyes open, a half-smile gives he me,
Then the eyes close, calmly close, and I speed forth to the darkness,

Resuming, marching, ever in darkness marching, on in the ranks,
The unknown road still marching.   25
1865

A Sight in Camp in the Daybreak
Gray and Dim

A sight in camp in the daybreak gray and dim,
As from my tent I emerge so early sleepless,
As slow I walk in the cool fresh air the path near by the hospital tent,
Three forms I see on stretchers lying, brought out there untended lying,
Over each the blanket spread, ample brownish woolen blanket,   5
Gray and heavy blanket, folding, covering all.

Curious I halt and silent stand,
Then with light fingers I from the face of the nearest the first just lift the blanket;
Who are you elderly man so gaunt and grim, with well-gray'd hair, and flesh
    all sunken about the eyes?
Who are you my dear comrade?   10

Then to the second I step—and who are you my child and darling?
Who are you sweet boy with cheeks yet blooming?

Then to the third—a face nor child nor old, very calm, as of beautiful
    yellow-white ivory;
Young man I think I know you—I think this face is the face of the Christ
    himself,
Dead and divine and brother of all, and here again he lies.   15
1865

The Wound-Dresser

1

An old man bending I come among new faces,
Years looking backward resuming in answer to children,
Come tell us old man, as from young men and maidens that love me,
(Arous'd and angry, I'd thought to beat the alarum, and urge relentless war,
But soon my fingers fail'd me, my face droop'd and I resign'd myself,   5
To sit by the wounded and soothe them, or silently watch the dead;)
Years hence of these scenes, of these furious passions, these chances,
Of unsurpass'd heroes, (was one side so brave? the other was equally brave;)
Now be witness again, paint the mightiest armies of earth,
Of those armies so rapid so wondrous what saw you to tell us?   10
What stays with you latest and deepest? of curious panics,
Of hard-fought engagements or sieges tremendous what deepest remains?

2

O maidens and young men I love and that love me,
What you ask of my days those the strangest and sudden your talking recalls,
Soldier alert I arrive after a long march cover'd with sweat and dust,   15
In the nick of time I come, plunge in the fight, loudly shout in the rush of
    successful charge,
Enter the captur'd works—yet lo, like a swift-running river they fade,
Pass and are gone they fade—I dwell not on soldiers' perils or soldier's joys,
(Both I remember well—many the hardships, few the joys, yet I was content.)

But in silence, in dreams' projections,   20
While the world of gain and appearance and mirth goes on,
So soon what is over forgotten, and waves wash the imprints off the sand,
With hinged knees returning I enter the doors, (while for you up there,
Whoever you are, follow without noise and be of strong heart.)

Bearing the bandages, water and sponge,   25
Straight and swift to my wounded I go,
Where they lie on the ground after the battle brought in,
Where their priceless blood reddens the grass the ground,
Or to the rows of the hospital tent, or under the roof'd hospital,
To the long rows of cots up and down each side I return,   30
To each and all one after another I draw near, not one do I miss,
An attendant follows holding a tray, he carries a refuse pail,
Soon to be fill'd with clotted rags and blood, emptied, and fill'd again.

I onward go, I stop,
With hinged knees and steady hand to dress wounds,   35
I am firm with each, the pangs are sharp yet unavoidable,
One turns to me his appealing eyes—poor boy! I never knew you,
Yet I think I could not refuse this moment to die for you, if that would save
    you.

3

On, and I go, (open doors of time! open hospital doors!)
The crush'd head I dress, (poor crazed hand tear not the bandage away,)   40
The neck of the cavalry-man with the bullet through and through I examine,
Hard the breathing rattles, quite glazed already the eye, yet life struggles hard,
(Come sweet death! be persuaded O beautiful death!
In mercy come quickly.)

From the stump of the arm, the amputated hand,   45
I undo the clotted lint, remove the slough, wash off the matter and blood,
Back on his pillow the soldier bends with curv'd neck and side-falling head,
His eyes are closed, his face is pale, he dares not look on the bloody stump,
And has not yet look'd on it.

I dress a wound in the side, deep, deep,   50
But a day or two more, for see the frame all wasted and sinking,
And the yellow-blue countenance see.

I dress the perforated shoulder, the foot with the bullet-wound,
Cleanse the one with a gnawing and putrid gangrene, so sickening, so offensive,
While the attendant stands behind aside me holding the tray and pail.   55

I am faithful, I do not give out,
The fractur'd thigh, the knee, the wound in the abdomen,
These and more I dress with impassive hand, (yet deep in my breast a fire, a
    burning flame.)

4

Thus in silence in dreams' projections,
Returning, resuming, I thread my way through the hospitals,   60
The hurt and wounded I pacify with soothing hand,
I sit by the restless all the dark night, some are so young,
Some suffer so much, I recall the experience sweet and sad,
(Many a soldier's loving arms about this neck have cross'd and rested,
Many a soldier's kiss dwells on these bearded lips.)   65
1865

Reconciliation

Word over all, beautiful as the sky,
Beautiful that war and all its deeds of carnage must in time be utterly lost,
That the hands of the sisters Death and Night incessantly softly wash again,
    and ever again, this soil'd world;
For my enemy is dead, a man divine as myself is dead,
I look where he lies white-faced and still in the coffin—I draw near,   5
Bend down and touch lightly with my lips the white face in the coffin.
1865–1866

from Memories of President Lincoln

When Lilacs Last in the Dooryard Bloom'd

1

When lilacs last in the dooryard bloom'd,
And the great star[40] early droop'd in the western sky in the night,
I mourn'd, and yet shall mourn with ever-returning spring.

Ever-returning spring, trinity sure to me you bring,
Lilac blooming perennial and drooping star in the west,   5
And thought of him I love.

40 i.e., the planet Venus.

2

O powerful western fallen star!
O shades of night—O moody, tearful night!
O great star disappear'd—O the black murk that hides the star!
O cruel hands that hold me powerless—O helpless soul of me!   10
O harsh surrounding cloud that will not free my soul.

3

In the dooryard fronting an old farm-house near the white-wash'd palings,
Stands the lilac-bush tall-growing with heart-shaped leaves of rich green,
With many a pointed blossom rising delicate, with the perfume strong I love,
With every leaf a miracle—and from this bush in the dooryard,   15
With delicate-color'd blossoms and heart-shaped leaves of rich green,
A sprig with its flower I break.

4

In the swamp in secluded recesses,
A shy and hidden bird is warbling a song.

Solitary the thrush,   20
The hermit withdrawn to himself, avoiding the settlements,
Sings by himself a song.

Song of the bleeding throat,
Death's outlet song of life, (for well dear brother I know,
If thou wast not granted to sing thou would'st surely die.)   25

5

Over the breast of the spring, the land, amid cities,
Amid lanes and through old woods, where lately the violets peep'd from the
    ground, spotting the gray debris,
Amid the grass in the fields each side of the lanes, passing the endless grass,
Passing the yellow-spear'd wheat, every grain from its shroud in the
    dark-brown fields uprisen,
Passing the apple-tree blows of white and pink in the orchards,   30
Carrying a corpse to where it shall rest in the grave,
Night and day journeys a coffin.

6

Coffin that passes through lanes and streets,
Through day and night with the great cloud darkening the land,
With the pomp of the inloop'd flags with the cities draped in black,   35
With the show of the States themselves as of crape-veil'd women standing,
With processions long and winding and the flambeaus of the night,
With the countless torches lit, with the silent sea of faces and the unbared heads,
With the waiting depot, the arriving coffin, and the sombre faces,

With dirges through the night, with the thousand voices rising strong and
    solemn,   40
With all the mournful voices of the dirges pour'd around the coffin,
The dim-lit churches and the shuddering organs—where amid these you
    journey,
With the tolling tolling bells' perpetual clang,
Here, coffin that slowly passes,
I give you my sprig of lilac.   45

7

(Nor for you, for one alone,
Blossoms and branches green to coffins all I bring,
For fresh as the morning, thus would I chant a song for you O sane and sacred
    death.

All over bouquets of roses,
O death, I cover you over with roses and early lilies,   50
But mostly and now the lilac that blooms the first,
Copious I break, I break the sprigs from the bushes,
With loaded arms I come, pouring for you,
For you and the coffins all of you O death.)

8

O western orb sailing the heaven,   55
Now I know what you must have meant as a month since I walk'd,
As I walk'd in silence the transparent shadowy night,
As I saw you had something to tell as you bent to me night after night,
As you droop'd from the sky low down as if to my side, (while the other stars
    all look'd on,)
As we wander'd together the solemn night, (for something I know not what
    kept me from sleep,)   60
As the night advanced, and I saw on the rim of the west how full you were of
    woe,
As I stood on the rising ground in the breeze in the cool transparent night,
As I watch'd where you pass'd and was lost in the netherward black of the
    night,
As my soul in its trouble dissatisfied sank, as where you sad orb,
Concluded, dropt in the night, and was gone.   65

9

Sing on there in the swamp,
O singer bashful and tender, I hear your notes, I hear your call,
I hear, I come presently, I understand you,
But a moment I linger, for the lustrous star has detain'd me,
The star my departing comrade holds and detains me.   70

10

O how shall I warble myself for the dead one there I loved?
And how shall I deck my song for the large sweet soul that has gone?
And what shall my perfume be for the grave of him I love?

Sea-winds blown from east and west,
Blown from the Eastern sea and blown from the Western sea, till there on
    the prairies meeting,   75
These and with these and the breath of my chant,
I'll perfume the grave of him I love.

11

O what shall I hang on the chamber walls?
And what shall the pictures be that I hang on the walls,
To adorn the burial-house of him I love?   80

Pictures of growing spring and farms and homes,
With the Fourth-month eve at sundown, and the gray smoke lucid and bright,
With floods of the yellow gold of the gorgeous, indolent, sinking sun, burning,
    expanding the air,
With the fresh sweet herbage under foot, and the pale green leaves of the trees
    prolific,
In the distance the flowing glaze, the breast of the river, with a wind-dapple
    here and there,   85
With ranging hills on the banks, with many a line against the sky, and shadows,
And the city at hand with dwellings so dense, and stacks of chimneys,
And all the scenes of life and the workshops, and the workmen homeward
    returning.

12

Lo, body and soul—this land,
My own Manhattan with spires, and the sparkling and hurrying tides, and
    the ships,   90
The varied and ample land, the South and the North in the light, Ohio's shores
    and flashing Missouri,
And ever the far-spreading prairies cover'd with grass and corn.

Lo, the most excellent sun so calm and haughty,
The violet and purple morn with just-felt breezes,
The gentle soft-born measureless light,   95
The miracle spreading bathing all, the fulfill'd noon,
The coming eve delicious, the welcome night and the stars,
Over my cities shining all, enveloping man and land.

13

Sing on, sing on you gray-brown bird,
Sing from the swamps, the recesses, pour your chant from the bushes,   100
Limitless out of the dusk, out of the cedars and pines.

Sing on dearest brother, warble your reedy song,
Loud human song, with voice of uttermost woe.

O liquid and free and tender!
O wild and loose to my soul—O wondrous singer!   105
You only I hear—yet the star holds me, (but will soon depart,)
Yet the lilac with mastering odor holds me.

14

Now while I sat in the day and look'd forth,
In the close of the day with its light and the fields of spring, and the farmers
    preparing their crops,
In the large unconscious scenery of my land with its lakes and forests,   110
In the heavenly aerial beauty, (after the perturb'd winds and the storms,)
Under the arching heavens of the afternoon swift passing, and the voices of
    children and women,
The many-moving sea-tides, and I saw the ships how they sail'd,
And the summer approaching with richness, and the fields all busy with labor,
And the infinite separate houses, how they all went on, each with its meals
    and minutia of daily usages,   115
And the streets how their throbbings throbb'd, and the cities pent—lo, then and
    there,
Falling upon them all and among them all, enveloping me with the rest,
Appear'd the cloud, appear'd the long black trail,
And I knew death, its thought, and the sacred knowledge of death.

Then with the knowledge of death as walking one side of me,   120
And the thought of death close-walking the other side of me,
And I in the middle as with companions, and as holding the hands of
    companions,
I fled forth to the hiding receiving night that talks not,
Down to the shores of the water, the path by the swamp in the dimness,
To the solemn shadowy cedars and ghostly pines so still.   125

And the singer so shy to the rest receiv'd me,
The gray-brown bird I know receiv'd us comrades three,
And he sang the carol of death, and a verse for him I love.

From deep secluded recesses,
From the fragrant cedars and the ghostly pines so still,   130
Came the carol of the bird.

And the charm of the carol rapt me,
As I held as if by their hands my comrades in the night,
And the voice of my spirit tallied the song of the bird.

Come lovely and soothing death,   135
Undulate round the world, serenely arriving, arriving,
In the day, in the night, to all, to each,
Sooner or later delicate death.

Prais'd be the fathomless universe,
For life and joy, and for objects and knowledge curious,   140
And for love, sweet love—but praise! praise! praise!
For the sure-enwinding arms of cool-enfolding death.

Dark mother always gliding near with soft feet,
Have none chanted for thee a chant of fullest welcome?
Then I chant it for thee, I glorify thee above all,   145
I bring thee a song that when thou must indeed come, come unfalteringly.

Approach strong deliveress,
When it is so, when thou hast taken them I joyously sing the dead,
Lost in the loving floating ocean of thee,
Laved in the flood of thy bliss O death.   150

From me to thee glad serenades,
Dances for thee I propose saluting thee, adornments and feastings for thee,
And the sights of the open landscape and the high-spread sky are fitting,
And life and the fields, and the huge and thoughtful night.

The night in silence under many a star,   155
The ocean shore and the husky whispering wave whose voice I know,
And the soul turning to thee O vast and well-veil'd death,
And the body gratefully nestling close to thee.

Over the tree-tops I float thee a song,
Over the rising and sinking waves, over the myriad fields and the prairies wide,   160
Over the dense-pack'd cities all and the teeming wharves and ways,
I float this carol with joy, with joy to thee O death.

15

To the tally of my soul,
Loud and strong kept up the gray-brown bird,
With pure deliberate notes spreading filling the night.   165

Loud in the pines and cedars dim,
Clear in the freshness moist and the swamp-perfume,
And I with my comrades there in the night.

While my sight that was bound in my eyes unclosed,
As to long panoramas of visions.   170

And I saw askant the armies,
I saw as in noiseless dreams hundreds of battle-flags,
Borne through the smoke of the battles and pierc'd with missiles I saw them,
And carried hither and yon through the smoke, and torn and bloody,
And at last but a few shreds left on the staffs, (and all in silence,)   175
And the staffs all splinter'd and broken.

I saw battle-corpses, myriads of them,
And the white skeletons of young men, I saw them,
I saw the debris and debris of all the slain soldiers of the war,
But I saw they were not as was thought,   180
They themselves were fully at rest, they suffer'd not,
The living remain'd and suffer'd, the mother suffer'd,
And the wife and the child and the musing comrade suffer'd,
And the armies that remain'd suffer'd.

16

Passing the visions, passing the night,   185
Passing, unloosing the hold of my comrades' hands,
Passing the song of the hermit bird and the tallying song of my soul,
Victorious song, death's outlet song, yet varying ever-altering song,
As low and wailing, yet clear the notes, rising and falling, flooding the night,
Sadly sinking and fainting, as warning and warning, and yet again bursting
        with joy,   190
Covering the earth and filling the spread of the heaven,
As that powerful psalm in the night I heard from recesses,
Passing, I leave thee lilac with heart-shaped leaves,
I leave thee there in the door-yard, blooming, returning with spring.

I cease from my song for thee,   195
From my gaze on thee in the west, fronting the west, communing with thee,
O comrade lustrous with silver face in the night.

Yet each to keep and all, retrievements out of the night,
The song, the wondrous chant of the gray-brown bird,
And the tallying chant, the echo arous'd in my soul,   200
With the lustrous and drooping star with the countenance full of woe,
With the holders holding my hand nearing the call of the bird,
Comrades mine and I in the midst, and their memory ever to keep, for the
        dead I loved so well,
For the sweetest, wisest soul of all my days and lands—and this for his dear
        sake,

Lilac and star and bird twined with the chant of my soul,   205
There in the fragrant pines and the cedars dusk and dim.
1865–1866

from **Autumn Rivulets**

There Was a Child Went Forth

There was a child went forth every day,
And the first object he look'd upon, that object he became,
And that object became part of him for the day or a certain part of the day,
Or for many years or stretching cycles of years.

The early lilacs became part of this child,   5
And grass and white and red morning-glories, and white and red clover, and
    the song of the phœbe-bird,
And the Third-month lambs and the sow's pink-faint litter, and the mare's foal
    and the cow's calf,
And the noisy brood of the barnyard or by the mire of the pond-side,
And the fish suspending themselves so curiously below there, and the beautiful
    curious liquid,
And the water-plants with their graceful flat heads, all became part of him.   10

The field-sprouts of Fourth-month and Fifth-month became part of him,
Winter-grain sprouts and those of the light-yellow corn, and the esculent roots
    of the garden,
And the apple-trees cover'd with blossoms and the fruit afterward, and
    wood-berries, and the commonest weeds by the road,
And the old drunkard staggering home from the outhouse of the tavern whence
    he had lately risen,
And the schoolmistress that pass'd on her way to the school,   15
And the friendly boys that pass'd, and the quarrelsome boys,
And the tidy and fresh-cheek'd girls, and the barefoot negro boy and girl,
And all the changes of city and country wherever he went.

His own parents, he that had father'd him and she that had conceiv'd him
    in her womb and birth'd him,
They gave this child more of themselves than that,   20
They gave him afterward every day, they became part of him.

The mother at home quietly placing the dishes on the supper-table,
The mother with mild words, clean her cap and gown, a wholesome odor
    falling off her person and clothes as she walks by,
The father, strong, self-sufficient, manly, mean, anger'd, unjust,
The blow, the quick loud word, the tight bargain, the crafty lure,   25
The family usages, the language, the company, the furniture, the yearning and
    swelling heart,

Affection that will not be gainsay'd, the sense of what is real, the thought if after
    all it should prove unreal,
The doubts of day-time and the doubts of night-time, the curious whether and
    how,
Whether that which appears so is so, or is it all flashes and specks?
Men and women crowding fast in the streets, if they are not flashes and specks
    what are they?   30
The streets themselves and the façades of houses, and goods in the windows,
Vehicles, teams, the heavy-plank'd wharves, the huge crossing at the ferries,
The village on the highland seen from afar at sunset, the river between,
Shadows, aureola and mist, the light falling on roofs and gables of white or brown
    two miles off,
The schooner near by sleepily dropping down the tide, the little boat
    slack-tow'd astern,   35
The hurrying tumbling waves, quick-broken crests, slapping,
The strata of color'd clouds, the long bar of maroon-tint away solitary by itself,
    the spread of purity it lies motionless in,
The horizon's edge, the flying sea-crow, the fragrance of salt marsh and shore
    mud,
These became part of that child who went forth every day, and who now goes,
    and will always go forth every day.
1855

Passage to India

1

Singing my days,
Singing the great achievements of the present,
Singing the strong light works of engineers,
Our modern wonders, (the antique ponderous Seven outvied,)
In the Old World the east the Suez canal,[41]   5
The New by its mighty railroad spann'd,
The seas inlaid with eloquent gentle wires;[42]
Yet first to sound, and ever sound, the cry with thee O soul,
The Past! the Past! the Past!

The Past—the dark unfathom'd retrospect!   10
The teeming gulf—the sleepers and the shadows!
The past—the infinite greatness of the past!
For what is the present after all but a growth out of the past?
(As a projectile form'd, impell'd, passing a certain line, still keeps on,
So the present, utterly form'd, impell'd by the past.)   15

---

[41] Opened in 1869.
[42] The transcontinental railroad link was com-
    pleted in 1869 and the Atlantic Cable suc-
    cessfully completed in 1866.

2

Passage O soul to India!
Eclaircise[43] the myths Asiatic, the primitive fables.

Not you alone proud truths of the world,
Nor you alone ye facts of modern science,
But myths and fables of eld, Asia's, Africa's fables,   20
The far-darting beams of the spirit, the unloos'd dreams,
The deep diving bibles and legends,
The daring plots of the poets, the elder religions;
O you temples fairer than lilies pour'd over by the rising sun!
O you fables spurning the known, eluding the hold of the known, mounting
     to heaven!   25
You lofty and dazzling towers, pinnacled, red as roses, burnish'd with gold!
Towers of fables immortal fashion'd from mortal dreams!
You too I welcome and fully the same as the rest!
You too with joy I sing.

Passage to India!   30
Lo, soul, seest thou not God's purpose from the first?
The earth to be spann'd, connected by network,
The races, neighbors, to marry and be given in marriage,
The oceans to be cross'd, the distant brought near,
The lands to be welded together.   35

A worship new I sing,
You captains, voyagers, explorers, yours,
You engineers, you architects, machinists, yours,
You, not for trade or transportation only,
But in God's name, and for thy sake O soul.   40

3

Passage to India!
Lo soul for thee of tableaus twain,
I see in one the Suez canal initiated, open'd,
I see the procession of steamships, the Empress Eugenie's[44] leading the van,
I mark from on deck the strange landscape, the pure sky, the level sand in the
     distance,   45
I pass swiftly the picturesque groups, the workmen gather'd,
The gigantic dredging machines.

In one again, different, (yet thine, all thine, O soul, the same,)
I see over my own continent the Pacific railroad surmounting every barrier,
I see continual trains of cars winding along the Platte carrying freight and
     passengers,   50

[43] French: "clarify."
[44] Empress Eugenie was the wife of Napoleon
     III.

I hear the locomotives rushing and roaring, and the shrill steam-whistle,
I hear the echoes reverberate through the grandest scenery in the world,
I cross the Laramie plains, I note the rocks in grotesque shapes, the buttes,
I see the plentiful larkspur and wild onions, the barren, colorless, sage-deserts,
I see in glimpses afar or towering immediately above me the great mountains,
    I see the Wind river and the Wahsatch mountains,   55
I see the Monument mountain and the Eagle's Nest, I pass the Promontory, I
    ascend the Nevadas,
I scan the noble Elk mountain and wind around its base,
I see the Humboldt range, I thread the valley and cross the river,
I see the clear waters of lake Tahoe, I see forests of majestic pines,
Or crossing the great desert, the alkaline plains, I behold enchanting mirages
    of waters and meadows,   60
Marking through these and after all, in duplicate slender lines,
Bridging the three or four thousand miles of land travel,
Tying the Eastern to the Western sea,
The road between Europe and Asia.

(Ah Genoese[45] thy dream! thy dream!   65
Centuries after thou art laid in thy grave,
The shore thou foundest verifies thy dream.)

4

Passage to India!
Struggles of many a captain, tales of many a sailor dead,
Over my mood stealing and spreading they come,   70
Like clouds and cloudlets in the unreach'd sky.

Along all history, down the slopes,
As a rivulet running, sinking now, and now again to the surface rising,
A ceaseless thought, a varied train—lo, soul, to thee, thy sight, they rise,
The plans, the voyages again, the expeditions;   75
Again Vasco de Gama sails forth,
Again the knowledge gain'd, the mariner's compass,
Lands found and nations born, thou born America,
For purpose vast, man's long probation fill'd,
Thou rondure of the world at last accomplish'd.   80

5

O vast Rondure, swimming in space,
Cover'd all over with visible power and beauty,
Alternate light and day and the teeming spiritual darkness,
Unspeakable high processions of sun and moon and countless stars above,
Below, the manifold grass and waters, animals, mountains, trees,   85

---

[45] i.e., Christopher Columbus.

With inscrutable purpose, some hidden prophetic intention,
Now first it seems my thought begins to span thee.

Down from the gardens of Asia descending radiating,
Adam and Eve appear, then their myriad progeny after them,
Wandering, yearning, curious, with restless explorations,   90
With questionings, baffled, formless, feverish, with never-happy hearts,
With that sad incessant refrain, *Wherefore unsatisfied soul?* and *Whither O
    mocking life?*

Ah who shall soothe these feverish children?
Who justify these restless explorations?
Who speak the secret of impassive earth?   95
Who bind it to us? what is this separate Nature so unnatural?
What is this earth to our affections? (unloving earth, without a throb to answer
    ours,
Cold earth, the place of graves.)

Yet soul be sure the first intent remains, and shall be carried out,
Perhaps even now the time has arrived.   100

After the seas are all cross'd, (as they seem already cross'd,)
After the great captains and engineers have accomplish'd their work,
After the noble inventors, after the scientists, the chemist, the geologist,
    ethnologist,
Finally shall come the poet worthy that name,
The true son of God shall come singing his songs.   105

Then not your deeds only O voyagers, O scientists and inventors, shall be
    justified,
All these hearts as of fretted children shall be sooth'd,
All affection shall be fully responded to, the secret shall be told,
All these separations and gaps shall be taken up and hook'd and link'd together,
The whole earth, this cold, impassive, voiceless earth, shall be completely
    justified,   110
Trinitas divine shall be gloriously accomplish'd and compacted by the true son
    of God, the poet,
(He shall indeed pass the straits and conquer the mountains,
He shall double the cape of Good Hope to some purpose,)
Nature and Man shall be disjoin'd and diffused no more,
The true son of God shall absolutely fuse them.   115

6

Year at whose wide-flung door I sing!
Year of the purpose accomplish'd!
Year of the marriage of continents, climates and oceans!
(No mere doge of Venice now wedding the Adriatic,)

I see O year in you the vast terraqueous globe given and giving all,   120
Europe to Asia, Africa join'd, and they to the New World,
The lands, geographies, dancing before you, holding a festival garland,
As brides and bridegrooms hand in hand.

Passage to India!
Cooling airs from Caucasus far, soothing cradle of man,   125
The river Euphrates flowing, the past lit up again.

Lo soul, the retrospect brought forward,
The old, most populous, wealthiest of earth's lands,
The streams of the Indus and the Ganges and their many affluents,
(I my shores of America walking to-day behold, resuming all,)   130
The tale of Alexander[46] on his warlike marches suddenly dying,
On one side China and on the other side Persia and Arabia,
To the south the great seas and the bay of Bengal,
The flowing literatures, tremendous epics, religions, castes,
Old occult Brahma interminably far back, the tender and junior Buddha,   135
Central and southern empires and all their belongings, possessors,
The wars of Tamerlane, the reign of Aurungzebe,
The traders, rulers, explorers, Moslems, Venetians, Byzantium, the Arabs,
    Portuguese,
The first travelers famous yet, Marco Polo, Batouta the Moor,
Doubts to be solv'd, the map incognita, blanks to be fill'd,   140
The foot of man unstay'd, the hands never at rest,
Thyself O soul that will not brook a challenge.

The mediæval navigators rise before me,
The world of 1492, with its awaken'd enterprise,
Something swelling in humanity now like the sap of the earth in spring,   145
The sunset splendor of chivalry declining.

And who art thou sad shade?
Gigantic, visionary, thyself a visionary,
With majestic limbs and pious beaming eyes,
Spreading around with every look of thine a golden world,   150
Enhuing it with gorgeous hues.

As the chief histrion,
Down to the footlights walks in some great scena,
Dominating the rest I see the Admiral himself,
(History's type of courage, action, faith,)   155
Behold him sail from Palos leading his little fleet,
His voyage behold, his return, his great fame,

[46] Alexander the Great (356–323 B.C.)

His misfortunes, calumniators, behold him a prisoner, chain'd,
Behold his dejection, poverty, death.

(Curious in time I stand, noting the efforts of heroes,   160
Is the deferment long? bitter the slander, poverty, death?
Lies the seed unreck'd for centuries in the ground? lo, to God's due occasion,
Uprising in the night, it sprouts, blooms,
And fills the earth with use and beauty.)

7

Passage indeed O soul to primal thought,   165
Not lands and seas alone, thy own clear freshness,
The young maturity of brood and bloom,
To realms of budding bibles.

O soul, repressless, I with thee and thou with me,
Thy circumnavigation of the world begin,   170
Of man, the voyage of his mind's return,
To reason's early paradise,
Back, back to wisdom's birth, to innocent intuitions,
Again with fair creation.

8

O we can wait no longer,   175
We too take ship O soul,
Joyous we too launch out on trackless seas,
Fearless for unknown shores on waves of ecstasy to sail,
Amid the wafting winds, (thou pressing me to thee, I thee to me, O soul,)
Caroling free, singing our song of God,   180
Chanting our chant of pleasant exploration.

With laugh and many a kiss,
(Let others deprecate, let others weep for sin, remorse, humiliation,)
O soul thou pleasest me, I thee.

Ah more than any priest O soul we too believe in God,   185
But with the mystery of God we dare not dally.

O soul thou pleasest me, I thee,
Sailing these seas or on the hills, or waking in the night,
Thoughts, silent thoughts, of Time and Space and Death, like waters flowing,
Bear me indeed as through the regions infinite,   190
Whose air I breathe, whose ripples hear, lave me all over,
Bathe me O God in thee, mounting to thee,
I and my soul to range in range of thee.

O Thou transcendent,
Nameless, the fibre and the breath,   195
Light of the light, shedding forth universes, thou centre of them,
Thou mightier centre of the true, the good, the loving,
Thou moral, spiritual fountain—affection's source—thou reservoir,
(O pensive soul of me—O thirst unsatisfied—waitest not there?
Waitest not haply for us somewhere there the Comrade perfect?)   200
Thou pulse—thou motive of the stars, suns, systems,
That, circling, move in order, safe, harmonious,
Athwart the shapeless vastnesses of space,
How should I think, how breathe a single breath, how speak, if, out of myself,
I could not launch, to those, superior universes?   205

Swiftly I shrivel at the thought of God,
At Nature and its wonders, Time and Space and Death,
But that I, turning, call to thee O soul, thou actual Me,
And lo, thou gently masterest the orbs,
Thou matest Time, smilest content at Death,   210
And fillest, swellest full the vastnesses of Space.

Greater than stars or suns,
Bounding O soul thou journeyest forth;
What love than thine and ours could wider amplify?
What aspirations, wishes, outvie thine and ours O soul?   215
What dreams of the ideal? What plans of purity, perfection, strength?
What cheerful willingness for others' sake to give up all?
For others' sake to suffer all?

Reckoning ahead O soul, when thou, the time achiev'd,
The seas all cross'd, weather'd the capes, the voyage done,   220
Surrounded, copest, frontest God, yieldest, the aim attain'd,
As fill'd with friendship, love complete, the Elder Brother found,
The Younger melts in fondness in his arms.

9

Passage to more than India!
Are thy wings plumed indeed for such far flights?   225
O soul, voyagest thou indeed on voyages like those?
Disportest thou on waters such as those?
Soundest below the Sanscrit and the Vedas?
Then have thy bent unleash'd.

Passage to you, your shores, ye aged fierce enigmas!   230
Passage to you, to mastership of you, ye strangling problems!
You, strew'd with the wrecks of skeletons, that, living, never reach'd you.

Passage to more than India!
O secret of the earth and sky!

Of you O waters of the sea! O winding creeks and rivers!   235
Of you O woods and fields! of you strong mountains of my land!
Of you O prairies! of you gray rocks!
O morning red! O clouds! O rain and snows!
O day and night, passage to you!

O sun and moon and all you stars! Sirius and Jupiter!   240
Passage to you!

Passage, immediate passage! the blood burns in my veins!
Away O soul! hoist instantly the anchor!
Cut the hawsers—haul out—shake out every sail!
Have we not stood here like trees in the ground long enough?   245
Have we not grovel'd here long enough, eating and drinking like mere brutes?
Have we not darken'd and dazed ourselves with books long enough?

Sail forth—steer for the deep waters only,
Reckless O soul, exploring, I with thee, and thou with me,
For we are bound where mariner has not yet dared to go,   250
And we will risk the ship, ourselves and all.

O my brave soul!
O farther farther sail!
O daring joy, but safe! are they not all the seas of God?
O farther, farther, farther sail!   255
1871

The Sleepers*

1

I wander all night in my vision,
Stepping with light feet, swiftly and noiselessly stepping and stopping,
Bending with open eyes over the shut eyes of sleepers,
Wandering and confused, lost to myself, ill-assorted, contradictory,
Pausing, gazing, bending, and stopping.   5

How solemn they look there, stretch'd and still,
How quiet they breathe, the little children in their cradles.

The wretched features of ennuyés,47 the white features of corpses, the livid faces
    of drunkards, the sick-gray faces of onanists,
The gash'd bodies on battle-fields, the insane in their strong-door'd rooms, the
    sacred idiots, the new-born emerging from gates, and the dying emerging
    from gates,
The night pervades them and infolds them.   10

---

* Untitled when first published in the 1855   47 French: "bored persons."
  edition of *Leaves of Grass*.

The married couple sleep calmly in their bed, he with his palm on the hip of
    the wife, and she with her palm on the hip of the husband,
The sisters sleep lovingly side by side in their bed,
The men sleep lovingly side by side in theirs,
And the mother sleeps with her little child carefully wrapt.

The blind sleep, and the deaf and dumb sleep,   15
The prisoner sleeps well in the prison, the runaway son sleeps,
The murderer that is to be hung next day, how does he sleep?
And the murder'd person, how does he sleep?

The female that loves unrequited sleeps,
And the male that loves unrequited sleeps,   20
The head of the money-maker that plotted all day sleeps,
And the enraged and treacherous dispositions, all, all sleep.

I stand in the dark with drooping eyes by the worst-suffering and the most
    restless,
I pass my hands soothingly to and fro a few inches from them,
The restless sink in their beds, they fitfully sleep.   25

Now I pierce the darkness, new beings appear,
The earth recedes from me into the night,
I saw that it was beautiful, and I see that what is not the earth is beautiful.

I go from bedside to bedside, I sleep close with the other sleepers each in turn,
I dream in my dream all the dreams of the other dreamers,   30
And I become the other dreamers.

I am a dance—play up there! the fit is whirling me fast!

I am the ever-laughing—it is new moon and twilight,
I see the hiding of douceurs,[48] I see nimble ghosts whichever way I look,
Cache[49] and cache again deep in the ground and sea, and where it is
    neither ground nor sea.   35

Well do they do their jobs those journeymen divine,
Only from me can they hide nothing, and would not if they could,
I reckon I am their boss and they make me a pet besides,
And surround me and lead me and run ahead when I walk,
To lift their cunning covers to signify me with stretch'd arms, and resume the
    way;   40

[48] French: "delights."
[49] Hide (from French *cacher*: "to hide").

Onward we move, a gay gang of blackguards! with mirth-shouting music and
   wild-flapping pennants of joy!

I am the actor, the actress, the voter, the politician,
The emigrant and the exile, the criminal that stood in the box,
He who has been famous and he who shall be famous after to-day,
The stammerer, the well-form'd person, the wasted or feeble person.   45

I am she who adorn'd herself and folded her hair expectantly,
My truant lover has come, and it is dark.

Double yourself and receive me darkness,
Receive me and my lover too, he will not let me go without him.

I roll myself upon you as upon a bed, I resign myself to the dusk.   50

He whom I call answers me and takes the place of my lover,
He rises with me silently from the bed.

Darkness, you are gentler than my lover, his flesh was sweaty and panting,
I feel the hot moisture yet that he left me.

My hands are spread forth, I pass them in all directions,   55
I would sound up the shadowy shore to which you are journeying.

Be careful darkness! already what was it touch'd me?
I thought my lover had gone, else darkness and he are one,
I hear the heart-beat, I follow, I fade away.

2

I descend my western course, my sinews are flaccid,   60
Perfume and youth course through me and I am their wake.

It is my face yellow and wrinkled instead of the old woman's,
I sit low in a straw-bottom chair and carefully darn my grandson's stockings.

It is I too, the sleepless widow looking out on the winter midnight,
I see the sparkles of starshine on the icy and pallid earth.   65

A shroud I see and I am the shroud, I wrap a body and lie in the coffin,
It is dark here under ground, it is not evil or pain here, it is blank here, for
   reasons.

(It seems to me that every thing in the light and air ought to be happy,
Whoever is not in his coffin and the dark grave let him know he has enough.)

3

I see a beautiful gigantic swimmer swimming naked through the eddies of the
    sea,   70
His brown hair lies close and even to his head, he strikes out with courageous
    arms, he urges himself with his legs,
I see his white body, I see his undaunted eyes,
I hate the swift-running eddies that would dash him head-foremost on the rocks.

What are you doing you ruffianly red-trickled waves?
Will you kill the courageous giant? will you kill him in the prime of his
    middle age?   75

Steady and long he struggles,
He is baffled, bang'd, bruis'd, he holds out while his strength holds out,
The slapping eddies are spotted with his blood, they bear him away, they roll him,
    swing him, turn him,
His beautiful body is borne in the circling eddies, it is continually bruis'd on
    rocks,
Swiftly and out of sight is borne the brave corpse.   80

4

I turn but do not extricate myself,
Confused, a past-reading, another, but with darkness yet.

The beach is cut by the razory ice-wind, the wreck-guns sound,
The tempest lulls, the moon comes floundering through the drifts.

I look where the ship helplessly heads end on, I hear the burst as she strikes,
    I hear the howls of dismay, they grow fainter and fainter.   85

I cannot aid with my wringing fingers,
I can but rush to the surf and let it drench me and freeze upon me.

I search with the crowd, not one of the company is wash'd to us alive,
In the morning I help pick up the dead and lay them in rows in a barn.

5

Now of the older war-days, the defeat at Brooklyn,[50]   90
Washington stands inside the lines, he stands on the intrench'd hills amid
    a crowd of officers,
His face is cold and damp, he cannot repress the weeping drops,

[50] In the battle of Long Island, August 1776.

He lifts the glass perpetually to his eyes, the color is blanch'd from his cheeks,
He sees the slaughter of the southern braves confided to him by their parents.

The same at last and at last when peace is declared,   95
He stands in the room of the old tavern,[51] the well-belov'd soldiers
    all pass through,
The officers speechless and slow draw near in their turns,
The chief encircles their necks with his arm and kisses them on the cheek,
He kisses lightly the wet cheeks one after another, he shakes hands and bids
    good-by to the army.

6

Now what my mother told me one day as we sat at dinner together,   100
Of when she was a nearly grown girl living home with her parents on the
    old homestead.

A red squaw came one breakfast-time to the old homestead,
On her back she carried a bundle of rushes for rush-bottoming chairs,
Her hair, straight, shiny, coarse, black, profuse, half-envelop'd her face,
Her step was free and elastic, and her voice sounded exquisitely as she spoke.   105

My mother look'd in delight and amazement at the stranger,
She look'd at the freshness of her tall-borne face and full and pliant limbs,
The more she look'd upon her she loved her,
Never before had she seen such wonderful beauty and purity,
She made her sit on a bench by the jamb of the fireplace, she cook'd food for
    her,   110
She had no work to give her, but she gave her remembrance and fondness.

The red squaw staid all the forenoon, and toward the middle of the afternoon
    she went away,
O my mother was loth to have her go away,
All the week she thought of her, she watch'd for her many a month,
She remember'd her many a winter and many a summer,   115
But the red squaw never came nor was heard of there again.

7

A show of the summer softness—a contact of something unseen—an amour of
    the light and air,
I am jealous and overwhelm'd with friendliness,
And will go gallivant with the light and air myself.

O love and summer, you are in the dreams and in me,   120
Autumn and winter are in the dreams, the farmer goes with his thrift,
The droves and crops increase, the barns are well-fill'd.

---

51 Fraunces Tavern in New York City.

Elements merge in the night, ships make tacks in the dreams,
The sailor sails, the exile returns home,
The fugitive returns unharm'd, the immigrant is back beyond months and years,   125
The poor Irishman lives in the simple house of his childhood with the well-known
    neighbors and faces,
They warmly welcome him, he is barefoot again, he forgets he is well off,
The Dutchman voyages home, and the Scotchman and Welshman voyage home,
    and the native of the Mediterranean voyages home,
To every port of England, France, Spain, enter well-fill'd ships,
The Swiss foots it toward his hills, the Prussian goes his way, the Hungarian his
    way, and the Pole his way,   130
The Swede returns, and the Dane and Norwegian return.

The homeward bound and the outward bound,
The beautiful lost swimmer, the ennuyé, the onanist, the female that loves
    unrequited, the money-maker,
The actor and actress, those through with their parts and those waiting to
    commence,
The affectionate boy, the husband and wife, the voter, the nominee that is
    chosen and the nominee that has fail'd,   135
The great already known and the great any time after to-day,
The stammerer, the sick, the perfect-form'd, the homely,
The criminal that stood in the box, the judge that sat and sentenced him, the
    fluent lawyers, the jury, the audience,
The laugher and weeper, the dancer, the midnight widow, the red squaw,
The consumptive, the erysipalite, the idiot, he that is wrong'd,   140
The antipodes, and every one between this and them in the dark,
I swear they are averaged now—one is no better than the other,
The night and sleep have liken'd them and restored them.

I swear they are all beautiful,
Every one that sleeps is beautiful, every thing in the dim light is beautiful,   145
The wildest and bloodiest is over, and all is peace.

Peace is always beautiful,
The myth of heaven indicates peace and night.

The myth of heaven indicates the soul,
The soul is always beautiful, it appears more or it appears less, it comes or it
    lags behind,   150
It comes from its embower'd garden and looks pleasantly on itself and encloses
    the world,
Perfect and clean the genitals previously jetting, and perfect and clean the womb
    cohering,
The head well-grown proportion'd and plumb, and the bowels and joints
    proportion'd and plumb.
The soul is always beautiful,
The universe is duly in order, every thing is in its place,   155
What has arrived is in its place and what waits shall be in its place,

What has arrived is in its place and what waits shall be in its place,
The twisted skull waits, the watery or rotten blood waits,
The child of the glutton or venerealee waits long, and the child of the drunkard
    waits long, and the drunkard himself waits long,
The sleepers that lived and died wait, the far advanced are to go on in their turns,
    and the far behind are to come on in their turns,
The diverse shall be no less diverse, but they shall flow and unite—they unite
    now.   160

8

The sleepers are very beautiful as they lie unclothed,
They flow hand in hand over the whole earth from east to west as they lie
    unclothed,
The Asiatic and African are hand in hand, the European and American are hand
    in hand,
Learn'd and unlearn'd are hand in hand, and male and female are hand in hand,
The bare arm of the girl crosses the bare breast of her lover, they press close
    without lust, his lips press her neck,   165
The father holds his grown or ungrown son in his arms with measureless love,
    and the son holds the father in his arms with measureless love,
The white hair of the mother shines on the white wrist of the daughter,
The breath of the boy goes with the breath of the man, friend is inarm'd by
    friend,
The scholar kisses the teacher and the teacher kisses the scholar, the wrong'd is
    made right,
The call of the slave is one with the master's call, and the master salutes the
    slave,   170
The felon steps forth from the prison, the insane becomes sane, the suffering of
    sick persons is reliev'd,
The sweatings and fevers stop, the throat that was unsound is sound, the lungs
    of the consumptive are resumed, the poor distress'd head is free,
The joints of the rheumatic move as smoothly as ever, and smoother than ever,
Stiflings and passages open, the paralyzed become supple,
The swell'd and convuls'd and congested awake to themselves in condition, 175
They pass the invigoration of the night and the chemistry of the night, and
    awake.

I too pass from the night,
I stay a while away O night, but I return to you again and love you.

Why should I be afraid to trust myself to you?
I am not afraid, I have been well brought forward by you,   180
I love the rich running day, but I do not desert her in whom I lay so long,
I know not how I came of you and I know not where I go with you, but I know
    I came well and shall go well.

I will stop only a time with the night, and rise betimes,
I will duly pass the day O my mother, and duly return to you.
1855

from Whispers of Heavenly Death

A Noiseless Patient Spider

A noiseless patient spider,
I mark'd where on a little promontory it stood isolated,
Mark'd how to explore the vacant vast surrounding,
It launch'd forth filament, filament, filament, out of itself,
Ever unreeling them, ever tirelessly speeding them.   5

And you O my soul where you stand,
Surrounded, detached, in measureless oceans of space,
Ceaselessly musing, venturing, throwing, seeking the spheres to connect them,
Till the bridge you will need be form'd, till the ductile anchor hold,
Till the gossamer thread you fling catch somewhere, O my soul.   10
1868

Emily Dickinson
1830–1886

Walt Whitman and Emily Dickinson are America's nineteenth-century poetic
geniuses; separately, they resisted the Anglophilia that had hobbled American verse in
genteel forms. Whitman invented American free verse unrhymed and unmeasured;
Dickinson invented a free form of England's most common poem, the hymn. Except
for a very few early experiments, Dickinson wrote in hymn meters all her life, shaping
her single form till it responded effortlessly to her intensity of perception and
expression.

Dickinson, brought up in conventional Protestantism, never abandoned the
metaphysical questions of her upbringing—questions of mortality, renunciation,
perfection, existential meaning. But she emptied them of specifically Christian import,
though she continued to employ Christian symbols, especially those of damnation,
salvation, crucifixion, and heaven. "Some keep the Sabbath going to Church— / I keep
it, staying at Home—" she wrote. Her poetry is frequently blasphemous, as when she
indicts God as the torturer who "scalps your naked Soul." She does not evade her
Puritan and Emersonian inheritance of personal ethical responsibility, but she
wrenches it powerfully to her own uses.

A second Dickinson, as powerful as the metaphysical one, is the observer of nature,
watching a bird eat a worm raw or coming upon a snake and feeling "Zero at the
Bone—." This Dickinson hears the "unobtrusive Mass" of the crickets and perceives "a

Druidic Difference" on the face of the world. She notices "a certain Slant of light, / Winter Afternoons"—a light that makes "Shadows—hold their breath." The New England seasons ("I see—New Englandly—," she said) are memorialized in her work in all their variety.

The third, and greatest, Dickinson is the psychological analyst. Herself subject to extremes of anxiety and depression, she never flinched from interrogating her own mental states, taming them (at least to some degree) by her fine-drawn descriptions of the horrors she experienced. When "a Plank in Reason, broke," or when "the Nerves sit ceremonious, like Tombs—," or when "Chaos—Stopless—cool" besets the soul, Dickinson watches, then reports. Though she concealed herself, in life, from others, she was nakedly exposed to herself.

There are other Dickinsons—the love poet, the social satirist, the observer of people, the poet of aesthetic reflection—each of them a considerable talent. The almost two thousand poems in the Dickinson canon can scarcely be fully present even to Dickinson critics, let alone to the common reader. A search through Dickinson's *Complete Poems* never fails to turn up new poems of great value.

And yet this great poet published only a dozen poems in her lifetime. It was not until 1955 that all her known poetry was published, and this was the first collection to reproduce Dickinson's texts as she wrote them, without many editorial changes; it was not until 1982 that her own arrangement of many of her poems in little books, or "fascicles," was made known in facsimile publication. Dickinson was perhaps discouraged by the criticism her poems received from Thomas Wentworth Higginson, an editor of the *Atlantic Monthly,* to whom she sent poems in 1862; but her friend Helen Hunt Jackson, a well-known author, could have helped to ensure that more poems were published had Dickinson been willing. Dickinson's personal reclusiveness forbade self-promotion, however, and she allowed her poems to accumulate instead in her bureau drawers.

Dickinson grew up in a well-to-do household and had the run of her father's library. Her father was the treasurer of Amherst College, and her grandfather had been one of its founders. She spent a single year at the South Hadley Female Seminary (later to become Mount Holyoke College) but did not remain; she experienced there the inability to believe in institutional religion that caused her to abandon attendance at the Congregational Church. After leaving school, Dickinson became increasingly unwilling to engage in social interchange outside her own house. Though she made brief visits to Boston, Philadelphia, and Washington, D.C., she spent her entire life in her father's house, eventually seeing no visitors. Her brother Austin, after his marriage, lived next door with his wife, the difficult "Sister Sue" to whom many of Dickinson's poems were addressed. Dickinson wrote hundreds of letters and poems yearly (366 poems in the single year 1862). Her neighbors, noting her elusiveness and her constant wearing of white, considered her eccentric. They had no idea of the practical purpose served by her withdrawal, which permitted her to escape the enormous labors usually required of single women, who were freely called on to attend the young, the sick, and the dying. Dickinson reserved her energies for her genius.

Dickinson's early poetry, when it is weak, displays hysteria, self-absorption, and a coy whimsicality. To watch her develop as a poet is to see the whimsicality relax, the hysteria become disciplined by intellectual analysis, and the self-absorption strengthen itself into meditation on the human lot. Her irony turns on herself as well as on the universe; her love of paradox deepens to an examination of the laws of necessity, creative and destructive at once. In manuscript, the smallest Dickinson poem spreads, in her enlarged handwriting, to fill the whole page on which it is written, as though each blank piece of paper were the brain, or the world, filled to the margins with a single mood or insight. Dickinson's bold calligraphy and her composition by phrase— each marked off by a dash with space before and after—puts emphasis on each stamp or impress of the mind in its analysis of experience. Slant rhymes and an oblique form of expression ensure the oddness of surface in Dickinson's poems; the resonant forms of her language stand for her conviction of the baffling eccentricity of life and thought. Though her poetry reflects her reading of many English poets (Shakespeare, Keats, Mrs. Browning) and of Emerson, she is the least imitative of American poets, turning the discursive certainties of writers and philosophers alike into her own preferred thematic form, the riddle. Enigma is her genre, and pain her topic; her anatomy of psychic skepticism remains one of the great documents of American nineteenth-century attitudes. The best measure of her success in verse is the way in which her poems make themselves remembered. Without any effort on our part to memorize them, we find we cannot forget her lines. Her fame has continued to grow. Her poems, once rewritten by others for public acceptability, are now known in their full power and self-assertion.

Reading Dickinson's Letters

Reading Emily Dickinson's often daily correspondence to both her family and friends enriches any careful consideration of her poetry. Her early letters to her brother Austin and to other family members reflect a lively and engaged mind, aware of and interested in the lives and activities of those about whom she cared a great deal. Her letters during this period are representative of the family correspondences which occupied all of the Dickinson children, and they are filled with a range of references to reading and current activities.

As Dickinson's poetic voice matured, she employed language in an increasingly personal grammatical structure, with the syntactical inversions and linguistic complexities of her poetry mirrored in the letter form, as though traditional language had ceased to answer adequately to her interior mind. These later letters reveal a woman capable of great—and enduring—friendship and deep passions, involved in an intricate series of family relationships which brought her into a continuing speculation about the formal aspects of each traditional form in which she found herself moving. The letters to Susan Gilbert included here are part of a much larger collection of letters from Dickinson to Susan (Gilbert) Dickinson, initially a close friend of Emily and later the wife of her brother Austin. Susan (Gilbert) Dickinson remained a constant presence in Emily's life.

While the language and often the grammar and syntax of Emily Dickinson's poetry and letters grew increasingly similar, her intentions for her poetry remained intensely private. The initial letter of April 15, 1862 to the publisher and abolitionist Thomas Wentworth Higginson represents Dickinson's efforts to elicit a response to her "Letters to the World," as she called her poetry. The correspondence between Dickinson and Higginson, and Higginson's letters to his wife detailing his visit to Dickinson's home in Amherst, Massachusetts, provide significant insights into Dickinson's poetic and creative life. As is the case with Dickinson's poems, all of her letters can be heavily annotated. Like the poems, Dickinson's letters often conceal as much as they reveal.

Further Reading:

G. F. Whicher, *This Was a Poet: A Critical Biography of Emily Dickinson,* 1939.

R. Chase, *Emily Dickinson,* 1951.

C. R. Anderson, *Emily Dickinson's Poetry,* 1960.

A. J. Gelpi, *Emily Dickinson: The Mind of the Poet,* 1965.

B. Lindberg-Seyersted, *The Voice of the Poet: Aspects of Style in the Poetry of Emily Dickinson,* 1968.

R. B. Sewall, *The Life of Emily Dickinson,* 1974.

S. Cameron, *Lyric Time: Dickinson & the Limits of Genre,* 1979.

K. Keller, *The Only Kangaroo Among the Beauty: Emily Dickinson and America,* 1979.

J. F. Diehl, *Dickinson and the Romantic Imagination,* 1981.

R. W. Franklin, *The Manuscript Books of Emily Dickinson,* 1981.

R. Porter, *Dickinson, the Modern Idiom,* 1981.

S. Juhasz, *The Undiscovered Continent: Emily Dickinson and the Space of the Mind,* 1983.

S. Howe, *My Emily Dickinson,* 1985.

C. Griffin Wolff, *Emily Dickinson,* 1986.

C. Miller, *Emily Dickinson: A Poet's Grammar,* 1987.

J. Dobson, *Dickinson and the Strategies of Reticence: The Woman Writer in Nineteenth-Century America,* 1989.

P. Bennett, *Emily Dickinson, Woman Poet,* 1990.

J. Loving, *Emily Dickinson: The Poet on the Second Story,* 1986.

J. Farr, *The Passion of Emily Dickinson,* 1992.

S. Cameron, *Choosing not Choosing: Dickinson's Fascicles,* 1992.

Texts:

The Poems of Emily Dickinson, ed. T. H. Johnson, 3 vols., 1953.

The Letters of Emily Dickinson, ed. T. H. Johnson and T. Ward, 1958.

Letters and Journals of Thomas Wentworth Higginson, ed. H. T. Higginson, 1921.

67

Success is counted sweetest
By those who ne'er succeed.
To comprehend a nectar
Requires sorest need.

Not one of all the purple Host   5
Who took the Flag today
Can tell the definition
So clear of Victory

As he defeated—dying—
On whose forbidden ear   10
The distant strains of triumph
Burst agonized and clear!
1878/1951

185

"Faith" is a fine invention
When Gentlemen can *see*—
But *microscopes* are prudent
In an Emergency.
1951

214

I taste a liquor never brewed—
From Tankards scooped in Pearl—
Not all the Frankfort Berries
Yield such an Alcohol!

Inebriate of Air—am I—   5
And Debauchee of Dew—
Reeling—thro endless summer days—
From inns of Molten Blue—

When "Landlords" turn the drunken Bee
Out of the Foxglove's door—   10
When Butterflies—renounce their "drams"—
I shall but drink the more!

Till Seraphs swing their snowy Hats—
And Saints—to windows run—
To see the little Tippler   15
From Manzanilla come!
1861/1951

216

[Draft 1]

Safe in their Alabaster Chambers—
Untouched by Morning
And untouched by Noon—
Sleep the meek members of the Resurrection—

Rafter of satin,   5
And Roof of stone.

Light laughs the breeze
In her Castle above them—
Babbles the Bee in a stolid Ear,
Pipe the Sweet Birds in ignorant cadence—   10
Ah, what sagacity perished here!
1859/1951

[Draft 2]

Safe in their Alabaster Chambers—
Untouched by Morning—
And untouched by Noon—
Lie the meek members of the Resurrection—
Rafter of Satin—and Roof of Stone!   5

Grand go the Years—in the Crescent—above
  them—
Worlds scoop their Arcs—
And Firmaments—row—
Diadems—drop—and Doges[1]—surrender—
Soundless as dots—on a Disc of Snow—   10
1861/1951

241

I like a look of Agony,
Because I know it's true—
Men do not sham Convulsion,
Nor simulate, a Throe—

The Eyes glaze once—and that is Death—   5
Impossible to feign
The Beads upon the Forehead
By homely Anguish strung.
1951

[1] Early chief magistrates of the Italian republics of Venice and Genoa; in this context,
rulers.

258

There's a certain Slant of light,
Winter Afternoons—
That oppresses, like the Heft
Of Cathedral Tunes—

Heavenly Hurt, it gives us—   5
We can find no scar,
But internal difference,
Where the Meanings, are—

None may teach it—Any—
'Tis the Seal Despair—   10
An imperial affliction
Sent us of the Air—

When it comes, the Landscape listens—
Shadows—hold their breath—
When it goes, 'tis like the Distance   15
On the look of Death—
1951

280

I felt a Funeral, in my Brain,
And Mourners to and fro
Kept treading—treading—till it seemed
That Sense was breaking through—

And when they all were seated,   5
A Service, like a Drum—
Kept beating—beating—till I thought
My Mind was going numb—

And then I heard them lift a Box
And creak across my Soul   10
With those same Boots of Lead, again,
Then Space—began to toll,

As all the Heavens were a Bell,
And Being, but an Ear,
And I, and Silence, some strange Race   15
Wrecked, solitary, here—

And then a Plank in Reason, broke,
And I dropped down, and down—
And hit a World, at every plunge,
And Finished knowing—then—   20
1951

303

The Soul selects her own Society—
Then—shuts the Door—
To her divine Majority—
Present no more—

Unmoved—she notes the Chariots—pausing—   5
At her low Gate—
Unmoved—an Emperor be kneeling
Upon her Mat—

I've known her—from an ample nation—
Choose One—   10
Then—close the Valves of her attention—
Like Stone—
1951

324

Some keep the Sabbath going to Church—
I keep it, staying at Home—
With a Bobolink for a Chorister—
And an Orchard, for a Dome—

Some keep the Sabbath in Surplice—   5
I just wear my Wings—
And instead of tolling the Bell, for Church,
Our little Sexton—sings.

God preaches, a noted Clergyman—
And the sermon is never long,   10
So instead of getting to Heaven at last—
I'm going, all along.
1951

338

I know that He exists.
Somewhere—in Silence—
He has hid his rare life
From our gross eyes.

'Tis an instant's play.   5
'Tis a fond Ambush—
Just to make Bliss
Earn her own surprise!

But—should the play
Prove piercing earnest—   10
Should the glee—glaze—
In Death's—stiff—stare—

Would not the fun
Look too expensive!
Would not the jest—   15
Have crawled too far!
1951

341

After great pain, a formal feeling comes—
The Nerves sit ceremonious, like Tombs—
The stiff Heart questions was it He, that bore,
And Yesterday, or Centuries before?

The Feet, mechanical, go round—   5
Of Ground, or Air, or Ought—
A Wooden way
Regardless grown,
A Quartz contentment, like a stone—

This is the Hour of Lead—   10
Remembered, if outlived,
As Freezing persons, recollect the Snow—
First—Chill—then Stupor—then the letting go—
1951

401

What Soft—Cherubic Creatures—
These Gentlewomen are—
One would as soon assault a Plush—
Or violate a Star—

Such Dimity Convictions— 5
A Horror so refined
Of freckled Human Nature—
Of Deity—ashamed—

It's such a common—Glory—
A Fisherman's—Degree— 10
Redemption—Brittle Lady—
Be so—ashamed of Thee—
1951

435

Much Madness is divinest Sense—
To a discerning Eye—
Much Sense—the starkest Madness—
'Tis the Majority
In this, as All, prevail— 5
Assent—and you are sane—
Demur—you're straightway dangerous—
And handled with a Chain—
1951

441

This is my letter to the World
That never wrote to Me—
The simple News that Nature told—
With tender Majesty

Her Message is committed 5
To Hands I cannot see—
For love of Her—Sweet—countrymen—
Judge tenderly—of Me
1951

448

This was a Poet—It is That
Distills amazing sense
From ordinary Meanings—
And Attar[1] so immense

From the familiar species   5
That perished by the Door—
We wonder it was not Ourselves
Arrested it—before—

Of Pictures, the Discloser—
The Poet—it is He—   10
Entitles Us—by Contrast—
To ceaseless Poverty—

Of Portion—so unconscious—
The Robbing—could not harm—
Himself—to Him—a Fortune—   15
Exterior—to Time—
1951

449

I died for Beauty—but was scarce
Adjusted in the Tomb
When One who died for Truth, was lain
In an adjoining Room—

He questioned softly "Why I failed"?   5
"For Beauty", I replied—
"And I—for Truth—Themself are One—
We Brethren, are", He said—

And so, as Kinsmen, met a Night—
We talked between the Rooms—   10
Until the Moss had reached our lips—
And covered up—our names—
1951

---

[1] Distilled fragrance, usually concentrated and
intense.

465

I heard a Fly buzz—when I died—
The Stillness in the Room
Was like the Stillness in the Air—
Between the Heaves of Storm—

The Eyes around—had wrung them dry—   5
And Breaths were gathering firm
For that last Onset—when the King
Be witnessed—in the Room—

I willed my Keepsakes—Signed away
What portion of me be   10
Assignable—and then it was
There interposed a Fly—

With Blue—uncertain stumbling Buzz—
Between the light—and me—
And then the Windows failed—and then   15
I could not see to see—
1951

501

This World is not Conclusion.
A Species stands beyond—
Invisible, as Music—
But positive, as Sound—
It beckons, and it baffles—   5
Philosophy—dont know—
And through a Riddle, at the last—
Sagacity, must go—
To guess it, puzzles scholars—
To gain it, Men have borne   10
Contempt of Generations
And Crucifixion, shown—
Faith slips—and laughs, and rallies—
Blushes, if any see—
Plucks at a twig of Evidence—   15
And asks a Vane, the way—
Much Gesture, from the Pulpit—
Strong Hallelujahs roll—

Narcotics cannot still the Tooth
That nibbles at the soul—   20
1951

536

The Heart asks Pleasure—first—
And then—Excuse from Pain—
And then—those little Anodynes
That deaden suffering—

And then—to go to sleep—   5
And then—if it should be
The will of its Inquisitor
The privilege to die—
1951

585

I like to see it lap the Miles—
And lick the Valleys up—
And stop to feed itself at Tanks—
And then—prodigious step

Around a Pile of Mountains—   5
And supercilious peer
In Shanties—by the sides of Roads—
And then a Quarry pare

To fit its sides
And crawl between   10
Complaining all the while
In horrid—hooting stanza—
Then chase itself down Hill—

And neigh like Boanerges—
Then—prompter than a Star   15
Stop—docile and omnipotent
At its own stable door—
1951

632

The Brain—is wider than the Sky—
For—put them side by side—
The one the other will contain
With ease—and You—beside—

The Brain is deeper than the sea—   5
For—hold them—Blue to Blue—
The one the other will absorb—
As Sponges—Buckets—do—

The Brain is just the weight of God—
For—Heft them—Pound for Pound—   10
And they will differ—if they do—
As Syllable from Sound—
1951

640

I cannot live with You—
It would be Life—
And Life is over there—
Behind the Shelf

The Sexton keeps the Key to—   5
Putting up
Our Life—His Porcelain—
Like a Cup—

Discarded of the Housewife—
Quaint—or Broke—   10
A newer Sevres[1] pleases—
Old Ones crack—

I could not die—with You—
For One must wait
To shut the Other's Gaze down—   15
You—could not—

---

[1] Porcelain made in the town of Sèvres,
France.

And I—Could I stand by
And see You—freeze—
Without my Right of Frost—
Death's privilege?   20

Nor could I rise—with You—
Because Your Face
Would put out Jesus'—
That New Grace

Glow plain—and foreign   25
On my homesick Eye—
Except that You than He
Shone closer by—

They'd judge Us—How—
For You—served Heaven—You know,   30
Or sought to—
I could not—

Because You saturated Sight—
And I had no more Eyes
For sordid excellence   35
As Paradise

And were You lost, I would be—
Though My Name
Rang loudest
On the Heavenly fame—   40

And were You—saved—
And I—condemned to be
Where You were not—
That self—were Hell to Me—

So We must meet apart—   45
You there—I—here—
With just the Door ajar
That Oceans are—and Prayer—
And that White Sustenance—
Despair—   50
1951

650

Pain—has an Element of Blank—
It cannot recollect
When it begun—or if there were
A time when it was not—

It has no Future—but itself—   5
Its Infinite contain
Its Past—enlightened to perceive
New Periods—of Pain.
1951

657

I dwell in Possibility—
A fairer House than Prose—
More numerous of Windows—
Superior—for Doors—

Of Chambers as the Cedars—   5
Impregnable of Eye—
And for an Everlasting Roof
The Gambrels of the Sky—

Of Visitors—the fairest—
For Occupation—This—   10
The spreading wide my narrow Hands
To gather Paradise—
1951

709

Publication—is the Auction
Of the Mind of Man—
Poverty—be justifying
For so foul a thing

Possibly—but We—would rather   5
From Our Garret go

White—Unto the White Creator—
Than invest—Our Snow—

Thought belong to Him who gave it—
Then—to Him Who bear   10
It's Corporeal illustration—Sell
The Royal Air—

In the Parcel—Be the Merchant
Of the Heavenly Grace—
But reduce no Human Spirit   15
To Disgrace of Price—
1951

712

Because I could not stop for Death—
He kindly stopped for me—
The Carriage held but just Ourselves—
And Immortality.

We slowly drove—He knew no haste   5
And I had put away
My labor and my leisure too,
For His Civility—

We passed the School, where Children strove
At Recess—in the Ring—   10
We passed the Fields of Gazing Grain—
We passed the Setting Sun—

Or rather—He passed Us—
The Dews drew quivering and chill—
For only Gossamer, my Gown—   15
My Tippet[1]—only Tulle—

We paused before a House that seemed
A Swelling of the Ground—
The Roof was scarcely visible—
The Cornice—in the Ground—   20

Since then—'tis Centuries—and yet
Feels shorter than the Day

---

[1] Short shoulder cape or scarf.

I first surmised the Horses' Heads
Were toward Eternity—
1951

721

Behind Me—dips Eternity—
Before Me—Immortality—
Myself—the Term between—
Death but the Drift of Eastern Gray,
Dissolving into Dawn away,   5
Before the West begin—

'Tis Kingdoms—afterward—they say—
In perfect—pauseless Monarchy—
Whose Prince—is Son of None—
Himself—His Dateless Dynasty—   10
Himself—Himself diversify—
In Duplicate divine[1]—

'Tis Miracle before Me—then—
'Tis Miracle behind—between—
A Crescent in the Sea—   15
With Midnight to the North of Her—
And Midnight to the South of Her—
And Maelstrom—in the Sky—
1951

754

My Life had stood—a Loaded Gun—
In Corners—till a Day
The Owner passed—identified—
And carried Me away—

And now We roam in Sovereign Woods—   5
And now We hunt the Doe—
And every time I speak for Him—
The Mountains straight reply—

[1] Reference to the Christian doctrine of the Trinity, which states that the Son issues from the Father, and the Holy Spirit from the union of Father and Son.

And do I smile, such cordial light
Upon the Valley glow—   10
It is as a Vesuvian[1] face
Had let its pleasure through—

And when at Night—Our good Day done—
I guard My Master's Head—
'Tis better than the Eider-Duck's   15
Deep Pillow[2]—to have shared—

To foe of His—I'm deadly foe—
None stir the second time—
On whom I lay a Yellow Eye—
Or an emphatic Thumb—   20

Though I than He—may longer live
He longer must—than I—
For I have but the power to kill,
Without—the power to die—
1951

764

Presentiment—is that long Shadow—on the Lawn—
Indicative that Suns go down—

The Notice to the startled Grass
That Darkness—is about to pass—
1951

986

A narrow Fellow in the Grass
Occasionally rides—
You may have met Him—did you not
His notice sudden is—

The Grass divides as with a Comb—   5
A spotted shaft is seen—
And then it closes at your feet
And opens further on—

---

[1] Reference to Mount Vesuvius, the famous   [2] i.e., filled with soft feathers.
volcano on the Bay of Naples.

He likes a Boggy Acre
A Floor too cool for Corn—   10
Yet when a Boy, and Barefoot—
I more than once at Noon
Have passed, I thought, a Whip lash
Unbraiding in the Sun
When stooping to secure it   15
It wrinkled, and was gone—

Several of Nature's People
I know, and they know me—
I feel for them a transport
Of cordiality—   20

But never met this Fellow
Attended, or alone
Without a tighter breathing
And Zero at the Bone—
1951

1052

I never saw a Moor—
I never saw the Sea—
Yet know I how the Heather looks
And what a Billow be.

I never spoke with God   5
Nor visited in Heaven—
Yet certain am I of the spot
As if the Checks[1] were given—
1951

1071

Perception of an object costs
Precise the Object's loss—
Perception in itself a Gain
Replying to its Price—

---

[1] Railway tickets.

The Object Absolute—is nought—   5
Perception sets it fair
And then upbraids a Perfectness
That situates so far—
1951

1078

The Bustle in a House
The Morning after Death
Is solemnest of industries
Enacted upon Earth—

The Sweeping up the Heart   5
And putting Love away
We shall not want to use again
Until Eternity.
1951

1125

Oh Sumptuous moment
Slower go
That I may gloat on thee—
'Twill never be the same to starve
Now I abundance see—   5

Which was to famish, then or now—
The difference of Day
Ask him unto the Gallows led—
With morning in the sky—
1945

1129

Tell all the Truth but tell it slant—
Success in Circuit lies
Too bright for our infirm Delight
The Truth's superb surprise

As Lightning to the Children eased   5
With explanation kind
The Truth must dazzle gradually
Or every man be blind—
1951

1463

A Route of Evanescence
With a revolving Wheel—
A Resonance of Emerald—
A Rush of Cochineal—
And every Blossom on the Bush   5
Adjusts its tumbled Head—
The mail from Tunis, probably,
An easy Morning's Ride—
1891

1540

As imperceptibly as Grief
The Summer lapsed away—
Too imperceptible at last
To seem like Perfidy—
A Quietness distilled   5
As Twilight long begun,
Or Nature spending with herself
Sequestered Afternoon—
The Dusk drew earlier in—
The Morning foreign shone—   10
A courteous, yet harrowing Grace,
As Guest, that would be gone—
And thus, without a Wing
Or service of a Keel
Our Summer made her light escape   15
Into the Beautiful.
1951

1545

The Bible is an antique Volume—
Written by faded Men
At the suggestion of Holy Spectres[1]—
Subjects—Bethlehem—
Eden—the ancient Homestead—   5

[1] The Holy Spirit is said to be the inspirer of
the authors of the Bible.

Satan—the Brigadier—
Judas—the Great Defaulter—
David—the Troubadour[2]—
Sin—a distinguished Precipice
Others must resist—   10
Boys that "believe" are very lonesome—
Other Boys are "lost"—
Had but the Tale a warbling Teller—
All the Boys would come—
Orpheus' Sermon captivated[3]—   15
It did not condemn—
1951

1624

Apparently with no surprise
To any happy Flower
The Frost beheads it at its play—
In accidental power—
The blonde Assassin passes on—   5
The Sun proceeds unmoved
To measure off another Day
For an Approving God.
1951

1651

A Word made Flesh[1] is seldom
And tremblingly partook[2]
Nor then perhaps reported
But have I not mistook
Each one of us has tasted   5
With ecstasies of stealth
The very food debated[3]
To our specific strength—

---

[2] Beginning in line 4 Dickinson enumerates, out of order, the fall of Satan and his rebel angels, the creation of Man in Eden, Original Sin and the Fall, the composition of the Psalms by King David, the birth of Jesus in Bethlehem, and the betrayal of Jesus by Judas.
[3] In mythology, when Orpheus played his lyre and sang, trees and rocks danced, and all the animals came to listen.

[1] "And the Word was made flesh and dwelt among us," are St. John's words for the Incarnation of Christ. (See John 1:14.)
[2] In the Christian rite of Holy Communion, believers "partake" of the bread and wine, symbols of Jesus' body and blood, respectively.
[3] Determined by discussion to be accurate.

A Word that breathes distinctly
Has not the power to die   10
Cohesive as the Spirit
It may expire if He—
"Made Flesh and dwelt among us"
Could condescension[4] be
Like this consent of Language   15
This loved Philology.
1951

1670

In Winter in my Room
I came upon a Worm—
Pink, lank and warm—
But as he was a worm
And worms presume   5
Not quite with him at home—
Secured him by a string
To something neighboring
And went along.

A Trifle afterward   10
A thing occurred
I'd not believe it if I heard
But state with creeeping blood—
A snake with mottles rare
Surveyed my chamber floor   15
In feature as the worm before
But ringed with power—

The very string with which
I tied him—too
When he was mean and new   20
That string was there—

I shrank—"How fair you are"!
Propitiation's claw—
"Afraid," he hissed
"Of me"?   25
"No cordiality"—
He fathomed me—

---

[4] Used theologically to signify Christ's descent
from the Godhead into flesh.

Then to a Rhythm *Slim*
Secreted in his Form
As Patterns swim   30
Projected him.

That time I flew
Both eyes his way
Lest he pursue
Nor ever ceased to run   35
Till in a distant Town
Towns on from mine
I set me down
This was a dream.
1914

1732

My life closed twice before its close—
It yet remains to see
If Immortality unveil
A third event to me

So huge, so hopeless to conceive   5
As these that twice befell.
Parting is all we know of heaven,
And all we need of hell.
1951

1760

Elysium[1] is as far as to
The very nearest Room
If in that Room a Friend await
Felicity or Doom—

What fortitude the Soul contains,   5
That it can so endure
The accent of a coming Foot—
The opening of a Door—
1951

---

[1] Mythological equivalent to the Christian
heaven.

To Austin Dickinson[1]   *17 October 1851*

We are waiting for breakfast, Austin, the meat and potato and a little pan of your favorite brown bread are keeping warm at the fire, while father goes for shavings.

    Everything has changed since my other letter—the doors are shut this morning, and all the kitchen wall is covered with chilly flies who are trying to warm themselves—poor things, they do not understand that there are no summer mornings remaining to them and me and they have a bewildered air which is really very droll, did'nt one feel *sorry* for them. You would say t'was a gloomy morning if you were sitting here—the frost has been severe and the few lingering leaves seem anxious to be going and wrap their faded cloaks more closely about them as if to shield them from the chilly northeast wind. The earth looks like some poor old lady who by dint of pains has bloomed e'en till *now*, yet in a forgetful moment a few silver hairs from out her cap come stealing, and she tucks them back so hastily and thinks nobody *sees*. The cows are going to pasture and little boys with their hands in their pockets are whistling to try to keep warm. Dont think that the sky will frown so the day when you come home! She will smile and look happy, and be full of sunshine *then*—and even *should* she frown upon her child returning, there is *another* sky ever serene and fair, and there is *another* sunshine, tho' it be darkness there—never mind faded forests, Austin, never mind silent fields—*here* is a little forest whose leaf is ever green, here is a *brighter* garden, where not a frost has been, in its unfading flowers I hear the bright bee hum, prithee, my Brother, into *my* garden come!

Your very aff
Sister.

To Susan Gilbert (Dickinson)[1]   *27 June 1852*

My Susie's last request; yes, darling, I grant it, tho' few, and fleet the days which separate us now—but six more weary days, but six more twilight evens, and my lone little fireside, my *silent* fireside is once more full.

    "We are seven, and one in heaven,"[2] we are *three* next Saturday, if *I* have *mine* and heaven has none. . . .

    Susie, will you indeed come home next Saturday, and be my own again, and kiss me as you used to? Shall I indeed behold you, not "darkly, but face to face"[3] or am I *fancying* so, and dreaming blessed dreams from which the day will wake me? I hope for you so much, and feel so eager for you, feel that I *cannot* wait, feel that *now* I must have you—that the expectation once more to see your face again, makes me feel hot and feverish, and my heart beats so fast—I go to sleep at night, and the first thing I know, I

---

[1] William Austin Dickinson (1829–1895), Emily Dickinson's brother. A prominent citizen of Amherst, Massachusetts, where he practiced law, Austin succeeded his father as treasurer of Amherst College in 1873.
[1] Susan Huntington Gilbert (Dickinson) (1830–1913), Emily Dickinson's closest friend in the 1850s. She married Emily's brother Austin in 1856. The couple lived next door to the Dickinson homestead.
[2] Refers to William Wordsworth's (1770–1850) poem "We Are Seven." In the poem, however, two are in heaven.
[3] Refers to the passage on love in Paul's first letter to Corinthians. Exhorting the believers to exhibit love, he reminds them that when Christ returns their confusion will be at an end: "For now we see through a glass, darkly: but then face to face: now I know in part; but then shall I know even as also I am known." I Cor. 13:12.

am sitting there wide awake, and clasping my hands tightly, and thinking of next Saturday, and "never a bit" of you.

Sometimes I must have Saturday before tomorrow comes, and I wonder if it w'd make any difference with God, to give it to me *today,* and I'd let him have Monday, to make him a Saturday; and then I feel so funnily, and wish the precious day would'nt come quite so soon, till I could know how to feel, and get my thoughts ready for it.

Why, Susie, it seems to me as if my absent Lover was coming home so soon—and my heart must be so busy, making ready for him.

While the minister this morning was giving an account of the Roman Catholic system, and announcing several facts which were usually startling, I was trying to make up my mind wh' of the two was prettiest to go and welcome *you* in, my fawn colored dress, or my blue dress. Just as I had decided by all means to wear the blue, down came the minister's fist with a terrible rap on the counter, and Susie, it scared me so, I hav'nt got over it yet, but I'm glad I reached a conclusion! I walked home from meeting with Mattie,[4] and *incidentally* quite, something was said of you, and I think one of us remarked that you would be here next Sunday; well—Susie—what it was *I* dont presume to know, but my gaiters[5] seemed to leave me, and I seemed to move on wings—and I move on wings now, Susie, on wings as white as snow, and as bright as the summer sunshine—because I am with you, and so few short days, you are with me at home. Be patient then, my Sister, for the hours will haste away, and Oh *so* soon! Susie, I write most hastily, and very carelessly too, for it is time for me to get the supper, and my mother is gone and besides, my darling, so near I seem to you, that I *disdain* this pen, and wait for a *warmer* language. With Vinnie's[6] love, and my love, I am once more

Your Emilie—

To T. W. Higginson[1]   15 April 1862

Mr Higginson,
    Are you too deeply occupied to say if my Verse is alive?
    The Mind is so near itself—it cannot see, distinctly—and I have none to ask—
    Should you think it breathed—and had you the leisure to tell me, I should feel quick gratitude—
    If I make the mistake—that you dared to tell me—would give me sincerer honor—toward you—
    I enclose my name—asking you, if you please—Sir—to tell me what is true?
    That you will not betray me—it is needless to ask—since Honor is it's own pawn—

---

4 Martha Isabella Gilbert (Smith) (1829–1895), Susan's slightly older sister.
5 High-topped shoes.
6 Lavinia Norcross Dickinson (1833–1899), Emily Dickinson's sister. Vinnie, like Emily, never married but lived at home. She survived Emily by twelve years, and was responsible for publishing the first volume of Dickinson's poems in 1890.
1 Thomas Wentworth Higginson (1823–1911), abolitionist and writer. "This first letter to Higginson, which begins a cor-

respondence that lasted until the month of her death, she wrote because she had just read his 'Letter to a Young Contributor,' the lead article in the *Atlantic Monthly* for April, offering practical advice to beginning writers. Instead of signing this letter, Dickinson enclosed a card with her name on it as well as four poems: 'Safe in their Alabaster Chambers,' 'The nearest Dream recedes unrealized,' 'We play at Paste,' and 'I'll tell you how the Sun rose.' " (Johnson's note)

To T. W. Higginson   *25 April 1862*

Mr Higginson,

Your kindness claimed earlier gratitude—but I was ill—and write today, from my pillow.

Thank you for the surgery[1]—it was not so painful as I supposed. I bring you others—as you ask—though they might not differ—

While my thought is undressed—I can make the distinction, but when I put them in the Gown—they look alike, and numb.

You asked how old I was? I made no verse—but one or two—until this winter—Sir—

I had a terror[2]—since September—I could tell to none—and so I sing, as the Boy does by the Burying Ground—because I am afraid—You inquire my Books—For Poets—I have Keats[3]—and Mr and Mrs Browning.[4] For Prose—Mr Ruskin[5]—Sir Thomas Browne[6]—and[7] the Revelations.[8] I went to school—but in your manner of the phrase—had no education. When a little Girl, I had a friend, who taught me Immortality[9]—but venturing too near, himself—he never returned—Soon after, my Tutor,[10] died—and for several years, my Lexicon—was my only companion—Then I found one more—but he was not contented I be his scholar—so he left the Land.

You ask of my Companions Hills—Sir—and the Sundown—and a Dog—large as myself, that my Father bought me—They are better than Beings—because they know—but do not tell—and the noise in the Pool, at Noon—excels my Piano. I have a Brother and Sister—My Mother does not care for thought—and Father,[11] too busy with his Briefs[12]—to notice what we do—He buys me many Books—but begs me not to read them—because he fears they joggle the Mind. They are religious—except me—and address an Eclipse, every morning—whom they call their "Father." But I fear my story fatigues you—I would like to learn—Could you tell me how to grow—or is it unconveyed—like Melody—or Witchcraft?

You speak of Mr Whitman[13]—I never read his Book—but was told that he was disgraceful—

[1] Might refer to Higginson's suggestions for cuts and revisions in her poems.

[2] There is much scholarly speculation about the details of this "terror" but no final resolution.

[3] English Romantic poet John Keats (1795–1821).

[4] English poets Robert (1812–1889) and Elizabeth Barrett Browning (1806–1861).

[5] John Ruskin (1819–1900) was an English social theorist and art critic.

[6] Sir Thomas Browne (1605–1682), English Renaissance physician, scientist, and philosopher.

[7] "Higginson's 'Letter to a Young Contributor' [which Dickinson had read in the *Atlantic Monthly*] quotes Ruskin and cites Sir Thomas Browne for vigor of style." (Johnson's note)

[8] The final, apocalyptic book of the Bible.

[9] "The friend who taught her 'Immortality' has generally been thought to be Benjamin Franklin Newton [who died in 1853]." (Johnson's note)

[10] Probably Leonard Humphrey (1824–1850), principal of Amherst Academy (1846–1847) at the time Dickinson attended it.

[11] Respectively: William Austin Dickinson (1829–1895), Lavinia Norcross Dickinson (1833–1899), Emily Norcross Dickinson (1804–1882) and Edward Dickinson (1803–1874).

[12] Edward Dickinson was a prominent Amherst lawyer. A brief is a legal document.

[13] Walt Whitman (1819–1892), American poet whose book *Leaves of Grass* was in its third (1860) edition at this time.

I read Miss Prescott's "Circumstance,"[14] but it followed me, in the Dark—so I avoided her—

Two Editors[15] of Journals came to my Father's House, this winter—and asked me for my Mind—and when I asked them "Why," they said I was penurious—and they, would use it for the World—

I could not weigh myself—Myself—

My size felt small—to me—I read your Chapters in the Atlantic[16]—and experienced honor for you—I was sure you would not reject a confiding question—

Is this—Sir—what you asked me to tell you?

Your friend,
E—Dickinson.

To T. W. Higginson   *7 June 1862*

Dear friend.

Your letter gave no Drunkenness, because I tasted Rum before—Domingo comes but once[1]—yet I have had few pleasures so deep as your opinion, and if I tried to thank you, my tears would block my tongue—

My dying Tutor told me that he would like to live till I had been a poet, but Death was much of Mob as I could master—then—And when far afterward—a sudden light on Orchards, or a new fashion in the wind troubled my attention—I felt a palsy, here—the Verses just relieve—

Your second letter surprised me, and for a moment, swung—I had not supposed it. Your first—gave no dishonor, because the True—are not ashamed—I thanked you for your justice—but could not drop the Bells whose jingling cooled my Tramp—Perhaps the Balm, seemed better, because you bled me,[2] first.

I smile when you suggest that I delay "to publish"—that being foreign to my thought, as Firmament to Fin—

If fame belonged to me, I could not escape her—if she did not, the longest day would pass me on the chase—and the approbation of my Dog, would forsake me—then—My Barefoot-Rank is better—

You think my gait "spasmodic"[3]—I am in danger—Sir—

You think me "uncontrolled"—I have no Tribunal.

---

14 "Harriet Prescott Spofford's 'Circumstance' was published in the *Atlantic Monthly* for May 1860." (Johnson's note)

15 "The two editors who recently had asked her for her mind may have been [Samuel] Bowles [1826–1878] and [Josiah Gilbert] Holland [1819–1881]." (Johnson's note)

16 The *Atlantic Monthly*, to which Higginson was a frequent contributor.

1 Santo Domingo, the capital of the Dominican Republic, a major producer of rum at this time. The analogy here is between tasting rum and earning praise.

2 Refers to the medical practice of drawing blood in order to cure disease. Here the allusion is to Higginson's proposed revisions of her poems. There is no evidence she incorporated his suggestions.

3 Probably refers to Higginson's critique of Dickinson's unique experiments with hymn meters.

Would you have time to be the "friend" you should think I need? I have a little shape—it would not crowd your Desk—nor make much Racket as the Mouse, that dents your Galleries—

If I might bring you what I do—not so frequent to trouble you—and ask you if I told it clear—'twould be control, to me—

The Sailor cannot see the North—but knows the Needle can—

The "hand you stretch me in the Dark," I put mine in, and turn away—I have no Saxon,[4] now—

As if I asked a common Alms,
And in my wondering hand
A Stranger pressed a Kingdom,
And I, bewildered, stand—
As if I asked the Orient
Had it for me a Morn—
And it should lift it's purple Dikes,
And shatter me with Dawn!

But, will you be my Preceptor, Mr Higginson?

Your friend
E Dickinson—

To T. W. Higginson   *July 1862*

Could you believe me—without? I had no portrait, now, but am small, like the Wren, and my Hair is bold, like the Chestnut Bur—and my eyes, like the Sherry in the Glass, that the Guest leaves—Would this do just as well?

It often alarms Father—He says Death might occur, and he has Molds of all the rest—but has no Mold of me, but I noticed the Quick wore off those things, in a few days, and forestall the dishonor—You will think no caprice of me—

You said "Dark." I know the Butterfly—and the Lizard—and the Orchis—

Are not those *your* Countrymen?

I am happy to be your scholar, and will deserve the kindness, I cannot repay.

If you truly consent, I recite, now—

Will you tell me my fault, frankly as to yourself, for I had rather wince, than die. Men do not call the surgeon, to commend—the Bone, but to set it, Sir, and fracture within, is more critical. And for this, Preceptor, I shall bring you—Obedience—the Blossom from my Garden, and every gratitude I know. Perhaps you smile at me. I could not stop for that—My Business is Circumference—An ignorance, not of Customs, but if caught with the Dawn—or the Sunset see me—Myself the only Kangaroo among the Beauty, Sir, if you please, it afflicts me, and I thought that instruction would take it away.

Because you have much business, beside the growth of me—you will appoint, yourself, how often I shall come—without your inconvenience. And if at any time— you regret you received me, or I prove a different fabric to that you supposed—you must banish me—

---

[4] "The phrase 'I have no Saxon' means 'Language fails me. . . .' " (Johnson's note)

When I state myself, as the Representative of the Verse—it does not mean—me—but a supposed person. You are true, about the "perfection."

Today, makes Yesterday mean.

You spoke of Pippa Passes—I never heard anybody speak of Pippa Passes[1]—before.

You see my posture is benighted.

To thank you, baffles me. Are you perfectly powerful? Had I a pleasure you had not, I could delight to bring it.

Your Scholar

To Susan Gilbert Dickinson　　　　　　　　　　　　　　　　　　*early October 1883*

Dear Sue—

The Vision of Immortal Life has been fulfilled—

How simply at the last the Fathom comes! The Passenger and not the Sea, we find surprises us—

Gilbert[1] rejoiced in Secrets—

His Life was panting with them—With what menace of Light he cried "Dont tell, Aunt Emily"! Now my ascended Playmate must instruct *me*. Show us, prattling Preceptor, but the way to thee!

He knew no niggard moment—His Life was full of Boon—The Playthings of the Dervish[2] were not so wild as his—

No crescent was this Creature—He traveled from the Full—

Such soar, but never set—

I see him in the Star, and meet his sweet velocity in everything that flies—His Life was like the Bugle, which winds itself away, his Elegy an echo—his Requiem ecstasy—

Dawn and Meridian in one.

Wherefore would he wait, wronged only of Night, which he left for us—

Without a speculation, our little Ajax[3] spans the whole—

Pass to thy Rendezvous of Light,
Pangless except for us—
Who slowly ford the Mystery
Which thou hast leaped across!

Emily.

---

[1] " 'Pippa Passes,' the first of the series in Browning's 'Bells and Pomegranates,' had been published in 1841. The letter enclosed four poems: 'Of Tribulation these are they,' 'Your Riches taught me poverty,' 'Some keep the Sabbath going to Church,' and 'Success is counted sweetest.' " (Johnson's note)

[1] Gilbert Dickinson (1875–1883), Emily's nephew and the youngest of Susan's and Austin's three children, died suddenly of typhoid fever on October 5, 1883.

[2] Dervishes were members of Muslim orders whose religious observances sometimes included howling and whirling.

[3] This could refer either to Ajax in Homer's *Iliad*, the warrior renowned for his bravery, or the warrior renowned for his speed.

To T. W. Higginson   *spring 1886*

"Mars[1] the sacred Loneliness"! What an Elegy! "From Mount Zion[2] below to Mount Zion above"! said President Humphrey of her Father[3]—Gabriel's[4] Oration would adorn his Child—

When she came the last time she had in her Hand as I entered, the "Choir invisible."[5]

"Superb," she said as she shut the Book, stooping to receive me, but fervor suffocates me. Thank you for "the Sonnet"[6]—I have lain it at her loved feet.

Not knowing when Herself may come
I open every Door,
Or has she Feathers, like a Bird,
Or Billows, like a Shore—

I think she would rather have stayed with us, but perhaps she will learn the Customs of Heaven, as the Prisoner of Chillon[7] of Captivity.

You asked had I read "the Notices."

I have been very ill, Dear friend, since November, bereft of Book and Thought, by the Doctor's reproof, but begin to roam in my Room now—

I think of you with absent Affection, and the Wife and Child I never have seen, Legend and Love in one—

Audacity of Bliss, said Jacob to the Angel[8] "I will not let thee go except I bless thee"—Pugilist and Poet, Jacob was correct—

Your Scholar—

<hr>

[1] Greek god of war. "Sometime during the winter Higginson had written, inquiring whether Emily Dickinson had read the notices about the death of Helen Jackson. [Helen Hunt Jackson (1830–1885), prominent poet and literary friend of Dickinson's.] Emily Dickinson replied as soon as she felt able to do so. The opening of the letter attempts to quote from Higginson's 'Decoration' (1874): 'And no stone, with feign'd distress,/Mocks the sacred loneliness.' " (Johnson's note)

[2] Hill in Jerusalem symbolizing the center of Jewish national life. Also a figure for heaven.

[3] "Helen Jackson's father, Professor Nathan Fiske, had died while on a trip to the Holy Land. On 30 March 1848, the Reverend Herman Humphrey published 'A Tribute to the Memory of Rev. Nathan W. Fiske . . .': 'In Jerusalem he died, on Mount Zion, and near the tomb of David was he buried . . . Who at death would not love to go up from Jerusalem below to Jerusalem above?' " (Johnson's note)

[4] In the biblical account of the birth of Jesus, the Archangel Gabriel announced to Mary that she would bear a son. (Luke 1:28)

[5] Refers to George Eliot's "The Choir Invisible."

[6] "Higginson's sonnet 'To the Memory of H.H.' was published in the May issue of the *Century Magazine* . . . The letter to Higginson suggests that she had received from him a transcript of his sonnet in advance of publication." (Johnson's note)

[7] "The Prisoner of Chillon," a poem by George Gordon, Lord Byron (1788–1824).

[8] Refers to the account in Genesis 32:24–26: "And Jacob was left alone; and there wrestled a man with him until the breaking of the day. And when he saw that he prevailed not against him . . . he said 'Let me go, for the day breaketh.' And he [Jacob] said 'I will not let thee go, except thou bless me.' " As a result of the encounter, God changed Jacob's name to Israel. Dickinson reverses the direction of the blessing.

from T. W. Higginson to his wife   *August 17, 1870*

I am stopping for dinner at White River Junction, dearest, & in a few hours shall be at Littleton thence to go to Bethlehem.[1] This morning at 9 I left Amherst & sent you a letter last night. I shall mail this at L. putting with it another sheet about E.D.[2] that is in my valise.

She said to me at parting "Gratitude is the only secret that cannot reveal itself."

I talked with Prest Stearns of Amherst[3] about her—& found him a very pleasant companion in the cars. Before leaving today, I got in to the Museums & enjoyed them much; saw a meteoric stone almost as long as my arm & weighing 436 lbs! a big slice of some other planet. It fell in Colorado. The collection of bird tracks of extinct birds in stone is very wonderful & unique & other good things. I saw Mr. Dickinson[4] this morning a little—thin dry & speechless—I saw what her life has been. Dr. S.[5] says her sister is proud of her.

I wd. have stolen a *totty* meteor, dear but they were under glass.

Mrs. Bullard[6] I have just met in this train with spouse & son—I shall ride up with her.

Some pretty glimpses of mts. but all is dry and burnt I never saw the river at Brattleboro[7] so low.

Did I say I staid at Sargents[8] in Boston & she still hopes for Newport.

This picture of Mrs Browning's[9] tomb is from E.D. "Timothy Titcomb" [Dr. Holland][10] gave it to her.

I think I will mail this here as I hv. found time to write so much. I miss you little woman & wish you were here but you'd hate travelling.

Ever

E D again

"Could you tell me what home is"

"I never had a mother. I suppose a mother is one to whom you hurry when you are troubled."

[1] White River Junction, Vermont is on the New Hampshire border. Littleton and Bethlehem are northern New Hampshire towns.

[2] Emily Dickinson.

[3] William Augustus Stearns (1805–1876), president of Amherst College from 1854 until his death.

[4] Edward Dickinson (1803–1874), Emily's father, prominent Amherst lawyer, treasurer of Amherst College from 1835–1872, and representative to the U.S. Congress from 1853–1855.

[5] Probably William Augustus Stearns (1805–1876), president of Amherst College.

[6] Perhaps the wife of Asa Bullard

(1804–1888), graduate of Amherst College, author and editor of religious publications, and general agent for the Congregational Sunday School and Publishing Society.

[7] The Connecticut River runs through Brattleboro, Vermont, and forms the border between that state and New Hampshire.

[8] The Reverend and Mrs. J. T. Sargent, whose house was a meeting place for the Boston Radical Club.

[9] Elizabeth Barrett Browning (1806–1861), English poet.

[10] Josiah Gilbert Holland (1819–1881), founder and editor of *Scribner's Monthly* and lifelong friend of Emily Dickinson.

"I never knew how to tell time by the clock till I was 15. My father thought he had taught me but I did not understand & I was afraid to say I did not & afraid to ask any one else lest he should know."

Her father was not severe I should think but remote. He did not wish them to read anything but the Bible. One day her brother brought home Kavanagh[11] hid it under the piano cover & made signs to her & they read it: her father at last found it & was displeased. Perhaps it was before this that a student of his was amazed that they had never heard of Mrs. [Lydia Maria] Child[12] & used to bring them books & hide in a bush by the door. They were then little things in short dresses with their feet on the rungs of the chair. After the first book she thought in ecstasy "This then is a book! And there are more of them!"

"Is it oblivion or absorption when things pass from our minds?"

Major Hunt[13] interested her more than any man she ever saw. She remembered two things he said—that her great dog "understood gravitation" & when he said he should come again "in a year. If I say a shorter time it will be longer."

When I said I would come again *some time* she said "Say in a long time, that will be nearer. Some time is nothing."

After long disuse of her eyes[14] she read Shakespeare & thought why is any other book needed.

I never was with any one who drained my nerve power so much. Without touching her, she drew from me. I am glad not to live near her. She often thought me *tired* & seemed very thoughtful of others.

[The postscript of a letter Higginson wrote his sisters (HCL) on Sunday, 21 August, adds:]

Of course I hv. enjoyed my trip very very much. In Amherst I had a nice aftn & evng with my singular poetic correspondent & the remarkable cabinets of the College.

[Recalling the interview twenty years later, Higginson wrote in the *Atlantic Monthly* LXVIII (October 1891) 453:]

The impression undoubtedly made on me was that of an excess of tension, and of an abnormal life. Perhaps in time I could have got beyond that somewhat overstrained relation which not my will, but her needs, had forced upon us. Certainly I should have been most glad to bring it down to the level of simple truth and every-day comradeship; but it was not altogether easy. She was much too enigmatical a being for me to solve in an hour's interview, and an instinct told me that the slightest attempt at direct cross-examination would make her withdraw into her shell; I could only sit still and watch, as one does in the woods; I must name my bird without a gun, as recommended by Emerson.[15]

[11] An idyllic romance (1849) by Henry Wadsworth Longfellow.

[12] Lydia Maria Child (1802–1880), American writer and abolitionist.

[13] Edward Bissell Hunt (?–1863), first husband of Helen Hunt Jackson.

[14] Refers to the eye ailment that required Dickinson to go to Boston for extended treatment in 1864.

[15] Ralph Waldo Emerson (1803–1883), prominent American poet, philosopher, and essayist.

Lewis Hine
Portrait of an Immigrant
Ellis Island, New York
gelatin-silver print: ca. 1915
(Courtesy George Eastman House)

The Literature of an Expanding Nation 1865–1912

The Paradox of Peace

At a cost of more than 600,000 lives, the Civil War put an end to chattel slavery—but not its heritage of social injustice—and vindicated the principle of Union. *United States* became a singular collective noun in postwar usage, instead of a plural one as before. The name now denoted a powerful young nation supposedly at peace with itself and dedicated to binding up its wounds. Whitman's image for the advent of peace was "Reconciliation . . . word over all, beautiful as the sky." But such sentiments, reflecting wishes rather than realities, belonged to what Emerson called "the optative mood" of American literature and spiritual history and found little support in the events of the period. The assassination of President Abraham Lincoln in 1865 was followed by the impeachment trial of his successor Andrew Johnson. Reconstruction politics often were a continuation of war by other means. For Whitman the democratic vistas of 1871 were marked by abandonment of principle, "hollowness of heart," "hypocrisy," "depravity," "robbery and scoundrelism": "What penetrating eye does not everywhere see through the mask? The spectacle is appalling." James Russell Lowell scanned "the festering news . . . of public scandal, private fraud" in what he called "the Land of Broken Promise."

Opportunism and Corruption

"There's millions in it," says Mark Twain's Colonel Beriah Sellers (*The Gilded Age*). "I've got the biggest scheme on earth—and I'll take you in; I've taken in every friend I've got that's ever stood by me, for there's enough for all, and to spare." A dealer in schemes involving mules, corn, bottled eyewash, and an illusory rail line serving Slouchburg, Hallelujah, and Corruptionville, the fictional Sellers typifies the promoter, a distinctive occupation of the period. The joining of the Union Pacific and Central Pacific rail lines at Promontory Point, Utah, in 1869 was a promoter's triumph. It fulfilled vision, purpose, engineering genius, and venture capitalism; passengers and goods traveled in less than a week across a nation whose separate parts were now bound to each other by three thousand miles of steel. The promoters of the transcontinental railroad, it was soon learned, had set up a construction company, Crédit Mobilier, that bilked the investing public of more than $20 million and, attempting to avoid exposure, bribed the vice president of the United States, Schuyler Colfax, along with members of the House and Senate. The Crédit Mobilier affair, which unraveled just before the general election of 1872, was not an isolated instance. On "Black Friday" in September 1869, the market collapsed after two sharpers, Jim Fisk and Jay Gould, tried to make a corner in gold. On "Black Friday" in 1873, an economy built on wildcat speculations fell on its face, ushering in the worst depression the United States had yet known. Crédit Mobilier was part of a cycle of abuses and reverses that darkened nearly every corner of national life.

The Reconstruction era had more than its share of memorably representative figures, among them Ulysses Grant, the North's supreme military hero. Men like General William Tecumseh Sherman had fought under Grant with "the faith a Christian has in his Savior." Grant's two terms in the White House, however, were notable for corruption, neglect, incompetence, and cronyism. America had "reverted to the stone age," Henry Adams lamented. "The progress of evolution from President Washington to President Grant was alone evidence enough to upset Darwin." In New York "Boss" William Tweed and his Tammany ring made off with somewhere between $30 million and $100 million in public funds.

The tutelary spirit of the Reconstruction era was not Lincoln but Benjamin Franklin, stripped for the most part of his irony, sense of play, heterodoxy, and free-ranging intellectual curiosity. In 1864 one of his biographers, the popular historian James Parton, counted 136 American towns named after Franklin; Ohio alone had nineteen. "I think I adequately appreciate the greatness of Washington," said Horace Greeley, the powerful editor of the *New York Tribune*, "yet I must place Franklin above him as the consummate type and flowering of human nature under the skies of colonial America." But it was not until 1868 that Franklin's *Autobiography*, long established as obligatory reading for his compatriots, was first published from a complete and authentic manuscript instead of a corrupt, partial source. This promoted a rediscovery and consequently a reinterpretation of the man in line with some of the dominant values of the era. Franklin's humble origins, dedication to self-improvement, and genius for business set an example for "Self-Made Men" (the title of Greeley's popular lecture) determined to acquire what the master showman P. T. Barnum called "The Art of Money-Getting." Barnum's best-selling autobiography, *Struggles and Triumphs,* suggests not only that his chief model was Franklin but that he regarded himself as the Franklin of humbug, harnessing credulity instead of lightning.

Franklin's gospel of getting on in the world, as it was then interpreted at face value, merged with practical Christianity, Emersonian self-reliance, and social Darwinism, which applied evolutionary theories of natural selection and the survival of the fittest to the daily race for bread, money, and status. The results of the merger could be seen in Horatio Alger's Ragged Dick books (1867 and after), lecture performances such as Henry Ward Beecher's "The Ministry of Wealth" and Thomas Wentworth Higginson's "The Natural Aristocracy of the Dollar," and "Acres of Diamonds," an inspirational address that Philadelphia Baptist clergyman Russell Conwell, founder of Temple University, delivered about six thousand times. "Opportunity is in your own backyard," Conwell said. "Money is power. Every good man and woman ought to strive for power, to do good with it when obtained."

Exposure and Reform

The most enduring label for the period that followed Lee's surrender at Appomattox and Lincoln's death comes from the novel Mark Twain wrote in 1873 with his Hartford neighbor, Charles Dudley Warner: *The Gilded Age*. It connotes vulgarity, boom times, specious glitter, and superficial glow. Since then, historians of the period have generated many other phrases that tend to scant the vitality and significant achievements of the times. A synoptic account compiled from book titles and verbal tags might read something like this: During a "tragic era" that was also an "age of negation," an "age of excess," and an "awkward age" and spanned several "brown decades," the American people, traveling "the road to reunion," were lured into "pragmatic acquiescence" and sedated by a bloodless "genteel tradition"; they created a cheap "chromo civilization" and watched complacently as "robber barons" devoured the nation's resources in a "great barbecue."

Labels aside, however, this was a dynamic era out of which emerged cultural and industrial maturity together with other lineaments of the United States in the coming century. Corruption and abuse brought on investigation and exposure; the beginnings of a reform, protest, and labor movement; and searching structural critiques such as Whitman's *Democratic Vistas* and Henry George's *Progress and Poverty* in the 1870s and, at the turn of the century, the economist and social theorist Thorstein Veblen's *The Theory of the Leisure Class*. Warring profiteers wasted money and labor, but the railroads were built all the same. Parvenus and vulgarians set a pattern for what Veblen called the "conspicuous consumption of valuable goods," but they did so by virtue of a social and economic mobility that made everyone a potential tycoon. Those who became tycoons amassed enormous private fortunes, but some of them—Andrew Carnegie and John D. Rockefeller, for example—also endowed universities and libraries and set up great private foundations dedicated to education, research, and public welfare.

The year 1876, the hundredth anniversary of the Declaration of Independence, offers a fair sampling of the varieties and vicissitudes of American life in the Gilded Age. At Little Bighorn, Montana, Sioux Indians led by Chiefs Sitting Bull and Crazy Horse annihilated Lieutenant Colonel George Armstrong Custer and his expeditionary force. Outlaw Jesse James reached the zenith of his career by robbing a stagecoach in Texas, a train in Missouri, and a bank in Minnesota. Evangelists Dwight Moody and Ira Sankey led a nationwide crusade to eradicate sin and reduce the future population of hell. President Grant's secretary of war and private secretary stood accused, respectively, of bribery and tax fraud. In a bitterly contested presidential election marked by fraud and violence, Rutherford B. Hayes of Ohio defeated Samuel J. Tilden of New York. Reconstruction, along with its program of protecting the political and economic rights of black freedmen, came to an end. ("The slave went free," W.E.B. Du Bois was to write, "stood a brief moment in the sun; then moved back again toward slavery.") Thomas Edison established his "invention factory" at Menlo Park, New Jersey. J. W. Draper took the first photographs of the solar spectrum. Alexander Graham Bell patented the telephone. Daniel Coit Gilman established Johns Hopkins, the first modern American university, and set national standards for graduate studies and advanced research. William James, then an instructor in physiology at Harvard, established the first American psychological laboratory. Professor Willard Gibbs of Yale published a paper on thermodynamics, "On the Equilibrium of Heterogeneous Substances," that remains one of the great creative achievements of nineteenth-century science.

Nearly 8 million visitors, equal to a sixth of the national population, passed through the turnstiles of the Centennial Exhibition at Philadelphia in 1876. Most of them were impressed by how far the United States had come during its first one hundred years toward fulfilling its mission to be the driving force as well as the light of the world. Dominating the exhibition was a forty-foot-high Corliss steam engine, which supplied power to the eight thousand presses, pumps, gins, mills, and lathes chugging away in Machinery Hall. "Yes, it is still in these things of iron and steel," said William Dean Howells, "that the national genius most freely speaks." But the national genius also spoke, if perhaps less freely, in other things and with a pronounced degree of distinction and purpose. Architect H. H. Richardson, painters Thomas Eakins, Winslow Homer, and Albert Pinkham Ryder, motion photography pioneer Eadweard Muybridge, and the Roeblings, father and son engineers and bridge builders, to name only a few, did their part in making what Lewis Mumford has called a "Buried Renaissance," "buried" because "the laval flow of industrialism after the war had swept over all the cities of the spirit, leaving here and there only an ashen ruin, standing erect in the crumbled landscape."

Labor unrest, on the rise since the Panic of 1873, peaked in 1877, a year of violence marked by riots and the use of federal troops to put down railroad strikes in West Virginia, Maryland, and Pennsylvania. In response, armories multiplied in cities all over America. Their crenellations, embrasures, and iron-studded sally ports suggested that the enemies of an economic society founded on steam, electricity, and dynamite were going to be repelled with crossbow, harquebus, and boiling oil. The age produced other public buildings that were anachronisms, eyesores, or swindles from their footings up. The Philadelphia city hall carried ornamentation about as far and as high as it could go. "Boss" William Tweed's Manhattan County Courthouse, a three-story iron-and-marble Palladian villa, cost taxpayers almost twice what Seward had paid for Alaska. Yet out of the same era came the Brooklyn Bridge, a structure of such purity and aspiration that it seemed to leap out of its century while fulfilling, at the same time, that century's passion for force and quantification. From the bridge's two majestic towers, together containing 85,159 cubic yards of masonry, hung four cables, each woven of 3,515 miles of wire and capable of supporting 24,621,780 pounds. The entire structure added up to an incomparably moving presence. "No one who has ever been upon it can ever forget it," said Mayor Seth Low of New York when the bridge was opened to traffic in 1883, thirteen years after construction began. "Not one shall see it and not feel prouder to be a man." In Hart Crane's epic celebration it was to be, quite simply, *The Bridge*.

The Old Order Gives Way

"If the tone of the American world is in some respects provincial, it is in none more so than in this matter of the exaggerated homage rendered to authorship," Henry James wrote in *Hawthorne* (1879). "In the United States at present authorship is a pedestal and literature is the fashion." These were signs of waning vitality, even stagnation, showing the need once again for those fresh currents of life and thought Margaret Fuller had called for thirty years earlier.

By the centennial year, Whitman, Melville, and Lowell, all born in 1819, were lapsing, respectively, into self-imitation, silence, and public service. Emily Dickinson, with Whitman the most important American poet of the century, was active during the 1860s, 1870s, and 1880s but remained a largely invisible literary presence (only half a dozen fugitive verses appeared in print) until the 1890s, when three volumes of her work were published posthumously. Of the older writers, Poe, Hawthorne, and Thoreau were dead. Whittier, Holmes, Longfellow, and Emerson, the last slipping into senility, were figures in a pantheon, objects of quasi-religious veneration. What Emerson once called "the Movement" and "the party of the Future" had become "the Establishment" and "the party of the Past" and now served as guardians and high priests of an official culture. The critic Tony Tanner has described this as a "culture of forms, frozen on the surface, hollow within; prohibitant rather than enabling; a series of habits adhered to by the imaginatively somnolent."

Yet there were signs that a new day had dawned. Local colorists celebrated the regional ambience and folkways of the Maine forests, Louisiana bayous, and Western mining camps. Realism asserted itself in frontier tales and the novels of William Dean Howells and Henry James. Naturalist writers such as Frank Norris and Stephen Crane would portray characters who were victims of circumstance and natural law instead of the free creatures of the Romantic tradition. And a literature of social protest and of America's oppressed races was about to emerge.

The Writer's Profession

A new class of professional writers, diverse in geographic and social origins and working under new professional conditions, emerged to make the nation's literature, a significant part of it regional in program and nature. Indicatively, William Dean Howells, the adoptive New Englander from the Midwest, was to leave the *Atlantic* to write for the *Century* and *Harper's*, both published in New York, where he eventually settled. But although this city became the nation's book and magazine publishing center, it was not necessarily where other writers chose to live and work. Among writers born during the three decades before the Civil War, Kate Chopin flourished in Saint Louis; San Francisco counted Mark Twain among its celebrities. This dispersal of centers of literary creation from the eastern seaboard augured a later generation of writers of the Midwest (Willa Cather, Sherwood Anderson, Sinclair Lewis, F. Scott Fitzgerald, Ernest Hemingway) and of the South (Katherine Anne Porter, William Faulkner, Thomas Wolfe, Zora Neale Hurston, Richard Wright).

Post–Civil War book publishing had become a two-tiered, two-culture system that reached overlapping but distinguishable classes of readers. "Trade" publishers—centered in New York, Boston, and Philadelphia—sold their books in bookstores to a primarily urban and educated audience, enjoyed prestige, and in turn conferred it on their authors. "Subscription" publishers, on the other hand, were merchandisers who employed door-to-door salesmen, armed with alluring prospectuses and binders' dummies, to work the towns and country districts; a broad, nonliterary audience—often tradesmen, farmers, and their families—ordered in advance of publication works of history, moral philosophy, patriotism, medical advice, and occasionally humor and fiction. "Anything but subscription publishing is printing for private circulation," Mark Twain said. He showed fellow writers like William Dean Howells, Thomas Bailey Aldrich, and George Washington Cable yet other avenues to income: the lecture circuit (later, public "readings"), the magazines, and the theater, with dramatizations of his novels. The career of letters had become a matter of business as well as craft and during the 1880s began to require the professional services of literary agents.

But if the rewards for American writers were now greater than they had been before the war, so were the risks and pitfalls of celebrity, the star system, and the box office. Transplanted from Albany to San Francisco, for a brief period in the early 1870s Bret Harte may have been the most famous writer in America. A pioneering local colorist, he helped create, in "The Luck of Roaring Camp" and other popular stories, the literary West, an imaginary region populated by sentimental gamblers, gallant badmen, and whores with middle-class hearts of gold, many of them speaking what Mel Brooks (in his western parody film, *Blazing Saddles*) was to call "frontier gibberish." At thirty-five Harte traveled east like a conqueror and signed a $10,000 contract with the *Atlantic Monthly,* only to begin a long slide into debt, disenchantment, mediocrity, and finally self-imposed exile in Europe and England. His career was a cautionary tale for writers.

In other ways, too, the post–Civil War era opened up vistas of regret as well as–opportunity for American writers. The world they inhabited, said Henry James, "was a more complicated place than it had hitherto seemed, the future more treacherous, success more difficult." Henry Adams, who lived into the twentieth century but thought of himself as a child of the eighteenth, felt like a ghost or revenant. Mark Twain's Connecticut Yankee mourns a "lost land . . . so fresh and new, so virgin" that progress and the industrial revolution had destroyed. Similarly, a significant number of writers attempted to preserve in fiction or memoir what seemed the idyllic simplicities of village life before the war and helped create a literary cult of childhood and innocence. Harriet Beecher Stowe's *Oldtown Folks,* Louisa May Alcott's *Little Women,* and Thomas Bailey Aldrich's *The Story of a Bad Boy* were all published between 1868 and 1870; *Tom Sawyer* appeared in 1876 and was a likely model for Howells's *A Boy's Town* (1890). Looking to the present, however, many writers discovered that the union of art and realism sparked literary controversies that opened up broader opportunities than their predecessors had known.

Getting at the "Real"

The novelists, social reformers, painters, journalists, photographers, philosophers, and plain folk who got worked up over the import of the terms *Realism, Naturalism,* and *Romance* (often coupled with *Idealism*) were not dealing in abstractions. They sensed how crucial it was to find more accurate means for expressing what they were experiencing in a rapidly expanding nation.

How one viewed the human in relation to reality was hotly contested. Idealists believed that the universe was run according to principles of absolute and eternal goodness and that humans were legatees of this cosmic contract. Romanticists put their faith in the ultimate triumph of the godlike human will. Contrary to that, Realists claimed that humans were no less and no more than mortals, their freedom of choice qualified and challenged by the power of outside pressures. Naturalists, finally, saw men and women as subjected to the indifferent forces of biology and environment lying beyond their control.

Leading writers and arbiters of literary taste like William Dean Howells were convinced that Realism was the only honest way to record what it was actually like to live everyday American life. Howells and his friends (Mark Twain and Henry James) and proteges (Stephen Crane and Sarah Orne Jewett) viewed Romanticism as an adversary of truth and common humanity. They felt that Romanticism, with its soft-focused views, preferred pretty emotions and denied the less savory facts cast up by the turmoil of late-nineteenth-century existence.

Clarence Darrow, famed trial lawyer, wrote in favor of Literary Realism, "The world has grown tired of preachers and sermons; to-day it asks for facts. It has grown tired of fairies and angels, and asks for flesh and blood. It looks on life as it exists to-day—both in its beauty and its horror, its joy and its sorrow. It wishes to see all; not only the prince and the millionaire, but the laborer and the beggar, the master and the slave." Ambrose "Bitter" Bierce, author, journalist, and resident cynic, held a more jaundiced view: "Realism is the art of depicting nature as it is seen by toads, the charm suffusing a landscape painted by a mole, or a story written by a measuring worm," he wrote. The Romanticists in return insisted on the validity of their approach, and so the debate was underway over who had the best access to the "real."

Both contestants had their strengths and weaknesses. Writing as a Realist could mean being expansive and exploratory or becoming boxed-in as a self-limited advocate of small home truths. A Romanticist might be a student of complex reality or merely one who glossed over the unpleasant. Just as Idealism could suggest either a profound examination of universal human concerns or a fantasy realm where one floated one's dreams of a perfect world, Romanticism also cut two ways—toward an escapism that twisted facts past recognition or toward a responsible exploration of psychological areas overlooked by the literal-minded.

Eventually, even stalwart champions of Literary Realism allowed certain kinds of romantic themes and techniques to infiltrate and energize their works. In his later years, Howells realized that the standoff between Realism and Romanticism was not quite as simple as he had once pictured it, and he began to probe the darker reaches of the psyche which had been the favorite stalking ground for the great American Romantics in the year prior to the Civil War.

All along, American writers had more to choose from than the schools of Realism or Romanticism. An author could follow the lead of the literary school of Naturalism that spilled over from the Continent in the 1890s. Stephen Crane, Jack London, and Theodore Dreiser each responded, however idiosyncratically, to the precepts of objective, scientific reporting set down in France by Émile Zola in *Le Roman Experimental* in 1880. Whatever the case, the consequences of this debate on what's real and how to show it were central to development within turn-of-the-century intellectual life, social conduct, and literary expression.

Writing About Lives on the Margin

For writers of color and of ethnic "otherness" it was crucial to position themselves in regard to the "facts" affecting their lives lived on the margin. Women who were consciously writing out of their engendered experiences also had to take vividly into account what the differing literary possibilities had to offer. Whether it was W.E.B. Du Bois seeking to express "the double consciousness" of African Americans who lived behind the veil of race or Charlotte Perkins Gilman and Kate Chopin whose stories released the intemperate forces lurking beneath smooth social surfaces—all had to consider with care what literary modes to call their own; particularly when it came to mounting a true literature of self-liberation.

Even at the time there was no single "Realism," "Romanticism," or "Naturalism," but one distinctive issue that differentiated these several modes of viewing the world and the roles taken by the individual. The difference was neither a matter of setting or theme—ugly, sordid events were a standard feature in Romance, Realism, as well as Naturalism—nor one of being true to life. The differences depended rather on the relative degree of individual choice allowed by Naturalists, Romanticists, and Realists to the characters whose lives they portrayed across a spectrum ranging from total freedom of will to tightly restricted subservience to inescapable forces of fate. In modern terms, these writers were consciously debating nature versus nurture, pitting inborn traits against socially conditioned reflexes.

Who in the United States did not face such an existential question? But for writers limited by race, gender, religion, or ethnicity in the choices they could make within America's political, cultural, or economic systems, it was a serious matter indeed for them to take up the literary mode that most accurately spoke to the burning issues of individual will and collective action.

The Writers' Challenge

During the 1890s and after, many writers also began to assume a definite sense of social obligation to their readers, even those who paid mind to matters of style and form and went with "the art for art's sake" crowd. These writers strove to write clearly and effectively about important personal and public issues out of the desire to help save American society from the enemies who lay within and without. Their stories probably would not directly bring about changes in the social attitudes of their readers, but still these writers wanted *to have an effect.*

They had to contend with an audience that preferred to be entertained, instructed, and (sometimes) rejuvenated by what they read. On occasion, members of the public seemed reluctant to face the realities singled out for their attention; more interested in being indulged than in being startled into emotional and intellectual life. But a marvelous thing happened. The writers whom we now think of as having contributed the best and most provocative literature of the fifty years between 1865 and 1915 got themselves published, read, and to some extent or another recognized as being of importance to the nation's cultural life.

What Is an "American"?

Many newcomers to American shores were stunned by New York City's harbor. New York was the ultimate modern city, resembling a modern machine, whose power equalled the massive Corliss engine (1877). In such a world of energies, the word *American* underwent severe testing. Questions rose over what constituted a "real" citizen of the United States. Whether it was a recent immigrant entering at any of the nation's borders or someone who had long (or always) resided on this continent, the religious preferences, cultural habits, racial and national antecedents, even the language and bodily mannerisms, of those designated as "the others" were scrutinized in the attempt to determine whether they could ever be considered "one of us." If advocates of the melting-pot theory put their faith in a massive process of assimilation, Nativists insisted that such types would remain forever "aliens."

The debate over who could claim the proud label "American" (native Anglo-Saxon stock only, or latecomers as well?) was complicated by the sense of national mission that reached its peak during the Spanish-American War and the takeover of the Philippines in 1898 and 1899. Members of the newly formed Anti-Imperialist League stepped in to say nay to this mood of expansionism (whether out of racist fears or from enlightened humanitarianism), but it became increasingly difficult to interpret America's proper role at home and abroad, just as it had always been hard to know how to "read" the features of the colossal Statue of Liberty that stood at the nation's portal as Emma Lazarus's Nurturing Mother.

For better or worse, whether at Ellis Island in New York or Angel Island in San Francisco, all the incoming millions were poised on the threshold of a new country. Some failed to meet the demands of the new forces that overwhelmed them; many did well over the long run. But the records are filled with examples of what it meant to be one of "the other half," bedded down on tenement shelves rented at five cents a spot per night. In comparison to the primitive life in a prairie house on the western frontier, life in the midst of the exploding populations of the large cities was hectic and complex. The psychologist William James, in a letter to H. G. Wells in 1906, wrote:

> Exactly that callousness to abstract justice is *the* sinister feature and, to me as well as to you, the incomprehensible feature of our U.S. civilization. . . . When the ordinary American hears of [legal injustices], instead of the idealist within him beginning to "see red" with the higher indignation, . . . he begins to pooh-pooh and minimize and tone down the thing, and breed excuses from his general fund of optimism and re-spect for expediency. "It's probably right enough"; "Scoundrelly," as you say, but un-derstandable, "from the point of view of parties interested"—but understandable in onlooking citizens only as a symptom of the moral flabbiness born of the exclusive worship of the bitch-goddess SUCCESS. That—with the squalid cash interpretation put on the word *success*—is our national disease.

How was one to know who was who in a society in which signs of recognition changed overnight? Could one distinguish friends from strangers in class terms, at least, by the houses they lived in? Henry James and Edith Wharton certainly knew how to make clear the distinctions between "new" and "old" money—differences between those who make a great show of their wealth and those who keep their possessions under wraps. In 1890 Jacob Riis, himself a recent immigrant from Denmark, attempted to do for the poor of the New York City slums what James and Wharton did for the well-to-do, albeit that what Riis "saw" through words and photographs was screened through his middle-class, Northern European values. Entirely different distinctions of class and race were addressed by W.E.B. Du Bois, Paul Laurence Dunbar, and Booker T. Washington, while the female imagination had to fight against being shunted to the attic-nursery, papered in yellow wallpaper, by males with the bad habit of calling those alien creatures, their wives, "little girl" and "blessed little goose."

Emerging Feminine Identities

The metamorphoses taking place within the species "young American woman" proved disturbing to many who witnessed new types of the female rushing into existence. Henry James and William Dean Howells initiated the type between the 1870s and 1880s. By the 1890s two of the most talked-about versions (favorites of the popular magazines and the Sunday newspaper supplements) were the "American heiress" and the "new woman."

Women as a sexual and social subclass were, by tradition, supposedly the most stable of all elements of American nineteenth-century middle-class life, fixed firmly within their sphere of home and hearth. In 1880 one of the many books of etiquette that taught Americans a proper "code of manners" stated flatly, "The power of a woman is in her refinement, gentleness and elegance; it is she who makes etiquette, and it is she who preserves the order and decency of society." But should a woman slip loose from the restraining influences of the home, she was transformed into that ancient aspect of Eve feared by "good society" and beloved by the tabloids.

There was no finer instance of the type of the femme fatale at the turn of the last century than Evelyn Nesbit, over whose tarnished innocence one man (her husband Harry Thaw) shot to death another man (her lover, the well-known architect Stanford White). The reporter for the *New York Evening World* covering the sensational murder trial of 1907 was agog over Nesbit's beauty—dangerous because it seemed so innocent.

It was a shock (of delight for some, of dismay for many) to realize there were still other forms of female behavior than those of the "eternal Evelyn" coming into play by the 1870s and after. New occupations brought native-born women (before and after marriage) into the work place, while factories and sweatshops relied on the labor supplied by the influx of immigrant women. Enhanced college programs for women of the upper classes and the burgeoning African American middle class introduced them to new ideas as well as to professional skills hitherto granted only to men. *The New York Journal* of March 22, 1896, headlined its alarm: "How Intellectual Work Destroys Beauty."

Women also pushed their way into politics. The suffrage movement made a widely publicized comeback in the 1880s after a relatively quiescent period in the years following the Civil War. The suffragists had no clear sailing, however. The right-to-vote advocates were criticized from without and within the movement. From outside their ranks, women as well as men feared the damage that social militancy might do to the sanctity of the home. From inside the world of political activism, working-class women charged the middle-class members of the movement with elitism and ineffectual action. However, women who did not do enough were less disturbing than women who did quite a lot. The immigrant woman was often viewed as a particular menace, her figure looming over the social horizon as a potential revolutionary force; but Carrie Nation with her axe, imaged as a "presidential impossibility," was most frightening of all—even more than Booker T. Washington who could be caricatured as a harmless ape.

The unknown quantity and qualities of the post-Reconstruction African American were viewed with ambivalence. In similar fashion, the mental and physical force released on society by women daunted those who were resistant to change and heartened those who looked forward to things being different, perhaps even better. On the one hand, the *New York Journal* let loose another blast in 1896, warning that females given to activism risked massive "disorganization of the nervous system," leading to "lines in the face, bad teeth, bad complexion, short sight and possibly hysteria, epilepsy, and insanity." On the other hand, *The Education of Henry Adams* studied the contrasting forces represented in the famous chapter, The Dynamo and the Virgin (1900). The male machine was the unit in power at the moment, but Adams had a presentiment that female energy, hitherto frustrated and wasted, was about to explode onto the American scene. Adams in his maleness was apprehensive of the consequences, but as a pupil and historian of modern times, he could hardly wait to see the results.

New Words, New Definitions

With changes marking almost every corner of American existence, it was inevitable that old words had new meanings forced upon them and that new phrases spun into being. The forty years between 1888 and 1928 witnessed the introduction of one new word out of every ten. As Mark Sullivan pointed out in his six-volume study *Our Times*, three thousand new words received official recognition between 1909 and 1927 alone. Most of these words reflected the discoveries taking place continually in physics, chemistry, and medicine and in the widening use of technology. But along with *X-ray, dynamo, telephone,* and *aeroplane* were words like *flivver, Kodak, movies, skyscraper, Coca Cola,* and *el*—slangier references to the new entities filling everyday lives.

Going west in the 1880s as a greenhorn, Samuel Clemens dragged along a massive dictionary in the stagecoach he rode out of St. Joseph, Missouri. Clemens, however, quickly found out that many of the words acceptable back east were of little use beyond the Mississippi. Words like *coyote* and *blind lead* were more to the point in his new life. The 1884 edition of *Adventures of Huckleberry Finn* was drummed off the shelf of the Concord, Massachusetts, library because it contained the ungrammatical sentences and lower-class language of a vagabond boy without genteel schooling. Writing under the pseudonym of Mark Twain, Clemens made the vernacular one of the strongest elements of the thrust toward literary independence that was well under way by the 1890s.

Mark Twain, William Dean Howells, and Henry James all introduced the flavor of colloquial speech into their fiction. Theodore Dreiser's city-dwellers and Stephen Crane's sailors talked like such people might talk. Sarah Orne Jewett accurately noted the linguistic mannerisms of rural characters from New England, just as Joel Chandler Harris and W.E.B. Du Bois provided the dialect of the Black Belt and as Kate Chopin pointed up the phrasings characteristic of Louisiana Creoles. As one result, the reading public was exposed to a variety of American speech distinctively unlike that of a "proper" literature derived from Boston or Great Britain.

So many new words! *Teddy bear* (inspired by the popular image of President Theodore Roosevelt), *she's a daisy,* and *ragtime* represented the simple pleasures of the

Rodney Thomson
Militants
(*Life*, 1913)

nursery, the holiday outing, and the music hall. Still other words were less innocent records of current social upheavals and maladies: *Jim Crow, carpetbagger, skid row, the Four Hundred, nabobs, the Pinkertons, sweatshop,* and *the Molly Maguires.* The influx of immigrants meant the incorporation of words from Yiddish, Polish, Gaelic, and Italian into the basic pool of Yankee speech. They also kicked up new terms of insult: *Yid, Polack, Mick, Dago.* American life was turning inside out, and the good and the bad found the vocabularies needed to express their cruder emotions and deepest needs in the crowded neighborhoods of the modern city.

Life's Presidential Impossibilities: Carrie Nation and Booker T. Washington (*Life*, 1904)

Older words were also redefined. On the battlefield in *The Red Badge of Courage*, Crane's Henry Fleming is forced to test accepted meanings for *heroism, glory,* and *patriotism.* African Americans in the South and the North and the slum dwellers in the cities had to reassess what it meant to live with the way words such as *values, equality,* and *freedom* were actually being used. Businessmen had to relearn what *individualism* and *business* signified in an economy where corporate organizations and new marketing techniques made the small, family-run company an anachronism. Faithful believers in American democracy had one set of definitions for *conservative, vote,* and *presidency;* Ambrose Bierce, dipping into his cynicism for *The Devil's Dictionary,* had others.

Home and the words that traditionally cluster around its values (*mother, wife, family, breadwinner*) were placed under the stress of still newer terms: *apartment, the working woman,* and *divorce. West, East, North,* and *South* were reassessed in light of what such labels meant to politicians dickering for votes, to bankers packaging far-flung mergers, to arbiters of culture attempting to create a national taste, to agronomists and economists trying to bring supply and demand into line, and to all those people piling onto the trains and wagons that moved them from one place to another in their search for a better life and true-blue American values. Chinese, Spanish, Yiddish, and Swedish contended for space on the streets and farms. The vocabularies of ragtime and the soul songs of the Black Belt made their way into the layers of languages by which Americans drew into contact.

A Nation Connected

New people, new places, new objects, new ideas, new types—all located in new patterns of interchange and communication. The Pullman car, the transcontinental railway, the electric trolley car, the transoceanic steamship, the bicycle, and the automobile were made possible by major advances in the technology of transportation. The telegraph, the Atlantic cable, and the telephone speeded the transport of messages.

A New Reading Public

But it was in the world of the printed page that many of the most startling innovations took place. Dozens of new magazines and newspapers appeared so quickly that it was hard to keep up with the blur of words and images. Advances in printing techniques increased the amount, the kind, and the quality of illustrations that could be included in books, journals, and newspapers. Photographs were in common use for public purposes by the late 1890s. More words and pictures could be printed faster, for the viewing of more people, than ever before.

Improved print and picture meant spreading contact through all layers of society. Farmers, factory workers, city dwellers (whether in the tenements, the big houses, or the new apartment complexes), ethnic groups, and people from every geographic region now had a newspaper or a magazine addressed expressly to them. At the same time special audiences were being singled out, methods for the standardization of production and consumption were also underway. A great deal of what went into print was couched in broadly nationalistic terms. The jarring headlines or the newest best-sellers that intrigued readers on one coast aroused the interest of audiences on the opposite coast and just about everyone in between.

Together with the widening of the general readership (aided by an increased access to public schools, land-grant colleges, and special-training courses—racially segregated or not) came a vertical thrust down through the layers of class. The so-called genteel readers once centered in Boston and radiating out from other established eastern communities had always possessed a selection of magazines that suited their tastes in the arts and in politics. Now brash new publications were supplying things to read all the way along the cultural slope to the shop girls and foreign-born mechanics.

Upper- and middle-class magazines prided themselves of being responsible to the intellectual and spiritual values of their readers, although sometimes this sense of social obligation defined itself as smug support of traditional views and as fear of change. The press aimed at the general populace was rather more cheerfully cynical about its role as critic of social ills and upholder of sacred truths. Editors of the large-circulation papers and magazines directed toward the working classes were unquestionably active in exposing national corruptions and local conniving since such stories (done up in bold headlines) did society both some good and sold like hotcakes. By the 1890s William

Randolph Hearst and Joseph Pulitzer refined the formulas for baying forth the latest sensations. Available facts were keyed up to make the stories splashier, or facts were doctored to bring stories—even wars—into existence.

Entertainment, instruction, and reform gave zest to the interconnecting worlds of journalism, magazine publication, and book sales, but there continued to be a deep split in tastes between different segments of the population. Van Wyck Brooks, the man who helped to popularize the terms *highbrow* and *lowbrow*, drove home the point that America was going through a cultural civil war:

> . . . on the one hand a quite unclouded, quite unhypocritical assumption of transcendent theory ("high ideals"); on the other a simultaneous acceptance of catchpenny realities. Between university ethic and business ethics, between American culture and American humor, between Good Government and Tammany [corruption], between academic pedantry and pavement slang, there is no community, no genial middle ground.

Along with all the other "strangers" (deemed so by virtue of race, heritage, economic status, region, and gender), those persons who lived by ideals were estranged from those who abided by the way things succeeded. This cultural division made itself felt in the way American writers and artists viewed their chances at effective expression in a nation where the business of being an American seemed mainly to be just that: *business.*

Thinking Hard and Writing Well

A distinguished group of thinkers populated the final decades of the nineteenth century who initiated original intellectual methods for resolving both age-old philosophical questions and the brand-new difficulties that rushed into existence. A great deal of hard thinking went on, especially from the 1880s onward, over matters of social justice and humanistic concerns.

Josiah Royce, George Santayana, William James, Charles Sanders Pierce, John Dewey as philosophers; Oliver Wendell Holmes, Jr. and Louis Brandeis as legal authorities; and Thorstein Veblen, Herbert Croly, Lester Frank Ward, Henry George, and W.E.B. Du Bois as economists, political scientists, and sociologists—all countered the slipshod notions and vicious ideologies, the *bad* thinking, that crowded the mental spaces of American life.

The men named here, as well as many others (women, too, like Jane Addams, Josephine Goldmark, and Florence Kelley), argued vigorously about such sharp-edged issues as how best to educate the young, to put equitable laws into practice, to ensure racial and economic fairness, to encourage ethical behavior, to initiate tax reforms, and to reshape democratic principles to fit the times. Overtly social questions battled for public attention alongside equally vital questions concerning freedom of choice, the existence of God or virtue, the ways by which the human mind works, how the bodily instincts function, and—above all—the nature of truths in an ambiguous universe and the means by which to signify them in language and in deeds.

The new schools of American philosophy and psychology saw to it that seemingly abstruse queries about materialism (emphasis on things and facts), idealism (concentration on ideas and principles), determinism (what you cannot control), and free will (the choices you can make) received recognition by thoughtful Americans as matters that concretely affected everyone's life. They wanted to stave off what many feared might take place: the loss of one's sense of humanity in a torrent of sensual impressions or the chance that humanity itself might be imprisoned within a massive mechanistic grid.

In 1890 William James mapped the terrain of the mind. It was *that* environment, he believed, out of which turn-of-the-century Americans had to make something good for themselves and their fellow citizens or go down in defeat. He wrote:

> Until quite recently all psychology, whether animistic or associationistic, was written on classic-academic lines. The consequence was that the human mind, as it is figured in this literature, was largely an abstraction. Its normal adult traits were recognized. A sort of sunlit terrace was exhibited on which it took its exercise. But where that terrace stopped, the mind stopped. . . . But of late years the terrace has been overrun by romantic improvers, and to pass to their work is like going from classic to gothic architecture, where few outlines are pure and where uncouth forms lurk in the shadows. A mass of mental phenomena are now seen in the shrubbery beyond the parapet. Fantastic, ignoble, hardly human, or frankly non-human are some of these new candidates for psychological description. The menagerie and the madhouse, the nursery, the prison, and the hospital, have been made to deliver up their material. The world of mind is shown as something infinitely more complex than was suspected; and whatever beauties it may still possess, it has lost at any rate the beauty of academic neatness.[1]

The soul was as important as the life of the mind and of the body, at least to idealists like Josiah Royce who still kept a toehold in a world of gross contingencies and materiality. Mind, body, or soul: the sense of *being human* had to make itself felt as an experienced fact; otherwise, life signified nothing. In *The Principles of Psychology*, William James hit it on the mark: "Millions of items of the outward order are present to my senses which never properly enter into my experience. Why? Because they have no *interest for me. My experience is what I agree to attend to.*"

From the 1860s onward Darwinism and its permutations affected the way Americans came to view their economic system (combativeness versus regulation in the marketplace), their religious beliefs (God versus chance as the master of the universe), their bodies (theirs to command versus control by inherited "tendencies"), and their physical surroundings (a living world imbued by spirit versus a conglomeration of geologic earth-masses). Herbert Spencer (champion of Social Darwinism) and Pierre and Marie Curie (discoverers of radium) were names that caught the interest of the public as much as those of inventors like Thomas Edison, industrialists like George Pullman and Henry Ford, and the builders of Chicago's skyscrapers and Brooklyn's bridge. The age was known as the Age of Energy. The forces set loose by the new sciences heartened some and dismayed others, but no one escaped their impact.

For many Americans, *being human* meant paying attention to the aesthetic side of life in order to offset the jolts of science, technology, and the business of buying and selling. The intrinsic value of literature, painting, music, architecture, the theater, and the decorative arts was reexamined (along with everything else) by the rising

---

[1] "The New Psychology" (William James, from "Frederic Myers' Service to Psychology," 1901).

generation of young writers and artists, who often felt they had to fight for attention in a society that seemed more interested in the Corliss engine, the Bessemer steel-processing method, and Standard Oil takeovers than in what artists had to express or how they expressed it.

The best of the writers who rode out the storms of late-nineteenth-century American life took on the task of dealing with puzzling and inevitable facts of nature. They did it in many ways. Such pluralism was all to the good as writers tried to record "the stream of thought" described by William James:

> Out of what is in itself an undistinguishable, swarming *continuum,* devoid of distinction or emphasis, our senses make for us, by attending to this motion and ignoring that, a world full of contrasts, of sharp accents, of abrupt changes of picturesque light and shade.[2]

It took the combined efforts of many minds and hearts to do justice to the facts of such a society. It was indeed fortunate that some of the best "products" coming out of this period were writers game to the need to represent what Henry James called "the complex fate" and what W.E.B. Du Bois called "the double consciousness" of being an American.

Further Reading:

L. Mumford, *The Brown Decades*, 1941.

F. L. Mott, *Golden Multitudes. The Story of Best Sellers in the United States*, 1947.

R. Hofstadter, *The Age of Reform*, 1955.

L. Ziff, *The American 1890s*, 1966.

R. H. Wiebe, *The Search for Order, 1877–1920*, 1967.

T. L. Hartshorne, *The Distorted Image. Changing Conceptions of the American Character Since Turner*, 1968.

N. Harris, ed., *The Land of Contrasts, 1880–1901*, 1970.

H. W. Morgan, ed., *The Gilded Age*, 1963/1970.

H. M. Jones, *The Age of Energy, Varieties of American Experience, 1865–1915*, 1971.

D. Aaron, *The Unwritten War*, 1973.

N. Harris, *Humbug: The Art of P. T. Barnum*, 1973.

D. Boorstin, *The Americans: The Democratic Experience*, 1974.

R. Ginger, *Age of Excess. The United States from 1877 to 1914*, 1965/1975.

J. Higham, *Strangers in the Land. Patterns of American Nativism, 1860–1925*, 1981.

R. E. Martin, *American Literature and the Universe of Force*, 1981.

E. Sundquist, ed., *American Realism. New Essays*, 1982.

A.Trachtenberg, *The Incorporation of America. Culture and Society in the Gilded Age*, 1982.

S. F. Fishkin, *From Fact to Fiction. Journalism and Imaginative Writing in America*, 1985.

C. P. Wilson, *The Labor of Words. Literary Professionals in the Progressive Era*, 1985.

R. Brodhead, *The School of Hawthorne*, 1986.

C. Tichi, *Shifting Gears. Technology, Literature, Culture in Modernist America*, 1987.

A. Kaplan, *The Social Construction of American Realism*, 1988.

S. Gillman, *Dark Twins. Imposture and Identity in Mark Twain's America*, 1989.

L. C. Mitchell, *Determined Fictions. American Literary Naturalism*, 1989.

M. Orvell, *The Real Thing. Imitation and Authenticity in American Culture, 1880–1940*, 1989.

M. Banta, *Taylored Lives. Narrative Productions in the Age of Taylor, Veblen, and Ford*, 1993.

M. D. Bell, *The Problems of American Realism. Studies in the Cultural History of a Literary Idea*, 1993.

R. W. Fox and T. J. J. Lears, ed., *The Power of Culture*, 1993.

A. Kaplan and D. Pease, ed., *Cultures of U.S. Imperialism*, 1993.

N. Silber, *The Romance of Reunion: Northerners and the South, 1865–1900*, 1993.

E. Sundquist, *To Wake the Nations. Race in the Making of American Literature*, 1993.

R. W. Fox and J. T. Kloppenberg, ed., *A Companion to American Thought*, 1995.

S. Blair, *Henry James and the Writing of Race and Nation*, 1996.

L. C. Mitchell, *Westerns: Making the Man in Fiction and Film*, 1996.

H. B. Wonham, ed., *Criticism and the Color Line*, 1996.

---

[2] William James, *The Principles of Psychology,* 1890.

Cultural Portfolio
The New Immigrants

The American Dream. The melting pot. Women with heads covered by wigs or babushkas. Bearded men carrying suitcases, disembarking from overcrowded ships at Ellis Island in New York's harbor. Wide-eyed stares from faces made in Russia, Norway, Macedonia, Poland, Ireland, Jamaica, Hungary, Sicily, Galicia, and Wales. These images of American immigrants captured by documentary photographs from turn-of-the-century New York City resonate with powerful cultural ideals that echo throughout late-nineteenth and early-twentieth century American literature. From as early as October 28, 1886, when Emma Lazarus's poem "The New Colossus," was inscribed on the pedestal of Frederic Bartholdi's Statue of Liberty, images of "the huddled masses yearning to breathe free" became synonymous with the ideals on which the United States—this nation of immigrants—is popularly believed to rest.

Although these vignettes tell only part of the ongoing story, they suggest the multitude of tales centering on all those who entered the United States through the vast and chaotic registry room of Ellis Island, the immigration station established in 1892 for the processing of shiploads of new arrivals from Europe; for the processing of passengers, that is, who had had to make the ocean crossing in steerage. (Immigrants able to afford first or second deck accommodations were serviced far more comfortably by the United States officials who boarded their ships in the harbor.) For the Chinese and other Asian immigrants, San Francisco's Angel Island was the Ellis Island of the West Coast, while New Orleans was the point of entry for most immigrants from countries to the south of the United States border.

Before Ellis Island became the primary gateway for Europeans entering the United States in the 1890s, the "old immigrants" from northern and central Europe and from Great Britain streamed into the New World through many points of entry—Boston, Philadelphia, and Baltimore, as well as New York. But the fact that Ellis Island should receive such prominence in America's cultural memory is not surprising. The twelve millions who passed through its screening processes between 1892 to 1924 became central actors in dramatic efforts to define and redefine what it meant to "be American."

Prior to the closing decades of the nineteenth century, emigres from the Scandinavian countries, from England, Wales, Scotland, and Ireland, and from Germany and France populated most of the states and territories of the North American continent. By 1907, however, more than 75 percent of the new arrivals came from southern and eastern Europe, enticed across the Atlantic in response to the promotional brochures and posters that flowed forth from promoters of the nation's rapidly developing industrial economy which avidly sought new sources of cheap labor to run its factory machines and build its railroads and cities. Henry Ford, for one, realized that he could only make a success of his Model-T automobile if he had immigrant workers on his assembly lines and immigrant consumers ready to purchase the cars they helped to make. Others were inspired to leave the Old Country as part of a process best described as chain immigration. First one member of a family immigrated, then—after earning enough money to pay for ship-passage—yet another member of the family crossed the Atlantic who, in turn, worked to save to buy steerage tickets for more relatives. Still others, particularly those crossing the Pacific from China, the Philippines, and Japan, came as contract laborers who worked for low wages for the company that paid their travel expenses. Not all who came during these peak years intended to stay on in the United States; some saw this country as a place of temporary employment that would provide them the financial means to enjoy better lives for themselves and their families after returning to the land of their birth.

Whatever the circumstances and motivations, those who arrived during the decades at either side of 1900 became the object of debates that grew in intensity over the role these "foreigners" should play in established American so-

On the Threshold of a New Country
(Scribners, March 1901)

ciety. Immigrants themselves were caught between the need to become part of a new culture for the sake of the benefits it had to offer and the desire to cling to the traditions and values of their past. They had to ask themselves whether they should risk being mocked with the label "greenhorn" if they preserved practices that held deep ethnic and religious significance, or whether they should turn their backs on the customs of the old country in order to blend into the American system. Had not America's storied opportunities for material advancement and its promise of political and religious freedoms been the reason they had left home in the first place? They had to decide which way to go: stick to what they had been back home or transform themselves into that new self—the "American."

At the same time the immigrants were experiencing these hopes and fears, political and cultural leaders in the United States expressed concern over the increasingly visible numbers of

people who seemed profoundly unlike themselves. More liberal commentators gave speeches and wrote articles and works of fiction calling attention to the vitality the immigrants had to offer, a home-grown culture that dared not become stagnantly reliant on its inherited traditions; they drew cartoons highlighting the hypocrisy of recent immigrants who wished to shut the doors on their fellow countrymen now that they had found success. Reactionaries stirred xenophobic fears by pointing out the sights that met Americans making their way through the packed jam of bodies crowding the byways of ethnic neighborhoods in the larger urban centers; they voiced warnings that poverty, crime, disease, and immorality were contaminating the ideal of a unified American way of life.

The newcomers tended to gravitate toward areas already settled by their family members and to other ethnic communities where they could share familiar values, customs, and languages. As Abraham Cahan described such a scene in *Yekl*, his tale of 1896, even the Jews gathered together in the ghetto of New York City's lower East Side were strangers in the midst of strangers.

It is one of the most densely populated spots on the face of the earth—a seething human sea fed by streams, streamlets, and rills of immigration flowing from all the Yiddish-speaking centers of Europe. Hardly a block but shelters Jews from every nook and corner of Russia, Poland, Galicia, Hungary, Roumania; Lithuanian Jews, Volhynian Jews, south Russian Jews, Bessarabian Jews; Jews crowded out of the 'pale of Jewish settlement'; Russified Jews expelled from Moscow, St. Petersburg, Kieff, or Saratoff; Jewish runaways from justice; Jewish refugees from crying political and economical injustice; people torn from a hard-gained foothold in life and from deep-rooted attachments by the caprice of intolerance or the wiles of demagoguery—innocent scapegoats of a guilty Government for its outraged populace to misspend its blind fury upon; students shut out from Russian universities, and come to these shores in quest of learning; artisans, merchants, teachers, rabbis, artists, beggars—all come in

"All those who enter here leave despair behind."
cartoon, 1903
(By courtesy of the Statue of Liberty National Monument)

THE TRIUMPHAL ARCH.

search of fortune. Nor is there a tenement house but harbors in its bosom specimens of all the whimsical metamorphoses wrought upon the children of Israel of the great modern exodus by the vicissitudes of life in this their Promised Land of today. You find there Jews born to plenty, whom the new conditions have delivered up to the clutches of penury; Jews reared in the straits of need, who have here risen to prosperity; good people morally degraded in the struggle for success amid an unwonted environment; moral outcasts lifted from the mire, purified, and imbued with self-respect; educated men and women with their intellectual polish tarnished in the inclement weather of adversity; ignorant sons of toil grown enlightened—in fine, people with all sorts of antecedents, tastes, habits, inclinations, and speaking all sorts of subdialects of the same jargon, thrown pellmell into one social caldron—a human hodgepodge with its component parts changed but not yet fused into one homogeneous whole.

Since most of the new arrivals had little money, in the beginning the housing they could afford was limited. Tenements characterized by crowded, often unsanitary conditions, packed by occupants from many nations and ethnic groups, spread over major sections of the urban landscape. These teeming neighborhoods became the focus for the anxiety felt by members of the American middle class who, assisted by the development of new railroad and subway systems, began to flee from the central city outward to the newly formed suburbs. Writers were drawn toward the subject of tenement life. Some like Lincoln Steffens and Upton Sinclair wrote with full sympathy; others like Jacob Riis (whose descriptions and photographs gave birth to the phrase "how the other half lives") wrote with concern but also out of horrified fascination over the physical squalor they witnessed in the city's slums and the moral degradation they thought they found.

Reformers like Jane Addams, who was active in the earliest Chicago settlement house movement, set to work in immigrant neighborhoods promoting projects for social betterment. As far back as Frederick Law Olmsted's plans for Central Park that opened great green vistas in the midst of New York City in 1859, civic leaders understood the necessity to provide public spaces that offered respite to immigrants from their crowded living conditions and aid in introducing them to their new home. And when Chicago turned the land that had been cleared for the 1893 Columbia Exposition into Jackson Park bordering Lake Michigan, and Coney Island developed a series of amusement centers in the late 1890s, they created new safety valves to relieve the growing urban crush.

Despite these earnest and well-intentioned moves to bring the immigrant population into the American mainstream, conservative sentiment prevailed in legislative bodies across the nation. Tensions between native-stock Americans and the new populations were not restricted to cities in the East and Midwest. In California areas dominated by Chinese, and in lesser numbers by Japanese workers, brought loud cries of protest from white citizens; this situation quickly led to the enactment of state legislation prohibiting Asians from owning or renting property; a series of Chinese Exclusion Acts starting in 1882 tried to put a stop to any Chinese entering the country.

With the Immigration Act of 1891 virtually all policies relating to immigrants, including control over the entry stations like Ellis and Angel Islands, passed from state to federal control. The earliest federal immigration laws had been relatively limited and selective. Convicts, prostitutes, and Chinese contract laborers were barred by laws passed in 1875, with lunatics, idiots, and paupers soon added to the list of nondesirables. Later legislation was more aggressive; it focused upon problems it associated with the so-called corrupting influence of racial mixtures, class tensions, and single working women adrift outside the home, and the fear that imported laborers would take jobs away from American-born workers.

The debate continued unabated. Liberal legislators spoke in favor of unrestricted immigration, motivated in large part by the perceived need to build up a vast supply of labor to support the burgeoning industrial complex. However, pro-immigration liberals lost ground to nativist groups such as the Immigration Restriction League.

The League had been founded in 1894 by Boston Brahmins drawn to social Darwinistic concepts of natural selection and heredity; in their view, the notion of "the survival of the fittest" threatened a take-over of the Anglo-Saxon base by immigrants who were morally inferior but capable of explosive reproductive powers. If the new arrivals were allowed to proliferate, the self-proclaimed cultural superiority of the native population faced extinction through genetic race-suicide. Thus came about the Immigration Act of 1917. Thirty-three categories of people—including illiterates—were now prohibited from settling in the United States. (Chauvinistic anxieties raised by the First World War helped exacerbate fears about the consequences of allowing too many non-Americans to infiltrate the nation's cultural base.) By 1921 the First Quota Act slashed total immigration to 350,000 people per year, signaling the end of the floodtide of immigration, while the Johnson-Reed Act of 1924 tapped the last nail into the coffin of immigrant aspirations.

As the public debates and resulting legislation indicate, the question of how best to "know" what is an American was even more difficult than getting to "be" a naturalized citizen. The pressures (social, economic, cultural) attending the years at the close of the nineteenth century were far stronger than those attending the question put by J. Hector St. John de Crèvecoeur[1] in 1782, in the famous chapter from his *Letters from an American Farmer*, titled "What Is an American?" For immigrants entering the North American continent one hundred years after de Crèvecoeur's query, this question often involved difficult personal decisions. For example, a Jewish laborer might have been pressed to decide whether to work on the sabbath as the sweatshop boss demanded, or whether to give honor to age-old religious practices over and above the getting of an American paycheck. For the political and cultural leaders holding down positions of power in American institutions and business companies, the question entailed nothing less than coming to terms with a new and revitalized understanding of national and personal identity. As varied as the immigrants and as the citizens of the nation who witnessed their arrival, the multiple answers to myriad questions regarding assimilation, acculturation, and cultural survival have not ended this crucial debate. Since 1900 new generations of new immigrants continue to open up new occasions for confronting this issue. We are still striving to understand the terms by which we are all involved in the exhilarating, demanding enterprise of *being* American.

Emma Lazarus, *The New Colossus*

Not like the brazen giant of Greek fame,
With conquering limbs astride from land to land;
Here at our sea-washed, sunset gates shall stand
A mighty woman with a torch, whose flame
Is the imprisoned lightning, and her name
Mother of Exiles. From her beacon-hand
Glows world-wide welcome; her mild eyes command
The air-bridged harbor that twin cities frame.
"Keep, ancient lands, your storied pomp!" cries she
With silent lips. "Give me your tired, your poor,
Your huddled masses yearning to breathe free,
The wretched refuse of your teeming shore.
Send these, the homeless, tempest-tossed to me:
I lift my lamp beside the golden door!"
1886

[1] Michel-Guillaume John de Crèvecoeur chose to anglicize his birthname, once he came to America. Thereafter, he used J. Hector St. John, the name by which he was known.

Lewis W. Hine
Tenement, Washington D.C.
gelatin silver print, 1908
(Courtesy George Eastman House)

from Henry James
The American Scene

The Terrible Little Ellis Island

. . . the facts of the terrible little Ellis Island,[2] the first harbour of refuge and stage of patience for the million or so of immigrants annually knocking at our official door. Before this door, which opens to them there only with a hundred forms and ceremonies, grindings and grumblings of the key, they stand appealing and waiting, marshalled, herded, divided, subdivided, sorted, sifted, searched, fumigated, for longer or shorter periods—the effect of all which prodigious process, an intendedly "scientific" feeding of the mill, is again to give the earnest observer a thousand more things to think of than he can pretend to retail. It is a drama that goes on, without a pause, day by day and year by year, this visible act of ingurgitation on the part of our body politic and social, and constituting really an appeal to amazement beyond that of any sword-swallowing or fire-swallowing of the circus. The wonder that one couldn't keep down was the thought that these two or three hours of one's own chance vision of the business were but as a tick or two of the mighty clock, the clock that never, never

[2] Ellis Island was opened in 1892 as the point of entry for the ever-increasing numbers of newly arrived immigrants.

"California, The Cornucopia of the World"
poster, 1870, Rand McNally & Co.
(Collection of the New-York Historical Society)

stops—least of all when it strikes, for a sign of so much winding-up, some louder hour of our national fate than usual. I think indeed that the simplest account of the action of Ellis Island on the spirit of any sensitive citizen who may have happened to "look in" is that he comes back from his visit not at all the same person that he went. He has eaten of the tree of knowledge, and the taste will be for ever in his mouth. Let not the unwary, therefore, visit Ellis Island.

1907

Berenice Abbott
Court of the First Model Tenements in New York
(Museum of the City of New York)

from Abraham Cahan, *The Rise of David Levinsky*

A Second Birth

The immigrant's arrival in his new home is like a second birth to him. Imagine a newborn babe in possession of a fully developed intellect. Would it ever forget its entry into the world? Neither does the immigrant ever forget his entry into a country which is, to him, a new world in the profoundest sense of the term in which he expects to pass the rest of his life. I conjure up the gorgeousness of the spectacle as it appeared to me on that clear June morning: the magnificent verdure of Staten Island, the tender blue of sea and sky, the dignified bustle of passing craft—above all, those floating, squatting, multitudinously windowed palaces which I subsequently learned to call ferries. It was all so utterly unlike anything I had ever seen or dreamed of before. It unfolded itself like a divine revelation. I was in a trance or in something closely resembling one.

1917

Lodgers in a Crowded Bayard Street Tenement—Five Cents a Spot
(Scribner's Monthly, 1889)

from Abraham Cahan, *The Rise of David Levinsky*

The Green One

The appearance of a newly arrived immigrant was still a novel spectacle on the East Side. Many of the passers-by paused to look at me with wistful smiles of curiosity. "There goes a green one!" some of them exclaimed. . . . As I went along I heard it again and again. Some of the passers-by would call me "greenhorn" in a tone of blighting gaiety, but these were an exception. For the most part it was "green one" and in a spirit of sympathetic interest. It hurt me, all the same. Even those glances that offered me a cordial welcome and good wishes had something self-complacent and condescending in them. "Poor fellow! he is a green one," these people seemed to say. "We are not, of course. We are Americanized."
1917

Angel Island*

People who enter this country
Come only because the family is poor,
Selling their fields and lands,
They wanted to come to the land of the Flowering Flag.
The family all looks to you.
Who is to understand it is the most difficult of difficulties!

from Lee Chew, *The Biography of a Chinaman*

The Chinese Laundryman

The Chinese laundryman does not learn his trade in China; there are no laundries in China. The women there do the washing in tubs and have no washboards or flat irons. All the Chinese laundrymen here were taught in the first place by American women, just as I was taught.

When I went to work for that American family I could not speak a word of English, and I did not know anything about housework. The family consisted of husband, wife and two children. They were very good to me and paid me $3.50 a week, of which I could save $3.

I did not know how to do anything, and I did not understand what the lady said to me, but she showed me how to cook, wash, iron, sweep, dust, make beds, wash dishes, clean windows, paint and brass, polish the knives and forks, etc., by doing the things herself and then overseeing my efforts to imitate her. She would take my hands and

* Poem inscribed by a Chinese immigrant on the barracks wall of the immigration detention center of Angel Island, San Francisco's "Ellis Island."

Arnold Genthe
"The Street of Gamblers (By Day)"—Chinatown
photograph, 1880
(California Historical Society, FN 23115)

show them how to do things. She and her husband and children laughed at me a great deal, but it was all good-natured. I was not confined to the house in the way servants are confined here, but when my work was done in the morning I was allowed to go out till lunchtime. People in California are more generous than they are here.

In six months I had learned how to do the work of our house quite well, and I was getting $5 a week and board, and putting away about $4.25 a week. I had also learned some English, and by going to a Sunday school I learned more English and something about Jesus, who was a great sage, and whose precepts are like those of Kong-foo-tsze.

It was twenty years ago when I came to this country, and I worked for two years as a servant, getting at the last $35 a month. I sent money home to comfort my parents, but tho I dressed well and lived well and had pleasure, going quite often to the Chinese theater and to dinner parties in Chinatown, I saved $50 in the first six months, $90 in the second, $120 in the third and $150 in the fourth. So I had $410 at the end of two years, and I was now ready to start in business.

When I first opened a laundry it was in company with a partner, who had been in the business for some years. We went to a town about 500 miles inland, where a railroad was building. We got a board shanty and worked for the men employed by the railroads. Our rent cost us $10 a month and food nearly $5 a week each, for all food was dear and we wanted the best of everything—we lived principally on rice, chickens, ducks, and pork, and did our own cooking. The Chinese take naturally to cooking. It cost us about $50 for our furniture and apparatus, and we made close upon $60 a week, which we divided between us. We had to put up with many insults and some frauds, as men would come in and claim parcels that did not belong to them, saying they had lost their tickets, and would fight if they did not get what they asked for. Sometimes we were taken before magistrates and fined for losing shirts that we had never seen. On the other hand, we were making money, and even after sending home $3 a week I was able to save about $15. When the railroad construction gang moved on we went with them. The men were rough and prejudiced against us, but not more so than in the big eastern cities. It is only lately in New York that the Chinese have been able to discontinue putting wire screens in front of their windows, and at the present time the street boys are still breaking the windows of Chinese laundries all over the city, while the police seem to think it a joke.

We were three years with the railroad, and then went to the mines, where we made plenty of money in gold dust, but had a hard time, for many of the miners were wild men who carried revolvers and after drinking would come into our place to shoot and steal shirts, for which we had to pay. One of these men hit his head hard against a flat iron and all the miners came and broke up our laundry, chasing us out of town. They were going to hang us. We lost all our property and $365 in money, which members of the mob must have found.

---

from Anzia Yezierska, *Bread Givers*

"Woman! when will you stop darkening the house with your worries?"

"When I'll have a man who does the worrying. Does it ever enter your head that the rent was not paid the second month? That to-day we're eating the last loaf of bread that the grocer trusted me?" Mother tried to squeeze the hard, stale loaf that nobody would buy for cash. "You're so busy working for Heaven that I have to suffer here such bitter hell."

We sat down to the table. With watering mouths and glistening eyes we watched Mother skimming off every bit of fat from the top soup into Father's big plate, leaving for us only the thin, watery part. We watched Father bite into the sour pickle which was special for him only; and waited, trembling with hunger, for our portion.

Father made his prayer, thanking God for the food. Then he said to Mother:

"What is there to worry about, as long as we have enough to keep the breath in our bodies? But the real food is God's Holy Torah." He shook her gently by the shoulder, and smiled down at her.

At Father's touch Mother's sad face turned into smiles. His kind look was like the sun shining on her.

"Shenah!" he called her by her first name, to show her he was feeling good. "I'll tell you a story that will cure you of all your worldly cares."

All faces turned to Father. Eyes widened, necks stretched, ears strained not to miss a word. The meal was forgotten as he began:

"Rabbi Chanina Ben Dosa was a starving, poor man who had to live on next to nothing. Once, his wife complained: 'We're so good, so pious, you give up nights and days in the study of the Holy Torah. Then why don't God provide for you at least enough to eat?' . . . 'Riches you want?' said Rabbi Chanina Ben Dosa. 'All right, woman. You shall have your wish.' . . . That very evening he went out into the fields to pray. Soon the heavens opened, and a Hand reached down to him and gave him a big chunk of gold. He brought it to his wife, and said: 'Go buy with this all the luxuries of the earth.' . . . She was so happy, as she began planning all she would buy next day. Then she fell asleep. And in her dream, she saw herself and her husband sitting with all the saints in Heaven. Each couple had a golden table between themselves. When the Good Angel put down for them their wine, their table shook so that half of it was spilled. Then she noticed that their table had a leg missing, and that is why it was so shaky. And the Good Angel explained to her that the chunk of gold that her husband had given her the night before was the missing leg of their table. As soon as she woke up, she begged her husband to pray to God to take back the gold he had given them. . . . 'I'll be happy and thankful to live in poverty, as long as I know that our reward will be complete in Heaven.'"

Mother licked up Father's every little word, like honey. Her eyes followed his shining eyes as he talked.

"*Nu, Shenah?*" He wagged his head. "Do you want gold on earth, or wine of Heaven?"

"I'm only a sinful woman," Mother breathed, gazing up at him. Her fingers stole a touch of his hand, as if he were the king of the world. "God be praised for the little we have. I'm willing to give up all my earthly needs for the wine of Heaven with you. But, *Moisheh*"—she nudged him by the sleeve—"God gave us children. They have a life to live yet, here, on earth. Girls have to get married. People point their fingers on me—a daughter, twenty-five years already, and not married yet. And no dowry to help her get married."

"Woman! Stay in your place!" His strong hand pushed her away from him. "You're smart enough to bargain with the fish-peddler. But I'm the head of this family. I give my daughters brains enough to marry when their time comes, without the worries of a dowry."

"*Nu*, you're the head of the family." Mother's voice rose in anger. "But what will you do if your books are thrown in the street?"

At the mention of his books, Father looked up quickly.

"What do you want me to do?"

"Take your things out from the front room to the kitchen, so I could rent your room to boarders. If we don't pay up the rent very soon, we'll all be in the street."

"I have to have a room for my books. Where will I put them?"

"I'll push my things out from under the bed. And you can pile up your books in the window to the top, because nothing but darkness comes through that window, anyway. I'll do anything, work the nails off my fingers, only to be free from the worry for rent."

"But where will I have quiet for my studies in this crowded kitchen? I have to be alone in a room to think with God."

"Only millionaires can be alone in America. By Zalmon the fish-peddler, they're squeezed together, twelve people, in one kitchen. The bedroom and the front room his wife rents out to boarders. If I could cook their suppers for them, I could even earn yet a few cents from their eating."

"Woman! Have your way. Take in your boarders, only to have peace in the house."

The next day, Mother and I moved Father's table and his chair with a back, and a cushion to sit on, into the kitchen.

Cartoon about the effect of the 1921 Quota Act
(Reproduced from the Collections of the Library of Congress)

Native American Assimilation and a Reemerging Tradition

Some races of men seem molded in wax, soft and melting, at once plastic and feeble. Some races, like some metals, combine the greatest flexibility with the greatest strength. But the Indian is hewn out of rock. You cannot change the form without destruction of the substance. Such, at least, has too often proved the case. Races of inferior energy have possessed a power of expansion and assimilation to which he is a stranger, and it is this fixed and rigid quality which has proved his ruin. He will not learn the arts of civilization, and he and his forest must perish together. The stern, unchanging features of his mind excite our admiration, from their very immutability; and we look with deep interest on the fate of this irreclaimable son of the wilderness, the child who will not be weaned from the breast of his rugged mother. And our interest increases when we discern in the unhappy wanderer, mingled among his vices, the germs of heroic virtues—a hand bountiful to bestow, as it is rapacious to receive, and, even in extreme famine, imparting its last morsel to a fellow-sufferer; a heart which, strong in friendship as in hate, thinks it not too much to lay down life for its chosen comrade; a soul true to its own idea of honor, and burning with an unquenchable thirst for greatness and renown.

> Francis Parkman, *The Conspiracy of Pontiac* (1851)

If the savage resists, civilization, with the ten commandments in one hand and the sword in the other, demands his immediate extermination.

> President Andrew Johnson, Message to Congress (1867)

The idea that a handful of wild, half-naked, thieving, plundering, murdering savages should be dignified with the sovereign attributes of nations, enter into solemn treaties, and claim a country five hundred miles wide by one thousand miles long as theirs in fee simple, because they hunted buffalo and antelope over it, might do for beautiful reading in Cooper's novels or Longfellow's *Hiawatha*, but is unsuited to the intelligence and justice of this age, or the natural rights of mankind.

> *United States v. Lucero* (1869)

So intimately has the Indian become associated with the government as ward of the nation, and so prominent a place among the questions of national policy does the much mooted "Indian question" occupy, that it behooves us no longer to study this problem from works of fiction, but to deal with it as it exists in reality. Stripped of the beautiful romance with which we have been so long willing to envelope him, transferred from the inviting pages of the novelist to the localities where we are compelled to meet with him, in his native village, on the war path, and when raiding upon our frontier settlements and lines of travel, the Indian forfeits his claim to the appellation of the "noble red man." We see him as he is, and, so far as all knowledge

Timothy O'Sullivan
Ruins of the White House, Canyon de Chelley
albumen print, 1873
(Courtesy George Eastman House)

goes, as he ever has been, a savage in every sense of the word; not worse, perhaps, than his white brother would be similarly born and bred, but one whose cruel and ferocious nature far exceeds that of any wild beast of the contact with the wild tribes will deny. Perhaps there are some who, as members of peace commissions or as wandering agents of some benevolent society, may have visited these tribes or attended with them at councils held for some pacific purpose, and who, by passing through the villages of the Indian while at peace, may imagine their opportunities for judging of the Indian nature all that could be desired. But the Indian, while he can seldom be accused of indulging in a great variety of wardrobe, can be said to have character capable of adapting itself to almost every occasion. He has one character, perhaps his most serviceable one, which he preserves carefully, and only airs it when making his appeal to the government or its agents for arms, ammunition, and license to employ them. This character is invariably paraded, and often with telling effect, when the motive is a peaceful one. Prominent chiefs invited to visit Washington invariably don this character, and in their "talks" with the "Great Father" and other less prominent personages they successfully contrive to exhibit but this one phase. Seeing under these or similar circumstances only, it is not surprising that by many the Indian is looked upon as a simple-minded "son of nature," desiring nothing beyond the privilege of roaming and hunting over the vast unsettled wilds of the West, inheriting and asserting but few native rights, and erroneous with that which regards the Indian as a creature possessing the human form but divested of all other attributes of humanity, and whose traits of character, habits, modes of life, disposition, and savage customs disqualify him from the exercise of all rights and privileges, even those pertaining to life itself.

General George Armstrong Custer, *My Life on the Plains* (1872)

As to our aboriginal or Indian population—the Aztec in the South, and many a tribe in the North and West—I know it seems to be agreed that they must gradually dwindle as time rolls on, and in a few generations more leave only a reminiscence, a blank. But I am not at all clear about that. As America, from its many far-back sources and current supplies, develops, adapts, entwines, faithfully identifies its own—are we to see it cheerfully accepting and using all the contributions of foreign lands from the whole outside globe—and then rejecting the only ones distinctively its own—the autochthonic ones?

Walt Whitman, letter to the city officials at Santa Fe, New Mexico (1883)

The allotment of lands in severalty, which began in land lust and is being carried to the bitter end by those who believe a Stone Age man can be developed into a citizen of the United States in single generation, is in violent antagonism to every wish and innate desire of the red man, and has failed of expected results, even among the Southern Cheyennes, where the land is rich and climate mild, because it presents a somber phase of civilized life.

The attempt to make the Sioux a greedy landowner, content to live the lonely life of the poor Western rancher, cut off from daily association with his fellows, is to me uselessly painful. If we would convert the primitive man to our ways, we must make our ways alluring.

Hamlin Garland, *The North American Review* (April 1902)

"Relinquish," McCaslin said. "Relinquish. You, the direct male descendant of him who saw the opportunity and took it, bought the land, took the land, got the land no matter how, out of the old grant, the first patent, when it was a wilderness of wild beasts and wilder men, and cleared it, translated it into something to bequeath to his children,

Edward S. Curtis
Princess Angeline
photogravure on Van Gelder paper, 1891
(Philadelphia Museum of Art: Purchased with funds from the
American Museum of Photography)

worthy of bequeathment for his descendants' ease and security and pride, and to
perpetuate his name and accomplishments. . . ."

"I can't repudiate it. It was never mine to repudiate. It was never Father's and Uncle
Buddy's to bequeath me to repudiate, because it was never Grandfather's to bequeath
them to bequeath me to repudiate, because it was never old Ikkemotubbe's to sell to
Grandfather for bequeathment and repudiation. Because it was never Ikkemotubbe's
fathers' fathers' to bequeath Ikkemotubbe to sell to Grandfather or any man because
on the instant when Ikkemotubbe discovered, realized, that he could sell it for money,
on that instant it ceased ever to have been his forever, father to father to father, and the
man who bought it bought nothing."

William Faulkner, *The Bear* (1942)

Seattle
1786–1866

Few Native Americans have had as enduring a presence in ordinary American life as Seattle, chief of the Suquamish and Dewamish tribes. The Pacific Northwest's largest city is named in his honor. He and his predecessors maintained amiable relations with white settlers and traders for several generations—relations that were strengthened by Seattle's conversion to Christianity in the 1830s. Intent on minimizing the possible conflicts between his people and the American government, Seattle was the first Native American to sign the Treaty of Port Elliott in 1855. That agreement provided Seattle's tribe with a reservation in what is now Washington State. In many respects, Seattle's public identity encapsulated the cumulative image white Americans had found it useful to cultivate—a trustworthy, noble "savage" who had been "civilized" by Christianity and the American government's "generosity."

In 1853 the Washington Territory was organized, and a plan for the city of Seattle was prepared. Two years later, Isaac Stevens, the governor of the territory, visited the city, seeking a pledge of cooperation from the Native Americans. Seattle willingly offered that, but his response to Stevens, printed here, sought assurances that his people would be treated humanely and that their cultural differences with the white settlers would be recognized and respected. The speech was recorded by Henry Smith, a physician fluent in the tribal languages. But the existing text appears to be corrupt; white American interpolations ("pale-face," "Happy Hunting Ground," and the like) suggest that Seattle's speech has been edited to make it conform to the settlers' highly romanticized, stereotypical view of Native Americans.

Further Reading:
E. G. Anderson, *Chief Seattle*, 1943.
W. C. Vanderwerth, *Indian Oratory*, 1971.

A. Rosenteil, *Red and White: Indian Views of the White Man*, 1983.

Text:
The Washington Historical Quarterly, 1931.

"Our People Are Ebbing Away
Like a Rapidly Receding Tide"*

Yonder sky that has wept tears of compassion upon my people for centuries untold, and which to us appears changeless and eternal, may change. Today is fair. Tomorrow it

---

* Speech delivered to Governor Isaac Stevens
  of the Oregon Territory, 1855.

may be overcast with clouds. My words are like the stars that never change. Whatever Seattle says the great chief at Washington[1] can rely upon with as much certainty as he can upon the return of the sun or the seasons. The White Chief says that Big Chief at Washington sends us greetings of friendship and good will. This is kind of him for we know he has little need of our friendship in return. His people are many. They are like the grass that covers vast prairies. My people are few. They resemble the scattering trees of a storm-swept plain. The Great—and I presume—good White Chief sends us word that he wishes to buy our lands but is willing to allow us enough to live comfortably. This indeed appears just, even generous, for the Red Man no longer has rights that he need respect, and the offer may be wise also, as we are no longer in need of an extensive country.

There was a time when our people covered the land as the waves of a wind-ruffled sea cover its shell-paved floor, but that time long since passed away with the greatness of tribes that are now but a mournful memory. I will not dwell on, nor mourn over, our untimely decay, nor reproach my pale face brothers with hastening it as we too may have been somewhat to blame.

Youth is impulsive. When our young men grow angry at some real or imaginary wrong, and disfigure their faces with black paint, it denotes that their hearts are black— and then they are often cruel and relentless, and our old men and old women are unable to restrain them. Thus it has ever been. Thus it was when the white man first began to push our forefathers westward. But let us hope that the hostilities between us may never return. We would have everything to lose and nothing to gain. Revenge by young braves is considered gain, even at the cost of their own lives, but old men who stay at home in times of war, and mothers who have sons to lose, know better.

Our good father at Washington—for I presume he is now our father as well as yours, since King George[2] has moved his boundaries further north—our great and good father, I say, sends us word that if we do as he desires he will protect us. His brave warriors will be to us a bristling wall of strength, and his wonderful ships of war will fill our harbors so that our ancient enemies far to the northward—the Hidas and Timpsions,[3] will cease to frighten our women, children and old men. Then in reality will he be our father and we his children. But can that ever be? Your God is not our God! Your God loves your people and hates mine. He folds his strong protecting arms lovingly about the pale face and leads him by the hand as a father leads his infant son—but He has forsaken His red children—if they are really His. Our God, the Great Spirit, seems also to have forsaken us. Your God makes your people wax strong every day. Soon they will fill all the land. Our people are ebbing away like a rapidly receding tide that will never return. The white man's God can not love our people or He would protect them. They seem to be orphans who can look nowhere for help. How then can we be brothers? How can your God become our God and renew our prosperity and awaken in us dreams of returning greatness. If we have a common Heavenly Father He must be partial—for He

---

[1] President Franklin Pierce.
[2] King of England during the American Revolution.

[3] i.e., the Haidas and Tsimshian, two Northwest Coast Indian groups living in what is now British Columbia, Canada.

came to His pale-face[4] children. We never saw Him. He gave you laws but had no word for His red children whose teeming multitudes once filled this vast continent as stars fill the firmament. No. We are two distinct races with separate origins and separate destinies. There is little in common between us.

To us the ashes of our ancestors are sacred and their resting place is hallowed ground. You wander far from the graves of your ancestors and seemingly without regret. Your religion was written on tables of stone by the iron finger of your God so that you could not forget. The Red Man could never comprehend nor remember it. Our religion is the traditions of our ancestors—the dreams of our old men, given them in the solemn hours of night by the Great Spirit; and the visions of our sachems, and is written in the hearts of our people.

Your dead cease to love you and the land of their nativity as soon as they pass the portals of the tomb and wander away beyond the stars. They are soon forgotten and never return. Our dead never forget the beautiful world that gave them being. They still love its verdant valleys, its murmuring rivers, its magnificent mountains, sequestered vales and verdant-lined lakes and bays, and ever yearn in tender, fond affection over the lonely hearted living, and often return from the Happy Hunting Ground to visit, guide, console and comfort them.

Day and night can not dwell together. The Red Man has ever fled the approach of the White Man as the morning mist flees before the rising sun.

However, your proposition seems fair, and I think that my folks will accept it and will retire to the reservation you offer them. Then we will dwell apart in peace for the words of the Great White Chief seem to be the voice of Nature speaking to my people out of dense darkness.

It matters little where we pass the remnant of our days. They will not be many. The Indian's night promises to be dark. Not a single star of hope hovers above his horizon. Sad-voiced winds moan in the distance. Grim Nemesis[5] seems to be on the Red Man's trail, and wherever he goes he will hear the approaching footsteps of his fell destroyer and prepare to stolidly meet his doom, as does the wounded doe that hears the approaching footsteps of the hunter.

A few more moons. A few more winters—and not one of the descendants of the mighty hosts that once moved over this broad land or lived in happy homes, protected by the Great Spirit, will remain to mourn over the graves of a people—once more powerful and hopeful than yours. But why should I mourn at the untimely fate of my people? Tribe follows tribe, and nation follows nation, like the waves of the sea. It is the order of nature, and regret is useless. Your time of decay may be distant—but it will surely come, for even the White Man whose God walked and talked with him as friend with friend, can not be exempt from the common destiny. We may be brothers after all. We will see.

We will ponder your proposition and when we decide we will let you know. But should we accept it, I here and now make this condition—that we will not be denied the

---

[4] This and terms that follow, such as "Happy Hunting Ground" and "a few more moons," suggest that the text has been heavily edited by white Americans to conform to stereotypes of Indian speech.

[5] Retribution.

privilege without molestation, of visiting at any time the tombs of our ancestors, friends and children. Every part of this soil is sacred, in the estimation of my people. Every hillside, every valley, every plain and grove, has been hallowed by some sad or happy event in days long vanished. Even the rocks, which seem to be dumb and dead as they swelter in the sun along the silent shore thrill with memories of stirring events connected with the lives of my people, and the very dust upon which you now stand responds more lovingly to their footsteps than to yours, because it is rich with the dust of our ancestors and our bare feet are conscious of the sympathetic touch. Our departed braves, fond mothers, glad, happy-hearted maidens, and even the little children who lived here and rejoiced here for a brief season, still love these sombre solitudes and at eventide they grow shadowy of returning spirits. And when the last Red Man shall have perished, and the memory of my tribe shall have become a myth among the white man, these shores will swarm with the invisible dead of my tribe, and when your children's children think themselves alone in the field, the store, the shop, upon the highway, or in the silence of the pathless woods, they will not be alone. In all the earth there is no place dedicated to solitude. At night when the streets of your cities and villages are silent and you think them deserted, they will throng with the returning hosts that once filled them and still love this beautiful land. The White Man will never be alone.

Let him be just and deal kindly with my people, for the dead are not powerless. Dead—I say? There is no death. Only a change of worlds.

1855/1931

Sarah Winnemucca Hopkins
1844–1891

Native American women helped for centuries to preserve and enrich their tribes' splendid traditions of oral literature. Yet as *writers* using English to chronicle their own lives as well as Native American history and culture, Indian women began to appear in print, albeit sporadically, only in the second half of the nineteenth century. Because they wrote primarily for white audiences interested in the "savage" world, these Native American women writers adopted the styles prevalent in the popular literature of the time—romantic, sentimental, and often fictional renditions of their lives, their tribes, and their contacts with white settlers and the American government. Sarah Winnemucca Hopkins' *Life Among the Piutes* (1883) is one of the most engaging examples of this relatively recent development in Native American literature.

Sarah Winnemucca Hopkins was born in northwestern Nevada, the granddaughter of Truckee and the daughter of Old Winnemucca, successive chiefs of the Paiute tribes. Because she was fluent in English at an early age, Hopkins was for much of her youth a liaison between her people and the white settlers in Nevada and later in Oregon, where many Paiutes had moved in response to the westward surge of frontier settlers. Increasing disenchantment with federal Indian policies prompted Hopkins to seek a broader public forum for the concerns of her people. In 1879 she began an extensive tour in the East that included more than three hundred lectures detailing the plight of the Paiutes and other Native Americans. After these heralded efforts and the publication of her book did not produce the results she had hoped for, she resettled in Nevada and opened a school for Paiute children on her brother's farm. Her poor health and inadequate finances could sustain the school only until 1887. She died in 1891.

Life Among the Piutes skillfully blends personal and tribal narrative to create an informative and at times harrowing account of the terrifying extremes the Paiutes were forced to undertake to preserve their families and culture.

Further Reading:

M. E. Gridley, *American Indian Women*, 1974.
W. F. Smith, Jr., "American Indian Autobiographies," *American Indian Quarterly*, 1975.
C.S. Fowler, "Sarah Winnemucca," in *American Indian Intellectuals*, ed. M. Liberty, 1976.
A. Krupat, "American Indian Autobiographies: Origins, Type, and function," *American Literature*, 1981.
G. W. Caulfield, *Sarah Winnemucca Hopkins of the Northern Paiutes*, 1983.
A.L. Brown Ruoff, "Three Nineteenth-Century American Indian Autobiographies," in A. L.

Brown Ruoff and J. W. Ward, eds. *Redefining American Literary History*, 1990.
W. C. Strange, "Story, Take Me Home: Instances of Resonance in Sarah Winnemucca Hopkins' *Life Among the Piutes*," in T. E. Schirer and F. Gilliard, eds. *Entering the 90's: The North American Experience: Proceedings from the Native American Studies Conference at Lake Superior University, Oct. 1989*, 1991.

Text:
Life Among the Piutes: Their Wrongs and Claims, 1883.

---

from Life Among the Piutes*

from **Chapter I: First Meeting of Piutes and Whites**

I was born somewhere near 1844, but am not sure of the precise time. I was a very small child when the first white people came into our country. They came like a lion, yes, like a roaring lion, and have continued so ever since, and I have never forgotten their first coming. My people were scattered at that time over nearly all the territory now known as Nevada. My grandfather was chief of the entire Piute nation, and was camped near Humboldt Lake,[1] with a small portion of his tribe, when a party travelling eastward from California was seen coming. When the news was brought to my grandfather, he asked what they looked like? When told that they had hair on their faces, and were white, he jumped up and clasped his hands together, and cried aloud,—

---

* i.e., Paiutes, two subgroups of the Shoshone-language Indians. The Southern Paiutes lived in southern Utah, Arizona, southern Nevada, and southeastern California. Hopkins was a member of the Northern Paiutes,

who lived in western Nevada, eastern Oregon, and east-central California.
[1] Lake in northwestern Nevada, also known as Humboldt Sink.

"My white brothers,—my long-looked-for white brothers have come at last!"

He immediately gathered some of his leading men, and went to the place where the party had gone into camp. Arriving near them, he was commanded to halt in a manner that was readily understood without an interpreter. Grandpa at once made signs of friendship by throwing down his robe and throwing up his arms to show them he had no weapons; but in vain,—they kept him at a distance. He knew not what to do. He had expected so much pleasure in welcoming his white brothers to the best in the land, that after looking at them sorrowfully for a little while, he came away quite unhappy. But he would not give them up so easily. He took some of his most trustworthy men and followed them day after day, camping near them at night, and travelling in sight of them by day, hoping in this way to gain their confidence. But he was disappointed, poor dear old soul!

I can imagine his feelings, for I have drank deeply from the same cup. When I think of my past life, and the bitter trials I have endured, I can scarcely believe I live, and yet I do; and, with the help of Him who notes the sparrow's fall, I mean to fight for my down-trodden race while life lasts.

Seeing they would not trust him, my grandfather left them, saying, "Perhaps they will come again next year." Then he summoned his whole people, and told them this tradition:—

"In the beginning of the world there were only four, two girls and two boys. Our forefather and mother were only two, and we are their children. You all know that a great while ago there was a happy family in this world. One girl and one boy were dark and the others were white. For a time they got along together without quarelling, but soon they disagreed, and there was trouble. They were cross to one another and fought, and our parents were very much grieved. They prayed that their children might learn better, but it did not do any good; and afterwards the whole household was made so unhappy that the father and mother saw that they must separate their children; and then our father took the dark boy and girl, and the white boy and girl, and asked them, 'Why are you so cruel to each other?' They hung down their heads, and would not speak. They were ashamed. He said to them, 'Have I not been kind to you all, and given you everything your hearts wished for? You do not have to hunt and kill your own game to live upon. You see, my dear children, I have the power to call whatsoever kind of game we want to eat; and I also have the power to separate my dear children, if they are not good to each other.' So he separated his children by a word. He said, 'Depart from each other, you cruel children;—go across the mighty ocean and do not seek each other's lives.'

"So the light girl and boy disappeared by that one word, and their parents saw them no more, and they were grieved, although they knew their children were happy. And by-and-by the dark children grew into a large nation; and we believe it is the one we belong to, and that the nation that sprung from the white children will some time send some one to meet us and heal all the old trouble. Now, the white people we saw a few days ago must certainly be our white brothers, and I want to welcome them. I want to love them as I love all of you. But they would not let me; they were afraid. But they will come again, and I want you one and all to promise that, should I not live to welcome them myself, you will not hurt a hair on their heads, but welcome them as I tried to do." . . .

The following spring, before my grandfather returned home, there was a great excitement among my people on account of fearful news coming from different tribes, that the people whom they called their white brothers were killing everybody that came in their way, and all the Indian tribes had gone into the mountains to save their lives. So my father told all his people to go into the mountains and hunt and lay up food for the coming winter. Then we all went into the mountains. There was a fearful story they told us children. Our mothers told us that the whites were killing everybody and eating them. So we were all afraid of them. Every dust that we could see blowing in the valleys we would say it was the white people. In the late fall my father told his people to go to the rivers and fish, and we all went to Humboldt River,[2] and the women went to work gathering wild seed, which they grind between the rocks. The stones are round, big enough to hold in the hands. The women did this when they got back, and when they had gathered all they could they put it in one place and covered it with grass, and then over the grass mud. After it is covered it looks like an Indian wigwam.

Oh, what a fright we all got one morning to hear some white people were coming. Every one ran as best they could. My poor mother was left with my little sister and me. Oh, I never can forget it. My poor mother was carrying my little sister on her back, and trying to make me run; but I was so frightened I could not move my feet, and while my poor mother was trying to get me along my aunt overtook us, and she said to my mother: "Let us bury our girls, or we shall all be killed and eaten up." So they went to work and buried us, and told us if we heard any noise not to cry out, for if we did they would surely kill us and eat us. So our mothers buried me and my cousin, planted sage bushes over our faces to keep the sun from burning them, and there we were left all day.

Oh, can any one imagine my feelings *buried alive*, thinking every minute that I was to be unburied and eaten up by the people that my grandfather loved so much? With my heart throbbing, and not daring to breathe, we lay there all day. It seemed that the night would never come. Thanks be to God! the night came at last. Oh, how I cried and said: "Oh, father, have you forgotten me? Are you never coming for me?" I cried so I thought my very heartstrings would break.

At last we heard some whispering. We did not dare to whisper to each other, so we lay still. I could hear their footsteps coming nearer and nearer. I thought my heart was coming right out of my mouth. Then I heard my mother say, " 'T is right here!" Oh, can any one in this world ever imagine what were my feelings when I was dug up by my poor mother and father? My cousin and I were once more happy in our mothers' and fathers' care, and we were taken to where all the rest were.

I was once buried alive; but my second burial shall be for ever, where no father or mother will come and dig me up. It shall not be with throbbing heart that I shall listen for coming footsteps. I shall be in the sweet rest of peace,—I, the chieftain's weary daughter. . . .

1883

---

[2] River flowing southwest into Humboldt Lake; it was an important route for immigrants traveling from Salt Lake City to central California.

Mark Twain
1835–1910

Mark Twain (born Samuel Langhorne Clemens) looked back with longing to what he recalled as the innocence, simplicity, and rectitude of pre-Gold Rush America. Yet no other writer partook so hungrily of the wealth, status, fame, and other rewards that the Gilded Age offered. A divided sensibility who alternately craved attention and solitude, he lived on the scale of a prince of industry or banking in New York, Hartford, and the great cities of Europe while his imagination remained tied to the drowsing villages of the Mississippi River valley. Out of such oppositions came one of the dominating prose styles of American literature, half a dozen of its classics, and an incomparably attractive public voice and personality.

Caught up in the westward tide of expansion, Samuel Clemens's parents, poor but blood-proud Virginia gentry, settled along what was then the southwestern frontier, first in the crossroads hamlet of Florida, Missouri, where he was born in 1835, and four years later in Hannibal. His father, a justice of the peace, failed in the law, shopkeeping, land speculation, and ventures in slave trading. The boy left school at twelve to earn his living; he worked in a printing office and wrote occasional newspaper items, burlesques, and humorous sketches. But he also realized the boyhood ambition he was to write about in *Old Times on the Mississippi*: In 1859, after two years of "cubbing," he earned a pilot's license and stood in princely grandeur in the wheelhouse of a river steamboat.

The coming of the Civil War put an end to this occupation and to commercial traffic on the river. Young Clemens spent a few grim weeks in the field as a Confederate irregular before going West to try his hand at prospecting in the Nevada Territory and California. While working as a reporter on the *Virginia City Territorial Enterprise,* he settled finally on his vocation as humorist: He was to learn that the punishing thing about laughter is that people refuse to take it seriously, even though, as he argued time and again, laughter was a supreme moral weapon. All his life he felt compelled to defend his profession, to segregate the noun *humorist* from the adjective *mere* and the synonym *clown.* Reciprocally, Americans of his time tended to cherish him as entertainer alone and, as soon as the smiles faded from their faces, trivialize his genius and irony, his moral passion and assaults on conventional wisdom.

In 1865, two years after Samuel Clemens's pseudonym "Mark Twain" appeared in print for the first time, he published "The Notorious Jumping Frog of Calaveras County." Although he once dismissed it as "a villainous backwoods sketch," the "Jumping Frog" is a brilliant experiment in narrative technique, point of view, and language. It points the way to the tales that make up much of *Roughing It* (1872), Mark Twain's account of his life in the West, and to *Adventures of Huckleberry Finn* (1885).

With *The Innocents Abroad* (1869), a humorous travel narrative that held Europe and the Holy Land up to American standards, Mark Twain first established himself as a popular author. His books, sold by door-to-door salesmen taking orders in advance of publication, reached a broad, nonliterary audience, typically the families of tradesmen, farmers, and small-town professionals. His royalties (he figured that *The Innocents*

Mark Twain
photograph, 1884
(Mark Twain Project)

Double signatures, Mark Twain and Samuel Clemens
(Courtesy of the author)

Abroad sold some 100,000 copies in two years) were supplemented by his earnings as one of the rising stars of the lecture circuit, successor to Artemus Ward. He owned and edited a daily newspaper in Buffalo, New York, and married Olivia Langdon, heiress to a coal fortune.

In 1871 they moved to Hartford, midway in values as well as distance between two literary capitals in transition, New York and Boston. They rented, and soon built, a house at Nook Farm, a tightly knit, high-minded enclave of writers and intellectuals that included Harriet Beecher Stowe and Charles Dudley Warner. *The Gilded Age* (1873), a satiric novel Mark Twain wrote in collaboration with Warner, fed rather than exorcised his growing anger at American society and institutions. In time he would be regarded as a spokesman for American democracy, for what he called "the mighty mass of the uncultivated" instead of "the thin top crust of humanity." But during the 1870s, believing that the American system had broken down, he raged against universal suffrage, the jury system, and what he saw as an "era of incredible rottenness." He crossed the Atlantic to "breathe the free air of Europe," indulge his worship of all things English (the English, in turn, lionized him), and write another travel book, *A Tramp Abroad* (1880). *The Gilded Age,* subtitled "A Tale of Today," had helped turn his mind toward the more malleable yesterdays of *Old Times on the Mississippi* (1875), *The Adventures of Tom Sawyer* (1876), and *The Prince and the Pauper* (1882), the last a concession to genteel taste.

In 1884, after eight years of intermittent struggles with plot problems, Mark Twain completed his masterpiece, *Adventures of Huckleberry Finn.* He wrote this realistic, satiric, yet lyrical novel in the southwestern vernacular from the first-person point of view of an unlettered boy at the bottom of the white social order. "It's the best book we've had," Ernest Hemingway wrote in 1935. T. S. Eliot said Mark Twain discovered "a new way of writing" that brought literary language "up to date." But though it has now been read in millions of copies and become a fixture in world literature, *Huckleberry Finn,* like Walt Whitman's *Leaves of Grass,* entered the world under a cloud of disapproval. Demanding refined language, exemplary heroes, and elevating morals, guardians of the genteel tradition inevitably found Mark Twain's book coarse, vulgar, and immoral. In 1885 the trustees of the Concord (Massachusetts) Public Library expelled the book from their shelves as "trash and suitable only for the slums." Today, *Huckleberry Finn,* a passionately humanitarian and antiracist book, often comes under fire because readers misunderstand Mark Twain's language, his portrayal of Jim, and the irony that frames and shapes the entire narrative.

At fifty it seemed that Mark Twain was blessed with everything: overflowing creative energies, as *Huckleberry Finn* demonstrated; domestic happiness; world fame and social eminence; friendships with Howells and other writers; wealth; and an eye-catching brick-and-brownstone mansion—part steamboat, part medieval stronghold, part cuckoo clock—that was one of Hartford's curiosities. He invested heavily in speculative business ventures. One was a New York subscription publishing house, Charles L. Webster & Company, which, in addition to Mark Twain's own books, issued *Personal Memoirs of U.S. Grant* (1885), a huge commercial success. It earned the general's widow about half a million dollars in royalties but misled Mark Twain into expecting even bigger bonanzas. Over the course of about fifteen years he also poured steadily increasing amounts of money and faith into James W. Paige's automatic typesetting machine, a device timely in concept but committed to impossibly expensive standards of perfection and hopeless competition with Ottmar Mergenthaler's superior Linotype.

Mark Twain in front of house in Hannibal
photograph, 1902
(Reproduced from the Collections of the Library of Congress)

The anarchic impulses unleashed in *A Connecticut Yankee in King Arthur's Court* (1889)—the book ends with a massacre and a rejection of new and old values alike—reflect Mark Twain's anguish and frustration during this period. After the final collapse of both typesetter and publishing house in 1894, he filed for bankruptcy. To pay off his debts he traveled to Australia, New Zealand, India, and South Africa on a yearlong lecture tour. He had settled in England to write a book about his journey around the world, *Following the Equator* (1897), when he learned by cable from Hartford that his favorite daughter had died of meningitis.

"It is one of the mysteries of our nature," Mark Twain was to reflect, "that a man, all unprepared, can receive a thunder-stroke like that and live." For a while he walked the edge of madness in a self-induced dream state that he hoped would reveal to him where and why he had gone wrong. He worked on a series of unfinished and perhaps unfinishable symbolic stories, voyage and dream narratives characterized by

Mark Twain's Hartford, Connecticut house, finished 1874
updated photograph
(Mark Twain House, Hartford, CT)

dislocations of time, place, and scale. These stories of the "Great Dark" (collected and published in 1967 as *Which Was the Dream?*) deal with guilt, responsibility, and identity. They are reminders that this humorist and realist, so anchored in the particularities and textures of day-to-day existence, also sailed the spectral seas of Poe, Hawthorne, and Melville.

To the end of his days Mark Twain argued that personality was merely a machine driven by self-interest and the craving for approval, a doctrine he elaborated in his "bible," *What Is Man?* (first published, anonymously, in 1906), and stated with remarkable concision in his essay, "Corn-Pone Opinions" (first published, posthumously, in 1923). Like *The Man That Corrupted Hadleyburg* (1899), much of his late work is marked by moral and logical clarity instead of a rich sprawl of incident and anecdote. To get his juices flowing he relied on progressively larger jolts of indignation directed at God, orthodox Christianity, Mary Baker Eddy (founder of Christian Science), imperialism, racism, lynching, the martial spirit, and conventional opinions in general. His preferred forms were polemics, satire, and, above all, personal reminiscence. Mark Twain's free-form autobiography, in manuscript a million words or more of written and dictated prose, is the major work of his last years. Its chief unifying principle is the accent and rhythm and attack of his voice.

Restored to financial health, Mark Twain moved back to the United States in 1900. (He had lived abroad for approximately half of the previous twenty-two years.) The ovation that welcomed him continued until his death in 1910. "The most conspicuous person on the planet," he was the idol of New York society and of plutocrats like the steelmaster Andrew Carnegie and Henry H. Rogers of the Standard Oil Trust; a spellbinding after-dinner speaker; a leading voice in the anti-imperialist movement; the most quotable public personality of his time; a master showman who wore white suits winter and summer, flaunted his shock of white hair, and made it a rule "never to smoke when asleep, and never to refrain when awake." In 1902 he revisited Missouri, "a great and beautiful country," for the last time and imagined Tom and Huck coming home to Hannibal old and withered. Five years later he journeyed to England to receive the degree of Doctor of Letters from Oxford University. "Emerson, Longfellow, Lowell, Holmes—" Howells wrote in his memoir, *My Mark Twain*, "I knew them all and all the rest of our sages, poets, seers, critics, humorists; they were like one another and like other literary men; but Clemens was sole, incomparable, the Lincoln of our literature."

Further Reading:

W. D. Howells, *My Mark Twain,* 1910.
A.B. Paine, *Mark Twain: A Biography,* 3 vols., 1912.
V. Brooks, *The Ordeal of Mark Twain,* 1920.
B. DeVoto, *Mark Twain's America,* 1932.
K. Andrews, *Nook Farm: Mark Twain's Hartford Circle,* 1950.
E. Branch, *The Literary Apprenticeship of Mark Twain,* 1950.
D. Wecter, *Sam Clemens of Hannibal,* 1952.

P. Fatout, *Mark Twain on the Lecture Circuit,* 1960.
W. Blair, *Mark Twain and Huck Finn,* 1960.
J. M. Cox, *Mark Twain: The Fate of Humor,* 1966.
J. Kaplan, *Mr. Clemens and Mark Twain,* 1966.
H. Hill, *Mark Twain, God's Fool,* 1973.
J. Steinbrink, *Getting To Be Mark Twain,* 1991.
S. F. Fishkin, *Was Huck Black? Mark Twain and African-American Voice,* 1993.

Texts:

"The Notorious Jumping Frog of Calaveras County," *Mark Twain's Sketches,* 1875.
"Fenimore Cooper's Literary Offenses," and "Corn-

Pone Opinions" from *The Writings of Mark Twain,* 37 vols., ed. A.B. Paine, 1922–1925.
Adventures of Huckleberry Finn, 1885.

Excite the *Laughter* of God's Creatures

I *have* had a "call" to literature, of a low order—*i.e.* humorous. It is nothing to be proud of, but it is my strongest suit, & if I were to listen to that maxim of stern *duty* which says that to do right you *must* multiply the one or the two or the three talents which the Almighty trusts to your keeping, I would long ago have ceased to meddle with things for which I was by nature unfitted & turned my attention to seriously scribbling to excite the *laughter* of God's creatures.

Mark Twain, Letter from San Francisco (October 19, 1865)

The Revised Catechism

What is the chief end of man?—to get rich. In what way?—dishonestly if we must; honestly if we can. Who is God, the one only and true? Money is God. Gold and Greenbacks and Stock—father, son, and the ghost of same—three persons in one; these are the true and only God, mighty and supreme: and William Tweed is his prophet.

Mark Twain, in the New York Tribune *(September 27, 1871)*

A Difference of Opinion

Training is everything. The peach was once a bitter almond; cauliflower is nothing but cabbage with a college education.

One of the most striking differences between a cat and a lie is that a cat has only nine lives.

As to the Adjective: when in doubt, strike it out.

It were not best we should all think alike; it is difference of opinion that makes horse-races.

Mark Twain, Pudd'nhead Wilson *(1894)*

It could probably be shown by facts and figures that there is no distinctly native American criminal class except Congress.

"*Classic.*" A book which people praise and don't read.

Everyone is a moon, and has a dark side which he never shows to anybody.

Mark Twain, Following the Equator *(1897)*

The Notorious Jumping Frog of Calaveras County

In compliance with the request of a friend of mine, who wrote me from the East, I called on good-natured, garrulous old Simon Wheeler, and inquired after my friend's friend, Leonidas W. Smiley, as requested to do, and I hereunto append the result. I have a lurking suspicion that *Leonidas W.* Smiley is a myth; that my friend never knew such a personage; and that he only conjectured that if I asked old Wheeler about him, it would remind him of his infamous *Jim* Smiley, and he would go to work and bore me to death with some exasperating reminiscence of him as long and as tedious as it should be useless to me. If that was the design, it succeeded.

I found Simon Wheeler dozing comfortably by the bar-room stove of the dilapidated tavern in the decayed mining camp of Angel's, and I noticed that he was fat and bald-headed, and had an expression of winning gentleness and simplicity upon his tranquil countenance. He roused up, and gave me good-day. I told him a friend of mine had commissioned me to make some inquiries about a cherished companion of his boyhood named *Leonidas W.* Smiley—*Rev. Leonidas W.* Smiley, a young minister of the Gospel, who he had heard was at one time a resident of Angel's Camp. I added that if Mr. Wheeler could tell me anything about this Rev. Leonidas W. Smiley, I would feel under many obligations to him.

Simon Wheeler backed me into a corner and blockaded me there with his chair, and then sat down and reeled off the monotonous narrative which follows this paragraph. He never smiled, he never frowned, he never changed his voice from the gentle-flowing key to which he tuned his initial sentence, he never betrayed the slightest suspicion of enthusiasm; but all through the interminable narrative there ran a vein of impressive earnestness and sincerity, which showed me plainly that, so far from his imagining that there was anything ridiculous or funny about this story, he regarded it as a really important matter, and admired its two heroes as men of transcendent genius in *finesse*. I let him go on in his own way, and never interrupted him once.

Rev. Leonidas W. H'm, Reverend Le—well, there was a feller here once by the name of *Jim* Smiley, in the winter of '49—or may be it was the spring of '50—I don't recollect exactly, somehow, though what makes me think it was one or the other is because I remember the big flume warn't finished when he first come to the camp; but any way, he was the curiosest man about always betting on anything that turned up you ever see, if he could get anybody to bet on the other side; and if he couldn't he'd change sides. Any way that suited the other man would suit *him*—any way just so's he got a bet, *he* was satisfied. But still he was lucky, uncommon lucky; he most always come out winner. He was always ready and laying for a chance; there couldn't be no solit'ry thing mentioned but that feller'd offer to bet on it, and take ary side you please, as I was just telling you. If there was a horse-race, you'd find him flush or you'd find him busted at the end of it; if there was a dog-fight, he'd bet on it; if there was a cat-fight, he'd bet on it; if there was a chicken-fight, he'd bet on it; why, if there was two birds setting on a fence, he would bet you which one would fly first; or if there was a camp-meeting, he would be there reg'lar to be on Parson Walker, which he judged to be the best exhorter about here, and so he was too, and a good man. If he even see a straddle-bug start to go anywheres, he would bet you how long it would take him to get to—to wherever he was going to, and if you took him up, he would foller that straddle-bug to Mexico but what he would find out where he was bound for and how long he was on the road. Lots of the boys here has seen that Smiley, and can tell you about him. Why, it never made no difference to *him*—he'd bet on *any* thing—the dangdest feller. Parson Walker's wife laid very sick once, for a good while, and it seemed as if they warn't going to save her; but one morning he come in, and Smiley up and asked him how she was, and he said she was considable better—thank the Lord for his inf'nit mercy—and coming on so smart that with the blessing of Prov'dence she'd get well yet; and Smiley, before he thought says, "Well, I'll resk two-and-a-half she don't anyway."

Thish-yer Smiley had a mare—the boys called her the fifteen-minute nag, but that was only in fun, you know, because of course she was faster than that—and he used to win money on that horse, for all she was so slow and always had the asthma, or the distemper, or the consumption, or something of that kind. They used to give her two or three hundred yards' start, and then pass her under way; but always at the fag-end of the race she'd get excited and desperate-like, and come cavorting and straddling up, and scattering her legs around limber, sometimes in the air, and sometimes out to one side amongst the fences, and kicking up m-o-r-e dust and raising m-o-r-e racket with her coughing and sneezing and blowing her nose—and *always* fetch up at the stand just about a neck ahead, as near as you could cipher it down.

And he had a little small bull-pup, that to look at him you'd think he warn't worth a cent but to set around and look ornery and lay for a chance to steal something. But as soon as money was up on him he was a different dog; his under-jaw'd begin to stick out like the fo'castle of a steamboat, and his teeth would uncover and shine like the furnaces. And a dog might tackle him and bully-rag him, and bite him, and throw him over his shoulder two or three times, and Andrew Jackson—which was the name of the pup—Andrew Jackson would never let on but what *he* was satisfied, and hadn't expected nothing else—and the bets being doubled and doubled on the other side all the time, till the money was all up; and then all of a sudden he would grab that other dog jest by the j'int of his hind leg and freeze to it—not chaw, you understand, but only just grip and hang on till they throwed up the sponge, if it was a year. Smiley always come out winner on that pup, till he harnessed a dog once that didn't have no hind legs, because they'd been sawed off in a circular saw, and when the thing had gone along far enough, and the money was all up, and he come to make a snatch for his pet holt, he see in a minute how he'd been imposed on, and how the other dog had him in the door, so to speak, and he 'peared surprised, and then he looked sorter discouraged-like, and didn't try no more to win the fight, and so he got shucked out bad. He give Smiley a look, as much as to say his heart was broke, and it was *his* fault, for putting up a dog that hadn't no hind legs for him to take holt of, which was his main dependence in a fight, and then he limped off a piece and laid down and died. It was a good pup, was that Andrew Jackson, and would have made a name for hisself if he'd lived, for the stuff was in him and he had genius—I know it, because he hadn't no opportunities to speak of, and it don't stand to reason that a dog could make such a fight as he could under them circumstances if he hadn't no talent. It always makes me feel sorry when I think of that last fight of his'n, and the way it turned out.

Well, thish-yer Smiley had rat-tarriers, and chicken cocks, and tom-cats and all them kind of things, till you couldn't rest, and you couldn't fetch nothing for him to bet on but he'd match you. He ketched a frog one day, and took him home, and said he cal'lated to educate him; and so he never done nothing for three months but set in his back-yard and learn that frog to jump. And you bet you he *did* learn him, too. He'd give him a little punch behind, and the next minute you'd see that frog whirling in the air like a doughnut—see him turn one summerset, or may be a couple, if he got a good start, and come down flat-footed and all right, like a cat. He got him up so in the ma'ter of ketching flies, and kep' him in practice so constant, that he'd nail a fly every time as fur as he could see him. Smiley said all a frog wanted was education, and he could do 'most anything—and I believe him. Why, I've seen him set Dan'l Webster down here on this floor—Dan'l Webster was the name of the frog—and sing out, "Flies, Dan'l, flies!" and quicker'n you could wink he'd spring straight up and snake a fly off'n the counter there, and flop down on the floor ag'in as solid as a gob of mud, and fall to scratching the side of his head with his hind foot as indifferent as if he hadn't no idea he'd been doin' any more'n any frog might do. You never see a frog so modest and straightfor'ard as he was, for all he was so gifted. And when it come to fair and square jumping on a dead level, he could get over more ground at one straddle than any animal of his breed you ever see. Jumping on a dead level was his strong suit, you understand; and when it come to that, Smiley would ante up money on him as long as he had a red. Smiley was monstrous proud of his frog, and well he might be, for fellers that had traveled and been everywheres, all said he laid over any frog that ever *they* see.

Well, Smiley kep' the beast in a little lattice box, and he used to fetch him down town sometimes and lay for a bet. One day a feller—a stranger in the camp, he was—come acrost him with his box, and says:

"What might it be that you've got in the box?"

And Smiley says, sorter indifferent-like, "It might be a parrot, or it might be a canary, maybe, but it ain't—it's only just a frog."

And the feller took it, and looked at it careful, and turned it round this way and that, and says, "H'm—so 'tis. Well, what's *he* good for?"

"Well," Smiley, says, easy and careless, "he's good enough for *one* thing, I should judge—he can outjump any frog in Calaveras county."

The feller took the box again, and took another long, particular look, and give it back to Smiley, and says, very deliberate, "Well," he says, "I don't see no p'ints about that frog that's any better'n any other frog."

"Maybe you don't," Smiley says. "Maybe you understand frogs and maybe you don't understand 'em; maybe you've had experience, and maybe you ain't only a amature, as it were. Anyways, I've got *my* opinion and I'll resk forty dollars that he can outjump any frog in Calaveras county."

And the feller studied a minute, and then says, kinder sad like, "Well, I'm only a stranger here, and I ain't got no frog; but if I had a frog, I'd bet you."

And then Smiley says, "That's all right—that's all right—if you'll hold my box a minute, I'll go and get you a frog." And so the feller took the box, and put up his forty dollars along with Smiley's, and set down to wait.

So he set there a good while thinking and thinking to hisself, and then he got the frog out and prized his mouth open and took a teaspoon and filled him full of quail shot— filled him pretty near up to his chin—and set him on the floor. Smiley he went to the swamp and slopped around in the mud for a long time, and finally he ketched a frog, and fetched him in, and give him to this feller, and says:

"Now, if you're ready, set him alongside of Dan'l, with his fore-paws just even with Dan'l's, and I'll give the word." Then he says, "One—two—three—*git!*" and him and the feller touched up the frogs from behind, and the new frog hopped off lively, but Dan'l give a heave, and hysted up his shoulders—so—like a Frenchman, but it warn't no use—he couldn't budge; he was planted as solid as a church, and he couldn't no more stir than if he was anchored out. Smiley was a good deal surprised, and he was disgusted too, but he didn't have no idea what the matter was, of course.

The feller took the money and started away; and when he was going out at the door, he sorted jerked his thumb over his shoulder—so—at Dan'l, and says again, very deliberate, "Well," he says, "*I* don't see no p'ints about that frog that's any better'n any other frog."

Smiley he stood scratching his head and looking down at Dan'l a long time, and at last he says, "I do wonder what in the nation that frog throw'd off for—I wonder if there ain't something the matter with him—he 'pears to look mighty baggy, somehow." And he ketched Dan'l by the nap of the neck, and hefted him, and says, "Why blame my cats if he don't weigh five pound!" and turned him upside down and he belched out a double handful of shot. And then he see how it was, and he was the maddest man—he set the frog down and took out after that feller, but he never ketched him. And—"

(Here Simon Wheeler heard his name called from the front yard, and got up to see what was wanted.) And turning to me as he moved away, he said: "Just set where you are, stranger, and rest easy—I ain't going to be gone a second."

But, by your leave, I did not think that a continuation of the history of the enterprising vagabond *Jim* Smiley would be likely to afford me much information concerning the Rev. *Leonidas W.* Smiley, and so I started away.

At the door I met the sociable Wheeler returning, and he button-holed me and recommenced:

"Well, thish-yer Smiley had a yaller one-eyed cow that didn't have no tail, only jest a short stump like a bannanner, and—"

However, lacking both time and inclination, I did not wait to hear about the afflicted cow, but took my leave.

1865

Fenimore Cooper's Literary Offenses

The Pathfinder and The Deerslayer *stand at the head of
Cooper's novels as artistic creations. There are others of his
works which contain parts as perfect as are to be found in
these, and scenes even more thrilling. Not one can be com-
pared with either of them as a finished whole.*
*The defects in both of these tales are comparatively slight.
They were pure works of art.*
Prof. Lounsbury

*The five tales reveal an extraordinary fullness of inven-
tion. . . .*
*One of the very greatest characters in fiction, Natty
Bumppo. . . .*
*The craft of the woodsman, the tricks of the trapper, all the
delicate art of the forest, were familiar to Cooper from his
youth up.*
Prof. Brander Matthews

*Cooper is the greatest artist in the domain of romantic fic-
tion yet produced by America.*
Wilkie Collins

It seems to me that it was far from right for the Professor of English Literature in Yale,
the Professor of English Literature in Columbia, and Wilkie Collins to deliver opinions
on Cooper's literature without having read some of it. It would have been much more
decorous to keep silent and let persons talk who have read Cooper.

Cooper's art has some defects. In one place in *Deerslayer,* and in the restricted space
of two-thirds of a page, Cooper has scored 114 offenses against literary art out of a possible 115. It breaks the record.

There are nineteen rules governing literary art in the domain of romantic fiction—
some say twenty-two. In *Deerslayer* Cooper violated eighteen of them. These eighteen
require:

1. That a tale shall accomplish something and arrive somewhere. But the *Deerslayer* tale accomplishes nothing and arrives in the air.
2. They require that the episodes of a tale shall be necessary parts of the tale, and
   shall help to develop it. But as the *Deerslayer* tale is not a tale, and accomplishes
   nothing and arrives nowhere, the episodes have no rightful place in the work,
   since there was nothing for them to develop.
3. They require that the personages in a tale shall be alive, except in the case of
   corpses, and that always the reader shall be able to tell the corpses from the
   others. But this detail has often been overlooked in the *Deerslayer* tale.
4. They require that the personages in a tale, both dead and alive, shall exhibit a
   sufficient excuse for being there. But this detail also has been overlooked in the
   Deerslayer tale.

5. They require that when the personages of a tale deal in conversation, the talk shall sound like human talk, and be talk such as human beings would be likely to talk in the given circumstances, and have a discoverable meaning, also a discoverable purpose, and a show of relevancy, and remain in the neighborhood of the subject in hand, and be interesting to the reader, and help out the tale, and stop when the people cannot think of anything more to say. But this requirement has been ignored from the beginning of the *Deerslayer* tale to the end of it.

6. They require that when the author describes the character of a personage in his tale, the conduct and conversation of that personage shall justify said description. But this law gets little or no attention in the *Deerslayer* tale, as Natty Bumppo's case will amply prove.

7. They require that when a personage talks like an illustrated, gilt-edged, tree-calf, hand-tooled, seven-dollar Friendship's Offering in the beginning of a paragraph, he shall not talk like a negro minstrel in the end of it. But this rule is flung down and danced upon in the *Deerslayer* tale.

8. They require that crass stupidities shall not be played upon the reader as "the craft of the woodsman, the delicate art of the forest," by either the author or the people in the tale. But this rule is persistently violated in the *Deerslayer* tale.

9. They require that the personages of a tale shall confine themselves to possibilities and let miracles alone; or, if they venture a miracle, the author must so plausibly set it forth as to make it look possible and reasonable. But these rules are not respected in the *Deerslayer* tale.

10. They require that the author shall make the reader feel a deep interest in the personages of his tale and in their fate; and that he shall make the reader love the good people in the tale and hate the bad ones. But the reader of the *Deerslayer* tale dislikes the good people in it, is indifferent to the others, and wishes they would all get drowned together.

11. They require that the characters in a tale shall be so clearly defined that the reader can tell beforehand what each will do in a given emergency. But in the Deerslayer tale this rule is vacated.

In addition to these larger rules there are some little ones. These require that the author shall

12. *Say* what he is proposing to say, not merely come near it.
13. Use the right word, not its second cousin.
14. Eschew surplusage.
15. Not omit necessary details.
16. Avoid slovenliness of form.
17. Use good grammar.
18. Employ a simple and straightforward style.

Even these seven are coldly and persistently violated in the *Deerslayer* tale.

Cooper's gift in the way of invention was not a rich endowment; but such as it was he liked to work it, he was pleased with the effects, and indeed he did some quite sweet things with it. In his little box of stage-properties he kept six or eight cunning devices, tricks, artifices for his savages and woodsmen to deceive and circumvent each other with, and he was never so happy as when he was working these innocent things and seeing them go. A favorite one was to make a moccasined person tread in the tracks of the moccasined enemy, and thus hide his own trail. Cooper wore out barrels and barrels of moccasins in working that trick. Another stage-property that he pulled out of his box pretty frequently was his broken twig. He prized his broken twig above all the rest of his effects, and worked it the hardest. It is a restful chapter in any book of his when somebody doesn't step on a dry twig and alarm all the reds and whites for two hundred yards around. Every time a Cooper person is in peril, and absolute silence is worth four dollars a minute, he is sure to step on a dry twig. There may be a hundred handier things to step on, but that wouldn't satisfy Cooper. Cooper requires him to turn out and find a dry twig; and if he can't do it, go and borrow one. In fact, the Leatherstocking Series ought to have been called the Broken Twig Series.

I am sorry there is not room to put in a few dozen instances of the delicate art of the forest, as practised by Natty Bumppo and some of the other Cooperian experts. Perhaps we may venture two or three samples. Cooper was a sailor—a naval officer; yet he gravely tells us how a vessel, driving toward a lee shore in a gale, is steered for a particular spot by her skipper because he knows of an *undertow* there which will hold her back against the gale and save her. For just pure woodcraft, or sailorcraft, or whatever it is, isn't that neat? For several years Cooper was daily in the society of artillery, and he ought to have noticed that when a cannon-ball strikes the ground it either buries itself or skips a hundred feet or so; skips again a hundred feet or so—and so on, till finally it gets tired and rolls. Now in one place he loses some "females"—as he always calls women—in the edge of a wood near a plain at night in a fog, on purpose to give Bumppo a chance to show off the delicate art of the forest before the reader. These mislaid people are hunting for a fort. They hear a cannon-blast, and a cannon-ball presently comes rolling into the wood and stops at their feet. To the females this suggests nothing. The case is very different with the admirable Bumppo. I wish I may never know peace again if he doesn't strike out promptly and *follow the track* of that cannon-ball across the plain through the dense fog and find the fort. Isn't it a daisy? If Cooper had any real knowledge of Nature's ways of doing things, he had a most delicate art in concealing the fact. For instance: one of his acute Indian experts, Chingachgook (pronounced Chicago, I think), has lost the trail of a person he is tracking through the forest. Apparently that trail is hopelessly lost. Neither you nor I could ever have guessed out the way to find it. It was very different with Chicago. Chicago was not stumped for long. He turned a running stream out of its course, and there, in the slush in its old bed, were that person's moccasin tracks. The current did not wash them away, as it would have done in all other like cases—no, even the eternal laws of Nature have to vacate when Cooper wants to put up a delicate job of woodcraft on the reader.

We must be a little wary when Brander Matthews tells us that Cooper's books "reveal an extraordinary fullness of invention." As a rule, I am quite willing to accept Brander Matthews's literary judgments and applaud his lucid and graceful phrasing of them; but that particular statement needs to be taken with a few tons of salt. Bless your heart, Cooper hadn't any more invention than a horse; and I don't mean a high-class horse, either; I mean a clothes-horse. It would be very difficult to find a really clever "situation" in Cooper's books, and still more difficult to find one of any kind which he has failed to render absurd by his handling of it. Look at the episodes of "the caves"; and at the celebrated scuffle between Maqua and those others on the table-land a few days later; and at Hurry Harry's queer water-transit from the castle to the ark; and at Deerslayer's half-hour with his first corpse; and at the quarrel between Hurry Harry and Deerslayer later; and at—but choose for yourself; you can't go amiss.

If Cooper had been an observer his inventive faculty would have worked better; not more interestingly, but more rationally, more plausibly. Cooper's proudest creations in the way of "situations" suffer noticeably from the absence of the observer's protecting gift. Cooper's eye was splendidly inaccurate. Cooper seldom saw anything correctly. He saw nearly all things as through a glass eye, darkly. Of course a man who cannot see the commonest little every-day matters accurately is working at a disadvantage when he is constructing a "situation." In the *Deerslayer* tale Cooper has a stream which is fifty feet wide where it flows out of a lake; it presently narrows to twenty as it meanders along for no given reason, and yet when a stream acts like that it ought to be required to explain itself. Fourteen pages later the width of the brook's outlet from the lake has suddenly shrunk thirty feet, and become "the narrowest part of the stream." This shrinkage is not accounted for. The stream has bends in it, a sure indication that it has alluvial banks and cuts them; yet these bends are only thirty and fifty feet long. If Cooper had been a nice and punctilious observer he would have noticed that the bends were oftener nine hundred feet long than short of it.

Cooper made the exit of that stream fifty feet wide, in the first place, for no particular reason; in the second place, he narrowed it to less than twenty to accommodate some Indians. He bends a "sapling" to the form of an arch over this narrow passage, and conceals six Indians in its foliage. They are "laying" for a settler's scow or ark which is coming up the stream on its way to the lake; it is being hauled against the stiff current by a rope whose stationary end is anchored in the lake; its rate of progress cannot be more than a mile an hour. Cooper describes the ark, but pretty obscurely. In the matter of dimensions "it was little more than a modern canal-boat." Let us guess, then, that it was about one hundred and forty feet long. It was of "greater breadth than common." Let us guess, then, that it was about sixteen feet wide. This leviathan had been prowling down bends which were but a third as long as itself, and scraping between banks where it had only two feet of space to spare on each side. We cannot too much admire this miracle. A low-roofed log dwelling occupies "two-thirds of the ark's length"—a dwelling ninety feet long and sixteen feet wide, let us say—a kind of vestibule train. The dwelling has two rooms—each forty-five feet long and sixteen feet wide, let us guess. One of them is the bedroom of the Hutter girls, Judith and Hetty; the other is the parlor in the daytime, at night it is papa's bedchamber. The ark is arriving at the stream's exit now, whose width has been reduced to less than twenty feet to accommodate the Indians—say to eighteen. There is a foot to spare on each side of the boat. Did the Indians notice that there was going to be a tight squeeze there? Did they notice that they could make money by climbing down out of that arched sapling and just stepping aboard when the ark scraped by? No, other Indians would have noticed these things, but Cooper's Indians never notice anything. Cooper thinks they are marvelous creatures for noticing, but he was almost always in error about his Indians. There was seldom a sane one among them.

The ark is one hundred and forty-feet long; the dwelling is ninety feet long. The idea of the Indians is to drop softly and secretly from the arched sapling to the dwelling as the ark creeps along under it at the rate of a mile an hour, and butcher the family. It will take the ark a minute and a half to pass under. It will take the ninety-foot dwelling a minute to pass under. Now, then, what did the six Indians do? It would take you thirty years to guess, and even then you would have to give it up, I believe. Therefore, I will tell you what the Indians did. Their chief, a person of quite extraordinary intellect for a Cooper Indian, warily watched the canal-boat as it squeezed along under him, and when he had got his calculations fined down to exactly the right shade, as he judged, he let go and dropped. And *missed the house!* That is actually what he did. He missed the house, and landed in the stern of the scow. It was not much of a fall, yet it knocked him silly. He lay there unconscious. If the house had been ninety-seven feet long he would have made the trip. The fault was Cooper's, not his. The error lay in the construction of the house. Cooper was no architect.

There still remained in the roost five Indians. The boat has passed under and is now out of their reach. Let me explain what the five did—you would not be able to reason it out for yourself. No. 1 jumped for the boat, but fell in the water astern of it. Then No. 2 jumped for the boat, but fell in the water still farther astern of it. Then No. 3 jumped for the boat, and fell a good way astern of it. Then No. 4 jumped for the boat, and fell in the water *away* astern. Then even No. 5 made a jump for the boat—for he was a Cooper Indian. In the matter of intellect, the difference between a Cooper Indian and the Indian that stands in front of the cigar-shop is not spacious. The scow episode is really a sublime burst of invention; but it does not thrill, because the inaccuracy of the details throws a sort of air of fictitiousness and general improbability over it. This comes of Cooper's inadequacy as an observer.

The reader will find some examples of Cooper's high talent for inaccurate observation in the account of the shooting-match in *The Pathfinder.*

> A common wrought nail was driven lightly into the target, its head having been first touched with paint.

The color of the paint is not stated—an important omission, but Cooper deals freely in important omissions. No, after all, it was not an important omission; for this nail-head is *a hundred yards from* the marksmen, and could not be seen by them at that distance, no matter what its color might be. How far can the best eyes see a common house-fly? A hundred yards? It is quite impossible. Very well; eyes that cannot see a house-fly that is a hundred yards away cannot see an ordinary nail-head at that distance, for the size of the two objects is the same. It takes a keen eye to see a fly or a nail-head at fifty yards—one hundred and fifty feet. Can the reader do it?

The nail was lightly driven, its head painted, and game called. Then the Cooper miracles began. The bullet of the first marksman chipped an edge of the nail-head; the next man's bullet drove the nail a little way into the target—and removed all the paint. Haven't the miracles gone far enough now? Not to suit Cooper; for the purpose of this whole scheme is to show off his prodigy, Deerslayer-Hawkeye-Long-Rifle-Leather-stocking-Pathfinder-Bumppo before the ladies.

> "Be all ready to clench it, boys!" cried out Pathfinder, stepping into his friend's tracks the instant they were vacant. "Never mind a new nail; I can see that, though the paint is gone, and what I can see I can hit at a hundred yards, though it were only a mosquito's eye. Be ready to clench!"

The rifle cracked, the bullet sped its way, and the head of the nail was buried in the wood, covered by the piece of flattened lead.

There, you see, is a man who could hunt flies with a rifle, and command a ducal salary in a Wild West show to-day if we had him back with us.

The recorded feat is certainly surprising just as it stands; but it is not surprising enough for Cooper. Cooper adds a touch. He has made Pathfinder do this miracle with another man's rifle; and not only that, but Pathfinder did not have even the advantage of loading it himself. He had everything against him, and yet he made that impossible shot; and not only made it, but did it with absolute confidence, saying, "Be ready to clench." Now a person like that would have undertaken that same feat with a brickbat, and with Cooper to help he would have achieved it, too.

Pathfinder showed off handsomely that day before the ladies. His very first feat was a thing which no Wild West show can touch. He was standing with the group of marks-men, observing—a hundred yards from the target, mind; one Jasper raised his rifle and drove the center of the bull's-eye. Then the Quartermaster fired. The target exhibited no result this time. There was a laugh. "It's a dead miss," said Major Lundie. Pathfinder waited an impressive moment or two; then said, in that calm, indifferent, know-it-all way of his, "No, Major, he has covered Jasper's bullet, as will be seen if any one will take the trouble to examine the target."

Wasn't it remarkable! How *could* he see that little pellet fly through the air and enter that distant bullet-hole? Yet that is what he did; for nothing is impossible to a Cooper person. Did any of those people have any deep-seated doubts about this thing? No; for that would imply sanity, and these were all Cooper people.

The respect for Pathfinder's skill and for his quickness and accuracy of sight [the italics are mine] was so profound and general, that the instant he made this declara-tion the spectators began to distrust their own opinions, and a dozen rushed to the target in order to ascertain the fact. There, sure enough, it was found that the Quar-termaster's bullet had gone through the hole made by Jasper's, and that, too, so accu-rately as to require a minute examination to be certain of the circumstance, which, however, was soon clearly established by discovering one bullet over the other in the stump against which the target was placed.

They made a "minute" examination; but never mind, how could they know that there were two bullets in that hole without digging the latest one out? For neither probe nor eyesight could prove the presence of any more than one bullet. Did they dig? No; as we shall see. It is the Pathfinder's turn now; he steps out before the ladies, takes aim, and fires.

But, alas! here is a disappointment; an incredible, an unimaginable disappoint-ment—for the target's aspect is unchanged; there is nothing there but that same old bullet-hole!

"If one dared to hint at such a thing," cried Major Duncan, "I should say that the Pathfinder has also missed the target!"

As nobody had missed it yet, the "also" was not necessary; but never mind about that, for the Pathfinder is going to speak.

"No, no, Major," said he, confidently, "that *would* be a risky declaration. I didn't load the piece, and can't say what was in it; but if it was lead, you will find the bullet driving down those of the Quartermaster and Jasper, else is not my name Pathfinder."

A shout from the target announced the truth of this assertion.

Is the miracle sufficient as it stands? Not for Cooper. The Pathfinder speaks again, as he "now slowly advances toward the stage occupied by the females":

"That's not all, boys, that's not all; if you find the target touched at all, I'll own to a miss. The Quartermaster cut the wood, but you'll find no wood cut by that last messenger."

The miracle is at last complete. He knew—doubtless *saw*—at the distance of a hundred yards—that his bullet had passed into the hole *without fraying the edges.* There were now three bullets in that one hole—three bullets embedded processionally in the body of the stump back of the target. Everybody knew this—somehow or other—and yet nobody had dug any of them out to make sure. Cooper is not a close observer, but he is interesting. He is certainly always that, no matter what happens. And he is more interesting when he is not noticing what he is about than when he is. This is a considerable merit.

The conversations in the Cooper books have a curious sound in our modern ears. To believe that such talk really ever came out of people's mouths would be to believe that there was a time when time was of no value to a person who thought he had something to say; when it was the custom to spread a two-minute remark out to ten; when a man's mouth was a rolling-mill, and busied itself all day long in turning four-foot pigs of thought into thirty-foot bars of conversational railroad iron by attenuation; when subjects were seldom faithfully stuck to, but the talk wandered all around and arrived nowhere; when conversations consisted mainly of irrelevancies, with here and there a relevancy, a relevancy with an embarrassed look, as not being able to explain how it got there.

Cooper was certainly not a master in the construction of dialogue. Inaccurate observation defeated him here as it defeated him in so many other enterprises of his. He even failed to notice that the man who talks corrupt English six days in the week must and will talk it on the seventh, and can't help himself. In the *Deerslayer* story he lets Deerslayer talk the showiest kind of book-talk sometimes, and at other times the basest of base dialects. For instance, when some one asks him if he has a sweetheart, and if so, where she abides, this is his majestic answer:

"She's in the forest—hanging from the boughs of the trees, in a soft rain—in the dew on the open grass—the clouds that float about in the blue heavens—the birds that sing in the woods—the sweet springs where I slake my thirst—and in all the other glorious gifts that come from God's Providence!"

And he preceded that, a little before, with this:

"It consarns me as all things that touches a fri'nd consarns a fri'nd."

And this is another of his remarks:

"If I was Injin born, now, I might tell of this, or carry in the scalp and boast of the expl'ite afore the whole tribe; or if my inimy had only been a bear"—[and so on].

We cannot imagine such a thing as a veteran Scotch Commander-in-Chief comporting himself in the field like a windy melodramatic actor, but Cooper could. On one occasion Alice and Cora were being chased by the French through a fog in the neighborhood of their father's fort:

"*Point de quartier aux coquins!*" cried an eager pursuer, who seemed to direct the operations of the enemy.

"Stand firm and be ready, my gallant 60ths!" suddenly exclaimed a voice above them; "wait to see the enemy; fire low, and sweep the glacis."

"Father! father" exclaimed a piercing cry from out the mist; "it is I! Alice! thy own Elsie! spare, O! save your daughters!"

"Hold!" shouted the former speaker, in the awful tones of parental agony, the sound reaching even to the woods, and rolling back in solemn echo.

" 'Tis she! God has restored me my children! Throw open the sally-port; to the field, 60ths, to the field! pull not a trigger, lest ye kill my lambs! Drive off these dogs of France with your steel!"

Cooper's word-sense was singularly dull. When a person has a poor ear for music he will flat and sharp right along without knowing it. He keeps near the tune, but it is *not* the tune. When a person has a poor ear for words, the result is a literary flatting and sharping; you perceive what he is intending to say, but you also perceive that he doesn't say it. This is Cooper. He was not a word-musician. His ear was satisfied with the *approximate* word. I will furnish some circumstantial evidence in support of this charge. My instances are gathered from half a dozen pages of the tale called *Deerslayer*. He uses "verbal" for "oral"; "precision" for "facility"; "phenomena" for "marvels"; "necessary" for "predetermined"; "unsophisticated" for "primitive"; "preparation" for "expectancy"; "rebuked" for "subdued"; "dependent on" for "resulting from"; "fact" for "condition"; "fact" for "conjecture"; "precaution" for "caution"; "explain" for "determine"; "mortified" for "disappointed"; "meretricious" for "factitious"; "materially" for "considerably"; "decreasing" for "deepening"; "increasing" for "disappearing"; "embedded" for "inclosed"; "treacherous" for "hostile"; "stood" for "stooped"; "softened" for "replaced"; "rejoined" for "remarked"; "situation" for "condition"; "different" for "differing"; "insensible" for "unsentient"; "brevity" for "celerity"; "distrusted" for "suspicious"; "mental imbecility" for "imbecility"; "eyes" for "sight"; "counteracting" for "opposing"; "funeral obsequies" for "obsequies."

There have been daring people in the world who claimed that Cooper could write English, but they are all dead now—all dead but Lounsbury. I don't remember that Lounsbury makes the claim in so many words, still he makes it, for he says that *Deerslayer* is a "pure work of art." Pure, in that connection, means faultless—faultless in all details—and language is a detail. If Mr. Lounsbury had only compared Cooper's English with the English which he writes himself—but it is plain that he didn't; and so it is likely that he imagines until this day that Cooper's is as clean and compact as his own. Now I feel sure, deep down in my heart, that Cooper wrote about the poorest English that exists in our language, and that the English of *Deerslayer* is the very worst that even Cooper ever wrote.

I may be mistaken, but it does seem to me that *Deerslayer* is not a work of art in any sense; it does seem to me that it is destitute of every detail that goes to the making of a work of art; in truth, it seems to me that *Deerslayer* is just simply a literary *delirium tremens*.

A work of art? It has no invention; it has no order, system, sequence, or result; it has no life-likeness, no thrill, no stir, no seeming of reality; its characters are confusedly drawn, and by their arts and words they prove that they are not the sort of people the author claims that they are; its humor is pathetic; its pathos is funny; its conversations are—oh! indescribable; its love-scenes odious; its English a crime against the language.

Counting these out, what is left is Art. I think we must all admit that.

1895

Corn-Pone Opinions

Fifty years ago, when I was a boy of fifteen and helping to inhabit a Missourian village on the banks of the Mississippi, I had a friend whose society was very dear to me because I was forbidden by my mother to partake of it. He was a gay and impudent and satirical and delightful young black man—a slave—who daily preached sermons from the top of his master's woodpile, with me for sole audience. He imitated the pulpit style of the several clergymen of the village, and did it well, and with fine passion and energy. To me he was a wonder. I believed he was the greatest orator in the United States and would some day be heard from. But it did not happen; in the distribution of rewards he was overlooked. It is the way, in this world.

He interrupted his preaching, now and then, to saw a stick of wood; but the sawing was a pretense—he did it with his mouth; exactly imitating the sound the bucksaw makes in shrieking its way through the wood. But it served its purpose; it kept his master from coming out to see how the work was getting along. I listened to the sermons from the open window of a lumber room at the back of the house. One of his texts was this:

"You tell me whar a man gits his corn pone, en I'll tell you what his 'pinions is."

I can never forget it. It was deeply impressed upon me. By my mother. Not upon my memory, but elsewhere. She had slipped in upon me while I was absorbed and not watching. The black philosopher's idea was that a man is not independent, and cannot afford views which might interfere with his bread and butter. If he would prosper, he must train with the majority; in matters of large moment, like politics and religion, he must think and feel with the bulk of his neighbors, or suffer damage in his social standing and in his business prosperities. He must restrict himself to corn-pone opinions—at least on the surface. He must get his opinions from other people; he must reason out none for himself; he must have no first-hand views.

I think Jerry was right, in the main, but I think he did not go far enough.

1. It was his idea that a man conforms to the majority view of his locality by calculation and intention.

This happens, but I think it is not the rule.

2. It was his idea that there is such a thing as a first-hand opinion; an original opinion; an opinion which is coldly reasoned out in a man's head, by a searching

analysis of the facts involved, with the heart unconsulted, and the jury room closed against outside influences. It may be that such an opinion has been born somewhere, at some time or other, but I suppose it got away before they could catch it and stuff it and put it in the museum.

I am persuaded that a coldly-thought-out and independent verdict upon a fashion in clothes, or manners, or literature, or politics, or religion, or any other matter that is projected into the field of our notice and interest, is a most rare thing—if it has indeed ever existed.

A new thing in costume appears—the flaring hoopskirt, for example—and the passers-by are shocked, and the irreverent laugh. Six months later everybody is reconciled; the fashion has established itself; it is admired, now, and no one laughs. Public opinion resented it before, public opinion accepts it now, and is happy in it. Why? Was the resentment reasoned out? Was the acceptance reasoned out? No. The instinct that moves to conformity did the work. It is our nature to conform; it is a force which not many can successfully resist. What is its seat? The inborn requirement of self-approval. We all have to bow to that; there are no exceptions. Even the woman who refuses from first to last to wear the hoopshirt comes under that law and is its slave; she could not wear the skirt and have her own approval; and that she *must* have, she cannot help herself. But as a rule our self-approval has its source in but one place and not elsewhere— the approval of other people. A person of vast consequences can introduce any kind of novelty in dress and the general world will presently adopt it—moved to do it, in the first place, by the natural instinct to passively yield to that vague something recognized as authority, and in the second place by the human instinct to train with the multitude and have its approval. An empress introduced the hoopskirt, and we know the result. A nobody introduced the bloomer, and we know the result. If Eve should come again, in her ripe renown, and reintroduce her quaint styles—well, we know what would happen. And we should be cruelly embarrassed, along at first.

The hoopskirt runs its course and disappears. Nobody reasons about it. One woman abandons the fashion; her neighbor notices this and follows her lead; this influences the next woman; and so on and so on, and presently the skirt has vanished out of the world, no one knows how nor why; nor cares, for that matter. It will come again, by and by; and in due course will go again.

Twenty-five years ago, in England, six or eight wine glasses stood grouped by each person's plate at a dinner party, and they were used, not left idle and empty; to-day there are but three or four in the group, and the average guest sparingly uses about two of them. We have not adopted this new fashion yet, but we shall do it presently. We shall not think it out; we shall merely conform, and let it go at that. We get our notions and habits and opinions from outside influences; we do not have to study them out.

Our table manners, and company manners, and street manners change from time to time, but the changes are not reasoned out; we merely notice and conform. We are creatures of outside influences; as a rule we do not think, we only imitate. We cannot invent standards that will stick; what we mistake for standards are only fashions, and perishable. We may continue to admire them, but we drop the use of them. We notice this in literature. Shakespeare is a standard, and fifty years ago we used to write tragedies which we couldn't tell from—from somebody else's; but we don't do it any more, now. Our prose standard, three quarters of a century ago, was ornate and diffuse;

some authority or other changed it in the direction of compactness and simplicity, and conformity followed, without argument. The historical novel starts up suddenly, and sweeps the land. Everybody writes one, and the nation is glad. We had historical novels before; but nobody read them, and the rest of us conformed—without reasoning it out. We are conforming in the other way, now, because it is another case of everybody.

The outside influences are always pouring in upon us, and we are always obeying their orders and accepting their verdicts. The Smiths like the new play; the Joneses go to see it, and they copy the Smith verdict. Morals, religions, politics, get their following from surrounding influences and atmospheres, almost entirely; not from study, not from thinking. A man must and will have his own approval first of all, in each and every moment and circumstance of his life—even if he must repent of a self-approved act the moment after its commission, in order to get his self-approval *again*: but, speaking in general terms, a man's self-approval in the large concerns of life has its source in the approval of the peoples about him, and not in a searching personal examination of the matter. Mohammedans are Mohammedans because they are born and reared among that sect, not because they have thought it out and can furnish sound reasons for being Mohammedans; we know why Catholics are Catholics; why Presbyterians are Presbyterians; why Baptists are Baptists; why Mormons are Mormons; why thieves are thieves; why monarchists are monarchists; why Republicans are Republicans and Democrats, Democrats. We know it is a matter of association and sympathy, not reasoning and examination; that hardly a man in the world has an opinion upon morals, politics, or religion which he got otherwise than through his associations and sympathies. Broadly speaking, there are none but corn-pone opinions. And broadly speaking, corn-pone stands for self-approval. Self-approval is acquired mainly from the approval of other people. The result is conformity. Sometimes conformity has a sordid business interest—the bread-and-butter interest—but not in most cases, I think. I think that in the majority of cases it is unconscious and not calculated; that it is born of the human being's natural yearning to stand well with his fellows and have their inspiring approval and praise—a yearning which is commonly so strong and so insistent that it cannot be effectually resisted, and must have its way.

A political emergency brings out the corn-pone opinion in fine force in its two chief varieties—the pocketbook variety, which has its origin in self-interest, and the bigger variety, the sentimental variety—the one which can't bear to be outside the pale; can't bear to be in disfavor; can't endure the averted face and the cold shoulder; wants to stand well with his friends, wants to be smiled upon, wants to be welcome, wants to hear the precious words, "*He's* on the right track!" Uttered, perhaps by an ass, but still an ass of high degree, an ass whose approval is gold and diamonds to a smaller ass, and confers glory and honor and happiness, and membership in the herd. For these gauds many a man will dump his life-long principles into the street, and his conscience along with them. We have seen it happen. In some millions of instances.

Men think they think upon great political questions, and they do; but they think with their party, not independently; they read its literature, but not that of the other side; they arrive at convictions, but they are drawn from a partial view of the matter in hand and are of no particular value. They swarm with their party, they feel with their party, they are happy in their party's approval; and where the party leads they will follow, whether for right and honor, or through blood and dirt and a mush of mutilated morals.

In our late canvass half of the nation passionately believed that in silver lay salvation, the other half as passionately believed that that way lay destruction. Do you believe that a tenth part of the people, on either side, had any rational excuse for having an opinion about the matter at all? I studied that mighty question to the bottom—came out empty. Half of our people passionately believe in high tariff, the other half believe otherwise. Does this mean study and examination, or only feeling? The latter, I think. I have deeply studied that question, too—and didn't arrive. We all do no end of feeling, and we mistake it for thinking. And out of it we get an aggregation which we consider a boon. Its name is Public Opinion. It is held in reverence. It settles everything. Some think it the Voice of God.

1923

Adventures of Huckleberry Finn

(Tom Sawyer's Comrade)

Scene: The Mississippi Valley
Time: Forty to Fifty Years Ago

NOTICE

PERSONS attempting to find a motive in this narrative will be prosecuted; persons attempting to find a moral in it will be banished; persons attempting to find a plot in it will be shot.

BY ORDER OF THE AUTHOR
PER G. G., CHIEF OF ORDNANCE.

Explanatory

In this book a number of dialects are used, to wit: the Missouri negro dialect; the extremest form of the back-woods South-Western dialect; the ordinary "Pike-County" dialect; and four modified varieties of this last. The shadings have not been done in a haphazard fashion, or by guess-work; but pains-takingly, and with the trustworthy guidance and support of personal familiarity with these several forms of speech.

I make this explanation for the reason that without it many readers would suppose that all these characters were trying to talk alike and not succeeding.

THE AUTHOR.

E. W. Kemble
The frontispiece of the first edition of
Adventures of Huckleberry Finn, *1885.*

Chapter I

You don't know about me, without you have read a book by the name of "The Adventures of Tom Sawyer," but that ain't no matter. That book was made by Mr. Mark Twain, and he told the truth, mainly. There was things which he stretched, but mainly he told the truth. That is nothing. I never seen anybody but lied, one time or another, without it was Aunt Polly, or the widow, or maybe Mary. Aunt Polly—Tom's Aunt Polly, she is—and Mary, and the Widow Douglas, is all told about in that book—which is mostly a true book; with some stretchers, as I said before.

Now the way that the book winds up, is this: Tom and me found the money that the robbers hid in the cave, and it made us rich. We got six thousand dollars apiece—all gold. It was an awful sight of money when it was piled up. Well, Judge Thatcher, he took it and put it out at interest, and it fetched us a dollar a day apiece, all the year round—more than a body could tell what to do with. The Widow Douglas, she took me for her son, and allowed she would sivilize me; but it was rough living in the house all the time, considering how dismal regular and decent the widow was in all her ways; and so when I couldn't stand it no longer, I lit out. I got into my old rags, and my sugar-hogshead again, and was free and satisfied. But Tom Sawyer, he hunted me up and said he was going to start a band of robbers, and I might join if I would go back to the widow and be respectable. So I went back.

The widow she cried over me, and called me a poor lost lamb, and she called me a lot of other names, too, but she never meant no harm by it. She put me in them new clothes again, and I couldn't do nothing but sweat and sweat, and feel all cramped up.

Well, then, the old thing commenced again. The widow rung a bell for supper, and you had to come to time. When you got to the table you couldn't go right to eating, but you had to wait for the widow to tuck down her head and grumble a little over the victuals, though there warn't really anything the matter with them. That is, nothing only everything was cooked by itself. In a barrel of odds and ends it is different; things get mixed up, and the juice kind of swaps around, and the things go better.

After supper she got out her book and learned me about Moses and the Bulrushers; and I was in a sweat to find out all about him; but by-and-by she let it out that Moses had been dead a considerable long time; so then I didn't care no more about him; because I don't take no stock in dead people.

Pretty soon I wanted to smoke, and asked the widow to let me. But she wouldn't. She said it was a mean practice and wasn't clean, and I must try to not do it any more. That is just the way with some people. They get down on a thing when they don't know nothing about it. Here she was a bothering about Moses, which was no kin to her, and no use to anybody, being gone, you see, yet finding a power of fault with me for doing a thing that had some good in it. And she took snuff too; of course that was all right, because she done it herself.

Her sister, Miss Watson, a tolerable slim old maid, with goggles on, had just come to live with her, and took a set at me now, with a spelling-book. She worked me middling hard for about an hour, and then the widow made her ease up. I couldn't stood it much longer. Then for an hour it was deadly dull, and I was fidgety. Miss Watson would say, "Dont put your feet up there, Huckleberry;" and "dont scrunch up like that, Huckleberry—set up straight;" and pretty soon she would say, "Don't gap and stretch like that, Huckleberry—why don't you try to behave?" Then she told me all about the bad place, and I said I wished I was there. She got mad, then, but I didn't mean no harm. All I wanted was to go somewheres; all I wanted was a change, I warn't particular. She said it was wicked to say what I said; said she wouldn't say it for the whole world; *she* was going to live so as to go to the good place. Well, I couldn't see no advantage in going where she was going, so I made up my mind I wouldn't try for it. But I never said so, because it would only make trouble, and wouldn't do no good.

Now she had got a start, and she went on and told me all about the good place. She said all a body would have to do there was to go around all day long with a harp and sing, forever and ever. So I didn't think much of it. But I never said so. I asked her if she reckoned Tom Sawyer would go there, and, she said, not by a considerable sight. I was glad about that, because I wanted him and me to be together.

Miss Watson she kept pecking at me, and it got tiresome and lonesome. By-and-by they fetched the niggers in and had prayers, and then everybody was off to bed. I went up to my room with a piece of candle and put it on the table. Then I set down in a chair by the window and tried to think of something cheerful, but it warn't no use. I felt so lonesome I most wished I was dead. The stars was shining, and the leaves rustled in the woods ever so mournful; and I heard an owl, away off, who-whooing about somebody that was dead, and a whippowill and a dog crying about somebody that was going to die; and the wind was trying to whisper something to me and I couldn't make out what it was, and so it made the cold shivers run over me. Then away out in the woods I heard that kind of a sound that a ghost makes when it wants to tell about something that's on its mind and can't make itself understood, and so can't rest easy in its grave and has to go about that way every night grieving. I got so down-hearted and scared, I did wish I had some company. Pretty soon a spider went crawling up my shoulder, and I flipped it off and it lit in the candle; and before I could budge it was all shriveled up. I didn't need anybody to tell me that that was an awful bad sign and would fetch me some bad luck, so I was scared and most shook the clothes off of me. I got up and turned around in my tracks three times and crossed my breast every time; and then I tied up a little lock of my hair with a thread to keep witches away. But I hadn't no confidence. You do that when you've lost a horse-shoe that you've found, instead of nailing it up over the door, but I hadn't ever heard anybody say it was any way to keep off bad luck when you'd killed a spider.

I set down again, a shaking all over, and got out my pipe for a smoke; for the house was all as still as death, now, and so the widow wouldn't know. Well, after a long time I heard the clock away off in the town go boom—boom—boom—twelve licks—and all still again—stiller than ever. Pretty soon I heard a twig snap, down in the dark amongst the trees—something was a stirring. I set still and listened. Directly I could just barely hear a "*me-yow! me-yow!*" down there. That was good! Says I, "*me-yow! me-yow!*" as soft as I could, and then I put out the light and scrambled out of the window onto the shed. Then I slipped down to the ground and crawled in amongst the trees. and sure enough there was Tom Sawyer waiting for me.

Chapter II

We went tip-toeing along a path amongst the trees back towards the end of the widow's garden, stooping down so as the branches wouldn't scrape our heads. When we was passing by the kitchen I fell over a root and made a noise. We scrouched down and laid still. Miss Watson's big nigger, named Jim, was setting in the kitchen door; we could see him pretty clear, because there was a light behind him. He got up and stretched his neck out about a minute, listening. Then he says,

"Who dah?"

He listened some more; then he come tip-toeing down and stood right between us; we could a touched him, nearly. Well, likely it was minutes and minutes that there warn't a sound, and we all there so close together. There was a place on my ankle that got to itching; but I dasn't scratch it; and then my ear begun to itch; and next my back, right between my shoulders. Seemed like I'd die if I couldn't scratch. Well, I've noticed that thing plenty of times since. If you are with the quality, or at a funeral, or trying to go to sleep when you ain't sleepy—if you are anywheres where it won't do for you to scratch, why you will itch all over in upwards of a thousand places. Pretty soon Jim says:

"Say—who is you? Whar is you? Dog my cats ef I didn' hear sumf'n. Well, I knows what I's gwyne to do. I's gwyne to set down here and listen tell I hears it agin."

So he set down on the ground betwixt me and Tom. He leaned his back up against a tree, and stretched his legs out till one of them most touched one of mine. My nose begun to itch. It itched till the tears come into my eyes. But I dasn't scratch. Then it begun to itch on the inside. Next I got to itching underneath. I didn't know how I was going to set still. This miserableness went on as much as six or seven minutes; but it seemed a sight longer than that. I was itching in eleven different places now. I reckoned I couldn't stand it more'n a minute longer, but I set my teeth hard and got ready to try. Just then Jim begun to breathe heavy; next he begun to snore—and then I was pretty soon comfortable again.

Tom he made a sign to me—kind of a little noise with his mouth—and we went creeping away on our hands and knees. When we was ten foot off, Tom whispered to me and wanted to tie Jim to the tree for fun; but I said no; he might wake and make a disturbance, and then they'd find out I warn't in. Then Tom said he hadn't got candles enough, and he would slip in the kitchen and get some more. I didn't want him to try. I said Jim might wake up and come. But Tom wanted to resk it; so we slid in there and got three candles, and Tom laid five cents on the table for pay. Then we got out, and I was in a sweat to get away; but nothing would do Tom but he must crawl to where Jim was, on his hands and knees, and play something on him. I waited, and it seemed a good while, everything was so still and lonesome.

As soon as Tom was back, we cut along the path, around the garden fence, and by-and-by fetched up on the steep top of the hill the other side of the house. Tom said he slipped Jim's hat off of his head and hung it on a limb right over him, and Jim stirred a little, but he didn't wake. Afterwards Jim said the witches bewitched him and put him in a trance, and rode him all over the State, and then set him under the trees again and hung his hat on a limb to show who done it. And next time Jim told it he said they rode him down to New Orleans; and after that, every time he told it he spread it more and more, till by-and-by he said they rode him all over the world, and tired him most to death, and his back was all over saddle-boils. Jim was monstrous proud about it, and he got so he wouldn't hardly notice the other niggers. Niggers would come miles to hear Jim tell about it, and he was more looked up to than any nigger in that country. Strange niggers would stand with their mouths open and look him all over, same as if he was a wonder. Niggers is always talking about witches in the dark by the kitchen fire; but whenever one was talking and letting on to know all about such things, Jim would happen in and say, "Hm! What you know 'bout witches?" and that nigger was corked up and had to take a back seat. Jim always kept that five-center piece around his neck with a string and said it was a charm the devil give to him with his own hands and told him he could cure anybody with it and fetch witches whenever he wanted to, just by saying something to it; but he never told what it was he said to it. Niggers would come from all around there and give Jim anything they had, just for a sight of that five-center piece; but they wouldn't touch it, because the devil had had his hand on it. Jim was most ruined, for a servant, because he got so stuck up on account of having seen the devil and been rode by witches.

Well, when Tom and me got to the edge of the hill-top, we looked away down into the village and could see three or four lights twinkling, where there was sick folks, may be; and the stars over us was sparkling ever so fine; and down by the village was the river, a whole mile broad, and awful still and grand. We went down the hill and found Jo Harper, and Ben Rogers, and two or three more of the boys, hid in the old tanyard. So we unhitched a skiff and pulled down the river two mile and a half, to the big scar on the hillside, and went ashore.

We went to a clump of bushes, and Tom made everybody swear to keep the secret, and then showed them a hole in the hill, right in the thickest part of the bushes. Then we lit the candles and crawled in on our hands and knees. We went about two hundred yards, and then the cave opened up. Tom poked about amongst the passages and pretty soon ducked under a wall where you wouldn't a noticed that there was a hole. We went along a narrow place and got into a kind of room, all damp and sweaty and cold, and there we stopped. Tom says:

"Now we'll start this band of robbers and call it Tom Sawyer's Gang. Everybody that wants to join has got to take an oath, and write his name in blood."

Everybody was willing. So Tom got out a sheet of paper that he had wrote the oath on, and read it. It swore every boy to stick to the band, and never tell any of the secrets; and if anybody done anything to any boy in the band, whichever boy was ordered to kill that person and his family must do it, and he mustn't eat and he mustn't sleep till he had killed them and hacked a cross in their breasts, which was the sign of the band. And nobody that didn't belong to the band could use that mark, and if he did he must be sued; and if he done it again he must be killed. And if anybody that belonged to the band told the secrets, he must have his throat cut, and then have his carcass burnt up and the ashes scattered all around, and his name blotted off of the list with blood and never mentioned again by the gang, but have a curse put on it and be forgot, forever.

Everybody said it was a real beautiful oath, and asked Tom if he got it out of his own head. He said, some of it, but the rest was out of pirate books, and robber books, and every gang that was high-toned had it.

Some thought it would be good to kill the *families* of boys that told the secrets. Tom said it was a good idea, so he took a pencil and wrote it in. Then Ben Rogers says:

"Here's Huck Finn, he hain't got no family—what you going to do 'bout him?"

"Well, hain't he got a father?" says Tom Sawyer.

"Yes, he's got a father, but you can't never find him, these days. He used to lay drunk with the hogs in the tanyard, but he hain't been seen in these parts for a year or more."

They talked it over, and they was going to rule me out, because they said every boy must have a family or somebody to kill, or else it wouldn't be fair and square for the others. Well, nobody could think of anything to do—everybody was stumped, and set still. I was most ready to cry; but all at once I thought of a way, and so I offered them Miss Watson—they could kill her. Everybody said:

"Oh, she'll do, she'll do. That's all right. Huck can come in."

Then they all stuck a pin in their fingers to get blood to sign with, and I made my mark on the paper.

"Now," says Ben Rogers, "what's the line of business of this Gang?"

"Nothing only robbery and murder," Tom said.

"But who are we going to rob? houses—or cattle—or—"

"Stuff! stealing cattle and such things ain't robbery, it's burglary," says Tom Sawyer. "We ain't burglars. That ain't no sort of style. We are highwaymen. We stop stages and carriages on the road, with masks on, and kill the people and take their watches and money."

"Must we always kill the people?"

"Oh, certainly. It's best. Some authorities think different, but mostly it's considered best to kill them. Except some that you bring to the cave here and keep them till they're ransomed."

"Ransomed? What's that?"

"I don't know. But that's what they do. I've seen it in books; and so of course that's what we've got to do."

"But how can we do it if we don't know what it is?"

"Why blame it all, we've *got* to do it. Don't I tell you it's in the books? Do you want to go to doing different from what's in the books, and get things all muddled up?"

"Oh, that's all very fine to *say*, Tom Sawyer, but how in the nation are these fellows going to be ransomed if we don't know how to do it to them? that's the thing *I* want to get at. Now what do you *reckon* it is?"

"Well I don't know. But per'aps if we keep them till they're ransomed, it means that we keep them till they're dead."

"Now, that's something *like*. That'll answer. Why couldn't you said that before? We'll keep them till they're ransomed to death—and a bothersome lot they'll be, too, eating up everything and always trying to get loose."

"How you talk, Ben Rogers. How can they get loose when there's a guard over them, ready to shoot them down if they move a peg?"

"A guard. Well, that *is* good. So somebody's got to set up all night and never get any sleep, just so as to watch them. I think that's foolishness. Why can't a body take a club and ransom them as soon as they get here?"

"Because it ain't in the books so—that's why. Now Ben Rogers, do you want to do things regular, or don't you?—that's the idea. Don't you reckon that the people that made the books knows what's the correct thing to do? Do you reckon *you* can learn 'em anything? Not by a good deal. No, sir, we'll just go on and ransom them in the regular way."

"All right. I don't mind; but I say it's a fool way, anyhow. Say—do we kill the women, too?"

"Well, Ben Rogers, if I was as ignorant as you I wouldn't let on. Kill the women? No—nobody ever saw anything in the books like that. You fetch them to the cave, and you're always as polite as pie to them; and by-and-by they fall in love with you and never want to go home any more."

"Well, if that's the way, I'm agreed, but I don't take no stock in it. Mighty soon we'll have the cave so cluttered up with women, and fellows waiting to be ransomed, that there won't be no place for the robbers. But go ahead, I ain't got nothing to say."

Little Tommy Barnes was asleep, now, and when they waked him up he was scared, and cried, and said he wanted to go home to his ma, and didn't want to be a robber any more.

So they all made fun of him, and called him cry-baby, and that made him mad, and he said he would go straight and tell all the secrets. But Tom give him five cents to keep quiet, and said we would all go home and meet next week and rob somebody and kill some people.

Ben Rogers said he couldn't get out much, only Sundays, and so he wanted to begin next Sunday; but all the boys said it would be wicked to do it on Sunday, and that settled the thing. They agreed to get together and fix a day as soon as they could, and then we elected Tom Sawyer first captain and Jo Harper second captain of the Gang, and so started home.

I clumb up the shed and crept into my window just before day was breaking. My new clothes was all greased up and clayey, and I was dog-tired.

Chapter III

Well, I got a good going-over in the morning, from old Miss Watson, on account of my clothes; but the widow she didn't scold, but only cleaned off the grease and clay and looked so sorry that I thought I would behave a while if I could. Then Miss Watson she took me in the closet and prayed, but nothing come of it. She told me to pray every day, and whatever I asked for I would get it. But it warn't so. I tried it. Once I got a fish-line, but no hooks. It warn't any good to me without hooks. I tried for the hooks three or four times, but somehow I couldn't make it work. By-and-by, one day, I asked Miss

Watson to try for me, but she said I was a fool. She never told me why, and I couldn't make it out no way.

I set down, one time, back in the woods, and had a long think about it. I says to myself, if a body can get anything they pray for, why don't Deacon Winn get back the money he lost on pork? Why can't the widow get back her silver snuff-box that was stole? Why can't Miss Watson fat up? No, says I to myself, there ain't nothing of it. I went and told the widow about it, and she said the thing a body could get by praying for it was "spiritual gifts." This was too many for me, but she told me what she meant—I must help other people, and do everything I could for other people, and look out for them all the time, and never think about myself. This was including Miss Watson, as I took it. I went out in the woods and turned it over in my mind a long time, but I couldn't see no advantage about it—except for the other people—so at last I reckoned I wouldn't worry about it any more, but just let it go. Sometimes the widow would take me one side and talk about Providence in a way to make a body's mouth water; but maybe next day Miss Watson would take hold and knock it all down again. I judged I could see that there was two Providences, and a poor chap would stand considerable show with the widow's Providence, but if Miss Watson's got him there warn't no help for him any more. I thought it all out, and reckoned I would belong to the widow's, if he wanted me, though I couldn't make out how he was agoing to be any better off then than what he was before, seeing I was so ignorant and so kind of low-down and ornery.

Pap he hadn't been seen for more than a year, and that was comfortable for me; I didn't want to see him no more. He used to always whale me when he was sober and could get his hands on me; though I used to take to the woods most of the time when he was around. Well, about this time he was found in the river drowned, about twelve mile above town, so people said. They judged it was him, anyway; and this drowned man was just his size, and was ragged, and had uncommon long hair—which was all like pap—but they couldn't make nothing out of the face, because it had been in the water so long it warn't much like a face at all. They said he was floating on his back in the water. They took him and buried him on the bank. But I warn't comfortable long, because I happened to think of something. I knowed mighty well that a drownded man don't float on his back, but on his face. So I knowed, then, that this warn't pap, but a woman dressed up in a man's clothes. So I was uncomfortable again. I judged the old man would turn up again by-and-by, though I wished he wouldn't.

We played robber now and then about a month, and then I resigned. All the boys did. We hadn't robbed nobody, we hadn't killed any people, but only just pretended. We used to hop out of the woods and go charging down on hog-drovers and women in carts taking garden stuff to market, but we never hived any of them. Tom Sawyer called the hogs "ingots," and he called the turnips and stuff "julery" and we would go to the cave and pow-wow over what we had done and how many people we had killed and marked. But I couldn't see no profit in it. One time Tom sent a boy to run about town with a blazing stick, which he called a slogan (which was the sign for the Gang to get together), and then he said he had got secret news by his spies that next day a whole parcel of Spanish merchants and rich A-rabs was going to camp in Cave Hollow with two hundred elephants, and six hundred camels, and over a thousand "sumter" mules, all loaded down with di'monds, and they didn't have only a guard of four hundred soldiers, and so we would lay in ambuscade, as he called it, and kill the lot and scoop the things. He said we must slick up our swords and guns, and get ready. He never could go after even a turnip-cart but he must have the swords and guns all scoured up for it; though they was only lath and broom-sticks, and you might scour at them till you rotted and then they warn't worth a mouthful of ashes more than what they was before. I didn't believe we could lick such a crowd of Spaniards and A-rabs, but I wanted to see the camels and elephants, so I was on hand next day, Saturday, in the ambuscade; and when we got the word, we rushed out of the woods and down the hill. But there warn't no Spaniards and A-rabs, and there warn't no camels nor no elephants. It warn't anything but a Sunday-school picnic, and only a primer-class at that. We busted it up, and chased the children up the hollow; but we never got anything but some doughnuts and jam, though Ben Rogers got a rag doll, and Jo Harper got a hymn-book and a tract; and then the teacher charged in and made us drop everything and cut. I didn't see no di'-monds, and I told Tom Sawyer so. He said there was loads of them there, anyway; and he said there was A-rabs there, too, and elephants and things. I said, why couldn't we see them, then? He said if I warn't so ignorant, but had read a book called "Don Quixote," I would know without asking. He said it was all done by enchantment. He said there was hundreds of soldiers there, and elephants and treasure, and so on, but we had enemies which he called magicians, and they had turned the whole thing into an infant Sunday school, just out of spite. I said, all right, then the thing for us to do was to go for the magicians. Tom Sawyer said I was a numskull.

"Why," says he, "a magician could call up a lot of genies, and they would hash you up like nothing before you could say Jack Robinson. They are as tall as a tree and as big around as a church."

"Well," I says, "s'pose we got some genies to help *us*—can't we lick the other crowd then?"

"How you going to get them?"

"I don't know. How do *they* get them?"

"Why they rub an old tin lamp or an iron ring, and then the genies come tearing in, with the thunder and lightning a-ripping around and the smoke a-rolling, and everything they're told to do they up and do it. They don't think nothing of pulling a shot tower up by the roots, and belting a Sunday-school superintendent over the head with it—or any other man."

"Who makes them tear around so?"

"Why, whoever rubs the lamp or the ring. They belong to whoever rubs the lamp or the ring, and they've got to do whatever he says. If he tells them to build a palace forty miles long, out of di'monds, and fill it full of chewing gum, or whatever you want, and fetch an emperor's daughter from China for you to marry, they've go to do it—and they've got to do it before sun-up next morning, too. And more—they've got to waltz that palace around over the country wherever you want it, you understand."

"Well," says I, "I think they are a pack of flatheads for not keeping the palace themselves 'stead of fooling them away like that. And what's more—if I was one of them I would see a man in Jericho before I would drop my business and come to him for the rubbing of an old tin lamp."

"How you talk, Huck Finn. Why, you'd *have* to come when he rubbed it, whether you wanted to or not."

"What, and I as high as a tree and as big as a church? All right, then; I *would* come; but I lay I'd make that man climb the highest tree there was in the country."

"Shucks, it ain't no use to talk to you, Huck Finn. You don't seem to know anything, somehow—perfect sap-head."

I thought all this over for two or three days, and then I reckoned I would see if there was anything in it. I got an old tin lamp and an iron ring and went out in the woods and rubbed and rubbed till I sweat like an Injun, calculating to build a palace and sell it; but it warn't no use, none of the genies come. So then I judged that all that stuff was only just one of Tom Sawyer's lies. I reckoned he believed in the A-rabs and the elephants, but as for me I think different. It had all the marks of a Sunday school.

Chapter IV

Well, three or four months run along, and it was well into the winter, now. I had been to school most all the time, and could spell, and read, and write just a little, and could say the multiplication table up to six times seven is thirty-five, and I don't reckon I could ever get any further than that if I was to live forever. I don't take no stock in mathematics, anyway.

At first I hated the school, but by-and-by I got so I could stand it. Whenever I got uncommon tired I played hookey, and the hiding I got next day done me good and cheered me up. So the longer I went to school the easier it got to be. I was getting sort of used to the widow's ways, too, and they warn't so raspy on me. Living in a house, and sleeping in a bed, pulled on me pretty tight, mostly, but before the cold weather I used to slide out and sleep in the woods, sometimes, and so that was a rest to me. I liked the old ways best, but I was getting so I liked the new ones, too, a little bit. The widow said I was coming along slow but sure, and doing very satisfactory. She said she warn't ashamed of me.

One morning I happened to turn over the salt-cellar at breakfast. I reached for some of it as quick as I could, to throw over my left shoulder and keep off the bad luck, but Miss Watson was in ahead of me, and crossed me off. She says, "Take your hands away, Huckleberry—what a mess you are always making." The widow put in a good word for me, but that warn't going to keep off the bad luck, I knowed that well enough. I started out, after breakfast, feeling worried and shaky, and wondering where it was going to fall on me, and what it was going to be. There is ways to keep off some kinds of bad luck, but this wasn't one of them kind; so I never tried to do anything, but just poked along low-spirited and on the watch-out.

I went down the front garden and clumb over the stile, where you go through the high board fence. There was an inch of new snow on the ground, and I seen somebody's tracks. They had come up from the quarry and stood around the stile a while, and then went on around the garden fence. It was funny they hadn't come in, after standing around so. I couldn't make it out. It was very curious, somehow. I was going to follow around, but I stooped down to look at the tracks first. I didn't notice anything at first, but next I did. There was a cross in the left boot-heel made with big nails, to keep off the devil.

I was up in a second and shinning down the hill. I looked over my shoulder every now and then, but I didn't see nobody. I was at Judge Thatcher's as quick as I could get there. He said:

"Why, my boy, you are all out of breath. Did you come for your interest?"

"No sir," I says, "is there some for me?"

"Oh, yes, a half-yearly is in, last night. Over a hundred and fifty dollars. Quite a fortune for you. You better let me invest it along with your six thousand, because if you take it you'll spend it."

"No sir," I says, "I don't want to spend it. I don't want it at all—nor the six thousand, nuther. I want you to take it; I want to give it to you—the six thousand and all."

He looked surprised. He couldn't seem to make it out. He says:

"Why, what can you mean, my boy?"

I says, "Don't you ask me no questions about it, please. You'll take it—won't you?" He says:

"Well I'm puzzled. Is something the matter?"

"Please take it," says I, "and don't ask me nothing—then I won't have to tell no lies."

He studied a while, and then he says:

"Oho-o. I think I see. You want to *sell* all your property to me—not give it. That's the correct idea."

Then he wrote something on a paper and read it over, and says:

"There—you see it says 'for a consideration.' That means I have bought it of you and paid you for it. Here's a dollar for you. Now, you sign it."

So I signed it, and left.

Miss Watson's nigger, Jim, had a hair-ball as big as your fist, which had been took out of the fourth stomach of an ox, and he used to do magic with it. He said there was a spirit inside of it, and it knowed everything. So I went to him that night and told him pap was here again, for I found his tracks in the snow. What I wanted to know, was, what he was going to do, and was he going to stay? Jim got out his hair-ball, and said something over it, and then he held it up and dropped it on the floor. It fell pretty solid, and only rolled about an inch. Jim tried it again, and then another time, and it acted just the same. Jim got down on his knees and put his ear against it and listened. But it warn't no use; he said it wouldn't talk. He said sometimes it wouldn't talk without money. I told him I had an old slick counterfeit quarter that warn't no good because the brass showed through the silver a little, and it wouldn't pass nohow, even if the brass didn't show, because it was so slick it felt greasy, and so that would tell on it every time. (I reckoned I wouldn't say nothing about the dollar I got from the judge.) I said it was pretty bad money, but maybe the hair-ball would take it, because maybe it wouldn't know the difference. Jim smelt it, and bit it, and rubbed it, and said he would manage so the hair-ball would think it was good. He said he would split open a raw Irish potato and stick the quarter in between and keep it there all night, and next morning you couldn't see no brass, and it wouldn't feel greasy no more, and so anybody in town would take it in a minute, let alone a hair-ball. Well, I knowed a potato would do that, before, but I had forgot it.

Jim put the quarter under the hair-ball and got down and listened again. This time he said the hair-ball was all right. He said it would tell my whole fortune if I wanted it to. I says, go on. So the hair-ball talked to Jim, and Jim told it to me. He says:

"Yo' ole father doan' know, yit, what he's a-gwyne to do. Sometimes he spec he'll go 'way, en den agin he spec he'll stay. De bes' way is to res' easy en let de ole man take his own way. Dey's two angels hoverin' roun' 'bout him. One uv 'em is white en shiny, en 'tother one is black. De white one gits him to go right, a little while, den de black one sail in en bust it all up. A body can't tell, yit, which one gwyne to fetch him at de las'.

But you is all right. You gwyne to have considable trouble in yo' life, en considable joy. Sometimes you gwyne to git hurt, en sometimes you gwyne to git sick; but every time you's gwyne to git well agin. Dey's two gals flyin' 'bout you in yo' life. One uv 'em's light en 'tother one is dark. One is rich en 'tother is po'. You's gwyne to marry de po' one fust en de rich one by-en-by. You wants to keep 'way fum de water as much as you kin, en don't run no resk, 'kase it's down in de bills dat you's gwyne to git hung."

When I lit my candle and went up to my room that night, there set pap, his own self!

E. W. Kemble
Pap
1885

"PAP."

Chapter V

I had shut the door to. Then I turned around, and there he was. I used to be scared of him all the time, he tanned me so much. I reckoned I was scared now, too; but in a minute I see I was mistaken. That is, after the first jolt, as you may say, when my breath sort of hitched—he being so unexpected; but right away after, I see I warn't scared of him worth bothering about.

He was most fifty, and he looked it. His hair was long and tangled and greasy, and hung down, and you could see his eyes shining through like he was behind vines. It was all black, no gray; so was his long, mixed-up whiskers. There warn't no color in his face, where his face showed; it was white; not like another man's white, but a white to make a body sick, a white to make a body's flesh crawl—a tree-toad white, a fish-belly white. As for his clothes—just rags, that was all. He had one ankle resting on 'tother knee; the boot on that foot was busted, and two of his toes stuck through, and he worked them now and then. His hat was laying on the floor; an old black slouch with the top caved in, like a lid.

I stood a-looking at him; he set there a-looking at me, with his chair tilted back a little. I set the candle down. I noticed the window was up; so he had clumb in by the shed. He kept a-looking me all over. By-and-by he says:

"Starchy clothes—very. You think you're a good deal of a big-bug, *don't* you?"

"Maybe I am, maybe I ain't," I says.

"Don't you give me none o' your lip," says he. "You've put on considerble many frills since I been away. I'll take you down a peg before I get done with you. You're educated, too, they say; can read and write. You think you're better'n your father, now, don't you, because he can't? *I'll* take it out of you. Who told you you might meddle with such hifalut'n foolishness, hey?—who told you you could?"

"The widow. She told me."

"The widow, hey?—and who told the widow she could put in her shovel about a thing that ain't none of her business?"

"Nobody never told her."

"Well, I'll learn her how to meddle. And looky here—you drop that school, you hear? I'll learn people to bring up a boy to put on airs over his own father and let on to be better'n what *he* is. You lemme catch you fooling around that school again, you hear? Your mother couldn't read, and she couldn't write, nuther, before she died. None of the family couldn't, before *they* died. *I* can't; and here you're a-swelling yourself up like this. I ain't the man to stand it—you hear? Say—lemme hear you read."

I took up a book and begun something about General Washington and the wars. When I'd read about a half a minute, he fetched the book a whack with his hand and knocked it across the house. He says:

"It's so. You can do it. I had my doubts when you told me. Now looky here; you stop that putting on frills. I won't have it. I'll lay for you, my smarty; and if I catch you about that school I'll tan you good. First you know you'll get religion, too. I never see such a son."

He took up a little blue and yaller picture of some cows and a boy, and says:

"What's this?"

"It's something they give me for learning my lessons good."

He tore it up, and says—

"I'll give you something better—I'll give you a cowhide."

He set there a-mumbling and a-growling a minute, and then he says—

"*Ain't* you a sweet-scented dandy, though? A bed; and bedclothes; and a look'n-glass; and a piece of carpet on the floor—and your own father got to sleep with the hogs in the tanyard. I never see such a son. I bet I'll take some o' these frills out o' you before I'm done with you. Why there ain't no end to your airs—they say you're rich. Hey?—how's that?"

"They lie—that's how."

"Looky here—mind how you talk to me; I'm a-standing about all I can stand, now—so don't gimme no sass. I've been in town two days, and I hain't heard nothing but about you bein' rich. I heard about it away down the river, too. That's why I come. You git me that money to-morrow—I want it."

"I hain't got no money."

"It's a lie. Judge Thatcher's got it. You git it. I want it."

"I hain't got no money, I tell you. You ask Judge Thatcher; he'll tell you the same."

"All right. I'll ask him; and I'll make him pungle, too, or I'll know the reason why. Say—how much you got in your pocket? I want it."

"I hain't got only a dollar, and I want that to—"

"It don't make no difference what you want it for—you just shell it out."

He took it and bit it to see if it was good, and then he said he was going down town to get some whisky; said he hadn't had a drink all day. When he had got out on the shed, he put his head in again, and cussed me for putting on frills and trying to be better than him; and when I reckoned he was gone, he come back and put his head in again, and told me to mind about that school, because he was going to lay for me and lick me if I didn't drop that.

Next day he was drunk, and he went to Judge Thatcher's and bullyragged him and tried to make him give up the money, but he couldn't, and then he swore he'd make the law force him.

The judge and the widow went to law to get the court to take me away from him and let one of them be my guardian; but it was a new judge that had just come, and he didn't know the old man; so he said courts mustn't interfere and separate families if they could help it; said he'd druther not take a child away from its father. So Judge Thatcher and the widow had to quit on the business.

That pleased the old man till he couldn't rest. He said he'd cowhide me till I was black and blue if I didn't raise some money for him. I borrowed three dollars from Judge Thatcher, and pap took it and got drunk and went a-blowing around and cussing and whooping and carrying on; and he kept it up all over town, with a tin pan, till most midnight; then they jailed him, and next day they had him before court, and jailed him again for a week. But he said *he* was satisfied; said he was boss of his son, and he'd make it warm for *him*.

When he got out the new judge said he was agoing to make a man of him. So he took him to his own house, and dressed him up clean and nice, and had him to breakfast and dinner and supper with the family, and was just old pie to him, so to speak. And after supper he talked to him about temperance and such things till the old man cried, and said he'd been a fool, and fooled away his life; but now he was agoing to turn over a new leaf and be a man nobody wouldn't be ashamed of, and he hoped the judge would help him and not look down on him. The judge said he could hug him for them words; so *he* cried, and his wife she cried again; pap said he'd been a man that had always been mis-understood before, and the judge said he believed it. The old man said that what a man wanted that was down, was sympathy; and the judge said it was so; so they cried again. And when it was bedtime, the old man rose up and held out his hand, and says:

"Look at it gentlemen, and ladies all; take ahold of it; shake it. There's a hand that was the hand of a hog; but it ain't so no more; it's the hand of a man that's started in on a new life, and 'll die before he'll go back. You mark them words—don't forget I said them. It's a clean hand now; shake it— don't be afeard."

So they shook it, one after the other, all around, and cried. The judge's wife she kissed it. Then the old man he signed a pledge—made his mark. The judge said it was the holiest time on record, or something like that. Then they tucked the old man into a beautiful room, which was the spare room, and in the night sometime he got powerful thirsty and clumb out onto the porch-roof and slid down a stanchion and traded his new coat for a jug of forty-rod, and clumb back again and had a good old time; and towards daylight he crawled out again, drunk as a fiddler, and rolled off the porch and broke his left arm in two places and was most froze to death when somebody found him after sun-up. And when they come to look at that spare room, they had to take soundings before they could navigate it.

The judge he felt kind of sore. He said he reckoned a body could reform the ole man with a shot-gun, maybe, but he didn't know no other way.

Chapter VI

Well, pretty soon the old man was up and around again, and then he went for Judge Thatcher in the courts to make him give up that money, and he went for me, too, for not stopping school. He catched me a couple of times and thrashed me, but I went to school just the same, and dodged him or out-run him most of the time. I didn't want to go to school much, before, but I reckoned I'd go now to spite pap. That law trial was a slow business; appeared like they warn't ever going to get started on it; so every now and then I'd borrow two or three dollars off of the judge for him, to keep from getting a cowhiding. Every time he got money he got drunk; and every time he got drunk he raised Cain around town; and every time he raised Cain he got jailed. He was just suited—this king of thing was right in his line.

He got to hanging around the widow's too much, and so she told him at last, that if he didn't quit using around there she would make trouble for him. Well, *wasn't* he mad? He said he would show who was Huck Finn's boss. So he watched out for me one day in the spring, and catched me, and took me up the river about three mile, in a skiff, and crossed over to the Illinois shore where it was woody and there warn't no houses but an old log hut in a place where the timber was so thick you couldn't find it if you didn't know where it was.

He kept me with him all the time, and I never got a chance to run off. We lived in that old cabin, and he always locked the door and put the key under his head, nights. He had a gun which he had stole, I reckon, and we fished and hunted, and that was what we lived on. Every little while he locked me in and went down to the shore, three miles, to the ferry, and traded fish and game for whisky and fetched it home and got drunk and had a good time, and licked me. The widow she found out where I was, by-and-by, and she sent a man over to try to get hold of me, but pap drove him off with the gun, and it warn't long after that till I was used to being where I was, and liked it, all but the cowhide part.

It was kind of lazy and jolly, laying off comfortable all day, smoking and fishing, and no books nor study. Two months or more run along, and my clothes got to be all rags and dirt, and I didn't see how I'd ever got to like it so well at the widow's, where you had to wash, and eat on a plate, and comb up, and go to bed and get up regular, and be forever bothering over a book and have old Miss Watson pecking at you all the time. I didn't want to go back no more. I had stopped cussing, because the widow didn't like it; but now I took to it again because pap hadn't no objections. It was pretty good times up in the woods there, take it all around.

But by-and-by pap got too handy with his hick'ry, and I couldn't stand it. I was all over welts. He got to going away so much, too, and locking me in. Once he locked me in and was gone three days. It was dreadful lonesome. I judged he had got drowned and I wasn't ever going to get out any more. I was scared. I made up my mind I would fix up some way to leave there. I had tried to get out of that cabin many a time, but I couldn't find no way. There warn't a window to it big enought for a dog to get through. I couldn't get up the chimbly, it was too narrow. The door was thick solid oak slabs. Pap was pretty careful not to leave a knife or anything in the cabin when he was away; I reckon I had hunted the place over as much as a hundred times; well, I was 'most all the time at it, because it was about the only way to put in the time. But this time I found something at last; I found an old rusty wood-saw without any handle; it was laid in between a rafter and the clapboards of the roof. I greased it up and went to work. There was an old horse-blanket nailed against the logs at the far end of the cabin behind the table, to keep the wind from blowing through the chinks and putting the candle out. I got under the table and raised the blanket and went to work to saw a section of the big bottom log out, big enough to let me through. Well, it was a good long job, but I was getting towards the end of it when I heard pap's gun in the woods. I got rid of the signs of my work, and dropped the blanket and hid my saw, and pretty soon pap come in.

Pap warn't in a good humor—so he was his natural self. He said he was down to town, and everything was going wrong. His lawyer said he reckoned he would win his lawsuit and get the money, if they ever got started on the trial; but then there was ways to put it off a long time, and Judge Thatcher knowed how to do it. And he said people allowed there'd be another trial to get me away from him and give me to the widow for my guardian, and they guessed it would win, this time. This shook me up considerable, because I didn't want to go back to the widow's any more and be so cramped up and sivilized, as they called it. Then the old man got to cussing, and cussed everything and everybody he could think of, and then cussed them all over again to make sure he hadn't skipped any, and after that he polished off with a kind of a general cuss all round, including a considerable parcel of people which he didn't know the names of, and so called them what's-his-name, when he got to them, and went right along with his cussing.

He said he would like to see the widow get me. He said he would watch out, and if they tried to come any such game on him he knowed of a place six or seven mile off, to stow me in, where they might hunt till they dropped and they couldn't find me. That made me pretty uneasy again, but only for a minute; I reckoned I wouldn't stay on hand till he got that chance.

The old man made me go to the skiff and fetch the things he had got. There was a fifty-pound sack of corn meal, and a side of bacon, ammunition, and a four-gallon jug of whisky, and an old book and two newspapers for wadding, besides some tow. I toted up a load, and went back and set down on the bow of the skiff to rest. I thought it all over, and I reckoned I would walk off with the gun and some lines, and take to the woods when I run away. I guessed I wouldn't stay in one place, but just tramp right across the country, mostly night times, and hunt and fish to keep alive, and so get so far away that the old man nor the widow couldn't ever find me any more. I judged I would saw out and leave that night if pap got drunk enough, and I reckoned he would. I got so full of it I didn't notice how long I was staying, till the old man hollered and asked me whether I was asleep or drownded.

I got the things all up to the cabin, and then it was about dark. While I was cooking supper the old man took a swig or two and got sort of warmed up, and went to ripping again. He had been drunk over in town, and laid in the gutter all night, and he was a sight to look at. A body would a thought he was Adam, he was just all mud. Whenever his liquor begun to work, he most always went for the govment. This time he says:

"Call this a govment! why, just look at it and see what it's like. Here's the law a-standing ready to take a man's son away from him—a man's own son, which he has had all the trouble and all the anxiety and all the expense of raising. Yes, just as that man has got that son raised at last, and ready to go to work and begin to do suthin' for *him* and give him a rest, the law up and goes for him. And they call *that* govment! That ain't all, nuther. The law backs that old Judge Thatcher up and helps him to keep me out o' my property. Here's what the law does. The law takes a man worth six thousand dollars and upards, and jams him into an old trap of a cabin like this, and lets him go round in clothes that ain't fitten for a hog. They call that govment! A man can't get his rights in a govment like this. Sometimes I've a mighty notion to just leave the country for good and all. Yes, and I *told* 'em so; I told old Thatcher so to his face. Lots of 'em heard me, and can tell what I said. Says I, for two cents I'd leave the blamed country and never come anear it agin. Them's the very words. I says, look at my hat—if you call it a hat—but the lid raises up and the rest of it goes down till it's below my chin, and then it ain't rightly a hat at all, but more like my head was shoved up through a jint o' stove-pipe. Look at it, says I—such a hat for me to wear—one of the wealthiest men in this town, if I could git my rights.

"Oh, yes, this is a wonderful govment, wonderful. Why, looky here. There was a free nigger there, from Ohio; a mulatter, most as white as a white man. He had the whitest shirt on you ever see, too, and the shiniest hat; and there ain't a man in that town that's got as fine clothes as what he had; and he had a gold watch and chain, and a silver-headed cane—the awfulest old gray-headed nabob in the State. And what do you think? they said he was a p'fessor in a college, and could talk all kinds of languages, and knowed everything. And that ain't the wust. They said he could *vote*, when he was at home. Well, that let me out. Thinks I, what is the country a-coming to? It was 'lection day, and I was just about to go and vote, myself, if I warn't too drunk to get there; but when they told me there was a State in this country where they'd let that nigger vote, I drawed out. I says I'll never vote again. Them's the very words I said; they all heard me; and the country may rot for all me—I'll never vote agin as long as I live. And to see the cool way of that nigger—why, he wouldn't a give me the road if I hadn't shoved him out o' the way. I says to the people, why ain't this nigger put up at auction and sold?—that's what I want to know. And what do you reckon they said? Why, they said he couldn't be sold till he'd been in the State six months, and he hadn't been there that long yet. There, now—that's a specimen. They call that a govment that can't sell a free nigger till he's been in the State six months. Here's a govment that calls itself a govment, and lets on to be a govment, and thinks it is a govment, and yet's got to set stock-still for six whole months before it can take ahold of a prowling, thieving, infernal, white-shirted free nigger, and—"

Pap was agoing on so, he never noticed where his old limber legs was taking him to, so he went head over heels over the tub of salt pork, and barked both shins, and the rest of his speech was all the hottest kind of language—mostly hove at the nigger and the govment, though he give the tub some, too, all along, here and there. He hopped around the cabin considerable, first on one leg and then on the other, holding first one shin and then the other one, and at last he let out with his left foot all of a sudden and fetched the tub a rattling kick. But it warn't good judgment, because that was the boot that had a couple of his toes leaking out of the front end of it; so now he raised a howl that fairly made a body's hair raise, and down he went in the dirt, and rolled there, and held his toes; and the cussing he done then laid over anything he had ever done previous. He said so his own self, afterwards. He had heard old Sowberry Hagan in his best days, and he said it laid over him, too; but I reckon that was sort of piling it on, maybe.

After supper pap took the jug, and said he had enough whisky there for two drunks and one delirium tremens. That was always his word. I judged he would be blind drunk in about an hour, and then I would steal the key, or saw myself out, one or 'tother. He drank, and drank, and tumbled down on his blankets, by-and-by; but luck didn't run my way. He didn't go sound asleep, but was uneasy. He groaned, and moaned, and thrashed around this way and that, for a long time. At last I got so sleepy I couldn't keep my eyes open, all I could do, and so before I knowed what I was about I was sound asleep, and the candle burning.

I don't know how long I was asleep, but all of a sudden there was an awful scream and I was up. There was pap, looking wild and skipping around every which way and yelling about snakes. He said they was crawling up his legs; and then he would give a jump and scream, and say one had bit him on the cheek—but I couldn't see no snakes. He started and run round and round the cabin, hollering "take him off! take him off! he's biting me on the neck!" I never see a man look so wild in the eyes. Pretty soon he was all fagged out, and fell down panting; then he rolled over and over, wonderful fast, kicking things every which way, and striking and grabbing at the air with his hands, and screaming, and saying there was devils ahold of him. He wore out, by-and-by, and laid still a while, moaning. Then he laid stiller, and didn't make a sound. I could hear the owls and the wolves, away off in the woods, and it seemed terrible still. He was laying over by the corner. By-and-by he raised up, part way, and listened, with his head to one side. He says very low:

"Tramp—tramp—tramp; that's the dead; tramp—tramp—tramp; they're coming after me; but I won't go—Oh, they're here! don't touch me—don't! hands off—they're cold; let go— Oh, let a poor devil alone!"

Then he went down on all fours and crawled off begging them to let him alone, and he rolled himself up in his blanket and wallowed in under the old pine table, still a-begging; and then he went to crying. I could hear him through the blanket.

By-and-by he rolled out and jumped up on his feet looking wild, and he see me and went for me. He chased me round and round the place, with a clasp-knife, calling me the Angel of Death and saying he would kill me and then I couldn't come for him no more. I begged, and told him I was only Huck, but he laughed *such* a screechy laugh, and roared and cussed, and kept on chasing me up. Once when I turned short and dodged under his arm he made a grab and got me by the jacket between my shoulders, and I thought I was gone; but I slid out of the jacket quick as lightning, and saved myself. Pretty soon he was all tired out, and dropped down with his back against the door, and said he would rest a minute and then kill me. He put his knife under him, and said he would sleep and get strong, and then he would see who was who.

So he dozed off, pretty soon. By-and-by I got the old split-bottom chair and clumb up, as easy as I could, not to make any noise, and got down the gun. I slipped the ramrod down it to make sure it was loaded, and then I laid it across the turnip barrel, pointing towards pap, and set down behind it to wait for him to stir. And how slow and still the time did drag along.

Chapter VII

"Git up! what you 'bout!"

I opened my eyes and looked around, trying to make out where I was. It was after sun-up, and I had been sound asleep. Pap was standing over me, looking sour—and sick, too. He says—

"What you doin' with this gun?"

I judged he didn't know nothing about what he had been doing, so I says:

"Somebody tried to get in, so I was laying for him."

"Why didn't you roust me out?"

"Well I tried to, but I couldn't; I couldn't budge you."

"Well, all right. Don't stand there palavering all day, but out with you and see if there's a fish on the lines for breakfast. I'll be along in a minute."

He unlocked the door and I cleared out, up the river bank. I noticed some pieces of limbs and such things floating down, and a sprinkling of bark; so I knowed the river had begun to rise. I reckoned I would have great times, now, if I was over at the town. The June rise used to be always luck for me; because as soon as that rise begins, here comes cord-wood floating down, and pieces of log rafts—sometimes a dozen logs together; so all you have to do is to catch them and sell them to the wood yards and the sawmill.

I went along up the bank with one eye out for pap and 'tother one out for what the rise might fetch along. Well, all at once, here comes a canoe; just a beauty, too, about thirteen or fourteen foot long, riding high like a duck. I shot head first off the bank, like a frog, clothes and all on, and struck out for the canoe. I just expected there'd be some-body laying down on it, because people often done that to fool folks, and when a chap had pulled a skiff out most to it they'd raise up and laugh at him. But it warn't so this time. It was a drift-canoe, sure enough, and I clumb in and paddled her ashore. Thinks I, the old man will be glad when he sees this—she's worth ten dollars. But when I got to shore pap wasn't in sight yet, and as I was running her into a little creek like a gully, all hung over with vines and willows, I struck another idea; I judged I'd hide her good, and then, stead of taking to the woods when I run off, I'd go down the river about fifty mile and camp in one place for good, and not have such a rough time tramping on foot.

It was pretty close to the shanty, and I thought I heard the old man coming, all the time; but I got her hid; and then I out and looked around a bunch of willows, and there was the old man down the path apiece just drawing a bead on a bird with his gun. So he hadn't seen anything.

When he got along, I was hard at it taking up a "trot" line. He abused me a little for being so slow, but I told him I fell in the river and that was what made me so long. I knowed he would see I was wet, and then he would be asking questions. We got five cat-fish off of the lines and went home.

While we laid off, after breakfast, to sleep up, both of us being about wore out, I got to thinking that if I could fix up some way to keep pap and the widow from trying to fol-low me, it would be a certainer thing than trusting to luck to get far enough off before they missed me; you see, all kinds of things might happen. Well, I didn't see no way for a while, but by-and-by pap raised up a minute, to drink another barrel of water, and he says:

"Another time a man comes a-prowling round here, you roust me out, you hear? That man warn't here for no good. I'd a shot him. Next time, you roust me out, you hear?"

Then he dropped down and went to sleep again—but what he had been saying give me the very idea I wanted. I says to myself, I can fix it now so nobody won't think of following me.

About twelve o'clock we turned out and went along up the bank. The river was coming up pretty fast, and lots of drift-wood going by on the rise. By-and-by, along comes part of a log raft—nine logs fast together. We went out with the skiff and towed it ashore. Then we had dinner. Anybody but pap would a waited and seen the day through, so as to catch more stuff; but that warn't pap's style. Nine logs was enough for one time; he must shove right over to town and sell. So he locked me in and took the skiff and started off towing the raft about half-past three. I judged he wouldn't come back that night. I waited till I reckoned he had got a good start, then I out with my saw and went to work on that log again. Before he was 'tother side of the river I was out of the hole; him and his raft was just a speck on the water away off yonder.

I took the sack of corn meal and took it to where the canoe was hid, and shoved the vines and branches apart and put it in; then I done the same with the side of bacon; then the whisky jug; I took all the coffee and sugar there was, and all the ammunition; I took the wadding; I took the bucket and gourd, I took a dipper and a tin cup, and my old saw and two blankets, and the skillet and the coffee-pot. I took fish-lines and matches and other things—everything that was worth a cent. I cleaned out the place. I wanted an axe, but there wasn't any, only the one out at the wood pile, and I knowed why I was going to leave that. I fetched out the gun, and now I was done.

I had wore the ground a good deal, crawling out of the hole and dragging out so many things. So I fixed that as good as I could from the outside by scattering dust on the place, which covered up the smoothness and the sawdust. Then I fixed the piece of log back into its place, and put two rocks under it and one against it to hold it there,—for it was bent up at that place, and didn't quite touch ground. If you stood four or five foot away and didn't know it was sawed, you wouldn't ever notice it; and besides, this was the back of the cabin and it warn't likely anybody would go fooling around there.

It was all grass clear to the canoe; so I hadn't left a track. I followed around to see. I stood on the bank and looked out over the river. All safe. So I took the gun and went up a piece into the woods and was hunting around for some birds, when I see a wild pig; hogs soon went wild in them bottoms after they had got away from the prairie farms. I shot this fellow and took him into camp.

I took the axe and smashed in the door—I beat it and hacked it considerable, a-doing it. I fetched the pig in and took him back nearly to the table and hacked into his throat with the ax, and laid him down on the ground to bleed—I say ground, because it *was* ground—hard packed, and no boards. Well, next I took an old sack and put a lot of big rocks in it,—all I could drag—and I started it from the pig and dragged it to the door and through the woods down to the river and dumped it in, and down it sunk, out of sight. You could easy see that something had been dragged over the ground. I did wish Tom Sawyer was there, I knowed he would take an interest in this kind of business, and throw in the fancy touches. Nobody could spread himself like Tom Sawyer in such a thing as that.

Well, last I pulled out some of my hair, and bloodied the ax good, and stuck it on the back side, and slung the ax in the corner. Then I took up the pig and held him to my breast with my jacket (so he couldn't drip) till I got a good piece below the house and then dumped him into the river. Now I thought of something else. So I went and got the bag of meal and my old saw out of the canoe and fetched them to the house. I took the bag to where it used to stand, and ripped a hole in the bottom of it with the saw, for there warn't no knives and forks on the place—pap done everything with his clasp-knife, about the cooking. Then I carried the sack about a hundred yards across the grass and through the willows east of the house, to a shallow lake that was five mile wide and full of rushes—and ducks too, you might say, in the season. There was a slough or a creek leading out of it on the other side, that went miles away, I don't know where, but it didn't go to the river. The meal sifted out and made a little track all the way to the lake. I dropped pap's whetstone there too, so as to look like it had been done by accident. Then I tied up the rip in the meal sack with a string, so it wouldn't leak no more, and took it and my saw to the canoe again.

It was about dark, now; so I dropped the canoe down the river under some willows that hung over the bank, and waited for the moon to rise. I made fast to a willow; then I took a bite to eat, and by-and-by laid down in the canoe to smoke a pipe and lay out a plan. I says to myself, they'll follow the track of that sackful of rocks to the shore and then drag the river for me. And they'll follow that meal track to the lake and go browsing down the creek that leads out of it to find the robbers that killed me and took the things. They won't ever hunt the river for anything but my dead carcass. They'll soon get tired of that, and won't bother no more about me. All right; I can stop anywhere I want to. Jackson's Island is good enough for me; I know that island pretty well, and nobody ever comes there. And then I can paddle over to town, nights, and slink around and pick up things I want. Jackson's Island's the place.

I was pretty tired, and the first thing I knowed, I was asleep. When I woke up I didn't know where I was, for a minute. I set up and looked around, a little scared. Then I remembered. The river looked miles and miles across. The moon was so bright I could a counted the drift logs that went a slipping along, black and still, hundreds of yards out from shore. Everything was dead quiet, and it looked late, and *smelt* late. You know what I mean—I don't know the words to put it in.

I took a good gap and a stretch, and was just going to unhitch and start, when I heard a sound away over the water. I listened. Pretty soon I made it out. It was that dull kind of a regular sound that comes from oars working in rowlocks when it's a still night. I peeped out through the willow branches, and there it was—a skiff, away across the water. I couldn't tell how many was in it. It kept-a-coming, and when it was abreast of me I see there warn't but one man in it. Thinks I, maybe it's pap, though I warn't expecting him. He dropped below me, with the current, and by-and-by he come a-swinging up shore in the easy water, and he went by so close I could a reached out the gun and touched him. Well, it *was* pap, sure enough—and sober, too, by the way he laid to his oars.

I didn't lose no time. The next minute I was a-spinning down stream soft but quick in the shade of the bank. I made two mile and a half, and then struck out a quarter of a mile or more towards the middle of the river, because pretty soon I would be passing the ferry landing and people might see me and hail me. I got out amongst the drift-wood and then laid down in the bottom of the canoe and let her float. I laid there and had a good rest and a smoke out of my pipe, looking away into the sky, not a cloud in it. The sky looks ever so deep when you lay down on your back in the moonshine; I never knowed it before. And how far a body can hear on the water such nights! I heard people talking at the ferry landing. I heard what they said, too, every word of it. One man said it was getting towards the long days and the short nights, now. 'Tother one said *this* warn't one of the short ones, he reckoned—and then they laughed, and he said it over again and they laughed again; then they waked up another fellow and told him, and laughed, but he didn't laugh; he ripped out something brisk and said let him alone. The first fellow said he 'lowed to tell it to his old woman—she would think it was pretty good; but he said that warn't nothing to some things he had said in his time. I heard one man say it was nearly three o'clock, and he hoped daylight wouldn't wait more than about a week longer. After that, the talk got further and further away, and I couldn't make out the words any more, but I could hear the mumble; and now and then a laugh, too, but it seemed a long ways off.

I was away below the ferry now. I rose up and there was Jackson's Island, about two mile and a half down stream, heavy-timbered and standing up out of the middle of the river, big and dark and solid, like a steamboat without any lights. There warn't any signs of the bar at the head—it was all under water, now.

It didn't take me long to get there. I shot past the head at a ripping rate, the current was so swift, and then I got into the dead water and landed on the side towards the Illinois shore. I run the canoe into a deep dent in the bank that I knowed about; I had to part the willow branches to get in; and when I made fast nobody could a seen the canoe from the outside.

I went up and set down on a log at the head of the island and looked out on the big river and the black driftwood, and away over to the town, three mile away, where there was three or four lights twinkling. A monstrous big lumber raft was about a mile up stream, coming along down, with a lantern in the middle of it. I watched it come creeping down, and when it was most abreast of where I stood I heard a man say, "Stern oars, there! heave her head to stabboard!" I heard that just as plain as if the man was by my side.

There was a little gray in the sky, now; so I stepped into the woods and laid down for a nap before breakfast.

Chapter VIII

The sun was up so high when I waked, that I judged it was after eight o'clock. I laid there in the grass and the cool shade, thinking about things and feeling rested and ruther comfortable and satisfied. I could see the sun out at one or two holes, but mostly it was big trees all about, and gloomy in there amongst them. There was freckled places on the ground where the light sifted down through the leaves, and the freckled places swapped about a little, showing there was a little breeze up there. A couple of squirrels set on a limb and jabbered at me very friendly.

I was powerful lazy and comfortable—didn't want to get up and cook breakfast. Well, I was dozing off again, when I thinks I hears a deep sound of "boom!" away up the river. I rouses up and rests on my elbow and listens; pretty soon I hears it again. I hopped up and went and looked out at a hole in the leaves, and I see a bunch of smoke laying on the water a long ways up—about abreast the ferry. And there was the ferry-boat full of people, floating along down. I knowed what was the matter, now, "Boom!" I see the white smoke squirt out of the ferry-boat's side. You see, they was firing cannon over the water, trying to make my carcass come to the top.

I was pretty hungry, but it warn't going to do for me to start a fire, because they might see the smoke. So I set there and watched the cannon-smoke and listened to the boom. The river was a mile wide, there, and it always looks pretty on a summer morning—so I was having a good enough time seeing them hunt for my remainders, if I only had a bite to eat. Well, then I happened to think how they always put quicksilver in loaves of bread and float them off because they always go right to the drownded carcass and stop there. So says I, I'll keep a lookout, and if any of them's floating around after me, I'll give them a show. I changed to the Illinois edge of the island to see what luck I could have, and I warn't disappointed. A big double loaf come along, and I most got it, with a long stick, but my foot slipped and she floated out further. Of course I was where the current set in the closest to the shore—I knowed enough for that. But by-and-by along comes another one, and this time I won. I took out the plug and shook out the little dab of quicksilver, and set my teeth in. It was "baker's bread"—what the quality eat—none of your low-down corn-pone.

I got a good place amongst the leaves, and set there on a log, munching the bread and watching the ferry-boat, and very well satisfied. And then something struck me. I says, now I reckon the widow or the parson or somebody prayed that this bread would find me, and here it has gone and done it. So there ain't no doubt but there is something in that thing. That is, there's something in it when a body like the widow or the parson prays, but it don't work for me, and I reckon it don't work for only just the right kind.

I lit a pipe and had a good long smoke and went on watching. The ferry-boat was floating with the current, and I allowed I'd have a chance to see who was aboard when she come along, because she would come in close, where the bread did. When she'd got pretty well along down towards me, I put out my pipe and went to where I fished out the bread, and laid down behind a log on the bank in a little open place. Where the log forked I could peep through.

By-and-by she come along, and she drifted in so close that they could a run out a plank and walked ashore. Most everybody was on the boat. Pap, and Judge Thatcher, and Bessie Thatcher, and Jo Harper, and Tom Sawyer, and his old Aunt Polly, and Sid and Mary, and plenty more. Everybody was talking about the murder, but the captain broke in and says:

"Look sharp, now; the current sets in the closest here, and maybe he's washed ashore and got tangled amongst the brush at the water's edge. I hope so, anyway."

I didn't hope so. They all crowded up and leaned over the rails, nearly in my face, and kept still, watching with all their might. I could see them first-rate, but they couldn't see me. Then the captain sung out:

"Stand away!" and the cannon let off such a blast right before me that it made me deef with the noise and pretty near blind with the smoke, and I judged I was gone. If they'd a had some bullets in, I reckon they'd a got the corpse they was after. Well, I see I warn't hurt, thanks to goodness. The boat floated on and went out of sight around the shoulder of the island. I could hear the booming, now and then, further and further off, and by-and-by after an hour, I didn't hear it no more. The island was three mile long. I judged they had got to the foot, and was giving it up. But they didn't yet a while. They turned around the foot of the island and started up the channel on the Missouri side, under steam, and booming once in a while as they went. I crossed over to that side and watched them. When they got abreast of the head of the island they quit shooting and dropped over to the Missouri shore and went home to the town.

I knowed I was all right now. Nobody else would come a-hunting after me. I got my traps out of the canoe and made me a nice camp in the thick woods. I made a kind of a tent out of my blankets to put my things under so the rain couldn't get at them. I catched a cat-fish and haggled him open with my saw, and towards sundown I started my camp fire and had supper. Then I set out a line to catch some fish for breakfast.

When it was dark I set by my camp fire smoking, and feeling pretty satisfied; but by-and-by it got sort of lonesome, and so I went and set on the bank and listened to the currents washing along, and counted the stars and drift-logs and rafts that come down, and then went to bed; there ain't no better way to put in time when you are lonesome; you can't stay so, you soon get over it.

And so for three days and nights. No difference—just the same thing. But the next day I went exploring around down through the island. I was boss of it; it all belonged to me, so to say, and I wanted to know all about it; but mainly I wanted to put in the time. I found plenty strawberries, ripe and prime; and green summer-grapes, and green razberries; and the green blackberries was just beginning to show. They would all come handy by-and-by, I judged.

Well, I went fooling along in the deep woods till I judged I warn't far from the foot of the island. I had my gun along, but I hadn't shot nothing; it was for protection; thought I would kill some game nigh home. About this time I mighty near stepped on a good sized snake, and it went sliding off through the grass and flowers, and I after it, trying to get a shot at it. I clipped along, and all of a sudden I bounded right on to the ashes of a camp fire that was still smoking.

My heart jumped up amongst my lungs. I never waited for to look further, but un-cocked my gun and went sneaking back on my tip-toes as fast as ever I could. Every now and then I stopped a second, amongst the thick leaves, and listened; but my breath come so hard I couldn't hear nothing else. I slunk along another piece further, then listened again; and so on, and so on; if I see a stump, I took it for a man; if I trod on a stick and broke it, it made me feel like a person had cut one of my breaths in two and I only got half, and the short half, too.

When I got to camp I warn't feeling very brash, there warn't much sand in my craw; but I says, this ain't no time to be fooling around. So I got all my traps into my canoe again so as to have them out of sight, and I put out the fire and scattered the ashes around to look like an old last year's camp, and then clumb a tree.

I reckon I was up in the tree two hours; but I didn't see nothing, I didn't hear nothing—I only *thought* I heard and seen as much as a thousand things. Well, I couldn't stay up there forever; so at last I got down, but I kept in the thick woods and on the lookout all the time. All I could get to eat was berries and what was left over from breakfast.

By the time it was night I was pretty hungry. So when it was good and dark, I slid out from shore before moonrise and paddled over to the Illinois bank—about a quarter of a mile. I went out in the woods and cooked a supper, and I had about made up my mind I would stay there all night, when I hear a *plunkety-plunk, plunkety-plunk,* and says to myself, horses coming; and next I hear people's voices. I got everything into the canoe as quick as I could, and then went creeping through the woods to see what I could find out. I hadn't got far when I hear a man say:

"We better camp here, if we can find a good place; the horses is about beat out. Let's look around."

I didn't wait, but shoved out and paddled away easy. I tied up in the old place, and reckoned I would sleep in the canoe.

I didn't sleep much. I couldn't, somehow, for thinking. And every time I waked up I thought somebody had me by the neck. So the sleep didn't do me no good. By-and-by I says to myself, I can't live this way; I'm agoing to find out who it is that's here on the island with me; I'll find it out or bust. Well, I felt better, right off.

So I took my paddle and slid out from shore just a step or two, and then let the canoe drop along down amongst the shadows. The moon was shining, and outside of the shadows it made it most as light as day. I poked along well onto an hour, everything still as rocks and sound asleep. Well by this time I was most down to the foot of the island. A little ripply, cool breeze begun to blow, and that was as good as saying the night was about done. I give her a turn with the paddle and brung her nose to shore; then I got my gun and slipped out and into the edge of the woods. I set down there on a log and looked out through the leaves. I see the moon go off watch and the darkness begin to blanket the river. But in a little while I see a pale streak over the tree-tops, and knowed the day was coming. So I took my gun and slipped off towards where I had run across that camp fire, stopping every minute or two to listen. But I hadn't no luck, somehow; I couldn't seem to find the place. But by-and-by, sure enough, I catched a glimpse of fire, away through the trees. I went for it, cautious and slow. By-and-by I was close enough to have a look, and there laid a man on the ground. It most give me the fan-tods. He had a blanket around his head, and his head was nearly in the fire. I set there behind a clump of bushes, in about six foot of him, and kept my eyes on him steady. It was getting gray daylight, now. Pretty soon he gapped, and stretched himself, and hove off the blanket, and it was Miss Watson's Jim! I bet I was glad to see him. I says:

"Hello, Jim!" and skipped out.

He bounced up and stared at me wild. Then he drops down on his knees, and puts his hands together and says:

"Doan' hurt me—don't! I hain't ever done no harm to a ghos'. I awluz liked dead people, en done all I could for 'em. You go en git in de river agin, whah you b'longs, en doan' do nuffin to Ole Jim, 'at 'uz awluz yo' fren'."

Well, I warn't long making him understand I warn't dead. I was ever so glad to see Jim. I warn't lonesome, now. I told him I warn't afraid of *him* telling the people where I was. I talked long, but he only set there and looked at me; never said nothing. Then I says:

"It's good daylight. Le's get breakfast. Make up your camp fire good."

"What's de use er makin' up de camp fire to cook strawbries en sich truck? But you got a gun, hain't you? Den we kin git sumfn better den strawbries."

"Strawberries and such truck," I says. "Is that what you live on?"

"I couldn' git nuffin else," he says.

"Why, how long you been on the island, Jim?"

"I come heah de night arter you's killed."

"What, all that time?"

"Yes-indeedy."

"And ain't you had nothing but that kind of rubbage to eat?"

"No, sah—nuffn else."

"Well, you must be most starved, ain't you?"

"I reck'n I could eat a hoss. I think I could. How long you ben on de islan'?"

"Since the night I got killed."

"No! W'y, what has you lived on? But you got a gun. Oh, yes, you got a gun. Dat's good. Now you kill sumfn en I'll make up de fire."

So we went over to where the canoe was, and while he built a fire in a grassy open place amongst the trees, I fetched meal and bacon and coffee, and coffee-pot and frying-pan, and sugar and tin cups, and the nigger was set back considerable, because he reckoned it was all done with witchcraft. I catched a good big cat-fish, too, and Jim cleaned him with his knife, and fried him.

When breakfast was ready, we lolled on the grass and eat it smoking hot. Jim laid it in with all his might, for he was most about starved. Then when we had got pretty well stuffed, we laid off and lazied.

By-and-by Jim says:

"But looky here, Huck, who wuz it dat 'uz killed in dat shanty, ef it warn't you?"

Then I told him the whole thing, and he said it was smart. He said Tom Sawyer couldn't get up no better plan than what I had. Then I says:

"How do you come to be here, Jim, and how'd you get here?"

He looked pretty uneasy, and didn't say nothing for a minute. Then he says:

"Maybe I better not tell."

"Why, Jim?"

"Well, dey's reasons. But you wouldn' tell on me ef I 'uz to tell you, would you, Huck?"

"Blamed if I would, Jim."

"Well, I b'lieve you, Huck. I—I *run off*."

"Jim!"

"But mind, you said you wouldn't tell—you know you said you wouldn't tell, Huck."

"Well, I did. I said I wouldn't, and I'll stick to it. Honest *injun* I will. People would call me a low down Ablitionist and despise me for keeping mum—but that don't make no difference. I ain't agoing to tell, and I ain't agoing back there anyways. So now, le's know all about it."

"Well, you see, it 'uz dis way. Ole Missus—dat's Miss Watson—she pecks on me all de time, en treats me pooty rough, but she awluz said she wouldn' sell me down to Orleans. But I noticed dey wuz a nigger trader roun' de place considable, lately, en I begin to git oneasy. Well, one night I creeps to de do', pooty late, en de do' warn't quite shet, en I hear ole missus tell de widder she gwyne to sell me down to Orleans, but she didn' want to, but she could git eight hund'd dollars for me, en it 'uz sich a big stack o' money she couldn' resis'. De widder she try to git her to say she wouldn' do it, but I never waited to hear de res'. I lit out mighty quick, I tell you.

"I tuck out en shin down de hill en 'spec to steal a skift 'long de sho' som'ers 'bove de town, but dey wuz people a-stirrin' yit, so I hid in de ole tumble-down cooper shop on de bank to wait for everybody to go 'way. Well, I wuz dah all night. Dey wuz somebody roun' all de time. 'Long 'bout six in de mawnin', skifts begin to go by, en 'bout eight er nine every skift dat went 'long wuz talkin' 'bout how yo' pap come over to de town en say you's killed. Dese las' skifts wuz full o' ladies en genlmen agoin' over for to see de place. Sometimes dey'd pull up at de sho' en take a res' b'fo' dey started acrost, so by de talk I got to know all 'bout de killin'. I 'uz powerful sorry you's killed, Huck, but I ain't no mo', now.

"I laid dah under de shavins all day. I 'uz hungry, but I warn't afeared; bekase I knowed ole missus en de widder wuz goin' to start to de camp-meetn' right arter breakfas' en be gone all day, en dey knows I goes off wid de cattle 'bout daylight, so dey wouldn' 'spec to see me roun' de place, en so dey wouldn' miss me tell arter dark in de evenin'. De yuther servants wouldn' miss me, kase dey'd shin out en take holiday, soon as de ole folks 'uz out'n de way.

"Well, when it come dark I tuck out up de river road, en went 'bout two mile er more to whah dey warn't no houses. I'd made up my mine 'bout what I's agwyne to do. You see ef I kep' on tryin' to git away afoot, de dogs 'ud track me; ef I stole a skift to cross over, dey'd miss dat skift, you see, en dey'd know 'bout whah I'd lan' on de yuther side en whah to pick up my track. So I says, a raff is what I's arter; it doan' *make* no track.

"I see a light a-comin' roun' de p'int, bymeby, so I wade' in en shove' a log ahead o' me, en swum more'n half-way acrost de river, en got in 'mongst de drift-wood, en kep' my head down low, en kinder swum agin de current tell de raff come along. Den I swum to de stern uv it, en tuck aholt. It clouded up en 'uz pooty dark for a little while. So I clumb up en laid down on de planks. De men 'uz all 'way yonder in de middle, whah de lantern wuz. De river wuz arisin' en day wuz a good current; so I reck'n'd 'at by fo' in de mawnin' I'd be twenty-five mile down de river, en den I'd slip in, jis' b'fo' daylight, en swim asho' en take to de woods on de Illinoi side.

"But I didn' have no luck. When we 'uz mos' down to de head er de islan', a man begin to come aft wid de lantern. I see it warn't no use fer to wait, so I slid overboad, en struck out fer de islan'. Well, I had a notion I could lan' mos' anywhers, but I couldn't—bank too bluff. I 'uz mos' to de foot er de islan' b'fo' I foun' a good place. I went into de woods en jedged I wouldn' fool wid raffs no mo', long as dey move de lantern roun' so. I had my pipe en a plug er dog-leg, en some matches in my cap, en day warn't wet, so I 'uz all right."

"And so you ain't had no meat nor bread to eat all this time? Why didn't you get mud-turkles?"

"How you gwyne to git'm? You can't slip up on um en grab um; en how's a body gwyne to hit um wid a rock? How could a body do it in de night? en I warn't gwyne to show mysef on de bank in de daytime."

"Well, that's so. You've had to keep in de woods all the time, of course. Did you hear 'em shooting the cannon?"

"Oh, yes. I knowed dey was arter you. I see um go by heah; watched um thoo de bushes."

Some young birds come along, flying a yard or two at a time and lighting. Jim said it was a sign it was going to rain. He said it was a sign when young chickens flew that way, and so he reckoned it was the same way when young birds done it. I was going to catch some of them, but Jim wouldn't let me. He said it was death. He said his father laid mighty sick once, and some of them catched a bird, and his old granny said his father would die, and he did.

And Jim said you musn't count the things you are going to cook for dinner, because that would bring bad luck. The same if you shook the table-cloth after sundown. And he said if a man owned a bee-hive, and that man died, the bees must be told about it before sun-up next morning, or else the bees would all weaken down and quit work and die. Jim said bees wouldn't sting idiots; but I didn't believe that, because I had tried them lots of times myself, and they wouldn't sting me.

I had heard about some of these things before, but not all of them. Jim knowed all kinds of signs. He said he knowed most everything. I said it looked to me like all the signs was about bad luck, and so I asked him if there warn't any good-luck signs. He says:

"Mighty few—an' *dey* ain' no use to a body. What you want to know when good luck's a-comin' for? want to keep it off?" And he said: "Ef you's got hairy arms en a hairy breas', it's a sign dat you's agwyne to be rich. Well, dey's some use in a sign like dat, 'kase it's so fur ahead. You see, maybe you's got to be po' a long time fust, en so you might git discourage' en kill yo'sef 'f you did n' know by de sign dat you gwyne to be rich bymeby."

"Have you got hairy arms and a hairy breast, Jim?"

"What's de use to ax dat question? don' you see I has?"

"Well, are you rich?"

"No, but I ben rich wunst, and gwyne to be rich agin. Wunst I had foteen dollars, but I tuck to specalat'n', en got busted out."

"What did you speculate in, Jim?"

"Well, fust I tackled stock."

"What kind of stock?"

"Why, live stock. Cattle, you know. I put ten dollars in a cow. But I ain' gwyne to resk no mo' money in stock. De cow up 'n' died on my han's."

"So you lost the ten dollars."

"No, I didn' lose it all. I on'y los' 'bout nine of it. I sole de hide en taller for a dollar en ten cents."

"You had five dollars and ten cents left. Did you speculate any more?"

"Yes. You know dat one-laigged nigger dat b'longs to old Misto Bradish? well, he sot up a bank, en say anybody dat put in a dollar would git fo' dollars mo' at de en' er de year. Well, all de niggers went in, but dey didn' have much. I wuz de on'y one dat had much. So I stuck out for mo' dan fo' dollars, en I said 'f I didn' git it I'd start a bank my-sef. Well o' course dat nigger want' to keep me out er de business, bekase he say dey warn't business 'nough for two banks, so he say I could put in my five dollars en he pay me thirty-five at de en' er de year.

"So I done it. Den I reck'n'd I'd inves' de thirty-five dollars right off en keep things a-movin'. Dey wuz a nigger name' Bob, dat had ketched a wood-flat, en his marster didn' know it; en I bought it off'n him en told him to take de thirty-five dollars when de en' er de year come; but somebody stole de wood-flat dat night, en nex' day de one-laigged nigger say de bank 's busted. So dey didn' none uv us git no money."

"What did you do with the ten cents, Jim?"

"Well, I 'uz gwyne to spen' it, but I had a dream, en de dream tole me to give it to a nigger name' Balum—Balum's Ass dey call him for short, he's one er dem chuckle-heads, you know. But he's lucky, dey say, en I see I warn't lucky. De dream say let Balum inves' de ten cents en he'd make a raise for me. Well, Balum he tuck de money, en when he wuz in church he hear de preacher say dat whoever give to de po' len' to de Lord, en boun' to git his money back a hund'd times. So Balum he tuck en give de ten cents to de po', en laid low to see what wuz gwyne to come of it."

"Well, what did come of it, Jim?"

"Nuff'n' never come of it. I couldn' manage to k'leck dat money no way; en Balum he couldn'. I ain' gwyne to len' no mo' money 'dout I see de security. Boun' to git yo' money back a hund'd times, de preacher says! Ef I could git de ten *cents* back, I'd call it squah, en be glad er de chanst."

"Well, it's all right, anyway, Jim, long as you're going to be rich again some time or other."

"Yes—en I's rich now, come to look at it. I owns mysef, en I's wuth eight hund'd dollars. I wisht I had de money, I wouldn' want no mo'."

Chapter IX

I wanted to go and look at a place right about the middle of the island, that I'd found when I was exploring; so we started, and soon got to it, because the island was only three miles long and a quarter of a mile wide.

This place was a tolerable long steep hill or ridge, about forty foot high. We had a rough time getting to the top, the sides was so steep and the bushes so thick. We tramped and clumb around all over it, and by-and-by found a good big cavern in the rock, most up to the top on the side towards Illinois. The cavern was as big as two or three rooms bunched together, and Jim could stand up straight in it. It was cool in there. Jim was for putting our traps in there, right away, but I said we didn't want to be climbing up and down there all the time.

Jim said if we had the canoe hid in a good place, and had all the traps in the cavern, we could rush there if anybody was to come to the island, and they would never find us without dogs. And besides, he said them little birds had said it was going to rain, and did I want the things to get wet?

So we went back and got the canoe and paddled up abreast the cavern, and lugged all the traps up there. Then we hunted up a place close by to hide the canoe in, amongst the thick willows. We took some fish off of the lines and set them again, and begun to get ready for dinner.

The door of the cavern was big enough to roll a hogshead in, and on one side of the door the floor stuck out a little bit and was flat and a good place to build a fire on. So we built it there and cooked dinner.

We spread the blankets inside for a carpet, and eat our dinner in there. We put all the other things handy at the back of the cavern. Pretty soon it darkened up and begun to thunder and lighten; so the birds was right about it. Directly it begun to rain, and it rained like all fury, too, and I never see the wind blow so. It was one of these regular summer storms. It would get so dark that it looked all blue-black outside, and lovely; and the rain would thrash along by so thick that the trees off a little ways looked dim and spider-webby; and here would come a blast of wind that would bend the trees down and turn up the pale underside of the leaves; and then a perfect ripper of a gust would follow along and set the branches to tossing their arms as if they was just wild; and next, when it was just about the bluest and blackest—*fst!* it was as bright as glory and you'd have a little glimpse of tree-tops a-plunging about, away off yonder in the storm, hundreds of yards further than you could see before; dark as sin again in a second, and now you'd hear the thunder let go with an awful crash and then go rumbling, grumbling, tumbling down the sky towards the under side of the world, like rolling empty barrels down stairs, where it's long stairs and they bounce a good deal, you know.

"Jim, this is nice," I says. "I wouldn't want to be nowhere else but here. Pass me along another hunk of fish and some hot corn-bread."

"Well, you wouldn't a ben here, 'f it hadn't a ben for Jim. You'd a ben down dah in de woods widout any dinner, en gittn' mos' drownded, too, dat you would, honey. Chickens knows when its gwyne to rain, en so do de birds, chile."

The river went on raising and raising for ten or twelve days, till at last it was over the banks. The water was three or four foot deep on the island in the low places and on the Illinois bottom. On that side it was a good many miles wide; but on the Missouri side it was the same old distance across—a half a mile—because the Missouri shore was just a wall of high bluffs.

Daytimes we paddled all over the island in the canoe. It was mighty cool and shady in the deep woods even if the sun was blazing outside. We went winding in and out amongst the trees; and sometimes the vines hung so thick we had to back away and go some other way. Well, on every old broken-down tree, you could see rabbits, and snakes, and such things; and when the island had been overflowed a day or two, they got so tame, on account of being hungry, that you could paddle right up and put your hand on them if you wanted to; but not the snakes and turtles—they would slide off in the water. The ridge our cavern was in, was full of them. We could a had pets enough if we'd wanted them.

One night we catched a little section of a lumber raft—nice pine planks. It was twelve foot wide and about fifteen or sixteen foot long, and the top stood above water six or seven inches, a solid level floor. We could see saw-logs go by in the daylight, sometimes, but we let them go; we didn't show ourselves in daylight.

Another night, when we was up at the head of the island, just before daylight, here comes a frame house down, on the west side. She was a two-story, and tilted over, considerable. We paddled out and got aboard—clumb in at an up-stairs window. But it was too dark to see yet, so we made the canoe fast and set in her to wait for daylight.

The light begun to come before we got to the foot of the island. Then we looked in at the window. We could make out a bed, and a table, and two old chairs, and lots of things around about on the floor; and there was clothes hanging against the wall. There was something laying on the floor in the far corner that looked like a man. So Jim says:

"Hello, you!"

But it didn't budge. So I hollered again, and then Jim says:

"De man ain't asleep—he's dead. You hold still—I'll go en see."

He went and bent down and looked, and says:

"It's a dead man. Yes, indeedy; naked, too. He's ben shot in de back. I reck'n he's ben dead two er three days. Come in, Huck, but doan' look at his face—it's too gashly."

I didn't look at him at all. Jim throwed some old rags over him, but he needn't done it; I didn't want to see him. There was heaps of old greasy cards scattered around over the floor, and old whisky bottles, and a couple of masks made out of black cloth; and all over the walls was the ignorantest kind of words and pictures, made with charcoal. There was two old dirty calico dresses, and a sun-bonnet, and some women's underclothes, hanging against the wall, and some men's clothing, too. We put the lot into the canoe; it might come good. There was a boy's old speckled straw hat on the floor; I took that too. And there was a bottle that had had milk in it; and it had a rag stopper for a baby to suck. We would a took the bottle, but it was broke. There was a seedy old chest, and an old hair trunk with the hinges broke. They stood open, but there warn't nothing left in them that was any account. The way things was scattered about, we reckoned the people left in a hurry and warn't fixed so as to carry off most of their stuff.

We got an old tin lantern, and a butcher knife without any handle, and a brannew Barlow knife worth two bits in any store, and a lot of tallow candles, and a tin candlestick, and a gourd, and a tin cup, and a ratty old bed-quilt off the bed, and a reticule with needles and pins and beeswax and buttons and thread and all such truck in it, and a hatchet and some nails, and a fish-line as thick as my little finger, with some monstrous hooks on it, and a roll of buckskin, and a leather dog-collar, and a horse-shoe, and some vials of medicine that didn't have no label on them; and just as we was leaving I found a tolerable good curry-comb, and Jim he found a ratty old fiddle-bow, and a wooden leg. The straps was broke off of it, but barring that, it was a good enough leg, though it was too long for me and not long enough for Jim, and we couldn't find the other one, though we hunted all around.

And so, take it all around, we made a good haul. When we was ready to shove off, we was a quarter of a mile below the island, and it was pretty broad day; so I made Jim lay down in the canoe and cover up with the quilt, because if he set up, people could tell he was a nigger a good ways off. I paddled over to the Illinois shore, and drifted down most a half a mile doing it. I crept up the dead water under the bank, and hadn't no accidents and didn't see nobody. We got home all safe.

Chapter X

After breakfast I wanted to talk about the dead man and guess out how he come to be killed, but Jim didn't want to. He said it would fetch bad luck; and besides, he said, he might come and ha'nt us; he said a man that warn't buried was more likely to go a-ha'nting around than one that was planted and comfortable. That sounded pretty reasonable, so I didn't say no more; but I couldn't keep from studying over it and wishing I knowed who shot the man, and what they done it for.

We rummaged the clothes we'd got, and found eight dollars in silver sewed up in the lining of an old blanket overcoat. Jim said he reckoned the people in that house stole the coat, because if they'd a knowed the money was there they wouldn't a left it. I said I reckoned they killed him, too; but Jim didn't want to talk about that. I says:

"Now you think it's bad luck; but what did you say when I fetched in the snake-skin that I found on the top of the ridge day before yesterday? You said it was the worst bad luck in the world to touch a snake-skin with my hands. Well, here's your bad luck! We've raked in all this truck and eight dollars besides. I wish we could have some bad luck like this every day, Jim."

"Never you mind, honey, never you mind. Don't you git too peart. It's a-comin'. Mind I tell you, it's a-comin'."

It did come, too. It was a Tuesday that we had that talk. Well, after dinner Friday, we was laying around in the grass at the upper end of the ridge, and got out of tobacco. I went to the cavern to get some, and found a rattlesnake in there. I killed him, and curled him up on the foot of Jim's blanket, ever so natural, thinking there'd be some fun when Jim found him there. Well, by night I forgot all about the snake, and when Jim flung himself down on the blanket while I struck a light, the snake's mate was there, and bit him.

He jumped up yelling, and the first thing the light showed was the varmint curled up and ready for another spring. I laid him out in a second with a stick, and Jim grabbed pap's whisky jug and begun to pour it down.

He was barefooted, and the snake bit him right on the heel. That all comes of my being such a fool as to not remember that wherever you leave a dead snake its mate always comes there and curls around it. Jim told me to chop off the snake's head and throw it away, and then skin the body and roast a piece of it. I done it, and he eat it and said it would help cure him. He made me take off the rattles and tie them around his wrist, too. He said that that would help. Then I slid out quiet and throwed the snakes clear away amongst the bushes; for I warn't going to let Jim find out it was all my fault, not if I could help it.

Jim sucked and sucked at the jug, and now and then he got out of his head and pitched around and yelled; but every time he come to himself he went to sucking at the jug again. His foot swelled up pretty big, and so did his leg; but by-and-by the drunk begun to come, and so I judged he was all right; but I'd druther been bit with a snake than pap's whisky.

Jim was laid up for four days and nights. Then the swelling was all gone and he was around again. I made up my mind I wouldn't ever take aholt of a snake-skin again with my hands, now that I see what had come of it. Jim said he reckoned I would believe him next time. And he said that handling a snake-skin was such awful bad luck that maybe we hadn't got to the end of it yet. He said he druther see the new moon over his left shoulder as much as a thousand times than take up a snake-skin in his hand. Well, I was getting to feel that way myself, though I've always reckoned that looking at the new moon over your left shoulder is one of the carelessest and foolishest things a body can do. Old Hank Bunker done it once, and bragged about it; and in less than two years he got drunk and fell off of the shot tower and spread himself out so that he was just a kind of a layer, as you may say; and they slid him edgeways between two barn doors for a coffin, and buried him so, so they say, but I didn't see it. Pap told me. But anyway, it all come of looking at the moon that way, like a fool.

Well, the days went along, and the river went down between its banks again; and about the first thing we done was to bait one of the big hooks with a skinned rabbit and set it and catch a cat-fish that was as big as a man, being six foot two inches long, and weighed over two hundred pounds. We couldn't handle him, of course; he would a flung us into Illinois. We just set there and watched him rip and tear around till he drownded. We found a brass button in his stomach, and a round ball, and lots of rubbage. We split the ball open with the hatchet, and there was a spool in it. Jim said he'd had it there a long time, to coat it over so and make a ball of it. It was as big a fish as was ever catched in the Mississippi, I reckon. Jim said he hadn't ever seen a bigger one. He would a been worth a good deal over at the village. They peddle out such a fish as that by the pound in the market house there; everybody buys some of him; his meat's as white as snow and makes a good fry.

Next morning I said it was getting slow and dull, and I wanted to get a stirring up, some way. I said I reckoned I would slip over the river and find out what was going on. Jim liked that notion; but he said I must go in the dark and look sharp. Then he studied it over and said, couldn't I put on some of them old things and dress up like a girl? That was a good notion, too. So we shortened up one of the calico gowns and I turned up my trowser-legs to my knees and got into it. Jim hitched it behind with the hooks, and it was a fair fit. I put on the sun-bonnet and tied it under my chin, and then for a body to look in and see my face was like looking down a joint of stove-pipe. Jim said nobody would know me, even in the daytime, hardly. I practiced around all day to get the hang of the things, and by-and-by I could do pretty well in them, only Jim said I didn't walk like a girl; and he said I must quit pulling up my gown to get at my britches pocket. I took notice, and done better.

I started up the Illinois shore in the canoe just after dark.

I started across to the town from a little below the ferry landing, and the drift of the current fetched me in at the bottom of the town. I tied up and started along the bank. There was a light burning in a little shanty that hadn't been lived in for a long time, and I wondered who had took up quarters there. I slipped up and peeped in at the window. There was a woman about forty year old in there, knitting by a candle that was on a pine table. I didn't know her face; she was a stranger, for you couldn't start a face in that town that I didn't know. Now this was lucky, because I was weakening; I was getting afraid I had come; people might know my voice and find me out. But if this woman had been in such a little town two days she could tell me all I wanted to know; so I knocked at the door, and made up my mind I wouldn't forget I was a girl.

Chapter XI

"Come in," says the woman, and I did. She says:

"Take a cheer."

I done it. She looked me all over with her little shiny eyes, and says:

"What might your name be?"

"Sarah Williams."

"Where 'bouts do you live? In this neighborhood?"

"No'm. In Hookerville, seven mile below. I've walked all the way and I'm all tired out."

"Hungry, too, I reckon. I'll find you something."

"No'm, I ain't hungry. I was so hungry I had to stop two mile below here at a farm; so I ain't hungry no more. It's what makes me so late. My mother's down sick, and out of money and everything, and I come to tell my uncle Abner Moore. He lives at the upper end of the town, she says. I hain't ever been here before. Do you know him?"

"No; but I don't know everybody yet. I haven't lived here quite two weeks. It's a considerable ways to the upper end of the town. You better stay here all night. Take off your bonnet."

"No," I says, "I'll rest a while, I reckon, and go on. I ain't afeard of the dark."

She said she wouldn't let me go by myself, but her husband would be in by-and-by, maybe in a hour and a half, and she'd send him along with me. Then she got to talking about her husband, and about her relations up the river, and her relations down the river, and about how much better off they used to was, and how they didn't know but they'd made a mistake coming to our town, instead of letting well alone—and so on and so on, till I was afeard *I* had made a mistake coming to her to find out what was going on in the town; but by-and-by she dropped onto pap and the murder, and then I was pretty willing to let her clatter right along. She told about me and Tom Sawyer finding the six thousand dollars (only she got it ten) and all about pap and what a hard lot he was, and what a hard lot I was, and at last she got down to where I was murdered. I says:

"Who done it? We've heard considerable about these goings on, down in Hookerville, but we don't know who 'twas that killed Huck Finn."

"Well, I reckon there's a right smart chance of people *here* that'd like to know who killed him. Some thinks old Finn done it himself."

"No—is that so?"

"Most everybody thought it at first. He'll never know how nigh he come to getting lynched. But before night they changed around and judged it was done by a runaway nigger named Jim."

"Why *he*—"

I stopped. I reckoned I better keep still. She run on, and never noticed I had put in at all.

"The nigger run off the very night Huck Finn was killed. So there's a reward out for him—three hundred dollars. And there's a reward out for old Finn too—two hundred dollars. You see, he come to town the morning after the murder, and told about it, and was out with 'em on the ferry-boat hunt, and right away after he up and left. Before night they wanted to lynch him, but he was gone, you see. Well, next day they found out the nigger was gone; they found out he hadn't ben seen sence ten o'clock the night the murder was done. So then they put it on him, you see, and while they was full of it, next day back comes old Finn and went boo-hooing to Judge Thatcher to get money to hunt for the nigger all over Illinois with. The judge give him some, and that evening he got drunk and was around till after midnight with a couple of mighty hard looking strangers, and then went off with them. Well, he hain't come back sence, and they ain't looking for him back till this thing blows over a little, for people thinks now that he killed his boy and fixed things so folks would think robbers done it, and then he'd get Huck's money without having to bother a long time with a lawsuit. People do say he warn't any too good to do it. Oh, he's sly, I reckon. If he don't come back for a year, he'll be all right. You can't prove anything on him, you know; everything will be quieted down then, and he'll walk into Huck's money as easy as nothing."

"Yes, I reckon so, 'm. I don't see nothing in the way of it. Has everybody quit thinking the nigger done it?"

"Oh, no, not everybody. A good many thinks he done it. But they'll get the nigger pretty soon, now, and maybe they can scare it out of him."

"Why, are they after him yet?"

"Well, you're innocent, ain't you? Does three hundred dollars lay around every day for people to pick up? Some folks thinks the nigger ain't far from here. I'm one of them—but I hain't talked it around. A few days ago I was talking with an old couple that lives next door in the log shanty, and they happened to say hardly anybody ever goes to that island over yonder that they call Jackson's Island. Don't anybody live there? says I. No, nobody, says they. I didn't say any more, but I done some thinking. I was pretty near certain I'd seen smoke over there, about the head of the island, a day or two before that, so I says to myself, like as not that nigger's hiding over there; anyway, says I, it's worth the trouble to give the place a hunt. I hain't seen any smoke sence, so I reckon maybe he's gone, if it was him; but husband's going over to see—him and another man. He was gone up the river; but he got back to-day and I told him as soon as he got here two hours ago."

I had got so uneasy I couldn't set still. I had to do something with my hands; so I took up a needle off of the table and went to threading it. My hands shook, and I was making a bad job of it. When the woman stopped talking, I looked up, and she was looking at me pretty curious, and smiling a little. I put down the needle and thread and let on to be interested—and I was, too—and says:

"Three hundred dollars is a power of money. I wish my mother could get it. Is your husband going over there to-night?"

"Oh, yes. He went up town with the man I was telling you of, to get a boat and see if they could borrow another gun. They'll go over after midnight."

"Couldn't they see better if they was to wait till daytime?"

"Yes. And couldn't the nigger see better, too? After midnight he'll likely be asleep, and they can slip around through the woods and hunt up his camp fire all the better for the dark, if he's got one."

"I didn't think of that."

The woman kept looking at me pretty curious, and I didn't feel a bit comfortable. Pretty soon she says:

"What did you say your name was, honey?"

"M—Mary Williams."

Somehow it didn't seem to me that I said it was Mary before, so I didn't look up; seemed to me I said it was Sarah; so I felt sort of cornered, and was afeared maybe I was looking it, too. I wished the woman would say something more; the longer she set still, the uneasier I was. But now she says:

"Honey, I thought you said it was Sarah when you first come in?"

"Oh, yes'm, I did. Sarah Mary Williams. Sarah's my first name. Some calls me Sarah, some calls me Mary."

"Oh, that's the way of it?"

"Yes'm."

I was feeling better, then, but I wished I was out of there, anyway. I couldn't look up yet.

Well, the woman fell to talking about how hard times was, and how poor they had to live, and how the rats was as free as if they owned the place, and so forth, and so on, and then I got easy again. She was right about the rats. You'd see one stick his nose out of a hole in the corner every little while. She said she had to have things handy to throw at them when she was alone, or they wouldn't give her no peace. She showed me a bar of lead, twisted up into a knot, and said she was a good shot with it generly, but she'd wrenched her arm a day or two ago, and didn't know whether she could throw true, now. But she watched for a chance, and directly she banged away at a rat, but she missed him wide, and said "Ouch!" it hurt her arm so. Then she told me to try for the next one. I wanted to be getting away before the old man got back, but of course I didn't let on. I got the thing, and the first rat that showed his nose I let drive, and if he'd a stayed where he was he'd a been a tolerable sick rat. She said that that was first-rate, and she reckoned I would hive the next one. She went and got the lump of lead and fetched it back and brought along a hank of yarn, which she wanted me to help her with. I held up my two hands and she put the hank over them and went on talking about her and her husband's matters. But she broke off to say:

"Keep your eye on the rats. You better have the lead in your lap, handy."

So she dropped the lump into my lap, just at that moment, and I clapped my legs together on it and she went on talking. But only about a minute. Then she took off the hank and looked me straight in the face, but very pleasant, and says:

"Come, now—what's your real name?"

"Wh-what, mum?"

"What's your real name? Is it Bill, or Tom, or Bob?—or what is it?"

I reckon I shook like a leaf, but I didn't know hardly what to do. But I says:

"Please to don't poke fun at a poor girl like me, mum. If I'm in the way, here, I'll—"

"No, you won't. Set down and stay where you are. I ain't going to hurt you, and I ain't going to tell on you, nuther. You just tell me your secret, and trust me. I'll keep it; and what's more, I'll help you. So'll my old man, if you want him to. You see, you're a runaway 'prentice—that's all. It ain't anything. There ain't any harm in it. You've been treated bad, and you made up your mind to cut. Bless you, child, I wouldn't tell on you. Tell me all about it, now—that's a good boy."

So I said it wouldn't be no use to try to play it any longer, and I would just make a clean breast and tell her everything, but she mustn't go back on her promise. Then I told her my father and mother was dead, and the law had bound me out to a mean old farmer in the country thirty mile back from the river, and he treated me so bad I couldn't stand it no longer; he went away to be gone a couple of days, and so I took my chance and stole some of his daughter's old clothes, and cleared out, and I had been three nights coming the thirty miles; I traveled nights, and hid day-times and slept, and the bag of bread and meat I carried from home lasted me all the way and I had a plenty. I said I believed my uncle Abner Moore would take care of me, and so that was why I struck out for this town of Goshen."

"Goshen, child? This ain't Goshen. This is St. Petersburg. Goshen's ten mile further up the river. Who told you this was Goshen?"

"Why, a man I met at day-break this morning, just as I was going to turn into the woods for my regular sleep. He told me when the roads forked I must take the right hand, and five mile would fetch me to Goshen."

"He was drunk I reckon. He told you just exactly wrong."

"Well, he did act like he was drunk, but it ain't no matter now. I got to be moving along. I'll fetch Goshen before day-light."

"Hold on a minute. I'll put you up a snack to eat. You might want it."

So she put me up a snack, and says:

"Say—when a cow's laying down, which end of her gets up first? Answer us prompt, now—don't stop to study over it. Which end gets up first?"

"The hind end, mum."

"Well, then, a horse?"

"The for'rard end, mum."

"Which side of a tree does the most moss grow on?"

"North side."

"If fifteen cows is browsing on a hillside, how many of them eats with their heads pointed the same direction?"

"The whole fifteen, mum."

"Well, I reckon you *have* lived in the country. I thought maybe you was trying to hocus me again. What's your real name, now?"

"George Peters, mum."

"Well, try to remember it, George. Don't forget and tell me it's Elexander before you go, and then get out by saying it's George Elexander when I catch you. And don't go about women in that old calico. You do a girl tolerable poor, but you might fool men, maybe. Bless you, child, when you set out to thread a needle, don't hold the thread still and fetch the needle up to it; hold the needle still and poke the thread at it—that's the way a woman most always does; but a man always does 'tother way. And when you throw at a rat or anything, hitch yourself up a tip-toe, and fetch your hand up over your head as awkard as you can, and miss your rat about six or seven foot. Throw stiff-armed from the shoulder, like there was a pivot there for it to turn on—like a girl; not from the wrist and elbow, with your arm out to one side, like a boy. And mind you, when a girl tries to catch anything in her lap, she throws her knees apart; she don't clap them together, the way you did when you catched the lump of lead. Why, I spotted you for a boy when you was threading the needle; and I contrived the other things just to make certain. Now trot along to your uncle, Sarah Mary Williams George Elexander Peters, and if you get into trouble you send word to Mrs. Judith Loftus, which is me, and I'll do what I can to get you out of it. Keep the river road, all the way, and next time you tramp, take shoes and socks with you. The river road's a rocky one, and your feet 'll be in a condition when you get to Goshen, I reckon."

I went up the bank about fifty yards, and then I doubled on my tracks and slipped back to where my canoe was, a good piece below the house. I jumped in and was off in a hurry. I went up stream far enough to make the head of the island, and then started across. I took off the sun-bonnet, for I didn't want no blinders on, then. When I was about the middle, I hear the clock begin to strike; so I stops and listens; the sound come faint over the water, but clear—eleven. When I struck the head of the island I never waited to blow, though I was most winded, but I shoved right into the timber where my old camp used to be, and started a good fire there on a high-and-dry spot.

Then I jumped in the canoe and dug out for a place a mile and a half below, as hard as I could go. I landed, and slopped through the timber and up the ridge and into the cavern. There Jim laid, sound asleep on the ground. I roused him out and says:

"Git up and hump yourself, Jim! There ain't a minute to lose. They're after us!"

Jim never asked no questions, he never said a word; but the way he worked for the next half an hour showed about how he was scared. By that time everything we had in the world was on our raft and she was ready to be shoved out from the willow cove where she was hid. We put out the camp fire at the cavern the first thing, and didn't show a candle outside after that.

I took the canoe out from shore a little piece and took a look, but if there was a boat around I couldn't see it, for stars and shadows ain't good to see by. Then we got out the raft and slipped along down in the shade, past the foot of the island dead still, never saying a word.

Chapter XII

It must a been close onto one o'clock when we got below the island at last, and the raft did seem to go mighty slow. If a boat was to come along, we was going to take to the canoe and break for the Illinois shore; and it was well a boat didn't come, for we hadn't ever thought to put the gun into the canoe, or a fishing-line or anything to eat. We was in ruther too much of a sweat to think of so many things. It warn't good judgment to put *everything* on the raft.

If the men went to the island, I just expect they found the camp fire I built, and watched it all night for Jim to come. Anyways, they stayed away from us, and if my building the fire never fooled them it warn't no fault of mine. I played it as low-down on them as I could.

When the first streak of day begun to show, we tied up to a tow-head in a big bend on the Illinois side, and hacked off cotton-wood branches with the hatchet and covered

E. W. Kemble
On the raft
1885

ON THE RAFT.

up the raft with them so she looked like there had been a cave-in in the bank there. A tow-head is a sand-bar that has cotton-woods on it as thick as harrow-teeth.

We had mountains on the Missouri shore and heavy timber on the Illinois side, and the channel was down the Missouri shore at that place, so we warn't afraid of anybody running across us. We laid there all day and watched the rafts and steamboats spin down the Missouri shore, and up-bound steamboats fight the big river in the middle. I told Jim all about the time I had jabbering with that woman; and Jim said she was a smart one, and if she was to start after us herself *she* wouldn't set down and watch a camp fire—no, sir, she'd fetch a dog. Well, then, I said, why couldn't she tell her husband to fetch a dog? Jim said he bet she did think of it by the time the men was ready to start, and he believed they must a gone up town to get a dog and so they lost all that time, or else we wouldn't be here on a tow-head sixteen or seventeen mile below the village—no, indeedy, we would be in that same old town again. So I said I didn't care what was the reason they didn't get us, as long as they didn't.

When it was beginning to come on dark, we poked our heads out of the cottonwood thicket and looked up, and down, and across; nothing in sight; so Jim took up some of the top planks of the raft and built a snug wigwam to get under in blazing weather and rainy, and to keep the things dry. Jim made a floor for the wigwam, and raised it a foot or more above the level of the raft, so now the blankets and all the traps was out of the reach of steamboat waves. Right in the middle of the wigwam we made a layer of dirt about five or six inches deep with a frame around it for to hold it to its place; this was to build a fire on in sloppy weather or chilly; the wigwam would keep it from being seen. We made an extra steering oar, too, because one of the others might get broke, on a snag or something. We fixed up a short forked stick to hang the old lantern on; because we must always light the lantern whenever we see a steamboat coming down stream, to keep from getting run over; but we wouldn't have to light it for upstream boats unless we see we was in what they call a "crossing;" for the river was pretty high yet, very low banks being still a little under water; so up-bound boats didn't always run the channel, but hunted easy water.

This second night we run between seven and eight hours, with a current that was making over four mile an hour. We catched fish, and talked, and we took a swim now and then to keep off sleepiness. It was kind of solemn, drifting down the big still river, laying on our backs looking up at the stars, and we didn't ever feel like talking loud, and it warn't often that we laughed, only a little kind of a low chuckle. We had mighty good weather, as a general thing, and nothing ever happened to us at all, that night, nor the next, nor the next.

Every night we passed towns, some of them away up on black hillsides, nothing but just a shiny bed of lights, not a house could you see. The fifth night we passed St. Louis, and it was like the whole world lit up. In St. Petersburg they used to say there was twenty or thirty thousand people in St. Louis, but I never believed it till I see that wonderful spread of lights at two o'clock that still night. There warn't a sound there; everybody was asleep.

Every night, now, I used to slip ashore, towards ten o'clock, at some little village, and buy ten or fifteen cents' worth of meal or bacon or other stuff to eat; and sometimes I lifted a chicken that warn't roosting comfortable, and took him along. Pap always said, take a chicken when you get a chance, because if you don't want him yourself you can easy find somebody that does, and a good deed ain't ever forgot. I never see pap when he didn't want the chicken himself, but that is what he used to say, anyway.

Mornings, before daylight, I slipped into corn fields and borrowed a watermelon, or a mushmelon, or a punkin, or some new corn, or things of that kind. Pap always said it warn't no harm to borrow things, if you was meaning to pay them back, sometime; but the widow said it warn't anything but a soft name for stealing, and no decent body would do it. Jim said he reckoned the widow was partly right and pap was partly right; so the best way would be for us to pick out two or three things from the list and say we wouldn't borrow them any more—then he reckoned it wouldn't be no harm to borrow the others. So we talked it over all one night, drifting along down the river, trying to make up our minds whether to drop the watermelons, or the cantelopes, or the mushmelons, or what. But towards daylight we got it all settled satisfactory, and concluded to drop crabapples and p'simmons. We warn't feeling just right, before that, but it was all comfortable now. I was glad the way it come out, too, because crabapples ain't ever good, and the p'simmons wouldn't be ripe for two or three months yet.

We shot a water-fowl, now and then, that got up too early in the morning or didn't go to bed early enough in the evening. Take it all around, we lived pretty high.

The fifth night below St. Louis we had a big storm after midnight, with a power of thunder and lightning, and the rain poured down in a solid sheet. We stayed in the wigwam and let the raft take care of itself. When the lightning glared out we could see a big straight river ahead, and high rocky bluffs on both sides. By-and-by says I, "Hel-*lo*, Jim, looky yonder!" It was a steamboat that had killed herself on a rock. We was drifting straight down for her. The lightning showed her very distinct. She was leaning over, with part of her upper deck above water, and you could see every little chimbly-guy clean and clear, and a chair by the big bell, with an old slouch hat hanging on the back of it when the flashes come.

Well, it being away in the night, and stormy, and all so mysterious-like, I felt just the way any other boy would a felt when I see that wreck laying there so mournful and lonesome in the middle of the river. I wanted to get aboard of her and slink around a little, and see what there was there. So I says:

"Le's land on her, Jim."

But Jim was dead against it, at first. He says:

"I doan' want to go fool'n 'long er no wrack. We's doin' blame' well, en we better let blame' well alone, as de good book says. Like as not dey's a watchman on dat wrack."

"Watchman your grandmother," I says; "there ain't nothing to watch but the texas and the pilot-house; and do you reckon anybody's going to resk his life for a texas and a pilot-house such a night as this, when it's likely to break up and wash off down the river any minute?" Jim couldn't say nothing to that, so he didn't try. "And besides," I says, "we might borrow something worth having, out of the captain's stateroom. Seegars, *I* bet you—and cost five cents apiece, solid cash. Steamboat captains is always rich, and get sixty dollars a month, and *they* don't care a cent what a thing costs, you know, long as they want it. Stick a candle in your pocket; I can't rest, Jim, till we give her a rummaging. Do you reckon Tom Sawyer would ever go by this thing? Not for pie, he wouldn't. He'd call it an adventure—that's what he'd call it; and he'd land on that wreck if it was his last act. And wouldn't he throw style into it?—wouldn't he spread himself, nor nothing? Why, you'd think it was Christopher C'lumbus discovering Kingdom-Come. I wish Tom Sawyer *was* here."

Jim he grumbled a little, but give in. He said we mustn't talk any more than we could help, and then talk mighty low. The lightning showed us the wreck again, just in time, and we fetched the starboard derrick, and made fast there.

The deck was high out, here. We went sneaking down the slope of it to labboard, in the dark, towards the texas, feeling our way slow with our feet, and spreading our hands out to fend off the guys, for it was so dark we couldn't see no sign of them. Pretty soon we struck the forward end of the skylight, and clumb onto it; and the next step fetched us in front of the captain's door, which was open, and by Jimminy, away down through the texas-hall we see a light! and all in the same second we seem to hear low voices in yonder!

Jim whispered and said he was feeling powerful sick, and told me to come along. I says, all right; and was going to start for the raft; but just then I heard a voice wail out and say:

"Oh, please don't, boys; I swear I won't ever tell!"

Another voice said, pretty loud:

"It's a lie, Jim Turner. You've acted this way before. You always want more'n your share of the truck, and you've always got it, too, because you've swore 't if you didn't you'd tell. But this time you've said it jest one time too many. You're the meanest, treacherousest hound in this country."

By this time Jim was gone for the raft. I was just a-biling with curiosity; and I says to myself, Tom Sawyer wouldn't back out now, and so I won't either; I'm agoing to see what's going on here. So I dropped on my hands and knees, in the little passage, and crept aft in the dark, till there warn't but about one stateroom betwixt me and the cross-hall of the texas. Then, in there I see a man stretched on the floor and tied hand

and foot, and two men standing over him, and one of them had a dim lantern in his hand, and the other one had a pistol. This one kept pointing the pistol at the man's head on the floor and saying—

"I'd *like* to! And I orter, too, a mean skunk!"

The man on the floor would shrivel up, and say: "Oh, please don't Bill—I hain't ever goin' to tell."

And every time he said that, the man with the lantern would laugh, and say:

"'Deed you *ain't*! You never said no truer thing 'n that, you bet you."

And once he said: "Hear him beg! and yit if we hadn't got the best of him and tied him, he'd a killed us both. And what *for*? Jist for noth'n. Jist because we stood on our *rights*—that's what for. But I lay you ain't agoin' to threaten nobody any more, Jim Turner. Put *up* that pistol, Bill."

Bill says:

"I don't want to, Jake Packard. I'm for killin' him—and didn't he kill old Hatfield jist the same way—and don't he deserve it?"

"But I don't *want* him killed, and I've got my reasons for it."

"Bless yo' heart for them words, Jake Packard! I'll never forget you, long's I live!" says the man on the floor, sort of blubbering.

Packard didn't take no notice of that, but hung up his lantern on a nail, and started towards where I was, there in the dark, and motioned Bill to come. I crawfished as fast as I could, about two yards, but the boat slanted so that I couldn't make very good time; so to keep from getting run over and catched I crawled into a stateroom on the upper side. The man come a-pawing along in the dark, and when Packard got to my stateroom, he says:

"Here—come in here."

And in he come, and Bill after him. But before they got in, I was up in the upper berth, cornered, and sorry I come. Then they stood there, with their hands on the ledge of the berth, and talked. I couldn't see them, but I could tell where they was, by the whisky they'd been having. I was glad I didn't drink whisky; but it wouldn't made much difference, anyway, because most of the time they couldn't a treed me because I didn't breathe. I was too scared. And besides, a body *couldn't* breathe, and hear such talk. They talked low and earnest. Bill wanted to kill Turner. He says:

"He's said he'll tell, and he will. If we was to give both our shares to him *now*, it wouldn't make no difference after the row, and the way we've served him. Shore's you're born, he'll turn State's evidence; now you hear *me*. I'm for putting him out of his troubles."

"So'm I," says Packard, very quiet.

"Blame it, I'd sorter begun to think you wasn't. Well, then, that's all right. Les' go and do it."

"Hold on a minute; I hain't had my say yit. You listen to me. Shooting's good, but there's quieter ways if the thing's *got* to be done. But what *I* say, is this; it ain't good sense to go court'n around after a halter, if you can git at what you're up to in some way that's jist as good and at the same time don't bring you into no resks. Ain't that so?"

"You bet it is. But how you goin' to manage it this time?"

"Well, my idea is this: we'll rustle around and gether up whatever pickins we've overlooked in the staterooms, and shove for shore and hide the truck. Then we'll wait.

Now I say it ain't agoin' to be more'n two hours befo' this wrack breaks up and washes off down the river. See? He'll be drownded, and won't have nobody to blame for it but his own self. I reckon that's a considerble sight better'n killin' of him. I'm unfavorable to killin' a man as long as you can git around it; it ain't good sense, it ain't good morals. Ain't I right?"

"Yes—I reck'n you are. But s'pose she *don't* break up and wash off?"

"Well, we can wait the two hours, anyway, and see, can't we?"

"All right, then; come along."

So they started, and I lit out, all in a cold sweat, and scrambled forward. It was dark as pitch there; but I said in a kind of a coarse whisper, "Jim!" and he answered up, right at my elbow, with a sort of a moan, and I says:

"Quick, Jim, it ain't no time for fooling around and moaning; there's a gang of murderers in yonder, and if we don't hunt up their boat and set her drifting down the river so these fellows can't get away from the wreck, there's one of 'em going to be in a bad fix. But if we find their boat we can put *all* of 'em in a bad fix—for the Sheriff'll get 'em. Quick—hurry! I'll hunt the labboard side, you hunt the stabboard. You start at the raft, and—"

"Oh, my lordy, lordy! *Raf'*? Dey ain' no raf' no mo', she done broke loose en gone!—'en here we is!"

Chapter XIII

Well, I catched my breath and most fainted. Shut up on a wreck with such a gang as that! But it warn't no time to be sentimentering. We'd *got* to find that boat, now—had to have it for ourselves. So we went a-quaking and shaking down the stabboard side, and slow work it was, too—seemed a week before we got to the stern. No sign of a boat. Jim said he didn't believe he could go any further—so scared he hadn't hardly any strength left, he said. But I said come on, if we get left on this wreck, we are in a fix, sure. So on we prowled, again. We struck for the stern of the texas, and found it, and then scrabbled along forwards on the skylight, hanging in from shutter to shutter, for the edge of the skylight was in the water. When we got pretty close to the cross-hall door, there was the skiff, sure enough! I could just barely see her. I felt ever so thankful. In another second I would a been aboard of her; but just then the door opened. One of the men stuck his head out, only about a couple of foot from me, and I thought I was gone; but he jerked it in again, and says:

"Heave that blame lantern out o' sight, Bill!"

He flung a bag of something into the boat, and then got in himself, and set down. It was Packard. Then Bill *he* come out and got in. Packard says, in a low voice:

"All ready—shove off!"

I couldn't hardly hang onto the shutters, I was so weak. But Bill says:

"Hold on—'d you go through him?"

"No. Didn't you?"

"No. So he's got his share o' the cash, yet."

"Well, then, come along—no use to take truck and leave money."

"Say—won't he suspicion what we're up to?"

"Maybe he won't. But we got to have it anyway. Come along."

So they got out and went in.

The door slammed to, because it was on the careened side; and in a half second I was in the boat, and Jim come a tumbling after me. I out with my knife and cut the rope, and away we went!

We didn't touch an oar, and we didn' speak nor whisper, nor hardly even breathe. We went gliding swift along, dead silent, past the tip of the paddle-box, and past the stern; then in a second or two more we was a hundred yards below the wreck, and the darkness soaked her up, every last sign of her, and we was safe, and knowed it.

When we was three or four hundred yards down stream, we see the lantern show like a little spark at the texas door, for a second, and we knowed by that that the rascals had missed their boat, and was beginning to understand that they was in just as much trouble, now, as Jim Turner was.

Then Jim manned the oars, and we took out after our raft. Now was the first time that I begun to worry about the men—I reckon I hadn't had time to before. I begun to think how dreadful it was, even for murderers, to be in such a fix. I says to myself, there ain't no telling but I might come to be a murderer myself, yet, and then how would *I* like it? So says I to Jim:

"The first light we see, we'll land a hundred yards below it or above it, in a place where it's a good hiding-place for you and the skiff, and then I'll go and fix up some kind of a yarn, and get somebody to go for that gang and get them out of their scrape, so they can be hung when their time comes."

But that idea was a failure; for pretty soon it begun to storm again, and this time worse than ever. The rain poured down, and never a light showed; everybody in bed, I reckon. We boomed along down the river, watching for lights and watching for our raft. After a long time the rain let up, but the clouds staid, and the lightning kept whimpering, and by-and-by a flash showed us a black thing ahead, floating, and we made for it.

It was the raft, and mighty glad was we to get aboard of it again. We seen a light, now, away down to the right, on shore. So I said I would go for it. The skiff was half full of plunder which that gang had stole, there on the wreck. We hustled it onto the raft in a pile, and I told Jim to float along down, and show a light when he judged he had gone about two mile, and keep it burning till I come; then I manned my oars and shoved for the light. As I got down towards it, three or four more showed—up on a hillside. It was a village. I closed in above the shore-light and laid on my oars and floated. As I went by, I see it was a lantern hanging on the jackstaff of a double-hull ferry-boat. I skimmed around for the watchman, a-wondering whereabouts he slept; and by-and-by I found him roosting on the bitts, forward, with his head down between his knees. I give his shoulder two or three little shoves, and begun to cry.

He stirred up, in a kind of a startlish way; but when he see it was only me, he took a good gap and stretch, and then he says:

"Hello, what's up? Don't cry, bub. What's the trouble?"

I says:

"Pap, and mam, and sis, and—"

Then I broke down. He says:

"Oh, dang it, now, *don't* take on so, we all has to have our troubles and this'n 'll come out all right. What's the matter with 'em?"

"They're—they're—are you the watchman of the boat?"

"Yes," he says, kind of pretty-well-satisfied like. "I'm the captain and the owner, and the mate, and the pilot, and watchman, and head deck-hand; and sometimes I'm the freight and passengers. I ain't as rich as old Jim Hornback, and I can't be so blame' generous and good to Tom, Dick, and Harry as what he is, and slam around money the way he does; but I've told him a many a time 't I wouldn't trade places with him; for, says I, a sailor's life's the life for me, and I'm derned if *I'd* live two mile out o' town, where there ain't nothing ever goin' on, not for all his spondulicks and as much more on top of it. Says I—"

I broke in and says:

"They're in an awful peck of trouble, and——"

"*Who* is?"

"Why, pap, and mam, and sis, and Miss Hooker; and if you'd take your ferry-boat and go up there—"

"Up where? Where are they?"

"On the wreck."

"What wreck?"

"Why, there ain't but one."

"What, you don't mean the *Walter Scott*?"

"Yes."

"Good land! what are they doin' *there*, for gracious sakes?"

"Well, they didn't go there a-purpose."

"I bet they didn't! Why, great goodness, there ain't no chance for 'em if they don't git off mighty quick! Why, how in the nation did they ever git into such a scrape?"

"Easy enough. Miss Hooker was a-visiting, up there to the town——"

"Yes, Booth's Landing—go on."

"She was a-visiting, there at Booth's Landing, and just in the edge of the evening she started over with her nigger woman in the horse-ferry, to stay all night at her friend's house, Miss What-you-may-call-her, I disremember her name, and they lost their steering-oar, and swung around and went a-floating down, stern-first, about two mile, and saddle-baggsed on the wreck, and the ferry man and the nigger woman and the horses as all lost, but Miss Hooker she made a grab and got aboard the wreck. Well, about an hour after dark, we come along down in our trading-scow, and it was so dark we didn't notice the wreck till we was right on it; and so *we* saddle-baggsed; but all of us was saved but Bill Whipple—and oh, he *was* the best cretur!—I most wish't it had been me, I do."

"My George! It's the beatenest thing I ever struck. And *then* what did you all do?"

"Well, we hollered and took on, but it's so wide there, we couldn't make nobody hear. So pap said somebody got to get ashore and get help somehow. I was the only one that could swim, so I made a dash for it, and Miss Hooker she said if I didn't strike help sooner, come here and hunt up her uncle, and he'd fix the thing. I made the land about a mile below, and been fooling along ever since, trying to get people to do something, but they said, 'What, in such a night and such a current? there ain't no sense in it; go for the steam-ferry.' Now if you'll go, and——"

"By Jackson, I'd *like* to, and blame it I don't know but I will; but who in the dingnation's agoin' to *pay* for it? Do you reckon your pap——"

"Why *that's* all right. Miss Hooker she told me, *particular*, that her uncle Hornback——"

"Great guns! is *he* her uncle? Looky here, you break for that light over yonder-way, and turn out west when you git there, and about a quarter of a mile out you'll come to the tavern; tell 'em to dart you out to Jim Hornback's and he'll foot the bill. And don't you fool around any, because he'll want to know the news. Tell him I'll have his niece all safe before he can get to town. Hump yourself, now; I'm agoing up around the corner here, to roust out my engineer."

I struck for the light, but as soon as he turned the corner I went back and got into my skiff and bailed her out and then pulled up shore in the easy water about six hundred yards, and tucked myself in among some woodboats; for I couldn't rest easy till I could see the ferry-boat start. But take it all around, I was feeling ruther comfortable on accounts of taking all this trouble for that gang, for not many would a done it. I wished the widow knowed about it. I judged she would be proud of me for helping these rapscallions, because rapscallions and dead beats is the kind the widow and good people takes the most interest in.

Well, before long, here comes the wreck, dim and dusky, sliding along down! A kind of cold shiver went through me, and then I struck out for her. She was very deep, and I see in a minute there warn't much chance for anybody being alive in her. I pulled all around her and hollered a little, but there wasn't any answer; all dead still. I felt a little bit heavy-hearted about the gang, but not much, for I reckoned if they could stand it, I could.

Then here comes the ferry-boat; so I shoved for the middle of the river on a long down-stream slant; and when I judged I was out of eye-reach, I laid on my oars, and looked back and see her go and smell around the wreck for Miss Hooker's remainders, because the captain would know her uncle Hornback would want them; and then pretty soon the ferry-boat give it up and went for shore, and I laid into my work and went a-booming down the river.

It did seem a powerful long time before Jim's light showed up; and when it did show, it looked like it was a thousand mile off. By the time I got there the sky was beginning to get a little gray in the east; so we struck for an island, and hid the raft, and sunk the skiff, and turned in and slept like dead people.

Chapter XIV

By-and-by, when we got up, we turned over the truck the gang had stole off of the wreck, and found boots, and blankets, and clothes, and all sorts of other things, and a lot of books, and a spyglass, and three boxes of seegars. We hadn't ever been this rich before, in neither of our lives. The seegars was prime. We laid off all the afternoon in the woods talking, and me reading the books, and having a general good time. I told Jim all about what happened inside the wreck, and at the ferry-boat; and I said these kinds of things was adventures; but he said he didn't want no more adventures. He said that when I went in the texas and he crawled back to get on the raft and found her gone, he nearly died; because he judged it was all up with *him*, anyway it could be fixed; for if he didn't get saved he would get drownded; and if he did get saved, whoever saved him would send him back home so as to get the reward, and then Miss Watson would sell him South, sure. Well, he was right; he was most always right; he had an uncommon level head, for a nigger.

I read considerable to Jim about kings, and dukes, and earls, and such, and how gaudy they dressed, and how much style they put on, and called each other your majesty, and your grace, and your lordship, and so on, 'stead of mister; and Jim's eyes bugged out, and he was interested. He says:

"I didn' know dey was so many un um. I hain't hearn 'bout none un um, skasely, but ole King Sollermun, onless you counts dem kings dat's in a pack er k'yards. How much do a king git?"

"Get?" I says; "why, they get a thousand dollars a month if they want it; they can have just as much as they want; everything belongs to them."

"*Ain'* dat gay? En what dey got to do, Huck?"

"*They* don't do nothing! Why how you talk. They just set around."

"No—is dat so?"

"Of course it is. They just set around. Except maybe when there's a war; then they go to the war. But other times they just lazy around; or go hawking—just hawking and sp— Sh!—d' you hear a noise?"

We skipped out and looked; but it warn't nothing but the flutter of a steamboat's wheel, away down coming around the point; so we come back.

"Yes," says I, "and other times, when things is dull, they fuss with the parlyment; and if everybody don't go just so he whacks their heads off. But mostly they hang round the harem."

"Roun' de which?"

"Harem."

"What's de harem?"

"The place where he keep his wives. Don't you know about the harem? Solomon had one; he had about a million wives."

"Why, yes, dat's so; I—I'd done forgot it. A harem's a bo'd'n-house, I reck'n. Mos' likely dey has rackety times in de nussery. En I reck'n de wives quarrels considable; en dat 'crease de racket. Yit dey say Sollermun de wises' man dat ever live'. I doan' take no stock in dat. Bekase why: would a wise man want to live in de mids' er sich a blimblammin' all de time? No—'deed he wouldn't. A wise man 'ud take en buil' a biler-factry; en den he could shet *down* de biler-factry when he want to res'."

"Well, but he *was* the wisest man, anyway; because the widow she told me so, her own self."

"I doan k'yer what de widder say, he *warn't* no wise man, nuther. He had some er de dad-fetchededs' ways I ever see. Does you know 'bout dat chile dat he 'uz gwyne to chop in two?"

"Yes, the widow told me all about it."

"*Well,* den! Warn' dat de beatenes' notion in der worl'? You jes' take en look at it a minute. Dah's de stump, dah—dat's one er de women; heah's you—dat's de yuther one; I's Sollermun; en dish-yer dollar bill's de chile. Bofe un you claims it. What does I do? Does I shin aroun' mongs' de neighbors en fine out which un you de bill *do* b'long to, en han' it over to de right one, all safe en soun', de way dat anybody dat had any gumption would? No—I take en whack de bill in *two,* en give half un it to you, en de yuther half to de yuther woman. Dat's de way Sollermun was gwyne to do wid de chile. Now I want to ast you: what's de use er dat half a bill?—can't buy noth'n wid it. En what use is a half a chile? I would'n give a dern for a million un um."

"But hang it, Jim, you've clean missed the point—blame it, you've missed it a thousand mile."

"Who? Me? Go 'long. Doan' talk to *me* 'bout yo' pints. I reck'n I knows sense when I sees it; en dey ain' no sense in sich doin's as dat. De 'spute warn't 'bout a half a chile, de 'spute was 'bout a whole chile; en de man dat think he kin settle a 'spute 'bout a whole chile wid a half a chile, doan' know enough to come in out'n de rain. Doan' talk to me 'bout Sollermun, Huck, I knows him by de back."

"But I tell you you don't get the point."

"Blame de pint! I reck'n I knows what I knows. En mine you, de *real* pint is down furder—it's down deeper. It lays in de way Sollermun was raised. You take a man dat's got on'y one or two chillen; is dat man gwyne to be waseful o' chillen? No, he ain't; he can't 'ford it. *He* know how to value 'em. But you take a man dat's got 'bout five million chillen runnin' roun' de house, en it's diffunt. *He* as soon chop a chile in two as a cat. Dey's plenty mo'. A chile er two, mo' er less, warn't no consekens to Sollermun, dad fetch him!"

I never see such a nigger. If he got a notion in his head once, there warn't no getting it out again. He was the most down on Solomon of any nigger I ever see. So I went to talking about other kings, and let Solomon slide. I told about Louis Sixteenth that got his head cut off in France long time ago; and about his little boy the dolphin, that would a been a king, but they took and shut him up in jail, and some say he died there.

"Po' little chap."

"But some says he got out and got away, and come to America."

"Dat's good! But he'll be pooty lonesome—dey ain' no kings here, is dey, Huck?"

"No."

"Den he cain't git no situation. What he gwyne to do?"

"Well, I don't know. Some of them gets on the police, and some of them learns people how to talk French."

"Why, Huck, doan' de French people talk de same way we does?"

"*No,* Jim; you couldn't understand a word they said—not a single word."

"Well, now, I be ding-busted! How do dat come?"

"*I* don't know; but it's so. I got some of their jabber out of a book. Spose a man was to come to you and say *Polly-voo-franzy*—what would you think?"

"I wouldn' think nuff'n; I'd take en bust him over de head. Dat is, if he warn't white. I wouldn't 'low no nigger to call me dat."

"Shucks, it ain't calling you anything. It's only saying do you know how to talk French."

"Well, den, why couldn't he *say* it?"

"Why, he *is* a-saying it. That's a Frenchman's *way* of saying it."

"Well, it's a blame ridicklous way, en I doan' want to hear no mo' 'bout it. Dey ain' no sense in it."

"Looky here, Jim; does a cat talk like we do?"

"No, a cat don't."

"Well, does a cow?"

"No, a cow don't, nuther."

"Does a cat talk like a cow, or a cow talk like a cat?"

"No, dey don't."

"It's natural and right for 'em to talk different from each other, ain't it?"

"'Course."

"And ain't it natural and right for a cat and a cow to talk different from *us*?"

"Why, mos' sholy it is."

"Well, then, why ain't it natural and right for a *Frenchman* to talk different from us? You answer me that."

"Is a cat a man, Huck?"

"No."

"Well, den, dey ain't no sense in a cat talkin' like a man. Is a cow a man? —er is a cow a cat?"

"No, she ain't either of them."

"Well, den, she ain't got no business to talk like either one er the yuther of 'em. Is a Frenchman a man?"

"Yes."

"*Well*, den! Dad blame it, why doan' he *talk* like a man? You answer me *dat*!"

I see it warn't no use wasting words—you can't learn a nigger to argue. So I quit.

Chapter XV

We judged that three nights more would fetch us to Cairo, at the bottom of Illinois, where the Ohio River comes in, and that was what we was after. We would sell the raft and get on a steamboat and go way up the Ohio amongst the free States, and then be out of trouble.

Well, the second night a fog begun to come on, and we made for a tow-head to tie to, for it wouldn't do to try to run in fog; but when I paddled ahead in the canoe, with the line, to make fast, there warn't anything but little saplings to tie to. I passed the line around one of them right on the edge of the cut bank, but there was a stiff current, and the raft come booming down so lively she tore it out by the roots and away went. I see the fog closing down, and it made me so sick and scared I couldn't budge for most a half a minute it seemed to me—and then there warn't no raft in sight; you couldn't see twenty yards. I jumped into the canoe and run back to the stern and grabbed the paddle and set her back a stroke. But she didn't come. I was in such a hurry I hadn't untied her. I got up and tried to untie her, but I was so excited my hands shook so I couldn't hardly do anything with them.

As soon as I got started I took out after the raft, hot and heavy, right down the tow-head. That was all right as far as it went, but the tow-head warn't sixty yards long, and the minute I flew by the foot of it I shot out into the solid white fog, and hadn't no more idea which way I was going than a dead man.

Thinks I, it won't do to paddle; first I know I'll run into the bank or a tow-head or something; I got to set still and float, and yet it's mighty fidgety business to have to hold your hands still at such a time. I whooped and listened. Away down there, somewheres, I hears a small whoop, and up comes my spirits. I went tearing after it, listening sharp to hear it again. The next time it come, I see I warn't heading for it but heading away to the right of it. And the next time, I was heading away to the left of it—and no gaining on it much, either, for I was flying around, this way and that and 'tother, but it was going straight ahead all the time.

I did wish the fool would think to beat a tin pan, and beat it all the time, but he never did, and it was the still places between the whoops that was making the trouble for me.

Well, I fought along, and directly I hears the whoop *behind* me. I was tangled good, now. That was somebody else's whoop, or else I was turned around.

I throwed the paddle down. I heard the whoop again; it was behind me yet, but in a different place; it kept coming, and kept changing its place, and I kept answering, till by-and-by it was in front of me again and I knowed the current had swung the canoe's head down stream and I was all right, if that was Jim and not some other raftsman hollering. I couldn't tell nothing about voices in a fog, for nothing don't look natural nor sound natural in a fog.

The whooping went on, and in about a minute I come a booming down on a cut bank with smoky ghosts of big trees on it, and the current throwed me off to the left and shot by, amongst a lot of snags that fairly roared, the current was tearing by them so swift.

In another second or two it was solid white and still again. I set perfectly still, then, listening to my heart thump, and I reckon I didn't draw a breath while it thumped a hundred.

I just give up, then: I knowed what the matter was. That cut bank was an island, and Jim had gone down 'tother side of it. It warn't no tow-head, that you could float by in ten minutes. It had the big timber of a regular island; it might be five or six mile long and more than a half a mile wide.

I kept quiet, with my ears cocked, about fifteen minutes, I reckon. I was floating along, of course, four or five mile an hour; but you don't ever think of that. No, you *feel* like you are laying dead still on the water; and if a little glimpse of a snag slips by, you don't think to yourself how fast *you're* going, but you catch your breath and think, my! how that snag's tearing along. If you think it ain't dismal and lonesome out in a fog that way, by yourself, in the night, you try it once—you'll see.

Next, for about a half an hour, I whoops now and then; at last I hears the answer a long ways off, and tries to follow it, but I couldn't do it, and directly I judged I'd got into a nest of tow-heads, for I had little dim glimpses of them on both sides of me, sometimes just a narrow channel between; and some that I couldn't see, I knowed was there, because I'd hear the wash of the current against the old dead brush and trash that hung over the banks. Well, I warn't long losing the whoops, down amongst the tow-heads; and I only tried to chase them a little while, anyway, because it was worse than chasing a Jack-o-lantern. You never knowed a sound dodge around so, and swap places so quick and so much.

I had to claw away from the bank pretty lively, four or five times, to keep from knocking the islands out of the river; and so I judged the raft must be butting into the bank every now and then, or else it would get further ahead and clear out of hearing—it was floating a little faster than what I was.

Well, I seemed to be in the open river again, by-and-by, but I couldn't hear no sign of a whoop nowheres. I reckoned Jim had fetched up on a snag, maybe, and it was all up with him. I was good and tired, so I laid down in the canoe and said I wouldn't bother no more. I didn't want to go to sleep, of course; but I was so sleepy I couldn't help it; so I thought I would take just one little cat-nap.

But I reckon it was more than a cat-nap, for when I waked up the stars was shining bright, the fog was all gone, and I was spinning down a big bend stern first. First I didn't know where I was; I thought I was dreaming; and when things begun to come back to me, they seemed to come up dim out of last week.

It was a monstrous big river here, with the tallest and the thickest kind of timber on both banks; just a solid wall, as well as I could see, by the stars. I looked away down stream, and seen a black speck on the water. I took out after it; but when I got to it it warn't nothing but a couple of saw-logs made fast together. Then I see another speck, and chased that; then another, and this time I was right. It was the raft.

When I got to it Jim was setting there with his head down between his knees, asleep, with his right arm hanging over the steering oar. The other oar was smashed off, and the raft was littered up with leaves and branches and dirt. So she'd had a rough time.

I made fast and laid down under Jim's nose on the raft, and begun to gap, and stretch my fists out against Jim, and says:

"Hello, Jim, have I been asleep? Why didn't you stir me up?"

"Goodness gracious, is dat you, Huck? En you ain' dead—you ain' drownded—you's back agin? It's too good for true, honey, it's too good for true. Lemme look at you, chile, lemme feel o' you. No, you ain' dead! you's back agin, 'live en soun', jis de same ole Huck—de same ole Huck, thanks to goodness!"

"What's the matter with you, Jim? You been a drinking?"

"Drinkin'? Has I ben a drinkin'? Has I had a chance to be a drinkin'?"

"Well, then, what makes you talk so wild?"

"How does I talk wild?"

"*How?* why, hain't you been talking about my coming back, and all that stuff, as if I'd been gone away?"

"Huck—Huck Fin, you look me in de eye; look me in de eye. *Hain't* you ben gone away?"

"Gone away? Why, what in the nation do you mean? *I* hain't been gone anywheres. Where would I go to?"

"Well, looky here, boss, dey's sumf'n wrong, dey is. Is I *me*, or who *is* I? Is I heah, or whah *is* I? Now dat's what I wants to know?"

"Well, I think you're here, plain enough, but I think you're a tangle-headed old fool, Jim."

"I is, is I? Well you answer me dis. Didn't you tote out de line in de canoe, fer to make fas' to de tow-head?"

"No, I didn't. What tow-head? I hain't seen no tow-head."

"You hain't seen no tow-head? Looky here—didn't de line pull loose en de raf' go a hummin' down de river, en leave you en de canoe behine in de fog?"

"What fog?"

"Why *de* fog. De fog dat's ben aroun' all night. En didn't you whoop, en didn't I whoop, tell we got mix' up in de islands en one un us got los' en 'tother one was jis' as good as los', 'kase he didn't know whah he wuz? En didn't I bust up agin a lot er dem islands en have a turrible time en mos' git drownded? Now ain' dat so, boss—ain't it so? You answer me dat."

"Well, this is too many for me, Jim. I hain't seen no fog, nor no islands, nor no troubles, nor nothing. I been setting here talking with you all night till you went to sleep about ten minutes ago, and I reckon I done the same. You couldn't a got drunk in that time, so of course you've been dreaming."

"Dad fetch it, how is I gwyne to dream all dat in ten minutes?"

"Well, hang it all, you did dream it, because there didn't any of it happen."

"But Huck, it's all jis' as plain to me as——"

"It don't make no difference how plain it is, there ain't nothing in it. I know, because I've been here all the time."

Jim didn't say nothing for about five minutes, but set there studying over it. Then he says:

"Well, den, I reck'n I did dream it, Huck; but dog my cats ef it ain't de powerfullest dream I ever see. En I hain't ever had no dream b'fo' dat's tired me like dis one."

"Oh, well, that's all right, because a dream does tire a body like everything, sometimes. But this one was a staving dream—tell me all about it, Jim."

So Jim went to work and told me the whole thing right through, just as it happened, only he painted it up considerable. Then he said he must start in and "'terpret" it, because it was sent for a warning. He said the first tow-head stood for a man that would try to do us some good, but the current was another man that would get us away from him. The whoops was warnings that would come to us every now and then, and if we didn't try hard to make out to understand them they'd just take us into bad luck, 'stead of keeping us out of it. The lot of tow-heads was troubles we was going to get into with quarrelsome people and all kinds of mean folks, but if we minded our business and didn't talk back and aggravate them, we would pull through and get out of the fog and into the big clear river, which was the free States, and wouldn't have no more trouble.

It had clouded up pretty dark just after I got onto the raft, but it was clearing up again, now.

"Oh, well, that's all interpreted well enough, as far as it goes, Jim," I says; "but what does *these* things stand for?"

It was the leaves and rubbish on the raft, and the smashed oar. You could see them first rate, now.

Jim looked at the trash, and then looked at me, and back at the trash again. He had got the dream fixed so strong in his head that he couldn't seem to shake it loose and get the facts back into its place again, right away. But when he did get the thing straightened around, he looked at me steady, without ever smiling, and says:

"What do dey stan' for? I's gwyne to tell you. When I got all wore out wid work, en wid de callin' for you, en went to sleep, my heart wuz mos' broke bekase you wuz los', en I didn't k'yer no mo' what become er me en de raf'. En when I wake up en fine you back agin', all safe en soun', de tears come en I could a got down on my knees en kiss' yo' foot I's so thankful. En all you wuz thinkin 'bout wuz how you could make a fool uv ole Jim wid a lie. Dat truck dah is *trash;* en trash is what people is dat puts dirt on de head er dey fren's en makes 'em ashamed."

Then he got up slow, and walked to the wigwam, and went in there, without saying anything but that. But that was enough. It made me feel so mean I could almost kissed *his* foot to get him to take it back.

It was fifteen minutes before I could work myself up to go and humble myself to a nigger—but I done it, and I warn't ever sorry for it afterwards, neither. I didn't do him no more mean tricks, and I wouldn't done that one if I'd a knowed it would make him feel that way.

Chapter XVI

We slept most all day, and started out at night, a little ways behind a monstrous long raft that was as long going by as a procession. She had four long sweeps at each end, so we judged she carried as many as thirty men, likely. She had five big wigwams aboard, wide apart, and an open camp fire in the middle, and a tall flag-pole at each end. There was a power of style about her. It *amounted* to something being a raftsman on such a craft as that.

We went drifting down into a big bend, and the night clouded up and got hot. The river was very wide, and was walled with solid timber on both sides; you couldn't see a break in it hardly ever, or a light. We talked about Cairo, and wondered whether we would know it when we got to it. I said likely we wouldn't, because I had heard say there warn't but about a dozen houses there, and if they didn't happen to have them lit up, how was we going to know we was passing a town? Jim said if the two big rivers joined together there, that would show. But I said maybe we might think we was passing the foot of an island and coming into the same old river again. That disturbed Jim—and me too. So the question was, what to do? I said, paddle ashore the first time a light showed, and tell them pap was behind, coming along with a trading-scow, and was a green hand at the business, and wanted to know how far it was to Cairo. Jim thought it was a good idea, so we took a smoke on it and waited.

There warn't nothing to do now, but to look out sharp for the town, and not pass it without seeing it. He said he'd be mighty sure to see it, because he'd be a free man the minute he seen it, but if he missed it he'd be in the slave country again and no more show for freedom. Every little while he jumps up and says:

"Dah she is!"

But it warn't. It was Jack-o-lanterns, or lightning-bugs; so he set down again, and went to watching, same as before. Jim said it made him all over trembly and feverish to be so close to freedom. Well, I can tell you it made me all over trembly and feverish, too, to hear him, because I begun to get it through my head that he *was* most free—and who was to blame for it? Why, *me*. I couldn't get that out of my conscience, no how nor no way. It got to troubling me so I couldn't rest; I couldn't stay still in one place. It hadn't ever come home to me before, what this thing was that I was doing. But now it did; and it staid with me, and scorched me more and more. I tried to make out to my-self that *I* warn't to blame, because *I* didn't run Jim off from his rightful owner; but it warn't no use, conscience up and says, every time, "But you knowed he was running for his freedom, and you could a paddled ashore and told somebody." That was so—I couldn't get around that, noway. That was where it pinched. Conscience says to me, "What had poor Miss Watson done to you, that you could see her nigger go off right under your eyes and never say one single word? What did that poor old woman do to you, that you could treat her so mean? Why, she tried to learn you your book, she tried to learn you your manners, she tried to be good to you every way she knowed how. *That's* what she done."

I got to feeling so mean and so miserable I most wished I was dead. I fidgeted up and down the raft, abusing myself to myself, and Jim was fidgeting up and down past me. We neither of us could keep still. Every time he danced around and says, "Dah's Cairo!" it went through me like a shot, and I thought if it *was* Cairo I reckoned I would die of miserableness.

Jim talked out loud all the time while I was talking to myself. He was saying how the first thing he would do when he got to a free State he would go to saving up money and never spend a single cent, and when he got enough he would buy his wife, which was owned on a farm close to where Miss Watson lived; and then they would both work to buy the two children, and if their master wouldn't sell them, they'd get an Ab'litionist to go and steal them.

It most froze me to hear such talk. He wouldn't ever dared to talk such talk in his life before. Just see what a difference it made in him the minute he judged he was about free. It was according to the old saying, "give a nigger an inch and he'll take an ell." Thinks I, this is what comes of my not thinking. Here was this nigger which I had as good as helped to run away, coming right out flat-footed and saying he would steal his children—children that belonged to a man I didn't even know; a man that hadn't ever done me no harm.

I was sorry to hear Jim say that, it was such a lowering of him. My conscience got to stirring me up hotter than ever, until at last I says to it, "Let up on me—it ain't too late, yet—I'll paddle ashore at the first light, and tell." I felt easy, and happy, and light as a feather, right off. All my troubles was gone. I went to looking out sharp for a light, and sort of singing to myself. By-and-by one showed. Jim sings out:

"We's safe, Huck, we's safe! Jump up and crack yo' heels, dat's de good ole Cairo at las', I jis knows it!"

I says:

"I'll take the canoe and go see, Jim. It mightn't be, you know."

He jumped and got the canoe ready, and put his old coat in the bottom for me to set on, and give me the paddle; and as I shoved off, he says:

"Pooty soon I'll be a-shout'n for joy, en I'll say, it's all on accounts o' Huck; I's a free man, en I couldn't ever ben free of it hadn't ben for Huck; Huck done it. Jim won't ever forgit you, Huck; you's de bes' fren' Jim's ever had; en you's de *only* fren' ole Jim's got now."

I was paddling off, all in a sweat to tell on him; but when he says this, it seemed to kind of take the tuck all out of me. I went along slow then, and I warn't right down certain whether I was glad I started or whether I warn't. When I was fifty yards off, Jim says:

"Dah you goes, de ole true Huck; de on'y white genlman dat ever kep' his promise to ole Jim."

Well, I just felt sick. But I says, I *got* to do it—I can't get *out* of it. Right then, along comes a skiff with two men in it, with guns, and they stopped and I stopped. One of them says:

"What's that, yonder?"

"A piece of a raft," I says.

"Do you belong on it?"

"Yes, sir."

"Any men on it?"

"Only one, sir."

"Well, there's five niggers run off to-night, up yonder above the head of the bend. Is your man white or black?"

I didn't answer up prompt. I tried to, but the words wouldn't come. I tried, for a second or two, to brace up and out with it, but I warn't man enough—hadn't the spunk of a rabbit. I see I was weakening; so I just give up trying, and up and says—

"He's white."

"I reckon we'll go and see for ourselves."

"I wish you would," says I, "because it's pap that's there, and maybe you'd help me tow the raft ashore where the light is. He's sick—and so is mam and Mary Ann."

"Oh, the devil! we're in a hurry, boy. But I s'pose we've got to. Come—buckle to your paddle, and let's get along."

I buckled to my paddle and they laid to their oars. When we had made a stroke or two, I says:

"Pap'll be mighty much obleeged to you, I can tell you. Everybody goes away when I want them to help me tow the raft ashore, and I can't do it by myself."

"Well, that's infernal mean. Odd, too. Say, boy, what's the matter with your father?"

"It's the—a—the—well, it ain't anything, much."

They stopped pulling. It warn't but a mighty little ways to the raft, now. One says:

"Boy, that a lie. What *is* the matter with your pap? Answer up square, now, and it'll be the better for you."

"I will, sir, I will, honest—but don't leave us, please. It's the—the—gentlemen, if you'll only pull ahead, and let me heave you the head-line, you won't have to come a-near the raft—please do."

"Set her back, John, set her back!" says one. They backed water. "Keep away, boy—keep to looard. Confound it, I just expect the wind has blowed it to us. Your pap's got the small-pox, and you know it precious well. Why didn't you come out and say so? Do you want to spread it all over?"

"Well," says I, a-blubbering, "I've told everybody before, and then they just went away and left us."

"Poor devil, there's something in that. We are right down sorry for you, but we—well, hang it, we don't want the small-pox, you see. Look here, I'll tell you what to do. Don't you try to land by yourself, or you'll smash everything to pieces. You float along down about twenty miles and you'll come to a town on the left-hand side of the river. It will be long after sun-up, then, and when you ask for help, you tell them your folks are all down with chills and fever. Don't be a fool again, and let people guess what is the matter. Now we're trying to do you a kindness; so you just put twenty miles between us, that's a good boy. It wouldn't do any good to land yonder where the light is—it's only a wood-yard. Say—I reckon your father's poor, and I'm bound to say he's in pretty hard luck. Here—I'll put a twenty dollar gold piece on this board, and you get it when it floats by. I feel mighty mean to leave you, but my kingdom! it won't do to fool with small-pox, don't you see?"

"Hold on, Parker," says the other man, "here's a twenty to put on the board for me. Good-bye, boy, you do as Mr. Parker told you, and you'll be all right."

"That's so, my boy—good-bye, good-bye. If you see any runaway niggers, you get help and nab them, and you can make some money by it."

"Good-bye, sir," says I, "I won't let no runaway niggers get by me if I can help it."

They went off, and I got aboard the raft, feeling bad and low, because I knowed very well I had done wrong, and I see it warn't no use for me to try to learn to do right; a body that don't get *started* right when he's little, ain't got no show—when the pinch comes there ain't nothing to back him up and keep him to his work, and so he gets beat. Then I thought a minute, and says to myself, hold on,—s'pose you'd a done right and give Jim up; would you felt better than what you do now? No, says I, I'd feel bad—I'd feel just the same way I do now. Well, then, says I, what's the use you learning to do right, when it's troublesome to do right and ain't no trouble to do wrong, and the wages is just the same? I was stuck. I couldn't answer that. So I reckoned I wouldn't bother no more about it, but after this always do whichever come handiest at the time.

I went into the wigwam; Jim warn't there. I looked all around; he warn't anywhere. I says:

"Jim!"

"Here I is, Huck. Is dey out o' sight yit? Don't talk loud."

He was in the river, under the stern oar, with just his nose out. I told him they was out of sight, so he come aboard. He says:

"I was a-listenin' to all de talk, en I slips into de river en was gwyne to shove for sho' if dey come aboard. Den I was gwyne to swim to de raf' agin when dey was gone. But lawsy, how you did fool 'em, Huck! Dat *wuz* de smartes' dodge! I tell you, chile, I 'speck it save' ole Jim—ole Jim ain't gwyne to forgit you for dat, honey."

Then we talked about the money. It was a pretty good raise, twenty dollars apiece. Jim said we could take deck passage on a steamboat now, and the money would last us as far as we wanted to go in the free States. He said twenty mile more warn't far for the raft to go, but he wished we was already there.

Towards daybreak we tied up, and Jim was mighty particular about hiding the raft good. Then he worked all day fixing things in bundles, and getting all ready to quit rafting.

That night about ten we hove in sight of the lights of a town away down in a left-hand bend.

I went off in the canoe, to ask about it. Pretty soon I found a man out in the river with a skiff, setting a trot-line. I ranged up and says:

"Mister, is that town Cairo?"

"Cairo? no. You must be a blame' fool."

"What town is it, mister?"

"If you want to know, go and find out. If you stay here botherin' around me for about a half a minute longer, you'll get something you won't want."

I paddled to the raft. Jim was awful disappointed, but I said never mind, Cairo would be the next place, I reckoned.

We passed another town before daylight, and I was going out again; but it was high ground, so I didn't go. No high ground about Cairo, Jim said. I had forgot it. We laid up for the day, on a tow-head tolerable close to the left-hand bank. I begun to suspicion something. So did Jim. I says:

"Maybe we went by Cairo in the fog that night."

He says:

"Doan' less' talk about it, Huck. Po' niggers can't have no luck. I awluz 'spected dat rattle-snake skin warn't done wid it's work."

"I wish I'd never seen that snake-skin, Jim—I do wish I'd never laid eyes on it."

"It ain't yo' fault, Huck; you didn' know. Don't you blame yo'self 'bout it."

When it was daylight, here was the clear Ohio water in shore, sure enough, and outside was the old regular Muddy! So it was all up with Cairo.

We talked it all over. It wouldn't do to take to the shore; we couldn't take the raft up the stream, of course. There warn't no way but to wait for dark, and start back in the canoe and take the chances. So we slept all day amongst the cotton-wood thicket, so as to be fresh for the work, and when we went back to the raft about dark the canoe was gone!

We didn't say a word for a good while. There warn't anything to say. We both knowed well enough it was some more work of the rattle-snake skin; so what was the use to talk about it? It would only look like we was finding fault, and that would be bound to fetch more bad luck—and keep on fetching it, too, till we knowed enough to keep still.

By-and-by we talked about what we better do, and found there warn't no way but just to go along down with the raft till we got a chance to buy a canoe to go back in. We warn't going to borrow it when there warn't anybody around, the way pap would do, for that might set people after us.

So we shoved out, after dark, on the raft.

Anybody that don't believe yet, that it's foolishness to handle a snake-skin, after all that that snake-skin done for us, will believe it now, if they read on and see what more it done for us.

The place to buy canoes is off of rafts laying up at shore. But we didn't see no rafts laying up; so we went along during three hours and more. Well, the night got gray, and ruther thick, which is the next meanest thing to fog. You can't tell the shape of the river, and you can't see no distance. It got to be very late and still, and then along comes a steamboat up the river. We lit the lantern, and judged she would see it. Up-stream boats didn't generly come close to us; they go out and follow the bars and hunt for easy water under the reefs; but nights like this they bull right up the channel against the whole river.

We could hear her pounding along, but we didn't see her good till she was close. She aimed right for us. Often they do that and try to see how close they can come without touching; sometimes the wheel bites off a sweep, and then the pilot sticks his head out and laughs, and thinks he's mighty smart. Well, here she comes, and we said she was going to try to shave us; but she didn't seem to be sheering off a bit. She was a big one, and she was coming in a hurry, too, looking like a black cloud with rows of glow-worms around it; but all of a sudden she bulged out, big and scary, with a long row of wide-open furnace doors shining like red-hot teeth, and her monstrous bows and guards hanging right over us. There was a yell at us, and a jingling of bells to stop the engines, a pow-wow of cussing, and whistling of steam—and as Jim went overboard on one side and I on the other, she come smashing straight through the raft.

I dived—and I aimed to find the bottom, too, for a thirty-foot wheel had got to go over me, and I wanted it to have plenty of room. I could always stay under water a minute; this time I reckon I staid under water a minute and a half. Then I bounced for the top in a hurry, for I was nearly busting. I popped out to my arm-pits and blowed the water out of my nose, and puffed a bit. Of course there was a booming current; and of course that boat started her engines again ten seconds after she stopped them, for they never cared much for raftsmen; so now she was churning along up the river, out of sight in the thick weather, though I could hear her.

I sung out for Jim about a dozen times, but I didn't get any answer; so I grabbed a plank that touched me while I was "treading water," and struck out for shore, shoving it ahead of me. But I made out to see that the drift of the current was towards the left-hand shore, which meant that I was in a crossing; so I changed off and went that way.

It was one of these long, slanting, two-mile crossings; so I was a good long time in getting over. I made a safe landing, and clum up the bank. I couldn't see but a little ways, but I went poking along over rough ground for a quarter of a mile or more, and then I run across a big old-fashioned double log house before I noticed it. I was going to rush by and get away, but a lot of dogs jumped out and went to howling and barking at me, and I knowed better than to move another peg.

Chapter XVII

In about half a minute somebody spoke out of a window, without putting his head out, and says:

"Be done, boys! Who's there?"

I says:

"It's me."

"Who's me?"

"George Jackson, sir."

"What do you want?"

"I don't want nothing, sir. I only want to go along by, but the dogs won't let me."

"What are you prowling around here this time of night, for—hey?"

"I warn't prowling around, sir; I fell overboard off of the steamboat."

"Oh, you did, did you? Strike a light there, somebody. What did you say your name was?"

"George Jackson, sir. I'm only a boy."

"Look here; if you're telling the truth, you needn't be afraid—nobody'll hurt you. But don't try to budge; stand right where you are. Rouse out Bob and Tom, some of you, and fetch the guns. George Jackson, is there anybody with you?"

"No, sir, nobody."

I heard the people stirring around in the house, now, and see a light. The man sung out:

"Snatch that light away, Betsy, you old fool—ain't you got any sense? Put it on the floor behind the front door. Bob, if you and Tom are ready, take your places."

"All ready."

"Now, George Jackson, do you know the Shepherdsons?"

"No, sir—I never heard of them."

"Well, that may be so, and it mayn't. Now, all ready. Step forward, George Jackson. And mind, don't you hurry—come mighty slow. If there's anybody with you, let him keep back—if he shows himself he'll be shot. Come along, now. Come slow; push the door open, yourself—just enough to squeeze in, d' you hear?"

I didn't hurry, I couldn't if I'd a wanted to. I took one slow step at a time, and there warn't a sound, only I thought I could hear my heart. The dogs were as still as the humans, but they followed a little behind me. When I got to the three log door-steps, I heard them unlocking and unbarring and unbolting. I put my hand on the door and pushed it a little and a little more, till somebody said, "There, that's enough—put your head in." I done it, but I judged they would take it off.

The candle was on the floor, and there they all was, looking at me, and me at them, for about a quarter of a minute. Three big men with guns pointed at me, which made me wince, I tell you; the oldest, gray and about sixty, the other two thirty or more—all of them fine and handsome—and the sweetest old gray-headed lady, and back of her two young women which I couldn't see right well. The old gentleman says:

"There—I reckon it's all right. Come in."

As soon as I was in, the old gentleman he locked the door and barred it and bolted it, and told the young men to come in with their guns, and they all went in a big parlor that had a new rag carpet on the floor, and got together in a corner that was out of range of the front windows—there warn't none on the side. They held the candle, and took a good look at me, and all said, "Why *he* ain't a Shepherdson—no, there ain't any Shepherdson about him." Then the old man said he hoped I wouldn't mind being searched for arms, because he didn't mean no harm by it—it was only to make sure. So he didn't pry into my pockets, but only felt outside with his hands, and said it was all right. He told me to make myself easy and at home, and tell all about myself; but the old lady says:

"Why bless you, Saul, the poor thing's as wet as he can be; and don't you reckon it may be he's hungry?"

"True for you, Rachel—I forgot."

So the old lady says:

"Betsy" (this was a nigger woman), "you fly around and get him something to eat, as quick as you can, poor thing; and one of you girls go and wake up Buck and tell him— Oh, here he is himself. Buck, take this little stranger and get the wet clothes off from him and dress him up in some of yours that's dry."

Buck looked about as old as me—thirteen or fourteen or along there, though he was a little bigger than me. He hadn't on anything but a shirt, and he was very frowsy-headed. He come in gaping and digging one fist into his eyes, and he was dragging a gun along with the other one. He says:

"Ain't they no Shepherdsons around?"

They said, no, 'twas a false alarm.

"Well," he says, "if they'd a ben some, I reckon I'd a got one."

They all laughed, and Bob says:

"Why, Buck, they might have scalped us all, you've been so slow in coming."

"Well, nobody come after me, and it ain't right. I'm always kep' down; I don't get no show."

"Never mind, Buck, my boy," says the old man, "you'll have show enough, all in good time, don't you fret about that. Go 'long with you now, and do as your mother told you."

When we got up stairs to his room, he got me a coarse shirt and a round-about and pants of his, and I put them on. While I was at it he asked me what my name was, but before I could tell him, he started to telling me about a blue jay and a young rabbit he had catched in the woods day before yesterday, and he asked me where Moses was when the candle went out. I said I didn't know; I hadn't heard about it before, no way.

"Well, guess," he says.

"How'm I going to guess," says I, "when I never heard tell about it before?"

"But you can guess, can't you? It's just as easy."

"*Which* candle?" I says.

"Why, any candle," he says.

"I don't know where he was," says I; "where was he?"

"Why he was in the *dark!* That's where he was!"

"Well, if you knowed where he was, what did you ask me for?"

"Why, blame it, it's a riddle, don't you see? Say, how long are you going to stay here? You got to stay always. We can just have booming times—they don't have no school now. Do you own a dog? I've got a dog—and he'll go in the river and bring out chips that you throw in. Do you like to comb up, Sundays, and all that kind of foolishness? You bet I don't, but ma she makes me. Confound these ole britches, I reckon I'd better put 'em on, but I'd ruther not, it's so warm. Are you all ready? All right—come along, old hoss."

Cold corn-pone, cold corn-beef, butter and butter-milk—that is what they had for me down there, and there ain't nothing better that ever I've come across yet. Buck and his ma and all of them smoked cob pipes, except the nigger woman, which was gone, and the two young women. They all smoked and talked, and I eat and talked. The young women had quilts around them, and their hair down their backs. They all asked me questions, and I told them how pap and me and all the family was living on a little farm down at the bottom of Arkansaw, and my sister Mary Ann run off and got married and never was heard of no more, and Bill went to hunt them and he warn't heard of no more, and Tom and Mort died, and then there warn't nobody but just me and pap left, and he was just trimmed down to nothing, on account of his troubles; so when he died I took what there was left, because the farm didn't belong to us, and started up the river, deck passage, and fell overboard; and that was how I come to be here. So they said I could have a home there as long as I wanted it. Then it was most daylight, and every-body went to bed, and I went to bed with Buck, and when I waked up in the morning, drat it all, I had forgot what my name was. So I laid there about an hour trying to think, and when Buck waked up, I says:

"Can you spell, Buck?"

"Yes," he says.

"I bet you can't spell my name," says I.

"I bet you what you dare I can," says he.

"All right," says I, "go ahead."

"G-o-r-g-e J-a-x-o-n—there now," he says.

"Well," says I, "you done it, but I didn't think you could. It ain't no slouch of a name to spell—right off without studying."

I set it down, private, because somebody might want *me* to spell it, next, and so I wanted to be handy with it and rattle it off like I was used to it.

It was a mighty nice family, and a mighty nice house, too. I hadn't seen no house out in the country before that was so nice and had so much style. It didn't have an iron latch on the front door, nor a wooden one with a buckskin string, but a brass knob to turn, the same as houses in a town. There warn't no bed in the parlor, not a sign of a bed; but heaps of parlors in towns has beds in them. There was a big fireplace that was bricked on the bottom, and the bricks was kept clean and red by pouring water on them and scrubbing them with another brick; sometimes they washed them over with red water-paint that they call Spanish-brown, same as they do in town. They had big brass dog-irons that could hold up a saw-log. There was a clock on the middle of the mantel-piece, with a picture of a town painted on the bottom half of the glass front, and a round place in the middle of it for the sun, and you could see the pendulum swing be-hind it. It was beautiful to hear that clock tick; and sometimes when one of these ped-dlers had been along and scoured her up and got her in good shape, she would start in and strike a hundred and fifty before she got tuckered out. They wouldn't took any money for her.

Well, there was a big outlandish parrot on each side of the clock, made out of some-thing like chalk, and painted up gaudy. By one of the parrots was a cat made of crock-ery, and a crockery dog by the other; and when you pressed down on them they squeaked, but didn't open their mouths nor look different nor interested. They squeaked through underneath. There was a couple of big wild-turkey-wing fans spread out behind those things. On a table in the middle of the room was a kind of a lovely crockery basket that had apples and oranges and peaches and grapes piled up in it which was much redder and yellower and prettier than real ones is, but they warn't real because you could see where pieces had got chipped off and showed the white chalk or whatever it was, underneath.

This table had a cover made out of beautiful oil-cloth, with a red and blue spread-eagle painted on it, and a painted border all around. It come all the way from Philadelphia, they said. There was some books too, piled up perfectly exact, on each corner of the table. One was a big family Bible, full of pictures. One was "Pilgrim's Progress," about a man that left his family it didn't say why. I read considerable in it now and then. The statements was interesting, but tough. Another was "Friendship's Offering," full of beautiful stuff and poetry; but I didn't read the poetry. Another was Henry Clay's Speeches, and another was Dr. Gunn's Family Medicine, which told you all about what to do if a body was sick or dead. There was a Hymn Book, and a lot of other books. And there was nice split-bottom chairs, and perfectly sound, too—not bagged down in the middle and busted, like an old basket.

They had pictures hung on the walls—mainly Washingtons and Lafayettes, and battles, and Highland Marys, and one called "Signing the Declaration." There was some that they called crayons, which one of the daughters which was dead made her own self when she was only fifteen years old. They was different from any pictures I ever see before; blacker, mostly, than is common. One was a woman in a slim black dress, belted small under the arm-pits, with bulges like a cabbage in the middle of the sleeves, and a large black scoop-shovel bonnet with a black veil, and white slim ankles crossed about with black tape, and very wee black slippers, like a chisel, and she was leaning pensive on a tombstone on her right elbow, under a weeping willow, and her other hand hanging down her side holding a white handkerchief and a reticule, and underneath the picture it said "Shall I Never See Thee More Alas." Another one was a young lady with her hair all combed up straight to the top of her head, and knotted there in front of a comb like a chair-back, and she was crying into a handkerchief and had a dead bird laying on its back in her other hand with its heels up, and underneath the picture it said "I Shall Never Hear Thy Sweet Chirrup More Alas." There was one where a young lady was at a window looking up at the moon, and tears running down her cheeks; and she had an open letter in one hand with black sealing-wax showing on one edge of it, and she was mashing a locket with a chain to it against her mouth, and underneath the picture it said "And Art Thou Gone Yes Thou Art Gone Alas." These was all nice pictures, I reckon, but I didn't somehow seem to take to them, because if ever I was down a little, they always give me the fan-tods. Everybody was sorry she died, because she had laid out a lot more of these pictures to do, and a body could see by what she had done what they had lost. But I reckoned, that with her disposition, she was having a better time in the graveyard. She was at work on what they said was her greatest picture when she took sick, and every day and every night it was her prayer to be allowed to live till she got it done, but she never got the chance. It was a picture of a young woman in a long white gown, standing on the rail of a bridge all ready to jump off, with her hair all down her back, and looking up to the moon, with the tears running down her face, and she had two arms folded across her breast, and two arms stretched out in front, and two more reaching up towards the moon—and the idea was, to see which pair would look best and then scratch out all the other arms; but, as I was saying, she died before she got her mind made up, and now they kept this picture over the head of the bed in her room, and every time her birthday come they hung flowers on it. Other times it was hid with a little curtain. The young woman in the picture had a kind of nice sweet face, but there was so many arms it made her look too spidery, seemed to me.

This young girl kept a scrap-book when she was alive, and used to paste obituaries and accidents and cases of patient suffering in it out of the *Presbyterian Observer,* and write poetry after them out of her own head. It was very good poetry. This is what she wrote about a boy by the name of Stephen Dowling Bots that fell down a well and was drownded:

ODE TO STEPHEN DOWLING BOTS, DEC'D.

And did young Stephen sicken,
    And did young Stephen die?
And did the sad hearts thicken,
    And did the mourners cry?

No; such was not the fate of
    Young Stephen Dowling Bots;
Though sad hearts round him thickened,
    'Twas not from sickness' shots.

No whooping-cough did rack his frame,
    Nor measles drear, with spots;
Not these impaired the sacred name
    Of Stephen Dowling Bots.

Despised love struck not with woe
    That head of curly knots,
Nor stomach troubles laid him low,
    Young Stephen Dowling Bots.

O no. Then list with tearful eye,
    Whilst I his fate do tell.
His soul did from this cold world fly,
    By falling down a well.

They got him out and emptied him;
    Alas it was too late;
His spirit was gone for to sport aloft
    In the realms of the good and great.

If Emmeline Grangerford could make poetry like that before she was fourteen, there ain't no telling what she could a done by-and-by. Buck said she could rattle off poetry like nothing. She didn't ever have to stop to think. He said she would slap down a line, and if she couldn't find anything to rhyme with it she would just scratch it out and slap down another one, and go ahead. She warn't particular, she could write about anything you choose to give her to write about, just so it was sadful. Every time a man died, or a woman died, or a child died, she would be on hand with her "tribute" before he was cold. She called them tributes. The neighbors said it was the doctor first, then Emmeline, then the undertaker—the undertaker never got in ahead of Emmeline but once, and then she hung fire on a rhyme for the dead person's name, which was Whistler. She warn't ever the same, after that; she never complained, but she kind of pined away and did not live long. Poor thing, many's the time I made myself go up to the little room that used to be hers and get out her poor old scrapbook and read in it when her pictures had been aggravating me and I had soured on her a little. I liked all that family, dead ones and all, and warn't going to let anything come between us. Poor Emmeline made poetry about all the dead people when she was alive, and it didn't seem right that there warn't nobody to make some about her, now she was gone; so I tried to sweat out a verse or two myself, but I couldn't seem to make it go, somehow. They kept Emmeline's room trim and nice and all the things fixed in it just the way she liked to have them when she was alive, and nobody ever slept there. The old lady took care of the room herself, though there was plenty of niggers, and she sewed there a good deal and read her Bible there, mostly.

Well, as I was saying about the parlor, there was beautiful curtains on the windows: white, with pictures painted on them, of castles with vines all down the walls, and cattle coming down to drink. There was a little old piano, too, that had tin pans in it, I reckon, and nothing was ever so lovely as to hear the young ladies sing, "The Last Link is Broken" and play "The Battle of Prague" on it. The walls of all the rooms was plastered, and most had carpets on the floors, and the whole house was whitewashed on the outside.

It was a double house, and the big open place betwixt them was roofed and floored, and sometimes the table was set there in the middle of the day, and it was a cool, comfortable place. Nothing couldn't be better. And warn't the cooking good, and just bushels of it too!

Chapter XVIII

Col. Grangerford was a gentleman, you see. He was a gentleman all over; and so was his family. He was well born, as the saying is, and that's worth as much in a man as it is in a horse, so the Widow Douglass said, and nobody ever denied that she was of the first aristocracy in our town; and pap he always said it, too, though he warn't no more quality than a mudcat, himself. Col. Grangerford was very tall and very slim, and had a darkish-paly complexion, not a sign of red in it anywheres; he was clean-shaved every morning, all over his thin face, and he had the thinnest kind of lips, and the thinnest kind of nostrils, and a high nose, and heavy eyebrows, and the blackest kind of eyes, sunk so deep back that they seemed like they was looking out of caverns at you, as you may say. His forehead was high, and his hair was black and straight, and hung to his shoulders. His hands was long and thin, and every day of his life he put on a clean shirt and a full suit from head to foot made out of linen so white it hurt your eyes to look at it; and on Sundays he wore a blue tail-coat with brass buttons on it. He carried a mahogany cane with a silver head to it. There warn't no frivolishness about him, not a bit, and he warn't ever loud. He was as kind as he could be—you could feel that, you know, and so you had confidence. Sometimes he smiled, and it was good to see; but when he straightened himself up like a liberty-pole, and the lightning begun to flicker out from under his eyebrows you wanted to climb a tree first, and find out what the matter was afterwards. He didn't ever have to tell anybody to mind their manners—everybody was always good mannered where he was. Everybody loved to have him around, too; he was sunshine most always—I mean he made it seem like good weather. When he turned into a cloud-bank it was awful dark for half a minute and that was enough; there wouldn't nothing go wrong again for a week.

When him and the old lady come down in the morning, all the family got up out of their chairs and give them good-day, and didn't set down again till they had set down. Then Tom and Bob went to the sideboard where the decanters was, and mixed a glass of bitters and handed it to him, and he held it in his hand and waited till Tom's and Bob's was mixed, and then they bowed and said "Our duty to you, sir, and madam;" and *they* bowed the least bit in the world and said thank you, and so they drank, all three, and Bob and Tom poured a spoonful of water on the sugar and the mite of whisky or apple brandy in the bottom of their tumblers, and give it to me and Buck, and we drank to the old people too.

Bob was the oldest, and Tom next. Tall, beautiful men with very broad shoulders and brown faces, and long black hair and black eyes. They dressed in white linen from head to foot, like the old gentleman, and wore broad Panama hats.

Then there was Miss Charlotte, she was twenty-five, and tall and proud and grand, but as good as she could be, when she warn't stirred up; but when she was, she had a look that would make you wilt in your tracks, like her father. She was beautiful.

So was her sister, Miss Sophia, but it was a different kind. She was gentle and sweet, like a dove, and she was only twenty.

Each person had their own nigger to wait on them—Buck, too. My nigger had a monstrous easy time, because I warn't used to having anybody do anything for me, but Buck's was on the jump most of the time.

This was all there was of the family, now; but there used to be more—three sons; they got killed; and Emmeline that died.

The old gentleman owned a lot of farms, and over a hundred niggers. Sometimes a stack of people would come there, horseback, from ten or fifteen mile around, and stay five or six days, and have such junketings round about and on the river, and dances and picnics in the woods, day-times, and balls at the house, nights. These people was mostly kin-folks of the family. The men brought their guns with them. It was a handsome lot of quality, I tell you.

There was another clan of aristocracy around there—five or six families—mostly of the name of Shepherdson. They was as high-toned, and well born, and rich and grand, as the tribe of Grangerfords. The Shepherdsons and the Grangerfords used the same steamboat landing, which was about two mile above our house; so sometimes when I went up there with a lot of our folks I used to see a lot of the Shepherdsons there, on their fine horses.

One day Buck and me was away out in the woods, hunting, and heard a horse coming. We was crossing the road. Buck says:

"Quick! Jump for the woods!"

We done it, and then peeped down the woods through the leaves. Pretty soon a splendid young man come galloping down the road, setting his horse easy and looking like a soldier. He had his gun across his pommel. I had seen him before. It was young Harney Shepherdson. I heard Buck's gun go off at my ear, and Harney's hat tumbled off from his head. He grabbed his gun and rode straight to the place where we was hid. But we didn't wait. We started through the woods on a run. The woods warn't thick, so I looked over my shoulder, to dodge the bullet, and twice I seen Harney cover Buck with his gun; and then he rode away the way he come—to get his hat, I reckon, but I couldn't see. We never stopped running till we got home. The old gentleman's eyes blazed a minute—'twas pleasure, mainly, I judged—then his face sort of smoothed down, and he says, kind of gentle:

"I don't like that shooting from behind a bush. Why didn't you step into the road, my boy?"

"The Shepherdsons don't father. They always take advantage."

Miss Charlotte she held her head up like a queen while Buck was telling his tale, and her nostrils spread and her eyes snapped. The two young men looked dark, but never said nothing. Miss Sophia she turned pale, but the color come back when she found the man warn't hurt.

Soon as I could get Buck down by the corn-cribs under the trees by ourselves, I says:

"Did you want to kill him, Buck?"

"Well, I bet I did."

"What did he do to you?"

"Him? He never done nothing to me."

"Well, then, what did you want to kill him for?"

"Why nothing—only it's on account of the feud."

"What's a feud?"

"Why, where was you raised? Don't you know what a feud is?"

"Never heard of it before—tell me about it."

"Well," says Buck, "a feud is this way. A man has a quarrel with another man, and kills him; then that other man's brother kills *him;* then the other brothers, on both sides, goes for one another; then the *cousins* chip in—and by-and-by everybody's killed off, and there ain't no more feud. But it's kind of slow, and takes a long time."

"Has this one been going on long, Buck?"

"Well I should *reckon!* it started thirty year ago, or som'ers along there. There was trouble 'bout something and then a lawsuit to settle it; and the suit went agin one of the men, and so he up and shot the man that won the suit—which he would naturally do, of course. Anybody would."

"What was the trouble about, Buck?—land?"

"I reckon maybe—I don't know."

"Well, who done the shooting?—was it a Grangerford or a Shepherdson?"

"Laws, how do *I* know? it was so long ago."

"Don't anybody know?"

"Oh, yes, pa knows, I reckon, and some of the other old folks; but they don't know, now, what the row was about in the first place."

"Has there been many killed, Buck?"

"Yes—right smart chance of funerals. But they don't always kill. Pa's got a few buck-shot in him; but he don't mind it 'cuz he don't weigh much anyway. Bob's been carved up some with a bowie, and Tom's been hurt once or twice."

"Has anybody been killed this year, Buck?"

"Yes, we got one and they got one. 'Bout three months ago, my cousin Bud, fourteen year old, was riding through the woods, on t'other side of the river, and didn't have no weapon with him, which was blame' foolishness, and in a lonesome place he hears a horse a-coming behind him, and sees old Baldy Shepherdson a-linkin' after him with his gun in his hand and his white hair a-flying in the wind; and 'stead of jumping off and taking to the brush, Bud 'lowed he could outrun him; so they had it, nip and tuck, for five mile or more, the old man a-gaining all the time; so at last Bud seen it warn't any use, so he stopped and faced around so as to have the bullet holes in front, you know, and the old man he rode up and shot him down. But he didn't git much chance to enjoy his luck, for inside of a week our folks laid *him* out."

"I reckon that old man was a coward, Buck."

"I reckon he *warn't* a coward. Not by a blame' sight. There ain't a coward amongst them Shepherdsons—not a one. And there ain't no cowards amongst the Grangerfords, either. Why, that old man kep' up his end in a fight one day, for a half an hour, against three Grangerfords, and come out winner. They was all a-horseback; he lit off of his horse and got behind a little wood-pile, and kep' his horse before him to stop the bullets; but the Grangerfords staid on their horses and capered around the old man, and peppered away at him, and he peppered away at them. Him and his horse both went home pretty leaky and crippled, but the Grangerfords had to be *fetched* home—and one of 'em was dead, and another died the next day. No, sir, if a body's out hunting for cowards, he don't want to fool away any time amongst them Shepherdsons, becuz they don't breed any of that *kind*."

Next Sunday we all went to church, about three mile, everybody a-horseback. The men took their guns along, so did Buck, and kept them between their knees or stood them handy against the wall. The Shepherdsons done the same. It was pretty ornery preaching—all about brotherly love, and such-like tiresomeness; but everybody said it was a good sermon, and they all talked it over going home, and had such a powerful lot to say about faith, and good works, and free grace, and preforeordestination, and I don't know what all, that it did seem to me to be one of the roughest Sundays I had run across yet.

About an hour after dinner everybody was dozing around, some in their chairs and some in their rooms, and it got to be pretty dull. Buck and a dog was stretched out on the grass in the sun, sound asleep. I went up to our room, and judged I would take a nap myself. I found that sweet Miss Sophia standing in her door, which was next to ours, and she took me in her room and shut the door very soft, and asked me if I liked her, and I said I did; and she asked me if I would do something for her and not tell anybody, and I said I would. Then she said she'd forgot her Testament, and left it in the seat at church, between two other books and would I slip out quiet and go there and fetch it to her, and not say nothing to nobody. I said I would. So I slid out and slipped off up the road, and there warn't anybody at the church, except maybe a hog or two, for there warn't any lock on the door, and hogs likes a puncheon floor in summer-time because it's cool. If you notice, most folks don't go to church only when they've got to; but a hog is different.

Says I to myself something's up—it ain't natural for a girl to be in such a sweat about a Testament; so I give it a shake, and out drops a little piece of paper with "*Half-past two*" wrote on it with a pencil. I ransacked it, but I couldn't find anything else. I couldn't make anything out of that, so I put the paper in the book again, and when I got home and up stairs, there was Miss Sophia in her door waiting for me. She pulled me in and shut the door; then she looked in the Testament till she found the paper, and as soon as she read it she looked glad; and before a body could think, she grabbed me and give me a squeeze, and said I was the best boy in the world, and not to tell anybody. She was mighty red in the face, for a minute, and her eyes lighted up and it made her powerful pretty. I was a good deal astonished, but when I got my breath I asked her what the paper was about, and she asked me if I had read it, and I said no, and she asked me if I could read writing, and I told her "no, only coarse-hand," and then she said the paper warn't anything but a book-mark to keep her place, and I might go and play now.

I went off down to the river, studying over this thing, and pretty soon I noticed that my nigger was following along behind. When we was out of sight of the house, he looked back and around a second, and then comes a-running, and says:

"Mars Jawge, if you'll come down into de swamp, I'll show you a whole stack o' water-moccasins."

Thinks I, that's might curious; he said that yesterday. He oughter know a body don't love water-moccasins enough to go around hunting for them. What is he up to anyway? So I says—

"All right, trot ahead."

I followed a half a mile, then he struck out over the swamp and waded ankle deep as much as another half mile. We come to a little flat piece of land which was dry and very thick with trees and bushes and vines, and he says—

"You shove right in dah, jist a few steps, Mars Jawge, dah's whah dey is. I's seed 'm befo', I don't k'yer to see 'em no mo'."

Then he slopped right along and went away, and pretty soon the trees hid him. I poked into the place a-ways, and come to a little open patch as big as a bedroom, all hung around with vines, and found a man laying there asleep—and by jings it was my old Jim!

I waked him up, and I reckoned it was going to be a grand surprise to him to see me again, but it warn't. He nearly cried, he was so glad, but he warn't surprised. Said he swum along behind me, that night, and heard me yell every time, but dasn't answer, because he didn't want nobody to pick *him* up, and take him into slavery again. Says he—

"I got hurt a little, en couldn't swim fas', so I wuz a considable ways behine you, towards de las'; when you landed I reck'ned I could ketch up wid you on de lan' 'dout havin' to shout at you, but when I see dat house I begin to go slow. I 'uz off too fur to hear what dey say to you—I wuz 'fraid o' de dogs—but when it uz all quiet agin, I knowed you's in de house, so I struck out for de woods to wait for day. Early in de mawnin' some er de niggers come along, gwyne to de fields, en dey tuck me en showed me dis place, whah de dogs can't track me on accounts o' de water, en dey brings me truck to eat every night, en tells me how you's a gitt'n along."

"Why didn't you tell my Jack to fetch me here sooner, Jim?"

"Well, 'twarn't no use to 'sturb you, Huck, tell we could do sumfn—but we's all right now. I ben a-buyin' pots en pans en vittles, as I got a chanst, en a patchin' up de raf', nights, when——"

"*What* raft, Jim?"

"Our ole raf'."

"You mean to say our old raft warn't smashed all to flinders?"

"No, she warn't. She was tore up a good deal—one en' of her was—but dey warn't no great harm done, on'y our traps was mos' all los'. Ef we hadn' dive' so deep en swum so fur under water, en de night hadn' ben so dark, en we warn't so sk'yerd, en ben sich punkin-heads, as de sayin' is, we'd a seed de raf'. But it's jis' as well we didn't, 'kase now she's all fixed up agin mos' as good as new, en we's got a new lot o' stuff, too, in de place o' what 'us los'."

"Why, how did you get hold of the raft again, Jim—did you catch her?"

"How I gwyne to ketch her, en I out in de woods? No, some er de niggers foun' her ketched on a snag, along heah in de ben', en dey hid her in a crick, 'mongst de willows, en dey wuz so much jawin' 'bout which un 'um she b'long to de mos', dat I come to heah 'bout it pooty soon, so I ups en settles de trouble by tellin' 'um she don't b'long to none uv um, but to you en me; en I ast 'm if dey gwyne to grab a young white genlman's propaty, en git a hid'n for it? Den I gin 'm ten cents apiece, en dey 'uz mighty well satis-fied, en wisht some mo' raf's 'ud come along en make 'm rich agin. Dey's mighty good to me, dese niggers is, en whatever I wants 'm to do fur me, I doan' have to ast 'm twice, honey. Dat Jack's a good nigger, en pooty smart."

"Yes, he is. He ain't ever told me you was here; told me to come, and he'd show me a lot of water-moccasins. If anything happens, *he* ain't mixed up in it. He can say he never seen us together, and it'll be the truth."

I don't want to talk much about the next day. I reckon I'll cut it pretty short. I waked up about dawn, and was agoing to turn over and go to sleep again, when I noticed how still it was—didn't seem to be anybody stirring. That warn't usual. Next I noticed that Buck was up and gone. Well, I gets up, a-wondering, and goes down stairs—nobody around; everything as still as a mouse. Just the same outside; thinks I, what does it mean? Down by the wood-pile I comes across my Jack, and says:

"What's it all about?"

Says he:

"Don't you know, Mars Jawge?"

"No," says I, "I don't."

"Well, den, Miss Sophia's run off! 'deed she has. She run off in de night, sometime—nobody don't know jis' when—run off to git married to dat young Harney Shepherd-son, you know—leastways, so dey 'spec. De fambly foun' it out, 'bout half an hour ago—maybe a little mo'—en' I *tell* you dey warn't no time los'. Sich another hurryin' up guns en hosses *you* never see! De women folks has gone for to stir up de relations, en ole Mars Saul en de boys tuck dey guns en rode up de river road for to try to ketch dat young man en kill him 'fo' he kin git acrost de river wid Miss Sophia. I reck'n dey's gwyne to be mighty rough times."

"Buck went off 'thout waking me up."

"Well I reck'n he *did*! Dey warn't gwyne to mix you up in it. Mars Buck he loaded up his gun en 'lowed he's gwyne to fetch home a Shepherdson or bust. Well, dey'll be plenty un 'm dah, I reck'n, en you bet you he'll fetch one ef he gits a chanst."

I took up the river road as hard as I could put. By-and-by I begin to hear guns a good ways off. When I come in sight of the log store and the wood-pile where the steamboats lands, I worked along under the trees and brush till I got to a good place, and then I clumb up into the forks of a cotton-wood that was out of reach, and watched. There was a wood-rank four foot high, a little ways in front of the tree, and first I was going to hide behind that; but maybe it was luckier I didn't.

There was four or five men cavorting around on their horses in the open place be-fore the log store, cussing and yelling, and trying to get at a couple of young chaps that was behind the wood-rank alongside of the steamboat landing—but they couldn't come it. Every time one of them showed himself on the river side of the wood-pile he got shot at. The two boys was squatting back to back behind the pile, so they could watch both ways.

By-and-by the men stopped cavorting around and yelling. They started riding towards the store; then up gets one of the boys, draws a steady bead over the wood-rank, and drops one of them out of his saddle. All the men jumped off of their horses and grabbed the hurt one and started to carry him to the store; and that minute the two boys started on the run. They got half-way to the tree I was in before the men noticed. Then the men see them, and jumped on their horses and took out after them. They gained on the boys, but it didn't do no good, the boys had too good a start; they got to the wood-pile that was in front of my tree, and slipped in behind it, and so they had the bulge on the men again. One of the boys was Buck, and the other was a slim young chap about nineteen years old.

The men ripped around awhile, and then rode away. As soon as they was out of sight, I sung out to Buck and told him. He didn't know what to make of my voice coming out of the tree, at first. He was awful surprised. He told me to watch out sharp and let him know when the men come in sight again; said they was up to some devilment or other—wouldn't be gone long. I wished I was out of that tree, but I dasn't come down. Buck begun to cry and rip, and 'lowed that him and his cousin Joe (that was the other young chap) would make up for this day, yet. He said his father and his two brothers was killed, and two or three of the enemy. Said the Shepherdsons laid for them, in ambush. Buck said his father and brothers ought to waited for their relations—the Shepherdsons was too strong for them. I asked him what was become of young Harney and Miss Sophia. He said they'd got across the river and was safe. I was glad of that; but the way Buck did take on because he didn't manage to kill Harney that day he shot at him—I hain't ever heard anything like it.

All of a sudden, bang! bang! bang! goes three or four guns—the men had slipped around through the woods and come in from behind without their horses! The boys jumped for the river—both of them hurt—and as they swum down the current the men run along the bank shooting at them and singing out, "Kill them, kill them!" It made me so sick I most fell out of the tree. I ain't agoing to tell *all* that happened—it would make me sick again if I was to do that. I wished I hadn't ever come ashore that night, to see such things. I ain't ever going to get shut of them—lots of times I dream about them.

I staid in the tree till it begun to get dark, afraid to come down. Sometimes I heard guns away off in the woods; and twice I seen little gangs of men gallop past the log store with guns; so I reckoned the trouble was still agoing on. I was mighty down-hearted; so I made up my mind I wouldn't ever go anear that house again, because I reckoned I was to blame, somehow. I judged that that piece of paper meant that Miss Sophia was to meet Harney somewheres at half-past two and run off; and I judged I ought to told her father about that paper and the curious way she acted, and then maybe he would a locked her up and this awful mess wouldn't ever happened.

When I got down out of the tree, I crept along down the river bank a piece, and found the two bodies laying in the edge of the water, and tugged at them till I got them ashore; then I covered up their faces, and got away as quick as I could. I cried a little when I was covering up Buck's face, for he was mighty good to me.

It was just dark, now. I never went near the house, but struck through the woods and made for the swamp. Jim warn't on his island, so I tramped off in a hurry for the crick, and crowded through the willows, red-hot to jump aboard and get out of that awful country—the raft was gone! My souls, but I was scared! I couldn't get my breath for most a minute. Then I raised a yell. A voice not twenty-five foot from me, says—

"Good lan'! is dat you, honey? Doan' make no noise."

It was Jim's voice—nothing ever sounded so good before. I run along the bank a piece and got aboard, and Jim he grabbed me and hugged me, he was so glad to see me. He says—

"Laws bless you, chile, I 'uz right down sho' you's dead agin. Jack's been heah, he say he reck'n you's ben shot, kase you didn' come home no mo'; so I's jes' dis minute a startin' de raf' down towards de mouf er de crick, so's to be all ready for to shove out en leave soon as Jack comes agin en tells me for certain you *is* dead. Lawsy, I's mighty glad to git you back agin, honey."

I says—

"All right—that's mighty good; they won't find me, and they'll think I've been killed, and floated down the river—there's something up there that'll help them to think so—so don't you lose no time, Jim, but just shove off for the big water as fast as ever you can."

I never felt easy till the raft was two mile below there and out in the middle of the Mississippi. Then we hung up our signal lantern, and judged that we was free and safe once more. I hadn't had a bite to eat since yesterday; so Jim he got out some corn-dodgers and buttermilk, and pork and cabbage, and greens—there ain't nothing in the world so good, when it's cooked right—and whilst I eat my supper, we talked, and had a good time. I was powerful glad to get away from the feuds, and so was Jim to get away from the swamp. We said there warn't no home like a raft, after all. Other places do seem so cramped up and smothery, but a raft don't. You feel mighty free and easy and comfortable on a raft.

Chapter XIX

Two or three days and nights went by; I reckon I might say they swum by, they slid along so quiet and smooth and lovely. Here is the way we put in the time. It was a monstrous big river down there—sometimes a mile and a half wide; we run nights, and laid up and hid day-times; soon as night was most gone, we stopped navigating and tied up—nearly always in the dead water under a towhead; and then cut young cotton-woods and willows and hid the raft with them. Then we set out the lines. Next we slid into the river and had a swim, so as to freshen up and cool off; then we set down on the sandy bottom where the water was about knee deep, and watched the daylight come. Not a sound, anywheres—perfectly still—just like the whole world was asleep, only sometimes the bull-frogs a-cluttering, maybe. The first thing to see, looking away over the water, was a kind of dull line—that was the woods on t'other side—you couldn't make nothing else out; then a pale place in the sky; then more paleness, spreading around; then the river softened up, away off, and warn't black any more, but gray; you could see little dark spots drifting along, ever so far away—trading scows, and such things; and long black streaks—rafts; sometimes you could hear a sweep screaking; or jumbled up voices, it was so still, and sounds come so far; and by-and-by you could see a streak on the water which you know by the look of the streak that there's a snag there in a swift current which breaks on it and makes that streak look that way; and you see the mist curl up off of the water, and the east reddens up, and the river, and you make out a log cabin in the edge of the woods, away on the bank on t'other side of the river, being a wood-yard, likely, and piled by them cheats so you can throw a dog through it anywheres; then the nice breeze springs up, and comes fanning you from over there, so cool and fresh, and sweet to smell, on account of the woods and the flowers; but sometimes not that way, because they've left dead fish laying around, gars, and such, and they do get pretty rank; and next you've got the full day, and everything smiling in the sun, and the song-birds just going it!

A little smoke couldn't be noticed, now, so we would take some fish off of the lines, and cook up a hot breakfast. And afterwards we would watch the lonesomeness of the river, and kind of lazy along, and by-and-by lazy off to sleep. Wake up, by-and-by, and look to see what done it, and maybe see a steamboat, coughing along up stream, so far off towards the other side you couldn't tell nothing about her only whether she was stern-wheel or side-wheel; then for about an hour there wouldn't be nothing to hear nor nothing to see—just solid lonesomeness. Next you'd see a raft sliding by, away off yonder, and maybe a galoot on it chopping, because they're most always doing it on a raft; you'd see the ax flash, and come down—you don't hear nothing; you see that ax go up again, and by the time it's above the man's head, then you hear the *k'chunk!*—it had took all that time to come over the water. So we would put in the day, lazying around, listening to the stillness. Once there was a thick fog, and the rafts and things that went by was beating tin pans so the steamboats wouldn't run over them. A scow or a raft went by so close we could hear them talking and cussing and laughing—heard them plain; but we couldn't see no sign of them; it made you feel crawly, it was like spirits carrying on that way in the air. Jim said he believed it was spirits; but I says:

"No, spirits wouldn't say, 'dern the dern fog.'"

Soon as it was night, out we shoved; when we got her out to about the middle, we let her alone, and let her float wherever the current wanted her to; then we lit the pipes, and dangled our legs in the water and talked about all kinds of things—we was always naked, day and night, whenever the mosquitoes would let us—the new clothes Buck's folks made for me was too good to be comfortable, and besides I didn't go much on clothes, nohow.

Sometimes we'd have that whole river all to ourselves for the longest time. Yonder was the banks and the islands, across the water; and maybe a spark—which was a candle in a cabin window—and sometimes on the water you could see a spark or two—on a raft or a scow, you know; and maybe you could hear a fiddle or a song coming over from one of them crafts. It's lovely to live on a raft. We had the sky, up there, all speckled with stars, and we used to lay on our backs and look up at them, and discuss about whether they was made, or only just happened—Jim he allowed they was made, but I allowed they happened; I judged it would have took too long to *make* so many. Jim said the moon could a *laid* them; well, that looked kind of reasonable, so I didn't say nothing against it, because I've seen a frog lay most as many, so of course it could be done. We used to watch the stars that fell, too, and see them streak down. Jim allowed they'd got spoiled and was hove out of the nest.

Once or twice of a night we would see a steamboat slipping along in the dark, and now and then she would belch a whole world of sparks up out of her chimbleys, and they would rain down in the river and look awful pretty; then she would turn a corner and her lights would wink out and her pow-wow shut off and leave the river still again; and by-and-by her waves would get to us, a long time after she was gone, and joggle the raft a bit, and after that you wouldn't hear nothing for you couldn't tell how long, except maybe frogs or something.

After midnight the people on shore went to bed, and then for two or three hours the shores was black—no more sparks in the cabin windows. These sparks was our clock—the first one that showed again meant morning was coming, so we hunted place to hide and tie up, right away.

One morning about day-break, I found a canoe and crossed over a chute to the main shore—it was only two hundred yards—and paddled about a mile up a crick amongst the cypress woods, to see if I couldn't get some berries. Just as I was passing a place where a kind of a cow-path crossed the crick, here comes a couple of men tearing up the path as tight as they could foot it. I thought I was a goner, for whenever anybody was after anybody I judged it was *me*—or maybe Jim. I was about to dig out from there in a hurry, but they was pretty close to me then, and sung out and begged me to save their lives—said they hadn't been doing nothing, and was being chased for it—said there was men and dogs a-coming. They wanted to jump right in, but I says—

"Don't you do it. I don't hear the dogs and horses yet; you've got time to crowd through the brush and get up the crick a little ways; then you take to the water and wade down to me and get in—that'll throw the dogs off the scent."

They done it, and soon as they was aboard I lit out for our tow-head, and in about five or ten minutes we heard the dogs and the men away off, shouting. We heard them come along towards the crick, but couldn't see them; they seemed to stop and fool around a while; then, as we got further and further away all the time, we couldn't hardly hear them at all; by the time we had left a mile of woods behind us and struck the river, everything was quiet, and we paddled over to the tow-head and hid in the cottonwoods and was safe.

One of these fellows was about seventy, or upwards, and had a bald head and very gray whiskers. He had an old battered-up slouch hat on, and a greasy blue woolen shirt, and ragged old blue jeans britches stuffed into his boot tops, and home-knit galluses—no, he only had one. He had an old long-tailed blue jeans coat with slick brass buttons, flung over his arm, and both of them had big fat ratty-looking carpet-bags.

The other fellow was about thirty and dressed about as ornery. After breakfast we all laid off and talked, and the first thing that come out was that these chaps didn't know one another.

"What got you into trouble?" says the baldhead to t'other chap.

"Well, I'd been selling an article to take the tartar off the teeth—and it does take it off, too, and generly the enamel along with it—but I staid about one night longer than I ought to, and was just in the act of sliding out when I ran across you on the trail this side of town, and you told me they were coming, and begged me to help you to get off. So I told you I was expecting trouble myself and would scatter out *with* you. That's the whole yarn—what's yourn?"

"Well, I'd ben a-runnin' a little temperance revival thar, 'bout a week, and was the pet of the women folks, big and little, for I was makin' it mighty warm for the rummies, I *tell* you, and takin' as much as five or six dollars a night—ten cents a head, children and niggers free—and business a growin' all the time; when somehow or another a little report got around, last night, that I had a way of puttin' in my time with a private jug, on the sly. A nigger rousted me out this mornin', and told me the people was getherin' on the quiet, with their dogs and horses, and they'd be along pretty soon and give me 'bout half an hour's start, and then run me down, if they could; and if they got me they'd tar and feather me and ride me on a rail, sure. I didn't wait for no breakfast—I warn't hungry."

"Old man," says the young one, "I reckon we might double-team it together; what do you think?"

"I ain't undisposed. What's your line—mainly?"

"Jour printer, by trade; do a little in patent medicines; theatre-actor—tragedy, you know; take a turn at mesmerism and phrenology when there's a chance; teach singing-geography school for a change; sling a lecture, sometimes—oh, I do lots of things—most anything that comes handy, so it ain't work. What's your lay?"

"I've done considerble in the doctoring way in my time. Layin' on o' hands is my best holt—for cancer, and paralysis, and sich things; and I k'n tell a fortune pretty good, when I've got somebody along to find out the facts for me. Preachin's my line, too; and workin' camp-meetin's; and missionaryin around."

Nobody never said anything for a while; then the young man hove a sigh and says—

"Alas!"

"What're you alassin' about?" says the baldhead.

"To think I should have lived to be leading such a life, and be degraded down into such company." And he begun to wipe the corner of his eye with a rag.

"Dern your skin, ain't the company good enough for you?" says the baldhead, pretty pert and uppish.

"Yes, it *is* good enough for me; it's as good as I deserve; for who fetched me so low, when I was so high? *I* did myself. I don't blame *you*, gentlemen—far from it; I don't blame anybody. I deserve it all. Let the cold world do its worst; one thing I know—there's a grave somewhere for me. The world may go on just as its always done, and take everything from me—loved ones, property, everything—but it can't take that. Some day I'll lie down in it and forget it all, and my poor broken heart will be at rest." He went on a-wiping.

"Drot your pore broken heart," says the baldhead; "what are you heaving your pore broken heart at *us* f'r? *We* hain't done nothing."

"No, I know you haven't. I ain't blaming you, gentlemen. I brought myself down—yes, I did it myself. It's right I should suffer—perfectly right—I don't make any moan."

"Brought you down from whar? Whar was you brought down from?"

"Ah, you would not believe me; the world never believes—let it pass—'tis no matter. The secret of my birth——"

"The secret of your birth? Do you mean to say——"

"Gentlemen," says the young man, very solemn, "I will reveal it to you, for I feel I may have confidence in you. By rights I am a duke!"

Jim's eyes bugged out when he heard that; and I reckon mine did, too. Then the baldhead says: "No! you can't mean it?"

"Yes. My great-grandfather, eldest son of the Duke of Bridgewater, fled to this country about the end of the last century, to breathe the pure air of freedom; married here, and died, leaving a son, his own father dying about the same time. The second son of the late duke seized the title and estates—the infant real duke was ignored. I am the lineal descendant of that infant—I am the rightful Duke of Bridgewater; and here am I, forlorn, torn from my high estate, hunted of men, despised by the cold world, ragged, worn, heart-broken, and degraded to the companionship of felons on a raft!"

Jim pitied him ever so much, and so did I. We tried to comfort him, but he said it warn't much use, he couldn't be much comforted; said if we was a mind to acknowledge him, that would do him more good than most anything else; so we said we would, if he would tell us how. He said we ought to bow, when we spoke to him, and say, "Your Grace," or "My Lord," or "Your Lordship"—and he wouldn't mind it if we called him plain "Bridgewater," which he said was a title, anyway, and not a name; and one of us ought to wait on him at dinner, and do any little thing for him he wanted done.

Well, that was all easy, so we done it. All through dinner Jim stood around and waited on him, and says, "Will yo' Grace have some o' dis, or some o' dat?" and so on, and a body could see it was mighty pleasing to him.

But the old man got pretty silent, by-and-by—didn't have much to say, and didn't look pretty comfortable over all that petting that was going on around that duke. He seemed to have something on his mind. So, along in the afternoon, he says:

"Looky here, Bilgewater," he says, "I'm nation sorry for you, but you ain't the only person that's had troubles like that."

"No?"

"No, you ain't. You ain't the only person that's ben snaked down wrongfully out'n a high place."

"Alas!"

"No, you ain't the only person that's had a secret of his birth." And by jings, *he* begins to cry.

"Hold! What do you mean?"

"Bilgewater, kin I trust you?" says the old man, still sort of sobbing.

"To the bitter death!" He took the old man by the hand and squeezed it, and says, "The secret of your being: speak!"

"Bilgewater, I am the late Dauphin!"

You bet you Jim and me stared, this time. Then the duke says:

"You are what?"

"Yes, my friend, it is too true—your eyes is lookin' at this very moment on the pore disappeared Dauphin, Looy the Seventeen, son of Looy the Sixteen and Marry Antonette."

"You! At your age! No! You mean you're the late Charlemagne; you must be six or seven hundred years old, at the very least."

"Trouble has done it, Bilgewater, trouble has done it; trouble has brung these gray hairs and this premature balditude. Yes, gentlemen, you see before you, in blue jeans and misery, the wanderin', exiled, trampled-on and sufferin' rightful King of France."

Well, he cried and took on so, that me and Jim didn't know hardly what to do, we was so sorry—and so glad and proud we'd got him with us, too. So we set in, like we done before with the duke, and tried to comfort *him*. But he said it warn't no use, nothing but to be dead and done with it all could do him any good; though he said it often made him feel easier and better for a while if people treated him according to his rights, and got down on one knee to speak to him, and always called him "Your Majesty," and waited on him first at meals, and didn't set down in his presence till he asked them. So

Jim and me set to majestying him, and doing this and that and t'other for him, and standing up till he told us we might set down. This done him heaps of good, and so he got cheerful and comfortable. But the duke kind of soured on him, and didn't look a bit satisfied with the way things was going; still, the king acted real friendly towards him, and said the duke's great-grandfather and all the other Dukes of Bilgewater was a good deal thought of by *his* father and was allowed to come to the palace considerable; but the duke staid huffy a good while, till by-and-by the king says:

"Like as not we got to be together a blamed long time, on this h-yer raft, Bilgewater, and so what's the use o' your bein' sour? It'll only make things oncomfortable. It ain't my fault I warn't born a duke, it ain't your fault you warn't born a king—so what's the use to worry? Make the best o' things the way you find 'em, says I—that's my motto. This ain't no bad thing that we've struck here—plenty grub and an easy life—come, give us your hand, Duke, and less all be friends."

The duke done it, and Jim and me was pretty glad to see it. It took away all the uncomfortableness, and we felt mighty good over it, because it would a been a miserable business to have any unfriendliness on the raft; for what you want, above all things, on a raft, is for everybody to be satisfied, and feel right and kind towards the others.

It didn't take me long to make up my mind that these liars warn't no kings nor dukes, at all, but just low-down humbugs and frauds. But I never said nothing, never let on; kept it to myself; it's the best way; then you don't have no quarrels, and don't get into no trouble. If they wanted us to call them kings and dukes, I hadn't no objections, 'long as it would keep peace in the family; and it warn't no use to tell Jim, so I didn't tell him. If I never learnt nothing else out of pap, I learnt that the best way to get along with his kind of people is to let them have their own way.

Chapter XX

They asked us considerable many questions; wanted to know what we covered up the raft that way for, and laid by in the day-time instead of running—was Jim a runaway nigger? Says I—

"Goodness sakes, would a runaway nigger run *south*?"

No, they allowed he wouldn't. I had to account for things some way, so I says:

"My folks was living in Pike County, in Missouri, where I was born, and they all died off but me and pa and my brother Ike. Pa, he 'lowed he'd break up and go down and live with Uncle Ben, who's got a little one-horse place on the river, forty-four mile below Orleans. Pa was pretty poor, and had some debts; so when he'd squared up there warn't nothing left but sixteen dollars and our nigger, Jim. That warn't enough to take us fourteen hundred mile, deck passage nor no other way. Well, when the river rose, pa had a streak of luck one day; he ketched this piece of a raft; so we reckoned we'd go down to Orleans on it. Pa's luck didn't hold out; a steamboat run over the forrard corner of the raft, one night, and we all went overboard and dove under the wheel; Jim and me come up, all right, but pa was drunk, and Ike was only four years old, so they never come up no more. Well, for the next day or two we had considerable trouble, because people was always coming out in skiffs and trying to take Jim away from me, saying they believed he was a runaway nigger. We don't run day-times no more, now; nights they don't bother us."

The duke says—

"Leave me alone to cipher out a way so we can run in the day-time if we want to. I'll think the thing over—I'll invent a plan that'll fix it. We'll let it alone for to-day, because of course we don't want to go by that town yonder in daylight—it mightn't be healthy."

Towards night it begun to darken up and look like rain; the heat lightning was squirting around, low down in the sky, and the leaves was beginning to shiver—it was going to be pretty ugly, it was easy to see that. So the duke and the king went to overhauling our wigwam, to see what the beds was like. My bed was a straw tick—better than Jim's, which was a corn-shuck tick; there's always cobs around about in a shuck tick, and they poke into you and hurt; and when you roll over, the dry shucks sound like you was rolling over in a pile of dead leaves; it makes such a rustling that you wake up. Well, the duke allowed he would take my bed; but the king allowed he wouldn't. He says—

"I should a reckoned the difference in rank would a sejested to you that a corn-shuck bed warn't just fitten for me to sleep on. Your Grace'll take the shuck bed yourself."

Jim and me was in a sweat again, for a minute, being afraid there was going to be some more trouble amongst them; so we was pretty glad when the duke says—

"'Tis my fate to be always ground into the mire under the iron heel of oppression. Misfortune has broken my once haughty spirit; I yield, I submit; 'tis my fate. I am alone in the world—let me suffer; I can bear it."

We got away as soon as it was good and dark. The king told us to stand well out towards the middle of the river, and not show a light till we got a long ways below the town. We come in sight of the little bunch of lights by-and-by—that was the town, you know—and slid by, about a half a mile out, all right. When we was three-quarters of a mile below, we hoisted up our signal lantern; and about ten o'clock it come on to rain and blow and thunder and lighten like everything; so the king told us to both stay on watch till the weather got better; then him and the duke crawled into the wigwam and turned in for the night. It was my watch below, till twelve, but I wouldn't a turned in, anyway, if I'd had a bed; because a body don't see such a storm as that every day in the week, not by a long sight. My souls, how the wind did scream along! And every second or two there'd come a glare that lit up the white-caps for a half a mile around, and you'd see the islands looking dusty through the rain, and the trees thrashing around in the wind; then comes a *h-wack!*—bum! bum! bumble-umble-um-bum-bum-bum-bum—and the thunder would go rumbling and grumbling away, and quit—and then *rip* comes another flash and another sockdolager. The waves most washed me off the raft, sometimes, but I hadn't any clothes on, and didn't mind. We didn't have no trouble about snags; the lightning was glaring and flittering around so constant that we could see them plenty soon enough to throw her head this way or that and miss them.

I had the middle watch, you know, but I was pretty sleepy by that time, so Jim he said he would stand the first half of it for me; he was always mighty good, that way, Jim was. I crawled into the wigwam, but the king and the duke had their legs sprawled around so there warn't no show for me; so I laid outside—I didn't mind the rain, because it was warm, and the waves warn't running so high, now. About two they come up again, though, and Jim was going to call me, but he changed his mind because he reckoned they warn't high enough yet to do any harm; but he was mistaken about that, for pretty soon all of a sudden along comes a regular ripper, and washed me overboard. It most killed Jim a-laughing. He was the easiest nigger to laugh that ever was, anyway.

I took the watch, and Jim he laid down and snored away; and by-and-by the storm let up for good and all; and the first cabin-light that showed, I rousted him out and we slid the raft into hiding-quarters for the day.

The king got out an old ratty deck of cards, after breakfast, and him and the duke played seven-up a while, five cents a game. Then they got tired of it, and allowed they would "lay out a campaign," as they called it. The duke went down into his carpet-bag and fetched up a lot of little printed bills, and read them out loud. One bill said "The celebrated Dr. Armand de Montalban of Paris," would "lecture on the Science of Phrenology" at such and such a place, on the blank day of blank, at ten cents admission, and "furnish charts of character at twenty-five cents apiece." The duke said that was *him*. In another bill he was the "world renowned Shaksperean tragedian, Garrick the Younger, of Drury Lane, London." In other bills he had a lot of other names and done other wonderful things, like finding water and gold with a "divining rod," "dissipating witch-spells," and so on. By-and-by he says—

"But the histrionic muse is the darling. Have you ever trod the boards, Royalty?"

"No," says the king.

"You shall, then, before you're three days older, Fallen Grandeur," says the duke. "The first good town we come to, we'll hire a hall and do the sword-fight in Richard III. and the balcony scene in Romeo and Juliet. How does that strike you?"

"I'm in, up to the hub, for anything that will pay, Bilgewater, but you see I don't know nothing about play-actn', and hain't ever seen much of it. I was too small when pap used to have 'em at the palace. Do you reckon you can learn me?"

"Easy!"

"All right. I'm jist a-freezn' for something fresh, anyway. Less commence, right away."

So the duke he told him all about who Romeo was, and who Juliet was, and said he was used to being Romeo, so the king could be Juliet.

"But if Juliet's such a young gal, Duke, my peeled head and my white whiskers is goin' to look oncommon odd on her, maybe."

"No, don't you worry—these country jakes won't ever think of that. Besides, you know, you'll be in costume, and that makes all the differences in the world; Juliet's in a balcony, enjoying the moonlight before she goes to bed, and she's got on her night-gown and her ruffled night-cap. Here are the costumes for the parts."

He got out two or three curtain-calico suits, which he said was meedyevil armor for Richard III. and t'other chap, and a long white cotton night-shirt and a ruffled night-cap to match. The king was satisfied; so the duke got out his book and read the parts over in the most splendid spread-eagle way, prancing around and acting at the same time, to show how it had got to be done; then he give the book to the king and told him to get his part by heart.

There was a little one-horse town about three mile down the bend, and after dinner the duke said he had ciphered out his idea about how to run in daylight without it being dangersome for Jim; so he allowed he would go down to the town and fix that thing. The king allowed he would go too, and see if he couldn't strike something. We was out of coffee, so Jim said I better go along with them in the canoe and get some.

When we got there, there warn't nobody stirring; streets empty, and perfectly dead and still, like Sunday. We found a sick nigger sunning himself in a back yard, and he said everybody that warn't too young or too sick or too old, was gone to camp-meeting, about two mile back in the woods. The king got the directions, and allowed he'd go and work that camp-meeting for all it was worth, and I might go, too.

The duke said what he was after was a printing office. We found it; a little bit of a concern, up over a carpenter shop—carpenters and printers all gone to the meeting, and no doors locked. It was a dirty, littered-up place, and had ink marks, and handbills with pictures of horses and runaway niggers on them, all over the walls. The duke shed his coat and said he was all right, now. So me and the king lit out for the camp-meeting.

We got there in about a half an hour, fairly dripping, for it was a most awful hot day. There was as much as a thousand people there, from twenty mile around. The woods was full of teams and wagons, hitched everywheres, feeding out of the wagon troughs and stomping to keep off the flies. There was sheds made out of poles and roofed over with branches, where they had lemonade and gingerbread to sell, and piles of watermelons and green corn and such-like truck.

The preaching was going on under the same kinds of sheds, only they was bigger and held crowds of people. The benches was made out of outside slabs of logs, with holes bored in the round side to drive sticks into for legs. They didn't have no backs. The preachers had high platforms to stand on, at one end of the sheds. The women had on sunbonnets; and some had linsey-woolsey frocks, some gingham ones, and a few of the young ones had on calico. Some of the young men was barefooted, and some of the children didn't have on any clothes but just a tow-linen shirt. Some of the old women was knitting, and some of the young folks was courting on the sly.

The first shed we come to, the preacher was lining out a hymn. He lined out two lines, everybody sung it, and it was kind of grand to hear it, there was so many of them and they done it in such a rousing way; then he lined out two more for them to sing— and so on. The people woke up more and more, and sung louder and louder; and towards the end, some begun to groan, and some begun to shout. Then the preacher began to preach; and begun in earnest, too; and went weaving first to one side of the platform and then the other, and then a leaning down over the front of it, with his arms and his body going all the time, and shouting his words out with all his might; and every now and then he would hold up his Bible and spread it open, and kind of pass it around this way and that, shouting, "It's the brazen serpent in the wilderness! Look upon it and live!" And people would shout out, "Glory—A-a-*men!*" And so he went on, and the people groaning and crying and saying amen:

"Oh, come to the mourners' bench! come, black with sin! (*amen!*) come, sick and sore! (*amen!*) come, lame and halt, and blind! (*amen!*) come, pore and needy, sunk in shame! (*a-a-men!*) come all that's worn, and soiled, and suffering!—come with a broken spirit! come with a contrite heart! come in your rags and sin and dirt! the waters that cleanse is free, the door of heaven stands open—oh, enter in and be at rest!" (*a-a-men! glory, glory hallelujah!*)

And so on. You couldn't make out what the preacher said, any more, on account of the shouting and crying. Folks got up, everywheres in the crowd, and worked their way, just by main strength, to the mourners' bench, with the tears running down their faces; and when all the mourners had got up there to the front benches in a crowd, they sung, and shouted, and flung themselves down on the straw, just crazy and wild.

Well, the first I knowed, the king got agoing; and you could hear him over everybody; and next he went a-charging up on to the platform and the preacher he begged him to speak to the people, and he done it. He told them he was a pirate—been a pirate for thirty years, out in the Indian Ocean, and his crew was thinned out considerable, last spring, in a fight, and he was home now, to take out some fresh men, and thanks to goodness he'd been robbed last night, and put ashore off of a steamboat without a cent, and he was glad of it, it was the blessedest thing that ever happened to him, because he was a changed man now, and happy for the first time in his life; and poor as he was, he was going to start right off and work his way back to the Indian Ocean and put in the rest of his life trying to turn the pirates into the true path; for he could do it better than anybody else, being acquainted with all the pirate crews in that ocean; and though it would take him a long time to get there, without money, he would get there anyway, and every time he convinced a pirate he would say to him, "Don't you thank me, don't you give me no credit, it all belongs to them dear people in Pokeville camp-meeting, natural brothers and benefactors of the race—and that dear preacher there, the truest friend a pirate ever had!"

And then he busted into tears, and so did everybody. Then somebody sings out, "Take up a collection for him, take up a collection!" Well, a half a dozen made a jump to do it, but somebody sings out, "Let *him* pass the hat around!" Then everybody said it, the preacher too.

So the king went all through the crowd with his hat, swabbing his eyes, and blessing the people and praising them and thanking them for being so good to the poor pirates away off there; and every little while the prettiest kind of girls, with the tears running down their cheeks, would up and ask him would he let them kiss him, for to remember him by; and he always done it; and some of them he hugged and kissed as many as five or six times—and he was invited to stay a week; and everybody wanted him to live in their houses, and said they'd think it was an honor; but he said as this was the last day of the camp-meeting he couldn't do no good, and besides he was in a sweat to get to the Indian Ocean right off and go to work on the pirates.

When we got back to the raft and he come to count up, he found he had collected eighty-seven dollars and seventy-five cents. And then he had fetched away a three-gallon jug of whisky, too, that he found under a wagon when we was starting home through the woods. The king said, take it all around, it laid over any day he'd ever put in in the missionarying line. He said it warn't no use talking, heathens don't amount to shucks, alongside of pirates, to work a camp-meeting with.

The duke was thinking *he'd* been doing pretty well, till the king come to show up, but after that he didn't think so so much. He had set up and printed off two little jobs for farmers, in that printing office—horse bills—and took the money, four dollars. And he had got in ten dollars worth of advertisements for the paper, which he said he would put in for four dollars if they would pay in advance—so they done it. The price of the paper was two dollars a year, but he took in three subscriptions for half a dollar apiece on condition of them paying him in advance; they were going to pay in cord-wood and onions, as usual, but he said he had just bought the concern and knocked down the price as low as he could afford it, and was going to run it for cash. He set up a little piece of poetry, which he made, himself, out of his own head—three verses—kind of sweet and saddish—the name of it was, "Yes, crush, cold world, this breaking heart"—and he left that all set up and ready to print in the paper and didn't charge nothing for it. Well, he took in nine dollars and a half, and said he'd done a pretty square day's work for it.

Then he showed us another little job he'd printed and hadn't charged for, because it was for us. It had a picture of a runaway nigger, with a bundle on a stick, over his shoulder, and "$200 reward" under it. The reading was all about Jim, and just described him to a dot. It said he run away from St. Jacques' plantation, forty mile below New Orleans, last winter, and likely went north, and whoever would catch him and send him back, he could have the reward and expenses.

"Now," says the duke, "after to-night we can run in the daytime if we want to. Whenever we see anybody coming, we can tie Jim hand and foot with a rope, and lay him in the wigwam and show this handbill and say we captured him up the river, and were too poor to travel on a steamboat, so we got this little raft on credit from our friends and are going down to get the reward. Handcuffs and chains would look still better on Jim, but it wouldn't go well with the story of us being so poor. Too much like jewelry. Ropes are the correct thing—we must preserve the unities, as we say on the boards."

We all said the duke was pretty smart, and there couldn't be no trouble about running daytimes. We judged we could make miles enough that night to get out of the reach of the pow-wow we reckoned the duke's work in the printing office was going to make in that little town—then we could boom right along, if we wanted to.

We laid low and kept still, and never shoved out till nearly ten o'clock; then we slid by, pretty wide away from the town, and didn't hoist our lantern till we was clear out of sight of it.

When Jim called me to take the watch at four in the morning, he says—

"Huck, does you reck'n we gwyne to run acrost any mo' kings on dis trip?"

"No," I says, "I reckon not."

"Well," says he, "dat's all right, den. I doan' mine one er two kings, but dat's enough. Dis one's powerful drunk, en de duke ain' much better."

I found Jim had been trying to get him to talk French, so he could hear what it was like; but he said he had been in this country so long, and had so much trouble, he'd forgot it.

Chapter XXI

It was after sun-up, now, but we went right on, and didn't tie up. The king and the duke turned out, by-and-by, looking pretty rusty; but after they'd jumped overboard and took a swim, it chippered them up a good deal. After breakfast the king he took a seat on a corner of the raft, and pulled off his boot and rolled up his britches, and let his legs dangle in the water, so as to be comfortable, and lit his pipe, and went to getting his Romeo and Juliet by heart. When he had got it pretty good, him and the duke begun to practice it together. The duke had to learn him over and over again, how to say every speech; and he made him sigh, and put his hand on his heart, and after while he said he done it pretty well; "only," he says, "you mustn't bellow out *Romeo!* that way, like a bull—you must say it soft, and sick, and languishy, so—R-o-o-meo! that is the idea; for Juliet's a dear sweet mere child of a girl, you know, and she don't bray like a jackass."

Well, next they got out a couple of long swords that the duke made out of oak laths, and begun to practice the sword-fight—the duke called himself Richard III.; and the way they laid on, and pranced around the raft was grand to see. But by-and-by the king tripped and fell overboard, and after that they took a rest, and had a talk about all kinds of adventures they'd had in other times along the river.

After dinner, the duke says:

"Well, Capet, we'll want to make this a first-class show, you know, so I guess we'll add a little more to it. We want a little something to answer encores with, anyway."

"What's onkores, Bilgewater?"

The duke told him, and then says:

"I'll answer by doing the Highland fling or the sailor's hornpipe; and you—well, let me see—oh, I've got it—you can do Hamlet's soliloquy."

"Hamlet's which?"

"Hamlet's soliloquy, you know; the most celebrated thing in Shakespeare. Ah, it's sublime, sublime! Always fetches the house. I haven't got it in the book—I've only got one volume—but I reckon I can piece it out from memory. I'll just walk up and down a minute, and see if I can call it back from recollection's vaults."

So he went to marching up and down, thinking, and frowning horrible every now and then; then he would hoist up his eyebrows; next he would squeeze his hand on his forehead and stagger back and kind of moan; next he would sigh, and next he'd let on to drop a tear. It was beautiful to see him. By-and-by he got it. He told us to give attention. Then he strikes a most noble attitude, with one leg shoved forwards, and his arms stretched away up, and his head tilted back, looking up at the sky; and then he begins to rip and rave and grit his teeth; and after that, all through his speech he howled, and spread around, and swelled up his chest, and just knocked the spots out of any acting ever *I* see before. This is the speech—I learned it, easy enough, while he was learning it to the king:

> To be, or not to be; that is the bare bodkin
> That makes calamity of so long life;
> For who would fardels bear, till Birnam Wood do come to Dunsinane,
> But that the fear of something after death
> Murders the innocent sleep,
> Great nature's second course,
> And makes us rather sling the arrows of outrageous fortune
> Than fly to others that we know not of.
> There's the respect must give us pause:
> Wake Duncan with thy knocking! I would thou couldst;
> For who would bear the whips and scorns of time,
> The oppressor's wrong, the proud man's contumely,
> The law's delay, and the quietus which his pangs might take,
> In the dead waste and middle of the night, when churchyards yawn
> In customary suits of solemn black,
> But that the undiscovered country from whose bourne no traveler returns,
> Breathes forth contagion on the world,
> And thus the native hue of resolution, like the poor cat i' the adage,
> Is sicklied o'er with care,
> And all the clouds that lowered o'er our housetops,
> With this regard their currents turn awry,
> And lose the name of action.
> 'Tis a consummation devoutly to be wished. But soft you, the fair Ophelia:
> Ope not thy ponderous and marble jaws,
> But get thee to a nunnery—go!

Well, the old man he liked that speech, and he mighty soon got it so he could do it first rate. It seemed like he was just born for it; and when he had his hand in and was excited, it was perfectly lovely the way he would rip and tear and rair up behind when he was getting it off.

The first chance we got, the duke he had some show bills printed; and after that, for two or three days as we floated along, the raft was a most uncommon lively place, for there warn't nothing but sword-fighting and rehearsing—as the duke called it—going on all the time. One morning, when we was pretty well down the State of Arkansaw, we come in sight of a little one-horse town in a big bend; so we tied up about three-quarters of a mile above it, in the mouth of a crick which was shut in like a tunnel by the cypress trees, and all of us but Jim took the canoe and went down there to see if there was any chance in that place for our show.

We struck it mighty lucky; there was going to be a circus there that afternoon, and the country people was already beginning to come in, in all kinds of old shackly wagons, and on horses. The circus would leave before night, so our show would have a pretty good chance. The duke he hired the court house, and we went around and stuck up our bills. They read like this:

Shaksperean Revival! ! !
Wonderful Attraction!
For One Night Only!
The world renowned tragedians,
David Garrick the younger, of Drury Lane Theatre, London,
and
Edmund Kean the elder, of the Royal Haymarket Theatre, White-
chapel, Pudding Lane, Piccadilly, London, and the
Royal Continental Theatres, in their sublime
Shaksperean Spectacle entitled
The Balcony Scene
in
Romeo and Juliet! ! !
Romeo . . . . Mr. Garrick.
Juliet . . . . Mr. Kean.
Assisted by the whole strength of the company!
New costumes, new scenery, new appointments!
Also:
The thrilling, masterly, and blood-curdling
Broad-sword conflict
In Richard III. ! ! !
Richard III . . . . Mr. Garrick.
Richmond . . . . Mr. Kean.
also:
(by special request,)
Hamlet's Immortal Soliloquy! !
By the Illustrious Kean!
Done by him 300 consecutive nights in Paris!
For One Night Only,
On account of imperative European engagements!
Admission 25 cents; children and servants, 10 cents.

Then we went loafing around the town. The stores and houses was most all old shackly dried-up frame concerns that hadn't ever been painted; they was set up three or four foot above ground on stilts, so as to be out of reach of the water when the river was overflowed. The houses had little gardens around them, but they didn't seem to raise hardly anything in them but jimpson weeds, and sunflowers, and ash-piles, and old curled-up boots and shoes, and pieces of bottles, and rags, and played-out tin-ware. The fences was made of different kinds of boards, nailed on at different times; and they leaned every which-way, and had gates that didn't generly have but one hinge—a leather one. Some of the fences had been whitewashed, some time or another, but the duke said it was in Clumbus's time, like enough. There was generly hogs in the garden, and people driving them out.

All the stores was along one street. They had white-domestic awnings in front, and the country people hitched their horses to the awning-posts. There was empty dry-goods boxes under the awnings, and loafers roosting on them all day long, whittling them with their Barlow knives; and chawing tobacco, and gaping and yawning and stretching—a mighty ornery lot. They generly had on yellow straw hats most as wide as an umbrella, but didn't wear no coats nor waistcoats; they called one another Bill, and Buck, and Hank, and Joe, and Andy, and talked lazy and drawly, and used considerable many cuss-words. There was as many as one loafer leaning up against every awning-post, and he most always had his hands in his britches pockets, except when he fetched them out to lend a chaw of tobacco or scratch. What a body was hearing amongst them, all the time was—

"Gimme a chaw 'v tobacker, Hank."

"Cain't—I hain't got but one chaw left. Ask Bill."

Maybe Bill he gives him a chaw; maybe he lies and says he ain't got none. Some of them kinds of loafers never has a cent in the world, nor a chaw of tobacco of their own. They get all their chawing by borrowing—they say to a fellow, "I wisht you'd len' me a chaw, Jack, I jist this minute give Ben Thompson the last chaw I had"—which is a lie, pretty much every time; it don't fool nobody but a stranger; but Jack ain't no stranger, so he says—

"*You* give him a chaw, did you? so did your sister's cat's grandmother. You pay me back the chaws you've awready borry'd off'n me, Lafe Buckner, then I'll loan you one or two ton of it, and won't charge you no back intrust, nuther."

"Well, I *did* pay you back some of it wunst."

"Yes, you did—'bout six chaws. You borry'd store tobacker and paid back nigger-head."

Store tobacco is flat black plug, but these fellows mostly chaws the natural leaf twisted. When they borrow a chaw, they don't generly cut it off with a knife, but they set the plug in between their teeth, and gnaw with their teeth and tug at the plug with their hands till they get it in two—then sometimes the one that owns the tobacco looks mournful at it when it's handed back, and says, sarcastic—

"Here, gimme the *chaw,* and you take the *plug.*"

All the streets and lanes was just mud, they warn't nothing else *but* mud—mud as black as tar, and nigh about a foot deep in some places; and two or three inches deep in *all* the places. The hogs loafed and grunted around, everywheres. You'd see a muddy sow and a litter of pigs come lazying along the street and whollop herself right down in the way, where folks had to walk around her, and she'd stretch out, and shut her eyes, and wave her ears, whilst the pigs was milking her, and look as happy as if she was on salary. And pretty soon you'd hear a loafer sing out, "Hi! *so* boy! sick him, Tige!" and away the sow would go, squealing most horrible, with a dog or two swinging to each ear, and three or four dozen more a-coming; and then you would see all the loafers get up and watch the thing out of sight, and laugh at the fun and look grateful for the noise. Then they'd settle back again till there was a dog-fight. There couldn't anything wake them up all over, and make them happy all over, like a dog-fight—unless it might be putting turpentine on a stray dog and setting fire to him, or tying a tin pan to his tail and see him run himself to death.

On the river front some of the houses was sticking out over the bank, and they was bowed and bent, and about ready to tumble in. The people had moved out of them. The bank was caved away under one corner of some others, and that corner was hanging over. People lived in them yet, but it was dangersome, because sometimes a strip of land as wide as a house caves in at a time. Sometimes a belt of land a quarter of a mile deep will start in and cave along and cave along till it all caves into the river in one summer. Such a town as that has to be always moving back, and back, and back, because the river's always gnawing at it.

The nearer it got to noon that day, the thicker and thicker was the wagons and horses in the streets, and more coming all the time. Families fetched their dinners with them, from the country, and eat them in the wagons. There was considerable whiskey drinking going on, and I seen three fights. By-and-by somebody sings out—

"Here comes old Boggs!—in from the country for his little old monthly drunk— here he comes, boys!"

All the loafers looked glad—I reckoned they was used to having fun out of Boggs. One of them says—

"Wonder who he's a gwyne to chaw up this time. If he'd a chawed up all the men he's ben a gwyne to chaw up in the last twenty year, he'd have considerble ruputation, now."

Another one says, "I wisht old Boggs 'd threaten me, 'cuz then I'd know I warn't gwyne to die for a thousan' year."

Boggs comes a-tearing along on his horse, whooping and yelling like an Injun, and singing out—

"Cler the track, thar. I'm on the waw-path, and the price uv coffins is a gwyne to raise."

He was drunk, and weaving about in his saddle; he was over fifty year old, and had a very red face. Everybody yelled at him, and laughed at him, and sassed him, and he sassed back, and said he'd attend to them and lay them out in their regular turns, but he couldn't wait now, because he'd come to town to kill old Colonel Sherburn, and his motto was, "meat first, and spoon vittles to top off on."

He see me, and rode up and says—

"Whar'd you come f'm, boy? You prepared to die?"

Then he rode on. I was scared; but a man says—

"He don't mean nothing; he's always a carryin' on like that, when he's drunk. He's the best-naturedest old fool in Arkansaw—never hurt nobody, drunk nor sober."

Boggs rode up before the biggest store in town and bent his head down so he could see under the curtain of the awning, and yells—

"Come out here, Sherburn! Come out and meet the man you've swindled. You're the houn' I'm after, and I'm a gwyne to have you, too!"

And so he went on, calling Sherburn everything he could lay his tongue to, and the whole street packed with people listening and laughing and going on. By-and-by a proud-looking man about fifty-five—and he was a heap the best dressed man in that town, too—steps out of the store, and the crowd drops back on each side to let him come. He says to Boggs, mighty ca'm and slow—he says:

"I'm tired of this; but I'll endure it till one o'clock. Till one o'clock, mind—no longer. If you open your mouth against me only once, after that time, you can't travel so far but I will find you."

Then he turns and goes in. The crowd looked mighty sober; nobody stirred, and there warn't no more laughing. Boggs rode off blackguarding Sherburn as loud as he could yell, all down the street; and pretty soon back he comes and stops before the store, still keeping it up. Some men crowded around him and tried to get him to shut up, but he wouldn't; they told him it would be one o'clock in about fifteen minutes, and so he *must* go home—he must go right away. But it didn't do no good. He cussed away, with all his might, and throwed his hat down in the mud and rode over it, and pretty soon away he went a-raging down the street again, with his gray hair a-flying. Everybody that could get a chance at him tried their best to coax him off of his horse so they could lock him up and get him sober; but it warn't no use—up the street he would tear again, and give Sherburn another cussing. By-and-by somebody says—

"Go for his daughter!—quick, go for his daughter; sometimes he'll listen to her. If anybody can persuade him, she can."

So somebody started on a run. I walked down street a ways, and stopped. In about five or ten minutes, here comes Boggs again—but not on his horse. He was a-reeling across the street towards me, bareheaded, with a friend on both sides of him aholt of his arms and hurrying him along. He was quiet, and looked uneasy; and he warn't hanging back any, but was doing some of the hurrying himself. Somebody sings out—

"Boggs!"

I looked over there to see who said it, and it was that Colonel Sherburn. He was standing perfectly still, in the street, and had a pistol raised in his right hand—not aiming it, but holding it out with the barrel tilted up towards the sky. The same second I see a young girl coming on the run, and two men with her. Boggs and the men turned round, to see who called him, and when they see the pistol the men jumped to one side, and the pistol barrel come down slow and steady to a level—both barrels cocked. Boggs throws up both of his hands, and says, "O Lord, don't shoot!" Bang! goes the first shot, and he staggers back clawing at the air—bang! goes the second one, and he tumbles backwards onto the ground, heavy and solid, with his arms spread out. That young girl screamed out, and comes rushing, and down she throws herself on her father, crying, and saying, "Oh, he's killed him, he's killed him!" The crowd closed up around them, and shouldered and jammed one another, with their necks stretched, trying to see, and people on the inside trying to shove them back, and shouting, "Back, back! give him air, give him air!"

Colonel Sherburn he tossed his pistol onto the ground, and turned around on his heels and walked off.

They took Boggs to a little drug store, the crowd pressing around, just the same, and the whole town following, and I rushed and got a good place at the window, where I was close to him and could see in. They laid him on the floor, and put one large Bible under his head, and opened another one and spread it on his breast—but they tore open his shirt first, and I seen where one of the bullets went in. He made about a dozen long gasps, his breast lifting the Bible up when he drawed in his breath, and letting it down again when he breathed it out—and after that he laid still; he was dead. Then they

Kemble.

THE DEATH OF BOGGS.

E. W. Kemble
The death of Boggs
1885

pulled his daughter away from him, screaming and crying, and took her off. She was about sixteen, and very sweet and gentle-looking, but awful pale and scared.

Well, pretty soon the whole town was there, squirming and scourging and pushing and shoving to get at the window and have a look, but people that had the places wouldn't give them up, and folks behind them was saying all the time, "Say, now, you've looked enough, you fellows; 'taint right and 'taint fair, for you to stay thar all the time, and never give nobody a chance; other folks has their rights as well as you."

There was considerable jawing back, so I slid out, thinking maybe there was going to be trouble. The streets was full, and everybody was excited. Everybody that seen the shooting was telling how it happened, and there was a big crowd packed around each one of these fellows, stretching their necks and listening. One long lanky man, with long hair and a big white fur stove-pipe hat on the back of his head, and a crooked-handled cane, marked out the places on the ground where Boggs stood, and where Sherburn stood, and the people following him around from one place t'other and watching every-thing he done, and bobbing their heads to show they understood, and stooping a little and resting their hands on their thighs to watch him mark the places on the ground with his cane; and then he stood up straight and stiff where Sherburn had stood, frown-ing and having his hat-brim down over his eyes, and sung out, "Boggs!" and then fetched his cane down slow to a level, and says "Bang!" staggered backwards, says "Bang!" again, and fell down flat on his back. The people that had seen the thing said he done it perfect; said it was just exactly the way it all happened. Then as much as a dozen people got out their bottles and treated him.

Well, by-and-by somebody said Sherburn ought to be lynched. In about a minute everybody was saying it; so away they went, mad and yelling, and snatching down every clothes-line they come to, to do the hanging with.

Chapter XXII

They swarmed up the street towards Sherburn's house, a-whooping and yelling and raging like Injuns, and everything had to clear the way or get run over and tromped to mush, and it was awful to see. Children was heeling it ahead of the mob, screaming and trying to get out of the way; and every window along the road was full of women's heads, and there was nigger boys in every tree, and bucks and wenches looking over every fence; and as soon as the mob would get nearly to them they would break and skaddle back out of reach. Lots of the women and girls was crying and taking on, scared most to death.

They swarmed up in front of Sherburn's palings as thick as they could jam together, and you couldn't hear yourself think for the noise. It was a little twenty-foot yard. Some sung out "Tear down the fence! tear down the fence!" Then there was a racket of ripping and tearing and smashing, and down she goes, and the front wall of the crowd begins to roll in like a wave.

Just then Sherburn steps out on to the roof of his little front porch, with a double-barrel gun in his hand, and takes his stand, perfectly ca'm and deliberate, not saying a word. The racket stopped, and the wave sucked back.

Sherburn never said a word—just stood there, looking down. The stillness was awful creepy and uncomfortable. Sherburn run his eye slow along the crowd; and wherever it struck, the people tried a little to outgaze him, but they couldn't; they dropped their eyes and looked sneaky. Then pretty soon Sherburn sort of laughed; not the pleasant kind, but the kind that makes you feel like when you are eating bread that's got sand in it.

Then he says, slow and scornful:

"The idea of *you* lynching anybody! It's amusing. The idea of you thinking you had pluck enough to lynch a *man!* Because you're brave enough to tar and feather poor friendless cast-out women that come along here, did that make you think you had grit enough to lay your hands on a *man?* Why, a *man's* safe in the hands of ten thousand of your kind—as long as it's day-time and you're not behind him.

"Do I know you? I know you clear through. I was born and raised in the South, and I've lived in the North; so I know the average all around. The average man's a coward. In the North he lets anybody walk over him that wants to, and goes home and prays for a humble spirit to bear it. In the South one man, all by himself, has stopped a stage full of men, in the day-time, and robbed the lot. Your newspapers call you a brave people so much that you think you *are* braver than any other people—whereas you're just *as* brave, and no braver. Why don't your juries hang murderers? Because they're afraid the man's friends will shoot them in the back, in the dark—and it's just what they *would* do.

"So they always acquit; and then a *man* goes in the night, with a hundred masked cowards at his back, and lynches the rascal. Your mistake is, that you didn't bring a man with you; that's one mistake, and the other is that you didn't come in the dark, and fetch your masks. You brought *part* of a man—Buck Harkness, there—and if you hadn't had him to start you, you'd a taken it out in blowing.

"You didn't want to come. The average man don't like trouble and danger. *You* don't like trouble and danger. But if only *half* a man—like Buck Harkness, there—shouts 'Lynch him, lynch him!' you're afraid to back down—afraid you'll be found out to be what you are—*cowards*—and so you raise a yell, and hang yourselves onto that half-a-man's coat tail, and come raging up here, swearing what big things you're going to do. The pitifulest thing out is a mob; that's what an army is—a mob; they don't fight with courage that's born in them, but with courage that's borrowed from their mass, and from their officers. But a mob without any *man* at the head of it, is *beneath* pitifulness. Now the thing for *you* to do, is to droop your tails and go home and crawl in a hole. If any real lynching's going to be done, it will be done in the dark, Southern fashion; and when they come they'll bring their masks, and fetch a *man* along. Now *leave*—and take your half-a-man with you"—tossing his gun up across his left arm and cocking it, when he says this.

The crowd washed back sudden, and then broke all apart and went tearing off every which way, and Buck Harkness he heeled it after them, looking tolerable cheap. I could a staid, if I'd a wanted to, but I didn't want to.

I went to the circus, and loafed around the back side till the watchman went by, and then dived in under the tent. I had my twenty-dollar gold piece and some other money, but I reckoned I better save it, because there ain't no telling how soon you are going to need it, away from home and amongst strangers, that way. You can't be too careful. I ain't opposed to spending money on circuses, when there ain't no other way, but there ain't no use in *wasting* it on them.

It was a real bully circus. It was the splendidest sight that ever was, when they all come riding in, two and two, a gentleman and lady, side by side, the men just in their drawers and under-shirts, and no shoes nor stirrups, and resting their hands on their thighs, easy and comfortable—there must a' been twenty of them—and every lady with a lovely complexion, and perfectly beautiful, and looking just like a gang of real sure-enough queens, and dressed in clothes that cost millions of dollars, and just littered with diamonds. It was a powerful fine sight; I never see anything so lovely. And then one by one they got up and stood, and went a-weaving around the ring so gentle and wavy and graceful, the men looking ever so tall and airy and straight, with their heads bobbing and skimming along, away up there under the tent-roof, and every lady's rose-leafy dress flapping soft and silky around her hips, and she looking like the most loveliest parasol.

And then faster and faster they went, all of them dancing, first one foot stuck out in the air and then the other, the horses leaning more and more, and the ring-master going round and round the centre-pole, cracking his whip and shouting "hi!—hi!" and the clown cracking jokes behind him; and by-and-by all hands dropped the reins, and every lady put her knuckles on her hips and every gentleman folded his arms, and then how the horses did lean over and hump themselves! And so, one after the other they all skipped off into the ring, and made the sweetest bow I ever see, and then scampered out, and everybody clapped their hands and went just about wild.

Well, all through the circus they done the most astonishing things; and all the time that clown carried on so it most killed the people. The ring-master couldn't ever say a word to him but he was back at him quick as a wink with the funniest things a body ever said; and how he ever *could* think of so many of them, and so sudden and so pat, was what I couldn't noway understand. Why, I couldn't a thought of them in a year. And by-and-by a drunk man tried to get into the ring—said he wanted to ride; said he could ride as well as anybody that ever was. They argued and tried to keep him out, but he wouldn't listen, and the whole show come to a standstill. Then the people begun to holler at him and make fun of him, and that made him mad, and he begun to rip and tear; so that stirred up the people, and a lot of men begun to pile down off of the benches and swarm towards the ring, saying, "Knock him down! throw him out!" and one or two women begun to scream. So, then, the ring-master he made a little speech, and said he hoped there wouldn't be no disturbance, and if the man would promise he wouldn't make no more trouble, he would let him ride, if he thought he could stay on the horse. So everybody laughed and said all right, and the man got on. The minute he was on, the horse begun to rip and tear and jump and cavort around, with two circus men hanging onto his bridle trying to hold him, and the drunk man hanging onto his neck, and his heels flying in the air every jump, and the whole crowd of people standing up shouting and laughing till the tears rolled down. And at last, sure enough, all the circus men could do, the horse broke loose, and away he went like the very nation, round and round the ring, with that sot laying down on him and hanging to his neck, with first one leg hanging most to the ground on one side, and then t'other one on t'other side, and the people just crazy. It warn't funny to me, though; I was all of a tremble to see his danger. But pretty soon he struggled up astraddle and grabbed the bridle, a-reeling this way and that; and the next minute he sprung up and dropped the bridle and stood! and the horse agoing like a house afire too. He just stood up there, a-sailing around as easy and comfortable as if he warn't ever drunk in his life—and then he begun to pull off his clothes and sling them. He shed them so thick they kind of clogged up the air, and altogether he shed seventeen suits. And then, there he was, slim and handsome, and dressed the gaudiest and prettiest you ever saw, and he lit into that horse with his whip and made him fairly hum—and finally skipped off, and made his bow and danced off to the dressing-room, and everybody just a-howling with pleasure and astonishment.

Then the ring-master he see how he had been fooled, and he *was* the sickest ring-master you ever see, I reckon. Why, it was one of his own men! He had got up that joke all out of his own head, and never let on to nobody. Well, I felt sheepish enough, to be took in so, but I wouldn't a been in that ring-master's place, not for a thousand dollars. I don't know; there may be bullier circuses than what that one was, but I never struck them yet. Anyways it was plenty good enough for *me*; and wherever I run across it, it can have all of *my* custom, every time.

Well, that night we had *our* show; but there warn't only about twelve people there; just enough to pay expenses. And they laughed all the time, and that made the duke mad; and everybody left, anyway, before the show was over, but one boy which was asleep. So the duke said these Arkansaw lunkheads couldn't come up to Shakspeare; what they wanted was low comedy—and may be something ruther worse than low comedy, he reckoned. He said he could size their style. So next morning he got some big sheets of wrapping-paper and some black paint, and drawed off some handbills and stuck them up all over the village. The bills said:

AT THE COURT HOUSE!

FOR 3 NIGHTS ONLY!

The World-Renowned Tragedians

DAVID GARRICK THE YOUNGER!

AND

EDMUND KEAN THE ELDER!

Of the London and Continental

Theatres,

In their Thrilling Tragedy of

THE KING'S CAMELOPARD

OR

THE ROYAL NONESUCH!!!

Admission 50 cents.

Then at the bottom was the biggest line of all—which said:

LADIES AND CHILDREN NOT ADMITTED.

"There," says he, "if that line don't fetch them, I dont know Arkansaw!"

Chapter XXIII

Well, all day him and the king was hard at it, rigging up a stage, and a curtain, and a row of candles for footlights; and that night the house was jam full of men in no time. When the place couldn't hold no more, the duke he quit tending door and went around the back way and come onto the stage and stood up before the curtain, and made a little speech, and praised up this tragedy, and said it was the most thrillingest one that ever was; and so he went on a-bragging about the tragedy and about Edmund Kean the Elder, which was to play the main principal part in it; and at last when he'd got everybody's expectations up high enough, he rolled up the curtain, and the next minute the king come a-prancing out on all fours, naked; and he was painted all over, ring-streaked-and-striped, all sorts of colors, as splendid as a rainbow. And—but never mind the rest of his outfit, it was just wild, but it was awful funny. The people most killed themselves laughing; and when the king got done capering, and capered off behind the scenes, they roared and clapped and stormed and haw-hawed till he come back and done it over again; and after that, they made him do it another time. Well, it would a made a cow laugh to see the shines that old idiot cut.

Then the duke he lets the curtain down, and bows to the people, and says the great tragedy will be performed only two nights more, on accounts of pressing London engagements, where the seats is all sold aready for it in Drury Lane; and then he makes them another bow, and says if he has succeeded in pleasing them and instructing them, he will be deeply obleeged if they will mention it to their friends and get them to come and see it.

Twenty people sings out:

"What, is it over? Is that *all?*"

The duke says yes. Then there was a fine time. Everybody sings out "sold," and rose up mad, and was agoing for that stage and them tragedians. But a big fine-looking man jumps up on a bench, and shouts:

"Hold on! Just a word, gentlemen." They stopped to listen. "We are sold—mighty badly sold, But we don't want to be the laughing-stock of this whole town, I reckon, and never hear the last of this thing as long as we live. *No.* What we want, is to go out of here quiet, and talk this show up, and sell the *rest* of the town! Then we'll all be in the same boat. Ain't that sensible?" ("You bet it is!—the jedge is right!" everybody sings out.) "All right, then—not a word about any sell. Go along home, and advise everybody to come and see the tragedy."

Next day you couldn't hear nothing around that town but how splendid that show was. House was jammed again, that night, and we sold this crowd the same way. When me and the king and duke got home to the raft, we all had a supper; and by-and-by, about midnight, they made Jim and me back her out and float her down the middle of the river and fetch her in and hide her about two mile below town.

The third night the house was crammed again—and they warn't new-comers, this time, but people that was at the show the other two nights. I stood by the duke at the door, and I see that every man that went in had his pockets bulging, or something muffled up under his coat—and I see it warn't no perfumery neither, not by a long sight. I smelt sickly eggs by the barrel, and rotten cabbages, and such things; and if I know the signs of a dead cat being around, and I bet I do, there was sixty-four of them went in. I shoved in there for a minute, but it was too various for me, I couldn't stand it. Well, when the place couldn't hold no more people, the duke he give a fellow a quarter and told him to tend door for him a minute, and then he started around for the stage door, I after him; but the minute we turned the corner and was in the dark, he says:

"Walk fast, now, till you get away from the houses, and then shin for the raft like the dickens was after you!"

I done it, and he done the same. We struck the raft at the same time, and in less than two seconds we was gliding down stream, all dark and still, and edging towards the middle of the river, nobody saying a word. I reckoned the poor king was in for a gaudy time of it with the audience; but nothing of the sort; pretty soon he crawls out from under the wigwam, and says:

"Well, how'd the old thing pan out this time, Duke?"

He hadn't been up town at all.

We never showed a light till we was about ten mile below that village. Then we lit up and had a supper, and the king and the duke fairly laughed their bones loose over the way they'd served them people. The dukes says:

"Greenhorns, flatheads! *I* knew the first house would keep mum and let the rest of the town get roped in; and I knew they'd lay for us the third night, and consider it was *their* turn now. Well, it *is* their turn, and I'd give something to know how much they'd take for it. I *would* just like to know how they're putting in their opportunity. They can turn it into a picnic, if they want to—they brought plenty provisions."

Them rapscallions took in four hundred and sixty-five dollars in that three nights. I never see money hauled in by the wagon-load like that, before.

By-and-by, when they was asleep and snoring, Jim says:

"Don't it 'sprise you, de way dem kings carries on, Huck?"

"No," I says, "it don't."

"Why don't it, Huck?"

"Well, it don't, because it's in the breed. I reckon they're all alike."

"But, Huck, dese kings o' ourn is regular rapscallions; dat's jist what dey is; dey's reglar rapscallions."

"Well, that's what I'm a-saying; all kings is mostly rapscallions, as fur as I can make out."

"Is dat so?"

"You read about them once—you'll see. Look at Henry the Eight; this'n 's a Sunday-School Superintendent to *him*. And look at Charles Second, and Louis Fourteen, and Louis Fifteen, and James Second, and Edward Second, and Richard Third, and forty more; besides all them Saxon heptarchies that used to rip around so in old times and raise Cain. My, you ought to seen old Henry the Eight when he was in bloom. He *was* a blossom. He used to marry a new wife every day, and chop off her head next morning. And he would do it just as indifferent as if he was ordering up eggs. 'Fetch up Nell Gwynn,' he says. They fetch her up. Next morning, 'Chop off her head!' And they chop it off. 'Fetch up Jane Shore,' he says; and up she comes. Next morning 'Chop off her head'—and they chop it off. 'Ring up Fair Rosamun.' Fair Rosamun answers the bell. Next morning, 'Chop off her head.' And he made every one of them tell him a tale every night; and he kept that up till he had hogged a thousand and one tales that way, and then he put them all in a book, and called it Domesday Book—which was a good name and stated the case. You don't know kings, Jim, but I know them; and this old rip of ourn is one of the cleanest I've struck in history. Well, Henry he takes a notion he wants to get up some trouble with this country. How does he go at it—give notice?—give the country a show? No. All of a sudden he heaves all the tea in Boston Harbor overboard, and whacks out a declaration of independence, and dares them to come on. That was *his* style—he never give anybody a chance. He had suspicions of his father, the Duke of Wellington. Well, what did he do?—ask him to show up? No—drownded him in a butt of mamsey, like a cat. Spose people left money laying around where he was—what did he do? He collared it. Spose he contracted to do a thing; and you paid him, and didn't set down there and see that he done it—what did he do? He always done the other thing. Spose he opened his mouth—what then? If he didn't shut it up powerful quick, he'd lose a lie, every time. That's the kind of a bug Henry was; and if we'd a had him along 'stead of our kings, he'd a fooled that town a heap worse than ourn done. I don't say that ourn is lambs, because they ain't, when you come right down to the cold facts; but they ain't nothing to *that* old ram, anyway. All I say is, kings is kings, and you got to make allowances. Take them all around, they're a mighty ornery lot. It's the way they're raised."

"But dis one do *smell* so like de nation, Huck."

"Well, they all do, Jim. *We* can't help the way a king smells; history don't tell no way."

"Now de duke, he's a tolerble likely man, in some ways."

"Yes, a duke's different. But not very different. This one's a middling hard lot, for a duke. When he's drunk, there ain't no near-sighted man could tell him from a king."

"Well, anyways, I doan' hanker for no mo' un um, Huck. Dese is all I kin stan'."

"It's the way I feel, too, Jim. but we've got them on our hands, and we got to remember what they are, and make allowances. Sometimes I wish we could hear of a country that's out of kings."

What was the use to tell Jim these warn't real kings and dukes? It wouldn't a done no good; and besides, it was just as I said; you couldn't tell them from the real kind.

I went to sleep, and Jim didn't call me when it was my turn. He often done that. When I waked up, just at day-break, he was setting there with his head down betwixt his knees, moaning and mourning to himself. I didn't take notice, nor let on. I knowed what it was about. He was thinking about his wife and his children, away up yonder, and he was low and homesick; because he hadn't ever been away from home before in his life; and I do believe he cared just as much for his people as white folks does for their'n. It don't seem natural, but I reckon it's so. He was often moaning and mourning that way, nights, when he judged I was asleep, and saying, "Po' little 'Lizabeth! po' little Johnny! its mighty hard; I spec' I ain't ever gwyne to see you no mo', no mo'!" He was a mighty good nigger, Jim was.

But this time I somehow got to talking to him about his wife and young ones; and by-and-by he says:

"What makes me feel so bad dis time, 'uz bekase I hear sumpn over yonder on de bank like a whack, er a slam, while ago, en it mine me er de time I treat my little 'Lizabeth so ornery. She warn't on'y 'bout fo' year ole, en she tuck de sk'yarlet-fever, en had a powful rough spell; but she got well, en one day she was a-stannin' aroun', en I says to her, I says:

"Shet de do'.'

"She never done it; jis' stood dah, kiner smilin' up at me. It make me mad; en I says agin, mighty loud, I says:

"'Doan' you hear me?—shet de do'!'

"She jis' stood de same way, kiner smilin' up. I was a-bilin'! I says:

"'I lay I *make* you mine!'

"En wid dat I fetch' her a slap side de head dat sont her a-sprawlin'. Den I went into de yuther room, en 'uz gone 'bout ten minutes; en when I come back, dah was dat do' a-stannin' open *yit*, en dat chile stannin' mos' right in it, a-lookin' down and mournin', en de tears runnin' down. My, but I *wuz* mad, I was agwyne for de chile, but jis' den—it was a do' dat open innerds—jis' den, 'long come de wind en slam it to, behine de chile, ker-*blam!*—en my lan', de chile never move'! My breff mos' hop outer me; en I feel so—so—I doan' know *how* I feel. I crope out, all a-tremblin', en crope aroun' en open de do' easy en slow, en poke my head in behine de chile, sof' en still, en all uv a sudden, I says pow! jis' as loud as I could yell. *She never budge!* Oh, Huck, I bust out a-cryin' en grab her up in my arms, en say, 'Oh, de po' little thing! de Lord God Amighty fogive po' ole Jim, kaze he never gwyne to fogive hisself as long's he live!' Oh, she was plumb deef en dumb, Huck, plumb deef en dumb—en I'd ben a-treat'n her so!"

Chapter XXIV

Next day, towards night, we laid up under a little willow tow-head out in the middle, where there was a village on each side of the river, and the duke and the king begun to lay out a plan for working them towns. Jim he spoke to the duke, and said he hoped it wouldn't take but a few hours, because it got mighty heavy and tiresome to him when he had to lay all day in the wigwam tied with the rope. You see, when we left him all alone we had to tie him, because if anybody happened on him all by himself and not tied, it wouldn't look much like he was a runaway nigger, you know. So the duke said it *was* kind of hard to have to lay roped all day, and he'd cipher out some way to get around it.

He was uncommon bright, the duke was, and he soon struck it. He dressed Jim up in King Lear's outfit—it was a long curtain calico gown, and a white horse-hair wig and whiskers; and then he took his theatre-paint and painted Jim's face and hands and ears and neck all over a dead dull solid blue, like a man that's been drownded nine days. Blamed if he warn't the horriblest looking outrage I ever see. Then the duke took and wrote out a sign on a shingle so—

Sick Arab—but harmless when not out of his head.

And he nailed that shingle to a lath, and stood the lath up four or five foot in front of the wigwam. Jim was satisfied. He said it was a sight better than laying tied a couple of years every day and trembling all over every time there was a sound. The duke told him to make himself free and easy, and if anybody ever come meddling around, he must hop out of the wigwam, and carry on a little, and fetch a howl or two like a wild beast, and he reckoned they would light out and leave him alone. Which was sound enough judgment; but you take the average man, and he wouldn't wait for him to howl. Why, he didn't only look like he was dead, he looked considerable more than that.

These rapscallions wanted to try the Nonesuch again, because there was so much money in it, but they judged it wouldn't be safe, because maybe the news might a worked along down by this time. They couldn't hit no project that suited, exactly; so at last the duke said he reckoned he'd lay off and work his brans an hour or two and see if he couldn't put up something on the Arkansaw village; and the king he allowed he would drop over to t'other village, without any plan, but just trust in Providence to lead him the profitable way—meaning the devil, I reckon. We had all bought store clothes where we stopped last; and now the king put his'n on, and he told me to put mine on. I done it, of course. The king's duds was all black, and he did look real swell and starchy. I never knowed how clothes could change a body before. Why, before, he looked like the orneriest old rip that ever was; but now, when he'd take off his new white beaver and make a bow and do a smile, he looked that grand and good and pious that you'd say he had walked right out of the ark, and maybe was old Leviticus himself. Jim cleaned up the canoe, and I got my paddle ready. There was a big steamboat laying at the shore away up under the point, about three mile above town—been there a couple of hours, taking on freight. Says the king:

"Seein' how I'm dressed, I reckon maybe I better arrive down from St. Louis or Cincinnati, or some other big place. Go for the steamboat, Huckleberry; we'll come down to the village on her."

I didn't have to be ordered twice, to go and take a steamboat ride. I fetched the shore a half a mile above the village, and then went scooting along the bluff bank in the easy water. Pretty soon we come to a nice innocent-looking young country jake setting on a log swabbing the sweat off of his face, for it was powerful warm weather; and he had a couple of big carpet-bags by him.

"Run her nose in shore," says the king. I done it. "Wher' you bound for, young man?"

"For the steamboat; going to Orleans."

"Git aboard," says the king. "Hold on a minute, my servant 'll he'p you with them bags. Jump out and he'p the gentleman, Adolphus"——meaning me, I see.

I done so, and then we all three started on again. The young chap was mighty thankful; said it was tough work toting his baggage such weather. He asked the king where he was going, and the king told him he'd come down the river and landed at the other village this morning, and now he was going up a few mile to see an old friend on a farm up there. The young fellow says:

"When I first see you, I says to myself, 'It's Mr. Wilks, sure, and he come mighty near getting here in time.' But then I says again, 'No, I reckon it ain't him, or else he wouldn't be paddling up the river.' You *ain't* him, are you?"

"No, my name's Blodgett—Elexander Blodgett—*Reverend* Elexander Blodgett, I spose I must say, as I'm one o' the Lord's poor servants. But still I'm jist as able to be sorry for Mr. Wilks for not arriving in time, all the same, if he's missed anything by it—which I hope he hasn't."

"Well, he don't miss any property by it, because he'll get that al right; but he's missed seeing his brother Peter die—which he mayn't mind, nobody can tell as to that—but his brother would a give anything in this world to see *him* before he died; never talked about nothing else all these three weeks; hadn't seen him since they was boys together—and hadn't ever seen his brother William at all—that's the deef and dumb one—William ain't more than thirty or thirty-five. Peter and George was the only ones that come out here; George was the married brother; him and his wife both died last year. Harvey and William's the only ones that's left now; and, as I was saying, they haven't got here in time."

"Did anybody send 'em word?"

"Oh, yes; a month or two ago, when Peter was first took; because Peter said then that he sorter felt like he warn't going to get well this time. You see, he was pretty old, and George's g'yirls was too young to be much company for him, except Mary Jane the red-headed one; and so he was kinder lonesome after George and his wife died, and didn't seem to care much to live. He most desperately wanted to see Harvey—and William too, for that matter—because he was one of them kind that can't bear to make a will. He left a letter behind for Harvey, and said he'd told in it where his money was hid, and how he wanted the rest of the property divided up so George's g'yirls would be all right—for George didn't leave nothing. And that letter was all they could get him to put a pen to."

"Why do you reckon Harvey didn't come? Wher' does he live?"

"Oh, he lives in England—Sheffield—preaches there—hasn't ever been in this country. He hasn't had any too much time—and besides he mightn't a got the letter at all, you know."

"Too bad, too bad he couldn't a lived to see his brothers, poor soul. You going to Orleans, you say?"

"Yes, but that ain't only a part of it. I'm going in a ship, next Wednesday, for Ryo Janeero, where my uncle lives."

"It's a pretty long journey. But it'll be lovely; I wisht I was agoing. Is Mary Jane the oldest? How old is the others?"

"Mary Jane's nineteen, Susan's fifteen, and Joanna's about fourteen—that's the one that gives herself to good works and has a hare-lip."

"Poor things! to be left alone in the cold world so."

"Well, they could be worse off. Old Peter had friends, and they ain't going to let them come to no harm. There's Hobson, the Babtis' preacher; and Deacon Lot Hovey, and Ben Rucker, and Abner Shackleford, and Levi Bell, the lawyer; and Dr. Robinson, and their wives, and the widow Bartley, and—well, there's a lot of them; but these are the ones that Peter was thickest with, and used to write about sometimes, when he wrote home; so Harvey'll know where to look for friends when he get's here."

Well, the old man he went on asking questions till he just fairly emptied that young fellow. Blamed if he didn't inquire about everybody and everything in that blessed town, and all about all the Wilkses; and about Peter's business—which was a tanner; and about George's—which was a carpenter; and about Harvey's—which was a dis-sentering minister; and so on, and so on. Then he says:

"What did you want to walk all the way up to the steamboat for?"

"Because she's a big Orleans boat, and I was afeard she mightn't stop there. When they're deep they won't stop for a hail. A Cincinnati boat will, but this is a St. Louis one."

"Was Peter Wilks well off?"

"Oh, yes, pretty well off. He had houses and land, and it's reckoned he left three or four thousand in cash hid up som'ers."

"When did you say he died?"

"I didn't say, but it was last night."

"Funeral to-morrow, likely?"

"Yes, 'bout the middle of the day."

"Well, it's all terrible sad; but we've all got to go, one time or another. So what we want to do is to be prepared; then we're all right."

"Yes, sir, it's the best way. Ma used to always say that."

When we struck the boat, she was about done loading, and pretty soon she got off. The king never said nothing about going aboard, so I lost my ride, after all. When the boat was gone, the king made me paddle up another mile to a lonesome place, and then he got ashore, and says:

"Now hustle back, right off, and fetch the duke up here, and the new carpet-bags. And if he's gone over to t'other side, go over there and git him. And tell him to git him-self up regardless. Shove along, now."

I see what *he* was up to; but I never said nothing, of course. When I got back with the duke, we hid the canoe and then they set down on a log, and the king told him every-thing, just like the young fellow had said it—every last word of it. And all the time he was a doing it, he tried to talk like an Englishman; and he done it pretty well too, for a slouch. I can't imitate him, and so I ain't agoing to try to; but he really done it pretty good. Then he says:

"How are you on the deef and dumb, Bilgewater?"

The duke said, leave him alone for that; said he had played a deef and dumb person on the histrionic boards. So then they waited for a steamboat.

About the middle of the afternoon a couple of little boats come along, but they didn't come from high enough up the river; but at last there was a big one, and they hailed her. She sent out her yawl, and we went aboard, and she was from Cincinnati; and when they found we only wanted to go four or five mile, they was booming mad, and give us a cussing, and said they wouldn't land us. But the king was ca'm. He says:

"If gentlemen kin afford to pay a dollar a mile apiece, to be took on and put off in a yawl, a steamboat kin afford to carry 'em, can't it?"

So they softened down and said it was all right; and when we got to the village, they yawled us ashore. About two dozen men flocked down, when they see the yawl a com-ing; and when the king says—

"Kin any of you gentlemen tell me wher' Mr. Peter Wilks lives?" they give a glance at one another, and nodded their heads, as much as to say, "What d' I tell you?" Then one of them says, kind of soft and gentle:

"I'm sorry, sir, but the best we can do is to tell you where he *did* live yesterday evening."

Sudden as winking, the ornery old cretur went all to smash, and fell up against the man, and put his chin on his shoulder, and cried down his back, and says:

"Alas, alas, our poor brother—gone, and we never got to see him; oh, it's too, *too* hard!"

Then he turns around, blubbering, and makes a lot of idiotic signs to the duke on his hands, and blamed if *he* didn't drop a carpet-bag and bust out a-crying. If they warn't the beatenest lot, them two frauds, that ever I struck.

Well, the men gethered around, and sympathized with them, and said all sorts of kind things to them, and carried their carpet-bags up the hill for them, and let them lean on them and cry, and told the king all about his brother's last moments, and the king he told it all over again on his hands to the duke, and both of them took on about that dead tanner like they'd lost the twelve disciples. Well, if ever I struck anything like it, I'm a nigger. It was enough to make a body ashamed of the human race.

Chapter XXV

The news was all over town in two minutes, and you could see the people tearing down on the run, from every which way, some of them putting on their coats as they come. Pretty soon we was in the middle of a crowd, and the noise of the tramping was like a soldier-march. The windows and door-yards was full; and every minute somebody would say, over a fence:

"Is it *them?*"

And somebody trotting along with the gang would answer back and say,

"You bet it is."

When we got to the house, the street in front of it was packed, and the three girls was standing in the door. Mary Jane *was* red-headed, but that don't make no difference, she was most awful beautiful, and her face and her eyes was all lit up like glory, she was so glad her uncles was come. The king he spread his arms, and Mary Jane she jumped for them, and the hare-lip jumped for the duke, and there they *had* it! Everybody most, leastways women, cried for joy to see them meet again at last and have such good times.

Then the king he hunched the duke, private—I see him do it—and then he looked around and see the coffin, over in the corner on two chairs; so then, him and the duke, with a hand across each other's shoulder, and t'other hand to their eyes, walked slow and solemn over there, everybody dropping back to give them room, and all the talk and noise stopping, people saying "Sh!" and all the men taking their hats off and drooping their heads, so you could a heard a pin fall. And when they got there, they bent over and looked in the coffin, and took one sight, and then they bust out a crying so you could a heard them to Orleans, most; and then they put their arms around each other's necks, and hung their chins over each other's shoulders; and then for three minutes, or maybe four, I never see two men leak the way they done. And mind you, everybody was doing the same; and the place was that damp I never see anything like it. Then one of them got on one side of the coffin, and t'other on t'other side, and they kneeled down and rested their foreheads on the coffin, and let on to pray all to theirselves. Well, when it come to that, it worked the crowd like you never see anything like it, and so everybody broke down and went to sobbing right out loud—the poor girls, too; and every woman, nearly, went up to the girls, without saying a word, and kissed them, solemn, on the forehead, and then put their hand on their head, and looked up towards the sky, with the tears running down, and then busted out and went off sobbing and swabbing, and give the next woman a show. I never see anything so disgusting.

Well, by-and-by the king he gets up and comes forward a little, and works himself up and slobbers out a speech, all full of tears and flapdoodle about its being a sore trial for him and his poor brother to lose the diseased, and to miss seeing diseased alive, after the long journey of four thousand mile, but its a trial that's sweetened and sanctified to us by this dear sympathy and these holy tears, and so he thanks them out of his heart and out of his brother's heart, because out of their mouths they can't, words being too weak and cold, and all that kind of rot and slush, till it was just sickening; and then he blubbers out a pious goody-goody Amen, and turns himself loose and goes to crying fit to bust.

And the minute the words was out of his mouth somebody over in the crowd struck up the doxolojer, and everybody joined in with all their might, and it just warmed you up and made you feel as good as church letting out. Music *is* a good thing; and after all that soul-butter and hogwash, I never see it freshen up things so, and sound so honest and bully.

Then the king begins to work his jaw again, and says how him and his nieces would be glad if a few of the main principal friends of the family would take supper here with them this evening, and help set up with the ashes of the diseased; and says if his poor brother laying yonder could speak, he knows who he would name, for they was names that was very dear to him, and mentioned often in his letters; and so he will name the same, to-wit, as follows, vizz:—Rev. Mr. Hobson, and Deacon Lot Hovey, and Mr. Ben Rucker, and Abner Shackleford, and Levi Bell, and Dr. Robinson, and their wives, and the widow Bartley.

Rev. Hobson and Dr. Robinson was down to the end of the town, a-hunting together; that is, I mean the doctor was shipping a sick man to t'other world, and the preacher was pinting him right. Lawyer Bell was away up to Louisville on some business. But the rest was on hand, and so they all come and shook hands with the king and thanked him and talked to him; and then they shook hands with the duke, and didn't say nothing but just kept a-smiling and bobbing their heads like a passel of sapheads whilst he made all sorts of signs with his hands and said "Goo-goo—goo-goo-goo," all the time, like a baby that can't talk.

So the king he blatted along, and managed to inquire about pretty much everybody and dog in town, by his name, and mentioned all sorts of little things that happened one time or another in the town, or to George's family, or to Peter; and he always let on that Peter wrote him the things, but that was a lie, he got every blessed one of them out of that young flathead that we canoed up to the steamboat.

Then Mary Jane she fetched the letter her father left behind, and the king he read it out loud and cried over it. It give the dwelling-house and three thousand dollars, gold, to the girls; and it give the tanyard (which was doing a good business), along with some other houses and land (worth about seven thousand), and three thousand dollars in gold to Harvey and William, and told where the six thousand cash was hid, down cellar.

So these two frauds said they'd go and fetch it up, and have everything square and above-board; and told me to come with a candle. We shut the cellar door behind us, and when they found the bag they spilt it out on the floor, and it was a lovely sight, all of them yaller-boys. My, the way the king's eyes did shine! He slaps the duke on the shoulder, and says:

"Oh, *this* ain't bully, nor noth'n! Oh, no, I reckon not! Why, Biljy, it beats the Nonesuch, *don't* it!"

The duke allowed it did. They pawed the yaller-boys, and sifted them through their fingers and let them jingle down on the floor; and the king says:

"It ain't no use talkin'; bein' brothers to a rich dead man, and representatives of furrin heirs that's got left, is the line for you and me, Bilge. Thish-yer comes of trust'n to Providence. It's the best way, in the long run. I've tried 'em all, and ther' ain't no better way."

Most everybody would a been satisfied with the pile, and took it on trust; but no, they must count it. So they counts it, and it comes out four hundred and fifteen dollars short. Says the king:

"Dern him, I wonder what he done with the four hundred and fifteen dollars?"

They worried over that a while, and ransacked all around for it. Then the duke says:

"Well, he was a pretty sick man, and likely he made a mistake—I reckon that's the way of it. The best way's to let it go, and keep still about it. We can spare it."

"Oh, shucks, yes, we can *spare* it. I don't k'yer noth'n 'bout that—it's the *count* I'm thinkin' about. We want to be awful square and open and above-board, here, you know. We want to lug this h-yer money up stairs and count it before everybody—then ther' ain't noth'n suspicious. But when the dead man says ther's six thous'n dollars, you know, we don't want to—"

"Hold on," says the duke. "Less make up the deffisit"—and he begun to haul out yaller-boys out of his pocket.

"It's a most amaz'n' good idea, duke—you *have* got a rattlin' clever head on you," says the king. "Blest if the old Nonesuch ain't a heppin' us out agin"—and *he* begun to haul out yaller-jackets and stack them up.

It most busted them, but they made up the six thousand clean and clear.

"Say," says the duke, "I got another idea. Le's go up stairs and count this money, and then take and *give it to the girls.*"

"Good land, duke, lemme hug you! It's the most dazzling idea 'at ever a man struck. You have cert'nly got the most astonishin' head I ever see. Oh, this is the boss dodge, ther' ain't no mistake 'bout it. Let 'em fetch along their suspicions now, if they want to—this'll lay 'em out."

When we got up stairs, everybody gethered around the table, and the king he counted it and stacked it up, three hundred dollars in a pile—twenty elegant little piles. Everybody looked hungry at it, and licked their chops. Then they raked it into the bag again, and I see the king begin to swell himself up for another speech. He says:

"Friends all, my poor brother that lays yonder, has done generous by them that's left behind in the vale of sorrers. He has done generous by these-yer poor little lambs that he loved and sheltered, and that's left fatherless and motherless. Yes, and we that knowed him, knows that he would a done *more* generous by 'em if he hadn't ben afeard o' woundin' his dear William and me. Now, *wouldn't* he? Ther' ain't no question 'bout it, in *my* mind. Well, then—what kind o' brothers would it be, that 'd stand in his way at sech a time? And what kind o' uncles would it be that 'd rob—yes, *rob*—sech poor sweet lambs as these 'at he loved so, at sech a time? If I know William—and I *think* I do—he—well, I'll jest ask him." He turns around and begins to make a lot of signs to the duke with his hands; and the duke he looks at him stupid and leather-headed a while, then all of a sudden he seems to catch his meaning, and jumps for the king, goo-gooing with all his might for joy, and hugs him about fifteen times before he lets up. Then the king says, "I knowed it; I reckon *that* 'll convince anybody the way *he* feels about it. Here, Mary Jane, Susan, Joanner, take the money—take it *all.* It's the gift of him that lays yonder, cold but joyful."

Mary Jane she went for him, Susan and the hare-lip went for the duke, and then such another hugging and kissing I never see yet. And everybody crowded up with the tears in their eyes, and most shook the hands off of them frauds, saying all the time:

"You *dear* good souls!—how *lovely!*—how *could* you!"

Well, then, pretty soon all hands got to talking about the diseased again, and how good he was, and what a loss he was, and all that; and before long a big iron-jawed man worked himself in there from outside, and stood a listening and looking, and not saying anything; and nobody saying anything to him either, because the king was talking and they was all busy listening. The king was saying—in the middle of something he'd started in on—

"—they bein' partickler friends o' the diseased. That's why they're invited here this evenin'; but to-morrow we want *all* to come—everybody; for he respected everybody, he liked everybody, and so it's fitten that his funeral orgiess h'd be public."

And so he went a-mooning on and on, liking to hear himself talk, and every little while he fetched in his funeral orgies again, till the duke he couldn't stand it no more; so he writes on a little scrap of paper, "*obsequies,* you old fool," and folds it up and goes to goo-gooing and reaching it over people's heads to him. The king he reads it, and puts it in his pocket, and says:

"Poor William, afflicted as he is, his *heart's* aluz right. Asks me to invite everybody to come to the funeral—wants me to make 'em all welcome. But he needn't a worried—it was jest what I was at."

Then he weaves along again, perfectly ca'm, and goes to dropping in his funeral orgies again every now and then, just like he done before. And when he done it the third time, he says:

"I say orgies, no because it's the common term, because it ain't—obsequies bein' the common term—but because orgies is the right term. Obsequies ain't used in England no more, now—it's gone out. We say orgies now, in England. Orgies is better, because it means the thing you're after, more exact. It's a word that's made up out'n the Greek *orgo,* outside, open, abroad; and the Hebrew *jessum,* to plant, cover up; hence *inter.* So, you see, funeral orgies is an open er public funeral."

He was the *worst* I ever struck. Well, the iron-jawed man he laughed right in his face. Everybody was shocked. Everybody says, "Why *doctor!*" and Abner Shackleford says:

"Why, Robinson, hain't you heard the news? This is Harvey Wilks."

The king he smiled eager, and shoved out his flapper, and says:

"*Is* it my poor brother's dear good friend and physician? I——"

"Keep your hands off of me!" says the doctor. "*You* talk like an Englishman—*don't* you? It's the worse imitation I ever heard. *You* Peter Wilks's brother. You're a fraud, that's what you are!"

Well, how they all took on! They crowded around the doctor, and tried to quiet him down, and tried to explain to him, and tell him how Harvey'd showed in forty ways that he *was* Harvey, and knowed everybody by name, and the names of the very dogs, and begged and *begged* him not to hurt Harvey's feelings and the poor girls' feelings, and all that; but it warn't no use, he stormed right along, and said any man that pretended to be an Englishman and couldn't imitate the lingo no better than what he did, was a fraud and a liar. The poor girls was hanging to the king and crying; and all of a sudden the doctor ups and turns on *them*. He says:

"I was your father's friend, and I'm your friend; and I warn you *as* a friend, and an honest one, that wants to protect you and keep you out of harm and trouble, to turn your backs on that scoundrel, and have nothing to do with him, the ignorant tramp, with his idiotic Greek and Hebrew as he calls it. He is the thinnest kind of an impostor—has come here with a lot of empty names and facts which he has picked up somewheres, and you take them for *proofs,* and are helped to fool yourselves by these foolish friends here, who ought to know better. Mary Jane Wilks, you know me for your friend, and for your unselfish friend, too. Now listen to me; turn this pitiful rascal out—I *beg* you to do it. Will you?"

Mary Jane straightened herself up, and my, but she was handsome! She says:

"*Here* is my answer." She hove up the bag of money and put it in the king's hands, and says, "Take this six thousand dollars, and invest for me and my sisters any way you want to, and don't give us no receipt for it."

Then she put her arm around the king on one side, and Susan and the harelip done the same on the other. Everybody clapped their hands and stomped on the floor like a perfect storm, whilst the king held up his head and smiled proud. The doctor says:

"All right, I wash *my* hands of the matter. But I warn you all that a time's coming when you're going to feel sick whenever you think of this day"—and away he went.

"All right, doctor," says the king, kinder mocking him, "we'll try and get 'em to send for you"—which made them all laugh, and they said it was a prime good hit.

Chapter XXVI

Well when they was all gone, the king he asks Mary Jane how they was off for spare rooms, and she said she had one spare room, which would do for Uncle William and she'd give her own room to Uncle Harvey, which was a little bigger, and she would turn into the room with her sisters and sleep on a cot; and up garret was a little cubby, with a pallet in it. The king said the cubby would do for his valley—meaning me.

So Mary Jane took us up, and she showed them their rooms, which was plain but nice. She said she'd have her frocks and a lot of other traps took out of her room if they was in Uncle Harvey's way, but he said they warn't. The frocks was hung along the wall, and before them was a curtain made out of calico that hung down to the floor. There was an old hair trunk in one corner, and a guitar box in another, and all sorts of little knick-knacks and jimcracks around, like girls brisken up a room with. The king said it was all the more homely and more pleasanter for these fixings, and so don't disturb them. The duke's room was pretty small, but plenty good enough, and so was my cubby.

That night they had a big supper, and all them men and women was there, and I stood behind the king and the duke's chairs and waited on them, and the niggers waited on the rest. Mary Jane she set at the head of the table, with Susan along side of her, and said how bad the biscuits was, and how mean the preserves was, and how ornery and tough the fried chickens was—and all that kind of rot, the way women always do for to force out compliments; and the people all knowed everything was tip-top, and said so—said "How *do* you get biscuits to brown so nice?" and "Where, for the land's sake *did* you get these amaz'n pickles?" and all that kind of humbug talky-talk, just the way people always does at a supper, you know.

And when it was all done, me and the hare-lip had supper in the kitchen off of the leavings, whilst the others was helping the niggers clean up the things. The hare-lip she got to pumping me about England, and blest if I didn't think the ice was getting mighty thin, sometimes. She says:

"Did you ever see the king?"

"Who? William Fourth? Well, I bet I have—he goes to our church." I knowed he was dead years ago, but I never let on. So when I says he goes to our church, she says:

"What—regular?"

"Yes—regular. His pew's right over opposite ourn—on 'tother side the pulpit."

"I thought he lived in London?"

"Well, he does. Where *would* he live?"

"But I thought *you* lived in Sheffield?"

I see I was up a stump. I had to let on to get choked with a chicken bone, so as to get time to think how to get down again. Then I says:

"I mean he goes to our church regular when he's in Sheffield. That's only in the summer-time, when he comes there to take the sea baths."

"Why, how you talk—Sheffield ain't on the sea."

"Well, who said it was?"

"Why, you did."

"I *didn't*, nuther."

"You did!"

"I didn't."

"You did."

"I never said nothing of the kind."

"Well, what *did* you say, then?"

"Said he come to take the sea *baths*—that's what I said."

"Well, then! how's he going to take the sea baths if it ain't on the sea?"

"Looky here," I says; "did you ever see any Congress water?"

"Yes."

"Well, did you have to go to Congress to get it?"

"Why, no."

"Well, neither does William Fourth have to go to the sea to get a sea bath."

"How does he get it, then?"

"Gets it the way people down here gets Congress-water—in barrels. There in the palace at Sheffield they've got furnaces, and he wants his water hot. They can't bile that amount of water away off there at the sea. They haven't got no conveniences for it."

"Oh, I see, now. You might a said that in the first place and saved time."

When she said that, I see I was out of the woods again, and so I was comfortable and glad. Next, she says:

"Do you go to church, too?"

"Yes—regular."

"Where do you set?"

"Why, in our pew."

"*Whose* pew?"

"Why, *ourn*—your Uncle Harvey's."

"His'n? What does *he* want with a pew?"

"Wants it to set in. What did you *reckon* he wanted with it?"

"Why, I thought he'd be in the pulpit."

Rot him, I forgot he was a preacher. I see I was up a stump again, so I played another chicken bone and got another think. Then I says:

"Blame it, do you suppose there ain't but one preacher to a church?"

"Why, what do they want with more?"

"What!—to preach before a king? I never see such a girl as you. They don't have no less than seventeen."

"Seventeen! My land! Why, I wouldn't set out such a string as that, not if I *never* got to glory. It must take 'em a week."

"Shucks, they don't *all* of 'em preach the same day—only *one* of 'em."

"Well, then, what does the rest of 'em do?"

"Oh, nothing much. Loll around, pass the plate—and one thing or another. But mainly they don't do nothing."

"Well, then, what are they *for?*"

"Why, they're for *style*. Don't you know nothing?"

"Well, I don't *want* to know no such foolishness as that. How is servants treated in England? Do they treat 'em better 'n we treat our niggers?"

"*No!* A servant ain't nobody there. They treat them worse than dogs."

"Don't they give 'em holidays, the way we do, Christmas and New Year's week, and Fourth of July?"

"Oh, just listen! A body could tell *you* hain't ever been to England, by that. Why, Hare-l—why, Joanna, they never see a holiday from year's end to year's end; never go to the circus, nor theatre, nor nigger shows, nor nowheres."

"Nor church?"

"Nor church."

"But *you* always went to church."

Well, I was gone up again. I forgot I was the old man's servant. But next minute I whirled in on a kind of an explanation how a valley was different from a common servant, and *had* to go to church whether he wanted to or not, and set with the family, on account of it's being the law. But I didn't do it pretty good, and when I got done I see she warn't satisfied. She says:

"Honest injun, now, hain't you been telling me a lot of lies?"

"Honest injun," says I.

"None of it at all?"

"None of it at all. Not a lie in it," says I.

"Lay your hand on this book and say it."

I see it warn't nothing but a dictionary, so I laid my hand on it and said it. So then she looked a little better satisfied, and says:

"Well, then, I'll believe some of it; but I hope to gracious if I'll believe the rest."

"What is it you won't believe, Joe?" says Mary Jane, stepping in with Susan behind her. "It ain't right nor kind for you to talk so to him, and him a stranger and so far from his people. How would you like to be treated so?"

"That's always your way, Maim—always sailing in to help somebody before they're hurt. I hain't done nothing to him. He's told some stretchers, I reckon; and I said I wouldn't swallow it all; and that's every bit and grain I *did* say. I reckon he can stand a little thing like that, can't he?"

"I don't care whether 'twas little or whether 'twas big, he's here in our house and a stranger, and it wasn't good of you to say it. If you was in his place, it would make you feel ashamed; and so you oughtn't to say a thing to another person that will make *them* feel ashamed."

"Why, Maim, he said——"

"It don't make no difference what he *said*—that ain't the thing. The thing is for you to treat him *kind,* and not be saying things to make him remember he ain't in his own country and amongst his own folks."

I says to myself, *this* is a girl that I'm letting that old reptile rob her of her money!

Then Susan *she* waltzed in; and if you'll believe me, she did give Hare-lip hark from the tomb!

Says I to myself, And this is *another* one that I'm letting him rob her of her money!

Then Mary Jane she took another inning, and went in sweet and lovely again—which was her way—but when she got done there warn't hardly anything left o' poor Hare-lip. So she hollered.

"All right, then," says the other girls, "you just ask his pardon."

She done it, too. And she done it beautiful. She done it so beautiful it was good to hear; and I wished I could tell her a thousand lies, so she could do it again.

I says to myself, this is *another* one that I'm letting him rob her of her money. And when she got through, they all jest laid theirselves out to make me feel at home and know I was amongst friends. I felt so ornery and low down and mean, that I says to myself, My mind's made up; I'll hive that money for them or bust.

So then I lit out—for bed, I said, meaning some time or another. When I got by myself, I went to thinking the thing over. I says to myself, shall I go to that doctor, private, and blow on these frauds? No—that won't do. He might tell who told him; then the king and the duke would make it warm for me. Shall I go, private, and tell Mary Jane? No—I dasn't do it. Her face would give them a hint, sure; they've got the money, and they'd slide right out and get away with it. If she was to fetch in help, I'd get mixed up in the business, before it was done with, I judge. No, there ain't no good way but one. I got to steal that money, somehow; and I got to steal it some way that they won't suspicion that I done it. They've got a good thing, here; and they ain't agoing to leave till they've played this family and this town for all they're worth, so I'll find a chance time enough. I'll steal it, and hide it; and by-and-by, when I'm away down the river, I'll write a letter and tell Mary Jane where it's hid. But I better hive it to-night, if I can, because the doctor maybe hasn't let up as much as he lets on he has; he might scare them out of here, yet.

So, thinks I, I'll go and search them rooms. Up stairs the hall was dark, but I found the duke's room, and started to paw around it with my hands; but I recollected it wouldn't be much like the king to let anybody else take care of that money but his own self; so then I went to his room and begun to paw around there. But I see I couldn't do nothing without a candle, and I dasn't light one, of course. So I judged I'd got to do the other thing—lay for them, and eavesdrop. About that time, I hears their footsteps coming, and was going to skip under the bed; I reached for it, but it wasn't where I thought it would be; but I touched the curtain that hid Mary Jane's frocks, so I jumped in behind that and snuggled in amongst the gowns, and stood there perfectly still.

They come in and shut the door; and the first thing the duke done was to get down and look under the bed. Then I was glad I hadn't found the bed when I wanted it. And yet, you know, it's kind of natural to hide under the bed when you are up to anything private. They sets down, then, and the king says:

"Well, what is it? and cut it middlin' short, because it's better for us to be down there a whoopin'-up the mournin', than up here givin' 'em a chance to talk us over."

"Well, this is it, Capet. I ain't easy; I ain't comfortable. That doctor lays on my mind. I wanted to know your plans. I've got a notion, and I think it's a sound one."

"What is it, duke?"

"That we better glide out of this, before three in the morning, and clip it down the river with what we've got. Specially, seeing we got it so easy—*given* back to us, flung at our heads, as you may say, when of course we allowed to have to steal it back. I'm for knocking off and lighting out."

That made me feel pretty bad. About an hour or two ago, it would a been a little different, but now it made me feel bad and disappointed. The king rips out and says:

"What! And not sell out the rest o' the property? March off like a passel o' fools and leave eight or nine thous'n' dollars' worth o' property layin' around jest sufferin' to be scooped in?—and all good salable stuff, too."

The duke he grumbled; said the bag of gold was enough, and he didn't want to go no deeper—didn't want to rob a lot of orphans of *everything* they had.

"Why, how you talk!" says the king. "We shan't rob 'em of nothing at all but jest this money. The people that *buys* the property is the suff'rers; because as soon's it's found out 'at we didn't own it—which won't be long after we've slid—the sale won't be valid, and it'll all go back to the estate. These-yer orphans 'll git their house back agin, and that's enough for *them;* they're young and spry, and k'n easy earn a livin'. *They* ain't agoing to suffer. Why, jest think—there's thous'n's and thous'n's that ain't nigh so well off. Bless you, *they* ain't got noth'n to complain of."

Well, the king he talked him blind; so at last he give in, and said all right, but said he believed it was blame foolishness to stay, and that doctor hanging over them. But the king says:

"Cuss the doctor! What do we k'yer for *him?* Hain't we got all the fools in town on our side? and ain't that a big enough majority in any town?"

So they got ready to go down stairs again. The duke says:

"I don't think we put that money in a good place."

That cheered me up. I'd begun to think I warn't going to get a hint of no kind to help me. The king says:

"Why?"

"Because Mary Jane 'll be in mourning from this out; and first you know the nigger that does up the rooms will get an order to box these duds up and put 'em away; and do you reckon a nigger can run across money and not borrow some of it?"

"Your head's level, agin, duke," says the king; and he come a fumbling under the curtain two or three foot from where I was. I stuck tight to the wall, and kept mighty still, though quivery; and I wondered what them fellows would say to me if they catched me; and I tried to think what I'd better do if they did catch me. But the king he got the bag before I could think more than about a half a thought, and he never suspicioned I was around. They took and shoved the bag through a rip in the straw tick that was under the feather bed, and crammed it in a foot or two amongst the straw and said it was all right, now, because a nigger only makes up the feather bed, and don't turn over the straw tick only about twice a year, and so it warn't in no danger of getting stole, now.

But I knowed better. I had it out of there before they was half-way down stairs. I groped along up to my cubby, and hid it there till I could get a chance to do better. I judged I better hide it outside of the house somewheres, because if they missed it they would give the house a good ransacking. I knowed that very well. Then I turned in, with my clothes all on; but I couldn't a gone to sleep, if I'd a wanted to, I was in such a sweat to get through with the business. By-and-by I heard the king and the duke come up; so I rolled off of my pallet and laid with my chin at the top of my ladder and waited to see if anything was going to happen. But nothing did.

So I held on till all the late sounds had quit and the early ones hadn't begun, yet; and then I slipped down the ladder.

Chapter XXVII

I crept to their doors and listened; they was snoring, so I tip-toed along, and got down stairs all right. There warn't a sound anywheres. I peeped through a crack of the dining-room door, and see the men that was watching the corpse all sound asleep on their chairs. The door was open into the parlor, where the corpse was laying, and there was a candle in both rooms. I passed along, and the parlor door was open; but I see there warn't nobody in there but the remainders of Peter; so I shoved on by; but the front door was locked, and the key wasn't there. Just then I heard somebody coming down the stairs, back behind me. I run in the parlor, and took a swift look around, and the only place I could see to hide the bag was in the coffin. The lid was shoved along about a foot, showing the dead man's face down in there, with a wet cloth over it, and his shroud on. I tucked the money-bag in under the lid, just down beyond where his hands was crossed, which made me creep, they was so cold, and then I run back across the room and in behind the door.

The person coming was Mary Jane. She went to the coffin, very soft, and kneeled down and looked in; then she put up her handkerchief and I see she begun to cry, though I couldn't hear her, and her back was to me. I slid out, and as I passed the dining-room I thought I'd make sure them watchers hadn't seen me; so I looked through the crack and everything was all right. They hadn't stirred.

I slipped up to bed, feeling ruther blue, on accounts of the thing playing out that way after I had took so much trouble and run so much resk about it. Says I, if it could stay where it is, all right; because when we get down the river a hundred mile or two, I could write back to Mary Jane, and she could dig him up again and get it; but that ain't the thing that's going to happen; the thing that's going to happen is, the money'll be found when they come to screw on the lid. Then the king'll get it again, and it'll be a long day before he gives anybody another chance to smouch it from him. Of course I *wanted* to slide down and get it out of there, but I dasn't try it. Every minute it was getting earlier, now, and pretty soon some of them watchers would begin to stir, and I might get catched—catched with six thousand dollars in my hands that nobody hadn't hired me to take care of. I don't wish to be mixed up in no such business as that, I says to myself.

When I got down stairs in the morning, the parlor was shut up, and the watchers was gone. There warn't nobody around but the family and the widow Bartley and our tribe. I watched their faces to see if anything had been happening, but I couldn't tell.

Towards the middle of the day the undertaker come, with his man, and they set the coffin in the middle of the room on a couple of chairs, and then set all our chairs in rows, and borrowed more from the neighbors till the hall and the parlor and the dining-room was full. I see the coffin lid was the way it was before, but I dasn't go to look in under it, with folks around.

Then the people begun to flock in, and the beats and the girls took seats in the front row at the head of the coffin, and for a half an hour the people filed around slow, in single rank, and looked down at the dead man's face a minute, and some dropped in a tear, and it was all very still and solemn, only the girls and the beats holding handkerchiefs to their eyes and keeping their heads bent, and sobbing a little. There warn't no other sound but the scraping of the feet on the floor, and blowing noses—because people always blows them more at a funeral than they do at other places except church.

When the place was packed full, the undertaker he slid around in his black gloves with his softy soothering ways, putting on the last touches, and getting people and things all ship-shape and comfortable, and making no more sound than a cat. He never spoke; he moved people around, he squeezed in late ones, he opened up passage-ways, and done it all with nods, and signs with his hands. Then he took his place over against the wall. He was the softest, glidingest, stealthiest man I ever see; and there warn't no more smile to him than there is to a ham.

They had borrowed a melodeum—a sick one; and when everything was ready, a young woman set down and worked it, and it was pretty skreeky and colicky, and everybody joined in and sung, and Peter was the only one that had a good thing, according to my notion. Then the Reverend Hobson opened up, slow and solemn, and begun to talk; and straight off the most outrageous row busted out in the cellar a body ever heard; it was only one dog, but he made a most powerful racket, and he kept it up, right along; the parson he had to stand there, over the coffin, and wait—you couldn't hear yourself think. It was right down awkward, and nobody didn't seem to know what to do. But pretty soon they see that long-legged undertaker make a sign to the preacher as much as to say, "Don't you worry—just depend on me." Then he stooped down and begun to glide along the wall, just his shoulders showing over the people's heads. So he glided along, and the pow-wow and racket getting more and more outrageous all the time; and at last, when he had gone around two sides of the room, he disappears down cellar. Then, in about two seconds we heard a whack, and the dog he finished up with a most amazing howl or two, and then everything was dead still, and the parson begun his solemn talk where he left off. In a minute or two here comes this undertaker's back and shoulders gliding along the wall again; and so he glided, and glided, around three sides of the room, and then rose up, and shaded his mouth with his hands, and stretched his neck out towards the preacher, over the people's heads, and says, in a kind of a coarse whisper, "*He had a rat!*" Then he drooped down and glided along the wall again to his place. You could see it was a great satisfaction to the people, because naturally they wanted to know. A little thing like that don't cost nothing, and it's just the little things that makes a man to be looked up to and liked. There warn't no more popular man in town than what that undertaker was.

Well, the funeral sermon was very good, but pison long and tiresome; and then the king he shoved in and got off some of his usual rubbage, and at last the job was through, and the undertaker begun to sneak up on the coffin with his screw-driver. I was in a sweat then, and watched him pretty keen. But he never meddled at all; just slid the lid along, as soft as mush, and screwed it down tight and fast. So there I was! I didn't know whether the money was in there, or not. So, says I, spose somebody has hogged that bag on the sly?—now how do *I* know whether to write to Mary Jane or not? 'Spose she dug him up and didn't find nothing—what would she think of me? Blame it, I says, I might get hunted up and jailed; I'd better lay low and keep dark, and not write at all; the thing's awful mixed, now; trying to better it, I've worsened it a hundred times, and I wish to goodness I'd just let it alone, dad fetch the whole business!

They buried him, and we come back home, and I went to watching faces again—I couldn't help it, and I couldn't rest easy. But nothing come of it; the faces didn't tell me nothing.

The king he visited around, in the evening, and sweetened every body up, and made himself ever so friendly; and he give out the idea that his congregation over in England would be in a sweat about him, so he must hurry and settle up the estate right away, and leave for home. He was very sorry he was so pushed, and so was everybody; they wished he could stay longer, but they said they could see it couldn't be done. And he said of course him and William would take the girls home with them; and that pleased every-body too, because then the girls would be well fixed, and amongst their own relations; and it pleased the girls, too—tickled them so they clean forgot they ever had a trouble in the world; and told him to sell out as quick as he wanted to, they would be ready. Them poor things was that glad and happy it made my heart ache to see them getting fooled and lied to so, but I didn't see no safe way for me to chip in and change the general tune.

Well, blamed if the king didn't bill the house and the niggers and all the property for auction straight off—sale two days after the funeral; but anybody could buy private be-forehand if they wanted to.

So the next day after the funeral, along about noontime, the girls' joy got the first jolt; a couple of nigger traders come along, and the king sold them the niggers reason-able, for three-day drafts as they called it, and away they went, the two sons up the river to Memphis, and their mother down the river to Orleans. I thought them poor girls and them niggers would break their hearts for grief; they cried around each other, and took on so it most made me down sick to see it. The girls said they hadn't ever dreamed of seeing the family separated or sold away from the town. I can't ever get it out of my memory, the sight of them poor miserable girls and niggers hanging around each other's necks and crying; and I reckon I couldn't a stood it all but would a had to bust out and tell on our gang if I hadn't knowed the sale warn't no account and the niggers would be back home in a week or two.

The thing made a big stir in the town, too, and a good many come out flat-footed and said it was scandalous to separate the mother and the children that way. It injured the frauds some; but the old fool he bulled right along, spite of all the duke could say or do, and I tell you the duke was powerful uneasy.

Next day was auction day. About broad-day in the morning, the king and the duke come up in the garret and woke me up, and I see by their look that there was trouble. The king says:

"Was you in my room night before last?"

"No, your majesty"—which was the way I always called him when nobody but our gang warn't around.

"Was you in there yesterday er last night?"

"No, your majesty."

"Honor bright, now—no lies."

"Honor bright, your majesty, I'm telling you the truth. I hain't been anear your room since Miss Mary Jane took you and the duke and showed it to you."

The duke says:

"Have you seen anybody else go in there?"

"No, your grace, not as I remember, I believe."

"Stop and think."

I studied a while, and see my chance, then I says:

"Well, I see the niggers go in there several times."

Both of them give a little jump; and looked like they hadn't ever expected it, and then like they *had*. Then the duke says:

"What, *all* of them?"

"No—leastways not all at once. That is, I don't think I ever see them all come *out* at once but just one time."

"Hello—when was that?"

"It was the day we had the funeral. In the morning. It warn't early, because I over-slept. I was just starting down the ladder, and I see them."

"Well, go on, *go on*—what did they do? How'd they act?"

"They didn't do nothing. And they didn't act anyway, much, as fur as I see. They tip-toed away; so I seen, easy enough, that they'd shoved in there to do up your majesty's room, or something, sposing you was up; and found you *warn't* up, and so they was hoping to slide out of the way of trouble without waking you up, if they hadn't already waked you up."

"Great guns, *this* is a go!" says the king; and both of them looked pretty sick, and tolerable silly. They stood there a thinking and scratching their heads, a minute, and then the duke he bust into a kind of a little raspy chuckle, and says:

"It does beat all, how neat the niggers played their hand. They let on to be *sorry* they was going out of this region! and I believed they *was* sorry. And so did you, and so did everybody. Don't ever tell *me* any more that a nigger ain't got any histrionic talent. Why, the way they played that thing, it would fool *anybody*. In my opinion there's a fortune in 'em. If I had capital and a theatre, I wouldn't want a better lay out than that—and here we've gone and sold 'em for a song. Yes, and ain't privileged to sing the song, yet. Say, where *is* that song?—that draft."

"In the bank for to be collected. Where *would* it be?"

"Well, *that's* all right then, thank goodness."

Says I, kind of timid-like:

"Is something gone wrong?"

The king whirls on me and rips out:

"None o' your business! You keep your head shet, and mind y'r own affairs—if you got any. Long as you're in this town, don't you forgit *that,* you hear?" Then he says to the duke, "We got to jest swaller it, and say noth'n: mum's the word for *us.*"

As they was starting down the ladder, the duke he chuckles again, and says:

"Quick sales *and* small profits! It's a good business—yes."

The king snarls around on him and says,

"I was trying to do for the best, in sellin' 'm out so quick. If the profits has turned out to be none, lackin' considable, and none to carry, is it my fault any more'n it's yourn?"

"Well, *they'd* be in this house yet, and we *wouldn't* if I could a got my advice listened to."

The king sassed back, as much as was safe for him, and then swapped around lit into *me* again. He give me down the banks for not coming and *telling* him I see the niggers come out of his room acting that way—said any fool would a *knowed* something was up. And then waltzed in and cussed *himself* a while; and said it all come of him not laying late and taking his natural rest that morning, and he'd be blamed if he'd ever do it again. So they went off a jawing; and I felt dreadful glad I'd worked it all off onto the niggers and yet hadn't done the niggers no harm by it.

Chapter XXVIII

By-and-by it was getting-up time; so I come down the ladder and started for down stairs, but as I come to the girls' room, the door was open, and I see Mary Jane setting by her old hair trunk, which was open and she'd been packing things in it—getting ready to go to England. But she had stopped now, with a folded gown in her lap, and had her face in her hands, crying. I felt awful bad to see it; of course anybody would. I went in there, and says:

"Miss Mary Jane, you can't abear to see people in trouble, and *I* can't—most always. Tell me about it."

So she done it. And it was the niggers—I just expected it. She said the beautiful trip to England was most about spoiled for her; she didn't know *how* she was ever going to be happy there, knowing the mother and the children warn't ever going to see each other no more—and then busted out bitterer than ever, and flung up her hands, and says:

"Oh, dear, dear, to think they ain't *ever* going to see each other any more!"

"But the *will*—and inside of two weeks—and I *know* it!" says I.

Laws it was out before I could think!—and before I could budge, she throws her arms around my neck, and told me to say it *again,* say it *again,* say it *again!*

I see I had spoke too sudden, and said too much, and was in a close place. I asked her to let me think a minute; and she set there, very impatient and excited, and handsome, but looking kind of happy and eased-up, like a person that's had a tooth pulled out. So I went to studying it out. I says to myself, I reckon a body that ups and tells the truth when he is in a tight place, is taking considerable many resks, though I ain't had no experience, and can't say for certain; but it looks so to me, anyway; and yet here's a case where I'm blest if it don't look to me like the truth is better, and actly *safer,* than a lie. I must lay it by in my mind, and think it over some time or other, it's so kind of strange and unregular. I never see nothing like it. Well, I says to myself at last, I'm agoing to chance it; I'll up and tell the truth this time, though it does seem most like setting down on a kag of powder and touching it off just to see where you'll go to. Then I says:

"Miss Mary Jane, is there any place out of town a little ways, where you could go and stay three or four days?"

"Yes—Mr. Lothrop's. Why?"

"Never mind why, yet. If I'll tell you how I know the niggers will see each other again—inside of two weeks—here in this house—and *prove* how I know it—will you go to Mr. Lothrop's and stay four days?"

"Four days!" she says; "I'll stay a year!"

"All right," I says, "I don't want nothing more out of *you* than just your word—I druther have it than another man's kiss-the-Bible." She smiled, and reddened up very sweet, and I says, "If you don't mind it, I'll shut the door—and bolt it."

Then I come back and set down again, and says:

"Don't you holler. Just set still, and take it like a man. I got to tell the truth, and you want to brace up, Miss Mary, because it's a bad kind, and going to be hard to take, but there ain't no help for it. These uncles of yourn ain't no uncles at all—they're a couple of frauds—regular dead-beats. There, now we're over the worst of it—you can stand the rest middling easy."

It jolted her up like everything, of course; but I was over the shoal water now, so I went right along, her eyes a blazing higher and higher all the time, and told her every blame thing, from where we first struck that young fool going up to the steamboat, clear through to where she flung herself onto the king's breast at the front door and he kissed her sixteen or seventeen times—and then up she jumps, with her face afire like sunset, and says:

"The brute! Come—don't waste a minute—not a *second*—we'll have them tarred and feathered, and flung in the river!"

Says I:

"Cert'nly. But do you mean, *before* you go to Mr. Lothrop's, or—"

"Oh," she says, "what am I *thinking* about!" she says, and set right down again. "Don't mind what I said—please don't—you *won't*, now, *will* you?" Laying her silky hand on mine in that kind of a way that I said I would die first. "I never thought, I was so stirred up," she says; "now go on, and I won't do so any more. You tell me what to do, and whatever you say, I'll do it."

"Well," I says, "it's a rough gang, them two frauds, and I'm fixed so I got to travel with them a while longer, whether I want to or not—I druther not tell you why—and if you was to blow on them this town would get me out of their claws, and I'd be all right, but there'd be another person that you don't know about who'd be in big trouble. Well, we got to save *him*, hain't we? Of course. Well, then, we won't blow on them."

Saying them words put a good idea in my head. I see how maybe I could get me and Jim rid of the frauds; get them jailed here, and then leave. But I didn't want to run the raft in day-time, without anybody aboard to answer questions but me; so I didn't want the plan to begin working till pretty late to-night. I says:

"Miss Mary Jane, I'll tell you what we'll do—and you won't have to stay at Mr. Lothrop's so long, nuther. How fur is it?"

"A little short of four miles—right out in the country, back here."

"Well, that'll answer. Now you go along out there, and lay low till nine or half-past, to-night, and then get them to fetch you home again—tell them you've thought of something. If you get here before eleven, put a candle in this window, and if I don't turn up, wait *till* eleven, and *then* if I don't turn up it means I'm gone, and out of the way, and safe. Then you come out and spread the news around, and get these beats jailed."

"Good," she says, "I'll do it."

"And if it just happens so that I don't get away, but get took up along with them, you must up and say I told you the whole thing beforehand, and you must stand by me all you can."

"Stand by you, indeed I will. They sha'n't touch a hair of your head!" she says, and I see her nostrils spread and her eyes snap when she said it, too.

"If I get away, I sha'n't be here," I says, "to prove these rapscallions ain't your uncles, and I couldn't do it if I *was* here. I could swear they was beats and bummers, that's all; though that's worth something. Well, there's others can do that better than what I can—and they're people that ain't going to be doubted as quick as I'd be. I'll tell you how to find them. Gimme a pencil and a piece of paper. There—'Royal Nonesuch, Bricksville.' Put it away, and don't lose it. When the court wants to find out something about these two, let them send up to Bricksville and say they've got the men that played the Royal Nonesuch, and ask for some witnesses—why, you'll have that entire town down here before you can hardly wink, Miss Mary. And they'll come a-biling, too."

I judged we had got everything fixed about right, now. So I says:

"Just let the auction go right along, and don't worry. Nobody don't have to pay for the things they buy till a whole day after the auction, on accounts of the short notice, and they ain't going out of this till they get that money—and the way we've fixed it the sale ain't going to count, and they ain't going to *get* no money. It's just like the way it was with the niggers—it warn't no sale, and the niggers will be back before long. Why, they can't collect the money for the *niggers,* yet—they're in the worst kind of a fix, Miss Mary."

"Well," she says, "I'll run down to breakfast now, and then I'll start straight for Mr. Lothrop's."

"'Deed, *that* ain't the ticket, Miss Mary Jane," I says, "by no manner of means; go *before* breakfast."

"Why?"

"What did you reckon I wanted you to go at all for, Miss Mary?"

"Well, I never thought—and come to think, I don't know. What was it?"

"Why, it's because you ain't one of these leather-face people. I don't want no better book that what your face is. A body can set down and read it off like coarse print. Do you reckon you can go and face your uncles, when they come to kiss you good-morning, and never—"

"There, there, don't! Yes, I'll go before breakfast—I'll be glad to. And leave my sisters with them?"

"Yes—never mind about them. They've got to stand it yet a while. They might suspicion something if all of you was to go. I don't want you to see them, nor your sisters, nor nobody in this town—if a neighbor was to ask how is your uncles this morning, your face would tell something. No, you go right along, Miss Mary Jane, and I'll fix it with all of them. I'll tell Miss Susan to give your love to your uncles and say you've went away for a few hours for to get a little rest and change, or to see a friend, and you'll be back to-night or early in the morning."

"Gone to see a friend is all right, but I won't have my love given to them."

"Well, then, it sha'n't be." It was well enough to tell *her* so—no harm in it. It was only a little thing to do, and no trouble; and it's the little things that smoothes people's roads the most, down here below; and it would make Mary Jane comfortable, and it wouldn't cost nothing. Then I says: "There's one more thing—that bag of money."

"Well, they've got that; and it makes me feel pretty silly to think *how* they got it."

"No, you're out, there. They hain't got it."

"Why, who's got it?"

"I wish I knowed, but I don't. I *had* it, because I stole it from them: and I stole it to give to you; and I know where I hid it, but I'm afraid it ain't there no more. I'm awful sorry, Miss Mary Jane, I'm just as sorry as I can be; but I done the best I could; I did, honest. I come nigh getting caught, and I had to shove it into the first place I come to, and run—and it warn't a good place."

"Oh, stop blaming yourself—it's too bad to do it, and I won't allow it—you couldn't help it; it wasn't your fault. Where did you hide it?"

I didn't want to set her to thinking about her troubles again; and I couldn't seem to get my mouth to tell her what would make her see that corpse laying in the coffin with that bag of money on his stomach. So for a minute I didn't say nothing—then I says:

"I'd ruther not *tell* you where I put it, Miss Mary Jane, if you don't mind letting me off; but I'll write it for you on a piece of paper, and you can read it along the road to Mr. Lothrop's, if you want to. Do you reckon that'll do?"

"Oh, yes."

So I wrote: "I put it in the coffin. It was in there when you was crying there, away in the night. I was behind the door, and I was mighty sorry for you, Miss Mary Jane."

It made my eyes water a little, to remember her crying there all by herself in the night, and them devils laying there right under her own roof, shaming her and robbing her; and when I folded it up and give it to her, I see the water come into her eyes, too; and she shook me by the hand, hard, and says:

"*Good*-bye—I'm going to do everything just as you've told me; and if I don't ever see you again, I sha'n't ever forget you, and I'll think of you a many and a many a time, and I'll *pray* for you, too!"—and she was gone.

Pray for me! I reckoned if she knowed me she'd take a job that was more nearer her size. But I bet she done it, just the same—she was just that kind. She had the grit to pray for Judus if she took the notion—there warn't no backdown to her, I judge. You may say what you want to, but in my opinion she had more sand in her than any girl I ever see; in my opinion she was just full of sand. It sounds like flattery, but it ain't no flattery. And when it comes to beauty—and goodness too—she lays over them all. I hain't ever seen her since that time that I see her go out of that door; no, I hain't ever seen her since, but I reckon I've thought of her a many and a many a million times, and of her saying she would pray for me; and if ever I'd a thought it would do any good for me to pray for *her,* blamed if I wouldn't a done it or bust.

Well, Mary Jane she lit out the back way, I reckon; because nobody see her go. When I struck Susan and the hare-lip, I says:

"What's the name of them people over on t'other side of the river that you all goes to see sometimes?"

They says:

"There's several; but it's the Proctors, mainly."

"That's the name," I says; "I most forgot it. Well, Miss Mary Jane she told me to tell you she's gone over there in a dreadful hurry—one of them's sick."

"Which one?"

"I don't know; leastways I kinder forgot; but I think it's—"

"Sakes alive, I hope it ain't *Hanner*?"

"I'm sorry to say it," I says, "but Hanner's the very one."

"My goodness—and she so well only last week! Is she took bad?"

"It ain't no name for it. They set up with her all night, Miss Mary Jane said, and they don't think she'll last many hours."

"Only think of that, now! What's the matter with her!"

I couldn't think of anything reasonable, right off that way, so I says: "Mumps."

"Mumps your granny! They don't set up with people that's got the mumps."

"They don't, don't they? You better bet they do with *these* mumps. These mumps is different. It's a new kind, Miss Mary Jane said."

"How's it a new kind?"

"Because it's mixed up with other things."

"What other things?"

"Well, measles, and whooping-cough, and erysiplas, and consumption, and yaller janders, and brain fever, and I don't know what all."

"My land! And they call it the *mumps*?"

"That's what Miss Mary Jane said."

"Well, what in the nation do they call it the *mumps* for?"

"Why, because it *is* the mumps. That's what it starts with."

"Well, ther' ain't no sense in it. A body might stump his toe, and take pison, and fall down the well, and break his neck, and bust his brains out, and somebody come along and ask what killed him, and some numskull up and say, 'Why, he stumped his *toe.*' Would ther' be any sense in that? *No.* And ther' ain't no sense in *this,* nuther. Is it ketching?"

"Is it *ketching?* Why, how you talk. Is a *harrow* catching?—in the dark? If you don't hitch onto one tooth, you're bound to on another, ain't you? And you can't get away with that tooth without fetching the whole harrow along, can you? Well, these kind of mumps is a kind of a harrow, as you may say—and it ain't no slouch of a harrow, nuther, you come to get it hitched on good."

"Well, it's awful, *I* think," says the hare-lip. "I'll go to Uncle Harvey and—"

"Oh, yes," I says, "I *would.* Of *course* I would. I wouldn't lose no time."

"Well, why wouldn't you?"

"Just look at it a minute, and maybe you can see. Hain't your uncles obleeged to get along home to England as fast as they can? And do you reckon they'd be mean enough to go off and leave you to go all that journey by yourselves? *You* know they'll wait for you. So fur, so good. Your uncle Harvey's a preacher, ain't he? Very well, then; is a *preacher* going to deceive a steamboat clerk? is he going to deceive a *ship clerk?*—so as to get them to let Miss Mary Jane go aboard? Now *you* know he ain't. What *will* he do, then? Why, he'll say, 'It's a great pity, but my church matters has got to get along the best way they can; for my niece has been exposed to the dreadful pluribus-unum mumps, and so it's my bounden duty to set down here and wait the three months it takes to show on her if she's got it.' But never mind, if you think it's best to tell your uncle Harvey—"

"Shucks, and stay fooling around here when we could all be having good times in England whilst we was waiting to find out whether Mary Jane's got it or not? Why, you talk like a muggins."

"Well, anyway, maybe you better tell some of the neighbors."

"Listen at that, now. You do beat all, for natural stupidness. Can't you *see* that *they'd* go and tell? Ther' ain't no way but just to not tell anybody at *all*."

"Well, maybe you're right—yes, I judge you *are* right."

"But I reckon we ought to tell Uncle Harvey she's gone out a while, anyway, so he wont be uneasy about her?"

"Yes, Miss Mary Jane she wanted you to do that. She says, 'Tell them to give Uncle Harvey and William my love and a kiss, and say I've run over the river to see Mr.—Mr.—what *is* the name of that rich family your uncle Peter used to think so much of?—I mean the one that—"

"Why, you must mean the Apthorps, ain't it?"

"Of course; bother them kind of names, a body can't ever seem to remember them, half the time, somehow. Yes, she said, say she has run over for to ask the Apthorps to be sure and come to the auction and buy this house, because she allowed her uncle Peter would ruther they had it than anybody else; and she's going to stick to them till they say they'll come, and then, if she ain't too tired, she's coming home; and if she is, she'll be home in the morning anyway. She said, don't say nothing about the Proctors, but only about the Apthorps—which'll be perfectly true, because she *is* going there to speak about their buying the house; I know it, because she told me so, herself."

"All right," they said, and cleared out to lay for their uncles, and give them the love and the kisses, and tell them the message.

Everything was all right now. The girls wouldn't say nothing because they wanted to go to England; and the king and the duke would ruther Mary Jane was off working for the auction than around in reach of Doctor Robinson. I felt very good; I judged I had done it pretty neat—I reckoned Tom Sawyer couldn't a done it no neater himself. Of course he would a throwed more style into it, but I can't do that very handy, not being brung up to it.

Well, they held the auction in the public square, along towards the end of the afternoon, and it strung along, and strung along, and the old man he was on hand and looking his level pisonest, up there longside of the auctioneer, and chipping in a little Scripture, now and then, or a little goody-goody saying, of some kind, and the duke he was around goo-gooing for sympathy all he knowed how, and just spreading himself generly.

But by-and-by the thing dragged through, and everything was sold. Everything but a little old trifling lot in the graveyard. So they'd got to work *that* off—I never see such a girafft as the king was for wanting to swallow *everything*. Well, whilst they was at it, a steamboat landed, and in about two minutes up comes a crowd a whooping and yelling and laughing and carrying on, and singing out:

"*Here's* your opposition line! here's your two sets o' heirs to old Peter Wilks—and you pays your money and you takes your choice!"

Chapter XXIX

They was fetching a very nice looking old gentleman along, and a nice looking younger one, with his right arm in a sling. And my souls, how the people yelled, and laughed, and kept it up. But I didn't see no joke about it, and I judged it would strain the duke and the king some to see any. I reckoned they'd turn pale. But no, nary a pale did *they* turn. The duke he never let on he suspicioned what was up, but just went a goo-gooing around, happy and satisfied, like a jug that's googling out buttermilk; and as for the king, he just gazed and gazed down sorrowful on them newcomers like it give him the stomach-ache in his very heart to think there could be such frauds and rascals in the world. Oh, he done it admirable. Lots of the principal people gethered around the king, to let him see they was on his side. That old gentleman that had just come looked all puzzled to death. Pretty soon he begun to speak, and I see, straight off, he pronounced *like* an Englishman, not the king's way, though the king's *was* pretty good, for an imitation. I can't give the old gent's words, nor I can't imitate him; but he turned around to the crowd, and says, about like this:

"This is a surprise to me which I wasn't looking for; and I'll acknowledge, candid and frank, I ain't very well fixed to meet it and answer it; for my brother and me has had misfortunes, he's broke his arm, and our baggage got put off at a town above here, last night in the night by a mistake. I am Peter Wilks's brother Harvey, and this is his brother William, which can't hear nor speak—and can't even make signs to amount to much, now't he's only got one hand to work them with. We are who we say we are; and in a day or two, when I get the baggage, I can prove it. But, up till then, I won't say nothing more, but go to the hotel and wait."

So him and the new dummy started off; and the king he laughs, and blethers out:

"Broke his arm—*very* likely *ain't* it?—and very convenient, too, for a fraud that's got to make signs, and hain't learnt how. Lost their baggage! That's *mighty* good!—and mighty ingenious—under the *circumstances!*"

So he laughed again; and so did everybody else, except three or four, or maybe half a dozen. One of these was that doctor; another one was a sharp looking gentleman, with a carpet-bag of the old-fashioned kind made out of carpet-stuff, that had just come off of the steamboat and was talking to him in a low voice, and glancing towards the king now and then and nodding their heads—it was Levi Bell, the lawyer that was gone up to Louisville; and another one was a big rough husky that come along and listened to all the old gentleman said, and was listening to the king now. And when the king got done, this husky up and says:

"Say, looky here; if you are Harvey Wilks, when'd you come to this town?"

"The day before the funeral, friend," says the king.

"But what time o' day?"

"In the evenin'—'bout an hour er two before sundown."

"*How'd* you come?"

"I come down on the *Susan Powell,* from Cincinnati."

"Well, then, how'd you come to be up at the Pint in the *mornin'*—in a canoe?"

"I warn't up at the Pint in the mornin'."

"It's a lie."

Several of them jumped for him and begged him not to talk that way to an old man and a preacher.

"Preacher be hanged, he's a fraud and a liar. He was up at the Pint that mornin'. I live up there, don't I? Well, I was up there, and he was up there. I *see* him there. He come in a canoe, along with Tim Collins and a boy."

The doctor he up and says:

"Would you know the boy again if you was to see him, Hines?"

"I reckon I would, but I don't know. Why, yonder he is, now. I know him perfectly easy."

It was me he pointed at. The doctor says:

"Neighbors, I don't know whether the new couple is frauds or not; but if *these* two ain't frauds, I am an idiot, that's all. I think it's our duty to see that they don't get away from here till we've looked into this thing. Come along, Hines; come along, the rest of you. We'll take these fellows to the tavern and affront them with t'other couple, and I reckon we'll find out *something* before we get through."

It was nuts for the crowd, though maybe not for the king's friends; so we all started. It was about sundown. The doctor he led me along by the hand, and was plenty kind enough, but he never let *go* my hand.

We all got in a big room in the hotel, and lit up some candles, and fetched in the new couple. First, the doctor says:

"I don't wish to be too hard on these two men, but *I* think they're frauds, and they may have complices that we don't know nothing about. If they have, won't the complices get away with that bag of gold Peter Wilks left? It ain't unlikely. If these men ain't frauds, they won't object to sending for that money and letting us keep it till they prove they're all right—ain't that so?"

Everybody agreed to that. So I judged they had our gang in a pretty tight place, right at the outstart. But the king he only looked sorrowful, and says:

"Gentlemen, I wish the money was there, for I ain't got no disposition to throw anything in the way of a fair, open, out-and-out investigation o' this misable business; but alas, the money ain't there; you k'n send and see, if you want to."

"Where is it, then?"

"Well, when my niece give it to me to keep for her, I took and hid it inside o' the straw tick o' my bed, not wishin' to bank it for the few days we'd be here, and considerin' the bed a safe place, we not bein' used to niggers, and suppos'n' 'em honest, like servants in England. The niggers stole it the very next mornin' after I had went down stairs; and when I sold 'em, I hadn't missed the money yit, so they got clean away with it. My servant here k'n tell you 'bout it gentlemen."

The doctor and several said "Shucks!" and I see nobody didn't altogether believe him. One man asked me if I see the niggers steal it. I said no, but I see them sneaking out of the room and hustling away, and I never thought nothing, only I reckoned they was afraid they had waked up my master and was trying to get away before he made trouble with them. That was all they asked me. Then the doctor whirls on me and says:

"Are *you* English too?"

I says yes; and him and some others laughed, and said, "Stuff!"

Well, then they sailed in on the general investigation, and there we had it, up an down, hour in, hour out, and nobody never said a word about supper, nor ever seemed to think about it—and so they kept it up, and kept it up; and it *was* the worst mixed-up thing you ever see. They made the king tell his yarn, and they made the old gentleman tell his'n; and anybody but a lot of prejudiced chuckleheads would a *seen* that the old gentleman was spinning truth and t'other one lies. And by-and-by they had me up to tell what I knowed. The king he give me a left-handed look out of the corner of his eye, and so I knowed enough to talk on the right side. I begun to tell about Sheffield, and how we lived there, and all about the English Wilkses, and so on; but I didn't get pretty fur till the doctor begun to laugh; and Levi Bell, the lawyer, says:

"Set down, my boy, I wouldn't strain myself, if I was you. I reckon you ain't used to lying, it don't seem to come handy; what you want is practice. You do it pretty awkward."

I didn't care nothing for the compliment, but I was glad to be let off, anyway.

The doctor he started to say something, and turns and says:

"If you'd been in town at first, Levi Bell—"

The king broke in and reached out his hand, and says:

"Why, is this my poor dead brother's old friend that he's wrote so often about?"

The lawyer and him shook hands, and the lawyer smiled and looked pleased, and they talked right along a while, and then got to one side and talked low; and at last the lawyer speaks up and says:

"That'll fix it. I'll take the order and send it, along with your brother's, and then they'll know it's all right."

So they got some paper and a pen, and the king he set down and twisted his head to one side, and chawed his tongue, and scrawled off something; and then they give the pen to the duke—and then for the first time, the duke looked sick. But he took the pen and wrote. So then the lawyer turns to the new old gentleman and says:

"You and your brother please write a line or two and sign your names."

The old gentleman wrote, but nobody couldn't read it. The lawyer looked powerful astonished, and says:

"Well, it beats *me*"—and snaked a lot of old letters out of his pocket, and examined them, and then examined the old man's writing, and then *them* again; and then says: "These old letters is from Harvey Wilks; and here's *these* two's handwritings, and anybody can see *they* didn't write them" (the king and the duke looked sold and foolish, I tell you, to see how the lawyer had took them in), "and here's *this* old gentleman's handwriting, and anybody can tell, easy enough, *he* didn't write them—fact is, the scratches he makes ain't properly *writing*, at all. Now here's some letters from—"

The new old gentleman says:

"If you please, let me explain. Nobody can read my hand but my brother there—so he copies for me. It's *his* hand you've got there, not mine."

"*Well!*" says the lawyer, "this *is* a state of things. I've got some of William's letters too; so if you'll get him to write a line or so we can com—"

"He *can't* write with his left hand," says the old gentleman. "If he could use his right hand, you would see that he wrote his own letters and mine too. Look at both, please—they're by the same hand."

The lawyer done it, and says:

"I believe it's so—and if it ain't so, there's a heap stronger resemblance than I'd noticed before, anyway. Well, well, well! I thought we was right on the track of a slution, but it's gone to grass, partly. But anyway, *one* thing is proved—*these* two ain't either of 'em Wilkses"—and he wagged his head towards the king and the duke.

Well, what do you think?—that muleheaded old fool wouldn't give in *then*! Indeed he wouldn't. Said it warn't no fair test. Said his brother William was the cussedest joker in the world, and hadn't *tried* to write—*he* see William was going to play one of his jokes the minute he put the pen to paper. And so he warmed up and went warbling and warbling right along, till he was actuly beginning to believe what he was saying, *himself*—but pretty soon the new old gentleman broke in, and says:

"I've thought of something. Is there anybody here that helped to lay out my br—helped to lay out the late Peter Wilks for burying?"

"Yes," says somebody, "me and Ab Turner done it. We're both here."

Then the old man turns towards the king, and says:

"Peraps this gentleman can tell me what was tatooed on his breast?"

Blamed if the king didn't have to brace up mighty quick, or he'd a squshed down like a bluff bank that the river has cut under, it took him so sudden—and mind you, it was a thing that was calculated to make most *anybody* sqush to get fetched such a solid one as that without any notice—because how was *he* going to know what was tatooed on the man? He whitened a little; he couldn't help it, and it was mighty still in there, and everybody bending a little forwards and gazing at him. Says I to myself, *Now* he'll throw up the sponge—there ain't no more use. Well, did he? A body can't hardly believe it, but he didn't. I reckon he thought he'd keep the thing up till he tired them people out, so they'd thin out, and him and the duke could break loose and get away. Anyway, he set there, and pretty soon he begun to smile, and says:

"Mf! It's a *very tough* question, *ain't* it! *Yes,* sir, I k'n tell you what's tatooed on his breast. It's jest a small, thin, blue arrow—that's what it is; and if you don't look clost, you can't see it. *Now* what do you say—hey?"

Well, *I* never see anything like that old blister for clean out-and-out cheek.

The new old gentleman turns brisk towards Ab Turner and his pard, and his eye lights up like he judged he'd got the king *this* time, and says:

"There—you've heard what he said! Was there any such mark on Peter Wilks's breast?"

Both of them spoke up and says:

"We didn't see no such mark."

"Good!" says the old gentleman. "Now, what you *did* see on his breast was a small dim P, and a B (which is an initial he dropped when he was young), and a W, with dashes between them; so: P—B—W"—and he marked them that way on a piece of paper. "Come—ain't that what you saw?"

Both of them spoke up again, and says:

"No, we *didn't*. We never seen any marks at all."

Well, everybody *was* in a state of mind, now; and they sings out:

"The whole *bilin'* of 'm 's frauds! Le's duck 'em! le's drown 'em! le's ride 'em on a rail!" and everybody was whooping at once, and there was a rattling pow-wow. But the lawyer he jumps on the table and yells, and says:

"Gentlemen—gentle*men*! Hear me just a word—just a *single* word—if you PLEASE! There's one way yet—let's go and dig up the corpse and look."

That took them.

"Hooray!" they all shouted, and was starting right off; but the lawyer and the doctor sung out:

"Hold on, hold on! Collar all these four men and the boy, and fetch *them* along, too!"

"We'll do it!" they all shouted: "and if we don't find them marks we'll lynch the whole gang!"

I *was* scared, now, I tell you. But there warn't no getting away, you know. They gripped us all, and marched us right along, straight for the graveyard, which was a mile and a half down the river, and the whole town at our heels, for we made noise enough, and it was only nine in the evening.

As we went by our house I wished I hadn't sent Mary Jane out of town; because now if I could tip her the wink, she'd light out and save me, and blow on our dead-beats.

Well, we swarmed along down the river road, just carrying on like wild-cats; and to make it more scary, the sky was darking up, and the lightning beginning to wink and flitter, and the wind to shiver amongst the leaves. This was the most awful trouble and most dangersome I ever was in; and I was kinder stunned; everything was going so different from what I had allowed for; stead of being fixed so I could take my own time, if I wanted to, and see all the fun, and have Mary Jane at my back to save me and set me free when the close-fit come, here was nothing in the world betwixt me and sudden death but just them tatoo-marks. If they didn't find them—

I couldn't bear to think about it; and yet, somehow, I couldn't think about nothing else. It got darker and darker, and it was a beautiful time to give the crowd the slip; but that big husky had me by the wrist—Hines—and a body might as well try to give Goliar the slip. He dragged me right along, he was so excited; and I had to run to keep up.

When they got there they swarmed into the graveyard and washed over it like an overflow. And when they got to the grave, they found they had about a hundred times as many shovels as they wanted, but nobody hadn't thought to fetch a lantern. But they sailed into digging, anyway, by the flicker of the lightning, and sent a man to the nearest house a half a mile off, to borrow one.

So they dug and dug, like everything; and it got awful dark, and the rain started, and the wind swished and swushed along, and the lightning come brisker and brisker, and the thunder boomed; but them people never took no notice of it, they was so full of this business; and one minute you could see everything and every face in that big crowd, and the shovelfuls of dirt sailing up out of the grave, and the next second the dark wiped it all out, and you couldn't see nothing at all.

At last they got out the coffin, and begun to unscrew the lid, and then such another crowding, and shouldering, and shoving as there was, to scourge in and get a sight, you never see; and in the dark, that way, it was awful. Hines he hurt my wrist dreadful, pulling and tugging so, and I reckon he clean forgot I was in the world, he was so excited and panting.

All of a sudden the lightning let go a perfect sluice of white glare, and somebody sings out:

"By the living jingo, here's the bag of gold on his breast!"

Hines let out a whoop, like everybody else, and dropped my wrist and give a big surge to bust his way in and get a look, and the way I lit out and shinned for the road in the dark, there ain't nobody can tell.

I had the road all to myself, and I fairly flew—leastways I had it all to myself except the solid dark, and the now-and-then glares, and the buzzing of the rain, and the thrashing of the wind, and the splitting of the thunder; and sure as you are born I did clip it along!

When I struck the town, I see there warn't nobody out in the storm, so I never hunted for no back streets, but humped it straight through the main one; and when I begun to get towards our house I aimed my eye and set it. No light there; the house all dark—which made me feel sorry and disappointed, I didn't know why. But at last, just as I was sailing by, *flash* comes the light in Mary Jane's window! and my heart swelled up sudden, like to bust; and the same second the house and all was behind me in the dark, and wasn't ever going to be before me no more in this world. She *was* the best girl I ever see, and had the most sand.

The minute I was far enough above the town to see I could make the towhead, I begun to look sharp for a boat to borrow; and the first time the lightning showed me one that wasn't chained, I snatched it and shoved. It was a canoe, and warn't fastened with nothing but a rope. The towhead was a rattling big distance off, away out there in the middle of the river, but I didn't lose no time; and when I struck the raft at last, I was so fagged I would a just laid down to blow and gasp if I could afforded it. But I didn't. As I sprung aboard I sung out:

"Out with you Jim, and set her loose! Glory be to goodness, we're shut of them!"

Jim lit out, and was a coming for me with both arms spread, he was so full of joy; but when I glimpsed him in the lightning, my heart shot up in my mouth, and I went overboard backwards; for I forgot he was old King Lear and a drownded A-rab all in one, and it most scared the livers and lights out of me. But Jim fished me out, and was going to hug me and bless me, and so on, he was so glad I was back and we was shut of the king and the duke, but I says:

"Not now—have it for breakfast, have it for breakfast! Cut loose and let her slide!"

So, in two seconds, away we went, a sliding down the river, and it *did* seem so good to be free again and all by ourselves on the big river and nobody to bother us. I had to skip around a bit, and jump up and crack my heels a few times, I couldn't help it; but about the third crack, I noticed a sound that I knowed mighty well—and held my breath and listened and waited—and sure enough, when the next flash busted out over the water, here they come!—and just a laying to their oars and making their skiff hum! It was the king and the duke.

So I wilted right down onto the planks, then, and give up; and it was all I could do to keep from crying.

Chapter XXX

When they got aboard, the king went for me, and shook me by the collar, and says:

"Tryin' to give us the slip, was ye, you pup! Tired of our company—hey?"

I says:

"No, your majesty, we warn't—*please* don't, your majesty!"

"Quick, then, and tell us what *was* your idea, or I'll shake the insides out o' you!"

"Honest, I'll tell you everything, just as it happened, your majesty. The man that had aholt of me was very good to me, and kept saying he had a boy about as big as me that died last year, and he was sorry to see a boy in such a dangerous fix; and when they was all took by surprise by finding the gold, and made a rush for the coffin, he lets go of me and whispers, 'Heel it now, or they'll hang ye, sure!' and I lit out. It didn't seem no good for *me* to stay—I couldn't do nothing, and I didn't want to be hung if I could get away. So I never stopped running till I found the canoe; and when I got here I told Jim to hurry, or they'd catch me and hang me yet, and said I was afeard you and the duke wasn't alive, now, and I was awful sorry, and so was Jim, and was awful glad when we see you coming, you may ask Jim if I didn't."

Jim said it was so; and the king told him to shut up, and said, "Oh, yes, it's *mighty* likely!" and shook me up again, and said he reckoned he'd drownd me. But the duke says:

"Leggo the boy, you old idiot! Would *you* a done any different? Did you inquire around for *him*, when you got loose? *I* don't remember it."

So the king let go of me, and begun to cuss that town and everybody in it. But the duke says:

"You better a blame sight give *yourself* a good cussing, for you're the one that's entitled to it most. You hain't done a thing, from the start, that had any sense in it, except coming out so cool and cheeky with that imaginary blue-arrow mark. That *was* bright—it was right down bully; and it was the thing that saved us. For if it hadn't been for that, they'd a jailed us till them Englishmen's baggage come—and then—the penitentiary, you bet! But that trick took 'em to the graveyard, and the gold done us a still bigger kindness; for if the excited fools hadn't let go all holts and made that rush to get a look, we'd a slept in our cravats to-night—cravats warranted to *wear,* too—longer than *we'd* need 'em."

They was still a minute—thinking—then the king says, kind of absent-minded like:

"Mf! And we reckoned the *niggers* stole it!"

That made me squirm!

"Yes," says the duke, kinder slow, and deliberate, and sarcastic, "*We* did."

After about a half a minute, the king drawls out:

"Leastways—*I* did."

The duke says, the same way:

"On the contrary—*I* did."

The king kind of ruffles up, and says:

"Looky here, Bilgewater, what'r you referrin' to?"

The duke says, pretty brisk:

"When it comes to that, maybe you'll let me ask, what was *you* referring to?"

"Shucks!" says the king, very sarcastic; "but *I* don't know—maybe you was asleep, and didn't know what you was about."

The duke bristles right up, now, and says:

"Oh, let *up* on this cussed nonsense—do you take me for a blame' fool? Don't you reckon *I* know who hid that money in that coffin?"

"*Yes,* sir! I know you *do* know—because you done it yourself!"

"It's a lie!"—and the duke went for him. The king sings out:

"Take y'r hands off!—leggo my throat!—I take it all back!"

The duke says:

"Well, you just own up, first, that you *did* hide that money there, intending to give me the slip one of these days, and come back and dig it up, and have it all to yourself."

"Wait jest a minute, duke—answer me this one question, honest and fair; if you didn't put the money there, say it, and I'll b'lieve you, and take back everything I said."

"You old scoundrel, I didn't, and you know I didn't. There, now!"

"Well, then, I b'lieve you. But answer me only jest this one more—now *don't* git mad; didn't you have it in your *mind* to hook the money and hide it?"

The duke never said nothing for a little bit; then he says:

"Well—I don't care if I *did,* I didn't *do* it, anyway. But you not only had it in mind to do it, but you *done* it."

"I wisht I may never die if I done it, duke, and that's honest. I won't say I warn't *goin'* to do it, because I *was;* but you—I mean somebody—got in ahead o' me."

"It's a lie! You done it, and you got to *say* you done it, or—"

The king begun to gurgle, and then he gasps out:

"'Nough!—*I own up!*"

I was very glad to hear him say that, it made me feel much more easier than what I was feeling before. So the duke took his hands off, and says:

"If you ever deny it again, I'll drown you. It's *well* for you to set there and blubber like a baby—it's fitten for you, after the way you've acted. I never see such an old ostrich for wanting to gobble everything—and I a trusting you all the time, like you was my own father. You ought to been ashamed of yourself to stand by and hear it saddled onto a lot of poor niggers and you never say a word for 'em. It makes me feel ridiculous to think I was soft enough to *believe* that rubbage. Cuss you, I can see, now, why you was so anxious to make up the deffesit—you wanted to get what money I'd got out of the Nonesuch and one thing or another, and scoop it *all!*"

The king says, timid, and still a snuffling:

"Why, duke, it was you that said make up the deffersit, it warn't me."

"Dry up! I don't want to hear no more *out* of you!" says the duke. "And *now* you see what you *got* by it. They've got all their own money back, and all of *ourn* but a shekel or two, *besides.* G'long to bed—and don't you deffersit *me* no more deffersits, long's *you* live!"

So the king sneaked into the wigwam, and took to his bottle for comfort; and before long the duke tackled *his* bottle; and so in about a half an hour they was as thick as thieves again, and the tighter they got, the lovinger they got; and went off a snoring in each other's arms. They both got powerful mellow, but I noticed the king didn't get mellow enough to forget to remember to not deny about hiding the money-bag again. That made me feel easy and satisfied. Of course when they got to snoring, we had a long gabble, and I told Jim everything.

Chapter XXXI

We dasn't stop again at any town for days and days; kept right along down the river. We was down south in the warm weather, now, and a mighty long ways from home. We begun to come to trees with Spanish moss on them, hanging down from the limbs like long gray beards. It was the first I ever see it growing, and it made the woods look solemn and dismal. So now the frauds reckoned they was out of danger, and they begun to work the villages again.

First they done a lecture on temperance; but they didn't make enough for them both to get drunk on. Then in another village they started a dancing school; but they didn't know no more how to dance than a kangaroo does; so the first prance they made, the general public jumped in and pranced them out of town. Another time they tried a go at yellocution; but they didn't yellocute long till the audience got up and give them a solid good cussing and made them skip out. They tackled missionarying, and mesmerizering, and doctoring, and telling fortunes, and a little of everything; but they couldn't seem to have no luck. So at last they got just about dead broke, and laid around the raft, as she floated along, thinking, and thinking, and never saying nothing, by the half a day at a time, and dreadful blue and desperate.

And at last they took a change, and begun to lay their heads together in the wigwam and talk low and confidential two or three hours at a time. Jim and me got uneasy. We didn't like the look of it. We judged they was studying up some kind of worse deviltry than ever. We turned it over and over, and at last we made up our minds they was going to break into somebody's house or store, or was going into the counterfeit-money business, or something. So then we was pretty scared, and made up an agreement that we wouldn't have nothing in the world to do with such actions, and if we ever got the least show we would give them the cold shake, and clear out and leave them behind. Well, early one morning we hid the raft in a good safe place about two mile below a little bit of a shabby village, named Pikesville, and the king he went ashore, and told us all to stay hid whilst he went up to town and smelt around to see if anybody had got any wind of the Royal Nonesuch there yet. ("House to rob, you *mean*," says I to myself; "and when you get through robbing it you'll come back here and wonder what's become of me and Jim and the raft—and you'll have to take it out in wondering.") And he said if he warn't back by midday, the duke and me would know it was all right, and we was to come along.

So we staid where we was. The duke he fretted and sweated around, and was in a mighty sour way. He scolded us for everything, and we couldn't seem to do nothing right; he found fault with every little thing. Something was a-brewing, sure. I was good and glad when midday come and no king; we could have a change, anyway—and maybe a chance for *the* change, on top of it. So me and the duke went up to the village, and hunted around there for the king, and by-and-by we found him in the back room of a little low doggery, very tight, and a lot of loafers bullyragging him for sport, and he a cussing and threatening with all his might, and so tight he couldn't walk, and couldn't do nothing to them. The duke he begun to abuse him for an old fool, and the king begun to sass back; and the minute they was fairly at it, I lit out, and shook the reefs out of my hind legs, and spun down the river road like a deer—for I see our chance; and I made up my mind that it would be a long day before they ever see me and Jim again. I got down there all out of breath but loaded up with joy, and sung out—

"Set her loose, Jim, we're all right, now!"

But there warn't no answer, and nobody come out of the wigwam. Jim was gone! I set up a shout—and then another—and then another one; and run this way and that in the woods, whooping and screeching; but it warn't no use—old Jim was gone. Then I set down and cried; I couldn't help it. But I couldn't set still long. Pretty soon I went out on the road, trying to think what I better do, and I run across a boy walking, and asked him if he'd seen a strange nigger, dressed so and so, and he says:

"Yes."

"Whereabouts?" says I.

"Down to Silas Phelps's place, two mile below here. He's a runaway nigger, and they've got him. Was you looking for him?"

"You bet I ain't! I run across him in the woods about an hour or two ago, and he said if I hollered he'd cut my livers out—and told me to lay down and stay where I was; and I done it. Been there ever since; afeard to come out."

"Well," he says, "you needn't be afeard no more, becuz they've got him. He run off f'm down South, som'ers."

"It's a good job they got him."

"Well, I *reckon!* There's two hunderd dollars reward on him. It's like picking up money out'n the road."

"Yes, it is—and *I* could a had it if I'd been big enough; I see him *first*. Who nailed him?"

"It was an old fellow—a stranger—and he sold out his chance in him for forty dollars, becuz he's got to go up the river and can't wait. Think o' that, now! You bet *I'd* wait, if it was seven year."

"That's me, every time," says I. "But maybe his chance ain't worth no more than that, if he'll sell it so cheap. Maybe there's something ain't straight about it."

"But it *is*, though—straight as a string. I see the handbill myself. It tells all about him, to a dot—paints him like a picture, and tells the plantation he's frum, below New*r*leans.

No-sirree-*bob,* they ain't no trouble 'bout *that* speculation, you bet you. Say, gimme a chaw tobacker, won't ye?"

I didn't have none, so he left. I went to the raft, and set down in the wigwam to think. But I couldn't come to nothing. I thought till I wore my head sore, but I couldn't see no way out of the trouble. After all this long journey, and after all we'd done for them scoundrels, here was it all come to nothing, everything all busted up and ruined, because they could have the heart to serve Jim such a trick as that, and make him a slave again all his life, and amongst strangers, too, for forty dirty dollars.

Once I said to myself it would be a thousand times better for Jim to be a slave at home where his family was, as long as he'd *got* to be a slave, and so I'd better write a letter to Tom Sawyer and tell him to tell Miss Watson where he was. But I soon give up that notion, for two things: she'd be mad and disgusted at his rascality and ungratefulness for leaving her, and so she'd sell him straight down the river again; and if she didn't, everybody naturally despises an ungrateful nigger, and they'd make Jim feel it all the time, and so he'd feel ornery and disgraced. And then think of *me!* It would get all around, that Huck Finn helped a nigger to get his freedom; and if I was to ever see anybody from that town again, I'd be ready to get down and lick his boots for shame. That's just the way: a person does a low-down thing, and then he don't want to take no consequences of it. Thinks as long as he can hide it, it ain't no disgrace. That was my fix exactly. The more I studied about this, the more my conscience went to grinding me, and the more wicked and low-down and ornery I got to feeling. And at last, when it hit me all of a sudden that here was the plain hand of Providence slapping me in the face and letting me know my wickedness was being watched all the time from up there in heaven, whilst I was stealing a poor old woman's nigger that hadn't ever done me no harm, and now was showing me there's One that's always on the lookout, and ain't agoing to allow no such miserable doings to go only just so fur and no further, I most dropped in my tracks I was so scared. Well, I tried the best I could to kinder soften it up somehow for myself, by saying I was brung up wicked, and so I warn't so much to blame; but something inside of me kept saying, "There was the Sunday school, you could a gone to it; and if you'd a done it they'd a learnt you, there, that people that acts as I'd been acting about that nigger goes to everlasting fire."

It made me shiver. And I about made up my mind to pray; and see if I couldn't try to quit being the kind of a boy I was, and be better. So I kneeled down. But the words wouldn't come. Why wouldn't they? It warn't no use to try and hide it from Him. Nor from *me,* neither. I knowed very well why they wouldn't come. It was because my heart warn't right; it was because I warn't square; it was because I was playing double. I was letting *on* to give up sin, but away inside of me I was holding on to the biggest one of all. I was trying to make my mouth *say* I would do the right thing and the clean thing, and go and write to that nigger's owner and tell where he was; but deep down in me I knowed it was a lie—and He knowed it. You can't pray a lie—I found that out.

So I was full of trouble, full as I could be; and didn't know what to do. At last I had an idea; and I says, I'll go and write the letter—and *then* see if I can pray. Why, it was astonishing, the way I felt as light as a feather, right straight off, and my troubles all gone. So I got a piece of paper and a pencil, all glad and excited, and set down and wrote:

Miss Watson your runaway nigger Jim is down here two mile below Pikesville and Mr. Phelps has got him and he will give him up for the reward if you send.

HUCK FINN.

I felt good and all washed clean of sin for the first time I had ever felt so in my life, and I knowed I could pray now. But I didn't do it straight off, but laid the paper down and set there thinking—thinking how good it was all this happened so, and how near I come to being lost and going to hell. And went on thinking. And got to thinking over our trip down the river; and I see Jim before me, all the time, in the day, and in the nighttime, sometimes moonlight, sometimes storms, and we a floating along, talking, and singing, and laughing. But somehow I couldn't seem to strike no places to harden me against him, but only the other kind. I'd see him standing my watch on top of his'n, stead of calling me, so I could go on sleeping; and see him how glad he was when I come back out of the fog; and when I come to him again in the swamp, up there where the feud was; and such-like times; and would always call me honey, and pet me, and do everything he could think of for me, and how good he always was; and at last I struck the time I saved him by telling the men we had small-pox aboard, and he was so grateful, and said I was the best friend old Jim ever had in the world, and the *only* one he's got now; and then I happened to look around, and see that paper.

It was a close place. I took it up, and held it in my hand. I was a trembling, because I'd got to decide, forever, betwixt two things, and I knowed it. I studied a minute, sort of holding my breath, and then says to myself:

"All right, then, I'll *go* to hell"—and tore it up.

It was awful thoughts, and awful words, but they was said. And I let them stay said; and never thought no more about reforming. I shoved the whole thing out of my head; and said I would take up wickedness again, which was in my line, being brung up to it, and the other warn't. And for a starter, I would go to work and steal Jim out of slavery again; and if I could think up anything worse, I would do that, too; because as long as I was in, and in for good, I might as well go the whole hog.

Then I set to thinking over how to get at it, and turned over considerable many ways in my mind; and at last fixed up a plan that suited me. So then I took the bearings of a woody island that was down the river a piece, and as soon as it was fairly dark I crept out with my raft and went for it, and hid it there, and then turned in. I slept the night through, and got up before it was light, and had my breakfast, and put on my store clothes, and tied up some others and one thing or another in a bundle, and took the canoe and cleared for shore. I landed below where I judged was Phelp's place, and hid my bundle in the woods, and then filled up the canoe with water, and loaded rocks into her and sunk her where I could find her again when I wanted her, about a quarter of a mile below a little steam sawmill that was on the bank.

Then I struck up the road, and when I passed the mill I see a sign on it, "Phelps's Sawmill," and when I come to the farm-houses, two or three hundred yards further along, I kept my eyes peeled, but didn't see nobody around, though it was good daylight, now. But I didn't mind, because I didn't want to see nobody just yet—I only wanted to get the lay of the land. According to my plan, I was going to turn up there from the village, not from below. So I just took a look, and shoved along, straight for town. Well, the very first man I see, when I got there, was the duke. He was sticking up a bill for the Royal Nonesuch—three-night performance—like that other time. *They* had the cheek, them frauds! I was right on him, before I could shirk. He looked astonished, and says:

"Hel-*lo!* Where'd *you* come from?" Then he says, kind of glad and eager, "Where's the raft?—got her in a good place?"

I says:

"Why, that's just what I was agoing to ask your grace."

Then he didn't look so joyful—and says:

"What was you idea for asking *me?*" he says.

"Well," I says, "when I see the king in that doggery yesterday, I says to myself, we can't get him home for hours, till he's soberer; so I went a loafing around town to put in the time, and wait. A man up and offered me ten cents to help him pull a skiff over the river and back to fetch a sheep, and so I went along; but when we was dragging him to the boat, and the man left me aholt of the rope and went behind him to shove him along, he was too strong for me, and jerked loose and run, and we after him. We didn't have no dog, and so we had to chase him all over the country till we tired him out. We never got him till dark, then we fetched him over, and I started down for the raft. When I got there and see it was gone, I says to myself, 'they've got into trouble and had to leave; and they've took my nigger, which the only nigger I've got in the world, and no I'm in a strange country, and ain't got no property no more, nor nothing, and no way to make my living;' so I set down and cried. I slept in the woods all night. But what *did* become of the raft then?—and Jim, poor Jim!"

"Blamed if *I* know—that is, what's become of the raft. That old fool had made a trade and got forty dollars, and when we found him in the doggery the loafers had matched half dollars with him and got every cent but what he'd spent for whisky; and when I got him home late last night and found the raft gone, we said, 'That little rascal has stole our raft and shook us, and run off down the river.'"

"I wouldn't shake my *nigger*, would I?—the only nigger I had in the world, and the only property."

"We never thought of that. Fact is, I reckon we'd come to consider him *our* nigger; yes, we did consider him so—goodness knows we had trouble enough for him. So when we see the raft was gone, and we flat broke, there warn't anything for it but to try the Royal Nonesuch another shake. And I've pegged along ever since, dry as a powderhorn. Where's that ten cents? Give it here."

I had considerable money, so I give him ten cents, but begged him to spend it for something to eat, and give me some, because it was all the money I had, and I hadn't had nothing to eat since yesterday. He never said nothing. The next minute he whirls on me and says:

"Do you reckon that nigger would blow on us? We'd skin him if he done that!"

"How can he blow? Hain't he run off?"

"No! That old fool sold him, and never divided with me, and the money's gone."

"*Sold* him?" I says, and begun to cry; "why, he was *my* nigger, and that was my money. Where is he?—I want my nigger."

"Well, you can't *get* your nigger, that's all—so dry up your blubbering. Looky here— do you think *you'd* venture to blow on us? Blamed if I think I'd trust you. Why, if you *was* to blow on us—"

He stopped, but I never see the duke look so ugly out of his eyes before. I went on a-whimpering, and says:

"I don't want to blow on nobody; and I ain't got no time to blow, nohow. I got to turn out and find my nigger."

He looked kinder bothered, and stood there with his bills fluttering on his arm, thinking, and wrinkling up his forehead. At last he says:

"I'll tell you something. We got to be here three days. If you'll promise you won't blow, and won't let the nigger blow, I'll tell you where to find him."

So I promised, and he says:

"A farmer by the name of Silas Ph—" and then he stopped. You see he started to tell me the truth; but when he stopped, that way, and begun to study and think again, I reckoned he was changing his mind. And so he was. He wouldn't trust me; he wanted to make sure of having me out of the way the whole three days. So pretty soon he says: "The man that bought him is named Abram Foster—Abram G. Foster—and he lives forty mile back here in the country, on the road to Lafayette."

"All right," I says, "I can walk it in three days. And I'll start this very afternoon."

"No you won't, you'll start *now;* and don't you lose any time about it, neither, nor do any gabbling by the way. Just keep a tight tongue in your head and move right along, and then you won't get into trouble with *us,* d'ye hear?"

That was the order I wanted, and that was the one I played for. I wanted to be left free to work my plans.

"So clear out," he says; "and you can tell Mr. Foster whatever you want to. Maybe you can get him to believe that Jim *is* your nigger—some idiots don't require documents—leastways I've heard there's such down South here. And when you tell him the handbill and the reward's bogus, maybe he'll believe you when you explain to him what the idea was for getting 'em out. Go 'long, now, and tell him anything you want to; but mind you don't work your jaw any *between* here and there."

So I left, and struck for the back country. I didn't look around, but I kinder felt like he was watching me. But I knowed I could tire him out at that. I went straight out in the country as much as a mile, before I stopped; then I doubled back through the woods towards Phelps's. I reckoned I better start in on my plan straight off, without fooling around, because I wanted to stop Jim's mouth till these fellows could get away. I didn't want no trouble with their kind. I'd seen all I wanted to of them, and wanted to get entirely shut of them.

Chapter XXXII

When I got there it was all still and Sunday-like, and hot and sunshiny—the hands was gone to the fields; and there was them kind of faint dronings of bugs and flies in the air that makes it seem so lonesome and like everybody's dead and gone; and if a breeze fans along and quivers the leaves, it makes you feel mournful, because you feel like it's spirits whispering—spirits that's been dead ever so many years—and you always think they're talking about *you.* As a general thing it makes a body wish *he* was dead, too, and done with it all.

Phelps's was one of these little one-horse cotton plantations; and they all look alike. A rail fence round a two-acre yard; a stile, made out of logs sawed off and up-ended, in steps, like barrels of a different length, to climb over the fence with, and for the women to stand on when they are going to jump onto a horse; some sickly grass-patches in the big yard, but mostly it was bare and smooth, like an old hat with the nap rubbed off; big double log house for the white folks—hewd logs, with the chinks stopped up with mud or mortar, and these mud-stripes been whitewashed some time or another; round-log kitchen, with a big broad, open but roofed passage joining it to the house; log smoke-house back of the kitchen; three little log nigger-cabins in a row t'other side the smoke-house; one little hut all by itself away down against the back fence, and some outbuild-ings down a piece the other side; ash-hopper, and big kettle to bile soap in, by the little hut; bench by the kitchen door, with bucket of water and a gourd; hound asleep there, in the sun; more hounds asleep, round about; about three shade-trees away off in a cor-ner; some currant bushes and gooseberry bushes in one place by the fence; outside of the fence a garden and a water-melon patch; then the cotton fields begins; and after the fields, the woods.

I went around and clumb over the back stile by the ash-hopper, and started for the kitchen. When I got a little ways, I heard the dim hum of a spinning-wheel wailing along up and sinking along down again; and then I knowed for certain I wished I was dead—for that *is* the lonesomest sound in the whole world.

I went right along, not fixing up any particular plan, but just trusting to Providence to put the right words in my mouth when the time come; for I'd noticed that Provi-dence always did put the right words in my mouth, if I left it alone.

When I got half-way, first one hound and then another got up and went for me, and of course I stopped and faced them, and kept still. And such another pow-wow as they made! In a quarter of a minute I was a kind of a hub of a wheel, as you may say—spokes made out of dogs—circle of fifteen of them packed together around me, with their necks and noses stretched up towards me, a barking and howling; and more a coming; you could see them sailing over fences and around corners from everywheres.

A nigger woman come tearing out of the kitchen with a rolling-pin in her hand, singing out, "Begone! *you* Tige! you Spot! begone, sah!" and she fetched first one and then another of them a clip and sent him howling, and then the rest followed; and the next second, half of them come back, wagging their tails around me, and making friends with me. There ain't no harm in a hound, nohow.

And behind the woman comes a little nigger girl and two little nigger boys, without anything on but tow-linen shirts, and they hung onto their mother's gown, and peeped out from behind her at me, bashful, the way they always do. And here comes the white woman running from the house, about forty-five or fifty years old, bareheaded, and her spinning-stick in her hand; and behind her comes her little white children, acting the same way the little niggers was doing. She was smiling all over so she could hardly stand—and says:

"It's *you,* at last!—*ain't* it?"

I out with a "Yes'm," before I thought.

She grabbed me and hugged me tight; and then gripped me by both hands and shook and shook; and the tears come in her eyes, and run down over; and she couldn't seem to hug and shake enough, and kept saying, "You don't look as much like your mother as I reckoned you would, but law sakes, I don't care for that, I'm *so* glad to see you! Dear, dear, it does seem like I could eat you up! Childern, it's your cousin Tom!—tell him howdy."

But they ducked their heads, and put their fingers in their mouths, and hid behind her. So she run on:

"Lize, hurry up and get him a hot breakfast, right away—or did you get your break-fast on the boat?"

I said I had got it on the boat. So then she started for the house, leading me by the hand, and the children tagging after. When we got there, she set me down in a split-bottomed chair, and set herself down on a little low stool in front of me, holding both of my hands, and says:

"Now I can have a *good* look at you; and laws-a-me, I've been hungry for it a many and a many a time, all these long years, and it's come at last! We been expecting you a couple of days and more. What's kep' you?—boat get aground?"

"Yes'm—she—"

"Don't say yes'm—say Aunt Sally. Where'd she get aground?"

I didn't rightly know what to say, because I didn't know whether the boat would be coming up the river or down. But I go a good deal on instinct; and my instinct said she would be coming up—from down towards Orleans. That did'nt help me much, though; for I didn't know the names of bars down that way. I see I'd got to invent a bar, or forget the name of the one we got aground on—or— Now I struck an idea, and fetched it out:

"It warn't the grounding—that didn't keep us back but a little. We blowed out a cylinder-head."

"Good gracious! anybody hurt?"

"No'm. Killed a nigger."

"Well, it's lucky; because sometimes people do get hurt. Two years ago last Christmas, your uncle Silas was coming up from Newrleans on the old *Lally Rook,* and she blowed out a cylinder-head and crippled a man. And I think he died afterwards. He was a Babtist. Your uncle Silas knowed a family in Baton Rouge that knowed his people very well. Yes, I remember, now he *did* die. Mortification set in, and they had to amputate him. But it didn't save him. Yes, it was mortification—that was it. He turned blue all over, and died in the hope of a glorious resurrection. They say he was a sight to look at. Your uncle's been up to the town every day to fetch you. And he's gone again, not more'n an hour ago; he'll be back any minute, now. You must a met him on the road, didn't you?—oldish man, with a—"

"No, I didn't see nobody, Aunt Sally. The boat landed just at daylight, and I left my baggage on the wharf-boat and went looking around the town and out a piece in the country, to put in the time and not get here too soon; and so I come down the back way."

"Who'd you give the baggage to?"

"Nobody."

"Why, child, it'll be stole!"

"Not where *I* hid it I reckon it won't," I says.

"How'd you get your breakfast so early on the boat?"

It was kinder thin ice, but I says:

"The captain see me standing around, and told me I better have something to eat before I went ashore; so he took me in the texas to the officers' lunch, and give me all I wanted."

I was getting so uneasy I couldn't listen good. I had my mind on the children all the time; I wanted to get them out to one side, and pump them a little, and find out who I was. But I couldn't get no show, Mrs. Phelps kept it up and run on so. Pretty soon she made the cold chills streak all down my back, because she says:

"But here we're a running on this way, and you hain't told me a word about Sis, nor any of them. Now I'll rest my works a little, and you start up yourn; just tell me *everything*—tell me all about 'm all—every one of 'm; and how they are, and what they're doing, and what they told you to tell me; and every last thing you can think of."

Well, I see I was up a stump—and up it good. Providence had stood by me this fur, all right, but I was hard and tight aground, now. I see it warn't a bit of use to try to go ahead—I'd *got* to throw up my hand. So I says to myself, here's another place where I got to resk the truth. I opened my mouth to begin; but she grabbed me and hustled me in behind the bed, and says:

"Here he comes! stick your head down lower—there, that'll do; you can't be seen, now. Don't you let on you're here. I'll play a joke on him. Childern, don't you say a word."

I see I was in a fix, now. But it warn't no use to worry; there warn't nothing to do but just hold still, and try and be ready to stand from under when the lightning struck.

I had just one little glimpse of the old gentleman when he come in, then the bed hid him. Mrs. Phelps she jumps for him and says:

"Has he come?"

"No," says her husband.

"Good-*ness* gracious!" she says, "what in the world *can* have become of him?"

"I can't imagine," says the old gentleman; "and I must say, it makes me dreadful uneasy."

"Uneasy!" she says, "I'm ready to go distracted! He *must* a come; and you've missed him along the road. I *know* it's so—something *tells* me so."

"Why Sally, I *couldn't* miss him along the road—*you* know that."

"But oh, dear, dear, what *will* Sis say! He must a come! You must a missed him. He—"

"Oh, don't distress me any more'n I'm already distressed. I don't know what in the world to make of it. I'm at my wit's end, and I don't mind acknowledging 't I'm right down scared. But there's no hope that he's come; for he *couldn't* come and me miss him. Sally, it's terrible—just terrible—something's happened to the boat, sure!"

"Why, Silas! Look yonder!—up the road!—ain't that somebody coming?"

He sprung to the window at the head of the bed, and that give Mrs. Phelps the chance she wanted. She stooped down quick, at the foot of the bed, and give me a pull, and out I come; and when he turned back from the window, there she stood, a-beaming and a-smiling like a house afire, and I standing pretty meek and sweaty alongside. The old gentleman stared, and says:

"Why, who's that?"

"Who do you reckon 't is?"

"I hain't no idea. Who *is* it?"

"It's *Tom Sawyer!*"

By jings, I most slumped through the floor. But there warn't no time to swap knives; the old man grabbed me by the hand and shook, and kept on shaking; and all the time, how the woman did dance around and laugh and cry; and then how they both did fire off questions about Sid, and Mary, and the rest of the tribe.

But if they was joyful, it warn't nothing to what I was; for it was like being born again, I was so glad to find out who I was. Well, they froze to me for two hours; and at last when my chin was so tired it couldn't hardly go, any more, I had told them more about my family—I mean the Sawyer family—than ever happened to any six Sawyer families. And I explained all about how we blowed out a cylinder-head at the mouth of White River and it took us three days to fix it. Which was all right, and worked first rate; because *they* didn't know but what it would take three days to fix it. If I'd a called it a bolt-head it would a done just as well.

Now I was feeling pretty comfortable all down one side, and pretty uncomfortable all up the other. Being Tom Sawyer was easy and comfortable; and it stayed easy and comfortable till by-and-by I hear a steamboat coughing along down the river—then I says to myself, spose Tom Sawyer come down on that boat?—and spose he steps in here, any minute, and sings out my name before I can throw him a wink to keep quiet? Well, I couldn't *have* it that way—it wouldn't do at all. I must go up the road and way-lay him. So I told the folks I reckoned I would go up to the town and fetch down my baggage. The old gentleman was for going along with me, but I said no, I could drive the horse myself, and I druther he wouldn't take no trouble about me.

Chapter XXXIII

So I started for town, in the wagon, and when I was half-way I see a wagon coming, and sure enough it was Tom Sawyer, and I stopped and waited till he come along. I says "Hold on!" and it stopped alongside, and his mouth opened up like a trunk, and staid so; and he swallowed two or three times like a person that's got a dry throat, and then says:

"I hain't ever done you no harm. You know that. So then, what you want to come back and ha'nt *me* for?"

I says:

"I hain't come back—I hain't been *gone*."

When he heard my voice, it righted him up some, but he warn't quite satisfied yet. He says:

"Don't you play nothing on me, because I wouldn't on you. Honest injun, now, you ain't a ghost?"

"Honest injun, I ain't," I says.

"Well—I—I—well, that ought to settle it, of course; but I can't somehow seem to understand it, no way. Looky here, warn't you ever murdered *at all?*"

"No. I warn't ever murdered at all—I played it on them. You come in here and feel of me if you don't believe me."

So he done it; and it satisfied him; and he was that glad to see me again, he didn't know what to do. And he wanted to know all about it right off; because it was a grand adventure, and mysterious, and so it hit him where he lived. But I said, leave it alone till by-and-by; and told his driver to wait, and we drove off a little piece, and I told him the kind of a fix I was in, and what did he reckon we better do? He said, let him alone a minute, and don't disturb him. So he thought and thought, and pretty soon he says:

"It's all right, I've got it. Take my trunk in your wagon, and let on it's your'n; and you turn back and fool along slow, so as to get to the house about the time you ought to; and I'll go towards town a piece, and take a fresh start, and get there a quarter or a half an hour after you; and you needn't let on to know me, at first."

I says:

"All right; but wait a minute. There's one more thing—a thing that *nobody* don't know but me. And that is, there's a nigger here that I'm a trying to steal out of slavery—and his name is *Jim*—old Miss Watson's Jim."

He says:

"What! Why Jim is—"

He stopped and went to studying. I says:

"*I* know what you'll say. You'll say it's dirty low-down business; but what if it is?—*I'm* low down; and I'm agoing to steal him, and I want you to keep mum and not let on. Will you?"

His eye lit up, and he says:

"I'll *help* you steal him!"

Well, I let go all holts then, like I was shot. It was the most astonishing speech I ever heard—and I'm bound to say Tom Sawyer fell, considerable, in my estimation. Only I couldn't believe it. Tom Sawyer a *nigger stealer!*

"Oh, shucks," I says, "you're joking."

"I ain't joking, either."

"Well, then," I says, "joking or no joking, if you hear anything said about a runaway nigger, don't forget to remember that *you* don't know nothing about him, and *I* don't know nothing about him."

Then we took the trunk and put it in my wagon, and he drove off his way, and I drove mine. But of course I forgot all about driving slow, on accounts of being glad and full of thinking; so I got home a heap too quick for that length of a trip. The old gentleman was at the door, and he says:

"Why, this is wonderful. Who ever would a thought it was in that mare to do it. I wish we'd a timed her. And she hain't sweated a hair—not a hair. It's wonderful. Why, I wouldn't take a hunderd dollars for that horse now; I wouldn't, honest; and yet I'd a sold her for fifteen before, and thought 'twas all she was worth."

That's all he said. He was the innocentest, best old soul I ever see. But it warn't surprising; because he warn't only just a farmer, he was a preacher, too, and had a little one-horse log church down back of the plantation, which he built it himself at his own expense, for a church and school-house, and never charged nothing for his preaching, and it was worth it, too. There was plenty other farmer-preachers like that, and done the same way, down South.

In about half an hour Tom's wagon drove up to the front stile, and Aunt Sally she see it through the window because it was only about fifty yards, and says:

"Why, there's somebody come! I wonder who 'tis? Why, I do believe it's a stranger. Jimmy" (that's one of the children), "run and tell Lize to put on another plate for dinner."

Everybody made a rush for the front door, because, of course, a stranger don't come *every* year, and so he lays over the yaller fever, for interest, when he does come. Tom was over the stile and starting for the house; the wagon was spinning up the road for the village, and we was all bunched in the front door. Tom had his store clothes on, and an audience—and that was always nuts for Tom Sawyer. In them circumstances it warn't no trouble to him to throw in an amount of style that was suitable. He warn't a boy to meeky along up that yard like a sheep; no, he come ca'm and important, like the ram. When he got afront of us, he lifts his hat ever so gracious and dainty, like it was the lid of a box that had butterflies asleep in it and he didn't want to disturb them, and says:

"Mr. Archibald Nichols, I presume?"

"No, my boy," says the old gentleman, "I'm sorry to say 't your driver has deceived you; Nichols's place is down a matter of three mile more. Come in, come in."

Tom he took a look back over his shoulder, and says, "Too late—he's out of sight."

"Yes, he's gone, my son, and you must come in and eat your dinner with us; and then we'll hitch up and take you down to Nichols's."

"Oh, I *can't* make you so much trouble; I couldn't think of it. I'll walk—I don't mind the distance."

"But we won't *let* you walk—it wouldn't be Southern hospitality to do it. Come right in."

"Oh, *do,*" says Aunt Sally; "it ain't a bit of trouble to us, not a bit in the world. You *must* stay. It's a long, dusty three mile, and we *can't* let you walk. And besides, I've already told 'em to put on another plate, when I see you coming; so you mustn't disappoint us. Come right in, and make yourself at home."

So Tom he thanked them very hearty and handsome, and let himself be persuaded, and come in; and when he was in, he said he was a stranger from Hicksville, Ohio, and his name was William Thompson—and he made another bow.

Well, he run on, and on, and on, making up stuff about Hicksville and everybody in it he could invent, and I getting a little nervous, and wondering how this was going to help me out of my scrape; and at last, still talking along, he reached over and kissed Aunt Sally right on the mouth, and then settled back again in his chair, comfortable, and was going on talking; but she jumped up and wiped it off with the back of her hand, and says:

"You owdacious puppy!"

He looked kind of hurt, and says:

"I'm surprised at you, m'am."

"You're s'rp— Why, what do you reckon *I* am? I've a good notion to take and—say, what do you mean by kissing me?"

He looked kind of humble, and says:

"I didn't mean nothing, m'am. I didn't mean no harm. I—I—thought you'd like it."

"Why, you born fool!" She took up the spinning-stick, and it looked like it was all she could do to keep from giving him a crack with it. "What made you think I'd like it?"

"Well, I don't know. Only, they—they—told me you would."

"*They* told you I would. Whoever told you's *another* lunatic. I never heard the beat of it. Who's *they?*"

"Why—everybody. They all said so, m'am."

It was all she could do to hold in; and her eyes snapped, and her fingers worked like she wanted to scratch him; and she says:

"Who's 'everybody?' Out with their names—or ther'll be an idiot short."

He got up and looked distressed, and fumbled his hat, and says:

"I'm sorry, and I warn't expecting it. They told me to. They all told me to. They all said kiss her; and said she'll like it. They all said it—every one of them. But I'm sorry, m'am, and I won't do it no more—I won't, honest."

"You won't, won't you? Well, I sh'd *reckon* you won't!"

"No'm, I'm honest about it; I won't ever do it again. Till you ask me."

"Till I *ask* you! Well, I never see the beat of it in my born days! I lay you'll be the Methusalem-numskull of creation before ever *I* ask you—or the likes of you."

"Well," he says, "it does surprise me so. I can't make it out, somehow. They said you would, and I thought you would. But—" He stopped and looked around slow, like he wished he could run across a friendly eye, somewhere's; and fetched up on the old gentleman's, and says, "Didn't *you* think she'd like me to kiss her, sir?"

"Why, no, I—I—well, no, I b'lieve I didn't."

Then he looks on around, the same way, to me—and says:

"Tom didn't *you* think Aunt Sally 'd open out her arms and say, 'Sid Sawyer—' "

"My land!" she says, breaking in and jumping for him, "you impudent young rascal, to fool a body so—" and was going to hug him, but he fended her off, and says:

"No, not till you've asked me, first."

So she didn't lose no time, but asked him; and hugged him and kissed him, over and over again, and then turned him over to the old man, and he took what was left. And after they got a little quiet again, she says:

"Why, dear me, I never see such a surprise. We warn't looking for *you,* at all, but only Tom. Sis never wrote to me about anybody coming but him."

"It's because it warn't *intended* for any of us to come but Tom," he says; "but I begged and begged, and at the last minute she let me come, too; so, coming down the river, me and Tom thought it would be a first-rate surprise for him to come here to the house first, and for me to by-and-by tag along and drop in and let on to be a stranger. But it was a mistake, Aunt Sally. This ain't no healthy place for a stranger to come."

"No—not impudent whelps, Sid. You ought to had your jaws boxed; I hain't been so put out since I don't know when. But I don't care, I don't mind the terms—I'd be willing to stand a thousand such jokes to have you here. Well, to think of that performance! I don't deny it, I was most putrified with astonishment when you give me that smack."

We had dinner out in that broad open passage betwixt the house and the kitchen; and there was things enough on that table for seven families—and all hot, too; none of your flabby tough meat that's laid in a cupboard in a damp cellar all night and tastes like a hunk of old cold cannibal in the morning. Uncle Silas he asked a pretty long blessing over it, but it was worth it; and it didn't cool it a bit, neither, the way I've seen them kind of interruptions do, lots of times.

There was a considerable good deal of talk, all the afternoon, and me and Tom was on the lookout all the time, but it warn't no use, they didn't happen to say nothing about any runaway nigger, and we was afraid to try to work up to it. But at supper, at night, one of the little boys says:

"Pa, mayn't Tom and Sid and me go to the show?"

"No," says the old man, "I reckon there ain't going to be any; and you couldn't go if there was; because the runaway nigger told Burton and me all about that scandalous show, and Burton said he would tell the people; so I reckon they've drove the owdacious loafers out of town before this time."

So there it was!—but *I* couldn't help it. Tom and me was to sleep in the same room and bed; so, being tired, we bid good-night and went up to bed, right after supper, and clumb out of the window and down the lightning-rod, and shoved for the town; for I didn't believe anybody was going to give the king and the duke a hint, and so, if I didn't hurry up and give them one they'd get into trouble sure.

On the road Tom he told me all about how it was reckoned I was murdered, and how pap disappeared, pretty soon, and didn't come back no more, and what a stir there was when Jim run away; and I told Tom all about our Royal Nonesuch rapscallions, and as much of the raft-voyage as I had time to; and as we struck into the town and up through the middle of it—it was as much as half-after eight, then—here comes a raging rush of people, with torches, and an awful whooping and yelling, and banging tin pans and blowing horns; and we jumped to one side to let them go by; and as they went by, I see they had the king and the duke astraddle of a rail—that is, I knowed it *was* the king and the duke, though they was all over tar and feathers, and didn't look like nothing in the world that was human—just looked like a couple of monstrous big soldier-plumes. Well, it made me sick to see it; and I was sorry for them poor pitiful rascals, it seemed like I couldn't ever feel any hardness against them any more in the world. It was a dreadful thing to see. Human beings *can* be awful cruel to one another.

We see we was too late—couldn't do no good. We asked some stragglers about it, and they said everybody went to the show looking very innocent; and laid low and kept dark till the poor old king was in the middle of his cavortings on the stage; then somebody gave a signal, and the house rose up and went for them.

So we poked along back home, and I warn't feeling so brash as I was before, but kind of ornery, and humble, and to blame, somehow—though *I* hadn't done nothing. But that's always the way; it don't make no difference whether you do right or wrong, a person's conscience ain't got no sense, and just goes for him *anyway*. If I had a yaller dog that didn't know no more than a person's conscience does, I would pison him. It takes up more room than all the rest of a person's insides, and yet ain't no good, nohow. Tom Sawyer he says the same.

Chapter XXXIV

We stopped talking, and got to thinking.

By-and-by Tom says:

"Looky, here, Huck, what fools we are, to not think of it before! I bet I know where Jim is."

"No! Where?"

"In that hut down by the ash-hopper. Why, looky here. When we was at dinner, didn't you see a nigger man go in there with some vittles?"

"Yes."

"What did you think the vittles was for?"

"For a dog."

"So'd I. Well, it wasn't for a dog."

"Why?"

"Because part of it was watermelon."

"So it was—I noticed it. Well, it does beat all, that I never thought about a dog not eating watermelon. It shows how a body can see and don't see at the same time."

"Well, the nigger unlocked the padlock when he went in, and he locked it again when he come out. He fetched uncle a key, about the time we got up from table—same key, I bet. Watermelon shows man, lock shows prisoner; and it ain't likely there's two prisoners on such a little plantation, and where the people's all so kind and good. Jim's the prisoner. All right—I'm glad we found it out detective fashion; I wouldn't give shucks for any other way. Now you work your mind and study out a plan to steal Jim, and I will study out one, too; and we'll take the one we like the best."

What a head for just a boy to have! If I had Tom Sawyer's head, I wouldn't trade it off to be a duke, nor mate of a steamboat, nor clown in a circus, nor nothing I can think of. I went to thinking out a plan, but only just to be doing something; I knowed very well where the right plan was going to come from. Pretty soon, Tom says:

"Ready?"

"Yes," I says.

"All right—bring it out."

"My plan is this," I says. "We can easy find out if it's Jim in there. Then get up my ca-noe to-morrow night, and fetch my raft over from the island. Then the first dark night that comes, steal the key out of the old man's britches, after he goes to bed, and shove off down the river on the raft, with Jim, hiding daytimes and running nights, the way me and Jim used to do before. Wouldn't that plan work?"

"*Work?* Why cert'nly, it would work, like rats a fighting. But it's too blame' simple; there ain't nothing *to* it. What's the good of a plan that ain't no more trouble than that? It's a mild as goose-milk. Why, Huck, it wouldn't make no more talk than breaking into a soap factory."

I never said nothing, because I warn't expecting nothing different; but I knowed mighty well that whenever he got *his* plan ready it wouldn't have none of them objec-tions to it.

And it didn't. He told me what it was, and I see in a minute it was worth fifteen of mine, for style, and would make Jim just as free a man as mine would, and maybe get us all killed besides. So I was satisfied, and said we would waltz in on it. I needn't tell what it was, here, because I knowed it wouldn't stay the way it was. I knowed he would be changing it around, every which way, as we went along, and heaving in new bullinesses wherever he got a chance. And that is what he done.

Well, one thing was dead sure; and that was, that Tom Sawyer was in earnest and was actuly going to help steal that nigger out of slavery. That was the thing that was too many for me. Here was a boy that was respectable, and well brung up; and had a char-acter to lose; and folks at home that had characters; and he was bright and not leather-headed; and knowing and not ignorant; and not mean, but kind; and yet here he was, without any more pride, or rightness, or feeling, than to stoop to this business, and make himself a shame, and his family a shame, before everybody. I *couldn't* understand it, no way at all. It was outrageous, and I knowed I ought to just up and tell him so; and so be his true friend, and let him quit the thing right where he was, and save himself. And I *did* start to tell him; but he shut me up, and says:

"Don't you reckon I know what I'm about? Don't I generly know what I'm about?"

"Yes."

"Didn't I *say* I was going to help steal the nigger?"

"Yes."

"*Well* then."

That's all he said, and that's all I said. It warn't no use to say any more; because when he said he'd do a thing, he always done it. But *I* couldn't make out how he was willing to go into this thing; so I just let it go, and never bothered no more about it. If he was bound to have it so, *I* couldn't help it.

When we got home, the house was all dark and still; so we went on down to the hut by the ash hopper, for to examine it. We went through the yard, so as to see what the hounds would do. They knowed us, and didn't make no more noise than country dogs is always doing when anything comes by in the night. When we got to the cabin, we took a look at the front and the two sides; and on the side I warn't acquainted with—which was the north side—we found a square window-hole, up tolerable high, with just one stout board nailed across it. I says:

"Here's the ticket. This hole's big enough for Jim to get through, if we wrench off the board."

Tom says:

"It's as simple as tit-tat-toe, three-in-a-row, and as easy as playing hooky. I should *hope* we can find a way that's a little more complicated than *that*, Huck Finn."

"Well, then," I says, "how'll it do to saw him out, the way I done before I was murdered, that time?"

"That's more *like*," he says. "It's real mysterious, and troublesome, and good," he says; "but I bet we can find a way that's twice as long. There ain't no hurry; le's keep on looking around."

Betwixt the hut and the fence, on the back side, was a lean-to, that joined the hut at the eaves, and was made out of plank. It was as long as the hut, but narrow—only about six foot wide. The door to it was at the south end, and was padlocked. Tom he went to the soap kettle, and searched around and fetched back the iron thing they lift the lid with; so he took it and prized out one of the staples. The chain fell down, and we opened the door and went in, and shut it, and struck a match, and see the shed was only built against the cabin and hadn't no connection with it; and there warn't no floor to the shed, nor nothing in it but some old rusty played-out hoes, and spades, and picks, and a crippled plow. The match went out, and so did we, and shoved in the staple again, and the door was locked as good as ever. Tom was joyful. He says:

"Now we're all right. We'll *dig* him out. It'll take about a week!"

Then we started for the house, and I went in the back door—you only have to pull a buckskin latch-string, they don't fasten the doors—but that warn't romantical enough for Tom Sawyer: no way would do him but he must climb up the lightning-rod. But after he got up half-way about three times, and missed fire and fell every time, and the last time most busted his brains out, he thought he'd got to give it up; but after he was rested, he allowed he would give her one more turn for luck, and this time he made the trip.

In the morning we was up at break of day, and down to the nigger cabins to pet the dogs and make friends with the nigger that fed Jim—if it *was* Jim that was being fed. The niggers was just getting through breakfast and starting for the fields; and Jim's nigger was piling up a tin pan with bread and meat and things; and whilst the others was leaving, the key come from the house.

This nigger had a good-natured, chuckle-headed face, and his wool was all tied up in little bunches with thread. That was to keep witches off. He said the witches was pestering him awful, these nights, and making him see all kinds of strange things, and hear all kinds of strange words and noises, and he didn't believe he was ever witched so long, before, in his life. He got so worked up, and got to running on so about his troubles, he forgot all about what he'd been agoing to do. So Tom says:

"What's the vittles for? Going to feed the dogs?"

The nigger kind of smiled around gradyly over his face, like when you heave a brickbat in a mud puddle, and he says:

"Yes, Mars Sid, *a* dog. Cur'us dog, too. Does you want to go en look at 'im?"

"Yes."

I hunched Tom, and whispers:

"You going, right here in the day-break? *That* warn't the plan."

"No, it warn't—but it's the plan *now*."

So, drat him, we went along, but I didn't like it much. When we got in, we couldn't hardly see anything, it was so dark; but Jim was there, sure enough, and could see us; and he sings out:

"Why, *Huck!* En good *lan'!* ain' dat Misto Tom?"

I just knowed how it would be; I just expected it. *I* didn't know nothing to do; and if I had, I couldn't a done it; because that nigger busted in and says:

"Why, de gracious sakes! do he know you genlmen?"

We could see pretty well, now. Tom he looked at the nigger, steady and kind of wondering, and says:

"Does *who* know us?"

"Why, dish-yer runaway nigger."

"I don't reckon he does; but what put that into your head?"

"What *put* it dar? Didn' he jis' dis minute sing out like he knowed you?"

Tom says, in a puzzled-up kind of way:

"Well, that's mighty curious. *Who* sung out? *When* did he sing out? *What* did he sing out?" And turns to me, perfectly c'am, and says, "Did *you* hear anybody sing out?"

Of course there warn't nothing to be said but the one thing; so I says:

"No; *I* ain't heard nobody say nothing."

Then he turns to Jim, and looks him over like he never see him before; and says:

"Did you sing out?"

"No, sah," says Jim; "*I* hain't said nothing, sah."

"Not a word?"

"No, sah, I hain't said a word."

"Did you ever see us before?"

"No, sah; not as *I* knows on."

So Tom turns to the nigger, which was looking wild and distressed, and says, kind of severe:

"What do you reckon's the matter with you, anyway? What made you think somebody sung out?"

"Oh, it's de dad-blame' witches, sah, en I wisht I was dead, I do. Dey's awluz at it, sah, en dey do mos' kill me, dey sk'yers me so. Please to don't tell nobody 'bout it sah, er ole Mars Silas he'll scole me; 'kase he say dey *ain't* no witches. I jis' wish to goodness he was heah now—*den* what would he say! I jis' bet he couldn' fine no way to git aroun' it *dis* time. But it's awluz jis' so; people dat's *sot,* stays sot; dey won't look into nothn' en fine it out f'r deyselves, en when *you* fine it out en tell um 'bout it, dey doan' b'lieve you."

Tom give him a dime, and said we wouldn't tell nobody; and told him to buy some more thread to tie up his wool with; and then looks at Jim, and says:

"I wonder if Uncle Silas is going to hang this nigger. If I was to catch a nigger that was ungrateful enough to run away, *I* wouldn't give him up, I'd hang him." And whilst the nigger stepped to the door to look at the dime and bite it to see if it was good, he whispers to Jim, and says:

"Don't ever let on to know us. And if you hear any digging going on nights, it's us: we're going to set you free."

Jim only had time to grab us by the hand and squeeze it, then the nigger come back, and we said we'd come again some time if the nigger wanted us to; and he said he would, more particular if it was dark, because the witches went for him mostly in the dark, and it was good to have folks around then.

Chapter XXXV

It would be most an hour, yet, till breakfast, so we left, and struck down into the woods; because Tom said we got to have *some* light to see how to dig by, and a lantern makes too much, and might get us into trouble; what we must have was a lot of them rotten chunks that's called fox-fire and just makes a soft kind of a glow when you lay them in a dark place. We fetched an armful and hid it in the weeds, and set down to rest, and Tom says, kind of dissatisfied:

"Blame it, this whole thing is just as easy and awkard as it can be. And so it makes it so rotten difficult to get up a difficult plan. There ain't no watchman to be drugged— now there *ought* to be a watchman. There ain't even a dog to give a sleeping-mixture to. And there's Jim chained by one leg, with a ten-foot chain, to the leg of his bed: why, all you got to do is to lift up the bedstead and slip off the chain. And Uncle Silas he trusts everybody; sends the key to the punkin-headed nigger, and don't send nobody to watch the nigger. Jim could a got out of that window hole before this, only there wouldn't be no use trying to travel with a ten-foot chain on his leg. Why, drat it, Huck, it's the stupidest arrangement I ever see. You got to invent *all* the difficulties. Well we can't help it, we got to do the best we can with the materials we've got. Anyhow, there's one thing— there's more honor in getting him out through a lot of difficulties and dangers, where there warn't one of them furnished to you by the people who it was their duty to furnish them, and you had to contrive them all out of your own head. Now look at just that one thing of the lantern. When you come down to the cold facts, we simply got to *let on* that a lantern's resky. Why, we could work with a torchlight procession if we wanted to, *I* believe. Now, whilst I think of it, we got to hunt up something to make a saw out of, the first chance we get."

"What do we want of a saw?"

"What do we *want* of it? Hain't we got to saw the leg of Jim's bed off, so as to get the chain loose?"

"Why, you just said a body could lift up the bedstead and slip the chain off."

"Well, if that ain't just like you, Huck Finn. You *can* get up the infant-schooliest ways of going at a thing. Why, hain't you ever read any books at all?—Baron Trenck, nor Casanova, nor Benvenuto Chelleeny, nor Henri IV., nor none of them heroes? Whoever heard of getting a prisoner loose in such an old-maidy way as that? No; the way all the best authorities does, is to saw the bed-leg in two, and leave it just so, and swallow the sawdust, so it can't be found, and put some dirt and grease around the sawed place so the very keenest seneskal can't see no sign of it's being sawed, and thinks the bed-leg is perfectly sound. Then, the night you're ready, fetch the leg a kick, down she goes; slip off your chain, and there you are. Nothing to do but hitch your rope-ladder to the battlements, shin down it, break your leg in the moat—because a rope-ladder is nineteen foot too short, you know—and there's your horses and your trusty vassles, and they scoop you up and fling you across a saddle and away you go, to your native Langudoc, or Navarre, or wherever it is. It's gaudy, Huck. I wish there was a moat to this cabin. If we get time, the night of the escape, we'll dig one."

I says:

"What do we want of a moat, when we're going to snake him out from under the cabin?"

But he never heard me. He had forgot me and everything else. He had his chin in his hand, thinking. Pretty soon, he sighs, and shakes his head; then sighs again, and says:

"No, it wouldn't do—there ain't necessity enough for it."

"For what?" I says.

"Why, to saw Jim's leg off," he says.

"Good land!" I says, "why, there ain't *no* necessity for it. And what would you want to saw his leg off for, anyway?"

"Well, some of the best authorities has done it. They couldn't get the chain off, so they just cut their hand off, and shoved. And a leg would be better still. But we got to let that go. There ain't necessity enough in this case; and besides, Jim's a nigger and wouldn't understand the reasons for it, and how it's the custom in Europe; so we'll let it go. But there's one thing—he can have a rope-ladder; we can tear up our sheets and make him a rope-ladder easy enough. And we can send it to him in a pie; it's mostly done that way. And I've et worse pies."

"Why, Tom Sawyer, how you talk," I says; "Jim ain't got no use for a rope-ladder."

"He *has* got use for it. How *you* talk, you better say; you don't know nothing about it. He's *got* to have a rope ladder; they all do."

"What in the nation can he *do* with it?"

"*Do* with it? He can hide it in his bed, can't he? That's what they all do; and *he's* got to, too. Huck, you don't ever seem to want to do anything that's regular; you want to be starting something fresh all the time. Spose he *don't* do nothing with it? ain't it there in his bed, for a clew, after he's gone? and don't you reckon they'll want clews? Of course they will. And you wouldn't leave them any? That would be a *pretty* howdy-do, *wouldn't* it! I never heard of such a thing."

"Well," I says, "if it's in the regulations, and he's got to have it, all right, let him have it; because I don't wish to go back on no regulations; but there's one thing, Tom Sawyer—if we go to tearing up our sheets to make Jim a rope-ladder, we're going to get into trouble with Aunt Sally, just as sure as you're born. Now, the way I look at it, a hickry-bark ladder don't cost nothing, and don't waste nothing, and is just as good to load up a pie with, and hide in a straw tick, as any rag ladder you can start; and as for Jim, he ain't had no experience, and so *he* don't care what kind of a—"

"Oh, shucks, Huck Finn, if I was as ignorant as you, I'd keep still—that's what *I'd* do. Who ever heard of a state prisoner escaping by a hickry-bark ladder? Why, it's perfectly ridiculous."

"Well, all right, Tom, fix it your own way; but if you'll take my advice, you'll let me borrow a sheet off of the clothes-line."

He said that would do. And that give him another idea, and he says:

"Borrow a shirt, too."

"What do we want of a shirt, Tom?"

"Want it for Jim to keep a journal on."

"Journal your granny—*Jim* can't write."

"Spose he *can't* write—he can make marks on the shirt, can't he, if we make him a pen out of an old pewter spoon or a piece of an old iron barrel-hoop?"

"Why, Tom, we can pull a feather out of a goose and make him a better one; and quicker, too."

"*Prisoners* don't have geese running around the donjon-keep to pull pens out of, you muggins. They *always* make their pens out of the hardest, toughest, troublesomest piece of old brass candlestick or something like that they can get their hands on; and it takes them weeks and weeks, and months and months to file it out, too, because they've got to do it by rubbing it on the wall. *They* wouldn't use a goose-quill if they had it. It ain't regular."

"Well, then, what'll we make him the ink out of?"

"Many makes it out of iron-rust and tears; but that's the common sort and women; the best authorities uses their own blood. Jim can do that; and when he wants to send any little common ordinary mysterious message to let the world know where he's captivated, he can write it on the bottom of a tin plate with a fork and throw it out of the window. The Iron Mask always done that, and it's a blame' good way, too."

"Jim ain't got no tin plates. They feed him in a pan."

"That ain't anything; we can get him some."

"Can't nobody *read* his plates."

"That ain't got nothing to *do* with it, Huck Finn. All *he's* got to do is to write on the plate and throw it out. You don't *have* to be able to read it. Why, half the time you can't read anything a prisoner writes on a tin plate, or anywhere else."

"Well, then, what's the sense in wasting the plates?"

"Why, blame it all, it ain't the *prisoner's* plates."

"But it's *somebody's* plates, ain't it?"

"Well, spos'n it is? What does the *prisoner* care whose—"

He broke off there, because we heard the breakfast-horn blowing. So we cleared out for the house.

Along during that morning I borrowed a sheet and a white shirt off of the clothes-line; and I found an old sack and put them in it, and we went down and got the fox-fire, and put that in too. I called it borrowing, because that was what pap always called it; but Tom said it warn't borrowing, it was stealing. He said we was representing prisoners; and prisoners don't care how they get a thing so they get it, and nobody don't blame them for it, either. It ain't no crime in a prisoner to steal the thing he needs to get away with, Tom said; it's his right; and so, as long as we was representing a prisoner, we had a perfect right to steal anything on this place we had the least use for, to get ourselves out of prison with. He said if we warn't prisoners it would be a very different thing, and nobody but a mean ornery person would steal when he warn't a prisoner. So we allowed we would steal everything there was that come handy. And yet he made a mighty fuss, one day, after that, when I stole a watermelon out of the nigger patch and eat it; and he made me go and give the niggers a dime, without telling them what it was for. Tom said that what he meant was, we could steal anything we *needed*. Well, I says, I needed the watermelon. But he said I didn't need it to get out of prison with, there's where the difference was. He said if I'd a wanted it to hide a knife in, and smuggle it to Jim to kill the seneskal with, it would a been all right. So I let it go at that, though I couldn't see no advantage in my representing a prisoner, if I got to set down and chaw over a lot of gold-leaf distinctions like that, every time I see a chance to hog a watermelon.

Well, as I was saying, we waited that morning till everybody was settled down to business, and nobody in sight around the yard; then Tom he carried the sack into the lean-to whilst I stood off a piece to keep watch. By-and-by he come out, and we went and set down on the wood-pile, to talk. He says:

"Everything's all right, now, except tools; and that's easy fixed."

"Tools?" I says.

"Yes."

"Tools for what?"

"Why, to dig with. We ain't agoing to *gnaw* him out, are we?"

"Ain't them old crippled picks and things in there good enough to dig a nigger out with?" I says.

He turns on me looking pitying enough to make a body cry, and says:

"Huck Finn, did you *ever* hear of a prisoner having picks and shovels, and all the modern conveniences in his wardrobe to dig himself out with? Now I want to ask you—if you got any reasonableness in you at all—what kind of a show would *that* give him to be a hero? Why, they might as well lend him the key, and done with it. Picks and shovels—why they wouldn't furnish 'em to a king."

"Well, then," I says, "if we don't want the picks and shovels, what do we want?"

"A couple of case-knives."

"To dig the foundations out from under the cabin with?"

"Yes."

"Confound it, it's foolish, Tom."

"It don't make no difference how foolish it is, it's the *right* way—and it's the regular way. And there ain't no *other* way, that ever *I* heard of, and I've read all the books that gives any information about these things. They always dig out with a case-knife—and not through dirt, mind you; generly it's through solid rock. And it takes them weeks and weeks and weeks, and for ever and ever. Why, look at one of them prisoners in the bottom dungeon of the Castle Deef, in the harbor of Marseilles, that dug himself out that way; how long was *he* at it, you reckon?"

"I don't know."

"Well, guess."

"I don't know. A month and a half?"

"*Thirty-seven year*—and he come out in China. *That's* the kind. I wish the bottom of *this* fortress was solid rock."

"*Jim* don't know nobody in China."

"What's *that* got to do with it? Neither did that other fellow. But you're always a-wandering off on a side issue. Why can't you stick to the main point?"

"All right—*I* don't care where he comes out, so he *comes* out; and Jim don't, either, I reckon. But there's one thing, anyway—Jim's too old to be dug out with a case-knife. He won't last."

"Yes he will *last,* too. You don't reckon it's going to take thirty-seven years to dig out through a *dirt* foundation, do you?"

"How long will it take, Tom?"

"Well, we can't resk being as long as we ought to, because it mayn't take very long for Uncle Silas to hear from down there by New Orleans. He'll hear Jim ain't from there. Then his next move will be to advertise Jim, or something like that. So we can't resk being as long digging him out as we ought to. By rights I reckon we ought to be a couple of years; but we can't. Things being so uncertain, what I recommend is this: that we really dig right in, as quick as we can; and after that, we can *let on,* to ourselves, that we was at it thirty-seven years. Then we can snatch him out and rush him away the first time there's an alarm. Yes, I reckon that'll be the best way."

"Now, there's *sense* in that," I says. "Letting on don't cost nothing; letting on ain't no trouble; and if it's any object, I don't mind letting on we was at it a hundred and fifty year. It wouldn't strain me none, after I got my hand in. So I'll mosey along now, and smouch a couple of case-knives."

"Smouch three," he says; "we want one to make a saw out of."

"Tom, if it ain't unregular and irreligious to sejest it," I says, "there's an old rusty saw-blade around yonder sticking under the weatherboarding behind the smoke-house."

He looked kind of weary and discouraged-like, and says:

"It ain't no use to try to learn you nothing, Huck. Run along and smouch the knives—three of them." So I done it.

Chapter XXXVI

As soon as we reckoned everybody was asleep, that night, we went down the lightning-rod, and shut ourselves up in the lean-to, and got out our pile of fox-fire, and went to work. We cleared everything out of the way, about four or five foot along the middle of the bottom log. Tom said he was right behind Jim's bed now, and we'd dig in under it, and when we got through there couldn't nobody in the cabin ever know there was any hole there, because Jim's counterpin hung down most to the ground, and you'd have to raise it up and look under to see the hole. So we dug and dug, with the case-knives, till most midnight; and then we was dog-tired, and our hands was blistered, and yet you couldn't see we'd done anything, hardly. At last I says:

"This ain't no thirty-seven year job, this is a thirty-eight year job, Tom Sawyer."

He never said nothing. But he sighed, and pretty soon he stopped digging, and then for a good little while I knowed he was thinking. Then he says:

"It ain't no use, Huck, it ain't agoing to work. If we was prisoners it would, because then we'd have as many years as we wanted, and no hurry; and we wouldn't get but a few minutes to dig, every day, while they was changing watches, and so our hands wouldn't get blistered, and we could keep it up right along, year in and year out, and do it right, and the way it ought to be done. But *we* can't fool along, we got to rush; we ain't got no time to spare. If we was to put in another night this way, we'd have to knock off for a week to let our hands get well—couldn't touch a case-knife with them sooner."

"Well, then, what we going to do, Tom?"

"I'll tell you. It ain't right, and it ain't moral, and I wouldn't like it to get out—but there ain't only just the one way; we got to dig him out with the picks, and *let on* it's case-knives."

"*Now* you're *talking!*" I says; "your head gets leveler and leveler all the time, Tom Sawyer," I says. "Picks is the thing, moral or no moral; and as for me, I don't care shucks for the morality of it, nohow. When I start in to steal a nigger, or a watermelon, or a Sunday-school book, I ain't no ways particular how it's done so it's done. What I want is my nigger; or what I want is my watermelon; or what I want is my Sunday-school book; and if a pick's the handiest thing, that's the thing I'm agoing to dig that nigger or that watermelon or that Sunday-school book out with; and I don't give a dead rat what the authorities thinks about it nuther."

"Well," he says, "there's excuse for picks and letting-on in a case like this; if it warn't so, I wouldn't approve of it, nor I wouldn't stand by and see the rules broke—because right is right, and wrong is wrong, and a body ain't got no business doing wrong when he ain't ignorant and knows better. It might answer for *you* to dig Jim out with a pick, *without* any letting-on, because you don't know no better; but it wouldn't for me, because I do know better. Gimme a case-knife."

He had his own by him, but I handed him mine. He flung it down, and says:

"Gimme a *case-knife*."

I didn't know just what to do—but then I thought. I scratched around amongst the old tools, and got a pick-ax and give it to him, and he took it and went to work, and never said a word.

He was always just that particular. Full of principle.

So then I got a shovel, and then we picked and shoveled, turn about, and made the fur fly. We stuck to it about a half an hour, which was as long as we could stand up; but we had a good deal of a hole to show for it. When I got up stairs, I looked out at the window and see Tom doing his level best with the lightning-rod, but he couldn't come it, his hands was so sore. At last he says:

"It ain't no use, it can't be done. What you reckon I better do? Can't you think up no way?"

"Yes," I says, "but I reckon it ain't regular. Come up the stairs, and let on it's a lightning-rod."

So he done it.

Next day Tom stole a pewter spoon and a brass candlestick in the house, for to make some pens for Jim out of, and six tallow candles; and I hung around the nigger cabins, and laid for a chance, and stole three tin plates. Tom said it wasn't enough; but I said nobody wouldn't ever see the plates that Jim throwed out, because they'd fall in the dog-fennel and jimpson weeds under the window-hole—then we could tote them back and he could use them over again. So Tom was satisfied. Then he says:

"Now, the thing to study out is, how to get the things to Jim."

"Take them in through the hole," I says, "when we get it done."

He only just looked scornful, and said something about nobody ever heard of such an idiotic idea, and then he went to studying. By-and-by he said he had ciphered out two or three ways, but there warn't no need to decide on any of them yet. Said we'd got to post Jim first.

That night we went down the lightning-rod a little after ten, and took one of the candles along, and listened under the window-hole, and heard Jim snoring; so we pitched it in, and it didn't wake him. Then we whirled in with the pick and shovel, and in about two hours and a half the job was done. We crept in under Jim's bed and into the cabin, and pawed around and found the candle and lit it, and stood over Jim a while, and found him looking hearty and healthy, and then we woke him up gentle and gradual. He was so glad to see us he most cried; and called us honey, and all the pet names he could think of; and was for having us hunt up a cold chisel to cut the chain off of his leg with, right away, and clearing out without losing any time. But Tom he showed him how unregular it would be, and set down and told him all about our plans, and how we could alter them in a minute any time there was an alarm; and not to be the least afraid, because we would see he got away, *sure*. So Jim he said it was all right, and we set there and talked over old times a while, and then Tom asked a lot of questions, and when Jim told him Uncle Silas come in every day or two to pray with him, and Aunt Sally come in to see if he was comfortable and had plenty to eat, and both of them was kind as they could be, Tom says:

"*Now* I know how to fix it. We'll send you some things by them."

I said, "Don't do nothing of the kind; it's one of the most jackass ideas I ever struck;" but he never paid no attention to me; went right on. It was his way when he'd got his plans set.

So he told Jim how we'd have to smuggle in the rope-ladder pie, and other large things, by Nat, the nigger that fed him, and he must be on the lookout, and not be surprised, and not let Nat see him open them; and we would put small things in uncle's coat pockets and he must steal them out; and we would tie things to aunt's apron strings or put them in her apron pocket, if we got a chance; and told him what they would be and what they was for. And told him how to keep a journal on the shirt with his blood, and all that. He told him everything. Jim he couldn't see no sense in the most of it, but he allowed we was white folks and knowed better than him; so he was satisfied, and said he would do it all just as Tom said.

Jim had plenty corn-cob pipes and tobacco; so we had a right down good sociable time; then we crawled out through the hole, and so home to bed, with hands that looked like they'd been chawed. Tom was in high spirits. He said it was the best fun he ever had in his life, and the most intellectual; and said if he only could see his way to it we would keep it up all the rest of our lives and leave Jim to our children to get out; for he believed Jim would come to like it better and better the more he got used to it. He said that in that way it could be strung out to as much as eighty year, and would be the best time on record. And he said it would make us all celebrated that had a hand in it.

In the morning we went out to the wood-pile and chopped up the brass candlestick into handy sizes, and Tom put them and the pewter spoon in his pocket. Then we went to the nigger cabins, and while I got Nat's notice off, Tom shoved a piece of candlestick into the middle of a corn-pone that was in Jim's pan, and we went along with Nat to see how it would work, and it just worked noble; when Jim bit into it it most mashed all his teeth out; and there warn't ever anything could a worked better. Tom said so himself. Jim he never let on but what it was only just a piece of rock or something like that that's always getting into bread, you know; but after that he never bit into nothing but what he jabbed his fork into it in three or four places, first.

And whilst we was a standing there in the dimmish light, here comes a couple of the hounds bulging in, from under Jim's bed; and they kept on piling in till there was eleven of them, and there warn't hardly room in there to get your breath. By jings, we forgot to fasten that lean-to door. The nigger Nat he only just hollered "witches!" once, and keeled over onto the floor amongst the dogs, and begun to groan like he was dying. Tom jerked the door open and flung out a slab of Jim's meat, and the dogs went for it, and in two seconds he was out himself and back again and shut the door, and I knowed he'd fixed the other door too. Then he went to work on the nigger, coaxing him and petting him, and asking him if he'd been imagining he saw something again. He raised up, and blinked his eyes around, and says:

"Mars Sid, you'll say I's a fool, but if I didn't b'lieve I see most a million dogs, er devils, er some'n, I wisht I may die right heah in dese tracks. I did, mos' sholy. Mars Sid, I *felt* um—I *felt* um, sah; dey was all over me. Dad fetch it, I jis' wisht I could git my han's on one er dem witches jis' wunst—on'y jis' wunst—it's all I'd ast. But mos'ly I wisht dey'd lemme 'lone, I does."

Tom says:

"Well, I tell you what *I* think. What makes them come here just at this runaway nigger's breakfast-time? It's because they're hungry; that's the reason. You make them a witch pie; that's the thing for *you* to do."

"But my lan', Mars Sid, how's *I* gwyne to make 'm a witch pie? I doan' know how to make it. I hain't ever hearn er sich a thing b'fo.'"

"Well, then, I'll have to make it myself."

"Will you do it, honey?—will you? I'll wusshup de groun' und' yo' foot, I will!"

"All right, I'll do it, seeing it's you, and you've been good to us and showed us the runaway nigger. But you got to be mighty careful. When we come around, you turn your back; and then whatever we've put in the pan, don't you let on you see it at all. And don't you look, when Jim unloads the pan—something might happen, I don't know what. And above all, don't you *handle* the witch-things."

"*Hannel* 'm Mars Sid? What *is* you a talkin' 'bout? I wouldn' lay de weight er my finger on um, not f'r ten hund'd thous'n' billion dollars, I wouldn't."

Chapter XXXVII

That was all fixed. So then we went away and went to the rubbage-pile in the back yard where they keep the old boots, and rags, and pieces of bottles, and wore-out tin things, and all such truck, and scratched around and found an old tin wash-pan and stopped up the holes as well as we could, to bake the pie in, and took it down cellar and stole it full of flour, and started for breakfast and found a couple of shingle-nails that Tom said would be handy for a prisoner to scrabble his name and sorrows on the dungeon walls with, and dropped one of them in Aunt Sally's apron pocket which was hanging on a chair, and t'other we stuck in the band of Uncle Silas's hat, what which was on the bureau, because we heard the children say their pa and ma was going to the runaway nigger's house this morning, and then went to breakfast, and Tom dropped the pewter spoon in Uncle Silas's coat pocket, and Aunt Sally wasn't come yet, so we had to wait a little while.

And when she come she was hot, and red, and cross, and couldn't hardly wait for the blessing; and then she went to sluicing out coffee with one hand and cracking the handiest child's head with her thimble with the other, and says:

"I've hunted high, and I've hunted low, and it does beat all, what *has* become of your other shirt."

My heart fell down amongst my lungs and livers and things, and a hard piece of corn-crust started down my throat after it and got me on the road with a cough and was shot across the table and took one of the children in the eye and curled him up like a fishing-worm, and let a cry out of him the size of a war-whoop, and Tom he turned kinder blue around the gills, and it all amounted to a considerable state of things for about a quarter of a minute or as much as that, and I would a sold out for half price if there was a bidder. But after that we was all right again—it was the sudden surprise of it that knocked us so kind of cold. Uncle Silas he says:

"It's most uncommon curious, I can't understand it. I know perfectly well I took it *off,* because—"

"Because you hain't got but one *on.* Just *listen* at the man! *I* know you took it off, and know it by a better way than your wool-gethering memory, too, because it was on the clo'es-line yesterday—I see it there myself. But it's gone—that's the long and the short of it, and you'll just have to change to a red flann'l one till I can get time to make a new one. And it'll be the third I've made in two years; it just keeps a body on the jump to keep you in shirts; and whatever you do manage to *do* with 'm all, is more'n *I* can make out. A body'd think you *would* learn to take some sort of care of 'em, at your time of life."

"I know it, Sally, and I do try all I can. But it oughtn't to be altogether my fault, because you know I don't see them nor have nothing to do with them except when they're on me; and I don't believe I've ever lost one of them *off* of me."

"Well, it ain't *your* fault if you haven't, Silas—you'd a done it if you could, I reckon. And the shirt ain't all that's gone, nuther. Ther's a spoon gone; and *that* ain't all. There was ten, and now ther's only nine. The calf got the shirt I reckon, but the calf never took the spoon, *that's* certain."

"Why, what else is gone, Sally?"

"Ther's six *candles* gone—that's what. The rats could a got the candles, and I reckon they did; I wonder they don't walk off with the whole place, the way you're always going to stop their holes and don't do it; and if they warn't fools they'd sleep in your hair, Silas—*you'd* never find it out; but you can't lay the *spoon* on the rats, and that I *know.*"

"Well, Sally, I'm in fault, and I acknowledge it; I've been remiss; but I won't let tomorrow go by without stopping up them holes."

"Oh, I wouldn't hurry, next year'll do. Matilda Angelina Araminta *Phelps!*"

Whack comes the thimble, and the child snatches her claws out of the sugar-bowl without fooling around any. Just then, the nigger woman steps onto the passage, and says:

"Missus, dey's a sheet gone."

"A *sheet* gone! Well, for the land's sake!"

"I'll stop up them holes *to-day,*" says Uncle Silas, looking sorrowful.

"Oh, *do* shet up!—spose the rats took the *sheet? Where's* it gone, Lize?"

"Clah to goodness I hain't no notion, Miss Sally. She wuz on de clo's-line yistiddy, but she done gone; she ain' dah no mo,' now."

"I reckon the world *is* coming to an end. I *never* see the beat of it, in all my born days. A shirt, and a sheet, and a spoon, and six can—"

"Missus," comes a young yaller wench, "dey's a brass cannelstick miss'n."

"Cler out from here, you hussy, er I'll take a skillet to ye!"

Well, she was just a biling. I begun to lay for a chance; I reckoned I would sneak out and go for the woods till the weather moderated. She kept a raging right along, running her insurrection all by herself, and everybody else mighty meek and quiet; and at last Uncle Silas, looking kind of foolish, fishes up that spoon out of his pocket. She stopped, with her mouth open and her hands up; and as for me, I wished I was in Jerusalem or somewheres. But not long; because she says:

"It's *just* as I expected. So you had it in your pocket all the time; and like as not you've *got* the other things there, too. How'd it get there?"

"I reely don't know, Sally," he says, kind of apologizing, "or you know I would tell. I was a-studying over my text in Acts Seventeen, before breakfast, and I reckon I put it in there, not noticing, meaning to put my Testament in, and it must be so, because my Testament ain't in, but I'll go and see, and if the Testament is where I had it, I'll know I didn't put it in, and that will show that I laid the Testament down and took up the spoon, and—"

"Oh, for the land's sake! Give a body a rest! Go 'long now, the whole kit and biling of ye; and don't come nigh me again till I've got back my peace of mind."

I'd a heard her, if she'd a said it to herself, let alone speaking it out; and I'd a got up and obeyed her, if I'd a been dead. As we was passing through the setting-room, the old man he took up his hat, and the shingle-nail fell out on the floor, and he just merely picked it up and laid it on the mantel-shelf, and never said nothing, and went out. Tom see him do it, and remembered about the spoon, and says:

"Well, it ain't no use to send things by *him* no more, he ain't reliable." Then he says: "But he done us a good turn with the spoon, anyway, without knowing it, and so we'll go and do him one without *him* knowing it—stop up his rat-holes."

There was a noble good lot of them, down cellar, and it took us a whole hour, but we done the job tight and good, and ship-shape. Then we heard steps on the stairs, and blowed out our light, and hid; and here comes the old man, with a candle in one hand and a bundle of stuff in t'other, looking as absent-minded as year before last. He went a mooning around, first to one rat-hole and then another, till he'd been to them all. Then he stood about five minutes, picking tallow-drip off of his candle and thinking. Then he turns off slow and dreamy towards the stairs, saying:

"Well, for the life of me I can't remember when I done it. I could show her now that I warn't to blame on account of the rats. But never mind—let it go. I reckon it wouldn't go no good."

And so he went on a mumbling up stairs, and then we left. He was a mighty nice old man. And always is.

Tom was a good deal bothered about what to do for a spoon, but he said we'd got to have it; so he took a think. When he had ciphered it out, he told me how we was to do; then we went and waited around the spoon-basket till we see Aunt Sally coming, and then Tom went to counting the spoons and laying them out to one side, and I slid one of them up my sleeve, and Tom says:

"Why, Aunt Sally, there ain't but nine spoons, *yet.*"

She says:

"Go 'long to your play, and don't bother me. I know better, I counted 'm myself."

"Well, I've counted them twice, Aunty, and *I* can't make but nine."

She looked out of all patience, but of course she come to count—anybody would.

"I declare to gracious ther' *ain't* but nine!" she says. "Why, what in the world—plague *take* the things, I'll count 'm again."

So I slipped back the one I had, and when she got done counting, she says:

"Hang the troublesome rubbage, ther's *ten,* now!" and she looked huffy and bothered both. But Tom says:

"Why, Aunty, *I* don't think there's ten."

"You numskull, didn't you see me *count* 'm?"

"I know, but—"

"Well, I'll count 'm *again.*"

So I smouched one, and they come out nine same as the other time. Well, she *was* in a tearing way—just a trembling all over, she was so mad. But she counted and counted, till she got that addled she'd start to count-in the *basket* for a spoon, sometimes; and so, three times they come out right, and three times they come out wrong. Then she grabbed up the basket and slammed it across the house and knocked the cat galley-west; and she said cle'r out and let her have some peace, and if we come bothering around her again betwixt that and dinner, she'd skin us. So we had the odd spoon; and dropped it in her apron pocket whilst she was a giving us our sailing-orders, and Jim got it all right, along with her shingle-nail, before noon. We was very well satisfied with this business, and Tom allowed it was worth twice the trouble it took, because he said *now* she couldn't ever count them spoons twice alike again to save her life; and wouldn't believe she'd counted them right, if she *did;* and said that after she'd about counted her head off, for the next three days, he judged she'd give it up and offer to kill anybody that wanted her to ever count them any more.

So we put the sheet back on the line, that night, and stole one out of her closet; and kept on putting it back and stealing it again, for a couple of days, till she didn't know how many sheets she had, any more, and said she didn't *care,* and warn't agoing to bullyrag the rest of her soul out about it, and wouldn't count them again not to save her life, she druther die first.

So we was all right now, as to the shirt and the sheet and the spoon and the candles, by the help of the calf and the rats and the mixed-up counting; and as to the candlestick, it warn't no consequence, it would blow over by-and-by.

But that pie was a job; we had no end of trouble with that pie. We fixed it up away down in the woods, and cooked it there; and we got it done at last, and very satisfactory, too; but not all in one day; and we had to use up three washpans full of flour, before we got through, and we got burnt pretty much all over, in places, and eyes put out with the smoke; because, you see, we didn't want nothing but a crust, and we couldn't prop it up right, and she would always cave in. But of course we thought of the right way at last; which was to cook the ladder, too, in the pie. So then we laid in with Jim, the second night, and tore up the sheet all in little strings, and twisted them together, and long before daylight we had a lovely rope, that you could a hung a person with. We let on it took nine months to make it.

And in the forenoon we took it down to the woods, but it wouldn't go in the pie. Being made of a whole sheet, that way, there was rope enough for forty pies, if we'd a wanted them, and plenty left over for soup, or sausage, or anything you choose. We could a had a whole dinner.

But we didn't need it. All we needed was just enough for the pie, and so we throwed the rest away. We didn't cook none of the pies in the washpan, afraid the solder would melt; but Uncle Silas he had a noble brass warming-pan which he thought considerable of, because it belonged to one of his ancestors with a long wooden handle that come over from England with William the Conqueror in the *Mayflower* or one of them early ships and was hid away up garret with a lot of other old pots and things that was valuable, not on account of being any account because they warn't, but on account of them being relicts, you know, and we snaked her out, private, and took her down there, but she failed on the first pies, because we didn't know how, but she come up smiling on the last one. We took and lined her with dough, and set her in the coals, and loaded her up with rag-rope, and put on a dough roof, and shut down the lid, and put hot embers on top, and stood off five foot, with the long handle, cool and comfortable, and in fifteen minutes she turned out a pie that was a satisfaction to look at. But the person that et it would want to fetch a couple of kags of toothpicks along, for if that rope-ladder wouldn't cramp him down to business, I don't know nothing what I'm talking about, and lay him in enough stomach-ache to last him till next time, too.

Nat didn't look, when we put the witch-pie in Jim's pan; and we put the three tin plates in the bottom of the pan under the vittles; and so Jim got everything all right, and as soon as he was by himself he busted into the pie and hid the rope-ladder inside of his straw tick, and scratched some marks on a tin plate and throwed it out of the window-hole.

Chapter XXXVIII

Making them pens was a distressid-tough job, and so was the saw; and Jim allowed the inscription was going to be the toughest of all. That's the one which the prisoner has to scrabble on the wall. But we had to have it; Tom said we'd *got* to; there warn't no case of a state prisoner not scrabbling his inscription to leave behind, and his coat of arms.

"Look at Lady Jane Grey," he says; "look at Gilford Dudley; look at old Northumberland! Why, Huck, spose it *is* considerble trouble?—what you going to do?—how you going to get around it? Jim's *got* to do his inscription and coat of arms. They all do."

Jim says:

"Why, Mars Tom, I hain't got no coat o' arms; I hain't got nuffn but dish-yer ole shirt, en you knows I got to keep de journal on dat."

"Oh, you don't understand, Jim; a coat of arms is very different."

"Well," I says, "Jim's right, anyway, when he says he hain't got no coat of arms, because he hain't."

"I reckon *I* knowed that," Tom says, "but you bet he'll have one before he goes out of this—because he's going out *right,* and there ain't going to be no flaws in his record."

So whilst me and Jim filed away at the pens on a brickbat apiece, Jim a making his'n out of the brass and I making mine out of the spoon, Tom set to work to think out the coat of arms. By-and-by he said he'd struck so many good ones he didn't hardly know which to take, but there was one which he reckoned he'd decide on. He says:

"On the scutcheon we'll have a bend *or* in the dexter base, a saltire *murrey* in the fess, with a dog, couchant, for common charge, and under his foot a chain embattled, for slavery, with a chevron *vert* in a chief engrailed, and three invected lines on a field *azure,* with the nombril points rampant on a dancette indented; crest, a runaway nigger, *sable,* with his bundle over his shoulder on a bar sinister: and a couple of gules for supporters, which is you and me; motto, *Maggiore fretta, minore atto.* Got it out of a book—means, the more haste, the less speed."

"Geewhillikins," I says, "but what does the rest of it mean?"

"We ain't got no time to bother over that," he says, "we got to dig in like all git-out."

"Well, anyway," I says, "what's *some* of it? What's a fess?"

"A fess—a fess is—*you* don't need to know what a fess is. I'll show him how to make it when he gets to it."

"Shucks, Tom," I says, "I think you might tell a person. What's a bar sinister?"

"Oh, *I* don't know. But he's got to have it. All the nobility does."

That was just his way. If it didn't suit him to explain a thing to you, he wouldn't do it. You might pump at him a week, it wouldn't make no difference.

He'd got all that coat of arms business fixed, so now he started in to finish up the rest of that part of the work, which was to plan out a mournful inscription—said Jim got to have one, like they all done. He made up a lot, and wrote them out on a paper, and read them off, so:

1. *Here a captive heart busted.*
2. *Here a poor prisoner, forsook by the world and friends, fretted out his sorrowful life.*

3.   *Here a lonely heart broke, and a worn spirit went to its rest, after thirty-seven years of solitary captivity.*

4.   *Here, homeless and friendless, after thirty-seven years of bitter captivity, perished a noble stranger, natural son of Louis XIV.*

Tom's voice trembled, whilst he was reading them, and he most broke down. When he got done, he couldn't no way make up his mind which one for Jim to scrabble onto the wall, they was all so good; but at last he allowed he would let him scrabble them all on. Jim said it would him a year to scrabble such a lot of truck onto the logs with a nail, and he didn't know how to make letters, besides; but Tom said he would block them out for him, and then he wouldn't have nothing to do but just follow the lines. Then pretty soon he says:

"Come to think, the logs ain't agoing to do; they don't have log walls in a dungeon: we got to dig the inscriptions into a rock. We'll fetch a rock."

Jim said the rock was worse than the logs; he said it would take him such a pison long time to dig them into a rock, he wouldn't ever get out. But Tom said he would let me help him do it. Then he took a look to see how me and Jim was getting along with the pens. It was most pesky tedious hard work and slow, and didn't give my hands no show to get well of the sores, and we didn't seem to make no headway, hardly. So Tom says:

"I know how to fix it. We got to have a rock for the coat of arms and mournful inscriptions, and we can kill two birds with that same rock. There's a gaudy big grindstone down at the mill, and we'll smouch it, and carve the things on it, and file out the pens and the saw on it, too."

It warn't no slouch of an idea; and it warn't no slouch of a grindstone nuther; but we allowed we'd tackle it. It warn't quite midnight, yet, so we cleared out for the mill, leaving Jim at work. We smouched the grindstone, and set out to roll her home, but it was a most nation tough job. Sometimes, do what we could, we couldn't keep her from falling over, and she come mighty near mashing us, every time. Tom said she was going to get one of us, sure, before we got through. We got her half way; and then we was plumb played out, and most drownded with sweat. We see it warn't no use, we got to go and fetch Jim. So he raised up his bed and slid the chain off of the bed-leg, and wrapt it round and round his neck, and we crawled out through our hole and down there, and Jim and me laid into that grindstone and walked her along like nothing; and Tom superintended. He could out-superintend any boy I ever see. He knowed how to do everything.

Our hole was pretty big, but it warn't big enough to get the grindstone through; but Jim he took the pick and soon made it big enough. Then Tom marked out them things on it with the nail, and set Jim to work on them, with the nail for a chisel and an iron bolt from the rubbage in the lean-to for a hammer, and told him to work till the rest of his candle quit on him, and then he could go to bed, and hide the grindstone under his straw tick and sleep on it. Then we helped him fix his chain back on the bed-leg, and was ready for bed ourselves. But Tom thought of something, and says:

"You got any spiders in here, Jim?"

"No, sah, thanks to goodness I hain't, Mars Tom."

"All right, we'll get you some."

"But bless you, honey, I doan' *want* none. I's afeard un um. I jis' 's soon have rattlesnakes aroun'."

Tom thought a minute or two, and says:

"It's a good idea. And I reckon it's been done. It *must* a been done; it stands to reason. Yes, it's a prime good idea. Where could you keep it?"

"Keep what, Mars Tom?"

"Why, a rattlesnake."

"De goodness gracious alive, Mars Tom! Why, if dey was a rattlesnake to come in heah, I'd take en bust right out thoo dat log wall, I would, wid my head."

"Why, Jim, you wouldn't be afraid of it, after a little. You could tame it."

"*Tame* it!"

"Yes—easy enough. Every animal is grateful for kindness and petting, and they wouldn't *think* of hurting a person that pets them. Any book will tell you that. You try—that's all I ask; just try for two or three days. Why, you can get him so, in a little while, that he'll love you; and sleep with you; and won't stay away from you a minute; and will let you wrap him round your neck and put his head in your mouth."

"*Please,* Mars Tom—*doan'* talk so! I can't *stan'* it! He'd *let* me shove his head in my mouf—fer a favor, hain't it? I lay he'd wait a pow'ful long time 'fo' I *ast* him. En mo' en dat, I doan' *want* him to sleep wid me."

"Jim, don't act so foolish. A prisoner's *got* to have some kind of a dumb pet, and if a rattlesnake hain't ever been tried, why, there's more glory to be gained in your being the first to ever try it than any other way you could ever think of to save your life."

"Why, Mars Tom, I doan' *want* no sich glory. Snake take 'n bite Jim's chin off, den *whah* is de glory? No, sah, I doan' want no sich doin's."

"Blame it, can't you *try?* I only *want* you to try—you needn't keep it up if it don't work."

"But de trouble all *done,* ef de snake bite me while I's a tryin' him. Mars Tom, I's willin' to tackle mos' anything 'at ain't onreasonable, but ef you en Huck fetches a rattlesnake in heah for me to tame, I's gwyne to *leave,* dat's *shore.*"

"Well, then, let it go, let it go, if you're so bullheaded about it. We can get you some garter-snakes and you can tie some buttons on their tails, and let on they're rattlesnakes, and I reckon that'll have to do."

"I k'n stan' *dem,* Mars Tom, but blame' 'f I couldn' get along widout um, I tell you dat. I never knowed b'fo', 't was so much bother and trouble to be a prisoner."

"Well, it *always* is, when it's done right. You got any rats around here?"

"No, sah, I hain't seed none."

"Well, we'll get you some rats."

"Why, Mars Tom, I doan' *want* no rats. Dey's de dad-blamedest creturs to sturb a body, en rustle roun' over 'im, en bite his feet, when he's tryin' to sleep, I ever see. No, sah, gimme g'yarter-snakes, 'f I's got to have 'm, but doan' gimme no rats, I ain' got no use f'r um, skasely."

"But Jim, you *got* to have 'em—they all do. So don't make no more fuss about it. Prisoners ain't ever without rats. There ain't no instance of it. And they train them, and pet them, and learn them tricks, and they get to be as sociable as flies. But you got to play music to them. You got anything to play music on?"

"I ain' got nuffn but a coase comb en a piece o' paper, en a juice-harp; but I reck'n dey wouldn' take no stock in a juice-harp."

"Yes they would. *They* don't care what kind of music 'tis. A jews-harp's plenty good enough for a rat. All animals likes music—in a prison they dote on it. Specially, painful music; and you can't get no other kind out of a jews-harp. It always interests them; they come out to see what's the matter with you. Yes, you're all right; you're fixed very well. You want to set on your bed, nights, before you go to sleep, and early in the mornings, and play our jews-harp; play The Last Link is Broken—that's the thing that'll scoop a rat, quicker'n anything else: and when you've played about two minutes, you'll see all the rats, and the snakes, and spiders, and things begin to feel worried about you, and come. And they'll just fairly swarm over you, and have a noble good time."

"Yes, *dey* will, I reck'n, Mars Tom, but what kine er time is *Jim* havin'? Blest if I kin see de pint. But I'll do it ef I got to. I reck'n I better keep de animals satisfied, en not have no trouble in de house."

Tom waited to think over, and see if there wasn't nothing else; and pretty soon he says:

"Oh—there's one thing I forgot. Could you raise a flower here, do you reckon?"

"I doan' know but maybe I could, Mars Tom; but it's tolable dark in heah, en I ain' got no use f'r no flower, nohow, en she'd be a pow'ful sight o' trouble."

"Well, you try it, anyway. Some other prisoners has done it."

"One er dem big cat-tail-lookin' mullen-stalks would grow in heah, Mars Tom, I reck'n, but she wouldn' be wuth half de trouble she'd coss."

"Don't you believe it. We'll fetch you a little one, and you plant it in the corner, over there, and raise it. And don't call it mullen, call it Pitchiola—that's its right name, when it's in a prison. And you want to water it with your tears."

"Why, I got plenty spring water, Mars Tom."

"You don't *want* spring water; you want to water it with your tears. It's the way they always do."

"Why, Mars Tom, I lay I kin raise one er dem mullen-stalks twyste wid spring water whiles another man's a *start'n* one wid tears."

"That ain't the idea. You *got* to do it with tears."

"She'll die on my han's, Mars Tom, she sholy will; kase I doan' skasely ever cry."

So Tom was stumped. But he studied it over, and then said Jim would have to worry along the best he could with an onion. He promised he would go to the nigger cabins and drop one, private, in Jim's coffee-pot, in the morning. Jim said he would 'jis' 's soon have tobacker in his coffee;" and found so much fault with it, and with the work and bother of raising the mullen, and jews-harping the rats, and petting and flattering up the snakes and spiders and things, on top of all the other work he had to do on pens, and inscriptions, and journals, and things, which made it more trouble and worry and responsibility to be a prisoner than anything he ever undertook, that Tom most lost all patience with him; and said he was just loadened down with more gaudier chances than a prisoner ever had in the world to make a name for himself, and yet he didn't know enough to appreciate them, and they was just about wasted on him. So Jim he was sorry, and said he wouldn't behave so no more, and then me and Tom shoved for bed.

Chapter XXXIX

In the morning we went up to the village and bought a wire rat trap and fetched it down, and unstopped the best rat hole, and in about an hour we had fifteen of the bulliest kind of ones; and then we took it and put it in a safe place under Aunt Sally's bed. But while we was gone for spiders, little Thomas Franklin Benjamin Jefferson Elexander Phelps found it there, and opened the door of it to see if the rats would come out, and they did; and Aunt Sally she come in, and when we got back she was a standing on top of the bed raising Cain, and the rats was doing what they could to keep off the dull times for her. So she took and dusted us both with the hickry, and we was as much as two hours catching another fifteen or sixteen, drat the meddlesome cub, and they warn't the likeliest, nuther, because the first haul was the pick of the flock. I never see a likelier lot of rats than what that first haul was.

We got a splendid stock of sorted spiders, and bugs, and frogs, and caterpillars, and one thing or another; and we like-to got a hornet's nest, but we didn't. The family was at home. We didn't give it right up, but staid with them as long as we could; because we allowed we'd tire them out or they'd got to tire us out, and they done it. Then we got allycumpain and rubbed on the places, and was pretty near all right again, but couldn't set down convenient. And so we went for the snakes, and grabbed a couple of dozen garters and housesnakes, and put them in a bag, and put it in our room, and by that time it was supper time, and a rattling good honest day's work; and hungry?—oh, no, I reckon not! And there warn't a blessed snake up there, when we went back—we didn't half tie the sack, and they worked out, somehow, and left. But it didn't matter much, because they was still on the premises somewheres. So we judged we could get some of them again. No, there warn't no real scarcity of snakes about the house for a considerble spell. You'd see them dripping from the rafters and places, every now and then; and they generly landed in your plate, or down the back of your neck, and most of the time when you didn't want them. Well, they was handsome, and striped, and there warn't no harm in a million of them: but that never made no difference to Aunt Sally, she despised snakes, be the breed what they might, and she couldn't stand them no way you could fix it; and every time one of them flopped down on her, it didn't make no difference what she was doing, she would just lay that work down and light out. I never see such a woman. And you could hear her whoop to Jericho. You couldn't get her to take aholt of one of them with the tongs. And if she turned over and found one in bed, she would scramble out and lift a howl that you would think the house was afire. She disturbed the old man so, that he said he could most wish there hadn't ever been no snakes created. Why, after every last snake had been gone clear out of the house for as much as a week, Aunt Sally warn't over it yet; she warn't near over it; when she was setting thinking about something, you could touch her on the back of her neck with a feather and she would jump right out of her stockings. It was very curious.. But Tom said all women was just so. He said they was made that way; for some reason or other.

We got a licking every time one of our snakes come in her way; and she allowed these lickings warn't nothing to what she would do if we ever loaded up the place again with them. I didn't mind the lickings, because they didn't amount to nothing; but I minded the trouble we had, to lay in another lot. But we got them laid in, and all the other things; and you never see a cabin as blithesome as Jim's was when they'd all swarm out for music and go for him. Jim didn't like the spiders, and the spiders didn't like Jim; and so they'd lay for him and make it mighty warm for him. And he said that between the rats, and the snakes, and the grindstone, there warn't no room in bed for him, skasely; and when there was, a body couldn't sleep, it was so lively, and it was always lively, he said, because *they* never all slept at one time, but took turn about, so when the snakes was asleep the rats was on deck, and when the rats turned in the snakes come on watch, so he always had one gang under him, in his way, and t'other gang having a circus over him, and if he got up to hunt a new place, the spiders would take a chance at him as he crossed over. He said if he ever got out, this time, he wouldn't ever be a prisoner again, not for a salary.

Well, by the end of three weeks, everything was in pretty good shape. The shirt was sent in early, in a pie, and every time a rat bit Jim he would get up and write a little in his journal whilst the ink was fresh; the pens was made, the inscriptions and so on was all carved on the grindstone; the bed-leg was sawed in two, and we had et up the sawdust, and it give us a most amazing stomach-ache. We reckoned we was all going to die, but didn't. It was the most undigestible sawdust I ever see; and Tom said the same. But as I was saying, we'd got all the work done, now, at last; and we was all pretty much fagged out, too, but mainly Jim. The old man had wrote a couple of times to the plantation below Orleans to come and get their runaway nigger, but hadn't got no answer, because there warn't no such plantation; so he allowed he would advertise Jim in the St. Louis and New Orleans papers; and when he mentioned the St. Louis ones, it give me the cold shivers, and I see we hadn't no time to lose. So Tom said, now for the nonnamous letters.

"What's them?" I says.

"Warnings to the people that something is up. Sometimes it's done one way, sometimes another. But there's always somebody spying around, that gives notice to the governor of the castle. When Louis XVI was going to light out of the Tooleries, a servant girl done it. It's a very good way, and so is the nonnamous letters. We'll use them both. And it's usual for the prisoner's mother to change clothes with him, and she stays in, and he slides out in her clothes. We'll do that too."

"But looky here, Tom, what do we want to *warn* anybody for, that something's up? Let them find it out for themselves—it's their lookout."

"Yes, I know; but you can't depend on them. It's the way they've acted from the very start—left us to do *everything*. They're so confiding and mullet-headed they don't take notice of nothing at all. So if we don't *give* them notice, there won't be nobody nor nothing to interfere with us, and so after all our hard work and trouble this escape 'll go off perfectly flat: won't amount to nothing—won't be nothing *to* it."

"Well, as for me, Tom, that's the way I'd like."

"Shucks," he says, and looked disgusted. So I says:

"But I ain't going to make no complaint. Anyway that suits you suits me. What you going to do about the servant-girl?"

"You'll be her. You slide in, in the middle of the night, and hook that yaller girl's frock."

"Why, Tom, that'll make trouble next morning; because of course she prob'ly hain't got any but that one."

"I know; but you don't want it but fifteen minutes, to carry the nonnamous letter and shove it under the front door."

"All right, then, I'll do it; but I could carry it just as handy in my own togs."

"You wouldn't look like a servant-girl *then*, would you?"

"No, but there won't be nobody to see what I look like, *anyway*."

"That ain't got nothing to do with it. The thing for us to do, is just to do our *duty*, and no worry about whether anybody *sees* us do it or not. Hain't you got no principle at all?"

"All right, I ain't saying nothing; I'm the servant-girl. Who's Jim's mother?"

"I'm his mother. I'll hook a gown from Aunt Sally."

"Well, then, you'll have to stay in the cabin when me and Jim leaves."

"Not much. I'll stuff Jim's clothes full of straw and lay it on his bed to represent his mother in disguise, and Jim 'll take the nigger woman's gown off of me and wear it, and we'll all evade together. When a prisoner of style escapes, it's called an evasion. It's always called so when a king escapes, f'rinstance. And the same with a king's son; it don't make no difference whether he's a natural one or an unnatural one."

So Tom he wrote the nonnamous letter, and I smouched the yaller wench's frock, that night, and put it on, and shoved it under the front door, the way Tom told me to. It said:

> *Beware.   Trouble is brewing.   Keep a sharp lookout.*
>
> UNKNOWN FRIEND.

Next night we stuck a picture which Tom drawed in blood, of a skull and cross-bones, on the front door; and next night another one of a coffin, on the back door. I never see a family in such a sweat. They couldn't a been worse scared if the place had a been full of ghosts laying for them behind everything and under the beds and shivering through the air. If a door banged, Aunt Sally she jumped, and said "ouch!" if anything fell, she jumped and said "ouch!" if you happened to touch her, when she warn't noticing, she done the same; she couldn't face noway and be satisfied, because she allowed there was something behind her every time—so she was always a whirling around, sudden, and saying "ouch," and before she'd get two-thirds around, she'd whirl back again, and say it again; and she was afraid to go to bed, but she dasn't set up. So the thing was working very well, Tom said; he said he never see a thing work more satisfactory. He said it showed it was done right.

So he said, now for the grand bulge! So the very next morning at the streak of dawn we got another letter ready, and was wondering what we better do with it, because we heard them say at supper they was going to have a nigger on watch at both doors all night. Tom he went down the lightning-rod to spy around; and the nigger at the back door was asleep, and he stuck it in the back of his neck and come back. This letter said:

> *Don't betray me, I wish to be your friend. There is a desperate gang of cutthroats from over in the Ingean Territory going to steal your runaway nigger to-night, and they have been trying to scare you so as you will stay in the house and not bother them. I am one of the gang, but have got relligion and wish to quit it and lead a honest life again, and will betray the helish design. They will sneak down from northards, along the fence, at midnight exact, with a false key, and go in the nigger's cabin to get him. I am to be off a piece and blow a tin horn if I see any danger; but stead of that, I will BA like a sheep soon as they get in and not blow at all; then whilst they are getting his chains loose, you slip there and lock them in, and can kill them at your leasure. Don't do anything but just the way I am telling you, if you do they will suspicion something and raise whoopjamboreehoo. I do not wish any reward but to know I have done the right thing.*
>
> UNKNOWN FRIEND.

Chapter XL

We was feeling pretty good, after breakfast, and took my canoe and went over the river a fishing, with a lunch, and had a good time, and took a look at the raft and found her all right, and got home late to supper, and found them in such a sweat and worry they didn't know which end they was standing on, and made us go right off to bed the minute we was done supper, and wouldn't tell us what the trouble was, and never let on a word about the new letter, but didn't need to, because we knowed as much about it as anybody did, and as soon as we was half up stairs and her back was turned, we slid for the cellar cupboard and loaded up a good lunch and took it up to our room and went to bed, and got up about half-past eleven, and Tom put on Aunt Sally's dress that he stole and was going to start with the lunch, but says:

"Where's the butter?"

"I laid out a hunk of it," I says, "on a piece of a corn-pone."

"Well, you *left* it laid out, then—it ain't here."

"We can get along without it," I says.

"We can get along *with* it, too," he says; "just you slide down cellar and fetch it. And then mosey right down the lightning-rod and come along. I'll go and stuff the straw into Jim's clothes to represent his mother in disguise, and be ready to *ba* like a sheep and shove soon as you get there."

So out he went, and down cellar went I. The hunk of butter, big as a person's fist, was where I had left it, so I took up the slab of corn-pone with it on, and blowed out my light, and started up stairs, very stealthy, and got up to the main floor all right, but here comes Aunt Sally with a candle, and I clapped the truck in my hat, and clapped my hat on my head, and the next second she see me; and she says:

"You been down cellar?"

"Yes'm."

"What you been doing down there?"

"Noth'n."

"*Noth'n!*"

"No'm."

"Well, then, what possessed you to go down there, this time of night?"

"I don't know'm."

"You don't *know?* Don't answer me that way, Tom, I want to know what you been *doing* down there?"

"I hain't been doing a single thing, Aunt Sally, I hope to gracious if I have."

I reckoned she'd let me go, now, and as a generl thing she would; but I spose there was so many strange things going on she was just in a sweat about every little thing that warn't yard-stick straight; so she says, very decided:

"You just march into that setting-room and stay there till I come. You been up to something you no business to, and I lay I'll find out what it is before *I'm* done with you."

So she went away as I opened the door and walked into the setting-room. My, but there was a crowd there! Fifteen farmers, and everyone of them had a gun. I was most powerful sick, and slunk to a chair and set down. They was setting around, some of them talking a little, in a low voice, and all of them fidgety and uneasy, but trying to look like they warn't; but I knowed they was, because they was always taking off their hats, and putting them on, and scratching their heads, and changing their seats, and fumbling with their buttons. I warn't easy myself, but I didn't take my hat off, all the same.

I did wish Aunt Sally would come, and get done with me, and lick me, if she wanted to, and let me get away and tell Tom how we'd overdone this thing, and what a thundering hornet's nest we'd got ourselves into, so we could stop fooling around, straight off, and clear out with Jim before these rips got out of patience and come for us.

At last she come, and begun to ask me questions, but I *couldn't* answer them straight, I didn't know which end of me was up; because these men was in such a fidget now, that some was wanting to start right *now* and lay for them desperadoes, and saying it warn't but a few minutes to midnight; and others was trying to get them to hold on and wait for the sheep-signal; and here was aunty pegging away at the questions, and me a shaking all over and ready to sink down in my tracks I was that scared; and the place getting hotter and hotter, and the butter beginning to melt and run down my neck and behind my ears; and pretty soon, when one of them says, "*I'm* for going and getting in the cabin *first,* and right *now,* and catching them when they come," I most dropped; and a streak of butter come a trickling down my forehead, and Aunt Sally she see it, and turns white as a sheet, and says:

"For the land's sake what *is* the matter with the child!—he's got the brain fever as shore as you're born, and they're oozing out!"

And everybody runs to see, and she snatches off my hat, and out comes the bread, and what was left of the butter, and she grabbed me, and hugged me, and says:

"Oh, what a turn you did give me! and how glad and grateful I am it ain't no worse; for luck's against us, and it never rains but it pours, and when I see that truck I thought we'd lost you, for I knowed by the color and all, it was just like your brains would be if— Dear, dear, whyd'nt you *tell* me that was what you'd been down there for, *I* wouldn't a cared. Now cler out to bed, and don't lemme see no more of you till morning!"

I was up stairs in a second, and down the lightning-rod in another one, and shinning through the dark for the lean-to. I couldn't hardly get my words out, I was so anxious; but I told Tom as quick as I could, we must jump for it, now, and not a minute to lose—the house full of men, yonder, with guns!

His eyes just blazed; and he says:

"No!—is that so? *Ain't* it bully! Why, Huck, if it was to do over again, I bet I could fetch two hundred! If we could put it off till—"

"Hurry! *hurry!*" I says. "Where's Jim?"

"Right at your elbow; if you reach out your arm you can touch him. He's dressed, and everything's ready. Now we'll slide out and give the sheep-signal."

But then we heard the tramp of men, coming to the door, and heard them begin to fumble with the padlock; and heard a man say:

"I *told* you we'd be too soon; they haven't come—the door is locked. Here, I'll lock some of you into the cabin and you lay for 'em in the dark and kill 'em when they come; and the rest scatter around a piece, and listen if you can hear 'em coming."

So in they come, but couldn't see us in the dark, and most trod on us whilst we was hustling to get under the bed. But we got under all right, and out through the hole, swift but soft—Jim first, me next, and Tom last, which was according to Tom's orders. Now we was in the lean-to, and heard trampings close by outside. So we crept to the door, and Tom stopped us there and put his eye to the crack, but couldn't make out nothing, it was so dark; and whispered and said he would listen for the steps to get further, and when he nudged us Jim must glide out first, and him last. So he set his ear to the crack and listened, and listened, and listened, and the steps a scraping around, out there, all the time; and at last he nudged us, and we slid out, and stooped down, not breathing, and not making the least noise, and slipped stealthy towards the fence, in Injun file, and got to it, all right, and me and Jim over it; but Tom's britches catched fast on a splinter on the top rail, and then he hear the steps coming, so he had to pull loose, which snapped the splinter and made a noise; and as he dropped in our tracks and started, somebody sings out:

"Who's that? Answer, or I'll shoot!"

"But we didn't answer; we just unfurled our heels and shoved. Then there was a rush, and a *bang, bang, bang!* and the bullets fairly whizzed around us! We heard them sing out:

"Here they are! They've broke for the river! after 'em, boys! And turn loose the dogs!"

So here they come, full tilt. We could hear them, because they wore boots, and yelled, but we didn't wear no boots, and didn't yell. We was in the path to the mill; and when they got pretty close onto us, we dodged into the bush and let them go by, and then dropped in behind them. They'd had all the dogs shut up, so they wouldn't scare off the robbers; but by this time somebody had let them loose, and here they come, making pow-wow enough for a million; but they was our dogs; so we stopped in our tracks till they catched up; and when they see it warn't nobody but us, and no excitement to offer them, they only just said howdy, and tore right ahead towards the shouting and clattering; and then we up steam again and whizzed along after them till we was nearly to the mill, and then struck up through the bush to where my canoe was tied, and hopped in and pulled for dear life towards the middle of the river, but didn't make no more noise than we was obleeged to. Then we struck out, easy and comfortable, for the island where my raft was; and we could hear them yelling and barking at each other all up and down the bank, till we was so far away the sounds got dim and died out. And when we stepped onto the raft, I says:

"*Now*, old Jim, you're a free man *again*, and I bet you won't ever be a slave no more."

"En a mighty good job it wuz, too, Huck. It 'uz planned beautiful, en it 'uz *done* beautiful; en dey ain't *nobody* kin git up a plan dat's mo' mixed-up en splendid den what dat one wuz."

We was all as glad as we could be, but Tom was the gladdest of all, because he had a bullet in the calf of his leg.

When me and Jim heard that, we didn't feel so brash as what we did before. It was hurting him considerble, and bleeding; so we laid him in the wigwam and tore up one of the duke's shirts for to bandage him, but he says:

"Gimme the rags, I can do it myself. Don't stop, now; don't fool around here, and the evasion booming along so handsome; man the sweeps, an set her loose! Boys, we done it elegant!—'deed we did. I wish *we'd* a had the handling of Louis XVI., there wouldn't a been no 'Son of Saint Louis, ascend to heaven!' wrote down in *his* biography: no, sir, we'd a whooped him over the *border*—that's what we'd a done with *him*—and done it just as slick as nothing at all, too. Man the sweeps—man the sweeps!"

But me and Jim was consulting—and thinking. And after we'd thought a minute, I says:

"Say it, Jim."

So he says:

"Well, den, dis is de way it look to me, Huck. Ef it wuz *him* dat 'uz bein' sot free, en one er de boys wuz to git shot, would he say, 'Go on en save me, nemmine 'bout a doctor f'r to save dis one? Is dat like Mars Tom Sawyer? Would he say dat? You *bet* he wouldn't! *Well*, den, is *Jim* gwyne to say it? No, sah—I doan' budge a step out'n dis place, 'dout a *doctor*; not if it's forty year!"

I knowed he was white inside, and I reckoned he's say what he did say—so it was all right, now, and I told Tom I was agoing for a doctor. He raised considerble row about it, but me and Jim stuck to it and wouldn't budge; so he was for crawling out and setting the raft loose himself; but we wouldn't let him. Then he give us a piece of his mind—but it didn't do no good.

So when he see me getting the canoe ready, he says:

"Well, then, if you're bound to go, I'll tell you the way to do, when you get to the village. Shut the door, and blindfold the doctor tight and fast, and make him swear to be silent as the grave, and put a purse full of gold in his hand, and then take and lead him all around the back alleys and everywheres, in the dark, and then fetch him here in the canoe, in a roundabout way amongst the islands, and search him and take his chalk away from him, and don't give it back to him till you get him back to the village, or else he will chalk this raft so he can find it again. It's the way they all do."

So I said I would, and left, and Jim was to hide in the woods when he see the doctor coming, till he was gone again.

Chapter XLI

The doctor was an old man; a very nice, kind-looking old man, when I got him up. I told him me and my brother was over on Spanish Island hunting, yesterday afternoon, and camped on a piece of a raft we found, and about midnight he must a kicked his gun in his dreams, for it went off and shot him in the leg, and we wanted him to go over there and fix it and not say nothing about it, nor let anybody know, because we wanted to come home this evening, and surprise the folks.

"Who is your folks?" he says.

"The Phelpses, down yonder."

"Oh," he says. And after a minute, he says: "How'd you say he got shot?"

"He had a dream," I says, "and it shot him."

"Singular dream," he says.

So he lit up his lantern, and got his saddle-bags, and we started. But when he see the canoe, he didn't like the look of her—said she was big enough for one, but didn't look pretty safe for two. I says:

"Oh, you needn't be afeard, sir, she carried the three of us, easy enough."

"What three?"

"Why, me and Sid, and—and—and *the guns;* that's what I mean."

"Oh," he says.

But he put his foot on the gunnel, and rocked her; and shook his head, and said he reckoned he'd look around for a bigger one. But they was all locked and chained; so he took my canoe, and said for me to wait till he come back, or I could hunt around further, or maybe I better go down home and get them ready for the surprise, if I wanted to. But I said I didn't; so I told him just how to find the raft, and then he started.

I struck an idea, pretty soon. I says to myself, spos'n he can't fix that leg just in three shakes of a sheep's tail, as the saying is? spos'n it takes him three or four days? What are we going to do?—lay around there till he lets the cat out of the bag? No, sir, I know what *I'll* do. I'll wait, and when he comes back, if he says he's got to go any more, I'll get down there, too, if I swim; and we'll take and tie him, and keep him, and shove out down the river; and when Tom's done with him, we'll give him what it's worth, or all we got, and then let him get ashore.

So then I crept into a lumber pile to get some sleep; and next time I waked up the sun was away up over my head! I shot out and went for the doctor's house, but they told me he'd gone away in the night, some time or other, and warn't back yet. Well, thinks I, that looks powerful bad for Tom, and I'll dig out for the island, right off. So way I shoved, and turned the corner, and nearly rammed my head into Uncle Silas's stomach! He says:

"Why, *Tom!* Where you been, all this time, you rascal?"

"*I* hain't been nowheres," I says, "only just hunting for the runaway nigger—me and Sid."

"Why, where ever did you go?" he says. "Your aunt's been mighty uneasy."

"She needn't," I says, "because we was all right. We followed the men and the dogs, but they out-run us, and we lost them; but we thought we heard them on the water, so we got a canoe and took out after them, and crossed over but couldn't find nothing of them; so we cruised along up-shore till we got kind of tired and beat out; and tied up the canoe and went to sleep, and never waked up till about an hour ago, then we paddled over here to hear the news, and Sid's at the post-office to see what he can hear, and I'm a branching out to get something to eat for us, and then we're going home."

So then we went to the post-office to get "Sid"; but just as I suspicioned, he warn't there; so the old man he got a letter out of the office, and we waited a while longer but Sid didn't come; so the old man said come along, let Sid foot it home, or canoe-it, when he got done fooling around—but we would ride. I couldn't get him to let me stay and wait for Sid; and he said there warn't no use in it, and I must come along, and let Aunt Sally see we was all right.

When we got home, Aunt Sally was that glad to see me she laughed and cried both, and hugged me, and give me one of them lickings of hern that don't amount to shucks, and said she'd serve Sid the same when he come.

And the place was plumb full of farmers and farmers' wives, to dinner; and such another clack a body never heard. Old Mrs. Hotchkiss was the worst; her tongue was agoing all the time. She says:

"Well, Sister Phelps, I've ransacked that-air cabin over an' I b'lieve the nigger was crazy. I says so to Sister Damrell—didn't I, Sister Damrell?—s'I, he's crazy, s'I—them's the very words I said. You all hearn me: he's crazy, s'I; everything shows it, s'I. Look at that-air grindstone, s'I; want to tell *me* 't any cretur 'ts in his right mind 's agoin' to scrabble all them crazy things onto a grindstone, s'I? Here sich 'n' sich a person busted his heart; 'n' here so 'n' so pegged along for thirty-seven year, 'n' all that—natcherl son o' Louis somebody, 'n' sich everlast'n rubbage. He's plumb crazy, s'I; it's what I says in the fust place, it's what I says in the middle, 'n' it's what I says last 'n' all the time—the nigger's crazy—crazy 's Neboodneezer, s'I."

"An' look at that-air ladder made out'n rags, Sister Hotchkiss," says old Mrs. Damrell, "what in the name o' goodness *could* he ever want of—"

"The very words I was a-sayin' no longer ago th'n this minute to Sister Utterback, 'n' she'll tell you so herself. Sh-she, look at that-air rag ladder, she-she; 'n' s'I, yes, *look* at it, s'I—what *could* he a wanted of it, s'I. Sh-she, Sister Hotchkiss, sh-she—"

"But how in the nation'd they ever *git* that grindstone *in* there, *anyway?* 'n' who dug that-air *hole?* 'n' who—"

"My very *words,* Brer Penrod! I was a-sayin'—pass that-air sasser o' m'lasses, won't ye?—I was a-sayin' to Sister Dunlap, jist this minute, how *did* they git that grindstone in there, s'I. Without *help,* mind you—'thout *help! Thar's* wher' 'tis. Don't tell *me,* s'I; there *wuz* help, s'I; 'n' ther' wuz a *plenty* help, too, s'I; ther's ben a *dozen* a-helpin' that nigger, 'n' I lay I'd skin every last nigger on this place, but *I'd* find out who done it, s'I; 'n' moreover, s'I—"

"A *dozen* says you!—*forty* couldn't a done everything that's been done. Look at them case-knife saws and things, how tedious they've been made; look at that bed-leg sawed off with 'm, a week's work for six men; look at that nigger made out'n straw on the bed; and look at—"

"You may *well* say it, Brer Hightower! It's jist as I was a-sayin' to Brer Phelps, his own self. S'e, what do *you* think of it, Sister Hotchkiss, s'e? think o' what, Brer Phelps, s'I? think o' that bed-leg sawed off that a way, s'e? *think* of it, s'I? I lay it never sawed *it-self* off, s'I—somebody *sawed* it, s'I; that's my opinion, take it or leave it, it mayn't be no 'count, s'I, but sich as 't is, it's my opinion, s'I, 'n' if anybody k'n start a better one, s'I, let him *do* it, s'I, that's all. I says to Sister Dunlap, s'I—"

"Why, dog my cats, they must a ben a house-full o'niggers in there every night for four weeks, to a done all that work, Sister Phelps. Look at that shirt—every last inch of it kivered over with secret African writ'n done with blood! Must a ben a raft uv 'm at it right along, all the time, amost. Why, I'd give two dollars to have it read to me; 'n' as for the niggers that wrote it, I 'low I'd take 'n' lash 'm t'll—"

"People to *help* him, Brother Marples! Well, I reckon you'd *think* so, if you'd a been in this house for a while back. Why, they've stole everything they could lay their hands on—and we a watching, all the time, mind you. They stole that shirt right off o' the line! and as for that sheet they made the rag ladder out of ther' ain't no telling how many times they *didn't* steal that; and flour, and candles, and candlesticks, and spoons, and the old warming-pan, and most a thousand things that I disremember, now, and my new calico dress; and me, and Silas, and my Sid and Tom on the constant watch day *and* night, as I was a telling you, and not a one of us could catch hide nor hair, nor sight nor sound of them; and here at the last minute, lo and behold you, they slides right in under our noses, and fools us, and not only fools *us* but the Injun Territory robbers too, and actuly gets *away* with that nigger, safe and sound, and that with sixteen men and twenty-two dogs right on their very heels at that very time! I tell you, it just bangs any-thing I ever *heard* of. Why, *sperits* couldn't a done better, and been no smarter. And I reckon they must a *been* sperits—because, *you* know our dogs, and ther' ain't no better; well, them dogs never even got on the *track* of 'm, once! You explain *that* to me, if you can!—*any* of you!"

"Well, it does beat—"

"Laws alive, I never—"

"So help me, I wouldn't a be—"

"*House* thieves as well as—"

"Goodnessgracioussakes, I'd a ben afeard to *live* in sich a—"

"'Fraid to *live!*—why, I was that scared I das'nt hardly go to bed, or get up, or lay down, or *set* down, Sister Ridgeway. Why, they'd steal the very—why, goodness sakes, you can guess what kind of a fluster *I* was in by the time midnight come, last night. I hope to gracious if I warn't afraid they'd steal some o' the family! I was just to that pass, I didn't have no reasoning faculties no more. It looks foolish enough, *now*, in the day-time; but I says to myself, there's my two poor boys asleep, 'way up stairs in that lone-some room, and I declare to goodness I was that uneasy 't I crep' up there and locked 'em in! I *did.* And anybody would. Because, you know, when you get scared, that way, and it keeps running on, and getting worse and worse, all the time, and your wits gets to addling, and you get to doing all sorts o' wild things, and by-and-by you think to yourself, spos'n *I* was a boy, and was away up there, and the door ain't locked, and you—" She stopped, looking kind of wondering, and then she turned her head around slow, and when her eye lit on me—I got up and took a walk.

Says I to myself, I can explain better how we come to not be in that room this morning, if I go out to one side and study over it a little. So I done it. But I dasn't go fur, or she'd a sent for me. And when it was late in the day, the people all went, and then I come in and told her the noise and shooting waked up me and "Sid," and the door was locked, and we wanted to see the fun, so we went down the lightning-rod, and both of us got hurt a little, and we didn't never want to try *that* no more. And then I went on and told her all what I told Uncle Silas before; and then she said she'd forgive us, and maybe it was all right enough anyway, and about what a body might expect of boys, for all boys was a pretty harum-scarum lot, as fur as she could see; and so, as long as no harm hadn't come of it, she judged she better put in her time being grateful we was alive and well and she had us still, stead of fretting over what was past and done. So then she kissed me, and patted me on the head, and dropped into a kind of a brown study; and pretty soon jumps up, and says:

"Why, lawsamercy, it's most night, and Sid not come yet! What *has* become of that boy?"

I see my chance; so I skips up and says:

"I'll run right up to town and get him," I says.

"No you won't," she says. "You'll stay right wher' you are; *one's* enough to be lost at a time. If he ain't here to supper, your uncle 'll go."

Well, he warn't there to supper; so right after supper uncle went.

He come back about ten, a little bit uneasy; hadn't run across Tom's track. Aunt Sally was a good *deal* uneasy; but Uncle Silas he said there warn't no occasion to be— boys will be boys, he said, and you'll see this one turn up in the morning, all sound and right. So she had to be satisfied. But she said she'd set up for him a while, anyway, and keep a light burning, so he could see it.

And then when I went up to bed she come up with me and fetched her candle, and tucked me in, and mothered me so good I felt mean, and like I couldn't look her in the face; and she set down on the bed and talked with me a long time, and said what a splendid boy Sid was, and didn't seem to want to ever stop talking about him; and kept asking me every now and then, if I reckoned he could a got lost, or hurt, or maybe drownded, and might be laying at this minute, somewhere, suffering or dead, and she not by him to help him, and so the tears would drip down, silent, and I would tell her that Sid was all right, and would be home in the morning, sure; and she would squeeze my hand, or maybe kiss me, and tell me to say it again, and keep on saying it, because it done her good, and she was in so much trouble. And when she was going away, she looked down in my eyes, so steady and gentle, and says:

"The door ain't going to be locked, Tom; and there's the window and the rod; but you'll be good, *won't* you? And you won't go? For *my* sake."

Laws knows I *wanted* to go, bad enough, to see about Tom, and was all intending to go; but after that, I wouldn't a went, not for kingdoms.

But she was on my mind, and Tom was on my mind; so I slept very restless. And twice I went down the rod, away in the night, and slipped around front, and see her setting there by her candle in the window with her eyes towards the road and the tears in them; and I wished I could do something for her, but I couldn't, only to swear that I wouldn't never do nothing to grieve her any more. And the third time, I waked up at dawn, and slid down, and she was there yet, and her candle was most out, and her old gray head was resting on her hand, and she was asleep.

Chapter XLII

The old man was up town again, before breakfast, but couldn't get no track of Tom; and both of them set at the table, thinking, and not saying nothing, and looking mournful, and their coffee getting cold, and not eating anything. And by-and-by the old man says:

"Did I give you the letter?"

"What letter?"

"The one I got yesterday out of the post-office."

"No, you didn't give me no letter."

"Well, I must a forgot it."

So he rummaged his pockets, and then went off somewheres where he had laid it down, and fetched it, and give it to her. She says:

"Why, it's from St. Petersburg—it's from Sis."

I allowed another walk would do me good; but I couldn't stir. But before she could break it open, she dropped it and run—for she see something. And so did I. It was Tom Sawyer on a mattress; and that old doctor; and Jim, in *her* calico dress, with his hands tied behind him; and a lot of people. I hid the letter behind the first thing that come handy, and rushed. She flung herself at Tom, crying, and says:

"Oh, he's dead, he's dead, I know he's dead!"

And Tom he turned his head a little, and muttered something or other, which showed he warn't in his right mind; then she flung up her hands, and says:

"He's alive, thank God! And that's enough!" and she snatched a kiss of him, and flew for the house to get the bed ready, and scattering orders right and left at the niggers and everybody else, as fast as her tongue could go, every jump of the way.

I followed the men to see what they was going to do with Jim; and the old doctor and Uncle Silas followed after Tom into the house. The men was very huffy, and some of them wanted to hang Jim, for an example to all the other niggers around there, so they wouldn't be trying to run away, like Jim done, and making such a raft of trouble, and keeping a whole family scared most to death for days and nights. But the others said, don't do it, it wouldn't answer at all, he ain't our nigger, and his owner would turn up and make us pay for him, sure. So that cooled them down a little, because the people that's always the most anxious for to hang a nigger that hain't done just right, is always the very ones that ain't the most anxious to pay for him when they've got their satisfaction out of him.

They cussed Jim considerble, though, and give him a cuff or two, side the head, once in a while, but Jim never said nothing, and he never let on to know me, and they took him to the same cabin, and put his own clothes on him, and chained him again, and not to no bed-leg, this time, but to a big staple drove into the bottom log, and chained his hands, too, and both legs, and said he warn't to have nothing but bread and water to eat, after this, till his owner come or he was sold at auction, because he didn't come in a certain length of time, and filled up our hole, and said a couple of farmers with guns must stand watch around about the cabin every night, and a bull-dog tied to the door in the day-time; and about this time they was through with the job and was tapering off with a kind of generl good-bye cussing, and then the old doctor comes and takes a look, and says:

"Don't be no rougher on him than you're obleeged to, because he ain't a bad nigger. When I got to where I found the boy, I see I couldn't cut the bullet out without some help, and he warn't in no condition for me to leave, to go and get help; and he got a little worse and a little worse, and after a long time he went out of his head, and wouldn't let me come anigh him, any more, and said if I chalked his raft he'd kill me, and no end of wild foolishness like that, and I see I couldn't do anything at all with him; so I says, I got to have *help*, somehow; and the minute I says it, out crawls this nigger from somewheres, and says he'll help, and he done it, too, and done it very well. Of course I judged he must be a runaway nigger, and there I *was!* and there I had to stick, right straight along all the rest of the day, and all night. It was a fix, I tell you! I had a couple of patients with the chills, and of course I'd of liked to run up to town and see them, but I dasn't, because the nigger might get away, and then I'd be to blame; and yet never a skiff come close enough for me to hail. So there I had to stick, plumb till daylight this morning; and I never see a nigger that was a better nuss or faithfuller, and yet he was resking his freedom to do it, and was all tired out, too, and I see plain enough he'd been worked main hard, lately. I liked the nigger for that; I tell you, gentlemen, a nigger like that is worth a thousand dollars—and kind treatment, too. I had everything I needed, and the boy was doing as well there as he would a done at home—better, maybe, because it was so quiet; but there I *was,* with both of 'm on my hands; and there I had to stick, till about dawn this morning; then some men in a skiff come by, and as good luck would have it, the nigger was setting by the pallet with his head propped on his knees, sound asleep; so I motioned them in, quiet, and they slipped up on him and grabbed him and tied him before he knowed what he was about, and we never had no trouble. And the boy being in a kind of a flighty sleep, too, we muffled the oars and hitched the raft on, and towed her over very nice and quiet, and the nigger never made the least row nor said a word, from the start. He ain't no bad nigger, gentlemen; that's what I think about him."

Somebody says:

"Well, it sounds very good, doctor, I'm obleeged to say."

Then the others softened up a little, too, and I was mighty thankful to that old doctor for doing Jim that good turn; and I was glad it was according to my judgment of him, too; because I thought he had a good heart in him and was a good man, the first time I see him. Then they all agreed that Jim had acted very well, and was deserving to have some notice took of it, and reward. So every one of them promised, right out and hearty, that they wouldn't cuss him no more.

Then they come out and locked him up. I hoped they was going to say he could have one or two of the chains took off, because they was rotten heavy, or could have meat and greens with his bread and water, but they didn't think of it, and I reckoned it warn't best for me to mix in, but I judged I'd get the doctor's yarn to Aunt Sally, somehow or other, as soon as I'd got through the breakers that was laying just ahead of me. Explanations, I mean, of how I forgot to mention about Sid being shot, when I was telling how him and me put in that dratted night paddling around hunting the runaway nigger.

But I had plenty time. Aunt Sally she stuck to the sick-room all day and all night; and every time I see Uncle Silas mooning around, I dodged him.

Next morning I heard Tom was a good deal better, and they said Aunt Sally was gone to get a nap. So I slips to the sick-room, and if I found him awake I reckoned we could put up a yarn for the family that would wash. But he was sleeping, and sleeping very peaceful, too; and pale, not fire-faced the way he was when he come. So I set down and laid for him to wake. In about a half an hour, Aunt Sally comes gliding in, and there I was, up a stump again! She motioned me to be still, and set down by me, and begun to whisper, and said we could all be joyful now, because all the symptoms was first rate, and he'd been sleeping like that for ever so long, and looking better and peacefuller all the time, and ten to one he'd wake up in his right mind.

So we set there watching, and by-and-by he stirs a bit, and opened his eyes very natural, and takes a look, and says:

"Hello, why I'm at *home!* How's that? "Where's the raft?"

"It's all right," I says.

"And *Jim?*"

"The same," I says, but couldn't say it pretty brash. But he never noticed, but says:

"Good! Splendid! *Now* we're all right and safe! Did you tell Aunty?"

I was going to say yes; but she chipped in and says:

"About what, Sid?"

"Why, about the way the whole thing was done."

"What whole thing?"

"Why, *the* whole thing. There ain't but one; how we set the runaway nigger free—me and Tom."

"Good land! Set the run— What *is* the child talking about? Dear, dear, out of his head again!"

"*No,* I ain't out of my HEAD; I know all what I'm talking about. We *did* set him free— me and Tom. We laid out to do it, and we *done* it. And we done it elegant, too." He'd got a start, and she never checked him up, just set and stared and stared, and let him clip along, and I see it warn't no use for *me* to put in. "Why, Aunty, it cost us a power of work—weeks of it—hours and hours, every night, whilst you was all asleep. And we had to steal candles, and the sheet, and the shirt, and your dress, and spoons, and tin plates, and case-knives, and the warming-pan, and the grindstone, and flour, and just no end of things, and you can't think what work it was to make the saws, and pens, and inscriptions, and one thing or another, and you can't think *half* the fun it was. And we had to make up the pictures of coffins and things, and nonnamous letters from the robbers, and get up and down the lightning-rod, and dig the hole into the cabin, and make the rope-ladder and send it in cooked up in a pie, and send in spoons and things to work with, in your apron pocket"—

"Mercy sakes!"

—"and load up the cabin with rats and snakes and so on, for company for Jim; and then you kept Tom here so long with the butter in his hat that you come near spiling the whole business, because the men come before we was out of the cabin, and we had to rush, and they heard us and let drive at us, and I got my share, and we dodged out of the path and let them go by, and when the dogs come they warn't interested in us, but went for the most noise, and we got our canoe, and made for the raft, and was all safe, and Jim was a free man, and we done it all by ourselves, and *wasn't* it bully, Aunty!"

"Well, I never heard the likes of it in all my born days! So it was *you*, you little rap-scallions, that's been making all this trouble, and turned everybody's wits clean inside out and scared us all most to death. I've as good a notion as ever I had in my life,to take it out o' you this very minute. To think, here I've been, night after night, a—*you* just get well once, you young scamp, and I lay I'll tan the Old Harry out o' both o' ye!"

But Tom, he *was* so proud and joyful, he just *couldn't* hold in, and his tongue just *went* it—she a-chipping in, and spitting fire all along, and both of them going it at once, like a cat-convention; and she says:

"*Well*, you get all the enjoyment you can out of it *now*, for mind I tell you if I catch you meddling with him again—"

"Meddling with *who?*" Tom says, dropping his smile and looking surprised.

"With *who?* Why, the runaway nigger, of course. Who'd you reckon?"

Tom looks at me very grave, and says:

"Tom, didn't you just tell me he was all right? Hasn't he got away?"

"*Him?*" says Aunt Sally; "the runaway nigger? 'Deed he hasn't. They've got him back, safe and sound, and he's in that cabin again, on bread and water, and loaded down with chains, till he's claimed or sold!"

Tom rose square up in bed, with his eye hot, and his nostrils opening and shutting like gills, and sings out to me:

"They hain't no *right* to shut him up! Shove!—and don't you lose a minute. Turn him loose! he ain't no slave; he's as free as any cretur that walks this earth!"

"What *does* the child mean?"

"I mean every word I *say*, Aunt Sally, and if somebody don't go, *I'll* go. I've knowed him all his life, and so has Tom, there. Old Miss Watson died two months ago, and she was ashamed she ever was going to sell him down the river, and *said* so; and she set him free in her will."

"Then what on earth did *you* want to set him free for, seeing he was already free?"

"Well, that *is* a question, I must say; and *just* like women! Why, I wanted the *adven-ture* of it; and I'd a waded neck-deep in blood to—goodness alive, AUNT POLLY!"

If she warn't standing right there, just inside the door, looking as sweet and con-tented as an angel half-full of pie, I wish I may never!

Aunt Sally jumped for her, and most hugged the head off of her, and cried over her, and I found a good enough place for me under the bed, for it was getting pretty sultry for *us*, seemed to me. And I peeped out, and in a little while Tom's Aunt Polly shook herself loose and stood there looking across at Tom over her spectacles—kind of grind-ing him into the earth, you know. And then she says:

"Yes, you *better* turn y'r head away—I would if I was you, Tom."

"Oh, deary me!" says Aunt Sally; "*is* he changed so? Why, that ain't *Tom* it's Sid; Tom's—Tom's—why, where is Tom? He was here a minute ago."

"You mean where's Huck *Finn*—that's what you mean! I reckon I hain't raised such a scamp as my Tom all these years, not to know him when I *see* him. That *would* be a pretty howdy-do. Come out from under that bed, Huck Finn."

So I done it. But not feeling brash.

Aunt Sally she was one of the mixed-upest looking persons I ever see; except one, and that was Uncle Silas, when he come in, and they told it all to him. It kind of made him drunk, as you may say, and he didn't know nothing at all the rest of the day, and preached a prayer-meeting sermon that night that give him a rattling ruputation, be-cause the oldest man in the world couldn't a understood it. So Tom's Aunt Polly, she told all about who I was, and what; and I had to up and tell how I was in such a tight place that when Mrs. Phelps took me for Tom Sawyer—she chipped in and says, "Oh, go on and call me Aunt Sally, I'm used to it, now, and 'tain't no need to change"—that when Aunt Sally took me for Tom Sawyer, I had to stand it—there warn't no other way, and I knowed he wouldn't mind, because it would be nuts for him, being a mystery, and he'd make an adventure out of it and be perfectly satisfied. And so it turned out, and he let on to be Sid, and made things as soft as he could for me.

And his Aunt Polly she said Tom was right about old Miss Watson setting Jim free in her will; and so, sure enough, Tom Sawyer had gone and took all that trouble and bother to set a free nigger free! and I couldn't ever understand, before, until that minute and that talk, how he *could* help a body set a nigger free, with his bringing-up.

Well, Aunt Polly she said that when Aunt Sally wrote to her that Tom and *Sid* had come, all right and safe, she says to herself:

"Look at that, now! I might have expected it, letting him go off that way without anybody to watch him. So now I got to go and trapse all the way down the river, eleven hundred mile, and find out what that creetur's up to, *this* time; as long as I couldn't seem to get any answer out of you about it."

"Why, I never heard nothing from you," says Aunt Sally.

"Well, I wonder! Why, I wrote to you twice, to ask you what you could mean by Sid being here."

"Well, I never got 'em, Sis."

Aunt Polly, she turns around slow and severe, and says:

"You, Tom!"

"Well—*what?*" he says, kind of pettish.

"Don't you what *me*, you impudent thing—hand out them letters."

"What letters?"

"*Them* letters. I be bound, if I have to take aholt of you I'll—"

"They're in the trunk. There, now. And they're just the same as they was when I got them out of the office. I hain't looked into them, I hain't touched them. But I knowed they'd make trouble, and I thought if you warn't in no hurry, I'd—"

"Well, you *do* need skinning, there ain't no mistake about it. And I wrote another one to tell you I was coming; and I spose he—"

"No, it come yesterday; I hain't read it yet, but *it's* all right, I've got that one."

I wanted to offer to bet two dollars she hadn't, but I reckoned maybe it was just as safe to not to. So I never said nothing.

Chapter the Last

The first time I catched Tom, private, I asked him what was his idea, time of the evasion?—what it was he'd planned to do if the evasion worked all right and he managed to set a nigger free that was already free before? And he said, what he had planned in his head, from the start, if we got Jim out all safe, was for us to run him down the river, on the raft, and have adventures plumb to the mouth of the river, and then tell him about his being free, and take him back up home on a steamboat, in style, and pay him for his lost time, and write word ahead and get out all the niggers around, and have them waltz him into town with a torchlight procession and a brass band, and then he would be a hero, and so would we. But I reckoned it was about as well the way it was.

We had Jim out of the chains in no time, and when Aunt Polly and Uncle Silas and Aunt Sally found out how good he helped the doctor nurse Tom, they made a heap of fuss over him, and fixed him up prime, and give him all he wanted to eat, and a good time, and nothing to do. And we had him up to the sick-room; and had a high talk; and Tom give Jim forty dollars for being prisoner for us so patient, and doing it up so good, and Jim was pleased most to death, and busted out, and says:

"*Dah,* now, Huck, what I tell you?—what I tell you up dah on Jackson islan'? I *tole* you I got a hairy breas', en what's de sign un it; en I *tole* you I ben rich wunst, en gwineter to be rich *agin;* en it's come true; en heah she *is! Dah,* now! doan' talk to *me—* signs is *signs,* mine I tell you; en I knowed jis' 's well 'at I 'uz gwineter be rich agin as I's a stannin' heah dis minute!"

And then Tom he talked along, and talked along, and says, le's all three slide out of here, one of these nights, and get an outfit, and go for howling adventures amongst the Injuns, over in the Territory, for a couple of weeks or two; and I says, all right, that suits me, but I aint got no money for to buy the outfit, and I reckon I couldn't get none from home, because it's likely pap's been back before now, and got it all away from Judge Thatcher and drunk it up.

"No he hain't," Tom says; "it's all there, yet—six thousand dollars and more; and your pap hain't ever been back since. Hadn't when I come away, anyhow."

Jim says, kind of solemn:

"He ain't a comin' back no mo', Huck."

I says:

"Why, Jim?"

"Nemmine why, Huck—but he ain't comin' back no mo'."

But I kept at him; so at last he says:

"Doan' you 'member de house dat was float'n down de river, en dey wuz a man in dah, kivered up, en I went in en unkivered him and didn' let you come in? Well, den, you k'n git yo' money when you wants it; kase dat wuz him."

Tom's most well, now, and got his bullet around his neck on a watch-guard for a watch, and is always seeing what time it is, and so there ain't nothing more to write about, and I am rotten glad of it, because if I'd a knowed what a trouble it was to make a book I wouldn't a tackled it and ain't agoing to no more. But I reckon I got to light out for the Territory ahead of the rest, because Aunt Sally she's going to adopt me and sivilize me and I can't stand it. I been there before.

THE END, YOURS TRULY HUCK FINN

1885

William Dean Howells
1837–1920

William Dean Howells is best remembered for his ability to recognize how good other writers were, not for his own merits. Rather than stressing the implications of his first name ("he who asserts his own will"), we tend to focus on *Dean,* picturing Howells as the person high up in the administrative order who oversees and evaluates others. From his place in "The Editor's Study" and "The Easy Chair," titles given the influential monthly essays he wrote for *Harper's* magazine, Howells served as America's foremost critic and editor from 1886 into the early years of the twentieth century. But his reputation as the acknowledged spokesman for middle-class literary values, the cautiousness of his approach to matters of sexuality, and the canniness with which he orchestrated his own career are misleading. They make Howells seem older and grayer than in fact he was.

Howells started out as a brash young man with a background in a printer's shop and local newspapers. He came out of Ohio to storm the genteel Eastern literary redoubts in much the manner of heroes of the nineteenth-century *Bildungsroman* (a novel in which climbers from the provinces make their energetic way upward to social and professional acclaim in the major centers of power). Another example of the same type is Mark Twain, a man Howells helped to attain the level of success he himself already enjoyed.

Oddly enough, we think of Mark Twain as the eternal boy, even after his hair went snowy white. But Twain and Howells were almost exact contemporaries and shared several of the same early experiences: printing-shop apprenticeship, jobs with regional newspapers, and moves to the East in 1866 after sitting out the Civil War in other places (for Twain, the Nevada Territory, as secretary to the governor's secretary; for Howells, a consulship in Venice). But Howells's early days were, probably even more than Twain's, given over to the pugnacious attempt to get ahead. Twain seems the more energetic because he let his wildness show, while Howells carefully kept his under cover. Howells's main chance came through his role as critic and editor, positions that called for him to reject the personal flamboyance Twain found useful to his role as humorist and iconoclast. But Howells's temperament put his psychic energies to work in controlling, not releasing, the extremes of emotion that lay concealed beneath the smooth surface of the polite young man from Ohio.

One of eight children, Howells was born to a humble family in Martin's Ferry, Ohio, somewhat shakily supported by the father's work as an itinerant printer and newspaper editor. Though poor and peripatetic in their shifts around Ohio during the early years of Howells's childhood, the family was close. Howells was strongly affected by his father's championing of various reform movements and by his own avid reading in the literary classics. He set to work at once to turn himself into a capable journalist and writer of occasional poems and sketches. By the time he was twenty-one, he had begun to make his mark in Ohio as a writer and editor for important newspapers in and around Cincinnati and Columbus—the *Gazette* and the *Ohio State Journal.*

Howells's ambitions exceeded what Ohio had to offer, however. In 1860 he made two crucial moves: He wrote a campaign biography for Abraham Lincoln's presidential candidacy, and he made a trip to New England to meet such literary celebrities as

Emerson, Holmes, Hawthorne, Lowell, and Thoreau. The Lincoln biography led to his appointment as American consul to Venice, and his visits with famous American writers gave him a glimpse into the nation's most prominent literary circle. The introductions he received to the Boston-Concord literary powers earned him early recognition for his talents and prepared the way, upon his return from Italy in 1865, for an assistant editorship at the country's most important journal, the *Atlantic Monthly,* where he was to become editor in chief in 1871. The *Atlantic* appointment was the start of what would be Howells's special fate: to be the arbiter of American letters and the judge of the careers of the next generation of writers.

From the time Howells settled in Boston, he began to pursue a second career as a novelist. The six novels he wrote while with the *Atlantic* not only helped him perfect his craft but also determined the kind of fiction he would urge on the American reading public, which heeded his judgments. Fiction had to be realistic, he maintained. It must give its attention to the details of the everyday lives of ordinary people. It must reject romanticized plots of passion and adventure to concentrate on stories of character and close observations of contemporary American life.

In 1881 Howells resigned his post with the *Atlantic* to free-lance. His first notable novel, *A Modern Instance,* appeared in 1882. *The Rise of Silas Lapham,* published in 1885, confirmed Howells's worth as a novelist. By 1886 he was back in an editor's chair, associated with *Harper's,* which had overtaken the *Atlantic* as the country's major literary arbiter. In 1889 he moved to New York, which had replaced Boston as the place where literary reputations were made or broken. Howells could work with the assurance that what he said for Realism and against the shoddily romantic would receive serious attention from a large, receptive, and international audience. Marked by the earnestness and commitment (as well as the humor and ironic touch) Howells brought to all his professional tasks, the essays and reviews he printed in the pages of *Harper's* helped make American literature what it became by 1900. The novels in the bookshops and lending libraries and in serial form in the popular magazines were no longer limited to the sentimental "weeper" or the historical costume romance.

This is not to suggest that the sentimental romance went out of style during Howells's day as the dean of American Realism; it flourished, but it did so in the face of the strong, new force in American writing that Howells made not only acceptable but respectable. White, middle-class readers could hardly think themselves in touch with the newest books if they were not familiar with the writings of such Americans as Hamlin Garland, Stephen Crane, and Frank Norris and with the names of such leading Continental writers as Tolstoy, Turgenev, Galdós, and Ibsen, as well as the Briton Thomas Hardy. Howells gave his editorial attention to American women writers—Sarah Orne Jewett, Mary E. Wilkins Freeman, Emily Dickinson, and Edith Wharton. He also encouraged new African American writers like Paul Laurence Dunbar and Charles Waddell Chesnutt. Howells took it on himself, early and late, to declare the central importance of Mark Twain and Henry James on the American cultural scene. Capable of appreciating their differing qualities as writers, Howells celebrated both the rowdiness of Twain's humor and the refined specialness of James's style. Part of Howells's talent was the ability to admire in others what he himself was unable to do. Certain literary leanings, differences in temperament, and deep-seated fears carried over from his childhood prevented Howells from speaking directly in his own fiction about the sex and violence that Stephen Crane and Frank Norris, for example, placed dead center in their works.

At the same time Howells helped several generations of Realists to get the notice they deserved, he continued to build up the bulk of his own writing. His most important essays and literary reminiscences trace the growth of the imaginative movement he himself helped to create: *Criticism and Fiction* (1891), *My Literary Passions* (1895), *Literary Friends and Acquaintances* (1900), and *My Mark Twain* (1910). Also noteworthy are his accounts of his youthful Ohio days, *A Boy's Town* (1890) and *My Year in a Log Cabin* (1893). In addition to *A Modern Instance* and *The Rise of Silas Lapham,* the foremost titles among his many novels are *Their Wedding Journey* (his first, 1878), *The Undiscovered Country* (1880), *Indian Summer* (1886), *A Hazard of New Fortunes* and *The Shadow of a Dream* (1890), *An Imperative Duty* (1892), *A Traveler from Altruria* (1894), *The Landlord at Lion's Head* (1897), *The Son of Royal Langbrith* (1904), and *The Leatherwood God* (1916). If all these titles were not enough, travel books, plays, and poems extended Howells's reach into other areas of writing.

Somehow there was time for other activities as well, both public and personal. On the political side, Howells took a number of courageous, well-publicized stands in the 1880s and 1890s: a forthright defense of the so-called Haymarket Anarchists in 1886, support of the founding of the NAACP, advocacy of socialism as the solution to the problem caused by the widening margin between the rich and the poor, encouragement of the suffragist movement, and criticism of the nation's imperialistic policies. On the private side, Howells, whose own psychological makeup had been vulnerable to jolts ever since young manhood, had to stave off further assaults to his mental stability, including breakdowns that came while he was at work on *A Modern Instance* in 1881 and 1882 and again in 1885 while completing *The Rise of Silas Lapham.*

The emotional history of Howells's wife and daughter Winifred was similar to that experienced by the Clemens household, as well as by the James and Adams families. It is a sad history—all too familiar to this period—of invalidism, nervous disorders, and early death. But Howells himself persevered, while trying to hold together the pieces of his family during Winny's illness in the 1880s, her death in 1889, and his wife's subsequent invalidism.

More and more honors were heaped upon his stocky body and graying head. Honorary degrees from Oxford, Princeton, Yale, and Columbia were bestowed on a man who had never had the chance back in Ohio to earn a regular grade-school education. By 1900 Howells commanded the literary scene. Over the next decade he was still deeply revered, but attention started to drift away from him toward the energetic young writers he had often been instrumental in getting started. By the 1920s Sinclair Lewis, H. L. Mencken, and other obstreperous young critics ridiculed Howells in a manner that was just as vigorous but less polite than the tone he had used as a young man to attack literary deadwood. By the 1930s the popularity of Melville and Poe was on the rise, while this honest Realist was shunted aside. Yet Howells's literary reputation began to regain attention in the 1940s as the concerns of the critics and historians turned once more toward the solid achievements of the post–Civil War generation.

Why is the praise that Howells gets sometimes begrudging? Certainly he introduced his readers to important "new" themes, something a literature requires if it is to keep pace with the events it tries to reflect. Among Howells's major themes are many that are still topical: the young American woman as a special type who sallies forth with somewhat reckless abandon to take on the world; the effects of divorce on couples in a society where admitting one's failures in marriage may be legally permissible but can be the cause of emotional devastation; the amorality of the business and professional classes, tenuously bound to the shaky morality of older values; the loss of religious certainties, with little of worth to replace them; the weakening position of "old families"; and the faltering relationships between parents and children. Howells portrays the shabby boredom of country life set against the more glamorous squalor and frenetic pace of city living; classes set against classes, both socially, in the drawing room, and economically, when strikers take to the street in protest; the shining veneer of manners that barely cover the fundamental crudity of people on the make. He is adept at the analysis of the female character and the discussion of the dream life that resists explanation by the most severe scientific scrutiny. Howells's main theme is the most modern theme of all: people at loose ends, displaced ethnically (with the "natives" drawing in their elbows in the presence of Irish, African Americans, and other "aliens") and psychically (men and women going it alone in their professions or their marriages).

In addition to the new areas Howells opened up to the novelists of Realism, he took a clear position on several ethical issues. For Howells the acts of the artist are moral acts. To see realistically is to meet the world honestly, even though it means giving up faith in abstract absolutes. To see romantically is to deceive and to be deceived, thereby to live without moral validation. He wished to reject fatalism because he believed choice is necessary so that people can be responsible for what they do. He also scorned self-isolation, excessive subjectivism, and the sentimentality of people—especially women—given over to self-sacrifice and lives ground down by excessive attention to "duty."

Howells knew his American scene, and he was careful to single out what was most characteristically "American" about it. Howells believed that ordinariness was fine; optimism and small appetites were the national traits. Without self-contradiction, he wrote stories about the way common people react when placed at the extremes possible in ordinary lives—drug addiction, madness, alcoholism, suicide, emotional incest, repressed sexuality, violent death. Without denying his statement that American literature does best with the "smiling aspects" of life, he lived and worked on the edge of his own pessimism and doubts. Howells did all these things, and handled these themes, because he was an ironist as well as a realist.

Irony is both Howells's greatest strength as an honest man and the source of the weakness that sapped his verve as a writer. We blame him most for not being exciting. But he would doubtless reply that he chose to keep himself and excitement apart. The love of novelty and the desire to set crazy things happening all at once, which attracts us to Mark Twain (because novelty and craziness pulled powerfully at Twain's imagination), were exactly what Howells tried to keep out of his life, his literature, and his pronouncements on the nature of Realism. Irony let him do this. It kept his fires banked, but it also held him to the truths of his life's intention: to re-create the American imagination in the image of his own self-limiting commitment to things exactly as they are.

Further Reading:
E. Cady, *The Road to Realism: The Early Years*, 1956.
E. Cady, *The Realist at War: The Mature Years*, 1958.
R. Hough, *The Quiet Rebel: Howells as Social Commentator*, 1959.
G. Carrington, *The Immense Complex Drama: The World and Art of the Howells' Novels*, 1966.

K. Vanderbilt, *The Achievement of William Dean Howells*, 1968.
K. Lynn, *William Dean Howells: An American Life*, 1971.
E. Sundquist, ed., *American Realism*, 1982.

E. Prioleau, *The Circle of Eros: Sexuality in the Work of Howells*, 1983.

A. Stein, *After the Vows Were Spoken*, 1985.

J. Crowley, *The Black Heart's Truth: The Early Career*, 1985.

R. Brodhead, *The School of Hawthorne*, 1986.

A. Kaplan, *The Social Construction of American Realism*, 1988.

E. Nettels, *Language, Race, and Social Class in Howells' America*, 1988.

J. Crowley, *The Mask of Fiction*, 1989.

J. Bassett, " 'A Heart of Ideality in My Realism': Howells' Early Criticism," *Papers on Language and Literature*, 25 (1989), 67–87.

Texts:

Criticism and Fiction, 1891.

"Editha" from *Between the Dark and the Daylight*, 1907.

The American Short Story

I am not sure that the Americans have not brought the short story nearer perfection in the all-round sense than almost any other people, and for reasons very simple and near at hand. It might be argued from the national hurry and impatience that it was a literary form peculiarly adapted to the American temperament, but I suspect that its extraordinary development among us is owing much more to more tangible facts. The success of American magazines, which is nothing less than prodigious, is only commensurate with their excellence. Their sort of success is not only from the courage to decide what ought to please, but from the knowledge of what does please; and it is probable that, aside from the pictures, it is the short stories which please the readers of our best magazines. The serial novels they must have, of course; but rather more of course they must have short stories, and by operation of the law of supply and demand, the short stories, abundant in quantity and excellent in quality, are forthcoming because they are wanted. By another operation of the same law, which political economists have more recently taken account of, the demand follows the supply, and short stories are sought for because there is a proven ability to furnish them, and people read them willingly because they are usually very good. The art of writing them is now so disciplined and diffused with us that there is no lack either for the magazines or for the newspaper "syndicates" which deal in them almost to the exclusion of the serials. In other countries the feuilleton[1] of the journals is a novel continued from day to day, but with us the papers, whether daily or weekly, now more rarely print novels, whether they get them at first hand from the writers, as a great many do, or through the syndicates, which purvey a vast variety of literary wares, chiefly for the Sunday editions of the city journals. In the country papers the short story takes place of the chapters of a serial which used to be given.

1891

William Dean Howells, from "The Nature of American Fiction,"
Criticism and Fiction, *1891.*

---

[1] The literary section of French newspapers.

Editha

The air was thick with the war[1] feeling, like the electricity of a storm which has not yet burst. Editha sat looking out into the hot spring afternoon, with her lips parted, and panting with the intensity of the question whether she could let him go. She had decided that she could not let him stay, when she saw him at the end of the still leafless avenue, making slowly up towards the house, with his head down and his figure relaxed. She ran impatiently out on the veranda, to the edge of the steps, and imperatively demanded greater haste of him with her will before she called aloud to him: "George!"

He had quickened his pace in mystical response to her mystical urgence, before he could have heard her; now he looked up and answered, "Well?"

"Oh, how united we are!" she exulted, and then she swooped down the steps to him. "What is it?" she cried.

"It's war," he said, and he pulled her up to him and kissed her.

She kissed him back intensely, but irrelevantly, as to their passion, and uttered from deep in her throat. "How glorious!"

"It's war," he repeated, without consenting to her sense of it; and she did not know just what to think at first. She never knew what to think of him; that made his mystery, his charm. All through their courtship, which was contemporaneous with the growth of the war feeling, she had been puzzled by his want of seriousness about it. He seemed to despise it even more than he abhorred it. She could have understood his abhorring any sort of bloodshed; that would have been a survival of his old life when he thought he would be a minister, and before he changed and took up the law. But making light of a cause so high and noble seemed to show a want of earnestness at the core of his being. Not but that she felt herself able to cope with a congenital defect of that sort, and make his love for her save him from himself. Now perhaps the miracle was already wrought in him. In the presence of the tremendous fact that he announced, all triviality seemed to have gone out of him; she began to feel that. He sank down on the top step, and wiped his forehead with his handkerchief, while she poured out upon him her question of the origin and authenticity of his news.

All the while, in her duplex emotioning, she was aware that now at the very beginning she must put a guard upon herself against urging him, by any word or act, to take the part that her whole soul willed him to take, for the completion of her ideal of him. He was very nearly perfect as he was, and he must be allowed to perfect himself. But he was peculiar, and he might very well be reasoned out of his peculiarity. Before her reasoning went her emotioning: her nature pulling upon his nature, her womanhood upon his manhood, without her knowing the means she was using to the end she was willing. She had always supposed that the man who won her would have done something to win her: she did not know what, but something. George Gearson had simply asked her for her love, on the way home from a concert, and she gave her love to him without, as it were, thinking. But now, it flashed upon her, if he could do something worthy to *have* won her—be a hero, *her* hero—it would be even better than if he had done it before asking her; it would be grander. Besides, she had believed in the war from the beginning.

[1] The Spanish-American War of 1898.

"But don't you see, dearest," she said, "that it wouldn't have come to this if it hadn't been in the order of Providence? And I call any war glorious that is for the liberation of people who have been struggling for years against the cruelest oppression. Don't you think so, too?"

"I suppose so," he returned languidly. "But war! Is it glorious to break the peace of the world?"

"That ignoble peace! It was no peace at all, with that crime and shame at our very gates." She was conscious of parroting the current phrases of the newspapers, but it was no time to pick and choose her words. She must sacrifice anything to the high ideal she had for him, and after a good deal of rapid argument she ended with the climax: "But now it doesn't matter about the how or why. Since the war has come, all that is gone. There are no two sides any more. There is nothing now but our country."

He sat with his eyes closed and his head leant back against the veranda, and he remarked, with a vague smile, as if musing aloud, "Our country—right or wrong."[2]

"Yes, right or wrong!" she returned, fervidly. "I'll go and get you some lemonade." She rose rustling, and whisked away; when she came back with two tall glasses of clouded liquid on a tray, and the ice clucking in them, he still sat as she had left him, and she said, as if there had been no interruption: "But there is no question of wrong in this case. I call it a sacred war. A war for liberty and humanity, if ever there was one. And I know you will see it just as I do, yet."

He took half the lemonade at a gulp, and he answered as he set the glass down: "I know you always have the highest ideal. When I differ from you I ought to doubt myself."

A generous sob rose in Editha's throat for the humility of a man, so very nearly perfect, who was willing to put himself below her.

Besides, she felt, more subliminally, that he was never so near slipping through her fingers as when he took that meek way.

"You shall not say that! Only, for once I happen to be right." She seized his hand in her two hands, and poured her soul from her eyes into his. "Don't you think so?" she entreated him.

He released his hand and drank the rest of his lemonade, and she added, "Have mine too," but he shook his head in answering, "I've no business to think so, unless I act so, too."

Her heart stopped a beat before it pulsed on with leaps that she felt in her neck. She had noticed that strange thing in men: they seemed to feel bound to do what they believed, and not think a thing was finished when they said it, as girls did. She knew what was in his mind, but she pretended not, as she said, "Oh, I am not sure," and then faltered.

He went on as if to himself, without apparently heeding her: "There's only one way of proving one's faith in a thing like this."

She could not say that she understood, but she did understand.

He went on again. "If I believed—if I felt as you do about this war—Do you wish me to feel as you do?"

Now she was really not sure; so she said: "George, I don't know what you mean."

---

[2] During an engagement with the British fleet in 1816, this phrase was coined by Stephen Decatur, the American naval hero.

He seemed to muse away from her as before. "There is a sort of fascination in it. I suppose that at the bottom of his heart every man would like at times to have his courage tested, to see how he would act."

"How can you talk in that ghastly way?"

"It *is* rather morbid. Still, that's what it comes to, unless you're swept away by ambition or driven by conviction. I haven't the conviction or the ambition, and the other thing is what it comes to with me. I ought to have been a preacher, after all; then I couldn't have asked it of myself, as I must, now I'm a lawyer. And you believe it's a holy war, Editha?" he suddenly addressed her. "Oh, I know you do! But you wish me to believe so, too?"

She hardly knew whether he was mocking or not, in the ironical way he always had with her plainer mind. But the only thing was to be outspoken with him.

"George, I wish you to believe whatever you think is true, at any and every cost. If I've tried to talk you into anything, I take it all back."

"Oh, I know that, Editha. I know how sincere you are, and how—I wish I had your undoubting spirit! I'll think it over; I'd like to believe as you do. But I don't, now; I don't, indeed. It isn't this war alone; though this seems peculiarly wanton and needless; but it's every war—so stupid; it makes me sick. Why shouldn't this thing have been settled reasonably?"

"Because," she said, very throatily again, "God meant it to be war."

"You think it was God? Yes, I suppose that is what people will say."

"Do you suppose it would have been war if God hadn't meant it?"

"I don't know. Sometimes it seems as if God had put this world into men's keeping to work it as they pleased."

"Now, George, that is blasphemy."

"Well, I won't blaspheme. I'll try to believe in your pocket Providence," he said, and then he rose to go.

"Why don't you stay to dinner?" Dinner at Balcom's Works was at one o'clock.

"I'll come back to supper, if you'll let me. Perhaps I shall bring you a convert."

"Well, you may come back, on that condition."

"All right. If I don't come, you'll understand."

He went away without kissing her, and she felt it a suspension of their engagement. It all interested her intensely; she was undergoing a tremendous experience, and she was being equal to it. While she stood looking after him, her mother came out through one of the long windows onto the veranda, with a catlike softness and vagueness.

"Why didn't he stay to dinner?"

"Because—because—war has been declared," Editha pronounced, without turning.

Her mother said, "Oh, my!" and then said nothing more until she had sat down in one of the large Shaker chairs[3] and rocked herself for some time. Then she closed whatever tacit passage of thought there had been in her mind with the spoken words: "Well, I hope *he* won't go."

"And *I* hope he *will*," the girl said, and confronted her mother with a stormy exaltation that would have frightened any creature less unimpressionable than a cat.

---

[3] Designed and manufactured by the Shakers,
members of a religious community noted for
the fine simplicity of their artifacts.

Her mother rocked herself again for an interval of cogitation. What she arrived at in speech was: "Well, I guess you've done a wicked thing, Editha Balcom."

The girl said, as she passed indoors through the same window her mother had come out by: "I haven't done anything—yet."

In her room, she put together all her letters and gifts from Gearson, down to the withered petals of the first flower he had offered, with that timidity of his veiled in that irony of his. In the heart of the packet she enshrined her engagement ring which she had restored to the pretty box he had brought it her in. Then she sat down, if not calmly yet strongly, and wrote:

"GEORGE:—I understood when you left me. But I think we had better emphasize your meaning that if we cannot be one in everything we had better be one in nothing. So I am sending these things for your keeping till you have made up your mind.

"I shall always love you, and therefore I shall never marry any one else. But the man I marry must love his country first of all, and be able to say to me,

'I could not love thee, dear, so much,
  Loved I not honor more.'[4]

"There is no honor above America with me. In this great hour there is no other honor.

"Your heart will make my words clear to you. I had never expected to say so much, but it has come upon me that I must say the utmost.

EDITHA."

She thought she had worded her letter well, worded it in a way that could not be bettered; all had been implied and nothing expressed.

She had it ready to send with the packet she had tied with red, white, and blue ribbon, when it occurred to her that she was not just to him, that she was not giving him a fair chance. He had said he would go and think it over, and she was not waiting. She was pushing, threatening, compelling. That was not a woman's part. She must leave him free, free, free. She could not accept for her country or herself a forced sacrifice.

In writing her letter she had satisfied the impulse from which it sprang; she could well afford to wait till he had thought it over. She put the packet and the letter by, and rested serene in the consciousness of having done what was laid upon her by her love itself to do, and yet used patience, mercy, justice.

She had her reward. Gearson did not come to tea, but she had given him till morning, when, late at night there came up from the village the sound of a fife and drum, with a tumult of voices, in shouting, singing, and laughing. The noise drew nearer and nearer; it reached the street end of the avenue; there it silenced itself, and one voice, the voice she knew best, rose over the silence. It fell; the air was filled with cheers; the fife and drum struck up, with the shouting, singing, and laughing again, but now retreating; and a single figure came hurrying up the avenue.

She ran down to meet her lover and clung to him. He was very gay, and he put his arm round her with a boisterous laugh. "Well, you must call me Captain now; or Cap, if you prefer; that's what the boys call me. Yes, we've had a meeting at the town-hall, and

---

[4] From the poem "To Lucasta, Going to the Wars," by Richard Lovelace (1618–1658).

everybody has volunteered; and they selected me for captain, and I'm going to the war, the big war, the glorious war, the holy war ordained by the pocket Providence that blesses butchery. Come along; let's tell the whole family about it. Call them from their downy beds, father, mother, Aunt Hitty, and all the folks!"

But when they mounted the veranda steps he did not wait for a larger audience; he poured the story out upon Editha alone.

"There was a lot of speaking, and then some of the fools set up a shout for me. It was all going one way, and I thought it would be a good joke to sprinkle a little cold water on them. But you can't do that with a crowd that adores you. The first thing I knew I was sprinkling hell-fire on them. 'Cry havoc, and let slip the dogs of war.'[5] That was the style. Now that it had come to the fight, there were no two parties; there was one country, and the thing was to fight to a finish as quick as possible. I suggested volunteering then and there, and I wrote my name first of all on the roster. Then they elected me— that's all. I wish I had some ice-water."

She left him walking up and down the veranda, while she ran for the ice-pitcher and a goblet, and when she came back he was still walking up and down, shouting the story he had told her to her father and mother, who had come out more sketchily dressed than they commonly were by day. He drank goblet after goblet of the ice-water without noticing who was giving it, and kept on talking, and laughing through his talk wildly. "It's astonishing," he said, "how well the worse reason looks when you try to make it appear the better. Why, I believe I was the first convert to the war in that crowd to-night! I never thought I should like to kill a man; but now I shouldn't care; and the smokeless powder lets you see the man drop that you kill. It's all for the country! What a thing it is to have a country that *can't* be wrong, but if it is, is right, anyway!"

Editha had a great, vital thought, an inspiration. She set down the ice-pitcher on the veranda floor, and ran up-stairs and got the letter she had written him. When at last he noisily bade her father and mother, "Well, good-night. I forgot I woke you up; I sha'n't want any sleep myself," she followed him down the avenue to the gate. There, after the whirling words that seemed to fly away from her thoughts and refuse to serve them, she made a last effort to solemnize the moment that seemed so crazy, and pressed the letter she had written upon him.

"What's this?" he said. "Want me to mail it?"

"No, no. It's for you. I wrote it after you went this morning. Keep it—keep it—and read it sometime—" She thought, and then her inspiration came: "Read it if ever you doubt what you've done, or fear that I regret your having done it. Read it after you've started."

They strained each other in embraces that seemed as ineffective as their words, and he kissed her face with quick, hot breaths that were so unlike him, that made her feel as if she had lost her old lover and found a stranger in his place. The stranger said: "What a gorgeous flower you are, with your red hair, and your blue eyes that look black now, and your face with the color painted out by the white moonshine! Let me hold you under the chin, to see whether I love blood, you tiger-lily!" Then he laughed Gearson's laugh, and released her, scared and giddy. Within her wilfulness she had been frightened by a sense of subtler force in him, and mystically mastered as she had never been before.

[5] Shakespeare's *Julius Caesar,* Act III, Sc. i, l. 273.

She ran all the way back to the house, and mounted the steps panting. Her mother and father were talking of the great affair. Her mother said: "Wa'n't Mr. Gearson in rather of an excited state of mind? Didn't you think he acted curious?"

"Well, not for a man who'd just been elected captain and had set 'em up for the whole of Company A," her father chuckled back.

"What in the world do you mean, Mr. Balcom? Oh! There's Editha!" She offered to follow the girl indoors.

"Don't come, mother!" Editha called, vanishing.

Mrs. Balcom remained to reproach her husband. "I don't see much of anything to laugh at."

"Well, it's catching. Caught it from Gearson. I guess it won't be much of a war, and I guess Gearson don't think so either. The other fellows will back down as soon as they see we mean it. I wouldn't lose any sleep over it. I'm going back to bed, myself."

Gearson came again next afternoon, looking pale and rather sick, but quite himself, even to his languid irony. "I guess I'd better tell you, Editha, that I consecrated myself to your god of battles last night by pouring too many libations to him down my own throat. But I'm all right now. One has to carry off the excitement, somehow."

"Promise me," she commanded, "that you'll never touch it again!"

"What! Not let the cannikin[6] clink? Not let the soldier drink? Well, I promise."

"You don't belong to yourself now; you don't even belong to *me*. You belong to your country, and you have a sacred charge to keep yourself strong and well for your country's sake. I have been thinking, thinking all night and all day long."

"You look as if you had been crying a little, too," he said, with his queer smile.

"That's all past. I've been thinking, and worshipping *you*. Don't you suppose I know all that you've been through, to come to this? I've followed you every step from your old theories and opinions."

"Well, you've had a long row to hoe."

"And I know you've done this from the highest motives—"

"Oh, there won't be much pettifogging to do till this cruel war is—"

"And you haven't simply done it for my sake. I couldn't respect you if you had."

"Well, then we'll say I haven't. A man that hasn't got his own respect intact wants the respect of all the other people he can corner. But we won't go into that. I'm in for the thing now, and we've got to face our future. My idea is that this isn't going to be a very protracted struggle; we shall just scare the enemy to death before it comes to a fight at all. But we must provide for contingencies, Editha. If anything happens to me—"

"Oh, George!" She clung to him, sobbing.

"I don't want you to feel foolishly bound to my memory. I should hate that, wherever I happened to be."

"I am yours, for time and eternity—time and eternity." She liked the words; they satisfied her famine for phrases.

"Well, say eternity; that's all right; but time's another thing; and I'm talking about time. But there is something! My mother! If anything happens—"

[6] Cup. The reference is to the tradition of a soldier's right to drink before battle, as described in Shakespeare's *Othello*, Act II, Sc. iii, ll. 71–75.

She winced, and he laughed, "You're not the bold soldier-girl of yesterday!" Then he sobered. "If anything happens, I want you to help my mother out. She won't like my doing this thing. She brought me up to think war a fool thing as well as a bad thing. My father was in the Civil War; all through it; lost his arm in it." She thrilled with the sense of the arm round her; what if that should be lost? He laughed as if divining her: "Oh, it doesn't run in the family, as far as I know!" Then he added, gravely: "He came home with misgivings about war, and they grew on him. I guess he and mother agreed between them that I was to be brought up in his final mind about it; but that was before my time. I only knew him from my mother's report of him and his opinions; I don't know whether they were hers first; but they were hers last. This will be a blow to her. I shall have to write and tell her—"

He stopped, and she asked: "Would you like me to write, too, George?"

"I don't believe that would do. No, I'll do the writing. She'll understand a little if I say that I thought the way to minimize it was to make war on the largest possible scale at once—that I felt I must have been helping on the war somehow if I hadn't helped keep it from coming, and I knew I hadn't; when it came, I had no right to stay out of it."

Whether his sophistries satisfied him or not, they satisfied her. She clung to his breast, and whispered, with closed eyes and quivering lips: "Yes, yes, yes!"

"But if anything should happen, you might go to her and see what you could do for her. You know? It's rather far off; she can't leave her chair—"

"Oh, I'll go, if it's the ends of the earth! But nothing will happen! Nothing *can!* I—"

She felt herself lifted with his rising, and Gearson was saying, with his arm still round her, to her father: "Well, we're off at once, Mr. Balcom. We're to be formally accepted at the capital, and then bunched up with the rest somehow, and sent into camp somewhere, and got to the front as soon as possible. We all want to be in the van, of course; we're the first company to report to the Governor. I came to tell Editha, but I hadn't got round to it."

She saw him again for a moment at the capital, in the station, just before the train started southward with his regiment. He looked well, in his uniform, and very soldierly, but somehow girlish, too, with his clean-shaven face and slim figure. The manly eyes and the strong voice satisfied her, and his preoccupation with some unexpected details of duty flattered her. Other girls were weeping and bemoaning themselves, but she felt a sort of noble distinction in the abstraction, the almost unconsciousness, with which they parted. Only at the last moment he said: "Don't forget my mother. It mayn't be such a walk-over as I supposed," and he laughed at the notion.

He waved his hand to her as the train moved off—she knew it among a score of hands that were waved to other girls from the platform of the car, for it held a letter which she knew was hers. Then he went inside the car to read it, doubtless, and she did not see him again. But she felt safe for him through the strength of what she called her love. What she called her God, always speaking the name in a deep voice and with the implication of a mutual understanding, would watch over him and keep him and bring him back to her. If with an empty sleeve, then he should have three arms instead of two, for both of hers should be his for life. She did not see, though, why she should always be thinking of the arm his father had lost.

There were not many letters from him, but they were such as she could have wished, and she put her whole strength into making hers such as she imagined he could have wished, glorifying and supporting him. She wrote to his mother glorifying him as their hero, but the brief answer she got was merely to the effect that Mrs. Gearson was not well enough to write herself, and thanking her for her letter by the hand of some one who called herself "Yrs truly, Mrs. W. J. Andrews."

Editha determined not to be hurt, but to write again quite as if the answer had been all she expected. Before it seemed as if she could have written, there came news of the first skirmish, and in the list of the killed, which was telegraphed as a trifling loss on our side, was Gearson's name. There was a frantic time of trying to make out that it might be, must be, some other Gearson; but the name and the company and the regiment and the State were too definitely given.

Then there was a lapse into depths out of which it seemed as if she never could rise again; then a lift into clouds far above all grief, black clouds, that blotted out the sun, but where she soared with him, with George—George! She had the fever that she expected of herself, but she did not die in it; she was not even delirious, and it did not last long. When she was well enough to leave her bed, her one thought was of George's mother, of his strangely worded wish that she should go to her and see what she could do for her. In the exaltation of the duty laid upon her—it buoyed her up instead of burdening her—she rapidly recovered.

Her father went with her on the long railroad journey from northern New York to western Iowa; he had business out at Davenport, and he said he could just as well go then as any other time; and he went with her to the little country town where George's mother lived in a little house on the edge of the illimitable cornfields, under trees pushed to a top of the rolling prairie. George's father had settled there after the Civil War, as so many other old soldiers had done; but they were Eastern people, and Editha fancied touches of the East in the June rose overhanging the front door, and the garden with early summer flowers stretching from the gate of the paling fence.

It was very low inside the house, and so dim, with the closed blinds, that they could scarcely see one another: Editha tall and black in her crapes which filled the air with smell of their dyes; her father standing decorously apart with his hat on his forearm, as at funerals; a woman rested in a deep arm-chair, and the woman who had let the strangers in stood behind the chair.

The seated woman turned her head round and up, and asked the woman behind her chair: "*Who* did you say?"

Editha, if she had done what she expected of herself, would have gone down on her knees at the feet of the seated figure and said, "I am George's Editha," for answer.

But instead of her own voice she heard that other woman's voice saying: "Well, I don't know as I *did* get the name just right. I guess I'll have to make a little more light in here," and she went and pushed two of the shutters ajar.

Then Editha's father said, in his public will-now-address-a few-remarks tone: "My name is Balcom, ma'am—Junius H. Balcom, of Balcom's Works, New York; my daughter—"

"Oh!" the seated woman broke in, with a powerful voice, the voice that always surprised Editha from Gearson's slender frame. "Let me see you. Stand round where the light can strike on your face," and Editha dumbly obeyed. "So, you're Editha Balcom," she sighed.

"Yes," Editha said, more like a culprit than a comforter.

"What did you come for?" Mrs. Gearson asked.

Editha's face quivered and her knees shook. "I came—because—because George—"
She could go no further.

"Yes," the mother said, "he told me he had asked you to come if he got killed. You
didn't expect that, I suppose, when you sent him."

"I would rather have died myself than done it!" Editha said, with more truth in her
deep voice than she ordinarily found in it. "I tried to leave him free—"

"Yes, that letter of yours, that came back with his other things, left him free."

Editha saw now where George's irony came from.

"It was not to be read before—unless—until—I told him so," she faltered.

"Of course, he wouldn't read a letter of yours, under the circumstances, till he
thought you wanted him to. Been sick?" the woman abruptly demanded.

"Very sick," Editha said, with self-pity.

"Daughter's life," her father interposed, "was almost despaired of, at one time."

Mrs. Gearson gave him no heed. "I suppose you would have been glad to die, such a
brave person as you! I don't believe *he* was glad to die. He was always a timid boy, that
way; he was afraid of a good many things; but if he was afraid he did what he made up
his mind to. I suppose he made up his mind to go, but I knew what it cost him by what
it cost me when I heard of it. I had been through *one* war before. When you sent him
you didn't expect he would get killed."

The voice seemed to compassionate Editha, and it was time. "No," she huskily
murmured.

"No, girls don't; women don't when they give their men up to their country. They
think they'll come marching back, somehow, just as gay as they went, or if it's an empty
sleeve, or even an empty pantaloon, it's all the more glory, and they're so much the
prouder of them, poor things!"

The tears began to run down Editha's face; she had not wept till then; but it was now
such a relief to be understood that the tears came.

"No, you didn't expect him to get killed," Mrs. Gearson repeated, in a voice which
was startlingly like George's again. "You just expected him to kill some one else, some
of those foreigners, that weren't there because they had any say about it, but because
they had to be there, poor wretches—conscripts, or whatever they call'em. You thought
it would be all right for my George, *your* George, to kill the sons of those miserable
mothers and the husbands of those girls that you would never see the faces of." The
woman lifted her powerful voice in a psalmlike note. "I thank my God he didn't live to
do it! I thank my God they killed him first, and that he ain't livin' with their blood on
his hands!" She dropped her eyes, which she had raised with her voice, and glared at
Editha. "What you got that black on for?" She lifted herself by her powerful arms so
high that her helpless body seemed to hang limp its full length. "Take it off, take it off,
before I tear it from your back!"

The lady who was passing the summer near Balcom's Works was sketching Editha's
beauty, which lent itself wonderfully to the effects of a colorist. It had come to that confidence which is rather apt to grow between artist and sitter, and Editha had told her
everything.

"To think of your having such tragedy in your life!" the lady said. She added: "I suppose there are people who feel that way about war. But when you consider the good this
war has done—how much it has done for the country! I can't understand such people,

for my part. And when you had come all the way out there to console her—got up out of a sick-bed! Well!"

"I think," Editha said, magnanimously, "she wasn't quite in her right mind; and so did papa."

"Yes," the lady said, looking at Editha's lips in nature and then at her lips in art, and giving an empirical touch to them in the picture. "But how dreadful of her! How per-fectly—excuse me—how *vulgar!*"

A light broke upon Editha in the darkness which she felt had been without a gleam of brightness for weeks and months. The mystery that had bewildered her was solved by the word; and from that moment she rose from grovelling in shame and self-pity, and began to live again in the ideal.

1905

Henry Adams
1838–1918

To be born a member of the Adams family, one of the few dynastic powers to descend from the days of the American Revolution, portends a special fate. It was an honor and a burden keenly felt by Henry Brooks Adams, great-grandson of John Adams and grandson of John Quincy Adams, second and sixth presidents of the United States, and member of the family whose existence had helped make the United States into a nation with its own separate fate to fulfill. When the family gardener observed to the child Henry, "You'll be thinkin' you'll be President too!" the "causality of the remark made so strong an impression on [Adams's] mind that he never forgot it." But Henry Adams learned that such steady patterns of cause and effect were no guarantees in the helter-skelter society in which he grew up.

Henry Adams did not become president, or anything near. The centers of public power had been closed after the 1828 election, when Andrew Jackson blocked John Quincy Adams's attempt to gain a second term in office. The brash new values of Jacksonian democracy did not favor the eighteenth-century Federalist principles of America's premier family. Henry Adams had to create a career out of *not* being president, out of not being one of *those* Adamses. But since he could hardly escape the consequences of the evolutionary process he studied so closely, he spent a lifetime testing what it meant to be the descendent of the Adamses and of the mythic Adam (the progenitor of all human history). He also had to work out the personal significance of having been flung into one century at a time when it was speeding headlong toward the next. Henry Adams would not, therefore, make his way into the nation's history as a statesman or politician or an industrial leader. Writing served as the shaping power of his career as he became simultaneously the historian and the autobiographer of himself, of the Adams family, and of all the children of Adam.

Henry Adams was born and raised in Boston, summered at the Adamses' country residence in nearby Quincy, graduated from Harvard, studied some law in Germany, traveled around Europe, and acted as secretary to his father when Lincoln named

Charles Francis Adams foreign minister to London during the Civil War years. After the war Adams, in his late twenties, knocked about for several years as a journalist writing on politics, economic matters, and historical events for the influential *Nation* and the *North American Review.* In 1870 Adams was cajoled into accepting a teaching post at Harvard. At the university he offered courses in medieval history to young men who might be unable to earn five dollars a day in the emerging commercial and industrial society with the information they got from his classes, however finely he honed their intellectual skills. He remained at Harvard until 1877 and developed an area of historical study where none had previously existed. (In the same way, his friend William James was just then teaching subjects at Harvard he had never taken as a student.)

The 1870s was a busy decade for Adams in other ways as well. He took on the editorship of the *North American Review* and used it as a forum to attack the political corruptions of the Gilded Age. In 1872 he married wealthy and clever Marion "Clover" Hooper of Boston. Adams had talent and energy to spare, together with enough of an independent income to assure him freedom to move from career to career or, as he would put it, from one kind of failed education to another.

Although Adams knew that he could never obtain political authority in the nation's capital, he decided he wanted to be where the power was. In 1877 he and Clover left New England and settled into the midst of "good" Washington, D.C., society. Here he could at least observe the nation's flaws and perhaps exert the influence of a sharp-eyed, caustic-tongued critic of the American scene.

Never an idler or quiescent observer, Adams launched himself into a full-time career as the historian of the Republic, especially of the period when the earlier Adamses had held center stage. His histories were actually extended biographies of the men who had, in addition to John Adams and John Quincy Adams, created a new country out of an old colony. Studies of Albert Gallatin (1879) and John Randolph (1882) joined with Adams's nine-volume *History of the United States of America During the Administrations of Thomas Jefferson and James Madison* (1889–1891) to give an overview of the period, one that is still considered essential to historical scholarship. He also published two anonymously written novels: *Democracy* (1880) and *Esther* (1884). Both novels make use of sensitive heroines to register the grievous flaws in American life that Adams and his wife found undermining confidence in the established beliefs—whether in government or in religion—that once gave Americans their sense of stability.

The growing loss of equilibrium on the public scene became almost unbearable for Adams when his wife committed suicide in 1885. Over and over he told his friends that he had died too, that what they saw in their midst was a dead man. The void caused by his wife's sudden death gave Adams a glimpse of "the supersensual chaos" that lay just below the surface of the elegant social world this husband and wife had shared. (Her suicide was an even greater shock than the one he had experienced as a young man when he stood at the bedside of his sister, dying terribly of lockjaw while the sun shone down upon the beauty of the world outside her window.) Marion's death also created a gap in the chronology Adams would give to his autobiography, *The Education of Henry Adams* (1918). When writing this, his most famous book, Adams deleted all mention of Marion or their marriage, omitting a twenty-year period in the chronology. But in actual life, the self-described "dead man" persevered.

Frenetic travel occupied Adams for several years after 1885. He and his friends zigzagged through Japan, Australia, the South Seas, Russia, the Middle East, as well as Europe, where he made almost annual trips. The habits of the student led him to continue his research into customs and artifacts of whatever cultures he came in contact with. *Historical Essays* about America was published in 1891, the same year as the final volume of *The History of the United States. Memoirs of Marau Taaroa,* about the Tahitian royal family, appeared in 1893.

As Adams's interests turned toward French history and culture, Paris and its environs became increasingly his home. The medievalist in him began to focus on the effects the Middle Ages had had on French civilization. Adams began to free himself from the weariness that had beset him since 1885 and to contemplate ways in which he might interpret his own era in terms of the past glories of Western culture. He hoped to be able to predict the future toward which he and his contemporaries were hurtling. He knew he could do nothing to control the social forces set loose by the new century. Perhaps he could learn how to interpret the laws that made it work. The cathedrals and religious monuments of northern France dedicated to the saints and the Virgin Mary attracted his imagination; so did the international expositions held in honor of the occult power of the dynamo, the most potent force of the new age of technology. *Mont-Saint-Michel and Chartres* (a "study of thirteenth-century unity") was completed and printed privately in 1904 and published in 1913. *The Education of Henry Adams* (a "study of twentieth-century multiplicity") was distributed to friends in 1907 but did not reach the hands of the general public until after Adams's death in 1918.

As Adams crisscrossed the ocean between the United States and the Continent during the final decade of his life, other writings occupied him. In 1901 Adams developed a theory of the future of human existence in "The Rule of Phase Applied to History." (With the increase in the quality of human consciousness, he noted, there was an alarming decline in the capacity of the mind to control the random forces of the universe.) While serving as the head of the American Historical Association, he gave an address that he later expanded into an essay, "A Letter to American Teachers of History" (1910), in which he argued that historical study must become more scientific and less impressionistic in its methods of research and interpretation. During an age increasingly scientific in temper and achievement, Adams thought history might become an anachronism through the acceleration of events marking the turn of the century. These two essays show Adams's continuing attempt to discover the kind of education that would permit him and his contemporaries to survive in a world of bewildering change.

In his sixties Adams turned to the study of X-rays, radiation, and thermodynamics. The new sciences were the essential education of the new age, an age neither his years at Harvard in the 1850s nor his subsequent experiences as a student of legal history, medieval philosophers, political skullduggery in London and Washington, nineteenth-century aesthetics, Darwinism, and the vagaries of the gold market had prepared him for.

Adams died the year the First World War came to its close. *The Education of Henry Adams* was published that year. It became an immediate best-seller and continues to hold its own as a masterpiece, though it has been more often praised than read. Among its fascinations are its power to foretell the course of future history: shaped by the ancient inertial weight of Russia in contention with China, by the nervous energy let loose by the New Woman, and by the explosive impersonality of the forces released by the new physics. The boy who had been born into the fourth decade of the nineteenth century with the assurance of meaning promised by his eighteenth-century mentality had lived long enough to face the fact that the twentieth century could not be mastered by any one of the forms of education available in the year 1900. The legacy Adams received from his distinguished Adams forebears had been insufficient. The value of the legacy that this childless man handed on to the children of Adam could come only from the records he had kept of trying, failing, and trying once again—those unending processes by which the new Adam might yet make sense out of a welter of experiences.

The reasons for the somewhat begrudging attention paid to Adams's writing are not hard to find. His works are perceived to be arduous to read as literary texts. Their author is often difficult to stomach as a man because of his egotism and petty snobberies. Poe and Thoreau also wrote hard texts; as for liking their personalities, if one were making out a list of America's most lovable writers, the names of Poe and Thoreau would probably not appear either. But Adams suffers from special kinds of distaste that are brought to the reading of his big book. He wrote stories of failure that strike readers as not only depressing but arrogant. Adams has also been attacked for being too rich and privileged, somehow protected from life's trials. Even his ironic responses to social and cosmic ills make him seem more narrowly conservative than the interesting mix he claimed for himself—"Christian conservative anarchist." And there is no clear way around the often nasty bigotry by which he expressed his fear that the United States would be overrun by alien cultures and the unformed masses.

Still, Adams's merits continue to make a place for him as one of the most important writers of the late nineteenth century—perhaps even, as a steadily increasing number of readers insist, one of the major figures in American letters. Adams helped to redefine *education,* a word that Americans, from the Puritans through Franklin, Emerson, Melville, Mark Twain, and DuBois have thought crucial for the nation's survival. Adams also made himself into a masterly commentator on the nature of autobiography. His predecessors are not only Augustine, Rousseau, and Franklin (figures he specifically mentions) but also John Woolman, Frederick Douglass, and Henry David Thoreau—Americans all. In a secular age, he asked important questions about what it is we are to celebrate: the Lord, technology, or the self. He emphasized the importance of the mind at work creating facts as well as interpreting them. As a prose stylist he took earthbound words out into cosmic spaces; he grounded pure abstractions in the concrete world of political, social, and personal events. Reluctant as he was to leave the comforting tidiness of his old-fashioned boyhood in Quincy, he let himself be hurtled into the anxieties of the dynamo age.

Adams stood between Thoreau, who knew the questions and the answers—though he was unable to live according to them in the fullest sense—and the legion of twentieth-century worriers with uncertain questions and no answers. Adams shared with Gertrude Stein the brave ability to admit that he was not even certain which questions to ask or whether there were any. Snobbish, self-deprecating, a bit neurotic, and partially insulated by wealth, Adams took advantage of his privileged view to give us, in stunning literary style and with the discipline of historical scholarship, the state of affairs of the world as he found it. Subsequent generations of readers have undergone the shock of discovering that his world and the future he speculated about with such energy are essentially their world and their future. The "modern" perspective Adams brought to the writing of history reveals what a personal and universal story it is. History, as Adams writes it, is the same thing as autobiography: an unending education in what it means to experience the twentieth century and beyond.

Further Reading:

H. Jordy, *Henry Adams: Scientific Historian,* 1952, 1963.

J. Conder, *A Formula of His Own: Henry Adams' Literary Experiment,* 1970.

J. Rowe, *Henry Adams and Henry James, The Emergence of the Modern Consciousness,* 1976.

E. Harbert, *The Force So Much Closer Home: Henry Adams and the Adams Family,* 1977.

W. Dusinberre, *Henry Adams: The Myth of Failure,* 1980. *Critical Essays on Henry Adams,* ed. E. Harbert, 1981.

J. Rowe, "Henry Adams," *Columbia Literary History of the United States,* 1988.

L. Hughson, *From Biography to History,* 1988.

E. Samuels, *Henry Adams,* 1989.

W. Decker, *The Literary Vocation of Henry Adams,* 1990.

R. Dawidoff, *The Genteel Tradition and the Sacred Rage,* 1992.

J. C. Rowe, ed., *New Essays on* The Education of Henry Adams, 1996.

B. D. Simpson, *The Political Education of Henry Adams,* 1996.

Text:

The Education of Henry Adams, 1974.

---

from The Education of Henry Adams[*]

Chapter XXV: The Dynamo and the Virgin (1900)

Until the Great Exposition of 1900[1] closed its doors in November, Adams haunted it, aching to absorb knowledge, and helpless to find it. He would have liked to know how much of it could have been grasped by the best-informed man in the world. While he was thus meditating chaos, Langley[2] came by, and showed it to him. At Langley's behest, the Exhibition dropped its superfluous rags and stripped itself to the skin, for Langley knew what to study, and why, and how; while Adams might as well have stood outside in the night, staring at the Milky Way. Yet Langley said nothing new, and taught nothing that one might not have learned from Lord Bacon,[3] three hundred years before; but though one should have known the "Advancement of Science" as well as one knew the "Comedy of Errors,"[4] the literary knowledge counted for nothing until some teacher should show how to apply it. Bacon took a vast deal of trouble in teaching King James I and his subjects, American or other, towards the year 1620, that true science was the development or economy of forces; yet an elderly American in 1900 knew neither the formula nor the forces; or even so much as to say to himself that his historical

---

[*] Adams began work on *The Education* in 1903, completed it by 1905, and sent out the first copy of a private printing early in 1907. The Massachusetts Historical Society brought out the first public edition in September 1918, after Adams's death in March of that year.

[1] On display at the Paris Exposition of 1900

was an array of the most recent advances in the technology of electric motors, transformers, and dynamos.

[2] Samuel Langley (1834–1906), American scientist.

[3] Francis Bacon (1561–1628), English scientist.

[4] Play by William Shakespeare.

business in the Exposition concerned only the economies or developments of force since 1893, when he began the study at Chicago.

Nothing in education is so astonishing as the amount of ignorance it accumulates in the form of inert facts. Adams had looked at most of the accumulations of art in the storehouses called Art Museums; yet he did not know how to look at the art exhibits of 1900. He had studied Karl Marx and his doctrines of history[5] with profound attention, yet he could not apply them at Paris. Langley, with the ease of a great master of experiment, threw out of the field every exhibit that did not reveal a new application of force, and naturally threw out, to begin with, almost the whole art exhibit. Equally, he ignored almost the whole industrial exhibit. He led his pupil directly to the forces. His chief interest was in new motors to make his airship feasible, and he taught Adams the astonishing complexities of the new Daimler motor,[6] and of the automobile, which, since 1893, had become a nightmare at a hundred kilometres an hour, almost as destructive as the electric tram which was only ten years older; and threatening to become as terrible as the locomotive steam-engine itself, which was almost exactly Adams's own age.

Then he showed his scholar the great hall of dynamos,[7] and explained how little he knew about electricity or force of any kind, even of his own special sun, which spouted heat in inconceivable volume, but which, as far as he knew, might spout less or more, at any time, for all the certainty he felt in it. To him, the dynamo itself was but an ingenious channel for conveying somewhere the heat latent in a few tons of poor coal hidden in a dirty engine-house carefully kept out of sight; but to Adams the dynamo became a symbol of infinity. As he grew accustomed to the great gallery of machines, he began to feel the forty-foot dynamos as a moral force, much as the early Christians felt the Cross. The planet itself seemed less impressive, in its old-fashioned, deliberate, annual or daily revolution, than this huge wheel, revolving within arm's-length at some vertiginous speed, and barely murmuring—scarcely humming an audible warning to stand a hair's-breadth further for respect of power—while it would not wake the baby lying close against its frame. Before the end, one began to pray to it; inherited instinct taught the natural expression of man before silent and infinite force. Among the thousand symbols of ultimate energy, the dynamo was not so human as some, but it was the most expressive.

Yet the dynamo, next to the steam-engine, was the most familiar of exhibits. For Adams's objects its value lay chiefly in its occult mechanism. Between the dynamo in the gallery of machines and the engine-house outside, the break of continuity amounted to abysmal fracture for a historian's objects. No more relation could he discover between the steam and the electric current than between the Cross and the cathedral. The forces were interchangeable if not reversible, but he could see only an absolute *fiat* in electricity as in faith. Langley could not help him. Indeed, Langley seemed to be worried by the same trouble, for he constantly repeated that the new forces were anarchical, and especially that he was not responsible for the new rays, that were little short of parricidal in their wicked spirit towards science. His own rays, with which he had

---

[5] Marx's *Das Kapital* was published in 1867.
[6] Invented by the German Gottlieb Daimler (1834–1900), one of the primary developers of the internal combustion engine.
[7] The first electrical generator had been developed in 1831 by the British inventor Michael

Faraday (1791–1867). By Adams's time the dynamo had come to stand for the forces of industrial society that lacked the personal humanity Adams associated with the Virgin Mary as worshipped during the Middle Ages.

doubled the solar spectrum, were altogether harmless and beneficent; but Radium denied its God[8]—or, what was to Langley the same thing, denied the truths of his Science. The force was wholly new. A historian who asked only to learn enough to be as futile as Langley or Kelvin,[9] made rapid progress under this teaching, and mixed himself up in the tangle of ideas until he achieved a sort of Paradise of ignorance vastly consoling to his fatigued senses. He wrapped himself in vibrations and rays which were new, and he would have hugged Marconi and Branly[10] had he met them, as he hugged the dynamo; while he lost his arithmetic in trying to figure out the equation between the discoveries and the economies of force. The economies, like the discoveries, were absolute, supersensual, occult; incapable of expression in horse-power. What mathematical equivalent could he suggest as the value of a Branly coherer? Frozen air, or the electric furnace, had some scale of measurement, no doubt, if somebody could invent a thermometer adequate to the purpose; but X-rays had played no part whatever in man's consciousness, and the atom itself had figured only as a fiction of thought. In these seven years man had translated himself into a new universe which had no common scale of measurement with the old. He had entered a supersensual world, in which he could measure nothing except by chance collisions of movements imperceptible to his senses, perhaps even imperceptible to his instruments, but perceptible to each other, and so to some known ray at the end of the scale. Langley seemed prepared for anything, even for an indeterminable number of universes interfused—physics stark mad in metaphysics.

Historians undertake to arrange sequences,—called stories, or histories—assuming in silence a relation of cause and effect. These assumptions, hidden in the depths of dusty libraries, have been astounding, but commonly unconscious and childlike; so much so, that if any captious critic were to drag them to light, historians would probably reply, with one voice, that they had never supposed themselves required to know what they were talking about. Adams, for one, had toiled in vain to find out what he meant. He had even published a dozen volumes of American history for no other purpose than to satisfy himself whether, by the severest process of stating, with the least possible comment, such facts as seemed sure, in such order as seemed rigorously consequent, he could fix for a familiar moment a necessary sequence of human movement. The result had satisfied him as little as at Harvard College. Where he saw sequence, other men saw something quite different, and no one saw the same unit of measure. He cared little about his experiments and less about his statesmen, who seemed to him quite as ignorant as himself and, as a rule, no more honest; but he insisted on a relation of sequence, and if he could not reach it by one method, he would try as many methods as science knew. Satisfied that the sequence of men led to nothing and that the sequence of their society could lead no further, while the mere sequence of time was artificial, and the sequence of thought was chaos, he turned at last to the sequence of force; and thus it happened that, after ten years' pursuit, he found himself lying in the Gallery of Machines at the Great Exposition of 1900, with his historical neck broken by the sudden irruption of forces totally new.

---

[8] Radium's radiation, caused by atomic disintegration, went beyond any conception of cosmic force previously known, even that disclosed by Langley in 1881 in his measurements of solar radiation.

[9] William Thomson, Lord Kelvin (1824–1907), British scientist.

[10] Guglielmo Marconi (1874–1937) and Edouard Branly (1846–1940), Italian inventor of the radio telegraph and French inventor of the method for detecting radio waves, respectively.

Since no one else showed much concern, an elderly person without other cares had no need to betray alarm. The year 1900 was not the first to upset schoolmasters. Copernicus and Galileo[11] had broken many professional necks about 1600; Columbus had stood the world on its head towards 1500; but the nearest approach to the revolution of 1900 was that of 310, when Constantine[12] set up the Cross. The rays that Langley disowned, as well as those which he fathered, were occult, supersensual, irrational; they were a revelation of mysterious energy like that of the Cross; they were what, in terms of medieval science, were called immediate modes of the divine substance.

The historian was thus reduced to his last resources. Clearly if he was bound to reduce all these forces to a common value, this common value could have no measure but that of their attraction on his own mind. He must treat them as they had been felt; as convertible, reversible, interchangeable attractions on thought. He made up his mind to venture it; he would risk translating rays into faith. Such a reversible process would vastly amuse a chemist,[13] but the chemist could not deny that he, or some of his fellow physicists, could feel the force of both. When Adams was a boy in Boston, the best chemist in the place had probably never heard of Venus except by way of scandal,[14] or of the Virgin except as idolatry; neither had he heard of dynamos or automobiles or radium; yet his mind was ready to feel the force of all, though the rays were unborn and the women were dead.

Here opened another totally new education, which promised to be by far the most hazardous of all. The knife-edge along which he must crawl, like Sir Lancelot[15] in the twelfth century, divided two kingdoms of force which had nothing in common but attraction. They were as different as a magnet is from gravitation, supposing one knew what a magnet was, or gravitation, or love. The force of the Virgin was still felt at Lourdes,[16] and seemed to be as potent as X-rays; but in America neither Venus nor Virgin ever had value as force—at most as sentiment. No American had ever been truly afraid of either.

This problem in dynamics gravely perplexed an American historian. The Woman had once been supreme; in France she still seemed potent, not merely as a sentiment, but as a force. Why was she unknown in America? For evidently America was ashamed of her, and she was ashamed of herself, otherwise they would not have strewn fig-leaves so profusely all over her. When she was a true force, she was ignorant of fig-leaves,[17] but the monthly-magazine-made American female had not a feature that would have been recognized by Adam. The trait was notorious, and often humorous, but anyone brought up among Puritans knew that sex was sin. In any previous age, sex was strength. Neither art nor beauty was needed. Everyone, even among Puritans, knew that

[11] Copernicus (1473–1543) and Galileo (1564–1642) reformed existing conceptions concerning the motion of the earth around the sun.

[12] Christianity was made the official religion of the Roman Empire in A.D. 313 upon the proclamation of Emperor Constantine I.

[13] Druggist.

[14] By way of the treatment of venereal disease, associated with Venus, the love goddess.

[15] Reference to one of the chivalric tales concerning Sir Lancelot's heroic deeds.

[16] Shrine in France dedicated to the healing powers of the Virgin Mary.

[17] According to Genesis, Eve went naked in Eden until the Fall. She then covered her body with leaves from the fig tree because of her sense of shame. Adams refers to the prudery about the unclothed female form common to American magazines of the period.

neither Diana of the Ephesians[18] nor any of the Oriental goddesses was worshipped for her beauty. She was goddess because of her force; she was the animated dynamo; she was reproduction—the greatest and most mysterious of all energies; all she needed was to be fecund. Singularly enough, not one of Adams's many schools of education had ever drawn his attention to the opening lines of Lucretius, though they were perhaps the finest in all Latin literature, where the poet invoked Venus exactly as Dante invoked the Virgin:—

"Quae quoniam rerum naturam *sola* gubernas."[19]

The Venus of Epicurean philosophy survived in the Virgin of the Schools:[20]—

"Donna, sei tanto grande, e tanto vali,
Che qual vuol grazia, e a te non ricorre,
Sua disianza vuol volar senz' ali."[21]

All this was to American thought as though it had never existed. The true American knew something of the facts, but nothing of the feelings; he read the letter, but he never felt the law. Before this historical chasm, a mind like that of Adams felt itself helpless; he turned from the Virgin to the Dynamo as though he were a Branly coherer. On one side, at the Louvre and at Chartres, as he knew by the record of work actually done and still before his eyes, was the highest energy ever known to man, the creator of four-fifths of his noblest art, exercising vastly more attraction over the human mind than all the steam-engines and dynamos ever dreamed of; and yet this energy was unknown to the American mind. An American Virgin would never dare command; an American Venus would never dare exist.

The question, which to any plain American of the nineteenth century seemed as remote as it did to Adams, drew him almost violently to study, once it was posed; and on this point Langleys were as useless as though they were Herbert Spencers[22] or dynamos. The idea survived only as art. There one turned as naturally as though the artist were himself a woman. Adams began to ponder, asking himself whether he knew of any American artist who had ever insisted on the power of sex, as every classic had always done; but he could think only of Walt Whitman; Bret Harte, as far as the magazine would let him venture; and one or two painters, for the flesh-tones. All the rest had used sex for sentiment, never for force; to them, Eve was a tender flower, and Herodias[23] an unfeminine horror. American art, like the American language and American education, was as far as possible sexless. Society regarded this victory over sex as its greatest triumph, and the historian readily admitted it, since the moral issue, for the

---

18 Fertility goddess.
19 From *De Rerum Natura* ("On the Nature of Things") by the Roman poet Lucretius (99?–55? B.C.): "Since thou alone dost govern the nature of things."
20 That is, as described by the medieval scholastic philosophers.
21 From Dante's *Divine Comedy* (*Paradiso* xxxiii, 13–15): "Lady [the Virgin], Thou art

so great and so worthy, / That one who desires grace and does not seek after thee, / Would have his wish to soar without wings."
22 Herbert Spencer (1820–1903): English advocate of social Darwinism.
23 The wife of King Herod, who had John the Baptist slain.

moment, did not concern one who was studying the relations of unmoral force. He cared nothing for the sex of the dynamo until he could measure its energy.

Vaguely seeking a clue, he wandered through the art exhibit, and, in his stroll, stopped almost every day before St. Gaudens's General Sherman,[24] which had been given the central post of honor. St. Gaudens himself was in Paris, putting on the work his usual interminable last touches, and listening to the usual contradictory suggestions of brother sculptors. Of all the American artists who gave to American art whatever life it breathed in the seventies, St. Gaudens was perhaps the most sympathetic, but certainly the most inarticulate. General Grant or Don Cameron[25] had scarcely less instinct of rhetoric than he. All the others—the Hunts, Richardson, John La Farge, Stanford White[26]—were exuberant; only St. Gaudens could never discuss or dilate on an emotion or suggest artistic arguments for giving to his work the forms that he felt. He never laid down the law or affected the despot, or became brutalized like Whistler[27] by the brutalities of his world. He required no incense; he was no egoist; his simplicity of thought was excessive; he could not imitate, or give any form but his own to the creations of his hand. No one felt more strongly than he the strength of other men, but the idea that they could affect him never stirred an image in his mind.

This summer his health was poor and his spirits were low. For such a temper, Adams was not the best companion, since his own gaiety was not *folle*;[28] but he risked going now and then to the studio on Mont Parnasse to draw him out for a stroll in the Bois de Boulogne,[29] or dinner as pleased his moods, and in return St. Gaudens sometimes let Adams go about in his company.

Once St. Gaudens took him down to Amiens, with a party of Frenchmen, to see the cathedral.[30] Not until they found themselves actually studying the sculpture of the western portal, did it dawn on Adams's mind that, for his purposes, St. Gaudens on that spot had more interest to him than the cathedral itself. Great men before great monuments express great truths, provided they are not taken too solemnly. Adams never tired of quoting the supreme phrase of his idol Gibbon, before the Gothic cathedrals: "I darted a contemptuous look on the stately monuments of superstition."[31] Even in the footnotes of his history, Gibbon had never inserted a bit of humor more human than this, and one would have paid largely for a photograph of the fat little historian, on the background of Notre Dame of Amiens, trying to persuade his readers—perhaps himself—that he was darting a contemptuous look on the stately monument, for which he felt in fact the respect which every man of his vast study and active mind always feels before objects wor-

---

[24] The statue of General William T. Sherman, Union general, was then on display in Paris; sculpted by Augustus Saint-Gaudens (1848–1907), it now stands at the edge of New York City's Central Park.

[25] James Donald Cameron (1833–1918), Pennsylvania senator and a man considered as inarticulate as President Grant, under whom he served as secretary of war.

[26] Well-known artists and architects of the period: William Morris Hunt (1824–1879); Richard Morris Hunt (1827–1895); Henry Richardson (1838–1886); John La Farge (1835–1910); Stanford White (1853–1906).

[27] James Abbott McNeil Whistler (1834–1903), who was apt to unloose vitriolic attacks against the artistic conventions of his day.

[28] French: "excessive" or "mad."

[29] Montparnasse was the Parisian artists' quarter; the Bois is a large park.

[30] The largest cathedral in France, dedicated to the Virgin Mary.

[31] English historian Edward Gibbon (1737–1794), author of *The Decline and Fall of the Roman Empire* (1776–1788), wrote this entry in his *French Journal* (February 21, 1763). Adams paraphrases here.

thy of it; but besides the humor, one felt also the relation. Gibbon ignored the Virgin, because in 1789 religious monuments were out of fashion. In 1900 his remark sounded fresh and simple as the green fields to ears that had heard a hundred years of other remarks, mostly no more fresh and certainly less simple. Without malice, one might find it more instructive than a whole lecture of Ruskin. One sees what one brings, and at that moment Gibbon brought the French Revolution. Ruskin[32] brought reaction against the Revolution. St. Gaudens had passed beyond all. He liked the stately monuments much more than he liked Gibbon or Ruskin; he loved their dignity; their unity; their scale; their lines; their lights and shadows; their decorative sculpture; but he was even less conscious than they of the force that created it all—the Virgin, the Woman—by whose genius "the stately monuments of superstition" were built, through which she was expressed. He would have seen more meaning in Isis with the cow's horns, at Edfoo,[33] who expressed the same thought. The art remained, but the energy was lost even upon the artist.

Yet in mind and person St. Gaudens was a survival of the 1500's; he bore the stamp of the Renaissance, and should have carried an image of the Virgin round his neck, or stuck in his hat, like Louis XI.[34] In mere time he was a lost soul that had strayed by chance into the twentieth century, and forgotten where it came from. He writhed and cursed at his ignorance, much as Adams did at his own, but in the opposite sense. St. Gaudens was a child of Benvenuto Cellini,[35] smothered in an American cradle. Adams was a quintessence of Boston, devoured by curiosity to think like Benvenuto. St. Gaudens's art was starved from birth, and Adams's instinct was blighted from babyhood. Each had but half of a nature, and when they came together before the Virgin of Amiens they ought both to have felt in her the force that made them one; but it was not so. To Adams she became more than ever a channel of force; to St. Gaudens she remained as before a channel of taste.

For a symbol of power, St. Gaudens instinctively preferred the horse, as was plain in his horse and Victory of the Sherman monument. Doubtless Sherman also felt it so. The attitude was so American that, for at least forty years, Adams had never realized that any other could be in sound taste. How many years had he taken to admit a notion of what Michael Angelo and Rubens[36] were driving at? He could not say; but he knew that only since 1895 had he begun to feel the Virgin or Venus as force, and not everywhere even so. At Chartres—perhaps at Lourdes—possibly at Cnidos if one could still find there the divinely naked Aphrodite of Praxiteles[37]—but otherwise one must look for force to the goddesses of Indian mythology. The idea died out long ago in the German and English stock. St. Gaudens at Amiens was hardly less sensitive to the force of the female energy than Matthew Arnold at the Grande Chartreuse.[38] Neither of them

[32] John Ruskin (1819–1900), English writer on art and architecture.

[33] At Edfu on the Nile, Adams had seen such a statue of the fertility goddess Isis.

[34] King of France from 1423 to 1483.

[35] I.e., of the Italian Renaissance. The sculptor and writer Benvenuto Cellini lived from 1500 to 1571.

[36] Both the Italian artist and the Flemish painter emphasized the human form in their depiction of religious themes.

[37] Famous statue of Venus of the fourth century B.C. by the renowned Greek sculptor Praxiteles.

[38] The English poet (1822–1888) wrote "Stanzas from the Grande Chartreuse" (1855) in expression of his sense of the loss of the faith once held by the members of this medieval monastic community.

felt goddesses as power—only as reflected emotion, human expression, beauty, purity, taste, scarcely even as sympathy. They felt a railway train as power; yet they, and all other artists, constantly complained that the power embodied in a railway train could never be embodied in art. All the steam in the world could not, like the Virgin, build Chartres.

Yet in mechanics, whatever the mechanicians might think, both energies acted as interchangeable forces on man, and by action on man all known force may be measured. Indeed, few men of science measured force in any other way. After once admitting that a straight line was the shortest distance between two points, no serious mathematician cared to deny anything that suited his convenience, and rejected no symbol, unproved or unproveable, that helped him to accomplish work. The symbol was force, as a compass-needle or a triangle was force, as the mechanist might prove by losing it, and nothing could be gained by ignoring their value. Symbol or energy, the Virgin had acted as the greatest force the Western world ever felt, and had drawn man's activities to herself more strongly than any other power, natural or supernatural, had ever done; the historian's business was to follow the track of the energy; to find where it came from and where it went to; its complex source and shifting channels; its values, equivalents, conversions. It could scarcely be more complex than radium; it could hardly be deflected, diverted, polarized, absorbed more perplexingly than other radiant matter. Adams knew nothing about any of them, but as a mathematical problem of influence on human progress, though all were occult, all reacted on his mind, and he rather inclined to think the Virgin easiest to handle.

The pursuit turned out to be long and tortuous, leading at last into the vast forests of scholastic science. From Zeno to Descartes, hand in hand with Thomas Aquinas, Montaigne, and Pascal,[39] one stumbled as stupidly as though one were still a German student of 1860.[40] Only with the instinct of despair could one force one's self into this old thicket of ignorance after having been repulsed at a score of entrances more promising and more popular. Thus far, no path had led anywhere, unless perhaps to an exceedingly modest living. Forty-five years of study had proved to be quite futile for the pursuit of power; one controlled no more force in 1900 than in 1850, although the amount of force controlled by society had enormously increased. The secret of education still hid itself somewhere behind ignorance, and one fumbled over it as feebly as ever. In such labyrinths, the staff is a force almost more necessary than the legs; the pen becomes a sort of blind-man's dog, to keep him from falling into the gutters. The pen works for itself, and acts like a hand, modelling the plastic material over and over again to the form that suits it best. The form is never arbitrary, but is a sort of growth like crystallization, as any artist knows too well; for often the pencil or pen runs into sidepaths and shapelessness, loses its relations, stops or is bogged. Then it has to return on its trail, and recover, if it can, its line of force. The result of a year's work depends more on what is struck out than on what is left in; on the sequence of the main lines of thought, than on their play or variety. Compelled once more to lean heavily on this

[39] Influential philosophers and mathematicians from the time of ancient Greece to the seventeenth century: Zeno of Elea (fifth century B.C.); René Descartes (1596–1650); St. Thomas Aquinas (1225?–1274); Michel de Montaigne (1533–1592); Blaise Pascal (1623–1662).

[40] Between 1858 and 1860 Adams studied in Germany.

support, Adams covered more thousands of pages with figures as formal as though they were algebra, laboriously striking out, altering, burning, experimenting, until the year had expired, the Exposition had long been closed, and winter drawing to its end, before he sailed from Cherbourg, on January 19, 1901, for home.

1905/1918

Henry James
1843–1916

Literary historians of the United States and Great Britain both claim Henry James as their own. Modernist critics say he is of no country at all because he possessed an imagination that is "international" in scope. A few, like Mark Twain (who would not read one of James's novels on a bet), are indifferent as to who claims him.

It is natural that a man who has attracted so many different views of his worth has been given so many identifying labels. James is "the expatriate," the man who lived, observed, and wrote *between* cultures. Still, although he resided abroad for the bulk of his mature years and became a British citizen in the last year of his life, James is also recognized for his intensely "American" consciousness and for the slant that American quality gave to his international themes. James is also "the critic" or, in his own words, "the restless analyst." One of the first major American critical theorists, he possessed a penetrating social intelligence of the kind needed to aid Americans in better understanding their collective strengths and weaknesses. In the words of recent criticism, James is "the androgyne of the imagination." Neither exclusively male nor female in his sensibilities, he preferred to sort people out in terms of their behavior, not their gender. James is "the celibate priest," the writer who willingly sacrifices everything on what he called the altar of art. Finally, and most important, James is known as "the Master"—the influential force who helped bring an end to the nineteenth-century novel based on external plots and public events and initiated twentieth-century views of fiction as inner dramas of consciousness.

James denied himself the elements of personality that come to a man through marriage and through making his permanent home in his native country. Yet it is striking to realize that James began his life as one of the most American of children. Gertrude Stein once teasingly observed that Henry James had to suffer the ignominy of having no last name, only two first names—that is, having no real family identity. But James was born in 1843 into a securely upper-middle-class home in New York City's fashionable Washington Square neighborhood. He was very much the member of a pronounced family group, headed by the sometimes benign, sometimes harmful domination of the senior Henry James—philosopher, visionary, lecturer, and writer. The second son in a family of five precociously alert children (including William, the psychologist and philosopher, and Alice, the youngest of the lot), the younger Henry James remained somewhat to the side until his father's death in 1882. At that time, he shook himself loose from the first label he had had to wear—"Henry James, Junior," the name he used to sign the literary pieces he had presented to the public since his emergence as a professional writer in 1864.

Until his twenty-first year, Henry James was usually in tow as his father moved the family from New York to Newport, Rhode Island, and Cambridge, Massachusetts, and on to England, France, Germany, and Switzerland—always in quest of the perfect spiritual and intellectual education. In his late teens, James studied painting and then the law during a brief stint at Harvard. But it was "the life of the imagination" to which he would apply himself. Without the aid or liability of advanced schooling, James's intelligence was shaped into an acutely sensuous responsiveness by the theaters, art galleries, landscape vistas, and city scenes through which the senior James marched his troop of children. The young James responded most of all to the intricate give-and-take he saw played out in the midst of the intensely social nucleus of the James family.

James sensed very early in his career that the choreographed shifts of relationship between his fictional men and women that would form the basis of his mature literary art required settings steeped in generations of cultural and historical expressiveness. To his mind, the right people for his fictional needs were available anywhere he turned his watchful eye, but the proper background for his characters' activities was generally missing in his native country. For this reason, James left America in 1876 to take up residence abroad. Finally settling in England, he dedicated his life to the only thing that mattered: studying people having "scenes" and learning how to "make scenes" in his fiction.

James never broke loose altogether from his ties to the United States, nor did he dismiss his family or his American friends. His decision to become a British citizen in 1915 was the result of the shock caused by the First World War, when he came to view England as standing alone against the enemies of Western culture. But James remained an American of the kind that Henry Adams, Gertrude Stein, Henry David Thoreau, and even Edgar Allan Poe also represented: observers and critics who stood somewhat to the side of the American scene. No wonder that he was valued by both James Baldwin and Ralph Ellison.

James had one of the longest and most sustained careers of any American writer, and he came to be considered one of the masters of fiction in Great Britain and the United States. In 1907 Scribner's publishing house began to put out the famous New York edition of his selected works in twenty-six volumes. James had not, however, leapt to fame overnight with the writing of a smashingly successful big book. With the exception of the relatively small popular success of *Daisy Miller* in 1879, that kind of fame always escaped him. Particularly at the very start of his career in the mid-1860s, James went through a long and often discouraging apprenticeship as a reviewer and writer of romantic tales, travel sketches, and what he later considered his "hideous" early attempts to write novels.

James's first notable appearance in print came in 1865 with a review of Walt Whitman's "Drum Taps," a collection of poems about the Civil War. (He did not care for it, but this early assessment of Whitman's poetry was revised sharply upward during his mature years.) His work as reviewer and writer of tales continued to appear in many of the more important journals of that period: the *North American Review,* the *Galaxy,* the *Nation,* and the newly formed *Atlantic Monthly.* James's first collection of stories was published in 1875, the same year that *Roderick Hudson* came out as an *Atlantic Monthly* serial; this was the novel he identified as the first serious expression of his powers as a writer of fiction. During that same decade, while on one of his frequent trips to the Continent, he met and conversed with Flaubert, Zola, Turgenev, and De Maupassant about literary matters. He also studied the works of his early favorites, Honoré de Balzac, the French chronicler of "the human comedy," and George Eliot, the English novelist. The late 1870s found James, settled in England and well into his chosen vocation, feeling increased confidence in his powers as a technician and storyteller. *The American* was published in 1877, quickly followed in 1878 by *The Europeans* and in 1879 by *Daisy Miller*. With *The Portrait of a Lady* in 1881, James completed his literary apprenticeship; he had fully arrived on the literary scene and was ready for the next stage of his developing career.

For the sake of convenience, students of James's career usually divide it into three periods. Analogous to the histories of the British monarchy, there is James I, James II, and James III (in the opinion of some of his detractors, James the Old Pretender). If *The Portrait of a Lady* stands out as the finest of James's early full-length novels (characteristic of the reign of James I), the middle period is highlighted by *The Bostonians, The Princess Casamassima* (both 1886), and *The Tragic Muse* (1889). None of these novels achieved the notoriety of *Daisy Miller*. James always longed for fame; at the same time, he trained his eye on the creation of a pure art. He wished to be free from compromises with the moral prudery of the public as well as the cheap sensationalism and easy sentimentality that brought big sales and wide publicity to lesser talents.

During the 1890s James turned to writing for the theater. There, he hoped, he would find the approval of the large theater-going public. But he encountered the same difficulties overcoming the theater audience's bent for superficiality as he had in capturing the attention of the readers of slickly presented fictions. This phase of his career was not the demoralizing failure it has sometimes been made to be. Yet clearly it was not a time of success. By 1895 James had returned to writing fiction, taking with him the skills of scenic presentation he had learned while trying his hand at drama. The loss in one area became a gain when he returned to writing novels and stories. Ten years of notable success followed as James wrote one after another intensely felt short tales, novellas, and long novels. Among his best known are "The Real Thing," "The Turn of the Screw," "The Beast in the Jungle," "The Aspern Papers," and "The Jolly Corner," as well as *The Spoils of Poynton* and *What Maisie Knew* in 1897 and *The Awkward Age* in 1899.

James's final period—the one that has made him one of the supreme masters of fiction in the minds of many and an overrated writer in the opinion of others—includes the three novels that were published in the years between 1902 and 1904: *The Wings of the Dove, The Ambassadors,* and *The Golden Bowl*. They were preceded and followed by the stylistic oddities of *The Sacred Fount* (1901), *The Sense of the Past,* and *The Ivory Tower,* the last two narratives remaining unfinished at the time of his death in 1916.

Any listing of James's major novels and novellas tends to overshadow two other areas of his productivity: the dozens of short stories he published throughout his fifty years as a writer and the great variety of nonfiction he wrote. In the latter grouping there are travel pieces, literary reviews, biographical descriptions, personal memoirs, and analyses of the social scene in the United States and abroad, including such memorable works as *The American Scene* (1907), *A Small Boy and Others* (1913), and *Notes of a Son and Brother* (1914). His reputation as a major influence on the art of the novel extends even further. The quantity and quality of his writings as a literary theorist must still be taken into account.

It was not that other American writers before Henry James paid no attention to the theory by which effective literary expression is formulated. Poe applied himself to this task. In varying degrees, Hawthorne and Whitman laid down principles of composition. And in James's own day, William Dean Howells was a constant commentator on the nature of literary composition. Hamlin Garland and Frank Norris also examined the matter of literary genres. But it was Henry James who over the years amassed a body of critical essays on both form and content that made him a major force in the definition of what prose fiction can do to create a sense of life on the page.

The Art of Fiction (1884), his notebooks, and the prefaces he supplied for each volume of the New York edition are but a few of the occasions he took to address, in public and in private, the long list of issues out of which modern literature has unfolded. James considered the essentially self-effacing role of the author who disappears inside the consciousnesses of his fictional characters or the generalized voice of the unseen narrator. He encouraged readers to give themselves willingly to a pleasureful encounter with complicated language and to delight in difficult syntax and ambiguities of verbal meaning. He experimented with the devices by which narrative time is compressed and expanded. He analyzed why emotion becomes intensified when the narrative is given over to one particularly alert fictional character whose singular point of view forms the story's drama. He refined the means for creating significant "scenes" out of barely perceptible incidents. Above all, James reiterated the importance of the literary techniques by which psychological complexities are revealed through the characters' responses to the environment that enfold them. Before James, writing good prose fiction had often been a happy accident; with James, writers and readers of literature alike became aware of fiction's conscious craft.

The same acute self-consciousness that Henry James lavished on his own and other writers' fiction provides the terms by which James himself can be assessed. Admired during his lifetime by a relatively small group of readers and fellow writers, James's loyal followers are matched by an equally intense group who find him infuriatingly or boringly difficult to read. The detail he gave to the nuances of individual consciousnesses within his stories seems liberating to many, stifling to some. Some see James responding to his characters with tender compassion for their frailties. To others he is a snob, a prude, an effete aesthete, and a social reactionary. The fact that many of the characters in his narratives are highly refined members of the leisured class, living and traveling far from American everyday doings, with all the Jamesian time in the world to linger with their exquisite consciousness, indicates for some that James was out of touch with his native land, his era, and real human life. Still others find in James's choice of subject and setting an inspired strategy for getting close to essential social and psychological concerns. These readers find their feelings mirrored by James's wide spectrum of human types—characters who discover they must (in the words of Lambert Strether, the hero of *The Ambassadors*) come to terms with what it means to live as though they were completely free, all the while remaining aware that they are gripped by binding limitations.

The value of James's influence on the art of fiction remains controversial. But all agree that, whether pernicious or inspiring, his influence has been immense and lasting. James remained convinced of his own greatness as a literary genius throughout his long devotion to his art. He would be pleased to know that his stamp is fixed on the face of fiction, altering the way we read about ourselves and others.

Further Reading:

F. Matthiessen, *Henry James: The Major Phase*, 1944.

D. Krook, *The Ordeal of Consciousness in Henry James*, 1962.

W. J. Stafford, ed., *James's Daisy Miller: The Story, the Play, the Critics*, 1963.

L. Holland, *The Expense of Vision: Essays on the Craft of Henry James*, 1964, 1982.

W. Veeder, *Henry James: The Lesson of the Master: Popular Fiction and Personal Style in the Nineteenth Century*, 1975.

J. Rowe, *Henry Adams and Henry James: The Emergence of a Modern Consciousness*, 1976.

R. Yeazell, *Language and Knowledge in the Late Novels of Henry James*, 1976.

M. Seltzer, *Henry James and the Art of Power*, 1984.

J. Rowe, *The Theoretical Dimensions of Henry James*, 1984.

L. Edel, *Henry James: A Life*, 1985.

M. Anesko, *"Friction in the Marketplace": James and the Profession of Authorship*, 1986.

W. Veeder, and S. Griffin, eds., *The Art of Criticism*, 1986.

R. Yeazell, "Henry James," *Columbia Literary History of the United States*, 1988.

D. Leeming, "Interview with James Baldwin on Henry James," *Leon Edel and Literary Art*, 1988.

R. Gale, *A Henry James Encyclopaedia*, 1989.

A. Habegger, *Henry James and the "Woman Business,"* 1989.

L. Boren, *Eurydice Reclaimed: Language, Gender, and Voice in Henry James*, 1989.

R. Hocks, *Henry James, Study of the Short Fiction*, 1990.

D. W. Fogel, *Daisy Miller: A Dark Comedy of Manners*, 1990.

W. Veeder, "Henry James and the Uses of the Feminine," *Out of Bounds: Male Writers and Gender*, 1990.

Posnock, Ross, *The Trial of Curiosity*, 1991.

P. Walton, *The Disruption of the Feminine in James*, 1992.

D. W. Fogel, ed., *A Companion to James Studies*, 1993.

V. R. Pollak, ed., *New Essays on Daisy Miller . . .*, 1993.

Text:

Daisy Miller from *The Novels and Tales of Henry James* (New York edition), 26 vols., 1907–1917.

Experience Is Never Limited

Experience is never limited, and it is never complete; it is an immense sensibility, a kind of huge spider-web of the finest silken threads suspended in the chamber of consciousness, and catching every air-borne particle in its tissue. It is the very atmosphere of the mind; and when the mind is imaginative . . . it takes to itself the faintest hints of life, it converts the very pulses of the air into revelations. . . . The power to guess the unseen from the seen, to trace the implication of things, to judge the whole piece by the pattern, the condition of feeling life in general so completely that you are well on your way to knowing any particular corner of it—this cluster of gifts may almost be said to constitute experience. . . . Therefore, if I should certainly say to a novice, "Write from experience and experience only," I should feel that this was rather a tantalizing monition if I were not careful immediately to add, "Try to be one of the people on whom nothing is lost!"

Henry James, from The Art of Fiction *(1884)*

The Real and the Romantic

. . . The real represents to my perception the things we cannot possibly *not* know, sooner or later, in one way or another; it being but one of the accidents of our hampered state, and one of the incidents of their quantity and number, that particular instances have not yet come our way. The romantic stands, on the other hand, for the things that, with all the facilities in the world, all the wealth and all the courage and all the wit and all the adventure, we never *can* directly know; the things that reach us only through the beautiful circuit and subterfuge of our thought and our desire.

Henry James, from Preface to The American *(1907)*

American Innocence Lost

. . . one may say that the Civil War marks an era in the history of the American mind. It introduced into the national consciousness a certain sense of proportion and relation, of the world being a more complicated place than it had hitherto seemed, the future more treacherous, success more difficult. At the rate at which things are going, it is obvious that good Americans will be more numerous than ever; but the good American, in days to come, will be a more critical person than his complacent and confident grandfather. He has eaten of the tree of knowledge. He will not, I think, be a sceptic, and still less, of course, a cynic; but he will be, without discredit to his well-known capacity for action, an observer. He will remember that the ways of the Lord are inscrutable, and that this is a world in which everything happens; and eventualities, as the late Emperor of the French used to say, will not find him intellectually unprepared. The good American of which Hawthorne was so admirable a specimen was not critical, and it was perhaps for this reason that Franklin Pierce seemed to him a very proper President. . . .

Henry James, from Hawthorne *(1879)*

Daisy Miller

from **Preface***

It was in Rome during the autumn of 1877; a friend then living there but settled now in a South less weighted with appeals and memories happened to mention—which she might perfectly not have done—some simple and uninformed American lady of the previous winter, whose young daughter, a child of nature and of freedom, accompanying her from hotel to hotel, had "picked up" by the wayside, with the best conscience in the world, a good-looking Roman, of vague identity, astonished at his luck, yet (so far

---

* James wrote this preface for the revised version of *Daisy Miller* published in 1909.

as might be, by the pair) all innocently, all serenely exhibited and introduced: this at least till the occurrence of some small social check, some interrupting incident, of no great gravity or dignity, and which I forget. I had never heard, save on this showing, of the amiable but not otherwise eminent ladies, who were n't in fact named, I think, and whose case had merely served to point a familiar moral; and it must have been just their want of salience that left a margin for the small pencil-mark inveterately signifying, in such connexions, "Dramatise, dramatise!" The result of my recognising a few months later the sense of my pencil-mark was the short chronicle of "Daisy Miller," which I indited in London the following spring and then addressed, with no conditions attached, as I remember, to the editor of a magazine that had its seat of publication at Philadelphia and had lately appeared to appreciate my contributions. That gentleman however (an historian of some repute) promptly returned me my missive, and with an absence of comment that struck me at the time as rather grim—as, given the circumstances, requiring indeed some explanation: till a friend to whom I appealed for light, giving him the thing to read, declared it could only have passed with the Philadelphian critic for "an outrage on American girlhood." This was verily a light, and of bewildering intensity; though I was presently to read into the matter a further helpful inference. To the fault of being outrageous this little composition added that of being essentially and preeminently a *nouvelle;*[1] a signal example in fact of that type, foredoomed at the best, in more cases than not, to editorial disfavour. If accordingly I was afterwards to be cradled, almost blissfully, in the conception that "Daisy" at least, among my productions, might approach "success," such success for example, on her eventual appearance, as the state of being promptly pirated in Boston—a sweet tribute I had n't yet received and was never again to know—the irony of things yet claimed its rights, I could n't but long continue to feel, in the circumstance that quite a special reprobation had waited on the first appearance in the world of the ultimately most prosperous child of my invention. So doubly discredited, at all events, this bantling met indulgence, with no great delay, in the eyes of my admirable friend the late Leslie Stephen and was published in two numbers of *The Cornhill Magazine* (1878).[2]

It qualified itself in that publication and afterwards as "a Study"; for reasons which I confess I fail to recapture unless they may have taken account simply of a certain flatness in my poor little heroine's literal denomination. Flatness indeed, one must have felt, was the very sum of her story; so that perhaps after all the attached epithet was meant but as a deprecation, addressed to the reader, of any great critical hope of stirring scenes. It provided for mere concentration, and on an object scant and superficially vulgar—from which, however, a sufficiently brooding tenderness might eventually extract a shy incongruous charm. I suppress at all events here the appended qualification—in view of the simple truth, which ought from the first to have been apparent to me, that my little exhibition is made to no degree whatever in critical but, quite inordinately and extravagantly, in poetical terms. It comes back to me that I was at a certain hour long afterwards to have reflected, in this connexion, on the characteristic free play of the

[1] Short prose narrative, one of James's favorite literary forms.
[2] British journal edited by Stephen, well-known writer and father of the writer Virginia Woolf.

whirligig of time. It was in Italy again—in Venice and in the prized society of an interesting friend, now dead, with whom I happened to wait, on the Grand Canal, at the animated water-steps of one of the hotels. The considerable little terrace there was so disposed as to make a salient stage for certain demonstrations on the part of two young girls, children *they,* if ever, of nature and of freedom, whose use of those resources, in the general public eye, and under our own as we sat in the gondola, drew from the lips of a second companion, sociably afloat with us, the remark that there before us, with no sign absent, were a couple of attesting Daisy Millers. Then it was that, in my charming hostess's prompt protest, the whirligig, as I have called it, at once betrayed itself. "How can you liken *those* creatures to a figure of which the only fault is touchingly to have transmuted so sorry a type and to have, by a poetic artifice, not only led our judgement of it astray, but made *any* judgement quite impossible?" With which this gentle lady and admirable critic turned on the author himself. "You *know* you quite falsified, by the turn you gave it, the thing you had begun with having in mind, the thing you had had, to satiety, the chance of 'observing': your pretty perversion of it, or your unprincipled mystification of our sense of it, does it really too much honour—in spite of which, none the less, as anything charming or touching always to that extent justifies itself, we after a fashion forgive and understand you. But why *waste* your romance? There are cases, too many, in which you 've done it again; in which, provoked by a spirit of observation at first no doubt sufficiently sincere, and with the measured and felt truth fairly twitching your sleeve, you have yielded to your incurable prejudice in favour of grace—to whatever it is in you that makes so inordinately for form and prettiness and pathos; not to say sometimes for misplaced drolling. Is it that you 've after all too much imagination? Those awful young women capering at the hotel-door, *they* are the real little Daisy Millers that were; whereas yours in the tale is such a one, more 's the pity, as—for pitch of the ingenuous, for quality of the artless—could n't possibly have been at all." My answer to all which bristled of course with more professions than I can or need report here; the chief of them inevitably to the effect that my supposedly typical little figure was of course pure poetry, and had never been anything else; since this is what helpful imagination, in however slight a dose, ever directly makes for. As for the original grossness of readers, I dare say I added, that was another matter—but one which at any rate had then quite ceased to signify. ....

Daisy Miller

I

At the little town of Vevey, in Switzerland, there is a particularly comfortable hotel; there are indeed many hotels, since the entertainment of tourists is the business of the place, which, as many travellers will remember, is seated upon the edge of a remarkably blue lake—a lake[3] that it behoves every tourist to visit. The shore of the lake presents an

---

[3] Lake Geneva.

unbroken array of establishments of this order, of every category, from the "grand ho-tel" of the newest fashion, with a chalk-white front, a hundred balconies, and a dozen flags flying from its roof, to the small Swiss pension of an elder day, with its name in-scribed in German-looking lettering upon a pink or yellow wall and an awkward sum-mer-house in the angle of the garden. One of the hotels at Vevey, however, is famous, even classical, being distinguished from many of its upstart neighbours by an air both of luxury and of maturity. In this region, through the month of June, American travellers are extremely numerous; it may be said indeed that Vevey assumes at that time some of the characteristics of an American watering-place. There are sights and sounds that evoke a vision, an echo, of Newport and Saratoga.[4] There is a flitting hither and thither of "stylish" young girls, a rustling of muslin flounces, a rattle of dance-music in the morning hours, a sound of high-pitched voices at all times. You receive an impression of these things at the excellent inn of the "Trois Couronnes,"[5] and are transported in fancy to the Ocean House or to Congress Hall.[6] But at the "Trois Couronnes," it must be added, there are other features much at variance with these suggestions: neat Ger-man waiters who look like secretaries of legation: Russian princesses sitting in the gar-den; little Polish boys walking about, held by the hand, with their governors; a view of the snowy crest of the Dent du Midi[7] and the picturesque towers of the Castle of Chillon.[8]

I hardly know whether it was the analogies or the differences that were uppermost in the mind of a young American, who, two or three years ago, sat in the garden of the "Trois Couronnes," looking about him rather idly at some of the graceful objects I have mentioned. It was a beautiful summer morning, and in whatever fashion the young American looked at things they must have seemed to him charming. He had come from Geneva the day before, by the little steamer, to see his aunt, who was staying at the ho-tel—Geneva having been for a long time his place of residence. But his aunt had a headache—his aunt had almost always a headache—and she was now shut up in her room smelling camphor, so that he was at liberty to wander about. He was some seven-and-twenty years of age; when his friends spoke of him they usually said that he was at Geneva "studying." When his enemies spoke of him they said—but after all he had no enemies: he was extremely amiable and generally liked. What I should say is simply that when certain persons spoke of him they conveyed that the reason of his spending so much time at Geneva was that he was extremely devoted to a lady who lived there—a foreign lady, a person older than himself. Very few Americans—truly I think none—had ever seen this lady, about whom there were some singular stories. But Winter-bourne had an old attachment for the little capital of Calvinism;[9] he had been put to school there as a boy and had afterwards even gone, on trial—trial of the grey old "Academy"[10] on the steep and stony hillside—to college there; circumstances which had led to his forming a great many youthful friendships. Many of these he had kept, and they were a source of great satisfaction to him.

---

[4] Fashionable resorts in Rhode Island and New York State, respectively.

[5] French: "Three Crowns."

[6] Hotels at Newport and Saratoga, respectively.

[7] Peak of Mont Blanc in the Swiss Alps.

[8] Medieval castle situated on the lake and the setting for "The Prisoner of Chillon" (1816) by Lord Byron.

[9] Bastion of John Calvin's Protestant reform activities between 1541 and 1564.

[10] University of Geneva.

After knocking at his aunt's door and learning that she was indisposed he had taken a walk about the town and then he had come in to his breakfast. He had now finished that repast, but was enjoying a small cup of coffee which had been served him on a little table in the garden by one of the waiters who looked like *attachés*. At last he finished his coffee and lit a cigarette. Presently a small boy came walking along the path—an urchin of nine or ten. The child, who was diminutive for his years, had an aged expression of countenance, a pale complexion and sharp little features. He was dressed in knicker-bockers and had red stockings that displayed his poor little spindle-shanks; he also wore a brilliant red cravat. He carried in his hand a long alpenstock, the sharp point of which he thrust into everything he approached—the flower-beds, the garden-benches, the trains of the ladies' dresses. In front of Winterbourne he paused, looking at him with a pair of bright and penetrating little eyes.

"Will you give me a lump of sugar?" he asked in a small sharp hard voice—a voice immature and yet somehow not young.

Winterbourne glanced at the light table near him, on which his coffee-service rested, and saw that several morsels of sugar remained. "Yes, you may take one," he answered; "but I don't think too much sugar good for little boys."

This little boy stepped forward and carefully selected three of the coveted fragments, two of which he buried in the pocket of his knickerbockers, depositing the other as promptly in another place. He poked his alpenstock, lance-fashion, into Winter-bourne's bench and tried to crack the lump of sugar with his teeth.

"Oh blazes; it's har-r-d!" he exclaimed, divesting vowel and consonants, pertinently enough, of any taint of softness.

Winterbourne had immediately gathered that he might have the honour of claiming him as a countryman. "Take care you don't hurt your teeth," he said paternally.

"I have n't got any teeth to hurt. They've all come out. I've only got seven teeth. Mother counted them last night, and one came out right afterwards. She said she'd slap me if any more came out. I can't help it. It's this old Europe. It's the climate that makes them come out. In America they did n't come out. It's these hotels."

Winterbourne was much amused. "If you eat three lumps of sugar your mother will certainly slap you," he ventured.

"She's got to give me some candy then," rejoined his young interlocutor. "I can't get any candy here—any American candy. American candy's the best candy."

"And are American little boys the best little boys?" Winterbourne asked.

"I don't know. *I'm* an American boy," said the child.

"I see you're one of the best!" the young man laughed.

"Are you an American man?" pursued this vivacious infant. And then on his friend's affirmative reply, "American men are the best," he declared with assurance.

His companion thanked him for the compliment, and the child, who had now got astride of his alpenstock, stood looking about him while he attacked another lump of sugar. Winterbourne wondered if he himself had been like this in his infancy, for he had been brought to Europe at about the same age.

"Here comes my sister!" cried his young compatriot. "She's an American girl, you bet!"

Winterbourne looked along the path and saw a beautiful young lady advancing. "American girls are the best girls," he thereupon cheerfully remarked to his visitor.

"My sister ain't the best!" the child promptly returned. "She's always blowing at me."[11]

"I imagine that's your fault, not hers," said Winterbourne. The young lady meanwhile had drawn near. She was dressed in white muslin, with a hundred frills and flounces and knots of pale-coloured ribbon. Bareheaded, she balanced in her hand a large parasol with a deep border of embroidery; and she was strikingly, admirably pretty. "How pretty they are!" thought our friend, who straightened himself in his seat as if he were ready to rise.

The young lady paused in front of his bench, near the parapet of the garden, which overlooked the lake. The small boy had now converted his alpenstock into a vaulting-pole, by the aid of which he was springing about in the gravel and kicking it up not a little. "Why Randolph," she freely began, "What *are* you doing?"

"I'm going up the Alps!" cried Randolph. "This is the way!" And he gave another extravagant jump, scattering the pebbles about Winterbourne's ears.

"That's the way they come down," said Winterbourne.

"He's an American man!" proclaimed Randolph in his harsh little voice.

The young lady gave no heed to this circumstance, but looked straight at her brother. "Well, I guess you'd better be quiet," she simply observed.

It seemed to Winterbourne that he had been in a manner presented. He got up and stepped slowly toward the charming creature, throwing away his cigarette. "This little boy and I have made acquaintance," he said with great civility. In Geneva, as he had been perfectly aware, a young man was n't at liberty to speak to a young unmarried lady save under certain rarely-occurring conditions; but here at Vevey what conditions could be better than these?—a pretty American girl coming to stand in front of you in a garden with all the confidence in life. This pretty American girl, whatever that might prove, on hearing Winterbourne's observation simply glanced at him; she then turned her head and looked over the parapet, at the lake and the opposite mountains. He wondered whether he had gone too far, but decided that he must gallantly advance rather than retreat. While he was thinking of something else to say the young lady turned again to the little boy, whom she addressed quite as if they were alone together. "I should like to know where you got that pole."

"I bought it!" Randolph shouted.

"You don't mean to say you're going to take it to Italy!"

"Yes, I'm going to take it t' Italy!" the child rang out.

She glanced over the front of her dress and smoothed out a knot or two of ribbon. Then she gave her sweet eyes to the prospect again. "Well, I guess you'd better leave it somewhere," she dropped after a moment.

"Are you going to Italy?" Winterbourne now decided very respectfully to enquire.

She glanced at him with lovely remoteness. "Yes, sir," she then replied. And she said nothing more.

"And are you—a—thinking of the Simplon?"[12] he pursued with a slight drop of assurance.

"I don't know," she said. "I suppose it's some mountain. Randolph, what mountain are we thinking of?"

---

[11] Slang for "criticizing me."

[12] Alpine pass between Switzerland and Italy.

"Thinking of?"—the boy stared.

"Why going right over."

"Going to where?" he demanded.

"Why right down to Italy"—Winterbourne felt vague emulations.

"I don't know," said Randolph. "I don't want to go t' Italy. I want to go to America."

"Oh Italy's a beautiful place!" the young man laughed.

"Can you get candy there?" Randolph asked of all the echoes.

"I hope not," said his sister. "I guess you've had enough candy, and mother thinks so too."

"I have n't had any for ever so long—for a hundred weeks!" cried the boy, still jumping about.

The young lady inspected her flounces and smoothed her ribbons again; and Winterbourne presently risked an observation on the beauty of the view. He was ceasing to be in doubt, for he had begun to perceive that she was really not in the least embarrassed. She might be cold, she might be austere, she might even be prim; for that was apparently—he had already so generalised—what the most "distant" American girls did: they came and planted themselves straight in front of you to show how rigidly unapproachable they were. There had n't been the slightest flush in her fresh fairness however; so that she was clearly neither offended nor fluttered. Only she was composed—he had seen that before too—of charming little parts that didn't match and that made no *ensemble*;[13] and if she looked another way when he spoke to her, and seemed not particularly to hear him, this was simply her habit, her manner, the result of her having no idea whatever of "form" (with such a tell-tale appendage as Randolph where in the world would she have got it?) in any such connexion. As he talked a little more and pointed out some of the objects of interest in the view, with which she appeared wholly unacquainted, she gradually, none the less, gave him more of the benefit of her attention; and then he saw that act unqualified by the faintest shadow of reserve. It was n't however what would have been called a "bold" front that she presented, for her expression was as decently limpid as the very cleanest water. Her eyes were the very prettiest conceivable, and indeed Winterbourne had n't for a long time seen anything prettier than his fair countrywoman's various features—her complexion, her nose, her ears, her teeth. He took a great interest generally in that range of effects and was addicted to noting and, as it were, recording them; so that in regard to this young lady's face he made several observations. It was n't at all insipid, yet at the same time was n't pointedly—what point, on earth, could she ever make?—expressive; and though it offered such a collection of small finenesses and neatnesses he mentally accused it—very forgivingly—of a want of finish. He thought nothing more likely than that its wearer would have had her own experience of the action of her charms, as she would certainly have acquired a resulting confidence; but even should she depend on this for her main amusement her bright sweet superficial little visage gave out neither mockery nor irony. Before long it became clear that, however these things might be, she was much disposed to conversation. She remarked to Winterbourne that they were going to Rome for the winter—she and her mother and Randolph. She asked him if he was a "real American"; she would n't have taken him for one; he seemed more like a German—this flower was gathered as

---

13 French: "harmonious whole."

from a large field of comparison—especially when he spoke. Winterbourne, laughing, answered that he had met Germans who spoke like Americans, but not, so far as he re-membered, any American with the resemblance she noted. Then he asked her if she might n't be more at ease should she occupy the bench he had just quitted. She an-swered that she liked hanging round, but she none the less resignedly, after a little, dropped to the bench. She told him she was from New York State—"if you know where that is"; but our friend really quickened this current by catching hold of her small slip-pery brother and making him stand a few minutes by his side.

"Tell me your honest name, my boy." So he artfully proceeded.

In response to which the child was indeed unvarnished truth. "Randolph C. Miller. And I'll tell you hers." With which he levelled his alpenstock at his sister.

"You had better wait till you're asked!" said this young lady quite at her leisure.

"I should like very much to know *your* name," Winterbourne made free to reply.

"Her name's Daisy Miller!" cried the urchin. "But that ain't her real name; that ain't her name on her cards."

"It's a pity you have n't got one of my cards!" Miss Miller quite as naturally remarked.

"Her real name's Annie P. Miller," the boy went on.

It seemed, all amazingly, to do her good. "Ask him *his* now"—and she indicated their friend.

But to this point Randolph seemed perfectly indifferent; he continued to supply in-formation with regard to his own family. "My father's name is Ezra B. Miller. My father ain't in Europe—he's in a better place than Europe." Winterbourne for a moment sup-posed this the manner in which the child had been taught to intimate that Mr. Miller had been removed to the sphere of celestial rewards. But Randolph immediately added: "My father's in Schenectady. He's got a big business. My father's rich, you bet."

"Well!" ejaculated Miss Miller, lowering her parasol and looking at the embroidered border. Winterbourne presently released the child, who departed, dragging his alpen-stock along the path. "He don't like Europe," said the girl as with an artless instinct for historic truth. "He wants to go back."

"To Schenectady, you mean?"

"Yes, he wants to go right home. He has n't got any boys here. There's one boy here, but he always goes round with a teacher. They won't let him play."

"And your brother has n't any teacher?" Winterbourne enquired.

It tapped, at a touch, the spring of confidence. "Mother thought of getting him one—to travel round with us. There was a lady told her of a very good teacher; an American lady—perhaps you know her—Mrs. Sanders. I think she came from Boston. She told her of this teacher, and we thought of getting him to travel round with us. But Randolph said he did n't want a teacher travelling round with us. He said he would n't have lessons when he was in the cars.[14] And we *are* in the cars about half the time. There was an English lady we met in the cars—I think her name was Miss Featherstone; per-haps you know her. She wanted to know why I did n't give Randolph lessons—give him 'instruction,' she called it. I guess he could give me more instruction than I could give him. He's very smart."

"Yes," said Winterbourne; "he seems very smart."

---

[14] Railway cars.

"Mother's going to get a teacher for him as soon as we get t' Italy. Can you get good teachers in Italy?"

"Very good, I should think," Winterbourne hastened to reply.

"Or else she's going to find some school. He ought to learn some more. He's only nine. He's going to college." And in this way Miss Miller continued to converse upon the affairs of her family and upon other topics. She sat there with her extremely pretty hands, ornamented with very brilliant rings, folded in her lap, and with her pretty eyes now resting upon those of Winterbourne, now wandering over the garden, the people who passed before her and the beautiful view. She addressed her new acquaintance as if she had known him a long time. He found it very pleasant. It was many years since he had heard a young girl talk so much. It might have been said of this wandering maiden who had come and sat down beside him upon a bench that she chattered. She was very quiet, she sat in a charming tranquil attitude; but her lips and her eyes were constantly moving. She had a soft slender agreeable voice, and her tone was distinctly sociable. She gave Winterbourne a report of her movements and intentions, and those of her mother and brother, in Europe, and enumerated in particular the various hotels at which they had stopped. "That English lady in the cars," she said—"Miss Featherstone—asked me if we did n't all live in hotels in America. I told her I had never been in so many hotels in my life as since I came to Europe. I've never seen so many—it's nothing but hotels." But Miss Miller made this remark with no querulous accent; she appeared to be in the best humour with everything. She declared that the hotels were very good when once you got used to their ways and that Europe was perfectly entrancing. She was n't disappointed—not a bit. Perhaps it was because she had heard so much about it before. She had ever so many intimate friends who had been there ever so many times, and that way she had got thoroughly posted. And then she had had ever so many dresses and things from Paris. Whenever she put on a Paris dress she felt as if she were in Europe.

"It was a kind of a wishing-cap," Winterbourne smiled.

"Yes," said Miss Miller at once and without examining this analogy; "it always made me wish I was here. But I need n't have done that for dresses. I'm sure they send all the pretty ones to America; you see the most frightful things here. The only thing I don't like," she proceeded, "is the society. There ain't any society—or if there is I don't know where it keeps itself. Do you? I suppose there's some society somewhere, but I have n't seen anything of it. I'm very fond of society and I've always had plenty of it. I don't mean only in Schenectady, but in New York. I used to go to New York every winter. In New York I had lots of society. Last winter I had seventeen dinners given me, and three of them were by gentlemen," added Daisy Miller. "I've more friends in New York than in Schenectady—more gentlemen friends; and more young lady friends too," she resumed in a moment. She paused again for an instant; she was looking at Winterbourne with all her prettiness in her frank gay eyes and in her clear rather uniform smile. "I've always had," she said, "a great deal of gentlemen's society."

Poor Winterbourne was amused and perplexed—above all he was charmed. He had never yet heard a young girl express herself in just this fashion; never at least save in cases where to say such things was to have at the same time some rather complicated consciousness about them. And yet was he to accuse Miss Daisy Miller of an actual or a potential *arrière-pensée*,[15] as they said at Geneva? He felt he had lived at Geneva so long as

---

[15] French: "ulterior motive."

to have got morally muddled; he had lost the right sense for the young American tone. Never indeed since he had grown old enough to appreciate things had he encountered a young compatriot of so "strong" a type as this. Certainly she was very charming, but how extraordinarily communicative and how tremendously easy! Was she simply a pretty girl from New York State—were they all like that, the pretty girls who had had a good deal of gentlemen's society? Or was she also a designing, an audacious, in short an expert young person? Yes, his instinct for such a question had ceased to serve him, and his reason could but mislead. Miss Daisy Miller looked extremely innocent. Some people had told him that after all American girls were exceedingly innocent, and others had told him that after all they were n't. He must on the whole take Miss Daisy Miller for a flirt—a pretty American flirt. He had never as yet had relations with representatives of that class. He had known here in Europe two or three women—persons older than Miss Daisy Miller and provided, for respectability's sake, with husbands—who were great coquettes; dangerous terrible women with whom one's light commerce might indeed take a serious turn. But this charming apparition was n't a coquette in that sense; she was very unsophisticated; she was only a pretty American flirt. Winterbourne was almost grateful for having found the formula that applied to Miss Daisy Miller. He leaned back in his seat; he remarked to himself that she had the finest little nose he had ever seen; he wondered what were the regular conditions and limitations of one's intercourse with a pretty American flirt. It presently became apparent that he was on the way to learn.

"Have you been to that old castle?" the girl soon asked, pointing with her parasol to the far-shining walls of the Château de Chillon.

"Yes, formerly, more than once," said Winterbourne. "You too, I suppose, have seen it?"

"No, we have n't been there. I want to go there dreadfully. Of course I mean to go there. I would n't go away from here without having seen that old castle."

"It's a very pretty excursion," the young man returned, "and very easy to make. You can drive, you know, or you can go by the little steamer."

"You can go in the cars," said Miss Miller.

"Yes, you can go in the cars," Winterbourne assented.

"Our courier[16] says they take you right up to the castle," she continued. "We were going last week, but mother gave out. She suffers dreadfully from dyspepsia. She said she could n't any more go—!" But this sketch of Mrs. Miller's plea remained unfinished. "Randolph would n't go either; he says he don't think much of old castles. But I guess we'll go this week if we can get Randolph."

"Your brother is n't interested in ancient monuments?" Winterbourne indulgently asked.

He now drew her, as he guessed she would herself have said, every time. "Why no, he says he don't care much about old castles. He's only nine. He wants to stay at the hotel. Mother's afraid to leave him alone, and the courier won't stay with him; so we have n't been to many places. But it will be too bad if we don't go up there." And Miss Miller pointed again at the Château de Chillon.

"I should think it might be arranged," Winterbourne was thus emboldened to reply. "Could n't you get some one to stay—for the afternoon—with Randolph?"

[16] Person hired to aid travelers with hotel
   reservations and luggage.

Miss Miller looked at him a moment, and then with all serenity, "I wish *you'd* stay with him!" she said.

He pretended to consider it. "I'd much rather go to Chillon with you."

"With me?" she asked without a shadow of emotion.

She did n't rise blushing, as a young person at Geneva would have done; and yet, conscious that he had gone very far, he thought it possible she had drawn back. "And with your mother," he answered very respectfully.

But it seemed that both his audacity and his respect were lost on Miss Daisy Miller. "I guess mother would n't go—for *you,*" she smiled. "And she ain't much *bent* on going, anyway. She don't like to ride round in the afternoon." After which she familiarly proceeded: "But did you really mean what you said just now—that you'd like to go up there?"

"Most earnestly I meant it," Winterbourne declared.

"Then we may arrange it. If mother will stay with Randolph I guess Eugenio will."

"Eugenio?" the young man echoed.

"Eugenio's our courier. He does n't like to stay with Randolph—he's the most fastidious man I ever saw. But he's a splendid courier. I guess he'll stay at home with Randolph if mother does, and then we can go to the castle."

Winterbourne reflected for an instant as lucidly as possible: "we" could only mean Miss Miller and himself. This prospect seemed almost too good to believe; he felt as if he ought to kiss the young lady's hand. Possibly he would have done so,—and quite spoiled his chance; but at this moment another person—presumably Eugenio—appeared. A tall handsome man, with superb whiskers and wearing a velvet morning-coat and a voluminous watch-guard, approached the young lady, looking sharply at her companion. "Oh Eugenio!" she said with the friendliest accent.

Eugenio had eyed Winterbourne from head to foot; he now bowed gravely to Miss Miller. "I have the honour to inform Mademoiselle that luncheon's on table."

Mademoiselle slowly rose. "See here, Eugenio, I'm going to that old castle anyway."

"To the Château de Chillon, Mademoiselle?" the courier enquired. "Mademoiselle has made arrangements?" he added in a tone that struck Winterbourne as impertinent.

Eugenio's tone apparently threw, even to Miss Miller's own apprehension, a slightly ironical light on her position. She turned to Winterbourne with the slightest blush. "You won't back out?"

"I shall not be happy till we go!" he protested.

"And you're staying in this hotel?" she went on. "And you're really American?"

The courier still stood there with an effect of offence for the young man so far as the latter saw in it a tacit reflexion on Miss Miller's behaviour and an insinuation that she "picked up" acquaintances. "I shall have the honour of presenting to you a person who'll tell you all about me," he said, smiling, and referring to his aunt.

"Oh well, we'll go some day," she beautifully answered; with which she gave him a smile and turned away. She put up her parasol and walked back to the inn beside Eugenio. Winterbourne stood watching her, and as she moved away, drawing her muslin furbelows over the walk, he spoke to himself of her natural elegance.

II

He had, however, engaged to do more than proved feasible in promising to present his aunt, Mrs. Costello, to Miss Daisy Miller. As soon as that lady had got better of her headache he waited on her in her apartment and, after a show of the proper solicitude about her health, asked if she had noticed in the hotel an American family—a mamma, a daughter and an obstreperous little boy.

"An obstreperous little boy and a preposterous big courier?" said Mrs. Costello. "Oh yes, I've noticed them. Seen them, heard them and kept out of their way." Mrs. Costello was a widow of fortune, a person of much distinction and who frequently intimated that if she had n't been so dreadfully liable to sick-headaches she would probably have left a deeper impress on her time. She had a long pale face, a high nose and a great deal of very striking white hair, which she wore in large puffs and over the top of her head. She had two sons married in New York and another who was now in Europe. This young man was amusing himself at Homburg[17] and, though guided by his taste, was rarely observed to visit any particular city at the moment selected by his mother for her appearance there. Her nephew, who had come to Vevey expressly to see her, was therefore more attentive than, as she said, her very own. He had imbibed at Geneva the idea that one must be irreproachable in all such forms. Mrs. Costello had n't seen him for many years and was now greatly pleased with him, manifesting her approbation by initiating him into many of the secrets of that social sway which, as he could see she would like him to think, she exerted from her stronghold in Forty-Second Street. She admitted that she was very exclusive, but if he had been better acquainted with New York he would see that one had to be. And her picture of the minutely hierarchical constitution of the society of that city, which she presented to him in many different lights, was, to Winterbourne's imagination, almost oppressively striking.

He at once recognized from her tone that Miss Daisy Miller's place in the social scale was low. "I'm afraid you don't approve of them," he pursued in reference to his new friends.

"They're horribly common"—it was perfectly simple. "They're the sort of Americans that one does one's duty by just ignoring."

"Ah you just ignore them?"—the young man took it in.

"I can't *not*, my dear Frederick. I would n't if I had n't to, but I have to."

"The little girl's very pretty," he went on in a moment.

"Of course she's very pretty. But she's of the last crudity."

"I see what you mean of course," he allowed after another pause.

"She has that charming look they all have," his aunt resumed. "I can't think where they pick it up; and she dresses in perfection—no, you don't know how well she dresses. I can't think where they get their taste."

"But, my dear aunt, she's not, after all, a Comanche savage."

"She is a young lady," said Mrs. Costello, "who has an intimacy with her mamma's courier?"

"An 'intimacy' with him?" Ah there it was!

"There's no other name for such a relation. But the skinny little mother's just as bad! They treat the courier as a familiar friend—as a gentleman and a scholar. I should n't wonder if he dines with them. Very likely they've never seen a man with such good manners, such fine clothes, so *like* a gentleman—or a scholar. He probably corresponds to the young lady's idea of a count. He sits with them in the garden of an evening. I think he smokes in their faces."

---

[17] German resort.

Winterbourne listened with interest to these disclosures; they helped him to make up his mind about Miss Daisy. Evidently she was rather wild. "Well," he said, "I'm not a courier and I did n't smoke in her face, and yet she was very charming to me."

"You had better have mentioned at first," Mrs. Costello returned with dignity, "that you had made her valuable acquaintance."

"We simply met in the garden and talked a bit."

"By appointment—no? Ah that's still to come! Pray what did you say?"

"I said I should take the liberty of introducing her to my admirable aunt."

"Your admirable aunt's a thousand times obliged to you."

"It was to guarantee my respectability."

"And pray who's to guarantee hers?"

"Ah you're cruel!" said the young man. "She's a very innocent girl."

"You don't say that as if you believed it," Mrs. Costello returned.

"She's completely uneducated," Winterbourne acknowledged, "but she's wonderfully pretty, and in short she's very nice. To prove I believe it I'm going to take her to the Château de Chillon."

Mrs. Costello made a wondrous face. "You two are going off there together? I should say it proved just the contrary. How long had you known her, may I ask, when this interesting project was formed? You have n't been twenty-four hours in the house."

"I had known her half an hour!" Winterbourne smiled.

"Then she's just what I supposed."

"And what do you suppose?"

"Why that she's a horror."

Our youth was silent for some moments. "You really think then," he presently began, and with a desire for trustworthy information, "you really think that—" But he paused again while his aunt waited.

"Think what, sir?"

"That she's the sort of young lady who expects a man sooner or later to—well, we'll call it carry her off?"

"I have n't the least idea what such young ladies expect a man to do. But I really consider you had better not meddle with little American girls who are uneducated, as you mildly put it. You've lived too long out of the country. You'll be sure to make some great mistake. You're too innocent."

"My dear aunt, not so much as that comes to!" he protested with a laugh and a curl of his moustache.

"You're too guilty then!"

He continued all thoughtfully to finger the ornament in question. "You won't let the poor girl know you then?" he asked at last.

"Is it literally true that she's going to the Château de Chillon with you?"

"I've no doubt she fully intends it."

"Then, my dear Frederick," said Mrs. Costello, "I must decline the honour of her acquaintance. I'm an old woman, but I'm not too old—thank heaven—to be honestly shocked!"

"But don't they all do these things—the little American girls at home?" Winterbourne enquired.

Mrs. Costello stared a moment. "I should like to see my granddaughters do them!" she then grimly returned.

This seemed to throw some light on the matter, for Winterbourne remembered to have heard his pretty cousins in New York, the daughters of this lady's two daughters, called "tremendous flirts." If therefore Miss Daisy Miller exceeded the liberal licence allowed to these young women it was probable she did go even by the American allowance rather far. Winterbourne was impatient to see her again, and it vexed, it even a little humiliated him, that he should n't by instinct appreciate her justly.

Though so impatient to see her again he hardly knew what ground he should give for his aunt's refusal to become acquainted with her; but he discovered promptly enough that with Miss Daisy Miller there was no great need of walking on tiptoe. He found her that evening in the garden, wandering about in the warm starlight after the manner of an indolent sylph and swinging to and fro the largest fan he had ever beheld. It was ten o'clock. He had dined with his aunt, had been sitting with her since dinner, and had just taken leave of her till the morrow. His young friend frankly rejoiced to renew their intercourse; she pronounced it the stupidest evening she had ever passed.

"Have you been all alone?" he asked with no intention of an epigram and no effect of her perceiving one.

"I've been walking round with mother. But mother gets tired walking round," Miss Miller explained.

"Has she gone to bed?"

"No, she does n't like to go to bed. She does n't sleep scarcely any—not three hours. She says she does n't know how she lives. She's dreadfully nervous. I guess she sleeps more than she thinks. She's gone somewhere after Randolph; she wants to try to get him to go to bed. He does n't like to go to bed."

The soft impartiality of her *constatations*,[18] as Winterbourne would have termed them, was a thing by itself—exquisite little fatalist as they seemed to make her. "Let us hope she'll persuade him," he encouragingly said.

"Well, she'll talk to him all she can—but he does n't like her to talk to him": with which Miss Daisy opened and closed her fan. "She's going to try to get Eugenio to talk to him. But Randolph ain't afraid of Eugenio. Eugenio's a splendid courier, but he can't make much impression on Randolph! I don't believe he'll go to bed before eleven." Her detachment from any invidious judgement of this was, to her companion's sense, inimitable; and it appeared that Randolph's vigil was in fact triumphantly prolonged, for Winterbourne attended her in her stroll for some time without meeting her mother. "I've been looking round for that lady you want to introduce me to," she resumed—"I guess she's your aunt." Then on his admitting the fact and expressing some curiosity as to how she had learned it, she said she had heard all about Mrs. Costello from the chambermaid. She was very quiet and very *comme il faut*;[19] she wore white puffs; she spoke to no one and she never dined at the common table. Every two days she had a headache. "I think that's a lovely description, headache and all!" said Miss Daisy, chattering along in her thin gay voice. "I want to know her ever so much. I know just what *your* aunt would be; I know I'd like her. She'd be very exclusive. I like a lady to be exclusive; I'm dying to be exclusive myself. Well, I guess we *are* exclusive, mother and I. We don't speak to any one—or they don't speak to us. I suppose it's about the same thing. Anyway, I shall be ever so glad to meet your aunt."

[18] French: "matter-of-fact conclusions."
[19] Attentive to the proprieties.

Winterbourne was embarrassed—he could but trump up some evasion. "She'd be most happy, but I'm afraid those tiresome headaches are always to be reckoned with."

The girl looked at him through the fine dusk. "Well, I suppose she does n't have a headache every day."

He had to make the best of it. "She tells me she wonderfully does." He did n't know what else to say.

Miss Miller stopped and stood looking at him. Her prettiness was still visible in the darkness; she kept flapping to and fro her enormous fan. "She does n't want to know me!" she then lightly broke out. "Why don't you say so? You need n't be afraid. *I'm* not afraid!" And she quite crowed for the fun of it.

Winterbourne distinguished however a wee false note in this: he was touched, shocked, mortified by it. "My dear young lady, she knows no one. She goes through life immured. It's her wretched health."

The young girl walked on a few steps in the glee of the thing. "You need n't be afraid," she repeated. "Why should she want to know me?" Then she paused again; she was close to the parapet of the garden, and in front of her was the starlit lake. There was a vague sheen on its surface, and in the distance were dimly-seen mountain forms. Daisy Miller looked out at these great lights and shades and again proclaimed a gay in-difference—"Gracious! she *is* exclusive!" Winterbourne wondered if she were seriously wounded and for a moment almost wished her sense of injury might be such as to make it becoming in him to reassure and comfort her. He had a pleasant sense that she would be all accessible to a respectful tenderness at that moment. He felt quite ready to sacri-fice his aunt—conversationally; to acknowledge she was a proud rude woman and to make the point that they need n't mind her. But before he had time to commit himself to this questionable mixture of gallantry and impiety, the young lady, resuming her walk, gave an exclamation in quite another tone. "Well, here's mother! I guess she *has n't* got Randolph to go to bed." The figure of a lady appeared, at a distance, very indis-tinct in the darkness; it advanced with a slow and wavering step and then suddenly seemed to pause.

"Are you sure it's your mother? Can you make her out in this thick dusk?" Winter-bourne asked.

"Well," the girl laughed, "I guess I know my own mother! And when she has got on my shawl too. She's always wearing my things."

The lady in question, ceasing now to approach, hovered vaguely about the spot at which she had checked her steps.

"I'm afraid your mother does n't see you," said Winterbourne. "Or perhaps," he added—thinking, with Miss Miller, the joke permissible—"perhaps she feels guilty about your shawl."

"Oh it's a fearful old thing!" his companion placidly answered. "I told her she could wear it if she did n't mind looking like a fright. She won't come here because she sees you."

"Ah then," said Winterbourne, "I had better leave you."

"Oh no—come on!" the girl insisted.

"I'm afraid your mother does n't approve of my walking with you."

She gave him, he thought, the oddest glance. "It is n't for me; it's for you—that is it's for *her*. Well, I don't know who it's for! But mother does n't like any of my gentlemen friends. She's right down timid. She always makes a fuss if I introduce a gentleman. But I *do* introduce them—almost always. If I did n't introduce my gentlemen friends to mother," Miss Miller added, in her small flat monotone, "I should n't think I was natural."

"Well, to introduce me," Winterbourne remarked, "you must know my name." And he proceeded to pronounce it.

"Oh my—I can't say all that!" cried his companion, much amused. But by this time they had come up to Mrs. Miller, who, as they drew near, walked to the parapet of the garden and leaned on it, looking intently at the lake and presenting her back to them. "Mother!" said the girl in a tone of decision—upon which the elder lady turned round. "Mr. Frederick Forsyth Winterbourne," said the latter's young friend, repeating his lesson of a moment before and introducing him very frankly and prettily. "Common" she might be, as Mrs. Costello had pronounced her; yet what provision was made by that epithet for her queer little native grace?

Her mother was a small spare light person, with a wandering eye, a scarce perceptible nose, and, as to make up for it, an unmistakeable forehead, decorated—but too far back, as Winterbourne mentally described it—with thin much-frizzled hair. Like her daughter Mrs. Miller was dressed with extreme elegance; she had enormous diamonds in her ears. So far as the young man could observe, she gave him no greeting—she certainly was n't looking at him. Daisy was near her, pulling her shawl straight. "What are you doing, poking round here?" this young lady enquired—yet by no means with the harshness of accent her choice of words might have implied.

"Well, I don't know"—and the new-comer turned to the lake again.

"I should n't think you'd want that shawl!" Daisy familiarly proceeded.

"Well—I do!" her mother answered with a sound that partook for Winterbourne of an odd strain between mirth and woe.

"Did you get Randolph to go to bed?" Daisy asked.

"No, I could n't induce him"—and Mrs. Miller seemed to confess to the same mild fatalism as her daughter. "He wants to talk to the waiter. He *likes* to talk to that waiter."

"I was just telling Mr. Winterbourne," the girl went on; and to the young man's ear her tone might have indicated that she had been uttering his name all her life.

"Oh yes!" he concurred—"I've the pleasure of knowing your son."

Randolph's mamma was silent; she kept her attention on the lake. But at last a sigh broke from her. "Well, I don't see how he lives!"

"Anyhow, it is n't so bad as it was at Dover,"[20] Daisy at least opined.

"And what occurred at Dover?" Winterbourne desired to know.

"He would n't go to bed at all. I guess he sat up all night—in the public parlour. He was n't in bed at twelve o'clock: it seemed as if he could n't budge."

"It was half-past twelve when *I* gave up," Mrs. Miller recorded with passionless accuracy.

It was of great interest to Winterbourne. "Does he sleep much during the day?"

"I guess he does n't sleep *very* much," Daisy rejoined.

"I wish he just *would!*" said her mother. "It seems as if he *must* make it up somehow."

"Well, I guess it's we that make it up. I think he's real tiresome," Daisy pursued.

---

[20] Town on the English side of the Channel.

After which, for some moments, there was silence. "Well, Daisy Miller," the elder lady then unexpectedly broke out, "I should n't think you'd want to talk against your own brother!"

"Well, he *is* tiresome, mother," said the girl, but with no sharpness of insistence.

"Well, he's only nine," Mrs. Miller lucidly urged.

"Well, he would n't go up to that castle, anyway," her daughter replied as for accommodation. "I'm going up there with Mr. Winterbourne."

To this announcement, very placidly made, Daisy's parent offered no response. Winterbourne took for granted on this that she opposed such a course; but he said to himself at the same time that she was a simple easily-managed person and that a few deferential protestations would modify her attitude. "Yes," he therefore interposed, "your daughter has kindly allowed me the honour of being her guide."

Mrs. Miller's wandering eyes attached themselves with an appealing air to her other companion, who, however, strolled a few steps further, gently humming to herself. "I presume you'll go in the cars," she then quite colourlessly remarked.

"Yes, or in the boat," said Winterbourne.

"Well, of course I don't know," Mrs. Miller returned. "I've never been up to that castle."

"It is a pity you should n't go," he observed, beginning to feel reassured as to her opposition. And yet he was quite prepared to find that as a matter of course she meant to accompany her daughter.

It was on this view accordingly that light was projected for him. "We've been thinking ever so much about going, but it seems as if we could n't. Of course Daisy—she wants to go round everywhere. But there's a lady here—I don't know her name—she says she should n't think we'd want to go to see castles *here;* she should think we'd want to wait till we got t' Italy. It seems as if there would be so many there," continued Mrs. Miller with an air of increasing confidence. "Of course we only want to see the principal ones. We visited several in England," she presently added.

"Ah yes, in England there are beautiful castles," said Winterbourne. "But Chillon here is very well worth seeing."

"Well, if Daisy feels up to it—" said Mrs. Miller in a tone that seemed to break under the burden of such conceptions. "It seems as if there's nothing she won't undertake."

"Oh I'm pretty sure she'll enjoy it!" Winterbourne declared. And he desired more and more to make it a certainty that he was to have the privilege of a *tête-à-tête*[21] with the young lady who was still strolling along in front of them and softly vocalising. "You're not disposed, madam," he enquired, "to make the so interesting excursion yourself?"

So addressed Daisy's mother looked at him an instant with a certain scared obliquity and then walked forward in silence. Then, "I guess she had better go alone," she said simply.

It gave him occasion to note that this was a very different type of maternity from that of the vigilant matrons who massed themselves in the forefront of social intercourse in the dark old city at the other end of the lake. But his meditations were interrupted by hearing his name very distinctly pronounced by Mrs. Miller's unprotected daughter. "Mr. Winterbourne!" she piped from a considerable distance.

---

[21] Intimate conversation.

"Mademoiselle!" said the young man.

"Don't you want to take me out in a boat?"

"At present?" he asked.

"Why of course!" she gaily returned.

"Well, Annie Miller!" exclaimed her mother.

"I beg you, madam, to let her go," he hereupon eagerly pleaded; so instantly had he been struck with the romantic side of this chance to guide through the summer starlight a skiff freighted with a fresh and beautiful young girl.

"I should n't think she'd want to," said her mother. "I should think she'd rather go indoors."

"I'm sure Mr. Winterbourne wants to *take* me," Daisy declared. "He's so awfully devoted!"

"I'll row you over to Chillon under the stars."

"I don't believe it!" Daisy laughed.

"Well!" the elder lady again gasped, as in rebuke of this freedom.

"You haven't spoken to me for half an hour," her daughter went on.

"I've been having some very pleasant conversation with your mother," Winterbourne replied.

"Oh pshaw! I want you to take me out in a boat!" Daisy went on as if nothing else had been said. They had all stopped and she had turned round and was looking at her friend. Her face wore a charming smile, her pretty eyes gleamed in the darkness, she swung her great fan about. No, he felt, it was impossible to be prettier than that.

"There are half a dozen boats moored at that landing-place," and he pointed to a range of steps that descended from the garden to the lake. "If you'll do me the honour to accept my arm we'll go and select one of them."

She stood there smiling; she threw back her head; she laughed as for the drollery of this. "I like a gentleman to be formal!"

"I assure you it's a formal offer."

"I was bound I'd make you say something," Daisy agreeably mocked.

"You see it's not very difficult," said Winterbourne. "But I'm afraid you're chaffing me."

"I think not, sir," Mrs. Miller shyly pleaded.

"Do then let me give you a row," he persisted to Daisy.

"It's quite lovely, the way you say that!" she cried in reward.

"It will be still more lovely to do it."

"Yes, it would be lovely!" But she made no movement to accompany him; she only remained an elegant image of free light irony.

"I guess you'd better find out what time it is," her mother impartially contributed.

"It's eleven o'clock, Madam," said a voice with a foreign accent out of the neighbouring darkness; and Winterbourne, turning, recognised the florid personage he had already seen in attendance. He had apparently just approached.

"Oh Eugenio," said Daisy, "I'm going out with Mr. Winterbourne in a boat!"

Eugenio bowed. "At this hour of the night, Mademoiselle?"

"I'm going with Mr. Winterbourne," she repeated with her shining smile. "I'm going this very minute."

"Do tell her she can't, Eugenio," Mrs. Miller said to the courier.

"I think you had better not go out in a boat, Mademoiselle," the man declared.

Winterbourne wished to goodness this pretty girl were not on such familiar terms with her courier; but he said nothing, and she meanwhile added to his ground. "I suppose you don't think it's proper! My!" she wailed; "Eugenio does n't think anything's proper."

"I'm nevertheless quite at your service," Winterbourne hastened to remark.

"Does Mademoiselle propose to go alone?" Eugenio asked of Mrs. Miller.

"Oh no, with this gentleman!" cried Daisy's mamma for reassurance.

"I *meant* alone with the gentleman." The courier looked for a moment at Winterbourne—the latter seemed to make out in his face a vague presumptuous intelligence as at the expense of their companions—and then solemnly and with a bow, "As Mademoiselle pleases!" he said.

But Daisy broke off at this. "Oh I hoped you'd make a fuss! I don't care to go now."

"Ah but I myself shall make a fuss if you don't go," Winterbourne declared with spirit.

"That's all I want—a little fuss!" With which she began to laugh again.

"Mr. Randolph has retired for the night!" the courier hereupon importantly announced.

"Oh Daisy, now we can go then!" cried Mrs. Miller.

Her daughter turned away from their friend, all lighted with her odd perversity. "Good-night—I hope you're disappointed or disgusted or something!"

He looked at her gravely, taking her by the hand she offered. "I'm puzzled, if you want to know!" he answered.

"Well, I hope it won't keep you awake!" she said very smartly; and, under the escort of the privileged Eugenio, the two ladies passed toward the house.

Winterbourne's eyes followed them; he was indeed quite mystified. He lingered beside the lake a quarter of an hour, baffled by the question of the girl's sudden familiarities and caprices. But the only very definite conclusion he came to was that he should enjoy deucedly "going off" with her somewhere.

Two days later he went off with her to the Castle of Chillon. He waited for her in the large hall of the hotel, where the couriers, the servants, the foreign tourists were lounging about and staring. It was n't the place he would have chosen for a tryst, but she had placidly appointed it. She came tripping downstairs, buttoning her long gloves, squeezing her folded parasol against her pretty figure, dressed exactly in the way that consorted best, to his fancy, with their adventure. He was a man of imagination and, as our ancestors used to say, of sensibility;[22] as he took in her charming air and caught from the great staircase her impatient confiding step the note of some small sweet strain of romance, not intense but clear and sweet, seemed to sound for their start. He could have believed he was *really* going "off" with her. He led her out through all the idle people assembled—they all looked at her straight and hard: she had begun to chatter as soon as she joined him. His preference had been that they should be conveyed to Chillon in a carriage, but she expressed a lively wish to go in the little steamer—there would be such a lovely breeze upon the water and they should see such lots of people. The sail was n't long, but Winterbourne's companion found time for many characteristic remarks and other demonstrations, not a few of which were, from the extremity of their candour, slightly disconcerting. To the young man himself their small excursion showed so for delightfully irregular and incongruously intimate that, even allowing for her habitual sense of freedom, he had some expectation of seeing her appear to find in it

22 Sensitive responses.

the same savour. But it must be confessed that he was in this particular rather disappointed. Miss Miller was highly animated, she was in the brightest spirits; but she was clearly not at all in a nervous flutter—as she should have been to match *his* tension; she avoided neither his eyes nor those of any one else; she neither coloured from an awkward consciousness when she looked at him nor when she saw that people were looking at herself. People continued to look at her a great deal, and Winterbourne could at least take pleasure in his pretty companion's distinguished air. He had been privately afraid she would talk loud, laugh overmuch, and even perhaps desire to move extravagantly about the boat. But he quite forgot his fears; he sat smiling with his eyes on her face while, without stirring from her place, she delivered herself of a great number of original reflexions. It was the most charming innocent prattle he had ever heard, for, by his own experience hitherto, when young persons were so ingenuous they were less articulate and when they were so confident were more sophisticated. If he had assented to the idea that she was "common," at any rate, *was* she proving so, after all, or was he simply getting used to her commonness? Her discourse was for the most part of what immediately and superficially surrounded them, but there were moments when it threw out a longer look or took a sudden straight plunge.

"What on *earth* are you solemn about?" she suddenly demanded, fixing her agreeable eyes on her friend's.

"*Am* I solemn?" he asked. "I had an idea I was grinning from ear to ear."

"You look as if you were taking me to a prayer-meeting or a funeral. If that's a grin your ears are very near together."

"Should you like me to dance a hornpipe on the deck?"

"Pray do, and I'll carry round your hat. It will pay the expenses of our journey."

"I never was better pleased in my life," Winterbourne returned.

She looked at him a moment, then let it renew her amusement. "I like to make you say those things. You're a queer mixture!"

In the castle, after they had landed, nothing could exceed the light independence of her humour. She tripped about the vaulted chambers, rustled her skirts in the corkscrew staircases, flirted back with a pretty little cry and a shudder from the edge of the oubliettes[23] and turned a singularly well-shaped ear to everything Winterbourne told her about the place. But he saw she cared little for mediæval history and that the grim ghosts of Chillon loomed but faintly before her. They had the good fortune to have been able to wander without other society than that of their guide; and Winterbourne arranged with this companion that they should n't be hurried—that they should linger and pause wherever they chose. He interpreted the bargain generously—Winterbourne on his side had been generous—and ended by leaving them quite to themselves. Miss Miller's observations were marked by no logical consistency; for anything she wanted to say she was sure to find a pretext. She found a great many, in the tortuous passages and rugged embrasures of the place, for asking her young man sudden questions about himself, his family, his previous history, his tastes, his habits, his designs, and for supplying information on corresponding points in her own situation. Of her own tastes, habits and designs the charming creature was prepared to give the most definite and indeed the most favourable account.

---

[23] Dungeon cells set below ground level with
   barred openings across the top.

"Well, I hope you know enough!" she exclaimed after Winterbourne had sketched for her something of the story of the unhappy Bonnivard.[24] "I never saw a man that knew so much!" The history of Bonnivard had evidently, as they say, gone into one ear and out of the other. But this easy erudition struck her none the less as wonderful, and she was soon quite sure she wished Winterbourne would travel with them and "go round" with them: they too in that case might learn something about something. "Don't you want to come and teach Randolph?" she asked; "I guess he'd improve with a gentleman teacher." Winterbourne was certain that nothing could possibly please him so much, but that he had unfortunately other occupations. "Other occupations? I don't believe a speck of it!" she protested. "What do you mean now? You're not in business." The young man allowed that he was not in business, but he had engagements which even within a day or two would necessitate his return to Geneva. "Oh bother!" she panted, "I don't believe it!" and she began to talk about something else. But a few moments later, when he was pointing out to her the interesting design of an antique fireplace, she broke out irrelevantly: "You don't mean to say you're going back to Geneva?"

"It is a melancholy fact that I shall have to report myself there to-morrow."

She met it with a vivacity that could only flatter him. "Well, Mr. Winterbourne, I think you're horrid!"

"Oh don't say such dreadful things!" he quite sincerely pleaded—"just at the last."

"The last?" the girl cried; "I call it the very first! I've half a mind to leave you here and go straight back to the hotel alone." And for the next ten minutes she did nothing but call him horrid. Poor Winterbourne was fairly bewildered; no young lady had as yet done him the honour to be so agitated by the mention of his personal plans. His companion, after this, ceased to pay any attention to the curiosities of Chillon or the beauties of the lake; she opened fire on the special charmer in Geneva whom she appeared to have instantly taken it for granted that he was hurrying back to see. How did Miss Daisy Miller know of that agent of his fate in Geneva? Winterbourne, who denied the existence of such a person, was quite unable to discover; and he was divided between amazement of the rapidity of her induction and amusement at the directness of her criticism. She struck him afresh, in all this, as an extraordinary mixture of innocence and crudity. "Does she never allow you more than three days at a time?" Miss Miller wished ironically to know. "Does n't she give you a vacation in summer? there's no one so hard-worked but they can get leave to go off somewhere at this season. I suppose if you stay another day she'll come right after you in the boat. Do wait over till Friday and I'll go down to the landing to see her arrive!" He began at last even to feel he had been wrong to be disappointed in the temper in which his young lady had embarked. If he had missed the personal accent, the personal accent was now making its appearance. It sounded very distinctly, toward the end, in her telling him she'd stop "teasing" him if he'd promise her solemnly to come down to Rome that winter.

"That's not a difficult promise to make," he hastened to acknowledge. "My aunt has taken an apartment in Rome from January and has already asked me to come and see her."

"I don't want you to come for your aunt," said Daisy; "I want you just to come for me." And this was the only allusion he was ever to hear her make again to his invidious

---

[24] François de Bonnivard (1465?–1570), Swiss patriot held prisoner in a castle for seven years; hero of Byron's poem.

kinswoman. He promised her that at any rate he would certainly come, and after this she forbore from teasing. Winterbourne took a carriage and they drove back to Vevey in the dusk; the girl at his side, her animation a little spent, was now quite distractingly passive.

In the evening he mentioned to Mrs. Costello that he had spent the afternoon at Chillon with Miss Daisy Miller.

"The Americans—of the courier?" asked this lady.

"Ah happily the courier stayed at home."

"She went with you all alone?"

"All alone."

Mrs. Costello sniffed a little at her smelling-bottle. "And that," she exclaimed, "is the little abomination you wanted me to know!"

III

Winterbourne, who had returned to Geneva the day after his excursion to Chillon, went to Rome toward the end of January. His aunt had been established there a considerable time and he had received from her a couple of characteristic letters. "Those people you were so devoted to last summer at Vevey have turned up here, courier and all," she wrote. "They seem to have made several acquaintances, but the courier continues to be the most *intime*.[25] The young lady, however, is also very intimate with various third-rate Italians, with whom she rackets about in a way that makes much talk. Bring me that pretty novel of Cherbuliez's—'Paule Méré'[26]—and don't come later than the 23d."

Our friend would in the natural course of events, on arriving in Rome, have presently ascertained Mrs. Miller's address at the American banker's and gone to pay his compliments to Miss Daisy. "After what happened at Vevey I certainly think I may call upon them," he said to Mrs. Costello.

"If after what happens—at Vevey and everywhere—you desire to keep up the acquaintance, you're very welcome. Of course you're not squeamish—a man may know every one. Men are welcome to the privilege!"

"Pray what is it then that 'happens'—here for instance?" Winterbourne asked.

"Well, the girl tears about alone with her unmistakeably low foreigners. As to what happens further you must apply elsewhere for information. She has picked up half a dozen of the regular Roman fortune-hunters of the inferior sort and she takes them about to such houses as she may put *her* nose into. When she comes to a party—such a party as she can come to—she brings with her a gentleman with a good deal of manner and a wonderful moustache."

"And where's the mother?"

"I have n't the least idea. They're very dreadful people."

Winterbourne thought them over in these new lights. "They're very ignorant—very innocent only, and utterly uncivilised. Depend on it they're not 'bad.' "

"They're hopelessly vulgar," said Mrs. Costello. "Whether or no being hopelessly vulgar is being 'bad' is a question for the metaphysicians. They're bad enough to blush for, at any rate; and for this short life that's quite enough."

The news that his little friend the child of nature of the Swiss lakeside was now surrounded by half a dozen wonderful moustaches checked Winterbourne's impulse to go

[25] French: "intimate."
[26] Novel by Victor Cherbuliez (1829–1899), published in 1864.

straightway to see her. He had perhaps not definitely flattered himself that he had made an ineffaceable impression upon her heart, but he was annoyed at hearing of a state of affairs so little in harmony with an image that had lately flitted in and out of his own meditations; the image of a very pretty girl looking out of an old Roman window and asking herself urgently when Mr. Winterbourne would arrive. If, however, he determined to wait a little before reminding this young lady of his claim to her faithful remembrance, he called with more promptitude on two or three other friends. One of these friends was an American lady who had spent several winters at Geneva, where she had placed her children at school. She was a very accomplished woman and she lived in Via Gregoriana.[27] Winterbourne found her in a little crimson drawing-room on a third floor; the room was filled with southern sunshine. He had n't been there ten minutes when the servant, appearing in the doorway, announced complacently "Madame Mila!" This announcement was presently followed by the entrance of little Randolph Miller, who stopped in the middle of the room and stood staring at Winterbourne. An instant later his pretty sister crossed the threshold; and then, after a considerable interval, the parent of the pair slowly advanced.

"I guess I know you!" Randolph broke ground without delay.

"I'm sure you know a great many things"—and his old friend clutched him all interestedly by the arm. "How's your education coming on?"

Daisy was engaged in some pretty babble with her hostess, but when she heard Winterbourne's voice she quickly turned her head with a "Well, I declare!" which he met smiling. "I told you I should come, you know."

"Well, I did n't believe it," she answered.

"I'm much obliged to you for that," laughed the young man.

"You might have come to see me then," Daisy went on as if they had parted the week before.

"I arrived only yesterday."

"I don't believe any such thing!" the girl declared afresh.

Winterbourne turned with a protesting smile to her mother, but this lady evaded his glance and, seating herself, fixed her eyes on her son. "We've got a bigger place than this," Randolph hereupon broke out. "It's all gold on the walls."

Mrs. Miller, more of a fatalist apparently than ever, turned uneasily in her chair. "I told you if I was to bring you you'd say something!" she stated as for the benefit of such of the company as might hear it.

"I told *you*!" Randolph retorted. "I tell *you*, sir!" he added jocosely, giving Winterbourne a thump on the knee. "It *is* bigger too!"

As Daisy's conversation with her hostess still occupied her Winterbourne judged it becoming to address a few words to her mother—such as "I hope you've been well since we parted at Vevey."

Mrs. Miller now certainly looked at him—at his chin. "Not very well, sir," she answered.

"She's got the dyspepsia," said Randolph. "I've got it too. Father's got it bad. But I've got it worst!"

This proclamation, instead of embarrassing Mrs. Miller, seemed to soothe her by reconstituting the environment to which she was most accustomed. "I suffer from the

27 Avenue in Rome.

liver," she amiably whined to Winterbourne. "I think it's this climate; it's less bracing than Schenectady, especially in the winter season. I don't know whether you know we reside at Schenectady. I was saying to Daisy that I certainly had n't found any one like Dr. Davis and I did n't believe I *would.* Oh up in Schenectady, he stands first; they think everything of Dr. Davis. He has so much to do, and yet there was nothing he would n't do for *me.* He said he never saw anything like my dyspepsia, but he was bound to get at it. I'm sure there was nothing he would n't try, and I did n't care what he did to me if he only brought me relief. He was just going to try something new, and I just longed for it, when we came right off. Mr. Miller felt as if he wanted Daisy to see Europe for herself. But I could n't help writing the other day that I supposed it was all right for Daisy, but that I did n't know as I *could* get on much longer without Dr. Davis. At Schenectady he stands at the very top; and there's a great deal of sickness there too. It affects my sleep."

Winterbourne had a good deal of pathological gossip with Dr. Davis's patient, during which Daisy chattered unremittingly to her own companion. The young man asked Mrs. Miller how she was pleased with Rome. "Well, I say I'm disappointed," she confessed. "We had heard so much about it—I suppose we had heard too much. But we could n't help that. We had been led to expect something different."

Winterbourne, however, abounded in reassurance. "Ah wait a little, and you'll grow very fond of it."

"I hate it worse and worse every day!" cried Randolph.

"You're like the infant Hannibal,"[28] his friend laughed.

"No I ain't—like any infant!" Randolph declared at a venture.

"Well, that's so—and you never *were!*" his mother concurred. "But we've seen places," she resumed, "that I'd put a long way ahead of Rome." And in reply to Winterbourne's interrogation, "There's Zürich—up there in the mountains," she instanced; "I think Zürich's real lovely, and we had n't heard half so much about it."

"The best place we've seen's the *City of Richmond!*" said Randolph.

"He means the ship," Mrs. Miller explained. "We crossed in that ship. Randolph had a good time on the *City of Richmond.*"

"It's the best place *I've* struck," the child repeated. "Only it was turned the wrong way."

"Well, we've got to turn the right way sometime," said Mrs. Miller with strained but weak optimism. Winterbourne expressed the hope that her daughter at least appreciated the so various interest of Rome, and she declared with some spirit that Daisy was quite carried away. "It's on account of the society—the society's splendid. She goes round everywhere; she has made a great number of acquaintances. Of course she goes round more than I do. I must say they've all been very sweet—they've taken her right in. And then she knows a great many gentlemen. Oh she thinks there's nothing like Rome. Of course it's a great deal pleasanter for a young lady if she knows plenty of gentlemen."

By this time Daisy had turned her attention again to Winterbourne, but in quite the same free form. "I've been telling Mrs. Walker how mean you were!"

"And what's the evidence you've offered?" he asked, a trifle disconcerted, for all his superior gallantry, by her inadequate measure of the zeal of an admirer who on his way down to Rome had stopped neither at Bologna nor at Florence, simply because of a certain sweet appeal to his fond fancy, not to say to his finest curiosity. He remembered

[28] Carthaginian general (243–183? B.C.), who
   bore a hatred of Rome from childhood on.

how a cynical compatriot had once told him that American women—the pretty ones, and this gave a largeness to the axiom—were at once the most exacting in the world and the least endowed with a sense of indebtedness.

"Why you were awfully mean up at Vevey," Daisy said. "You would n't do most anything. You would n't stay there when I asked you."

"Dearest young lady," cried Winterbourne, with generous passion, "have I come all the way to Rome only to be riddled by your silver shafts?"

"Just hear him say that!"—and she gave an affectionate twist to a bow on her hostess's dress. "Did you ever hear anything so quaint?"

"So 'quaint,' my dear?" echoed Mrs. Walker more critically—quite in the tone of a partisan of Winterbourne.

"Well, I don't know"—and the girl continued to finger her ribbons. "Mrs. Walker, I want to tell you something."

"Say, mother-r," broke in Randolph with his rough ends to his words, "I tell you you've got to go. Eugenio'll raise something!"

"I'm not afraid of Eugenio," said Daisy with a toss of her head. "Look here, Mrs. Walker," she went on, "you know I'm coming to your party."

"I'm delighted to hear it."

"I've got a lovely dress."

"I'm very sure of that."

"But I want to ask a favour—permission to bring a friend."

"I shall be happy to see any of your friends," said Mrs. Walker, who turned with a smile to Mrs. Miller.

"Oh they're not my friends," cried that lady, squirming in shy repudiation. "It seems as if they did n't take to *me*—I never spoke to one of them!"

"It's an intimate friend of mine, Mr. Giovanelli," Daisy pursued without a tremor in her young clearness or a shadow on her shining bloom.

Mrs. Walker had a pause and gave a rapid glance at Winterbourne. "I shall be glad to see Mr. Giovanelli," she then returned.

"He's just the finest kind of Italian," Daisy pursued with the prettiest serenity. "He's a great friend of mine and the handsomest man in the world—except Mr. Winterbourne! He knows plenty of Italians, but he wants to know some Americans. It seems as if he was crazy about Americans. He's tremendously bright. He's perfectly lovely!"

It was settled that this paragon should be brought to Mrs. Walker's party, and then Mrs. Miller prepared to take her leave. "I guess we'll go right back to the hotel," she remarked with a confessed failure of the larger imagination.

"You may go back to the hotel, mother," Daisy replied, "but I'm just going to walk round."

"She's going to go it with Mr. Giovanelli," Randolph unscrupulously commented.

"I'm going to go it on the Pincio,"[29] Daisy peaceably smiled, while the way that she "condoned" these things almost melted Winterbourne's heart.

"Alone, my dear—at this hour?" Mrs. Walker asked. The afternoon was drawing to a close—it was the hour for the throng of carriages and of contemplative pedestrians. "I don't consider it's safe, Daisy," her hostess firmly asserted.

---

[29] Roman hill with a panoramic vista.

"Neither do I then," Mrs. Miller thus borrowed confidence to add. "You'll catch the fever as sure as you live. Remember what Dr. Davis told you!"

"Give her some of that medicine before she starts in," Randolph suggested.

The company had risen to its feet; Daisy, still showing her pretty teeth, bent over and kissed her hostess. "Mrs. Walker, you're too perfect," she simply said. "I'm not going alone; I'm going to meet a friend."

"Your friend won't keep you from catching the fever even if it *is* his own second nature," Mrs. Miller observed.

"Is it Mr. Giovanelli that's the dangerous attraction?" Mrs. Walker asked without mercy.

Winterbourne was watching the challenged girl; at this question his attention quickened. She stood there smiling and smoothing her bonnet-ribbons; she glanced at Winterbourne. Then, while she glanced and smiled, she brought out all affirmatively and without a shade of hesitation: "Mr. Giovanelli—the beautiful Giovanelli."

"My dear young friend"—and, taking her hand, Mrs. Walker turned to pleading—"don't prowl off to the Pincio at this hour to meet a beautiful Italian."

"Well, he speaks first-rate English," Mrs. Miller incoherently mentioned.

"Gracious me," Daisy piped up, "I don't want to do anything that's going to affect my health—or my character either! There's an easy way to settle it." Her eyes continued to play over Winterbourne. "The Pincio's only a hundred yards off, and if Mr. Winterbourne were as polite as he pretends he'd offer to walk right in with me!"

Winterbourne's politeness hastened to proclaim itself, and the girl gave him gracious leave to accompany her. They passed downstairs before her mother, and at the door he saw Mrs. Miller's carriage drawn up, with the ornamental courier whose acquaintance he had made at Vevey seated within. "Goodbye, Eugenio," cried Daisy; "I'm going to take a walk!" The distance from Via Gregoriana to the beautiful garden at the other end of the Pincian Hill is in fact rapidly traversed. As the day was splendid, however, and the concourse of vehicles, walkers and loungers numerous, the young Americans found their progress much delayed. This fact was highly agreeable to Winterbourne, in spite of his consciousness of his singular situation. The slow-moving, idly-gazing Roman crowd bestowed much attention on the extremely pretty young woman of English race who passed through it, with some difficulty, on his arm; and he wondered what on earth had been in Daisy's mind when she proposed to exhibit herself unattended to its appreciation. His own mission, to her sense, was apparently to consign her to the hands of Mr. Giovanelli; but, at once annoyed and gratified, he resolved that he would do no such thing.

"Why haven't you been to see me?" she meanwhile asked. "You can't get out of that."

"I've had the honour of telling you that I've only just stepped out of the train."

"You must have stayed in the train a good while after it stopped!" she derisively cried. "I suppose you were asleep. You've had time to go to see Mrs. Walker."

"I knew Mrs. Walker—" Winterbourne began to explain.

"I know where you knew her. You knew her at Geneva. She told me so. Well, you knew me at Vevey. That's just as good. So you ought to have come." She asked him no other question than this; she began to prattle about her own affairs. "We've got splendid rooms at the hotel; Eugenio says they're the best rooms in Rome. We're going to stay all winter—if we don't die of the fever; and I guess we'll stay then! It's a great deal nicer than I thought; I thought it would be fearfully quiet—in fact I was sure it would be deadly pokey. I foresaw we should be going round all the time with one of those dreadful old men who explain about the pictures and things. But we only had about a week of that, and now I'm enjoying myself. I know ever so many people, and they're all so charming. The society's extremely select. There are all kinds—English and Germans and Italians. I think I like the English best. I like their style of conversation. But there are some lovely Americans. I never saw anything so hospitable. There's something or other every day. There's not much dancing—but I must say I never thought dancing was everything. I was always fond of conversation. I guess I'll have plenty at Mrs. Walker's—her rooms are so small." When they had passed the gate of the Pincian Gardens Miss Miller began to wonder where Mr. Giovanelli might be. "We had better go straight to that place in front, where you look at the view."

Winterbourne at this took a stand. "I certainly shan't help you to find him."

"Then I shall find him without you," Daisy said with spirit.

"You certainly won't leave me!" he protested.

She burst into her familiar little laugh. "Are you afraid you'll get lost—or run over? But there's Giovanelli leaning against that tree. He's staring at the women in the carriages: did you ever see anything so cool?"

Winterbourne descried hereupon at some distance a little figure that stood with folded arms and nursing its cane. It had a handsome face, a hat artfully poised, a glass in one eye and a nosegay in its buttonhole. Daisy's friend looked at it a moment and then said: "Do you mean to speak to that thing?"

"Do I mean to speak to him? Why you don't suppose I mean to communicate by signs!"

"Pray understand then," the young man returned, "that I intend to remain with you."

Daisy stopped and looked at him without a sign of troubled consciousness, with nothing in her face but her charming eyes, her charming teeth and her happy dimples. "Well, she's a cool one!" he thought.

"I don't like the way you say that," she declared. "It's too imperious."

"I beg your pardon if I say it wrong. The main point's to give you an idea of my meaning."

The girl looked at him more gravely, but with eyes that were prettier than ever. "I've never allowed a gentleman to dictate to me or to interfere with anything I do."

"I think that's just where your mistake has come in," he retorted. "You should sometimes listen to a gentleman—the right one."

At this she began to laugh again. "I do nothing but listen to gentlemen! Tell me if Mr. Giovanelli is the right one."

The gentleman with the nosegay in his bosom had now made out our two friends and was approaching Miss Miller with obsequious rapidity. He bowed to Winterbourne as well as to the latter's compatriot; he seemed to shine, in his coxcombical way, with the desire to please and the fact of his own intelligent joy, though Winterbourne thought him not a bad-looking fellow. But he nevertheless said to Daisy: "No, he's not the right one."

She had clearly a natural turn for free introductions: she mentioned with the easiest grace the name of each of her companions to the other. She strolled forward with one of them on either hand; Mr. Giovanelli, who spoke English very cleverly—Winterbourne afterwards learned that he had practised the idiom upon a great many American heiresses—addressed her a great deal of very polite nonsense. He had the best possible manners, and the young American, who said nothing, reflected on that depth of Italian subtlety, so strangely opposed to Anglo-Saxon simplicity, which enables people to show a smoother surface in proportion as they're more acutely displeased. Giovanelli of course had counted upon something more intimate—he had not bargained for a party of three; but he kept his temper in a manner that suggested far-stretching intentions. Winterbourne flattered himself he had taken his measure. "He's anything but a gentleman," said the young American; "he is n't even a very plausible imitation of one. He's a music-master or a penny-a-liner[30] or a third-rate artist. He's awfully on his good behaviour, but damn his fine eyes!" Mr. Giovanelli had indeed great advantages; but it was deeply disgusting to Daisy's other friend that something in her should n't have instinctively discriminated against such a type. Giovanelli chattered and jested and made himself agreeable according to his honest Roman lights. It was true that if he was an imitation the imitation was studied. "Nevertheless," Winterbourne said to himself, "a nice girl ought to know!" And then he came back to the dreadful question of whether this *was* in fact a nice girl. Would a nice girl—even allowing for her being a little American flirt—make a rendezvous with a presumbably low-lived foreigner? The rendezvous in this case indeed had been in broad daylight and in the most crowded corner of Rome; but was n't it possible to regard the choice of these very circumstances as a proof more of vulgarity than of anything else? Singular though it may seem, Winterbourne was vexed that the girl, in joining her *amoroso*,[31] should n't appear more impatient of his own company, and he was vexed precisely because of his inclination. It was impossible to regard her as a wholly unspotted flower—she lacked a certain indispensable fineness; and it would therefore much simplify the situation to be able to treat her as the subject of one of the visitations known to romancers as "lawless passions." That she should seem to wish to get rid of him would have helped him to think more lightly of her, just as to be able to think more lightly of her would have made her less perplexing. Daisy at any rate continued on this occasion to present herself as an inscrutable combination of audacity and innocence.

She had been walking some quarter of an hour, attended by her two cavaliers and responding in a tone of very childish gaiety, as it after all struck one of them, to the pretty speeches of the other, when a carriage that had detached itself from the revolving train drew up beside the path. At the same moment Winterbourne noticed that his friend Mrs. Walker—the lady whose house he had lately left—was seated in the vehicle and was beckoning to him. Leaving Miss Miller's side, he hastened to obey her summons—and all to find her flushed, excited, scandalised. "It's really too dreadful"—she earnestly appealed to him. "That crazy girl must n't do this sort of thing. She must n't walk here with you two men. Fifty people have remarked her."

Winterbourne—suddenly and rather oddly rubbed the wrong way by this—raised his grave eyebrows. "I think it's a pity to make too much fuss about it."

"It's a pity to let the girl ruin herself!"

"She's very innocent," he reasoned in his own troubled interest.

"She's very reckless," cried Mrs. Walker, "and goodness knows how far—left to itself—it may go. Did you ever," she proceeded to enquire, "see anything so blatantly imbecile as the mother? After you had all left me just now I could n't sit still for thinking of it. It seemed too pitiful not even to attempt to save them. I ordered the carriage and put on my bonnet and came here as quickly as possible. Thank heaven I've found you!"

---

[30] Low-paid hack writer.   [31] Italian: "lover"; "admirer."

"What do you propose to do with us?" Winterbourne uncomfortably smiled.

"To ask her to get in, to drive her about here for half an hour—so that the world may see she's not running absolutely wild—and then take her safely home."

"I don't think it's a very happy thought," he said after reflexion, "but you're at liberty to try."

Mrs. Walker accordingly tried. The young man went in pursuit of their young lady who had simply nodded and smiled, from her distance, at her recent patroness in the carriage and then had gone her way with her own companion. On learning, in the event, that Mrs. Walker had followed her, she retraced her steps, however, with a perfect good grace and with Mr. Giovanelli at her side. She professed herself "enchanted" to have a chance to present this gentleman to her good friend, and immediately achieved the introduction; declaring with it, and as if it were of as little importance, that she had never in her life seen anything so lovely as that lady's carriage-rug.

"I'm glad you admire it," said her poor pursuer, smiling sweetly. "Will you get in and let me put it over you?"

"Oh no, thank you!"—Daisy knew her mind. "I'll admire it ever so much more as I see you driving round with it."

"Do get in and drive round *with* me," Mrs. Walker pleaded.

"That would be charming, but it's so fascinating just as I am!"—with which the girl radiantly took in the gentlemen on either side of her.

"It may be fascinating, dear child, but it's not the custom here," urged the lady of the victoria,[32] leaning forward in this vehicle with her hands devoutly clasped.

"Well, it ought to be then!" Daisy imperturbably laughed. "If I did n't walk I'd expire."

"You should walk with your mother, dear," cried Mrs. Walker with a loss of patience.

"With my mother dear?" the girl amusedly echoed. Winterbourne saw she scented interference. "My mother never walked ten steps in her life. And then, you know," she blandly added, "I'm more than five years old."

"You're old enough to be more reasonable. You're old enough, dear Miss Miller, to be talked about."

Daisy wondered to extravagance. "Talked about? What do you mean?"

"Come into my carriage and I'll tell you."

Daisy turned shining eyes again from one of the gentlemen beside her to the other. Mr. Giovanelli was bowing to and fro, rubbing down his gloves and laughing irresponsibly; Winterbourne thought the scene the most unpleasant possible. "I don't think I want to know what you mean," the girl presently said. "I don't think I should like it."

Winterbourne only wished Mrs. Walker would tuck up her carriage-rug and drive away; but this lady, as she afterwards told him, did n't feel she could "rest there." "Should you prefer being thought a very reckless girl?" she accordingly asked.

"Gracious me!" exclaimed Daisy. She looked again at Mr. Giovanelli, then she turned to her other companion. There was a small pink flush in her cheek; she was tremendously pretty. "Does Mr. Winterbourne think," she put to him with a wonderful bright intensity of appeal, "that—to save my reputation—I ought to get into the carriage?"

It really embarrassed him; for an instant he cast about—so strange was it to hear her speak that way of her "reputation." But he himself in fact had to speak in accordance

---

[32] Horse-drawn carriage.

with gallantry. The finest gallantry here was surely just to tell her the truth; and the truth, for our young man, as the few indications I have been able to give have made him known to the reader, was that his charming friend should listen to the voice of civilised society. He took in again her exquisite prettiness and then said the more distinctly: "I think you should get into the carriage."

Daisy gave the rein to her amusement. "I never heard anything so stiff! If this is improper, Mrs. Walker," she pursued, "then I'm *all* improper, and you had better give me right up. Good-bye; I hope you'll have a lovely ride!"—and with Mr. Giovanelli, who made a triumphantly obsequious salute, she turned away.

Mrs. Walker sat looking after her, and there were tears in Mrs. Walker's eyes. "Get in here, sir," she said to Winterbourne, indicating the place beside her. The young man answered that he felt bound to accompany Miss Miller; whereupon the lady of the victoria declared that if he refused her this favour she would never speak to him again. She was evidently wound up. He accordingly hastened to overtake Daisy and her more faithful ally, and, offering her his hand, told her that Mrs. Walker had made a stringent claim on his presence. He had expected her to answer with something rather free, something still more significant of the perversity from which the voice of society, through the lips of their distressed friend, had so earnestly endeavoured to dissuade her. But she only let her hand slip, as she scarce looked at him, through his slightly awkward grasp; while Mr. Giovanelli, to make it worse, bade him farewell with too emphatic a flourish of the hat.

Winterbourne was not in the best possible humour as he took his seat beside the author of his sacrifice. "That was not clever of you," he said candidly, as the vehicle mingled again with the throng of carriages.

"In such a case," his companion answered, "I don't want to be clever—I only want to be *true*!"

"Well, your truth has only offended the strange little creature—it has only put her off."

"It has happened very well"—Mrs. Walker accepted her work. "If she's so perfectly determined to compromise herself the sooner one knows it the better—one can act accordingly."

"I suspect she meant no great harm, you know," Winterbourne maturely opined.

"So I thought a month ago. But she has been going too far."

"What has she been doing?"

"Everything that's not done here. Flirting with any man she can pick up; sitting in corners with mysterious Italians; dancing all the evening with the same partners; receiving visits at eleven o'clock at night. Her mother melts away when the visitors come."

"But her brother," laughed Winterbourne, "sits up till two in the morning."

"He must be edified by what he sees. I'm told that at their hotel every one's talking about her and that a smile goes round among the servants when a gentleman comes and asks for Miss Miller."

"Ah we need n't mind the servants!" Winterbourne compassionately signified. "The poor girl's only fault," he presently added, "is her complete lack of education."

"She's naturally indelicate," Mrs. Walker, on her side, reasoned. "Take that example this morning. How long had you known her at Vevey?"

"A couple of days."

"Imagine then the taste of her making it a personal matter that you should have left the place!"

He agreed that taste was n't the strong point of the Millers—after which he was silent for some moments; but only at last to add: "I suspect, Mrs. Walker, that you and I have lived too long at Geneva!" And he further noted that he should be glad to learn with what particular design she had made him enter her carriage.

"I wanted to enjoin on you the importance of your ceasing your relations with Miss Miller; that of your not appearing to flirt with her; that of your giving her no further opportunity to expose herself; that of your in short letting her alone."

"I'm afraid I can't do anything quite so enlightened as *that*," he returned. "I like her awfully, you know."

"All the more reason you should n't help her to make a scandal."

"Well, there shall be nothing scandalous in my attentions to her," he was willing to promise.

"There certainly will be in the way she takes them. But I've said what I had on my conscience," Mrs. Walker pursued. "If you wish to rejoin the young lady I'll put you down. Here, by the way, you have a chance."

The carriage was engaged in that part of the Pincian drive which overhangs the wall of Rome and overlooks the beautiful Villa Borghese.[33] It is bordered by a large parapet, near which are several seats. One of these, at a distance, was occupied by a gentleman and a lady, toward whom Mrs. Walker gave a toss of her head. At the same moment these persons rose and walked to the parapet. Winterbourne had asked the coachman to stop; he now descended from the carriage. His companion looked at him a moment in silence and then, while he raised his hat, drove majestically away. He stood where he had alighted; he had turned his eyes toward Daisy and her cavalier. They evidently saw no one; they were too deeply occupied with each other. When they reached the low garden-wall they remained a little looking off at the great flat-topped pine-clusters of Villa Borghese; then the girl's attendant admirer seated himself familiarly on the broad ledge of the wall. The western sun in the opposite sky sent out a brilliant shaft through a couple of cloud-bars; whereupon the gallant Giovanelli took her parasol out of her hands and opened it. She came a little nearer and he held the parasol over her; then, still holding it, he let it so rest on her shoulder that both of their heads were hidden from Winterbourne. This young man stayed but a moment longer; then he began to walk. But he walked—not toward the couple united beneath the parasol, rather toward the residence of his aunt Mrs. Costello.

IV

He flattered himself on the following day that there was no smiling among the servants when he at least asked for Mrs. Miller at her hotel. This lady and her daughter, however, were not at home; and on the next day after, repeating his visit, Winterbourne again was met by a denial. Mrs. Walker's party took place on the evening of the third day, and

[33] Former summer palace of the Borghese family and now a museum, located in a public park.

in spite of the final reserves that had marked his last interview with that social critic our young man was among the guests. Mrs. Walker was one of those pilgrims from the younger world who, while in contact with the elder, make a point, in their own phrase, of studying European society; and she had on this occasion collected several specimens of diversely-born humanity to serve, as might be, for text-books. When Winterbourne arrived the little person he desired most to find was n't there; but in a few moments he saw Mrs. Miller come in alone, very shyly and ruefully. This lady's hair, above the dead waste of her temples, was more frizzled than ever. As she approached their hostess Winterbourne also drew near.

"You see I've come all alone," said Daisy's unsupported parent. "I'm so frightened I don't know what to do; it's the first time I've ever been to a party alone—especially in this country. I wanted to bring Randolph or Eugenio or some one, but Daisy just pushed me off by myself. I ain't used to going round alone."

"And does n't your daughter intend to favour us with her society?" Mrs. Walker impressively enquired.

"Well, Daisy's all dressed," Mrs. Miller testified with that accent of the dispassionate, if not of the philosophic, historian with which she always recorded the current incidents of her daughter's career. "She got dressed on purpose before dinner. But she has a friend of hers there; that gentleman—the handsomest of the Italians—that she wanted to bring. They've got going at the piano—it seems as if they could n't leave off. Mr. Giovanelli does sing splendidly. But I guess they'll come before very long," Mrs. Miller hopefully concluded.

"I'm sorry she should come—in that particular way," Mrs. Walker permitted herself to observe.

"Well, I told her there was no use in her getting dressed before dinner if she was going to wait three hours," returned Daisy's mamma. "I did n't see the use of her putting on such a dress as that to sit round with Mr. Giovanelli."

"This is most horrible!" said Mrs. Walker, turning away and addressing herself to Winterbourne. "*Elle s'affiche, la malheureuse.*[34] It's her revenge for my having ventured to remonstrate with her. When she comes I shan't speak to her."

Daisy came after eleven o'clock, but she was n't, on such an occasion, a young lady to wait to be spoken to. She rustled forward in radiant loveliness, smiling and chattering, carrying a large bouquet and attended by Mr. Giovanelli. Every one stopped talking and turned and looked at her while she floated up to Mrs. Walker. "I'm afraid you thought I never was coming, so I sent mother off to tell you. I wanted to make Mr. Giovanelli practise some things before he came; you know he sings beautifully, and I want you to ask him to sing. This is Mr. Giovanelli; you know I introduced him to you; he's got the most lovely voice and he knows the most charming set of songs. I made him go over them this evening on purpose; we had the greatest time at the hotel." Of all this Daisy delivered herself with the sweetest brightest loudest confidence, looking now at her hostess and now at all the room, while she gave a series of little pats, round her very white shoulders, to the edges of her dress. "Is there any one I know?" she as undiscourageably asked.

---

[34] French: "She's making a spectacle of herself, poor girl."

"I think every one knows you!" said Mrs. Walker as with a grand intention; and she gave a very cursory greeting to Mr. Giovanelli. This gentleman bore himself gallantly; he smiled and bowed and showed his white teeth, he curled his moustaches and rolled his eyes and performed all the proper functions of a handsome Italian at an evening party. He sang, very prettily, half a dozen songs, though Mrs. Walker afterwards declared that she had been quite unable to find out who asked him. It was apparently not Daisy who had set him in motion—this young lady being seated a distance from the piano and though she had publicly, as it were, professed herself his musical patroness or guarantor, giving herself to gay and audible discourse while he warbled.

"It's a pity these rooms are so small; we can't dance," she remarked to Winterbourne as if she had seen him five minutes before.

"I'm not sorry we can't dance," he candidly returned. "I'm incapable of a step."

"Of course you're incapable of a step," the girl assented. "I should think your legs *would* be stiff cooped in there so much of the time in that victoria."

"Well, they were very restless three days ago," he amicably laughed; "all they really wanted was to dance attendance on you."

"Oh my other friend—my friend in need—stuck to me; he seems more at one with his limbs than you are—I'll say that for him. But did you ever hear anything so cool," Daisy demanded, "as Mrs. Walker's wanting me to get into her carriage and drop poor Mr. Giovanelli, and under the pretext that it was proper? People have different ideas! It would have been most unkind; he had been talking about that walk for ten days."

"He shouldn't have talked about it at all," Winterbourne decided to make answer on this: "he would never have proposed to a young lady of this country to walk about the streets of Rome with him."

"About the streets?" she cried with her pretty stare. "Where then would he have proposed to her to walk? The Pincio ain't the streets either, I guess; and I besides, thank goodness, am not a young lady of this country. The young ladies of this country have a dreadfully pokey time of it, by what I can discover; I don't see why I should change my habits for *such* stupids."

"I'm afraid your habits are those of a ruthless flirt," said Winterbourne with studied severity.

"Of course they are!"—and she hoped, evidently, by the manner of it, to take his breath away. "I'm a fearful frightful flirt! Did you ever hear of a nice girl that wasn't? But I suppose you'll tell me now I'm not a nice girl."

He remained grave indeed under the shock of her cynical profession. "You're a very nice girl, but I wish you'd flirt with me, and me only."

"Ah thank you, thank you very much: you're the last man I should think of flirting with. As I've had the pleasure of informing you, you're too stiff."

"You say that too often," he resentfully remarked.

Daisy gave a delighted laugh. "If I could have the sweet hope of making you angry I'd say it again."

"Don't do that—when I'm angry I'm stiffer than ever. But if you won't flirt with me do cease at least to flirt with your friend at the piano. They don't," he declared as in full sympathy with "them," "understand that sort of thing here."

"I thought they understood nothing else!" Daisy cried with startling world-knowledge.

"Not in young unmarried women."

"It seems to me much more proper in young unmarried than in old married ones," she retorted.

"Well," said Winterbourne, "when you deal with natives you must go by the custom of the country. American flirting is a purely American silliness; it has—in its ineptitude of innocence—no place in *this* system. So when you show yourself in public with Mr. Giovanelli and without your mother—"

"Gracious, poor mother!"—and she made it beautifully unspeakable.

Winterbourne had a touched sense for this, but it did n't alter his attitude. "Though *you* may be flirting Mr. Giovanelli is n't—he means something else."

"He is n't preaching at any rate," she returned. "And if you want very much to know, we're neither of us flirting—not a little speck. We're too good friends for that. We're real intimate friends."

He was to continue to find her thus at moments inimitable. "Ah," he then judged, "if you're in love with each other it's another affair altogether!"

She had allowed him up to this point to speak so frankly that he had no thought of shocking her by the force of his logic; yet she now none the less immediately rose, blushing visibly and leaving him mentally to exclaim that the name of little American flirts was incoherent. "Mr. Giovanelli at least," she answered, sparing but a single small queer glance for it, a queerer small glance, he felt, than he had ever yet had from her—"Mr. Giovanelli never says to me such very disagreeable things."

It had an effect on him—he stood staring. The subject of their contention had finished singing; he left the piano, and his recognition of what—a little awkwardly—did n't take place in celebration of this might nevertheless have been an acclaimed operatic tenor's series of repeated ducks before the curtain. So he bowed himself over to Daisy. "Won't you come to the other room and have some tea?" he asked—offering Mrs. Walker's slightly thin refreshment as he might have done all the kingdoms of the earth.

Daisy at last turned on Winterbourne a more natural and calculable light. He was but the more muddled by it, however, since so inconsequent a smile made nothing clear—it seemed at the most to prove in her a sweetness and softness that reverted instinctively to the pardon of offences. "It has never occurred to Mr. Winterbourne to offer me any tea," she said with her finest little intention of torment and triumph.

"I've offered you excellent advice," the young man permitted himself to growl.

"I prefer weak tea!" cried Daisy, and she went off with the brilliant Giovanelli. She sat with him in the adjoining room, in the embrasure of the window, for the rest of the evening. There was an interesting performance at the piano, but neither of these conversers gave heed to it. When Daisy came to take leave of Mrs. Walker this lady conscientiously repaired the weakness of which she had been guilty at the moment of the girl's arrival—she turned her back straight on Miss Miller and left her to depart with what grace she might. Winterbourne happened to be near the door; he saw it all. Daisy turned very pale and looked at her mother, but Mrs. Miller was humbly unconscious of any rupture of any law or of any deviation from any custom. She appeared indeed to have felt an incongruous impulse to draw attention to her own striking conformity. "Good-night, Mrs. Walker," she said; "we've had a beautiful evening. You see if I let Daisy come to parties without me I don't want her to go away without me." Daisy turned away, looking with a small white prettiness, a blighted grace, at the circle near the door: Winterbourne saw that for the first moment she was too much shocked and puzzled even for indignation. He on his side was greatly touched.

"That was very cruel," he promptly remarked to Mrs. Walker.

But this lady's face was also as a stone. "She never enters my drawing-room again."

Since Winterbourne then, hereupon, was not to meet her in Mrs. Walker's drawing-room he went as often as possible to Mrs. Miller's hotel. The ladies were rarely at home, but when he found them the devoted Giovanelli was always present. Very often the glossy little Roman, serene in success, but not unduly presumptuous, occupied with Daisy alone the florid salon enjoyed by Eugenio's care, Mrs. Miller being apparently ever of the opinion that discretion is the better part of solicitude. Winterbourne noted, at first with surprise, that Daisy on these occasions was neither embarrassed nor annoyed by his own entrance; but he presently began to feel that she had no more surprises for him and that he really liked, after all, not making out what she was "up to." She showed no displeasure for the interruption of her *tête-à-tête* with Giovanelli; she could chatter as freshly and freely with two gentlemen as with one, and this easy flow had ever the same anomaly for her earlier friend that it was so free without availing itself of its freedom. Winterbourne reflected that if she was seriously interested in the Italian it was odd she should n't take more trouble to preserve the sanctity of their interviews, and he liked her the better for her innocent-looking indifference and her inexhaustible gaiety. He could hardly have said why, but she struck him as a young person not formed for a troublesome jealousy. Smile at such a betrayal though the reader may, it was a fact with regard to the women who had hitherto interested him that, given certain contingencies, Winterbourne could see himself afraid—literally afraid—of these ladies. It pleased him to believe that even were twenty other things different and Daisy should love him and he should know it and like it, he would still never be afraid of Daisy. It must be added that this conviction was not altogether flattering to her: it represented that she was nothing every way if not light.

But she was evidently very much interested in Giovanelli. She looked at him whenever he spoke; she was perpetually telling him to do this and to do that; she was constantly chaffing and abusing him. She appeared completely to have forgotten that her other friend had said anything to displease her at Mrs. Walker's entertainment. One Sunday afternoon, having gone to Saint Peter's with his aunt, Winterbourne became aware that the young woman held in horror by that lady was strolling about the great church under escort of her coxcomb of the Corso.[35] It amused him, after a debate, to point out the exemplary pair—even at the cost, as it proved, of Mrs. Costello's saying when she had taken them in through her eye-glass: "That's what makes you so pensive in these days, eh?"

"I had n't the least idea I was pensive," he pleaded.

"You're very much preoccupied; you're always thinking of something."

"And what is it," he asked, "that you accuse me of thinking of?"

"Of that young lady's, Miss Baker's, Miss Chandler's—what's her name?—Miss Miller's intrigue with that little barber's block."

"Do you call it an intrigue," he asked—"an affair that goes on with such peculiar publicity?"

"That's their folly," said Mrs. Costello, "it's not their merit."

[35] Roman street.

"No," he insisted with a hint perhaps of the preoccupation to which his aunt had alluded—"I don't believe there's anything to be called an intrigue."

"Well"—and Mrs. Costello dropped her glass—"I've heard a dozen people speak of it: they say she's quite carried away by him."

"They're certainly as thick as thieves," our embarrassed young man allowed.

Mrs. Costello came back to them, however, after a little; and Winterbourne recognized in this a further illustration—than that supplied by his own condition—of the spell projected by the case. "He's certainly very handsome. One easily sees how it is. She thinks him the most elegant man in the world, the finest gentleman possible. She has never seen anything like him—he's better even than the courier. It was the courier probably who introduced him, and if he succeeds in marrying the young lady the courier will come in for a magnificent commission."

"I don't believe she thinks of marrying him," Winterbourne reasoned, "and I don't believe he hopes to marry her."

"You may be very sure she thinks of nothing at all. She romps on from day to day, from hour to hour, as they did in the Golden Age. I can imagine nothing more vulgar," said Mrs. Costello, whose figure of speech scarcely went on all fours. "And at the same time," she added, "depend upon it she may tell you any moment that she is 'engaged.' "

"I think that's more than Giovanelli really expects," said Winterbourne.

"And who is Giovanelli?"

"The shiny— but, to do him justice, not greasy—little Roman. I've asked questions about him and learned something. He's apparently a perfectly respectable little man. I believe he's in a small way a *cavaliere avvocato*.[36] But he does n't move in what are called the first circles. I think it really not absolutely impossible the courier introduced him. He's evidently immensely charmed with Miss Miller. If she thinks him the finest gentleman in the world, he, on his side, has never found himself in personal contact with such splendour, such opulence, such personal daintiness, as this young lady's. And then she must seem to him wonderfully pretty and interesting. Yes, he can't really hope to pull it off. That must appear to him too impossible a piece of luck. He has nothing but his handsome face to offer, and there's a substantial, a possibly explosive Mr. Miller in that mysterious land of dollars and six-shooters. Giovanelli's but too conscious that he has n't a title to offer. If he were only a count or a *marchese*![37] What on earth can he make of the way they've taken him up?"

"He accounts for it by his handsome face and thinks Miss Miller a young lady *qui se passe ses fantaisies!*"[38]

"It's very true," Winterbourne pursued, "that Daisy and her mamma have n't yet risen to that stage of—what shall I call it—of culture, at which the idea of catching a count or a *marchese* begins. I believe them intellectually incapable of that conception."

"Ah but the *cavaliere avvocato* does n't believe them!" cried Mrs. Costello.

Of the observation excited by Daisy's "intrigue" Winterbourne gathered that day at Saint Peter's sufficient evidence. A dozen of the American colonists in Rome came to talk with his relative, who sat on a small portable stool at the base of one of the great pilasters. The vesper-service was going forward in splendid chants and organ-tones in the adjacent choir, and meanwhile, between Mrs. Costello and her friends, much was said

---

[36] Italian: "lawyer from the upper classes."
[37] Marquis; one of noble rank.

[38] French: "who submits to her caprices."

about poor little Miss Miller's going really "too far." Winterbourne was not pleased with what he heard; but when, coming out upon the great steps of the church, he saw Daisy, who had emerged before him, get into an open cab with her accomplice and roll away through the cynical streets of Rome, the measure of her course struck him as simply there to take. He felt very sorry for her—not exactly that he believed she had completely lost her wits, but because it was painful to see so much that was pretty and undefended and natural sink so low in human estimation. He made an attempt after this to give a hint to Mrs. Miller. He met one day in the Corso a friend—a tourist like himself—who had just come out of the Doria Palace, where he had been walking through the beautiful gallery. His friend "went on" for some moments about the great portrait of Innocent X, by Velasquez,[39] suspended in one of the cabinets of the palace; and then said: "And in the same cabinet, by the way, I enjoyed sight of an image of a different kind; that little American who's so much more a work of nature than of art and whom you pointed out to me last week." In answer to Winterbourne's enquiries his friend narrated that the little American—prettier now than ever—was seated with a companion in the secluded nook in which the papal presence is enshrined.

"All alone?" the young man heard himself disingenuously ask.

"Alone with a little Italian who sports in his button-hole a stack of flowers. The girl's a charming beauty, but I thought I understood from you the other day that she's a young lady *du meilleur monde*."[40]

"So she is!" said Winterbourne; and having assured himself that his informant had seen the interesting pair but ten minutes before, he jumped into a cab and went to call on Mrs. Miller. She was at home, but she apologised for receiving him in Daisy's absence.

"She's gone out somewhere with Mr. Giovanelli. She's always going round with Mr. Giovanelli."

"I've noticed they're intimate indeed," Winterbourne concurred.

"Oh it seems as if they could n't live without each other!" said Mrs. Miller. "Well, he's a real gentleman anyhow. I guess I have the joke on Daisy—that she *must* be engaged!"

"And how does your daughter *take* the joke?"

"Oh she just says she ain't. But she might as *well* be!" this philosophic parent resumed. "She goes on as if she was. But I've made Mr. Giovanelli promise to tell me if Daisy don't. I'd want to write to Mr. Miller about it—wouldn't you?"

Winterbourne replied that he certainly should; and the state of mind of Daisy's mamma struck him as so unprecedented in the annals of parental vigilance that he recoiled before the attempt to educate at a single interview either her conscience or her wit.

After this Daisy was never at home and he ceased to meet her at the houses of their common acquaintance, because, as he perceived, these shrewd people had quite made up their minds as to the length she must have gone. They ceased to invite her, intimating that they wished to make, and make strongly, for the benefit of observant Europeans, the point that though Miss Daisy Miller was a pretty American girl all right, her behaviour was n't pretty at all—was in fact regarded by her compatriots as quite monstrous. Winterbourne wondered how she felt about all the cold shoulders that were turned upon her, and sometimes found himself suspecting with impatience that she

---

[39] Diego Rodriguez de Silva y Velasquez (1599–1660), Spanish painter of the portrait of Pope Innocent X.

[40] French: "of the best society."

simply did n't feel and did n't know. He set her down as hopelessly childish and shallow, as such mere giddiness and ignorance incarnate as was powerless either to heed or to suffer. Then at other moments he could n't doubt that she carried about in her elegant and irresponsible little organism a defiant, passionate, perfectly observant consciousness of the impression she produced. He asked himself whether the defiance would come from the consciousness of innocence or from her being essentially a young person of the reckless class. Then it had to be admitted, he felt, that holding fast to a belief in her "innocence" was more and more but a matter of gallantry too fine-spun for use. As I have already had occasion to relate, he was reduced without pleasure to this chopping of logic and vexed at his poor fallibility, his want of instinctive certitude as to how far her extravagance was generic and national and how far it was crudely personal. Whatever it was he had helplessly missed her, and now it was too late. She was "carried away" by Mr. Giovanelli.

A few days after his brief interview with her mother he came across her at that supreme seat of flowering desolation known as the Palace of the Cæsars.[41] The early Roman spring had filled the air with bloom and perfume, and the rugged surface of the Palatine was muffled with tender verdure. Daisy moved at her ease over the great mounds of ruin that are embanked with mossy marble and paved with monumental inscriptions. It seemed to him he had never known Rome so lovely as just then. He looked off at the enchanting harmony of line and colour that remotely encircles the city—he inhaled the softly humid odours and felt the freshness of the year and the antiquity of the place reaffirm themselves in deep interfusion. It struck him also that Daisy had never showed to the eye for so utterly charming; but this had been his conviction on every occasion of their meeting. Giovanelli was of course at her side, and Giovanelli too glowed as never before with something of the glory of his race.

"Well," she broke out upon the friend it would have been such mockery to designate as the latter's rival, "I should think you'd be quite lonesome!"

"Lonesome?" Winterbourne resignedly echoed.

"You're always going round by yourself. Can't you get any one to walk with you?"

"I'm not so fortunate," he answered, "as your gallant companion."

Giovanelli had from the first treated him with distinguished politeness; he listened with a deferential air to his remarks; he laughed punctiliously at his pleasantries; he attached such importance as he could find terms for to Miss Miller's cold compatriot. He carried himself in no degree like a jealous wooer; he had obviously a great deal of tact; he had no objection to any one's expecting a little humility of him. It even struck Winterbourne that he almost yearned at times for some private communication in the interest of his character for common sense; a chance to remark to him as another intelligent man that, bless him, *he* knew how extraordinary was their young lady and did n't flatter himself with confident—at least *too* confident and too delusive—hopes of matrimony and dollars. On this occasion he strolled away from his charming charge to pluck a sprig of almond-blossom which he carefully arranged in his button-hole.

"I know why you say that," Daisy meanwhile observed. "Because you think I go round too much with *him!*" And she nodded at her discreet attendant.

"Every one thinks so—if you care to know," was all Winterbourne found to reply.

[41] Roman palace, now in ruins, on the Palatine Hill.

"Of course I care to know!"—she made this point with much expression. "But I don't believe a word of it. They're only pretending to be shocked. They don't really care a straw what I do. Besides, I don't go round so much."

"I think you'll find they do care. They'll show it—disagreeably," he took on himself to state.

Daisy weighed the importance of that idea. "How—disagreeably?"

"Have n't you noticed anything?" he compassionately asked.

"I've noticed *you*. But I noticed you've no more 'give' than a ramrod the first time ever I saw you."

"You'll find at least that I've more 'give' than several others," he patiently smiled.

"How shall I find it?"

"By going to see the others."

"What will they do to me?"

"They'll show you the cold shoulder. Do you know what that means?"

Daisy was looking at him intently; she began to colour. "Do you mean as Mrs. Walker did the other night?"

"Exactly as Mrs. Walker did the other night."

She looked away at Giovanelli, still titivating with his almond-blossom. Then with her attention again on the important subject: "I should n't think you'd let people be so unkind!"

"How can I help it?"

"I should think you'd want to say something."

"I do want to say something"—and Winterbourne paused a moment. "I want to say that your mother tells me she believes you engaged."

"Well, I guess she does," said Daisy very simply.

The young man began to laugh. "And does Randolph believe it?"

"I guess Randolph does n't believe anything." This testimony to Randolph's scepticism excited Winterbourne to further mirth, and he noticed that Giovanelli was coming back to them. Daisy, observing it as well, addressed herself again to her countryman. "Since you've mentioned it," she said, "I *am* engaged." He looked at her hard—he had stopped laughing. "You don't believe it!" she added.

He asked himself, and it was for a moment like testing a heart-beat; after which, "Yes, I believe it!" he said.

"Oh no, you don't," she answered. "But *if* you possibly do," she still more perversely pursued—"well, I ain't!"

Miss Miller and her constant guide were on their way to the gate of the enclosure, so that Winterbourne, who had but lately entered, presently took leave of them. A week later on he went to dine at a beautiful villa on the Cælian Hill, and, on arriving, dismissed his hired vehicle. The evening was perfect, and he promised himself the satisfaction of walking home beneath the Arch of Constantine and past the vaguely-lighted monuments of the Forum.[42] Above was a moon half-developed, whose radiance was not brilliant but veiled in a thin cloud-curtain that seemed to diffuse and equalise it. When on his return from the villa at eleven o'clock he approached the dusky circle of

[42] Remnants of ancient constructions from the
time of imperial Rome.

the Colosseum the sense of the romantic in him easily suggested that the interior, in such an atmosphere, would well repay a glance. He turned aside and walked to one of the empty arches, near which, as he observed, an open carriage—one of the little Roman street-cabs—was stationed. Then he passed in among the cavernous shadows of the great structure and emerged upon the clear and silent arena. The place had never seemed to him more impressive. One half of the gigantic circus was in deep shade while the other slept in the luminous dusk. As he stood there he began to murmur Byron's famous lines out of "Manfred";[43] but before he had finished his quotation he remembered that if nocturnal meditation thereabouts was the fruit of a rich literary culture it was none the less deprecated by medical science. The air of other ages surrounded one; but the air of other ages, coldly analysed, was no better than a villainous miasma. Winterbourne sought, however, toward the middle of the arena, a further reach of vision, intending the next moment a hasty retreat. The great cross in the centre was almost obscured; only as he drew near did he make it out distinctly. He thus also distinguished two persons stationed on the low steps that formed its base. One of these was a woman seated; her companion hovered before her.

Presently the sound of the woman's voice came to him distinctly in the warm night-air. "Well, he looks at us as one of the old lions or tigers may have looked at the Christian martyrs!" These words were winged with their accent, so that they fluttered and settled about him in the darkness like vague white doves. It was Miss Daisy Miller who had released them for flight.

"Let us hope he's not very hungry"—the bland Giovanelli fell in with her humour. "He'll have to take *me* first; you'll serve for dessert."

Winterbourne felt himself pulled up with final horror now—and, it must be added, with final relief. It was as if a sudden clearance had taken place in the ambiguity of the poor girl's appearances and the whole riddle of her contradictions had grown easy to read. She was a young lady about the *shades* of whose perversity a foolish puzzled gentleman need no longer trouble his head or his heart. That once questionable quantity *had* no shades—it was a mere black little blot. He stood there looking at her, looking at her companion too, and not reflecting that though he saw them vaguely he himself must have been more brightly presented. He felt angry at all his shiftings of view—he felt ashamed of all his tender little scruples and all his witless little mercies. He was about to advance again, and then again checked himself; not from the fear of doing her injustice, but from a sense of the danger of showing undue exhilaration for this disburdenment of cautious criticism. He turned away toward the entrance of the place; but as he did so he heard Daisy speak again.

"Why it was Mr. Winterbourne! He saw me and he cuts me dead!"

What a clever little reprobate she was, he was amply able to reflect at this, and how smartly she feigned, how promptly she sought to play off on him, a surprised and injured innocence! But nothing would induce him to cut her either "dead" or to within any measurable distance even of the famous "inch" of her life. He came forward again and went toward the great cross. Daisy had got up and Giovanelli lifted his hat. Winterbourne had now begun to think simply of the madness, on the ground of exposure and

---

[43] Lord Byron's verse drama of 1817.

infection, of a frail young creature's lounging away such hours in a nest of malaria. What if she *were* the most plausible of little reprobates? That was no reason for her dying of the *perniciosa*.[44] "How long have you been 'fooling round' here?" he asked with conscious roughness.

Daisy, lovely in the sinister silver radiance, appraised him a moment, roughness and all. "Well, I guess all the evening." She answered with spirit and, he could see even then, with exaggeration. "I never saw anything so quaint."

"I'm afraid," he returned, "you'll not think a bad attack of Roman fever very quaint. This is the way people catch it. I wonder," he added to Giovanelli, "that you, a native Roman, should countenance such extraordinary rashness."

"Ah," said this seasoned subject, "for myself I have no fear."

"Neither have I—for you!" Winterbourne retorted in French. "I'm speaking for this young lady."

Giovanelli raised his well-shaped eyebrows and showed his shining teeth, but took his critic's rebuke with docility. "I assured Mademoiselle it was a grave indiscretion, but when was Mademoiselle ever prudent?"

"I never was sick, and I don't mean to be!" Mademoiselle declared. "I don't look like much, but I'm healthy! I was bound to see the Colosseum by moonlight—I would n't have wanted to go home without *that*; and we've had the most beautiful time, have n't we, Mr. Giovanelli? If there has been any danger Eugenio can give me some pills. Eugenio has got some splendid pills."

"*I* should advise you then," said Winterbourne, "to drive home as fast as possible and take one!"

Giovanelli smiled as for the striking happy thought. "What you say is very wise. I'll go and make sure the carriage is at hand." And he went forward rapidly.

Daisy followed with Winterbourne. He tried to deny himself the small fine anguish of looking at her, but his eyes themselves refused to spare him, and she seemed moreover not in the least embarrassed. He spoke no word; Daisy chattered over the beauty of the place: "Well, I *have* seen the Colosseum by moonlight—that's one thing I can rave about!" Then noticing her companion's silence she asked him why he was so stiff—it had always been her great word. He made no answer, but he felt his laugh an immense negation of stiffness. They passed under one of the dark archways; Giovanelli was in front with the carriage. Here Daisy stopped a moment, looking at her compatriot. "*Did* you believe I was engaged the other day?"

"It does n't matter now what I believed the other day!" he replied with infinite point.

It was a wonder how she did n't wince for it. "Well, what do you believe now?"

"I believe it makes very little difference whether you're engaged or not!"

He felt her lighted eyes fairly penetrate the thick gloom of the vaulted passage—as if to seek some access to him she had n't yet compassed. But Giovanelli, with a graceful inconsequence, was at present all for retreat. "Quick, quick; if we get in by midnight we're quite safe!"

Daisy took her seat in the carriage and the fortunate Italian placed himself beside her. "Don't forget Eugenio's pills!" said Winterbourne as he lifted his hat.

[44] Malaria, known locally as "the Roman fever."

"I don't care," she unexpectedly cried out for this, "whether I have Roman fever or not!" On which the cab-driver cracked his whip and they rolled across the desultory patches of antique pavement.

Winterbourne—to do him justice, as it were—mentioned to no one that he had encountered Miss Miller at midnight in the Colosseum with a gentleman; in spite of which deep discretion, however, the fact of the scandalous adventure was known a couple of days later, with a dozen vivid details, to every member of the little American circle, and was commented accordingly. Winterbourne judged thus that the people about the hotel had been thoroughly empowered to testify, and that after Daisy's return there would have been an exchange of jokes between the porter and the cab-driver. But the young man became aware at the same moment of how thoroughly it had ceased to ruffle him that the little American flirt should be "talked about" by low-minded menials. These sources of current criticism a day or two later abounded still further: the little American flirt was alarmingly ill and the doctors now in possession of the scene. Winterbourne, when the rumour came to him, immediately went to the hotel for more news. He found that two or three charitable friends had preceded him and that they were being entertained in Mrs. Miller's salon by the all-efficient Randolph.

"It's going round at night that way, you bet—that's what has made her so sick. She's always going round at night. I should n't think she'd want to—it's so plaguey dark over here. You can't see anything over here without the moon's right up. In America they don't go round by the moon!" Mrs. Miller meanwhile wholly surrendered to her genius for unapparent uses; her salon knew her less than ever, and she was presumably now at least giving her daughter the advantage of her society. It was clear that Daisy was dangerously ill.

Winterbourne constantly attended for news from the sick-room, which reached him, however, but with worrying indirectness, though he once had speech, for a moment, of the poor girl's physician and once saw Mrs. Miller, who, sharply alarmed, struck him as thereby more happily inspired than he could have conceived and indeed as the most noiseless and light-handed of nurses. She invoked a good deal the remote shade of Dr. Davis, but Winterbourne paid her the compliment of taking her after all for less monstrous a goose. To this indulgence indeed something she further said perhaps even more insidiously disposed him. "Daisy spoke of you the other day quite pleasantly. Half the time she does n't know what she's saying, but that time I think she did. She gave me a message—she told me to tell you. She wanted you to know she never was engaged to that handsome Italian who was always round. I'm sure I'm very glad; Mr. Giovanelli has n't been near us since she was taken ill. I thought he was so much of a gentleman, but I don't call that very polite! A lady told me he was afraid I had n't approved of his being round with her so much evenings. Of course it ain't as if their evenings were as pleasant as ours—since *we* don't seem to feel that way about the poison. I guess I *don't* see the point now; but I suppose he knows I'm a lady and I'd scorn to raise a fuss. Anyway, she wants you to realise she ain't engaged. I don't know why she makes so much of it, but she said to me three times 'Mind you tell Mr. Winterbourne.' And then she told me to ask if you remembered the time you went up to that castle in Switzerland. But I said I would n't give any messages as *that*. Only if she ain't engaged I guess I'm glad to realise it too."

But, as Winterbourne had originally judged, the truth on this question had small actual relevance. A week after this the poor girl died; it had been indeed a terrible case of the *perniciosa*. A grave was found for her in the little Protestant cemetery, by an angle of the wall of imperial Rome, beneath the cypresses and the thick spring-flowers. Winterbourne stood there beside it with a number of other mourners; a number larger than the scandal excited by the young lady's career might have made probable. Near him stood Giovanelli, who came nearer still before Winterbourne turned away. Giovanelli, in decorous mourning, showed but a whiter face; his button-hole lacked its nosegay and he had visibly something urgent—and even to distress—to say, which he scarce knew how to "place." He decided at last to confide it with a pale convulsion to Winterbourne. "She was the most beautiful young lady I ever saw, and the most amiable." To which he added in a moment: "Also—naturally!—the most innocent."

Winterbourne sounded him with hard dry eyes, but presently repeated his words, "The most innocent?"

"The most innocent!"

It came somehow so much too late that our friend could only glare at its having come at all. "Why the devil," he asked, "did you take her to that fatal place?"

Giovanelli raised his neat shoulders and eyebrows to within suspicion of a shrug. "For myself I had no fear; and *she*—she did what she liked."

Winterbourne's eyes attached themselves to the ground. "She did what she liked!"

It determined on the part of poor Giovanelli a further pious, a further candid, confidence. "If she had lived I should have got nothing. She never would have married me."

It had been spoken as if to attest, in all sincerity, his disinterestedness, but Winterbourne scarce knew what welcome to give it. He said, however, with a grace inferior to his friend's: "I dare say not."

The latter was even by this not discouraged. "For a moment I hoped so. But no. I'm convinced."

Winterbourne took it in; he stood staring at the raw protuberance among the April daisies. When he turned round again his fellow mourner had stepped back.

He almost immediately left Rome, but the following summer he again met his aunt Mrs. Costello at Vevey. Mrs. Costello extracted from the charming old hotel there a value that the Miller family had n't mastered the secret of. In the interval Winterbourne had often thought of the most interesting member of that trio—of her mystifying manners and her queer adventure. One day he spoke of her to his aunt—said it was on his conscience he had done her injustice.

"I'm sure I don't know"—that lady showed caution. "How did your injustice affect her?"

"She sent me a message before her death which I did n't understand at the time. But I've understood it since. She would have appreciated one's esteem."

"She took an odd way to gain it! But do you mean by what you say," Mrs. Costello asked, "that she would have reciprocated one's affection?"

As he made no answer to this she after a little looked round at him—he had n't been directly within sight; but the effect of that was n't to make her repeat her question. He spoke, however, after a while. "You were right in that remark that you made last summer. I was booked to make a mistake. I've lived too long in foreign parts." And this time she herself said nothing.

Nevertheless he soon went back to live at Geneva, whence there continue to come the most contradictory accounts of his motives of sojourn: a report that he's "studying" hard—an intimation that he's much interested in a very clever foreign lady.

1909

Alice James
1848–1892

It may be odd to give special recognition to a woman whose only accomplishment was that she died well. And for what purpose does one feature the relatively unknown member of a distinguished family of males? But Alice James is not a superfluous footnote to the lives of her older brothers. The diary she kept during the final two years of her invalidism recounts her drawn-out anticipation of "the grand mortuary moment" of death and what it meant to be a James who was *not* William, the famous philosopher-psychologist, or Henry, the famous novelist-critic. But she recorded other matters as well: in the main, "the resistance we bring to life," which promised the only true form of immortality that any of the Jameses, brothers and sister, could count on.

Alice James was the youngest of the five children of Henry James, Sr., and his wife Mary. Born in New York in 1848, she was preceded by William (1842), Henry, Jr. (1843), Garth Wilkinson (1845), and Robertson (1846). The senior James was a writer and lecturer on utopian schemes, a student of the writings of the mystic Emanuel Swedenborg, and an early socialist. The imprint he left on his brood of highly intelligent and sensitive children was simultaneously indulgent and demanding, liberating and restrictive. The mother's cultivated acts of self-effacement offered her daughter no lessons in independence. As the only girl, Alice James was reared in a demandingly masculine setting that seemed to make no room for her unique talents.

Alice James's girlhood and young womanhood sound like the lives of other well-brought-up young women of upper-middle-class families of the post–Civil War period, but with the addition of the darker edge of nervousness that worked against her ability to function with so-called normalcy. Her father and brothers also suffered from acute nervous disturbances at different periods in their lives, but they were able to come to better terms with their condition, perhaps because they, as males, had more chances to combat "the horrors." Active careers provided acceptable ways of expressing their ideas and their feelings. Hysteria and nervous collapse for Alice began in 1868, attacks that reappeared with increasing frequency. The family consulted a series of doctors, who prescribed the newest mind-cure treatments (electricity, motorpathy, and, later, hypnosis). To some degree Alice James's symptoms parallel those that marred the lives of Emily Dickinson, Elizabeth Barrett Browning, and the women who consulted that new Viennese doctor, Sigmund Freud. The causes of Alice's symptoms were too complex to be disentangled completely. The results stand out clearly.

In 1878, when Alice James deliberated killing herself, her father wisely gave his permission. This made it impossible for her to do so, since she would be responsible for such an act. The remainder of Alice James's life was given over, in the words of the critic Ruth Yeazell, to "a covert career in mortality," though she did not take to her bed as an invalid until 1884. In 1890 Alice James decided to keep a diary. She wished to write down her thoughts about her life from the perspective of her bedroom. This decision came after she went to live in England under the protective eyes of her brother Henry, by then a permanent British resident, and her friend Katharine Loring, who lived with her and cared for her until her death in 1892.

Alice James's existence seems strange and essentially tragic, but it was more than that. No public deeds or great poetry of the kind that Emily Dickinson wrote in her self-incarceration in the family house in Amherst were forthcoming. She dedicated her life instead to an analysis of consciousness. Her own consciousness was often fervid and intense—alternating between Whitmanesque exuberance ("I lay in a meadow until the unwrinkled serenity entered into my bones and made me one with the browsing kine, the still greenery, the drifting clouds, and the swooping birds") and a self-absorption about her ailments so great that, at times, she was transformed into a great headache. Still, she drew the world outside into her invalid's room. She asked questions, read newspapers and journals, made jokes. The Irish question about home rule, Henry's attempts to win acclaim in the popular theater, William's accomplishments as a celebrated thinker, and the lives of the London poor all found welcome room in her mind. They kept her alert, responsive, and amused until the day in 1892 when this sometimes difficult and snobbish, often unhappy, but always *interested* woman died, having achieved (as she wrote to William) "significance for myself."

Further Reading:

A. Burr, ed., *Alice James: Her Brothers, Her Journals*, 1934.

F. Matthiessen, ed., *The James Family*, 1961.

J. Strouse, *Alice James: A Biography*, 1980.

R. Yeazell, ed., *The Death and Letters of Alice James*, 1981.

J. Gunn, "The Autobiographical Occupation: Alice James's Diary and the Decoration of Space," *Auto-Biography Studies* 4 (1988), 37–45.

R. W. B. Lewis, *The Jameses: A Family Narrative*, 1991.

L. Anderson, *Women and Autobiography in the 20th Century*, 1997.

Text:

The Diary of Alice James, ed. L. Edel, 1964.

---

from The Diary of Alice James

[May 31, 1889]

I think that if I get into the habit of writing a bit about what happens, or rather doesn't happen, I may lose a little of the sense of loneliness and desolation which abides with me. My circumstances allowing of nothing but the ejaculation of one-syllabled reflections, a written monologue by that most interesting being, *myself*, may have its yet to be discovered consolations. I shall at least have it all my own way and it may bring relief as an outlet to that geyser of emotions, sensations, speculations and reflections which ferments perpetually within my poor old carcass for its sins; so here goes, my first Journal! . . .

[June 18, 1890]

I remember so distinctly the first time I was conscious of a purely intellectual process. 'Twas the summer of '56 which we spent in Boulogne and the parents of Mlle. Marie Boningue our governess had a *campagne*[1] on the outskirts and invited us to spend the day, perhaps Marie's fête-day.[2] A large and shabby calèche came for us into which we were packed, save Wm.;[3] all I can remember of the drive was a never-ending ribbon of dust stretching in front and the anguish greater even than usual of Wilky's and Bob's[4] heels grinding into my shins. Marie told us that her father had a scar upon his face caused by a bad scald in his youth and we must be sure and not look at him as he was very sensitive. How I remember the painful conflict between sympathy and the desire to look and the fear that my baseness should be discovered by the good man as he sat at the head of the table in charge of a big frosted-cake, sprinkled o'er with those pink and white worms in which lurk the caraway seed. How easy 'twould be to picture one's youth as a perpetual escape from that abhorred object!—I wonder if it is a blight upon children still?—But to arrive at the first flowering of me Intellect! We were turned into the garden to play, a sandy or rather dusty expanse with nothing in it, as I remember, but two or three scrubby apple-trees, from one of which hung a swing. As time went on Wilky and Bob disappeared, not to my grief, and the Boningues. Harry was sitting in the swing and I came up and stood near by as the sun began to slant over the desolate expanse, as the dready h[ou]rs, with that endlessness which they have for infancy, passed, when Harry suddenly exclaimed: "This might certainly be called pleasure under difficulties!" The stir of my whole being in response to the substance and exquisite, *original* form of this remark almost makes my heart beat now with the sisterly pride which was then awakened and it came to me in a flash, the higher nature of this appeal to the mind, as compared to the rudimentary solicitations which usually produced my childish explosions of laughter; and I can also feel distinctly the sense of self-satisfaction in that I could not only perceive, but appreciate this subtlety, as if I had acquired a new sense, a sense whereby to measure intellectual things, wit as distinguished from giggling, for example.

[July 28, 1890]

I lay in a meadow until the unwrinkled serenity entered into my bones and made me one with the browsing kine, the still greenery, the drifting clouds, and the swooping birds.

[October 26, 1890]

William uses an excellent expression when he says in his paper on the "Hidden Self"[5] that the nervous victim "abandons" certain portions of his consciousness. It may be the

---

[1] French: "little country house."
[2] Birthday or name day.
[3] William James (1842–1910).
[4] Wilky: Garth Wilkinson James (1845–1883); Bob: Robertson James (1846–1910).

[5] The essay "The Hidden Self," which appeared in *Scribner's,* March 1890, discusses the state of consciousness experienced in hysterics.

word commonly used by his kind. It is just the right one at any rate, altho' I have never unfortunately been able to abandon my consciousness and get five minutes' rest. I have passed thro' an infinite succession of conscious abandonments and in looking back now I see how it began in my childhood, altho' I wasn't conscious of the necessity until '67 or '68 when I broke down first, acutely, and had violent turns of hysteria. As I lay prostrate after the storm with my mind luminous and active and susceptible of the clearest, strongest impressions, I saw so distinctly that it was a fight simply between my body and my will, a battle in which the former was to be triumphant to the end. Owing to some physical weakness, excess of nervous susceptibility, the moral power *pauses,* as it were for a moment, and refuses to maintain muscular sanity, worn out with the strain of its constabulary functions. As I used to sit immovable reading in the library with waves of violent inclination suddenly invading my muscles taking some one of their myriad forms such as throwing myself out of the window, or knocking off the head of the benignant pater as he sat with his silver locks, writing at his table, it used to seem to me that the only difference between me and the insane was that I had not only all the horrors and suffering of insanity but the duties of doctor, nurse, and strait-jacket imposed upon me, too. Conceive of never being without the sense that if you let yourself go for a moment your mechanism will fall into pie and that at some given moment you must abandon it all, let the dykes break and the flood sweep in, acknowledging yourself abjectly impotent before the immutable laws. When all one's moral and natural stock in trade is a temperament forbidding the abandonment of an inch or the relaxation of a muscle, 'tis a never-ending fight. When the fancy took me of a morning at school to *study* my lessons by way of variety instead of shirking or wiggling thro' the most impossible sensations of upheaval, violent revolt in my head overtook me so that I had to "abandon" my brain, as it were. So it has always been, anything that sticks of itself is free to do so, but conscious and continuous cerebration is an impossible exercise and from just behind the eyes my head feels like a dense jungle into which no ray of light has ever penetrated. So, with the rest, you abandon the pit of your stomach, the palms of your hands, the soles of your feet, and refuse to keep them sane when you find in turn one moral impression after another producing despair in the one, terror in the other, anxiety in the third and so on until life becomes one long flight from remote suggestion and complicated eluding of the multifold traps set for your undoing.

Ambrose Bierce
1842–1914

An account of Ambrose Bierce's life reads like one of the fantastic stories he wrote, down to the fact that there is no explanation provided for its ending. One day in 1912 he disappeared without a trace in Mexico. Rumors persist that he was killed there during the insurrection led by Pancho Villa's forces. Such a dramatic and mysterious conclusion would probably have pleased Bierce the storyteller; this ending to an existence marked by personal torment and family disasters would confirm the pessimism that earned him the nickname "Bitter Bierce."

The youngest of nine children of parents whose religious fanaticism turned him against both his family and their faith, Bierce was born in rural southeastern Ohio and raised on a farm in Indiana. Like Mark Twain, William Dean Howells and Joel Chandler Harris (all born within ten years of one another), Bierce had early training as a printer's apprentice. As with so many other figures in American literature, he had little schooling. One year at the Kentucky Military Institute was his only attempt at formal education. He enlisted in the Union army as a drummer boy when the Civil War began, fought in several major battles, and rose in rank to lieutenant. At the war's end, he moved west, taking with him memories of the often brutal and always unhappy years of his childhood as well as the military horrors he had seen at first hand. By 1866 Bierce was settled into a journalist's life in San Francisco, where he worked alongside other young men (including Mark Twain, Bret Harte, and Joaquin Miller) who were making the newspaper world their entrance into the larger literary world. Then Bierce and his bride went to London to live for four years. There he learned new devices of satire and made his reputation for slash-and-cut journalism. As defined in *The Devil's Dictionary* of 1906, his views of marriage ("The state or condition of a community consisting of a master, a mistress, and two slaves, making in all, two"), religion ("A daughter of Hope and Fear, explaining to Ignorance the nature of the Unknowable"), and life ("A spiritual pickle preserving the body from decay") were bitingly sardonic, but his own experiences gave him sufficient cause for such reactions. Divorce, the suicide of friends, the murder of one son in a brawl, the death by alcoholism of another son, and the endless warfare carried out with relatives deepened his already pronounced cynicism into nihilism. But his savage way with words, his pungent black humor, and his apt critiques of topical follies and universal human stupidity won him immense popularity.

In 1876 Bierce returned to California, eventually to write for the *San Francisco Examiner,* published by William Randolph Hearst, and to pour forth a variety of essays, reviews, political polemics, social commentaries, and works of fiction. Considered a major representative of post–Civil War literary realism, though he himself detested this mode, Bierce was also a master of the grotesque and the tale of the supernatural. In *Tales of Soldiers and Civilians* (1891) and *Can Such Things Be?* (1893), Bierce made clear with frightening vividness that he believed the ultimate reality lay in people's futile attempts to beat a cosmic system commanded by an impersonal fate.

When Bierce disappeared in 1912, the tradition he shared with many other writers did not vanish with him. Herman Melville had possessed "the darkness," and so did Bierce's contemporaries, Mark Twain and Stephen Crane—as would Ernest Hemingway, Nathanael West, and Thomas Pynchon in later generations. All were young men who confronted an unkind universe and made of it the stuff of a literary realism that seemed true in relation to its madness. The bad, mad, bitter man from San Francisco helped show American writers the way to hell.

Further Reading:

C. Grattan, *Bitter Bierce: A Mystery of American Letters,* 1929.

C. McWilliams, *Ambrose Bierce: A Biography,* 1929, 1967.

F. D. Walker, *Ambrose Bierce, the Wickedest Man in San Francisco,* 1941.

P. Fatout, *Ambrose Bierce, the Devil's Lexicographer,* 1951.

S. Woodruff, *The Short Stories of Ambrose Bierce: A Study in Polarity*, 1964.

G. Barrett and T. Erskine, eds., *From Fiction to Film: Ambrose Bierce's "An Occurrence at Owl Creek Bridge,"* 1973.

C. N. Davidson, *Critical Essays on Ambrose Bierce*, 1982.

Text:
Tales of Soldiers and Civilians, 1892.
See also *Collected Works of Ambrose Bierce*, 12 vols., ed. W. Neale, 1909–1912.

An Occurrence at Owl Creek Bridge

I

A man stood upon a railroad bridge in northern Alabama, looking down into the swift water twenty feet below. The man's hands were behind his back, the wrists bound with a cord. A rope loosely encircled his neck. It was attached to a stout cross-timber above his head, and the slack fell to the level of his knees. Some loose boards laid upon the sleepers[1] supporting the metals of the railway supplied a footing for him and his executioners—two private soldiers of the Federal army, directed by a sergeant, who in civil life may have been a deputy sheriff. At a short remove upon the same temporary platform was an officer in the uniform of his rank, armed. He was a captain. A sentinel at each end of the bridge stood with his rifle in the position known as "support," that is to say, vertical in front of the left shoulder, the hammer resting on the forearm thrown straight across the chest—a formal and unnatural position, enforcing an erect carriage of the body. It did not appear to be the duty of these two men to know what was occurring at the center of the bridge; they merely blockaded the two ends of the foot plank which traversed it.

Beyond one of the sentinels, nobody was in sight; the railroad ran straight away into a forest for a hundred yards, then, curving, was lost to view. Doubtless there was an outpost farther along. The other bank of the stream was open ground—a gentle acclivity crowned with a stockade of vertical tree trunks, loopholed for rifles, with a single embrasure through which protruded the muzzle of a brass cannon commanding the bridge. Midway of the slope between bridge and fort were the spectators—a single company of infantry in line, at "parade rest," the butts of the rifles on the ground, the barrels inclining slightly backward against the right shoulder, the hands crossed upon the stock. A lieutenant stood at the right of the line, the point of his sword upon the ground, his left hand resting upon his right. Excepting the group of four at the center of the bridge, not a man moved. The company faced the bridge, staring stonily, motion-

---

[1] Railroad ties.

less. The sentinels, facing the banks of the stream, might have been statues to adorn the bridge. The captain stood with folded arms, silent, observing the work of his subordinates, but making no sign. Death is a dignitary who when he comes announced is to be received with formal manifestations of respect, even by those most familiar with him. In the code of military etiquette silence and fixity are forms of deference.

The man who was engaged in being hanged was apparently about thirty-five years of age. He was a civilian, if one might judge from his dress, which was that of a planter. His features were good—a straight nose, firm mouth, broad forehead, from which his long, dark hair was combed straight back, falling behind his ears to the collar of his well-fitting frock coat. He wore a mustache and pointed beard, but no whiskers: his eyes were large and dark gray, and had a kindly expression which one would hardly have expected in one whose neck was in the hemp. Evidently this was no vulgar assassin. The liberal military code makes provision for hanging many kinds of people, and gentlemen are not excluded.

The preparations being complete, the two private soldiers stepped aside and each drew away the plank upon which he had been standing. The sergeant turned to the captain, saluted, and placed himself immediately behind that officer, who in turn moved apart one pace. These movements left the condemned man and the sergeant standing on the two ends of the same plank, which spanned three of the crossties of the bridge. The end upon which the civilian stood almost, but not quite, reached a fourth. This plank had been held in place by the weight of the captain; it was now held by that of the sergeant. At a signal from the former, the latter would step aside, the plank would tilt, and the condemned man go down between two ties. The arrangement commended itself to his judgment as simple and effective. His face had not been covered nor his eyes bandaged. He looked a moment at his "unsteadfast footing," then let his gaze wander to the swirling water of the stream racing madly beneath his feet. A piece of dancing driftwood caught his attention and his eyes followed it down the current. How slowly it appeared to move! What a sluggish stream!

He closed his eyes in order to fix his last thoughts upon his wife and children. The water, touched to gold by the early sun, the brooding mists under the banks at some distance down the stream, the fort, the soldiers, the piece of drift—all had distracted him. An now he became conscious of a new disturbance. Striking through the thought of his dear ones was a sound which he could neither ignore nor understand, a sharp, distinct, metallic percussion like the stroke of a blacksmith's hammer upon the anvil; it had the same ringing quality. He wondered what it was, and whether immeasurably distant or near by—it seemed both. Its recurrence was regular, but as slow as the tolling of a death knell. He awaited each stoke with impatience and—he knew not why—apprehension. The intervals of silence grow progressively longer; the delays became maddening. With their greater infrequency the sounds increased in strength and sharpness. They hurt his ear like the thrust of a knife; he feared he would shriek. What he heard was the ticking of his watch.

He unclosed his eyes, and saw again the water below him. "If I could free my hands," he thought, "I might throw off the noose and spring into the stream. By diving I could evade the bullets, and, swimming vigorously, reach the bank, take to the woods, and get away home. My home, thank God, is as yet outside their lines; my wife and little ones are still beyond the invader's farthest advance."

As these thoughts, which have here to be set down in words, were flashed into the doomed man's brain rather than evolved from it, the captain nodded to the sergeant. The sergeant stepped aside.

II

Peyton Farquhar was a well-to-do planter of an old and highly respected Alabama family. Being a slave owner and like other slave owners a politician, he was naturally an original secessionist and ardently devoted to the Southern cause. Circumstances of an imperious nature, which it is unnecessary to relate here, had prevented him from taking service with the gallant army which had fought the disastrous campaigns ending with the fall of Corinth,[2] and he chafed under the inglorious restraint, longing for the release of his energies, the larger life of the soldier, the opportunity for distinction. That opportunity, he felt, would come, as it comes to all in war time. Meanwhile he did what he could. No service was too humble for him to perform in aid of the South, no adventure too perilous for him to undertake if consistent with the character of a civilian who was at heart a soldier, and who in good faith and without too much qualification assented to at least a part of the frankly villainous dictum that all is fair in love and war.

One evening while Farquhar and his wife were sitting on a rustic bench near the entrance to his grounds, a gray-clad soldier rode up to the gate and asked for a drink of water. Mrs. Farquhar was only too happy to serve him with her own white hands. While she was gone to fetch the water, her husband approached the dusty horseman and inquired eagerly for news from the front.

"The Yanks are repairing the railroads," said the man, "and are getting ready for another advance. They have reached the Owl Creek bridge, put it in order, and built a stockade on the north bank. The commandant has issued an order, which is posted everywhere, declaring that any civilian caught interfering with the railroad, its bridges, tunnels, or trains will be summarily hanged. I saw the order."

"How far is it to the Owl Creek bridge?" Farquhar asked.

"About thirty miles."

"Is there no force on this side the creek?"

"Only a picket post half a mile out, on the railroad, and a single sentinel at this end of the bridge."

"Suppose a man—a civilian and student of hanging—should elude the picket post and perhaps get the better of the sentinel," said Farquhar, smiling, "what could he accomplish?"

The soldier reflected, "I was there a month ago," he replied. "I observed that the flood of last winter had lodged a great quantity of driftwood against the wooden pier at this end of the bridge. It is now dry and would burn like tow."

The lady had now brought the water, which the soldier drank. He thanked her ceremoniously, bowed to her husband, and rode away. An hour later, after nightfall, he repassed the plantation, going northward in the direction from which he had come. He was a Federal scout.

---

[2] The Union army seized Corinth, Mississippi, in the spring of 1862 during the Battle of Shiloh.

III

As Peyton Farquhar fell straight downward through the bridge he lost consciousness and was as one already dead. From this state he was awakened—ages later, it seemed to him—by the pain of a sharp pressure upon his throat, followed by a sense of suffocation. Keen, poignant agonies seemed to shoot from his neck downward through every fiber of his body and limbs. These pains appeared to flash along well-defined lines a ramification and to beat with an inconceivably rapid periodicity. They seemed like streams of pulsating fire heating him to an intolerable temperature. As to his head, he was conscious of nothing but a feeling of fullness—of congestion. These sensations were unaccompanied by thought. The intellectual part of his nature was already effaced: he had power only to feel, and feeling was torment. He was conscious of motion. Encompassed in a luminous cloud, of which he was now merely the fiery heart, without material substance, he swung through unthinkable arcs of oscillation, like a vast pendulum. Then all at once, with terrible suddenness, the light about him shot upward with the noise of a loud plash; a frightful roaring was in his ears, and all was cold and dark. The power of thought was restored; he knew that the rope had broken and he had fallen into the stream. There was no additional strangulation; the noose about his neck was already suffocating him and kept the water from his lungs. To die of hanging at the bottom of a river! —the idea seemed to him ludicrous. He opened his eyes in the darkness and saw about him a gleam of light, but how distant, how inaccessible! He was still sinking, for the light became fainter and fainter until it was a mere glimmer. Then it began to grow and brighten, and he knew that he was rising toward the surface—knew it with reluctance, for he was now very comfortable. "To be hanged and drowned," he thought, "this is not so bad; but I do not wish to be shot. No, I will not be shot, that is not fair."

He was not conscious of an effort, but a sharp pain in his wrist apprised him that he was trying to free his hands. He gave the struggle his attention, as an idler might observe the feat of a juggler, without interest in the outcome. What splendid effort! —what magnificent, what super-human strength! Ah, that was a fine endeavor! Bravo! The cord fell away; his arms parted and floated upward, the hands dimly seen on each side in the growing light. He watched them with a new interest as first one and then the other pounced upon the noose at his neck. They tore it away and thrust it fiercely aside, its undulations resembling those of a water snake. "Put it back, put it back!" He thought he shouted these words to his hands, for the undoing of the noose had been succeeded by the direst pang that he had yet experienced. His neck arched horribly; his brain was on fire; his heart, which had been fluttering faintly, gave a great leap, trying to force itself out at his mouth. His whole body was racked and wrenched with an insupportable anguish! But his disobedient hands gave no heed to the command. They beat the water vigorously with quick downward strokes, forcing him to the surface. He felt his head emerge; his eyes were blinded by the sunlight; his chest expanded convulsively, and with a supreme and crowning agony his lungs engulfed a great draught of air, which instantly he expelled in a shriek!

He was now in full possession of his physical senses. They were, indeed, preternaturally keen and alert. Something in the awful disturbance of his organic system had so exalted and refined them that they made record of things never before perceived. He felt the ripples upon his face and heard their separate sounds as they struck. He looked at the forest on the bank of the stream, saw the individual trees, the leaves and the veining of each leaf—saw the very insects upon them: the locusts, the brilliant-bodied flies, the gray spiders stretching their webs from twig to twig. He noted the prismatic colors in all the dewdrops upon a million blades of grass. The humming of the gnats that danced above the eddies of the stream, the beating the dragonflies' wings, the strokes of the water spiders' legs, like oars which had lifted their boat—all these made audible music. A fish slid along beneath his eyes and he heard the rush of its body parting the water.

He had come to the surface facing down the stream; in a moment the visible world seemed to wheel slowly round, himself at the pivotal point, and he saw the bridge, the fort, the soldiers upon the bridge, the captain, the sergeant, the two privates, his executioners. They were in silhouette against the blue sky. They shouted and gesticulated, pointing at him. The captain had drawn his pistol, but did not fire; the others were unarmed. Their movements were grotesque and horrible, their forms gigantic.

Suddenly, he heard a sharp report and something struck the water smartly within a few inches of his head, spattering his face with spray. He heard the second report, and saw one of the sentinels with his rifle at his shoulder, a light cloud of blue smoke rising from the muzzle. The man in the water saw the eye of the man on the bridge gazing into his own through the sights of the rifle. He observed that it was a gray eye and remembered having read that gray eyes were keenest, and that all famous marksmen had them. Nevertheless, this one had missed.

A counterswirl had caught Farquhar and turned him half round; he was again looking into the forest on the bank opposite the fort. The sound of a clear, high voice in a monotonous singsong now rang out behind him and came across the water with distinctness that pierced and subdued all other sounds, even the beating of the ripples in his ears. Although no soldier, he had frequented camps enough to know the dread significance of the deliberate, drawling, aspirated chant; the lieutenant on shore was taking part in the morning's work. How coldly and pitilessly—with what an even, calm intonation, presaging and enforcing tranquillity in the men—with what accurately measured intervals fell those cruel words:

"Attention, company! . . . . shoulder arms! . . . Ready! . . . Aim! . . . Fire!"

Farquhar dived—dived as deeply as he could. The water roared in his ears like the voice of Niagara, yet he heard the dulled thunder of the volley and, rising again toward the surface, met shining bits of metal, singularly flattened, oscillating slowly downward. Some of them touched him on the face and hands, then fell way, continuing their descent. One lodged between his collar and his neck; it was uncomfortably warm and he snatched it out.

As he rose to the surface, gasping for breath, he saw that he had been a long time under water; he was perceptibly farther downstream—nearer to safety. The soldiers had almost finished reloading; the metal ramrods flashed all at once in the sunshine as they were drawn from the barrels, turned in the air, and thrust into their sockets. The two sentinels fired again, independently and ineffectually.

The hunted man saw all this over his shoulder; he was now swimming vigorously with the current. His brain was energetic as his arms and legs; he thought with the rapidity of lightning.

"The officer," he reasoned, "will not make that martinet's error a second time. It is as easy to dodge a volley as a single shot. He has probably already given the command to fire at will. God help me, I cannot dodge them all!"

An appalling plash within two yards of him was followed by a loud, rushing sound, *diminuendo*,[3] which seemed to travel back through the air to the fort and died in an explosion which stirred the very river to its deeps! A rising sheet of water, which curved over him, fell down upon him, blinded him, strangled him! The cannon had taken a hand in the game. As he shook his head free from the commotion of the smitten water, he heard the deflected shot humming through the air ahead, and in an instant it was cracking and smashing the branches in the forest beyond.

"They will not do that again," he thought; "the next time they will use a charge of grape.[4] I must keep my eye upon the gun; the smoke will apprise me—the report arrives too late; it lags behind the missile. That is a good gun."

Suddenly he felt himself whirled round and round—spinning like a top. The water, the banks, the forests, the now distant bridge, fort, and men—all were commingled and blurred. Objects were represented by their colors only; circular horizontal streaks of color—that was all he saw. He had been caught in a vortex and was being whirled on with a velocity of advance and gyration which made him giddy and sick. In a few moments he was flung upon the gravel at the foot of the left bank of the stream—the southern bank—and behind a projecting point which concealed him from his enemies. The sudden arrest of his motion, the abrasion of one of his hands on the gravel, restored him, and he wept with delight. He dug his fingers into the sand, threw it over himself in handfuls, and audibly blessed it. It looked like gold, like diamonds, rubies, emeralds; he could think of nothing beautiful which it did not resemble. The trees upon the bank were giant garden plants; he noted a definite order in their arrangement, inhaled the fragrance of their blooms. A strange, roseate light shone through the spaces among their trunks and the wind made in their branches the music of aeolian harps. He had no wish to perfect his escape—was content to remain in that enchanting spot until retaken.

A whiz and rattle of grapeshot among the branches high above his head roused him from his dream. The baffled cannoneer had fired him a random farewell. He sprang to his feet, rushed up the sloping bank, and plunged into the forest.

All that day he traveled, laying his course by the rounding sun. The forest seemed interminable; nowhere did he discover a break in it, not even a woodman's road. He had not known that he lived in so wild a region. There was something uncanny in the revelation.

By nightfall he was fatigued, footsore, famishing. The thought of his wife and children urged him on. At last he found a road which led him in what he knew to be the right direction. It was wide and straight as a city street, yet it seemed untraveled. No fields bordered it, no dwelling anywhere. Not so much as the barking of a dog suggested human habitation. The black bodies of the great trees formed a straight wall on both sides, terminating on the horizon in a point, like a diagram in a lesson in perspective. Overhead, as he looked up through this rift in the wood, shone great golden stars looking unfamiliar and grouped in strange constellations. He was sure they were arranged in some order which had a secret and malign significance. The wood on either side was

---

[3] Dying away in volume.
[4] Grapeshot; cannon charge made up of clusters of iron balls.

full of singular noises, among which—once, twice, and again—he distinctly heard whispers in an unknown tongue.

His neck was in pain and lifting his hand to it he found it horribly swollen. He knew that it had a circle of black where the rope had bruised it. His eyes felt congested; he could no longer close them. His tongue was swollen with thirst; he relieved its fever by thrusting it forward from between his teeth into the cool air. How softly the turf had carpeted the untraveled avenue—he could no longer feel the roadway beneath his feet!

Doubtless, despite his suffering, he had fallen asleep while walking, for now he sees another scene—perhaps he has merely recovered from a delirium. He stands at the gate of his own home. All is as he left it, and all bright and beautiful in the morning sunshine. He must have traveled the entire night. As he pushes open the gate and passes up the wide white walk, he sees a flutter of female garments; his wife, looking fresh and cool and sweet, steps down from the veranda to meet him. At the bottom of the steps she stands waiting, with a smile of ineffable joy, an attitude of matchless grace and dignity. Ah, how beautiful she is! He springs forward with extended arms. As he is about to clasp her, he feels a stunning blow upon the back of the neck; a blinding white light blazes all about him with a sound like the shock of a cannon—then all is darkness and silence!

Peyton Farquhar was dead; his body, with a broken neck, swung gently from side to side beneath the timbers of the Owl Creek bridge.

1888–1891

Cultural Portfolio
Oral Traditions and
Turn-of-the-Century Literature

Despite being figured even at the time as a harbinger of modernity, the Civil War did not radically alter the centrality of oral traditions and other folkways in the lives of many Americans. Especially in rural areas across the nation, storytelling persisted in familial and communal contexts as a valued form of entertainment. Thus, folksongs and sayings, such as proverbs, riddles, and family lore, continued to pass from person to person and from generation to generation through the end of the nineteenth century. European Americans, such as those living in the mountains of Appalachia, still sang the ballads and lullabies of the past, while African Americans, usually drawing on their just recently ended heritage of slavery, sang spirituals and the blues and told tales of how John got the best of Ole Massa yet again. In all-male spheres of the West, cowboys, miners, and loggers frequently sang of their lonesomeness as well as retold tall tales of adventure and sexual prowess. Whether immigrants, typically from northern, eastern, or southern Europe during this era, found their new homes in teeming cities such as New York or Philadelphia or in the open spaces of the Midwest, these persons often clung to songs and stories of their homelands when confronted with unfamiliar English. And, as they had for thousands of years, Native American cultures remained rooted in oral tradition, even as they faced ever more deadly and disheartening conflicts with encroaching European Americans.

And yet these American oral traditions could not help but be reshaped by the nation's radical changes after the war. Industrialization, sharp increases in urban and suburban populations, and technological advances in print culture all seemingly worked to remove persons from agrarian communities typically associated with oral traditions. At the same time, however, cities often created new venues for the oral transmission of stories and songs. In the 1890s, for instance, public libraries in the North began sponsoring "story hours" for young patrons. This so-called Progressive Era similarly saw the creation and widespread use of national parks, church camps, and summer camps, all of which helped to foster the transmission of camp lore, such as ghost stories, among urban and suburban middle- and upper-class youth. And it was not until this period that some of the nation's most enduring folk heroes were created. Stories surrounding John Henry arose only in the 1870s, while those of Paul Bunyan emerged in the 1880s and 1890s, and those of Casey Jones appeared after the turn of the century. The fame of these figures was often contingent, however, on their stories being printed in newspapers and magazines and then reentering oral tradition.

There was a sense, nevertheless, that the nation's oral traditions of the past were rapidly vanishing in the face of modernity. To combat this perceived loss, scholars and literary figures sought to instigate a systematic recording of American folklore. This impulse was not, however, completely new. Throughout the century there had been concerted efforts to "capture" disappearing Native American oral culture. In the 1830s Henry Rowe Schoolcraft, the "father of American folklore," compiled a collection of Native American narratives he had gathered while an Indian agent on the northwestern frontier. This sort of collecting continued under the guidance of John Wesley Powell, head of the Bureau of American Ethnology from 1879 until 1902. The folklife of African Americans drew similar interest, although serious study was not begun until after the Civil War. As with the collecting of Native American materials, white researchers' ethnocentrism tempered the gathering of African American stories and songs. When, for example, Lucy McKim, William Francis Allen, and Charles Pickard Ware published *Slave Songs of the United States* in 1867, they felt compelled to judge the various songs as either "civilized" or "barbaric."

While the American Folklore Society did not fully escape this pitfall, it did bring unprecedented serious attention to American oral traditions. Founded in 1888 in Cambridge, Massachusetts, by Francis James Child, William Wells Newell, Daniel Garrison Brinton, and Franz Boas, among others, the society devoted itself to "the collection of the fast-vanishing Folk-Lore in America" and "the study of the general subject," to be published in the *Journal of American Folklore* begun that same year. Despite including literary figures like Mark Twain and Joel Chandler Harris among its charter members, the society largely worked from an anthropological focus. In an implicit critique of this emphasis, Union veteran Fletcher S. Bassett organized the Chicago Folk-Lore Society in 1892 with a more literary focus. Although this society published its own journal, the *Folk-Lorist,* and even sponsored the International Folk-Lore Congress at the 1893 Columbian Exposition in Chicago, it ultimately proved short-lived after Bassett's death later that same year. Nevertheless, the Chicago Folk-Lore Society, the American Folklore Society, and the American Dialect Society, founded in 1890, reflect the relative explosion of folklore studies during the years surrounding the turn of the century. By the 1920s, major collections of songs, sayings, and stories had been gathered for several prominent racial, ethnic, and regional groups of the country, as typified by Francis James Child's *The English and Scottish Popular Ballads* (1882–1898), Emma Bell Miles's *The Spirit of the Mountains* (1905), John Lomax's *Cowboy Songs and Other Frontier Ballads* (1910), and John C. Campbell's *The Southern Highlander and His Homeland* (1921). Thus, when Zora Neale Hurston, under direction of Franz Boas, collected African American tales and sayings from her native Florida in the 1920s and published them in *Mules and Men* (1935), she was making an important contribution to an already well-established field of study.

At the same time that this academic study was being organized, many of the nation's writers were increasingly turning to oral traditions for their plots and characters. Earlier writers, such as Washington Irving, James Fenimore Cooper, and the Old Southwest humorists had already mined their respective regions' folktales as literary sources, but after the Civil War this interest in capturing "local color"—the dialects, speech patterns, folkways, and other ostensibly realistic details of a given geography—became acute. And yet, for all of the regional differences

that this sort of writing sought to reflect, certain communalities emerged. None was more pervasive than the shared figure of the storyteller. Again and again stories featured a teller who was often as colorful and nuanced as the tale. He—and increasingly she—could both create humor through quaint dialect, mispronunciations, and earthy language and allow for the expression of exacting social criticism. In the North, for instance, Harriet Beecher Stowe's lazy Sam Lawson deflated pompous New England ministers, while Marietta Holley's bustling, ever-practical Josiah Allen's Wife satirized women's lachrymose sentimentalism. In the South Charles W. Chesnutt's Uncle Julius benignly established the wit and intelligence of African Americans, while George Washington Harris's sadistic mountaineer Sut Lovingood expressed dark sentiments concerning human nature worthy in their pessimism of Herman Melville or Mark Twain.

These writers reflected an understanding of the nation as more subtly regionalized than merely through the designations of North, West, and South. Sarah Orne Jewett's "Down East" fiction, often set in Maine and drawing on maritime folkways and sayings, is differently accented from that of Stowe's New England tales, just as Twain's *Huckleberry Finn* (1884) depicts a far different West in St. Petersburg, Missouri, from that offered in Owen Wister's *The Virginian,* his myth-codifying 1902 novel of Wyoming cowpunchers. It was the South, however, that was perhaps the most variegated region. Thomas Nelson Page's aristocratic Virginia bears little resemblance to Mary Noailles Murfree's Tennessee mountains, and neither is like the Louisiana bayous and New Orleans streets of Kate Chopin, Grace King, and George Washington Cable.

The South was also that region perceived as being the richest in oral tradition, and its literary expressions throughout the late nineteenth century were often closely linked to its native tales and songs. The reasons for this wealth of folklore are numerous, as southern historian and biographer Douglas Southall Freeman suggested in the late 1940s. For him five distinctive qualities shaped southern folklore and oral traditions after the Civil War: "the British stock, the presence of the Negro almost everywhere, the persistence of the Confederate tradition, the dominance of staple agriculture, and a climate that supplies outdoor themes for stories more appropriately told under a shade tree than from a chimney corner." Of these, the presence of African Americans in particular found its way into southern fiction of the day. In *Uncle Remus: His Songs and His Sayings* (1880), for instance, Joel Chandler Harris rehearses African American proverbs and tales of animal trickster figures, ones that bear striking parallels to earlier Cherokee stories from the same region. At the same time, national African American leaders such as W.E.B. Du Bois sought to reclaim southern black folkways and, in the case of the "sorrow songs," to theorize their importance in most African Americans' heritage of slavery. Thus, Du Bois's *The Souls of Black Folk* (1903) uses these songs to gloss each chapter and ends with a deliberate focus on the songs themselves.

For southern whites, tales of the Confederacy and its defeat often played a similar role in helping to create a sense of community during times of hardship. Freeman clarifies: "For close to two generations the war of 1861–65 was the greatest fact in Southern life. Conversation of the elders gravitated to the heroes and the horrors of that conflict. . . . It was much more a matter of parental duty to see that a son knew the southern estimates of casualties in the principal battles than that he remembered with precision the provoking differences between seven times eight and nine times six." Because at least two generations of Southerners grew up hearing these stories and debates, many of the writers of the Southern Renaissance drew directly on familial lore of the era preserved through oral tradition. Novels such as Stark Young's *So Red the Rose* (1934), Margaret Mitchell's *Gone With the Wind* (1936), and William Faulkner's *The Unvanquished* (1938) all testify to the power of these stories to shape their hearers' consciousnesses and establish once again that, as the nation passed through the final years of the nineteenth century and entered into the twentieth, its literature remained profoundly impacted by oral traditions.

---

from # Franz Boas, *et. al., The Journal of American Folk-Lore*

On the Field and Work of a Journal of American Folk-Lore

A proposal to establish a Folk-Lore Society in America was made in the form of a circular letter, dated at Cambridge, Mass., May 5, 1887, and subscribed with seventeen names. This invitation was repeated in a second letter, issued in October, bearing 104 signatures, representing various parts of the United States and Canada. In consequence, the number of signers having reached the necessary number, the American Folk-Lore Society was organized at Cambridge, January 4, 1888. In the proposals in question, the objects to be accomplished are stated in the following terms: —

It is proposed to form a society for the study of Folk-Lore, of which the principal object shall be to establish a Journal, of a scientific character, designed: —

    (1) For the collection of the fast-vanishing remains of Folk-Lore in America, namely:

        (*a*) Relics of Old English Folk-Lore (ballads, tales, superstitions, dialect, etc.).
        (*b*) Lore of Negroes in the Southern States of the Union.
        (*c*) Lore of the Indian Tribes of North America (myths, tales, etc.).
        (*d*) Lore of French Canada, Mexico, etc.

    (2) For the study of the general subject, and publication of the results of special students in this department.

In the first number of a journal established in conformity with this definition, it may be proper briefly to outline the services which a journal of American folk-lore may hope to accomplish in each of the departments above indicated.

As to Old English lore, the early settlers, in the colonies peopled from Great Britain, not only brought with them the oral traditions of the mother country, but clung to those traditions with the usual tenacity of emigrants transported to a new land. It is certain that up to a recent date, abundant and interesting collections could everywhere have been made. But traditional lore was unprized: the time for its preservation, on both sides of the Atlantic, was suffered to elapse, and what now remains is sufficient to stimulate, rather than satisfy, curiosity.

As respects old ballads—the first branch of English lore named—the prospect of obtaining much of value is not flattering. In the seventeenth century, the time for the composition of these had almost passed; and they had, in a measure, been superseded by inferior rhymes of literary origin, diffused by means of broadsides and song-books, or by popular doggerels, which may be called ballads, but possess little poetic interest. Still, genuine ballads continued to be sung in the colonies; a few have been recorded which have obviously been transmitted from generation to generation by oral tradition. Many of the best Scotch and Irish ballad-singers, who have preserved, in their respective dialects, songs which were once the property of the English-speaking race, have emigrated to this country; and it is possible that something of value may be obtained from one or other of these sources.

For the collection of ancient nursery tales the prospects are more hopeful; scarcely a single such tale has been recorded in America, yet it is certain that, until within a very few years, they existed in great abundance. Fairy tales, beast fables, jests, by scores, were on the lips of mothers and nurses. If they have perished in neglect, the case is very little better in the old country. Because it so happened that the brothers Grimm were the first to collect popular tales, even intelligent people suppose that such stories are peculiarly German, being unaware that their own grandparents (frequently their parents) were amused by similar narratives, which had the great advantage of being traditional and idiomatic. There is reason to hope that some of these may be saved from oblivion.

Superstitions, which possess their own interest, and which supply material to the psychologist for studying the problems of mind-history, survive in abundance. The belief in witchcraft lingers, not only in remote valleys of Virginia and Tennessee, but in the neighborhood of Eastern cities. Faith in signs and omens, prejudices in respect to colors of dress and costume, belief in lucky days and inherited methods of work, continue in some measure to influence conduct.

The minor elements of folk-lore are still remembered. The games of children, attended by song and rhyme, have been shown to be as numerous and ancient as in the most primitive part of the old world. Proverbs, riddles, racy sayings, peculiar expressions, having that attraction of freshness and quaintness which belongs only to the unwritten word, are here and there to be heard. But all these relate to the quiet past: if they are not gathered while there is time, they will soon be absorbed into the uniformity of the written language.

Finally, the older and more retired towns frequently have their local dialect, quaint expressions and terms peculiar to a neighborhood, and which sometimes indicate what district of the mother country sent forth a swarm to make the new hive.

If local historical societies are concerned to rescue from the dust of letters and pamphlets scraps of personal information, genealogies and records of buildings, which seem unimportant to a stranger, yet are recognized as locally useful, by preserving the historical reminiscences of the place, and making up a stock of information which in the aggregate may be valuable to the historian of American life, certainly these remains of a tradition which was once the inheritance of every speaker of the English tongue ought not to be allowed to perish.

The second division of folk-lore indicated is that belonging to the American negroes. It is but within a few years that attention has been called to the existence among these of a great number of tales relating to animals, which have been preserved in an interesting collection. The origin of these stories, many of which are common to a great part of the world, has not been determined. In the interest of comparative research, it is desirable that variants be recorded, and that the record should be rendered as complete as possible. It is also to be wished that thorough studies were made of negro music and songs. Such inquiries are becoming difficult, and in a few years will be impossible. Again, the great mass of beliefs and superstitions which exist among this people need attention, and present interesting and important psychological problems, connected with the history of a race who, for good or ill, are henceforth an indissoluble part of the body politic of the United States.

The collection of the third kind of American folk-lore—the traditions of the Indian tribes—will be generally regarded as the most promising and important part of the work to be accomplished. Here the investigator has to deal with whole nations, scattered over a continent, widely separated in language, custom, and belief. The harvest does not consist of scattered gleanings, the relics of a crop once plentiful, but, unhappily, allowed to perish ungarnered; on the contrary, it remains to be gathered, if not in the original abundance, still in ample measure. Systems of myth, rituals, feasts, sacred customs, games, songs, tales, exist in such profusion that volumes would be required to contain the lore of each separate tribe.

It is scarcely necessary to point out that, in this department, collection of folk-lore is not an amusement for leisure, but an important and essential part of history. It is even more desirable for the newer States and Territories to preserve memorials of the life of the original owners of the soil than to record minute details of the settlement. If historical societies are maintained for the latter purpose, the former will be considered no less interesting even by the grandchildren of the present generation. The people of the Eastern States would give much if their ancestors had kept a record of the Indian legends which once belonged to every lake, river, and rock. One race cannot with impunity erase the beliefs and legends of its predecessor. To destroy these is to deprive the imagination of its natural food; to neglect them is to incur the reproach of descendants, who will wonder at and lament the dulness and barbarism of their fathers. To take a wider view, humanity is a whole, the study of which is rendered possible only by records of every part of that whole.

There is, no doubt, another side. The habits and ideas of primitive races include much that seems to us cruel and immoral, much that it might be thought well to leave unrecorded. But this would be a superficial view. What is needed is not an anthology of customs and beliefs, but a complete representation of the savage mind in its rudeness as well as its intelligence, its licentiousness as well as its fidelity.

A great change is about to take place in the condition of the Indian tribes, and what is to be done must be done quickly. For the sake of the Indians themselves, it is necessary that they should be allowed opportunities for civilization; for our sake and for the future, it is desirable that a complete history should remain of what they have been, since their picturesque and wonderful life will soon be absorbed and lost in the uniformity of the modern world.

It is to be hoped that measures may be taken for systematizing and completing collection, by sending competent persons to reside among the tribes for the express purpose of collecting their lore, and by providing means for the publication of these researches. This task must be left to the generosity of local societies and private individuals. All that a single journal can hope to accomplish is to print a few articles of limited extent, to stimulate inquiry, keep a record of progress, and furnish abstracts of investigations.

The fourth department of labor named consists of fields too many and various to be here particularized, every one of which offers an ample field to the investigator.

In the second place, this journal has been established, not only to promote collection, but to forward the study of the general subject. It is obvious that the study of American folk-lore, at least in some of its branches, cannot be pursued without taking into account the folk-lore of other continents. For example, the lore of the English in America can neither be understood nor collected without reference to that of the mother country; while the latter, again, is but part of a common European stock; and the folk-lore of Europe, in its turn, is variously related to that of other continents. While, therefore, this journal is primarily concerned with American tradition, it will occasionally go beyond the limits of the continent when any good purpose can be attained by so doing. At the same time, it is obviously more important to gather materials which may form the basis of later study than to pursue comparison with insufficient materials; especially as the collection must be accomplished at once, if at all, while the comparison may safely be postponed.

In conformity with the spirit of modern scholarship, much attention has been given to the supposed origin of certain widely diffused systems of myth and custom, as well as to the general problems of the subject: the editors will endeavor to keep the readers of this journal informed of such views of this sort as seem to possess sufficient scientific status to make them worth recording. In regard, however, to comparative investigations, such as may be expected in a special journal, it appears to the editors that these, in order to be of utility, should be limited to a particular theme, should be free from controversial reference, treated solely with a view to the elucidation of the theme in hand, and should follow the narrow path of historical criticism, rather than diverge into the broad fields of philosophic speculation.

The editors hope in the course of time to furnish, in its various divisions, a complete bibliography of American folk-lore, to which already belongs an extensive literature.

It is obvious that the ability of a journal to forward the ends mentioned will, in a measure, depend on its circulation; and it is to be hoped that members of the Society will bear in mind the desirability of extending its influence, by bringing its plans to the notice of friends whom they may think likely to be interested.

1888

Harriet Beecher Stowe, *Sam Lawson's Oldtown Fireside Stories*

from **The Minister's Housekeeper**

"Wal, to be sure, Mis' Carryl looked up to him in spirituals, and thought all the world on him; for there warn't a smarter minister no where 'round. Why, when he preached on decrees and election, they used to come clear over from South Parish, and West Sherburne, and Old Town to hear him; and there was sich a row o' waggins tied along by the meetin'-house that the stables was all full, and all hitchin'-posts was full clean up

Darley
"Do, do tell us a story."
from *Sam Lawson's Oldtown Fireside Stories,*
1892

Darley
Sam Lawson
from *Sam Lawson's
Oldtown Fireside Stories*,
1892

SAM LAWSON.

to the tavern, so that folks said the doctor made the town look like a gineral trainin'-day a Sunday.

"He was gret on texts, the doctor was. When he hed a p'int to prove, he'd jest go thro' the Bible, and drive all the texts ahead o' him like a flock o' sheep; and then, if there was a text that seemed gin him, why, he'd come out with his Greek and Hebrew, and kind o' chase it 'round a spell, jest as ye see a fellar chase a contrary bell-wether, and make him jump the fence arter the rest. I tell you, there wa'n't no text in the Bible that could stand agin the doctor when his blood was up. The year arter the doctor was app'inted to preach the 'lection sermon in Boston, he made such a figger that the Brattle-street Church sent a committee right down to see if they couldn't get him to Boston; and then the Sherburne folks, they up and raised his salary; ye see, there ain't nothin' wakes folks up like somebody else's wantin' wakes folks up like somebody else's wantin' what you've got. Wal, that fall they made him a Doctor o' Divinity at Cambridge College, and so they sot more by him than ever."

1872

Marietta Holley (Josiah Allen's Wife), *My Opinions and Betsey Bobbet's*

from **A Day of Trouble**

After the father drove off, the first dive the biggest twin made was at the clock, he crep' up to that, and broke off the pendulum, so it haint been since, while I was a hangin' thier cloaks in the bedroom. And while I was a puttin' thier little oversocks under the stove to dry, the littlest one clim' up and sot down in a pail of maple syrup, and while I was a wringin' him out, the biggest one dove under the bed, at Josiah's tin trunk where he keeps a lot of old papers, and come a creepin' out, drawin' it after him like a hand-sled. There was a gography in it, and a Fox'es book of martyrs, and a lot of other such light reading' and I let the twins have 'em to recreate themselves on, and it kep 'em still most a minute.

I hadn't much more'n got my eye offen that Fox'es book of Martyrs—when there appeared before 'em a still more mournful sight, it was Betsey Bobbett come to spend the day....

I see she had got over bein' mad about the surprise party, for she smiled on me once or twice, and as she looked at the twins, she smiled 2 times on each of 'em, which made 4 and says she in tender tones,

"You deah little motherless things." Then she tried to kiss 'em. But the biggest one gripped her by her false hair, which was flax, and I should think by a careless estimate, that he pulled out about enough to make half a knot of thread. The little one didn't do much harm, only I think he loosened her teeth a little, he hit her pretty near the mouth, and I thought as she arose she slipped 'em back in thier place. But she only said,

"Sweet, sweet little things, how ardent and impulsive they are, so like thier deah Pa."

She took out her work, and says she, "I have come to spend the day. I saw thier deah Pa bringin' the deah little twins in heah, and I thought maybe I could comfort the precious little motherless things some, if I should come over heah. If there is any object upon the earth, Josiah Allen's wife, that appeals to a feelin' heart, it is the sweet little children of widowers. I cannot remember the time when I did not want to comfort them, and thier deah Pa's. I have always felt that it was woman's highest speah, her only mission to soothe, to cling, to smile, to coo. I have always felt it, and for yeah's back it has been a growin' on me. I feel that you do not feel as I do in this matter, you do not feel that is woman's greatest privilege, her crowning blessing, to soothe lacerations, to be a sort of a poultice to the noble, manly breast when it is torn with the cares of life."

This was too much, in the agitated frame of mind I then was.

"Am I a poultice Betsey Bobbet; do I look like one?—am I in the condition to be one?" I cried turnin' my face, red and drippin' with prespiration towards her, and then attacked one of Josiah's shirt sleeves agin. "What has my sect done" says I, as I wildly rubbed his shirt sleeves, "That they have got to be lacerator soothers, when they have got everything else under the sun to do?" Here I stirred down the preserves that was a runnin' over, and turned a pail full of syrup into the sugar kettle. "Everybody says that men are stronger than women, and why should they be treated as if they was glass china, liable to break all to pieces if they haint handled careful. And if they have got to be soothed," says I in an agitated tone, caused by my emotions (and by pumpin' 6 pails

1617

of water to fill up the biler), "Why don't they get men to sooth'em? They have as much agin time as wimmen have; evenin's they don't have anything else to do, they might jest as well be a soothin' each other as to be a hangin' round grocery stores, or settin' by the fire whittlin'."

I see I was frightenin' her by my delerious tone and I continued more mildly, as I stirred down the strugglin' sugar with one hand—removed a cake from the oven with the other—watched my apple preserves with a eagle vision, and listened intently to the voice of the twins, who was playin' in the woodhouse.

"I had jest as soon soothe lacerations as not, Betsey, if I hadn't everything else to do. I had jest as lives set down and smile at Josiah by the hour, but who would fry him nut cakes? I could smoothe down his bald head affectionately, but who would do off this batch of sugar? I could coo at him day in and day out, but who would skim milk—wash pans—get vittles—wash and iron—and patch and scour—and darn and fry—and make and mend—and bake and bile while I was a cooin', tell me?" says I.

Betsey spoke not, but quailed, and I continued—

"Women haint any stronger than men, naturally; thier backs and thier nerves haint made of any stouter timber; their hearts are jest as liable to ache as men's are; so with their heads; and after doin a hard day's work when she is jest ready to drop down, a little smilin' and cooin' would do a woman jest as much good as a man. Not what," I repeated in the firm tone of principle "Not but what I am willin' to coo, if I only had time."
1873

Eastern European
Jewish Oral Tradition*

Yiddish Proverbs

A blind horse makes straight for the pit.
Send a lazy man for the Angel of Death.
The tavern can't corrupt a good man, the synagogue can't reform a bad one.
A wise man hears one word and understands two.
There are more alms for a cripple than for a scholar.
A job is fine but interferes with your time.
A man should live if only to satisfy his curiosity.
"For example" is no proof.
When a fool goes to the baths, he forgets to wash his face.
A fool grows without rain.
Your health comes first—you can always hang yourself later.
Every Jew can be a cantor, but he is usually hoarse.
If God were living on earth, people would break His windows.

* From *A Treasury of Yiddish Stories,* edited by Irving Howe and Eliezer Greenberg; proverbs translated from Yiddish by Isadore Goldstick.

If you can't bite, don't show your teeth.

If you dance at every wedding you will weep for every death.

A Jew's joy is not without fright.

If the ass had horns and the ox knew his strength, the world would be done for.

The rabbi drains the bottle and tells the others to be gay.

Truth rests with God alone, and a little with me.

God never told anyone to be stupid.

God loves the poor and helps the rich.

"For dust thou art, and unto dust thou shalt return" —betwixt and between, a drink
comes in handy.

Shrouds are made without pockets.

If the horse had anything to say he would speak up.

Mark Twain, *How to Tell a Story*

The Humorous Story an American Development.—Its Difference from Comic and Witty Stories.

I do not claim that I can tell a story as it ought to be told. I only claim to know how a
story ought to be told, for I have been almost daily in the company of the most expert
story-tellers for many years.

There are several kinds of stories, but only one difficult kind—the humorous. I will
talk mainly about that one. The humorous story is American, the comic story is English, the witty story is French. The humorous story depends for its effect upon the *manner* of the telling; the comic story and the witty story upon the *matter*.

The humorous story may be spun out to great length, and may wander around as
much as it pleases, and arrive nowhere in particular; but the comic and witty stories must
be brief and with a point. The humorous story bubbles gently along, the others burst.

The humorous story is strictly a work of art—high and delicate art—and only an
artist can tell it; but no art is necessary in telling the comic and the witty story; anybody
can do it. The art of telling a humorous story—understand, I mean by word of mouth,
not print—was created in America, and has remained at home.

The humorous story is told gravely; the teller does his best to conceal the fact that he even
dimly suspects that there is anything funny about it; but the teller of the comic story tells you
beforehand that it is one of the funniest things he has ever heard, then tells it with eager delight, and is the first person to laugh when he gets through. And sometimes, if he has had
good success, he is so glad and happy that he will repeat the "nub" of it and glance around
from face to face, collecting applause, and then repeat it again. It is a pathetic thing to see.

Very often, of course, the rambling and disjointed humorous story finishes with a
nub, point, snapper, or whatever you like to call it. Then the listener must be alert, for
in many cases the teller will divert attention from that nub by dropping it in a carefully
casual and indifferent way, with the pretence that he does not know it is a nub.

Artemus Ward used that trick a good deal; then when the belated audience presently
caught the joke he would look up with innocent surprise, as if wondering what they had

found to laugh at. Dan Setchell used it before him, Nye and Riley and others use it to-day.

But the teller of the comic story does not slur the nub; he shouts it at you—every time. And when he prints it, in England, France, Germany, and Italy, he italicizes it, puts some whooping exclamation-points after it, and sometimes explains it in a parenthesis. All of which is very depressing, and makes one want to renounce joking and lead a better life.

Let me set down an instance of the comic method, using an anecdote which has been popular all over the world for twelve or fifteen hundred years. The teller tells it in this way:

In the course of a certain battle a soldier whose leg has been shot off appealed to another soldier who was hurrying by to carry him to the rear, informing him at the same time of the loss which he had sustained; whereupon the generous son of Mars, shouldering the unfortunate, proceeded to carry out his desire. The bullets and cannon-balls were flying in all directions, and presently one of the latter took the wounded man's head off—without, however, his deliverer being aware of it. In no long time he was hailed by an officer, who said:

"Where are you going with that carcass?"

"To the rear, sir—he's lost his leg!"

"His leg, forsooth?" responded the astonished officer; "you mean his head, you booby."

Whereupon the soldier dispossessed himself of his burden, and stood looking down upon it in great perplexity. At length he said:

"It is true, sir, just as you have said." Then after a pause he added, "*But he* TOLD *me* IT WAS HIS LEG! ! ! ! !"

Here the narrator bursts into explosion after explosion of thunderous horselaughter, repeating that nub from time to time through his gaspings and shriekings and suffocatings.

It takes only a minute and a half to tell that in its comic-story form; and isn't worth the telling, after all. Put into the humorous-story form it takes ten minutes, and is about the funniest thing I have ever listened to—as James Whitcomb Riley tells it.

He tells it in the character of a dull-witted old farmer who has just heard it for the first time, thinks it is unspeakably funny, and is trying to repeat it to a neighbor. But he can't remember it; so he gets all mixed up and wanders helplessly round and round, putting in tedious details that don't belong in the tale and only retard it; taking them out conscientiously and putting in others that are just as useless; making minor mistakes now and then and stopping to correct them and explain how he came to make them; remembering things which he forgot to put in their proper place and going back to put them in there; stopping his narrative a good while in order to try to recall the name of the soldier that was hurt, and finally remembering that the soldier's name was not mentioned, and remarking placidly that the name is of no real importance, anyway—better, of course, if one knew it, but not essential, after all—and so on, and so on, and so on.

The teller is innocent and happy and pleased with himself, and has to stop every little while to hold himself in and keep from laughing outright; and does hold in, but his body quakes in a jelly-like way with interior chuckles; and at the end of the ten minutes the audience have laughed until they are exhausted, and the tears are running down their faces.

The simplicity and innocence and sincerity and unconsciousness of the old farmer are perfectly simulated, and the result is a performance which is thoroughly charming and delicious. This is art—and fine and beautiful, and only a master can compass it; but a machine could tell the other story.

To string incongruities and absurdities together in a wandering and sometimes purposeless way, and seem innocently unaware that they are absurdities, is the basis of the American art, if my position is correct. Another feature is the slurring of the point. A third is the dropping of a studied remark apparently without knowing it, as if one were thinking aloud. The fourth and last is the pause.

Artemus Ward dealt in numbers three and four a good deal. He would begin to tell with great animation something which he seemed to think was wonderful; then lose confidence, and after an apparently absent-minded pause add an incongruous remark in a soliloquizing way; and that was the remark intended to explode the mine—and it did.

For instance, he would say eagerly, excitedly, "I once knew a man in New Zealand who hadn't a tooth in his head" —here his animation would die out; a silent, reflective pause would follow, then he would say dreamily, and as if to himself, "and yet that man could beat a drum better than any man I ever saw."

The pause is an exceedingly important feature in any kind of story, and a frequently recurring feature, too. It is a dainty thing, and delicate, and also uncertain and treacherous; for it must be exactly the right length—no more and no less—or it fails of its purpose and makes trouble. If the pause is too short the impressive point is passed, and the audience have had time to divine that a surprise is intended—and then you can't surprise them, of course.

On the platform I used to tell a negro ghost story that had a pause in front of the snapper on the end, and that pause was the most important thing in the whole story. If I got it the right length precisely, I could spring the finishing ejaculation with effect enough to make some impressible girl deliver a startled little yelp and jump out of her seat—and that was what I was after. This story was called "The Golden Arm," and was told in this fashion. You can practise with it yourself—and mind you look out for the pause and get it right.

The Golden Arm

Once 'pon a time dey wuz a monsus mean man, en he live 'way out in de prairie all 'lone by hisself, 'cep'n he had a wife. En bimeby she died, en he tuck en toted her way out dah in de prairie en buried her. Well, she had a golden arm—all solid gold, fum de shoulder down. He wuz pow'ful mean—pow'ful; en dat night he couldn't sleep, caze he want dat golden arm so bad.

When it come midnight he couldn't stan' it no mo'; so he git up, he did, en tuck his lanern en shoved out thoo de storm en dug her up en got de golden arm; en he bent his head down 'gin de win', en plowed en plowed en plowed thoo de snow. Den all on a sudden he stop (make a considerable pause here, and look startled, and take a listening attitude) en say: "My *lan'*, what's dat!"

En he listen—en listen—en de win' say (set your teeth together and imitate the wailing and wheezing singsong of the wind), "Bzzz-z-zzz" —en den, way back yonder whah de grave is, he hear a *voice!* —he hear a voice all mix' up in de win'—can't hardly tell'em 'part —"Bzzz-zz—W-h-o—g-o-t—m-y—g-o-l-d-e-n *arm?* —zzz—zzz—W-h-o g-o-t m-y g-o-l-d-e-n *arm?* (You must begin to shiver violently now.)

En he begin to shiver en shake, en say, "Oh, my! *Oh*, my lan'!" en de win' blow de lantern out, en de snow en sleet blow in his face en mos' choke him, en he start a-plowin' knee-deep towards home mos' dead, he so sk'yerd—en pooty soon he hear de voice agin, en (pause) it 'us comin' *after* him! "Bzzz—zzz—zzz—W-h-o—g-o-t—m-y—g-o-l-d-e-n—*arm?*"

When he git to de pasture he hear it agin—closter now, en a-*comin'*! —a-comin' back dah in de dark en de storm—(repeat the wind and the voice). When he git to de house he rush upstairs en jump in de bed en kiver up, head and years, en lay dah shiv-erin' en shakin'—en den way out dah he hear it *agin!* —en a-*comin'*! En bimeby he hear (pause—awed, listening attitude) —pat—pat—pat—*hit's a-comin' up-stairs!* Den he hear de latch, en he *know* it's in de room!

Den pooty soon he know it's *a-stannin' by de bed!* (Pause.) Den—he know it's *a-bendin' down over him*—en he cain't skasely git his breath! Den—den—he seem to feel someth'n *c-o-l-d*, right down 'most agin his head! (Pause.)

Den de voice say, *right at his year*—"W-h-o—g-o-t—m-y—g-o-l-d-e-n *arm?*" (You must wait it out very plaintively and accusingly; then you stare steadily and impressively into the face of the farthest-gone auditor—a girl, preferably—and let that awe-inspiring pause begin to build itself in the deep hush. When it has reached exactly the right length, jump suddenly at that girl and yell, "*You've* got it!")

If you've got the *pause* right, she'll fetch a dear little yelp and spring right out of her shoes. But you *must* get the pause right; and you will find it the most troublesome and aggravating and uncertain thing you ever undertook.)
1895

Owen Wister, *The Virginian*

from *Chapter 16: The Game and the Nation—Last Act*

"Speakin' of bites," spoke up a new man, "how's that?" He held up his thumb.

"My!" breathed Scipio. "Must have been a lion."

The man wore a wounded look. "I was huntin' owl eggs for a botanist from Boston," he explained to me.

"Chiropodist, weren't he?" said Scipio. "Or maybe a sonnabulator?"

"No, honest," protested the man with the thumb, so that I was sorry for him, and begged him to go on.

"I'll listen to you," I assured him. And I wondered why this politeness of mine should throw one or two of them into stifled mirth. Scipio, on the other hand, gave me a disgusted look and sat back sullenly for a moment, and then took himself out on the platform, where the Virginian was lounging.

"The young feller wore knee-pants and ever so thick spectacles with a half-moon cut in 'em," resumed the narrator, "and he carried a tin box strung to a strap I took for his lunch till it flew open on him and a horn toad hustled out. Then I was sure he was a botanist—or whatever yu' say they're called. Well, he would have owl eggs—them little prairie-owl that some claim can turn their head clean around and keep a-watchin' yu', only that's non-sense. We was ridin' through that prairie-dog town, used to be on the flat just after yu' crossed the south fork of Powder River on the Buffalo trail, and I said I'd dig an owl nest out for him if he was willin' to camp till I'd dug it. I wanted to know about them owls some myself—if they did live with the dogs and snakes, yu' know," he broke off, appealing to me.

"Oh, yes," I told him eagerly.

"So while the botanist went glarin' around the town with his glasses to see if he could spot a prairie-dog and an owl usin' the same hole, I was diggin' in a hole I'd seen an owl run down. And that's what I got." He held up his thumb again.

"The snake!" I exclaimed.

"Yes, sir. Mr. Rattler was keepin' house that day. Took me right there. I hauled him out of the hole hangin' to me. Eight rattles."

"Eight!" said I. "A big one."

"Yes, sir. Thought I was dead. But the woman—"

"The woman?" said I.

"Yes, woman. Didn't I tell yu' the botanist had his wife along? Well, he did. And she acted better than the man, for he was losin' his head, and shoutin' he had no whiskey, and he didn' guess his knife was sharp enough to amputate my thumb, and none of us chewed, and the doctor was twenty miles away, and if he had only remembered to bring his ammonia—well, he was screeching out 'most everything he knew in the world and without arranging it any, neither. But she just clawed his pocket and burrowed and kep' yelling. 'Give him the stone, Augustus!' And she whipped out one of them Injun medicine-stones, —first one I ever seen, —and she clapped it on to my thumb, and it started in right away."

"What did it do?" said I.

"Sucked. Like blotting-paper does. Soft and funny it was, and gray. They get 'em from elks' stomachs, yu' know. And when it had sucked the poison out of the wound, off it falls off my thumb by itself! And I thanked the woman for saving my life that capable and keeping her head that cool. I never knowed how excited she had been till afterward. She was awful shocked."

"I suppose she started to talk when the danger was over," said I, with deep silence around me.

"No; she didn't say nothing to me. But when her next child was born, it had eight rattles."

Din now rose in the caboose. They rocked together. The enthusiast beat his knee tumultuously. And I joined them. Who could help it? It had been so well conducted from the imperceptible beginning. Fact and falsehood blended with such perfect art. And this last, an effect so new made with such world-old material!

1902

---

from George Washington Harris, *Sut Lovingood: Yarns Spun by a Nat'ral Born Durn'd Fool*

"I hates ole Onsightly Peter, jis' caze he didn't seem tu like tu hear me narrate las' night; that's human nater the yeath over, an' yeres more univarsal onregenerit human nater: ef ever yu dus enything tu eny body wifout cause, yu hates em allers arterwards, an' sorter wants tu hurt em agin. An' yere's anuther human nater: ef enything happens sum feller,

I don't keer ef he's yure bes' frien, an' I don't keer how sorry yu is fur him, thars a streak ove satisfackshun 'bout like a sowin thread a-runnin all thru yer sorrer. Yu may be shamed ove hit, but durn me ef hit ain't thar. Hit will show like the white cottin chain in mean cassinett; brushin hit onder only hides hit. An' yere's a littil more; no odds how good yu is tu yung things, ur how kine yu is in treatin em, when yu sees a littil long laiged lamb a-shakin hits tail, an' a dancin staggerinly onder hits mam a-huntin fur the tit, ontu hits knees, yer fingers *will* itch to seize that ar tail, an' fling the littil ankshus son ove a mutton over the fence amung the blackberry briars, not tu hurt hit, but jis' tu dis-apint hit. Ur say, a littil calf, a-buttin fus' under the cow's fore-laigs, an' then the hine, wif the pint ove hits tung stuck out, makin suckin moshuns, not yet old enuf tu know the bag aind ove hits mam frum the hookin aind, don't yu want tu kick hit on the snout, hard enough tu send hit backwards, say fifteen foot, jis' tu show hit that buttin won't allers fetch milk? Ur a baby even rubbin hits heels apas' each uther, a-rootin an' a-snifflin arter the breas', an' the mam duin her bes' tu git hit out, over the hem ove her clothes, don't yu feel hungry tu gin hit jis' one 'cussion cap slap, rite ontu the place what sum day'll fit a saddil, ur a sowin cheer, tu show hit what's atwixt hit an' the grave; that hit stans a pow'ful chance not tu be fed every time hits hungry, ur in a hurry?"

1867

Cherokee Oral Tradition

The Rabbitt and the Tar Wolf

First Version

Once there was such a long spell of dry weather that there was no more water in the creeks and springs, and the animals held a council to see what to do about it. They decided to dig a well, and all agreed to help except the Rabbit, who was a lazy fellow, and said, "I don't need to dig for water. The dew on the grass is enough for me." The others did not like this, but they went to work together and dug their well.

They noticed that the Rabbit kept sleek and lively, although it was still dry weather and the water was getting low in the well. They said, "That tricky Rabbit steals our water at night," so they made a wolf of pine gum and tar and set it up by the well to scare the thief. That night the Rabbit came, as he had been coming every night, to drink enough to last him all next day. He saw the queer black thing by the well and said, "Who's there?" but the tar wolf said nothing. He came nearer, but the wolf never moved, so he grew braver and said, "Get out of my way or I'll strike you." Still the wolf never moved and the Rabbit came up and struck it with his paw, but the gum held his foot and it stuck fast. Now he was angry and said, "Let me go or I'll kick you." Still the wolf said nothing. Then the Rabbit struck again with his hind foot, so hard that it was caught in the gum and he could not move, and there he stuck until the animals came for water in the morning. When they found who the thief was they had great sport over him for a while and then got ready to kill him, but as soon as he was unfastened from the tar wolf he managed to get away.

1624

Second Version

Once upon a time there was such a severe drought that all streams of water and all lakes were dried up. In this emergency the beasts assembled together to devise means to procure water. It was proposed by one to dig a well. All agreed to do so except the hare. She refused because it would soil her tiny paws. The rest, however, dug their well and were fortunate enough to find water. The hare beginning to suffer and thirst, and having no right to the well, was thrown upon her wits to procure water. She determined, as the easiest way, to steal from the public well. The rest of the anmals, suprised to find that the hare was so well supplied with water, asked her where she got it. She replied that she arose betimes in the morning and gathered the dewdrops. However the wolf and the fox suspected her of theft and hit on the following plan to detect her:

They made a wolf of tar and placed it near the well. On the following night the hare came as usual after her supply of water. On seeing the tar wolf she demanded who was there. Receiving no answer she repeated the demand, threatening to kick the wolf if he did not reply. She receiving no reply kicked the wolf, and by this means adhered to the tar and was caught. When the fox and wolf got hold of her they consulted what it was best to do with her. One proposed cutting her head off. This the hare protested would be useless, as it had often been tried without hurting her. Other methods were proposed for dispatching her, all of which she said would be useless. At last it was proposed to let her loose to perish in a thicket. Upon this the hare affected great uneasiness and pleaded hard for life. Her enemies, however, refused to listen and she was accordingly let loose. As soon, however, as she was out of reach of her enemies, she gave a whoop, and bounding away she exclaimed: "This is where I live."

1900

---

from Joel Chandler Harris, *Uncle Remus: His Songs and Sayings*

II: The Wonderful Tar-Baby Story

"Didn't the fox *never* catch the rabbit, Uncle Remus?" asked the little boy the next evening.

"He come mighty nigh it, honey, sho's you born—Brer Fox did. One day atter Brer Rabbit fool 'im wid dat calamus root, Brer Fox went ter wuk en got 'im some tar, en mix it wid some turkentime, en fix up a contrapsun wat he call a Tar-Baby, en he tuck dish yer Tar-Baby en he sot 'er in de big road, en den he lay off in de bushes fer to see wat de news wuz gwineter be. En he didn't hatter wait long, nudder, kaze bimeby here come Brer Rabbit pacin' down de road—lippity-clippity, clippity-lippity—dez ez sassy ez a jay-bird. Brer Fox, he lay low. Brer Rabbit come prancin' 'long twel he spy de Tar-Baby, en den he fotch up on his behime legs like he wuz 'stonished. De Tar-Baby, she sot dar, she did, en Brer Fox, he lay low.

" 'Mawnin'!' sez Brer Rabbit, sezee—'nice wedder dis mawnin',' sezee.

"Tar-Baby ain't sayin' nothin', en Brer Fox, he lay low.

" 'How duz yo' sym'tums seem ter segashuate?' sez Brer Rabbit, sezee.

"Brer Fox, he wink his eye slow, en lay low, en de Tar-Baby, she ain't sayin' nothin'.

" 'How you come on, den? Is you deaf?' sez Brer Rabbit, sezee. 'Kaze if you is, I kin holler louder,' sezee.

Frederick S. Church and James H. Moser
Uncle Remus
from *Uncle Remus: His Songs and Sayings*
1880

"Tar-Baby stay still, en Brer Fox, he lay low.

" 'Youer stuck up, dat's w'at you is,' says Brer Rabbit, sezee, 'en I'm gwineter kyore you, dat's w'at I'm a gwineter do,' sezee.

"Brer Fox, he sorter chuckle in his stummuck, he did, but Tar-Baby ain't sayin' nothin'.

" 'I'm gwineter larn you howter talk ter 'specttubble fokes ef hit's de las' ack,' sez Brer Rabbit, sezee. 'Ef you don't take off dat hat en tell me howdy, I'm gwinteter bus' you wide open,' sezee.

"Tar-Baby stay still, en Brer Fox, he lay low.

"Brer Rabbit keep on axin' 'im, en de Tar-Baby, she keep on sayin' nothin', twel present'y Brer Rabbit draw back wid his fis', he did, en blip he tuck 'er side er de head. Right dar's whar he broke his merlasses jug. His fis' stuck, en he can't pull loose. De tar hilt 'im. But Tar-Baby, she stay still, en Brer Fox, he lay low.

" 'Ef you don't lemme loose, I'll knock you agin,' sez Brer Rabbit, sezee, en wid dat he fotch 'er a wipe wid de udder han', en dat stuck. Tar-Baby, she ain't sayin' nothin', en Brer Fox, he lay low.

" 'Tu'n me loose, fo' I kick de natal stuffin' outen you,' sez Brer Rabbit, sezee, but de Tar-Baby, she ain't sayin' nothin'. She des hilt on, en den Brer Rabbit lose de use er his feet in de same way. Brer Fox, he lay low. Den Brer Rabbit squall out dat ef de Tar-Baby don't tu'n 'im loose he butt 'er cranksided. En den he butted, en his head got stuck. Den Brer Fox, he sa'ntered fort', lookin' des ez innercent ez one er yo' mammy's mockin'-birds.

" 'Howdy, Brer Rabbit,' sez Brer Fox, sezee. 'You look sorter stuck up dis mawnin',' sezee, en den he rolled on de groun', en laughed en laughed twel he couldn't laugh no mo'. 'I speck you'll take dinner wid me dis time, Brer Rabbit. I done laid in some calamus root, en I ain't gwineter take no skuse,' sez Brer Fox, sezee."

Here Uncle Remus paused, and drew a two-pound yam out of the ashes.

"Did the fox eat the rabbit?" asked the little boy to whom the story had been told.

"Dat's all de fur de tale goes," replied the old man. "He mout, en den agin he moutent. Some say Jedge B'ar come 'long en loosed 'im —some say he didn't. I hear Miss Sally callin'. You better run 'long."

1880

Frederick S. Church and
James H. Moser
*The Tarbaby and
Brer Rabbit*
from *Uncle Remus:
His Songs and Sayings*
1880

IV: How Mr. Rabbit Was Too Sharp For Mr. Fox

"Uncle Remus" said the little boy one evening, when he had found the old man with little or nothing to do, "did the fox kill and eat the rabbit when he caught him with the Tar-Baby?"

"Law, honey, ain't I tell you 'bout dat?" replied the old darkey, chuckling slyly. "I 'clar ter grashus I ought er tole you dat, but ole man Nod wuz ridin' on my eyeleds 'twel a leetle mo'n I'd a dis'member'd my own name, en den on to dat here come yo' mammy hollerin' atter you.

"W'at I tell you w'en I fus' begin? I tole you Brer Rabbit wuz a monstus soon beas'; leas'ways dat's w'at I laid out fer ter tel you. Well, den, honey, don't you go en make no udder kalkalashuns, kaze in dem days Brer Rabbit en his fambly wuz at de head er de gang w'en enny racket wuz on han', en dar de stayed. 'Fo' you begins fer ter wipe yo' eyes 'bout Brer Rabbit, you wait en see whar'bouts Brer Rabbit gwineter fetch up at. But dat's needer yer ner dar.

"W'en Brer Fox fine Brer Rabbit mixt up wid de Tar-Baby, he feel mighty good, en he roll on de groun' en laff. Bimeby he up'n say, sezee:

" 'Well, I speck I got you dis time, Brer Rabbit,' sezee; 'maybe I ain't, but I speck I is. You been runnin' roun' here sassin' atter me a mighty long time, but I speck you done come ter de een'er de row. You bin cuttin' up yo' capers en bouncin' 'roun' in dis naberhood ontwel you come ter b'leeve yo'se'f de boss er de whole gang. En den youer allers some'rs whar you got no bizness,' sez Brer Fox, sezee. 'Who ax you fer ter come en strike up a 'quaintence wid dish yer Tar-Baby? En who stuck you up dar whar yu iz? Nobody in de roun' worril. Yu des tuck en jam yo'se'f on dat Tar-Baby widout waitin' fer enny invite,' sez Brer Fox, sezee, 'en dar you is, en dar you'll stay twel I fixes up a bresh-pile and fires her up, kaze I'm gwineter bobbycue you dis day, sho,' sez Brer Fox, sezee.

"Den Brer Rabbit talk mighty 'umble.

" 'I don't keer w'at you do wid me, Brer Fox,' sezee, 'so you don't fling me in dat brier-patch. Roas' me, Brer Fox,' sezee, 'but don't fling me in dat brier-patch,' sezee.

" 'Hit's so much trouble fer ter kindle a fier,' sez Brer Fox, sezee, 'dat I speck I'll hatter hang you,' sezee.

" 'Hang me des ez high as you please, Brer Fox,' sez Brer Rabbit, sezee, 'but do fer de Lord's sake don't fling me in dat brier-pach,' sezee.

" 'I ain't got no string,' sez Brer Fox, sezee, 'en now I speck I'll hatter drown you,' sezee.

" 'Drown me des ez deep ez you please, Brer Fox,' sez Brer Rabbit, sezee, 'but do don't fling me in dat brier-patch,' sezee.

" 'Dey ain't no water nigh,' sez Brer Fox, sezee, 'en now I speck I'll hatter skin you,' sezee.

" 'Skin me, Brer Fox,' sez Brer Rabbit, sezee, 'snatch out my eyeballs, t'ar out my years by de roots, en cut off my legs,' sezee, 'but do please, Brer Fox, don't fling me in dat brier-patch,' sezee.

"Co'se Brer Fox wanter hurt Brer Rabbit bad ez he kin, so he cotch 'im by de behime legs en slung 'im right in de middle er de brier-patch. Dar wuz a considerbul flutter whar Brer Rabbit struck de bushes, en Brer Fox sorter hang 'roun' fer ter see w'at wuz gwineter happen. Bimeby he hear somebody call 'im, en way up de hill he see Brer Rabbit settin' cross-legged on a chinkapin log koamin' de pitch outen his har wid a chip. Den Brer Fox know dat he bin swop off mighty bad. Brer Rabbit wuz bleedzed fer ter fling back some er his sass, en he holler out:

" 'Bred en bawn in a brier-patch, Brer Fox—bred en bawn in a brier-patch!' en wid dat he skip out des ez lively ez a cricket in de embers."

1880

---

from Zora Neale Hurston, *Mules and Men*

from **Chapter V**

Going back home Ole Massa said: "Well, John, you done made me vast rich so I goin' to Philly-Me-York and won't be back in three weeks. I leave everything in yo' charge."

So Ole Massa and his wife got on de train and John went to de depot with 'em and seen 'em off on de train bid 'em goodbye. Then he hurried on back to de plantation. Ole Massa and Ole Miss got off at de first station and made it on back to see whut John was doin'.

John went back and told de niggers, "Massa's gone to Philly-Me-York and left everything in my charge. Ah want one of you niggers to git on a mule and ride three miles north, and another one three miles west and another one three miles south and another one three miles east. Tell everybody to come here—there's gointer be a ball here tonight. The rest of you go into de lot and kill hogs until you can walk on 'em."

So they did. John goes in and dressed up in Ole Massa's swaller-tail clothes, put on his collar and tie; got a box of cigars and put under his arm, and one cigar in his mouth.

When de crowd come John said: "Y'all kin dance and Ah'm goin' to call figgers."

So he got Massa's biggest rockin' chair and put it up in Massa's bed and then he got up in de bed in de chair and begin to call figgers:

"Hands up!" "Four circle right." "Half back." "Two ladies change." He was puffing his cigar all de time.

'Bout this time John seen a white couple come in but they looked so trashy he figgered they was piney woods crackers, so he told 'em to g'wan out in de kitchen and git some barbecue and likker and to stay out there where they belong. So he went callin' figgers agin. De git Fiddles was raisin' cain over in de corner and John was callin' for de new set:

"Choose yo' parters." "Couples to yo' places like horses to de traces." "Sashay all." "Sixteen hands up." "Swing Miss Sally 'round and 'round and bring her back to me!"

Just as he went to say "Four hands up," he seen Ole Massa comin' out the kitchen wipin' the dirt off his face.

Ole Massa said: "John, just look whut you done done! I'm gointer take you to that persimmon tree and break yo' neck for this—killing up all my hogs and havin' all these niggers in my house."

John ast, "Ole Massa, Ah know you gointer kill me, but can Ah have a word with my friend Jack before you kill me?"

"Yes, John, but have it quick."

So John called Jack and told him; says: "Ole Massa is gointer hang me under that persimmon tree. Now you get three matches and get in the top of the tree. Ah'm gointer pray and when you hear me ast God to let it lightning Ah want you to strike matches."

Jack went on out to the tree. Ole Massa brought John on out with the rope around his neck and put it over a limb.

"Now, John," said Massa, "have you got any last words to say?"

"Yes sir, Ah want to pray."

"Pray and pray damn quick. I'm clean out of patience with you, John."

So John knelt down. "Oh Lord, here Ah am at de foot of de persimmon tree. If you're gointer destroy Old Massa tonight, with his wife and chillun and everything he got, lemme see it lightnin'."

Jack up the tree, struck a match. Ole Massa caught hold of John and said: "John, don't pray no more."

John said: "Oh yes, turn me loose so Ah can pray. O Lord, here Ah am tonight callin' on Thee and Thee alone. If you are gointer destroy Ole Massa tonight, his wife and chillun and all he got, Ah want to see it lightnin' again."

Jack struck another match and Ole Massa started to run. He give John his freedom and a heap of land and stock. He run so fast that it took a express train running at the rate of ninety miles an hour and six months to bring him back, and that's how come niggers got they freedom today.

1935

African American Spirituals

Steal Away to Jesus

Steal away, steal away, steal away to Jesus,
Steal away, steal away home,
I ain't got long to stay here.

My Lord, He calls me,
He calls me by the thunder,

5

The trumpet sounds within-a my soul,
I ain't got long to stay here.

Steal away, steal away, steal away to Jesus,
Steal away, steal away home,
I ain't got long to stay here.   10

Green trees a-bending,
Po' sinner stands a-trembling,
The trumpet sounds within-a my soul,
I ain't got long to stay here.

Steal away, steal away, steal away to Jesus,   15
Steal away, steal away home,
I ain't got long to stay here.

Go Down Moses

Go down, Moses,
Way down in Egyptland
Tell old Pharaoh
To let my people go.

When Israel was in Egyptland   5
Let my people go
Oppressed so hard they could not stand
Let my people go.

Go down, Moses,
Way down in Egyptland   10
Tell old Pharaoh
"Let my people go."

"Thus saith the Lord," bold Moses said,
"Let my people go;
If not I'll smite your first-born dead   15
Let my people go.

"No more shall they in bondage toil,
    Let my people go;
Let them come out with Egypt's spoil,
    Let my people go."   20
The Lord told Moses what to do
    Let my people go;

To lead the children of Israel through,
  Let my people go.

Go down, Moses,
  Way down in Egyptland,
Tell old Pharaoh,
  "Let my people go!"

W. E. B. Du Bois, *The Souls of Black Folk*

from **Chapter XIV: Of the Sorrow Songs**

What are these songs, and what do they mean? I know little of music and can say nothing in technical phase, but I know something of men, and knowing them, I know that these songs are the articulate message of the slave to the world. They tell us in these eager days that life was joyous to the black slave, careless and happy. I can easily believe this of some, of many. But not all the past South, though it rose from the dead, can gainsay the heart-touching witness of these songs. They are the music of an unhappy people, of the children of disappointment; they tell of death and suffering and unvoiced longing toward a truer world, of misty wanderings and hidden ways.

The songs are indeed the siftings of centuries; the music is far more ancient than the words, and in it we can trace here and there signs of development. My grandfather's grandmother was seized by an evil Dutch trader two centuries ago; and coming to the valleys of the Hudson and Housatonic, black, little, and lithe, she shivered and shrank in the harsh north winds, looked longingly at the hills, and often crooned a heathen melody to the child between her knees. . . . The child sang it to his children and they to their children's children, and so two hundred years it has travelled down to us and we sing it to our children, knowing as little as our fathers what its words may mean, but knowing well the meaning of its music.

This was primitive African music; it may be seen in larger form in the strange chant which heralds "The Coming of John":

"You may bury me in the East,
You may bury me in the West,
But I'll hear the trumpet sound in that morning,"

—the voice of exile.

Ten master songs, more or less, one may pluck from this forest of melody—songs of undoubted Negro origin and wide popular currency, and songs peculiarly characteristic of the slave. One of these I have just mentioned. Another whose strains begin this book is "Nobody knows the trouble I've seen." When, struck with a sudden poverty, the United States refused to fulfill its promises of land to the freedmen, a brigadier-general went down to the Sea Islands to carry the news. An old woman on the outskirts of the throng began singing this song; all the mass joined with her, swaying. And the soldier wept.

The third song is the cradle-song of death which all men know, —"Swing low, sweet chariot," —whose bars begin the life story of "Alexander Crummell." Then there is the song of many waters, "Roll, Jordan, roll," a mighty chorus with minor cadences. There were many songs of the fugitive like that which opens "The Wings of Atalanta," and the more familiar "Been a-listening." The seventh is the song of the End and the Beginning—"My Lord, what a mourning! when the stars begin to fall"; a strain of this is placed before "The Dawn of Freedom." The song of groping—"My way's cloudy" —begins "The Meaning of Progresss"; the ninth is the song of this chapter—"Wrestlin' Jacob, the day is a-breaking,"—a pæan of hopeful strife. The last master song is the song of songs—"Steal away," —sprung from "The Faith of the Fathers."

There are many others of the Negro folk-songs as striking and characteristic as these, as, for instance, the three strains in the third, eighth, and ninth chapters; and others I am sure could easily make a selection on more scientific principles. There are, too, songs that seem to be a step removed from the more primitive types: there is the maze-like medley, "Bright sparkles," one phrase of which heads "The Black Belt"; the Eastern carol, "Dust, dust and ashes"; the dirge, "My mother's took her flight and gone home"; and that burst of melody hovering over "The Passing of the First-Born" —"I hope my mother will be there in that beautiful world on high."

These represent a third step in the development of the slave song, of which "You may bury me in the East" is the first, and songs like "March on" (chapter six) and "Steal away" are the second. The first is African music, the second Afro-American, while the third is a blending of Negro music with the music heard in the foster land. The result is still distinctively Negro and the method of blending original, but the elements are both Negro and Caucasian. One might go further and find a fourth step in this development, where the songs of white America have been distinctively influenced by the slave songs or have incorporated whole phrases of Negro melody, as "Swanee River" and "Old Black Joe." Side by side, too, with the growth has gone the debasements and imitations—the Negro "minstrel" songs, many of the "gospel" hymns, and some of the contemporary "coon" songs, —a mass of music in which the novice may easily lose himself and never find the real Negro melodies.

In these songs, I have said, the slave spoke to the world. Such a message is naturally veiled and half articulate. Words and music have lost each other and new and cant phrases of a dimly understood theology have displaced the older sentiment. Once in a while we catch a strange word of an unknown tongue, as the "Mighty Myo," which figures as a river of death; more often slight words or mere doggerel are joined to music of singular sweetness. Purely secular songs are few in number, partly because many of them were turned into hymns by a change of words, partly because the frolics were seldom heard by the stranger, and the music less often caught. Of nearly all the songs, however, the music is distinctly sorrowful. The ten master songs I have mentioned tell in word and music of trouble and exile, of strife and hiding; they grope toward some unseen power and sigh for rest in the End.

1903

Ballads and Work Songs

John Henry

When John Henry was a little fellow,
 You could hold him in the palm of your hand,
He said to his pa, "When I grow up
 I'm gonna be a steel-driving man.
  Gonna be a steel-driving man."   5

When John Henry was a little baby,
 Setting on his mammy's knee,
He said "The Big Bend Tunnel on the C. & O. Road
 Is gonna be the death of me,
  Gonna be the death of me."   10

One day his captain told him,
 How he had bet a man
That John Henry would beat his stream-drill down,
 Cause John Henry was the best in the land,
  John Henry was the best in the land.   15

John Henry kissed his hammer,
 White man turned on steam,
Shaker held John Henry's trusty steel,
 Was the biggest race the world had ever seen,
  Lord, biggest race the world ever seen.   20

John Henry on the right side
 The steam drill on the left,
"Before I'll let your steam drill beat me down,
 I'll hammer my fool self to death,
  Hammer my fool self to death."   25

John Henry walked in the tunnel,
 His captain by his side,
The mountain so tall, John Henry so small,
 He laid down his hammer and he cried,
  Laid down his hammer and he cried.   30

Captain heard a mighty rumbling,
 Said "The mountain must be caving in,"
John Henry said to the captain,
 "It's my hammer swinging in de wind,
  "My hammer swinging in de wind."   35

John Henry said to his shaker,
  "Shaker, you'd better pray;
For if ever I miss this piece of steel,
    Tomorrow'll be your burial day,
      Tomorrow'll be your burial day."   40

John Henry said to his shaker,
  "Lordy, shake it while I sing,
I'm pulling my hammer from my shoulders down,
    Great Gawdamighty, how she ring,
      Great Gawdamighty, how she ring!"   45

John Henry said to his captain,
  "Before I ever leave town,
Gimme one mo' drink of dat tom-cat gin,
    And I'll hammer dat steam driver down,
      I'll hammer dat steam driver down."   50

John Henry said to his captain,
  "Before I ever leave town,
Gimme a twelve-pound hammer wid a whale-bone handle,
    And I'll hammer dat steam driver down,
      I'll hammer dat steam drill on down."   55

John Henry said to his captain,
  "A man ain't nothin' but a man,
But before I'll let dat steam drill beat me down,
    I'll die wid my hammer in my hand,
      Die wid my hammer in my hand."   60

The man that invented the steam drill
  He thought he was mighty fine,
John Henry drove down fourteen feet,
    While the steam drill only made nine,
      Steam drill only made nine.   65

"Oh, lookaway over yonder, captain,
  You can't see like me,"
He gave a long and loud and lonesome cry,
    "Lawd, a hammer be the death of me,
      A hammer be the death of me!"   70

John Henry had a little woman,
  Her name was Polly Ann,
John Henry took sick, she took his hammer,
    She hammered like a natural man,
      Lawd, she hammered like a natural man.   75

John Henry hammering on the mountain
   As the whistle blew for half-past two,
The last words his captain heard him say,
    "I've done hammered my insides in two,
      Lawd, I've hammered my insides in two."   80

The hammer that John Henry swung
   It weighed over twelve pound,
He broke, a rib in his left hand side
   And his intrels fell on the ground,
     And his intrels fell on the ground.   85

John Henry, O, John Henry,
   His blood is running red,
Fell right down with his hammer to the ground,
   Said, "I beat him to the bottom but I'm dead,
     Lawd, beat him to the bottom but I'm dead."   90

When John Henry was laying there dying,
   The people all by his side,
The very last words they heard him say,
   "Give me a cool drink of water 'fore I die,
     Cool drink of water 'fore I die."   95

John Henry had a little woman,
   The dress she wore was red,
She went down the track, and she never looked back,
   Going where her man fell dead,
     Going where her man fell dead.   100

John Henry had a little woman,
   The dress she wore was blue,
De very last words she said to him,
   "John Henry, I'll be true to you,
     John Henry, I'll be true to you."   105

"Who's gonna shoes yo' little feet,
   Who's gonna glove yo' hand,
Who's gonna kiss yo' pretty, pretty cheek,
   Now you done lost yo' man?
     Now you done lost yo' man?"   110

"My mammy's gonna shoes my little feet,
   Pappy gonna glove my hand,
My sister's gonna kiss my pretty, pretty cheek,
   Now I done lost my man,
     Now I done lost my man."   115

They carried him down by the river,
   And buried him in the sand,
And everybody that passed that way,
   Said, "There lies that steel-driving man,
     There lies a steel-driving man."   120

They took John Henry to the river,
   And buried him in the sand,
And every locomotive come a-roaring by,
   Says "There lies that steel-drivin' man,
     Lawd, there lies a *steel*-drivin' man."   125

Some say he came from Georgia,
   And some from Alabam,
But its wrote on the rock at the Big Bend Tunnel,
   That he was an East Virginia man,
     Lord, Lord, an East Virginia man.   130

Dave McCarn, *Cotton Mill Colic*

When you buy clothes on easy terms
The collectors treat you like measly worms.
One dollar down, and then Lord knows
If you don't make a payment they'll take your clothes.
When you go to bed you can't sleep;   5
You owe so much at the end of the week.
   No use to colic, they're all that way
   Pecking at your door till they get your pay.
   I'm a-gonna starve, everybody will
   'Cause you can't make a living at a cotton mill.   10

When you go to work you work like the devil
At the end of the week you're not on the level.
Payday comes, you pay your rent;
When you get through you've not got a cent.
To buy fat-back meat, pinto beans;   15
Now and then you get turnip greens.
   No use to colic, we're all that way,
   Can't get the money to move away.
   I'm a-gonna starve, everybody will
   'Cause you can't make a living at a cotton mill.   20
Twelve dollars a week is all we get
How in the heck can we live on that?
I've got a wife and fourteen kids

We all have to sleep on two bedsteads.
Patches on my britches, holes in my hat, 25
Ain't had a shave since my wife got fat.
    No use to colic, every day at noon
    The kids get to crying in a different time.
    I'm a-gonna starve, nobody will
    'Cause you can't make a living at a cotton mill. 30

They run a few days and then they stand
Just to keep down the working man;
We can't make it, we never will
As long as we stay at a lousy mill.
The poor are getting poorer, the rich are getting rich 35
If I don't starve I'm a son of a gun.
    No use to colic, no use to rave;
    We'll never rest till we're in our grave.
    I'm a-gonna starve, nobody will
    'Cause you can't make a living at a cotton mill. 40

1926

Unidentified Photographer
Confederate Veterans
1905
(Photographic Archives, University of Louisville, Neg. #86.15)

Margaret Mitchell, *Gone With the Wind*

from **Chapter XLI**

Whenever two former Confederates met anywhere, there was never but one topic of conversation, and where a dozen or more gathered together, it was a foregone conclusion that the war would be spiritedly refought. And always the word "if" had the most prominent part in the talk.

"If England had recognized us—" "If Jeff Davis had commandeered all the cotton and gotten it to England before the blockade tightened—" "If Longstreet had obeyed orders at Gettysburg—" "If Jeb Stuart hadn't been away on that raid when Marse Bob needed him—" "If we hadn't lost Stonewall Jackson—" "If Vicksburg hadn't fallen—" "If we could have held on another year—" And always: "If they hadn't replaced Johnston with Hood—" or "If they'd put Hood in command at Dalton instead of Johnston—"

If! If! The soft drawling voices quickened with an old excitement as they talked in the quiet darkness—infantryman, cavalryman, cannoneer, evoking memories of the days when life was ever at high tide, recalling the fierce heat of their midsummer in this forlorn sunset of their winter.

"They don't talk of anything else," thought Scarlett. "Nothing but the war. Always the war. And they'll never talk of anything but the war. No, not until they die."

She looked about, seeing little boys lying in the crooks of their fathers' arms, breath coming fast, eyes glowing, as they heard of midnight stories and wild cavalry dashes and flags planted on enemy breastworks. They were hearing drums and bugles and the Rebel yell, seeing footsore men going by in the rain with torn flags slanting.

"And these children will never talk of anything else either. They'll think it was wonderful and glorious to fight the Yankees and come home blind and crippled—or not come home at all. They all like to remember the war, to talk about it. But I don't. I don't even like to think about it. I'd forget it all if I could—oh, if I only could!"

1936

Sarah Orne Jewett
1849–1909

There is a direct line of influence from the inspiration taken by Sarah Orne Jewett from the regional stories of Harriet Beecher Stowe down to the impetus given by Jewett's writings to the young Mary Eleanor Wilkins Freeman and later to Willa Cather, who became one of Jewett's editors. With the exception of Cather, all these women were reared in New England. They gained almost immediate recognition for their talent to create literary annotations of a tight-knit way of life and a tradition of moral rigor that changed rapidly during their lifetimes. Of this group, Jewett's field of vision stands out for its attention to New England customs and local settings, made universal through its accounting of a people bound to family and community.

One of three daughters of a local practitioner and professor of medicine at Bowdoin College, Sarah Orne Jewett was born in South Berwick, Maine, a coastal town where her grandfather had been the leading sea captain and shipowner. In "The Custom House," preface to *The Scarlet Letter,* written in 1849–1850, Nathaniel Hawthorne could look back on the declining fortunes of once bustling Massachusetts port towns such as Salem. By the time of Jewett's adolescence in the 1860s, the shift from a maritime and entrepreneurial economic system to industrial America had already taken place. Spurred by her reading of Harriet Beecher Stowe's account of Maine coast life, *The Pearl of Orr's Island* (1862), and by the trips she made with her doctor-father on his buggy rounds to rural patients, Jewett decided in her teens to act as a literary amanuensis for the lives of the people of that region.

Jewett's earliest pieces, published under various pseudonyms, were written at the age of fourteen. These stories were often luridly overplotted in the manner of the popular fiction of the time, but she soon included local legends and observations of speech patterns and social mannerisms. Too sickly to receive a regular education, she read a great deal in the books of her father's library, with his constant encouragement. Most of all, she "read" the lives of people who were shaped both by the natural conditions of the villages, farms, and seaports of Maine and by the social complications introduced into a world that no longer seemed small enough to be manageable and pleasing.

By the age of twenty, Sarah Orne Jewett had had her story "Mr. Bruce" accepted by William Dean Howells for publication in the *Atlantic Monthly.* Her first collection of stories appeared as *Deephaven* (1877). In response to the praise she received for work that appeared in the country's best magazines (the *Atlantic, Harper's,* and *Scribner's*), she published more than twenty volumes of stories over the years, culminating in 1896 with *The Country of the Pointed Firs,* her single best collection.

Even more than Mary E. Wilkins Freeman, who was markedly the reporter of present moments, Jewett became a recorder of times in the process of being lost forever—the "was" of her remembered childhood. She did not write rustic idylls about a perfect time and place, but in celebrating the modest pleasures and virtues of rural lives she proved how capable an unmarried woman from a sheltered background could be as the keeper of the literary annals of small-town New England. There was a large audience for such writing in her day. Later generations were reminded of a world they had never experienced personally; through Jewett, Americans came to believe they still possessed it as part of their national heritage.

Further Reading:

F. Matthiessen, *Sarah Orne Jewett,* 1960.

R. Cary, ed., *Appreciation of Sarah Orne Jewett: 29 Interpretive Essays,* 1973.

J. Donovan, *Sarah Orne Jewett,* 1980.

P. Westbrook, *Acres of Flint: Sarah Orne Jewett and Her Contemporaries,* 1981.

L. Renza, *"A White Heron" and the Question of Minor Literature,* 1984.

G. Nagel, ed., *Critical Essays on Sarah Orne Jewett,* 1984.

K. Griffith, "Sylvia as Hero in Jewett's 'White Heron," *Colby Library Quarterly* 21 (1985), 22–27.

S. Sherman, *Sarah Orne Jewett,* 1989.

M. Pennell, "A New Spiritual Biography: Domesticity and Sorority in the Fiction of Jewett," *Studies in American Fiction* 18 (1990), 193–206.

E. Ammons, *Conflicting Stories,* 1991.

M. S. Mobley, *Folk Roots and Mythic Wings in Jewett and Toni Morrison,* 1991.

M. Roman, *Sarah Orne Jewett: Reconstructing Gender,* 1992.

P. Blanchard. *Sarah Orne Jewett,* 1994.

Text:

"A White Heron" from *A White Heron and Other Stories,* 1884, 1914.

A White Heron

I

The woods were already filled with shadows one June evening, just before eight o'clock, though a bright sunset still glimmered faintly among the trunks of the trees. A little girl was driving home her cow, a plodding, dilator6y, provoking creature in her behavior, but a valued companion for all that. They were going away from whatever light there was, and striking deep into the woods, but their feet were familiar with the path, and it was no matter whether their eyes could see it or not.

There was hardly a night the summer through when the old cow could be found waiting at the pasture bars; on the contrary, it was her greatest pleasure to hide herself away among the huckleberry bushes, and though she wore a loud bell she had made the discovery that if one stood perfectly still it would not ring. So Sylvia had to hunt for her until she found her, and call Co'! Co'! with never an answering Moo, until her childish patience was quite spent. If the creature had not given good milk and plenty of it, the case would have seemed very different to her owners. Besides, Sylvia had all the time there was, and very little use to make of it. Sometimes in pleasant weather it was a consolation to look upon the cow's pranks as an intelligent attempt to play hide and seek, and as the child had no playmates she lent herself to this amusement with a good deal of zest. Though this chase had been so long that the wary animal herself had given an unusual signal of her whereabouts, Sylvia had only laughed when she came upon Mistress Moolly at the swamp-side, and urged her affectionately homeward with a twig of birch leaves. The old cow was not inclined to wander farther, she even turned in the right direction for once as they left the pasture, and stepped along the road at a good pace. She was quite ready to be milked now, and seldom stopped to browse. Sylvia wondered what her grandmother would say because they were so late. It was a great while since she had left home at half-past five o'clock, but everybody knew the difficulty of making this errand a short one. Mrs. Tilley had chased the hornéd torment too many summer evenings herself to blame any one else for lingering, and was only thankful as she waited that she had Sylvia, nowadays, to give such valuable assistance. The good woman suspected that Sylvia loitered occasionally on her own account; there never was such a child for straying about out-of-doors since the world was made! Everybody said that it was a good change for a little maid who had tried to grow for eight years in a crowded manufacturing town, but, as for Sylvia herself, it seemed as if she never had been alive at all before she came to live at the farm. She thought often with wistful compassion of a wretched geranium that belonged to a town neighbor.

" 'Afraid of folks,' " old Mrs. Tilley said to herself, with a smile, after she had made the unlikely choice of Sylvia from her daughter's houseful of children, and was returning to the farm. " 'Afraid of folks,' they said! I guess she won't be troubled no great with 'em up to the old place!" When they reached the door of the lonely house and stopped to unlock it, and the cat came to purr loudly, and rub against them, a deserted pussy, indeed, but fat with young robins, Sylvia whispered that this was a beautiful place to live in, and she never should wish to go home.

The companions followed the shady woodroad, the cow taking slow steps and the child very fast ones. The cow stopped long at the brook to drink, as if the pasture were not half a swamp, and Sylvia stood still and waited, letting her bare feet cool themselves in the shoal water, while the great twilight moths struck softly against her. She waded on through the brook as the cow moved away, and listened to the thrushes with a heart that beat fast with pleasure. There was a stirring in the great boughs overhead. They were full of little birds and beasts that seemed to be wide awake, and going about their world, or else saying good-night to each other in sleepy twitters. Sylvia herself felt sleepy as she walked along. However, it was not much farther to the house, and the air was soft and sweet. She was not often in the woods so late as this, and it made her feel as if she were a part of the gray shadows and the moving leaves. She was just thinking how long it seemed since she first came to the farm a year ago, and wondering if everything went on in the noisy town just the same as when she was there, the thought of the great red-faced boy who used to chase and frighten her made her hurry along the path to escape from the shadow of the trees.

Suddenly this little woods-girl is horror-stricken to hear a clear whistle not very far away. Not a bird's-whistle, which would have a sort of friendliness, but a boy's whistle, determined, and somewhat aggressive. Sylvia left the cow to whatever sad fate might await her, and stepped discreetly aside into the bushes, but she was just too late. The enemy had discovered her, and called out in a very cheerful and persuasive tone, "Halloa, little girl, how far is it to the road?" and trembling Sylvia answered almost inaudibly, "A good ways."

She did not dare to look boldly at the tall young man, who carried a gun over his shoulder, but she came out of her bush and again followed the cow, while he walked alongside.

"I have been hunting for some birds," the stranger said kindly, "and I have lost my way, and need a friend very much. Don't be afraid," he added gallantly. "Speak up and tell me what your name is, and whether you think I can spend the night at your house, and go out gunning early in the morning."

Sylvia was more alarmed than before. Would not her grandmother consider her much to blame? But who could have foreseen such an accident as this? It did not seem to be her fault, and she hung her head as if the stem of it were broken, but managed to answer "Sylvy," with much effort when her companion again asked her name.

Mrs. Tilley was standing in the doorway when the trio came into view. The cow gave a loud moo by way of explanation.

"Yes, you'd better speak up for yourself, you old trial! Where'd she tucked herself away this time, Sylvy?" But Sylvia kept an awed silence; she knew by instinct that her grandmother did not comprehend the gravity of the situation. She must be mistaking the stranger for one of the farmer-lads of the region.

The young man stood his gun beside the door, and dropped a lumpy game-bag beside it; then he bade Mrs. Tilley good-evening, and repeated his wayfarer's story, and asked if he could have a night's lodging.

"Put me anywhere you like," he said. "I must be off early in the morning, before day; but I am very hungry, indeed. You can give me some milk at any rate, that's plain."

"Dear sakes, yes," responded the hostess, whose long slumbering hospitality seemed to be easily awakened. "You might fare better if you went out to the main road a mile or so, but you're welcome to what we've got. I'll milk right off, and you make yourself at home. You can sleep on husks or feathers," she proffered graciously. "I raised them all myself. There's good pasturing for geese just below here towards the ma'sh. Now step round and set a plate for the gentleman, Sylvy!" And Sylvia promptly stepped. She was glad to have something to do, and she was hungry herself.

It was a surprise to find so clean and comfortable a little dwelling in this New England wilderness. The young man had known the horrors of its most primitive housekeeping, and the dreary squalor of that level of society which does not rebel at the companionship of hens. This was the best thrift of an old-fashioned farmstead, though on such a small scale that it seemed like a hermitage. He listened eagerly to the old woman's quaint talk, he watched Sylvia's pale face and shining gray eyes with ever growing enthusiasm, and insisted that this was the best supper he had eaten for a month, and afterward the new-made friends sat down in the door-way together while the moon came up.

Soon it would be berry-time, and Sylvia was a great help at picking. The cow was a good milker, though a plaguy thing to keep track of, the hostess gossiped frankly, adding presently that she had buried four children, so Sylvia's mother, and a son (who might be dead) in California were all the children she had left. "Dan, my boy, was a great hand to go gunning," she explained sadly. "I never wanted for pa'tridges or gray squer'ls while he was to home. He's been a great wand'rer, I expect, and he's no hand to write letters. There, I don't blame him, I'd ha' seen the world myself if it had been so I could."

"Sylvy takes after him," the grandmother continued affectionately, after a minute's pause. "There ain't a foot o' ground she don't know her way over, and the wild creaturs counts her one o' themselves. Squer'ls she'll tame to come an' feed right out o' her hands, and all sorts o' birds. Last winter she got the jaybirds to bangeing here, and I believe she 'd a' scanted herself of her own meals to have plenty to throw out amongst 'em, if I had n't kep' watch. Anything but crows, I tell her, I'm willin' to help support— though Dan he had a tamed one o' them that did seem to have reason same as folks. It was round here a good spell after he went away. Dan an' his father they did n't hitch,— but he never held up his head ag'in after Dan had dared him an' gone off."

The guest did not notice this hint of family sorrows in his eager interest in some-thing else.

"So Sylvy knows all about birds, does she?" he exclaimed, as he looked round at the little girl who sat, very demure but increasingly sleepy, in the moonlight. "I am making a collection of birds myself. I have been at it ever since I was a boy." (Mrs. Tilley smiled.) "There are two or three very rare ones I have been hunting for these five years. I mean to get them on my own ground if they can be found."

"Do you cage 'em up?" asked Mrs. Tilley doubtfully, in response to this enthusiastic announcement.

"Oh no, they 're stuffed and preserved, dozens and dozens of them," said the ornithol-ogist, "and I have shot or snared every one myself. I caught a glimpse of a white heron a few miles from here on Saturday, and I have followed it in this direction. They have never been found in this district at all. The little white heron, it is," and he turned again to look at Sylvia with the hope of discovering that the rare bird was one of her acquaintances.

But Sylvia was watching a hop-toad in the narrow footpath.

"You would know the heron if you saw it," the stranger continued eagerly. "A queer tall white bird with soft feathers and long thin legs. And it would have a nest perhaps in the top of a high tree, made of sticks, something like a hawk's nest."

Sylvia's heart gave a wild beat; she knew that strange white bird, and had once stolen softly near where it stood in some bright green swamp grass, away over at the other side of the woods. There was an open place where the sunshine always seemed strangely yel-low and hot, where tall, nodding rushes grew, and her grandmother had warned her that she might sink in the soft black mud underneath and never be heard of more. Not far beyond were the salt marshes just this side the sea itself, which Sylvia wondered and dreamed much about, but never had seen, whose great voice could sometimes be heard above the noise of the woods on stormy nights.

"I can't think of anything I should like so much as to find that heron's nest," the handsome stranger was saying. "I would give ten dollars to anybody who could show it to me," he added desperately, "and I mean to spend my whole vacation hunting for it if need be. Perhaps it was only migrating, or had been chased out of its own region by some bird of prey."

Mrs. Tilley gave amazed attention to all this, but Sylvia still watched the toad, not di-vining, as she might have done at some calmer time, that the creature wished to get to its hole under the door-step, and was much hindered by the unusual spectators at that hour of the evening. No amount of thought, that night, could decide how many wished-for treasures the ten dollars, so lightly spoken of, would buy.

The next day the young sportsman hovered about the woods, and Sylvia kept him com-pany, having lost her first fear of the friendly lad, who proved to be most kind and sym-pathetic. He told her many things about the birds and what they knew and where they lived and what they did with themselves. And he gave her a jack-knife, which she thought as great a treasure as if she were a desert-islander. All day long he did not once make her troubled or afraid except when he brought down some unsuspecting singing creature from its bough. Sylvia would have liked him vastly better without his gun; she could not understand why he killed the very birds he seemed to like so much. But as the day waned, Sylvia still watched the young man with loving admiration. She had never seen anybody so charming and delightful; the woman's heart, asleep in the child, was vaguely thrilled by a dream of love. Some premonition of that great power stirred and swayed these young creatures who traversed the solemn woodlands with soft-footed silent care. They stopped to listen to a bird's song; they pressed forward again eagerly, parting the branches—speaking to each other rarely and in whispers; the young man going first and Sylvia following, fascinated, a few steps behind, with her gray eyes dark with excitement.

She grieved because the longed-for white heron was elusive, but she did not lead the guest, she only followed, and there was no such thing as speaking first. The sound of her own unquestioned voice would have terrified her—it was hard enough to answer yes or no when there was need of that. At last evening began to fall, and they drove the cow home together, and Sylvia smiled with pleasure when they came to the place where she heard the whistle and was afraid only the night before.

II

Half a mile from home, at the farther edge of the woods, where the land was highest, a great pine-tree stood, the last of its generation. Whether it was left for a boundary mark, or for what reason, no one could say; the woodchoppers who had felled its mates were dead and gone long ago, and a whole forest of sturdy trees, pines and oaks and maples, had grown again. But the stately head of this old pine towered above them all and made a landmark for sea and shore miles and miles away. Sylvia knew it well. She had always believed that whoever climbed to the top of it could see the ocean; and the little girl had often laid her hand on the great rough trunk and looked up wistfully at those dark boughs that the wind always stirred, no matter how hot and still the air might be below. Now she thought of the tree with a new excitement, for why, if one climbed it at break of day could not one see all the world, and easily discover from whence the white heron flew, and mark the place, and find the hidden nest?

What a spirit of adventure, what wild ambition! What fancied triumph and delight and glory for the later morning when she could make known the secret! It was almost too real and too great for the childish heart to bear.

All night the door of the little house stood open and the whippoorwills came and sang upon the very step. The young sportsman and his old hostess were sound asleep, but Sylvia's great design kept her broad awake and watching. She forgot to think of sleep. The short summer night seemed as long as the winter darkness, and at last when the whippoorwills ceased, and she was afraid the morning would after all come too soon, she stole out of the house and followed the pasture path through the woods, hastening toward the open ground beyond, listening with a sense of comfort and companionship to the drowsy twitter of a half-awakened bird, whose perch she had jarred in passing. Alas, if the great wave of human interest which flooded for the first time this dull little life should sweep away the satisfactions of an existence heart to heart with nature and the dumb life of the forest!

There was the huge tree asleep yet in the paling moonlight, and small and silly Sylvia began with utmost bravery to mount to the top of it, with tingling, eager blood coursing the channels of her whole frame, with her bare feet and fingers, that pinched and held like bird's claws to the monstrous ladder reaching up, up, almost to the sky itself. First she must mount the white oak tree that grew alongside, where she was almost lost among the dark branches and the green leaves heavy and wet with dew; a bird fluttered off its nest, and a red squirrel ran to and fro and scolded pettishly at the harmless housebreaker. Sylvia felt her way easily. She had often climbed there, and knew that higher still one of the oak's upper branches chafed against the pine trunk, just where its lower boughs were set close together. There, when she made the dangerous pass from one tree to the other, the great enterprise would really begin.

She crept out along the swaying oak limb at last, and took the daring step across into the old pine-tree. The way was harder than she thought; she must reach far and hold fast, the sharp dry twigs caught and held her and scratched her like angry talons, the pitch made her thin little fingers clumsy and stiff as she went round and round the tree's great stem, higher and higher upward. The sparrows and robins in the woods below were beginning to wake and twitter to the dawn, yet it seemed much lighter there aloft in the pine-tree, and the child knew she must hurry if her project were to be of any use.

The tree seemed to lengthen itself out as she went up, and to reach farther and farther upward. It was like a great main-mast to the voyaging earth; it must truly have been amazed that morning through all its ponderous frame as it felt this determined spark of human spirit wending its way from higher branch to branch. Who knows how steadily the least twigs held themselves to advantage this light, weak creature on her way! The old pine must have loved his new dependent. More than all the hawks, and bats, and moths, and even the sweet voiced thrushes, was the brave, beating heart of the solitary gray-eyed child. And the tree stood still and frowned away the winds that June morning while the dawn grew bright in the east.

Sylvia's face was like a pale star, if one had seen it from the ground, when the last thorny bough was past, and she stood trembling and tired but wholly triumphant, high in the treetop. Yes, there was the sea with the dawning sun making a golden dazzle over it, and toward that glorious east flew two hawks with slow-moving pinions. How low they looked in the air from that height when one had only seen them before far up, and dark against the blue sky. Their gray feathers were as soft as moths; they seemed only a little way from the tree, and Sylvia felt as if she too could go flying away among the clouds. Westward, the woodlands and farms reached miles and miles into the distance; here and there were church steeples, and white villages, truly it was a vast and awesome world!

The birds sang louder and louder. At last the sun came up bewildering bright. Sylvia could see the white sails of ships out at sea, and the clouds that were purple and rose-colored and yellow at first began to fade away. Where was the white heron's nest in the sea of green branches, and was this wonderful sight and pageant of the world the only reward for having climbed to such a giddy height? Now look down again, Sylvia, where the green marsh is set among the shining birches and dark hemlocks; there where you saw the white heron once you will see him again; look, look! a white spot of him like a single floating feather comes up from the dead hemlock and grows larger, and rises, and comes close at last, and goes by the landmark pine with steady sweep of wing and out-stretched slender neck and crested head. And wait! wait! do not move a foot or a finger, little girl, do not send an arrow of light and consciousness from your two eager eyes, for the heron has perched on a pine bough not far beyond yours, and cries back to his mate on the nest and plumes his feathers for the new day!

The child gives a long sigh a minute later when a company of shouting cat-birds comes also to the tree, and vexed by their fluttering and lawlessness the solemn heron goes away. She knows his secret now, the wild, light, slender bird that floats and wavers, and goes back like an arrow presently to his home in the green world beneath. Then

Sylvia, well satisfied, makes her perilous way down again, not daring to look far below the branch she stands on, ready to cry sometimes because her fingers ache and her lamed feet slip. Wondering over and over again what the stranger would say to her, and what he would think when she told him how to find his way straight to the heron's nest.

"Sylvy, Sylvy!" called the busy old grandmother again and again, but nobody answered, and the small husk bed was empty and Sylvia had disappeared.

The guest waked from a dream, and remembering his day's pleasure hurried to dress himself that might it sooner begin. He was sure from the way the shy little girl looked once or twice yesterday that she had at least seen the white heron, and now she must really be made to tell. Here she comes now, paler than ever, and her worn old frock is torn and tattered, and smeared with pine pitch. The grandmother and the sportsman stand in the door together and question her, and the splendid moment has come to speak of the dead hemlock-tree by the green marsh.

But Sylvia does not speak after all, though the old grandmother fretfully rebukes her, and the young man's kind, appealing eyes are looking straight in her own. He can make them rich with money; he has promised it, and they are poor now. He is so well worth making happy, and he waits to hear the story she can tell.

No, she must keep silence! What is it that suddenly forbids her and makes her dumb? Has she been nine years growing and now, when the great world for the first time puts out a hand to her, must she thrust it aside for a bird's sake? The murmur of the pine's green branches is in her ears, she remembers how the white heron came flying through the golden air and how they watched the sea and the morning together, and Sylvia cannot speak; she cannot tell the heron's secret and give its life away.

Dear loyalty, that suffered a sharp pang as the guest went away disappointed later in the day, that could have served and followed him and loved him as a dog loves! Many a night Sylvia heard the echo of his whistle haunting the pasture path as she came home with the loitering cow. She forgot even her sorrow at the sharp report of his gun and the sight of thrushes and sparrows dropping silent to the ground, their songs hushed and their pretty feathers stained and wet with blood. Were the birds better friends than their hunter might have been,—who can tell? Whatever treasures were lost to her, woodlands and summer-time, remember! Bring your gifts and graces and tell your secrets to this lonely country child!

1884, 1914

Kate Chopin
1851–1904

To the age of nineteen, Katherine O'Flaherty experienced both the pleasures and the boring aimlessness that came to her as a belle caught up in the social swirl of St. Louis, a city flourishing in the aftermath of Civil War prosperity. Her father, an immigrant from Ireland, was a successful businessman; her mother was from an old Creole family that had settled in St. Louis. Her upbringing was Catholic, affluent, and "French" in its adherence to pious convent education, society balls, and French language and culture. Kate Chopin's later remarks about that period of giddy girlhood make clear that both nuns and debutantes lived lives of fantasy that excluded "real life." Real life is what Katherine O'Flaherty confronted in 1870 when she became Mrs. Oscar Chopin (pronounced in the French way, as in the name of the pianist Frédéric Chopin). She went to live in New Orleans, then, after business reversals, to a rural community near the cotton plantation owned by her husband's family. By 1884 she was back again in St. Louis, a widow with six children. Although she was not in financial want, Kate Chopin took up the literary career she had contemplated years earlier—the one she had been too busy raising her family to enter upon.

Kate Chopin set to work to learn how to write acceptable works of fiction. For her models of stories, sketches, and poetry she drew upon French writers—her contemporaries Émile Zola and Guy de Maupassant as well as the eighteenth-century literary and intellectual figure Madame de Staël. But what influenced her most were her experiences among the diverse cultures of Louisiana. Her fiction took as its home ground the lives of Creoles (descendants of the first French and Spanish settlers in the territory), Cajuns (progeny of the French immigrants who had been ignominiously expelled from Canada by the British conquerors in the eighteenth century), and the African Americans and Native Americans of mixed blood who lived throughout Louisiana.

The history of Kate Chopin's reception by the reading public is a revealing one. The publication in 1894 of *Bayou Folk,* a collection of tales of rural life, earned her critical acceptance. *A Night in Acadie* (1897) confirmed her popularity as a teller of stories. Her readers were pleased by her attention to local customs and dialects. (They had taken in the same way to the tales of New England written by Mary Wilkins Freeman and Sarah Orne Jewett, which exerted a similar appeal with different material.) Newspapers and important national magazines, such as the newly formed *Vogue* and the well-established *Century,* featured her work. She had already written two novels of slight merit when *The Awakening* appeared in 1899. Almost immediately, her previously appreciative audience rose against her, not surprising when one realizes that the same middle-class readership had been unable to accept Stephen Crane's *Maggie, A Girl of the Streets* in 1893 and would reject Theodore Dreiser's *Sister Carrie* when it appeared in 1900.

Chopin had long been a loyal reader of Walt Whitman's *Leaves of Grass,* and the portrayal in *The Awakening* of Edna Pontellier's aroused sensuousness is indeed Whitmanesque. The young woman's increasing resentment of the constrictions imposed by married life and her flirtations with an attractive roué brought condemnation to the novel and its author; both were dropped from libraries and genteel society. Naturally upset by her fall from favor, Kate Chopin attempted little more writing before her death five years later.

The Awakening was rediscovered in the 1950s. What was once called bad behavior for a woman is now seen as good writing about a woman's turbulent feelings. During Chopin's lifetime, readers may have been drawn to her piquant tales of the exotic yet recognizably human types found in Creole and Cajun culture, but there was hardly approbation for her novel. Today appreciation comes easily to *The Awakening,* while her brief, almost anecdotal stories continue to surprise readers with their arresting portraits of passionate lives.

Further Reading:

P. Seyersted, *Kate Chopin: A Critical Biography,* 1969, 1980. *Southern Studies,* Special Issue, 1984.

R. Franklin, "*The Awakening* and the Failure of Psyche," *American Literature* 56 (1984), 510–26.

A. Stein, *After the Vows Were Spoken,* 1985.

W. Martin, ed., *New Essays on* The Awakening, 1988.

B. Koloski, ed., *Approaches to Teaching Chopin's* The Awakening, 1988.

P. Seyersted, "American Girl from Howells to Chopin," *Arbeiten ans Anglistik und Amerikanistik* 13 (1988), 183–92.

S. Harris, *19th-Century American Women's Novels,* 1990.

M. Papke, *Verging on the Abyss: Social Fiction and Chopin and Wharton,* 1990.

E. Toth, *Kate Chopin,* 1990.

E. Ammons, *Conflicting Stories,* 1991.

B. Bender, " 'The Teeth of Desire': *The Awakening* and *The Descent of Man,*" *American Literature* 63 (1991), 459–73.

K. Kearns, "The Nullification of Edna Pontellier," *American Literature* 63 (1991), 62–88.

E. Showalter, *Sister's Choice,* 1991.

M. Hoder-Salmon, *Kate Chopin's* The Awakening: *Screenplay as Interpretation,* 1992.

N. A. Walker, ed., *The Awakening* [text, biographical and historical contexts, critical history, critical essays], 1993.

Text:
The Awakening, 1899.

The Awakening

I

A green and yellow parrot, which hung in a cage outside the door, kept repeating over and over:

"*Allez vous-en! Allez vous-en!*[1] *Sapristi!*[2] That's all right!"

He could speak a little Spanish, and also a language which nobody understood, unless it was the mocking-bird that hung on the other side of the door, whistling his fluty notes out upon the breeze with maddening persistence.

Mr. Pontellier, unable to read his newspaper with any degree of comfort, arose with an expression and an exclamation of disgust. He walked down the gallery and across the narrow "bridges" which connected the Lebrun cottages one with the other. He had been seated before the door of the main house. The parrot and the mocking-bird were the property of Madame Lebrun, and they had the right to make all the noise they wished. Mr. Pontellier had the privilege of quitting their society when they ceased to be entertaining.

He stopped before the door of his own cottage, which was the fourth one from the main building and next to the last. Seating himself in a wicker rocker which was there, he once more applied himself to the task of reading the newspaper. The day was Sunday; the

---

[1] "Go away!"
[2] Mild form of "Damn it!"

paper was a day old. The Sunday papers had not yet reached Grand Isle. He was already acquainted with the market reports, and he glanced restlessly over the editorials and bits of news which he had not had time to read before quitting New Orleans the day before.

Mr. Pontellier wore eye-glasses. He was a man of forty, of medium height and rather slender build; he stooped a little. His hair was brown and straight, parted on one side. His beard was neatly and closely trimmed.

Once in a while he withdrew his glance from the newspaper and looked about him. There was more noise than ever over at the house. The main building was called "the house," to distinguish it from the cottages. The chattering and whistling birds were still at it. Two young girls, the Farival twins, were playing a duet from "Zampa"[3] upon the piano. Madame Lebrun was bustling in and out, giving orders in a high key to a yard-boy whenever she got inside the house, and directions in an equally high voice to a dining-room servant whenever she got outside. She was a fresh, pretty woman, clad always in white with elbow sleeves. Her starched skirts crinkled as she came and went. Farther down, before one of the cottages, a lady in black was walking demurely up and down, telling her beads. A good many persons of the *pension*[4] had gone over to the *Chênière Caminada* in Beaudelet's lugger to hear mass. Some young people were out under the water-oaks playing croquet. Mr. Pontellier's two children were there—sturdy little fellows of four and five. A quadroon nurse followed them about with a far-away, meditative air.

Mr. Pontellier finally lit a cigar and began to smoke, letting the paper drag idly from his hand. He fixed his gaze upon a white sunshade that was advancing at snail's pace from the beach. He could see it plainly between the gaunt trunks of the water-oaks and across the stretch of yellow camomile. The gulf looked far away, melting hazily into the blue of the horizon. The sunshade continued to approach slowly. Beneath its pink-lined shelter were his wife, Mrs. Pontellier, and young Robert Lebrun. When they reached the cottage, the two seated themselves with some appearance of fatigue upon the upper step of the porch, facing each other, each leaning against a supporting post.

"What folly! to bathe at such an hour in such heat!" exclaimed Mr. Pontellier. He himself had taken a plunge at daylight. That was why the morning seemed long to him.

"You are burnt beyond recognition," he added, looking at his wife as one looks at a valuable piece of personal property which has suffered some damage. She held up her hands, strong, shapely hands, and surveyed them critically, drawing up her lawn sleeves above the wrists. Looking at them reminded her of her rings, which she had given to her husband before leaving for the beach. She silently reached out to him, and he, understanding, took the rings from his vest pocket and dropped them into her open palm. She slipped them upon her fingers; then clasping her knees, she looked across at Robert and began to laugh. The rings sparkled upon her fingers. He sent back an answering smile.

"What is it?" asked Pontellier, looking lazily and amused from one to the other. It was some utter nonsense; some adventure out there in the water, and they both tried to relate it at once. It did not seem half so amusing when told. They realized this, and so did Mr. Pontellier. He yawned and stretched himself. Then he got up, saying he had half a mind to go over to Klein's hotel and play a game of billiards.

"Come go along, Lebrun," he proposed to Robert. But Robert admitted quite frankly that he preferred to stay where he was and talk to Mrs. Pontellier.

---

[3] From the French opera-comique (1831) by Louis Herold (1791–1833).

[4] Small residential hotel.

"Well, send him about his business when he bores you, Edna," instructed her husband as he prepared to leave.

"Here, take the umbrella," she exclaimed, holding it out to him. He accepted the sunshade, and lifting it over his head descended the steps and walked away.

"Coming back to dinner?" his wife called after him. He halted a moment and shrugged his shoulders. He felt in his vest pocket; there was a ten-dollar bill there. He did not know; perhaps he would return for the early dinner and perhaps he would not. It all depended upon the company which he found over at Klein's and the size of "the game." He did not say this, but she understood it, and laughed, nodding good-by to him.

Both children wanted to follow their father when they saw him starting out. He kissed them and promised to bring them back bonbons and peanuts.

II

Mrs. Pontellier's eyes were quick and bright; they were a yellowish brown, about the color of her hair. She had a way of turning them swiftly upon an object and holding them there as if lost in some inward maze of contemplation or thought.

Her eyebrows were a shade darker than her hair. They were thick and almost horizontal, emphasizing the depth of her eyes. She was rather handsome than beautiful. Her face was captivating by reason of a certain frankness of expression and a contradictory subtle play of features. Her manner was engaging.

Robert rolled a cigarette. He smoked cigarettes because he could not afford cigars, he said. He had a cigar in his pocket which Mr. Pontellier had presented him with, and he was saving it for his after-dinner smoke.

This seemed quite proper and natural on his part. In coloring he was not unlike his companion. A clean-shaved face made the resemblance more pronounced than it would otherwise have been. There rested no shadow of care upon his open countenance. His eyes gathered in and reflected the light and languor of the summer day.

Mrs. Pontellier reached over for a palm-leaf fan that lay on the porch and began to fan herself, while Robert sent between his lips light puffs from his cigarette. They chatted incessantly: about the things around them; their amusing adventure out in the water—it had again assumed its entertaining aspect; about the wind, the trees, the people who had gone to the *Chênière;* about the children playing croquet under the oaks, and the Farival twins, who were now performing the overture to "The Poet and the Peasant."[5] Robert talked a good deal about himself. He was very young, and did not know any better. Mrs. Pontellier talked a little about herself for the same reason. Each was interested in what the other said. Robert spoke of his intention to go to Mexico in the autumn, where fortune awaited him. He was always intending to go to Mexico, but some way never got there. Meanwhile he held on to his modest position in a mercantile house in New Orleans, where an equal familiarity with English, French and Spanish gave him no small value as a clerk and correspondent.

He was spending his summer vacation, as he always did, with his mother at Grand Isle. In former times, before Robert could remember, "the house" had been a summer

[5] Popular piece by Franz von Suppe, Austrian composer (1819–95).

luxury of the Lebruns. Now, flanked by its dozen or more cottages, which were always filled with exclusive visitors from the *"Quartier Français,"*[6] it enabled Madame Lebrun to maintain the easy and comfortable existence which appeared to be her birthright.

Mrs. Pontellier talked about her father's Mississippi plantation and her girlhood home in the old Kentucky blue-grass country. She was an American woman, with a small infusion of French which seemed to have been lost in dilution. She read a letter from her sister, who was away in the East, and who had engaged herself to be married. Robert was interested, and wanted to know what manner of girls the sisters were, what the father was like, and how long the mother had been dead.

When Mrs. Pontellier folded the letter it was time for her to dress for the early dinner.

"I see Léonce isn't coming back," she said, with a glance in the direction whence her husband had disappeared. Robert supposed he was not, as there were a good many New Orleans club men over at Klein's.

When Mrs. Pontellier left him to enter her room, the young man descended the steps and strolled over toward the croquet players, where, during the half-hour before dinner, he amused himself with the little Pontellier children, who were very fond of him.

III

It was eleven o'clock that night when Mr. Pontellier returned from Klein's hotel. He was in an excellent humor, in high spirits, and very talkative. His entrance awoke his wife, who was in bed and fast asleep when he came in. He talked to her while he undressed, telling her anecdotes and bits of news and gossip that he had gathered during the day. From his trousers pockets he took a fistful of crumpled bank notes and a good deal of silver coin, which he piled on the bureau indiscriminately with keys, knife, handkerchief, and whatever else happened to be in his pockets. She was overcome with sleep, and answered him with little half utterances.

He thought it very discouraging that his wife, who was the sole object of his existence, evinced so little interest in things which concerned him, and valued so little his conversation.

Mr. Pontellier had forgotten the bonbons and peanuts for the boys. Notwithstanding he loved them very much, and went into the adjoining room where they slept to take a look at them and make sure that they were resting comfortably. The result of his investigation was far from satisfactory. He turned and shifted the youngsters about in bed. One of them began to kick and talk about a basket full of crabs.

Mr. Pontellier returned to his wife with the information that Raoul had a high fever and needed looking after. Then he lit a cigar and went and sat near the open door to smoke it.

Mrs. Pontellier was quite sure Raoul had no fever. He had gone to bed perfectly well, she said, and nothing had ailed him all day. Mr. Pontellier was too well acquainted with fever symptoms to be mistaken. He assured her the child was consuming at that moment in the next room.

He reproached his wife with her inattention, her habitual neglect of the children. If it was not a mother's place to look after children, whose on earth was it? He himself had

---

[6] Old French section of New Orleans.

his hands full with his brokerage business. He could not be in two places at once; making a living for his family on the street, and staying at home to see that no harm befell them. He talked in a monotonous, insistent way.

Mrs. Pontellier sprang out of bed and went into the next room. She soon came back and sat on the edge of the bed, leaning her head down on the pillow. She said nothing, and refused to answer her husband when he questioned her. When his cigar was smoked out he went to bed, and in half a minute he was fast asleep.

Mrs. Pontellier was by that time thoroughly awake. She began to cry a little, and wiped her eyes on the sleeve of her *peignoir*.[7] Blowing out the candle, which her husband had left burning, she slipped her bare feet into a pair of satin *mules*[8] at the foot of the bed and went out on the porch, where she sat down in the wicker chair and began to rock gently to and fro.

It was then past midnight. The cottages were all dark. A single faint light gleamed out from the hallway of the house. There was no sound abroad except the hooting of an old owl in the top of a water-oak, and the everlasting voice of the sea, that was not uplifted at that soft hour. It broke like a mournful lullaby upon the night.

The tears came so fast to Mrs. Pontellier's eyes that the damp sleeve of her *peignoir* no longer served to dry them. She was holding the back of her chair with one hand; her loose sleeve had slipped almost to the shoulder of her uplifted arm. Turning, she thrust her face, streaming and wet, into the bend of her arm, and she went on crying there, not caring any longer to dry her face, her eyes, her arms. She could not have told why she was crying. Such experiences as the foregoing were not uncommon in her married life. They seemed never before to have weighed much against the abundance of her husband's kindness and a uniform devotion which had come to be tacit and self-understood.

An indescribable oppression, which seemed to generate in some unfamiliar part of her consciousness, filled her whole being with a vague anguish. It was like a shadow, like a mist passing across her soul's summer day. It was strange and unfamiliar; it was a mood. She did not sit there inwardly upbraiding her husband, lamenting at Fate, which had directed her footsteps to the path which they had taken. She was just having a good cry all to herself. The mosquitoes made merry over her, biting her firm, round arms and nipping at her bare insteps.

The little stinging, buzzing imps succeeded in dispelling a mood which might have held her there in the darkness half a night longer.

The following morning Mr. Pontellier was up in good time to take the rockaway which was to convey him to the steamer at the wharf. He was returning to the city to his business, and they would not see him again at the Island till the coming Saturday. He had regained his composure, which seemed to have been somewhat impaired the night before. He was eager to be gone, as he looked forward to a lively week in Carondelet Street.

Mr. Pontellier gave his wife half of the money which he had brought away from Klein's hotel the evening before. She liked money as well as most women, and accepted it with no little satisfaction.

"It will buy a handsome wedding present for Sister Janet!" she exclaimed, smoothing out the bills as she counted them one by one.

"Oh! we'll treat Sister Janet better than that, my dear," he laughed, as he prepared to kiss her good-by.

---

[7] Dressing gown.   [8] Slippers.

The boys were tumbling about, clinging to his legs, imploring that numerous things be brought back to them. Mr. Pontellier was a great favorite, and ladies, men, children, even nurses, were always on hand to say good-by to him. His wife stood smiling and waving, the boys shouting, as he disappeared in the old rockaway down the sandy road.

A few days later a box arrived for Mrs. Pontellier from New Orleans. It was from her husband. It was filled with *friandises*,[9] with luscious and toothsome bits—the finest of fruits, *patés*,[10] a rare bottle or two, delicious syrups, and bonbons in abundance.

Mrs. Pontellier was always very generous with the contents of such a box; she was quite used to receiving them when away from home. The *patés* and fruit were brought to the dining-room; the bonbons were passed around. And the ladies, selecting with dainty and discriminating fingers and a little greedily, all declared that Mr. Pontellier was the best husband in the world. Mrs. Pontellier was forced to admit that she knew of none better.

IV

It would have been a difficult matter for Mr. Pontellier to define to his own satisfaction or any one else's wherein his wife failed in her duty toward their children. It was something which he felt rather than perceived, and he never voiced the feeling without subsequent regret and ample atonement.

If one of the little Pontellier boys took a tumble whilst at play, he was not apt to rush crying to his mother's arms for comfort; he would more likely pick himself up, wipe the water out of his eyes and the sand out of his mouth, and go on playing. Tots as they were, they pulled together and stood their ground in childish battles with doubled fists and uplifted voices, which usually prevailed against the other mother-tots. The quadroon[11] nurse was looked upon as a huge encumbrance, only good to button up waists and panties and to brush and part hair; since it seemed to be a law of society that hair must be parted and brushed.

In short, Mrs. Pontellier was not a mother-woman. The mother-women seemed to prevail that summer at Grand Isle. It was easy to know them, fluttering about with extended, protecting wings when any harm, real or imaginary, threatened their precious brood. They were women who idolized their children, worshiped their husbands, and esteemed it a holy privilege to efface themselves as individuals and grow wings as ministering angels.

Many of them were delicious in the rôle; one of them was the embodiment of every womanly grace and charm. If her husband did not adore her, he was a brute, deserving of death by slow torture. Her name was Adèle Ratignolle. There are no words to describe her save the old ones that have served so often to picture the bygone heroine of romance and the fair lady of our dreams. There was nothing subtle or hidden about her charms; her beauty was all there, flaming and apparent: the spun-gold hair that comb nor confining pin could restrain; the blue eyes that were like nothing but sapphires; two lips that pouted, that were so red one could only think of cherries or some other delicious crimson fruit in looking at them. She was growing a little stout, but it did not

---

[9] Delicacies.
[10] Pastries.
[11] According to the race-arithmetic practiced at this time, the term indicates that the woman is one-fourth African American.

seem to detract an iota from the grace of every step, pose, gesture. One would not have wanted her white neck a mite less full or her beautiful arms more slender. Never were hands more exquisite than hers, and it was a joy to look at them when she threaded her needle or adjusted her gold thimble to her taper middle finger as she sewed away on the little night-drawers or fashioned a bodice or a bib.

Madame Ratignolle was very fond of Mrs. Pontellier, and often she took her sewing and went over to sit with her in the afternoons. She was sitting there the afternoon of the day the box arrived from New Orleans. She had possession of the rocker, and she was busily engaged in sewing upon a diminutive pair of nightdrawers.

She had brought the pattern of the drawers for Mrs. Pontellier to cut out—a marvel of construction, fashioned to enclose a baby's body so effectually that only two small eyes might look out from the garment, like an Eskimo's. They were designed for winter wear, when treacherous drafts came down chimneys and insidious currents of deadly cold found their way through key-holes.

Mrs. Pontellier's mind was quite at rest concerning the present material needs of her children, and she could not see the use of anticipating and making winter night garments the subject of her summer meditations. But she did not want to appear unamiable and uninterested, so she had brought forth newspapers, which she spread upon the floor of the gallery, and under Madame Ratignolle's directions she had cut a pattern of the impervious garment.

Robert was there, seated as he had been the Sunday before, and Mrs. Pontellier also occupied her former position on the upper step, leaning listlessly against the post. Beside her was a box of bonbons, which she held out at intervals to Madame Ratignolle.

That lady seemed at a loss to make a selection, but finally settled upon a stick of nougat, wondering if it were not too rich; whether it could possibly hurt her. Madame Ratignolle had been married seven years. About every two years she had a baby. At that time she had three babies, and was beginning to think of a fourth one. She was always talking about her "condition." Her "condition" was in no way apparent, and no one would have known a thing about it but for her persistence in making it the subject of conversation.

Robert started to reassure her, asserting that he had known a lady who had subsisted upon nougat during the entire—but seeing the color mount into Mrs. Pontellier's face he checked himself and changed the subject.

Mrs. Pontellier, though she had married a Creole, was not thoroughly at home in the society of Creoles; never before had she been thrown so intimately among them. There were only Creoles that summer at Lebrun's. They all knew each other, and felt like one large family, among whom existed the most amicable relations. A characteristic which distinguished them and which impressed Mrs. Pontellier most forcibly was their entire absence of prudery. Their freedom of expression was at first incomprehensible to her, though she had no difficulty in reconciling it with a lofty chastity which in the Creole woman seems to be inborn and unmistakable.

Never would Edna Pontellier forget the shock with which she heard Madame Ratignolle relating to old Monsieur Farival the harrowing story of one of her *accouchements*,[12] withholding no intimate detail. She was growing accustomed to like shocks,

---

[12] When a woman goes into labor to give birth.

but she could not keep the mounting color back from her cheeks. Oftener than once her coming had interrupted the droll story with which Robert was entertaining some amused group of married women.

A book had gone the rounds of the *pension*. When it came her turn to read it, she did so with profound astonishment. She felt moved to read the book in secret and solitude, though none of the others had done so—to hide it from view at the sound of approaching footsteps. It was openly criticised and freely discussed at table. Mrs. Pontellier gave over being astonished, and concluded that wonders would never cease.

V

They formed a congenial group sitting there that summer afternoon—Madame Ratignolle sewing away, often stopping to relate a story or incident with much expressive gesture of her perfect hands; Robert and Mrs. Pontellier sitting idle, exchanging occasional words, glances or smiles which indicated a certain advanced stage of intimacy and *camaraderie*.[13]

He had lived in her shadow during the past month. No one thought anything of it. Many had predicted that Robert would devote himself to Mrs. Pontellier when he arrived. Since the age of fifteen, which was eleven years before, Robert each summer at Grand Isle had constituted himself the devoted attendant of some fair dame or damsel. Sometimes it was a young girl, again a widow; but as often as not it was some interesting married woman.

For two consecutive seasons he lived in the sunlight of Mademoiselle Duvigné's presence. But she died between summers; then Robert posed as an inconsolable, prostrating himself at the feet of Madame Ratignolle for whatever crumbs of sympathy and comfort she might be pleased to vouchsafe.

Mrs. Pontellier liked to sit and gaze at her fair companion as she might look upon a faultless Madonna.

"Could any one fathom the cruelty beneath that fair exterior?" murmured Robert. "She knew that I adored her once, and she let me adore her. It was 'Robert, come; go; stand up; sit down; do this; do that; see if the baby sleeps; my thimble, please, that I left God knows where. Come and read Daudet to me while I sew.'"

"*Par example!*[14] I never had to ask. You were always there under my feet, like a troublesome cat."

"You mean like an adoring dog. And just as soon as Ratignolle appeared on the scene, then it *was* like a dog. '*Passez! Adieu! Allez vous-en!*'"[15]

"Perhaps I feared to make Alphonse jealous," she interjoined, with excessive naïveté. That made them all laugh. The right hand jealous of the left! The heart jealous of the soul! But for that matter, the Creole husband is never jealous; with him the gangrene passion is one which has become dwarfed by disuse.

Meanwhile Robert, addressing Mrs. Pontellier, continued to tell of his one time hopeless passion for Madame Ratignolle; of sleepless nights, of consuming flames till the very sea sizzled when he took his daily plunge. While the lady at the needle kept up a little running, contemptuous comment:

---

[13] Comradeship.
[14] For instance.

[15] Go! Goodbye! Go away!

"Blagueur—farceur—gros bête va!"[16]

He never assumed this serio-comic tone when alone with Mrs. Pontellier. She never knew precisely what to make of it; at that moment it was impossible for her to guess how much of it was jest and what proportion was earnest. It was understood that he had often spoken words of love to Madame Ratignolle, without any thought of being taken seriously. Mrs. Pontellier was glad he had not assumed a similar role toward herself. It would have been unacceptable and annoying.

Mrs. Pontellier had brought her sketching materials, which she sometimes dabbled with in an unprofessional way. She liked the dabbling. She felt in it satisfaction of a kind which no other employment afforded her.

She had long wished to try herself on Madame Ratignolle. Never had that lady seemed a more tempting subject than at that moment, seated there like some sensuous Madonna, with the gleam of the fading day enriching her splendid color.

Robert crossed over and seated himself upon the step below Mrs. Pontellier, that he might watch her work. She handled her brushes with a certain ease and freedom which came, not from long and close acquaintance with them, but from a natural aptitude. Robert followed her work with close attention, giving forth little ejaculatory expressions of appreciation in French, which he addressed to Madame Ratignolle.

"Mais ce n'est pas mal! Elle s'y connait, elle a de la force, oui."[17]

During his oblivious attention he once quietly rested his head against Mrs. Pontellier's arm. As gently she repulsed him. Once again he repeated the offense. She could not but believe it to be thoughtlessness on his part; yet that was no reason she should submit to it. She did not remonstrate, except again to repulse him quietly but firmly. He offered no apology.

The picture completed bore no resemblance to Madame Ratignolle. She was greatly disappointed to find that it did not look like her. But it was a fair enough piece of work, and in many respects satisfying.

Mrs. Pontellier evidently did not think so. After surveying the sketch critically she drew a broad smudge of paint across its surface, and crumpled the paper between her hands.

The youngsters came tumbling up the steps, the quadroon following at the respectful distance which they required her to observe. Mrs. Pontellier made them carry her paints and things into the house. She sought to detain them for a little talk and some pleasantry. But they were greatly in earnest. They had only come to investigate the contents of the bonbon box. They accepted without murmuring what she chose to give them, each holding out two chubby hands scoop-like, in the vain hope that they might be filled; and then away they went.

The sun was low in the west, and the breeze soft and languorous that came up from the south, charged with the seductive odor of the sea. Children, freshly befurbelowed, were gathering for their games under the oaks. Their voices were high and penetrating.

Madame Ratignolle folded her sewing, placing thimble, scissors and thread all neatly together in the roll, which she pinned securely. She complained of faintness. Mrs. Pontellier flew for the cologne water and a fan. She bathed Madame Ratignolle's face with cologne, while Robert plied the fan with unnecessary vigor.

---

[16] You joker, you fool, go away!

[17] But it's not bad. She knows herself. She has strength.

The spell was soon over, and Mrs. Pontellier could not help wondering if there were not a little imagination responsible for its origin, for the rose tint had never faded from her friend's face.

She stood watching the fair woman walk down the long line of galleries with the grace and majesty which queens are sometimes supposed to possess. Her little ones ran to meet her. Two of them clung about her white skirts, the third she took from its nurse and with a thousand endearments bore it along in her own fond, encircling arms. Though, as everybody well knew, the doctor had forbidden her to lift so much as a pin!

"Are you going bathing?" asked Robert of Mrs. Pontellier. It was not so much a question as a reminder.

"Oh, no," she answered, with a tone of indecision. "I'm tired; I think not." Her glance wandered from his face away toward the Gulf, whose sonorous murmur reached her like a loving but imperative entreaty.

"Oh, come!" he insisted. "You mustn't miss your bath. Come on. The water must be delicious; it will not hurt you. Come."

He reached up for her big, rough straw hat that hung on a peg outside the door, and put it on her head. They descended the steps, and walked away together toward the beach. The sun was low in the west and the breeze was soft and warm.

VI

Edna Pontellier could not have told why, wishing to go to the beach with Robert, she should in the first place have declined, and in the second place have followed in obedience to one of the two contradictory impulses which impelled her.

A certain light was beginning to dawn dimly within her,—the light which, showing the way, forbids it.

At that early period it served but to bewilder her. It moved her to dreams, to thoughtfulness, to the shadowy anguish which had overcome her the midnight when she had abandoned herself to tears.

In short, Mrs. Pontellier was beginning to realize her position in the universe as a human being, and to recognize her relations as an individual to the world within and about her. This may seem like a ponderous weight of wisdom to descend upon the soul of a young woman of twenty-eight—perhaps more wisdom than the Holy Ghost is usually pleased to vouchsafe to any woman.

But the beginning of things, of a world especially, is necessarily vague, tangled, chaotic, and exceedingly disturbing. How few of us ever emerge from such beginning! How many souls perish in its tumult!

The voice of the sea is seductive; never ceasing, whispering, clamoring, murmuring, inviting the soul to wander for a spell in abysses of solitude; to lose itself in mazes of inward contemplation.

The voice of the sea speaks to the soul. The touch of the sea is sensuous, en-folding the body in its soft, close embrace.

VII

Mrs. Pontellier was not a woman given to confidences, a characteristic hitherto contrary to her nature. Even as a child she had lived her own small life all within herself. At a very early period she had apprehended instinctively the dual life—that outward existence which conforms, the inward life which questions.

That summer at Grand Isle she began to loosen a little the mantle of reserve that had always enveloped her. There may have been—there must have been—influences, both subtle and apparent, working in their several ways to induce her to do this; but the most obvious was the influence of Adèle Ratignolle. The excessive physical charm of the Creole had first attracted her, for Edna had a sensuous susceptibility to beauty. Then the candor of the woman's whole existence, which every one might read, and which formed so striking a contrast to her own habitual reserve—this might have furnished a link. Who can tell what metals the gods use in forging the subtle bond which we call sympathy, which we might as well call love.

The two women went away one morning to the beach together, arm in arm, under the huge white sunshade. Edna had prevailed upon Madame Ratignolle to leave the children behind, though she could not induce her to relinquish a diminutive roll of needlework, which Adèle begged to be allowed to slip into the depths of her pocket. In some unaccountable way they had escaped from Robert.

The walk to the beach was no inconsiderable one, consisting as it did of a long, sandy path, upon which a sporadic and tangled growth that bordered it on either side made frequent and unexpected inroads. There were acres of yellow camomile reaching out on either hand. Further away still, vegetable gardens abounded, with frequent small plantations of orange or lemon trees intervening. The dark green clusters glistened from afar in the sun.

The women were both of goodly height, Madame Ratignolle possessing the more feminine and matronly figure. The charm of Edna Pontellier's physique stole insensibly upon you. The lines of her body were long, clean and symmetrical; it was a body which occasionally fell into splendid poses; there was no suggestion of the trim, stereotyped fashion-plate about it. A casual and indiscriminating observer, in passing, might not cast a second glance upon the figure. But with more feeling and discernment he would have recognized the noble beauty of its modeling, and the graceful severity of poise and movement, which made Edna Pontellier different from the crowd.

She wore a cool muslin that morning—white, with a waving vertical line of brown running through it; also a white linen collar and the big straw hat which she had taken from the peg outside the door. The hat rested any way on her yellow-brown hair, that waved a little, was heavy, and clung close to her head.

Madame Ratignolle, more careful of her complexion, had twined a gauze veil about her head. She wore dogskin gloves, with gauntlets that protected her wrists. She was dressed in pure white, with a fluffiness of ruffles that became her. The draperies and fluttering things which she wore suited her rich, luxuriant beauty as a greater severity of line could not have done.

There were a number of bath-houses along the beach, of rough but solid construction, built with small, protecting galleries facing the water. Each house consisted of two compartments, and each family at Lebrun's possessed a compartment for itself, fitted out with all the essential paraphernalia of the bath and whatever other conveniences the owners might desire. The two women had no intention of bathing; they had just strolled down to the beach for a walk and to be alone and near the water. The Pontellier and Ratignolle compartments adjoined one another under the same roof.

Mrs. Pontellier had brought down her key through force of habit. Unlocking the door of her bathroom she went inside, and soon emerged, bringing a rug, which she spread upon the floor of the gallery, and two huge hair pillows covered with crash, which she placed against the front of the building.

The two seated themselves there in the shade of the porch, side by side, with their backs against the pillows and their feet extended. Madame Ratignolle removed her veil, wiped her face with a rather delicate handkerchief, and fanned herself with the fan which she always carried suspended somewhere about her person by a long, narrow ribbon. Edna removed her collar and opened her dress at the throat. She took the fan from Madame Ratignolle and began to fan both herself and her companion. It was very warm, and for a while they did nothing but exchange remarks about the heat, the sun, the glare. But there was a breeze blowing, a choppy, stiff wind that whipped the water into froth. It fluttered the skirts of the two women and kept them for a while engaged in adjusting, readjusting, tucking in, securing hair-pins and hatpins. A few persons were sporting some distance away in the water. The beach was very still of human sound at that hour. The lady in black was reading her morning devotions on the porch of a neighboring bath-house. Two young lovers were exchanging their hearts' yearnings beneath the children's tent, which they had found unoccupied.

Edna Pontellier, casting her eyes about, had finally kept them at rest upon the sea. The day was clear and carried the gaze out as far as the blue sky went; there were a few white clouds suspended idly over the horizon. A lateen sail was visible in the direction of Cat Island, and others to the south seemed almost motionless in the far distance.

"Of whom—of what are you thinking?" asked Adèle of her companion, whose countenance she had been watching with a little amused attention, arrested by the absorbed expression which seemed to have seized and fixed every feature into a statuesque repose.

"Nothing," returned Mrs. Pontellier, with a start, adding at once: "How stupid! But it seems to me it is the reply we make instinctively to such a question. Let me see," she went on, throwing back her head and narrowing her fine eyes till they shone like two vivid points of light. "Let me see. I was really not conscious of thinking of anything; but perhaps I can retrace my thoughts."

"Oh! never mind!" laughed Madame Ratignolle. "I am not quite so exacting. I will let you off this time. It is really too hot to think, especially to think about thinking."

"But for the fun of it," persisted Edna. "First of all, the sight of the water stretching so far away, those motionless sails against the blue sky, made a delicious picture that I just wanted to sit and look at. The hot wind beating in my face made me think—without any connection that I can trace—of a summer day in Kentucky, of a meadow that seemed as big as the ocean to the very little girl walking through the grass, which was higher than her waist. She threw out her arms as if swimming when she walked, beating the tall grass as one strikes out in the water. Oh, I see the connection now!"

"Where were you going that day in Kentucky, walking through the grass?"

"I don't remember now. I was just walking diagonally across a big field. My sunbonnet obstructed the view. I could see only the stretch of green before me, and I felt as if I must walk on forever, without coming to the end of it. I don't remember whether I was frightened or pleased. I must have been entertained.

"Likely as not it was Sunday," she laughed; "and I was running away from prayers, from the Presbyterian service, read in a spirit of gloom by my father that chills me yet to think of."

"And have you been running away from prayers ever since, *ma chère?*"[18] asked Madame Ratignolle, amused.

"No! oh, no!" Edna hastened to say. "I was a little unthinking child in those days, just following a misleading impulse without question. On the contrary, during one period of my life religion took a firm hold upon me; after I was twelve and until—until—why, I suppose until now, though I never thought much about it—just driven along by habit. But do you know," she broke off, turning her quick eyes upon Madame Ratignolle and leaning forward a little so as to bring her face quite close to that of her companion, "sometimes I feel this summer as if I were walking through the green meadow again; idly, aimlessly, unthinking and unguided."

Madame Ratignolle laid her hand over that of Mrs. Pontellier, which was near her. Seeing that the hand was not withdrawn, she clasped it firmly and warmly. She even stroked it a little, fondly, with the other hand, murmuring in an undertone, "*Pauvre chérie.*"[19]

The action was at first a little confusing to Edna, but she soon lent herself readily to the Creole's gentle caress. She was not accustomed to an outward and spoken expression of affection, either in herself or in others. She and her younger sister, Janet, had quarreled a good deal through force of unfortunate habit. Her older sister, Margaret, was matronly and dignified, probably from having assumed matronly and housewifely responsibilities too early in life, their mother having died when they were quite young. Margaret was not effusive; she was practical. Edna had had an occasional girl friend, but whether accidentally or not, they seemed to have been all of one type—the self-contained. She never realized that the reverse of her own character had much, perhaps everything, to do with this. Her most intimate friend at school had been one of rather exceptional intellectual gifts, who wrote fine-sounding essays, which Edna admired and strove to imitate; and with her she talked and glowed over the English classics, and sometimes held religious and political controversies.

Edna often wondered at one propensity which sometimes had inwardly disturbed her without causing any outward show or manifestation on her part. At a very early age—perhaps it was when she traversed the ocean of waving grass—she remembered that she had been passionately enamored of a dignified and sadeyed cavalry officer who visited her father in Kentucky. She could not leave his presence when he was there, nor remove her eyes from his face, which was something like Napoleon's, with a lock of black hair falling across the forehead. But the cavalry officer melted imperceptibly out of her existence.

At another time her affections were deeply engaged by a young gentleman who visited a lady on a neighboring plantation. It was after they went to Mississippi to live. The young man was engaged to be married to the young lady, and they sometimes called upon Margaret, driving over of afternoons in a buggy. Edna was a little miss, just merging into her teens; and the realization that she herself was nothing, nothing, nothing to the engaged young man was a bitter affliction to her. But he, too, went the way of dreams.

She was a grown young woman when she was overtaken by what she supposed to be the climax of her fate. It was when the face and figure of a great tragedian began to haunt

---

[18] My dear one.   [19] Poor dear.

her imagination and stir her senses. The persistence of the infatuation lent it an aspect of genuineness. The hopelessness of it colored it with the lofty tones of a great passion.

The picture of the tragedian stood enframed upon her desk. Any one may possess the portrait of a tragedian without exciting suspicion or comment. (This was a sinister reflection which she cherished.) In the presence of others she expressed admiration for his exalted gifts, as she handed the photograph around and dwelt upon the fidelity of the likeness. When alone she sometimes picked it up and kissed the cold glass passionately.

Her marriage to Léonce Pontellier was purely an accident, in this respect resembling many other marriages which masquerade as the decrees of Fate. It was in the midst of her secret great passion that she met him. He fell in love, as men are in the habit of doing, and pressed his suit with an earnestness and an ardor which left nothing to be desired. He pleased her; his absolute devotion flattered her. She fancied there was a sympathy of thought and taste between them in which fancy she was mistaken. Add to this the violent opposition of her father and her sister Margaret to her marriage with a Catholic, and we need seek no further for the motives which led her to accept Monsieur Pontellier for her husband.

The acme of bliss which would have been a marriage with the tragedian, was not for her in this world. As the devoted wife of a man who worshiped her, she felt she would take her place with a certain dignity in the world of reality, closing the portals forever behind her upon the realm of romance and dreams.

But it was not long before the tragedian had gone to join the cavalry officer and the engaged young man and a few others; and Edna found herself face to face with the realities. She grew fond of her husband, realizing with some unaccountable satisfaction that no trace of passion or excessive and fictitious warmth colored her affection, thereby threatening its dissolution.

She was fond of her children in an uneven, impulsive way. She would sometimes gather them passionately to her heart; she would sometimes forget them. The year before they had spent part of the summer with their grandmother Pontellier in Iberville. Feeling secure regarding their happiness and welfare, she did not miss them except with an occasional intense longing. Their absence was a sort of relief, though she did not admit this, even to herself. It seemed to free her of a responsibility which she had blindly assumed and for which Fate had not fitted her.

Edna did not reveal so much as all this to Madame Ratignolle that summer day when they sat with faces turned to the sea. But a good part of it escaped her. She had put her head down on Madame Ratignolle's shoulder. She was flushed and felt intoxicated with the sound of her own voice and the unaccustomed taste of candor. It muddled her like wine, or like a first breath of freedom.

There was the sound of approaching voices. It was Robert, surrounded by a troop of children, searching for them. The two little Pontelliers were with him, and he carried Madame Ratignolle's little girl in his arms. There were other children beside, and two nurse-maids followed, looking disagreeable and resigned.

The women at once rose and began to shake out their draperies and relax their muscles. Mrs. Pontellier threw the cushions and rug into the bath-house. The children all scampered off to the awning, and they stood there in a line, gazing upon the intruding lovers, still exchanging their vows and sighs. The lovers got up, with only a silent protest, and walked slowly away somewhere else.

The children possessed themselves of the tent, and Mrs. Pontellier went over to join them.

Madame Ratignolle begged Robert to accompany her to the house; she complained of cramp in her limbs and stiffness of the joints. She leaned draggingly upon his arm as they walked.

VIII

"Do me a favor, Robert," spoke the pretty woman at his side, almost as soon as she and Robert had started on their slow, homeward way. She looked up in his face, leaning on his arm beneath the encircling shadow of the umbrella which he had lifted.

"Granted; as many as you like," he returned, glancing down into her eyes that were full of thoughtfulness and some speculation.

"I only ask for one; let Mrs. Pontellier alone."

"*Tiens!*" he exclaimed, with a sudden, boyish laugh. "*Voilà que Madame Ratignolle est jalouse!*"[20]

"Nonsense! I'm in earnest; I mean what I say. Let Mrs. Pontellier alone."

"Why?" he asked; himself growing serious at his companion's solicition.

"She is not one of us; she is not like us. She might make the unfortunate blunder of taking you seriously."

His face flushed with annoyance, and taking off his soft hat he began to beat it impatiently against his leg as he walked. "Why shouldn't she take me seriously?" he demanded sharply. "Am I a comedian, a clown, a jack-in-the-box? Why shouldn't she? You Creoles! I have no patience with you! Am I always to be regarded as a feature of an amusing programme? I hope Mrs. Pontellier does take me seriously. I hope she has discernment enough to find in me something besides the *blagueur.*[21] If I thought there was any doubt—"

"Oh, enough, Robert!" she broke into his heated outburst. "You are not thinking of what you are saying. You speak with about as little reflection as we might expect from one of those children down there playing in the sand. If your attentions to any married women here were ever offered with any intention of being convincing, you would not be the gentleman we all know you to be, and you would be unfit to associate with the wives and daughters of the people who trust you."

Madame Ratignolle had spoken what she believed to be the law and the gospel. The young man shrugged his shoulders impatiently.

"Oh! well! That isn't it," slamming his hat down vehemently upon his head. "You ought to feel that such things are not flattering to say to a fellow."

"Should our whole intercourse consist of an exchange of compliments? *Ma foi!*"[22]

"It isn't pleasant to have a woman tell you—" he went on, unheedingly, but breaking off suddenly: "Now if I were like Arobin—you remember Alcée Arobin and that story of the consul's wife at Biloxi?" And he related the story of Alcée Arobin and the consul's wife; and another about the tenor of the French Opera, who received letters which

---

[20] Indeed! It's that Madame Ratignolle is jealous.

[21] Humbug.

[22] Indeed, yes!

should never have been written; and still other stories, grave and gay, till Mrs. Pontellier and her possible propensity for taking young men seriously was apparently forgotten.

Madame Ratignolle, when they had regained her cottage, went in to take the hour's rest which she considered helpful. Before leaving her, Robert begged her pardon for the impatience—he called it rudeness—with which he had received her well-meant caution.

"You made one mistake, Adèle," he said, with a light smile; "there is no earthly possibility of Mrs. Pontellier ever taking me seriously. You should have warned me against taking myself seriously. Your advice might then have carried some weight and given me subject for some reflection. *Au revoir.* But you look tired," he added, solicitously. "Would you like a cup of bouillon? Shall I stir you a toddy? Let me mix you a toddy with a drop of Angostura."

She acceded to the suggestion of bouillon, which was grateful and acceptable. He went himself to the kitchen, which was a building apart from the cottages and lying to the rear of the house. And he himself brought her the golden-brown bouillon, in a dainty Sèvres cup, with a flaky cracker or two on the saucer.

She thrust a bare, white arm from the curtain which shielded her open door, and received the cup from his hands. She told him he was a *bon garçon,*[23] and she meant it. Robert thanked her and turned away toward "the house."

The lovers were just entering the grounds of the *pension.* They were leaning toward each other as the water-oaks bent from the sea. There was not a particle of earth beneath their feet. Their heads might have been turned upside-down, so absolutely did they tread upon blue ether. The lady in black, creeping behind them, looked a trifle paler and more jaded than usual. There was no sign of Mrs. Pontellier and the children. Robert scanned the distance for any such apparition. They would doubtless remain away till the dinner hour. The young man ascended to his mother's room. It was situated at the top of the house, made up of odd angles and a queer, sloping ceiling. Two broad dormer windows looked out toward the Gulf, and as far across it as a man's eye might reach. The furnishings of the room were light, cool, and practical.

Madame Lebrun was busily engaged at the sewing-machine. A little black girl sat on the floor, and with her hands worked the treadle of the machine. The Creole woman does not take any chances which may be avoided of imperiling her health.

Robert went over and seated himself on the broad sill of one of the dormer windows. He took a book from his pocket and began energetically to read it, judging by the precision and frequency with which he turned the leaves. The sewing-machine made a resounding clatter in the room; it was of a ponderous, by-gone make. In the lulls, Robert and his mother exchanged bits of desultory conversation.

"Where is Mrs. Pontellier?"

"Down at the beach with the children."

"I promised to lend her the Goncourt. Don't forget to take it down when you go; it's there on the bookshelf over the small table." Clatter, clatter, clatter, bang! for the next five or eight minutes.

"Where is Victor going with the rockaway[24]?"

"The rockaway? Victor?"

"Yes; down there in front. He seems to be getting ready to drive away somewhere."

"Call him." Clatter, clatter!

Robert uttered a shrill, piercing whistle which might have been heard back at the wharf.

"He won't look up."

Madame Lebrun flew to the window. She called "Victor!" She waved a handkerchief and called again. The young fellow below got into the vehicle and started the horse off at a gallop.

Madame Lebrun went back to the machine, crimson with annoyance. Victor was the younger son and brother—a *tête montée*,[25] with a temper which invited violence and a will which no ax could break.

"Whenever you say the word I'm ready to thrash any amount of reason into him that he's able to hold."

"If your father had only lived!" Clatter, clatter, clatter, clatter, bang! It was a fixed belief with Madame Lebrun that the conduct of the universe and all things pertaining thereto would have been manifestly of a more intelligent and higher order had not Monsieur Lebrun been removed to other spheres during the early years of their married life.

"What do you hear from Montel?" Montel was a middle-aged gentleman whose vain ambition and desire for the past twenty years had been to fill the void which Monsieur Lebrun's taking off had left in the Lebrun household. Clatter, clatter, bang, clatter!

"I have a letter somewhere," looking in the machine drawer and finding the letter in the bottom of the work-basket. "He says to tell you he will be in Vera Cruz the beginning of next month"—clatter, clatter!—"and if you still have the intention of joining him"—bang! clatter, clatter, bang!

"Why didn't you tell me so before, mother? You know I wanted—" Clatter, clatter, clatter!

"Do you see Mrs. Pontellier starting back with the children? She will be in late to luncheon again. She never starts to get ready for luncheon till the last minute." Clatter, clatter! "Where are you going?"

"Where did you say the Goncourt was?"

IX

Every light in the hall was ablaze; every lamp turned as high as it could be without smoking the chimney or threatening explosion. The lamps were fixed at intervals against the wall, encircling the whole room. Some one had gathered orange and lemon branches, and with these fashioned graceful festoons between. The dark green of the branches stood out and glistened against the white muslin curtains which draped the windows, and which puffed, floated, and flapped at the capricious will of a stiff breeze that swept up from the Gulf.

It was Saturday night a few weeks after the intimate conversation held between Robert and Madame Ratignolle on their way from the beach. An unusual number of husbands, fathers, and friends had come down to stay over Sunday; and they were being suitably entertained by their families, with the material help of Madame Lebrun. The dining tables had all been removed to one end of the hall, and the chairs ranged about

[25] Excitable temperment.

in rows and in clusters. Each little family group had had its say and exchanged its domestic gossip earlier in the evening. There was now an apparent disposition to relax; to widen the circle of confidences and give a more general tone to the conversation.

Many of the children had been permitted to sit up beyond their usual bedtime. A small band of them were lying on their stomachs on the floor looking at the colored sheets of the comic papers which Mr. Pontellier had brought down. The little Pontellier boys were permitting them to do so, and making their authority felt.

Music, dancing, and a recitation or two were the entertainments furnished, or rather, offered. But there was nothing systematic about the programme, no appearance of prearrangement nor even premeditation.

At an early hour in the evening the Farival twins were prevailed upon to play the piano. They were girls of fourteen, always clad in the Virgin's colors, blue and white, having been dedicated to the Blessed Virgin at their baptism. They played a duet from "Zampa," and at the earnest solicitation of every one present followed it with the overture to "The Poet and the Peasant."

"*Allez vous-en! Sapristi!*" shrieked the parrot outside the door. He was the only being present who possessed sufficient candor to admit that he was not listening to these gracious performances for the first time that summer. Old Monsieur Farival, grandfather of the twins, grew indignant over the interruption and insisted upon having the bird removed and consigned to regions of darkness. Victor Lebrun objected; and his decrees were as immutable as those of Fate. The parrot fortunately offered no further interruption to the entertainment, the whole venom of his nature apparently having been cherished up and hurled against the twins in that one impetuous outburst.

Later a young brother and sister gave recitations, which every one present had heard many times at winter evening entertainments in the city.

A little girl performed a skirt dance in the center of the floor. The mother played her accompaniments and at the same time watched her daughter with greedy admiration and nervous apprehension. She need have had no apprehension. The child was mistress of the situation. She had been properly dressed for the occasion in black tulle and black silk tights. Her little neck and arms were bare, and her hair, artificially crimped, stood out like fluffy black plumes over her head. Her poses were full of grace, and her little black-shod shoes twinkled as they shot out and upward with a rapidity and suddenness which were bewildering.

But there was no reason why every one should not dance. Madame Ratignolle could not, so it was she who gaily consented to play for the others. She played very well, keeping excellent waltz time and infusing an expression into the strains which was indeed inspiring. She was keeping up her music on account of the children, she said; because she and her husband both considered it a means of brightening the home and making it attractive.

Almost every one danced but the twins, who could not be induced to separate during the brief period when one or the other should be whirling around the room in the arms of a man. They might have danced together, but they did not think of it.

The children were sent to bed. Some went submissively; others with shrieks and protests as they were dragged away. They had been permitted to sit up till after the ice-cream, which naturally marked the limit of human indulgence.

The ice-cream was passed around with cake—gold and silver cake arranged on platters in alternate slices; it had been made and frozen during the afternoon back of the kitchen by two black women, under the supervision of Victor. It was pronounced a great success—excellent if it had only contained a little less vanilla or a little more sugar, if it had been frozen a degree harder, and if the salt might have been kept out of portions of it. Victor was proud of his achievement, and went about recommending it and urging every one to partake of it to excess.

After Mrs. Pontellier had danced twice with her husband, once with Robert, and once with Monsieur Ratignolle, who was thin and tall and swayed like a reed in the wind when he danced, she went out on the gallery and seated herself on the low windowsill, where she commanded a view of all that went on in the hall and could look out toward the Gulf. There was a soft effulgence in the east. The moon was coming up, and its mystic shimmer was casting a million lights across the distant, restless water.

"Would you like to hear Mademoiselle Reisz play?" asked Robert, coming out on the porch where she was. Of course Edna would like to hear Mademoiselle Reisz play; but she feared it would be useless to entreat her.

"I'll ask her," he said. "I'll tell her that you want to hear her. She likes you. She will come." He turned and hurried away to one of the far cottages, where Mademoiselle Reisz was shuffling away. She was dragging a chair in and out of her room, and at intervals objecting to the crying of a baby, which a nurse in the adjoining cottage was endeavoring to put to sleep. She was a disagreeable little woman, no longer young, who had quarreled with almost every one, owing to a temper which was self-assertive and a disposition to trample upon the rights of others. Robert prevailed upon her without any too great difficulty.

She entered the hall with him during a lull in the dance. She made an awkward, imperious little bow as she went in. She was a homely woman, with a small weazened face and body and eyes that glowed. She had absolutely no taste in dress, and wore a batch of rusty black lace with a bunch of artificial violets pinned to the side of her hair.

"Ask Mrs. Pontellier what she would like to hear me play," she requested of Robert. She sat perfectly still before the piano, not touching the keys, while Robert carried her message to Edna at the window. A general air of surprise and genuine satisfaction fell upon every one as they saw the pianist enter. There was a settling down, and a prevailing air of expectancy everywhere. Edna was a trifle embarrassed at being thus singled out for the imperious little woman's favor. She would not dare to choose, and begged that Mademoiselle Reisz would please herself in her selections.

Edna was what she herself called very fond of music. Musical strains, well rendered, had a way of evoking pictures in her mind. She sometimes liked to sit in the room of mornings when Madame Ratignolle played or practiced. One piece which that lady played Edna had entitled "Solitude." It was a short, plaintive, minor strain. The name of the piece was something else, but she called it "Solitude." When she heard it there came before her imagination the figure of a man standing beside a desolate rock on the seashore. He was naked. His attitude was one of hopeless resignation as he looked toward a distant bird winging its flight away from him.

Another piece called to her mind a dainty young woman clad in an Empire gown, taking mincing dancing steps as she came down a long avenue between tall hedges. Again, another reminded her of children at play, and still another of nothing on earth but a demure lady stroking a cat.

The very first chords which Mademoiselle Reisz struck upon the piano sent a keen tremor down Mrs. Pontellier's spinal column. It was not the first time she had heard an artist at the piano. Perhaps it was the first time she was ready, perhaps the first time her being was tempered to take an impress of the abiding truth.

She waited for the material pictures which she thought would gather and blaze before her imagination. She waited in vain. She saw no pictures of solitude, of hope, of longing, or of despair. But the very passions themselves were aroused within her soul, swaying it, lashing it, as the waves daily beat upon her splendid body. She trembled, she was choking, and the tears blinded her.

Mademoiselle had finished. She arose, and bowing her stiff, lofty bow, she went away, stopping for neither thanks nor applause. As she passed along the gallery she patted Edna upon the shoulder.

"Well, how did you like my music?" she asked. The young woman was unable to answer; she pressed the hand of the pianist convulsively. Mademoiselle Reisz perceived her agitation and even her tears. She patted her again upon the shoulder as she said:

"You are the only one worth playing for. Those others? Bah!" and she went shuffling and sidling on down the gallery toward her room.

But she was mistaken about "those others." Her playing had aroused a fever of enthusiasm. "What passion!" "What an artist!" "I have always said no one could play Chopin[26] like Mademoiselle Reisz!" "That last prelude! Bon Dieu![27] It shakes a man!"

It was growing late, and there was a general disposition to disband. But some one, perhaps it was Robert, thought of a bath at that mystic hour and under that mystic moon.

X

At all events Robert proposed it, and there was not a dissenting voice. There was not one but was ready to follow when he led the way. He did not lead the way, however, he directed the way; and he himself loitered behind with the lovers, who had betrayed a disposition to linger and hold themselves apart. He walked between them, whether with malicious or mischievous intent was not wholly clear, even to himself.

The Pontelliers and Ratignolles walked ahead; the women leaning upon the arms of their husbands. Edna could hear Robert's voice behind them, and could sometimes hear what he said. She wondered why he did not join them. It was unlike him not to. Of late he had sometimes held away from her for an entire day, redoubling his devotion upon the next and the next, as though to make up for hours that had been lost. She missed him the days when some pretext served to take him away from her, just as one misses the sun on a cloudy day without having thought much about the sun when it was shining.

The people walked in little groups toward the beach. They talked and laughed; some of them sang. There was a band playing down at Klein's hotel, and the strains reached them faintly, tempered by the distance. There were strange, rare odors abroad—a tangle of the sea smell and of weeds and damp, new-plowed earth, mingled with the heavy perfume of a field of white blossoms somewhere near. But the night sat lightly upon the sea and the land. There was no weight of darkness; there were no shadows. The white light of the moon had fallen upon the world like the mystery and the softness of sleep.

---

[26] Frédéric Chopin (1810–49), Polish-born composer who lived in France, where his performances as a concert pianist greatly influenced the Romantic style.

[27] Good God!

Most of them walked into the water as though into a native element. The sea was quiet now, and swelled lazily in broad billows that melted into one another and did not break except upon the beach in little foamy crests that coiled back like slow, white serpents.

Edna had attempted all summer to learn to swim. She had received instructions from both the men and women; in some instances from the children. Robert had pursued a system of lessons almost daily; and he was nearly at the point of discouragement in realizing the futility of his efforts. A certain ungovernable dread hung about her when in the water, unless there was a hand near by that might reach out and reassure her.

But that night she was like the little tottering, stumbling, clutching child, who of a sudden realizes its powers, and walks for the first time alone, boldly and with over-confidence. She could have shouted for joy. She did shout for joy, as with a sweeping stroke or two she lifted her body to the surface of the water.

A feeling of exultation overtook her, as if some power of significant import had been given her to control the working of her body and her soul. She grew daring and reckless, overestimating her strength. She wanted to swim far out, where no woman had swum before.

Her unlooked-for achievement was the subject of wonder, applause, and admiration. Each one congratulated himself that his special teachings had accomplished this desired end.

"How easy it is!" she thought. "It is nothing," she said aloud; "why did I not discover before that it was nothing. Think of the time I have lost splashing about like a baby!" She would not join the groups in their sports and bouts, but intoxicated with her newly conquered power, she swam out alone.

She turned her face seaward to gather in an impression of space and solitude, which the vast expanse of water, meeting and melting with the moonlit sky, conveyed to her excited fancy. As she swam she seemed to be reaching out for the unlimited in which to lose herself.

Once she turned and looked toward the shore, toward the people she had left there. She had not gone any great distance—that is, what would have been a great distance for an experienced swimmer. But to her unaccustomed vision the stretch of water behind her assumed the aspect of a barrier which her unaided strength would never be able to overcome.

A quick vision of death smote her soul, and for a second of time appalled and enfeebled her senses. But by an effort she rallied her staggering faculties and managed to regain the land.

She made no mention of her encounter with death and her flash of terror, except to say to her husband, "I thought I should have perished out there alone."

"You were not so very far, my dear; I was watching you," he told her.

Edna went at once to the bath-house, and she had put on her dry clothes and was ready to return home before the others had left the water. She started to walk away alone. They all called to her and shouted to her. She waved a dissenting hand, and went on, paying no further heed to their renewed cries which sought to detain her.

"Sometimes I am tempted to think that Mrs. Pontellier is capricious," said Madame Lebrun, who was amusing herself immensely and feared that Edna's abrupt departure might put an end to the pleasure.

"I know she is," assented Mr. Pontellier; "sometimes, not often."

Edna had not traversed a quarter of the distance on her way home before she was overtaken by Robert.

"Did you think I was afraid?" she asked him, without a shade of annoyance.

"No; I knew you weren't afraid."

"Then why did you come? Why didn't you stay out there with the others?"

"I never thought of it."

"Thought of what?"

"Of anything. What difference does it make?"

"I'm very tired," she uttered, complainingly.

"I know you are."

"You don't know anything about it. Why should you know? I never was so exhausted in my life. But it isn't unpleasant. A thousand emotions have swept through me to-night. I don't comprehend half of them. Don't mind what I'm saying; I am just thinking aloud. I wonder if I shall ever be stirred again as Mademoiselle Reisz's playing moved me to-night. I wonder if any night on earth will ever again be like this one. It is like a night in a dream. The people about me are like some uncanny, half-human beings. There must be spirits abroad to-night."

"There are," whispered Robert. "Didn't you know this was the twenty-eighth of August?"

"The twenty-eighth of August?"

"Yes. On the twenty-eighth of August, at the hour of midnight, and if the moon is shining—the moon must be shining—a spirit that has haunted these shores for ages rises up from the Gulf. With its own penetrating vision the spirit seeks some one mortal worthy to hold him company, worthy of being exalted for a few hours into realms of the semi-celestials. His search has always hitherto been fruitless, and he has sunk back, disheartened, into the sea. But to-night he found Mrs. Pontellier. Perhaps he will never wholly release her from the spell. Perhaps she will never again suffer a poor, unworthy earthling to walk in the shadow of her divine presence."

"Don't banter me," she said, wounded at what appeared to be his flippancy. He did not mind the entreaty, but the tone with its delicate note of pathos was like a reproach. He could not explain; he could not tell her that he had penetrated her mood and understood. He said nothing except to offer her his arm, for by her own admission, she was exhausted. She had been walking alone with her arms hanging limp, letting her white skirts trail along the dewy path. She took his arm, but she did not lean upon it. She let her hand lie listlessly, as though her thoughts were elsewhere—somewhere in advance of her body, and she was striving to overtake them.

Robert assisted her into the hammock which swung from the post before her door out to the trunk of a tree.

"Will you stay out here and wait for Mr. Pontellier?" he asked.

"I'll stay out here. Good-night."

"Shall I get you a pillow?"

"There's one here," she said, feeling about, for they were in the shadow.

"It must be soiled; the children have been tumbling it about."

"No matter." And having discovered the pillow, she adjusted it beneath her head. She extended herself in the hammock with a deep breath of relief. She was not a supercilious or an over-dainty woman. She was not much given to reclining in the hammock, and when she did so it was with no cat-like suggestion of voluptuous ease, but with a beneficent repose which seemed to invade her whole body.

"Shall I stay with you till Mr. Pontellier comes?" asked Robert, seating himself on the outer edge of one of the steps and taking hold of the hammock rope which was fastened to the post.

"If you wish. Don't swing the hammock. Will you get my white shawl which I left on the window-sill over at the house?"

"Are you chilly?"

"No; but I shall be presently."

"Presently?" he laughed. "Do you know what time it is? How long are you going to stay out here?"

"I don't know. Will you get the shawl?"

"Of course I will," he said, rising. He went over to the house, walking along the grass. She watched his figure pass in and out of the strips of moonlight. It was past midnight. It was very quiet.

When he returned with the shawl she took it and kept it in her hand. She did not put it around her.

"Did you say I should stay till Mr. Pontellier came back?"

"I said you might if you wished to."

He seated himself again and rolled a cigarette, which he smoked in silence. Neither did Mrs. Pontellier speak. No multitude of words could have been more significant than those moments of silence, or more pregnant with the first-felt throbbings of desire.

When the voices of the bathers were heard approaching, Robert said good-night. She did not answer him. He thought she was asleep. Again she watched his figure pass in and out of the strips of moonlight as he walked away.

XI

"What are you doing out here, Edna? I thought I should find you in bed," said her husband, when he discovered her lying there. He had walked up with Madame Lebrun and left her at the house. His wife did not reply.

"Are you asleep?" he asked, bending down close to look at her.

"No." Her eyes gleamed bright and intense, with no sleepy shadows, as they looked into his.

"Do you know it is past one o'clock? Come on," and he mounted the steps and went into their room.

"Edna!" called Mr. Pontellier from within, after a few moments had gone by.

"Don't wait for me," she answered. He thrust his head through the door.

"You will take cold out there," he said, irritably. "What folly is this? Why don't you come in?"

"It isn't cold; I have my shawl."

"The mosquitoes will devour you."

"There are no mosquitoes."

She heard him moving about the room; every sound indicating impatience and irritation. Another time she would have gone in at his request. She would, through habit, have yielded to his desire; not with any sense of submission or obedience to his compelling wishes, but unthinkingly, as we walk, move, sit, stand, go through the daily treadmill of the life which has been portioned out to us.

"Edna, dear, are you not coming in soon?" he asked again, this time fondly, with a note of entreaty.

"No; I am going to stay out here."

"This is more than folly," he blurted out. "I can't permit you to stay out there all night. You must come in the house instantly."

With a writhing motion she settled herself more securely in the hammock. She perceived that her will had blazed up, stubborn and resistant. She could not at that moment have done other than denied and resisted. She wondered if her husband had ever spoken to her like that before, and if she had submitted to his command. Of course she had; she remembered that she had. But she could not realize why or how she should have yielded, feeling as she then did.

"Léonce, go to bed," she said. "I mean to stay out here. I don't wish to go in, and I don't intend to. Don't speak to me like that again; I shall not answer you."

Mr. Pontellier had prepared for bed, but he slipped on an extra garment. He opened a bottle of wine, of which he kept a small and select supply in a buffet of his own. He drank a glass of the wine and went out on the gallery and offered a glass to his wife. She did not wish any. He drew up the rocker, hoisted his slippered feet on the rail, and proceeded to smoke a cigar. He smoked two cigars; then he went inside and drank another glass of wine. Mrs. Pontellier again declined to accept a glass when it was offered to her. Mr. Pontellier once more seated himself with elevated feet, and after a reasonable interval of time smoked some more cigars.

Edna began to feel like one who awakens gradually out of a dream, a delicious, grotesque, impossible dream, to feel again the realities pressing into her soul. The physical need for sleep began to overtake her; the exuberance which had sustained and exalted her spirit left her helpless and yielding to the conditions which crowded her in.

The stillest hour of the night had come, the hour before dawn, when the world seems to hold its breath. The moon hung low, and had turned from silver to copper in the sleeping sky. The old owl no longer hooted, and the water-oaks had ceased to moan as they bent their heads.

Edna arose, cramped from lying so long and still in the hammock. She tottered up the steps, clutching feebly at the post before passing into the house.

"Are you coming in, Léonce?" she asked, turning her face toward her husband.

"Yes, dear," he answered, with a glance following a misty puff of smoke. "Just as soon as I have finished my cigar."

XII

She slept but a few hours. They were troubled and feverish hours, disturbed with dreams that were intangible, that eluded her, leaving only an impression upon her half-awakened senses of something unattainable. She was up and dressed in the cool of the early morning. The air was invigorating and steadied somewhat her faculties. However, she was not seeking refreshment or help from any source, either external or from within. She was blindly following whatever impulse moved her, as if she had placed herself in alien hands for direction, and freed her soul of responsibility.

Most of the people at this early hour were still in bed and asleep. A few, who intended to go over to the *Chênière* for mass, were moving about. The lovers, who had laid their plans the night before, were already strolling toward the wharf. The lady in black, with her Sunday prayer-book, velvet and gold-clasped, and her Sunday silver beads, was following them at no great distance. Old Monsieur Farival was up, and was more than half inclined to do anything that suggested itself. He put on his big straw hat, and taking his umbrella from the stand in the hall, followed the lady in black, never overtaking her.

The little negro girl who worked Madame Lebrun's sewing-machine was sweeping the galleries with long, absent-minded strokes of the broom. Edna sent her up into the house to awaken Robert.

"Tell him I am going to the *Chênière*. The boat is ready; tell him to hurry."

He had soon joined her. She had never sent for him before. She had never asked for him. She had never seemed to want him before. She did not appear conscious that she had done anything unusual in commanding his presence. He was apparently equally unconscious of anything extraordinary in the situation. But his face was suffused with a quiet glow when he met her.

They went together back to the kitchen to drink coffee. There was no time to wait for any nicety of service. They stood outside the window and the cook passed them their coffee and a roll, which they drank and ate from the window-sill. Edna said it tasted good. She had not thought of coffee nor of anything. He told her he had often noticed that she lacked forethought.

"Wasn't it enough to think of going to the *Chênière* and waking you up?" she laughed. "Do I have to think of everything?—as Léonce says when he's in a bad humor. I don't blame him; he'd never be in a bad humor if it weren't for me."

They took a short cut across the sands. At a distance they could see the curious procession moving toward the wharf—the lovers, shoulder to shoulder, creeping; the lady in black, gaining steadily upon them; old Monsieur Farival, losing ground inch by inch, and a young barefooted Spanish girl, with a red kerchief on her head and a basket on her arm, bringing up the rear.

Robert knew the girl, and he talked to her a little in the boat. No one present understood what they said. Her name was Mariequita. She had a round, sly, piquant face and pretty black eyes. Her hands were small, and she kept them folded over the handle of her basket. Her feet were broad and coarse. She did not strive to hide them. Edna looked at her feet, and noticed the sand and slime between her brown toes.

Beaudelet grumbled because Mariequita was there, taking up so much room. In reality he was annoyed at having old Monsieur Farival, who considered himself the better sailor of the two. But he would not quarrel with so old a man as Monsieur Farival, so he quarreled with Mariequita. The girl was deprecatory at one moment, appealing to Robert. She was saucy the next, moving her head up and down, making "eyes" at Robert and making "mouths" at Beaudelet.

The lovers were all alone. They saw nothing, they heard nothing. The lady in black was counting her beads for the third time. Old Monsieur Farival talked incessantly of what he knew about handling a boat, and of what Beaudelet did not know on the same subject.

Edna liked it all. She looked Mariequita up and down, from her ugly brown toes to her pretty black eyes, and back again.

"Why does she look at me like that?" inquired the girl of Robert.

"Maybe she thinks you are pretty. Shall I ask her?"

"No. Is she your sweetheart?"

"She's a married lady, and has two children."

"Oh! well! Francisco ran away with Sylvano's wife, who had four children. They took all his money and one of the children and stole his boat."

"Shut up!"

"Does she understand?"

"Oh, hush!"

"Are those two married over there—leaning on each other?"

"Of course not," laughed Robert.

"Of course not," echoed Mariequita, with a serious, confirmatory bob of the head.

The sun was high up and beginning to bite. The swift breeze seemed to Edna to bury the sting of it into the pores of her face and hands. Robert held his umbrella over her.

As they went cutting sidewise through the water, the sails bellied taut, with the wind filling and overflowing them. Old Monsieur Farival laughed sardonically at something as he looked at the sails, and Beaudelet swore at the old man under his breath.

Sailing across the bay to the *Chênière Caminada*, Edna felt as if she were being borne away from some anchorage which had held her fast, whose chains had been loosening—had snapped the night before when the mystic spirit was abroad, leaving her free to drift whithersoever she chose to set her sails. Robert spoke to her incessantly; he no longer noticed Mariequita. The girl had shrimps in her bamboo basket. They were covered with Spanish moss. She beat the moss down impatiently, and muttered to herself sullenly.

"Let us go to Grande Terre to-morrow?" said Robert in a low voice.

"What shall we do there?"

"Climb up the hill to the old fort and look at the little wriggling gold snakes, and watch the lizards sun themselves."

She gazed away toward Grande Terre and thought she would like to be alone there with Robert, in the sun, listening to the ocean's roar and watching the slimy lizards writhe in and out among the ruins of the old fort.

"And the next day or the next we can sail to the Bayou Brulow," he went on.

"What shall we do there?"

"Anything—cast bait for fish."

"No; we'll go back to Grande Terre. Let the fish alone."

"We'll go wherever you like," he said. "I'll have Tonie come over and help me patch and trim my boat. We shall not need Beaudelet nor any one. Are you afraid of the pirogue?"

"Oh, no."

"Then I'll take you some night in the pirogue when the moon shines. Maybe your Gulf spirit will whisper to you in which of these islands the treasures are hidden—direct you to the very spot, perhaps."

"And in a day we should be rich!" she laughed. "I'd give it all to you, the pirate gold and every bit of treasure we could dig up. I think you would know how to spend it. Pirate gold isn't a thing to be hoarded or utilized. It is something to squander and throw to the four winds, for the fun of seeing the golden specks fly."

"We'd share it, and scatter it together," he said. His face flushed.

They all went together up to the quaint little Gothic church of Our Lady of Lourdes, gleaming all brown and yellow with paint in the sun's glare.

Only Beaudelet remained behind, tinkering at his boat, and Mariequita walked away with her basket of shrimps, casting a look of childish ill-humor and reproach at Robert from the corner of her eye.

XIII

A feeling of oppression and drowsiness overcame Edna during the service. Her head began to ache, and the lights on the altar swayed before her eyes. Another time she might have made an effort to regain her composure; but her one thought was to quit the stifling atmosphere of the church and reach the open air. She arose, climbing over Robert's feet with a muttered apology. Old Monsieur Farival, flurried, curious, stood up, but upon seeing that Robert had followed Mrs. Pontellier, he sank back into his seat. He whispered an anxious inquiry of the lady in black, who did not notice him or reply, but kept her eyes fastened upon the pages of her velvet prayer-book.

"I felt giddy and almost overcome," Edna said, lifting her hands instinctively to her head and pushing her straw hat up from her forehead. "I couldn't have stayed through the service." They were outside in the shadow of the church. Robert was full of solicitude.

"It was folly to have thought of going in the first place, let alone staying. Come over to Madame Antoine's; you can rest there." He took her arm and led her away, looking anxiously and continuously down into her face.

How still it was, with only the voice of the sea whispering through the reeds that grew in the salt-water pools! The long line of little gray, weather-beaten houses nestled peacefully among the orange trees. It must always have been God's day on that low, drowsy island, Edna thought. They stopped, leaning over a jagged fence made of sea-drift, to ask for water. A youth, a mild-faced *Acadian*,[28] was drawing water from the cistern, which was nothing more than a rusty buoy, with an opening on one side, sunk in the ground. The water which the youth handed to them in a tin pail was not cold to taste, but it was cool to her heated face, and it greatly revived and refreshed her.

Madame Antoine's cot was at the far end of the village. She welcomed them with all the native hospitality, as she would have opened her door to let the sunlight in. She was fat, and walked heavily and clumsily across the floor. She could speak no English, but when Robert made her understand that the lady who accompanied him was ill and desired to rest, she was all eagerness to make Edna feel at home and to dispose of her comfortably.

The whole place was immaculately clean, and the big, four-posted bed, snow-white, invited one to repose. It stood in a small side room which looked out across a narrow grass plot toward the shed, where there was a disabled boat lying keel upward.

Madame Antoine had not gone to mass. Her son Tonie had, but she supposed he would soon be back, and she invited Robert to be seated and wait for him. But he went

---

[28] Native of Louisiana, reputed to have been
transported South from Canada; also called
"Cajuns."

and sat outside the door and smoked. Madame Antoine busied herself in the large front room preparing dinner. She was boiling mullets over a few red coals in the huge fireplace.

Edna, left alone in the little side room, loosened her clothes, removing the greater part of them. She bathed her face, her neck and arms in the basin that stood between the windows. She took off her shoes and stockings and stretched herself in the very center of the high, white bed. How luxurious it felt to rest thus in a strange, quaint bed, with its sweet country odor of laurel lingering about the sheets and mattress! She stretched her strong limbs that ached a little. She ran her fingers through her loosened hair for a while. She looked at her round arms as she held them straight up and rubbed them one after the other, observing closely, as if it were something she saw for the first time, the fine, firm quality and texture of her flesh. She clasped her hands easily above her head, and it was thus she fell asleep.

She slept lightly at first, half awake and drowsily attentive to the things about her. She could hear Madame Antoine's heavy, scraping tread as she walked back and forth on the sanded floor. Some chickens were clucking outside the windows, scratching for bits of gravel in the grass. Later she half heard the voices of Robert and Tonie talking under the shed. She did not stir. Even her eyelids rested numb and heavily over her sleepy eyes. The voices went on—Tonie's slow, Acadian drawl, Robert's quick, soft, smooth French. She understood French imperfectly unless directly addressed, and the voices were only part of the other drowsy, muffled sounds lulling her senses.

When Edna awoke it was with the conviction that she had slept long and soundly. The voices were hushed under the shed. Madame Antoine's step was no longer to be heard in the adjoining room. Even the chickens had gone elsewhere to scratch and cluck. The mosquito bar was drawn over her; the old woman had come in while she slept and let down the bar. Edna arose quietly from the bed, and looking between the curtains of the window, she saw by the slanting rays of the sun that the afternoon was far advanced. Robert was out there under the shed, reclining in the shade against the sloping keel of the overturned boat. He was reading from a book. Tonie was no longer with him. She wondered what had become of the rest of the party. She peeped out at him two or three times as she stood washing herself in the little basin between the windows.

Madame Antoine had laid some coarse, clean towels upon a chair, and had placed a box of *poudre de riz*[29] within easy reach. Edna dabbed the powder upon her nose and cheeks as she looked at herself closely in the little distorted mirror which hung on the wall above the basin. Her eyes were bright and wide awake and her face glowed.

When she had completed her toilet she walked into the adjoining room. She was very hungry. No one was there. But there was a cloth spread upon the table that stood against the wall, and a cover was laid for one, with a crusty brown loaf and a bottle of wine beside the plate. Edna bit a piece from the brown loaf, tearing it with her strong, white teeth. She poured some of the wine into the glass and drank it down. Then she went softly out of doors, and plucking an orange from the low-hanging bough of a tree, threw it at Robert, who did not know she was awake and up.

An illumination broke over his whole face when he saw her and joined her under the orange tree.

---

[29] Rice powder used for the complexion.

"How many years have I slept?" she inquired. "The whole island seems changed. A new race of beings must have sprung up, leaving only you and me as past relics. How many ages ago did Madame Antoine and Tonie die? and when did our people from Grand Isle disappear from the earth?"

He familiarly adjusted a ruffle upon her shoulder.

"You have slept precisely one hundred years. I was left here to guard your slumbers; and for one hundred years I have been out under the shed reading a book. The only evil I couldn't prevent was to keep a broiled fowl from drying up."

"If it has turned to stone, still will I eat it," said Edna, moving with him into the house. "But really, what has become of Monsieur Farival and the others?"

"Gone hours ago. When they found that you were sleeping they thought it best not to awake you. Any way, I wouldn't have let them. What was I here for?"

"I wonder if Léonce will be uneasy!" she speculated, as she seated herself at table.

"Of course not; he knows you are with me," Robert replied, as he busied himself among sundry pans and covered dishes which had been left standing on the hearth.

"Where are Madame Antoine and her son?" asked Edna.

"Gone to Vespers, and to visit some friends, I believe. I am to take you back in Tonie's boat whenever you are ready to go."

He stirred the smoldering ashes till the broiled fowl began to sizzle afresh. He served her with no mean repast, dripping the coffee anew and sharing it with her. Madame Antoine had cooked little else than the mullets, but while Edna slept Robert had foraged the island. He was childishly gratified to discover her appetite, and to see the relish with which she ate the food which he had procured for her.

"Shall we go right away?" she asked, after draining her glass and brushing together the crumbs of the crusty loaf.

"The sun isn't as low as it will be in two hours," he answered.

"The sun will be gone in two hours."

"Well, let it go; who cares!"

They waited a good while under the orange trees, till Madame Antoine came back, panting, waddling, with a thousand apologies to explain her absence. Tonie did not dare to return. He was shy, and would not willingly face any woman except his mother.

It was very pleasant to stay there under the orange trees, while the sun dipped lower and lower, turning the western sky to flaming copper and gold. The shadows lengthened and crept out like stealthy, grotesque monsters across the grass.

Edna and Robert both sat upon the ground—that is, he lay upon the ground beside her, occasionally picking at the hem of her muslin gown.

Madame Antoine seated her fat body, broad and squat, upon a bench beside the door. She had been talking all the afternoon, and had wound herself up to the story-telling pitch.

And what stories she told them! But twice in her life she had left the *Chênière Caminada*, and then for the briefest span. All her years she had squatted and waddled there upon the island, gathering legends of the Baratarians and the sea. The night came on, with the moon to lighten it. Edna could hear the whispering voices of dead men and the click of muffled gold.

When she and Robert stepped into Tonie's boat, with the red lateen sail, misty spirit forms were prowling in the shadows and among the reeds, and upon the water were phantom ships, speeding to cover.

XIV

The youngest boy, Etienne, had been very naughty, Madame Ratignolle said, as she delivered him into the hands of his mother. He had been unwilling to go to bed and had made a scene; whereupon she had taken charge of him and pacified him as well as she could. Raoul had been in bed and asleep for two hours.

The youngster was in his long white nightgown, that kept tripping him up as Madame Ratignolle led him along by the hand. With the other chubby fist he rubbed his eyes, which were heavy with sleep and ill humor. Edna took him in her arms, and seating herself in the rocker, began to coddle and caress him, calling him all manner of tender names, soothing him to sleep.

It was not more than nine o'clock. No one had yet gone to bed but the children.

Léonce had been very uneasy at first, Madame Ratignolle said, and had wanted to start at once for the *Chênière*. But Monsieur Farival had assured him that his wife was only overcome with sleep and fatigue, that Tonie would bring her safely back later in the day; and he had thus been dissuaded from crossing the bay. He had gone over to Klein's, looking up some cotton broker whom he wished to see in regard to securities, exchanges, stocks, bonds, or something of the sort, Madame Ratignolle did not remember what. He said he would not remain away late. She herself was suffering from heat and oppression, she said. She carried a bottle of salts and a large fan. She would not consent to remain with Edna, for Monsieur Ratignolle was alone, and he detested above all things to be left alone.

When Etienne had fallen asleep Edna bore him into the back room, and Robert went and lifted the mosquito bar that she might lay the child comfortably in his bed. The quadroon had vanished. When they emerged from the cottage Robert bade Edna goodnight.

"Do you know we have been together the whole livelong day, Robert—since early this morning?" she said at parting.

"All but the hundred years when you were sleeping. Goodnight."

He pressed her hand and went away in the direction of the beach. He did not join any of the others, but walked alone toward the Gulf.

Edna stayed outside, awaiting her husband's return. She had no desire to sleep or to retire; nor did she feel like going over to sit with the Ratignolles, or to join Madame Lebrun and a group whose animated voices reached her as they sat in conversation before the house. She let her mind wander back over her stay at Grand Isle; and she tried to discover wherein this summer had been different from any and every other summer of her life. She could only realize that she herself—her present self—was in some way different from the other self. That she was seeing with different eyes and making the acquaintance of new conditions in herself that colored and changed her environment, she did not yet suspect.

She wondered why Robert had gone away and left her. It did not occur to her to think he might have grown tired of being with her the livelong day. She was not tired, and she felt that he was not. She regretted that he had gone. It was so much more natural to have him stay when he was not absolutely required to leave her.

As Edna waited for her husband she sang low a little song that Robert had sung as they crossed the bay. It began with "Ah! *Si tu savais*," and every verse ended with "*si tu savais*."[30]

---

[30] If you knew.

Robert's voice was not pretentious. It was musical and true. The voice, the notes, the whole refrain haunted her memory.

XV

When Edna entered the dining-room one evening a little late, as was her habit, an unusually animated conversation seemed to be going on. Several persons were talking at once, and Victor's voice was predominating, even over that of his mother. Edna had returned late from her bath, had dressed in some haste, and her face was flushed. Her head, set off by her dainty white gown, suggested a rich, rare blossom. She took her seat at table between old Monsieur Farival and Madame Ratignolle.

As she seated herself and was about to begin to eat her soup, which had been served when she entered the room, several persons informed her simultaneously that Robert was going to Mexico. She laid her spoon down and looked about her bewildered. He had been with her, reading to her all the morning, and had never even mentioned such a place as Mexico. She had not seen him during the afternoon; she had heard some one say he was at the house, upstairs with his mother. This she had thought nothing of, though she was surprised when he did not join her later in the afternoon, when she went down to the beach.

She looked across at him, where he sat beside Madame Lebrun, who presided. Edna's face was a blank picture of bewilderment, which she never thought of disguising. He lifted his eyebrows with the pretext of a smile as he returned her glance. He looked embarrassed and uneasy.

"When is he going?" she asked of everybody in general, as if Robert were not there to answer for himself.

"Tonight!" "This very evening!" "Did you ever!" "What possesses him!" were some of the replies she gathered, uttered simultaneously in French and English.

"Impossible!" she exclaimed. "How can a person start off from Grand Isle to Mexico at a moment's notice, as if he were going over to Klein's or to the wharf or down to the beach?"

"I said all along I was going to Mexico; I've been saying so for years!" cried Robert, in an excited and irritable tone, with the air of a man defending himself against a swarm of stinging insects.

Madame Lebrun knocked on the table with her knife handle.

"Please let Robert explain why he is going, and why he is going to-night," she called out. "Really, this table is getting to be more and more like Bedlam every day, with everybody talking at once. Sometimes—I hope God will forgive me—but positively, sometimes I wish Victor would lose the power of speech."

Victor laughed sardonically as he thanked his mother for her holy wish, of which he failed to see the benefit to anybody, except that it might afford her a more ample opportunity and license to talk herself.

Monsieur Farival thought that Victor should have been taken out in mid-ocean in his earliest youth and drowned. Victor thought there would be more logic in thus disposing of old people with an established claim for making themselves universally obnoxious. Madame Lebrun grew a trifle hysterical; Robert called his brother some sharp, hard names.

"There's nothing much to explain, mother," he said; though he explained, nevertheless—looking chiefly at Edna—that he could only meet the gentleman whom he intended to join at Vera Cruz by taking such and such a steamer, which left New Orleans on such a day; that Beaudelet was going out with his lugger-load of vegetables that night, which gave him an opportunity of reaching the city and making his vessel in time.

"But when did you make up your mind to all this?" demanded Monsieur Farival.

"This afternoon," returned Robert, with a shade of annoyance.

"At what time this afternoon?" persisted the old gentleman, with nagging determination, as if he were cross-questioning a criminal in a court of justice.

"At four o'clock this afternoon, Monsieur Farival," Robert replied, in a high voice and with a lofty air, which reminded Edna of some gentleman on the stage.

She had forced herself to eat most of her soup, and now she was picking the flaky bits of a *court bouillon* with her fork.

The lovers were profiting by the general conversation on Mexico to speak in whispers of matters which they rightly considered were interesting to no one but themselves. The lady in black had once received a pair of prayer-beads of curious workmanship from Mexico, with very special indulgence attached to them, but she had never been able to ascertain whether the indulgence extended outside the Mexican border. Father Fochel of the Cathedral had attempted to explain it; but he had not done so to her satisfaction. And she begged that Robert would interest himself, and discover, if possible, whether she was entitled to the indulgence accompanying the remarkably curious Mexican prayer-beads.

Madame Ratignolle hoped that Robert would exercise extreme caution in dealing with the Mexicans, who, she considered, were a treacherous people, unscrupulous and revengeful. She trusted she did them no injustice in thus condemning them as a race. She had known personally but one Mexican, who made and sold excellent tamales, and whom she would have trusted implicitly, so soft-spoken was he. One day he was arrested for stabbing his wife. She never knew whether he had been hanged or not.

Victor had grown hilarious, and was attempting to tell an anecdote about a Mexican girl who served chocolate one winter in a restaurant in Dauphine Street. No one would listen to him but old Monsieur Farival, who went into convulsions over the droll story.

Edna wondered if they had all gone mad, to be talking and clamoring at that rate. She herself could think of nothing to say about Mexico or the Mexicans.

"At what time do you leave?" she asked Robert.

"At ten," he told her. "Beaudelet wants to wait for the moon."

"Are you all ready to go?"

"Quite ready. I shall only take a hand-bag, and shall pack my trunk in the city."

He turned to answer some question put to him by his mother, and Edna, having finished her black coffee, left the table.

She went directly to her room. The little cottage was close and stuffy after leaving the outer air. But she did not mind; there appeared to be a hundred different things demanding her attention indoors. She began to set the toilet-stand to rights, grumbling at the negligence of the quadroon, who was in the adjoining room putting the children to bed. She gathered together stray garments that were hanging on the backs of chairs, and put each where it belonged in closet or bureau drawer. She changed her gown for a more comfortable and commodious wrapper. She rearranged her hair, combing and brushing it with unusual energy. Then she went in and assisted the quadroon in getting the boys to bed.

They were very playful and inclined to talk—to do anything but lie quiet and go to sleep. Edna sent the quadroon away to her supper and told her she need not return. Then she sat and told the children a story. Instead of soothing it excited them, and added to their wakefulness. She left them in heated argument, speculating about the conclusion of the tale which their mother promised to finish the following night.

The little black girl came in to say that Madame Lebrun would like to have Mrs. Pontellier go and sit with them over at the house till Mr. Robert went away. Edna returned answer that she had already undressed, that she did not feel quite well, but perhaps she would go over to the house later. She started to dress again, and got as far advanced as to remove her *peignoir*. But changing her mind once more she resumed the *peignoir*, and went outside and sat down before her door. She was overheated and irritable, and fanned herself energetically for a while. Madame Ratignolle came down to discover what was the matter.

"All that noise and confusion at the table must have upset me," replied Edna, "and moreover, I hate shocks and surprises. The idea of Robert starting off in such a ridiculously sudden and dramatic way! As if it were a matter of life and death! Never saying a word about it all morning when he was with me."

"Yes," agreed Madame Ratignolle. "I think it was showing us all—you especially—very little consideration. It wouldn't have surprised me in any of the others; those Lebruns are all given to heroics. But I must say I should never have expected such a thing from Robert. Are you not coming down? Come on, dear; it doesn't look friendly."

"No," said Edna, a little sullenly. "I can't go to the trouble of dressing again; I don't feel like it."

"You needn't dress; you look all right; fasten a belt around your waist. Just look at me!"

"No," persisted Edna; "but you go on. Madame Lebrun might be offended if we both stayed away."

Madame Ratignolle kissed Edna goodnight, and went away, being in truth rather desirous of joining in the general and animated conversation which was still in progress concerning Mexico and the Mexicans.

Somewhat later Robert came up, carrying his handbag.

"Aren't you feeling well?" he asked.

"Oh, well enough. Are you going right away?"

He lit a match and looked at his watch. "In twenty minutes," he said. The sudden and brief flare of the match emphasized the darkness for a while. He sat down upon a stool which the children had left out on the porch.

"Get a chair," said Edna.

"This will do," he replied. He put on his soft hat and nervously took it off again, and wiping his face with his handkerchief, complained of the heat.

"Take the fan," said Edna, offering it to him.

"Oh, no! Thank you. It does no good; you have to stop fanning some time, and feel all the more uncomfortable afterward."

"That's one of the ridiculous things which men always say. I have never known one to speak otherwise of fanning. How long will you be gone?"

"Forever, perhaps. I don't know. It depends upon a good many things."

"Well, in case it shouldn't be forever, how long will it be?"

"I don't know."

"This seems to me perfectly preposterous and uncalled for. I don't like it. I don't understand your motive for silence and mystery, never saying a word to me about it this morning." He remained silent, not offering to defend himself. He only said, after a moment:

"Don't part from me in an ill-humor. I never knew you to be out of patience with me before."

"I don't want to part in any ill-humor," she said. "But can't you understand? I've grown used to seeing you, to having you with me all the time, and your action seems unfriendly, even unkind. You don't even offer an excuse for it. Why, I was planning to be together, thinking of how pleasant it would be to see you in the city next winter."

"So was I," he blurted. "Perhaps that's the—" He stood up suddenly and held out his hand. "Good-by, my dear Mrs. Pontellier; good-by. You won't—I hope you won't completely forget me." She clung to his hand, striving to detain him.

"Write to me when you get there, won't you, Robert?" she entreated.

"I will, thank you. Good-by."

How unlike Robert! The merest acquaintance would have said something more emphatic than "I will, thank you; good-by," to such a request.

He had evidently already taken leave of the people over at the house, for he descended the steps and went to join Beaudelet, who was out there with an oar across his shoulder waiting for Robert. They walked away in the darkness. She could only hear Beaudelet's voice; Robert had apparently not even spoken a word of greeting to his companion.

Edna bit her handkerchief convulsively, striving to hold back and to hide, even from herself as she would have hidden from another, the emotion which was troubling—tearing—her. Her eyes were brimming with tears.

For the first time she recognized anew the symptoms of infatuation which she had felt incipiently as a child, as a girl in her earliest teens, and later as a young woman. The recognition did not lessen the reality, the poignancy of the revelation by any suggestion or promise of instability. The past was nothing to her; offered no lesson which she was willing to heed. The future was a mystery which she never attempted to penetrate. The present alone was significant; was hers, to torture her as it was doing then with the biting conviction that she had lost that which she had held, that she had been denied that which her impassioned, newly awakened being demanded.

XVI

"Do you miss your friend greatly?" asked Mademoiselle Reisz one morning as she came creeping up behind Edna, who had just left her cottage on her way to the beach. She spent much of her time in the water since she had acquired finally the art of swimming. As their stay at Grand Isle drew near its close, she felt that she could not give too much time to a diversion which afforded her the only real pleasurable moments that she knew. When Mademoiselle Reisz came and touched her upon the shoulder and spoke to her, the woman seemed to echo the thought which was ever in Edna's mind; or, better, the feeling which constantly possessed her.

Robert's going had some way taken the brightness, the color, the meaning out of everything. The conditions of her life were in no way changed, but her whole existence was dulled, like a faded garment which seems to be no longer worth wearing. She sought him everywhere—in others whom she induced to talk about him. She went up in the mornings to Madame Lebrun's room, braving the clatter of the old sewing-machine. She sat there and chatted at intervals as Robert had done. She gazed around the room at the pictures and photographs hanging upon the wall, and discovered in some corner an old family album, which she examined with the keenest interest, appealing to Madame Lebrun for enlightenment concerning the many figures and faces which she discovered between its pages.

There was a picture of Madame Lebrun with Robert as a baby, seated in her lap, a round-faced infant with a fist in his mouth. The eyes alone in the baby suggested the man. And that was he also in kilts, at the age of five, wearing long curls and holding a whip in his hand. It made Edna laugh, and she laughed, too, at the portrait in his first long trousers; while another interested her, taken when he left for college, looking thin, long-faced, with eyes full of fire, ambition and great intentions. But there was no recent picture, none which suggested the Robert who had gone away five days ago, leaving a void and wilderness behind him.

"Oh, Robert stopped having his pictures taken when he had to pay for them himself! He found wiser use for his money, he says," explained Madame Lebrun. She had a letter from him, written before he left New Orleans. Edna wished to see the letter, and Madame Lebrun told her to look for it either on the table or the dresser, or perhaps it was on the mantelpiece.

The letter was on the bookshelf. It possessed the greatest interest and attraction for Edna; the envelope, its size and shape, the post-mark, the handwriting. She examined every detail of the outside before opening it. There were only a few lines, setting forth that he would leave the city that afternoon, that he had packed his trunk in good shape, that he was well, and sent her his love and begged to be affectionately remembered to all. There was no special message to Edna except a postscript saying that if Mrs. Pontellier desired to finish the book which he had been reading to her, his mother would find it in his room, among other books there on the table. Edna experienced a pang of jealousy because he had written to his mother rather than to her.

Every one seemed to take for granted that she missed him. Even her husband, when he came down the Saturday following Robert's departure, expressed regret that he had gone.

"How do you get on without him, Edna?" he asked.

"It's very dull without him," she admitted. Mr. Pontellier had seen Robert in the city, and Edna asked him a dozen questions or more. Where had they met? On Carondelet Street, in the morning. They had gone "in" and had a drink and a cigar together. What had they talked about? Chiefly about his prospects in Mexico, which Mr. Pontellier thought were promising. How did he look? How did he seem—grave, or gay, or how? Quite cheerful, and wholly taken up with the idea of his trip, which Mr. Pontellier found altogether natural in a young fellow about to seek fortune and adventure in a strange, queer country.

Edna tapped her foot impatiently, and wondered why the children persisted in playing in the sun when they might be under the trees. She went down and led them out of the sun, scolding the quadroon for not being more attentive.

It did not strike her as in the least grotesque that she should be making of Robert the object of conversation and leading her husband to speak of him. The sentiment which she entertained for Robert in no way resembled that which she felt for her husband, or had ever felt, or ever expected to feel. She had all her life long been accustomed to harbor thoughts and emotions which never voiced themselves. They had never taken the form of struggles. They belonged to her and were her own, and she entertained the conviction that she had a right to them and that they concerned no one but herself. Edna had once told Madame Ratignolle that she would never sacrifice herself for her children, or for any one. Then had followed a rather heated argument; the two women did not appear to understand each other or to be talking the same language. Edna tried to appease her friend, to explain.

"I would give up the unessential; I would give my money, I would give my life for my children; but I wouldn't give myself. I can't make it more clear; it's only something which I am beginning to comprehend, which is revealing itself to me."

"I don't know what you would call the essential, or what you mean by the unessential," said Madame Ratignolle, cheerfully; "but a woman who would give her life for her children could do no more than that—your Bible tells you so. I'm sure I couldn't do more than that."

"Oh, yes you could!" laughed Edna.

She was not surprised at Mademoiselle Reisz's question the morning that lady, following her to the beach, tapped her on the shoulder and asked if she did not greatly miss her young friend.

"Oh, good morning, Mademoiselle; is it you? Why, of course I miss Robert. Are you going down to bathe?"

"Why should I go down to bathe at the very end of the season when I haven't been in the surf all summer," replied the woman, disagreeably.

"I beg your pardon," offered Edna, in some embarrassment, for she should have remembered that Mademoiselle Reisz's avoidance of the water had furnished a theme for much pleasantry. Some among them thought it was on account of her false hair, or the dread of getting the violets wet, while others attributed it to the natural aversion for water sometimes believed to accompany the artistic temperament. Mademoiselle offered Edna some chocolates in a paper bag, which she took from her pocket, by way of showing that she bore no ill feeling. She habitually ate chocolates for their sustaining quality; they contained much nutriment in small compass, she said. They saved her from starvation, as Madame Lebrun's table was utterly impossible; and no one save so impertinent a woman as Madame Lebrun could think of offering such food to people and requiring them to pay for it.

"She must feel very lonely without her son," said Edna, desiring to change the subject. "Her favorite son, too. It must have been quite hard to let him go."

Mademoiselle laughed maliciously.

"Her favorite son! Oh, dear! Who could have been imposing such a tale upon you? Aline Lebrun lives for Victor, and for Victor alone. She has spoiled him into the worthless creature he is. She worships him and the ground he walks on. Robert is very well in a way, to give up all the money he can earn to the family, and keep the barest pittance for himself. Favorite son, indeed! I miss the poor fellow myself, my dear. I liked to see him and to hear him about the place—the only Lebrun who is worth a pinch of salt. He comes to see me often in the city. I like to play to him. That Victor! hanging would be too good for him. It's a wonder Robert hasn't beaten him to death long ago."

"I thought he had great patience with his brother," offered Edna, glad to be talking about Robert, no matter what was said.

"Oh! he thrashed him well enough a year or two ago," said Mademoiselle. "It was about a Spanish girl, whom Victor considered that he had some sort of claim upon. He met Robert one day talking to the girl, or walking with her, or bathing with her, or carrying her basket—I don't remember what;—and he became so insulting and abusive that Robert gave him a thrashing on the spot that has kept him comparatively in order for a good while. It's about time he was getting another."

"Was her name Mariequita?" asked Edna.

"Mariequita—yes, that was it; Mariequita. I had forgotten. Oh, she's a sly one, and a bad one, that Mariequita!"

Edna looked down at Mademoiselle Reisz and wondered how she could have listened to her venom so long. For some reason she felt depressed, almost unhappy. She had not intended to go into the water; but she donned her bathing suit, and left Mademoiselle alone, seated under the shade of the children's tent. The water was growing cooler as the season advanced. Edna plunged and swam about with an abandon that thrilled and invigorated her. She remained a long time in the water, half hoping that Mademoiselle Reisz would not wait for her.

But Mademoiselle waited. She was very amiable during the walk back, and raved much over Edna's appearance in her bathing suit. She talked about music. She hoped that Edna would go to see her in the city, and wrote her address with the stub of a pencil on a piece of card which she found in her pocket.

"When do you leave?" asked Edna.

"Next Monday; and you?"

"The following week," answered Edna, adding, "It has been a pleasant summer, hasn't it, Mademoiselle?"

"Well," agreed Mademoiselle Reisz, with a shrug, "rather pleasant, if it hadn't been for the mosquitoes and the Farival twins."

XVII

The Pontelliers possessed a very charming home on Esplanade Street in New Orleans. It was a large, double cottage, with a broad front veranda, whose round, fluted columns supported the sloping roof. The house was painted a dazzling white; the outside shutters, or jalousies, were green. In the yard, which was kept scrupulously neat, were flowers and plants of every description which flourishes in South Louisiana. Within doors the appointments were perfect after the conventional type. The softest carpets and rugs covered the floors; rich and tasteful draperies hung at doors and windows. There were paintings, selected with judgment and discrimination, upon the walls. The cut glass, the silver, the heavy damask which daily appeared upon the table were the envy of many women whose husbands were less generous than Mr. Pontellier.

Mr. Pontellier was very fond of walking about his house examining its various appointments and details, to see that nothing was amiss. He greatly valued his possessions, chiefly because they were his, and derived genuine pleasure from contemplating a painting, a statuette, a rare lace curtain—no matter what—after he had bought it and placed it among his household gods.

On Tuesday afternoons—Tuesday being Mrs. Pontellier's reception day—there was a constant stream of callers—women who came in carriages or in the street cars, or walked when the air was soft and distance permitted. A light-colored mulatto boy, in dress coat and bearing a diminutive silver tray for the reception of cards, admitted them. A maid, in white fluted cap, offered the callers liqueur, coffee, or chocolate, as they might desire. Mrs. Pontellier, attired in a handsome reception gown, remained in the drawing-room the entire afternoon receiving her visitors. Men sometimes called in the evening with their wives.

This had been the programme which Mrs. Pontellier had religiously followed since her marriage, six years before. Certain evenings during the week she and her husband attended the opera or sometimes the play.

Mr. Pontellier left his home in the mornings between nine and ten o'clock, and rarely returned before half-past six or seven in the evening—dinner being served at half-past seven.

He and his wife seated themselves at table one Tuesday evening, a few weeks after their return from Grand Isle. They were alone together. The boys were being put to bed; the patter of their bare, escaping feet could be heard occasionally, as well as the pursuing voice of the quadroon, lifted in mild protest and entreaty. Mrs. Pontellier did not wear her usual Tuesday reception gown; she was in ordinary house dress. Mr. Pontellier, who was observant about such things, noticed it, as he served the soup and handed it to the boy in waiting.

"Tired out, Edna? Whom did you have? Many callers?" he asked. He tasted his soup and began to season it with pepper, salt, vinegar, mustard—everything within reach.

"There were a good many," replied Edna, who was eating her soup with evident satisfaction. "I found their cards when I got home; I was out."

"Out!" exclaimed her husband, with something like genuine consternation in his voice as he laid down the vinegar cruet and looked at her through his glasses. "Why, what could have taken you out on Tuesday? What did you have to do?"

"Nothing. I simply felt like going out, and I went out."

"Well, I hope you left some suitable excuse," said her husband, somewhat appeased, as he added a dash of cayenne pepper to the soup.

"No, I left no excuse. I told Joe to say I was out, that was all."

"Why, my dear, I should think you'd understand by this time that people don't do such things; we've got to observe *les convenances* if we ever expect to get on and keep up with the procession. If you felt that you had to leave home this afternoon, you should have left some suitable explanation for your absence.

"This soup is really impossible; it's strange that woman hasn't learned yet to make a decent soup. Any free-lunch stand in town serves a better one. Was Mrs. Belthrop here?"

"Bring the tray with the cards, Joe. I don't remember who was here."

The boy retired and returned after a moment, bringing the tiny silver tray, which was covered with ladies' visiting cards. He handed it to Mrs. Pontellier.

"Give it to Mr. Pontellier," she said.

Joe offered the tray to Mr. Pontellier, and removed the soup.

Mr. Pontellier scanned the names of his wife's callers, reading some of them aloud, with comments as he read.

" 'The Misses Delasidas.' I worked a big deal in futures for their father this morning; nice girls; it's time they were getting married. 'Mrs. Belthrop.' I tell you what it is, Edna; you can't afford to snub Mrs. Belthrop. Why, Belthrop could buy and sell us ten times over. His business is worth a good, round sum to me. You'd better write her a note. 'Mrs. James Highcamp.' Hugh! the less you have to do with Mrs. Highcamp, the better.

'Madame Laforcé.' Came all the way from Carrolton, too, poor old soul. 'Miss Wiggs,' 'Mrs. Eleanor Boltons.' " He pushed the cards aside.

"Mercy!" exclaimed Edna, who had been fuming. "Why are you taking the thing so seriously and making such a fuss over it?"

"I'm not making any fuss over it. But it's just such seeming trifles that we've got to take seriously; such things count."

The fish was scorched. Mr. Pontellier would not touch it. Edna said she did not mind a little scorched taste. The roast was in some way not to his fancy, and he did not like the manner in which the vegetables were served.

"It seems to me," he said, "we spend money enough in this house to procure at least one meal a day which a man could eat and retain his self-respect."

"You used to think the cook was a treasure," returned Edna, indifferently.

"Perhaps she was when she first came; but cooks are only human. They need looking after, like any other class of persons that you employ. Suppose I didn't look after the clerks in my office, just let them run things their own way; they'd soon make a nice mess of me and my business."

"Where are you going?" asked Edna, seeing that her husband arose from table without having eaten a morsel except a taste of the highly-seasoned soup.

"I'm going to get my dinner at the club. Good night." He went into the hall, took his hat and stick from the stand, and left the house.

She was somewhat familiar with such scenes. They had often made her very unhappy. On a few previous occasions she had been completely deprived of any desire to finish her dinner. Sometimes she had gone into the kitchen to administer a tardy rebuke to the cook. Once she went to her room and studied the cookbook during an entire evening, finally writing out a menu for the week, which left her harassed with a feeling that, after all, she had accomplished no good that was worth the name.

But that evening Edna finished her dinner alone, with forced deliberation. Her face was flushed and her eyes flamed with some inward fire that lighted them. After finishing her dinner she went to her room, having instructed the boy to tell any other callers that she was indisposed.

It was a large, beautiful room, rich and picturesque in the soft, dim light which the maid had turned low. She went and stood at an open window and looked out upon the deep tangle of the garden below. All the mystery and witchery of the night seemed to have gathered there amid the perfumes and the dusky and tortuous outlines of flowers and foliage. She was seeking herself and finding herself in just such sweet, half-darkness which met her moods. But the voices were not soothing that came to her from the darkness and the sky above and the stars. They jeered and sounded mournful notes without promise, devoid even of hope. She turned back into the room and began to walk to and fro down its whole length, without stopping, without resting. She carried in her hands a thin handkerchief, which she tore into ribbons, rolled into a ball, and flung from her. Once she stopped, and taking off her wedding ring, flung it upon the carpet. When she saw it lying there, she stamped her heel upon it, striving to crush it. But her small boot heel did not make an indenture, not a mark upon the little glittering circlet.

In a sweeping passion she seized a glass vase from the table and flung it upon the tiles of the hearth. She wanted to destroy something. The crash and clatter were what she wanted to hear.

A maid, alarmed at the din of breaking glass, entered the room to discover what was the matter.

"A vase fell upon the hearth," said Edna. "Never mind; leave it till morning."

"Oh! You might get some of the glass in your feet, ma'am," insisted the young woman, picking up bits of the broken vase that were scattered upon the carpet. "And here's your ring, ma'am, under the chair."

Edna held out her hand, and taking the ring, slipped it upon her finger.

XVIII

The following morning Mr. Pontellier, upon leaving for his office, asked Edna if she would not meet him in town in order to look at some new fixtures for the library.

"I hardly think we need new fixtures, Léonce. Don't let us get anything new; you are too extravagant. I don't believe you ever think of saving or putting by."

"The way to become rich is to make money, my dear Edna, not to save it," he said. He regretted that she did not feel inclined to go with him and select new fixtures. He kissed her good-by, and told her she was not looking well and must take care of herself. She was unusually pale and very quiet.

She stood on the front veranda as he quitted the house, and absently picked a few sprays of jessamine that grew upon a trellis near by. She inhaled the odor of the blossoms and thrust them into the bosom of her white morning gown. The boys were dragging along the banquette a small "express wagon," which they had filled with blocks and sticks. The quadroon was following them with little quick steps, having assumed a fictitious animation and alacrity for the occasion. A fruit vender was crying his wares in the street.

Edna looked straight before her with a self-absorbed expression upon her face. She felt no interest in anything about her. The street, the children, the fruit vender, the flowers growing there under her eyes, were all part and parcel of an alien world which had suddenly become antagonistic.

She went back into the house. She had thought of speaking to the cook concerning her blunders of the previous night; but Mr. Pontellier had saved her that disagreeable mission, for which she was so poorly fitted. Mr. Pontellier's arguments were usually convincing with those whom he employed. He left home feeling quite sure that he and Edna would sit down that evening, and possibly a few subsequent evenings, to a dinner deserving of the name.

Edna spent an hour or two in looking over some of her old sketches. She could see their shortcomings and defects, which were glaring in her eyes. She tried to work a little, but found she was not in the humor. Finally she gathered together a few of the sketches—those which she considered the least discreditable; and she carried them with her when, a little later, she dressed and left the house. She looked handsome and distinguished in her street gown. The tan of the seashore had left her face, and her forehead was smooth, white, and polished beneath her heavy, yellow-brown hair. There were a few freckles on her face, and a small, dark mole near the under lip and one on the temple, half-hidden in her hair.

As Edna walked along the street she was thinking of Robert. She was still under the spell of her infatuation. She had tried to forget him, realizing the inutility of remembering. But the thought of him was like an obsession, ever pressing itself upon her. It was not that she dwelt upon details of their acquaintance, or recalled in any special or peculiar way his personality; it was his being, his existence, which dominated her thought, fading sometimes as if it would melt into the mist of the forgotten, reviving again with an intensity which filled her with an incomprehensible longing.

Edna was on her way to Madame Ratignolle's. Their intimacy, begun at Grand Isle, had not declined, and they had seen each other with some frequency since their return to the city. The Ratignolles lived at no great distance from Edna's home, on the corner of a side street, where Monsieur Ratignolle owned and conducted a drug store which enjoyed a steady and prosperous trade. His father had been in the business before him, and Monsieur Ratignolle stood well in the community and bore an enviable reputation for integrity and clear-headedness. His family lived in commodious apartments over the store, having an entrance on the side within the *porte cochère*.[31] There was something which Edna thought very French, very foreign, about their whole manner of living. In the large and pleasant salon which extended across the width of the house, the Ratignolles entertained their friends once a fortnight with a *soirée musicale*,[32] sometimes diversified by cardplaying. There was a friend who played upon the 'cello. One brought his flute and another his violin, while there were some who sang and a number who performed upon the piano with various degrees of taste and agility. The Ratignolles' *soirées musicales* were widely known, and it was considered a privilege to be invited to them.

Edna found her friend engaged in assorting the clothes which had returned that morning from the laundry. She at once abandoned her occupation upon seeing Edna, who had been ushered without ceremony into her presence.

" 'Cité can do it as well as I; it is really her business," she explained to Edna, who apologized for interrupting her. And she summoned a young black woman, whom she instructed, in French, to be very careful in checking off the list which she handed her. She told her to notice particularly if a fine linen handkerchief of Monsieur Ratignolle's, which was missing last week, had been returned; and to be sure to set to one side such pieces as required mending and darning.

Then placing an arm around Edna's waist, she led her to the front of the house, to the salon, where it was cool and sweet with the odor of great roses that stood upon the hearth in jars.

Madame Ratignolle looked more beautiful than ever there at home, in a negligé which left her arms almost wholly bare and exposed the rich, melting curves of her white throat.

"Perhaps I shall be able to paint your picture some day," said Edna with a smile when they were seated. She produced the roll of sketches and started to unfold them. "I believe I ought to work again. I feel as if I wanted to be doing something. What do you think of them? Do you think it worth while to take it up again and study some more? I might study for a while with Laidpore."

She knew that Madame Ratignolle's opinion in such a matter would be next to valueless, that she herself had not alone decided, but determined; but she sought the words of praise and encouragement that would help her to put heart into her venture.

"Your talent is immense, dear!"

---

[31] Covered entryway.
[32] Evening party devoted to musical performances.

"Nonsense!" protested Edna, well pleased.

"Immense, I tell you," persisted Madame Ratignolle, surveying the sketches one by one, at close range, then holding them at arm's length, narrowing her eyes, and dropping her head on one side. "Surely, this Bavarian peasant is worthy of framing; and this basket of apples! never have I seen anything more lifelike. One might almost be tempted to reach out a hand and take one."

Edna could not control a feeling which bordered upon complacency at her friend's praise, even realizing, as she did, its true worth. She retained a few of the sketches, and gave all the rest to Madame Ratignolle, who appreciated the gift far beyond its value and proudly exhibited the pictures to her husband when he came up from the store a little later for his midday dinner.

Mr. Ratignolle was one of those men who are called the salt of the earth. His cheerfulness was unbounded, and it was matched by his goodness of heart, his broad charity, and common sense. He and his wife spoke English with an accent which was only discernible through its un-English emphasis and a certain carefulness and deliberation. Edna's husband spoke English with no accent whatever. The Ratignolles understood each other perfectly. If ever the fusion of two human beings into one has been accomplished on this sphere it was surely in their union.

As Edna seated herself at table with them she thought, "Better a dinner of herbs," though it did not take her long to discover that it was no dinner of herbs, but a delicious repast, simple, choice, and in every way satisfying.

Monsieur Ratignolle was delighted to see her, though he found her looking not so well as at Grand Isle, and he advised a tonic. He talked a good deal on various topics, a little politics, some city news and neighborhood gossip. He spoke with an animation and earnestness that gave an exaggerated importance to every syllable he uttered. His wife was keenly interested in everything he said, laying down her fork the better to listen, chiming in, taking the words out of his mouth.

Edna felt depressed rather than soothed after leaving them. The little glimpse of domestic harmony which had been offered her, gave her no regret, no longing. It was not a condition of life which fitted her, and she could see in it but an appalling and hopeless ennui. She was moved by a kind of commiseration for Madame Ratignolle,—a pity for that colorless existence which never uplifted its possessor beyond the region of blind contentment, in which no moment of anguish ever visited her soul, in which she would never have the taste of life's delirium. Edna vaguely wondered what she meant by "life's delirium." It had crossed her thought like some unsought, extraneous impression.

XIX

Edna could not help but think that it was very foolish, very childish, to have stamped upon her wedding ring and smashed the crystal vase upon the tiles. She was visited by no more outbursts, moving her to such futile expedients. She began to do as she liked and to feel as she liked. She completely abandoned her Tuesdays at home, and did not return the visits of those who had called upon her. She made no ineffectual efforts to conduct her household *en bonne ménagère*,[33] going and coming as it suited her fancy, and, so far as she was able, lending herself to any passing caprice.

---

[33] Like a good housekeeper.

Mr. Pontellier had been a rather courteous husband so long as he met a certain tacit submissiveness in his wife. But her new and unexpected line of conduct completely bewildered him. It shocked him. Then her absolute disregard for her duties as a wife angered him. When Mr. Pontellier became rude, Edna grew insolent. She had resolved never to take another step backward.

"It seems to me the utmost folly for a woman at the head of a household, and the mother of children, to spend in an atelier days which would be better employed contriving for the comfort of her family."

"I feel like painting," answered Edna. "Perhaps I shan't always feel like it."

"Then in God's name paint! but don't let the family go to the devil. There's Madame Ratignolle; because she keeps up her music, she doesn't let everything else go to chaos. And she's more of a musician than you are a painter."

"She isn't a musician, and I'm not a painter. It isn't on account of painting that I let things go."

"On account of what, then?"

"Oh! I don't know. Let me alone; you bother me."

It sometimes entered Mr. Pontellier's mind to wonder if his wife were not growing a little unbalanced mentally. He could see plainly that she was not herself. That is, he could not see that she was becoming herself and daily casting aside that fictitious self which we assume like a garment with which to appear before the world.

Her husband let her alone as she requested, and went away to his office. Edna went up to her atelier[34]—a bright room in the top of the house. She was working with great energy and interest, without accomplishing anything, however, which satisfied her even in the smallest degree. For a time she had the whole household enrolled in the service of art. The boys posed for her. They thought it amusing at first, but the occupation soon lost its attractiveness when they discovered that it was not a game arranged especially for their entertainment. The quadroon sat for hours before Edna's palette, patient as a savage, while the house-maid took charge of the children, and the drawing-room went undusted. But the house-maid, too, served her term as model when Edna perceived that the young woman's back and shoulders were molded on classic lines, and that her hair, loosened from its confining cap, became an inspiration. While Edna worked she sometimes sang low the little air, "Ah! si tu savais!"[35]

It moved her with recollections. She could hear again the ripple of the water, the flapping sail. She could see the glint of the moon upon the bay, and could feel the soft, gusty beating of the hot south wind. A subtle current of desire passed through her body, weakening her hold upon the brushes and making her eyes burn.

There were days when she was very happy without knowing why. She was happy to be alive and breathing, when her whole being seemed to be one with the sunlight, the color, the odors, the luxuriant warmth of some perfect Southern day. She liked then to wander alone into strange and unfamiliar places. She discovered many a sunny, sleepy corner, fashioned to dream in. And she found it good to dream and to be alone and unmolested.

There were days when she was unhappy, she did not know why,—when it did not seem worth while to be glad or sorry, to be alive or dead; when life appeared to her like a grotesque pandemonium and humanity like worms struggling blindly toward in-

---

[34] Studio.   [35] Ah, if you knew.

evitable annihilation. She could not work on such a day, nor weave fancies to stir her pulses and warm her blood.

XX

It was during such a mood that Edna hunted up Mademoiselle Reisz. She had not forgotten the rather disagreeable impression left upon her by their last interview; but she nevertheless felt a desire to see her—above all, to listen while she played upon the piano. Quite early in the afternoon she started upon her quest for the pianist. Unfortunately she had mislaid or lost Mademoiselle Reisz's card, and looking up her address in the city directory, she found that the woman lived on Bienville Street, some distance away. The directory which fell into her hands was a year or more old, however, and upon reaching the number indicated, Edna discovered that the house was occupied by a respectable family of mulattoes who had *chambres garnies*[36] to let. They had been living there for six months, and knew absolutely nothing of a Mademoiselle Reisz. In fact, they knew nothing of any of their neighbors; their lodgers were all people of the highest distinction, they assured Edna. She did not linger to discuss class distinctions with Madame Pouponne, but hastened to a neighboring grocery store, feeling sure that Mademoiselle would have left her address with the proprietor.

He knew Mademoiselle Reisz a good deal better than he wanted to know her, he informed his questioner. In truth she did not want to know her at all, or anything concerning her—the most disagreeable and unpopular woman who ever lived in Bienville Street. He thanked heaven she had left the neighborhood, and was equally thankful that he did not know where she had gone.

Edna's desire to see Mademoiselle Reisz had increased tenfold since these unlooked-for obstacles had arisen to thwart it. She was wondering who could give her the information she sought, when it suddenly occurred to her that Madame Lebrun would be the one most likely to do so. She knew it was useless to ask Madame Ratignolle, who was on the most distant terms with the musician, and preferred to know nothing concerning her. She had once been almost as emphatic in expressing herself upon the subject as the corner grocer.

Edna knew that Madame Lebrun had returned to the city, for it was the middle of November. And she also knew where the Lebruns lived, on Chartres Street.

Their home from the outside looked like a prison, with iron bars before the door and lower windows. The iron bars were a relic of the old *régime,* and no one had ever thought of dislodging them. At the side was a high fence enclosing the garden. A gate or door opening upon the street was locked. Edna rang the bell at this side garden gate, and stood upon the banquette, waiting to be admitted.

It was Victor who opened the gate for her. A black woman, wiping her hands upon her apron, was close at his heels. Before she saw them Edna could hear them in altercation, the woman—plainly an anomaly—claiming the right to be allowed to perform her duties, one of which was to answer the bell.

Victor was surprised and delighted to see Mrs. Pontellier, and he made no attempt to conceal either his astonishment or his delight. He was a dark-browned, good-looking

[36] Furnished apartments.

youngster of nineteen, greatly resembling his mother, but with ten times her impetuos-
ity. He instructed the black woman to go at once and inform Madame Lebrun that Mrs.
Pontellier desired to see her. The woman grumbled a refusal to do part of her duty
when she had not been permitted to do it all, and started back to her interrupted task of
weeding the garden. Whereupon Victor administered a rebuke in the form of a volley of
abuse, which, owing to its rapidity and incoherence, was all but incomprehensible to
Edna. Whatever it was, the rebuke was convincing, for the woman dropped her hoe and
went mumbling into the house.

Edna did not wish to enter. It was very pleasant there on the side porch, where there
were chairs, a wicker lounge, and a small table. She seated herself, for she was tired from
her long tramp; and she began to rock gently and smooth out the folds of her silk parasol. Victor drew up his chair beside her. He at once explained that the black woman's
offensive conduct was all due to imperfect training, as he was not there to take her in
hand. He had only come up from the island the morning before, and expected to return
next day. He stayed all winter at the island; he lived there, and kept the place in order
and got things ready for the summer visitors.

But a man needed occasional relaxation, he informed Mrs. Pontellier, and every now
and again he drummed up a pretext to bring him to the city. My! but he had had a time
of it the evening before! He wouldn't want his mother to know, and he began to talk in
a whisper. He was scintillant with recollections. Of course, he couldn't think of telling
Mrs. Pontellier all about it, she being a woman and not comprehending such things.
But it all began with a girl peeping and smiling at him through the shutters as he passed
by. Oh! but she was a beauty! Certainly he smiled back, and went up and talked to her.
Mrs. Pontellier did not know him if she supposed he was one to let an opportunity like
that escape him. Despite herself, the youngster amused her. She must have betrayed in
her look some degree of interest or entertainment. The boy grew more daring, and Mrs.
Pontellier might have found herself, in a little while, listening to a highly colored story
but for the timely appearance of Madame Lebrun.

That lady was still clad in white, according to her custom of the summer. Her eyes
beamed an effusive welcome. Would not Mrs. Pontellier go inside? Would she partake
of some refreshment? Why had she not been there before? How was that dear Mr. Pontellier and how were those sweet children? Had Mrs. Pontellier ever known such a
warm November?

Victor went and reclined on the wicker lounge behind his mother's chair, where he
commanded a view of Edna's face. He had taken her parasol from her hands while he
spoke to her, and he now lifted it and twirled it above him as he lay on his back. When
Madame Lebrun complained that it was *so* dull coming back to the city; that she saw *so*
few people now; that even Victor, when he came up from the island for a day or two,
had *so* much to occupy him and engage his time; then it was that the youth went into
contortions on the lounge and winked mischievously at Edna. She somehow felt like a
confederate in crime, and tried to look severe and disapproving.

There had been but two letters from Robert, with little in them, they told her. Victor
said it was really not worth while to go inside for the letters, when his mother entreated
him to go in search of them. He remembered the contents, which in truth he rattled off
very glibly when put to the test.

One letter was written from Vera Cruz and the other from the City of Mexico. He
had met Montel, who was doing everything toward his advancement. So far, the finan-

cial situation was no improvement over the one he had left in New Orleans, but of course the prospects were vastly better. He wrote of the City of Mexico, the buildings, the people and their habits, the conditions of life which he found there. He sent his love to the family. He inclosed a check to his mother, and hoped she would affectionately remember him to all his friends. That was about the substance of the two letters. Edna felt that if there had been a message for her, she would have received it. The despondent frame of mind in which she had left home began again to overtake her, and she remembered that she wished to find Mademoiselle Reisz.

Madame Lebrun knew where Mademoiselle Reisz lived. She gave Edna the address, regretting that she would not consent to stay and spend the remainder of the afternoon, and pay a visit to Mademoiselle Reisz some other day. The afternoon was already well advanced.

Victor escorted her out upon the banquette, lifted her parasol, and held it over her while he walked to the car with her. He entreated her to bear in mind that the disclosures of the afternoon were strictly confidential. She laughed and bantered him a little, remembering too late that she should have been dignified and reserved.

"How handsome Mrs. Pontellier looked!" said Madame Lebrun to her son.

"Ravishing!" he admitted. "The city atmosphere has improved her. Some way she doesn't seem like the same woman."

XXI

Some people contended that the reason Mademoiselle Reisz always chose apartments up under the roof was to discourage the approach of beggars, peddlars and callers. There were plenty of windows in her little front room. They were for the most part dingy, but as they were nearly always open it did not make so much difference. They often admitted into the room a good deal of smoke and soot; but at the same time all the light and air that there was came through them. From her windows could be seen the crescent of the river, the masts of ships and the big chimneys of the Mississippi steamers. A magnificent piano crowded the apartment. In the next room she slept, and in the third and last she harbored a gasoline stove on which she cooked her meals when disinclined to descend to the neighboring restaurant. It was there also that she ate, keeping her belongings in a rare old buffet, dingy and battered from a hundred years of use.

When Edna knocked at Mademoiselle Reisz's front room door and entered, she discovered that person standing beside the window, engaged in mending or patching an old prunella gaiter. The little musician laughed all over when she saw Edna. Her laugh consisted of a contortion of the face and all the muscles of the body. She seemed strikingly homely, standing there in the afternoon light. She still wore the shabby lace and the artificial bunch of violets on the side of her head.

"So you remembered me at last," said Mademoiselle. "I had said to myself, 'Ah, bah! she will never come.' "

"Did you want me to come?" asked Edna with a smile.

"I had not thought much about it," answered Mademoiselle. The two had seated themselves on a little bumpy sofa which stood against the wall. "I am glad, however, that you came. I have the water boiling back there, and was just about to make some coffee. You will drink a cup with me. And how is *la belle dame?*[37] Always handsome!

---

[37] Beautiful woman.

always healthy! always contented!" She took Edna's hand between her strong wiry fingers, holding it loosely without warmth, and executing a sort of double theme upon the back and palm.

"Yes," she went on; "I sometimes thought: 'She will never come. She promised as those women in society always do, without meaning it. She will not come.' For I really don't believe you like me, Mrs. Pontellier."

"I don't know whether I like you or not," replied Edna, gazing down at the little woman with a quizzical look.

The candor of Mrs. Pontellier's admission greatly pleased Mademoiselle Reisz. She expressed her gratification by repairing forthwith to the region of the gasoline stove and rewarding her guest with the promised cup of coffee. The coffee and the biscuit accompanying it proved very acceptable to Edna, who had declined refreshment at Madame Lebrun's and was now beginning to feel hungry. Mademoiselle set the tray which she brought in upon a small table near at hand, and seated herself once again on the lumpy sofa.

"I have had a letter from your friend," she remarked, as she poured a little cream into Edna's cup and handed it to her.

"My friend?"

"Yes, your friend Robert. He wrote to me from the City of Mexico."

"Wrote to *you?*" repeated Edna in amazement, stirring her coffee absently.

"Yes, to me. Why not? Don't stir all the warmth out of your coffee; drink it. Though the letter might as well have been sent to you; it was nothing but Mrs. Pontellier from beginning to end."

"Let me see it," requested the young woman, entreatingly.

"No; a letter concerns no one but the person who writes it and the one to whom it is written."

"Haven't you just said it concerned me from beginning to end?"

"It was written about you, not to you. 'Have you seen Mrs. Pontellier? How is she looking?' he asks. 'As Mrs. Pontellier says,' or 'as Mrs. Pontellier once said.' 'If Mrs. Pontellier should call upon you, play for her that Impromptu of Chopin's, my favorite. I heard it here a day or two ago, but not as you play it. I should like to know how it affects her,' and so on, as if he supposed we were constantly in each other's society."

"Let me see the letter."

"Oh, no."

"Have you answered it?"

"No."

"Let me see the letter."

"No, and again, no."

"Then play the Impromptu for me."

"It is growing late; what time do you have to be home?"

"Time doesn't concern me. Your question seems a little rude. Play the Impromptu."

"But you have told me nothing of yourself. What are you doing?"

"Painting!" laughed Edna. "I am becoming an artist. Think of it!"

"Ah! an artist! You have pretensions, Madame."

"Why pretensions? Do you think I could not become an artist?"

"I do not know you well enough to say. I do not know your talent or your temperament. To be an artist includes much; one must possess many gifts—absolute gifts—

which have not been acquired by one's own effort. And, moreover, to succeed, the artist must possess the courageous soul."

"What do you mean by the courageous soul?"

"Courageous, *ma foi!* The brave soul. The soul that dares and defies."

"Show me the letter and play for me the Impromptu. You see that I have persistence. Does that quality count for anything in art?"

"It counts with a foolish old woman whom you have captivated," replied Mademoiselle, with her wriggling laugh.

The letter was right there at hand in the drawer of the little table upon which Edna had just placed her coffee cup. Mademoiselle opened the drawer and drew forth the letter, the topmost one. She placed it in Edna's hands, and without further comment arose and went to the piano.

Mademoiselle played a soft interlude. It was an improvisation. She sat low at the instrument, and the lines of her body settled into ungraceful curves and angles that gave it an appearance of deformity. Gradually and imperceptibly the interlude melted into the soft opening minor chords of the Chopin Impromptu.

Edna did not know when the Impromptu began or ended. She sat in the sofa corner reading Robert's letter by the fading light. Mademoiselle had glided from the Chopin into the quivering love-notes of Isolde's song, and back again to the Impromptu with its soulful and poignant longing.

The shadows deepened in the little room. The music grew strange and fantastic—turbulent, insistent, plaintive and soft with entreaty. The shadows grew deeper. The music filled the room. It floated out upon the night, over the housetops, the crescent of the river, losing itself in the silence of the upper air.

Edna was sobbing, just as she had wept one midnight at Grand Isle when strange, new voices awoke in her. She arose in some agitation to take her departure. "May I come again, Mademoiselle?" she asked at the threshold.

"Come whenever you feel like it. Be careful; the stairs and landings are dark; don't stumble."

Mademoiselle reëntered and lit a candle. Robert's letter was on the floor. She stooped and picked it up. It was crumpled and damp with tears. Mademoiselle smoothed the letter out, restored it to the envelope, and replaced it in the table drawer.

XXII

One morning on his way into town Mr. Pontellier stopped at the house of his old friend and family physician, Doctor Mandelet. The Doctor was a semi-retired physician, resting, as the saying is, upon his laurels. He bore a reputation for wisdom rather than skill—leaving the active practice of medicine to his assistants and younger contemporaries—and was much sought for in matters of consultation. A few families, united to him by bonds of friendship, he still attended when they required the services of a physician. The Pontelliers were among these.

Mr. Pontellier found the Doctor reading at the open window of his study. His house stood rather far back from the street, in the center of a delightful garden, so that it was quiet and peaceful at the old gentleman's study window. He was a great reader. He stared up disapprovingly over his eye-glasses as Mr. Pontellier entered, wondering who had the temerity to disturb him at that hour of the morning.

"Ah, Pontellier! Not sick, I hope. Come and have a seat. What news do you bring this morning?" He was quite portly, with a profusion of gray hair, and small blue eyes which age had robbed of much of their brightness but none of their penetration.

"Oh! I'm never sick, Doctor. You know that I come of tough fiber—of that old Creole race of Pontelliers that dry up and finally blow away. I came to consult—no, not precisely to consult—to talk to you about Edna. I don't know what ails her."

"Madame Pontellier not well?" marveled the Doctor. "Why, I saw her—I think it was a week ago—walking along Canal Street, the picture of health, it seemed to me."

"Yes, yes; she seems quite well," said Mr. Pontellier, leaning forward and whirling his stick between his two hands; "but she doesn't act well. She's odd, she's not like herself. I can't make her out, and I thought perhaps you'd help me."

"How does she act?" inquired the doctor.

"Well, it isn't easy to explain," said Mr. Pontellier, throwing himself back in his chair. "She lets the housekeeping go to the dickens."

"Well, well; women are not all alike, my dear Pontellier. We've got to consider—"

"I know that; I told you I couldn't explain. Her whole attitude—toward me and everybody and everything—has changed. You know I have a quick temper, but I don't want to quarrel or be rude to a woman, especially my wife; yet I'm driven to it, and feel like ten thousand devils after I've made a fool of myself. She's making it devilishly uncomfortable for me," he went on nervously. "She's got some sort of notion in her head concerning the eternal rights of women; and—you understand—we meet in the morning at the breakfast table."

The old gentleman lifted his shaggy eyebrows, protruded his thick nether lip, and tapped the arms of his chair with his cushioned fingertips.

"What have you been doing to her, Pontellier?"

"Doing! *Parbleu!*"[38]

"Has she," asked the Doctor, with a smile, "has she been associating of late with a circle of pseudo-intellectual women—super-spiritual superior beings? My wife has been telling me about them."

"That's the trouble," broke in Mr. Pontellier, "she hasn't been associating with any one. She has abandoned her Tuesdays at home, has thrown over all her acquaintances, and goes tramping about by herself, moping in the street-cars, getting in after dark. I tell you she's peculiar. I don't like it; I feel a little worried over it."

This was a new aspect for the Doctor. "Nothing hereditary?" he asked, seriously. "Nothing peculiar about her family antecedents, is there?"

"Oh, no, indeed! She comes of sound old Presbyterian Kentucky stock. The old gentleman, her father, I have heard, used to atone for his week-day sins with his Sunday devotions. I know for a fact, that his race horses literally ran away with the prettiest bit of Kentucky farming land I ever laid eyes upon. Margaret—you know Margaret—she has all the Presbyterianism undiluted. And the youngest is something a vixen. By the way, she gets married in a couple of weeks from now."

"Send your wife up to the wedding," exclaimed the Doctor, foreseeing a happy solution. "Let her stay among her own people for a while; it will do her good."

38 To be sure.

"That's what I want her to do. She won't go to the marriage. She says a wedding is one of the most lamentable spectacles on earth. Nice thing for a woman to say to her husband!" exclaimed Mr. Pontellier, fuming anew at the recollection.

"Pontellier," said the Doctor, after a moment's reflection, "let your wife alone for a while. Don't bother her, and don't let her bother you. Woman, my dear friend, is a very peculiar and delicate organism—a sensitive and highly organized woman, such as I know Mrs. Pontellier to be, is especially peculiar. It would require an inspired psychologist to deal successfully with them. And when ordinary fellows like you and me attempt to cope with their idiosyncrasies the result is bungling. Most women are moody and whimsical. This is some passing whim of your wife, due to some cause or causes which you and I needn't try to fathom. But it will pass happily over, especially if you let her alone. Send her around to see me."

"Oh! I couldn't do that; there'd be no reason for it," objected Mr. Pontellier.

"Then I'll go around and see her," said the Doctor. "I'll drop in to dinner some evening *en bon ami.*"[39]

"Do! by all means," urged Mr. Pontellier. "What evening will you come? Say Thursday. Will you come Thursday?" he asked, rising to take his leave.

"Very well; Thursday. My wife may possibly have some engagement for me Thursday. In case she has, I shall let you know. Otherwise, you may expect me."

Mr. Pontellier turned before leaving to say:

"I am going to New York on business very soon. I have a big scheme on hand, and want to be on the field proper to pull the ropes and handle the ribbons. We'll let you in on the inside if you say so, Doctor," he laughed.

"No, I thank you, my dear sir," returned the Doctor. "I leave such ventures to you younger men with the fever of life still in your blood."

"What I wanted to say," continued Mr. Pontellier, with his hand on the knob; "I may have to be absent a good while. Would you advise me to take Edna along?"

"By all means, if she wishes to go. If not, leave her here. Don't contradict her. The mood will pass, I assure you. It may take a month, two, three months—possibly longer, but it will pass; have patience."

"Well, good-by, *à jeudi,*"[40] said Mr. Pontellier, as he let himself out.

The Doctor would have liked during the course of conversation to ask, "Is there any man in the case?" but he knew his Creole too well to make such a blunder as that.

He did not resume his book immediately, but sat for a while meditatively looking out into the garden.

XXIII

Edna's father was in the city, and had been with them several days. She was not very warmly or deeply attached to him, but they had certain tastes in common, and when together they were companionable. His coming was in the nature of a welcome disturbance; it seemed to furnish a new direction for her emotions.

He had come to purchase a wedding gift for his daughter, Janet, and an outfit for himself in which he might make a creditable appearance at her marriage. Mr. Pontellier

---

[39] Like a friend.   [40] Until Thursday.

had selected the bridal gift, as every one immediately connected with him always deferred to his taste in such matters. And his suggestions on the question of dress—which too often assumes the nature of a problem—were of inestimable value to his father-in-law. But for the past few days the old gentleman had been upon Edna's hands, and in his society she was becoming acquainted with a new set of sensations. He had been a colonel in the Confederate army, and still maintained, with the title, the military bearing which had always accompanied it. His hair and mustache were white and silky, emphasizing the rugged bronze of his face. He was tall and thin, and wore his coats padded, which gave a fictitious breadth and depth to his shoulders and chest. Edna and her father looked very distinguished together, and excited a good deal of notice during their perambulations. Upon his arrival she began by introducing him to her atelier and making a sketch of him. He took the whole matter very seriously. If her talent had been tenfold greater than it was, it would not have surprised him, convinced as he was that he had bequeathed to all of his daughters the germs of a masterful capability, which only depended upon their own efforts to be directed toward successful achievement.

Before her pencil he sat rigid and unflinching, as he had faced the cannon's mouth in days gone by. He resented the intrusion of the children, who gaped with wondering eyes at him, sitting so stiff up there in their mother's bright atelier. When they drew near he motioned them away with an expressive action of the foot, loath to disturb the fixed lines of his countenance, his arms, or his rigid shoulders.

Edna, anxious to entertain him, invited Mademoiselle Reisz to meet him, having promised him a treat in her piano playing; but Mademoiselle declined the invitation. So together they attended a *soirée musicale* at the Ratignolles'. Monsieur and Madame Ratignolle made much of the Colonel, installing him as the guest of honor and engaging him at once to dine with them the following Sunday, or any day which he might select. Madame coquetted with him in the most captivating and naïve manner, with eyes, gestures, and a profusion of compliments, till the Colonel's old head felt thirty years younger on his padded shoulders. Edna marveled, not comprehending. She herself was almost devoid of coquetry.

There were one or two men whom she observed at the *soirée musicale;* but she would never have felt moved to any kittenish display to attract their notice—to any feline or feminine wiles to express herself toward them. Their personality attracted her in an agreeable way. Her fancy selected them, and she was glad when a lull in the music gave them an opportunity to meet her and talk with her. Often on the street the glance of strange eyes had lingered in her memory, and sometimes had disturbed her.

Mr. Pontellier did not attend these *soirées musicales.* He considered them *bourgeois,* and found more diversion at the club. To Madame Ratignolle he said the music dispensed at her *soirées* was too "heavy," too far beyond his untrained comprehension. His excuse flattered her. But she disapproved of Mr. Pontellier's club, and she was frank enough to tell Edna so.

"It's a pity Mr. Pontellier doesn't stay home more in the evenings. I think you would be more—well, if you don't mind my saying it—more united, if he did."

"Oh! dear no!" said Edna, with a blank look in her eyes. "What should I do if he stayed home? We wouldn't have anything to say to each other."

She had not much of anything to say to her father, for that matter; but he did not antagonize her. She discovered that he interested her, though she realized that he might not interest her long; and for the first time in her life she felt as if she were thoroughly acquainted with him. He kept her busy serving him and ministering to his wants. It amused her to do so. She would not permit a servant or one of the children to do anything for him which she might do herself. Her husband noticed, and thought it was the expression of a deep filial attachment which he had never suspected.

The Colonel drank numerous "toddies" during the course of the day, which left him, however, imperturbed. He was an expert at concocting strong drinks. He had even invented some, to which he had given fantastic names, and for whose manufacture he required diverse ingredients that it devolved upon Edna to procure for him.

When Doctor Mandelet dined with the Pontelliers on Thursday he could discern in Mrs. Pontellier no trace of that morbid condition which her husband had reported to him. She was excited and in a manner radiant. She and her father had been to the race course, and their thoughts when they seated themselves at table were still occupied with the events of the afternoon, and their talk was still of the track. The Doctor had not kept pace with turf affairs. He had certain recollections of racing in what he called "the good old times" when the Lecompte stables flourished, and he drew upon this fund of memories so that he might not be left out and seem wholly devoid of the modern spirit. But he failed to impose upon the Colonel, and was even far from impressing him with this trumped-up knowledge of bygone days. Edna had staked her father on his last venture, with the most gratifying results to both of them. Besides, they had met some very charming people, according to the Colonel's impressions. Mrs. Mortimer Merriman and Mrs. James Highcamp, who were there with Alcée Arobin, had joined them and had enlivened the hours in a fashion that warmed him to think of.

Mr. Pontellier himself had no particular leaning toward horse racing, and was even rather inclined to discourage it as a pastime, especially when he considered the fate of that blue-grass farm in Kentucky. He endeavored, in a general way, to express a particular disapproval, and only succeeded in arousing the ire and opposition of his father-in-law. A pretty dispute followed, in which Edna warmly espoused her father's cause and the Doctor remained neutral.

He observed his hostess attentively from under his shaggy brows, and noted a subtle change which had transformed her from the listless woman he had known into a being who, for the moment, seemed palpitant with the forces of life. Her speech was warm and energetic. There was no repression in her glance or gesture. She reminded him of some beautiful, sleek animal waking up in the sun.

The dinner was excellent. The claret was warm and the champagne was cold, and under their beneficent influence the threatened unpleasantness melted and vanished with the fumes of the wine.

Mr. Pontellier warmed up and grew reminiscent. He told some amusing plantation experiences, recollections of old Iberville and his youth, when he hunted 'possum in company with some friendly darky; thrashed the pecan trees, shot the grosbec, and roamed the woods and fields in mischievous idleness.

The Colonel, with little sense of humor and of the fitness of things, related a somber episode of those dark and bitter days, in which he had acted a conspicuous part and always formed a central figure. Nor was the Doctor happier in his selection, when he told the old, ever new and curious story of the waning of a woman's love, seeking strange, new channels, only to return to its legitimate source after days of fierce unrest. It was one of the many little human documents which had been unfolded to him during his long career as a physician. The story did not seem especially to impress Edna. She had one of her own to tell, of a woman who paddled away with her lover one night in a pirogue[41] and never came back. They were lost amid the Baratarian Islands,[42] and no one ever heard of them or found trace of them from that day to this. It was a pure invention. She said that Madame Antoine had related it to her. That, also, was an invention. Perhaps it was a dream she had had. But every glowing word seemed real to those who listened. They could feel the hot breath of the Southern night; they could hear the long sweep of the pirogue through the glistening moonlit water, the beating of birds' wings, rising startled from among the reeds in the salt-water pools; they could see the faces of the lovers, pale, close together, rapt in oblivious forgetfulness, drifting into the unknown.

The champagne was cold, and its subtle fumes played fantastic tricks with Edna's memory that night.

Outside, away from the glow of the fire and the soft lamplight, the night was chill and murky. The Doctor doubled his old-fashioned cloak across his breast as he strode home through the darkness. He knew his fellow-creatures better than most men; knew that inner life which so seldom unfolds itself to unanointed eyes. He was sorry he had accepted Pontellier's invitation. He was growing old, and beginning to need rest and an imperturbed spirit. He did not want the secrets of other lives thrust upon him.

"I hope it isn't Arobin," he muttered to himself as he walked. "I hope to heaven it isn't Alcée Arobin."

XXIV

Edna and her father had a warm, and almost violent dispute upon the subject of her refusal to attend her sister's wedding. Mr. Pontellier declined to interfere, to interpose either his influence or his authority. He was following Doctor Mandelet's advice, and letting her do as she liked. The Colonel reproached his daughter for her lack of filial kindness and respect, her want of sisterly affection and womanly consideration. His arguments were labored and unconvincing. He doubted if Janet would accept any excuse—forgetting that Edna had offered none. He doubted if Janet would ever speak to her again, and he was sure Margaret would not.

Edna was glad to be rid of her father when he finally took himself off with his wedding garments and his bridal gifts, with his padded shoulders, his Bible reading, his "toddies" and ponderous oaths.

Mr. Pontellier followed him closely. He meant to stop at the wedding on his way to New York and endeavor by every means which money and love could devise to atone somewhat for Edna's incomprehensible action.

"You are too lenient, too lenient by far, Léonce," asserted the Colonel. "Authority, coercion are what is needed. Put your foot down good and hard; the only way to manage a wife. Take my word for it."

The Colonel was perhaps unaware that he had coerced his own wife into her grave. Mr. Pontellier had a vague suspicion of it which he thought it needless to mention at that late day.

Edna was not so consciously gratified at her husband's leaving home as she had been over the departure of her father. As the day approached when he was to leave her for a comparatively long stay, she grew melting and affectionate, remembering his many acts

---

[41] Small canoe-shaped boat used to navigate Louisiana swamps. [42] In the Louisiana bayou country.

of consideration and his repeated expressions of an ardent attachment. She was solicitous about his health and his welfare. She bustled around, looking after his clothing, thinking about heavy underwear, quite as Madame Ratignolle would have done under similar circumstances. She cried when he went away, calling him her dear, good friend, and she was quite certain she would grow lonely before very long and go to join him in New York.

But after all, a radiant peace settled upon her when she at last found herself alone. Even the children were gone. Old Madame Pontellier had come herself and carried them off to Iberville with their quadroon. The old madame did not venture to say she was afraid they would be neglected during Léonce's absence; she hardly ventured to think so. She was hungry for them—even a little fierce in her attachment. She did not want them to be wholly "children of the pavement," she always said when begging to have them for a space. She wished them to know the country, with its streams, its fields, its woods, its freedom, so delicious to the young. She wished them to taste something of the life their father had lived and known and loved when he, too, was a little child.

When Edna was at last alone, she breathed a big, genuine sigh of relief. A feeling that was unfamiliar but very delicious came over her. She walked all through the house, from one room to another, as if inspecting it for the first time. She tried the various chairs and lounges, as if she had never sat and reclined upon them before. And she perambulated around the outside of the house, investigating, looking to see if windows and shutters were secure and in order. The flowers were like new acquaintances; she approached them in a familiar spirit, and made herself at home among them. The garden walks were damp, and Edna called to the maid to bring out her rubber sandals. And there she stayed, and stooped, digging around the plants, trimming, picking dead, dry leaves. The children's little dog came out, interfering, getting in her way. She scolded him, laughed at him, played with him. The garden smelled so good and looked so pretty in the afternoon sunlight. Edna plucked all the bright flowers she could find, and went into the house with them, she and the little dog.

Even the kitchen assumed a sudden interesting character which she had never before perceived. She went in to give directions to the cook, to say that the butcher would have to bring much less meat, that they would require only half their usual quantity of bread, of milk and groceries. She told the cook that she herself would be greatly occupied during Mr. Pontellier's absence, and she begged her to take all thought and responsibility of the larder upon her own shoulders.

That night Edna dined alone. The candelabra, with a few candles in the center of the table, gave all the light she needed. Outside the circle of light in which she sat, the large dining-room looked solemn and shadowy. The cook, placed upon her mettle, served a delicious repast—a luscious tenderloin broiled *à point*.[43] The wine tasted good; the *marron glacé*[44] seemed to be just what she wanted. It was so pleasant, too, to dine in a comfortable *peignoir*.

She thought a little sentimentally about Léonce and the children, and wondered what they were doing. As she gave a dainty scrap or two to the doggie, she talked intimately to him about Etienne and Raoul. He was beside himself with astonishment and delight over these companionable advances, and showed his appreciation by his little quick, snappy barks and a lively agitation.

---

[43] Exactly right.   [44] Glazed chestnuts.

Then Edna sat in the library after dinner and read Emerson until she grew sleepy. She realized that she had neglected her reading, and determined to start anew upon a course of improving studies, now that her time was completely her own to do with as she liked.

After a refreshing bath, Edna went to bed. And as she snuggled comfortably beneath the eiderdown a sense of restfulness invaded her, such as she had not known before.

XXV

When the weather was dark and cloudy Edna could not work. She needed the sun to mellow and temper her mood to the sticking point. She had reached a stage when she seemed to be no longer feeling her way, working, when in the humor, with sureness and ease. And being devoid of ambition, and striving not toward accomplishment, she drew satisfaction from the work in itself.

On rainy or melancholy days Edna went out and sought the society of the friends she had made at Grand Isle. Or else she stayed indoors and nursed a mood with which she was becoming too familiar for her own comfort and peace of mind. It was not despair; but it seemed to her as if life were passing by, leaving its promise broken and unfulfilled. Yet there were other days when she listened, was led on and deceived by fresh promises which her youth held out to her.

She went again to the races, and again. Alcée Arobin and Mrs. Highcamp called for her one bright afternoon in Arobin's drag. Mrs. Highcamp was a worldly but unaffected, intelligent, slim, tall blonde woman in the forties, with an indifferent manner and blue eyes that stared. She had a daughter who served her as a pretext for cultivating the society of young men of fashion. Alcée Arobin was one of them. He was a familiar figure at the race course, the opera, the fashionable clubs. There was a perpetual smile in his eyes, which seldom failed to awaken a corresponding cheerfulness in any one who looked into them and listened to his good-humored voice. His manner was quiet, and at times a little insolent. He possessed a good figure, a pleasing face, not overburdened with depth of thought or feeling; and his dress was that of the conventional man of fashion.

He admired Edna extravagantly, after meeting her at the races with her father. He had met her before on other occasions, but she had seemed to him unapproachable until that day. It was at his instigation that Mrs. Highcamp called to ask her to go with them to the Jockey Club to witness the turf event of the season.

There were possibly a few track men out there who knew the race horse as well as Edna, but there was certainly none who knew it better. She sat between her two companions as one having authority to speak. She laughed at Arobin's pretensions, and deplored Mrs. Highcamp's ignorance. The race horse was a friend and intimate associate of her childhood. The atmosphere of the stables and the breath of the blue grass paddock revived in her memory and lingered in her nostrils. She did not perceive that she was talking like her father as the sleek geldings ambled in review before them. She played for very high stakes, and fortune favored her. The fever of the game flamed in her cheeks and eyes, and it got into her blood and into her brain like an intoxicant. People turned their heads to look at her, and more than one lent an attentive ear to her utterances, hoping thereby to secure the elusive but ever-desired "tip." Arobin caught the contagion of excitement which drew him to Edna like a magnet. Mrs. Highcamp remained, as usual, unmoved, with her indifferent stare and uplifted eyebrows.

Edna stayed and dined with Mrs. Highcamp upon being urged to do so. Arobin also remained and sent away his drag.

The dinner was quiet and uninteresting, save for the cheerful efforts of Arobin to enliven things. Mrs. Highcamp deplored the absence of her daughter from the races, and tried to convey to her what she had missed by going to the "Dante reading"[45] instead of joining them. The girl held a geranium leaf up to her nose and said nothing, but looked knowing and noncommittal. Mr. Highcamp was a plain, bald-headed man, who only talked under compulsion. He was unresponsive. Mrs. Highcamp was full of delicate courtesy and consideration toward her husband. She addressed most of her conversation to him at table. They sat in the library after dinner and read the evening papers together under the droplight; while the younger people went into the drawing-room near by and talked.

Miss Highcamp played some selections from *Grieg*[46] upon the piano. She seemed to have apprehended all of the composer's coldness and none of his poetry. While Edna listened she could not help wondering if she had lost her taste for music.

When the time came for her to go home, Mr. Highcamp grunted a lame offer to escort her, looking down at his slippered feet with tactless concern. It was Arobin who took her home. The car ride was long, and it was late when they reached Esplanade Street. Arobin asked permission to enter for a second to light his cigarette—his match safe was empty. He filled his match safe, but did not light his cigarette until he left her, after she had expressed her willingness to go to the races with him again.

Edna was neither tired nor sleepy. She was hungry again, for the Highcamp dinner, though of excellent quality, had lacked abundance. She rummaged in the larder and brought forth a slice of Gruyère and some crackers. She opened a bottle of beer which she found in the ice-box. Edna felt extremely restless and excited. She vacantly hummed a fantastic tune as she poked at the wood embers on the hearth and munched a cracker.

She wanted something to happen—something, anything; she did not know what. She regretted that she had not made Arobin stay a half hour to talk over the horses with her. She counted the money she had won. But there was nothing else to do, so she went to bed, and tossed there for hours in a sort of monotonous agitation.

In the middle of the night she remembered that she had forgotten to write her regular letter to her husband; and she decided to do so next day and tell him about her afternoon at the Jockey Club. She lay wide awake composing a letter which was nothing like the one which she wrote next day. When the maid awoke her in the morning Edna was dreaming of Mr. Highcamp playing the piano at the entrance of a music store on Canal Street, while his wife was saying to Alcée Arobin, as they boarded an Esplanade Street car:[47]

"What a pity that so much talent has been neglected! but I must go."

When, a few days later, Alcée Arobin again called for Edna in his drag, Mrs. Highcamp was not with him. He said they would pick her up. But as that lady had not been apprised of his intention of picking her up, she was not at home. The daughter was just leaving the house to attend the meeting of a branch Folk Lore Society, and regretted that she could not accompany them. Arobin appeared nonplused, and asked Edna if there were any one else she cared to ask.

---

[45] Literary gathering for the purpose of discussing the poetry of Dante Alighieri (1265–1321), author of *The Divine Comedy*.

[46] Edvard Grieg (1843–1907), Norwegian composer.

[47] Horse-drawn trolley.

She did not deem it worth while to go in search of any of the fashionable acquaintances from whom she had withdrawn herself. She thought of Madame Ratignolle, but knew that her fair friend did not leave the house, except to take a languid walk around the block with her husband after nightfall. Mademoiselle Reisz would have laughed at such a request from Edna. Madame Lebrun might have enjoyed the outing, but for some reason Edna did not want her. So they went alone, she and Arobin.

The afternoon was intensely interesting to her. The excitement came back upon her like a remittent fever. Her talk grew familiar and confidential. It was no labor to become intimate with Arobin. His manner invited easy confidence. The preliminary stage of becoming acquainted was one which he always endeavored to ignore when a pretty and engaging woman was concerned.

He stayed and dined with Edna. He stayed and sat beside the wood fire. They laughed and talked; and before it was time to go he was telling her how different life might have been if he had known her years before. With ingenuous frankness he spoke of what a wicked, ill-disciplined boy he had been, and impulsively drew up his cuff to exhibit upon his wrist the scar from a saber cut which he had received in a duel outside of Paris when he was nineteen. She touched his hand as she scanned the red cicatrice on the inside of his white wrist. A quick impulse that was somewhat spasmodic impelled her fingers to close in a sort of clutch upon his hand. He felt the pressure of her pointed nails in the flesh of his palm.

She arose hastily and walked toward the mantel.

"The sight of a wound or scar always agitates and sickens me," she said. "I shouldn't have looked at it."

"I beg your pardon," he entreated, following her; "it never occurred to me that it might be repulsive."

He stood close to her, and the effrontery in his eyes repelled the old, vanishing self in her, yet drew all her awakening sensuousness. He saw enough in her face to impel him to take her hand and hold it while he said his lingering good night.

"Will you go to the races again?" he asked.

"No," she said. "I've had enough of the races. I don't want to lose all the money I've won, and I've got to work when the weather is bright, instead of—"

"Yes; work; to be sure. You promised to show me your work. What morning may I come up to your atelier? To-morrow?"

"No!"

"Day after?"

"No, no."

"Oh, please don't refuse me! I know something of such things. I might help you with a stray suggestion or two."

"No. Good night. Why don't you go after you have said good night? I don't like you," she went on in a high, excited pitch, attempting to draw away her hand. She felt that her words lacked dignity and sincerity, and she knew that he felt it.

"I'm sorry you don't like me. I'm sorry I offended you. How have I offended you? What have I done? Can't you forgive me?" And he bent and pressed his lips upon her hand as if he wished never more to withdraw them.

"Mr. Arobin," she complained, "I'm greatly upset by the excitement of the afternoon; I'm not myself. My manner must have misled you in some way. I wish you to go, please." She spoke in a monotonous, dull tone. He took his hat from the table, and stood with eyes turned from her, looking into the dying fire. For a moment or two he kept an impressive silence.

"Your manner has not misled me, Mrs. Pontellier," he said finally. "My own emotions have done that. I couldn't help it. When I'm near you, how could I help it? Don't think anything of it, don't bother, please. You see, I go when you command me. If you wish me to stay away, I shall do so. If you let me come back, I—oh! you will let me come back?"

He cast one appealing glance at her, to which she made no response. Alcée Arobin's manner was so genuine that it often deceived even himself.

Edna did not care or think whether it were genuine or not. When she was alone she looked mechanically at the back of her hand which he had kissed so warmly. Then she leaned her head down on the mantelpiece. She felt somewhat like a woman who in a moment of passion is betrayed into an act of infidelity, and realizes the significance of the act without being wholly awakened from its glamour. The thought was passing vaguely through her mind, "What would he think?"

She did not mean her husband; she was thinking of Robert Lebrun. Her husband seemed to her now like a person whom she had married without love as an excuse.

She lit a candle and went up to her room. Alcée Arobin was absolutely nothing to her. Yet his presence, his manners, the warmth of his glances, and above all the touch of his lips upon her hand had acted like a narcotic upon her.

She slept a languorous sleep, interwoven with vanishing dreams.

XXVI

Alcée Arobin wrote Edna an elaborate note of apology, palpitant with sin-cerity. It embarrassed her; for in a cooler, quieter moment it appeared to her absurd that she should have taken his action so seriously, so dramatically. She felt sure that the significance of the whole occurrence had lain in her own self-consciousness. If she ignored his note it would give undue importance to a trivial affair. If she replied to it in a serious spirit it would still leave in his mind the impression that she had in a susceptible moment yielded to his influence. After all, it was no great matter to have one's hand kissed. She was provoked at his having written the apology. She answered in as light and bantering a spirit as she fancied it deserved, and said she would be glad to have him look in upon her at work whenever he felt the inclination and his business gave him the opportunity.

He responded at once by presenting himself at her home with all his disarming naïveté. And then there was scarcely a day which followed that she did not see him or was not reminded of him. He was prolific in pretexts. His attitude became one of good-humored subservience and tacit adoration. He was ready at all times to submit to her moods, which were as often kind as they were cold. She grew accustomed to him. They became intimate and friendly by imperceptible degrees, and then by leaps. He some-times talked in a way that astonished her at first and brought the crimson into her face; in a way that pleased her at last, appealing to the animalism that stirred impatiently within her.

There was nothing which so quieted the turmoil of Edna's senses as a visit to Made-moiselle Reisz. It was then, in the presence of that personality which was offensive to her, that the woman, by her divine art, seemed to reach Edna's spirit and set it free.

It was misty, with heavy, lowering atmosphere, one afternoon, when Edna climbed the stairs to the pianist's apartments under the roof. Her clothes were dripping with moisture. She felt chilled and pinched as she entered the room. Mademoiselle was poking at a rusty stove that smoked a little and warmed the room indifferently. She was endeavoring to heat a pot of chocolate on the stove. The room looked cheerless and dingy to Edna as she entered. A bust of Beethoven, covered with a hood of dust, scowled at her from the mantelpiece.

"Ah! here comes the sunlight!" exclaimed Mademoiselle, rising from her knees before the stove. "Now it will be warm and bright enough; I can let the fire alone."

She closed the stove door with a bang, and approaching, assisted in removing Edna's dripping mackintosh.

"You are cold; you look miserable. The chocolate will soon be hot. But would you rather have a taste of brandy? I have scarcely touched the bottle which you brought me for my cold." A piece of red flannel was wrapped around Mademoiselle's throat; a stiff neck compelled her to hold her head on one side.

"I will take some brandy," said Edna, shivering as she removed her gloves and overshoes. She drank the liquor from the glass as a man would have done. Then flinging herself upon the uncomfortable sofa she said, "Mademoiselle, I am going to move away from my house on Esplanade Street."

"Ah!" ejaculated the musician, neither surprised nor especially interested. Nothing ever seemed to astonish her very much. She was endeavoring to adjust the bunch of violets which had become loose from its fastening in her hair. Edna drew her down upon the sofa, and taking a pin from her own hair, secured the shabby artificial flowers in their accustomed place.

"Aren't you astonished?"

"Passably. Where are you going? to New York? to Iberville? to your father in Mississippi? where?"

"Just two steps away," laughed Edna, "in a little four-room house around the corner. It looks so cozy, so inviting and restful, whenever I pass by; and it's for rent. I'm tired looking after that big house. It never seemed like mine, anyway—like home. It's too much trouble. I have to keep too many servants. I am tired bothering with them."

"That is not your true reason, *ma belle.*[48] There is no use in telling me lies. I don't know your reason, but you have not told me the truth." Edna did not protest or endeavor to justify herself.

"The house, the money that provides for it, are not mine. Isn't that enough reason?"

"They are your husband's," returned Mademoiselle, with a shrug and a malicious elevation of the eyebrows.

"Oh! I see there is no deceiving you. Then let me tell you: It is a caprice. I have a little money of my own from my mother's estate, which my father sends me by driblets. I won a large sum this winter on the races, and I am beginning to sell my sketches. Laidpore is more and more pleased with my work; he says it grows in force and individuality. I cannot judge of that myself, but I feel that I have gained in ease and confidence. However, as I said, I have sold a good many through Laidpore. I can live in the tiny house for little or nothing, with one servant. Old Celestine, who works occasionally for me, says she will come stay with me and do my work. I know I shall like it, like the feeling of freedom and independence."

[48] My pretty one.

"What does your husband say?"

"I have not told him yet. I only thought of it this morning. He will think I am demented, no doubt. Perhaps you think so."

Mademoiselle shook her head slowly. "Your reason is not yet clear to me," she said.

Neither was it quite clear to Edna herself; but it unfolded itself as she sat for a while in silence. Instinct had prompted her to put away her husband's bounty in casting off her allegiance. She did not know how it would be when he returned. There would have to be an understanding, an explanation. Conditions would some way adjust themselves, she felt; but whatever came, she had resolved never again to belong to another than herself.

"I shall give a grand dinner before I leave the old house!" Edna exclaimed. "You will have to come to it, Mademoiselle. I will give you everything that you like to eat and to drink. We shall sing and laugh and be merry for once." And she uttered a sigh that came from the very depths of her being.

If Mademoiselle happened to have received a letter from Robert during the interval of Edna's visits, she would give her the letter unsolicited. And she would seat herself at the piano and play as her humor prompted her while the young woman read the letter.

The little stove was roaring; it was red-hot, and the chocolate in the tin sizzled and sputtered. Edna went forward and opened the stove door, and Mademoiselle rising, took a letter from under the bust of Beethoven and handed it to Edna.

"Another! so soon!" she exclaimed, her eyes filled with delight. "Tell me, Mademoiselle, does he know that I see his letters?"

"Never in the world! He would be angry and would never write to me again if he thought so. Does he write to you? Never a line. Does he send you a message? Never a word. It is because he loves you, poor fool, and is trying to forget you, since you are not free to listen to him or to belong to him."

"Why do you show me his letters, then?"

"Haven't you begged for them? Can I refuse you anything? Oh! you cannot deceive me," and Mademoiselle approached her beloved instrument and began to play. Edna did not at once read the letter. She sat holding it in her hand, while the music penetrated her whole being like an effulgence, warming and brightening the dark places of her soul. It prepared her for joy and exultation.

"Oh!" she exclaimed, letting the letter fall to the floor. "Why did you not tell me?" She went and grasped Mademoiselle's hands up from the keys. "Oh! unkind! malicious! Why did you not tell me?"

"That he was coming back? No great news, *ma foi*. I wonder he did not come long ago."

"But when, when?" cried Edna, impatiently. "He does not say when."

"He says 'very soon.' You know as much about it as I do; it is all in the letter."

"But why? Why is he coming? Oh, if I thought—" and she snatched the letter from the floor and turned the pages this way and that way, looking for the reason, which was left untold.

"If I were young and in love with a man," said Mademoiselle, turning on the stool and pressing her wiry hands between her knees as she looked down at Edna, who sat on the floor holding the letter, "it seems to me he would have to be some *grand esprit;*[49] a

49 Noble spirit.

man with lofty aims and ability to reach them; one who stood high enough to attract the notice of his fellow-men. It seems to me if I were young and in love I should never deem a man of ordinary caliber worthy of my devotion."

"Now it is you who are telling lies and seeking to deceive me, Mademoiselle; or else you have never been in love, and know nothing about it. Why," went on Edna, clasping her knees and looking up into Mademoiselle's twisted face, "do you suppose a woman knows why she loves? Does she select? Does she say to herself: 'Go to! Here is a distinguished statesman with presidential possibilities; I shall proceed to fall in love with him.' Or, 'I shall set my heart upon this musician, whose fame is on every tongue?' Or, 'This financier, who controls the world's money markets?' "

"You are purposely misunderstanding me, *ma reine*.[50] Are you in love with Robert?"

"Yes," said Edna. It was the first time she had admitted it, and a glow overspread her face, blotching it with red spots.

"Why?" asked her companion. "Why do you love him when you ought not to?"

Edna, with a motion or two, dragged herself on her knees before Mademoiselle Reisz, who took the glowing face between her two hands.

"Why? Because his hair is brown and grows away from his temples; because he opens and shuts his eyes, and his nose is a little out of drawing; because he has two lips and a square chin, and a little finger which he can't straighten from having played baseball too energetically in his youth. Because—"

"Because you do, in short," laughed Mademoiselle. "What will you do when he comes back?" she asked.

"Do? Nothing, except feel glad and happy to be alive."

She was already glad and happy to be alive at the mere thought of his return. The murky, lowering sky, which had depressed her a few hours before, seemed bracing and invigorating as she splashed through the streets on her way home.

She stopped at a confectioner's and ordered a huge box of bonbons for the children in Iberville. She slipped a card in the box, on which she scribbled a tender message and sent an abundance of kisses.

Before dinner in the evening Edna wrote a charming letter to her husband, telling him of her intention to move for a while into the little house around the block, and to give a farewell dinner before leaving, regretting that he was not there to share it, to help her out with the menu and assist her in entertaining the guests. Her letter was brilliant and brimming with cheerfulness.

XXVII

"What is the matter with you?" asked Arobin that evening. "I never found you in such a happy mood." Edna was tired by that time, and was reclining on the lounge before the fire.

"Don't you know the weather prophet has told us we shall see the sun pretty soon?"

"Well, that ought to be reason enough," he acquiesced. "You wouldn't give me another if I sat here all night imploring you." He sat close to her on a low tabouret, and as he spoke his fingers lightly touched the hair that fell a little over her forehead. She liked the touch of his fingers through her hair, and closed her eyes sensitively.

[50] My queen.

"One of these days," she said, "I'm going to pull myself together for a while and think—try to determine what character of a woman I am; for, candidly, I don't know. By all the codes which I am acquainted with, I am a devilishly wicked specimen of the sex. But some way I can't convince myself that I am. I must think about it."

"Don't. What's the use? Why should you bother thinking about it when I can tell you what manner of woman you are." His fingers strayed occasionally down to her warm, smooth cheeks and firm chin, which was growing a little full and double.

"Oh, yes! You will tell me that I am adorable; everything that is captivating. Spare yourself the effort."

"No; I shan't tell you anything of the sort, though I shouldn't be lying if I did."

"Do you know Mademoiselle Reisz?" she asked irrelevantly.

"The pianist? I know her by sight. I've heard her play."

"She says queer things sometimes in a bantering way that you don't notice at the time and you find yourself thinking about afterward."

"For instance?"

"Well, for instance, when I left her to-day, she put her arms around me and felt my shoulder blades, to see if my wings were strong, she said. 'The bird that would soar above the level plain of tradition and prejudice must have strong wings. It is a sad spectacle to see the weaklings bruised, exhausted, fluttering back to earth.'"

"Whither would you soar?"

"I'm not thinking of any extraordinary flights. I only half comprehend her."

"I've heard she's partially demented," said Arobin.

"She seems to me wonderfully sane," Edna replied.

"I'm told she's extremely disagreeable and unpleasant. Why have you introduced her at a moment when I desired to talk of you?"

"Oh! talk of me if you like," cried Edna, clasping her hands beneath her head; "but let me think of something else while you do."

"I'm jealous of your thoughts to-night. They're making you a little kinder than usual; but some way I feel as if they were wandering, as if they were not here with me." She only looked at him and smiled. His eyes were very near. He leaned upon the lounge with an arm extended across her, while the other hand still rested upon her hair. They continued silently to look into each other's eyes. When he leaned forward and kissed her, she clasped his head, holding his lips to hers.

It was the first kiss of her life to which her nature had really responded. It was a flaming torch that kindled desire.

XXVIII

Edna cried a little that night after Arobin left her. It was only one phase of the multitudinous emotions which had assailed her. There was with her an overwhelming feeling of irresponsibility. There was the shock of the unexpected and the unaccustomed. There was her husband's reproach looking at her from the external things around her which he had provided for her external existence. There was Robert's reproach making itself felt by a quicker, fiercer, more overpowering love, which had awakened within her toward him. Above all, there was understanding. She felt as if a mist had been lifted from her eyes, enabling her to look upon and comprehend the significance of life, that monster made up of beauty and brutality. But among the conflicting sensations which assailed her, there was neither shame nor remorse. There was a dull pang of regret because it was not the kiss of love which had inflamed her, because it was not love which had held this cup of life to her lips.

XXIX

Without even waiting for an answer from her husband regarding his opinion or wishes in the matter, Edna hastened her preparations for quitting her home on Esplanade Street and moving into the little house around the block. A feverish anxiety attended her every action in that direction. There was no moment of deliberation, no interval of repose between the thought and its fulfillment. Early upon the morning following those hours passed in Arobin's society, Edna set about securing her new abode and hurrying her arrangements for occupying it. Within the precincts of her home she felt like one who has entered and lingered within the portals of some forbidden temple in which a thousand muffled voices bade her begone.

Whatever was her own in the house, everything which she had acquired aside from her husband's bounty, she caused to be transported to the other house, supplying simple and meager deficiencies from her own resources.

Arobin found her with rolled sleeves, working in company with the house-maid when he looked in during the afternoon. She was splendid and robust, and had never appeared handsomer than in the old blue gown, with a red silk handkerchief knotted at random around her head to protect her hair from the dust. She was mounted upon a high step-ladder, unhooking a picture from the wall when he entered. He had found the front door open, and had followed his ring by walking in unceremoniously.

"Come down!" he said. "Do you want to kill yourself?" She greeted him with affected carelessness, and appeared absorbed in her occupation.

If he had expected to find her languishing, reproachful, or indulging in sentimental tears, he must have been greatly surprised.

He was no doubt prepared for any emergency, ready for any one of the foregoing attitudes, just as he bent himself easily and naturally to the situation which confronted him.

"Please come down," he insisted, holding the ladder and looking up at her.

"No," she answered; "Ellen is afraid to mount the ladder. Joe is working over at the 'pigeon house'—that's the name Ellen gives it, because it's so small and looks like a pigeon house—and some one has to do this."

Arobin pulled off his coat, and expressed himself ready and willing to tempt fate in her place. Ellen brought him one of her dust-caps, and went into contortions of mirth, which she found it impossible to control, when she saw him put it on before the mirror as grotesquely as he could. Edna herself could not refrain from smiling when she fastened it at his request. So it was he who in turn mounted the ladder, unhooking pictures and curtains, and dislodging ornaments as Edna directed. When he had finished he took off his dust-cap and went out to wash his hands.

Edna was sitting on the tabouret, idly brushing the tips of a feather duster along the carpet when he came in again.

"Is there anything more you will let me do?" he asked.

"That is all," she answered. "Ellen can manage the rest." She kept the young woman occupied in the drawing-room, unwilling to be left alone with Arobin.

"What about the dinner?" he asked; "the grand event, the *coup d'état?*"[51]

"It will be day after to-morrow. Why do you call it the *'coup d'état?'* Oh! it will be very fine; all my best of everything—crystal, silver and gold, Sèvres, flowers, music, and champagne to swim in. I'll let Léonce pay the bills. I wonder what he'll say when he sees the bills."

"And you ask me why I call it a *coup d'état?*" Arobin had put on his coat, and he stood before her and asked if his cravat was plumb. She told him it was, looking no higher than the tip of his collar.

"When do you go to the 'pigeon house?'—with all due acknowledgment to Ellen."

"Day after to-morrow, after the dinner. I shall sleep there."

"Ellen, will you very kindly get me a glass of water?" asked Arobin. "The dust in the curtains, if you will pardon me for hinting such a thing, has parched my throat to a crisp."

"While Ellen gets the water," said Edna, rising, "I will say good-by and let you go. I must get rid of this grime, and I have a million things to do and think of."

"When shall I see you?" asked Arobin, seeking to detain her, the maid having left the room.

"At the dinner, of course. You are invited."

"Not before?—not to-night or to-morrow morning or to-morrow noon or night? or the day after morning or noon? Can't you see yourself, without my telling you, what an eternity it is?"

He had followed her into the hall and to the foot of the stairway, looking up at her as she mounted with her face half turned to him.

"Not an instant sooner," she said. But she laughed and looked at him with eyes that at once gave him courage to wait and made it torture to wait.

XXX

Though Edna had spoken of the dinner as a very grand affair, it was in truth a very small affair and very select, in so much as the guests invited were few and were selected with discrimination. She had counted upon an even dozen seating themselves at her round mahogany board, forgetting for the moment that Madame Ratignolle was to the last degree *souffrante*[52] and unpresentable, and not foreseeing that Madame Lebrun would send a thousand regrets at the last moment. So there were only ten, after all, which made a cozy, comfortable number.

There were Mr. and Mrs. Merriman, a pretty, vivacious little woman in the thirties; her husband, a jovial fellow, something of a shallow-pate, who laughed a good deal at other people's witticisms, and had thereby made himself extremely popular. Mrs. High-camp had accompanied them. Of course, there was Alcée Arobin; and Mademoiselle Reisz had consented to come. Edna had sent her a fresh bunch of violets with black lace trimmings for her hair. Monsieur Ratignolle brought himself and his wife's excuses. Victor Lebrun, who happened to be in the city, bent upon relaxation, had accepted with alacrity. There was a Miss Mayblunt, no longer in her teens, who looked at the world through lorgnettes and with the keenest interest. It was thought and said that she was intellectual; it was suspected of her that she wrote under a *nom de guerre*.[53] She had

[51] The climactic occasion.
[52] Unwell.

[53] Assumed name.

come with a gentleman by the name of Gouvernail, connected with one of the daily papers, of whom nothing special could be said, except that he was observant and seemed quiet and inoffensive. Edna herself made the tenth, and at half-past eight they seated themselves at table, Arobin and Monsieur Ratignolle on either side of their hostess.

Mrs. Highcamp sat between Arobin and Victor Lebrun. Then came Mrs. Merriman, Mr. Gouvernail, Miss Mayblunt, Mr. Merriman, and Mademoiselle Reisz next to Monsieur Ratignolle.

There was something extremely gorgeous about the appearance of the table, an effect of splendor conveyed by a cover of pale yellow satin under strips of lace-work. There were wax candles in massive brass candelabra, burning softly under yellow silk shades; full, fragrant roses, yellow and red, abounded. There were silver and gold, as she had said there would be, and crystal which glittered like the gems which the women wore.

The ordinary stiff dining chairs had been discarded for the occasion and replaced by the most commodious and luxurious which could be collected throughout the house. Mademoiselle Reisz, being exceedingly diminutive, was elevated upon cushions, as small children are sometimes hoisted at table upon bulky volumes.

"Something new, Edna?" exclaimed Miss Mayblunt, with lorgnette directed toward a magnificent cluster of diamonds that sparkled, that almost sputtered, in Edna's hair, just over the center of her forehead.

"Quite new; 'brand' new, in fact; a present from my husband. It arrived this morning from New York. I may as well admit that this is my birthday, and that I am twenty-nine. In good time I expect you to drink my health. Meanwhile, I shall ask you to begin with this cocktail, composed—would you say 'composed?'" with an appeal to Miss Mayblunt—"composed by my father in honor of Sister Janet's wedding."

Before each guest stood a tiny glass that looked and sparkled like a garnet gem.

"Then, all things considered," spoke Arobin, "it might not be amiss to start out by drinking the Colonel's health in the cocktail which he composed, on the birthday of the most charming of women—the daughter whom he invented."

Mr. Merriman's laugh at this sally was such a genuine outburst and so contagious that it started the dinner with an agreeable swing that never slackened.

Miss Mayblunt begged to be allowed to keep her cocktail untouched before her, just to look at. The color was marvelous! She could compare it to nothing she had ever seen, and the garnet lights which it emitted were unspeakably rare. She pronounced the Colonel an artist, and stuck to it.

Monsieur Ratignolle was prepared to take things seriously: the *mets*, the *entre-mets*,[54] the service, the decorations, even the people. He looked up from his pompono and inquired of Arobin if he were related to the gentleman of that name who formed one of the firm of Laitner and Arobin, lawyers. The young man admitted that Laitner was a warm personal friend, who permitted Arobin's name to decorate the firm's letterheads and to appear upon a shingle that graced Perdido Street.

"There are so many inquisitive people and institutions abounding," said Arobin, "that one is really forced as a matter of convenience these days to assume the virtue of an occupation if he has it not."

Monsieur Ratignolle stared a little, and turned to ask Mademoiselle Reisz if she considered the symphony concerts up to the standard which had been set the previous win-

---

[54] Main food courses, side-dishes.

ter. Mademoiselle Reisz answered Monsieur Ratignolle in French, which Edna thought a little rude, under the circumstances, but characteristic. Mademoiselle had only disagreeable things to say of the symphony concerts, and insulting remarks to make of all the musicians of New Orleans, singly and collectively. All her interest seemed to be centered upon the delicacies placed before her.

Mr. Merriman said that Mr. Arobin's remark about inquisitive people reminded him of a man from Waco the other day at the St. Charles Hotel—but as Mr. Merriman's stories were always lame and lacking point, his wife seldom permitted him to complete them. She interrupted him to ask if he remembered the name of the author whose book she had bought the week before to send to a friend in Geneva. She was talking "books" with Mr. Gouvernail and trying to draw from him his opinion upon current literary topics. Her husband told the story of the Waco man privately to Miss Mayblunt, who pretended to be greatly amused and to think it extremely clever.

Mrs. Highcamp hung with languid but unaffected interest upon the warm and impetuous volubility of her left-hand neighbor, Victor Lebrun. Her attention was never for a moment withdrawn from him after seating herself at table; and when he turned to Mrs. Merriman, who was prettier and more vivacious than Mrs. Highcamp, she waited with easy indifference for an opportunity to reclaim his attention. There was the occasional sound of music, of mandolins, sufficiently removed to be an agreeable accompaniment rather than an interruption to the conversation. Outside the soft, monotonous splash of a fountain could be heard; the sound penetrated into the room with the heavy odor of jessamine that came through the open windows.

The golden shimmer of Edna's satin gown spread in rich folds on either side of her. There was a soft fall of lace encircling her shoulders. It was the color of her skin, without the glow, the myriad living tints that one may sometimes discover in vibrant flesh. There was something in her attitude, in her whole appearance when she leaned her head against the high-backed chair and spread her arms, which suggested the regal woman, the one who rules, who looks on, who stands alone.

But as she sat there amid her guests, she felt the old ennui overtaking her; the hopelessness which so often assailed her, which came upon her like an obsession, like something extraneous, independent of volition. It was something which announced itself; a chill breath that seemed to issue from some vast cavern wherein discords wailed. There came over her the acute longing which always summoned into her spiritual vision the presence of the beloved one, overpowering her at once with a sense of the unattainable.

The moments glided on, while a feeling of good fellowship passed around the circle like a mystic cord, holding and binding these people together with jest and laughter. Monsieur Ratignolle was the first to break the pleasant charm. At ten o'clock he excused himself. Madame Ratignolle was waiting for him at home. She was *bien souffrante,* and she was filled with vague dread, which only her husband's presence could allay.

Mademoiselle Reisz arose with Monsieur Ratignolle, who offered to escort her to the car. She had eaten well; she had tasted the good, rich wines, and they must have turned her head, for she bowed pleasantly to all as she withdrew from table. She kissed Edna upon the shoulder, and whispered: *"Bonne nuit, ma reine; soyez sage."*[55] She had been a little bewildered upon rising, or rather, descending from her cushions, and Monsieur Ratignolle gallantly took her arm and led her away.

---

[55] Good night, my queen; sleep well.

Mrs. Highcamp was weaving a garland of roses, yellow and red. When she had finished the garland, she laid it lightly upon Victor's black curls. He was reclining far back in the luxurious chair, holding a glass of champagne to the light.

As if a magician's wand had touched him, the garland of roses transformed him into a vision of Oriental beauty. His cheeks were the color of crushed grapes, and his dusky eyes glowed with a languishing fire.

"*Sapristi!*" exclaimed Arobin.

But Mrs. Highcamp had one more touch to add to the picture. She took from the back of her chair a white silken scarf, with which she had covered her shoulders in the early part of the evening. She draped it across the boy in graceful folds, and in a way to conceal his black, conventional evening dress. He did not seem to mind what she did to him, only smiled, showing a faint gleam of white teeth, while he continued to gaze with narrowing eyes at the light through his glass of champagne.

"Oh! to be able to paint in color rather than in words!" exclaimed Miss Mayblunt, losing herself in a rhapsodic dream as she looked at him.

> " 'There was a graven image of Desire
> Painted with red blood on a ground of gold.' "

murmured Gouvernail, under his breath.

The effect of the wine upon Victor was to change his accustomed volubility into silence. He seemed to have abandoned himself to a reverie, and to be seeing pleasing visions in the amber bead.

"Sing," entreated Mrs. Highcamp. "Won't you sing to us?"

"Let him alone," said Arobin.

"He's posing," offered Mr. Merriman; "let him have it out."

"I believe he's paralyzed," laughed Mrs. Merriman. And leaning over the youth's chair, she took the glass from his hand and held it to his lips. He sipped the wine slowly, and when he had drained the glass she laid it upon the table and wiped his lips with her little filmy handkerchief.

"Yes, I'll sing for you," he said, turning in his chair toward Mrs. Highcamp. He clasped his hands behind his head, and looking up at the ceiling began to hum a little, trying his voice like a musician tuning an instrument. Then, looking at Edna, he began to sing:

"Ah! si tu savais!"

"Stop!" she cried, "don't sing that. I don't want you to sing it," and she laid her glass so impetuously and blindly upon the table as to shatter it against a caraffe. The wine spilled over Arobin's legs and some of it trickled down upon Mrs. Highcamp's black gauze gown. Victor had lost all idea of courtesy, or else he thought his hostess was not in earnest, for he laughed and went on:

> "Ah! si tu savais
> Ce que tes yeux me disent"—[56]

---

[56] Ah, if you knew what your eyes tell me.

"Oh! you mustn't! you mustn't," exclaimed Edna, and pushing back her chair she got up, and going behind him placed her hand over his mouth. He kissed the soft palm that pressed upon his lips.

"No, no, I won't, Mrs. Pontellier. I didn't know you meant it," looking up at her with caressing eyes. The touch of his lips was like a pleasing sting to her hand. She lifted the garland of roses from his head and flung it across the room.

"Come, Victor; you've posed long enough. Give Mrs. Highcamp her scarf."

Mrs. Highcamp undraped the scarf from about him with her own hands. Miss Mayblunt and Mr. Gouvernail suddenly conceived the notion that it was time to say good night. And Mr. and Mrs. Merriman wondered how it could be so late.

Before parting from Victor, Mrs. Highcamp invited him to call upon her daughter, who she knew would be charmed to meet him and talk French and sing French songs with him. Victor expressed his desire and intention to call upon Miss Highcamp at the first opportunity which presented itself. He asked if Arobin were going his way. Arobin was not.

The mandolin players had long since stolen away. A profound stillness had fallen upon the broad, beautiful street. The voices of Edna's disbanding guests jarred like a discordant note upon the quiet harmony of the night.

XXXI

"Well?" questioned Arobin, who had remained with Edna after the others had departed.

"Well," she reiterated, and stood up, stretching her arms, and feeling the need to relax her muscles after having been so long seated.

"What next?" he asked.

"The servants are all gone. They left when the musicians did. I have dismissed them. The house has to be closed and locked, and I shall trot around to the pigeon house, and shall send Celestine over in the morning to straighten things up."

He looked around, and began to turn out some of the lights.

"What about upstairs?" he inquired.

"I think it is all right; but there may be a window or two unlatched. We had better look; you might take a candle and see. And bring me my wrap and hat on the foot of the bed in the middle room."

He went up with the light, and Edna began closing doors and windows. She hated to shut in the smoke and the fumes of the wine. Arobin found her cape and hat, which he brought down and helped her to put on.

When everything was secured and the lights put out, they left through the front door, Arobin locking it and taking the key, which he carried for Edna. He helped her down the steps.

"Will you have a spray of jessamine?" he asked, breaking off a few blossoms as he passed.

"No; I don't want anything."

She seemed disheartened, and had nothing to say. She took his arm, which he offered her, holding up the weight of her satin train with the other hand. She looked down, noticing the black line of his leg moving in and out so close to her against the yellow shimmer of her gown. There was the whistle of a railway train somewhere in the distance, and the midnight bells were ringing. They met no one in their short walk.

The "pigeon-house" stood behind a locked gate, and a shallow *parterre*[57] that had been somewhat neglected. There was a small front porch, upon which a long window and the front door opened. The door opened directly into the parlor; there was no side entry. Back in the yard was a room for servants, in which old Celestine had been ensconced.

Edna had left a lamp burning low upon the table. She had succeeded in making the room look habitable and homelike. There were some books on the table and a lounge near at hand. On the floor was a fresh matting, covered with a rug or two; and on the walls hung a few tasteful pictures. But the room was filled with flowers. These were a surprise to her. Arobin had sent them, and had had Celestine distribute them during Edna's absence. Her bedroom was adjoining, and across a small passage were the dining-room and kitchen.

Edna seated herself with every appearance of discomfort.

"Are you tired?" he asked.

"Yes, and chilled, and miserable. I feel as if I had been wound up to a certain pitch—too tight—and something inside of me had snapped." She rested her head against the table upon her bare arm.

"You want to rest," he said, "and to be quiet. I'll go; I'll leave you and let you rest."

"Yes," she replied.

He stood up beside her and smoothed her hair with his soft, magnetic hand. His touch conveyed to her a certain physical comfort. She could have fallen quietly asleep there if he had continued to pass his hand over her hair. He brushed the hair upward from the nape of her neck.

"I hope you will feel better and happier in the morning," he said. "You have tried to do too much in the past few days. The dinner was the last straw; you might have dispensed with it."

"Yes," she admitted; "it was stupid."

"No, it was delightful; but it has worn you out." His hand had strayed to her beautiful shoulders, and he could feel the response of her flesh to his touch. He seated himself beside her and kissed her lightly upon the shoulder.

"I thought you were going away," she said, in an uneven voice.

"I am, after I have said good night."

"Good night," she murmured.

He did not answer, except to continue to caress her. He did not say good night until she had become supple to his gentle, seductive entreaties.

XXXII

When Mr. Pontellier learned of his wife's intention to abandon her home and take up her residence elsewhere, he immediately wrote her a letter of unqualified disapproval and remonstrance. She had given reasons which he was unwilling to acknowledge as adequate. He hoped she had not acted upon her rash impulse; and he begged her to consider first, foremost, and above all else, what people would say. He was not dreaming of scandal when he uttered this warning; that was a thing which would never have entered into his mind to consider in connection with his wife's name or his own. He was simply

57 Flower garden.

thinking of his financial integrity. It might get noised about that the Pontelliers had met with reverses, and were forced to conduct their *ménage* on a humbler scale than heretofore. It might do incalculable mischief to his business prospects.

But remembering Edna's whimsical turn of mind of late, and foreseeing that she had immediately acted upon her impetuous determination, he grasped the situation with his usual promptness and handled it with his well-known business tact and cleverness.

The same mail which brought to Edna his letter of disapproval carried instructions—the most minute instructions—to a well-known architect concerning the remodeling of his home, changes which he had long contemplated, and which he desired carried forward during his temporary absence.

Expert and reliable packers and movers were engaged to convey the furniture, carpets, pictures—everything movable, in short—to places of security. And in an incredibly short time the Pontellier house was turned over to the artisans. There was to be an addition—a small snuggery; there was to be frescoing, and hardwood flooring was to be put into such rooms as had not yet been subjected to this improvement.

Furthermore, in one of the daily papers appeared a brief notice to the effect that Mr. and Mrs. Pontellier were contemplating a summer sojourn abroad, and that their handsome residence on Esplanade Street was undergoing sumptuous alterations, and would not be ready for occupancy until their return. Mr. Pontellier had saved appearances!

Edna admired the skill of his maneuver, and avoided any occasion to balk his intentions. When the situation as set forth by Mr. Pontellier was accepted and taken for granted, she was apparently satisfied that it should be so.

The pigeon-house pleased her. It at once assumed the intimate character of a home, while she herself invested it with a charm which it reflected like a warm glow. There was with her a feeling of having descended in the social scale, with a corresponding sense of having risen in the spiritual. Every step which she took toward relieving herself from obligations added to her strength and expansion as an individual. She began to look with her own eyes; to see and to apprehend the deeper undercurrents of life. No longer was she content to "feed upon opinion" when her own soul had invited her.

After a little while, a few days, in fact, Edna went up and spent a week with her children in Iberville. They were delicious February days, with all the summer's promise hovering in the air.

How glad she was to see the children! She wept for very pleasure when she felt their little arms clasping her; their hard, ruddy cheeks pressed against her own glowing cheeks. She looked into their faces with hungry eyes that could not be satisfied with looking. And what stories they had to tell their mother! About the pigs, the cows, the mules! About riding to the mill behind Gluglu; fishing back in the lake with their Uncle Jasper; picking pecans with Lidie's little black brood, and hauling chips in their express wagon. It was a thousand times more fun to haul real chips for old lame Susie's real fire than to drag painted blocks along the banquette on Esplanade Street!

She went with them herself to see the pigs and the cows, to look at the darkies laying the cane, to thrash the pecan trees, and catch fish in the back lake. She lived with them a whole week long, giving them all of herself, and gathering and filling herself with their young existence. They listened, breathless, when she told them the house in Esplanade Street was crowded with workmen, hammering, nailing, sawing, and filling the place with clatter. They wanted to know where their bed was; what had been done with their rocking-horse; and where did Joe sleep, and where had Ellen gone, and the cook? But, above all, they were fired with a desire to see the little house around the block. Was there any place to play? Were there any boys next door? Raoul, with pessimistic foreboding, was convinced that there were only girls next door. Where would they sleep, and where would papa sleep? She told them the fairies would fix it all right.

The old Madame was charmed with Edna's visit, and showered all manner of delicate attentions upon her. She was delighted to know that the Esplanade Street house was in a dismantled condition. It gave her the promise and pretext to keep the children indefinitely.

It was with a wrench and a pang that Edna left her children. She carried away with her the sound of their voices and the touch of their cheeks. All along the journey homeward their presence lingered with her like the memory of a delicious song. But by the time she had regained the city the song no longer echoed in her soul. She was again alone.

XXXIII

It happened sometimes when Edna went to see Mademoiselle Reisz that the little musician was absent, giving a lesson or making some small necessary household purchase. The key was always left in a secret hiding-place in the entry, which Edna knew. If Mademoiselle happened to be away, Edna would usually enter and wait for her return.

When she knocked at Mademoiselle Reisz's door one afternoon there was no response; so unlocking the door, as usual, she entered and found the apartment deserted, as she had expected. Her day had been quite filled up, and it was for a rest, for a refuge, and to talk about Robert, that she sought out her friend.

She had worked at her canvas—a young Italian character study—all the morning, completing the work without the model; but there had been many interruptions, some incident to her modest housekeeping, and others of a social nature.

Madame Ratignolle had dragged herself over, avoiding the too public thoroughfares, she said. She complained that Edna had neglected her much of late. Besides, she was consumed with curiosity to see the little house and the manner in which it was conducted. She wanted to hear all about the dinner party; Monsieur Ratignolle had left *so* early. What had happened after he left? The champagne and grapes which Edna sent over were *too* delicious. She had so little appetite; they had refreshed and toned her stomach. Where on earth was she going to put Mr. Pontellier in that little house, and the boys? And then she made Edna promise to go to her when her hour of trial overtook her.

"At any time—any time of the day or night, dear," Edna assured her.

Before leaving Madame Ratignolle said:

"In some way you seem to me like a child, Edna. You seem to act without a certain amount of reflection which is necessary in this life. That is the reason I want to say you mustn't mind if I advise you to be a little careful while you are living here alone. Why don't you have some one come and stay with you? Wouldn't Mademoiselle Reisz come?"

"No; she wouldn't wish to come, and I shouldn't want her always with me."

"Well, the reason—you know how evil-minded the world is—some one was talking of Alcée Arobin visiting you. Of course, it wouldn't matter if Mr. Arobin had not such a dreadful reputation. Monsieur Ratignolle was telling me that his attentions alone are considered enough to ruin a woman's name."

"Does he boast of his successes?" asked Edna, indifferently, squinting at her picture.

"No, I think not. I believe he is a decent fellow as far as that goes. But his character is so well known among the men. I shan't be able to come back and see you; it was very, very imprudent to-day."

"Mind the step!" cried Edna.

"Don't neglect me," entreated Madame Ratignolle; "and don't mind what I said about Arobin, or having some one to stay with you."

"Of course not," Edna laughed. "You may say anything you like to me." They kissed each other good-by. Madame Ratignolle had not far to go, and Edna stood on the porch a while watching her walk down the street.

Then in the afternoon Mrs. Merriman and Mrs. Highcamp had made their "party call." Edna felt that they might have dispensed with the formality. They had also come to invite her to play *vingt-et-un*[58] one evening at Mrs. Merriman's. She was asked to go early, to dinner, and Mr. Merriman or Mr. Arobin would take her home. Edna accepted in a half-hearted way. She sometimes felt very tired of Mrs. Highcamp and Mrs. Merriman.

Late in the afternoon she sought refuge with Mademoiselle Reisz, and stayed there alone, waiting for her, feeling a kind of repose invade her with the very atmosphere of the shabby, unpretentious little room.

Edna sat at the window, which looked out over the housetops and across the river. The window frame was filled with pots of flowers, and she sat and picked the dry leaves from a rose geranium. The day was warm, and the breeze which blew from the river was very pleasant. She removed her hat and laid it on the piano. She went on picking the leaves and digging around the plants with her hat pin. Once she thought she heard Mademoiselle Reisz approaching. But it was a young black girl, who came in, bringing a small bundle of laundry, which she deposited in the adjoining room, and went away.

Edna seated herself at the piano, and softly picked out with one hand the bars of a piece of music which lay open before her. A half-hour went by. There was the occasional sound of people going and coming in the lower hall. She was growing interested in her occupation of picking out the aria, when there was a second rap at the door. She vaguely wondered what these people did when they found Mademoiselle's door locked.

"Come in," she called, turning her face toward the door. And this time it was Robert Lebrun who presented himself. She attempted to rise; she could not have done so without betraying the agitation which mastered her at sight of him, so she fell back upon the stool, only exclaiming, "Why, Robert!"

He came and clasped her hand, seemingly without knowing what he was saying or doing.

"Mrs. Pontellier! How do you happen—oh! how well you look! Is Mademoiselle Reisz not here? I never expected to see you."

"When did you come back?" asked Edna in an unsteady voice, wiping her face with her handkerchief. She seemed ill at ease on the piano stool, and he begged her to take the chair by the window. She did so, mechanically, while he seated himself on the stool.

"I returned day before yesterday," he answered, while he leaned his arm on the keys, bringing forth a crash of discordant sound.

"Day before yesterday!" she repeated, aloud; and went on thinking to herself, "day before yesterday," in a sort of an uncomprehending way. She had pictured him seeing

---

[58] "Twenty-one"; a card game.

her at the very first hour, and he had lived under the same sky since day before yester-day; while only by accident had he stumbled upon her. Mademoiselle must have lied when she said, "Poor fool, he loves you."

"Day before yesterday," she repeated, breaking off a spray of Mademoiselle's gera-nium; "then if you had not met me here today you wouldn't—when—that is, didn't you mean to come and see me?"

"Of course, I should have gone to see you. There have been so many things—" he turned the leaves of Mademoiselle's music nervously. "I started in at once yesterday with the old firm. After all there is as much chance for me here as there was there—that is, I might find it profitable some day. The Mexicans were not very congenial."

So he had come back because the Mexicans were not congenial; because business was as profitable here as there; because of any reason, and not because he cared to be near her. She remembered the day she sat on the floor, turning the pages of his letter, seeking the reason which was left untold.

She had not noticed how he looked—only feeling his presence; but she turned delib-erately and observed him. After all, he had been absent but a few months, and was not changed. His hair—the color of hers—waved back from his temples in the same way as before. His skin was not more burned than it had been at Grand Isle. She found in his eyes, when he looked at her for one silent moment, the same tender caress, with an added warmth and entreaty which had not been there before—the same glance which had penetrated to the sleeping places of her soul and awakened them.

A hundred times Edna had pictured Robert's return, and imagined their first meet-ing. It was usually at her home, whither he had sought her out at once. She always fan-cied him expressing or betraying in some way his love for her. And here, the reality was that they sat ten feet apart, she at the window, crushing geranium leaves in her hand and smelling them, he twirling around on the piano stool, saying:

"I was very much surprised to hear of Mr. Pontellier's absence; it's a wonder Made-moiselle Reisz did not tell me; and your moving—mother told me yesterday. I should think you would have gone to New York with him, or to Iberville with the children, rather than be bothered here with housekeeping. And you are going abroad, too, I hear. We shan't have you at Grand Isle next summer; it won't seem—do you see much of Mademoiselle Reisz? She often spoke of you in the few letters she wrote."

"Do you remember that you promised to write to me when you went away?" A flush overspread his whole face.

"I couldn't believe that my letters would be of any interest to you."

"That is an excuse; it isn't the truth." Edna reached for her hat on the piano. She ad-justed it, sticking the hat pin through the heavy coil of hair with some deliberation.

"Are you not going to wait for Mademoiselle Reisz?" asked Robert.

"No; I have found when she is absent this long, she is liable not to come back till late." She drew on her gloves, and Robert picked up his hat.

"Won't you wait for her?" asked Edna.

"Not if you think she will not be back till late," adding, as if suddenly aware of some discourtesy in his speech, "and I should miss the pleasure of walking home with you." Edna locked the door and put the key back in its hiding-place.

They went together, picking their way across muddy streets and sidewalks encumbered with the cheap display of small tradesmen. Part of the distance they rode in the car, and after disembarking, passed the Pontellier mansion, which looked broken and half torn asunder. Robert had never known the house, and looked at it with interest.

"I never knew you in your home," he remarked.

"I am glad you did not."

"Why?" She did not answer. They went on around the corner, and it seemed as if her dreams were coming true after all, when he followed her into the little house.

"You must stay and dine with me, Robert. You see I am all alone, and it is so long since I have seen you. There is so much I want to ask you."

She took off her hat and gloves. He stood irresolute, making some excuse about his mother who expected him; he even muttered something about an engagement. She struck a match and lit the lamp on the table; it was growing dusk. When he saw her face in the lamp-light, looking pained, with all the soft lines gone out of it, he threw his hat aside and seated himself.

"Oh! you know I want to stay if you will let me!" he exclaimed. All the softness came back. She laughed, and went and put her hand on his shoulder.

"This is the first moment you have seemed like the old Robert. I'll go tell Celestine." She hurried away to tell Celestine to set an extra place. She even sent her off in search of some added delicacy which she had not thought of for herself. And she recommended great care in dripping the coffee and having the omelet done to a proper turn.

When she reëntered, Robert was turning over magazines, sketches, and things that lay upon the table in great disorder. He picked up a photograph, and exclaimed:

"Alcée Arobin! What on earth is his picture doing here?"

"I tried to make a sketch of his head one day," answered Edna, "and he thought the photograph might help me. It was at the other house. I thought it had been left there. I must have packed it up with my drawing materials."

"I should think you would give it back to him if you have finished with it."

"Oh! I have a great many such photographs. I never think of returning them. They don't amount to anything." Robert kept on looking at the picture.

"It seems to me—do you think his head worth drawing? Is he a friend of Mr. Pontellier's? You never said you knew him."

"He isn't a friend of Mr. Pontellier's; he's a friend of mine. I always knew him—that is, it is only of late that I know him pretty well. But I'd rather talk about you, and know what you have been seeing and doing and feeling out there in Mexico." Robert threw aside the picture.

"I've been seeing the waves and the white beach of Grand Isle; the quiet, grassy street of the *Chênière;* the old fort at Grande Terre. I've been working like a machine, and feeling like a lost soul. There was nothing interesting."

She leaned her head upon her hand to shade her eyes from the light.

"And what have you been seeing and doing and feeling all these days?" he asked.

"I've been seeing the waves and the white beach of Grand Isle; the quiet, grassy street of the *Chênière Caminada;* the old sunny fort at Grande Terre. I've been working with a little more comprehension than a machine and still feeling like a lost soul. There was nothing interesting."

"Mrs. Pontellier, you are cruel," he said, with feeling, closing his eyes and resting his head back in his chair. They remained in silence till old Celestine an-nounced dinner.

XXXIV

The dining-room was very small. Edna's round mahogany would have almost filled it. As it was there was but a step or two from the little table to the kitchen, to the mantel, the small buffet, and the side door that opened out on the narrow brick-paved yard.

A certain degree of ceremony settled upon them with the announcement of dinner. There was no return to personalities. Robert related incidents of his sojourn in Mexico, and Edna talked of events likely to interest him, which had occurred during his absence. The dinner was of ordinary quality, except for the few delicacies which she had sent out to purchase. Old Celestine, with a bandana *tignon*[59] twisted about her head, hobbled in and out, taking a personal interest in everything; and she lingered occasionally to talk patois with Robert, whom she had known as a boy.

He went out to a neighboring cigar stand to purchase cigarette papers, and when he came back he found that Celestine had served the black coffee in the parlor.

"Perhaps I shouldn't have come back," he said. "When you are tired of me, tell me to go."

"You never tire me. You must have forgotten the hours and hours at Grand Isle in which we grew accustomed to each other and used to being together."

"I have forgotten nothing at Grand Isle," he said, not looking at her, but rolling a cigarette. His tobacco pouch, which he laid upon the table, was a fantastic embroidered silk affair, evidently the handiwork of a woman.

"You used to carry your tobacco in a rubber pouch," said Edna, picking up the pouch and examining the needlework.

"Yes; it was lost."

"Where did you buy this one? In Mexico?"

"It was given to me by a Vera Cruz girl; they are very generous," he replied, striking a match and lighting his cigarette.

"They are very handsome, I suppose, those Mexican women; very picturesque, with their black eyes and their lace scarfs."

"Some are; others are hideous. Just as you find women everywhere."

"What was she like—the one who gave you the pouch? You must have known her very well."

"She was very ordinary. She wasn't of the slightest importance. I knew her well enough."

"Did you visit at her house? Was it interesting? I should like to know and hear about the people you met, and the impressions they made on you."

"There are some people who leave impressions not so lasting as the imprint of an oar upon the water."

"Was she such a one?"

"It would be ungenerous for me to admit that she was of that order and kind." He thrust the pouch back in his pocket, as if to put away the subject with the trifle which had brought it up.

Arobin dropped in with a message from Mrs. Merriman, to say that the card party was postponed on account of the illness of one of her children.

"How do you do, Arobin?" said Robert, rising from the obscurity.

[59] Scarf.

"Oh! Lebrun. To be sure! I heard yesterday you were back. How did they treat you down in Mexique?"

"Fairly well."

"But not well enough to keep you there. Stunning girls, though, in Mexico. I thought I should never get away from Vera Cruz when I was down there a couple of years ago."

"Did they embroider slippers and tobacco pouches and hatbands and things for you?" asked Edna.

"Oh! my! no! I didn't get so deep in their regard. I fear they made more impression on me than I made on them."

"You were less fortunate than Robert, then."

"I am always less fortunate than Robert. Has he been imparting tender confidences?"

"I've been imposing myself long enough," said Robert, rising, and shaking hands with Edna. "Please convey my regards to Mr. Pontellier when you write."

He shook hands with Arobin and went away.

"Fine fellow, that Lebrun," said Arobin when Robert had gone. "I never heard you speak of him."

"I knew him last summer at Grand Isle," she replied. "Here is that photograph of yours. Don't you want it?"

"What do I want with it? Throw it away." She threw it back on the table.

"I'm not going to Mrs. Merriman's," she said. "If you see her, tell her so. But perhaps I had better write. I think I shall write now, and say that I am sorry her child is sick, and tell her not to count on me."

"It would be a good scheme," acquiesced Arobin. "I don't blame you; stupid lot!"

Edna opened the blotter, and having procured paper and pen, began to write the note. Arobin lit a cigar and read the evening paper, which he had in his pocket.

"What is the date?" she asked. He told her.

"Will you mail this for me when you go out?"

"Certainly." He read to her little bits out of the newspaper, while she straightened things on the table.

"What do you want to do?" he asked, throwing aside the paper. "Do you want to go out for a walk or a drive or anything? It would be a fine night to drive."

"No; I don't want to do anything but just be quiet. You go away and amuse yourself. Don't stay."

"I'll go away if I must; but I shan't amuse myself. You know that I only live when I am near you."

He stood up to bid her good night.

"Is that one of the things you always say to women?"

"I have said it before, but I don't think I ever came so near meaning it," he answered with a smile. There were no warm lights in her eyes; only a dreamy, absent look.

"Good night. I adore you. Sleep well," he said, and he kissed her hand and went away.

She stayed alone in a kind of reverie—a sort of stupor. Step by step she lived over every instant of the time she had been with Robert after he had entered Mademoiselle Reisz's door. She recalled his words, his looks. How few and meager they had been for her hungry heart! A vision—a transcendently seductive vision of a Mexican girl arose before her. She writhed with a jealous pang. She wondered when he would come back. He had not said he would come back. She had been with him, had heard his voice and touched his hand. But some way he had seemed nearer to her off there in Mexico.

XXXV

The morning was full of sunlight and hope. Edna could see before her no denial—only the promise of excessive joy. She lay in bed awake, with bright eyes full of speculation. "He loves you, poor fool." If she could but get that conviction firmly fixed in her mind, what mattered about the rest? She felt she had been childish and unwise the night before in giving herself over to despondency. She recapitulated the motives which no doubt explained Robert's reserve. They were not insurmountable; they would not hold if he really loved her; they could not hold against her own passion, which he must come to realize in time. She pictured him going to his business that morning. She even saw how he was dressed; how he walked down one street, and turned the corner of another; saw him bending over his desk, talking to people who entered the office, going to his lunch, and perhaps watching for her on the street. He would come to her in the afternoon or evening, sit and roll his cigarette, talk a little, and go away as he had done the night before. But how delicious it would be to have him there with her! She would have no regrets, nor seek to penetrate his reserve if he still chose to wear it.

Edna ate her breakfast only half dressed. The maid brought her a delicious printed scrawl from Raoul, expressing his love, asking her to send him some bonbons, and telling her they had found that morning ten tiny white pigs all lying in a row beside Lidie's big white pig.

A letter also came from her husband, saying he hoped to be back early in March, and then they would get ready for that journey abroad which he had promised her so long, which he felt now fully able to afford; he felt able to travel as people should, without any thought of small economies—thanks to his recent speculations in Wall Street.

Much to her surprise she received a note from Arobin, written at midnight from the club. It was to say good morning to her, to hope she had slept well, to assure her of his devotion, which he trusted she in some faintest manner returned.

All these letters were pleasing to her. She answered the children in a cheerful frame of mind, promising them bonbons, and congratulating them upon their happy find of the little pigs.

She answered her husband with friendly evasiveness,—not with any fixed design to mislead him, only because all sense of reality had gone out of her life; she had abandoned herself to Fate, and awaited the consequences with indifference.

To Arobin's note she made no reply. She put it under Celestine's stove-lid.

Edna worked several hours with much spirit. She saw no one but a picture dealer, who asked her if it were true that she was going abroad to study in Paris.

She said possibly she might, and he negotiated with her for some Parisian studies to reach him in time for the holiday trade in December.

Robert did not come that day. She was keenly disappointed. He did not come the following day, nor the next. Each morning she awoke with hope, and each night she was a prey to despondency. She was tempted to seek him out. But far from yielding to the impulse, she avoided any occasion which might throw her in his way. She did not go to Mademoiselle Reisz's nor pass by Madame Lebrun's, as she might have done if he had still been in Mexico.

When Arobin, one night, urged her to drive with him, she went—out to the lake, on the Shell Road. His horses were full of mettle, and even a little unmanageable. She liked the rapid gait at which they spun along, and the quick, sharp sound of the horses' hoofs

on the hard road. They did not stop anywhere to eat or to drink. Arobin was not needlessly imprudent. But they ate and they drank when they regained Edna's little dining-
room—which was comparatively early in the evening.

It was late when he left her. It was getting to be more than a passing whim with
Arobin to see her and be with her. He had detected the latent sensuality, which unfolded under his delicate sense of her nature's requirements like a torpid, torrid, sensitive blossom.

There was no despondency when she fell asleep that night; nor was there hope when
she awoke in the morning.

XXXVI

There was a garden out in the suburbs; a small, leafy corner, with a few green tables under the orange trees. An old cat slept all day on the stone step in the sun, and an old *mulatresse*[60] slept her idle hours away in her chair at the open window, till some one happened to knock on one of the green tables. She had milk and cream cheese to sell, and
bread and butter. There was no one who could make such excellent coffee or fry a
chicken so golden brown as she.

The place was too modest to attract the attention of people of fashion, and so quiet
as to have escaped the notice of those in search of pleasure and dissipation. Edna had
discovered it accidentally one day when the high-board gate stood ajar. She caught sight
of a little green table, blotched with the checkered sunlight that filtered through the
quivering leaves overhead. Within she had found the slumbering *mulatresse,* the drowsy
cat, and a glass of milk which reminded her of the milk she had tasted in Iberville.

She often stopped there during her perambulations; sometimes taking a book with
her, and sitting an hour or two under the trees when she found the place deserted. Once
or twice she took a quiet dinner there alone, having instructed Celestine beforehand to
prepare no dinner at home. It was the last place in the city where she would have expected to meet any one she knew.

Still she was not astonished when, as she was partaking of a modest dinner late in the
afternoon, looking into an open book, stroking the cat, which had made friends with
her—she was not greatly astonished to see Robert come in at the tall garden gate.

"I am destined to see you only by accident," she said, shoving the cat off the chair
beside her. He was surprised, ill at ease, almost embarrassed at meeting her thus so
unexpectedly.

"Do you come here often?" he asked.

"I almost live here," she said.

"I used to drop in very often for a cup of Catiche's good coffee. This is the first time
since I came back."

"She'll bring you a plate, and you will share my dinner. There's always enough for
two—even three." Edna had intended to be indifferent and as reserved as he when she
met him; she had reached the determination by a laborious train of reasoning, incident
to one of her despondent moods. But her resolve melted when she saw him before her,
seated there beside her in the little garden, as if a designing Providence had led him into
her path.

[60] Mulatto woman.

"Why have you kept away from me, Robert?" she asked, closing the book that lay open upon the table.

"Why are you so personal, Mrs. Pontellier? Why do you force me to idiotic subterfuges?" he exclaimed with sudden warmth. "I suppose there's no use telling you I've been very busy, or that I've been sick, or that I've been to see you and not found you at home. Please let me off with any one of these excuses."

"You are the embodiment of selfishness," she said. "You save yourself something—I don't know what—but there is some selfish motive, and in sparing yourself you never consider for a moment what I think, or how I feel your neglect and indifference. I suppose this is what you would call unwomanly; but I have got into a habit of expressing myself. It doesn't matter to me, and you may think me unwomanly if you like."

"No; I only think you cruel, as I said the other day. Maybe not intentionally cruel; but you seem to be forcing me into disclosures which can result in nothing; as if you would have me bare a wound for the pleasure of looking at it, without the intention or power of healing it."

"I'm spoiling your dinner, Robert; never mind what I say. You haven't eaten a morsel."

"I only came in for a cup of coffee." His sensitive face was all disfigured with excitement.

"Isn't this a delightful place?" she remarked. "I am so glad it has never actually been discovered. It is so quiet, so sweet, here. Do you notice there is scarcely a sound to be heard? It's so out of the way; and a good walk from the car. However, I don't mind walking. I always feel so sorry for women who don't like to walk; they miss so much—so many rare little glimpses of life; and we women learn so little of life on the whole.

"Catiche's coffee is always hot. I don't know how she manages it, here in the open air. Celestine's coffee gets cold bringing it from the kitchen to the dining-room. Three lumps! How can you drink it so sweet? Take some of the cress with your chop; it's so biting and crisp. Then there's the advantage of being able to smoke with your coffee out here. Now, in the city—aren't you going to smoke?"

"After a while," he said, laying a cigar on the table.

"Who gave it to you?" she laughed.

"I bought it. I suppose I'm getting reckless; I bought a whole box." She was determined not to be personal again and make him uncomfortable.

The cat made friends with him, and climbed into his lap when he smoked his cigar. He stroked her silky fur, and talked a little about her. He looked at Edna's book, which he had read; and he told her the end, to save her the trouble of wading through it, he said.

Again he accompanied her back to her home; and it was after dusk when they reached the little "pigeon-house." She did not ask him to remain, which he was grateful for, as it permitted him to stay without the discomfort of blundering through an excuse which he had no intention of considering. He helped her to light the lamp; then she went into her room to take off her hat and to bathe her face and hands.

When she came back Robert was not examining the pictures and magazines as before; he sat off in the shadow, leaning his head back on the chair as if in a reverie. Edna lingered a moment beside the table, arranging the books there. Then she went across the room to where he sat. She bent over the arm of his chair and called his name.

"Robert," she said, "are you asleep?"

"No," he answered, looking up at her.

She leaned over and kissed him—a soft, cool, delicate kiss, whose voluptuous sting penetrated his whole being—then she moved away from him. He followed, and took her in his arms, just holding her close to him. She put her hand up to his face and pressed his cheek against her own. The action was full of love and tenderness. He sought her lips again. Then he drew her down upon the sofa beside him and held her hand in both of his.

"Now you know," he said, "now you know what I have been fighting against since last summer at Grand Isle; what drove me away and drove me back again."

"Why have you been fighting against it?" she asked. Her face glowed with soft lights.

"Why? Because you were not free; you were Léonce Pontellier's wife. I couldn't help loving you if you were ten times his wife; but so long as I went away from you and kept away I could help telling you so." She put her free hand up to his shoulder, and then against his cheek, rubbing it softly. He kissed her again. His face was warm and flushed.

"There in Mexico I was thinking of you all the time, and longing for you."

"But not writing to me," she interrupted.

"Something put into my head that you cared for me; and I lost my senses. I forgot everything but a wild dream of your some way becoming my wife."

"Your wife!"

"Religion, loyalty, everything would give way if only you cared."

"Then you must have forgotten that I was Léonce Pontellier's wife."

"Oh! I was demented, dreaming of wild, impossible things, recalling men who had set their wives free, we have heard of such things."

"Yes, we have heard of such things."

"I came back full of vague, mad intentions. And when I got here—"

"When you got here you never came near me!" She was still caressing his cheek.

"I realized what a cur I was to dream of such a thing, even if you had been willing."

She took his face between her hands and looked into it as if she would never withdraw her eyes more. She kissed him on the forehead, the eyes, the cheeks, and the lips.

"You have been a very, very foolish boy, wasting your time dreaming of impossible things when you speak of Mr. Pontellier setting me free! I am no longer one of Mr. Pontellier's possessions to dispose of or not. I give myself where I choose. If he were to say, 'Here, Robert, take her and be happy; she is yours,' I should laugh at you both."

His face grew a little white. "What do you mean?" he asked.

There was a knock at the door. Old Celestine came in to say that Madame Ratignolle's servant had come around the back way with a message that Madame had been taken sick and begged Mrs. Pontellier to go to her immediately.

"Yes, yes," said Edna, rising; "I promised. Tell her yes—to wait for me. I'll go back with her."

"Let me walk over with you," offered Robert.

"No," she said; "I will go with the servant." She went into her room to put on her hat, and when she came in again she sat once more upon the sofa beside him. He had not stirred. She put her arms about his neck.

"Good-by, my sweet Robert. Tell me good-by." He kissed her with a degree of passion which had not before entered into his caress, and strained her to him.

"I love you," she whispered, "only you; no one but you. It was you who awoke me last summer out of a life-long, stupid dream. Oh! you have made me so unhappy with your indifference. Oh! I have suffered, suffered! Now you are here we shall love each other, my Robert. We shall be everything to each other. Nothing else in the world is of any consequence. I must go to my friend; but you will wait for me? No matter how late; you will wait for me, Robert?"

"Don't go; don't go! Oh! Edna, stay with me," he pleaded. "Why should you go? Stay with me, stay with me."

"I shall come back as soon as I can; I shall find you here." She buried her face in his neck, and said good-by again. Her seductive voice, together with his great love for her, had enthralled his senses, had deprived him of every impulse but the longing to hold her and keep her.

XXXVII

Edna looked in at the drug store. Monsieur Ratignolle was putting up a mixture himself, very carefully, dropping a red liquid into a tiny glass. He was grateful to Edna for having come; her presence would be a comfort to his wife. Madame Ratignolle's sister, who had always been with her at such trying times, had not been able to come up from the plantation, and Adèle had been inconsolable until Mrs. Pontellier so kindly promised to come to her. The nurse had been with them at night for the past week, as she lived a great distance away. And Dr. Mandelet had been coming and going all the afternoon. They were then looking for him any moment.

Edna hastened upstairs by a private stairway that led from the rear of the store to the apartments above. The children were all sleeping in a back room. Madame Ratignolle was in the salon, whither she had strayed in her suffering impatience. She sat on the sofa, clad in an ample white *peignoir,* holding a handkerchief tight in her hand with a nervous clutch. Her face was drawn and pinched, her sweet blue eyes haggard and unnatural. All her beautiful hair had been drawn back and plaited. It lay in a long braid on the sofa pillow, coiled like a golden serpent. The nurse, a comfortable looking *Griffe* woman in white apron and cap, was urging her to return to her bedroom.

"There is no use, there is no use," she said at once to Edna. "We must get rid of Mandelet; he is getting too old and careless. He said he would be here at half-past seven; now it must be eight. See what time it is, Joséphine."

The woman was possessed of a cheerful nature, and refused to take any situation too seriously, especially a situation with which she was so familiar. She urged Madame to have courage and patience. But Madame only set her teeth hard into her under lip, and Edna saw the sweat gather in beads on her white forehead. After a moment or two she uttered a profound sigh and wiped her face with the handkerchief rolled in a ball. She appeared exhausted. The nurse gave her a fresh handkerchief, sprinkled with cologne water.

"This is too much!" she cried. "Mandelet ought to be killed! Where is Alphonse? Is it possible I am to be abandoned like this—neglected by every one?"

"Neglected, indeed!" exclaimed the nurse. Wasn't she there? And here was Mrs. Pontellier leaving, no doubt, a pleasant evening at home to devote to her? And wasn't Monsieur Ratignolle coming that very instant through the hall? And Joséphine was quite sure she had heard Doctor Mandelet's coupé. Yes, there it was, down at the door.

Adèle consented to go back to her room. She sat on the edge of a little low couch next to her bed.

Doctor Mandelet paid no attention to Madame Ratignolle's upbraidings. He was accustomed to them at such times, and was too well convinced of her loyalty to doubt it.

He was glad to see Edna, and wanted her to go with him into the salon and entertain him. But Madame Ratignolle would not consent that Edna should leave her for an instant. Between agonizing moments, she chatted a little, and said it took her mind off her sufferings.

Edna began to feel uneasy. She was seized with a vague dread. Her own like experiences seemed far away, unreal, and only half remembered. She recalled faintly an ecstasy of pain, the heavy odor of chloroform, a stupor which had deadened sensation, and an awakening to find a little new life to which she had given being, added to the great unnumbered multitude of souls that come and go.

She began to wish she had not come; her presence was not necessary. She might have invented a pretext for staying away; she might even invent a pretext now for going. But Edna did not go. With an inward agony, with a flaming, outspoken revolt against the ways of Nature, she witnessed the scene of torture.

She was still stunned and speechless with emotion when later she leaned over her friend to kiss her and softly say good-by. Adèle, pressing her cheek, whispered in an exhausted voice: "Think of the children, Edna. Oh think of the children! Remember them!"

XXXVIII

Edna still felt dazed when she got outside in the open air. The Doctor's coupé had returned for him and stood before the *porte cochère.*[60] She did not wish to enter the coupé, and told Doctor Mandelet she would walk; she was not afraid, and would go alone. He directed his carriage to meet him at Mrs. Pontellier's, and he started to walk home with her.

Up—away up, over the narrow street between the tall houses, the stars were blazing. The air was mild and caressing, but cool with the breath of spring and the night. They walked slowly, the Doctor with a heavy, measured tread and his hands behind him; Edna, in an absent-minded way, as she had walked one night at Grand Isle, as if her thoughts had gone ahead of her and she was striving to overtake them.

"You shouldn't have been there, Mrs. Pontellier," he said. "That was no place for you. Adèle is full of whims at such times. There were a dozen women she might have had with her, unimpressionable women. I felt that it was cruel, cruel. You shouldn't have gone."

"Oh, well!" she answered, indifferently. "I don't know that it matters after all. One has to think of the children some time or other; the sooner the better."

"When is Léonce coming back?"

"Quite soon. Some time in March."

"And you are going abroad?"

"Perhaps—no, I am not going. I'm not going to be forced into doing things. I don't want to go abroad. I want to be let alone. Nobody has any right—except children, perhaps—and even then, it seems to me—or it did seem—" She felt that her speech was voicing the incoherency of her thoughts, and stopped abruptly.

"The trouble is," sighed the Doctor, grasping her meaning intuitively, "that youth is given up to illusions. It seems to be a provision of Nature; a decoy to secure mothers for the race. And Nature takes no account of moral consequences, of arbitrary conditions which we create, and which we feel obliged to maintain at any cost."

[60] Covered carriage entrance.

"Yes," she said. "The years that are gone seem like dreams—if one might go on sleeping and dreaming—but to wake up and find—oh! well! perhaps it is better to wake up after all, even to suffer, rather than to remain a dupe to illusions all one's life."

"It seems to me, my dear child," said the Doctor at parting, holding her hand, "you seem to me to be in trouble. I am not going to ask for your confidence. I will only say that if ever you feel moved to give it to me, perhaps I might help you. I know I would understand, and I tell you there are not many who would—not many, my dear."

"Some way I don't feel moved to speak of things that trouble me. Don't think I am ungrateful or that I don't appreciate your sympathy. There are periods of despondency and suffering which take possession of me. But I don't want anything but my own way. That is wanting a good deal, of course, when you have to trample upon the lives, the hearts, the prejudices of others—but no matter—still, I shouldn't want to trample upon the little lives. Oh! I don't know what I'm saying, Doctor. Good night. Don't blame me for anything."

"Yes, I will blame you if you don't come and see me soon. We will talk of things you never have dreamt of talking about before. It will do us both good. I don't want you to blame yourself, whatever comes. Good night, my child."

She let herself in at the gate, but instead of entering she sat upon the step of the porch. The night was quiet and soothing. All the tearing emotion of the last few hours seemed to fall away from her like a somber, uncomfortable garment, which she had but to loosen to be rid of. She went back to that hour before Adèle had sent for her; and her senses kindled afresh in thinking of Robert's words, the pressure of his arms, and the feeling of his lips upon her own. She could picture at that moment no greater bliss on earth than possession of the beloved one. His expression of love had already given him to her in part. When she thought that he was there at hand, waiting for her, she grew numb with the intoxication of expectancy. It was so late; he would be asleep perhaps. She would awaken him with a kiss. She hoped he would be asleep that she might arouse him with her caresses.

Still, she remembered Adèle's voice whispering, "Think of the children; think of them." She meant to think of them; that determination had driven into her soul like a death wound—but not to-night. To-morrow would be time to think of everything.

Robert was not waiting for her in the little parlor. He was nowhere at hand. The house was empty. But he had scrawled on a piece of paper that lay in the lamplight:

"I love you. Good-by—because I love you."

Edna grew faint when she read the words. She went and sat on the sofa. Then she stretched herself out there, never uttering a sound. She did not sleep. She did not go to bed. The lamp sputtered and went out. She was still awake in the morning, when Celestine unlocked the kitchen door and came in to light the fire.

XXXIX

Victor, with hammer and nails and scraps of scantling, was patching a corner of one of the galleries. Mariequita sat near by, dangling her legs, watching him work, and handing him nails from the tool-box. The sun was beating down upon them. The girl had covered her head with her apron folded into a square pad. They had been talking for an hour or more. She was never tired of hearing Victor describe the dinner at Mrs. Pontellier's. He exaggerated every detail, making it appear a veritable Lucullean feast. The flowers were in tubs, he said. The champagne was quaffed from huge golden goblets. Venus rising from the foam could have presented no more entrancing a spectacle than Mrs. Pontellier, blazing with beauty and diamonds at the head of the board, while the other women were all of them youthful houris, possessed of incomparable charms.

She got it into her head that Victor was in love with Mrs. Pontellier, and he gave her evasive answers, framed so as to confirm her belief. She grew sullen and cried a little, threatening to go off and leave him to his fine ladies. There were a dozen men crazy about her at the *Chênière;* and since it was the fashion to be in love with married people, why, she could run away any time she liked to New Orleans with Célina's husband.

Célina's husband was a fool, a coward, and a pig, and to prove it to her, Victor intended to hammer his head into a jelly the next time he encountered him. This assurance was very consoling to Mariequita. She dried her eyes, and grew cheerful at the prospect.

They were still talking of the dinner and the allurements of city life when Mrs. Pontellier herself slipped around the corner of the house. The two youngsters stayed dumb with amazement before what they considered to be an apparition. But it was really she in flesh and blood, looking tired and a little travel-stained.

"I walked up from the wharf," she said, "and heard the hammering. I supposed it was you, mending the porch. It's a good thing. I was always tripping over those loose planks last summer. How dreary and deserted everything looks!"

It took Victor some little time to comprehend that she had come in Beaudelet's lugger, that she had come alone, and for no purpose but to rest.

"There's nothing fixed up yet, you see. I'll give you my room; it's the only place."

"Any corner will do," she assured him.

"And if you can stand Philomel's cooking," he went on, "though I might try to get her mother while you are here. Do you think she would come?" turning to Mariequita.

Mariequita thought that perhaps Philomel's mother might come for a few days, and money enough.

Beholding Mrs. Pontellier make her appearance, the girl had at once suspected a lovers' rendezvous. But Victor's astonishment was so genuine, and Mrs. Pontellier's indifference so apparent, that the disturbing notion did not lodge long in her brain. She contemplated with the greatest interest this woman who gave the most sumptuous dinners in America, and who had all the men in New Orleans at her feet.

"What time will you have dinner?" asked Edna. "I'm very hungry; but don't get anything extra."

"I'll have it ready in little or no time," he said, bustling and packing away his tools. "You may go to my room to brush up and rest yourself. Mariequita will show you."

"Thank you," said Edna. "But, do you know, I have a notion to go down to the beach and take a good wash and even a little swim, before dinner?"

"The water is too cold!" they both exclaimed. "Don't think of it."

"Well, I might go down and try—dip my toes in. Why, it seems to me the sun is hot enough to have warmed the very depths of the ocean. Could you get me a couple of towels? I'd better go right away, so as to be back in time. It would be a little too chilly if I waited till this afternoon."

Mariequita ran over to Victor's room, and returned with some towels, which she gave to Edna.

"I hope you have fish for dinner," said Edna, as she started to walk away; "but don't do anything extra if you haven't."

"Run and find Philomel's mother," Victor instructed the girl. "I'll go to the kitchen and see what I can do. By Gimminy! Women have no consideration! She might have sent me word."

Edna walked on down to the beach rather mechanically, not noticing anything special except that the sun was hot. She was not dwelling upon any particular train of thought. She had done all the thinking which was necessary after Robert went away, when she lay awake upon the sofa till morning.

She had said over and over to herself: "To-day it is Arobin; to-morrow it will be some one else. It makes no difference to me, it doesn't matter about Léonce Pontellier—but Raoul and Etienne!" She understood now clearly what she had meant long ago when she said to Adèle Ratignolle that she would give up the unessential, but she would never sacrifice herself for her children.

Despondency had come upon her there in the wakeful night, and had never lifted. There was no one thing in the world that she desired. There was no human being whom she wanted near her except Robert; and she even realized that the day would come when he, too, and the thought of him would melt out of her existence, leaving her alone. The children appeared before her like antagonists who had overcome her; who had overpowered and sought to drag her into the soul's slavery for the rest of her days. But she knew a way to elude them. She was not thinking of these things when she walked down to the beach.

The water of the Gulf stretched out before her, gleaming with the million lights of the sun. The voice of the sea is seductive, never ceasing, whispering, clamoring, murmuring, inviting the soul to wander in abysses of solitude. All along the white beach, up and down, there was no living thing in sight. A bird with a broken wing was beating the air above, reeling, fluttering, circling disabled down, down to the water.

Edna had found her old bathing suit still hanging, faded, upon its accustomed peg.

She put it on, leaving her clothing in the bath-house. But when she was there beside the sea, absolutely alone, she cast the unpleasant, pricking garments from her, and for the first time in her life she stood naked in the open air, at the mercy of the sun, the breeze that beat upon her, and the waves that invited her.

How strange and awful it seemed to stand naked under the sky! how delicious! She felt like some new-born creature, opening its eyes in a familiar world that it had never known.

The foamy wavelets curled up to her white feet, and coiled like serpents about her ankles. She walked out. The water was chill, but she walked on. The water was deep, but she lifted her white body and reached out with a long, sweeping stroke. The touch of the sea is sensuous, enfolding the body in its soft, close embrace.

She went on and on. She remembered the night she swam far out, and recalled the terror that seized her at the fear of being unable to regain the shore. She did not look back now, but went on and on, thinking of the blue-grass meadow that she had traversed when a little child, believing that it had no beginning and no end.

Her arms and legs were growing tired.

She thought of Léonce and the children. They were a part of her life. But they need not have thought that they could possess her, body and soul. How Mademoiselle Reisz would have laughed, perhaps sneered, if she knew! "And you call yourself an artist! What pretensions, Madame! The artist must possess the courageous soul that dares and defies."

Exhaustion was pressing upon and overpowering her.

"Good-by—because I love you." He did not know; he did not understand. He would never understand. Perhaps Doctor Mandelet would have understood if she had seen him—but it was too late; the shore was far behind her, and her strength was gone.

She looked into the distance, and the old terror flamed up for an instant, then sank again. Edna heard her father's voice and her sister Margaret's. She heard the barking of an old dog that was chained to the sycamore tree. The spurs of the cavalry officer clanged as he walked across the porch. There was the hum of bees, and the musky odor of pinks filled the air.

1899

Charlotte Perkins Gilman
1860–1935

Charlotte Perkins Gilman is now studied primarily by social historians interested in her advocacy of women's rights, her often astute comments concerning the relation of female households to male economies, and her active career as a lecturer and writer on a large number of sociological themes. But she is largely ignored as a writer of specifically literary works; her fiction is combed to see what it reveals about social issues. However, one of her stories, "The Yellow Wallpaper," has been celebrated by two diverse groups: fans of horror tales and feminist critics. This ability to write a story with great personal intensity and to convert an unhappy bit of autobiography into a memorable fiction came once in Gilman's long career as a polemicist and social critic, but once was enough.

From her father's family, Charlotte Perkins inherited the approved attitudes toward female domesticity, but out of her mother's experience she formed more complex views toward family love, wifehood, and mothering.

Charlotte Anne Perkins, born in Hartford, Connecticut, was directly connected through her father to Lyman and Henry Ward Beecher, Catherine Beecher, and Harriet Beecher Stowe. The Beechers were famous for their ability to talk and to write about matters of religious piety and social reform and the need to affirm the values of middle-class America while correcting its ills. The various activities of the Beecher women can be interpreted as being against slavery in one form or another. At the same time—and this is the paradox that marked Gilman's own career—the Beechers upheld the supposedly enslaving institutions of hearth, home, and marriage.

However much a Beecher, Charlotte Perkins's father (himself an educated and influential writer) left his wife soon after the birth of his daughter. He remained aloof for the rest of his life from the ill fortune of his wife, who was left alone to support two children. Charlotte afterward attempted to gain her father's favor but was constantly thwarted. She had to experience the poverty and instability of a girlhood spent on the move as her mother wandered from place to place in search of a home she never found.

At twenty-four, after studying art and spending some time as an art teacher, Charlotte Perkins married Charles Stetson, an artist. When her only child was born the next year, 1885, she fell into a deep depression. At the urging of her husband she became a patient of S. Weir Mitchell, a famous Philadelphia physician who had evolved a cure for female nervous disorders in the 1870s. Mitchell's treatment consisted of total bed rest and the enforced isolation of the patient from all activities, physical and mental. Mitchell had some success with his procedures, and his emphasis on the need for the complete moral reliance of patient on physician paralleled the principles of Freudian analysis that were being introduced in Vienna. But these facts are overshadowed by the effect his treatment had on Charlotte Stetson; it was to drive her almost insane. She escaped this fate by fleeing both physician and husband for California, breaking free from these two men's well-intentioned domination over her mind and body. Not until 1892 was she able to take this bitter experience and convert it into her story "The Yellow Wallpaper," written with the purpose of exposing one of the ways by which women are reduced to the state of helpless children.

Charlotte Perkins accomplished a great deal besides writing one famous story. She developed several careers—first as a writer and then as a lecturer on issues of woman suffrage, socialism, and trade unionism. In 1900 she entered upon a successful marriage to George Gilman, her first cousin and another Beecher descendant. But marriage did not stay her hand as a critic of male society. Her best-known books (which the feminist movement has revived) are *Women and Economics* (1899), *The Home: Its Work and Influence* (1903), and *The Man-Made World, or Our Androcentric Culture* (1911). Her autobiography, *The Living of Charlotte Perkins Gilman,* was published posthumously in 1935, the year she committed suicide in order to avoid the final torments of inoperable cancer.

Notwithstanding the questions of choice that arise from Gilman's final act, it is fortunate that, back in 1885, she was able, in spite of the terrible psychic experiences of that period, to will herself a different fate than that suffered by the tormented narrator in her story "The Yellow Wallpaper." She was able to end the mad repetition of defeat and despair that sent her nameless victim crawling around and around the edges of the wallpaper. In contrast, Gilman was able to break out of the room and those secrets and go on through a lifetime of considerable achievement.

Further Reading:

M. Hill, *Charlotte Perkins Gilman: The Making of a Radical Feminist,* 1980.

W. Veeder, "Who Is Jane? The Intricate Feminism of Gilman," *American Quarterly* 44 (1988), 40–79.

P. Allen, *Building Domestic Liberty: Gilman's Architectural Feminism,* 1988.

E. Ammons, *Conflicting Stories,* 1991.

C. Golden, ed., *The Captive Imagination: Casebook on* The Yellow Wallpaper, 1992.

J. B. Karpinski, ed., *Critical Essays on C. P. Gilman,* 1992.

D. D. Knight, ed., *The Diaries of C. P. Gilman,* 1994.

Text:

"The Yellow Wallpaper" from *The Charlotte Perkins Gilman Reader,* 1980.

The Yellow Wallpaper

It is very seldom that mere ordinary people like John and myself secure ancestral halls for the summer.

A colonial mansion, a hereditary estate, I would say a haunted house and reach the height of romantic felicity—but that would be asking too much of fate!

Still I will proudly declare that there is something queer about it.

Else, why should it be let so cheaply? And why have stood so long untenanted?

John laughs at me, of course, but one expects that.

John is practical in the extreme. He has no patience with faith, an intense horror of superstition, and he scoffs openly at any talk of things not to be felt and seen and put down in figures.

John is a physician, and *perhaps*—(I would not say it to a living soul, of course, but this is dead paper and a great relief to my mind)—*perhaps* that is one reason I do not get well faster.

You see, he does not believe I am sick! And what can one do?

If a physician of high standing, and one's own husband, assures friends and relatives that there is really nothing the matter with one but temporary nervous depression—a slight hysterical tendency—what is one to do?

My brother is also a physician, and also of high standing, and he says the same thing.

So I take phosphates or phosphites—whichever it is—and tonics, and air and exercise, and journeys, and am absolutely forbidden to "work" until I am well again.

Personally, I disagree with their ideas.

Personally, I believe that congenial work, with excitement and change, would do me good.

But what is one to do?

I did write for a while in spite of them; but it *does* exhaust me a good deal—having to be so sly about it, or else meet with heavy opposition.

I sometimes fancy that in my condition, if I had less opposition and more society and stimulus—but John says the very worst thing I can do is to think about my condition, and I confess it always makes me feel bad.

So I will let it alone and talk about the house.

The most beautiful place! It is quite alone, standing well back from the road, quite three miles from the village. It makes me think of English places that you read about, for there are hedges and walls and gates that lock, and lots of separate little houses for the gardeners and people.

There is a *delicious* garden! I never saw such a garden—large and shady, full of box-bordered paths, and lined with long grape-covered arbors with seats under them.

There were greenhouses, but they are all broken now.

There was some legal trouble, I believe, something about the heirs and co-heirs; anyhow, the place has been empty for years.

That spoils my ghostliness, I am afraid, but I don't care—there is something strange about the house—I can feel it.

I even said so to John one moonlight evening, but he said what I felt was a draught, and shut the window.

I get unreasonably angry with John sometimes. I'm sure I never used to be so sensitive. I think it is due to this nervous condition.

But John says if I feel so I shall neglect proper self-control; so I take pains to control myself—before him, at least, and that makes me very tired.

I don't like our room a bit. I wanted one downstairs that opened onto the piazza and had roses all over the window, and such pretty old-fashioned chintz hangings! But John would not hear of it.

He said there was only one window and not room for two beds, and no near room for him if he took another.

He is very careful and loving, and hardly lets me stir without special direction.

I have a schedule prescription for each hour in the day; he takes all care from me, and so I feel basely ungrateful not to value it more.

He said he came here solely on my account, that I was to have perfect rest and all the air I could get. "Your exercise depends on your strength, my dear," said he, "and your food somewhat on your appetite; but air you can absorb all the time." So we took the nursery at the top of the house.

It is a big, airy room, the whole floor nearly, with windows that look all ways, and air and sunshine galore. It was nursery first, and then playroom and gymnasium, I should judge, for the windows are barred for little children, and there are rings and things in the walls.

The paint and paper look as if a boys' school had used it. It is stripped off—the paper—in great patches all around the head of my bed, about as far as I can reach, and in a great place on the other side of the room low down. I never saw a worse paper in my life. One of those sprawling, flamboyant patterns committing every artistic sin.

It is dull enough to confuse the eye in following, pronounced enough constantly to irritate and provoke study, and when you follow the lame uncertain curves for a little distance they suddenly commit suicide—plunge off at outrageous angles, destroy themselves in unheard-of contradictions.

The color is repellent, almost revolting: a smouldering unclean yellow, strangely faded by the slow-turning sunlight. It is a dull yet lurid orange in some places, a sickly sulphur tint in others.

No wonder the children hated it! I should hate it myself if I had to live in this room long.

There comes John, and I must put this away—he hates to have me write a word.

We have been here two weeks, and I haven't felt like writing before, since that first day.

I am sitting by the window now, up in this atrocious nursery, and there is nothing to hinder my writing as much as I please, save lack of strength.

John is away all day, and even some nights when his cases are serious.

I am glad my case is not serious!

But these nervous troubles are dreadfully depressing.

John does not know how much I really suffer. He knows there is no reason to suffer, and that satisfies him.

Of course it is only nervousness. It does weigh on me so not to do my duty in any way!

I meant to be such a help to John, such a real rest and comfort, and here I am a comparative burden already!

Nobody would believe what an effort it is to do what little I am able—to dress and entertain, and order things.

It is fortunate Mary is so good with the baby. Such a dear baby!

And yet I *cannot* be with him, it makes me so nervous.

I suppose John never was nervous in his life. He laughs at me so about this wallpaper!

At first he meant to repaper the room, but afterward he said that I was letting it get the better of me, and that nothing was worse for a nervous patient than to give way to such fancies.

He said that after the wallpaper was changed it would be the heavy bedstead, and then the barred windows, and then that gate at the head of the stairs, and so on.

"You know the place is doing you good," he said, "and really, dear, I don't care to renovate the house just for a three months' rental."

"Then do let us go downstairs," I said. "There are such pretty rooms there."

Then he took me in his arms and called me a blessed little goose, and said he would go down cellar, if I wished, and have it whitewashed into the bargain.

But he is right enough about the beds and windows and things.

It is as airy and comfortable a room as anyone need wish, and, of course, I would not be so silly as to make him uncomfortable just for a whim.

I'm really getting quite fond of the big room, all but that horrid paper.

Out of one window I can see the garden—those mysterious deep-shaded arbors, the riotous old-fashioned flowers, and bushes and gnarly trees.

Out of another I get a lovely view of the bay and a little private wharf belonging to the estate. There is a beautiful shaded lane that runs down there from the house. I always fancy I see people walking in these numerous paths and arbors, but John has cautioned me not to give way to fancy in the least. He says that with my imaginative power and habit of story-making, a nervous weakness like mine is sure to lead to all manner of excited fancies, and that I ought to use my will and good sense to check the tendency. So I try.

I think sometimes that if I were only well enough to write a little it would relieve the press of ideas and rest me.

But I find I get pretty tired when I try.

It is so discouraging not to have any advice and companionship about my work. When I get really well, John says we will ask Cousin Henry and Julia down for a long visit; but he says he would as soon put fireworks in my pillow-case as to let me have those stimulating people about now.

I wish I could get well faster.

But I must not think about that. This paper looks to me as if it *knew* what a vicious influence it had!

There is a recurrent spot where the pattern lolls like a broken neck and two bulbous eyes stare at you upside down.

I get positively angry with the impertinence of it and the ever-lastingness. Up and down and sideways they crawl, and those absurd unblinking eyes are everywhere. There is one place where two breadths didn't match, and the eyes go all up and down the line, one a little higher than the other.

I never saw so much expression in an inanimate thing before, and we all know how much expression they have! I used to lie awake as a child and get more entertainment and terror out of blank walls and plain furniture than most children could find in a toy-store.

I remember what a kindly wink the knobs of our big old bureau used to have, and there was one chair that always seemed like a strong friend.

I used to feel that if any of the other things looked too fierce I could always hop into that chair and be safe.

The furniture in this room is no worse than inharmonious, however, for we had to bring it all from downstairs. I suppose when this was used as a playroom they had to take the nursery things out, and no wonder! I never saw such ravages as the children have made here.

The wallpaper, as I said before, is torn off in spots, and it sticketh closer than a brother—they must have had perseverance as well as hatred.

Then the floor is scratched and gouged and splintered, the plaster itself is dug out here and there, and this great heavy bed, which is all we found in the room, looks as if it had been through the wars.

But I don't mind it a bit—only the paper.

There comes John's sister. Such a dear girl as she is, and so careful of me! I must not let her find me writing.

She is a perfect and enthusiastic housekeeper, and hopes for no better profession. I verily believe she thinks it is the writing which made me sick!

But I can write when she is out, and see her a long way off from these windows.

There is one that commands the road, a lovely shaded winding road, and one that just looks off over the country. A lovely country, too, full of great elms and velvet meadows.

This wallpaper has a kind of sub-pattern in a different shade, a particularly irritating one, for you can only see it in certain lights, and not clearly then.

But in the places where it isn't faded and where the sun is just so—I can see a strange, provoking, formless sort of figure that seems to skulk about behind that silly and conspicuous front design.

There's sister on the stairs!

Well, the Fourth of July is over! The people are all gone, and I am tired out. John thought it might do me good to see a little company, so we just had Mother and Nellie and the children down for a week.

Of course I didn't do a thing. Jennie sees to everything now.

But it tired me all the same.

John says if I don't pick up faster he shall send me to Weir Mitchell[1] in the fall.

But I don't want to go there at all. I had a friend who was in his hands once, and she says he is just like John and my brother, only more so!

Besides, it is such an undertaking to go so far.

I don't feel as if it was worthwhile to turn my hand over for anything, and I'm getting dreadfully fretful and querulous.

I cry at nothing, and cry most of the time.

Of course I don't when John is here, or anybody else, but when I am alone.

And I am alone a good deal just now. John is kept in town very often by serious cases, and Jennie is good and lets me alone when I want her to.

So I walk a little in the garden or down that lovely lane, sit on the porch under the roses, and lie down up here a good deal.

---

[1] American physician famous for his treatment of "neurotic females" by means of enforced bed rest and isolation. Herself a highly dissatisfied patient of Mitchell, Gilman intended this story as an attack against his methods.

I'm getting really fond of the room in spite of the wallpaper. Perhaps *because* of the wallpaper.

It dwells in my mind so!

I lie here on this great immovable bed—it is nailed down, I believe—and follow that pattern about by the hour. It is as good as gymnastics, I assure you. I start, we'll say, at the bottom, down in the corner over there where it has not been touched, and I determine for the thousandth time that I *will* follow that pointless pattern to some sort of a conclusion.

I know a little of the principle of design, and I know this thing was not arranged on any laws of radiation, or alternation, or repetition, or symmetry, or anything else that I ever heard of.

It is repeated, of course, by the breadths, but not otherwise.

Looked at in one way, each breadth stands alone; the bloated curves and flourishes—a kind of "debased Romanesque"[2] with delirium tremens—go waddling up and down in isolated columns of fatuity.

But, on the other hand, they connect diagonally, and the sprawling outlines run off in great slanting waves of optic horror, like a lot of wallowing sea-weeds in full chase.

The whole thing goes horizontally, too, at least it seems so, and I exhaust myself trying to distinguish the order of its going in that direction.

They have used a horizontal breadth for a frieze, and that adds wonderfully to the confusion.

There is one end of the room where it is almost intact, and there, when the crosslights fade and the low sun shines directly upon it, I can almost fancy radiation after all—the interminable grotesque seems to form around a common center and rush off in headlong plunges of equal distraction.

It makes me tired to follow it. I will take a nap, I guess.

I don't know why I should write this.

I don't want to.

I don't feel able.

And I know John would think it absurd. But I must say what I feel and think in some way—it is such a relief!

But the effort is getting to be greater than the relief.

Half the time now I am awfully lazy, and lie down ever so much. John says I mustn't lose my strength, and has me take cod liver oil and lots of tonics and things, to say nothing of ale and wine and rare meat.

Dear John! He loves me very dearly, and hates to have me sick. I tried to have a real earnest reasonable talk with him the other day, and tell him how I wish he would let me go and make a visit to Cousin Henry and Julia.

But he said I wasn't able to go, nor able to stand it after I got there; and I did not make out a very good case for myself, for I was crying before I had finished.

It is getting to be a great effort for me to think straight. Just this nervous weakness, I suppose.

And dear John gathered me up in his arms, and just carried me upstairs and laid me on the bed, and sat by me and read to me till it tired my head.

---

[2] Style of architecture and decoration originating in the eleventh and twelfth centuries, here debased to ugliness.

He said I was his darling and his comfort and all he had, and that I must take care of myself for his sake, and keep well.

He says no one but myself can help me out of it, that I must use my will and self-control and not let any silly fancies run away with me.

There's one comfort—the baby is well and happy, and does not have to occupy this nursery with the horrid wallpaper.

If we had not used it, that blessed child would have! What a fortunate escape! Why, I wouldn't have a child of mine, an impressionable little thing, live in such a room for worlds.

I never thought of it before, but it is lucky that John kept me here after all; I can stand it so much easier than a baby, you see.

Of course I never mention it to them any more—I am too wise—but I keep watch for it all the same.

There are things in that wallpaper that nobody knows about but me, or ever will.

Behind that outside pattern the dim shapes get clearer every day.

It is always the same shape, only very numerous.

And it is like a woman stooping down and creeping about behind that pattern. I don't like it a bit. I wonder—I begin to think—I wish John would take me away from here!

It is so hard to talk with John about my case, because he is so wise, and because he loves me so.

But I tried it last night.

It was moonlight. The moon shines in all around just as the sun does.

I hate to see it sometimes, it creeps so slowly, and always comes in by one window or another.

John was asleep and I hated to waken him, so I kept still and watched the moonlight on that undulating wallpaper till I felt creepy.

The faint figure behind seemed to shake the pattern, just as if she wanted to get out.

I got up softly and went to feel and see if the paper *did* move, and when I came back John was awake.

"What is it, little girl?" he said. "Don't go walking about like that—you'll get cold."

I thought it was a good time to talk, so I told him that I really was not gaining here, and that I wished he would take me away.

"Why, darling!" said he. "Our lease will be up in three weeks, and I can't see how to leave before.

"The repairs are not done at home, and I cannot possibly leave town just now. Of course, if you were in any danger, I could and would, but you really are better, dear, whether you can see it or not. I am a doctor, dear, and I know. You are gaining flesh and color, your appetite is better, I feel really much easier about you."

"I don't weigh a bit more," said I, "nor as much; and my appetite may be better in the evening when you are here but it is worse in the morning when you are away!"

"Bless her little heart!" said he with a big hug. "She shall be as sick as she pleases! But now let's improve the shining hours by going to sleep, and talk about it in the morning!"

"And you won't go away?" I asked gloomily.

"Why, how can I, dear? It is only three weeks more and then we will take a nice little trip of a few days while Jennie is getting the house ready. Really, dear, you are better!"

"Better in body perhaps—" I began, and stopped short, for he sat up straight and looked at me with such a stern, reproachful look that I could not say another word.

"My darling," said he, "I beg of you, for my sake and for our child's sake, as well as for your own, that you will never for one instant let that idea enter your mind! There is nothing so dangerous, so fascinating, to a temperament like yours. It is a false and foolish fancy. Can you not trust me as a physician when I tell you so?"

So of course I said no more on that score, and we went to sleep before long. He thought I was asleep first, but I wasn't, and lay there for hours trying to decide whether that front pattern and the back pattern really did move together or separately.

On a pattern like this, by daylight, there is a lack of sequence, a defiance of law, that is a constant irritant to a normal mind.

The color is hideous enough, and unreliable enough, and infuriating enough, but the pattern is torturing.

You think you have mastered it, but just as you get well under way in following, it turns a back-somersault and there you are. It slaps you in the face, knocks you down, and tramples upon you. It is like a bad dream.

The outside pattern is a florid arabesque, reminding one of a fungus. If you can imagine a toadstool in joints, an interminable string of toadstools, budding and sprouting in endless convolutions—why, that is something like it.

That is, sometimes!

There is one marked peculiarity about this paper, a thing nobody seems to notice but myself, and that is that it changes as the light changes.

When the sun shoots in through the east window—I always watch for that first long, straight ray—it changes so quickly that I never can quite believe it.

That is why I watch it always.

By moonlight—the moon shines in all night when there is a moon—I wouldn't know it was the same paper.

At night in any kind of light, in twilight, candlelight, lamplight, and worst of all by moonlight, it becomes bars! The outside pattern, I mean, and the woman behind it is as plain as can be.

I didn't realize for a long time what the thing was that showed behind, that dim subpattern, but now I am quite sure it is a woman.

By daylight she is subdued, quiet. I fancy it is the pattern that keeps her so still. It is so puzzling. It keeps me quiet by the hour.

I lie down ever so much now. John says it is good for me, and to sleep all I can.

Indeed he started the habit by making me lie down for an hour after each meal.

It is a very bad habit, I am convinced, for you see, I don't sleep.

And that cultivates deceit, for I don't tell them I'm awake—oh, no!

The fact is I am getting a little afraid of John.

He seems very queer sometimes, and even Jennie has an inexplicable look.

It strikes me occasionally, just as a scientific hypothesis, that perhaps it is the paper!

I have watched John when he did not know I was looking, and come into the room suddenly on the most innocent excuses, and I've caught him several times *looking at the paper!* And Jennie too. I caught Jennie with her hand on it once.

She didn't know I was in the room, and when I asked her in a quiet, a very quiet voice, with the most restrained manner possible, what she was doing with the paper, she turned around as if she had been caught stealing, and looked quite angry—asked me why I should frighten her so!

Then she said that the paper stained everything it touched, that she had found yellow smooches on all my clothes and John's and she wished we would be more careful!

Did not that sound innocent? But I know she was studying that pattern, and I am determined that nobody shall find it out but myself!

Life is very much more exciting now than it used to be. You see, I have something more to expect, to look forward to, to watch. I really do eat better, and am more quiet than I was.

John is so pleased to see me improve! He laughed a little the other day, and said I seemed to be flourishing in spite of my wallpaper.

I turned it off with a laugh. I had no intention of telling him it was *because* of the wallpaper—he would make fun of me. He might even want to take me away.

I don't want to leave now until I have found it out. There is a week more, and I think that will be enough.

I'm feeling so much better!

I don't sleep much at night, for it is so interesting to watch developments; but I sleep a good deal during the daytime.

In the daytime it is tiresome and perplexing.

There are always new shoots on the fungus, and new shades of yellow all over it. I cannot keep count of them, though I have tried conscientiously.

It is the strangest yellow, that wallpaper! It makes me think of all the yellow things I ever saw—not beautiful ones like buttercups, but old, foul, bad yellow things.

But there is something else about that paper—the smell! I noticed it the moment we came into the room but with so much air and sun it was not bad. Now we have had a week of fog and rain, and whether the windows are open or not, the smell is here.

It creeps all over the house.

I find it hovering in the dining-room, skulking in the parlor, hiding in the hall, lying in wait for me on the stairs.

It gets into my hair.

Even when I go to ride, if I turn my head suddenly and surprise it—there is that smell!

Such a peculiar odor, too! I have spent hours in trying to analyze it, to find what it smelled like.

It is not bad—at first—and very gentle, but quite the subtlest, most enduring odor I ever met.

In this damp weather it is awful. I wake up in the night and find it hanging over me.

It used to disturb me at first. I thought seriously of burning the house—to reach the smell.

But now I am used to it. The only thing I can think of that it is like is the *color* of the paper! A yellow smell.

There is a very funny mark on this wall, low down, near the mopboard. A streak that runs round the room. It goes behind every piece of furniture, except the bed, a long, straight, even *smooch,* as if it had been rubbed over and over.

I wonder how it was done and who did it, and what they did it for. Round and round and round—round and round and round—it makes me dizzy!

I really have discovered something at last.

Through watching so much at night, when it changes so, I have finally found out.

The front pattern *does* move—and no wonder! The woman behind shakes it!

Sometimes I think there are a great many women behind, and sometimes only one, and she crawls around fast, and her crawling shakes it all over.

Then in the very bright spots she keeps still, and in the very shady spots she just takes hold of the bars and shakes them hard.

And she is all the time trying to climb through. But nobody could climb through that pattern—it strangles so; I think that is why it has so many heads.

They get through, and then the pattern strangles them off and turns them upside down, and makes their eyes white!

If those heads were covered or taken off it would not be half so bad.

I think that woman gets out in the daytime!

And I'll tell you why—privately—I've seen her!

I can see her out of every one of my windows!

It is the same woman, I know, for she is always creeping, and most women do not creep by daylight.

I see her in that long shaded lane, creeping up and down. I see her in those dark grape arbors, creeping all around the garden.

I see her on that long road under the trees, creeping along, and when a carriage comes she hides under the blackberry vines.

I don't blame her a bit. It must be very humiliating to be caught creeping by daylight!

I always lock the door when I creep by daylight. I can't do it at night, for I know John would suspect something at once.

And John is so queer now that I don't want to irritate him. I wish he would take another room! Besides, I don't want anybody to get that woman out at night but myself.

I often wonder if I could see her out of all the windows at once.

But, turn as fast as I can, I can only see out of one at one time.

And though I always see her, she *may* be able to creep faster than I can turn! I have watched her sometimes away off in the open country, creeping as fast as a cloud shadow in a wind.

If only that top pattern could be gotten off from the under one! I mean to try it, little by little.

I have found out another funny thing, but I shan't tell it this time! It does not do to trust people too much.

There are only two more days to get this paper off, and I believe John is beginning to notice. I don't like the look in his eyes.

And I heard him ask Jennie a lot of professional questions about me. She had a very good report to give.

She said I slept a good deal in the daytime.

John knows I don't sleep very well at night, for all I'm so quiet!

He asked me all sorts of questions, too, and pretended to be very loving and kind.

As if I couldn't see through him!

Still, I don't wonder he acts so, sleeping under this paper for three months.

It only interests me, but I feel sure John and Jennie are affected by it.

  •   •   •   •   •

Hurrah! This is the last day, but it is enough. John is to stay in town over night, and won't be out until this evening.

Jennie wanted to sleep with me—the sly thing; but I told her I should undoubtedly rest better for a night all alone.

That was clever, for really I wasn't alone a bit! As soon as it was moonlight and that poor thing began to crawl and shake the pattern, I got up and ran to help her.

I pulled and she shook. I shook and she pulled, and before morning we had peeled off yards of that paper.

A strip about as high as my head and half around the room.

And then when the sun came and that awful pattern began to laugh at me, I declared I would finish it today!

We go away tomorrow, and they are moving all my furniture down again to leave things as they were before.

Jennie looked at the wall in amazement, but I told her merrily that I did it out of pure spite at the vicious thing.

She laughed and said she wouldn't mind doing it herself, but I must not get tired.

How she betrayed herself that time!

But I am here, and no person touches this paper but Me—not *alive!*

She tried to get me out of the room—it was too patent! But I said it was so quiet and empty and clean now that I believed I would lie down again and sleep all I could, and not to wake me even for dinner—I would call when I woke.

So now she is gone, and the servants are gone, and the things are gone, and there is nothing left but that great bedstead nailed down, with the canvas mattress we found on it.

We shall sleep downstairs tonight, and take the boat home tomorrow.

I quite enjoy the room, now it is bare again.

How those children did tear about here!

This bedstead is fairly gnawed!

But I must get to work.

I have locked the door and thrown the key down into the front path.

I don't want to go out, and I don't want to have anybody come in, till John comes.

I want to astonish him.

I've got a rope up here that even Jennie did not find. If that woman does get out, and tries to get away, I can tie her!

But I forgot I could not reach far without anything to stand on!

This bed will *not* move!

I tried to lift and push it until I was lame, and then I got so angry I bit off a little piece at one corner—but it hurt my teeth.

Then I peeled off all the paper I could reach standing on the floor. It sticks horribly and the pattern just enjoys it! All those strangled heads and bulbous eyes and waddling fungus growths just shriek with derision!

I am getting angry enough to do something desperate. To jump out of the window would be admirable exercise, but the bars are too strong even to try.

Besides I wouldn't do it. Of course not. I know well enough that a step like that is improper and might be misconstrued.

I don't like to *look* out of the windows even—there are so many of those creeping women, and they creep so fast.

I wonder if they all come out of that wallpaper as I did?

But I am securely fastened now by my well-hidden rope—you don't get *me* out in the road there!

I suppose I shall have to get back behind the pattern when it comes night, and that is hard!

It is so pleasant to be out in this great room and creep around as I please!

I don't want to go outside. I won't, even if Jennie asks me to.

For outside you have to creep on the ground, and everything is green instead of yellow.

But here I can creep smoothly on the floor, and my shoulder just fits in that long smooch around the wall, so I cannot lose my way.

Why, there's John at the door!

It is no use, young man, you can't open it!

How he does call and pound!

Now he's crying to Jennie for an axe.

It would be a shame to break down that beautiful door!

"John, dear!" said I in the gentlest voice. "The key is down by the front steps, under a plantain leaf!"

That silenced him for a few moments.

Then he said, very quietly indeed, "Open the door, my darling!"

"I can't," said I. "The key is down by the front door under a plantain leaf!" And then I said it again, several times, very gently and slowly, and said it so often that he had to go and see, and he got it of course, and came in. He stopped short by the door.

"What is the matter?" he cried. "For God's sake, what are you doing!"

I kept on creeping just the same, but I looked at him over my shoulder.

"I've got out at last," said I, "in spite of you and Jane. And I've pulled off most of the paper, so you can't put me back!"

Now why should that man have fainted? But he did, and right across my path by the wall, so that I had to creep over him every time!

1892

Why I Wrote "The Yellow Wallpaper"

Many and many a reader has asked that. When the story first came out, in the *New England Magazine* about 1891, a Boston physician made protest in *The Transcript.* Such a story ought not to be written, he said; it was enough to drive anyone mad to read it.

Another physician, in Kansas I think, wrote to say that it was the best description of incipient insanity he had ever seen, and—begging my pardon—had I been there?

Now the story of the story is this:

For many years I suffered from a severe and continuous nervous breakdown tending to melancholia—and beyond. During about the third year of this trouble I went, in devout faith and some faint stir of hope, to a noted specialist in nervous diseases, the best known in the country. This wise man put me to bed and applied the rest cure, to which a still good physique responded so promptly that he concluded there was nothing much the matter with me, and sent me home with solemn advice to 'live as domestic a life as far as possible,' to 'have but two hours' intellectual life a day,' and 'never to touch pen, brush or pencil again, as long as I lived.' This was in 1887.

I went home and obeyed those directions for some three months, and came so near the border line of utter mental ruin that I could see over.

Then, using the remnants of intelligence that remained, and helped by a wise friend, I cast the noted specialist's advice to the winds and went to work again—work, the normal life of every human being; work, in which is joy and growth and service, without which one is a pauper and a parasite; ultimately recovering some measure of power.

Being naturally moved to rejoicing by this narrow escape, I wrote *The Yellow Wallpaper,* with its embellishments and additions to carry out the ideal (I never had hallucinations or objections to my mural decorations) and sent a copy to the physician who so nearly drove me mad. He never acknowledged it.

The little book is valued by alienists and as a good specimen of one kind of literature. It has to my knowledge saved one woman from a similar fate—so terrifying her family that they let her out into normal activity and she recovered.

But the best result is this. Many years later I was told that the great specialist had admitted to friends of his that he had altered his treatment of neurasthenia since reading *The Yellow Wallpaper.*

It was not intended to drive people crazy, but to save people from being driven crazy, and it worked.

Charlotte Perkins Gilman, Forerunner, 4 (October 1913), 271.

RELATED VOICES

Deciding to Publish "The Yellow Wallpaper"

It wanted at least two generations to freeze our young blood with Mrs. Perkins Gilman's story of *The Yellow Wallpaper,* which Horace Scudder (then of *The Atlantic* said in refusing it that it was so terribly good that it ought never to be printed. But terrible and too wholly dire as it was, I could not rest until I had corrupted the editor of *The New England Magazine* into publishing it. Now that I have got it into my collection here, I shiver over it as much as I did when I first read the manuscript . . .

William Dean Howells, "A Reminiscent Introduction,"
The Great Modern American Stories (1921).

Note: Horace Scudder's original remarks to Howells at the time he turned down the story for *The Atlantic Monthly:* "I could not forgive myself if I made others as miserable as I have made myself!"

Edith Wharton
1862–1937

There are many reasons why Mrs. Teddy Wharton (born Edith Newbold Jones) might not have become what she did, an important figure in American literature, a formidably acute recorder of social mores both here and abroad, and a sharp-minded organizer of both her own complex professional career and of relief agencies to aid refugees during the First World War. Edith Wharton was born into "old money"—that stratum of New York society that could take education, cultural refinement, and deference to class for granted. She never experienced the economic deprivations that drove, for example, Theodore Dreiser and Hamlin Garland on an upward scramble, nor did she know the uncertainties of the literary world that prompted William Dean Howells and Stephen Crane to run fast and far. As a woman of wealth and position, she could have remained throughout her lifetime essentially like many of the fictional characters in her stories and novels, characters who exist trivially in terms of glittering social events that mask their discontent and unsatisfied lives. This is not what happened, however. Slowly at first, but then with increasing momentum, Edith Wharton began to write about her life, not merely to acquiesce to its deadlier rhythms.

Edith Jones grew up in New York City, with interludes spent traveling abroad. Educated by a succession of governesses, she attained an early fluency in both foreign languages and the European outlook. This training was considered appropriate to a young woman in a patrician social circle that defined itself in terms of England and the Continent—not with any Whitmanesque democracy that lay somewhere vaguely west and north of Manhattan's chic avenues. She "came out" into society at eighteen according to the rigid rituals of her class—the class she later analyzed as rigorously as an anthropologist might the courtship habits of Fiji islanders. In the same year she also brought out some poems in the *Atlantic Monthly*. Printed anonymously, her poems signified little more than the fact that yet another young lady of good breeding believed she had something to say.

At twenty-three Edith Jones became the wife of Edward Wharton, a man of impeccable Boston ancestors. They settled into a childless, busy life. Edith Wharton threw her energies into being a society matron in New York, Newport, and Paris, and later at a large house she had built in the Massachusetts Berkshires. Marriage with Teddy (as this amiable but increasingly unstable man was known to his friends) lasted for twenty-eight generally unhappy years; it ended at last with a divorce in 1913 after his mental condition deteriorated into insanity. The decision to leave her husband pained Edith Wharton greatly. Their divorce was concluded in the courts after she proved him guilty of adultery. Everything in her nature that clung to tradition recoiled at this morally objectionable step, which she regarded as an act against "family."

She had made other, even more momentous choices than divorce prior to 1913. If the outward shows of Wharton's life continued to present her as a woman of leisure with the public style of a perennial hostess, she had long since begun to turn her private hours over to writing. Her first collection of short stories appeared in 1899 under the apt title *The Great Inclination;* it was a success that both amazed her and freed her to throw herself with even greater resolve into learning her craft. The novel *The Valley of Decision* followed in 1902, and another collection, *The Descent of Man,* in 1904. Her reputation was assured with *The House of Mirth* in 1905. From then on, Mrs. Teddy Wharton the society lady had a formidable competitor—Edith Wharton the acclaimed writer.

Wharton took up permanent residence in France in 1907. Personal and professional needs made her crave a more cosmopolitan setting than the United States could give her. Her writings poured forth, including three more collections of short stories, the last of which showed her skill at tales of the supernatural: *The Hermit and the Wild Woman and Other Stories* (1908), *Xingu and Other Stories* (1916), and *Tales of Men and Ghosts* (1910). The content of her work was by no means made up of the details of cosmopolitan society. The harshly bitter lives endured in the villages and farm areas of New England caught her attention and resulted in two powerful novels, *Ethan Frome* (1911) and *Summer* (1917). *The Custom of the Country* (1913) and *The Age of Innocence* (1920) returned Wharton to the city and to scenes of elegant society, her skill for satire still intact. Her targets continued to be both the "old society" and the "new society." The former was in the grip of outmoded values that gave idealistic young men and women little chance to survive under the new conditions. The latter was controlled by parvenues whose combative, often morally shabby actions undercut family, continuity, professional probity, and personal loyalties.

When World War I began, Wharton assumed the causes of France and Belgium as her own. She emerged from the war invigorated by the successes she had had organizing war relief programs for refugees as well as compiling several books of propaganda for the Allies.

By her midfifties Wharton had returned to her career as a literary figure. *The Age of Innocence* won her the Pulitzer Prize in 1920. *The Writing of Fiction* (1925) presented her views of her craft, and the autobiographical *A Backward Glance* (1934) revealed as much of her self as she chose. Kept out of her memoirs were mention of the difficult times she had spent as her mother's slighted child, the unhappiness of her marriage, and the brief but passionate affair she had had with an old friend, Morton Fullerton. Admitted were anecdotes of her friendships with Henry James, Sinclair Lewis, and Jean Cocteau.

Edith Wharton died in France, a member of a distinguished expatriate generation. The generation that came after—peopled by Hemingway, Stein, Dos Passos, and Fitzgerald—was also, in its own way, rebellious against convention and analytical about the mores of a newly evolving society. The life and writings of Edith Wharton might seem too special and too protected to this new throng in Paris, but she first explored some of the same literary territory settled by these later writers.

There are a number of points at which Edith Wharton's novels and stories align with those of her contemporaries. Living socially above the rank and file of Americans did not mean that Wharton existed beyond the absorptions and anxieties expressed by others. The extent to which human behavior is shaped by forces of environment and breeding is a major motif in Wharton's narratives, just as it was in those of Mark Twain, Frank Norris, and Theodore Dreiser. The manners that distinguish one group from another in a supposedly classless America called upon her powers as a social analyst, just as attention to manners absorbed Henry James and William Dean Howells in their fiction. Wharton paid the cost for sitting in judgment of her own country, just as did Henry James and Henry Adams. The annals of small-town life and the tragedies that come from the narrowing of individual aspirations are recorded in Wharton's *Ethan Frome* and *Summer,* as they were in the fiction of Sarah Orne Jewett and Mary Wilkins Freeman. A woman's experience of personal displacement and her longings to break free are presented as clearly in Wharton's stories as in those by Kate Chopin. The sharp-tongued critique of people who act like asses and rascals is as apparent in Wharton's satires as in Mark Twain's. In addition, both Wharton and Twain wrote, on occasion, reminiscences of the past that reveal their wistfulness over the loss of old values and simpler times.

Whatever the similarities between the well-bred lady from New York, Newport, and Paris and her literary contemporaries, Edith Wharton was her own woman. She frequently expressed her annoyance over being described as the too slavish pupil of Henry James. James was a friend and confidant, but she made it plain that she was not dependent on his example as a writer. Wharton's lucidity of style, her treatment of the inner life, and her eye and ear for cultural nuances are identifiably her own. She had served an arduous apprenticeship to her craft and to her life, and her strengths and weaknesses as a writer are to be credited to her alone. Now, with ever increasing interest, recent criticism is establishing Edith Wharton's place in American literary history. She is winning attention not only as a writer but also as a woman who wrote effectively about the toll taken on women in turn-of-the-century society and on the men who shared in their common fate.

Further Reading:

B. Nevius, *Edith Wharton: A Study of Her Fiction,* 1953.
I. Home, ed., *Edith Wharton: A Collection of Critical Essays,* 1962.
M. Bell, *Edith Wharton and Henry James,* 1965.
G. Kellogg, *The Two Lives of Edith Wharton: The Woman and Her Work,* 1965.
R. W. B. Lewis, *Edith Wharton,* 1975.
C. Wolff, *A Feast of Words: The Triumph of Edith Wharton,* 1977.
E. Ammons, *Edith Wharton's Argument with America,* 1980.
J. Fryer, *Felicitous Space,* 1986.
R. Lewis and N. Lewis, *Letters of Edith Wharton,* 1988.

A. Kaplan, *The Social Construction of American Realism,* 1988.
M. Papke, *Verging on the Abyss: Social Fiction of Chopin and Wharton,* 1990.
S. Goodman, *Edith Wharton's Women: Friends and Rivals,* 1990.
J. Goodwyn, *Wharton: Traveller in the Land of Letters,* 1990.
E. Showalter, *Sister's Choice,* 1991.
S. Benstock, *No Gifts From Chance: A Biography,* 1994.
E. E. Fracasso, *Edith Wharton's Prisoners of Consciousness,* 1994.
M. Bell, ed., *The Cambridge Companion to Edith Wharton,* 1995.

Texts:
"The Other Two" from *The Collected Stories of Edith Wharton,* 2 vols., 1968.

The Other Two

I

Waythorn, on the drawing-room hearth, waited for his wife to come down to dinner.

It was their first night under his own roof, and he was surprised at his thrill of boyish agitation. He was not so old, to be sure—his glass gave him little more than the five-

and-thirty years to which his wife confessed—but he had fancied himself already in the temperate zone; yet here he was listening for her step with a tender sense of all it symbolised, with some old trail of verse about the garlanded nuptial door-posts floating through his enjoyment of the pleasant room and the good dinner just beyond it.

They had been hastily recalled from their honeymoon by the illness of Lily Haskett, the child of Mrs. Waythorn's first marriage. The little girl, at Waythorn's desire, had been transferred to his house on the day of her mother's wedding, and the doctor, on their arrival, broke the news that she was ill with typhoid, but declared that all the symptoms were favourable. Lily could show twelve years of unblemished health, and the case promised to be a light one. The nurse spoke as reassuringly, and after a moment of alarm Mrs. Waythorn had adjusted herself to the situation. She was very fond of Lily—her affection for the child had perhaps been her decisive charm in Waythorn's eyes—but she had the perfectly balanced nerves which her little girl had inherited, and no woman ever wasted less tissue in unproductive worry. Waythorn was therefore quite prepared to see her come in presently, a little late because of a last look at Lily, but as serene and well-appointed as if her good-night kiss had been laid on the brow of health. Her composure was restful to him; it acted as ballast to his somewhat unstable sensibilities. As he pictured her bending over the child's bed he thought how soothing her presence must be in illness: her very step would prognosticate recovery.

His own life had been a gray one, from temperament rather than circumstance, and he had been drawn to her by the unperturbed gaiety which kept her fresh and elastic at an age when most women's activities are growing either slack or febril. He knew what was said about her; for, popular as she was, there had always been a faint undercurrent of detraction. When she had appeared in New York, nine or ten years earlier, as the pretty Mrs. Haskett whom Gus Varick had unearthed somewhere—was it in Pittsburg or Utica?—society, while promptly accepting her, had reserved the right to cast a doubt on its own indiscrimination. Enquiry, however, established her undoubted connection with a socially reigning family, and explained her recent divorce as the natural result of a runaway match at seventeen; and as nothing was known of Mr. Haskett it was easy to believe the worst of him.

Alice Haskett's remarriage with Gus Varick was a passport to the set whose recognition she coveted, and for a few years the Varicks were the most popular couple in town. Unfortunately the alliance was brief and stormy, and this time the husband had his champions. Still, even Varick's stanchest supporters admitted that he was not meant for matrimony, and Mrs. Varick's grievances were of a nature to bear the inspection of the New York courts. A New York divorce is in itself a diploma of virtue, and in the semi-widowhood of this second separation Mrs. Varick took on an air of sanctity, and was allowed to confide her wrongs to some of the most scrupulous ears in town. But when it was known that she was to marry Waythorn there was a momentary reaction. Her best friends would have preferred to see her remain in the role of the injured wife, which was as becoming to her as crape to a rosy complexion. True, a decent time had elapsed, and it was not even suggested that Waythorn had supplanted his predecessor. People shook their heads over him, however, and one grudging friend, to whom he affirmed that he took the step with his eyes open, replied oracularly: "Yes—and with your ears shut."

Waythorn could afford to smile at these innuendoes. In the Wall Street phrase, he had "discounted" them. He knew that society has not yet adapted itself to the consequences of divorce, and that till the adaptation takes place every woman who uses the freedom the law accords her must be her own social justification. Waythorn had an amused confidence in his wife's ability to justify herself. His expectations were fulfilled, and before the wedding took place Alice Varick's group had rallied openly to her support. She took it all imperturbably: she had a way of surmounting obstacles without seeming to be aware of them, and Waythorn looked back with wonder at the trivialities over which he had worn his nerves thin. He had the sense of having found refuge in a richer, warmer nature than his own, and his satisfaction, at the moment, was humourously summed up in the thought that his wife, when she had done all she could for Lily, would not be ashamed to come down and enjoy a good dinner.

The anticipation of such enjoyment was not, however, the sentiment expressed by Mrs. Waythorn's charming face when she presently joined him. Though she had put on her most engaging teagown she had neglected to assume the smile that went with it, and Waythorn thought he had never seen her look so nearly worried.

"What is it?" he asked. "Is anything wrong with Lily?"

"No; I've just been in and she's still sleeping." Mrs. Waythorn hesitated. "But something tiresome has happened."

He had taken her two hands, and now perceived that he was crushing a paper between them.

"This letter?"

"Yes—Mr. Haskett has written—I mean his lawyer has written."

Waythorn felt himself flush uncomfortably. He dropped his wife's hands.

"What about?"

"About seeing Lily. You know the courts—"

"Yes, yes," he interrupted nervously.

Nothing was known about Haskett in New York. He was vaguely supposed to have remained in the outer darkness from which his wife had been rescued, and Waythorn was one of the few who were aware that he had given up his business in Utica and followed her to New York in order to be near his little girl. In the days of his wooing, Waythorn had often met Lily on the doorstep, rosy and smiling, on her way "to see papa."

"I am so sorry," Mrs. Waythorn murmured.

He roused himself. "What does he want?"

"He wants to see her. You know she goes to him once a week."

"Well—he doesn't expect her to go to him now, does he?"

"No—he has heard of her illness; but he expects to come here."

"*Here?*"

Mrs. Waythorn reddened under his gaze. They looked away from each other.

"I'm afraid he has the right. . . . You'll see. . . ." She made a proffer of the letter.

Waythorn moved away with a gesture of refusal. He stood staring about the softly lighted room, which a moment before had seemed so full of bridal intimacy.

"I'm so sorry," she repeated. "If Lily could have been moved—"

"That's out of the question," he returned impatiently.

"I suppose so."

Her lip was beginning to tremble, and he felt himself a brute.

"He must come, of course," he said. "What is—his day?"

"I'm afraid—to-morrow."

"Very well. Send a note in the morning."

The butler entered to announce dinner.

Waythorn turned to his wife. "Come—you must be tired. It's beastly, but try to forget about it," he said, drawing her hand through his arm.

"You're so good, dear. I'll try," she whispered back.

Her face cleared at once, and as she looked at him across the flowers, between the rosy candle-shades, he saw her lips waver back into a smile.

"How pretty everything is!" she sighed luxuriously.

He turned to the butler. "The champagne at once, please. Mrs. Waythorn is tired."

In a moment or two their eyes met above the sparkling glasses. Her own were quite clear and untroubled: he saw that she had obeyed his injunction and forgotten.

II

Waythorn, the next morning, went down town earlier than usual. Haskett was not likely to come till the afternoon, but the instinct of flight drove him forth. He meant to stay away all day—he had thoughts of dining at his club. As his door closed behind him he reflected that before he opened it again it would have admitted another man who had as much right to enter it as himself, and the thought filled him with a physical repugnance.

He caught the "elevated"[1] at the employés' hour, and found himself crushed between two layers of pendulous humanity. At Eighth Street the man facing him wriggled out, and another took his place. Waythorn glanced up and saw that it was Gus Varick. The men were so close together that it was impossible to ignore the smile of recognition on Varick's handsome overblown face. And after all—why not? They had always been on good terms, and Varick had been divorced before Waythorn's attentions to his wife began. The two exchanged a word on the perennial grievance of the trains, and when a seat at their side was miraculously left empty the instinct of self-preservation made Waythorn slip into it after Varick.

The latter drew the stout man's breath of relief. "Lord—I was beginning to feel like a pressed flower." He leaned back, looking unconcernedly at Waythorn. "Sorry to hear that Sellers is knocked out again."

"Sellers?" echoed Waythorn, starting at his partner's name.

Varick looked surprised. "You didn't know he was laid up with the gout?"

"No. I've been away—I only got back last night," Waythorn felt himself reddening in anticipation of the other's smile.

"Ah—yes; to be sure. And Sellers's attack came on two days ago. I'm afraid he's pretty bad. Very awkward for me, as it happens, because he was just putting through a rather important thing for me."

"Ah?" Waythorn wondered vaguely since when Varick had been dealing in "important things." Hitherto he had dabbled only in the shallow pools of speculation, with which Waythorn's office did not usually concern itself.

It occurred to him that Varick might be talking at random, to relieve the strain of their propinquity. That strain was becoming momentarily more apparent to Waythorn, and when, at Cortlandt Street, he caught sight of an acquaintance and had a sudden vision of the picture he and Varick must present to an initiated eye, he jumped up with a muttered excuse.

"I hope you'll find Sellers better," said Varick civilly, and he stammered back: "If I can be of any use to you—" and let the departing crowd sweep him to the platform.

[1] Elevated railway.

At his office he heard that Sellers was in fact ill with the gout, and would probably not be able to leave the house for some weeks.

"I'm sorry it should have happened so, Mr. Waythorn," the senior clerk said with affable significance. "Mr. Sellers was very much upset at the idea of giving you such a lot of extra work just now."

"Oh, that's no matter," said Waythorn hastily. He secretly welcomed the pressure of additional business, and was glad to think that, when the day's work was over, he would have to call at his partner's on the way home.

He was late for luncheon, and turned in at the nearest restaurant instead of going to his club. The place was full, and the waiter hurried him to the back of the room to capture the only vacant table. In the cloud of cigar-smoke Waythorn did not at once distinguish his neighbours: but presently, looking about him, he saw Varick seated a few feet off. This time, luckily, they were too far apart for conversation, and Varick, who faced another way, had probably not even seen him; but there was an irony in their renewed nearness.

Varick was said to be fond of good living, and as Waythorn sat despatching his hurried luncheon he looked across half enviously at the other's leisurely degustation of his meal. When Waythorn first saw him he had been helping himself with critical deliberation to a bit of Camembert at the ideal point of liquefaction, and now, the cheese removed, he was just pouring his *café double*[2] from its little two-storied earthen pot. He poured slowly, his ruddy profile bent above the task, and one beringed white hand steadying the lid of the coffee-pot; then he stretched his other hand to the decanter of cognac at his elbow, filled a liqueur-glass, took a tentative sip, and poured the brandy into his coffee-cup.

Waythorn watched him in a kind of fascination. What was he thinking of—only of the flavour of the coffee and the liqueur? Had the morning's meeting left no more trace in his thoughts than on his face? Had his wife so completely passed out of his life that even this odd encounter with her present husband, within a week after her remarriage, was no more than an incident in his day? And as Waythorn mused, another idea struck him: had Haskett ever met Varick as Varick and he had just met? The recollection of Haskett perturbed him, and he rose and left the restaurant, taking a circuitous way out to escape the placid irony of Varick's nod.

It was after seven when Waythorn reached home. He thought the footman who opened the door looked at him oddly.

"How is Miss Lily?" he asked in haste.

"Doing very well, sir. A gentleman—"

"Tell Barlow to put off dinner for half an hour," Waythorn cut him off, hurrying upstairs.

He went straight to his room and dressed without seeing his wife. When he reached the drawing-room she was there, fresh and radiant. Lily's day had been good; the doctor was not coming back that evening.

At dinner Waythorn told her of Sellers's illness and of the resulting complications. She listened sympathetically, adjuring him not to let himself be overworked, and asking vague feminine questions about the routine of the office. Then she gave him the chronicle of Lily's day; quoted the nurse and doctor, and told him who had called to inquire.

[2] Strong coffee.

He had never seen her more serene and unruffled. It struck him, with a curious pang, that she was very happy in being with him, so happy that she found a childish pleasure in rehearsing the trivial incidents of her day.

After dinner they went to the library, and the servant put the coffee and liqueurs on a low table before her and left the room. She looked singularly soft and girlish in her rosy pale dress, against the dark leather of one of his bachelor armchairs. A day earlier the contrast would have charmed him.

He turned away now, choosing a cigar with affected deliberation.

"Did Haskett come?" he asked, with his back to her.

"Oh, yes—he came."

"You didn't see him, of course?"

She hesitated a moment. "I let the nurse see him."

That was all. There was nothing more to ask. He swung round toward her, applying a match to his cigar. Well, the thing was over for a week, at any rate. He would try not to think of it. She looked up at him, a trifle rosier than usual, with a smile in her eyes.

"Ready for your coffee, dear?"

He leaned against the mantelpiece, watching her as she lifted the coffee-pot. The lamplight struck a gleam from her bracelets and tipped her soft hair with brightness. How light and slender she was, and how each gesture flowed into the next! She seemed a creature all compact of harmonies. As the thought of Haskett receded, Waythorn felt himself yielding again to the joy of possessorship. They were his, those white hands with their flitting motions, his the light haze of hair, the lips and eyes. . . .

She set down the coffee-pot, and reached for the decanter of cognac, measured off a liqueur-glass and poured it into his cup.

Waythorn uttered a sudden exclamation.

"What is the matter?" she said, startled.

"Nothing; only—I don't take cognac in my coffee."

"Oh, how stupid of me," she cried.

Their eyes met, and she blushed a sudden agonised red.

III

Ten days later, Mr. Sellers, still house-bound, asked Waythorn to call on his way down town.

The senior partner, with his swaddled foot propped up by the fire, greeted his associate with an air of embarrassment.

"I'm sorry, my dear fellow; I've got to ask you to do an awkward thing for me."

Waythorn waited, and the other went on, after a pause apparently given to the arrangement of his phrases: "The fact is, when I was knocked out I had just gone into a rather complicated piece of business for—Gus Varick."

"Well?" said Waythorn, with an attempt to put him at his ease.

"Well—it's this way: Varick came to me the day before my attack. He had evidently had an inside tip from somebody, and had made about a hundred thousand. He came to me for advice, and I suggested his going in with Vanderlyn."

"Oh, the deuce!" Waythorn exclaimed. He saw in a flash what had happened. The investment was an alluring one, but required negotiation. He listened quietly while

Sellers put the case before him, and, the statement ended, he said: "You think I ought to see Varick?"

"I'm afraid I can't as yet. The doctor is obdurate. And this thing can't wait. I hate to ask you, but no one else in the office knows the ins and outs of it."

Waythorn stood silent. He did not care a farthing for the success of Varick's venture, but the honour of the office was to be considered, and he could hardly refuse to oblige his partner.

"Very well," he said, "I'll do it."

That afternoon, apprised by telephone, Varick called at the office. Waythorn, waiting in his private room, wondered what the others thought of it. The newspapers, at the time of Mrs. Waythorn's marriage, had acquainted their readers with every detail of her previous matrimonial ventures, and Waythorn could fancy the clerks smiling behind Varick's back as he was ushered in.

Varick bore himself admirably. He was easy without being undignified, and Waythorn was conscious of cutting a much less impressive figure. Varick had no experience of business, and the talk prolonged itself for nearly an hour while Waythorn set forth with scrupulous precision the details of the proposed transaction.

"I'm awfully obliged to you," Varick said as he rose. "The fact is I'm not used to having much money to look after, and I don't want to make an ass of myself—" He smiled, and Waythorn could not help noticing that there was something pleasant about his smile. "It feels uncommonly queer to have enough cash to pay one's bills. I'd have sold my soul for it a few years ago!"

Waythorn winced at the illusion. He had heard it rumoured that a lack of funds had been one of the determining causes of the Varick separation, but it did not occur to him that Varick's words were intentional. It seemed more likely that the desire to keep clear of embarrassing topics had fatally drawn him into one. Waythorn did not wish to be outdone in civility.

"We'll do the best we can for you," he said. "I think this is a good thing you're in."

"Oh, I'm sure it's immense. It's awfully good of you—" Varick broke off, embarrassed. "I suppose the thing's settled now—but if—"

"If anything happens before Sellers is about, I'll see you again," said Waythorn quietly. He was glad, in the end, to appear the more self-possessed of the two.

The course of Lily's illness ran smooth, and as the days passed Waythorn grew used to the idea of Haskett's weekly visit. The first time the day came round, he stayed out late, and questioned his wife as to the visit on his return. She replied at once that Haskett had merely seen the nurse downstairs, as the doctor did not wish any one in the child's sick-room till after the crisis.

The following week Waythorn was again conscious of the recurrence of the day, but had forgotten it by the time he came home to dinner. The crisis of the disease came a few days later, with a rapid decline of fever, and the little girl was pronounced out of danger. In the rejoicing which ensued the thought of Haskett passed out of Waythorn's mind, and one afternoon, letting himself into the house with a latch-key, he went straight to his library without noticing a shabby hat and umbrella in the hall.

In the library he found a small effaced-looking man with a thinnish gray beard sitting on the edge of a chair. The stranger might have been a piano-tuner, or one of those mysteriously efficient persons who are summoned in emergencies to adjust some detail of the domestic machinery. He blinked at Waythorn through a pair of gold-rimmed spectacles and said mildly: "Mr. Waythorn, I presume? I am Lily's father."

Waythorn flushed. "Oh—" he stammered uncomfortably. He broke off, disliking to appear rude. Inwardly he was trying to adjust the actual Haskett to the image of him projected by his wife's reminiscences. Waythorn had been allowed to infer that Alice's first husband was a brute.

"I am sorry to intrude," said Haskett, with his over-the-counter politeness.

"Don't mention it," returned Waythorn, collecting himself. "I suppose the nurse has been told?"

"I presume so. I can wait," said Haskett. He had a resigned way of speaking, as though life had worn down his natural powers of resistance.

Waythorn stood on the threshold, nervously pulling off his gloves.

"I'm sorry you've been detained. I will send for the nurse," he said; and as he opened the door he added with an effort: "I'm glad we can give you a good report of Lily." He winced as the *we* slipped out, but Haskett seemed not to notice it.

"Thank you, Mr. Waythorn. It's been an anxious time for me."

"Ah, well, that's past. Soon she'll be able to go to you." Waythorn nodded and passed out. In his own room he flung himself down with a groan. He hated the woman-ish sensibility which made him suffer so acutely from the grotesque chances of life. He had known when he married that his wife's former husbands were both living, and that amid the multiplied contacts of modern existence there were a thousand chances to one that he would run against one or the other, yet he found himself as much disturbed by his brief encounter with Haskett as though the law had not obligingly removed all diffi-culties in the way of their meeting.

Waythorn sprang up and began to pace the room nervously. He had not suffered half as much from his two meetings with Varick. It was Haskett's presence in his own house that made the situation so intolerable. He stood still, hearing steps in the passage.

"This way, please," he heard the nurse say. Haskett was being taken upstairs, then: not a corner of the house but was open to him. Waythorn dropped into another chair, staring vaguely ahead of him. On his dressing-table stood a photograph of Alice, taken when he had first known her. She was Alice Varick then—how fine and exquisite he had thought her! Those were Varick's pearls about her neck. At Waythorn's insistence they had been returned before her marriage. Had Haskett ever given her any trinkets—and what had become of them, Waythorn wondered? He realised suddenly that he knew very little of Haskett's past or present situation; but from the man's appearance and manner of speech he could reconstruct with curious precision the surroundings of Alice's first marriage. And it startled him to think that she had, in the background of her life, a phase of existence so different from anything with which he had connected her. Varick, whatever his faults, was a gentleman, in the conventional, traditional sense of the term: the sense which at that moment seemed, oddly enough, to have most meaning to Waythorn. He and Varick had the same social habits, spoke the same lan-guage, understood the same allusions. But this other man . . . it was grotesquely upper-most in Waythorn's mind that Haskett had worn a made-up tie attached with an elastic. Why should that ridiculous detail symbolise the whole man? Waythorn was exasperated by his own paltriness, but the fact of the tie expanded, forced itself on him, became as it were the key to Alice's past. He could see her, as Mrs. Haskett, sitting in a "front parlour" furnished in plush, with a pianola,[3] and a copy of "Ben Hur"[4] on the centre-table. He could see her going to the theatre with Haskett—or perhaps even to a "Church Sociable"—she in a "picture hat" and Haskett in a black frock-coat, a little creased, with the made-up tie on an elastic. On the way home they would stop and look at the illuminated shop-windows, lingering over the photographs of New York actresses. On Sunday afternoons Haskett would take her for a walk, pushing Lily ahead of them in a white enamelled perambulator, and Waythorn had a vision of the people they would stop and talk to. He could fancy how pretty Alice must have looked, in a dress adroitly constructed from the hints of a New York fashion-paper, and how she must have looked down on the other women, chafing at her life, and secretly feeling that she belonged in a bigger place.

For the moment his foremost thought was one of wonder at the way in which she had shed the phase of existence which her marriage with Haskett implied. It was as if her whole aspect, every gesture, every inflection, every allusion, were a studied negation of that period of her life. If she had denied being married to Haskett she could hardly have stood more convicted of duplicity than in this obliteration of the self which had been his wife.

Waythorn started up, checking himself in the analysis of her motives. What right had he to create a fantastic effigy of her and then pass judgment on it? She had spoken vaguely of her first marriage as unhappy, had hinted, with becoming reticence, that Haskett had wrought havoc among her young illusions. . . . It was a pity for Waythorn's peace of mind that Haskett's very inoffensiveness shed a new light on the nature of those illusions. A man would rather think that his wife has been brutalised by her first husband than that the process has been reversed.

IV

"Mr. Waythorn, I don't like that French governess of Lily's."

Haskett, subdued and apologetic, stood before Waythorn in the library, revolving his shabby hat in his hand.

Waythorn, surprised in his armchair over the evening paper, stared back perplexedly at his visitor.

"You'll excuse my asking to see you," Haskett continued. "But this is my last visit, and I thought if I could have a word with you it would be a better way than writing to Mrs. Waythorn's lawyer."

Waythorn rose uneasily. He did not like the French governess either; but that was irrelevant.

"I am not so sure of that," he returned stiffly; "but since you wish it I will give your message to—my wife." He always hesitated over the possessive pronoun in addressing Haskett.

The latter sighed. "I don't know as that will help much. She didn't like it when I spoke to her."

Waythorn turned red. "When did you see her?" he asked.

---

[3] An automatic piano player.
[4] Best-selling novel (1880) by General Lew

Wallace (1827–1905). Like the pianola, suggestive of lower-middle-class tastes.

"Not since the first day I came to see Lily—right after she was taken sick. I remarked to her then that I didn't like the governess."

Waythorn made no answer. He remembered distinctly that, after that first visit, he had asked his wife if she had seen Haskett. She had lied to him then, but she had respected his wishes since; and the incident cast a curious light on her character. He was sure she would not have seen Haskett that first day if she had divined that Waythorn would object, and the fact that she did not divine it was almost as disagreeable to the latter as the discovery that she had lied to him.

"I don't like the woman," Haskett was repeating with mild persistency. "She ain't straight, Mr. Waythorn—she'll teach the child to be underhand. I've noticed a change in Lily—she's too anxious to please—and she don't always tell the truth. She used to be the straightest child, Mr. Waythorn—" He broke off, his voice a little thick. "Not but what I want her to have a stylish education," he ended.

Waythorn was touched. "I'm sorry, Mr. Haskett; but frankly, I don't quite see what I can do."

Haskett hesitated. Then he laid his hat on the table, and advanced to the hearth-rug, on which Waythorn was standing. There was nothing aggressive in his manner, but he had the solemnity of a timid man resolved on a decisive measure.

"There's just one thing you can do, Mr. Waythorn," he said. "You can remind Mrs. Waythorn that, by the decree of the courts, I am entitled to have a voice in Lily's bringing up." He paused, and went on more deprecatingly: "I'm not the kind to talk about enforcing my rights, Mr. Waythorn. I don't know as I think a man is entitled to rights he hasn't known how to hold on to; but this business of the child is different. I've never let go there—and I never mean to."

The scene left Waythorn deeply shaken. Shamefacedly, in indirect ways, he had been finding out about Haskett; and all that he had learned was favourable. The little man, in order to be near his daughter, had sold out his share in a profitable business in Utica, and accepted a modest clerkship in a New York manufacturing house. He boarded in a shabby street and had few acquaintances. His passion for Lily filled his life. Waythorn felt that this exploration of Haskett was like groping about with a dark-lantern in his wife's past; but he saw now that there were recesses his lantern had not explored. He had never enquired into the exact circumstances of his wife's first matrimonial rupture. On the surface all had been fair. It was she who had obtained the divorce, and the court had given her the child. But Waythorn knew how many ambiguities such a verdict might cover. The mere fact that Haskett retained a right over his daughter implied an unsuspected compromise. Waythorn was an idealist. He always refused to recognise unpleasant contingencies till he found himself confronted with them, and then he saw them followed by a special train of consequences. His next days were thus haunted, and he determined to try to lay the ghosts by conjuring them up in his wife's presence.

When he repeated Haskett's request a flame of anger passed over her face; but she subdued it instantly and spoke with a slight quiver of outraged motherhood.

"It is very ungentlemanly of him," she said.

The word grated on Waythorn. "That is neither here nor there. It's a bare question of rights."

She murmured: "It is not as if he could ever be a help to Lily—"

Waythorn flushed. This was even less to his taste. "The question is," he repeated, "what authority has he over her?"

She looked downward, twisting herself a little in her seat. "I am willing to see him—I thought you objected," she faltered.

In a flash he understood that she knew the extent of Haskett's claims. Perhaps it was not the first time she had resisted them.

"My objecting has nothing to do with it," he said coldly; "if Haskett has a right to be consulted you must consult him."

She burst into tears, and he saw that she expected him to regard her as a victim.

Haskett did not abuse his rights. Waythorn had felt miserably sure that he would not. But the governess was dismissed, and from time to time the little man demanded an interview with Alice. After the first outburst she accepted the situation with her usual adaptability. Haskett had once reminded Waythorn of the piano-tuner, and Mrs. Waythorn, after a month or two, appeared to class him with that domestic familiar. Waythorn could not but respect the father's tenacity. At first he had tried to cultivate the suspicion that Haskett might be "up to" something, that he had an object in securing a foothold in the house. But in his heart Waythorn was sure of Haskett's single-mindedness; he even guessed in the latter a mild contempt for such advantages as his relation with the Waythorns might offer. Haskett's sincerity of purpose made him invulnerable, and his successor had to accept him as a lien on the property.

Mr. Sellers was sent to Europe to recover from his gout, and Varick's affairs hung on Waythorn's hands. The negotiations were prolonged and complicated; they necessitated frequent conferences between the two men, and the interests of the firm forbade Waythorn's suggesting that his client should transfer his business to another office.

Varick appeared well in the transaction. In moments of relaxation his coarse streak appeared, and Waythorn dreaded his geniality; but in the office he was concise and clear-headed, with a flattering deference to Waythorn's judgment. Their business relations being so affably established, it would have been absurd for the two men to ignore each other in society. The first time they met in a drawing-room, Varick took up their intercourse in the same easy key, and his hostess's grateful glance obliged Waythorn to respond to it. After that they ran across each other frequently, and one evening at a ball Waythorn, wandering through the remoter rooms, came upon Varick seated beside his wife. She coloured a little, and faltered in what she was saying; but Varick nodded to Waythorn without rising, and the latter strolled on.

In the carriage, on the way home, he broke out nervously: "I didn't know you spoke to Varick."

Her voice trembled a little. "It's the first time—he happened to be standing near me; I didn't know what to do. It's so awkward, meeting everywhere—and he said you had been very kind about some business."

"That's different," said Waythorn.

She paused a moment. "I'll do just as you wish," she returned pliantly. "I thought it would be less awkward to speak to him when we meet."

Her pliancy was beginning to sicken him. Had she really no will of her own—no theory about her relation to these men? She had accepted Haskett—did she mean to accept Varick? It was "less awkward," as she had said, and her instinct was to evade difficulties or to circumvent them. With sudden vividness Waythorn saw how the instinct had developed. She was "as easy as an old shoe"—a shoe that too many feet had worn. Her elasticity was the result of tension in too many different directions. Alice Haskett—Alice Varick—Alice Waythorn—she had been each in turn, and had left hanging to each name a little of her privacy, a little of her personality, a little of the inmost self where the unknown god abides.

"Yes—it's better to speak to Varick," said Waythorn wearily.

V

The winter wore on, and society took advantage of the Waythorns' acceptance of Varick. Harassed hostesses were grateful to them for bridging over a social difficulty, and Mrs. Waythorn was held up as a miracle of good taste. Some experimental spirits could not resist the diversion of throwing Varick and his former wife together, and there were those who thought he found a zest in the propinquity. But Mrs. Waythorn's conduct remained irreproachable. She neither avoided Varick nor sought him out. Even Waythorn could not but admit that she had discovered the solution of the newest social problem.

He had married her without giving much thought to that problem. He had fancied that a woman can shed her past like a man. But now he saw that Alice was bound to hers both by the circumstances which forced her into continued relation with it, and by the traces it had left on her nature. With grim irony Waythorn compared himself to a member of a syndicate. He held so many shares in his wife's personality and his predecessors were his partners in the business. If there had been any element of passion in the transaction he would have felt less deteriorated by it. The fact that Alice took her change of husbands like a change of weather reduced the situation to mediocrity. He could have forgiven her for blunders, for excesses; for resisting Haskett, for yielding to Varick; for anything but her acquiescence and her tact. She reminded him of a juggler tossing knives; but the knives were blunt and he knew they would never cut her.

And then, gradually, habit formed a protecting surface for his sensibilities. If he paid for each day's comfort with the small change of his illusions, he grew daily to value the comfort more and set less store upon the coin. He had drifted into a dulling propinquity with Haskett and Varick and he took refuge in the cheap revenge of satirising the situation. He even began to reckon up the advantages which accrued from it, to ask himself if it were not better to own a third of a wife who knew how to make a man happy than a whole one who had lacked opportunity to acquire the art. For it *was* an art, and made up, like all others, of concessions, eliminations and embellishments; of lights judiciously thrown and shadows skilfully softened. His wife knew exactly how to manage the lights, and he knew exactly to what training she owed her skill. He even tried to trace the source of his obligations, to discriminate between the influences which had combined to produce his domestic happiness: he perceived that Haskett's commonness had made Alice worship good breeding, while Varick's liberal construction of the marriage bond had taught her to value the conjugal virtues; so that he was directly indebted to his predecessors for the devotion which made his life easy if not inspiring.

From this phase he passed into that of complete acceptance. He ceased to satirise himself because time dulled the irony of the situation and the joke lost its humour with its sting. Even the sight of Haskett's hat on the hall table had ceased to touch the springs of epigram. The hat was often seen there now, for it had been decided that it was better for Lily's father to visit her than for the little girl to go to his boarding-house. Waythorn, having acquiesced in this arrangement, had been surprised to find how little difference it made. Haskett was never obtrusive, and the few visitors who met him on the stairs were unaware of his identity. Waythorn did not know how often he saw Alice, but with himself Haskett was seldom in contact.

One afternoon, however, he learned on entering that Lily's father was waiting to see him. In the library he found Haskett occupying a chair in his usual provisional way. Waythorn always felt grateful to him for not leaning back.

"I hope you'll excuse me, Mr. Waythorn," he said rising. "I wanted to see Mrs. Waythorn about Lily, and your man asked me to wait here till she came in."

"Of course," said Waythorn, remembering that a sudden leak had that morning given over the drawing-room to the plumbers.

He opened his cigar-case and held it out to his visitor, and Haskett's acceptance seemed to mark a fresh stage in their intercourse. The spring evening was chilly, and Waythorn invited his guest to draw up his chair to the fire. He meant to find an excuse to leave Haskett in a moment; but he was tired and cold, and after all the little man no longer jarred on him.

The two were enclosed in the intimacy of their blended cigar-smoke when the door opened and Varick walked into the room. Waythorn rose abruptly. It was the first time that Varick had come to the house, and the surprise of seeing him, combined with the singular inopportuneness of his arrival, gave a new edge to Waythorn's blunted sensibilities. He stared at his visitor without speaking.

Varick seemed too preoccupied to notice his host's embarrassment.

"My dear fellow," he exclaimed in his most expansive tone, "I must apologise for tumbling in on you in this way, but I was too late to catch you down town, and so I thought—"

He stopped short, catching sight of Haskett, and his sanguine colour deepened to a flush which spread vividly under his scant blond hair. But in a moment he recovered himself and nodded slightly. Haskett returned the bow in silence, and Waythorn was still groping for speech when the footman came in carrying a tea-table.

The intrusion offered a welcome vent to Waythorn's nerves. "What the deuce are you bringing this here for?" he said sharply.

"I beg your pardon, sir, but the plumbers are still in the drawing-room, and Mrs. Waythorn said she would have tea in the library." The footman's perfectly respectful tone implied a reflection on Waythorn's reasonableness.

"Oh, very well," said the latter resignedly, and the footman proceeded to open the folding tea-table and set out its complicated appointments. While this interminable process continued the three men stood motionless, watching it with a fascinated stare, till Waythorn, to break the silence, said to Varick: "Won't you have a cigar?"

He held out the case he had just tendered to Haskett, and Varick helped himself with a smile. Waythorn looked about for a match, and finding none, proffered a light from his own cigar. Haskett, in the background, held his ground mildly, examining his cigar-tip now and then, and stepping forward at the right moment to knock its ashes into the fire.

The footman at last withdrew, and Varick immediately began: "If I could just say half a word to you about this business—"

"Certainly," stammered Waythorn; "in the dining-room—"

But as he placed his hand on the door it opened from without, and his wife appeared on the threshold.

She came in fresh and smiling, in her street dress and hat, shedding a fragrance from the boa[5] which she loosened in advancing.

"Shall we have tea in here, dear?" she began; and then she caught sight of Varick. Her smile deepened, veiling a slight tremor of surprise.

"Why, how do you do?" she said with a distinct note of pleasure.

As she shook hands with Varick she saw Haskett standing behind him. Her smile faded for a moment, but she recalled it quickly, with a scarcely perceptible side-glance at Waythorn.

"How do you do, Mr. Haskett?" she said, and shook hands with him a shade less cordially.

The three men stood awkwardly before her, till Varick, always the most self-possessed, dashed into an explanatory phrase.

"We—I had to see Waythorn a moment on business," he stammered, brick-red from chin to nape.

Haskett stepped forward with his air of mild obstinacy. "I am sorry to intrude; but you appointed five o'clock—" he directed his resigned glance to the timepiece on the mantel.

She swept aside their embarrassment with a charming gesture of hospitality.

"I'm so sorry—I'm always late; but the afternoon was so lovely." She stood drawing off her gloves, propitiatory and graceful, diffusing about her a sense of ease and familiarity in which the situation lost its grotesqueness. "But before talking business," she added brightly, "I'm sure every one wants a cup of tea."

She dropped into her low chair by the tea-table, and the two visitors, as if drawn by her smile, advanced to receive the cups she held out.

She glanced about for Waythorn, and he took the third cup with a laugh.

1904

Booker T. Washington
1856–1915

There has been a dramatic shift in Booker T. Washington's reputation since the turn of the century. His celebration as the almost mythic "Moses of his race" before World War I and his dismissal by African American militants during the civil rights struggles of the 1960s as an Uncle Tom reveal the changing nature of African American activism in America. Washington's contributions and his failings are being reassessed, but regardless of controversy about the man himself, his life and writings can hardly be dismissed. His

---

[5] Long scarf of fur or feathers worn around a
woman's neck or shoulders.

autobiography alone confirms this. First published serially in the magazine *Outlook*, edited by the white liberal Lyman Abbott, Washington's *Up from Slavery* appeared in book form in 1901. Washington's life story caught the imagination of a large American audience. Whites in particular saw Washington as representing the "best" kind of black and the "right" kind of success. The period between the close of the Civil War and World War I has been called "the era of Booker T. Washington." In 1902, W. E. B. Du Bois, one of Washington's severest critics, could freely admit that Washington was "the one recognized spokesman of his ten million fellows and one of the most notable figures in a nation of seventy millions." What is currently in question is Washington's role in African American history, not in whites' versions of that history.

Booker T. Washington was the son of an unidentified white slaveowner and a slave woman, born on an unknown date sometime in 1856 in Hale's Ford, Virginia. He did not even acquire a last name until he started school and took his stepfather's first name as his surname. After the end of the Civil War, he moved with his mother and stepfather to Malden, West Virginia, where he grew up poor. Consumed by the desire to get an education, he made the five-hundred-mile trek by foot and rail to Virginia's Hampton Institute, a school set up for the education of impoverished African Americans. This incident forms one of the most vivid chapters in his tale of self-willed success. Out of his early experiences, Washington became a committed advocate of self-discipline and self-help (the very virtues that, in Benjamin Franklin's work ethic, could enable any poor boy to realize "the American dream").

Determined to succeed, Washington moved in 1881 to the Tuskegee Institute in Alabama, a manual arts school established after the Civil War to train African Americans. He became the head of the institute, an effective fund-raiser, and promoter of its work in the Deep South, where lynchings and racial injustice were still common practice, despite the attempt of many whites to better the lot of the former slaves. In 1895 Washington earned national attention with his speech known as "The Atlanta Compromise." In this address he urged a moderate policy of reconciliation between aspiring African Americans and nervous whites. Let African Americans be given every means to improve their condition economically by learning useful trades, Washington urged, and they would be content to overlook the white community's failure to provide fundamental political rights. A practical man, Washington advocated a plan of compromise and trade-offs to secure his people the best chance to survive under difficult economic conditions. The assurance of jobs and living wages came first; social equality would come later. He knew the facts of power in a nation where animosity toward all minority groups was on the rise in the 1890s and where an essentially mercantile society responded to the appeal of money and management principles better than it did to suggestions that the moral fabric of the nation was being destroyed by inequality. Guest at a dinner given by President Theodore Roosevelt (not without riling many), recipient of an honorary degree from Harvard, praised by African Americans and whites alike, Washington shrewdly did what he could to make African Americans' lives more bearable.

When Washington is taken on his own terms, his autobiographical account of how clever, energetic boys go upward and onward in the face of practical contingencies has an undeniable impact on the imagination. He knew his times and used them well. He provided a model for African American aspiration by his habit of seizing from history the essential economic principles that led to material advancement while glossing over whatever might threaten the achievement of social and political equality.

Further Reading:

H. Hawkins, ed., *Booker T. Washington and His Critics, Black Leadership in Crisis*, 1962.

A. Meier, *Negro Thought in America, 1880–1915: Racial Ideologies in the Age of Booker T. Washington*, 1963.

R. Brisbane, *The Black Vanguard*, 1970.

A. Bontemps, *Young Booker: Booker T. Washington's Early Days*, 1972.

L. Harlan, *Booker T. Washington: The Making of a Black Leader, 1856–1901*, 1972.

L. Harlan, *Booker T. Washington: The Wizard of Tuskegee, 1901–1915*, 1983.

R. M. Franklin, *Liberating Visions*, 1990.

L. Patterson, *B. T. Washington*, 1991.

J. Neyland, *B. T. Washington*, 1992.

A. Schroeder, *B. T. Washington*, 1992.

V. L. Denton, *B. T. Washington and The Adult Education Movement*, 1993.

Text:
Up from Slavery, 1901.

Up from Slavery

Chapter III: The Struggle for an Education

One day, while at work in the coal-mine, I happened to overhear two miners talking about a great school for coloured people somewhere in Virginia. This was the first time that I had ever heard anything about any kind of school or college that was more pretentious than the little coloured school in our town.

In the darkness of the mine I noiselessly crept as close as I could to the two men who were talking. I heard one tell the other that not only was the school established for the members of my race, but that opportunities were provided by which poor but worthy students could work out all or a part of the cost of board, and at the same time be taught some trade or industry.

As they went on describing the school, it seemed to me that it must be the greatest place on earth, and not even Heaven presented more attractions for me at that time than did the Hampton Normal and Agricultural Institute in Virginia, about which these men were talking. I resolved at once to go to that school, although I had no idea where it was, or how many miles away, or how I was going to reach it; I remembered only that I was on fire constantly with one ambition, and that was to go to Hampton. This thought was with me day and night.

After hearing of the Hampton Institute, I continued to work for a few months longer in the coal-mine. While at work there, I heard of a vacant position in the household of General Lewis Ruffner, the owner of the salt-furnace and coal-mine. Mrs. Viola Ruffner, the wife of General Ruffner, was a "Yankee" woman from Vermont. Mrs. Ruffner had a reputation all through the vicinity for being very strict with her servants, and especially with the boys who tried to serve her. Few of them had remained with her more than two or three weeks. They all left with the same excuse: she was too strict. I decided, however, that I would rather try Mrs. Ruffner's house than remain in the coal-mine, and so my mother applied to her for the vacant position. I was hired at a salary of $5 per month.

I had heard so much about Mrs. Ruffner's severity that I was almost afraid to see her, and trembled when I went into her presence. I had not lived with her many weeks, however, before I began to understand her. I soon began to learn that, first of all, she wanted everything kept clean about her, that she wanted things done promptly and systematically, and that at the bottom of everything she wanted absolute honesty and frankness. Nothing must be sloven or slipshod; every door, every fence, must be kept in repair.

I cannot now recall how long I lived with Mrs. Ruffner before going to Hampton, but I think it must have been a year and a half. At any rate, I here repeat what I have said more than once before, that the lessons that I learned in the home of Mrs. Ruffner were as valuable to me as any education I have ever gotten anywhere since. Even to this day I never see bits of paper scattered around a house or in the street that I do not want to pick them up at once. I never see a filthy yard that I do not want to clean it, a paling off of a fence that I do not want to put it on, an unpainted or unwhitewashed house that I do not want to paint or whitewash it, or a button off one's clothes, or a grease-spot on them or on a floor, that I do not want to call attention to it.

From fearing Mrs. Ruffner I soon learned to look upon her as one of my best friends. When she found that she could trust me she did so implicitly. During the one or two winters that I was with her she gave me an opportunity to go to school for an hour in the day during a portion of the winter months, but most of my studying was done at night, sometimes alone, sometimes under some one whom I could hire to teach me. Mrs. Ruffner always encouraged and sympathized with me in all my efforts to get an education. It was while living with her that I began to get together my first library. I secured a dry-goods box, knocked out one side of it, put some shelves in it, and began putting into it every kind of book that I could get my hands upon, and called it my "library."

Notwithstanding my success at Mrs. Ruffner's I did not give up the idea of going to the Hampton Institute. In the fall of 1872 I determined to make an effort to get there, although, as I have stated, I had no definite idea of the direction in which Hampton was, or of what it would cost to go there. I do not think that any one thoroughly sympathized with me in my ambition to go to Hampton unless it was my mother, and she was troubled with a grave fear that I was starting out on a "wild-goose chase." At any rate, I got only a half-hearted consent from her that I might start. The small amount of money that I had earned had been consumed by my stepfather and the remainder of the family, with the exception of a very few dollars, and so I had very little with which to buy clothes and pay my travelling expenses. My brother John helped me all that he could, but of course that was not a great deal, for his work was in the coal-mine, where he did not earn much, and most of what he did earn went in the direction of paying the household expenses.

Perhaps the thing that touched and pleased me most in connection with my starting for Hampton was the interest that many of the older coloured people took in the matter. They had spent the best days of their lives in slavery, and hardly expected to live to see the time when they would see a member of their race leave home to attend a boarding-school. Some of these older people would give me a nickel, others a quarter, or a handkerchief.

Finally the great day came, and I started for Hampton. I had only a small, cheap satchel that contained what few articles of clothing I could get. My mother at the time was rather weak and broken in health. I hardly expected to see her again, and thus our parting was all the more sad. She, however, was very brave through it all. At that time there were no through trains connecting that part of West Virginia with eastern Virginia. Trains ran only a portion of the way, and the remainder of the distance was travelled by stage-coaches.

The distance from Malden to Hampton is about five hundred miles. I had not been away from home many hours before it began to grow painfully evident that I did not have enough money to pay my fare to Hampton. One experience I shall long remember. I had been travelling over the mountains most of the afternoon in an old-fashioned stage-coach, when, late in the evening, the coach stopped for the night at a common, unpainted house called a hotel. All the other passengers except myself were whites. In my ignorance I supposed that the little hotel existed for the purpose of accommodating the passengers who travelled on the stage-coach. The difference that the colour of one's skin would make I had not thought anything about. After all the other passengers had been shown rooms and were getting ready for supper, I shyly presented myself before the man at the desk. It is true I had practically no money in my pocket with which to pay for bed or food, but I had hoped in some way to beg my way into the good graces of the landlord, for at that season in the mountains of Virginia the weather was cold, and I wanted to get indoors for the night. Without asking as to whether I had any money, the man at the desk firmly refused to even consider the matter of providing me with food or lodging. This was my first experience in finding out what the colour of my skin meant. In some way I managed to keep warm by walking about, and so got through the night. My whole soul was so bent upon reaching Hampton that I did not have time to cherish any bitterness toward the hotel-keeper.

By walking, begging rides both in wagons and in the cars, in some way, after a number of days, I reached the city of Richmond, Virginia, about eighty-two miles from Hampton. When I reached there, tired, hungry, and dirty, it was late in the night. I had never been in a large city, and this rather added to my misery. When I reached Richmond, I was completely out of money. I had not a single acquaintance in the place, and, being unused to city ways, I did not know where to go. I applied at several places for lodging, but they all wanted money, and that was what I did not have. Knowing nothing else better to do, I walked the streets. In doing this I passed by many foodstands where fried chicken and half-moon apple pies were piled high and made to present a most tempting appearance. At that time it seemed to me that I would have promised all that I expected to possess in the future to have gotten hold of one of those chicken legs or one of those pies. But I could not get either of these, nor anything else to eat.

I must have walked the streets till after midnight. At last I became so exhausted that I could walk no longer. I was tired, I was hungry, I was everything but discouraged. Just about the time when I reached extreme physical exhaustion, I came upon a portion of a street where the board sidewalk was considerably elevated. I waited for a few minutes, till I was sure that no passers-by could see me, and then crept under the sidewalk and lay for the night upon the ground, with my satchel of clothing for a pillow. Nearly all night I could hear the tramp of feet over my head. The next morning I found myself somewhat refreshed but I was extremely hungry, because it had been a long time since I had had sufficient food. As soon as it became light enough for me to see my surroundings I noticed that I was near a large ship, and that this ship seemed to be unloading a cargo of pig iron. I went at once to the vessel and asked the captain to permit me to help unload the vessel in order to get money for food. The captain, a white man, who seemed to be kind-hearted, consented. I worked long enough to earn money for my breakfast, and it seems to me, as I remember it now, to have been about the best breakfast that I have ever eaten.

My work pleased the captain so well that he told me if I desired I could continue working for a small amount per day. This I was very glad to do. I continued working on this vessel for a number of days. After buying food with the small wages I received there was not much left to add to the amount I must get to pay my way to Hampton. In order to economize in every way possible, so as to be sure to reach Hampton in a reasonable time, I continued to sleep under the same sidewalk that gave me shelter the first night I was in Richmond. Many years after that the coloured citizens of Richmond very kindly tendered me a reception at which there must have been two thousand people present. This reception was held not far from the spot where I slept the first night I spent in that city, and I must confess that my mind was more upon the sidewalk that first gave me shelter than upon the reception, agreeable and cordial as it was.

When I had saved what I considered enough money with which to reach Hampton, I thanked the captain of the vessel for his kindness, and started again. Without any unusual occurrence I reached Hampton, with a surplus of exactly fifty cents with which to begin my education. To me it had been a long, eventful journey; but the first sight of the large, three-story, brick school building seemed to have rewarded me for all that I had undergone in order to reach the place. If the people who gave the money to provide that building could appreciate the influence the sight of it had upon me, as well as upon thousands of other youths, they would feel all the more encouraged to make such gifts. It seemed to me to be the largest and most beautiful building I had ever seen. The sight of it seemed to give me new life. I felt that a new kind of existence had now begun—that life would now have a new meaning. I felt that I had reached the promised land, and I resolved to let no obstacle prevent me from putting forth the highest effort to fit myself to accomplish the most good in the world.

As soon as possible after reaching the grounds of the Hampton Institute, I presented myself before the head teacher for assignment to a class. Having been so long without proper food, a bath and change of clothing, I did not, of course, make a very favourable impression upon her, and I could see at once that there were doubts in her mind about the wisdom of admitting me as a student. I felt that I could hardly blame her if she got the idea that I was a worthless loafer or tramp. For some time she did not refuse to admit me, neither did she decide in my favour, and I continued to linger about her, and to impress her in all the ways I could with my worthiness. In the meantime I saw her admitting other students, and that added greatly to my discomfort, for I felt, deep down in my heart, that I could do as well as they, if I could only get a chance to show what was in me.

After some hours had passed, the head teacher said to me: "The adjoining recitation-room needs sweeping. Take the broom and sweep it."

It occurred to me at once that here was my chance. Never did I receive an order with more delight. I knew that I could sweep, for Mrs. Ruffner had thoroughly taught me how to do that when I lived with her.

I swept the recitation-room three times. Then I got a dusting-cloth and I dusted it four times. All the woodwork around the walls, every bench, table, and desk, I went over four times with my dusting-cloth. Besides, every piece of furniture had been moved and every closet and corner in the room had been thoroughly cleaned. I had the feeling that in a large measure my future depended upon the impression I made upon the teacher in the cleaning of that room. When I was through, I reported to the head teacher. She was a "Yankee" woman who knew just where to look for dirt. She went into the room and inspected the floor and closets; then she took her handkerchief and rubbed it on the woodwork about the walls, and over the table and benches. When she was unable to find one bit of dirt on the floor, or a particle of dust on any of the furniture, she quietly remarked, "I guess you will do to enter this institution."

I was one of the happiest souls on earth. The sweeping of that room was my college examination, and never did any youth pass an examination for entrance into Harvard or Yale that gave him more genuine satisfaction. I have passed several examinations since then, but I have always felt that this was the best one I ever passed.

I have spoken of my own experience in entering the Hampton Institute. Perhaps few, if any, had anything like the same experience that I had, but about that same period there were hundreds who found their way to Hampton and other institutions after experiencing something of the same difficulties that I went through. The young men and women were determined to secure an education at any cost.

The sweeping of the recitation-room in the manner that I did it seems to have paved the way for me to get through Hampton. Miss Mary F. Mackie, the head teacher, offered me a position as janitor. This, of course, I gladly accepted, because it was a place where I could work out nearly all the cost of my board. The work was hard and taxing, but I stuck to it. I had a large number of rooms to care for, and had to work late into the night, while at the same time I had to rise by four o'clock in the morning, in order to build the fires and have a little time in which to prepare my lessons. In all my career at Hampton, and ever since I have been out in the world, Miss Mary F. Mackie, the head teacher to whom I have referred, proved one of my strongest and most helpful friends. Her advice and encouragement were always helpful and strengthening to me in the darkest hour.

I have spoken of the impression that was made upon me by the buildings and general appearance of the Hampton Institute, but I have not spoken of that which made the greatest and most lasting impression upon me, and that was a great man—the noblest, rarest human being that it has ever been my privilege to meet. I refer to the late General Samuel C. Armstrong.

It has been my fortune to meet personally many of what are called great characters, both in Europe and America, but I do not hesitate to say that I never met any man who, in my estimation, was the equal of General Armstrong. Fresh from the degrading influences of the slave plantation and the coal-mines, it was a rare privilege for me to be permitted to come into direct contact with such a character as General Armstrong. I shall always remember that the first time I went into his presence he made the impression upon me of being a perfect man: I was made to feel that there was something about him that was superhuman. It was my privilege to know the General personally from the time I entered Hampton till he died, and the more I saw of him the greater he grew in my estimation. One might have removed from Hampton all the buildings, class-rooms, teachers, and industries, and given the men and women there the opportunity of coming into daily contact with General Armstrong, and that alone would have been a liberal education. The older I grow, the more I am convinced that there is no education which one can get from books and costly apparatus that is equal to that which can be gotten from contact with great men and women. Instead of studying books so constantly, how I wish that our schools and colleges might learn to study men and things!

General Armstrong spent two of the last six months of his life in my home at Tuskegee. At that time he was paralyzed to the extent that he had lost control of his body and voice in a very large degree. Notwithstanding his affliction, he worked almost constantly night and day for the cause to which he had given his life. I never saw a man who so completely lost sight of himself. I do not believe he ever had a selfish thought. He was just as happy in trying to assist some other institution in the South as he was when working for Hampton. Although he fought the Southern white man in the Civil War, I never heard him utter a bitter word against him afterward. On the other hand, he was constantly seeking to find ways by which he could be of service to the Southern whites.

It would be difficult to describe the hold that he had upon the students at Hampton, or the faith they had in him. In fact, he was worshipped by his students. It never occurred to me that General Armstrong could fail in anything that he undertook. There is almost no request that he could have made that would not have been complied with. When he was a guest at my home in Alabama, and was so badly paralyzed that he had to be wheeled about in an invalid's chair, I recall that one of the General's former students had occasion to push his chair up a long, steep hill that taxed his strength to the utmost. When the top of the hill was reached, the former pupil, with a glow of happiness on his face, exclaimed, "I am so glad that I have been permitted to do something that was real hard for the General before he dies!" While I was a student at Hampton, the dormitories became so crowded that it was impossible to find room for all who wanted to be admitted. In order to help remedy the difficulty the General conceived the plan of putting up tents to be used as rooms. As soon as it became known that General Armstrong would be pleased if some of the older students would live in the tents during the winter, nearly every student in school volunteered to go.

I was one of the volunteers. The winter that we spent in those tents was an intensely cold one, and we suffered severely—how much I am sure General Armstrong never knew, because we made no complaints. It was enough for us to know that we were pleasing General Armstrong, and that we were making it possible for an additional number of students to secure an education. More than once, during a cold night, when a stiff gale would be blowing, our tent was lifted bodily, and we would find ourselves in the open air. The General would usually pay a visit to the tents early in the morning, and his earnest, cheerful, encouraging voice would dispel any feeling of despondency.

I have spoken of my admiration for General Armstrong, and yet he was but a type of that Christlike body of men and women who went into the Negro schools at the close of the war by the hundreds to assist in lifting up my race. The history of the world fails to show a higher, purer, and more unselfish class of men and women than those who found their way into those Negro schools.

Life at Hampton was a constant revelation to me; was constantly taking me into a new world. The matter of having meals at regular hours, of eating on a tablecloth, using a napkin, the use of the bath-tub and of the tooth-brush, as well as the use of sheets upon the bed, were all new to me.

I sometimes feel that almost the most valuable lesson I got at the Hampton Institute was in the use and value of the bath. I learned there for the first time some of its value, not only in keeping the body healthy, but in inspiring self-respect and promoting virtue. In all my travels in the South and elsewhere since leaving Hampton I have always in some way sought my daily bath. To get it sometimes when I have been the guest of my own people in a single-roomed cabin has not always been easy to do, except by slipping away to some stream in the woods. I have always tried to teach my people that some provision for bathing should be a part of every house.

For some time, while a student at Hampton, I possessed but a single pair of socks, but when I had worn these till they became soiled, I would wash them at night and hang them by the fire to dry, so that I might wear them again the next morning.

The charge for my board at Hampton was ten dollars per month. I was expected to pay a part of this in cash and to work out the remainder. To meet this cash payment, as I have stated, I had just fifty cents when I reached the institution. Aside from a very few dollars that my brother John was able to send me once in a while, I had no money with which to pay my board. I was determined from the first to make my work as janitor so valuable that my services would be indispensable. This I succeeded in doing to such an extent that I was soon informed that I would be allowed the full cost of my board in return for my work. The cost of tuition was seventy dollars a year. This, of course, was wholly beyond my ability to provide. If I had been compelled to pay the seventy dollars for tuition, in addition to providing for my board, I would have been compelled to leave the Hampton school. General Armstrong, however, very kindly got Mr. S. Griffitts Morgan, of New Bedford, Mass., to defray the cost of my tuition during the whole time that I was at Hampton. After I finished the course at Hampton and had entered upon my lifework at Tuskegee, I had the pleasure of visiting Mr. Morgan several times.

After having been for a while at Hampton, I found myself in difficulty because I did not have books and clothing. Usually, however, I got around the trouble about books by borrowing from those who were more fortunate than myself. As to clothes, when I reached Hampton I had practically nothing. Everything that I possessed was in a small hand satchel. My anxiety about clothing was increased because of the fact that General Armstrong made a personal inspection of the young men in ranks, to see that their clothes were clean. Shoes had to be polished, there must be no buttons off the clothing, and no grease-spots. To wear one suit of clothes continually, while at work and in the schoolroom, and at the same time keep it clean, was rather a hard problem for me to solve. In some way I managed to get on till the teachers learned that I was in earnest and meant to succeed, and then some of them were kind enough to see that I was partly supplied with second-hand clothing that had been sent in barrels from the North. These barrels proved a blessing to hundreds of poor but deserving students. Without them I question whether I should ever have gotten through Hampton.

When I first went to Hampton I do not recall that I had ever slept in a bed that had two sheets on it. In those days there were not many buildings there, and room was very precious. There were seven other boys in the same room with me; most of them, however, students who had been there for some time. The sheets were quite a puzzle to me. The first night I slept under both of them, and the second night I slept on top of both of them; but by watching the other boys I learned my lesson in this, and have been trying to follow it ever since and to teach it to others.

I was among the youngest of the students who were in Hampton at that time. Most of the students were men and women—some as old as forty years of age. As I now recall the scene of my first year, I do not believe that one often has the opportunity of coming into contact with three or four hundred men and women who were so tremendously in earnest as these men and women were. Every hour was occupied in study or work. Nearly all had had enough actual contact with the world to teach them the need of education. Many of the older ones were, of course, too old to master the text-books very thoroughly, and it was often sad to watch their struggles; but they made up in earnestness much of what they lacked in books. Many of them were as poor as I was, and, besides having to wrestle with their books, they had to struggle with a poverty which prevented their having the necessities of life. Many of them had aged parents who were dependent upon them, and some of them were men who had wives whose support in some way they had to provide for.

The great and prevailing idea that seemed to take possession of every one was to prepare himself to lift up the people at his home. No one seemed to think of himself. And the officers and teachers, what a rare set of human beings they were! They worked for the students night and day, in season and out of season. They seemed happy only when they were helping the students in some manner. Whenever it is written—and I hope it will be—the part that the Yankee teachers played in the education of the Negroes immediately after the war will make one of the most thrilling parts of the history of this country. The time is not far distant when the whole South will appreciate this service in a way that it has not yet been able to do.

Chapter XIV: The Atlanta Exposition Address[1]

The Atlanta Exposition, at which I had been asked to make an address as a representative of the Negro race, as stated in the last chapter, was opened with a short address from Governor Bullock. After other interesting exercises, including an invocation from Bishop Nelson, of Georgia, a dedicatory ode by Albert Howell, Jr., and addresses by the President of the Exposition and Mrs. Joseph Thompson, the President of the Woman's Board, Governor Bullock introduced me with the words, "We have with us to-day a representative of Negro enterprise and Negro civilization."

When I arose to speak, there was considerable cheering, especially from the coloured people. As I remember it now, the thing that was uppermost in my mind was the desire to say something that would cement the friendship of the races and bring about hearty coöperation between them. So far as my outward surroundings were concerned, the only thing that I recall distinctly now is that when I got up, I saw thousands of eyes looking intently into my face. The following is the address which I delivered:—

MR. PRESIDENT AND GENTLEMEN OF THE BOARD OF DIRECTORS AND CITIZENS.

One-third of the population of the South is of the Negro race. No enterprise seeking the material, civil, or moral welfare of this section can disregard this element of our population and reach the highest success. I but convey to you, Mr. President and Directors, the sentiment of the masses of my race when I say that in no way have the value and manhood of the American Negro been more fittingly and generously recognized than by the managers of this magnificent Exposition at every stage of its progress. It is a recognition that will do more to cement the friendship of the two races than any occurrence since the dawn of our freedom.

---

[1] Delivered on September 18, 1895 before an audience of 2,000 at an exposition held in Atlanta, Georgia. This was the speech which brought Washington into national prominence. Because of the "compromise" he proposed for striking a balance between the aspirations of African Americans and the fears of whites, he became a figure of controversy.

Not only this, but the opportunity here afforded will awaken among us a new era of industrial progress. Ignorant and inexperienced, it is not strange that in the first years of our new life we began at the top instead of at the bottom; that a seat in Congress or the state legislature was more sought than real estate or industrial skill; that the political convention of stump speaking had more attractions than starting a dairy farm or truck garden.

A ship lost at sea for many days suddenly sighted a friendly vessel. From the mast of the unfortunate vessel was seen a signal, "Water, water; we die of thirst!" The answer from the friendly vessel at once came back, "Cast down your bucket where you are." A second time the signal, "Water, water; send us water!" ran up from the distressed vessel, and was answered, "Cast down your bucket where you are." And a third and fourth signal for water was answered, "Cast down your bucket where you are." The captain of the distressed vessel, at last heeding the injunction, cast down his bucket, and it came up full of fresh, sparkling water from the mouth of the Amazon River. To those of my race who depend on bettering their condition in a foreign land or who underestimate the importance of cultivating friendly relations with the Southern white man, who is their next-door neighbour, I would say: "Cast down your bucket where you are"—cast it down in making friends in every manly way of the people of all races by whom we are surrounded.

Cast it down in agriculture, mechanics, in commerce, in domestic service, and in the professions. And in this connection it is well to bear in mind that whatever other sins the South may be called to bear, when it comes to business, pure and simple, it is in the South that the Negro is given a man's chance in the commercial world, and in nothing is this Exposition more eloquent than in emphasizing this chance. Our greatest danger is that in the great leap from slavery to freedom we may overlook the fact that the masses of us are to live by the productions of our hands, and fail to keep in mind that we shall prosper in proportion as we learn to dignify and glorify common labour and put brains and skill into the common occupations of life; shall prosper in proportion as we learn to draw the line between the superficial and the substantial, the ornamental gewgaws of life and the useful. No race can prosper till it learns that there is as much dignity in tilling a field as in writing a poem. It is at the bottom of life we must begin, and not at the top. Nor should we permit our grievances to overshadow our opportunities.

To those of the white race who look to the incoming of those of foreign birth and strange tongue and habits for the prosperity of the South, were I permitted I would repeat what I say to my own race, "Cast down your bucket where you are." Cast it down among the eight millions of Negroes whose habits you know, whose fidelity and love you have tested in days when to have proved treacherous meant the ruin of your firesides. Cast down your bucket among these people who have, without strikes and labour wars, tilled your fields, cleared your forests, builded your railroads and cities, and brought forth treasures from the bowels of the earth, and helped make possible this magnificent representation of the progress of the South. Casting down your bucket among my people, helping and encouraging them as you are doing on these grounds, and to education of head, hand, and heart, you will find that they will buy your surplus land, make blossom the waste places in your fields, and run your factories. While doing this, you can be sure in the future, as in the past, that you and your families will be surrounded by the most patient, faithful, law-abiding, and unresentful people that the world has seen. As we have proved our loyalty to you in the past, in nursing your children, watching by the sick-bed of your mothers and fathers, and often following them with tear-dimmed eyes to their graves, so in the future, in our humble way, we shall stand by you with a devotion that no foreigner can approach, ready to lay down our lives, if need be, in defence of yours, interlacing our industrial, commercial, civil, and religious life with yours in a way that shall make the interests of both races one. In all things that are purely social we can be as separate as the fingers, yet one as the hand in all things essential to mutual progress.

There is no defence or security for any of us except in the highest intelligence and development of all. If anywhere there are efforts tending to curtail the fullest growth of the Negro, let these efforts be turned into stimulating, encouraging, and making him the most useful and intelligent citizen. Effort or means so invested will pay a thousand per cent interest. These efforts will be twice blessed—"blessing him that gives and him that takes."[2]

There is no escape through law of man or God from the inevitable:—

The laws of changeless justice bind
  Oppressor with oppressed;
And close as sin and suffering joined
  We march to fate abreast.[3]

Nearly sixteen millions of hands will aid you in pulling the load upward, or they will pull against you the load downward. We shall constitute one-third and more of the ignorance and crime of the South, or one-third its intelligence and progress; we shall contribute one-third to the business and industrial prosperity of the South, or we shall prove a veritable body of death, stagnating, depressing, retarding every effort to advance the body politic.

Gentlemen of the Exposition, as we present to you our humble effort at an exhibition of our progress, you must not expect overmuch. Starting thirty years ago with ownership here and there in a few quilts and pumpkins and chickens (gathered from miscellaneous sources), remember the path that has led from these to the inventions and production of agricultural implements, buggies, steam-engines, newspapers, books, statuary, carving, paintings, the management of drug-stores and banks, has not been trodden without contact with thorns and thistles. While we take pride in what we exhibit as a result of our independent efforts, we do not for a moment forget that our part in this exhibition would fall far short of your expectations but for the constant help that has come to our educational life, not only from the Southern states, but especially from Northern philanthropists, who have made their gifts a constant stream of blessing and encouragement.

The wisest among my race understand that the agitation of questions of social equality is the extremest folly, and that progress in the enjoyment of all the privileges that will come to us must be the result of severe and constant struggle rather than of artificial forcing. No race that has anything to contribute to the markets of the world is long in any degree ostracized. It is important and right that all privileges of the law be ours, but it is vastly more important that we be prepared for the exercises of these privileges. The opportunity to earn a dollar in a factory just now is worth infinitely more than the opportunity to spend a dollar in an opera-house.

In conclusion, may I repeat that nothing in thirty years has given us more hope and encouragement, and drawn us so near to you of the white race, as this opportunity offered by the Exposition; and here bending, as it were, over the altar that represents the results of the struggles of your race and mine, both starting practically

---

[2] Shakespeare's play *The Merchant of Venice*, Act IV, Sc. i, l. 1670.

[3] "Song of the Negro Boatmen" by John Greenleaf Whittier (1807–1892), New England abolitionist poet.

empty-handed three decades ago, I pledge that in your effort to work out the great and intricate problem which God has laid at the doors of the South, you shall have at all times the patient, sympathetic help of my race; only let this be constantly in mind, that, while from representations in these buildings of the product of field, of forest, of mine, of factory, letters, and art, much good will come, yet far above and be-yond material benefits will be that higher good, that, let us pray God, will come, in a blotting out of sectional differences and racial animosities and suspicions, in a determination to administer absolute justice, in a willing obed-ience among all classes to the mandates of law. This, this coupled with our material prosperity, will bring into our beloved South a new heaven and a new earth.

The first thing that I remember, after I had finished speaking, was that Governor Bullock rushed across the platform and took me by the hand, and that others did the same. I received so many and such hearty congratulations that I found it difficult to get out of the building. I did not appreciate to any degree, however, the impression which my address seemed to have made, until the next morning, when I went into the business part of the city. As soon as I was recognized, I was surprised to find myself pointed out and surrounded by a crowd of men who wished to shake hands with me. This was kept up on every street on to which I went, to an extent which embarrassed me so much that I went back to my boarding-place. The next morning I returned to Tuskegee. At the station in Atlanta, and at almost all of the stations at which the train stopped between that city and Tuskegee, I found a crowd of people anxious to shake hands with me.

The papers in all parts of the United States published the address in full, and for months afterward there were complimentary editorial references to it. Mr. Clark Howell, the editor of the Atlanta *Constitution,* telegraphed to a New York paper, among other words, the following, "I do not exaggerate when I say that Professor Booker T. Washington's address yesterday was one of the most notable speeches, both as to character and as to the warmth of its reception, ever delivered to a Southern audience. The address was a revelation. The whole speech is a platform upon which blacks and whites can stand with full justice to each other."

The Boston *Transcript* said editorially: "The speech of Booker T. Washington at the Atlanta Exposition, this week, seems to have dwarfed all the other proceedings and the Exposition itself. The sensation that it has caused in the press has never been equalled."

I very soon began receiving all kinds of propositions from lecture bureaus, and editors of magazines and papers, to take the lecture platform, and to write articles. One lecture bureau offered me fifty thousand dollars, or two hundred dollars a night and expenses, if I would place my services at its disposal for a given period. To all these communications I replied that my life-work was at Tuskegee; and that whenever I spoke it must be in the interests of the Tuskegee school and my race, and that I would enter into no arrangements that seemed to place a mere commercial value upon my services.

Some days after its delivery I sent a copy of my address to the President of the United States, the Hon. Grover Cleveland.[4] I received from him the following autograph reply:—

---

4 At this time Grover Cleveland (1837–1908) was serving his second term as president (1893–1897); he had formerly served between 1885 and 1889.

GRAY GABLES, BUZZARD'S BAY, MASS.,
October 6, 1895.

BOOKER T. WASHINGTON, ESQ.:

MY DEAR SIR: I thank you for sending me a copy of your address delivered at the Atlanta Exposition.

I thank you with much enthusiasm for making the address. I have read it with intense interest, and I think the Exposition would be fully justified if it did not do more than furnish the opportunity for its delivery. Your words cannot fail to delight and encourage all who wish well for your race; and if our coloured fellow-citizens do not from your utterances gather new hope and form new determinations to gain every valuable advantage offered them by their citizenship, it will be strange indeed.

Yours very truly,

GROVER CLEVELAND.

Later I met Mr. Cleveland, for the first time, when, as President, he visited the Atlanta Exposition. At the request of myself and others he consented to spend an hour in the Negro Building, for the purpose of inspecting the Negro exhibit and of giving the coloured people in attendance an opportunity to shake hands with him. As soon as I met Mr. Cleveland I became impressed with his simplicity, greatness, and rugged honesty. I have met him many times since then, both at public functions and at his private residence in Princeton, and the more I see of him the more I admire him. When he visited the Negro Building in Atlanta he seemed to give himself up wholly, for that hour, to the coloured people. He seemed to be as careful to shake hands with some old coloured "auntie" clad partially in rags, and to take as much pleasure in doing so, as if he were greeting some millionnaire. Many of the coloured people took advantage of the occasion to get him to write his name in a book or on a slip of paper. He was as careful and patient in doing this as if he were putting his signature to some great state document.

Mr. Cleveland has not only shown his friendship for me in many personal ways, but has always consented to do anything I have asked of him for our school. This he has done, whether it was to make a personal donation or to use his influence in securing the donations of others. Judging from my personal acquaintance with Mr. Cleveland, I do not believe that he is conscious of possessing any colour prejudice. He is too great for that. In my contact with people I find that, as a rule, it is only the little, narrow people who live for themselves, who never read good books, who do not travel, who never open up their souls in a way to permit them to come into contact with other souls— with the great outside world. No man whose vision is bounded by colour can come into contact with what is highest and best in the world. In meeting men, in many places, I have found that the happiest people are those who do the most for others; the most miserable are those who do the least. I have also found that few things, if any, are capable of making one so blind and narrow as race prejudice. I often say to our students, in the course of my talks to them on Sunday evenings in the chapel, that the longer I live and the more experience I have of the world, the more I am convinced that, after all, the one thing that is most worth living for—and dying for, if need be—is the opportunity of making some one else more happy and more useful.

The coloured people and the coloured newspapers at first seemed to be greatly pleased with the character of my Atlanta address, as well as with its reception. But after the first burst of enthusiasm began to die away, and the coloured people began reading the speech in cold type, some of them seemed to feel that they had been hypnotized.

They seemed to feel that I had been too liberal in my remarks toward the Southern whites, and that I had not spoken out strongly enough for what they termed the "rights" of the race. For a while there was a reaction, so far as a certain element of my own race was concerned, but later these reactionary ones seemed to have been won over to my way of believing and acting.

While speaking of changes in public sentiment, I recall that about ten years after the school at Tuskegee was established, I had an experience that I shall never forget. Dr. Lyman Abbott,[5] then the pastor of Plymouth Church, and also editor of the *Outlook* (then the *Christian Union*), asked me to write a letter for his paper giving my opinion of the exact condition, mental and moral, of the coloured ministers in the South, as based upon my observations. I wrote the letter, giving the exact facts as I conceived them to be. The picture painted was a rather black one—or, since I am black, shall I say "white"? It could not be otherwise with a race but a few years out of slavery, a race which had not had time or opportunity to produce a competent ministry.

What I said soon reached every Negro minister in the country, I think, and the letters of condemnation which I received from them were not few. I think that for a year after the publication of this article every association and every conference or religious body of any kind, of my race, that met, did not fail before adjourning to pass a resolution condemning me, or calling upon me to retract or modify what I had said. Many of these organizations went so far in their resolutions as to advise parents to cease sending their children to Tuskegee. One association even appointed a "missionary" whose duty it was to warn the people against sending their children to Tuskegee. This missionary had a son in the school, and I noticed that, whatever the "missionary" might have said or done with regard to others, he was careful not to take his son away from the institution. Many of the coloured papers, especially those that were the organs of religious bodies, joined in the general chorus of condemnation or demands for retraction.

During the whole time of the excitement, and through all the criticism, I did not utter a word of explanation or retraction. I knew that I was right, and that time and the sober second thought of the people would vindicate me. It was not long before the bishops and other church leaders began to make a careful investigation of the conditions of the ministry, and they found out that I was right. In fact, the oldest and most influential bishop in one branch of the Methodist Church said that my words were far too mild. Very soon public sentiment began making itself felt, in demanding a purifying of the ministry. While this is not yet complete by any means, I think I may say, without egotism, and I have been told by many of our most influential ministers, that my words had much to do with starting a demand for the placing of a higher type of men in the pulpit. I have had the satisfaction of having many who once condemned me thank me heartily for my frank words.

The change of the attitude of the Negro ministry, so far as regards myself, is so complete that at the present time I have no warmer friends among any class than I have among the clergymen. The improvement in the character and life of the Negro ministers is one of the most gratifying evidences of the progress of the race. My experience with them, as well as other events in my life, convince me that the thing to do, when one

5 American clergyman, editor, author, and leader of "liberal" Protestantism (1835–1922).

feels sure that he has said or done the right thing, and is condemned, is to stand still and keep quiet. If he is right, time will show it.

In the midst of the discussion which was going on concerning my Atlanta speech, I received the letter which I give below, from Dr. Gilman, the President of Johns Hopkins University, who had been made chairman of the judges of award in connection with the Atlanta Exposition:—

JOHNS HOPKINS UNIVERSITY, BALTIMORE,
President's Office, September 30, 1895.

DEAR MR. WASHINGTON: Would it be agreeable to you to be one of the Judges of Award in the Department of Education at Atlanta? If so, I shall be glad to place your name upon the list. A line by telegraph will be welcomed.

Yours very truly,
D. C. GILMAN.

I think I was even more surprised to receive this invitation than I had been to receive the invitation to speak at the opening of the Exposition. It was to be a part of my duty, as one of the jurors, to pass not only upon the exhibits of the coloured schools, but also upon those of the white schools. I accepted the position, and spent a month in Atlanta in performance of the duties which it entailed. The board of jurors was a large one, consisting in all of sixty members. It was about equally divided between Southern white people and Northern white people. Among them were college presidents, leading scientists and men of letters, and specialists in many subjects. When the group of jurors to which I was assigned met for organization, Mr. Thomas Nelson Page,[6] who was one of the number, moved that I be made secretary of that division, and the motion was unanimously adopted. Nearly half of our division were Southern people. In performing my duties in the inspection of the exhibits of white schools I was in every case treated with respect, and at the close of our labours I parted from my associates with regret.

I am often asked to express myself more freely than I do upon the political condition and the political future of my race. These recollections of my experience in Atlanta give me the opportunity to do so briefly. My own belief is, although I have never before said so in so many words, that the time will come when the Negro in the South will be accorded all the political rights which his ability, character, and material possessions entitle him to. I think, though, that the opportunity to freely exercise such political rights will not come in any large degree through outside or artificial forcing, but will be accorded to the Negro by the Southern white people themselves, and that they will protect him in the exercise of those rights. Just as soon as the South gets over the old feeling that it is being forced by "foreigners," or "aliens," to do something which it does not want to do, I believe that the change in the direction that I have indicated is going to begin. In fact, there are indications that it is already beginning in a slight degree.

Let me illustrate my meaning. Suppose that some months before the opening of the

---

[6] Southern writer of regional literature and diplomat (1853–1922).

Atlanta Exposition there had been a general demand from the press and public platform outside the South that a Negro be given a place on the opening programme, and that a Negro be placed upon the board of jurors of award. Would any such recognition of the race have taken place? I do not think so. The Atlanta officials went as far as they did because they felt it to be a pleasure, as well as a duty, to reward what they considered merit in the Negro race. Say what we will, there is something in human nature which we cannot blot out, which makes one man, in the end, recognize and reward merit in another, regardless of colour or race.

I believe it is the duty of the Negro—as the greater part of the race is already doing—to deport himself modestly in regard to political claims, depending upon the slow but sure influences that proceed from the possession of property, intelligence, and high character for the full recognition of his political rights. I think that the according of the full exercise of political rights is going to be a matter of natural, slow growth, not an over-night, gourd-vine affair. I do not believe that the Negro should cease voting, for a man cannot learn the exercise of self-government by ceasing to vote any more than a boy can learn to swim by keeping out of the water, but I do believe that in his voting he should more and more be influenced by those of intelligence and character who are his next-door neighbours.

I know coloured men who, through the encouragement, help, and advice of Southern white people, have accumulated thousands of dollars' worth of property, but who, at the same time, would never think of going to those same persons for advice concerning the casting of their ballots. This, it seems to me, is unwise and unreasonable, and should cease. In saying this I do not mean that the Negro should truckle, or not vote from principle, for the instant he ceases to vote from principle he loses the confidence and respect of the Southern white man even.

I do not believe that any state should make a law that permits an ignorant and poverty-stricken white man to vote, and prevents a black man in the same condition from voting. Such a law is not only unjust, but it will react, as all unjust laws do, in time; for the effect of such a law is to encourage the Negro to secure education and property, and at the same time it encourages the white man to remain in ignorance and poverty. I believe that in time, through the operation of intelligence and friendly race relations, all cheating at the ballot box in the South will cease. It will become apparent that the white man who begins by cheating a Negro out of his ballot soon learns to cheat a white man out of his, and that the man who does this ends his career of dishonesty by the theft of property or by some equally serious crime. In my opinion, the time will come when the South will encourage all of its citizens to vote. It will see that it pays better, from every standpoint, to have healthy, vigorous life than to have that political stagnation which always results when one-half of the population has no share and no interest in the Government.

As a rule, I believe in universal, free suffrage, but I believe that in the South we are confronted with peculiar conditions that justify the protection of the ballot in many of the states, for a while at least, either by an educational test, a property test, or by both combined; but whatever tests are required, they should be made to apply with equal and exact justice to both races.

1900

W. E. B. Du Bois
1868–1963

"The Niagara Movement" (the militant declaration of the need for African Americans to demand equal rights) or "The Atlanta Compromise" (the placating request that whites allow African Americans to remain quietly on the underside of American society in exchange for the promise of a moderate livelihood)—these are the two positions taken by the best-known and most articulate African American leaders at the turn of the century, W. E. B. Du Bois and Booker T. Washington. Both men made a major difference in the directions taken in racial matters after the Civil War; but whereas Washington was once the figure favored by the majority of whites and African Americans before World War I, today it is clearly Du Bois who enjoys the greatest approval.

Du Bois did not start out as an activist, nor did he have to struggle to survive, as did Washington, who had been born a slave. Du Bois had the good fortune to grow up under social conditions that allowed him time to reflect on the status of African Americans in post–Civil War America and to develop the ideas that formed his later radicalism. Du Bois was born and raised in Great Barrington, Massachusetts, an amalgam, in his own words, of "a flood of Negro blood, a strain of French, a bit of Dutch, but thank God! no 'Anglo Saxon.' " His childhood was pleasant, if poor, marred only—but influentially—by the shock he had in grade school when he learned he was considered different from his fellow students because of his color.

Du Bois attended Fisk University in Nashville, Tennessee, and then went on to Harvard, where he graduated cum laude in 1890. While at Harvard, he attended classes conducted by the country's major philosophers, William James, George Santayana, and Josiah Royce. However reputable an institution Fisk was, it could not have provided Du Bois the association with prominent educators he gained at Harvard.

Du Bois remained at Harvard for two years of graduate school, then moved on to two more years of study on a fellowship at the University of Berlin. Thereafter, Du Bois interleaved his teaching position at Wilberforce University with the completion of a doctoral dissertation on the slave trade, published in the first volume of the *Harvard Historical Studies* series in 1896. Du Bois also taught at the University of Pennsylvania but moved in 1897 to Atlanta University, an African American institution more receptive to his interest in African American sociology.

During the late 1890s Du Bois was shaken out of his life as a scholar. In a time of violent racism, scarred by 3,500 lynchings between 1885 and 1910, Du Bois became increasingly active, both as a writer and as a political figure, working in concert with the most aggressive of the African American leaders. American society appeared to offer his people only two choices: follow the lead of Booker T. Washington, whose 1895 speech at the Atlanta Exposition counseled the acceptance of the status quo as the price for living in peace, though not with justice, or follow the lead of Du Bois, whose 1903 publication, *The Souls of Black Folk,* challenged Washington's position, advocated political radicalism, and provided an "autobiography" for African Americans to counter Washington's own Horatio Alger–like myth of material success.

From 1910 into the 1930s, Du Bois edited *The Crisis,* the journal of the National Association for the Advancement of Colored People, and crisis was the psychological condition he worked hard to instill in the minds of both African Americans and whites. Having left Atlanta for New York in 1910, he saw that he could address large audiences on an ever broadening series of issues. His subsequent movement toward an "international" solution to the universal problem of race eventually led him into the Communist Party in 1961. He left the United States in 1963 for Ghana, where he applied for citizenship just before he died.

The nature of Du Bois's life's work is represented by certain expressions he reiterated in his writings and speeches: "the veil" (cast by whites, whose sense of revulsion toward "people of color" kept the latter safely "invisible"—the probable source for the title of Ralph Ellison's novel, *Invisible Man*), "the problem" (racism, the great issue the twentieth century has had to face), "the souls" (possessed by a people whose heritage of suffering must not be negated by bribes of semiskilled jobs and subsistence wages), and "crisis" (what the entire world society had to pass through before justice could be brought to everyone). Du Bois learned well the political fact that rhetoric and effective literary style can make the difference when major social changes hang in the balance. Du Bois's cosmopolitan education enabled him to respond in more complex ways to a complex social world than was possible for Booker T. Washington, whose focus remained on the needs of a rural southern past.

Further Reading:

F. Broderick, *W. E. B. Du Bois: A Negro Leader's Time of Crisis,* 1959.

E. Rudwick, *W. E. B. Du Bois: A Study in Minority Group Leadership,* 1968.

C. Contee, *W. E. B. Du Bois and African Naturalism, 1914–45,* 1970.

A. Rampersad, *The Art and Imagination of W. E. B. Du Bois,* 1976.

W. Andrews, *W. E. B. Du Bois,* 1985.

A. Appiah, "The Uncompleted Argument: DuBois and the Illusion of Race," *Critical Inquiry* 12 (1985), 21–37.

M. Marable, "The Black Truth of W. E. B. Du Bois: Sociocultural and Political Dimensions of Black Religion," *Southern Quarterly* 23 (1985), 15–33.

W. Cain, "Du Bois' Autobiography and the Politics of Literature," *Black American Literature Forum* 24 (1990), 266–313.

D. Blight, "Up From 'Twoness': Douglass and the Meaning of Du Bois' Concept of Double Consciousness," *Canadian Review of American Studies* 21 (1990), 301–19.

D. L. Lewis, *W. E. B. Du Bois: Biography of a Race,* 1993.

E. Sundquist, *To Wake the Nations: Race in American Literature and Culture,* 1993.

K. E. Byerman, *Seizing the Word,* 1994.

S. Zamir, *Dark Voices: Du Bois and American Thought,* 1995.

E. J. Sundquist, ed., *The Oxford W. E. B. Du Bois Reader,* 1996.

Text:

From *The Thought and Writings of W. E. B. Du Bois, The Seventh Son,* 2 vols., 1971.

The Souls of Black Folk

from *Chapter 1: This Double-Consciousness*

After the Egyptian and Indian, the Greek and Roman, the Teuton and the Mongolian, the Negro is a sort of seventh son, born with a veil, and gifted with second-sight in this American world—a world which yields him no true self-consciousness, but only lets him see himself through the revelation of the other world. It is a peculiar sensation, this double-consciousness, this sense of always looking at one's self through the eyes of others, of measuring one's soul by the tape of a world that looks on in amused contempt and pity. One ever feels his twoness—an American, a Negro; two souls, two thoughts, two unreconciled strivings; two warring ideals in one dark body, whose dogged strength alone keeps it from being torn asunder.

The history of the American Negro is the history of this strife,—this longing to attain self-conscious manhood, to merge his double self into a better and truer self. In this merging he wishes neither of the older selves to be lost. He would not Africanize America, for America has much to teach the world and Africa. He would not bleach his Negro soul in a flood of white Americanism, for he knows that Negro blood has a message for the world. He simply wishes to make it possible for a man to be both a Negro and an American, without being cursed and spit upon by his fellows, without having the doors of opportunity closed roughly in his face.

Chapter III: Of Mr. Booker T. Washington and Others

From birth till death enslaved; in word, in deed, unmanned!
. . . .
Hereditary bondsmen! Know ye not
Who would be free themselves must strike the blow?[1]

Byron

Easily the most striking thing in the history of the American Negro since 1876[2] is the ascendancy of Mr. Booker T. Washington. It began at the time when war memories and ideals were rapidly passing; a day of astonishing commercial development was dawning; a sense of doubt and hesitation overtook the freedmen's sons,—then it was that his leading began. Mr. Washington came, with a single definite programme, at the psychological moment when the nation was a little ashamed of having bestowed so much sentiment on Negroes, and was concentrating its energies on Dollars. His programme of industrial education, conciliation of the South, and submission and silence as to civil and political rights, was not wholly original; the Free Negroes from 1830 up to war-time had striven to build industrial schools, and the American Missionary Association had

[1] From George Gordon, Lord Byron's *Childe Harold's Pilgrimage* (1812), Canto II.
[2] The year federal troops departed the South and the Reconstruction policy of support for African American political power was ended.

from the first taught various trades; and Price[3] and others had sought a way of honorable alliance with the best of the Southerners. But Mr. Washington first indissolubly linked these things; he put enthusiasm, unlimited energy, and perfect faith into this programme, and changed it from a by-path into a veritable Way of Life. And the tale of the methods by which he did this is a fascinating study of human life.

It startled the nation to hear a Negro advocating such a programme after many decades of bitter complaint; it startled and won the applause of the South, it interested and won the admiration of the North; and after a confused murmur of protest, it silenced if it did not convert the Negroes themselves.

To gain the sympathy and coöperation of the various elements comprising the white South was Mr. Washington's first task; and this, at the time Tuskegee[4] was founded, seemed, for a black man, well-nigh impossible. And yet ten years later it was done in the word spoken at Atlanta: "In all things purely social we can be as separate as the five fingers, and yet one as the hand in all things essential to mutual progress." This "Atlanta Compromise"[5] is by all odds the most notable thing in Mr. Washington's career. The South interpreted it in different ways: the radicals received it as a complete surrender of the demand for civil and political equality; the conservatives, as a generously conceived working basis for mutual understanding. So both approved it, and to-day its author is certainly the most distinguished Southerner since Jefferson Davis,[6] and the one with the largest personal following.

Next to this achievement comes Mr. Washington's work in gaining place and consideration in the North. Others less shrewd and tactful had formerly essayed to sit on these two stools and had fallen between them; but as Mr. Washington knew the heart of the South from birth and training, so by singular insight he intuitively grasped the spirit of the age which was dominating the North. And so thoroughly did he learn the speech and thought of triumphant commercialism, and the ideals of material prosperity, that the picture of a lone black boy poring over a French grammar amid the weeds and dirt of a neglected home soon seemed to him the acme of absurdities. One wonders what Socrates and St. Francis of Assisi would say to this.[7]

And yet this very singleness of vision and thorough oneness with his age is a mark of the successful man. It is as though Nature must needs make men narrow in order to give them force. So Mr. Washington's cult has gained unquestioning followers, his work has wonderfully prospered, his friends are legion, and his enemies are confounded. To-day he stands as the one recognized spokesman of his ten million fellows, and one of the most notable figures in a nation of seventy millions. One hesitates, therefore, to criticise a life which, beginning with so little, has done so much. And yet the

---

[3] Thomas Frederick Price (1860–1919), Roman Catholic priest and editor, a founder of the American Missionary Association.

[4] Tuskegee Institute, Alabama, founded and built by Washington.

[5] In his 1895 speech, delivered at the Atlanta Exposition, Washington proposed that African Americans be given vocational training in lieu of guaranteed civil rights; his intent was to promote racial stability by en-

suring that African Americans would receive the skills needed to obtain steady work.

[6] An influential senator from Mississippi prior to the war, Davis became president of the Confederacy (1861–1865).

[7] Reference to the Greek philosopher and the founder of the Franciscan order, whose humble circumstances failed to detract from their wisdom.

time is come when one may speak in all sincerity and utter courtesy of the mistakes and shortcomings of Mr. Washington's career, as well as of his triumphs, without being thought captious or envious, and without forgetting that it is easier to do ill than well in the world.

The criticism that has hitherto met Mr. Washington has not always been of this broad character. In the South especially has he had to walk warily to avoid the harshest judgments,—and naturally so, for he is dealing with the one subject of deepest sensitiveness to that section. Twice—once when at the Chicago celebration of the Spanish-American War he alluded to the color-prejudice that is "eating away the vitals of the South," and once when he dined with President Roosevelt[8]—has the resulting Southern criticism been violent enough to threaten seriously his popularity. In the North the feeling has several times forced itself into words, that Mr. Washington's counsels of submission overlooked certain elements of true manhood, and that his educational programme was unnecessarily narrow. Usually, however, such criticism has not found open expression, although, too, the spiritual sons of the Abolitionists have not been prepared to acknowledge that the schools founded before Tuskegee, by men of broad ideals and self-sacrificing spirit, were wholly failures or worthy of ridicule. While, then, criticism has not failed to follow Mr. Washington, yet the prevailing public opinion of the land has been but too willing to deliver the solution of a wearisome problem into his hands, and say, "If that is all you and your race ask, take it."

Among his own people, however, Mr. Washington has encountered the strongest and most lasting opposition, amounting at times to bitterness, and even to-day continuing strong and insistent even though largely silenced in outward expression by the public opinion of the nation. Some of this opposition is, of course, mere envy; the disappointment of displaced demagogues and the spite of narrow minds. But aside from this, there is among educated and thoughtful colored men in all parts of the land a feeling of deep regret, sorrow, and apprehension at the wide currency and ascendancy which some of Mr. Washington's theories have gained. These same men admire his sincerity of purpose, and are willing to forgive much to honest endeavor which is doing something worth the doing. They coöperate with Mr. Washington as far as they conscientiously can; and, indeed, it is no ordinary tribute to this man's tact and power that, steering as he must between so many diverse interests and opinions, he so largely retains the respect of all.

But the hushing of the criticism of honest opponents is a dangerous thing. It leads some of the best of the critics to unfortunate silence and paralysis of effort, and others to burst into speech so passionately and intemperately as to lose listeners. Honest and earnest criticism from those whose interests are most nearly touched,—criticism of writers by readers, of government by those governed, of leaders by those led,—this is the soul of democracy and the safeguard of modern society. If the best of the American Negroes receive by outer pressure a leader whom they had not recognized before, manifestly there is here a certain palpable gain. Yet there is also irreparable loss,—a loss of that peculiarly valuable education which a group receives when by search and criticism

---

[8] Theodore Roosevelt (1858–1919), when president of the United States (1901–1909), invited Washington to dinner, an incident that evoked severe criticism around the country.

it finds and commissions its own leaders. The way in which this is done is at once the most elementary and the nicest problem of social growth. History is but the record of such group-leadership; and yet how infinitely changeful is its type and character! And of all types and kinds, what can be more instructive than the leadership of a group within a group?—that curious double movement where real progress may be negative and actual advance be relative retrogression. All this is the social student's inspiration and despair.

Now in the past the American Negro has had instructive experience in the choosing of group leaders, founding thus a peculiar dynasty which in the light of present conditions is worth while studying. When sticks and stones and beasts form the sole environment of a people, their attitude is largely one of determined opposition to and conquest of natural forces. But when to earth and brute is added an environment of men and ideas, then the attitude of the imprisoned group may take three main forms,—a feeling of revolt and revenge; an attempt to adjust all thought and action to the will of the greater group; or, finally, a determined effort at self-realization and self-development despite environing opinion. The influence of all of these attitudes at various times can be traced in the history of the American Negro, and in the evolution of his successive leaders.

Before 1750, while the fire of African freedom still burned in the veins of the slaves, there was in all leadership or attempted leadership but the one motive of revolt and revenge,—typified in the terrible Maroons, the Danish blacks, and Cato of Stono, and veiling all the Americas in fear of insurrection.[9] The liberalizing tendencies of the latter half of the eighteenth century brought, along with kindlier relations between black and white, thoughts of ultimate adjustment and assimilation. Such aspiration was especially voiced in the earnest songs of Phyllis, in the martyrdom of Attucks, the fighting of Salem and Poor, the intellectual accomplishments of Banneker and Derham, and the political demands of the Cuffes.[10]

Stern financial and social stress after the war cooled much of the previous humanitarian ardor. The disappointment and impatience of the Negroes at the persistence of slavery and serfdom voiced itself in two movements. The slaves in the South, aroused undoubtedly by vague rumors of the Haytian revolt, made three fierce attempts at insurrection,—in 1800 under Gabriel in Virginia, in 1822 under Vesey in Carolina, and in 1831 again in Virginia under the terrible Nat Turner.[11] In the Free States, on the other hand, a new and curious attempt at self-development was made. In Philadelphia and New York color-prescription led to a withdrawal of Negro communicants from white churches and the formation of a peculiar socio-religious institution among the Negroes known as the African Church,—an organization still living and controlling in its various branches over a million of men.

---

[9] Reference to the slave insurrections in the West Indies and South Carolina during the seventeenth and eighteenth centuries, which caused consternation among slave owners.

[10] Phyllis: Phillis Wheatley (ca. 1753–1784), a slave poet; Attucks: Crispus Attucks (ca. 1723–1770), slain leader of the "Boston Massacre" against the British troops; Salem and Poor: Peter Salem and Salem Poor, African American soldiers during the American Revolution; Banneker: Benjamin

Banneker (1731–1806), African American astronomer and mathematician; Derham: James Derham (b. 1762), first acknowledged African American physician; Cuffes: Paul Cuffe (1759–1817), African American leader in the movement to resettle African Americans in Africa.

[11] Gabriel Prosser, Denmark Vesey, and Nat Turner were slaves who led insurrections in 1800, 1822, and 1831, respectively; all were quelled and the leaders hanged.

Walker's wild appeal[12] against the trend of the times showed how the world was changing after the coming of the cotton-gin. By 1830 slavery seemed hopelessly fastened on the South, and the slaves thoroughly cowed into submission. The free Negroes of the North, inspired by the mulatto immigrants from the West Indies, began to change the basis of their demands; they recognized the slavery of slaves, but insisted that they themselves were freemen, and sought assimilation and amalgamation with the nation on the same terms with other men. Thus, Forten and Purvis of Philadelphia, Shad of Wilmington, Du Bois of New Haven, Barbadoes of Boston,[13] and others, strove singly and together as men, they said, not as slaves; as "people of color," not as "Negroes." The trend of the times, however, refused them recognition save in individual and exceptional cases, considered them as one with all the despised blacks, and they soon found themselves striving to keep even the rights they formerly had of voting and working and moving as freemen. Schemes of migration and colonization arose among them; but these they refused to entertain, and they eventually turned to the Abolition movement as a final refuge.

Here, led by Remond, Nell, Wells-Brown, and Douglass,[14] a new period of self-assertion and self-development dawned. To be sure, ultimate freedom and assimilation was the ideal before the leaders, but the assertion of the manhood rights of the Negro by himself was the main reliance, and John Brown's raid[15] was the extreme of its logic. After the war and emancipation, the great form of Frederick Douglass, the greatest of American Negro leaders, still led the host. Self-assertion, especially in political lines, was the main programme, and behind Douglass came Elliot, Bruce, and Langston, and the Reconstruction politicians, and, less conspicuous but of greater social significance Alexander Crummell and Bishop Daniel Payne.[16]

Then came the Revolution of 1876, the suppression of the Negro votes, the changing and shifting of ideals, and the seeking of new lights in the great night. Douglass, in his old age, still bravely stood for the ideals of his early manhood,—ultimate assimilation *through* self-assertion, and on no other terms. For a time Price arose as a new leader, destined, it seemed, not to give up, but to re-state the old ideals in a form less repugnant to the white South. But he passed away in his prime. Then came the new leader. Nearly all the former ones had become leaders by the silent suffrage of their fellows, had sought to lead their own people alone, and were usually, save Douglass, little known outside their race. But Booker T. Washington arose as essentially the leader not of one race but of two,—a compromiser between the South, the North, and the Negro. Naturally the

---

12 Antislavery pamphlet by the African American leader David Walker (1785–1830).

13 A roster of notable African American political leaders in the prewar years: James Forten (1766–1842); Robert Purvis (1810–1898); Abraham Shadd; Alexander Du Bois (1803–1887), grandfather of W. E. B. Du Bois; and James G. Barbadoes.

14 Remond: Charles Lenox Remond (1810–1873); Nell: William Cooper Nell (1816–1874); Wells-Brown: William Wells-Brown (1816?–1884); Douglass: Frederick Douglass (1817–1895).

15 The federal arsenal at Harper's Ferry, Virginia, was attacked by Brown and his followers on October 16, 1859, with the purpose of instigating a mass revolt of all slaves.

16 Elliot: Robert Brown Elliot (1842–1884); Bruce: Blanche K. Bruce (1841–1898); Langston: John Mercer Langston (1829–1897); Crummell: Alexander Crummell (1819–1898); Payne: Daniel Alexander Payne (1811–1893), African American congressman, senator, lawyer, clergyman, and educator, active after the end of the war.

Negroes resented, at first bitterly, signs of compromise which surrendered their civil and political rights, even though this was to be exchanged for larger chances of economic development. The rich and dominating North, however, was not only weary of the race problem, but was investing largely in Southern enterprises, and welcomed any method of peaceful coöperation. Thus, by national opinion, the Negroes began to recognize Mr. Washington's leadership; and the voice of criticism was hushed.

Mr. Washington represents in Negro thought the old attitude of adjustment and submission; but adjustment at such a peculiar time as to make his programme unique. This is an age of unusual economic development, and Mr. Washington's programme naturally takes an economic cast, becoming a gospel of Work and Money to such an extent as apparently almost completely to overshadow the higher aims of life. Moreover, this is an age when the more advanced races are coming in closer contact with the less developed races, and the race-feeling is therefore intensified; and Mr. Washington's programme practically accepts the alleged inferiority of the Negro races. Again, in our own land, the reaction from the sentiment of war time has given impetus to race-prejudice against Negroes, and Mr. Washington withdraws many of the high demands of Negroes as men and American citizens. In other periods of intensified prejudice all the Negro's tendency to self-assertion has been called forth; at this period a policy of submission is advocated. In the history of nearly all other races and peoples the doctrine preached at such crises has been that manly self-respect is worth more than lands and houses, and that a people who voluntarily surrender such respect, or cease striving for it, are not worth civilizing.

In answer to this, it has been claimed that the Negro can survive only through submission. Mr. Washington distinctly asks that black people give up, at least for the present, three things,—

First, political power,

Second, insistence on civil rights,

Third, higher education of Negro youth,— and concentrate all their energies on industrial education, the accumulation of wealth, and the conciliation of the South. This policy has been courageously and insistently advocated for over fifteen years, and has been triumphant for perhaps ten years. As a result of this tender of the palm-branch, what has been the return? In these years there have occurred:

1. The disfranchisement of the Negro.
2. The legal creation of a distinct status of civil inferiority for the Negro.
3. The steady withdrawal of aid from institutions for the higher training of the Negro.

These movements are not, to be sure, direct results of Mr. Washington's teachings; but his propaganda has, without a shadow of doubt, helped their speedier accomplishment. The question then comes: Is it possible, and probable, that nine millions of men can make effective progress in economic lines if they are deprived of political rights, made a servile caste, and allowed only the most meagre chance for developing their exceptional men? If history and reason give any distinct answer to these questions, it is an emphatic *No*. And Mr. Washington thus faces the triple paradox of his career:

1. He is striving nobly to make Negro artisans business men and property-owners; but it is utterly impossible, under modern competitive methods, for working-

men and property-owners to defend their rights and exist without the right of
suffrage.

2. He insists on thrift and self-respect, but at the same time counsels a silent
submission to civic inferiority such as is bound to sap the manhood of any race
in the long run.
3. He advocates common-school[17] and industrial training, and depreciates
institutions of higher learning; but neither the Negro common-schools, nor
Tuskegee itself, could remain open a day were it not for teachers trained in
Negro colleges, or trained by their graduates.

This triple paradox in Mr. Washington's position is the object of criticism by two
classes of colored Americans. One class is spiritually descended from Toussaint the Savior,[18] through Gabriel, Vesey, and Turner, and they represent the attitude of revolt and
revenge; they hate the white South blindly and distrust the white race generally, and so
far as they agree on definite action, think that the Negro's only hope lies in emigration
beyond the borders of the United States. And yet, by the irony of fate, nothing has more
effectually made this programme seem hopeless than the recent course of the United
States toward weaker and darker peoples in the West Indies, Hawaii, and the Philippines—for where in the world may we go and be safe from lying and brute force?

The other class of Negroes who cannot agree with Mr. Washington has hitherto said
little aloud. They deprecate the sight of scattered counsels, of internal disagreement;
and especially they dislike making their just criticism of a useful and earnest man an excuse for a general discharge of venom from small-minded opponents. Nevertheless, the
questions involved are so fundamental and serious that it is difficult to see how men
like the Grimkés, Kelly Miller, J. W. E. Bowen,[19] and other representatives of this group,
can much longer be silent. Such men feel in conscience bound to ask of this nation
three things:

1. The right to vote.
2. Civic equality.
3. The education of youth according to ability.

They acknowledge Mr. Washington's invaluable service in counselling patience and
courtesy in such demands; they do not ask that ignorant black men vote when ignorant
whites are debarred, or that any reasonable restrictions in the suffrage should not be applied; they know that the low social level of the mass of the race is responsible for much
discrimination against it, but they also know, and the nation knows, that relentless
color-prejudice is more often a cause than a result of the Negro's degradation; they seek
the abatement of this relic of barbarism, and not its systematic encouragement and
pampering by all agencies of social power from the Associated Press to the Church of
Christ. They advocate, with Mr. Washington, a broad system of Negro common

[17] Public schools offering free instruction at
the precollege level.
[18] Pierre Dominique Toussaint (1743–1803),
later called Toussaint L'Ouverture, African
American leader of the slave revolt that resulted in Haitian independence.

[19] Archibald Grimké (1849–1930) and Francis
Grimké (1850–1937); Kelly Miller
(1863–1939); J. W. E. Bowen (1855–1933).

schools supplemented by thorough industrial training; but they are surprised that a man of Mr. Washington's insight cannot see that no such educational system ever has rested or can rest on any other basis than that of the well-equipped college and university, and they insist that there is a demand for a few such institutions throughout the South to train the best of the Negro youth as teachers, professional men, and leaders.

This group of men honor Mr. Washington for his attitude of conciliation toward the white South; they accept the "Atlanta Compromise" in its broadest interpretation; they recognize, with him, many signs of promise, many men of high purpose and fair judgment, in this section; they know that no easy task has been laid upon a region already tottering under heavy burdens. But, nevertheless, they insist that the way to truth and right lies in straightforward honesty, not in indiscriminate flattery; in praising those of the South who do well and criticising uncompromisingly those who do ill; in taking advantage of the opportunities at hand and urging their fellows to do the same, but at the same time in remembering that only a firm adherence to their higher ideals and aspirations will ever keep those ideals within the realm of possibility. They do not expect that the free right to vote, to enjoy civic rights, and to be educated, will come in a moment; they do not expect to see the bias and prejudices of years disappear at the blast of a trumpet; but they are absolutely certain that the way for a people to gain their reasonable rights is not by voluntarily throwing them away and insisting that they do not want them; that the way for a people to gain respect is not by continually belittling and ridiculing themselves; that, on the contrary, Negroes must insist continually, in season and out of season, that voting is necessary to modern manhood, that color discrimination is barbarism, and that black boys need education as well as white boys.

In failing thus to state plainly and unequivocally the legitimate demands of their people, even at the cost of opposing an honored leader, the thinking classes of American Negroes would shirk a heavy responsibility,—a responsibility to themselves, a responsibility to the struggling masses, a responsibility to the darker races of men whose future depends so largely on this American experiment, but especially a responsibility to this nation,—this common Fatherland. It is wrong to aid and abet a national crime simply because it is unpopular not to do so. The growing spirit of kindliness and reconciliation between the North and South after the frightful difference of a generation ago ought to be a source of deep congratulation to all, and especially those whose mistreatment caused the war; but if that reconciliation is to be marked by the industrial slavery and civic death of those same black men, with permanent legislation into a position of inferiority, then those black men, if they are really men, are called upon by every consideration of patriotism and loyalty to oppose such a course by all civilized methods, even though such opposition involves disagreement with Mr. Booker T. Washington. We have no right to sit silently by while the inevitable seeds are sown for a harvest of disaster to our children, black and white.

First, it is the duty of black men to judge the South discriminatingly. The present generation of Southerners are not responsible for the past, and they should not be blindly hated or blamed for it. Furthermore, to no class is the indiscriminate endorsement of the recent course of the South toward Negroes more nauseating than to the best thought of the South. The South is not "solid"; it is a land in the ferment of social change, wherein forces of all kinds are fighting for supremacy; and to praise the ill the South is to-day perpetrating is just as wrong as to condemn the good. Discriminating and broad-minded criticism is what the South needs,—needs it for the sake of her own white sons and daughters, and for the insurance of robust, healthy mental and moral development.

To-day even the attitude of the Southern whites toward the blacks is not, as so many assume, in all cases the same; the ignorant Southerner hates the Negro, the workingmen fear his competition, the money-makers wish to use him as a laborer, some of the educated see a menace in his upward development, while others—usually the sons of the masters—wish to help him to rise. National opinion has enabled this last class to maintain the Negro common schools, and to protect the Negro partially in property, life, and limb. Through the pressure of the money-makers, the Negro is in danger of being reduced to semi-slavery, especially in the country districts; the workingmen, and those of the educated who fear the Negro, have united to disfranchise him, and some have urged his deportation; while the passions of the ignorant are easily aroused to lynch and abuse any black man. To praise this intricate whirl of thought and prejudice is nonsense; to inveigh indiscriminately against "the South" is unjust; but to use the same breath in praising Governor Aycock, exposing Senator Morgan, arguing with Mr. Thomas Nelson Page, and denouncing Senator Ben Tillman, is not only sane, but the imperative duty of thinking black men.[20]

It would be unjust to Mr. Washington not to acknowledge that in several instances he has opposed movements in the South which were unjust to the Negro; he sent memorials to the Louisiana and Alabama constitutional conventions, he has spoken against lynching, and in other ways has openly or silently set his influence against sinister schemes and unfortunate happenings. Notwithstanding this, it is equally true to assert that on the whole the distinct impression left by Mr. Washington's propaganda is, first, that the South is justified in its present attitude toward the Negro because of the Negro's degradation; secondly, that the prime cause of the Negro's failure to rise more quickly is his wrong education in the past; and, thirdly, that his future rise depends primarily on his own efforts. Each of these propositions is a dangerous half-truth. The supplementary truths must never be lost sight of: first, slavery and race-prejudice are potent if not sufficient causes of the Negro's position; second, industrial and common-school training were necessarily slow in planting because they had to await the black teachers trained by higher institutions,—it being extremely doubtful if any essentially different development was possible, and certainly a Tuskegee was unthinkable before 1880; and, third, while it is a great truth to say that the Negro must strive and strive mightily to help himself, it is equally true that unless his striving be not simply seconded, but rather aroused and encouraged by the initiative of the richer and wiser environing group, he cannot hope for great success.

In his failure to realize and impress this last point, Mr. Washington is especially to be criticised. His doctrine has tended to make the whites, North and South, shift the burden of the Negro problem to the Negro's shoulders and stand aside as critical and rather pessimistic spectators; when in fact the burden belongs to the nation, and the hands of none of us are clean if we bend not our energies to righting these great wrongs.

The South ought to be led, by candid and honest criticism, to assert her better self and do her full duty to the race she has cruelly wronged and is still wronging. The

---

[20] Aycock, Morgan, Page, and Tillman were white leaders who took various positions regarding African American suffrage in postwar affairs.

North—her co-partner in guilt—cannot salve her conscience by plastering it with gold. We cannot settle this problem by diplomacy and suaveness, by "policy" alone. If worse come to worst, can the moral fibre of this country survive the slow throttling and murder of nine millions of men?

The black men of America have a duty to perform, a duty stern and delicate,—a forward movement to oppose a part of the work of their greatest leader. So far as Mr. Washington preaches Thrift, Patience, and Industrial Training for the masses, we must hold up his hands and strive with him, rejoicing in his honors and glorying in the strength of this Joshua[21] called of God and of man to lead the headless host. But so far as Mr. Washington apologizes for injustice, North or South, does not rightly value the privilege and duty of voting, belittles the emasculating effects of caste distinctions, and opposes the higher training and ambition of our brighter minds,—so far as he, the South, or the Nation, does this,—we must unceasingly and firmly oppose them. By every civilized and peaceful method we must strive for the rights which the world accords to men, clinging unwaveringly to those great words which the sons of the Fathers would fain forget: "We hold these truths to be self-evident: That all men are created equal; that they are endowed by their Creator with certain unalienable rights; that among these are life, liberty, and the pursuit of happiness."

Chapter VII: Of the Black Belt

> *I am black but comely, O ye daughters of Jerusalem,*
> *As the tents of Kedar, as the curtains of Solomon.*
> *Look not upon me, because I am black,*
> *Because the sun hath looked upon me:*
> *My mother's children were angry with me;*
> *They made me the keeper of the vineyards;*
> *But mine own vineyard have I not kept.*

The Song of Solomon[22]

Out of the North the train thundered, and we woke to see the crimson soil of Georgia stretching away bare and monotonous right and left. Here and there lay straggling, unlovely villages, and lean men loafed leisurely at the depots; then again came the stretch of pines and clay. Yet we did not nod, nor weary of the scene; for this is historic ground. Right across our track, three hundred and sixty years ago, wandered the cavalcade of Hernando de Soto,[23] looking for gold and the Great Sea; and he and his footsore captives disappeared yonder in the grim forests to the west. Here sits Atlanta, the city of a hundred hills, with something Western, something Southern, and something quite its own, in its busy life. Just this side Atlanta is the land of the Cherokees and to the southwest, not far from where Sam Hose[24] was crucified, you may stand on a spot

---

[21] Israelite leader who assumed the task of guiding the Jews in their flight from the Egyptians into the Promised Land after the death of Moses.

[22] Song of Songs 1:5–6.

[23] Spanish explorer and discoverer of the Mississippi River (1500?–1542).

[24] African American accused of rape, tortured, and burned alive in Palmetto, Georgia, in 1899.

which is to-day the centre of the Negro problem,—the centre of those nine million men who are America's dark heritage from slavery and the slave-trade.

Not only is Georgia thus the geographical focus of our Negro population, but in many other respects, both now and yesterday, the Negro problems have seemed to be centered in this State. No other State in the Union can count a million Negroes among its citizens,—a population as large as the slave population of the whole Union in 1800; no other State fought so long and strenuously to gather this host of Africans. Oglethorpe[25] thought slavery against law and gospel; but the circumstances which gave Georgia its first inhabitants were not calculated to furnish citizens over-nice in their ideas about rum and slaves. Despite the prohibitions of the trustees, these Georgians, like some of their descendants, proceeded to take the law into their own hands; and so pliant were the judges, and so flagrant the smuggling, and so earnest were the prayers of Whitefield,[26] that by the middle of the eighteenth century all restrictions were swept away, and the slave-trade went merrily on for fifty years and more.

Down in Darien, where the Delegal riots took place some summers ago, there used to come a strong protest against slavery from the Scotch Highlanders; and the Moravians[27] of Ebenezer did not like the system. But not till the Haytian Terror of Toussaint was the trade in men even checked; while the national statute of 1808 did not suffice to stop it. How the Africans poured in!—fifty thousand between 1790 and 1810, and then, from Virginia and from smugglers, two thousand a year for many years more. So the thirty thousand Negroes of Georgia in 1790 were doubled in a decade,—were over a hundred thousand in 1810, had reached two hundred thousand in 1820, and half a million at the time of the war. Thus like a snake the black population writhed upward.

But we must hasten on our journey. This that we pass as we near Atlanta is the ancient land of the Cherokees,—that brave Indian nation which strove so long for its fatherland, until Fate and the United States Government drove them beyond the Mississippi. If you wish to ride with me you must come into the "Jim Crow Car."[28] There will be no objection,—already four other white men, and a little white girl with her nurse, are in there. Usually the races are mixed in there; but the white coach is all white. Of course this car is not so good as the other, but it is fairly clean and comfortable. The discomfort lies chiefly in the hearts of those four black men yonder—and in mine.

We rumble south in quite a business-like way. The bare red clay and pines of Northern Georgia begin to disappear, and in their place appears a rich rolling land, luxuriant, and here and there well tilled. This is the land of the Creek Indians; and a hard time the Georgians had to seize it. The towns grow more frequent and more interesting, and brand-new cotton mills rise on every side. Below Macon the world grows darker; for now we approach the Black Belt,—that strange land of shadows, at which even slaves paled in the past, and whence come now only faint and half-intelligible murmurs to the world beyond. The "Jim Crow Car" grows larger and a shade better; three rough field-hands and two or three white loafers accompany us, and the newsboy still spreads his

---

[25] James Edward Oglethorpe (1696–1785), English founder of the Georgia colony and antislavery crusader.

[26] George Whitefield (1711–1770), English Methodist preacher.

[27] Protestant sect founded by John Huss around 1722.

[28] Jim Crow laws were tightened during the 1890s to enforce racial segregation in public places.

wares at one end. The sun is setting, but we can see the great cotton country as we enter it,—the soil now dark and fertile, now thin and gray, with fruit-trees and dilapidated buildings,—all the way to Albany.

At Albany, in the heart of the Black Belt, we stop. Two hundred miles south of Atlanta, two hundred miles west of the Atlantic, and one hundred miles north of the Great Gulf lies Dougherty County, with ten thousand Negroes and two thousand whites. The Flint River winds down from Andersonville, and, turning suddenly at Albany, the county-seat, hurries on to join the Chattahoochee and the sea. Andrew Jackson knew the Flint well, and marched across it once to avenge the Indian Massacre at Fort Mims.[29] That was in 1814, not long before the battle of New Orleans;[30] and by the Creek treaty that followed this campaign, all Dougherty County, and much other rich land, was ceded to Georgia. Still, settlers fought shy of this land, for the Indians were all about, and they were unpleasant neighbors in those days. The panic of 1837, which Jackson bequeathed to Van Buren,[31] turned the planters from the impoverished lands of Virginia, the Carolinas, and east Georgia, toward the West. The Indians were removed to Indian Territory, and settlers poured into these coveted lands to retrieve their broken fortunes. For a radius of a hundred miles about Albany, stretched a great fertile land, luxuriant with forests of pine, oak, ash, hickory, and poplar; hot with the sun and damp with the rich black swamp-land; and here the corner-stone of the Cotton Kingdom was laid.

Albany is to-day a wide-streeted, placid, Southern town, with a broad sweep of stores and saloons, and flanking rows of homes,—whites usually to the north, and blacks to the south. Six days in the week the town looks decidedly too small for itself, and takes frequent and prolonged naps. But on Saturday suddenly the whole county disgorges itself upon the place, and a perfect flood of black peasantry pours through the streets, fills the stores, blocks the sidewalks, chokes the thoroughfares, and takes full possession of the town. They are black, sturdy, uncouth country folk, good-natured and simple, talkative to a degree, and yet far more silent and brooding than the crowds of the Rhinepfalz,[32] or Naples, or Cracow. They drink considerable quantities of whiskey, but do not get very drunk; they talk and laugh loudly at times, but seldom quarrel or fight. They walk up and down the streets, meet and gossip with friends, stare at the shop windows, buy coffee, cheap candy, and clothes, and at dusk drive home—happy? well no, not exactly happy, but much happier than as though they had not come.

Thus Albany is a real capital,—a typical Southern county town, the centre of the life of ten thousand souls; their point of contact with the outer world, their centre of news and gossip, their market for buying and selling, borrowing and lending, their fountain of justice and law. Once upon a time we knew country life so well and city life so little, that we illustrated city life as that of a closely crowded country district. Now the world has well-nigh forgotten what the country is, and we must imagine a little city of black people scattered far and wide over three hundred lonesome square miles of land, with-

---

29 Before Jackson (1767–1845) became the seventh president (serving from 1829 to 1837), he had led troops against the Native Americans in the southern colonies.

30 Jackson emerged as a national hero for his victory in this battle fought during the War of 1812.

31 Martin Van Buren (1782–1862), who succeeded Jackson as president, entered office during a time of national financial troubles.

32 Territory in Germany; the Palatinate.

out train or trolley, in the midst of cotton and corn, and wide patches of sand and gloomy soil.

It gets pretty hot in Southern Georgia in July,—a sort of dull, determined heat that seems quite independent of the sun; so it took us some days to muster courage enough to leave the porch and venture out on the long country roads, that we might see this unknown world. Finally we started. It was about ten in the morning, bright with a faint breeze, and we jogged leisurely southward in the valley of the Flint. We passed the scattered box-like cabins of the brick-yard hands, and the long tenement-row facetiously called "The Ark," and were soon in the open country, and on the confines of the great plantations of other days. There is the "Joe Fields place"; a rough old fellow was he, and had killed many a "nigger" in his day. Twelve miles his plantation used to run,—a regular barony. It is nearly all gone now; only straggling bits belong to the family, and the rest has passed to Jews and Negroes. Even the bits which are left are heavily mortgaged, and, like the rest of the land, tilled by tenants. Here is one of them now,—a tall brown man, a hard worker and a hard drinker, illiterate, but versed in farmlore, as his nodding crops declare. This distressingly new board house is his, and he has just moved out of yonder moss-grown cabin with its one square room.

From the curtains in Benton's house, down the road, a dark comely face is staring at the strangers; for passing carriages are not every-day occurrences here. Benton is an intelligent yellow man with a good-sized family, and manages a plantation blasted by the war and now the broken staff of the widow. He might be well-to-do, they say; but he carouses too much in Albany. And the half-desolate spirit of neglect born of the very soil seems to have settled on these acres. In times past there were cotton-gins and machinery here; but they have rotted away.

The whole land seems forlorn and forsaken. Here are the remnants of the vast plantations of the Sheldons, the Pellots, and the Rensons; but the souls of them are passed. The houses lie in half ruin, or have wholly disappeared; the fences have flown, and the families are wandering in the world. Strange vicissitudes have met these whilom masters. Yonder stretch the wide acres of Bildad Reasor; he died in war-time, but the upstart overseer hastened to wed the widow. Then he went, and his neighbors too, and now only the black tenant remains; but the shadow-hand of the master's grand-nephew or cousin or creditor stretches out of the gray distance to collect the rack-rent remorselessly, and so the land is uncared-for and poor. Only black tenants can stand such a system, and they only because they must. Ten miles we have ridden to-day and have seen no white face.

A resistless feeling of depression falls slowly upon us, despite the gaudy sunshine and the green cottonfields. This, then, is the Cotton Kingdom,—the shadow of a marvellous dream. And where is the King? Perhaps this is he,—the sweating ploughman, tilling his eighty acres with two lean mules, and fighting a hard battle with debt. So we sit musing, until, as we turn a corner on the sandy road, there comes a fairer scene suddenly in view,—a neat cottage snugly ensconced by the road, and near it a little store. A tall bronzed man rises from the porch as we hail him, and comes out to our carriage. He is six feet in height, with a sober face that smiles gravely. He walks too straight to be a tenant,—yes, he owns two hundred and forty acres. "The land is run down since the boom-days of eighteen hundred and fifty," he explains, and cotton is low. Three black tenants live on his place, and in his little store he keeps a small stock of tobacco, snuff, soap, and soda, for the neighborhood. Here is his gin-house with new machinery just installed. Three hundred bales of cotton went through it last year. Two children he has sent away to school. Yes, he says sadly, he is getting on, but cotton is down to four cents; I know how Debt sits staring at him.

Wherever the King may be, the parks and palaces of the Cotton Kingdom have not wholly disappeared. We plunge even now into great groves of oak and towering pine, with an undergrowth of myrtle and shrubbery. This was the "home-house" of the Thompsons,—slave-barons who drove their coach and four in the merry past. All is silence now, and ashes, and tangled weeds. The owner put his whole fortune into the rising cotton industry of the fifties, and with the falling prices of the eighties he packed up and stole away. Yonder is another grove, with unkempt lawn, great magnolias, and grass-grown paths. The Big House stands in half-ruin, its great front door staring blankly at the street, and the back part grotesquely restored for its black tenant. A shabby, well-built Negro he is, unlucky and irresolute. He digs hard to pay rent to the white girl who owns the remnant of the place. She married a policeman, and lives in Savannah.

Now and again we come to churches. Here is one now,—Shepherd's, they call it,—a great white-washed barn of a thing, perched on stilts of stone, and looking for all the world as though it were just resting here a moment and might be expected to waddle off down the road at almost any time. And yet it is the centre of a hundred cabin homes; and sometimes, of a Sunday, five hundred persons from far and near gather here and talk and eat and sing. There is a school-house near,—a very airy, empty shed; but even this is an improvement, for usually the school is held in the church. The churches vary from log-huts to those like Shepherd's, and the schools from nothing to this little house that sits demurely on the county line. It is a tiny plank-house, perhaps ten by twenty, and has within a double row of rough unplaned benches, resting mostly on legs, sometimes on boxes. Opposite the door is a square home-made desk. In one corner are the ruins of a stove, and in the other a dim blackboard. It is the cheerfulest schoolhouse I have seen in Dougherty, save in town. Back of the schoolhouse is a lodge-house two stories high and not quite finished. Societies meet there,—societies "to care for the sick and bury the dead"; and these societies grow and flourish.

We had come to the boundaries of Dougherty, and were about to turn west along the county-line, when all these sights were pointed out to us by a kindly old man, black, white-haired, and seventy. Forty-five years he had lived here, and now supports himself and his old wife by the help of the steer tethered yonder and the charity of his black neighbors. He shows us the farm of the Hills just across the county line in Baker,—a widow and two strapping sons, who raised ten bales (one need not add "cotton" down here) last year. There are fences and pigs and cows, and the soft-voiced, velvet-skinned young Memnon, who sauntered half-bashfully over to greet the strangers, is proud of his home. We turn now to the west along the county line. Great dismantled trunks of pines tower above the green cotton-fields, cracking their naked gnarled fingers toward the border of living forest beyond. There is little beauty in this region, only a sort of crude abandon that suggests power,—a naked grandeur, as it were. The houses are bare and straight; there are no hammocks or easy-chairs, and few flowers. So when, as here at Rawdon's, one sees a vine clinging to a little porch, and home-like windows peeping over the fences, one takes a long breath. I think I never before quite realized the place of the Fence in civilization. This is the Land of the Unfenced, where crouch on either hand scores of ugly one-room cabins, cheerless and dirty. Here lies the Negro problem in its naked dirt and penury. And here are no fences. But now and then the criss-cross rails or straight palings break into view, and then we know a touch of culture is near. Of course Harrison Gohagen,—a quiet yellow man, young, smooth-faced, and diligent,—of course he is lord of some hundred acres, and we expect to see a vision of well-kept rooms and fat beds and laughing children. For has he not fine fences? And those over yonder, why should they build fences on the rack-rented land? It will only increase their rent.

On we wind, through sand and pines and glimpses of old plantations, till there creeps into sight a cluster of buildings,—wood and brick, mills and houses, and scattered cabins. It seemed quite a village. As it came nearer and nearer, however, the aspect changed: the buildings were rotten, the bricks were falling out, the mills were silent, and the store was closed. Only in the cabins appeared now and then a bit of lazy life. I could imagine the place under some weird spell, and was half-minded to search out the princess. An old ragged black man, honest, simple, and improvident, told us the tale. The Wizard of the North—the Capitalist—had rushed down in the seventies to woo this coy dark soil. He bought a square mile or more, and for a time the field-hands sang, the gins groaned, and the mills buzzed. Then came a change. The agent's son embezzled the funds and ran off with them. Then the agent himself disappeared. Finally the new agent stole even the books, and the company in wrath closed its business and its houses, refused to sell, and let houses and furniture and machinery rust and rot. So the Waters-Loring plantation was stilled by the spell of dishonesty, and stands like some gaunt rebuke to a scarred land.

Somehow that plantation ended our day's journey; for I could not shake off the influence of that silent scene. Back toward town we glided, past the straight and thread-like pines, past a dark tree-dotted pond where the air was heavy with a dead sweet perfume. White slender-legged curlews flitted by us, and the garnet blooms of the cotton looked gay against the green and purple stalks. A peasant girl was hoeing in the field, white-turbaned and black-limbed. All this we saw, but the spell still lay upon us.

How curious a land is this,—how full of untold story, of tragedy and laughter, and the rich legacy of human life; shadowed with a tragic past, and big with future promise! This is the Black Belt of Georgia. Dougherty County is the west end of the Black Belt, and men once called it the Egypt of the Confederacy. It is full of historic interest. First there is the Swamp, to the west, where the Chickasawhatchee flows sullenly southward. The shadow of an old plantation lies at its edge, forlorn and dark. Then comes the pool; pendent gray moss and brackish waters appear, and forests filled with wildfowl. In one place the wood is on fire, smouldering in dull red anger; but nobody minds. Then the swamp grows beautiful; a raised road, built by chained Negro convicts, dips down into it, and forms a way walled and almost covered in living green. Spreading trees spring from a prodigal luxuriance of undergrowth; great dark green shadows fade into the black background, until all is one mass of tangled semi-tropical foliage, marvellous in its weird savage splendor. Once we crossed a black silent stream, where the sad trees and writhing creepers, all glinting fiery yellow and green, seemed like some vast cathedral,—some green Milan[33] builded of wildwood. And as I crossed, I seemed to see again that fierce tragedy of seventy years ago. Osceola,[34] the Indian-Negro chieftain, had risen in the swamps of Florida, vowing vengeance. His war-cry reached the red Creeks of

[33] The cathedral of Milan, Italy, is one of the largest church structures in Europe.   [34] Chief of the Seminoles (1804?–1838).

Dougherty, and their war-cry rang from the Chattahoochee to the sea. Men and women and children fled and fell before them as they swept into Dougherty. In yonder shadows a dark and hideously painted warrior glided stealthily on,—another and another, until three hundred had crept into the treacherous swamp. Then the false slime closing about them called the white men from the east. Waist-deep, they fought beneath the tall trees, until the war-cry was hushed and the Indians glided back into the west. Small wonder the wood is red.

Then came the black slaves. Day after day the clank of chained feet marching from Virginia and Carolina to Georgia was heard in these rich swamp lands. Day after day the songs of the callous, the wail of the motherless, and the muttered curses of the wretched echoed from the Flint to the Chickasawhatchee, until by 1860 there had risen in West Dougherty perhaps the richest slave kingdom the modern world ever knew. A hundred and fifty barons commanded the labor of nearly six thousand negroes, held sway over farms with ninety thousand acres of tilled land, valued even in times of cheap soil at three millions of dollars. Twenty thousand bales of ginned cotton went yearly to England, New and Old; and men that came there bankrupt made money and grew rich. In a single decade the cotton output increased four-fold and the value of lands was tripled. It was the heyday of the *nouveau riche,* and a life of careless extravagance reigned among the masters. Four and six bob-tailed thoroughbreds rolled their coaches to town; open hospitality and gay entertainment were the rule. Parks and groves were laid out, rich with flower and vine, and in the midst stood the low wide-halled "big house," with its porch and columns and great fire-places.

And yet with all this there was something sordid, something forced,—a certain feverish unrest and recklessness; for was not all this show and tinsel built upon a groan? "This land was a little Hell," said a ragged, brown, and grave-faced man to me. We were seated near a roadside blacksmith-shop, and behind was the bare ruin of some master's home. "I've seen niggers drop dead in the furrow, but they were kicked aside, and the plough never stopped. And down in the guard-house, there's where the blood ran."

With such foundations a kingdom must in time sway and fall. The masters moved to Macon and Augusta, and left only the irresponsible overseers on the land. And the result is such ruin as this, the Lloyd "home-place":—great waving oaks, a spread of lawn, myrtles and chestnuts, all ragged and wild; a solitary gate-post standing where once was a castle entrance; an old rusty anvil lying amid rotting bellows and wood in the ruins of a blacksmith shop; a wide rambling old mansion, brown and dingy, filled now with the grandchildren of the slaves who once waited on its tables; while the family of the master has dwindled to two lone women, who live in Macon and feed hungrily off the remnants of an earldom. So we ride on, past phantom gates and falling homes,—past the once flourishing farms of the Smiths, the Gandys, and the Lagores,—and find all dilapidated and half ruined, even there where a solitary white woman, a relic of other days, sits alone in state among miles of Negroes and rides to town in her ancient coach each day.

This was indeed the Egypt of the Confederacy,—the rich granary whence potatoes and corn and cotton poured out to the famished and ragged Confederate troops as they battled for a cause lost long before 1861. Sheltered and secure, it became the place of refuge for families, wealth, and slaves. Yet even then the hard ruthless rape of the land began to tell. The red-clay sub-soil already had begun to peer above the loam. The harder the slaves were driven the more careless and fatal was their farming. Then came the revolution of war and Emancipation, the bewilderment of Reconstruction,—and now, what is the Egypt of the Confederacy, and what meaning has it for the nation's weal or woe?

It is a land of rapid contrasts and of curiously mingled hope and pain. Here sits a pretty blue-eyed quadroon hiding her bare feet; she was married only last week, and yonder in the field is her dark young husband, hoeing to support her, at thirty cents a day without board. Across the way is Gatesby, brown and tall, lord of two thousand acres shrewdly won and held. There is a store conducted by his black son, a blacksmith shop, and a ginnery. Five miles below here is a town owned and controlled by one white New Englander. He owns almost a Rhode Island county, with thousands of acres and hundreds of black laborers. Their cabins look better than most, and the farm, with machinery and fertilizers, is much more business-like than any in the county, although the manager drives hard bargains in wages. When now we turn and look five miles above, there on the edge of town are five houses of prostitutes,—two of blacks and three of whites; and in one of the houses of the whites a worthless black boy was harbored too openly two years ago; so he was hanged for rape. And here, too, is the high whitewashed fence of the "stockade," as the county prison is called; the white folks say it is ever full of black criminals,—the black folks say that only colored boys are sent to jail, and they not because they are guilty, but because the State needs criminals to eke out its income by their forced labor.

The Jew is the heir of the slave-baron in Dougherty; and as we ride westward, by wide stretching cornfields and stubby orchards of peach and pear, we see on all sides within the circle of dark forest a Land of Canaan.[35] Here and there are tales of projects for money-getting, born in the swift days of Reconstruction,[36]—"improvement" companies, wine companies, mills and factories; nearly all failed, and the Jew fell heir. It is a beautiful land, this Dougherty, west of the Flint. The forests are wonderful, the solemn pines have disappeared, and this is the "Oakey Woods," with its wealth of hickories, beeches, oaks, and palmettos. But a pall of debt hangs over the beautiful land; the merchants are in debt to the wholesalers, the planters are in debt to the merchants, the tenants owe the planters, and laborers bow and bend beneath the burden of it all. Here and there a man has raised his head above these murky waters. We passed one fenced stock-farm, with grass and grazing cattle, that looked very homelike after endless corn and cotton. Here and there are black freeholders: there is the gaunt dull-black Jackson, with his hundred acres. "I says, 'Look up! If you don't look up you can't get up,' " remarks Jackson, philosophically. And he's gotten up. Dark Carter's neat barns would do credit to New England. His master helped him to get a start, but when the black man died last fall the master's sons immediately laid claim to the estate. "And them white folks will get it, too," said my yellow gossip.[37]

I turn from these well-tended acres with a comfortable feeling that the Negro is rising. Even then, however, the fields, as we proceed, begin to redden and the trees disappear. Rows of old cabins appear filled with renters and laborers,—cheerless, bare, and

[35] The land God told Moses was promised to the Israelites upon their flight from bondage in Egypt; roughly equivalent to today's nation of Israel.

[36] The period between 1867 and 1877, during which the federal government initiated the process by which the Southern states were brought back into the Union; a time of great social, economic, and political change.

[37] Mulatto informant.

dirty, for the most part, although here and there the very age and decay makes the scene picturesque. A young black fellow greets us. He is twenty-two, and just married. Until last year he had good luck renting; then cotton fell, and the sheriff seized and sold all he had. So he moved here, where the rent is higher, the land poorer, and the owner inflexible; he rents a forty-dollar mule for twenty dollars a year. Poor lad!—a slave at twenty-two. This plantation, owned now by a Russian Jew, was a part of the famous Bolton estate. After the war it was for many years worked by gangs of Negro convicts,—and black convicts then were even more plentiful than now; it was a way of making Negroes work, and the question of guilt was a minor one. Hard tales of cruelty and mistreatment of the chained freemen are told, but the county authorities were deaf until the free-labor market was nearly ruined by wholesale migration. Then they took the convicts from the plantations, but not until one of the fairest regions of the "Oakey Woods" had been ruined and ravished into a red waste, out of which only a Yankee or his like could squeeze more blood from debt-cursed tenants.

No wonder that Luke Black, slow, dull, and discouraged, shuffles to our carriage and talks hopelessly. Why should he strive? Every year finds him deeper in debt. How strange that Georgia, the world-heralded refuge of poor debtors, should bind her own to sloth and misfortune as ruthlessly as ever England did! The poor land groans with its birth-pains, and brings forth scarcely a hundred pounds of cotton to the acre, where fifty years ago it yielded eight times as much. Of this meagre yield the tenant pays from a quarter to a third in rent, and most of the rest in interest on food and supplies bought on credit. Twenty years yonder sunken-cheeked, old black man has labored under that system, and now, turned day-laborer, is supporting his wife and boarding himself on his wages of a dollar and a half a week, received only part of the year.

The Bolton convict farm formerly included the neighboring plantation. Here it was that the convicts were lodged in the great log prison still standing. A dismal place it still remains, with rows of ugly huts filled with surly ignorant tenants. "What rent do you pay here?" I inquired. "I don't know,—what is it, Sam?" "All we make," answered Sam. It is a depressing place,—bare, unshaded, with no charm of past association, only a memory of forced human toil,—now, then, and before the war. They are not happy, these black men whom we meet throughout this region. There is little of the joyous abandon and playfulness which we are wont to associate with the plantation Negro. At best, the natural good-nature is edged with complaint or has changed into sullenness and gloom. And now and then it blazes forth in veiled but hot anger. I remember one big red-eyed black whom we met by the road-side. Forty-five years he had labored on this farm, beginning with nothing, and still having nothing. To be sure, he had given four children a common-school training, and perhaps if the new fence-law had not allowed unfenced crops in West Dougherty he might have raised a little stock and kept ahead. As it is, he is hopelessly in debt, disappointed, and embittered. He stopped us to inquire after the black boy in Albany, whom it was said a policeman had shot and killed for loud talking on the sidewalk. And then he said slowly: "Let a white man touch me, and he dies; I don't boast this,—I don't say it around loud, or before the children,—but I mean it. I've seen them whip my father and my old mother in them cotton-rows till the blood ran; by—" and we passed on.

Now Sears, whom we met next lolling under the chubby oak-trees, was of quite different fibre. Happy?—Well, yes; he laughed and flipped pebbles, and thought the world was as it was. He had worked here twelve years and has nothing but a mortgaged mule.

Children? Yes, seven; but they hadn't been to school this year,—couldn't afford books and clothes, and couldn't spare their work. There go part of them to the fields now,— three big boys astride mules, and a strapping girl with bare brown legs. Careless ignorance and laziness here, fierce hate and vindictiveness there;—these are the extremes of the Negro problem which we met that day, and we scarce knew which we preferred.

Here and there we meet distinct characters quite out of the ordinary. One came out of a piece of newly cleared ground, making a wide detour to avoid the snakes. He was an old, hollow-cheeked man, with a drawn and characterful brown face. He had a sort of self-contained quaintness and rough humor impossible to describe; a certain cynical earnestness that puzzled one. "The niggers were jealous of me over on the other place," he said, "and so me and the old woman begged this piece of woods, and I cleared it up myself. Made nothing for two years, but I reckon I've got a crop now." The cotton looked tall and rich, and we praised it. He curtsied low, and then bowed almost to the ground, with an imperturbable gravity that seemed almost suspicious. Then he continued, "My mule died last week,"—a calamity in this land equal to a devastating fire in town,—"but a white man loaned me another." Then he added, eyeing us, "Oh, I gets along with white folks." We turned the conversation. "Bears? deer?" he answered, "well, I should say there were," and he let fly a string of brave oaths, as he told hunting-tales of the swamp. We left him standing still in the middle of the road looking after us, and yet apparently not noticing us.

The Whistle place, which includes his bit of land, was bought soon after the war by an English syndicate, the "Dixie Cotton and Corn Company." A marvellous deal of style their factor put on, with his servants and coach-and-six; so much so that the concern soon landed in inextricable bankruptcy. Nobody lives in the old house now, but a man comes each winter out of the North and collects his high rents. I know not which are the more touching,—such old empty houses, or the homes of the masters' sons. Sad and bitter tales lie hidden back of those white doors,—tales of poverty, of struggle, of disappointment. A revolution such as that of '63 is a terrible thing; they that rose rich in the morning often slept in paupers' beds. Beggars and vulgar speculators rose to rule over them, and their children went astray. See yonder sad-colored house, with its cabins and fences and glad crops! It is not glad within; last month the prodigal son of the struggling father wrote home from the city for money. Money! Where was it to come from? And so the son rose in the night and killed his baby, and killed his wife, and shot himself dead. And the world passed on.

I remember wheeling around a bend in the road beside a graceful bit of forest and a singing brook. A long low house faced us, with porch and flying pillars, great oaken door, and a broad lawn shining in the evening sun. But the window-panes were gone, the pillars were worm-eaten, and the moss-grown roof was falling in. Half curiously I peered through the unhinged door, and saw where, on the wall across the hall, was written in once gay letters a faded "Welcome."

Quite a contrast to the southwestern part of Dougherty County is the northwest. Soberly timbered in oak and pine, it has none of that half-tropical luxuriance of the southwest. Then, too, there are fewer signs of a romantic past, and more of systematic modern land-grabbing and money-getting. White people are more in evidence here, and farmer and hired labor replace to some extent the absentee landlord and rack-rented tenant. The crops have neither the luxuriance of the richer land nor the signs of neglect so often seen, and there were fences and meadows here and there. Most of this land was poor, and beneath the notice of the slave-baron, before the war. Since then his nephews and the poor whites and the Jews have seized it. The returns of the farmer are too small to allow much for wages, and yet he will not sell off small farms. There is the Negro Sanford; he has worked fourteen years as overseer on the Ladson place, and "paid out enough for fertilizers to have bought a farm," but the owner will not sell off a few acres.

Two children—a boy and a girl—are hoeing sturdily in the fields on the farm where Corliss works. He is smooth-faced and brown, and is fencing up his pigs. He used to run a successful cotton-gin, but the Cotton Seed Oil Trust has forced the price of ginning so low that he says it hardly pays him. He points out a stately old house over the way as the home of "Pa Willis." We eagerly ride over, for "Pa Willis" was the tall and powerful black Moses who led the Negroes for a generation, and led them well. He was a Baptist preacher, and when he died two thousand black people followed him to the grave; and now they preach his funeral sermon each year. His widow lives here,—a weazened, sharp-featured little woman, who curtsied quaintly as we greeted her. Further on lives Jack Delson, the most prosperous Negro farmer in the county. It is a joy to meet him—a great broad-shouldered, handsome black man, intelligent and jovial. Six hundred and fifty acres he owns, and has eleven black tenants. A neat and tidy home nestled in a flower-garden, and a little store stands beside it.

We pass the Munson place, where a plucky white widow is renting and struggling; and the eleven hundred acres of the Sennet plantation, with its Negro overseer. Then the character of the farms begins to change. Nearly all the lands belong to Russian Jews; the overseers are white, and the cabins are bare board-houses scattered here and there. The rents are high, and day-laborers and "contract" hands abound. It is a keen, hard struggle for living here, and few have time to talk. Tired with the long ride, we gladly drive into Gillonsville. It is a silent cluster of farm-houses standing on the cross-roads, with one of its stores closed and the other kept by a Negro preacher. They tell great tales of busy times at Gillonsville before all the railroads came to Albany; now it is chiefly a memory. Riding down the street, we stop at the preacher's and seat ourselves before the door. It was one of those scenes one cannot soon forget:—a wide, low, little house, whose motherly roof reached over and sheltered a snug little porch. There we sat, after the long hot drive, drinking cool water,—the talkative little store-keeper who is my daily companion; the silent old black woman patching pantaloons and saying never a word; the ragged picture of helpless misfortune who called in just to see the preacher; and finally the neat matronly preacher's wife, plump, yellow, and intelligent. "Own land?" said the wife; "well, only this house." Then she added quietly, "We did buy seven hundred acres up yonder, and paid for it; but they cheated us out of it. Sells was the owner." "Sells!" echoed the ragged misfortune, who was leaning against the balustrade and listening, "he's a regular cheat. I worked for him thirty-seven days this spring, and he paid me in cardboard checks which were to be cashed at the end of the month. But he never cashed them,—kept putting me off. Then the sheriff came and took my mule and corn and furniture—" "Furniture?" I asked; "but furniture is exempt from seizure by law." "Well, he took it just the same," said the hard-faced man.

1903

Paul Laurence Dunbar
1872–1906

"Irrespective of these facts," William Dean Howells judged (and praised) the literary art he found in Dunbar's collection of poems, *Lyrics of Lowly Life*. But what were "these facts" that Howells preferred to disregard? In his words, Howells elected not "to care for the work of a poet because he is black, because his father and mother were slaves, because he was, before and after he began to write poems, an elevator-boy." He, in fact, elected to like it because the writing was very good, not for reasons of patronizing white liberalism.

On the one hand, his universalizing of the creative act beyond the factors of race, origin, and condition was an admirable position for Howells, the benevolent literary dictator of his day, to have taken. On the other hand, it was problematic in its obliteration of the personal histories that lie behind works of art. Such a stance certainly created problems for Dunbar as he went through his decade of fame within the white literary community, stretching between the 1896 publication of *Lyrics of Lowly Life* and his death of tuberculosis in 1906.

Both Dunbar's parents had been born into slavery. His father had escaped north to Canada; his mother, freed during the Civil War, came to Ohio where she met her future husband. Dayton, Ohio, was Dunbar's birthplace. His first poem was printed in the local Dayton newspaper when he was sixteen. Upon graduating from high school, he supported himself with menial jobs but continued to press forward with his writing. In 1892 *Oak and Ivy* was published at his expense, followed by a series of public readings throughout the Midwest. Mainstream magazines (*Century, Mumsey's*) began to accept his poems, however his real breakthrough came after Howells singled out his poetry for special mention in *Harper's Weekly*. *Lyrics of the Hearthside* appeared in 1899, and *Lyrics of Love and Laughter* in 1903. Dunbar's output during the final decade of his life also included several collections of stories, four novels (only *The Sport of the Gods* focused upon a black man's experiences), and active participation on the lecture circuit.

In addition to his mentor William Dean Howells, Dunbar became acquainted with such preeminent white figures as George Washington Cable, Theodore Roosevelt, and James Whitcomb Riley (whose popular verses in Hoosier dialect helped create an audience receptive to Dunbar's own employment of an African American dialect). These connections eased Dunbar's entree into the public scene, but far more vital to his sense of his own heritage were his associations with Frederick Douglass at the 1893 Columbia Exposition in Chicago, Booker T. Washington, W. E. B. Du Bois, and James Weldon Johnson. For Dunbar's was a divided life, his achievements hedged about because the decade in which he was trying so hard to express himself with force were the years that have been named "the nadir" of "the Negro in American thought."

Current scholarship is reviving interest in Dunbar's role as a seminal figure in the founding of the African American poetic tradition. The previously held notion that he was just another African American who "sold out" is also being revised. Today there is far greater understanding of the constraints that the 1890s and early 1900s placed upon persons of color attempting to find wide readership and their need to make it in the "white marketplace" if they were to be heard at all. Furthermore, recognition is now given to the success of many of Dunbar's lyrics in getting past the onus of "the plantation tradition." "Blues energies" are found in Dunbar's use of the mythic. The dialect format of "The Ante-Bellum Sermon" is admired for its satiric bite that goes well beyond self-limiting pathos and humor, as James Weldon Johnson once characterized the dialect mode. Dunbar's polished use of traditional poetic forms now is given the appreciation it deserves. The tradition of the obituary ode stands strongly behind "Frederick Douglass" and the ballad tradition adds force to "Black Sampson of Brandywine" and "The Haunted Oak."

There is no question that Dunbar learned to cut corners and make adjustments to what he wanted to say about the African American experience and how he could say it, but his art often goes beyond the poetry "which does not think or feel black" that Howells found in Dunbar's lyrics.

Further Reading:

H. Baker, *Blues, Ideology, and Afro-American Litera-
ture,* 1985.
K. Ensslen, "The Status of Black Poetry from 1865
to 1914," *American Poetry Between
Tradition and Modernism,* 1985.
P. Revell, *Paul Laurence Dunbar,* 1987.

Texts:

"Frederick Douglass," "We Wear the Mask" from
Lyrics of Lowly Life, 1896.
"Sympathy" from *Lyrics of the Hearthside,* 1899.
See also *The Complete Poems of Paul Laurence Dun-
bar,* 1913.

Frederick Douglass

A hush is over all the teeming lists,
 And there is pause, a breath-space in the strife;
A spirit brave has passed beyond the mists
 And vapors that obscure the sun of life.
And Ethiopia, with bosom torn,   5
Laments the passing of her noblest born.

She weeps for him a mother's burning tears—
 She loved him with a mother's deepest love.
He was her champion thro' direful years,
 And held her weal all other ends above.   10
When Bondage held her bleeding in the dust,
He raised her up and whispered, "Hope and Trust."

For her his voice, a fearless clarion, rung
 That broke in warning on the ears of men;
For her the strong bow of his power he strung,   15

And sent his arrows to the very den
Where grim Oppression held his bloody place
And gloated o'er the mis'ries of a race.

And he was no soft-tongued apologist;
   He spoke straightforward, fearlessly uncowed;   20
The sunlight of his truth dispelled the mist,
   And set in bold relief each dark hued cloud;
To sin and crime he gave their proper hue,
And hurled at evil what was evil's due.

Through good and ill report he cleaved his way   25
   Right onward, with his face set toward the heights,
Nor feared to face the foeman's dread array,—
   The lash of scorn, the sting of petty spites.
He dared the lightning in the lightning's track,
And answered thunder with his thunder back.   30

When men maligned him, and their torrent wrath
   In furious imprecations o'er him broke,
He kept his counsel as he kept his path;
   'T was for his race, not for himself he spoke.
He knew the import of his Master's call,   35
And felt himself too mighty to be small.

No miser in the good he held was he,—
   His kindness followed his horizon's rim.
His heart, his talents, and his hands were free
   To all who truly needed aught of him.   40
Where poverty and ignorance were rife,
He gave his bounty as he gave his life.

The place and cause that first aroused his might
   Still proved its power until his latest day.
In Freedom's lists and for the aid of Right   45
   Still in the foremost rank he waged the fray;
Wrong lived; his occupation was not gone.
He died in action with his armor on!

We weep for him, but we have touched his hand,
   And felt the magic of his presence nigh,   50
The current that he sent throughout the land,
   The kindling spirit of his battle-cry.
O'er all that holds us we shall triumph yet,
And place our banner where his hopes were set!

Oh, Douglass, thou hast passed beyond the shore,   55
   But still thy voice is ringing o'er the gale!

Thou'st taught thy race how high her hopes may soar,
    And bade her seek the heights, nor faint, nor fail.
She will not fail, she heeds thy stirring cry,
She knows thy guardian spirit will be nigh,   60
And, rising from beneath the chast'ning rod,
She stretches out her bleeding hands to God!
1896

We Wear the Mask

We wear the mask that grins and lies,
It hides our cheeks and shades our eyes,—
This debt we pay to human guile;
With torn and bleeding hearts we smile,
And mouth with myriad subtleties.   5

Why should the world be overwise,
In counting all our tears and sighs?
Nay, let them only see us, while
    We wear the mask.

We smile, but, O great Christ, our cries   10
To thee from tortured souls arise.
We sing, but oh the clay is vile
Beneath our feet, and long the mile;
But let the world dream otherwise,
    We wear the mask!   15
1896

Sympathy

I know what the caged bird feels, alas!
    When the sun is bright on the upland
        slopes;
When the wind stirs soft through the springing
        grass,
And the river flows like a stream of glass;
    When the first bird sings and the first bud
        opens,   5

And the faint perfume from its chalice steals—
I know what the caged bird feels!

I know why the caged bird beats his wing
   Till its blood is red on the cruel bars;
For he must fly back to his perch and cling   10
When he fain would be on the bough a-swing;
   And a pain still throbs in the old, old scars
And they pulse again with a keener sting—
I know why he beats his wing!
I know why the caged bird sings, ah me,   15
   When his wing is bruised and his bosom
      sore,—
When he beats his bars and he would be free;
It is not a carol of joy or glee,
   But a prayer that he sends from his heart's
      deep core,
But a plea, that upward to Heaven he flings—   20
I know why the caged bird sings!
1899

Edwin Arlington Robinson
1869–1935

The poets who preceded Edwin Arlington Robinson—Bryant, Whittier, Longfellow, and James Russell Lowell—have been grouped as "the fireside poets," and the name conveys their acceptability to the genteel tradition. Unlike these poets, Robinson had the lonely courage not to write conventionally pleasing verse. Instead he wrote lyrics stemming directly from his doomed sense of life. He was, in the existential bleakness of his vision, a forerunner of the disillusioned generation that created the modernist movement in art.

One of Robinson's brothers was an alcoholic, one a doctor addicted to drugs, and Robinson himself became an alcoholic. His father's business had failed, and it was only through local benefactors that Robinson managed to spend two years (like Robert Frost later) as a special student at Harvard. When he left Harvard, he returned home to Gardiner, Maine, where, trapped, unemployed, and in the force of his twenties, he wrote his most memorable poems. Robinson first anatomized his village (under the name "Tilbury Town") and its cast of local failures and eccentrics in the 1897 collection of poems *Children of the Night*. The most famous of his characters—the hopeless, backward-looking Miniver Cheevy and the immaculately dressed but suicidal Richard Cory—are perhaps self-caricatures who bear a special lyric force in their cruel self-satire. Nearing thirty, Robinson moved to New York, where he lived the rest of his life, although after 1911 he spent the summers in New Hampshire at the MacDowell Colony for artists. He never married.

In 1922 Robinson's *Collected Poems* was awarded the Pulitzer Prize. In his maturity, he was known chiefly for his long, Tennysonian poems on Arthurian themes, *Merlin* (1917), *Lancelot* (1920), and *Tristram* (1927), which have not aged well. He also wrote long psychological studies of character, among them *Cavender's House* (1929) and *Matthis at the Door* (1931). George Crabbe rather than Tennyson was Robinson's true English precursor. Crabbe's "hard, human pulse," his "plain excellence and stubborn skill," as Robinson called them, were Robinson's own aesthetic strengths. His brisk quatrains, the stern blank verse of his satires, his death-knell rhymes in "Eros Turannos"—"confusion, illusion, seclusion" or "striven, given, driven"—are marks of his care in composing.

Robinson's achievement in verse is now perceived, paradoxically, through the work of Robert Frost, who learned everything Robinson had to teach and brought it to rhythmic and lyric perfection. Without Robinson, we can scarcely imagine Frost's existence. Robinson's dark, sardonic nature appealed to Frost's grim side, and he also taught Frost how to be a regional poet. Robinson's revelation of the spoiled erotic life allowed Frost to draw aside curtains of privacy, and his insight into the tragic dramas enacted in rural life gave Frost one of his chief topics. When we look at Robinson now, we feel he must have been reading Frost; but the debt goes the other way.

Further Reading:

Y. Winters, *Edwin Arlington Robinson,* 1946.
E. Fussell, *Edwin Arlington Robinson,* 1954.
E. Barnard, ed., *Edwin Arlington Robinson: Centenary Essays,* 1973.

G. Lensing, "Robinson: the Sad, Wry Poet," *American Poetry Between Tradition and Modernism,* 1985.
H. Bloom, ed., *Edward Arlington Robinson,* 1988.

Text:
Collected Poems, 1940.

Richard Cory

Whenever Richard Cory went down town,
We people on the pavement looked at him:
He was a gentleman from sole to crown,
Clean favored, and imperially slim.

And he was always quietly arrayed,   5
And he was always human when he talked;
But still he fluttered pulses when he said,
"Good-morning," and he glittered when he walked.

And he was rich—yes, richer than a king—
And admirably schooled in every grace: 10

In fine, we thought that he was everything
To make us wish that we were in his place.

So on we worked, and waited for the light,
And went without the meat, and cursed the bread;
And Richard Cory, one calm summer night,   15
Went home and put a bullet through his head.
1896

Miniver Cheevy

Miniver Cheevy, child of scorn,
   Grew lean while he assailed the seasons;
He wept that he was ever born,
   And he had reasons.

Miniver loved the days of old   5
   When swords were bright and steeds were prancing;
The vision of a warrior bold
   Would set him dancing.

Miniver sighed for what was not,
   And dreamed, and rested from his labors;   10
He dreamed of Thebes[1] and Camelot,[2]
   And Priam's[3] neighbors.

Miniver mourned the ripe renown
   That made so many a name so fragrant;
He mourned Romance, now on the town,   15
   And Art, a vagrant.

Miniver loved the Medici,[4]
   Albeit he had never seen one;
He would have sinned incessantly
   Could he have been one.   20

Miniver cursed the commonplace
   And eyed a khaki suit with loathing;
He missed the mediæval grace
   Of iron clothing.

[1] City in Greece made famous by Homer and the Greek tragedians.
[2] Site of King Arthur's court.
[3] Priam was king of Troy. (The Trojan War is described in Homer's *Iliad*.)
[4] One of the ruling families of the Italian Renaissance.

Miniver scorned the gold he sought,   25
    But sore annoyed was he without it;
Miniver thought, and thought, and thought,
    And thought about it.

Miniver Cheevy, born too late,
    Scratched his head and kept on thinking;   30
Miniver coughed, and called it fate,
    And kept on drinking.
1910

Eros Turannos*

She fears him, and will always ask
    What fated her to choose him;
She meets in his engaging mask
    All reasons to refuse him;
But what she meets and what she fears   5
Are less than are the downward years,
Drawn slowly to the foamless weirs
    Of age, were she to lose him.

Between a blurred sagacity
    That once had power to sound him,   10
And Love, that will not let him be
    The Judas that she found him,
Her pride assuages her almost,
As if it were alone the cost.—
He sees that he will not be lost,   15
    And waits and looks around him.

A sense of ocean and old trees
    Envelops and allures him;
Tradition, touching all he sees,
    Beguiles and reassures him;   20
And all her doubts of what he says
Are dimmed with what she knows of days—
Till even prejudice delays
    And fades, and she secures him.

The falling leaf inaugurates   25
    The reign of her confusion;

* Greek: "Love, the Ruler."

The pounding wave reverberates
   The dirge of her illusion;
And home, where passion lived and died,
Becomes a place where she can hide,   30
While all the town and harbor side
   Vibrate with her seclusion.

We tell you, tapping on our brows,
   The story as it should be,—
As if the story of a house   35
   Were told, or ever could be;
We'll have no kindly veil between
Her visions and those we have seen,—
As if we guessed what hers have been,
   Or what they are or would be.   40

Meanwhile we do no harm; for they
   That with a god have striven,
Not hearing much of what we say,
   Take what the god has given;
Though like waves breaking it may be,   45
Or like a changed familiar tree,
Or like a stairway to the sea
   Where down the blind are driven.

1916

Mr. Flood's Party

Old Eben Flood, climbing alone one night
Over the hill between the town below
And the forsaken upland hermitage
That held as much as he should ever know
On earth again of home, paused warily.   5
The road was his with not a native near;
And Eben, having leisure, said aloud,
For no man else in Tilbury Town to hear:

"Well, Mr. Flood, we have the harvest moon
Again, and we may not have many more;   10
The bird is on the wing, the poet says,
And you and I have said it here before.
Drink to the bird." He raised up to the light
The jug that he had gone so far to fill,

And answered huskily: "Well, Mr. Flood,   15
Since you propose it, I believe I will."

Alone, as if enduring to the end
A valiant armor of scarred hopes outworn,
He stood there in the middle of the road
Like Roland's ghost winding a silent horn.[1]   20
Below him, in the town among the trees,
Where friends of other days had honored him,
A phantom salutation of the dead
Rang thinly till old Eben's eyes were dim.

Then, as a mother lays her sleeping child   25
Down tenderly, fearing it may awake,
He set the jug down slowly at his feet
With trembling care, knowing that most things break;
And only when assured that on firm earth
It stood, as the uncertain lives of men   30
Assuredly did not, he paced away,
And with his hand extended paused again:

"Well, Mr. Flood, we have not met like this
In a long time; and many a change has come
To both of us, I fear, since last it was   35
We had a drop together. Welcome home!"
Convivially returning with himself,
Again he raised the jug up to the light;
And with an acquiescent quaver said:
"Well, Mr. Flood, if you insist, I might.   40

"Only a very little, Mr. Flood—
For auld lang syne. No more, sir; that will do."
So, for the time, apparently it did,
And Eben evidently thought so too;
For soon amid the silver loneliness   45
Of night he lifted up his voice and sang,
Secure, with only two moons listening,
Until the whole harmonious landscape rang—

"For auld lang syne." The weary throat gave out,
The last word wavered, and the song was done.   50
He raised again the jug regretfully
And shook his head, and was again alone.

[1] A reference to the anonymous eleventh century French poem *Chanson de Roland.* Roland, one of Charlemagne's commanders, who was to blow his horn if he needed support, proudly waited too long and died along with thousands of his troops.

There was not much that was ahead of him,
And there was nothing in the town below—
Where strangers would have shut the many doors   55
That many friends had opened long ago.
1920

Stephen Crane
1871–1900

At nineteen Stephen Crane was best known for his skill as a baseball player. Any other distinctions while briefly a college student were negligible. Within ten years Crane was dead of tuberculosis, acclaimed as a journalist and as the author of *The Red Badge of Courage* (1894), the novel that alone assures his place in American fiction.

Between 1890 and 1900 Crane worked as a free-lance newspaper reporter observing life in New York's slums and as a correspondent reporting on often violent events taking place in Mexico, the American West, Cuba, and Greece. Because the role of the journalist and correspondent was made increasingly glamorous by the "romantic wars" of the 1890s, Crane became a celebrity. He lived in England in manorial splendor he could not afford with his common-law wife, the former madam of the Hotel de Dream in Jacksonville, Florida. He was the friend of writers of great importance, including Joseph Conrad, H. G. Wells, and Henry James. Throughout all this commotion—public and personal—Stephen Crane feverishly wrote the ten volumes of material that make up his collected literary works.

The youngest of fourteen children, Crane was born in Newark, New Jersey, the son of a Methodist minister. The peripatetic nature of the father's ministry moved the Crane family from one small town to another in New Jersey and New York State. After Crane's abortive visits to the classrooms of Lafayette College in Pennsylvania and Syracuse University in New York, he turned full-time to the newspaper life. Crane had had some experience in the business, first as a boy working for his older brother's press bureau, then as the local correspondent of the *New York Tribune* while still a student at Syracuse University. Once he left college at the age of twenty, he had a living to earn and a good idea of how he was to do it.

Crane went to New York in 1891, held a post on the *New York Herald,* lost it, and turned to free-lance writing. He only infrequently sold filler stories to city papers that saw little merit in pieces reporting on what it feels like to live in the slums; exposés in the manner of the muckrakers were preferred. Crane lived hand to mouth, hanging about in the company of medical students and art students, with occasional stints back home in New Jersey. He knew from experience what being poor is like, and he brought to his studies of Bowery life a keenness of observation beyond that possible to the casually curious.

Maggie, a Girl of the Streets was completed in 1893 when Crane was twenty-one. Established publishers had no use for this portrayal of Irish immigrants hanging on to a Bowery existence. In contrast, Jacob Riis's *How the Other Half Lives* (1890) had quickly acquired a receptive readership for its straightforward account of the fetid places where the city's discards lived, perhaps because Riis's approach was patently that of the social reformer. Crane's fictional narrative of the short, dreary, dream-deluded life of Maggie, a young girl who goes "on the toif" as a streetwalker and ends drowned in the East River, was not so obviously uplifting. In an 1896 review of the republished version of *Maggie,* Frank Norris vividly described Crane's camera-eye techniques as "scores and scores of tiny flashlight photographs, instantaneous, caught as it were, on the run." But respectable readers in 1893 preferred the didacticism of the actual photographs Riis had used to dramatize his appeals for aid and reform of the poor to Crane's seemingly impersonal, amoral, sensational effects. *Maggie* came out under the pseudonym Johnston Smith and received little attention. But what attention it got mattered. Hamlin Garland and William Dean Howells recognized Crane's talent and became his mentors—Garland through his praise in *Crumbling Idols* (1894) and Howells in reviews placed in the *Philadelphia Press* (1893) and *Harper's Weekly* (1895).

Late in 1894 Crane's novel *The Red Badge of Courage* appeared as a syndicated feature in some 750 small newspapers across the country. Early the next year the *Philadelphia Press,* part of the chain that had printed *The Red Badge of Courage,* posted their hot young property on writing assignments out West. (From these experiences Crane would write "The Bride Comes to Yellow Sky" and "The Blue Hotel" in 1897.) In May 1895 his first collection of poems, *The Black Riders,* was published to unfavorable reviews. His experimentations in poetic form and the dark mood of his vision were too unconventional for popular acceptance. But in October 1895 *The Red Badge of Courage* was brought out by Appleton's, an important press, and Crane knew what it was like to be famous. Readers immediately took to the vivid tale of Civil War combat written by a young man born ten years after that war had been fought. Unlike *Maggie,* it created a stir among readers who were eager to read realistic accounts of Civil War battles but were uneasy with accounts of daily slum warfare. The serial publication of "Battles and Leaders of the Civil War" (published in four volumes in 1887 and 1888 by *Century* magazine) had roused public interest in the events of the war. Crane could count on excited attention from this moment on for anything he wrote or did.

For Crane, 1896 and 1897 were exceedingly productive years. *Maggie* was republished in 1896 by Appleton's under the eye of the writer-critic Frank Norris. The language of the original edition was cleaned up to meet current tastes in the printed word, and the novel received the approval it had failed to win in 1893. Also published in 1896 were *The Little Regiment,* a collection of Civil War stories, and *George's Mother,* the psychological account of the death-grip solicitude of a mother for her son. During the winter of 1896–1897 Crane was assigned to Cuba to cover the insurrection that led to the military confrontation in 1898 between Spain and the United States. He met and formed a permanent liaison with Cora Taylor of the Hotel de Dream. Early in 1897 he experienced the surprise of having the ship he was aboard sunk from under him as it headed for Cuba—an incident he immediately wrote up as a newspaper report and then developed into the short story "The Open Boat." In the midst of this activity, he published *The Third Violet,* a partly autobiographical novel about a young painter. By the summer of 1897, Crane was off to the Greco-Turkish war front, from whence he sent dispatches to American and British papers. By year's end he and Cora had gone to England to live.

Crane was once again in the Caribbean in 1898, reporting on the battles of the Spanish-American War for the famous Pulitzer paper, the *New York World.* By 1899 he had returned to England, already ill with tuberculosis and deep in debt. Over the next twelve months, Crane worked hard to earn the money he and Cora needed. He published *The Whilomville Stories* and *Wounds in the Rain;* prepared a second collection of poems, *War Is Kind;* completed the novel *Active Service;* wrote articles on major war battles published posthumously as *Great Battles of the World;* and pushed through the writing of twenty-five chapters of yet another novel, *The O'Ruddy.* Taken by Cora to a German sanatorium in the desperate hope that his illness could be arrested, Crane died on June 5, 1900.

That Crane was a literary prodigy is obvious. That he furnished American literature with a group of memorable tales and one novel-length masterwork is not at issue. The *kind* of writing Crane produced is what sparks controversy. Crane examined the inevitable conflict between self-made images that comfort and external facts that undercut romantic visions. But in his literary methods, was he primarily a realist, a naturalist, or an impressionist? Crane was a rebel against everything considered correct by the society he had left behind at twenty. The bohemian life he followed, the woman he lived with, and the material he wrote about all tell us this. But was he attempting to judge conventional society as a realist does, did he prefer to analyze its elements coolly in the manner of the naturalist, or was he most interested in imprinting impression-istic images for their own sake on his readers' minds?

The ironic tone that pervades Crane's narratives makes it difficult to determine his motives. Sometimes he appears hardly more than a very clever young man, and a rather cold one, who closes out the chance of getting at profound human feelings. At times Crane's compassion for those who yield to the stress of constant threats to their lives seems offset by a certain glibness. Those are the moments when he seems to be displaying what he knows (and his readers do not). At other times Crane appears to be trapped in unquestioned dreams of heroic male action. Consider for example, the problematic conclusion of *The Red Badge of Courage.* The young soldier Henry Fleming is now certain he knows the value of heroic action, but do the narrator's remarks in the closing sentences put the boy's certainty in doubt? Many of the endings Crane gives his stories are troublesome. They strike us as sophomoric exercises in facile cleverness—as with Mary Johnson's lament for her injured "goodness" in *Maggie,* the cash-register sign that flips up at the conclusion of "The Blue Hotel," Scratchy Wilson's double-take response to the news that the town marshal had gone and "got hisself married," and the final parade of small-town hypocrisies in "The Monster."

But Crane's imaginative force cannot be denied; nor can the way he finds apt images to encode human behavior. We detect in his writings the same discoveries made by William James's new psychology and by the theories of Charles Darwin and Herbert Spencer, which emphasize how susceptible we are to forces of inherited habits and environmental pressures. In one sense, *The Red Badge of Courage* is a determinist's primer about fears and falsehoods, but Crane manages to avoid trapping this story of a young soldier facing combat and his inner self in the doctrinaire. The novel is a very human tale, not a scientific treatise.

Crane lived quickly and wrote fast. His writing may have outrun his mind's ability or his heart's capacity to cut past the upper layers of that emotional cuticle where people under stress display their desires and terrors. But without question, Crane's reporter's eye is unfailingly accurate in its notations, just as his artist's touch is apparent in the images he has left permanently in his readers' memory.

Further Reading:

J. Berryman, *Stephen Crane,* 1950, 1962.

E. Cady, *Stephen Crane,* 1962, 1980.

M. Bassan, ed. *Stephen Crane: A Collection of Critical Essays,* 1967.

R. Stallman, *Stephen Crane: A Biography,* 1968.

R. Weatherford, *The Growth of Stephen Crane's Literary Reputation,* 1970.

J. Katz, ed. *Stephen Crane in Transition: Centenary Essays,* 1972.

M. Holton, *Cylinder of Vision: The Fiction and Journalistic Writing of Stephen Crane,* 1972.

J. Nagel, *Stephen Crane and Literary Impressionism,* 1980.

E. Sundquist, ed., *American Realism,* 1982.

M. Fried, *Realism, Writing, Disfiguration: On Thomas Eakins and Stephen Crane,* 1987.

A. Kaplan, *The Social Construction of American Realism,* 1988.

L. Mitchell, *Determined Fictions,* 1989.

C. Benfey, *The Double Life of Stephen Crane,* 1992.

S. Wertheim, *The Crane Log,* 1994.

Texts:

"The Open Boat," from *The Works of Stephen Crane,* 10 vols., 1969–1976.

Poems from *Black Riders and Other Lines,* 1895.

The Open Boat

*A Tale Intended to Be After the Fact. Being the Experience of Four Men from the Sunk Steamer Commodore**

I

None of them knew the color of the sky. Their eyes glanced level, and were fastened upon the waves that swept toward them. These waves were of the hue of slate, save for the tops, which were of foaming white, and all of the men knew the colors of the sea.

---

* Crane was on board the *Commodore* bound for Cuba to cover the revolution as a correspondent when the ship (carrying arms for the combatants) was sunk January 2, 1897, off the Florida coast. Together with four other men, Crane spent almost thirty hours in a dinghy before making a safe landing at Daytona. The New York *Press* ran Crane's account of his experiences on January 7. By June he had published his fictional version in *Scribner's Magazine* as "The Open Boat."

The horizon narrowed and widened, and dipped and rose, and at all times its edge was jagged with waves that seemed thrust up in points like rocks.

Many a man ought to have a bath-tub larger than the boat which here rode upon the sea. These waves were most wrongfully and barbarously abrupt and tall, and each froth-top was a problem in small boat navigation.

The cook squatted in the bottom and looked with both eyes at the six inches of gun-wale which separated him from the ocean. His sleeves were rolled over his fat forearms, and the two flaps of his unbuttoned vest dangled as he bent to bail out the boat. Often he said: "Gawd! That was a narrow clip." As he remarked it he invariably gazed eastward over the broken sea.

The oiler, steering with one of the two oars in the boat, sometimes raised himself suddenly to keep clear of water that swirled in over the stern. It was a thin little oar and it seemed often ready to snap.

The correspondent, pulling at the other oar, watched the waves and wondered why he was there.

The injured captain, lying in the bow, was at this time buried in that profound dejection and indifference which comes, temporarily at least, to even the bravest and most enduring when, willy nilly, the firm fails, the army loses, the ship goes down. The mind of the master of a vessel is rooted deep in the timbers of her, though he command for a day or a decade, and this captain had on him the stern impression of a scene in the grays of dawn of seven turned faces, and later a stump of a top-mast with a white ball on it that slashed to and fro at the waves, went low and lower, and down. Thereafter there was something strange in his voice. Although steady, it was deep with mourning, and of a quality beyond oration or tears.

"Keep' er a little more south, Billie," said he.

" 'A little more south,' sir," said the oiler in the stern.

A seat in this boat was not unlike a seat upon a bucking broncho, and, by the same token, a broncho is not much smaller. The craft pranced and reared, and plunged like an animal. As each wave came, and she rose for it, she seemed like a horse making at a fence outrageously high. The manner of her scramble over these walls of water is a mystic thing, and, moreover, at the top of them were ordinarily these problems in white water, the foam racing down from the summit of each wave, requiring a new leap, and a leap from the air. Then, after scornfully bumping a crest, she would slide, and race, and splash down a long incline and arrive bobbing and nodding in front of the next menace.

A singular disadvantage of the sea lies in the fact that after successfully surmounting one wave you discover that there is another behind it just as important and just as nervously anxious to do something effective in the way of swamping boats. In a ten-foot dingey one can get an idea of the resources of the sea in the line of waves that is not probable to the average experience, which is never at sea in a dingey. As each salty wall of water approached, it shut all else from the view of the men in the boat, and it was the final outburst of the ocean, the last effort of the grim water. There was a terrible grace in the move of the waves, and they came in silence, save for the snarling of the crests.

In the wan light, the faces of the men must have been gray. Their eyes must have glinted in strange ways as they gazed steadily astern. Viewed from a balcony, the whole thing would doubtlessly have been weirdly picturesque. But the men in the boat had no time to see it, and if they had had leisure there were other things to occupy their minds. The sun swung steadily up the sky, and they knew it was broad day because the color of the sea changed from slate to emerald-green, streaked with amber lights, and the foam was like tumbling snow. The process of the breaking day was unknown to them. They were aware only of this effect upon the color of the waves that rolled toward them.

In disjointed sentences the cook and the correspondent argued as to the difference between a life-saving station and a house of refuge. The cook had said: "There's a house of refuge just north of the Mosquito Inlet Light, and as soon as they see us, they'll come off in their boat and pick us up."

"As soon as who see us?" said the correspondent.

"The crew," said the cook.

"Houses of refuge don't have crews," said the correspondent. "As I understand them, they are only places where clothes and grub are stored for the benefit of ship-wrecked people. They don't carry crews."

"Oh, yes, they do," said the cook.

"No, they don't," said the correspondent.

"Well, we're not there yet, anyhow," said the oiler, in the stern.

"Well," said the cook, "perhaps it's not a house of refuge that I'm thinking of as be-ing near Mosquito Inlet Light. Perhaps it's a life-saving station."

"We're not there yet," said the oiler, in the stern.

II

As the boat bounced from the top of each wave, the wind tore through the hair of the hatless men, and as the craft plopped her stern down again the spray slashed past them. The crest of each of these waves was a hill, from the top of which the men surveyed, for a moment, a broad tumultuous expanse, shining and wind-riven. It was probably splendid. It was probably glorious, this play of the free sea, wild with lights of emerald and white and amber.

"Bully good thing it's an on-shore wind," said the cook. "If not, where would we be? Wouldn't have a show."

"That's right," said the correspondent.

The busy oiler nodded his assent.

Then the captain, in the bow, chuckled in a way that expressed humor, contempt, tragedy, all in one. "Do you think we've got much of a show, now, boys?" said he.

Whereupon the three were silent, save for a trifle of hemming and hawing. To ex-press any particular optimism at this time they felt to be childish and stupid, but they all doubtless possessed this sense of the situation in their mind. A young man thinks doggedly at such times. On the other hand, the ethics of their condition was decidedly against any open suggestion of hopelessness. So they were silent.

"Oh, well," said the captain, soothing his children, "we'll get ashore all right."

But there was that in his tone which made them think, so the oiler quoth: "Yes! If this wind holds!"

The cook was bailing. "Yes! If we don't catch hell in the surf."

Canton flannel gulls flew near and far. Sometimes they sat down on the sea, near patches of brown sea-weed that rolled over the waves with a movement like carpets on a line in a gale. The birds sat comfortably in groups, and they were envied by some in the dingey, for the wrath of the sea was no more to them than it was to a covey of prairie chickens a thousand miles inland. Often they came very close and stared at the men with black bead-like eyes. At these times they were uncanny and sinister in their unblinking scrutiny, and the men hooted angrily at them, telling them to be gone. One came, and evidently decided to alight on the top of the captain's head. The bird flew parallel to the boat and did not circle, but made short sidelong jumps in the air in chicken-fashion. His black eyes were wistfully fixed upon the captain's head. "Ugly brute," said the oiler to the bird. "You look as if you were made with a jack-knife." The cook and the correspondent swore darkly at the creature. The captain naturally wished to knock it away with the end of the heavy painter, but he did not dare do it, because anything resembling an emphatic gesture would have capsized this freighted boat, and so with his open hand, the captain gently and carefully waved the gull away. After it had been discouraged from the pursuit the captain breathed easier on account of his hair, and others breathed easier because the bird struck their minds at this time as being somehow grewsome and ominous.

In the meantime the oiler and the correspondent rowed. And also they rowed.

They sat together in the same seat, and each rowed an oar, then the oiler took both oars; then the correspondent took both oars; then the oiler; then the correspondent. They rowed and they rowed. The very ticklish part of the business was when the time came for the reclining one in the stern to take his turn at the oars. By the very last star of truth, it is easier to steal eggs from under a hen than it was to change seats in the dingey. First the man in the stern slid his hand along the thwart and moved with care, as if he were of Sèvres. Then the man in the rowing seat slid his hand along the other thwart. It was all done with the most extraordinary care. As the two sidled past each other, the whole party kept watchful eyes on the coming wave, and the captain cried: "Look out now! Steady there!"

The brown mats of sea-weed that appeared from time to time were like islands, bits of earth. They were travelling, apparently, neither one way nor the other. They were, to all intents, stationary. They informed the men in the boat that it was making progress slowly toward the land.

The captain, rearing cautiously in the bow, after the dingey soared on a great swell, said that he had seen the light-house at Mosquito Inlet. Presently the cook remarked that he had seen it. The correspondent was at the oars, then, and for some reason he too wished to look at the light-house, but his back was toward the far shore and the waves were important, and for some time he could not seize an opportunity to turn his head. But at last there came a wave more gentle than the others, and when at the crest of it he swiftly scoured the western horizon.

"See it?" said the captain.

"No," said the correspondent, slowly. "I didn't see anything."

"Look again," said the captain. He pointed. "It's exactly in that direction."

At the top of another wave, the correspondent did as he was bid, and this time his eyes chanced on a small still thing on the edge of the swaying horizon. It was precisely like the point of a pin. It took an anxious eye to find a light-house so tiny.

"Think we'll make it, Captain?"

"If this wind holds and the boat don't swamp, we can't do much else," said the captain.

The little boat, lifted by each towering sea, and splashed viciously by the crests, made progress that in the absence of sea-weed was not apparent to those in her. She seemed just a wee thing wallowing, miraculously, top-up, at the mercy of five oceans. Occasionally, a great spread of water, like white flame, swarmed into her.

"Bail her, cook," said the captain, serenely.

"All right, Captain," said the cheerful cook.

III

It would be difficult to describe the subtle brotherhood of men that was here established on the seas. No one said that it was so. No one mentioned it, but it dwelt in the boat, and each man felt it warm him. They were a captain, an oiler, a cook, and a correspondent, and they were friends, friends in a more curiously ironbound degree than may be common. The hurt captain, lying against the water-jar in the bow, spoke always in a low voice and calmly but he could never command a more ready and swiftly obedient crew than the motley three of the dingey. It was more than a mere recognition of what was best for the common safety. There was surely in it a quality that was personal and heartfelt. And after this devotion to the commander of the boat there was this comradeship that the correspondent, for instance, who had been taught to be cynical of men, knew even at the time was the best experience of his life. But no one said that it was so. No one mentioned it.

"I wish we had a sail," remarked the captain. "We might try my overcoat on the end of an oar and give you two boys a chance to rest." So the cook and the correspondent held the mast and spread wide the overcoat, the oiler steered, and the little boat made good way with her new rig. Sometimes the oiler had to scull sharply to keep a sea from breaking into the boat, but otherwise sailing was a success.

Meanwhile the light-house had been growing slowly larger. It had now almost assumed color, and appeared like a little gray shadow in the sky. The man at the oars could not be prevented from turning his head rather often to try for a glimpse of this little gray shadow.

At last, from the top of each wave the men in the tossing boat could see land. Even as the light-house was an upright shadow on the sky, this land seemed but a long black shadow on the sea. It certainly was thinner than paper. "We must be about opposite New Smyrna," said the cook, who had coasted this shore often in schooners. "Captain, by the way, I believe they abandoned that life-saving station there about a year ago."

"Did they?" said the captain.

The wind slowly died away. The cook and the correspondent were not now obliged to slave in order to hold high the oar. But the waves continued their old impetuous swooping at the dingey, and the little craft, no longer under way, struggled woundily over them. The oiler or the correspondent took the oars again.

Shipwrecks are *apropos* of nothing. If men could only train for them and have them occur when the men had reached pink condition, there would be less drowning at sea. Of the four in the dingey none had slept any time worth mentioning for two days and two nights previous to embarking in the dingey, and in the excitement of clambering about the deck of a foundering ship they had also forgotten to eat heartily.

For these reasons, and for others, neither the oiler nor the correspondent was fond of rowing at this time. The correspondent wondered ingenuously how in the name of all that was sane could there be people who thought it amusing to row a boat. It was not an amusement; it was a diabolical punishment, and even a genius of mental aberrations could never conclude that it was anything but a horror to the muscles and a crime against the back. He mentioned to the boat in general how the amusement of rowing struck him, and the weary-faced oiler smiled in full sympathy. Previously to the foundering, by the way, the oiler had worked double-watch in the engine-room of the ship.

"Take her easy, now, boys," said the captain. "Don't spend yourselves. If we have to run a surf you'll need all your strength, because we'll sure have to swim for it. Take your time."

Slowly the land arose from the sea. From a black line it became a line of black and a line of white—trees and sand. Finally, the captain said that he could make out a house on the shore. "That's the house of refuge, sure," said the cook. "They'll see us before long, and come out after us."

The distant light-house reared high. "The keeper ought to be able to make us out now, if he's looking through a glass," said the captain. "He'll notify the life-saving people."

"None of those other boats could have got ashore to give word of the wreck," said the oiler, in a low voice. "Else the life-boat would be out hunting us."

Slowly and beautifully the land loomed out of the sea. The wind came again. It had veered from the northeast to the southeast. Finally, a new sound struck the ears of the men in the boat. It was the low thunder of the surf on the shore. "We'll never be able to make the light-house now," said the captain. "Swing her head a little more north, Billie."

" 'A little more north,' sir," said the oiler.

Whereupon the little boat turned her nose once more down the wind, and all but the oarsman watched the shore grow. Under the influence of this expansion doubt and direful apprehension was leaving the minds of the men. The management of the boat was still most absorbing, but it could not prevent a quiet cheerfulness. In an hour, perhaps, they would be ashore.

Their back-bones had become thoroughly used to balancing in the boat and they now rode this wild colt of a dingey like circus men. The correspondent thought that he had been drenched to the skin, but happening to feel in the top pocket of his coat, he found therein eight cigars. Four of them were soaked with seawater; four were perfectly scatheless. After a search, somebody produced three dry matches, and thereupon the four waifs rode impudently in their little boat, and with an assurance of an impending rescue shining in their eyes, puffed at the big cigars and judged well and ill of all men. Everybody took a drink of water.

IV

"Cook," remarked the captain, "there don't seem to be any signs of life about your house of refuge."

"No," replied the cook. "Funny they don't see us!"

A broad stretch of lowly coast lay before the eyes of the men. It was dunes topped with dark vegetation. The roar of the surf was plain, and sometimes they could see the white lip of a wave as it spun up the beach. A tiny house was blocked out black upon the sky. Southward, the slim light-house lifted its little gray length.

Tide, wind, and waves were swinging the dingey northward. "Funny they don't see us," said the men.

The surf's roar was here dulled, but its tone was, nevertheless, thunderous and mighty. As the boat swam over the great rollers, the men sat listening to this roar. "We'll swamp sure," said everybody.

It is fair to say here that there was not a life-saving station within twenty miles in either direction, but the men did not know this fact and in consequence they made dark and opprobrious remarks concerning the eyesight of the nation's life-savers. Four scowling men sat in the dingey and surpassed records in the invention of epithets.

"Funny they don't see us."

The light-heartedness of a former time had completely faded. To their sharpened minds it was easy to conjure pictures of all kinds of incompetency and blindness and indeed, cowardice. There was the shore of the populous land, and it was bitter and bitter to them that from it came no sign.

"Well," said the captain, ultimately, "I suppose we'll have to make a try for ourselves. If we stay out here too long, we'll none of us have strength left to swim after the boat swamps."

And so the oiler, who was at the oars, turned the boat straight for the shore. There was a sudden tightening of muscles. There was some thinking.

"If we don't all get ashore—" said the captain. "If we don't all get ashore, I suppose you fellows know where to send news of my finish?"

They then briefly exchanged some addresses and admonitions. As for the reflections of the men, there was a great deal of rage in them. Perchance they might be formulated thus: "If I am going to be drowned—if I am going to be drowned—if I am going to be drowned, why, in the name of the seven mad gods who rule the sea, was I allowed to come thus far and contemplate sand and trees? Was I brought here merely to have my nose dragged away as I was about to nibble the sacred cheese of life? It is preposterous. If this old ninny-woman, Fate, cannot do better than this, she should be deprived of the management of men's fortunes. She is an old hen who knows not her intention. If she has decided to drown me, why did she not do it in the beginning and save me all this trouble. The whole affair is absurd. . . . But, no, she cannot mean to drown me. She dare not drown me. She cannot drown me. Not after all this work." Afterward the man might have had an impulse to shake his fist at the clouds. "Just you drown me, now, and then hear what I call you!"

The billows that came at this time were more formidable. They seemed always just about to break and roll over the little boat in a turmoil of foam. There was a preparatory and long growl in the speech of them. No mind unused to the sea would have concluded that the dingey could ascend these sheer heights in time, the shore was still afar, the oiler was a wily surfman. "Boys," he said, swiftly, "she won't live three minutes more and we're too far out to swim. Shall I take her to sea again, Captain?"

"Yes! Go ahead!" said the captain.

This oiler, by a series of quick miracles, and fast and steady oarsmanship, turned the boat in the middle of the surf and took her safely to sea again.

There was a considerable silence as the boat bumped over the furrowed sea to deeper water. Then somebody in gloom spoke. "Well, anyhow, they must have seen us from the shore by now."

The gulls went in slanting flight up the wind toward the gray desolate east. A squall, marked by dingy clouds, and clouds brick-red, like smoke from a burning building, appeared from the southeast.

"What do you think of those life-saving people? Ain't they peaches?"

"Funny they haven't seen us."

"Maybe they think we're out here for sport! Maybe they think we're fishin'. Maybe they think we're damned fools."

It was a long afternoon. A changed tide tried to force them southward, but wind and wave said northward. Far ahead, where coastline, sea, and sky formed their mighty angle, there were little dots which seemed to indicate a city on the shore.

"St. Augustine?"

The captain shook his head. "Too near Mosquito Inlet."

And the oiler rowed, and then the correspondent rowed. Then the oiler rowed. It was a weary business. The human back can become the seat of more aches and pains than are registered in books for the composite anatomy of a regiment. It is a limited area, but it can become the theatre of innumerable muscular conflicts, tangles, wrenches, knots, and other comforts.

"Did you ever like to row, Billie?" asked the correspondent.

"No," said the oiler. "Hang it."

When one exchanged the rowing-seat for a place in the bottom of the boat, he suffered a bodily depression that caused him to be careless of everything save an obligation to wiggle one finger. There was cold sea-water swashing to and fro in the boat, and he lay in it. His head, pillowed on a thwart, was within an inch of the swirl of a wave crest, and sometimes a particularly obstreperous sea came in-board and drenched him once more. But these matters did not annoy him. It is almost certain that if the boat had capsized he would have tumbled comfortably out upon the ocean as if he felt sure that it was a great soft mattress.

"Look! There's a man on the shore!"

"Where?"

"There! See 'im? See 'im?"

"Yes, sure! He's walking along."

"Now he's stopped. Look! He's facing us!"

"He's waving at us!"

"So he is! By thunder!"

"Ah, now, we're all right! Now we're all right! There'll be a boat out here for us in half an hour."

"He's going on. He's running. He's going up to that house there."

The remote beach seemed lower than the sea, and it required a searching glance to discern the little black figure. The captain saw a floating stick and they rowed to it. A bath-towel was by some weird chance in the boat, and, tying this on the stick, the captain waved it. The oarsman did not dare turn his head, so he was obliged to ask questions.

"What's he doing now?"

"He's standing still again. He's looking, I think. . . . There he goes again. Toward the house. . . . Now he's stopped again."

"Is he waving at us?"

"No, not now! he was, though."

"Look! There comes another man!"

"He's running."

"Look at him go, would you."

"Why, he's on a bicycle. Now he's met the other man. They're both waving at us. Look!"

"There comes something up the beach."

"What the devil is that thing?"

"Why, it looks like a boat."

"Why, certainly it's a boat."

"No, it's on wheels."

"Yes, so it is. Well, that must be the life-boat. They drag them along shore on a wagon."

"That's the life-boat, sure."

"No, by ———, it's—it's an omnibus."

"I tell you it's a life-boat."

"It is not! It's an omnibus. I can see it plain. See? One of those big hotel omnibuses."

"By thunder, you're right. It's an omnibus, sure as fate. What do you suppose they are doing with an omnibus? Maybe they are going around collecting the life-crew, hey?"

"That's it, likely. Look! There's a fellow waving a little black flag. He's standing on the steps of the omnibus. There come those other two fellows. Now they're all talking together. Look at the fellow with the flag. Maybe he ain't waving it!"

"That ain't a flag, is it? That's his coat. Why, certainly, that's his coat."

"So it is. It's his coat. He's taken it off and is waving it around his head. But would you look at him swing it!"

"Oh, say, there isn't any life-saving station there. That's just a winter resort hotel omnibus that has brought over some of the boarders to see us drown."

"What's that idiot with the coat mean? What's he signaling, anyhow?"

"It looks as if he were trying to tell us to go north. There must be a life-saving station up there."

"No! He thinks we're fishing. Just giving us a merry hand. See? Ah, there, Willie."

"Well, I wish I could make something out of those signals. What do you suppose he means?"

"He don't mean anything. He's just playing."

"Well, if he'd just signal us to try the surf again, or to go to sea and wait, or go north, or go south, or go to hell—there would be some reason in it. But look at him. He just stands there and keeps his coat revolving like a wheel. The ass!"

"There come more people."

"Now there's quite a mob. Look! Isn't that a boat?"

"Where? Oh, I see where you mean. No, that's no boat."

"That fellow is still waving his coat."

"He must think we like to see him do that, why don't he quit it. It don't mean anything."

"I don't know. I think he is trying to make us go north. It must be that there's a life-saving station there somewhere."

"Say, he ain't tired yet. Look at 'im wave."

"Wonder how long he can keep that up. He's been revolving his coat ever since he caught sight of us. He's an idiot. Why aren't they getting men to bring a boat out. A fishing boat—one of those big yawls—could come out here all right. Why don't he do something?"

"Oh, it's all right, now."

"They'll have a boat out here for us in less than no time, now that they've seen us."

A faint yellow tone came into the sky over the low land. The shadows on the sea slowly deepened. The wind bore coldness with it, and the men began to shiver.

"Holy smoke!" said one, allowing his voice to express his impious mood, "if we keep on monkeying out here! If we've got to flounder out here all night!"

"Oh, we'll never have to stay here all night! don't you worry. They've seen us now, and it won't be long before they'll come chasing out after us."

The shore grew dusky. The man waving a coat blended gradually into the gloom, and it swallowed in the same manner the omnibus and the group of people. The spray, when it dashed uproariously over the side, made the voyagers shrink and swear like men who were being branded.

"I'd like to catch the chump who waved the coat. I feel like soaking him one, just for luck."

"Why? What did he do?"

"Oh, nothing, but then he seemed so damned cheerful."

In the meantime the oiler rowed, and then the correspondent rowed, and then the oiler rowed. Gray-faced and bowed forward, they mechanically, turn by turn, plied the leaden oars. The form of the light-house had vanished from the southern horizon, but finally a pale star appeared, just lifting from the sea. The streaked saffron in the west passed before the all-merging darkness, and the sea to the east was black. The land had vanished, and was expressed only by the low and drear thunder of the surf.

"If I am going to be drowned—if I am going to be drowned—if I am going to be drowned, why, in the name of the seven mad gods who rule the sea, was I allowed to come thus far and contemplate sand and trees? Was I brought here merely to have my nose dragged away as I was about to nibble the sacred cheese of life?"

The patient captain, drooped over the water-jar, was sometimes obliged to speak to the oarsman.

"Keep her head up! Keep her head up!"

" 'Keep her head up,' sir." The voices were weary and low.

This was surely a quiet evening. All save the oarsman lay heavily and listlessly in the boat's bottom. As for him, his eyes were just capable of noting the tall black waves that swept forward in a most sinister silence, save for an occasional subdued growl of a crest.

The cook's head was on a thwart, and he looked without interest at the water under his nose. He was deep in other scenes. Finally he spoke. "Billie," he murmured, dreamfully, "what kind of pie do you like best?"

V

"Pie," said the oiler and the correspondent, agitatedly. "Don't talk about those things, blast you!"

"Well," said the cook, "I was just thinking about ham sandwiches, and—"

A night on the sea in an open boat is a long night. As darkness settled finally, the shine of the light, lifting from the sea in the south, changed to full gold. On the northern horizon a new light appeared, a small bluish gleam on the edge of the waters. These two lights were the furniture of the world. Otherwise there was nothing but waves.

Two men huddled in the stern, and distances were so magnificent in the dingey that the rower was enabled to keep his feet partly warmed by thrusting them under his companions. Their legs indeed extended far under the rowing-seat until they touched the feet of the captain forward. Sometimes, despite the efforts of the tired oarsman, a wave came piling into the boat, an icy wave of the night, and the chilling water soaked them anew. They would twist their bodies for a moment and groan, and sleep the dead sleep once more, while the water in the boat gurgled about them as the craft rocked.

The plan of the oiler and the correspondent was for one to row until he lost the ability, and then arouse the other from his sea-water couch in the bottom of the boat.

The oiler plied the oars until his head drooped forward, and the overpowering sleep blinded him. And he rowed yet afterward. Then he touched a man in the bottom of the boat, and called his name. "Will you spell me for a little while?" he said, meekly.

"Sure, Billie," said the correspondent, awakening and dragging himself to a sitting position. They exchanged places carefully, and the oiler, cuddling down in the sea-water at the cook's side, seemed to go to sleep instantly.

The particular violence of the sea had ceased. The waves came without snarling. The obligation of the man at the oars was to keep the boat headed so that the tilt of the rollers would not capsize her, and to preserve her from filling when the crests rushed past. The black waves were silent and hard to be seen in the darkness. Often one was almost upon the boat before the oarsman was aware.

In a low voice the correspondent addressed the captain. He was not sure that the captain was awake, although this iron man seemed to be always awake. "Captain, shall I keep her making for that light north, sir?"

The same steady voice answered him. "Yes. Keep it about two points off the port bow."

The cook had tied a life-belt around himself in order to get even the warmth which this clumsy cork contrivance could donate, and he seemed almost stove-like when a rower, whose teeth invariably chattered wildly as soon as he ceased his labor, dropped down to sleep.

The correspondent, as he rowed, looked down at the two men sleeping under foot. The cook's arm was around the oiler's shoulders, and, with their fragmentary clothing and haggard faces, they were the babes of the sea, a grotesque rendering of the old babes in the wood.

Later he must have grown stupid at his work, for suddenly there was a growling of water, and a crest came with a roar and a swash into the boat, and it was a wonder that it did not set the cook afloat in his life-belt. The cook continued to sleep, but the oiler sat up, blinking his eyes and shaking with the new cold.

"Oh, I'm awful sorry, Billie," said the correspondent, contritely.

"That's all right, old boy," said the oiler, and lay down again and was asleep.

Presently it seemed that even the captain dozed, and the correspondent thought that he was the one man afloat on all the oceans. The wind had a voice as it came over the waves, and it was sadder than the end.

There was a long, loud swishing astern of the boat, and a gleaming trail of phosphorescence, like blue flame, was furrowed on the black waters. It might have been made by a monstrous knife.

Then there came a stillness, while the correspondent breathed with the open mouth and looked at the sea.

Suddenly there was another swish and another long flash of bluish light, and this time it was alongside the boat, and might almost have been reached with an oar. The correspondent saw an enormous fin speed like a shadow through the water, hurling the crystalline spray and leaving the long glowing trail.

The correspondent looked over his shoulder at the captain. His face was hidden, and he seemed to be asleep. He looked at the babes of the sea. They certainly were asleep. So, being bereft of sympathy, he leaned a little way to one side and swore softly into the sea.

But the thing did not then leave the vicinity of the boat. Ahead or astern, on one side or the other, at intervals long or short, fled the long sparkling streak, and there was to be heard the whiroo of the dark fin. The speed and power of the thing was greatly to be admired. It cut the water like a gigantic and keen projectile.

The presence of this biding thing did not affect the man with the same horror that it would if he had been a picknicker. He simply looked at the sea dully and swore in an undertone.

Nevertheless, it is true that he did not wish to be alone with the thing. He wished one of his companions to awaken by chance and keep him company with it. But the captain hung motionless over the water-jar and the oiler and the cook in the bottom of the boat were plunged in slumber.

VI

"If I am going to be drowned—if I am going to be drowned—if I am going to be drowned, why, in the name of the seven mad gods who rule the sea, was I allowed to come thus far and contemplate sand and trees?"

During this dismal night, it may be remarked that a man would conclude that it was really the intention of the seven mad gods to drown him, despite the abominable injustice of it. For it was certainly an abominable injustice to drown a man who had worked so hard, so hard. The man felt it would be a crime most unnatural. Other people had drowned at sea since galleys swarmed with painted sails, but still—

When it occurs to a man that nature does not regard him as important, and that she feels she would not maim the universe by disposing of him, he at first wishes to throw bricks at the temple, and he hates deeply the fact that there are no bricks and no temples. Any visible expression of nature would surely be pelleted with his jeers.

Then, if there be no tangible thing to hoot he feels, perhaps, the desire to confront a personification and indulge in pleas, bowed to one knee, and with hands supplicant, saying: "Yes, but I love myself."

A high cold star on a winter's night is the word he feels that she says to him. Thereafter he knows the pathos of his situation.

The men in the dingey had not discussed these matters, but each had, no doubt, reflected upon them in silence and according to his mind. There was seldom any expression upon their faces save the general one of complete weariness. Speech was devoted to the business of the boat.

To chime the notes of his emotion, a verse mysteriously entered the correspondent's head. He had even forgotten that he had forgotten this verse, but it suddenly was in his mind.

A soldier of the Legion lay dying in Algiers,
There was lack of woman's nursing, there was dearth of woman's tears;

But a comrade stood beside him, and he took that comrade's hand,
And he said: "I never more shall see my own, my native land."[1]

In his childhood, the correspondent had been made acquainted with the fact that a soldier of the legion lay dying in Algiers, but he had never regarded it as important. Myriads of his school-fellows had informed him of the soldier's plight, but the dinning had naturally ended by making him perfectly indifferent. He had never considered it his affair that a soldier of the Legion lay dying in Algiers, nor had it appeared to him as a matter for sorrow. It was less to him than the breaking of a pencil's point.

Now, however, it quaintly came to him as a human, living thing. It was no longer merely a picture of a few throes in the breast of a poet, meanwhile drinking tea and warming his feet at the grate; it was an actuality—stern, mournful, and fine.

The correspondent plainly saw the soldier. He lay on the sand with his feet out straight and still. While his pale left hand was upon his chest in an attempt to thwart the going of his life, the blood came between his fingers. In the far Algerian distance, a city of low square forms was set against a sky that was faint with the last sunset hues. The correspondent, plying the oars and dreaming of the slow and slower movements of the lips of the soldier, was moved by a profound and perfectly impersonal comprehension. He was sorry for the soldier of the Legion who lay dying in Algiers.

The thing which had followed the boat and waited had evidently grown bored at the delay. There was no longer to be heard the slash of the cut-water, and there was no longer the flame of the long trail. The light in the north still glimmered, but it was apparently no nearer to the boat. Sometimes the boom of the surf rang in the correspondent's ears, and he turned the craft seaward then and rowed harder. Southward, some one had evidently built a watch-fire on the beach. It was too low and too far to be seen, but it made a shimmering, roseate reflection upon the bluff back of it, and this could be discerned from the boat. The wind came stronger, and sometimes a wave suddenly raged out like a mountain-cat and there was to be seen the sheen and sparkle of a broken crest.

The captain, in the bow, moved on his water-jar and sat erect. "Pretty long night," he observed to the correspondent. He looked at the shore. "Those life-saving people take their time."

"Did you see that shark playing around?"

"Yes, I saw him. He was a big fellow, all right."

"Wish I had known you were awake."

Later the correspondent spoke into the bottom of the boat.

"Billie!" There was a slow and gradual disentanglement. "Billie, will you spell me?"

"Sure," said the oiler.

As soon as the correspondent touched the cold comfortable seawater in the bottom of the boat, and had huddled close to the cook's life-belt he was deep in sleep, despite the fact that his teeth played all the popular airs. This sleep was so good to him that it was but a moment before he heard a voice call his name in a tone that demonstrated the last stages of exhaustion. "Will you spell me?"

"Sure, Billie."

---

[1] Crane's rendition of lines from a poem by Caroline E. S. Norton, "Bingen on the Rhine" (1883).

The light in the north had mysteriously vanished, but the correspondent took his course from the wide-awake captain.

Later in the night they took the boat farther out to sea, and the captain directed the cook to take one oar at the stern and keep the boat facing the seas. He was to call out if he should hear the thunder of the surf. This plan enabled the oiler and the correspondent to get respite together. "We'll give those boys a chance to get into shape again," said the captain. They curled down and, after a few preliminary chatterings and trembles, slept once more the dead sleep. Neither knew they had bequeathed to the cook the company of another shark, or perhaps the same shark.

As the boat caroused on the waves, spray occasionally bumped over the side and gave them a fresh soaking, but this had no power to break their repose. The ominous slash of the wind and the water affected them as it would have affected mummies.

"Boys," said the cook, with the notes of every reluctance in his voice, "she's drifted in pretty close. I guess one of you had better take her to sea again." The correspondent, aroused, heard the crash of the toppled crests.

As he was rowing, the captain gave him some whiskey and water, and this steadied the chills out of him. "If I ever get ashore and anybody shows me even a photograph of an oar—"

At last there was a short conversation.

"Billie. . . . Billie, will you spell me?"

"Sure," said the oiler.

VII

When the correspondent again opened his eyes, the sea and the sky were each of the gray hue of the dawning. Later, carmine and gold was painted upon the waters. The morning appeared finally, in its splendor, with a sky of pure blue, and the sunlight flamed on the tips of the waves.

On the distant dunes were set many little black cottages, and a tall white wind-mill reared above them. No man, nor dog, nor bicycle appeared on the beach. The cottages might have formed a deserted village.

The voyagers scanned the shore. A conference was held in the boat. "Well," said the captain, "if no help is coming, we might better try a run through the surf right away. If we stay out here much longer we will be too weak to do anything for ourselves at all." The others silently acquiesced in this reasoning. The boat was headed for the beach. The correspondent wondered if none ever ascended the tall wind-tower, and if then they never looked seaward. This tower was a giant, standing with its back to the plight of the ants. It represented in a degree, to the correspondent, the serenity of nature amid the struggles of the individual—nature in the wind, and nature in the vision of men. She did not seem cruel to him then, nor beneficent, nor treacherous, nor wise. But she was indifferent, flatly indifferent. It is, perhaps, plausible that a man in this situation, impressed with the unconcern of the universe, should see the innumerable flaws of his life and have them taste wickedly in his mind and wish for another chance. A distinction between right and wrong seems absurdly clear to him, then, in this new ignorance of the grave-edge, and he understands that if he were given another opportunity he would mend his conduct and his words, and be better and brighter during an introduction, or at a tea.

"Now, boys," said the captain, "she is going to swamp sure. All we can do is to work her in as far as possible, and then when she swamps, pile out and scramble for the beach. Keep cool now, and don't jump until she swamps sure."

The oiler took the oars. Over his shoulders he scanned the surf. "Captain," he said, "I think I'd better bring her about, and keep her head-on to the seas and back her in."

"All right, Billie," said the captain. "Back her in." The oiler swung the boat then and, seated in the stern, the cook and the correspondent were obliged to look over their shoulders to contemplate the lonely and indifferent shore.

The monstrous inshore rollers heaved the boat high until the men were again enabled to see the white sheets of water scudding up the slanted beach. "We won't get in very close," said the captain. Each time a man could wrest his attention from the rollers, he turned his glance toward the shore, and in the expression of the eyes during this contemplation there was a singular quality. The correspondent, observing the others, knew that they were not afraid, but the full meaning of their glances was shrouded.

As for himself, he was too tired to grapple fundamentally with the fact. He tried to coerce his mind into thinking of it, but the mind was dominated at this time by the muscles, and the muscles said they did not care. It merely occurred to him that if he should drown it would be a shame.

There were no hurried words, no pallor, no plain agitation. The men simply looked at the shore. "Now, remember to get well clear of the boat when you jump," said the captain.

Seaward the crest of a roller suddenly fell with a thunderous crash, and the long white comber came roaring down upon the boat.

"Steady now," said the captain. The men were silent. They turned their eyes from the shore to the comber and waited. The boat slid up the incline, leaped at the furious top, bounced over it, and swung down the long back of the wave. Some water had been shipped and the cook bailed it out.

But the next crest crashed also. The tumbling boiling flood of white water caught the boat and whirled it almost perpendicular. Water swarmed in from all sides. The correspondent had his hands on the gunwale at this time, and when the water entered at that place he swiftly withdrew his fingers, as if he objected to wetting them.

The little boat, drunken with this weight of water, reeled and snuggled deeper into the sea.

"Bail her out, cook! Bail her out," said the captain.

"All right, Captain," said the cook.

"Now, boys, the next one will do for us, sure," said the oiler. "Mind to jump clear of the boat."

The third wave moved forward, huge, furious, implacable. It fairly swallowed the dingey, and almost simultaneously the men tumbled into the sea. A piece of life-belt had lain in the bottom of the boat, and as the correspondent went overboard he held this to his chest with his left hand.

The January water was icy, and he reflected immediately that it was colder than he had expected to find it off the coast of Florida. This appeared to his dazed mind as a fact important enough to be noted at the time. The coldness of the water was sad; it was tragic. This fact was somehow so mixed and confused with his opinion of his own situation that it seemed almost a proper reason for tears. The water was cold.

When he came to the surface he was conscious of little but the noisy water. Afterward he saw his companions in the sea. The oiler was ahead in the race. He was swimming strongly and rapidly. Off to the correspondent's left, the cook's great white and corked back bulged out of the water, and in the rear the captain was hanging with his one good hand to the keel of the overturned dingey.

There is a certain immovable quality to a shore, and the correspondent wondered at it amid the confusion of the sea.

It seemed also very attractive, but the correspondent knew that it was a long journey, and he paddled leisurely. The piece of life-preserver lay under him, and sometimes he whirled down the incline of a wave as if he were on a hand-sled.

But finally he arrived at a place in the sea where travel was beset with difficulty. He did not pause swimming to inquire what manner of current had caught him, but there his progress ceased. The shore was set before him like a bit of scenery on a stage, and he looked at it and understood with his eyes each detail of it.

As the cook passed, much farther to the left, the captain was calling to him, "Turn over on your back, cook! Turn over on your back and use the oar."

"All right, sir." The cook turned on his back, and paddling with an oar, went ahead as if he were a canoe.

Presently the boat also passed to the left of the correspondent with the captain clinging with one hand to the keel. He would have appeared like a man raising himself to look over a board fence, if it were not for the extraordinary gymnastics of the boat. The correspondent marvelled that the captain could still hold it.

They passed on, nearer to shore—the oiler, the cook, the captain—and following them went the water-jar, bouncing gayly over the seas.

The correspondent remained in the grip of this strange new enemy—a current. The shore, with its white slope of sand and its green bluff, topped with little silent cottages, was spread like a picture before him. It was very near to him then, but he was impressed as one who in a gallery looks at a scene from Brittany or Holland.

He thought: "I am going to drown? Can it be possible? Can it be possible? Can it be possible?" Perhaps an individual must consider his own death to be the final phenomenon of nature.

But later a wave perhaps whirled him out of this small deadly current, for he found suddenly that he could again make progress toward the shore. Later still, he was aware that the captain, clinging with one hand to the keel of the dingey, had his face turned away from the shore and toward him, and was calling his name. "Come to the boat! Come to the boat!"

In his struggle to reach the captain and the boat, he reflected that when one gets properly wearied, drowning must really be a comfortable arrangement, a cessation of hostilities accompanied by a large degree of relief, and he was glad of it, for the main thing in his mind for some moments had been horror of the temporary agony. He did not wish to be hurt.

Presently he saw a man running along the shore. He was undressing with most remarkable speed. Coat, trousers, shirt, everything flew magically off him.

"Come to the boat," called the captain.

"All right, Captain." As the correspondent paddled, he saw the captain let himself down to bottom and leave the boat. Then the correspondent performed his one little marvel of the voyage. A large wave caught him and flung him with ease and supreme speed completely over the boat and far beyond it. It struck him even then as an event in gymnastics, and a true miracle of the sea. An overturned boat in the surf is not a plaything to a swimming man.

The correspondent arrived in water that reached only to his waist, but his condition did not enable him to stand for more than a moment. Each wave knocked him into a heap, and the under-tow pulled at him.

Then he saw the man who had been running and undressing, and undressing and running, come bounding into the water. He dragged ashore the cook, and then waded toward the captain, but the captain waved him away, and sent him to the correspondent. He was naked, naked as a tree in winter, but a halo was about his head, and he shone like a saint. He gave a strong pull, and a long drag, and a bully heave at the correspondent's hand. The correspondent, schooled in the minor formulae, said: "Thanks, old man." But suddenly the man cried: "What's that?" He pointed a swift finger. The correspondent said: "Go."

In the shallows, face downward, lay the oiler. His forehead touched sand that was periodically, between each wave, clear of the sea.

The correspondent did not know all that transpired afterward.

When he achieved safe ground he fell, striking the sand with each particular part of his body. It was as if he had dropped from a roof, but the thud was grateful to him.

It seems that instantly the beach was populated with men with blankets, clothes, and flasks, and women with coffee-pots and all the remedies sacred to their minds. The welcome of the land to the men from the sea was warm and generous, but a still and dripping shape was carried slowly up the beach, and the land's welcome for it could only be the different and sinister hospitality of the grave.

When it came night, the white waves paced to and fro in the moonlight, and the wind brought the sound of the great sea's voice to the men on shore, and they felt that they could then be interpreters.

1897

---

from Black Riders and Other Lines

VIII

I looked here
I looked there
No where could I see my love.
And—this time—
She was in my heart.   5
Truly then I have no complaint
For 'though she be fair and fairer
She is none so fair as she
In my heart.

XXIV

I saw a man pursuing the horizon;
Round and round they sped.
I was disturbed at this;
I accosted the man.
"It is futile," I said,   5
"You can never——"

"You lie," he cried,
And ran on.

XLVI

Many red devils ran from my heart
And out upon the page.
They were so tiny
The pen could mash them.
And many struggled in the ink.   5
It was strange
To write in this red muck
Of things from my heart.

1895

Theodore Dreiser
1871–1945

By the end of the nineteenth century, Indiana had become a major center of literary
production, able to satisfy the needs of a large body of readers across the country.
There had been General Lew Wallace's best-selling novel *Ben Hur,* about early
Christians in Rome and Palestine, to provide the uplift of religious inspiration mixed
with the romance of exotic times and places. There were the down-home humor and
sentiment of James Whitcomb Riley's verses and the popular satires of George Ade
and, later, Chic Sale. Best of all, there was Booth Tarkington, "the gentleman from
Indiana," who provided middle-class parlors with the novels (such as *Seventeen*) and
magazine pieces (the Penrod stories) that extolled the pleasures and pain of growing
up as a boy in Indianapolis. Tarkington's Indiana (closely observed, with wit and good
nature) was a nice place to be a boy and a dandy place to be a rich and famous author
(especially one who could, as Tarkington did, also turn out such popular historical
romances as *Monsieur Beaucaire* and astute comedies of manners like *The Magnificent*

Ambersons). This Indiana, however, was not the one that Theodore Herman Albert Dreiser knew. He grew up poor and unhappy, the son of German immigrant parents, in Terre Haute, a rough river town.

Dreiser's imagination was midwestern through and through. It was not the Tarkington imagination, however. Dreiser was closer to the Hoosier author of an earlier generation, Edward Eggleston, who had portrayed the seamier, more violent sides of life when Indiana had been little more than a scattering of frontier settlements. Yet Dreiser's novels are most correctly associated with the Chicago school of Realism. Just as New York began to replace Boston as the primary center for work and culture by the 1880s, Indianapolis (locale for easygoing realism and genteel romancing) was displaced by Chicago in the 1890s and early 1900s. That boom city was both the literal place and the symbolic setting for lives and literature that dramatized the naturalistic principles that Dreiser's writings commandingly represent; for Dreiser, to live in Chicago was to experience the forces of environment and physical urges emphasized by his fiction.

Chicago was not the only place to stimulate Dreiser's imagination or to offer an arena for his struggles. Dreiser was a wanderer by nature; he characterized himself as a "cosmic waif." Like others of his generation, he felt buffeted by a willful and indifferent universe. He was always sympathetic toward his unhappy fictional characters because he felt himself to be as bereft as they. He took up lodgings in St. Louis, Pittsburgh, Cleveland, Chicago, and New York. He visited the Soviet Union for eleven weeks in 1927–1928. He acted as journalist, editor, and novelist—whatever his temporary stops called upon him to do. His brother Paul became a popular songwriter with the hit "On the Banks of the Wabash"—a nostalgic bit of "down-home" melody—but home was a place neither Theodore Dreiser nor his fictional characters ever had.

Dreiser had experienced almost too much family life when he was growing up. His family, especially his sisters with their wayward lives and illegitimate children, furnished him with ideas for the stories he would write. But it was not the life Booth Tarkington gave to his boys, Penrod or Sam. The bare, though hardly barren, facts of Dreiser's life are easy to review. He was the twelfth of thirteen children. His father (severe, a religious fanatic, and often out of work) and his mother (absorbed in her family, sympathetic, and illiterate) were unable to stave off the ruin and squalor that beset them. By the age of fifteen, Dreiser was on his own, living off small jobs he scared up around Terre Haute. A year at Indiana University followed in 1889 after a high school teacher who believed in him gave him money for further schooling. But Dreiser was eager to put as much distance between himself and his childhood as possible. As it had for other young men of the period, journalism offered a way out. From 1892 on, Dreiser gained experience on newspapers around the Midwest before heading for New York. He supplemented his street knowledge as best he could with the contemporary literature that most appealed to him—the evolutionary theories of scientific and social determinism grounded on the work of Charles Darwin, Thomas Huxley, and Herbert Spencer.

The year 1900 saw the publication—and quick demise—of Dreiser's first novel, *Sister Carrie,* based in part on the elopement of one of his sisters and a story of the embezzlement of company funds that filled the newspapers at that time. *Sister Carrie* dropped from sight almost as soon as the publishers released it; because, as the story goes, the publisher's wife found it shocking. Only recently has the full story of the tampering with Dreiser's novel come to light with the scholarly publication of the original manuscript. Dreiser had not only to suffer the evisceration of his original ideas but also to witness the disappearance from public view of the resulting bowdlerization.

Deeply disappointed by the failure of *Sister Carrie,* for which his royalties came to $68.40, Dreiser moved on to write a group of short stories. A nervous breakdown followed, debilitating him until 1904, the year he started to work for several magazines, including the Butterick publication *The Delineator.* In 1907 *Sister Carrie* was reissued and began both to receive the attention it deserved and to exert an influence on American literature's turn toward naturalism. *Jennie Gerhardt* was published in 1911; once again the plot came to Dreiser by way of a sister's experience as a rich man's mistress. In 1912 Dreiser brought out the first of three novels known as the Cowperwood trilogy: *The Financier,* followed by *The Titan* (1914) and *The Stoic* (posthumously published in 1947). A journalist by nature, Dreiser continued to base his fiction on contemporary figures whose stories were played out in the newspapers. (In the case of the Cowperwood novels, he modeled his hero on a well-known financial swashbuckler, Charles T. Yerkes.) By these means he dramatized the methods by which clever, ruthless entrepreneurs were taking control of the American system.

Autobiographical books followed: *The "Genius"* (1915) was a fictionalized version of Dreiser's early efforts as a writer; *A Book About Myself,* also known as *Newspaper Days* (1922), and *Dawn* (1931) were straightforward autobiographies. But it was the 1925 publication of *An American Tragedy,* based on an actual murder trial, that earned him the recognition he had been lumbering toward ever since his early days in Terre Haute.

Politics received most of Dreiser's attention in the last decades of his life. It is revealing that he simultaneously became a member of the Communist Party and a Quaker. He was a naive thinker and a somewhat confused social reformer, but to the end he tried to find a way out for individuals and social groups who wanted to escape the deadening grip of a mechanistic determinism that he both believed in and yearned to modify. Dreiser's example helps explain why American naturalism took a different approach to the universe from that upheld by Continental writers who worked from principles, based on their appraisal of human behavior, that attempted to be as clinically objective as any derived by laboratory observation of rats in a test cage.

Dreiser did his "homework" in the nineteenth-century evolutionary theory that had replaced Divine Providence with biology. He was a practicing journalist trained to report empirical facts. He was also a full-fledged participant in a literary movement that attempted to replace the self-delusions of romanticized fictions with honest, sobering accounts of how people react to real events. But Dreiser had to add hope to what he saw, however tragic the scene. This was how he expressed his own desires for happiness, material success, and sexual triumphs.

As Dreiser traveled around the United States—a country in the process of changing before his eyes—he wanted to be able to define the changes he witnessed as progress toward something better. He needed to associate the longings that frustrated his fictional characters and himself with the necessary birth pangs of a soul on its upward ascent. Dreiser once stopped in the middle of an outburst about the quiet farmlands of the Midwest, with their promise of stability and calm, and exclaimed, "But I have seen Pittsburgh!" That is, he had seen firsthand the hectic lives of people who worked silhouetted against the fires of the blast furnaces of the Pennsylvanian steel mills that gave the lie to an agricultural America. But if he contrasted the picture of Pittsburgh with the Ohio farmlands, he kept American ideals and rural idylls in his memory.

Carrie Meeber and George Hurstwood in *Sister Carrie* pass one another along the lines of ascent and descent that take the one to a celebrity's suite at the new Waldorf-Astoria and the other to suicide in a flophouse and a pauper's grave. In *An American Tragedy* Clyde Griffiths goes to his death for the murder of one young woman because of his longing for another, richer, more glamorous girl. His foolish dream of wealth is matched by the folly of his romantic desire for perfect love. Frank Cowperwood's life expresses his faith that he can take command of the machine that brings him financial success and sexual prowess. He rejects the notion that he can be broken by the mechanisms of a "hot" society and a "cold" universe. Money, sex, and power as the way (however abortive) to go "home" became major themes in twentieth-century literature, precisely because Dreiser made them important. His books and his life frequently demonstrate how freedom of choice and fulfillment of one's yearnings are often denied. But this did not stop him. He kept on writing as much about the power of desire as about the inevitability of defeat.

Further Reading:

F. Matthiessen, *Theodore Dreiser,* 1951.

A. Kazin and C. Shapiro, eds. *The Stature of Theodore Dreiser: A Critical Survey of the Man and His Work,* 1955.

J. McAleer, *Theodore Dreiser: An Introduction and Interpretation,* 1968.

R. Lehan, *Theodore Dreiser: His World and His Novels,* 1969.

E. Moers, *Two Dreisers,* 1969.

D. Pizer, ed. *Critical Essays on Theodore Dreiser,* 1981.

E. Sundquist, ed. *American Realism,* 1982.

D. Pizer, *Realism and Naturalism,* rev. ed., 1984.

J. Howard, *Form and History in American Literary Naturalism,* 1985.

P. Fisher, *Hard Facts,* 1985.

S. Fishkin, *From Fact to Fiction,* 1985.

A. Kaplan, *The Social Reconstruction of American Realism,* 1988.

W. Michaels, *The Gold Standard and the Logic of Naturalism,* 1987.

S. Misruchi, *The Power of Historical Knowledge,* 1988.

L. Mitchell, *Determined Fictions,* 1989.

R. Lingeman, *Theodore Dreiser.* 2 vols, 1986, 1990.

P. L. Gerber, *Theodore Dreiser Revisited,* 1992.

Text:
"He Got a Ride," from *Theodore Dreiser, Journalism.* vol. 1.

He Got a Ride

Either a most diabolical outrage was yesterday committed upon one of St. Louis' prominent merchants, Mr. Austin M. Nelson, president of the A. M. Nelson Paint Company, or the police of the Third District have been guilty of gross negligence in a matter of serious criminal import. A very serious accusation, by implication at least, was made against Mr. Nelson by officers of the Third District yesterday afternoon, and that gentleman was carted off from the rear of a vacant dwelling at 601 North Levee in a hoodlum wagon, accompanied by an unknown negro girl about 9 years of age. The arrest of Mr. Nelson was the cause of a scene of excitement, and was attended by sensational features. At the Third District Station, where Mr. Nelson was arraigned before

Captain Joyce, the latter official saw fit to set him at liberty and discharge the negro girl without taking either her name or address.

The whole exciting incident occurred at 3 o'clock yesterday afternoon in the rear of 601 North Levee. The rear of North Levee street is partially an alley and partially a business street, which the City Directory gives as Commercial street. At that number on North Levee, which lies between Washington avenue and Lucas avenue, a plain, faded two-story brick stands. Just south of it the tunnel passes out into the bridge. South of this tunnel, facing on Washington avenue and with its west wall forming a portion of the Commercial alley line, stands a three-story brick structure that backs close up against the Eads tunnel as though trying to crowd it out. It is very old, very musty and unoccupied, except for the garret-like third floor, which some colored children playing below said was occupied by one Mrs. Clark, colored. The second floor has long been vacant, as well as the ground floor, which has long since been a Levee saloon. The walls of the place are much smoked and dingy, the floor rotten and bulging from damp in places. The entrance to the upper floor is by a covered rear stairway of black rotten wood, which is decidedly dark and filthy. It was on the second floor landing of this stairway that Mr. Nelson was found by Officers Callaghan and McInerny of the Third District. With him was the now untraceable negro girl, 9 years old, who is supposed by some neighbors to live in the vicinity of Sixth and Cerre streets. The two officers named were standing on the Levee, near Lucas avenue, when a stranger came forward and informed them that he had observed a strange man going up the stairway in question in company with a negro girl. He hinted at a monstrous crime and the two officers started to go with him. By the time they reached Commercial street and Lucas avenue Officer Kirhen joined them and the three proceeded towards the dark stairway. The neighborhood in question is a mixture of wholesale houses and dwellings. The class of residents there is decidedly conglomerate and, according to the police, very "hard." The progress of the officers south through Commercial street attracted a crowd that grew to fully 500 people, who somehow had got the idea that a great outrage had been perpetrated and passed the word about until the crowd became a mob following and centering about the bluecoats. When the officers came to the stairway all three entered and soon returned with Mr. Nelson and the girl, the latter carrying a lemon basket. Then some one in the crowd yelled, "Lynch him!" This cry was taken up and repeated, coupled with the assertion, "If it was a nigger, he'd soon be swinging to a lamp post." The excitement was increasing as the crowd swelled, and the situation was looking very serious when the patrol wagon arrived and the two prisoners were hauled away.

Among those who saw the policemen ascend the steps and reappear with Mr. Nelson was John Harrison, a boarder of the St. Louis Hotel, which is near by, at the northeast corner of Main and Lucas avenue. Last evening he said to a *Republic* reporter:

"I saw the policemen bring a man out of that stairway; also a negro girl. People around said the man's name was Nelson. When the policemen got him out in the light one of them said, 'What's your name?' The man was awfully nervous. He fidgeted about and finally pulled out a business card. He said he was president of that company. The officer cursed him and said: 'Well, you come along.' Nelson looked very old and wore a seersucker coat and vest and a straw hat—as I remember."

A number of other people corroborated John Harrison's testimony, namely, John Camien, a tailor at 14 Lucas avenue, and his employes, as well as the employes of other firms, who witnessed the arrest from the rear doors of business houses that open out into Commercial street.

Mrs. Potter, a colored woman, living at 601 North Levee, said that her father had seen the officers bring Nelson from the stairway and had heard the negro child state that she lived near the corner of Sixth and Cerre streets.

Mrs. Potter had seen the policemen and Nelson together at the patrol box near the corner of the Levee and Lucas avenue, and had seen the couple bundled into the patrol wagon. There was a big crowd and considerable excitement.

A *Republic* reporter having gathered these facts proceeded to the Third District Police Station, where Mr. Nelson and the girl had been conveyed. There Captain Joyce was found complacently reading.

"Where is Mr. Nelson?" was asked.

"What Mr. Nelson?" queried the Captain.

"Why, the Austin M. Nelson who was brought in here from the Levee with a negro child."

Captain Joyce gazed thoughtfully away for a moment and then said: "Yes, I believe there was such a man in here."

"Where is he now?"

"Why, I set him free. There was nothing to the case. The man is a prominent business man and can be found any time. There's nothing to the case."

"Didn't the officers charge attempted rape?"

"No, sir."

"Did you question the child any or investigate the case?"

"I heard her story. There's nothing in the case; the officers didn't charge anything especially."

"What was the child's name?"

"I don't know."

"Where does she live?"

"I can't tell. I didn't consider the case worth investigating. You are endeavoring to make a sensation out of nothing."

"Have you made out an official report?"

"Oh, no; there isn't anything to the whole matter. Mr. Nelson is a prominent business man. He couldn't be accused of anything like that."

"How did Mr. Nelson explain his presence in that stairway?"

"He said the girl called him up and wanted a dime. That's all."

Further explanation could not be had of Captain Joyce, nor would he discuss the very remarkable conduct of his officers in forcing such a prominent man as Mr. A. M. Nelson to submit to the ignominy of arrest and a ride through the streets in the patrol wagon, when the case was of such a trivial character that the first glance of the Captain's eagle eye showed him there was "nothing in it."

Later Mr. Nelson was visited at his residence, No. 4055 Delmar avenue. He was out driving, but returned at 8:30 P.M. He wore the seersucker coat and vest and the straw hat described by the people about Lucas and Commercial street. When accosted he was smoking a pipe on his front stoop.

"You were engaged in a rather unpleasant affair this afternoon, Mr. Nelson, were you not?"

"Yes," confidentially drawled Mr. Nelson.

"You were conveyed in a patrol wagon to the Third District, were you not, in company with a negro girl, 9 years old?"

"Yes."

"Will you state how you came to be up the dark stairway in the rear of the store at Washington avenue and Commercial street?"

"Why," said Mr. Nelson, "I was passing by there at 8 o'clock to-day and I met a little colored girl with a basket. She stepped into that doorway and as I passed called me. I didn't know what she wanted and so I went toward her. She went up the stairs and when she got into a dark corner she exposed her person and wanted to know whether I would give her a dime. When I heard this I came right down."

"You had never seen the girl before, had you?"

"No."

"Do you know who sent the policemen after you?"

"No."

Mr. Nelson expressed the fear that if the story was printed someone might misjudge him, but expressed no resentment toward the police for giving him a free ride, but it is not improbable that the action of the officers in the case will be laid before the Police Board in the shape of a complaint, or Captain Joyce may discipline his subordinates, who certainly acted in a very injudicious manner if the case is as plain a one as Captain Joyce seems to consider it.

The Nelson Paint Company occupies a four-story brick structure at Nos. 701 and 703 North Second street. The negro child could not be located in the neighborhood given as her home.

1983

Jack London
1876–1916

One of the most popular and most highly paid writers of his time, Jack London was born in San Francisco on January 12, 1876, the illegitimate son of William Henry Chaney, an itinerant astrologer, and Flora Wellman, a spiritualist. He took the name of his stepfather, John London, an unsuccessful rancher who moved the family to Oakland in 1886. As London records in his autobiography, *John Barleycorn* (1913), he quit Oakland High School at fourteen and began a life of odd jobs, heavy drinking, and daring adventures: He earned money as an oyster pirate in San Francisco Bay, worked long hours in a cannery, frequented the Oakland libraries and saloons, and sailed as an able-bodied seaman to Japan. In 1894 he tramped halfway across the country with Kelley's Industrial Army, a California group of unemployed who staged a protest march on Washington. This experience not only led to his long embrace of socialism but also impelled him, especially after being arrested for vagrancy in Buffalo, New York, to begin what he called his "frantic pursuit of knowledge." In 1896 he enrolled as a special student at the University of California at Berkeley, but after a semester he decided he would rather spend the winter prospecting for gold in the Klondike. He found no gold;

instead he returned with experiences and material he would mine for a lifetime as a writer. His first collection of short stories, *The Son of the Wolf*, appeared in 1900.

Three years later he published a best-selling novel, *The Call of the Wild*, in which he attempted to enter into the consciousness of an animal: "There is an ecstasy that marks the summit of life and beyond which life cannot rise. . . . This ecstasy comes when one is most alive, and it comes as a complete forgetfulness that one is alive." London believed that such elemental and ecstatic forms of consciousness could also be attained by people, though mainly in moments of violent struggle with forces larger than themselves.

Though the drama of extremely reduced states of consciousness, as depicted in such famous London stories as "To Build a Fire," informs much of his writing, there is another side to London's work, one more dependent on Marxist economics than Darwinian biology. A year before *Call of the Wild* appeared, London spent six weeks disguised as an out-of-work American sailor roaming the slums of London's East End while he gathered material for the one book he claimed to love the most, *People of the Abyss* (1903). An indictment of capitalism and the class system, the book revealed an intellectual conflict in the writer that would become increasingly strained in his later work. London never satisfactorily reconciled his intense desire for social justice with his equally intense belief in the survival of the powerful. If his Marxism was tainted by an almost ferocious faith in individualism and racial superiority ("I am first of all a white man and only then a socialist"), his Darwinism was diluted by his affection for the underdog and his collectivist sympathies. Throughout his career, he alternated between the rugged individualism of Theodore Roosevelt and the quest for solidarity of Eugene Debs.

The main difficulty with London's personal philosophy, however, was not his inability to reconcile Darwin and Marx but his inability to extend his thoughts past their crudest formulations. He once wrote in a letter:

> I assert, with Hobbes, that it is impossible to separate thought from matter that thinks.
> I assert, with Bacon, that all human understanding arises from the world of sensations.
> I assert, with Locke, that all human ideas are due to the functions of the senses.
> I assert, with Kant, the mechanical origin of the universe, and that creation is a natural and historical process.
> I assert, with Laplace, that there is no need of the hypothesis of a Creator.

This manifesto typifies the blunt style of London's thinking. He tended to see ideas in much the same way that he saw nature—as elemental forces to be reckoned with. Yet, like Rudyard Kipling, whom he greatly admired, London was a natural storyteller. In its narrative energy and mythic power, London's best writing transcends whatever philosophical slogans he set out to portray.

During the height of his popularity as a novelist, London continued to lead a strenuous and adventurous life. After completing one of his most successful novels, *The Sea Wolf*, in 1904, he went to Japan and Korea to cover the Russo-Japanese War for the Hearst papers. In 1905 he ran unsuccessfully for the second time as the Socialist candidate for mayor of Oakland. He published another successful novel, *White Fang*, in 1906 and wrote one of his most highly respected books, the semiautobiographical novel *Martin Eden*, in 1908 and 1909 while sailing his homemade yacht to the South Pacific. When the Mexican Revolution broke out in 1914, he rushed to Veracruz as a correspondent for *Collier's*. In 1915, exhausted and in failing health, he traveled to

Hawaii, where during the day he produced hack work to keep up his dwindling fortune (he had made over a million dollars from his writing) and at night read Freud and Jung. Back in California, suffering from acute uremia, he injected a larger dose of painkilling morphine than he had been accustomed to and died early in the morning of November 22, 1916.

Further Reading:

J. McClintock, *White Logic: Jack London's Short Stories*, 1975.

A. Sinclair, *Jack: A Biography of Jack London*, 1977.

C. Johnson, *Jack London—An American Radical?* 1984

D. Pizer, *Realism and Naturalism*. rev. ed, 1984.

J. Howard, *Form and History in American Literary Naturalism*, 1985.

E. Labor, *et al*, eds. *Letters of Jack London*, 1988.

L. Mitchell, *Determined Fictions*, 1989.

W. Cain, "Socialism, Power, and the Fate of Style: London in His Letters," *American Literary History* 3 (1991), 603–13.

J. Auerbach, *Male Call: Becoming Jack London*, 1996.

L. Cassuto and J. C. Reesman, ed. *Rereading Jack London*, 1996.

Text:
From *Lost Face*, 1910.

To Build a Fire*

Day had broken cold and gray, exceedingly cold and gray, when the man turned aside from the main Yukon trail and climbed the high earth-bank, where a dim and little-travelled trail led eastward through the fat spruce timberland. It was a steep bank, and he paused for breath at the top, excusing the act to himself by looking at his watch. It was nine o'clock. There was no sun nor hint of sun, though there was not a cloud in the sky. It was a clear day, and yet there seemed an intangible pall over the face of things, a subtle gloom that made the day dark, and that was due to the absence of sun. This fact did not worry the man. He was used to the lack of sun. It had been days since he had seen the sun, and he knew that a few more days must pass before that cheerful orb, due south, would just peep above the sky line and dip immediately from view.

The man flung a look back along the way he had come. The Yukon lay a mile wide and hidden under three feet of ice. On top of this ice were as many feet of snow. It was all pure white, rolling in gentle undulations where the ice jams of the freeze-up had formed. North and south, as far as his eye could see, it was unbroken white, save for a dark hairline that curved and twisted from around the spruce-covered island to the south, and that curved and twisted away into the north, where it disappeared behind another spruce-covered island. This dark hairline was the trail—the main trail—that led south five hundred miles to the Chilcoot Pass, Dyea, and salt water; and that led north seventy miles to Dawson, and still on to the north a thousand miles to Nulato, and finally to St. Michael, on Bering Sea, a thousand miles and half a thousand more.

But all this—the mysterious, far-reaching hairline trail, the absence of sun from the sky, the tremendous cold, and the strangeness and weirdness of it all—made no impression on the man. It was not because he was long used to it. He was a newcomer in the

---

* An earlier version of this story first appeared in *Youth's Companion* in May 1902.

land, a *chechaquo,* and this was his first winter. The trouble with him was that he was without imagination. He was quick and alert in the things of life, but only in the things, and not in the significances. Fifty degrees below zero meant eighty-odd degrees of frost. Such fact impressed him as being cold and uncomfortable, and that was all. It did not lead him to meditate upon his frailty as a creature of temperature, and upon man's frailty in general, able only to live within certain narrow limits of heat and cold; and from there on it did not lead him to the conjectural field of immortality and man's place in the universe. Fifty degrees below zero stood for a bite of frost that hurt and that must be guarded against by the use of mittens, ear flaps, warm moccasins, and thick socks. Fifty degrees below zero was to him just precisely fifty degrees below zero. That there should be anything more to it than that was a thought that never entered his head.

As he turned to go on, he spat speculatively. There was a sharp, explosive crackle that startled him. He spat again. And again, in the air, before it could fall to the snow, the spittle crackled. He knew that at fifty below spittle crackled on the snow, but this spittle had crackled in the air. Undoubtedly it was colder than fifty below—how much colder he did not know. But the temperature did not matter. He was bound for the old claim on the left fork of Henderson Creek, where the boys were already. They had come over across the divide from the Indian Creek country, while he had come the roundabout way to take a look at the possibilities of getting out logs in the spring from the islands in the Yukon. He would be in to camp by six o'clock; a bit after dark, it was true, but the boys would be there, a fire would be going, and a hot supper would be ready. As for lunch, he pressed his hand against the protruding bundle under his jacket. It was also under his shirt, wrapped up in a handkerchief and lying against the naked skin. It was the only way to keep the biscuits from freezing. He smiled agreeably to himself as he thought of those biscuits, each cut open and sopped in bacon grease, and each enclosing a generous slice of fried bacon.

He plunged in among the big spruce trees. The trail was faint. A foot of snow had fallen since the last sled had passed over, and he was glad he was without a sled, travelling light. In fact, he carried nothing but the lunch wrapped in the handkerchief. He was surprised, however, at the cold. It certainly was cold, he concluded, as he rubbed his numb nose and cheekbones with his mittened hand. He was a warm-whiskered man, but the hair on his face did not protect the high cheekbones and the eager nose that thrust itself aggressively into the frosty air.

At the man's heels trotted a dog, a big native husky, the proper wolf dog, gray-coated and without any visible or temperamental difference from its brother, the wild wolf. The animal was depressed by the tremendous cold. It knew that it was no time for travelling. Its instinct told it a truer tale than was told to the man by the man's judgment. In reality, it was not merely colder than fifty below zero; it was colder than sixty below, than seventy below. It was seventy-five below zero. Since the freezing point is thirty-two above zero, it meant that one hundred and seven degrees of frost obtained. The dog did not know anything about thermometers. Possibly in its brain there was no sharp consciousness of a condition of very cold such as was in the man's brain. But the brute had its instinct. It experienced a vague but menacing apprehension that subdued it and made it slink along at the man's heels, and that made it question eagerly every unwonted movement of the man as if expecting him to go into camp or to seek shelter somewhere and build a fire. The dog had learned fire, and it wanted fire, or else to burrow under the snow and cuddle its warmth away from the air.

The frozen moisture of its breathing had settled on its fur in a fine powder of frost, and especially were its jowls, muzzle, and eyelashes whitened by its crystalled breath. The man's red beard and mustache were likewise frosted, but more solidly, the deposit taking the form of ice and increasing with every warm, moist breath he exhaled. Also, the man was chewing tobacco, and the muzzle of ice held his lips so rigidly that he was unable to clear his chin when he expelled the juice. The result was that a crystal beard of the color and solidity of amber was increasing its length on his chin. If he fell down it would shatter itself, like glass, into brittle fragments. But he did not mind the appendage. It was the penalty all tobacco chewers paid in that country, and he had been out before in two cold snaps. They had not been so cold as this, he knew, but by the spirit thermometer at Sixty Mile he knew they had been registered at fifty below and at fifty-five.

He held on through the level stretch of woods for several miles, crossed a wide flat of nigger heads, and dropped down a bank to the frozen bed of a small stream. This was Henderson Creek, and he knew he was ten miles from the forks. He looked at his watch. It was ten o'clock. He was making four miles an hour, and he calculated that he would arrive at the forks at half-past twelve. He decided to celebrate that event by eating his lunch there.

The dog dropped in again at his heels, with a tail drooping discouragement, as the man swung along the creek bed. The furrow of the old sled trail was plainly visible, but a dozen inches of snow covered the marks of the last runners. In a month no man had come up or down that silent creek. The man held steadily on. He was not much given to thinking, and just then particularly he had nothing to think about save that he would eat lunch at the forks and that at six o'clock he would be in camp with the boys. There was nobody to talk to; and, had there been, speech would have been impossible because of the ice muzzle on his mouth. So he continued monotonously to chew tobacco and to increase the length of his amber beard.

Once in a while the thought reiterated itself that it was very cold and that he had never experienced such cold. As he walked along he rubbed his cheekbones and nose with the back of his mittened hand. He did this automatically, now and again changing hands. But, rub as he would, the instant he stopped his cheekbones went numb, and the following instant the end of his nose went numb. He was sure to frost his cheeks; he knew that, and experienced a pang of regret that he had not devised a nose strap of the sort Bud wore in cold snaps. Such a strap passed across the cheeks, as well, and saved them. But it didn't matter much, after all. What were frosted cheeks? A bit painful, that was all; they were never serious.

Empty as the man's mind was of thoughts, he was keenly observant, and he noticed the changes in the creek, the curves and bends and timber jams, and always he sharply noted where he placed his feet. Once, coming around a bend, he shied abruptly, like a startled horse, curved away from the place where he had been walking, and retreated several paces back along the trail. The creek he knew was frozen clear to the bottom—no creek could contain water in that arctic winter—but he knew also that there were springs that bubbled out from the hillsides and ran along under the snow and on top the ice of the creek. He knew that the coldest snaps never froze these springs, and he knew likewise their danger. They were traps. They hid pools of water under the snow that might be three inches deep, or three feet. Sometimes a skin of ice half an inch thick covered them, and in turn was covered by the snow. Sometimes there were alternate layers of water and ice skin, so that when one broke through he kept on breaking through for a while, sometimes wetting himself to the waist.

That was why he had shied in such panic. He had felt the give under his feet and heard the crackle of a snow-hidden ice skin. And to get his feet wet in such a temperature meant trouble and danger. At the very least it meant delay, for he would be forced to stop and build a fire, and under its protection to bare his feet while he dried his socks and moccasins. He stood and studied the creek bed and its banks, and decided that the flow of water came from the right. He reflected awhile, rubbing his nose and cheeks, then skirted to the left, stepping gingerly and testing the footing for each step. Once clear of the danger, he took a fresh chew of tobacco and swung along at his four-mile gait.

In the course of the next two hours he came upon several similar traps. Usually the snow above the hidden pools had a sunken, candied appearance that advertised the danger. Once again, however, he had a close call; and once, suspecting danger, he compelled the dog to go on in front. The dog did not want to go. It hung back until the man shoved it forward, and then it went quickly across the white, unbroken surface. Suddenly it broke through, floundered to one side, and got away to firmer footing. It had wet its forefeet and legs, and almost immediately the water that clung to it turned to ice. It made quick efforts to lick the ice off its legs, then dropped down in the snow and began to bite out the ice that had formed between the toes. This was matter of instinct. To permit the ice to remain would mean sore feet. It did not know this. It merely obeyed the mysterious prompting that arose from the deep crypts of its being. But the man knew, having achieved a judgment on the subject, and he removed the mitten from his right hand and helped tear out the ice particles. He did not expose his fingers more than a minute, and was astonished at the swift numbness that smote them. It certainly was cold. He pulled on the mitten hastily, and beat the hand savagely across his chest.

At twelve o'clock the day was at its brightest. Yet the sun was too far south on its winter journey to clear the horizon. The bulge of the earth intervened between it and Henderson Creek, where the man walked under a clear sky at noon and cast no shadow. At half-past twelve, to the minute, he arrived at the forks of the creek. He was pleased at the speed he had made. If he kept it up, he would certainly be with the boys by six. He unbuttoned his jacket and shirt and drew forth his lunch. The action consumed no more than a quarter of a minute, yet in that brief moment the numbness laid hold of the exposed fingers. He did not put the mitten on, but, instead, struck the fingers a dozen sharp smashes against his leg. Then he sat down on a snow-covered log to eat. The sting that followed upon the striking of his fingers against his leg ceased so quickly that he was startled. He had had no chance to take a bit of biscuit. He struck the fingers repeatedly and returned them to the mitten, baring the other hand for the purpose of eating. He tried to take a mouthful, but the ice muzzle prevented. He had forgotten to build a fire and thaw out. He chuckled at his foolishness, and as he chuckled he noted the numbness creeping into the exposed fingers. Also, he noted that the stinging which had first come to his toes when he sat down was already passing away. He wondered whether the toes were warm or numb. He moved them inside the moccasins and decided that they were numb.

He pulled the mitten on hurriedly and stood up. He was a bit frightened. He stamped up and down until the stinging returned into the feet. It certainly was cold, was his thought. That man from Sulphur Creek had spoken the truth when telling how cold it sometimes got in the country. And he had laughed at him at the time! That showed one must not be too sure of things. There was no mistake about it, it was cold. He strode up and down, stamping his feet and threshing his arms, until reassured by the returning warmth. Then he got out matches and proceeded to make a fire. From the undergrowth, where high water of the previous spring had lodged a supply of seasoned twigs, he got his firewood. Working carefully from a small beginning, he soon had a roaring fire, over which he thawed the ice from his face and in the protection of which he ate his biscuits. For the moment the cold of space was outwitted. The dog took satisfaction in the fire, stretching out close enough for warmth and far enough away to escape being singed.

When the man had finished, he filled his pipe and took his comfortable time over a smoke. Then he pulled on his mittens, settled the ear flaps of his cap firmly about his ears, and took the creek trail up the left fork. The dog was disappointed and yearned back toward the fire. This man did not know cold. Possibly all the generations of his ancestry had been ignorant of cold, of real cold, of cold one hundred and seven degrees below freezing point. But the dog knew; all its ancestry knew, and it had inherited the knowledge. And it knew that it was not good to walk abroad in such fearful cold. It was the time to lie snug in a hole in the snow and wait for a curtain of cloud to be drawn across the face of outer space whence this cold came. On the other hand, there was no keen intimacy between the dog and the man. The one was the toil slave of the other, and the only caresses it had ever received were the caresses of the whip lash and of harsh and menacing throat sounds that threatened the whip lash. So the dog made no effort to communicate its apprehension to the man. It was not concerned in the welfare of the man; it was for its own sake that it yearned back toward the fire. But the man whistled, and spoke to it with the sound of whip lashes, and the dog swung in at the man's heels and followed after.

The man took a chew of tobacco and proceeded to start a new amber beard. Also, his moist breath quickly powdered with white his mustache, eyebrows, and lashes. There did not seem to be so many springs on the left fork of the Henderson, and for half an hour the man saw no signs of any. And then it happened. At a place where there were no signs, where the soft, unbroken snow seemed to advertise solidity beneath, the man broke through. It was not deep. He wet himself halfway to the knees before he floundered out to the firm crust.

He was angry, and cursed his luck aloud. He had hoped to get into camp with the boys at six o'clock, and this would delay him an hour, for he would have to build a fire and dry out his footgear. This was imperative at that low temperature—he knew that much; and he turned aside to the bank, which he climbed. On top, tangled in the underbrush about the trunks of several small spruce trees, was a highwater deposit of dry firewood—sticks and twigs, principally, but also larger portions of seasoned branches and fine, dry, last year's grasses. He threw down several large pieces on top of the snow. This served for a foundation and prevented the young flame from drowning itself in the snow it otherwise would melt. The flame he got by touching a match to a small shred of birch bark that he took from his pocket. This burned even more readily than paper. Placing it on the foundation, he fed the young flame with wisps of dry grass and with the tiniest dry twigs.

He worked slowly and carefully, keenly aware of his danger. Gradually, as the flame grew stronger, he increased the size of the twigs with which he fed it. He squatted in the snow, pulling the twigs out from their entanglement in the brush and feeding directly to the flame. He knew there must be no failure. When it is seventy-five below zero, a man must not fail in his first attempt to build a fire—that is, if his feet are wet. If his feet are dry, and he fails, he can run along the trail for half a mile and restore his circulation. But the circulation of wet and freezing feet cannot be restored by running when it is seventy-five below. No matter how fast he runs, the wet feet will freeze the harder. All this the man knew. The old-timer on Sulphur Creek had told him about it the previous fall, and now he was appreciating the advice. Already all sensation had gone out of his feet. To build the fire he had been forced to remove his mittens, and the fingers had quickly gone numb. His pace of four miles an hour had kept his heart pumping blood to the surface of his body and to all the extremities. But the instant he stopped, the action of the pump eased down. The cold of space smote the unprotected tip of the planet, and he, being on that unprotected tip, received the full force of the blow. The blood of his body recoiled before it. The blood was alive, like the dog, and like the dog it wanted to hide away and cover itself up from the fearful cold. So long as he walked four miles an hour, he pumped that blood, willy-nilly, to the surface; but now it ebbed away and sank down into the recesses of his body. The extremities were the first to feel its absence. His wet feet froze the faster, and his exposed fingers numbed the faster, though they had not yet begun to freeze. Nose and cheeks were already freezing, while the skin of all his body chilled as it lost its blood.

But he was safe. Toes and nose and cheeks would be only touched by the frost, for the fire was beginning to burn with strength. He was feeding it with twigs the size of his finger. In another minute he would be able to feed it with branches the size of his wrist, and then he could remove his wet footgear, and, while it dried, he could keep his naked feet warm by the fire, rubbing them at first, of course, with snow. The fire was a success. He was safe. He remembered the advice of the old-timer on Sulphur Creek, and smiled. The old-timer had been very serious in laying down the law that no man must travel alone in the Klondike after fifty below. Well, here he was; he had had the accident; he was alone; and he had saved himself. Those old-timers were rather womanish, some of them, he thought. All a man had to do was to keep his head, and he was all right. Any man who was a man could travel alone. But it was surprising, the rapidity with which his cheeks and nose were freezing. And he had not thought his fingers could go lifeless in so short a time. Lifeless they were, for he could scarcely make them move together to grip a twig, and they seemed remote from his body and from him. When he touched a twig, he had to look and see whether or not he had hold of it. The wires were pretty well down between him and his finger ends.

All of which counted for little. There was the fire, snapping and crackling and promising life with every dancing flame. He started to untie his moccasins. They were coated with ice; the thick German socks were like sheaths of iron halfway to the knees; and the moccasin strings were like rods of steel all twisted and knotted as by some conflagration. For a moment he tugged with his numb fingers, then, realizing the folly of it, he drew his sheath knife.

But before he could cut the strings, it happened. It was his own fault or, rather, his mistake. He should not have built the fire under the spruce tree. He should have built it in the open. But it had been easier to pull the twigs from the brush and drop them directly on the fire. Now the tree under which he had done this carried a weight of snow on its boughs. No wind had blown for weeks, and each bough was fully freighted. Each time he had pulled a twig he had communicated a slight agitation to the tree—an imperceptible agitation, so far as he was concerned, but an agitation sufficient to bring about the disaster. High up in the tree one bough capsized its load of snow. This fell on the boughs beneath, capsizing them. This process continued, spreading out and involving the whole tree. It grew like an avalanche, and it descended without warning upon the man and the fire, and the fire was blotted out! Where it had burned was a mantle of fresh and disordered snow.

The man was shocked. It was as though he had just heard his own sentence of death. For a moment he sat and stared at the spot where the fire had been. Then he grew very calm. Perhaps the old-timer on Sulphur Creek was right. If he had only had a trail mate he would have been in no danger now. The trail mate could have built the fire. Well, it was up to him to build the fire over again, and this second time there must be no failure. Even if he succeeded, he would most likely lose some toes. His feet must be badly frozen by now, and there would be some time before the second fire was ready.

Such were his thoughts, but he did not sit and think them. He was busy all the time they were passing through his mind. He made a new foundation for a fire, this time in the open, where no treacherous tree could blot it out. Next he gathered dry grasses and tiny twigs from the highwater flotsam. He could not bring his fingers together to pull them out, but he was able to gather them by the handful. In this way he got many rotten twigs and bits of green moss that were undesirable, but it was the best he could do. He worked methodically, even collecting an armful of the larger branches to be used later when the fire gathered strength. And all the while the dog sat and watched him, a certain yearning wistfulness in its eyes, for it looked upon him as the fire provider, and the fire was slow in coming.

When all was ready, the man reached in his pocket for a second piece of birch bark. He knew the bark was there, and, though he could not feel it with his fingers, he could hear its crisp rustling as he fumbled for it. Try as he would, he could not clutch hold of it. And all the time, in his consciousness, was the knowledge that each instant his feet were freezing. This thought tended to put him in a panic, but he fought against it and kept calm. He pulled on his mittens with his teeth, and threshed his arms back and forth, beating his hands with all his might against his sides. He did this sitting down, and he stood up to do it; and all the while the dog sat in the snow, its wolf brush of a tail curled around warmly over its forefeet, its sharp wolf ears pricked forward intently as it watched the man. And the man, as he beat and threshed with his arms and hands, felt a great surge of envy as he regarded the creature that was warm and secure in its natural covering.

After a time he was aware of the first faraway signals of sensation in his beaten fingers. The faint tingling grew stronger till it evolved into a stinging ache that was excruciating, but which the man hailed with satisfaction. He stripped the mitten from his right hand and fetched forth the birch bark. The exposed fingers were quickly going numb again. Next he brought out his bunch of sulphur matches. But the tremendous cold had already driven the life out of his fingers. In his effort to separate one match from the others, the whole bunch fell in the snow. He tried to pick it out of the snow, but failed. The dead fingers could neither touch nor clutch. He was very careful. He drove the thought of his freezing feet, and nose, and cheeks, out of his mind, devoting his whole soul to the matches. He watched, using the sense of vision in place of that of touch, and when he saw his fingers on each side the bunch, he closed them—that is, he willed to close them, for the wires were down, and the fingers did not obey. He pulled the mitten on the right hand, and beat it fiercely against his knee. Then, with both mittened hands, he scooped the bunch of matches, along with much snow, into his lap. Yet he was no better off.

After some manipulation he managed to get the bunch between the heels of his mittened hands. In this fashion he carried it to his mouth. The ice crackled and snapped when by a violent effort he opened his mouth. He drew the lower jaw in, curled the upper lip out of the way, and scraped the bunch with his upper teeth in order to separate a match. He succeeded in getting one, which he dropped on his lap. He was no better off. He could not pick it up. Then he devised a way. He picked it up in his teeth and scratched it on his leg. Twenty times he scratched before he succeeded in lighting it. As it flamed he held it with his teeth to the birch bark. But the burning brimstone went up his nostrils and into his lungs, causing him to cough spasmodically. The match fell into the snow and went out.

The old-timer on Sulphur Creek was right, he thought in the moment of controlled despair that ensued: after fifty below, a man should travel with a partner. He beat his hands, but failed in exciting any sensation. Suddenly he bared both hands, removing the mittens with his teeth. He caught the whole bunch between the heels of his hands. His arm muscles not being frozen enabled him to press the hand heels tightly against the matches. Then he scratched the bunch along his leg. It flared into flame, seventy sulphur matches at once! There was no wind to blow them out. He kept his head to one side to escape the strangling fumes, and held the blazing bunch to the birch bark. As he so held it, he became aware of sensation in his hand. His flesh was burning. He could smell it. Deep down below the surface he could feel it. The sensation developed into pain that grew acute. And still he endured it, holding the flame of the matches clumsily to the bark that would not light readily because his own burning hands were in the way, absorbing most of the flame.

At last, when he could endure no more, he jerked his hands apart. The blazing matches fell sizzling into the snow, but the birch bark was alight. He began laying dry grasses and the tiniest twigs on the flame. He could not pick and choose, for he had to lift the fuel between the heels of his hands. Small pieces of rotten wood and green moss clung to the twigs, and he bit them off as well as he could with his teeth. He cherished the flame carefully and awkwardly. It meant life, and it must not perish. The withdrawal of blood from the surface of his body now made him begin to shiver, and he grew more awkward. A large piece of green moss fell squarely on the little fire. He tried to poke it out with his fingers, but his shivering frame made him poke too far, and he disrupted the nucleus of the little fire, the burning grasses and tiny twigs separating and scattering. He tried to poke them together again, but in spite of the tenseness of the effort, his shivering got away with him, and the twigs were hopelessly scattered. Each twig gushed a puff of smoke and went out. The fire provider had failed. As he looked apathetically about him, his eyes chanced on the dog, sitting across the ruins of the fire from him, in the snow, making restless, hunching movements, slightly lifting one forefoot and then the other, shifting its weight back and forth on them with wistful eagerness.

The sight of the dog put a wild idea into his head. He remembered the tale of the man, caught in a blizzard, who killed a steer and crawled inside the carcass, and so was saved. He would kill the dog and bury his hands in the warm body until the numbness went out of them. Then he could build another fire. He spoke to the dog, calling it to him; but in his voice was a strange note of fear that frightened the animal, who had never known the man to speak in such way before. Something was the matter, and its suspicious nature sensed danger—it knew not what danger, but somewhere, somehow, in its brain arose an apprehension of the man. It flattened its ears down at the sound of the man's voice, and its restless, hunching movements and the liftings and shiftings of its forefeet became more pronounced; but it would not come to the man. He got on his hands and knees and crawled toward the dog. This unusual posture again excited suspicion, and the animal sidled mincingly away.

The man sat up in the snow for a moment and struggled for calmness. Then he pulled on his mittens, by means of his teeth, and got upon his feet. He glanced down at first in order to assure himself that he was really standing up, for the absence of sensation in his feet left him unrelated to the earth. His erect position in itself started to drive the webs of suspicion from the dog's mind; and when he spoke peremptorily, with the sound of whip lashes in his voice, the dog rendered its customary allegiance and came to him. As it came within reaching distance, the man lost his control. His arms flashed out to the dog, and he experienced genuine surprise when he discovered that his hands could not clutch, that there was neither bend nor feeling in the fingers. He had forgotten for the moment that they were frozen and that they were freezing more and more. All this happened quickly, and before the animal could get away, he encircled its body with his arms. He sat down in the snow, and in this fashion held the dog, while it snarled and whined and struggled.

But it was all he could do, hold its body encircled in his arms and sit there. He realized that he could not kill the dog. There was no way to do it. With his helpless hands he could neither draw nor hold his sheath knife nor throttle the animal. He released it, and it plunged wildly away, with tail between its legs, and still snarling. It halted forty feet away and surveyed him curiously, with ears sharply pricked forward.

The man looked down at his hands in order to locate them, and found them hanging on the ends of his arms. It struck him as curious that one should have to use his eyes in order to find out where his hands were. He began threshing his arms back and forth, beating the mittened hands against his sides. He did this for five minutes, violently, and his heart pumped enough blood up to the surface to put a stop to his shivering. But no sensation was aroused in the hands. He had an impression that they hung like weights on the ends of his arms, but when he tried to run the impression down, he could not find it.

A certain fear of death, dull and oppressive, came to him. This fear quickly became poignant as he realized that it was no longer a mere matter of freezing his fingers and toes, or of losing his hands and feet, but that it was a matter of life and death with the chances against him. This threw him into a panic, and he turned and ran up the creek bed along the old, dim trail. The dog joined in behind and kept up with him. He ran blindly, without intention, in fear such as he had never known in his life. Slowly, as he plowed and floundered through the snow, he began to see things again—the banks of the creek, the old timber jams, the leafless aspens, and the sky. The running made him feel better. He did not shiver. Maybe, if he ran on, his feet would thaw out; and, anyway, if he ran far enough, he would reach camp and the boys. Without doubt he would lose some fingers and toes and some of his face; but the boys would take care of him, and save the rest of him when he got there. And at the same time there was another thought in his mind that said he would never get to the camp and the boys; that it was too many miles away, that the freezing had too great a start on him, and that he would soon be stiff and dead. This thought he kept in the background and refused to consider. Sometimes it pushed itself forward and demanded to be heard, but he thrust it back and strove to think of other things.

It struck him as curious that he could run at all on feet so frozen that he could not feel them when they struck the earth and took the weight of his body. He seemed to himself to skim along above the surface, and to have no connection with the earth. Somewhere he had once seen a winged Mercury, and he wondered if Mercury felt as he felt when skimming over the earth.

His theory of running until he reached camp and the boys had one flaw in it: he lacked the endurance. Several times he stumbled, and finally he tottered, crumpled up, and fell. When he tried to rise, he failed. He must sit and rest, he decided, and next time he would merely walk and keep on going. As he sat and regained his breath, he noted that he was feeling quite warm and comfortable. He was not shivering, and it even seemed that a warm glow had come to his chest and trunk. And yet, when he touched his nose or cheeks, there was no sensation. Running would not thaw them out. Nor would it thaw out his hands and feet. Then the thought came to him that the frozen portions of his body must be extending. He tried to keep this thought down, to forget it, to think of something else; he was aware of the panicky feeling that it caused, and he was afraid of the panic. But the thought asserted itself, and persisted, until it produced a vision of his body totally frozen. This was too much, and he made another wild run along the trail. Once he slowed down to a walk, but the thought of the freezing extending itself made him run again.

And all the time the dog ran with him, at his heels. When he fell down a second time, it curled its tail over its forefeet and sat in front of him, facing him, curiously eager and intent. The warmth and security of the animal angered him, and he cursed it till it flattened down its ears appeasingly. This time the shivering came more quickly upon the man. He was losing in his battle with the frost. It was creeping into his body from all sides. The thought of it drove him on, but he ran no more than a hundred feet, when he staggered and pitched headlong. It was his last panic. When he had recovered his breath and control, he sat up and entertained in his mind the conception of meeting death with dignity. However, the conception did not come to him in such terms. His idea of it was that he had been making a fool of himself, running around like a chicken with its head cut off—such was the simile that occurred to him. Well, he was bound to freeze anyway, and he might as well take it decently. With this new-found peace of mind came the first glimmerings of drowsiness. A good idea, he thought, to sleep off to death. It was like taking an anesthetic. Freezing was not so bad as people thought. There were lots worse ways to die.

He pictured the boys finding his body next day. Suddenly he found himself with them, coming along the trail and looking for himself. And, still with them, he came around a turn in the trail and found himself lying in the snow. He did not belong with himself any more, for even then he was out of himself, standing with the boys and looking at himself in the snow. It certainly was cold, was his thought. When he got back to the States he could tell the folks what real cold was. He drifted on from this to a vision of the old-timer on Sulphur Creek. He could see him quite clearly, warm and comfortable, and smoking a pipe.

"You were right, old hoss; you were right," the man mumbled to the old-timer of Sulphur Creek.

Then the man drowsed off into what seemed to him the most comfortable and satisfying sleep he had ever known. The dog sat facing him and waiting. The brief day drew to a close in a long, slow twilight. There were no signs of a fire to be made, and, besides, never in the dog's experience had it known a man to sit like that in the snow and make no fire. As the twilight drew on, its eager yearning for the fire mastered it, and with a great lifting and shifting of forefeet, it whined softly, then flattened its ears down in anticipation of being chidden by the man. But the man remained silent. Later the dog whined loudly. And still later it crept close to the man and caught the scent of death. This made the animal bristle and back away. A little longer it delayed, howling under the stars that leaped and danced and shone brightly in the cold sky. Then it turned and trotted up the trail in the direction of the camp it knew, where were the other food providers and fire providers.

1908

Zitkala Ša (Gertrude Simmons Bonnin)
1876–1938

Zitkala Ša, or Red Bird, as she called herself, became a writer and political activist despite formidable obstacles: she was a woman, a Dakota Sioux, born poor and in captivity on a reservation. Instead of remaining silent, segregated, and submissive, however, she vigorously pursued her own education and autonomy, and later lobbied for legal, political, and economic rights for all Native Americans.

Born February 22, 1876, as Gertrude Simmons, Zitkala Ša was eight years old when she left her traditional life in South Dakota for a Quaker missionary school in Wabash, Indiana. Because her older brother had been educated in the East and the missionaries promised her such sweet (and in her narrative, symbolic) treats as red apples and a ride on an "iron horse," Simmons wanted to follow his example.

No sooner had she seen her mother recede in the distance, however, than she realized tearfully what she had left behind. The contrast between her quiet life in tune with nature and her Sioux community against the severe work ethic of the missionaries is the subject of the included selections. They come from the first two chapters of her *Impressions of an Indian Childhood*, portions of which were first published in 1900 in the *Atlantic Monthly*.

Zitkala Ša described her seven-year old self as the secure daughter of a mother who cultivated "my wild freedom and overflowing spirits. She taught me no fear save that of intruding myself upon others."

During her first year away, she found that freedom imperiled. A week after recovering from a fever which killed several of her Indian classmates, she said she "was testing the chains which tightly bound my individuality like a mummy for burial."

In a later chapter, "An Indian Teacher Among Indians," she chronicles the casual brutality inflicted on Native Americans by the colonizers: a drunken doctor sending them to early graves; an opium-addicted teacher at the head of a class; a sadistic educator calling an Indian brave a "government pauper." Such experiences kindled rage, she wrote, and at that stage of her "evolution," raised an important cultural and philosophical question: "Does real life or long-lasting death lie beneath this semblance of civilization?"

Given its multiple perspectives, Zitkala Ša's autobiography thus becomes a modern story of the perennial outsider who passes painfully from one culture to another, who is angry and indignant, yet an active observer, not a victim.

Zitkala Ša left her teaching to study violin at the Boston Conservatory of Music. She visited Paris as a violin soloist and in 1913 co-wrote an opera, *Sun Dance*. During these early years of the twentieth century she also was at work on her autobiography as well as on stories for *Harper's Monthly*. In 1902 she married Raymon Talefase Bonnin, a Sioux who worked for the Indian Service. They settled on the Uintah and Ouray Reservation in Utah where she bore a son, Raymond.

Zitkala Ša became involved with the Society of American Indians, the first lobbying group of its kind to be managed by Native Americans. She was elected secretary of the society in 1916 and moved to Washington, D.C., where she also organized the National Council of American Indians on which she served as president until her death in 1938.

As Mary Young notes in her critical biography of Bonnin in *Notable American Women*, Zitkala Ša's most effective work was done with the General Federation of Women's Clubs, which she persuaded to establish an Indian Welfare Committee. The federation was successful in improving the treatment of American Indians and in preserving certain aspects of Native American cultures. It may have been through her work with the women's clubs that she was introduced to Helen Keller and other influential American women. Keller's laudatory letter about her second book, *American Indian Stories* (1921), was often reprinted. Keller called Zitkala Ša's writing the "low voice of a curiously colored seashell which is only for those ears that are bent with compassion to hear it." That writing was infused with a love for nature, shared by the Transcendental writers of European origins such as Emerson and Thoreau. For Zitkala Ša, nature was a place where "the voice of the Great Spirit is heard in birds, waters, flowers" while "his fluttering robe is the universe with spangles of oscillating brilliants of sun, moon and stars."

Her 1921 collection of Indian stories was the last of her literary efforts. An essay on "America's Indian Problem" is appended to that edition of her *Impressions of an Indian Childhood*. In that politically astute article from *Edict* magazine, the great irony of the European displacement of the Native Americans was not lost on Zitkala Ša:

> America was divided between the powers of Europe and the aborigines were dispossessed of their country. The barbaric rule of might from which the paleface had fled hither for refuge caught up with him again and in this melée the hospitable native suffered legal disability.

Zitkala Ša spent the remainder of her life addressing those legal disabilities.

Impressions of an Indian Childhood*

I: My Mother

A wigwam of weather-stained canvas stood at the base of some irregularly ascending hills. A footpath wound its was gently down the sloping land till it reached the broad river bottom; creeping through the long swamp grasses that bent over it on either side, it came out on the edge of the Missouri.

Here, morning, noon, and evening, my mother came to draw water from the muddy stream for our household use. Always, when my mother started for the river, I stopped my play to run along with her. She was only of medium height. Often she was sad and silent, at which times her full arched lips were compressed into hard and bitter lines, and shadows fell under her black eyes. Then I clung to her hand and begged to know what made the tears fall.

"Hush; my little daughter must never talk about my tears;" and smiling through them, she patted my head and said, "Now let me see how fast you can run to-day." Whereupon I tore away at my highest possible speed, with my long black hair blowing in the breeze.

I was a wild little girl of seven. Loosely clad in a slip of brown buckskin, and light-footed with a pair of soft moccasins on my feet, I was as free as the wind that blew my hair, and no less spirited than a bounding deer. These were my mother's pride,—my wild freedom and overflowing spirits. She taught me no fear save that of intruding myself upon others.

Having gone many paces ahead I stopped, panting for breath, and laughing with glee as my mother watched my every movement. I was not wholly conscious of myself, but was more keenly alive to the fire within. It was as if I were the activity, and my hands and feet were only experiments for my spirit to work upon.

Returning from the river, I tugged beside my mother, with my hand upon the bucket I believed I was carrying. One time, on such a return, I remember a bit of conversation we had. My grown-up cousin, Warca-Ziwin (Sunflower), who was then seventeen, always went to the river alone for water for her mother. Their wigwam was not far from ours; and I saw her daily going to and from the river. I admired my cousin greatly. So I said: "Mother, when I am tall as my cousin Warca-Ziwin, you shall not have to come for water. I will do it for you."

With a strange tremor in her voice which I could not understand, she answered, "If the paleface does not take away from us the river we drink."

"Mother, who is this bad paleface?" I asked.

"My little daughter, he is a sham,—a sickly sham! The bronzed Dakota is the only real man."

---

* *Impressions of an Indian Childhood* first appeared in the *Atlantic Monthly* for January of 1900.

I looked up into my mother's face while she spoke; and seeing her bite her lips. I knew she was unhappy. This aroused revenge in my small soul. Stamping my foot on the earth, I cried aloud, "I hate the paleface that makes my mother cry!"

Setting the pail of water on the ground, my mother stopped, and stretching her left hand out on the level with my eyes, she placed her other arm about me; she pointed to the hill where my uncle and my only sister lay buried.

"There is what the paleface has done! Since then your father too has been buried in a hill nearer the rising sun. We were once very happy. But the paleface has stolen our lands and driven us hither. Having defrauded us of our land, the paleface forced us away.

"Well, it happened on the day we moved camp that your sister and uncle were both very sick. Many others were ailing, but there seemed to be no help. We traveled many days and nights; not in the grand happy way that we moved camp when I was a little girl, but we were driven, my child, driven like a herd of buffalo. With every step, your sister, who was not as large as you are now, shrieked with the painful jar until she was hoarse with crying. She grew more and more feverish. Her little hands and cheeks were burning hot. Her little lips were parched and dry, but she would not drink the water I gave her. Then I discovered that her throat was swollen and red. My poor child, how I cried with her because the Great Spirit had forgotten us!

"At last, when we reached this western country, on the first weary night your sister died. And soon your uncle died also, leaving a widow and an orphan daughter, your cousin Warca-Ziwin. Both your sister and uncle might have been happy with us to-day, had it not been for the heartless paleface."

My mother was silent the rest of the way to our wigwam. Though I saw no tears in her eyes, I knew that was because I was with her. She seldom wept before me.

II: The Legends

During the summer days, my mother built her fire in the shadow of our wigwam.

In the early morning our simple breakfast was spread upon the grass west of our tepee. At the farthest point of the shade my mother sat beside her fire, toasting a savory piece of dried meat. Near her, I sat upon my feet, eating my dried meat with unleavened bread, and drinking strong black coffee.

The morning meal was our quiet hour, when we two were entirely alone. At noon, several who chanced to be passing by stopped to rest, and to share our luncheon with us, for they were sure of our hospitality.

My uncle, whose death my mother ever lamented, was one of our nation's bravest warriors. His name was on the lips of old men when talking of the proud feats of valor; and it was mentioned by younger men, too, in connection with deeds of gallantry. Old women praised him for his kindness toward them; young women held him up as an ideal to their sweethearts. Every one loved him, and my mother worshiped his memory. Thus it happened that even strangers were sure of welcome in our lodge, if they but asked a favor in my uncle's name.

Though I heard many strange experiences related by these wayfarers, I loved best the evening meal, for that was the time old legends were told. I was always glad when the sun hung low in the west, for then my mother sent me to invite the neighboring old men and women to eat supper with us. Running all the way to the wigwams, I halted shyly at the entrances. Sometimes I stood long moments without saying a word. It was not any fear that made me so dumb when out upon such a happy errand; nor was it that I wished to withhold the invitation, for it was all I could do to observe this very proper silence. But it was a sensing of the atmosphere, to assure myself that I should not hinder other plans. My mother used to say to me, as I was almost bounding away for the old people: "Wait a moment before you invite any one. If other plans are being discussed, do not interfere, but go elsewhere."

The old folks knew the meaning of my pauses; and often they coaxed my confidence by asking, "What do you seek, little granddaughter?"

"My mother says you are to come to our tepee this evening," I instantly exploded, and breathed the freer afterwards.

"Yes, yes, gladly, gladly I shall come!" each replied. Rising at once and carrying their blankets across one shoulder, they flocked leisurely from their various wigwams toward our dwelling.

My mission done, I ran back, skipping and jumping with delight. All out of breath, I told my mother almost the exact words of the answers to my invitation. Frequently she asked, "What were they doing when you entered their tepee?" This taught me to remember all I saw at a single glance. Often I told my mother my impressions without being questioned.

While in the neighboring wigwams sometimes an old Indian woman asked me, "What is your mother doing?" Unless my mother had cautioned me not to tell, I generally answered her questions without reserve.

At the arrival of our guests I sat close to my mother, and did not leave her side without first asking her consent. I ate my supper in quiet, listening patiently to the talk of the old people, wishing all the time that they would begin the stories I loved best. At last, when I could not wait any longer, I whispered in my mother's ear, "Ask them to tell an Iktomi[1] story, mother."

Soothing my impatience, my mother said aloud, "My little daughter is anxious to hear your legends." By this time all were through eating, and the evening was fast deepening into twilight.

As each in turn began to tell a legend. I pillowed my head in my mother's lap; and lying flat upon my back, I watched the stars as they peeped down upon me, one by one. The increasing interest of the tale aroused me, and I sat up eagerly listening for every word. The old women made funny remarks, and laughed so heartily that I could not help joining them.

The distant howling of a pack of wolves or the hooting of an owl in the river bottom frightened me, and I nestled into my mother's lap. She added some dry sticks to the fire, and the bright flames heaped up into the faces of the old folks as they sat around in a great circle.

On such an evening, I remember the glare of the fire shone on a tattooed star upon the brow of the old warrior who was telling a story. I watched him curiously as he made his unconscious gestures. The blue star upon his bronzed forehead was a puzzle to me. Looking about, I saw two parallel lines on the chin of one of the old women. The rest had none. I examined my mother's face, but found no sign there.

[1] Spider (Sioux, literal trans.); sometimes used to mean trickster.

After the warrior's story was finished, I asked the old women the meaning of the blue lines on her chin, looking all the while out of the corners of my eyes at the warrior with the star on his forehead. I was a little afraid that he would rebuke me for my boldness.

Here the old woman began: "Why, my grandchild, they are signs,—secret signs I dare not tell you. I shall, however, tell you a wonderful story about a woman who had a cross tattooed upon each of her cheeks."

It was a long story of a woman whose magic power lay hidden behind the marks upon her face. I fell asleep before the story was completed.

Ever after that night I felt suspicious of tattooed people. Wherever I saw one I glanced furtively at the mark and round about it, wondering what terrible magic power was covered there.

It was rarely that such a fearful story as this one was told by the camp fire. Its impression was so acute that the picture still remains vividly clear and pronounced.

III: The Beadwork

Soon after breakfast, mother sometimes began her beadwork. On a bright clear day, she pulled out the wooden pegs that pinned the skirt of our wigwam to the ground, and rolled the canvas part way up on its frame of slender poles. Then the cool morning breezes swept freely through our dwelling, now and then wafting the perfume of sweet grasses from newly burnt prairie.

Untying the long tasseled strings that bound a small brown buckskin bag, my mother spread upon a mat beside her bunches of colored beads, just as an artist arranges the paints upon his palette. On a lapboard she smoothed out a double sheet of soft white buckskin; and drawing from a beaded case that hung on the left of her wide belt a long, narrow blade, she trimmed the buckskin into shape. Often she worked upon small moccasins for her small daughters. Then I became intensely interested in her designing. With a proud, beaming face, I watched her work. In imagination, I saw myself walking in a new pair of snugly fitting moccasins. I felt the envious eyes of my playmates upon the pretty red beads decorating my feet.

Close beside my mother I sat on a rug, with a scrap of buckskin in one hand and an awl in the other. This was the beginning of my practical observation lessons in the art of beadwork. From a skein of finely twisted threats of silvery sinews my mother pulled out a single one. With an awl she pierced the buckskin, and skillfully threaded it with the white sinew. Picking up the tiny beads one by one, she stung them with the point of her thread, always twisting it carefully after every stitch.

It took many trials before I learned how to knot my sinew thread on the point of my finger, as I saw her do. Then the next difficulty was in keeping my thread stiffly twisted, so that I could easily string my beads upon it. My mother required of me original designs for my lessons in beading. At first I frequently ensnared many a sunny hour into working a long design. Soon I learned from self-inflicted punishment to refrain from drawing complex patterns, for I had to finish whatever I began.

After some experience I usually drew easy and simple crosses and squares. These were some of the set forms. My original designs were not always symmetrical nor sufficiently characteristic, two faults with which my mother had little patience. The quietness of her oversight made me feel strongly responsible and dependent upon my own

judgment. She treated me as a dignified little individual as long as I was on my good behavior; and how humiliated I was when some boldness of mine drew forth a rebuke
from her!

In the choice of colors she left me to my own taste. I was pleased with an outline of
yellow upon a background of dark blue, or a combination of red and myrtle-green.
There was another of red with a bluish gray that was more conventionally used. When I
became a little familiar with designing and the various pleasing combinations of color, a
harder lesson was given me. It was the sewing on, instead of beads, some tinted porcu-
pine quills, moistened and flattened between the nails of the thumb and forefinger. My
mother cut off the prickly ends and burned them at once in the centre fire. These sharp
points were poisonous, and worked into the flesh wherever they lodged. For this reason,
my mother said, I should not do much alone in quills until I was as tall as my cousin
Warca-Ziwin.

Always after these confining lessons I was wild with surplus spirits, and found joyous
relief in running loose in the open again. Many a summer afternoon, a party of four or
five of my playmates roamed over the hills with me. We each carried a light sharpened
rod about four feet long, with which we pried up certain sweet roots. When we had
eaten all the choice roots we chanced upon, we shouldered our rods and strayed off into
patches of a stalky plant under whose yellow blossoms we found little crystal drops of
gum. Drop by drop we gathered this nature's rockcandy, until each of us could boast of
a lump the size of a small bird's egg. Soon satiated with its woody flavor, we tossed away
our gum, to return again to the sweet roots.

I remember well how we used to exchange our necklaces, beaded belts, and sometimes even our moccasins. We pretended to offer them as gifts to one another. We delighted in impersonating our own mothers. We talked of things we had heard them say
in their conversations. We imitated their various manners, even to the inflection of
their voices. In the lap of the prairie we seated ourselves upon our feet; and leaning our
painted cheeks in the palms of our hands, we rested our elbows on our knees, and bent
forward as old women were most accustomed to do.

. . . that he would bite my fingers. So I was as content as he to keep the corn between
us. Every morning he came for more corn. Some evenings I have seen him creeping about
our grounds; and when I gave a sudden whoop of recognition, he ran quickly out of sight.

When mother had dried all the corn she wished, then she sliced great pumpkins into
thin rings; and these she doubled and linked together into long chains. She hung them
on a pole that stretched between two forked posts. The wind and sun soon thoroughly
dried the chains of pumpkin. Then she packed them away in a case of thick and still
buckskin.

In the sun and wind she also dried many wild fruits,—cherries, berries, and plums.
But chiefest among my early recollections of autumn is that one of the corn drying and
the ground squirrel.

I have few memories of winter days, at this period of my life, though many of the
summer. There is one only which I can recall.

Some missionaries gave me a little bag of marbles. They were all sizes and colors.
Among them were some of colored glass. Walking with my mother to the river, on a
late winter day, we found great chunks of ice piled all along the bank. The ice on the
river was floating in huge pieces. As I stood beside one large block, I noticed for the first
time the colors of the rainbow in the crystal ice. Immediately I thought of my glass

marbles at home. With my bare fingers I tried to pick out some of the colors, for they seemed so near the surface. But my fingers began to sting with the intense cold, and I had to bite them hard to keep from crying.

From that day on, for many a moon, I believed that glass marbles had river ice inside of them.

VII: The Big Red Apples

The first turning away from the easy, natural flow of my life occurred in an early spring. It was in my eighth year; in the month of March, I afterward learned. At this age I knew but one language, and that was my mother's native tongue.

From some of my playmates I heard that two paleface missionaries were in our village. They were from that class of white men who wore big hats and carried large hearts, they said. Running direct to my mother, I began to question her why these two strangers were among us. She told me, after I had teased much, that they had come to take away Indian boys and girls to the East. My mother did not seem to want me to talk about them. But in a day or two, I gleaned many wonderful stories from my playfellows concerning the strangers.

"Mother, my friend Judéwin is going home with the missionaries. She is going to a more beautiful country than ours; the palefaces told her so!" I said wistfully, wishing in my heart that I too might go.

Mother sat in a chair, and I was hanging on her knee. Within the last two seasons my big brother Dawée had returned from a three years' education in the East, and his coming back influenced my mother to take a farther step from her native way of living. First it was a change from the buffalo skin to the white man's canvas that covered our wigwam. Now she had given up her wigwam of slender poles, to live, a foreigner, in a home of clumsy logs.

"Yes, my child, several others besides Judéwin are going away with the palefaces. Your brother said the missionaries had inquired about his little sister," she said, watching my face very closely.

My heart thumped so hard against my breast, I wondered if she could hear it.

"Did he tell them to take me, mother?" I asked, fearing lest Dawée had forbidden the palefaces to see me, and that my hope of going to the Wonderland would be entirely blighted.

With a sad, slow smile, she answered: "There! I knew you were wishing to go, because Judéwin has filled your ears with the white men's lies. Don't believe a word they say! Their words are sweet, but, my child, their deeds are bitter. You will cry for me, but they will not even soothe you. Stay with me, my little one! Your brother Dawée says that going East, away from your mother, is too hard an experience for his baby sister."

Thus my mother discouraged my curiosity about the lands beyond our eastern horizon; for it was not yet an ambition for Letters that was stirring me. But on the following day the missionaries did come to our very house. I spied them coming up the footpath leading to our cottage. A third man was with them, but he was not my brother Dawée. It was another, young interpreter, a paleface who had a smattering of the Indian language. I was ready to run out to meet them, but I did not dare to displease my mother. With great glee, I jumped up and down on our ground floor. I begged my mother to open the door, that they would be sure to come to us. Alas! They came, they saw, and they conquered!

Judéwin told me of the great tree where grew red, red apples; and how we could reach out our hands and pick all the red apples we could eat. I had never seen apple trees. I had never tasted more than a dozen red apples in my life; and when I heard of the orchards of the East, I was eager to roam among them. The missionaries smiled into my eyes, and patted my head. I wondered how mother could say such hard words against them.

"Mother, ask them if little girls may have all the red apples they want, when they go East," I whispered aloud, in my excitement.

The interpreter heard me, and answered: "Yes, little girl, the nice red apples are for those who pick them; and you will have a ride on the iron horse if you go with these good people."

I had never seen a train, and he knew it.

"Mother, I'm going East! I like big red apples, and I want to ride on the iron horse! Mother, say yes!" I pleaded.

My mother said nothing. The missionaries waited in silence; and my eyes began to blur with tears, though I struggled to choke them back. The corners of my mouth twitched, and my mother saw me.

"I am not ready to give you any word," she said to them. "To-morrow I shall send you my answer by my son."

With this they left us. Alone with my mother, I yielded to my tears, and cried aloud, shaking my head so as not to hear what she was saying to me. This was the first time I had ever been so unwilling to give up my own desire that I refused to hearken to my mother's voice.

There was a solemn silence in our home that night. Before I went to bed I begged the Great Spirit to make my mother willing I should go with the missionaries.

The next morning came, and my mother called me to her side. 'My daughter, do you still persist in wishing to leave your mother?" she asked.

"Oh, mother, it is not that I wish to leave you, but I want to see the wonderful Eastern land," I answered.

My dear old aunt came to our house that morning, and I heard her say, "Let her try it."

I hope that, as usual, my aunt was pleading on my side. My brother Dawée came for mother's decision. I dropped my play, and crept close to my aunt.

"Yes, Dawée, my daughter, though she does not understand what it all means, is anxious to go. She will need an education when she is grown, for then there will be fewer real Dakotas, and many more palefaces. This tearing her away, so young, from her mother is necessary, if I would have her an educated woman. The palefaces, who owe us a large debt for stolen lands, have begun to pay a tardy justice in offering some education to our children. But I know my daughter must suffer keenly in this experiment. For her sake, I dread to tell you my reply to the missionaries. Go, tell them that they may take my little daughter, and that the Great Spirit shall not fail to reward them according to their hearts."

Wrapped in my heavy blanket, I walked with my mother to the carriage that was soon to take us to the iron horse. I was happy. I met my playmates, who were also wearing their best thick blankets. We showed one another our new beaded moccasins, and the width of the belts that girdled our new dresses. Soon we were being drawn rapidly away by the white man's horses. When I saw the lonely figure of my mother vanish in the distance, a sense of regret settled heavily upon me. I felt suddenly weak, as if I might fall limp to the ground. I was in the hands of strangers whom my mother did not fully trust. I no longer felt free to be myself, or to voice my own feelings. The tears trickled down my cheeks, and I buried my face in the folds of my blanket. Now the first step, parting me from my mother, was taken, and all my belated tears availed nothing.

Having driven thirty miles to the ferryboat, we crossed the Missouri in the evening. Then riding again a few miles eastward, we stopped before a massive brick building. I looked at it in amazement, and with a vague misgiving, for in our village I had never seen so large a house. Trembling with fear and distrust of the palefaces, my teeth chattering from the chilly ride, I crept noiselessly in my soft moccasins along the narrow hall, keeping very close to the bare wall. I was as frightened and bewildered as the captured young of a wild creature.

1900

from School Days

II: The Cutting of My Long Hair

The first day in the land of apples was a bitter-cold one; for the snow still covered the ground, and the trees were bare. A large bell rang for breakfast, its loud metallic voice crashing through the belfry overhead and into our sensitive ears. The annoying clatter of shoes on bare floors gave us no peace. The constant clash of harsh noises, with an undercurrent of many voices murmuring an unknown tongue, made a bedlam within which I was securely tied. And though my spirit tore itself in struggling for its lost freedom, all was useless.

A paleface woman, with white hair, came up after us. We were placed in a line of girls who were marching into the dining room. These were Indian girls, in stiff shoes and closely clinging dresses. The small girls wore sleeved aprons and shingled hair. As I walked noiselessly in my soft moccasins, I felt like sinking to the floor, for my blanket had been stripped from my shoulder. I looked hard at the Indian girls, who seemed not to care that they were even more immodestly dressed than I, in their tightly fitting clothes. While we marched in, the boys entered at an opposite door. I watched for the three young braves who came in our party. I spied them in the rear ranks, looking as uncomfortable as I felt.

A small bell was tapped, and each of the pupils drew a chair from under the table. Supposing this act meant they were to be seated, I pulled out mine and at once slipped into it from one side. But when I turned my head, I saw that I was the only one seated, and all the rest at our table remained standing. Just as I began to rise, looking shyly around to see how chairs were to be used, a second bell was sounded. All were seated at last, and I had to crawl back into my chair again. I heard a man's voice at one end of the hall, and I looked around to see him. But all the others hung their heads over their plates. As I glanced at the long chain of tables, I caught the eyes of a paleface woman upon me. Immediately I dropped my eyes, wondering why I was so keenly watched by the strange woman. The man ceased his mutterings, and then a third bell was tapped.

Every one picked up his knife and fork and began eating. I began crying instead, for by this time I was afraid to venture anything more.

But this eating by formula was not the hardest trial in that first day. Late in the morning, my friend Judéwin gave me a terrible warning. Judéwin knew a few words of English; and she had overhead the paleface woman talk about cutting our long, heavy hair. Our mothers had taught us that only unskilled warriors who were captured had their hair shingled by the enemy. Among our people, short hair was worn by mourners, and shingled hair by cowards!

We discussed our fate some moments, and when Judéwin said, "We have to submit, because they are strong," I rebelled.

"No, I will not submit! I will struggle first!" I answered.

I watched my chance, and when no one noticed I disappeared. I crept up the stairs as quietly as I could in my squeaking shoes,—my moccasins had been exchanged for shoes. Along the hall I passed, without knowing whither I was going. Turning aside to an open door, I found a large room with three white beds in it. The windows were covered with dark green curtains, which made the room very dim. Thankful that no one was there, I directed my steps toward the corner farthest from the door. On my hands and knees I crawled under the bed, and cuddled myself in the dark corner.

From my hiding place I peered out, shuddering with fear whenever I heard footsteps near by. Though in the hall loud voices were calling my name, and I knew that even Judéwin was searching for me, I did not open my mouth to answer. Then the steps were quickened and the voices became excited. The sounds came nearer and nearer. Women and girls entered the room. I held my breath and watched them open closet doors and peep behind large trunks. Some one threw up the curtains, and the room was filled with sudden light. What caused them to stoop and look under the bed I do not know. I remember being dragged out, though I resisted by kicking and scratching wildly. In spite of myself, I was carried downstairs and tied fast in a chair.

I cried aloud, shaking my head all the while until I felt the cold blades of the scissors against my neck, and heard them gnaw off one of my thick braids. Then I lost my spirit. Since the day I was taken from my mother I had suffered extreme indignites. People had stared at me. I had been tossed about in the air like a wooden puppet. And now my long hair was shingled like a coward's! In my anguish I moaned for my mother, but no one came to comfort me. Not a soul reasoned quietly with me, as my own mother used to do; for now I was only one of many little animals driven by a herder.

III: The Snow Episode

A short time after our arrival we three Dakotas were playing in the snowdrift. We were all still deaf to the English language, excepting Judéwin, who always heard such puzzling things. One morning we learned through her ears that we were forbidden to fall lengthwise in the snow, as we had been doing, to see our own impressions. However, before many hours we had forgotten the order, and were having great sport in the snow, when a shrill voice called us. Looking up, we saw an imperative hand beckoning us into the house. We shook the snow off ourselves, and started toward the woman as slowly as we dared.

Judéwin said: "Now the paleface is angry with us. She is going to punish us for falling into the snow. If she looks straight into your eyes and talks loudly, you must wait until she stops. Then, after a tiny pause, say, 'No.' " The rest of the way we practiced upon the little word "no."

As it happened, Thowin was summoned to judgment first. The door shut behind her with a click.

Judéwin and I stood silently listening at the keyhole. The paleface woman talked in very severe tones. Her words fell from her lips like crackling embers, and her inflection ran up like the small end of a switch. I understood her voice better than the things she was saying. I was certain we had made her very impatient with us. Judéwin heard enough of the words to realize all too late that she had taught us the wrong reply.

"Oh, poor Thowin!" she gasped, as she put both hands over her ears.

Just then I heard Thowin's tremulous answer, "No."

With an angry exclamation, the woman gave her a hard spanking. Then she stopped to say something. Judéwin said it was this: "Are you going to obey my word the next time?"

Thowin answered again with the only word at her command, "No."

This time the woman meant her blows to smart, for the poor frightened girl shrieked at the top of her voice. In the midst of the whipping the blows ceased abruptly, and the woman asked another question: "Are you going to fall in the snow again?"

Thowin gave her bad password another trial. We heard her say feebly, "No! No!"

With this the women hid away her half-worn slipper, and led the child out, stroking her black shorn head. Perhaps it occurred to her that brute force is not the solution for such a problem. She did nothing to Judéwin nor to me. She only returned to us our unhappy comrade, and left us alone in the room.

During the first two or three seasons misunderstandings as ridiculous as this one of the snow episode frequently took place, bringing unjustifiable frights and punishments into our little lives.

Within a year I was able to express myself somewhat in broken English. As soon as I comprehended a part of what was said and done, a mischievous spirit of revenge possessed me. One day I was called in from my play for some misconduct. I had disregarded a rule which seemed to me very needlessly binding. I was sent into the kitchen to mash the turnips for dinner. It was noon, and steaming dishes were hastily carried into the dinning-room. I hated turnips, and their odor which came from the brown jar was offensive to me. With fire in my heart, I took the wooden tool that the paleface woman held out to me. I stood upon a step, and, grasping the handle with both hands, I bent in hot rage over the turnips. I worked my vengeance upon them. All were so busily occupied that no one noticed me. I saw that the turnips were in a pulp, and that further beating could not improve them; but the order was, "Mash these turnips," and mash them I would! I renewed my energy; and as I sent the masher into the bottom of the jar, I felt a satisfying sensation that the weight of my body had gone into it.

Just here a paleface woman came up to my table. As she looked into the jar, she shoved my hands roughly aside. I stood fearless and angry. She placed her red hands upon the rim of the jar. Then she gave one lift and stride away from the table. But lo! the pulpy contents fell through the crumbled bottom to the floor! She spared me no scolding phrases that I had earned. I did not heed them. I felt triumphant in my revenge, though deep within me I was a wee bit sorry to have broken the jar.

As I sat eating my dinner, and saw that no turnips were served, I whooped in my heart for having once asserted the rebellion within me.

V: Iron Routine

A loud-clamoring bell awakened us at half-past six in the cold winter mornings. From happy dreams of Western rolling lands and unlassoed freedom we tumbled out upon chilly bare floors back again into a paleface day. We had short time to jump into our shoes and clothes, and wet our eyes with icy water, before a small hand bell was vigorously rung for roll call.

There were too many drowsy children and too numerous orders for the day to waste a moment in any apology to nature for giving her children such a shock in the early morning. We rushed downstairs, bounding over two high steps at a time, to land in the assembly room.

A paleface woman, with a yellow-covered roll book open on her arm and a gnawed pencil in her hand, appeared at the door. Her small, tired face was coldly lighted with a pair of large gray eyes.

She stood still in a halo of authority, while over the rim of her spectacles her eyes pried nervously about the room. Having glanced at her long list of names and called out the first one, she tossed up her chin and peered through the crystals of her spectacles to make sure of the answer "Here."

Relentlessly her pencil black-marked our daily records if we were not present to respond to our names, and no chum of ours had done it successfully for us. No matter if a dull headache or the painful cough of slow consumption had delayed the absentee, there was only time enough to mark the tardiness. It was next to impossible to leave the iron routine after the civilizing machine had once begun its day's buzzing; and as it was inbred in me to suffer in silence rather than to appeal to the ears of one whose open eyes could not see my pain, I have many times trudged in the day's harness heavy-footed, like a dumb sick brute.

Once I lost a dear classmate. I remember well how she used to mope along at my side, until one morning she could not raise her head from her pillow. At her deathbed I stood weeping, as the paleface woman sat near her moistening the dry lips. Among the folds of the bedclothes I saw the open pages of the white man's Bible. The dying Indian girl talked disconnectedly of Jesus the Christ and the paleface who was cooling her swollen hands and feet.

I grew bitter, and censured the woman for cruel neglect of our physical ills. I despised the pencils that moved automatically, and the one teaspoon which dealt out, from a large bottle, healing to a row of variously ailing Indian children. I blamed the hard-working, well-meaning, ignorant woman who was inculcating in our hearts her superstitious ideas. Though I was sullen in all my little troubles, as soon as I felt better I was ready again to smile upon the cruel woman. Within a week I was again actively testing the chains which tightly bound my individuality like a mummy for burial.

The melancholy of those black days has left so long a shadow that it darkens the path of years that have since gone by.

Walker Evans
Brooklyn Bridge
photograph, ca. 1928
(The J. Paul Getty Museum,
Los Angeles)

Georgia O'Keeffe
Brooklyn Bridge
oil on masonite, 1948
(The Brooklyn Museum of Art,
Bequest of Mary Childs Draper;
77.11)

The Literature of
a New Century
1912–1945

American writers of the early twentieth century worked
in a culture of striking contrasts and tensions. Expanding
railway systems as well as new means of communication
were bringing the nation closer together; and, with other
industries, they were also producing large fortunes that
spurred growth, increasing the nation's exuberance and
expansiveness. "The old nations of the earth creep at a
snail's pace," Andrew Carnegie wrote in 1886, while the
American "Republic thunders past with the rush of the
express." Following the Civil War, the nation had begun
an era of expansion designed to "tame the West" and
make it safe for settlers by destroying or displacing
Native Americans. The result was a series of "Indian
Wars," beginning in the late 1860s and lasting through
the 1880s, that left memories that defeated Native
Americans recounted in songs and stories on the
"reservations" where they were confined and that the
victors recounted in Buffalo Bill's Wild West Show,
scores of novels, and, later, scores of movies. Similarly,
the legacies of the "peculiar institution" of slavery,
wiped out by the Civil War, were carried into the
twentieth century not only in the "Jim Crow" laws of the
South and established patterns of segregation in the
North but also as living memories of thousands of
people who had been born into slavery, some of whom,
including Caroline Barr (1840–1940)—to whom
William Faulkner later dedicated *Go Down, Moses*
(1942)—lived well into the twentieth century. Yet the
confidence of the nation that Carnegie reflected survived

these and other historical complications as though unfazed. For it was underwritten not only by economic and industrial expansion but also by a double conviction, implicit in Carnegie's words, that the future belonged to the "New World" and that the dominant force in the "New World" was the United States.

In a famous address delivered at a meeting of the American Historical Association in 1893, held in Chicago during the World's Columbian Exposition, Frederick Jackson Turner announced that American democracy drew its force not from its European heritage of exploration but from its renewing frontier experience of conquest. Twenty years later, on June 17, 1914, roughly two months before the "guns of August" shattered the peace of Europe and began the twentieth century's first "Great War"—a war that would change the lives of many writers represented in this anthology—Turner reiterated his celebrated announcement: "American Democracy was born of no theorist's dream: it was not carried in the *Susan Constant* to Virginia, nor in the *Mayflower* to Plymouth. It came stark and strong and full of life out of the American forest, and it gained new strength each time it touched a new frontier."

New World; New Writers

To live on the edge of civilization, or, more precisely, in a civilized nation whose western frontier bordered "the wild," was, then, from an American point of view to feel more blessed than deprived, and this sentiment held sway, at least part of the time, even among writers who drew inspiration from ancient as well as recent texts. Writing in the mid-nineteenth century, Henry David Thoreau captured one dimension of this tension: "I love the wild not less than the good." A few years later, Huck Finn carried related sentiments with him when he decided "to light out for the Territory ahead of the rest." Later still, several characters of Jack London and Ernest Hemingway as well as Willa Cather's Tiny Soderball in *My Antonia* carried them into the twentieth century by tying physical and even spiritual renewal to contact with, or re-immersion in, nature. Other writers, including F. Scott Fitzgerald, associated both the New World's new culture and its lingering ambivalence about culture itself with what Henry James called the peculiar "importance of the individual in the American world."

Yet writers and artists also tended, perhaps more than most Americans, to be suspicious of the nation's claims to special moral and social authority. To them, furthermore, both the sense of cultural inferiority vis-à-vis Europe and the legacies of violence and guilt associated with the nation's celebration of the frontier as the shaping force in its history—themes that Carnegie's story of "triumphant democracy" either transformed or buried—were carried as special burdens. For some, the burdens stemmed primarily from the violent "taming" of a once "New World"; for others they were associated primarily with the violent wars waged against that world's original inhabitants and with the destruction of their cultures; and for others it was associated with the contradictions bound up in celebrating one's own freedom while profiting from the segregation or the enslavement of other human beings. Sitting Bull (c.1834–1891), the nation's most prominent Native American, was a contemporary of Walt Whitman (1819–1892) and Emily Dickinson (1830–1886)—and so was Frederick Douglass (1818–1895), the nation's most prominent former slave. During the two decades in which these four famous Americans died, many of the outstanding writers of the first half of the twentieth century were born, including, to name a few, William

Carlos Williams, Ezra Pound, Marianne Moore, T. S. Eliot, F. Scott Fitzgerald, William Faulkner, and Ernest Hemingway. Like surviving Native Americans, furthermore, young African American writers—including Langston Hughes, Countee Cullen, Jean Toomer, Helene Johnson, Richard Wright, and Zora Neale Hurston—were told, not that their culture was inferior to Europe's, but that they had no culture at all; and further, that their only hope of becoming "literary" lay in imitating white cultural traditions that demeaned them in the rare instances in which they did not ignore them.

The great accomplishment of American literature of the early twentieth century, and especially of the years between the outbreak of the new century's first "Great War" in 1914 and the end of its second "Great War" in 1945, was to equal if not surpass the literary achievements of the great countries of Europe, not with a few scattered writers of genius like Whitman, Dickinson, James and Wharton from the Atlantic seaboard, but with scores of writers from a wide range of social classes born in Idaho (Pound), Missouri (Eliot and Hughes), Illinois (Hemingway), Ohio (Hart Crane and Sherwood Anderson), Minnesota (Fitzgerald), Georgia (Georgia Douglas Johnson), Kentucky (Robert Penn Warren), Florida (Hurston), Tennessee (John Crowe Ransom and Allen Tate), Mississippi (Faulkner, Eudora Welty, and Richard Wright), and Texas (Katherine Anne Porter). "The Middle West," Ford Madox Ford wrote from Paris in the early twenties, "was seething with literary impulse." During the thirties and forties the same thing became true of the South. Earlier, from the late nineteenth century into the twentieth, great waves of immigration from southern and eastern Europe had transformed American society; and increasingly in the twentieth century, immigrants and the children of immigrants began to enrich as well as change the nation's literature. Gertrude Stein, Nathanael West, Henry Roth, and Anzia Yezierska became the nation's first major Jewish writers. Working alongside other writers, many of them born poor, female, and black, these writers helped to transform American literature. Following the example of Mark Twain, they made use of different versions of colloquial American English—gathered from the cadences of folk tales and sermons, from voices heard in kitchens and churches in the rural midwest or around livery stables and courthouses in the rural South, or on the streets and in the flats of Chicago and New York.

One feature of the literary flowering that followed was a striking democratization of American literature that freed it from its heavy reliance on standard diction and English pentameter. Writers borrowed from the rhythms of blues and the syncopation of jazz as well as from settings and traditions that previously had been thought inappropriate for prose and inconceivable for poetry. And they brought with them the experiences as well as the words of dispossessed domestic servants, laborers, and sharecroppers. What Pound said of Frost in a review of *North of Boston*—that he was "putting New England rural life into verse"—could with modifications of locale and genre have been said of many other writers of the time. We see the results of such breaks with tradition in Cummings's poems, freed of capital letters and traditional punctuation and opened up to new words; in Hughes's vignettes of Harlem life; in Williams's proletarian portraits; in the voices of Hurston's resilient black women; as well as in Frost's poems about the people, the rocky soil, and the weather of New England. With these literary appropriations of local and colloquial traditions, furthermore, American literature became a counterforce to the cultural homogenization fostered by new media such as the radio and movies.

The Great War

Another development that challenged centralization stemmed from a sense of disillusionment fueled, first, by disclosures of the terrible human costs of the Great War and the botched peace of Versailles, and then by the mounting disenchantment among writers with the materialism of the booming twenties. The Great War had begun as a crusade to save civilization—"The world must be made safe for democracy," said President Wilson. But it had ended by deepening doubt and fostering cynicism. "That's what you all are. . . . You are a lost generation," Gertrude Stein said to Ernest Hemingway, as one of the war's young survivors. And even those who had not seen the war's horrors began to share in the disillusionment once it became clear, as Frederick Lewis Allen noted in *Only Yesterday* (1931), that "the new day so sonorously heralded by the optimists and propagandists of war-time had turned into night before it ever arrived," leaving people in an "uncertain blackness," not knowing "which way to turn."

People had died, Ezra Pound wrote in "Hugh Selwyn Mauberley," "For an old bitch gone in the teeth, / For a botched civilization." One source of disillusionment was the magnitude of the slaughter: 48,000 killed, 2,900 missing, 56,000 dead from disease for the United States; 947,000 killed for England; 1,200,000 killed for Austria-Hungary; 1,400,000 killed for France; 1,700,000 killed for Russia; and 1,800,000 killed for Germany. After the war was over, a milestone of sorts was reached when nations began summarizing casualties in figures rounded to the nearest 1,000, or 10,000, or even 100,000. A second source of disillusionment came with realization that the heinous deeds of one side had been followed by heinous deeds of the other and that no nation had behaved honorably. To the contrary, as a young Winston Churchill put it, "All the horrors of all the ages" had been brought together, thrusting "whole populations . . . into the midst of them," until no nation had been willing to draw "the line at any deed which they thought could help them win." And a third sobering realization lay in how little had been achieved by such unprecedented sacrifice and slaughter—namely, a Europe decimated, depleted, and debt-ridden, still racked with old animosities, now intensified, as well as increased inflation and mounting political unrest. "I was always embarrassed," Fredric Henry says in Hemingway's *A Farewell to Arms* (1929), "by the words *sacred, glorious,* and *sacrifice* and the expression *in vain*. We had heard them . . . and read them . . . and I had seen nothing sacred, and the things that were glorious had no glory and the sacrifices were like the stockyards at Chicago if nothing was done with the meat except to bury it. There were many words that you could not stand to hear and finally only the names of places had dignity." Later, in a novel called *Company K* (1933), William March of Alabama, who had been awarded the Distinguished Service Cross, the Navy Cross, and the Croix de guerre in the Great War, created a letter, written by a commanding officer to a bereaved mother, that captures with unusual force the lingering bitterness left by the war. "Dear Madam," it begins, "your son, Francis, died needlessly in Belleau Wood," and "at the time of his death he was crawling with vermin," his "feet were swollen and rotten and they stank," and he was living "like a frightened animal, cold and hungry," until "a piece of shrapnel hit him and he died in agony, slowly," suffering for "three full hours screaming and cursing by turns," with "nothing to hold on to," since he had already learned that everything you had "taught [him] to believe . . . under the meaningless names of honor, courage and patriotism, were all lies."

The Age of Business and Frolic

People emptied of beliefs remained rare, of course, even when the Great War ended in disillusionment. Once peace was declared, many American writers returned to their pencils and typewriters and began composing works that disclose a deep fascination with the details of modern life as well as deep ambivalences toward its materialism, its hypocrisies, its lack of felt community, and its lack of respect for art. Politics in general and reform in particular, allied as they were with the good hope discredited by the war, survived among some writers, including John Dos Passos, Genevieve Taggard, and Jean Toomer. But the political enthusiasms that had enlivened the "Lyric Years" before the Great War were in near eclipse by the mid-1920s, replaced by an intense and at times almost frenetic exuberance that was increasingly secular. The Jazz Age, Fitzgerald announced, was an age of miracles, art, excess, and satire that "had no interest in politics at all." "The great problems of the world—social, political, economic, and theological—do not concern me in the slightest," said the drama critic George Jean Nathan. "What concerns me alone is myself, and the interests of a few close friends. For all I care the rest of the world may go to hell at today's sunset." Social concerns and reform politics would not mount much of a comeback among writers until the 1930s. In the meantime, some writers, including Mencken and Nathan, turned to wit and satire, while others, including James G. Huneker, turned to aestheticism, hoping to find in art a substitute for religion. Some highbrows, Ben Hecht remarked, talked of art with reverence previously saved for dead grandmothers.

At its best, however, the aestheticism of the twenties fostered engagement, not flight. Its concern for craftsmanship and its stress on experimentation manifested themselves in the widening of literary traditions on which writers drew and in the introduction of new voices and rhythms as well as innovations in style and form. Even when it fostered a desire to isolate literature from overt political concerns, it also expressed a need to find in art creative responses to the malaise and disillusionment that writers saw around them and felt within. What they sought in their literary experiments were new ways of saying "no" to a still fragmented yet suddenly skeptical and even cynical world from which the gods seemed suddenly to have departed, taking with them familiar forms of hope and consolation and leaving in their wake new slogans and gadgets. "To see the gods dispelled in mid-air and dissolve like clouds is one of the great human experiences," Wallace Stevens wrote. For though "It was their annihilation . . . it left us feeling that in a measure, we, too, had been annihilated."

The outpouring of literary and artistic experimentation that followed was one of the richest and most varied in history. In some moments, it constituted something like a direct address to the disillusionment that Stevens and others thought of as forming the philosophical base of modernist literature. "In an age of disbelief, or what is the same thing, in a time that is largely humanistic, in one sense or another, it is for the poet to supply the satisfactions of belief," Stevens wrote, "in his manner and in his style." In others, it featured a determination to alter the literary landscape by bringing into it the voices of people who had previously been excluded and even despised. Soon writers were composing poems and stories, to borrow from Hughes's list, about "women domestics, workers on Florida roads, poor black students wanting to shatter the darkness of ignorance and prejudice, and . . . the sharecroppers of Mississippi." The prose and poetry of the period featured a much more diverse range of scenes and settings, urban and rural, sophisticated and primitive, than had previously been seen.

Some works came out of enclaves established by artists; others were written in virtual isolation by American writers living and working in France, Italy, Spain, England, Mexico, and Cuba as well as cities like Atlanta, New Orleans, Memphis, Nashville, Chicago, Washington, D.C., and New York; and small towns like Eatonville, Florida, and Oxford, Mississippi.

During these years, the United States experienced, first, a period of unprecedented prosperity, and, then, the most severe depression in its history. Between 1920 and 1929, national income rose from $59.4 billion to $87.2 billion, enabling the nation to achieve the highest standard of living the world had ever known. By early 1929, the United States accounted for 34.4 percent of total world production, compared with 39.6 percent for Great Britain, France, Germany, Russia, and Japan combined—a domination never before approached. Over this same period, the number of telephones rose from less than 1.4 million to more than 20.2 million, and the number of automobiles produced rose from 4,000 to 4.8 million. In the autumn of 1920, Americans heard their first radio broadcast; in 1929, they spent $852 million purchasing radios. Meanwhile, movies, baseball, and boxing were becoming big businesses, making stars of Rudolph Valentino and Greta Garbo and heroes of Babe Ruth and Jack Dempsey. In 1922, roughly 40 million people attended movies; by the decade's end an average of 100 million were buying tickets each week. Although several parts of the country remained rural and agricultural, and though the South remained poor throughout the twenties, a new pattern of life—urban, industrial, commercial, affluent, and increasingly secular—was clearly being established. Dominant first in the Northeast, it spread across the upper Midwest toward the Pacific. Eventually, it triumphed even in the South.

Writers and artists participated in several parts of the remaking of American culture and led in a few. Although the era created competing diversions—radios, movies, and spectator sports, among them—it also spurred the growth of advertising, encouraging the development of new magazines and new publishing firms, including Viking (1925). With magazines and publishers competing for their works, writers were able to make more money and reach more readers than ever before. Fitzgerald's first novel, *This Side of Paradise* (1920), sold more than 40,000 copies in its first year. After 1927, when *The Jazz Singer* transformed the use of sound in motion pictures, Hollywood began offering lucrative contracts to writers, including, to name a few, Fitzgerald, Faulkner, Dashiell Hammett, and Nathanael West. Yet many writers remained ambivalent about the nation's headlong rush to make money, even when they found themselves drawn to it, just as they felt cynical about Prohibition, the nation's newest form of Puritanism, in which hundreds of licensed saloons were replaced by thousands of illegal "speakeasies," many of them controlled by organized crime. Soon, casual lawlessness as well as drinking was accepted as a sign of sophistication. Like the Red Scare of 1919, the Palmer Raids of 1920 encouraged illegal as well as legal expressions of hostility toward "aliens," "anarchists," and "communists," promoting cynicism among artists and writers. The long, divisive trial and execution of Nicola Sacco and Bartolomeo Vanzetti (1920–1927) further polarized the nation, as did the National Origins Act of 1924, which halted immigration from Asia and restricted immigration from southern and eastern Europe. Vigilante groups of "concerned" citizens—most notably, the Ku Klux Klan, whose membership rose from 5 thousand in 1920 to 5 million in 1925—began organizing "to protect" the country by persecuting and even lynching members of political, religious, and racial minorities. Meanwhile, the nation moved, without much notice, from the cronyism and corruption of Warren Harding's administration (1920–1923) to the stern asceticism of Calvin Coolidge's (1923–1929), as though to reinforce the impression that its only shared commitment was to "a businessman's government" that knew how to promote economic growth. "What is the finest game? Business. The soundest science? Business. The fullest education? Business. The fairest opportunity? Business. The cleanest philanthropy? Business. The sanest religion? Business," wrote Edward Earl Purington in 1921, as though he were speaking for the nation as well as to it.

Racism and Sexism

Like materialism and nativism, sexism and racism also flourished. In 1920, after nearly a century of work and protest, women won the right to vote, but what followed was neither the reconstitution of society that women had hoped for nor the disintegration of it that their largely male opponents had predicted. The new votes produced little discernible change in political life. And, with no compelling goal to focus on, their movement declined, leaving many women disillusioned. Established writers like Wharton and Cather continued to publish; and younger ones like Hurston, Moore, Porter, and Welty began to emerge. But many women, in Paris as well as the United States, encountered in male writers sentiments distressingly similar to those expressed by the novelist Joseph Hergesheimer in "The Feminine Nuisance in American Literature," which was delivered as a lecture at Yale and then published as an essay in the *Yale Review* in 1921—namely, more suspicion and hostility than affirmation. Meanwhile, racism flourished even more openly and widely—both in appeals to racial pride, particularly among so-called Nordics or Aryans, and in appeals to racial fear of the "darker" immigrants from southern and eastern Europe as well as all African Americans. In books like *The Passing of the Great Race* (1916) and *The Rising Tide of Color* (1920), written by men bearing the resonant names of Madison Grant and Lothrop Stoddard, two flawed and even contradictory arguments developed side by side, one suggesting that "Aryans" constituted a superior race that had risen to positions of power and prestige solely on the basis of innate intellectual and moral superiority that manifested themselves in disciplined habits and hard work that led to social, economic, and political success; and a second suggesting that members of this naturally superior and socially empowered race were somehow suddenly and even seriously threatened by members of lazy, undisciplined, and hopelessly inferior "darker" races who were somehow, despite their inferior abilities and status, about to take over the world. The real work of such books was not logical argumentation, of course; it was the dissemination of alarmist and even inflammatory rhetoric. Yet they found a ready audience among readers whose ideas resembled those expressed by Tom Buchanan in *The Great Gatsby* (1925). Referring to a book called *The Rise of the Colored Empires* "by this man Goddard," which "everybody ought to read," Tom says he has become terribly pessimistic about the future of "the white race" because Goddard has figured "the whole thing" out—"It's all scientific stuff; it's been proved," Tom adds—that if we, who are now "the dominant race" don't "watch out . . . these other races will have control of things" and we "will be utterly submerged."

An Alienated Generation

"Feeling like aliens" in their own country, as Malcolm Cowley put it in *Exile's Return*, many writers, musicians, and other artists began sailing for Europe "as soon as they had money enough to pay for their steamer tickets." Only a few—Eliot, Pound, Stein, and Wright, among them—became permanent expatriates, but many made trips, some for extended stays. Others gravitated toward the enclaves that sprang up in Atlanta, New Orleans, Memphis, Chicago, and Washington, D.C., as well as Harlem and Greenwich Villlage in New York. Faulkner lived for a time in New Orleans, then sailed for Europe, where he spent time in Italy, England, and especially France before returning to live and work in relative isolation in Oxford, Mississippi. Sooner or later, many writers, including Yezierska, Faulkner, and Fitzgerald, spent some time working in Hollywood. But even writers who shared in the country's prosperity and participated in its highjinks, as Fitzgerald did, felt uncomfortable with the crass worship of money that seemed to doom each "new generation . . . more than the last" to what Fitzgerald called "the fear of poverty and the worship of success." "I would say," Faulkner remarked, "that in our culture there is really no place for the artist." A favorite story among writers of the period recalled the day, considerably more complicated in fact than in reports of it, when a thirty-six year-old man named Sherwood Anderson walked out of his successful paint factory in Elyria, Ohio, hoping to find meaning in art. "I hardly know what I can teach," Anderson wrote his brother Karl, "except anti-success."

Many of the same poets and fiction writers who transformed the literary landscape of the United States also played major roles in the international development of literary modernism, which featured as one of its themes what Lionel Trilling, in *Freud and the Crisis of Our Culture* (1955), called "the self in its standing quarrel with culture": "In its essence literature is concerned with the self; and the particular concern of the literature of the last two centuries has been with the self in its standing quarrel with" a culture that has failed to meet its "legitimate demands," thus provoking as well as authorizing writers to express the bitter discontent of its most sensitive and thoughtful members. In their campaign against priggishness and censorship, Randolph Bourne, Van Wyck Brooks, and H. L. Mencken made *puritan* an epithet for people who fear pleasure and love power, and *puritanism* a scapegoat for most known forms of blindness, greed, and repression. Eliot, Stein, Hemingway, Pound, and Wright became prominent voices in literary affairs in London and Paris, in part by making colloquial American English a resource for modern literary experimentation, a move Hemingway identified specifically as a legacy of Mark Twain. In 1930, when the Swedish Academy awarded the Nobel Prize in literature to Sinclair Lewis, the first American to receive it, the secretary of the Academy said of Lewis, he "is an American. He writes the new language—American—as one of the representatives of a hundred and twenty million souls" who have created the "new American literature." During the twenties and thirties, books of American writers were marketed widely in England and Europe, and some were published there before they were published in the United States. Faulkner, among others, gained recognition in France before he gained it in the United States. Yet the efforts of writers to make more use of the resources of colloquial American English coincided with and even reinforced their efforts to develop an "international style" that, like the colloquial, had as one of its chief targets the pentameter that they associated with established English models.

English writers, especially of the Renaissance and the nineteenth century, continued to influence American writers, but increasingly the dominant revisionary mood embraced colloquial voices and traditions in one motion and international voices and traditions in another.

The Making of American Modernists

We sometimes speak of poets like Cummings, Hughes, Frost, Eliot, Moore, Pound, and Stevens and of fiction writers like Anderson, Fitzgerald, Hemingway, Faulkner, Hurston, Welty, and Wright, among others, as Modernists, as though they form some common school. But readers encountering these writers for the first time are likely to be struck by their differences. For one thing they shared was a radical spirit of experimentation in style, form, subject matter, and language so that even when their efforts resemble one another on some counts, they differ on others. They differ, for example, in their sense of which earlier writers had become oppressive; of what forgotten voices they hoped to reclaim; and how they hoped to declare their own independence. In one motion, they expanded the nature-anchored contemplative–meditative tradition of Emerson; in another they expanded the colloquial tradition of Mark Twain by introducing into poetry a wide range of colloquial voices that had already been brought into fiction. They thus introduced the slang, the dialects, the rhythms, and even the previously forbidden words of the regions, ethnic groups or classes that they knew best, from the rural South as well as from the streets of Chicago and New York; and from the countrysides of the Midwest and New England. At the same time, though in a distinctly different motion, they cultivated in poetry and prose a broadly "international style." Working in different languages, different traditions, and different places, scattered writers seemed to be gathering "from the air," to borrow from Pound's Canto LXXXI, "a live tradition" that could help them to make things new in a world in which so many things, including many words, seemed worn, abused, crass, or deceitful. They drew from many sources, including recent French poets (Baudelaire, Laforgue, Apollinaire, and Mallarmé, for example); Italian poets of a more distant past (Guido Cavalcanti, for example, as well as Dante and Petrarch); and novelists like Cervantes, Melville, Dostoevsky, Flaubert, Twain, James, and Conrad. With Eliot, they reached out to the religious poetry of the Indian Upanishads; with Pound they reached back to Anglo-Saxon and Latin models and out to Chinese literature and philosophy. Books provided one means of gathering and disseminating this "international style," including some that belong to what Baudelaire called the "sublime literature" of despair. But so did letters, conversations, and especially "little magazines." *The Dial,* based in New York, and *Poetry,* based in Chicago, to take two prominent examples, played crucial roles in bringing news of avant-garde developments, in painting as well as poetry and prose, to the United States; and they also provided places where the experimental work of new writers could be published. Such magazines sprang up in virtually every literary enclave in the United States and abroad. In them, writers examined the consequences of the quickened pace of urban life and the flood of modern technological inventions on the moods of people and on the landscape, whether in celebration, dismay, or alarm. In little magazines associated with the Southern Agrarians, most notably *The Fugitive,* writers sought to find new ways of saying "Yes" to the traditions they valued and "No" to everything about the industrial, commercial, and secular drift of the nation.

From the Crash to the New Deal

A variety of prominent public figures—such as Charlie Chaplin, Isadora Duncan, Buffalo Bill, and Presidents Harding, Coolidge, and Roosevelt—and a variety of prominent public events—such as the trial and execution of Sacco and Vanzetti (1920–1927), the Scopes trial of 1925; and the trial of the "Scottsboro 'boys,' " (1931–1937)—engaged the attention of writers and entered the literature of the time. Yet it was not until the crash of 1929 brought what Fitzgerald called "history's most expensive orgy" to a halt, replacing it with the Great Depression of the 1930s, that any event came close to matching the impact of the Great War on literary culture. For the crash struck with an abruptness and a force that remain hard to comprehend. In December 1928, President Coolidge assured the nation that it had never "met with a more pleasing prospect," and for the next several months, investors continued to push "the Great Bull Market" up. In 1923, sales on the New York Stock Exchange had topped 235 million shares for the first time; late in 1928, shortly before Coolidge told the nation what it wanted to believe, sales passed 1.1 billion shares. Then, less than a year later, the market broke: Industrials lost 228 points between early September and early November, a decline of 50 percent; and by 1932, they had fallen from a high of 452 to a low of 58.

As confidence, reserves, and income plummeted, unemployment, bankruptcies, and suicides rose. Yet for writers already skeptical of the nation's infatuation with money, the shock was mixed with "a sense of relief," as Malcolm Cowley put it, like that felt "on coming out of a room too full of talk and people into the sunlight of the winter streets." By appealing to political and social idealism, Franklin Delano Roosevelt became the first president since Woodrow Wilson to capture the attention of writers and make reform politics respectable. Concern with stylistic and formal literary experimentation continued, but now it was charged by a sense of urgency about social-political issues that had earlier been seen only in writers like Johnson, Hughes, Crane, Moore, and Williams. Soon some older writers and scores of younger ones were writing as though determined to prove, as Alfred Kazin later observed, that they could move "the streets, the stockyards, the hiring halls into literature" and thus make their "radical strength . . . carry on the experimental impulse of modern literature."

By becoming the heyday of documentary literature in America, the 1930s enlarged the nation's sense of what "literature" might be. It yielded not only books like Ruth McKenny's *Industrial Valley* and George Leighton's *Five Cities* but also a series of striking collaborations between writers and photographers, including Dorothea Lange's and Paul S. Taylor's *An American Exodus: A Record of Human Erosion in the Thirties*, Erskine Caldwell's and Margaret Bourke-White's *You Have Seen Their Faces*, Richard Wright's and Edwin Rosskam's *12 Million Black Voices*, and James Agee's and Walker Evans's *Let Us Now Praise Famous Men*. In these and other collaborative books, writers and photographers sought to record the suffering of the poor and also to endow it with meaning by grounding it in a stoic dignity and a will to survive. At the same time, a new interest in the idea of "culture" manifested itself in frequent use of phrases like the "American Dream" and the "American way of life" as well as a broad-scale effort to record and preserve the past, much of it carried out by New Deal initiatives such as the Federal Writers' Project (FWP) and the Federal Theater Project (FTP). During its four-year existence, the FTP employed nearly 13,000 people and presented more than 42,000 performances, ranging from *Macbeth* to W.E.B. Du Bois's *Haiti,* one of several productions that Martin Dies's House Un-American Activities Committee condemned. Conrad Aiken, Saul Bellow, Arna Bontemps, Erskine Caldwell, Ralph Ellison, Margaret Walker, Eudora Welty, Edmund Wilson, Richard Wright, and Frank Yerby were among hundreds of writers employed on federal projects that produced guidebooks to the people—land, history, and culture—of each of the forty-eight states and Alaska. Richard Wright's *Uncle Tom's Children* (1938) won a prize from *Story* magazine for the best work by an FWP writer. Pare Lorentz's documentary film *The River,* which influenced both Steinbeck and Faulkner, was produced by the Farm Security Administration (FSA).

Social Criticism and Marxism

Although the documentary movement of the thirties produced uneven works of art, several of its achievements were important. It reinforced the sense that the nation and its literature had done and were doing too little for "the people." It gave new energy to forms of radicalism that had not been heard since before World War I. At a time when the nation's sense of confidence was badly shaken, it enlarged one of the needs it set out to meet—namely, the need to recover, in Kazin's phrase, a sense of "America *as an idea.*" By producing a series of creative works in which words and photographs were juxtaposed, it stimulated examinations of the complex relations between the scenes of life, on one side, and forms of perception and expression, on the other. Finally, it gave new resonance to an idea that dated back to Plato—that human creativity begins with a sense of place. Some of the fiction of the time, including the "naturalistic" works of James T. Farrell, relied heavily on a logic of reiteration that manifested itself in an accumulation of similar scenes. But works like those of Lange and Taylor, Bourke-White and Caldwell, and Wright and Rosskam accomplished more than some naturalistic novels. Photographers of the 1930s tended to think of cameras as passive instruments for recording "the truth of the times." Their aim was to document the crippling effects of poverty on the suddenly visible poor—like a farmer interviewed and photographed by Lange and Taylor who described himself as "burned out, blowed out, eat out, tractored out." But in their efforts to record what Agee called "the cruel radiance of what is"—in images of black "native sons," white sharecroppers, marginalized women, and "hyphenated-Americans"—they created as well as recorded. As a result, their works share important qualities not only with fiction writers like Faulkner, Hurston, and Wright, but also with the misshapen characters we encounter in Nathanael West's *Miss Lonelyhearts,* urban though they are, or those in Edward Dahlberg's *Bottom Dogs* (1930) or Jack Conroy's *The Disinherited* (1933). Soon new forms of cultural analysis, some of them influenced by Marxist critiques of political and cultural institutions, began gaining currency, provoking some Americans to wonder whether their economic system ("free enterprise capitalism") might not be at odds with their political system ("egalitarian democracy"). "Thousands were convinced and hundreds of thousands were half-persuaded that no simple operation would save us," Cowley wrote; "there had to be the complete renovation of society that Karl Marx had prophesied in 1848. Unemployment would be ended, war and fascism would vanish from the earth, but only after the revolution." "There is a song that says, 'the time ain't long.' That song is right. Something has got to change in America—and change soon," Langston Hughes added in "To Negro Writers" (1935). "We want an America that will be ours, a world that will be ours—we Negro workers and white workers! Black writers and white! We'll make that world."

Although some writers of the thirties permitted their writing to become propagandistic, others as different as Dos Passos, Hughes, Hurston, West, and Wright did not. Some of their characters—rootless vagabonds and defiant criminals, crippled or deformed outcasts, people of mixed or uncertain racial identity, or of conflicted and ambiguous sexual identity—belong to the margins of society. Others, finding themselves trapped on worn-out farms, in tenements, or in ghettos, begin to feel a kind of hopelessness that compounds the hardships they encounter. Some titles of novels—including Edward Dahlberg's *Bottom Dogs,* Jack Conroy's *The Disinherited,* and Tess Slesinger's *The Unpossessed* (1934), for example—convey a sense of different moods of the times. Yet the thirties yielded prose and poetry of lasting value, including Stevens's *Ideas of Order* (1935), Faulkner's *Light in August* (1932) and *Absalom, Absalom!* (1936), and Hemingway's *For Whom the Bell Tolls* (1940), as well as the fine early work of Porter and Welty, new work by Cummings, Eliot, and Pound, and much of the finest work of West, Dos Passos, Hurston, Williams, and Wright, among others.

The Second World War

As early as 1933, when Adolph Hitler's *Mein Kampf* was reviewed by the *New York Times,* it was clear that Hitler's ambitions went beyond what he thought of as the reunification of Germany to what he thought of as its purification. Yet no one realized how far his ambitions would reach until he and his allies began intervening in the affairs of their neighbors and then began invading them. In 1935, Italy conquered Ethiopia; and in 1936, civil war broke out in Spain, with Russia intervening on one side, Germany and Italy on the other, in a conflict that galvanized the attention of many writers in England and Europe as well as the United States, including André Malraux, George Orwell, W. H. Auden, Stephen Spender, Dos Passos, and Hemingway. In 1938, when Germany invaded Austria, it became clear that Hitler was nearer the beginning of his planned aggressions than the end. Meanwhile, Japan was intensifying hostilities against China, quickening the flow of refugees from Asia as well as Europe, and with it, the flow of warnings and appeals. In the late thirties, however, with 10 million United States workers still unemployed, the nation's attention remained fixed on its own problems. In 1940, Hemingway published a novel based on his experiences as a war corespondent in Spain; and in its title, *For Whom the Bell Tolls,* borrowed from John Donne, he suggested that the bells tolling for the people of Europe were tolling for people of the rest of the world as well. But *America First* was the name of one of several strong isolationist organizations in the country; and its very different message, favoring isolationism and opposing all entangling alliances, appealed to many Americans.

Even with Hitler's horrific persecution of Jews escalating and the flow of refugees increasing—scholars, artists, writers, and musicians, including Albert Einstein, Hannah Arendt, Thomas Mann, and Vladimir Nabokov—the United States remained determined in its isolationism. During 1941, however, as hostilities in Europe escalated and relations between the United States and Japan worsened, isolationism became less viable. Then, on 7 December 1941, when a large force of Japanese aircraft carriers launched an air attack at Pearl Harbor, inflicting heavy damage on armed forces of the United States, it came to a halt. We "have learned a terrible lesson," President Roosevelt announced two days later. To accomplish "the great task that is before us," we must abandon "once and for all the illusion that we can ever again isolate ourselves from the rest of Humanity."

Over the next several months the nation left the Great Depression behind it by rapidly enlarging its economy to include military production—which more than doubled in 1942, and by the end of 1943 had reached a level that exceeded the country's total gross national product when President Roosevelt first took office in 1933. Required to play a far more decisive role in the century's second "great war" than it had in the first, the United States successfully launched major efforts both in Europe and in Asia. In the process it regained its sense of confidence and shared purpose. With employment and wages rising, strikes and protests dropped dramatically. Virtually the only thing that marred the first half of the decade of the forties, beyond the substantial casualties inflicted by the war itself, was the decision to arrest 80,000 Japanese-American citizens, denying them their constitutionally guaranteed rights, as well as 40,000 legal immigrants who had been denied citizenship only because of their national origin. Classified as "enemy aliens," these people were moved through "reception centers," such as the one hastily constructed at the Santa Anita racetrack in Los Angeles, to migrant labor camps constructed in remote places farther inland.

Later, as details of the wreckage that Japan had inflicted on Asia began to emerge and, especially, as details not only of the damage inflicted by Germany on Europe but especially of the atrocities inflicted by Germany on those judged to be "social undesirables," including Gypsies, homosexuals and especially the Jews of Europe, became known—more than 6 million men, women, and children annihilated in gas chambers, in medical and military "experimental" stations, in crematoriums and torture chambers, in detention centers and concentration camps—World War II came to be regarded as a "great crusade." Looking back on his own incarceration, in a book titled *Night* (1958), Elie Wiesel recalls the scene of his paralyzing fear during the last night of his father's life. "There was silence all around, broken only by groans" of the imprisoned and dying and the SS officers "giving orders." From the bunk below him the young boy hears his father begging for water, then hears an officer "shouting at him to be quiet" and hitting him "on the head with his truncheon." Paralyzed with fear, he remains still until after "roll call," when he gets down to see his father's face, then crawls back into his bunk. It was January 28, 1945, he tells us, and it was the last time he saw father. For, at dawn the next morning, he finds "another invalid" in his father's bunk and knows that they have taken his father "to the crematory," though he "may still have been breathing." Reflecting what we have learned, in part from him, to call "the guilt of the survivor," Wiesel tells us that "no prayers" were spoken at his father's grave and that no candles were lit in his memory. "I did not weep, and it pained me that I could not weep. But I had no more tears."

"There," wrote Colonel William W. Quinn, who led United States troops in rescu-ing survivors of Dachau, "our troops found sights, sounds, and strenches horrible be-yond belief, cruelties so enormous as to be incomprehensible to the normal mind."

Due in part to its magnitude, the century's second great war became a preemptive force that seemed to put everything else on hold for its duration, and in this sense it was "bad for writing," as Faulkner wrote his agent in 1944. Saul Bellow, John Cheever, James Dickey, Joseph Heller, James Jones, and Norman Mailer, among many others, served in one or another of the armed forces, and Hemingway served again as a war correspondent. Having tried and failed to get into the fray, Faulkner joined the small army of writers gathered in Hollywood to work on screenplays about Nazi spies and allied heroes. Once the war was over, however, these and many other writers were quick to pick up their pencils or pull out their typewriters and began producing short stories, novels, plays, and poems as well as screenplays, in some of which we hear echoes of the disillusionment that had followed World War I, though none of them matches it. More prevalent in them is a sense of the war as a "grand crusade" in which "right" and "might" had again been united. Later, as the nation's sense of shared purpose began to fade, a note of something like nostalgia entered its literature. But even in the immediate aftermath of the war, while the victory parades were still fresh memories, notes of doubt began to be heard, stemming primarily from the two related events that had hastened the war's end, saving the lives of many American soldiers—namely, the dropping of atomic bombs on Hiroshima and Nagasaki.

The Dawn of Postmodernism

More than any war in history, World War II was a war of technology—of new developments in synthetic rubber, radar, microwaves, and rockets, as well as advances in building trucks, ships, planes, and a variety of new aiming and tracking devices as well as new weapons. But the most stunning advance in weaponry had begun before the United States entered the war, when, in the summer of 1939, following a meeting with a group of physicists that included Albert Einstein and Enrico Fermi, President Roosevelt established the Advisory Committee on Uranium. Six years later, on 16 July 1945, the United States tested the world's first atomic bomb. Then, on the mornings of August 6 and 9, it dropped bombs on Hiroshima and Nagasaki, bringing the century's second great war to an end. The bomb, the President of the United States announced, "had more power than twenty thousand tons of TNT" and carried more than two thousand times the blast power of the largest bomb ever before used in the history of warfare—the "British Grand Slam."

Given the dramatic manner of the war's ending, it scarcely seemed strange that one of the first of many books to come out of the war, John Hersey's *Hiroshima* (1946), should focus on the events that brought it to an end, when, "At exactly fifteen minutes past eight in the morning, on August 6, 1945, Japanese time," Hersey writes, an "atomic bomb flashed above Hiroshima," and "a tremendous flash of light cut across the sky," turning what had begun as another "cool and pleasant morning" into a memory so traumatic that the few survivors of the bombing who did not lapse into silence would feel compelled to fall back "on primitive, childish terms" when they tried to discuss it. Three days and three hours later, at 11:02 A.M. Japanese time, the people of Nagasaki joined the people of Hiroshima, Hersey continues, as "objects" of the first two great experiments in the use of atomic power, although it would be "several days before the survivors of Hiroshima knew that they had company." For these events, almost as much as the Holocaust and the interrelated acts of aggression that precipitated the war itself, helped to make World War II another memory that would not go away. Literary appropriation of it continued through the 1940s, with James Gould Cozzens's *Guard of Honor* and Norman Mailer's *The Naked and the Dead;* to the 1950s, with Harriette Arnow's *The Dollmaker,* which focuses on the "home front," James Jones's *From Here to Eternity,* Herman Wouk's *The Caine Mutiny,* and Thomas Berger's *Crazy in Berlin;* to the 1970s, with Joseph Heller's *Catch-22* and Thomas Pynchon's *Gravity's Rainbow.*

American literature of the modernist period began before the century's first great war and ended some time during its second great war. Marked by humor and playfulness as well as high seriousness and great boldness of spirit, it introduced technical and formal experiments that redefined the languages as well as the forms of literature. Yet it also demonstrated an unparalleled willingness to confront a host of grave social problems having to do with ethnicity, gender, race, poverty, and disease, as well as war. One thing that writers of the first half of the twentieth century had inherited from writers of the nineteenth century, besides skepticism about sufficiency of material progress, was belief in freedom that manifested itself in a willingness to blur or even dissolve restrictions and rules governing life as well as art. Yet, the freedom American modernists celebrate in their writing, including the freedom to reject customs governing traditional poetry and fiction, is paid for by sacrifices reflected in the losses that their poems and stories confront and in a sense enact. Like all great innovative moves in literature, furthermore, their innovations were at once technical and thematic; they involved what W. H. Auden called "new styles of architecture" and at the same time gave expression to "a change of heart." We can recognize versions of this double move, to take a few examples, in Frost's couplings of new "sentence sounds" with his adaptations of ancient stoicism; in Eliot's and Pound's experiments in "free verse" that allowed them to bring disparate elements and voices into the same poem; in the spare diction and spare rhythms of Hemingway's prose; in Hughes's and Hurston's literary appropriations of African American vernacular as well as African American experiences and ordeals; and in the wide range of styles, voices, agonies, and humor that we encounter in Faulkner's fiction. We can also tell much about both the predicaments and the creative responses of these and other writers represented in this anthology from the striking frequency with which their poems, stories, and novels come to us as works pieced together from scattered fragments—or put another way, as works that strive for a kind of unity and closure that they can never fully achieve. In several important respects, the longer poems of American modernism—Eliot's "The Waste Land," Pound's *Cantos,* Williams's "Paterson," Crane's "The Bridge," and Stevens's "Notes Toward a Supreme Fiction"—have more in common with Whitman's "Song of Myself" than with the great long poems of Milton and Wordsworth. They range in diction from "high" to "low"; they make free use of techniques that we associate with "collage" in modern art and techniques that we associate with "montage" in film; and they are by turn serious, farcical, philosophical, and anecdotal. Like many other works of the period, they remain unpredictable in form as well as diction in part because they strive for a sense of unity and closure that they approximate yet finally forego. Confrontations and experiments with discontinuity also run through the fiction of the period, as we see most clearly in the broken or discontinuous narratives we encounter in Stein's *Three Lives,* Anderson's *Winesburg, Ohio,* Hemingway's *In Our Time,* Wright's *Uncle Tom's Children,* and Faulkner's *Go Down, Moses,* to name a few.

By the end of the modernist period, the traditionally elevated and genteel language of American literature had been replaced by vocabularies and dialects as diverse as the artists who used them. So, too, had the scenes and subjects, the manners and mores, the dreams and horrors they presented. Writers of this era wrote, of course, for reasons and under pressures as varied as the works they created. Looking back, however, from the end of the century they helped to begin, it seems almost as if they wrote for us to fulfill Walt Whitman's prediction, in "Song of the Exposition," that the "universal Muse" would come finally to these shores as an "illustrious émigré" of many voices, to give expression to "wide geographies, manifold, different, distant." And it is certain that in their varied ways they contributed to a remarkable outpouring of innovative expression that was marked both by their willingness to confront grave social and moral problems and by their willingnesses to undertake daring stylistic and formal experiments in poetry and in fiction.

Further Reading:

F. L. Allen, *Only Yesterday,* 1931.

S. Brown, *Negro Poetry and Drama,* 1937.

M. Cowley, *After the Genteel Tradition: American Writing, 1910–1930,* 1937.

A. Kazin, *On Native Ground: An Interpretation of Modern American Prose Literature,* 1942.

H. Gregory and M. Zaturenska, *A History of American Poetry, 1900–1940,* 1946.

L. Trilling, *The Liberal Imagination,* 1950.

M. Cowley, *Exile's Return: A Narrative of Ideas,* 1934, 1951.

L. Brogan, *Achievement in American Poetry, 1900–1950.*

E. Wilson, *The Shores of Light: A Literary Chronicle of the Twenties and Thirties,* 1952.

F. J. Hoffman, *The Twenties: American Writing in the Postwar Decade,* 1955.

R. Hofstadter, *The Age of Reform: From Bryan to FDR,* 1955.

L. Trilling, *The Opposing Self,* 1955.

L. Trilling, *Freud and the Crisis of our Culture,* 1956.

W. Leuchtenburg, *The Perils of Prosperity: 1914–1932,* 1958.

W. Morris, *The Territory Ahead,* 1958.

D. Aaron, *Writers on the Left,* 1961.

R. H. Pearce, *The Continuity of American Poetry,* 1961.

M. Cowley, *After the Genteel Tradition: American Writers 1910–1930,* rev. ed., 1964.

W. Berthoff, *The Ferment of Realism: American Literature 1884–1919,* 1965.

H. Miller, *Poets of Reality,* 1965.

R. Bridgman, *The Colloquial Style in America,* 1966.

E. Margolies, *Native Sons: A Critical Study of Twentieth-Century Negro Authors,* 1968.

J. Mazzaro, *Modern American Poetry,* 1970.

R. Sklar, ed., *The Plastic Age: 1917–1930,* 1970.

L. Huggins, *Harlem Renaissance,* 1971.

H. Kenner, *The Pound Era,* 1971.

R. Miller, *Black American Literature: 1760 to the Present,* 1971.

W. Susman, ed., *Culture and Commitment: 1929–1945,* 1973.

A. Gelpi, *The Tenth Muse: The Psyche of the American Poet,* 1975.

E. S. Watts, *The Poetry of American Women from 1632 to 1945,* 1977.

R. Stepto, *From Behind the Veil: A Study of Afro-American Narrative,* 1979.

R. H. King, *A Southern Renaissance: The Cultural Awakening of the American: 1930–1955,* 1980.

H. Vendler, *Part of Nature, Part of Us: Modern American Poets,* 1980.

D. L. Lewis, *When Harlem Was in Vogue,* 1981.

P. Johnson, *Modern Times: The World from the Twenties to the Eighties,* 1983.

D. E. Stanford, *Revolution and Convention in Modern Poetry,* 1983.

V. A. Kramer, ed., *The Harlem Renaissance: Re-examined,* 1987.

C. Nelson, *Repression and Recovery: Modern American Poetry and the Politics of Cultural Memory, 1910–1945,* 1989.

L. Hughes, ed., *Black Magic: A Pictorial History of the African-American in the Performing Arts,* 1990.

F. Lentricchia, *Modernist Quartet,* 1994.

D. Minter, *A Cultural History of the American Novel: Henry James to William Faulkner,* 1994.

Willa Cather
1873–1947

The old settlements of Virginia and the new lands of Nebraska formed the bedding ground for Willa Cather's talents; so did the layers of memory she found elsewhere across the North American continent, from New Mexico to Canada. Cather was born on the family farm in the hills of Virginia; she lived there until she was nine, when she moved with her parents to Nebraska. After several farming ventures there proved unsuccessful, the Cathers decided to live in the small town of Red Cloud. A young community, Red Cloud nevertheless offered the usual mix of frontier activities. It was flavored by the customs of newcomers from Scandinavia, Germany, and Central Europe as well as by "eastern cultivation" based on classical languages, music, and literature.

Willa Cather was graduated from the University of Nebraska in 1895, then returned East to Pittsburgh. She supported herself first as a journalist and later as a high school teacher. By 1900 she was placing stories and poems in such well-known, large-circulation magazines as *McClure's* and *Cosmopolitan. April Twilight,* a collection of poems, appeared in 1903; it was followed in 1905 by *The Troll Garden,* a grouping of short stories. On the move again, she arrived in New York in 1906 and worked as managing editor of *McClure's* until 1912, the publication date of her first novel, *Alexander's Bridge.* She decided to support herself solely by writing fiction. The appreciation commanded by her earliest work continued and grew, and her decision to be a full-time professional writer proved to be a wise one.

Until 1912 Willa Cather had only hovered around her childhood experiences in Nebraska as possible material for her writings. The next five years saw a burst of literary activity stimulated by those memories, three novels that make clear her affinity for recording dreams of an ordered life whose every moment had significance. They show her mind stimulated by the ahistorical, semimythic landscapes of Nebraska and Arizona. *O Pioneers!* (1913), *Song of the Lark* (1915), and *My Ántonia* (1918) reveal the aspirations of young men and women on the frontier who try to trick defeat and betrayal with their hopes and unflinching will.

Youth and the Bright Medusa, a collection of stories, emerged in 1920. In 1922, the year her war novel, *One of Ours,* was published, Cather's writing career and personal life faltered when the woman she loved got married. She regained her psychic strength, however, and over the next five years wrote three more novels: *A Lost Lady* (1923), *The Professor's House* (1925), and *Death Comes for the Archbishop* (1927). *Shadows on the Rock* followed in 1931, as did other books of less note. Throughout the 1920s and early 1930s she received a number of awards, confirming her place as an important literary voice.

The twin roles of religious faith and memory are strong forces in Willa Cather's fiction. The human need for illusion, dreams, and a vision of a world that lies beyond the material frame permeates her accounts of characters whose lives are made greater, though not necessarily happier, by their insistence on linking their present desires with the aspirations experienced by previous generations. Repeatedly, she portrays the psychological patterns of those who make pilgrimages of the spirit into virginal territories, either geographical or spiritual. Her confirmation as a Protestant Episcopalian in 1922 made her especially responsive to the traditions of Roman Catholicism that had led priests into the frontier areas of New Mexico and French Canada. Priests and pioneers shared the same tradition of heart's longings that are central to much of her fiction.

Cather specifically rejected the realism she associated with a journalist's itemization of facts. She worked more closely with the modernist writers of her generation, who approached their subjects by means of suggestion and the power of descriptive language. But however oblique her treatment, Cather's analysis of why we dream of something better and of how those dreams result in courage and not in defeat makes her narratives of hopeful immigrants and sensitive carriers of culture seem accurate deep down at the bone of truth.

Further Reading:

D. Daiches, *Willa Cather: A Critical Introduction,* 1951, 1962.
J. Randall, *The Landscape and the Looking Glass: Willa Cather's Search for Value,* 1960, 1973.
D. Van Ghent, *Willa Cather,* 1964.
J. Schroeter, ed., *Willa Cather and Her Critics,* 1967.
J. Woodress, *Willa Cather: Her Life and Art,* 1970.
D. McFarland, *Willa Cather's Imagination,* 1972.
M. Arnold, *Willa Cather's Short Fiction,* 1984.
J. Murphy, *Critical Essays on Willa Cather,* 1984.
S. O'Brien, " 'The Thing Not Named': Willa Cather As a Lesbian Writer," *Signs* 9 (1984), 576–99.
J. Fryer, *Felicitous Space,* 1986.

S. Rosowski, *The Voyage Perilous,* 1986.
———, "Writing Against Silences," *Studies in the Novel* 21 (1989), 60–77.
J. Woodress, *Cather: A Literary Life,* 1987.
S. O'Brien, *Cather: The Emerging Voice,* 1987.
Literature and Belief, Special Issue, 1988.
J. Middleton, *Cather's Modernism,* 1990.
H. Lee, *Cather: Double Lives,* 1990.
M. Skaggs, *After the World Broke in Two,* 1990.
Murphy, *et al.,* eds., *Cather: Family, Community and History,* J. 1990.
E. Ammons, *Conflicting Stories,* 1991.

Text:
"Neighbour Rosicky" from *Obscure Destinies,* 1930.

Neighbour Rosicky

I

When Doctor Burleigh told neighbour Rosicky he had a bad heart, Rosicky protested.

"So? No, I guess my heart was always pretty good. I got a little asthma, maybe. Just a awful short breath when I was pitchin' hay last summer, dat's all."

"Well now, Rosicky, if you know more about it than I do, what did you come to me for? It's your heart that makes you short of breath, I tell you. You're sixty-five years old, and you've always worked hard, and your heart's tired. You've got to be careful from now on, and you can't do heavy work any more. You've got five boys at home to do it for you."

The old farmer looked up at the Doctor with a gleam of amusement in his queer triangular-shaped eyes. His eyes were large and lively, but the lids were caught up in the middle in a curious way, so that they formed a triangle. He did not look like a sick man. His brown face was creased but not wrinkled, he had a ruddy colour in his smooth-shaven cheeks and in his lips, under his long brown moustache. His hair was thin and ragged around his ears, but very little grey. His forehead, naturally high and crossed by deep parallel lines, now ran all the way up to his pointed crown. Rosicky's face had the habit of looking interested,—suggested a contented disposition and a reflective quality that was gay rather than grave. This gave him a certain detachment, the easy manner of an onlooker and observer.

"Well, I guess you ain't got no pills fur a bad heart, Doctor Ed. I guess the only thing is fur me to git me a new one."

Doctor Burleigh swung round in his desk-chair and frowned at the old farmer. "I think if I were you I'd take a little care of the old one, Rosicky."

Rosicky shrugged. "Maybe I don't know how. I expect you mean fur me not to drink my coffee no more."

"I wouldn't, in your place. But you'll do as you choose about that. I've never yet been able to separate a Bohemian[1] from his coffee or his pipe. I've quit trying. But the sure thing is you've got to cut out farm work. You can feed the stock and do chores about the barn, but you can't do anything in the fields that makes you short of breath."

"How about shelling corn?"

"Of course not!"

Rosicky considered with puckered brows.

"I can't make my heart go no longer'n it wants to, can I, Doctor Ed?"

"I think it's good for five or six years yet, maybe more, if you'll take the strain off it. Sit around the house and help Mary. If I had a good wife like yours, I'd want to stay around the house."

His patient chuckled. "It ain't no place fur a man. I don't like no old man hanging round the kitchen too much. An' my wife, she's a awful hard worker her own self."

"That's it; you can help her a little. My Lord, Rosicky, you are one of the few men I know who has a family he can get some comfort out of; happy dispositions, never quarrel among themselves, and they treat you right. I want to see you live a few years and enjoy them."

"Oh, they're good kids, all right," Rosicky assented.

The Doctor wrote him a prescription and asked him how his oldest son, Rudolph, who had married in the spring, was getting on. Rudolph had struck out for himself, on rented land. "And how's Polly? I was afraid Mary mightn't like an American daughter-in-law, but it seems to be working out all right."

"Yes, she's a fine girl. Dat widder woman bring her daughters up very nice. Polly got lots of spunk, an' she got some style, too. Da's nice, for young folks to have some style." Rosicky inclined his head gallantly. His voice and his twinkly smile were an affectionate compliment to his daughter-in-law.

"It looks like a storm, and you'd better be getting home before it comes. In town in the car?" Doctor Burleigh rose.

"No, I'm in de wagon. When you got five boys, you ain't got much chance to ride round in de Ford. I ain't much for cars, noway."

"Well, it's a good road out to your place; but I don't want you bumping around in a wagon much. And never again on a hay-rake, remember!"

---

[1] Native of Bohemia, a province of Czechoslovakia.

Rosicky placed the Doctor's fee delicately behind the desk-telephone, looking the other way, as if this were an absent-minded gesture. He put on his plush cap and his corduroy jacket with a sheepskin collar, and went out.

The Doctor picked up his stethoscope and frowned at it as if he were seriously annoyed with the instrument. He wished it had been telling tales about some other man's heart, some old man who didn't look the Doctor in the eye so knowingly, or hold out such a warm brown hand when he said good-bye. Doctor Burleigh had been a poor boy in the country before he went away to medical school; he had known Rosicky almost ever since he could remember, and he had a deep affection for Mrs. Rosicky.

Only last winter he had had such a good breakfast at Rosicky's, and that when he needed it. He had been out all night on a long, hard confinement case[2] at Tom Marshall's,—a big rich farm where there was plenty of stock and plenty of feed and a great deal of expensive farm machinery of the newest model, and no comfort whatever. The woman had too many children and too much work, and she was no manager. When the baby was born at last, and handed over to the assisting neighbour woman, and the mother was properly attended to, Burleigh refused any breakfast in that slovenly house, and drove his buggy—the snow was too deep for a car—eight miles to Anton Rosicky's place. He didn't know another farm-house where a man could get such a warm welcome, and such good strong coffee with rich cream. No wonder the old chap didn't want to give up his coffee!

He had driven in just when the boys had come back from the barn and were washing up for breakfast. The long table, covered with a bright oilcloth, was set out with dishes waiting for them, and the warm kitchen was full of the smell of coffee and hot biscuit and sausage. Five big handsome boys, running from twenty to twelve, all with what Burleigh called natural good manners,—they hadn't a bit of the painful self-consciousness he himself had to struggle with when he was a lad. One ran to put his horse away, another helped him off with his fur coat and hung it up, and Josephine, the youngest child and the only daughter, quickly set another place under her mother's direction.

With Mary, to feed creatures was the natural expression of affection,—her chickens, the calves, her big hungry boys. It was a rare pleasure to feed a young man whom she seldom saw and of whom she was as proud as if he belonged to her. Some country housekeepers would have stopped to spread a white cloth over the oilcloth, to change the thick cups and plates for their best china, and the wooden-handled knives for plated ones. But not Mary.

"You must take us as you find us, Doctor Ed. I'd be glad to put out my good things for you if you was expected, but I'm glad to get you any way at all."

He knew she was glad,—she threw back her head and spoke out as if she were announcing him to the whole prairie. Rosicky hadn't said anything at all; he merely smiled his twinkling smile, put some more coal on the fire, and went into his own room to pour the Doctor a little drink in a medicine glass. When they were all seated, he watched his wife's face from his end of the table and spoke to her in Czech. Then, with the instinct of politeness which seldom failed him, he turned to the Doctor and said slyly; "I was just tellin' her not to ask you no questions about Mrs. Marshall till you eat some breakfast. My wife, she's terrible fur to ask questions."

---

[2] i.e., the delivery of a baby.

The boys laughed, and so did Mary. She watched the Doctor devour her biscuit and sausage, too much excited to eat anything herself. She drank her coffee and sat taking in everything about her visitor. She had known him when he was a poor country boy, and was boastfully proud of his success, always saying: "What do people go to Omaha for, to see a doctor, when we got the best one in the State right here?" If Mary liked people at all, she felt physical pleasure in the sight of them, personal exultation in any good fortune that came to them. Burleigh didn't know many women like that, but he knew she was like that.

When his hunger was satisfied, he did, of course, have to tell them about Mrs. Marshall, and he noticed what a friendly interest the boys took in the matter.

Rudolph, the oldest one (he was still living at home then), said: "The last time I was over there, she was lifting them big heavy milk-cans, and I knew she oughtn't to be doing it."

"Yes, Rudolph told me about that when he come home, and I said it wasn't right," Mary put in warmly. "It was all right for me to do them things up to the last, for I was terrible strong, but that woman's weakly. And do you think she'll be able to nurse it, Ed?" She sometimes forgot to give him the title she was so proud of. "And to think of your being up all night and then not able to get a decent breakfast! I don't know what's the matter with such people."

"Why, Mother," said one of the boys, "if Doctor Ed had got breakfast there, we wouldn't have him here. So you ought to be glad."

"He knows I'm glad to have him, John, any time. But I'm sorry for that poor woman, how bad she'll feel the Doctor had to go away in the cold without his breakfast."

"I wish I'd been in practice when these were getting born." The doctor looked down the row of close-clipped heads. "I missed some good breakfasts by not being."

The boys began to laugh at their mother because she flushed so red, but she stood her ground and threw up her head. "I don't care, you wouldn't have got away from this house without breakfast. No doctor ever did. I'd have had something ready fixed that Anton could warm up for you."

The boys laughed harder than ever, and exclaimed at her: "I'll bet you would!" "She would, that!"

"Father, did you get breakfast for the doctor when we were born?"

"Yes, and he used to bring me my breakfast, too, mighty nice. I was always awful hungry!" Mary admitted with a guilty laugh.

While the boys were getting the Doctor's horse, he went to the window to examine the house plants. "What do you do to your geraniums to keep them blooming all winter, Mary? I never pass this house that from the road I don't see your windows full of flowers."

She snapped off a dark red one, and a ruffled new green leaf, and put them in his buttonhole. "There, that looks better. You look too solemn for a young man, Ed. Why don't you git married? I'm worried about you. Settin' at breakfast, I looked at you real hard, and I seen you've got some grey hairs already."

"Oh, yes! They're coming. Maybe they'd come faster if I married."

"Don't talk so. You'll ruin your health eating at the hotel. I could send your wife a nice loaf of nut bread, if you only had one. I don't like to see a young man getting grey. I'll tell you something, Ed; you make some strong black tea and keep it handy in a bowl, and every morning just brush it into your hair, an' it'll keep the grey from showin' much. That's the way I do!"

Sometimes the Doctor heard the gossipers in the drug-store wondering why Rosicky didn't get on faster. He was industrious, and so were his boys, but they were rather free and easy, weren't pushers, and they didn't always show good judgment. They were comfortable, they were out of debt, but they didn't get much ahead. Maybe, Doctor Burleigh reflected, people as generous and warm-hearted and affectionate as the Rosickys never got ahead much; maybe you couldn't enjoy your life and put it into the bank, too.

II

When Rosicky left Doctor Burleigh's office he went into the farm-implement store to light his pipe and put on his glasses and read over the list Mary had given him. Then he went into the general merchandise place next door and stood about until the pretty girl with the plucked eyebrows, who always waited on him, was free. Those eyebrows, two thin India-ink strokes, amused him, because he remembered how they used to be. Rosicky always prolonged his shopping by a little joking; the girl knew the old fellow admired her, and she liked to chaff with him.

"Seems to me about every other week you buy ticking, Mr. Rosicky, and always the best quality," she remarked as she measured off the heavy bolt with red stripes.

"You see, my wife is always makin' goose-fedder pillows, an' de thin stuff don't hold in dem little down-fedders."

"You must have lots of pillows at your house."

"Sure. She makes quilts of dem, too. We sleeps easy. Now she's makin' a fedder quilt for my son's wife. You know Polly, that married my Rudolph. How much my bill, Miss Pearl?"

"Eight eighty-five."

"Chust make it nine, and put in some candy fur de women."

"As usual. I never did see a man buy so much candy for his wife. First thing you know, she'll be getting too fat."

"I'd like dat. I ain't much fur all dem slim women like what de style is now."

"That's one for me, I suppose, Mr. Bohunk!" Pearl sniffed and elevated her India-ink strokes.

When Rosicky went out to his wagon, it was beginning to snow,—the first snow of the season, and he was glad to see it. He rattled out of town and along the highway through a wonderfully rich stretch of country, the finest farms in the county. He admired this High Prairie, as it was called, and always liked to drive through it. His own place lay in a rougher territory, where there was some clay in the soil and it was not so productive. When he bought his land, he hadn't the money to buy on High Prairie; so he told his boys, when they grumbled, that if their land hadn't some clay in it, they wouldn't own it at all. All the same, he enjoyed looking at these fine farms, as he enjoyed looking at a prize bull.

After he had gone eight miles, he came to the graveyard, which lay just at the edge of his own hay-land. There he stopped his horses and sat still on his wagon seat, looking about at the snowfall. Over yonder on the hill he could see his own house, crouching low, with the clump of orchard behind and the windmill before, and all down the gentle hill-slope the rows of pale gold cornstalks stood out against the white field. The snow was falling over the cornfield and the pasture and the hay-land, steadily, with very little wind,—a nice dry snow. The graveyard had only a light wire fence about it and was all overgrown with long red grass. The fine snow, settling into this red grass and upon the few little evergreens and the headstones, looked very pretty.

It was a nice graveyard, Rosicky reflected, sort of snug and homelike, not cramped or mournful,—a big sweep all round it. A man could lie down in the long grass and see the complete arch of the sky over him, hear the wagons go by; in summer the mowing-machine rattled right up to the wire fence. And it was so near home. Over there across the cornstalks his own roof and windmill looked so good to him that he promised himself to mind the Doctor and take care of himself. He was awful fond of his place, he admitted. He wasn't anxious to leave it. And it was a comfort to think that he would never have to go farther than the edge of his own hayfield. The snow, falling over his barnyard and the graveyard, seemed to draw things together like. And they were all old neighbours in the graveyard, most of them friends; there was nothing to feel awkward or embarrassed about. Embarrassment was the most disagreeable feeling Rosicky knew. He didn't often have it,—only with certain people whom he didn't understand at all.

Well, it was a nice snowstorm; a fine sight to see the snow falling so quietly and graciously over so much open country. On his cap and shoulders, on the horses' backs and manes, light, delicate, mysterious it fell; and with it a dry cool fragrance was released into the air. It meant rest for vegetation and men and beasts, for the ground itself; a season of long nights for sleep, leisurely breakfasts, peace by the fire. This and much more went through Rosicky's mind, but he merely told himself that winter was coming, clucked to his horses, and drove on.

When he reached home, John, the youngest boy, ran out to put away his team for him, and he met Mary coming up from the outside cellar with her apron full of carrots. They went into the house together. On the table, covered with oilcloth figured with clusters of blue grapes, a place was set, and he smelled hot coffee-cake of some kind. Anton never lunched in town; he thought that extravagant, and anyhow he didn't like the food. So Mary always had something ready for him when he got home.

After he was settled in his chair, stirring his coffee in a big cup, Mary took out of the oven a pan of *kolache* stuffed with apricots, examined them anxiously to see whether they had got too dry, put them beside his plate, and then sat down opposite him.

Rosicky asked her in Czech if she wasn't going to have any coffee.

She replied in English, as being somehow the right language for transacting business: "Now what did Doctor Ed say, Anton? You tell me just what."

"He said I was to tell you some compliments, but I forgot 'em." Rosicky's eyes twinkled.

"About you, I mean. What did he say about your asthma?"

"He says I ain't got no asthma." Rosicky took one of the little rolls in his broad brown fingers. The thickened nail of his right thumb told the story of his past.

"Well, what is the matter? And don't try to put me off."

"He don't say nothing much, only I'm a little older, and my heart ain't so good like it used to be."

Mary started and brushed her hair back from her temples with both hands as if she were a little out of her mind. From the way she glared, she might have been in a rage with him.

"He says there's something the matter with your heart? Doctor Ed says so?"

"Now don't yell at me like I was a hog in de garden, Mary. You know I always did like to hear a woman talk soft. He didn't say anything de matter wid my heart, only it ain't so young like it used to be, an' he tell me not to pitch hay or run de corn-sheller."

Mary wanted to jump up, but she sat still. She admired the way he never under any circumstances raised his voice or spoke roughly. He was city-bred, and she was country-bred; she often said she wanted her boys to have their papa's nice ways.

"You never have no pain there, do you? It's your breathing and your stomach that's been wrong. I wouldn't believe nobody but Doctor Ed about it. I guess I'll go see him myself. Didn't he give you no advice?"

"Chust to take it easy like, an' stay round de house dis winter. I guess you got some carpenter work for me to do. I kin make some new shelves for you, and I want dis long time to build a closet in de boys' room and make dem two little fellers keep dere clo'es hung up."

Rosicky drank his coffee from time to time, while he considered. His moustache was of the soft long variety and came down over his mouth like the teeth of a buggy-rake over a bundle of hay. Each time he put down his cup, he ran his blue handkerchief over his lips. When he took a drink of water, he managed very neatly with the back of his hand.

Mary sat watching him intently, trying to find any change in his face. It is hard to see anyone who has become like your own body to you. Yes, his hair had got thin, and his high forehead had deep lines running from left to right. But his neck, always clean shaved except in the busiest seasons, was not loose or baggy. It was burned a dark reddish brown, and there were deep creases in it, but it looked firm and full of blood. His cheeks had a good colour. On either side of his mouth there was a half-moon down the length of his cheek, not wrinkles, but two lines that had come there from his habitual expression. He was shorter and broader than when she married him; his back had grown broad and curved, a good deal like the shell of an old turtle, and his arms and legs were short.

He was fifteen years older than Mary, but she had hardly ever thought about it before. He was her man, and the kind of man she liked. She was rough, and he was gentle,—city-bred, as she always said. They had been shipmates on a rough voyage and had stood by each other in trying times. Life had gone well with them because, at bottom, they had the same ideas about life. They agreed, without discussion, as to what was most important and what was secondary. They didn't often exchange opinions, even in Czech,—it was as if they had thought the same thought together. A good deal had to be sacrificed and thrown overboard in a hard life like theirs, and they had never disagreed as to the things that could go. It had been a hard life, and a soft life, too. There wasn't anything brutal in the short, broad-backed man with the three-cornered eyes and the forehead that went on to the top of his skull. He was a city man, a gentle man, and though he had married a rough farm girl, he had never touched her without gentleness.

They had been at one accord not to hurry through life, not to be always skimping and saving. They saw their neighbours buy more land and feed more stock than they did, without discontent. Once when the creamery agent came to the Rosickys to persuade them to sell him their cream, he told them how much money the Fasslers, their nearest neighbours, had made on their cream last year.

"Yes," said Mary, "and look at them Fassler children! Pale, pinched little things, they look like skimmed milk. I'd rather put some colour into my children's faces than put money into the bank."

The agent shrugged and turned to Anton.

"I guess we'll do like she says," said Rosicky.

III

Mary very soon got into town to see Doctor Ed, and then she had a talk with her boys and set a guard over Rosicky. Even John, the youngest, had his father on his mind. If Rosicky went to throw hay down from the loft, one of the boys ran up the ladder and took the fork from him. He sometimes complained that though he was getting to be an old man, he wasn't an old woman yet.

That winter he stayed in the house in the afternoons and carpentered, or sat in the chair between the window full of plants and the wooden bench where the two pails of drinking-water stood. This spot was called "Father's corner," though it was not a corner at all. He had a shelf there, where he kept his Bohemian papers and his pipes and tobacco, and his shears and needles and thread and tailor's thimble. Having been a tailor in his youth, he couldn't bear to see a woman patching at his clothes, or at the boys'. He liked tailoring, and always patched all the overalls and jackets and work shirts. Occasionally he made over a pair of pants one of the older boys had outgrown, for the little fellow.

While he sewed, he let his mind run back over his life. He had a good deal to remember, really; life in three countries. The only part of his youth he didn't like to remember was the two years he had spent in London, in Cheapside, working for a German tailor who was wretchedly poor. Those days, when he was nearly always hungry, when his clothes were dropping off him for dirt, and the sound of a strange language kept him in continual bewilderment, had left a sore spot in his mind that wouldn't bear touching.

He was twenty when he landed at Castle Garden[3] in New York, and he had a protector who got him work in a tailor shop in Vesey Street, down near the Washington Market. He looked upon that part of his life as very happy. He became a good workman, he was industrious, and his wages were increased from time to time. He minded his own business and envied nobody's good fortune. He went to night school and learned to read English. He often did overtime work and was well paid for it, but somehow he never saved anything. He couldn't refuse a loan to a friend, and he was self-indulgent. He liked a good dinner, and a little went for beer, a little for tobacco; a good deal went to the girls. He often stood through an opera on Saturday nights; he could get standing-room for a dollar. Those were the great days of opera in New York, and it gave a fellow something to think about for the rest of the week. Rosicky had a quick ear, and a childish love of all the stage splendour; the scenery, the costumes, the ballet. He usually went with a chum, and after the performance they had beer and maybe some oysters somewhere. It was a fine life; for the first five years or so it satisfied him completely. He was never hungry or cold or dirty, and everything amused him: a fire, a dog fight, a parade, a storm, a ferry ride. He thought New York the finest, richest, friendliest city in the world.

Moreover, he had what he called a happy home life. Very near the tailor shop was a

---

[3] Entry point for immigrants, replaced in 1892 by Ellis Island.

small furniture-factory, where an old Austrian, Loeffler, employed a few skilled men and made unusual furniture, most of it to order, for the rich German housewives up-town. The top floor of Loeffler's five-storey factory was a loft, where he kept his choice lumber and stored the odd pieces of furniture left on his hands. One of the young work-men he employed was a Czech, and he and Rosicky became fast friends. They per-suaded Loeffler to let them have a sleeping-room in one corner of the loft. They bought good beds and bedding and had their pick of the furniture kept up there. The loft was low-pitched, but light and airy, full of windows, and good-smelling by reason of the fine lumber put up there to season. Old Loeffler used to go down to the docks and buy wood from South America and the East from the sea captains. The young men were as foolish about their house as a bridal pair. Zichec, the young cabinet-maker, devised every sort of convenience, and Rosicky kept their clothes in order. At night and on Sun-days, when the quiver of machinery underneath was still, it was the quietest place in the world, and on summer nights all the sea winds blew in. Zichec often practised on his flute in the evening. They were both fond of music and went to the opera together. Rosicky thought he wanted to live like that for ever.

But as the years passed, all alike, he began to get a little restless. When spring came round, he would begin to feel fretted, and he got to drinking. He was likely to drink too much of a Saturday night. On Sunday he was languid and heavy, getting over his spree. On Monday he plunged into work again. So he never had time to figure out what ailed him, though he knew something did. When the grass turned green in Park Place, and the lilac hedge at the back of Trinity churchyard put out its blossoms,[4] he was tor-mented by a longing to run away. That was why he drank too much; to get a temporary illusion of freedom and wide horizons.

Rosicky, the old Rosicky, could remember as if it were yesterday the day when the young Rosicky found out what was the matter with him. It was on a Fourth of July after-noon, and he was sitting in Park Place in the sun. The lower part of New York was empty. Wall Street, Liberty Street, Broadway, all empty. So much stone and asphalt with nothing going on, so many empty windows. The emptiness was intense, like the stillness in a great factory when the machinery stops and the belts and bands cease running. It was too great a change, it took all the strength out of one. Those blank buildings, without the stream of life pouring through them, were like empty jails. It struck young Rosicky that this was the trouble with big cities; they built you in from the earth itself, cemented you away from any contact with the ground. You lived in an unnatural world, like the fish in an aquar-ium, who were probably much more comfortable than they ever were in the sea.

On that very day he began to think seriously about the articles he had read in the Bo-hemian papers, describing prosperous Czech farming communities in the West. He be-lieved he would like to go out there as a farm hand; it was hardly possible that he could ever have land of his own. His people had always been workmen; his father and grand-father had worked in shops. His mother's parents had lived in the country, but they rented their farm and had a hard time to get along. Nobody in his family had ever owned any land,—that belonged to a different station of life altogether. Anton's mother died when he was little, and he was sent into the country to her parents. He stayed with them until he was twelve, and formed those ties with the earth and the farm animals

---

[4] In the area at the southern end of Manhattan.

and growing things which are never made at all unless they are made early. After his grandfather died, he went back to live with his father and stepmother, but she was very hard on him, and his father helped him to get passage to London.

After that Fourth of July day in Park Place, the desire to return to the country never left him. To work on another man's farm would be all he asked; to see the sun rise and set and to plant things and watch them grow. He was a very simple man. He was like a tree that has not many roots, but one tap-root that goes down deep. He subscribed for a Bohemian paper printed in Chicago, then for one printed in Omaha. His mind got farther and farther west. He began to save a little money to buy his liberty. When he was thirty-five, there was a great meeting in New York of Bohemian athletic societies, and Rosicky left the tailor shop and went home with the Omaha delegates to try his fortune in another part of the world.

IV

Perhaps the fact that his own youth was well over before he began to have a family was one reason why Rosicky was so fond of his boys. He had almost a grandfather's indulgence for them. He had never had to worry about any of them—except, just now, a little about Rudolph.

On Saturday night the boys always piled into the Ford, took little Josephine, and went to town to the moving-picture show. One Saturday morning they were talking at the breakfast table about starting early that evening, so that they would have an hour or so to see the Christmas things in the stores before the show began. Rosicky looked down the table.

"I hope you boys ain't disappointed, but I want you to let me have de car tonight. Maybe some of you can go in with de neighbours."

Their faces fell. They worked hard all week, and they were still like children. A new jackknife or a box of candy pleased the older ones as much as the little fellow.

"If you and Mother are going to town," Frank said, "maybe you could take a couple of us along with you, anyway."

"No, I want to take de car down to Rudolph's, and let him an' Polly go in to de show. She don't git into town enough, an' I'm afraid she's gettin' lonesome, an' he can't afford no car yet."

That settled it. The boys were a good deal dashed. Their father took another piece of apple-cake and went on: "Maybe next Saturday night de two little fellers can go along wid dem."

"Oh, is Rudolph going to have the car every Saturday night?"

Rosicky did not reply at once; then he began to speak seriously: "Listen, boys; Polly ain't lookin' so good. I don't like to see nobody lookin' sad. It comes hard fur a town girl to be a farmer's wife. I don't want no trouble to start in Rudolph's family. When it starts, it ain't so easy to stop. An American girl don't git used to our ways all at once. I like to tell Polly she and Rudolph can have the car every Saturday night till after New Year's, if it's all right with you boys."

"Sure it's all right, Papa," Mary cut in. "And it's good you thought about that. Town girls is used to more than country girls. I lay awake nights, scared she'll make Rudolph discontented with the farm."

The boys put as good a face on it as they could. They surely looked forward to their

Saturday nights in town. That evening Rosicky drove the car the half-mile down to Rudolph's new, bare little house.

Polly was in a short-sleeved gingham dress, clearing away the supper dishes. She was a trim, slim little thing, with blue eyes and shingled yellow hair, and her eyebrows were reduced to a mere brush-stroke, like Miss Pearl's.

"Good evening, Mr. Rosicky. Rudolph's at the barn, I guess." She never called him father, or Mary mother. She was sensitive about having married a foreigner. She never in the world would have done it if Rudolph hadn't been such a handsome, persuasive fellow and such a gallant lover. He had graduated in her class in the high school in town, and their friendship began in the ninth grade.

Rosicky went in, though he wasn't exactly asked. "My boys ain't goin' to town tonight, an' I brought de car over fur you two to go in to de picture show."

Polly, carrying dishes to the sink, looked over her shoulder at him. "Thank you. But I'm late with my work tonight, and pretty tired. Maybe Rudolph would like to go in with you."

"Oh, I don't go to de shows! I'm too old-fashioned. You won't feel so tired after you ride in de air a ways. It's a nice clear night, an' it ain't cold. You go an' fix yourself up, Polly, an' I'll wash de dishes an' leave everything nice fur you."

Polly blushed and tossed her bob. "I couldn't let you do that, Mr. Rosicky. I wouldn't think of it."

Rosicky said nothing. He found a bib apron on a nail behind the kitchen door. He slipped it over his head and then took Polly by her two elbows and pushed her gently toward the door of her own room. "I washed up de kitchen many times for my wife, when de babies was sick or somethin'. You go an' make yourself look nice. I like you to look prettier'n any of dem town girls when you go in. De young folks must have some fun, an' I'm goin' to look out fur you, Polly."

That kind, reassuring grip on her elbows, the old man's funny bright eyes, made Polly want to drop her head on his shoulder for a second. She restrained herself, but she lingered in his grasp at the door of her room, murmuring tearfully: "You always lived in the city when you were young, didn't you? Don't you ever get lonesome out here?"

As she turned round to him, her hand fell naturally into his, and he stood holding it and smiling into her face with his peculiar, knowing, indulgent smile without a shadow of reproach in it. "Dem big cities is all right fur de rich, but dey is terrible hard fur de poor."

"I don't know. Sometimes I think I'd like to take a chance. You lived in New York, didn't you?"

"An' London. Da's bigger still. I learned my trade dere. Here's Rudolph comin', you better hurry."

"Will you tell me about London some time?"

"Maybe. Only I ain't no talker, Polly. Run an' dress yourself up."

The bedroom door closed behind her, and Rudolph came in from the outside, looking anxious. He had seen the car and was sorry any of his family should come just then. Supper hadn't been a very pleasant occasion. Halting in the doorway, he saw his father in a kitchen apron, carrying dishes to the sink. He flushed crimson and something flashed in his eye. Rosicky held up a warning finger.

"I brought de car over fur you an' Polly to go to de picture show, an' I made her let me finish here so you won't be late. You go put on a clean shirt, quick!"

"But don't the boys want the car, Father?"

"Not tonight dey don't." Rosicky fumbled under his apron and found his pants pocket. He took out a silver dollar and said in a hurried whisper: "You go an' buy dat girl some ice cream an' candy tonight, like you was courtin'. She's awful good friends wid me."

Rudolph was very short of cash, but he took the money as if it hurt him. There had been a crop failure all over the county. He had more than once been sorry he'd married this year.

In a few minutes the young people came out, looking clean and a little stiff. Rosicky hurried them off, and then he took his own time with the dishes. He scoured the pots and pans and put away the milk and swept the kitchen. He put some coal in the stove and shut off the draughts, so the place would be warm for them when they got home late at night. Then he sat down and had a pipe and listened to the clock tick.

Generally speaking, marrying an American girl was certainly a risk. A Czech should marry a Czech. It was lucky that Polly was the daughter of a poor widow woman; Rudolph was proud, and if she had a prosperous family to throw up at him, they could never make it go. Polly was one of four sisters, and they all worked; one was book-keeper in the bank, one taught music, and Polly and her younger sister had been clerks, like Miss Pearl. All four of them were musical, had pretty voices, and sang in the Methodist choir, which the eldest sister directed.

Polly missed the sociability of a store position. She missed the choir, and the company of her sisters. She didn't dislike housework, but she disliked so much of it. Rosicky was a little anxious about this pair. He was afraid Polly would grow so discontented that Rudy would quit the farm and take a factory job in Omaha. He had worked for a winter up there, two years ago, to get money to marry on. He had done very well, and they would always take him back at the stockyards. But to Rosicky that meant the end of everything for his son. To be a landless man was to be a wage-earner, a slave, all your life; to have nothing, to be nothing.

Rosicky thought he would come over and do a little carpentering for Polly after the New Year. He guessed she needed jollying. Rudolph was a serious sort of chap, serious in love and serious about his work.

Rosicky shook out his pipe and walked home across the fields. Ahead of him the lamplight shone from his kitchen windows. Suppose he were still in a tailor shop on Vesey Street, with a bunch of pale, narrow-chested sons working on machines, all coming home tired and sullen to eat supper in a kitchen that was a parlour also; with another crowded, angry family quarrelling just across the dumb-waiter shaft, and squeaking pulleys at the windows where dirty washings hung on dirty lines above a court full of old brooms and mops and ash-cans. . . .

He stopped by the windmill to look up at the frosty winter stars and draw a long breath before he went inside. That kitchen with the shining windows was dear to him; but the sleeping fields and bright stars and the noble darkness were dearer still.

V

On the day before Christmas the weather set in very cold; no snow, but a bitter, biting wind that whistled and sang over the flat land and lashed one's face like fine wires. There was baking going on in the Rosicky kitchen all day, and Rosicky sat inside, making over a coat that Albert had outgrown into an overcoat for John. Mary had a big red geranium in bloom for Christmas, and a row of Jerusalem cherry trees, full of berries. It was the first year she had ever grown these; Doctor Ed brought her the seeds from Omaha when he went to some medical convention. They reminded Rosicky of plants he had seen in England; and all afternoon, as he stitched, he sat thinking about those two years in London, which his mind usually shrank from even after all this while.

He was a lad of eighteen when he dropped down into London, with no money and no connexions except the address of a cousin who was supposed to be working at a confectioner's. When he went to the pastry shop, however, he found that the cousin had gone to America. Anton tramped the streets for several days, sleeping in doorways and on the Embankment,[5] until he was in utter despair. He knew no English, and the sound of the strange language all about him confused him. By chance he met a poor German tailor who had learned his trade in Vienna, and could speak a little Czech. This tailor, Lifschnitz, kept a repair shop in a Cheapside basement, underneath a cobbler. He didn't much need an apprentice, but he was sorry for the boy and took him in for no wages but his keep and what he could pick up. The pickings were supposed to be coppers given you when you took work home to a customer. But most of the customers called for their clothes themselves, and the coppers that came Anton's way were very few. He had, however, a place to sleep. The tailor's family lived upstairs in three rooms; a kitchen, a bedroom, where Lifschnitz and his wife and five children slept, and a living-room. Two corners of this living-room were curtained off for lodgers; in one Rosicky slept on an old horsehair sofa, with a feather quilt to wrap himself in. The other corner was rented to a wretched, dirty boy, who was studying the violin. He actually practised there. Rosicky was dirty, too. There was no way to be anything else. Mrs. Lifschnitz got the water she cooked and washed with from a pump in a brick court, four flights down. There were bugs in the place, and multitudes of fleas, though the poor woman did the best she could. Rosicky knew she often went empty to give another potato or a spoonful of dripping to the two hungry, sad-eyed boys who lodged with her. He used to think he would never get out of there, never get a clean shirt to his back again. What would he do, he wondered, when his clothes actually dropped to pieces and the worn cloth wouldn't hold patches any longer?

It was still early when the old farmer put aside his sewing and his recollections. The sky had been a dark grey all day, with not a gleam of sun, and the light failed at four o'clock. He went to shave and change his shirt while the turkey was roasting. Rudolph and Polly were coming over for supper.

After supper they sat round in the kitchen, and the younger boys were saying how sorry they were it hadn't snowed. Everybody was sorry. They wanted a deep snow that would lie long and keep the wheat warm, and leave the ground soaked when it melted.

"Yes, sir!" Rudolph broke out fiercely; "if we have another dry year like last year, there's going to be hard times in this country."

Rosicky filled his pipe. "You boys don't know what hard times is. You don't owe nobody, you got plenty to eat an' keep warm, an' plenty water to keep clean. When you got them, you can't have it very hard."

---

5 The region of London alongside the Thames River.

Rudolph frowned, opened and shut his big right hand, and dropped it clenched upon his knee. "I've got to have a good deal more than that, Father, or I'll quit this farming gamble. I can always make good wages railroading, or at the packing house, and be sure of my money."

"Maybe so," his father answered dryly.

Mary, who had just come in from the pantry and was wiping her hands on the roller towel, thought Rudy and his father were getting too serious. She brought her darning-basket and sat down in the middle of the group.

"I ain't much afraid of hard times, Rudy," she said heartily. "We've had a plenty, but we've always come through. Your father wouldn't never take nothing very hard, not even hard times. I got a mind to tell you a story on him. Maybe you boys can't hardly remember the year we had that terrible hot wind, that burned everything up on the Fourth of July? All the corn an' the gardens. An' that was in the days when we didn't have alfalfa yet,—I guess it wasn't invented.

"Well, that very day your father was out cultivatin' corn, and I was here in the kitchen makin' plum preserves. We had bushels of plums that year. I noticed it was terrible hot, but it's always hot in the kitchen when you're preservin', an' I was too busy with my plums to mind. Anton come in from the field about three o'clock, an' I asked him what was the matter.

" 'Nothin',' he says, 'but it's pretty hot, an' I think I won't work no more today.' He stood round for a few minutes, an' then he says: 'Ain't you near through? I want you should git up a nice supper for us tonight. It's Fourth of July.'

"I told him to git along, that I was right in the middle of preservin', but the plums would taste good on hot biscuit. 'I'm goin' to have fried chicken, too,' he says, and he went off an' killed a couple. You three oldest boys was little fellers, playin' round outside, real hot an' sweaty, an' your father took you to the horse tank down by the windmill an' took off your clothes an' put you in. Them two box-elder trees was little then, but they made shade over the tank. Then he took off all his own clothes, an' got in with you. While he was playin' in the water with you, the Methodist preacher drove into our place to say how all the neighbours was goin' to meet at the schoolhouse that night, to pray for rain. He drove right to the windmill, of course, and there was your father and you three with no clothes on. I was in the kitchen door, an' I had to laugh, for the preacher acted like he ain't never seen a naked man before. He surely was embarrassed, an' your father couldn't git to his clothes; they was all hangin' up on the windmill to let the sweat dry out of 'em. So he laid in the tank where he was, an' put one of you boys on top of him to cover him up a little, an' talked to the preacher.

"When you got through playin' in the water, he put clean clothes on you and a clean shirt on himself, an' by that time I'd begun to get supper. He says: 'It's too hot in here to eat comfortable. Let's have a picnic in the orchard. We'll eat our supper behind the mulberry hedge, under them linden trees.'

"So he carried our supper down, an' a bottle of my wild-grape wine, an' everything tasted good, I can tell you. The wind got cooler as the sun was goin' down, and it turned out pleasant, only I noticed how the leaves was curled up on the linden trees. That made me think, an' I asked your father if that hot wind all day hadn't been terrible hard on the gardens an' the corn.

" 'Corn,' he says, 'there ain't no corn.'

" 'What you talkin' about?' I said. 'Ain't we got forty acres?'

" 'We ain't got an ear,' he says, 'nor nobody else ain't got none. All the corn in this country was cooked by three o'clock today, like you'd roasted it in an oven.'

" 'You mean you won't get no crop at all?' I asked him. I couldn't believe it, after he'd worked so hard.

" 'No crop this year,' he says. 'That's why we're havin' a picnic. We might as well enjoy what we got.'

"An' that's how your father behaved, when all the neighbours was so discouraged they couldn't look you in the face. An' we enjoyed ourselves that year, poor as we was, an' our neighbours wasn't a bit better off for bein' miserable. Some of 'em grieved till they got poor digestions and couldn't relish what they did have."

The younger boys said they thought their father had the best of it. But Rudolph was thinking that, all the same, the neighbours had managed to get ahead more, in the fifteen years since that time. There must be something wrong about his father's way of doing things. He wished he knew what was going on in the back of Polly's mind. He knew she liked his father, but he knew, too, that she was afraid of something. When his mother sent over coffee-cake or prune tarts or a loaf of fresh bread, Polly seemed to regard them with a certain suspicion. When she observed to him that his brothers had nice manners, her tone implied that it was remarkable they should have. With his mother she was stiff and on her guard. Mary's hearty frankness and gusts of good humour irritated her. Polly was afraid of being unusual or conspicuous in any way, of being "ordinary," as she said!

When Mary had finished her story, Rosicky laid aside his pipe.

"You boys like me to tell you about some of dem hard times I been through in London?" Warmly encouraged, he sat rubbing his forehead along the deep creases. It was bothersome to tell a long story in English (he nearly always talked to the boys in Czech), but he wanted Polly to hear this one.

"Well, you know about dat tailor shop I worked in in London? I had one Christmas dere I ain't never forgot. Times was awful bad before Christmas; de boss ain't got much work, an' have it awful hard to pay his rent. It ain't so much fun, bein' poor in a big city like London, I'll say! All de windows is full of good t'ings to eat, an' all de pushcarts in de streets is full, an' you smell 'em all de time, an' you ain't got no money,—not a damn bit. I didn't mind de cold so much, though I didn't have no overcoat, chust a short jacket I'd outgrowed so it wouldn't meet on me, an' my hands was chapped raw. But I always had a good appetite, like you all know, an' de sight of dem pork pies in de windows was awful fur me!

"Day before Christmas was terrible foggy dat year, an' dat fog gits into your bones and makes you all damp like. Mrs. Lifschnitz didn't give us nothin' but a little bread an' drippin' for supper, because she was savin' to try for to give us a good dinner on Christmas Day. After supper de boss say I can go an' enjoy myself, so I went into de streets to listen to de Christmas singers. Dey sing old songs an' make very nice music, an' I run round after dem a good ways, till I got awful hungry. I t'ink maybe if I go home, I can sleep till mornin' an' forget my belly.

"I went into my corner real quiet, and roll up in my fedder quilt. But I ain't got my head down, till I smell somet'ing good. Seem like it git stronger an' stronger, an' I can't git to sleep noway. I can't understand dat smell. Dere was a gas light in a hall across de court, dat always shine in at my window a little. I got up an' look round. I got a little wooden box in my corner fur a stool, 'cause I ain't got no chair. I picks up dat box, and under it dere is a roast goose on a platter! I can't believe my eyes. I carry it to de window where de light comes in, an' touch it and smell it to find out, an' den I taste it to be sure. I say, I will eat chust one little bite of dat goose, so I can go to sleep, and tomorrow I won't eat none at all. But I tell you, boys, when I stop, one half of dat goose was gone!"

The narrator bowed his head, and the boys shouted. But little Josephine slipped behind his chair and kissed him on the neck beneath his ear.

"Poor little Papa, I don't want him to be hungry!"

"Da's long ago, child. I ain't never been hungry since I had your mudder to cook fur me."

"Go on and tell us the rest, please," said Polly.

"Well, when I come to realize what I done, of course, I felt terrible. I felt better in de stomach, but very bad in de heart. I set on my bed wid dat platter on my knees, an' it all come to me; how hard dat poor woman save to buy dat goose, and how she get some neighbour to cook it dat got more fire, an' how she put it in my corner to keep it away from dem hungry children. Dey was a old carpet hung up to shut my corner off, an' de children wasn't allowed to go in dere. An' I know she put it in my corner because she trust me more'n she did de violin boy. I can't stand it to face her after I spoil de Christmas. So I put on my shoes and go out into de city. I tell myself I better throw myself in de river; but I guess I ain't dat kind of a boy.

"It was after twelve o'clock, an' terrible cold, an' I start out to walk about London all night. I walk along de river awhile, but dey was lots of drunks all along; men, and women too. I chust move along to keep away from de police. I git onto de Strand, an' den over to New Oxford Street,[6] where dere was a big German restaurant on de ground floor, wid big windows all fixed up fine, an' I could see de people havin' parties inside. While I was lookin' in, two men and two ladies come out, laughin' and talkin' and feelin' happy about all dey been eatin' an' drinkin', and dey was speakin' Czech,—not like de Austrians, but like de home folks talk it.

"I guess I went crazy, an' I done what I ain't never done before nor since. I went right up to dem gay people an' begun to beg dem: 'Fellow-countrymen, for God's sake give me money enough to buy a goose!'

"Dey laugh, of course, but de ladies speak awful kind to me, an' dey take me back into de restaurant and give me hot coffee and cakes, an' make me tell all about how I happened to come to London, an' what I was doin' dere. Dey take my name and where I work down on paper, an' both of dem ladies give me ten shillings.

"De big market at Covent Garden ain't very far away, an' by dat time it was open. I go dere an' buy a big goose an' some pork pies, an' potatoes and onions, an' cakes an' oranges fur de children,—all I could carry! When I git home, everybody is still asleep. I pile all I bought on de kitchen table, an' go in an' lay down on my bed, an' I ain't waken up till I hear dat woman scream when she come out into her kitchen. My goodness, but she was surprise! She laugh an' cry at de same time, an' hug me and waken all de children. She ain't stop fur no breakfast; she git de Christmas dinner ready dat morning, and we all sit down an' eat all we can hold. I ain't never seen dat violin boy have all he can hold before.

---

[6] Fashionable area of London with shops, theaters, and restaurants.

"Two three days after dat, de two men come to hunt me up, an' dey ask my boss, and he give me a good report an' tell dem I was a steady boy all right. One of dem Bohemians was very smart an' run a Bohemian newspaper in New York, an' de odder was a rich man, in de importing business, an' dey been travelling togedder. Dey told me how t'ings was easier in New York, an' offered to pay my passage when dey was goin' home soon on a boat. My boss say to me: 'You go. You ain't got no chance here, an' I like to see you git ahead, fur you always been a good boy to my woman, and fur dat fine Christmas dinner you give us all.' An' da's how I got to New York."

That night when Rudolph and Polly, arm in arm, were running home across the fields with the bitter wind at their backs, his heart leaped for joy when she said she thought they might have his family come over for supper on New Year's Eve. "Let's get up a nice supper, and not let your mother help at all; make her be company for once."

"That would be lovely of you, Polly," he said humbly. He was a very simple, modest boy, and he, too, felt vaguely that Polly and her sisters were more experienced and worldly than his people.

VI

The winter turned out badly for farmers. It was bitterly cold, and after the first light snows before Christmas there was no snow at all,—and no rain. March was as bitter as February. On those days when the wind fairly punished the country, Rosicky sat by his window. In the fall he and the boys had put in a big wheat planting, and now the seed had frozen in the ground. All that land would have to be ploughed up and planted over again, planted in corn. It had happened before, but he was younger then, and he never worried about what had to be. He was sure of himself and of Mary; he knew they could bear what they had to bear, that they would always pull through somehow. But he was not so sure about the young ones, and he felt troubled because Rudolph and Polly were having such a hard start.

Sitting beside his flowering window while the panes rattled and the wind blew in under the door, Rosicky gave himself to reflection as he had not done since those Sundays in the loft of the furniture-factory in New York, long ago. Then he was trying to find what he wanted in life for himself; now he was trying to find what he wanted for his boys, and why it was he so hungered to feel sure they would be here, working this very land, after he was gone.

They would have to work hard on the farm, and probably they would never do much more than make a living. But if he could think of them as staying here on the land, he wouldn't have to fear any great unkindness for them. Hardships, certainly; it was a hardship to have the wheat freeze in the ground when seed was so high; and to have to sell your stock because you had no feed. But there would be other years when everything came along right, and you caught up. And what you had was your own. You didn't have to choose between bosses and strikers, and go wrong either way. You didn't have to do with dishonest and cruel people. They were the only things in his experience he had found terrifying and horrible; the look in the eyes of a dishonest and crafty man, of a scheming and rapacious woman.

In the country, if you had a mean neighbour, you could keep off his land and make him keep off yours. But in the city, all the foulness and misery and brutality of your neighbours was part of your life. The worst things he had come upon in his journey through the world were human,—depraved and poisonous specimens of man. To this day he could recall certain terrible faces in the London streets. There were mean people everywhere, to be sure, even in their own country town here. But they weren't tempered, hardened, sharpened, like the treacherous people in cities who live by grinding or cheating or poisoning their fellow-men. He had helped to bury two of his fellow-workmen in the tailoring trade, and he was distrustful of the organized industries that see one out of the world in big cities. Here, if you were sick, you had Doctor Ed to look after you; and if you died, fat Mr. Haycock, the kindest man in the world, buried you.

It seemed to Rosicky that for good, honest boys like his, the worst they could do on the farm was better than the best they would be likely to do in the city. If he'd had a mean boy, now, one who was crooked and sharp and tried to put anything over on his brothers, then town would be the place for him. But he had no such boy. As for Rudolph, the discontented one, he would give the shirt off his back to anyone who touched his heart. What Rosicky really hoped for his boys was that they could get through the world without ever knowing much about the cruelty of human beings. "Their mother and me ain't prepared them for that," he sometimes said to himself.

These thoughts brought him back to a grateful consideration of his own case. What an escape he had had, to be sure! He, too, in his time, had had to take money for repair work from the hand of a hungry child who let it go so wistfully; because it was money due his boss. And now, in all these years, he had never had to take a cent from anyone in bitter need,—never had to look at the face of a woman become like a wolf's from struggle and famine. When he thought of these things, Rosicky would put on his cap and jacket and slip down to the barn and give his work-horses a little extra oats, letting them eat it out of his hand in their slobbery fashion. It was his way of expressing what he felt, and made him chuckle with pleasure.

The spring came warm, with blue skies,—but dry, dry as a bone. The boys began ploughing up the wheat-fields to plant them over in corn. Rosicky would stand at the fence corner and watch them, and the earth was so dry it blew up in clouds of brown dust that hid the horses and the sulky plough and the driver. It was a bad outlook.

The big alfalfa-field that lay between the home place and Rudolph's came up green, but Rosicky was worried because during that open windy winter a great many Russian thistle plants had blown in there and lodged. He kept asking the boys to rake them out; he was afraid their seed would root and "take the alfalfa." Rudolph said that was nonsense. The boys were working so hard planting corn, their father felt he couldn't insist about the thistles, but he set great store by that big alfalfa field. It was a feed you could depend on,—and there was some deeper reason, vague, but strong. The peculiar green of that clover woke early memories in old Rosicky, went back to something in his childhood in the old world. When he was a little boy, he had played in fields of that strong blue-green colour.

One morning, when Rudolph had gone to town in the car, leaving a work-team idle in his barn, Rosicky went over to his son's place, put the horses to the buggy-rake, and set about quietly raking up those thistles. He behaved with guilty caution, and rather enjoyed stealing a march on Doctor Ed, who was just then taking his first vacation in seven years of practice and was attending a clinic in Chicago. Rosicky got the thistles raked up, but did not stop to burn them. That would take some time, and his breath was pretty short, so he thought he had better get the horses back to the barn.

He got them into the barn and to their stalls, but the pain had come on so sharp in his chest that he didn't try to take the harness off. He started for the house, bending lower with every step. The cramp in his chest was shutting him up like a jack-knife. When he reached the windmill, he swayed and caught at the ladder. He saw Polly coming down the hill, running with the swiftness of a slim greyhound. In a flash she had her shoulder under his armpit.

"Lean on me, Father, hard! Don't be afraid. We can get to the house all right."

Somehow they did, though Rosicky became blind with pain; he could keep on his legs, but he couldn't steer his course. The next thing he was conscious of was lying on Polly's bed, and Polly bending over him wringing out bath towels in hot water and putting them on his chest. She stopped only to throw coal into the stove, and she kept the tea-kettle and the black pot going. She put these hot applications on him for nearly an hour, she told him afterwards, and all that time he was drawn up stiff and blue, with the sweat pouring off him.

As the pain gradually loosed its grip, the stiffness went out of his jaws, the black circles round his eyes disappeared, and a little of his natural colour came back. When his daughter-in-law buttoned his shirt over his chest at last, he sighed.

"Da's fine, de way I feel now, Polly. It was a awful bad spell, an' I was so sorry it all come on you like it did."

Polly was flushed and excited. "Is the pain really gone? Can I leave you long enough to telephone over to your place?"

Rosicky's eyelids fluttered. "Don't telephone, Polly. It ain't no use to scare my wife. It's nice and quiet here, an' if I ain't too much trouble to you, just let me lay still till I feel like myself. I ain't got no pain now. It's nice here."

Polly bent over him and wiped the moisture from his face. "Oh, I'm so glad it's over!" she broke out impulsively. "It just broke my heart to see you suffer so, Father."

Rosicky motioned her to sit down on the chair where the tea-kettle had been, and looked up at her with that lively affectionate gleam in his eyes. "You was awful good to me, I won't never forgit dat. I hate it to be sick on you like dis. Down at de barn I say to myself, dat young girl ain't had much experience in sickness, I don't want to scare her, an' maybe she's got a baby comin' or somet'ing."

Polly took his hand. He was looking at her so intently and affectionately and confidingly; his eyes seemed to caress her face, to regard it with pleasure. She frowned with her funny streaks of eyebrows, and then smiled back at him.

"I guess maybe there is something of that kind going to happen. But I haven't told anyone yet, not my mother or Rudolph. You'll be the first to know."

His hand pressed hers. She noticed that it was warm again. The twinkle in his yellow-brown eyes seemed to come nearer.

"I like mighty well to see dat little child, Polly," was all he said. Then he closed his eyes and lay half-smiling. But Polly sat still, thinking hard. She had a sudden feeling that nobody in the world, not her mother, not Rudolph, or anyone, really loved her as much as old Rosicky did. It perplexed her. She sat frowning and trying to puzzle it out. It was as if Rosicky had a special gift for loving people, something that was like an ear for music or an eye for colour. It was quiet, unobtrusive; it was merely there. You saw it in his eyes,—perhaps that was why they were merry. You felt it in his hands, too. After he dropped off to sleep, she sat holding his warm, broad, flexible brown hand. She had never seen another in the least like it. She wondered if it wasn't a kind of gypsy hand, it was so alive and quick and light in its communications,—very strange in a farmer. Nearly all the farmers she knew had huge lumps of fists, like mauls,[7] or they were knotty and bony and uncomfortable-looking, with stiff fingers. But Rosicky's was like quicksilver, flexible, muscular, about the colour of a pale cigar, with deep, deep creases across the palm. It wasn't nervous, it wasn't a stupid lump; it was a warm brown human hand, with some cleverness in it, a great deal of generosity, and something else which Polly could only call "gypsy-like,"—something nimble and lively and sure, in the way that animals are.

Polly remembered that hour long afterwards; it had been like an awakening to her. It seemed to her that she had never learned so much about life from anything as from old Rosicky's hand. It brought her to herself; it communicated some direct and untranslatable message.

When she heard Rudolph coming in the car, she ran out to meet him.

"Oh, Rudy, your father's been awful sick! He raked up those thistles he's been worrying about, and afterwards he could hardly get to the house. He suffered so I was afraid he was going to die."

Rudolph jumped to the ground. "Where is he now?"

"On the bed. He's asleep. I was terribly scared, because, you know, I'm so fond of your father." She slipped her arm through his and they went into the house. That afternoon they took Rosicky home and put him to bed, though he protested that he was quite well again.

The next morning he got up and dressed and sat down to breakfast with his family. He told Mary that his coffee tasted better than usual to him, and he warned the boys not to bear any tales to Doctor Ed when he got home. After breakfast he sat down by his window to do some patching and asked Mary to thread several needles for him before she went to feed her chickens,—her eyes were better than his, and her hands steadier. He lit his pipe and took up John's overalls. Mary had been watching him anxiously all morning, and as she went out of the door with her bucket of scraps, she saw that he was smiling. He was thinking, indeed, about Polly, and how he might never have known what a tender heart she had if he hadn't got sick over there. Girls nowadays didn't wear their heart on their sleeve. But now he knew Polly would make a fine woman after the foolishness wore off. Either a woman had that sweetness at her heart or she hadn't. You couldn't always tell by the look of them; but if they had that, everything came out right in the end.

After he had taken a few stitches, the cramp began in his chest, like yesterday. He put his pipe cautiously down on the window-sill and bent over to ease the pull. No use,—he had better try to get to his bed if he could. He rose and groped his way across the familiar floor, which was rising and falling like the deck of a ship. At the door he fell. When Mary came in, she found him lying there, and the moment she touched him she knew that he was gone.

Doctor Ed was away when Rosicky died, and for the first few weeks after he got home he was hard driven. Every day he said to himself that he must get out to see that family that had lost their father. One soft, warm moonlight night in early summer he started

---

[7] Heavy mallets.

for the farm. His mind was on other things, and not until his road ran by the graveyard did he realize that Rosicky wasn't over there on the hill where the red lamplight shone, but here, in the moonlight. He stopped his car, shut off the engine, and sat there for a while.

A sudden hush had fallen on his soul. Everything here seemed strangely moving and significant, though signifying what, he did not know. Close by the wire fence stood Rosicky's mowing-machine, where one of the boys had been cutting hay that afternoon; his own work-horses had been going up and down there. The new-cut hay perfumed all the night air. The moonlight silvered the long, billowy grass that grew over the graves and hid the fence; the few little evergreens stood out black in it, like shadows in a pool. The sky was very blue and soft, the stars rather faint because the moon was full.

For the first time it struck Doctor Ed that this was really a beautiful graveyard. He thought of city cemeteries; acres of shrubbery and heavy stone, so arranged and lonely and unlike anything in the living world. Cities of the dead, indeed; cities of the forgotten, of the "put away." But this was open and free, this little square of long grass which the wind for ever stirred. Nothing but the sky overhead, and the many-coloured fields running on until they met that sky. The horses worked here in summer; the neighbours passed on their way to town; and over yonder, in the cornfield, Rosicky's own cattle would be eating fodder as winter came on. Nothing could be more undeathlike than this place; nothing could be more right for a man who had helped to do the work of great cities and had always longed for the open country and had got to it at last. Rosicky's life seemed to him complete and beautiful.

1928/1930

Robert Frost
1875–1963

Robert Frost is the best known of our modern American poets: His poems find their way into high school textbooks and into popular memory far more quickly than do the poems of his contemporaries. In part, Frost's popularity may be due to the apparent simplicity of his subject matter, but it is surely more profoundly due to his uncanny feeling for what he called "sentence sounds," the sounds and syntactic patterns into which the American language naturally falls. Frost's lines are remembered without effort: "The land was ours before we were the land's"; "But I have promises to keep"; "Nothing gold can stay"; "Earth's the right place for love"; "Good fences make good neighbors." Frost's immense talent as a reader of his own work made him something of a national institution; the gravel-voiced old man with a shock of white hair who was seen on television reading "The Gift Outright" at John F. Kennedy's inauguration in 1961 was already a figure known to most viewers. But they also knew his work; he was probably the one living poet whose poetry had touched them in school.

Frost's gift for an intimate lyricism was learned in part from Whitman; "You come too" (from "The Pasture") was an invitation that Whitman had often extended to his readers. Whitman's patriotism, too, finds a kindred echo in Frost's faith in the continuity of American principle, evident in a poem like "Immigrants," where every immigrant ship is said to have the *Mayflower* as its convoy. And Emerson, the ancestor of both Whitman and Frost, stands behind Frost's resolute transcendental confidence that we can stay—anchor—our minds on something like a star.

And yet these American ancestors do not fully account for Frost. Since Lionel Trilling first emphasized the darker side of Frost's imagination, critics have increasingly seen how many-sided Frost is. Biographers have drawn links between the events of Frost's own life—a Gothic chronicle of disasters—and the poetry. Frost's father, a transplanted easterner, died in San Francisco when Frost was eleven. (Frost's mother returned to New Hampshire, and Frost took the region for his own.) But it was not only the early death of his father that convinced Frost of the evil in existence. His own first child died in infancy; his only son committed suicide; one daughter died after childbirth, and another was mentally ill; his embittered wife refused on her deathbed to admit him to her room. The "rage" that Frost saw in the natural order ("Once by the Pacific") had for him its counterpart in the social order, where any "flower" could be subverted; the poem "The Subverted Flower" suggests a fundamental incompatibility between male sexual desire and female fear and disgust. In many of his grimmer poems (like "Design") Frost comes close to Thomas Hardy in suspecting that the universe may be governed by a malevolent God or, worse, not governed at all—by anyone.

Like many American writers, Frost had to expatriate himself to find his first success. Before he went to England in 1912 at the age of thirty-eight, he had been writing poetry for a long time. He had been class poet at his graduation in 1892 from high school in Lawrence, Massachusetts, where his future wife, Elinor White, was co-valedictorian with him. Frost went on to Dartmouth but dropped out after only one term. He continued to write while working at odd jobs—bobbin boy at a cotton mill, cobbler, schoolteacher, journalist. In 1897 he came to Harvard for two years as a special student, where he carried on the study of Latin that he had begun in high school. At Harvard he attended the philosophy lectures of George Santayana and read William James; their skepticism and pragmatism influenced the philosophical temper of his poetry. In 1899 his grandfather bought a farm for him in Derry, New Hampshire; but though Frost lived there and worked the farm for ten years, he was no nearer to publishing a book. After three more years of teaching at Pinkerton Academy in Derry, Frost left for England, where he published his first volume, *A Boy's Will* (1913). The title comes from Longfellow: "A boy's will is the wind's will, / And the thoughts of youth are long, long thoughts." In choosing this title, Frost made explicit his own derivation from and competition with Longfellow, New England's regional poet, and in fact Longfellow's "Schooner Hesperus" and "Hiawatha" have now been displaced in our literary history by Frost's regional poetry of New Hampshire.

In England, Frost met Ezra Pound, who helped publish Frost's second book, *North of Boston* (1914), a volume containing several of Frost's most stunning poems, including "Mending Wall," "Home Burial," and "After Apple-Picking." His reputation made, Frost returned to the United States to take a teaching position at Amherst College in 1917, though he taught there only intermittently. His many other teaching stints and his poetry readings, together with his royalties, supported Frost for the rest of his life. He was far more popular, and more successful financially, than the majority of his contemporaries.

Frost's poems tend to fall, formally speaking, into two groups: the long blank-verse poems like "Home Burial," often embodying some form of New England rural suffering, and the short, exquisite, rhymed lyrics, including philosophical sonnets like "Design." The narratives, which reopen a vein already worked by Edwin Arlington Robinson, represent the strains of life lived under pinched, emotionally thwarting conditions. They are a powerful corrective to the European pastoral tradition that represents nature as bountiful and gracious and man's life in nature as healing and joyful. They are also a corrective to the optimistic Emersonian view of nature as an authentic teacher. After reading the harsh accusations in "Home Burial," no reader can continue to think nature or domesticity merciful. The troglodytic farmer in "Mending Wall" is more a savage than a noble savage.

Frost's songlike lyrics ("Reluctance" or "Stopping by Woods on a Snowy Evening") stem directly from the most musical of English poems (Shakespeare's songs, Keats's odes, Shelley's choruses); his more philosophical lyrics are given their sternness by Horace and Lucretius. Frost's long reading in the Latin poets is visible not merely in his use of hendecasyllabics (eleven-syllable lines) in "For Once, Then, Something," but more powerfully in his pre-Christian view of nature. In repudiating the Christian tradition of a sacramental nature in favor of a nature enigmatic ("The Most of It"), elusive ("For Once, Then, Something"), or unreadable ("Time Out"), Frost adds to his nature poetry a metaphysical element of philosophic commentary. But his deftness of touch ("If design govern in a thing so small") retains his poetry within a colloquial tradition, just as his reliance on rhyme (he objected to free verse, saying it was like playing tennis without a net) retains his poetry within the tradition of the European lyric.

Frost represents a powerful antithesis to the modernist poetic represented by Pound and Eliot. As they face Europe, he faces America; as they assume and display learning, he is only obliquely allusive; as they write free verse, he writes in meter; as they lament a fragmented culture, he records a culture that can still muster a living, if forgotten, tradition. No one has better incorporated American speed into verse; Frost was delighted when he wrote, as a final line to "The Pauper Witch of Grafton," "I might have, but it doesn't seem as if"—a line that, in its vernacular lilt, could never have closed a British poem. In his grimly comic, sometimes even mischievous poetry, Frost preserved a vein of American humor that we are more likely to associate with prose like Twain's. And in his essays on poetry—aphoristic, pithy, and profound—Frost is one of the best theorists of a skeptical, questioning modern poetry that settles for no easy answers.

Further Reading:

L. R. Thompson, *Fire and Ice: The Art and Thought of Robert Frost,* 1942.

S. Cox, *A Swinger of Birches,* 1957.

R. L. Cook, *The Dimensions of Robert Frost,* 1959.

J. F. Lynan, *The Pastoral Art of Robert Frost,* 1960.

R. Squires, *The Major Themes of Robert Frost,* 1963.

R. Brower, *The Poetry of Robert Frost,* 1963.

P. L. Gerber, *Robert Frost,* 1966.

L. R. Thompson, *Robert Frost: The Early Years,* 1966.

L. R. Thompson, *Robert Frost: The Years of Triumph,* 1970.

F. Lentricchia, *Robert Frost: Modern Poetics and the Landscape of Self,* 1975.

L. R. Thompson and R. H. Winnick, *Robert Frost: The Later Years,* 1976.

F. Lentricchia and M. C. Lentricchia, *Robert Frost: A Bibliography,* 1976.

R. Poirier, *Robert Frost: The Work of Knowing,* 1977.

L. Wagner, *Robert Frost: The Critical Reception,* 1977.

J. C. Kemp, *Robert Frost and New England,* 1979.

L. R. Thompson, *Robert Frost,* 1981.

P. L. Gerber, ed., *Critical Essays on Robert Frost,* 1982.

D. Bromwich, *A Choice of Inheritance: Self and Community from Edmund Burke to Robert Frost,* 1989.

P. Van Egmond, *Robert Frost: A Reference Guide,* 1991.

Texts:

The Poetry of Robert Frost, ed. E. C. Lathem, 1969 (punctuation corrected from *The Selected Poems of Robert Frost,* 1963).

See also *Selected Letters of Robert Frost,* ed. L. R. Thompson, 1964.

Selected Prose of Robert Frost, ed. H. Cox and E. C. Lathem, 1966.

Mending Wall

Something there is that doesn't love a wall,[1]
That sends the frozen-ground-swell under it
And spills the upper boulders in the sun,
And makes gaps even two can pass abreast.
The work of hunters is another thing: 5
I have come after them and made repair
Where they have left not one stone on a stone,
But they would have the rabbit out of hiding,
To please the yelping dogs. The gaps I mean,
No one has seen them made or heard them made,   10
But at spring mending-time we find them there.
I let my neighbor know beyond the hill;
And on a day we meet to walk the line
And set the wall between us once again.
We keep the wall between us as we go.   15
To each the boulders that have fallen to each.
And some are loaves and some so nearly balls
We have to use a spell to make them balance:
"Stay where you are until our backs are turned!"
We wear our fingers rough with handling them.   20
Oh, just another kind of outdoor game,
One on a side. It comes to little more:
There where it is we do not need the wall:
He is all pine and I am apple orchard.
My apple trees will never get across   25
And eat the cones under his pines, I tell him.
He only says, "Good fences make good neighbors."
Spring is the mischief in me, and I wonder
If I could put a notion in his head:

---

[1] It is frost (a pun on Frost himself) that is inimical to walls.

"*Why* do they make good neighbors? Isn't it   30
Where there are cows? But here there are no cows.
Before I built a wall I'd ask to know
What I was walling in or walling out,
And to whom I was like to give offense.
Something there is that doesn't love a wall,   35
That wants it down." I could say "Elves" to him,
But it's not elves exactly, and I'd rather
He said it for himself. I see him there,
Bringing a stone grasped firmly by the top
In each hand, like an old-stone savage armed.   40
He moves in darkness as it seems to me,
Not of woods only and the shade of trees.
He will not go behind his father's saying,
And he likes having thought of it so well
He says again, "Good fences make good neighbors."   45
1914

The Road Not Taken

Two roads diverged in a yellow wood,
And sorry I could not travel both
And be one traveler, long I stood
And looked down one as far as I could
To where it bent in the undergrowth;   5

Then took the other, as just as fair,
And having perhaps the better claim,
Because it was grassy and wanted wear;
Though as for that the passing there
Had worn them really about the same,   10

And both that morning equally lay
In leaves no step had trodden black.
Oh, I kept the first for another day!
Yet knowing how way leads on to way,
I doubted if I should ever come back.   15

I shall be telling this with a sigh
Somewhere ages and ages hence:
Two roads diverged in a wood, and I—

I took the one less traveled by,
And that has made all the difference.   20
1916

The Oven Bird

There is a singer everyone has heard,
Loud, a mid-summer and a mid-wood bird,
Who makes the solid tree trunks sound again.
He says that leaves are old and that for flowers
Mid-summer is to spring as one to ten.   5
He says the early petal-fall is past
When pear and cherry bloom went down in
    showers
On sunny days a moment overcast;
And comes that other fall we name the fall.
He says the highway dust is over all.   10
The bird would cease and be as other birds
But that he knows in singing not to sing.
The question that he frames in all but words
Is what to make of a diminished thing.
1916

After Apple-Picking

My long two-pointed ladder's sticking through a tree
Toward heaven still,
And there's a barrel that I didn't fill
Beside it, and there may be two or three
Apples I didn't pick upon some bough.   5
But I am done with apple-picking now.
Essence of winter sleep is on the night,
The scent of apples: I am drowsing off.
I cannot rub the strangeness from my sight
I got from looking through a pane of glass   10
I skimmed this morning from the drinking trough

And held against the world of hoary grass.
It melted, and I let it fall and break.
But I was well
Upon my way to sleep before it fell,   15
And I could tell
What form my dreaming was about to take.
Magnified apples appear and disappear,
Stem end and blossom end,
And every fleck of russet showing clear.   20
My instep arch not only keeps the ache,
It keeps the pressure of a ladder-round.
I feel the ladder sway as the boughs bend.
And I keep hearing from the cellar bin
The rumbling sound   25
Of load on load of apples coming in.
For I have had too much
Of applie-picking: I am overtired
Of the great harvest I myself desired.
There were ten thousand thousand fruit to touch,   30
Cherish in hand, lift down, and not let fall.
For all
That struck the earth,
No matter if not bruised or spiked with stubble,
Went surely to the cider-apple heap   35
As of no worth.
One can see what will trouble
This sleep of mine, whatever sleep it is.
Were he not gone,
The woodchuck could say whether it's like his   40
Long sleep, as I describe its coming on,
Or just some human sleep.

Birches

When I see birches bend to left and right
Across the lines of straighter darker trees,
I like to think some boy's been swinging them.
But swinging doesn't bend them down to stay
As ice storms do. Often you must have seen them   5
Loaded with ice a sunny winter morning
After a rain. They click upon themselves
As the breeze rises, and turn many-colored
As the stir cracks and crazes their enamel.
Soon the sun's warmth makes them shed crystal shells   10

Shattering and avalanching on the snow crust—
Such heaps of broken glass to sweep away
You'd think the inner dome of heaven had fallen.
They are dragged to the withered bracken[1] by the load,
And they seem not to break; though once they are bowed   15
So low for long, they never right themselves:
You may see their trunks arching in the woods
Years afterwards, trailing their leaves on the ground
Like girls on hands and knees that throw their hair
Before them over their heads to dry in the sun.   20
But I was going to say when Truth broke in
With all her matter of fact about the ice storm
I should prefer to have some boy bend them
As he went out and in to fetch the cows—
Some boy too far from town to learn baseball,   25
Whose only play was what he found himself,
Summer or winter, and could play alone.
One by one he subdued his father's trees
By riding them down over and over again
Until he took the stiffness out of them,   30
And not one but hung limp, not one was left
For him to conquer. He learned all there was
To learn about not launching out too soon
And so not carrying the tree away
Clear to the ground. He always kept his poise   35
To the top branches, climbing carefully
With the same pains you use to fill a cup
Up to the brim, and even above the brim.
Then he flung outward, feet first, with a swish,
Kicking his way down through the air to the ground.   40
So was I once myself a swinger of birches.
And so I dream of going back to be.
It's when I'm weary of considerations,
And life is too much like a pathless wood
Where your face burns and tickles with the cobwebs   45
Broken across it, and one eye is weeping
From a twig's having lashed across it open.
I'd like to get away from earth awhile
And then come back to it and begin over.
May no fate willfully misunderstand me   50
And half grant what I wish and snatch me away
Not to return. Earth's the right place for love:
I don't know where it's likely to go better.
I'd like to go by climbing a birch tree,
And climb black branches up a snow-white trunk   55

[1] Fern.

Toward heaven, till the tree could bear no more,
But dipped its top and set me down again.
That would be good both going and coming back.
One could do worse than be a swinger of birches.
1916

Stopping by Woods on a Snowy Evening

Whose woods these are I think I know.
His house is in the village, though;
He will not see me stopping here
To watch his woods fill up with snow.

My little horse must think it queer   5
To stop without a farmhouse near
Between the woods and frozen lake
The darkest evening of the year.

He gives his harness bells a shake
To ask if there is some mistake.   10
The only other sound's the sweep
Of easy wind and downy flake.

The woods are lovely, dark and deep,
But I have promises to keep,
And miles to go before I sleep,   15
And miles to go before I sleep.
1923

Once by the Pacific

The shattered water made a misty din.
Great waves looked over others coming in,
And thought of doing something to the shore
That water never did to land before.
The clouds were low and hairy in the skies,   5
Like locks blown forward in the gleam of eyes.
You could not tell, and yet it looked as if
The shore was lucky in being backed by cliff,
The cliff in being backed by continent;

It looked as if a night of dark intent 10
Was coming, and not only a night, an age.
Someone had better be prepared for rage.
There would be more than ocean-water broken
Before God's last *Put out the Light* was spoken.[1]
1928

Desert Places

Snow falling and night falling fast, oh, fast
In a field I looked into going past,
And the ground almost covered smooth in snow,
But a few weeds and stubble showing last.

The woods around it have it—it is theirs. 5
All animals are smothered in their lairs.
I am too absent-spirited to count;
The loneliness includes me unawares.

And lonely as it is, that loneliness
Will be more lonely ere it will be less— 10
A blanker whiteness of benighted[1] snow
With no expression, nothing to express.

They cannot scare me with their empty spaces
Between stars—on stars where no human race is.
I have it in me so much nearer home 15
To scare myself with my own desert places.
1936

Design*

I found a dimpled spider, fat and white,
On a white heal-all,[1] holding up a moth

---

[1] God's first words in Genesis are, "Let there be Light."
[1] Ignorant; overtaken by spiritual and physical darkness.

* The argument from design (order in nature) was often urged as a proof for the existence of God.
[1] A flower, normally blue.

Like a white piece of rigid satin cloth—
Assorted characters of death and blight
Mixed ready to begin the morning right,   5
Like the ingredients of a witches' broth—
A snow-drop spider, a flower like a froth,[2]
And dead wings carried like a paper kite.

What had that flower to do with being white,
The wayside blue and innocent heal-all?   10
What brought the kindred spider to that height,
Then steered the white moth thither in the night?
What but design of darkness to appall?—
If design govern in a thing so small.

1936

The Most of It

He thought he kept the universe alone;
For all the voice in answer he could wake
Was but the mocking echo of his own
From some tree-hidden cliff across the lake.
Some morning from the boulder-broken beach   5
He would cry out on life, that what it wants
Is not its own love back in copy speech,
But counter-love, original response.
And nothing ever came of what he cried
Unless it was the embodiment that crashed   10
In the cliff's talus[1] on the other side,
And then in the far-distant water splashed,
But after a time allowed for it to swim,
Instead of proving human when it neared
And someone else additional to him,   15
As a great buck it powerfully appeared,
Pushing the crumpled water up ahead,
And landed pouring like a waterfall,
And stumbled through the rocks with horny tread,
And forced the underbrush—and that was all.   20

1942

---

[2] In the octave (first eight lines), Frost complicates his task by using the only four common words ending with the sound ŏth; he also continues the octave rhyme sound *ite* in the sestet (last six lines).

[1] Slope.

Directive

Back out of all this now too much for us,
Back in a time made simple by the loss
Of detail, burned, dissolved, and broken off
Like graveyard marble sculpture in the weather,
There is a house that is no more a house   5
Upon a farm that is no more a farm
And in a town that is no more a town.
The road there, if you'll let a guide direct you
Who only has at heart your getting lost,
May seem as if it should have been a quarry—   10
Great monolithic knees the former town
Long since gave up pretense of keeping covered.
And there's a story in a book about it:
Besides the wear of iron wagon wheels
The ledges show lines ruled southeast-northwest,   15
The chisel work of an enormous Glacier
That braced his feet against the Arctic Pole.
You must not mind a certain coolness from him
Still said to haunt this side of Panther Mountain.
Nor need you mind the serial ordeal   20
Of being watched from forty cellar holes
As if by eye pairs out of forty firkins.
As for the woods' excitement over you
That sends light rustle rushes to their leaves,
Charge that to upstart inexperience.   25
Where were they all not twenty years ago?
They think too much of having shaded out
A few old pecker-fretted apple trees.
Make yourself up a cheering song of how
Someone's road home from work this once was,   30
Who may be just ahead of you on foot
Or creaking with a buggy load of grain.
The height of the adventure is the height
Of country where two village cultures faded
Into each other. Both of them are lost.   35
And if you're lost enough to find yourself
By now, pull in your ladder road behind you
And put a sign up CLOSED to all but me.
Then make yourself at home. The only field
Now left's no bigger than a harness gall.   40
First there's the children's house of make-believe,
Some shattered dishes underneath a pine,
The playthings in the playhouse of the children.

Weep for what little things could make them glad.
Then for the house that is no more a house,   45
But only a belilaced cellar hole,
Now slowly closing like a dent in dough.
This was no playhouse but a house in earnest.
Your destination and your destiny's
A brook that was the water of the house,   50
Cold as a spring as yet so near its source,
Too lofty and original to rage.
(We know the valley streams that when aroused
Will leave their tatters hung on barb and thorn.)
I have kept hidden in the instep arch   55
Of an old cedar at the waterside
A broken drinking goblet like the Grail
Under a spell so the wrong ones can't find it,
So can't get saved, as Saint Mark says they mustn't.
(I stole the goblet from the children's playhouse.)   60
Here are your waters and your watering place.
Drink and be whole again beyond confusion.
1947

The Figure a Poem Makes

The figure a poem makes. It begins in delight and ends in wisdom. The figure is the same as for love. No one can really hold that the ecstasy should be static and stand still in one place. It begins in delight, it inclines to the impulse, it assumes direction with the first line laid down, it runs a course of lucky events, and ends in a clarification of life—not necessarily a great clarification, such as sects and cults are founded on, but in a momentary stay against confusion. It has denouement. It has an outcome that though unforeseen was predestined from the first image of the original mood—and indeed from the very mood. It is but a trick poem and no poem at all if the best of it was thought of first and saved for the last. It finds its own name as it goes and discovers the best waiting for it in some final phrase at once wise and sad—the happy-sad blend of the drinking song.

Robert Frost from "The Figure a Poem Makes" (1939)[1]

Susan Keating Glaspell
1876–1948

Susan Keating Glaspell was born in Davenport, Iowa, on 1 July 1876, roughly forty years after her family arrived in the nation's heartland as pioneers, and three days

[1] From "The Figure a Poem Makes" in *Selected Prose* of Robert Frost,   Edward C. Latham, ed., 1963, pp. 393–396.

before her country celebrated its first centenary. Following her graduation from the local high school, Glaspell began working as a reporter on the Davenport *Morning Republican*. Later she worked on the town's *Weekly Outlook* as society editor. But she soon tired of her first writing ventures and left Davenport to attend Drake University, from which she graduated in 1899.

Following a brief stint writing for the Des Moines *Daily News*, Glaspell returned to Davenport to concentrate on writing fiction. In 1902, she moved to Chicago where she took graduate courses at the newly established University of Chicago, became involved in the Chicago Renaissance, and continued writing, with increasing success. Her first novel, *The Glory of the Conquered* (1909), brought her considerable attention. A second novel, *The Visioning*, followed in 1911, and a year later a collection of stories called *Lifted Masks*.

Although most of Glaspell's early work now seems strained or sentimental, some of it—stories like "Contrary to Precedent," for example—show a sharp-edged talent for evoking the poignancy and significance of the commonplace. Given their indifference to the commonplace, an indifference reinforced by a false sense of their own importance, Glaspell's men rarely become strong characters. Some of them seem childish, others blustery, and others falsely busy. Unable, as it were, to see the trees for the forest, they typically misread the forest of which they claim to be the masters. Glaspell's female characters, by contrast, whom her male characters regularly treat with a combination of condescension and feigned tolerance, see their world more deeply because they see its particulars more clearly.

Having returned to Davenport and then left on a trip that took her to Paris, Glaspell again returned to Davenport and in 1913 married a wealthy, prominent, Harvard-educated, recently divorced man named George Cram Cook. A year later Glaspell and Cook moved to Provincetown, Massachusetts, where they founded the Provincetown Players, hoping to create an ideal community based on Cook's highly spiritualized theory of drama. Over the next several years, writers like Eugene O'Neill, Edna St. Vincent Millay, and John Reed joined them in their endeavor. O'Neill's first play, *Bound East for Cardiff*, was staged at the Wharf Theater in Provincetown in 1916, and *The Emperor Jones* opened at the Provincetown Playhouse in 1920.

During these same years, Glaspell flourished as a writer of fiction, in novels like *Fidelity* (1915), and even more as a writer of drama. Between 1914 and 1921, she wrote ten plays, including two written in collaboration with Cook, which the Provincetown Players produced. Among these, *The People* (1917), *Woman's Honor* (1918), and *The Verge* (1921) all bear in interesting ways on Glaspell's most important themes, which revolve around the place of women in a world dominated by men. But the play she named *Trifles* (1916), together with the story "A Jury of Her Peers," which she based on the play, are now regarded as her most powerful and compelling works.

In 1922 Glaspell and Cook moved to Greece, still looking for a more perfect world. But Glaspell missed Provincetown, and two years later, when Cook died, she returned to Massachusetts, and began writing prose again, first in *The Road to the Temple* (1927), a biography of Cook, and then in several novels, including *Brook Evans* (1928), *Fugitive's Return* (1929), and *Ambrose Holt and Family* (1931). In 1930 her play *Alison's House*, based on Emily Dickinson's life, won her a Pulitzer Prize. But neither it nor any of her later work quite matched the force of *Trifles*. She died in Provincetown, scene of her best years as well as some of her loneliest, on 27 July 1948.

Further Reading:

K. Alkalay-Gut, " 'A Jury of Her Peers': The Importance of *Trifles*." *Studies in Short Fiction* 21 (1984), 1–9.

E. Hedges, "Small Things Reconsidered: Susan Glaspell's 'A Jury of Her Peers.' " *Women's Studies* 12 (1986), 89–110.

V. Makowsky, "Susan Glaspell," L. Baechler and A. W. Litz, eds., *Modern American Women Writers*, 1991.

Beverly A. Smith, "Women's Work—Trifles? The Skill and Insights of Playwright Susan Glaspell." *International Journal of Women's Studies* 5 (1982), 172–184.

Arthur E. Waterman, *Susan Glaspell*, 1966.

Text:

"Trifles" from *Plays*, 1920.

Trifles

First Performed by the Provincetown Players at the Wharf Theatre, Provincetown, Mass., August 8, 1916

Original Cast

George Henderson, County Attorney—Robert Rogers

Henry Peters, Sheriff—Robert Conville

Lewis Hale, A Neighboring Farmer—George Cram Cook

Mrs. Peters—Alice Hall

Mrs. Hale—Susan Glaspell

Scene

The kitchen in the now abandoned farmhouse of John Wright, a gloomy kitchen, and left without having been put in order—unwashed pans under the sink, a loaf of bread outside the bread-box, a dish-towel on the table—other signs of incompleted work. At the rear the outer door opens and the Sheriff comes in followed by the County Attorney and Hale. The Sheriff and Hale are men in middle life, the County Attorney is a young man; all are much bundled up and go at once to the stove. They are followed by the two women—the Sheriff's wife first; she is a slight wiry woman, a thin nervous face. Mrs. Hale is larger and would or-

dinarily be called more comfortable looking, but she is disturbed now and looks fearfully about as she enters. The women have come in slowly, and stand close together near the door.

County Attorney: (Rubbing his hands.) This feels good. Come up to the fire, ladies.

Mrs. Peters: (After taking a step forward.) I'm not—cold.

Sheriff: (Unbuttoning his overcoat and stepping away from the stove as if to mark the be-ginning of official business.) Now, Mr. Hale, before we move things about, you ex-plain to Mr. Henderson just what you saw when you came here yesterday morning.

County Attorney: By the way, has anything been moved? Are things just as you left them yesterday?

Sheriff: (Looking about.) It's just the same. When it dropped below zero last night I thought I'd better send Frank out this morning to make a fire for us—no use get-ting pneumonia with a big case on, but I told him not to touch anything except the stove—and you know Frank.

County Attorney: Somebody should have been left here yesterday.

Sheriff: Oh—yesterday. When I had to send Frank to Morris Center for that man who went crazy—I want you to know I had my hands full yesterday. I knew you could get back from Omaha by today and as long as I went over everything here myself—

County Attorney: Well, Mr. Hale, tell just what happened when you came here yester-day morning.

Hale: Harry and I had started to town with a load of potatoes. We came along the road from my place and as I got here I said, "I'm going to see if I can't get John Wright to go in with me on a party telephone." I spoke to Wright about it once before and he put me off, saying folks talked too much anyway, and all he asked was peace and quiet—I guess you know about how much he talked himself; but I thought maybe if I went to the house and talked about it before his wife, though I said to Harry that I didn't know as what his wife wanted made much difference to John—

County Attorney: Let's talk about that later, Mr. Hale. I do want to talk about that, but tell now just what happened when you got to the house.

Hale: I didn't hear or see anything; I knocked at the door, and still it was all quiet inside. I knew they must be up, it was past eight o'clock. So I knocked again, and I thought I heard somebody say, "Come in." I wasn't sure, I'm not sure yet, but I opened the door—this door *(indicating the door by which the two women are still standing)* and there in that rocker—*(pointing to it)* sat Mrs. Wright.

(They all look at the rocker.)

County Attorney: What—was she doing?

Hale: She was rockin' back and forth. She had her apron in her hand and was kind of—pleating it.

County Attorney: And how did she—look?

Hale: Well, she looked queer.

County Attorney: How do you mean—queer?

Hale: Well, as if she didn't know what she was going to do next. And kind of done up.

County Attorney: How did she seem to feel about your coming?

Hale: Why, I don't think she minded—one way or other. She didn't pay much atten-tion. I said, "How do, Mrs. Wright, it's cold, ain't it?" And she said, "Is it?"—and went on kind of pleating at her apron. Well, I was surprised; she didn't ask me to come up to the stove, or to set down, but just sat there, not even looking at me, so I said, "I want to see John." And then she—laughed. I guess you would call it a laugh. I thought of Harry and the team outside, so I said a little sharp: "Can't I see John?" "No," she says, kind o' dull like. "Ain't he home?" says I. "Yes," says she, "he's home." "Then why can't I see him?" I asked her, out of patience. " 'Cause he's dead," says she. "*Dead?*" says I. She just nodded her head, not getting a bit excited, but rockin' back and forth. "Why—where is he?" says I, not knowing what to say. She just pointed upstairs—like that (*himself pointing to the room above*). I got up, with the idea of going up there. I walked from there to here—then I says, "Why, what did he die of?" "He died of a rope round his neck," says she, and just went on pleatin' at her apron. Well, I went out and called Harry. I thought I might—need help. We went upstairs and there he was lyin'—

County Attorney: I think I'd rather have you go into that upstairs, where you can point it all out. Just go on now with the rest of the story.

Hale: Well, my first thought was to get that rope off. It looked . . . (*Stops, his face twitches*) . . . but Harry, he went up to him, and he said, "No, he's dead all right, and we'd better not touch anything." So we went back downstairs. She was still sitting that same way. "Has anybody been notified?" I asked. "No," says she, unconcerned. "Who did this, Mrs. Wright?" said Harry. He said it business-like—and she stopped pleatin' of her apron. "I don't know," she says. "You don't *know?*" says Harry. "No," says she. "Weren't you sleepin' in the bed with him?" says Harry. "Yes," says she, "but I was on the inside." "Somebody slipped a rope round his neck and strangled him and you didn't wake up?" says Harry. "I didn't wake up," she said after him. We must 'a looked as if we didn't see how that could be, for after a minute she said, "I sleep sound." Harry was going to ask her more questions but I said maybe we ought to let her tell her story first to the coroner, or the sheriff, so Harry went fast as he could to Rivers' place, where there's a telephone.

County Attorney: And what did Mrs. Wright do when she knew that you had gone for the coroner?

Hale: She moved from that chair to this one over here (*Pointing to a small chair in the corner*) and just sat there with her hands held together and looking down. I got a feeling that I ought to make come conversation, so I said I had come in to see if John wanted to put in a telephone, and at that she started to laugh, and then she stopped and looked at me—scared. (*The County Attorney, who has had his notebook out, makes a note.*) I dunno, maybe it wasn't scared. I wouldn't like to say it was. Soon Harry got back, and then Dr. Lloyd came, and you, Mr. Peters, and so I guess that's all I know that you don't.

County Attorney: (*Looking around.*) I guess we'll go upstairs first—and then out to the barn and around there. (*To the Sheriff.*) You're convinced that there was nothing important here—nothing that would point to any motive.

Sheriff: Nothing here but kitchen things.

(*The County Attorney, after again looking around the kitchen, opens the door of a cupboard closet. He gets up on a chair and looks on a shelf. Pulls his hand away, sticky.*)

County Attorney: Here's a nice mess.

(The women draw nearer.)

Mrs. Peters: *(To the other woman.)* Oh, her fruit; it did freeze. *(To the Lawyer.)* She worried about that when it turned so cold. She said the fire'd go out and her jars would break.

Sheriff: Well, can you beat the women! Held for murder and worryin' about her preserves.

County Attorney: I guess before we're through she may have something more serious than preserves to worry about.

Hale: Well, women are used to worrying over trifles.

(The two women move a little closer together.)

County Attorney: *(With the gallantry of a young politician.)* And yet, for all their worries, what would we do without the ladies?

(The women do not unbend. He goes to the sink, takes a dipperful of water from the pail and pouring it into a basin, washes his hands. Starts to wipe them on the roller-towel, turns it for a cleaner place.)

Dirty towels! *(Kicks his foot against the pans under the sink.)* Not much of a housekeeper, would you say, ladies?

Mrs. Hale: *(Stiffly.)* There's a great deal of work to be done on a farm.

County Attorney: To be sure. And yet *(With a little bow to her)* I know there are some Dickson county farmhouses which do not have such roller towels.

(He gives it a pull to expose its full length again.)

Mrs. Hale: Those towels get dirty awful quick. Men's hands aren't always as clean as they might be.

County Attorney: Ah, loyal to your sex, I see. But you and Mrs. Wright were neighbors. I suppose you were friends, too.

Mrs. Hale: *(Shaking her head.)* I've not seen much of her of late years. I've not been in this house—it's more than a year.

County Attorney: And why was that? You didn't like her?

Mrs. Hale: I liked her all well enough. Farmers' wives have their hands full, Mr. Henderson. And then—

County Attorney: Yes—?

Mrs. Hale: *(Looking about.)* It never seemed a very cheerful place.

County Attorney: No—it's not cheerful. I shouldn't say she had the homemaking instinct.

Mrs. Hale: Well, I don't know as Wright had, either.

County Attorney: You mean that they didn't get on very well?

Mrs. Hale: No, I don't mean anything. But I don't think a place'd be any cheerfuller for John Wright's being in it.

County Attorney: I'd like to talk more of that a little later. I want to get the lay of things upstairs now.

(He goes to the left, where three steps lead to a stair door.)

Sheriff: I suppose anything Mrs. Peters does'll be all right. She was to take in some clothes for her, you know, and a few little things. We left in such a hurry yesterday.

County Attorney: Yes, but I would like to see what you take, Mrs. Peters, and keep an eye out for anything that might be of use to us.

Mrs. Peters: Yes, Mr. Henderson.

(The women listen to the men's steps on the stairs, then look about the kitchen.)

Mrs. Hale: I'd hate to have men coming into my kitchen, snooping around and criticising.

(She arranges the pans under sink which the Lawyer had shoved out of place.)

Mrs. Peters: Of course it's no more than their duty.

Mrs. Hale: Duty's all right, but I guess that deputy sheriff that came out to make the fire might have got a little of this on. *(Gives the roller towel a pull.)* Wish I'd thought of that sooner. Seems mean to talk about her for not having things slicked up when she had to come away in such a hurry.

Mrs. Peters:

(Who has gone to a small table in the left rear corner of the room, and lifted one end of a towel that covers a pan.)

She had bread set.

(Stands still.)

Mrs. Hale:

(Eyes fixed on a loaf of bread beside the breadbox, which is on a low shelf at the other side of the room. Moves slowly toward it.)

She was going to put this in there. *(Picks up loaf, then abruptly drops it. In a manner of returning to familiar things.)* It's a shame about her fruit. I wonder if it's all gone. *(Gets up on the chair and looks.)* I think there's some here that's all right, Mrs. Peters. Yes— here; *(Holding it toward the window)* this is cherries, too. *(Looking again.)* I declare I believe that's the only one. *(Gets down, bottle in her hand. Goes to the sink and wipes it off on the outside.)* She'll feel awful bad after all her hard work in the hot weather. I remember the afternoon I put up my cherries last summer.

(She puts the bottle on the big kitchen table, center of the room. With a sigh, is about to sit down in the rocking-chair. Before she is seated realizes what chair it is; with a slow look at it, steps back. The chair which she has touched rocks back and forth.)

Mrs. Peters: Well, I must get those things from the front room closet. *(She goes to the door at the right, but after looking into the other room, steps back.)* You coming with me, Mrs. Hale? You could help me carry them.

(They go in the other room; reappear, Mrs. Peters carrying a dress and skirt, Mrs. Hale following with a pair of shoes.)

Mrs. Peters: My, it's cold in there.

(She puts the clothes on the big table, and hurries to the stove.

Mrs. Hale: *(Examining the skirt.)* Wright was close. I think maybe that's why she kept so much to herself. She didn't even belong to the Ladies Aid. I suppose she felt she couldn't do her part, and then you don't enjoy things when you feel shabby. She used to wear pretty clothes and be lively, when she was Minnie Foster, one of the town girls singing in the choir. But that—oh, that was thirty years ago. This all you was to take in?

Mrs. Peters: She said she wanted an apron. Funny thing to want, for there isn't much to get you dirty in jail, goodness knows. But I suppose just to make her feel more natural. She said they was in the top drawer in this cupboard. Yes, here. And then her little shawl that always hung behind the door. *(Opens stair door and looks.)* Yes, here it is.

(Quickly shuts door leading upstairs.)

Mrs. Hale:

(Abruptly moving toward her.)

Mrs. Peters?
Mrs. Peters: Yes, Mrs. Hale?
Mrs. Hale: Do you think she did it?
Mrs. Peters:

(In a frightened voice.)

Oh, I don't know.
Mrs. Hale: Well, I don't think she did. Asking for an apron and her little shawl. Worrying about her fruit.

Mrs. Peters:

(Starts to speak, glances up, where footsteps are heard in the room above. In a low voice.)

Mr. Peters says it looks bad for her. Mr. Henderson is awful sarcastic in a speech and he'll make fun of her sayin' she didn't wake up.

Mrs. Hale: Well, I guess John Wright didn't wake when they was slipping that rope under his neck.

Mrs. Peters: No, it's strange. It must have been done awful crafty and still. They say it was such a—funny way to kill a man, rigging it all up like that.

Mrs. Hale: That's just what Mr. Hale said. There was a gun in the house. He says that's what he can't understand.

Mrs. Peters: Mr. Henderson said coming out that what was needed for the case was a motive; something to show anger, or—sudden feeling.

Mrs. Hale: (Who is standing by the table.) Well, I don't see any signs of anger around here. *(She puts her hand on the dish towel which lies on the table, stands looking down at table, one half of which is clean, the other half messy.)* It's wiped to here. *(Makes a move as if to finish work, then turns and looks at loaf of bread outside the breadbox. Drops towel. In that voice of coming back to familiar things.)* Wonder how they are finding things upstairs. I hope she had it a little more red-up up there. You know, it seems kind of *sneaking.* Locking her up in town and then coming out here and trying to get her own house to turn against her!

Mrs. Peters: But Mrs. Hale, the law is the law.

Mrs. Hale: I s'pose 'tis. *(Unbuttoning her coat.)* Better loosen up your things, Mrs. Peters. You won't feel them when you go out.

(Mrs. Peters takes off her fur tippet, goes to hang it on hook at back of room, stands looking at the under part of the small corner table.)

Mrs. Peters: She was piecing a quilt.

(She brings the large sewing basket and they look at the bright pieces.)

Mrs. Hale: It's log cabin pattern. Pretty, isn't it? I wonder if she was goin' to quilt it or just knot it?

(Footsteps have been heard coming down the stairs. The Sheriff enters followed by Hale and the County Attorney.)

Sheriff: They wonder if she was going to quilt it or just knot it!

(The men laugh, the women look abashed.)

County Attorney: (Rubbing his hands over the stove.) Frank's fire didn't do much up there, did it? Well, let's go out to the barn and get that cleared up.

(The men go outside.)

Mrs. Hale: *(Resentfully.)* I don't know as there's anything so strange, our takin' up our time with little things while we're waiting for them to get the evidence. *(She sits down at the big table smoothing out a block with decision.)* I don't see as it's anything to laugh about.

Mrs. Peters: *(Apologetically.)* Of course they've got awful important things on their minds.

(Pulls up a chair and joins Mrs. Hale at the table.)

Mrs. Hale: *(Examining another block.)* Mrs. Peters, look at this one. Here, this is the one she was working on, and look at the sewing! All the rest of it has been so nice and even. And look at this! It's all over the place! Why, it looks as if she didn't know what she was about!

(After she has said this they look at each other, then start to glance back at the door. After an instant Mrs. Hale has pulled at a knot and ripped the sewing.)

Mrs. Peters: Oh, what are you doing, Mrs. Hale?

Mrs. Hale: *(Mildly.)* Just pulling out a stitch or two that's not sewed very good. *(Threading a needle.)* Bad sewing always made me fidgety.

Mrs. Peters: *(Nervously.)* I don't think we ought to touch things.

Mrs. Hale: I'll just finish up this end. *(Suddenly stopping and leaning forward.)* Mrs. Peters?

Mrs. Peters: Yes, Mrs. Hale?

Mrs. Hale: What do you suppose she was so nervous about?

Mrs. Peters: Oh—I don't know. I don't know as she was nervous. I sometimes sew awful queer when I'm just tired. *(Mrs. Hale starts to say something, looks at Mrs. Peters, then goes on sewing.)* Well I must get these things wrapped up. They may be through sooner than we think. *(Putting apron and other things together.)* I wonder where I can find a piece of paper, and string.

Mrs. Hale: In that cupboard, maybe.

Mrs. Peters: *(Looking in cupboard.)* Why, here's a bird-cage. *(Holds it up.)* Did she have a bird, Mrs. Hale?

Mrs. Hale: Why, I don't know whether she did or not—I've not been here for so long. There was a man around last year selling canaries cheap, but I don't know as she took one; maybe she did. She used to sing real pretty herself.

Mrs. Peters: *(Glancing around.)* Seems funny to think of a bird here. But she must have had one, or why would she have a cage? I wonder what happened to it.

Mrs. Hale: I s'pose maybe the cat got it.

Mrs. Peters: No, she didn't have a cat. She's got that feeling some people have about cats—being afraid of them. My cat got in her room and she was real upset and asked me to take it out.

Mrs. Hale: My sister Bessie was like that. Queer, ain't it?

Mrs. Peters: (Examining the cage.) Why, look at this door. It's broke. One hinge is
  pulled apart.
Mrs. Hale: (Looking too.) Looks as if someone must have been rough with it.
Mrs. Peters: Why, yes.

(She brings the cage forward and puts it on the table.)

Mrs. Hale: I wish if they're going to find any evidence they'd be about it. I don't like
  this place.
Mrs. Peters: But I'm awful glad you came with me, Mrs. Hale. It would be lonesome for
  me sitting here alone.
Mrs. Hale: It would, wouldn't it? *(Dropping her sewing.)* But I tell you what I do wish,
  Mrs. Peters. I wish I had come over sometimes when *she* was here. I—*(Looking
  around the room)*—wish I had.
Mrs. Peters: But of course you were awful busy, Mrs. Hale—your house and your children.
Mrs. Hale: I could've come. I stayed away because it weren't cheerful—and that's why I
  ought to have come. I—I've never liked this place. Maybe because it's down in a
  hollow and you don't see the road. I dunno what it is, but it's a lonesome place and
  always was. I wish I had come over to see Minnie Foster sometimes. I can see now—

(Shakes her head.)

Mrs. Peters: Well, you mustn't reproach yourself, Mrs. Hale. Somehow we just don't see
  how it is with other folks until—something comes up.
Mrs. Hale: Not having children makes less work—but it makes a quiet house, and
  Wright out to work all day, and no company when he did come in. Did you know
  John Wright, Mrs. Peters?
Mrs. Peters: Not to know him; I've seen him in town. They say he was a good man.
Mrs. Hale: Yes—good; he didn't drink, and kept his word as well as most, I guess, and
  paid his debts. But he was a hard man, Mrs. Peters. Just to pass the time of day
  with him— *(Shivers.)* Like a raw wind that gets to the bone. *(Pauses, her eye
  falling on the cage.)* I should think she would 'a wanted a bird. But what do you
  suppose went with it?
Mrs. Peters: I don't know, unless it got sick and died.

(She reaches over and swings the broken door, swings it again, both women watch it.)

Mrs. Hale: You weren't raised round here, were you? *(Mrs. Peters shakes her head.)* You
  didn't know—her?
Mrs. Peters: Not till they brought her yesterday.
Mrs. Hale: She—come to think of it, she was kind of like a bird herself—real sweet and
  pretty, but kind of timid and—fluttery. How—she—did—change.

(Silence; then as if struck by a happy thought and relieved to get back to every day things.)

Tell you what, Mrs. Peters, why don't you take the quilt in with you? It might take up
her mind.

Mrs. Peters: Why, I think that's a real nice idea, Mrs. Hale. There couldn't possibly be any objection to it, could there? Now, just what would I take? I wonder if her patches are in here—and her things.

(They look in the sewing basket.)

Mrs. Hale: Here's some red. I expect this has got sewing things in it. *(Brings out a fancy box.)* What a pretty box. Looks like something somebody would give you. Maybe her scissors are in here. *(Opens box. Suddenly puts her hand to her nose.)* Why— *(Mrs. Peters bends nearer, then turns her face away.)* There's something wrapped up in this piece of silk.

Mrs. Peters: Why, this isn't her scissors.

Mrs. Hale: (Lifting the silk.) Oh, Mrs. Peters—its— *(Mrs. Peters bends closer.)*

Mrs. Peters: It's the bird.

Mrs. Hale: (Jumping up.) But, Mrs. Peters—look at it! It's neck! Look at its neck! It's all—other side *to*.

Mrs. Peters: Somebody—wrung—its—neck.

(Their eyes meet. A look of growing comprehension, of horror. Steps are heard outside. Mrs. Hale slips box under quilt pieces, and sinks into her chair. Enter Sheriff and County Attorney. Mrs. Peters rises.)

County Attorney: (As one turning from serious things to little pleasantries.) Well, ladies, have you decided whether she was going to quilt it or knot it?

Mrs. Peters: We think she was going to—knot it.

County Attorney: Well, that's interesting, I'm sure. *(Seeing the bird-cage.)* Has the bird flown?

Mrs. Hale: (Putting more quilt pieces over the box.) We think the—cat got it.

County Attorney: (Preoccupied.) Is there a cat?

(Mrs. Hale glances in a quick covert way at Mrs. Peters.)

Mrs. Peters: Well, not *now*. They're superstitious, you know. They leave.

County Attorney: (To Sheriff Peters, continuing an interrupted conversation.) No sign at all of anyone having come from the outside. Their own rope. Now let's go up again and go over it piece by piece. *(They start upstairs.)* It would have to have been someone who knew just the—

(Mrs. Peters sits down. The two women sit there not looking at one another, but as if peering into something and at the same time holding back. When they talk now it is in the manner of feeling their way over strange ground, as if afraid of what they are saying, but as if they can not help saying it.)

Mrs. Hale: She liked the bird. She was going to bury it in that pretty box.

Mrs. Peters: (In a whisper.) When I was a girl—my kitten—there was a boy took a hatchet, and before my eyes—and before I could get there—*(Covers her face an instant.)* If they hadn't held me back I would have—*(Catches herself, looks upstairs where steps are heard, falters weakly)*—hurt him.

Mrs. Hale: (With a slow look around her.) I wonder how it would seem never to have had any children around. *(Pause.)* No, Wright wouldn't like the bird—a thing that sang. She used to sing. He killed that, too.

Mrs. Peters: (Moving uneasily.) We don't know who killed the bird.

Mrs. Hale: I knew John Wright.

Mrs. Peters: It was an awful thing was done in this house that night, Mrs. Hale. Killing a man while he slept, slipping a rope around his neck that choked the life out of him.

Mrs. Hale: His neck. Choked the life out of him.

(Her hand goes out and rests on the bird-cage.)

Mrs. Peters: (With rising voice.) We don't know who killed him. We don't *know*.

Mrs. Hale: (Her own feeling not interrupted.) If there'd been years and years of nothing, then a bird to sing to you, it would be awful—still, after the bird was still.

Mrs. Peters: (Something within her speaking.) I know what stillness is. When we homesteaded in Dakota, and my first baby died—after he was two years old, and me with no other then—

Mrs. Hale: (Moving.) How soon do you suppose they'll be through, looking for the evidence?

Mrs. Peters: I know what stillness is. *(Pulling herself back.)* The law has got to punish crime, Mrs. Hale.

Mrs. Hale: (Not as if answering that.) I wish you'd seen Minnie Foster when she wore a white dress with blue ribbons and stood up there in the choir and sang. *(A look around the room.)* Oh, I *wish* I'd come over here once in a while! That was a crime! That was a crime! Who's going to punish that?

Mrs. Peters: (Looking upstairs.) We mustn't—take on.

Mrs. Hale: I might have known she needed help! I know how things can be—for women. I tell you, it's queer, Mrs. Peters. We live close together and we live far apart. We all go through the same things—it's all just a different kind of the same thing. *(Brushes her eyes, noticing the bottle of fruit, reaches out for it.)* If I was you I wouldn't tell her her fruit was gone. Tell her it *ain't*. Tell her it's all right. Take this in to prove it to her. She—she may never know whether it was broke or not.

Mrs. Peters: (Takes the bottle, looks about for something to wrap it in; takes petticoat from the clothes brought from the other room, very nervously begins winding this around the bottle. In a false voice.) My, it's a good thing the men couldn't hear us. Wouldn't they just laugh! Getting all stirred up over a little thing like a—dead canary. As if that could have anything to do with—with—wouldn't they *laugh*!

(The men are heard coming down stairs.)

Mrs. Hale: (Under her breath.) Maybe they would—maybe they wouldn't.

County Attorney: No, Peters, it's all perfectly clear except a reason for doing it. But you know juries when it comes to women. If there was some definite thing. Something to show—something to make a story about—a thing that would connect up with this strange way of doing it—

(The women's eyes meet for an instant. Enter Hale from outer door.)

Hale: Well, I've got the team around. Pretty cold out there.

County Attorney: I'm going to stay here a while by myself. *(To the Sheriff.)* You can send Frank out for me, can't you? I want to go over everything. I'm not satisfied that we can't do better.

Sheriff: Do you want to see what Mrs. Peters is going to take in?

(The Lawyer goes to the table, picks up the apron, laughs.)

County Attorney: Oh, I guess they're not very dangerous things the ladies have picked out. *(Moves a few things about, disturbing the quilt pieces which cover the box. Steps back.)* No, Mrs. Peters doesn't need supervising. For that matter, a sheriff's wife is married to the law. Ever think of it that way, Mrs. Peters?

Mrs. Peters: Not—just that way.

Sheriff: *(Chuckling.)* Married to the law. *(Moves toward the other room.)* I just want you to come in here a minute, George. We ought to take a look at these windows.

County Attorney: *(Scoffingly.)* Oh, windows!

Sheriff: We'll be right out, Mr. Hale.

(Hale goes outside. The Sheriff follows the County Attorney into the other room. Then Mrs. Hale rises, hands tight together, looking intensely at Mrs. Peters, whose eyes make a slow turn, finally meeting Mrs. Hale's. A moment Mrs. Hale holds her, then her own eyes point the way to where the box is concealed. Suddenly Mrs. Peters throws back quilt pieces and tries to put the box in the bag she is wearing. It is too big. She opens box, starts to take bird out, cannot touch it, goes to pieces, stands there helpless. Sound of a knob turning in the other room. Mrs. Hale snatches the box and puts it in the pocket of her big coat. Enter County Attorney and Sheriff.)

County Attorney: *(Facetiously.)* Well, Henry, at least we found out that she was not going to quilt it. She was going to—what is it you call it, ladies?

Mrs. Hale: *(Her hand against her pocket.)* We call it—knot it, Mr. Henderson.

(CURTAIN)

1916

Sherwood Anderson
1876–1941

Sherwood Anderson was born on September 13, 1876, in Camden, Ohio, a small town near the Kentucky border. During the first eighteen years of his life, his family moved from one Ohio town to the next, as his father, a harness maker and inveterate storyteller whom Anderson described as a "colorful no account," shifted from job to job. Anderson's formal education was brief and spotty. As a boy he worked at many jobs—as a newsboy, a housepainter, a stableboy, a farmhand, and a laborer in a bicycle factory. At fourteen, when his mother died, he dropped out of school altogether. When he was eighteen, his family settled in Clyde, Ohio, the town that he would later imaginatively transform into Winesburg, Ohio, the fictional setting that ensured his literary reputation. In 1896, however, after only two years in Clyde, Anderson moved to Chicago, where he worked as a warehouse laborer. In 1898 he enlisted in the army during the Spanish-American War and served briefly in Cuba. Back from the army, he drifted into business, first as an advertising copywriter in Chicago and later as the manager of two paint firms in Ohio. By 1904, when he married the first of his four wives, he was living the life of a successful businessman.

At the same time, Anderson was secretly writing fiction and building toward a crisis. Everything came to a head on November 27, 1912, when suddenly, in the middle of dictating a letter, he walked out of his office in Elyria, Ohio, and disappeared for several days. He turned up in Cleveland disturbed, disheveled, and disoriented. He later dramatized this apparently confused gesture as an artistic repudiation of the business world. It also became an integral part of his literary achievement. The critic Clifton Fadiman remarked of Anderson that "the dramatization of this moment is his major contribution to the interpretation of American life. . . . He is obsessed with the experience of sudden self-discovery."

Having recovered from his nervous collapse, Anderson moved again to Chicago, hoping this time to combine a career writing advertising copy with a career writing fiction. But he was now moving steadily toward art. He was reading receptively the work of Sigmund Freud, D. H. Lawrence, and Gertrude Stein. He was also receiving encouragement from some of the leading figures of the Chicago "Renaissance," including Theodore Dreiser, Ben Hecht, Floyd Dell, and Carl Sandburg. Soon he began publishing verse and short fiction in *The Little Review, Poetry, The Masses,* and *The Seven Arts.* In 1916 he published his first novel, *Windy McPherson's Son,* an autobiographical story based on memories of his father and his own recent disillusionment with the world of business. A second novel, *Marching Men* (1917), dealt with a militant brotherhood of industrial workers. In 1918 Anderson published a volume of poems in the Carl Sandburg manner, *Mid-American Chants.*

In the late fall of 1915 Anderson began writing the 23 tales that would compose the only one of his books still regarded as a major achievement, *Winesburg, Ohio* (1919). By the middle of the next year he had finished most of "The Tales and the Persons" that make up his "Book of the Grotesque." Thematically, Anderson's Winesburg tales (the name of the fictional town suggests a combination of the dreamy and the mundane) anticipate the wasteland image explored by T. S. Eliot, Ernest Hemingway, F. Scott Fitzgerald, and Nathanael West. The truncation of life that his characters experience becomes a kind of living death. Their senses seem anesthetized, their sensibilities numbed, their spirits shrunken. Though the feeling of small-town paralysis derived directly from Anderson's experiences, *Winesburg, Ohio* was structurally indebted to such collections as Ivan Turgenev's *A Sportsman's Sketches* (1852), James Joyce's *Dubliners* (1914), and particularly Edgar Lee Masters's *Spoon River Anthology* (1915). Anderson acknowledged the influence of Gertrude Stein's *Three Lives* (1909)— "She is making new, strange and to my ears sweet combinations of words"—in the development of his repetitive, colloquial prose style. So deliberately did Anderson resist fancy writing ("I have had a great fear of phrase-making") that his prose might be said to approach a poetry of inarticulation. Nearly all of his characters struggle at self-expression and, as stories like "Hands" and "Mother" clearly reveal, live in a conversational world of unfocused feelings and awkward silences.

Winesburg, Ohio has had an enormous influence on the development of the American short story. Its sequential pattern anticipates such collections as Jean Toomer's *Cane*, Ernest Hemingway's *In Our Time*, William Faulkner's *Go Down, Moses*, and more recently, John Barth's *Lost in the Funhouse*. Its preoccupation with American eccentrics and "grotesques" foreshadowed the characterizations of such later short-story writers as Flannery O'Connor and Carson McCullers. And its spare poetry of ordinary American speech anticipates the recent working-class tales of Raymond Carver and Bobbie Ann Mason. Anderson also demonstrated in his stories and critical essays an aesthetic resistance to the literary slickness of contrived plots: No Americans, he wrote, "lived, felt, or talked as the average American novel makes them live, feel, or talk and as for the plot short stories of the magazines—those bastard children of de Maupassant, Poe, and O. Henry—it was certain that there were no plot stories ever lived in any life."

As much as any writer of his time, Anderson combined the fate of being a flawed writer ("For all my egotism," he remarked late in his life, "I know I am but a minor figure") and a major force ("He was the father of my generation of American writers and the tradition of American writing which our successors will carry on," remarked William Faulkner). None of Anderson's subsequent books had the literary impact of *Winesburg, Ohio,* though collections of short stories such as *The Triumph of the Egg* (1921), *Horses and Men* (1923), and *Death in the Woods and Other Stories* (1933) contain a number of excellent tales. Anderson continued to write novels, the most successful of which is *Poor White* (1920), the story of an aspiring midwestern inventor who realizes that his industrial genius is destroying the environment. His later novels include *Many Marriages* (1923), *Dark Laughter* (1925), *Beyond Desire* (1932), and *Kit Brandon* (1936). Anderson also published several collections of essays on American industrial and rural conditions, *Perhaps Women* (1931), *Puzzled America* (1935), and *Home Town* (1940), and a collection of literary profiles, *No Swank* (1934).

In the summer of 1922, a year after he had traveled to Europe and met Gertrude Stein, Anderson was finally able to give up copywriting. In 1924 he moved with his third wife to Marion, Virginia, where he edited two local newspapers, one Democratic and the other Republican. He collected his editorials in *Hello, Towns* (1929). In 1941, while on a State Department goodwill tour of South America, he died of peritonitis caused by his accidentally having swallowed a fragment of a toothpick at a cocktail party.

One explanation of the discrepancy between Anderson's achievement and his influence has to do with his origins. Many critics and readers were easterners who nevertheless believed, as Van Wyck Brooks put it, "that the heart of America lay in the West" and that "Sherwood was the essence of his West." A second explanation lies in the overriding importance of the theme and scene that Anderson sought to explore: the loneliness of the modern world as manifested in the social, cultural, and spiritual impoverishment of small-town America. The isolation that haunts Anderson's characters is religious as well as social; felt as a form of orphanhood, a kind of ultimate separation, it leads them almost inevitably to flight that is undertaken as a kind of return. The struggle his characters wage, they wage in the name of reestablishing ties with a community, a family, or a self that they have somehow lost. A third explanation lies in Anderson's capacity for deliberate self-dramatization. Like Walt Whitman, Anderson viewed himself as a composite of us all; he was the American as writer. In the tales he told about himself, in his three volumes of autobiographical writing, *A Story-Teller's Story* (1924), *Tar: A Midwest Childhood* (1926), and the posthumous *Sherwood Anderson's Memoirs* (1942), and in his letters, he insisted on mixing his life and art, on making himself into a fictional character for his time as well as for himself. In this, too, his motives were mixed: They were social and even didactic as well as personal and artistic. Anderson wanted to teach us, among other things, the value of dropping out and breaking away. "I hardly know what I can teach except anti-success," he wrote his brother Karl in 1931. Most of all, Anderson wanted to teach us that the purpose of art, like the purpose of love, is self-transcendence. "I think the whole glory of writing lies in the fact that it forces us out of ourselves and into the lives of others," he said later in his life. "In the end the real writer becomes a lover."

Further Reading:
I. Howe, *Sherwood Anderson*, 1951.
R. Burbank, *Sherwood Anderson*, 1964.
B. Weber, *Sherwood Anderson*, 1964.

R. L. White, ed., *The Achievement of Sherwood Anderson: Essays in Criticism*, 1966.

Text:
"The Egg" from *The Triumph of the Egg*, 1921.

The Egg*

My father was, I am sure, intended by nature to be a cheerful, kindly man. Until he was thirty-four years old he worked as a farm-hand for a man named Thomas Butterworth whose place lay near the town of Bidwell, Ohio. He had then a horse of his own and on Saturday evenings drove into town to spend a few hours in social intercourse with other farm-hands. In town he drank several glasses of beer and stood about in Ben Head's saloon—crowded on Saturday evenings with visiting farm-hands. Songs were sung and glasses thumped on the bar. At ten o'clock father drove home along a lonely country road, made his horse comfortable for the night and himself went to bed, quite happy in his position in life. He had at that time no notion of trying to rise in the world.

It was in the spring of his thirty-fifth year that father married my mother, then a country school-teacher, and in the following spring I came wriggling and crying into the world. Something happened to the two people. They became ambitious. The American passion for getting up in the world took possession of them.

It may have been that mother was responsible. Being a school-teacher she had no doubt read books and magazines. She had, I presume, read of how Garfield, Lincoln, and other Americans rose from poverty to fame and greatness and as I lay beside her—in the days of her lying-in—she may have dreamed that I would some day rule men and

---

* First published in 1920 in *The Dial* as "The Triumph of the Egg."

cities. At any rate she induced father to give up his place as a farm-hand, sell his horse and embark on an independent enterprise of his own. She was a tall silent woman with a long nose and troubled grey eyes. For herself she wanted nothing. For father and myself she was incurably ambitious.

The first venture into which the two people went turned out badly. They rented ten acres of poor stony land on Griggs's Road, eight miles from Bidwell, and launched into chicken raising. I grew into boyhood on the place and got my first impressions of life there. From the beginning they were impressions of disaster and if, in my turn, I am a gloomy man inclined to see the darker side of life, I attribute it to the fact that what should have been for me the happy joyous days of childhood were spent on a chicken farm.

One unversed in such matters can have no notion of the many and tragic things that can happen to a chicken. It is born out of an egg, lives for a few weeks as a tiny fluffy thing such as you will see pictured on Easter cards, then becomes hideously naked, eats quantities of corn and meal bought by the sweat of your father's brow, gets diseases called pip, cholera, and other names, stands looking with stupid eyes at the sun, becomes sick and dies. A few hens and now and then a rooster, intended to serve God's mysterious ends, struggle through to maturity. The hens lay eggs out of which come other chickens and the dreadful cycle is thus made complete. It is all unbelievably complex. Most philosophers must have been raised on chicken farms. One hopes for so much from a chicken and is so dreadfully disillusioned. Small chickens, just setting out on the journey of life, look so bright and alert and they are in fact so dreadfully stupid. They are so much like people they mix one up in one's judgments of life. If disease does not kill them they wait until your expectations are thoroughly aroused and then walk under the wheels of a wagon—to go squashed and dead back to their maker. Vermin infest their youth, and fortunes must be spent for curative powders. In later life I have seen how a literature has been built up on the subject of fortunes to be made out of the raising of chickens. It is intended to be read by the gods who have just eaten of the tree of the knowledge of good and evil. It is a hopeful literature and declares that much may be done by simple ambitious people who own a few hens. Do not be led astray by it. It was not written for you. Go hunt for gold on the frozen hills of Alaska, put your faith in the honesty of a politician, believe if you will that the world is daily growing better and that good will triumph over evil, but do not read and believe the literature that is written concerning the hen. It was not written for you.

I, however, digress. My tale does not primarily concern itself with the hen. If correctly told it will center on the egg. For ten years my father and mother struggled to make our chicken farm pay and then they gave up that struggle and began another. They moved into the town of Bidwell, Ohio and embarked in the restaurant business. After ten years of worry with incubators that did not hatch, and with tiny—and in their own way lovely—balls of fluff that passed on into semi-naked pullethood and from that into dead henhood, we threw all aside and packing our belongings on a wagon drove down Griggs's Road toward Bidwell, a tiny caravan of hope looking for a new place from which to start on our upward journey through life.

We must have been a sad looking lot, not, I fancy, unlike refugees fleeing from a battlefield. Mother and I walked in the road. The wagon that contained our goods had been borrowed for the day from Mr. Albert Griggs, a neighbor. Out of its sides stuck the legs of cheap chairs and at the back of the pile of beds, tables, and boxes filled with kitchen utensils was a crate of live chickens, and on top of that the baby carriage in which I had been wheeled about in my infancy. Why we stuck to the baby carriage I don't know. It was unlikely other children would be born and the wheels were broken. People who have few possessions cling tightly to those they have. That is one of the facts that make life so discouraging.

Father rode on top of the wagon. He was then a bald-headed man of forty-five, a little fat and from long association with mother and the chickens he had become habitually silent and discouraged. All during our ten years on the chicken farm he had worked as a laborer on neighboring farms and most of the money he had earned had been spent for remedies to cure chicken diseases, on Wilmer's White Wonder Cholera Cure or Professor Bidlow's Egg Producer or some other preparations that mother found advertised in the poultry papers. There were two little patches of hair on father's head just above his ears. I remember that as a child I used to sit looking at him when he had gone to sleep in a chair before the stove on Sunday afternoons in the winter. I had at that time already begun to read books and have notions of my own and the bald path that led over the top of his head was, I fancied, something like a broad road, such a road as Caesar might have made on which to lead his legions out of Rome and into the wonders of an unknown world. The tufts of hair that grew above father's ears were, I thought, like forests. I fell into a half-sleeping, half-waking state and dreamed I was a tiny thing going along the road into a far beautiful place where there were no chicken farms and where life was a happy eggless affair.

One might write a book concerning our flight from the chicken farm into town. Mother and I walked the entire eight miles—she to be sure that nothing fell from the wagon and I to see the wonders of the world. On the seat of the wagon beside father was his greatest treasure. I will tell you of that.

On a chicken farm where hundreds and even thousands of chickens come out of eggs surprising things sometimes happen. Grotesques are born out of eggs as out of people. The accident does not often occur—perhaps once in a thousand births. A chicken is, you see, born that has four legs, two pairs of wings, two heads or what not. The things do not live. They go quickly back to the hand of their maker that has for a moment trembled. The fact that the poor little things could not live was one of the tragedies of life to father. He had some sort of notion that if he could but bring into henhood or roosterhood a five-legged hen or a two-headed rooster his fortune would be made. He dreamed of taking the wonder about to county fairs and of growing rich by exhibiting it to other farm-hands.

At any rate he saved all the little monstrous things that had been born on our chicken farm. They were preserved in alcohol and put each in its own glass bottle. These he had carefully put into a box and on our journey into town it was carried on the wagon seat beside him. He drove the horses with one hand and with the other clung to the box. When we got to our destination the box was taken down at once and the bottles removed. All during our days as keepers of a restaurant in the town of Bidwell, Ohio, the grotesques in their little glass bottles sat on a shelf back of the counter. Mother sometimes protested but father was a rock on the subject of his treasure. The grotesques were, he declared, valuable. People, he said, liked to look at strange and wonderful things.

Did I say that we embarked in the restaurant business in the town of Bidwell, Ohio? I exaggerated a little. The town itself lay at the foot of a low hill and on the shore of a small river. The railroad did not run through the town and the station was a mile away to the north at a place called Pickleville. There had been a cider mill and pickle factory at the station, but before the time of our coming they had both gone out of business. In the morning and in the evening busses came down to the station along a road called Turner's Pike from the hotel on the main street of Bidwell. Our going to the out of the way place to embark in the restaurant business was mother's idea. She talked of it for a year and then one day went off and rented an empty store building opposite the railroad station. It was her idea that the restaurant would be profitable. Travelling men, she said, would be always waiting around to take trains out of town and town people would come to the station to await incoming trains. They would come to the restaurant to buy pieces of pie and drink coffee. Now that I am older I know that she had another motive in going. She was ambitious for me. She wanted me to rise in the world, to get into a town school and become a man of the towns.

At Pickleville father and mother worked hard as they always had done. At first there was the necessity of putting our place into shape to be a restaurant. That took a month. Father built a shelf on which he put tins of vegetables. He painted a sign on which he put his name in large red letters. Below his name was the sharp command—"EAT HERE"—that was so seldom obeyed. A show case was bought and filled with cigars and tobacco. Mother scrubbed the floor and the walls of the room. I went to school in the town and was glad to be away from the farm and from the presence of the discouraged, sad-looking chickens. Still I was not very joyous. In the evening I walked home from school along Turner's Pike and remembered the children I had seen playing in the town school yard. A troop of little girls had gone hopping about and singing. I tried that. Down along the frozen road I went hopping solemnly on one leg. "Hippity Hop To The Barber Shop," I sang shrilly. Then I stopped and looked doubtfully about. I was afraid of being seen in my gay mood. It must have seemed to me that I was doing a thing that should not be done by one who, like myself, had been raised on a chicken farm where death was a daily visitor.

Mother decided that our restaurant should remain open at night. At ten in the evening a passenger train went north past our door followed by a local freight. The freight crew had switching to do in Pickleville and when the work was done they came to our restaurant for hot coffee and food. Sometimes one of them ordered a fried egg. In the morning at four they returned north-bound and again visited us. A little trade began to grow up. Mother slept at night and during the day tended the restaurant and fed our boarders while father slept. He slept in the same bed mother had occupied during the night and I went off to the town of Bidwell and to school. During the long nights, while mother and I slept, father cooked meats that were to go into sandwiches for the lunch baskets of our boarders. Then an idea in regard to getting up in the world came into his head. The American spirit took hold of him. He also became ambitious.

In the long nights when there was little to do father had time to think. That was his undoing. He decided that he had in the past been an unsuccessful man because he had not been cheerful enough and that in the future he would adopt a cheerful outlook on life. In the early morning he came upstairs and got into bed with mother. She woke and the two talked. From my bed in the corner I listened.

It was father's idea that both he and mother should try to entertain the people who came to eat at our restaurant. I cannot now remember his words, but he gave the impression of one about to become in some obscure way a kind of public entertainer.

When people, particularly young people from the town of Bidwell, came into our place, as on very rare occasions they did, bright entertaining conversation was to be made. From father's words I gathered that something of the jolly inn-keeper effect was to be sought. Mother must have been doubtful from the first, but she said nothing discouraging. It was father's notion that a passion for the company of himself and mother would spring up in the breasts of the younger people of the town of Bidwell. In the evening bright happy groups would come singing down Turner's Pike. They would troop shouting with joy and laughter into our place. There would be song and festivity. I do not mean to give the impression that father spoke so elaborately of the matter. He was as I have said an uncommunicative man. "They want some place to go. I tell you they want some place to go," he said over and over. That was as far as he got. My own imagination has filled in the blanks.

For two or three weeks this notion of father's invaded our house. We did not talk much, but in our daily lives tried earnestly to make smiles take the place of glum looks. Mother smiled at the boarders and I, catching the infection, smiled at our cat. Father became a little feverish in his anxiety to please. There was no doubt, lurking somewhere in him, a touch of the spirit of the showman. He did not waste much of his ammunition on the railroad men he served at night but seemed to be waiting for a young man or woman from Bidwell to come in to show what he could do. On the counter in the restaurant there was a wire basket kept always filled with eggs, and it must have been before his eyes when the idea of being entertaining was born in his brain. There was something pre-natal about the way eggs kept themselves connected with the development of his idea. At any rate an egg ruined his new impulse in life. Late one night I was awakened by a roar of anger coming from father's throat. Both mother and I sat upright in our beds. With trembling hands she lighted a lamp that stood on a table by her head. Downstairs the front door of our restaurant went shut with a bang and in a few minutes father tramped up the stairs. He held an egg in his hand and his hand trembled as though he were having a chill. There was a half insane light in his eyes. As he stood glaring at us I was sure he intended throwing the egg at either mother or me. Then he laid it gently on the table beside the lamp and dropped on his knees beside mother's bed. He began to cry like a boy and I, carried away by his grief, cried with him. The two of us filled the little upstairs room with our wailing voices. It is ridiculous, but of the picture we made I can remember only the fact that mother's hand continually stroked the bald path that ran across the top of his head. I have forgotten what mother said to him and how she induced him to tell her of what had happened downstairs. His explanation also has gone out of my mind. I remember only my own grief and fright and the shiny path over father's head glowing in the lamp light as he knelt by the bed.

As to what happened downstairs. For some unexplainable reason I know the story as well as though I had been a witness to my father's discomfiture. One in time gets to know many unexplainable things. On that evening young Joe Kane, son of a merchant of Bidwell, came to Pickleville to meet his father, who was expected on the ten o'clock evening train from the South. The train was three hours late and Joe came into our place to loaf about and to wait for its arrival. The local freight train came in and the freight crew were fed. Joe was left alone in the restaurant with father.

From the moment he came into our place the Bidwell young man must have been puzzled by my father's actions. It was his notion that father was angry at him for hanging around. He noticed that the restaurant keeper was apparently disturbed by his presence and he thought of going out. However, it began to rain and he did not fancy the long walk to town and back. He bought a five-cent cigar and ordered a cup of coffee. He had a newspaper in his pocket and took it out and began to read. "I'm waiting for the evening train. It's late," he said apologetically.

For a long time father, whom Joe Kane had never seen before, remained silently gazing at his visitor. He was no doubt suffering from an attack of stage fright. As so often happens in life he had thought so much and so often of the situation that now confronted him that he was somewhat nervous in its presence.

For one thing, he did not know what to do with his hands. He thrust one of them nervously over the counter and shook hands with Joe Kane. "How-de-do," he said. Joe Kane put his newspaper down and stared at him. Father's eye lighted on the basket of eggs that sat on the counter and he began to talk. "Well," he began hesitatingly, "well, you have heard of Christopher Columbus, eh?" He seemed to be angry. "That Christopher Columbus was a cheat," he declared emphatically. "He talked of making an egg stand on its end. He talked, he did, and then he went and broke the end of the egg."

My father seemed to his visitor to be beside himself at the duplicity of Christopher Columbus. He muttered and swore. He declared it was wrong to teach children that Christopher Columbus was a great man when, after all, he cheated at the critical moment. He had declared he would make an egg stand on end and then when his bluff had been called he had done a trick. Still grumbling at Columbus, father took an egg from the basket on the counter and began to walk up and down. He rolled the egg between the palms of his hands. He smiled genially. He began to mumble words regarding the effect to be produced on an egg by the electricity that comes out of the human body. He declared that without breaking its shell and by virtue of rolling it back and forth in his hands he could stand the egg on its end. He explained that the warmth of his hands and the gentle rolling movement he gave the egg created a new centre of gravity, and Joe Kane was mildly interested. "I have handled thousands of eggs," father said. "No one knows more about eggs than I do."

He stood the egg on the counter and it fell on its side. He tried the trick again and again, each time rolling the egg between the palms of his hands and saying the words regarding the wonders of electricity and the laws of gravity. When after a half hour's effort he did succeed in making the egg stand for a moment he looked up to find that his visitor was no longer watching. By the time he had succeeded in calling Joe Kane's attention to the success of his effort the egg had again rolled over and lay on its side.

Afire with the showman's passion and at the same time a good deal disconcerted by the failure of his first effort, father now took the bottles containing the poultry monstrosities down from their place on the shelf and began to show them to his visitor. "How would you like to have seven legs and two heads like this fellow?" he asked, exhibiting the most remarkable of his treasures. A cheerful smile played over his face. He reached over the counter and tried to slap Joe Kane on the shoulder as he had seen men do in Ben Head's saloon when he was a young farm-hand and drove to town on Saturday evenings. His visitor was made a little ill by the sight of the body of the terribly deformed bird floating in the alcohol in the bottle and got up to go. Coming from behind the counter father took hold of the young man's arm and led him back to his seat. He grew a little angry and for a moment had to turn his face away and force himself to smile. Then he put the bottles back on the shelf. In an outburst of generosity he fairly compelled Joe Kane to have a fresh cup of coffee and another cigar at his expense. Then he took a pan and filling it with vinegar, taken from a jug that sat beneath the counter, he declared himself about to do a new trick. "I will heat this egg in this pan of vinegar," he said. "Then I will put it through the neck of a bottle without breaking the shell. When the egg is inside the bottle it will resume its normal shape and the shell will become hard again. Then I will give the bottle with the egg in it to you. You can take it about with you wherever you go. People will want to know how you got the egg in the bottle. Don't tell them. Keep them guessing. That is the way to have fun with this trick."

Father grinned and winked at his visitor. Joe Kane decided that the man who confronted him was mildly insane but harmless. He drank the cup of coffee that had been given him and began to read his paper again. When the egg had been heated in vinegar father carried it on a spoon to the counter and going into a back room got an empty bottle. He was angry because his visitor did not watch him as he began to do his trick, but nevertheless went cheerfully to work. For a long time he struggled, trying to get the egg to go through the neck of the bottle. He put the pan of vinegar back on the stove, intending to reheat the egg, then picked it up and burned his fingers. After a second bath in the hot vinegar the shell of the egg had been softened a little but not enough for his purpose. He worked and worked and a spirit of desperate determination took possession of him. When he thought that at last the trick was about to be consummated the delayed train came in at the station and Joe Kane started to go nonchalantly out at the door. Father made a last desperate effort to conquer the egg and make it do the thing that would establish his reputation as one who knew how to entertain guests who came into his restaurant. He worried the egg. He attempted to be somewhat rough with it. He swore and the sweat stood out on his forehead. The egg broke under his hand. When the contents spurted over his clothes, Joe Kane, who had stopped at the door, turned and laughed.

A roar of anger rose from my father's throat. He danced and shouted a string of inarticulate words. Grabbing another egg from the basket on the counter, he threw it, just missing the head of the young man as he dodged through the door and escaped.

Father came upstairs to mother and me with an egg in his hand. I do not know what he intended to do. I imagine he had some idea of destroying it, of destroying all eggs, and that he intended to let mother and me see him begin. When, however, he got into the presence of mother something happened to him. He laid the egg gently on the table and dropped on his knees by the bed as I have already explained. He later decided to close the restaurant for the night and to come upstairs and get into bed. When he did so he blew out the light and after much muttered conversation both he and mother went to sleep. I suppose I went to sleep also, but my sleep was troubled. I awoke at dawn and for a long time looked at the egg that lay on the table. I wondered why eggs had to be and why from the egg came the hen who again laid the egg. The question got into my blood. It has stayed there, I imagine, because I am the son of my father. At any rate, the problem remains unsolved in my mind. And that, I conclude, is but another evidence of the complete and final triumph of the egg—at least as far as my family is concerned.

1920

Carl Sandburg
1878–1967

With his fellow Chicago poet Edgar Lee Masters, Carl Sandburg was one of the early rebels of the modern period, reacting against the genteel tradition in the name of Walt Whitman and America. Writing in free verse and about such unpoetic subjects as the vigorous, even violent poor of Chicago, the "Hog Butcher for the World," he sought to be a poet of the people in the Whitman tradition. Sandburg was strongly populist in his political sympathies; he celebrated grass-roots American characters and circumstances, often in poems that drew clearly on Whitman for their verse technique. "Chicago," for example, teems with people and attempts to recreate, in a modern and stridently vitalist way, the energy of Whitman's chants. His main concern as a poet was the vivid presentation of unrefined reality, and poems like "Fog" resemble the work of the Imagists in their brevity, their juxtaposition of images to catch objective reality, and their clean, simple language. Sandburg characteristically wrote other kinds of poems as well—most notably poems of social protest, such as "Graceland," and emotional, reflective poems, such as "Cool Tombs" and "Grass."

Carl Sandburg was born in 1878 to a family of Swedish immigrants in Illinois, where his father was employed in the railroad yards. Raised in poverty, Sandburg was forced to quit school at the age of thirteen to earn money at a variety of odd jobs— milkman, porter, dishwasher. After the Spanish-American war, in which he volunteered for the army and was sent to Puerto Rico, he enrolled in Lombard College, supporting himself while there by working for the local fire department; he left abruptly in 1902 without graduating. He again found work of various sorts, including a stint as salesman of stereoscopic photographs. He even spent some time riding the rails with hoboes and served a short jail term in Pittsburgh. His experiences helped reinforce his strong populist convictions, and in 1907 and 1908 he worked for the Social Democratic party as journalist and organizer. Meanwhile he was trying to settle down, and in 1908 he married the sister of the photographer Edward Steichen.

In 1914 Harriet Monroe published a group of his poems, entitled "Chicago Poems," in *Poetry;* two years later a book with the same title appeared. It marked the start of Sandburg's fame, which by the end of his life was considerable. *Cornhuskers* appeared in 1918, followed by *Smoke and Steel* (1920), *Slabs of the Sunburnt West* (1922), and *The People, Yes* (1936). His six-volume biography of Abraham Lincoln (1940) earned him the Pulitzer Prize for history. Other prose writings include children's stories (beginning with *Rootabaga Stories,* 1922), historical commentary (*Storm over the Land,* 1942, and *Home Front Memos,* 1943), and a novel (*Remembrance Rock,* 1950). The poet who toured the country, reading and singing folksongs while accompanying himself on guitar, interspersing his performances with homespun philosophizing, became a celebrated public figure. He was asked to be a candidate for the presidency in 1940, and his birthplace was made a museum that same year; his 75th birthday was declared Carl Sandburg Day by the governor of Illinois. Sandburg received the Presidential Medal of Freedom in 1964.

He was not admired, on the whole, by his fellow poets. Ezra Pound once suggested that the University of Pennsylvania set up a fellowship for creative ability; he had Sandburg in mind as a possible recipient, for he feared Sandburg would remain imperfect for lack of culture. William Carlos Williams also criticized Sandburg's artlessness, but Frost's observation, after their first meeting, was the most acid:

> We've been having a dose of Carl Sandburg. He's another person I find it hard to do justice to. He was possibly [three] hours in town and he spent one of those washing his white hair and toughening his expression for his public performance. His mandolin pleased some people, his poetry a very few, and his infantile talk none. His affectations have almost buried him out of sight. He is probably the most artificial and studied ruffian the world has had.

Often as artless in life as he appeared to be in his writing, Sandburg had walked away from that meeting feeling that a friendship had begun. "Met Frost," he wrote, "about the strongest, loneliest, friendliest personality among the poets today; I'm going to write him once a year; and feel the love of him every day."

In a tradition in which the poet as primitive occupies a central, if complicated, place, Sandburg might have become an important figure. But, from Whitman on, to be "one of the roughs," to be artless in American literature, has been a creation of highly self-conscious art. By those standards Sandburg was lacking. Where others sought to create the illusion of unsophisticated spontaneity, Sandburg *was* artistically unsophisticated; almost paradoxically, he therefore seemed, at least to an observer like Frost, affected. Behind Pound's and Williams's apparently casual Imagist poems lay an almost obsessive concern with craft and, in Pound's case in particular, considerable acquaintance with the literary past that he sought to make new. Behind Whitman's chants of America lay far more than the desire to present American figures in all their vitality. The Americans Whitman wrote of, including himself in his own complicated self-portrayal, were part of a comprehensive vision of divine, natural, social, and psychological reality, and Whitman's language ranged from the demotic to the sublime in his attempt to give flesh to this vision. Against that achievement, Sandburg's work as a whole seems notable primarily for its part in the modernist revolution in literature. It is best appreciated for the real power of some of the individual poems, where Sandburg achieved a memorable freshness and vigor of expression.

Further Reading:

B. Weirick, *From Whitman to Sandburg*, 1924.
K. Detzer, *Carl Sandburg*, 1941.
H. Durnell, *The America of Carl Sandburg*, 1945.
R. Crowder, *Carl Sandburg*, 1964.
J. Haas, *Carl Sandburg*, 1967.
N. Callahan, *Carl Sandburg, Lincoln of Our Literature*, 1969.

G. W. Allen, *Carl Sandburg*, 1972.
N. Callahan, *Carl Sandburg: His Life and Works*, 1987.
P. Niven, *Carl Sandburg: A Biography*, 1991.

Text:

Complete Poems, 1950.

Chicago

Hog Butcher for the World,
Tool Maker, Stacker of Wheat,
Player with Railroads and the Nation's Freight Handler;
Stormy, husky, brawling,
City of the Big Shoulders: 5

They tell me you are wicked and I believe them, for I have seen your painted women
    under the gas lamps luring the farm boys.
And they tell me you are crooked and I answer: Yes, it is true I have seen the gunman
    kill and go free to kill again.
And they tell me you are brutal and my reply is: On the faces of women and children I
    have seen the marks of wanton hunger.
And having answered so I turn once more to those who sneer at this my city, and I give
    them back the sneer and say to them:
Come and show me another city with lifted head singing so proud to be alive and
    coarse and strong and cunning.   10
Flinging magnetic curses amid the toil of piling job on job, here is a tall bold slugger set
    vivid against the little soft cities;
Fierce as a dog with tongue lapping for action, cunning as a savage pitted
  against the wilderness,
    Bareheaded,
    Shoveling,
    Wrecking,   15
    Planning,
    Building, breaking, rebuilding,
Under the smoke, dust all over his mouth, laughing with white teeth,
Under the terrible burden of destiny laughing as a young man laughs,
Laughing even as an ignorant fighter laughs who has never lost a battle,   20
Bragging and laughing that under his wrist is the pulse, and under his ribs the heart of
    the people,
          Laughing!
Laughing the stormy, husky, brawling laughter of Youth, half-naked, sweating, proud
    to be Hog Butcher, Tool Maker, Stacker of Wheat, Player with Railroads and
    Freight Handler to the Nation.

1914

Fog

        The fog comes
        on little cat feet.

It sits looking
over harbor and city
on silent haunches 5
and then moves on.
1916

Cool Tombs

When Abraham Lincoln was shoveled into the tombs, he forgot the copperheads[1]
and the assassin . . . in the dust, in the cool tombs.

And Ulysses Grant lost all thought of con men and Wall Street, cash and
collateral turned ashes . . . in the dust, in the cool tombs.

Pocahontas' body, lovely as a poplar, sweet as a red haw[2] in November or a 5
pawpaw[3] in May, did she wonder? does she remember? . . . in the dust, in
the cool tombs?

Take any streetful of people buying clothes and groceries, cheering a hero or
throwing confetti and blowing tin horns . . . tell me if the lovers are losers . . .
tell me if any get more than the lovers . . . in the dust . . . in the cool tombs. 10
1918

Wallace Stevens
1879–1955

Wallace Stevens's extraordinary first book, *Harmonium* (1923), is one of those books,
like T. S. Eliot's *Prufrock and Other Observations* and Marianne Moore's *Observations,*
by which we have come to define American modernism. Each of these collections
struck a clear new note in formal terms; each was in some way self-displaying.
Stevens's book was not a success; even in 1931, when it was reprinted in an expanded
form, it had only a *succès d'estime*. It was full of odd poems with odd names, like
"Thirteen Ways of Looking at a Blackbird" and "Metaphors of a Magnifico." These
strange-looking poems did not at all resemble the other poems in the volume, which
were recognizably in a traditional vein, with reminiscences of Wordsworth, Keats,
Browning, and Tennyson. Even the seemingly conventional poems, however, had

---

[1] Copperhead: species of poisonous snake, but
here a derogatory epithet for Northerners
who sided with the Confederacy during the
Civil War.

[2] Hawthorn berry.

[3] Fruit of the pawpaw tree, much like papaya.

strange titles like "Le Monocle de Mon Oncle" and "The Comedian as the Letter C." The book did contain one conventionally named poem in a conventional style— "Sunday Morning." But this poem, soon to become very famous, was unconventional in theme; it was a bold declaration of the death of God. In the poem a sensuous aestheticism and agnosticism became substitutes for religious observance.

At least one of those who read the second edition of *Harmonium* when it appeared in the depths of the Great Depression found it shocking that the poet was not addressing the social ills of the day. Stanley Burnshaw's criticism of *Harmonium* in *The New Masses* stung Stevens into his attempts, in *Owl's Clover* (1936) and *Parts of a World* (1942), to treat social issues, including the war in Ethiopia and World War II. But these poems achieved no real stylistic success, and Stevens remained, for the rest of his career, preeminently a poet of the inner life. Nonetheless, Stevens never lost his concern with the social function of poetry, that "postcard from a volcano" addressed to future generations.

Stevens's nature was both religious and romantic; yet the two beliefs he had wholeheartedly entered into, religion and romantic love, both turned out, in his eyes, to be delusory. By these striking evidences of the mind's capacity to delude itself he was led to meditate on the ways that the mind constructs objects and worlds responsive to desire, then sees them shatter and dissolve. The inadequacy of the world to our desire, coupled with our apparently incorrigible pursuit of belief and desire, gave Stevens the great paradox on which he was to brood all his life, the incommensurability of desire and its object. For him, the imagination was what desired; "reality" was what the imagination constructed as a response to desire. "Reality" therefore changes always, as desire is frustrated and a new fictive construct must be shaped yet once again. In this way, new political states are constructed after the collapse of old ones, new art forms are invented when the old become withered, and a new religion replaces the stale religion of the past. Stevens's skepticism about these successive reconstructions of reality comes from his taking the long historical view of the psyche's inner life.

At the same time, though Stevens held seriously to the absolute power of the imagination in the construction of the self and culture, he could treat his theme with gaiety, mockery, and brio. Many of the short poems in *Harmonium* are what we would now call "conceptual art"—the originality of the idea behind them, rather than the linguistic execution, gives them their poetic energy. "Anecdote of the Jar" is such a poem, in its witty reversal of Keats's "Ode on a Grecian Urn." The British poet may have an illustrated marble urn in the British Museum, but the American poet has only a bare gray stoneware jar in the Tennessee wilderness. And whereas the British poet can write in opulent stanzas derived from Shakespeare and the sonnet, the American poet cannot find any diction or stanza form that he is comfortable in. In this respect, Stevens's laconic wit is often turned against himself as the clumsy American trying to utter "heavenly labials in a world of gutturals." In the many volumes following *Harmonium,* Stevens's seriousness of subject and gaiety of treatment continue to create a style peculiar to him, in which he deepens his exploration of the inner life of desire.

During his life as a poet, Stevens carried on a parallel life as a lawyer and insurance executive. He was the son of a Reading, Pennsylvania, lawyer who sent all three of his sons to law school. After three years at Harvard, where he wrote poetry and was president of the literary magazine, Stevens left without taking a degree; his father would not pay for a final year, as only three years of college were required for admission at some law schools. Since the Harvard Law School required four years of college, Stevens could not be admitted there; instead, he entered New York Law School, but after graduation he was relatively unsuccessful in his first professional jobs. At this time in New York, Stevens associated with other young poets, especially his Harvard classmate Alfred Kreymborg, who edited a journal called *Others*. In the *Others* group Stevens met William Carlos Williams and Marianne Moore, a lifelong friend. But as Stevens's professional duties increased, he drifted away from literary society; his move to Hartford, Connecticut, in 1916 removed him from the New York scene. He eventually became a very successful insurance lawyer; at his death he was a vice-president of the Hartford Accident and Indemnity Company.

From 1916 to his death in 1955, Stevens lived in Hartford, and although he made many business trips in America, he never went to Europe. His chief literary life, aside from poetry, took place through correspondence with friends and students of his poetry. His marriage to Elsie Kachel seems to have been unhappy. They had one child, born in 1924, named by Stevens, because her birth came near Christmas, Holly Bright.

By the end of his life, Stevens was recognized as a major poet. His *Collected Poems* (1955) won the National Book Award and a Pulitzer Prize. Although Stevens's daughter has published, in *The Palm at the End of the Mind* (1971), a group of his poems arranged in chronological order, the *Collected Poems* remains the way to know Stevens, to read the poems as he himself arranged them in successive volumes. To Stevens, his *Collected Poems*, when he saw them bound, seemed like the whole world in reduced form, like the terrestrial globe used in geography classes. The volume was "the planet on the table," and he, as poet, was like Shakespeare's airy spirit Ariel: "Ariel was glad he had written his poems."

In 1951 Stevens published a remarkable collection of essays, *The Necessary Angel*. Here, and in essays published after his death in *Opus Posthumous* (1957), he displays the outlines of his theory of poetry. Stevens saw poetry as an "accuracy with respect to the structure of reality"; it was formed by the pressure of the mind against the outside pressure of reality. Imagination was for him a "third planet," comparable in power to the sun and moon, allowing us to see the world in a personal way, different with each mood. Poetry is "the gaiety of language," "a holiday in reality"; but it is also a voice, speaking in "ghostlier demarcations, keener sounds," "of ourselves and of our origins." Stevens's most concise view of the poet's role in society appears in the poem "Academic Discourse at Havana," where he says of the poet:

> As part of nature he is part of us.
> His rarities are ours: may they be fit
> And reconcile us to our selves in those
> True reconcilings, dark, pacific words,
> And the adroiter harmonies of their fall.

Stevens showed American poetry a new way of being American—not by regionalism (though he wrote memorable poems about Connecticut), not by patriotism, not through use of the common vernacular, but by an adaptation of English literature to the American language. In his long poems he invented a new pentameter, freer in its metric than the English model, returning to Whitman's largeness of motion. And in his skeptical, ironic, and whimsical humor he lightens into modern American speculativeness the seriousness of English discursive verse.

Further Reading:

F. Kermode, *Wallace Stevens,* 1961.

J. G. Benziger, *Images of Eternity,* 1962.

A. Brown and R. Haller, eds., *The Achievement of Wallace Stevens,* 1962.

D. Fuchs, *The Comic Spirit of Wallace Stevens,* 1962.

G. Cambon, *The Inclusive Flame,* 1963.

J. J. Enck, *Wallace Stevens: Images and Judgments,* 1964.

H. Wells, *Introduction to Wallace Stevens,* 1964.

J. N. Riddell, *The Clairvoyant Eye,* 1965.

E. P. Nasser, *Wallace Stevens: An Anatomy of Figuration,* 1965.

F. Doggett, *Stevens' Poetry of Thought,* 1966.

H. J. Stern, *Wallace Stevens: Art of Uncertainty,* 1966.

R. Buttel, *Wallace Stevens: The Making of "Harmonium,"* 1967.

R. Sukenick, *Wallace Stevens: Musing the Obscure,* 1967.

J. Baird, *The Dome and the Rock: Structure in the Poetry of Wallace Stevens,* 1968.

W. Burney, *Wallace Stevens,* 1968.

H. Vendler, *On Extended Wings: Wallace Stevens' Longer Poems,* 1969.

R. Blessing, *Wallace Stevens's "Whole Harmonium,"* 1970.

S. F. Morse, *Wallace Stevens: Poetry as Life,* 1970.

M. Benamou, *Wallace Stevens and the Symbolist Imagination,* 1972.

W. A. Litz, *Introspective Voyage: The Poetic Development of Wallace Stevens,* 1972.

L. Beckett, *Wallace Stevens,* 1977.

H. Bloom, *Wallace Stevens: The Poems of Our Climate,* 1977.

H. Stevens, *Souvenirs and Prophecies: The Young Wallace Stevens,* 1977.

S. B. Weston, *Wallace Stevens: An Introduction,* 1977.

F. Doggett, *Wallace Stevens: The Making of a Poem,* 1980.

F. Doggett and R. Buttel, eds., *Wallace Stevens: A Celebration,* 1980.

H. Vendler, *Wallace Stevens: Words Chosen out of Desire,* 1985.

E. Cook, *Poetry, Word-Play, and Word-War in Wallace Stevens,* 1988.

F. Lentricchia, *Ariel and the Police: Michel Foucault, William James, and Wallace Stevens,* 1988.

A. Filreis, *Wallace Stevens and the Actual Word,* 1991.

Text:

The Palm at the End of the Mind, ed. H. Stevens, 1971.

Sunday Morning

I

Complacencies of the peignoir, and late
Coffee and oranges in a sunny chair,[1]
And the green freedom of a cockatoo
Upon a rug mingle to dissipate
The holy hush of ancient sacrifice.[2]   5
She dreams a little, and she feels the dark
Encroachment of that old catastrophe,

---

[1] The agnostic lady does not attend a Sunday church service; instead, she remains in her peignoir and breakfasts.

[2] The death of Jesus.

As a calm darkens among water-lights.
The pungent oranges and bright, green wings
Seem things in some procession of the dead,   10
Winding across wide water, without sound.
The day is like wide water, without sound,
Stilled for the passing of her dreaming feet
Over the seas, to silent Palestine,
Dominion of the blood and sepulchre[3]   15

II

Why should she give her bounty to the dead?
What is divinity if it can come
Only in silent shadows and in dreams?
Shall she not find in comforts of the sun,
In pungent fruit and bright, green wings, or else   20
In any balm or beauty of the earth,
Things to be cherished like the thought of heaven?
Divinity must live within herself:
Passions of rain, or moods in falling snow;
Grievings in loneliness, or unsubdued   25
Elations when the forest blooms; gusty
Emotions on wet roads on autumn nights;
All pleasures and all pains, remembering
The bough of summer and the winter branch.
These are the measures destined for her soul.   30

III

Jove[4] in the clouds had his inhuman birth.
No mother suckled him, no sweet land gave
Large-mannered motions to his mythy mind.
He moved among us, as a muttering king,
Magnificent, would move among his hinds,   35
Until our blood, commingling, virginal,[5]
With heaven, brought such requital to desire
The very hinds[6] discerned it, in a star.
Shall our blood fail? Or shall it come to be
The blood of paradise? And shall the earth   40
Seem all of paradise that we shall know?
The sky will be much friendlier then than now,
A part of labor and a part of pain,

---

[3] The passion and entombment of Jesus.
[4] In mythology, the king of the gods.
[5] Like the Virgin Mary, impregnated by the
Holy Spirit.

[6] The shepherds who saw the Christmas star.

And next in glory to enduring love,
Not this dividing and indifferent blue.   45

IV

She says, "I am content when wakened birds,
Before they fly, test the reality
Of misty fields, by their sweet questionings;
But when the birds are gone, and their warm fields
Return no more, where, then, is paradise?"   50
There is not any haunt of prophecy,
Nor any old chimera[7] of the grave,
Neither the golden underground,[8] nor isle
Melodious,[9] where spirits gat them home,
Nor visionary south, nor cloudy palm[10]   55
Remote on heaven's hill, that has endured
As April's green endures; or will endure
Like her remembrance of awakened birds,
Or her desire for June and evening, tipped
By the consummation of the swallow's wings.   60

V

She says, "But in contentment I still feel
The need of some imperishable bliss."
Death is the mother of beauty; hence from her,
Alone, shall come fulfilment to our dreams
And our desires. Although she strews the leaves   65
Of sure obliteration on our paths,
The path sick sorrow took, the many paths
Where triumph rang its brassy phrase, or love
Whispered a little out of tenderness,
She makes the willow shiver in the sun   70
For maidens who were wont to sit and gaze
Upon the grass, relinquished to their feet.
She causes boys to pile new plums and pears
On disregarded plate.[11] The maidens taste
And stray impassioned in the littering leaves.   75

---

[7] Ghost, illusion.
[8] The Elysian fields, in mythology the heaven of heroes.
[9] Avalon, where King Arthur was taken after death.

[10] The palm was the reward given to Christian martyrs in heaven.
[11] Silver dishes.

VI

Is there no change of death in paradise?
Does ripe fruit never fall? Or do the boughs
Hang always heavy in that perfect sky,
Unchanging, yet so like our perishing earth,
With rivers like our own that seek for seas   80
They never find, the same receding shores
That never touch with inarticulate pang?
Why set the pear upon those river-banks
Or spice the shores with odors of the plum?
Alas, that they should wear our colors there,   85
The silken weavings of our afternoons,
And pick the strings of our insipid lutes!
Death is the mother of beauty, mystical,
Within whose burning bosom we devise
Our earthly mothers waiting, sleeplessly.   90

VII

Supple and turbulent, a ring of men
Shall chant in orgy on a summer morn
Their boisterous devotion to the sun,
Not as a god, but as a god might be,
Naked among them, like a savage source.   95
Their chant shall be a chant of paradise,
Out of their blood, returning to the sky;
And in their chant shall enter, voice by voice,
The windy lake wherein their lord delights,
The trees, like serafin,[12] and echoing hills,   100
That choir among themselves long afterward.
They shall know well the heavenly fellowship
Of men that perish and of summer morn.
And whence they came and whither they shall go
The dew upon their feet shall manifest.   105

VIII

She hears, upon that water without sound,
A voice that cries, "The tomb in Palestine
Is not the porch of spirits lingering.[13]

---

[12] Seraphim; angels.
[13] When Jesus' friends went to the sepulcher,
they found that the door-stone had been
rolled away and the tomb was empty. An
angel sat on the stone and said, "He is not
here, for he is risen" (Matthew 28:2–6;
Mark 16:4–6). (In Luke 24:1–6 and in John
20:11–12, there are two angels at the tomb.)

It is the grave of Jesus, where he lay."
We live in an old chaos of the sun,   110
Or old dependency of day and night,
Or island solitude, unsponsored, free,
Of that wide water, inescapable.
Deer walk upon our mountains, and the quail
Whistle about us their spontaneous cries;   115
Sweet berries ripen in the wilderness;
And, in the isolation of the sky,
At evening, casual flocks of pigeons make
Ambiguous undulations as they sink,
Downward to darkness, on extended wings.   120
1923

Thirteen Ways of Looking at a Blackbird

I

Among twenty snowy mountains,
The only moving thing
Was the eye of the blackbird.

II

I was of three minds,
Like a tree   5
In which there are three blackbirds.

III

The blackbird whirled in the autumn winds.
It was a small part of the pantomime.

IV

A man and a woman
Are one.   10
A man and a woman and a blackbird
Are one.

V

I do not know which to prefer,
The beauty of inflections
Or the beauty of innuendoes,   15
The blackbird whistling
Or just after.

VI

Icicles filled the long window
With barbaric glass.
The shadow of the blackbird   20
Crossed it, to and fro.
The mood
Traced in the shadow
An indecipherable cause.

VII

O thin men of Haddam,[1]   25
Why do you imagine golden birds?
Do you not see how the blackbird
Walks around the feet
Of the women about you?

VIII

I know noble accents   30
And lucid, inescapable rhythms;
But I know, too,
That the blackbird is involved
In what I know.

IX

When the blackbird flew out of sight,   35
It marked the edge
Of one of many circles.

X

At the sight of blackbirds
Flying in a green light,

---

[1] Town in Connecticut.

Even the bawds of euphony[2]   40
Would cry out sharply.

XI

He rode over Connecticut
In a glass coach.
Once a fear pierced him,
In that he mistook   45
The shadow of his equipage
For blackbirds.

XII

The river is moving.
The blackbird must be flying.

XIII

It was evening all afternoon.   50
It was snowing
And it was going to snow.
The blackbird sat
In the cedar-limbs.
1923

Anecdote of the Jar

I placed a jar in Tennessee,
And round it was, upon a hill.
It made the slovenly wilderness
Surround that hill.

The wilderness rose up to it,   5
And sprawled around, no longer wild.
The jar was round upon the ground
And tall and of a port in air.

It took dominion everywhere.
The jar was gray and bare.   10

[2] Those touting harmony as the highest
aesthetic virtue.

It did not give of bird or bush,
Like nothing else in Tennessee.
1923

The Emperor of Ice-Cream

Call the roller of big cigars,
The muscular one, and bid him whip
In kitchen cups concupiscent curds.
Let the wenches dawdle in such dress
As they are used to wear, and let the boys   5
Bring flowers in last month's newspapers.
Let be be finale of seem.
The only emperor is the emperor of ice-cream.

Take from the dresser of deal.
Lacking the three glass knobs, that sheet   10
On which she embroidered fantails once
And spread it so as to cover her face.
If her horny feet protrude, they come
To show how cold she is, and dumb.
Let the lamp affix its beam.   15
The only emperor is the emperor of ice-cream.

The Idea of Order at Key West

She sang beyond the genius of the sea.
The water never formed to mind or voice,
Like a body wholly body, fluttering
Its empty sleeves; and yet its mimic motion
Made constant cry, caused constantly a cry,   5
That was not ours although we understood,
Inhuman, of the veritable ocean.

The sea was not a mask. No more was she.
The song and water were not medleyed sound
Even if what she sang was what she heard,   10
Since what she sang was uttered word by word.
It may be that in all her phrases stirred

The grinding water and the gasping wind;
But it was she and not the sea we heard.

For she was the maker of the song she sang.   15
The ever-hooded, tragic-gestured sea
Was merely a place by which she walked to sing.
Whose spirit is this? we said, because we knew
It was the spirit that we sought and knew
That we should ask this often as she sang.   20

If it was only the dark voice of the sea
That rose, or even colored by many waves;
If it was only the outer voice of sky
And cloud, of the sunken coral water-walled,
However clear, it would have been deep air,   25
The heaving speech of air, a summer sound
Repeated in a summer without end
And sound alone. But it was more than that,
More even than her voice, and ours, among
The meaningless plungings of water and the wind,   30
Theatrical distances, bronze shadows heaped
On high horizons, mountainous atmospheres
Of sky and sea.
                    It was her voice that made
The sky acutest at its vanishing.   35
She measured to the hour its solitude.
She was the single artificer of the world
In which she sang. And when she sang, the sea,
Whatever self it had, became the self
That was her song, for she was the maker. Then we,   40
As we beheld her striding there alone,
Knew that there never was a world for her
Except the one she sang and, singing, made.

Ramon Fernandez,[1] tell me, if you know,
Why, when the singing ended and we turned   45
Toward the town, tell why the glassy lights,
The lights in the fishing boats at anchor there,
As the night descended, tilting in the air,
Mastered the night and portioned out the sea,
Fixing emblazoned zones and fiery poles,[2]   50
Arranging, deepening, enchanting night.

---

[1] Stevens said that he invented this name.
[2] The zones and poles are like those geographers invent to demarcate the terrestrial globe.

Oh! Blessed rage for order, pale Ramon,
The maker's rage to order words of the sea,
Words of the fragrant portals, dimly-starred,
And of ourselves and of our origins,   55
In ghostlier demarcations, keener sounds.
1936

The Poem That Took the Place of a Mountain

There it was, word for word,
The poem that took the place of a mountain.

He breathed its oxygen,
Even when the book lay turned in the dust of his table.

It reminded him how he had needed   5
A place to go to in his own direction,

How he had recomposed the pines,
Shifted the rocks and picked his way among clouds,

For the outlook that would be right,
Where he would be complete in an unexplained completion: 10

The exact rock where his inexactness
Would discover, at last, the view toward which they had edged,

Where he could lie and, gazing down at the sea,
Recognize his unique and solitary home.

From "Adagia"

All poetry is experimental poetry.

Poetry is a purging of the world's poverty and change and evil and death. It is a present perfecting, a satisfaction in the irremediable poverty of life.

Wallace Stevens, from "Adagia" (1957)

Anzia Yezierska
1880?–1970

It is not certain just when Yezierska was born in Russian-occupied Poland, or where; nor is it known precisely when she arrived in America with her parents and nine brothers and sisters. The very facts that most people take for granted as identifying marks of their existence are lost in Yezierska's case. Even her birth-name was taken from her in the New World, replaced for a time by the "Hattie Mayer" that was given to her when she passed through Ellis Island.

But very early Yezierska started to assert herself. She resisted the strictures against a woman choosing a life of her own, imposed by her father, a man of the old faith of the Old Country. She resumed her original name of Anzia Yezierska. She toiled in the sweatshops of the Lower East Side, strove to learn English, and pushed her way up and out of the home conditions stifling the aspirations that stirred her ambitious heart.

Yezierska managed to advance from manual labor to various teaching posts, through the aid of a sympathetic settlement worker and of Harriet Rodman, whose feminist views had given focus to Yezierska's rebellious nature. She felt a growing need to express herself in the right language about what it takes to batter down the barriers that separate the immigrant "greenhorn" from the New World's promises of "the beautifulness"; just as urgent, she wanted to express what it meant for the women of her generation and her culture to resist whatever restricted their choices. And so, after two failed marriages, she began to concentrate on her writing, with her first story published in 1915.

Yezierska's meeting with John Dewey, Columbia University professor of philosophy and his era's most prominent innovator of educational theory, came in 1917. This encounter led to a brief romance; more importantly, because of Dewey's encouragement and support, their association had a long-term impact upon her career as a writer.

Yezierska had her moment of fame when "The Fat of the Land" appeared in *Best Short Stories of 1919*, and *Hungry Hearts*, her own collection of stories, was published in 1920. Two movies were made of her stories and of her first novel *Salome of the Tenements* (1922). Her stay in Hollywood, however, tore her loose from contact with those whom she called "my own people"—a contact essential to her best work, and so she came back to New York.

The publication of *Children of Loneliness* (1923), *Bread Givers* (1925), *Arrogant Beggar* (1927), *All I Could Never Be* (1932) eventually was followed by her autobiography *Red Ribbon on a White Horse* (1950). Involved in the WPA Writer's Project throughout the 1930s, she thereafter continued to write in spurts and appeared occasionally as a lecturer, but by the time she died in 1970 at nearly ninety, Yezierska's name had largely been erased from the literary scene.

Yezierska's importance as a writer of the immigrant experience is currently being rediscovered. Even more attention is being paid to the "Blut-und-Eisen" (blood and iron) of her stories about a woman's struggle to make a name and a life for herself. A pioneer in her use of dialect to image sharply the intense emotions that burn in the soul of Yiddish culture, she has been described as one who "dipped her pen in her heart." As a Jew she had been born an outsider in Russian Poland. As an immigrant to the New World, she became an outsider to American society. As a woman she chose to escape outside the control of her father's rigid notions about a daughter's place. Always an outsider, she continued to strive through the intensity of her language to write a bridge of emotions that might link "America and I"—and "I" as the Woman—with the rest of humankind.

Further Reading:
C. Schoen, *Anzia Yezierska*, 1982.   L. Henriksen, *Anzia Yezierska. A Writer's Life*, 1988.
S. Girgus, *The New Covenant*, 1984.   E. Ammons, *Conflicting Stories*, 1991.

Text:
"America and I" from *Children of Loneliness*, 1923.

America and I

As one of the dumb, voiceless ones I speak. One of the millions of immigrants beating, beating out their hearts at your gates for a breath of understanding.

Ach! America! From the other end of the earth from where I came, America was a land of living hope, woven of dreams, aflame with longing and desire.

Choked for ages in the airless oppression of Russia, the Promised Land rose up—wings for my stifled spirit—sunlight burning through my darkness—freedom singing to me in my prison—deathless songs tuning prison-bars into strings of a beautiful violin.

I arrived in America. My young, strong body, my heart and soul pregnant with the unlived lives of generations clamoring for expression.

What my mother and father and their mother and father never had a chance to give out in Russia, I would give out in America. The hidden sap of centuries would find release; colors that never saw light—songs that died unvoiced—romance that never had a chance to blossom in the black life of the Old World.

In the golden land of flowing opportunity I was to find my work that was denied me in the sterile village of my forefathers. Here I was to be free from the dead drudgery for bread that held me down in Russia. For the first time in America, I'd cease to be a slave of the belly. I'd be a creator, a giver, a human being! My work would be the living joy of fullest self-expression.

But from my high visions, my golden hopes, I had to put my feet down on earth. I had to have food and shelter. I had to have the money to pay for it.

I was in America, among the Americans, but not of them. No speech, no common language, no way to win a smile of understanding from them, only my young, strong body and my untried faith. Only my eager, empty hands, and my full heart shining from my eyes!

God from the world! Here I was with so much richness in me, but my mind was not wanted without the language. And my body, unskilled, untrained, was not even wanted in the factory. Only one of two chances was left open to me: the kitchen, or minding babies.

My first job was as a servant in an Americanized family. Once, long ago, they came from the same village from where I came. But they were so well-dressed, so well-fed, so successful in America, that they were ashamed to remember their mother tongue.

"What were to be my wages?" I ventured timidly, as I looked up to the well-fed, well-dressed "American" man and woman.

They looked at me with a sudden coldness. What have I said to draw away from me their warmth? Was it so low from me to talk of wages? I shrank back into myself like a low-down bargainer. Maybe they're so high up in well-being they can't any more understand my low thoughts for money.

From his rich height the man preached down to me that I must not be so grabbing for wages. Only just landed from the ship and already thinking about money when I should be thankful to associate with "Americans."

The woman, out of her smooth, smiling fatness assured me that this was my chance for a summer vacation in the country with her two lovely children. My great chance to learn to be a civilized being, to become an American by living with them.

So, made to feel that I was in the hands of American friends, invited to share with them their home, their plenty, their happiness, I pushed out from my head the worry for wages. Here was my first chance to begin my life in the sunshine, after my long darkness. My laugh was all over my face as I said to them: "I'll trust myself to you. What I'm worth you'll give me." And I entered their house like a child by the hand.

The best of me I gave them. Their house cares were my house cares. I got up early. I worked till late. All that my soul hungered to give I put into the passion with which I scrubbed floors, scoured pots, and washed clothes. I was so grateful to mingle with the American people, to hear the music of the American language, that I never knew tiredness.

There was such a freshness in my brains and such a willingness in my heart that I could go on and on——not only with the work of the house, but work with my head—— learning new words from the children, the grocer, the butcher, the iceman. I was not even afraid to ask for words from the policeman on the street. And every new word made me see new American things with American eyes. I felt like a Columbus, finding new worlds through every new word.

But words alone were only for the inside of me. The outside of me still branded me for a steerage immigrant. I had to have clothes to forget myself that I'm a stranger yet. And so I had to have money to buy these clothes.

The month was up. I was so happy! Now I'd have money. *My own, earned* money. Money to buy a new shirt on my back——shoes on my feet. Maybe yet an American dress and hat!

Ach! How high rose my dreams! How plainly I saw all that I would do with my visionary wages shining like a light over my head!

In my imagination I already walked in my new American clothes. How beautiful I looked as I saw myself like a picture before my eyes! I saw how I would throw away my immigrant rags tied up in my immigrant shawl. With money to buy——free money in my hands——I'd show them that I could look like an American in a day.

Like a prisoner in his last night in prison, counting the seconds that will free him from his chains, I trembled breathlessly for the minute I'd get the wages in my hand.

Before dawn I rose.

I shined up the house like a jewel-box.

I prepared breakfast and waited with my heart in my mouth for my lady and gentleman to rise. At last I heard them stirring. My eyes were jumping out of my head to them when I saw them coming in and seating themselves by the table.

Like a hungry cat rubbing up to its boss for meat, so I edged and simpered around them as I passed them the food. Without my will, like a beggar, my hand reached out to them.

The breakfast was over. And no word yet from my wages.

"*Gottuniu!*"[1] I thought to myself. "Maybe they're so busy with their own things they forgot it's the day for my wages. Could they who have everything know what I was to do with my first American dollars? How could they, soaking in plenty, how could they feel the longing and the fierce hunger in me, pressing up through each visionary dollar? How could they know the gnawing ache of my avid fingers for the feel of my own, earned dollars? *My* dollars that I could spend like a free person. *My* dollars that would make me feel with everybody alike!"

Breakfast was long past.

Lunch came. Lunch past.

Oi-i weh![2] Not a word yet about my money.

It was near dinner. And not a word yet about my wages.

I began to set the table. But my head—it swam away from me. I broke a glass. The silver dropped from my nervous fingers. I couldn't stand it any longer. I dropped everything and rushed over to my American lady and gentleman.

"*Oi weh!* The money—my money—my wages!" I cried breathlessly.

Four cold eyes turned on me.

"Wages? Money?" The four eyes turned into hard stone as they looked me up and down. "Haven't you a comfortable bed to sleep, and three good meals a day? You're only a month here. Just came to America. And you already think about money. Wait till you're worth any money. What use are you without knowing English? You should be glad we keep you here. It's like a vacation for you. Other girls pay money yet to be in the country."

It went black for my eyes. I was so choked no words came to my lips. Even the tears went dry in my throat.

I left. Not a dollar for all my work.

For a long, long time my heart ached and ached like a sore wound. If murderers would have robbed me and killed me it wouldn't have hurt me so much. I couldn't think through my pain. The minute I'd see before me how they looked at me, the words they said to me—then everything began to bleed in me. And I was helpless.

For a long, long time the thought of ever working in an "American" family made me tremble with fear, like the fear of wild wolves. No—never again would I trust myself to an "American" family, no matter how fine their language and how sweet their smile.

It was blotted out in me all trust in friendship from "Americans." But the life in me still burned to live. The hope in me still craved to hope. In darkness, in dirt, in hunger and want, but only to live on!

There had been no end to my day—working for the "American" family.

Now rejecting false friendships from higher-ups in America, I turned back to the Ghetto. I worked on a hard bench with my own kind on either side of me. I knew before I began what my wages were to be. I knew what my hours were to be. And I knew the feeling of the end of the day.

[1] Oh, my God!
[2] Alas!

From the outside my second job seemed worse than the first. It was in a sweatshop[3] of a Delancey Street basement, kept up by an old, wrinkled woman that looked like a black witch of greed. My work was sewing on buttons. While the morning was still dark I walked into a dark basement. And darkness met me when I turned out of the basement.

Day after day, week after week, all the contact I got with America was handling dead buttons. The money I earned was hardly enough to pay for bread and rent. I didn't have a room to myself. I didn't even have a bed. I slept on a mattress on the floor in a rat-hole of a room occupied by a dozen other immigrants. I was always hungry—oh, so hungry! The scant meals I could afford only sharpened my appetite for real food. But I felt myself better off than working in the "American" family, where I had three good meals a day and a bed to myself. With all the hunger and darkness of the sweatshop, I had at least the evening to myself. And all night was mine. When all were asleep, I used to creep up on the roof of the tenement and talk out my heart in silence to the stars in the sky.

"Who am I? What am I? What do I want with my life? Where is America? Is there an America? What is this wilderness in which I'm lost?"

I'd hurl my questions and then think and think. And I could not tear it out of me, the feeling that America must be somewhere, somehow—only I couldn't find it—*my America,* where I would work for love and not for a living. I was like a thing following blindly after something far off in the dark!

"Oi weh!" I'd stretch out my hand up in the air. "My head is so lost in America! What's the use of all my working if I'm not in it? Dead buttons is not me."

Then the busy season started in the shop. The mounds of buttons grew and grew. The long day stretched out longer. I had to begin with the buttons earlier and stay with them till later in the night. The old witch turned into a huge greedy maw for wanting more and more buttons.

For a glass of tea, for a slice of herring over black bread, she would buy us up to stay another and another hour, till there seemed no end to her demands.

One day, the light of self-assertion broke into my cellar darkness.

"I don't want the tea. I don't want your herring," I said with terrible boldness. "I only want to go home. I only want the evening to myself!"

"You fresh mouth, you!" cried the old witch. "You learned already too much in America. I want no clock-watchers in my shop. Out you go!"

I was driven out to cold and hunger. I could no longer pay for my mattress on the floor. I no longer could buy the bite in the mouth. I walked the streets. I knew what it is to be alone in a strange city, among strangers.

But I laughed through my tears. So I learned too much already in America because I wanted the whole evening to myself? Well America has yet to teach me still more: how to get not only the whole evening to myself, but a whole day a week like the American workers.

That sweat-shop was a bitter memory but a good school. It fitted me for a regular factory. I could walk in boldly and say I could work at something, even if it is was only sewing on buttons.

---

[3] Workroom set up in tenement building where workers did piecework under contract to the "sweater," often laboring under unsavory physical conditions for inadequate pay.

Gradually, I became a trained worker. I worked in a light, airy factory, only eight hours a day. My boss was no longer a sweater and a blood-squeezer. The first freshness of the morning was mine. And the whole evening was mine. All day Sunday was mine.

Now I had better food to eat. I slept on a better bed. Now, I even looked dressed up like the American-born. But inside of me I knew that I was not yet an American. I choked with longing when I met an American-born, and I could say nothing.

Something cried dumb in me. I couldn't help it. I didn't know what it was I wanted. I only knew I wanted. I wanted. Like the hunger in the heart that never gets food.

An English class for foreigners started in our factory. The teacher had such a good, friendly face, her eyes looked so understanding, as if she could see right into my heart. So I went to her one day for an advice:

"I don't know what is with me the matter," I began. "I have no rest in me. I never yet done what I want."

"What is it you want to do, child?" she asked me.

"I want to do something with my head, my feelings. All day long, only with my hands I work."

"First you must learn English." She patted me as if I was not yet grown up. "Put your mind on that, and then we'll see."

So for a time I learned the language. I could almost begin to think with English words in my head. But in my heart the emptiness still hurt. I burned to give, to give something, to do something, to be something. The dead work with my hands was killing me. My work left only hard stones on my heart.

Again I went to our factory teacher and cried out to her: "I know already to read and write the English language, but I can't put it into words what I want. What is it in me so different that can't come out?"

She smiled at me down from her calmness as if I were a little bit out of my head. "What *do you want* to do?"

"I feel. I see. I hear. And I want to think it out. But I'm like dumb in me. I only feel I'm different—different from everybody."

She looked at me close and said nothing for a minute. "You ought to join one of the social clubs of the Women's Association," she advised.

"What's the Women's Association?" I implored greedily.

"A group of American women who are trying to help the working-girl find herself. They have a special department for immigrant girls like you."

I joined the Women's Association. On my first evening there they announced a lecture: "The Happy Worker and His Work," by the Welfare director of the United Mills Corporation.

"Is there such a thing as a happy worker at his work?" I wondered. "Happiness is only by working at what you love. And what poor girl can ever find it to work at what she loves? My old dreams about my America rushed through my mind. Once I thought that in America everybody works for love. Nobody has to worry for a living. Maybe this welfare man came to show me the *real* America that till now I sought in vain.

With a lot of polite words the head lady of the Women's Association introduced a higher-up that looked like the king of kings of business. Never before in my life did I ever see a man with such a sureness in his step, such power in his face, such friendly positiveness in his eye as when he smiled upon us.

"Efficiency is the new religion of business," he began. "In big business houses, even in up-to-date factories, they no longer take the first comer and give him any job that happens to stand empty. Efficiency begins at the employment office. Experts are hired for the one purpose, to find out how best to fit the worker to his work. It's economy for the boss to make the worker happy." And then he talked a lot more on efficiency in educated language that was over my head.

I didn't know exactly what it meant—efficiency—but if it was to make the worker happy at his work, then that's what I had been looking for since I came to America. I only felt from watching him that he was happy by his job. And as I looked on this clean, well-dressed, successful one, who wasn't ashamed to say he rose from an office-boy, it made me feel that I, too, could lift myself up for a person.

He finished his lecture, telling us about the Vocational-Guidance Center that the Women's Association started.

The very next evening I was at the Vocational-Guidance Center. There I found a young, college-looking woman. Smartness and health shining from her eyes! She, too, looked as if she knew her way in America. I could tell at the first glance: here is a person that is happy by what she does.

"I feel you'll understand me," I said right away.

She leaned over with pleasure in her face: "I hope I can."

"I want to work by what's in me. Only, I don't know what's in me. I only feel I'm different."

She gave me a quick, puzzled look from the corner of her eyes. "What are you doing now?"

"I'm the quickest shirtwaist hand on the floor. But my heart wastes away by such work. I think and think, and my thoughts can't come out."

"Why don't you think out your thoughts in shirtwaists? You could learn to be a designer. Earn more money."

"I don't want to look on waists. If my hands are sick from waists, how could my head learn to put beauty into them?"

"But you must earn your living at what you know, and rise slowly from job to job."

I looked at her office sign: "Vocational Guidance." "What's your vocational guidance?" I asked. "How to rise from job to job—how to earn more money?"

The smile went out from her eyes. But she tried to be kind yet. "What *do* you want?" she asked, with a sigh of last patience.

"I want America to want me."

She fell back in her chair, thunderstruck with my boldness. But yet, in a low voice of educated self-control, she tried to reason with me:

"You have to *show* that you have something special for America before America has need of you."

"But I never had a chance to find out what's in me, because I always had to work for a living. Only, I feel it's efficiency for America to find out what's in me so different, so I could give it out by my work."

Her eyes half closed as they bored through me. Her mouth opened to speak, but no words came from her lips. So I flamed up with all that was choking in me like a house on fire:

"America gives free bread and rent to criminals in prison. They got grand houses with sunshine, fresh air, doctors and teachers, even for the crazy ones. Why don't they have free boarding-schools for immigrants—strong people—willing people? Here you see us burning up with something different, and America turns her head away from us."

Her brows lifted and dropped down. She shrugged her shoulders away from me with the look of pity we give to cripples and hopeless lunatics.

"America is no Utopia. First you must become efficient in earning a living before you can indulge in your poetic dreams."

I went away from the vocational-guidance office with all the air out of my lungs. All the light out of my eyes. My feet dragged after me like dead wood.

Till now there had always lingered a rosy veil of hope over my emptiness, a hope that a miracle would happen. I would open up my eyes some day and suddenly find the America of my dreams. As a young girl hungry for love sees always before her eyes the picture of lover's arms around her, so I saw always in my heart the vision of Utopian America.

But now I felt that the America of my dreams never was and never could be. Reality had hit me on the head as with a club. I felt that the America that I sought was nothing but a shadow—an echo—a chimera of lunatics and crazy immigrants.

Stripped of all illusion, I looked about me. The long desert of wasting days of drudgery stared me in the face. The drudgery that I had lived through, and the endless drudgery still ahead of me rose over me like a withering wilderness of sand. In vain were all my cryings, in vain were all frantic efforts of my spirit to find the living waters of understanding for my perishing lips. Sand, sand was everywhere. With every seeking, every reaching out I only lost myself deeper and deeper in a vast sea of sand.

I knew now the American language. And I knew now, if I talked to the Americans from morning till night, they could not understand what the Russian soul of me wanted. They could not understand *me* any more than if I talked to them in Chinese. Between my soul and the American soul were worlds of difference that no words could bridge over. What was that difference? What made the Americans so far apart from me?

I began to read the American history. I found from the first pages that America started with a band of Courageous Pilgrims. They had left their native country as I had left mine. They had crossed an unknown ocean and landed in an unknown country, as I.

But the great difference between the first Pilgrims and me was that they expected to make America, build America, create their own world of liberty. I wanted to find it ready made.

I read on. I delved deeper down into the American history. I saw how the Pilgrim Fathers came to a rocky desert country, surrounded by Indian savages on all sides. But undaunted, they pressed on—through danger—through famine, pestilence, and want—they pressed on. They did not ask the Indians for sympathy, for understanding. They made no demands on anybody, but on their own indomitable spirit of persistence.

And I—I was forever begging a crumb of sympathy, a gleam of understanding from strangers who could not sympathize, who could not understand.

I, when I encountered a few savage Indian scalpers, like the old witch of the sweatshop, like my "Americanized" countryman, who cheated me of my wages—I, when I found myself on the lonely, untrodden path through which all seekers of the new world must pass, I lost heart and said: "There is no America!"

Then came a light—a great revelation! I saw America—a big idea—a deathless hope—a world still in the making. I saw that it was the glory of America that it was not yet finished. And I, the last comer, had her share to give, small or great, to the making of America, like those Pilgrims who came in the *Mayflower*.

Fired up by this revealing light, I began to build a bridge of understanding between the American-born and myself. Since their life was shut out from such as me, I began to open up my life and the lives of my people to them. And life draws life. In only writing about the Ghetto I found America.

Great chances have come to me. But in my heart is always a deep sadness. I feel like a man who is sitting down to a secret table of plenty, while his near ones and dear ones are perishing before his eyes. My very joy in doing the work I love hurts me like secret guilt, because all about me I see so many with my longings, my burning eagerness, to do and to be, wasting their days in drudgery they hate, merely to buy bread and pay rent. And America is losing all that richness of the soul.

The Americans of to-morrow, the America that is every day nearer coming to be, will be too wise, too open-hearted, too friendly-handed, to let the least last-comer at their gates knock in vain with his gifts unwanted.

1923

William Carlos Williams
1883–1963

William Carlos Williams was long viewed as the homespun poet for the technological age. A New Jersey physician, he was mistaken for a hobbyist-poet jotting verses at odd moments between patients. Only with the 1946 publication of Book One of his modern industrial-age American epic, *Paterson,* did readers begin to appreciate Williams's achievement as a major twentieth-century American writer. Thereafter, students, young poets, and critics looked closely and with increasing admiration at his formally innovative books of poetry, fiction, drama, and criticism. Dr. Williams had been writing in relative obscurity since before 1920. At last, at midcentury, his readers caught up with the poet and began to realize that Williams deserved the recognition and honor already accorded to the select group of twentieth-century American poets that included T. S. Eliot, Robert Frost, and Wallace Stevens.

His *Autobiography* (1951) presents young Billy Williams as an all-American boy playing baseball and pranks, but in several ways his youth was not typically American. Williams was born in 1883 in Rutherford, a northern New Jersey town across the Meadowlands from New York City. He was the elder son of William George and Raquel Helene Hoheb Williams. His father, an Englishman earning his living as a traveling salesman in the Caribbean and in Latin America, had met Helene, of Basque and Jewish origins, in Puerto Rico. After their marriage he settled with her in Rutherford, where neither had friends or family. "Imagine," Williams later wrote of the town in the 1880s, "no sewers, no water supply, no gas even, not even a trolley car. The sidewalks were of wood." Williams's father was periodically away on business, while his mother, knowing little English, was somewhat reclusive in the town. More difficult still, there was mental disorder in the family. His father's brother, Uncle Godwin, who lived with them, terrified young Billy with his erratic behavior. Helene herself was subject periodically to seizures combined with changes of voice, which embarrassed and doubtless frightened the child.

Yet Williams's parents were a cultured couple. As a young woman, his mother had studied art in the *beaux arts* tradition in Paris, and throughout her life she conveyed her love of all things European, especially art, which Williams later considered studying. His father passed along his literary interests to the boy by reading aloud from the African-American poet Paul Laurence Dunbar, from Gilbert and Sullivan, and from a collection of English Romantic and Victorian poets, including Keats. The household was bilingual in English and Spanish, and in boyhood the Williams sons, including Billy's younger brother Edgar, took music lessons and tasted life abroad, including a year of school in Switzerland and several months in Paris. This family background has proved significant to Williams's readers, who continue to discover important strains of European artistic influence in writing that is self-professedly American.

Ambitious for his sons' education, George Williams sent them, at considerable financial sacrifice, to Horace Mann High School in New York City, a two-hour daily commute each way. With the family's blessing, Edgar, evidently the academically superior student, prepared to study architecture, while William was readied for a career in dentistry. At the turn of the century, college work was not required for admission to some American medical schools, and Williams entered the School of Medicine at the University of Pennsylvania in Philadelphia following his graduation from high school. In retrospect, it was a happy choice. Within the year he had transferred from dentistry into medicine. Meanwhile, in a moment crucial for his life as a writer, he met the aspiring artist Charles Demuth, the young poet H. D. (Hilda Doolittle), and a graduate student, Ezra Pound, who became his lifelong friend and critic.

Through medical school and his interning years in New York (1902–1909), Williams, an earnest and dutiful young man, remained a Sunday painter and sustained his literary ambitions. Unknown to him then, his medical education, emphasizing rapid diagnosis and note-taking on cases, would later become an integral part of his poetic practice. In those early years, however, Williams still wrote well-meant clichés ("the only way to be truly happy is to make others happy") that echoed the Christian liberalism of his Rutherford culture. His first book, *Poems* (1909), self-published, was ambitious but sentimental and derivative—"bad Keats" he later called it. At that point poetry was his haven, a respite from the daily experience of blood and childbirth, roach-infested laboratories and disease.

At twenty-six, while a medical intern, Williams began the courtship of Charlotte Herman, the daughter of a prosperous German-American printer in Rutherford whose family became the subject of Williams's Stecher trilogy of novels (*White Mule*, 1937; *In the Money*, 1940; *The Build-Up*, 1952). When she refused him, Williams immediately proposed to her quieter, plainer, younger sister Florence. Williams and "Flossie" became informally engaged in 1909, just before he left for a year of postgraduate medical study in Leipzig, Germany. He also visited Pound in London and saw his brother Ed, who was studying architecture at the American Academy in Rome. After touring in Spain, Williams returned to America to begin medical practice in his hometown. He married Flossie in December 1912, and within two years had a mortgage, the first of two infant sons, and a practice that included evening office hours and house calls. Nonetheless, he determined to continue his literary life.

Manhattan, Rutherford, and their surroundings thereafter became Williams's main compass points. The Rutherford area provided abundant material for his writing, while an hour's drive away in a Model-T Ford, a wide circle of cosmopolitan artists and writers in New York kept him abreast of the contemporary movement in the arts known as modernism. In 1913, the year in which Pound arranged for the publication of Williams's second book of poems, *The Tempers,* Williams probably learned of the latest European work of artists like Matisse, Cézanne, and Braque, whose works were displayed at the New York Armory. By the midteens, Williams had affiliated with the *Others* group of artists and writers and had met Marianne Moore, Wallace Stevens, and Marcel Duchamp, who were revolutionizing the arts through their efforts to break down and restructure space and time.

But the cultural influences on Williams were broad-based. One was the efficiency movement of the 1910s, which was meant to encourage more productive labor and which taught Americans to think in ever finer, more precise subdivisions of time and motion. Even as Williams criticized this glorification of speed, he was writing prodigiously and sustaining a busy, multifaceted life.

Williams's break with traditional forms and subject matter came with *Al Que Quiere!* ("To Him Who Wants It!"), a book of iconoclastic lyrics, and with *Kora in Hell: Improvisations* (1920). *Kora* was an experimental montage of passages written "automatically" to tap subconscious funds of poetic energy; portions of unpremeditated writing were coupled with Williams's commentary on them. *Kora* appeared in the same issues of *The Little Review* that carried James Joyce's *Ulysses,* a work that was to influence Williams profoundly, as it did numerous other American writers. (Williams met Joyce in 1924, while on sabbatical in Europe with Flossie.)

The 1920s were an especially prolific period for Williams. Continuously experimenting in form, he spoke in the voice that is unmistakably his. Often angry and irreverent in tone, it was defiant of all conventions—formal, political, and religious. A self-consciously American poet, he was angered by—and jealous of—T. S. Eliot, whose insistence on the British tradition Williams thought retrograde. During those years, various small presses published many of Williams's most lasting works, including *Spring and All* (1923), which combined prose and poetry, *The Great American Novel* (1923), and *In the American Grain* (1925), a personal revision of American history and culture. Williams always remained innovative. He believed the repetition of familiar forms to be a kind of living death for a poet.

During the Great Depression, Williams published a collection of short stories aptly entitled *The Knife of the Times* (1932) and saw two major collections of poems through the press. From the wartime 1940s, as successive books of his long poem *Paterson* appeared and his reputation grew, Williams began to suffer health problems. Through heart attacks and strokes he continued, with the tireless help of Flossie, to read, write, travel, and lecture. Two major works, *The Desert Music* (1954) and *Pictures from Brueghel* (1962) came from the efforts of those years, as he struggled toward a flexible verse form he called the variable foot.

By now Williams was earning prestigious prizes for his poetry. Still he resolutely encouraged the younger poets who wrote him letters and appeared on his Rutherford doorstep. He never forgot how hard it was to make his way or how difficult his isolation had often been. He remarked in 1950, "I think the artist, generally speaking, feels lonely. Perhaps his recourse to art, in any form, comes from his essential loneliness. He is usually in rebellion against the world."

Further Reading:

J. H. Miller, *Poets of Reality*, 1965.

J. Guimond, *The Art of William Carlos Williams*, 1968.

S. Paul, *The Music of Survival*, 1968.

B. Dijkstra, *The Hieroglyphics of a New Speech*, 1969.

J. Breslin, *William Carlos Williams*, 1970.

J. Conarroe, *William Carlos Williams' "Paterson,"* 1970.

B. Sankey, *A Companion to William Carlos Williams' "Paterson,"* 1971.

D. Tashjian, *William Carlos Williams and the American Scene, 1920–1940*, 1978.

P. Mariani, *William Carlos Williams*, 1981.

C. Terrell, ed., *William Carlos Williams: Man and Poet*, 1983.

V. Kutzinski, *Against the American Grain, Myth and History in William Carlos Williams, Jay Wright and Nicolás Guillen*, 1987.

P. Schmidt, *William Carlos Williams, the Arts and Literary Tradition*, 1988.

T. Whitaker, *William Carlos Williams*. 1989.

R. Callan, *William Carlos Williams and Transcendentalism*, 1992.

Texts:

The Collected Earlier Poems of William Carlos Williams, 1966.

The Collected Later Poems of William Carlos Williams, 1967.

Queen Anne's Lace*

Her body is not so white as
anemone petals nor so smooth—nor
so remote a thing. It is a field
of the wild carrot taking
the field by force; the grass   5
does not raise above it.
Here is no question of whiteness,
white as can be, with a purple mole
at the center of each flower.
Each flower is a hand's span   10
of her whiteness. Wherever
his hand has lain there is
a tiny purple blemish. Each part

* The wild carrot; its flower is composed of
multiple white blossoms, giving a lacelike
appearance.

is a blossom under his touch
to which the fibres of her being   15
stem one by one, each to its end,
until the whole field is a
white desire, empty, a single stem,
a cluster, flower by flower,
a pious wish to whiteness gone over—   20
or nothing.
1921

Spring and All

By the road to the contagious hospital
under the surge of the blue
mottled clouds driven from the
northeast—a cold wind. Beyond, the
waste of broad, muddy fields   5
brown with dried weeds, standing and fallen

patches of standing water
the scattering of tall trees

All along the road the reddish
purplish, forked, upstanding, twiggy   10
stuff of bushes and small trees
with dead, brown leaves under them
leafless vines—

Lifeless in appearance, sluggish
dazed spring approaches—   15

They enter the new world naked,
cold, uncertain of all
save that they enter. All about them
the cold, familiar wind—

Now the grass, tomorrow   20
the stiff curl of wildcarrot leaf
One by one objects are defined—
It quickens: clarity, outline of leaf

But now the stark dignity of
entrance—Still, the profound change   25

has come upon them: rooted they
grip down and begin to awaken
1923

The Red Wheelbarrow

so much depends
upon

a red wheel
barrow

glazed with rain   5
water

beside the white
chickens
1923

This Is Just to Say

I have eaten
the plums
that were in
the icebox

and which   5
you were probably
saving
for breakfast

Forgive me
they were delicious   10
so sweet
and so cold
1934

The Yachts

contend in a sea which the land partly encloses
shielding them from the too-heavy blows
of an ungoverned ocean which when it chooses

tortures the biggest hulls, the best man knows
to pit against its beatings, and sinks them pitilessly.   5
Mothlike in mists, scintillant in the minute

brilliance of cloudless days, with broad bellying sails
they glide to the wind tossing green water
from their sharp prows while over them the crew crawls

ant-like, solicitously grooming them, releasing,   10
making fast as they turn, lean far over and having
caught the wind again, side by side, head for the mark.

In a well guarded arena of open water surrounded by
lesser and greater craft which, sycophant, lumbering
and flittering follow them, they appear youthful, rare   15

as the light of a happy eye, live with the grace
of all that in the mind is fleckless, free and
naturally to be desired. Now the sea which holds them

is moody, lapping their glossy sides, as if feeling
for some slightest flaw but fails completely.   20
Today no race. Then the wind comes again. The yachts

move, jockeying for a start, the signal is set and they
are off. Now the waves strike at them but they are too
well made, they slip through, though they take in canvas.

Arms with hands grasping seek to clutch at the prows.   25
Bodies thrown recklessly in the way are cut aside.
It is a sea of faces about them in agony, in despair

until the horror of the race dawns staggering the mind,
the whole sea become an entanglement of watery bodies
lost to the world bearing what they cannot hold. Broken,   30

beaten, desolate, reaching from the dead to be taken up
they cry out, failing, failing! their cries rising
in waves still as the skillful yachts pass over.
1935

A Machine Made of Words

A poem is a small (or large) machine made of words. When I say there's nothing sentimental about a poem I mean that there can be no part, as in any other machine, that is redundant.

Prose may carry a load of ill-defined matter like a ship. But poetry is the machine which drives it, pruned to a perfect economy. As in all machines its movement is intrinsic, undulant, a physical more than a literary character. In a poem this movement is distinguished in each case by the character of the speech from which it arises. . . .

There is no poetry of distinction without formal invention, for it is in the intimate form that works of art achieve their exact meaning, in which they most resemble the machine, to give language its highest dignity, its illumination in the environment to which it is native.

William Carlos Williams from "Introduction" to the Wedge *(1944)*

Ezra Pound
1885–1972

Ezra Pound set himself the goal of knowing by the age of thirty "more about poetry than any man living." Accomplished and influential as a poet and—perhaps more notably—as critic, translator, and literary entrepreneur, he pursued his many-sided literary career with ambition and intensity. There can be "no doubt," a reviewer remarked, "as to his vitality and his determination to burst his way into Parnassus." He remains one of the writers most responsible for the modernist revolution in English poetry and prose.

Pound was born in Hailey, Idaho, and raised in Philadelphia in middle-class circumstances. At Hamilton College and the University of Pennsylvania, he specialized in medieval and Renaissance literature in Spanish, Italian, French, and Latin, including a "special study" of Martial, Catullus, and Tacitus. By the time he received his M.A. in 1906, he had "spatted with nearly everybody" and decided against continuing toward the Ph.D. A short period teaching at Wabash College ("the last or at least sixth circle of desolation") only confirmed him in his often heated contempt of American college professors. Dismissed abruptly after a scandal about keeping a woman overnight in his room, Pound traveled to Venice. There he began his lifelong struggle to live for and, wherever possible, on his writing.

In Venice, he had his first book, *A Lume Spento* (1908), published, but at his own expense. He tried working as a gondolier (he was not strong enough) and, briefly, as a publicist for a friend ("the greatest livin' she pianist") before moving in 1908 to London, "the place for poetry." He immediately began to transform English literature—without, however, sacrificing his pleasure in ostentatiously playing the raw and vital American. He frequently cultivated, in speech and writing, a parodic version of the American language; he also was an occasional self-appointed expert on native manners, as when, at lunch with the novelists D. H. Lawrence and Ford Madox Ford, he demonstrated, in a suitably barbaric fashion, how an American ate an apple.

In London, Pound entered a milieu of poets dedicated to writing what, he determined, had already been written in language that was already worn. He responded with poetry that was at once conservative and revolutionary. His famous rallying cry—"make it new!"—meant not a break with the past, but remaining faithful to the spirit of the past while attempting to modernize it, to rediscover its vigor through the creation of new forms. This was something that, Pound vehemently believed, most did not do, because of the sterile academism of most scholarship and the formulaic rhetoric of conventional literary styles. Pound was thus a maverick iconoclast who denounced both the academic scholarship and conventional verse of his day; he was, at the same time, however eccentrically, a passionately learned, even bookish writer. These apparently contradictory tendencies account for much of the energy in an early poem like "Sestina: Altaforte," which is in the difficult sestina form, on a historical subject, and in the tradition of the dramatic monologue associated with Robert Browning. Despite all this indebtedness to literary tradition and history, Pound sought to project himself into the speaker so completely that he became him, and to make thereby a poem that was not archaizing but vitally alive—so alive that when Pound read the poem at a poets' dinner at the Tour Eiffel restaurant, the management put a screen around his table.

Pound's success in infusing the books he touched and the history he recounted with immediacy and passion was so great that some have seen in his intense immersion in experience a sort of mysticism. The English writer and artist Wyndham Lewis observed that Pound "has really walked with Sophocles beside the Aegean; he has *seen* the Florence of Cavalcanti." When Pound continually exhorted himself and others that "every literaryism, every book word, fritters away a scrap of the reader's patience, a scrap of his sense of your sincerity," he did so with an evangelist's intensity. Literature was for him an intensification of life, and he treated his own lapses into "literaryisms"—his poems that echoed the dead letter of an old language rather than the living spirit of the past—with as much severity as he did those of others. After Ford Madox Ford looked through the copy of Pound's third book of poetry, *Canzoni* (1911), he rolled on the floor of his room in mock horror at the book's artificial language. That roll, Pound wrote, "saved me at least two years, perhaps more."

Pound's engagement with the past throughout his career encompassed a wide variety of literary traditions and historical eras, from classical Greece and Rome to medieval Europe, ancient China, and eighteenth-century America. The result was frequently poetry studded with covert references, difficult to the point of inaccessibility. Yet part of the reason for this difficulty was Pound's increasing exploration of an essentially simple poetic technique. At the beginning of his career he called it the technique of the "luminous detail"; later it became the "ideogrammatic method." In his early work it meant to evoke by means of a few, spare words, used without narrative context, moments of transcendent beauty. Later, employed with greater compression and allusiveness, the same technique could evoke the "intelligence of a period."

The first uses of the technique were purely literary. The luminous detail was essential to the Imagist movement in poetry, of which Pound was the originator and, for a little while, the leader. Under the banner of Imagism, he advocated poetry that eschewed all rhetoric and "emotional slither," that would be, objectively and concretely, an image—which Pound defined as "that which presents an intellectual and emotional 'complex' in an instant of time." The Imagist poem showed with as much immediacy as possible a luminous moment; it sought to owe little or nothing, therefore, to narrative or expository structures. When, shortly after defining the Imagist poem, Pound discovered Ernest Fenellosa's essay on the Chinese written character, he was able to extend the implications of the Imagist aesthetic considerably. In that essay, Fenellosa argued that Chinese characters were pictographs and that Chinese poetry was a succession of these "concrete pictures." Poetry of this sort could, Pound felt, in its presentation of a succession of luminous moments, approach the grammarless immediacy of perception, an ontological ideal that remained crucial to his poetry throughout his career. In 1914 Pound joined Wyndham Lewis in founding the Vorticism movement, which stood in essence for an aggressive version of these ideas.

The short Imagist poem "In a Station of the Metro" is representative, in compressed form, of Pound's technique. Pound presents concretely a moment of perception. The language is economical, free of "emotional slither." And, thanks to the unexplained juxtaposition of the two lines—a juxtaposition that avoids the use of logical and narrative connectives—the poem approaches, Pound would maintain, the grammarless immediacy of nature. Reality, the poem implies, is a construction of such relationships, and poetic perception is a succession of moments in which those relationships become luminously manifest.

By the end of the decade, Pound was the author of a number of books of poetry, of which *Personae* (1909), *Ripostes* (1912), and *Lustra* (1915) are the most important. The best poems from the latter two were later added to an expanded version of *Personae*. Pound also distinguished himself during this time as one of the century's outstanding, though sometimes controversial, translators of poetry. The most famous of his translations are those from the Chinese, done from the notes of Fenellosa and collected under the title *Cathay* (1915), and from the Latin poet Propertius, published as *Homage to Sextus Propertius* (1917).

With the appearance in 1920 of *Hugh Selwyn Mauberley: Life and Contacts* and the first sections of the poem that was to occupy him for the rest of his life, *The Cantos*, it was clear that Pound had decisively expanded on and complicated his poetic technique. With his friends T. S. Eliot and James Joyce, he shared the ambition to exploit and to overcome the often depressing, often comic disparity between ancient and modern cultures by writing an epic for the modern world. Increasingly concerned with the relationships of art and society, Pound began working in longer, more complex forms. *Hugh Selwyn Mauberley* was a sequence of short, crisp cameos; it was, Pound wrote, "a study in form, an attempt to condense the James novel." *The Cantos*, by contrast, were not condensations but a finally unending, encyclopedic long poem in open form, one that could include, however chaotically, all that was on Pound's mind, from personal anecdotes to literary allusions of an enormous variety and range. Both these works extended the technique of the luminous detail. It became, in the *Mauberley* poems, more decisively a historiographical technique, as details, allusions, and fragments of quotations were inserted in the separate sections of the poem as means of evoking the whole flavor of the society and era from which they came. Once again, narrative structure, though hard to avoid, was suppressed wherever possible. In *The Cantos* this technique of often cryptic, fragmented, and highly allusive references was vastly extended, and narrative and expository structure was more daringly put aside. The result is a poem of greater flexibility and difficulty, if one that finally lacks the coherence of an overall design.

While Pound was attempting to establish his own career as a poet, he was passionately interested in the careers of other writers. Indeed, his own work was often overshadowed by that of the writers he admired and worked on behalf of. Pound was as passionately generous as he was egoistic. He attempted to aid, practically and artistically, an astonishing number of the century's most important writers. A short list would include Lawrence, Joyce, Eliot, Lewis, William Butler Yeats, William Carlos Williams, Robert Frost, and Ernest Hemingway. He served as corresponding editor in Europe for Harriet Monroe's Chicago-based *Poetry*, the literary magazine most responsible for exporting the modernist revolution to America, and as editor or contributing editor for numerous other magazines. He once made unauthorized changes in some poems that Yeats had entrusted to him for submission to *Poetry*; once Yeats got over his shock, he sought Pound's help in modernizing his style. Pound acted as an editor for Eliot's *Waste Land*, cutting a number of lines and passages from it. Pound also tried to help Eliot at one point by setting up a fund to enable his friend to stop working in a bank and to devote himself to writing poetry full-time. On numerous occasions, Pound helped writers financially from his own pocket. He encouraged other writers even when their achievements made him jealous (*The Waste Land* evoked from Pound the response "Complimenti, you bitch. I am wracked by the seven jealousies") or when he detested them, as he did Lawrence.

Between 1915 and 1920, as Pound worked on the *Mauberley* poems and the beginning of *The Cantos*, he became a committed social critic and theorist. The *Mauberley* poems show vividly how Pound's bitter reaction to World War I, which convinced him of the bankruptcy of Western history, helped launch him on his ultimately disastrous career as social analyst and critic. "There died a myriad, / And of the best, among them, / For an old bitch gone in the teeth / For a botched civilization," he wrote in Section V; among the best who were killed, he was doubtless thinking of his friend the sculptor Henri Gaudier-Brzeska, who died at the front in 1915. But the crucial point in Pound's transformation into a passionately engaged social critic came with his discovery of the economic theories of Major C. H. Douglas. Pound felt he had discovered in them the answer to many of the evils of the current system. In particular, he saw in Douglas's theories of social credit the basis for a monetary system that would change the disenfranchised position of the artist in the modern commercial world. Governments would grant citizens social credit for work done. They would consider, in doing so, the inherent and social value of the work that went into making something; the laws of the marketplace, the laws of cost, supply, and demand would be set aside. Pound threw himself as passionately into the fray as social critic as he had as literary critic. "Usurers"—a category which for Pound consisted of capitalists, Jews, and bankers—acted against the common good. As a prose work like *Jefferson and Mussolini* (1935) illustrates, he made them the targets of repeated virulent attacks.

Pound left England for France in 1921. Dissatisfied there, he moved in 1924 to Rapallo, Italy, where he stayed until the end of World War II. He became more and more obsessed with his missionary role as social critic, turning his enormous vigor in that direction in letters, essays, and poems. He met Mussolini in 1933 and was greatly impressed; Mussolini had found Pound's *A Draft of XXX Cantos* "entertaining," and Pound saw in Mussolini someone who had outdone the aesthetes in their own field. Feeling that Fascist Italy was a nation that was likely to adopt his economic theories, Pound supported it more and more vigorously. The most notorious form of that support was his broadcasting a regular program on Rome Radio in which he discussed both aesthetic and political matters and propagandized for Fascism even after America had entered the war. In 1939 he wrote, "Usury is the cancer of the world, and only the surgeon's knife of Fascism can cut it out of the life of the nations." His support of Fascism included an equally strenuous anti-Semitism.

At the end of the war Pound was imprisoned in an American camp for prisoners of war at Pisa. He was first put in a cage that had been reinforced with heavy steel, where he was exposed to the weather. After three weeks, he became so thin and weak that he was transferred to a tent in the medical compound. There, on the dispensary typewriter, he wrote (along with letters for other prisoners) what many regard as his best poems, *The Pisan Cantos*. At the end of six months he was taken to America to stand trial for treason. Declared legally insane, he was transferred to St. Elizabeth's mental hospital in Washington, D.C., where he was incarcerated for thirteen years. At last, after receiving the Bollingen Prize for poetry and after work on his behalf by a number of writers, including Frost, Hemingway, Archibald MacLeish, and the ever-faithful Eliot, he was released to return to Italy. He died in 1972, last of the great leaders of the modernist movement.

Though he spent his formative years as an artist in England and lived abroad most of his life, and though he uttered, on more than one occasion, the sentiment that "residence in America is most revolting to think of," Pound remains a distinctively American author. Like Walt Whitman, the poet he likened to a "pig-headed father" in "Pact," Pound was pig-headed, exhibitionistic, and egoistic, yet equally generous in both his attachments and his commitment to the renewal of poetry in his age. He wrote poetry that was as indecorous as it was sublime, in the way that Whitman's verse had echoed for Emerson both the Bhagavad-Gita and the *New York Herald*. And Pound spent the bulk of his poetic career working on a long poem in the Whitmanesque tradition. *The Cantos* has been variously assessed, by Pound and others, as a success or a failure in its accomplishment; it is, at least in ambition, based on an epic model and frequently messianic in impulse. Confused and confusing, it is often capricious in its use of juxtaposition without structural connection, the technique that Pound came to label in later years the ideogrammatic method. In its confusion, however, *The Cantos* too, like Walt Whitman's "Song of Myself," contains multitudes—of ideas, insights, characters, and events—from the wide-ranging play of Pound's sometimes nobly impassioned, sometimes violently satiric personality. Though the theater of the poems is not the American scene and circumstance but world history, it was here that Pound came closest to living up to the egotism of his early comment about Whitman: "I honor him for he prophesized me." Pound's place as critic, aesthetician, and central figure in the tradition of American poetry is still disputed. But though his work is variously assessed, none would deny Pound's importance to the modernist movement: as literary entrepreneur, generous publicist for the work of others, and literary journalist.

Further Reading:

C. Norman, *Ezra Pound*, 1960.
L. Dembo, *The Confucian Odes of Ezra Pound*, 1963.
G. Dekker, *The Cantos of Ezra Pound*, 1963.
N. de Nagy, *Ezra Pound's Poetics and Literary Tradition*, 1966.
K. L. Goodwin, *The Influence of Ezra Pound*, 1966.
J. Cornell, *The Trial of Ezra Pound*, 1966.
N. Stock, *Reading the Cantos*, 1967.
T. H. Jackson, *The Early Poetry of Ezra Pound*, 1968.
W. Yip, *Ezra Pound's Cathay*, 1969.
E. Hesse, ed., *New Approaches to Ezra Pound*, 1969.
N. Stock, *The Life of Ezra Pound*, 1970.
M. de Rachewiltz, *Discretions*. 1971.
C. Brooke-Rose, *A ZBC of Ezra Pound*, 1971.
H. Kenner, *The Pound Era*, 1972.
D. Davie, *Ezra Pound*, 1976.
R. Bush, *The Genesis of Pound's Cantos*, 1976.
J. Wilhelm, *The Later Cantos of Ezra Pound*, 1977.
M. Alexander, *The Poetic Achievement of Ezra Pound*, 1979.
M. S. Bernstein, *The Tale of the Tribe: Ezra Pound and Modern Verse Epic*, 1980.
W. Flory, *Ezra Pound and the Cantos*, 1980.
G. Kearn, *Guide to Ezra Pound's Selected Cantos*, 1980.

C. Terrell, *A Companion to the Cantos of Ezra Pound*, 1980.
P. Ackroyd, *Ezra Pound and His World*, 1981.
I. F. A. Bell, *Critic as Scientist: The Modernist Poetics of Ezra Pound*, 1981.
C. Froula, *A Guide to Ezra Pound's Selected Poems*, 1982.
E. Fuller Torrey, *The Roots of Treason: Ezra Pound and the Secret of St. Elizabeth's*, 1983.
N. Stock, *The Life of Ezra Pound*, 1982.
H. Kenner, *The Poetry of Ezra Pound*, 1985.
M. Perloff, *The Dance of the Intellect: Studies in the Poetry of the Pound Tradition*, 1985.
J. Laughlin, *Pound as Wuz: Essays and Lectures on Ezra Pound*, 1987.
K. V. Lindberg, *Reading Pound Reading: Modernism after Nietzsche*, 1987.
J. Tytell, *Ezra Pound: The Solitary Volcano*, 1987.
J. McGann, *Towards a Literature of Knowledge*, 1989.
L. Rainey, *Ezra Pound and the Monument of Culture*, 1990.
K. Ruthven, *Ezra Pound as Literary Critic*, 1990.
S. Hamilton, *Ezra Pound and the Symbolist Inheritance*, 1992.

Texts:

Personae, 1949.
The Cantos of Ezra Pound, 1970.
See also *The Letters of Ezra Pound, 1907–1941*, ed. D. D. Paige, 1950.

Pound/Joyce: Letters and Essays, ed. F. Read, 1967.

The River-Merchant's Wife: A Letter*

While my hair was still cut straight across my forehead
I played about the front gate, pulling flowers.
You came by on bamboo stilts, playing horse,
You walked about my seat, playing with blue plums.
And we went on living in the village of Chokan: 5
Two small people, without dislike or suspicion.

---

* Adapted from the Chinese of Li Po (700?–762). Ernest Fenollosa (1853–1908), an American orientalist and collector, made the translation from which Pound worked.

At fourteen I married My Lord you.
I never laughed, being bashful.
Lowering my head, I looked at the wall.
Called to, a thousand times, I never looked back.   10

At fifteen I stopped scowling,
I desired my dust to be mingled with yours
Forever and forever and forever.
Why should I climb the look out?

At sixteen you departed,   15
You went into far Ku-to-yen, by the river of swirling eddies,
And you have been gone five months.
The monkeys make sorrowful noise overhead.

You dragged your feet when you went out.
By the gate now, the moss is grown, the different mosses,   20
Too deep to clear them away!
The leaves fall early this autumn, in wind.
The paired butterflies are already yellow with August
Over the grass in the West garden;
They hurt me. I grow older.   25
If you are coming down through the narrows of the river Kiang,
Please let me know beforehand,
And I will come out to meet you
              As far as Cho-fu-Sa.

1915

A Pact

I make a pact with you, Walt Whitman—
I have detested you long enough.
I come to you as a grown child
Who has had a pig-headed father;
I am old enough now to make friends.   5
It was you that broke the new wood,
Now is a time for carving.
We have one sap and one root—
Let there be commerce between us.

1916

In a Station of the Metro*

The apparition of these faces in the crowd;
Petals on a wet, black bough.
1916

from Hugh Selwyn Mauberley
(Life and Contacts)

"Vocat œstus in umbram"[1]
NEMESIANUS, *Ec. IV*

I: *E. P. Ode pour l'Election de Son Sepulchre*[2]

For three years, out of key with his time,
He strove to resuscitate the dead art
Of poetry; to maintain "the sublime"
In the old sense. Wrong from the start—

No, hardly, but seeing he had been born   5
In a half savage country, out of date;
Bent resolutely on wringing lilies from the acorn;
Capaneus;[3] trout for factitious bait;

῍Ιδμεν γάρ τοι πάνθ᾿,῾όσ᾿ ᾿ενὶ Τροίη[4]
Caught in the unstopped ear;   10
Giving the rocks small lee-way
The chopped seas held him, therefore, that year.

His true Penelope was Flaubert,[5]
He fished by obstinate isles;
Observed the elegance of Circe's[6] hair   15
Rather than the mottoes on sun-dials.

---

* The Paris subway.
[1] Latin: "Heat summons us into the shade."
From the fourth *Eclogue* of Nemesianus,
Roman poet (fl. A.D. 283).
[2] Adaptation of the title of an ode by the
French Renaissance poet Pierre de Ronsard
(1524–1585), *On the Selection of His Tomb.*
[3] One of the Seven against Thebes, struck by
lightning for his rebellion.
[4] From the song the Sirens sang (*Odyssey*

12.189): "For we know all the toils [en-
dured] in wide Troy." Odysseus stopped his
comrades' ears with wax so they would not
be seduced by the song.
[5] Penelope: Odysseus' faithful wife; Flaubert:
Gustave Flaubert (1821–1880), French
novelist who cultivated "the right word," *le
mot juste.*
[6] Circe: Enchantress with whom Odysseus
remained for a year.

Unaffected by "the march of events,"
He passed from men's memory in *l'an trentiesme*
De son eage;[7] the case presents
No adjunct to the Muses' diadem.   20

IV

These fought in any case,
and some believing,
                    pro domo,[8] in any case . . .

Some quick to arm,
some for adventure,   65
some from fear of weakness,
some from fear of censure,
some for love of slaughter, in imagination,
learning later . . .
some in fear, learning love of slaughter;   70

Died some, pro patria,
                    non "dulce" non
                    "et decor" . . .[9]
walked eye-deep in hell
believing in old men's lies, then unbelieving
came home, home to a lie,   75
home to many deceits,
home to old lies and new infamy;
usury age-old and age-thick
and liars in public places.

Daring as never before, wastage as never before.   80
Young blood and high blood,
fair cheeks, and fine bodies;

fortitude as never before

frankness as never before,
disillusions as never told in the old days,   85
hysterias, trench confessions,
laughter out of dead bellies.

---

[7] "His thirtieth year." Adapted from *The Testament* of François Villon, French Renaissance poet.
[8] Latin: "for the home."

[9] "For the homeland, not sweetly, not gloriously." Adapted from Horace: "Dulce et decorum est pro patria mori" (*Odes*, III, ii, 13).

V

There died a myriad,
And of the best, among them,   90
For an old bitch gone in the teeth,
For a botched civilization,
Charm, smiling at the good mouth,
Quick eyes gone under earth's lid,

For two gross of broken statues,   95
For a few thousand battered books.
1920

---

from The Cantos

from XLV

With *Usura*[1]

With usura hath no man a house of good stone
each block cut smooth and well fitting
that design might cover their face,
with usura   5
hath no man a painted paradise on his church wall
harpes et luz[2]
or where virgin receiveth message
and halo projects from incision,
with usura   10
seeth no man Gonzaga[3] his heirs and his concubines
no picture is made to endure nor to live with
but it is made to sell and sell quickly
with usura, sin against nature,
is thy bread ever more of stale rags   15
is thy bread dry as paper,
with no mountain wheat, no strong flour
with usura the line grows thick
with usura is no clear demarcation
and no man can find site for his dwelling.   20

---

[1] Latin: "usury," exorbitant interest paid for money borrowed; more generally, avarice of all sorts.
[2] French: "harps and lutes," from Jacques Villon's prayer for his mother.
[3] Luigi Gonzaga (1267–1360), ruler of Mantua.

Stonecutter is kept from his stone
weaver is kept from his loom
WITH USURA
wool comes not to market
sheep bringeth no gain with usura   25
Usura is a murrain,[4] usura
blunteth the needle in the maid's hand
and stoppeth the spinner's cunning. Pietro Lombardo[5]
came not by usura
Duccio[6] came not by usura   30
nor Pier della Francesca;[7] Zuan Bellin'[8] not by usura
nor was 'La Calunnia'[9] painted.
Came not by usura Angelico;[10] came not Ambrogio Praedis,[11]
Came no church of cut stone signed: *Adamo me fecit.*[12]
Not by usura St Trophime[13]   35
Not by usura Saint Hilaire,[14]
Usura rusteth the chisel
It rusteth the craft and the craftsman
It gnaweth the thread in the loom
None learneth to weave gold in her pattern;   40
Azure hath a canker by usura; cramoisi[15] is unbroidered
Emerald findeth no Memling[16]
Usura slayeth the child in the womb
It stayeth the young man's courting
It hath brought palsey to bed, lyeth   45
between the young bride and her bridegroom
                    CONTRA NATURAM[17]
They have brought whores for Eleusis[18]
Corpses are set to banquet
at behest of usura.   50
1937

---

[4] Disease.
[5] Italian sculptor (1435–1515).
[6] Sienese painter (1260?–1318?).
[7] Florentine painter (1420?–1492).
[8] Giovanni Bellini (1430?–1516), Venetian painter.
[9] Italian: "Calumny," painting by Sandro Botticelli (1445?–1510).
[10] Fra Angelico (1387?–1455), Florentine painter.
[11] Ambrogio de Predis (1455?–1506), Italian painter.

[12] Latin: "Adam made me," the inscription by the architect on the Church of San Zeno Maggiore in Verona.
[13] Church in Arles, France.
[14] Church in Poitiers, France.
[15] Crimson cloth.
[16] Hans Memling (1430?–1495), Flemish painter.
[17] Latin: "against nature."
[18] Shrine of Demeter, the mother goddess.

from LXXXI

Libretto

Yet
Ere the season died a-cold
Borne upon a zephyr's shoulder
I rose through the aureate sky

> *Lawes and Jenkyns guard thy rest*
> *Dolmetsch ever be thy guest,*

Has he tempered the viol's wood
To enforce   both the grave   and the acute?
Has he curved us the bowl of the lute?

> *Lawes and Jenkyns guard thy rest*
> *Dolmetsch ever be thy guest,*

Hast 'ou fashioned so airy a mood
    To draw up leaf from the root?
Hast 'ou found   a cloud   so light
    As seemed neither mist nor shade?

> Then resolve me, tell me aright
> If Waller sang or Dowland played.

> Your eyen two wol sleye me sodenly
> I may the beauté of hem nat susteyne

And for 180 years almost nothing.

Ed ascoltando al leggier mormorio
    there came new sublety of eyes into my tent,
whether of spirit or hypostasis,
    but what the blindfold hides
or at carneval
                nor any pair showed anger
    Saw but the eyes and stance between the eyes,
colour, diastasis,
    careless or unaware it had not the
   whole tent's room
nor was place for the full Εἰδὼς
interpass, penetrate
    casting but shade beyond the other lights
        sky's clear
        night's sea
        green of the mountain pool
        shone from the unmasked eyes in half-mask's space.

What thou lovest well remains,
                                     the rest is dross
What thou lov'st well shall not be reft from thee
What thou lov'st well is thy true heritage
Whose world, or mine or theirs.
                              or is it of none?
First came the seen, then thus the palpable
        Elysium, though it were in the halls of hell,
What thou lovest well is thy true heritage
What thou lov'st well shall not be reft from thee.

The ant's a centaur in his dragon world.
Pull down thy vanity, it is not man
Made courage, or made order, or made grace,
        Pull down thy vanity, I say pull down.
Learn of the green world what can be thy place
In scaled invention or true artistry.
Pull down thy vanity.
                        Paquin pull down!
The green casque has outdone your elegance.

"Master thyself, then others shall thee beare"
        Pull down thy vanity
Thou art a beaten dog beneath the hail,
A swollen magpie in a fitful sun,
Half black half white
Nor knowst'ou wing from tail
Pull down thy vanity
                How mean thy hates
Fostered in falsity,
                Pull down thy vanity,
Rathe to destroy, niggard in charity,
Pull down thy vanity,
                I say pull down.
But to have done instead of not doing
                this is not vanity
To have, with decency, knocked
That a Blunt should open
                To have gathered from the air a live tradition
or from a fine old eye the unconquered flame
This is not vanity.
        Here error is all in the not done,
all in the diffidence that faltered . . .
1948

Hilda Doolittle
(1886–1961)

Hilda Doolittle, whom we know as H. D., was born in Bethlehem, Pennsylvania. Her mother, Helen Wolle Doolittle, was a member of one of Bethlehem's most prominent Moravian families. Her father, Charles Leander Doolittle, was a professor of mathematics and astronomy at Lehigh University and, beginning in 1895, at the University of Pennsylvania. In 1902 H. D. entered Friends' Central School, an exclusive Philadelphia preparatory school, where she did distinguished work in Greek, Latin, French, and German. But around 1905, when she entered Bryn Mawr, her hold on herself as a model daughter and student loosened, and then gave way entirely.

Looking back, H. D. thought of herself as caught between two kinds of intelligence, "my father's science and my mother's art." But the tensions that made her life as a student impossible had their roots in parental and social expectations that both governed and reinforced Bryn Mawr's authoritarian approach to educating gifted young women. In 1906, shortly before the end of her third semester, she quit. Except for one brief stint two years later at the University of Pennsylvania, her formal education was over.

In 1901, shortly before she entered Friends' Central School, H.D. met Ezra Pound at a Halloween costume ball. She was fifteen, and he was a sixteen-year-old freshman at the University of Pennsylvania. Both were hungry readers, ready talkers, and aspiring writers. Over the next several years, the two of them moved in and out of several "engagements," in a relationship that was both complicated and intensified by parental opposition, competing ambitions, and conflicted sexual desires. In 1910, Frances Josepha Gregg arrived on the scene and became deeply involved, first with H. D., who fell in love with her, and then with Pound, with whom she fell in love. H. D. wrote her first poems for Gregg, and in 1911, when Pound sailed for England, H. D. and Gregg followed. Later, after H. D.'s poems began attracting attention, her relations with Pound and Gregg cooled. But she had discovered a pattern—of emotionally charged, somewhat restrained bisexuality—that worked for her; subsequently, men like Richard Aldington and D. H. Lawrence took Pound's place, and women like Bryher (Winifred Ellerman) took Gregg's. And she had found in London the only place she ever liked unequivocally. Even after the Great War, when Paris became the indisputable capital of the literary world, H. D. continued to prefer London.

H. D.'s revisionary writings in prose and especially in poetry explore tensions between public and private spheres as tensions between submission and resistance, compliance and rebellion. Her contributions to Imagism, Vorticism, and other such movements mark her as a pioneer of modern poetry. Having appeared in little magazines and anthologies, her poems were collected in *Sea Garden* (1916). Later, following the Great War, in collections such as *Hymen* (1921), her style became more boldly meditative—a blend of what she called "vision of the womb and vision of the brain." During the 30s, when she underwent psychoanalysis with Sigmund Freud, she wrote prose as well as poetry, including the novellas *Kora and Ka* (1934) and *Nights* (1935). From that time until her death in 1961, she continued to experiment with fiction, nonfiction, and poetry. In 1960, in accepting an Award of Merit from the

American Academy of Arts and Letters, she balanced the reticence she had retained with the confidence she had won. "Winged words make their own spiral; caught up in them, we are lost, or found. . . . This winged victory belongs to the poem, not the poet. But to share in the making of a poem is the privilege of the poet." A year later, diminished by a series of ailments, she died shortly after publication of her epic poem *Helen in Egypt*.

Further Reading:

S. Friedman, *Psyche Reborn: The Emergence of H. D.*, 1981.

B. Guest, *Herself Defined: The Poet H. D. and Her World*, 1984.

R. DuPlessis, *H. D.: The Career of that Struggle*, 1986.

S. Friedman, *Penelope's Web: H. D.'s Fictions and the Engendering of Modernism*, 1991.

Text:
Collected Poems: 1912–1944, 1983, ed. L. Martz.

Sea Rose

Rose, harsh rose,
marred and with stint of petals,
meagre flower, thin,
sparse of leaf,

more precious   5
than a wet rose
single on a stem—
you are caught in the drift.

Stunted, with small leaf,
you are flung on the sand,   10
you are lifted
in the crisp sand
that drives in the wind.

Can the spice-rose
drip such acrid fragrance   15
hardened in a leaf?
1916

Oread*

Whirl up, sea—
whirl your pointed pines,
splash your great pines
on our rocks,
hurl your green over us,   5
cover us with your pools of fir.
1924

Helen†

All Greece hates
the still eyes in the white face,
the lustre as of olives
where she stands,
and the white hands.   5

All Greece reviles
the wan face when she smiles,
hating it deeper still
when it grows wan and white,
remembering past enchantments   10
and past ills.

Greece sees unmoved,
God's daughter, born of love,
the beauty of cool feet
and slenderest knees,   15
could love indeed the maid,
only if she were laid,
white ash amid funereal cypresses.
1924

---

* A nymph of the mountains and hills.
† Beautiful wife of Menelaus whose abduction
  by Paris brought on the Trojan War.

Robinson Jeffers
1887–1962

Robinson Jeffers was a poet of long forms who remained a poetic conservative, choosing traditional narrative over the innovative open form of Walt Whitman's "Song of Myself." Yet, as much as Whitman, Jeffers worked to articulate with evangelical intensity a vision of America and the cosmos, a vision that was at once religious, historical, psychological, and scientific in its points of reference. He differed from Whitman in depicting his primitive American characters against the background of classical tragedy rather than the epic tradition; he once professed to be pleased by a description of himself as "striding morosely over the hills with a copy of Aeschylus in one hand and a shilling shocker in the other."

Jeffers was born in 1887 to a prosperous family in Pittsburgh, Pennsylvania. His father, a Presbyterian preacher and theologian who taught at Western Theological Seminary, could afford to send his son to study in Switzerland and Germany. After graduation in 1905 from Occidental College (his family having moved west to Long Beach, California, in 1903), the young Jeffers began work on an M.A. at the University of Southern California, studied in Zurich in 1906, and returned to U.S.C. as a medical student in 1907.

At U.S.C. Jeffers met Una Call Kuster, who was then married to a prominent Los Angeles lawyer. It was the first of what he later called the two "accidents that changed and directed my life." As their relationship deepened and grew to trouble them both, Jeffers broke away to study forestry in Washington State; but within an hour of his return to California in 1911, he saw Una in the street, and their relationship recommenced. In a last attempt to save the marriage, her husband persuaded her to spend a year abroad; it did not succeed. In 1913 Una divorced Kuster and married Jeffers. Years later, Jeffers touchingly acknowledged his personal debt to Una with a characteristically self-deprecating tribute: "My nature is cold and undiscriminating; she excited and focused it, gave it eyes and nerves and sympathies. She never saw any of my poems until they were typed, yet by her presence and conversation she has coauthored every one of them." Una also served, as Jeffers wrote in 1953, in many practical ways as a mediator between him and the world, something that his extreme shyness made necessary.

In 1914, aided by a modest inheritance, Jeffers settled in Carmel, California. Happening upon that region was the second of the two accidents that directed his life. There, Jeffers wrote, he "could see people living—amid magnificent unspoiled scenery—essentially as they did in the Idylls, or the Sagas, or in Homer's Ithaca." The region was to furnish much of both the settings and the spirit of his major poetry. In 1919 he started work on Tor House and Hawk Tower, the stone buildings that became his lifelong home. As Jeffers "helped the mason shift and place the wave and wind-worn granite," Una wrote, he became "aware of strengths in himself unknown before." In a poem published in 1951, "The Old Stonemason," Jeffers linked working with stone with some of the major preoccupations of his poetry, the strength that allows one to struggle out of the "tidewash" of human passions and illusions, and the ability to face the "enormous inhuman beauty of things." In 1924 Jeffers's first major work, *Tamar and Other Poems,* was privately published; it was reissued with the narrative "Roan Stallion" in 1925. The success of these poems marked the beginning of his public career as a poet and his emerging identity as a sort of cult figure. From the nature of his poetry, which was often sensational, tragic, and philosophical (he also, though less frequently, philosophized in prose), it was not difficult to picture him as a solitary, brooding, prophetic figure who, from his rugged house overlooking the Pacific, wrote of the suicidal passions of a self-deluded mankind.

By now the pattern of the rest of his reclusive, outwardly uneventful life was set. With Una to manage his limited contact with the public world, he could stay in the seclusion he so required, a seclusion that had less to do with the misanthropy many readers have found in his works than it did with Jeffers's shyness and extreme self-protectiveness. When he did have contact with others, he showed himself consistently to be a conscientious and considerate man. Though a stoical detachment from the passions of mankind was an important theme and a heroic posture in much of his poetry, Jeffers's personal need for solitude had humbler and tenderer roots. As Una remarked, "Many people work best, I think, when they are stimulated by outside influences and clashing with other minds, but not my husband, who gets quite *numb* when he cannot pursue his own quiet and solitary way." So shy of contact was he that once, when Una was away, he hid in the bedroom with their dog to avoid two strangers who had knocked at the door. The great tragedy of his life was Una's death in 1950. The "passage of time does not make it more endurable," he wrote a year later, in refusing an invitation to give a reading in Chicago. He died after years of illness in 1962.

Jeffers's work consists primarily of two kinds of poems. Long tragic narratives like *Tamar* and "Roan Stallion" and, later, *The Women at Point Sur, Cawdor, Thurso's Landing,* and *Give Your Heart to the Hawks* are complemented by short meditative lyrics, typically set on the dramatic Pacific coastline. In all his poems, Jeffers saw himself as an exponent of what he called "inhumanism," a philosophy so austere and forbidding that it has, along with the sensationalistic plots of his longer works, limited Jeffers's appeal. His view of the world, molded as it was by the disillusionment that followed World War I, was as prophetically stern as his domestic life was quiet and devoted. He believed that "man is a part of nature, but a nearly infinitesimal part; the human race will cease after a while and leave no trace, but the great splendors of nature will go on." Most fear to face this truth, Jeffers believed; as a result, the life of the bulk of humankind is characterized by "immoderate racial introversion," with "ninety-odd percent of people's activities turned in on other people instead of outward on the world." Human social and historical concerns, he believed, are blind and vain. They isolate humankind as a species from awareness of the far greater, inhuman beauty of the cosmos it inhabits. Jeffers occasionally took comfort in the thought of the extinction of the human race, when nature will have purified itself of man. More frequently, he condemned his fellows for their many forms of self-degradation. Jeffers interpreted such differing phenomena as urbanization and world war as signs of the self-destructive self-preoccupation of the species, and he could sound quite strident, even foolish in his condemnations. He once described the life of the masses with disgust as "this horrible entwining of people libidinously listening to *crooners,* etc." His work frequently uses the theme of incest to express symbolically how the species causes its own suffering by turning away from the grandeur of nonhuman nature to focus its energies and passions on itself.

Against this collective degradation, lonely individuals of a higher sort could stand out in bold relief insofar as they sought the triumph of an extreme and painful self-transcendence. In such moments, moments that usually came in the midst of a great tragedy that burned away the all-too-human in them, a few of Jeffers's heroes were capable of looking directly on inhuman reality in all its terrible beauty. For Jeffers, this was the equivalent of looking directly at God. In these moments his characters found in themselves an austere, stony stoicism. Jeffers once wrote a characteristically stern version of the biblical commandments: One must love God with all one's heart and soul and one's neighbor as oneself—"as much as that, but as *little* as that."

Further Reading:

L. Powell, *Robinson Jeffers, The Man and His Work,* 1934, 1940.

R. Gilbert, *Shine, Perishing Republic: Robinson Jeffers and the Tragic Sense in Modern Poetry,* 1936.

R. Squires, *The Loyalties of Robinson Jeffers,* 1956, 1963.

M. C. Monjian, *Robinson Jeffers, a Study in Inhumanism,* 1958.

M. Bennett, *The Stone Mason of Tor House: The Life and Work of Robinson Jeffers,* 1966.

Brother Antonius (W. Everson), *Robinson Jeffers: Fragments of an Older Fury,* 1968.

A. B. Coffin, *Robinson Jeffers: Poet of Inhumanism,* 1970.

R. Brophy, *Robinson Jeffers: Myth, Ritual, and Symbol in the Narrative Poems,* 1973.

J. Shebl, *In This Wild Water,* 1976.

W. Nolte, *Rock and Hawk: Robinson Jeffers and the Romantic Agony,* 1978.

R. Zaller, ed., *The Cliffs of Solitude: A Reading of Robinson Jeffers,* 1983.

Robert Zaller, ed., *Centennial Essays for Robinson Jeffers,* 1991.

J. Karman, *Robinson Jeffers: Poet of California,* 1987.

W. Everson, *The Excesses of God: Robinson Jeffers as a Religious Figure,* 1988.

Texts:

"Boats in a Fog" from *The Selected Poetry of Robinson Jeffers,* 1959.

"Hurt Hawks" from *Robinson Jeffers: Selected Poems,* 1965.

See also *The Selected Letters of Robinson Jeffers, 1897–1962,* ed. A. Ridgeway, 1968.

Boats in a Fog

Sports and gallantries, the stage, the arts, the antics of dancers,
The exuberant voices of music,
Have charm for children but lack nobility; it is bitter earnestness
That makes beauty; the mind
Knows, grown adult.
           A sudden fog-drift muffled the ocean,   5
A throbbing of engines moved in it,
At length, a stone's throw out, between the rocks and the vapor,
One by one moved shadows
Out of the mystery, shadows, fishing-boats, trailing each other
Following the cliff for guidance,   10
Holding a difficult path between the peril of the sea-fog
And the foam on the shore granite.

One by one, trailing their leader, six crept by me,
Out of the vapor and into it,
The throb of their engines subdued by the fog, patient and cautious,   15
Coasting all round the peninsula
Back to the buoys in Monterey[1] harbor. A flight of pelicans
Is nothing lovelier to look at;
The flight of the planets is nothing nobler; all the arts lose virtue
Against the essential reality   20
Of creatures going about their business among the equally
Earnest elements of nature.
1925

Hurt Hawks

I

The broken pillar of the wing jags from the clotted shoulder,
The wing trails like a banner in defeat,
No more to use the sky forever but live with famine
And pain a few days: cat nor coyote
Will shorten the week of waiting for death, there is game without talons.   5
He stands under the oak-bush and waits
The lame feet of salvation; at night he remembers freedom
And flies in a dream, the dawns ruin it.
He is strong and pain is worse to the strong, incapacity is worse.
The curs of the day come and torment him   10
At distance, no one but death the redeemer will humble that head,
The intrepid readiness, the terrible eyes.
The wild God of the world is sometimes merciful to those
That ask mercy, not often to the arrogant.
You do not know him, you communal people, or you have forgotten him;   15
Intemperate and savage, the hawk remembers him;
Beautiful and wild, the hawks, and men that are dying, remember him.

II

I'd sooner, except the penalties, kill a man than a hawk; but the
  great redtail
Had nothing left but unable misery
From the bone too shattered for mending, the wing that trailed
  under his talons when he moved.   20

---

[1] California coastal town just to the north of
Carmel, the site of Jeffers's Tor House.

We had fed him six weeks, I gave him freedom,
He wandered over the foreland hill and returned in the evening,
   asking for death,
Not like a beggar, still eyed with the old
Implacable arrogance. I gave him the lead gift in the twilight.
   What fell was relaxed,   25
Owl-downy, soft feminine feathers; but what
Soared: the fierce rush: the night-herons by the flooded river
   cried fear at its rising
Before it was quite unsheathed from reality.
1928

Marianne Moore
1887–1972

Marianne Moore, by the end of her long life, was treated somewhat as a lovable mascot to be patronized by those who thought her eccentricities (the black tricorn hat or her love of the Brooklyn Dodgers) charming. This latter image obscured the real person, the clever and scornful writer who came on the literary scene praised by T. S. Eliot, in 1921. Moore's clear and avant-garde intelligence made *The Dial*, under her editorship (1925–1929), the magazine anyone interested in new art and writing in the 1920s had to read. In her poetry, she was a precise artist for whom a few words sketched an ethical problem, an exotic animal, or a landscape.

    Moore was born within a year of Emily Dickinson's death; it was not, in fact, until Moore was in her twenties that Dickinson's art was understood and her rank as a major poet established. Moore looked to Dickinson as a model, but looked even more to various English sources, especially George Herbert, John Bunyan, and other religious writers. She had been brought up in strict Presbyterianism, and the strong ethical bent that this training produced in her remained in lifelong tension (at first productive, later destructive) with her appreciation of the multiplicity and aesthetic diversity of life's natural and human products. She gazed at lizards and medieval tapestries with equal interest; she relished the lore of bestiaries and newspaper quotations, advertising copy and guidebooks, fashion reporting and the Bible. But her moral side urged the strictness of principles, the plainness of axioms, and the geometry of the righteous life. Her relish she called "gusto," her love of the plain style she called "sincerity," and in the antiphony between "gusto" and "sincerity" her poetry takes form.

    The form it takes is both strict and free. Moore would write out a stanza until the phrases all fell right and the lines were satisfactory. Then she would create other stanzas on the model of the first, counting the syllables in each line of the original stanza and replicating that number in subsequent stanzas. She insisted that she wrote by stanzas, not in syllabic lines. By fixing a relatively inflexible number of syllables in each line, she established the rule of control that a poet needs for ingenious invention to be pressed into service. Though many of her poems are written in free verse, the elegant and quirky motion of her syllabic poems (including "The Fish" and "Poetry") made her famous.

Moore's father went insane before she was born; she never knew him. For the first seven years of her life she lived with her mother and her elder brother in the house of her maternal grandparents in St. Louis. Her mother took a teaching job and moved the family to Carlisle, Pennsylvania; there they continued the intense closeness reflected in their subsequent lives. Moore lived with her mother all her life and remained closely attached to her brother. Moore graduated from Bryn Mawr College; her grades were not good enough for her to major in English—an ironic fate—so she majored in biology, beginning that training of the eye that, together with the act of the commenting mind, gave her second book its punning title, *Observations* (1924).

In fact, that book contained mostly poems reprinted from her first book, *Poems* (1921), published (without her knowledge or permission) by two of her friends, American writers living in London, Winifred Bryher and Hilda Doolittle. Moore's poems had already appeared in such American avant-garde journals as *Poetry* and *Others.* She was moving in a circle that included Alfred Kreymborg (the editor of *Others*), Wallace Stevens, William Carlos Williams, and various painters and sculptors. She was thought beautiful by many who knew her, but marriage (which it takes "all one's criminal ingenuity to avoid") was something she turned away from, though her long poem "Marriage" shows she had considered both its seductions and its rewards. Her mother's bitter experience may have deterred her, or, like Emily Dickinson, she may have reserved her attention for her work.

"One detects creative power," wrote Moore, "by its capacity to conquer one's detachment." To read Moore's best pages is to find one's detachment conquered as one is drawn into an odd, unpredictable, satiric, learned mind, offering "neatness of finish! neatness of finish!" side by side with the sprawling grandeur of "an octopus of ice"—as Moore called the many-armed glacier covering Mt. Rainier. A great deal of Moore's creative power was spent, as in "An Octopus," thinking about America, both critically and approvingly. Her symbol for America is Mt. Rainier itself—enormous, half threat, half invitation, hospitable to all sorts of enterprising and hardy mountain fauna but at the same time the site of terrible geographic, climatic, and aesthetic extremes. Moore was tart when she looked at American failings: Against the American disposition to listen to "snake-charming controversialists" she argued that "it is one thing to change one's mind, / another to eradicate it." Against those who saw in New York only a commercial center she argued "it is not the plunder, / but 'accessibility to experience.' " Against Anglophiles she argued that excellence "has never been confined to one locality." She hated the "half limping and half-ladyfied" rhetoric of diplomats; she scoffed at those who complacently announced that woman was "circumscribed by a / heritage of blindness and native / incompetence." Generally, the prejudiced, in Moore's poetry, condemn themselves; their words, quoted back at them and embedded in Moore's surgical cleanness of style, resound in foolishness. Moore's habit of quoting, however, extended far beyond the satirical quoting of the words of fools; she collected with the temperament of a magpie all sorts of things to quote. The Rosenbach Foundation Museum in Philadelphia preserves her living room; its drawers are full of the accumulation of a lifetime—conversation notebooks in which she recorded sayings (especially of her mother and brother) and files of clippings. Her poems are mosaics, or collages; many pieces are arranged until they fit together. The impossible ideal hovering under the surface is that of an assemblage so perfect that it would need no authorially supplied connective tissue.

The aesthetic pleasures to be found in Moore are those of exquisite appositeness, lightness of touch combined with depth of feeling, ingenuity and surprise, and conversational urbanity and wit. In her later years her morality ("this is mortality, / this is eternity") and her whimsy ("O to be a dragon") disturbed the delicate balance maintained in the best of her poetry, but *Observations* remains, like T. S. Eliot's *Prufrock and Other Observations* and Wallace Stevens's *Harmonium*, one of the treasures of American modernist writing.

Further Reading:

F. Engel, *Marianne Moore*, 1964.
J. Garrigue, *Marianne Moore*, 1965.
A. K. Weatherhead, *The Edge of the Image: Marianne Moore, William Carlos Williams, and Some Other Poets*, 1967.
G. W. Nitchie, *Marianne Moore: An Introduction to the Poetry*, 1969.
C. Tomlinson, ed., *Marianne Moore: A Collection of Critical Essays*, 1969.

D. Hall, *Marianne Moore: The Cage and the Animal*, 1970.
C. S. Abbot, *Marianne Moore: A Reference Guide*, 1980.
B. Costello, *Marianne Moore: Imaginary Possessions*, 1981.
J. Parisi, ed., *Marianne Moore: The Art of a Modernist*, 1990.
P. Willis, *Marianne Moore: Woman and Poet*, 1990.

Texts:

"Poetry" from *Collected Poems*, 1951.
All other selections from *The Complete Poems of Marianne Moore*, 1981.

See also *A Marianne Moore Reader*, 1961.

Poetry*

I, too, dislike it: there are things that are important beyond all this fiddle.
    Reading it, however, with a perfect contempt for it, one discovers in
    it after all, a place for the genuine.
        Hands that can grasp, eyes
        that can dilate, hair that can rise   5
            if it must, these things are important not because a

high-sounding interpretation can be put upon them but because they are
    useful. When they become so derivative as to become unintelligible,
    the same thing may be said for all of us, that we
        do not admire what   10
        we cannot understand: the bat
            holding on upside down or in quest of something to

* This poem was revised several times and in the end (1967) reduced to its first two sentences. The version here is from *Collected Poems* (1951).

eat, elephants pushing, a wild horse taking a roll, a tireless wolf under
 a tree, the immovable critic twitching his skin like a horse that feels a flea,
  the base-   15
ball fan, the statistician—
  nor is it valid
   to discriminate against 'business documents and

school-books';[1] all these phenomena are important. One must make a
 distinction
however: when dragged into prominence by half poets, the result is not
  poetry,   20
nor till the poets among us can be
  'literalists of
   the imagination'[2]—above
    insolence and triviality and can present

for inspection, 'imaginary gardens with real toads in them', shall we have 25
 it. In the meantime, if you demand on the one hand,
 the raw material of poetry in
  all its rawness[3] and
  that which is on the other hand
   genuine, you are interested in poetry.   30
1921

The Fish

  wade
  through black jade.[1]
   Of the crow-blue mussel-shells, one keeps
   adjusting the ash-heaps;[2]
    opening and shutting itself like   5

[1] Moore's note: "*Diary of Tolstoy* (Dutton), p. 84. 'Where the boundary between prose and poetry lies, I shall never be able to understand. The question is raised in manuals of style, yet the answer to it lies beyond me. Poetry is verse; prose is not verse. Or else poetry is everything with the exception of business documents and school books.' "

[2] Moore's note: "*Yeats: Ideas of Good and Evil* (A. H. Bullen), p. 182. 'The limitation of his view was from the very intensity of his vision; he was a too literal realist of imagination, as others are of nature; and because he believed that the figures seen by the mind's eye, when exalted by inspiration, were "eternal existences," symbols of divine essences, he hated every grace of style that might obscure their lineaments.' "

[3] Moore saved a clipping from *The Spectator* (London) for May 10, 1913, in which a contributor, called "C," asked why the Greek Anthology still charms us, says: "All [of its poems] appeal to emotions which endure for all time, and which, it has been aptly said, are the true raw material of poetry."

[1] The ocean waters.

[2] I.e., the heaps of mussels look like lumps of burnt coal.

an
injured fan.
   The barnacles which encrust the side
   of the wave, cannot hide
      there for the submerged shafts of the   10

sun,
split like spun
   glass, move themselves with spotlight swiftness
   into the crevices—
      in and out, illuminating   15

the
turquoise sea
   of bodies. The water drives a wedge
   of iron through the iron edge
      of the cliff; whereupon the stars,[3]   20

pink
rice-grains, ink-
   bespattered jelly-fish, crabs like green
   lilies, and submarine
      toadstools, slide each on the other.   25

All
external
   marks of abuse are present on this
   defiant edifice—
      all the physical features of   30

ac-
cident—lack
   of cornice, dynamite grooves, burns, and
   hatchet strokes, these things stand
      out on it; the chasm-side is   35

dead.
Repeated
   evidence has proved that it can live
   on what can not revive
      its youth. The sea grows old in it.   40
   1924

---

[3] Starfish.

A Grave

Man looking into the sea,
taking the view from those who have as much right to it as you have to it
    yourself,
it is human nature to stand in the middle of a thing,
but you cannot stand in the middle of this;
the sea has nothing to give but a well excavated grave.   5
The firs stand in a procession, each with an emerald turkey-foot at the top,
reserved as their contours, saying nothing;
repression, however, is not the most obvious characteristic of the sea;
the sea is a collector, quick to return a rapacious look.
There are others besides you who have worn that look—   10
whose expression is no longer a protest; the fish no longer investigate them
for their bones have not lasted:
men lower nets, unconscious of the fact that they are desecrating a grave,
and row quickly away—the blades of the oars
moving together like the feet of water-spiders as if there were no such
    thing as death.   15
The wrinkles progress among themselves in a phalanx—beautiful under
    networks of foam,
and fade breathlessly while the sea rustles in and out of the seaweed;
the birds swim through the air at top speed, emitting cat-calls as heretofore—
the tortoise-shell scourges about the feet of the cliffs, in motion beneath
    them;
and the ocean, under the pulsation of lighthouses and noise of bell-buoys, 20
advances as usual, looking as if it were not that ocean in which dropped
    things are bound to sink—
in which if they turn and twist, it is neither with volition nor consciousness.
1924

The Monkeys

winked too much and were afraid of snakes. The zebras,
                          supreme in
    their abnormality; the elephants with their fog-colored skin
      and strictly practical appendages
        were there, the small cats; and the parakeet—   5
          trivial and humdrum on examination, destroying
        bark and portions of the food it could not eat.

I recall their magnificence, now not more magnificent
than it is dim. It is difficult to recall the ornament,
   speech, and precise manner of what one might   10
      call the minor acquaintances twenty
         years back; but I shall not forget him—that Gilgamesh
                          among
   the hairy carnivora—that cat with the

wedge-shaped, slate-gray marks on its forelegs and the resolute   15
                                          tail,
astringently remarking, "They have imposed on us with their pale
   half-fledged protestations, trembling about
      in inarticulate frenzy, saying
         it is not for us to understand art; finding it   20
   all so difficult, examining the thing

as if it were inconceivably arcanic, as symmetrically
frigid as if it had been carved out of chrysoprase
   or marble—strict with tension, malignant
      in its power over us and deeper   25
        than the sea when it proffers flattery in exchange for
                            hemp,
   rye, flax, horses, platinum, timber, and fur."

1921

T. S. Eliot
1888–1965

T. S. Eliot's *The Waste Land,* like Walt Whitman's "Song of Myself," changed the course of American literary history. Eliot's long poem, published in 1922, consolidated the despair felt throughout Europe after World War I and thus spoke for the collapse of a whole culture. Its fragments of civilization seemed like the rubbish heap of history. But it was the exquisite musicality of the poem, its instantly memorable lines, that made it haunt the literary imagination.

The poet of *The Waste Land* was an expatriate American living in London. At the time he wrote the poem he had been driven, by fears of a permanent breakdown, to psychiatric treatment in Lausanne. There, in the midst of polyglot Switzerland, in the center of Europe, he looked inward to his own nervous collapse and outward to the fragmentation of Europe. But behind the European voices and landscapes of this famous poem lay an American story. In fact, Eliot had originally begun his poem with a scene in Boston's Scollay Square (the home of brothels and burlesque shows). In deleting his original opening scene and affixing instead an opening unmistakably European, Eliot turned his back on the New World and placed himself resolutely in the Old.

Eliot's family had come to the United States from England, and the pull back to family origins in East Coker, Somersetshire, is given its due in the second poem of his later sequence, *Four Quartets.* Eliot's own branch of the family had moved from Gloucester, Massachusetts, to St. Louis, where Eliot's grandfather founded Washington University in 1853. Eliot's father made money manufacturing bricks from Mississippi clay; it was Eliot's mother (author of a long verse-drama on Savonarola, which her son paid to have published) who sponsored the literary education of the poet. Eliot was a brilliantly successful student at Harvard (1906–1910 as an undergraduate studying literature, 1911–1914 as a graduate student in Sanskrit and philosophy). Though he completed a Ph.D. dissertation on the work of the skeptical idealist philosopher F. H. Bradley, Eliot never took the degree. He was studying at Oxford when World War I broke out; by the time it ended, when he could have returned to America to defend the dissertation, he had married and had chosen poetry over the academic life.

The marriage was unhappy from the beginning. Eliot's wife, Vivien Haight-Wood, was constantly ill with an assortment of maladies, in part psychosomatic but nonetheless agonizing. Eliot's father, disapproving of the marriage, changed his will and died leaving Eliot only the income, not the capital, from his share of the estate. It was after his father's death, the punishment of the will, and a London visit by his mother and sister that Eliot experienced the breakdown preceding the composition of *The Waste Land.*

With the recovery of his health, a change of job from banking to publishing (at Faber & Faber), and the publication of *The Waste Land* in *The Criterion* (a journal that he edited), Eliot's life found renewed stability. In 1932 he obtained a legal separation from his wife, whose condition had considerably worsened and who eventually died in a mental hospital in 1947. After World War II, Eliot lived for over ten years in London with John Hayward, a bibliophile, editor, and reviewer who was confined to a wheelchair by muscular dystrophy. In 1957, at age sixty-eight, Eliot married Valerie Fletcher, for many years his secretary at Faber.

Eliot's sensibility sometimes seems, to use Ezra Pound's term, a "vortex" into which the whole of modern culture was absorbed. Even as an undergraduate, Eliot adopted the irony and *ennui* of the French poets Charles Baudelaire and Jules Laforgue, whom he had discovered through Arthur Symons's influential book, *The Symbolist Movement in Literature.* In "The Love Song of J. Alfred Prufrock" the French influence is brilliantly crossed with a Tennysonian music and a Browningesque dramatic monologue. Eliot's surrealism, combining the etherized patient, the catlike fog, the butt-ends of days, and the impaled Prufrock wriggling on the wall, was something altogether new in American poetry, far from the inert Imagism of Amy Lowell and equally far from the pieties of the nineteenth-century "fireside poets."

Prufrock and Other Observations (1917) is, like Wallace Stevens's *Harmonium* (1923) and Marianne Moore's *Observations* (1924), one of the landmarks of American modernism. It was followed rapidly by *Gerontion* (1919), *Poems* (1920), and *Poems 1909–1925,* which contained *The Waste Land.* These books remain Eliot's chief poetic achievement. In them we see Eliot's most striking lyric invention, a play of voices deployed almost as instruments in an orchestra, as he drew into lyric the vocal theatricality he had found in Elizabethan and Jacobean drama. Eliot's original title for *The Waste Land* had been "He do the police in different voices," a quotation from

Dickens's *Our Mutual Friend,* describing a character who would read aloud newspaper accounts of police-blotter business, giving all the characters different dramatic voicings. Escaping from "personality" (the lyric self of the conventional lyric speaker), Eliot found freedom in multiplying his poetic voices, both in *The Waste Land* and in his later plays.

At the same time, Eliot was becoming the most brilliant literary critic in English since Coleridge. As assistant editor of *The Egoist* from 1917 to 1919 and editor of *The Criterion* for seventeen years (1922–1939), he wrote the essays collected in *The Sacred Wood* (1920), *Homage to Dryden* (1924), and *For Lancelot Andrewes* (1928). Eliot's essays took up polemical positions in the service of his own theory of poetry, projecting his own "dissociation of sensibility" back into the post-metaphysical poets, defending the macabre extremes of tension in the Jacobeans, and (after his conversion to Anglicanism in 1927) arguing for the glories of Anglican literature (Lancelot Andrewes, George Herbert). Eliot's most influential essay, "Tradition and the Individual Talent," published in *The Sacred Wood,* repudiates both the avant-garde conviction that modern poetry should break utterly from the past and the Wordsworthian definition of poetry as "emotion recollected in tranquillity." It argues that the modern poet cannot succeed without a profound incorporation of the literature of the past. It argues as well that the poet is a medium, serving as a catalyst for new combinations of language, and that the poet must therefore escape from individual personality and emotion in composing poetry. In turning away from biographical and historical information and toward language and style in his essays on individual poets (Milton, Herbert), Eliot gave a new direction to the practice of literary criticism. The so-called New Criticism, advocated in England by I. A. Richards and in the United States by such followers of Eliot as Allen Tate and John Crowe Ransom, brought a new sophistication, after the manner of Eliot, to the analysis of poetry.

Eliot's valuing of complexity, irony, and paradox, his powerful sense of the unity of a literary work, and his conviction that the work provided an "objective correlative" for the state of mind of its creator pervaded his critical writing in the 1920s. In later essays Eliot's political views became increasingly conservative until, in 1934, in a book he later retracted, *After Strange Gods* (based on lectures given at the University of Virginia), he argued against the desirability of "any large number of free-thinking Jews" in any Christian society. Eliot, who remained in many ways a Victorian intellectual preoccupied with the dissolution of social consensus and Christian belief, was pained by the increasing democratization of society and the increasing secularism of education. Both of these, he thought, entailed the loss of the fabric of common culture he believed indispensable to literature and government alike.

Though Eliot was acquainted with the avant-garde English writers of Bloomsbury, he could not greet with any joy their enthusiasm for change, reflected in Virginia Woolf's statement that in 1910 the world had changed, had become modern. His own balance was too precarious to welcome any external disruptions. Eliot may have displayed a failure of nerve in being unable to embrace social change, but that change found no more sensitive seismographer than its horrified poet-witness.

Eliot's major work after *The Waste Land* was the sequence now known as *Four Quartets* ("Burnt Norton," "East Coker," "The Dry Salvages," and "Little Gidding"). The first was written in 1935, the others during World War II; they were published together in the United States in 1943. They should be read, in part, as war poems, as well as poems having a relation, as Eliot said, to "the four seasons and the four elements." In wartime, Eliot's confidence in the value of writing was momentarily shaken: "It is hard . . . to feel confident that morning after morning spent fiddling with words and rhythms is justified activity—especially as there is never any certainty that the whole thing won't have to be scrapped."

Yet Eliot's career as a writer continued, not only in the autobiographical and historical accounts of temporal mutability in the *Quartets* but also in a series of plays. He had earlier composed *Sweeney Agonistes* (1926–1927), a brilliant adaptation of vaudeville rhythms; *Murder in the Cathedral* (1935), a dramatization of the temptation of Thomas à Becket; and *The Family Reunion* (1939), a play about marital guilt. After the *Quartets,* Eliot wrote more plays—*The Cocktail Party* (1949), which introduced a psychiatrist into a drama of Christian expiation of guilt; *The Confidential Clerk* (1953); and *The Elder Statesman* (1959). Only the first of these succeeded on the stage.

In 1948 Eliot was awarded the Nobel Prize for literature. His reputation fluctuated even during his lifetime, and it will require the publication of manuscripts, letters, and other such documents before a full history of his significance and influence can be written. He is indubitably the greatest writer of modern free verse in America and the greatest of our literary critics, a man whose taste set the taste of his era. Eliot's conviction that he was witnessing the death of culture, conveyed most powerfully in his myths of historical decline, gripped his first auditors. More skeptical readers may believe his later ironic statement that *The Waste Land* represented merely "a personal grudge," a catastrophe of the inner life rather than of the life of civilization. Those readers will see it as one of the great lyrics of a crisis in consciousness, an American long poem to be ranked with Milton's "Lycidas" and Wordsworth's "Ode: On the Intimations of Immortality" as a comprehensive account of the human predicament.

Further Reading:

F. R. Leavis, *New Bearings in English Poetry, 1932.*
F. O. Matthiessen, *The Achievement of T. S. Eliot,* 1935, 1947.
L. Unger, ed., *T. S. Eliot: A Selected Critique,* 1948.
E. Drew, *T. S. Eliot: The Design of His Poetry,* 1949.
H. Gardner, *The Art of T. S. Eliot,* 1949.
D. E. S. Maxwell, *The Poetry of T. S. Eliot,* 1952.
G. Williamson, *A Reader's Guide to T. S. Eliot,* 1953.
G. Smith, *T. S. Eliot's Poetry and Plays,* 1956.
H. Kenner, *The Invisible Poet: T. S. Eliot,* 1959.
D. E. Jones, *The Plays of T. S. Eliot,* 1960.
K. Smidt, *Poetry and Belief in the Work of T. S. Eliot,* 1961.
A. G. George, *T. S. Eliot: His Mind and Art,* 1962.
P. R. Headings, *T. S. Eliot,* 1964.
H. Howarth, *Notes of Some Figures Behind T. S. Eliot,* 1964.
L. Unger, *T. S. Eliot: Monuments and Patterns,* 1966.
H. Blamires, *Word Unheard: A Guide Through Eliot's Four Quartets,* 1969.
A. Austin, *T. S. Eliot: The Literary and Social Criticism,* 1971.
B. Bergonzi, *T. S. Eliot,* 1971.
G. Patterson, *T. S. Eliot: Poems in the Making,* 1971.
R. Sencourt, *T. S. Eliot: A Memoir,* 1971.

R. Kirk, *Eliot and His Age,* 1972.
R. Kojecky, *T. S. Eliot's Social Criticism,* 1972.
J. D. Margolis, *T. S. Eliot's Intellectual Development,* 1972.
B. Rajan, *The Overwhelming Question: A Study of the Poetry of T. S. Eliot,* 1976.
S. Spender, *T. S. Eliot,* 1976.
D. Traversi, *T. S. Eliot: The Longer Poems,* 1976.
H. Gardner, *The Composition of the "Four Quartets,"* 1977.
L. Gordon, *Eliot's Early Years,* 1977.
J. E. Miller, *T. S. Eliot's Personal Waste Land,* 1977.
D. Newton-DeMolina, ed., *The Literary Criticism of T. S. Eliot: New Essays,* 1977.
N. Frye, *T. S. Eliot,* 1981.
C. Behr, *T. S. Eliot: A Chronology of His Life and Works,* 1982.
E. K. Hay, *T. S. Eliot's Negative Way,* 1982.
R. Bush, *T. S. Eliot: A Study in Character and Style,* 1983.
R. Bush, ed., *T. S. Eliot: The Modernist in History,* 1991.
T. Sharpe, *T. S. Eliot: A Literary Life,* 1991.

Texts:
Selections from *Complete Poems and Plays,* 1962.

The Love Song of J. Alfred Prufrock

S'io credesse che mia risposta fosse
A persona che mai tornasse al mondo,
Questa fiamma staria senza piu scosse.
Ma perciocche giammai di questo fondo
Non torno vivo alcun, s'i'odo il vero,
Senza tema d'infamia it rispondo.[1]

Let us go then, you and I,
When the evening is spread out against the sky
Like a patient etherised upon a table;
Let us go, through certain half-deserted streets,
The muttering retreats   5
Of restless nights in one-night cheap hotels
And sawdust restaurants with oyster-shells:
Streets that follow like a tedious argument
Of insidious intent
To lead you to an overwhelming question . . .   10
Oh, do not ask, "What is it?"
Let us go and make our visit.

    In the room the women come and go
Talking of Michelangelo.

    The yellow fog that rubs its back upon the window-panes,   15
The yellow smoke that rubs its muzzle on the window-panes,
Licked its tongue into the corners of the evening,
Lingered upon the pools that stand in drains,
Let fall upon its back the soot that falls from chimneys,
Slipped by the terrace, made a sudden leap,   20
And seeing that it was a soft October night,
Curled once about the house, and fell asleep.

    And indeed there will be time
For the yellow smoke that slides along the street,
Rubbing its back upon the window-panes;   25
There will be time, there will be time
To prepare a face to meet the faces that you meet;

---

[1] From Dante's *Inferno*, XXVII, 61–66. Guido da Montefeltro speaks, after Dante questions him: "If I thought that my reply were to be to someone who would ever return to the world, this flame would be still, without further motion. But since no one has ever returned alive from this depth, if what I hear is true, I answer you without fear of shame." In the poem, Prufrock speaks, similarly, an inner truth to an unnamed "you."

There will be time to murder and create,
And time for all the works and days[2] of hands
That lift and drop a question on your plate;   30
Time for you and time for me,
And time yet for a hundred indecisions,
And for a hundred visions and revisions,
Before the taking of a toast and tea.

    In the room the women come and go   35
Talking of Michelangelo.

    And indeed there will be time
To wonder, "Do I dare?" and, "Do I dare?"
Time to turn back and descend the stair,
With a bald spot in the middle of my hair—   40
(They will say: "How his hair is growing thin!")
My morning coat, my collar mounting firmly to the chin,
My necktie rich and modest, but asserted by a simple pin—
(They will say: "But how his arms and legs are thin!")
Do I dare   45
Disturb the universe?
In a minute there is time
For decisions and revisions which a minute will reverse.

    For I have known them all already, known them all—
Have known the evenings, mornings, afternoons,   50
I have measured out my life with coffee spoons;
I know the voices dying with a dying fall
Beneath the music from a farther room.
    So how should I presume?

    And I have known the eyes already, known them all—   55
The eyes that fix you in a formulated phrase,
And when I am formulated, sprawling on a pin,
When I am pinned and wriggling on the wall,
Then how should I begin
To spit out all the butt-ends of my days and ways?   60
    And how should I presume?

    And I have known the arms already, known them all—
Arms that are braceleted and white and bare
(But in the lamplight, downed with light brown hair!)
Is it perfume from a dress   65
That makes me so digress?
Arms that lie along a table, or wrap about a shawl.

---

[2] The Greek poet Hesiod (eighth century B.C.)
wrote *Works and Days,* a georgic poem.

And should I then presume?
And how should I begin?
    . . . . .

Shall I say, I have gone at dusk through narrow streets   70
And watched the smoke that rises from the pipes
Of lonely men in shirt-sleeves, leaning out of windows? . . .

I should have been a pair of ragged claws
Scuttling across the floors of silent seas.
     . . . . .

And the afternoon, the evening, sleeps so peacefully!   75
Smoothed by long fingers,
Asleep . . . tired . . . or it malingers,
Stretched on the floor, here beside you and me.
Should I, after tea and cakes and ices,
Have the strength to force the moment to its crisis?   80
But though I have wept and fasted, wept and prayed,
Though I have seen my head (grown slightly bald) brought in upon a platter,[3]
I am no prophet—and here's no great matter;
I have seen the moment of my greatness flicker,
And I have seen the eternal Footman hold my coat, and snicker,   85
And in short, I was afraid.

And would it have been worth it, after all,
After the cups, the marmalade, the tea,
Among the porcelain, among some talk of you and me,
Would it have been worth while,   90
To have bitten off the matter with a smile,
To have squeezed the universe into a ball
To roll it toward some overwhelming question,
To say: "I am Lazarus, come from the dead,[4]
Come back to tell you all, I shall tell you all"—   95
If one, settling a pillow by her head,
    Should say: "That is not what I meant at all.
    That is not it, at all."

And would it have been worth it, after all,
Would it have been worth while,   100
After the sunsets and the dooryards and the sprinkled streets,
After the novels, after the teacups, after the skirts that trail along the floor—
And this, and so much more?—
It is impossible to say just what I mean!
But as if a magic lantern threw the nerves in patterns on a screen: 105

---

[3] The head of John the Baptist was delivered   [4] Lazarus was raised from the dead by Jesus
on a platter to Salome (Matthew 14:1–11).   (John 11:1–44).

Would it have been worth while
If one, settling a pillow or throwing off a shawl,
And turning toward the window, should say:
   "That is not it at all,
   That is not what I meant, at all."   110
      . . . . .

No! I am not Prince Hamlet,[5] nor was meant to be;
Am an attendant lord, one that will do
To swell a progress,[6] start a scene or two,
Advise the prince; no doubt, an easy tool,
Deferential, glad to be of use,   115
Politic, cautious, and meticulous;
Full of high sentence,[7] but a bit obtuse;
At times, indeed, almost ridiculous—
Almost, at times, the Fool.

     I grow old . . . I grow old . . .   120
I shall wear the bottoms of my trousers rolled.

     Shall I part my hair behind? Do I dare to eat a peach?
I shall wear white flannel trousers, and walk upon the beach.
I have heard the mermaids singing, each to each.

I do not think that they will sing to me.   125

I have seen them riding seaward on the waves
Combing the white hair of the waves blown back
When the wind blows the water white and black.

We have lingered in the chambers of the sea
By sea-girls wreathed with seaweed red and brown   130
Till human voices wake us, and we drown.
1917

Gerontion

    Thou hast nor youth nor age
    But as it were an after dinner sleep
    Dreaming of both.

Here I am, an old man in a dry month,
Being read to by a boy, waiting for rain.

---

5 i.e., Prufrock will be, not like Hamlet the
hero, but rather like Polonius, a fussy court
advisor.

6 Royal procession.
7 Sententiousness.

I was neither at the hot gates
Nor fought in the warm rain
Nor knee deep in the salt marsh, heaving a cutlass,   5
Bitten by flies, fought.
My house is a decayed house,
And the jew squats on the window sill, the owner,
Spawned in some estaminet of Antwerp,
Blistered in Brussels, patched and peeled in London.   10
The goat coughs at night in the field overhead;
Rocks, moss, stonecrop, iron, merds.
The woman keeps the kitchen, makes tea,
Sneezes at evening, poking the peevish gutter.
                        I an old man,   15
A dull head among windy spaces.

    Signs are taken for wonders. "We would see a sign!"
The word within a word, unable to speak a word,
Swaddled with darkness. In the juvescence of the year
Came Christ the tiger   20

    In depraved May, dogwood and chestnut, flowering judas,
To be eaten, to be divided, to be drunk
Among whispers; by Mr. Silvero
With caressing hands, at Limoges
Who walked all night in the next room;   25

    By Hakagawa, bowing among the Titians;
By Madame de Tornquist, in the dark room
Shifting the candles; Fräulein von Kulp
Who turned in the hall, one hand on the door.   30
    Vacant shuttles
Weave the wind. I have no ghosts,
An old man in a draughty house
Under a windy knob.

    After such knowledge, what forgiveness? Think now
History has many cunning passages, contrived corridors   35
And issues, deceives with whispering ambitions,
Guides us by vanities. Think now
She gives when our attention is distracted
And what she gives, gives with such supple confusions
That the giving famishes the craving. Gives too late   40
What's not believed in, or if still believed,
In memory only, reconsidered passion. Gives too soon
Into weak hands, what's thought can be dispensed with
Till the refusal propagates a fear. Think
Neither fear nor courage saves us. Unnatural vices   45
Are fathered by our heroism. Virtues

Are forced upon us by our impudent crimes.
These tears are shaken from the wrath-bearing tree.

   The tiger springs in the new year. Us he devours. Think at last
We have not reached conclusion, when I   50
Stiffen in a rented house. Think at last
I have not made this show purposelessly
And it is not by any concitation
Of the backward devils.
I would meet you upon this honestly.   55
I that was near your heart was removed therefrom
To lose beauty in terror, terror in inquisition.
I have lost my passion: why should I need to keep it
Since what is kept must be adulterated?
I have lost my sight, smell, hearing, taste and touch: 60
How should I use them for your closer contact?

   These with a thousand small deliberations
Protract the profit of their chilled delirium,
Excite the membrane, when the sense has cooled,
With pungent sauces, multiply variety   65
In a wilderness of mirrors. What will the spider do,
Suspend its operations, will the weevil
Delay? De Bailhache, Fresca, Mrs. Cammel, whirled
Beyond the circuit of the shuddering Bear
In fractured atoms. Gull against the wind, in the windy straits   70
Of Belle Isle, or running on the Horn,
White feathers in the snow, the Gulf claims,
And an old man driven by the Trades
To a sleepy corner.

            Tenants of the house,   75
Thoughts of a dry brain in a dry season.
1920

The Waste Land

The Waste Land was printed first in 1922 in *The Criterion* and *The Dial;* when it was expanded to book form later that year, Eliot added notes. "In the early poems," said Eliot at seventy-six in a *Paris Review* interview, "it was a question of . . . having more to say than one knew how to say. . . . In *The Waste Land,* I wasn't even bothering whether I understood what I was saying." In his thirties Eliot was perhaps writing under the compulsions of extreme marital unhappiness and self-disgust, yet his agile and retentive mind was not quite so unconscious as he later suggested.

The Waste Land is based on a few well-known literary and aesthetic sources, most of them myths manipulated so that they yield unhappy endings (the death of the vegetation god; the death of the father; shipwreck; the devastation of the land when its king, symbolically wounded in the thigh, is impotent). Eliot also found for his poem myths that already had unhappy endings: the destruction of Valhalla through human greed, dramatized by Wagner in *The Ring of the Nibelung;* the death of the cities that symbolize civilization (Jerusalem, Athens, Alexandria, Rome, London); and the death of cultures, like that of Renaissance England personified in Queen Elizabeth. These myths are for Eliot macrocosmic cultural versions of the death of personal love between man and wife and the death of generosity and freedom in the heart. *The Waste Land* sees history—both universal history and personal history—as unredeemable on its own terms.

Sexual malaise lies at the heart of *The Waste Land.* The neurasthenic upper-class couple driven mad by each other's presence are paired, in "A Game of Chess," with a squalid lower-class couple whose marriage is foundering because of bad teeth, abortion, and sexual infidelity. Girls at Margate are seduced and abandoned, just as Philomela was raped and tortured long ago; Tristan sees only a blank sea instead of Isolde; Ophelia goes mad after Hamlet's desertion. Sexual squalor appears in the joyless affair of the typist and the "young man carbuncular," in Sweeney's vulgar conjunction with Mrs. Porter, and in the unsavory offer of a homosexual weekend by Mr. Eugenides. Women become surreal seducers surrounded by bats with baby faces. Salome, enraged by John the Baptist's persistence in speaking of Jesus from the cistern in which he is imprisoned, takes revenge for his rejection of her by ordering his execution.

The central figure in the poem, one who has "foresuffered all," is Tiresias, the prophet who had experienced sexuality as both man and woman. The androgynous voice of this "old man with wrinkled female breasts" mediates this poem, so full of loathing for the sexual principle.

The poem is also an elegy. It begins with the ritual of the burial of the dead, and at its nerve center we see the immemorial topic of elegy, the death of the beautiful young man, "Phlebas, who was once handsome and tall as you." (Eliot had dedicated *Prufrock and Other Observations* to the memory of Jean Verdenal, a young doctor he had known in Paris, who had drowned during World War I.) The elegiac subject is also multiple—the "so many" undone by death, the drowned Phoenician Sailor, the Hanged Man, the corpse planted in the garden, "the king my brother's wreck," and "the king my father's death before him."

Against the twin horrors of sexuality and death, Eliot sets certain luminous fragments of value—the young steersman's love song to his Irish love, Spenser's refrain in his betrothal song, Ophelia's poignant "goodnight" spoken in madness, the Rhinemaidens' ecstatic water song, the repentance of St. Augustine, the Buddha's fire sermon. He asserts also the consolatory powers of literature; he has shored fragments of literature as his only bulwark against his ruins. Seen in this way, the poem is an assemblage of what Matthew Arnold called "touchstones," those lines of literature that move us deeply and against which we test other lines for greatness. In these closing "touchstones," the poem reminds itself of the chant of salvation (sung by boy sopranos in Wagner's *Parsifal*), when the grail knight cures the impotent king and restores the land to fertility. It invokes a Dantesque purgation in the refining fire and recalls a sonnet in which the disinherited speaker ("El Desdichado") says that he is the inconsolable widower whose beloved has died, whose tower is ruined. It invokes ideas of madness and vengeance in its allusion to *The Spanish Tragedy*. In finding lines of poetry appropriate to his own disinherited and mad state, to his dead father's cruelty and his own sexual failure, Eliot condensed his wide and polyglot reading to "touchstones," ending with one line of sexual longing ("The swallow has its mate; when shall I be as the swallow?") and one line of ethical and religious Buddhist resignation ("Give. Sympathize. Control. Peace. Peace. Peace.").

This collage of literary fragments, this archaeological heap of literary ruins, is the mirror of Eliot's acute inspection of his own spiritual and literary predicament. How could he forge a new literature out of the ruins of European culture? The refusal here to end with a Christian solution marks only one resting place of Eliot's long mental and aesthetic journey. It is, however, deservedly, the most famous pause in his career. In spite of its initial difficulty, *The Waste Land* has rapidly become domesticated in our literature, its combination of the ferociously colloquial and a stylized exaltation of diction setting a new level of literary daring.

The manuscript of *The Waste Land* was edited by Ezra Pound into its present form, gaining him Eliot's grateful dedication as "the better craftsman." But it should not be forgotten that Eliot could have edited it himself—as he did previous and subsequent poems—and that its glories are his invention. Its music is so pervasive that long stretches resound in the mind long after the pages are closed. At a time of suicidal grief—the epigraph, after all, says "I want to die"—Eliot raised himself, in this one poem, to a fury of self-analysis and cultural polemic that remains unsurpassed in modern literature.

The Waste Land*

"Nam Sibyllam quidem Cumigo ipse oculis meis vidi in ampulla pendere, et cum illi pueri dicerent: Σίβνλλα τί θέλεις; respondebat illa: ἀποθανεῖν θέλω."[1]

For Ezra Pound
il miglior fabbro.[2]

I. The Burial of the Dead [3]

April is the cruellest month, breeding
Lilacs out of the dead land, mixing

---

* Eliot's notes are printed after the text of the poem. His notes are referred to in parentheses in the footnotes that follow by an E followed by the section number of the poem in Roman numerals and the line number in Arabic, e.g., (E.,II,32).

[1] "For I myself saw with my own eyes the Cumaean Sibyl hanging in a bottle, and when the boys said to her, 'Sibyl, what do you want?,' she would reply, 'I want to die' " (Petronius, *Satyricon*, XLVIII). The Sibyl, in requesting longevity from Apollo, had forgotten to ask for perpetual youth and had therefore shriveled with age.

[2] "The better craftsman" (Dante, *Purgatorio*, XXVI, 117). Eliot's tribute to Pound, whose editorial help can be seen in the facsimile *Waste Land* (1971), which transcribes the original manuscript of the poem.

[3] Title of the funeral service in the Anglican *Book of Common Prayer*.

Memory and desire, stirring
Dull roots with spring rain.
Winter kept us warm, covering   5
Earth in forgetful snow, feeding
A little life with dried tubers.
Summer surprised us, coming over the Starnbergersee[4]
With a shower of rain; we stopped in the colonnade,
And went on in sunlight, into the Hofgarten,[5]   10
And drank coffee, and talked for an hour.
Bin gar keine Russin, stamm' aus Litauen, echt deutsch.[6]
And when we were children, staying at the archduke's,
My cousin's, he took me out on a sled,
And I was frightened. He said, Marie,   15
Marie, hold on tight. And down we went.
In the mountains, there you feel free.
I read, much of the night, and go south in the winter.

   What are the roots that clutch, what branches grow
Out of this stony rubbish? Son of man,[7]   20
You cannot say, or guess, for you know only
A heap of broken images, where the sun beats,
And the dead tree gives no shelter, the cricket no relief,[8]
And the dry stone no sound of water. Only
There is shadow under this red rock,   25
(Come in under the shadow of this red rock),[9]
And I will show you something different from either
Your shadow at morning striding behind you
Or your shadow at evening rising to meet you;
I will show you fear in a handful of dust.[10]   30
     Frisch weht der Wind
     Der Heimat zu
     Mein Irisch Kind,
     Wo weilest du?[11]
"You gave me hyacinths first a year ago;   35
"They called me the hyacinth girl."
—Yet when we came back, late, from the Hyacinth garden,

---

4 Lake near Munich.
5 Park in Munich.
6 German: "I'm not Russian at all, I come from Lithuania, pure German."
7 God's address to the prophet Ezekiel (E.,I,20).
8 "The grasshopper shall be a burden" in old age, when "desire shall fail," says the Preacher in Ecclesiastes (E.,I,23).
9 Cf. Isaiah 32:1–2, where the coming of the Messiah will be "as the shadow of a great rock in a weary land."
10 "Dust thou art, and unto dust thou shalt return," as in the funeral service.
11 From Richard Wagner's opera *Tristan und Isolde* (E.,I,34), the young steersman's lyric song: "The wind blows fresh / To the homeland / My Irish girl, / Where are you waiting?"

Your arms full, and your hair wet, I could not
Speak, and my eyes failed, I was neither
Living nor dead, and I knew nothing,   40
Looking into the heart of light, the silence.
Oed' und leer das Meer.[12]

    Madame Sosostris, famous clairvoyante,
Had a bad cold, nevertheless
Is known to be the wisest woman in Europe,   45
With a wicked pack of cards.[13] Here, said she,
Is your card, the drowned Phoenician Sailor,
(Those are pearls that were his eyes.[14] Look!)
Here is Belladonna, the Lady of the Rocks,
The lady of situations.   50
Here is the man with three staves, and here the Wheel,
And here is the one-eyed merchant, and this card,
Which is blank, is something he carries on his back,
Which I am forbidden to see. I do not find
The Hanged Man. Fear death by water.   55
I see crowds of people, walking round in a ring.
Thank you. If you see dear Mrs. Equitone,
Tell her I bring the horoscope myself:
One must be so careful these days.

    Unreal City,   60
Under the brown fog of a winter dawn,
A crowd flowed over London Bridge, so many,
I had not thought death had undone so many.[15]
Sighs, short and infrequent, were exhaled,
And each man fixed his eyes before his feet.   65
Flowed up the hill and down King William Street,
To where Saint Mary Woolnoth[16] kept the hours
With a dead sound on the final stroke of nine.
There I saw one I knew, and stopped him, crying: "Stetson!
"You who were with me in the ships at Mylae![17]   70
"That corpse you planted last year in your garden,
"Has it begun to sprout? Will it bloom this year?
"Or has the sudden frost disturbed its bed?
"Oh keep the Dog far hence, that's friend to men,

---

[12] "Empty and barren the sea" (E.,I, 42), Tristan's lament as he lies dying, thinking that he will die before Isolde arrives.

[13] Tarot cards, used to tell fortunes (E., I, 46).

[14] From Shakespeare's *The Tempest* (Act I, Sc. ii, l. 398); said of a drowned father.

[15] Quoted from Dante's *Inferno* (E.,I,63).

[16] London church.

[17] Naval battle (260 B.C.) in which the Romans defeated the Carthaginians.

"Or with his nails he'll dig it up again![18]   75
"You! hypocrite lecteur!—mon semblable,—mon frère!"[19]

II. A Game of Chess [20]

The Chair she sat in, like a burnished throne,
Glowed on the marble,[21] where the glass
Held up by standards wrought with fruited vines
From which a golden Cupidon[22] peeped out   80
(Another hid his eyes behind his wing)
Doubled the flames of sevenbranched candelabra
Reflecting light upon the table as
The glitter of her jewels rose to meet it,
From satin cases poured in rich profusion;   85
In vials of ivory and coloured glass
Unstoppered, lurked her strange synthetic perfumes,
Unguent, powdered, or liquid—troubled, confused
And drowned the sense in odours; stirred by the air
That freshened from the window, these ascended   90
In fattening the prolonged candle-flames,
Flung their smoke into the laquearia,[23]
Stirring the pattern on the coffered ceiling.
Huge sea-wood fed with copper
Burned green and orange, framed by the coloured stone,   95
In which sad light a carvèd dolphin swam.
Above the antique mantel was displayed
As though a window gave upon the sylvan scene[24]
The change of Philomel,[25] by the barbarous king
So rudely forced; yet there the nightingale   100
Filled all the desert with inviolable voice
And still she cried, and still the world pursues,
"Jug Jug"[26] to dirty ears.

[18] An echo from the play *The White Devil* (1612) by John Webster. The original reads: "But keep the wolf far thence, that's foe to men, / For with his nails he'll dig them up again" (Act V, Sc. iv, ll. 97–98).

[19] Quote from Baudelaire's poem "Au Lecteur"("To the Reader"): "Hypocrite reader!—my double,—my brother!" (E.,I,76).

[20] Title of a play by Thomas Middleton (1627) about a marriage of convenience.

[21] Echo of a passage in Shakespeare's *Antony and Cleopatra* (Act II, Sc. ii, ll. 196–197), referring to Cleopatra's barge: "The barge she sat in, like a burnish'd throne, / Burn'd on the water."

[22] Statue of Cupid, god of love in Roman mythology.

[23] Paneled ceiling as described in a passage in Virgil's *Aeneid* telling of Dido's welcome of Aeneas to Carthage. When Aeneas left her, Dido committed suicide (E.,II,92).

[24] Allusion to the Garden of Eden in John Milton's *Paradise Lost* (IV, 140).

[25] Ovid, in the *Metamorphoses,* retells the story of the rape of Philomel by her brother-in-law Tereus; he cut out her tongue, but the gods, in compensation, turned her into a nightingale.

[26] Conventional Elizabethan rendering of the nightingale's song.

And other withered stumps of time
Were told upon the walls; staring forms   105
Leaned out, leaning, hushing the room enclosed.
Footsteps shuffled on the stair.
Under the firelight, under the brush, her hair
Spread out in fiery points
Glowed into words, then would be savagely still.   110

    "My nerves are bad to-night. Yes, bad. Stay with me.
"Speak to me. Why do you never speak. Speak.
    "What are you thinking of? What thinking? What?
"I never know what you are thinking. Think."

    I think we are in rats' alley   115
Where the dead men lost their bones.

    "What is that noise?"
                           The wind under the door.

"What is that noise now? What is the wind doing?"
                       Nothing again nothing.   120
                                    "Do
"You know nothing? Do you see nothing? Do you remember
"Nothing?"

         I remember
Those are pearls that were his eyes.   125
"Are you alive, or not? Is there nothing in your head?"
                                  But

O O O O that Shakespeherian Rag—
It's so elegant
So intelligent[27]   130
"What shall I do now? What shall I do?"
"I shall rush out as I am, and walk the street
"With my hair down, so. What shall we do to-morrow?
"What shall we ever do?"
                       The hot water at ten.   135
And if it rains, a closed car at four.
And we shall play a game of chess,
Pressing lidless eyes and waiting for a knock upon the door.

    When Lil's husband got demobbed,[28] I said—
I didn't mince my words, I said to her myself,   140

---

[27] Lines adapted from a popular song, "That Shakesperian Rag."

[28] Demobilized from the army (slang).

HURRY UP PLEASE ITS TIME[29]

Now Albert's coming back, make yourself a bit smart.
He'll want to know what you done with that money he gave you
To get yourself some teeth. He did, I was there.
You have them all out, Lil, and get a nice set,   145
He said, I swear, I can't bear to look at you.
And no more can't I, I said, and think of poor Albert,
He's been in the army four years, he wants a good time,
And if you don't give it him, there's others will, I said.
Oh is there, she said. Something o' that, I said.   150
Then I'll know who to thank, she said, and give me a straight look.
HURRY UP PLEASE ITS TIME
If you don't like it you can get on with it, I said.
Others can pick and choose if you can't.
But if Albert makes off, it won't be for lack of telling.   155
You ought to be ashamed, I said, to look so antique.
(And her only thirty-one.)
I can't help it, she said, pulling a long face,
It's them pills I took, to bring it off,[30] she said.
(She's had five already, and nearly died of young George.)   160
The chemist[31] said it would be all right, but I've never been the same.
You are a proper fool, I said.
Well, if Albert won't leave you alone, there it is, I said,
What you get married for if you don't want children?
HURRY UP PLEASE ITS TIME   165
Well, that Sunday Albert was home, they had a hot gammon,[32]
And they asked me in to dinner, to get the beauty of it hot—
HURRY UP PLEASE ITS TIME
HURRY UP PLEASE ITS TIME
Goonight Bill. Goodnight Lou. Goonight May. Goonight.   170
Ta ta. Goonight. Goonight.
Good night, ladies, good night, sweet ladies, good night, good night.[33]

III. The Fire Sermon[34]

The river's tent is broken: the last fingers of leaf
Clutch and sink into the wet bank. The wind
Crosses the brown land, unheard. The nymphs are departed.   175
Sweet Thames, run softly, till I end my song.[35]
The river bears no empty bottles, sandwich papers,

---

[29] English pubkeeper's announcement of closing time.
[30] I.e., to cause an abortion.
[31] In England: "pharmacist."
[32] Bacon.
[33] From Ophelia's mad speech, after Hamlet has repudiated her (Shakespeare's *Hamlet*, Act IV, Sc. ii, ll. 72–74).

[34] Title of a sermon by the Buddha, denouncing the fires of passion, hatred, and infatuation with which the senses burn (E.,III,308).
[35] From Edmund Spenser's "Prothalamion," a nuptial eulogy describing a wedding party on the river Thames, including nymphs and swans.

Silk handkerchiefs, cardboard boxes, cigarette ends
Or other testimony of summer nights. The nymphs are departed.
And their friends, the loitering heirs of city directors;[36]   180
Departed, have left no addresses.
By the waters of Leman I sat down and wept . . .[37]
Sweet Thames, run softly till I end my song,
Sweet Thames, run softly, for I speak not loud or long.
But at my back in a cold blast I hear[38]   185
The rattle of the bones, and chuckle spread from ear to ear.
A rat crept softly through the vegetation
Dragging its slimy belly on the bank
While I was fishing in the dull canal
On a winter evening round behind the gashouse   190
Musing upon the king my brother's wreck
And on the king my father's death before him.[39]
White bodies naked on the low damp ground
And bones cast in a little low dry garret,
Rattled by the rat's foot only, year to year.   195
But at my back from time to time I hear
The sound of horns and motors, which shall bring
Sweeney to Mrs. Porter in the spring.[40]
O the moon shone bright on Mrs. Porter
And on her daughter   200
They wash their feet in soda water
Et O ces voix d'enfants, chantant dans la coupole![41]

    Twit twit twit
Jug jug jug jug jug jug
So rudely forc'd.   205
Tereu[42]

[36] The "city" is London's financial district.

[37] Echo of Psalm 137, lamenting the Jews' exile from Jerusalem: "By the rivers of Babylon, there we sat down, yea, we wept, when we remembered Zion." Eliot substitutes "Leman," the French name for Lake Geneva. (Eliot was hospitalized in Lausanne, Switzerland, while writing *The Waste Land*.)

[38] Adapted from "To His Coy Mistress" by Andrew Marvell (1621–1678): "But at my back I always hear / Time's wingèd chariot hurrying near."

[39] Adapted from Shakespeare's *Tempest* (Act I, Sc. ii, ll. 389–391), as Ferdinand laments his father's presumed death: "Sitting on a bank, / Weeping against the king my father's wreck, / This music crept by me upon the waters."

[40] Sweeney, as in Eliot's other poems, represents vulgar humanity. Mrs. Porter and her daughter appear in a bawdy song from World War I. The allusion (E.,III,197) is to a poem by John Day (1574–1640?) that mentions Actaeon's violation of the goddess Diana's privacy as he spied on her as she was bathing, an offense that was punished by death.

[41] French: "And O those treble voices, singing in the dome!" This is the closing line of the sonnet "Parsifal" by Paul Verlaine (1844–1896). In Wagner's opera *Parsifal,* the voices of boy sopranos are heard up high, from the wings, in the final affirmation of Parsifal's salvation once he has defeated the seductress Kundry, thereby preserving his sexual purity.

[42] A reprise of the nightingale's song and the story of Philomel and Tereus.

    Unreal City
Under the brown fog of a winter noon
Mr. Eugenides, the Smyrna[43] merchant
Unshaven, with a pocket full of currants   210
C.i.f. London:[44] documents at sight,
Asked me in demotic[45] French
To luncheon at the Cannon Street Hotel[46]
Followed by a weekend at the Metropole.

    At the violet hour, when the eyes and back   215
Turn upward from the desk, when the human engine waits
Like a taxi throbbing waiting,
I Tiresias, though blind, throbbing between two lives,[47]
Old man with wrinkled female breasts, can see
At the violet hour, the evening hour that strives   220
Homeward, and brings the sailor home from sea,[48]
The typist home at teatime, clears her breakfast, lights
Her stove, and lays out food in tins.
Out of the window perilously spread
Her drying combinations[49] touched by the sun's last rays,   225
On the divan are piled (at night her bed)
Stockings, slippers, camisoles, and stays.[50]
I Tiresias, old man with wrinkled dugs[51]
Perceived the scene, and foretold the rest—
I too awaited the expected guest.   230
He, the young man carbuncular,[52] arrives,
A small house agent's clerk, with one bold stare,
One of the low on whom assurance sits
As a silk hat on a Bradford millionaire.[53]
The time is now propitious, as he guesses,   235
The meal is ended, she is bored and tired,
Endeavours to engage her in caresses
Which still are unreproved, if undesired.
Flushed and decided, he assaults at once;
Exploring hands encounter no defence;   240
His vanity requires no response,

---

[43] Turkish port.
[44] "Carriage and insurance free" to London.
[45] Vulgar.
[46] Presumably, a homosexual assignation in a luxury hotel in Brighton.
[47] Tiresias, a blind prophet, had been transformed into a woman for seven years; when asked by the gods who had greater pleasure in sex, men or women, he answered that it was women (E.,III,218).

[48] The allusion is to Sappho's poem (CXLIX) on the evening star, which brings all things home that the morning had dispersed.
[49] Underwear.
[50] Corsets.
[51] Breasts.
[52] i.e., suffering from acne.
[53] A *nouveau riche* industrialist from Bradford, Yorkshire.

And makes a welcome of indifference.
(And I Tiresias have foresuffered all
Enacted on this same divan or bed;
I who have sat by Thebes below the wall   245
And walked among the lowest of the dead.)[54]
Bestows one final patronising kiss,
And gropes his way, finding the stairs unlit . . .

    She turns and looks a moment in the glass,
Hardly aware of her departed lover;   250
Her brain allows one half-formed thought to pass:
"Well now that's done: and I'm glad it's over."
When lovely woman stoops to folly and
Paces about her room again, alone,
She smoothes her hair with automatic hand,   255
And puts a record on the gramophone.[55]

    "This music crept by me upon the waters"
And along the Strand,[56] up Queen Victoria Street.
O City city, I can sometimes hear
Beside a public bar in Lower Thames Street,   260
The pleasant whining of a mandoline
And a clatter and a chatter from within
Where fishmen lounge at noon: where the walls
Of Magnus Martyr[57] hold
Inexplicable splendour of Ionian white and gold.   265

      The river sweats
    Oil and tar
    The barges drift
    With the turning tide
    Red sails   270
    Wide
    To leeward, swing on the heavy spar.
    The barges wash
    Drifting logs
    Down Greenwich reach[58]   275

---

54 Tiresias lived in Thebes, and in the afterlife in Hades.

55 Echo of *The Vicar of Wakefield* by Oliver Goldsmith (1728–1774), in which Olivia recalls her seduction: "When lovely woman stoops to folly, / And finds too late that men betray, / What charm can soothe her melancholy? / What art can wash her guilt away?"

56 London street.

57 London church built by the famous architect Sir Christopher Wren (1632–1723) (E.,III,264).

58 Along the Thames River at Greenwich.

        Past the Isle of Dogs.[59]
               Weialala leia
               Wallala leialala[60]

        Elizabeth and Leicester[61]
        Beating oars   280
        The stern was formed
        A gilded shell
        Red and gold
        The brisk swell
        Rippled both shores   285
        Southwest wind
        Carried down stream
        The peal of bells
        White towers
               Weialala leia   290
               Wallala leialala

      "Trams[62] and dusty trees.
    Highbury bore me. Richmond and Kew
    Undid me.[63] By Richmond I raised my knees
    Supine on the floor of a narrow canoe."   295
      "My feet are at Moorgate,[64] and my heart
    Under my feet. After the event
    He wept. He promised 'a new start.'
    I made no comment. What should I resent?"

      "On Margate Sands.[65]   300
    I can connect
    Nothing with nothing.
    The broken fingernails of dirty hands.
    My people humble people who expect
    Nothing."   305
          la la

---

59 Peninsula in the Thames opposite Greenwich where Queen Elizabeth I was born.

60 From the song of the Rhinemaidens in
Wagner's *Ring* cycle. These are the river
nymphs who open the tetralogy and who
repossess their Rhinegold at the end.

61 Queen Elizabeth I and Robert Dudley, earl
of Leicester. The account of their boat ride
on the Thames (E.,III,279) is drawn from
an incident, retold by the Spanish ambassador, in which Elizabeth and Leicester
joked about their marrying. Of course no
marriage took place.

62 Streetcars.

63 Highbury, Richmond, and Kew are areas
near London. The passage rephrases Dante's
"Siena bore me; Maremma undid me"
(E.,III,64).

64 Slum in East London.

65 Resort on the Thames estuary.

To Carthage then I came[66]

Burning burning burning burning[67]

O Lord Thou pluckest me out[68]

O Lord Thou pluckest   310

burning

IV. Death by Water[69]

Phlebas the Phoenician, a fortnight dead,
Forgot the cry of gulls, and the deep sea swell
And the profit and loss.
                                        A current under sea   315
Picked his bones in whispers. As he rose and fell
He passed the stages of his age and youth
Entering the whirlpool.
                                        Gentile or Jew
O you who turn the wheel and look to windward,   320
Consider Phlebas, who was once handsome and tall as you.

V. What the Thunder Said[70]

After the torchlight red on sweaty faces
After the frosty silence in the gardens
After the agony in stony places
The shouting and the crying   325
Prison and palace and reverberation
Of thunder of spring over distant mountains
He who was living is now dead[71]
We who were living are now dying
With a little patience   330

      Here is no water but only rock
Rock and no water and the sandy road

66 From the *Confessions* of St. Augustine; in
   Carthage, Augustine continued his life of
   sexual sin (E.,III,309).
67 From the Buddha's Fire Sermon.
68 St. Augustine (*Confessions*) thanks God for
   having plucked him out of the life of sin.
69 Eliot had dedicated his first volume of verse
   to the memory of his French friend Jean

Verdenal, who had drowned. (See Madame
Sosostris's warning [I, 55].)
70 The thunder is the voice of God in the
   Indian *Upanishads* (E.,V,402).
71 The opening of this section recalls Jesus'
   agony in the Garden of Gethsemane, his betrayal by Judas, his judging by Pontius Pilate in the palace, and his death.

The road winding above among the mountains
Which are mountains of rock without water
If there were water we should stop and drink   335
Amongst the rock one cannot stop or think
Sweat is dry and feet are in the sand
If there were only water amongst the rock
Dead mountain mouth of carious[72] teeth that cannot spit
Here one can neither stand nor lie nor sit   340
There is not even silence in the mountains
But dry sterile thunder without rain
There is not even solitude in the mountains
But red sullen faces sneer and snarl
From doors of mudcracked houses   345
     If there were water

 And no rock
 If there were rock
 And also water
 And water   350
 A spring
 A pool among the rock
 If there were the sound of water only
 Not the cicada
 And dry grass singing   355
 But sound of water over a rock
 Where the hermit-thrush sings in the pine trees
 Drip drop drip drop drop drop drop
 But there is no water

 Who is the third who walks always beside you?[73]   360
When I count, there are only you and I together
But when I look ahead up the white road
There is always another one walking beside you
Gliding wrapt in a brown mantle, hooded
I do not know whether a man or a woman   365
—But who is that on the other side of you?

 What is that sound high in the air
Murmur of maternal lamentation
Who are those hooded hordes swarming
Over endless plains, stumbling in cracked earth   370
Ringed by the flat horizon only
What is the city over the mountains
Cracks and reforms and bursts in the violet air
Falling towers

---

[72] Decayed.
[73] Eliot suggests here the hallucinations of Antarctic explorers; he also recalls (E.,V, introductory note) Christ's accompanying, unrecognized, two disciples to Emmaus after his resurrection.

Jerusalem Athens Alexandria   375
Vienna London
Unreal

    A woman drew her long black hair out tight
And fiddled whisper music on those strings
And bats with baby faces in the violet light   380
Whistled, and beat their wings
And crawled head downward down a blackened wall
And upside down in air were towers
Tolling reminiscent bells, that kept the hours
And voices singing out of empty cisterns and exhausted wells.   385

    In this decayed hole among the mountains
In the faint moonlight, the grass is singing
Over the tumbled graves, about the chapel
There is the empty chapel,[74] only the wind's home.
It has no windows, and the door swings,   390
Dry bones can harm no one.
Only a cock stood on the rooftree
Co co rico co co rico
In a flash of lightning. Then a damp gust
Bringing rain   395

    Ganga[75] was sunken, and the limp leaves
Waited for rain, while the black clouds
Gathered far distant, over Himavant.[76]
The jungle crouched, humped in silence.
Then spoke the thunder   400
DA
Datta:[77] what have we given?
My friend, blood shaking my heart
The awful daring of a moment's surrender
Which an age of prudence can never retract   405
By this, and this only, we have existed
Which is not to be found in our obituaries
Or in memories draped by the beneficent spider
Or under seals broken by the lean solicitor
In our empty rooms   410
DA
Dayadhvam:[78] I have heard the key
Turn in the door once and turn once only

---

[74] In Arthurian legend, the Chapel Perilous, where the Grail knights prayed before they set out to find the Holy Grail.

[75] The Ganges, India's sacred river.

[76] The Himalayas.

[77] Sanskrit for "give," the first word of the thunder in the Upanishads.

[78] Sanskrit: "sympathize."

We think of the key, each in his prison
Thinking of the key, each confirms a prison
Only at nightfall, aethereal rumours
Revive for a moment a broken Coriolanus[79]
DA
Damyata:[80] The boat responded
Gaily, to the hand expert with sail and oar
The sea was calm, your heart would have responded
Gaily, when invited, beating obedient
To controlling hands

                I sat upon the shore
Fishing,[81] with the arid plain behind me
Shall I at least set my lands in order?[82]
London Bridge is falling down falling down falling down
Poi s'ascose nel foco che gli affina[83]
Quando fiam uti chelidon[84]—O swallow swallow
Le Prince d'Aquitaine à la tour abolie[85]
These fragments I have shored against my ruins
Why then Ile fit you. Hieronymo's mad againe.[86]
Datta. Dayadhvam. Damyata.
        Shantih shantih shantih[87]
1922

415
420
425
430

Notes on "The Waste Land"[88]

Not only the title, but the plan and a good deal of the incidental symbolism of the poem were suggested by Miss Jessie L. Weston's book on the Grail legend: *From Ritual to*

[79] Shakespeare's tragic hero who betrayed his own country and then betrayed the opposite camp.

[80] Sanskrit: "Control yourselves."

[81] Eliot's note refers to the Fisher King of the Grail legend (E.,V,425).

[82] Allusion to God's command in Isaiah 38:1: "Set thine house in order: for thou shalt die, and not live."

[83] In the *Purgatorio* (*Purgatory*) of Dante's *Divine Comedy,* the Provençal poet Arnaut Daniel implores Dante's regard: "Then he hid himself in the fire that refines them."

[84] "When will I be like the swallow" (and have a mate and be able to sing again)? From the late Latin poem *Pervigilium Veneris* (*The Vigil of Venus*), a love complaint (E.,V,429).

[85] French: "The prince of Aquitaine of the ruined tower." From the sonnet "El Desdichado" ("The Disinherited Son") by Gérard de Nerval (1808–1855). The passage

reads: "I am the man of shadows, the widower, unconsoled, / The prince of Aquitaine of the ruined tower, / My only star is dead, and my starry lute / Bears the black sun of melancholia."

[86] Lines from Elizabethan playwright Thomas Kyd's revenge play *The Spanish Tragedy.* "I'll suit your wish," says the bereaved father Hieronymo, agreeing to write a play by means of which, even though mad, he revenges himself for the murder of his son and then kills himself.

[87] Sanskrit: the formal ending of an Upanishad; equivalent, says Eliot, to "the peace which passeth understanding" (E.,v.,434).

[88] In its original appearance in journals in both England and America, *The Waste Land* had no notes. When it appeared as a separate publication, Eliot was asked to fill out the pages and added the notes.

Romance (Cambridge). Indeed, so deeply am I indebted, Miss Weston's book will elucidate the difficulties of the poem much better than my notes can do; and I recommend it (apart from the great interest of the book itself) to any who think such elucidation of the poem worth the trouble. To another work of anthropology I am indebted in general, one which has influenced our generation profoundly; I mean *The Golden Bough*;[89] I have used especially the two volumes *Adonis, Attis, Osiris*.[90] Anyone who is acquainted with these works will immediately recognise in the poem certain references to vegetation ceremonies.

I. The Burial of the Dead

Line 20. Cf. Ezekiel II, i.

    23. Cf. Ecclesiastes XII, v.

    31. V. Tristan und Isolde, I, verses 5–8.

    42. Id. III, verse 24.

    46. I am not familiar with the exact constitution of the Tarot pack of cards, from which I have obviously departed to suit my own convenience. The Hanged Man, a member of the traditional pack, fits my purpose in two ways: because he is associated in my mind with the Hanged God of Frazer, and because I associate him with the hooded figure in the passage of the disciples to Emmaus in Part V. The Phoenician Sailor and the Merchant appear later; also the "crowds of people," and Death by Water is executed in Part IV. The Man with Three Staves (an authentic member of the Tarot pack) I associate, quite arbitrarily, with the Fisher King himself.

    60.   Cf. Baudelaire:

        "Fourmillante cité, cité pleine de reves,

        "Où le spectre en plein jour raccroche le passant."[91]

    63.   Cf. Inferno III, 55–57:

             "si lunga tratta

        di gente, ch'io non avrei mai creduto

        che morte tanta n'avesse disfatta."[92]

    64.   Cf. Inferno IV, 25–27:

        "Quivi, secondo che per ascoltare,

        "non avea pianto, ma' che di sospiri,

        "che l'aura eterna facevan tremare."[93]

    68. A phenomenon which I have often noticed.

    74. Cf. the Dirge in Webster's *White Devil*.

    76. V. Baudelaire, Preface to *Fleurs du Mal*.

---

[89] Sir James Frazer's compendium of myths and religions (1890).

[90] Vegetation gods who die and are reborn.

[91] From "Les Sept Vieillards" ("The Seven Old Men") of Charles Baudelaire (1821–1867): "Swarming city, city of dreams, / Where in broad daylight a ghost accosts the passerby."

[92] Dante: "such a long train / of people, that I would never have believed / that death had undone so many."

[93] Dante: "Here, as far as hearing could ascertain, / was no complaint, except for sighs, / that made the eternal air tremble."

II. A Game of Chess

77. Cf. *Antony and Cleopatra*, II, ii, l. 190.

92. Laquearia. V. *Aeneid*, I, 726:

dependent lychni laquearibus aureis incensi / et noctem flammis funalia

vincunt.[94]

98. Sylvan scene. V. Milton, *Paradise Lost*, IV, 140.

99. V. Ovid, *Metamorphoses*, VI, Philomela.

100. Cf. Part III, l. 204.

115. Cf. Part III, l. 195.

118. Cf. Webster: "Is the wind in that door still?"[95]

126. Cf. Part I, l. 37, 48.

138. Cf. the game of chess in Middleton's *Women beware Women*.[96]

III. The Fire Sermon

176. V. Spenser, *Prothalamion*.

192. Cf. *The Tempest*, I, ii.

196. Cf. Marvell, *To His Coy Mistress*.

197. Cf. Day, *Parliament of Bees*:

"When of the sudden, listening, you shall hear,

"A noise of horns and hunting, which shall bring

"Actaeon to Diana in the spring,

"Where all shall see her naked skin . . ."

199. I do not know the origin of the ballad from which these lines are taken: it was reported to me from Sydney, Australia.

202. V. Verlaine, *Parsifal*.

210. The currants were quoted at a price "carriage and insurance free to London"; and the Bill of Lading etc. were to be handed to the buyer upon payment of the sight draft.

218. Tiresias, although a mere spectator and not indeed a "character," is yet the most important personage in the poem, uniting all the rest. Just as the one-eyed merchant, seller of currants, melts into the Phoenician Sailor, and the latter is not wholly distinct from Ferdinand Prince of Naples,[97] so all the women are one woman, and the two sexes meet in Tiresias. What Tiresias *sees*, in fact, is the substance of the poem. The whole passage from Ovid is of great anthropological interest:

. . . Cum Iunone iocos et 'maior vestra profecto est

Quam, quae contingit maribus,' dixisse, 'voluptas.'

Illa negat; placuit quae sit sententia docti

Quaerere Tiresiae: venus huic erat utraque nota.

---

[94] "Lighted lamps hang from the gold-paneled ceiling, and flaming torches vanquish the night."

[95] In John Webster's play *The Devil's Law-Case* (1623) this is said of a dying man, meaning "Is there still breath coming from his mouth?"

[96] In this play by Thomas Middleton (1657), a guardian plays a game of chess while her ward is seduced.

[97] In Shakespeare's The Tempest.

Nam duo magnorum viridi coeuntia silva
Corpora serpentum baculi violaverat ictu
Deque viro factus, mirabile, femina septem
Egerat autumnos; octavo rursus eosdem
Vidit et 'est vestrae si tanta potentia plagae,'
Dixit 'ut auctoris sortem in contraria mutet,
Nunc quoque vos feriam!' percussis anguibus isdem
Forma prior rediit genetivaque venit imago.
Arbiter hic igitur sumptus de lite iocosa
Dicta Iovis firmat; gravius Saturnia iusto
Nec pro materia fertur doluisse suique
Iudicis aeterna damnavit lumina nocte,
At pater omnipotens (neque enim licet inrita cuiquam
Facta dei fecisse deo) pro lumine adempto
Scire futura dedit poenamque levavit honore.[98]

221. This may not appear as exact as Sappho's lines, but I had in mind the "long-shore" or "dory" fisherman, who returns at nightfall.

253. V. Goldsmith, the song in *The Vicar of Wakefield.*

257. V. *The Tempest,* as above.

264. The interior of St. Magnus Martyr is to my mind one of the finest among Wren's interiors. See *The Proposed Demolition of Nineteen City Churches:* (P. S. King & Son, Ltd.).

266. The Song of the (three) Thames-daughters begins here. From line 292 to 306 inclusive they speak in turn. V. *Götterdämmerung,* III, i: the Rhine-daughters.

279. V. Froude, *Elizabeth,* Vol. I, ch. iv, letter of De Quadra to Philip of Spain:

"In the afternoon we were in a barge, watching the games on the river. (The queen) was alone with Lord Robert and myself on the poop, when they began to talk nonsense, and went so far that Lord Robert at last said, as I was on the spot there was no reason why they should not be married if the queen pleased."

293. Cf. *Purgatorio,* V, 133:

"Ricorditi di me, che son la Pia;
"Siena mi fe', disfecemi Maremma."[99]

---

[98] The passage Eliot quotes is from Ovid's *Metamorphoses* II, 421–43: "Jove said jestingly to Juno: 'You wives have greater pleasure in love than husbands.' She denied it. It pleased them to ask the opinion of the learned Tiresias, who knew both sorts of love. For once, with a blow of his staff, he had separated two copulating snakes in the forest, and was miraculously changed instantly from a man into a woman, remaining so for seven years. In the eighth year he saw the same snakes again and said, 'If striking you is so powerful that it changes the sex of the one dealing the blow, then I will now strike you again.' As soon as he struck them, his former shape and masculine form were restored. As arbiter of the jesting quarrel, he supported Jove's opinion. Juno, disturbed by the decision, decreed that he should be condemned to eternal blindness. But the omnipotent god (since no god can undo what has been done by another god) gave him the power to know the future, with this honor redeeming his loss of sight."

[99] La Pia, born in Siena, was murdered by her husband in his castle at Maremma: "Remember me, who am La Pia; / Siena made me, Maremma undid me."

307. V. St. Augustine's *Confessions:* "to Carthage then I came, where a cauldron of unholy loves sang all about mine ears."

308. The complete text of the Buddha's Fire Sermon (which corresponds in importance to the Sermon on the Mount) from which these words are taken, will be found translated in the late Henry Clarke Warren's *Buddhism in Translation* (Harvard Oriental Series). Mr. Warren was one of the great pioneers of Buddhist studies in the Occident.

309. From St. Augustine's *Confessions* again. The collocation of these two representatives of eastern and western asceticism, as the culmination of this part of the poem, is not an accident.

V. What the Thunder Said

In the first part of Part V three themes are employed: the journey to Emmaus, the approach to the Chapel Perilous (see Miss Weston's book) and the present decay of Eastern Europe.

357. This is *Turdus aonalaschkae pallasii,* the hermit-thrush which I have heard in Quebec Province. Chapman says (*Handbook of Birds of Eastern North America*) "it is most at home in secluded woodland and thickety retreats.... Its notes are not remarkable for variety or volume, but in purity and sweetness of tone and exquisite modulation they are unequalled." Its "water-dripping song" is justly celebrated.

360. The following lines were stimulated by the account of one of the Antarctic expeditions (I forget which, but I think one of Shackleton's): it was related that the party of explorers, at the extremity of their strength, had the constant delusion that there was *one more member* than could actually be counted.

367–77. Cf. Hermann Hesse, *Blick ins Chaos:* "Schon ist halb Europa, schon ist zumindest der halbe Osten Europas auf dem Wege zum Chaos, fährt betrunken im heiligem Wahn am Abgrund entlang und singt dazu, singt betrunken und hymnisch wie Dmitri Karamasoff sang. Ueber diese Lieder lacht der Bürger beleidigt, der Heilige und Seher hört sie mit Tränen."[100]

402. "Datta, dayadhvam, damyata" (Give, sympathise, control). The fable of the meaning of the Thunder is found in the *Brihadaranyaka—Upanishad,* 5, 1. A translation is found in Deussen's *Sechzig Upanishads des Veda,* p. 489.

408. Cf. Webster, *The White Devil,* V, vi:

> "... they'll remarry
>
> Ere the worm pierce your winding-sheet, ere the spider
>
> Make a thin curtain for your epitaphs."

412. Cf. *Inferno,* XXXIII, 46:

> "ed io senti chiavar l'uscio di sotto
>
> all'orribile torre."[101]

Also F. H. Bradley, *Appearance and Reality,* p. 346.

---

[100] "Already half of Europe, already at least half of Eastern Europe, is on the way to chaos, traveling drunken in a sort of holy ecstasy, headlong toward the abyss, singing the while, singing drunken hymns, as Dmitri Karamazov sang. The offended bourgeois laughs at these songs; the saint and the seer hear them with tears."

[101] Ugolino was imprisoned with his children, and they starved to death: "And I heard the key turn below in the door / of the horrible tower."

"My external sensations are no less private to myself than are my thoughts or my feelings. In either case my experience falls within my own circle, a circle closed on the outside; and, with all its elements alike, every sphere is opaque to the others which surround it. . . . In brief, regarded as an existence which appears in a soul, the whole world for each is peculiar and private to that soul."

425. V. Weston: *From Ritual to Romance;* chapter on the Fisher King.

428. V. *Purgatorio*, XXVI, 148.

  " 'Ara vos prec per aquella valor

   'que vos guida al som de l'escalina,

   'sovegna vos a temps de ma dolor.'

    Poi s'ascose nel foco che gli affina."[102]

429. V. *Pervigilium Veneris.* Cf. Philomela in Parts II and III.

430. V. Gérard de Nerval, Sonnet *El Desdichado.*

432. V. Kyd's *Spanish Tragedy.*

434. Shantih. Repeated as here, a formal ending to an Upanishad. "The peace which passeth understanding" is our equivalent to this word.

1922

The Hollow Men

A penny for the Old Guy

I

We are the hollow men
We are the stuffed men
Leaning together
Headpiece filled with straw. Alas!
Our dried voices, when   5
We whisper together
Are quiet and meaningless
As wind in dry grass
Or rats' feet over broken glass
In our dry cellar   10

  Shape without form, shade without colour,
  Paralysed force, gesture without motion;

  Those who have crossed
  With direct eyes, to death's other Kingdom

---

[102] The speaker is the troubadour poet Arnaut Daniel: " 'I pray you now, by the goodness / that guides you to the top of the staircase, / remember my suffering in due time.' / Then he hid himself in the fire that refines them."

Remember us—if at all—not as lost   15
Violent souls, but only
As the hollow men
The stuffed men.

II

Eyes I dare not meet in dreams
In death's dream kingdom   20
These do not appear:
There, the eyes are
Sunlight on a broken column
There, is a tree swinging
And voices are   25
In the wind's singing
More distant and more solemn
Than a fading star.

Let me be no nearer
In death's dream kingdom   30
Let me also wear
Such deliberate disguises
Rat's coat, crowskin, crossed staves
In a field
Behaving as the wind behaves   35
No nearer—

Not that final meeting
In the twilight kingdom

III

This is the dead land
This is cactus land   40
Here the stone images
Are raised, here they receive
The supplication of a dead man's hand
Under the twinkle of a fading star.

Is it like this   45
In death's other kingdom
Waking alone
At the hour when we are
Trembling with tenderness
Lips that would kiss   50
Form prayers to broken stone.

IV

The eyes are not here
There are no eyes here
In this valley of dying stars
In this hollow valley   55
This broken jaw of our lost kingdoms

   In this last of meeting places
We grope together
And avoid speech
Gathered on this beach of the tumid river   60

   Sightless, unless
The eyes reappear
As the perpetual star
Multifoliate rose
Of death's twilight kingdom   65
The hope only
Of empty men.

V

Here we go round the prickly pear
Prickly pear prickly pear
Here we go round the prickly pear   70
At five o'clock in the morning.

   Between the idea
And the reality
Between the motion
And the act   75
Falls the Shadow

              For Thine is the Kingdom

   Between the conception
And the creation
Between the emotion   80
And the response
Falls the Shadow

              Life is very long

   Between the desire
And the spasm   85
Between the potency
And the existence
Between the essence

And the descent
Falls the Shadow   90
                                     For Thine is the Kingdom

For Thine is
Life is
For Thine is the

This is the way the world ends   95
This is the way the world ends
This is the way the world ends
Not with a bang but a whimper.
1925

---

from Tradition and the Individual Talent

We dwell with satisfaction upon the poet's difference from his predecessors, especially his immediate predecessors; we endeavour to find something that can be isolated in order to be enjoyed. Whereas if we approach a poet without this prejudice we shall often find that not only the best, but the most individual parts of his work may be those in which the dead poets, his ancestors, assert their immortality most vigorously. And I do not mean the impressionable period of adolescence, but the period of full maturity.

Yet if the only form of tradition, of handing down, consisted in following the ways of the immediate generation before us in a blind or timid adherence to its successes, 'tradition' should positively be discouraged. We have seen many such simple currents soon lost in the sand; and novelty is better than repetition. Tradition is a matter of much wider significance. It cannot be inherited, and if you want it you must obtain it by great labour. It involves, in the first place, the historical sense, which we may call nearly indispensable to anyone who would continue to be a poet beyond his twenty-fifth year; and the historical sense involves a perception, not only of the pastness of the past, but of its presence; the historical sense compels a man to write not merely with his own generation in his bones, but with a feeling that the whole of the literature of Europe from Homer and within it the whole of the literature of his own country has a simultaneous existence and composes a simultaneous order. This historical sense, which is a sense of the timeless as well as of the temporal and of the timeless and of the temporal together, is what makes a writer traditional. And it is at the same time what makes a writer most acutely conscious of his place in time, of his own contemporaneity.

No poet, no artist of any art, has his complete meaning alone. His significance, his appreciation in the appreciation of his relation to the dead poets and artists. You cannot value him alone; you must set him, for contrast and comparison, among the dead. I mean this as a principle of aesthetic, not merely historical, criticism. The necessity that he shall conform, that he shall cohere, is not onesided; what happens when a new work of art is created is something that happens simultaneously to all the works of art which preceded it. The existing monuments form an ideal order among themselves, which is modified by the introduction of the new (the really new) work of art among them. The

existing order is complete before the new work arrives; for order to persist after the su-
pervention of novelty, the *whole* existing order must be, if ever so slightly, altered; and
so the relations, proportions, values of each work of art toward the whole are readjusted;
and this is conformity between the old and the new. Whoever has approved this idea of
order, of the form or European, of English literature will not find it preposterous that
the past should be altered by the present as much as the present is directed by the past.
And the poet who is aware of this will be aware of great difficulties and responsibilities.

In a peculiar sense he will be aware also that he must inevitably be judged by the standards of the past. I say judged, not amputated by them; not judged to be as good as, or
worse or better than, the dead; and certainly not judged by the canons of dead critics. It
is a judgment, a comparison, in which two things are measured by each other. To conform merely would be for the new work not really to conform at all; it would not be new,
and would therefore not be a work of art. And we do not quite say that the new is more
valuable because it fits in; but its fitting in is a test of its value—a test, it is true, which
can only be slowly and cautiously applied, for we are none of us infallible judges of conformity. We say: it appears to conform, and is perhaps individual, or it appears individual, and may conform; but we are hardly likely to find that it is one and not the other.

To proceed to a more intelligible exposition of the relation of the poet to the past: he
can neither take the past as a lump, an indiscriminate bolus, nor can he form himself
wholly on one or two private admirations, nor can he form himself wholly upon one
preferred period. The first course is inadmissible, the second is an important experience
of youth, and the third is a pleasant and highly desirable supplement. The poet must be
very conscious of the main current, which does not at all flow invariably through the
most distinguished reputations. He must be quite aware of the obvious fact that art
never improves, but that the material of art is never quite the same. He must be aware
that the mind of Europe—the mind of his own country—a mind which he learns in
time to be much more important than his own private mind—is a mind which changes,
and that this change is a development which abandons nothing *en route,* which does not
superannuate either Shakespeare, or Homer, or the rock drawing of the Magdalenian
draughtsmen. That this development, refinement perhaps, complication certainly, is
not, from the point of view of the artist, any improvement. Perhaps not even an improvement from the point of view of the psychologist or not to the extent which we
imagine; perhaps only in the end based upon a complication in economics and machinery. But the difference between the present and the past is that the conscious present is
an awareness of the past in a way and to an extent which the past's awareness of itself
cannot show.

1919

Eugene O'Neill
1888–1953

Nobel Prize–winning playwright Eugene Gladstone O'Neill was born in a Broadway
hotel room, in the center of New York's theater district, and grew up in the world of
the American theater. "You might say I started as a trouper," he once reported. "I knew

only actors and the stage. My mother nursed me in the wings and in dressing rooms." His father, James O'Neill, was an extremely successful, Irish-born actor who played the lead in over 6,000 performances of *The Count of Monte Cristo,* a melodrama based on Alexandre Dumas's famous novel. By his late teens O'Neill had begun to despise the popular Victorian theater that his father represented. Later he would set out to create a new dramatic style and idiom—to completely transform the American stage.

O'Neill was educated in Catholic boarding schools and private academies. His only regular home in childhood was in New London, Connecticut, where his family lived during the summer, and where he grew to love both the sea and the gritty waterfront life of sailors and saloons. He entered Princeton in 1906, but collegiate life soon clashed with his hard-drinking, rebellious behavior, and he was suspended in his first year. He spent several years "just drifting" and in 1909 was secretly married against the wishes of both his and his wife's parents. A few months later he embarked on the experiences as a seaman that would provide him with much of the material for his later plays. He sailed to Honduras to prospect for gold and spent two years before the mast, sailing to Buenos Aires, England, and South Africa.

On his return, divorced and the father of a two-year-old son, O'Neill hung around disreputable New York waterfront backrooms, several of which became settings for later plays; passed a few months on tour with his father's company; and found a position as a reporter for a New London newspaper, where he contributed local news items and light verse. Toward the end of 1912, however, he was hospitalized for six months with tuberculosis. The event proved to be a turning point in his life. While recovering in a Connecticut sanitorium, he started to read drama seriously—especially Strindberg, Ibsen, and the Greek tragic poets—and decided to become a playwright. In the summer of 1914 he applied to George Pierce Baker's famous drama workshop at Harvard ("because I want to be an artist or nothing") to study for one year as a special student, and that same year he published his first book, *Thirst, and Other One-Act Plays.*

After a semester at Harvard, O'Neill moved to Greenwich Village, where he became a leading member of two avant-garde groups, the Provincetown Players and the Greenwich Village Theatre, both of which helped to lay the foundation for the modern "little theater" movement. On July 28, 1916, O'Neill's first play, *Bound East for Cardiff,* was produced at the Wharf Theatre in Provincetown, Massachusetts. Written in 1914 and included as a writing sample with his Harvard application, this one-act play showed O'Neill's gift for evoking a powerful atmosphere and his keen ear for the vernacular. These two elements, voice and atmosphere, became prominent features of every O'Neill stage production.

In 1918 O'Neill remarried and, despite severe bouts of alcoholism, began working on longer plays. His first full-length play, *Beyond the Horizon,* was produced in New York in 1920 and won a Pulitzer Prize. *The Emperor Jones* was also staged in 1920 and a year later O'Neill won his second Pulitzer Prize for *Anna Christie.* To O'Neill, however, *Anna Christie* seemed a backward-looking work, full of "Broadway tricks," rather than a new theatrical form designed to get beneath conventional dramatic surfaces—"behind life," as he put it.

Following *Anna Christie,* O'Neill began a period of restless experimentation and colossal productivity. The early 1920s brought the deaths in close succession of his father, mother, and brother and were marred by his own continued drinking problems

*Paul Robeson as Emperor Jones, in the Eugene O'Neill play
adapted by DuBose Haywood and directed by Dudley
Murphy for United Artists release.*
(Culver Pictures, Inc.)

and a deteriorating marriage. Yet twenty of his plays were produced on New York stages. These included a series of experimental plays: *The Hairy Ape* (1922), *All God's Chillun Got Wings* (1924), *Desire Under the Elms* (1924), *The Great God Brown* (1926), and the nine-act *Strange Interlude* (1928), which won him a third Pulitzer Prize. With *Strange Interlude* O'Neill achieved a new dramatic language, one that stressed breakdowns in communication, with private voices submerged beneath social voices. A stage direction from the play offers an indication of the "interior dialogue" that O'Neill was striving for: "They stare straight ahead and remain motionless. They speak, ostensibly one to the other, but showing by their tone it is a thinking aloud to oneself, and neither appears to hear what the other has said." In 1929 O'Neill, recovered from his alcoholism, divorced his second wife and married the actress Carlotta Monterey in France, where they were to live for several years. Two years later, The Theatre Guild produced one of O'Neill's most ambitious plays, *Mourning Becomes Electra,* a trilogy that focuses on the passions of an old New England family at the conclusion of the Civil War.

O'Neill's later drama turned increasingly to personal memories. *Ah, Wilderness!* (1933), which featured George M. Cohan, is a domestic comedy—O'Neill called it a "comedy of recollection"—about a rebellious adolescent growing up, like O'Neill himself, in a turn-of-the-century Connecticut family. In *The Iceman Cometh* (1946), O'Neill delved back into his New York waterfront days. Set in a backroom world of drunk and hopeless individuals, the four and one-half hour drama climaxes in an astonishing soliloquy, perhaps the longest in American drama. The last of O'Neill's plays to be produced on Broadway during his lifetime, *The Iceman Cometh* achieved greater success during its revival in the 1950s than in its first production, and it is now among his most widely acclaimed works.

In 1932 O'Neill and his wife moved to Sea Island, Georgia. Four years later he was awarded the Nobel Prize. As his health continued to decline, he moved, first to California, where he lived in relative seclusion, and then to New York. During this period he wrote several plays, all of which were produced in Sweden after his death in 1953. Of these, the most impressive is another four and one-half hour play, *Long Day's Journey into Night,* for which O'Neill received posthumously his fourth Pulitzer Prize. An intense, autobiographical drama concerning a writer's miserly father, drug-addicted mother, and alcoholic brother, *Long Day's Journey into Night* is probably O'Neill's finest work. After seeing a London production of the play, T. S. Eliot called it "one of the most moving plays I have ever seen." The critic Brendan Gill considered it "the finest play written in English in my lifetime." The play opened in New York in 1956 and has been successfully revived twice on Broadway, most recently in 1986. An experimental drama that blends fantasy and reality against an incessant beat of drums, *The Emperor Jones*—the drama of an African American Pullman car porter who makes himself emperor of a West Indies island—established O'Neill as America's most promising playwright. O'Neill claimed that he got the idea from a story he heard about a president of Haiti who predicted that he would never be killed by a lead bullet. First performed on November 1, 1920 in New York City by the Provincetown players, the play was an immediate sensation. In 1933 it was made into both an enormously successful opera and, with Paul Robeson playing the role of Brutus Jones, a popular motion picture. Three other plays received posthumous premieres: *A Touch of the Poet, Hughie,* and *More Stately Mansions.*

Further Reading:

B. H. Clark, *Eugene O'Neill: The Man and His Plays,* 1947.
E. Engel, *The Haunted Heroes of Eugene O'Neill,* 1953.
D. Alexander, *The Tempering of Eugene O'Neill,* 1962.
A. and B. Gelb, *O'Neill,* 1962, 1973.
J. Raleigh, *The Plays of Eugene O'Neill,* 1965.
L. Schaeffer, *O'Neill, Son and Playwright,* 1968.
L. Chabrowe, *Ritual and Pathos: The Theater of O'Neill,* 1976.
E. Griffin, ed., *Eugene O'Neill: A Collection of Criticism,* 1976.

M. Manheim, *Eugene O'Neill's New Language of Kinship,* 1982.
V. Floyd, *The Plays of Eugene O'Neill: A New Assessment,* 1985.
J. Barlow, *Final Acts: The Creation of Three Late O'Neill Plays,* 1985.
T. Bogard, *Contour in Time: The Plays of Eugene O'Neill,* rev. ed., 1987.
L. Porter, *The Banished Prince: Time, Memory, and Ritual in the Late Plays of Eugene O'Neill,* 1988.

Text:
The Emperor Jones, 1920.

The Emperor Jones

Characters

Brutus Jones, Emperor

Henry Smithers, a Cockney trader

An Old Native Woman

Lem, a Native Chief

Soldiers, Adherents of Lem

The Little Formless Fears; Jeff;
The Negro Convicts; The Prison Guard;
The Planters; The Auctioneer; The Slaves;
The Congo Witch-Doctor;
The Crocodile God

The action of the play takes place on an island in the West Indies as yet not self-deter-mined by White Marines. The form of native government is, for the time being, an Empire.

Scenes

Scene I: In the palace of the Emperor Jones. Afternoon.
Scene II: The edge of the Great Forest. Dusk.
Scene III: In the Forest. Night.
Scene IV: In the Forest. Night.
Scene V: In the Forest. Night.
Scene VI: In the Forest. Night.
Scene VII: In the Forest. Night.
Scene VIII: Same as Scene Two—the edge of the Great Forest. Dawn.

Scene One

The audience chamber in the palace of the Emperor—a spacious, high-ceilinged room with bare, white-washed walls. The floor is of white tiles. In the rear, to the left of center, a wide archway giving out on a portico with white pillars. The palace is evidently situated on high ground for beyond the portico nothing can be seen but a vista of distant hills, their summits crowned with thick groves of palm trees. In the right wall, center, a smaller arched doorway leading to the living quarters of the palace. The room is bare of furniture with the exception of one huge chair made of uncut wood which stands at center, its back to rear. This is very apparently the Emperor's throne. It is painted a dazzling, eye-smiting scarlet. There is a brilliant orange cushion on the seat and another smaller one is placed on the floor to serve as a foot-stool. Strips of matting, dyed scarlet, lead from the foot of the throne to the two entrances.

It is late afternoon but the sunlight still blazes yellowly beyond the portico and there is an oppressive burden of exhausting heat in the air.

As the curtain rises, a native negro woman sneaks in cautiously from the entrance on the right. She is very old, dressed in cheap calico, bare-footed, a red bandana handkerchief covering all but a few stray wisps of white hair. A bundle bound in colored cloth is carried over her shoulder on the end of a stick. She hesitates beside the doorway, peering back as if in extreme dread of being discovered. Then she begins to glide noiselessly, a step at a time, toward the doorway in the rear. At this moment, Smithers appears beneath the portico.

Smithers is a tall, stoop-shouldered man about forty. His bald head, perched on a long neck with an enormous Adam's apple, looks like an egg. The tropics have tanned his naturally pasty face with its small, sharp features to a sickly yellow, and native rum has painted his pointed nose to a startling red. His little, washy-blue eyes are red-rimmed and dart about him like a ferret's. His expression is one of unscrupulous meanness, cowardly and dangerous. He is dressed in a worn riding suit of dirty white drill, puttees, spurs, and wears a white cork helmet. A cartridge belt with an automatic revolver is around his waist. He carries a riding whip in his hand. He sees the woman and stops to watch her suspiciously. Then, making up his mind, he steps quickly on tiptoe into the room. The woman, looking back over her shoulder continually, does not see him until it is too late. When she does Smithers springs forward and grabs her firmly by the shoulder. She struggles to get away, fiercely but silently.

Smithers: (*tightening his grasp—roughly*) Easy! None o' that, me birdie. You can't wriggle out, now I got me 'ooks on yer.

Woman: (*seeing the uselessness of struggling, gives way to frantic terror, and sinks to the ground, embracing his knees supplicatingly*) No tell him! No tell him, Mister!

Smithers: (*with great curiosity*) Tell 'im? (*then scornfully*) Oh, you mean 'is bloomin' Majesty. What's the gaime, any 'ow? What are you sneakin' away for? Been stealin' a bit, I s'pose. (*He taps her bundle with his riding whip significantly.*)

Woman: (*shaking her head vehemently*) No, me no steal.

Smithers: Bloody liar! But tell me what's up. There's somethin' funny goin' on. I smelled it in the air first thing I got up this mornin'. You blacks are up to some devilment. This palace of 'is is like a bleedin' tomb. Where's all the 'ands? (*The woman keeps sullenly silent. Smithers raises his whip threateningly.*) Ow, yer won't, won't yer? I'll show yer what's what.

Woman: (*coweringly*) I tell, Mister. You no hit. They go—all go. (*She makes a sweeping gesture toward the hills in the distance.*)

Smithers: Run away—to the 'ills?

Woman: Yes, Mister. Him Emperor—Great Father. (*She touches her forehead to the floor with a quick mechanical jerk.*) Him sleep after eat. Then they go—all go. Me old woman. Me left only. Now me go too.

Smithers: (*his astonishment giving way to an immense, mean satisfaction*) Ow! So that's the ticket! Well, I know bloody well wot's in the air—when they runs orf to the 'ills. The tom-tom 'll be thumping out there bloomin' soon. (*with extreme vindictiveness*) And I'm bloody glad of it, for one! Serve 'im right! Puttin' on airs, the stinkin' nigger! 'Is Majesty! Gawd blimey! I only 'opes I'm there when they takes 'im out to shoot 'im. (*suddenly*) 'E's still 'ere all right, ain't 'e?

Woman: Him sleep.

Smithers: 'E's bound to find out soon as 'e wakes up. 'E's cunnin' enough to know when 'is time's come. (*He goes to the doorway on right and whistles shrilly with his fingers in his mouth. The old woman springs to her feet and runs out of the doorway, rear. Smithers goes after her, reaching for his revolver.*) Stop or I'll shoot! (*then stopping— indifferently*) Pop orf then, if yer like, yer black cow. (*He stands in the doorway, looking after her.*)

(*Jones enters from the right. He is a tall, powerfully-built, full-blooded negro of middle age. His features are typically negroid, yet there is something decidedly distinctive about his face—an underlying strength of will, a hardy, self-reliant confidence in himself that inspires respect. His eyes are alive with a keen, cunning intelligence. In manner he is shrewd, suspicious, evasive. He wears a light blue uniform coat, sprayed with brass buttons, heavy gold chevrons on his shoulders, gold braid on the collar, cuffs, etc. His pants are bright red with a light blue stripe down the side. Patent leather laced boots with brass spurs, and a belt with a long-barreled, pearl-handled revolver in a holster complete his make up. Yet there is something not altogether ridiculous about his grandeur. He has a way of carrying it off.*)

Jones: (*not seeing anyone—greatly irritated and blinking sleepily—shouts*) Who dare whistle dat way in my palace? Who dare wake up de Emperor? I'll git de hide frayled off some o' you niggers sho'!

Smithers: (*showing himself—in a manner half-afraid and half-defiant*) It was me whistled to yer. (*as Jones frowns angrily*) I got news for yer.

Jones: (*putting on his suavest manner, which fails to cover up his contempt for the white man*) Oh, it's you, Mister Smithers. (*He sits down on his throne with easy dignity.*) What news you got to tell me?

Smithers: (*coming close to enjoy his discomfiture*) Don't yer notice nothin' funny today?

Jones: (*coldly*) Funny? No. I ain't perceived nothin' of de kind!

Smithers: Then yer ain't so foxy as I thought yer was. Where's all your court? (*sarcastically*) the Generals and the Cabinet Ministers and all?

Jones: (*imperturbably*) Where dey mostly runs to minute I closes my eyes—drinkin' rum and talkin' big down in de town. (*sarcastically*) How come you don't know dat? Ain't you sousin' with 'em most every day?

Smithers: (*stung but pretending indifference—with a wink*) That's part of the day's work. I got ter—ain't I—in my business?

Jones: (*contemptuously*) Yo' business!

Smithers: (*imprudently enraged*) Gawd blimey, you was glad enough for me ter take yer in on it when you landed here first. You didn't 'ave no 'igh and mighty airs in them days!

Jones: (*his hand going to his revolver like a flash—menacingly*) Talk polite, white man! Talk polite, you heah me! I'm boss heah now, is you fergettin'? (*The Cockney seems about to challenge this last statement with the facts but something in the other's eyes holds and cows him.*)

Smithers: (*in a cowardly whine*) No 'arm meant, old top.

Jones: (*condescendingly*) I accepts yo' apology. (*lets his hand fall from his revolver*) No use'n you rakin' up ole times. What I was den is one thing. What I is now 's another. You didn't let me in on yo' crooked work out o' no kind feelin's dat time. I done de dirty work fo' you—and most o' de brain work, too, fo' dat matter—and I was wu'th money to you, dat's de reason.

Smithers: Well, blimey, I give yer a start, didn't I?—when no one else would. I wasn't afraid to 'ire you like the rest was—'count of the story about your breakin' jail back in the States.

Jones: No, you didn't have no s'cuse to look down on me fo' dat. You been in jail you'self more'n once.

Smithers: (*furiously*) It's a lie! (*then trying to pass it off by an attempt at scorn*) Garn! Who told yer that fairy tale?

Jones: Dey's some tings I ain't got to be tole. I kin see 'em in folk's eyes. (*then after a pause—meditatively*) Yes, you sho' give me a start. And it didn't take long from dat time to git dese fool, woods' niggers right where I wanted dem. (*with pride*) From stowaway to Emperor in two years! Dat's goin' some!

Smithers: (*with curiosity*) And I bet you got yer pile o' money 'id safe some place.

Jones: (*with satisfaction*) I sho' has! And it's in a foreign bank where no pusson don't ever git it out but me no matter what come. You didn't s'pose I was holdin' down dis Emperor job for de glory in it, did you? Sho'! De fuss and glory part of it, dat's only to turn de heads o' de low-flung, bush niggers dat's here. Dey wants de big circus show for deir money. I gives it to 'em an' I gits de money. (*with a grin*) De long green, dat's me every time! (*then rebukingly*) But you ain't got no kick agin me, Smithers. I'se paid you back all you done for me many times. Ain't I pertected you and winked at all de crooked tradin' you been doin' right out in de broad day? Sho' I has—and me makin' laws to stop it at de same time! (*He chuckles.*)

Smithers: (*grinning*) But, meanin' no 'arm, you been grabbin' right and left yourself, ain't yer? Look at the taxes you've put on 'em! Blimey! You've squeezed 'em dry!

Jones: (*chuckling*) No, dey ain't *all* dry yet. I'se still heah, ain't I?

Smithers: (*smiling at his secret thought*) They're dry right now, you'll find out. (*changing the subject abruptly*) And as for me breakin' laws, you've broke 'em all yerself just as fast as yer made 'em.

Jones: Ain't I de Emperor? De laws don't go for him. (*judicially*) You heah what I tells you, Smithers. Dere's little stealin' like you does, and dere's big stealin' like I does. For de little stealin' dey gits you in jail soon or late. For de big stealin' dey makes you Emperor and puts you in de Hall o' Fame when you croaks. (*reminiscently*) If dey's one thing I learns in ten years on de Pullman ca's listenin' to de white quality talk, it's dat same fact. And when I gits a chance to use it I winds up Emperor in two years.

Smithers: (*unable to repress the genuine admiration of the small fry for the large*) Yes, yer turned the bleedin' trick, all right. Blimey, I never seen a bloke 'as 'ad the bloomin' luck you 'as.

Jones: (*severely*) Luck? What you mean—luck?

Smithers: I suppose you'll say as that swank about the silver bullet ain't luck—and that was what first got the fool blacks on yer side the time of the revolution, wasn't it?

Jones: (*with a laugh*) Oh, dat silver bullet! Sho' was luck! But I makes dat luck, you heah? I loads de dice! Yessuh! When dat murderin' nigger ole Lem hired to kill me takes aim ten feet away and his gun misses fire and I shoots him dead, what you heah me say?

Smithers: You said yer'd got a charm so's no lead bullet'd kill yer. You was so strong only a silver bullet could kill yer, you told 'em. Blimey, wasn't that swank for yer—and plain, fat-'eaded luck?

Jones: (*proudly*) I got brains and I uses 'em quick. Dat ain't luck.

Smithers: Yer know they wasn't 'ardly liable to get no silver bullets. And it was luck 'e didn't 'it you that time.

Jones: (*laughing*) And dere all dem fool bush niggers was kneelin' down and bumpin' deir heads on de ground like I was a miracle out o' de Bible. Oh Lawd, from dat time on I has dem all eatin' out of my hand. I cracks de whip and dey jumps through.

Smithers: (*with a sniff*) Yankee bluff done it.

Jones: Ain't a man's talkin' big what makes him big—long as he makes folks believe it? Sho', I talks large when I ain't got nothin' to back it up, but I ain't talkin' wild just de same. I knows I kin fool 'em—I *knows* it—and dat's backin' enough fo' my game. And ain't I got to learn deir lingo and teach some of dem English befo' I kin talk to 'em? Ain't dat wuk? You ain't never learned ary word er it, Smithers, in de ten years you been heah, dough you knows it's money in you' pocket tradin' wid 'em if you does. But you'se too shiftless to take de trouble.

Smithers: (*flushing*) Never mind about me. What's this I've 'eard about yer really 'avin' a silver bullet moulded for yourself?

Jones: It's playin' out my bluff. I has de silver bullet moulded and I tells 'em when de time comes I kills myself wid it. I tells 'em dat's 'cause I'm de on'y man in de world big enuff to git me. No use'n deir tryin'. And dey falls down and bumps deir heads. (*He laughs.*) I does dat so's I kin take a walk in peace widout no jealous nigger gun-nin' at me from behind de trees.

Smithers: (*astonished*) Then you 'ad it made—'onest?

Jones: Sho' did. Heah she be. (*He takes out his revolver, breaks it, and takes the silver bul-let out of one chamber.*) Five lead an' dis silver baby at de last. Don't she shine pretty? (*He holds it in his hand, looking at it admiringly, as if strangely fascinated.*)

Smithers: Let me see. (*reaches out his hand for it*)

Jones: (*harshly*) Keep yo' hands whar dey b'long, white man. (*He replaces it in the cham-ber and puts the revolver back on his hip.*)

Smithers: (*snarling*) Gawd blimey! Think I'm a bleedin' thief, you would.

Jones: No, 'tain't dat. I knows you'se scared to steal from me. On'y I ain't 'lowin' nary body to touch dis baby. She's my rabbit's foot.

Smithers: (*sneering*) A bloomin' charm, wot? (*venomously*) Well, you'll need all the bloody charms you 'as before long, s' 'elp me!

Jones: (*judicially*) Oh, I'se good for six months yit 'fore dey gits sick o' my game. Den, when I sees trouble comin', I makes my getaway.

Smithers: Ho! You got it all planned, ain't yer?

Jones: I ain't no fool. I knows dis Emperor's time is sho't. Dat why I make hay when de sun shine. Was you thinkin' I'se aimin' to hold down dis job for life? No, suh! What good is gittin' money if you stays back in dis raggedy country? I wants action when I spends. And when I sees dese niggers gittin' up deir nerve to tu'n me out, and I'se got all de money in sight, I resigns on de spot and beats it quick.

Smithers: Where to?

Jones: None o' yo' business.

Smithers: Not back to the bloody States, I'll lay my oath.

Jones: (*suspiciously*) Why don't I? (*then with an easy laugh*) You mean 'count of dat story 'bout me breakin' from jail back dere? Dat's all talk.

Smithers: (*skeptically*) Ho, yes!

Jones: (*sharply*) You ain't 'sinuatin' I'se a liar, is you?

Smithers: (*hastily*) No, Gawd strike me! I was only thinkin' o' the bloody lies you told the blacks 'ere about killin' white men in the States.

Jones: (*angered*) How come dey're lies?

Smithers: You'd 'ave been in jail if you 'ad, wouldn't yer then? (*with venom*) And from what I've 'eard, it ain't 'ealthy for a black to kill a white man in the States. They burns 'em in oil, don't they?

Jones: (*with cool deadliness*) You mean lynchin' 'd scare me? Well, I tells you, Smithers, maybe I does kill one white man back dere. Maybe I does. And maybe I kills another right heah 'fore long if he don't look out.

Smithers: (*trying to force a laugh*) I was on'y spoofin' yer. Can't yer take a joke? And you was just sayin' you'd never been in jail.

Jones: (*in the same tone—slightly boastful*) Maybe I goes to jail dere for gettin' in an argument wid razors ovah a crap game. Maybe I gits twenty years when dat colored man die. Maybe I gits in 'nother argument wid de prison guard was overseer ovah us when we're wukin' de road. Maybe he hits me wid a whip and I splits his head wid a shovel and runs away and files de chain off my leg and gits away safe. Maybe I does all dat an' maybe I don't. It's a story I tells you so's you knows I'se de kind of man dat if you evah repeats one word of it, I ends yo' stealin' on dis yearth mighty damn quick!

Smithers: (*terrified*) Think I'd peach on yer? Not me! Ain't I always been yer friend?

Jones: (*suddenly relaxing*) Sho' you has—and you better be.

Smithers: (*recovering his composure—and with it his malice*) And just to show yer I'm yer friend, I'll tell yer that bit o' news I was goin' to.

Jones: Go ahead! Shoot de piece. Must be bad news from de happy way you look.

Smithers: (*warningly*) Maybe it's gettin' time for you to resign—with that bloomin' silver bullet, wot? (*He finishes with a mocking grin.*)

Jones: (*puzzled*) What's dat you say? Talk plain.

Smithers: Ain't noticed any of the guards or servants about the place today, I 'aven't.

Jones: (*carelessly*) Dey're all out in de garden sleepin' under de trees. When I sleeps, dey sneaks a sleep, too, and I pretends I never suspicions it. All I got to do is to ring de bell and dey come flyin', makin' a bluff dey was wukin' all de time.

Smithers: (*in the same mocking tone*) Ring the bell now an' you'll bloody well see what I means.

Jones: (*startled to alertness, but preserving the same careless tone*) Sho' I rings. (*He reaches below the throne and pulls out a big, common dinner bell which is painted the same vivid scarlet as the throne. He rings this vigorously—then stops to listen. Then he goes to both doors, rings again, and looks out.*)

Smithers: (*watching him with malicious satisfaction, after a pause—mockingly*) The bloody ship is sinkin' an' the bleedin' rats 'as slung their 'ooks.

Jones: (*in a sudden fit of anger flings the bell clattering into a corner*) Low-flung, woods' niggers! (*Then catching Smithers' eye on him, he controls himself and suddenly bursts into a low chuckling laugh.*) Reckon I overplays my hand dis once! A man can't take de pot on a bob-tailed flush all de time. Was I sayin' I'd sit in six months mo'? Well, I'se changed my mind den. I cashes in and resigns de job of Emperor right dis minute.

Smithers: (*with real admiration*) Blimey, but you're a cool bird, and no mistake.

Jones: No use'n fussin'. When I knows de game's up I kisses it good-by widout no long waits. Dey've all run off to de hills, ain't dey?

Smithers: Yes—every bleedin' man jack of 'em.

Jones: Den de revolution is at de post. And de Emperor better git his feet smokin' up de trail. (*He starts for the door in rear.*)

Smithers: Goin' out to look for your 'orse? Yer won't find any. They steals the 'orses first thing. Mine was gone when I went for 'im this mornin'. That's wot first give me a suspicion of wot was up.

Jones: (*alarmed for a second, scratches his head, then philosophically*) Well, den I hoofs it. Feet, do yo' duty! (*He pulls out a gold watch and looks at it.*) Three-thuty. Sundown's at six-thuty or dereabouts. (*puts his watch back—with cool confidence*) I got plenty o' time to make it easy.

Smithers: Don't be so bloomin' sure of it. They'll be after you 'ot and 'eavy. Ole Lem is at the bottom o' this business an' 'e 'ates you like 'ell. 'E'd rather do for you than eat 'is dinner, 'e would!

Jones: (*scornfully*) Dat fool no-count nigger! Does you think I'se scared o' him? I stands him on his thick head more'n once befo' dis, and I does it again if he comes in my way—(*fiercely*) And dis time I leave him a dead nigger fo' sho'!

Smithers: You'll 'ave to cut through the big forest—an' these blacks 'ere can sniff and follow a trail in the dark like 'ounds. You'd 'ave to 'ustle to get through that forest in twelve hours even if you knew all the bloomin' trails like a native.

Jones: (*with indignant scorn*) Look-a-heah, white man! Does you think I'se a natural bo'n fool? Give me credit fo' havin' some sense, fo' Lawd's sake! Don't you s'pose I'se looked ahead and made sho' of all de chances? I'se gone out in dat big forest, pretendin' to hunt, so many times dat I knows it high an' low like a book. I could go through on dem trails wid my eyes shut. (*with great contempt*) Think dese ign'rent bush niggers dat ain't got brains enuff to know deir own names even can catch Brutus Jones? Huh, I s'pects not! Not on yo' life! Why, man, de white men went after me wid bloodhounds where I come from an' I jes' laughs at 'em. It's a shame to fool dese black trash around heah, dey're so easy. You watch me, man. I'll make dem look sick, I will. I'll be 'cross de plain to de edge of de forest by time dark comes. Once in de woods in de night, dey got a swell chance o' findin' dis baby! Dawn tomorrow I'll be out at de oder side and on de coast whar dat French gunboat is stayin'. She picks me up, takes me to Martinique when she go dar, and dere I is safe wid a mighty big bankroll in my jeans. It's easy as rollin' off a log.

Smithers: (*maliciously*) But s'posin' somethin' 'appens wrong 'an they do nab yer?

Jones: (*decisively*) Dey don't—dat's de answer.

Smithers: But, just for argument's sake—what'd you do?

Jones: (*frowning*) I'se got five lead bullets in dis gun good enuff fo' common bush niggers—and after dat I got de silver bullet left to cheat 'em out o' gittin' me.

Smithers: (*jeeringly*) Ho, I was fergettin' that silver bullet. You'll bump yourself orf in style, won't yer? Blimey!

Jones: (*gloomily*) You kin bet yo' whole roll on one thing, white man. Dis baby plays out his string to de end and when he quits, he quits wid a bang de way he ought. Silver bullet ain't none too good for him when he go, dat's a fac'! (*then shaking off his nervousness—with a confident laugh*) Sho'! What is I talkin' about? Ain't come to dat yit and I never will—not wid trash niggers like dese yere. (*boastfully*) Silver bullet bring me luck anyway. I kin outguess, outrun, outfight, an' outplay de whole lot o' dem all ovah de board any time o' de day er night! You watch me! (*From the distant hills comes the faint, steady thump of a tom-tom, low and vibrating. It starts at a rate exactly corresponding to normal pulse beat—72 to the minute—and continues at a gradually accelerating rate from this point uninterruptedly to the very end of the play. Jones starts at the sound. A strange look of apprehension creeps into his face for a moment as he listens. Then he asks, with an attempt to regain his most casual manner*) What's dat drum beatin' fo'?

Smithers: (*with a mean grin*) For you. That means the bleedin' ceremony 'as started. I've 'eard it before and I knows.

Jones: Cer'mony? What cer'mony?

Smithers: The blacks is 'oldin' a bloody meetin', 'avin' a war dance, gettin' their courage worked up b'fore they starts after you.

Jones: Let dem! Dey'll sho' need it!

Smithers: And they're there 'oldin' their 'eathen religious service—makin' no end of devil spells and charms to 'elp 'em against your silver bullet. (*He guffaws loudly.*) Blimey, but they're balmy as 'ell!

Jones: (*a tiny bit awed and shaken in spite of himself*) Huh! Takes more'n dat to scare dis chicken!

Smithers: (*scenting the other's feeling—maliciously*) Ternight when it's pitch black in the forest, they'll 'ave their pet devils and ghosts 'oundin' after you. You'll find yer bloody 'air 'll be standin' on end before termorrow mornin'. (*seriously*) It's a bleedin' queer place, that stinkin' forest, even in daylight. Yer don't know what might 'appen in there, it's that rotten still. Always sends the cold shivers down my back minute I gets in it.

Jones: (*with a contemptuous sniff*) I ain't no chicken-liver like you is. Trees an' me, we'se friends, and dar's a full moon comin' bring me light. And let dem po' niggers make all de fool spells dey'se a min' to. Does yo' s'pect I'se silly enuff to b'lieve in ghosts an' ha'nts an' all dat ole woman's talk? G'long, white man! You ain't talkin' to me. (*with a chuckle*) Doesn't you know dey's got to do wid a man was member in good standin' o' de Baptist Church? Sho' I was dat when I was porter on de Pullmans, befo' I gits into my little trouble. Let dem try deir heathen tricks. De Baptist Church done pertect me and land dem all in hell. (*then with more confident satisfaction*) And I's got little silver bullet o' my own, don't forgit!

Smithers: Ho! You 'aven't give much 'eed to your Baptist Church since you been down 'ere. I've 'eard myself you 'ad turned yer coat an' was takin' up with their blarsted witchdoctors, or whatever the 'ell yer calls the swine.

Jones: (*vehemently*) I pretends to! Sho' I pretends! Dat's part o' my game from de fust. If I finds out dem niggers believes dat black is white, den I yells it out louder 'n deir loudest. It don't git me nothin' to do missionary work for de Baptist Church. I'se after de coin, an' I lays my Jesus on de shelf for de time bein'. (*stops abruptly to look at his watch—alertly*) But I ain't got de time to waste on no more fool talk wid you.

I'se gwine away from heah dis secon'. (*He reaches in under the throne and pulls out an expensive Panama hat with a bright multi-colored band and sets it jauntily on his head.*) So long, white man! (*with a grin*) See you in jail sometime, maybe!

Smithers: Not me, you won't. Well, I wouldn't be in yer bloody boots for no bloomin' money, but 'ere's wishin' yer luck just the same.

Jones: (*contemptuously*) You're de frightenedest man evah I see! I tells you I'se safe's 'f I was in New York City. It takes dem niggers from now to dark to git up de nerve to start somethin'. By dat time, I'se got a head start dey never kotch up wid.

Smithers: (*maliciously*) Give my regards to any ghosts yer meets up with.

Jones: (*grinning*) If dat ghost got money, I'll tell him never ha'nt you less'n he wants to lose it.

Smithers: (*flattered*) Garn! (*then curiously*) Ain't yer takin' no luggage with yer?

Jones: I travels light when I wants to move fast. And I got tinned grub buried on de edge o' de forest. (*boastfully*) Now say dat I don't look ahead an' use my brains! (*with a wide, liberal gesture*) I will all dat's left in de palace to you—and you better grab all you kin sneak away wid befo' dey gits here.

Smithers: (*gratefully*) Righto—and thanks ter yer. (*as Jones walks toward the door in rear—cautioningly*) Say! Look 'ere, you ain't goin' out that way, are yer?

Jones: Does you think I'd slink out de back door like a common nigger? I'se Emperor yit, ain't I? And de Emperor Jones leaves de way he comes, and dat black trash don't dare stop him—not yit, leastways. (*He stops for a moment in the doorway, listening to the far-off but insistent beat of the tom-tom.*) Listen to dat roll-call, will you? Must be mighty big drum carry dat far. (*then with a laugh*) Well, if dey ain't no whole brass band to see me off, I sho' got de drum part of it. So long, white man. (*He puts his hands in his pockets and with studied carelessness, whistling a tune, he saunters out of the doorway and off to the left.*)

Smithers: (*looks after him with a puzzled admiration*) 'E's got 'is bloomin' nerve with 'im, s'elp me! (*then angrily*) Ho—the bleedin' nigger—puttin' on 'is bloody airs! I 'opes they nabs 'im an' gives 'im what's what!

(Curtain)

Scene Two

The end of the plain where the Great Forest begins. The foreground is sandy, level ground dotted by a few stones and clumps of stunted bushes cowering close against the earth to escape the buffeting of the trade wind. In the rear the forest is a wall of darkness dividing the world. Only when the eye becomes accustomed to the gloom can the outlines of separate trunks of the nearest trees be made out, enormous pillars of deeper blackness. A somber monotone of wind lost in the leaves moans in the air. Yet this sound serves but to intensify the impression of the forest's relentless immobility, to form a background throwing into relief its brooding, implacable silence.

Jones enters from the left, walking rapidly. He stops as he nears the edge of the forest, looks around him quickly, peering into the dark as if searching for some familiar landmark. Then, apparently satisfied that he is where he ought to be, he throws himself on the ground, dog-tired.

Well, heah I is. In de nick o' time, too! Little mo' an' it'd be blacker'n de ace of spades heahabouts. (*He pulls a bandana handkerchief from his hip pocket and mops off his perspiring face.*) Sho'! Gimme air! I'se tuckered out sho' 'nuff. Dat soft Emperor job ain't no trainin' fo' a long hike ovah dat plain in de brilin' sun. (*then with a chuckle*) Cheer up, nigger, de worst is yet to come. (*He lifts his head and stares at the forest. His chuckle peters out abruptly. In a tone of awe*) My goodness, look at dem woods, will you? Dat no-count Smithers said dey'd be black an' he sho' called de turn. (*Turning away from them quickly and looking down at his feet, he snatches at a chance to change the subject—solicitously*) Feet, you is holdin' up yo' end fine an' I sutinly hopes you ain't blisterin' none. It's time you git a rest. (*He takes off his shoes, his eyes studiously avoiding the forest. He feels of the soles of his feet gingerly.*) You is still in de pink—on'y a little mite feverish. Cool yo'selfs. Remember you done got a long journey yit befo' you. (*He sits in a weary attitude, listening to the rhythmic beating of the tom-tom. He grumbles in a loud tone to cover up a growing uneasiness*) Bush niggers! Wonder dey wouldn't git sick o' beatin' dat drum. Sound louder, seem like. I wonder if dey's startin' after me? (*He scrambles to his feet, looking back across the plain.*) Couldn't see dem now, nohow, if dey was hundred feet away. (*then shaking himself like a wet dog to get rid of these depressing thoughts*) Sho', dey's miles an' miles behind. What you gittin' fidgety about? (*But he sits down and begins to lace up his shoes in great haste, all the time muttering reassuringly.*) You know what? Yo' belly is empty, dat's what's de matter wid you. Come time to eat! Wid nothin' but wind on yo' stumach, o' course you feels jiggedy. Well, we eats right heah an' now soon's I gits dese pesky shoes laced up. (*He finishes lacing up his shoes.*) Dere! Now le's see! (*gets on his hands and knees and searches the ground around him with his eyes*) White stone, white stone, where is you? (*He sees the first white stone and crawls to it—with satisfaction*) Heah you is! I knowed dis was de right place. Box of grub, come to me. (*He turns over the stone and feels in under it—in a tone of dismay*) Ain't heah! Gorry, is I in de right place or isn't I? Dere's 'nother stone. Guess dat's it. (*He scrambles to the next stone and turns it over.*) Ain't heah, neither! Grub, whar is you? Ain't heah. Gorry, has I got to go hungry into dem woods—all de night? (*While he is talking he scrambles from one stone to another, turning them over in frantic haste. Finally, he jumps to his feet excitedly.*) Is I lost de place? Must have! But how dat happen when I was followin' de trail across de plain in broad daylight? (*almost plaintively*) I'se hungry, I is! I gotta git my feed. Whar's my strength gonna come from if I doesn't? Gorry, I gotta find dat grub high an' low somehow! Why it come dark so quick like dat? Can't see nothin'. (*He scratches a match on his trousers and peers about him. The rate of the beat of the far-off tom-tom increases perceptibly as he does so. He mutters in a bewildered voice*) How come all dese white stones come heah when I only remembers one? (*Suddenly, with a frightened gasp, he flings the match on the ground and stamps on it.*) Nigger, is you gone crazy mad? Is you lightin' matches to show dem whar you is? Fo' Lawd's sake, use yo' haid. Gorry, I'se got to be careful! (*He stares at the plain behind him apprehensively, his hand on his revolver.*) But how come all dese white stones? And whar's dat tin box o' grub I hid all wrapped up in oilcloth?

(*While his back is turned, the Little Formless Fears creep out from the deeper blackness of the forest. They are black, shapeless, only their glittering little eyes can be seen. If they have any describable form at all it is that of a grubworm about the size of a creeping child. They move noiselessly, but with deliberate, painful effort, striving to raise themselves on end, failing and sinking prone again. Jones turns about to face the forest. He stares up at the tops of the trees, seeking vainly to discover his whereabouts by their conformation.*)

Can't tell nothin' from dem trees! Gorry, nothin' 'round heah looks like I evah seed it befo'. I'se done lost de place sho' 'nuff! (*with mournful foreboding*) It's mighty queer! It's mighty queer! (*with sudden forced defiance—in an angry tone*) Woods, is you tryin' to put somethin' ovah on me?

(*From the formless creatures on the ground in front of him comes a tiny gale of low mocking laughter like a rustling of leaves. They squirm upward toward him in twisted attitudes. Jones looks down, leaps backward with a yell of terror, yanking out his revolver as he does so—in a quavering voice*) What's dat? Who's dar? What is you? Git away from me befo' I shoots you up! You don't?—

(*He fires. There is a flash, a loud report, then silence broken only by the far-off, quickened throb of the tom-tom. The formless creatures have scurried back into the forest. Jones remains fixed in his position, listening intently. The sound of the shot, the reassuring feel of the revolver in his hand, have somewhat restored his shaken nerve. He addresses himself with renewed confidence.*)

Dey're gone. Dat shot fix 'em. Dey was only little animals—little wild pigs, I reckon. Dey've maybe rooted out yo' grub an' eat it. Sho', you fool nigger, what you think dey is—ha'nts? (*excitedly*) Gorry, you give de game away when you fire dat shot. Dem niggers heah dat fo' su'tin! Time you beat it in de woods widout no long waits. (*He starts for the forest—hesitates before the plunge—then urging himself in with manful resolution*) Git in, nigger! What you skeered at? Ain't nothin' dere but de trees! Git in! (*He plunges boldly into the forest.*)

Scene Three

In the forest. The moon has just risen. Its beams, drifting through the canopy of leaves, make a barely perceptible, suffused, eerie glow. A dense low wall of underbrush and creepers is in the nearer foreground, fencing in a small triangular clearing. Beyond this is the massed blackness of the forest like an encompassing barrier. A path is dimly discerned leading down to the clearing from left, rear, and winding away from it again toward the right. As the scene opens nothing can be distinctly made out. Except for the beating of the tom-tom, which is a trifle louder and quicker than at the close of the previous scene, there is silence, broken every few seconds by a queer, clicking sound. Then gradually the figure of the negro, Jeff, can be discerned crouching on his haunches at the rear of the triangle. He is middle-aged, thin, brown in color, is dressed in a Pullman porter's uniform and cap. He is throwing a pair of dice on the ground before him, picking them up, shaking them, casting them out with the regular, rigid, mechanical movements of an automaton. The heavy, plodding footsteps of someone approaching along the trail from the left are heard and Jones' voice, pitched on a slightly higher key and strained in a cheery effort to overcome its own tremors.

De moon's risen. Does you heah dat, nigger? You gits more light from dis out. No mo' buttin' yo' fool head agin' de trunks an' scratchin' de hide off yo' legs in de bushes. Now you sees whar yo'se gwine. So cheer up! From now on you has a snap. (*He steps just to the rear of the triangular clearing and mops off his face on his sleeve. He has lost his Panama hat. His face is scratched, his brilliant uniform shows several large rents.*) What time's it gittin' to be, I wonder? I dassent light no match to find out. Phoo'. It's wa'm an' dat's a fac'! (*wearily*) How long I been makin' tracks in dese woods? Must be hours an' hours. Seems like fo'evah! Yit can't be, when de moon's jes' riz. Dis am a long night fo' yo', yo' Majesty! (*with a mournful chuckle*) Majesty! Der ain't much majesty 'bout dis baby now. (*with attempted cheerfulness*) Never min'. It's all part o' de game. Dis night come to an end like everything else. And when you gits dar safe and has dat bankroll in yo' hands you laughs at all dis. (*He starts to whistle but checks himself abruptly.*) What yo' whistlin' for, you po' dope! Want all de worl' to heah you? (*He stops talking to listen.*) Heah dat ole drum! Sho' gits nearer from de sound. Dey's packin' it along wid 'em. Time fo' me to move. (*He takes a step forward, then stops—worriedly*) What's dat odder queer clickety sound I heah? Dere it is! Sound close! Sound like—sound like—Fo' God sake, sound like some nigger was shootin' crap! (*frightenedly*) I better beat it quick when I gits dem notions. (*He walks quickly into the clear space—then stands transfixed as he sees Jeff—in a terrified gasp*) Who dar? Who dat? Is dat you, Jeff? (*starting toward the other, forgetful for a moment of his surroundings and really believing it is a living man that he sees—in a tone of happy relief*) Jeff! I'se sho' mighty glad to see you! Dey tol' me you done died from dat razor cut I gives you. (*stopping suddenly, bewilderedly*) But how you come to be heah, nigger? (*He stares fascinatedly at the other who continues his mechanical play with the dice. Jones' eyes begin to roll wildly. He stutters*) Ain't you gwine—look up—can't you speak to me? Is you—is you—a ha'nt? (*He jerks out his revolver in a frenzy of terrified rage.*) Nigger, I kills you dead once. Has I got to kill you ag'in? You take it den. (*He fires. When the smoke clears away Jeff has disappeared. Jones stands trembling—then with a certain reassurance*) He's gone, anyway. Ha'nt or not ha'nt, dat shot fix him. (*The beat of the far-off tom-tom is perceptibly louder and more rapid. Jones becomes conscious of it—with a start, looking back over his shoulder*) Dey's gittin' near! Dey's comin' fast! And heah I is shootin' shots to let 'em knows jes' whar I is! Oh, Gorry, I'se got to run. (*Forgetting the path he plunges wildly into the underbrush in the rear and disappears in the shadow.*)

Scene Four

In the forest. A wide dirt road runs diagonally from right, front, to left, rear. Rising sheer on both sides the forest walls it in. The moon is now up. Under its light the road glimmers ghastly and unreal. It is as if the forest had stood aside momentarily to let the road pass through and accomplish its veiled purpose. This done, the forest will fold in upon itself again and the road will be no more. Jones stumbles in from the forest on the right. His uniform is ragged and torn. He looks about him with numbed surprise when he sees the road, his eyes blinking in the bright moonlight. He flops down exhaustedly and pants heavily for a while. Then with sudden anger

I'm meltin' wid heat! Runnin' an' runnin' an' runnin'! Damn dis heah coat! Like a straitjacket! (*He tears off his coat and flings it away from him, revealing himself stripped to the waist.*) Dere! Dat's better! Now I kin breathe! (*looking down at his feet, the spurs catch his eye*) And to hell wid dese high-fangled spurs. Dey're what's been a-trippin' me up an' breakin' my neck. (*He unstraps them and flings them away disgustedly.*) Dere! I gits rid o' dem frippety Emperor trappin's an' I travels lighter. Lawd! I'se tired! (*after a pause, listening to the insistent beat of the tom-tom in the distance*) I must 'a' put some distance between myself an' dem—runnin' like dat—and yit—dat damn drum sounds jes' de same—nearer, even. Well, I guess I a'most holds my lead anyhow. Dey won't never catch up. (*with a sigh*) If on'y my fool legs stands up. Oh, I'se sorry I evah went in for dis. Dat Emperor job is sho' hard to shake. (*He looks around him suspiciously.*) How'd dis road evah git heah? Good level road, too. I never remembers seein' it befo'. (*shaking his head apprehensively*) Dese woods is sho' full o' de queerest things at night. (*with a sudden terror*) Lawd God, don't let me see no more o' dem ha'nts! Dey gits my goat! (*then trying to talk himself into confidence*) Ha'nts! You fool nigger, dey ain't no such things! Don't de Baptist parson tell you dat many time? Is you civilized, or is you like dese ign'rent black niggers heah? Sho'! Dat was all in yo' own head. Wasn't nothin' dere. Wasn't no Jeff! Know what? You jus' get seein' dem things 'cause yo' belly's empty and you's sick wid hunger inside. Hunger 'fects yo' head and yo' eyes. Any fool know dat. (*then pleading fervently*) But bless God, I don't come across no more o' dem, whatever dey is! (*then cautiously*) Rest! Don't talk! Rest! You needs it. Den you gits on yo' way again. (*looking at the moon*) Night's half gone a'most. You hits de coast in de mawning! Den you's all safe.

(*From the right forward a small gang of negroes enter. They are dressed in striped convict suits, their heads are shaven, one leg drags limpingly, shackled to a heavy ball and chain. Some carry picks, the others shovels. They are followed by a white man dressed in the uniform of a prison guard. A Winchester rifle is slung across his shoulders and he carries a heavy whip. At a signal from the guard they stop on the road opposite where Jones is sitting. Jones, who has been staring up at the sky, unmindful of their noiseless approach, suddenly looks down and sees them. His eyes pop out, he tries to get to his feet and fly, but sinks back, too numbed by fright to move. His voice catches in a choking prayer.*)

Lawd Jesus!

(*The prison guard cracks his whip—noiselessly—and at that signal all the convicts start to work on the road. They swing their picks, they shovel, but not a sound comes from their labor. Their movements, like those of Jeff in the preceding scene, are those of automatons,— rigid, slow, and mechanical. The prison guard points sternly at Jones with his whip, motions him to take his place among the other shovelers. Jones gets to his feet in a hypnotized stupor. He mumbles subserviently*)

Yes, suh! Yes, suh! I'se comin'.

(*As he shuffles, dragging one foot, over to his place, he curses under his breath with rage and hatred.*)

God damn yo' soul, I gits even wid you yit, sometime.

(*As if there were a shovel in his hands he goes through weary, mechanical gestures of digging up dirt, and throwing it to the roadside. Suddenly the guard approaches him angrily, threateningly. He raises his whip and lashes Jones viciously across the shoulders with it. Jones winces with pain and cowers abjectly. The guard turns his back on him and walks away contemptuously. Instantly Jones straightens up. With arms upraised as if his shovel were a club in his hands he springs murderously at the unsuspecting guard. In the act of crashing down his shovel on the white man's skull, Jones suddenly becomes aware that his hands are empty. He cries despairingly*)

Whar's my shovel? Gimme my shovel 'til I splits his damn head! (*appealing to his fellow convicts*) Gimme a shovel, one o' you, fo' God's sake!

(*They stand fixed in motionless attitudes, their eyes on the ground. The guard seems to wait expectantly, his back turned to the attacker. Jones bellows with baffled, terrified rage, tugging frantically at his revolver.*)

I kills you, you white debil, if it's de last thing I evah does! Ghost or debil, I kill you agin!

(*He frees the revolver and fires point blank at the guard's back. Instantly the walls of the forest close in from both sides, the road and the figures of the convict gang are blotted out in an enshrouding darkness. The only sounds are a crashing in the underbrush as Jones leaps away in mad flight and the throbbing of the tom-tom, still far distant, but increased in volume of sound and rapidity of beat.*)

Scene Five

A large circular clearing, enclosed by the serried ranks of gigantic trunks of tall trees whose tops are lost to view. In the center is a big dead stump worn by time into a curious resemblance to an auction block. The moon floods the clearing with a clear light. Jones forces his way in through the forest on the left. He looks wildly about the clearing with hunted, fearful glances. His pants are in tatters, his shoes cut and misshapen, flapping about his feet. He slinks cautiously to the stump in the center and sits down in a tense position, ready for instant flight. Then he holds his head in his hands and rocks back and forth, moaning to himself miserably.

Oh Lawd, Lawd! Oh Lawd, Lawd! (*Suddenly he throws himself on his knees and raises his clasped hands to the sky—in a voice of agonized pleading*) Lawd Jesus, heah my prayer! I'se a po' sinner, a po' sinner! I knows I done wrong, I knows it! When I cotches Jeff cheatin' wid loaded dice my anger overcomes me and I kills him dead! Lawd, I done wrong! When dat guard hits me wid de whip, my anger overcomes me, and I kills him dead. Lawd, I done wrong! And down heah whar dese fool bush niggers raises me up to the seat o' de mighty, I steals all I could grab. Lawd, I done wrong! I knows it! I'se sorry! Forgive me, Lawd! Forgive dis po' sinner! (*then beseeching terrifiedly*) And keep dem away, Lawd! Keep dem away from me! And stop dat drum soundin' in my ears! Dat begin to sound ha'nted, too. (*He gets to his feet, evidently slightly reassured by his prayer—with attempted confidence*) De Lawd'll preserve me from dem ha'nts after dis. (*sits down on the stump again*) I ain't skeered o' real men. Let dem come. But dem odders—(*He shudders—then looks down at his feet, working his toes inside the shoes—with a groan*) Oh, my po' feet! Dem shoes ain't no use no more 'ceptin' to hurt. I'se better off widout dem. (*He unlaces them and pulls them off—holds the wrecks of the shoes in his hands and regards them mournfully.*) You was real, A-one patin' leather, too. Look at you now. Emperor, you'se gittin' mighty low!

(*He sighs dejectedly and remains with bowed shoulders, staring down at the shoes in his hands as if reluctant to throw them away. While his attention is thus occupied, a crowd of figures silently enter the clearing from all sides. All are dressed in Southern costumes of the period of the fifties of the last century. There are middle-aged men who are evidently well-to-do planters. There is one spruce, authoritative individual—the auctioneer. There is a crowd of curious spectators, chiefly young belles and dandies who have come to the slave-*

market for diversion. All exchange courtly greetings in dumb show and chat silently to-gether. There is something stiff, rigid, unreal, marionettish about their movements. They group themselves about the stump. Finally a batch of slaves is led in from the left by an at-tendant—three men of different ages, two women, one with a baby in her arms, nursing. They are placed to the left of the stump, besides Jones.

(The white planters look them over appraisingly as if they were cattle, and exchange judgments on each. The dandies point with their fingers and make witty remarks. The belles titter bewitchingly. All this in silence save for the ominous throb of the tom-tom. The auctioneer holds up his hand, taking his place at the stump. The groups strain forward at-tentively. He touches Jones on the shoulder peremptorily, motioning for him to stand on the stump—the auction block.

(Jones looks up, sees the figures on all sides, looks wildly for some opening to escape, sees none, screams and leaps madly to the top of the stump to get as far away from them as pos-sible. He stands there, cowering, paralyzed with horror. The auctioneer begins his silent spiel. He points to Jones, appeals to the planters to see for themselves. Here is a good field hand, sound in wind and limb as they can see. Very strong still in spite of his being middle-aged. Look at that back. Look at those shoulders. Look at the muscles in his arms and his sturdy legs. Capable of any amount of hard labor. Moreover, of a good disposition, intelli-gent and tractable. Will any gentleman start the bidding? The planters raise their fingers, make their bids. They are apparently all eager to possess Jones. The bidding is lively, the crowd interested. While this has been going on, Jones has been seized by the courage of des-peration. He dares to look down and around him. Over his face abject terror gives way to mystification, to gradual realization—stutteringly)

What you all doin', white folks? What's all dis? What you all lookin' at me fo'? What you doin' wid me, anyhow? (*suddenly convulsed with raging hatred and fear*) Is dis a auc-tion? Is you sellin' me like dey uster befo' de war? (*jerking out his revolver just as the auc-tioneer knocks him down to one of the planters—glaring from him to the purchaser*) And *you* sells me? And *you* buys me? I shows you I's a free nigger, damn yo' souls! (*He fires at the auctioneer and at the planter with such rapidity that the two shots are almost simulta-neous. As if this were a signal the walls of the forest fold in. Only blackness remains and si-lence broken by Jones as he rushes off, crying with fear—and by the quickened, ever louder beat of the tom-tom.*)

Scene Six

A cleared space in the forest. The limbs of the trees meet over it forming a low ceiling about five feet from the ground. The interlocked ropes of creepers reaching upward to en-twine the tree trunks give an arched appearance to the sides. The space thus enclosed is like the dark, noisome hold of some ancient vessel. The moonlight is almost completely shut out and only a vague wan light filters through. There is the noise of someone ap-proaching from the left, stumbling and crawling through the undergrowth. Jones' voice is heard between chattering moans.

Oh, Lawd, what I gwine do now? Ain't got no bullet left on'y de silver one. If mo' o' dem ha'nts come after me, how I gwine skeer dem away? Oh, Lawd, on'y de silver one left—an' I gotta save dat fo' luck. If I shoots dat one I'm a goner sho'! Lawd, it's black heah! Whar's de moon? Oh, Lawd, don't dis night evah come to an end! (*By the sounds, he is feeling his way cautiously forward.*) Dere! Dis feels like a clear space. I gotta lie down an' rest. I don't care if dem niggers does cotch me. I gotta rest.

(*He is well forward now where his figure can be dimly made out. His pants have been so torn away that what is left of them is no better than a breech cloth. He flings himself full length, face downward on the ground, panting with exhaustion. Gradually it seems to grow lighter in the enclosed space and two rows of seated figures can be seen behind Jones. They are sitting in crumpled, despairing attitudes, hunched, facing one another with their backs touching the forest walls as if they were shackled to them. All are negroes, naked save for loin cloths. At first they are silent and motionless. Then they begin to sway slowly forward toward each other and back again in unison, as if they were laxly letting themselves follow the long roll of a ship at sea. At the same time, a low, melancholy murmur rises among them, increasing gradually by rhythmic degrees which seem to be directed and controlled by the throb of the tom-tom in the distance, to a long, tremulous wail of despair that reaches a certain pitch, unbearably acute, then falls by slow gradations of tone into silence and is taken up again. Jones starts, looks up, sees the figures, and throws himself down again to shut out the sight. A shudder of terror shakes his whole body as the wail rises up about him again. But the next time, his voice, as if under some uncanny compulsion, starts with the others. As their chorus lifts he rises to a sitting posture similar to the others, swaying back and forth. His voice reaches the highest pitch of sorrow, of desolation. The light fades out, the other voices cease, and only darkness is left. Jones can be heard scrambling to his feet and running off, his voice sinking down the scale and receding as he moves farther and farther away in the forest. The tom-tom beats louder, quicker, with a more insistent, triumphant pulsation.*)

Scene Seven

The foot of a gigantic tree by the edge of a great river. A rough structure of boulders, like an altar, is by the tree. The raised river bank is in the nearer background. Beyond this the surface of the river spreads out, brilliant and unruffled in the moonlight, blotted out and merged into a veil of bluish mist in the distance. Jones' voice is heard from the left rising and falling in the long, despairing wail of the chained slaves, to the rhythmic beat of the tom-tom. As his voice sinks into silence, he enters the open space. The expression of his face is fixed and stony, his eyes have an obsessed glare, he moves with a strange deliberation like a sleep-walker or one in a trance. He looks around at the tree, the rough stone altar, the moonlit surface of the river beyond, and passes his hand over his head with a vague gesture of puzzled bewilderment. Then, as if in obedience to some obscure impulse, he sinks into a kneeling, devotional posture before the altar. Then he seems to come to himself partly, to have an uncertain realization of what he is doing, for he straightens up and stares about him horrifiedly—in an incoherent mumble

What—what is I doin'? What is—dis place? Seems like I know dat tree—an' dem stones—an' de river. I remember—seems like I been heah befo'. (*tremblingly*) Oh, Gorry, I'se skeered in dis place! I'se skeered. Oh, Lawd, perfect dis sinner!

(*Crawling away from the altar, he cowers close to the ground, his face hidden, his shoulders heaving with sobs of hysterical fright. From behind the trunk of the tree, as if he had sprung out of it, the figure of the Congo witch-doctor appears. He is wizened and old, naked except for the fur of some small animal tied about his waist, its bushy tail hanging down in front. His body is stained all over a bright red. Antelope horns are on each side of his head, branching upward. In one hand he carries a bone rattle, in the other a charm stick with a bunch of white cockatoo feathers tied to the end. A great number of glass beads and bone ornaments are about his neck, ears, wrists, and ankles. He struts noiselessly with a queer prancing step to a position in the clear ground between Jones and the altar. Then with a preliminary, summoning stamp of his foot on the earth, he begins to dance and to chant. As if in response to his summons the beating of the tom-tom grows to a fierce, exultant boom whose throbs seem to fill the air with vibrating rhythm. Jones looks up, starts to spring to his feet, reaches a half-kneeling, half-squatting position and remains rigidly fixed there, paralyzed with awed fascination by this new apparition. The witch-doctor sways, stamping with his foot, his bone rattle clicking the time. His voice rises and falls in a weird, monotonous croon, without articulate word divisions. Gradually his dance becomes clearly one of a narrative in pantomime, his croon is an incantation, a charm to allay the fierceness of some implacable deity demanding sacrifice. He flees, he is pursued by devils, he hides, he flees again. Ever wilder and wilder becomes his flight, nearer and nearer draws the pursuing evil, more and more the spirit of terror gains possession of him. His croon, rising to intensity, is punctuated by shrill cries. Jones has become completely hypnotized. His voice joins in the incantation, in the cries, he beats time with his hands and sways his body to and fro from the waist. The whole spirit and meaning of the dance has entered into him, has become his spirit. Finally the theme of the pantomime halts on a howl of despair, and is taken up again in a note of savage hope. There is a salvation. The forces of evil demand sacrifice. They must be appeased. The witch-doctor points with his wand to the sacred tree, to the river beyond, to the altar, and finally to Jones with a ferocious command. Jones seems to sense the meaning of this. It is he who must offer himself for sacrifice. He beats his forehead abjectly to the ground, moaning hysterically)*

Mercy, Oh Lawd! Mercy! Mercy on dis po' sinner.

(The witch-doctor springs to the river bank. He stretches out his arms and calls to some God within its depths. Then he starts backward slowly, his arms remaining out. A huge head of a crocodile appears over the bank and its eyes, glittering greenly, fasten upon Jones. He stares into them fascinatedly. The witch-doctor prances up to him, touches him with his wand, motions with hideous command toward the waiting monster. Jones squirms on his belly nearer and nearer, moaning continually)

Mercy, Lawd! Mercy!

(The crocodile heaves more of his enormous hulk onto the land. Jones squirms toward him. The witch-doctor's voice shrills out in furious exultation, the tom-tom beats madly. Jones cries out in a fierce, exhausted spasm of anguished pleading)

Lawd, save me! Lawd Jesus, heah my prayer!
(Immediately, in answer to his prayer, comes the thought of the one bullet left him. He snatches at his hip, shouting defiantly)
De silver bullet! You don't git me yit!

(He fires at the green eyes in front of him. The head of the crocodile sinks back behind the river bank, the witch-doctor springs behind the sacred tree and disappears. Jones lies with his face to the ground, his arms outstretched, whimpering with fear as the throb of the tom-tom fills the silence about him with a somber pulsation, a baffled but revengeful power.)

Scene Eight

Dawn. Same as Scene Two, the dividing line of forest and plain. The nearest tree trunks are dimly revealed but the forest behind them is still a mass of glooming shadow. The tom-tom seems on the very spot, so loud and continuously vibrating are its beats. Lem enters from the left, followed by a small squad of his soldiers, and by the Cockney trader, Smithers. Lem is a heavy-set, ape-faced old savage of the extreme African type, dressed only in a loin cloth. A revolver and cartridge belt are about his waist. His soldiers are in different degrees of rag-concealed nakedness. All wear broad palm-leaf hats. Each one carries a rifle. Smithers is the same as in Scene One. One of the soldiers, evidently a tracker, is peering about keenly on the ground. He points to the spot where Jones entered the forest. Lem and Smithers come to look.

Smithers: *(after a glance, turns away in disgust)* That's where 'e went in right enough. Much good it'll do yer. 'E's miles orf by this an' safe to the Coast, damn 's 'ide! I tole yer yer'd lose 'im, didn't I?—wastin' the 'ole bloomin' night beatin' yer bloody drum and castin' yer silly spells! Gawd blimey, wot a pack!

Lem: *(gutturally)* We cotch him. *(He makes a motion to his soldiers who squat down on their haunches in a semi-circle.)*

Smithers: *(exasperatedly)* Well, ain't yer goin' in an' 'unt 'im in the woods? What the 'ell's the good of waitin'?

Lem: *(imperturbably—squatting down himself)* We cotch him.

Smithers: *(turning away from him contemptuously)* Aw! Garn! 'E's a better man than the lot o' you put together. I 'ates the sight o' 'im but I'll say that for 'im. *(A sound comes from the forest. The soldiers jump to their feet, cocking their rifles alertly. Lem remains sitting with an imperturbable expression, but listening intently. He makes a quick signal with his hand. His followers creep quickly into the forest, scattering so that each enters at a different spot.)*

Smithers: You ain't thinkin' that would be 'im, I 'ope?

Lem: *(calmly)* We cotch him.

Smithers: Blarsted fat 'eads! *(then after a second's thought—wonderingly)* Still an' all, it might 'appen. If 'e lost 'is bloody way in these stinkin' woods 'e'd likely turn in a circle without 'is knowin' it.

Lem: *(peremptorily)* Sssh! *(The reports of several rifles sound from the forest, followed a second later by savage, exultant yells. The beating of the tom-tom abruptly ceases. Lem looks up at the white man with a grin of satisfaction.)* We cotch him. Him dead.

Smithers: *(with a snarl)* 'Ow d'yer know it's 'im an' 'ow d'yer know 'e's dead?

Lem: My mens dey got um silver bullets. Lead bullet no kill him. He got um strong charm. I cook um money, make um silver bullet, make um strong charm, too.

Smithers: *(astonished)* So that's wot you was up to all night, wot? You was scared to put after 'im till you'd moulded silver bullets, eh?

Lem: *(simply stating a fact)* Yes. Him got strong charm. Lead no good.

Smithers: (slapping his thigh and guffawing) Haw-haw! If yer don't beat all 'ell! (*then recovering himself—scornfully*) I'll bet yer it ain't 'im they shot at all, yer bleedin' looney!

Lem: (calmly) Dey come bring him now. (*The soldiers come out of the forest, carrying Jones' limp body. He is dead. They carry him to Lem, who examines his body with great satisfaction.*)

Smithers: leans over his shoulder—in a tone of frightened awe) Well, they did for yer right enough, Jonesey, me lad! Dead as a 'erring! (*mockingly*) Where's yer 'igh an' mighty airs now, yer bloomin' Majesty? (*then with a grin*) Silver bullets! Gawd blimey, but yer died in the 'eighth o' style, any'ow!

(Curtain)

Katherine Anne Porter
1890–1980

Katherine Anne Porter was born Callie Porter on May 15, 1890, in a simple L-shaped log cabin in Indian Creek, Texas, a small frontier community. She received, as she put it, a "fragmentary, but strangely useless and ornamental education" in various convent schools. Looking back, she saw herself as having been taught not at "schools at all but by five writers: Henry James, James Joyce, W. B. Yeats, T. S. Eliot, and Ezra Pound." Throughout her life, she spread misrepresentations, concoctions, and fabrications about her family and childhood, evoking a grand family plantation and distinguished ancestry that bore little resemblance to the actualities of the hard, uprooted life she experienced but considerable resemblance to elements of the stories she wrote.

During her long life, Porter lived in towns all over Texas and in cities throughout the United States—Denver, Chicago, New Orleans, New York, and Washington, to name a few—where she worked on newspapers and later held teaching positions. She also lived in Mexico, where she was politically active, as well as Belgium, Switzerland, France, and Germany. Approaching forty, she reported "that she had had four husbands and thirty-seven lovers." Over the last half of her life, there were two more husbands and many more lovers, including several after she reached the age of seventy. "Love," she said, is "purely a creation of the human imagination": it is the "most important example of how the imagination continually outruns the creature it inhabits." In addition to men, Porter collected furs, jewels, fine silver and china, antique furniture, gossip, and fables.

Porter's need to glamorize and enhance the facts of her life emerged early and lasted as long as she lived. Her finest fiction, however, which clearly sprang in part from needs like those expressed in her fabrications, was largely concentrated in the middle years of her life, especially the decade of the 1930s. "I went to Europe in 1931 an unknown," she later remarked, "and returned to find myself a celebrity." This success was based on two collections of stories and short novels, *Flowering Judas* (published in 1930 and augmented in 1935) and *Noon Wine* (1937). Her critical reputation was enhanced by *Pale Horse, Pale Rider: Three Short Novels* (1938) and *The Leaning Tower and Other Stories* (1944). In his review of *The Leaning Tower*, Edmund Wilson admitted that Porter was "baffling" to him and struggled to formulate the "elusive" quality that made her "absolutely a first-rate artist":

> These stories are not illustrations of anything that is reducible to a moral law or a political or social analysis or even a principle of human behavior. What they show us are human relations in their constantly shifting phases and in the moments of which their existence is made. There is no place for general reflections; you are to live through the experience as the characters do.

Like Sherwood Anderson, Porter believed that the short story did not require a "plot." The writer, she said, "needed *first* a *theme,* and then a point of view, a certain knowledge of human nature and strong feeling about it, and style—that is to say, his own special way of telling a thing that makes it precisely his own and no one else's." As Eudora Welty pointed out in a review of *The Collected Stories of Katherine Anne Porter* (1965), she cared nothing for conventionally dramatic construction: "The suspense— so acute and so real—in Katherine Anne Porter's work never did depend for its life on disclosure of the happenings of the narrative . . . but in the writing of the story, which becomes one single long sustained moment for the reader."

Even in Porter's finest work we observe a tension between a desire to confront and disclose the significance of her experience and a countervailing desire to disguise and conceal that significance. The conflict between these impulses sometimes results in a rarefied, ethereal prose, as though Porter were reaching for the timeless and the universal before making sufficient contact with the local and the immediate. Both her aestheticism and her evasiveness, her reluctance to confront fully the significances lurking in her own experience of the world she knew best, occasionally limit her achievement. In works such as "Old Mortality" and "The Jilting of Granny Weatherall," however, she masters the tension between her sense of herself as a stylist seeking timelessness and universality and her sense of herself as a storyteller drawing upon perceptions and memories of local scenes and human actions.

Porter's only novel, *Ship of Fools,* which she wrote laboriously over a thirty-year period, appeared in 1962 and attracted considerable attention, in part because it had been so long awaited. The novel, an account of a voyage from Veracruz, Mexico, to Bremerhaven, Germany, in 1931, before the Nazi regime, explores the wreckage of modern civilization by focusing on the often vicious private histories and behavior of the ship's passengers. The vision of the book is a bleak one and apparently derives from Porter's longstanding belief that art offered the only hope, however small and fragile, in a darkening world. In 1940 she wrote in an introduction to a new edition of *Flowering Judas:* "All the conscious and recollected years of my life have been lived to this day under the heavy threat of world catastrophe, and most of the energies of my mind and spirit have been spent in the effort to grasp the meaning of those threats, to trace them to their sources and to understand the logic of this majestic and terrible failure of the life of man in the Western world." In 1952 Porter published *The Days Before: Collected Essays and Occasional Writings,* a volume that was expanded in 1970; the essays range from an interpretation of nuclear fear to a profile of Jacqueline

Kennedy. Katherine Anne Porter died on September 18, 1980, in the Carriage Hill Nursing Center in Silver Spring, Maryland.

Further Reading:

H. J. Mooney, *The Fiction and Criticism of Katherine Anne Porter*, 1962.
R. B. West, Jr., *Katherine Anne Porter*, 1963.
E. Welty, "The Eye of the Story," *Yale Review*, December 1965.

J. Givner, *Katherine Anne Porter: A Life*, 1982.
J. Tanner, *The Texas Legacy of Katherine Anne Porter*, 1991.
Flowering Judas, 1935.

Text:

"The Jilting of Granny Weatherall," from *Flowering Judas and Other Stories*, 1935.

The Jilting of Granny Weatherall

She flicked her wrist neatly out of Doctor Harry's pudgy careful fingers and pulled the sheet up to her chin. The brat ought to be in knee breeches. Doctoring around the country with spectacles on his nose! "Get along now, take your schoolbooks and go. There's nothing wrong with me."

Doctor Harry spread a warm paw like a cushion on her forehead where the forked green vein danced and made her eyelids twitch. "Now, now, be a good girl, and we'll have you up in no time."

"That's no way to speak to a woman nearly eighty years old just because she's down. I'd have you respect your elders, young man."

"Well, Missy, excuse me." Doctor Harry patted her cheek. "But I've got to warn you, haven't I? You're a marvel, but you must be careful or you're going to be good and sorry."

"Don't tell me what I'm going to be. I'm on my feet now, morally speaking. It's Cornelia. I had to go to bed to get rid of her."

Her bones felt loose, and floated around in her skin, and Doctor Harry floated like a balloon around the foot of the bed. He floated and pulled down his waistcoat and swung his glasses on a cord. "Well, stay where you are, it certainly can't hurt you."

"Get along and doctor your sick," said Granny Weatherall. "Leave a well woman alone. I'll call for you when I want you. . . . Where were you forty years ago when I pulled through milk-leg and double pneumonia? You weren't even born. Don't let Cornelia lead you on," she shouted, because Doctor Harry appeared to float up to the ceiling and out. "I pay my own bills, and I don't throw my money away on nonsense!"

She meant to wave good-by, but it was too much trouble. Her eyes closed of themselves, it was like a dark curtain drawn around the bed. The pillow rose and floated under her, pleasant as a hammock in a light wind. She listened to the leaves rustling outside the window. No, somebody was swishing newspapers: no, Cornelia and Doctor Harry were whispering together. She leaped broad awake, thinking they whispered in her ear.

"She was never like this, *never* like this!" "Well, what can we expect?" "Yes, eighty years old. . . ."

Well, and what if she was? She still had ears. It was like Cornelia to whisper around doors. She always kept things secret in such a public way. She was always being tactful and kind. Cornelia was dutiful; that was the trouble with her. Dutiful and good: "So good and dutiful," said Granny, "that I'd like to spank her." She saw herself spanking Cornelia and making a fine job of it.

"What'd you say, Mother?"

Granny felt her face tying up in hard knots.

"Can't a body think, I'd like to know?"

"I thought you might want something."

"I do. I want a lot of things. First off, go away and don't whisper."

She lay and drowsed, hoping in her sleep that the children would keep out and let her rest a minute. It had been a long day. Not that she was tired. It was always pleasant to snatch a minute now and then. There was always so much to be done, let me see: tomorrow.

Tomorrow was far away and there was nothing to trouble about. Things were finished somehow when the time came; thank God there was always a little margin over for peace: then a person could spread out the plan of life and tuck in the edges orderly. It was good to have everything clean and folded away, with the hair brushes and tonic bottles sitting straight on the white embroidered linen: the day started without fuss and the pantry shelves laid out with rows of jelly glasses and brown jugs and white stone-china jars with blue whirligigs and words painted on them: coffee, tea, sugar, ginger, cinnamon, allspice: and the bronze clock with the lion on top nicely dusted off. The dust that lion could collect in twenty-four hours! The box in the attic with all those letters tied up, well, she'd have to go through that tomorrow. All those letters—George's letters and John's letters and her letters to them both—lying around for the children to find afterwards made her uneasy. Yes, that would be tomorrow's business. No use to let them know how silly she had been once.

While she was rummaging around she found death in her mind and it felt clammy and unfamiliar. She had spent so much time preparing for death there was no need for bringing it up again. Let it take care of itself now. When she was sixty she had felt very old, finished, and went around making farewell trips to see her children and grandchildren, with a secret in her mind: This is the very last of your mother, children! Then she made her will and came down with a long fever. That was all just a notion like a lot of other things, but it was lucky too, for she had once for all got over the idea of dying for a long time. Now she couldn't be worried. She hoped she had better sense now. Her father had lived to be one hundred and two years old and had drunk a noggin of strong hot toddy on his last birthday. He told the reporters it was his daily habit, and he owed his long life to that. He had made quite a scandal and was very pleased about it. She believed she'd just plague Cornelia a little.

"Cornelia! Cornelia!" No footsteps, but a sudden hand on her cheek. "Bless you, where have you been?"

"Here, mother."

"Well, Cornelia, I want a noggin of hot toddy."

"Are you cold, darling?"

"I'm chilly, Cornelia. Lying in bed stops the circulation. I must have told you that a thousand times."

Well, she could just hear Cornelia telling her husband that Mother was getting a little childish and they'd have to humor her. The thing that most annoyed her was that Cornelia thought she was deaf, dumb, and blind. Little hasty glances and tiny gestures tossed around her and over her head saying, "Don't cross her, let her have her way, she's eighty years old," and she sitting there as if she lived in a thin glass cage. Sometimes Granny almost made up her mind to pack up and move back to her own house where nobody could remind her every minute that she was old. Wait, wait, Cornelia, till your own children whisper behind your back!

In her day she had kept a better house and had got more work done. She wasn't too old yet for Lydia to be driving eighty miles for advice when one of the children jumped the track, and Jimmy still dropped in and talked things over: "Now, Mammy, you've a good business head, I want to know what you think of this? . . ." Old. Cornelia couldn't change the furniture around without asking. Little things, little things! They had been so sweet when they were little. Granny wished the old days were back again with the children young and everything to be done over. It had been a hard pull, but not too much for her. When she thought of all the food she had cooked, and all the clothes she had cut and sewed, and all the gardens she had made—well, the children showed it. There they were, made out of her, and they couldn't get away from that. Sometimes she wanted to see John again and point to them and say, Well, I didn't do so badly, did I? But that would have to wait. That was for tomorrow. She used to think of him as a man, but now all the children were older than their father, and he would be a child beside her if she saw him now. It seemed strange and there was something wrong in the idea. Why, he couldn't possibly recognize her. She had fenced in a hundred acres once, digging the post holes herself and clamping the wires with just a negro boy to help. That changed a woman. John would be looking for a young woman with the peaked Spanish comb in her hair and the painted fan. Digging post holes changed a woman. Riding country roads in the winter when women had their babies was another thing: sitting up nights with sick horses and sick negroes and sick children and hardly ever losing one. John, I hardly ever lost one of them! John would see that in a minute, that would be something he could understand, she wouldn't have to explain anything!

It made her feel like rolling up her sleeves and putting the whole place to rights again. No matter if Cornelia was determined to be everywhere at once, there were a great many things left undone on this place. She would start tomorrow and do them. It was good to be strong enough for everything, even if all you made melted and changed and slipped under your hands, so that by the time you finished you almost forgot what you were working for. What was it I set out to do? she asked herself intently, but she could not remember. A fog rose over the valley, she saw it marching across the creek swallowing the trees and moving up the hill like an army of ghosts. Soon it would be at the near edge of the orchard, and then it was time to go in and light the lamps. Come in, children, don't stay out in the night air.

Lighting the lamps had been beautiful. The children huddled up to her and breathed like little calves waiting at the bars in the twilight. Their eyes followed the match and watched the flame rise and settle in a blue curve, then they moved away from her. The lamp was lit, they didn't have to be scared and hang on to mother any more. Never, never, never more. God, for all my life I thank Thee. Without Thee, my God, I could never have done it. Hail, Mary, full of grace.

I want you to pick all the fruit this year and see that nothing is wasted. There's always someone who can use it. Don't let good things rot for want of using. You waste life when you waste good food. Don't let things get lost. It's bitter to lose things. Now, don't let me get to thinking, not when I am tired and taking a little nap before supper. . . .

The pillow rose about her shoulders and pressed against her heart and the memory was being squeezed out of it: oh, push down the pillow, somebody: it would smother her if she tried to hold it. Such a fresh breeze blowing and such a green day with no threats in it. But he had not come, just the same. What does a woman do when she has put on the white veil and set out the white cake for a man and he doesn't come? She tried to remember. No, I swear he never harmed me but in that. He never harmed me but in that . . . and what if he did? There was the day, the day, but a whirl of dark smoke rose and covered it, crept up and over into the bright field where everything was planted so carefully in orderly rows. That was hell, she knew hell when she saw it. For sixty years she had prayed against remembering him and against losing her soul in the deep pit of hell, and now the two things were mingled in one and the thought of him was a smoky cloud from hell that moved and crept in her head when she had just got rid of Doctor Harry and was trying to rest a minute. Wounded vanity, Ellen, said a sharp voice in the top of her mind. Don't let your wounded vanity get the upper hand of you. Plenty of girls get jilted. You were jilted, weren't you? Then stand up to it. Her eyelids wavered and let in streamers of blue-gray light like tissue paper over her eyes. She must get up and pull the shades down or she'd never sleep. She was in bed again and the shades were not down. How could that happen? Better turn over, hide from the light, sleeping in the light gave you nightmares. "Mother, how do you feel now?" and a sting-ing wetness on her forehead. But I don't like having my face washed in cold water!

Hapsy? George? Lydia? Jimmy? No, Cornelia, and her features were swollen and full of little puddles. "They're coming, darling, they'll all be here soon." Go wash your face, child, you look funny.

Instead of obeying, Cornelia knelt down and put her head on the pillow. She seemed to be talking but there was no sound. "Well, are you tongue-tied? Whose birthday is it? Are you going to give a party?"

Cornelia's mouth moved urgently in strange shapes. "Don't do that, you bother me, daughter."

"Oh, no, Mother. Oh, no. . . ."

Nonsense. It was strange about children. They disputed your every word. "No what, Cornelia?"

"Here's Doctor Harry."

"I won't see that boy again. He just left five minutes ago."

"That was this morning, Mother. It's night now. Here's the nurse."

"This is Doctor Harry, Mrs. Weatherall. I never saw you look so young and happy!"

"Ah, I'll never be young again—but I'd be happy if they'd let me lie in peace and get rested."

She thought she spoke up loudly, but no one answered. A warm weight on her fore-head, a warm bracelet on her wrist, and a breeze went on whispering, trying to tell her something. A shuffle of leaves in the everlasting hand of God, He blew on them and they danced and rattled. "Mother, don't mind, we're going to give you a little hypoder-mic." "Look here, daughter, how do ants get in this bed? I saw sugar ants yesterday." Did you send for Hapsy too?

It was Hapsy she really wanted. She had to go a long way back through a great many rooms to find Hapsy standing with a baby on her arm. She seemed to herself to be Hapsy also, and the baby on Hapsy's arm was Hapsy and himself and herself, all at once, and there was no surprise in the meeting. Then Hapsy melted from within and turned flimsy as gray gauze and the baby was a gauzy shadow, and Hapsy came up close and said, "I thought you'd never come," and looked at her very searchingly and said, "You haven't changed a bit!" They leaned forward to kiss, when Cornelia began whispering from a long way off, "Oh, is there anything you want to tell me? Is there anything I can do for you?"

Yes, she had changed her mind after sixty years and she would like to see George. I want you to find George. Find him and be sure to tell him I forgot him. I want him to know I had my husband just the same and my children and my house like any other woman. A good house too and a good husband that I loved and fine children out of him. Better than I hoped for even. Tell him I was given back everything he took away and more. Oh, no, oh, God, no, there was something else besides the house and the man and the children. Oh, surely they were not all? What was it? Something not given back. . . . Her breath crowded down under her ribs and grew into a monstrous frightening shape with cutting edges; it bored up into her head, and the agony was unbelievable: Yes, John, get the Doctor now, no more talk, my time has come.

When this one was born it should be the last. The last. It should have been born first, for it was the one she had truly wanted. Everything came in good time. Nothing left out, left over. She was strong, in three days she would be as well as ever. Better. A woman needed milk in her to have her full health.

"Mother, do you hear me?"

"I've been telling you—"

"Mother, Father Connolly's here."

"I went to Holy Communion only last week. Tell him I'm not so sinful as all that."

"Father just wants to speak to you."

He could speak as much as he pleased. It was like him to drop in and inquire about her soul as if it were a teething baby, and then stay on for a cup of tea and a round of cards and gossip. He always had a funny story of some sort, usually about an Irishman who made his little mistakes and confessed them, and the point lay in some absurd thing he would blurt out in the confessional showing his struggles between native piety and original sin. Granny felt easy about her soul. Cornelia, where are your manners? Give Father Connolly a chair. She had her secret comfortable understanding with a few favorite saints who cleared a straight road to God for her. All as surely signed and sealed as the papers for the new Forty Acres. Forever . . . heirs and assigns forever. Since the day the wedding cake was not cut, but thrown out and wasted. The whole bottom dropped out of the world, and there she was blind and sweating with nothing under her feet and the walls falling away. His hand had caught her under the breast, she had not fallen, there was the freshly polished floor with the green rug on it, just as before. He had cursed like a sailor's parrot and said, "I'll kill him for you." Don't lay a hand on him, for my sake leave something to God. "Now, Ellen, you must believe what I tell you. . . ."

So there was nothing, nothing to worry about any more, except sometimes in the night one of the children screamed in a nightmare, and they both hustled out shaking and hunting for the matches and calling, "There, wait a minute, here we are!" John, get the doctor now, Hapsy's time has come. But there was Hapsy standing by the bed in a white cap. "Cornelia, tell Hapsy to take off her cap. I can't see her plain."

Her eyes opened very wide and the room stood out like a picture she had seen somewhere. Dark colors with the shadows rising towards the ceiling in long angles. The tall black dresser gleamed with nothing on it but John's picture, enlarged from a little one, with John's eyes very black when they should have been blue. You never saw him, so how do you know how he looked? But the man insisted the copy was perfect, it was very rich and handsome. For a picture, yes, but it's not my husband. The table by the bed had a linen cover and a candle and a crucifix. The light was blue from Cornelia's silk lampshades. No sort of light at all, just frippery. You had to live forty years with kerosene lamps to appreciate honest electricity. She felt very strong and she saw Doctor Harry with a rosy nimbus around him.

"You look like a saint, Doctor Harry, and I vow that's as near as you'll ever come to it."

"She's saying something."

"I heard you, Cornelia. What's all this carrying-on?"

"Father Connolly's saying—"

Cornelia's voice staggered and bumped like a cart in a bad road. It rounded corners and turned back again and arrived nowhere. Granny stepped up in the cart very lightly and reached for the reins, but a man sat beside her and she knew him by his hands, driving the cart. She did not look in his face, for she knew without seeing, but looked instead down the road where the trees leaned over and bowed to each other and a thousand birds were singing a Mass. She felt like singing too, but she put her hand in the bosom of her dress and pulled out a rosary, and Father Connolly murmured Latin in a very solemn voice and tickled her feet. My God, will you stop that nonsense? I'm a married woman. What if he did run away and leave me to face the priest by myself? I found another a whole world better. I wouldn't have exchanged my husband for anybody except St. Michael himself, and you may tell him that for me with a thank you in the bargain.

Light flashed on her closed eyelids, and a deep roaring shook her. Cornelia, is that lightning? I hear thunder. There's going to be a storm. Close all the windows. Call the children in. . . . "Mother, here we are, all of us." "Is that you, Hapsy?" "Oh, no, I'm Lydia. We drove as fast as we could." Their faces drifted above her, drifted away. The rosary fell out of her hands and Lydia put it back. Jimmy tried to help, their hands fumbled together, and Granny closed two fingers around Jimmy's thumb. Beads wouldn't do, it must be something alive. She was so amazed her thoughts ran round and round. So, my dear Lord, this is my death and I wasn't even thinking about it. My children have come to see me die. But I can't, it's not time. Oh, I always hated surprises. I wanted to give Cornelia the amethyst set—Cornelia, you're to have the amethyst set, but Hapsy's to wear it when she wants, and, Doctor Harry, do shut up. Nobody sent for you. Oh, my dear Lord, do wait a minute. I meant to do something about the Forty Acres, Jimmy doesn't need it and Lydia will later on, with that worthless husband of hers. I meant to finish the altar cloth and send six bottles of wine to Sister Borgia for her dyspepsia. I want to send six bottles of wine to Sister Borgia, Father Connolly, now don't let me forget.

Cornelia's voice made short turns and tilted over and crashed. "Oh, Mother, oh, Mother, oh, Mother. . . ."

"I'm not going, Cornelia. I'm taken by surprise. I can't go."

You'll see Hapsy again. What about her? "I thought you'd never come." Granny made a long journey outward, looking for Hapsy. What if I don't find her? What then? Her heart sank down and down, there was no bottom to death, she couldn't come to the end of it. The blue light from Cornelia's lampshade drew into a tiny point in the center of her brain, it flickered and winked like an eye, quietly it fluttered and dwindled. Granny lay curled down within herself, amazed and watchful, staring at the point of light that was herself; her body was now only a deeper mass of shadow in an endless darkness and this darkness would curl around the light and swallow it up. God, give a sign!

For the second time there was no sign. Again no bridegroom and the priest in the house. She could not remember any other sorrow because this grief wiped them all away. Oh, no, there's nothing more cruel than this—I'll never forgive it. She stretched herself with a deep breath and blew out the light.

1929

Zora Neale Hurston
ca. 1891–1960

Zora Neale Hurston was reared in Eatonville, Florida, a town she described as "the first [incorporated] Negro community" and "the first attempt at organized self-government on the part of Negroes in America." After her mother's death in 1904, her father placed her in a school in Jacksonville. Later, when want of money forced her father to remove her from school, she joined a traveling Gilbert and Sullivan troupe as a maid, hoping to save money so that she could return to school. Near the end of her life, Hurston entered another period of wandering: She worked again as a maid, then as a librarian, a part-time teacher, and a reporter. On January 28, 1960, she died in the County Welfare Home in Fort Pierce, Florida. Between her troubled beginnings and her lonely end, however, during the 1920s, the 1930s, and into the 1940s, Hurston lived a remarkably full and varied life, one she autobiographically recorded in one of her finest books, *Dust Tracks on the Road* (1942).

In 1918 Hurston entered Howard University, where she began to write. Later she won a scholarship to Barnard College, where she was the first African American woman to be admitted and where she continued to write. She also began to cultivate an interest in anthropology. By the time she graduated, she had attracted the attention of Columbia University's distinguished anthropologist Franz Boas, with whom she worked off and on for more than ten years. From 1928 to 1931 she collected folklore throughout the South and in 1935 published *Mules & Men*, anthropological stories of voodoo among southern African Americans. In 1937 and 1938, sponsored by two successive Guggenheim fellowships, she did field research in Jamaica, Haiti, and Bermuda, investigations that led to another book of anthropology, *Tell My Horse* (1938). Later still, she collected folklore in Florida for the Works Progress Administration. "Voodooism" and "black magic" became abiding interests, as did the oral folk literature of the African American South and the Caribbean. "She was always getting scholarships and things from wealthy white people," Langston Hughes recalled, "some of whom simply paid her just to sit around and represent the Negro race for them. . . . She was full of side-splitting anecdotes, humorous tales, and tragicomic stories, remembered out of her life in the South as a daughter of a travelling minister of God."

In part because she was a flamboyant, charismatic woman, and especially because she was a remarkably gifted writer, Hurston played a major role in the Harlem Renaissance during the late 1920s and the early 1930s. No writer of the period did more than she to show the glamor, the excitement, and the promise that enabled American cities to draw hundreds of thousands of African American people to them. And none did more than she to expose the loneliness, emptiness, and brutality that people often found once they had reached their destinations. Her deeper subject, however, one embedded in the move of people from the farms and villages to the cities, lay in the strength and wisdom that people found in the folkways, the music, and the stories they carried with them. Many of these themes were explored in a series of novels: *Jonah's Gourd Vine* (1934), a narrative based on the lives of her parents; *Moses, Man of the Mountain* (1939), a re-creation and reinterpretation of the Old Testament Hebrews in the form of Negro folktales; and *Seraph on the Suwanee* (1948), the story of a young African American woman's failed efforts to free herself from a sense of inferiority inculcated by her racist and sexist society.

Hurston's finest writings are rooted in cultural traditions created by African American Southerners, including their folklore and folk music, their sermons, spirituals, and blues. Before they moved to Florida, Hurston's parents, John Hurston and Lucy Potts Hurston, were tenant farmers in Alabama. In Eatonville, her father worked as a carpenter and was thrice elected mayor. But it was as a preacher and storyteller of rare rhetorical gifts that he seemed to his daughter most compelling. Her mother, on the other hand, she remembered as a spunky and even defiant woman who was denied place and voice even in Eatonville. "She depended on me for voice," Hurston later remarked.

"Voice," both as a means of self-expression and as a sign and mode of social power, and thus as intricately connected both to subjectivity or selfhood and to social status, figures prominently in Hurston's best fiction, including *Their Eyes Were Watching God*. This stress—coupled with the conviction that folk traditions of African American Southerners potentially provided resources even to African American women—gave Hurston a point of view so distinctly and powerfully her own that she seldom pleased many readers, and for a time seemed to please none at all. More recently, however, the same writings which once were viewed as politically naive have come to be regarded as crucial instances of the long African American tradition of subversive "signifying" which stands at the center of the music as well as the literature of African Americans, as a means of preserving and passing on from one generation to the next what Henry Louis Gates has called "peculiarly black texts of being." As a result, the severe decline in reputation that Hurston suffered, from the 1940s through the 1950s, to her lonely death in 1960, has given way to widening recognition that, in the words of Alice Walker, she was indeed "before her time" in presenting African American people, including African American women, "as complete, complex, undiminished human beings. . . ."

Further Reading:
L. Hughes, *The Big Sea*, 1940.
A. Rayson, "The Novels of Zora Neale Hurston," *Studies in Black Literature*, Winter 1974.
A. Walker, "In Search of Zora Neale Hurston," *Ms. Magazine*, March 1975.
R. E. Hemenway, *Zora Neale Hurston: A Literary Biography*, 1977.

B. Johnson, "Metaphor, Metonymy, and Voice in Zora Neale Hurston's *Their Eyes Were Watching God*," in H. Gates, ed., *Black Literature and Literary Theory*, 1984.
C. Wall, "Zora Neale Hurston," in L. Baechler and A. W. Litz, eds., *African American Writers*, 1991.

Text:
"The Gilded Six-Bits" and "Spunk" from *The Complete Stories* by Zora Neale Hurston, eds., H. L. Gates, Jr. and S. Lemke 1995.

The Gilded Six–Bits

It was a Negro yard around a Negro house in a Negro settlement that looked to the payroll of the G and G Fertilizer works for its support.

But there was something happy about the place. The front yard was parted in the middle by a sidewalk from gate to doorstep, a sidewalk edged on either side by quart bottles driven neck down to the ground on a slant. A mess of homey flowers planted without a plan but blooming cheerily from their helter-skelter places. The fence and house were whitewashed. The porch and steps scrubbed white.

The front door stood open to the sunshine so that the floor of the front room could finish drying after its weekly scouring. It was Saturday. Everything clean from the front gate to the privy house. Yard raked so that the strokes of the rake would make a pattern. Fresh newspaper cut in fancy-edge on the kitchen shelves.

Missie May was bathing herself in the galvanized washtub in the bedroom. Her dark-brown skin glistened under the soapsuds that skittered down from her wash rag. Her stiff young breasts thrust forward aggressively like broad-based cones with the tips lacquered in black.

She heard men's voices in the distance and glanced at the dollar clock on the dresser. "Humph! Ah'm way behind time t'day! Joe gointer be heah 'fore Ah git mah clothes on if Ah don't make haste."

She grabbed the clean meal sack at hand and dried herself hurriedly and began to dress. But before she could tie her slippers, there came the ring of singing metal on wood. Nine times.

Missie May grinned with delight. She had not seen the big tall man come stealing in the gate and creep up the walk grinning happily at the joyful mischief he was about to commit. But she knew that it was her husband throwing silver dollars in the door for her to pick up and pile beside her plate at dinner. It was this way every Saturday afternoon. The nine dollars hurled into the open door, he scurried to a hiding place behind the cape jasmine bush and waited.

Missie May promptly appeared at the door in mock alarm.

"Who dat chunkin' money in mah do'way?" she demanded. No answer from the yard. She leaped off the porch and began to search the shrubbery. She peeped under the porch and hung over the gate to look up and down the road. While she did this, the man behind the jasmine darted to the chinaberry tree. She spied him and gave chase.

"Nobody ain't gointer be chunkin' money at me and Ah not do'em nothing'," she shouted in mock anger. He ran around the house with Missie May at his heels. She overtook him at the kitchen door. He ran inside but could not close it after him before she crowded in and locked with him in a rough and tumble. For several minutes the two were a furious mass of male and female energy. Shouting, laughing, twisting, turning, and Joe trying, but not too hard, to get away.

"Missie May, take yo' hand out mah pocket!" Joe shouted out between laughs.

"Ah ain't, Joe, not lessen you gwine gimme whateve' it is good you got in yo' pocket. Turn it go Joe, do Ah'll tear yo' clothes."

"Go on tear 'em. You de one dat pushes de needles round heah. Move yo' hand, Missie May."

"Lemme git dat paper sack out yo' pocket. Ah bet its candy kisses."

"Tain't. Move yo' hand. Woman ain't got no business in a man's clothes nohow. Go 'way."

Missie May gouged way down and gave an upward jerk and triumphed.

"Unhhunh! Ah got it. It 'tis so candy kisses. Ah knowed you had somethin' for me in yo' clothes. Now Ah got to see whut's in every pocket you got."

Joe smiled indulgently and let his wife go through all of his pockets and take out the things that he had hidden there for her to find. She bore off the chewing gum, the cake of sweet soap, the pocket handkerchief as if she had wrested them from him, as if they had not been bought for the sake of this friendly battle.

"Whew! dat play-fight done got me all warmed up," Joe exclaimed. "Got me some water in de kittle?"

"Yo' water is on de fire and yo' clean things is cross de bed. Hurry up and wash yo'self and git changed so we kin eat. Ah'm hongry." As Missie said this, she bore the steaming kettle into the bedroom.

"You ain't hongry, sugar," Joe contradicted her. "Youse jes'a little empty. Ah'm de one whut's hongry. Ah could eat up camp meetin,' back off'ssociation, and drink Jurdan dry. Have it on de table when Ah git out de tub."

"Don't you mess wid mah business, man. You git in yo' clothes. Ah'm a real wife, not no dress and breath. Ah might not look lak one, but if you burn me, you won't git a thing but wife ashes."

Joe splashed in the bedroom and Missie May fanned around in the kitchen. A fresh red and white checked cloth on the table. Big pitcher of buttermilk beaded with pale drops of butter from the churn. Hot fried mullet, crackling bread, ham hocks atop a mound of string beans and new potatoes, and perched on the window-sill a pone of spicy potato pudding.

Very little talk during the meal but that little consisted of banter that pretended to deny affection but in reality flaunted it. Like when Missie May reached for a second helping of the tater pone. Joe snatched it out of her reach. After Missie May had made two or three unsuccessful grabs at the pan, she begged, "Aw, Joe gimme some mo' dat tater pone."

"Nope, sweetenin' is for us men-folks. Y'all pritty li'l frail eels don't need nothin' lak dis. You too sweet already."

"Please, Joe."

"Naw, naw. Ah don't want you to git no sweeter than whut you is already. We goin' down de road a li'l piece t'night so you go put on yo' Sunday-go-to-meetin' things."

Missie May looked at her husband to see if he was playing some prank. "Sho' nuff, Joe?"

"Yeah. We goin' to de ice cream parlor."

"Where de ice cream parlor at, Joe?"

"A new man done come heah from Chicago and he done got a place and took and opened it up for a ice cream parlor, and bein' as it's real swell, Ah wants you to be one de first ladies to walk in dere and have some set down."

"Do Jesus, Ah ain't knowed nothin' 'bout it. Who de man done it?"

"Mister Otis D. Slemmons, of spots and places—Memphis, Chicago, Jacksonville, Philadelphia and so on."

"Dat heavy-set man wid his mouth full of gold teeths?"

"Yeah. Where did you see 'im at?"

"Ah went down to de sto' tuh git a box of lye and Ah seen 'im standin' on de corner talkin' to some of de mens, and Ah come on back and went to scrubbin' de floor, and he passed and tipped his hat whilst Ah was scourin' de steps. Ah thought Ah never seen *him* befo'."

Joe smiled pleasantly. "Yeah, he's up to date. He got de finest clothes Ah ever seen on a colored man's back."

"Aw, he don't look no better in his clothes than you do in yourn. He got a puzzlegut on 'im and he so chuckle-headed, he got a pone behind his neck."

Joe looked down at his own abdomen and said wistfully, "Wisht Ah had a build on me lak he got. He ain't puzzlegutted, honey. He jes' got a corperation. Dat make 'm look lak a rich white man. All rich mens is got some belly on 'em."

"Ah seen de pitchers of Henry Ford and he's a spare-built man and Rockefeller look lak he ain't got but one gut. But Ford and Rockefeller and dis Slemmons and all de rest kin be as many-gutted as dey please, ah'm satisfied wid you jes' lak you is, baby. God took pattern after a pine tree and built you noble. Youse a pritty still man, and if Ah knowed any way to make you mo' pritty still Ah'd take and do it."

Joe reached over gently and toyed with Missie May's ear. "You jes' say dat cause you love me, but Ah know Ah can't hold no light to Otis D. Slemmons. Ah ain't never been nowhere and Ah ain't got nothin' but you."

"How you know dat, Joe."

"He tole us so himself."

"Dat don't make it so. His mouf is cut cross-ways, ain't it? Well, he kin lie jes' lak anybody els."

"Good Lawd, Missie! You womens sho' is hard to sense into things. He's got a five-dollar gold piece for a stick-pin and he got a ten-dollar gold piece on his watch chain and his mouf is jes' crammed full of gold teethes. Sho' wisht it wuz mine. And whut make it so cool, he got money 'cumulated. And womens give it all to 'im."

"Ah don't see whut de womens see on 'im. Ah wouldn't give 'im a wink if de sheriff wuz after 'im."

"Well, he tole us how de white womens in Chicago give 'im all dat gold money. So he don't 'low nobody to touch it at all. Not even put dey finger on it. Dey tole 'im not to. You kin make 'miration at it, but don't tetch it."

"Whyn't he stay up dere where dey so crazy 'bout 'im?"

"Ah reckon dey done made 'im vast-rich and he wants to travel some. He say dey wouldn't leave 'im hit a lick of work. He got mo' lady people crazy 'bout him than he kin shake a stick at."

"Joe, Ah hates to see you so dumb. Dat stray nigger jes' tell y'all anything and y'all b'lieve it."

"Go 'head on now, honey and put on yo' clothes. He talkin' 'bout his pritty womens—Ah want 'im to see *mine*."

Missie May went off to dress and Joe spent the time trying to make his stomach punch out like Slemmons's middle. He tried the rolling swagger of the stranger, but found that his tall bone-and-muscle stride fitted ill with it. He just had time to drop back into his seat before Missie May came in dressed to go.

On the way home that night Joe was exultant. "Didn't Ah say ole Otis was swell? Can't he talk Chicago talk? Wuzn't dat funny whut he said when great big fat ole Ida Armstrong come in? He asted me, " 'Who is dat broad wid de forte shake?' Dat's a new word. Us always thought forty was a set of figgers but he showed us where it means a whole heap of things. Sometimes he don't say forty, he jes' say thirty-eight and two and dat mean de same thing. Know whut he tole me when Ah was payin' for our ice cream? He say, 'Ah have to hand it to you, Joe. Dat wife of yours is jes' thirty-eight and two. Yessuh, she's forte!' Ain't he killin'?"

"He'll do in case of a rush. But he sho' is got uh heap uh gold on 'im. Dat's de first time Ah ever seed gold money. It lookted good on him sho' nuff, but it'd look a whole heap better on you."

"Who, me? Missie May was youse crazy! Where would a po' man lak me git gold money from?"

Missie May was silent for a minute, then she said, "Us might find some goin' long de road some time. Us could."

"Who would be losin' gold money 'round heah? We ain't even seen none dese white folks wearin' no gold money on dey watch chain. You must be figgeren' Mister Packard or Mister Cadillac goin' pass through heah . . ."

"You don't know whut been lost 'round heah. Maybe somebody way back in memorial times lost they gold money and went on off and it ain't never been found. And then if we wuz to find it, you could wear some 'thout havin' no gang of womens lak dat Slemmons say he got."

Joe laughed and hugged her. "Don't be so wishful 'bout me. Ah'm satisfied de way Ah is. So long as Ah be yo' husband, ah don't keer 'bout nothin' else. Ah'd ruther all de other womens in de world to be dead than for you to have de toothache. Less we go to bed and git our night rest."

It was Saturday night once more before Joe could parade his wife in Slemmons' ice cream parlor again. He worked the night shift and Saturday was his only night off. Every other evening around six o'clock he left home, and dying dawn saw him hustling home around the lake where the challenging sun flung a flaming sword from east to west across the trembling water.

That was the best part of life—going home to Missie May. Their whitewashed house, the mock battle on Saturday, the dinner and ice cream parlor afterwards, church on Sunday nights when Missie outdressed any woman in town—all, everything was right.

One night around eleven the acid ran out at the G and G. The foreman knocked off the crew and let the steam die down. As Joe rounded the lake on his way home, a lean moon rode the lake in a silver boat. If anybody had asked Joe about the moon on the lake, he would have said he hadn't paid it any attention. But he saw it with his feelings. It made him yearn painfully for Missie. Creation obsessed him. He thought about children. They had been married for more than a year now. They had money put away. They ought to be making little feet for shoes. A little boy child would be about right.

He saw a dim light in the bedroom and decided to come in through the kitchen door. He could wash the fertilizer dust off himself before presenting himself to Missie May. It would be nice for her not to know that he was there until he slipped into his place in bed and hugged her back. She always liked that.

He eased the kitchen door open slowly and silently, but when he went to set his dinner bucket on the table he bumped it into a pile of dishes, and something crashed to the floor. He heard his wife gasp in fright and hurried to reassure her.

"Iss me, honey. Don't get skeered."

There was a quick, large movement in the bedroom. A rustle, a thud, and a stealthy silence. The light went out.

What? Robbers? Murderers? Some varmint attacking his helpless wife, perhaps? He struck a match, threw himself on guard and stepped over the door-sill into the bedroom.

The great belt on the wheel of Time slipped and eternity stood still. By the match light he could see the man's legs fighting with his breeches in his frantic desire to get them on. He had both chance and time to kill the intruder in his helpless condition—half-in and half-out of his pants—but he was too weak to take action. The shapeless enemies of humanity that live in the hours of Time had waylaid Joe. He was assaulted in his weakness. Like Samson awakening after his haircut. So he just opened his mouth and laughed.

The match went out and he struck another and lit the lamp. A howling wind raced across his heart, but underneath its fury he heard his wife sobbing and Slemmons pleading for his life. Offering to buy it with all that he had. "Please, suh, don't kill me. Sixty-two dollars at de sto' gold money."

Joe just stood. Slemmons looked at the window, but it was screened. Joe stood out like a rough-backed mountain between him and the door. Barring him from escape, from sunrise, from life.

He considered a surprise attack upon the big clown that stood there laughing like a chessy cat. But before his fist could travel an inch, Joe's own rushed out to crush him like a battering ram. Then Joe stood over him.

"Git into yo' damn rags, Slemmons, and dat quick."

Slemmons scambled to his feet and into his vest and coat. As he grabbed his hat, Joe's fury overrode his intentions and he grabbed at Slemmons with his left hand and struck at him with his right. The right landed. The left grazed the front of his vest. Slemmons was knocked a somersault into the kitchen and fled through the open door. Joe found himself alone with Missie May, with the golden watch charm clutched in his left fist. A short bit of broken chain dangled between his fingers.

Missie May was sobbing. Wails of weeping without words. Joe stood, and after awhile she found out that he had something in his hand. And then he stood and felt without thinking and without seeing with his natural eyes. Missie May kept on crying and Joe kept on feeling so much, and not knowing what to do with all his feelings, he put Slemmons' watch charm in his pants pocket and took a good laugh and went to bed.

"Missie May, whut you crying for?"

"Cause Ah love you so hard and Ah know you don't love *me* no mo'."

Joe sank his face into the pillow for a spell, then he said huskily, "You don't know de feelings of dat yet, Missie May."

"Oh Joe, honey, he said he wuz gointer gimme dat gold money and he jes' kept on after me—"

Joe was very still and silent for a long time. Then he said, "Well, don't cry no mo', Missie May. Ah got yo' gold piece for you."

The hours went past on their rusty ankles. Joe still and quiet on one bed-rail and Missie May wrung dry of sobs on the other. Finally the sun's tide crept upon the shore of night and drowned all its hours. Missie May with her face stiff and streaked towards the window saw the dawn come into her yard. It was day. Nothing more. Joe wouldn't be coming home as usual. No need to fling open the front door and sweep off the porch, making it nice for Joe. Never no more breakfast to cook; no more washing and starching of Joe's jumper-jackets and pants. No more nothing. So why get up?

With this strange man in her bed, she felt embarrassed to get up and dress. She decided to wait till he had dressed and gone. Then she would get up, dress quickly and be gone forever beyond reach of Joe's looks and laughs. But he never moved. Red light turned to yellow, then white.

From beyond the no-man's land between them came a voice. A strange voice that yesterday had been Joe's.

"Missie May, ain't you gonna fix me no breakfus'?"

She sprang out of bed. "Yeah, Joe. Ah didn't reckon you wuz hongry."

No need to die today. Joe needed her for a few more minutes anyhow.

Soon there was a roaring fire in the cook stove. Water bucket full and two chickens killed. Joe loved fried chicken and rice. She didn't deserve a thing and good Joe was letting her cook him some breakfast. She rushed hot biscuits to the table as Joe took his seat.

He ate with his eyes on his plate. No laughter, no banter.

"Missie May, you ain't eatin' yo' breakfus'."

"Ah don't choose none, Ah thank yuh."

His coffee cup was empty. She sprang to refill it. When she turned from the stove and bent to set the cup beside Joe's plate, she saw the yellow coin on the table between them.

She slumped into her seat and wept into her arms.

Presently Joe said calmly, "Missie May, you cry too much. Don't look back lak Lot's wife and turn to salt."

The sun, the hero of every day, the impersonal old man that beams as brightly on death as on birth, came up every morning and raced across the blue dome and dipped into the sea of fire every evening. Water ran down hill and birds nested.

Missie knew why she didn't leave Joe. She couldn't. She loved him too much. But she couldn't understand why Joe didn't leave her. He was polite, even kind at times, but aloof.

There were no more Saturday romps. No ringing silver dollars to stack beside her plate. No pockets to rifle. In fact the yellow coin in his trousers was like a monster hiding in the cave of his pockets to destroy her.

She often wondered if he still had it, but nothing could have induced her to ask nor yet to explore his pockets to see for herself. Its shadow was in the house whether or no.

One night Joe came home around midnight and complained of pains in the back. He asked Missie to rub him down with liniment. It had been three months since Missie had touched his body and it all seemed strange. But she rubbed him. Grateful for the chance. Before morning, youth triumphed and Missie exulted. But the next day, as she joyfully made up their bed, beneath her pillow she found the piece of money with the bit of chain attached.

Alone to herself, she looked at the thing with loathing, but look she must. She took it into her hands with trembling and saw first thing that it was no gold piece. It was a gilded half-dollar. Then she knew why Slemmons had forbidden anyone to touch his gold. He trusted village eyes at a distance not to recognize his stick-pin as a gilded quarter, and his watch charm as a four-bit piece.

She was glad at first that Joe had left it there. Perhaps he was through with her punishment. They were man and wife again. Then another thought came clawing at her. He had come home to buy from her as if she were any woman in the long house. Fifty cents for her love. As if to say that he could pay as well as Slemmons. She slid the coin into his Sunday pants pocket and dressed herself and left his house.

Halfway between her house and the quarters she met her husband's mother, and after a short talk she turned and went back home. If she had not the substance of marriage, she had the outside show. Joe must leave *her*. She let him see she didn't want his old gold four-bits too.

She saw no more of the coin for some time though she knew that Joe could not help finding it in his pocket. But his health kept poor, and he came home at least every ten days to be rubbed.

The sun swept around the horizon, trailing its robes of weeks and days. One morning as Joe came in from work, he found Missie May chopping wood. Without a word he took the ax and chopped a huge pile before he stopped.

"You ain't got no business choppin' wood, and you know it."

"How come? Ah been choppin' it for de last longest."

"Ah ain't blind. You makin' feet for shoes."

"Won't you be glad to have a li'l baby chile, Joe?"

"You know dat 'thout astin' me."

"Iss gointer be a boy chile and de very spit of you."

"You reckon, Missie May?"

"Who else could it look lak?"

Joe said nothing, but he thrust his hand deep into his pocket and fingered something there.

It was almost six months later Missie May took to bed and Joe went and got his mother to come wait on the house.

Missie May delivered a fine boy. Her travail was over when Joe came in from work one morning. His mother and the old women were drinking great bowls of coffee around the fire in the kitchen.

The minute Joe came into the room his mother called him aside.

"How did Missie May make out?" he asked quickly.

"Who, dat gal? She strong as a ox. She gointer have plenty mo'. We done fixed her wid de sugar and lard to sweeten her for de nex' one."

Joe stood silent awhile.

"You ain't ast 'bout de baby, Joe. You oughter be mightly proud cause he sho' is de spittin' image of yuh, son. Dat's yourn all right, if you never git another one, dat un is yourn. And you know Ah'm mighty proud too, son, cause Ah never thought well of you marryin' Missie May cause her ma used tuh fan her foot 'round right smart and Ah been mighty skeered dat Missie May wuz gointer git misput on her road."

Joe said nothing. He fooled around the house till late in the day then just before he went to work, he went and stood at the foot of the bed and asked his wife how she felt. He did this every day during the week.

On Saturday he went to Orlando to make his market. It had been a long time since he had done that.

Meat and lard, meal and flour, soap and starch. Cans of corn and tomatoes. All the staples. He fooled around town for awhile and bought bananas and apples. Way after while he went around to the candy store.

"Hello, Joe," the clerk greeted him. "Ain't seen you in a long time."

"Nope, Ah ain't been heah. Been 'round spots and places."

"Want some of them molasses kisses you always buy?"

"Yessuh," He threw the gilded half-dollar on the counter. "Will dat spend?"

"Whut is it, Joe? Well, I'll be doggone! A gold-plated four-bit piece. Where'd you git it, Joe?"

"Offen a stray nigger dat come through Eatonville. He had it on his watch chain for a charm—goin' 'round making out iss gold money. Ha ha! He had a quarter on his tie pin and it wuz all golded up too. Tryin' to fool people. Makin' out he so rich and everything. Ha! Ha! Tryin' to tole off folkses wives from home."

"How did you git it, Joe? Did he fool you, too?"

"Who, me? Naw suh! He ain't fooled me none. Know whut Ah done? He come 'round me wid his smart talk. Ah hauled off and knocked 'im down and took his old four-bits 'way from 'im. Gointer buy my wife some good ole 'lasses kisses wid it. Gimme fifty cents worth of dem candy kisses." "Fifty cents buys a mightly lot of candy kisses, Joe. Why don't you split it up and take some chocolate bars, too. They eat good, too."

"Yessuh, dey do, but Ah wants all dat in kisses. Ah got a li'l boy chile home now. Tain't a week old yet, but he kin suck a sugar tit and maybe eat one them kisses hisself."

Joe got his candy and left the store. The clerk turned to the next customer. "Wisht I could be like these darkies. Laughin' all the time. Nothin' worries 'em."

Back in Eatonville, Joe reached his own front door. There was the ring of singing metal on wood. Fifteen times. Missie May couldn't run to the door, but she crept there as quickly as she could.

"Joe Banks, Ah hear you chunkin' money in mah do'way. You wait till Ah got mah strength back and Ah'm gointer fix you for dat."

Spunk

A GIANT OF a brown-skinned man sauntered up the one street of the village and out into the palmetto thickets with a small pretty woman clinging lovingly to his arm.

"Looka theah, folkses!" cried Elijah Mosley, slapping his leg gleefully. "Theah they go, big as a life an' brassy as tacks."

All the loungers in the store tried to walk to the door with an air of nonchalance but with small success.

"Now pee-eople!" Walter Thomas gasped. "Will you look at 'em!"

"But that's one thing Ah likes about Spunk Banks—he ain't skeered of nothin' on God's green footstools—*nothin'*! He rides that log down at saw-mill jus' like he struts 'round wid another man's wife—jus' don't give a kitty. When Tes' Miller got cut to giblets on the circle-saw, Spunk steps right up and starts riding'. The rest of us was skeered to go near it."

A round-shouldered figure in overalls much too large came nervously in the door and the talking ceased. The men looked at each other and winked.

"Gimme some soda-water. Sass'prilla Ah reckon," the newcomer ordered, and stood far down the counter near the open pickled pig-feet tub to drink it.

Elijah nudged Walter and turned with mock gravity to the new-comer.

"Say, Joe, how's everything up yo' way? How's yo' wife?"

Joe started and all but dropped the bottle he was holding. He swallowed several times painfully and his lips trembled.

"Aw 'Lige, you oughtn't to do nothin' like that," Walter grumbled. Elijah ignored him.

"She jus' passed heah a few minutes ago goin' thata way," with a wave of his hand in the direction of the woods.

Now Joe knew his wife had passed that way. He knew that the men lounging in the general store had seen her, moreover, he knew that the men knew *he* knew. He stood there silent for a long moment staring blankly, with his Adam's apple twitching nervously up and down his throat. One could actually *see* the pain he was suffering, his eyes, his face, his hands and even the dejected slump of his shoulders. He set the bottle down upon the counter. He didn't bang it, just eased it out of his hand silently and fiddled with his suspender buckle.

"Well, Ah'm goin' after her to-day. Ah'm goin' an' fetch her back. Spunk's done gone too fur."

He reached deep down into his trouser pocket and drew out a hollow ground razor, large and shiny, and passed his moistened thumb back and forth over the edge.

"Talkin' like a man, Joe. 'Course that's *yo'* fambly affairs, but Ah like to see grit in anybody."

Joe Kanty laid down a nickel and stumbled out into the street.

Dusk crept in from the woods. Ike Clarke lit the swinging oil lamp that was almost immediately surrounded by candleflies. The men laughed boisterously behind Joe's back as they watched him shamble woodward.

"You oughtn't to said whut you did to him, Lige—look how it worked him up," Walter chided.

"And Ah hope it did work him up. Tain't even decent for a man to take and take like he do."

"Spunk will sho' kill him."

"Aw, Ah doan know. You never kin tell. He might turn him up an' spank him fur gettin' in the way, but Spunk wouldn't shoot no unarmed man. Dat razor he carried outa heah ain't gonna run Spunk down an' cut him, an' Joe ain't got the nerve to go up to Spunk with it knowing he totes that Army .45. He makes that break outa heah to bluff us. He's gonna hide that razor behind the first palmetto root an' sneak back home to bed. Don't tell me nothin' 'bout that rabbit-foot colored man. Didn't he meet Spunk an' Lena face to face one day las' week an' mumble sumthin' to Spunk 'bout lettin' his wife alone?"

"What did Spunk say?" Walter broke in, "Ah like him fine but tain't right the way he carris on wid Lena Kanty, jus' 'cause Joe's timid 'bout fightin'."

"You wrong theah, Walter. Tain't 'cause Joe's timid at all, it's 'cause Spunk wants Lena. If Joe was a passle of wile cats Spunk would tackle the job just the same. He'd go af-ter *anything* he wanted the same way. As Ah wuz sayin' a minute ago, he tole Joe right to his face that Lena was his. 'Call her and see if she'll come. A woman knows her boss an' she answers when he calls.' 'Lena, ain't I yo' husband?' Joe sorter whines out. Lena looked at him real disgusted but she don't answer and she don't move outa her tracks. Then Spunk reaches out an' takes hold of her arm an' says: 'Lena, youse mine. From now on Ah works for you an' fights for you an' Ah never wants you to look to nobody for a crumb of bread, a stitch of close or a shingle to go over yo' head, but *me* long as Ah live. Ah'll git the lumber foh owah house to-morrow. Go home an' get yo' things together!'

" 'Thass mah house,' Lena speaks up. 'Papa gimme that.'

" 'Well,' says Spunk, 'doan give up whut's yours, but when youse inside doan forgit youse mine, an' let no other man git outa his place wid you!'

"Lena looked up at him with her eyes so full of love that they wuz runnin' over, an' Spunk seen it an' Joe seen it too, and his lip started to tremblin' and his Adam's apple was galloping up and down his neck like a race horse. Ah bet he's wore out half a dozen Adam's apples since Spunk's been on the job with Lena. That's all he'll do. He'll be back heah after while swallowin' an' workin' his lips like he wants to say somethin' an' can't."

"But didn't he do *nothin'* to stop 'em?"

"Nope, not a frazzlin' thing—jus' stood there. Spunk took Lena's arm and walked off jus' like nothin' ain't happened and he stood there gazin' after them till they was outa sight. Now you know a woman don't want no man like that. I'm jus' waitin' to see whut he's goin' to say when he gits back."

II

But Joe Kanty never came back, never. The men in the store heard the sharp report of a pistol somewhere distant in the palmetto thicket and soon Spunk came walking leisurely, with his big black Stetson set at the same rakish angle and Lena clinging to his arm, came walking right into the general store. Lena wept in a frightened manner.

"Well," Spunk announced calmly, "Joe come out there wid a meat axe an' made me kill him."

He sent Lena home and led the men back to Joe—crumpled and limp with his right hand still clutching his razor.

"See mah back? Mah close cut clear through. He sneaked up an' tried to kill me from the back, but Ah got him, an' got him good, first shot," Spunk said.

The men glared at Elijah, accusingly.

"Take him up an' plant him in Stony Lonesome," Spunk said in a careless voice. "Ah didn't wanna shoot him but he made me do it. He's a dirty coward, jumpin' on a man from behind."

Spunk turned on his heel and sauntered away to where he knew his love wept in fear for him and no man stopped him. At the general store later on, they all talked of locking him up until the sheriff should come from Orlando, but no one did anything but talk.

A clear case of self-defense, the trial was a short one, and Spunk walked out of the court house to freedom again. He could work again, ride the dangerous log-carriage that fed the singing, snarling, biting circle-saw; he could stroll the soft dark lanes with his guitar. He was free to roam the woods again; he was free to return to Lena. He did all of these things.

III

"Whut you reckon, Walt?" Elijah asked one night later. "Spunk's gittin' ready to marry Lena!"

"Naw! Why, Joe ain't had time to git cold yit. Nohow Ah didn't figger Spunk was the marryin' kind."

"Well, he is," rejoined Elijah. "He done moved most of Lena's things—and her along wid 'em—over to the Bradley house. He's buying it. Jus' like Ah told yo' all right in heah the night Joe wuz kilt. Spunk's crazy 'bout Lena. He don't want folks to keep on talkin' 'bout her—thass reason he's rushin' so. Funny thing 'bout that bob-cat, wan't it?"

"What bob-cat, 'Lige? Ah ain't heered 'bout none."

"Ain't cher? Well, night befo' las' as they was goin' to bed, a big black bob-cat, black all over, you hear me, *black*, walked round and round that house and howled like forty, an' when Spunk got his gun an' went to the winder to shoot it, he says it stood right still an' looked him in the eye, an' howled right at him. The thing got Spunk so nervoused up he couldn't shoot. But Spunk says twan't no bob-cat nohow. He says it was Joe done sneaked back from Hell!"

"Humph!" sniffed Walter, "he oughter be nervous after what he done. Ah reckon Joe came back to dare him to marry Lena, or to come out an' fight. Ah bet he'll be back time and again, too. Know what Ah think? Joe wuz a braver man than Spunk."

There was a general shout of derision from the group.

"Thass a fact," went on Walter. "Lookit whut he done; took a razor an' went out to fight a man he knowed toted a gun an' wuz a crack shot, too; 'nother thing Joe wuz skeered of Spunk, skeered plumb stiff! But he went jes' the same. It took him a long time to get his nerve up. Tain't nothin' for Spunk to fight when he ain't skeered of nothin'. Now, Joe's done come back to have it out wid the man that's got all he ever had. Y'all know Joe ain't never had nothin' nor wanted nothin' besides Lena. It musta been a h'ant cause ain't nobody never seen no black bob-cat."

" 'Nother thing," cut in one of the men, "Spunk wuz cussin' a blue streak to-day 'cause he 'lowed dat saw wuz wobblin'—almos' got 'im once. The machinist come, looked it over an' said it wuz alright. Spunk musta been leanin' t'wards it some. Den he claimed somebody pushed 'im but twan't nobody close to 'im. Ah wuz glad when knockin' off time come. I'm skeered of dat man when he gits hot. He'd beat you full of button holes as quick as he's look atcher."

IV

The men gathered the next evening in a different mood, no laughter. No badinage this time.

"Look, 'Lige, you goin' to set up wid Spunk?"

"Naw, Ah reckon not, Walter. Tell yuh the truth, Ah'm a li'l bit skittish. Spunk died too wicket—died cussin' he did. You know he thought he was done outa life."

"Good Lawd, who'd he think done it?"

"Joe."

"Joe Kanty? How come?"

"Walter, Ah b'leeve Ah will walk up thata way an' set. Lena would like it Ah reckon."

"But whut did he say, 'Lige?"

Elijah did not answer until they had left the lighted store and were strolling down the dark street.

"Ah wuz loadin' a wagon wid scantlin' right near the saw when Spunk fell on the carriage but 'fore Ah could git to him the saw got him in the body—awful sight. Me an' Skint Miller got him off but it was too late. Anybody could see that. The fust thing he said wuz: 'He pushed me, 'Lige—the dirty hound pushed me in the back!'—he was spittin' blood at ev'ry breath. We laid him on the sawdust pile with his face to the East so's he could die easy. He helt mah han' till the last, Walter, and said: 'It was Joe, 'Lige . . . the dirty sneak shoved me . . . he didn't dare come to mah face . . . but Ah'll git the son-of-a-wood louse soon's Ah get there an' make hell too hot for him . . . Ah felt him shove me . . . !' Thass how he died."

"If spirits kin fight, there's a powerful tussle goin' on somewhere ovah Jordan 'cause Ah b'leeve Joe's ready for Spunk an' ain't skeered any more—yas, Ah b'leeve Joe pushed 'im mahself."

They had arrived at the house. Lena's lamentations were deep and loud. She had filled the room with magnolia blossoms that gave off a heavy sweet odor. The keepers of the wake tipped about whispering in frightened tones. Everyone in the village was there, even old Jeff Kanty, Joe's father, who a few hours before would have been afraid to come within ten feet of him, stood leering triumphantly down upon the fallen giant as if his fingers had been the teeth of steel that laid him low.

The cooling board consisted of three sixteen-inch boards on saw horses, a dingy sheet was his shroud.

The women ate heartily of the funeral baked meats and wondered who would be Lena's next. The men whispered coarse conjectures between guzzles of whiskey.

Edna St. Vincent Millay
1892–1950

Edna St. Vincent Millay was born in Rockland, Maine, the first of three daughters of Cora Buzzelle Millay and Henry Tolman Millay, a school administrator. In 1900, her mother divorced her father, took up work as a practical nurse to help support her family, and moved to Camden, Maine, where she firmly established music and literature as the dominant interests of her daughters' lives. By 1909, when Edna graduated from high school, she had studied piano seriously for several years and had published several poems in *St. Nicholas,* a children's magazine.

Three years later, Millay entered two poems—"Renaissance," later retitled "Renascence," and "Interim"—in a competition sponsored by a magazine called *The Lyric Year.* When "Renascence" won the competition, Millay began attracting enthusiastic sponsors; and in 1913 she entered Vassar College, where she continued to write poetry and acquired a lasting interest in the theater.

In 1917 Millay graduated from Vassar, moved to New York, and published her first book, *Renascence and Other Poems,* which includes "Interim" as well as "Renascence," several other lyric poems, and several Shakespearean and Petrarchan sonnets. Two years later, she wrote and directed a play, *Aria da Capo,* for the Provincetown Players. In 1920, a second book, *A Few Figs from Thistles,* followed. Together, these three early works established four concerns that continued to engage Millay: traditional forms of lyric poetry as defined principally by Shakespeare, Donne, Marvell, Milton, Wordsworth, Coleridge, Keats, and Browning; the force of nature and the charm of "local color," as defined chiefly by her memories of growing up along the Maine coast; dramatic literature, particularly as it opened itself to active political concerns and authorized dramatic readings of her own poetry; and the fate of women who feel compelled to compete on equal terms with men not only socially, politically, and literarily but sexually as well.

Millay had been reared in a secure female household, and she had been encouraged by her mother at every turn. But nothing in her early training prepared her for coping with the new and difficult concept of womanhood that she felt bound to explore. Some sense of what lay before her entered "Interim." A firmer sense appears in "Witch-Wife" and the last sonnet in *Renascence and Other Poems,* where the poet's need of sanctuary is clear: "alone out of my life I kept/Unto myself, lest anyone know me quite." But it made its first boastful appearance in the playful poems of *A Few Figs from Thistles,* which begins with the famous multivoiced declaration. "My candle burns at both ends," and then moves through a range of female voices, some resigned, some confused, and some rebellious. Some of the poems in *Second April* (1921), which followed *A Few Figs from Thistles,* look back to Maine's coastline; others reach out toward free verse. But in the twelve sonnets with which *Second April* closes, cynicism and lyricism merge, particularly where "love" is concerned.

With *Second April,* Millay's reputation as a romantic, flamboyant public figure was fixed. When she died in 1950, her reputation as a poet had declined—hurt by the dated idiom in which she wrote; by the public image she and others had created; and by her effort to engage the anguish of World War II directly in books like *Poem and Prayer for an Invading Army* (1944). Recently, however, her work has begun to attract fresh attention, grounded in recognition of the striking ways in which it anticipates both the "new formalism" of the 1970s and 1980s and the rise of feminism.

Further Reading:

J. Gould, *The Poet and Her Book: A Biography of Edna St. Vincent Millay,* 1969.

N. Brittin, *Edna St. Vincent Millay,* 1967, 1982.

D. Fried, "Andromeda Unbound: Gender and Genre in Millay's Sonnets," *Twentieth Century Literature,* 32:1–22 (Spring 1986).

S. Clark, "The Unwarranted Discourse: Sentimental Community, Modernist Women, and the Case of Millay," *Genre,* 20:133–152 (Summer 1987).

Text:

Collected Sonnets of Edna St. Vincent Millay, 1988.

Euclid alone has looked on Beauty bare.
Let all who prate of Beauty hold their peace,
And lay them prone upon the earth and cease
To ponder on themselves, the while they stare
At nothing, intricately drawn nowhere   5
In shapes of shifting lineage; let geese
Gabble and hiss, but heroes seek release
From dusty bondage into luminous air.
O blinding hour, O holy, terrible day,
When first the shaft into his vision shone   10
Of light anatomized! Euclid alone
Has looked on Beauty bare. Fortunate they
Who, though once only and then but far away,
Have heard her massive sandal set on stone.
1923

Love is not all: it is not meat nor drink
Nor slumber nor a roof against the rain;
Nor yet a floating spar to men that sink
And rise and sink and rise and sink again;
Love can not fill the thickened lung with breath,   5
Nor clean the blood, nor set the fractured bone;
Yet many a man is making friends with death
Even as I speak, for lack of love alone.
It well may be that in a difficult hour,
Pinned down by pain and moaning for release,   10
Or nagged by want past resolution's power,
I might be driven to sell your love for peace,

Or trade the memory of this night for food.
It well may be. I do not think I would.
1931

Jean Toomer
1894–1967

For a time, the poet and novelist Jean Toomer was regarded as the most talented writer
of the "Harlem Renaissance," a literary movement of African American writers who
had congregated in New York City in the early 1920s and had transformed Harlem
into the intellectual and cultural center. The group included an impressive number of
painters, photographers, and musicians, as well as such writers as Langston Hughes,
Countee Cullen, Zora Neale Hurston, and Claude McKay. In its magazines and
anthologies, the movement promoted the creative work of the "New Negro," of whom
Jean Toomer was thought to be one of the outstanding examples in literature. He was
so highly regarded not only because he wrote truthfully and sensitively about African
American life but because he did so, as one member of the movement put it, "without
the surrender or compromise of the artist's vision."

Jean Toomer was born in Washington, D.C., in 1894. His father was Nathan
Toomer, an African American planter, and his mother was the daughter of P. B. S.
Pinchback, a Reconstruction governor of Louisiana whose own racial background was
apparently mixed. Toomer's early years were severely complicated by his father's
desertion in 1895, when Toomer was only one year old; they were perhaps even more
severely complicated by what Toomer later termed his "racial composition and
position." From early on, his life took him back and forth between what he later
described as the "white" world and the "black" in a land where life itself was viewed
"as if it were divided into white and black." "In my body were many bloods, some
dark blood, all blended . . . ," he wrote. "I was . . . either a new type of man or the very
oldest." He once claimed seven blood strains ("French, Dutch, Welsh, Negro, German,
Jewish, and Indian"). Yet at other times Toomer doubted "whether there is any
colored blood in me or not." Both of his marriages were to white women—the first to
a promising writer who was a descendant of the Puritan poet Anne Bradstreet.

Toomer lived for several years in New Rochelle, New York, then moved back to
Washington, where he finished high school. He then enrolled at the University of
Wisconsin but abandoned his studies there after a year and wandered about—all the
while working at odd jobs, studying, and writing—to Chicago, New York,
Massachusetts, Wisconsin again, and New Jersey. Returning to Washington, he began
to write more concertedly. In 1921 he moved to Sparta, Georgia, near his father's
original home, and took a job briefly as a teacher at the Georgia Normal and Industrial
Institute. It was there that he conceived and began *Cane* (1923), the book that
established him as an important literary figure.

During the early 1920s Toomer contributed regularly to such leading African

American journals as *The Crisis* and *Opportunity* and to such experimental magazines as *Broom, The Little Review,* and *The Double Dealer.* The experimental nature of his work, and particularly his interest in combining dramatic and narrative sketches, drew praise from a wide range of writers, including Sherwood Anderson, Allen Tate, and Hart Crane. Shortly after publishing *Cane,* Toomer became intrigued by the Russian spiritual teacher George Gurdjieff, who believed that through proper discipline and meditation an individual could achieve cosmic consciousness. Toomer traveled to France in the summer of 1926 to study at the Gurdjieff Institute and returned to Harlem prepared to set up classes in the philosophy of "Unitism." Looking back, Longston Hughes described this period in Toomer's life with a blend of humor and sorrow. People in Harlem, Hughes wrote in *The Big Sea* (1940), "had to work all day to make a living" and so turned out to be reluctant converts:

> Their advance toward cosmic consciousness was slow and their hope of achieving awareness distant indeed. . . . So Jean Toomer shortly left his Harlem group and went downtown to drop the seeds of Gurdjieff in less dark and poverty-stricken fields. . . . From downtown New York, Toomer carried Gurdjieff to Chicago's Gold Coast—and the Negroes lost one of the most talented of all their writers—the author of the beautiful book of prose and verse, *Cane.*

Though Toomer disappeared from the literary scene, he continued to write poetry, plays, essays, and fiction, much of it going unpublished. Works such as *Essentials* (1931) and *Portage Potential* (1932) reflect his mounting interests in different forms of mystical philosophy (he became deeply involved in Quaker pietism) and poetry, while the long poem *Blue Meridian* (1936) reflects his continuing effort artistically to resolve the problems generated by racial tensions in America. But Toomer's literary reputation still rests primarily on the book conceived during the four months he lived near his father's home in Georgia.

In *Cane,* Toomer draws heavily on the folk songs, the folktales, and the syncopated rhythms of the language of the African American people he encountered in Georgia. By mixing poems with both dramatic and prose sketches, he not only created one of the distinctive literary experiments of the 1920s but also fashioned a work of lasting historical and artistic significance. Historically, *Cane* played a major role in the efforts of African American writers to enlarge the cultural life of African American people in America. Artistically, it celebrates the power of exotic and primitive impulses to triumph over the tyranny of culture. What holds these two different aspects of Toomer's achievement together is his celebration of a freedom that is physical and psychic as well as aesthetic.

Further Reading:

H. M. Gloster, *Negro Voices in American Fiction,* 1948.

A. Bontemps, "The Negro Renaissance: Jean Toomer and the Harlem Writers of the 1920's" in *Anger and Beyond: The Negro Writer in the United States,* ed. H. Hill, 1966.

D. T. Turner, *In a Minor Chord: Three Afro-American Writers and Their Search for Identity,* 1971.

N. Y. McKay, *Jean Toomer, Artist,* 1984.

Text:

"Blood-Burning Moon" from *Cane,* 1923.

from Cane

Blood-Burning Moon

1

Up from the skeleton stone walls, up from the rotting floor boards and the solid hand-hewn beams of oak of the pre-war cotton factory, dusk came. Up from the dusk the full moon came. Glowing like a fired pine-knot, it illumined the great door and soft showered the Negro shanties aligned along the single street of factory town. The full moon in the great door was an omen. Negro women improvised songs against its spell.

Louisa sang as she came over the crest of the hill from the white folks' kitchen. Her skin was the color of oak leaves on young trees in fall. Her breasts, firm and up-pointed like ripe acorns. And her singing had the low murmur of winds in fig trees. Bob Stone, younger son of the people she worked for, loved her. By the way the world reckons things, he had won her. By measure of that warm glow which came into her mind at thought of him, he had won her. Tom Burwell, whom the whole town called Big Boy, also loved her. But working in the fields all day, and far away from her, gave him no chance to show it. Though often enough of evenings he had tried to. Somehow, he never got along. Strong as he was with hands upon the ax or plow, he found it difficult to hold her. Or so he thought. But the fact was that he held her to factory town more firmly than he thought for. His black balanced, and pulled against, the white of Stone, when she thought of them. And her mind was vaguely upon them as she came over the crest of the hill, coming from the white folks' kitchen. As she sang softly at the evil face of the full moon.

A strange stir was in her. Indolently, she tried fix upon Bob or Tom as the cause of it. To meet Bob in the canebrake as she was going to do an hour or so later, was nothing new. And Tom's proposal which she felt on its way to her could be indefinitely put off. Separately, there was no unusual significance to either one. But for some reason, they jumbled when her eyes gazed vacantly at the rising moon. And from the jumble came the stir that was strangely within her. Her lips trembled. The slow rhythm of her song grew agitant and restless. Rusty black and tan spotted hounds, lying in the dark corners of porches or prowling around back yards, put their noses in the air and caught its tremor. They began plaintively to yelp and howl. Chickens woke up and cackled. Intermittently, all over the countryside dogs barked and roosters crowed as if heralding a weird dawn or some ungodly awakening. The women sang lustily. Their songs were cotton-wads to stop their ears. Louisa came down into factory town and sank wearily upon the step before her home. The moon was rising towards a thick cloud-bank which soon would hide it.

> Red nigger moon. Sinner!
> Blood-burning moon. Sinner!
> Come out that fact'ry door.

2

Up from the deep dusk of a cleared spot on the edge of the forest a mellow glow arose and spread fan-wise into the low-hanging heavens. And all around the air was heavy with the scent of boiling cane. A large pile of cane-stalks lay like ribboned shadows upon the ground. A mule, harnessed to a pole, trudged lazily round and round the pivot of the grinder. Beneath a swaying oil lamp, a Negro alternately whipped out at the mule, and fed cane-stalks to the grinder. A fat boy waddled pails of fresh ground juice between the grinder and the boiling stove. Steam came from the copper boiling pan. The scent of cane came from the copper pan and drenched the forest and the hill that sloped to factory town, beneath its fragrance. It drenched the men in circle seated around the stove. Some of them chewed at the white pulp of stalks, but there was no need for them to, if all they wanted was to taste the cane. One tasted it in factory town. And from factory town one could see the soft haze thrown by the glowing stove upon the low-hanging heavens.

Old David Georgia stirred the thickening syrup with a long ladle, and ever so often drew it off. Old David Georgia tended his stove and told tales about the white folks, about moonshining and cotton picking, and about sweet nigger gals, to the men who sat there about his stove to listen to him. Tom Burwell chewed cane-stalk and laughed with the others till someone mentioned Louisa. Till some one said something about Louisa and Bob Stone, about the silk stockings she must have gotten from him. Blood ran up Tom's neck hotter than the glow that flooded from the stove. He sprang up. Glared at the men and said, "She's my gal." Will Manning laughed. Tom strode over to him. Yanked him up and knocked him to the ground. Several of Manning's friends got up to fight for him. Tom whipped out a long knife and would have cut them to shreds if they hadnt ducked into the woods. Tom had had enough. He nodded to Old David Georgia and swung down the path to factory town. Just then, the dogs started barking and the roosters began to crow. Tom felt funny. Away from the fight, away from the stove, chill got to him. He shivered. He shuddered when he saw the full moon rising towards the cloud-bank. He who didnt give a godam for the fears of old women. He forced his mind to fasten on Louisa. Bob Stone. Better not be. He turned into the street and saw Louisa sitting before her home. He went towards her, ambling, touched the brim of a marvelously shaped, spotted, felt hat, said he wanted to say something to her, and then found that he didnt know what he had to say, or if he did, that he couldnt say it. He shoved his big fists in his overalls, grinned, and started to move off.

"Youall want me, Tom?"

"Thats what us wants, sho, Louisa."

"Well, here I am—"

"An here I is, but that aint ahelpin none, all th same."

"You wanted to say something? . . ."

"I did that, sho. But words is like th spots on dice: no matter how y fumbles em, there's times when they jes wont come. I dunno why. Seems like th love I feels fo yo done stole m tongue. I got it now. Whee! Louisa, honey, I oughtnt tell y, I feel I oughtnt cause yo is young an goes t church an I has had other gals, but Louisa I sho do love y. Lil gal, Ise watched y from them first days when youall sat right here befo yo door befo th well an sang sometimes in a way that like t broke m heart. Ise carried y with me into th fields, day after day, an after that, an I sho can plow when yo is there, an I can pick cotton. Yassur! Come near beatin Barlo yesterday. I sho did. Yassur! An next if ole Stone'll trust me, I'll have a farm. My own. My bales will buy yo what y gets from white folks now. Silk stockings an purple dresses—course I dont believe what some folks been whisperin as t how y gets them things now. White folks always did do for niggers what they likes. An they jes cant help alikin yo, Louisa. Bob Stone likes y. Course he does. But not th way folks is awhisperin. Does he, hon?"

"I dont know what you mean, Tom."

"Course y dont. Ise already cut two niggers. Had t hon, t tell em so. Niggers always tryin t make somethin out a nothin. An then besides, white folks aint up t them tricks so much nowadays. Godam better not be. Leastawise not with yo. Cause I wouldnt stand f it. Nassur."

"What would you do, Tom?"

"Cut him jes like I cut a nigger."

"No, Tom—"

"I said I would an there aint no mo to it. But that aint th talk f now. Sing, honey Louisa, an while I'm listenin t y I'll be makin love."

Tom took her hand in his. Against the tough thickness of his own, hers felt soft and small. His huge body slipped down to the step beside her. The full moon sank upward into the deep purple of the cloud-bank. An old woman brought a lighted lamp and hung it on the common well whose bulky shadow squatted in the middle of the road, opposite Tom and Louisa. The old woman lifted the well-lid, took hold the chain, and began drawing up the heavy bucket. As she did so, she sang. Figures shifted, restlesslike, between lamp and window in the front rooms of the shanties. Shadows of the figures fought each other on the gray dust of the road. Figures raised the windows and joined the old women in song. Louisa and Tom, the whole street, singing:

> Red nigger moon. Sinner!
> Blood-burning moon. Sinner!
> Come out that fact'ry door.

3

Bob Stone sauntered from his veranda out into the gloom of fir trees and magnolias. The clear white of his skin paled, and the flush of his cheeks turned purple. As if to balance this outer change, his mind became consciously a white man's. He passed the house with its huge open hearth which, in the days of slavery, was the plantation cookery. He saw Louisa bent over that hearth. He went in as a master should and took her. Direct, honest, bold. None of this sneaking that he had to go through now. The contrast was repulsive to him. His family had lost ground. Hell no, his family still owned the niggers, practically. Damned if they did, or he wouldnt have to duck around so. What would they think if they knew? His mother? His sister? He shouldnt mention them, shouldnt think of them in this connection. There in the dusk he blushed at doing so. Fellows about town were all right, but how about his friends up North? He could see them incredible, repulsed. They didnt know. The thought first made him laugh. Then, with their eyes still upon him, he began to feel embarrassed. He felt the need of explaining things to them. Explain hell. They wouldnt understand, and moreover, who ever heard of a Southerner getting on his knees to any Yankee, or anyone. No sir. He was going to see Louisa to-night, and love her. She was lovely—in her way. Nigger way. What way was that? Damned if he knew. Must know. He's known her long enough to know.

Was there something about niggers that you couldnt know? Listening to them at church didnt tell you anything. Looking at them didnt tell you anything. Talking to them didnt tell you anything—unless it was gossip, unless they wanted to talk. Of course, about farming, and licker, and craps—but those werent nigger. Nigger was something more. How much more? Something to be afraid of, more? Hell no. Who ever heard of being afraid of a nigger? Tom Burwell. Cartwell had told him that Tom went with Louisa after she reached home. No sir. No nigger had ever been with his girl. He'd like to see one try. Some position for him to be in. Him, Bob Stone, of the old Stone family, in a scrap with a nigger over a nigger girl. In the good old days . . . Ha! Those were the days. His family had lost ground. Not so much, though. Enough for him to have to cut through old Lemon's canefield by way of the woods, that he might meet her. She was worth it. Beautiful nigger gal. Why nigger? Why not, just gal? No, it was because she was nigger that he went to her. Sweet . . . The scent of boiling cane came to him. Then he saw the rich glow of the stove. He heard the voices of the men circled around it. He was about to skirt the clearing when he heard his own name mentioned. He stopped. Quivering. Leaning against a tree, he listened.

"Bad nigger. Yassur, he sho is one bad nigger when he gets started."

"Tom Burwell's been on th gang three times fo cuttin men."

"What y think he's agwine t do t Bob Stone?"

"Dunno yet. He aint found out. When he does—Baby!"

"Aint no tellin."

"Young Stone aint no quitter an I ken tell y that. Blood of th old uns in his veins."

"Thats right. He'll scrap, sho."

"Be gettin too hot f niggers round this away."

"Shut up, nigger. Y dont know what y talkin bout."

Bob Stone's ears burned as though he had been holding them over the stove. Sizzling heat welled up within him. His feet felt as if they rested on red-hot coals. They stung him to quick movement. He circled the fringe of the glowing. Not a twig cracked beneath his feet. He reached the path that led to factory town. Plunged furiously down it. Halfway along, a blindness within him veered him aside. He crashed into the bordering canebrake. Cane leaves cut his face and lips. He tasted blood. He threw himself down and dug his fingers in the ground. The earth was cool. Cane-roots took the fever from his hands. After a long while, or so it seemed to him, the thought came to him that it must be time to see Louisa. He got to his feet and walked calmly to their meeting place. No Louisa. Tom Burwell had her. Veins in his forehead bulged and distended. Saliva moistened the dried blood on his lips. He bit down on his lips. He tasted blood. Not his own blood; Tom Burwell's blood. Bob drove through the cane and out again upon the road. A hound swung down the path before him towards factory town. Bob couldnt see it. The dog loped aside to let him pass. Bob's blind rushing made him stumble over it. He fell with a thud that dazed him. The hound yelped. Answering yelps came from all over the countryside. Chickens cackled. Roosters crowed, heralding the bloodshot eyes of southern awakening. Singers in the town were silenced. They shut their windows down. Palpitant between the rooster crows, a chill hush settled upon the huddled forms of Tom and Louisa. A figure rushed from the shadow and stood before them. Tom popped to his feet.

"Whats y want?"

"I'm Bob Stone."

"Yassur—an I'm Tom Burwell. Whats y want?"

Bob lunged at him. Tom side-stepped, caught him by the shoulder, and flung him to the ground. Straddled him.

"Let me up."

"Yassur—but watch yo doins, Bob Stone."

A few dark figures, drawn by the sound of scuffle, stood about them. Bob sprang to his feet.

"Fight like a man, Tom Burwell, an I'll lick y."

Again he lunged. Tom side-stepped and flung him to the ground. Straddled him. "Get off me, you godam nigger you."

"Yo sho has started somethin now. Get up."

Tom yanked him up and began hammering at him. Each blow sounded as if it smashed into a precious, irreplaceable soft something. Beneath them, Bob staggered back. He reached in his pocket and whipped out a knife.

"Thats my game, sho."

Blue flash, a steel blade slashed across Bob Stone's throat. He had a sweetish sick feeling. Blood began to flow. Then he felt a sharp twitch of pain. He let his knife drop. He slapped one hand against his neck. He pressed the other on top of his head as if to hold it down. He groaned. He turned, and staggered towards the crest of the hill in the direction of white town. Negroes who had seen the fight slunk into their homes and blew the lamps out. Louisa, dazed, hysterical, refused to go indoors. She slipped, crumbled, her body loosely propped against the woodwork of the well. Tom Burwell leaned against it. He seemed rooted there.

Bob reached Broad Street. White men rushed up to him. He collapsed in their arms.

"Tom Burwell. . . ."

White men like ants upon a forage rushed about. Except for the taut hum of their moving, all was silent. Shotguns, revolvers, rope, kerosene, torches. Two high-powered cars with glaring search-lights. They came together. The taut hum rose to a low roar. Then nothing could be heard but the flop of their feet in the thick dust of the road. The moving body of their silence preceded them over the crest of the hill into factory town. It flattened the Negroes beneath it. It rolled to the wall of the factory, where it stopped. Tom knew that they were coming. He couldnt move. And then he saw the search-lights of the two cars glaring down on him. A quick shock went through him. He stiffened. He started to run. A yell went up from the mob. Tom wheeled about and faced them. They poured down on him. They swarmed. A large man with dead-white face and flabby cheeks came to him and almost jabbed a gun-barrel through his guts.

"Hands behind y, nigger."

Tom's wrists were bound. The big man shoved him to the well. Burn him over it, and when the woodwork caved in, his body would drop to the bottom. Two deaths for a godam nigger. Louisa was driven back. The mob pushed in. Its pressure, its momentum was too great. Drag him to the factory. Wood and stakes already there. Tom moved in the direction indicated. But they had to drag him. They reached the great door. Too many to get in there. The mob divided and flowed around the walls to either side. The big man shoved him through the door. The mob pressed in from the sides. Taut humming. No words. A stake was sunk into the ground. Rotting floor boards piled around it. Kerosene poured on the rotting floor boards. Tom bound to the stake. His breast was bare. Nails scratches let little lines of blood trickle down and mat into the hair. His face, his eyes were set and stony. Except for irregular breathing, one would have thought him already dead. Torches were flung onto the pile. A great flare muffled in black smoke shot upward. The mob yelled. The mob was silent. Now Tom could be seen within the flames. Only his head, erect, lean like a blackened stone. Stench of burning flesh soaked the air. Tom's eyes popped. His head settled downward. The mob yelled. Its yell echoed against the skeleton stone walls and sounded like a hundred yells. Like a hundred mobs yelling. Its yell thudded against the thick front wall and fell back. Ghost of a yell slipped through the flames and out the great door of the factory. It fluttered like a dying thing down the single street of factory town. Louisa, upon the step before her home, did not hear it, but her eyes opened slowly. They saw the full moon glowing in the great door. The full moon, an evil thing, an omen, soft showering the homes of folks she knew. Where were they, these people? She'd sing, and perhaps they'd come out and join her. Perhaps Tom Burwell would come. At any rate, the full moon in the great door was an omen which she must sing to:

> Red nigger moon. Sinner!
> Blood-burning moon. Sinner!
> Come out that fact'ry door.

1923

Cultural Portfolio
The Harlem Renaissance

"The 1920s," Langston Hughes wrote in his autobiography *The Big Sea* (1940), "were the years of Manhattan's black Renaissance." And, although no specific date can be set for its beginning, the Harlem Renaissance now clearly stands as one of the most diverse and extraordinary outpourings of creative energy—in music and dance as well as poetry and prose—in the history of American culture. Published in the middle of the decade, Alain Locke's important anthology *The New Negro* (1925) served a double purpose: it reminded readers that a long, painful history lay behind the new writing of black Americans, and it announced that a new age of creative achievement had dawned. By 1925, the creative energies of black Americans gathered in Harlem had already found expression in many forms, including Jean Toomer's *Cane* (1923), and they had already begun spilling out of Harlem's flats, clubs, cafes, music halls, and theaters onto its sidewalks and streets. As a result, announcements such as those found in *The New Negro* possessed the force of observation rather than mere proclamation. Something like Harlem's ferment had occurred earlier on New York's Lower Eastside, in the last decade of the nineteenth century and the first two decades of the twentieth, when Jewish refugees from Europe began creating a vital intellectual community and a vital literature, much of it written in Yiddish. On a smaller scale, something like it happened again in the 1950s and 1960s when disillusioned young people from across America began congregating in San Francisco. But Harlem was different from these and other such communities because its refugees were different. The disenchantment of the young people of the 1950s and 1960s had little in common with the troubles that the refugees gathered in Harlem had endured. And, unlike the heavy memories that Europe's refugees carried with them to the United States, the painful memories that black Americans carried with them in their search for a "promised land" were so intensely and even uniquely American that they were certain to encounter versions of them even in Harlem.

Yet it was more than memories of old atrocities and fresh reminders of entrenched prejudice and injustice that made Harlem a magnet and turned it into a scene of striking creativity. It was hope of a kind that was new to black Americans—of making a new start by creating a world unlike any that they had ever directly known. As word spread, the cast of players became more diverse. People came from farms and plantations, and from villages, towns, and cities scattered across the United States. A few even came from beyond the nation's borders. Langston Hughes was born in Joplin, Missouri, grew up mainly in Lawrence, Kansas, and lived in Cleveland, Mexico, and Washington, D.C., before his first year in New York, 1921–1922; Zora Neale Hurston grew up in Eatonville, Florida, and went to school in Washington, D.C., before she arrived in New York in January 1925; Nella Larsen had either lived, attended school, or worked in Chicago, Nashville, and Denmark before she arrived in New York in 1915; Claude McKay, born in Jamaica, had traveled widely in the Soviet Union, Europe, and Africa before he began living and working in New York; and James Weldon Johnson had been born and reared in Jacksonville, Florida, and educated at Atlanta University before he moved to New York. Yet these are but a few of the thousands of talented, hopeful, hungry black Americans who helped to create, on a grander scale, what others were creating in New Orleans, Memphis, Kansas City, St. Louis, Chicago, and Detroit—namely, a "critical mass" of musicians, including composers, improvising instrumentalists, and vocalists; of actors and actresses; of painters and sculptors; and of writers of poetry, fiction, history, and journalism. In the process, they also attracted and educated a growing community of listeners, viewers, and readers.

Working together—stimulated, supported, and challenged by other artists and by an expanding audience—the makers of the Harlem Renaissance began creating a tradition of endurance and triumph out of a heritage of pain,

Bill Robinson, Lena Horne, and Cab Calloway in a scene from the 20th Century-Fox Production, "Stormy Weather" (Culver Pictures, Inc.)

humiliation, and deprivation, punctuated by atrocities as well as abuses. In the process they not only created works of lasting value; they also inspired and enabled people to make new beginnings. For, as works such as James Weldon Johnson's *Black Manhattan* (1930) make clear, the achievements of the Harlem Renaissance reached well beyond its immediate boundaries. And they included, as Johnson notes, defiantly building toward an enlarged life, of "greater and greater things," for all black Americans, first, by creating and, then, by making visible and accessible a cultural heritage that they could call their own. Strangely, however, in many unexpected ways the achievements of the Harlem Renaissance also became a remarkable enrichment of the larger culture of the United States that it set out to challenge—and that it challenges still. For among the many things that the works of the Harlem Renaissance make visible to us are these: the myriad means, legal and illegal, that the

dominant "white" culture of the United States has employed, first, in seeking to control all definitions of the "place" of black Americans within American society; second, in seeking to control their access to the wealth that their talents and labor helped to create; and third, in seeking to discourage, control, and judge their efforts to create a culture of their own. Yet, despite the formidable difficulties they faced, the builders of the Harlem Renaissance repeatedly discovered, as Langston Hughes noted in "The Negro Artist and the Racial Mountain" (June 23, 1926), that for those who were no longer afraid there existed "a wealth of colorful, distinctive material,"—"a great field of unused material ready" for art—that was more than sufficient for "a lifetime of creative work."

In the process of saving their heritage and bequeathing it to others, the musicians, actors, artists, and writers who created the Harlem Renaissance showed that they knew what it

Josephine Baker in the Folies Bergere
(Culver Pictures, Inc.)

meant to keep on "keepin' on," as an old phrase went. Many of them had lived versions of the experiences that they recorded in songs and recounted in stories, plays, and poems. And in exploring their experiences, they not only discovered and reclaimed a wealth of material for their art; they also found waiting for them what Hughes describes, in "The Negro Artist and the Racial Mountain," as a sustaining "heritage of rhythm and warmth" and a sustaining legacy not only of endurance but, ultimately, of triumph. In addition, however, they also discovered new versions of the old stories that other people in their nation's much-mixed history had lived, were living, or would later live—including stories of migrations from the soil of farms, plantations, and ranches to the sidewalks of cities and the walls of factories, shops, and office buildings—some of them stories of triumph, others of disaster, and others of frustration and disappointment, tilting toward despair, when their newly discovered world fell short of their dreams. "For where," as Claude Brown later put it, in the Foreword to *Manchild in the Promised Land* (1965), "does one run to when he's already in the promised land?"

No group of people battling the forces arrayed against the black Americans who created the Harlem Renaissance could hope to gain a total victory. For some the Harlem Renaissance fell short of its great promise. For others, it offered new beginnings. For many it became another version of the great yet mixed American success story. But as we look back on their achievements, from our vantage point at the end of the twentieth century, a few things at least are clear:

First, black Americans transformed and enriched the lives of countless people; and, second, they enriched the culture of the United States immeasurably in dramatic performances, in instrumental and vocal music, and in dance as well as in poetry and fiction, thereby permanently altering its cultural landscape. In music, for example, they gave us instrumentalists like Duke Ellington, Fats Waller, and Fletcher Henderson and vocalists like Leon Bibb, Josh White, Odetta, Marian Anderson, and Paul Robeson. In dance, they added stars like Josephine Baker, the daughter of a St. Louis washerwoman, who went from being a waitress in New York, to being a dancer in the chorus of *Shuffle Along,* at the Sixty-Third Street Music Hall, to being a star of international reknown in Paris's Folies Bergeres. In theater they made possible two important productions of Eugene O'Neill's *The Emperor Jones,* first at its opening in 1920, with a cast that featured several black actors; then, in a revival in 1925, with Paul Robeson making a triumphant appearance in the title role. And in poetry and fiction they gave us, among many others, the selections represented in this anthology. A richer, more diverse literary and artistic "renaissance," American culture has yet to produce.

THIS VOLUME
IS DEDICATED
TO THE
YOUNGER GENERATION

O, rise, shine for Thy Light is a' com-ing.
(Traditional.)

Dedication page from The New Negro: An Interpretation

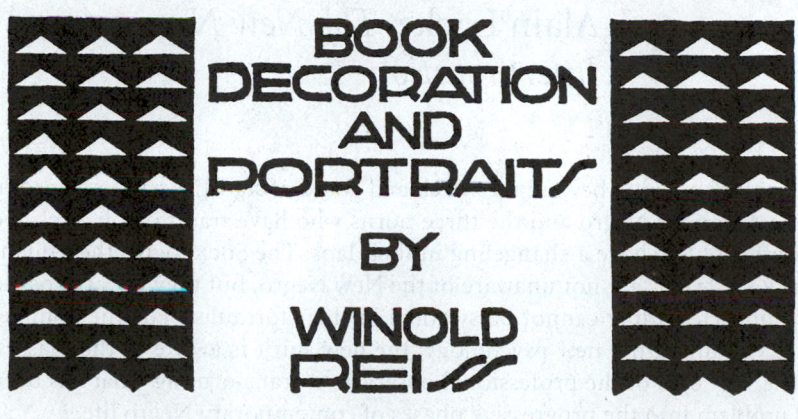

THE NEW NEGRO
AN INTERPRETATION

EDITED BY ALAIN LOCKE

BOOK
DECORATION
AND
PORTRAITS
BY
WINOLD REISS

ALBERT AND CHARLES BONI
NEW YORK   1925

Winold Reiss
Title page of The New Negro: An Interpretation, *edited
by Alain Locke*
block print, 1925

THE NEW NEGRO

Winold Reiss
Opening page of The New Negro: An Interpretation
block print

from Alain Locke, *The New Negro: An Interpretation*

In the last decade something beyond the watch and guard of statistics has happened in the life of the American Negro and the three norns who have traditionally presided over the Negro problem have a changeling in their laps. The Sociologist, the Philanthropist, the Race-leader are not unaware of the New Negro, but they are at a loss to account for him. He simply cannot be swathed in their formulae. For the younger generation is vibrant with a new psychology; the new spirit is awake in the masses, and under the very eyes of the professional observers is transforming what has been a perennial problem into the progressive phases of contemporary Negro life.

Could such a metamorphosis have taken place as suddenly as it has appeared to? The answer is no; not because the New Negro is not here, but because the Old Negro had long become more of a myth than a man. The Old Negro, we must remember, was a creature of moral debate and historical controversy. His has been a stock figure perpetuated as an historical fiction partly in innocent sentimentalism, partly in deliberate reactionism. The Negro himself has contributed his share to this through a sort of protective social mimicry forced upon him by the adverse circumstances of dependence. So for generations in the mind of America, the Negro has been more of a formula than a human being—a something to be argued about, condemned or defended, to be "kept down," or "in his place," or "helped up," to be worried with or worried over, harassed or patronized, a social bogey or a social burden. The thinking Negro even has been induced to share this same general attitude, to focus his attention on controversial issues, to see himself in the distorted perspective of a social problem. His shadow, so to speak, has been more real to him than his personality. Through having had to appeal from the unjust stereotypes of his oppressors and traducers to those of his liberators, friends and benefactors he has had to subscribe to the traditional positions from which his case has been viewed. Little true social or self-understanding has or could come from such a situation.

But while the minds of most of us, black and white, have thus burrowed in the trenches of the Civil War and Reconstruction, the actual march of development has simply flanked these positions, necessitating a sudden reorientation of view. We have not been watching in the right direction; set North and South on a sectional axis, we have not noticed the East till the sun has us blinking.

Recall how suddenly the Negro spirituals revealed themselves; suppressed for generations under the stereotypes of Wesleyan hymn harmony, secretive, half-ashamed, until the courage of being natural brought them out—and behold, there was folk-music. Similarly the mind of the Negro seems suddenly to have slipped from under the tyranny of social intimidation and to be shaking off the psychology of imitation and implied inferiority. By shedding the old chrysalis of the Negro problem we are achieving something like a spiritual emancipation. Until recently, lacking self-understanding, we have been almost as much of a problem to ourselves as we still are to others. But the decade that found us with a problem has left us with only a task. The multitude perhaps feels as yet only a strange relief and a new vague urge, but the thinking few know that in the reaction the vital inner grip of prejudice has been broken.

With this renewed self-respect and self-dependence, the life of the Negro community is bound to enter a new dynamic phase, the buoyancy from within compensating for whatever pressure there may be of conditions from without. The migrant masses, shifting from countryside to city, hurdle several generations of experience at a leap, but more important, the same thing happens spiritually in the life-attitudes and self-expression of the Young Negro, in his poetry, his art, his education and his new outlook, with the additional advantage, of course, of the poise and greater certainty of knowing what it is all about. From this comes the promise and warrant of a new leadership. . . .

Take Harlem as an instance of this. Here in Manhattan is not merely the largest Negro community in the world, but the first concentration in history of so many diverse elements of Negro life. It has attracted the African, the West Indian, the Negro American; has brought together the Negro of the North and the Negro of the South; the man from the city and the man from the town and village; the peasant, the student, the business man, the professional man, artist, poet, musician, adventurer and worker, preacher and criminal, exploiter and social outcast. Each group has come with its own separate motives and for its own special ends, but their greatest experience has been the finding of one another. Proscription and prejudice have thrown these dissimilar elements into a common area of contact and interaction. Within this area, race sympathy and unity have determined a further fusing of sentiment and experience. So what began in terms of segregation becomes more and more, as its elements mix and react, the laboratory of a great race-welding. Hitherto, it must be admitted that American Negroes have been a race more in name than in fact, or to be exact, more in sentiment than in experience. The chief bond between them has been that of a common condition rather than a common consciousness; a problem in common rather than a life in common. In Harlem, Negro life is seizing upon its first chances for group expression and self-determination. It is—or promises at least to be—a race capital. That is why our comparison is taken with those nascent centers of folk-expression and self-determination which are playing a creative part in the world to-day. Without pretense to their political significance, Harlem has the same rôle to play for the New Negro as Dublin has had for the New Ireland or Prague for the New Czechoslovakia. . . .

from James Weldon Johnson,
*God's Trombones**

Listen!—Listen!
All you sons of Pharaoh.
Who do you think can hold God's people
When the Lord God himself has said,
Let my people go?

from Langston Hughes, *The Negro Artist
and the Racial Mountain*

One of the most promising of the young Negro poets said to me once, "I want to be a poet—not a Negro poet," meaning, I believe, "I want to write like a white poet"; meaning subconsciously, "I would like to be a white poet"; meaning behind that, "I would like to be white." And I was sorry the young man said that, for no great poet has ever been afraid of being himself. And I doubted then that, with his desire to run away spiritually from his race, this boy would ever be a great poet. But this is the mountain standing in the way of any true Negro art in America—this urge within the race toward whiteness, the desire to pour racial individuality into the mold of American standardization, and to be as little Negro and as much American as possible.

But let us look at the immediate background of this young poet. His family is of what I suppose one would call the Negro middle class: people who are by no means rich yet never uncomfortable nor hungry—smug, contented, respectable folk, members of the Baptist church. The father goes to work every morning. He is a chief steward at a large white club. The mother sometimes does fancy sewing or supervises parties for the rich families of the town. The children go to a mixed school. In the home they read white papers and magazines. And the mother often says "Don't be like niggers" when the children are bad. A frequent phrase from the father is, "Look how well a white man does things." And so the word white comes to be unconsciously a symbol of all the virtues. It holds for the children beauty, morality, and money. The whisper of "I want to be white" runs silently through their minds. This young poet's home is, I believe, a fairly typical home of the colored middle class. One sees immediately how difficult it would be for an artist born in such a home to interest himself in interpreting the beauty of his own people. He is never taught to see that beauty. He is taught rather not to see it, or if he does, to be ashamed of it when it is not according to Caucasian patterns.

For racial culture the home of a self-styled "high-class" Negro has nothing better to offer. Instead there will perhaps be more aping of things white than in a less cultured or less wealthy home. The father is perhaps a doctor, lawyer, land-owner, or politician. The mother may be a social worker, or a teacher, or she may do nothing and have a maid. Father is often dark but he has usually married the lightest woman he could find. The family attend a fashionable church where few really colored faces are to be found. And they themselves draw a

---

* Reprinted is the final stanza of *"Let My People Go."*

Aaron Douglas
Drawing from James Weldon Johnson's poem, "Let My People Go"
from God's Trombones.

(Aldis Family Papers, Special Collections, The University Library,
University of Illinois at Chicago)

color line. In the North they go to white theaters and white movies. And in the South they have at least two cars and a house "like white folks." Nordic manners, Nordic faces, Nordic hair, Nordic art (if any), and an Episcopal heaven. A very high mountain indeed for the would-be racial artist to climb in order to discover himself and his people.

But then there are the low-down folks, the so-called common element, and they are the majority—may the Lord be praised! The people who have their nip of gin on Saturday nights and are not too important to themselves or the community, or too well fed, or too learned to watch the lazy world go round. They live on Seventh Street in Washington or State Street in Chicago and they do not particularly care whether they are like white folks or anybody else. Their joy runs, bang! into ecstasy. Their religion soars to a shout. Work maybe a little today, rest a little tomorrow. Play awhile. Sing awhile. O, let's dance! These common people are not afraid of spirituals, as for a long time their more intellectual brethren were, and jazz is their child. They furnish a wealth of colorful, distinctive material for any artist because they still hold their own individuality in the face of American standardizations. And perhaps these common people will give to the world its truly great Negro artist, the one who is not afraid to be himself. Whereas the better-class Negro would tell the artist what to do, the people at least let him alone when he does appear. And they are not ashamed of him—if they know he exists at all. And they accept what beauty is their own without question.

Certainly there is, for the American Negro artist who can escape the restrictions the more advanced among his own group would put upon him, a great field of unused material ready for his art. Without going outside his race, and even among the better classes with their "white" culture and conscious American manners, but still Negro enough to be different, there is sufficient matter to furnish a black artist with a lifetime of creative work. And when he chooses to touch on the relations between Negroes and whites in this country with their innumerable overtones and undertones, surely, and especially for literature and the drama, there is an inexaustible supply of themes at hand. To these the Negro artist can give his racial individuality, his heritage of rhythm and warmth, and his incongruous humor that so often, as in the Blues, becomes ironic laughter mixed with tears. But let us look again at the mountain.

(Aldis Family Papers, Special Collections, The University Library, University of Illinois at Chicago)

A prominent Negro clubwoman in Philadelphia paid eleven dollars to hear Raquel Meller sing Andalusian popular songs. But she told me a few weeks before she would not think of going to hear "that woman," Clara Smith, a great black artist, sing Negro folksongs. And many an upper-class Negro church, even now, would not dream of employing a spiritual in its services. The drab melodies in white folks' hymnbooks are much to be preferred. "We want to worship the Lord correctly and quietly. We don't believe in 'shouting.' Let's be dull like the Nordics," they say, in effect.

The road for the serious black artist, then, who would produce a racial art is most certainly rocky and the mountain is high. Until recently he received almost no encouragement for his work from either white or colored people. The fine novels of Chestnutt go out of print with neither race noticing their passing. The quaint charm and humor of Dunbar's dialect verse brought to him, in his day, largely the same kind of encouragement one would give a sideshow freak (A colored man writing poetry! How odd!) or a clown (How amusing!).

The present vogue in things Negro, although it may do as much harm as good for the budding colored artist, has at least done this: it has brought him forcibly to the attention of his own people among whom for so long, unless the other race had noticed him beforehand, he was a prophet with little honor. I understand that Charles Gilpin acted for years in Negro theaters without any special acclaim from his own, but when Broadway gave him eight curtain calls, Negroes, too, began to beat a tin pan in his honor. I know a young colored writer, a manual worker by day, who had been writing well for the colored magazines for some years, but it was not until he recently broke into the white publications and his first book was accepted by a prominent New York publisher that the "best" Negroes in his city took the trouble to discover that he lived there. Then almost immediately they decided to give a grand dinner for him. But the society ladies were careful to whisper to his mother that perhaps she'd better not come. They were not sure she would have an evening gown.

The Negro artist works against an undertow of sharp criticism and misunderstanding from his own group and unintentional bribes from the whites. "O, be respectable, write about nice people, show how good we are," say the Negroes. "Be stereotyped, don't go too far, don't shatter our illusions about you, don't amuse us too seriously. We will pay you," say the whites. Both would have told Jean Toomer not to write "Cane." The colored people did not praise it. The white people did not buy it. Most of the colored people who did read "Cane" hate it. They are afraid of it. Although the critics gave it good reviews the public remained indifferent. Yet (excepting the work of Du Bois) "Cane" contains the finest prose written by a Negro in America. And like the singing of Robeson, it is truly racial.

But in spite of the Nordicized Negro intelligentsia and the desire of some white editors we have an honest American Negro literature already with us. Now I await the rise of the Negro theater. Our folk music, having achieved world-wide fame, offers itself to the genius of the great individual American Negro composer who is to come. And within the next decade I expect to see the work of a growing school of colored artists who paint and model the beauty of dark faces and create with new technique the expressions of their own soul-world. And the Negro dancers who will dance like flame and the singers who will continue to carry our songs to all who listen—they will be with us in even greater numbers tomorrow.

Most of my own poems are racial in theme and treatment, derived from the life I know. In many of them I try to grasp and hold some of the meanings and rhythms of jazz. I am sincere as I know how to be in these poems and yet after every reading I answer questions like these from my own people: Do you think Negroes should always write about Negroes? I wish you wouldn't read some of your poems to white folks. How do you find anything interesting in a place like a cabaret? Why do you write about black people? You aren't black. What makes you do so many jazz poems?

But jazz to me is one of the inherent expressions of Negro life in America: the eternal tom-tom beating in the Negro soul—the tom-tom of revolt against weariness in a white world, a world of subway trains, and work, work, work; the tom-tom of joy and laughter, and pain swallowed in a smile. Yet the Philadelphia clubwoman is ashamed to say that her race created it and she does not like me to write about it. The old subconscious "white is best" runs through her mind. Years of study under white teachers, a lifetime of white books, pictures, and papers, and white manners, morals, and Puritan standards made her dislike the spirituals. And now she turns up her nose at jazz and all its manifestations—likewise almost everything else distinctly racial. She doesn't care for the Winold Reiss portraits of Negroes because they are "too Negro." She does not want a true picture of herself from anybody. She wants the artist to flatter her, to make the white world believe that all Negroes are as smug and as near white in soul as she wants to be. But, to my mind, it is the duty of the younger Negro artist, if he accepts any duties at all from outsiders, to change through the force of his art that old whispering "I want to be white," hidden in the aspirations of his people, to "Why should I want to be white? I am a Negro—and beautiful!"

So I am ashamed for the black poet who says, "I want to be a poet, not a Negro poet," as though his own racial world were not as interesting as any other world. I am ashamed, too, for the colored artist who runs from the painting of Negro faces to the painting of sunsets after the manner of the academicians because he fears the strange un-whiteness of his own features. An artist must be free to choose what he does, certainly, but he must also never be afraid to do what he might choose.

Let the blare of Negro jazz bands and the bellowing voice of Bessie Smith singing Blues penetrate the closed ears of the colored near-intellectuals until they listen and perhaps understand. Let Paul Robeson singing Water Boy, and Rudolph Fisher writing about the streets of Harlem, and Jean Toomer holding the heart of Georgia in his hands, and Aaron Douglas drawing strange black fantasies cause the smug Negro middle class to turn from their white, respectable, ordinary books and papers to catch a glimmer of their own beauty. We younger Negro artists who create now intend to express our individual dark-skinned selves without fear or shame. If white people are pleased we are glad. If they are not, it doesn't matter. We know we are beautiful. And ugly too. The tom-tom cries and the tom-tom laughs. If colored people are pleased we are glad. If they are not, their displeasure doesn't matter either. We build our temples for tomorrow, strong as we know how, and we stand on top of the mountain, free within ourselves.

Georgia Douglas Johnson
(1880–1966)

The Heart of a Woman

The heart of a woman goes forth with the dawn
As a lone bird, soft winging, so restlessly on;
Afar o'er life's turrets and vales does it roam
In the wake of those echoes the heart calls home.

The heart of a woman falls back with the night,   5
And enters some alien cage in its plight,
And tries to forget it has dreamed of the stars
While it breaks, breaks, breaks on the sheltering bars.
1918

Smothered Fires

A woman with a burning flame
 Deep covered through the years
With ashes—ah! she hid it deep,
 And smothered it with tears.

Sometimes a baleful light would rise   5
 From out the dusky bed,
And then the woman hushed it quick
 To slumber on, as dead.

At last the weary war was done,
    The tapers were alight,   10
And with a sigh of victory
    She breathed a soft—goodnight!
1918

Motherhood

Don't knock on my door, little child,
I cannot let you in;
You know not what a world this is
Of cruelty and sin.
Wait in the still eternity   5
Until I come to you.
The world is cruel, cruel, child,
I cannot let you through.

Don't knock at my heart, little one,
I cannot bear the pain   10
Of turning deaf ears to your call,
Time and time again.
You do not know the monster men
Inhabiting the earth.
Be still, be still, my precious child,   15
I cannot give you birth.
1922

Zora Neale Hurston
(ca. 1891–1960)

Sweat

It was eleven o'clock of a Spring night in Florida. It was Sunday. Any other night, Delia Jones would have been in bed for two hours by this time. But she was a washwoman, and Monday morning meant a great deal to her. So she collected the soiled clothes on Saturday when she returned the clean things. Sunday night after church, she sorted and put the white things to soak. It saved her almost a half-day's start. A great hamper in the bedroom held the clothes that she brought home. It was so much neater than a number of bundles lying around.

    She squatted on the kitchen floor beside the great pile of clothes, sorting them into small heaps according to color, and humming a song in a mournful key, but wondering through it all where Sykes, her husband, had gone with her horse and buckboard.

Just then something long, round, limp and black fell upon her shoulders and slithered to the floor beside her. A great terror took hold of her. It softened her knees and dried her mouth so that it was a full minute before she could cry out or move. Then she saw that it was the big bull whip her husband liked to carry when he drove.

She lifted her eyes to the door and saw him standing there bent over with laughter at her fright. She screamed at him.

"Sykes, what you throw dat whip on me like dat? You know it would skeer me— looks just like a snake, an' you knows how skeered Ah is of snakes."

"Course Ah knowed it! That's how come Ah done it." He slapped his leg with his hand and almost rolled on the ground in his mirth. "If you such a big fool dat you got to have a fit over a earth worm or a string, Ah don't keer how bad Ah skeer you."

"You ain't got no business doing it. Gawd knows it's a sin. Some day Ah'm gointuh drop dead from some of yo' foolishness. 'Nother thing, where you been wid mah rig? Ah feeds dat pony. He ain't fuh you to be drivin' wid no bull whip."

"You sho' is one aggravatin' nigger woman!" he declared and stepped into the room. She resumed her work and did not answer him at once. "Ah done tole you time and again to keep them white folks' clothes outa dis house."

He picked up the whip and glared at her. Delia went on with her work. She went out into the yard and returned with a galvanized tub and set it on the washbench. She saw that Sykes had kicked all of the clothes together again, and now stood in her way truculently, his whole manner hoping, *praying*, for an argument. But she walked calmly around him and commenced to re-sort the things.

"Next time, Ah'm gointer kick 'em outdoors," he threatened as he struck a match along the leg of his corduroy breeches.

Delia never looked up from her work, and her thin, stooped shoulders sagged further.

"Ah ain't for no fuss t'night Sykes. Ah just come from taking sacrament at the church house."

He snorted scornfully. "Yeah, you just come from de church house on a Sunday night, but heah you is gone to work on them clothes. You ain't nothing but a hypocrite. One of them amen-corner Christians—sing, whoop, and shout, then come home and wash white folks' clothes on the Sabbath."

He stepped roughly upon the whitest pile of things, kicking them helter-skelter as he crossed the room. His wife gave a little scream of dismay, and quickly gathered them together again.

"Sykes, you quit grindin' dirt into these clothes! How can Ah git through by Sat'day if Ah don't start on Sunday?"

"Ah don't keer if you never git through. Anyhow, Ah done promised Gawd and a couple of other men, Ah ain't gointer have it in mah house. Don't gimme no lip neither, else Ah'll throw'em out and put mah fist up side yo' head to boot."

Delia's habitual meekness seemed to slip from her shoulders like a blown scarf. She was on her feet; her poor little body, her bare knuckly hands bravely defying the strapping hulk before her.

"Looka heah, Sykes, you done gone too fur. Ah been married to you fur fifteen years, and Ah been takin' in washin' fur fifteen years. Sweat, sweat, sweat! Work and sweat, cry and sweat, pray and sweat!"

"What's that got to do with me?" he asked brutally.

"What's it got to do with you, Sykes? Mah tub of suds is filled yo' belly with vittles more times than yo' hands is filled it. Mah sweat is done paid for this house and Ah reckon Ah kin keep on sweatin' in it."

She seized the iron skillet from the stove and struck a defensive pose, which act surprised him greatly, coming from her. It cowed him and he did not strike her as he usually did.

"Naw you won't," she panted, "that ole snaggle-toothed black woman you runnin' with ain't comin' heah to pile up on *mah* sweat and blood. You ain't paid for nothin' on this place, and Ah'm gointer stay right heah till Ah'm toted out foot foremost."

"Well, you better quit gittin' me riled up, else they'll be totin' you out sooner than you expect. Ah'm so tired of you Ah don't know whut to do. Gawd! How Ah hates skinny wimmen!"

A little awed by this new Delia, he sidled out of the door and slammed the back gate after him. He did not say where he had gone, but she knew too well. She knew very well that he would not return until nearly daybreak also. Her work over, she went on to bed but not to sleep at once. Things had come to a pretty pass!

She lay awake, gazing upon the debris that cluttered their matrimonial trail. Not an image left standing along the way. Anything like flowers had long ago been drowned in the salty stream that had been pressed from her heart. Her tears, her sweat, her blood. She had brought love to the union and he had brought a longing after the flesh. Two months after the wedding, he had given her the first brutal beating. She had the memory of his numerous trips to Orlando with all of his wages when he had returned to her penniless, even before the first year had passed. She was young and soft then, but now she thought of her knotty, muscled limbs, her harsh knuckly hands, and drew herself up into an unhappy little ball in the middle of the big feather bed. Too late now to hope for love, even if it were not Bertha it would be someone else. This case differed from the others only in that she was bolder than the others. Too late for everything except her little home. She had built it for her old days, and planted one by one the trees and flowers there. It was lovely to her, lovely.

Somehow, before sleep came, she found herself saying aloud: "Oh well, whatever goes over the Devil's back, is got to come under his belly. Sometime or ruther, Sykes, like everybody else, is gointer reap his sowing." After that she was able to build a spiritual earthworks against her husband. His shells could no longer reach her. AMEN. She went to sleep and slept until he announced his presence in bed by kicking her feet and rudely snatching the covers away.

"Gimme some kivah heah, an' git yo' damn foots over on yo' own side! Ah oughter mash you in yo' mouf fuh drawing dat skillet on me."

Delia went clear to the rail without answering him. A triumphant indifference to all that he was or did.

II

The week was as full of work for Delia as all other weeks, and Saturday found her behind her little pony, collecting and delivering clothes.

It was a hot, hot day near the end of July. The village men on Joe Clarke's porch even chewed cane listlessly. They did not hurl the cane-knots as usual. They let them dribble over the edge of the porch. Even conversation had collapsed under the heat.

"Heah come Delia Jones," Jim Merchant said, as the shaggy pony came 'round the bend of the road toward them. The rusty buckboard was heaped with baskets of crisp, clean laundry.

"Yep," Joe Lindsay agreed. "Hot or col', rain or shine, jes' ez reg'lar ez de weeks roll roun' Delia carries 'em an' fetches 'em on Sat'day."

"She better if she wanter eat," said Moss. "Syke Jones ain't wuth de shot an' powder hit would tek tuh kill 'em. Not to *huh* he ain't."

"He sho' ain't," Walter Thomas chimed in. "It's too bad, too, cause she wuz a right pretty li'l trick when he got huh. Ah'd uh mah'ied huh mahself if he hadnter beat me to it."

Delia nodded briefly at the men as she drove past.

"Too much knockin' will ruin *any* 'oman. He done beat huh 'nough tuh kill three women, let 'lone change they looks," said Elijah Moseley. "How Syke kin stommuck dat big black greasy Mogul he's layin' roun' wid, gits me. Ah swear dat eight-rock couldn't kiss a sardine can Ah done thowed out de back do' 'way las' yeah."

"Aw, she's fat, thass how come. He's allus been crazy 'bout fat women," put in Merchant. "He'd a' been tied up wid one long time ago if he could a' found one tuh have him. Did Ah tell yuh 'bout him come sidlin' roun' *mah* wife—bringin' her a basket uh peecans outa his yard fuh a present? Yessir, mah wife! She tol' him tuh take 'em right straight back home, 'cause Delia works so hard ovah dat washtub she reckon everything on de place taste lak sweat an' soapsuds. Ah jus' wisht Ah'd a' caught 'im 'roun' dere! Ah'd a' made his hips ketch on fiah down dat shell road."

"Ah know he done it, too. Ah sees 'im grinnin' at every 'oman dat passes," Walter Thomas said. "But even so, he useter eat some mighty big hunks uh humble pie tuh git dat li'l 'oman he got. She wuz ez prity ez a speckled pup! Dat wuz fifteen years ago. He useter be so skeered uh losin' huh, she could make him do some part of a husband's duty. Dey never wuz de same in de mind."

"There oughter be a law about him," said Lindsay. "He ain't fit tuh carry guts tuh a bear."

Clarke spoke for the first time. "Tain't no law on earth dat kin make a man be decent if it ain't in 'im. There's plenty men dat takes a wife lak dey do a joint uh sugar-cane. It's round, juicy an' sweet when dey gits it. But dey squeeze an' grind, squeeze an' grind an' wring tell dey wring every drop uh pleasure dat's in 'em out. When dey's satisfied dat dey is wrung dry, dey treats 'em jes' lak dey do a cane-chew. Dey throws 'em away. Dey knows whut dey is doin' while dey is at it, an' hates theirselves fuh it but they keeps on hangin' after huh tell she's empty. Den dey hates uh fuh bein' a cane-chew an' in de way."

"We oughter take Syke an' dat stray 'oman uh his'n down in Lake Howell swamp an' lay on de rawhide till they cain't say Lawd a' mussy. He allus wuz uh ovahbearin niggah, but since dat white 'oman from up north done teached 'im how to run a automobile, he done got too beggety to live—an' we oughter kill 'im," Old Man Anderson advised.

A grunt of approval went around the porch. But the heat was melting their civic virtue and Elijah Moseley began to bait Joe Clarke.

"Come on, Joe, git a melon outa dere an' slice it up for yo' customers. We'se all sufferin' wid de heat. De bear's done got *me!*"

"Thass right, Joe, a watermelon is jes' whut Ah needs tuh cure de eppizudicks," Walter Thomas joined forces with Moseley. "Come on dere, Joe. We all is steady customers an' you ain't set us up in a long time. Ah chooses dat long, bowlegged Floridy favorite."

"A god, an' be dough. You all gimme twenty cents and slice away," Clarke retorted. "Ah needs a col' slice m'self. Heah, everybody chip in. Ah'll lend y'all mah meat knife."

The money was all quickly subscribed and the huge melon brought forth. At that moment, Sykes and Bertha arrived. A determined silence fell on the porch and the melon was put away again.

Merchant snapped down the blade of his jackknife and moved toward the store door.

"Come on in Joe, an' gimme a slab uh sow belly an' uh pound uh coffee—almost fuhgot 'twas Sat'day. Got to git on home." Most of the men left also.

Just then Delia drove past on her way home, as Sykes was ordering magnificently for Bertha. It pleased him for Delia to see.

"Git whutsoever yo' heart desires, Honey. Wait a minute, Joe. Give huh two bottles uh strawberry soda-water, uh quart parched ground-peas, an' a block uh chewin' gum."

With all this they left the store, with Sykes reminding Bertha that this was his town and she could have it if she wanted it.

The men returned soon after they left, and held their watermelon feast.

"Where did Syke Jones git da 'oman from nohow?" Lindsay asked.

"Ovah Apopka. Guess dey musta been cleanin' out de town when she lef'. She don't look lak a thing but a hunk un liver wid hair on it."

"Well, she sho' kin squall," Dave Carter contributed. "When she gits ready tuh laff, she jes' opens huh mouf an' latches it back tuh de las' notch. No ole granpa alligator down in Lake Bell ain't got nothin' on huh."

III

Bertha had been in town three months now. Sykes was still paying her room-rent at Della Lewis'—the only house in town that would have taken her in. Sykes took her frequently to Winter Park to 'stomps'. He still assured her that he was the swellest man in the state.

"Sho' you kin have dat li'l ole house soon's Ah git dat 'oman outa dere. Everything b'longs tuh me an' you sho' kin have it. Ah sho' 'bominates uh skinny 'oman. Lawdy, you sho' is got one portly shape on you! You kin git *anything* you wants. Dis is *mah* town an' you sho' kin have it."

Delia's work-worn knees crawled over the earth in Gethsemane and up the rocks of Calvary many, many times during these months. She avoided the villagers and meeting places in her efforts to be blind and deaf. But Bertha nullified this to a degree, by coming to Delia's house to call Sykes out to her at the gate.

Delia and Sykes fought all the time now with no peaceful interludes. They slept and ate in silence. Two or three times Delia had attempted a timid friendliness, but she was repulsed each time. It was plain that the breaches must remain agape.

The sun had burned July to August. The heat streamed down like a million hot arrows, smiting all things living upon the earth. Grass withered, leaves browned, snakes went blind in shedding and men and dogs went mad. Dog days!

Delia came home one day and found Sykes there before her. She wondered, but started to go on into the house without speaking, even though he was standing in the kitchen door and she must enter stoop under his arm or ask him to move. He made no room for her. She noticed a soap box beside the steps, but paid no particular attention to it, knowing that he must have brought it there. As she was stooping to pass under his outstretched arm, he suddenly pushed her backward, laughingly.

"Look in de box dere Delia, Ah done brung yuh somethin'!"

She nearly fell upon the box in her stumbling, and when she saw what it held, she all but fainted outright.

"Syke! Syke, mah Gawd! You take dat rattlesnake 'way from heah! You *gottuh*. Oh Jesus, have mussy!"

"Ah ain't got tuh do nuthin' uh de kin'—fact is Ah ain't got tuh do nothin' but die. Tain't no use uh you puttin' on airs makin' out lak you skeered uh dat snake—he's gointer stay right heah tell he die. He wouldn't bite me cause Ah knows how tuh handle 'im. Nohow he wouldn't risk breakin' out his fangs 'gin *yo* skinny laigs."

"Naw, now Syke, don't keep dat thing' round tryin' tuh skeer me tuh death. You knows Ah'm even feared uh earth worms. Thass de biggest snake Ah evah did see. Kill 'im Syke, please."

"Doan ast me tuh do nothin' fuh yuh. Goin' 'round tryin' tuh be so damn asterperious. Naw, Ah ain't gonna kill it. Ah think uh damn sight mo' uh him dan you! Dat's a nice snake an' anybody doan lak 'im kin jes' hit de grit."

The village soon heard that Sykes had the snake, and came to see and ask questions.

"How de hen-fire did you ketch dat six-foot rattler, Syke?" Thomas asked.

"He's full uh frogs so he cain't hardly move, thass how Ah eased up on 'm. But Ah'm a snake charmer an' knows how tuh handle 'em. Shux, dat ain't nothin'. Ah could ketch one eve'y day if Ah so wanted tuh."

"Whut he needs is a heavy hick'ry club leaned real heavy on his head. Dat's de bes' way tuh charm a rattlesnake."

"Naw, Walt, y'all jes' don't understand dese diamon' backs lak Ah do," said Sykes in a superior tone of voice.

The village agreed with Walter, but the snake stayed on. His box remained by the kitchen door with its screen wire covering. Two or three days later it had digested its meal of frogs and literally came to life. It rattled at every movement in the kitchen or the yard. One day as Delia came down the kitchen steps she saw his chalky-white fangs curved like scimitars hung in the wire meshes. This time she did not run away with averted eyes as usual. She stood for a long time in the doorway in a red fury that grew bloodier for every second that she regarded the creature that was her torment.

That night she broached the subject as soon as Sykes sat down to the table.

"Syke, Ah wants you tuh take dat snake 'way fum heah. You done starved me an' Ah put up widcher, you done beat me an Ah took dat, but you done kilt all mah insides bringin' dat varmint heah."

Sykes poured out a saucer full of coffee and drank it deliberately before he answered her.

"A whole lot Ah keer 'bout how you feels inside uh out. Dat snake ain't goin' no damn wheah till Ah gits ready fuh 'im tuh go. So fur as beatin' is concerned, yuh ain't took near all dat you gointer take ef yuh stay 'round *me*."

Delia pushed back her plate and got up from the table. "Ah hates you, Sykes," she said calmly. "Ah hates you tuh de same degree dat Ah useter love yuh. Ah done took an' took till mah belly is full up tuh mah neck. Dat's de reason Ah got mah letter fum de church an' moved mah membership tuh Woodbridge—so Ah don't haftuh take no sacrament wid yuh. Ah don't wantuh see yuh' round me atall. Lay 'round wid dat 'oman all yuh wants tuh, but gwan 'way fum me an' mah house. Ah hates yuh lak uh suck-egg dog."

Sykes almost let the huge wad of corn bread and collard greens he was chewing fall out of his mouth in amazement. He had a hard time whipping himself up to the proper fury to try to answer Delia.

"Well, Ah'm glad you does hate me. Ah'm sho' tiahed uh you hangin' ontuh me. Ah don't want yuh. Look at yuh stringey ole neck! Yo' rawbony laigs an' arms is enough tuh cut uh man tuh death. You looks jes' lak de devvul's doll-baby tuh *me*. You cain't hate me no worse dan Ah hates you. Ah been hatin' *you* fuh years."

"Yo' ole black hide don't look lak nothin' tuh me, but uh passle uh wrinkled up rubber, wid yo' big ole yeahs flappin' on each side lak uh paih uh buzzard wings. Don't think Ah'm gointuh be run 'way fum mah house neither. Ah'm goin' tuh de white folks 'bout *you*, mah young man, de very nex' time you lay yo' han's on me. Mah cup is done run ovah." Delia said this with no signs of fear and Sykes departed from the house, threatening her, but made not the slightest move to carry out any of them.

That night he did not return at all, and the next day being Sunday, Delia was glad she did not have to quarrel before she hitched up her pony and drove the four miles to Woodbridge.

She stayed to the night service—'love feast'—which was very warm and full of spirit. In the emotional winds her domestic trials were borne far and wide so that she sang as she drove homeward,

> *Jurden water, black an' col*
> *Chills de body, not de soul*
> *An' Ah wantah cross Jurden in uh calm time.*

She came from the barn to the kitchen door and stopped.

"Whut's de mattah, ol' Satan, you ain't kickin' up yo' racket?" She addressed the snake's box. Complete silence. She went on into the house with a new hope in its birth struggles. Perhaps her threat to go to the white folks had frightened Sykes! Perhaps he was sorry! Fifteen years of misery and suppression had brought Delia to the place where she would hope *anything* that looked towards a way over or through her wall of inhibitions.

She felt in the match-safe behind the stove at once for a match. There was only one there.

"Dat niggah wouldn't fetch nothin' heah tuh save his rotten neck, but he kin run thew whut Ah brings quick enough. Now he done toted off nigh on tuh haff uh box uh matches. He done had dat 'oman heah in mah house, too."

Nobody but a woman could tell how she knew this even before she struck the match. But she did and it put her into a new fury.

Presently she brought in the tubs to put the white things to soak. This time she decided she need not bring the hamper out of the bedroom; she would go in there and do the sorting. She picked up the pot-bellied lamp and went in. The room was small and the hamper stood hard by the foot of the white iron bed. She could sit and reach through the bedposts—resting as she worked.

"*Ah wantah cross Jurden in uh calm time.*" She was singing again. The mood of the 'love feast' had returned. She threw back the lid of the basket almost gaily. Then, moved by both horror and terror, she sprang back toward the door. *There lay the snake in the basket!* He moved sluggishly at first, but even as she turned round and round, jumped up and down in an insanity of fear, he began to stir vigorously. She saw him pouring his awful beauty from the basket upon the bed, then she seized the lamp and ran as fast as she could to the kitchen. The wind from the open door blew out the light and the darkness added to her terror. She sped to the darkness of the yard, slamming the door after her before she thought to set down the lamp. She did not feel safe even on the ground, so she climbed up in the hay barn.

There for an hour or more she lay sprawled upon the hay a gibbering wreck.

Finally she grew quiet, and after that came coherent thought. With this stalked through her a cold, bloody rage. Hours of this. A period of introspection, a space of retrospection, then a mixture of both. Out of this an awful calm.

"Well, Ah done de bes' An could. If things ain't right, Gawd knows tain't mah fault."

She went to sleep—a twitch sleep—and woke up to a faint gray sky. There was a loud hollow sound below. She peered out. Sykes was at the wood-pile, demolishing a wire-covered box.

He hurried to the kitchen door, but hung outside there some minutes before he entered, and stood some minutes more inside before he closed it after him.

The gray in the sky was spreading. Delia descended without fear now, and crouched beneath the low bedroom window. The drawn shade shut out the dawn, shut in the night. But the thin walls held back no sound.

"Dat ol' scratch is woke up now!" She mused at the tremendous whirr inside, which every woodsman knows, is one of the sound illusions. The rattler is a ventriloquist. His whirr sounds to the right, to the left, straight ahead, behind, close under foot—everywhere but where it is. Woe to him who guesses wrong unless he is prepared to hold up his end of the argument! Sometimes he strikes without rattling at all.

Inside, Sykes heard nothing until he knocked a pot lid off the stove while trying to reach the match-safe in the dark. He had emptied his pockets at Bertha's.

The snake seemd to wake up under the stove and Sykes made a quick leap into the bedroom. In spite of the gin he had had, his head was clearing now.

"Mah Gawd!" he chattered, "ef Ah could on'y strack uh light!"

The rattling ceased for a moment as he stood paralyzed. He waited. It seemed that the snake waited also.

"Oh, fuh de light! Ah thought he'd be too sick"—Sykes was muttering to himself when the whirr began again, closer, right underfoot this time. Long before this, Sykes' ability to think had been flattened down to primitive instinct and he leaped—onto the bed.

Outside Delia heard a cry that might have come from a maddened chimpanzee, a stricken gorilla. All the terror, all the horror, all the rage that man possibly could express, without a recognizable human sound.

A tremendous stir inside there, another series of animal screams, the intermittent whirr of the reptile. The shade torn violently down from the window, letting in the red dawn, a huge brown hand seizing the window stick, great dull blows upon the wooden floor punctuating the gibberish of sound long after the rattle of the snake had abruptly subsided. All this Delia could see and hear from her place beneath the window, and it made her ill. She crept over to the four-o'clocks and stretched herself on the cool earth to recover.

She lay there. "Delia, Delia!" She could hear Sykes calling in a most despairing tone as one who expected no answer. The sun crept on up, and he called. Delia could not move—her legs had gone flabby. She never moved, he called, and the sun kept rising.

"Mah Gawd!" She heard him moan, "Mah Gawd fum Heben!" She heard him stumbling about and got up from her flower-bed. The sun was growing warm. As she approached the door she heard him call out hopefully, "Delia, is dat you Ah heah?"

She saw him on his hands and knees as soon as she reached the door. He crept an inch or two toward her—all that he was able, and she saw his horribly swollen neck and his one open eye shining with hope. A surge of pity too strong to support bore her away from that eye that must, could not, fail to see the tubs. He would see the lamp. Orlando with its doctors was too far. She could scarcely reach the chinaberry tree, where she waited in the growing heat while inside she knew the cold river was creeping up and up to extinguish that eye which must know by now that she knew.

1926

Sterling A. Brown
(1901–1989)

Ma Rainey

I

When Ma Rainey
Comes to town,
Folks from anyplace
Miles aroun',
From Cape Girardeau,   5
Poplar Bluff,
Flocks in to hear
Ma do her stuff;
Comes flivverin' in,
Or ridin' mules,   10
Or packed in trains,
Picknickin' fools. . . .
That's what it's like,
Fo' miles on down,
To New Orleans delta   15
An' Mobile town,
When Ma hits
Anywheres aroun'.

II

Dey comes to hear Ma Rainey from de little river settlements,
From blackbottom cornrows and from lumber camps;   20
Dey stumble in de hall, jes a-laughin' an' a-cacklin',
Cheerin' lak roarin' water, lak wind in river swamps.

An' some jokers keeps deir laughs a-goin' in de crowded aisles,
An' some folks sits dere waitin' wid deir aches an' miseries,
Till Ma comes out before dem, a-smilin' gold-toofed smiles   25
An' Long Boy ripples minors on de black an' yellow keys.

III

O Ma Rainey,
Sing yo' song;
Now you's back
Whah you belong,   30
Git way inside us,
Keep us strong. . . .

O Ma Rainey,
Li'l an' low;
Sing us 'bout de hard luck   35
Roun' our do';
Sing us 'bout de lonesome road
We mus' go. . . .

IV

I talked to a fellow, an' the fellow say,
"She jes' catch hold of us, somekindaway.   40
She sang Backwater Blues one day:

    'It rained fo' days an' de skies was dark as night,
    Trouble taken place in de lowlands at night.

    'Thundered an' lightened an' the storm begin to roll
    Thousan's of people ain't got no place to go.   45

    'Den I went an' stood upon some high ol' lonesome hill,
    An' looked down on the place where I used to live.

An' den de folks, dey natchally bowed dey heads an' cried,
Bowed dey heavy heads, shet dey moufs up tight an' cried,
An' Ma lef' de stage, an' followed some de folks outside."   50

Dere wasn't much more de fellow say:
She jes' gits hold of us dataway.
1932

Slim in Hell

I

Slim Greer went to heaven;
    St. Peter said, "Slim,
You been a right good boy."
    An' he winked at him.
        "You been a travelin' rascal   5
        In yo' day.
        You kin roam once mo';
        Den you comes to stay.

"Put dese wings on yo' shoulders,
    An' save yo' feet."   10
Slim grin, and he speak up
    "Thankye, Pete."

        Den Peter say, "Go
        To Hell an' see,

All dat is doing, and　　　　　　　　15
　　Report to me.

"Be sure to remember
　　How everything go."
Slim say, "I be seein' yuh
　　On de late watch, bo."　　　　　　20

　　Slim got to cavortin',
　　　　Swell as you choose,
　　Like Lindy in de "Spirit
　　　　Of St. Louis Blues!"

He flew an' he flew,　　　　　　　　25
　　Till at last he hit
A hangar wid de sign readin'
　　DIS IS IT.

　　Den he parked his wings,
　　　　An' strolled aroun'　　　　　30
　　Gettin' used to his feet
　　　　On de solid ground.

II

Big bloodhound came aroarin'
　　Like Niagry Falls,
Sicked on by white devils　　　　　35
　　In overhalls.

Now Slim warn't scared,
　　Cross my heart, it's a fac',
An' de dog went on a bayin'
　　Some po' devil's track.　　　　　40

　　Den Slim saw a mansion
　　　　An' walked right in;
　　De Devil looked up
　　　　Wid a sickly grin.

"Suttinly didn't look　　　　　　　45
　　Fo' you, Mr. Greer,
How it happen you comes
　　To visit here?"

　　Slim say—"Oh, jes' thought
　　　　I'd drap by a spell."　　　　50
　　"Feel at home, seh, an' here's
　　　　De keys to Hell."

Den he took Slim around
  An' showed him people
Raisin' hell as high as
  De First Church Steeple.

    Lots of folks fightin'
      At de roulette wheel,
    Like old Rampart Street,
      Or leastwise Beale.

Showed him bawdy houses
  An' cabarets,
Slim thought of New Orleans
  An' Memphis days.

    Each devil was busy
      Wid a devilish broad,
    An' Slim cried, "Lawdy,
      Lawd, Lawd, Lawd."

Took him in a room
  Where Slim see
De preacher wid a brownskin
  On each knee.

    Showed him giant stills,
      Going everywhere
    Wid a passel of devils,
      Stretched dead drunk there.

Den he took him to de furnace
  Dat some devils was firing,
Hot as hell, an' Slim start
  A mean presspirin';

    White devils wid pitchforks
      Threw black devils on,
    Slim thought he'd better
      Be gittin' along.

An' he say—"Dis makes
  Me think of home—
Vicksburg, Little Rock, Jackson,
  Waco, and Rome."

    Den de devil gave Slim
      De big Ha-Ha;
    An' turned into a cracker,
      Wid a sheriff's star.

Slim ran fo' his wings,
  Lit out from de groun'
Hauled it back to St. Peter,
  Safety boun'.   95

III

St. Peter said, "Well,
  You got back quick.
How's de devil? An' what's
  His latest trick?"   100

An' Slim say, "Peter,
  I really cain't tell,
De place was Dixie
  Dat I took for Hell."

Then Peter say, "You must   105
  Be crazy, I vow,
Where'n hell dja think Hell *was*,
  Anyhow?

"Git on back to de yearth,
  Cause I got de fear,   110
You'se a leetle too dumb,
  Fo' to stay up here . . ."
    1932

Remembering Nat Turner

(For R. C. L.)[1]

We saw a bloody sunset over Courtland, once Jerusalem,
As we followed the trail that old Nat took
When he came out of Cross Keys down upon Jerusalem,
In his angry stab for freedom a hundred years ago.
The land was quiet, and the mist was rising,   5
Out of the woods and the Nottaway swamp,
Over Southampton the still night fell,
As we rode down to Cross Keys where the march began.

When we got to Cross Keys, they could tell us little of him,
The Negroes had only the faintest recollections: 10

---

[1] Rayford C. Logan, the eminent historian,
whose teaching at Howard University over-
lapped with Brown's.

"I ain't been here so long, I come from up roun' Newsome;
Yassah, a town a few miles up de road,
The old folks who coulda told you is all dead an' gone.
I heard something, sometime; I doan jis remember what.
'Pears lak I heard that name somewheres or other.   15
So he fought to be free. Well. You doan say."

An old white woman recalled exactly
How Nat crept down the steps, axe in his hand,
After murdering a woman and child in bed,
"Right in this here house at the head of these stairs"   20
(In a house built long after Nat was dead).
She pointed to a brick store where Nat was captured,
(Nat was taken in the swamp, three miles away)
With his men around him, shooting from the windows
(She was thinking of Harpers Ferry and old John Brown).   25
She cackled as she told how they riddled Nat with bullets
(Nat was tried and hanged at Courtland, ten miles away).
She wanted to know why folks would come miles
Just to ask about an old nigger fool.
        "Ain't no slavery no more, things is going all right, 30
Pervided thar's a good goober market this year.
We had a sign post here with printing on it,
But it rotted in the hole, and thar it lays,
And the nigger tenants split the marker for kindling.
Things is all right, now, ain't no trouble with the niggers   35
Why they make this big to-do over Nat?"

As we drove from Cross Keys back to Courtland,
Along the way that Nat came down upon Jerusalem,
A watery moon was high in the cloud-filled heavens,
The same moon he dreaded a hundred years ago.   40
The tree they hanged Nat on is long gone to ashes,
The trees he dodged behind have rotted in the swamps.

The bus for Miami and the trucks boomed by,
And touring cars, their heavy tires snarling on the pavement.
Frogs piped in the marshes, and a hound bayed long,   45
And yellow lights glowed from the cabin windows.

As we came back the way that Nat led his army,
Down from Cross Keys, down to Jerusalem,
We wondered if his troubled spirit still roamed the Nottaway,
Or if it fled with the cock-crow at daylight,   50
Or lay at peace with the bones in Jerusalem,
Its restlessness stifled by Southampton clay.

We remembered the poster rotted through and falling,
The marker split for kindling a kitchen fire.
1939

Countee Cullen
(1903–1946)

Yet Do I Marvel

I doubt not God is good, well-meaning, kind,
And did He stoop to quibble could tell why
The little buried mole continues blind,
Why flesh that mirrors Him must some day die,
Make plain the reason tortured Tantalus[1]   5
Is baited by the fickle fruit, declare
If merely brute caprice dooms Sisyphus[2]
To struggle up a never-ending stair.
Inscrutable His ways are, and immune
To catechism by a mind too strewn   10
With petty cares to slightly understand
What awful brain compels His awful hand.
Yet do I marvel at this curious thing:
To make a poet black, and bid him sing!
1947

Incident

(For Eric Walrond)

Once riding in old Baltimore,
    Heart-filled, head-filled with glee,
I saw a Baltimorean
    Keep looking straight at me.

Now I was eight and very small,   5
    And he was no whit bigger,
And so I smiled, but he poked out
    His tongue, and called me, "Nigger."
I saw the whole of Baltimore
    From May until December;   10
Of all the things that happened there
    That's all that I remember.
1947

---

[1] Tantalus was tortured in Hades by hunger and thirst; when he tried to reach fruit above him, it drew away.

[2] Sisyphus, in Hades, was doomed to continually push a rock up a hill and then see it roll to the bottom again.

Heritage

(For Harold Jackman)

What is Africa to me:
Copper sun or scarlet sea,
Jungle star or jungle track,
Strong bronzed men, or regal black
Women from whose loins I sprang   5
When the birds of Eden sang?
One three centuries removed
From the scenes his fathers loved,
Spicy grove, cinnamon tree,
What is Africa to me?   10

So I lie, who all day long
Want no sound except the song
Sung by wild barbaric birds
Goading massive jungle herds,
Juggernauts of flesh that pass   15
Trampling tall defiant grass
Where young forest lovers lie,
Plighting troth beneath the sky.
So I lie, who always hear,
Though I cram against my ear   20
Both my thumbs, and keep them there,
Great drums throbbing through the air.
So I lie, whose fount of pride,
Dear distress, and joy allied,
Is my somber flesh and skin,   25
With the dark blood dammed within
Like great pulsing tides of wine
That, I fear, must burst the fine
Channels of the chafing net
Where they surge and foam and fret.   30

Africa? A book one thumbs
Listlessly, till slumber comes.
Unremembered are her bats
Circling through the night, her cats
Crouching in the river reeds,   35
Stalking gentle flesh that feeds
By the river brink; no more
Does the bugle-throated roar
Cry that monarch claws have leapt
From the scabbards where they slept.   40
Silver snakes that once a year
Doff the lovely coats you wear,

Seek no covert in your fear
Lest a mortal eye should see;
What's your nakedness to me? 45
Here no leprous flowers rear
Fierce corollas[1] in the air;
Here no bodies sleek and wet,
Dripping mingled rain and sweat,
Tread the savage measures of 50
Jungle boys and girls in love.
What is last year's snow[2] to me,
Last year's anything? The tree
Budding yearly must forget
How its past arose or set— 55
Bough and blossom, flower, fruit,
Even what shy bird with mute
Wonder at her travail there,
Meekly labored in its hair.
One three centuries removed 60
From the scenes his fathers loved,
Spicy grove, cinnamon tree,
What is Africa to me?

So I lie, who find no peace
Night or day, no slight release 65
From the unremittent beat
Made by cruel padded feet
Walking through my body's street.
Up and down they go, and back,
Treading out a jungle track. 70
So I lie, who never quite
Safely sleep from rain at night—
I can never rest at all
When the rain begins to fall;
Like a soul gone mad with pain 75
I must match its weird refrain;
Ever must I twist and squirm,
Writhing like a baited worm,
While its primal measures drip
Through my body, crying, "Strip! 80
Doff this new exuberance.
Come and dance the Lover's Dance!"
In an old remembered way
Rain works on me night and day.

---

[1] Crowns of petals.
[2] An echo of the French poet François Villon (1431–1463?), whose famous refrain from "La Ballade des Dames du Temps Jadis" is "Où sont les neiges d'antan?"

Quaint, outlandish heathen gods   85
Black men fashion out of rods,
Clay, and brittle bits of stone,
In a likeness like their own,
My conversion came high-priced;
I belong to Jesus Christ,   90
Preacher of humility;
Heathen gods are naught to me.

Father, Son, and Holy Ghost,
So I make an idle boast;
Jesus of the twice-turned cheek,   95
Lamb of God, although I speak
With my mouth thus, in my heart
Do I play a double part.
Ever at Thy glowing altar
Must my heart grow sick and falter,   100
Wishing He I served were black,
Thinking then it would not lack
Precedent of pain to guide it,
Let who would or might deride it;
Surely then this flesh would know   105
Yours had borne a kindred woe.
Lord, I fashion dark gods, too,
Daring even to give You
Dark despairing features where,
Crowned with dark rebellious hair,   110
Patience wavers just so much as
Mortal grief compels, while touches
Quick and hot, of anger, rise
To smitten cheek and weary eyes.
Lord, forgive me if my need   115
Sometimes shapes a human creed.
All day long and all night through,
One thing only must I do:
Quench my pride and cool my blood,
Lest I perish in the flood.   120
Lest a hidden ember set
Timber that I thought was wet
Burning like the dryest flax,
Melting like the merest wax,
Lest the grave restore its dead.   125
Not yet has my heart or head
In the least way realized
They and I are civilized.
1947

Helene Johnson
(1907–?)

Sonnet to a Negro in Harlem

You are disdainful and magnificent—
Your perfect body and your pompous gait,
Your dark eyes flashing solemnly with hate,
Small wonder that you are incompetent
To imitate those whom you so despise—   5
Your shoulders towering high above the throng,
Your head thrown back in rich, barbaric song,
Palm trees and mangoes stretched before your eyes.
Let others toil and sweat for labor's sake
And wring from grasping hands their meed of gold.   10
Why urge ahead your supercilious feet?
Scorn will efface each footprint that you make.
I love your laughter arrogant and bold.
You are too splendid for this city street.
1923

What Do I Care for Morning

What do I care for morning,
For a shivering aspen tree,
For sunflowers and sumac
Opening greedily?
What do I care for morning,   5
For the glare of the rising sun,
For a sparrow's noisy prating,
For another day begun?
Give me the beauty of evening,
The cool consummation of night,   10

And the moon like a love-sick lady,
Listless and wan and white.
Give me a little valley,
Huddled beside a hill,
Like a monk in a monastery,   15
Safe and contented and still.
Give me the white road glistening,
A strand of the pale moon's hair,

And the tall hemlocks towering,
Dark as the moon is fair.   20
Oh what do I care for morning,
Naked and newly born—
Night is here, yielding and tender—
What do I care for dawn!
1927

Remember Not

Remember not the promises we made
In this same garden many moons ago.
You must forget them. I would have it so
Old vows are like old flowers as they fade
And vaguely vanish in a feeble death.   5
There is no reason why your hands should clutch
At pretty yesterdays. There is not much
Of beauty in me now. And though my breath
Is quick, my body sentient, my heart
Attuned to romance as before, you must   10
Not, through mistaken chivalry, pretend
To love me still. There is no mortal art
Can overcome Time's deep, corroding rust.
Let Love's beginning expiate Love's end.
1931

Langston Hughes, *The Big Sea*

from When the Negro was in Vogue

The 1920's were the years of Manhattan's black Renaissance. It began with *Shuffle Along, Running Wild,* and the Charleston. Perhaps some people would say even with *The Emperor Jones,* Charles Gilpin, and the tom-toms at the Provincetown. But certainly it was the musical revue, *Shuffle Along,* that gave a scintillating send-off to that Negro vogue in Manhattan, which reached its peak just before the crash of 1929, the crash that sent Negroes, white folks, and all rolling down the hill toward the Works Progress Administration.

    Shuffle Along was a honey of a show. Swift, bright, funny, rollicking, and gay, with a dozen danceable, singable tunes. Besides, look who were in it: The now famous choir director, Hall Johnson, and the composer, William Grant Still, were a part of the orchestra. Eubie Blake and Noble Sissle wrote the music and played and acted in the show. Miller and Lyles were the comics. Florence Mills skyrocketed to fame in the second act. Trixie Smith sang "He May Be Your Man But He Comes to See Me Sometimes." And Caterina Jarboro, now a European prima donna, and the internationally celebrated Josephine Baker were merely in the chorus. Everybody was in the audience—including me. People came back to see it innumerable times. It was always packed.

To see *Shuffle Along* was the main reason I wanted to go to Columbia. When I saw it, I was thrilled and delighted. From then on I was in the gallery of the Cort Theatre every time I got a chance. That year, too, I saw Katharine Cornell in *A Bill of Divorcement*, Margaret Wycherly in *The Verge*, Maugham's *The Circle* with Mrs. Leslie Carter, and the Theatre Guild production of Kaiser's *From Morn Till Midnight*. But I remember *Shuffle Along* best of all. It gave just the proper push—a pre-Charleston kick—to that Negro vogue of the 20's, that spread to books, African sculpture, music, and dancing.

Put down the 1920's for the rise of Roland Hayes, who packed Carnegie Hall, the rise of Paul Robeson in New York and London, of Florence Mills over two continents, of Rose McClendon in Broadway parts that never measured up to her, the booming voice of Bessie Smith and the low moan of Clara on thousands of records, and the rise of the grand comedienne of song, Ethel Waters, singing: "Charlie's elected now! He's in right for sure!" Put down the 1920's for Louis Armstrong and Gladys Bentley and Josephine Baker.

White people began to come to Harlem in droves. For several years they packed the expensive Cotton Club on Lenox Avenue. But I was never there, because the Cotton Club was a Jim Crow club for gangsters and monied whites. They were not cordial to Negro patronage, unless you were a celebrity like Bojangles. So Harlem Negroes did not like the Cotton Club and never appreciated its Jim Crow policy in the very heart of their dark community. Nor did ordinary Negroes like the growing influx of whites toward Harlem after sundown, flooding the little cabarets and bars where formerly only colored people laughed and sang, and where now the strangers were given the best ringside tables to sit and stare at the Negro customers—like amusing animals in a zoo.

The Negroes said: "We can't go downtown and sit and stare at you in your clubs. You won't even let us in your clubs." But they didn't say it out loud—for Negroes are practically never rude to white people. So thousands of whites came to Harlem night after night, thinking the Negroes loved to have them there, and firmly believing that all Harlemites left their houses at sundown to sing and dance in cabarets, because most of the whites saw nothing but the cabarets, not the houses.

Some of the owners of Harlem clubs, delighted at the flood of white patronage, made the grievous error of barring their own race, after the manner of the famous Cotton Club. But most of these quickly lost business and folded up, because they failed to realize that a large part of the Harlem attraction for downtown New Yorkers lay in simply watching the colored customers amuse themselves. And the smaller clubs, of course, had no big floor shows or a name band like the Cotton Club, where Duke Ellington usually held forth, so, without black patronage, they were not amusing at all.

Some of the small clubs, however, had people like Gladys Bentley, who was something worth discovering in those days, before she got famous, acquired an accompanist, specially written material, and conscious vulgarity. But for two or three amazing years, Miss Bentley sat, and played a big piano all night long, literally all night, without stopping—singing songs like "The St. James Infirmary," from ten in the evening until dawn, with scarcely a break between the notes, sliding from one song to another, with a powerful and continuous underbeat of jungle rhythm. Miss Bentley was an amazing exhibition of musical energy—a large, dark, masculine lady, whose feet pounded the floor while her fingers pounded the keyboard—a perfect piece of African sculpture, animated by her own rhythm.

But when the place where she played became too well known, she began to sing with an accompanist, became a star, moved to a larger place, then downtown, and is now in Hollywood. The old magic of the woman and the piano and the night and the rhythm being one is gone. But everything goes, one way or another. The '20's are gone and lots of fine things in Harlem night life have disappeared like snow in the sun—since it became utterly commercial, planned for the downtown tourist trade, and therefore dull. . . .

All of us know that the gay and sparkling life of the so-called Negro Renaissance of the '20's was not so gay and sparkling beneath the surface as it looked. Carl Van Vechten, in the character of Byron in *Nigger Heaven,* captured some of the bitterness and frustration of literary Harlem that Wallace Thurman later so effectively poured into his *Infants of the Spring*—the only novel by a Negro about that fantastic period when Harlem was in vogue. . . .

Then it was that house-rent parties began to flourish—and not always to raise the rent either. But, as often as not, to have a get-together of one's own, where you could do the black-bottom with no stranger behind you trying to do it, too. Non-theatrical, non-intellectual Harlem was an unwilling victim of its own vogue. It didn't like to be stared at by white folks. But perhaps the downtowners never knew this—for the cabaret owners, the entertainers, and the speakeasy proprietors treated them fine—as long as they paid.

The Saturday night rent parties that I attended were often more amusing than any night club, in small apartments where God knows who lived—because the guests seldom did—but where the piano would often be augmented by a guitar, or an odd cornet, or somebody with a pair of drums walking in off the street. And where awful bootleg whiskey and good fried fish or steaming chitterling were sold at very low prices. And the dancing and singing and impromptu entertaining went on until dawn came in at the windows.

These parties, often termed whist parties or dances, were usually announced by brightly colored cards stuck in the grille of apartment house elevators. Some of the cards were highly entertaining in themselves:

We got yellow girls, we've got black and tan
Will you have a good time? - YEAH MAN !

A Social Whist Party

—GIVEN BY—
MARY WINSTON
147 West 145th Street   Apt. 5

SATURDAY EVE., MARCH 19th, 1932

GOOD MUSIC   **REFRESHMENTS**

Railroad Men's Ball

AT CANDY'S PLACE

FRIDAY, SATURDAY & SUNDAY,

April 29-30, May 1, 1927

Black Wax, says change your mind and say they
do and he will give you a hearing, while MEAT
HOUSE SLIM, laying in the bin
killing all good men.

L. A. Vaugh, *President*

OH BOY — OH JOY

The Eleven Brown Skins

of the

Evening Shadow Social Club

are giving their

Second Annual St. Valentine Dance

Saturday evening, Feb. 18th, 1928

At 129 West 136th Street, New York City

Good Music — Refreshments Served

Subscription — 25 Cents

---

*Some wear pajamas, some wear pants, what does it matter
just so you can dance, at*

A Social Whist Party

GIVEN BY

Mr. & Mrs. Brown

AT 258 w. 115th street, APT. 9

SATURDAY EVE., SEPT. 14, 1929

The music is sweet and everything good to eat!

Almost every Saturday night when I was in Harlem I went to a house-rent party. I wrote lots of poems about house-rent parties, and ate thereat many a fried fish and pig's foot—with liquid refreshments on the side. I met ladies' maids and truck drivers, laundry workers and shoe shine boys, seamstresses and porters. I can still hear their laughter in my ears, hear the soft slow music, and feel the floor shaking as the dancers danced.

from Harlem Literati

The summer of 1926, I lived in a rooming house on 137th Street, where Wallace Thurman and Harcourt Tynes also lived. Thurman was then managing editor of the *Messenger,* a Negro magazine that had a curious career. It began by being very radical, racial, and socialistic, just after the war. I believe it received a grant from the Garland Fund in its early days. Then it later became a kind of Negro society magazine and a plugger for Negro business, with photographs of prominent colored ladies and their nice homes in it. A. Phillip Randolph, now President of the Brotherhood of Sleeping Car Porters, Chandler Owen, and George S. Schuyler were connected with it. Schuyler's editorials, à la Mencken, were the most interesting things in the magazine, verbal brickbats that said sometimes one thing, sometimes another, but always vigorously. I asked Thurman what kind of magazine the *Messenger* was, and he said it reflected the policy of whoever paid off best at the time.

Anyway, the *Messenger* bought my first short stories. They paid me ten dollars a story. Wallace Thurman wrote me that they were very bad stories, but better than any others they could find, so he published them. . . .

During the summer of 1926, Wallace Thurman, Zora Neale Hurston, Aaron Douglas, John P. Davis, Bruce Nugent, Gwendolyn Bennett, and I decided to publish "a Negro quarterly of the arts" to be called *Fire*—the idea being that it would burn up a lot of the old, dead conventional Negro-white ideas of the past, *épater le bourgeois* into a realization of the existence of the younger Negro writers and artists, and provide us with an outlet for publication not available in the limited pages of the small Negro magazines then existing, the *Crisis, Opportunity,* and the *Messenger*—the first two being house organs of inter-racial organizations, and the latter being God knows what. . . .

None of the older Negro intellectuals would have anything to do with *Fire*. Dr. DuBois in the *Crisis* roasted it. The Negro press called it all sorts of bad names, largely because of a green and purple story by Bruce Nugent, in the Oscar Wilde tradition, which we had included. Rean Graves, the critic for the *Baltimore Afro-American,* began his review by saying: "I have just tossed the first issue of *Fire* into the fire." Commenting upon various of our contributors, he said: "Aaron Douglas who, in spite of himself and the meaningless grotesqueness of his creations, has gained a reputation as an artist, is permitted to spoil three perfectly good pages and a cover with his pen and ink hudge pudge. Countee Cullen has written a beautiful poem in his 'From a Dark Tower,' but tries his best to obscure the thought in superfluous sentences. Langston Hughes displays his usual ability to say nothing in many words."

So *Fire* had plenty of cold water thrown on it by the colored critics. The white critics (except for an excellent editorial in the *Bookman* for November, 1926) scarcely noticed it at all. We had no way of getting it distributed to bookstands or news stands. Bruce Nugent took it around New York on foot and some of the Greenwich Village bookshops put it on display, and sold it for us. But then Bruce, who had no job, would collect the money and, on account of salary, eat it up before he got back to Harlem.

Finally, irony of ironies, several hundred copies of *Fire* were stored in the basement of an apartment where an actual fire occurred and the bulk of the whole issue was burned up. Even after that Thurman had to go on paying the printer.

Now *Fire* is a collector's item, and very difficult to get, being mostly ashes. . . .

Harlem was like a great magnet for the Negro intellectual, pulling him from everywhere. Or perhaps the magnet was New York—but once in New York, he had to live in Harlem, for rooms were hardly to be found elsewhere unless one could pass for white or Mexican or Eurasian and perhaps live in the Village—which always seemed to me a very arty locale, in spite of the many real artists and writers who lived there. Only a few of the New Negroes lived in the Village, Harlem being their real stamping ground.

The wittiest of these New Negroes of Harlem, whose tongue was flavored with the sharpest and saltiest humor, was Rudolph Fisher, whose stories appeared in the *Atlantic Monthly*. His novel, *Walls of Jericho,* captures but slightly the raciness of his own conversation. He was a young medical doctor and X-ray specialist, who always frightened me a little, because he could think of the most incisively clever things to say—and I could never think of anything to answer. He and Alain Locke together were great for intellectual wise-cracking. The two would fling big and witty words about with such swift and punning innuendo that an ordinary mortal just sat and looked wary for fear of being caught in a net of witticisms beyond his cultural ken. I used to wish I could talk like Rudolph Fisher. Besides being a good writer, he was an excellent singer, and had sung with Paul Robeson during their college days. But I guess Fisher was too brilliant and too talented to stay long on this earth. During the same week, in December, 1934, he and Wallace Thurman both died.

Thurman died of tuberculosis in the charity ward at Bellevue Hospital, having just flown back to New York from Hollywood.

1940

E. E. Cummings
1894–1962

Cummings belongs to the part of the modernist movement that wanted to experiment with the visual appearance of the printed page. Both Guillaume Apollinaire and Stéphane Mallarmé in France had scattered typography over the page, and Cummings adopted their inventions (which would later engender "concrete poetry") to his own purposes. Numbers and letters fall like confetti down his pages, giving his *Collected Poems* the look of a volume printed by a tipsy typesetter. Cummings's typographical experiments arose in part from his visual gifts. He was a painter all his life, and his sophisticated and humorous paintings and drawings are still regularly shown in museums. But his experiments arose perhaps even more from his wish to upset the predictability of the printed page and the expectations of conventional readers.

Cummings was born in Cambridge, Massachusetts, the child of cultured parents. His father was a Congregational minister and professor at Harvard, but it was chiefly his mother, to whom Cummings was devoted all his life, who encouraged her son's writing. It seems likely that a good deal of Cummings's wish to shock stemmed originally from his repudiation of his father's way of life. For all Cummings's protestations of filial piety in "my father moved through dooms of love," he was irritated by his father's unremitting seriousness, so alien to his own volatile temperament; the role of *enfant terrible* was one Cummings never tired of playing.

Cummings's father taught English and social ethics at Harvard, and Cummings himself graduated from Harvard in 1915 and took an M.A. in literature there the following year. At Harvard, through knowledgeable friends like Scofield Thayer and Witter Bynner, Cummings discovered new art and music. At his Harvard graduation, having won the privilege of delivering one of the commencement "parts" (or speeches), Cummings praised cubist painting and Stravinsky's music. He knew such tastes were opposed by the majority of his teachers and fellow students. In his writing he continually pitted the values of what he scornfully called "mostpeople" against the bohemian tastes of the artist.

Cummings went off to France in 1917 as a volunteer ambulance driver for the Red Cross. Through his own unconventional behavior, he was suspected of being a spy and was detained, with his friend Slater Brown, for three months in a French internment camp. His father wrote letters to friends in Washington pleading for intervention on his son's behalf; through the influence of President Woodrow Wilson, Cummings was freed. He described his imprisonment in *The Enormous Room* (1922), the book that first brought him fame.

Cummings lived in France from 1921 to 1923, where he was exposed to a bohemian culture that he imitated when he finally settled, in 1924, in New York's Greenwich Village, where he spent the rest of his life writing and painting. His mother helped to support him until she died. Cummings married three times and had a daughter by his first wife, who concealed Cummings's paternity from the child because she had remarried and wished the child to believe that her second husband was the father. Cummings acknowledged his daughter when she was in her twenties, and they became affectionately attached to each other.

Cummings's first poems were published in *The Dial* in 1920. In his lifetime, his most frequently anthologized poems were those in which he was most sentimental. But his greatest gift was as a satirist. He could take the measure of literary falsity, patriotic cant, or intellectual humbug with a scathing phrase; he scorned conventional verbal and political pieties and conventional standards of behavior. He preached a neo-paganism of untroubled sexual pleasure, childlike egotism, and irrepressible impudence; a myth of spontaneity animated his aesthetic. Of course, the ingenuity visible in his poems about the grasshopper and the falling leaf demonstrates how unspontaneous such compositions actually are. An acrobat of words, Cummings scorned discursive logic and political strategy. If this world did not suit, "there's a hell / of a good universe next door; let's go." He establishes only two poles of thought, ignorance and belief; there is, to him, something suspect about the middle ground of learning, on the one hand, and skepticism, on the other.

In American literary history, Cummings ranks as a memorable documentary writer because of *The Enormous Room* and *Eimi* (1933), his account of travels in Russia after the rise of Stalin (whom he hated). Both books are vivid in rapidly noted sensory detail and irrepressibly energetic in style. Cummings's early poetry remains a body of inventive and ebullient work, raising provocative aesthetic questions. Is something that cannot be read aloud a poem? If so, what do we mean by the word *poem?* Can a poem incorporate slang, obscenity, advertising jargon, dialect? Is all language material for poetry? Must the line be the unit of the poem? Does the eye have as much right to the poem as the ear? Is the sonnet dead or can it be resuscitated? Can satiric lyrics be written in puritanical America? These questions are still relevant.

Cummings's wish to believe that all people are at heart alike in love and that all desires are simple ones led him into a conventional sentimentalizing of the erotic life. But his capacity for play in language and for vivid satire of America and its institutions ensures him a permanent place in American literature.

Further Reading:

C. Norman, *The Magic Maker, E. E. Cummings,* 1958.

N. Friedman, *E. E. Cummings: The Art of His Poetry,* 1960.

N. Friedman, *E. E. Cummings: The Growth of a Writer,* 1964.

B. A. Marks, *E. E. Cummings,* 1964.

R. E. Wegner, *The Poetry and Prose of E. E. Cummings,* 1965.

E. Triem, *E. E. Cummings,* 1969.

B. K. Dumas, *A Remembrance of Miracles,* 1974.

G. Lane, *I Am: A Study of E. E. Cummings' Poems,* 1976.

P. Lauter, *E. E. Cummings,* 1976.

R. Kidder, *E. E. Cummings: An Introduction to the Poetry,* 1979.

R. S. Kennedy, *Dreams in the Mirror: A Biography of E. E. Cummings,* 1980.

K. McBride, ed., *A Concordance to the Poems of E. E. Cummings,* 1982.

Text:

Complete Poems, 1972.

See also *Selected Letters of E. E. Cummings,* eds. F. W. Dupee and G. Stade, 1969.

[in Just-]

in Just-
spring   when the world is mud-
luscious the little
lame balloonman

whistles   far   and wee   5

and eddieandbill come
running from marbles and
piracies and it's
spring

when the world is puddle-wonderful   10

the queer
old balloonman whistles
far   and   wee
and bettyandisbel come dancing

from hop-scotch and jump-rope and   15
it's
spring
and
      the

            goat-footed[1]   20

balloonMan   whistles
far
and
wee
1923

---

[1] Characteristic of Pan, ancient Greek god of
woods and shepherds.

[the Cambridge ladies who live in furnished souls]

the Cambridge ladies who live in furnished souls
are unbeautiful and have comfortable minds
(also, with the church's protestant blessings
daughters, unscented shapeless spirited)
they believe in Christ and Longfellow,[1] both dead,   5
are invariably interested in so many things—
at the present writing one still finds
delighted fingers knitting for the is it Poles?
perhaps. While permanent faces coyly bandy
scandal of Mrs. N and Professor D   10
. . . . the Cambridge ladies do not care, above
Cambridge if sometimes in its box of
sky lavender and cornerless, the
moon rattles like a fragment of angry candy
1923

["next to of course god america i]

"next to of course god america i
love you land of the pilgrims' and so forth oh
say can you see by the dawn's early my
country 'tis of centuries come and go
and are no more what of it we should worry   5
in every language even deafanddumb
thy sons acclaim your glorious name by gorry
by jingo by gee by gosh by gum
why talk of beauty what could be more beautiful than these heroic happy dead   10
who rushed like lions to the roaring slaughter
they did not stop to think they died instead
then shall the voice of liberty be mute?"

He spoke. And drank rapidly a glass of water
1926

---

[1] Henry Wadsworth Longfellow (1807–1882),
   Cambridge poet and Harvard professor.

[my sweet old etcetera]

my sweet old etcetera
aunt lucy during the recent

war could and what
is more did tell you just
what everybody was fighting   5

for,
my sister

isabel created hundreds
(and
hundreds) of socks not to   10
mention shirts fleaproof earwarmers

etcetera wristers etcetera, my
mother hoped that

i would die etcetera
bravely of course my father used   15
to become hoarse talking about how it was
a privilege and if only he
could meanwhile my

self etcetera lay quietly
in the deep mud et   20

cetera
(dreaming,
et
    cetera, of
Your smile   25
eyes knees and of your Etcetera)
1926

[i sing of Olaf glad and big]

i sing of Olaf glad and big
whose warmest heart recoiled at war:
a conscientious object-or

his wellbelovéd colonel(trig
westpointer most succinctly bred)   5
took erring Olaf soon in hand;
but—though an host of overjoyed
noncoms(first knocking on the head
him)do through icy waters roll
that helplessness which others stroke   10
with brushes recently employed
anent this muddy toiletbowl,
while kindred intellects evoke
allegiance per blunt instruments—
Olaf(being to all intents   15
a corpse and wanting any rag
upon what God unto him gave)
responds, without getting annoyed
"I will not kiss your fucking flag"

straightway the silver bird looked grave   20
(departing hurriedly to shave)

but—though all kinds of officers
(a yearning nation's blueeyed pride)
their passive prey did kick and curse
until for wear their clarion   25
voices and boots were much the worse,
and egged the firstclassprivates on
his rectum wickedly to tease
by means of skilfully applied
bayonets roasted hot with heat—   30
Olaf(upon what were once knees)
does almost ceaselessly repeat
"there is some shit I will not eat"

our president, being of which
assertions duly notified   35
threw the yellowsonofabitch
into a dungeon, where he died
Christ(of His mercy infinite)
i pray to see; and Olaf, too

preponderatingly because   40
unless statistics lie he was
more brave than me:more blond than you.
1931

[anyone lived in a pretty how town]

anyone lived in a pretty how town
(with up so floating many bells down)
spring summer autumn winter
he sang his didn't he danced his did.

Women and men(both little and small)   5
cared for anyone not at all
they sowed their isn't they reaped their same
sun moon stars rain

children guessed(but only a few
and down they forgot as up they grew   10
autumn winter spring summer)
that noone loved him more by more

when by now and tree by leaf
she laughed his joy she cried his grief
bird by snow and stir by still   15
anyone's any was all to her

someones married their everyones
laughed their cryings and did their dance
(sleep wake hope and then)they
said their nevers they slept their dream   20

stars rain sun moon
(and only the snow can begin to explain
how children are apt to forget to remember
with up so floating many bells down)

one day anyone died i guess   25
(and noone stooped to kiss his face)
busy folk buried them side by side
little by little and was by was

all by all and deep by deep   30
and more by more they dream their sleep
noone and anyone earth by april
wish by spirit and if by yes.

Women and men(both dong and ding)
summer autumn winter spring   35

reaped their sowing and went their came
sun moon stars rain
1940

[what a proud dreamhorse]

what a proud dreamhorse pulling(smoothloomingly)through
(stepp)this(ing)crazily seething of this
raving city screamingly street wonderful

flowers And o the Light thrown by Them opens

sharp holes in dark places paints eye touches hands with new-   5
ness and these startled whats are a(piercing clothes thoughts kiss
-ing wishes bodies)squirm-of-frightened shy are whichs small
its hungry for Is for Love Spring thirsty for happens
only and beautiful
         there is a ragged beside the who limps   10
man crying silence upward
         —to have tasted Beautiful to have known
Only to have smelled Happens—skip dance kids hop point at
red blue yellow violet white orange green-
ness   15

    o what a proud dreamhorse moving(whose feet
almost walk air). now who stops. Smiles.he
            stamps
1935

F. Scott Fitzgerald
1896–1940

Francis Scott Key Fitzgerald belonged, as Edmund Wilson once noted, as much to "the middle west of large cities and country clubs" as Sinclair Lewis belonged to "the middle west of the prairies and little towns." Born in St. Paul, Minnesota, on September 24, 1896, Fitzgerald was descended on his father's side from a socially prominent family of once-prosperous landowners and legislators, including the author of "The Star-Spangled Banner," and on his mother's from a family of newly prosperous and still thriving Irish immigrants. The former, he later noted, possessed "that series of reticences and obligations that go under the poor old shattered word 'breeding,' " while the latter "had the money." From this divided heritage, Fitzgerald acquired not only a deep ambivalence toward both status and money but also a sense of entanglement in America's history. "I look out at it," he once said of that history, "and I think it is the most beautiful history in the world. It is the history of me and my people. . . . It is the history of all aspiration—not just the American dream but the human dream." Yet Fitzgerald's hold on his heritage, as on almost everything, remained precarious. "That was always my experience," he observed near the end of his life, "a poor boy in a rich town; a poor boy in a rich boy's school; a poor boy in a rich man's club."

From St. Paul, Fitzgerald went on to Princeton and New York and Paris and Hollywood. No major writer of his time lived so extravagant a version of success, and none experienced a more devastating version of failure. He was at once a striking embodiment and a scathing critic of his age, primarily because he possessed, as his friend John Peale Bishop remarked, "the rare faculty of being able to experience romantic and ingenuous emotions and a half hour later regard them with satiric detachment." Many of Fitzgerald's emotions, like those of his age, derived from the almost religious awe that he felt toward the idealization of great wealth and the romanticization of sexual love, by both of which he felt simultaneously attracted and repulsed, enchanted and offended. At the same time, however, his fiction discloses a preoccupation with and a sensitivity to social class that is unusual in American fiction. In both his writing and his life, Fitzgerald continually demonstrated the tensions of a divided consciousness. Toward the end of his life, in a series of remarkably personal and vulnerable essays about his "crack-up," he said that "the test of a first-rate intelligence is the ability to hold two opposed ideas in the mind at the same time, and still retain the ability to function."

At a Catholic prep school in New Jersey and then at Princeton, where poor examination scores barely qualified him for admission "with conditions," Fitzgerald sacrificed academic achievement to social success. Years later, in "The Crack-up" (1936), he wrote that "it seemed a romantic business to be a successful literary man— you were not ever going to be as famous as a movie star but what note you had was probably longer-lived—you were never going to have the power of a man of strong political or religious convictions but you were certainly more independent." At Princeton, he compiled a dismal scholastic record—he was in academic trouble every semester—yet managed to distinguish himself socially and intellectually through his writing. He wrote clever plots and lyrics for Triangle Club shows (in one he played a glamorous show girl, and a photograph of him in costume appeared in the *New York Times*), along with short stories, poems, and plays for literary and humor magazines.

In 1917 Fitzgerald eased himself out of Princeton, where he had fallen a year behind because of poor grades, by accepting a commission in the U.S. Infantry. That winter, at Fort Leavenworth, Kansas (where his platoon captain was Dwight David Eisenhower), Fitzgerald began a novel, *The Romantic Egoist*, which, after several drafts and rejections, was eventually salvaged as *This Side of Paradise* (1920). Working hard on the novel, he kept at it while in the army, including a tour in Montgomery, Alabama (he never got overseas), and then after the army while working briefly in New York and living at his parents' house in St. Paul—because he optimistically equated its publication with both literary and romantic success. While stationed in Montgomery, he had fallen in love with a recent high school graduate, a beautiful, high-spirited, talented, precariously balanced debutante named Zelda Sayre. "If I stopped working to finish the novel," Fitzgerald later wrote, "I lost the girl." With the publication of *This Side of Paradise,* an autobiographical novel set in Princeton, Fitzgerald not only won Zelda's hand but also made himself a cultural hero to the "flappers and philosophers" of the era he named "the Jazz Age." A whole generation of college students listened to Fitzgerald as one might listen to an oracle.

The novel proved to be an immediate sensation; it sold over 40,000 copies in its first year and made Fitzgerald an overnight celebrity. It also immensely improved his income: "Counting the bag, I found that in 1919 I had made $800 by writing, that in 1920 I had made $18,000 [from] stories, picture rights, and book. My story price had gone from $30 to $1,000." Fitzgerald had been publishing his short stories since the spring of 1919, first in H. L. Mencken's *The Smart Set* and later in the mass-circulation *Saturday Evening Post,* where he published story after story for the next seventeen years. Though Fitzgerald remains one of the finest American short-story writers, he often expressed contempt for the form—"I don't enjoy it & just do it for the money"— and considered the novel as the best expression of his art. Nevertheless, Fitzgerald would publish in his lifetime four significant collections of stories: *Flappers and Philosophers* (1920), *Tales of the Jazz Age* (1922), *All the Sad Young Men* (1926) (which featured "The Rich Boy" as the lead story), and *Taps at Reveille* (1935). Several collections of stories were also published posthumously. Edmund Wilson, who met Fitzgerald at Princeton and who became one his closest friends, had warned Fitzgerald after reading *This Side of Paradise* that he was in danger of becoming a "very popular trashy novelist." In selling scores of stories to popular magazines over the years, Fitzgerald, it is apparent, did not always heed Wilson's warning.

After their marriage in April 1920, Fitzgerald and Zelda set out on a life together that was glamorous, extravagant, emotionally stormy, and usually good publicity. Through the 1920s and into the 1930s they dressed fashionably, stayed in expensive hotels, swam in public fountains, and danced on restaurant tables. They partied for nights at a time, drank excessively, and enjoyed being evicted from public places, all the while spending money even more rapidly than Fitzgerald could earn it. A second novel, *The Beautiful and Damned,* a story of moral and sexual dissolution partly stimulated by the fast style of the Fitzgeralds' marriage, appeared in 1922 and received many disappointing reviews. Between 1922 and 1924 Fitzgerald lived in Great Neck, Long Island, where he became friends with Ring Lardner and where he tried his hand at an unsuccessful play, *The Vegetable* (1923). In 1924 the Fitzgeralds sailed for an extended European trip, during which Fitzgerald met Gertrude Stein and Ezra Pound and began a tense, competitive friendship with Ernest Hemingway. In 1925 Fitzgerald published his finest novel, *The Great Gatsby,* which has continued to exercise a remarkable hold on both the popular and the academic imagination. Three movies have been based on it, and scores of critical articles have been written about it. The novel is about the mysterious, fabulously wealthy Jay Gatsby, who throws lavish parties at his Long Island estate and who tries to relive a previous idyllic romance. For all his vulgarity, Gatsby possesses "some heightened sensitivity to the promises of life . . . an extraordinary gift for hope, a romantic readiness." The enormous popularity of the book derives in part from its focus on two of Fitzgerald's favorite themes, love and money, while its enormous critical success derives from Fitzgerald's ability to imbue a popular subject with cultural myth and literary seriousness.

Fitzgerald returned to the United States in December 1926 and spent a few months scriptwriting in Hollywood. The Fitzgeralds then settled outside of Wilmington, Delaware, where they tried to piece their lives together. Zelda felt unproductive and frustrated; Fitzgerald's drinking had reached dangerous proportions. In the summer of 1928 they returned to Paris, where Zelda, always a talented dancer and desperately searching for an independent identity, tried too late to find a creative outlet in ballet. Two years later, while on another trip to Europe, Zelda suffered the first of a series of mental breakdowns that forced her to spend most of the last seventeen years of her life in sanatoriums. By 1931, when the Fitzgeralds returned to America, the Great Depression was deepening and Fitzgerald was experiencing an abrupt reversal of fortune. Guilt-ridden and depressed by Zelda's collapse, humbled by his own rising self-doubts, he began drinking more and writing less.

In 1932 Zelda Fitzgerald published a novel, *Save Me the Waltz,* which she had written while she was receiving treatment at the Johns Hopkins clinic. Two years later Fitzgerald published *Tender Is the Night,* the story of an alcoholic American psychiatrist who falls in love with and disastrously marries one of his wealthy patients. (The book's title comes from "Ode to a Nightingale," one of several Keats poems that had long exerted a powerful influence on Fitzgerald's fiction.) But nothing could revitalize Fitzgerald's financial situation. The royalties on works that had earned hundreds of thousands of dollars in the 1920s brought him a total of $50 in 1932 and 1933. Sorely in debt, he returned to Hollywood in 1937 on a lucrative contract as a scriptwriter. But his effort to translate his genius for narrative fiction into screenplays also failed. Although he worked on numerous scripts, he managed to receive only one screen credit over the next two years. His drinking binges continued to get him in trouble with the studios, and he gradually drifted into free-lance jobs. In 1940, at the age of forty-four, he died in Hollywood of a heart attack at the home of the journalist Sheilah Graham. His new novel—Fitzgerald liked to think of it as "a Western"—about a self-made Hollywood producer, *The Last Tycoon,* remained unfinished. Over the next eight years, Zelda continued to struggle with bouts of severe depression. In 1947, she was burned to death in a North Carolina hospital fire.

"I am not a great man," Fitzgerald said to his daughter, near the end of his life, "but sometimes I think the impersonal and objective quality of my talent and the sacrifices of it, in pieces, to preserve its essential value has some sort of epic grandeur." At the time of his death, Fitzgerald's reputation, like his income, had fallen very low. In the years since, however, readers have discovered, in *The Great Gatsby, Tender Is the Night,* and a handful of stories, including "Winter Dreams," works of permanent value. At its best, the lyricism of his prose arises from and is interlaced with dramatic situations that disclose something of the emptiness and something of the hope of our world. The critic Lionel Trilling regarded Fitzgerald as "perhaps the last notable writer to affirm the Romantic fantasy, descended from the Renaissance, of personal ambition or heroism, of life committed to, or thrown away for, some ideal of self."

Further Reading:

K. Eble, *F. Scott Fitzgerald,* 1963.

W. Goldhurst, *F. Scott Fitzgerald and His Contemporaries,* 1963.

A. Mizener, *The Far Side of Paradise,* rev. ed., 1965.

J. F. Callahan, *The Illusions of a Nation: Myth and History in the Novels of F. Scott Fitzgerald,* 1972.

M. J. Bruccoli, *Some Sort of Epic Grandeur: The Life of F. Scott Fitzgerald*, 1981.

R. Lehan, The Great Gatsby: *The Limits of Wonder*, 1990.

Text:

"Winter Dreams" from *All the Sad Young Men*, 1926.

Winter Dreams*

I

Some of the caddies were poor as sin and lived in one-room houses with a neurasthenic cow in the front yard, but Dexter Green's father owned the second best grocery-store in Black Bear—the best one was "The Hub," patronized by the wealthy people from Sherry Island—and Dexter caddied only for pocket-money.

In the fall when the days became crisp and gray, and the long Minnesota winter shut down like the white lid of a box, Dexter's skis moved over the snow that hid the fairways of the golf course. At these times the country gave him a feeling of profound melancholy—it offended him that the links should lie in enforced fallowness, haunted by ragged sparrows for the long season. It was dreary, too, that on the trees where the gay colors fluttered in summer there were now only the desolate sand-boxes knee-deep in crusted ice. When he crossed the hills the wind blew cold as misery, and if the sun was out he tramped with his eyes squinted up against the hard dimensionless glare.

In April the winter ceased abruptly. The snow ran down into Black Bear Lake scarcely tarrying for the early golfers to brave the season with red and black balls. Without elation, without an interval of moist glory, the cold was gone.

Dexter knew that there was something dismal about this Northern spring, just as he knew there was something gorgeous about the fall. Fall made him clinch his hands and tremble and repeat idiotic sentences to himself, and make brisk abrupt gestures of command to imaginary audiences and armies. October filled him with hope which November raised to a sort of ecstatic triumph, and in this mood the fleeting brilliant impressions of the summer at Sherry Island were ready grist to his mill. He became a golf champion and defeated Mr. T. A. Hedrick in a marvellous match played a hundred times over the fairways of his imagination, a match each detail of which he changed about untiringly—sometimes he won with almost laughable ease, sometimes he came up magnificently from behind. Again, stepping from a Pierce-Arrow automobile, like Mr. Mortimer Jones, he strolled frigidly into the lounge of the Sherry Island Golf Club—or perhaps, surrounded by an admiring crowd, he gave an exhibition of fancy diving from the spring-board of the club raft. . . . Among those who watched him in open-mouthed wonder was Mr. Mortimer Jones.

And one day it came to pass that Mr. Jones—himself and not his ghost—came up to Dexter with tears in his eyes and said that Dexter was the — — best caddy in the club,

* "Winter Dreams" was first published in 1926 in a collection of Fitzgerald short stories titled *All the Sad Young Men*. Like Dexter Green of "Winter Dreams" (and like Nick Carraway of *The Great Gatsby*), F. Scott Fitzgerald (1896–1940) was born in the upper Midwest and educated in the East at an Ivy League school. He lived in New York City, on Long Island, in Paris, and in Hollywood.

and wouldn't he decide not to quit if Mr. Jones made it worth his while, because every other — — caddy in the club lost one ball a hole for him—regularly——

"No, sir," said Dexter decisively, "I don't want to caddy any more." Then, after a pause: "I'm too old."

"You're not more than fourteen. Why the devil did you decide just this morning that you wanted to quit? You promised that next week you'd go over to the state tournament with me."

"I decided I was too old."

Dexter handed in his "A Class" badge, collected what money was due him from the caddy master, and walked home to Black Bear Village.

"The best — — caddy I ever saw," shouted Mr. Mortimer Jones over a drink that afternoon. "Never lost a ball! Willing! Intelligent! Quiet! Honest! Grateful!"

The little girl who had done this was eleven—beautifully ugly as little girls are apt to be who are destined after a few years to be inexpressibly lovely and bring no end of misery to a great number of men. The spark, however, was perceptible. There was a general ungodliness in the way her lips twisted down at the corners when she smiled, and in the—Heaven help us!—in the almost passionate quality of her eyes. Vitality is born early in such women. It was utterly in evidence now, shining through her thin frame in a sort of glow.

She had come eagerly out on to the course at nine o'clock with a white linen nurse and five small new golf-clubs in a white canvas bag which the nurse was carrying. When Dexter first saw her she was standing by the caddy house, rather ill at ease and trying to conceal the fact by engaging her nurse in an obviously unnatural conversation graced by startling and irrelevant grimaces from herself.

"Well, it's certainly a nice day, Hilda," Dexter heard her say. She drew down the corners of her mouth, smiled, and glanced furtively around, her eyes in transit falling for an instant on Dexter.

Then to the nurse:

"Well, I guess there aren't very many people out here this morning, are there?"

The smile again—radiant, blatantly artificial—convincing.

"I don't know what we're supposed to do now," said the nurse, looking nowhere in particular.

"Oh, that's all right. I'll fix it up."

Dexter stood perfectly still, his mouth slightly ajar. He knew that if he moved forward a step his stare would be in her line of vision—if he moved backward he would lose his full view of her face. For a moment he had not realized how young she was. Now he remembered having seen her several times the year before—in bloomers.

Suddenly, involuntarily, he laughed, a short abrupt laugh—then, startled by himself, he turned and began to walk quickly away.

"Boy!"

Dexter stopped.

"Boy——"

Beyond question he was addressed. Not only that, but he was treated to that absurd smile, that preposterous smile—the memory of which at least a dozen men were to carry into middle age.

"Boy, do you know where the golf teacher is?"

"He's giving a lesson."

"Well, do you know where the caddy-master is?"

"He isn't here yet this morning."

"Oh." For a moment this baffled her. She stood alternately on her right and left foot.

"We'd like to get a caddy," said the nurse. "Mrs. Mortimer Jones sent us out to play golf, and we don't know how without we get a caddy."

Here she was stopped by an ominous glance from Miss Jones, followed immediately by the smile.

"There aren't any caddies here except me," said Dexter to the nurse, "and I got to stay here in charge until the caddy-master gets here."

"Oh."

Miss Jones and her retinue now withdrew, and at a proper distance from Dexter became involved in a heated conversation, which was concluded by Miss Jones taking one of the clubs and hitting it on the ground with violence. For further emphasis she raised it again and was about to bring it down smartly upon the nurse's bosom, when the nurse seized the club and twisted it from her hands.

"You damn little mean old *thing!*" cried Miss Jones wildly.

Another argument ensued. Realizing that the elements of comedy were implied in the scene, Dexter several times began to laugh, but each time restrained the laugh before it reached audibility. He could not resist the monstrous conviction that the little girl was justified in beating the nurse.

The situation was resolved by the fortuitous appearance of the caddy-master, who was appealed to immediately by the nurse.

"Miss Jones is to have a little caddy, and this one says he can't go."

"Mr. McKenna said I was to wait here till you came," said Dexter quickly.

"Well, he's here now." Miss Jones smiled cheerfully at the caddy-master. Then she dropped her bag and set off at a haughty mince toward the first tee.

"Well?" The caddy-master turned to Dexter. "What you standing there like a dummy for? Go pick up the young lady's clubs."

"I don't think I'll go out to-day," said Dexter.

"You don't——"

"I think I'll quit."

The enormity of his decision frightened him. He was a favorite caddy, and the thirty dollars a month he earned through the summer were not to be made elsewhere around the lake. But he had received a strong emotional shock, and his perturbation required a violent and immediate outlet.

It is not so simple as that, either. As so frequently would be the case in the future, Dexter was unconsciously dictated to by his winter dreams.

II

Now, of course, the quality and the seasonability of these winter dreams varied, but the stuff of them remained. They persuaded Dexter several years later to pass up a business course at the State university—his father, prospering now, would have paid his way—for the precarious advantage of attending an older and more famous university in the East, where he was bothered by his scanty funds. But do not get the impression, because his winter dreams happened to be concerned at first with musings on the rich, that there was anything merely snobbish in the boy. He wanted not association with glittering things and glittering people—he wanted the glittering things themselves. Often he reached out for the best without knowing why he wanted it—and sometimes he ran up against the mysterious denials and prohibitions in which life indulges. It is with one of those denials and not with his career as a whole that this story deals.

He made money. It was rather amazing. After college he went to the city from which Black Bear Lake draws its wealthy patrons. When he was only twenty-three and had been there not quite two years, there were already people who liked to say: "Now *there's* a boy——" All about him rich men's sons were peddling bonds precariously, or investing patrimonies precariously, or plodding through the two dozen volumes of the "George Washington Commercial Course," but Dexter borrowed a thousand dollars on his college degree and his confident mouth, and bought a partnership in a laundry.

It was a small laundry when he went into it, but Dexter made a specialty of learning how the English washed fine woolen golf-stockings without shrinking them, and within a year he was catering to the trade that wore knickerbockers. Men were insisting that their Shetland hose and sweaters go to his laundry, just as they had insisted on a caddy who could find golf-balls. A little later he was doing their wives' lingerie as well—and running five branches in different parts of the city. Before he was twenty-seven he owned the largest string of laundries in his section of the country. It was then that he sold out and went to New York. But the part of his story that concerns us goes back to the days when he was making his first big success.

When he was twenty-three Mr. Hart—one of the gray-haired men who liked to say "Now there's a boy"—gave him a guest card to the Sherry Island Golf Club for a weekend. So he signed his name one day on the register, and that afternoon played golf in a foursome with Mr. Hart and Mr. Sandwood and Mr. T. A. Hedrick. He did not consider it necessary to remark that he had once carried Mr. Hart's bag over this same links, and that he knew every trap and gully with his eyes shut—but he found himself glancing at the four caddies who trailed them, trying to catch a gleam or gesture that would remind him of himself, that would lessen the gap which lay between his present and his past.

It was a curious day, slashed abruptly with fleeting, familiar impressions. One minute he had the sense of being a trespasser—in the next he was impressed by the tremendous superiority he felt toward Mr. T. A. Hedrick, who was a bore and not even a good golfer any more.

Then, because of a ball Mr. Hart lost near the fifteenth green, an enormous thing happened. While they were searching the stiff grasses of the rough there was a clear call of "Fore!" from behind a hill in their rear. And as they all turned abruptly from their search a bright new ball sliced abruptly over the hill and caught Mr. T. A. Hedrick in the abdomen.

"By Gad!" cried Mr. T. A. Hedrick, "they ought to put some of these crazy women off the course. It's getting to be outrageous."

A head and a voice came up together over the hill:

"Do you mind if we go through?"

"You hit me in the stomach!" declared Mr. Hedrick wildly.

"Did I?" The girl approached the group of men. "I'm sorry. I yelled 'Fore!' "

Her glance fell casually on each of the men—then scanned the fairway for her ball.

"Did I bounce into the rough?"

It was impossible to determine whether this question was ingenuous or malicious. In a moment, however, she left no doubt, for as her partner came up over the hill she called cheerfully:

"Here I am! I'd have gone on the green except that I hit something."

As she took her stance for a short mashie shot, Dexter looked at her closely. She wore a blue gingham dress, rimmed at throat and shoulders with a white edging that accentuated her tan. The quality of exaggeration, of thinness, which had made her passionate eyes and down-turning mouth absurd at eleven, was gone now. She was arrestingly beautiful. The color in her cheeks was centred like the color in a picture—it was not a "high" color, but a sort of fluctuating and feverish warmth, so shaded that it seemed at any moment it would recede and disappear. This color and the mobility of her mouth gave a continual impression of flux, of intense life, of passionate vitality—balanced only partially by the sad luxury of her eyes.

She swung her mashie impatiently and without interest, pitching the ball into a sand-pit on the other side of the green. With a quick, insincere smile and a careless "Thank you!" she went on after it.

"That Judy Jones!" remarked Mr. Hedrick on the next tee, as they waited—some moments—for her to play on ahead. "All she needs is to be turned up and spanked for six months and then to be married off to an old-fashioned cavalry captain."

"My God, she's good-looking!" said Mr. Sandwood, who was just over thirty.

"Good-looking!" cried Mr. Hedrick contemptuously, "she always looks as if she wanted to be kissed! Turning those big cow-eyes on every calf in town!"

It was doubtful if Mr. Hedrick intended a reference to the maternal instinct.

"She'd play pretty good golf if she'd try," said Mr. Sandwood.

"She has no form," said Mr. Hedrick solemnly.

"She has a nice figure," said Mr. Sandwood.

"Better thank the Lord she doesn't drive a swifter ball," said Mr. Hart, winking at Dexter.

Later in the afternoon the sun went down with a riotous swirl of gold and varying blues and scarlets, and left the dry, rustling night of Western summer. Dexter watched from the veranda of the Golf Club, watched the even overlap of the waters in the little wind, silver molasses under the harvest-moon. Then the moon held a finger to her lips and the lake became a clear pool, pale and quiet. Dexter put on his bathing-suit and swam out to the farthest raft, where he stretched dripping on the wet canvas of the springboard.

There was a fish jumping and a star shining and the lights around the lake were gleaming. Over on a dark peninsula a piano was playing the songs of last summer and of summers before that—songs from "Chin-Chin" and "The Count of Luxemburg" and "The Chocolate Soldier"—and because the sound of a piano over a stretch of water had always seemed beautiful to Dexter he lay perfectly quiet and listened.

The tune the piano was playing at that moment had been gay and new five years before when Dexter was a sophomore at college. They had played it at a prom once when he could not afford the luxury of proms, and he had stood outside the gymnasium and listened. The sound of the tune precipitated in him a sort of ecstasy and it was with that ecstasy he viewed what happened to him now. It was a mood of intense appreciation, a sense that, for once, he was magnificently attuned to life and that everything about him was radiating a brightness and a glamour he might never know again.

A low, pale oblong detached itself suddenly from the darkness of the Island, spitting forth the reverberated sound of a racing motor-boat. Two white streamers of cleft water rolled themselves out behind it and almost immediately the boat was beside him, drowning out the hot tinkle of the piano in the drone of its spray. Dexter raising himself on his arms was aware of a figure standing at the wheel, of two dark eyes regarding him over the lengthening space of water—then the boat had gone by and was sweeping in an immense and purposeless circle of spray round and round in the middle of the lake. With equal eccentricity one of the circles flattened out and headed back toward the raft.

"Who's that?" she called, shutting off her motor. She was so near now that Dexter could see her bathing-suit, which consisted apparently of pink rompers.

The nose of the boat bumped the raft, and as the latter tilted rakishly he was precipitated toward her. With different degrees of interest they recognized each other.

"Aren't you one of those men we played through this afternoon?" she demanded.

He was.

"Well, do you know how to drive a motor-boat? Because if you do I wish you'd drive this one so I can ride on the surf-board behind. My name is Judy Jones"—she favored him with an absurd smirk—rather, what tried to be a smirk, for, twist her mouth as she might, it was not grotesque, it was merely beautiful—"and I live in a house over there on the Island, and in that house there is a man waiting for me. When he drove up at the door I drove out of the dock because he says I'm his ideal."

There was a fish jumping and a star shining and the lights around the lake were gleaming. Dexter sat beside Judy Jones and she explained how her boat was driven. Then she was in the water, swimming to the floating surf-board with a sinuous crawl. Watching her was without effort to the eye, watching a branch waving or a sea-gull flying. Her arms, burned to butternut, moved sinuously among the dull platinum ripples, elbow appearing first, casting the forearm back with a cadence of falling water, then reaching out and down, stabbing a path ahead.

They moved out into the lake; turning, Dexter saw that she was kneeling on the low rear of the now uptilted surf-board.

"Go faster," she called, "fast as it'll go."

Obediently he jammed the lever forward and the white spray mounted at the bow. When he looked around again the girl was standing up on the rushing board, her arms spread wide, her eyes lifted toward the moon.

"It's awful cold," she shouted. "What's your name?"

He told her.

"Well, why don't you come to dinner to-morrow night?"

His heart turned over like the fly-wheel of the boat, and, for the second time, her casual whim gave a new direction to his life.

III

Next evening while he waited for her to come down-stairs, Dexter peopled the soft deep summer room and the sun-porch that opened from it with the men who had already loved Judy Jones. He knew the sort of men they were—the men who when he first went to college had entered from the great prep schools with graceful clothes and the deep tan of healthy summers. He had seen that, in one sense, he was better than these men. He was newer and stronger. Yet in acknowledging to himself that he wished his children to be like them he was admitting that he was but the rough, strong stuff from which they eternally sprang.

When the time had come for him to wear good clothes, he had known who were the best tailors in America, and the best tailors in America had made him the suit he wore this evening. He had acquired that particular reserve peculiar to his university, that set it off from other universities. He recognized the value to him of such a mannerism and he had adopted it; he knew that to be careless in dress and manner required more confidence than to be careful. But carelessness was for his children. His mother's name had been Krimslich. She was a Bohemian of the peasant class and she had talked broken English to the end of her days. Her son must keep to the set patterns.

At a little after seven Judy Jones came down-stairs. She wore a blue silk afternoon dress, and he was disappointed at first that she had not put on something more elaborate. This feeling was accentuated when, after a brief greeting, she went to the door of a butler's pantry and pushing it open called: "You can serve dinner, Martha." He had rather expected that a butler would announce dinner, that there would be a cocktail. Then he put these thoughts behind him as they sat down side by side on a lounge and looked at each other.

"Father and mother won't be here," she said thoughtfully.

He remembered the last time he had seen her father, and he was glad the parents were not to be here to-night—they might wonder who he was. He had been born in Keeble, a Minnesota village fifty miles farther north, and he always gave Keeble as his home instead of Black Bear Village. Country towns were well enough to come from if they weren't inconveniently in sight and used as footstools by fashionable lakes.

They talked of his university, which she had visited frequently during the past two years, and of the near-by city which supplied Sherry Island with its patrons, and whither Dexter would return next day to his prospering laundries.

During dinner she slipped into a moody depression which gave Dexter a feeling of uneasiness. Whatever petulance she uttered in her throaty voice worried him. Whatever she smiled at—at him, at a chicken liver, at nothing—it disturbed him that her smile could have no root in mirth, or even in amusement. When the scarlet corners of her lips curved down, it was less a smile than an invitation to a kiss.

Then, after dinner, she led him out on the dark sun-porch and deliberately changed the atmosphere.

"Do you mind if I weep a little?" she said.

"I'm afraid I'm boring you," he responded quickly.

"You're not. I like you. But I've just had a terrible afternoon. There was a man I cared about, and this afternoon he told me out of a clear sky that he was poor as a church-mouse. He'd never even hinted it before. Does this sound horribly mundane?"

"Perhaps he was afraid to tell you."

"Suppose he was," she answered. "He didn't start right. You see, if I'd thought of him as poor—well, I've been mad about loads of poor men, and fully intended to marry them all. But in this case, I hadn't thought of him that way, and my interest in him wasn't strong enough to survive the shock. As if a girl calmly informed her fiancé that she was a widow. He might not object to widows, but——"

"Let's start right," she interrupted herself suddenly. "Who are you, anyhow?"

For a moment Dexter hesitated. Then:

"I'm nobody," he announced. "My career is largely a matter of futures."

"Are you poor?"

"No," he said frankly, "I'm probably making more money than any man my age in the Northwest. I know that's an obnoxious remark, but you advised me to start right."

There was a pause. Then she smiled and the corners of her mouth drooped and an almost imperceptible sway brought her closer to him, looking up into his eyes. A lump rose in Dexter's throat, and he waited breathless for the experiment, facing the unpredictable compound that would form mysteriously from the elements of their lips. Then he saw—she communicated her excitement to him, lavishly, deeply, with kisses that were not a promise but a fulfillment. They aroused in him not hunger demanding renewal but surfeit that would demand more surfeit . . . kisses that were like charity, creating want by holding back nothing at all.

It did not take him many hours to decide that he had wanted Judy Jones ever since he was a proud, desirous little boy.

IV

It began like that—and continued, with varying shades of intensity, on such a note right up to the dénouement. Dexter surrendered a part of himself to the most direct and unprincipled personality with which he had ever come in contact. Whatever Judy wanted, she went after with the full pressure of her charm. There was no divergence of method, no jockeying for position or premeditation of effects—there was very little mental side to any of her affairs. She simply made men conscious to the highest degree of her physical loveliness. Dexter had no desire to change her. Her deficiencies were knit up with a passionate energy that transcended and justified them.

When, as Judy's head lay against his shoulder that first night, she whispered, "I don't know what's the matter with me. Last night I thought I was in love with a man and tonight I think I'm in love with you——"—it seemed to him a beautiful and romantic thing to say. It was the exquisite excitability that for the moment he controlled and owned. But a week later he was compelled to view this same quality in a different light. She took him in her roadster to a picnic supper, and after supper she disappeared, likewise in her roadster, with another man. Dexter became enormously upset and was scarcely able to be decently civil to the other people present. When she assured him that she had not kissed the other man, he knew she was lying—yet he was glad that she had taken the trouble to lie to him.

He was, as he found before the summer ended, one of a varying dozen who circulated about her. Each of them had at one time been favored above all others—about half of them still basked in the solace of occasional sentimental revivals. Whenever one showed signs of dropping out through long neglect, she granted him a brief honeyed hour, which encouraged him to tag along for a year or so longer. Judy made these forays upon the helpless and defeated without malice, indeed half unconscious that there was anything mischievous in what she did.

When a new man came to town every one dropped out—dates were automatically cancelled.

The helpless part of trying to do anything about it was that she did it all herself. She was not a girl who could be "won" in the kinetic sense—she was proof against cleverness, she was proof against charm; if any of these assailed her too strongly she would immediately resolve the affair to a physical basis, and under the magic of her physical splendor the strong as well as the brilliant played her game and not their own. She was entertained only by the gratification of her desires and by the direct exercise of her own charm. Perhaps from so much youthful love, so many youthful lovers, she had come, in self-defense, to nourish herself wholly from within.

Succeeding Dexter's first exhilaration came restlessness and dissatisfaction. The helpless ecstasy of losing himself in her was opiate rather than tonic. It was fortunate for his work during the winter that those moments of ecstasy came infrequently. Early in their acquaintance it had seemed for a while that there was a deep and spontaneous mutual attraction—that first August, for example—three days of long evenings on her dusky veranda, of strange wan kisses through the late afternoon, in shadowy alcoves or behind the protecting trellises of the garden arbors, of mornings when she was fresh as a dream and almost shy at meeting him in the clarity of the rising day. There was all the ecstasy of an engagement about it, sharpened by his realization that there was no engagement. It was during those three days that, for the first time, he had asked her to marry him. She said "maybe some day," she said "kiss me," she said "I'd like to marry you," she said "I love you"—she said—nothing.

The three days were interrupted by the arrival of a New York man who visited at her house for half September. To Dexter's agony, rumor engaged them. The man was the son of the president of a great trust company. But at the end of a month it was reported that Judy was yawning. At a dance one night she sat all evening in a motor-boat with a local beau, while the New Yorker searched the club for her frantically. She told the local beau that she was bored with her visitor, and two days later he left. She was seen with him at the station, and it was reported that he looked very mournful indeed.

On this note the summer ended. Dexter was twenty-four, and he found himself increasingly in a position to do as he wished. He joined two clubs in the city and lived at one of them. Though he was by no means an integral part of the stag-lines at these clubs, he managed to be on hand at dances where Judy Jones was likely to appear. He could have gone out socially as much as he liked—he was an eligible young man, now, and popular with down-town fathers. His confessed devotion to Judy Jones had rather solidified his position. But he had no social aspirations and rather despised the dancing men who were always on tap for the Thursday or Saturday parties and who filled in at dinners with the younger married set. Already he was playing with the idea of going East to New York. He wanted to take Judy Jones with him. No disillusion as to the world in which she had grown up could cure his illusion as to her desirability.

Remember that—for only in the light of it can what he did for her be understood.

Eighteen months after he first met Judy Jones he became engaged to another girl. Her name was Irene Scheerer, and her father was one of the men who had always believed in Dexter. Irene was light-haired and sweet and honorable, and a little stout, and she had two suitors whom she pleasantly relinquished when Dexter formally asked her to marry him.

Summer, fall, winter, spring, another summer, another fall—so much he had given of his active life to the incorrigible lips of Judy Jones. She had treated him with interest, with encouragement, with malice, with indifference, with contempt. She had inflicted on him the innumerable little slights and indignities possible in such a case—as if in revenge for having ever cared for him at all. She had beckoned him and yawned at him and beckoned him again and he had responded often with bitterness and narrowed eyes. She had brought him ecstatic happiness and intolerable agony of spirit. She had caused him untold inconvenience and not a little trouble. She had insulted him, and she had ridden over him, and she had played his interest in her against his interest in his work—for fun. She had done everything to him except to criticise him—this she had not done—it seemed to him only because it might have sullied the utter indifference she manifested and sincerely felt toward him.

When autumn had come and gone again it occurred to him that he could not have Judy Jones. He had to beat this into his mind but he convinced himself at last. He lay awake at night for a while and argued it over. He told himself the trouble and the pain she had caused him, he enumerated her glaring deficiencies as a wife. Then he said to himself that he loved her, and after a while he fell asleep. For a week, lest he imagined her husky voice over the telephone or her eyes opposite him at lunch, he worked hard and late, and at night he went to his office and plotted out his years.

At the end of a week he went to a dance and cut in on her once. For almost the first time since they had met he did not ask her to sit out with him or tell her that she was lovely. It hurt him that she did not miss these things—that was all. He was not jealous when he saw that there was a new man to-night. He had been hardened against jealousy long before.

He stayed late at the dance. He sat for an hour with Irene Scheerer and talked about books and about music. He knew very little about either. But he was beginning to be master of his own time now, and he had a rather priggish notion that he—the young and already fabulously successful Dexter Green—should know more about such things.

That was in October, when he was twenty-five. In January, Dexter and Irene became engaged. It was to be announced in June, and they were to be married three months later.

The Minnesota winter prolonged itself interminably, and it was almost May when the winds came soft and the snow ran down into Black Bear Lake at last. For the first time in over a year Dexter was enjoying a certain tranquillity of spirit. Judy Jones had been in Florida, and afterward in Hot Springs, and somewhere she had been engaged, and somewhere she had broken it off. At first, when Dexter had definitely given her up, it had made him sad that people still linked them together and asked for news of her, but when he began to be placed at dinner next to Irene Scheerer people didn't ask him about her any more—they told him about her. He ceased to be an authority on her.

May at last. Dexter walked the streets at night when the darkness was damp as rain, wondering that so soon, with so little done, so much of ecstasy had gone from him. May one year back had been marked by Judy's poignant, unforgivable, yet forgiven turbulence—it had been one of those rare times when he fancied she had grown to care for him. That old penny's worth of happiness he had spent for this bushel of content. He knew that Irene would be no more than a curtain spread behind him, a hand moving among gleaming teacups, a voice calling to children . . . fire and loveliness were gone, the magic of nights and the wonder of the varying hours and seasons . . . slender lips, down-turning, dropping to his lips and bearing him up into a heaven of eyes. . . . The thing was deep in him. He was too strong and alive for it to die lightly.

In the middle of May when the weather balanced for a few days on the thin bridge that led to deep summer he turned in one night at Irene's house. Their engagement was to be announced in a week now—no one would be surprised at it. And to-night they would sit together on the lounge at the University Club and look on for an hour at the dancers. It gave him a sense of solidity to go with her—she was so sturdily popular, so intensely "great."

He mounted the steps of the brownstone house and stepped inside.

"Irene," he called.

Mrs. Scheerer came out of the living-room to meet him.

"Dexter," she said, "Irene's gone up-stairs with a splitting headache. She wanted to go with you but I made her go to bed."

"Nothing serious, I——"

"Oh, no. She's going to play golf with you in the morning. You can spare her for just one night, can't you, Dexter?"

Her smile was kind. She and Dexter liked each other. In the living-room he talked for a moment before he said good-night.

Returning to the University Club, where he had rooms, he stood in the doorway for a moment and watched the dancers. He leaned against the doorpost, nodded at a man or two—yawned.

"Hello, darling."

The familiar voice at his elbow startled him. Judy Jones had left a man and crossed the room to him—Judy Jones, a slender enamelled doll in cloth of gold: gold in a band at her head, gold in two slipper points at her dress's hem. The fragile glow of her face seemed to blossom as she smiled at him. A breeze of warmth and light blew through the room. His hands in the pockets of his dinner-jacket tightened spasmodically. He was filled with a sudden excitement.

"When did you get back?" he asked casually.

"Come here and I'll tell you about it."

She turned and he followed her. She had been away—he could have wept at the wonder of her return. She had passed through enchanted streets, doing things that were like provocative music. All mysterious happenings, all fresh and quickening hopes, had gone away with her, come back with her now.

She turned in the doorway.

"Have you a car here? If you haven't, I have."

"I have a coupé."

In then, with a rustle of golden cloth. He slammed the door. Into so many cars she had stepped—like this—like that—her back against the leather, so—her elbow resting on the door—waiting. She would have been soiled long since had there been anything to soil her—except herself—but this was her own self outpouring.

With an effort he forced himself to start the car and back into the street. This was nothing, he must remember. She had done this before, and he had put her behind him, as he would have crossed a bad account from his books.

He drove slowly down-town and, affecting abstraction, traversed the deserted streets of the business section, peopled here and there where a movie was giving out its crowd or where consumptive or pugilistic youth lounged in front of pool halls. The clink of glasses and the slap of hands on the bars issued from saloons, cloisters of glazed glass and dirty yellow light.

She was watching him closely and the silence was embarrassing, yet in this crisis he could find no casual word with which to profane the hour. At a convenient turning he began to zigzag back toward the University Club.

"Have you missed me?" she asked suddenly.

"Everybody missed you."

He wondered if she knew of Irene Scheerer. She had been back only a day—her absence had been almost contemporaneous with his engagement.

"What a remark!" Judy laughed sadly—without sadness. She looked at him searchingly. He became absorbed in the dashboard.

"You're handsomer than you used to be," she said thoughtfully. "Dexter, you have the most rememberable eyes."

He could have laughed at this, but he did not laugh. It was the sort of thing that was said to sophomores. Yet it stabbed at him.

"I'm awfully tired of everything, darling." She called every one darling, endowing the endearment with careless, individual comraderie. "I wish you'd marry me."

The directness of this confused him. He should have told her now that he was going to marry another girl, but he could not tell her. He could as easily have sworn that he had never loved her.

"I think we'd get along," she continued, on the same note, "unless probably you've forgotten me and fallen in love with another girl."

Her confidence was obviously enormous. She had said, in effect, that she found such a thing impossible to believe, that if it were true he had merely committed a childish indiscretion—and probably to show off. She would forgive him, because it was not a matter of any moment but rather something to be brushed aside lightly.

"Of course you could never love anybody but me," she continued, "I like the way you love me. Oh, Dexter, have you forgotten last year?"

"No, I haven't forgotten."

"Neither have I!"

Was she sincerely moved—or was she carried along by the wave of her own acting?

"I wish we could be like that again," she said, and he forced himself to answer:

"I don't think we can."

"I suppose not. . . . I hear you're giving Irene Scheerer a violent rush."

There was not the faintest emphasis on the name, yet Dexter was suddenly ashamed.

"Oh, take me home," cried Judy suddenly; "I don't want to go back to that idiotic dance—with those children."

Then, as he turned up the street that led to the residence district, Judy began to cry quietly to herself. He had never seen her cry before.

The dark street lightened, the dwellings of the rich loomed up around them, he stopped his coupé in front of the great white bulk of the Mortimer Joneses' house, somnolent, gorgeous, drenched with the splendor of the damp moonlight. Its solidity startled him. The strong walls, the steel of the girders, the breadth and beam and pomp of it were there only to bring out the contrast with the young beauty beside him. It was sturdy to accentuate her slightness—as if to show what a breeze could be generated by a butterfly's wing.

He sat perfectly quiet, his nerves in wild clamor, afraid that if he moved he would find her irresistibly in his arms. Two tears had rolled down her wet face and trembled on her upper lip.

"I'm more beautiful than anybody else," she said brokenly, "why can't I be happy?" Her moist eyes tore at his stability—her mouth turned slowly downward with an exquisite sadness: "I'd like to marry you if you'll have me, Dexter. I suppose you think I'm not worth having, but I'll be so beautiful for you, Dexter."

A million phrases of anger, pride, passion, hatred, tenderness fought on his lips. Then a perfect wave of emotion washed over him, carrying off with it a sediment of wisdom, of convention, of doubt, of honor. This was his girl who was speaking, his own, his beautiful, his pride.

"Won't you come in?" He heard her draw in her breath sharply.

Waiting.

"All right," his voice was trembling, "I'll come in."

V

It was strange that neither when it was over nor a long time afterward did he regret that night. Looking at it from the perspective of ten years, the fact that Judy's flare for him endured just one month seemed of little importance. Nor did it matter that by his yielding he subjected himself to a deeper agony in the end and gave serious hurt to Irene Scheerer and to Irene's parents, who had befriended him. There was nothing sufficiently pictorial about Irene's grief to stamp itself on his mind.

Dexter was at bottom hard-minded. The attitude of the city on his action was of no importance to him, not because he was going to leave the city, but because any outside attitude on the situation seemed superficial. He was completely indifferent to popular opinion. Nor, when he had seen that it was no use, that he did not possess in himself the power to move fundamentally or to hold Judy Jones, did he bear any malice toward her. He loved her, and he would love her until the day he was too old for loving—but he could not have her. So he tasted the deep pain that is reserved only for the strong, just as he had tasted for a little while the deep happiness.

Even the ultimate falsity of the grounds upon which Judy terminated the engagement that she did not want to "take him away" from Irene—Judy who had wanted nothing else—did not revolt him. He was beyond any revulsion or any amusement.

He went East in February with the intention of selling out his laundries and settling in New York—but the war came to America in March and changed his plans. He returned to the West, handed over the management of the business to his partner, and went into the first officers' training-camp in late April. He was one of those young thousands who greeted the war with a certain amount of relief, welcoming the liberation from webs of tangled emotion.

VI

This story is not his biography, remember, although things creep into it which have nothing to do with those dreams he had when he was young. We are almost done with them and with him now. There is only one more incident to be related here, and it happens seven years farther on.

It took place in New York, where he had done well—so well that there were no barriers too high for him. He was thirty-two years old, and, except for one flying trip immediately after the war, he had not been West in seven years. A man named Devlin from Detroit came into his office to see him in a business way, and then and there this incident occurred, and closed out, so to speak, this particular side of his life.

"So you're from the Middle West," said the man Devlin with careless curiosity. "That's funny—I thought men like you were probably born and raised on Wall Street.

You know—wife of one of my best friends in Detroit came from your city. I was an usher at the wedding."

Dexter waited with no apprehension of what was coming.

"Judy Simms," said Devlin with no particular interest; "Judy Jones she was once."

"Yes, I knew her." A dull impatience spread over him. He had heard, of course, that she was married—perhaps deliberately he had heard no more.

"Awfully nice girl," brooded Devlin meaninglessly, "I'm sort of sorry for her."

"Why?" Something in Dexter was alert, receptive, at once.

"Oh, Lud Simms has gone to pieces in a way. I don't mean he ill-uses her, but he drinks and runs around——"

"Doesn't she run around?"

"No. Stays at home with her kids."

"Oh."

"She's a little too old for him," said Devlin.

"Too old!" cried Dexter. "Why, man, she's only twenty-seven."

He was possessed with a wild notion of rushing out into the streets and taking a train to Detroit. He rose to his feet spasmodically.

"I guess you're busy," Devlin apologized quickly. "I didn't realize——"

"No, I'm not busy," said Dexter, steadying his voice. "I'm not busy at all. Not busy at all. Did you say she was—twenty-seven? No, I said she was twenty-seven."

"Yes, you did," agreed Devlin dryly.

"Go on, then. Go on."

"What do you mean?"

"About Judy Jones."

Devlin looked at him helplessly.

"Well, that's—I told you all there is to it. He treats her like the devil. Oh, they're not going to get divorced or anything. When he's particularly outrageous she forgives him. In fact, I'm inclined to think she loves him. She was a pretty girl when she first came to Detroit."

A pretty girl! The phrase struck Dexter as ludicrous.

"Isn't she—a pretty girl, any more?"

"Oh, she's all right."

"Look here," said Dexter, sitting down suddenly. "I don't understand. You say she was a 'pretty girl' and now you say she's 'all right.' I don't understand what you mean—Judy Jones wasn't a pretty girl, at all. She was a great beauty. Why, I knew her, I knew her. She was——"

Devlin laughed pleasantly.

"I'm not trying to start a row," he said. "I think Judy's a nice girl and I like her. I can't understand how a man like Lud Simms could fall madly in love with her, but he did." Then he added: "Most of the women like her."

Dexter looked closely at Devlin, thinking wildly that there must be a reason for this, some insensitivity in the man or some private malice.

"Lots of women fade just like *that*," Devlin snapped his fingers. "You must have seen it happen. Perhaps I've forgotten how pretty she was at her wedding. I've seen her so much since then, you see. She has nice eyes."

A sort of dullness settled down upon Dexter. For the first time in his life he felt like getting very drunk. He knew that he was laughing loudly at something Devlin had said, but he did not know what it was or why it was funny. When, in a few minutes, Devlin went he lay down on his lounge and looked out the window at the New York sky-line into which the sun was sinking in dull lovely shades of pink and gold.

He had thought that having nothing else to lose he was invulnerable at last—but he knew that he had just lost something more, as surely as if he had married Judy Jones and seen her fade away before his eyes.

The dream was gone. Something had been taken from him. In a sort of panic he pushed the palms of his hands into his eyes and tried to bring up a picture of the waters lapping on Sherry Island and the moonlit veranda, and gingham on the golf-links and the dry sun and the gold color of her neck's soft down. And her mouth damp to his kisses and her eyes plaintive with melancholy and her freshness like new fine linen in the morning. Why, these things were no longer in the world! They had existed and they existed no longer.

For the first time in years the tears were streaming down his face. But they were for himself now. He did not care about mouth and eyes and moving hands. He wanted to care, and he could not care. For he had gone away and he could never go back any more. The gates were closed, the sun was gone down, and there was no beauty but the gray beauty of steel that withstands all time. Even the grief he could have borne was left behind in the country of illusion, of youth, of the richness of life, where his winter dreams had flourished.

"Long ago," he said, "long ago, there was something in me, but now that thing is gone. Now that thing is gone, that thing is gone. I cannot cry. I cannot care. That thing will come back no more."

1922

William Faulkner
1897–1962

Eudora Welty said that to be a writer in Mississippi after Faulkner was like living next door to a mountain. Brilliant and erratic (even after he won the Nobel Prize in 1949, he was still capable of producing work his editors hesitated to publish), Faulkner is today generally regarded as the greatest twentieth-century American writer of fiction, and his work is routinely ranked with the literary achievements of Hawthorne, Melville, Twain, and James. Although Faulkner's novels and tales have been frequently described as difficult and obscure, his explanation of them was simple: He wrote, he said in his Nobel Prize acceptance speech, of "the problems of the human heart in conflict with itself which alone can make good writing because only that is worth writing about, worth the agony and the sweat."

Born on September 25, 1897, in New Albany, Mississippi, Faulkner soon moved with his family to Oxford, Mississippi, where he lived most of his life. He grew up with legends about his ancestors, most notably his great-grandfather, William Clark Falkner, a lawyer and a Civil War colonel prominent in the region for his colorful exploits, his political influence and wealth, his keen sense of honor, and his popular romantic novel, *The White Rose of Memphis* (1881). "When I was a little boy," Faulkner said, "there'd be sometimes twenty or thirty people in the house, mostly relatives, . . . some maybe coming for overnight and staying on for months, swapping stories about the family and about the past, while I sat in a corner and listened. That's where I got my books." The Faulkner family had made its money in railroad and banking enterprises during the post–Civil War era, but after the family railroad was sold in 1902, Faulkner's father ran a livery stable, then a hardware store, and eventually became business manager of the University of Mississippi.

A good student in his early years, Faulkner soon became restive in school and was often truant. Though he liked to read, draw, and write poetry, he attended classes during his last two years of high school mainly to play football. In 1915 he dropped out of school for good, planning to work in his grandfather's bank. For two years he frequented the University of Mississippi campus, writing poems and submitting his drawings to student publications. Distressed when his childhood sweetheart decided to marry another man, Faulkner tried to enlist in the U.S. Army, only to be told that he was too small (he was five feet five and a half inches tall). In the spring of 1918 he moved to New Haven, Connecticut, to be close to an Oxford friend, Phil Stone, who was attending Yale Law School and who had already begun to encourage and promote Faulkner's literary talents. Later that year Faulkner changed the spelling of his name from Falkner to Faulkner and enlisted with the Royal Air Force in Canada. After spending several months in Toronto, he returned to Oxford dressed in an officer's uniform and armed with dramatic tales of his adventures in the skies over France.

As a veteran, Faulkner was allowed in the fall of 1919 to enroll as a special student at the University of Mississippi, where he studied French and wrote for University periodicals. He had a poem accepted by *The New Republic*, and his first published short story, an aviation tale, appeared in the college newspaper. But Faulkner soon found college little more to his liking than high school had been, and after a year and a half he again dropped out. He continued to read, write, and sketch while working for brief intervals as a salesman in a New York City bookstore and as a carpenter, a house painter, and a university postmaster in Oxford, earning for himself a reputation as a ne'er-do-well. "Count No Count," the people of Oxford called him.

During his early years as a writer, Faulkner thought of himself as a poet (he would later describe himself as a "failed poet"). His reading continued to range widely, from French and English poetry of the nineteenth and early twentieth centuries to Cervantes and Shakespeare, Fielding and Dickens, Hawthorne and Melville, Balzac, Conrad, and Joyce. But most of his early writing is poetry, much of it written in the pastoral mode and all of it full not only of echoes but of borrowed words and borrowed sentiments, taken especially from the Romantics, particularly John Keats; from the Victorians, particularly Alfred Lord Tennyson; from the aesthetes and decadents of the late nineteenth and early twentieth centuries, particularly Algernon Charles Swinburne and A. E. Housman; and from his own contemporaries, particularly T. S. Eliot. In 1924, with the energetic help of his friend Phil Stone, who acted from time to time as critic, editor, agent, and publicist, Faulkner published his first book, a slim volume of poetry called—in echo of Hawthorne—*The Marble Faun*. Stone also wrote the book's preface, promoting Faulkner as a promising local celebrity, "a man steeped in the soil of his native land, a Southerner by every instinct, and, more than that, a Mississippian."

The first major turning point in Faulkner's career came in the fall of 1924, when he visited New Orleans and met Sherwood Anderson, whose writing he admired; at the time, Faulkner thought Conrad's *Heart of Darkness* and Anderson's "I'm a Fool" the two best stories he had ever read. The following year, he spent several months with Anderson, discussing books, spinning yarns, and drinking, while he contributed to the new literary magazine, *The Double Dealer,* and wrote sketches of New Orleans for the *Times-Picayune* (these were collected in 1968 as *New Orleans Sketches*). With Anderson's encouragement, Faulkner was turning increasingly to prose. While in New Orleans he finished *Soldiers' Pay* (1926), a novel about the homecoming of a badly scarred and dying air force veteran. In the summer of 1925 Faulkner traveled to Europe, visiting Italy, Switzerland, France, and England. Upon his return, he alternated between Oxford and New Orleans.

In 1927 Faulkner brought out his second novel, *Mosquitoes,* a story about a sophisticated New Orleans literary crowd on a yachting expedition that is written in the "conversational" mode Aldous Huxley had made fashionable in the 1920s. It is, however, in the work that followed *Mosquitoes,* the work set in his mythical Mississippi county, Yoknapatawpha, that Faulkner established the special themes—having to do with the complexities of sexual, familial, social, and racial identities and the force and burden of the past—that would eventually make him famous. In writing a book originally called *Flags in the Dust* but published as *Sartoris* (1929), Faulkner made the discovery that marked the second turning point in his career: "I discovered that my own little postage stamp of native soil was worth writing about and that I would never live long enough to exhaust it, and that by sublimating the actual into the apocryphal I might have complete liberty to use whatever talent I might have to its absolute top. I opened up a gold mine of other people, so I created a cosmos of my own." In *Sartoris,* a novel about the history of several generations of a distinguished Mississippi family, modeled in part on his own family, Faulkner introduced many of the characters and themes he would work with in his fiction throughout his career.

In the best of the Yoknapatawpha fiction, Faulkner created works unequaled in America in this century. Of his twenty novels, fifteen are set in Yoknapatawpha County, a location based on Lafayette County in northern Mississippi. *The Sound and the Fury* (1929), one of the great twentieth-century novels, treats the economic and emotional deterioration of the Compson family in four magnificent chapters, each one dramatizing a different consciousness with a different conception of time and language. The famous opening chapter, for example, is narrated by Benjy Compson, a thirty-three-year-old idiot, as his mind alternates between sense impressions and memories. No less innovative in its narrative method is Faulkner's next novel, *As I Lay Dying* (1930), which he wrote while working the night shift in a University of Mississippi boiler room. The novel, told from the multiple perspectives of fifteen "interior monologues," moves between horror and comedy as it recounts the adventures of a poor white family's efforts to fulfill the mother's wish to have her body decently buried in her hometown. Plot summary can give no sense of Faulkner's stylistic achievement in these books and those that were to follow. Trying to capture the effect on the reader of Faulkner's narrative technique, Jean-Paul Sartre wrote:

> Faulkner's vision of the world can be compared to that of a man sitting in a convert-
> ible looking backward. At every moment shadows emerge on his right, and on his left

flickering and quavering points of light, which become trees, men, and cars only when they are seen in perspective. The past here gains a surrealistic quality; its outline is hard, clear, and immutable. The indefinable and elusive present is helpless before it; it is full of holes through which past things, fixed, motionless, and silent, invade it.

In 1929 Faulkner finally succeeded in marrying his childhood sweetheart, not long after she had divorced her first husband and moved back to Oxford with her two children. The following year he bought and restored an antebellum mansion; he was also beginning to sell his fiction to national magazines. In 1931 he published *Sanctuary,* the tale of a collegiate "flapper," Temple Drake, who gets involved with criminals, drugs, and prostitution. Following *Sanctuary,* the first of his novels to enjoy any commercial success, Faulkner immediately wrote several of his finest novels. In 1932 he published *Light in August,* a story of sexual passion, racism, and religious fanaticism that traces the parallel destinies of two wandering orphans—a pregnant country girl, Lena Grove, who is searching for her fleeing lover, and a presumed murderer, Joe Christmas, who is eventually shot and castrated. In *Absalom, Absalom!* (1936), Faulkner explored the intricate family history of a poor white man, Thomas Sutpen, whose dream of founding a dynasty in Mississippi ends in the tragic ruin of almost everyone involved. In 1938 Faulkner collected seven stories concerning the Sartoris family in *The Unvanquished.* He also published two non-Yoknapatawpha books during this period: *Pylon* (1935), a novel that grew out of Faulkner's flying lessons in 1933 and that traces the adventures of barnstorming airplane pilots, and *Wild Palms* (1939), a novel with two stories arranged in alternating chapters—one the tale of two doomed lovers and the other the story of a convict caught in a flood.

In 1940 Faulkner completed *The Hamlet,* the story of a grasping and rising family of poor whites, the Snopeses, who are described as "just Snopes, like colonies of rats or termites." Faulkner later added two more episodic novels about the Snopes family, *The Town* (1957) and *The Mansion* (1959), the three books usually being referred to as the Snopes trilogy. In 1942 Faulkner completed *Go Down, Moses,* which explores the history of the racially mixed McCaslin family. Faulkner frequently incorporated stories into his novels. "Spotted Horses," for example, evolved into a section of *The Hamlet.* Many stories, furthermore, deal with characters who also appear in the novels. The Compsons of "That Evening Sun," for example, are the central characters in *The Sound and the Fury.*

Because of his complex narrative methods and his morally oriented subject matter, Faulkner did not greatly interest sociologically minded critics during the Depression years; by the mid-1940s, of all his books, only *Sanctuary* remained in print. During the late 1940s and the early 1950s, however, a reappraisal of Faulkner's achievement began, spurred in part by the publication in 1948 of *Intruder in the Dust,* a "detective" story about an elderly African American man who refuses to "act like a nigger" and whose surprising innocence in a murder case leaves him a "tyrant over the whole county's white conscience." In 1950, shortly after the appearance of his *Collected Stories,* Faulkner learned that he had won the Nobel Prize for literature. In the early 1950s he made several trips to Europe and lectured frequently on college campuses. In 1954 he published *The Fable,* a dense allegory that takes place during the false armistice of 1918. The novel won both the National Book Award and the Pulitzer Prize. A month before his death from a heart attack in 1962, Faulkner published his last novel, *The Reivers,* a nostalgic and comic story based on events remembered from his childhood.

Although Faulkner's finest fiction deals with one imaginary county in Mississippi, it explores the whole of human experience, a fact recognized when Faulkner received the Nobel Prize. No American writer of his time has exerted wider influence. His fiction has been translated into many languages, and it has exercised a deep, varied influence on writers not only in Europe, especially France, but throughout South America and even Japan, where he traveled on a State Department trip in 1955. In his work readers have discovered a feeling for the American South—and for the South's history—that bespeaks a concern for human beings both in the modern world and in some larger, more inclusive realm as well. In addition, readers have recognized that Faulkner's work is strikingly innovative in structure, form, and style. In its rhetorical extravagance and its dry understatement, in its rich allusions and intricate design, readers have found themselves amply challenged and amply rewarded. "The study of Faulkner," said Robert Penn Warren, "is the most challenging single task in contemporary American literature for criticism to undertake. Here is a novelist who, in mass of work, in scope of material, in range of effect, in reportorial accuracy and symbolic subtlety, in philosophical weight can be put beside the masters of our own past literature."

Shortly before Faulkner died on July 6, 1962, he wrote in a letter to a friend that he had finally gotten "some perspective on all that I have done. I mean, the work apart from me, the work which I did, apart from what I am. . . . And now I realise for the first time what an amazing gift I had. . . . I don't know where it came from." Though Faulkner sometimes feared that words bore too little relation to life, his fiction demonstrates the power of words—their power to serve, as one of his characters puts it, as a "meager and fragile thread . . . by which the little surface corners and edges of men's secret and solitary lives may be joined for an instant now and then," and their power, as another of his characters puts it, when brought "into a happy conjunction" to "produce something that lives."

Further Reading:

C. Brooks, *William Faulkner: The Yoknapatawpha Country*, 1963.

J. Blotner, *Faulkner: A Biography*, 1974.

D. Kartiganer, *The Fragile Thread: The Meaning of Form in Faulkner's Novels*, 1979.

D. Minter, *William Faulkner: His Life and Work*, 1980.

R. H. Brodhead, ed., *Faulkner: New Perspectives*, 1983.

T. Davis, *Faulkner's "Negro": Art and the Southern Context*, 1983.

W. Wadlington, *Reading Faulknerian Tragedy*, 1987.

W. Morris, with B. Morris, *Reading Faulkner*, 1989.

A. Bleikasten, *The Ink of Melancholy: Faulkner's Novels from "The Sound and the Fury" to "Light in August,"* 1990.

Texts:

"Spotted Horses" from *Uncollected Stories of William Faulkner*, 1979.

"That Evening Sun" from *Collected Stories*, 1976.

Spotted Horses

I

Yes, sir. Flem Snopes has filled that whole country full of spotted horses. You can hear folks running them all day and all night, whooping and hollering, and the horses running back and forth across them little wooden bridges ever now and then kind of like thunder. Here I was this morning pretty near half way to town, with the team ambling along and me setting in the buckboard about half asleep, when all of a sudden something come swurging up outen the bushes and jumped the road clean, without touching hoof to it. It flew right over my team, big as a billboard and flying through the air like a hawk. It taken me thirty minutes to stop my team and untangle the harness and the buckboard and hitch them up again.

That Flem Snopes. I be dog if he ain't a case, now. One morning about ten years ago, the boys was just getting settled down on Varner's porch for a little talk and tobacco, when here come Flem out from behind the counter, with his coat off and his hair all parted, like he might have been clerking for Varner for ten years already. Folks all knowed him; it was a big family of them about five miles down the bottom. That year, at least. Share-cropping. They never stayed on any place over a year. Then they would move on to another place, with the chap or maybe the twins of that year's litter. It was a regular nest of them. But Flem. The rest of them stayed tenant farmers, moving ever year, but here come Flem one day, walking out from behind Jody Varner's counter like he owned it. And he wasn't there but a year or two before folks knowed that, if him and Jody was both still in that store in ten years more, it would be Jody clerking for Flem Snopes. Why, that fellow could make a nickel where it wasn't but four cents to begin with. He skun me in two trades, myself, and the fellow that can do that, I just hope he'll get rich before I do; that's all.

All right. So here Flem was, clerking at Varner's, making a nickel here and there and not telling nobody about it. No, sir. Folks never knowed when Flem got the better of somebody lessen the fellow he beat told it. He'd just set there in the store-chair, chewing his tobacco and keeping his own business to hisself, until about a week later we'd find out it was somebody else's business he was keeping to hisself—provided the fellow he trimmed was mad enough to tell it. That's Flem.

We give him ten years to own ever thing Jody Varner had. But he never waited no ten years. I reckon you-all know that gal of Uncle Billy Varner's, the youngest one; Eula. Jody's sister. Ever Sunday ever yellow-wheeled buggy and curried riding horse in that country would be hitched to Bill Varner's fence, and the young bucks setting on the porch, swarming around Eula like bees around a honey pot. One of these here kind of big, soft-looking gals that could giggle richer than plowed new-ground. Wouldn't none of them leave before the others, and so they would set there on the porch until time to go home, with some of them with nine and ten miles to ride and then get up tomorrow and go back to the field. So they would all leave together and they would ride in a clump down to the creek ford and hitch them curried horses and yellow-wheeled buggies and get out and fight one another. Then they would get in the buggies again and go on home.

Well, one day about a year ago, one of them yellow-wheeled buggies and one of them curried saddle-horses quit this country. We heard they was heading for Texas. The next day Uncle Billy and Eula and Flem come in to town in Uncle Bill's surrey, and when they come back, Flem and Eula was married. And on the next day we heard that two more of them yellow-wheeled buggies had left the country. They mought have gone to Texas, too. It's a big place.

Anyway, about a month after the wedding, Flem and Eula went to Texas, too. They was gone pretty near a year. Then one day last month, Eula come back, with a baby. We figgered up, and we decided that it was as well-growed a three-months-old baby as we ever see. It can already pull up on a chair. I reckon Texas makes big men quick, being a big place. Anyway, if it keeps on like it started, it'll be chewing tobacco and voting time it's eight years old.

And so last Friday here come Flem himself. He was on a wagon with another fellow. The other fellow had one of these two-gallon hats and a ivory-handled pistol and a box of gingersnaps sticking out of his hind pocket, and tied to the tail-gate of the wagon was about two dozen of them Texas ponies, hitched to one another with barbed wire. They was colored like parrots and they was quiet as doves, and ere a one of them would kill you quick as a rattlesnake. Nere a one of them had two eyes the same color, and nere a one of them had ever see a bridle, I reckon; and when that Texas man got down offen the wagon and walked up to them to show how gentle they was, one of them cut his vest clean offen him, same as with a razor.

Flem had done already disappeared; he had went on to see his wife, I reckon, and to see if that ere baby had done gone on to the field to help Uncle Billy plow maybe. It was the Texas man that taken the horses on to Mrs. Littlejohn's lot. He had a little trouble at first, when they come to the gate, because they hadn't never see a fence before, and when he finally got them in and taken a pair of wire cutters and unhitched them and got them into the barn and poured some shell corn into the trough, they durn nigh tore down the barn. I reckon they thought that shell corn was bugs, maybe. So he left them in the lot and he announced that the auction would begin at sunup to-morrow.

That night we was setting on Mrs. Littlejohn's porch. You-all mind the moon was nigh full that night, and we could watch them spotted varmints swirling along the fence and back and forth across the lot same as minnows in a pond. And then now and then they would all kind of huddle up against the barn and rest themselves by biting and kicking one another. We would hear a squeal, and then a set of hoofs would go Bam! against the barn, like a pistol. It sounded just like a fellow with a pistol, in a nest of cat-tymounts, taking his time.

II

It wasn't ere a man knowed yet if Flem owned them things or not. They just knowed one thing: that they wasn't never going to know for sho if Flem did or not, or if maybe he didn't just get on that wagon at the edge of town, for the ride or not. Even Eck Snopes didn't know, Flem's own cousin. But wasn't nobody surprised at that. We knowed that Flem would skin Eck quick as he would ere a one of us.

They was there by sunup next morning, some of them come twelve and sixteen miles, with seed-money tied up in tobacco sacks in their overalls, standing along the fence, when the Texas man come out of Mrs. Littlejohn's after breakfast and clumb onto the gate post with that ere white pistol butt sticking outen his hind pocket. He taken a new box of gingersnaps outen his pocket and bit the end offen it like a cigar and spit out the paper, and said the auction was open. And still they was coming up in wagons and a horse- and mule-back and hitching the teams across the road and coming to the fence. Flem wasn't nowhere in sight.

But he couldn't get them started. He begun to work on Eck, because Eck holp him last night to get them into the barn and feed them that shell corn. Eck got out just in time. He come outen that barn like a chip on the crest of a busted dam of water, and clumb into the wagon just in time.

He was working on Eck when Henry Armstid come up in his wagon. Eck was saying he was skeered to bid on one of them, because he might get it, and the Texas man says, "Them ponies? Them little horses?" He clumb down offen the gate post and went toward the horses. They broke and run, and him following them, kind of chirping to them, with his hand out like he was fixing to catch a fly, until he got three or four of them cornered. Then he jumped into them, and then we couldn't see nothing for a while because of the dust. It was a big cloud of it, and them blare-eyed, spotted things swoaring outen it twenty foot to a jump, in forty directions without counting up. Then the dust settled and there they was, that Texas man and the horse. He had its head twisted clean around like a owl's head. Its legs was braced and it was trembling like a new bride and groaning like a saw mill, and him holding its head wrung clean around on its neck so it was snuffing sky. "Look it over," he says, with his heels dug too and that white pistol sticking outen his pocket and his neck swole up like a spreading adder's until you could just tell what he was saying, cussing the horse and talking to us all at once: "Look him over, the fiddleheaded son of fourteen fathers. Try him, buy him; you will get the best—" Then it was all dust again, and we couldn't see nothing but spotted hide and mane, and that ere Texas man's boot-heels like a couple of walnuts on two strings, and after a while that two-gallon hat come sailing out like a fat old hen crossing a fence.

When the dust settled again, he was just getting outen the far fence corner, brushing himself off. He come and got his hat and brushed it off and come and clumb onto the gate post again. He was breathing hard. He taken the gingersnap box outen his pocket and et one, breathing hard. The hammer-head horse was still running round and round the lot like a merry-go-round at a fair. That was when Henry Armstid come shoving up to the gate in patched overalls and one of them dangle-armed shirts of hisn. Hadn't nobody noticed him until then. We was all watching the Texas man and the horses. Even Mrs. Littlejohn; she had done come out and built a fire under the wash-pot in her back yard, and she would stand at the fence a while and then go back into the house and come out again with a arm full of wash and stand at the fence again. Well, here come Henry shoving up, and then we see Mrs. Armstid right behind him, in that ere faded wrapper and sunbonnet and them tennis shoes. "Git on back to that wagon," Henry says.

"Henry," she says.

"Here, boys," the Texas man says; "make room for missus to git up and see. Come on, Henry," he says; "here's your chance to buy that saddle-horse missus has been wanting. What about ten dollars, Henry?"

"Henry," Mrs. Armstid says. She put her hand on Henry's arm. Henry knocked her hand down.

"Git on back to that wagon, like I told you," he says.

Mrs. Armstid never moved. She stood behind Henry, with her hands rolled into her dress, not looking at nothing. "He hain't no more despair than to buy one of them things," she says. "And us not five dollars ahead of the pore house, he hain't no more despair." It was the truth, too. They ain't never made more than a bare living offen that place of theirs, and them with four chaps and the very clothes they wears she earns by weaving by the firelight at night while Henry's asleep.

"Shut your mouth and git on back to that wagon," Henry says. "Do you want I taken a wagon stake to you here in the big road?"

Well, that Texas man taken one look at her. Then he begun on Eck again, like Henry wasn't even there. But Eck was skeered. "I can git me a snapping turtle or a water moccasin for nothing. I ain't going to buy none."

So the Texas man said he would give Eck a horse. "To start the auction, and because you holp me last night. If you'll start the bidding on the next horse," he says, "I'll give you that fiddle-head horse."

I wish you could have seen them, standing there with their seed-money in their pockets, watching that Texas man give Eck Snopes a live horse, all fixed to call him a fool if he taken it or not. Finally Eck says he'll take it. "Only I just starts the bidding," he says. "I don't have to buy the next one lessen I ain't overtopped." The Texas man said all right, and Eck bid a dollar on the next one, with Henry Armstid standing there with his mouth already open, watching Eck and the Texas man like a mad-dog or something. "A dollar," Eck says.

The Texas man looked at Eck. His mouth was already open too, like he had started to say something and what he was going to say had up and died on him. "A dollar?" he says. "One dollar? You mean, *one* dollar, Eck?"

"Durn it," Eck says; "two dollars, then."

Well, sir, I wish you could a seen that Texas man. He taken out that gingersnap box and held it up and looked into it, careful, like it might have been a diamond ring in it, or a spider. Then he threwed it away and wiped his face with a bandanna. "Well," he says. "Well. Two dollars. Two dollars. Is your pulse all right, Eck?" he says. "Do you have ager-sweats at night, maybe?" he says. "Well," he says, "I got to take it. But are you boys going to stand there and see Eck get two horses at a dollar a head?"

That done it. I be dog if he wasn't nigh as smart as Flem Snopes. He hadn't no more than got the words outen his mouth before here was Henry Armstid, waving his hand. "Three dollars," Henry says. Mrs. Armstid tried to hold him again. He knocked her hand off, shoving up to the gate post.

"Mister," Mrs. Armstid says, "we got chaps in the house and not corn to feed the stock. We got five dollars I earned my chaps a-weaving after dark, and him snoring in the bed. And he hain't no more despair."

"Henry bids three dollars," the Texas man says. "Raise him a dollar, Eck, and the horse is yours."

"Henry," Mrs. Armstid says.

"Raise him, Eck," the Texas man says.

"Four dollars," Eck says.

"Five dollars," Henry says, shaking his fist. He shoved up right under the gate post. Mrs. Armstid was looking at the Texas man too.

"Mister," she says, "if you take that five dollars I earned my chaps a-weaving for one of them things, it'll be a curse onto you and yourn during all the time of man."

But it wasn't no stopping Henry. He had shoved up, waving his fist at the Texas man. He opened it; the money was in nickels and quarters, and one dollar bill that looked like a cow's cud. "Five dollars," he says. "And the man that raises it'll have to beat my head off, or I'll beat hisn."

"All right," the Texas man says. "Five dollars is bid. But don't you shake your hand at me."

III

It taken till nigh sundown before the last one was sold. He got them hotted up once and the bidding got up to seven dollars and a quarter, but most of them went around three or four dollars, him setting on the gate post and picking the horses out one at a time by mouth-word, and Mrs. Littlejohn pumping up and down at the tub and stopping and coming to the fence for a while and going back to the tub again. She had done got done too, and the wash was hung on the line in the back yard, and we could smell supper cooking. Finally they was all sold; he swapped the last two and the wagon for a buckboard.

We was all kind of tired, but Henry Armstid looked more like a mad-dog than ever. When he bought, Mrs. Armstid had went back to the wagon, setting in it behind them two rabbit-sized, bone-pore mules, and the wagon itself looking like it would fall all to pieces soon as the mules moved. Henry hadn't even waited to pull it outen the road; it was still in the middle of the road and her setting in it, not looking at nothing, ever since this morning.

Henry was right up against the gate. He went up to the Texas man. "I bought a horse and I paid cash," Henry says. "And yet you expect me to stand around here until they are all sold before I can get my horse. I'm going to take my horse outen that lot."

The Texas man looked at Henry. He talked like he might have been asking for a cup of coffee at the table. "Take your horse," he says.

Then Henry quit looking at the Texas man. He begun to swallow, holding onto the gate. "Ain't you going to help me?" he says.

"It ain't my horse," the Texas man says.

Henry never looked at the Texas man again, he never looked at nobody. "Who'll help me catch my horse?" he says. Never nobody said nothing. "Bring the plowline," Henry says. Mrs. Armstid got outen the wagon and brought the plowline. The Texas man got down offen the post. The woman made to pass him, carrying the rope.

"Don't you go in there, missus," the Texas man says.

Henry opened the gate. He didn't look back. "Come on here," he says.

"Don't you go in there, missus," the Texas man says.

Mrs. Armstid wasn't looking at nobody, neither, with her hands across her middle, holding the rope. "I reckon I better," she says. Her and Henry went into the lot. The horses broke and run. Henry and Mrs. Armstid followed.

"Get him into the corner," Henry says. They got Henry's horse cornered finally, and Henry taken the rope, but Mrs. Armstid let the horse get out. They hemmed it up again, but Mrs. Armstid let it get out again, and Henry turned and hit her with the rope. "Why didn't you head him back?" Henry says. He hit her again. "Why didn't you?" It was about that time I looked around and see Flem Snopes standing there.

It was the Texas man that done something. He moved fast for a big man. He caught the rope before Henry could hit the third time, and Henry whirled and made like he would jump at the Texas man. But he never jumped. The Texas man went and taken Henry's arm and led him outen the lot. Mrs. Armstid come behind them and the Texas man taken some money outen his pocket and he give it into Mrs. Armstid's hand. "Get him into the wagon and take him on home," the Texas man says, like he might have been telling them he enjoyed his supper.

Then here come Flem. "What's that for, Buck?" Flem says.

"Thinks he bought one of them ponies," the Texas man says. "Get him on away, missus."

But Henry wouldn't go. "Give him back that money," he says. "I bought that horse and I aim to have him if I have to shoot him."

And there was Flem, standing there with his hands in his pockets, chewing, like he had just happened to be passing.

"You take your money and I take my horse," Henry says. "Give it back to him," he says to Mrs. Armstid.

"You don't own no horse of mine," the Texas man says. "Get him on home, missus."

Then Henry seen Flem. "You got something to do with these horses," he says. "I bought one. Here's the money for it." He taken the bill outen Mrs. Armstid's hand. He offered it to Flem. "I bought one. Ask him. Here. Here's the money," he says, giving the bill to Flem.

When Flem taken the money, the Texas man dropped the rope he had snatched outen Henry's hand. He had done sent Eck Snopes's boy up to the store for another box of gingersnaps, and he taken the box outen his pocket and looked into it. It was empty and he dropped it on the ground. "Mr. Snopes will have your money for you to-mor-row," he says to Mrs. Armstid. "You can get it from him to-morrow. He don't own no horse. You get him into the wagon and get him on home." Mrs. Armstid went back to the wagon and got in. "Where's that ere buckboard I bought?" the Texas man says. It was after sundown then. And then Mrs. Littlejohn come out on the porch and rung the supper bell.

IV

I come on in and et supper. Mrs. Littlejohn would bring in a pan of bread or something, then she would go out to the porch a minute and come back and tell us. The Texas man had hitched his team to the buckboard he had swapped them last two horses for, and him and Flem had gone, and then she told that the rest of them that never had ropes had went back to the store with I. O. Snopes to get some ropes, and wasn't nobody at the gate but Henry Armstid, and Mrs. Armstid setting in the wagon in the road, and Eck Snopes and that boy of hisn. "I don't care how many of them fool men gets killed by them things," Mrs. Littlejohn says, "but I ain't going to let Eck Snopes take that boy into that lot again." So she went down to the gate, but she come back without the boy or Eck neither.

"It ain't no need to worry about that boy," I says. "He's charmed." He was right be-hind Eck last night when Eck went to help feed them. The whole drove of them jumped clean over that boy's head and never touched him. It was Eck that touched him. Eck snatched him into the wagon and taken a rope and frailed the tar outen him.

So I had done et and went to my room and was undressing, long as I had a long trip to make next day; I was trying to sell a machine to Mrs. Bundren up past Whiteleaf; when Henry Armstid opened that gate and went in by hisself. They couldn't make him wait for the balance of them to get back with their ropes. Eck Snopes said he tried to make Henry wait, but Henry wouldn't do it. Eck said Henry walked right up to them and that when they broke, they run clean over Henry like a hay-mow breaking down. Eck said he snatched that boy of hisn out of the way just in time and that them things went through that gate like a creek flood and into the wagons and teams hitched side the road, busting wagon tongues and snapping harness like it was fishing-line, with Mrs. Armstid still setting in their wagon in the middle of it like something carved outen wood. Then they scattered, wild horses and tame mules with pieces of harness and sin-gle trees dangling offen them, both ways up and down the road.

"There goes ourn, paw!" Eck says his boy said. "There it goes, into Mrs. Littlejohn's house." Eck says it run right up the steps and into the house like a boarder late for supper. I reckon so. Anyway, I was in my room, in my underclothes, with one sock on and one sock in my hand, leaning out the window when the commotion busted out, when I heard something run into the melodeon in the hall; it sounded like a railroad engine. Then the door to my room come sailing in like when you throw a tin bucket top into the wind and I looked over my shoulder and see something that looked like a fourteen-foot pinwheel a-blaring its eyes at me. It had to blare them fast, because I was already done jumped out the window.

I reckon it was anxious, too. I reckon it hadn't never seen barbed wire or shell corn before, but I know it hadn't never seen underclothes before, or maybe it was a sewing-machine agent it hadn't never seen. Anyway, it swirled and turned to run back up the hall and outen the house, when it met Eck Snopes and that boy just coming in, carrying a rope. It swirled again and run down the hall and out the back door just in time to meet Mrs. Littlejohn. She had just gathered up the clothes she had washed, and she was coming onto the back porch with a armful of washing in one hand and a scrubbing-board in the other, when the horse skidded up to her, trying to stop and swirl again. It never taken Mrs. Littlejohn no time a-tall.

"Git outen here, you son," she says. She hit it across the face with the scrubbing-board; that ere scrubbing-board split as neat as ere a axe could have done it, and when the horse swirled to run back up the hall, she hit it again with what was left of the scrubbing-board, not on the head this time. "And stay out," she says.

Eck and that boy was half-way down the hall by this time. I reckon that horse looked like a pinwheel to Eck too. "Git to hell outen here, Ad!" Eck says. Only there wasn't time. Eck dropped flat on his face, but the boy never moved. The boy was about a yard tall maybe, in overhalls just like Eck's; that horse swoared over his head without touching a hair. I saw that, because I was just coming back up the front steps, still carrying that ere sock and still in my underclothes, when the horse come onto the porch again. It taken one look at me and swirled again and run to the end of the porch and jumped the banisters and the lot fence like a hen-hawk and lit in the lot running and went out the gate again and jumped eight or ten upside-down wagons and went on down the road. It was a full moon then. Mrs. Armstid was still setting in the wagon like she had done been carved outen wood and left there and forgot.

That horse. It ain't never missed a lick. It was going about forty miles a hour when it come to the bridge over the creek. It would have had a clear road, but it so happened that Vernon Tull was already using the bridge when it got there. He was coming back from town; he hadn't heard about the auction; him and his wife and three daughters and Mrs. Tull's aunt, all setting in chairs in the wagon bed, and all asleep, including the mules. They waked up when the horse hit the bridge one time, but Tull said the first he knew was when the mules tried to turn the wagon around in the middle of the bridge and he seen that spotted varmint run right twixt the mules and run up the wagon tongue like a squirrel. He said he just had time to hit it across the face with his whip-stock, because about that time the mules turned the wagon around on that ere one-way bridge and that horse clumb across one of the mules and jumped down onto the bridge again and went on, with Vernon standing up in the wagon and kicking at it.

Tull said the mules turned in the harness and clumb back into the wagon too, with Tull trying to beat them out again, with the reins wrapped around his wrist. After that he says all he seen was overturned chairs and womenfolks' legs and white drawers shining in the moonlight, and his mules and that spotted horse going on up the road like a ghost.

The mules jerked Tull outen the wagon and drug him a spell on the bridge before the reins broke. They thought at first that he was dead, and while they was kneeling around him, picking the bridge splinters outen him, here come Eck and that boy, still carrying the rope. They was running and breathing a little hard. "Where'd he go?" Eck says.

V

I went back and got my pants and shirt and shoes on just in time to go and help get Henry Armstid outen the trash in the lot. I be dog if he didn't look like he was dead, with his head hanging back and his teeth showing in the moonlight, and a little rim of white under his eyelids. We could still hear them horses, here and there; hadn't none of them got more than four-five miles away yet, not knowing the country, I reckon. So we could hear them and folks yelling now and then: "Whooey. Head him!"

We toted Henry into Mrs. Littlejohn's. She was in the hall; she hadn't put down the armful of clothes. She taken one look at us, and she laid down the busted scrubbing-board and taken up the lamp and opened a empty door. "Bring him in here," she says.

We toted him in and laid him on the bed. Mrs. Littlejohn set the lamp on the dresser, still carrying the clothes. "I'll declare, you men," she says. Our shadows was way up the wall, tiptoeing too; we could hear ourselves breathing. "Better get his wife," Mrs. Littlejohn says. She went out, carrying the clothes.

"I reckon we had," Quick says. "Go get her, somebody."

"Whyn't you go?" Winterbottom says.

"Let Ernest git her," Durley says. "He lives neighbors with them."

Ernest went to fetch her. I be dog if Henry didn't look like he was dead. Mrs. Littlejohn come back, with a kettle and some towels. She went to work on Henry, and then Mrs. Armstid and Ernest come in. Mrs. Armstid come to the foot of the bed and stood there, with her hands rolled into her apron, watching what Mrs. Littlejohn was doing, I reckon.

"You men git outen the way," Mrs. Littlejohn says. "Git outside," she says. "See if you can't find something else to play with that will kill some more of you."

"Is he dead?" Winterbottom says.

"It ain't your fault if he ain't," Mrs. Littlejohn says. "Go tell Will Varner to come up here. I reckon a man ain't so different from a mule, come long come short. Except maybe a mule's got more sense."

We went to get Uncle Billy. It was a full moon. We could hear them, now and then, four mile away: "Whooey. Head him." The country was full of them, one on ever wooden bridge in the land, running across it like thunder: "Whooey. There he goes. Head him."

We hadn't got far before Henry begun to scream. I reckon Mrs. Littlejohn's water had brung him to; anyway, he wasn't dead. We went on to Uncle Billy's. The house was dark. We called to him, and after a while the window opened and Uncle Billy put his head out, peart as a peckerwood, listening. "Are they still trying to catch them durn rabbits?" he says.

He come down, with his britches on over his night-shirt and his suspenders dangling, carrying his horse-doctoring grip. "Yes, sir," he says, cocking his head like a woodpecker; "they're still a-trying."

We could hear Henry before we reached Mrs. Littlejohn's. He was going Ah-Ah-Ah. We stopped in the yard. Uncle Billy went on in. We could hear Henry. We stood in the yard, hearing them on the bridges, this-a-way and that: "Whooey. Whooey."

"Eck Snopes ought to caught hisn," Ernest says.

"Looks like he ought," Winterbottom said.

Henry was going Ah-Ah-Ah steady in the house; then he begun to scream. "Uncle Billy's started," Quick says. We looked into the hall. We could see the light where the door was. Then Mrs. Littlejohn come out.

"Will needs some help," she says. "You, Ernest. You'll do." Ernest went into the house.

"Hear them?" Quick said. "That one was on Four Mile bridge." We could hear them; it sounded like thunder a long way off; it didn't last long:

"Whooey."

We could hear Henry: "Ah-Ah-Ah-Ah-Ah."

"They are both started now," Winterbottom says. "Ernest too."

That was early in the night. Which was a good thing, because it taken a long night for folks to chase them things right and for Henry to lay there and holler, being as Uncle Billy never had none of this here chloryfoam to set Henry's leg with. So it was considerate in Flem to get them started early. And what do you reckon Flem's com-ment was?

That's right. Nothing. Because he wasn't there. Hadn't nobody see him since that Texas man left.

VI

That was Saturday night. I reckon Mrs. Armstid got home about daylight, to see about the chaps. I don't know where they thought her and Henry was. But lucky the oldest one was a gal, about twelve, big enough to take care of the little ones. Which she did for the next two days. Mrs. Armstid would nurse Henry all night and work in the kitchen for hern and Henry's keep, and in the afternoon she would drive home (it was about four miles) to see to the chaps. She would cook up a pot of victuals and leave it on the stove, and the gal would bar the house and keep the little ones quiet. I would hear Mrs. Littlejohn and Mrs. Armstid talking in the kitchen. "How are the chaps making out?" Mrs. Littlejohn says.

"All right," Mrs. Armstid says.

"Don't they git skeered at night?" Mrs. Littlejohn says.

"Ina May bars the door when I leave," Mrs. Armstid says. "She's got the axe in bed with her. I reckon she can make out."

I reckon they did. And I reckon Mrs. Armstid was waiting for Flem to come back to town; hadn't nobody seen him until this morning; to get her money the Texas man said Flem was keeping for her. Sho. I reckon she was.

Anyway, I heard Mrs. Armstid and Mrs. Littlejohn talking in the kitchen this morning while I was eating breakfast. Mrs. Littlejohn had just told Mrs. Armstid that Flem was in town. "You can ask him for that five dollars," Mrs. Littlejohn says.

"You reckon he'll give it to me?" Mrs. Armstid says.

Mrs. Littlejohn was washing dishes, washing them like a man, like they was made out of iron. "No," she says. "But asking him won't do no hurt. It might shame him. I don't reckon it will, but it might."

"If he wouldn't give it back, it ain't no use to ask," Mrs. Armstid says.

"Suit yourself," Mrs. Littlejohn says. "It's your money."

I could hear the dishes.

"Do you reckon he might give it back to me?" Mrs. Armstid says. "That Texas man said he would. He said I could get it from Mr. Snopes later."

"Then go and ask him for it," Mrs. Littlejohn says.

I could hear the dishes.

"He won't give it back to me," Mrs. Armstid says.

"All right," Mrs. Littlejohn says. "Don't ask him for it, then."

I could hear the dishes; Mrs. Armstid was helping. "You don't reckon he would, do you?" she says. Mrs. Littlejohn never said nothing. It sounded like she was throwing the dishes at one another. "Maybe I better go and talk to Henry about it," Mrs. Armstid says.

"I would," Mrs. Littlejohn says. I be dog if it didn't sound like she had two plates in her hands, beating them together. "Then Henry can buy another five-dollar horse with it. Maybe he'll buy one next time that will out and out kill him. If I thought that, I'd give you back the money, myself."

"I reckon I better talk to him first," Mrs. Armstid said. Then it sounded like Mrs. Littlejohn taken up all the dishes and throwed them at the cook-stove, and I come away.

That was this morning. I had been up to Bundren's and back, and I thought that things would have kind of settled down. So after breakfast, I went up to the store. And there was Flem, setting in the store-chair and whittling, like he might not have ever moved since he come to clerk for Jody Varner. I. O. was leaning in the door, in his shirt sleeves and with his hair parted too, same as Flem was before he turned the clerking job over to I. O. It's a funny thing about them Snopes: they all looks alike, yet there ain't ere a two of them that claims brothers. They're always just cousins, like Flem and Eck and Flem and I. O. Eck was there too, squatting against the wall, him and that boy, eating cheese and crackers outen a sack; they told me that Eck hadn't been home a-tall. And that Lon Quick hadn't got back to town, even. He followed his horse clean down to Samson's Bridge, with a wagon and a camp outfit. Eck finally caught one of hisn. It run into a blind lane at Freeman's and Eck and the boy taken and tied their rope across the end of the lane, about three foot high. The horse come to the end of the lane and whirled and run back without ever stopping. Eck says it never seen the rope a-tall. He says it looked just like one of these here Christmas pinwheels. "Didn't it try to run again?" I says.

"No," Eck says, eating a bite of cheese offen his knife blade. "Just kicked some."

"Kicked some?" I says.

"It broke its neck," Eck says.

Well, they was squatting there, about six of them, talking, talking at Flem; never nobody knowed yet if Flem had ere a interest in them horses or not. So finally I come right out and asked him. "Flem's done skun all of us so much," I says, "that we're proud of him. Come on, Flem," I says, "how much did you and that Texas man make offen them horses? You can tell us. Ain't nobody here but Eck that bought one of them; the others ain't got back to town yet, and Eck's your own cousin; he'll be proud to hear, too. How much did you-all make?"

They was all whittling, not looking at Flem, making like they was studying. But you could a heard a pin drop. And I. O. He had been rubbing his back up and down on the door, but he stopped now, watching Flem like a pointing dog. Flem finished cutting the sliver offen his stick. He spit across the porch, into the road. " 'Twarn't none of my horses," he says.

I. O. cackled, like a hen, slapping his legs with both hands. "You boys might just as well quit trying to get ahead of Flem," he said.

Well, about that time I see Mrs. Armstid come outen Mrs. Littlejohn's gate, coming up the road. I never said nothing. I says, "Well, if a man can't take care of himself in a trade, he can't blame the man that trims him."

Flem never said nothing, trimming at the stick. He hadn't seen Mrs. Armstid. "Yes, sir," I says. "A fellow like Henry Armstid ain't got nobody but hisself to blame."

"Course he ain't," I. O. says. He ain't seen her, neither. "Henry Armstid's a born fool. Always is been. If Flem hadn't a got his money, somebody else would."

We looked at Flem. He never moved. Mrs. Armstid come on up the road.

"That's right," I says. "But, come to think of it, Henry never bought no horse." We looked at Flem; you could a heard a match drop. "That Texas man told her to get that five dollars back from Flem next day. I reckon Flem's done already taken that money to Mrs. Littlejohn's and give it to Mrs. Armstid."

We watched Flem. I. O. quit rubbing his back against the door again. After a while Flem raised his head and spit across the porch, into the dust. I. O. cackled, just like a hen. "Ain't he a beating fellow, now?" I. O. says.

Mrs. Armstid was getting closer, so I kept on talking, watching to see if Flem would look up and see her. But he never looked up. I went on talking about Tull, about how he was going to sue Flem, and Flem setting there, whittling his stick, not saying nothing else after he said they wasn't none of his horses.

Then I. O. happened to look around. He seen Mrs. Armstid. "Pssst!" he says. Flem looked up. "Here she comes!" I. O. says. "Go out the back. I'll tell her you done went in to town to-day."

But Flem never moved. He just set there, whittling, and we watched Mrs. Armstid come up onto the porch, in that ere faded sunbonnet and wrapper and them tennis shoes that made a kind of hissing noise on the porch. She come onto the porch and stopped, her hands rolled into her dress in front, not looking at nothing.

"He said Saturday," she says, "that he wouldn't sell Henry no horse. He said I could get the money from you."

Flem looked up. The knife never stopped. It went on trimming off a sliver same as if he was watching it. "He taken that money off with him when he left," Flem says.

Mrs. Armstid never looked at nothing. We never looked at her, neither, except that boy of Eck's. He had a half-et cracker in his hand, watching her, chewing.

"He said Henry hadn't bought no horse," Mrs. Armstid says. "He said for me to get the money from you today."

"I reckon he forgot about it," Flem said. "He taken that money off with him Saturday." He whittled again. I. O. kept on rubbing his back, slow. He licked his lips. After a while the woman looked up the road, where it went on up the hill, toward the graveyard. She looked up that way for a while, with that boy of Eck's watching her and I. O. rubbing his back slow against the door. Then she turned back toward the steps.

"I reckon it's time to get dinner started," she says.

"How's Henry this morning, Mrs. Armstid?" Winterbottom says.

She looked at Winterbottom; she almost stopped. "He's resting, I thank you kindly," she says.

Flem got up, outen the chair, putting his knife away. He spit across the porch. "Wait a minute, Mrs. Armstid," he says. She stopped again. She didn't look at him. Flem went on into the store, with I. O. done quit rubbing his back now, with his head craned after Flem, and Mrs. Armstid standing there with her hands rolled into her dress, not looking at nothing. A wagon come up the road and passed; it was Freeman, on the way to town. Then Flem come out again, with I. O. still watching him. Flem had one of these little striped sacks of Jody Varner's candy; I bet he still owes Jody that nickel, too. He put the sack into Mrs. Armstid's hand, like he would have put it into a hollow stump. He spit again across the porch. "A little sweetening for the chaps," he says.

"You're right kind," Mrs. Armstid says. She held the sack of candy in her hand, not looking at nothing. Eck's boy was watching the sack, the half-et cracker in his hand; he wasn't chewing now. He watched Mrs. Armstid roll the sack into her apron. "I reckon I better get on back and help with dinner," she says. She turned and went back across the porch. Flem set down in the chair again and opened his knife. He spit across the porch again, past Mrs. Armstid where she hadn't went down the steps yet. Then she went on, in that ere sunbonnet and wrapper all the same color, back down the road toward Mrs. Littlejohn's. You couldn't see her dress move, like a natural woman walking. She looked like a old snag still standing up and moving along on a high water. We watched her turn in at Mrs. Littlejohn's and go outen sight. Flem was whittling. I. O. begun to rub his back on the door. Then he begun to cackle, just like a durn hen.

"You boys might just as well quit trying," I. O. says. "You can't git ahead of Flem. You can't touch him. Ain't he a sight, now?"

I be dog if he ain't. If I had brung a herd of wild cattymounts into town and sold them to my neighbors and kinfolks, they would have lynched me. Yes, sir.

1931

That Evening Sun*

I

Monday is no different from any other weekday in Jefferson now. The streets are paved now, and the telephone and electric companies are cutting down more and more of the shade trees—the water oaks, the maples and locusts and elms—to make room for iron poles bearing clusters of bloated and ghostly and bloodless grapes, and we have a city laundry which makes the rounds on Monday morning, gathering the bundles of clothes into bright-colored, specially-made motor cars: the soiled wearing of a whole week now flees apparitionlike behind alert and irritable electric horns, with a long diminishing noise of rubber and asphalt like tearing silk, and even the Negro women who still take in white people's washing after the old custom, fetch and deliver it in automobiles.

But fifteen years ago, on Monday morning the quiet, dusty, shady streets would be full of Negro women with, balanced on their steady, turbaned heads, bundles of clothes

---

* Probably an echo of "I hate to see that evening sun go down," from the 1914 song "St. Louis Blues" by W. C. Handy.

tied up in sheets, almost as large as cotton bales, carried so without touch of hand between the kitchen door of the white house and the blackened washpot beside a cabin door in Negro Hollow.

Nancy would set her bundle on the top of her head, then upon the bundle in turn she would set the black straw sailor hat which she wore winter and summer. She was tall, with a high, sad face sunken a little where her teeth were missing. Sometimes we would go a part of the way down the lane and across the pasture with her, to watch the balanced bundle and the hat that never bobbed nor wavered, even when she walked down into the ditch and up the other side and stooped through the fence. She would go down on her hands and knees and crawl through the gap, her head rigid, uptilted, the bundle steady as a rock or a balloon, and rise to her feet again and go on.

Sometimes the husbands of the washing women would fetch and deliver the clothes, but Jesus never did that for Nancy, even before father told him to stay away from our house, even when Dilsey was sick and Nancy would come to cook for us.

And then about half the time we'd have to go down the lane to Nancy's cabin and tell her to come on and cook breakfast. We would stop at the ditch, because father told us to not have anything to do with Jesus—he was a short black man, with a razor scar down his face—and we would throw rocks at Nancy's house until she came to the door, leaning her head around it without any clothes on.

"What yawl mean, chunking my house?" Nancy said. "What you little devils mean?"

"Father says for you to come on and get breakfast," Caddy said. "Father says it's over a half an hour now, and you've got to come this minute."

"I aint studying no breakfast," Nancy said. "I going to get my sleep out."

"I bet you're drunk," Jason said. "Father says you're drunk. Are you drunk, Nancy?"

"Who says I is?" Nancy said. "I got to get my sleep out. I aint studying no breakfast."

So after a while we quit chunking the cabin and went back home. When she finally came, it was too late for me to go to school. So we thought it was whisky until that day they arrested her again and they were taking her to jail and they passed Mr Stovall. He was the cashier in the bank and a deacon in the Baptist church, and Nancy began to say:

"When you going to pay me, white man? When you going to pay me, white man? It's been three times now since you paid me a cent—" Mr Stovall knocked her down, but she kept on saying, "When you going to pay me, white man? It's been three times now since—" until Mr Stovall kicked her in the mouth with his heel and the marshal caught Mr Stovall back, and Nancy lying in the street, laughing. She turned her head and spat out some blood and teeth and said, "It's been three times now since he paid me a cent."

That was how she lost her teeth, and all that day they told about Nancy and Mr Stovall, and all that night the ones that passed the jail could hear Nancy singing and yelling. They could see her hands holding to the window bars, and a lot of them stopped along the fence, listening to her and to the jailer trying to make her stop. She didn't shut up until almost daylight, when the jailer began to hear a bumping and scraping upstairs and he went up there and found Nancy hanging from the window bar. He said that it was cocaine and not whisky, because no nigger would try to commit suicide unless he was full of cocaine, because a nigger full of cocaine wasn't a nigger any longer.

The jailer cut her down and revived her; then he beat her, whipped her. She had hung herself with her dress. She had fixed it all right, but when they arrested her she didn't have on anything except a dress and so she didn't have anything to tie her hands with and she couldn't make her hands let go of the window ledge. So the jailer heard the noise and ran up there and found Nancy hanging from the window, stark naked, her belly already swelling out a little, like a little balloon.

When Dilsey was sick in her cabin and Nancy was cooking for us, we could see her apron swelling out; that was before father told Jesus to stay away from the house. Jesus was in the kitchen, sitting behind the stove, with his razor scar on his black face like a piece of dirty string. He said it was a watermelon that Nancy had under her dress.

"It never come off of your vine, though," Nancy said.

"Off of what vine?" Caddy said.

"I can cut down the vine it did come off of," Jesus said.

"What makes you want to talk like that before these chillen?" Nancy said. "Whyn't you go on to work? You done et. You want Mr Jason to catch you hanging around his kitchen, talking that way before these chillen?"

"Talking what way?" Caddy said. "What vine?"

"I cant hang around white man's kitchen," Jesus said. "But white man can hang around mine. White man can come in my house, but I cant stop him. When white man want to come in my house, I aint got no house. I cant stop him, but he cant kick me outen it. He cant do that."

Dilsey was still sick in her cabin. Father told Jesus to stay off our place. Dilsey was still sick. It was a long time. We were in the library after supper.

"Isn't Nancy through in the kitchen yet?" mother said. "It seems to me that she has had plenty of time to have finished the dishes."

"Let Quentin go and see," father said. "Go and see if Nancy is through, Quentin. Tell her she can go on home."

I went to the kitchen. Nancy was through. The dishes were put away and the fire was out. Nancy was sitting in a chair, close to the cold stove. She looked at me.

"Mother wants to know if you are through," I said.

"Yes," Nancy said. She looked at me. "I done finished." She looked at me.

"What is it?" I said. "What is it?"

"I aint nothing but a nigger," Nancy said. "It aint none of my fault."

She looked at me, sitting in the chair before the cold stove, the sailor hat on her head. I went back to the library. It was the cold stove and all, when you think of a kitchen being warm and busy and cheerful. And with a cold stove and the dishes all put away, and nobody wanting to eat at that hour.

"Is she through?" mother said.

"Yessum," I said.

"What is she doing?" mother said.

"She's not doing anything. She's through."

"I'll go and see," father said.

"Maybe she's waiting for Jesus to come and take her home," Caddy said.

"Jesus is gone," I said. Nancy told us how one morning she woke up and Jesus was gone.

"He quit me," Nancy said. "Done gone to Memphis, I reckon. Dodging them city *po-lice* for a while, I reckon."

"And a good riddance," father said. "I hope he stays there."

"Nancy's scaired of the dark," Jason said.

"So are you," Caddy said.

"I'm not," Jason said.

"Scairy cat," Caddy said.

"I'm not," Jason said.

"You, Candace!" mother said. Father came back.

"I am going to walk down the lane with Nancy," he said. "She says that Jesus is back."

"Has she seen him?" mother said.

"No. Some Negro sent her word that he was back in town. I wont be long."

"You'll leave me alone, to take Nancy home?" mother said. "Is her safety more precious to you than mine?"

"I wont be long," father said.

"You'll leave these children unprotected, with that Negro about?"

"I'm going too," Caddy said. "Let me go, Father."

"What would he do with them, if he were unfortunate enough to have them?" father said.

"I want to go, too," Jason said.

"Jason!" mother said. She was speaking to father. You could tell that by the way she said the name. Like she believed that all day father had been trying to think of doing the thing she wouldn't like the most, and that she knew all the time that after a while he would think of it. I stayed quiet, because father and I both knew that mother would want him to make me stay with her if she just thought of it in time. So father didn't look at me. I was the oldest. I was nine and Caddy was seven and Jason was five.

"Nonsense," father said. "We wont be long."

Nancy had her hat on. We came to the lane. "Jesus always been good to me," Nancy said. "Whenever he had two dollars, one of them was mine." We walked in the lane. "If I can just get through the lane," Nancy said, "I be all right then."

The lane was always dark. "This is where Jason got scared on Hallowe'en," Caddy said.

"I didn't," Jason said.

"Cant Aunt Rachel do anything with him?" father said. Aunt Rachel was old. She lived in a cabin beyond Nancy's, by herself. She had white hair and she smoked a pipe in the door, all day long; she didn't work any more. They said she was Jesus' mother. Sometimes she said she was and sometimes she said she wasn't any kin to Jesus.

"Yes, you did," Caddy said. "You were scairder than Frony. You were scairder than T.P. even. Scairder than niggers."

"Cant nobody do nothing with him," Nancy said. "He say I done woke up the devil in him and aint but one thing going to lay it down again."

"Well, he's gone now," father said. "There's nothing for you to be afraid of now. And if you'd just let white men alone."

"Let what white men alone?" Caddy said. "How let them alone?"

"He aint gone nowhere," Nancy said. "I can feel him. I can feel him now, in this lane. He hearing us talk, every word, hid somewhere, waiting. I aint seen him, and I aint going to see him again but once more, with that razor in his mouth. That razor on that string down his back, inside his shirt. And then I aint going to be even surprised."

"I wasn't scaired," Jason said.

"If you'd behave yourself, you'd have kept out of this," father said. "But it's all right now. He's probably in St. Louis now. Probably got another wife by now and forgot all about you."

"If he has, I better not find out about it," Nancy said. "I'd stand there right over them, and every time he wropped her, I'd cut that arm off. I'd cut his head off and I'd slit her belly and I'd shove—"

"Hush," father said.

"Slit whose belly, Nancy?" Caddy said.

"I wasn't scaired," Jason said. "I'd walk right down this lane by myself."

"Yah," Caddy said. "You wouldn't dare to put your foot down in it if we were not here too."

II

Dilsey was still sick, so we took Nancy home every night until mother said, "How much longer is this going on? I to be left alone in this big house while you take home a frightened Negro?"

We fixed a pallet in the kitchen for Nancy. One night we waked up, hearing the sound. It was not singing and it was not crying, coming up the dark stairs. There was a light in mother's room and we heard father going down the hall, down the back stairs, and Caddy and I went into the hall. The floor was cold. Our toes curled away from it while we listened to the sound. It was like singing and it wasn't like singing, like the sounds that Negroes make.

Then it stopped and we heard father going down the back stairs, and we went to the head of the stairs. Then the sound began again, in the stairway, not loud, and we could see Nancy's eyes halfway up the stairs, against the wall. They looked like cat's eyes do, like a big cat against the wall, watching us. When we came down the steps to where she was, she quit making the sound again, and we stood there until father came back up from the kitchen, with his pistol in his hand. He went back down with Nancy and they came back with Nancy's pallet.

We spread the pallet in our room. After the light in mother's room went off, we could see Nancy's eyes again. "Nancy," Caddy whispered, "are you asleep, Nancy?"

Nancy whispered something. It was oh or no, I dont know which. Like nobody had made it, like it came from nowhere and went nowhere, until it was like Nancy was not there at all; that I had looked so hard at her eyes on the stairs that they had got printed on my eyeballs, like the sun does when you have closed your eyes and there is no sun. "Jesus," Nancy whispered. "Jesus."

"Was it Jesus?" Caddy said. "Did he try to come into the kitchen?"

"Jesus," Nancy said. Like this: Jeeeeeeeeeeeeeeeesus, until the sound went out, like a match or a candle does.

"It's the other Jesus she means," I said.

"Can you see us, Nancy?" Caddy whispered. "Can you see our eyes too?"

"I aint nothing but a nigger," Nancy said. "God knows. God knows."

"What did you see down there in the kitchen?" Caddy whispered. "What tried to get in?"

"God knows," Nancy said. We could see her eyes. "God knows."

Dilsey got well. She cooked dinner. "You'd better stay in bed a day or two longer," father said.

"What for?" Dilsey said. "If I had been a day later, this place would be to rack and ruin. Get on out of here now, and let me get my kitchen straight again."

Dilsey cooked supper too. And that night, just before dark, Nancy came into the kitchen.

"How do you know he's back?" Dilsey said. "You aint seen him."

"Jesus is a nigger," Jason said.

"I can feel him," Nancy said. "I can feel him laying yonder in the ditch."

"Tonight?" Dilsey said. "Is he there tonight?"

"Dilsey's a nigger too," Jason said.

"You try to eat something," Dilsey said.

"I dont want nothing," Nancy said.

"I aint a nigger," Jason said.

"Drink some coffee," Dilsey said. She poured a cup of coffee for Nancy. "Do you know he's out there tonight? How come you know it's tonight?"

"I know," Nancy said. "He's there, waiting. I know. I done lived with him too long. I know what he is fixing to do fore he know it himself."

"Drink some coffee," Dilsey said. Nancy held the cup to her mouth and blew into the cup. Her mouth pursed out like a spreading adder's, like a rubber mouth, like she had blown all the color out of her lips with blowing the coffee.

"I aint a nigger," Jason said. "Are you a nigger, Nancy?"

"I hellborn, child," Nancy said. "I wont be nothing soon. I going back where I come from soon."

III

She began to drink the coffee. While she was drinking, holding the cup in both hands, she began to make the sound again. She made the sound into the cup and the coffee sploshed out onto her hands and her dress. Her eyes looked at us and she sat there, her elbows on her knees, holding the cup in both hands, looking at us across the wet cup, making the sound. "Look at Nancy," Jason said. "Nancy cant cook for us now. Dilsey's got well now."

"You hush up," Dilsey said. Nancy held the cup in both hands, looking at us, making the sound, like there were two of them: one looking at us and the other making the sound. "Whyn't you let Mr Jason telefoam the marshal?" Dilsey said. Nancy stopped then, holding the cup in her long brown hands. She tried to drink some coffee again, but it sploshed out of the cup, onto her hands and her dress, and she put the cup down. Jason watched her.

"I cant swallow it," Nancy said. "I swallows but it wont go down me."

"You go down to the cabin," Dilsey said. "Frony will fix you a pallet and I'll be there soon."

"Wont no nigger stop him," Nancy said.

"I aint a nigger," Jason said. "Am I, Dilsey?"

"I reckon not," Dilsey said. She looked at Nancy. "I dont reckon so. What you going to do, then?"

Nancy looked at us. Her eyes went fast, like she was afraid there wasn't time to look, without hardly moving at all. She looked at us, at all three of us at one time. "You member that night I stayed in yawls' room?" she said. She told about how we waked up early the next morning, and played. We had to play quiet, on her pallet, until father woke up and it was time to get breakfast. "Go and ask your maw to let me stay here tonight," Nancy said. "I wont need no pallet. We can play some more."

Caddy asked mother. Jason went too. "I cant have Negroes sleeping in the bedrooms," mother said. Jason cried. He cried until mother said he couldn't have any dessert for three days if he didn't stop. Then Jason said he would stop if Dilsey would make a chocolate cake. Father was there.

"Why dont you do something about it?" mother said. "What do we have officers for?"

"Why is Nancy afraid of Jesus?" Caddy said. "Are you afraid of father, mother?"

"What could the officers do?" father said. "If Nancy hasn't seen him, how could the officers find him?"

"Then why is she afraid?" mother said.

"She says he is there. She says she knows he is there tonight."

"Yet we pay taxes," mother said. "I must wait here alone in this big house while you take a Negro woman home."

"You know that I am not lying outside with a razor," father said.

"I'll stop if Dilsey will make a chocolate cake," Jason said. Mother told us to go out and father said he didn't know if Jason would get a chocolate cake or not, but he knew what Jason was going to get in about a minute. We went back to the kitchen and told Nancy.

"Father said for you to go home and lock the door, and you'll be all right," Caddy said. "All right from what, Nancy? Is Jesus mad at you?" Nancy was holding the coffee cup in her hands again, her elbows on her knees and her hands holding the cup between her knees. She was looking into the cup. "What have you done that made Jesus mad?" Caddy said. Nancy let the cup go. It didn't break on the floor, but the coffee spilled out, and Nancy sat there with her hands still making the shape of the cup. She began to make the sound again, not loud. Not singing and not unsinging. We watched her.

"Here," Dilsey said. "You quit that, now. You get ahold of yourself. You wait here. I going to get Versh to walk home with you." Dilsey went out.

We looked at Nancy. Her shoulders kept shaking, but she quit making the sound. We watched her. "What's Jesus going to do to you?" Caddy said. "He went away."

Nancy looked at us. "We had fun that night I stayed in yawls' room, didn't we?"

"I didn't," Jason said. "I didn't have any fun."

"You were asleep in mother's room," Caddy said. "You were not there."

"Let's go down to my house and have some more fun," Nancy said.

"Mother wont let us," I said. "It's too late now."

"Dont bother her," Nancy said. "We can tell her in the morning. She wont mind."

"She wouldn't let us," I said.

"Dont ask her now," Nancy said. "Dont bother her now."

"She didn't say we couldn't go," Caddy said.

"We didn't ask," I said.

"If you go, I'll tell," Jason said.

"We'll have fun," Nancy said. "They won't mind, just to my house. I been working for yawl a long time. They won't mind."

"I'm not afraid to go," Caddy said. "Jason is the one that's afraid. He'll tell."

"I'm not," Jason said.

"Yes, you are," Caddy said. "You'll tell."

"I won't tell," Jason said. "I'm not afraid."

"Jason ain't afraid to go with me," Nancy said. "Is you, Jason?"

"Jason is going to tell," Caddy said. The lane was dark. We passed the pasture gate. "I bet if something was to jump out from behind that gate, Jason would holler."

"I wouldn't," Jason said. We walked down the lane. Nancy was talking loud.

"What are you talking so loud for, Nancy?" Caddy said.

"Who; me?" Nancy said. "Listen at Quentin and Caddy and Jason saying I'm talking loud."

"You talk like there was five of us here," Caddy said. "You talk like father was here too."

"Who; me talking loud, Mr Jason?" Nancy said.

"Nancy called Jason 'Mister,'" Caddy said.

"Listen how Caddy and Quentin and Jason talk," Nancy said.

"We're not talking loud," Caddy said. "You're the one that's talking like father—"

"Hush," Nancy said; "hush, Mr Jason."

"Nancy called Jason 'Mister' aguh—"

"Hush," Nancy said. She was talking loud when we crossed the ditch and stooped through the fence where she used to stoop through with the clothes on her head. Then we came to her house. We were going fast then. She opened the door. The smell of the house was like the lamp and the smell of Nancy was like the wick, like they were waiting for one another to begin to smell. She lit the lamp and closed the door and put the bar up. Then she quit talking loud, looking at us.

"What're we going to do?" Caddy said.

"What do yawl want to do?" Nancy said.

"You said we would have some fun," Caddy said.

There was something about Nancy's house; something you could smell besides Nancy and the house. Jason smelled it, even. "I don't want to stay here," he said. "I want to go home."

"Go home, then," Caddy said.

"I don't want to go by myself," Jason said.

"We're going to have some fun," Nancy said.

"How?" Caddy said.

Nancy stood by the door. She was looking at us, only it was like she had emptied her eyes, like she had quit using them. "What do you want to do?" she said.

"Tell us a story," Caddy said. "Can you tell a story?"

"Yes," Nancy said.

"Tell it," Caddy said. We looked at Nancy. "You don't know any stories."

"Yes," Nancy said. "Yes, I do."

She came and sat in a chair before the hearth. There was a little fire there. Nancy built it up, when it was already hot inside. She built a good blaze. She told a story. She talked like her eyes looked, like her eyes watching us and her voice talking to us did not belong to her. Like she was living somewhere else, waiting somewhere else. She was outside the cabin. Her voice was inside and the shape of her, the Nancy that could stoop under a barbed wire fence with a bundle of clothes balanced on her head as though without weight, like a balloon, was there. But that was all. "And so this here queen come walking up to the ditch, where that bad man was hiding. She was walking up to the ditch, and she say, 'If I can just get past this here ditch,' was what she say . . ."

"What ditch?" Caddy said. "A ditch like that one out there? Why did a queen want to go into a ditch?"

"To get to her house," Nancy said. She looked at us. "She had to cross the ditch to get into her house quick and bar the door."

"Why did she want to go home and bar the door?" Caddy said.

IV

Nancy looked at us. She quit talking. She looked at us. Jason's legs stuck straight out of his pants where he sat on Nancy's lap. "I don't think that's a good story," he said. "I want to go home."

"Maybe we had better," Caddy said. She got up from the floor. "I bet they are looking for us right now." She went toward the door.

"No," Nancy said. "Don't open it." She got up quick and passed Caddy. She didn't touch the door, the wooden bar.

"Why not?" Caddy said.

"Come back to the lamp," Nancy said. "We'll have fun. You don't have to go."

"We ought to go," Caddy said. "Unless we have a lot of fun." She and Nancy came back to the fire, the lamp.

"I want to go home," Jason said. "I'm going to tell."

"I know another story," Nancy said. She stood close to the lamp. She looked at Caddy, like when your eyes look up at a stick balanced on your nose. She had to look down to see Caddy, but her eyes looked like that, like when you are balancing a stick.

"I won't listen to it," Jason said. "I'll bang on the floor."

"It's a good one," Nancy said. "It's better than the other one."

"What's it about?" Caddy said. Nancy was standing by the lamp. Her hand was on the lamp, against the light, long and brown.

"Your hand is on that hot globe," Caddy said. "Don't it feel hot to your hand?"

Nancy looked at her hand on the lamp chimney. She took her hand away, slow. She stood there, looking at Caddy, wringing her long hand as though it were tied to her wrist with a string.

"Let's do something else," Caddy said.

"I want to go home," Jason said.

"I got some popcorn," Nancy said. She looked at Caddy and then at Jason and then at me and then at Caddy again. "I got some popcorn."

"I don't like popcorn," Jason said. "I'd rather have candy."

Nancy looked at Jason. "You can hold the popper." She was still wringing her hand; it was long and limp and brown.

"All right," Jason said. "I'll stay a while if I can do that. Caddy can't hold it. I'll want to go home again if Caddy holds the popper."

Nancy built up the fire. "Look at Nancy putting her hands in the fire," Caddy said. "What's the matter with you, Nancy?"

"I got popcorn," Nancy said. "I got some." She took the popper from under the bed. It was broken. Jason began to cry.

"Now we can't have any popcorn," he said.

"We ought to go home, anyway," Caddy said. "Come on, Quentin."

"Wait," Nancy said; "wait. I can fix it. Don't you want to help me fix it?"

"I don't think I want any," Caddy said. "It's too late now."

"You help me, Jason," Nancy said. "Don't you want to help me?"

"No," Jason said. "I want to go home."

"Hush," Nancy said; "hush. Watch. Watch me. I can fix it so Jason can hold it and pop the corn." She got a piece of wire and fixed the popper.

"It won't hold good," Caddy said.

"Yes, it will," Nancy said. "Yawl watch. Yawl help me shell some corn."

The popcorn was under the bed too. We shelled it into the popper and Nancy helped Jason hold the popper over the fire.

"It's not popping," Jason said. "I want to go home."

"You wait," Nancy said. "It'll begin to pop. We'll have fun then." She was sitting close to the fire. The lamp was turned up so high it was beginning to smoke.

"Why don't you turn it down some?" I said.

"It's all right," Nancy said. "I'll clean it. Yawl wait. The popcorn will start in a minute."

"I don't believe it's going to start," Caddy said. "We ought to start home, anyway. They'll be worried."

"No," Nancy said. "It's going to pop. Dilsey will tell um yawl with me. I been working for yawl long time. They won't mind if yawl at my house. You wait, now. It'll start popping any minute now."

Then Jason got some smoke in his eyes and he began to cry. He dropped the popper into the fire. Nancy got a wet rag and wiped Jason's face, but he didn't stop crying.

"Hush," she said. "Hush." But he didn't hush. Caddy took the popper out of the fire.

"It's burned up," she said. "You'll have to get some more popcorn, Nancy."

"Did you put all of it in?" Nancy said.

"Yes," Caddy said. Nancy looked at Caddy. Then she took the popper and opened it and poured the cinders into her apron and began to sort the grains, her hands long and brown, and we watching her.

"Haven't you got any more?" Caddy said.

"Yes," Nancy said; "yes. Look. This here ain't burnt. All we need to do is—"

"I want to go home," Jason said. "I'm going to tell."

"Hush," Caddy said. We all listened. Nancy's head was already turned toward the barred door, her eyes filled with red lamplight. "Somebody is coming," Caddy said.

Then Nancy began to make that sound again, not loud, sitting there above the fire, her long hands dangling between her knees; all of a sudden water began to come out on her face in big drops, running down her face, carrying in each one a little turning ball of firelight like a spark until it dropped off her chin. "She's not crying," I said.

"I ain't crying," Nancy said. Her eyes were closed. "I ain't crying. Who is it?"

"I don't know," Caddy said. She went to the door and looked out. "We've got to go now," she said. "Here comes father."

"I'm going to tell," Jason said. "Yawl made me come."

The water still ran down Nancy's face. She turned in her chair. "Listen. Tell him. Tell him we going to have fun. Tell him I take good care of yawl until in the morning. Tell him to let me come home with yawl and sleep on the floor. Tell him I won't need no pallet. We'll have fun. You member last time how we had so much fun?"

"I didn't have fun," Jason said. "You hurt me. You put smoke in my eyes. I'm going to tell."

V

Father came in. He looked at us. Nancy did not get up.

"Tell him," she said.

"Caddy made us come down here," Jason said. "I didn't want to."

Father came to the fire. Nancy looked up at him. "Can't you go to Aunt Rachel's and stay?" he said. Nancy looked up at father, her hands between her knees. "He's not here," father said. "I would have seen him. There's not a soul in sight."

"He in the ditch," Nancy said. "He waiting in the ditch yonder."

"Nonsense," father said. He looked at Nancy. "Do you know he's there?"

"I got the sign," Nancy said.

"What sign?"

"I got it. It was on the table when I come in. It was a hog-bone, with blood meat still on it, laying by the lamp. He's out there. When yawl walk out that door, I gone."

"Gone where, Nancy?" Caddy said.

"I'm not a tattletale," Jason said.

"Nonsense," father said.

"He out there," Nancy said. "He looking through that window this minute, waiting for yawl to go. Then I gone."

"Nonsense," father said. "Lock up your house and we'll take you on to Aunt Rachel's."

" 'Twont do no good," Nancy said. She didn't look at father now, but he looked down at her, at her long, limp, moving hands. "Putting it off wont do no good."

"Then what do you want to do?" father said.

"I don't know," Nancy said. "I can't do nothing. Just put it off. And that don't do no good. I reckon it belong to me. I reckon what I going to get ain't no more than mine."

"Get what?" Caddy said. "What's yours?"

"Nothing," father said. "You all must get to bed."

"Caddy made me come," Jason said.

"Go on to Aunt Rachel's," father said.

"It won't do no good," Nancy said. She sat before the fire, her elbows on her knees, her long hands between her knees. "When even your own kitchen wouldn't do no good. When even if I was sleeping on the floor in the room with your chillen, and the next morning there I am, and blood—"

"Hush," father said. "Lock the door and put out the lamp and go to bed."

"I scared of the dark," Nancy said. "I scared for it to happen in the dark."

"You mean you're going to sit right here with the lamp lighted?" father said. Then Nancy began to make the sound again, sitting before the fire, her long hands between her knees. "Ah, damnation," father said. "Come along, chillen. It's past bedtime."

"When yawl go home, I gone," Nancy said. She talked quieter now, and her face looked quiet, like her hands. "Anyway, I got my coffin money saved up with Mr. Love-lady." Mr. Lovelady was a short, dirty man who collected the Negro insurance, coming around to the cabins or the kitchens every Saturday morning, to collect fifteen cents. He and his wife lived at the hotel. One morning his wife committed suicide. They had a child, a little girl. He and the child went away. After a week or two he came back alone. We would see him going along the lanes and the back streets on Saturday mornings.

"Nonsense," father said. "You'll be the first thing I'll see in the kitchen tomorrow morning."

"You'll see what you'll see, I reckon," Nancy said. "But it will take the Lord to say what that will be."

VI

We left her sitting before the fire.

"Come and put the bar up," father said. But she didn't move. She didn't look at us again, sitting quietly there between the lamp and the fire. From some distance down the lane we could look back and see her through the open door.

"What, Father?" Caddy said. "What's going to happen?"

"Nothing," father said. Jason was on father's back, so Jason was the tallest of all of us. We went down into the ditch. I looked at it, quiet. I couldn't see much where the moonlight and the shadows tangled.

"If Jesus is hid here, he can see us, can't he?" Caddy said.

"He's not there," father said. "He went away a long time ago."

"You made me come," Jason said, high; against the sky it looked like father had two heads, a little one and a big one. "I didn't want to."

We went up out of the ditch. We could still see Nancy's house and the open door, but we couldn't see Nancy now, sitting before the fire with the door open, because she was tired. "I just done got tired," she said. "I just a nigger. It ain't no fault of mine."

But we could hear her, because she began just after we came up out of the ditch, the sound that was not singing and not unsinging. "Who will do our washing now, Father?" I said.

"I'm not a nigger," Jason said, high and close above father's head.

"You're worse," Caddy said, "you are a tattletale. If something was to jump out, you'd be scairder than a nigger."

"I wouldn't," Jason said.

"You'd cry," Caddy said.

"Caddy," father said.

"I wouldn't!" Jason said.

"Scairy cat," Caddy said.

"Candace!" father said.

1931

Barn Burning

The store in which the Justice of the Peace's court was sitting smelled of cheese. The boy, crouched on his nail keg at the back of the crowded room, knew he smelled cheese, and more: from where he sat he could see the ranked shelves close-packed with the solid, squat, dynamic shapes of tin cans whose labels his stomach read, not from the lettering which meant nothing to his mind but from the scarlet devils and the silver curve of fish—this, the cheese which he knew he smelled and the hermetic meat which his intestines believed he smelled coming in intermittent gusts momentary and brief between the other constant one, the smell and sense just a little of fear because mostly of despair and grief, the old fierce pull of blood. He could not see the table where the Justice sat and before which his father and his father's enemy (*our enemy* he thought in that despair; *ourn! mine and hisn both! He's my father!*) stood, but he could hear them, the two of them that is, because his father had said no word yet:

"But what proof have you, Mr. Harris?"

"I told you. The hog got into my corn. I caught it up and sent it back to him. He had no fence that would hold it. I told him so, warned him. The next time I put the hog in my pen. When he came to get it I gave him enough wire to patch up his pen. The next time I put the hog up and kept it. I rode down to his house and saw the wire I gave him still rolled on to the spool in his yard. I told him he could have the hog when he paid me a dollar pound fee. That evening a nigger came with the dollar and got the hog. He was a strange nigger. He said, 'He say to tell you wood and hay kin burn.' I said, 'What?' 'That whut he say to tell you,' the nigger said. 'Wood and hay kin burn.' That night my barn burned. I got the stock out but I lost the barn."

"Where is the nigger? Have you got him?"

"He was a strange nigger, I tell you. I don't know what became of him."

"But that's not proof. Don't you see that's not proof?"

"Get that boy up here. He knows." For a moment the boy thought too that the man meant his older brother until Harris said, "Not him. The little one. The boy," and, crouching, small for his age, small and wiry like his father, in patched and faded jeans even too small for him, with straight, uncombed, brown hair and eyes gray and wild as storm scud, he saw the men between himself and the table part and become a lane of grim faces, at the end of which he saw the Justice, a shabby, collarless, graying man in spectacles, beckoning him. He felt no floor under his bare feet; he seemed to walk beneath the palpable weight of the grim turning faces. His father, stiff in his black Sunday coat donned not for the trial but for the moving, did not even look at him. *He aims for me to lie,* he thought, again with that frantic grief and despair. *And I will have to do hit.*

"What's your name, boy?" the Justice said.

"Colonel Sartoris Snopes," the boy whispered.

"Hey?" the Justice said. Talk louder. Colonel Sartoris? I reckon anybody named for Colonel Sartoris in this country can't help but tell the truth, can they?" The boy said nothing. *Enemy! Enemy!* he thought; for a moment he could not even see, could not see that the Justice's face was kindly nor discern that his voice was troubled when he spoke to the man named Harris: "Do you want me to question this boy?" But he could hear, and during those subsequent long seconds while there was absolutely no sound in the crowded little room save that of quiet and intent breathing it was as if he had swung outward at the end of a grape vine, over a ravine, and at the top of the swing had been caught in a prolonged instant of mesmerized gravity, weightless in time.

"No!" Harris said violently, explosively. "Damnation! Send him out of here!" Now time, the fluid world, rushed beneath him again, the voices coming to him again through the smell of cheese and sealed meat, the fear and despair and the old grief of blood:

"This case is closed. I can't find against you, Snopes, but I can give you advice. Leave this country and don't come back to it."

His father spoke for the first time, his voice cold and harsh, level, without emphasis: "I aim to. I don't figure to stay in a country among people who …" he said something unprintable and vile, addressed to no one.

"That'll do," the Justice said. "Take your wagon and get out of this country before dark. Case dismissed."

His father turned, and he followed the stiff black coat, the wiry figure walking a little stiffly from where a Confederate provost's man musket ball had taken him in the heel on a stolen horse thirty years ago, followed the two backs now, since his older brother had appeared from somewhere in the crowd, no taller than the father but thicker, chewing tobacco steadily, between the two lines of grim-faced men and out of the store and across the worn gallery and down the sagging steps and among the dogs and half-grown boys in the mild May dust, where as he passed a voice hissed:

"Barn burner!"

Again he could not see, whirling; there was a face in a red haze, moonlike, bigger than the full moon, the owner of it half again his size, he leaping in the red haze toward the face, feeling no blow, feeling no shock when his head struck the earth, scrabbling up and leaping again, feeling no blow this time either and tasting no blood, scrabbling up to see the other boy in full flight and himself already leaping into pursuit as his father's hand jerked him back, the harsh, cold voice speaking above him: "Go get in the wagon."

It stood in a grove of locusts and mulberries across the road. His two hulking sisters in their Sunday dresses and his mother and her sister in calico and sunbonnets were already in it, sitting on and among the sorry residue of the dozen and more movings which even the boy could remember—the battered stove, the broken beds and chairs, the clock inlaid with mother-of-pearl, which would not run, stopped at some fourteen minutes past two o'clock of a dead and forgotten day and time, which had been his mother's dowry. She was crying, though when she saw him she drew her sleeve across her face and began to descend from the wagon. "Get back," the father said.

"He's hurt. I got to get some water and wash his . . ."

"Get back in the wagon," his father said. He got in too, over the tail-gate. His father mounted to the seat where the older brother already sat and struck the gaunt mules two savage blows with the peeled willow, but without heat. It was not even sadistic; it was exactly that same quality which in later years would cause his descendants to over-run the engine before putting a motor car into motion, striking and reining back in the same movement. The wagon went on, the store with its quiet crowd of grimly watching men dropped behind; a curve in the road hid it. *Forever* he thought. *Maybe he's done satisfied now, now that he has . . .* stopping himself, not to say it aloud even to himself. His mother's hand touched his shoulder.

"Does hit hurt" she said.

"Naw," he said. "Hit don't hurt. Lemme be."

"Can't you wipe some of the blood off before hit dries?"

"I'll wash to-night," he said. "Lemme be, I tell you."

The wagon went on. He did not know where they were going. None of them ever did or ever asked, because it was always somewhere, always a house of sorts waiting for them a day or two days or even three days away. Likely his father had already arranged to make a crop on another farm before he . . . Again he had to stop himself. He (the father) always did. There was something about his wolflike independence and even courage when the advantage was at least neutral which impressed strangers, as if they got from his latent ravening ferocity not so much a sense of dependability as a feeling that his ferocious conviction in the rightness of his own actions would be of advantage to all whose interest lay with his.

That night they camped, in a grove of oaks and beeches where a spring ran. The nights were still cool and they had a fire against it, of a rail lifted from a nearby fence and cut into lengths—a small fire, neat, niggard almost, a shrewd fire, such fires were his father's habit and custom always, even in freezing weather. Older, the boy might have remarked this and wondered why not a big one; why should not a man who had not only seen the waste and extravagance of war, but who had in his blood an inherent voracious prodigality with material not his own, have burned everything in sight? Then he might have gone a step farther and thought that that was the reason: that niggard blaze was the living fruit of nights passed during those four years in the woods hiding from all men, blue or gray, with his strings of horses (captured horses, he called them). And older still, he might have divined the true reason: that the element of fire spoke to some deep mainspring of his father's being, as the element of steel or of powder spoke to other men, as the one weapon for the preservation of integrity, else breath were not worth the breathing, and hence to be regarded with respect and used with discretion.

But he did not think this now and he had seen those same niggard blazes all his life. He merely ate his supper beside it and was already half asleep over his iron plate when his father called him, and once more he followed the stiff back, the stiff and ruthless limp, up the slope and on to the starlit road where, turning, he could see his father against the stars but without face or depth—a shape black, flat, and bloodless as though cut from tin in the iron folds of the frockcoat which had not been made for him, the voice harsh like tin and without heat like tin:

"You were fixing to tell them. You would have told him." He didn't answer. His father struck him with the flat of his hand on the side of the head, hard but without heat, exactly as he had struck the two mules at the store, exactly as he would strike either of them with any stick in order to kill a horse fly, his voice still without heat or anger: "You're getting to be a man. You got to learn. You got to learn to stick to your own blood or you ain't going to have any blood to stick to you. Do you think either of them, any man there this morning, would? Don't you know all they wanted was a chance to get at me because they knew I had them beat? Eh?" Later, twenty years later, he was to tell himself, "If I had said they wanted only truth, justice, he would have hit me again." But now he said nothing. He was not crying. He just stood there. "Answer me," his father said.

"Yes," he whispered. His father turned.

"Get on to bed. We'll be there tomorrow."

To-morrow they were there. In the early afternoon the wagon stopped before a paintless two-room house identical almost with the dozen others it had stopped before even in the boy's ten years, and again, as on the other dozen occasions, his mother and aunt got down and began to unload the wagon, although his two sisters and his father and brother had not moved.

"Likely hit ain't fitten for hawgs," one of the sisters said.

"Nevertheless, fit it will and you'll hog it and like it," his father said. "Get out of them chairs and help your Ma unload."

The two sisters got down, big, bovine, in a flutter of cheap ribbons; one of them drew from the jumbled wagon bed a battered lantern, the other a worn broom. His father handed the reins to the older son and began to climb stiffly over the wheel. "When they get unloaded, take the team to the barn and feed them." Then he said, and at first the boy thought he was still speaking to his brother: "Come with me."

"Me?" he said.

"Yes," his father said. "You."

"Abner," his mother said. His father paused and looked back—the harsh level stare beneath the shaggy, graying, irascible brows.

"I reckon I'll have a word with the man that aims to begin to-morrow owning me body and soul for the next eight months."

They went back up the road. A week ago—or before last night, that is—he would have asked where they were going, but not now. His father had struck him before last night but never before had he paused afterward to explain why; it was as if the blow and the following calm, outrageous voice still rang, repercussed, divulging nothing to him save the terrible handicap of being young, the light weight of his few years, just heavy enough to prevent his soaring free of the world as it seemed to be ordered but not heavy enough to keep him footed solid in it, to resist it and try to change the course of its events.

Presently he could see the grove of oaks and cedars and the other flowering trees and shrubs where the house would be, though not the house yet. They walked beside a fence massed with honeysuckle and Cherokee roses and came to a gate swinging open between two brick pillars, and now, beyond a sweep of drive, he saw the house for the first time and at that instant he forgot his father and the terror and despair both, and even when he remembered his father again (who had not stopped) the terror and despair did not return. Because, for all the twelve movings, they had sojourned until now in a poor country, a land of small farms and fields and houses, and he had never seen a house like this before. *Hit's big as a courthouse* he thought quietly, with a surge of peace and joy whose reason he could not have thought into words, being too young for that: *They are safe from him. People whose lives are a part of this peace and dignity are beyond his touch, be no more to them than a buzzing wasp: capable of stinging for a little moment but that's all; the spell of this peace and dignity rendering even the barns and stable and cribs which belong to it impervious to the puny flames he might contrive . . .* this, the peace and joy, ebbing for an instant as he looked again at the stiff black back, the stiff and implacable limp of the figure which was not dwarfed by the house, for the reason that it had never looked big anywhere and which now, against the serene columned backdrop, had more than ever that impervious quality of something cut ruthlessly from tin, depthless, as though, sidewise to the sun, it would cast no shadow. Watching him, the boy remarked the absolutely undeviating course which his father held and saw the stiff foot come squarely down in a pile of fresh droppings where a horse had stood in the drive and which his father could have avoided by a simple change of stride. But it ebbed only for a moment, though he could not have thought this into words either, walking on in the spell of the house, which he could ever want but without envy, without sorrow, certainly never with that ravening and jealous rage which unknown to him walked in the ironlike black coat before him: *Maybe he will feel it too. Maybe it will even change him now from what maybe he couldn't help but be.*

They crossed the portico. Now he could hear his father's stiff foot as it came down on the boards with clocklike finality, a sound out of all proportion to the displacement of the body it bore and which was not dwarfed either by the white door before it, as though it had attained to a sort of vicious and ravening minimum not to be dwarfed by anything—the flat, wide, black hat, the formal coat of broadcloth which had once been black but which had now that friction-glazed greenish cast of the bodies of old house flies, the lifted sleeve which was too large, the lifted hand like a curled claw. The door opened so promptly that the boy knew the Negro must have been watching them all the time, an old man with neat grizzled hair, in a linen jacket, who stood barring the door with his body, saying, "Wipe yo foots, white man, fo you come in here. Major ain't home nohow."

"Get out of my way, nigger," his father said, without heat too, flinging the door back and the Negro also and entering, his hat still on his head. And now the boy saw the prints of the stiff foot on the doorjamb and saw them appear on the pale rug behind the machinelike deliberation of the foot which seemed to bear (or transmit) twice the weight which the body compassed. The Negro was shouting "Miss Lula! Miss Lula!" somewhere behind them, then the boy, deluged as though by a warm wave by a suave turn of carpeted stair and a pendant glitter of chandeliers and a mute gleam of gold frames, heard the swift feet and saw her too, a lady—perhaps he had never seen her like before either—in a gray, smooth gown with lace at the throat and an apron tied at the waist and the sleeves turned back, wiping cake or biscuit dough from her hands with a towel as she came up the hall, looking not at his father at all but at the tracks on the blond rug with an expression of incredulous amazement.

"I tried," the Negro cried. "I tole him to . . ."

"Will you please go away?" she said in a shaking voice. "Major de Spain is not at home. Will you please go away?"

His father had not spoken again. He did not speak again. He did not even look at her. He just stood stiff in the center of the rug, in his hat, the shaggy iron-gray brows twitching slightly above the pebble-colored eyes as he appeared to examine the house with brief deliberation. Then with the same deliberation he turned; the boy watched him pivot on the good leg and saw the stiff foot drag round the arc of the turning, leaving a final long and fading smear. His father never looked at it, he never once looked down at the rug. The Negro held the door. It closed behind them, upon the hysteric and indistinguishable woman-wail. His father stopped at the top of the steps and scraped his boot clean on the edge of it. At the gate he stopped again. He stood for a moment, planted stiffly on the stiff foot, looking back at the house. "Pretty and white, ain't it?" he said. "That's sweat. Nigger sweat. Maybe it ain't white enough yet to suit him. Maybe he wants to mix some white sweat with it."

Two hours later the boy was chopping wood behind the house within which his mother and aunt and the two sisters (the mother and aunt, not the two girls, he knew that; even at this distance and muffled by walls the flat loud voices of the two girls emanated an incorrigible idle inertia) were setting up the stove to prepare a meal, when he heard the hooves and saw the linen-clad man on a fine sorrel mare, whom he recognized even before he saw the rolled rug in front of the Negro youth following on a fat bay carriage horse—a suffused, angry face vanishing, still at full gallop, beyond the corner of the house where his father and brother were sitting in the two tilted chairs; and a moment later, almost before he could have put the axe down, he heard the hooves again and watched the sorrel mare go back out of the yard, already galloping again. Then his father began to shout one of the sisters' names, who presently emerged backward from the kitchen door dragging the rolled rug along the ground by one end while the other sister walked behind it.

"If you ain't going to tote, go on and set up the wash pot," the first said.

"You, Sarty!" the second shouted. "Set up the wash pot!" His father appeared at the door, framed against that shabbiness, as he had been against that other bland perfection, impervious to either, the mother's anxious face at his shoulder.

"Go on," the father said. "Pick it up." The two sisters stooped, broad, lethargic; stooping, they presented an incredible expanse of pale cloth and a flutter of tawdry ribbons.

"If I thought enough of a rug to have to git hit all the way from France I wouldn't keep hit where folks coming in would have to tromp on hit," the first said. They raised the rug.

"Abner," the mother said. "Let me do it."

"You go back and git dinner," his father said. "I'll tend to this."

From the woodpile through the rest of the afternoon the boy watched them, the rug spread flat in the dust beside the bubbling wash-pot, the two sisters stooping over it with that profound and lethargic reluctance, while the father stood over them in turn, implacable and grim, driving them though never raising his voice again. He could smell the harsh homemade lye they were using; he saw his mother come to the door once and look toward them with an expression not anxious now but very like despair; he saw his father turn, and he fell to with the axe and saw from the corner of his eye his father raise from the ground a flattish fragment of field stone and examine it and return to the pot, and this time his mother actually spoke: "Abner. Abner. Please don't. Please, Abner."

Then he was done too. It was dusk; the whippoorwills had already begun. He could smell coffee from the room where they would presently eat the cold food remaining from the mid-afternoon meal, though when he entered the house he realized they were having coffee again probably because there was a fire on the hearth, before which the rug now lay spread over the backs of the two chairs. The tracks of his father's foot were gone. Where they had been were now long, water-cloudy scoriations resembling the sporadic course of a lilliputian mowing machine.

It still hung there while they ate the cold food and then went to bed, scattered without order or claim up and down the two rooms, his mother in one bed, where his father would later lie, the older brother in the other, himself, the aunt, and the two sisters on pallets on the floor. But his father was not in bed yet. The last thing the boy remembered was the depthless, harsh silhouette of the hat and coat bending over the rug and it seemed to him that he had not even closed his eyes when the silhouette was standing over him, the fire almost dead behind it, the stiff foot prodding him awake. "Catch up the mule," his father said.

When he returned with the mule his father was standing in the black door, the rolled rug over his shoulder. "Ain't you going to ride?" he said.

"No. Give me your foot."

He bent his knee into his father's hand, the wiry, surprising power flowed smoothly, rising, he rising with it, on to the mule's bare back (they had owned a saddle once; the boy could remember it though not when or where) and with the same effortlessness his father swung the rug up in front of him. Now in the starlight they retraced the afternoon's path, up the dusty road rife with honeysuckle, through the gate and up the black tunnel of the drive to the lightless house, where he sat on the mule and felt the rough warp of the rug drag across his thighs and vanish.

"Don't you want me to help" he whispered. His father did not answer and now he heard again that stiff foot striking the hollow portico with that wooden and clocklike deliberation, that outrageous overstatement of the weight it carried. The rug, hunched, not flung (the boy could tell that even in the darkness) from his father's shoulder struck the angle of wall and floor with a sound unbelievably loud, thunderous, then the foot again, unhurried and enormous; a light came on in the house and the boy sat, tense, breathing steadily and quietly and just a little fast, though the foot itself did not increase its beat at all, descending the steps now; now the boy could see him.

"Don't you want to ride now?" he whispered. "We kin both ride now," the light within the house altering now, flaring up and sinking. *He's coming down the stairs now,* he thought. He had already ridden the mule up beside the horse block; presently his father was up behind him and he doubled the reins over and slashed the mule across the neck, but before the animal could begin to trot the hard, thin arm came round him, the hard, knotted hand jerking the mule back to a walk.

In the first red rays of the sun they were in the lot, putting plow gear on the mules. This time the sorrel mare was in the lot before he heard it at all, the rider collarless and even bareheaded, trembling, speaking in a shaking voice as the woman in the house had done, his father merely looking up once before stooping again to the hame he was buckling, so that the man on the mare spoke to his stooping back:

"You must realize you have ruined that rug. Wasn't there anybody here, any of your women . . ." he ceased, shaking, the boy watching him, the older brother leaning now in the stable door, chewing, blinking slowly and steadily at nothing apparently. "It cost a hundred dollars. But you never had a hundred dollars. You never will. So I'm going to charge you twenty bushels of corn against your crop. I'll add it in your contract and when you come to the commissary you can sign it. That won't keep Mrs. de Spain quiet but maybe it will teach you to wipe your feet off before you enter her house again."

Then he was gone. The boy looked at his father, who still had not spoken or even looked up again, who was now adjusting the logger-head in the hame.

"Pap," he said. His father looked at him—the inscrutable face, the shaggy brows beneath which the gray eyes glinted coldly. Suddenly the boy went toward him, fast, stopping as suddenly. "You done the best you could!" he cried. "If he wanted hit done different why didn't he wait and tell you how? He won't git no twenty bushels! He won't git none! We'll gether hit and hide hit! I kin watch . . ."

"Did you put the cutter back in that straight stock like I told you?"

"No, sir," he said.

"Then go do it."

That was Wednesday. During the rest of that week he worked steadily, at what was within his scope and some which was beyond it, with an industry that did not need to be driven nor even commanded twice; he had this from his mother, with the difference that some at least of what he did he liked to do, such as splitting wood with the half-size axe which his mother and aunt had earned, or saved money somehow, to present him with at Christmas. In company with the two older women (and on one afternoon, even one of the sisters), he built pens for the shoat and the cow which were a part of his father's contract with the landlord, and one afternoon, his father being absent, gone somewhere on one of the mules, he went to the field.

They were running a middle buster now, his brother holding the plow straight while he handled the reins, and walking beside the straining mule, the rich black soil shearing cool and damp against his bare ankles, he thought *Maybe this is the end of it. Maybe even that twenty bushels that seems hard to have to pay for just a rug will be a cheap price for him to stop forever and always from being what he used to be;* thinking, dreaming now, so that his brother had to speak sharply to him to mind the mule: *Maybe he even won't collect the twenty bushels. Maybe it will all add up and balance and vanish—corn, rug, fire;*

the terror and grief, the being pulled two ways like between two teams of horses—gone, done with for ever and ever.

Then it was Saturday; he looked up from beneath the mule he was harnessing and saw his father in the black coat and hat. "Not that," his father said. "The wagon gear." And then, two hours later, sitting in the wagon bed behind his father and brother on the seat, the wagon accomplished a final curve, and he saw the weathered paintless store with its tattered tobacco- and patent-medicine posters and the tethered wagons and saddle animals below the gallery. He mounted the gnawed steps behind his father and brother, and there again was the lane of quiet, watching faces for the three of them to walk through. He saw the man in spectacles sitting at the plank table and he did not need to be told this was a Justice of the Peace; he sent one glare of fierce, exultant, partisan defiance at the man in collar and cravat now, whom he had seen but twice before in his life, and that on a galloping horse, who now wore on his face an expression not of rage but of amazed unbelief which the boy could not have known was at the incredible circumstance of being sued by one of his own tenants, and came and stood against his father and cried at the Justice: "He ain't done it! He ain't burnt . . ."

"Go back to the wagon," his father said.

"Burnt?" the Justice said. "Do I understand this rug was burned too?"

"Does anybody here claim it was?" his father said. "Go back to the wagon." But he did not, he merely retreated to the rear of the room, crowded as that other had been, but not to sit down this time, instead, to stand pressing among the motionless bodies, listening to the voices:

"And you claim twenty bushels of corn is too high for the damage you did to the rug?"

"He brought the rug to me and said he wanted the tracks washed out of it. I washed the tracks out and took the rug back to him."

"But you didn't carry the rug back to him in the same condition it was in before you made the tracks on it."

His father did not answer, and now for perhaps half a minute there was no sound at all save that of breathing, the faint, steady suspiration of complete and intent listening.

"You decline to answer that, Mr. Snopes?" Again his father did not answer. "I'm going to find against you, Mr. Snopes. I'm going to find that you were responsible for the injury to Major de Spain's rug and hold you liable for it. But twenty bushels of corn seems a little high for a man in your circumstances to have to pay. Major de Spain claims it cost a hundred dollars. October corn will be worth about fifty cents. I figure that if Major de Spain can stand a ninety-five dollar loss on something he paid cash for, you can stand a five-dollar loss you haven't earned yet. I hold you in damages to Major de Spain to the amount of ten bushels of corn over and above your contract with him, to be paid to him out of your crop at gathering time. Court adjourned."

It had taken no time hardly, the morning was but half begun. He thought they would return home and perhaps back to the field, since they were late, far behind all other farmers. But instead his father passed on behind the wagon, merely indicating with his hand for the older brother to follow with it, and crossed the road toward the blacksmith shop opposite, pressing on after his father, overtaking him, speaking, whispering up at the harsh, calm face beneath the weathered hat: "He won't git no ten bushels neither. He won't git one. We'll . . ." until his father glanced for an instant down at him, the face absolutely calm, the grizzled eyebrows tangled above the cold eyes, the voice almost pleasant, almost gentle:

"You think so? Well, we'll wait till October anyway."

The matter of the wagon—the setting of a spoke or two and the tightening of the tires—did not take long either, the business of the tires accomplished by driving the wagon into the spring branch behind the shop and letting it stand there, the mules nuzzling into the water from time to time, and the boy on the seat with the idle reins, looking up the slope and through the sooty tunnel of the shed where the slow hammer rang and where his father sat on an upended cypress bolt, easily, either talking or listening, still sitting there when the boy brought the dripping wagon up out of the branch and halted it before the door.

"Take them on to the shade and hitch," his father said. He did so and returned . His father and the smith and a third man squatting on his heels inside the door were talking, about crops and animals; the boy, squatting too in the ammoniac dust and hoofparings and scales of rust, heard his father tell a long and unhurried story out of the time before the birth of the older brother even when he had been a professional horsetrader. And then his father came up beside him where he stood before a tattered last year's circus poster on the other side of the store, gazing rapt and quiet at the scarlet horses, the incredible poisings and convolutions of tulle and tights and the painted leers of comedians, and said, "It's time to eat."

But not at home. Squatting beside his brother against the front wall, he watched his father emerge from the store and produce from a paper sack a segment of cheese and divide it carefully and deliberately into three with his pocket knife and produce crackers from the same sack. They all three squatted on the gallery and ate, slowly, without talking; then in the store again, they drank from a tin dipper tepid water smelling of the cedar bucket and of living beech trees. And still they did not go home. It was a horse lot this time, a tall rail fence upon and along which men stood and sat and out of which one by one horses were led, to be walked and trotted and then cantered back and forth along the road while the slow swapping and buying went on and the sun began to slant westward, they—the three of them—watching and listening, the older brother with his muddy eyes and his steady, inevitable tobacco, the father commenting now and then on certain of the animals, to no one in particular.

It was after sundown when they reached home. They ate supper by lamplight, then, sitting on the doorstep, the boy watched the night fully accomplish, listening to the whippoorwills and the frogs, when he heard his mother's voice: "Abner! No! No! Oh, God. Oh, God. Abner!" and he rose, whirled, and saw the altered light through the door where a candle stub now burned in a bottle neck on the table and his father, still in the hat and coat, at once formal and burlesque as though dressed carefully for some shabby and ceremonial violence, emptying the reservoir of the lamp back into the five-gallon kerosene can from which it had been filled, while the mother tugged at his arm until he shifted the lamp to the other hand and flung her back, not savagely or viciously, just hard, into the wall, her hands flung out against the wall for balance, her mouth open and in her face the same quality of hopeless despair as had been in her voice. Then his father saw him standing in the door.

"Go to the barn and get that can of oil we were oiling the wagon with," he said. The boy did not move. Then he could speak.

"What . . ." he cried. "What are you . . ."

"Go get that oil," his father said. "Go."

Then he was moving, running, outside the house, toward the stable: this the old habit, the old blood which he had not been permitted to choose for himself, which had been bequeathed him willy nilly and which had run for so long (and who knew where, battening on what of outrage and savagery and lust) before it came to him. *I could keep on*, he thought. *I could run on and on and never look back, never need to see his face again. Only I can't. I can't*, the rusted can in his hand now, the liquid sploshing in it as he ran back to the house and into it, into the sound of his mother's weeping in the next room, and handed the can to his father.

"Ain't you going to even send a nigger?" he cried. "At least you sent a nigger before!"

This time his father didn't strike him. The hand came even faster than the blow had, the same hand which had set the can on the table with almost excruciating care flashing from the can toward him too quick for him to follow it, gripping him by the back of his shirt and on to tiptoe before he had seen it quit the can, the face stooping at him in breathless and frozen ferocity, the cold, dead voice speaking over him to the older brother who leaned against the table, chewing with that steady, curious, sidewise motion of cows:

"Empty the can into the big one and go on. I'll catch up with you."

"Better tie him up to the bedpost," the brother said.

"Do like I told you," the father said. Then the boy was moving, his bunched shirt and the hard, bony hand between his shoulder-blades, his toes just touching the floor, across the room and into the other one, past the sisters sitting with spread heavy thighs in the two chairs over the cold hearth, and to where his mother and aunt sat side by side on the bed, the aunt's arms about his mother's shoulders.

"Hold him," the father said. The aunt made a startled movement. "Not you," the father said. "Lennie. Take hold of him. I want to see you do it." His mother took him by the wrist. "You'll hold him better than that. If he gets loose don't you know what he is going to do? He will go up yonder." He jerked his head toward the road. "Maybe I'd better tie him."

"I'll hold him," his mother whispered.

"See you do then." Then his father was gone, the stiff foot heavy and measured upon the boards, ceasing at last.

Then he began to struggle. His mother caught him in both arms, he jerking and wrenching at them. He would be stronger in the end, he knew that. But he had no time to wait for it. "Lemme go!" he cried. "I don't want to have to hit you!"

"Let him go!" the aunt said. "If he don't go, before God, I am going up there myself!"

"Don't you see I can't?" his mother cried. "Sarty! Sarty! No! No! Help me, Lizzie!"

Then he was free. His aunt grasped at him but it was too late. He whirled, running, his mother stumbled forward on to her knees behind him, crying to the nearer sister: "Catch him, Net! Catch him!" But that was too late too, the sister (the sisters were twins, born at the same time, yet either of them now gave the impression of being, encompassing as much living meat and volume and weight as any other two of the family) not yet having begun to rise from the chair, her head, face, alone merely turned, presenting to him in the flying instant an astonishing expanse of young female features untroubled by any surprise even, wearing only an expression of bovine interest. Then he was out of the room, out of the house, in the mild dust of the starlit road and the heavy rifeness of honeysuckle, the pale ribbon unspooling with terrific slowness under his running feet, reaching the gate at last and turning in, running, his heart and lungs drumming, on up the drive toward the lighted house, the lighted door. He did not knock, he burst in, sobbing for breath, incapable for the moment of speech; he saw the astonished face of the Negro in the linen jacket without knowing when the Negro had appeared.

"De Spain!" he cried, panted. "Where's . . ." then he saw the white man too emerging from a white door down the hall. "Barn!" he cried. "Barn!"

"What?" the white man said. "Barn?"

"Yes!" the boy cried. "Barn!"

"Catch him!" the white man shouted.

But it was too late this time too. The Negro grasped his shirt, but the entire sleeve, rotten with washing, carried away, and he was out that door too and in the drive again, and had actually never ceased to run even while he was screaming into the white man's face.

Behind him the white man was shouting, "My horse! Fetch my horse!" and he thought for an instant of cutting across the park and climbing the fence into the road, but he did not know the park nor how high the vine-massed fence might be and he dared not risk it. So he ran on down the drive, blood and breath roaring; presently he was in the road again though he could not see it. He could not hear either: the galloping mare was almost upon him before he heard her, and even then he held his course, as if the very urgency of his wild grief and need must in a moment more find him wings, waiting until the ultimate instant to hurl himself aside and into the weed-choked roadside ditch as the horse thundered past and on, for an instant in furious silhouette against the stars, the tranquil early summer night sky which, even before the shape of the horse and rider vanished, stained abruptly and violently upward: a long, swirling roar incredible and soundless, blotting the stars, and he springing up and into the road again, running again, knowing it was too late yet still running even after he heard the shot and, an instant later, two shots, pausing now without knowing he had ceased to run, crying "Pap! Pap!," running again before he knew he had begun to run, stumbling, tripping over something and scrabbling up again without ceasing to run, looking backward over his shoulder at the glare as he got up, running on among the invisible trees, panting, sobbing, "Father! Father!"

At midnight he was sitting on the crest of a hill. He did not know it was midnight and he did not know how far he had come. But there was no glare behind him now and he sat now, his back toward what he had called home for four days anyhow, his face toward the dark woods which he would enter when breath was strong again, small, shaking steadily in the chill darkness, hugging himself into the remainder of his thin, rotten shirt, the grief and despair now no longer terror and fear but just grief and despair. *Father. My father,* he thought. "He was brave!" he cried suddenly, aloud but not loud, no more than a whisper: "He was! He was a Colonel Sartoris' cav'ry!" not knowing that his father had gone to that war a private in the fine old European sense, wearing no uniform, admitting the authority of and giving fidelity to no man or army or flag, going to war as Malbrouck himself did: for booty—it meant nothing and less than nothing to him if it were enemy booty or his own.

The slow constellations wheeled on. It would be dawn and then sun-up after a while and he would be hungry. But that would be to-morrow and now he was only cold, and walking would cure that. His breathing was easier now and he decided to get up and go on, and then he found that he had been asleep because he knew it was almost dawn, the night almost over. He could tell that from the whippoorwills. They were everywhere now among the dark trees below him, constant and inflectioned and ceaseless, so that, as the instant for giving over to the day birds drew nearer and nearer, there was no interval at all between them. He got up. He was a little stiff, but walking would cure that too as it would the cold, and soon there would be the sun. He went on down the hill, toward the dark woods within which the liquid silver voices of the birds called unceasing—the rapid and urgent beating of the urgent and quiring heart of the late spring night. He did not look back.

Cultural Portfolio
The Southern Renaissance

The remarkable outpouring of writing—in experimental collaborations of writers and photographers and in cultural and literary criticism as well as poetry and fiction—that we know as the "Southern Renaissance" reached its peak during the 1930s and early 1940s. In its broader form, the literary reemergence of the South might be said to date from the novels of Ellen Glasgow, including *The Deliverance* (1904), which used satiric means to debunk Southern myth-making about the "Lost Cause," and *Barren Ground* (1925), perhaps her finest novel, which focuses especially on the roles of women in the South. In its more concerted form, however, the Southern Renaissance dates from 1922 with the publication of the first issue of a magazine called *The Fugitive,* a collaborative venture of a group of writers gathered in and around Nashville, Tennessee, and Vanderbilt University. For, although *The Fugitive* lasted only three years, it was followed by another collaborative publication, put together by the same group of writers, slightly enlarged, in the form of a manifesto titled *I'll Take My Stand* (1930). Led by the poet-critic John Crowe Ransom, the group included Donald Davidson, a poet and cultural critic; Allen Tate and Robert Penn Warren, both of whom wrote poetry and fiction as well as literary criticism; Cleanth Brooks, a literary critic; and the novelist Stark Young, author of *So Red the Rose* (1934).

With the exception of Young, who came from Mississippi, the named writers came from the border states of Kentucky and Tennessee. They had met in and around Vanderbilt, where they came under the influence of Ransom. Known both as the "Fugitives" and as the "Southern Agrarians," they tended, especially in their early work, to be self-consciously "traditional" in style, "conservative" in values and themes, and "defensive" in tone. For they thought of themselves as besieged defenders of a simpler, more tranquil, traditional, and contemplative way of life that dated back to Rome and to Greece but was now dis-

appearing in other parts of the world, including other parts of the United States, and was endangered even in the South. What they feared as well as condemned was a way of life that they associated not only with the streets, flats, and skyscrapers of cities but also with industrialization and commercialism or more broadly with the "modern" and "the cult of the new," and thus with "secularism" and "materialism," which is to say, the way of life that they thought of as already dominating and corrupting the rest of the nation and as threatening the South.

In their double-edged undertaking—their defense and celebration of the South and its "traditional" and "Agrarian" values, on one side, and their attack on "modern" secularism and materialism, on the other—the "Southern Agrarians" contributed significantly to a literary "Renaissance" of the 1930s that was almost as surprising as the Harlem Renaissance of the 1920s. The South had, of course, a literary tradition that reached back through Mark Twain and Edgar Allen Poe to Thomas Jefferson, William Byrd, and their contemporaries. And novelists like James Branch Cabell as well as Glasgow had extended that tradition into the twentieth century. But much of the nation and parts of the world had been schooled by writers like H. L. Mencken, who in 1920 published an essay on the culture of the South, bearing the provocative title "The Sahara of the Bozart," in which he compared the South to the Gobi Desert and other places that he thought of as cultural and literary wastelands. Indeed, it was in part against such attacks that the Southern Agrarians addressed defense. In fact, however, the Southern Renaissance that began in the late twenties was from the outset much broader and more varied than Ransom and his followers either understood or desired. Indeed, in retrospect it is clear that their defense and celebration of the South and its "agrarian" traditions and values was both more and less than a defense of the South: "more" because, in addition to mounting a defense of the South's literary culture, it also constituted an attempt to claim for themselves and others who resembled them the right to define the South and its traditions; and "less" because, in retrospect at least, it is clear that it ignored much of what was happening in the South's several literary scenes. Cabell and Glasgow, both Virginians, were well-established writers before the Southern Agrarians launched their defense of the South; Zora Neale Hurston of Florida had played an important role in the Harlem Renaissance; and a talented group of writers, including Sherwood Anderson, had congregated in New Orleans, where William Faulkner wrote his first novel, *Soldiers' Pay* (1926). In 1929, one year before publication of *I'll Take My Stand,* two major novels had emerged from the South— Faulkner's *The Sound and the Fury,* his third novel and his first great novel, and Thomas Wolfe's *Look Homeward, Angel,* his first and finest novel.

In short, as a remarkable cultural flowering, the Southern Renaissance had begun before the Southern Agrarians announced their "stand"; and it had begun as a flowering that no one could harness, let alone lay claim to own. Furthermore, it owed much of its rise to national and even international attention to an ironic coincidence of events over which no one had much control, especially writers from the South. For, when the Great Crash of October 1929 hit, bringing the greatest speculative binge in the nation's history to an end, it not only plunged the nation into the steepest and deepest economic decline in its history; it also made the South's considerable experience with want, privation, fear, and failure suddenly seem far more pertinent to the nation as a whole than it ever had before. With established writers like Sherwood Anderson and Theodore Dreiser, both of whom came from the Midwest, the heart of the heart of the country, writing books bearing titles like *Puzzled America* (1935) and *Tragic America* (1931), it suddenly became clear that the nation as a whole might have reason more carefully and less condescendingly to study some of the negative lessons on which Southerners had reason to think of themselves as resident experts. As a result, both Southern history and Southern literature began rapidly to acquire greater resonance and authority than they had ever before possessed. For many of the poems, stories, and novels being written in the South carried with them one version or another of what we might call, borrowing the title of C. Vann Woodward's celebrated book on the subject, *The Burden of Southern History* (1968). They engaged and inscribed, contested and confronted, as painful burdens that could no longer be denied, the South's long, shameful, "un-American" experiences with failure and guilt—failure associated with intimate experiences with poverty and privation as well as defeat in a bitter, bloody war that had ended in surrender and occupation; and guilt associated with the systematic denial of liberty and equal opportunity to other human beings, together with the systematic exploitation of them, first, through the institution of slavery and, then, through the institutions of segregation.

In short, from its inception, the Southern Renaissance drew its force from a wide range of writers, many of whom had little or no contact with the Fugitives and no part in the creation of the version of the South's heritage, traditions, and mission that the Agrarians themselves unevenly espoused. These writers included, to name a few not already mentioned, James Agee, Evelyn Scott, and T. S. Stribling of Tennessee; Erskine Caldwell, Carson McCullers, and Flannery O'Connor of Georgia; Zora Neale Hurston of Florida; Eudora Welty and Richard Wright of Mississippi; and Katherine Anne Porter of Texas. Furthermore, though they remained fundamentally Southern, many of these writers moved far beyond the forms of denial that characterized some of the early statements of the Fugitives. Stepping outside the legends of the Old South, they brought attention to a wide range of social, human problems, and they did so in astonishingly rich and varied poems, stories, and novels. As it turned out, furthermore, the broader Southern Renaissance clearly changed the Fugitives more than the Fugitives shaped it. The intellectual and imaginative landscapes, and thus, the poetry, fiction, and criticism, of several of the most prominent of the Southern Agrarians altered as the broader Southern Renaissance gained national and international attention— Ransom's more than Donaldson's, Tate's more than Ransom's, Brooks's more than Tate's, and

Warren's more than Brooks's. For, as it spread, the Southern Renaissance became both an unruly movement that no one owned and a force capable of changing as well as challenging those drawn to it, in part by virtue of its ability to attract, inspire, and enable writers far more varied—in class, race, and ethnicity; in gender and sexual orientation; in experience, interests and abilities—than any of the original Fugitives could possibly have foreseen. Indeed, we need only look, to take a few examples, at the fiction of Faulkner, Welty, Hurston, and Wright and at three extraordinary experimental collaborations between photographers and writers—namely, James Agee's and Walker Evan's *Let Us Now Praise Famous Men* (1941); Erskine Caldwell's and Margaret Bourke-White's *You Have Seen Their Faces* (1937); and Richard Wright's and Edwin Roskam's *Twelve Million Black Voices* (1941)—to recognize the unexpected and enduring force of the Southern Renaissance.

---

from W. J. Cash, *The Mind of the South*

The end of the decade [of the twenties] saw Thomas Wolfe and William Faulkner tower into view almost simultaneously. The thirties opened with Erskine Caldwell's *Tobacco Road.* And thereafter the multiplication of Southern writers would go on at such a pace until in 1939 the South actually produced more books of measurable importance than any other section of the country, until anybody who fired off a gun in the region was practically certain to kill an author.

The makers of this new literature differed widely in their viewpoints and interests, of course. . . . [But] not a few of [them] . . . showed a marked tendency to react to a new extreme, and as they sloughed off the old imperative to use their writings as a vehicle for glorifying and defending Dixie, to take more or less actively to hating and denouncing the South. . . .

In reality they hated the South a good deal less than they said and thought. Rather, so far as their hatred was not mere vain profession designed to invite attention to their own superior perception, they hated it with the exasperated hate of a lover who cannot persuade the object of his affections to his desire. . . .

All these men remained fundamentally Southern. . . . And their hate and anger against the South was both a defense mechanism . . . and a sort of reverse embodiment of the old sentimentality itself. . . .

[Yet], however much the new Southern authors might differ in their approach to their material, and regardless of what faults they might still display, nearly all of them had decisively escaped from the old Southern urge to turn the country into Never-Never Land, [and] nearly all of them stood, intellectually at least, pretty decisively outside the legend; and so were able to contribute to the region its first literature of any bulk and importance. And at the same time, in one measure or another, [they were able] to cast light on the Southern social scene and direct attention to Southern social problems.

1941

from Thomas Wolfe, *Look Homeward, Angel*

Epigraph

. . . a stone, a leaf, an unfound door; of a stone, a leaf, a door. And of all the forgotten faces.

Naked and alone we came into exile. In her dark womb we did not know our mother's face; from the prison of her flesh have we come into the unspeakable and incommunicable prison of this earth.

Which of us has known his brother? Which of us has looked into his father's heart? Which of us has not remained forever prison-pent? Which of us is not forever a stranger and alone?

O waste of loss, in the hot mazes, lost, among bright stars on this most weary unbright cinder, lost! Remembering speechlessly we seek the great forgotten language, the lost lane-end into heaven, a stone, a leaf, an unfound door. Where? When?

O lost, and by the wind grieved, ghost, come back again.

1929

from William Faulkner, *The Sound and the Fury*

Through the fence, between the curling flower spaces, I could see them hitting. They were coming toward where the flag was and I went along the fence. Luster was hunting in the grass by the flower tree. They took the flag out, and they were hitting. Then they put the flag back and they went to the table, and he hit and the other hit. Then they went on, and I went along the fence. Luster came away from the flower tree and we went along the fence and they stopped and we stopped and I looked through the fence while Luster was hunting in the grass.

"Here, caddie." He hit. They went away across the pasture. I held to the fence and watched them going away.

"Listen at you, now." Luster said. "Aint you something, thirty three years old, going on that way. After I done went all the way to town to buy you that cake. Hush up that moaning. Aint you going to help me find that quarter so I can go to the show tonight."

They were hitting little, across the pasture. I went back along the fence to where the flag was. It flapped on the bright grass and the trees.

"Come on." Luster said. "We done looked there. They aint no more coming right now. Les go down to the branch and find that quarter before them niggers finds it."

It was red, flapping on the pasture. Then there was a bird slanting and tilting on it. Luster threw. The flag flapped on the bright grass and the trees. I held to the fence.

"Shut up that moaning." Luster said. "I cant make them come if they aint coming, can I. If you dont hush up, mammy aint going to have no birthday for you. If you dont hush, you know what I going to do. I going to eat that cake all up. Eat them candles, too. Eat all them thirty three candles. Come on, les go down to the branch. I got to find my quarter. Maybe we can find one of they balls. Here. Here they is. Way over yonder.

2186

See." He came to the fence and pointed his arm. "See them. They aint coming back here no more. Come on."

We went along the fence and came to the garden fence, where our shadows were. My shadow was higher than Luster's on the fence. We came to the broken place and went through it.

"Wait a minute." Luster said. "You snagged on the nail again. Cant you never crawl through here without snagging on that nail."

Caddy uncaught me and we crawled through. Uncle Maury said to not let anybody see us, so we better stoop over, Caddy said. Stoop over, Benjy. Like this, see. We stooped over and crossed the garden, where the flowers rasped and rattled against us. The ground was hard. We climbed the fence, where the pigs were grunting and snuffing. I expect they're sorry because one of them got killed today, Caddy said. The ground was hard, churned and knotted.

Keep your hands in your pockets, Caddy said. Or they'll get froze. You dont want your hands froze on Christmas, do you. . . .
1929

Two Writers' Beginnings

Richard Wright

from *Black Boy*
A Record of Childhood and Youth

Now, how could I find out about this Mencken? There was a huge library near the riverfront, but I knew that Negroes were not allowed to patronize its shelves any more than they were the parks and playgrounds of the city. I had gone into the library several times to get books for the white men on the job. Which of them would now help me to get books? And how could I read them without causing concern to the white men with whom I worked? I had so far been successful in hiding my thoughts and feelings from them, but I knew that I would create hostility if I went about this business of reading in a clumsy way.

I weighed the personalities of the men on the job. . . .

There remained only one man whose attitude did not fit into an anti-Negro category, for I had heard the white men refer to him as a "Pope lover." He was an Irish Catholic and was hated by the white Southerners. I knew that he read books, because I had got him volumes from the library several times. Since he, too, was an object of hatred, I felt that he might refuse me but would hardly betray me. I hesitated, weighing and balancing the imponderable realities.

One morning I paused before the Catholic fellow's desk.

"I want to ask you a favor," I whispered to him.

"What is it?"

"I want to read. I can't get books from the library. I wonder if you'd let me use your card?"

He looked at me suspiciously.

"My card is full most of the time," he said.

"I see," I said and waited, posing my question silently.

"You're not trying to get me into trouble, are you, boy?" he asked, staring at me.

"Oh, no, sir."

"What book do you want?"

"A book by H. L. Mencken."

"Which one?"

"I don't know. Has he written more than one?"

"He has written several."

"I didn't know that."

"What makes you want to read Mencken?"

"Oh, I just saw his name in the newspaper," I said.

"It's good of you to want to read," he said. "But you ought to read the right things."

I said nothing. Would he want to supervise my reading?

"Let me think," he said. "I'll figure out something."

I turned from him and he called me back. He stared at me quizzically.

"Richard, don't mention this to the other white men," he said.

"I understand," I said. "I won't say a word."

A few days later he called me to him.

"I've got a card in my wife's name," he said. "Here's mine."

"Thank you, sir."

"Do you think you can manage it?"

"I'll manage fine," I said.

"If they suspect you, you'll get in trouble," he said.

"I'll write the same kind of notes to the library that you wrote when you sent me for books," I told him. "I'll sign your name."

He laughed.

"Go ahead. Let me see what you get," he said.

That afternoon I addressed myself to forging a note. Now, what were the names of books written by H. L. Mencken? I did not know any of them. I finally wrote what I thought would be a foolproof note: *Dear Madam: Will you please let this nigger boy*—I used the word "nigger" to make the librarian feel that I could not possibly be the author of the note—*have some books by H. L. Mencken?* I forged the white man's name.

I entered the library as I had always done when on errands for whites, but I felt that I would somehow slip up and betray myself. I doffed my hat, stood a respectful distance from the desk, looked as unbookish as possible, and waited for the white patrons to be taken care of. When the desk was clear of people, I still waited. The white librarian looked at me.

"What do you want, boy?"

As though I did not possess the power of speech, I stepped forward and simply handed her the forged note, not parting my lips.

"What books by Mencken does he want?" she asked.

"I don't know, ma'am," I said, avoiding her eyes.

"Who gave you this card?"

"Mr. Falk," I said.

"Where is he?"

"He's at work, at the M—— Optical Company," I said. "I've been in here for him before."

"I remember," the woman said. "But he never wrote notes like this."

Oh, God, she's suspicious. Perhaps she would not let me have the books? If she had turned her back at that moment, I would have ducked out the door and never gone back. Then I thought of a bold idea.

"You can call him up, ma'am," I said, my heart pounding.

"You're not using these books, are you?" she asked pointedly.

"Oh, no, ma'am. I can't read."

"I don't know what he wants by Mencken," she said under her breath.

I knew now that I had won; she was thinking of other things and the race question had gone out of her mind. She went to the shelves. Once or twice she looked over her shoulder at me, as though she was still doubtful. Finally she came forward with two books in her hand.

"I'm sending him two books," she said. "But tell Mr. Falk to come in next time, or send me the names of the books he wants. I don't know what he wants to read."

I said nothing. She stamped the card and handed me the books. Not daring to glance at them, I went out of the library, fearing that the woman would call me back for further questioning. A block away from the library I opened one of the books and read a title: *A Book of Prefaces*. I was nearing my nineteenth birthday and I did not know how to pronounce the word "preface." I thumbed the pages and saw strange names. I shook my head, disappointed. I looked at the other book; it was called *Prejudices*. I knew what that word meant; I had heard it all my life. And right off I was on guard against Mencken's books. Why would a man want to call a book *Prejudices*? The word was so stained with all my memories of racial hate that I would not conceive of anybody using it for a title. Perhaps I had made a mistake about Mencken? A man who had prejudices must be wrong.

When I showed the books to Mr. Falk, he looked at me and frowned.

"That librarian might telephone you," I warned him.

"That's all right," he said. "But when you're through reading those books, I want you to tell me what you get out of them."

That night in my rented room, while letting the hot water run over my can of pork and beans in the sink, I opened *A Book of Prefaces* and began to read. I was jarred and shocked by the style, the clear, clean, sweeping sentences. Why did he write like that? And how did one write like that? I pictured the man as a raging demon, slashing with his pen, consumed with hate, denouncing everything American, extolling everything European or German, laughing at the weaknesses of people, mocking God, authority. What was this? I stood up, trying to realize what reality lay behind the meaning of the words . . . Yes, this man was fighting, fighting with words. He was using words as a weapon, using them as one would use a club. Could words be weapons? Well, yes, for here they were. Then, maybe, perhaps, I could use them as a weapon? No. It frightened me. I read on and what amazed me was not what he said, but how on earth anybody had the courage to say it.

Occasionally I glanced up to reassure myself that I was alone in the room. Who were these men about whom Mencken was talking so passionately? Who was Anatole France? Joseph Conrad? Sinclair Lewis, Sherwood Anderson, Dostoevski, George Moore, Gustave Flaubert, Maupassant, Tolstoy, Frank Harris, Mark Twain, Thomas Hardy, Arnold Bennett, Stephen Crane, Zola, Norris, Gorky, Bergson, Ibsen, Balzac, Bernard Shaw, Dumas, Poe, Thomas Mann, O. Henry, Dreiser, H. G. Wells, Gogol, T. S. Eliot, Gide, Baudelaire, Edgar Lee Masters, Stendhal, Turgenev, Huneker, Nietzsche, and scores of others? Were these men real? Did they exist or had they existed? And how did one pronounce their names?

1945

from *American Hunger*

Color hate defined the place of black life as below that of white life; and the black man, responding to the same dreams as the white man, strove to bury within his heart his awareness of this difference because it made him lonely and afraid. Hated by whites and being an organic part of the culture that hated him, the black man grew in turn to hate in himself that which others hated in him. But pride would make him hide his self-hate, for he would not want whites to know that he was so thoroughly conquered by them that his total life was conditioned by their attitude; but in the act of hiding his self-hate, he could not help but hate those who evoked his self-hate in him. So each part of his day would be consumed in a war with himself, a good part of his energy would be spent in keeping control of his unruly emotions, emotions which he had not wished to have, but could not help having. Held at bay by the hate of others, preoccupied with his own feelings, he was continuously at war with reality. He became inefficient, less able to see and judge the objective world. And when he reached that state, the white people looked at him and laughed and said:

"Look, didn't I tell you niggers were that way?"

To solve this tangle of balked emotion, I loaded the empty part of the ship of my personality with fantasies of ambition to keep it from toppling over into the sea of senselessness. Like any other American, I dreamed of going into business and making money; I dreamed of working for a firm that would allow me to advance until I reached an important position; I even dreamed of organizing secret groups of blacks to fight all whites. . . . And if the blacks would not agree to organize, then they would have to be fought. I would end up again with self-hate, but it was now a self-hate that was projected outward upon other blacks. Yet I knew—with that part of my mind that the whites had given me—that none of my dreams was possible. Then I would hate myself for allowing my mind to dwell upon the unattainable. Thus the circle would complete itself.

Slowly I began to forge in the depths of my mind a mechanism that repressed all the dreams and desires that the Chicago streets, the newspapers, the movies were evoking in me. I was going through a second childhood; a new sense of the limit of the possible was being born in me. What could I dream of that had the barest possibility of coming true? I could think of nothing. And, slowly, it was upon exactly that nothingness that my mind began to dwell, that constant sense of wanting without having, of being hated without reason. A dim notion of what life meant to a Negro in America was coming to consciousness in me, not in terms of external events, lynchings, Jim Crowism, and the endless brutalities, but in terms of crossed-up feeling, of psyche pain. I sensed that Negro life was a sprawling land of unconscious suffering, and there were but few Negroes who knew the meaning of their lives, who could tell their story.

1977

---

from Eudora Welty, *A Sweet Devouring*

When I used to ask my mother which we were, rich or poor, she refused to tell me. I was then nine years old and of course what I was dying to hear was that we were poor. I was reading a book called *Five Little Peppers* and my heart was set on baking a cake for my mother in a stove with a hole in it. Some version of rich, crusty old Mr. King—up till that time not living on our street—was sure to come down the hill in his wheel chair and rescue me if anything went wrong. But before I could start a cake at all I had to find out if we were poor, and poor *enough;* and my mother wouldn't tell me, she said she was too busy. I couldn't wait too long; I had to go on reading and soon Polly Pepper got into more trouble, some that was a little harder on her and easier on me.

Trouble, the backbone of literature, was still to me the original property of the fairy tale, and as long as there was plenty of trouble for everybody and the rewards for it were falling in the right spots, reading was all smooth sailing. At that age a child reads with higher appetite and gratification, and with those two stars sailing closer together, than ever again in his growing up. The home shelves had been providing me all along with the usual books, and I read them with love—but snap, I finished them. I read everything just alike—snap. I even came to the *Tales from Maria Edgeworth* and went right ahead, without feeling the bump—then. It *was* noticeable that when her characters suffered she punished them for it, instead of rewarding them as a reader had rather been led to hope. In her stories, the children had to make their choice between being unhappy and good about it and being unhappy and bad about it, and then she helped them to choose wrong. In *The Purple Jar,* it will be remembered, there was the little girl being taken through the shops by her mother and her downfall coming when she chooses to buy something beautiful instead of something necessary. The purple jar, when the shop sends it out, proves to have been purple only so long as it was filled with purple water, and her mother knew it all the time. They don't deliver the water. That's only the cue for stones to start coming through the hole in the victim's worn-out shoe. She bravely agrees she must keep walking on stones until such time as she is offered another choice between the beautiful and the useful. Her father tells her as far as he is concerned she can stay in the house. If I had been at all easy to disappoint, that story would have disappointed me. Of course I did feel what is the good of walking on rocks if they are going to let the water out of the jar too? And it seemed to me that even the illustrator fell down on the characters in that book, not alone Maria Edgeworth, for when a rich, crusty old gentleman gave Simple Susan a guinea for some kind deed she'd done him, there was a picture of the transaction and where was the guinea? I couldn't make out a feather. But I liked *reading* the book all right—except that I finished it.

My mother took me to the Public Library and introduced me: "Let her have any book she wants, except *Elsie Dinsmore.*" I looked for the book I couldn't have and it was a row. That was how I learned about the Series books. The *Five Little Peppers* belonged, so did *The Wizard of Oz,* so did *The Little Colonel,* so did *The Green Fairy Book.* There were many of everything, generations of everybody, instead of one. I wasn't coming to the end of reading, after all—I was saved.

Our library in those days was a big rotunda lined with shelves. A copy of *V. V.'s Eyes* seemed to follow you wherever you went, even after you'd read it. I didn't know what I liked, I just knew what there was a lot of. After *Randy's Spring* there came *Randy's Summer, Randy's Fall* and *Randy's Winter.* True, I didn't care very much myself for her spring, but it didn't occur to me that I might not care for her summer, and then her summer didn't prejudice me against her fall, and I still had hopes as I moved on to her winter. I was disappointed in her whole year as it turned out, but a thing like that didn't keep me from wanting to read every word of it. The pleasures of reading itself—who doesn't remember?—were like those of a Christmas cake, a sweet devouring. The "Randy Books" failed chiefly in being so soon over. Four seasons doesn't make a series.

All that summer I used to put on a second petticoat (our librarian wouldn't let you past the front door if she could see through you), ride my bicycle up the hill and "through the Capitol" (short cut) to the library with my two read books in the basket (two was the limit you could take out at one time when you were a child and also as long as you lived), and tiptoe in ("Silence") and exchange them for two more in two minutes. Selection was no object. I coasted the two new books home, jumped out of my petticoat, read (I suppose I ate and bathed and answered questions put to me), then in all hope put my petticoat back on and rode those two books back to the library to get my next two.

The librarian was the lady in town who wanted to be it. She called me by my full name and said: "Does your mother know where you are? You know good and well the fixed rule of this library: *Nobody is going to come running back here with any book on the same day they took it out.* Get both those things out of here and don't come back till tomorrow. And I can practically see through you."

1969

Three Poets

John Crowe Ransom

Bells for John Whiteside's Daughter

There was such speed in her little body,
And such lightness in her footfall,
It is no wonder her brown study
Astonishes us all.

Her wars were bruited in our high window.   5
We looked among orchard trees and beyond
Where she took arms against her shadow,
Or harried unto the pond

The lazy geese, like a snow cloud
Dripping their snow on the green grass,   10
Tricking and stopping, sleepy and proud,
Who cried in goose, Alas,

For the tireless heart within the little
Lady with rod that made them rise
From their noon apple-dreams and scuttle   15
Goose-fashion under the skies!

But now go the bells, and we are ready,
In one house we are sternly stopped
To say we are vexed at her brown study,
Lying so primly propped.   20
1924

Piazza Piece

—I am a gentleman in a dustcoat trying
To make you hear. Your ears are soft and small
And listen to an old man not at all,
They want the young men's whispering and sighing.
But see the roses on your trellis dying   5
And hear the spectral singing of the moon;
For I must have my lovely lady soon,
I am a gentleman in a dustcoat trying.

—I am a lady young in beauty waiting
Until my truelove comes, and then we kiss.   10
But what grey man among the vines is this
Whose words are dry and faint as in a dream?
Back from my trellis, Sir, before I scream!
I am a lady young in beauty waiting.
1927

The Equilibrists

Full of her long white arms and milky skin
He had a thousand times remembered sin.
Alone in the press of people traveled he,
Minding her jacinth, and myrrh, and ivory.

Mouth he remembered: the quaint orifice   5
From which came heat that flamed upon the kiss,
Till cold words came down spiral from the head,
Grey doves from the officious tower illsped.

Body: it was a white field ready for love,
On her body's field, with the gaunt tower above,   10
The lilies grew, beseeching him to take,
If he would pluck and wear them, bruise and break.

Eyes talking: Never mind the cruel words,
Embrace my flowers, but not embrace the swords.
But what they said, the doves came straightway flying 15
And unsaid: Honor, Honor, they came crying.

Importunate her doves. Too pure, too wise,
Clambering on his shoulder, saying, Arise,
Leave me now, and never let us meet,
Eternal distance now command thy feet.   20

Predicament indeed, which thus discovers
Honor among thieves, Honor between lovers.
O such a little word is Honor, they feel!
But the grey word is between them cold as steel.

At length I saw these lovers fully were come   25
Into their torture of equilibrium;
Dreadfully had forsworn each other, and yet
They were bound each to each, and they did not forget.

And rigid as two painful stars, and twirled
About the clustered night their prison world,   30
They burned with fierce love always to come near,
But Honor beat them back and kept them clear.

Ah, the strict lovers, they are ruined now!
I cried in anger. But with puddled brow
Devising for those gibbeted and brave   35
Came I descanting: Man, what would you have?

For spin your period out, and draw your breath,
A kinder sæculum[1] begins with Death.
Would you ascend to Heaven and bodiless dwell?
Or take your bodies honorless to Hell?   40

In Heaven you have heard no marriage is,
No white flesh tinder to your lecheries,
Your male and female tissue sweetly shaped
Sublimed away, and furious blood escaped.

Great lovers lie in Hell, the stubborn ones   45
Infatuate of the flesh upon the bones;
Stuprate,[2] they rend each other when they kiss,
The pieces kiss again, no end to this.

[1] World.
[2] Violated.

But still I watched them spinning, orbited nice.
Their flames were not more radiant than their ice.   50
I dug in the quiet earth and wrought the tomb
And made these lines to memorize their doom:—

EPITAPH

Equilibrists lie here; stranger, tread light;
Close, but untouching in each other's sight;   55
Mouldered the lips and ashy the tall skull.
Let them lie perilous and beautiful.
1927

Allen Tate, *Ode to the Confederate Dead*

Row after row with strict impunity
The headstones yield their names to the element,
The wind whirrs without recollection;
In the riven troughs the splayed leaves
Pile up, of nature the casual sacrament   5
To the seasonal eternity of death;
Then driven by the fierce scrutiny
Of heaven to their election in the vast breath,
They sough[1] the rumour of mortality.

Autumn is desolation in the plot   10
Of a thousand acres where these memories grow
From the inexhaustible bodies that are not
Dead, but feed the grass row after rich row.
Think of the autumns that have come and gone!—
Ambitious November with the humors of the year,   15
With a particular zeal for every slab,
Staining the uncomfortable angels that rot
On the slabs, a wing chipped here, an arm there:
The brute curiosity of an angel's stare
Turns you, like them, to stone,   20
Transforms the heaving air
Till plunged to a heavier world below
You shift your sea-space blindly
Heaving, turning like the blind crab.

Dazed by the wind, only the wind   25
The leaves flying, plunge

[1] Sigh.

You know who have waited by the wall
The twilight certainty of an animal,
Those midnight restitutions of the blood
You know—the immitigable pines, the smoky frieze   30
Of the sky, the sudden call: you know the rage,
The cold pool left by the mounting flood,
Of muted Zeno and Parmenides.[2]
You who have waited for the angry resolution
Of those desires that should be yours tomorrow,   35
You know the unimportant shrift of death
And praise the vision
And praise the arrogant circumstance
Of those who fall
Rank upon rank, hurried beyond decision—   40
Here by the sagging gate, stopped by the wall.

> Seeing, seeing only the leaves
> Flying, plunge and expire

Turn your eyes to the immoderate past,
Turn to the inscrutable infantry rising   45
Demons out of the earth—they will not last.
Stonewall, Stonewall,[3] and the sunken fields of hemp,
Shiloh, Antietam, Malvern Hill, Bull Run.[4]
Lost in that orient of the thick-and-fast
You will curse the setting sun.   50

> Cursing only the leaves crying
> Like an old man in a storm

You hear the shout, the crazy hemlocks point
With troubled fingers to the silence which
Smothers you, a mummy, in time.   55

> The hound bitch
Toothless and dying, in a musty cellar
Hears the wind only.

> Now that the salt of their blood
Stiffens the saltier oblivion of the sea,   60
Seals the malignant purity of the flood,
What shall we who count our days and bow
Our heads with a commemorial woe
In the ribboned coats of grim felicity,
What shall we say of the bones, unclean,   65

---

[2] Greek philosophers of the fifth century B.C.
who denied the reality of change and
believed in the permanence of "being."

[3] Confederate general Stonewall Jackson
(1824–1863).

[4] Shiloh; Antietam; Malvern Hill; Bull Run:
battles of the Civil War.

Whose verdurous anonymity will grow?
The ragged arms, the ragged heads and eyes
Lost in these acres of the insane green?
The gray lean spiders come, they come and go;
In a tangle of willows without light   70
The singular screech-owl's tight
Invisible lyric seeds the mind
With the furious murmur of their chivalry.

    We shall say only the leaves
    Flying, plunge and expire   75

We shall say only the leaves whispering
In the improbable mist of nightfall
That flies on multiple wing;
Night is the beginning and the end
And in between the ends of distraction   80
Waits mute speculation, the patient curse
That stones the eyes, or like the jaguar leaps
For his own image in a jungle pool, his victim.
What shall we say who have knowledge
Carried to the heart? Shall we take the act   85
To the grave? Shall we, more hopeful, set up the grave
In the house? The ravenous grave?

                        Leave now
The shut gate and the decomposing wall:
The gentle serpent, green in the mulberry bush,   90
Riots with his tongue through the hush—
Sentinel of the grave who counts us all!
1930

Robert Penn Warren, *Bearded Oaks*

The oaks, how subtle and marine,
Bearded, and all the layered light
Above them swims; and thus the scene,
Recessed, awaits the positive night.

So, waiting, we in the grass now lie   5
Beneath the languorous tread of light:
The grasses, kelp-like, satisfy
The nameless motions of the air.

Upon the floor of light, and time,
Unmurmuring, of polyp made,   10

We rest; we are, as light withdraws,
Twin atolls on a shelf of shade.

Ages to our construction went,
Dim architecture, hour by hour:
And violence, forgot now, lent   15
The present stillness all its power.

The storm of noon above us rolled,
Of light the fury, furious gold,
The long drag troubling us, the depth:
Dark is unrocking, unrippling, still.   20

Passion and slaughter, ruth, decay
Descent, minutely whispering down,
Silted down swaying streams, to lay
Foundation for our voicelessness.

All our debate is voiceless here,   25
As all our rage, the rage of stone;
If hope is hopeless, then fearless fear,
And history is thus undone.

Our feet once wrought the hollow street
With echo when the lamps were dead   30
At windows, once our headlight glare
Disturbed the doe that, leaping, fled.

I do not love you less that now
The caged heart makes iron stroke,
Or less that all that light once gave   35
The graduate dark should now revoke.

We live in time so little time
And we learn all so painfully,
That we may spare this hour's term
To practice for eternity.   40
1942

Two Collaborations

from Erskine Caldwell and Margaret Bourke-White, *You Have Seen Their Faces*

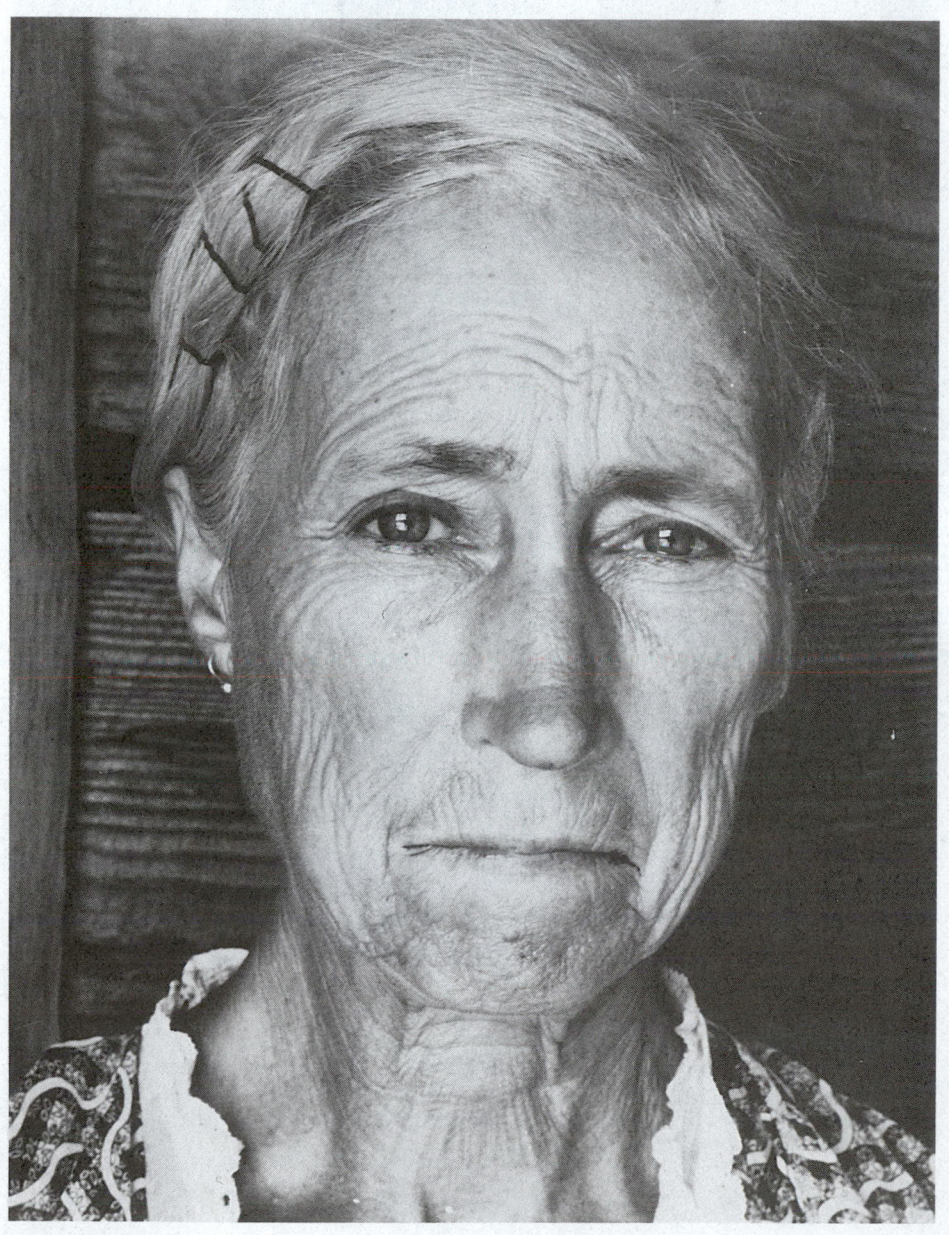

Margaret Bourke-White
Resident of Locket, Georgia, ca. 1937
from You Have Seen Their Faces
(© Margaret Bourke-White Estate, courtesy *Life Magazine*)

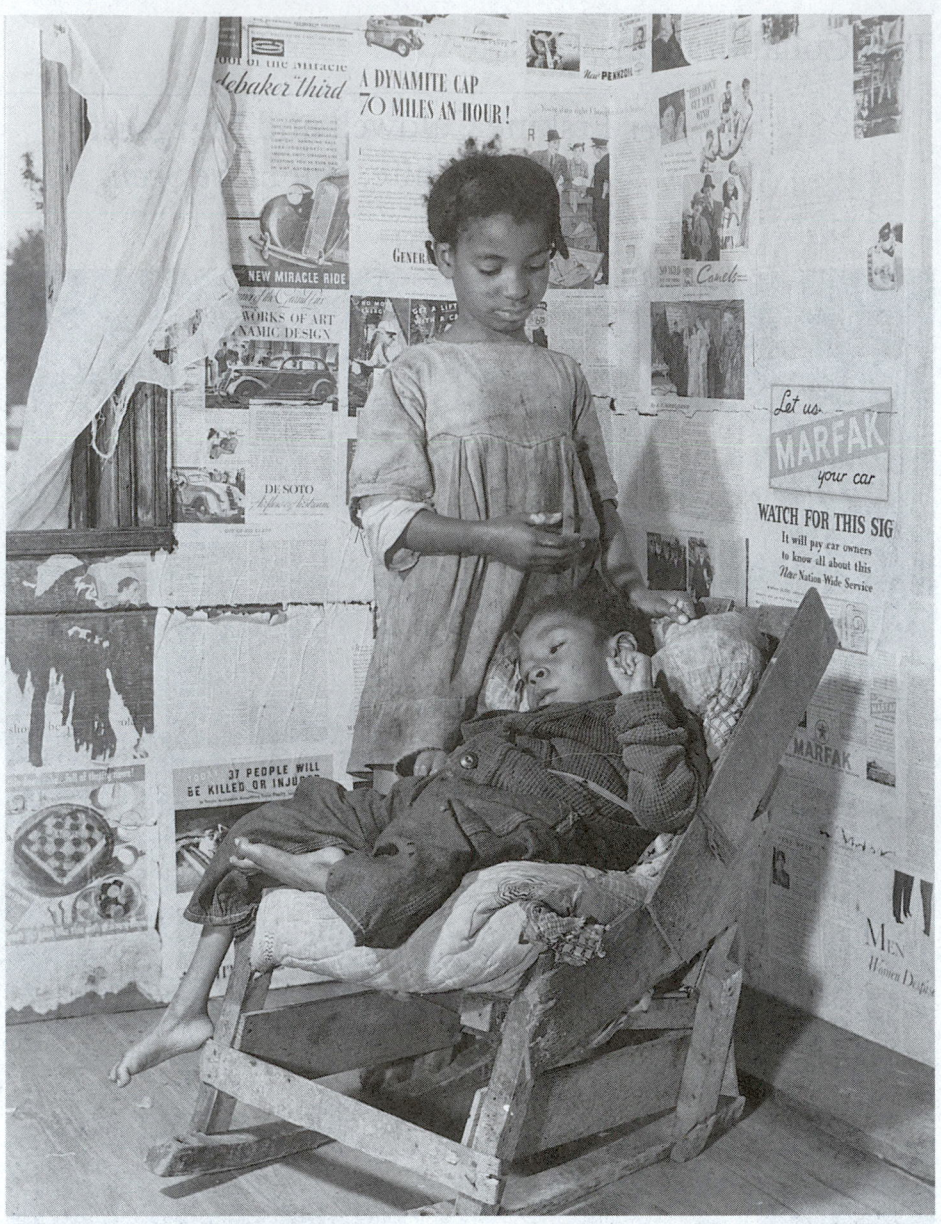

Margaret Bourke-White
Belmont, Florida: "Little brother began shrivel-
ing up eleven years ago,"
from You Have Seen Their Faces
(© Margaret Bourke-White Estate,
courtesy *Life Magazine*)

Margaret Bourke-White
Marion Junction, Alabama
from You Have Seen Their Faces
(© Margaret Bourke-White Estate,
courtesy *Life Magazine*)

from James Agee and Walker Evans,
Let Us Now Praise Famous Men

Lamplight here, and lone, late: the odor is of pine that has stood shut on itself through the heat of a hot day: the odor of an attic at white noon: and all of the walls save that surface within immediate touch of the lamp, where like water slept in lantern light the grain in so sharply discerned in its retirement beyond the sleep of the standing shape of pines, and the pastings and pinnings of sad ornaments, are a most dim scarce-color of grayed silver breathed in yellow red which is the hue and haze in the room; and above me, black: where, beyond bones of rafters underlighted, a stomach sucked against the spine in fear, the roof draws up its peak: and this is a frightening dark, which has again to do with an attic: for it is the darkness that stands just up the stairs, sucking itself out of sight of the light, from an attic door left ajar, noticed on your way to bed, and re-membered after you are there: so that I muse what not quite creatures and what not quite forms are suspended like bats above and behind my bent head; and how far down

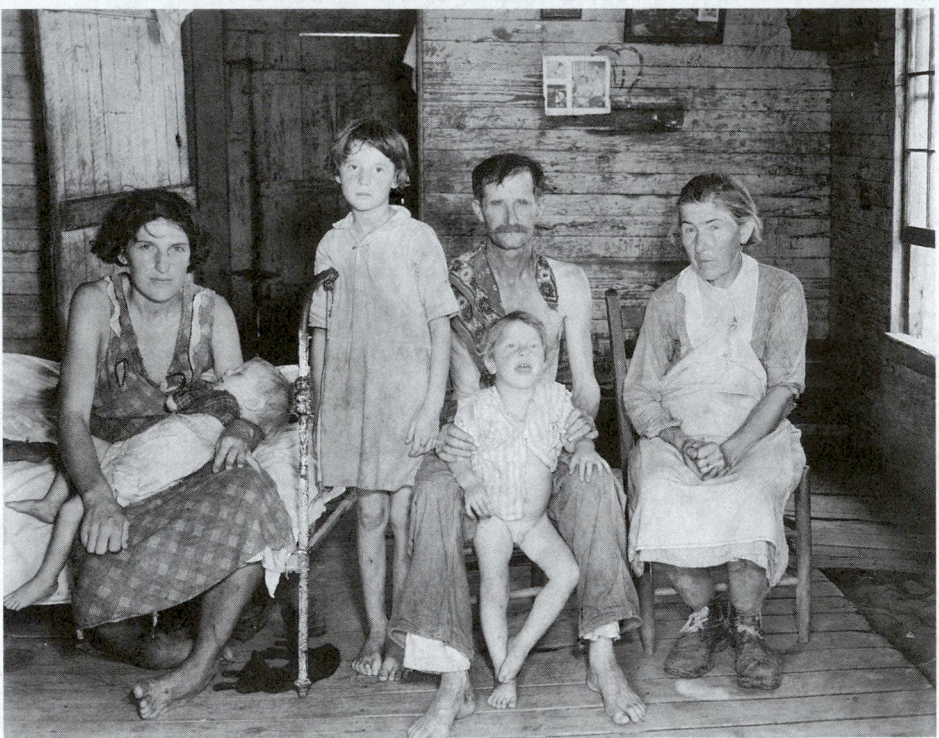

Walker Evans
Family
from Let Us Now Praise Famous Men
(Reproduced from the Collections of the Library of Congress)

Walker Evans
Woman and Baby
from Let Us Now Praise Famous Men
(Reproduced from the Collections of the Library of Congress)

in their clustered weight they are stealing while my eyes are on this writing; and how skillfully swiftly they suck themselves back upward into the dark when I turn my head: and above all, why they should be so coy, who, with one slather of cold membranes drooping, could slap out light and have me: and who own me since all time's beginning. Yet this mere fact of thinking holds them at distance, as crucifixes demons, so lightly and well that I am almost persuaded of being merely fanciful; in which exercise I would be theirs most profoundly beyond rescue, not knowing, and not fearing, I am theirs.

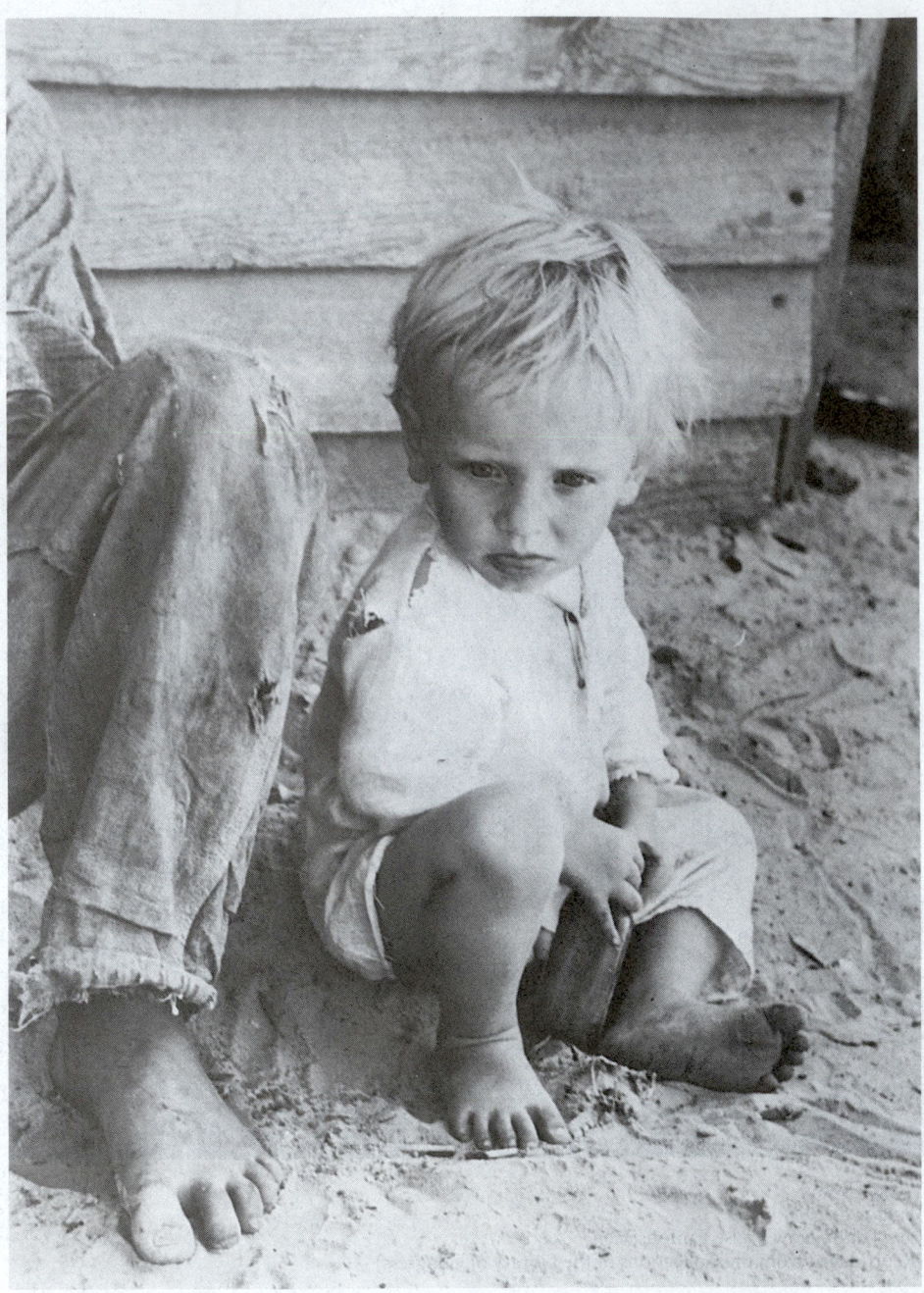

Walker Evans
Little Boy
from Let Us Now Praise Famous Men
(Reproduced from the Collections of the Library of Congress)

Above that shell and carapace, more frail against heaven than fragilest membrane of glass, nothing, straight to the terrific stars: whereof all heaven is chalky; and of whom the nearest is so wild a reach my substance wilts to think on: and we, this Arctic flower snow-rooted, last matchflame guarded on a windy plain, are seated among these stars alone: none to turn to, none to make us known; a little country settlement so deep, so lost in shelve and shade of dew, no one so much as laughs at us. Small wonder how pitiably we love our home, cling in her skirts at night, rejoice in her wide star-seducing smile, when every star strikes us sick with the fright: do we really exist at all?

> This world is not my home, I'm, only passing through,
> My treasures and my hopes, are, all, beyond the sky,
> I've many, friends, and kindreds, that's gone along before,
> And I can't, feel, at home, in this world, any, more.

And thus, too, these families, not otherwise than with every family in the earth, how each, apart, how inconceivably lonely, sorrowful, and remote! Not one other on earth, nor in any dream, that can care so much what comes to them, so that even as they sit at the lamp and eat their supper, the joke they are laughing at could not be so funny to anyone else; and the littlest child who stands on the bench solemnly, with food glitter-ing all over his cheeks in the lamplight, this littlest child I speak of is not there, he is of another family, and it is a different woman who wipes the food from his cheeks and takes his weight upon her thighs and against her body and who feeds him, and lets his weight slacken against her in his heavying sleep; and the man who puts another soaked cloth to the skin cancer on his shoulder; it is his wife who is looking on, and his child who lies sunken along the floor with his soft mouth broad open and his nakedness up like a rolling dog, asleep: and the people next up the road cannot care in the same say, not for any of it: for they are absorbed upon themselves: and the negroes down beyond the spring have drawn their shutters tight, the lamplight pulses like wounded honey through the seams into the soft night, and there is laughter: but nobody else cares. All over the whole round earth and in the settlements, the towns, and the great iron stones of cities, people are drawn inward within their little shells of rooms, and are to be seen in their wondrous and pitful actions through the surfaces of their lighted windows by thousands, by millions, little golden aquariums, in chairs, reading, setting tables, sewing, playing cards, not talking, talking, laughing inaudibly, mixing drinks, at radio dials, eating, in shirt-sleeves, carefully dressed, courting, teasing, loving, seducing, un-dressing, leaving the room empty in its empty light, alone and writing a letter urgently, in couples married, in separate chairs, in family parties, in gay parties, preparing for bed, preparing for sleep: and none can care, beyond that room; and none can be cared for, by any beyond that room: and it is small wonder they are drawn together so cow-ardly close, and small wonder in what dry agony of despair a mother may fasten her talons and her vampire mouth upon the soul of her struggling son and drain him empty, light as a locust shell: and wonder only that an age that has borne its children and must lose and has lost them, and lost life, can bear further living; but so it is.

1941

Hart Crane
1899–1932

In his short life, Hart Crane left a small legacy of highly worked and powerfully thought-through poems in which the legacy of the modernist French poets Rimbaud and Mallarmé first entered our literature. Like Rimbaud in his "Bateau Ivre," Crane wrote a poetry of headlong momentum, his precipitous current flowing, like the Mississippi, toward a revelatory ocean. Like Mallarmé, Crane pressed syntax to its utmost compression, and by transferred epithets and periphrases he made up a heady texture rich with music and light. Crane's poems name Emily Dickinson, Herman Melville, and Walt Whitman as his predecessors, but Robert Lowell was right in calling Crane "the Shelley of our age"; Crane had learned from Shelley the ecstatic hope and incandescent love that opposed themselves to skepticism and irony, which they both nonetheless knew well.

Nothing in Crane's life or background explains his meteoric poetic genius. He was born in Cleveland, Ohio, of unhappily married parents, who were divorced when he was seventeen. Crane's businessman father, a candy manufacturer, hoped that his son would enter his business. Crane's predatory mother, from whom he had eventually to cut himself off, bound her son ever more tightly to her. Crane's schooling was interrupted by his mother's insisting he accompany her on trips; lacking enough credits at the end of high school to enter college, Crane took jobs in advertising, first in Cleveland and then New York. The jobs bored him, but as he moved, he found friends. In New York these included Sherwood Anderson, Allen Tate, and Gorham Munson, editor of *The Pagan,* where in 1916 Crane had published a poem. In Cleveland again, from 1919 to 1921, while working for his father, Crane made the acquaintance of other artists, who recognized him as one of their own.

Crane returned to New York, where he published his first collection, *White Buildings,* in 1926 and began work on *The Bridge* (he had already completed *Voyages,* his love sequence for Emil Opffer, a sailor with whom he shared an apartment with a view of the Brooklyn Bridge). Grants from the philanthropist Otto Kahn, as well as money from his family and friends, enabled Crane to live without steady work. But already Crane's drinking and his search for homosexual liaisons in dock bars were proving dangerous.

Crane's uncontrollable alcoholism proved so destructive that it led him to his early suicide. Toward the end of his life there was a chaotic period in Mexico, where he attempted to forsake his lifelong homosexuality by beginning an affair with Peggy Cowley (previously married to the critic Malcolm Cowley). In Mexico, Crane was imprisoned for disturbing the peace. In 1932 he set sail for New York but jumped into the Gulf of Mexico, the last impulsive act of an impulsive life.

Although the surface of Crane's poetry is difficult, behind his opaque texture lie careful reasons for his choice of words, as his patient letters to his friends show and as close reading will confirm. He had epic ambitions (fulfilled only partly by his sequence *The Bridge*), and many of his poems attempt epic scope within a lyric compass as they retell a decisive journey or voyage. They do this with a profound commitment to modernity.

The modern poet must, Crane thought, "absorb the machine." In opposing himself to Eliot's more conservative Europeanizing of American poetry, Crane looked resolutely not eastward to Europe but westward to America's frontiers. In *The Bridge,* Crane connects the bridge, the technological symbol of the machine age, to the dance of Pocahontas, to Whitman's mapping of the American continent, to the hoboes riding the freight trains, and to New Yorkers in the subway. Each portion of the sequence has its own form, ranging from first-person monologue to third-person description to second-person colloquy; the sequence employs both rhyme and free verse. In recognizing the Indian dance as the primal American aesthetic and religious form, and, later, in wanting to write an epic called *The Conquistadors,* Crane demonstrated his conviction that the present is constructed upon the past. America, he thought, must retain historical memory, not the memory of Europe so much as the memory of what has occurred on American soil. And unlike Pound and Frost, he turned not only to the New England past but to Spanish sources. *The Bridge* included not only political events (Columbus's voyage) but also aesthetic ones, from *Rip Van Winkle* to the works of Poe.

In 1930, after the publication of *The Bridge* (to mixed reviews), Crane received a Guggenheim fellowship and traveled to Mexico, but it became increasingly difficult for him to write. In the brief peaceful period with Peggy Cowley, he completed his last lyric, "The Broken Tower." In it what Crane called "the logic of metaphor" appears fully coherent, and the poem becomes an example of the sort of verse that would assemble itself into one great organized "single new word, never before spoken." At their best, Crane's assimilative powers produce a poetry that is at once rapidly cumulative and disintegrating, in which atmospheres dissolve as fast as they are created. This instability of essence in Crane affronted conservative critics, among them Yvor Winters, who argued that Crane's suicide was the logical result of his Emersonian and Whitmanesque individualism.

Crane's ambition was halted by his rapidly worsening alcoholism. But he left, besides the uneven *Bridge,* many exquisite smaller pieces (from the tender "Chaplinesque" to the symphonic *Voyages*) by which he will be remembered, and in his essays and letters he bequeathed a strict body of working aesthetic theory. Its chief tenet is the forsaking of a discursive or expository appearance to the poem. The logic of the poem must be impeccable, but it is not the explanatory or instructional logic of versified prose. Instead, the logic of the poem is associational, governed by the succession of feelings acted out by the words of the poem. Crane often uses transferred epithets—for example, "adagios of islands"—to combine two ideas—here, moving slowly (as in a musical adagio) and an ocean voyage through islands. Such writing conveys much information in a small compass, and subsequent poets (especially Robert Lowell in his sonnets and Allen Ginsberg in his telegraphic descriptions) have learned to write in Crane's rapid notation. In turning poetry away from the instructional and toward the associational, Crane taught other poets how to render brilliant impressions, in language duplicating the dazzling multiplicity of human sensations and thoughts.

Further Reading:

B. Weber, *Hart Crane: A Biographical and Critical Study,* 1948, 1970.
V. Quinn, *Hart Crane,* 1963.
R. W. B. Lewis, *The Poetry of Hart Crane,* 1969.

J. E. Unterecker, *Voyager: A Life of Hart Crane,* 1969.
S. Paul, *Hart's Bridge,* 1972.
M. D. Uroff, *Hart Crane: The Patterns of His Poetry,* 1974.

P. Horton, *Hart Crane*, 1976.
R. Sugg, *Hart Crane's* The Bridge, 1976.
H. Nilsen, *Hart Crane's Divided Vision: An Analysis of* The Bridge, 1980.
D. R. Clark, *Critical Essays on Hart Crane*, 1982.
A. Trachtenberg, *Hart Crane: A Collection of Critical Essays*, 1982.

J. Schwartz, *Hart Crane: A Reference Guide*, 1983.
H. Bloom, ed., *Hart Crane: Modern Critical Views*, 1986.
T. Yingling, *Hart Crane and the Homosexual Text*, 1990.
L. Hammer, *Hart Crane and Allen Tate: Janus-Faced Modernism*, 1993.

Text:
The Complete Poems and Selected Letters and Prose of Hart Crane, ed. B. Weber, 1966.

See also *The Letters of Hart Crane, 1916–1932*, ed. B. Weber, 1952, 1965.

Black Tambourine

The interests of a black man in a cellar
Mark tardy judgment on the world's closed door.
Gnats toss in the shadow of a bottle,
And a roach spans a crevice in the floor.

Æsop, driven to pondering, found   5
Heaven with the tortoise and the hare;
Fox brush and sow ear top his grave
And mingling incantations on the air.

The black man, forlorn in the cellar,
Wanders in some mid-kingdom, dark, that lies,   10
Between his tambourine, stuck on the wall,
And, in Africa, a carcass quick with flies.
1926

Chaplinesque*

We make our meek adjustments,
Contented with such random consolations
As the wind deposits
In slithered and too ample pockets.

For we can still love the world, who find   5
A famished kitten on the step, and know
Recesses for it from the fury of the street,
Or warm torn elbow coverts.

* In the manner of Charles Chaplin.

We will sidestep, and to the final smirk
Dally the doom of that inevitable thumb   10
That slowly chafes its puckered index toward us,
Facing the dull squint with what innocence
And what surprise!

And yet these fine collapses are not lies
More than the pirouettes of any pliant cane;   15
Our obsequies are, in a way, no enterprise.
We can evade you, and all else but the heart:
What blame to us if the heart live on.

The game enforces smirks; but we have seen
The moon in lonely alleys make   20
A grail of laughter of an empty ash can,
And through all sound of gaiety and quest
Have heard a kitten in the wilderness.
1926

At Melville's Tomb*

Often beneath the wave, wide from this ledge
The dice of drowned men's bones he saw bequeath
An embassy. Their numbers as he watched,
Beat on the dusty shore and were obscured.

And wrecks passed without sound of bells,   5
The calyx[1] of death's bounty giving back
A scattered chapter, livid hieroglyph,
The portent wound in corridors of shells.

Then in the circuit calm of one vast coil,
Its lashings charmed and malice reconciled,   10
Frosted eyes there were that lifted altars;
And silent answers crept across the stars.

Compass, quadrant and sextant[2] contrive
No farther tides . . . High in the azure steeps
Monody[3] shall not wake the mariner.   15
This fabulous shadow only the sea keeps.
1926

---

* Written in memory of Herman Melville
(1819–1891), author of *Moby Dick* (1851).
The poem imitates the French convention of
the poem at the tomb of the artist-predeces-
sor.

[1] Used metaphorically of the vortex made in
   the ocean by a sinking ship.
[2] Instruments used in navigation.
[3] Ode sung by one voice.

Voyages

I

Above the fresh ruffles of the surf
Bright striped urchins flay each other with sand.
They have contrived a conquest for shell shucks,
And their fingers crumble fragments of baked weed
Gaily digging and scattering.   5

And in answer to their treble interjections
The sun beats lightning on the waves,
The waves fold thunder on the sand;
And could they hear me I would tell them:

O brilliant kids, frisk with your dog,   10
Fondle your shells and sticks, bleached
By time and the elements; but there is a line
You must not cross nor ever trust beyond it
Spry cordage[1] of your bodies to caresses
Too lichen-faithful from too wide a breast.   15
The bottom of the sea is cruel.

II

—And yet this great wink of eternity,
Of rimless floods, unfettered leewardings,
Samite[2] sheeted and processioned where
Her undinal[3] vast belly moonward bends,   20
Laughing the wrapt inflections of our love;

Take this Sea, whose diapason[4] knells
On scrolls of silver snowy sentences,
The sceptred terror of whose sessions rends
As her demeanors motion well or ill,   25
All but the pieties of lovers' hands.

And onward, as bells off San Salvador
Salute the crocus lustres of the stars,
In these poinsettia meadows of her tides,—
Adagios[5] of islands, O my Prodigal,   30
Complete the dark confessions her veins spell.

---

[1] Ropes in the rigging of a ship.
[2] Medieval silk fabric, threaded with gold or silver. (Cf. Tennyson's *Morte d'Arthur*, where the hand from the water claiming Arthur's sword is "clothed in white samite.")

[3] Referring to waves (from Latin *unda*: "wave").
[4] Entire compass of musical tones.
[5] Slow movements, as in music.

Mark how her turning shoulders wind the hours,
And hasten while her penniless rich palms
Pass superscription of bent foam and wave,—
Hasten, while they are true,—sleep, death, desire,   35
Close round one instant in one floating flower.

Bind us in time, O Seasons clear, and awe.
O minstrel galleons of Carib fire,
Bequeath us to no earthly shore until
Is answered in the vortex of our grave   40
The seal's wide spindrift[6] gaze toward paradise.

III

Infinite consanguinity[7] it bears—
This tendered theme of you that light
Retrieves from sea plains where the sky
Resigns a breast that every wave enthrones;   45
While ribboned water lanes I wind
Are laved and scattered with no stroke
Wide from your side, whereto this hour
The sea lifts, also, reliquary hands.

And so, admitted through black swollen gates   50
That must arrest all distance otherwise,—
Past whirling pillars and lithe pediments,
Light wrestling there incessantly with light,
Star kissing star through wave on wave unto
Your body rocking!
                            and where death, if shed,   55
Presumes no carnage, but this single change,—
Upon the steep floor flung from dawn to dawn
The silken skilled transmemberment[8] of song;

Permit me voyage, love, into your hands . . .
1926

---

from The Bridge

To Brooklyn Bridge

How many dawns, chill from his rippling rest
The seagull's wings shall dip and pivot him,

---

[6] Sea spray.
[7] Blood relation.

[8] Word invented by Crane, made up of *trans-mutation* and *dismemberment*.

Shedding white rings of tumult, building high
Over the chained bay waters Liberty—

Then, with inviolate curve, forsake our eyes   5
As apparitional as sails that cross
Some page of figures to be filed away;
—Till elevators drop us from our day . . .

I think of cinemas, panoramic sleights
With multitudes bent toward some flashing scene   10
Never disclosed, but hastened to again,
Foretold to other eyes on the same screen;

And Thee, across the harbor, silver-paced
As though the sun took step of thee, yet left
Some motion ever unspent in thy stride,—   15
Implicitly thy freedom staying thee!

Out of some subway scuttle, cell or loft
A bedlamite¹ speeds to thy parapets,
Tilting there momently, shrill shirt ballooning,
A jest falls from the speechless caravan.   20

Down Wall,² from girder into street noon leaks,
A rip-tooth of the sky's acetylene;
All afternoon the cloud-flown derricks turn . . .
Thy cables breathe the North Atlantic still.

And obscure as that heaven of the Jews,   25
Thy guerdon³ . . . Accolade⁴ thou dost bestow
Of anonymity time cannot raise:
Vibrant reprieve and pardon thou dost show.

O harp and altar, of the fury fused,
(How could mere toil align thy choiring strings!)   30
Terrific threshold of the prophet's pledge,
Prayer of pariah,⁵ and the lover's cry,—

---

¹ Madman.   ⁴ Award of special merit.
² Wall Street in New York City.   ⁵ Outcast.
³ Reward.

Again the traffic lights that skim thy swift
Unfractioned idiom, immaculate sigh of stars,
Beading thy path—condense eternity: 35
And we have seen night lifted in thine arms.

Under thy shadow by the piers I waited;
Only in darkness is thy shadow clear.
The City's fiery parcels all undone,
Already snow submerges an iron year . . .   40

O Sleepless as the river under thee,
Vaulting the sea, the prairies' dreaming sod,
Unto us lowliest sometime sweep, descend
And of the curveship lend a myth to God.
1930

I Am Concerned with the Future of America

I am concerned with the Future of America, but not because I think that America has
any so-called par value as a state or as a group of people. . . . It is only because I feel
persuaded that here are destined to be discovered certain as yet undefined spiritual
quantities, perhaps a new hierarchy of faith not to be developed so completely elsewhere. And in this process I like to feel myself as a potential factor; certainly I must
speak in its terms and what discoveries I may make are situated in its experience.

Hart Crane, from "General Aims and Theories" (1937)

Ernest Hemingway
1899–1961

No other major American writer has ever equaled the popular success and worldwide
reputation of Ernest Hemingway. During his lifetime he attained the status of an
international celebrity; his activities were reported by gossip columnists along with the
disport of the movie stars and the athletes he became friends with. His prose style
became one of the most recognizable literary "trademarks" of all time and is still
widely imitated and parodied.

Hemingway was born on July 21, 1899, in Oak Park, Illinois, a suburb just west of
Chicago. His father was a prosperous physician; his mother, a devoted member of the
Congregational church who, having tried to pursue a career as an opera singer, taught
music. In high school Hemingway participated in several organized sports, including
football and boxing. He played the cello in the school orchestra (his mother hoped he

would become a cellist) and wrote for the school's newspaper and literary magazine. But the most intense of his early experiences, if we may judge by the memories he carried with him, centered on the hunting and fishing he did with his father near the family cottage on the upper peninsula of northern Michigan. There, under his father's tutelage, he learned things he never forgot—the ritual of the hunt and the code of the hunter, lessons that stressed the primacy of elemental physical confrontations and the importance of physical prowess, physical endurance, and physical courage. His father, who committed suicide in 1928, gave Hemingway his first fishing rod at age two and his first gun at age ten: "I am so pleased and proud you have grown to be such a fine big manly fellow," he wrote his son in 1915.

In 1917, having finished high school, Hemingway decided to forgo college. Setting out on his own, he found work as a cub reporter on the Kansas City *Star,* where he began cultivating the restrained yet vigorous prose style that later, when he shaped it into literature under the influence of Sherwood Anderson, Ezra Pound, and Gertrude Stein, would make him famous. Though he enjoyed newspaper work, he soon left it for Europe, drawn by the first of several wars in which he would serve. Rejected by the army because of an eye defect, he volunteered for the Red Cross ambulance corps. In 1918, after a brief stay in France, he entered active duty in Italy, where he was severely wounded by the explosion of a mortar shell. Throughout his life he wore a platinum kneecap and bore numerous shrapnel scars. Yet the experience proved exhilarating as well as traumatic. "Wounds don't matter," he wrote his family jauntily in a letter from a Milan hospital that was published in the Oak Park newspaper; "I wouldn't mind being wounded again so much because I know just what it is like . . . and it does give you an awfully satisfactory feeling to be wounded." Wounds—physical and psychic— would play a significant role not only in Hemingway's writing but also in his life. Remarkably accident-prone, he was repeatedly injured—in car crashes, plane crashes, shooting mishaps, freak accidents, and fires. Nearly everywhere he went—Italy, Spain, France, England, Africa, Montana, Idaho, the Florida Keys, Cuba—something happened, making his scarred body a personal geography of wounds.

After the war Hemingway returned home, decorated by the Italians for conspicuous valor. For the next two years he tried to resume the life he had left behind. He hunted and fished with friends in northern Michigan and began writing for the Toronto *Star.* But he could not adjust to the United States and Canada and itched to return to Europe. He would always be attacked by critics for not concentrating on the "American scene" ("Difference with us guys," he wrote Faulkner, "is I always lived out of country"), and most of his writing is set in other countries. In 1921 he married the first of his four wives and left the United States to join the growing band of self-exiled artists and writers who were gathering in Paris.

Paris attracted Americans such as Hemingway not only because it was the exciting center of a modernist revolution in art and literature but also because of its more liberal moral climate, the availability of liquor (Prohibition had gone into effect in the United States in 1919), and the highly favorable exchange rate. Back in the spring of 1921 Hemingway had met Sherwood Anderson, and it was through Anderson's courteous letters of introduction that the younger midwestern writer met Gertrude Stein and Ezra Pound. Later, Hemingway would get to know John Dos Passos, James Joyce (whose *Ulysses* he considered a "most goddamn wonderful book"), and F. Scott

Fitzgerald. Though all of these writers in one way or another helped Hemingway launch his literary career, he ended up quarreling—at times nastily—with nearly everyone who had helped him.

"That's what you are, that's what you all are," Gertrude Stein said to Hemingway, speaking of those who had survived the war. "You are a lost generation." And it was in part a sense of loss, disillusionment, and disenchantment that Hemingway shared with the other expatriates in Paris. The Great War, like the grand words used to justify it, seemed to him a terrible betrayal. He was beginning to discover in violence and the consequences of violence one of his major themes and in war and its aftermath one of his favorite settings. The violence of the modern world, ritualized in hunting, fishing, and bullfighting (in which he saw a combination of "valor and art"), began to preoccupy his imagination. At the same time, he continued to write articles as the European correspondent of the Toronto *Star:* He interviewed Mussolini, covered the Greco-Turkish War, and wrote about crime. In 1923 he published his first book, *Three Stories and Ten Poems,* and returned to Toronto, where he resumed newspaper work and where his first child was born.

A year later Hemingway was back in Paris, trying to support a family on his meager income from journalism and publishing short stories in small literary journals. One of his early stories, "My Old Man," was selected for an anthology of the best stories of 1923, though the editor of the volume consistently misspelled Hemingway's name. Gradually, however, Hemingway was building a reputation as a meticulous craftsman. His stories, he warned a publisher, "are written so tight and so hard that the alteration of a word can throw an entire story out of key." In 1925 he published *In Our Time,* a story sequence that included several stories set in the Michigan of his boyhood. A year earlier he had published a slightly different collection in Paris under the lowercase title *in our time.* The main sequence of stories, which concludes with "Big Two-Hearted River, Parts I and II," is introduced and interspersed with a series of brief and elliptically related interchapters that begins with the violence of the Turkish War and concludes with the violence of bullfighting and political execution.

Although, as its title indicates, Hemingway clearly intended *In Our Time* to have the immediacy and impact of journalism, its style is far from the representational realism of modern reporting. In a 1958 interview, Hemingway expressed his literary concern in a way that shows how his art both depends on and radically departs from conventional "realism": "From things that have happened and from things as they exist and from all the things that you know and all those that you cannot know, you make something through your invention that is not a representation but a whole new thing truer than any thing true and alive." The two parts of "Big Two-Hearted River" are firmly grounded in Hemingway's firsthand knowledge of fishing the Fox River north of Seney, Michigan, yet, as he said to Gertrude Stein, in writing the story he was "trying to do the country like Cézanne," a reference to Cézanne's now famous landscape paintings of the Provence countryside, which became the creative force behind cubism.

By 1926 Hemingway had grown increasingly annoyed at critical references to his artistic indebtedness to Sherwood Anderson. As a response, he published an insensitive and even vicious parody of Anderson called *The Torrents of Spring,* a book that is widely regarded as one of his weakest efforts. Yet in the same year he published *The Sun Also Rises,* which brought him international fame and is still widely regarded as the best of his novels. *The Sun Also Rises* centers on a group of heavy-drinking, tough-talking, and hard-living expatriates and is narrated by an American reporter in Paris. For many readers, *The Sun Also Rises* perfectly captured the postwar mood of the "lost generation;" to emphasize the point, Hemingway used Gertrude Stein's phrase as an epigraph to the book. A second collection of stories, *Men Without Women*, followed in 1927, and two years later his second serious novel, *A Farewell to Arms*, the story of an American ambulance officer in Italy who is seriously wounded and falls in love with a British nurse. After discovering that she is pregnant, he deserts the service and escapes with her to Switzerland, where for a few idyllic months in the mountains they find a "separate peace" that is disastrously shattered when both mother and infant die in childbirth.

In 1930, at the suggestion of John Dos Passos, Hemingway bought a house in Key West, Florida. By this time he was married for a second time, was sporting a full beard, weighed a burly 208 pounds, and was already referring to himself as "Papa." It was a persona he would use for the rest of his life. In Key West, Hemingway developed a lifelong passion for sailing and deep-sea fishing. "A sportsman," James Joyce had called him, "and ready to live the life he writes about. He would never have written it if his body had not allowed him to live it." In his writing and behavior, Hemingway consistently promoted a conventionally "masculine" way of life; for a biographical sketch, he once listed his hobbies as "skiing, fishing, shooting, and drinking." Yet even during his life, his insistently male performances, though good for publicity, were the subject of critical ridicule. Edmund Wilson had been among the first to praise Hemingway's early stories. In the Key West Hemingway, however, "the Hemingway of the handsome photographs with the sportsman's tan and the outdoor grin, with the ominous resemblance to Clark Gable, who poses with giant marlin which he has just hauled in," Wilson saw an "arrogant, belligerent and boastful" man who was "certainly the worst-invented character to be found in the author's work."

For all his public posturing, however, Hemingway continued to write. In 1932 he published a now classic book about bullfighting, *Death in the Afternoon*, which contains much of what can be called the author's "philosophy of life"—his fascination with danger and death and his unswerving commitment to honor, valor, and a quality of style he called "grace under pressure." Another excellent collection of short stories, *Winner Take Nothing*, appeared in 1933, and in 1935 Hemingway used the experiences gathered on African safaris to write *The Green Hills of Africa*, a book that blends literary commentary and travel description with a metaphysics of big-game hunting. Out of his African experience also came two of his finest stories, "The Snows of Kilimanjaro" and "The Short Happy Life of Francis Macomber."

Throughout the 1930s Hemingway was criticized by leftist critics for ignoring progressive causes and retreating into a hedonistic sporting life. Hemingway was always suspicious of politically motivated fiction: "There is no left and right in writing," he claimed; "there is only good and bad writing." Yet in his next book, *To Have and Have Not* (1937), his only novel that uses an American setting, Hemingway created the hard-bitten, pragmatic hero Harry Morgan, a Florida fishing boat captain who fights a separate war against the Depression by smuggling rum from Cuba to Key West. Morgan's often-quoted dying words—"One man alone ain't got no bloody f——ing chance"—appealed to "socially aware" readers who were perhaps too eager to see in the book a statement of Hemingway's social conscience. In 1936 Hemingway went to Spain with Dos Passos to work on an anti-Fascist documentary film, *The Spanish Earth*. His journalistic coverage of the civil war in Spain provided him with the material for a play called *The Fifth Column* (1938) and a novel called *For Whom the Bell Tolls* (1940), an enormously popular story about an American academic, Robert Jordan, who teams up with a small group of peasant guerrillas and heroically sacrifices his life in what proves to be a losing cause.

In 1940, married for the third time, Hemingway moved to an estate in Cuba, where he fished for marlin, drank excessively, raised fighting cocks, and played lavish host to actors and actresses, matadors, fighters, politicos, and an assortment of international celebrities. When the United States entered the Second World War, Hemingway volunteered his prized fishing vessel for antisubmarine duty. In 1944, as a war correspondent, he participated in the Normandy invasion and eventually took such an "active" role with the U.S. Army's 4th Infantry Division in France and Germany that he was awarded the Bronze Star. After the war, he married again and spent time in Venice, the city that served as the setting for one of his most poorly received novels, the idyllic romance, *Across the River and into the Trees* (1950). He returned to Cuba and started working on a long "sea novel" that he had much difficulty with and that eventually was published posthumously as *Islands in the Stream* (1970). In 1952, however, Hemingway selected one long self-contained section of that novel and published it as *The Old Man and the Sea*—a parable-like tale of an old Cuban fisherman who catches a giant marlin but is unable to keep the sharks from mutilating it before he can get it safely to shore. This novella became Hemingway's biggest-selling book, won him the Pulitzer Prize, and led directly to his being awarded the Nobel Prize in 1954.

During the final years of his life, Hemingway made several trips to Spain and engaged in another African safari, during which he barely survived back-to-back plane crashes. But his health was giving out. As political tension mounted in Cuba, he left his estate and moved to Ketchum, Idaho, where he underwent both medical and psychiatric treatment. In 1960 he used some notes and reportage that had survived from the 1920s as the basis for a collection of reminiscences, *A Moveable Feast*, which appeared posthumously in 1964. In 1961 he found himself unable to write one sentence for a volume to be presented to President John F. Kennedy: "It just won't come any more," he said. "How simple the writing of literature would be," he had written in his Nobel Prize acceptance speech, "if it were only necessary to write in another way what has been well written."

A sense of loss and the threat of violence had informed almost everything Hemingway wrote. In a deceptively simple, spare, disciplined prose (he said of *In Our Time*, "There is no writing in it that anybody with a high-school education cannot read"), he labored to find ways of restoring the force of words that had lost their edge. His heroes bear scars that are psychological as well as physical, and they carry with them memories of violence as well as premonitions of death. Facing a disordered, hypocritical world, they seek to discover some code by which to live, some style for comporting themselves in reality. Their cause, that of finding some way gracefully to endure the pain and accept the futility of life without cant or illusion, is based on the assumption that learning how to live life can sometimes help us to understand it. On July 2, 1961, in Ketchum, Idaho, Hemingway chose, as his father had before him, to end his own life violently. He pressed a double-barreled shotgun to his forehead and pulled both triggers.

Further Reading:

J. K. M. McCaffrey, ed., *Ernest Hemingway: The Man and His Work,* 1950.

P. Young, *Ernest Hemingway,* rev. ed., 1966.

C. Baker, *Ernest Hemingway: A Life Story,* 1969.

A. Burgess, *Ernest Hemingway and His World,* 1978.

K. Lynn, *Hemingway,* 1987.

Text:

"Soldier's Home" from *In Our Time,* 1925.

Soldier's Home

Krebs went to the war from a Methodist college in Kansas. There is a picture which shows him among his fraternity brothers, all of them wearing exactly the same height and style collar. He enlisted in the Marines in 1917 and did not return to the United States until the second division returned from the Rhine in the summer of 1919.

There is a picture which shows him on the Rhine with two German girls and another corporal. Krebs and the corporal look too big for their uniforms. The German girls are not beautiful. The Rhine does not show in the picture.

By the time Krebs returned to his home town in Oklahoma the greeting of heroes was over. He came back much too late. The men from the town who had been drafted had all been welcomed elaborately on their return. There had been a great deal of hysteria. Now the reaction had set in. People seemed to think it was rather ridiculous for Krebs to be getting back so late, years after the war was over.

At first Krebs, who had been at Belleau Wood, Soissons, the Champagne, St. Mihiel, and in the Argonne did not want to talk about the war at all. Later he felt the need to talk but no one wanted to hear about it. His town had heard too many atrocity stories to be thrilled by actualities. Krebs found that to be listened to at all he had to lie, and after he had done this twice he, too, had a reaction against the war and against talking about it. A distaste for everything that had happened to him in the war set in because of the lies he had told. All of the times that had been able to make him feel cool and clear inside himself when he thought of them; the times so long back when he had done the one thing, the only thing for a man to do, easily and naturally, when he might have done something else, now lost their cool, valuable quality and then were lost themselves.

His lies were quite unimportant lies and consisted in attributing to himself things other men had seen, done, or heard of, and stating as facts certain apocryphal incidents familiar to all soldiers. Even his lies were not sensational at the pool room. His acquaintances, who had heard detailed accounts of German women found chained to machine guns in the Argonne forest and who could not comprehend, or were barred by their patriotism from interest in, any German machine gunners who were not chained, were not thrilled by his stories.

Krebs acquired the nausea in regard to experience that is the result of untruth or exaggeration, and when he occasionally met another man who had really been a soldier and they talked a few minutes in the dressing room at a dance he fell into the easy pose of the old soldier among other soldiers: that he had been badly, sickeningly frightened all the time. In this way he lost everything.

During this time, it was late summer, he was sleeping late in bed, getting up to walk down town to the library to get a book, eating lunch at home, reading on the front porch until he became bored, and then walking down through the town to spend the hottest hours of the day in the cool dark of the pool room. He loved to play pool.

In the evening he practiced on his clarinet, strolled down town, read, and went to bed. He was still a hero to his two young sisters. His mother would have given him breakfast in bed if he had wanted it. She often came in when he was in bed and asked him to tell her about the war, but her attention always wandered. His father was noncommittal.

Before Krebs went away to the war he had never been allowed to drive the family motor car. His father was in the real estate business and always wanted the car to be at his command when he required it to take clients out into the country to show them a piece of farm property. The car always stood outside the First National Bank building where his father had an office on the second floor. Now, after the war, it was still the same car.

Nothing was changed in the town except that the young girls had grown up. But they lived in such a complicated world of already defined alliances and shifting feuds that Krebs did not feel the energy or the courage to break into it. He liked to look at them, though. There were so many good-looking young girls. Most of them had their hair cut short. When he went away only little girls wore their hair like that or girls that were fast. They all wore sweaters and shirt waists with round Dutch collars. It was a pattern. He liked to look at them from the front porch as they walked on the other side of the street. He liked to watch them walking under the shade of the trees. He liked the round Dutch collars above their sweaters. He liked their silk stockings and flat shoes. He liked their bobbed hair and the way they walked.

When he was in town their appeal to him was not very strong. He did not like them when he saw them in the Greek's ice cream parlor. He did not want them themselves really. They were too complicated. There was something else. Vaguely he wanted a girl but he did not want to have to work to get her. He would have liked to have a girl but he did not want to have to spend a long time getting her. He did not want to get into the intrigue and the politics. He did not want to have to do any courting. He did not want to tell any more lies. It wasn't worth it.

He did not want any consequences. He did not want any consequences ever again. He wanted to live along without consequences. Besides he did not really need a girl. The army had taught him that. It was all right to pose as though you had to have a girl. Nearly everybody did that. But it wasn't true. You did not need a girl. That was the funny thing. First a fellow boasted how girls mean nothing to him, that he never thought of them, that they could not touch him. Then a fellow boasted that he could not get along without girls, that he had to have them all the time, that he could not go to sleep without them.

That was all a lie. It was all a lie both ways. You did not need a girl unless you thought about them. He learned that in the army. Then sooner or later you always got one. When you were really ripe for a girl you always got one. You did not have to think about it. Sooner or later it would come. He had learned that in the army.

Now he would have liked a girl if she had come to him and not wanted to talk. But here at home it was all too complicated. He knew he could never get through it all again. It was not worth the trouble. That was the thing about French girls and German girls. There was not all this talking. You couldn't talk much and you did not need to talk. It was simple and you were friends. He thought about France and then he began to think about Germany. On the whole he had liked Germany better. He did not want to leave Germany. He did not want to come home. Still, he had come home. He sat on the front porch.

He liked the girls that were walking along the other side of the street. He liked the look of them much better than the French girls or the German girls. But the world they were in was not the world he was in. He would like to have one of them. But it was not worth it. They were such a nice pattern. He liked the pattern. It was exciting. But he would not go through all the talking. He did not want one badly enough. He liked to look at them all, though. It was not worth it. Not now when things were getting good again.

He sat there on the porch reading a book on the war. It was a history and he was reading about all the engagements he had been in. It was the most interesting reading he had ever done. He wished there were more maps. He looked forward with a good feeling to reading all the really good histories when they would come out with good detail maps. Now he was really learning about the war. He had been a good soldier. That made a difference.

One morning after he had been home about a month his mother came into his bedroom and sat on the bed. She smoothed her apron.

"I had a talk with your father last night, Harold," she said, "and he is willing for you to take the car out in the evenings."

"Yeah?" said Krebs, who was not fully awake. "Take the car out? Yeah?"

"Yes. Your father has felt for some time that you should be able to take the car out in the evenings whenever you wished but we only talked it over last night."

"I'll bet you made him," Krebs said.

"No. It was your father's suggestion that we talk the matter over."

"Yeah. I'll bet you made him," Krebs sat up in bed.

"Will you come down to breakfast, Harold?" his mother said.

"As soon as I get my clothes on," Krebs said.

His mother went out of the room and he could hear her frying something downstairs while he washed, shaved, and dressed to go down into the dining-room for breakfast. While he was eating breakfast his sister brought in the mail.

"Well, Hare," she said. "You old sleepyhead. What do you ever get up for?"

Krebs looked at her. He liked her. She was his best sister.

"Have you got the paper?" he asked.

She handed him the Kansas City *Star* and he shucked off its brown wrapper and opened it to the sporting page. He folded the *Star* open and propped it against the water pitcher with his cereal dish to steady it, so he could read while he ate.

"Harold," his mother stood in the kitchen doorway, "Harold, please don't muss up the paper. Your father can't read his *Star* if it's been mussed."

"I won't muss it," Krebs said.

His sister sat down at the table and watched him while he read.

"We're playing indoor over at school this afternoon," she said. "I'm going to pitch."

"Good," said Krebs. "How's the old wing?"

"I can pitch better than lots of the boys. I tell them all you taught me. The other girls aren't much good."

"Yeah?" said Krebs.

"I tell them all you're my beau. Aren't you my beau, Hare?"

"You bet."

"Couldn't your brother really be your beau just because he's your brother?"

"I don't know."

"Sure you know. Couldn't you be my beau, Hare, if I was old enough and if you wanted to?"

"Sure. You're my girl now."

"Am I really your girl?"

"Sure."

"Do you love me?"

"Uh, huh."

"Will you love me always?"

"Sure."

"Will you come over and watch me play indoor?"

"Maybe."

"Aw, Hare, you don't love me. If you loved me, you'd want to come over and watch me play indoor."

Krebs's mother came into the dining-room from the kitchen. She carried a plate with two fried eggs and some crisp bacon on it and a plate of buckwheat cakes.

"You run along, Helen," she said. "I want to talk to Harold."

She put the eggs and bacon down in front of him and brought in a jug of maple syrup for the buckwheat cakes. Then she sat down across the table from Krebs.

"I wish you'd put down the paper a minute, Harold," she said.

Krebs took down the paper and folded it.

"Have you decided what you are going to do yet, Harold?" his mother said, taking off her glasses.

"No," said Krebs.

"Don't you think it's about time?" His mother did not say this in a mean way. She seemed worried.

"I hadn't thought about it," Krebs said.

"God has some work for everyone to do," his mother said. "There can be no idle hands in His Kingdom."

"I'm not in His Kingdom," Krebs said.

"We are all of us in His Kingdom."

Krebs felt embarrassed and resentful as always.

"I've worried about you so much, Harold," his mother went on. "I know the temptations you must have been exposed to. I know how weak men are. I know what your own dear grandfather, my own father, told us about the Civil War and I have prayed for you. I pray for you all day long, Harold."

Krebs looked at the bacon fat hardening on his plate.

"Your father is worried, too," his mother went on. "He thinks you have lost your ambition, that you haven't got a definite aim in life. Charley Simmons, who is just your age, has a good job and is going to be married. The boys are all settling down; they're all determined to get somewhere; you can see that boys like Charley Simmons are on their way to being really a credit to the community."

Krebs said nothing.

"Don't look that way, Harold," his mother said. "You know we love you and I want to tell you for your own good how matters stand. Your father does not want to hamper your freedom. He thinks you should be allowed to drive the car. If you want to take some of the nice girls out riding with you, we are only too pleased. We want you to enjoy yourself. But you are going to have to settle down to work, Harold. Your father doesn't care what you start in at. All work is honorable as he says. But you've got to make a start at something. He asked me to speak to you this morning and then you can stop in and see him at his office."

"Is that all?" Krebs said.

"Yes. Don't you love your mother, dear boy?"

"No," Krebs said.

His mother looked at him across the table. Her eyes were shiny. She started crying.

"I don't love anybody," Krebs said.

It wasn't any good. He couldn't tell her, he couldn't make her see it. It was silly to have said it. He had only hurt her. He went over and took hold of her arm. She was crying with her head in her hands.

"I didn't mean it," he said. "I was just angry at something. I didn't mean I didn't love you."

His mother went on crying. Krebs put his arm on her shoulder.

"Can't you believe me, mother?"

His mother shook her head.

"Please, please, mother. Please believe me."

"All right," his mother said chokily. She looked up at him. "I believe you, Harold."

Krebs kissed her hair. She put her face up to him.

"I'm your mother," she said. "I held you next to my heart when you were a tiny baby."

Krebs felt sick and vaguely nauseated.

"I know, Mummy," he said. "I'll try and be a good boy for you."

"Would you kneel and pray with me, Harold?" his mother asked.

They knelt down beside the dining-room table and Krebs's mother prayed.

"Now, you pray, Harold," she said.

"I can't," Krebs said.

"Try, Harold."

"I can't."

"Do you want me to pray for you?"

"Yes."

So his mother prayed for him and then they stood up and Krebs kissed his mother and went out of the house. He had tried so to keep his life from being complicated. Still, none of it had touched him. He had felt sorry for his mother and she had made him lie. He would go to Kansas City and get a job and she would feel all right about it. There would be one more scene maybe before he got away. He would not go down to his father's office. He would miss that one. He wanted his life to go smoothly. It had just gotten going that way. Well, that was all over now, anyway. He would go over to the schoolyard and watch Helen play indoor baseball.

1925

Langston Hughes
1902–1967

Langston Hughes's short stories won him an enormous audience among the African American population. The stories, like the poems, showed the average struggle of ordinary African Americans in their everyday lives. The edge of bitter humor animating Hughes's work does not take away from its essential comedy; his satire of both white and African American, while establishing with perfect clarity the extent of social injustice in America, creates a cast of characters who are resourceful and hapless, courageous and foolish, altruistic and self-serving.

Hughes's realistic descriptions in verse and prose of the life of poor African Americans earned him hatred and condemnation from black intellectuals who wished African American writing to be improving, to show African American life only at its best. When his second book of poetry, *Fine Clothes to the Jew* (1929), appeared, the headline in the widely circulated African American newspaper *The Amsterdam News* was "Langston Hughes—The Sewer Dweller."

Hughes's father, who had left his wife shortly after his son's birth, disavowed all connection with African Americans and went to live in Mexico, where Hughes lived with him in his adolescent years. Hughes grew to hate his father and, reversing his father's attitude, decided to immerse himself in the life of African Americans, to write about the entire community:

> Workers, roustabouts, and singers, and job hunters on Lenox Avenue in New York, or Seventh Street in Washington or South State in Chicago—people up today and down tomorrow, working this week and fired the next, beaten and baffled, but determined not to be wholly beaten, buying furniture on the installment plan, filling the house with roomers to help pay the rent, hoping to get a new suit for Easter—and pawning that suit before the Fourth of July.

James Langston Hughes dropped his first name, which he shared with his father, and adopted his middle name, his mother's maiden name, for his writing career.

After an unsuccessful year at Columbia University, Hughes dropped out of school, but he later received the A.B. from Lincoln University in Pennsylvania, an all-black college. In his long writing life he was able to support himself by his writing and his public readings. Besides poems and short stories, he wrote novels, children's books, plays, nonfiction, opera libretti, and lyrics for musicals, notably for Kurt Weill's *Street Scene* (1948). He was in the center of the group making up the Harlem Renaissance in the 1920s. At that time, Negro intellectuals took on as a self-conscious task the construction of an aesthetic and intellectual culture for African Americans. Hughes was drawn into the group by Dr. Alain Locke, who had included some of Hughes's poems in his 1925 anthology *The New Negro*. Hughes was also sponsored by the poet Vachel Lindsay and the novelist Carl Van Vechten. Eventually Hughes set out on his own, reading widely to southern audiences, traveling to Russia, reporting the Spanish Civil War for the *Baltimore Afro-American,* and translating García Lorca and Gabriela

Mistral. He was a force for the establishing of African American theaters; he anthologized his fellow African American writers.

The fullness of Hughes's literary achievement will only be seen when his collected works have been compiled; he left his mark on every phase of literary activity in America. His writing created a new audience for poetry—the African American community, who, in spite of the criticism of African American intellectuals and moralists, saw in Hughes's direct, frank, open verse a reflection of their music and their language, their social debasement and their persistent hope and despair. In drawing on the poems of Carl Sandburg to make his own verse, Hughes continued a populist tradition in American poetry, one that depends as much on the spoken word as on the written page. In his "documentary, journalistic, and topical" poems (as he described them), Hughes reached the hearts of his listeners and validated a poetry with a strong oral base. The "Beat" poets—especially Allen Ginsberg in his blues chants—continued Hughes's emphasis on the spoken or sung poem, and subsequent African American poets have emphasized the colloquial vigor of African American speech as Hughes himself did, transforming it into poetry.

Further Reading:

D. C. Dickinson, *A Bio-Bibliography of Langston Hughes, 1902–1967*, 1967.

J. Emanuel, *Langston Hughes*, 1967.

C. H. Rollins, *Black Troubadour*, 1970.

T. B. O'Daniel, ed., *Langston Hughes, Black Genius*, 1971.

O. Jemie, *Langston Hughes: An Introduction to the Poetry*, 1976.

R. K. Barksdale, *Langston Hughes: The Poet and His Critics*, 1977.

E. P. Myers, *Langston Hughes*, 1981.

F. Berry, *Langston Hughes: Before and After Harlem*, 1983.

A. Rampersad, *The Life of Langston Hughes*, 2v., 1986–1988.

Texts:

Selected Poems, 1959.

See also *I Wonder as I Wander: An Autobiographical Journey*, 1956.

The Langston Hughes Reader, 1958.

The Negro Speaks of Rivers

I've known rivers:
I've known rivers ancient as the world and older than the flow of human blood in
    human veins.

My soul has grown deep like the rivers.

I bathed in the Euphrates when dawns were young.
I built my hut near the Congo and it lulled me to sleep.
I looked upon the Nile and raised the pyramids above it.   5
I heard the singing of the Mississippi when Abe Lincoln went down to New
    Orleans, and I've seen its muddy bosom turn all golden in the sunset.

I've known rivers:
Ancient, dusky rivers.

My soul has grown deep like the rivers.   10
1926

The Weary Blues

Droning a drowsy syncopated tune,
Rocking back and forth to a mellow croon,
    I heard a Negro play.
Down on Lenox Avenue the other night
By the pale dull pallor of an old gas light   5
    He did a lazy sway. . . .
    He did a lazy sway. . . .
To the tune o' those Weary Blues.
With his ebony hands on each ivory key
He made that poor piano moan with melody.   10
    O Blues!
Swaying to and fro on his rickety stool
He played that sad raggy tune like a musical fool.
    Sweet Blues!
Coming from a black man's soul.   15
    O Blues!
In a deep song voice with a melancholy tone
I heard that Negro sing, that old piano moan—
    "Ain't got nobody in all this world,
    Ain't got nobody but ma self.   20
    I's gwine to quit ma frownin'
    And put ma troubles on the shelf."
Thump, thump, thump, went his foot on the floor.
He played a few chords then he sang some more—
    "I got the Weary Blues   25
    And I can't be satisfied.
    Got the Weary Blues
    And can't be satisfied—
    I ain't happy no mo'
    And I wish that I had died."   30
And far into the night he crooned that tune.

The stars went out and so did the moon.
The singer stopped playing and went to bed

While the Weary Blues echoed through his head.
He slept like a rock or a man that's dead.   35
1926

I, Too

I, too, sing America.

I am the darker brother.
They send me to eat in the kitchen
When company comes,
But I laugh,   5
And eat well,
And grow strong.
Tomorrow,
I'll be at the table
When company comes.   10
Nobody'll dare
Say to me,
"Eat in the kitchen,"
Then.

Besides,   15
They'll see how beautiful I am
And be ashamed—

I, too, am America.
1932

Dream Boogie

Good morning, daddy!
Ain't you heard
The boogie-woogie rumble
Of a dream deferred?

Listen closely: 5
You'll hear their feet
Beating out and beating out a——

You think
It's a happy beat?

Listen to it closely: 10
Ain't you heard
something underneath
like a——

What did I say?

Sure,   15
I'm happy!
Take it away!

Hey, pop!
Re-bop!
Mop!   20
Y-e-a-h!
What don't bug
them white kids
sure bugs me:
We knows everybody   25
ain't free!

Some of these young ones is cert'ly bad——
One batted a hard ball right through my window
and my gold fish et the glass.

What's written down   30
for white folks
ain't for us a-tall:
"Liberty And Justice——
Huh—For All."

Oop-pop-a-da!   35
Skee! Daddle-de-do!
Be-bop!

Salt'peanuts!

De-dop!
1951

Theme for English B

The instructor said,

> *Go home and write*
> *a page tonight.*
> *And let that page come out of you——*
> *Then, it will be true.*   5

I wonder if it's that simple?

I am twenty-two, colored, born in Winston-Salem.
I went to school there, then Durham, then here
to this college on the hill above Harlem.

I am the only colored student in my class.   10
The steps from the hill lead down into Harlem,
through a park, then I cross St. Nicholas,
Eighth Avenue, Seventh, and I come to the Y,
the Harlem Branch Y, where I take the elevator
up to my room, sit down, and write this page: 15

It's not easy to know what is true for you or me
at twenty-two, my age. But I guess I'm what
I feel and see and hear. Harlem, I hear you:
hear you, hear me—we two—you, me, talk on this page.
(I hear New York, too.) Me—who?   20

Well, I like to eat, sleep, drink, and be in love.
I like to work, read, learn, and understand life.
I like a pipe for a Christmas present,
or records—Bessie,[1] bop, or Bach.
I guess being colored doesn't make me *not* like   25
the same things other folks like who are other races.

So will my page be colored that I write?
Being me, it will not be white.
But it will be
a part of you, instructor.   30

You are white——
yet a part of me, as I am a part of you.

---

[1] Bessie Smith (1898?–1937), black blues
singer.

That's American.
Sometimes perhaps you don't want to be a part of me.
Nor do I often want to be a part of you.   35
But we are, that's true!
As I learn from you,
I guess you learn from me——
although you're older—and white——
and somewhat more free.   40

This is my page for English B.
1951

Richard Wright
1908–1960

Richard Wright was born into an impoverished African American sharecropper family on a cotton plantation near Natchez, Mississippi, on September 4, 1908. His father deserted the family when Wright was five years old, and when he was ten his mother suffered the first of a series of strokes that left her partially paralyzed. As a child Wright was shuttled about among various relatives and spent some time in an orphanage. A good student, he graduated from Smith-Robinson High School in Jackson, Mississippi, in 1925 and moved to Memphis, where he took menial jobs and began writing. Two years later he moved to Chicago, then in 1937 to New York City. In 1947 he moved to Paris, where he lived as an expatriate until his fatal heart attack on November 28, 1960.

Although each of the places Wright lived marked his life, none marked it more deeply than Mississippi, which inspired the characteristic tone of anguish and anger that we find in all his best work. The deprivation that Wright felt in the Deep South was partly physical—he was often hungry, and he was always poor. But it was also psychological, intellectual, and spiritual. Both his mother and his maternal grandmother, who helped raise him, were rigidly moralistic and believed in harsh corporal punishment. In the society around him, the threat of far worse forms of violence was constant. In the schools he attended, education was not only limited but restrictive. In Memphis he once tried to get books from the library by forging a note from a white borrower: *"Dear Madam:"* he later wrote in "The Library Card," *"Will you please let this nigger boy . . . have some books by H. L. Mencken?"* The deception reflects not only the iconoclastic role Mencken later came to play for Wright but also the sense Wright had of having been deliberately denied access to the books he most needed. An avid reader, Wright often turned to books for the emotional fulfillment he could not find in life: "It had been only through books," he wrote, ". . . that I had managed to keep myself alive."

After his move to Chicago, Wright worked as a porter, a dishwasher, a salesman for a disreputable burial insurance agency, and as a postal worker. With the onset of the Depression, he was forced to go on relief and work as a street sweeper before gravitating toward the Federal Negro Theater and the Federal Writer's Project, both of which were sponsored by the WPA. Wright also became active in radical politics; he began writing poetry for leftist journals, and in 1933 he joined the Chicago John Reed Club shortly before officially becoming a member of the Communist party. In 1935 Wright began to contribute articles and reviews to the intellectual and politically radical journal, *The New Masses.*

With his move to New York City in 1937, Wright became Harlem editor of the Communist newspaper *The Daily Worker* and soon began writing the books that made him famous. That year he finished his first novel, *Lawd Today,* an experimental work (not published until 1963) about twenty-four hours in the life of a middle-class Chicago African American that Wright self-consciously modeled after James Joyce's *Ulysses* and John Dos Passos's *U.S.A.* A year later Wright published his first book, *Uncle Tom's Children: Four Novellas,* a collection of stories that viscerally concern racial prejudice, African American resistance, and violence in the Deep South. Wright said of one of the stories, "Long Black Song," that he was influenced by both Gertrude Stein and Ernest Hemingway as he tried to find a way to handle serious social issues in a simple, naturalistic style. In 1940, while on a Guggenheim fellowship, Wright published *Native Son,* the grim, nightmarish tale of a young African American man who accidentally murders the liberal daughter of his white employer. As Theodore Dreiser had done with *An American Tragedy* (1925), Wright based his story on an actual murder case; like Dreiser's, Wright's intentions were more literary than documentary. He wanted, he wrote, to put the case of the Negro squarely into American literary tradition:

> We do have in the Negro the embodiment of a past, tragic enough to appease the spiritual hunger of even a [Henry] James and we have in the oppression of the Negro a shadow athwart our national life dense and heavy enough to satisfy even the gloomy broodings of a Hawthorne. And if Poe were alive, he would not have to invent horror; horror would invent him.

An enormous publishing success, *Native Son* was the first book written by an African American to be selected for the Book of the Month Club.

In 1941 Wright wrote the text for *Twelve Million Black Voices,* a book that combined words and pictures to express the "folk history of the Negro in the United States." The following year, while giving a talk at Fisk University on growing up African American in America, Wright decided to compose his autobiography:

> It was not half-way through my speech that it crashed upon me that I was saying things that whites had forbidden Negroes to say. . . . Later, I learned that I had accidentally blundered into the secret, black, hidden core of race relations in the United States. That core is this: nobody is ever expected to speak honestly about this problem.

The result of his autobiographical efforts was another best-selling book, *Black Boy* (1945), which contained the story of his life up until his move to Chicago. Deleted at the time were several chapters dealing with his life in Chicago and his increasing disenchantment with the Communist party; this material was eventually published posthumously as *American Hunger* (1977). Wright had left the Communist party in

1944, following a bitter struggle in which the party accused him of harboring anti-Stalinist sentiments and resisting party discipline.

In the spring of 1946 Wright and his family visited France for several months on the invitation of Gertrude Stein. The Wrights returned to Paris in 1947, where they settled permanently and where Wright, by now a vehement anti-Communist, met Jean-Paul Sartre and immersed himself in existentialist philosophy. Wright's work had long concerned itself with such issues as freedom, alienation, dread, and identity through violence ("When a man kills, it's for something. . . . I didn't know I was really alive in this world until I felt things hard enough to kill for 'em," says the hero of *Native Son*), but in his later work, such as *The Outsider* (1953), *Savage Holiday* (1954), and *The Long Dream* (1958), philosophy became a more explicit part of his fiction. These novels focus on heroes who, finding themselves cut off from the world around them as well as from the past, determine to make virtues of isolation and rootlessness. Throughout the 1950s Wright also traveled extensively in an attempt to understand the origins and legacy of African American slavery: *Black Power: A Report of Reactions in a Land of Pathos* (1954) is an account of a trip to the Gold Coast (Ghana); *The Color Curtain* (1956) reports on his coverage of a conference in Indonesia; and *Pagan Spain* (1957) is an attempt to find answers to the history of slavery in the paradoxes of Spanish culture. In 1957 Wright also brought out a collection of his European lectures on politics, racism, and African American literature. A collection of short stories, *Eight Men,* was published posthumously in 1961.

Wright's early works focus on the large demographic shift of African American people from the rural South toward the urban North. His heroes struggle against accepting both the "place" of powerlessness and the "role" of subservience and silence that their society has assigned them. Since this struggle often leads Wright's heroes into defiance that society regards as criminal—and sometimes leads them directly into criminality—they characteristically find themselves threatened by social rejection as well as terrible punishment. Both of these threats, one psychological, the other physical, haunt Wright's characters as they attempt to force people who occupy positions of power and prestige to see, hear, and acknowledge them. It was a struggle Wright himself continually endured: "I had elected," he wrote in *American Hunger,* "in my fevered search for honorable adjustment to the American scene, not to submit and in doing so I had embraced the daily horror of anxiety, of tension, of eternal disquiet."

Further Reading:

J. Baldwin, "Everybody's Protest Novel," in *Notes of a Native Son,* 1955.

I. Howe, "Black Boys and Native Sons," in *A World More Attractive,* 1963.

R. Ellison, "Richard Wright's Blues," in *Shadow and Act,* 1964.

C. Webb, *Richard Wright: A Biography,* 1968.

D. McCall, *The Example of Richard Wright,* 1969.

R. Macksey and F. Moorer, eds., *Richard Wright: A Collection of Critical Essays,* 1984.

J. A. Joyce, *Richard Wright's Art of Tragedy,* 1986.

Texts:
"Long Black Song" from *Uncle Tom's Children,* 1940.

Long Black Song

I

Go t sleep, baby
Papas gone t town
Go t sleep, baby
The suns goin down
Go t sleep, baby
Yo candys in the sack
Go t sleep, baby
Papas comin back . . .

Over and over she crooned, and at each lull of her voice she rocked the wooden cradle with a bare black foot. But the baby squalled louder, its wail drowning out the song. She stopped and stood over the cradle, wondering what was bothering it, if its stomach hurt. She felt the diaper; it was dry. She lifted it up and patted its back. Still it cried, longer and louder. She put it back into the cradle and dangled a string of red beads before its eyes. The little black fingers clawed them away. She bent over, frowning, murmuring: "Whuts the mattah, chile? Yuh wan some watah?" She held a dripping gourd to the black lips, but the baby turned its head and kicked its legs. She stood a moment, perplexed. Whuts wrong wid that chile? She ain never carried on like this this tima day. She picked it up and went to the open door. "See the sun, baby?" she asked, pointing to a big ball of red dying between the branches of trees. The baby pulled back and strained its round black arms and legs against her stomach and shoulders. She knew it was tired; she could tell by the halting way it opened its mouth to draw in air. She sat on a wooden stool, unbuttoned the front of her dress, brought the baby closer and offered it a black teat.

"Don baby wan suppah?" It pulled away and went limp, crying softly, piteously, as though it would never stop. Then it pushed its fingers against her breasts and wailed. Lawd, chile, what yuh wan? Yo ma cant hep yuh less she knows whut yuh wan. Tears gushed; four white teeth flashed in red gums; the little chest heaved up and down and round black fingers stretched floorward. Lawd, chile, whuts wrong wid yuh? She stooped slowly, allowing her body to be guided by the downward tug. As soon as the little fingers touched the floor the wail quieted into a broken sniffle. She turned the baby loose and watched it crawl toward a corner. She followed and saw the little fingers reach for the tail-end of an old eight-day clock. "Yuh wan tha ol clock?" She dragged the clock into the center of the floor. The baby crawled after it, calling, "Ahh!" Then it raised its hands and beat on the top of the clock Bink! Bink! Bink! "Naw, yuhll hurt yo hans!" She held the baby and looked around. It cried and struggled. "Wait, baby!" She fetched a small stick from the top of a rickety dresser. "Here," she said, closing the little fingers about it. "Beat wid this, see?" She heard each blow landing squarely on top of the clock. Bang! Bang! Bang! And with each bang the baby smiled and said, "Ahh!" Mabbe thall keep yuh quiet erwhile. Mabbe Ah kin git some res now. She stood in the doorway. Lawd, tha chiles a pain! She mus be teethin. Er something . . .

She wiped sweat from her forehead with the bottom of her dress and looked out over the green fields rolling up the hillsides. She sighed, fighting a feeling of loneliness. Lawd, its sho hard t pass the days wid Silas gone. Been mos a week now since he took the wagon outta here. Hope ain nothin wrong. He must be buyin a heapa stuff there in Colwatah t be stayin all this time. Yes; maybe Silas would remember and bring that fiveyard piece of red calico she wanted. Oh, Lawd! Ah *hope* he don fergit it!

She saw green fields wrapped in the thickening gloam. It was as if they had left the earth, those fields, and were floating slowly skyward. The afterglow lingered, red, dying, somehow tenderly sad. And far away, in front of her, earth and sky met in a soft swoon of shadow. A cricket chirped, sharp and lonely; and it seemed she could hear it chirping long after it had stopped. Silas oughta c mon soon. Ahm tireda staying here by mahsef.

Loneliness ached in her. She swallowed, hearing Bang! Bang! Bang! Tom been gone t war mos a year now. N tha ol wars over n we ain heard nothing yit. Lawd, don let Tom be dead! She frowned into the gloam and wondered about that awful war so far away. They said it was over now. Yeah, Gawd had t stop em fo they killed everybody. She felt that merely to go so far away from home was a kind of death in itself. Just to go that far away was to be killed. Nothing good could come from men going miles across the sea to fight. N how come they wanna kill each other? How come they wanna make blood? Killing was not what men ought to do. Shucks! she thought.

She sighed, thinking of Tom, hearing Bang! Bang! Bang! She saw Tom, saw his big black smiling face; her eyes went dreamily blank, drinking in the red afterglow. Yes, God; it could have been Tom instead of Silas who was having her now. Yes; it could have been Tom she was loving. She smiled and asked herself, Lawd, Ah wondah how would it been wid Tom? Against the plush sky she saw a white bright day and a green cornfield and she saw Tom walking in his overalls and she was with Tom and he had his arm about her waist. She remembered how weak she had felt feeling his fingers sinking into the flesh of her hips. Her knees had trembled and she had had a hard time trying to stand up and not just sink right there to the ground. Yes; that was what Tom had wanted her to do. But she had held Tom up and he had held her up; they had held each other up to keep from slipping to the ground there in the green cornfield. Lawd! Her breath went and she passed her tongue over her lips. But that was not as exciting as that winter evening when the grey skies were sleeping and she and Tom were coming home from church down dark Lover's Lane. She felt the tips of her teats tingling and touching the front of her dress as she remembered how he had crushed her against him and hurt her. She had closed her eyes and was smelling the acrid scent of dry October leaves and had gone weak in his arms and had felt she could not breathe any more and had torn away and run, run home. And the sweet ache which had frightened her then was stealing back to her loins now with the silence and the cricket calls and the red afterglow and Bang! Bang! Bang! Lawd, Ah wondah how would it been wid Tom?

She stepped out on the porch and leaned against the wall of the house. Sky sang a red song. Fields whispered a green prayer. And song and prayer were dying in silence and shadow. Never in all her life had she been so much alone as she was now. Days were never so long as these days; and nights were never so empty as these nights. She jerked her head impatiently, hearing Bang! Bang! Bang! Shucks! she thought. When Tom had gone something had ebbed so slowly that at first she had not noticed it. Now she felt all of it as though the feeling had no bottom. She tried to think just how it had happened. Yes; there had been all her life the long hope of white bright days and the deep desire of dark black nights and then Tom had gone. Bang! Bang! Bang! There had been laughter and eating and singing and the long gladness of green cornfields in summer. There had been cooking and sewing and sweeping and the deep dream of sleeping grey skies in winter. Always it had been like that and she had been happy. But no more. The happiness of those days and nights, of those green cornfields and grey skies had started to go from her when Tom had gone to war. His leaving had left an empty black hole in her heart, a black hole that Silas had come in and filled. But not quite. Silas had not quite filled that hole. No; days and nights were not as they were before.

She lifted her chin, listening. She had heard something, a dull throb like she had heard that day Silas had called her outdoors to look at the airplane. Her eyes swept the sky. But there was no plane. Mabbe its behin the house? She stepped into the yard and looked upward through paling light. There were only a few big wet stars trembling in the east. Then she heard the throb again. She turned, looking up and down the road. The throb grew louder, droning; and she heard Bang! Bang! Bang! There! A car! Wondah whuts a car doin coming out here? A black car was winding over a dusty road, coming toward her. Mabbe some white mans bringing Silas home wida loada goods? But, Lawd, Ah *hope* its no trouble! The car stopped in front of the house and a white man got out. Wondah whut he wans? She looked at the car, but could not see Silas. The white man was young; he wore a straw hat and had no coat. He walked toward her with a huge black package under his arm.

"Well, howre yuh today, Aunty?"

"Ahm well. How yuh?"

"Oh, so-so. Its sure hot today, hunh?"

She brushed her hand across her forehead and sighed.

"Yeah; it is kinda warm."

"You busy?"

"Naw, Ah ain doin nothin."

"Ive got something to show you. Can I sit here, on your porch?"

"Ah reckon so. But, Mistah, Ah ain got no money."

"Haven't you sold your cotton yet?"

"Silas gone t town wid it now."

"Whens he coming back?"

"Ah don know. Ahm waitin fer im."

She saw the white man take out a handkerchief and mop his face. Bang! Bang! Bang! He turned his head and looked through the open doorway, into the front room.

"Whats all that going on in there?"

She laughed.

"Aw, thas jus Ruth."

"Whats she doing?"

"She beatin tha ol clock."

"Beating a *clock*?"

She laughed again.

"She wouldnt go t sleep so Ah give her tha ol clock t play wid."

The white man got up and went to the front door; he stood a moment looking at the black baby hammering on the clock. Bang! Bang! Bang!

"But why let her tear your clock up?"

"It ain no good."

"You could have it fixed."

"We ain got no money t be fixin' no clocks."

"Haven't you got a clock?"

"Naw."

"But how do you keep time?"

"We git erlong widout time."

"But how do you know when to get up in the morning?"

"We jus git up, thas all."

"But how do you know what time it is when you get up?"

"We git up wid the sun."

"And at night, how do you tell when its night?"

"It gits dark when the sun goes down."

"Haven't you ever had a clock?"

She laughed and turned her face toward the silent fields. "Mistah, we don need no clock."

"Well, this beats everything! I don't see how in the world anybody can live without time."

"We just don need no time, Mistah."

The white man laughed and shook his head; she laughed and looked at him. The white man was funny. Jus like lil boy. Astin how do Ah know when t git up in the mawnin! She laughed again and mused on the baby, hearing Bang! Bang! Bang! She could hear the white man breathing at her side; she felt his eyes on her face. She looked at him; she saw he was looking at her breasts. Hes jus lika lil boy. Acks like he cant understand *nothin!*

"But you need a clock," the white man insisted. "Thats what Im out here for. Im selling clocks and graphophones. The clocks are made right into the graphophones, a nice sort of combination, hunh? You can have music and time all at once. Ill show you . . ."

"Mistah, we don need no clock!"

"You dont have to buy it. It wont cost you anything just to look."

He unpacked the big black box. She saw the strands of his auburn hair glinting in the afterglow. His back bulged against his white shirt as he stooped. He pulled out a square brown graphophone. She bent forward, looking. Lawd, but its pretty! She saw the face of a clock under the horn of the graphophone. The gilt on the corners sparkled. The color in the wood glowed softly. It reminded her of the light she saw sometimes in the baby's eyes. Slowly she slid a finger over a beveled edge; she wanted to take the box into her arms and kiss it.

"Its eight o'clock," he said.

"Yeah?"

"It only costs fifty dollars. And you dont have to pay for it all at once. Just five dollars down and five dollars a month."

She smiled. The white man was just like a little boy. Jus like a chile. She saw him grinding the handle of the box.

There was a sharp, scratching noise; then she moved nervously, her body caught in the ringing coils of music.

When the trumpet of the Lord shall sound . . .

She rose on circling waves of white bright days and dark black nights.

. . . and time shall be no more . . .

Higher and higher she mounted.

And the morning breaks . . .

Earth fell far behind, forgotten.

. . . eternal, bright and fair . . .

Echo after echo sounded.

When the saved of the earth shall gather . . .

Her blood surged like the long gladness of summer.

. . . over the other shore . . .

Her blood ebbed like the deep dream of sleep in winter.

And when the roll is called up yonder . . .

She gave up, holding her breath.

I'll be there . . .

A lump filled her throat. She leaned her back against a post, trembling, feeling the rise and fall of days and nights, of summer and winter; surging, ebbing, leaping about her, beyond her, far out over the fields to where earth and sky lay folded in darkness. She wanted to lie down and sleep, or else leap up and shout. When the music stopped she felt herself coming back, being let down slowly. She sighed. It was dark now. She looked into the doorway. The baby was sleeping on the floor. Ah gotta git up n put tha chile t bed, she thought.

"Wasnt that pretty?"

"It wuz pretty, awright."

"When do you think your husbands coming back?"

"Ah don know, Mistah."

She went into the room and put the baby into the cradle. She stood again in the doorway and looked at the shadowy box that had lifted her up and carried her away. Crickets called. The dark sky had swallowed up the earth, and more stars were hanging, clustered, burning. She heard the white man sigh. His face was lost in shadow. She saw him rub his palms over his forehead. *Hes just lika lil boy.*

"Id like to see your husband tonight," he said. "Ive got to be in Lilydale at six o'clock in the morning and I wont be back through here soon. I got to pick up my buddy over there and we're heading North."

She smiled into the darkness. He was just like a little boy. A little boy selling clocks.

"Yuh sell them things alla time?" she asked.

"Just for the summer," he said. "I go to school in winter. If I can make enough money out of this Ill go to Chicago to school this fall . . ."

"Whut yuh gonna be?"

"*Be?* What do you mean?"

"Whut yuh goin to school fer?"

"Im studying science."

"Whuts tha?"

"Oh, er . . ." He looked at her. "Its about why things are as they are."

"Why things is as they *is?*"

"Well, its something like that."

"How come yuh wanna study tha?"

"Oh, you wouldnt understand."

She sighed.

"Naw, Ah guess Ah wouldnt."

"Well, I reckon Ill be getting along," said the white man. "Can I have a drink of water?"

"Sho. But we ain got nothin but well-watah, n yuhll have t come n git."

"Thats all right."

She slid off the porch and walked over the ground with bare feet. She heard the shoes of the white man behind her, falling to the earth in soft whispers. It was dark now. She led him to the well, groped her way, caught the bucket and let it down with a rope; she heard a splash and the bucket grew heavy. She drew it up, pulling against its weight, throwing one hand over the other, feeling the cool wet of the rope on her palms.

"Ah don git watah outa here much," she said, a little out of breath. "Silas gits the watah mos of the time. This buckets too heavy fer me."

"Oh, wait! Ill help!"

His shoulder touched hers. In the darkness she felt his warm hands fumbling for the rope.

"Where is it?"

"Here."

She extended the rope through the darkness. His fingers touched her breasts.

"Oh!"

She said it in spite of herself. He would think she was thinking about that. And he was a white man. She was sorry she had said that.

"Wheres the gourd?" he asked. "Gee, its dark!"

She stepped back and tried to see him.

"Here."

"I cant see!" he said, laughing.

Again she felt his fingers on the tips of her breasts. She backed away, saying nothing this time. She thrust the gourd out from her. Warm fingers met her cold hands. He had the gourd. She heard him drink; it was the faint, soft music of water going down a dry throat, the music of water in a silent night. He sighed and drank again.

"I was thirsty," he said. "I hadnt had any water since noon."

She knew he was standing in front of her; she could not see him, but she felt him. She heard the gourd rest against the wall of the well. She turned, then felt his hands full on her breasts. She struggled back.

"Naw, Mistah!"

"Im not going to hurt you!"

White arms were about her, tightly. She was still. But hes a *white* man. A *white* man. She felt his breath coming hot on her neck and where his hands held her breasts the flesh seemed to knot. She was rigid, poised; she swayed backward, then forward. She caught his shoulders and pushed.

"Naw, naw . . . Mistah, Ah cant do that!"

She jerked away. He caught her hand.

"Please . . ."

"Lemme go!"

She tried to pull her hand out of his and felt his fingers tighten. She pulled harder, and for a moment they were balanced, one against the other. Then he was at her side again, his arms about her.

"I wont hurt you! I wont hurt you . . ."

She leaned backward and tried to dodge his face. Her breasts were full against him; she gasped, feeling the full length of his body. She held her head far to one side; she knew he was seeking her mouth. His hands were on her breasts again. A wave of warm blood swept into her stomach and loins. She felt his lips touching her throat and where he kissed it burned.

"Naw, naw . . ."

Her eyes were full of the wet stars and they blurred, silver and blue. Her knees were loose and she heard her own breathing; she was trying to keep from falling. But hes a *white* man! A *white* man! Naw! Naw! And still she would not let him have her lips; she kept her face away. Her breasts hurt where they were crushed against him and each time she caught her breath she held it and while she held it it seemed that if she would let it go it would kill her. Her knees were pressed hard against his and she clutched the upper parts of his arms, trying to hold on. Her loins ached. She felt her body sliding.

"Gawd . . ."

He helped her up. She could not see the stars now; her eyes were full of the feeling that surged over her body each time she caught her breath. He held her close, breathing into her ear; she straightened, rigidly, feeling that she had to straighten or die. And then her lips felt his and she held her breath and dreaded ever to breathe again for fear of the feeling that would sweep down over her limbs. She held tightly, hearing a mountain tide of blood beating against her throat and temples. Then she gripped him, tore her face away, emptied her lungs in one long despairing gasp and went limp. She felt his hand; she was still, taut, feeling his hand, then his fingers. The muscles in her legs flexed and she bit her lips and pushed her toes deep into the wet dust by the side of the well and tried to wait and tried to wait until she could wait no longer. She whirled away from him and a streak of silver and blue swept across her blood. The wet ground cooled her palms and knee-caps. She stumbled up and ran, blindly, her toes flicking warm, dry dust. Her numbed fingers grabbed at a rusty nail in the post at the porch and she pushed ahead of hands that held her breasts. Her fingers found the door-facing; she moved into the darkened room, her hands before her. She touched the cradle and turned till her knees hit the bed. She went over, face down, her fingers trembling in the crumpled folds of his shirt. She moved and moved again and again, trying to keep ahead of the warm flood of blood that sought to catch her. A liquid metal covered her and she rode on the curve of white bright days and dark black nights and the surge of the long gladness of summer and the ebb of the deep dream of sleep in winter till a high red wave of hotness drowned her in a deluge of silver and blue and boiled her blood and blistered her flesh *bangbangbang* . . .

II

"Yuh bettah go," she said.

She felt him standing by the side of the bed, in the dark. She heard him clear his throat. His belt-buckle tinkled.

"Im leaving that clock and graphophone," he said.

She said nothing. In her mind she saw the box glowing softly, like the light in the baby's eyes. She stretched out her legs and relaxed.

"You can have it for forty instead of fifty. Ill be by early in the morning to see if your husbands in."

She said nothing. She felt the hot skin of her body growing steadily cooler.

"Do you think hell pay ten on it? Hell only owe thirty then."

She pushed her toes deep into the quilt, feeling a night wind blowing through the door. Her palms rested lightly on top of her breasts.

"Do you think hell pay ten on it?"

"Hunh?"

"Hell pay ten, wont he?"

"Ah don know," she whispered.

She heard his shoe hit against a wall; footsteps echoed on the wooden porch. She started nervously when she heard the roar of his car; she followed the throb of the motor till she heard it when she could hear it no more, followed it till she heard it roaring faintly in her ears in the dark and silent room. Her hands moved on her breasts and she was conscious of herself, all over; she felt the weight of her body resting heavily on shucks. She felt the presence of fields lying out there covered with night. She turned over slowly and lay on her stomach, her hands tucked under her. From somewhere came a creaking noise. She sat upright, feeling fear. The wind sighed. Crickets called. She lay down again, hearing shucks rustle. Her eyes looked straight up in the darkness and her blood sogged. She had lain a long time, full of a vast peace, when a far away tinkle made her feel the bed again. The tinkle came through the night; she listened, knowing that soon she would hear the rattle of Silas' wagon. Even then she tried to fight off the sound of Silas' coming, even then she wanted to feel the peace of night filling her again; but the tinkle grew louder and she heard the jangle of a wagon and the quick trot of horses. Thas Silas! She gave up and waited. She heard horses neighing. Out of the window bare feet whispered in the dust, then crossed the porch, echoing in soft booms. She closed her eyes and saw Silas come into the room in his dirty overalls as she had seen him come in a thousand times before.

"Yuh sleep, Sarah?"

She did not answer. Feet walked across the floor and a match scratched. She opened her eyes and saw Silas standing over her with a lighted lamp. His hat was pushed far back on his head and he was laughing.

"Ah reckon yuh thought Ah waznt never comin back, hunh? Cant yuh wake up? See, Ah got that red cloth yuh wanted . . ." He laughed again and threw the red cloth on the mantel.

"Yuh hongry?" she asked.

"Naw, Ah kin make out till mawnin." Shucks rustled as he sat on the edge of the bed. "Ah got two hundred n fifty fer mah cotton."

"Two hundred n fifty?"

"Nothin different! N guess whut Ah done?"

"Whut?"

"Ah bought ten mo acres o lan. Got em from ol man Burgess. Paid im a hundred n fifty dollahs down. Ahll pay the rest next year ef things go erlong awright. Ahma have t git a man t hep me nex spring . . ."

"Yuh mean hire somebody?"

"Sho, hire somebody! Whut yuh think? Ain tha the way the white folks do? Ef yuhs gonna git anywheres yuhs gotta do just like they do." He paused. "Whut yuh been doin since Ah been gone?"

"Nothin. Cookin, cleanin, n . . ."

"How Ruth?"

"She awright." She lifted her head. "Silas, yuh git any lettahs?"

"Naw. But Ah heard Tom wuz in town."

"In *town?*"

She sat straight up.

"Yeah, thas whut the folks wuz sayin at the sto."

"Back from the war?"

"Ah ast erroun t see ef Ah could fin im. But Ah couldnt."

"Lawd, Ah wish hed c mon home."

"Them white folks shos glad the wars over. But things wuz kinda bad there in town. Everywhere Ah looked wuznt nothin but black n white soljers. N them white folks beat up a black soljer yestiddy. He was jus in from France. Wuz still wearin his soljers suit. They claimed he sassed a white woman . . ."

"Who wuz he?"

"Ah don know. Never saw im befo."

"Yuh see An Peel?"

"Naw."

"Silas!" she said reprovingly.

"Aw, Sarah, Ah jus couldnt git out there."

"Whut else yuh bring sides the cloth?"

"Ah got yuh some high-top shoes." He turned and looked at her in the dim light of the lamp. "Woman, ain yuh glad Ah bought yuh some shoes n cloth?" He laughed and lifted his feet to the bed. "Lawd, Sarah, yuhs sho sleepy, ain yuh?"

"Bettah put tha lamp out, Silas . . ."

"Aw . . ." He swung out of the bed and stood still for a moment. She watched him, then turned her face to the wall.

"Whuts that by the windah?" he asked.

She saw him bending over and touching the graphophone with his fingers.

"Thasa graphophone."

"Where yuh git it from?"

"A man lef it here."

"When he bring it?"

"Today."

"But how come he t leave it?"

"He says hell be out here in the mawnin to see ef yuh wans t buy it."

He was on his knees, feeling the wood and looking at the gilt on the edges of the box. He stood up and looked at her.

"Yuh ain never said yuh wanted one of these things."

She said nothing.

"Where wuz the man from?"

"Ah don know."

"He white?"

"Yeah."

He put the lamp back on the mantel. As he lifted the globe to blow out the flame, his hand paused.

"Whos hats this?"

She raised herself and looked. A straw hat lay bottom upwards on the edge of the mantel. Silas picked it up and looked back to the bed, to Sarah.

"Ah guess its the white mans. He must a lef it . . ."

"Whut he doin *in our room*?"

"He wuz talkin t me bout that graphophone."

She watched him go to the window and stoop again to the box. He picked it up, fumbled with the price-tag and took the box to the light.

"Whut this thing cos?"

"Forty dollahs."

"But its marked fifty here."

"Oh, Ah means he said fifty . . ."

He took a step toward the bed.

"Yuh lyin t me!"

"Silas!"

He heaved the box out of the front door; there was a smashing, tinkling noise as it bounded off the front porch and hit the ground. "Whut in hell yuh lie t me fer?"

"Yuh broke the box!"

"Ahma break yo Gawddam neck ef yuh don stop lyin t me!"

"Silas, Ah ain lied t yuh!"

"Shut up, Gawddammit! Yuh did!"

He was standing by the bed with the lamp trembling in his hand. She stood on the other side, between the bed and the wall.

"How come yuh tell me that thing cos *forty* dollahs when it cos *fifty*?"

"Thas whut he tol me."

"How come he take *ten* dollars off fer yuh?"

"He ain took nothin off fer me, Silas!"

"Yuh lyin t me! N yuh lied t me bout Tom, too!"

She stood with her back to the wall, her lips parted, looking at him silently, steadily. Their eyes held for a moment. Silas looked down, as though he were about to believe her. Then he stiffened.

"Whos this?" he asked, picking up a short, yellow pencil from the crumpled quilt.

She said nothing. He started toward her.

"Yuh wan me t take mah raw-hide whip n make yuh talk?"

"Naw, naw, Silas! Yuh wrong! He wuz figgerin wid tha pencil!"

He was silent a moment, his eyes searching her face.

"Gawddam yo black soul t hell, don yuh try lyin t me! Ef yuh start layin wid white men Ahll hosswhip yuh t a incha yo life. Shos theres a Gawd in Heaven Ah will! From sunup t sundown Ah works mah guts out t pay them white trash bastards whut Ah owe em, n then Ah comes n fins they been in mah house! Ah cant go into their houses, n yuh know Gawddam well Ah cant! They don have no mercy on no black folks; wes jus like dirt under their feet! Fer ten years Ah slaves lika dog t git mah farm free, givin ever penny Ah kin t em, n then Ah comes n fins they been in mah house . . ." He was speechless with outrage. "If yuh wans t eat at mah table yuhs gonna keep them white trash bastards out, yuh hear? Tha white ape kin come n git tha damn box n Ah ain gonna pay im a cent! He had no bisness leavin it here, n yuh had no bisness lettin im! Ahma tell tha sonofabitch something when he comes out here in the mawnin, so hep me Gawd! Now git back in tha bed!"

She slipped beneath the quilt and lay still, her face turned to the wall. Her heart thumped slowly and heavily. She heard him walk across the floor in his bare feet. She heard the bottom of the lamp as it rested on the mantel. She stiffened when the room darkened. Feet whispered across the floor again. The shucks rustled from Silas' weight as he sat on the edge of the bed. She was still, breathing softly. Silas was mumbling. She felt sorry for him. In the darkness it seemed that she could see the hurt look on his black face. The crow of a rooster came from far away, came so faintly that it seemed she had not heard it. The bed sank and the shucks cried out in dry whispers; she knew Silas had stretched out. She heard him sigh. Then she jumped because he jumped. She could feel the tenseness of his body; she knew he was sitting bolt upright. She felt his hands fumbling jerkily under the quilt. Then the bed heaved amid a wild shout of shucks and Silas' feet hit the floor with a loud boom. She snatched herself to her elbows, straining her eyes in the dark, wondering what was wrong now. Silas was moving about, cursing under his breath.

"Don wake Ruth up!" she whispered.

"Ef yuh say one mo word t me Ahma slap yuh inter a black spasm!"

She grabbed her dress, got up and stood by the bed, the tips of her fingers touching the wall behind her. A match flared in yellow flame; Silas' face was caught in a circle of light. He was looking downward, staring intently at a white wad of cloth balled in his hand. His black cheeks were hard, set; his lips were tightly pursed. She looked closer; she saw that the white cloth was a man's handkerchief. Silas' fingers loosened; she heard the handkerchief hit the floor softly, damply. The match went out.

"Yuh little bitch!"

Her knees gave. Fear oozed from her throat to her stomach. She moved in the dark toward the door, struggling with the dress, jamming it over her head. She heard the thick skin of Silas' feet swish across the wooden planks.

"Ah got mah raw-hide whip n Ahm takin yuh t the barn!"

She ran on tiptoe to the porch and paused, thinking of the baby. She shrank as something whined through the air. A red streak of pain cut across the small of her back and burned its way into her body, deeply.

"Silas!" she screamed.

She grabbed for the post and fell in dust. She screamed again and crawled out of reach.

"Git t the barn, Gawddammit!"

She scrambled up and ran through the dark, hearing the baby cry. Behind her leather thongs hummed and feet whispered swiftly over the dusty ground.

"C mere, yuh bitch! C mere, Ah say!"

She ran to the road and stopped. She wanted to go back and get the baby, but she dared not. Not as long as Silas had that whip. She stiffened, feeling that he was near.

"Yuh jus as well c mon back n git yo beatin!"

She ran again, slowing now and then to listen. If she only knew where he was she would slip back into the house and get the baby and walk all the way to Aunt Peel's.

"Yuh ain comin back in mah house till Ah beat yuh!"

She was sorry for the anger she knew he had out there in the field. She had a bewildering impulse to go to him and ask him not to be angry; she wanted to tell him that there was nothing to be angry about; that what she had done did not matter; that she was sorry; that after all she was his wife and still loved him. But there was no way she could do that now; if she went to him he would whip her as she had seen him whip a horse.

"Sarah! Sarah!"

His voice came from far away. Ahm goin git Ruth. Back through dust she sped, going on her toes, holding her breath.

"Saaaarah!"

From far off his voice floated over the fields. She ran into the house and caught the baby in her arms. Again she sped through dust on her toes. She did not stop till she was so far away that his voice sounded like a faint echo falling from the sky. She looked up; the stars were paling a little. Mus be gittin near mawnin. She walked now, letting her feet sink softly into the cool dust. The baby was sleeping; she could feel the little chest swelling against her arm. She looked up again; the sky was solid black. Its gittin near mawnin. Ahma take Ruth t An Peels. N mabbe Ahll fin Tom . . . But she could not walk all that distance in the dark. Not now. Her legs were tired. For a moment a memory of surge and ebb rose in her blood; she felt her legs straining, upward. She sighed. Yes, she would go to the sloping hillside back of the garden and wait until morning. Then she would slip away. She stopped, listened. She heard a faint, rattling noise. She imagined Silas' kicking or throwing the smashed graphophone. Hes mad! Hes sho mad! Aw, Lawd! . . . She stopped stock still, squeezing the baby till it whimpered. What would happen when that white man came out in the morning? She had forgotten him. She would have to head him off and tell him. Yeah, cause Silas jus mad ernuff t kill! Lawd, hes mad ernuff t kill!

III

She circled the house widely, climbing a slope, groping her way, holding the baby high in her arms. After awhile she stopped and wondered where on the slope she was. She remembered there was an elm tree near the edge; if she could find it she would know. She groped farther, feeling with her feet. Ahm gittin los! And she did not want to fall with the baby. Ahma stop here, she thought. When morning came she would see the car of the white man from this hill and she would run down the road and tell him to go back; and then there would be no killing. Dimly she saw in her mind a picture of men killing and being killed. White men killed the black and black men killed the white. White men killed the black men because they could, and the black men killed the white men to keep from being killed. And killing was blood. Lawd, Ah wish Tom wuz here. She shuddered, sat on the ground and watched the sky for signs of morning. Mabbe Ah oughta walk on down the road? Naw . . . Her legs were tired. Again she felt her body straining. Then she saw Silas holding the white man's handkerchief. She heard it hit the floor, softly, damply. She was sorry for what she had done. Silas was as good to her as any black man could be to a black woman. Most of the black women worked in the fields as croppers. But Silas had given her her own home, and that was more than many others had done for their women. Yes, she knew how Silas felt. Always he had said he was as good as any white man. He had worked hard and saved his money and bought a farm so he could grow his own crops like white men. Silas hates white folks! Lawd, he sho hates em!

The baby whimpered. She unbuttoned her dress and nursed her in the dark. She looked toward the east. There! A tinge of grey hovered. It wont be long now. She could see ghostly outlines of trees. Soon she would see the elm, and by the elm she would sit till it was light enough to see the road.

The baby slept. Far off a rooster crowed. Sky deepened. She rose and walked slowly down a narrow, curving path and came to the elm tree. Standing on the edge of a slope, she saw a dark smudge in a sea of shifting shadows. That was her home. Wondah how come Silas didnt light the lamp? She shifted the baby from her right hip to her left, sighed, struggled against sleep. She sat on the ground again, caught the baby close and leaned against the trunk of a tree. Her eye-lids drooped and it seemed that a hard, cold hand caught hold of her right leg or was it her left leg—she did not know which—and began to drag her over a rough litter of shucks and when she strained to see who it was that was pulling her no one was in sight but far ahead was darkness and it seemed that out of the darkness some force came and pulled her like a magnet and she went sliding along over a rough bed of screeching shucks and it seemed that a wild fear made her want to scream but when she opened her mouth to scream she could not scream and she felt she was coming to a wide black hole and again she made ready to scream and then it was too late for she was already over the wide black hole falling falling falling . . .

She awakened with a start and blinked her eyes in the sunshine. She found she was clutching the baby so hard that it had begun to cry. She got to her feet, trembling from fright of the dream, remembering Silas and the white man and Silas' running her out of the house and the white man's coming. Silas was standing in the front yard; she caught her breath. Yes, she had to go and head that white man off! Naw! She could not do that, not with Silas standing there with that whip in his hand. If she tried to climb any of those slopes he would see her surely. And Silas would never forgive her for something like that. If it were anybody but a white man it would be different.

Then, while standing there on the edge of the slope looking wonderingly at Silas striking the whip against his overall-leg—and then, while standing there looking—she froze. There came from the hills a distant throb. Lawd! The baby whimpered. She loosened her arms. The throb grew louder, droning. Hes comin fas! She wanted to run to Silas and beg him not to bother the white man. But he had that whip in his hand. She should not have done what she had done last night. This was all her fault. Lawd, ef anything happens t im its mah blame . . . Her eyes watched a black car speed over the crest of a hill. She should have been out there on the road instead of sleeping here by the tree. But it was too late now. Silas was standing in the yard; she saw him turn with a nervous jerk and sit on the edge of the porch. He was holding the whip stiffly. The car came to a stop. A door swung open. A white man got out. Thas im! She saw another white man in the front seat of the car. N thats his buddy . . . The white man who had gotten out walked over the ground, going to Silas. They faced each other, the white man standing up and Silas sitting down; like two toy men they faced each other. She saw Silas point the whip to the smashed graphophone. The white man looked down and took a quick step backward. The white man's shoulders were bent and he shook his head from left to right. Then Silas got up and they faced each other again; like two dolls, a white doll and a black doll, they faced each other in the valley below. The white man pointed his finger into Silas' face. Then Silas' right arm went up; the whip flashed. The white man turned, bending, flinging his hands to shield his head. Silas' arm rose and fell, rose and fell. She saw the white man crawling in dust, trying to get out of reach. She screamed when she saw the other white man get out of the car and run to Silas. Then all three were on the ground, rolling in dust, grappling for the whip. She clutched the baby and ran. Lawd! Then she stopped, her mouth hanging open. Silas had broken loose and was running toward the house. She knew he was going for his gun.

"Silas!"

Running, she stumbled and fell. The baby rolled in the dust and bawled. She grabbed it up and ran again. The white men were scrambling for their car. She reached level ground, running. Hell be killed! Then again she stopped. Silas was on the front porch, aiming a rifle. One of the white men was climbing into the car. The other was standing, waving his arms, shouting at Silas. She tried to scream, but choked; and she could not scream till she heard a shot ring out.

"Silas!"

One of the white men was on the ground. The other was in the car. Silas was aiming again. The car started, running in a cloud of dust. She fell to her knees and hugged the baby close. She heard another shot, but the car was roaring over the top of the southern hill. Fear was gone now. Down the slope she ran. Silas was standing on the porch, holding his gun and looking at the fleeing car. Then she saw him go to the white man lying in dust and stoop over him. He caught one of the man's legs and dragged the body into the middle of the road. Then he turned and came slowly back to the house. She ran, holding the baby, and fell at his feet.

"Silas!"

IV

"Git up, Sarah!"

His voice was hard and cold. She lifted her eyes and saw blurred black feet. She wiped tears away with dusty fingers and pulled up. Something took speech from her and she stood with bowed shoulders. Silas was standing still, mute; the look on his face condemned her. It was as though he had gone far off and had stayed a long time and had come back changed even while she was standing there in the sunshine before him. She wanted to say something, to give herself. She cried.

"Git the chile up, Sarah!"

She lifted the baby and stood waiting for him to speak, to tell her something to change all this. But he said nothing. He walked toward the house. She followed. As she attempted to go in, he blocked the way. She jumped to one side as he threw the red cloth outdoors to the ground. The new shoes came next. Then Silas heaved the baby's cradle. It hit the porch and a rocker splintered; the cradle swayed for a second, then fell to the ground, lifting a cloud of brown dust against the sun. All of her clothes and the baby's clothes were thrown out.

"Silas!"

She cried, seeing blurred objects sailing through the air and hearing them hit softly in the dust.

"Git you things n go!"

"Silas!"

"Ain no use yuh sayin *nothin* now!"

"But theyll kill yuh!"

"There ain nothin Ah kin do. N there ain nothin yuh kin do. Yuh done done too Gawddam much awready. Git yo things n go!"

"Theyll kill yuh, Silas!"

He pushed her off the porch.

"GIT YO THINGS N GO T AN PEELS!"

"Les *both* go, Silas!"

"Ahm stayin here till they come back!"

She grabbed his arm and he slapped her hand away. She dropped to the edge of the porch and sat looking at the ground.

"Go way," she said quietly. "Go way fo they comes. Ah didnt mean no harm . . ."

"Go way fer whut?"

"Theyll *kill* yuh . . ."

"It don make no difference." He looked out over the sunfilled fields. "Fer ten years Ah slaved mah life out t git mah farm free . . ." His voice broke off. His lips moved as though a thousand words were spilling silently out of his mouth, as though he did not have breath enough to give them sound. He looked to the sky, and then back to the dust. "Now, its all gone. *Gone* . . . Ef Ah run erway, Ah ain got nothin. Ef Ah stay n fight, Ah ain got nothin. It dont make no difference which way Ah go. Gawd! Gawd, Ah wish all them white folks wuz dead! *Dead,* Ah tell yuh! Ah wish Gawd would kill em *all!*"

She watched him run a few steps and stop. His throat swelled. He lifted his hands to his face; his fingers trembled. Then he bent to the ground and cried. She touched his shoulders.

"Silas!"

He stood up. She saw he was staring at the white man's body lying in the dust in the middle of the road. She watched him walk over to it. He began to talk to no one in particular; he simply stood over the dead white man and talked out of his life, out of a deep and final sense that now it was all over and nothing could make any difference.

"The white folks ain never gimme a chance! They ain never give no black man a chance! There ain nothin in yo whole life yuh kin keep from em! They take yo lan! They take yo freedom! They take yo women! N then they take yo life!" He turned to her, screaming. "N then Ah gits stabbed in the back by mah own blood! When mah eyes is on the white folks to keep em from killin me, mah own blood trips me up!" He knelt in the dust again and sobbed; after a bit he looked to the sky, his face wet with tears. "Ahm gonna be hard like they is! So hep me, Gawd, Ah'm gonna be *hard!* When they come fer me Ahm gonna *be here!* N when they git me outta here theys gonna *know Ahm gone!* Ef Gawd lets me live Ahm gonna make em *feel* it!" He stopped and tried to get his breath. "But, Lawd, Ah don wanna be this way! I don mean nothin! Yuh die ef yuh fight! Yuh die ef yuh don fight! Either way yuh die n it don mean nothin . . ."

He was lying flat on the ground, the side of his face deep in dust. Sarah stood nursing the baby with eyes black and stony. Silas pulled up slowly and stood again on the porch.

"Git on t An Peels, Sarah!"

A dull roar came from the south. They both turned. A long streak of brown dust was weaving down the hillside.

"Silas!"

"Go on cross the fiels, Sarah!"

"We kin *both* go! Git the hosses!"

He pushed her off the porch, grabbed her hand, and led her to the rear of the house, past the well, to where a path led up a slope to the elm tree.

"Silas!"

"Yuh git on fo they ketch yuh too!"

Blind from tears, she went across the swaying fields, stumbling over blurred grass. It ain no use! She knew it was now too late to make him change his mind. The calves of her legs knotted. Suddenly her throat tightened, aching. She stopped, closed her eyes and tried to stem a flood of sorrow that drenched her. Yes, killing of white men by black men and killing of black men by white men went on in spite of the hope of white bright days and the desire of dark black nights and the long gladness of green corn-fields in summer and the deep dream of sleepy grey skies in winter. And when killing started it went on, like a river flowing. Oh, she felt sorry for Silas! Silas. . . . He was fol-lowing that long river of blood. Lawd, how come he wans t stay there like tha? And he did not want to die; she knew he hated dying by the way he talked of it. Yet he followed the old river of blood, knowing that it meant nothing. He followed it, cursing and whimpering. But he followed it. She stared before her at the dry, dusty grass. Some-how, men, black men and white men, land and houses, green cornfields and grey skies, gladness and dreams, were all a part of that which made life good. Yes, somehow, they were linked, like the spokes in a spinning wheel. She felt they were. She knew they were. She felt it when she breathed and knew it when she looked. But she could not say how; she could not put her finger on it and when she thought hard about it it became all mixed up, like milk spilling suddenly. Or else it knotted in her throat and chest in a hard, aching lump, like the one she felt now. She touched her face to the baby's face and cried again.

There was a loud blare of auto horns. The growing roar made her turn round. Silas was standing, seemingly unafraid, leaning against a post of the porch. The long line of cars came speeding in clouds of dust. Silas moved toward the door and went in. Sarah ran down the slope a piece, coming again to the elm tree. Her breath was slow and hard.

The cars stopped in front of the house. There was a steady drone of motors and drifting clouds of dust. For a moment she could not see what was happening. Then on all sides white men with pistols and rifles swarmed over the fields. She dropped to her knees, unable to take her eyes away, unable, it seemed, to breathe. A shot rang out. A white man fell, rolling over, face downward.

"Hes gotta gun!"

"Git back!"

"Lay down!"

The white men ran back and crouched behind cars. Three more shots came from the house. She looked, her head and eyes aching. She rested the baby in her lap and shut her eyes. Her knees sank into the dust. More shots came, but it was no use looking now. She knew it all by heart. She could feel it happening even before it happened. There were men killing and being killed. Then she jerked up, being compelled to look.

"Burn the bastard out!"

"Set the sonofabitch on fire!"

"Cook the coon!"

"Smoke im out!"

She saw two white men on all fours creeping past the well. One carried a gun and the other a red tin can. When they reached the back steps the one with the tin can crept under the house and crept out again. Then both rose and ran. Shots. One fell. A yell went up. A yellow tongue of fire licked out from under the back steps.

"Burn the nigger!"

"C mon out, nigger, n git yos!"

She watched from the hill-slope; the back steps blazed. The white men fired a steady stream of bullets. Black smoke spiraled upward in the sunshine. Shots came from the house. The white men crouched out of sight, behind their cars.

"Make up your mind, nigger!"

"C mon out er burn, yuh black bastard!"

"Yuh think yuhre white now, nigger?"

The shack blazed, flanked on all sides by whirling smoke filled with flying sparks. She heard the distant hiss of flames. White men were crawling on their stomachs. Now and then they stopped, aimed, and fired into the bulging smoke. She looked with a tense numbness; she looked, waiting for Silas to scream, or run out. But the house crackled and blazed, spouting yellow plumes to the blue sky. The white men shot again, sending a hail of bullets into the furious pillars of smoke. And still she could not see Silas running out, or hear his voice calling. Then she jumped, standing. There was a loud crash; the roof caved in. A black chimney loomed amid crumbling wood. Flames roared and black smoke billowed, hiding the house. The white men stood up, no longer afraid. Again she waited for Silas, waited to see him fight his way out, waited to hear his call. Then she breathed a long, slow breath, emptying her lungs. She knew now. Silas had killed as many as he could and stayed on to burn, had stayed without a murmur. She filled her lungs with a quick gasp as the walls fell in; the house was hidden by eager plumes of red. She turned and ran with the baby in her arms, ran blindly across the fields, crying, "Naw, Gawd!"

1938

Eudora Welty
b. 1909

Admirers of Eudora Welty's fiction have always been in good company: Ford Madox Ford, Katherine Anne Porter, and Robert Penn Warren were among her earliest supporters. Like those who have followed them, they praised Welty's fiction for its evocative sense of place and even more for its compelling and honest presentation of human experience on all levels. Welty's most recent novel, *The Optimist's Daughter* (1972), focuses primarily on the social elite of a modern southern town, while her early, famous short story, "A Worn Path," is a realistic and uncondescending account of an old African American woman's strength and dignity. Convinced that "to write honestly and with all our powers is the least we can do, and the most," Welty persists in confronting the flaws she sees in her characters and her region, but she does so without bitterness. She brings to life "the turn of mind, the nature of temperament, of a privileged observer," but "owing to the way I became so," she has remarked, "it turned out that I became the loving kind."

A native of Jackson, Mississippi, where she has lived most of her life, Eudora Welty was born on April 13, 1909. She attended the Mississippi State College for Women for two years before transferring to the University of Wisconsin, from which she was graduated in 1929. She then enrolled at the Columbia University Graduate School of Business to study advertising. "As certain as I was of wanting to be a writer," she says, "I was certain of *not* wanting to be a teacher." After two years in New York, she returned to Jackson, where she worked in advertising with a local radio station and a state commission on tourism and as a society correspondent for a Memphis newspaper. As a publicist for the Works Progress Administration in the early 1930s, she took a series of photographs on southern rural poverty, some of which were exhibited in a one-woman show at the Museum of Modern Art in 1973. In 1936 she published her first short story, "Death of a Travelling Salesman," and followed it in rapid succession with two collections of stories, *A Curtain of Green and Other Stories* (1941) and *The Wide Net* (1943). Her first novel, *The Robber Bridegroom,* a fairy-tale-like story, appeared in 1942. Other novels, all dealing with various aspects of Mississippi life, include the story of a modern plantation family in *Delta Wedding* (1946), the comic first-person narrative of small-town life in *The Ponder Heart* (1954), and the complex tale of a large rural family in *Losing Battles* (1970), her most ambitious book. Her most recent work, *One Writer's Beginnings,* a collection of three autobiographical pieces, appeared in 1984. She has published additional collections of short stories—some realistic and others more fantastic—as well as several collections of essays on criticism and fictional theory, including *Place in Fiction* (1957) and *The Eye of the Story* (1977). Although *The Optimist's Daughter* has received widespread popular and critical acclaim, Welty remains best known for her finely crafted and often extremely funny short stories, which were published in 1980 as *The Collected Stories of Eudora Welty.*

Welty's fiction draws heavily on her deep knowledge of her region and her keen powers of observation. She has said that her imagination is predominantly visual, yet her ear for dialect matches her mastery of descriptive detail. Welty's major achievement, however, lies in her ability to reach through detailed surfaces to less tangible dimensions of reality. In "Why I Live at the P.O.," for example, Sister's obsessive monologue reveals not only the comic interaction of her extended family, nor merely her own deep-rooted feelings of alienation and lost opportunity, but also a sense of the mystery of human relationships. Like many southern writers, Welty is known for the creation of "grotesque" characters. Her characters, including Sister, are often physically, mentally, or emotionally handicapped and are thus at odds with their community. Yet even as they show the pain that isolation inflicts, they also show a freedom that a small, tightly-knit community does not permit.

In an early story, Welty describes a young girl who often looks at the world through a frame that she makes with her fingers. A frame, as Welty has since observed, not only involves focus and distance and selection; it also involves a viewer's values and commitments, her preferences, even her beliefs. The "frame through which I viewed the world changed too, with time," she has written recently, in *One Writer's Beginnings.* "Greater than scene, I came to see, is situation. Greater than situation is implication. Greater than all of these is a single, entire human being, who will never be confined in any frame." Over the years, Welty has concentrated on refining her frame, believing that the integrity of a work largely determines its quality. She makes her stories, she says, not directly out of her own life nor directly out of the lives of other people but out of "the *whole* fund of my feelings, my responses to the real experiences of my own life, to the relationships that formed and changed it, that I have given most of myself to." She writes of familiar themes—the power of the community and the power of the past in shaping the lives of individuals, the power of love and the power of memory, and the pain of loneliness and the pain of loss. Yet the character she feels closest to is the spinster piano teacher Miss Eckhart in "June Recital": "What I have put into her is my passion for my own life work, my own art. Exposing yourself to risk is a truth Miss Eckhart and I had in common. What animates and possesses me is what drives Miss Eckhart, the love of her art and the love of giving it, the desire to give it until there is no more left."

Further Reading:

R. P. Warren, "The Love and Separateness in Miss Welty," *Selected Essays,* 1958.

L. D. Rubin, Jr., "The Golden Apples of the Sun," in *The Faraway Country: Writers of the Modern South,* 1963.

M. Kreyling, *Eudora Welty's Achievement of Order,* 1980.

P. Yeager, "Because a Fire Was in My Head: Eudora Welty and the Dialogic Imagination," *PMLA* 99(1984), 955–73.

H. Bloom, ed., *Eudora Welty,* 1986.

D. Trouard, ed., *Eudora Welty: Eye of the Storyteller,* 1989.

Text:

"Why I Live at the P. O." from *Collected Stories,* 1980.

Why I Live at the P.O.

I was getting along fine with Mama, Papa-Daddy and Uncle Rondo until my sister Stella-Rondo just separated from her husband and came back home again. Mr. Whitaker! Of course I went with Mr. Whitaker first, when he first appeared here in China Grove, taking "Pose Yourself" photos, and Stella-Rondo broke us up. Told him I was one-sided. Bigger on one side than the other, which is a deliberate, calculated false-hood: I'm the same. Stella-Rondo is exactly twelve months to the day younger than I am and for that reason she's spoiled.

She's always had anything in the world she wanted and then she'd throw it away. Papa-Daddy gave her this gorgeous Add-a-Pearl necklace when she was eight years old and she threw it away playing baseball when she was nine, with only two pearls.

So as soon as she got married and moved away from home the first thing she did was separate! From Mr. Whitaker! This photographer with the popeyes she said she trusted. Came home from one of those towns up in Illinois and to our complete surprise brought this child of two.

Mama said she like to made her drop dead for a second. "Here you had this mar-velous blonde child and never so much as wrote your mother a word about it," says Mama. "I'm thoroughly ashamed of you." But of course she wasn't.

Stella-Rondo just calmly takes off this *hat*, I wish you could see it. She says, "Why, Mama, Shirley-T.'s adopted. I can prove it."

"How?" says Mama, but all I says was, "H'm!" There I was over the hot stove, trying to stretch two chickens over five people and a completely unexpected child into the bar-gain, without one moment's notice.

"What do you mean—'H'm!'?" says Stella-Rondo, and Mama says, "I heard that, Sister."

I said that oh, I didn't mean a thing, only that whoever Shirley-T. was, she was the spit-image of Papa-Daddy if he'd cut off his beard, which of course he'd never do in the world. Papa-Daddy's Mama's papa and sulks.

Stella-Rondo got furious! She said, "Sister, I don't need to tell you you got a lot of nerve and always did have and I'll thank you to make no future reference to my adopted child whatsoever."

"Very well," I said. "Very well, very well. Of course I noticed at once she looks like Mr. Whitaker's side too. That frown. She looks like a cross between Mr. Whitaker and Papa-Daddy."

"Well, all I can say is she isn't."

"She looks exactly like Shirley Temple to me," says Mama, but Shirley-T. just ran away from her.

So the first thing Stella-Rondo did at the table was turn Papa-Daddy against me.

"Papa-Daddy," she says. He was trying to cut up his meat. "Papa-Daddy!" I was taken completely by surprise. Papa-Daddy is about a million years old and's got this long-long beard. "Papa-Daddy, Sister says she fails to understand why you don't cut off your beard."

So Papa-Daddy l-a-y-s down his knife and fork! He's real rich. Mama says he is, he says he isn't. So he says, "Have I heard correctly? You don't understand why I don't cut off my beard?"

"Why," I says, "Papa-Daddy, of course I understand, I did not say any such of a thing, the idea!"

He says, "Hussy!"

I says, "Papa-Daddy, you know I wouldn't any more want you to cut off your beard than the man in the moon. It was the farthest thing from my mind! Stella-Rondo sat there and made that up while she was eating breast of chicken."

But he says, "So the postmistress fails to understand why I don't cut off my beard. Which job I got you through my influence with the government. 'Bird's nest'—is that what you call it?"

Not that it isn't the next to smallest P.O. in the entire state of Mississippi.

I says, "Oh, Papa-Daddy," I says, "I didn't say any such of a thing, I never dreamed it was a bird's nest, I have always been grateful though this is the next to smallest P.O. in the state of Mississippi, and I do not enjoy being referred to as a hussy by my own grandfather."

But Stella-Rondo says, "Yes, you did say it too. Anybody in the world could of heard you, that had ears."

"Stop right there," says Mama, looking at *me*.

So I pulled my napkin straight back through the napkin ring and left the table.

As soon as I was out of the room Mama says, "Call her back, or she'll starve to death," but Papa-Daddy says, "This is the beard I started growing on the Coast when I was fifteen years old." He would of gone on till nightfall if Shirley-T. hadn't lost the Milky Way she ate in Cairo.

So Papa-Daddy says, "I am going out and lie in the hammock, and you can all sit here and remember my words: I'll never cut off my beard as long as I live, even one inch, and I don't appreciate it in you at all." Passed right by me in the hall and went straight out and got in the hammock.

It would be a holiday. It wasn't five minutes before Uncle Rondo suddenly appeared in the hall in one of Stella-Rondo's flesh-colored kimonos, all cut on the bias, like something Mr. Whitaker probably thought was gorgeous.

"Uncle Rondo!" I says. "I didn't know who that was! Where are you going?"

"Sister," he says, "get out of my way, I'm poisoned."

"If you're poisoned stay away from Papa-Daddy," I says. "Keep out of the hammock. Papa-Daddy will certainly beat you on the head if you come within forty miles of him. He thinks I deliberately said he ought to cut off his beard after he got me the P.O., and I've told him and told him and told him, and he acts like he just don't hear me. Papa-Daddy must of gone stone deaf."

"He picked a fine day to do it then," says Uncle Rondo, and before you could say "Jack Robinson" flew out in the yard.

What he'd really done, he'd drunk another bottle of that prescription. He does it every single Fourth of July as sure as shooting, and it's horribly expensive. Then he falls over in the hammock and snores. So he insisted on zigzagging right on out to the hammock, looking like a half-wit.

Papa-Daddy woke up with this horrible yell and right there without moving an inch he tried to turn Uncle Rondo against me. I heard every word he said. Oh, he told Uncle Rondo I didn't learn to read till I was eight years old and he didn't see how in the world I ever got the mail put up at the P.O., much less read it all, and he said if Uncle Rondo could only fathom the lengths he had gone to get me that job! And he said on the other hand he thought Stella-Rondo had a brilliant mind and deserved credit for getting out of town. All the time he was just lying there swinging as pretty as you please and looping out his beard, and poor Uncle Rondo was *pleading* with him to slow down the hammock, it was making him as dizzy as a witch to watch it. But that's what Papa-Daddy likes about a hammock. So Uncle Rondo was too dizzy to get turned against me for the time being. He's Mama's only brother and is a good case of a one-track mind. Ask anybody. A certified pharmacist.

Just then I heard Stella-Rondo raising the upstairs window. While she was married she got this peculiar idea that it's cooler with the windows shut and locked. So she has to raise the window before she can make a soul hear her outdoors.

So she raises the window and says, *"Oh!"* You would have thought she was mortally wounded.

Uncle Rondo and Papa-Daddy didn't even look up, but kept right on with what they were doing. I had to laugh.

I flew up the stairs and threw the door open! I says, "What in the wide world's the matter, Stella-Rondo? You mortally wounded?"

"No," she says, "I am not mortally wounded but I wish you would do me the favor of looking out that window there and telling me what you see."

So I shade my eyes and look out the window.

"I see the front yard," I says.

"Don't you see any human beings?" she says.

"I see Uncle Rondo trying to run Papa-Daddy out of the hammock," I says. "Nothing more. Naturally, it's so suffocating-hot in the house, with all the windows shut and locked, everybody who cares to stay in their right mind will have to go out and get in the hammock before the Fourth of July is over."

"Don't you notice anything different about Uncle Rondo?" asks Stella-Rondo.

"Why, no, except he's got on some terrible-looking flesh-colored contraption I wouldn't be found dead in, is all I can see," I says.

"Never mind, you won't be found dead in it, because it happens to be part of my trousseau, and Mr. Whitaker took several dozen photographs of me in it," says Stella-Rondo. "What on earth could Uncle Rondo *mean* by wearing part of my trousseau out in the broad open daylight without saying so much as 'Kiss my foot,' *knowing* I only got home this morning after my separation and hung my negligee up on the bathroom door, just as nervous as I could be?"

"I'm sure I don't know, and what do you expect me to do about it?" I says. "Jump out the window?"

"No, I expect nothing of the kind. I simply declare that Uncle Rondo looks like a fool in it, that's all," she says. "It makes me sick to my stomach."

"Well, he looks as good as he can," I says. "As good as anybody in reason could." I stood up for Uncle Rondo, please remember. And I said to Stella-Rondo, "I think I would do well not to criticize so freely if I were you and came home with a two-year-old child I had never said a word about, and no explanation whatever about my separation."

"I asked you the instant I entered this house not to refer one more time to my adopted child, and you gave me your word of honor you would not," was all Stella-Rondo would say, and started pulling out every one of her eyebrows with some cheap Kress tweezers.

So I merely slammed the door behind me and went down and made some green-tomato pickle. Somebody had to do it. Of course Mama had turned both the Negroes loose; she always said no earthly power could hold one anyway on the Fourth of July, so she wouldn't even try. It turned out that Jaypan fell in the lake and came within a very narrow limit of drowning.

So Mama trots in. Lifts up the lid and says, "H'm! Not very good for your Uncle Rondo in his precarious condition, I must say. Or poor little adopted Shirley-T. Shame on you!"

That made me tired. I says, "Well, Stella-Rondo had better thank her lucky stars it was her instead of me came trotting in with that very peculiar-looking child. Now if it had been me that trotted in from Illinois and brought a peculiar-looking child of two, I shudder to think of the reception I'd of got, much less controlled the diet of an entire family."

"But you must remember, Sister, that you were never married to Mr. Whitaker in the first place and didn't go up to Illinois to live," says Mama, shaking a spoon in my face. "If you had I would of been just as overjoyed to see you and your little adopted girl as I was to see Stella-Rondo, when you wound up with your separation and came on back home."

"You would not," I says.

"Don't contradict me, I would," says Mama.

But I said she couldn't convince me though she talked till she was blue in the face. Then I said, "Besides, you know as well as I do that that child is not adopted."

"She most certainly is adopted," says Mama, stiff as a poker.

I says, "Why, Mama, Stella-Rondo had her just as sure as anything in this world, and just too stuck up to admit it."

"Why, Sister," said Mama. "Here I thought we were going to have a pleasant Fourth of July, and you start right out not believing a word your own baby sister tells you!"

"Just like Cousin Annie Flo. Went to her grave denying the facts of life," I remind Mama.

"I told you if you ever mentioned Annie Flo's name I'd slap your face," says Mama, and slaps my face.

"All right, you wait and see," I says.

"I," says Mama, "I prefer to take my children's word for anything when it's humanly possible." You ought to see Mama, she weighs two hundred pounds and has real tiny feet.

Just then something perfectly horrible occurred to me.

"Mama," I says, "can that child talk?" I simply had to whisper! "Mama, I wonder if that child can be—you know—in any way? Do you realize," I says, "that she hasn't spoken one single, solitary word to a human being up to this minute? This is the way she looks," I says, and I looked like this.

Well, Mama and I just stood there and stared at each other. It was horrible!

"I remember well that Joe Whitaker frequently drank like a fish," says Mama. "I believed to my soul he drank *chemicals*." And without another word she marches to the foot of the stairs and calls Stella-Rondo.

"Stella-Rondo? O-o-o-o-o! Stella-Rondo!"

"What?" says Stella-Rondo from upstairs. Not even the grace to get up off the bed.

"Can that child of yours talk?" asks Mama.

Stella-Rondo says, "Can she what?"

"Talk! Talk!" says Mama. "Burdyburdyburdyburdy!"

So Stella-Rondo yells back, "Who says she can't talk?"

"Sister says so," says Mama.

"You didn't have to tell me, I know whose word of honor don't mean a thing in this house," says Stella-Rondo.

And in a minute the loudest Yankee voice I ever heard in my life yells out, "OE'm Pop-OE the Sailor-r-r Ma-a-an!" and then somebody jumps up and down in the upstairs hall. In another second the house would of fallen down.

"Not only talks, she can tap-dance!" calls Stella-Rondo. "Which is more than some people I won't name can do."

"Why, the little precious darling thing!" Mama says, so surprised. "Just as smart as she can be!" Starts talking baby talk right there. Then she turns on me. "Sister, you ought to be thoroughly ashamed! Run upstairs this instant and apologize to Stella-Rondo and Shirley-T."

"Apologize for what?" I says. "I merely wondered if the child was normal, that's all. Now that she's proved she is, why, I have nothing further to say."

But Mama just turned on her heel and flew out, furious. She ran right upstairs and hugged the baby. She believed it was adopted. Stella-Rondo hadn't done a thing but turn her against me from upstairs while I stood there helpless over the hot stove. So that made Mama, Papa-Daddy and the baby all on Stella-Rondo's side.

Next, Uncle Rondo.

I must say that Uncle Rondo has been marvelous to me at various times in the past and I was completely unprepared to be made to jump out of my skin, the way it turned out. Once Stella-Rondo did something perfectly horrible to him—broke a chain letter from Flanders Field—and he took the radio back he had given her and gave it to me. Stella-Rondo was furious! For six months we all had to call her Stella instead of Stella-Rondo, or she wouldn't answer. I always thought Uncle Rondo had all the brains of the entire family. Another time he sent me to Mammoth Cave, with all expenses paid.

But this would be the day he was drinking that prescription, the Fourth of July.

So at supper Stella-Rondo speaks up and says she thinks Uncle Rondo ought to try to eat a little something. So finally Uncle Rondo said he would try a little cold biscuits and ketchup, but that was all. So *she* brought it to him.

"Do you think it wise to disport with ketchup in Stella-Rondo's flesh-colored kimono?" I says. Trying to be considerate! If Stella-Rondo couldn't watch out for her trousseau, somebody had to.

"Any objections?" asks Uncle Rondo, just about to pour out all the ketchup.

"Don't mind what she says, Uncle Rondo," says Stella-Rondo. "Sister has been devoting this solid afternoon to sneering out my bedroom window at the way you look."

"What's that?" says Uncle Rondo. Uncle Rondo has got the most terrible temper in the world. Anything is liable to make him tear the house down if it comes at the wrong time.

So Stella-Rondo says, "Sister says, 'Uncle Rondo certainly does look like a fool in that pink kimono!' "

Do you remember who it was really said that?

Uncle Rondo spills out all the ketchup and jumps out of his chair and tears off the kimono and throws it down on the dirty floor and puts his foot on it. It had to be sent all the way to Jackson to the cleaners and re-pleated.

"So that's your opinion of your Uncle Rondo, is it?" he says. "I look like a fool, do I? Well, that's the last straw. A whole day in this house with nothing to do, and then to hear you come out with a remark like that behind my back!"

"I didn't say any such of a thing, Uncle Rondo," I says, "and I'm not saying who did, either. Why, I think you look all right. Just try to take care of yourself and not talk and eat at the same time," I says. "I think you better go lie down."

"Lie down my foot," says Uncle Rondo. I ought to of known by that he was fixing to do something perfectly horrible.

So he didn't do anything that night in the precarious state he was in—just played Casino with Mama and Stella-Rondo and Shirley-T. and gave Shirley-T. a nickel with a head on both sides. It tickled her nearly to death, and she called him "Papa." But at 6:30 A.M. the next morning, he threw a whole five-cent package of some unsold one-inch firecrackers from the store as hard as he could into my bedroom and they every one went off. Not one bad one in the string. Anybody else, there'd be one that wouldn't go off.

Well, I'm just terribly susceptible to noise of any kind, the doctor has always told me I was the most sensitive person he had ever seen in his whole life, and I was simply prostrated. I couldn't eat! People tell me they heard it as far as the cemetery, and old Aunt Jep Patterson, that had been holding her own so good, thought it was Judgment Day and she was going to meet her whole family. It's usually so quiet here.

And I'll tell you it didn't take me any longer than a minute to make up my mind what to do. There I was with the whole entire house on Stella-Rondo's side and turned against me. If I have anything at all I have pride.

So I just decided I'd go straight down to the P.O. There's plenty of room there in the back, I says to myself.

Well! I made no bones about letting the family catch on to what I was up to. I didn't try to conceal it.

The first thing they knew, I marched in where they were all playing Old Maid and pulled the electric oscillating fan out by the plug, and everything got real hot. Next I snatched the pillow I'd done the needlepoint on right off the davenport from behind Papa-Daddy. He went "Ugh!" I beat Stella-Rondo up the stairs and finally found my charm bracelet in her bureau drawer under a picture of Nelson Eddy.

"So that's the way the land lies," says Uncle Rondo. There he was, piecing on the ham. "Well, Sister, I'll be glad to donate my army cot if you got any place to set it up, providing you'll leave right this minute and let me get some peace." Uncle Rondo was in France.

"Thank you kindly for the cot and 'peace' is hardly the word I would select if I had to resort to firecrackers at 6:30 A.M. in a young girl's bedroom," I says back to him. "And as to where I intend to go, you seem to forget my position as postmistress of China Grove, Mississippi," I says. "I've always got the P.O."

Well, that made them all sit up and take notice.

I went out front and started digging up some four-o'clocks to plant around the P.O.

"Ah-ah-ah!" says Mama, raising the window. "Those happen to be my four-o'clocks. Everything planted in that star is mine. I've never known you to make anything grow in your life."

"Very well," I says. "But I take the fern. Even you, Mama, can't stand there and deny that I'm the one watered that fern. And I happen to know where I can send in a box top and get a packet of one thousand mixed seeds, no two the same kind, free."

"Oh, where?" Mama wants to know.

But I says, "Too late. You 'tend to your house, and I'll 'tend to mine. You hear things like that all the time if you know how to listen to the radio. Perfectly marvelous offers. Get anything you want free."

So I hope to tell you I marched in and got that radio, and they could of all bit a nail in two, especially Stella-Rondo, that it used to belong to, and she well knew she couldn't get it back, I'd sue for it like a shot. And I very politely took the sewing-machine motor I helped pay the most on to give Mama for Christmas back in 1929, and a good big calendar, with the first-aid remedies on it. The thermometer and the Hawaiian ukulele certainly were rightfully mine, and I stood on the step-ladder and got all my watermelon-rind preserves and every fruit and vegetable I'd put up, every jar. Then I began to pull the tacks out of the bluebird wall vases on the archway to the dining room.

"Who told you you could have those, Miss Priss?" says Mama, fanning as hard as she could.

"I bought 'em and I'll keep track of 'em," I says. "I'll tack 'em up one on each side the post-office window, and you can see 'em when you come to ask me for your mail, if you're so dead to see 'em."

"Not I! I'll never darken the door to that post office again if I live to be a hundred," Mama says. "Ungrateful child! After all the money we spent on you at the Normal."[1]

"Me either," says Stella-Rondo. "You can just let my mail lie there and *rot,* for all I care. I'll never come and relieve you of a single, solitary piece."

"I should worry," I says. "And who you think's going to sit down and write you all those big fat letters and postcards, by the way? Mr. Whitaker? Just because he was the only man ever dropped down in China Grove and you got him—unfairly—is he going to sit down and write you a lengthy correspondence after you come home giving no rhyme nor reason whatsoever for your separation and no explanation for the presence of that child? I may not have your brilliant mind, but I fail to see it."

So Mama says, "Sister, I've told you a thousand times that Stella-Rondo simply got homesick, and this child is far too big to be hers," and she says, "Now, why don't you all just sit down and play Casino?"

Then Shirley-T. sticks out her tongue at me in this perfectly horrible way. She has no more manners than the man in the moon. I told her she was going to cross her eyes like that some day and they'd stick.

"It's too late to stop me now," I says. "You should have tried that yesterday. I'm going to the P.O. and the only way you can possibly see me is to visit me there."

So Papa-Daddy says, "You'll never catch me setting foot in that post office, even if I should take a notion into my head to write a letter some place." He says, "I won't have you reachin' out of that little old window with a pair of shears and cuttin' off any beard of mine. I'm too smart for you!"

"We all are," says Stella-Rondo.

---

[1] i.e., normal school, which trained teachers, chiefly for the elementary grades.

But I said, "If you're so smart, where's Mr. Whitaker?"

So then Uncle Rondo says, "I'll thank you from now on to stop reading all the orders I get on postcards and telling everybody in China Grove what you think is the matter with them," but I says, "I draw my own conclusions and will continue in the future to draw them." I says, "If people want to write their inmost secrets on penny postcards, there's nothing in the wide world you can do about it, Uncle Rondo."

"And if you think we'll ever *write* another postcard you're sadly mistaken," says Mama.

"Cutting off your nose to spite your face then," I says. "But if you're all determined to have no more to do with the U.S. mail, think of this: What will Stella-Rondo do now, if she wants to tell Mr. Whitaker to come after her?"

"Wah!" says Stella-Rondo. I knew she'd cry. She had a conniption fit right there in the kitchen.

"It will be interesting to see how long she holds out," I says. "And now—I am leaving."

"Good-bye," says Uncle Rondo.

"Oh, I declare," says Mama, "to think that a family of mine should quarrel on the Fourth of July, or the day after, over Stella-Rondo leaving old Mr. Whitaker and having the sweetest little adopted child! It looks like we'd all be glad!"

"Wah!" says Stella-Rondo, and has a fresh conniption fit.

"*He* left *her*—you mark my words," I says. "That's Mr. Whitaker. I know Mr. Whitaker. After all, I knew him first. I said from the beginning he'd up and leave her. I foretold every single thing that's happened."

"Where did he go?" asks Mama.

"Probably to the North Pole, if he knows what's good for him," I says.

But Stella-Rondo just bawled and wouldn't say another word. She flew to her room and slammed the door.

"Now look what you've gone and done, Sister," says Mama. "You go apologize."

"I haven't got time, I'm leaving," I says.

"Well, what are you waiting around for?" asks Uncle Rondo.

So I just picked up the kitchen clock and marched off, without saying "Kiss my foot" or anything, and never did tell Stella-Rondo good-bye.

There was a girl going along on a little wagon right in front.

"Girl," I says, "come help me haul these things down the hill, I'm going to live in the post office."

Took her nine trips in her express wagon. Uncle Rondo came out on the porch and threw her a nickel.

And that's the last I've laid eyes on any of my family or my family laid eyes on me for five solid days and nights. Stella-Rondo may be telling the most horrible tales in the world about Mr. Whitaker, but I haven't heard them. As I tell everybody, I draw my own conclusions.

But oh, I like it here. It's ideal, as I've been saying. You see, I've got everything cater-cornered, the way I like it. Hear the radio? All the war news. Radio, sewing machine, book ends, ironing board and that great big piano lamp—peace, that's what I like. But-ter-bean vines planted all along the front where the strings are.

Of course, there's not much mail. My family are naturally the main people in China Grove, and if they prefer to vanish from the face of the earth, for all the mail they get or the mail they write, why, I'm not going to open my mouth. Some of the folks here in town are taking up for me and some turned against me. I know which is which. There are always people who will quit buying stamps just to get on the right side of Papa-Daddy.

But here I am, and here I'll stay. I want the world to know I'm happy.

And if Stella-Rondo should come to me this minute, on bended knees, and *attempt* to explain the incidents of her life with Mr. Whitaker, I'd simply put my fingers in both my ears and refuse to listen.

1941

Robert Rauschenberg
Estate
oil and printer's ink, 1963
(Philadelphia Museum of Art; Given by the Friends of the Philadelphia Museum of Art)

The Literature Since Midcentury 1945 –Present

Contemporary Literature

The course of American literature at midcentury was radically affected by World War II. Randall Jarrell's "The Death of the Ball Turret Gunner," Robert Lowell's "Memories of West Street and Lepke," Gwendolyn Brooks' *Negro Hero*, Norman Mailer's *The Naked and the Dead*, and Joseph Heller's *Catch-22* are but a few of the major literary responses to the war which drove American literature in new directions. However, the events and developments of the aftermath of the war transformed the literature in even more substantial ways.

One such development was the new-found confidence and clarity with which the United States saw its position in the world. Confidence came with victory and with pushing the Depression into the annals of history. Clarity was achieved as well when it became abundantly clear after the war that the United States was a global superpower, and clear, too, who the nation's enemy was: the Soviet Union and communism. Confidence and clarity together generated fresh forms of patriotism and a new resolve to defend democracy, throughout the world if necessary. When these postwar resolves led to McCarthyism in the 1950s and hastened the nation's costly commitments to war in Korea and later in Vietnam, they proved to be disastrous and regrettable. When they challenged the nation to live up to its best ideals, including those expressed in the Declaration of Independence and the Constitution, major changes came about in the workplace and in political and civil rights. American writers throughout this period (Ralph Ellison and Arthur Miller, for example, at the beginning; Tim O'Brien, Michael S. Harper, and Leslie Marmon Silko, for example, currently) have seen both sides of the postwar national resolve and have created a literature charged with the tensions inherent in this circumstance.

The changed status of immigrants, indigenous minorities (obviously Native Americans, but after four hundred years of comparable attenuated citizenship African Americans have a claim to this category, too), and women has also energized American literature in fresh ways. The after-years of World War II produced major shifts in immigration policies, creating an immigrant population that was no longer arriving mainly from Europe. As many thousands of people were arriving from all of Asia and Latin America, as well as Mexico and the Caribbean, American literature gained new stories and tropes, often expressed in fresh comminglings of English with other languages. In the past fifty years, Native Americans strengthened their ties to the rural, sometimes sacred, spaces which writers like N. Scott Momaday and Louis Erdrich limned, yet founded major urban communities which would inspire writers including Wendy Rose and Susan Power. African Americans entered into a rich period of literary production, marked at first by major contributions from Ralph Ellison, James Baldwin, Gwendolyn Brooks and Robert Hayden. New formations of urban black America, created by the great migration of the World War II years, prompted new themes, characters, and settings, but also new interpretations of the African American past. The civil rights advances had a similar effect: Toni Morrison, Ernest Gaines, and Alice Walker are among the writers who emerged during the most momentous civil rights struggles to write of how a certain history vibrates in the contemporary African American scene. American women writers have always had a footing, though not always an equal one, in the national literary enterprise. Social change for American women in the last fifty years helped create a culture in which women writers are taken far more seriously, and not just read by widely taught. In contrast to only a few decades ago, no one today is surprised when a woman wins a major literary prize, or when a scholarly study of women writers garners awards.

American literature also developed in striking ways because the literature as a whole came to be seen differently and taught differently in the last fifty years, certainly in the last thirty of them. American literature has gained parity with British literature in many curriculums, including those of colleges and universities. Literature faculties, here and abroad, have determined that they must include American literature specialists, including scholars of Native American, Asian American, and African American literatures. Starting in the late 1940s, colleges and universities began to develop the first American Studies programs, in which new, sometimes interdisciplinary approaches to the study of American literature were forged. The era has thus been the one in which *both* English departments and American Studies programs, frequently with differing approaches and concerns, have generated the academic discussion of American literature.

The generation of midcentury writers (or "since midcentury" writers) is usefully seen as comprising two groups: the "first postwar generation" of writers who had published before the war (e.g., William Faulkner) or were poised to publish right after the war (Saul Bellow, Elizabeth Bishop, Robert Lowell, etc.); and the "second postwar generation" of writers who were younger and who started publishing in the 1960s or

1970s. This latter group was "postwar" in multiple senses of the term: some writers had seen all three midcentury wars (WW II, Korea, Vietnam), not just one. Both generations of midcentury writers deserve a mention in their own right.

The First Postwar Generation

World War II was in many ways "bad for writing," William Faulkner wrote his agent in 1944. Impelled in part by the magnitude of the war and its political implications, and in part by the horror of the Holocaust that accompanied it, the twentieth century's second "Great War" continued to dominate the world consciousness for nearly two decades after its conclusion. As it turned out, however, the cataclysmic event that hastened its end—the dropping of the first atomic bombs—deepened the impact of the war and reinforced a brutal lesson: sooner or later, nations will do whatever their weapons make possible. For several younger writers and few older ones, the influence of the war was direct. Saul Bellow served in the merchant marine, John Cheever and Normal Mailer in the United States Army, Ernest Hemingway once again as a war correspondent. Having failed to get a commission, Faulkner spent considerable time in Hollywood, working on screenplays about Nazi spies or great Allied heroes.

Once the war was over, however, and veterans began coming home hoping to find jobs or to go to college, they carried with them stories of their generation's great adventure. Literary appropriation of the war began in the 1940s, with John Hersey's *Hiroshima* (1946), James Gould Gozzens's *Guard of Honor* (1948), and Norman Mailer's *The Naked and the Dead* (1948); and it continued through the 1950s with Herman Wouk's *The Caine Mutiny* (1951), to the 1960s with Joseph Heller's *Catch-22* (1961), and the 1970s with Thomas Pynchon's *Gravity's Rainbow* (1973). A few works, including Harriette Arnow's *The Dollmaker* (1954), focused on the "home front," as it came to be called. Marked by exuberance as well as irony, these works specialize in humor darkened by anger, a tone that would come to mark much of the literature (as well as the"postmodern" visual arts and theater) of the second half of the twentieth century.

Some of the fiction written after World War II echoes the disillusionment that floated in the wake of World War I, but it seldom matches it. Before long, writers like Norman Mailer began looking back nostalgically on the sense of unity and purpose fostered by the war, because divisions that had remained submerged during the war effort began to surface almost before the victory celebrations stopped. Strikes and slowed production were rampant; women and other marginalized citizens felt betrayed when they were expected to step aside and let returning servicemen replace them in the work force. Only for African Americans, did World War II mark a clear, if modest turning point. In February, 1945, Richard Wright's *Black Boy* became a Book-of-the-Month Club selection. In 1947, Jackie Robinson, the son of sharecroppers and the grandson of slaves, signed a contract with the Brooklyn Dodgers organization and became the first black man to cross the color line in professional sports. The next year President Truman integrated the United States armed services in which African Americans had fought so valiantly in segregated units. In 1954, the Supreme Court struck down segregation in the public schools and Martin Luther King, Jr., organized a successful bus boycott in Montgomery, Alabama.

More powerful, however, than either the disappointments or the reforms of American life in the late 1940s and early 1950s was the strong sense of conformity that rolled across the land. The nation's economy remained generally strong, and despite frustrations, expectations remained high. This emerging sense of national unity was bolstered by a series of aggressive acts by the Soviet Union. Having already occupied Poland, the Soviet Union overran Hungry in April 1947 and a year later, Czechoslovakia. Winston Churchill warned that an "iron curtain" had descended, separating East from West, thus reinforcing the dominant centripetal forces at work in the United States between 1945 and 1960. In an essay called "This Age of Conformity" (1954), Irving Howe described the tendency of writers to endorse America's "claim to a unique and immaculate destiny" as dangerous. But unity and its corollary, conformity, remained the most powerful forces of the age, particularly during the Eisenhower years (1953–1961). David Reisman's sociological study, *The Lonely Crowd* (1950)—which traced the rise of "other-directed people," people whose actions are based less on internal convictions than on responses to "the signals" provided by their peers—became a classic of the age, anticipating Sloan Wilson's novel *The Man in the Gray Flannel Suit* (1955), as well as William S. Whyte's sociological analysis *The Organization Man* (1956). Such insights about image and its manipulation have become standard "principles" of political campaigns since the late 1970s.

With the rise of conformity came clear political dangers, as Senator Joseph McCarthy (Republican, Wisconsin) promptly began to prove. Between February 1950, when he made his first dramatic accusations and December 1954 when he was censured by the Senate, McCarthy headed an anti-Communist inquisition that dominated the American political scene as few events have. In the process, he accused hundreds of people—composers like Aaron Copland, writers like Howard Fast and Lillian Hellman—of being either Communists, Communist sympathizers, or Communist dupes. "McCarthyism" tested the nation's commitment to civil liberties, its tolerance for dissent, and its respect for freedom of conscience. Among the direct literary responses to the ordeal, the most notable was Arthur Miller's play *The Crucible* (1953). Despite "McCarthyism" and the alarming pressures it embodied, however, the 1950s still managed to produce an impressive literary culture and a poetry of a quiet formality, as well as a lively counterculture, led by the "beat generation."

Following such poets as Allen Ginsberg and Lawrence Ferlinghetti and such prose writers as Jack Kerouac, the beats made the City Lights Book Store in the North Beach area of San Francisco famous as both a gathering place and publishing location. College students across the country listened to recordings of Ginsberg reading "Howl," although one of the striking features of the counterculture of the 1950s was the extent to which the considerable political potential of its music, fiction, and poetry remained quiescent until the next decade.

The generation of poets who flourished after World War II—poets as diverse as Robert Lowell and Elizabeth Bishop, John Berryman and John Ashbery, Ginsberg and A. R. Ammons, Adrienne Rich and James Wright—had one thing in common: they had to define themselves against the achievements of their modernist predecessors. American poetics and aesthetics had been broadly defined by the first generation of twentieth-century American poets. T. S. Eliot and Ezra Pound had made American poetry international and had established free verse as the modernist mode. Robert Frost had established a national poetry sturdily American in syntax and local accent, while William Carlos Williams had created an innovative, "industrial age" poetry of hard-edged realism. Langston Hughes, among other writers of the Harlem

Renaissance, had claimed poetic value for the African American vernacular and urban culture. Wallace Stevens, possibly the most elusive of the modernists, had brought philosophic skepticism into American poetry and had found an ironic and syntactically elaborate meditative style for his subject. The poets after World War II seem, in retrospect, more American and less European than most of these poetic forebearers. With the rise of America as a world power, fewer poets believed in the inferiority of American literature to Europe's.

The dominant European influence on the poets of the first post–World War II generation was not a poet, but the psychoanalyst Sigmund Freud. Freud's model for the organization of the inner life (the superego, the id, and the ego) emphasized dark and unruly drives, driven underground only to erupt disastrously in violence or madness. Such a model appealed to a generation who had just experienced World War II. But more significantly, many poets of this generation underwent psychoanalysis; the work of their therapy, recalling influential incidents and fantasies of childhood and youth, soon appeared in their poetry. Theodore Roethke, Randall Jarrell, John Berryman, Robert Lowell, Anne Sexton, and Sylvia Plath all made poetry out of the family constellation described in psychoanalytic terms. Lowell's *Life Studies* (1959) was an anatomy of the family; Berryman's *77 Dream Songs* showed the id (renamed Henry) in full force; and Plath's "Daddy" (1966) became the most famous poem exposing the dark underside of the family romance. "Confessions" were made not only on the analyst's couch, but also on the printed page.

If Freud was the chief external influence on American poetry after 1945, there was nonetheless a continuing influence of foreign poetry as well. The cross-fertilization of American literature that took place in this generation imported Arthur Rimbaud (through John O'Hara and Ashbery), Rainer Maria Rilke and Herman Hesse (through Jarrell and Wright), Pablo Neruda and other South American poets (through Robert Bly and Elizabeth Bishop). Although poets after 1945 interested themselves in foreign poetry, they did not, in the manner of Eliot and Pound, adopt European modes of speech. Pound's archaisms and Eliot's anglicisms were purged from the new American poetry. The foreign poets were silently absorbed into the American vernacular; only the new structures of lyric and new kinds of imagery made apparent the presence of European, South American or Asian poetic influence. There was very little attempt at an international speaking voice; even when the perspective of the poet was global as in Lowell or Ginsberg. That perspective was expressed in indigenous American tones.

And the tones became increasingly varied. Whitman, in the nineteenth century, had represented himself as the channel for the "varied carols" of America. He implied a hope that one day the silent voices would be able to speak for themselves, and in the second half of this century they have begun to fulfill his prophecy. Through Ginsberg, for example, the American immigrant voice entered American poetry in a powerful way. In his long sequence "Kaddish," Ginsberg presented the life of his mother, a Jewish immigrant from Russia, as typical of the unbearable strain put on the psyche by such a violent break in experience. Ginsberg's rich social documentation marked a new era in American lyric poetry; in "Howl" and the volumes that followed it in quick succession, Jews, beatniks, war protesters, and urban gays and lesbians all appeared in vivid, believable form.

In 1949, Gwendolyn Brooks received the Pulitzer Prize for poetry. This adknowledgment of an African-American woman's voice and subject matter marked a new appreciation for diversity in American poetry and a reaction against the modernist impersonality of voice. This new appreciation suggested a shift from the conventional view of American poetry as a descendant of English poetry, to one that embraced the wider view that American poetry was also the poetry of the first inhabitants of this country. The resurgence of Native American poetry as a source of inspiration, especially in the work of Gary Snyder and Joy Harjo, has been an impetus to Native Americans to claim their own written literature and to advance it.

An increased regional diversity also entered American poetry after World War II as, for the first time, a strong poetic school was founded by Ferlinghetti and others on the West Coast. Universities increasingly became the base for literary journals and poetry readings and writers-in-residence. T. S. Eliot's occasional visits from England drew huge throngs. Frost spoke as the official poet at the 1960 presidential inauguration of John F. Kennedy. In support of various political causes, poets including Ginsberg and Denise Levertov and Adrienne Rich also drew large audiences all across the country. Poetry no longer seemed a monopoly of New England.

Various "schools" of poetry also formed. The "New York school" (including John Ashbery, Frank O'Hara, and Kenneth Koch) had close relationships with painters, especially the abstract expressionists. They turned inward toward a spontaneous rendering of imaginative moments, in contrast to both the political fierceness of Pound and the elegiac solemnity of Eliot. A complicated and more elusive school was that of the "Black Mountain poets," headquartered at the avant-garde Black Mountain College in North Carolina where the poet Charles Olson was rector. The best-known members of the group, besides Olson, were Robert Creeley, Robert Duncan, and Denise Levertov; their progeny include today's "language poets" and their more traditional exemplar, the metaphysical poet Jorie Graham. Although associated with such experimenters as the dancer Merce Cunningham, composer John Cage, and painters including Franz Kline, Josef Albers, and Robert Rauschenberg, all the Black Mountain poets derived from Pound and his method of historical collage: One fragment of historical information is placed against another, over and over, until a jagged accumulation is achieved. The much more popular Beats forged a poetry characterized by a linguistic freedom that included words commonly considered obscene. Perhaps more disturbing to the common reader was the open admission in poetry, by Ginsberg and others, of the use of drugs, of gay experiences, of promiscuity in sexual life, and of disillusionment with politics, the United States government, and its policies.

The Second Postwar Generation and Vietnam

The years between the assassination of John F. Kennedy (November 1963) and the final withdrawal of American troops from Vietnam (April 1975) unmoored everyone living in the United States, especially the thoughtful young. Allen J. Matusow called his history of these convulsive years *The Unraveling of America.* In an essay published in July 1984, literary critic Benjamin DeMott referred to them as "the killer decade."

Such assessments of American society of the late 1960s and early 1970s may now strike readers as excessive, particularly in light of the political and social reactions that followed; the marshalling of the "great, silent majority" against protest during the Nixon era; the brief resurgence of liberalism during the post-Watergate administration of Jimmy Carter; the illusory prosperity and apparent unity of conservatives during the Reagan-Bush era; the confusion about policy and the congressional stalemates of the Clinton administration.

Many forces worked to shift the United States from the heyday of hippies to that of yuppies and beyond. Social protests against the Vietnam war, simultaneously with movements to expand rights for women and racial and sexual minorities, left protesters exhausted and, in many cases, with no fixed political or ideological values. Self-absorption slowly replaced social engagement and by the 1980s, "careerism" occupied even members of the counterculture. By the 1990s the pursuit of money, power, and status became an increasingly global phenomenon in a world culture dominated by multinational corporations and American media. Even the counterculture of the 1960s and 1970s had celebrated self-gratification, however. In indulging individual needs and desires (for "Drugs, Sex, and Rock 'n Roll" as Eric Bogosian named one his monologues), the counterculture did not stop to wonder whether unbridling the erotic will might reinforce a similar unbridling of the economic will, and with it the will to power.

As the millennium approaches, major issues—the Equal Rights Amendment, genetic cloning, artificial intelligence, and the spread of AIDS—have fueled many a debate, but never again have the young people of America become as much engaged as in the civil rights movement and the Vietnam protests. And similarly, no single overriding issue presently engages the imaginations of the nation's writers.

As the cultural situation in America has changed, writers play a diminished role in the public arena. Writers continue to come from every region (Philip Levine from Detroit; Michael S. Harper from Brooklyn; Leslie Marmon Silko from Albuquerque; Alice Walker from Eatonton, Georgia.) Sexually and racially, the American literary scene is more varied than ever before. For the first time in history, women are publishing much of the most interesting work. Novelist Toni Morrison became the first African American woman to win the Nobel Prize for literature. And countering the trend away from public engagement, she has since edited timely and provocative anthologies of essays responding to widely televised, racially charged events such as the Clarence Thomas-Anita Hill hearings and the O. J. Simpson trial. Writers continue to show concern for a large and varied set of social and political issues, but no writer of the 1970s, 1980s, and 1990s, except perhaps Morrison, has played the social role that H. L. Mencken played in the 1920s, that John Dos Passos played in the 1930s, or that Norman Mailer, James Baldwin, and Allen Ginsberg played in the 1960s.

Related to this diminished role is a deepening anxiety about literature's increasing marginality. Nothing in public discourse, including the direct challenges of Norman Mailer and the essays of Toni Morrison, has effectively countered the impression that reporters have replaced writers as primary witnesses to the disorders and adventures of contemporary history. The interpenetration of literature with other media, including movies, television, and music, continues to accelerate, especially in stage performances that blend the rehearsed and the improvised in music, dance, poetry, prose, and drama. But such "impure" literary forms reflect more than a loss of faith in literature; the influence of contemporary music (improvised and composed) can be felt in the looser, freer structures of much contemporary fiction and poetry. Such "voices" are meant to be heard, not simply read.

As the lines between poetry and prose, fiction and nonfiction continue to blur, there has been a resurgence of nonfictional forms such as the memoir. *Angela's Ashes,* for example, Frank McCourt's account of growing up poor in Limerick, Ireland, won the 1996 Pulitzer Prize for biography. Another prose form which has become popular is the kind of highly personal, imaginative reporting represented by Wayne Koestenbaum in his book on Jacqueline Kennedy Onassis, *Jackie Under My Skin;* or the meditative memoirs written by Annie Dillard, *Pilgrim at Tinker Creek,* and Kathleen Norris's *The Cloister Walk,* both related to the transcendentalist tradition of Emerson and Thoreau. Courses in literary nonfiction have proliferated in university literature and writing programs, even as self-conscious experimentation in fiction (like that practiced by John Barth and Robert Coover) has lost ground in recent years. Writers are no longer so certain that literary realism can master social realities by transmuting them into novels. These signs of uncertainty about the cultural role of art and the vocation of the artist are underscored by advances in telecommunications and digital technology during the last several years. And recent cutbacks in funding generated by congressional opposition to both the National Endowment for the Arts and the National Endowment for the Humanities have underscored the sense that writers, like other artists, are increasingly at the mercy of an American cultural marketplace dominated by commercial electronic media.

One of the dominant, disturbing themes of the fiction of the last two decades, that of impassivity, of internal blankness that merges with interpersonal blankness, of selves as coexisting deserts, draws support from philosophy as well as history. Several contemporary philosophers, Michael Foucault and Jacques Derrida, for example, reinforce the wrenching experiences of the Vietnam era in at least one important way: They extend the web of suspicion to include language and art as well as human feeling. Henry James thought of the artist as occupying a "sacred office," and he could and did speak of the terrible possibility of betraying that office. In much contemporary writing, such responsiveness is viewed as another dubious bourgeois creation of the self-interested, sentimental and mindlessly optimistic nineteenth century. In Joan Didion's novel *Play It As It Lays* (1970), for instance, we encounter a character so completely modern that nothing moves her. Asked what she wants, she replies, "Nothing"; asked what she feels, she again replies, "Nothing." Such characters are skeptical of everything but they are most deeply skeptical of the notion that human beings ever believed or doubted passionately, ever felt wonder before the mysterious, or ever experienced sympathy, compassion, or love. In such fiction, all human values are threatened, and the capacity, or even the desire, for the human feeling of wonder is imperiled.

Still within the diverse range of recent American fiction there are signs that reports of the death of feeling and vulnerability are exaggerated. Such signs appear in the stories of Maxine Hong Kingston, Leslie Silko, and Alice Walker, for whom heritage and race and gender have continued to bear heavily on individual existence; in the works of Reginald McKnight and Raymond Carver; and Tim O'Brien's "The Things They Carried," a wrenching story about Vietnam. Similarly, a range of literary works from Melvin Dixon's poem "Heartbeats" to Tony Kushner's two-part theatrical epic "Angels in America" have given vivid imaginative life to the AIDS epidemic and have extended empathy toward those infected and those who care for and about them.

Irony, the predominant tone of all the postmodern arts, still dominates the tone of contemporary fiction, just as it dominated the inward-turning and ironic stance of poetry in the 1970s. Such writers clearly remain skeptical about the possibility of bringing imaginative form to the damaged lives they see around them. Yet they continue to draw on diverse traditions and to find in those traditions new creative strengths. Oral history, myth, folk tale, and legend are strong forces in the fiction of Silko and Morrison, both of whom are sensitive to states of consciousness more primal than Western rationalism. Although most contemporary writers no longer adhere to the grand ideologies of Freudian analysis and Marxist doctrine, many are on friendly terms with science and technology, and attitude presaged by Thomas Pynchon. Minority writers continue to explore their own indigenous traditions, often juxtaposing generational responses to change as in Walker's short story, "Everyday Use," and in poems such as Wendy Rose's "Vanishing Point: Urban Indian," Albert Rios's "Mi Abuelo" (my grandfather), Cathy Song's "The Lost Sister," and Rita Dove's "Possum."

In an increasingly fragmented, decentered world, contemporary American literature continues to reveal the moral authority of those at the margins. In a related development, American literary culture continues to become more international. Fresh attention is being paid to writers representing not just the myriad cultures within the United States (Stuart Dybek's Polish America, the South of Bobbie Ann Mason and Andrew Hudgins, Li-Young Lee's Indonesian/Chinese America, etc.) but also more global sources. In one development, the literary culture is now far more attentive to the various literatures in English throughout the world: writers like Chinua Achebe and Wole Soyinka from Africa, R. K. Narayan and Salman Rushdie from India, and Derek Walcott and Jamaica Kincaid from the Caribbean are now thoroughly a part of our reading and literary studies. In another development, American literary culture is more and more aware of the eastern European writers. Philip Roth, for example, as general editor of the excellent series, "Writers from the Other Europe," has helped bring writers of eastern Europe such as Milan Kundera and Czeslaw Milosz into the literary world of the United States. And then there are the Latin American writers whom we have been reading avidly for at least the past two decades: Jorge Amado, Jorge Luis Borges, and Gabriel Garcia Marquez (just to name three) are now as important to American literature as are any writers from England or Europe.

American literature in our time is becoming both different and more American. We really cannot talk any more just about the lives of the expatriates or of the side careers of some writers as translators as the most authentic evidence of the international dimensions to American writing. Just as we hear different languages, different voices, on the streets, in buses and stores, in the walkways of universities and malls, so, too, do we "hear" a new American literature full of fresh words, new musicalities, new takes on the literary traditions of Old and New World English. This last point is perhaps the most important: the new writers, wherever they might be from here or abroad, are magnificiently conversant with the traditions of literature in English. If they sound different, it is not because they have not been exposed to the literature, but rather because they have a different respect for it. American contemporary writers already share a special history. While theirs is not the first generation to reside in a culturally diverse America, arguably theirs is the first to embody that diversity and to produce a pluralistic literary vision and practice.

Although our contemporary American writers clearly bear witness to the pain and confusion of recent history, and to the threat that history presents to our literature and to our capacity for human feeling, such writers also bear witness and testify to the promise of contemporary life. In the sheer diversity of their voices, they open American literature to new perspectives and heritages. They present for our inspection new models of human possibility. They seek to reflect our shared life and our inner lives—however wonderful or terrible. And as writers have always done, they revitalize for this generation the language and imaginative forms by which we know, and name, ourselves.

Theodore Roethke
1908–1963

Theodore Roethke's childhood intimacy with the world of his father's greenhouse provided a rich vein of poetic material, from which his most individual poems issued. American poets (except for Whitman) have traditionally been bookish; the soil has been relatively absent from our verse. Roethke knew swamp and soil, cuttings and roots, the dark life of plants in the earth before their time for blossoming. He knew, too, the authoritarian structure of the greenhouse, where his German grandfather and his father ruled with an iron hand; there he was helpless, small, frightened, "the lost son."

The voice of the child he was is Roethke's most notable poetic invention (imitated, since he invented it, by poets as various as Robert Lowell, Anne Sexton, and Sylvia Plath). Of course, Roethke did not entirely invent this child voice; he learned it in part from William Blake, whose *Songs of Innocence* first memorably introduced the voice of the child into poetry in English. But Roethke's child has, so to speak, studied Freud and discovered his unconscious. His preconscious language is full of brilliant linguistic and poetic invention; its quick, elusive rhythms and slippery sounds convey the daring investigations of the bewildered child.

Roethke's greenhouse poems occur in the volume *The Lost Son* (1948). His volumes subsequent to *Praise to the End!* (1952) and *The Waking* (1953) became both more formal (with many imitations of William Butler Yeats and T. S. Eliot) and more prolix in their use of free verse, while still containing some lyrics of terse power, especially some short bitter poems about confinement for mental illness.

Roethke was born in Saginaw, Michigan, and educated at the University of Michigan; he spent most of his teaching life (1948–1963) at the University of Washington in Seattle, where he served as mentor to many younger poets and creative writing students, including James Wright. Roethke's successive breakdowns and recurrent alcoholism made his life increasingly difficult until his early death in his fifties.

His influence on the emergence of West Coast writing was a powerful one, and his advocacy of formal prosody (both in his own work and in his teaching) was one of the countermeasures against the domination by free verse of the American poetic scene. Though he was a large, powerfully built man, the truest self for which he found a voice was the small soul that trembled in childhood before the mysteries of nature.

Further Reading:

R. J. Mills, Jr., *Theodore Roethke*, 1963.
A. Stein, ed., *Theodore Roethke: Essays on the Poetry*, 1965.
A. Seagar, *The Glass House: The Life of Theodore Roethke*, 1968.
J. LaBelle, *The Echoing Wood of Theodore Roethke*, 1976.

H. Williams, *"The Edge Is What I Have": Theodore Roethke and After*, 1977.
J. Parini, *Theodore Roethke: An American Romantic*, 1979.
P. Balakian, *Theodore Roethke's Far Fields*, 1989.
D. Bogen, *Theodore Roethke and the Writing Process*, 1991.

Text:
Collected Poems, 1966.

Cuttings

Sticks-in-a-drowse droop over sugary loam,
Their intricate stem-fur dries;
But still the delicate slips keep coaxing up water;
The small cells bulge;

One nub of growth   5
Nudges a sand-crumb loose,
Pokes through a musty sheath
Its pale tendrilous horn.
1948

Cuttings
(later)

This urge, wrestle, resurrection of dry sticks,
Cut stems struggling to put down feet,
What saint strained so much,
Rose on such lopped limbs to a new life?

I can hear, underground, that sucking and sobbing,   5
In my veins, in my bones I feel it,—
The small waters sweeping upward,
The tight grains parting at last.
When sprouts break out,

Slippery as fish,
I quail, lean to beginnings, sheath-wet.   10
1948

My Papa's Waltz

The whiskey on your breath
Could make a small boy dizzy;
But I hung on like death:
Such waltzing was not easy.

We romped until the pans   5
Slid from the kitchen shelf;
My mother's countenance
Could not unfrown itself.

The hand that held my wrist
Was battered on one knuckle: 10
At every step you missed
My right ear scraped a buckle.

You beat time on my head
With a palm caked hard by dirt,
Then waltzed me off to bed   15
Still clinging to your shirt.
1948

The Lost Son

1. The Flight

At Woodlawn I heard the dead cry:
I was lulled by the slamming of iron,
A slow drip over stones,
Toads brooding wells.
All the leaves stuck out their tongues;   5
I shook the softening chalk of my bones,
Saying,
Snail, snail, glister me forward,
Bird, soft-sigh me home,

Worm, be with me.   10
This is my hard time.

Fished in an old wound,
The soft pond of repose;
Nothing nibbled my line,
Not even the minnows came.   15

Sat in an empty house
Watching shadows crawl,
Scratching.
There was one fly.

Voice, come out of the silence.   20
Say something.
Appear in the form of a spider
Or a moth beating the curtain.

Tell me:
Which is the way I take;   25
Out of what door do I go,
Where and to whom?

      Dark hollows said, lee to the wind,
      The moon said, back of an eel,
      The salt said, look by the sea,
      Your tears are not enough praise,   30
      You will find no comfort here,
      In the kingdom of bang and blab.

      Running lightly over spongy ground,
      Past the pasture of flat stones,
      The three elms,   35
      The sheep strewn on a field,
      Over a rickety bridge
      Toward the quick-water, wrinkling and rippling.

      Hunting along the river,   40
      Down among the rubbish, the bug-riddled foliage,
      By the muddy pond-edge, by the bog-holes,
      By the shrunken lake, hunting, in the heat of summer.

The shape of a rat?
      It's bigger than that.   45
      It's less than a leg
      And more than a nose,
      Just under the water
      It usually goes.

It is soft like a mouse?   50
Can it wrinkle its nose?
Could it come in the house
On the tips of its toes?

   Take the skin of a cat
   And the back of an eel,
   Then roll them in grease,—   55
   That's the way it would feel.

   It's sleek as an otter
   With wide webby toes
   Just under the water   60
   It usually goes.

2. The Pit

Where do the roots go?
   Look down under the leaves.
Who put the moss there?
   These stones have been here too long.   65
Who stunned the dirt into noise?
   Ask the mole, he knows.
I feel the slime of a wet nest.
   Beware Mother Mildew.
Nibble again, fish nerves.   70

3. The Gibber

At the wood's mouth,
By the cave's door,
I listened to something
I had heard before.

Dogs of the groin   75
Barked and howled,
The sun was against me,
The moon would not have me.

The weeds whined,
The snakes cried,   80
The cows and briars
Said to me: Die.

What a small song. What slow clouds. What dark water.
Hath the rain a father? All the caves are ice. Only the snow's here.
I'm cold. I'm cold all over. Rub me in father and mother.   85

Fear was my father, Father Fear.
His look drained the stones.

> What gliding shape
> Beckoning through halls,
> Stood poised on the stair,   90
> Fell dreamily down?

> From the mouths of jugs
> Perched on many shelves,
> I saw substance flowing
> That cold morning.   95

> Like a slither of eels
> That watery cheek
> As my own tongue kissed
> My lips awake.

Is this the storm's heart? The ground is unstilling itself.   100
My veins are running nowhere. Do the bones cast out their fire?
Is the seed leaving the old bed? These buds are live as birds.
Where, where are the tears of the world?
Let the kisses resound, flat like a butcher's palm;
Let the gestures freeze; our doom is already decided.   105
All the windows are burning! What's left of my life?
I want the old rage, the lash of primordial milk!
Goodbye, goodbye, old stones, the time-order is going,
I have married my hands to perpetual agitation,
I run, I run to the whistle of money.   110

> Money money money
> Water water water

> How cool the grass is.
> Has the bird left?
> The stalk still sways.   115
> Has the worm a shadow?
> What do the clouds say?

> These sweeps of light undo me.
> Look, look, the ditch is running white!
> I've more veins than a tree!   120
> Kiss me, ashes, I'm falling through a dark swirl.

4. The Return

> The way to the boiler was dark,
> Dark all the way,

Over slippery cinders
Through the long greenhouse.   125

The roses kept breathing in the dark.
They had many mouths to breathe with.
My knees made little winds underneath
Where the weeds slept.

There was always a single light   130
Swinging by the fire-pit,
Where the fireman pulled out roses,
The big roses, the big bloody clinkers.

Once I stayed all night.
Snow.   135
The light in the morning came slowly over the white
There were many kinds of cool
Air.
Then came steam.

Pipe-knock.   140

Scurry of warm over small plants.
Ordnung! ordnung![1]
Papa is coming!

A fine haze moved off the leaves;
Frost melted on far panes;   145
The rose, the chrysanthemum turned toward the light.
Even the hushed forms, the bent yellow weeds
Moved in a slow up-sway.

5. "It Was Beginning Winter"

It was beginning winter,
An in-between time,   150
The landscape still party brown:
The bones of weeds kept swinging in the wind,
Above the blue snow.

It was beginning winter,
The light moved slowly over the frozen field,   155
Over the dry seed-crowns,
The beautiful surviving bones
Swinging in the wind.

---

[1] German: "Order, order!"

Light traveled over the wide field;
Stayed.
The weeds stopped swinging.   160
The mind moved, not alone,
Though the clear air, in the silence.

    Was it light?
    Was it light within?   165
    Was it light within light?
    Stillness becoming alive,
    Yet still?

A lively understandable spirit
Once entertained you.
It will come again.   170
Be still.
Wait.

1948

Elegy for Jane

My student, thrown by a horse

    I remember the neckcurls, limp and damp as tendrils:
    And her quick look, a sidelong pickerel smile;
    And how, once startled into talk, the light syllables leaped for her,
    And she balanced in the delight of her thought,
    A wren, happy, tail into the wind,   5
    Her song trembling the twigs and small branches.
    The shade sang with her;
    The leaves, their whispers turned to kissing;
    And the mold sang in the bleached valleys under the rose.

    Oh, when she was sad, she cast herself down into such a pure depth,   10
    Even a father could not find her:
    Scraping her cheek against straw;
    Stirring the clearest water.

    My sparrow, you are not here,
    Waiting like a fern, making a spiny shadow.   15
    The sides of wet stones cannot console me,
    Nor the moss, wound with the last light.

If only I could nudge you from this sleep,
My maimed darling, my skittery pigeon.
Over this damp grave I speak the words of my love: 20
I, with no rights in this matter,
Neither father nor lover.
1953

The Waking

I wake to sleep, and take my waking slow.
I feel my fate in what I cannot fear.
I learn by going where I have to go.

We think by feeling. What is there to know?
I hear my being dance from ear to ear.   5
I wake to sleep, and take my waking slow.

Of those so close beside me, which are you?
God bless the Ground! I shall walk softly there,
And learn by going where I have to go.

Light takes the Tree; but who can tell us how?   10
The lowly worm climbs up a winding stair;
I wake to sleep, and take my waking slow.

Great Nature has another thing to do
To you and me; so take the lively air,
And, lovely, learn by going where to go.   15

This shaking keeps me steady. I should know.
What falls away is always. And is near.
I wake to sleep, and take my waking slow.
I learn by going where I have to go.
1953

Elizabeth Bishop
1911–1979

Elizabeth Bishop's poetry is that of a skeptic who looks on everything she sees with the
eye of estrangement. Bishop was, in effect, orphaned early. Her father died before she

was a year old, and her mother had a breakdown that led to insanity and permanent commitment to an asylum when Bishop was five. Bishop was raised in Massachusetts by an aunt but spent summers until she was thirteen with her grandparents in Nova Scotia. After graduating from Vassar (in the class commemorated by Mary McCarthy in *The Group*), she lived for some time in Key West; she also lived in France and Mexico. Eventually, during a trip to Brazil, she renewed acquaintance with Lota de Macedo Soares, with whom she lived for the next nineteen years. She then returned to the United States and during the last years of her life taught at Harvard. Bishop's continual geographic displacements reinforced her sense of homelessness and lack of parents. In effect, she was always piecing together a world out of unfamiliar elements.

Bishop's career unfolded slowly. In college, she wrote imitations of Hopkins and Herbert, but even in these bits of pastiche her humor and self-scrutiny are already evident. Her first book, *North and South* (1946), shows her as an accomplished poet aware already of her major metaphor, the resemblance between a map and a poem. Each represents—but in an arbitrary, schematic, and conventionalized way—a reality independent of its charting. Maps and poems both distort in the service of representation; both are miniature versions of the world. Bishop also poses, in her first book, questions of spirit and flesh, truth and nature, and establishes her polarities of North and South—polarities that also dominate her later books. *A Cold Spring* (1955), *Questions of Travel* (1965), and *Geography III* (1976), which followed the *Collected Poems* of 1969. One of her last uses of geographic polarities occurs in the splendid late poem "Crusoe in England," where Robinson Crusoe, back in England, laments the loss of his distant tropical island and of his friend Friday.

Bishop's first critics compared her to Marianne Moore, who was for a long time Bishop's poetic mentor; Bishop had met Moore through the librarian at Vassar. But in fact Bishop's roots go back to the religious poetry of the seventeenth-century poet George Herbert, to Protestant hymnody, and to the plain style of William Cowper and William Wordsworth. Bishop's skepticism unfolds against the backdrop of a lost religious faith. The seriality of existence without a religious meaning, ending only in the dust of the grave appalls her: "Why couldn't we have seen this old Nativity while we were at it?" she asks, reproducing in the Christmas scene that "family with pets" that she had never had. But nostalgia is powerless against the icy truth of human solitude in the universe. Bishop's tableau of the fishhouses, in the poem named for them, is inhabited by three solitaries: the Wordsworthian fisherman, Bishop herself, and the single seal. Bishop's solitary "total immersion" in knowledge—"dark, salt, clear, moving, utterly free"—stands against the permanent inscrutability of the world.

In her experiments in reproducing the thought processes of a child, an animal, a tourist, or an exile, Bishop invents a language lucid in its simple diction but surreal in its bewildered disjunction of space and time. While she retained an interested in rhyme and formal patterns (one of her last poems was the villanelle "One Art"), she began early to introduce natural speech rhythms and slant rhymes to her stanzas. Her naturalness earned Robert Lowell's admiration; he dedicated "Skunk Hour" to her, saying that he had learned from "The Armadillo" how to loosen up his own lines. Lowell and Bishop remained close friends; "North Haven," her elegy for him, expresses not only her loss but also their aesthetic difference. Lowell, a copious writer, revised constantly, treating even his printed work as manuscript, while Bishop, a perfectionist, kept poems unpublished for years while she sought the *mot juste* to fill a gap.

In an American literature largely preoccupied with the transcendental, the emblematic, the Christian, and the chauvinistic, Bishop's skeptical, observant, and ironic tone (learned in part from Emily Dickinson) comes as a welcome note. Her gaze takes in the whole hemisphere, from Cape Breton to Rio de Janeiro. Though she sees the dangers of travel—the exploitative cruelty of the conquistadors, the superficiality of tourist experience—in the end she values those questions that are provoked only by travel; and values as well, almost against her will, the resulting lessons in skepticism and loss.

Further Reading:

L. Schwartz and S. Estess, *Elizabeth Bishop and Her Art*, 1982.

R. Parker, *The Unbeliever: The Poetry of Elizabeth Bishop*, 1988.

B. Costello, *Elizabeth Bishop: Questions of Mastery*, 1991.

L. Goldensohn, *Elizabeth Bishop: The Biography of a Poetry*, 1991.

B. Millier, *Elizabeth Bishop: Life and the Memory of It*, 1993.

G. Fountain and P. Brazeau, eds., *Remembering Elizabeth Bishop: An Oral Biography*, 1994.

S. McCabe, *Elizabeth Bishop: Her Poetics of Loss*, 1994.

M. Lombardi, *The Body and The Song: Elizabeth Bishop's Poetics*, 1995.

Text:

Complete Poems, 1982.

The Fish

I caught a tremendous fish
and held him beside the boat
half out of water, with my hook
fast in a corner of his mouth,
He didn't fight.   5
He hadn't fought at all.
He hung a grunting weight,
battered and venerable
and homely. Here and there
his brown skin hung in strips   10
like ancient wallpaper,
and its pattern of darker brown
was like wallpaper:
shapes like full-blown roses
stained and lost through age.   15
He was speckled with barnacles,
fine rosettes of lime,
and infested
with tiny white sea-lice,
and underneath two or three   20
rags of green weed hung down.
While his gills were breathing in
the terrible oxygen

—the frightening gills,
fresh and crisp with blood,   25
that can cut so badly—
I thought of the coarse white flesh
packed in like feathers,
the big bones and the little bones,
the dramatic reds and blacks   30
of his shiny entrails,
and the pink swim-bladder
like a big peony.
I looked into his eyes
which were far larger than mine   35
but shallower, and yellowed,
the irises backed and packed
with tarnished tinfoil
seen through the lenses
of old scratched isinglass.   40
They shifted a little, but not
to return my stare.
—It was more like the tipping
of an object toward the light.
I admired his sullen face,   45
the mechanism of his jaw,
and then I saw
that from his lower lip
—if you could call it a lip—
grim, wet, and weaponlike,   50
hung five old pieces of fish-line,
or four and a wire leader
with the swivel still attached,
with all their five big hooks
grown firmly in his mouth.   55
A green line, frayed at the end
where he broke it, two heavier lines,
and a fine black thread
still crimped from the strain and snap
when it broke and he got away.   60
Like medals with their ribbons
frayed and wavering,
a five-haired bread of wisdom
trailing from his aching jaw.
I stared and stared   65
and victory filled up
the little rented boat,
from the pool of bilge
where oil had spread a rainbow
around the rusted engine   70

to the bailer rusted orange,
the sun-cracked thwarts,
the oarlocks on their strings,
the gunnels—until everything
was rainbow, rainbow, rainbow!　　　　　　　　　75
And I let the fish go.
1946

At the Fishhouses

Although it is a cold evening,
down by one of the fishhouses
an old man sits netting,
his net, in the gloaming almost invisible
a dark purple-brown,　　　　　　　　　　　　5
and his shuttle worn and polished.
The air smells so strong of codfish
it makes one's nose run and one's eyes water.
The five fishhouses have steeply peaked roofs
and narrow, cleated gangplanks slant up　　　10
to storerooms in the gables
for the wheelbarrows to be pushed up and down on.
All is silver: the heavy surface of the sea,
swelling slowly as if considering spilling over,
is opaque, but the silver of the benches,　　　15
the lobster pots, and masts, scattered
among the wild jagged rocks,
is of an apparent translucence
like the small old buildings with an emerald moss
growing on their shoreward walls.　　　　　　20
The big fish tubs are completely lined
with layers of beautiful herring scales
and the wheelbarrows are similarly plastered
with creamy iridescent costs of mail,
with small iridescent flies crawling on them.　25
Up on the little slope behind the houses,
set in the sparse bright sprinkle of grass,
is an ancient wooden capstan,[1]
cracked, with two long bleached handles
and some melancholy stains, like dried blood,　30
where the ironwork has rusted.

---

[1] Machine for raising weights by winding cable around a vertical rotating drum.

The old man accepts a Lucky Strike.
He was a friend of my grandfather.
We talk of the decline in the population
and of codfish and herring   35
while he waits for a herring boat to come in.
There are sequins on his vest and on his thumb.
He has scraped the scales, the principal beauty,
from unnumbered fish with the black old knife,
the blade of which is almost worn away.   40

Down at the water's edge, at the place
where they haul up the boats, up the long ramp
descending into the water, thin silver
tree trunks are laid horizontally
across the gray stones, down and down   45
at intervals of four or five feet.
Cold dark deep and absolutely clear,
element bearable to no mortal,
to fish and to seals . . . One seal particularly
I have seen here evening after evening.   50
He was curious about me. He was interested in music;
like me a believer in total immersion,[2]
so I used to sing him Baptist hymns.
I also sang "A Mighty Fortress Is Our God."[3]
He stood up in the water and regarded me   55
steadily, moving his head a little,
Then he would disappear, then suddenly emerge
almost in the same spot, with a sort of shrug
as if it were against his better judgment.
Cold dark deep and absolutely clear,   60
the clear gray icy water . . . Back, behind us,
the dignified tall firs begin.
Bluish, associating with their shadows,
a million Christmas trees stand
waiting for Christmas. The water seems suspended   65
above the rounded gray and blue-gray stones.
I have seen it over and over, the same sea, the same,
slightly, indifferently swinging above the stones,
icily free above the stones,
above the stones and then the world.   70
If you should dip your hand in,
your wrist would ache immediately,
your bones would begin to ache and your hand would burn
as if the water were a transmutation of fire

---

2 Form of baptism practiced by some Christian sects.

3 Hymn of which the original German version
was written by Martin Luther (1483–1546).

that feeds on stones and burns with a dark gray flame.   75
If you tasted it, it would first taste bitter,
then briny, then surely burn your tongue.
It is like what we imagine knowledge to be:
dark, salt, clear, moving, utterly free,
drawn from the cold hard mouth   80
of the world, derived from the rocky breasts
forever, flowing and drawn, and since
our knowledge is historical, flowing, and flown.
1955

Questions of Travel

There are too many waterfalls here; the crowded streams
hurry too rapidly down to the sea,
and the pressure of so many clouds on the mountaintops
makes them spill over the sides in soft slow-motion,
turning to waterfalls under our very eyes.   5
—For if those streaks, those mile-long, shiny, tearstains,
aren't waterfalls yet,
in a quick age or so, as ages go here,
they probably will be.
But if the streams and clouds keep travelling, travelling,   10
the mountains look like the hulls of capsized ships,
slime-hung and barnacled.

Think of the long trip home.
Should we have stayed at home and thought of here?
Where should we be today?   15
Is it right to be watching strangers in a play
in this strangest of theatres?
What childishness is it that while there's breath of life
in our bodies, we are determined to rush
to see the sun the other way around?   20
The tiniest green hummingbird in the world?
To stare at some inexplicable old stonework,
inexplicable and impenetrable,
at any view,
instantly seen and always, always delightful?   25
Oh, must we dream our dreams
and have them, too?
And have we room
for one more folded sunset, still quite warm?

But surely it would have been a pity   30
not to have seen the trees along this road,
really exaggerated in their beauty,
not to have seen them gesturing
like noble pantomimists, robed in pink.
—Not to have had to stop for gas and heard   35
the sad, two-noted, wooden tune
of disparate wooden clogs
carelessly clacking over
a grease-stained filling-station floor.
(In another country the clogs would all be tested.   40
Each pair there would have identical pitch.)
—A pity not to have heard
the other, less primitive music of the fat brown bird
who sings above the broken gasoline pump
in a bamboo church of Jesuit baroque:[1]   45
three towers, five silver crosses.
—Yes, a pity not to have pondered,
blurr'dly and inconclusively,
on what connection can exist for centuries
between the crudest wooden footwear   50
and, careful and finicky,
the whittled fantasies of wooden cages.
—Never to have studied history in
the weak calligraphy of songbirds' cages.
—And never to have had to listen to rain   55
so much like politicians' speeches:
two hours of unrelenting oratory
and then a sudden golden silence
in which the traveller takes a notebook, writes:

"Is it lack of imagination that makes us come   60
to imagined places, not just stay at home?
Or could Pascal[2] have been not entirely right
about just sitting quietly in one's room?

Continent, city, country, society:
the choice is never wide and never free.   65
And here, or there . . . No. Should we have stayed at home,
wherever that may be?"
1965

---

[1] Style of architecture introduced into South
America in the seventeenth century by Jesuit
missionaries.

[2] Blaise Pascal, French philosopher
(1623–1662).

Sestina

September rain falls on the house.
In the failing light, the old grandmother
sits in the kitchen with the child
beside the Little Marvel Stove,
reading the jokes from the almanac,   5
laughing and talking to hide her tears.

She thinks that her equinoctial[1] tears
and the rain that beats on the roof of the house
were both foretold by the almanac,
but only known to a grandmother.   10
The iron kettle sings on the stove.
She cuts some bread and says to the child,

It's time for tea now; but the child
is watching the teakettle's small hard tears
dance like mad on the hot black stove,   15
the way the rain must dance on the house.
Tidying up, the old grandmother
hangs up the clever almanac

on its string. Bird-like, the almanac
hovers half open above the child,   20
hovers above the old grandmother
and her teacup full of dark brown tears.
She shivers and says she thinks the house
feels chilly, and puts more wood in the stove.

It was to be, says the Marvel Stove.   25
I know what I know, says the almanac.
With crayons the child draws a rigid house
and a winding pathway. Then the child
puts in a man with buttons like tears
and shows it proudly to the grandmother.   30

But secretly, while the grandmother
busies herself about the stove,
the little moons fall down like tears
from between the pages of the almanac

---

[1] At the time of the (autumn) equinox; an
oblique reference to September rain.

into the flower bed the child   35
has carefully placed in the front of the house.

Time to plant tears, says the almanac.
The grandmother sings to the marvellous stove
and the child draws another inscrutable house.
1965

In the Waiting Room

In Worcester, Massachusetts,
I went with Aunt Consuelo
to keep her dentist's appointment
and sat and waited for her
in the dentist's waiting room.   5
It was winter. It got dark
early. The waiting room
was full of grown-up people,
arctics and overcoats,
lamps and magazines.   10
My aunt was inside
what seemed like a long time
and while I waited I read
the *National Geographic*
(I could read) and carefully   15
studied the photographs:
the inside of a volcano,
black, and full of ashes;
then it was spilling over
in rivulets of fire.   20
Osa and Martin Johnson[1]
dressed in riding breeches,
laced boots, and pith helmets.
A dead man slung on a pole
—"Long Pig,"[2] the caption said.   25
Babies with pointed heads
wound round and round with string;
black, naked women with necks
wound round and round with wire
like the necks of light bulbs.   30
Their breasts were horrifying.

---

[1] Osa Johnson (1894–1953) and Martin Johnson (1884–1937), tropical explorers and authors of travel books.

[2] Name given by cannibals to a dead man to be eaten.

I read it right straight through.
I was too shy to stop.
And then I looked at the cover:
the yellow margins, the date.   35

Suddenly, from inside,
came an *oh!* of pain
—Aunt Consuelo's voice—
not very loud or long.
I wasn't at all surprised;   40
even then I knew she was
a foolish, timid woman.
I might have been embarrassed,
but wasn't. What took me
completely by surprise   45
was that it was *me:*
my voice, in my mouth.
Without thinking at all
I was my foolish aunt,
I—we—were falling, falling,   50
our eyes glued to the cover
of the *National Geographic,*
February, 1918.

I said to myself: three days
and you'll be seven years old.   55
I was saying it to stop
the sensation of falling off
the round, turning world
into cold, blue-black space.
But I felt: you are an *I,*   60
you are an *Elizabeth,*
you are one of *them.*
Why should you be one, too?
I scarcely dared to look
to see what it was I was.   65
I gave a sidelong glance
—I couldn't look any higher—
at shadowy gray knees,
trousers and skirts and boots
and different pairs of hands   70
lying under the lamps.
I knew that nothing stranger
had ever happened, that nothing
stranger could ever happen.
Why should I be my aunt,   75
or me, or anyone?

What similarities—
boots, hands, the family voice
I felt in my throat, or even
the *National Geographic*   80
and those awful hanging breasts—
held us all together
or made us all just one?
How—I didn't know any
word for it—how "unlikely" . . .   85
How had I come to be here,
like them, and overhear
a cry of pain that could have
got loud and worse but hadn't?

The waiting room was bright   90
and too hot. It was sliding
beneath a big black wave,
another, and another.

Then I was back in it.
The War was on. Outside,   95
in Worcester, Massachusetts,
were night and slush and cold,
and it was still the fifth
of February, 1918.
1976

One Art

The art of losing isn't hard to master;
so many things seem filled with the intent
to be lost that their loss is no disaster.

Lose something every day. Accept the fluster
of lost door keys, the hour badly spent.   5
The art of losing isn't hard to master.

Then practice losing farther, losing faster:
places, and names, and where it was you meant
to travel. None of these will bring disaster.

I lost my mother's watch. And look! my last, or   10
next-to-last, of three loved houses went.
The art of losing isn't hard to master.

I lost two cities, lovely ones. And, vaster,
some realms I owned, two rivers, a continent.
I miss them, but it wasn't a disaster.   15

—Even losing you (the joking voice, a gesture
I love) I shan't have lied. It's evident
the art of losing's not too hard to master
though it may look like (*Write it!*) like disaster.
1976

Tennessee Williams
1911–1983

Tennessee Williams's first successful play, *The Glass Menagerie,* made its debut on December 26, 1944 in Chicago; reviewers hailed it as an outstanding example of Williams's mastery of lyric drama. Originally conceived as a film script and entitled *The Gentleman Caller,* this "memory play" drew heavily on the circumstances of William's own life, thinly disguised in the presence of the narrator Tom, and was presented as a compelling series of wistful vignettes about loneliness and personal difficulty. After a limited but highly successful run in Chicago, *The Glass Menagerie* played to larger and even more enthusiastic audiences on Broadway, where it won the New York Drama Critics' Circle Award. Since those early acclaimed productions, *The Glass Menagerie* has enjoyed numerous revivals, both in the United States and abroad. The play is considered by many critics as the most accomplished and significant of Williams's major works.

Despite the early success of *The Glass Menagerie,* Tennessee Williams's critical reputation has wavered over the years. His first recognized work, *Battle of Angels,* was assailed at its 1940 opening in Boston. One critic charged it with giving "the audience the sensation of having been dunked in mire." However, with *The Glass Menagerie,* Williams created an indelible presence for himself in the American theater. Soon he was providing gossip columnists with extravagant incidents from his troubled and unconventional personal life.

Born in Columbus, Mississippi, in 1911, Thomas Lanier Williams was descended on his father's side from "pioneer Tennessee stock" and on his mother's from early Quaker "settlers of Nantucket Island in New England," a mix of "Cavalier" and "Puritan" he later saw as a possible source "for the conflicting impulses I often represent in the people I write about." During his early years Williams lived in several Mississippi towns and in Nashville, Tennessee, with his mother, his older sister Rose, and his grandfather, an Episcopalian minister. In his early adolescence, his family made what he later described as "a tragic move" to St. Louis, where his father, a traveling salesman, had accepted an appointment as the manager of a shoe company.

Neither my sister nor I could adjust ourselves to life in a midwestern city. The school-children made fun of our southern speech and manners. I remember gangs of kids following me home yelling "Sissy!" and home was not a very pleasant refuge. It was a perpetually dim little apartment in a wilderness of identical brick and concrete structures with no grass and no trees nearer than the park.

It was also a place where his parents seemed constantly to quarrel and where his father, disappointed at not having a more athletic son, began calling his son "Miss Nancy." Soon Williams's frail physical and psychological condition weakened into partial paralysis in his legs. His sister Rose, suffering comparable pressures, experienced a mental breakdown that culminated when a suitor died—circumstances similar to those that form the narrative basis for his one-act play *Portrait of a Madonna,* an early version of what later developed into *A Streetcar Named Desire.*

Early in his troubled life, writing became Williams's sanctuary:

At the age of fourteen I discovered writing as an escape from a world of reality in which I felt acutely uncomfortable. It immediately became my place of retreat, my cave, my refuge.

At age eleven Williams had his own typewriter; at fourteen he garnered recognition with a first-place award (and $25.00) in a nationwide writing contest sponsored by the prestigious *Smart Set* magazine. After high school, he studied briefly at the University of Missouri, then worked in "a clerical job in the shoe company that employed my father." They were two years of "indescribable torment to me as an individual but of immense value to me as a writer for they gave me first-hand knowledge of what it meant to be a small wage earner in a hopelessly routine job." Williams continued to write—often late into the night—without regard for his poor health. After recuperating from another nervous collapse, he lived briefly with his grandparents in Memphis and then returned to college, first at Washington University in St. Louis, where he wrote and produced several plays, and then at the University of Iowa, where he took a B.A. in 1938, with a major in playwriting.

In the years following graduation, Williams traveled and lived briefly in Chicago, St. Louis, Mexico, Los Angeles, New Orleans, and New York, experiencing the kind of life he was so often to present on stage: lonely and uncertain, trapped in a painful past, and struggling to survive in a world essentially indifferent to personal illusions. During this period he also changed his name. Thomas Lanier Williams was, he observed,

a nice enough name, perhaps a little too nice. . . . It sounds like it might belong to the son of a writer who turns out sonnet sequences to Spring. . . . Under that name I published a good deal of lyric poetry which was a bad imitation of Edna Millay. When I grew up I realized this poetry wasn't much good and I felt the name had been compromised so I changed it to Tennessee Williams, the justification being mainly that the Williamses had fought the Indians for Tennessee and I had already discovered that the life of a young writer was going to be something similar to the dilemma of a stockade against a band of savages.

Williams supported himself mainly through odd jobs, including working as a scriptwriter at MGM studios, running the night elevator in a large hotel, and ushering at the Strand Theater on Broadway. "All the while I kept on writing, writing, not with any hope of making a living at it but because I found no other means of expressing things that seemed to demand expression."

By 1945, however, with *The Glass Menagerie* written and produced, Williams began to enjoy both critical praise, including a New York Drama Critics Circle Award, and financial rewards. In its first appearance on Broadway, *The Glass Menagerie* ran for 561 performances. In 1947 Williams won a Pulitzer Prize as well as a second Drama Critics Circle Award for *A Streetcar Named Desire*, which ran for 855 performances. *The Rose Tattoo*, with 300 performances, followed in 1951, and four years later *Cat On a Hot Tin Roof* earned Williams a third Drama Critics Circle Award and a second Pulitzer Prize. In 1953 the play *Camino Real* provoked controversy that was rekindled in 1956 when the film *Baby Doll* was released. These in turn were followed by well-received stage and film versions of *Suddenly Last Summer* (1958), *Sweet Bird of Youth* (1959), and *The Night of the Iguana* (1961), which is widely recognized as Williams's last important play. Although he continued to write until quite close to his death in 1983, none of his later plays received the acclaim of his earlier works.

Williams wrote about such subjects as murder, rape, homosexuality, nymphomania and drug and alcohol addiction at a time when many of these subjects were still regarded as too controversial for the American stage. But his characters transcend their exaggerated roles—neurotics, victims, would-be artists, and outsiders. However sensational his strong characters and captivating plots, Williams continually aimed at "theater poetry" in his dramatic renditions of fear, anxiety, loneliness, and suffering. At his best, such as in *The Glass Menagerie*, Williams reached remarkable heights of lyric power and originality.

During his last twenty years, Williams's depression became, in his own words, "almost clinical," and alcohol and drugs began to dominate his life. In the 1970s Williams published a string of theatrical failures, two works of fiction (*Eight Mortal Ladies Possessed* and *Noise and the World of Reason*), and a collection of poems (*Androgyne, Mon Amour*), along with his collected essays (*Where I Live*, 1978) and his *Memoirs* (1975). By the time of his death, only the extravagances of his personal life succeeded in bringing his name to public attention.

Further Reading:

N. Tischler, *Tennessee Williams: Rebellious Puritan*, 1961.
J. Tharpe, ed., *Tennessee Williams: A Tribute*, 1977.
S. L. Falk, *Tennessee Williams*, 2nd ed., 1978.
F. Hirsch, *A Portrait of the Artist: The Plays of Tennessee Williams*, 1979.
F. H. Londre, *Tennessee Williams*, 1979.

J. S. McCann, *The Critical Reputation of Tennessee Williams: A Reference Guide*, 1983.
D. Rader, *Tennessee, Cry of the Heart*, 1983.
D. Williams and S. Mead, *Tennessee Williams: An Intimate Biography*, 1983.
D. Spoto, *The Kindness of Strangers: The Life of Tennessee Williams*, 1985.

Text:
The Glass Menagerie, 1973

The Glass Menagerie

List of Characters

Amanda Wingfield, the mother.—A little woman of great but confused vitality clinging frantically to another time and place. Her characterization must be carefully created, not copied from type. She is not paranoiac, but her life is paranoia. There is much to admire in Amanda, and as much to love and pity as there is to laugh at. Certainly she has endurance and a kind of heroism, and though her foolishness makes her unwittingly cruel at times, there is tenderness in her slight person.

Laura Wingfield, her daughter.—Amanda, having failed to establish contact with reality, continues to live vitally in her illusions, but Laura's situation is even graver. A childhood illness has left her crippled, one leg slightly shorter than the other, and held in a brace. This defect need not be more than suggested on the stage. Stemming from this, Laura's separation increases till she is like a piece of her own glass collection, too exquisitely fragile to move from the shelf.

Tom Wingfield, her son.—And the narrator of the play. A poet with a job in a warehouse. His nature is not remorseless, but to escape from a trap he has to act without pity.

Jim O'Connor, the gentleman caller.—A nice, ordinary, young man.

Scene: An alley in St. Louis.
Part 1: Preparation for a Gentleman Caller.
Part 2: The Gentleman Calls.
Time: Now and the Past.

Scene 1

The Wingfield apartment is in the rear of the building, one of those vast hive-like conglomerations of cellular living-units that flower as warty growths in overcrowded urban centers of lower middle-class population and are symptomatic of the impulse of this largest and fundamentally enslaved section of American society to avoid fluidity and differentiation and to exist and function as one interfused mass of automatism.

The apartment faces an alley and is entered by a fire-escape, a structure whose name is a touch of accidental poetic truth, for all of these huge buildings are always burning with the slow and implacable fires of human desperation. The fire escape is included in the set—that is, the landing of it and steps descending from it.

The scene is memory and is therefore non-realistic. Memory takes a lot of poetic license. It omits some details; others are exaggerated, according to the emotional value of the articles it touches, for memory is seated predominantly in the heart. The interior is therefore rather dim and poetic.

At the rise of the curtain, the audience is faced with the dark, grim rear wall of the Wingfield tenement. This building, which runs parallel to the footlights, is flanked on both sides by dark, narrow alleys which run into murky canyons of tangled clotheslines, garbage cans and the sinister latticework of neighboring fire-escapes. It is up and down these side alleys that exterior entrances and exits are made, during the play. At the end of Tom's opening commentary, the dark tenement wall slowly reveals (by means of a transparency) the interior of the ground floor Wingfield apartment.

Downstage is the living room, which also serves as a sleeping room for Laura, the sofa unfolding to make her bed. Upstage, center, and divided by a wide arch or second proscenium with transparent faded portieres (or second curtain), is the dining room. In an old-fashioned what-not in the living room are seen scores of transparent glass animals. A blown-up photograph of the father hangs on the wall of the living room, facing the audience, to the left of the archway. It is the face of a very handsome young man in a doughboy's First World War cap. He is gallantly smiling, ineluctably smiling, as if to say, "I will be smiling forever."

The audience hears and sees the opening scene in the dining room through both the transparent fourth wall of the building and the transparent gauze portieres of the diningroom arch. It is during this revealing scene that the fourth wall slowly ascends, out of sight.

This transparent exterior wall is not brought down again until the very end of the play, during Tom's final speech.

The narrator is an undisguised convention of the play. He takes whatever license with dramatic convention as is convenient to his purposes.

Tom enters dressed as a merchant sailor from alley, stage left, and strolls across the front of the stage to the fire-escape. There he stops and lights a cigarette. He addresses the audience.

Tom: Yes, I have tricks in my pocket, I have things up my sleeve. But I am the opposite of a stage magician. He gives you illusion that has the appearance of truth. I give you truth in the pleasant disguise of illusion. To begin with, I turn back time. I reverse it to that quaint period, the thirties, when the huge middle class of America was matriculating in a school for the blind. Their eyes had failed them, or they had failed their eyes, and so they were having their fingers pressed forcibly down on the fiery Braille alphabet of a dissolving economy. In Spain there was revolution. Here there was only shouting and confusion. In Spain there was Guernica. Here there were disturbances of labor, sometimes pretty violent, in otherwise peaceful cities such as Chicago, Cleveland, Saint Louis. . . . This is the social background of the play.

(Music.)

The play is memory. Being a memory play, it is dimly lighted, it is sentimental, it is not realistic. In memory everything seems to happen to music. That explains the fiddle

in the wings. I am the narrator of the play, and also a character in it. The other characters are my mother, Amanda, my sister, Laura, and a gentleman caller who appears in
the final scenes. He is the most realistic character in the play, being an emissary from a
world of reality that we were somehow set apart from. But since I have a poet's weakness for symbols, I am using this character also as a symbol; he is the long delayed but
always expected something that we live for. There is a fifth character in the play who
doesn't appear except in this larger-than-life photograph over the mantel. This is our
father who left us a long time ago. He was a telephone man who fell in love with long
distances; he gave up his job with the telephone company and skipped the light fantastic
out of town. . . . The last we heard of him was a picture post-card from Mazatlan, on the
Pacific coast of Mexico, containing a message of two words—"Hello—Good-bye!" and
no address. I think the rest of the play will explain itself. . . .

Amanda's voice becomes audible through the portieres.

(Legend on Screen: "Où Sont Les Neiges.")

*He divides the portieres and enters the upstage area. Amanda and Laura are seated at a
drop-leaf table. Eating is indicated by gestures without food or utensils. Amanda faces the
audience. Tom and Laura are seated in profile. The interior has lit up softly and through
the scrim we see Amanda and Laura seated at the table in the upstage area.*

Amanda: (calling). Tom?
Tom: Yes, Mother.
Amanda: We can't say grace until you come to the table!
Tom: Coming, Mother. (*He bows slightly and withdraws, reappearing a few moments
   later in his place at the table.*)
Amanda: (to her son). Honey, don't *push* with your *fingers.* If you have to push with
   something, the thing to push with is a crust of bread. And chew—chew! Animals
   have sections in their stomachs which enable them to digest food without mastication, but human beings are supposed to chew their food before they swallow it
   down. Eat food leisurely, son, and really enjoy it. A well-cooked meal has lots of
   delicate flavors that have to be held in the mouth for appreciation. So chew your
   food and give your salivary glands a chance to function!

(Tom deliberately lays his imaginary fork down and pushes his chair back from the table.)

Tom: I haven't enjoyed one bite of this dinner because of your constant directions on
   how to eat it. It's you that makes me rush through meals with your hawk-like at-
   tention to every bite I take. Sickening—spoils my appetite—all this discussion of
   animals' secretion—salivary glands—mastication!
Amanda: (lightly). Temperament like a Metropolitan star! (*He rises and crosses down-
   stage.*) You're not excused from the table.
Tom: I am getting a cigarette.
Amanda: You smoke too much. (*Laura rises.*)
Laura: I'll bring in the blanc mange.
(He remains standing with his cigarette by the portieres during the following.)
Amanda: (rising). No, sister, no, sister—you be the lady this time and I'll be the darky.

Laura: I'm already up.

Amanda: Resume your seat, little sister—I want you to stay fresh and pretty—for gentlemen callers!

Laura: I'm not expecting any gentlemen callers.

Amanda: (*crossing out to kitchenette. Airily*). Sometimes they come when they are least expected! Why, I remember one Sunday afternoon in Blue Mountain—(*Enters kitchenette.*)

Tom: I know what's coming!

Laura: Yes. But let her tell it.

Tom: Again?

Laura: She loves to tell it.

(*Amanda returns with bowl of dessert.*)

Amanda: One Sunday afternoon in Blue Mountain—your mother received—*seventeen!*—gentlemen callers! Why, sometimes there weren't chairs enough to accommodate them all. We had to send the nigger over to bring in folding chairs from the parish house.

Tom: (*remaining at portieres*). How did you entertain those gentlemen callers?

Amanda: I understood the art of conversation!

Tom: I bet you could talk.

Amanda: Girls in those days *knew* how to talk, I can tell you.

Tom: Yes?

(*Image: Amanda as a Girl on a Porch Greeting Callers.*)

Amanda: They knew how to entertain their gentlemen callers. It wasn't enough for a girl to be possessed of a pretty face and a graceful figure—although I wasn't slighted in either respect. She also needed to have a nimble wit and a tongue to meet all occasions.

Tom: What did you talk about?

Amanda: Things of importance going on in the world! Never anything coarse or common or vulgar. (*She addresses Tom as though he were seated in the vacant chair at the table though he remains by portieres. He plays this scene as though he held the book.*) My callers were gentlemen—all! Among my callers were some of the most prominent young planters of the Mississippi Delta—planters and sons of planters!

(*Tom motions for music and a spot of light on Amanda. Her eyes lift, her face glows, her voice becomes rich and elegiac.*)

(*Screen Legend: "Où Sont Les Neiges."*)

There was young Champ Laughlin who later became vice-president of the Delta Planters Bank. Hadley Stevenson who was drowned in Moon Lake and left his widow one hundred and fifty thousand in Government bonds. There were the Cutrere brothers, Wesley and Bates. Bates was one of my bright particular beaux! He got in a quarrel with that wild Wainright boy. They shot it out on the floor of Moon Lake Casino. Bates was shot through the stomach. Died in the ambulance on his way to Memphis. His widow was also well provided for, came into eight or ten thousand acres, that's all. She married him on the rebound—never loved her—carried my picture on him the night he died! And there was that boy that every girl in the Delta had set her cap for! That beautiful, brilliant young Fitzhugh boy from Green County!

Tom: What did he leave his widow?

Amanda: He never married! Gracious, you talk as though all of my old admirers had turned up their toes to the daisies!

Tom: Isn't this the first you mentioned that still survives?

Amanda: That Fitzhugh boy went North and made a fortune—came to be known as the Wolf of Wall Street! He had the Midas touch, whatever he touched turned to gold! And I could have been Mrs. Duncan J. Fitzhugh, mind you! But—I picked your *father!*

Laura: (*rising*). Mother, let me clear the table.

Amanda: No dear, you go in front and study your typewriter chart. Or practice your shorthand a little. Stay fresh and pretty!—It's almost time for our gentlemen callers to start arriving. (*She flounces girlishly toward the kitchenette.*) How many do you suppose we're going to entertain this afternoon?

(*Tom throws down the paper and jumps up with a groan.*)

Laura: (*alone in the dining room*). I don't believe we're going to receive any, Mother.

Amanda: (*reappearing, airily*). What? No one—not one? You must be joking! (*Laura nervously echoes her laugh. She slips in a fugitive manner through the half-open portieres and draws them gently behind her. A shaft of very clear light is thrown on her face against the faded tapestry of the curtains.*) (*Music: "The Glass Menagerie" Under Faintly.*) (*Lightly*) Not one gentleman caller? It can't be true! There must be a flood, there must have been a tornado!

Laura: It isn't a flood, it's not a tornado, Mother. I'm just not popular like you were in Blue Mountain. . . . (*Tom utters another groan. Laura glances at him with a faint, apologetic smile. Her voice catching a little*) Mother's afraid I'm going to be an old maid.

(*The Scene Dims Out with "Glass Menagerie" Music.*)

Scene 2
"Laura, Haven't You Ever Liked Some Boy?"

On the dark stage the screen is lighted with the image of blue roses. Gradually Laura's figure becomes apparent and the screen goes out. The music subsides. Laura is seated in the delicate ivory chair at the small clawfoot table. She wears a dress of soft violet material for a kimono—her hair tied back from her forehead with a ribbon. She is washing and polishing her collection of glass.

   Amanda appears on the fire-escape steps. At the sound of her ascent, Laura catches her breath, thrusts the bowl of ornaments away and seats herself stiffly before the diagram of the typewriter keyboard as though it held her spellbound. Something has happened to Amanda. It is written in her face as she climbs to the landing: a look that is grim and hopeless and a little absurd.

She has on one of those cheap or imitation velvety-looking cloth coats with imitation fur collar. Her hat is five or six years old, one of those dreadful cloche hats that were worn in the late twenties, and she is clasping an enormous black patent-leather pocketbook with nickel clasp and initials. This is her full-dress outfit, the one she usually wears to the D.A.R.

Before entering she looks through the door. She purses her lips, opens her eyes wide, rolls them upward and shakes her head. Then she slowly lets herself in the door. Seeing her mother's expression Laura touches her lips with a nervous gesture.

Laura: Hello, Mother, I was—(*She makes a nervous gesture toward the chart on the wall. Amanda leans against the shut door and stares at Laura with a martyred look.*)

Amanda: Deception? Deception? (*She slowly removes her hat and gloves, continuing the swift suffering stare. She lets the hat and gloves fall on the floor—a bit of acting.*)

Laura: (shakily). How was the D.A.R. meeting? (*Amanda slowly opens her purse and removes a dainty white handkerchief which she shakes out delicately and delicately touches to her lips and nostrils.*) Didn't you go to the D.A.R. meeting, Mother?

Amanda: (faintly, almost inaudibly).—No.—No. (*Then more forcibly*) I did not have the strength—to go to the D.A.R. In fact, I did not have the courage! I waited to find a hole in the ground and hide myself in it forever! (*She crosses slowly to the wall and removes the diagram of the typewriter keyboard. She holds it in front of her for a second, staring at it sweetly and sorrowfully—then bites her lips and tears it in two pieces.*)

Laura: (faintly). Why did you do that, Mother? (*Amanda repeats the same procedure with the chart of the Gregg Alphabet.*) Why are you—

Amanda: Why? Why? How old are you, Laura?

Laura: Mother, you know my age.

Amanda: I thought that you were an adult; it seems that I was mistaken. (*She crosses slowly to the sofa and sinks down and stares at Laura.*)

Laura: Please don't stare at me, Mother.

(*Amanda closes her eyes and lowers her head. Count ten.*)

Amanda: What are we going to do, what is going to become of us, what is the future?

(*Count ten.*)

Laura: Has something happened, Mother? (*Amanda draws a long breath and takes out the handkerchief again. Dabbing process.*) Mother, has—something happened?

Amanda: I'll be all right in a minute. I'm just bewildered—(*count five*)—by life. . . .

Laura: Mother, I wish that you would tell me what's happened.

Amanda: As you know, I was supposed to be inducted into my office at the D.A.R. this afternoon. (*Image: A Swarm of Typewriters.*) But I stopped off at Rubicam's Business College to speak to your teachers about your having a cold and ask them what progress they thought you were making down there.

Laura: Oh. . . .

Amanda: I went to the typing instructor and introduced myself as your mother. She didn't know who you were. Wingfield, she said. We don't have any such student enrolled at the school! I assured her she did, that you had been going to classes since early in January. "I wonder," she said, "if you could be talking about that terribly shy little girl who dropped out of school after only a few days' attendance?" "No," I said, "Laura, my daughter, has been going to school every day for the past six weeks!" "Excuse me," she said. She took the attendance book out and there was your name, unmistakably printed, and all the dates you were absent until they decided that you had dropped out of school. I still said, "No, there must have been some mistake! There must have been some mix-up in the records!" And she said, "No—I remember her perfectly now. Her hand shook so that she couldn't hit the right keys! The first time we gave a speed-test, she broke down completely—was sick at the stomach and almost had to be carried into the wash-room! After that morning she never showed up any more. We phoned the house but never got any answer"—while I was working at Famous and Barr, I suppose, demonstrating those—Oh! I felt so weak I could barely keep on my feet. I had to sit down while they got me a glass of water! Fifty dollars' tuition, all of our plans—my hopes and ambitions for you—just gone up the spout, just gone up the spout like that. (*Laura draws a long breath and gets awkwardly to her feet. She crosses to the victrola and winds it up.*) What are you doing?

Laura: Oh! (*She releases the handle and returns to her seat.*)

Amanda: Laura, where have you been going when you've gone out pretending that you were going to business college?

Laura: I've just been going out walking.

Amanda: That's not true.

Laura: It is. I just went walking.

Amanda: Walking? Walking? In winter? Deliberately courting pneumonia in that light coat? Where did you walk to, Laura?

Laura: It was the lesser of two evils, Mother. (*Image: Winter Scene in Park.*) I couldn't go back up. I—threw up—on the floor!

Amanda: From half past seven till after five thirty every day you mean to tell me you walked around in the park, because you wanted to make me think that you were still going to Rubicam's Business College?

Laura: It wasn't as bad as it sounds. I went inside places to get warmed up.

Amanda: Inside where?

Laura: I went in the art museum and the birdhouses at the Zoo. I visited the penguins every day! Sometimes I did without lunch and went to the movies. Lately I've been spending most of my afternoons in the Jewel-box, that big glass house where they raise the tropical flowers.

Amanda: You did all this to deceive me, just for the deception? (*Laura looks down.*) Why?

Laura: Mother, when you're disappointed, you get that awful suffering look on your face, like the picture of Jesus' mother in the museum!

Amanda: Hush!

Laura: I couldn't face it.

(*Pause. A whisper of strings.*)

(*Legend: "The Crust of Humility."*)

Amanda: (*hopelessly fingering the huge pocketbook*). So what are we going to do the rest of our lives? Stay home and watch the parades go by? Amuse ourselves with the glass menagerie, darling? Eternally play those worn-out phonograph records your father left as a painful reminder of him? We won't have a business career—we've given that up because it gave us nervous indigestion! (*Laughs wearily.*) What is there left but dependency all our lives? I know so well what becomes of unmarried women who aren't prepared to occupy a position. I've seen such pitiful cases in the South—barely tolerated spinsters living upon the grudging patronage of sister's husband or brother's wife!—stuck away in some little mousetrap of a room—encouraged by one inlaw to visit another—little birdlike women without any nest—eating the crust of humility all their life! Is that the future that we've mapped out for ourselves? I swear it's the only alternative I can think of! It isn't a very pleasant alternative, is it? Of course—some girls *do marry*. (*Laura twists her hands nervously.*) Haven't you ever liked some boy?

Laura: Yes. I liked one once. (*Rises.*) I came across his picture a while ago.

Amanda: (*with some interest*). He gave you his picture?

Laura: No, it's in the year-book.

Amanda: (*disappointed*). Oh—a high-school boy.

(*Screen Image: Jim as a High-School Hero Bearing a Silver Cup.*)

Laura: Yes. His name was Jim. (*Laura lifts the heavy annual from the clawfoot table.*) Here he is in *The Pirates of Penzance*.

Amanda: (*absently*). The what?

Laura: The operetta the senior class put on. He had a wonderful voice and we sat across the aisle from each other Mondays, Wednesdays and Fridays in the Aud. Here he is with the silver cup for debating! See his grin?

Amanda: (*absently*). He must have had a jolly disposition.

Laura: He used to call me—Blue Roses.

(*Image: Blue Roses.*)

Amanda: Why did he call you such a name as that?

Laura: When I had that attack of pleurosis—he asked me what was the matter when I came back. I said pleurosis—he thought that I said Blue Roses! So that's what he always called me after that. Whenever he saw me, he'd holler, "Hello, Blue Roses!" I didn't care for the girl that he went out with. Emily Meisenbach. Emily was the best-dressed girl at Soldan. She never struck me, though, as being sincere. . . . It says in the Personal Section—they're engaged. That's—six years ago! They must be married by now.

Amanda: Girls that aren't cut out for business careers usually wind up married to some nice man. (*Gets up with a spark of revival.*) Sister, that's what you'll do!

(*Laura utters a startled, doubtful laugh. She reaches quickly for a piece of glass.*)

Laura: But, Mother—

Amanda: Yes? (*Crossing to photograph.*)

Laura: (*in a tone of frightened apology*) I'm—crippled!

(*Image: Screen.*)

Amanda: Nonsense! Laura, I've told you never, never to use that word. Why, you're not crippled, you just have a little defect—hardly noticeable, even! When people have some slight disadvantage like that, they cultivate other things to make up for it—develop charm—and vivacity—and—*charm!* That's all you have to do! (*She turns again to the photograph.*) One thing your father had *plenty of*—was *charm!*

(*Tom motions to the fiddle in the wings.*)

(*The Scene Fades Out with Music.*)

Scene 3
(*Legend on the Screen: "After the Fiasco—"*)

Tom speaks from the fire-escape landing.

Tom: After the fiasco at Rubicam's Business College, the idea of getting a gentleman caller for Laura began to play a more important part in Mother's calculations. It became an obsession. Like some archetype of the universal unconscious, the image of the gentleman caller haunted our small apartment. . . . (*Image: Young Man at Door with Flowers.*) An evening at home rarely passed without some allusion to this image, this specter, this hope. . . . Even when he wasn't mentioned, his presence hung in Mother's preoccupied look and in my sister's frightened, apologetic manner—hung like a sentence passed upon the Wingfields! Mother was a woman of action as well as words. She began to take logical steps in the planned direction. Late that winter and in the early spring—realizing that extra money would be needed to properly feather the nest and plume the bird—she conducted a vigorous campaign on the telephone, roping in subscribers to one of those magazines for matrons called The *Home-maker's Companion,* the type of journal that features the serialized sublimations of ladies of letters who think in terms of delicate cup-like breasts, slim, tapering waists, rich, creamy thighs, eyes like wood-smoke in autumn, fingers that soothe and caress like strains of music, bodies as powerful as Etruscan sculpture.

(*Screen Image: Glamor Magazine Cover.*)

(*Amanda enters with phone on long extension cord. She is spotted in the dim stage.*)

Amanda: Ida Scott? This is Amanda Wingfield! We *missed* you at the D.A.R. last Monday! I said to myself: She's probably suffering with that sinus condition! How is that sinus condition? Horrors! Heaven have mercy!—You're a Christian martyr, yes, that's what you are, a Christian martyr! Well, I just now happened to notice that your subscription to the *Companion's* about to expire! Yes, it expires with the next issue, honey!—just when that wonderful new serial by Bessie Mae Hopper is getting off to such an exciting start. Oh, honey, it's something that you can't miss! You remember how *Gone With the Wind* took everybody by storm? You simply couldn't go out if you hadn't read it. All everybody *talked* was Scarlett O'Hara. Well, this is a book that critics already compare to *Gone With the Wind*. It's the *Gone With the Wind* of the post-World War generation!—What?—Burning? Oh, honey, don't let them burn, go take a look in the oven and I'll hold the wire! Heavens—I think she's hung up!

(Dim Out.)

(Legend on Screen: "You Think I'm in Love with Continental Shoemakers?")

(Before the stage is lighted, the violent voices of Tom and Amanda are heard. They are quarreling behind the portieres. In front of them stands Laura with clenched hands and panicky expression. A clear pool of light on her figure throughout this scene.)

Tom: What in Christ's name am I—
Amanda: (shrilly) Don't you use that—
Tom: Supposed to do!
Amanda: Expression! Not in my—
Tom: Ohhh!
Amanda: Presence! Have you gone out of your senses?
Tom: I have, that's true, *driven* out!
Amanda: What is the matter with you, you—big—big—IDIOT!
Tom: Look—I've got *no thing*, no single thing—
Amanda: Lower your voice!
Tom: In my life here that I can call my OWN! Everything is—
Amanda: Stop that shouting!
Tom: Yesterday you confiscated my books! You had the nerve to—
Amanda: I took that horrible novel back to the library—yes! That hideous book by that
    insane Mr. Lawrence. *(Tom laughs wildly.)* I cannot control the output of diseased
    minds or people who cater to them—*(Tom laughs still more wildly.)* BUT I WON'T
    ALLOW SUCH FILTH BROUGHT INTO MY HOUSE! No, no, no, no, no!
Tom: House, house! Who pays rent on it, who makes a slave of himself to—
Amanda: (fairly screeching) Don't you DARE to—
Tom: No, no, *I* mustn't say things! *I've* got to just—
Amanda: Let me tell you—
Tom: I don't want to hear any more! *(He tears the portieres open. The upstage area is lit
    with a turgid smoky red glow.)*

*Amanda's hair is in metal curlers and she wears a very old bathrobe, much too large for her
slight figure, a relic of the faithless Mr. Wingfield. An upright typewriter and a wild disarray of manuscripts are on the drop-leaf table. The quarrel was probably precipitated by
Amanda's interruption of his creative labor. A chair lying overthrown on the floor. Their
gesticulating shadows are cast on the ceiling by the fiery glow.*

Amanda: You *will* hear more, you—
Tom: No, I won't hear more, I'm going out!
Amanda: You come right back in—
Tom: Out, out out! Because I'm—
Amanda: Come back here, Tom Wingfield! I'm not through talking to you!
Tom: Oh, go—
Laura: (desperately) Tom!
Amanda: You're going to listen, and no more insolence from you! I'm at the end of my
    patience! *(He comes back toward her.)*

Tom: What do you think I'm at? Aren't I supposed to have any patience to reach the end of, Mother? I know, I know. It seems unimportant to you, what I'm *doing*—what I *want* to do—having a little *difference* between them! You don't think that—

Amanda: I think you've been doing things that you're ashamed of. That's why you act like this. I don't believe that you go every night to the movies. Nobody goes to the movies night after night. Nobody in their right minds goes to the movies as often as you pretend to. People don't go to the movies at nearly midnight, and movies don't let out at two A.M. Come in stumbling. Muttering to yourself like a maniac! You get three hours' sleep and then go to work. Oh, I can picture the way you're doing down there. Moping, doping, because you're in no condition.

Tom: (*wildly*) No, I'm in no condition!

Amanda: What right have you got to jeopardize your job? Jeopardize the security of us all? How do you think we'd manage if you were—

Tom: Listen! You think I'm crazy *about* the *warehouse?* (*He bends fiercely toward her slight figure.*) You think I'm in love with the Continental Shoemakers? You think I want to spend fifty-five *years* down there in that—*celotex interior!* with—*fluorescent—tubes!* Look! I'd rather somebody picked up a crowbar and battered out my brains than go back mornings! I *go!* Every time you come in yelling that God damn *"Rise and Shine!" "Rise and Shine!"* I say to myself *"How lucky dead* people are!" But I get up. I *go!* For sixty-five dollars a month I give up all that I dream of doing and being *ever!* And you say self—*self's* all I ever think of. Why, listen, if self is what I thought of, Mother, I'd be where he is—GONE! (*Pointing to father's picture.*) As far as the system of transportation reaches! (*He starts past her. She grabs his arm.*) Don't grab at me, Mother!

Amanda: Where are you going?

Tom: I'm going to the *movies!*

Amanda: I don't believe that lie!

Tom: (*crouching toward her, overtowering her tiny figure. She backs away, gasping*) I'm going to opium dens! Yes, opium dens, dens of vice and criminals' hang-outs, Mother. I've joined the Hogan gang, I'm a hired assassin, I carry a tommy-gun in a violin case! I run a string of cat-houses in the Valley! They call me Killer, Killer Wingfield, I'm leading a double-life, a simple, honest warehouse worker by day, by night a dynamic *czar* of the *underworld, Mother.* I go to gambling casinos, I spin away fortunes on the roulette table! I wear a patch over one eye and a false mustache, sometimes I put on green whiskers. On those occasions they call me—*El Diablo!* Oh, I could tell you things to make you sleepless! My enemies plan to dynamite this place. They're going to blow us all sky-high some night! I'll be glad, very happy, and so will you! You'll go up, up on a broomstick, over Blue Mountain with seventeen gentlemen callers! You ugly—babbling old—*witch.* . . . (*He goes through a series of violent, clumsy movements, seizing his overcoat, lunging to the door, pulling it fiercely open. The women watch him, aghast. His arm catches in the sleeve of the coat as he struggles to pull it on. For a moment he is pinioned by the bulky garment. With an outraged groan he tears the coat off again, splitting the shoulders of it, and hurls it across the room. It strikes against the shelf of Laura's glass collection, there is a tinkle of shattering glass. Laura cries out as if wounded.*)

(*Music Legend: "The Glass Menagerie."*)

Laura: (shrilly) My glass!—menagerie. . . . (She covers her face and turns away.)

(But Amanda is still stunned and stupefied by the "ugly witch" so that she barely notices this occurrence. Now she recovers her speech.)

Amanda: (in an awful voice) I won't speak to you—until you apologize! (She crosses through portieres and draws them together behind her. Tom is left with Laura. Laura clings weakly to the mantel with her face averted. Tom stares at her stupidly for a moment. Then he crosses to shelf. Drops awkwardly to his knees to collect the fallen glass, glancing at Laura as if he would speak but couldn't.)

("The Glass Menagerie" steals in as the Scene Dims Out.)

Scene 4

The interior is dark. Faint light in the alley. A deep-voiced bell in a church is tolling the hour by five as the scene commences.

Tom appears at the top of the alley. After each solemn boom of the bell in the tower, he shakes a little noise-maker or rattle as if to express the tiny spasm of man in contrast to the sustained power and dignity of the Almighty. This and the unsteadiness of his advance make it evident that he has been drinking.

As he climbs the few steps to the fire-escape landing light steals up inside. Laura appears in night-dress, observing Tom's empty bed in the front room.

Tom fishes in his pockets for the door-key, removing a motley assortment of articles in the search, including a perfect shower of movie-ticket stubs and an empty bottle. At last he finds the key, but just as he is about to insert it, it slips from his fingers. He strikes a match and crouches below the door.

Tom: (bitterly) One crack—and it falls through!

(Laura opens the door.)

Laura: Tom! Tom, what are you doing?
Tom: Looking for a door-key.
Laura: Where have you been all this time?
Tom: I have been to the movies.
Laura: All this time at the movies?
Tom: There was a very long program. There was a Garbo picture and a Mickey Mouse and a travelogue and a newsreel and a preview of coming attractions. And there was an organ solo and a collection for the milk-fund—simultaneously—which ended up in a terrible fight between a fat lady and an usher!
Laura: (innocently) Did you have to stay through everything?
Tom: Of course! And, oh, I forgot! There was a big stage show! The headliner on this stage show was Malvolio the Magician. He performed wonderful tricks, many of them, such as pouring water back and forth between pitchers. First it turned to wine and then it turned to beer and then it turned to whiskey. I know it was whiskey it finally turned into because he needed somebody to come up out of the audience to help him, and I came up—both shows! It was Kentucky Straight Bour-

bon. A very generous fellow, he gave souvenirs. (*He pulls from his back pocket a shimmering rainbow-colored scarf.*) He gave me this. This is his magic scarf. You can have it, Laura. You wave it over a canary cage and you get a bowl of gold-fish. You wave it over the goldfish bowl and they fly away canaries. . . . But the wonderfulest trick of all was the coffin trick. We nailed him into a coffin and he got out of the coffin without removing one nail. (*He has come inside.*) There is a trick that would come in handy for me—get me out of this 2 by 4 situation! (*Flops onto bed and starts removing shoes.*)

Laura: Tom—Shhh!

Tom: What you shushing me for?

Laura: You'll wake up Mother.

Tom: Goody, goody! Pay 'er back for all those "Rise an' Shines." (*Lies down, groaning.*) You know it don't take much intelligence to get yourself into a nailed-up coffin, Laura. But who in hell ever got himself out of one without removing one nail?

(*As if in answer, the father's grinning photograph lights up.*)

(*Scene Dims Out.*)

Immediately following: The church bell is heard striking six. At the sixth stroke the alarm clock goes off in Amanda's room, and after a few moments we hear her calling: "Rise and Shine! Rise and Shine! Laura, go tell your brother to rise and shine!"

Tom: (*sitting up slowly*) I'll rise—but I won't shine.

(*The light increases.*)

Amanda: Laura, tell your brother his coffee is ready.

(*Laura slips into front room.*)

Laura: Tom! it's nearly seven. Don't make Mother nervous. (*He stares at her stupidly. Beseechingly*) Tom, speak to Mother this morning. Make up with her, apologize, speak to her!

Tom: She won't to me. It's her that started not speaking.

Laura: If you just say you're sorry she'll start speaking.

Tom: Her not speaking—is that such a tragedy?

Laura: Please—please!

Amanda: (*calling from kitchenette*) Laura, are you going to do what I asked you to do, or do I have to get dressed and go out myself?

Laura: Going, going—soon as I get on my coat! (*She pulls on a shapeless felt hat with nervous, jerky movement, pleadingly glancing at Tom. Rushes awkwardly for coat. The coat is one of Amanda's, inaccurately made-over, the sleeves too short for Laura.*) Butter and what else?

Amanda: (*entering upstage*) Just butter. Tell them to charge it.

Laura: Mother, they make such faces when I do that.

Amanda: Sticks and stones may break my bones, but the expression of Mr. Garfinkel's face won't harm me! Tell your brother his coffee is getting cold.

Laura: (*at door*) Do what I asked you, will you, will you, Tom?

(He looks sullenly away.)

Amanda: Laura, go now or just don't go at all!
Laura: *(rushing out).* Going—going! *(A second later she cries out. Tom springs up and crosses to the door. Amanda rushes anxiously in. Tom opens the door.)*
Tom: Laura?
Laura: I'm all right. I slipped, but I'm all right.
Amanda: *(peering anxiously after her).* If anyone breaks a leg on those fire-escape steps, the landlord ought to be sued for every cent he possesses! *(She shuts door. Remembers she isn't speaking and returns to other room.)*

(As Tom enters listlessly for his coffee, she turns her back to him and stands rigidly facing the window on the gloomy gray vault of the areaway. Its light on her face with its aged but childish features is cruelly sharp, satirical as a Daumier print.)

(Music Under: "Ave Maria.")

(Tom glances sheepishly but sullenly at her averted figure and slumps at the table. The coffee is scalding hot; he sips it and gasps and spits it back in the cup. At his gasp, Amanda catches her breath and half turns. Then catches herself and turns back to window.
   Tom blows on his coffee, glancing sidewise at his mother. She clears her throat. Tom clears his. He starts to rise. Sinks back down again, scratches his head, clears his throat again. Amanda coughs. Tom raises his cup in both hands to blow on it, his eyes staring over the rim of it at his mother for several moments. Then he slowly sets the cup down and awkwardly and hesitantly rises from the chair.)

Tom: *(hoarsely)* Mother. I—I apologize. Mother. *(Amanda draws a quick, shuddering breath. Her face works grotesquely. She breaks into childlike tears.)* I'm sorry for what I said, for everything that I said, I didn't mean it.
Amanda: *(sobbingly)* My devotion has made me a witch and so I make myself hateful to my children!
Tom: No, you *don't.*
Amanda: I worry so much, don't sleep, it makes me nervous!
Tom: *(gently)* I understand that.
Amanda: I've had to put up a solitary battle all these years. But you're my right-hand bower! Don't fall down, don't fail!
Tom: *(gently)* I try, Mother.
Amanda: *(with great enthusiasm)* Try and you will SUCCEED! *(The notion makes her breathless.)* Why, you—you're just *full* of natural endowments! Both of my children—they're *unusual* children! Don't you think I know it? I'm so—*proud!* Happy and—feel I've—so much to be thankful for but—Promise me one thing, son!
Tom: What, Mother?
Amanda: Promise, son, you'll—never be a drunkard!
Tom: *(turns to her grinning)* I will never be a drunkard, Mother.
Amanda: That's what frightened me so, that you'd be drinking! Eat a bowl of Purina!
Tom: Just coffee, Mother.
Amanda: Shredded wheat biscuit?

Tom: No. No, Mother, just coffee.

Amanda: You can't put in a day's work on an empty stomach. You've got ten minutes—don't gulp! Drinking too-hot liquids makes cancer of the stomach. . . . Put cream in.

Tom: No, thank you.

Amanda: To cool it.

Tom: No! No, thank you, I want it black.

Amanda: I know, but it's not good for you. We have to do all that we can to build ourselves up. In these trying times we live in, all that we have to cling to is each other. . . . That's why it's so important to—Tom, I—I sent out your sister so I could discuss something with you. If you hadn't spoken I would have spoken to you. (*Sits down.*)

Tom: (*gently*) What is it, Mother, that you want to discuss?

Amanda: Laura!

(*Tom puts his cup down slowly.*)

(*Legend on Screen: "Laura."*)

(*Music: "The Glass Menagerie."*)

Tom: —Oh.—Laura . . .

Amanda: (*touching his sleeve*) You know how Laura is. So quiet but—still water runs deep! She notices things and I think she—broods about them. (*Tom looks up.*) A few days ago I came in and she was crying.

Tom: What about?

Amanda: You.

Tom: Me?

Amanda: She has an idea that you're not happy here.

Tom: What gave her that idea?

Amanda: What gives her any idea? However, you do act strangely. I—I'm not criticizing, understand *that!* I know your ambitions do not lie in the warehouse, that like everybody in the whole wide world—you've had to—make sacrifices, but—Tom— Tom—life's not easy, it calls for—Spartan endurance! There's so many things in my heart that I cannot describe to you! I've never told you but I—*loved* your father. . . .

Tom: (*gently*) I know that, Mother.

Amanda: And you—when I see you taking after his ways! Staying out late—and—well, you *had* been drinking the night you were in that—terrifying condition! Laura says that you hate the apartment and that you go out nights to get away from it! Is that true, Tom?

Tom: No. You say there's so much in your heart that you can't describe to me. That's true of me, too. There's so much in my heart that I can't describe to *you!* So let's respect each other's—

Amanda: But, why—why, Tom—are you always so *restless?* Where do you go to, nights?

Tom: I—go to the movies.

Amanda: Why do you go to the movies so much, Tom?

Tom: I go to the movies because—I like adventure. Adventure is something I don't have
   much of at work, so I go to the movies.
Amanda: But, Tom, you go to the movies *entirely too much!*
Tom: I like a lot of adventure.

(*Amanda looks baffled, then hurt. As the familiar inquisition resumes he becomes hard and
impatient again. Amanda slips back into her querulous attitude toward him.*)

(*Image on Screen: Sailing Vessel with Jolly Roger.*)

Amanda: Most young men find adventure in their careers.
Tom: Then most young men are not employed in a warehouse.
Amanda: The world is full of young men employed in warehouses and offices and facto-
   ries.
Tom: Do all of them find adventure in their careers?
Amanda: They do or they do without it! Not everybody has a craze for adventure.
Tom: Man is by instinct a lover, a hunter, a fighter, and none of those instincts are given
   much play at the warehouse!
Amanda: Man is by instinct! Don't quote instinct to me! Instinct is something that peo-
   ple have got away from! It belongs to animals! Christian adults don't want it!
Tom: What do Christian adults want, then, Mother?
Amanda: Superior things! Things of the mind and the spirit! Only animals have to satisfy
   instincts! Surely your aims are somewhat higher than theirs! Than monkeys—pigs—
Tom: I reckon they're not.
Amanda: You're joking. However, that isn't what I wanted to discuss.
Tom: (*rising*) I haven't much time.
Amanda: (*pushing his shoulders*) Sit down.
Tom: You want me to punch in red at the warehouse, Mother?
Amanda: You have five minutes. I want to talk about Laura.

(*Legend: "Plans and Provisions."*)

Tom: All right! What about Laura?
Amanda: We have to be making plans and provisions for her. She's older than you, two
   years, and nothing has happened. She just drifts along doing nothing. It frightens
   me terribly how she just drifts along.
Tom: I guess she's the type that people call home girls.
Amanda: There's no such type, and if there is, it's a pity! That is unless the home is hers,
   with a husband!
Tom: What?
Amanda: Oh, I can see the handwriting on the wall as plain as I see the nose in front of
   my face! It's terrifying! More and more you remind me of your father! He was out
   all hours without explanation—Then *left! Good-bye!* And me with the bag to hold.
   I saw that letter you got from the Merchant Marine. I know what you're dreaming
   of. I'm not standing here blindfolded. Very well, then. Then *do* it! But not till
   there's somebody to take your place.
Tom: What do you mean?

Amanda: I mean that as soon as Laura has got somebody to take care of her, married, a home of her own, independent—why, then you'll be free to go wherever you please, on land, on sea, whichever way the wind blows! But until that time you've got to look out for your sister. I don't say me because I'm old and don't matter! I say for your sister because she's young and dependent. I put her in business college—a dismal failure! Frightened her so it made her sick to her stomach. I took her over to the Young People's League at the church. Another fiasco. She spoke to nobody, nobody spoke to her. Now all she does is fool with those pieces of glass and play those worn-out records. What kind of a life is that for a girl to lead!

Tom: What can I do about it?

Amanda: Overcome selfishness! Self, self, self is all that you ever think of! (*Tom springs up and crosses to get his coat. It is ugly and bulky. He pulls on a cap with earmuffs.*) Where is your muffler? Put your wool muffler on! (*He snatches it angrily from the closet and tosses it around his neck and pulls both ends tight.*) Tom! I haven't said what I had in mind to ask you.

Tom: I'm too late to—

Amanda: (*catching his arms very importunately. Then shyly.*) Down at the warehouse, aren't there some—nice young men?

Tom: No!

Amanda: There *must* be—*some*.

Tom: Mother—

(*Gesture.*)

Amanda: Find out one that's clean-living—doesn't drink and—ask him out for sister!

Tom: What?

Amanda: For *sister*! To *meet*! Get acquainted!

Tom: (*stamping to door*). Oh, my go-osh!

Amanda: Will you? (*He opens door. Imploringly*) Will you? (*He starts down.*) Will you? Will you, dear?

Tom: (*calling back*). YES!

(*Amanda closes the door hesitantly and with a troubled but faintly hopeful expression.*)

(*Screen Image: Glamor Magazine Cover.*)

(*Spot Amanda at phone.*)

Amanda: Ella Cartwright? This is Amanda Wingfield! How are you, honey? How is that kidney condition? (*Count five.*) Horrors! (*Count five.*) You're a Christian martyr, yes, honey, that's what you are, a Christian martyr! Well, I just happened to notice in my little red book that your subscription to the *Companion* has just run out! I knew that you wouldn't want to miss out on the wonderful serial starting in this new issue. It's by Bessie Mae Hopper, the first thing she's written since *Honeymoon for Three.* Wasn't that a strange and interesting story? Well, this one is even lovelier, I believe. It has a sophisticated society background. It's all about the horsey set on Long Island!

(Fade Out.)

Scene 5
(Legend on Screen: "Annunciation.") Fade with music.

It is early dusk of a spring evening. Supper has just been finished in the Wingfield apartment. Amanda and Laura in light-colored dresses are removing dishes from the table, in the upstage area, which is shadowy, their movements formalized almost as a dance or ritual, their moving forms as pale and silent as moths. Tom, in white shirt and trousers, rises from the table and crosses toward the fire-escape.

Amanda: *(as he passes her)* Son, will you do me a favor?

Tom: What?

Amanda: Comb your hair! You look so pretty when your hair is combed! *(Tom slouches on sofa with evening paper. Enormous caption "Franco Triumphs.")* There is only one respect in which I would like you to emulate your father.

Tom: What respect is that?

Amanda: The care he always took of his appearance. He never allowed himself to look untidy. *(He throws down the paper and crosses to fire-escape.)* Where are you going?

Tom: I'm going out to smoke.

Amanda: You smoke too much. A pack a day at fifteen cents a pack. How much would that amount to in a month? Thirty times fifteen is how much, Tom? Figure it out and you will be astounded at what you could save. Enough to give you a night-school course in accounting at Washington U! Just think what a wonderful thing that would be for you, son!

(Tom is unmoved by the thought.)

Tom: I'd rather smoke. *(He steps out on landing, letting the screen door slam.)*

Amanda: *(sharply).* I know! That's the tragedy of it. . . . *(Alone, she turns to look at her husband's picture.)*

(Dance Music: "All the World Is Waiting for the Sunrise!")

Tom: *(to the audience).* Across the alley from us was the Paradise Dance Hall. On evenings in spring the windows and doors were open and the music came out-doors. Sometimes the lights were turned out except for a large glass sphere that hung from the ceiling. It would turn slowly about and filter the dusk with delicate rainbow colors. Then the orchestra played a waltz or a tango, something that had a slow and sensuous rhythm. Couples would come outside, to the relative privacy of the alley. You could see them kissing behind ashpits and telephone poles. This was the compensation for lives that passed like mine, without any change or adventure. Adventure and change were imminent in this year. They were waiting around the corner for all these kids. Suspended in the mist over Berchtesgaden, caught in the folds of Chamberlain's umbrella—In Spain there was Guernica! But here there was only hot swing music and liquor, dance halls, bars, and movies, and sex that hung in the gloom like a chandelier and flooded the world with brief, deceptive rainbows. . . . All the world was waiting for bombardments!

(*Amanda turns from the picture and comes outside.*)

Amanda: (*sighing*). A fire-escape landing's a poor excuse for a porch. (*She spreads a newspaper on a step and sits down, gracefully and demurely as if she were settling into a swing on a Mississippi veranda.*) What are you looking at?

Tom: The moon.

Amanda: Is there a moon this evening?

Tom: It's rising over Garfinkel's Delicatessen.

Amanda: So it is! A little silver slipper of a moon. Have you made a wish on it yet?

Tom: Um-hum.

Amanda: What did you wish for?

Tom: That's a secret.

Amanda: A secret, huh? Well, I won't tell mine either. I will be just as mysterious as you.

Tom: I bet I can guess what yours is.

Amanda: Is my head so transparent?

Tom: You're not a sphinx.

Amanda: No, I don't have secrets. I'll tell you what I wished for on the moon. Success and happiness for my precious children! I wish for that whenever there's a moon, and when there isn't a moon, I wish for it, too.

Tom: I thought perhaps you wished for a gentleman caller.

Amanda: Why do you say that?

Tom: Don't you remember asking me to fetch one?

Amanda: I remember suggesting that it would be nice for your sister if you brought home some nice young man from the warehouse. I think I've made that suggestion more than once.

Tom: Yes, you have made it repeatedly.

Amanda: Well?

Tom: We are going to have one.

Amanda: What?

Tom: A gentleman caller!

(*The Annunciation Is Celebrated with Music.*)

(*Amanda rises.*)

(*Image on Screen: Caller with Bouquet.*)

Amanda: You mean you have asked some nice young man to come over?

Tom: Yep. I've asked him to dinner.

Amanda: You really did?

Tom: I did!

Amanda: You did, and did he—*accept?*

Tom: He did!

Amanda: Well, well—well, well! That's—lovely!

Tom: I thought that you would be pleased.

Amanda: It's definite, then?

Tom: Very definite.

Amanda: Soon?

Tom: Very soon.

Amanda: For heaven's sake, stop putting on and tell me some things, will you?

Tom: What things do you want me to tell you?

Amanda: Naturally I would like to know when he's *coming!*

Tom: He's coming tomorrow.

Amanda: *Tomorrow?*

Tom: Yep. Tomorrow.

Amanda: But, Tom!

Tom: Yes, Mother?

Amanda: Tomorrow gives me no time!

Tom: Time for what?

Amanda: Preparations! Why didn't you phone me at once, as soon as you asked him, the minute that he accepted? Then, don't you see, I could have been getting ready!

Tom: You don't have to make any fuss.

Amanda: Oh, Tom, Tom, Tom, of course I have to make a fuss! I want things nice, not sloppy! Not thrown together. I'll certainly have to do some fast thinking, won't I?

Tom: I don't see why you have to think at all.

Amanda: You just don't know. We can't have a gentleman caller in a pig-sty! All my wedding silver has to be polished, the monogrammed table linen ought to be laundered! The windows have to be washed and fresh curtains put up. And how about clothes? We have to *wear* something, don't we?

Tom: Mother, this boy is no one to make a fuss over!

Amanda: Do you realize he's the first young man we've had introduced to your sister? It's terrible, dreadful, disgraceful that poor little sister has never received a single gentleman caller! Tom, come inside! (*She opens the screen door.*)

Tom: What for?

Amanda: I want to ask you some things.

Tom: If you're going to make such a fuss, I'll call it off, I'll tell him not to come.

Amanda: You certainly won't do anything of the kind. Nothing offends people worse than broken engagements. It simply means I'll have to work like a Turk! We won't be brilliant, but we'll pass inspection. Come on inside. (*Tom follows, groaning.*) Sit down.

Tom: Any particular place you would like me to sit?

Amanda: Thank heavens I've got that new sofa! I'm also making payments on a floor lamp I'll have sent out! And put the chintz covers on, they'll brighten things up! Of course I'd hoped to have these walls re-papered. . . . What is the young man's name?

Tom: His name is O'Connor.

Amanda: That, of course, means fish—tomorrow is Friday! I'll have that salmon loaf—with Durkee's dressing! What does he do? He works at the warehouse?

Tom: Of course! How else would I—

Amanda: Tom, he—doesn't drink?

Tom: Why do you ask me that?

Amanda: Your father *did!*

Tom: Don't get started on that!

Amanda: He *does* drink, then?

Tom: Not that I know of!

Amanda: Make sure, be certain! The last thing I want for my daughter's a boy who drinks!

Tom: Aren't you being a little premature? Mr. O'Connor has not yet appeared on the scene!

Amanda: But will tomorrow. To meet your sister, and what do I know about his character? Nothing! Old maids are better off than wives of drunkards!

Tom: Oh, my God!

Amanda: Be still!

Tom: (*leaning forward to whisper*) Lots of fellows meet girls whom they don't marry!

Amanda: Oh, talk sensibly, Tom—and don't be sarcastic! (*She has gotten a hairbrush.*)

Tom: What are you doing?

Amanda: I'm brushing that cow-lick down! What is this young man's position at the warehouse?

Tom: (*submitting grimly to the brush and the interrogation*). This young man's position is that of a shipping clerk, Mother.

Amanda: Sounds to me like a fairly responsible job, the sort of a job *you* would be in if you just had more *get-up*. What is his salary? Have you got any idea?

Tom: I would judge it to be approximately eighty-five dollars a month.

Amanda: Well—not princely, but——

Tom: Twenty more than I make.

Amanda: Yes, how well I know! But for a family man, eighty-five dollars a month is not much more than you can just get by on. . . .

Tom: Yes, but Mr. O'Connor is not a family man.

Amanda: He might be, mightn't he? Some time in the future?

Tom: I see. Plans and provisions.

Amanda: You are the only young man that I know of who ignores the fact that the future becomes the present, the present the past, and the past turns into everlasting regret if you don't plan for it!

Tom: I will think that over and see what I can make of it.

Amanda: Don't be supercilious with your mother! Tell me some more about this— what do you call him?

Tom: James D. O'Connor. The D. is for Delaney.

Amanda: Irish on *both* sides! *Gracious!* And doesn't drink?

Tom: Shall I call him up and ask him right this minute?

Amanda: The only way to find out about those things is to make discreet inquiries at the proper moment. When I was a girl in Blue Mountain and it was suspected that a young man drank, the girl whose attentions he had been receiving, if any girl *was,* would sometimes speak to the minister of his church, or rather her father would if her father was living, and sort of feel him out on the young man's character. That is the way such things are discreetly handled to keep a young woman from making a tragic mistake!

Tom: Then how did you happen to make a tragic mistake?

Amanda: That innocent look of your father's had everyone fooled! He *smiled*—the world was *enchanted!* No girl can do worse than put herself at the mercy of a handsome appearance! I hope that Mr. O'Connor is not too good-looking.

Tom: No, he's not too good-looking. He's covered with freckles and hasn't too much
    of a nose.
Amanda: He's not right-down homely, though?
Tom: Not right-down homely. Just medium homely, I'd say.
Amanda: Character's what to look for in a man.
Tom: That's what I've always said, Mother.
Amanda: You've never said anything of the kind and I suspect you would never give it
    a thought.
Tom: Don't be suspicious of me.
Amanda: At least I hope he's the type that's up and coming.
Tom: I think he really goes in for self-improvement.
Amanda: What reason have you to think so?
Tom: He goes to night school.
Amanda: (*beaming*) Splendid! What does he do, I mean study?
Tom: Radio engineering and public speaking!
Amanda: Then he has visions of being advanced in the world! Any young man who
    studies public speaking is aiming to have an executive job some day! And radio en-
    gineering? A thing for the future! Both of these facts are very illuminating. Those
    are the sort of things that a mother should know concerning any young man who
    comes to call on her daughter. Seriously or—not.
Tom: One little warning. He doesn't know about Laura. I didn't let on that we had dark
    ulterior motives. I just said, why don't you come have dinner with us? He said okay
    and that was the whole conversation.
Amanda: I bet it was! You're eloquent as an oyster. However, he'll know about Laura
    when he gets here. When he sees how lovely and sweet and pretty she is, he'll thank
    his lucky stars he was asked to dinner.
Tom: Mother, you mustn't expect too much of Laura.
Amanda: What do you mean?
Tom: Laura seems all those things to you and me because she's ours and we love her.
    We don't even notice she's crippled any more.
Amanda: Don't say crippled! You know that I never allow that word to be used!
Tom: But face facts, Mother. She is and—that's not all—
Amanda: What do you mean "not all"?
Tom: Laura is very different from other girls.
Amanda: I think the difference is all to her advantage.
Tom: Not quite all—in the eyes of others—strangers—she's terribly shy and lives in a
    world of her own and those things make her seem a little peculiar to people outside
    the house.
Amanda: Don't say peculiar.
Tom: Face the facts. She is.

(*The Dance-Hall Music Changes to a Tango That Has a Minor and Somewhat Ominous
Tone.*)

Amanda: In what way is she peculiar—may I ask?
Tom: (*gently*) She lives in a world of her own—a world of—little glass ornaments,
    Mother. . . . (*Gets up. Amanda remains holding brush, looking at him, troubled.*) She

plays old phonograph records and—that's about all—(*He glances at himself in the mirror and crosses to door.*)

Amanda: (*sharply*) Where are you going?

Tom: I'm going to the movies. (*Out screen door.*)

Amanda: Not to the movies, every night to the movies! (*Follows quickly to screen door.*) I don't believe you always go to the movies! (*He is gone. Amanda looks worriedly after him for a moment. Then vitality and optimism return and she turns from the door. Crossing to portieres.*) Laura! Laura! (*Laura answers from kitchenette.*)

Laura: Yes, Mother.

Amanda: Let those dishes go and come in front! (*Laura appears with dish towel. Gaily*) Laura, come here and make a wish on the moon!

Laura: (*entering*) Moon—moon?

Amanda: A little silver slipper of a moon. Look over your left shoulder, Laura, and make a wish! (*Laura looks faintly puzzled as if called out of sleep. Amanda seizes her shoulders and turns her at angle by the door.*) Now! Now, darling, *wish!*

Laura: What shall I wish for, Mother?

Amanda: (*her voice trembling and her eyes suddenly filling with tears*) Happiness! Good Fortune!

(*The violin rises and the stage dims out.*)

Scene 6
(*Image: High School Hero.*)

Tom: And so the following evening I brought Jim home to dinner. I had known Jim slightly in high school. In high school Jim was a hero. He had tremendous Irish good nature and vitality with the scrubbed and polished look of white chinaware. He seemed to move in a continual spotlight. He was a star in basketball, captain of the debating club, president of the senior class and the glee club and he sang the male lead in the annual light operas. He was always running or bounding, never just walking. He seemed always at the point of defeating the law of gravity. He was shooting with such velocity through his adolescence that you would logically expect him to arrive at nothing short of the White House by the time he was thirty. But Jim apparently ran into more interference after his graduation from Soldan. His speed had definitely slowed. Six years after he left high school he was holding a job that wasn't much better than mine.

(*Image: Clerk.*) *He was the only one at the warehouse with whom I was on friendly terms. I was valuable to him as someone who could remember his former glory, who had seen him win basketball games and the silver cup in debating. He knew of my secret practice of retiring to a cabinet of the washroom to work on poems when business was slack in the warehouse. He called me Shakespeare. And while the other boys in the warehouse regarded me with suspicious hostility, Jim took a humorous attitude toward me. Gradually his attitude affected the others, their hostility wore off and they also began to smile at me as people smile at an oddly fashioned dog who trots across their path at some distance.*

I knew that Jim and Laura had known each other at Soldan, and I had heard Laura speak admiringly of his voice. I didn't know if Jim remembered her or not. In high school

Laura had been as unobtrusive as Jim had been astonishing. If he did remember Laura, it was not as my sister for when I asked him to dinner, he grinned and said, "You know, Shakespeare, I never thought of you as having folks!"

He was about to discover that I did. . . .

(*Light upstage.*)

(Legend on Screen: "The Accent of a Coming Foot.")

(Friday evening. It is about five o'clock of a late spring evening which comes "scattering poems in the sky." A delicate lemony light is in the Wingfield apartment. Amanda has worked like a Turk in preparation for the gentleman caller. The results are astonishing. The new floor lamp with its rose-silk shade is in place, a colored paper lantern conceals the broken light fixture in the ceiling, new billowing white curtains are at the windows, chintz covers are on chairs and sofa, a pair of new sofa pillows make their initial appearance.

Open boxes and tissue paper are scattered on the floor.

Laura stands in the middle with lifted arms while Amanda crouches before her, adjusting the hem of the new dress, devout and ritualistic. The dress is colored and designed by memory. The arrangement of Laura's hair is changed; it is softer and more becoming. A fragile, unearthly prettiness has come out in Laura: she is like a piece of translucent glass touched by light, given a momentary radiance, not actual, not lasting.)

Amanda: (*impatiently*) Why are you trembling?
Laura: Mother, you've made me so nervous!
Amanda: How have I made you nervous?
Laura: By all this fuss! You make it seem so important!
Amanda: I don't understand you, Laura. You couldn't be satisfied with just sitting home, and yet whenever I try to arrange something for you, you seem to resist it. (*She gets up.*) Now take a look at yourself. No, wait! Wait just a moment—I have an idea!
Laura: What is it now?

(Amanda produces two powder puffs which she wraps in handkerchiefs and stuffs in Laura's bosom.)

Laura: Mother, what are you doing?
Amanda: They call them "Gay Deceivers"!
Laura: I won't wear them!
Amanda: You will!
Laura: Why should I?
Amanda: Because, to be painfully honest, your chest is flat.
Laura: You make it seem like we were setting a trap.
Amanda: All pretty girls are a trap, a pretty trap, and men expect them to be.

(Legend: "A Pretty Trap.")

Now look at yourself, young lady. This is the prettiest you will ever be! I've got to fix myself now! You're going to be surprised by your mother's appearance! (*She crosses through portieres, humming gaily.*)

(*Laura moves slowly to the long mirror and stares solemnly at herself. A wind blows the white curtains inward in a slow, graceful motion and with a faint, sorrowful sighing.*)

Amanda: (*offstage*) It isn't dark enough yet. (*She turns slowly before the mirror with a troubled look.*)

(*Legend on Screen: "This Is My Sister: Celebrate Her with Strings!" Music.*)

Amanda: (*laughing, off*) I'm going to show you something. I'm going to make a spectacular appearance!
Laura: What is it, Mother?
Amanda: Possess your soul in patience—you will see! Something I've resurrected from that old trunk! Styles haven't changed so terribly much after all. . . . (*She parts the portieres.*) Now just look at your mother! (*She wears a girlish frock of yellowed voile with a blue silk sash. She carries a bunch of jonquils—the legend of her youth is nearly revived. Feverishly*) This is the dress in which I led the cotillion. Won the cakewalk twice at Sunset Hill, wore one spring to the Governor's ball in Jackson! See how I sashayed around the ballroom, Laura? (*She raises her skirt and does a mincing step around the room.*) I wore it on Sundays for my gentlemen callers! I had it on the day I met your father—I had malaria fever all that spring. The change of climate from East Tennessee to the Delta—weakened resistance—I had a little temperature all the time—not enough to be serious—just enough to make me restless and giddy! Invitations poured in parties all over the Delta!—"Stay in bed," said Mother, "you have fever!"—but I just wouldn't.—I took quinine but kept on going, going!—Evenings, dances!—Afternoons, long, long rides! Picnics—lovely!—So lovely, that country in May.—All lacy with dogwood, literally flooded with jonquils!—That was the spring I had the craze for jonquils. Jonquils became an absolute obsession. Mother said, "Honey, there's no more room for jonquils." And still I kept bringing in more jonquils. Whenever, wherever I saw them, I'd say, "Stop! Stop! I see jonquils!" I made the young men help me gather the jonquils! It was a joke, Amanda and her jonquils! Finally there were no more vases to hold them, every available space was filled with jonquils. No vases to hold them? All right, I'll hold them myself! And then I—(*She stops in front of the picture.*)

(*Music.*) met your father! Malaria fever and jonquils and then—this—boy. . . . (*She switches on the rose-colored lamp.*) I hope they get here before it starts to rain. (*She crosses upstage and places the jonquils in bowl on table.*) I gave your brother a little extra change so he and Mr. O'Connor could take the service car home.

Laura: (*with altered look*) What did you say his name was?

Amanda: O'Connor.
Laura: What is his first name?
Amanda: I don't remember. Oh, yes, I do. It was—Jim!

(*Laura sways slightly and catches hold of a chair.*)

(*Legend on Screen: "Not Jim!"*)

Laura: (*faintly*) Not—Jim!
Amanda: Yes, that was it, it was Jim! I've never known a Jim that wasn't nice!

(*Music: Ominous.*)

Laura: Are you sure his name is Jim O'Connor?
Amanda: Yes. Why?
Laura: Is he the one that Tom used to know in high school?
Amanda: He didn't say so. I think he just got to know him at the warehouse.
Laura: There was a Jim O'Connor we both knew in high school—(*Then, with effort.*) If
that is the one that Tom is bringing to dinner—you'll have to excuse me, I won't
come to the table.
Amanda: What sort of nonsense is this?
Laura: You asked me once if I'd ever liked a boy. Don't you remember I showed you
this boy's picture?
Amanda: You mean the boy you showed me in the year book?
Laura: Yes, that boy.
Amanda: Laura, Laura, were you in love with that boy?
Laura: I don't know, Mother. All I know is I couldn't sit at the table if it was him!
Amanda: It won't be him! It isn't the least bit likely. But whether it is or not, you will
come to the table. You will not be excused.
Laura: I'll have to be, Mother.
Amanda: I don't intend to humor your silliness, Laura. I've had too much from you and
your brother, both! So just sit down and compose yourself till they come. Tom has
forgotten his key so you'll have to let them in, when they arrive.
Laura: (*panicky*) Oh, Mother—*you* answer the door!
Amanda: (*lightly*) I'll be in the kitchen—busy!
Laura: Oh, Mother, please answer the door, don't make me do it!
Amanda: (*crossing into kitchenette*) I've got to fix the dressing for the salmon. Fuss,
fuss—silliness!—over a gentleman caller!

(*Door swings shut. Laura is left alone.*)

(*Legend: "Terror!"*)

(*She utters a low moan and turns off the lamp—sits stiffly on the edge of the sofa, knotting
her fingers together.*)

(*Legend on Screen: "The Opening of a Door!"*)

(*Tom and Jim appear on the fire-escape steps and climb to landing. Hearing their approach, Laura rises with a panicky gesture. She retreats to the portieres.*
The doorbell. Laura catches her breath and touches her throat. Low drums.)

Amanda: (*calling*) Laura, sweetheart! The door!

(*Laura stares at it without moving.*)

Jim: I think we just beat the rain.
Tom: Uh-huh. (*He rings again, nervously. Jim whistles and fishes for a cigarette.*)
Amanda: (*very, very gaily*) Laura, that is your brother and Mr. O'Connor! Will you let them in, darling?

(*Laura crosses toward kitchenette door.*)

Laura: (*breathlessly*) Mother—you go to the door!

(*Amanda steps out of the kitchenette and stares furiously at Laura. She points imperiously at the door.*)

Laura: Please, please!
Amanda: (*in a fierce whisper*) What is the matter with you, you silly thing?
Laura: (*desperately*) Please, you answer it, *please!*
Amanda: I told you I wasn't going to humor you, Laura. Why have you chosen this moment to lose your mind?
Laura: Please, please, please, you go!
Amanda: You'll have to go to the door because I can't!
Laura: (*despairingly*) I can't either!
Amanda: Why?
Laura: I'm *sick!*
Amanda: I'm sick, too—of your nonsense! Why can't you and your brother be normal people? Fantastic whims and behavior! (*Tom gives a long ring.*) Preposterous goings on! Can you give me one reason—(*Calls out lyrically.*) COMING! JUST ONE SECOND!— why should you be afraid to open a door? Now you answer it, Laura!
Laura: Oh, oh, oh . . . (*She returns through the portieres. Darts to the victrola and winds it frantically and turns it on.*)
Amanda: Laura Wingfield, you march right to that door!
Laura: Yes—yes, Mother!

(*A faraway, scratchy rendition of "Dardanella" softens the air and gives her strength to move through it. She slips to the door and draws it cautiously open. Tom enters with the caller, Jim O'Connor.*)

Tom: Laura, this is Jim. Jim, this is my sister, Laura.
Jim: (*stepping inside*) I didn't know that Shakespeare had a sister!
Laura: (*retreating stiff and trembling from the door*). How—how do you do?
Jim: (*heartily extending his hand*) Okay!

(Laura touches it hesitantly with hers.)

Jim: Your hand's *cold,* Laura!

Laura: Yes, well—I've been playing the victrola. . . .

Jim: Must have been playing classical music on it! You ought to play a little hot swing music to warm you up!

Laura: Excuse me—I haven't finished playing the victrola. . . .

(She turns awkwardly and hurries into the front room. She pauses a second by the victrola. Then catches her breath and darts through the portieres like a frightened deer.)

Jim: (grinning) What was the matter?

Tom: Oh—with Laura? Laura is—terribly shy.

Jim: Shy, huh? It's unusual to meet a shy girl nowadays. I don't believe you ever mentioned you had a sister.

Tom: Well, now you know. I have one. Here is the *Post Dispatch.* You want a piece of it?

Jim: Uh-huh.

Tom: What piece? The comics?

Jim: Sports! *(Glances at it.)* Ole Dizzy Dean is on his bad behavior.

Tom: (disinterest) Yeah? *(Lights cigarette and crosses back to fire-escape door.)*

Jim: Where are *you* going?

Tom: I'm going out on the terrace.

Jim: (goes after him) You know, Shakespeare—I'm going to sell you a bill of goods!

Tom: What goods?

Jim: A course I'm taking.

Tom: Huh?

Jim: In public speaking! You and me, we're not the warehouse type.

Tom: Thanks—that's good news. But what has public speaking got to do with it?

Jim: It fits you for—executive positions!

Tom: Awww.

Jim: I tell you it's done a helluva lot for me.

(Image: Executive at Desk.)

Tom: In what respect?

Jim: In every! Ask yourself what is the difference between you an' me and men in the office down front? Brains?—No!—Ability?—No! Then what? Just one little thing—

Tom: What is that one little thing?

Jim: Primarily it amounts to—social poise! Being able to square up to people and hold your own on any social level!

Amanda: (off stage) Tom?

Tom: Yes, Mother?

Amanda: Is that you and Mr. O'Connor?

Tom: Yes, Mother.

Amanda: Well, you just make yourselves comfortable in there.

Tom: Yes, Mother.

Amanda: Ask Mr. O'Connor if he would like to wash his hands.

Jim: Aw—no—no—thank you—I took care of that at the warehouse. Tom—

Tom: Yes?

Jim: Mr. Mendoza was speaking to me about you.

Tom: Favorably?

Jim: What do you think?

Tom: Well—

Jim: You're going to be out of a job if you don't wake up.

Tom: I am waking up—

Jim: You show no signs.

Tom: The signs are interior.

(Image on Screen: The Sailing Vessel with Jolly Roger Again.)

Tom: I'm planning to change. (*He leans over the rail speaking with quiet exhilaration. The incandescent marquees and signs of the first-run movie houses light his face from across the alley. He looks like a voyager.*) I'm right at the point of committing myself to a future that doesn't include the warehouse and Mr. Mendoza or even a night-school course in public speaking.

Jim: What are you gassing about?

Tom: I'm tired of the movies.

Jim: Movies!

Tom: Yes, movies! Look at them—(*A wave toward the marvels of Grand Avenue.*) All of those glamorous people—having adventures—hogging it all, gobbling the whole thing up! You know what happens? People go to the *movies* instead of *moving!* Hollywood characters are supposed to have all the adventures for everybody in America, while everybody in America sits in a dark room and watches them have them! Yes, until there's a war. That's when adventure becomes available to the masses! *Everyone's* dish, not only Gable's! Then the people in the dark room come out of the dark room to have some adventures themselves—Goody, goody—It's our turn now, to go to the South Sea Island—to make a safari—to be exotic, far-off—But I'm not patient. I don't want to wait till then. I'm tired of the *movies* and I am *about* to move!

Jim: (*incredulously*) Move?

Tom: Yes.

Jim: When?

Tom: Soon!

Jim: Where? Where?

(Theme Three: Music Seems to Answer the Question, While Tom Thinks It Over. He Searches Among His Pockets.)

Tom: I'm starting to boil inside. I know I seem dreamy, but inside—well, I'm boiling! Whenever I pick up a shoe, I shudder a little thinking how short life is and what I am doing!—Whatever that means. I know it doesn't mean shoes—except as something to wear on a traveler's feet! (*Finds paper.*) Look—

Jim: What?

Tom: I'm a member.

Jim: (*reading*) The Union of Merchant Seamen.

Tom: I paid my dues this month, instead of the light bill.

Jim: You will regret it when they turn the lights off.

Tom: I won't be here.

Jim: How about your mother?

Tom: I'm like my father. The bastard son of a bastard! See how he grins? And he's been absent going on sixteen years!

Jim: You're just talking, you drip. How does your mother feel about it?

Tom: Shhh—Here comes Mother! Mother is not acquainted with my plans!

Amanda: (*enters portieres*) Where are you all?

Tom: On the terrace, Mother.

(*They start inside. She advances to them. Tom is distinctly shocked at her appearance. Even Jim blinks a little. He is making his first contact with girlish Southern vivacity and in spite of the night-school course in public speaking is somewhat thrown off the beam by the unexpected outlay of social charm. Certain responses are attempted by Jim but are swept aside by Amanda's gay laughter and chatter. Tom is embarrassed but after the first shock Jim reacts very warmly. Grins and chuckles, is altogether won over.*)

(*Image: Amanda as a Girl.*)

Amanda: (*coyly smiling, shaking her girlish ringlets*) Well, well, well, so this is Mr. O'Connor. Introductions entirely unnecessary. I've heard so much about you from my boy. I finally said to him, Tom—good gracious!—why don't you bring this paragon to supper? I'd like to meet this nice young man at the warehouse!—Instead of just hearing him sing your praises so much! I don't know why my son is so stand-offish—that's not Southern behavior! Let's sit down and—I think we could stand a little more air in here! Tom, leave the door open. I felt a nice fresh breeze a moment ago. Where has it gone? Mmm, so warm already! And not quite summer, even. We're going to burn up when summer really gets started. However, we're having—we're having a very light supper. I think light things are better fo' this time of year. The same as light clothes are. Light clothes an' light food are what warm weather calls fo'. You know our blood gets so thick during th' winter—it takes a while fo' us to *adjust* ou'selves!—when the season changes . . . It's come so quick this year. I wasn't prepared. All of a sudden—heavens! Already summer!—I ran to the trunk an' pulled out this light dress—Terribly old! Historical almost! But feels so good—so good an' co-ol, y'know. . . .

Tom: Mother—

Amanda: Yes, honey?

Tom: How about—supper?

Amanda: Honey, you go ask Sister if supper is ready! You know that Sister is in full charge of supper! Tell her you hungry boys are waiting for it. (*To Jim*) Have you met Laura?

Jim: She—

Amanda: Let you in? Oh, good, you've met already! It's rare for a girl as sweet an' pretty as Laura to be domestic! But Laura is, thank heavens, not only pretty but also very domestic. I'm not at all. I never was a bit. I never could make a thing but angelfood cake. Well, in the South, we had so many servants. Gone, gone, gone. All vestiges of gracious living! Gone completely! I wasn't prepared for what the future brought me. All of my gentlemen callers were sons of planters and so of course I assumed that I would be married to one and raise my family on a large piece of land with plenty of servants. But man proposes—and woman accepts the proposal!— To vary that old, old saying a little bit—I married no planter! I married a man who worked for the telephone company!—that gallantly smiling gentleman over there! (*Points to the picture.*) A telephone man who—fell in love with long distance!— Now he travels and I don't even know where!—But what am I going on for about my—tribulations! Tell me yours—I hope you don't have any! Tom?

Tom: (*returning*) Yes, Mother?

Amanda: Is supper nearly ready?

Tom: It looks to me like supper is on the table.

Amanda: Let me look—(*She rises prettily and looks through portieres.*) Oh, lovely—But where is Sister?

Tom: Laura is not feeling well and she says that she thinks she'd better not come to the table.

Amanda: What?—Nonsense!—Laura? Oh, Laura!

Laura: (*off stage, faintly*) Yes, Mother.

Amanda: You really must come to the table. We won't be seated until you come to the table! Come in, Mr. O'Connor. You sit over there and I'll—Laura? Laura Wingfield! You're keeping us waiting, honey! We can't say grace until you come to the table!

(*The back door is pushed weakly open and Laura comes in. She is obviously quite faint, her lips trembling, her eyes wide and staring. She moves unsteadily toward the table.*)

(*Legend: "Terror!"*)

(*Outside a summer storm is coming abruptly. The white curtains billow inward at the windows and there is a sorrowful murmur and deep blue dusk. Laura suddenly stumbles—She catches at a chair with a faint moan.*)

Tom: Laura!

Amanda: Laura! (*There is a clap of thunder.*) (*Legend: "Ah!"*) (*Despairingly*) Why, Laura, you *are* sick, darling! Tom, help your sister into the living room, dear! Sit in the living room, Laura—rest on the sofa. Well! (*To the gentleman caller*) Standing over the hot stove made her ill! I told her that it was just too warm this evening, but— (*Tom comes back in. Laura is on the sofa.*) Is Laura all right now?

Tom: Yes.

Amanda: What *is* that? Rain? A nice cool rain has come up! (*She gives the gentleman caller a frightened look.*) I think we may—have grace—now . . . (*Tom looks at her stupidly.*) Tom, honey—you say grace!

Tom: Oh . . . "For these and all thy mercies—" (*They bow their heads, Amanda stealing a nervous glance at Jim. In the living room Laura, stretched on the sofa, clenches her hands to her lips, to hold back a shuddering sob.*) God's Holy Name be praised—

(*The Scene Dims Out.*)

Scene 7
A Souvenir

Half an hour later. Dinner is just being finished in the upstage area which is concealed by the drawn portieres.

As the curtain rises Laura is still huddled upon the sofa, her feet drawn under her, her head resting on a pale blue pillow, her eyes wide and mysteriously watchful. The new floor lamp with its shade of rose-colored silk gives a soft, becoming light to her face, bringing out the fragile, unearthly prettiness which usually escapes attention. There is a steady murmur of rain, but it is slackening and stops soon after the scene begins; the air outside becomes pale and luminous as the moon breaks out.

A moment after the curtain rises, the lights in both rooms flicker and go out.

Jim: Hey, there, Mr. Light Bulb!

(Amanda laughs nervously.)

(Legend: "Suspension of a Public Service.")

Amanda: Where was Moses when the lights went out? Ha-ha. Do you know the answer
    to that one, Mr. O'Connor?

Jim: No, Ma'am, what's the answer?

Amanda: In the dark! *(Jim laughs appreciatively.)* Everybody sit still. I'll light the can-
    dles. Isn't it lucky we have them on the table? Where's a match? Which of you gen-
    tlemen can provide a match?

Jim: Here.

Amanda: Thank you, sir.

Jim: Not at all, Ma'am!

Amanda: I guess the fuse has burnt out. Mr. O'Connor, can you tell a burnt-out fuse? I
    know I can't and Tom is a total loss when it comes to mechanics. *(Sound: Getting
    Up: Voices Recede a Little to Kitchenette.)* Oh, be careful you don't bump into some-
    thing. We don't want our gentleman caller to break his neck. Now wouldn't that be
    a fine howdy-do?

Jim: Ha-ha! Where is the fuse-box?

Amanda: Right here next to the stove. Can you see anything?

Jim: Just a minute.

Amanda: Isn't electricity a mysterious thing? Wasn't it Benjamin Franklin who tied a
    key to a kite? We live in such a mysterious universe, don't we? Some people say that
    science clears up all the mysteries for us. In my opinion it only creates more! Have
    you found it yet?

Jim: No, Ma'am. All these fuses look okay to me.

Amanda: Tom!

Tom: Yes, Mother?

Amanda: That light bill I gave you several days ago. The one I told you we got the no-
    tices about?

Tom: Oh.—Yeah.

(Legend: "Ha!")

Amanda: You didn't neglect to pay it by any chance?

Tom: Why, I—

Amanda: Didn't! I might have known it!

Jim: Shakespeare probably wrote a poem on that light bill, Mrs. Wingfield.

Amanda: I might have known better than to trust him with it! There's such a high price for negligence in this world!

Jim: Maybe the poem will win a ten-dollar prize.

Amanda: We'll just have to spend the remainder of the evening in the nineteenth century, before Mr. Edison made the Mazda lamp!

Jim: Candlelight is my favorite kind of light.

Amanda: That shows you're romantic! But that's no excuse for Tom. Well, we got through dinner. Very considerate of them to let us get through dinner before they plunged us into everlasting darkness, wasn't it, Mr. O'Connor?

Jim: Ha-ha!

Amanda: Tom, as a penalty for your carelessness you can help me with the dishes.

Jim: Let me give you a hand.

Amanda: Indeed you will not!

Jim: I ought to be good for something.

Amanda: Good for something? (*Her tone is rhapsodic.*) You? Why, Mr. O'Connor, nobody, *nobody's* given me this much entertainment in years—as you have!

Jim: Aw, now, Mrs. Wingfield!

Amanda: I'm not exaggerating, not one bit! But Sister is all by her lonesome. You go keep her company in the parlor! I'll give you this lovely old candelabrum that used to be on the altar at the church of the Heavenly Rest. It was melted a little out of shape when the church burnt down. Lightning struck it one spring. Gypsy Jones was holding a revival at the time and he intimated that the church was destroyed because the Episcopalians gave card parties.

Jim: Ha-ha.

Amanda: And how about coaxing Sister to drink a little wine? I think it would be good for her! Can you carry both at once?

Jim: Sure. I'm Superman!

Amanda: Now, Thomas, get into this apron!

(*The door of kitchenette swings closed on Amanda's gay laughter; the flickering light approaches the portieres. Laura sits up nervously as he enters. Her speech at first is low and breathless from the almost intolerable strain of being alone with a stranger.*)

(*Legend: "I Don't Suppose You Remember Me at All!"*)

(*In her first speeches in this scene, before Jim's warmth overcomes her paralyzing shyness, Laura's voice is thin and breathless as though she has run up a steep flight of stairs. Jim's attitude is gently humorous. In playing this scene it should be stressed that while the incident is apparently unimportant, it is to Laura the climax of her secret life.*)

Jim: Hello, there, Laura.

Laura: (*faintly*) Hello. (*She clears her throat.*)

Jim: How are you feeling now? Better?

Laura: Yes. Yes, thank you.

Jim: This is for you. A little dandelion wine. (*He extends it toward her with extravagant gallantry.*)

Laura: Thank you.

Jim: Drink it—but don't get drunk! (*He laughs heartily. Laura takes the glass uncertainly; laughs shyly.*) Where shall I set the candles?

Laura: Oh—oh, anywhere . . .

Jim: How about here on the floor? Any objections?

Laura: No.

Jim: I'll spread a newspaper under to catch the drippings. I like to sit on the floor. Mind if I do?

Laura: Oh, no.

Jim: Give me a pillow?

Laura: What?

Jim: A pillow!

Laura: Oh . . . (*Hands him one quickly.*)

Jim: How about you? Don't you like to sit on the floor?

Laura: Oh—yes.

Jim: Why don't you, then?

Laura: I—will.

Jim: Take a pillow! (*Laura does. Sits on the other side of the candelabrum. Jim crosses his legs and smiles engagingly at her.*) I can't hardly see you sitting way over there.

Laura: I can—see you.

Jim: I know, but that's not fair, I'm in the limelight. (*Laura moves her pillow closer.*) Good! Now I can see you! Comfortable?

Laura: Yes.

Jim: So am I. Comfortable as a cow. Will you have some gum?

Laura: No, thank you.

Jim: I think that I will indulge, with your permission. (*Musingly unwraps it and holds it up.*) Think of the fortune made by the guy that invented the first piece of chewing gum. Amazing, huh? The Wrigley Building is one of the sights of Chicago.—I saw it summer before last when I went up to the Century of Progress. Did you take in the Century of Progress?

Laura: No, I didn't.

Jim: Well, it was quite a wonderful exposition. What impressed me most was the Hall of Science. Gives you an idea of what the future will be in America, even more wonderful than the present time is! (*Pause. Smiling at her*) Your brother tells me you're shy. Is that right, Laura?

Laura: I—don't know.

Jim: I judge you to be an old-fashioned type of girl. Well, I think that's a pretty good type to be. Hope you don't think I'm being too personal—do you?

Laura: (*hastily, out of embarrassment*). I believe I *will* take a piece of gum, if you—don't mind. (*Clearing her throat*) Mr. O'Connor, have you—kept up with your singing?

Jim: Singing? Me?

Laura: Yes. I remember what a beautiful voice you had.

Jim: When did you hear me sing?

(Voice Offstage in the Pause.)

Voice: *(offstage).*
        O blow, ye winds, heigh-ho,
        A-roving I will go!
        I'm off to my love
        With a boxing glove—
        Ten thousand miles away!

Jim: You say you've heard me sing?

Laura: Oh, yes! Yes, very often . . . I—don't suppose you remember me—at all?

Jim: *(smiling doubtfully).* You know I have an idea I've seen you before. I had that idea soon as you opened the door. It seemed almost like I was about to remember your name. But the name that I started to call you—wasn't a name! And so I stopped myself before I said it.

Laura: Wasn't it—Blue Roses?

Jim: *(springs up, grinning)* Blue Roses! My gosh, yes—Blue Roses! That's what I had on my tongue when you opened the door! Isn't it funny what tricks your memory plays? I didn't connect you with the high school somehow or other. But that's where it was; it was high school. I didn't even know you were Shakespeare's sister! Gosh, I'm sorry.

Laura: I didn't expect you to. You—barely knew me!

Jim: But we did have a speaking acquaintance, huh?

Laura: Yes, we—spoke to each other.

Jim: When did you recognize me?

Laura: Oh, right away!

Jim: Soon as I came in the door?

Laura: When I heard your name I thought it was probably you. I knew that Tom used to know you a little in high school. So when you came in the door—Well, then I was—sure.

Jim: Why didn't you *say* something, then?

Laura: *(breathlessly)* I didn't know what to say, I was—too surprised!

Jim: For goodness' sakes! You know, this sure is funny!

Laura: Yes! Yes, isn't it, though . . .

Jim: Didn't we have a class in something together?

Laura: Yes, we did.

Jim: What class was that?

Laura: It was—singing—Chorus!

Jim: Aw!

Laura: I sat across the aisle from you in the Aud.

Jim: Aw.

Laura: Mondays, Wednesdays and Fridays.

Jim: Now I remember—you always came in late.

Laura: Yes, it was so hard for me, getting upstairs. I had that brace on my leg—it clumped so loud!

Jim: I never heard any clumping.

Laura: (*wincing at the recollection*). To me it sounded like—thunder!

Jim: Well, well, well. I never even noticed.

Laura: And everybody was seated before I came in. I had to walk in front of all those people. My seat was in the back row. I had to go clumping all the way up the aisle with everyone watching!

Jim: You shouldn't have been self-conscious.

Laura: I know, but I was. It was always such a relief when the singing started.

Jim: Aw, yes, I've placed you now! I used to call you Blue Roses. How was it that I got started calling you that?

Laura: I was out of school a little while with pleurosis. When I came back you asked me what was the matter. I said I had pleurosis—you thought I said Blue Roses. That's what you always called me after that!

Jim: I hope you didn't mind.

Laura: Oh, no—I liked it. You see, I wasn't acquainted with many—people. . . .

Jim: As I remember you sort of stuck by yourself.

Laura: I—I—never had much luck at—making friends.

Jim: I don't see why you wouldn't.

Laura: Well, I—started out badly.

Jim: You mean being—

Laura: Yes, it sort of—stood between me—

Jim: You shouldn't have let it!

Laura: I know, but it did, and—

Jim: You were shy with people!

Laura: I tried not to be but never could—

Jim: Overcome it?

Laura: No, I—I never could!

Jim: I guess being shy is something you have to work out of kind of gradually.

Laura: (*sorrowfully*) Yes—I guess it—

Jim: Takes time!

Laura: Yes

Jim: People are not so dreadful when you know them. That's what you have to remember! And everybody has problems, not just you, but practically everybody has got some problems. You think of yourself as having the only problems, as being the only one who is disappointed. But just look around you and you will see lots of people as disappointed as you are. For instance, I hoped when I was going to high school that I would be further along at this time, six years later, than I am now—You remember that wonderful write-up I had in *The Torch*?

Laura: Yes! (*She rises and crosses to table.*)

Jim: It said I was bound to succeed in anything I went into! (*Laura returns with the annual.*) Holy Jeez! *The Torch*! (*He accepts it reverently. They smile across it with mutual wonder. Laura crouches beside him and they begin to turn through it. Laura's shyness is dissolving in his warmth.*)

Laura: Here you are in *Pirates of Penzance*!

Jim: (*wistfully*). I sang the baritone lead in that operetta.

Laura: (*rapidly*) So—beautifully!

Jim: (*protesting*). Aw—

Laura: Yes, yes—beautifully—beautifully!

Jim: You heard me?

Laura: All three times!

Jim: No!

Laura: Yes!

Jim: All three performances?

Laura: (*looking down*). Yes.

Jim: Why?

Laura: I—wanted to ask you to—autograph my program.

Jim: Why didn't you ask me to?

Laura: You were always surrounded by your own friends so much that I never had a chance to.

Jim: You should have just—

Laura: Well, I—thought you might think I was—

Jim: Thought I might think you was—what?

Laura: Oh—

Jim: (*with reflective relish*). I was beleaguered by females in those days.

Laura: You were terribly popular!

Jim: Yeah—

Laura: You had such a—friendly way—

Jim: I was spoiled in high school.

Laura: Everybody—liked you!

Jim: Including you?

Laura: I—yes, I—I did, too—(*She gently closes the book in her lap.*)

Jim: Well, well, well!—Give me that program, Laura. (*She hands it to him. He signs it with a flourish.*) There you are—better late than never!

Laura: Oh, I—what a—surprise!

Jim: My signature isn't worth very much right now. But some day—maybe—it will increase in value! Being disappointed is one thing and being discouraged is something else. I am disappointed but I'm not discouraged. I'm twenty-three years old. How old are you?

Laura: I'll be twenty-four in June.

Jim: That's not old age!

Laura: No, but—

Jim: You finished high school?

Laura: (*with difficulty*). I didn't go back.

Jim: You mean you dropped out?

Laura: I made bad grades in my final examinations. (*She rises and replaces the book and the program. Her voice strained.*) How is—Emily Meisenbach getting along?

Jim: Oh, that kraut-head!

Laura: Why do you call her that?

Jim: That's what she was.

Laura: You're not still—going with her?

Jim: I never see her.

Laura: It said in the Personal Section that you were—engaged!

Jim: I know, but I wasn't impressed by that—propaganda!

Laura: It wasn't—the truth?

Jim: Only in Emily's optimistic opinion!

Laura: Oh—

(*Legend: "What Have You Done Since High School?"*)

Jim lights a cigarette and leans indolently back on his elbows smiling at Laura with a warmth and charm which light her inwardly with altar candles. She remains by the table and turns in her hands a piece of glass to cover her tumult.

Jim: (*after several reflective puffs on a cigarette*). What have you done since high school? (*She seems not to hear him.*) Huh? (*Laura looks up.*) I said what have you done since high school, Laura?
Laura: Nothing much.
Jim: You must have been doing something these six long years.
Laura: Yes.
Jim: Well, then, such as what?
Laura: I took a business course at business college—
Jim: How did that work out?
Laura: Well, not very—well—I had to drop out, it gave me—indigestion—

(*Jim laughs gently.*)

Jim: What are you doing now?
Laura: I don't do anything—much. Oh, please don't think I sit around doing nothing! My glass collection takes up a good deal of my time. Glass is something you have to take good care of.
Jim: What did you say—about glass?
Laura: Collection I said—I have one—(*She clears her throat and turns away again, acutely shy.*)
Jim: (*abruptly*) You know what I judge to be the trouble with you? Inferiority complex! Know what that is? That's what they call it when someone low-rates himself! I understand it because I had it, too. Although my case was not so aggravated as yours seems to be. I had it until I took up public speaking, developed my voice, and learned that I had an aptitude for science. Before that time I never thought of myself as being outstanding in any way whatsoever! Now I've never made a regular study of it, but I have a friend who says I can analyze people better than doctors that make a profession of it. I don't claim that to be necessarily true, but I can sure guess a person's psychology, Laura! (*Takes out his gum.*) Excuse me, Laura. I always take it out when the flavor is gone. I'll use this scrap of paper to wrap it in. I know how it is to get it stuck on a shoe. Yep—that's what I judge to be your principal trouble. A lack of confidence in yourself as a person. You don't have the proper amount of faith in yourself. I'm basing that fact on a number of your remarks and also on certain observations I've made. For instance that clumping you thought was so awful in high school. You say that you even dreaded to walk into class. You see what you did? You dropped out of school, you gave up an education because of a clump, which as far as I know was practically nonexistent! A little physical defect is what you have. Hardly noticeable even! Magnified thousands of times by imagination! You know what my strong advice to you is? Think of yourself as *superior* in some way!

Laura: In what way would I think?

Jim: Why, man alive, Laura! Just look about you a little. What do you see? A world full of common people! All of 'em born and all of 'em going to die! Which of them has one-tenth of your good points! Or mine! Or anyone else's, as far as that goes— Gosh! Everybody excels in some one thing. Some in many! (*Unconsciously glances at himself in the mirror.*) All you've got to do is discover in *what!* Take me, for instance. (*He adjusts his tie at the mirror.*) My interest happens to lie in electrodynamics. I'm taking a course in radio engineering at night school, Laura, on top of a fairly responsible job at the warehouse. I'm taking that course and studying public speaking.

Laura: Ohhhh.

Jim: Because I believe in the future of television! (*Turning back to her.*) I wish to be ready to go up right along with it. Therefore I'm planning to get in on the ground floor. In fact, I've already made the right connections and all that remains is for the industry itself to get under way! Full steam—(*His eyes are starry.*) Knowledge— Zzzzzp! *Money*—Zzzzzp! *Power!* That's the cycle democracy is built on! (*His attitude is convincingly dynamic. Laura stares at him, even her shyness eclipsed in her absolute wonder. He suddenly grins.*) I guess you think I think a lot of myself!

Laura: No—o-o-o, I—

Jim: Now how about you? Isn't there something you take more interest in than anything else?

Laura: Well, I do—as I said—have my—glass collection—

(A peal of girlish laughter from the kitchen.)

Jim: I'm not right sure I know what you're talking about. What kind of glass is it?

Laura: Little articles of it, they're ornaments mostly! Most of them are little animals made out of glass, the tiniest little animals in the world. Mother calls them a glass menagerie! Here's an example of one, if you'd like to see it! This one is one of the oldest. It's nearly thirteen. (*He stretches out his hand.*) (*Music: "The Glass Menagerie."*) Oh, be careful—if you breathe, it breaks!

Jim: I'd better not take it. I'm pretty clumsy with things.

Laura: Go on. I trust you with him! (*Places it in his palm.*) There now—you're holding him gently! Hold him over the light, he loves the light! You see how the light shines through him?

Jim: It sure does shine!

Laura: I shouldn't be partial, but he is my favorite one.

Jim: What kind of a thing is this one supposed to be?

Laura: Haven't you noticed the single horn on his forehead?

Jim: A unicorn, huh?

Laura: Mmm-hmmm!

Jim: Unicorns, aren't they extinct in the modern world?

Laura: I know!

Jim: Poor little fellow, he must feel sort of lonesome.

Laura: (*smiling*). Well, if he does he doesn't complain about it. He stays on a shelf with some horses that don't have horns and all of them seem to get along nicely together.

Jim: How do you know?

Laura: (*lightly*) I haven't heard any arguments among them!

Jim: (*grinning*) No arguments, huh? Well, that's a pretty good sign! Where shall I set him?

Laura: Put him on the table. They all like a change of scenery once in a while!

Jim: (*stretching*) Well, well, well, well—Look how big my shadow is when I stretch!

Laura: Oh, oh, yes—it stretches across the ceiling!

Jim: (*crossing to door*) I think it's stopped raining. (*Opens fire-escape door.*) Where does
   the music come from?

Laura: From the Paradise Dance Hall across the alley.

Jim: How about cutting the rug a little, Miss Wingfield?

Laura: Oh, I—

Jim: Or is your program filled up? Let me have a look at it. (*Grasps imaginary card.*)
   Why, every dance is taken! I'll just have to scratch some out. (*Waltz Music: "La
   Golondrina."*) Ahhh, a waltz! (*He executes some sweeping turns by himself then holds
   his arms toward Laura.*)

Laura: (*breathlessly*) I—can't dance!

Jim: There you go, that inferiority stuff!

Laura: I've never danced in my life!

Jim: Come on, try!

Laura: Oh, but I'd step on you!

Jim: I'm not made out of glass.

Laura: How—how—how do we start?

Jim: Just leave it to me. You hold your arms out a little.

Laura: Like this?

Jim: A little bit higher. Right. Now don't tighten up, that's the main thing about it—relax.

Laura: (*laughing breathlessly*) It's hard not to.

Jim: Okay.

Laura: I'm afraid you can't budge me.

Jim: What do you bet I can't? (*He swings her into motion.*)

Laura: Goodness, yes, you can!

Jim: Let yourself go, now, Laura, just let yourself go.

Laura: I'm—

Jim: Come on!

Laura: Trying!

Jim: Not so stiff—Easy does it!

Laura: I know but I'm—

Jim: Loosen th' backbone! There now, that's a lot better.

Laura: Am I?

Jim: Lots, lots better! (*He moves her about the room in a clumsy waltz.*)

Laura: Oh, my!

Jim: Ha-ha!

Laura: Goodness, yes you can!

Jim: Ha-ha-ha! (*They suddenly bump into the table, Jim stops.*) What did we hit on?

Laura: Table.

Jim: Did something fall off it? I think—

Laura: Yes.

Jim: I hope that it wasn't the little glass horse with the horn!

Laura: Yes.

Jim: Aw, aw, aw. Is it broken?

Laura: Now it is just like all the other horses.

Jim: It's lost its—

Laura: Horn! It doesn't matter. Maybe it's a blessing in disguise.

Jim: You'll never forgive me. I bet that that was your favorite piece of glass.

Laura: I don't have favorites much. It's no tragedy, Freckles. Glass breaks so easily. No matter how careful you are. The traffic jars the shelves and things fall off them.

Jim: Still I'm awfully sorry that I was the cause.

Laura: (*smiling*). I'll just imagine he had an operation. The horn was removed to make him feel less—freakish! (*They both laugh.*) Now he will feel more at home with the other horses, the ones that don't have horns . . .

Jim: Ha-ha, that's very funny! (*Suddenly serious*) I'm glad to see that you have a sense of humor. You know—you're—well—very different! Surprisingly different from anyone else I know! (*His voice becomes soft and hesitant with a genuine feeling.*) Do you mind me telling you that? (*Laura is abashed beyond speech.*) You make me feel sort of—I don't know how to put it! I'm usually pretty good at expressing things, but— This is something that I don't know how to say! (*Laura touches her throat and clears it—turns the broken unicorn in her hands.*) (*Even softer*) Has anyone ever told you that you were pretty? (*Pause: Music.*) (*Laura looks up slowly, with wonder, and shakes her head.*) Well, you are! In a very different way from anyone else. And all the nicer because of the difference, too. (*His voice becomes low and husky. Laura turns away, nearly faint with the novelty of her emotions.*) I wish that you were my sister. I'd teach you to have some confidence in yourself. The different people are not like other people, but being different is nothing to be ashamed of. Because other people are not such wonderful people. They're one hundred times one thousand. You're one times one! They walk all over the earth. You just stay here. They're common as—weeds, but—you—well, you're—*Blue Roses!*

(*Image on Screen: Blue Roses.*)

(*Music Changes.*)

Laura: But blue is wrong for—roses . . .

Jim: It's right for you—You're—pretty!

Laura: In what respect am I pretty?

Jim: In all respects—believe me! Your eyes—your hair—are pretty! Your hands are pretty! (*He catches hold of her hand.*) You think I'm making this up because I'm invited to dinner and have to be nice. Oh, I could do that! I could put on an act for you, Laura, and say lots of things without being very sincere. But this time I am. I'm talking to you sincerely. I happened to notice you had this inferiority complex that keeps you from feeling comfortable with people. Somebody needs to build your confidence up and make you proud instead of shy and turning away and— blushing—Somebody ought to—ought to—*kiss* you, Laura!

(*His hand slips slowly up her arm to her shoulder.*) (*Music Swells Tumultuously.*) (*He suddenly turns her about and kisses her on the lips. When he releases her Laura sinks on the sofa with a bright, dazed look. Jim backs away and fishes in his pocket for a cigarette.*) (*Legend on Screen: "Souvenir."*) Stumble-john! (*He lights the cigarette, avoiding her look.*

There is a peal of girlish laughter from Amanda in the kitchen. Laura slowly raises and opens her hand. It still contains the little broken glass animal. She looks at it with a tender, bewildered expression.)

Stumble-john! I shouldn't have done that—That was way off the beam. You don't smoke, do you? (*She looks up, smiling, not hearing the question. He sits beside her a little gingerly. She looks at him speechlessly—waiting. He coughs decorously and moves a little farther aside as he considers the situation and senses her feelings, dimly, with perturbation. Gently*) Would you—care for a—mint? (*She doesn't seem to hear him but her look grows brighter even.*) Peppermint—Life Saver? My pocket's a regular drug store—wherever I go . . . (*He pops a mint in his mouth. Then gulps and decides to make a clean breast of it. He speaks slowly and gingerly.*) Laura, you know, if I had a sister like you, I'd do the same thing as Tom. I'd bring out fellows—introduce her to them. The right type of boys of a type to—appreciate her. Only—well—he made a mistake about me. Maybe I've got no call to be saying this. That may not have been the idea in having me over. But what if it was? There's nothing wrong about that. The only trouble is that in my case—I'm not in a situation to—do the right thing. I can't take down your number and say I'll phone. I can't call up next week and—ask for a date. I thought I had better explain the situation in case you misunderstood it and—hurt your feelings. . . . (*Pause. Slowly, very slowly, Laura's look changes, her eyes returning slowly from his to the ornament in her palm.*)

(Amanda utters another gay laugh in the kitchen.)

Laura: (*faintly*) You—won't—call again?
Jim: No, Laura, I can't. (*He rises from the sofa.*) As I was just explaining, I've—got strings on me, Laura, I've—been going steady! I go out all the time with a girl named Betty. She's a home-girl like you, and Catholic, and Irish, and in a great many ways we—get along fine. I met her last summer on a moonlight boat trip up the river to Alton, on the *Majestic*. Well—right away from the start it was—love! (*Legend: Love!*) (*Laura sways slightly forward and grips the arm of the sofa. He fails to notice, now enrapt in his own comfortable being.*) Being in love has made a new man of me! (*Leaning stiffly forward, clutching the arm of the sofa, Laura struggles visibly with her storm. But Jim is oblivious, she is a long way off.*) The power of love is really pretty tremendous! Love is something that—changes the whole world, Laura! (*The storm abates a little and Laura leans back. He notices her again.*) It happened that Betty's aunt took sick, she got a wire and had to go to Centralia. So Tom—when he asked me to dinner—I naturally just accepted the invitation, not knowing that you—that he—that I—(*He stops awkwardly.*) Huh—I'm a stumble-john! (*He flops back on the sofa. The holy candles in the altar of Laura's face have been snuffed out! There is a look of almost infinite desolation. Jim glances at her uneasily.*) I wish that you would—say something. (*She bites her lip which was trembling and then bravely smiles. She opens her hand again on the broken glass ornament. Then she gently takes his hand and raises it level with her own. She carefully places the unicorn in the palm of his hand, then pushes his fingers closed upon it.*) What are you—doing that for? You want me to have him?—Laura? (*She nods.*) What for?

Laura: A—souvenir . . .

(She rises unsteadily and crouches beside the victrola to wind it up.)

(Legend on Screen: "Things Have a Way of Turning Out So Badly.")

(Or Image: "Gentleman Caller Waving Good-Bye—Gaily.")

(At this moment Amanda rushes brightly back in the front room. She bears a pitcher of fruit punch in an old-fashioned cut-glass pitcher and a plate of macaroons. The plate has a gold border and poppies painted on it.)

Amanda: Well, well, well! Isn't the air delightful after the shower? I've made you children a little liquid refreshment. *(Turns gaily to the gentleman caller.)* Jim, do you
know that song about lemonade?

> "Lemonade, lemonade
> Made in the shade and stirred with a spade—
> Good enough for any old maid!"

Jim: *(uneasily)* Ha-ha! No—I never heard it.
Amanda: Why, Laura! You look so serious!
Jim: We were having a serious conversation.
Amanda: Good! Now you're better acquainted!
Jim: *(uncertainly).* Ha-ha! Yes.
Amanda: You modern young people are much more serious-minded than my genera-
tion. I was so gay as a girl!
Jim: You haven't changed, Mrs. Wingfield.
Amanda: Tonight I'm rejuvenated! The gaiety of the occasion, Mr. O'Connor! *(She
tosses her head with a peal of laughter. Spills lemonade.)* Oooo! I'm baptizing myself!
Jim: Here—let me—
Amanda: *(setting the pitcher down.)* There now. I discovered we had some maraschino
cherries. I dumped them in, juice and all!
Jim: You shouldn't have gone to that trouble, Mrs. Wingfield.
Amanda: Trouble, trouble? Why it was loads of fun! Didn't you hear me cutting up in
the kitchen? I bet your ears were burning! I told Tom how outdone with him I was
for keeping you to himself so long a time! He should have brought you over much,
much sooner! Well, now that you've found your way, I want you to be a very frequent caller! Not just occasional but all the time. Oh, we're going to have a lot of
gay times together! I see them coming! Mmm, just breathe that air! So fresh, and
the moon's so pretty! I'll skip back out—I know where my place is when young
folks are having a—serious conversation!
Jim: Oh, don't go out, Mrs. Wingfield. The fact of the matter is I've got to be going.
Amanda: Going, now? You're joking! Why, it's only the shank of the evening, Mr.
O'Connor!
Jim: Well, you know how it is.

Amanda: You mean you're a young workingman and have to keep workingmen's hours. We'll let you off early tonight. But only on the condition that next time you stay later. What's the best night for you? Isn't Saturday night the best night for you workingmen?

Jim: I have a couple of time-clocks to punch, Mrs. Wingfield. One at morning, another one at night!

Amanda: My, but you *are* ambitious! You work at night, too?

Jim: No, Ma'am, not work but—Betty! (*He crosses deliberately to pick up his hat. The band at the Paradise Dance Hall goes into a tender waltz.*)

Amanda: Betty? Betty? Who's—Betty! (*There is an ominous cracking sound in the sky.*)

Jim: Oh, just a girl. The girl I go steady with! (*He smiles charmingly. The sky falls.*)

(*Legend: "The Sky Falls."*)

Amanda: (*a long-drawn exhalation*) Ohhhh . . . Is it a serious romance, Mr. O'Connor?

Jim: We're going to be married the second Sunday in June.

Amanda: Ohhhh—how nice! Tom didn't mention that you were engaged to be married.

Jim: The cat's not out of the bag at the warehouse yet. You know how they are. They call you Romeo and stuff like that. (*He stops at the oval mirror to put on his hat. He carefully shapes the brim and the crown to give a discreetly dashing effect.*) It's been a wonderful evening, Mrs. Wingfield. I guess this is what they mean by Southern hospitality.

Amanda: It really wasn't anything at all.

Jim: I hope it don't seem like I'm rushing off. But I promised Betty I'd pick her up at the Wabash depot, an' by the time I get my jalopy down there her train'll be in. Some women are pretty upset if you keep 'em waiting.

Amanda: Yes, I know—The tyranny of women! (*Extends her hand.*) Goodbye, Mr. O'Connor. I wish you luck—and happiness—and success! All three of them, and so does Laura!—Don't you, Laura?

Laura: Yes!

Jim: (*taking her hand*) Goodbye, Laura. I'm certainly going to treasure that souvenir. And don't you forget the good advice I gave you. (*Raises his voice to a cheery shout.*) So long, Shakespeare! Thanks again, ladies—Good night!

(*He grins and ducks jauntily out. Still bravely grimacing, Amanda closes the door on the gentleman caller. Then she turns back to the room with a puzzled expression. She and Laura don't dare to face each other. Laura crouches beside the victrola to wind it.*)

Amanda: (*faintly*) Things have a way of turning out so badly. I don't believe that I would play the victrola. Well, well—well—Our gentleman caller was engaged to be married! Tom!

Tom: (*from back*) Yes, Mother?

Amanda: Come in here a minute. I want to tell you something awfully funny.

Tom: (*enters with macaroon and a glass of the lemonade*) Has the gentleman caller gotten away already?

Amanda: The gentleman caller has made an early departure. What a wonderful joke you played on us!

Tom: How do you mean?

Amanda: You didn't mention that he was engaged to be married.

Tom: Jim? Engaged?

Amanda: That's what he just informed us.

Tom: I'll be jiggered! I didn't know about that.

Amanda: That seems very peculiar.

Tom: What's peculiar about it?

Amanda: Didn't you call him your best friend down at the warehouse?

Tom: He is, but how did I know?

Amanda: It seems extremely peculiar that you wouldn't know your best friend was going to be married!

Tom: The warehouse is where I work, not where I know things about people!

Amanda: You don't know things anywhere! You live in a dream; you manufacture illusions! (*He crosses to door.*) Where are you going?

Tom: I'm going to the movies.

Amanda: That's right, now that you've had us make such fools of ourselves. The effort,
the preparations, all the expense! The new floor lamp, the rug, the clothes for
Laura! All for what? To entertain some other girl's fiancé! Go to the movies, go!
Don't think about us, a mother deserted, an unmarried sister who's crippled and
has no job! Don't let anything interfere with your selfish pleasure! Just go, go, go—
to the movies!

Tom: All right, I will! The more you shout about my selfishness to me the quicker I'll go,
and I won't go to the movies!

Amanda: Go, then! Then go to the moon—you selfish dreamer!

*Tom smashes his glass on the floor. He plunges out on the fire-escape, slamming the door.
Laura screams—cut by door.*

*Dance-hall music up. Tom goes to the rail and grips it desperately, lifting his face in the
chill white moonlight penetrating the narrow abyss of the alley.*

(*Legend on Screen: "And So Good-Bye . . ."*)

(*Tom's closing speech is timed with the interior pantomime. The interior scene is played as
though viewed through sound-proof glass. Amanda appears to be making a comforting
speech to Laura who is huddled upon the sofa. Now that we cannot hear the mother's
speech, her silliness is gone and she has dignity and tragic beauty. Laura's dark hair hides
her face until at the end of the speech she lifts it to smile at her mother. Amanda's gestures
are slow and graceful, almost dancelike, as she comforts the daughter. At the end of her
speech she glances a moment at the father's picture—then withdraws through the portieres.
At close of Tom's speech, Laura blows out the candles, ending the play.*)

Tom: I didn't go to the moon, I went much further—for time is the longest distance between two places—Not long after that I was fired for writing a poem on the lid of a
shoe-box. I left Saint Louis. I descended the steps of this fire-escape for a last time
and followed, from then on, in my father's footsteps, attempting to find in motion
what was lost in space—I traveled around a great deal. The cities swept about me

like dead leaves, leaves that were brightly colored but torn away from the branches. I would have stopped, but I was pursued by something. It always came upon me unawares, taking me altogether by surprise. Perhaps it was a familiar bit of music. Perhaps it was only a piece of transparent glass—Perhaps I am walking along a street at night, in some strange city, before I have found companions. I pass the lighted window of a shop where perfume is sold. The window is filled with pieces of colored glass, tiny transparent bottles in delicate colors, like bits of a shattered rainbow. Then all at once my sister touches my shoulder. I turn around and look into her eyes . . . Oh, Laura, Laura, I tried to leave you behind me, but I am more faithful than I intended to be! I reach for a cigarette, I cross the street, I run into the movies or a bar, I buy a drink, I speak to the nearest stranger—anything that can blow your candles out! (*Laura bends over the candles.*)—for nowadays the world is lit by lightning! Blow out your candles, Laura—and so goodbye . . .

(*She blows the candles out.*)

(*The Scene Dissolves.*)

Robert Hayden
1913–1980

Robert Hayden's two most ambitious poems directly confront the intolerable social evil of slavery by retelling the history of slave rebellions. "Middle Passage" recounts the seizure of the slave ship *Amistad* by Cinquez, one of the slaves being transported in the "middle passage" from Africa to America. "Runagate Runagate" retells the 1849 escape from slavery of Harriet Tubman, who subsequently led more than three hundred slaves to freedom. Hayden's form of protest poetry is solidly rooted in historical antecedents, as though to argue that one cannot write about the phenomenon of racism without understanding its historical causes. In this way he differs both from the African American writers who confined themselves to the contemporary plight of African Americans in American society and from those who tried to write conventional "English" poetry on conventional themes.

Hayden was a learned poet. He received a B.A. from Detroit City College (now Wayne State University) in 1942, at the age of twenty-nine, but he had already won the Hopwood Award for poetry at the University of Michigan in 1938 and in 1942, and had published his first book, *Heart-Shaped in the Dust,* in 1940. After returning to Michigan to take an M.A., he taught at Fisk University for twenty-three years, eventually leaving Fisk to become professor of English at Michigan, where he taught until his death.

Hayden's poems appeared, after 1940, in successive arrestingly named volumes: *A Ballad of Remembrance* (1962), *Words in Mourning Time* (1970), *The Night-Blooming Cereus* (1972), *Angle of Ascent* (1975), and *American Journal* (1978). His poetry ranged through many subjects and forms; it was marked by a consistent experimentation in voices, allusiveness, patterns on the page, and choice of speaker. He wished to avoid writing agitprop verse, and his career offers an implicit rebuke to an aesthetic that would disregard the importance of form in art. Hayden once said:

> I write poetry because I prefer it to prose, for one thing. Because, for another, I'm driven, impelled to make patterns of words in the special ways that poetry demands. . . . I suppose I could say, with fear of contradicting myself later, that writing poetry is one way I have of coming to grips with both inner and external realities. I also think of my writing as a form of prayer—a prayer for illumination, perfection.

Hayden's example has been important for such subsequent African American poets as Michael Harper and Rita Dove. The poetic implicit in his work, and theirs, is a reconstructive one: The contemporary African American poet must speak not only for living African Americans but also for all the dead African Americans deprived of voice. The voice of the living, it suggests, cannot be properly vocal if it does not know its own antecedents. It will be thin if it speaks out of the present alone, depriving the present of the very past that constituted it. The past of slavery, peculiar to African Americans, is preserved, Hayden's poetry suggests, in the consciousness and imagination of African Americans, and a poetry that represents it is bound to falsify. Michael Harper's allusions to African American history and Rita Dove's recreations of slave voices are attempts to enlarge and consolidate Hayden's model—a poetic language committed to adequate historical self-knowledge.

At the same time, Hayden was a vigorous commentator on the general American scene. In the late poem "American Journal" he adopted the voice of a visiting alien from outer space, reporting on America:

> There among them the americans this baffling
> multi people extremes and variegations their
> noise relentless their almost frightening
> energy . . .

As he studies these "charming savages enlightened primitives brash / new corners lately sprung up in our galaxy," the alien commentator takes precisely the very tone that whites have often used historically about African Americans. Hayden's ironic social mirror silently shows American society in a devastating light. In 1985, Hayden's *Collected Poems* appeared, making widely available once again the work of a neglected American poet.

Further Reading:
M. Harper, *Remembering Robert Hayden," Michigan Quarterly Review,* Winter 1982.
J. Hatcher, *From the Auroral Darkness: The Life and Poetry of Robert Hayden,* 1984.
R. B. Miller, ed., *Black Poets Between Worlds, 1940–1960,* 1986.
V. Kutzinski, *"Changing Permanences," Callaloo,* Winter 1986.
P. Williams, *Robert Hayden: A Critical Analysis of His Poetry,* 1987.

Text:
Collected Poems, 1985.

Homage to the Empress of the Blues

Because there was a man somewhere in a candystripe silk shirt,
gracile and dangerous as a jaguar and because a woman moaned
for him in sixty-watt gloom and mourned him Faithless Love
Twotiming Love Oh Love Oh Careless Aggravating Love,

    She came out on the stage in yards of pearls, emerging like   5
    a favorite scenic view, flashed her golden smile and sang.

Because grey laths began somewhere to show from underneath
torn hurdygurdy lithographs of dollfaced heaven;
and because there were those who feared alarming fists of snow
on the door and those who feared the riot-squad of statistics,   10

    She came out on the stage in ostrich feathers, beaded satin,
    and shone that smile on us and sang.

1966

Those Winter Sundays

Sundays too my father got up early
and put his clothes on in the blueblack cold,
then with cracked hands that ached
from labor in the weekday weather made
banked fires blaze. No one ever thanked him.   5

I'd wake and hear the cold splintering, breaking.
When the rooms were warm, he'd call,
and slowly I would rise and dress,
fearing the chronic angers of that house,

Speaking indifferently to him,   10
who had driven out the cold
and polished my good shoes as well.
What did I know, what did I know
of love's austere and lonely offices?

1966

A Letter from Phillis Wheatley

London, 1773

Dear Obour
  Our crossing was without
event. I could not help, at times,
reflecting on that first—my Destined—
voyage long ago (I yet   5
have some remembrance of its Horrors)
and marvelling at God's Ways.
    Last evening, her Ladyship presented me
to her illustrious Friends.
I scarce could tell them anything   10
of Africa, though much of Boston
and my hope of Heaven. I read
my latest Elegies to them.
"O Sable Muse!" the Countess cried,
embracing me, when I had done.   15
I held back tears, as is my wont,
and there were tears in Dear
Nathaniel's eyes.
    At supper—I dined apart
like captive Royalty—   20
the Countess and her Guests promised
signatures affirming me
True Poetess, albeit once a slave.
Indeed, they were most kind, and spoke,
moreover, of presenting me   25
at Court (I thought of Pocahontas)—
an Honor, to be sure, but one,
I should, no doubt, as Patriot decline.
    My health is much improved;
I feel I may, if God so Wills,   30
entirely recover here.
Idyllic England! Alas, there is
no Eden without its Serpent. Under
the chiming Complaisance I hear him Hiss;
I see his flickering tongue   35
when foppish would-be Wits
murmur of the Yankee Pedlar
and his Cannibal Mockingbird.
    Sister, forgive th'intrusion of
my Sombreness—Nocturnal Mood   40
I would not share with any save

your trusted Self. Let me disperse,
in closing, such unseemly Gloom
by mention of an Incident
you may, as I, consider Droll: 45
Today, a little Chimney Sweep,
his face and hands with soot quite Black,
staring hard at me, politely asked:
"Does you, M'lady, sweep chimneys too?"
I was amused, but dear Nathaniel   50
(ever Solicitous) was not.
     I pray the Blessings of our Lord
and Saviour Jesus Christ be yours
Abundantly. In His Name,
     Phillis   55
1985

RELATED VOICES

A Letter to Obour Tanner from Phillis Wheatley

To Obour Tanner, in New Port.

Boston, Oct. 30, 1773.

Dear Obour,—I rec'd your most kind epistles of Augt 27th, & Oct. 13th, by a young man of your acquaintance, for which I am oblig'd to you. I hear of your welfare with pleasure; but this acquaints you that I am at present indispos'd by a cold, & since my arrival have been visited by the asthma.

Your observations on our dependence on the Deity, & your hopes that my wants will be supply'd from his fulness which is in Christ Jesus, is truly worthy of your self. I can't say but my voyage to England has conduced to the recovery (in a great measure) of my health. The friends I found there among the nobility and gentry, their benevolent conduct towards me, the unexpected and unmerited civility and complaisance with which I was treated by all, fills me with astonishment. I can scarcely realize it. This I humbly hope has the happy effect of lossening me in my own esteem. Your reflections on the sufferings of the Son of God, & the inestimable price of our immortal souls, plainly demonstrates the sensations of a soul united to Jesus. What you observe of Esau is true of all mankind, who, (left to themselves) would sell their heavenly birth rights for a few moments of sensual pleasure, whose wages at last (dreadful wages!) is eternal condemnation. Dear Obour, let us not sell our birthright for a thousand worlds, which indeed would be as dust upon the balance. The God of the seas and dry land, has graciously brought me home in safety. Join with me in thanks to him for so great a mercy, & that it may excite me to praise him with cheerfulness, to persevere in Grace & Faith, & in the knowledge of our Creator and Redeemer,—that my heart may be fill'd with gratitude. I should have been pleas'd greatly to see Miss West, as I imagine she knew you. I have been very busy ever since my arrival, or should

> have now wrote a more particular account of my voyage, but must submit that
> satisfaction to some other opportunity. I am Dear friend,
>
> Most affectionately ever yours,
>
> PHILLIS WHEATLEY.
>
> My mistress has been very sick above 14 weeks, & confined to her bed the
> whole time, but is I hope somewhat better now.
>
> The young man by whom this is handed you seems to me to be a very clever
> man, knows you very well, & is very complaisant and agreeable.   P.W.
>
> I enclose Proposals for my book, and beg you'd use your interest to get sub-
> scriptions, as it is for my benefit.

Tillie Olsen
b. 1913

Tillie Olsen was fifteen years old when she paid ten cents for a water-soaked copy of
the April 1861 issue of the *Atlantic Monthly* in an Omaha used-book store. In this
sixty-seven-year-old magazine, she read an excerpt from Rebecca Harding Davis's
anonymously published *Life in the Iron Mills* and learned, as she reports in *Silences*,
that "literature can be made out of the lives of despised people." Although some
readers have praised Olsen as a great prose stylist, most are convinced that the power
of her work turns on its eloquent rendering of the pain and the possibility of the lives
of the "despised"—the white working-class women and men who together with their
African American brothers and sisters populate the world of her fiction.

Born Tillie Lerner to Russian immigrant parents in Omaha, Nebraska, Olsen
received more formal education than most women during the Depression. She
completed the eleventh grade and, as she has reported, used the local public library as
her college classroom. At the age of nineteen she began working on what to date has
been her only novel. Within a short time, however, she put the manuscript aside and
lost it. Years later, having accidentally recovered it, she decided to reconstruct and
finish it. Published in 1974 as *Yonnonido: From the Thirties,* the book recounts the
impoverished odyssey, anguished relations, and eventual survival of an unflinchingly
hopeful mother and daughter. Above all, as one reviewer puts it, *Yonnonido*
demonstrates Olsen's profound understanding of "what a great weight poor women
carry" as well as a "deep sympathy for the restlessness and degraded pride" of working-
class men.

Olsen's first publications—a few poems and a short story ("The Iron Throat," later
the opening chapter of *Yonnonido*)—appeared in the initial volume of the *Partisan
Review* in 1934. That same year *The New Republic* printed her autobiographical essay

"Thousand-Dollar Vagrant." After this promising beginning, however, Olsen dropped from sight. For the next twenty-two years she published nothing. Having married Jack Olsen, a printer, in 1936, she spent the next two decades trying to write while also rearing four children and working—not only as a typist-transcriber for a dairy-equipment company but also, as she notes in *Silences,* "full time on temporary jobs, a Kelly, a Western Agency girl (girl!), wandering from office to office, always hoping to manage two, three writing months ahead." Time in which to write came as "stolen moments" on a bus or on the job, she reports, or more often in "the deep night hours for as long as I could stay awake, after the kids were in bed, after the household tasks were done, sometimes during. It is no accident," she adds, "that the first work I considered publishable began: 'I stand here ironing, and what you asked me moves tormented back and forth with the iron.' "

"Eventually," however, Olsen reports, "there was time." The story that begins "I stand here ironing," reprinted here, was written in 1953 and 1954 and first published under the title "Help Her to Believe" in a small magazine, *The Pacific Spectator.* Its theme (how women contend with familial trauma) and its style (lyric rhythms cast in achingly beautiful terms) mark all of Olsen's best work. Retitled "I Stand Here Ironing," the story was included in what is to date Olsen's only collection of fiction, *Tell Me a Riddle* (1961). In that same year, the title story of the collection won the O. Henry Award for best American short story. Since then, Olsen's stories have been reprinted in numerous anthologies, and her contributions—as a writer, critic, teacher, and feminist—have received wide recognition. When *Tell Me a Riddle* was reissued in 1971, it earned even greater praise, as work comparable to Faulkner's "The Bear" and Melville's "Benito Cereno" in the way in which it "carries us through despair to a renewal of hope."

In recent years Tillie Olsen has received numerous honors and awards, including Guggenheim and Radcliffe fellowships, a National Endowment for the Arts grant, and several honorary degrees. She has also been writer-in-residence or visiting professor at several colleges and universities, including Amherst, Stanford, Massachusetts Institute of Technology, and the University of Massachusetts at Boston.

In 1972 Olsen revived Rebecca Harding Davis's *Life in the Iron Mills,* to which she had been so indebted in her youth. Reissued by the Feminist Press, *Life in the Iron Mills* now carries with it an incisive "biographical interpretation" written by Olsen. Olsen's most important recent book is *Silences* (1978), a collection of finely woven pieces concerned, as Olsen has noted, "with the relationship of circumstances—including class, color, sex, the times, climate into which one is born—to the creation of literature." The poet Adrienne Rich has hailed *Silences* as a "prose poem" that is enriched not only by "Olsen's unique connection and resonance with other writers" but also by its explorations of the "losses, the empty spaces, she, above all, has been equipped to recognize."

Although Olsen's body of work is relatively small, her influence on other writers has been large. Margaret Atwood has written of the "reverence" with which other women writers regard Olsen's work. And Alice Walker has observed that there have been few other writers "who manage in their work and in their sharing of their understanding to actually help us to live, to work, to create, day by day." Compelling on many counts, Olsen's work is especially unforgettable for its poor, forgotten female characters—

archetypal in their ordinariness—who struggle to claim a dignified place for themselves in circumstances that nurture but also restrain the creative self.

Further Reading:

C. Stimpson, *"Tillie Olsen: Witness as Servant," Polit,* Fall 1977.

M. Atwood, *"Obstacle Course," New York Times Book Review,* July 30, 1978.

M. Pearlman and A. H. P. Werlock, *Tillie Olsen,* 1991.

M. Faulkner, *Protest and Possibility in the Writing of Tillie Olsen,* 1993.

K. H. Nelson and N. Huse, *The Critical Response to Tillie Olsen,* 1994.

N. R. Roberts, *Three Radical Women Writers,* 1995.

Text:

"I Stand Here Ironing" from *Tell Me a Riddle,* 1961.

I Stand Here Ironing

I stand here ironing, and what you asked me moves tormented back and forth with the iron.

"I wish you would manage the time to come in and talk with me about your daughter. I'm sure you can help me understand her. She's a youngster who needs help and whom I'm deeply interested in helping."

"Who needs help." Even if I came, what good would it do? You think because I am her mother I have a key, or that in some way you could use me as a key? She has lived for nineteen years. There is all that life that has happened outside of me, beyond me.

And when is there time to remember, to sift, to weigh, to estimate, to total? I will start and there will be an interruption and I will have to gather it all together again. Or I will become engulfed with all I did or did not do, with what should have been and what cannot be helped.

She was a beautiful baby. The first and only one of our five that was beautiful at birth. You do not guess how new and uneasy her tenancy in her now-loveliness. You did not know her all those years she was thought homely, or see her poring over her baby pictures, making me tell her over and over how beautiful she had been—and would be, I would tell her—and was now, to the seeing eye. But the seeing eyes were few or nonexistent. Including mine.

I nursed her. They feel that's important nowadays. I nursed all the children, but with her, with all the fierce rigidity of first motherhood, I did like the books then said. Though her cries battered me to trembling and my breasts ached with swollenness, I waited till the clock decreed.

Why do I put that first? I do not even know if it matters, or if it explains anything.

She was a beautiful baby. She blew shining bubbles of sound. She loved motion, loved light, loved color and music and textures. She would lie on the floor in her blue overalls patting the surface so hard in ecstasy her hands and feet would blur. She was a miracle to me, but when she was eight months old I had to leave her daytimes with the woman downstairs to whom she was no miracle at all, for I worked or looked for work and for Emily's father, who "could no longer endure" (he wrote in his good-bye note) "sharing want with us."

I was nineteen. It was the pre-relief, pre-WPA world of the depression. I would start running as soon as I got off the streetcar, running up the stairs, the place smelling sour, and awake or asleep to startle awake, when she saw me she would break into a clogged weeping that could not be comforted, a weeping I can hear yet.

After a while I found a job hashing at night so I could be with her days, and it was better. But it came to where I had to bring her to his family and leave her.

It took a long time to raise the money for her fare back. Then she got chicken pox and I had to wait longer. When she finally came, I hardly knew her, walking quick and nervous like her father, looking like her father, thin, and dressed in a shoddy red that yellowed her skin and glared at the pockmarks. All the baby loveliness gone.

She was two. Old enough for nursery school they said, and I did not know then what I know now—the fatigue of the long day, and the lacerations of group life in nurseries that are only parking places for children.

Except that it would have made no difference if I had known. It was the only place there was. It was the only way we could be together, the only way I could hold a job.

And even without knowing, I knew. I knew the teacher that was evil because all these years it has curdled into my memory, the little boy hunched in the corner, her rasp, "why aren't you outside, because Alvin hits you? that's no reason, go out, scaredy." I knew Emily hated it even if she did not clutch and implore "don't go Mommy" like the other children, mornings.

She always had a reason why we should stay home. Momma, you look sick, Momma. I feel sick. Momma, the teachers aren't there today, they're sick. Momma, we can't go, there was a fire there last night. Momma, it's a holiday today, no school, they told me.

But never a direct protest, never rebellion. I think of our others in their three-, four-year-oldness—the explosions, the tempers, the denunciations, the demands—and I feel suddenly ill. I put the iron down. What in me demanded that goodness in her? And what was the cost, the cost to her of such goodness?

The old man living in the back once said in his gentle way: "You should smile at Emily more when you look at her." What *was* in my face when I looked at her? I loved her. There were all the acts of love.

It was only with the others I remembered what he said, and it was the face of joy, and not of care or tightness or worry I turned to them—too late for Emily. She does not smile easily, let alone almost always as her brothers and sisters do. Her face is closed and sombre, but when she wants, how fluid. You must have seen it in her pantomimes, you spoke of her rare gift for comedy on the stage that rouses a laughter out of the audience so dear they applaud and applaud and do not want to let her go.

Where does it come from, that comedy? There was none of it in her when she came back to me that second time, after I had had to send her away again. She had a new daddy now to learn to love, and I think perhaps it was a better time.

Except when we left her alone nights, telling ourselves she was old enough.

"Can't you go some other time, Mommy, like tomorrow?" she would ask. "Will it be just a little while you'll be gone? Do you promise?"

The time we came back, the front door open, the clock on the floor in the hall. She rigid awake. "It wasn't just a little while. I didn't cry. Three times I called you, just three times, and then I ran downstairs to open the door so you could come faster. The clock talked loud. I threw it away, it scared me what it talked."

She said the clock talked loud again that night I went to the hospital to have Susan. She was delirious with the fever that comes before red measles, but she was fully conscious all the week I was gone and the week after we were home when she could not come near the new baby or me.

She did not get well. She stayed skeleton thin, not wanting to eat, and night after night she had nightmares. She would call for me, and I would rouse from exhaustion to sleepily call back: "You're all right, darling, go to sleep, it's just a dream," and if she still called, in a sterner voice, "now go to sleep, Emily, there's nothing to hurt you." Twice, only twice, when I had to get up for Susan anyhow, I went in to sit with her.

Now when it is too late (as if she would let me hold and comfort her like I do the others) I get up and go to her at once at her moan or restless stirring. "Are you awake, Emily? Can I get you something?" And the answer is always the same: "No, I'm all right, go back to sleep, Mother."

They persuaded me at the clinic to send her away to a convalescent home in the country where "she can have the kind of food and care you can't manage for her, and you'll be free to concentrate on the new baby." They still send children to that place. I see pictures on the society page of sleek young women planning affairs to raise money for it, or dancing at the affairs, or decorating Easter eggs or filling Christmas stockings for the children.

They never have a picture of the children so I do not know if the girls still wear those gigantic red bows and the ravaged looks on the every other Sunday when parents can come to visit "unless otherwise notified"—as we were notified the first six weeks.

Oh it is a handsome place, green lawns and tall trees and fluted flower beds. High up on the balconies of each cottage the children stand, the girls in their red bows and white dresses, the boys in white suits and giant red ties. The parents stand below shrieking up to be heard and the children shriek down to be heard, and between them the invisible wall "Not To Be Contaminated by Parental Germs or Physical Affection."

There was a tiny girl who always stood hand in hand with Emily. Her parents never came. One visit she was gone. "They moved her to Rose College," Emily shouted in explanation. "They don't like you to love anybody here."

She wrote once a week, the labored writing of a seven-year-old. "I am fine. How is the baby. If I write my letter nicly I will have a star. Love." There never was a star. We wrote every other day, letters she could never hold or keep but only hear read—once. "We simply do not have room for children to keep any personal possessions," they patiently explained when we pieced one Sunday's shrieking together to plead how much it would mean to Emily, who loved so to keep things, to be allowed to keep her letters and cards.

Each visit she looked frailer. "She isn't eating," they told us.

(They had runny eggs for breakfast or mush with lumps, Emily said later, I'd hold it in my mouth and not swallow. Nothing ever tasted good, just when they had chicken.)

It took us eight months to get her released home, and only the fact that she gained back so little of her seven lost pounds convinced the social worker.

I used to try to hold and love her after she came back, but her body would stay stiff, and after a while she'd push away. She ate little. Food sickened her, and I think much of life too. Oh she had physical lightness and brightness, twinkling by on skates, bouncing like a ball up and down up and down over the jump rope, skimming over the hill; but these were momentary.

She fretted about her appearance, thin and dark and foreign-looking at a time when every little girl was supposed to look or thought she should look a chubby blonde replica of Shirley Temple. The doorbell sometimes rang for her, but no one seemed to come and play in the house or be a best friend. Maybe because we moved so much.

There was a boy she loved painfully through two school semesters. Months later she told me how she had taken pennies from my purse to buy him candy. "Licorice was his favorite and I brought him some every day, but he still liked Jennifer better'n me. Why, Mommy?" The kind of question for which there is no answer.

School was a worry to her. She was not glib or quick in a world where glibness and quickness were easily confused with ability to learn. To her overworked and exasperated teachers she was an overconscientious "slow learner" who kept trying to catch up and was absent entirely too often.

I let her be absent, though sometimes the illness was imaginary. How different from my now-strictness about attendance with the others. I wasn't working. We had a new baby, I was home anyhow. Sometimes, after Susan grew old enough, I would keep her home from school, too, to have them all together.

Mostly Emily had asthma, and her breathing, harsh and labored, would fill the house with a curiously tranquil sound. I would bring the two old dresser mirrors and her boxes of collections to her bed. She would select beads and single earrings, bottle tops and shells, dried flowers and pebbles, old postcards and scraps, all sorts of oddments; then she and Susan would play Kingdom, setting up landscapes and furniture, peopling them with action.

Those were the only times of peaceful companionship between her and Susan. I have edged away from it, that poisonous feeling between them, that terrible balancing of hurts and needs I had to do between the two, and did so badly, those earlier years.

Oh there are conflicts between the others too, each one human, needing, demanding, hurting, taking—but only between Emily and Susan, no, Emily toward Susan that corroding resentment. It seems so obvious on the surface, yet it is not obvious. Susan, the second child, Susan, golden- and curly-haired and chubby, quick and articulate and assured, everything in appearance and manner Emily was not; Susan, not able to resist Emily's precious things, losing or sometimes clumsily breaking them; Susan telling jokes and riddles to company for applause while Emily sat silent (to say to me later: that was *my* riddle, Mother, I told it to Susan); Susan, who for all the five years' difference in age was just a year behind Emily in developing physically.

I am glad for that slow physical development that widened the difference between her and her contemporaries, though she suffered over it. She was too vulnerable for that terrible world of youthful competition, of preening and parading, of constant measuring of yourself against every other, of envy, "If I had that copper hair," "If I had that skin. . . ." She tormented herself enough about not looking like the others, there was enough of the unsureness, the having to be conscious of words before you speak, the constant caring—what are they thinking of me? without having it all magnified by the merciless physical drives.

Ronnie is calling. He is wet and I change him. It is rare there is such a cry now. That time of motherhood is almost behind me when the ear is not one's own but must always be racked and listening for the child cry, the child call. We sit for a while and I hold him, looking out over the city spread in charcoal with its soft aisles of light. *"Shoogily,"* he breathes and curls closer. I carry him back to bed, asleep. *Shoogily.* A funny word, a family word, inherited from Emily, invented by her to say: *comfort.*

In this and other ways she leaves her seal, I say aloud. And startle at my saying it. What do I mean? What did I start to gather together, to try and make coherent? I was at the terrible, growing years. War years. I do not remember them well. I was working, there were four smaller ones now, there was not time for her. She had to help be a mother, and housekeeper, and shopper. She had to set her seal. Mornings of crisis and near hysteria trying to get lunches packed, hair combed, coats and shoes found, everyone to school or Child Care on time, the baby ready for transportation. And always the paper scribbled on by a smaller one, the book looked at by Susan then mislaid, the homework not done. Running out to that huge school where she was one, she was lost, she was a drop; suffering over the unpreparedness, stammering and unsure in her classes.

There was so little time left at night after the kids were bedded down. She would struggle over books, always eating (it was in those years she developed her enormous appetite that is legendary in our family) and I would be ironing, or preparing food for the next day, or writing V-mail to Bill, or tending the baby. Sometimes, to make me laugh, or out of her despair, she would imitate happenings or types at school.

I think I said once: "Why don't you do something like this in the school amateur show?" One morning she phoned me at work, hardly understandable through the weeping: "Mother, I did it. I won, I won; they gave me first prize; they clapped and clapped and wouldn't let me go."

Now suddenly she was Somebody, and as imprisoned in her difference as she had been in anonymity.

She began to be asked to perform at other high schools, even in colleges, then at city and statewide affairs. The first one we went to, I only recognized her that first moment when thin, shy, she almost drowned herself into the curtains. Then: Was this Emily? The control, the command, the convulsing and deadly clowning, the spell, then the roaring, stamping audience, unwilling to let this rare and precious laughter out of their lives.

Afterwards: You ought to do something about her with a gift like that—but without money or knowing how, what does one do? We have left it all to her, and the gift has as often eddied inside, clogged and clotted, as been used and growing.

She is coming. She runs up the stairs two at a time with her light graceful step, and I know she is happy tonight. Whatever it was that occasioned your call did not happen today.

"Aren't you ever going to finish the ironing, Mother? Whistler painted his mother in a rocker. I'd have to paint mine standing over an ironing board." This is one of her communicative nights and she tells me everything and nothing as she fixes herself a plate of food out of the icebox.

She is so lovely. Why did you want me to come in at all? Why were you concerned? She will find her way.

She starts up the stairs to bed. "Don't get me up with the rest in the morning." "But I thought you were having midterms." "Oh, those," she comes back in, kisses me, and says quite lightly, "in a couple of years when we'll all be atom-dead they won't matter a bit."

She has said it before. She *believes* it. But because I have been dredging the past, and all that compounds a human being is so heavy and meaningful in me, I cannot endure it tonight.

I will never total it all. I will never come in to say: She was a child seldom smiled at. Her father left me before she was a year old. I had to work her first six years when there was work, or I sent her home and to his relatives. There were years she had care she hated. She was dark and thin and foreign-looking in a world where the prestige went to blondeness and curly hair and dimples, she was slow where glibness was prized. She was a child of anxious, not proud, love. We were poor and could not afford for her the soil of easy growth. I was a young mother, I was a distracted mother. There were the other children pushing up, demanding. Her younger sister seemed all that she was not. There were years she did not want me to touch her. She kept too much in herself, her life was such she had to keep too much in herself. My wisdom came too late. She has much to her and probably nothing will come of it. She is a child of her age, of depression, of war, of fear.

Let her be. So all that is in her will not bloom—but in how many does it? There is still enough left to live by. Only help her to know—help make it so there is cause for her to know—that she is more than this dress on the ironing board, helpless before the iron.

1953–1954/1956

Ralph Ellison
1914–1994

When Ralph Ellison published *Invisible Man* in 1952, he was thirty-eight years old. At that time he had published a number of reviews primarily in "little magazines" and radical periodicals, most notably *The New Masses.* He had also published several stories, including "Slick Gonna Learn," "That I had the Wings," "In a Strange Country," "Flying Home," and "King of the Bingo Game." Twelve years after *Invisible Man,* he published *Shadow and Act* (1964), a work that includes several distinguished essays. Since the mid 1950s he had been at work on a second novel, several parts of which have been published. The winner of several prizes when it was published, including the National Book Award for 1953, *Invisible Man* has been widely praised. In a poll of two hundred authors, critics, and editors conducted by *Book Week,* it was selected as the "most distinguished work" published in the United States between 1945 and 1965.

Ralph Waldo Ellison was born in Oklahoma City on March 1, 1914. His father, Lewis Ellison, a native of South Carolina, worked both as a construction foreman and as an independent businessman selling ice and coal. His mother, Ida Milsap Ellison, a native of Mississippi, worked as a maid. Three years after Ellison's birth, his father died, but despite the ensuing poverty, Ellison's family managed to keep him in school, where he was drawn particularly to the study of music, sacred and secular, classical and jazz. By 1933, when he left home to enter Tuskegee Institute, Ellison had had twelve years' instruction in playing the soprano saxophone and several brass instruments. At Tuskegee he studied literature, painting, and photography but still concentrated on music, hoping to become a composer. Forced by lack of funds to quit school after three years, he left for New York, where he worked as a receptionist, file clerk, and factory hand while also playing music and trying to compose it. He also experimented briefly with photography and sculpture. As he came under the influence of Richard Wright and Langston Hughes, however, he began reading more widely, especially the works of the great modernists. In André Malraux he found an interesting merging of literature and politics. In T. S. Eliot's *The Waste Land* he found something that reminded him of the rhythms and allusional density he heard in African American music but often missed in African American writing. Soon Ellison was also writing. Hoping to combine a commitment to art with a commitment to politics, he found himself working for the WPA Federal Writer's Project and at the same time writing reviews and stories for radical magazines. For a brief period in 1942 and 1943 he was managing editor of *The Negro Quarterly*, a "Review of Negro Life and Culture" that regularly published leftist artists and scholars.

Ellison's political concerns derived in part from the example of his mother, who had been an ardent supporter of Eugene Debs's Socialist party, and they were intensified by his mother's death in 1937. By the time he began writing *Invisible Man* in 1945, however, most organized forms of radical politics had begun to seem to him too restrictive. More and more he was convinced that literature, like music, could capture the revolutionary implications of African American life only by discovering techniques commensurate with the complexities of that life. With this emerging conviction came a new mode of fiction that combined elements of "social realism" with elements of "surrealism." In addition to music, which continued strongly to influence his writing, Ellison began to infuse his fiction with African American folklore out of a conviction that African American folklore captured and conveyed the sense of African American experience "with a complexity of vision that seldom gets into our writing." As he labored to write his way through these interrelated shifts, Ellison also began to move away from short fiction toward the novel as his appropriate form. The novel, he says, "is a form which attempts to deal with the contradictions of life and ambivalence and ambiguities of values." On a personal level, the novel seemed to him to provide a means of discovering some deeper, "more universal meaning" in his own experience— in "remembered conversations" and "local customs." Beyond that, on broader social and political levels, the novel seemed to him to provide a way of discovering "the heroic component" of the experience of African Americans in America. "Let's not forget," he states in *Shadow and Act*, "that the great tragedies not only treat of negative matters, of violence, brutalities, defeats, but they treat them within a context of man's will to act, to challenge reality and to snatch triumph from the teeth of destruction."

Further Reading:

J. Hersey, ed., *Ralph Ellison: A Collection of Critical Essays*, 1974.

R. Stepto, *From Behind the Veil: A Study of Afro-American Literature*, 1979.

A. Nadel, *Invisible Criticism: Ralph Ellison and the American Canon*, 1988.

R. O'Meally, *The Craft of Ralph Ellison*, 1980.

———, ed., *New Essays on Invisible Man*, 1988.

J. G. Watts, *Heroism and the Black Intellectual: Ralph Ellison, Politics, and Afro-American Intellectual Life*, 1994.

M. Graham and A. Singh, eds., *Conversations with Ralph Ellison*, 1995.

E. Sundquist, ed. *Cultural Contexts for Ralph Ellison's* Invisible Man, 1995.

Text:
"The Battle Royal" from *Invisible Man*, 1952.

The Battle Royal

It goes a long way back, some twenty years. All my life I had been looking for something, and everywhere I turned someone tried to tell me what it was. I accepted their answers too, though they were often in contradiction and even self-contradictory. I was naïve. I was looking for myself and asking everyone except myself questions which I, and only I, could answer. It took me a long time and much painful boomeranging of my expectations to achieve a realization everyone else appears to have been born with: That I am nobody but myself. But first I had to discover that I am an invisible man!

And yet I am no freak of nature, nor of history. I was in the cards, other things having been equal (or unequal) eighty-five years ago. I am not ashamed of my grandparents for having been slaves. I am only ashamed of myself for having at one time been ashamed. About eighty-five years ago they were told that they were free, united with others of our country in everything pertaining to the common good, and, in everything social, separate like the fingers of the hand. And they believed it. They exulted in it. They stayed in their place, worked hard, and brought up my father to do the same. But my grandfather is the one. He was an odd old guy, my grandfather, and I am told I take after him. It was he who caused the trouble. On his deathbed he called my father to him and said, "Son, after I'm gone I want you to keep up the good fight. I never told you, but our life is a war and I have been a traitor all my born days, a spy in the enemy's country ever since I give up my gun back in the Reconstruction. Live with your head in the lion's mouth. I want you to overcome 'em with yeses, undermine 'em with grins, agree 'em to death and destruction, let 'em swoller you till they vomit or bust wide open." They thought the old man had gone out of his mind. He had been the meekest of men. The younger children were rushed from the room, the shades drawn and the flame of the lamp turned so low that it sputtered on the wick like the old man's breathing. "Learn it to the younguns," he whispered fiercely; then he died.

But my folks were more alarmed over his last words than over his dying. It was as though he had not died at all, his words caused so much anxiety. I was warned emphatically to forget what he had said and, indeed, this is the first time it has been mentioned outside the family circle. It had a tremendous effect upon me, however. I could never be sure of what he meant. Grandfather had been a quiet old man who never made any trouble, yet on his deathbed he had called himself a traitor and a spy, and he had spoken of his meekness as a dangerous activity. It became a constant puzzle which lay unanswered in the back of my mind. And whenever things went well for me I remembered my grandfather and felt guilty and uncomfortable. It was as though I was carrying out his advice in spite of myself. And to make it worse, everyone loved me for it. I was praised by the most lily-white men of the town. I was considered an example of desirable conduct—just as my grandfather had been. And what puzzled me was that the old man had defined it as *treachery*. When I was praised for my conduct I felt a guilt that in some way I was doing something that was really against the wishes of the white folks, that if they had understood they would have desired me to act just the opposite, that I should have been sulky and mean, and that that really would have been what they wanted, even though they were fooled and thought they wanted me to act as I did. It made me afraid that some day they would look upon me as a traitor and I would be lost. Still I was more afraid to act any other way because they didn't like that at all. The old man's words were like a curse. On my graduation day I delivered an oration in which I showed that humility was the secret, indeed, the very essence of progress. (Not that I believed this—how could I, remembering my grandfather?—I only believed that it worked.) It was a great success. Everyone praised me and I was invited to give the speech at a gathering of the town's leading white citizens. It was a triumph for our whole community.

It was in the main ballroom of the leading hotel. When I got there I discovered that it was on the occasion of a smoker, and I was told that since I was to be there anyway I might as well take part in the battle royal to be fought by some of my schoolmates as part of the entertainment. The battle royal came first.

All of the town's big shots were there in their tuxedoes, wolfing down the buffet foods, drinking beer and whiskey and smoking black cigars. It was a large room with a high ceiling. Chairs were arranged in neat rows around three sides of a portable boxing ring. The fourth side was clear, revealing a gleaming space of polished floor. I had some misgivings over the battle royal, by the way. Not from a distaste for fighting, but because I didn't care too much for the other fellows who were to take part. They were tough guys who seemed to have no grandfather's curse worrying their minds. No one could mistake their toughness. And besides, I suspected that fighting a battle royal might detract from the dignity of my speech. In those pre-invisible days I visualized myself as a potential Booker T. Washington. But the other fellows didn't care too much for me either, and there were nine of them. I felt superior to them in my way, and I didn't like the manner in which we were all crowded together into the servants' elevator. Nor did they like my being there. In fact, as the warmly lighted floors flashed past the elevator we had words over the fact that I, by taking part in the fight, had knocked one of their friends out of a night's work.

We were led out of the elevator through a rococo hall into an anteroom and told to get into our fighting togs. Each of us was issued a pair of boxing gloves and ushered out into the big mirrored hall, which we entered looking cautiously about us and whispering, lest we might accidentally be heard above the noise of the room. It was foggy with cigar smoke. And already the whiskey was taking effect. I was shocked to see some of the most important men of the town quite tipsy. They were all there—bankers, lawyers, judges, doctors, fire chiefs, teachers, merchants. Even one of the more fashionable pastors. Something we could not see was going on up front. A clarinet was vibrating sensuously and the men were standing up and moving eagerly forward. We were a small tight group, clustered together, our bare upper bodies touching and shining with anticipatory sweat; while up front the big shots were becoming increasingly excited over something we still could not see. Suddenly I heard the school superintendent, who had told me to come, yell, "Bring up the shines, gentlemen! Bring up the little shines!"

We were rushed up to the front of the ballroom, where it smelled even more strongly of tobacco and whiskey. Then we were pushed into place. I almost wet my pants. A sea of faces, some hostile, some amused, ringed around us, and in the center, facing us, stood a magnificent blonde—stark naked. There was dead silence. I felt a blast of cold air chill me. I tried to back away, but they were behind me and around me. Some of the boys stood with lowered heads, trembling. I felt a wave of irrational guilt and fear. My teeth chattered, my skin turned to goose flesh, my knees knocked. Yet I was strongly attracted and looked in spite of myself. Had the price of looking been blindness, I would

have looked. The hair was yellow like that of a circus kewpie doll, the face heavily powdered and rouged, as though to form an abstract mask, the eyes hollow and smeared a
cool blue, the color of a baboon's butt. I felt a desire to spit upon her as my eyes
brushed slowly over her body. Her breasts were firm and round as the domes of East Indian temples, and I stood so close as to see the fine skin texture and beads of pearly perspiration glistening like dew around the pink and erected buds of her nipples. I wanted
at one and the same time to run from the room, to sink through the floor, or go to her
and cover her from my eyes and the eyes of the others with my body; to feel the soft
thighs, to caress her and destroy her, to love her and murder her, to hide from her, and
yet to stroke where below the small American flag tattooed upon her belly her thighs
formed a capital V. I had a notion that of all in the room she saw only me with her impersonal eyes.

And then she began to dance, a slow sensuous movement; the smoke of a hundred
cigars clinging to her like the thinnest of veils. She seemed like a fair bird-girl girdled in
veils calling to me from the angry surface of some gray and threatening sea. I was transported. Then I became aware of the clarinet playing and the big shots yelling at us. Some
threatened us if we looked and others if we did not. On my right I saw one boy faint.
And now a man grabbed a silver pitcher from a table and stepped close as he dashed ice
water upon him and stood him up and forced two of us to support him as his head hung
and moans issued from his thick bluish lips. Another boy began to plead to go home.
He was the largest of the group, wearing dark red fighting trunks much too small to
conceal the erection which projected from him as though in answer to the insinuating
low-registered moaning of the clarinet. He tried to hide himself with his boxing gloves.

And all the while the blonde continued dancing, smiling faintly at the big shots who
watched her with fascination, and faintly smiling at our fear. I noticed a certain merchant who followed her hungrily, his lips loose and drooling. He was a large man who
wore diamond studs in a shirtfront which swelled with the ample paunch underneath,
and each time the blonde swayed her undulating hips he ran his hand through the thin
hair of his bald head and, with his arms upheld, his posture clumsy like that of an intoxicated panda, wound his belly in a slow and obscene grind. This creature was completely hypnotized. The music had quickened. As the dancer flung herself about with a
detached expression on her face, the men began reaching out to touch her. I could see
their beefy fingers sink into the soft flesh. Some of the others tried to stop them and she
began to move around the floor in graceful circles, as they gave chase, slipping and sliding over the polished floor. It was mad. Chairs went crashing, drinks were spilt, as they
ran laughing and howling after her. They caught her just as she reached a door, raised
her from the floor, and tossed her as college boys are tossed at a hazing, and above her
red, fixed-smiling lips I saw the terror and disgust in her eyes, almost like my own terror
and that which I saw in some of the other boys. As I watched, they tossed her twice and
her soft breasts seemed to flatten against the air and her legs flung wildly as she spun.
Some of the more sober ones helped her to escape. And I started off the floor, heading
for the anteroom with the rest of the boys.

Some were still crying and in hysteria. But as we tried to leave we were stopped and
ordered to get into the ring. There was nothing to do but what we were told. All ten of
us climbed under the ropes and allowed ourselves to be blindfolded with broad bands
of white cloth. One of the men seemed to feel a bit sympathetic and tried to cheer us up
as we stood with our backs against the ropes. Some of us tried to grin. "See that boy

over there?" one of the men said. "I want you to run across at the bell and give it to him right in the belly. If you don't get him, I'm going to get you. I don't like his looks." Each of us was told the same. The blindfolds were put on. Yet even then I had been going over my speech. In my mind each word was as bright as flame. I felt the cloth pressed into place, and frowned so that it would be loosened when I relaxed.

But now I felt a sudden fit of blind terror. I was unused to darkness. It was as though I had suddenly found myself in a dark room filled with poisonous cottonmouths. I could hear the bleary voices yelling insistently for the battle royal to begin.

"Get going in there!"

"Let me at that big nigger!"

I strained to pick up the school superintendent's voice, as though to squeeze some security out of that slightly more familiar sound.

"Let me at those black sonsabitches!" someone yelled.

"No, Jackson, no!" another voice yelled. "Here, somebody, help me hold Jack."

"I want to get at that ginger-colored nigger. Tear him limb from limb," the first voice yelled.

I stood against the ropes trembling. For in those days I was what they called ginger-colored, and he sounded as though he might crunch me between his teeth like a crisp ginger cookie.

Quite a struggle was going on. Chairs were being kicked about and I could hear voices grunting as with a terrific effort. I wanted to see, to see more desperately than ever before. But the blindfold was tight as a thick skin-puckering scab and when I raised my gloved hands to push the layers of white aside a voice yelled, "Oh, no you don't, black bastard! Leave that alone!"

"Ring the bell before Jackson kills him a coon!" someone boomed in the sudden silence. And I heard the bell clang and the sound of the feet scuffling forward.

A glove smacked against my head. I pivoted, striking out stiffly as someone went past, and felt the jar ripple along the length of my arm to my shoulder. Then it seemed as though all nine of the boys had turned upon me at once. Blows pounded me from all sides while I struck out as best I could. So many blows landed upon me that I wondered if I were not the only blindfolded fighter in the ring, or if the man called Jackson hadn't succeeded in getting me after all.

Blindfolded, I could no longer control my motions. I had no dignity. I stumbled about like a baby or a drunken man. The smoke had become thicker and with each new blow it seemed to sear and further restrict my lungs. My saliva became like hot bitter glue. A glove connected with my head, filling my mouth with warm blood. It was everywhere. I could not tell if the moisture I felt upon my body was sweat or blood. A blow landed hard against the nape of my neck. I felt myself going over, my head hitting the floor. Streaks of blue light filled the black world behind the blindfold. I lay prone, pretending that I was knocked out, but felt myself seized by hands and yanked to my feet. "Get going, black boy! Mix it up!" My arms were like lead, my head smarting from blows. I managed to feel my way to the ropes and held on, trying to catch my breath. A glove landed in my mid-section and I went over again, feeling as though the smoke had become a knife jabbed into my guts. Pushed this way and that by the legs milling around me, I finally pulled erect and discovered that I could see the black, sweat-washed forms weaving in the smoky-blue atmosphere like drunken dancers weaving to the rapid drum-like thuds of blows.

Everyone fought hysterically. It was complete anarchy. Everybody fought everybody else. No group fought together for long. Two, three, four, fought one, then turned to fight each other, were themselves attacked. Blows landed below the belt and in the kidney, with the gloves open as well as closed, and with my eye partly opened now there was not so much terror. I moved carefully, avoiding blows, although not too many to attract attention, fighting from group to group. The boys groped about like blind, cautious crabs crouching to protect their mid-sections, their heads pulled in short against their shoulders, their arms stretched nervously before them, with their fists testing the smoke-filled air like the knobbed feelers of hypersensitive snails. In one corner I glimpsed a boy violently punching the air and heard him scream in pain as he smashed his hand against a ring post. For a second I saw him bent over holding his hand, then going down as a blow caught his unprotected head. I played one group against the other, slipping in and throwing a punch then stepping out of range while pushing the others into the melee to take the blows blindly aimed at me. The smoke was agonizing and there were no rounds, no bells at three minute intervals to relieve our exhaustion. The room spun round me, a swirl of lights, smoke, sweating bodies surrounded by tense white faces. I bled from both nose and mouth, the blood spattering upon my chest.

The men kept yelling, "Slug him, black boy! Knock his guts out!"

"Uppercut him! Kill him! Kill that big boy!"

Taking a fake fall, I saw a boy going down heavily beside me as though we were felled by a single blow, saw a sneaker-clad foot shoot into his groin as the two who had knocked him down stumbled upon him. I rolled out of range, feeling a twinge of nausea.

The harder we fought the more threatening the men became. And yet, I had begun to worry about my speech again. How would it go? Would they recognize my ability? What would they give me?

I was fighting automatically when suddenly I noticed that one after another of the boys was leaving the ring. I was surprised, filled with panic, as though I had been left alone with an unknown danger. Then I understood. The boys had arranged it among themselves. It was the custom for the two men left in the ring to slug it out for the winner's prize. I discovered this too late. When the bell sounded two men in tuxedoes leaped into the ring and removed the blindfold. I found myself facing Tatlock, the biggest of the gang. I felt sick at my stomach. Hardly had the bell stopped ringing in my ears than it clanged again and I saw him moving swiftly toward me. Thinking of nothing else to do I hit him smash on the nose. He kept coming, bringing the rank sharp violence of stale sweat. His face was a black blank of a face, only his eyes alive—with hate of me and aglow with a feverish terror from what had happened to us all. I became anxious. I wanted to deliver my speech and he came at me as though he meant to beat it out of me. I smashed him again and again, taking his blows as they came. Then on a sudden impulse I struck him lightly and as we clinched, I whispered, "Fake like I knocked you out, you can have the prize."

"I'll break your behind," he whispered hoarsely.

"For *them*?"

"For *me*, sonofabitch!"

They were yelling for us to break it up and Tatlock spun me half around with a blow, and as a joggled camera sweeps in a reeling scene, I saw the howling red faces crouching tense beneath the cloud of blue-gray smoke. For a moment the world wavered, unraveled, flowed, then my head cleared and Tatlock bounced before me. That fluttering shadow before my eyes was his jabbing left hand. Then falling forward, my head against his damp shoulder, I whispered,

"I'll make it five dollars more."

"Go to hell!"

But his muscles relaxed a trifle beneath my pressure and I breathed, "Seven?"

"Give it to your ma," he said, ripping me beneath the heart.

And while I still held him I butted him and moved away. I felt myself bombarded with punches. I fought back with hopeless desperation. I wanted to deliver my speech more than anything else in the world, because I felt that only these men could judge truly my ability, and now this stupid clown was ruining my chances. I began fighting carefully now, moving in to punch him and out again with my greater speed. A lucky blow to his chin and I had him going too—until I heard a loud voice yell, "I got my money on the big boy."

Hearing this, I almost dropped my guard. I was confused: Should I try to win against the voice out there? Would not this go against my speech, and was not this a moment for humility, for nonresistance? A blow to my head as I danced about sent my right eye popping like a jack-in-the-box and settled my dilemma. The room went red as I fell. It was a dream fall, my body languid and fastidious as to where to land, until the floor became impatient and smashed up to meet me. A moment later I came to. An hypnotic voice said FIVE emphatically. And I lay there, hazily watching a dark red spot of my own blood shaping itself into a butterfly, glistening and soaking into the soiled gray world of the canvas.

When the voice drawled TEN I was lifted up and dragged to a chair. I sat dazed. My eye pained and swelled with each throb of my pounding heart and I wondered if now I would be allowed to speak. I was wringing wet, my mouth still bleeding. We were grouped along the wall now. The other boys ignored me as they congratulated Tatlock and speculated as to how much they would be paid. One boy whimpered over his smashed hand. Looking up front, I saw attendants in white jackets rolling the portable ring away and placing a small square rug in the vacant space surrounded by chairs. Perhaps, I thought, I will stand on the rug to deliver my speech.

Then the M.C. called to us, "Come on up here boys and get your money."

We ran forward to where the men laughed and talked in their chairs, waiting. Everyone seemed friendly now.

"There it is on the rug," the man said. I saw the rug covered with coins of all dimensions and a few crumpled bills. But what excited me, scattered here and there, were the gold pieces.

"Boys, it's all yours," the man said. "You get all you grab."

"That's right, Sambo," a blond man said, winking at me confidentially.

I trembled with excitement, forgetting my pain. I would get the gold and the bills, I thought. I would use both hands. I would throw my body against the boys nearest me to block them from the gold.

"Get down around the rug now," the man commanded, "and don't anyone touch it until I give the signal."

"This ought to be good," I heard.

As told, we got around the square rug on our knees. Slowly the man raised his freckled hand as we followed it upward with our eyes.

I heard, "These niggers look like they're about to pray!"

Then, "Ready," the man said. "Go!"

I lunged for a yellow coin lying on the blue design of the carpet, touching it and sending a surprised shriek to join those rising around me. I tried frantically to remove my hand but could not let go. A hot, violent force tore through my body, shaking me like a wet rat. The rug was electrified. The hair bristled up on my head as I shook myself free. My muscles jumped, my nerves jangled, writhed. But I saw that this was not stopping the other boys. Laughing in fear and embarrassment, some were holding back and scooping up the coins knocked off by the painful contortions of the others. The men roared above us as we struggled.

"Pick it up, goddamnit, pick it up!" someone called like a bass-voiced parrot. "Go on, get it!"

I crawled rapidly around the floor, picking up the coins, trying to avoid the coppers and to get greenbacks and the gold. Ignoring the shock by laughing, as I brushed the coins off quickly, I discovered that I could contain the electricity—a contradiction, but it works. Then the men began to push us onto the rug. Laughing embarrassedly, we struggled out of their hands and kept after the coins. We were all wet and slippery and hard to hold. Suddenly I saw a boy lifted into the air, glistening with sweat like a circus seal, and dropped, his wet back landing flush upon the charged rug, heard him yell and saw him literally dance upon his back, his elbows beating a frenzied tattoo upon the floor, his muscles twitching like the flesh of a horse stung by many flies. When he finally rolled off, his face was gray and no one stopped him when he ran from the floor amid booming laughter.

"Get the money," the M.C. called. "That's good hard American cash!"

And we snatched and grabbed, snatched and grabbed. I was careful not to come too close to the rug now, and when I felt the hot whiskey breath descend upon me like a cloud of foul air I reached out and grabbed the leg of a chair. It was occupied and I held on desperately.

"Leggo, nigger! Leggo!"

The huge face wavered down to mine as he tried to push me free. But my body was slippery and he was too drunk. It was Mr. Colcord, who owned a chain of movie houses and "entertainment palaces." Each time he grabbed me I slipped out of his hands. It became a real struggle. I feared the rug more than I did the drunk, so I held on, surprising myself for a moment by trying to topple *him* upon the rug. It was such an enormous idea that I found myself actually carrying it out. I tried not to be obvious, yet when I grabbed his leg, trying to tumble him out of the chair, he raised up roaring with laughter, and, looking at me with soberness dead in the eye, kicked me viciously in the chest. The chair leg flew out of my hand and I felt myself going and rolled. It was as though I had rolled through a bed of hot coals. It seemed a whole century would pass before I would roll free, a century in which I was seared through the deepest levels of my body to the fearful breath within me and the breath seared and heated to the point of explosion. It'll all be over in a flash, I thought as I rolled clear. It'll all be over in a flash.

But not yet, the men on the other side were waiting, red faces swollen as though from apoplexy as they bent forward in their chairs. Seeing their fingers coming toward me I rolled away as a fumbled football rolls off the receiver's fingertips, back into the coals. That time I luckily sent the rug sliding out of place and heard the coins ringing against the floor and the boys scuffling to pick them up and the M.C. calling, "All right, boys, that's all. Go get dressed and get your money."

I was limp as a dish rag. My back felt as though it had been beaten with wires.

When we had dressed the M.C. came in and gave us each five dollars, except Tatlock, who got ten for being last in the ring. Then he told us to leave. I was not to get a chance to deliver my speech, I thought. I was going out into the dim alley in despair when I was stopped and told to go back. I returned to the ballroom, where the men were pushing back their chairs and gathering in groups to talk.

The M.C. knocked on a table for quiet. "Gentlemen," he said, "we almost forgot an important part of the program. A most serious part, gentlemen. This boy was brought here to deliver a speech which he made at his graduation yesterday . . ."

"Bravo!"

"I'm told that he is the smartest boy we've got out there in Greenwood. I'm told that he knows more big words than a pocket-sized dictionary."

Much applause and laughter.

"So now, gentlemen, I want you to give him your attention."

There was still laughter as I faced them, my mouth dry, my eye throbbing. I began slowly, but evidently my throat was tense, because they began shouting, "Louder! Louder!"

"We of the younger generation extol the wisdom of that great leader and educator," I shouted, "who first spoke these flaming words of wisdom: 'A ship lost at sea for many days suddenly sighted a friendly vessel. From the mast of the unfortunate vessel was seen a signal: "Water, water; we die of thirst!" The answer from the friendly vessel came back: "Cast down your bucket where you are." The captain of the distressed vessel, at last heeding the injunction, cast down his bucket, and it came up full of fresh sparkling water from the mouth of the Amazon River.' And like him I say, and in his words, 'To those of my race who depend upon bettering their condition in a foreign land, or who underestimate the importance of cultivating friendly relations with the Southern white man, who is his next-door neighbor, I would say: "Cast down your bucket where you are"—cast it down in making friends in every manly way of the people of all races by whom we are surrounded . . .' "

I spoke automatically and with such fervor that I did not realize that the men were still talking and laughing until my dry mouth, filling up with blood from the cut, almost strangled me. I coughed, wanting to stop and go to one of the tall brass, sand-filled spittoons to relieve myself, but a few of the men, especially the superintendent, were listening and I was afraid. So I gulped it down, blood, saliva and all, and continued. (What powers of endurance I had during those days! What enthusiasm! What a belief in the rightness of things!) I spoke even louder in spite of the pain. But still they talked and still they laughed, as though deaf with cotton in dirty ears. So I spoke with greater emotional emphasis. I closed my ears and swallowed blood until I was nauseated. The speech seemed a hundred times as long as before, but I could not leave out a single word. All had to be said, each memorized nuance considered, rendered. Nor was that all. Whenever I uttered a word of three or more syllables a group of voices would yell for me to repeat it. I used the phrase "social responsibility" and they yelled:

"What's that word you say, boy?"

"Social responsibility," I said.

"What?"

"Social . . ."

"Louder."

"... responsibility."

"More!"

"Respon———"

"Repeat!"

"———sibility."

The room filled with the uproar of laughter until, no doubt, distracted by having to gulp down my blood, I made a mistake and yelled a phrase I had often seen denounced in newspaper editorials, heard debated in private.

"Social . . ."

"What?" they yelled.

". . . equality———"

The laughter hung smokelike in the sudden stillness. I opened my eyes, puzzled. Sounds of displeasure filled the room. The M.C. rushed forward. They shouted hostile phrases at me. But I did not understand.

A small dry mustached man in the front row blared out, "Say that slowly, son!"

"What, sir?"

"What you just said!"

"Social responsibility, sir," I said.

"You weren't being smart, were you, boy?" he said, not unkindly.

"No, sir!"

"You sure that about 'equality' was a mistake?"

"Oh, yes, sir," I said. "I was swallowing blood."

"Well, you had better speak more slowly so we can understand. We mean to do right by you, but you've got to know your place at all times. All right, now, go on with your speech."

I was afraid. I wanted to leave but I wanted also to speak and I was afraid they'd snatch me down.

"Thank you, sir," I said, beginning where I had left off, and having them ignore me as before.

Yet when I finished there was a thunderous applause. I was surprised to see the superintendent come forth with a package wrapped in white tissue paper, and, gesturing for quiet, address the men.

"Gentlemen, you see that I did not overpraise this boy. He makes a good speech and some day he'll lead his people in the proper paths. And I don't have to tell you that that is important in these days and times. This is a good, smart boy, and so to encourage him in the right direction, in the name of the Board of Education I wish to present him a prize in the form of this . . ."

He paused, removing the tissue paper and revealing a gleaming calfskin brief case.

". . . in the form of this first-class article from Shad Whitmore's shop."

"Boy," he said, addressing me, "take this prize and keep it well. Consider it a badge of office. Prize it. Keep developing as you are and some day it will be filled with important papers that will help shape the destiny of your people."

I was so moved that I could hardly express my thanks. A rope of bloody saliva forming a shape like an undiscovered continent drooled upon the leather and I wiped it quickly away. I felt an importance that I had never dreamed.

"Open it and see what's inside," I was told.

My fingers a-tremble, I complied, smelling the fresh leather and finding an official-looking document inside. It was a scholarship to the state college for Negroes. My eyes filled with tears and I ran awkwardly off the floor.

I was overjoyed; I did not even mind when I discovered that the gold pieces I had scrambled for were brass pocket tokens advertising a certain make of automobile.

When I reached home everyone was excited. Next day the neighbors came to congratulate me. I even felt safe from grandfather, whose deathbed curse usually spoiled my triumphs. I stood beneath his photograph with my brief case in hand and smiled triumphantly into his stolid black peasant's face. It was a face that fascinated me. The eyes seemed to follow everywhere I went.

That night I dreamed I was at a circus with him and that he refused to laugh at the clowns no matter what they did. Then later he told me to open my brief case and read what was inside and I did, finding an official envelope stamped with the state seal; and inside the envelope I found another and another, endlessly, and I thought I would fall of weariness. "Them's years," he said. "Now open that one." And I did and in it I found an engraved document containing a short message in letters of gold. "Read it," my grandfather said. "Out loud!"

"To Whom It May Concern," I intoned. "Keep This Nigger-Boy Running."

I awoke with the old man's laughter ringing in my ears.

(It was a dream I was to remember and dream again for many years after. But at that time I had no insight into its meaning. First I had to attend college.)

1952

Randall Jarrell
1914–1965

Randall Jarrell (the accent is on the second syllable) was a divided soul, half critic, half poet. By the time of his early death (he walked either by accident or design into the path of a car on a freeway), he was the best-known critic of poetry in America, serving as poetry editor of *The Nation* (1946) and writing brilliantly witty essays on American poetry from Whitman to Elizabeth Bishop. His essay on Whitman helped restore Whitman to the American pantheon of poets, he understood Marianne Moore better than anyone else, and he greeted (from his privileged position as Robert Lowell's college roommate) Lowell's first book of verse, *Lord Weary's Castle* (1946), as the achievement of a major poet. It was his own poetic sensibility, of course, that made Jarrell's criticism so acute; he saw into the workings of verse with a poet's eye. And his criticism was also a reflection of his rapid, abrasive, allusive, and mercurial conversation that made willing hearers of his gifted friends—Lowell, Peter Taylor, John Berryman. Jarrell's critical books—*Poetry and the Age* (1953), *A Sad Heart at the Supermarket* (1962), and *The Third Book of Criticism* (1971)—brought American poetry reviewing from a generally depressing exhibition of puffery to the level of a high accomplishment.

Yet Jarrell's own heart was with his poetry, where he wrote chiefly with a yearning pity for the fallibility, weakness, and sadness of human beings. He could insert himself with uncanny insight into the mind of his characters. That Keatsian degree of empathy may have been what led him to major in psychology at Vanderbilt; Freud was to become one of his major intellectual points of reference. In going to Vanderbilt, Jarrell was remaining in Nashville, where he had been born and had lived since the age of twelve. Yet the impressionable years of his early childhood had been spent in California, and a deep nostalgia for Hollywood, where he had lived for a year with his grandparents, never left him. He called it his "lost world" in the reminiscent title poem of his last book (1965), and its movie lots, with their temporary fantasy constructions, were for him symbols of the imagination.

Jarrell took an M.A. in English from Vanderbilt in 1938 and, except for his military service from 1942 to 1946, spent the rest of his life teaching in various colleges, notably Kenyon, the University of Texas, Sarah Lawrence, Princeton, and the Women's College of the University of North Carolina (1947–1965, with occasional interruptions). Jarrell first became known for his poignant war poetry. He had served in the air force in World War II, and his first volumes, *Little Friend, Little Friend* (1945) and *Losses* (1948), show soldiers as pitiful high school boys plunged, unequipped and ignorant, into war, bombing, and death. In 1965, after a long and brilliant career, Jarrell was hospitalized for a nervous breakdown; he died not long thereafter. His *Complete Poems* appeared posthumously, in 1969.

Jarrell liked the English blank verse line, adapted (via the example of Frost) to American speech rhythms; he was also capable (as in "Next Day") of beautiful inventions in stanza form and rhyme scheme. He had an eye for the poetry of the ordinary ("Moving from Cheer to Joy, from Joy to All"), and his rendering of the pathos of a young soldier, of a woman in a supermarket or at a zoo, of a girl falling asleep over her homework, is exact and touching.

Further Reading:

Randall Jarrell, 1914–1965, ed. R. Lowell, P. Taylor, and R. P. Warren, 1967.
K. Shapiro, *Randall Jarrell,* 1967.
The Achievement of Randall Jarrell, ed. F. Hoffman, 1970.
S. Ferguson, *The Poetry of Randall Jarrell,* 1971.
M. L. Rosenthal, *Randall Jarrell,* 1972.
H. Hagenbuchle, *The Black Goddess: A Study of the Archetypal Feminine in the Poetry of Randall Jarrell,* 1975.

B. Quinn, *Randall Jarrell,* 1981.
S. Ferguson, *Critical Essays on Randall Jarrell,* 1983.
R. Flynn, *Randall Jarrell and the Lost World of Childhood,* 1990.
W. Pritchard, *Randall Jarrell: A Literary Life,* 1990.

Texts:

Complete Poems, 1969.
See also *Poetry and the Age,* 1953.
Pictures from an Institution, 1954.

A Sad Heart at the Supermarket, 1962.
The Third Book of Criticism, 1969.

The Death of the Ball Turret* Gunner

From my mother's sleep I fell into the State,
And I hunched in its belly till my wet fur froze.
Six miles from earth, loosed from its dream of life,
I woke to black flak and the nightmare fighters.
When I died they washed me out of the turret with a hose.   5
1955

The Woman at the Washington Zoo

The saris¹ go by me from the embassies.

Cloth from the moon. Cloth from another planet.
They look back at the leopard like the leopard.

And I. . . .
       this print of mine, that has kept its color   5
Alive through so many cleanings; this dull null
Navy I wear to work, and wear from work, and so
To my bed, so to my grave, with no
Complaints, no comment: neither from my chief,
The Deputy Chief Assistant, nor his chief—   10
Only I complain. . . . this serviceable
Body that no sunlight dyes, no hand suffuses
But, dome-shadowed, withering among columns,
Wavy beneath fountains—small, far-off, shining
In the eyes of animals, these beings trapped   15
As I am trapped but not, themselves, the trap,
Aging, but without knowledge of their age,
Kept safe here, knowing not of death, for death—
Oh, bars of my own body, open, open!

---

* A *ball turret* was a revolvable plexiglass sphere set into the underside of a B-17 or B-24 bomber, from which a man, in a crouched position, could fire a mounted .50 caliber machine gun at other aircraft aloft.

¹ Long flowing garments worn by women of India.

The world goes by my cage and never sees me. 20
And there come not to me, as come to these,
The wild beasts, sparrows pecking the llamas' grain,
Pigeons settling on the bears' bread, buzzards
Tearing the meat the flies have clouded. . . .
                       Vulture, 25
When you come for the white rat that the foxes left,
Take off the red helmet of your head, the black
Wings that have shadowed me, and step to me as man:
The wild brother at whose feet the white wolves fawn,
To whose hand of power the great lioness 30
Stalks, purring. . . .
                 You know what I was,
You see what I am: change me, change me!
1960

Robert Lowell
1917–1977

Robert Lowell's poems are so various in theme and form that it is difficult to believe they were all written by the same man. With *Lord Weary's Castle* (1946), he burst on the literary scene as a "Roman Catholic poet," writing a poetry of social protest in icily formal meters swelling with Miltonic rage; with *Day by Day* (1977), he left the American literary scene as a Horatian poet of quiet stoicism, writing verse "day by day." In having the daring to break his own aesthetic several times over, Lowell helped to reshape twentieth-century poetry. His poetic powers, trained in Greek and Latin and developed further by "imitations" of many famous European poems, were formidable.

    The accident of Lowell's quasi-aristocratic birth determined his poetic life; he was a Lowell first, and a husband, lover, father, teacher, or political protester second. The other determinant of his life was his recurrent manic-depressive illness, which caused a part of almost every year of his adult life to be spent in confinement in an asylum. In the last ten years of his life his condition was stabilized by lithium. But the uncertainty of his behavior made it for a long time impossible for him to be regularly employed; his family income luckily made that unnecessary. His large poetic output has yet to be fully absorbed by critics and the public.

    Robert Lowell's father was a vacant and inept man who made the mistake of leaving the navy, at his wife's insistence, to take up stockbroking. The firm kept him on for his name and social connections, but he had, according to his son's memoir, *91 Revere Street,* no clients. Lowell's mother, a Winslow by birth, was intelligent, possessive, and domineering. After an unsuccessful two years at Harvard, Lowell fled his parents and, advised by Ford Madox Ford, went off to Kenyon College to study under John Crowe Ransom. There he succeeded brilliantly, majored in classics, and was valedictorian of his class.

Lowell married the novelist Jean Stafford (all three of his wives were writers) and for a brief period became a Roman Catholic (the one thing that would most enrage his Puritan-descended family). After attempting to enlist in the navy during World War II and being refused for bad eyesight, he decided on pacifist grounds to become a conscientious objector, flouting the family naval tradition. Finally, in full mania, he wrote a letter to President Roosevelt ("I made my manic statement"), explaining his choice of conscientious objector status. After spending several months in jail, Lowell was released. Lowell's first marriage ended after bouts of drinking, insanity, and infidelity. His second, more stable marriage was to the writer Elizabeth Hardwick, who enabled him to survive moves, breakdowns, and hospitalizations. He entered psychoanalytic therapy, and the reflection on his past entailed by therapy is visible in *Life Studies* (1960), a book of pitilessly naked portraits of his family.

These poems were written in a new laconic free verse (retaining some underpinnings of rhyme) that Lowell ascribed to the influence of both Elizabeth Bishop's natural cadences and the new oral poetry of the Beats. In writing *Life Studies,* Lowell was continuing the historical portraiture of his Puritan stock that had begun in his early poems about the Winslows (whom he scandalously called "Indian killers") and Jonathan Edwards (to whom, as a Puritan intellectual of crisis mentality, he was very much drawn). *Life Studies* also records Lowell's repudiation of Roman Catholicism; here, in a symbolic decision, he leaves Rome and travels "Beyond the Alps" to Paris.

Life Studies was excoriated by Lowell's old mentor Allen Tate, who said the poems were not poetry. Seeing Lowell's agnostic stance, Catholics regretted losing an apologist. Young poets, on the other hand, recognized that Lowell had crystallized a new plain style into form. But no sooner had Lowell consolidated that free-verse style in *For the Union Dead* (1964) than he confused the reading world (he was by this time a much-read poet here and abroad) by publishing the formal Marvellian poems of *Near the Ocean* (1967). He next poured out an apparently inexhaustible stream of unrhymed sonnets, first as *Notebook 1967–68,* next (augmented and revised) as *Notebook* (1970), next rearranged and split in two as *History* and *For Lizzie and Harriet* (1973). At the same time, he published a coda in *The Dolphin* (1973), a set of sonnets about his third marriage, in England, to Lady Caroline Blackwood, a journalist and novelist.

The sonnets are full of events, public and private, that took place during their composition; they are also full of allusiveness. Often they seemed unreadable to those who did not possess Lowell's learning and could not know the events of his private life. For those who liked them, the sonnets seemed yet another form of Lowellesque energy—as though the poet had determined to put into his poetry his entire complex mind, not simply some selection from it. The sonnets often resemble, in diction, the denser passages of Milton or Shakespeare. As they are clarified by time and annotation, they will be better understood. In their political dimension, they represent a gripping testimony to one intellectual's revulsion at the Vietnam War, the March on the Pentagon in 1967 (in which Lowell participated), and the state of government and society in America in the late 1960s.

It might be said that all of Lowell's writing was driven into being by some cause or belief—religious, political, or historical. The consistent linking of his own family's history with the history of the United States made Lowell see, for most of his life, every political event as one intimately addressed to himself. And he viewed the Puritan theocratic obsessions, toward which he felt both admiration and revulsion, as a form of familial legacy. But when he broke his style for the last time in *Day by Day*, he abandoned all fictions of battle and now saw his past religious and political positions chiefly as constructs of his own embattled psyche. In the brief hope that he could be, with the help of lithium, an ordinary person, he had moved to England in 1970, entered his last marriage, and had a son. The early idyll of the new marriage, the recurrence of his mental illness, and the unhappiness of the later years in England are all reflected in the new, spare free verse of *Day by Day*, a verse that is pared to the bone, dry and plangent at once in its anticipation of death. Lowell died of a heart attack in a taxicab in New York City shortly before he was due to return to Harvard, where he had been teaching literature and writing for several years.

Lowell wrote occasional prose (not yet collected) and several plays. He adapted Melville's *Benito Cereno*, three stories by Hawthorne, and Thomas Morton's 1637 *New Canaan* for the stage under the title *The Old Glory* (1965); he translated Racine's *Phèdre* (1961) and Aeschylus' *Prometheus Bound* (1969). In times of depression, when he could not write poetry, he turned to translation. Eventually, his practice in translating was to turn the foreign original into a poem that could have been written by himself. These extraordinary "translations" were collected under the title *Imitations* (1961), and, for all their willfulness, raised the level of both translation and the theory of translation in America.

However, Lowell will be judged, finally, by his revolutionizing of American poetry. He took it from the formal patterns of Tate and Ransom into a new era of boldly revolutionary free verse, then into a torrential new formality. Finally, he invented, in *Day by Day*, a new kind of lyric—wayward, structurally free, and intimate—that reflects formally his abandonment of transcendence and teleology in favor of an unforced perception of earthly transience.

Further Reading:

H. Staples, *Robert Lowell: The First Twenty Years*, 1961.

T. Parkinson, ed., *Robert Lowell: A Collection of Critical Essays*, 1968.

M. Perloff, *The Poetic Art of Robert Lowell*, 1973.

S. Yenser, *Circle to Circle: The Poetry of Robert Lowell*, 1975.

J. Meyers, ed., *Manic Power: Robert Lowell and His Circle*, 1987.

P. Hobsbaum, *A Reader's Guide to Robert Lowell*, 1988.

P. Mariani, *Lost Puritan: A Life of Robert Lowell*, 1994.

H. Vendler, *The Given and The Made: Strategies of Poetic Definition*, 1995.

Texts:

"Memories of West Street and Lepke" and "Skunk Hour" from *Life Studies*, 1959.

"For the Union Dead" from *For the Union Dead*, 1964.

"History" from *History*, 1973.

"For John Berryman" and "Epilogue" from *Day by Day*, 1977.

Memories of West Street and Lepke

Only teaching on Tuesdays, book-worming
in pajamas fresh from the washer each morning,
I hog a whole house on Boston's
"hardly passionate Marlborough Street,"   5
where even the man
scavenging filth in the back alley trash cans,
has two children, a beach wagon, a helpmate,
and is a "young Republican."
I have a nine months' daughter,
young enough to be my granddaughter.   10
Like the sun she rises in her flame-flamingo infants' wear.

These are the tranquillized *Fifties,*
and I am forty. Ought I to regret my seedtime?
I was a fire-breathing Catholic C.O.,
and made my manic statement,   15
telling off the state and president, and then
sat waiting sentence in the bull pen
beside a Negro boy with curlicues
of marijuana in his hair.

Given a year,   20
I walked on the roof of the West Street Jail, a short
enclosure like my school soccer court,
and saw the Hudson River once a day
through sooty clothesline entanglements
and bleaching khaki tenements.   25
Strolling, I yammered metaphysics with Abramowitz,
a jaundice-yellow ("it's really tan")
and fly-weight pacifist,
so vegetarian,
he wore rope shoes and preferred fallen fruit.   30
He tried to convert Bioff and Brown,
the Hollywood pimps, to his diet.
Hairy, muscular, suburban,
wearing chocolate double-breasted suits,
they blew their tops and beat him black and blue.   35

I was so out of things, I'd never heard
of the Jehovah's Witnesses.
"Are you a C.O.?" I asked a fellow jailbird.
"No," he answered, "I'm a J.W."
He taught me the "hospital tuck,"   40

and pointed out the T-shirted back
of *Murder Incorporated's* Czar Lepke,
there piling towels on a rack,
or dawdling off to his little segregated cell full
of things forbidden the common man: 45
a portable radio, a dresser, two toy American
flags tied together with a ribbon of Easter palm.
Flabby, bald, lobotomized,
he drifted in a sheepish calm,
where no agonizing reappraisal   50
jarred his concentration on the electric chair—
hanging like an oasis in his air
of lost connections. . . .
1959

Skunk Hour

(For Elizabeth Bishop)

Nautilus Island's[1] hermit
heiress still lives through winter in her Spartan cottage;
her sheep still graze above the sea.
Her son's a bishop. Her farmer
is first selectman in our village;   5
she's in her dotage.

Thirsting for
the hierarchic privacy
of Queen Victoria's century,
she buys up all   10
the eyesores facing her shore,
and lets them fall.

The season's ill—
we've lost our summer millionaire,
who seemed to leap from an L. L. Bean[2]   15
catalogue. His nine-knot yawl

---

[1] In Maine, near Castine, where Lowell often
spent summers.

[2] Store in Freeport, Maine, specializing in
outdoor clothing and camping goods.

was auctioned off to lobstermen.
A red fox stain[3] covers Blue Hill.

And now our fairy
decorator brightens his shop for fall;   20
his fishnet's filled with orange cork,
orange, his cobbler's bench and awl;
there is no money in his work,
he'd rather marry.

One dark night,   25
my Tudor[4] Ford climbed the hill's skull;
I watched for love-cars. Lights turned down,
they lay together, hull to hull,
where the graveyard shelves on the town. . . .
My mind's not right.   30

A car radio bleats,
"Love, O careless Love. . . ." I hear
my ill-spirit sob in each blood cell,
as if my hand were at its throat. . . .
I myself am hell;[5]   35
nobody's here—

only skunks, that search
in the moonlight for a bite to eat.
They march on their soles up Main Street:
white stripes, moonstruck eyes' red fire   40
under the chalk-dry and spar spire
of the Trinitarian Church.

I stand on top
of our back steps and breathe the rich air—
a mother skunk with her column[6] of kittens swills the garbage pail.   45
She jabs her wedge-head in a cup
of sour cream, drops her ostrich tail,
and will not scare.

1960

---

[3] The autumn leaves.
[4] Make of two-door Ford.
[5] "Myself am hell," Satan says in Milton's
  Paradise Lost, IV, 75.

[6] A military formation.

For the Union Dead*

"Relinquunt Omnia Servare Rem Publicam."[1]

The old South Boston Aquarium stands
in a Sahara of snow now. Its broken windows are boarded.
The bronze weathervane cod[2] has lost half its scales.
The airy tanks are dry.

Once my nose crawled like a snail on the glass;   5
my hand tingled
to burst the bubbles
drifting from the noses of the cowed, compliant fish.

My hand draws back. I often sigh still
for the dark downward and vegetating kingdom   10
of the fish and reptile. One morning last March,
I pressed against the new barbed and galvanized

fence on the Boston Common.[3] Behind their cage,
yellow dinosaur steamshovels were grunting
as they cropped up tons of mush and grass   15
to gouge their underworld garage.[4]

Parking spaces luxuriate like civic
sandpiles in the heart of Boston.
A girdle of orange, Puritan-pumpkin colored girders
braces the tingling Statehouse,   20

shaking over the excavations, as it faces Colonel Shaw
and his bell-cheeked Negro infantry
on St. Gaudens' shaking Civil War relief,
propped by a plank splint against the garage's earthquake.

---

* Soldiers who died fighting for the North in
the Civil War. The poem is written about a
bronze bas-relief opposite the Massachusetts
State House on Beacon Street, in Boston; the
monument, by Augustus St. Gaudens
(1848–1897), commemorates Colonel
Robert Gould Shaw (1837–1863), who commanded the first all-Negro regiment in the
North, and who was killed while leading an
attack on Fort Wagner in South Carolina.
The monument represents Shaw on horseback flanked by Negro foot soldiers.

[1] Lowell has changed the inscription on the
monument from singular to plural, so that it
reads: "They leave everything behind to
serve the Republic."
[2] Codfish, the symbol of Boston.
[3] Park facing the State House.
[4] The construction of the garage beneath the
Common was attended by graft and corruption.

Two months after marching through Boston,   25
half the regiment was dead;
at the dedication,
William James[5] could almost hear the bronze Negroes breathe.

Their monument sticks like a fishbone
in the city's throat.   30
Its Colonel is as lean
as a compass-needle.

He has an angry wrenlike vigilance,
a greyhound's gentle tautness;
he seems to wince at pleasure,   35
and suffocate for privacy.

He is out of bounds now. He rejoices in man's lovely,
peculiar power to choose life and die—
when he leads his black soldiers to death,
he cannot bend his back.   40

On a thousand small town New England greens,[6]
the old white churches hold their air
of sparse, sincere rebellion; frayed flags
quilt the graveyards of the Grand Army of the Republic.

The stone statues of the abstract Union Soldier   45
grow slimmer and younger each year—
wasp-waisted, they doze over muskets
and muse through their sideburns . . .

Shaw's father wanted no monument
except the ditch,   50
where his son's body was thrown
and lost with his "niggers."[7]

The ditch is nearer.
There are no statues for the last war[8] here;

---

[5] Philosopher and psychologist (1842–1910); the allusion is to a letter.
[6] Lowell is thinking of the village green in Castine.
[7] Shaw's father could have had his son's body brought home (officers had that privilege, while infantry were buried where they fell), but he refused, knowing his son's affection for his men.

[8] Perhaps the Korean War (1950–1953); or, as Lowell's mention of Hiroshima suggests, World War II, which ended with the dropping of the atom bomb; the exploitation of the survival of the safe for advertising purposes is a sign of callousness, while the use in the advertisement of the phrase "Rock of Ages," normally a reference to Christ, proclaims the collapse of religion.

on Boylston Street, a commercial photograph   55
shows Hiroshima boiling

over a Mosler Safe, the "Rock of Ages"
that survived the blast. Space is nearer.
When I crouch[9] to my television set,
the drained faces of Negro school-children[10] rise like balloons.   60

Colonel Shaw
is riding on his bubble,
he waits
for the blessèd break.

The Aquarium is gone. Everywhere,   65
giant finned cars nose forward like fish;
a savage servility
slides by on grease.
1964

History

History has to live with what was here,
clutching and close to fumbling all we had—
it is so dull and gruesome how we die,
unlike writing, life never finishes.
Abel was finished; death is not remote,   5
a flash-in-the-pan electrifies the skeptic,
his cows crowding like skulls against high-voltage wire,
his baby crying all night like a new machine.
As in our Bibles, white-faced, predatory,
the beautiful mist-drunken hunter's moon ascends—   10
a child could give it a face: two holes, two holes,
my eyes, my mouth, between them a skull's no-nose—
O there's a terrifying innocence in my face
drenched with the silver salvage of the mornfrost.
1973

---

9 The posture of a "savage" worshipping a
   "god."

10 Schools in the South were being forcibly
    desegregated in 1960.

For John Berryman

(After reading his last Dream Song)[1]

The last years we only met
when you were on the road,
and lit up for reading
your battering *Dream*—
audible, deaf . . .   5
in another world then as now.
I used to want to live
to avoid your elegy.
Yet really we had the same life,
the generic one   10
our generation offered
(*Les Maudits*[2]—the compliment
each American generation
pays itself in passing):
first students, then with our own,   15
our galaxy of grands maîtres,[3]
our fifties' fellowships
to Paris, Rome and Florence,
veterans of the Cold War[4] not the War—
all the best of life . . .   20
then daydreaming to drink at six,
waiting for the iced fire,
even the feel of the frosted glass,
like waiting for a girl . . .
if you had waited.   25
We asked to be obsessed with writing,
and we were.

Do you wake dazed like me,
and find your lost glasses in a shoe?

Something so heavy lies on my heart—   30
there, still here, the good days
when we sat by a cold lake in Maine,
talking about the *Winter's Tale,*

---

[1] The poet John Berryman, Lowell's contemporary, committed suicide in 1972 after episodes of acute alcoholism and mental breakdown; the sequence of lyrics called *The Dream Songs* became Berryman's major poetic undertaking.

[2] The *poète maudit* (French: "accursed poet" or "damned poet") was a cliché of the later nineteenth century.

[3] "Great teachers" (poetic mentors).

[4] Diplomatic estrangement between the United States and Russia during the 1950s.

Leontes' jealousy[5]
in Shakespeare's broken syntax.   35
You got there first.
Just the other day,
I discovered how we differ—humor . . .
even in this last *Dream Song,*
to mock your catlike flight   40
from home and classes—
to leap from the bridge.

Girls will not frighten the frost from the grave.[6]

To my surprise, John,
I pray *to* not for you,   45
think of you not myself,
smile and fall asleep.
1977

Epilogue*

Those blessed structures, plot and rhyme—
why are they no help to me now
I want to make
something imagined, not recalled?
I hear the noise of my own voice: 5
The painter's vision is not a lens,
it trembles to caress the light.
But sometimes everything I write
with the threadbare art of my eye
seems a snapshot,   10
lurid, rapid, garish, grouped,
heightened from life,
yet paralyzed by fact.
All's misalliance.
Yet why not say what happened?   15
Pray for the grace of accuracy

---

[5] In Shakespeare's *The Winner's Tale,* Leontes
orders his wife killed, unreasonably suspecting her of infidelity.
[6] Lowell is recalling the last two lines from a
song in *The Sad Shepherd* by Ben Jonson
(1572/3–1637): " 'Except Love's fires the
virtue have, / To fright the frost out of the
grave.' "
* This is the closing poem in Lowell's last volume of poetry, *Day by Day* (1977).

Vermeer[1] gave to the sun's illumination
stealing like the tide across a map
to his girl solid with yearning.
We are poor passing facts,   20
warned by that to give
each figure in the photograph
his living name.
1977

Gwendolyn Brooks
b. 1917

For Gwendolyn Brooks, "poets who happen to be Negroes are twice-tried. They have to write poetry, and they have to remember that they are Negroes." This double consciousness—at once restive, protective, and in part aggressive—continues to mark Brooks's impassioned life and distinguished verse.

Gwendolyn Brooks was born in Topeka, Kansas, on June 17, 1917, and raised on Chicago's South Side, where she was taken at the age of one month. Chicago remains her home and the setting for most of her poetry. She graduated from Englewood High School in 1934 and from Wilson Junior College in 1936. Soon after, she supported herself at various jobs, including newspaper and magazine work.

Brooks reports that she has written poetry "since about seven, at which time my parents expressed most earnest confidence that I would one day be a writer." She published her first poem, "Eventide," at the age thirteen, in what was then a popular children's magazine, *American Childhood.* By the age of seventeen she was a frequent contributor to the weekly *Chicago Defender,* which was also publishing the work of Langston Hughes and James Weldon Johnson, both of whom encouraged her to dedicate herself to writing poetry. Johnson introduced her to the great modern poets, including T. S. Eliot and Ezra Pound, and in Hughes she discovered, as she explains, a man who "believed in the beauty of blackness" long before it became the "fashion." Hughes, she notes, was also someone who "loved literature . . . not fearfully, not with awe," but with deep devotion, and not as "his private inch" but as a "great acreage." "The plantings of others," she says, "he not only welcomed but busily enriched." And in Hughes's self-announced literary purpose—"to explain and illuminate the Negro condition in America"—Gwendolyn Brooks found ample motivation to sustain her own poetic efforts.

Gwendolyn Brooks practiced her art with the help ;and encouragement of other writers at the poetry workshop in Chicago's South Side Community Art Center, and in

---

[1] Jan Vermeer (1632–1675), Dutch painter; the painting in question, *Girl Reading a Letter,* has in the background a map hanging on the wall on which light shines from an open casement, which the girl reading the letter is facing in profile.

1944 she was published for the first time in *Poetry: A Magazine of Verse.* Within a year she published her first volume of poetry, *A Magazine of Verse.* Within a year she published her first volume of poetry, *A Street in Bronzeville,* which soon earned her a series of honors and awards, including a Guggenheim fellowship and a $1,000 prize from the American Academy of Arts and Letters. In that same year, *Mademoiselle* magazine named her one of ten women of the year. *A Street in Bronzeville* offers a compelling portrait of America's African American urban poor. In writing the volume she hoped, as she explains, "that people would recognize instantly that Negroes are just like other people; they have the same hates and loves and fears, the same tragedies and triumphs and deaths, as people of any race or religion or nationality."

In *Annie Allen* (1949), a powerful three-part verse narrative recounting a young African American girl's coming to consciousness during World War II, Brooks displayed a remarkable sensitivity to the psychological pressures of the passage from childhood to marriage and maturity. In 1950 she was awarded the Pulitzer Prize for Poetry, and later she was officially named Poet Laureate of Illinois, a title previously held by Carl Sandburg. A volume of children's verse, *Bronzeville Boys and Girls,* followed in 1956, as did frequent contributions to many of the nation's most prestigious and popular literary journals. She published *Bean Eaters* in 1960 and *Selected Poems* in 1963. Each of Brooks's early volumes is marked by a delicate tension between sentiment and objectivity, between traditional poetic forms and contemporary African American idiom. Counterbalancing the lyric impulses in these early poems are tough-minded and at times humorous views of what Langston Hughes called the "soul world."

Since the Second Black Writer's Conference (1967), Gwendolyn Brooks's work has responded more directly—and forcefully—to racial and feminist issues. The poems of *In the Mecca* (1968), for example, focus on the daily pain and suffering of ghetto life and express more explicitly her anger and rage at the deprivation of African American experience. These same urgent concerns are extended in *Riot* (1969), *The Wall* (n.d.), *Family Pictures* (1970), and *Aloneness* (1971). Among her more recent volumes are *Aurora* (1972) and *Beckonings* (1975).

In 1972 she published a collection of autobiographical essays, *Report from Part One.* She has also written a novella, *Maud Martha* (1953), about a young African American woman's disillusioning romance in Chicago. Throughout her work, Brooks reminds her readers of the personal "cost" of being African American in white America.

Brooks has taught writing at numerous colleges and universities, including Chicago's Columbia College, Elmhurst College, and the University of Wisconsin. She is also the recipient of several honorary degrees and has lectured and read her poetry throughout the United States, from small rural colleges to the Library of Congress. She continues to advise young poets "to live richly with your eyes open, and heart, too."

Brooks's poetry is distinguished by what she calls the "concentration, the crush" of the painful and joyful realities of ordinary people in familiar situations. Echoing Walt Whitman, she once defined her task as a poet as that of vivifying fact, not merely contemporary fact but universal fact, mindful that "the universal wears contemporary clothing very well."

Further Reading:

T. C. Bambara, "Report From Part One," *New York Times Book Review,* January 7, 1973.

H. A. Baker, *Singers of Daybreak: Studies in Black American Literature,* 1974.

H. B. Shaw, *Gwendolyn Brooks,* 1980.

D. Melhem, *Gwendolyn Brooks: Poetry and the Heroic Voice,* 1987.

M. Mootry and G. Smith, eds., *A Life Distilled: Gwendolyn Brooks, Her Poetry and Fiction,* 1987.

G. Kent, *A Life of Gwendolyn Brooks,* 1990.

S. C. Wright, ed., *On Gwendolyn Brooks: Reliant Contemplation,* 1996.

Text:

Selected Poems, 1963.

from A Street in Bronzeville

Kitchenette Building

We are things of dry hours and the involuntary plan.
Grayed in, and gray. "Dream" makes a giddy sound, not strong
Like "rent," "feeding a wife," "satisfying a man."

But could a dream send up through onion fumes
Its white and violet, fight with fried potatoes
And yesterday's garbage ripening in the hall,   5
Flutter, or sing an aria down these rooms

Even if we were willing to let it in,
Had time to warm it, keep it very clean,
Anticipate a message, let it begin?   10

We wonder. But not well! not for a minute!
Since Number Five is out of the bathroom now,
We think of lukewarm water, hope to get in it.
1945

The Mother

Abortions will not let you forget.
You remember the children you got that you did not get,
The damp small pulps with a little or with no hair,
The singers and workers that never handled the air.
You will never neglect or beat   5
Them, or silence or buy with a sweet.
You will never wind up the sucking-thumb
Or scuttle off ghosts that come.
You will never leave them, controlling your luscious sigh,
Return for a snack of them, with gobbling mother-eye.   10

I have heard in the voices of the wind the voices of my dim killed children.
I have contracted. I have eased
My dim dears at the breasts they could never suck.
I have said, Sweets, if I sinned, if I seized
Your luck   15
And your lives from your unfinished reach,
If I stole your births and your names,
Your straight baby tears and your games,
Your stilted or lovely loves, your tumults, your marriages, aches, and your
    deaths,
If I poisoned the beginnings of your breaths,   20
Believe that even in my deliberateness I was not deliberate.
Though why should I whine,
Whine that the crime was other than mine?—
Since anyhow you are dead.
Or rather, or instead,   25
You were never made.
But that too, I am afraid,
Is faulty: oh, what shall I say, how is the truth to be said?
You were born, you had body, you died.
It is just that you never giggled or planned or cried.   30

Believe me, I loved you all.
Believe me, I knew you, though faintly, and I loved, I loved you
All.
1945

Negro Hero

to suggest Dorie Miller[1]

I HAD to kick their law into their teeth in order to save them.
However I have heard that sometimes you have to deal
Devilishly with drowning men in order to swim them to shore.
Or they will haul themselves and you to the trash and the fish beneath.

---

[1] Dorie Miller was a messman aboard the U.S.S. Arizona during the attack on Pearl Harbor, 7 December 1941. Though assigned to kitchen duties (as were most black sailors then), Miller manned a gun and shot down four attacking planes. He was later awarded the Navy Cross.

(When I think of this, I do not worry about a few   5
Chipped teeth.)

It is good I gave glory, it is good I put gold on their name.
Or there would have been spikes in the afterward hands.
But let us speak only of my success and the pictures in the Caucasian dailies
As well as the Negro weeklies. For I am a gem.   10
(They are not concerned that it was hardly The Enemy my fight was against.
But them.)

It was a tall time. And of course my blood was
Boiling about in my head and straining and howling and singing me on.
Of course I was rolled on wheels of my boy itch to get at the gun.   15
Of course all the delicate rehearsal shots of my childhood massed in mirage
    before me.
Of course I was child
And my first swallow of the liquor of battle bleeding black air dying and
    demon noise
Made me wild.

It was kinder than that, though, and I showed like a banner my kindness.   20
I loved. And a man will guard when he loves.
Their white-gowned democracy was my fair lady.
With her knife lying cold, I straight, in the softness of her sweet-flowing
    sleeve.
But for the sake of the dear smiling mouth and the stuttered promise I toyed
    with my life.
I threw back!—I would not remember   25
Entirely the knife.

Still—am I good enough to die for them, is my blood bright enough to be
    spilled,
Was my constant back-question—are they clear
On this? Or do I intrude even now?
Am I clean enough to kill for them, do they wish me to kill   30
For them or is my place while death licks his lips and strides to them
In the galley still?

(In a southern city a white man said
Indeed, I'd rather be dead;
Indeed, I'd rather be shot in the head   35
Or ridden to waste on the back of a flood
Than saved by the drop of a black man's blood.)
Naturally, the important thing is, I helped to save them, them and a part of
    their democracy.

Even if I had to kick their law into their teeth in order to do that for them.
And I am feeling well and settled in myself because I believe it was a good
   job,   40
Despite this possible horror: that they might prefer the
Preservation of their law in all its sick dignity and their knives
To the continuation of their creed
And their lives.

1945

A Bronzeville Mother Loiters in Mississippi. Meanwhile, a Mississippi Mother Burns Bacon.

From the first it had been like a
Ballad. It had the beat inevitable. It had the blood.
A wildness cut up, and tied in little bunches,
Like the four-line stanzas of the ballads she had never quite
Understood—the ballads they had set her to, in school.   5
Herself: the milk-white main, the "maid mild"
Of the ballad. Pursued
By the Dark Villain. Rescued by the Fine Prince.
The Happiness-Ever-After.
That was worth anything.   10
It was good to be a "maid mild."
That made the breath go fast.

Her bacon burned. She
Hastened to hide it in the step-on can, and
Drew more strips from the meat case. The eggs and sour-milk biscuits   15
Did well. She set out a jar
Of her new quince preserve.
. . . But there was a something about the matter of the Dark Villain.
He should have been older, perhaps.
The hacking down of a villain was more fun to think about   20
When his menace possessed undisputed breadth, undisputed height,
And a harsh kind of vice.
And best of all, when his history was cluttered
With the bones of many eaten knights and princesses.

The fun was disturbed, then all but nullified   25
When the Dark Villain was a blackish child
Of fourteen, with eyes still too young to be dirty,
And a mouth too young to have lost every reminder
Of its infant softness.

That boy must have been surprised! For   30
These were grown-ups. Grown-ups were supposed to be wise.
And the Fine Prince—and that other—so tall, so broad, so
Grown! Perhaps the boy had never guessed
That the trouble with grown-ups was that under the magnificent shell of
     adulthood, just under,
Waited the baby full of tantrums.   35
It occurred to her that there may have been something
Ridiculous in the picture of the Fine Prince
Rushing (rich with the breadth and height and
Mature solidness whose lack, in the Dark Villain, was impressing her,
Confronting her more and more as this first day after the trial   40
And acquittal wore on) rushing
With the heavy companion to hack down (unhorsed)
That little foe.
So much had happened, she could not remember now what that foe had
     done
Against her, or if anything had been done.   45
The one thing in the world that she did know and knew
With terrifying clarity was that her composition
Had disintegrated. That, although the pattern prevailed,
The breaks were everywhere. That she could think
Of no thread capable of the necessary   50
Sew-work.

She made the babies sit in their places at the table.
Then, before calling Him, she hurried
To the mirror with her comb and lipstick. It was necessary
To be more beautiful that ever.
The beautiful wife.   55
For sometimes she fancied he looked at her as though
Measuring her. As if he considered, Had she been worth It?
Had *she* been worth the blood, the cramped cries, the little stuttering
     bravado,
The gradual dulling of those Negro eyes.   60
The sudden, overwhelming *little-boyness* in that barn?
Whatever she might feel or half-feel, the lipstick necessity was something
     apart. He must never conclude
That she had not been worth It.

He sat down, the Fine Prince, and
Began buttering a biscuit. He looked at his hands.   65
He twisted in his chair, he scratched his nose.
He glanced again, almost secretly, at his hands.
More papers were in from the North, he mumbled. More meddling
     headlines.
With their pepper-words, "bestiality," and "barbarism," and "Shocking."   70

The half-sneers he had mastered for the trial worked across
His sweet and pretty face.

What he'd like to do, he explained, was kill them all.
The time lost. The unwanted frame.
Still, it had been fun to show those intruders   75
A thing or two. To show that snappy-eyed mother,
That sassy, Northern, brown-black—

Nothing could stop Mississippi.
He knew that. Big Fella
Knew that.   80
And, what was so good, Mississippi knew that.
Nothing and nothing could stop Mississippi.
They could send in their petitions, and scar
Their newspapers with bleeding headlines. Their governors
Could appeal to Washington . . .   85

"What I want," the older baby said, "is 'lasses on my jam."
Whereupon the younger baby
Picked up the molasses pitcher and threw
The molasses in his brother's face. Instantly
The Fine Prince learned across the table and slapped   90
The small and smiling criminal.

She did not speak. When the Hand
Came down and away, and she could look at her child,
At her baby-child,
She could think only of blood.   95
Surely her baby's cheek
Had disappeared, and in its place, surely,
Hung a heaviness, a lengthening red, a red that had no end.
She shook her head. It was not true, of course.
It was not true at all. The   100
Child's face was as always, the
Color of the paste in her paste-jar.

She left the table, to the tune of the children's lamentations, which were
    shriller
Than ever. She
Looked out of a window. She said not a word. *That*   105
Was one of the new Somethings—
The fear,
Tying her as with iron.

Suddenly she felt his hands upon her. He had followed her
To the window. The children were whimpering now.   110

Such bits of tots. And she, their mother,
Could not protect them. She looked at her shoulders, still
Gripped in the claim of his hands. She tried, but could not resist the idea
That a red ooze was seeping, spreading darkly, thickly, slowly,
Over her white shoulders, her own shoulders,   115
And over all of Earth and Mars.

He whispered something to her, did the Fine Prince, something
About love, something about love and night and intention.
She heard no hoof-beat of the horse and saw no flash of the shining steel.

He pulled her face around to meet   120
His, and there it was, close close,
For the first time in all those days and nights.
His mouth, wet and red,
So very, very, very red,
Closed over hers.   125

Then a sickness heaved within her. The courtroom Coca-Cola,
The courtroom beer and hate and sweat and drone,
Pushed like a wall against her. She wanted to bear it.
But his mouth would not go away and neither would the
Decapitated exclamation points in that Other Woman's eyes.   130

She did not scream.
She stood there.
But a hatred for him burst into glorious flower,
And its perfume enclasped them—big,
Bigger than all magnolias.   135

The last bleak news of the ballad.
The rest of the rugged music.
The last quatrain.
1960

The Last Quatrain of the Ballad of Emmett Till*

after the murder,
after the burial

---

* In September 1955 fourteen-year-old Emmett Louis Till, a black Chicagoan, was abducted from a Mississippi home and brutally murdered. Two white males charged with the crime were later acquitted by an all-white jury. The events brought national attention to the emerging civil rights movement.

    Emmett's mother is a pretty-faced thing;
        the tint of pulled taffy.
    She sits in a red room,   5
        drinking black coffee.
    She kisses her killed boy.
          And she is sorry.
    Chaos in windy grays
        through a red prairie.   10
    1960

The Blackstone Rangers*

I. As Seen by Disciplines

Thirty at the corner.
Black, raw, ready.
Sores in the city
that do not want to heal.   5

II. The Leaders

Jeff. Gene. Geronimo. And Bop.
They cancel, cure and curry.
Hardly the dupes of the downtown thing
the cold bonbon,
the rhinestone thing. And hardly   10
in a hurry.
Hardly Belafonte, King,
Black Jesus, Stokely, Malcolm X or Rap.
Bungled trophies.
Their country is a Nation on no map.   15

Jeff, Gene, Geronimo and Bop
in the passionate noon,
in bewitching night
are the detailed men, the copious men.
They curry, cure,   20
they cancel, cancelled images whose Concerts
are not divine, vivacious; the different tins

---

* A tough Chicago gang. Blackstone Avenue is
 on Chicago's southside.

are intense last entries; pagan argument;
translations of the night.

The Blackstone bitter bureaus   25
(bureaucracy is footloose) edit, fuse
unfashionable damnations and descent;
and exulting, monstrous hand on monstrous hand,
construct, strangely, a monstrous pearl or grace.

III. Gang Girls
A Rangerette

Gang Girls are sweet exotics.   30
Mary Ann
uses the nutrients of her orient,
but sometimes sighs for Cities of blue and jewel
beyond her Ranger rim of Cottage Grove.[1]
(Bowery Boys, Disciples, Whip-Birds will   35
dissolve no margins, stop no savory sanctities.)

Mary is
a rose in a whiskey glass.
Mary's
Februaries shudder and are gone. Aprils   40
fret frankly, lilac hurries on.
Summer is a hard irregular ridge.
October looks away.
And that's the Year!
        Save for her bugle-love.   45
Save for the bleat of not-obese devotion.
Save for Somebody Terribly Dying, under
the philanthropy of robins. Save for his Ranger
bringing
an amount of rainbow in a string-drawn bag.   50
"Where did you get the diamond?" Do not ask:
but swallow, straight, the spirals of his flask
and assist him at your zipper; pet his lips
and help him clutch you.
Love's another departure.   55
Will there be any arrivals, confirmations?
Will there be gleaning?

---

[1] A south side avenue; the western boundary
("rim") of the Blackstone Ranger territory
or turf.

Mary, the Shakedancer's child
from the rooming-flat, pants carefully, peers at
her laboring lover. . . .   60
    Mary! Mary Ann!
Settle for sandwiches! settle for stocking caps!
for sudden blood, aborted carnival,
the props and niceties of non-loneliness—
the rhymes of Leaning.   65
1968

Young Afrikans

of the **furious**

Who take Today and jerk it out of joint
have made new underpinnings and a Head.

Blacktime is time for chimeful
poemhood
but they decree a   5
Jagged chiming now.

If there are flowers flowers
must come out to the road. Rowdy!—
knowing where wheels and people are,
knowing where whips and screams are,   10
knowing where deaths are, where the kind kills are.

As for that other kind of kindness,
if there is milk it must be mindful.
The milkofhumankindness must be mindful
as wily wines.   15
Must be fine fury.
Must be mega, must be main.

Taking Today (to jerk it out of joint)
the hardheroic maim the
leechlike-as-usual who use,   20
adhere to, carp, and harm.

And they await,
across the Changes and the spiraling dead,
our Black revival, our Black vinegar,
our hands, and our hot blood.   25
1981

Richard Wilbur
b. 1921

Richard Wilbur's verse combines a Latin elegance and wit with the New England skepticism and wisdom we associate with Robert Frost (whom Wilbur met as an undergraduate at Amherst College). Wilbur's first book, *The Beautiful Changes and Other Poems* (1947), published when he was in his twenties, reflected his war service in Italy and France (1943–1945) and his admiration for the landscape and architecture of Europe. The book drew immediate critical praise, and Wilbur's poetry has continued to attract readers who see the continuity of American poetry with the formal verse of the English past. The rougher line of American verse, from Emerson through Whitman to Ashbery, insists on discontinuity, rupture, and spontaneity, whereas the Europeanized tradition exemplified by Stevens, Frost, Merrill, and Wilbur values continuity, gradualism, and musicality.

Wilbur's alignment with Europe arises, in part, from his affiliation with Eliot as a "civilized poet" and from his superb command of French. He has translated Molière into excellent English verse for the stage; he was one of the lyricists for Leonard Bernstein's musical version of *Candide* (1956).

Unlike the *poètes maudits* ("accursed poets") of the modern tradition like Baudelaire and Rimbaud, who emphasize the role of the poet as social outcast, Wilbur, who has remained a Christian believer, considers himself "a poet-citizen rather than an alienated artist. . . . Poetry is sterile unless it arises from a sense of community, or, at least, from the hope of community." By meditating on the conflicts like those between sensual pleasure and transcendence or between the stationary and the restless, the poet, says Wilbur, is "acknowledging the contradictions that inhere in life." The chief contradiction is that between "the tangible world and the institutions of the spirit." Though Wilbur's use of stanzaic structures and regular meters reflects his attachment to poetic tradition, his genial, understated American voice has naturalized older English forms into new indigenous ones. His intricately musical meditative writing continues, in a secular vein, the reflective verse of such seventeenth-century religious poets as George Herbert and Thomas Traherne. Wilbur, the son of a painter, writes poetry of the eye, but he wishes to find, behind the eye, the workings of the soul.

Wilbur served as Poet Laureate in 1987. He has taught at Harvard (where he took an M.A.), at Wellesley, at Wesleyan, and at Smith. His poems were collected in 1963; since then, he has published *Walking to Sleep* (1969), *The Mind-Reader* (1976), and another collection, *New and Collected Poems* (1988), which won a Pulitzer Prize in 1989. His essays have been collected in *Responses: Prose Pieces, 1948–1976* (1976) and *The Catbird's Song: Prose Pieces 1963–1995* (1997).

Further Reading:

D. L. Hill, *Richard Wilbur*, 1967.

H. Stevens, *Richard Wilbur*, 1977.

W. Salinger, ed., *Richard Wilbur's Creation*, 1983.

F. Bixler, *Richard Wilbur: A Reference Guide*, 1991.

B. Michelson, *Wilbur's Poetry: Music in a Scattering Time*, 1991.

R. Edgecombe, *A Reader's Guide to the Poetry of Richard Wilbur*, 1995.

J. Hougen, *Ecstasy Within Discipline: The Poetry of Richard Wilbur*, 1995.

Texts:
"Love Calls Us to the Things of This World" from *Things of This World*, 1956.
"Playboy" from *Walking to Sleep*, 1969.

"The Writer" and "Cottage Street" from *The Mind-Reader*, 1976

Love Calls Us to the Things of This World

The eyes open to a cry of pulleys,
And spirited from sleep, the astounded soul
Hangs for a moment bodiless and simple
As false dawn.
                Outside the open window   5
The morning air is all awash with angels.

Some are in bed-sheets, some are in blouses
Some are in smocks: but truly there they are.
Now they are rising together in calm swells
Of halcyon feeling, filling whatever they wear   10
With the deep joy of their impersonal breathing;
    Now they are flying in place, conveying
The terrible speed of their omnipresence, moving
And staying like white water; and now of a sudden
They swoon down into so rapt a quiet   15
That nobody seems to be there.
                   The soul shrinks

From all that it is about to remember,
From the punctual rape of every blessed day,
And cries,   20
"Oh, let there be nothing on earth but laundry,
Nothing but rosy hands in the rising steam
And clear dances done in the sight of heaven."
    Yet, as the sun acknowledges
With a warm look the world's hunks and colors,   25
The soul descends once more in bitter love
To accept the waking body, saying now
In a change voice as the man yawns and rises,

"Bring them down from their muddy gallows;
Let there be clean linen for the blacks of thieves;   30
Let lovers go fresh and sweet to be undone,
And the heaviest nuns walk in a pure floating
Of dark habits,
                keeping their difficult balance."

1956

Playboy*

High on his stockroom ladder like a dunce
The stock-boy sits, and studies like a sage
The subject matter of one glossy page,
As lost in curves as Archimedes once.

Sometimes, without a glance, he feeds himself.   5
The left hand, like a mother-bird in flight,
Brings him a sandwich for a sidelong bite,
And then returns it to a dusty shelf.

What so engrosses him? The wild décor
Of this pink-papered alcove into which   10
A naked girl has stumbled, with its rich
Welter of pelts and pillows on the floor,

Amidst which, kneeling in a supple pose,
She lifts a goblet in her father hand,
As if about to toast a flower-stand   15
Above which hovers an exploding rose

Fired from a long-necked crystal vase that rests
Upon a tasseled and vermilion cloth
One taste of which would shrivel up a moth?
Or is he pondering her perfect breasts?   20

Nothing escapes him of her body's grace
Or of her floodlit skin, so sleek and warm
And yet so strangely like a uniform,
But what now grips his fancy is her face,

And how the cunning picture holds her still   25
At just that smiling instant when her soul,
Grown sweetly faint, and swept beyond control,
Consents to his inexorable will.
1969

* The popular American pinup magazine but
also possibly a reference to the fantasy described in the poem.

The Writer

In her room at the prow of the house
Where light breaks, and the windows are tossed with linden,
My daughter is writing a story.

I pause in the stairwell, hearing
From her shut door a commotion of typewriter-keys   5
Like a chain hauled over a gunwale.

Young as she is, the stuff
Of her life is a great cargo, and some of it heavy:
I wish her a lucky passage.

But now it is she who pauses,   10
As if to reject my thought and its easy figure.
A stillness greatens, in which

The whole house seems to be thinking,
And then she is at it again with a bunched clamor
Of strokes, and again is silent.   15

I remember the dazed starling
Which was trapped in that very room, two years ago;
How we stole in, lifted a sash

And retreated, not to affright it;
And how for a helpless hour, though the crack of the door,   20
We watched the sleek, wild, dark

And iridescent creature
Batter against the brilliance, drop like a glove
To the hard floor, or the desk-top,

And wait then, humped and bloody,   25
For the wits to try it again; and how our spirits
Rose when, suddenly sure,

It lifted off from a chair-back,
Beating a smooth course for the right window
And clearing the sill of the world.   30

It is always a matter, my darling,
Of life or death, as I had forgotten. I wish
What I wished you before, but harder.
1976

Cottage Street, 1953

Framed in her phoenix fire-screen, Edna Ward
Bends to the tray of Canton,[1] pouring tea
For frightened Mrs. Plath; then, turning toward
The pale, slumped daughter, and my wife, and me,

Asks if we would prefer it weak or strong.   5
Will we have milk or lemon, she enquires?
The visit seems already strained and long.
Each in his turn, we tell her our desires.

It is my office to exemplify
The published poet in his happiness,   10
Thus cheering Sylvia, who has wished to die;[2]
But half-ashamed, and impotent to bless,

I am a stupid life-guard who has found,
Swept to his shallows by the tide, a girl
Who, far from shore, has been immensely drowned.   15
And stares through water now with eyes of pearl.

How large is her refusal; and how slight
The genteel chat whereby we recommend
Life, of a summer afternoon, despite
The brewing dusk which hints that it may end.   20

And Edna Ward shall die in fifteen years,
After her eight-and-eighty summers of
Such grace and courage as permit no tears,
The thin hand reaching out, the last word *love*,

Outliving Sylvia who, condemned to live,   25
Shall study for a decade, as she must,
To state at last her brilliant negative
In poems free and helpless and unjust.
1976

---

[1] Blue-and-white patterned Chinese-export
porcelain ware; in this case, the tea service.
[2] The poet Sylvia Plath (1932–1963) attempted suicide after her junior year at
Smith College. Later, she died by suicide.

Denise Levertov
b. 1923

Born in Essex, England, Denise Levertov was raised in a family deeply concerned with both the divine and the political, concerns hauntingly evoked in her riveting poetry. Her father and mother, descended from a Hasidic rabbi and a Welsh mystic, respectively, chose to educate their daughter privately; she studied French, art, and ballet, while her crusading parents spoke in favor of the League of Nations union and assisted German and Austrian refugees after 1933. Levertov served as a nurse during World War II, after which she married author Mitchell Goodman (from whom she's now divorced), and emigrated to the United States in 1948. She taught at Brandeis University, City College of New York, Drew, M.I.T., Tufts University, and Vassar before completing her career in the English and Creative Writing departments at Stanford.

In 1946, Levertov wrote her first collection of verse *Poetry: The Double Image* in stanzaic form, but switched to free verse in her later collections of poetry, including *Here and Now* (1957), *The Sorrow Dance* (1966), and *The Freeing of the Dust* (1975). Her early verse was most evidently influenced by the poetry and theory of William Carlos Williams, and the "Black Mountain School" of poetry, of which she is often classified as a member. Levertov's poetry exhibits a keen concern with the crafting of each word in an attempt to make the common and everyday extraordinary. In the title poem of the 1964 collection, *O Taste and See: New Poems,* she exhorts, "The world is/not with us enough./O Taste and See." Levertov uses unusual, often jarring, language and syntax to weld the mystical and the human, the social and the political, with the natural and the lyric. After 1965, with the United States' growing involvement in the Vietnam War, Levertov's poetry began to take on a more sharp, political edge, utilizing the themes of death, war, nuclear proliferation, mysticism, and motherhood to prod the reader into greater social consciousness, if not overt political action: "Tolerance, what crimes/are committed in your name."

Levertov won an Elmer Holmes Bobst Award in 1983, and has also received a Guggenheim Fellowship, the Lenore Marshall Prize for poetry, the Morton Dauwen Zabel Award, as well as honors from both the National Institute of Arts and Letters and the National Endowment for the Arts. Her more recent collections of poetry, *Candles in Babylon* (1982), *Oblique Prayers* (1984), and *Breathing the Water* (1987), vividly expressed the contemporary dilemmas involved in facing international poverty, racism, sexism, and environmental decay in a humane and ultimately divine manner. It is Levertov's sense of outrage and awe at the horror and magic around us that ultimately remains: "Every day, every day I hear/enough to fill/a year of nights with wondering."

Further Reading:

L. Wagner, *Denise Levertov,* 1967.
W. Slaughter, *The Imagination's Tongue: Denise Levertov's Poetics,* 1981.

H. Marten, *Understanding Denise Levertov,* 1988.
L. Wagner-Martin, ed., *Critical Essays on Denise Levertov,* 1990.

A. Gelpi, ed., *Denise Levertov: Selected Criticism,* 1993.
A. Rodgers, *Denise Levertov: The Poetry of Engagement,* 1993.

L. Kinnahan, *Poetics of the Feminine,* 1994.
C. Bloom and B. Docherty, eds., *American Poetry:
The Modernist Ideal,* 1995.

Text:
With Eyes at the Back of Our Heads, 1959.
O Taste and See: New Poems, 1964.

Pleasures

I like to find
what's not found
at once, but lies

within something of another nature,
in repose, distinct.   5
Gull feathers of glass, hidden

in white pulp: the bones of squid
which I pull out and lay
blade by blade on the draining board—

    tapered as if for swiftness, to piece   10
    the heart, but fragile, substance
    belying design.   Or a fruit, *mamey,*

cased in rough brown peel, the flesh
rose-amber, and the seed:
the seed a stone of wood, carved and   15

polished, walnut-colored, formed
like a brazilnut, but large,
large enough to fill
the hungry palm of a hand.

I like the juicy stem of grass that grows   20
within the coarser leaf folded round,
and the butteryellow glow

in the narrow flute from which the morning-glory
opens blue and cool on a hot morning
1959

The Ache of Marriage

The ache of marriage:

thigh and tongue, beloved,
are heavy with it,
it throbs in the teeth

We look for communion   5
and are turned away, beloved,
each and each

It is leviathan and we
in its belly
looking for joy, some joy   10
not to be known outside it
two by two in the ark of
the ache of it.
1964

O Taste and See

The world is
not with us enough.
O taste and see[1]

the subway Bible poster said,
meaning **The Lord,** meaning   5
if anything all that lives
to the imagination's tongue,

grief, mercy, language,
tangerine, weather, to
breathe them, bite,   10
savor, chew, swallow, transform

---

[1] Psalms 34:8 "O taste and see that the Lord is
good."

into our flesh our
deaths, crossing the street, plum, quince,
living in the orchard and being

hungry, and plucking   15
the fruit.
1964

Where Is the Angel?

Where is the angel for me to wrestle?
No diving snow in the glass bubble,
but mild September.

Outside, the stark shadows
menace, and fling their huge arms about   5
unheard. I breathe

a tepid air, the blur
of asters, of brown fern and gold-dust
seems to murmur,

and that's what I hear, only that.   10
Such clear walls of curved glass:
I see the violent gesticulations

and feel—no, not nothing. But in this
gentle haze, nothing commensurate.
It is pleasant in here. History   15

mouths, volume turned off. A band of iron,
like they put round a split tree,
circles my heart. In here

it is pleasant, but when I open
my mouth to speak, I too   20
am soundless. Where is the angel

to wrestle with me and wound
not my thigh but my throat,
so cures and blessings flow storming out

and the glass shatters, and the iron sunders?   25
1989

Norman Mailer
b. 1923

Norman Mailer was born in Long Branch, New Jersey, on January 31, 1923, and grew up in Brooklyn, New York. At Harvard College he studied aeronautical engineering but also spent much of his time writing. In 1941 he won *Story* magazine's annual award for college fiction. Two years later he left Harvard with an honors degree in engineering, joined the army, and headed for the Philippines as a rifleman in the 112th Cavalry.

Mailer's first novel, *The Naked and the Dead* (1948), the account of an American invasion of a small Pacific island held by the Japanese, drew directly on his military experiences and is generally considered one of the finest novels to come out of the Second World War. An enormous success, it gave Mailer an immediate literary reputation. In the early 1950s Mailer settled in New York City and, as he says in his first collection of essays, *Advertisements for Myself* (1959), resolved to make "a revolution in the consciousness of our time." He set about doing so through fiction, essays, journalism, and publishing. His second novel, *Barbary Shore* (1951), grew out of his reflections on the difficulties that necessarily surround reform politics in a world where all values seem to have gone dead. *The Deer Park* (1955), his third novel, in which he pays literary dues to Ernest Hemingway and F. Scott Fitzgerald, is still regarded as one of the best novels yet written about Hollywood. In 1959 Mailer attempted through a long essay, "The White Negro," to define the existential characteristics of "hip," a style of thought and behavior that he opposed to the "square" and that he believed typified the most desirable mode of contemporary consciousness. In 1953 he became a coeditor of *Dissent* and a year later helped found *The Village Voice*.

During the 1960s and early 1970s Mailer's work became increasingly political as he began to explore more deeply the various sources of power in America. He published two collections of essays on politics and culture, *The Presidential Papers* (1963) and *Cannibals and Christians* (1966). He wrote *An American Dream* in 1965, a novel about a war hero, excongressman, and friend of John F. Kennedy who murders his socially prominent wife and then apparently purges himself clean—a baptism by fire—by a deliberate immersion into what he bleakly sees as his country's cultural disintegration. In 1967 he published his fifth novel, *Why Are We in Vietnam?*, a contemporary tall tale that examines American violence through the pulsating narrative voice of an eighteen-year-old Dallas disc jockey. But much of Mailer's best work of the period was in the budding genre of "New Journalism"—writing that combined a sense of the occasions and objectivity of journalism with many of the techniques and freedoms of fiction. In 1968 Mailer wrote one of his finest books (it won both the Pulitzer Prize and the National Book Award), *The Armies of the Night,* which he subtitled *History as a Novel/The Novel as History* and which deals with his experiences in the 1967 peace march on the Pentagon to protest the Vietnam War. In the same vein he wrote about the presidential conventions of 1968 and 1972 in *Miami and the Siege of Chicago: An Informal History of the Republican and Democratic Conventions of 1968* (1969) and *St. George and the Godfather* (1972). In 1968 he published a collection of earlier political essays, *The Idol and the Octopus: Political Writings on the Kennedy and Johnson*

Administrations, and in the same year reinforced his political theme by running as an independent candidate for mayor of New York City.

Like Yeats's poetry, Mailer's prose grows out of a dialectic between a fascination with his own life and a matching fascination with the life of his times. Mailer is often seen trying to balance a desire to be a public figure—a performer, an oracle, and a celebrity—with the desire to be a serious man of letters. His writing, too, draws heavily on his abiding concern for the American culture—for its heroes and heroines, its gadgets and gimmicks, its aberrations and achievements, and above all its spiritual endangerment as it seeks to open up new worlds and yet find enduring values. In recent years he has written a number of books that investigate various aspects of contemporary American society and culture: the space program and first moon landing in *Of a Fire on the Moon* (1970), a personal polemic against feminism and the women's movement in *The Prisoner of Sex* (1971), a biographical essay on Marilyn Monroe in *Marilyn* (1973), an interpretation of urban graffiti in *The Faith of Graffiti* (1974), a report of a famous Muhammad Ali championship bout in *The Fight* (1975), and a searching account of a convicted murderer's Utah background in *The Executioner's Song* (1979). In keeping with his remarkable versatility, Mailer has also written a long novel set in the Egypt of the Pharaohs, *Ancient Evenings* (1983), and a murder mystery, *Tough Guys Don't Dance* (1984), and *Harlot's Ghost* (1991).

Both controversy and acclaim have greeted Mailer's efforts to make the tension between his art and his life as compellingly interesting to others as it is to himself. Even so, both his work and his career surely stand among the more remarkable achievements of our time. For more than thirty years now he has displayed an artistic restlessness—deriving from what he once described as an instinctive feeling that "the best way to grow was not to write one novel after another but to move from activity to activity"—that has carried him from one telling experiment to another. As much as any writer of his time, he has reached beyond familiar attitudes, themes, styles, and modes into new areas and so has broadened literature in our time. Furthermore, though he has sometimes simplified and reduced the realities of modern American life, he has also, at his best, brought unusual imaginative force, and unusually supple prose, to bear on them. "I suppose," he once remarked,

> that the virtue I should like most to achieve as a writer is to be genuinely disturbing . . .
> to see life . . . as others do not see it, or only partially see it, and therefore open for the
> reader that literary experience . . . of having one's experience enlarged, one's percep-
> tions deepened, and one's illusions about oneself rendered even more untenable. For
> me, this is the highest function of art, precisely that it is disturbing, that it does not let
> man rest.

Further Reading:

R. Poirier, *Norman Mailer,* 1973.
R. Solotaroff, *Down Mailer's Way,* 1974.
P. Manso, ed., *Mailer: His Life and Times,* 1985.
J. Wenke, *Mailer's America,* 1987.

J. Lennon, ed., *Conversations with Mailer,* 1988.
C. Rollyson, *The Lives of Norman Mailer: A Biography,* 1991.

Text:

*The Armies of the Night: History as a Novel/The
Novel as History,* 1968.

---

from The Armies of the Night*

Book I: History as a Novel:
The Steps of the Pentagon

from **Part I: Thursday Evening**

5: Toward a Theater of Ideas

The guests were beginning to leave the party for the Ambassador, which was two blocks away. Mailer did not know this yet, but the audience there had been waiting almost an hour. They were being entertained by an electronic folk rock guitar group, so presumably the young were more or less happy, and the middle-aged dim. Mailer was feeling the high sense of clarity which accompanies the light show of the aurora borealis when it is projected upon the inner universe of the chest, the lungs, and the heart. He was happy. On leaving, he had appropriated a coffee mug and filled it with bourbon. The fresh air illumined the bourbon, gave it a cerebrative edge; words entered his brain with the agreeable authority of fresh minted coins. Like all good professionals, he was stimulated by the chance to try a new if related line of work. Just as professional football players love sex because it is so close to football, so he was fond of speaking in public because it was thus near to writing. An extravagant analogy? Consider that a good half of writing consists of being sufficiently sensitive to the moment to reach for the next promise which is usually hidden in some word or phrase just a shift to the side of one's conscious intent. (Consciousness, that blunt tool, bucks in the general direction of the truth; instinct plucks the feather. Cheers!) Where public speaking is an exercise from prepared texts to demonstrate how successfully a low order of consciousness can beat upon the back of a collective flesh, public speaking being, therefore, a sullen expression of human possibility metaphorically equal to a bugger on his victim, speaking-in-public (as Mailer liked to describe any speech which was more or less improvised, impromptu, or dangerously written) was an activity like writing; one had to trick or seize or submit to the grace of each moment, which, except for those unexpected and sometimes well-deserved moments when consciousness and grace came together (and one felt on the consequence, heroic) were usually occasions of some mystery. The pleasure of speaking in public was the sensitivity it offered: with every phrase one was better or worse, close or less close to the existential promise of truth, *it feels true,* which hovers on good occasions like a presence between speaker and audience. Sometimes one was better, and worse, at the same moment; so strategic choices on the continuation of the attack would soon have to be decided, a moment to know the blood of the gambler in oneself.

Intimations of this approaching experience, obviously one of Mailer's preferred pleasures in life, at least when he did it well, were now connected to the professional sense of intrigue at the new task: tonight he would be both speaker and master of cere-

---

* *The Armies of the Night* is based on the
march to the Pentagon in October 1967 in
opposition to the Vietnam War.

monies. The two would conflict, but interestingly. Already he was looking in his mind for kind even celebrative remarks about Paul Goodman[1] which would not violate every reservation he had about Goodman's dank glory. But he had it. It would be possible with no violation of truth to begin by saying that the first speaker looked very much like Nelson Algren,[2] because in fact the first speaker was Paul Goodman, and both Nelson Algren and Paul Goodman looked like old cons. Ladies and Gentlemen, without further ado let me introduce one of young America's favorite old cons, Paul Goodman! (It would not be necessary to add that where Nelson Algren looked like the sort of skinny old con who was in on every make in the joint, and would sign away Grandma's farm to stay in the game, Goodman looked like the sort of old con who had first gotten into trouble in the YMCA, and hadn't spoken to anyone since.)

All this while, Mailer had in clutch *Why Are We In Vietnam?* He had neglected to bring his own copy to Washington and so had borrowed the book from his hostess on the promise he would inscribe it. (Later he was actually to lose it—working apparently on the principle that if you cannot make a hostess happy, the next best charity is to be so evil that the hostess may dine out on tales of your misconduct.) But the copy of the book is now noted because Mailer, holding it in one hand and the mug of whisky in the other, was obliged to notice on entering the Ambassador Theater that he had an overwhelming urge to micturate. The impulse to pass urine, being for some reason more difficult to restrain when both hands are occupied, there was no thought in the Master of Ceremonies' mind about the alternatives—he would have to find The Room before he went on stage.

That was not so immediately simple as one would have thought. The twenty guests from the party, looking a fair piece subdued under the fluorescent lights, had therefore the not unhaggard look of people who have arrived an hour late at the theater. No matter that the theater was by every evidence sleazy (for neighborhood movie houses built on the dream of the owner that some day Garbo or Harlow or Lombard would give a look in, aged immediately they were not used for movies anymore) no matter, the guests had the uneasiness of very late arrivals. Apologetic, they were therefore in haste for the speakers to begin.

Mailer did not know this. He was off already in search of The Room, which, it developed was up on the balcony floor. Imbued with the importance of his first gig as Master of Ceremonies, he felt such incandescence of purpose that he could not quite conceive it necessary to notify de Grazia[3] he would be gone for a minute. Incandescence is the *satori*[4] of the Romantic spirit which spirit would insist—this is the essence of the Romantic—on accelerating time. The greater the power of any subjective state, the more total is a Romantic's assumption that everyone understands exactly what he is about to do, therefore waste not a moment by stopping to tell them.

---

[1] American poet and cultural critic (1911–1972), and author of *Growing Up Absurd* (1959).

[2] Contemporary American novelist (b. 1909) and author of *The Man With the Golden Arm* (1949).

[3] Ed de Grazia, one of the organizers of the march.

[4] State of spiritual enlightenment sought in Zen Buddhism.

Flush with his incandescence, happy in all the anticipations of liberty which this Götterdämmerung[5] of a urination was soon to provide, Mailer did not know, but he had already and unwitting to himself metamorphosed into the Beast. Wait and see!

He was met on the stairs by a young man from *Time* magazine, a stringer presumably, for the young man lacked that I-am-damned look in the eye and rep tie of those whose work for *Time* has become a life addiction. The young man had a somewhat ill-dressed look, a map showed on his skin of an old adolescent acne, and he gave off the unhappy furtive presence of a fraternity member on probation for the wrong thing, some grievous mis-deposit of vomit, some hanky panky with frat-house tickets.

But the Beast was in a great good mood. He was soon to speak; that was food for all. So the Beast greeted the *Time* man with the geniality of a surrogate Hemingway unbending for the Luce-ites (Loo-sights was the pun) made some genial cryptic remark or two about finding Herr John, said cheerfully in answer to why he was in Washington that he had come to protest the war in Vietnam, and taking a sip of bourbon from the mug he kept to keep all fires idling right, stepped off into the darkness of the top balcony floor, went through a door into a pitch-black men's room, and was alone with his need. No chance to find the light switch for he had no matches, he did not smoke. It was therefore a matter of locating what's what with the probing of his toes. He found something finally which seemed appropriate, and pleased with the precision of these generally unused senses in his feet, took aim between them at a point twelve inches ahead, and heard in the darkness the sound of his water striking the floor. Some damn mistake had been made, an assault from the side doubtless instead of the front, the bowl was relocated now, and Master of Ceremonies breathed deep of the great reveries of this utterly non-Sisyphian release—at last!!—and thoroughly enjoyed the next forty-five seconds, being left on the aftermath not a note depressed by the condition of the premises. No, he was off on the Romantic's great military dream, which is: seize defeat, convert it to triumph. Of course, pissing on the floor was bad; very bad; the attendant would probably gossip to the police (if the *Time* man did not sniff it out first) and The Uniformed in turn would report it to The Press who were sure to write about the scandalous condition in which this meeting had left the toilets. And all of this contretemps merely because the management, bitter with their lost dream of Garbo and Harlow and Lombard, were now so pocked and stingy they doused the lights. (Out of such stuff is a novelist's brain.)

Well, he could convert this deficiency to an asset. From gap to gain is very American. He would confess straight out to all aloud that he was the one who wet the floor in the men's room, he alone! While the audience was recovering from the existential anxiety of encountering an orator who confessed to such a crime, he would be able—their attention now riveted—to bring them up to a contemplation of deeper problems, of, indeed, the deepest problems, the most chilling alternatives, and would from there seek to bring them back to a restorative view of man. Man might be a fool who peed in the wrong pot, man was also a scrupulous servant of the self-damaging admission; man was therefore a philosopher who possessed the magic stone; he could turn loss to philo-

---

[5] German: "twilight of the gods." Hence, catastrophic and grandiose like the Wagnerian opera of that title.

sophical gain, and so illumine the deeps, find the poles, and eventually learn to cultivate his most special fool's garden: *satori,* incandescence, and the hard gem-like flame of bourbon burning in the furnaces of metabolism.

Thus composed, illumined by these first stages of Emersonian transcendence, Mailer left the men's room, descended the stairs, entered the back of the orchestra, all opening remarks held close file in his mind like troops ranked in order before the parade, and then suddenly, most suddenly saw, with a cancerous swoop of albatross wings, that de Grazia was on the stage, was acting as M.C., was—no calling it back—launched into the conclusion of a gentle stammering stumbling—small orator, de Grazia!—introduction of Paul Goodman. All lost! The magnificent opening remarks about the forces gathered here to assemble on Saturday before the Pentagon, this historic occasion, let us hold it in our mind and focus on a puddle of passed water on the floor above and see if we assembled here can as leftists and proud dissenters contain within our minds the grandeur of the two—all lost!—no chance to do more than pick up later—later! after de Grazia and Goodman had finished dead-assing the crowd. Traitor de Grazia! Sicilian de Grazia!

As Mailer picked his way between people sitting on the stone floor (orchestra seats had been removed—the movie house was a dance hall now with a stage) he made a considerable stir in the orchestra. Mailer had been entering theaters for years, mounting stages—now that he had put on weight, it would probably have been fair to say that he came to the rostrum like a poor man's version of Orson Welles, some minor note of the same contemplative presence. A titter and rise of expectation followed him. He could not resist its appeal. As he passed de Grazia, he scowled, threw a look from Lower Shakespearia "Èt tu Bruté," and proceeded to slap the back of his hand against de Grazia's solar plexus. It was not a heavy blow, but then de Grazia was not a heavy man; he wilted some hint of an inch. And the audience pinched off a howl, squeaked on their squeal. It was not certain to them what had taken place.

Picture the scene two minutes later from the orchestra floor. Paul Goodman, now up at the microphone with no podium or rostrum, is reading the following lines:

> . . . these days my contempt
> for the misrulers of my country
> is icy and my indignation raucous.

It is impossible to tell what he is reading. Off at the wing of the stage where the others are collected—stout Macdonald, noble Lowell, beleaguered de Grazia, and Mailer, Prince of Bourbon, the acoustics are atrocious. One cannot hear a word the speaker is saying. Nor are there enough seats. If de Grazia and Macdonald are sitting in folding chairs, Mailer is squatting on his haunches, or kneeling on one knee like a player about to go back into the ball game. Lowell has the expression on his face of a dues payer who is just about keeping up with the interest on some enormous debt. As he sits on the floor with his long arms clasped mournfully about his long Yankee legs, "I am here," says his expression, "but I do not have to pretend I like what I see." The hollows in his cheeks give a hint of the hanging judge. Lowell is of a good weight, not too heavy, not too light, but the hollows speak of the great Puritan gloom in which the country was founded—man was simply not good enough for God.

At this moment, it is hard not to agree with Lowell. The cavern of the theater seems to resonate behind the glare of the footlights, but this is no resonance of a fine bass voice—it is rather electronics on the march. The public address system hisses, then rings in a random chorus of electronic music, sounds of cerebral mastication from some horror machine of Outer Space (where all that electricity doubtless comes from, child!) then a hum like the squeak in the hinges of the gates of Hell—we are in the penumbra of psychedelic netherworlds, ghost-odysseys from the dead brain cells of adolescent trysts with LSD, some ultrapurple spotlight from the balcony (not ultraviolet—ultrapurple, deepest purple one could conceive) there out in the dark like some neon eye of the night, the media is the message, and the message is purple, speaks of the monarchies of Heaven, madnesses of God, and clam-vaults of people on a stone floor. Mailer's senses are now tuned to absolute pitch or sheer error—he marks a ballot for absolute pitch—he is certain there is a profound pall in the audience. Yes, they sit there, stricken, inert, in terror of what Saturday will bring, and so are unable to rise to a word the speaker is offering them. It will take dynamite to bring life. The shroud of burned-out psychedelic dreams is in this audience, Cancer Gulch with open maw—and Mailer thinks of the vigor and the light (from marijuana?) in the eyes of those American soldiers in Vietnam who have been picked by the newsreel cameras to say their piece, and the happy healthy never unintelligent faces of all those professional football players he studies so assiduously on television come Sunday (he has neglected to put his bets in this week) and wonders how they would poll out on sentiment for the war.

HAWKS 95   DOVES 6

NFL Footballers Approve Vietnam War

Doubtless. All the healthy Marines, state troopers, professional athletes, movie stars, rednecks, sensuous life-loving Mafia, cops, mill workers, city officials, nice healthy-looking easy-grafting politicians full of the light (from marijuana?) in their eye of a life they enjoy—yes, they would be for the war in Vietnam. Arrayed against them as hard-core troops: an elite! the Freud-ridden embers of Marxism, good old American anxiety strata—the urban middle-class with their proliferated monumental adenoidal resentments, their secret slavish love for the oncoming hegemony of the computer and the suburb, yes, they and their children, by the sheer ironies, the sheer ineptitude, the *kinks* of history, were now being compressed into more and more militant stands, their resistance to the war some hopeless melange, somehow firmed, of Pacifism and closet Communism. And their children—on a freak-out from the suburbs to a love-in on the Pentagon wall.

It was the children in whom Mailer had some hope, a gloomy hope. These mad middle-class children with their lobotomies from sin, their nihilistic embezzlement of all middle-class moral funds, their innocence, their lust for apocalypse, their unbelievable indifference to waste: twenty generations of buried hopes perhaps engraved in their chromosomes, and now conceivably burning like faggots in the secret inquisitional fires of LSD. It was a devil's drug—designed by the Devil to consume the love of the best, and leave them liver-wasted, weeds of the big city. If there had been a player piano, Mailer might have put in a quarter to hear "In the Heart of the City Which Has No Heart."

Yes, these were the troops: middle-class cancer-pushers and drug-gutted flower children. And Paul Goodman to lead them. Was he now reading this?

Once American faces
were beautiful to me
but now they look cruel
and as if they had narrow thoughts.

Not much poetry, but well put prose. And yet there was always Goodman's damnable tolerance for all the varieties of sex. Did he know nothing of evil or entropy? Sex was the superhighway to your own soul's entropy if it was used without a constant sharpening of the taste. And orgies? What did Goodman know of orgies, real ones, not lib-lab college orgies to carry out the higher program of the Great Society, but real ones with murder in the air, and witches on the shoulder. The collected Tory in Mailer came roaring to the surface like a cocked hat in a royal coach.

"When Goodman finishes, I'm going to take over as M.C.," he whispered to de Grazia. (The revery we have just attended took no more in fact than a second. Mailer's melancholy assessment of the forces now mounting in America took place between two consecutive lines of Goodman's poem—not because Mailer cerebrated that instantly, but because he had had the revery many a time before—he had to do no more than sense the audience, whisper Cancer Gulch to himself and the revery went by with a mental ch-ch-ch Click! reviewed again.) In truth, Mailer was now in a state. He had been prepared to open the evening with apocalyptic salvos to announce the real gravity of the situation, and the intensely peculiar American aspect of it—which is that the urban and suburban middle class were to be offered on Saturday an opportunity for glory—what other nation could boast of such option for its middle class? Instead—lost. The benignity and good humor of his planned opening remarks now subjugated to the electronic hawking and squabbling and *hum* of the P.A., the maniacal necessity to *wait* was on this hiatus transformed into a violent concentration of purpose, all intentions reversed. He glared at de Grazia. "How could you do this?" he whispered to his ear.

De Grazia looked somewhat confused at the intensity. Meetings to de Grazia were obviously just meetings, assemblages of people who coughed up for large admissions or kicked in for the pitch; at best, some meetings were less boring than others. De Grazia was much too wise and guilty-spirited to brood on apocalypse. "I couldn't find you," he whispered back.

"You didn't trust me long enough to wait one minute?"

"We were over an hour late," de Grazia whispered again. "We had to begin."

Mailer was all for having the conversation right then on stage: to hell with reciprocal rights and polite incline of the ear to the speaker. The Beast was ready to grapple with the world. "Did you think I wouldn't show up?" he asked de Grazia.

"Well, I was wondering."

In what sort of mumbo-jumbo of promise and betrayal did de Grazia live? How could de Grazia ever suppose he would not show up? He had spent his life showing up at the most boring and onerous places. He gave a blast of his eyes to de Grazia. But Macdonald gave a look at Mailer, as if to say, "You're creating a disturbance."

Now Goodman was done.

Mailer walked to the stage. He did not have any idea any longer of what he would say, his mind was empty, but in a fine calm, taking for these five instants a total rest. While there was no danger of Mailer ever becoming a demagogue since if the first idea he offered could appeal to a mob, the second in compensation would be sure to enrage them, he might nonetheless have made a fair country orator, for he loved to speak, he loved in fact to holler, and liked to hear a crowd holler back. (Of how many New York intellectuals may that be said?)

"I'm here as your original M.C., temporarily displaced owing to a contretemps"— which was pronounced purposefully as contretempse—"in the men's room," he said into the microphone for opening, but the gentle high-strung beast of a device pushed into a panic by the electric presence of a real Beast, let loose a squeal which shook the welds in the old foundation of the Ambassador. Mailer immediately decided he had had enough of public address systems, electronic fields of phase, impedance, and spooks in the circuitry. A hex on collaborating with Cancer Gulch. He pushed the microphone away, squared off before the audience. "Can you hear me?" he bellowed.

"Yes."

"Can you hear me in the balcony?"

"Yes."

"Then let's do away with electronics," he called out.

Cries of laughter came back. A very small pattern of applause. (Not too many on his side for electrocuting the public address system, or so his orator's ear recorded the vote.)

"Now I missed the beginning of this occasion, or I would have been here to introduce Paul Goodman, for which we're all sorry, right?"

Confused titters. Small reaction.

"What are you, dead-heads?" he bellowed at the audience. "Or are you all"—here he put on his false Irish accent—"in the nature of becoming dead ahsses?" Small laughs. A whistle or two. "No," he said, replying to the whistles, "I invoke these dead asses as part of the gravity of the occasion. The middle class plus one hippie surrealistic symbolic absolutely insane March on the Pentagon, bless us all," beginning of a big applause which offended Mailer for it came on "bless" and that was too cheap a way to win votes, "bless us all—shit!" he shouted, "I'm trying to say the middle class plus shit, I mean plus revolution, is equal to one big collective dead ass." Some yells of approval, but much shocked curious rather stricken silence. He had broken the shank of his oratorical charge. Now he would have to sweep the audience together again. (Perhaps he felt like a surgeon delivering a difficult breech—nothing to do but plunge to the elbows again.)

"To resume our exposition," a good warm titter, then a ripple of laughter, not unsympathetic to his ear; the humor had been unwitting, but what was the life of an orator without some bonus? "To resume this orderly marshalling of concepts"—a conscious attempt at humor which worked less well; he was beginning to recognize for the first time that bellowing without a mike demanded a more forthright style—"I shall now *engage* in confession." More Irish accent. (He blessed Brendan Behan for what he had learned from him.) "A public speaker may offer you two opportunities. Instruction or confession." Laughter now. "Well, you're all college heads, so my instruction would be as pearls before—I dare not say it." Laughs. Boos. A voice from the balcony: "Come on, Norman, say something!"

"Is there a black man in the house?" asked Mailer. He strode up and down the stage pretending to peer at the audience. But in fact they were illumined just well enough to emphasize one sad discovery—if black faces there were they were certainly not in plenty. "Well ah'll just have to be the *impromptu* Black Power for tonight. Woo-eeeeee!

Woo-eeeeee! HMmmmmmm." He grunted with some partial success, showing hints of Cassius Clay. "Get your white butts moving."

"The confession. The confession!" screamed some adolescents from up front.

He came to a stop, shifted his voice. Now he spoke in a relaxed tone. "The confession, yeah!" Well, at least the audience was awake. He felt as if he had driven away some sepulchral phantoms of a variety which inhabited the profound middle-class schist. Now to charge the center of vested spookery.

"Say," he called out into the semidarkness with the ultrapurple light coming off the psychedelic lamp on the rail of the balcony, and the spotlights blaring against his eyes, "say," all happiness again, "I think of Saturday, and that March and do you know, fellow carriers of the holy unendurable grail, for the first time in my life I don't know whether I have the piss or the shit scared out of me most." It was an interesting concept, thought Mailer, for there was a difference between the two kinds of fear—pursue the thought, he would, in quieter times—"we are up, face this, all of you, against an existential situation—we do not know how it is going to turn out, and what is even more inspiring of dread is that the government doesn't know either."

Beginning of a real hand, a couple of rebel yells. "We're going to try to stick it up the government's ass," he shouted, "right into the sphincter of the Pentagon." Wild yells and chills of silence from different reaches of the crowd. Yeah, he was cooking now. "Will reporters please get every word accurately," he called out dryly to warm the chill.

But humor may have been too late. *The New Yorker* did not have strictures against the use of sh*t for nothing; nor did Dwight Macdonald love *The New Yorker* for nothing, he also had strictures against sh*t's metaphorical associations. Mailer looked to his right to see Macdonald approaching, a book in his hands, arms at his side, a sorrowing look of concern in his face. "Norman," said Macdonald quietly, "I can't possibly follow you after all this. Please introduce me, and get it over with."

Mailer was near to stricken. On the one hand interrupted on a flight; on the other, he had fulfilled no duty whatsoever as M.C. He threw a look at Macdonald which said: give me this. I'll owe you one.

But de Grazia was there as well. "Norman, let me be M.C. now," he said.

They were being monstrous unfair, thought Mailer. They didn't understand what he had been doing, how good he had been, what he would do next. Fatal to walk off now—the verdict would claim he was unbalanced. Still, he could not hold the stage by force. That was unthinkably worse.

For the virtuous, however, deliverance (like buttercups) pops up everywhere. Mailer now took the microphone and turned to the audience. He was careful to speak in a relaxed voice. "We are having a disagreement about the value of the proceedings. Some think de Grazia should resume his post as Master of Ceremonies. I would like to keep the position. It is an existential moment. We do not know how it will turn out. So let us vote on it." Happy laughter from the audience at these comic effects. Actually Mailer did not believe it was an existential situation any longer. He reckoned the vote would be well in his favor. "Will those," he asked, "who are in favor of Mr. de Grazia succeeding me as Master of Ceremonies please say aye."

A good sound number said aye.

Now for the ovation. "Will those opposed to this, please say no." The no's to Mailer's lack of pleasure were no greater in volume. "It seems the ayes and no's are about equal," said Mailer. (He was thinking to himself that he had posed the issue all wrong—the ayes should have been reserved for those who would keep him in office.) "Under the circumstances," he announced, "I will keep the chair." Laughter at this easy cheek. He stepped into the middle of such laughter. "You have all just learned an invaluable political lesson." He waved the microphone at the audience. "In the absence of a definitive vote, the man who holds the power, keeps it."

"Hey, de Grazia," someone yelled from the audience, "why do you let him have it?"

Mailer extended the microphone to de Grazia who smiled sweetly into it. "Because if I don't," he said in a gentle voice, "he'll beat the shit out of me." The dread word had been used again.

"Please, Norman," said Macdonald retreating.

So Mailer gave his introduction to Macdonald. It was less than he would have attempted if the flight had not been grounded, but it was certainly respectable. Under the military circumstances, it was a decent cleanup operation. For about a minute he proceeded to introduce Macdonald as a man with whom one might seldom agree, but could never disrespect because he always told the truth as he saw the truth, a man therefore of the most incorruptible integrity. "Pray heaven, I am right," said Mailer to himself, and walked past Macdonald who was on his way to the mike. Both men nodded coolly to each other.

In the wing, visible to the audience, Paul Goodman sat on a chair clearly avoiding any contaminatory encounter with The Existentialist. De Grazia gave his "It's tough all over" smile. Lowell sat in a mournful hunch on the floor, his eyes peering over his glasses to scrutinize the metaphysical substance of his boot, now hide? now machine? now, where the joining and to what? foot to boot, boot to earth—cease all speculations as to what was in Lowell's head. "The one mind a novelist cannot enter is the mind of a novelist superior to himself," said once to Mailer by Jean Malaquais. So, by corollary, the one mind a minor poet may not enter . . .

Lowell looked most unhappy. Mailer, minor poet, had often observed that Lowell had the most disconcerting mixture of strength and weakness in his presence, a blending so dramatic in its visible sign of conflict that one had to assume he would be sensationally attractive to women. He had something untouchable, all insane in its force; one felt immediately there were any number of causes for which the man would be ready to die, and for some he would fight, with an axe in his hand and a Cromwellian light in his eye. It was even possible that physically he was very strong—one couldn't tell at all—he might be fragile, he might have the sort of farm mechanic's strength which could manhandle the rear axle and differential off a car and into the back of a pickup. But physical strength or no, his nerves were all too apparently delicate. Obviously spoiled by everyone for years, he seemed nonetheless to need the spoiling. These nerves—the nerves of a consummate poet—were not tuned to any battering. The squalls of the mike, now riding up a storm on the erratic piping breath of Macdonald's voice, seemed to tear along Lowell's back like a gale. He detested tumult—obviously. And therefore saw everything which was hopeless in a rife situation: the dank middle-class depths of the audience, the strident squalor of the mike, the absurdity of talent gathered to raise money—for what, dear God? who could finally know what this March might convey, or worse, purvey, and worst of all—to be associated now with Mailer's butcher boy attack. Lowell's eyes looked up from the shoe, and passed one withering glance by the novelist, saying much, saying, "Every single bad thing I have ever heard about you is not exaggerated."

Mailer, looking back, thought bitter words he would not say: "You, Lowell, beloved poet of many, what do you know of the dirt and the dark deliveries of the necessary? What do you know of dignity hard-achieved, and dignity lost through innocence, and dignity lost by sacrifice for a cause one cannot name. What do you know about getting fat against your will, and turning into a clown of an arriviste baron when you would rather be an eagle or a count, or rarest of all, some natural aristocrat from these damned democratic states. No, the only subject we share, you and I, is that species of perception which shows that if we are not very loyal to our unendurable and most exigent inner light, then some day we may burn. How dare you condemn me! You know the diseases which inhabit the audience in this accursed psychedelic house. How dare you scorn the explosive I employ?"

And Lowell with a look of the greatest sorrow as if all this *mess* were finally too shapeless for the hard Protestant smith of his own brain, which would indeed burst if it could not forge his experience into the iron edge of the very best words and the most unsinkable relation of words, now threw up his eyes like an epileptic as if turned out of orbit by a turn of the vision—and fell backward, his head striking the floor with no last instant hesitation to cushion the blow, but like a baby, downright sudden, savagely to himself, as if from the height of a foot he had taken a pumpkin and dropped it splat on the floor. "There, much-regarded, much-protected brain, you have finally taken a blow," Lowell might have said to himself, for he proceeded to lie there, resting quietly, while Macdonald went on reading from "The White Man's Burden," Lowell seeming as content as if he had just tested the back of his cranium against a policeman's club. What a royal head they had all to lose!

1968

James Baldwin
1924–1987

"An artist," says James Baldwin, "is here not to give you answers but to ask you questions." In his long career as a novelist, essayist, and civil rights activist, Baldwin's questions have most often taken the form of moral alternatives. In both his fiction and his essays, he deals with controversial subjects, posing questions about race, politics, sex, and love that address the sources of human suffering and human joy. Baldwin's characters succeed through knowledge that is hard won, and they are usually closest to triumph in moments of maximum risk.

James Baldwin was born on August 2, 1924, in Harlem. Three years later his mother, Emma Jones, married David Baldwin, a preacher whom Baldwin later admitted was the only person he had ever hated. Baldwin and his eight brothers and sisters grew up in abject poverty in the Harlem ghetto, and Baldwin says of himself that he "wanted to become rich and famous simply so no one could evict my family again." In 1938 he was converted and became a preacher at the Fireside Pentecostal Assembly, experiences that form the basis for his first novel, *Go Tell It on the Mountain* (1953). In

1942 he graduated from high school and left the ministry, convinced that religion provided inadequate answers to the problems of poor African Americans. That same year he began a ten-year struggle to write *Go Tell It on the Mountain.* "In a sense," he said, "I wrote to redeem my father. I had to understand the forces, the experience, the life that shaped him before I could grow up myself, before I could become a writer." While working on the novel, he moved to Greenwich Village, where he met Richard Wright. With Wright's help, he received a Eugene Saxton fellowship and began writing essays and reviews for *The Nation* and *Commentary.* In 1948 he published his first short story, "Previous Condition," and received a Rosenwald fellowship, which allowed him to move to Paris where he remained for the next nine years.

The publication of *Go Tell It on the Mountain* marked Baldwin's emergence as a major writer. He followed it with a collection of essays, *Notes of a Native Son* (1955), and the controversial novel *Giovanni's Room* (1956), which deals with a young, white homosexual's attempt to accept himself as he is. Over the next several years Baldwin's work moved back and forth between efforts to deal with the racial situation in America—*Another Country* (1962) and *The Fire Next Time* (1963)—and efforts to deal with the subject of homosexuality—*Tell Me How Long the Train's Been Gone* (1965). In "Sonny's Blues," which was first published in *Going to Meet the Man* (1965), as in his novel *Just Above My Head* (1979), Baldwin presents an older brother's account of his relationship with a younger brother who is a musician. In the story as well as the novel, Baldwin uses music to explore the relationship of art to life.

Baldwin has always thought of writing—of art—as a public act. Writing, he says, "involves, after all, disturbing the peace." For him, artists are revolutionaries not simply as a result of their perspectives but also as a result of the potential their work has to effect social change. Yet the artist's role is not simply to affirm political rhetoric: "You got to be aware that a slogan is only a slogan," for "what you have to do is insist on complexity which people in the battle don't want to think about."

Baldwin's own involvement in the civil rights movement began with his return from France in 1957; by 1962 he had become a nationally recognized leader for the movement. In "Fifth Avenue, Uptown: A Letter from Harlem" (1960) he says that "it is a terrible, an inexorable, law that one cannot deny the humanity of another without diminishing one's own: in the face of one's victim, one sees himself." To "be a Negro in this country," he says, "and to be relatively conscious is to be in a rage almost all the time."

In his fiction, as well as in his essays and speeches, Baldwin consistently depicts the political, economic, and social injustice he sees in American society, but he also affirms the importance of accepting the past, both personal and collective, even when it involves pain. Accepting "one's past—one's history—is not the same thing as drowning in it, it is learning how to use it." In his work, religion tends to reinforce oppression while art serves as a bridge between people, as music does in "Sonny's Blues." Like art, love is almost always a liberating force in Baldwin's work, even though in its less socially acceptable forms, such as interracial or homosexual love, it can also cause intense pain. "You write," Baldwin says,

> in order to change the world, knowing perfectly well that you probably can't, but also knowing that literature is indispensable to the world. In some way, your aspirations and concern for a single man in fact do begin to change the world. The world changes

according to the way people see it, and if you alter, even by a millimeter, the way a person looks or people look at reality, then you can change it.

Further Reading:

F. Eckman, *The Furious Passage of James Baldwin,* 1966.

K. Kinnamon, ed., *James Baldwin: A Collection of Critical Essays,* 1979.

C. Sylvander, *James Baldwin,* 1980.

T. Harris, *Black Women in the Fiction of James Baldwin,* 1985.

H. Porter, *Stealing the Fire: The Art and Protest of James Baldwin,* 1989.

Q. Troupe, ed., *James Baldwin: The Legacy,* 1989.

J. Campbell, *Talking at the Gates: A Life of James Baldwin,* 1991.

D. Leeming, *James Baldwin: A Biography,* 1994.

Text:

"Sonny's Blues" from *Going to Meet the Man,* 1965.

Sonny's Blues

I read about it in the paper, in the subway, on my way to work. I read it, and I couldn't believe it, and I read it again. Then perhaps I just stared at it, at the newsprint spelling out his name, spelling out the story. I stared at it in the swinging lights of the subway car, and in the faces and bodies of the people, and in my own face, trapped in the darkness which roared outside.

It was not to be believed and I kept telling myself that, as I walked from the subway station to the high school. And at the same time I couldn't doubt it. I was scared, scared for Sonny. He became real to me again. A great block of ice got settled in my belly and kept melting there slowly all day long, while I taught my classes algebra. It was a special kind of ice. It kept melting, sending trickles of ice water all up and down my veins, but it never got less. Sometimes it hardened and seemed to expand until I felt my guts were going to come spilling out or that I was going to choke or scream. This would always be at a moment when I was remembering some specific thing Sonny had once said or done.

When he was about as old as the boys in my classes his face had been bright and open, there was a lot of copper in it; and he'd had wonderfully direct brown eyes, and great gentleness and privacy. I wondered what he looked like now. He had been picked up, the evening before, in a raid on an apartment downtown, for peddling and using heroin.

I couldn't believe it: but what I mean by that is that I couldn't find any room for it anywhere inside me. I had kept it outside me for a long time. I hadn't wanted to know. I had had suspicions, but I didn't name them, I kept putting them away. I told myself that Sonny was wild, but he wasn't crazy. And he'd always been a good boy, he hadn't ever turned hard or evil or disrespectful, the way kids can, so quick, so quick, especially in Harlem. I didn't want to believe that I'd ever see my brother going down, coming to nothing, all that light in his face gone out, in the condition I'd already seen so many others. Yet it had happened and here I was, talking about algebra to a lot of boys who might, every one of them for all I knew, be popping off needles every time they went to the head. Maybe it did more for them than algebra could.

I was sure that the first time Sonny had ever had horse, he couldn't have been much older than these boys were now. These boys, now, were living as we'd been living then, they were growing up with a rush and their heads bumped abruptly against the low ceiling of their actual possibilities. They were filled with rage. All they really knew were two darknesses, the darkness of their lives, which was now closing in on them, and the darkness of the movies, which had blinded them to that other darkness, and in which they now, vindictively, dreamed, at once more together than they were at any other time, and more alone.

When the last bell rang, the last class ended, I let out my breath. It seemed I'd been holding it for all that time. My clothes were wet—I may have looked as though I'd been sitting in a steam bath, all dressed up, all afternoon. I sat alone in the classroom a long time. I listened to the boys outside, downstairs, shouting and cursing and laughing. Their laughter struck me for perhaps the first time. It was not the joyous laughter which—God knows why—one associates with children. It was mocking and insular, its intent was to denigrate. It was disenchanted, and in this, also, lay the authority of their curses. Perhaps I was listening to them because I was thinking about my brother and in them I heard my brother. And myself.

One boy was whistling a tune, at once very complicated and very simple, it seemed to be pouring out of him as though he were a bird, and it sounded very cool and moving through all that harsh, bright air, only just holding its own through all those other sounds.

I stood up and walked over to the window and looked down into the courtyard. It was the beginning of the spring and the sap was rising in the boys. A teacher passed through them every now and again, quickly, as though he or she couldn't wait to get out of that courtyard, to get those boys out of their sight and off their minds. I started collecting my stuff. I thought I'd better get home and talk to Isabel.

The courtyard was almost deserted by the time I got downstairs. I saw this boy standing in the shadow of a doorway, looking just like Sonny. I almost called his name. Then I saw that it wasn't Sonny, but somebody we used to know, a boy from around our block. He'd been Sonny's friend. He'd never been mine, having been too young for me, and, anyway, I'd never liked him. And now, even though he was a grown-up man, he still hung around that block, still spent hours on the street corners, was always high and raggy. I used to run into him from time to time and he'd often work around to asking me for a quarter or fifty cents. He always had some real good excuse, too, and I always gave it to him, I don't know why.

But now, abruptly, I hated him. I couldn't stand the way he looked at me, partly like a dog, partly like a cunning child. I wanted to ask him what the hell he was doing in the school courtyard.

He sort of shuffled over to me, and he said, "I see you got the papers. So you already know about it."

"You mean about Sonny? Yes, I already know about it. How come they didn't get you?"

He grinned. It made him repulsive and it also brought to mind what he'd looked like as a kid. "I wasn't there. I stay away from them people."

"Good for you." I offered him a cigarette and I watched him through the smoke. "You come all the way down here just to tell me about Sonny?"

"That's right." He was sort of shaking his head and his eyes looked strange, as though they were about to cross. The bright sun deadened his damp dark brown skin and it made his eyes look yellow and showed up the dirt in his kinked hair. He smelled funky. I moved a little away from him and I said, "Well, thanks. But I already know about it and I got to get home."

"I'll walk you a little ways," he said. We started walking. There were a couple of kids still loitering in the courtyard and one of them said goodnight to me and looked strangely at the boy beside me.

"What're you going to do?" he asked me. "I mean, about Sonny?"

"Look. I haven't seen Sonny for over a year, I'm not sure I'm going to do anything. Anyway, what the hell *can* I do?"

"That's right," he said quickly, "ain't nothing you can do. Can't much help old Sonny no more, I guess."

It was what I was thinking and so it seemed to me he had no right to say it.

"I'm surprised at Sonny, though," he went on—he had a funny way of talking, he looked straight ahead as though he were talking to himself—"I thought Sonny was a smart boy, I thought he was too smart to get hung."

"I guess he thought so too," I said sharply, "and that's how he got hung. And now about you? You're pretty goddamn smart, I bet."

Then he looked directly at me, just for a minute. "I ain't smart," he said. "If I was smart, I'd have reached for a pistol a long time ago."

"Look. Don't tell *me* your sad story, if it was up to me, I'd give you one." Then I felt guilty—guilty, probably, for never having supposed that the poor bastard *had* a story of his own, much less a sad one, and I asked, quickly, "What's going to happen to him now?"

He didn't answer this. He was off by himself some place. "Funny thing," he said, and from his tone we might have been discussing the quickest way to get to Brooklyn, "when I saw the papers this morning, the first thing I asked myself was if I had anything to do with it. I felt sort of responsible."

I began to listen more carefully. The subway station was on the corner, just before us, and I stopped. He stopped, too. We were in front of a bar and he ducked slightly, peering in, but whoever he was looking for didn't seem to be there. The juke box was blasting away with something black and bouncy and I half watched the barmaid as she danced her way from the juke box to her place behind the bar. And I watched her face as she laughingly responded to something someone said to her, still keeping time to the music. When she smiled one saw the little girl, one sensed the doomed, still-struggling woman beneath the battered face of the semi-whore.

"I never *give* Sonny nothing," the boy said finally, "but a long time ago I come to school high and Sonny asked me how it felt." He paused, I couldn't bear to watch him, I watched the barmaid, and I listened to the music which seemed to be causing the pavement to shake. "I told him it felt great." The music stopped, the barmaid paused and watched the juke box until the music began again. "It did."

All this was carrying me some place I didn't want to go. I certainly didn't want to know how it felt. It filled everything, the people, the houses, the music, the dark, quick-silver barmaid, with menace; and this menace was their reality.

"What's going to happen to him now?" I asked again.

"They'll send him away some place and they'll try to cure him." He shook his head. "Maybe he'll even think he's kicked the habit. Then they'll let him loose"—he gestured, throwing his cigarette into the gutter. "That's all."

"What do you mean, that's *all*?"

But I knew what he meant.

"I *mean*, that's *all*." He turned his head and looked at me, pulling down the corners of his mouth. "Don't you know what I mean?" he asked, softly.

"How the hell *would* I know what you mean?" I almost whispered it, I don't know why.

"That's right," he said to the air, "how would *he* know what I mean?" He turned toward me again, patient and calm, and yet I somehow felt him shaking, shaking as though he were going to fall apart. I felt that ice in my guts again, the dread I'd felt all afternoon; and again I watched the barmaid, moving about the bar, washing glasses, and singing. "Listen. They'll let him out and then it'll just start all over again. That's what I mean."

"You mean—they'll let him out. And then he'll just start working his way back in again. You mean he'll never kick the habit. Is that what you mean?"

"That's right," he said, cheerfully. "*You* see what I mean."

"Tell me," I said it last, "why does he want to die? He must want to die, he's killing himself, why does he want to die?"

He looked at me in surprise. He licked his lips. "He don't want to die. He wants to live. Don't nobody want to die, ever."

Then I wanted to ask him—too many things. He could not have answered, or if he had, I could not have borne the answers. I started walking. "Well, I guess it's none of my business."

"It's going to be rough on old Sonny," he said. We reached the subway station. "This is your station?" he asked. I nodded. I took one step down. "Damn!" he said, suddenly. I looked up at him. He grinned again. "Damn it if I didn't leave all my money home. You ain't got a dollar on you, have you? Just for a couple of days, is all."

All at once something inside gave and threatened to come pouring out of me. I didn't hate him any more. I felt that in another moment I'd start crying like a child.

"Sure," I said. "Don't sweat." I looked in my wallet and didn't have a dollar, I only had a five. "Here," I said. "That hold you?"

He didn't look at it—he didn't want to look at it. A terrible, closed look came over his face, as though he were keeping the number on the bill a secret from him and me. "Thanks," he said, and now he was dying to see me go. "Don't worry about Sonny. Maybe I'll write him or something."

"Sure," I said. "You do that. So long."

"Be seeing you," he said. I went on down the steps.

And I didn't write Sonny or send him anything for a long time. When I finally did, it was just after my little girl died, he wrote me back a letter which made me feel like a bastard.

Here's what he said:

Dear brother,

You don't know how much I needed to hear from you. I wanted to write you many a time but I dug how much I must have hurt you and so I didn't write. But now I feel like a man who's been trying to climb up out of some deep, real deep and funky hole and just saw the sun up there, outside. I got to get outside.

I can't tell you much about how I got here. I mean I don't know how to tell you. I guess I was afraid of something or I was trying to escape from something and you know I have never been very strong in the head (smile). I'm glad Mama and Daddy are dead and can't see what's happened to their son and I swear if I'd known what I was doing I would never have hurt you so, you and a lot of other fine people who were nice to me and who believed in me.

I don't want you to think it had anything to do with me being a musician. It's more than that. Or maybe less than that. I can't get anything straight in my head down here and I try not to think about what's going to happen to me when I get outside again. Sometime I think I'm going to flip and *never* get outside and sometime I think I'll come straight back. I tell you one thing, though, I'd rather blow my brains out than go through this again. But that's what they all say, so they tell me. If I tell you when I'm coming to New York and if you could meet me, I sure would appreciate it. Give my love to Isabel and the kids and I was sure sorry to hear about little Gracie. I wish I could be like Mama and say the Lord's will be done, but I don't know it seems to me that trouble is the one thing that never does get stopped and I don't know what good it does to blame it on the Lord. But maybe it does some good if you believe it.

Your brother,
Sonny

Then I kept in constant touch with him and I sent him whatever I could and I went to meet him when he came back to New York. When I saw him many things I thought I had forgotten came flooding back to me. This was because I had begun, finally, to wonder about Sonny, about the life that Sonny lived inside. This life, whatever it was, had made him older and thinner and it had deepened the distant stillness in which he had always moved. He looked very unlike my baby brother. Yet, when he smiled, when we shook hands, the baby brother I'd never known looked out from the depths of his private life, like an animal waiting to be coaxed into the light.

"How you been keeping?" he asked me.

"All right. And you?"

"Just fine." He was smiling all over his face. "It's good to see you again."

"It's good to see you."

The seven years' difference in our ages lay between us like a chasm: I wondered if these years would ever operate between us as a bridge. I was remembering, and it made it hard to catch my breath, that I had been there when he was born; and I had heard the first words he had ever spoken. When he started to walk, he walked from our mother straight to me. I caught him just before he fell when he took the first steps he ever took in this world.

"How's Isabel?"

"Just fine. She's dying to see you."

"And the boys?"

"They're fine, too. They're anxious to see their uncle."

"Oh, come on. You know they don't remember me."

"Are you kidding? Of course they remember you."

He grinned again. We got into a taxi. We had a lot to say to each other, far too much to know how to begin.

As the taxi began to move, I asked, "You still want to go to India?"

He laughed. "You still remember that. Hell, no. This place is Indian enough for me."

"It used to belong to them," I said.

And he laughed again. "They damn sure knew what they were doing when they got rid of it."

Years ago, when he was around fourteen, he'd been all hipped on the idea of going to India. He read books about people sitting on rocks, naked, in all kinds of weather, but mostly bad, naturally, and walking barefoot through hot coals and arriving at wisdom. I used to say that it sounded to me as though they were getting away from wisdom as fast as they could. I think he sort of looked down on me for that.

"Do you mind," he asked, "if we have the driver drive alongside the park? On the west side—I haven't seen the city in so long."

"Of course not," I said. I was afraid that I might sound as though I were humoring him, but I hoped he wouldn't take it that way.

So we drove along, between the green of the park and the stony, lifeless elegance of hotels and apartment buildings, toward the vivid, killing streets of our childhood. These streets hadn't changed, though housing projects jutted up out of them now like rocks in the middle of a boiling sea. Most of the houses in which we had grown up had vanished, as had the stores from which we had stolen, the basements in which we had first tried sex, the rooftops from which we had hurled tin cans and bricks. But houses exactly like the houses of our past yet dominated the landscape, boys exactly like the boys we once had been found themselves smothering in these houses, came down into the streets for light and air and found themselves encircled by disaster. Some escaped the trap, most didn't. Those who got out always left something of themselves behind, as some animals amputate a leg and leave it in the trap. It might be said, perhaps, that I had escaped, after all, I was a school teacher; or that Sonny had, he hadn't lived in Harlem for years. Yet, as the cab moved uptown through streets which seemed, with a rush, to darken with dark people, and as I covertly studied Sonny's face, it came to me that what we both were seeking through our separate cab windows was that part of ourselves which had been left behind. It's always at the hour of trouble and confrontation that the missing member aches.

We hit 110th Street and started rolling up Lenox Avenue. And I'd known this avenue all my life, but it seemed to me again, as it had seemed on the day I'd first heard about Sonny's trouble, filled with a hidden menace which was its very breath of life.

"We almost there," said Sonny.

"Almost." We were both too nervous to say anything more.

We live in a housing project. It hasn't been up long. A few days after it was up it seemed uninhabitably new, now, of course, it's already rundown. It looks like a parody of the good, clean, faceless life—God knows the people who live in it do their best to make it a parody. The beat-looking grass lying around isn't enough to make their lives green, the hedges will never hold out the streets, and they know it. The big windows fool no one, they aren't big enough to make space out of no space. They don't bother with the windows, they watch the TV screen instead. The playground is most popular with the children who don't play at jacks, or skip rope, or roller skate, or swing, and they can be found in it after dark. We moved in partly because it's not too far from where I teach, and partly for the kids; but it's really just like the houses in which Sonny and I grew up. The same things happen, they'll have the same things to remember. The moment Sonny and I started into the house I had the feeling that I was simply bringing him back into the danger he had almost died trying to escape.

Sonny has never been talkative. So I don't know why I was sure he'd be dying to talk to me when supper was over the first night. Everything went fine, the oldest boy remembered him, and the youngest boy liked him, and Sonny had remembered to bring something for each of them; and Isabel, who is really much nicer than I am, more open and giving, had gone to a lot of trouble about dinner and was genuinely glad to see him. And she's always been able to tease Sonny in a way that I haven't. It was nice to see her face so vivid again and to hear her laugh and watch her make Sonny laugh. She wasn't, or, anyway, she didn't seem to be, at all uneasy or embarrassed. She chatted as though there were no subject which had to be avoided and she got Sonny past his first, faint stiffness. And thank God she was there, for I was filled with that icy dread again. Everything I did seemed awkward to me, and everything I said sounded freighted with hidden meaning. I was trying to remember everything I'd heard about dope addiction and I couldn't help watching Sonny for signs. I wasn't doing it out of malice. I was trying to find out something about my brother. I was dying to hear him tell me he was safe.

"Safe!" my father grunted, whenever Mama suggested trying to move to a neighborhood which might be safer for children. "Safe, hell! Ain't no place safe for kids, nor nobody."

He always went on like this, but he wasn't, ever, really as bad as he sounded, not even on weekends, when he got drunk. As a matter of fact, he was always on the lookout for "something a little better," but he died before he found it. He died suddenly, during a drunken weekend in the middle of the war, when Sonny was fifteen. He and Sonny hadn't ever got on too well. And this was partly because Sonny was the apple of his father's eye. It was because he loved Sonny so much and was frightened for him, that he was always fighting with him. It doesn't do any good to fight with Sonny. Sonny just moves back, inside himself, where he can't be reached. But the principal reason that they never hit it off is that they were so much alike. Daddy was big and rough and loud-talking, just the opposite of Sonny, but they both had—that same privacy.

Mama tried to tell me something about this, just after Daddy died. I was home on leave from the army.

This was the last time I ever saw my mother alive. Just the same, this picture gets all mixed up in my mind with pictures I had of her when she was younger. The way I always see her is the way she used to be on a Sunday afternoon, say, when the old folks were talking after the big Sunday dinner. I always see her wearing pale blue. She'd be sitting on the sofa. And my father would be sitting in the easy chair, not far from her. And the living room would be full of church folks and relatives. There they sit, in chairs all around the living room, and the night is creeping up outside, but nobody knows it yet. You can see the darkness growing against the windowpanes and you hear the street noises every now and again, or maybe the jangling beat of a tambourine from one of the churches close by, but it's real quiet in the room. For a moment nobody's talking, but every face looks darkening, like the sky outside. And my mother rocks a little from the waist, and my father's eyes are closed. Everyone is looking at something a child can't see. For a minute they've forgotten the children. Maybe a kid is lying on the rug, half asleep. Maybe somebody's got a kid in his lap and is absent-mindedly stroking the kid's head. Maybe there's a kid, quiet and big-eyed, curled up in a big chair in the corner. The silence, the darkness coming, and the darkness in the faces frightens the child obscurely. He hopes that the hand which strokes his forehead will never stop—will never die. He hopes that there will never come a time when the old folks won't be sitting around the living room, talking about where they've come from, and what they've seen, and what's happened to them and their kinfolk.

But something deep and watchful in the child knows that this is bound to end, is already ending. In a moment someone will get up and turn on the light. Then the old folks will remember the children and they won't talk any more that day. And when light fills the room, the child is filled with darkness. He knows that every time this happens he's moved just a little closer to that darkness outside. The darkness outside is what the old folks have been talking about. It's what they've come from. It's what they endure. The child knows that they won't talk any more because if he knows too much about what's happened to *them,* he'll know too much too soon, about what's going to happen to *him.*

The last time I talked to my mother, I remember I was restless. I wanted to get out and see Isabel. We weren't married then and we had a lot to straighten out between us.

There Mama sat, in black, by the window. She was humming an old church song, *Lord, you brought me from a long ways off.* Sonny was out somewhere. Mama kept watching the streets.

"I don't know," she said, "if I'll ever see you again, after you go off from here. But I hope you'll remember the things I tried to teach you."

"Don't talk like that," I said, and smiled. "You'll be here a long time yet."

She smiled, too, but she said nothing. She was quiet for a long time. And I said, "Mama, don't you worry about nothing. I'll be writing all the time, and you be getting the checks. . . ."

"I want to talk to you about your brother," she said, suddenly. "If anything happens to me he ain't going to have nobody to look out for him."

"Mama," I said, "ain't nothing going to happen to you *or* Sonny. Sonny's all right. He's a good boy and he's got good sense."

"It ain't a question of his being a good boy," Mama said, "nor of his having good sense. It ain't only the bad ones, nor yet the dumb ones that gets sucked under." She stopped, looking at me. "Your Daddy once had a brother," she said, and she smiled in a way that made me feel she was in pain. "You didn't never know that, did you?"

"No," I said, "I never knew that," and I watched her face.

"Oh, yes," she said, "your Daddy had a brother." She looked out of the window again. "I know you never saw your Daddy cry. But *I* did—many a time, through all these years."

I asked her, "What happened to his brother? How come nobody's ever talked about him?"

This was the first time I ever saw my mother look old.

"His brother got killed," she said, "when he was just a little younger than you are now. I knew him. He was a fine boy. He was maybe a little full of the devil, but he didn't mean nobody no harm."

Then she stopped and the room was silent, exactly as it had sometimes been on those Sunday afternoons. Mama kept looking out into the streets.

"He used to have a job in the mill," she said, "and, like all young folks, he just liked to perform on Saturday nights. Saturday nights, him and your father would drift around to different place, go to dances and things like that, or just sit around with people they knew, and your father's brother would sing, he had a fine voice, and play along with himself on his guitar. Well, this particular Saturday night, him and your father was coming home from some place, and they were both a little drunk and there was a moon that night, it was bright like day. Your father's brother was feeling kind of good, and he was whistling to himself, and he had his guitar slung over his shoulder. They was coming down a hill and beneath them was a road that turned off from the highway. Well, your father's brother, being always kind of frisky, decided to run down this hill, and he did, with that guitar banging and clanging behind him, and he ran across the road, and he was making water behind a tree. And your father was sort of amused at him and he was still coming down the hill, kind of slow. Then he heard a car motor and that same minute his brother stepped from behind the tree, into the road, in the moonlight. And he started to cross the road. And your father started to run down the hill, he says he don't know why. This car was full of white men. They was all drunk, and when they seen your father's brother they let out a great whoop and holler and they aimed the car straight at him. They was having fun, they just wanted to scare him, the way they do sometimes, you know. But they was drunk. And I guess the boy, being drunk, too, and scared, kind of lost his head. By the time he jumped it was too late. Your father says he heard his brother scream when the car rolled over him, and he heard the wood of that guitar when it give, and he heard them strings go flying, and he heard them white men shouting, and the car kept on a-going and it ain't stopped till this day. And, time your father got down the hill, his brother weren't nothing but blood and pulp."

Tears were gleaming on my mother's face. There wasn't anything I could say.

"He never mentioned it," she said, "because I never let him mention it before you children. Your Daddy was like a crazy man that night and for many a night thereafter. He says he never in his life seen anything as dark as that road after the lights of that car had gone away. Weren't nothing, weren't nobody on that road, just your Daddy and his brother and that busted guitar. Oh, yes. Your Daddy never did really get right again. Till the day he died he weren't sure but that every white man he saw was the man that killed his brother."

She stopped and took out her handkerchief and dried her eyes and looked at me.

"I ain't telling you all this," she said, "to make you scared or bitter or to make you hate nobody. I'm telling you this because you got a brother. And the world ain't changed."

I guess I didn't want to believe this. I guess she saw this in my face. She turned away from me, toward the window again, searching those streets.

"But I praise my Redeemer," she said at last, "that He called your Daddy home before me. I ain't saying it to throw no flowers at myself, but, I declare, it keeps me from feeling too cast down to know I helped your father get safely through this world. Your father always acted like he was the roughest, strongest man on earth. And everybody took him to be like that. But if he hadn't had *me* there—to see his tears!"

She was crying again. Still, I couldn't move. I said, "Lord, Lord, Mama, I didn't know it was like that."

"Oh, honey," she said, "there's a lot that you don't know. But you are going to find it out." She stood up from the window and came over to me. "You got to hold on to your brother," she said, "and don't let him fall, no matter what it looks like is happening to him and no matter how evil you gets with him. You going to be evil with him many a time. But don't you forget what I told you, you hear?"

"I won't forget," I said. "Don't you worry, I won't forget. I won't let nothing happen to Sonny."

My mother smiled as though she were amused at something she saw in my face. Then, "You may not be able to stop nothing from happening. But you got to let him know you's *there.*"

Two days later I was married, and then I was gone. And I had a lot of things on my mind and I pretty well forgot my promise to Mama until I got shipped home on a special furlough for her funeral.

And, after the funeral, with just Sonny and me alone in the empty kitchen, I tried to find out something about him.

"What do you want to do?" I asked him.

"I'm going to be a musician," he said.

For he had graduated, in the time I had been away, from dancing to the juke box to finding out who was playing what, and what they were doing with it, and he had bought himself a set of drums.

"You mean, you want to be a drummer?" I somehow had the feeling that being a drummer might be all right for other people but not for my brother Sonny.

"I don't think," he said, looking at me very gravely, "that I'll ever be a good drummer. But I think I can play a piano."

I frowned. I'd never played the role of the older brother quite so seriously before, had scarcely ever, in fact, *asked* Sonny a damn thing. I sensed myself in the presence of something I didn't really know how to handle, didn't understand. So I made my frown a little deeper as I asked: "What kind of musician do you want to be?"

He grinned. "How many kinds do you think there are?"

"Be *serious,*" I said.

He laughed, throwing his head back, and then looked at me. "I *am* serious."

"Well, then, for Christ's sake, stop kidding around and answer a serious question. I mean, do you want to be a concert pianist, you want to play classical music and all that, or—or what?" Long before I finished he was laughing again. "For Christ's *sake,* Sonny!"

He sobered, but with difficulty. "I'm sorry. But you sound so—*scared!*" and he was off again.

"Well, you may think it's funny now, baby, but it's not going to be so funny when you have to make your living at it, let me tell you *that.*" I was furious because I knew he was laughing at me and I didn't know why.

"No," he said, very sober now, and afraid, perhaps, that he'd hurt me, "I don't want to be a classical pianist. That isn't what interests me. I mean"—he paused, looking hard at me, as though his eyes would help me to understand, and then gestured helplessly, as though perhaps his hand would help—"I mean, I'll have a lot of studying to do, and I'll have to study *everything,* but, I mean, I want to play *with*—jazz musicians." He stopped. "I want to play jazz," he said.

Well, the word had never before sounded as heavy, as real, as it sounded that afternoon in Sonny's mouth. I just looked at him and I was probably frowning a real frown by this time. I simply couldn't see why on earth he'd want to spend his time hanging around nightclubs, clowning around on bandstands, while people pushed each other around a dance floor. It seemed—beneath him, somehow. I had never thought about it before, had never been forced to, but I suppose I had always put jazz musicians in a class with what Daddy called "good-time people."

"Are you *serious?*"

"Hell, *yes,* I'm serious."

He looked more helpless than ever, and annoyed, and deeply hurt.

I suggested, helpfully: "You mean—like Louis Armstrong?"

His face closed as though I'd struck him. "No. I'm not talking about none of that old-time, down home crap."

"Well, look, Sonny, I'm sorry, don't get mad. I just don't altogether get it, that's all. Name somebody—you know, a jazz musician you admire."

"Bird."

"Who?"

"Bird! Charlie Parker! Don't they teach you nothing in the goddamn army?"

I lit a cigarette. I was surprised and then a little amused to discover that I was trembling. "I've been out of touch," I said. "You'll have to be patient with me. Now. Who's this Parker character?"

"He's just one of the greatest jazz musicians alive," said Sonny, sullenly, his hands in his pockets, his back to me. "Maybe *the* greatest," he added, bitterly, "that's probably why *you* never heard of him."

"All right," I said, "I'm ignorant. I'm sorry. I'll go out and buy all the cat's records right away, all right?"

"It don't," said Sonny, with dignity, "make any difference to me. I don't care what you listen to. Don't do me no favors."

I was beginning to realize that I'd never seen him so upset before. With another part of my mind I was thinking that this would probably turn out to be one of those things kids go through and that I shouldn't make it seem important by pushing it too hard. Still, I didn't think it would do any harm to ask: "Doesn't all this take a lot of time? Can you make a living at it?"

He turned back to me and half leaned, half sat, on the kitchen table. "Everything takes time," he said, "and—well, yes, sure, I can make a living at it. But what I don't seem to be able to make you understand is that it's the only thing I want to do."

"Well, Sonny," I said, gently, "you know people can't always do exactly what they *want* to do—"

"*No,* I don't know that," said Sonny, surprising me. "I think people *ought* to do what they want to do, what else are they alive for?"

"You getting to be a big boy," I said desperately, "it's time you started thinking about your future."

"I'm thinking about my future," said Sonny, grimly. "I think about it all the time."

I gave up. I decided, if he didn't change his mind, that we could always talk about it later. "In the meantime," I said, "you got to finish school." We had already decided that he'd have to move in with Isabel and her folks. I knew this wasn't the ideal arrangement because Isabel's folks are inclined to be dicty[1] and they hadn't especially wanted Isabel to marry me. But I didn't know what else to do. "And we have to get you fixed up at Isabel's."

There was a long silence. He moved from the kitchen table to the window. "That's a terrible idea. You know it yourself."

---

[1] Snobbish or bossy.

"Do you have a *better* idea?"

He just walked up and down the kitchen for a minute. He was as tall as I was. He had started to shave. I suddenly had the feeling that I didn't know him at all.

He stopped at the kitchen table and picked up my cigarettes. Looking at me with a kind of mocking, amused defiance, he put one between his lips. "You mind?"

"You smoking already?"

He lit the cigarette and nodded, watching me through the smoke. "I just wanted to see if I'd have the courage to smoke in front of you." He grinned and blew a great cloud of smoke to the ceiling. "It was easy." He looked at my face. "Come on, now. I bet you was smoking at my age, tell the truth."

I didn't say anything but the truth was on my face, and he laughed. But now there was something very strained in his laugh. "Sure. And I bet that ain't all you was doing."

He was frightening me a little. "Cut the crap," I said. "We already decided that you was going to go and live at Isabel's. Now what's got into you all of a sudden?"

"*You* decided it," he pointed out. "*I* didn't decide nothing." He stopped in front of me, leaning against the stove, arms loosely folded. "Look, brother. I don't want to stay in Harlem no more, I really don't." He was very earnest. He looked at me, then over toward the kitchen window. There was something in his eyes I'd never seen before, some thoughtfulness, some worry all his own. He rubbed the muscle of one arm. "It's time I was getting out of here."

"Where do you want to *go*, Sonny?"

"I want to join the army. Or the navy, I don't care. If I say I'm old enough, they'll believe me."

Then I got mad. It was because I was so scared. "You must be crazy. You goddamn fool, what the hell do you want to go and join the *army* for?"

"I just told you. To get out of Harlem."

"Sonny, you haven't even finished *school*. And if you really want to be a musician, how do you expect to study if you're in the *army*?"

He looked at me, trapped, and in anguish. "There's ways. I might be able to work out some kind of deal. Anyway, I'll have the G.I. Bill when I come out."

"*If* you come out." We stared at each other. "Sonny, please. Be reasonable. I know the setup is far from perfect. But we got to do the best we can."

"I ain't learning nothing in school," he said. "Even when I go." He turned away from me and opened the window and threw his cigarette out into the narrow alley. I watched his back. "At least, I ain't learning nothing you'd want me to learn." He slammed the window so hard I thought the glass would fly out, and turned back to me. "And I'm sick of the stink of these garbage cans!"

"Sonny," I said, "I know how you feel. But if you don't finish school now, you're going to be sorry later that you didn't." I grabbed him by the shoulders. "And you only got another year. It ain't so bad. And I'll come back and I swear I'll help you do *whatever* you want to do. Just try to put up with it till I come back. Will you please do that? For me?"

He didn't answer and he wouldn't look at me.

"Sonny. You hear me?"

He pulled away. "I hear you. But you never hear anything *I* say."

I didn't know what to say to that. He looked out of the window and then back at me. "OK," he said, and sighed. "I'll try."

Then I said, trying to cheer him up a little, "They got a piano at Isabel's. You can practice on it."

And as a matter of fact, it did cheer him up for a minute. "That's right," he said to himself. "I forgot that." His face relaxed a little. But the worry, the thoughtfulness, played on it still, the way shadows play on a face which is staring into the fire.

But I thought I'd never hear the end of that piano. At first, Isabel would write me, saying how nice it was that Sonny was so serious about his music and how, as soon as he came in from school, or wherever he had been when he was supposed to be at school, he went straight to that piano and stayed there until suppertime. And, after supper, he went back to that piano and stayed there until everybody went to bed. He was at the piano all day Saturday and all day Sunday. Then he bought a record player and started playing records. He'd play one record over and over again, all day long sometimes, and he'd improvise along with it on the piano. Or he'd play one section of the record, one chord, one change, one progression, then he'd do it on the piano. Then back to the record. Then back to the piano.

Well, I really don't know how they stood it. Isabel finally confessed that it wasn't like living with a person at all, it was like living with sound. And the sound didn't make any sense to her, didn't make any sense to any of them—naturally. They began, in a way, to be afflicted by this presence that was living in their home. It was as though Sonny were some sort of god, or monster. He moved in an atmosphere which wasn't like theirs at all. They fed him and he ate, he washed himself, he walked in and out of their door; he certainly wasn't nasty or unpleasant or rude, Sonny isn't any of those things; but it was as though he were all wrapped up in some cloud, some fire, some vision all his own; and there wasn't any way to reach him.

At the same time, he wasn't really a man yet, he was still a child, and they had to watch out for him in all kinds of ways. They certainly couldn't throw him out. Neither did they dare to make a great scene about that piano because even they dimly sensed, as I sensed, from so many thousands of miles away, that Sonny was at that piano playing for his life.

But he hadn't been going to school. One day a letter came from the school board and Isabel's mother got it—there had, apparently, been other letters but Sonny had torn them up. This day, when Sonny came in, Isabel's mother showed him the letter and asked where he'd been spending his time. And she finally got it out of him that he'd been down in Greenwich Village, with musicians and other characters, in a white girl's apartment. And this scared her and she started to scream at him and what came up, once she began—though she denies it to this day—was what sacrifices they were making to give Sonny a decent home and how little he appreciated it.

Sonny didn't play the piano that day. By evening, Isabel's mother had calmed down but then there was the old man to deal with, and Isabel herself. Isabel says she did her best to be calm but she broke down and started crying. She says she just watched Sonny's face. She could tell, by watching him, what was happening with him. And what was happening was that they penetrated his cloud, they had reached him. Even if their fingers had been a thousand times more gentle than human fingers ever are, he could hardly help feeling that they had stripped him naked and were spitting on that nakedness. For he also had to see that his presence, that music, which was life or death to him, had been torture for them and that they had endured it, not at all for his sake, but only for mine. And Sonny couldn't take that. He can take it a little better today than he could then but he's still not very good at it and, frankly, I don't know anybody who is.

The silence of the next few days must have been louder than the sound of all the music ever played since time began. One morning, before she went to work, Isabel was in his room for something and she suddenly realized that all of his records were gone. And she knew for certain that he was gone. And he was. He went as far as the navy would carry him. He finally sent me a postcard from some place in Greece and that was the first I knew that Sonny was still alive. I didn't see him any more until we were both back in New York and the war had long been over.

He was a man by then, of course, but I wasn't willing to see it. He came by the house from time to time, but we fought almost every time we met. I didn't like the way he carried himself, loose and dreamlike all the time, and I didn't like his friends, and his music seemed to be merely an excuse for the life he led. It sounded just that weird and disordered.

Then we had a fight, a pretty awful fight, and I didn't see him for months. By and by I looked him up, where he was living, in a furnished room in the Village, and I tried to make it up. But there were lots of other people in the room and Sonny just lay on his bed, and he wouldn't come downstairs with me, and he treated these other people as though they were his family and I weren't. So I got mad and then he got mad, and then I told him that he might just as well be dead as live the way he was living. Then he stood up and he told me not to worry about him any more in life, that he *was* dead as far as I was concerned. Then he pushed me to the door and the other people looked on as though nothing were happening, and he slammed the door behind me. I stood in the hallway, staring at the door. I heard somebody laugh in the room and then the tears came to my eyes. I started down the steps, whistling to keep from crying, I kept whistling to myself, *You going to need me, baby, one of these cold, rainy days.*

I read about Sonny's trouble in the spring. Little Grace died in the fall. She was a beautiful little girl. But she only lived a little over two years. She died of polio and she suffered. She had a slight fever for a couple of days, but it didn't seem like anything and we just kept her in bed. And we would certainly have called the doctor, but the fever dropped, she seemed to be all right. So we thought it had just been a cold. Then, one day, she was up, playing, Isabel was in the kitchen fixing lunch for the two boys when they'd come in from school, and she heard Grace fall down in the living room. When you have a lot of children you don't always start running when one of them falls, unless they start screaming or something. And, this time, Grace was quiet. Yet, Isabel says that when she heard that *thump* and then that silence, something happened in her to make her afraid. And she ran to the living room and there was little Grace on the floor, all twisted up, and the reason she hadn't screamed was that she couldn't get her breath. And when she did scream, it was the worst sound, Isabel says, that she'd ever heard in all her life, and she still hears it sometimes in her dreams. Isabel will sometimes wake me up with a low, moaning, strangled sound and I have to be quick to awaken her and hold her to me and where Isabel is weeping against me seems a mortal wound.

I think I may have written Sonny the very day that little Grace was buried. I was sitting in the living room in the dark, by myself, and I suddenly thought of Sonny. My trouble made his real.

One Saturday afternoon, when Sonny had been living with us, or, anyway, been in our house, for nearly two weeks, I found myself wandering aimlessly about the living room, drinking from a can of beer, and trying to work up the courage to search Sonny's room. He was out, he was usually out whenever I was home, and Isabel had taken the children to see their grandparents. Suddenly I was standing still in front of the living room window, watching Seventh Avenue. The idea of searching Sonny's room made me still. I scarcely dared to admit to myself what I'd be searching for. I didn't know what I'd do if I found it. Or if I didn't.

On the sidewalk across from me, near the entrance to a barbecue joint, some people were holding an old-fashioned revival meeting. The barbecue cook, wearing a dirty white apron, his conked hair[2] reddish and metallic in the pale sun, and a cigarette between his lips, stood in the doorway, watching them. Kids and older people paused in their errands and stood there, along with some older men and a couple of very tough-looking women who watched everything that happened on the avenue, as though they owned it, or were maybe owned by it. Well, they were watching this, too. The revival was being carried on by three sisters in black, and a brother. All they had were their voices and their Bibles and a tambourine. The brother was testifying and while he testified two of the sisters stood together, seeming to say, amen, and the third sister walked around with the tambourine outstretched and a couple of people dropped coins into it. Then the brother's testimony ended and the sister who had been taking up the collection dumped the coins into her palm and transferred them to the pocket of her long black robe. Then she raised both hands, striking the tambourine against the air, and then against one hand, and she started to sing. And the two other sisters and the brother joined in.

It was strange, suddenly, to watch, though I had been seeing these street meetings all my life. So, of course, had everybody else down there. Yet, they paused and watched and listened and I stood still at the window. *"Tis the old ship of Zion,"* they sang, and the sister with the tambourine kept a steady, jangling beat, *"it has rescued many a thousand!"* Not a soul under the sound of their voices was hearing this song for the first time, not one of them had been rescued. Nor had they seen much in the way of rescue work being done around them. Neither did they especially believe in the holiness of the three sisters and the brother, they knew too much about them, knew where they lived, and how. The woman with the tambourine, whose voice dominated the air, whose face was bright with joy, was divided by very little from the woman who stood watching her, a cigarette between her heavy, chapped lips, her hair a cuckoo's nest, her face scarred and swollen from many beatings, and her black eyes glittering like coal. Perhaps they both knew this, which was why, when, as rarely, they addressed each other, they addressed each other as Sister. As the singing filled the air the watching, listening faces underwent a change, the eyes focusing on something within; the music seemed to soothe a poison out of them; and time seemed, nearly, to fall away from the sullen, belligerent, battered faces, as though they were fleeing back to their first condition, while dreaming of their last. The barbecue cook half shook his head and smiled, and dropped his cigarette and disappeared into his joint. A man fumbled in his pockets for change and stood holding it in his hand impatiently, as though he had just remembered a pressing appointment further up the avenue. He looked furious. Then I saw Sonny, standing on the edge of

[2] Hair that has been straightened and coated heavily with grease.

the crowd. He was carrying a wide, flat notebook with a green cover, and it made him look, from where I was standing, almost like a schoolboy. The coppery sun brought out the copper in his skin, he was very faintly smiling, standing very still. Then the singing stopped, the tambourine turned into a collection plate again. The furious man dropped in his coins and vanished, so did a couple of the women, and Sonny dropped some change in the plate, looking directly at the woman with a little smile. He started across the avenue, toward the house. He has a slow, loping walk, something like the way Harlem hipsters walk, only he's imposed on this his own half-beat. I had never really noticed it before.

I stayed at the window, both relieved and apprehensive. As Sonny disappeared from my sight, they began singing again. And they were still singing when his key turned in the lock.

"Hey," he said.

"Hey, yourself. You want some beer?"

"No. Well, maybe." But he came up to the window and stood beside me, looking out. "What a warm voice," he said.

They were singing *If I could only hear my mother pray again!*

"Yes," I said, "and she can sure beat that tambourine."

"But what a terrible song," he said, and laughed. He dropped his notebook on the sofa and disappeared into the kitchen. "Where's Isabel and the kids?"

"I think they went to see their grandparents. You hungry?"

"No." He came back into the living room with his can of beer. "You want to come some place with me tonight?"

I sensed, I don't know how, that I couldn't possibly say no. "Sure. Where?"

He sat down on the sofa and picked up his notebook and started leafing through it. "I'm going to sit in with some fellows in a joint in the Village."

"You mean, you're going to play, tonight?"

"That's right." He took a swallow of his beer and moved back to the window. He gave me a sidelong look. "If you can stand it."

"I'll try," I said.

He smiled to himself and we both watched as the meeting across the way broke up. The three sisters and the brother, heads bowed, were singing *God be with you till we meet again.* The faces around them were very quiet. Then the song ended. The small crowd dispersed. We watched the three women and the lone man walk slowly up the avenue.

"When she was singing before," said Sonny, abruptly, "her voice reminded me for a minute of what heroin feels like sometimes—when it's in your veins. It makes you feel sort of warm and cool at the same time. And distant. And—and sure." He sipped his beer, very deliberately not looking at me. I watched his face. "It makes you feel—in control. Sometimes you've got to have that feeling."

"Do you?" I sat down slowly in the easy chair.

"Sometimes." He went to the sofa and picked up his notebook again. "Some people do."

"In order," I asked, "to play?" And my voice was very ugly, full of contempt and anger.

"Well"—he looked at me with great, troubled eyes, as though, in fact, he hoped his eyes would tell me things he could never otherwise say—"they *think* so. And *if* they think so—!"

"And what do *you* think?" I asked.

He sat on the sofa and put his can of beer on the floor. "I don't know," he said, and I couldn't be sure if he were answering my question or pursuing his thoughts. His face didn't tell me. "It's not so much to *play*. It's to *stand* it, to be able to make it at all. On any level." He frowned and smiled: "In order to keep from shaking to pieces."

"But these friends of yours," I said, "they seem to shake themselves to pieces pretty goddamn fast."

"Maybe." He played with the notebook. And something told me that I should curb my tongue, that Sonny was doing his best to talk, that I should listen. "But of course you only know the ones that've gone to pieces. Some don't—or at least they haven't *yet* and that's just about all *any* of us can say." He paused. "And then there are some who just live, really, in hell, and they know it and they see what's happening and they go right on. I don't know." He sighed, dropped the notebook, folded his arms. "Some guys, you can tell from the way they play, they on something *all* the time. And you can see that, well, it makes something real for them. But of course," he picked up his beer from the floor and sipped it and put the can down again, "they *want* to, too, you've got to see that. Even some of them that say they don't—*some,* not all."

"And what about you?" I asked—I couldn't help it. "What about you? Do *you* want to?"

He stood up and walked to the window and remained silent for a long time. Then he sighed. "Me," he said. Then: "While I was downstairs before, on my way here, listening to that woman sing, it struck me all of a sudden how much suffering she must have had to go through—to sing like that. It's *repulsive* to think you have to suffer that much."

I said: "But there's no way not to suffer—is there, Sonny?"

"I believe not," he said and smiled, "but that's never stopped anyone from trying." He looked at me. "Has it?" I realized, with this mocking look, that there stood between us, forever, beyond the power of time or forgiveness, the fact that I had held silence—so long!—when he had needed human speech to help him. He turned back to the window. "No, there's no way not to suffer. But you try all kinds of ways to keep from drowning in it, to keep on top of it, and to make it seem—well, like *you.* Like you did something, all right, and now you're suffering for it. You know?" I said nothing. "Well you know," he said, impatiently, "why *do* people suffer? Maybe it's better to do something to give it a reason, *any* reason."

"But we just agreed," I said, "that there's no way not to suffer. Isn't it better, then, just to—take it?"

"But nobody just takes it," Sonny cried, "that's what I'm telling you! *Everybody* tries not to. You're just hung up on the *way* some people try—it's not *your* way!"

The hair on my face began to itch, my face felt wet. "That's not true," I said, "that's not true. I don't give a damn what other people do, I don't even care how they suffer. I just care how *you* suffer." And he looked at me. "Please believe me," I said, "I don't want to see you—die—trying not to suffer."

"I won't," he said, flatly, "die trying not to suffer. At least, not any faster than anybody else."

"But there's no need," I said, trying to laugh, "is there? in killing yourself."

I wanted to say more, but I couldn't. I wanted to talk about will power and how life could be—well, beautiful. I wanted to say that it was all within; but was it? or, rather, wasn't that exactly the trouble? And I wanted to promise that I would never fail him again. But it would all have sounded—empty words and lies.

So I made the promise to myself and prayed that I would keep it.

"It's terrible sometimes, inside," he said, "that's what's the trouble. You walk these streets, black and funky and cold, and there's not really a living ass to talk to, and there's nothing shaking, and there's no way of getting it out—that storm inside. You can't talk it and you can't make love with it, and when you finally try to get with it and play it, you realize *nobody's* listening. So *you've* got to listen. You got to find a way to listen."

And then he walked away from the window and sat on the sofa again, as though all the wind had suddenly been knocked out of him. "Sometimes you'll do *anything* to play, even cut your mother's throat." He laughed and looked at me. "Or your brother's." Then he sobered. "Or your own." Then: "Don't worry. I'm all right now and I think I'll *be* all right. But I can't forget—where I've been. I don't mean just the physical place I've been, I mean where I've *been*. And *what* I've been."

"What have you been, Sonny?" I asked.

He smiled—but sat sideways on the sofa, his elbow resting on the back, his fingers playing with his mouth and chin, not looking at me. "I've been something I didn't recognize, didn't know I could be. Didn't know anybody could be." He stopped, looking inward, looking helplessly young, looking old. "I'm not talking about it now because I feel *guilty* or anything like that—maybe it would be better if I did, I don't know. Anyway, I can't really talk about it. Not to you, not to anybody," and now he turned and faced me. "Sometimes, you know, and it was actually when I was most *out* of the world, I felt that I was in it, that I was *with* it, really, and I could play or I didn't really have to *play*, it just came out of me, it was there. And I don't know how I played, thinking about it now, but I know I did awful things, those times, sometimes, to people. Or it wasn't that I *did* anything to them—it was that they weren't real." He picked up the beer can; it was empty; he rolled it between his palms: "And other times—well, I needed a fix, I needed to find a place to lean, I needed to clear a space to *listen*—and I couldn't find it, and I—went crazy, I did terrible things to *me*, I was terrible *for* me." He began pressing the beer can between his hands, I watched the metal begin to give. It glittered, as he played with it, like a knife, and I was afraid he would cut himself, but I said nothing. "Oh well. I can never tell you. I was all by myself at the bottom of something, stinking and sweating and crying and shaking, and I smelled it, you know? *my* stink, and I thought I'd die if I couldn't get away from it and yet, all the same, I knew that everything I was doing was just locking me in with it. And I didn't know," he paused, still flattening the beer can, "I didn't know, I still *don't* know, something kept telling me that maybe it was good to smell your own stink, but I didn't think that *that* was what I'd been trying to do—and—who can stand it?" and he abruptly dropped the ruined beer can, looking at me with a small, still smile, and then rose, walking to the window as though it were the lodestone rock. I watched his face, he watched the avenue, "I couldn't tell you when Mama died—but the reason I wanted to leave Harlem so bad was to get away from drugs. And then, when I ran away, that's what I was running from—really. When I came back, nothing had changed, *I* hadn't changed, I was just—older." And he stopped, drumming with his fingers on the windowpane. The sun had vanished, soon darkness would fall. I watched his face. "It can come again," he said, almost as though speaking to himself. Then he turned to me. "It can come again," he repeated. "I just want you to know that."

"All right," I said, at last. "So it can come again. All right."

He smiled, but the smile was sorrowful. "I had to try to tell you," he said.

"Yes," I said. "I understand that."

"You're my brother," he said, looking straight at me, and not smiling at all.

"Yes," I repeated, "yes. I understand that."

He turned back to the window, looking out. "All that hatred down there," he said, "all that hatred and misery and love. It's a wonder it doesn't blow the avenue apart."

We went to the only nightclub on a short, dark street, downtown. We squeezed through the narrow, chattering, jam-packed bar to the entrance of the big room, where the bandstand was. And we stood there for a moment, for the lights were very dim in this room and we couldn't see. Then, "Hello, boy," said a voice and an enormous black man, much older than Sonny or myself, erupted out of all that atmospheric lighting and put an arm around Sonny's shoulder. "I been sitting right here," he said, "waiting for you."

He had a big voice, too, and heads in the darkness turned toward us.

Sonny grinned and pulled a little away, and said, "Creole, this is my brother. I told you about him."

Creole shook my hand. "I'm glad to meet you, son," he said, and it was clear that he was glad to meet me *there,* for Sonny's sake. And he smiled, "You got a real musician in *your* family," and he took his arm from Sonny's shoulder and slapped him, lightly, affectionately, with the back of his hand.

"Well. Now I've heard it all," said a voice behind us. This was another musician, and a friend of Sonny's, a coal-black, cheerful-looking man, built close to the ground. He immediately began confiding to me, at the top of his lungs, the most terrible things about Sonny, his teeth gleaming like a lighthouse and his laugh coming up out of him like the beginning of an earthquake. And it turned out that everyone at the bar knew Sonny, or almost everyone; some were musicians, working there, or nearby, or not working, some were simply hangers-on, and some were there to hear Sonny play. I was introduced to all of them and they were all very polite to me. Yet, it was clear that, for them, I was only Sonny's brother. Here, I was in Sonny's world. Or, rather: his kingdom. Here, it was not even a question that his veins bore royal blood.

They were going to play soon and Creole installed me, by myself, at a table in a dark corner. Then I watched them, Creole, and the little black man, and Sonny, and the others, while they horsed around, standing just below the bandstand. The light from the bandstand spilled just a little short of them and, watching them laughing and gesturing and moving about, I had the feeling that they, nevertheless, were being most careful not to step into that circle of light too suddenly: that if they moved into the light too suddenly, without thinking, they would perish in flame. Then, while I watched, one of them, the small, black man, moved into the light and crossed the bandstand and started fooling around with his drums. Then—being funny and being, also, extremely ceremonious—Creole took Sonny by the arm and led him to the piano. A woman's voice called Sonny's name and a few hands started clapping. And Sonny, also being funny and being ceremonious, and so touched, I think, that he could have cried, but neither hiding it nor showing it, riding it like a man, grinned, and put both hands to his heart and bowed from the waist.

Creole then went to the bass fiddle and a lean, very bright-skinned brown man jumped up on the bandstand and picked up his horn. So there they were, and the atmosphere on the bandstand and in the room began to change and tighten. Someone stepped up to the microphone and announced them. Then there were all kinds of murmurs. Some people at the bar shushed others. The waitress ran around, frantically getting in the last orders, guys and chicks got closer to each other, and the lights on the bandstand, on the quartet, turned to a kind of indigo. Then they all looked different there. Creole looked about him for the last time, as though he were making certain that all his chickens were in the coop, and then he—jumped and struck the fiddle. And there they were.

All I know about music is that not many people ever really hear it. And even then, on the rare occasions when something opens within, and the music enters, what we mainly hear, or hear corroborated, are personal, private, vanishing evocations. But the man who creates the music is hearing something else, is dealing with the roar rising from the void and imposing order on it as it hits the air. What is evoked in him, then, is of another order, more terrible because it has no words, and triumphant, too, for that same reason. And his triumph, when he triumphs, is ours. I just watched Sonny's face. His face was troubled, he was working hard, but he wasn't with it. And I had the feeling that, in a way, everyone on the bandstand was waiting for him, both waiting for him and pushing him along. But as I began to watch Creole, I realized that it was Creole who held them all back. He had them on a short rein. Up there, keeping the beat with his whole body, wailing on the fiddle, with his eyes half closed, he was listening to everything, but he was listening to Sonny. He was having a dialogue with Sonny. He wanted Sonny to leave the shoreline and strike out for the deep water. He was Sonny's witness that deep water and drowning were not the same thing—he had been there, and he knew. And he wanted Sonny to know. He was waiting for Sonny to do the things on the keys which would let Creole know that Sonny was in the water.

And, while Creole listened, Sonny moved, deep within, exactly like someone in torment. I had never before thought of how awful the relationship must be between the musician and his instrument. He has to fill it, this instrument, with the breath of life, his own. He has to make it do what he wants it to do. And a piano is just a piano. It's made out of so much wood and wires and little hammers and big ones, and ivory. While there's only so much you can do with it, the only way to find this out is to try; to try and make it do everything.

And Sonny hadn't been near a piano for over a year. And he wasn't on much better terms with his life, not the life that stretched before him now. He and the piano stammered, started one way, got scared, stopped; started another way, panicked, marked time, started again; then seemed to have found a direction, panicked again, got stuck. And the face I saw on Sonny I'd never seen before. Everything had been burned out of it, and, at the same time, things usually hidden were being burned in, by the fire and fury of the battle which was occurring in him up there.

Yet, watching Creole's face as they neared the end of the first set, I had the feeling that something had happened, something I hadn't heard. Then they finished, there was scattered applause, and then, without an instant's warning, Creole started into something else, it was almost sardonic, it was *Am I Blue.* And, as though he commanded, Sonny began to play. Something began to happen. And Creole let out the reins. The dry, low, black man said something awful on the drums, Creole answered, and the drums talked back. Then the horn insisted, sweet and high, slightly detached perhaps, and Creole listened, commenting now and then, dry, and driving, beautiful and calm and old.

Then they all came together again, and Sonny was part of the family again. I could tell this from his face. He seemed to have found, right there beneath his fingers, a damn brand-new piano. It seemed that he couldn't get over it. Then, for awhile, just being happy with Sonny, they seemed to be agreeing with him that brand-new pianos certainly were a gas.

Then Creole stepped forward to remind them that what they were playing was the blues. He hit something in all of them, he hit something in me, myself, and the music tightened and deepened, apprehension began to beat the air. Creole began to tell us what the blues were all about. They were not about anything very new. He and his boys up there were keeping it new, at the risk of ruin, destruction, madness, and death, in order to find new ways to make us listen. For, while the tale of how we suffer, and how we are delighted, and how we may triumph is never new, it always must be heard. There isn't any other tale to tell, it's the only light we've got in all this darkness.

And this tale, according to that face, that body, those strong hands on those strings, has another aspect in every country, and a new depth in every generation. Listen, Creole seemed to be saying, listen. Now these are Sonny's blues. He made the little black man on the drums know it, and the bright, brown man on the horn. Creole wasn't trying any longer to get Sonny in the water. He was wishing him Godspeed. Then he stepped back, very slowly, filling the air with the immense suggestion that Sonny speak for himself.

Then they all gathered around Sonny and Sonny played. Every now and again one of them seemed to say, amen. Sonny's fingers filled the air with life, his life. But that life contained so many others. And Sonny went all the way back, he really began with the spare, flat statement of the opening phrase of the song. Then he began to make it his. It was very beautiful because it wasn't hurried and it was no longer a lament. I seemed to hear with what burning he had made it his, with what burning we had yet to make it ours, how we could cease lamenting. Freedom lurked around us and I understood, at last, that he could help us to be free if we would listen, that he would never be free until we did. Yet, there was no battle in his face now. I heard what he had gone through, and would continue to go through until he came to rest in earth. He had made it his: that long line, of which we knew only Mama and Daddy. And he was giving it back, as everything must be given back, so that, passing through death, it can live forever. I saw my mother's face again, and felt, for the first time, how the stones of the road she had walked on must have bruised her feet. I saw the moonlit road where my father's brother died. And it brought something else back to me, and carried me past it, I saw my little girl again and felt Isabel's tears again, and I felt my own tears begin to rise. And I was yet aware that this was only a moment, that the world waited outside, as hungry as a tiger, and that trouble stretched above us, longer than the sky.

Then it was over. Creole and Sonny let out their breath, both soaking wet, and grinning. There was a lot of applause and some of it was real. In the dark, the girl came by and I asked her to take drinks to the bandstand. There was a long pause, while they talked up there in the indigo light and after awhile I saw the girl put a Scotch and milk on top of the piano for Sonny. He didn't seem to notice it, but just before they started playing again, he sipped from it and looked toward me, and nodded. Then he put it back on top of the piano. For me, then, as they began to play again, it glowed and shook above my brother's head like the very cup of trembling.

1957

Letter to My Nephew on the One-Hundredth Anniversary of the Emancipation

Dear James:

I have begun this letter five times and torn it up five times. I keep seeing your face, which is also the face of your father and my brother. Like him, you are tough, dark, vulnerable, moody—with a very definitive tendency to sound truculent because you want no one to think you are soft. You may be like your grandfather in this, I don't know, but certainly both you and your father resemble him very much physically. Well, he is dead, he never saw you, and he had a terrible life; he was defeated long before he died because, at the bottom of his heart, he really believed what white people said about him. This is one of the reasons that he became so holy. I am sure that your father has told you something about all that. Neither you nor your father exhibit any tendency towards holiness: you really *are* of another era, part of what happened when the Negro left the land and came into what the late E. Franklin Frazier called "the cities of destruction." You can only be destroyed by believing that you really are what the white world calls a *nigger.* I tell you this because I love you, and please don't you ever forget it.

I have known both of you all your lives, have carried your Daddy in my arms and on my shoulders, kissed and spanked him and watched him learn to walk. I don't know if you've known anybody from that far back; if you've loved anybody that long, first as an infant, then as a child, then as a man, you gain a strange perspective on time and human pain and effort. Other people cannot see what I see whenever I look into your father's face, for behind your father's face as it is today are all those other faces which were his. Let him laugh and I see a cellar your father does not remember and a house he does not remember and I hear in his present laughter his laughter as a child. Let him curse and I remember him falling down the cellar steps, and howling, and I remember, with pain, his tears, which my hand or your grandmother's so easily wiped away. But no one's hand can wipe away those tears he sheds invisibly today, which one hears in his laughter and in his speech and in his songs. I know what the world has done to my brother and how narrowly he has survived it. And I know, which is much worse, and this is the crime of which I accuse my country and my countrymen, and for which neither I nor time nor history will ever forgive them, that they have destroyed and are destroying hundreds of thousands of lives and do not know it and do not want to know it. One can be, indeed one must strive to become, tough and philosophical concerning destruction and death, for this is what most of mankind has been best at since we have heard of man. (But remember: *most* of mankind is not *all* of mankind.) But it is not permissible that the authors of devastation should also be innocent. It is the innocence which constitutes the crime.

Now, my dear namesake, these innocent and well-meaning people, your countrymen, have caused you to be born under conditions not very far removed from those described for us by Charles Dickens in the London of more than a hundred years ago. (I hear the chorus of the innocents screaming, "No! This is not true! How *bitter* you are!"—but I am writing this letter to *you,* to try to tell you something about how to handle *them,* for most of them do not yet really know that you exist. I *know* the conditions under which you were born, for I was there. Your countrymen were *not* there, and haven't made it yet. Your grandmother was also there, and no one has ever accused her of being bitter. I suggest that the innocents check with her. She isn't hard to find. Your countrymen don't know that *she* exists, either, though she has been working for them all their lives.)

Well, you were born, here you came, something like fifteen years ago; and though your father and mother and grandmother, looking about the streets through which they were carrying you, staring at the walls into which they brought you, had every reason to be heavyhearted, yet they were not. For here you were, Big James, named for me—you were a big baby, I was not—here you were: to be loved. To be loved, baby, hard, at once, and forever, to strengthen you against the loveless world. Remember that: I know how black it looks today, for you. It looked bad that day, too, yes, we were trembling. We have not stopped trembling yet, but if we had not loved each other none of us would have survived. And now you must survive because we love you, and for the sake of your children and your children's children.

This innocent country set you down in a ghetto in which, in fact, it intended that you should perish. Let me spell out precisely what I mean by that, for the heart of the matter is here, and the root of my dispute with my country. You were born where you were born and faced the future that you faced because you were black and *for no other reason.* The limits of your ambition were, thus, expected to be set forever. You were born into a society which spelled out with brutal clarity, and in as many ways as possible, that you were a worthless human being. You were not expected to aspire to excellence: you were expected to make peace with mediocrity. Wherever you have turned, James, in your short time on this earth, you have been told where you could go and what you could do (and *how* you could do it) and where you could live and whom you could marry. I know your countrymen do not agree with me about this, and I hear them saying, "You exaggerate." They do not know Harlem, and I do. So do you. Take no one's word for anything, including mine—but trust your experience. Know whence you came. If you know whence you came, there is really no limit to where you can go. The details and symbols of your life have been deliberately constructed to make you believe what white people say about you. Please try to remember that what they believe, as well as what they do and cause you to endure, does not testify to your inferiority but to their inhumanity and fear. Please try to be clear, dear James, through the storm which rages about your youthful head today, about the reality which lies behind the words *acceptance* and *integration.* There is no reason for you to try to become like white people and there is no basis whatever for their impertinent assumption that *they* must accept *you.* The really terrible thing, old buddy, is that *you* must accept *them.* And I mean that very seriously. You must accept them and accept them with love. For these innocent people have no other hope. They are, in effect, still trapped in a history which they do not understand; and until they understand it, they cannot be released from it. They have had to believe for many years, and for innumerable reasons, that black men are inferior to white men. Many of them, indeed, know better, but as you will discover, people find it very difficult to act on what they know. To act is to be committed, and to be committed is to be in danger. In this case, the danger, in the minds of most white Americans, is the loss of their identity. Try to imagine how you would feel if you woke up one morning to find the sun shining and all the stars aflame. You would be frightened because it is out of the order of nature. Any upheaval in the universe is terrifying because it so profoundly attacks one's sense of one's own reality. Well, the black man has functioned in the white man's world as a fixed star, as an immovable pillar: and as he moves out of his place, heaven and earth are shaken to their foundations. You, don't be afraid. I said that it was intended that you should perish in the ghetto, perish by never being allowed to go behind the white man's definition, by never being allowed to spell your proper name. You have, and many of us have, defeated this intention; and, by a terrible law, a terrible paradox, those innocents who believed that your imprisonment made them safe are losing their grasp of reality. But these men are your brothers—your lost, younger brothers. And if the word *integration* means anything, this is what it means: that we, with love, shall force our brothers to see themselves as they are, to cease fleeing from reality and begin to change it. For this is your home, my friend, do not be driven from it; great men have done great things here, and will again, and we can make America what America must become. It will be hard, James, but you come from sturdy, peasant stock, men who picked cotton and dammed rivers and built railroads, and, in the teeth of the most terrifying odds, achieved an unassailable and monumental dignity. You come from a long line of great poets, some of the greatest poets since Homer. One of them said, *The very time I thought I was lost, My dungeon shook and my chains fell off.*

You know, and I know, that the country is celebrating one hundred years of freedom one hundred years too soon. We cannot be free until they are free. God bless you, James and Godspeed.

Your uncle,
James

1962

Flannery O'Connor
1925–1964

"Fiction," Flannery O'Connor wrote, "can transcend its limitations only by staying within them." That paradox informed her entire career as well. She was a determined regionalist whose work never lapses into a comfortable provinciality, a devout Catholic who found her themes and characters in the "Christ-haunted" southern Protestant Bible belt, and, for much of her adult life, a confined invalid who could be as resistant to sentimentality and what she called "hazy compassion" as the most hard-boiled detective novelist. Like such earlier southern regionalists as George Washington Harris, she wanted nothing to do with mansions, magnolias, and mockingbirds, and like Harris, too, she shaped her stories around moments of unexpected comic violence. Yet unlike Harris, her literary commitment to comedy and violence never seems gratuitous but rather was deeply rooted in religious and aesthetic convictions. "My subject in fiction," she said, "is the action of grace in territory held largely by the devil."

Mary Flannery O'Connor was born in Savannah, Georgia, on March 25, 1925. Her family moved when she was twelve to Milledgeville, Georgia, where she graduated from the Women's College of Georgia. She studied creative writing at the State University of Iowa, earning an M.F.A. in 1947. In 1948 she was invited to join Yaddo, the prestigious writer's colony in Saratoga Springs, New York, but resigned, along with her new friends Robert Lowell and Elizabeth Hardwick, over the internal handling of a political incident. She lived for a few months in New York City and then spent a year with the writers Sally and Robert Fitzgerald at their Connecticut home.

In 1950, after she learned that she was dying of lupus, an incurable tubercular disease that had killed her father, she returned to Milledgeville to live with her mother on the family dairy farm. Her first novel, *Wise Blood*, the story of a young Tennessee religious fanatic who preaches a Church Without Christ, appeared in 1952. It was followed by a collection of ten short stories, *A Good Man Is Hard to Find* (1955). She published her second novel, another grotesque tale of religious aberration, *The Violent Bear It Away*, in 1960. Suffering from acute anemia, Flannery O'Connor underwent what may have been an ill-advised operation to remove a benign tumor. The operation reactivated the lupus, and she died in Milledgeville on August 3, 1964. Her second collection of stories, *Everything That Rises Must Converge* (its title derives from the Catholic theologian Teilhard de Chardin), appeared in 1965.

Flannery O'Connor hated abstraction. "The first and most obvious characteristic of fiction is that it deals with reality, through what can be seen, heard, smelt, tasted, and touched." Following the great Catholic philosopher, St. Thomas Aquinas, she believed that human knowledge begins through the senses. She disliked critical abstractions as well, feeling that a good story must resist sociological, psychological, philosophical, or religious paraphrase. She recalled that once after a reading of her short story "A Good Man Is Hard to Find," an earnest teacher began asking her questions:

> "Miss O'Connor," he said, "why was the Misfit's hat *black*?" I said most countrymen in Georgia wore black hats. He looked pretty disappointed. Then he said, "Miss O'Connor, the Misfit represents Christ, does he not?" "He does not," I said. He looked crushed. "Well, Miss O'Connor," he said, "what is the significance of the Misfit's hat?" I said it was to cover his head; and after that he left me alone. Anyway, that's what's happening to the teaching of literature.

Her irritation with the questions has less to do with a dislike for symbolism than with a dislike for a symbol-hunting mentality that thinks it has "understood" a story when it has completely discarded the work's literal level and discovered, as in an algebraic equation, what every detail "stands for."

In Flannery O'Connor's own critical articles, collected posthumously in *Mystery and Manners* (1969), she is always careful to respect the essential mystery of art. She saw the preservation of mystery as fundamental to both art and religion: "Christian dogma," she claimed, "is about the only thing left in the world that surely guards and respects mystery." The novelist's sense of mystery, she believed, grows out of a recognition of the world's incompleteness; the writer's profound sense of something lacking in the world gives serious fiction its value and meaning. In one of her finest essays, "Some Aspects of the Grotesque in Southern Fiction," she expressed this belief in a way that bears directly on her own literary achievement: For a certain kind of writer, she noted, "the meaning of a story does not begin except at a depth where adequate motivation and adequate psychology and the various determinations have been exhausted. Such a writer will be interested in what we don't understand rather than in what we do."

Further Reading:

J. Hendin, *The World of Flannery O'Connor*, 1970.

J. May, *The Pruning Word: The Parables of Flannery O'Connor*, 1976.

C. Schloss, *Flannery O'Connor's Dark Comedies*, 1980.

M. Friedman and B. Clark, eds., *Critical Essays on Flannery O'Connor*, 1985.

E. Kessler, *Flannery O'Connor and the Language of Apocalypse*, 1986

R. Brinkmeyer, *The Art and Vision of Flannery O'Connor*, 1989.

R. Coles, *Flannery O'Connor's South*, 1980, rev. 1993.

S. Rath and M. N. Shaw, eds., *Flannery O'Connor: New Perspectives*, 1996.

Text:

"A Good Man Is Hard to Find" from *The Complete Stories*, 1971.

A Good Man Is Hard to Find

The grandmother didn't want to go to Florida. She wanted to visit some of her connections in east Tennessee and she was seizing every chance to change Bailey's mind. Bailey was the son she lived with, her only boy. He was sitting on the edge of his chair at the table, bent over the orange sports section of the *Journal*. "Now look here, Bailey," she said, "see here, read this," and she stood with one hand on her thin hip and the other rattling the newspaper at his bald head. "Here this fellow that calls himself The Misfit is aloose from the Federal Pen and headed toward Florida and you read here what it says he did to these people. Just you read it. I wouldn't take my children in any direction with a criminal like that aloose in it. I couldn't answer to my conscience if I did."

Bailey didn't look up from his reading so she wheeled around then and faced the children's mother; a young woman in slacks, whose face was as broad and innocent as a cabbage and was tied around with a green headkerchief that had two points on the top like rabbit's ears. She was sitting on the sofa, feeding the baby his apricots out of a jar. "The children have been to Florida before," the old lady said. "You all ought to take them somewhere else for a change so they would see different parts of the world and be broad. They never have been to east Tennessee."

The children's mother didn't seem to hear her, but the eight-year-old boy, John Wesley, a stocky child with glasses, said, "If you don't want to go to Florida, why dontcha stay at home?" He and the little girl, June Star, were reading the funny papers on the floor.

"She wouldn't stay at home to be queen for a day," June Star said without raising her yellow head.

"Yes, and what would you do if this fellow, The Misfit, caught you?" the grandmother asked.

"I'd smack his face," John Wesley said.

"She wouldn't stay at home for a million bucks," June Star said. "Afraid she'd miss something. She has to go everywhere we go."

"All right, Miss," the grandmother said. "Just remember that the next time you want me to curl your hair."

June Star said her hair was naturally curly.

The next morning the grandmother was the first one in the car, ready to go. She had her big black valise that looked like the head of a hippopotamus in one corner, and underneath it she was hiding a basket with Pitty Sing, the cat, in it. She didn't intend for the cat to be left alone in the house for three days because he would miss her too much and she was afraid he might brush against one of the gas burners and accidentally asphyxiate himself. Her son, Bailey, didn't like to arrive at a motel with a cat.

She sat in the middle of the back seat with John Wesley and June Star on either side of her. Bailey and the children's mother and the baby sat in the front and they left Atlanta at eight forty-five with the mileage on the car at 55890. The grandmother wrote this down because she thought it would be interesting to say how many miles they had been when they got back. It took them twenty minutes to reach the outskirts of the city.

The old lady settled herself comfortably, removing her white cotton gloves and putting them up with her purse on the shelf in front of the back window. The children's mother still had on slacks and still had her head tied up in a green kerchief, but the grandmother had on a navy blue straw sailor hat with a bunch of white violets on the brim and a navy blue dress with a small white dot in the print. Her collar and cuffs were white organdy trimmed with lace and at her neckline she had pinned a purple spray of cloth violets containing a sachet. In case of an accident, anyone seeing her dead on the highway would know at once that she was a lady.

She said she thought it was going to be a good day for driving, neither too hot nor too cold, and she cautioned Bailey that the speed limit was fifty-five miles an hour and that the patrolmen hid themselves behind bill-boards and small clumps of trees and sped out after you before you had a chance to slow down. She pointed out interesting details of the scenery: Stone Mountain; the blue granite that in some places came up to both sides of the highway; the brilliant red clay banks slightly streaked with purple; and the various crops that made rows of green lace-work on the ground. The trees were full of silver-white sunlights and the meanest of them sparkled. The children were reading comic magazines and their mother had gone back to sleep.

"Let's go through Georgia fast so we won't have to look at it much," John Wesley said.

"If I were a little boy," said the grandmother, "I wouldn't talk about my native state that way. Tennessee has the mountains and Georgia has the hills."

"Tennessee is just a hillbilly dumping ground," John Wesley said, "and Georgia is a lousy state too."

"You said it," June Star said.

"In my time," said the grandmother, folding her thin veined fingers, "children were more respectful of their native states and their parents and everything else. People did right then. Oh look at the cute little pickaninny!" she said and pointed to a Negro child standing in the door of a shack. "Wouldn't that make a picture, now?" she asked and they all turned and looked at the little Negro out of the back window. He waved.

"He didn't have any britches on," June Star said.

"He probably didn't have any," the grandmother explained. "Little niggers in the country don't have things like we do. If I could paint, I'd paint that picture," she said.

The children exchanged comic books.

The grandmother offered to hold the baby and the children's mother passed him over the front seat to her. She set him on her knee and bounced him and told him about the things they were passing. She rolled her eyes and screwed up her mouth and stuck her leathery thin face into his smooth bland one. Occasionally he gave her a faraway smile. They passed a large cotton field with five or six graves fenced in the middle of it, like a small island. "Look at the graveyard!" the grandmother said, pointing it out. "That was the old family burying ground. That belonged to the plantation."

"Where's the plantation?" John Wesley asked.

"Gone With the Wind," said the grandmother. "Ha. Ha."

When the children finished all the comic books they had brought, they opened the lunch and ate it. The grandmother ate a peanut butter sandwich and an olive and would not let the children throw the box and the paper napkins out the window. When there was nothing else to do they played a game by choosing a cloud and making the other two guess what shape it suggested. John Wesley took one the shape of a cow and June Star guessed a cow and John Wesley said, no, an automobile, and June Star said he didn't play fair, and they began to slap each other over the grandmother.

The grandmother said she would tell them a story if they would keep quiet. When she told a story, she rolled her eyes and waved her head and was very dramatic. She said once when she was a maiden lady she had been courted by a Mr. Edgar Atkins Teagarden from Jasper, Georgia. She said he was a very good-looking man and a gentleman and that he brought her a watermelon every Saturday afternoon with his initials cut in it, E.A.T. Well, one Saturday, she said, Mr. Teagarden brought the watermelon and there was nobody at home and he left it on the front porch and returned in his buggy to Jasper, but she never got the watermelon, she said, because a nigger boy ate it when he saw the initials, E.A.T.! This story tickled John Wesley's funny bone and he giggled and giggled but June Star didn't think it was any good. She said she wouldn't marry a man that just brought her a watermelon on Saturday. The grandmother said she would have done well to marry Mr. Teagarden because he was a gentleman and had bought Coca-Cola stock when it first came out and that he had died only a few years ago, a very wealthy man.

They stopped at The Tower for barbecued sandwiches. The Tower was a part-stucco and part-wood filling station and dance hall set in a clearing outside of Timothy. A fat man named Red Sammy Butts ran it and there were signs stuck here and there on the building and for miles up and down the highway saying, TRY RED SAMMY'S FAMOUS BARBECUE. NONE LIKE FAMOUS RED SAMMY'S! RED SAM! THE FAT BOY WITH THE HAPPY LAUGH. A VETERAN! RED SAMMY'S YOUR MAN!

Red Sammy was lying on the bare ground outside The Tower with his head under a truck while a gray monkey about a foot high, chained to a small chinaberry tree, chattered nearby. The monkey sprang back into the tree and got on the highest limb as soon as he saw the children jump out of the car and run toward him.

Inside, The Tower was a long dark room with a counter at one end and tables at the other and dancing space in the middle. They all sat down at a broad table next to the nickelodeon and Red Sam's wife, a tall burnt-brown woman with hair and eyes lighter than her skin, came and took their order. The children's mother put a dime in the machine and played "The Tennessee Waltz," and the grandmother said that tune always made her want to dance. She asked Bailey if he would like to dance but he only glared at her. He didn't have a naturally sunny disposition like she did and trips made him nervous. The grandmother's brown eyes were very bright. She swayed her head from side to side and pretended she was dancing in her chair. June Star said play something she could tap to so the children's mother put in another dime and played a fast number and June Star stepped out onto the dance floor and did her tap routine.

"Ain't she cute?" Red Sam's wife said, leaning over the counter. "Would you like to come be my little girl?"

"No, I certainly wouldn't," June Star said. "I wouldn't live in a broken-down place like this for a million bucks!" and she ran back to the table.

"Ain't she cute?" the woman repeated, stretching her mouth politely.

"Aren't you ashamed?" hissed the grandmother.

Red Sam came in and told his wife to quit lounging on the counter and hurry up with these people's order. His khaki trousers reached just to his hip bones and his stomach hung over them like a sack of meal swaying under his shirt. He came over and sat down at a table nearby and let out a combination sigh and yodel. "You can't win," he said. "You can't win," and he wiped his sweating red face off with a gray handkerchief. "These days you don't know who to trust," he said. "Ain't that the truth?"

"People are certainly not nice like they used to be," said the grandmother.

"Two fellers come in here last week," Red Sammy said, "driving a Chrysler. It was an old beat-up car but it was a good one and these boys looked all right to me. Said they worked at the mill and you know I let them fellers charge the gas they bought? Now why did I do that?"

"Because you're a good man!" the grandmother said at once.

"Yes'm, I suppose so," Red Sam said as if he were struck with this answer.

His wife brought the orders, carrying the five plates all at once without a tray, two in each hand and one balanced on her arm. "It isn't a soul in this green world of God's that you can trust," she said. "And I don't count nobody out of that, not nobody," she repeated, looking at Red Sammy.

"Did you read about that criminal, The Misfit, that's escaped?" asked the grandmother.

"I wouldn't be a bit surprised if he didn't attack this place right here," said the woman. "If he hears about it being here, I wouldn't be none surprised to see him. If he hears it's two cent in the cash register, I wouldn't be a tall surprised if he. . . . "

"That'll do," Red Sam said. "Go bring these people their Co'-Colas," and the woman went off to get the rest of the order.

"A good man is hard to find," Red Sammy said. "Everything is getting terrible. I remember the day you could go off and leave your screen door unlatched. Not no more."

He and the grandmother discussed better times. The old lady said that in her opinion Europe was entirely to blame for the way things were now. She said the way Europe acted you would think we were made of money and Red Sam said it was no use talking about it, she was exactly right. The children ran outside into the white sunlight and looked at the monkey in the lacy chinaberry tree. He was busy catching fleas on himself and biting each one carefully between his teeth as if it were a delicacy.

They drove off again into the hot afternoon. The grandmother took cat naps and woke up every few minutes with her own snoring. Outside of Toombsboro she woke up and recalled an old plantation that she had visited in this neighborhood once when she was a young lady. She said the house had six white columns across the front and that there was an avenue of oaks leading up to it and two little wooden trellis arbors on either side in front where you sat down with your suitor after a stroll in the garden. She recalled exactly which road to turn off to get to it. She knew that Bailey would not be willing to lose any time looking at an old house, but the more she talked about it, the more she wanted to see it once again and find out if the little twin arbors were still standing. "There was a secret panel in this house," she said craftily, not telling the truth but wishing that she were, "and the story went that all the family silver was hidden in it when Sherman[1] came through but it was never found. . . . "

"Hey!" John Wesley said. "Let's go see it! We'll find it! We'll poke all the wood work and find it! Who lives there? Where do you turn off at? Hey Pop, can't we turn off there?"

"We never have seen a house with a secret panel!" June Star shrieked. "Let's go to the house with the secret panel! Hey, Pop, can't we go see the house with the secret panel!"

"It's not far from here, I know," the grandmother said. "It wouldn't take over twenty minutes."

Bailey was looking straight ahead. His jaw was as rigid as a horseshoe. "No," he said.

The children began to yell and scream that they wanted to see the house with the secret panel. John Wesley kicked the back of the front seat and June Star hung over her mother's shoulder and whined desperately into her ear that they never had any fun even on their vacation, that they could never do what THEY wanted to do. The baby began to scream and John Wesley kicked the back of the seat so hard that his father could feel the blows in his kidney.

"All right!" he shouted and drew the car to a stop at the side of the road. "Will you all shut up? Will you all just shut up for one second? If you don't shut up, we won't go anywhere."

"It would be very educational for them," the grandmother murmured.

"All right," Bailey said, "but get this. This is the only time we're going to stop for anything like this. This is the one and only time."

"The dirt road that you have to turn down is about a mile back," the grandmother directed. "I marked it when we passed."

"A dirt road," Bailey groaned.

After they had turned around and were headed toward the dirt road, the grandmother recalled other points about the house, the beautiful glass over the front doorway and the candle lamp in the hall. John Wesley said that the secret panel was probably in the fireplace.

"You can't go inside this house," Bailey said. "You don't know who lives there."

"While you all talk to the people in front, I'll run around behind and get in a window," John Wesley suggested.

"We'll all stay in the car," his mother said.

They turned onto the dirt road and the car raced roughly along in a swirl of pink dust. The grandmother recalled the times when there were no paved roads and thirty miles was a day's journey. The dirt road was hilly and there were sudden washes in it and sharp curves on dangerous embankments. All at once they would be on a hill, look-

---

[1] William Tecumseh Sherman, the Union general who marched his troops through Atlanta to the Georgia coast in the winter of 1864.

ing down over the blue tops of trees for miles around, then the next minute, they would be in a red depression with the dust-coated trees looking down on them.

"This place had better turn up in a minute," Bailey said, "or I'm going to turn around."

The road looked as if no one had traveled on it in months.

"It's not much farther," the grandmother said and just as she said it, a horrible thought came to her. The thought was so embarrassing that she turned red in the face and her eyes dilated and her feet jumped up, upsetting her valise in the corner. The instant the valise moved, the newspaper top she had over the basket under it rose with a snarl and Pitty Sing, the cat, sprang onto Bailey's shoulder.

The children were thrown to the floor and their mother, clutching the baby, was thrown out the door onto the ground; the old lady was thrown into the front seat. The car turned over once and landed right-side-up in a gulch on the side of the road. Bailey remained in the driver's seat with the cat—gray-striped with a broad white face and an orange nose—clinging to his neck like a caterpillar.

As soon as the children saw they could move their arms and legs, they scrambled out of the car, shouting, "We've had an ACCIDENT!" The grandmother was curled up under the dashboard, hoping she was injured so that Bailey's wrath would not come down on her all at once. The horrible thought she had had before the accident was that the house she had remembered so vividly was not in Georgia but in Tennessee.

Bailey removed the cat from his neck with both hands and flung it out the window against the side of a pine tree. Then he got out of the car and started looking for the children's mother. She was sitting against the side of the red gutted ditch, holding the screaming baby, but she only had a cut down her face and a broken shoulder. "We've had an ACCIDENT!" the children screamed in a frenzy of delight.

"But nobody's killed," June Star said with disappointment as the grandmother limped out of the car, her hat still pinned to her head but the broken front brim standing up at a jaunty angle and the violet spray hanging off the side. They all sat down in the ditch, except the children, to recover from the shock. They were all shaking.

"Maybe a car will come along," said the children's mother hoarsely.

"I believe I have injured an organ," said the grandmother, pressing her side, but no one answered her. Bailey's teeth were clattering. He had on a yellow sport shirt with bright blue parrots designed in it and his face was as yellow as the shirt. The grandmother decided that she would not mention that the house was in Tennessee.

The road was about ten feet above and they could see only the tops of the trees on the other side of it. Behind the ditch they were sitting in there were more woods, tall and dark and deep. In a few minutes they saw a car some distance away on top of a hill, coming slowly as if the occupants were watching them. The grandmother stood up and waved both arms dramatically to attract their attention. The car continued to come on slowly, disappeared around a bend and appeared again, moving even slower on top of the hill they had gone over. It was a big black battered hearselike automobile. There were three men in it.

It came to a stop just over them and for some minutes, the driver looked down with a steady expressionless gaze to where they were sitting, and didn't speak. Then he turned his head and muttered something to the other two and they got out. One was a fat boy in black trousers and a red sweat shirt with a silver stallion embossed on the front of it. He moved around on the right side of them and stood staring, his mouth partly open in a kind of loose grin. The other had on khaki pants and a blue striped coat and a gray hat pulled down very low, hiding most of his face. He came around slowly on the left side. Neither spoke.

The driver got out of the car and stood by the side of it, looking down at them. He was an older man than the other two. His hair was just beginning to gray and he wore silver-rimmed spectacles that gave him a scholarly look. He had a long creased face and didn't have on any shirt or undershirt. He had on blue jeans that were too tight for him and was holding a black hat and a gun. The two boys also had guns.

"We've had an ACCIDENT!" the children screamed.

The grandmother had the peculiar feeling that the bespectacled man was someone she knew. His face was as familiar to her as if she had known him all her life but she could not recall who he was. He moved away from the car and began to come down the embankment, placing his feet carefully so that he wouldn't slip. He had on tan and white shoes and no socks, and his ankles were red and thin. "Good afternoon," he said. "I see you all had you a little spill."

"We turned over twice!" said the grandmother.

"Oncet," he corrected. "We see it happen. Try their car and see will it run, Hiram," he said quietly to the boy with the gray hat.

"What you got that gun for?" John Wesley asked. "Whatcha gonna do with that gun?"

"Lady," the man said to the children's mother, "would you mind calling them children to sit down by you? Children make me nervous. I want all you to sit down right together there where you're at."

"What are you telling us what to do for?" June Star asked.

Behind them the line of woods gaped like a dark open mouth. "Come here," said their mother.

"Look here now," Bailey began suddenly, "we're in a predicament! We're in. . . ."

The grandmother shrieked. She scrambled to her feet and stood staring.

"You're The Misfit!" she said. "I recognized you at once!"

"Yes'm," the man said, smiling slightly as if he were pleased in spite of himself to be known, "but it would have been better for all of you, lady, if you hadn't of reckernized me."

Bailey turned his head sharply and said something to his mother that shocked even the children. The old lady began to cry and The Misfit reddened.

"Lady," he said, "don't you get upset. Sometimes a man says things he don't mean. I don't reckon he meant to talk to you thataway."

"You wouldn't shoot a lady, would you?" the grandmother said and removed a clean handkerchief from her cuff and began to slap at her eyes with it.

The Misfit pointed the toe of his shoe into the ground and made a little hole and then covered it up again. "I would hate to have to," he said.

"Listen," the grandmother almost screamed, "I know you're a good man. You don't look a bit like you have common blood. I know you must come from nice people!"

"Yes mam," he said, "finest people in the world." When he smiled he showed a row of strong white teeth. "God never made a finer woman than my mother and my daddy's heart was pure gold," he said. The boy with the red sweat shirt had come around behind them and was standing with his gun at his hip. The Misfit squatted down on the ground. "Watch them children, Bobby Lee," he said. "You know they make me nervous." He looked at the six of them huddled together in front of him and he seemed to be embarrassed as if he couldn't think of anything to say. "Ain't a cloud in the sky," he remarked, looking up at it. "Don't see no sun but don't see no cloud neither."

"Yes, it's a beautiful day," said the grandmother. "Listen," she said, "you shouldn't call yourself The Misfit because I know you're a good man at heart. I can just look at you and tell."

"Hush!" Bailey yelled. "Hush! Everybody shut up and let me handle this!" He was squatting in the position of a runner about to sprint forward but he didn't move.

"I pre-chate that, lady," The Misfit said and drew a little circle in the ground with the butt of his gun.

"It'll take a half a hour to fix this here car," Hiram called, looking over the raised hood of it.

"Well, first you and Bobby Lee get him and that little boy to step over yonder with you," The Misfit said, pointing to Bailey and John Wesley. "The boys want to ask you something," he said to Bailey. "Would you mind stepping back in them woods there with them?"

"Listen," Bailey began, "we're in a terrible predicament! Nobody realizes what this is," and his voice cracked. His eyes were as blue and intense as the parrots in his shirt and he remained perfectly still.

The grandmother reached up to adjust her hat brim as if she were going to the woods with him but it came off in her hand. She stood staring at it and after a second she let it fall on the ground. Hiram pulled Bailey up by the arm as if he were assisting an old man. John Wesley caught hold of his father's hand and Bobby Lee followed. They went off toward the woods and just as they reached the dark edge, Bailey turned and supporting himself against a gray naked pine trunk, he shouted, "I'll be back in a minute, Mamma, wait on me!"

"Come back this instant!" his mother shrilled but they all disappeared into the woods.

"Bailey Boy!" the grandmother called in a tragic voice but she found she was looking at The Misfit squatting on the ground in front of her. "I just know you're a good man," she said desperately. "You're not a bit common!"

"Nome, I ain't a good man," The Misfit said after a second as if he had considered her statement carefully, "but I ain't the worst in the world neither. My daddy said I was a different breed of dog from my brothers and sisters. 'You know,' Daddy said, 'it's some that can live their whole life without asking about it and it's others has to know why it is, and this boy is one of the latters. He's going to be into everything!'" He put on his black hat and looked up suddenly and then away deep into the woods as if he were embarrassed again. "I'm sorry, I don't have on a shirt before you ladies," he said, hunching his shoulders slightly. "We buried our clothes that we had on when we escaped and we're just making do until we can get better. We borrowed these from some folks we met," he explained.

"That's perfectly all right," the grandmother said. "Maybe Bailey has an extra shirt in his suitcase."

"I'll look and see terrectly," The Misfit said.

"Where are they taking him?" the children's mother screamed.

"Daddy was a card himself," The Misfit said. "You couldn't put anything over on him. He never got in trouble with the Authorities though. Just had the knack of handling them."

"You could be honest too if you'd only try," said the grandmother. "Think how wonderful it would be to settle down and live a comfortable life and not have to think about somebody chasing you all the time."

The Misfit kept scratching in the ground with the butt of his gun as if he were thinking about it. "Yes'm, somebody is always after you," he murmured.

The grandmother noticed how thin his shoulder blades were just behind his hat because she was standing up looking down on him. "Do you ever pray?" she asked.

He shook his head. All she saw was the black hat wiggle between his shoulder blades. "Nome," he said.

There was a pistol shot from the woods, followed closely by another. Then silence. The old lady's head jerked around. She could hear the wind move through the tree tops like a long satisfied insuck of breath. "Bailey Boy!" she called.

"I was a gospel singer for a while," The Misfit said. "I been most everything. Been in the arm service, both land and sea, at home and abroad, been twict married, been an undertaker, been with the railroads, plowed Mother Earth, been in a tornado, seen a man burnt alive oncet," and he looked up at the children's mother and the little girl who were sitting close together, their faces white and their eyes glassy; "I even seen a woman flogged," he said.

"Pray, pray," the grandmother began, "pray, pray. . . . "

"I never was a bad boy that I remember of," The Misfit said in an almost dreamy voice, "but somewheres along the line I done something wrong and got sent to the penitentiary. I was buried alive," and he looked up and held her attention to him by a steady stare.

"That's when you should have started to pray," she said. "What did you do to get sent to the penitentiary that first time?"

"Turn to the right, it was a wall," The Misfit said, looking up again at the cloudless sky. "Turn to the left, it was a wall. Look up it was a ceiling, look down it was a floor. I forget what I done, lady. I set there and set there, trying to remember what it was I done and I ain't recalled it to this day. Oncet in a while, I would think it was coming to me, but it never come."

"Maybe they put you in by mistake," the old lady said vaguely.

"Nome," he said. "It wasn't no mistake. They had the papers on me."

"You must have stolen something," she said.

The Misfit sneered slightly. "Nobody had nothing I wanted," he said. "It was a head-doctor at the penitentiary said what I had done was kill my daddy but I known that for a lie. My daddy died in nineteen ought nineteen of the epidemic flu[2] and I never had a thing to do with it. He was buried in the Mount Hopewell Baptist churchyard and you can go there and see for yourself."

"If you would pray," the old lady said, "Jesus would help you."

"That's right," The Misfit said.

"Well then, why don't you pray?" she asked trembling with delight suddenly.

---

[2] I.e., the worldwide flu epidemic of 1919.

"I don't want no hep," he said. "I'm doing all right by myself."

Bobby Lee and Hiram came ambling back from the woods. Bobby Lee was dragging a yellow shirt with bright blue parrots in it.

"Throw me that shirt, Bobby Lee," The Misfit said. The shirt came flying at him and landed on his shoulder and he put it on. The grandmother couldn't name what the shirt reminded her of. "No, lady," The Misfit said while he was buttoning it up, "I found out the crime don't matter. You can do one thing or you can do another, kill a man or take a tire off his car, because sooner or later you're going to forget what it was you done and just be punished for it."

The children's mother had begun to make heaving noises as if she couldn't get her breath. "Lady," he asked, "would you and that little girl like to step off yonder with Bobby Lee and Hiram and join your husband?"

"Yes, thank you," the mother said faintly. Her left arm dangled helplessly and she was holding the baby, who had gone to sleep, in the other. "Hep that lady up, Hiram," The Misfit said as she struggled to climb out of the ditch, "and Bobby Lee, you hold onto that little girl's hand."

"I don't want to hold hands with him," June Star said. "He reminds me of a pig."

The fat boy blushed and laughed and caught her by the arm and pulled her off into the woods after Hiram and her mother.

Alone with The Misfit, the grandmother found that she had lost her voice. There was not a cloud in the sky nor any sun. There was nothing around her but woods. She wanted to tell him that he must pray. She opened and closed her mouth several times before anything came out. Finally she found herself saying, "Jesus. Jesus," meaning, Jesus will help you, but the way she was saying it, it sounded as if she might be cursing.

"Yes'm," The Misfit said as if he agreed. "Jesus thrown everything off balance. It was the same case with Him as with me except He hadn't committed any crime and they could prove I had committed one because they had the papers on me. Of course," he said, "they never shown me my papers. That's why I sign myself now. I said long ago, you get you a signature and sign everything you do and keep a copy of it. Then you'll know what you done and you can hold up the crime to the punishment and see do they match and in the end you'll have something to prove you ain't been treated right. I call myself The Misfit," he said, "because I can't make what all I done wrong fit what all I gone through in punishment."

There was a piercing scream from the woods, followed closely by a pistol report. "Does it seem right to you, lady, that one is punished a heap and another ain't punished at all?"

"Jesus!" the old lady cried. "You've got good blood! I know you wouldn't shoot a lady! I know you come from nice people! Pray! Jesus, you ought not to shoot a lady. I'll give you all the money I've got!"

"Lady," The Misfit said, looking beyond her far into the woods, "there never was a body that give the undertaker a tip."

There were two more pistol reports and the grandmother raised her head like a parched old turkey hen crying for water and called, "Bailey Boy, Bailey Boy!" as if her heart would break.

"Jesus was the only One that ever raised the dead," The Misfit continued, "and He shouldn't have done it. He thrown everything off balance. If He did what He said, then it's nothing for you to do but throw away everything and follow Him, and if He didn't then it's nothing for you to do but enjoy the few minutes you got left the best way you can—by killing somebody or burning down his house or doing some other meanness to him. No pleasure but meanness," he said and his voice had become almost a snarl.

"Maybe He didn't raise the dead," the old lady mumbled, not knowing what she was saying and feeling so dizzy that she sank down in the ditch with her legs twisted under her.

"I wasn't there so I can't say He didn't," The Misfit said. "I wisht I had of been there," he said, hitting the ground with his fist. "It ain't right I wasn't there because if I had of been there I would of known. Listen lady," he said in a high voice, "if I had of been there I would of known and I wouldn't be like I am now." His voice seemed about to crack and the grandmother's head cleared for an instant. She saw the man's face twisted close to her own as if he were going to cry and she murmured, "Why, you're one of my babies. You're one of my own children!" She reached out and touched him on the shoulder. The Misfit sprang back as if a snake had bitten him and shot her three times through the chest. Then he put his gun down on the ground and took off his glasses and began to clean them.

Hiram and Bobby Lee returned from the woods and stood over the ditch, looking down at the grandmother who half sat and half lay in a puddle of blood with her legs crossed under her like a child's and her face smiling up at the cloudless sky.

Without his glasses, The Misfit's eyes were red-rimmed and pale and defenseless-looking. "Take her off and throw her where you thrown the others," he said, picking up the cat that was rubbing itself against his leg.

"She was a talker, wasn't she?" Bobby Lee said, sliding down the ditch with a yodel.

"She would of been a good woman," The Misfit said, "if it had been somebody there to shoot her every minute of her life."

"Some fun!" Bobby Lee said.

"Shut up, Bobby Lee," The Misfit said. "It's no real pleasure in life."

1953

Allen Ginsberg
1926–1997

Allen Ginsberg brought a raw new power into American poetry with the publication of *Howl* (1956). It was a recognizable descendant of *Leaves of Grass*, but Whitman's poetry had been out of favor during the ascendancy of the difficult and "European" poetry of Eliot, Pound, and Stevens. Ginsberg had crossed Whitman's long lines with the long lines of the Hebrew psalms and Whitman's protests against gentility with the Hebrew prophets' denunciations of their society. In the relatively quiet 1950s, Ginsberg's excoriation of America rang out with explosive force: "I saw the best minds of my generation destroyed by madness, starving hysterical naked. . . ."

Yet Ginsberg's declamations, considering his early life, were not surprising. As we learn from "Kaddish" and other poems, he had grown up in a milieu of protest, among

Jewish socialists and communists, in Paterson, New Jersey. The faith that rhetoric and political action can be effective was bred into him, and it might have been predicted that William Blake, the English protest-poet, would become Ginsberg's favorite writer. Blake's hatred of the forces of repression found expression in both small lyrics (the *Songs of Innocence* and *Experience*) and in giant mythic narratives like *Jerusalem*. Ginsberg, too, writes both songs and long journey poems, and he has never turned aside from his stance of protest.

Allen Ginsberg saw at close hand the enormous psychic strain endured by American immigrant populations. In his elegy for his mother, Naomi, the long poem entitled "Kaddish" (after the Hebrew prayer for the dead), Ginsberg traces Naomi's life from her first arrival in America from Russia through her brief idyllic youth in the Young People's Socialist League and on to her marriage and long decline into paranoia, confinement in an asylum, eventual lobotomy, and death. Naomi's life became for Ginsberg a paradigm of all the lives of the suffering poor, the confined, and the oppressed. Ginsberg's openly proclaimed homosexuality, which made him a criminal in the eyes of the law, reinforced his belief that the legal system is unnecessarily oppressive, directed by American fundamentalist morality rather than by a concern for public order.

Large public issues—the stockpiling of nuclear bombs, the Korean and Vietnam wars, FBI wiretappings, racism, ecology—continue to enter Ginsberg's poems, but the poetry contains as well Ginsberg's ruefully humorous account of his private life—his travels, his sexual history, his experiments with drugs, his interest in Buddhism, his mourning for his father.

Ginsberg's father was a high school teacher of English and a writer of inept conventional verse (Ginsberg gave poetry readings jointly with his father in the later years of his father's life, as if to demonstrate that family solidarity outweighs aesthetic compatibility). Ginsberg's mother ("from whose pained head I first took Vision," says Ginsberg) may have been his muse, but in his father's verse he found his introduction to English poetry. Ginsberg went to Columbia University, was expelled as a sophomore for writing an obscene phrase in the dust on his dormitory windowpane, lived for a while with William Burroughs and Jack Kerouac, reentered Columbia, and graduated in 1948. Shortly after graduation, implicated in a friend's thefts because the stolen goods had been stored in his apartment, Ginsberg pleaded insanity to avoid imprisonment and was confined for eight months in the Columbia Psychiatric Institute. In the early 1950s, in San Francisco, he met the poets who were to be known collectively with him as the Beat generation—Kenneth Rexroth, Lawrence Ferlinghetti, and Gary Snyder. The City Lights Press, founded by Ferlinghetti, published Ginsberg's verse from *Howl* until 1985, including such volumes as *Reality Sandwiches* (1963), *Planet News* (1968), *The Fall of America* (1973) and *Mind Breaths* (1977). In 1985 Harper & Row issued Ginsberg's *Collected Poems;* the volume *White Shroud* followed in 1986.

Ginsberg's return to the oral tradition in poetry had far-reaching effects, as did his allegiance to the line of poetry stretching from Whitman through Williams. (As one New Jersey poet to another, Williams had encouraged Ginsberg's early verse, and contributed an introduction to *Howl;* he had even included letters from Ginsberg in *Paterson*.) Even such formal poets as Robert Lowell became conscious, by the example of the beat poets, of the necessity of incorporating in poetry the rhythms of American speech. The uninhibited poetry readings Ginsberg has given—which have included, over the years, occasional nakedness, references to drugs, chants with a harmonium and finger cymbals, the reading aloud of sexual diaries, Buddhist mantras, and audience participation—immensely changed the nature of the poetry reading as a communal occasion. Ginsberg's humorous and candid poetry suggested that self-revelation need not be shaming or self-abasing and that political protest need not be dour or hateful. His spiritual evolution—his repudiation of drugs, his travels in India, his adoption of Buddhism—appears in his poetry as a dramatic thread giving continuity to the whole. Right up until his death in 1997, he remained a powerful presence in American poetry and was probably the only living American poet whose name was known throughout the world.

Further Reading:

J. Kramer, *Allen Ginsberg in America*, 1970.

J. Tytell, *Naked Angels: The Lives and Literature of the Beat Generation*, 1976.

P. C. Portuges, *The Visionary Poetics of Allen Ginsberg*, 1978.

T. Merrill, *Allen Ginsberg*, 1969, rev. 1988.

B. Miles, *Ginsberg: A Biography*, 1990.

M. Schumacher, *Dharma Lion: A Biography of Allen Ginsberg*, 1992.

C. Bloom and B. Docherty, eds., *American Poetry: The Modernist Ideal*, 1995.

Text:
Collected Poems: 1947–1980, 1984.

---

from Howl

for Carl Solomon

I

I saw the best minds of my generation destroyed by madness, starving hysterical
    naked,
dragging themselves through the negro streets at dawn looking for an angry fix,
angelheaded hipsters burning for the ancient heavenly connections to the starry
    dynamo in the machinery of night,
who poverty and tatters and hollow-eyed and high sat up smoking in the
    supernatural darkness of cold-water flats floating across the tops of cities
    contemplating jazz,
who bared their brains to Heaven under the El and saw Mohammedan angels
    staggering on tenement roofs illuminated,   5
who passed through universities with radiant cool eyes hallucinating Arkansas
    and Blake-light tragedy among the scholars of war,
who were expelled from the academies for crazy & publishing obscene odes on
    the windows of the skull,[1]
who cowered in unshaven rooms in underwear, burning their money in
    wastebaskets and listening to the Terror through the wall,

---

[1] Ginsberg was expelled from Columbia University for writing an obscenity in the dust on his dormitory windowpane.

who got busted in their pubic beards returning through Laredo with a belt of
    marijuana for New York,

who ate fire in paint hotels or drank turpentine in Paradise Alley,[2] death, or
    purgatoried their torsos night after night   10

with dreams, with drugs, with waking nightmares, alcohol and cock and
    endless balls,

incomparable blind streets of shuddering cloud and lightning in the mind leaping
    toward poles of Canada & Paterson, illuminating all the motionless
    world of Time between,

Peyote solidities of halls, backyard green tree cemetery dawns, wine drunkenness
    over the rooftops, storefront boroughs of teahead joyride neon blinking
    traffic light, sun and moon and tree vibrations in the roaring winter dusks of
    Brooklyn, ashcan rantings and kind king light of mind,

who chained themselves to subways for the endless ride from Battery to holy
    Bronx on benzedrine until the noise of wheels and children brought them
    down shuddering mouth-wracked and battered bleak of brain all drained of
    brilliance in the drear light of Zoo,

who sank all night in submarine light of Bickford's floated out and sat through
    the stale beer afternoon in desolate Fugazzi's, listening to the crack of doom
    on the hydrogen jukebox,   15

who talked continuously seventy hours from park to pad to bar to Bellevue to
    museum to the Brooklyn Bridge,

a lost battalion of platonic conversationalists jumping down the stoops off fire
    escapes off windowsills off Empire State out of the moon,

yacketayakking screaming vomiting whispering facts and memories and
    anecdotes and eyeball kicks and shocks of hospitals and jails and wars,

whole intellects disgorged in total recall for seven days and nights with brilliant
    eyes, meat for the Synagogue cast on the pavement,

who vanished into nowhere Zen New Jersey leaving a trail of ambiguous
    picture postcards of Atlantic City Hall,   20

suffering Eastern sweats and Tangerian bone-grindings and migraines of China
    under junk-withdrawal of Newark's bleak furnished room,

who wandered around and around at midnight in the railroad yard wondering
    where to go, and went, leaving no broken hearts,

who lit cigarettes in boxcars boxcars boxcars racketing through snow toward
    lonesome farms in grandfather night,

who studied Plotinus Poe St. John of the Cross telepathy and bop kaballa
    because the cosmos instinctively vibrated at their feet in Kansas,

who loned it through the streets of Idaho seeking visionary indian angels who were
    visionary indian angels,   25

who thought they were only mad when Baltimore gleamed in supernatural
    ecstasy,

who jumped in limousines with the Chinaman of Oklahoma on the impulse of
    winter midnight streetlight smalltown rain,

---

[2] Ginsberg's note: "A slum courtyard N.Y.
    Lower East Side, site of [the writer Jack] Ker-
    ouac's *Subterraneans*, 1958."

who lounged hungry and lonesome through Houston seeking jazz or sex or soup,
and followed the brilliant Spaniard to converse about America and Eternity,
a hopeless task, and so took ship to Africa,

who disappeared into the volcanoes of Mexico leaving behind nothing but the
shadow of dungarees and the lava and ash of poetry scattered in fireplace
Chicago,

who reappeared on the West Coast investigating the F.B.I. in beards and shorts
with big pacifist eyes sexy in their dark skin passing out incomprehensible
leaflets,   30

who burned cigarette holes in their arms protesting the narcotic tobacco haze
of Capitalism,

who distributed Supercommunist pamphlets in Union Square weeping and
undressing while the sirens of Los Alamos wailed them down, and wailed
down Wall, and the Staten Island ferry also wailed,

who broke down crying in white gymnasiums naked and trembling before the
machinery of other skeletons,

who bit detectives in the neck and shrieked with delight in policecars for
committing no crime but their own wild cooking pederasty and
intoxication,

who howled on their knees in the subway and were dragged off the roof
waving genitals and manuscripts,   35

who let themselves be fucked in the ass by saintly motorcyclists, and screamed
with joy,

who blew and were blown by those human seraphim, the sailors, caresses of
Atlantic and Caribbean love,

who balled in the morning in the evenings in rosegardens and the grass of
public parks and cemeteries scattering their semen freely to whomever come
who may,

who hiccupped endlessly trying to giggle but wound up with a sob behind a
partition in a Turkish Bath when the blonde & naked angel came to pierce
them with a sword,

who lost their loveboys to the three old shrews of fate the one eyed shrew of
the heterosexual dollar the one eyed shrew that winks out of the womb and
the one eyed shrew that does nothing but sit on her ass and snip the
intellectual golden threads of the craftsman's loom,   40

who copulated ecstatic and insatiate with a bottle of beer a sweetheart a package
of cigarettes a candle and fell off the bed, and continued along the floor and
down the hall and ended fainting on the wall with a vision of ultimate cunt
and come eluding the last gyzym of consciousness,

who sweetened the snatches of a million girls trembling in the sunset, and were
red eyed in the morning but prepared to sweeten the snatch of the sunrise,
flashing buttocks under barns and naked in the lake,

who went out whoring through Colorado in myriad stolen night-cars, N.C.,[3]

---

[3] Neal Cassady, a friend of Ginsberg and Jack
Kerouac, who appears as the character Dean
Moriarty in Kerouac's novel *On the Road*.

secret hero of these poems, cocksman and Adonis of Denver—joy to the
    memory of his innumerable lays of girls in empty lots & diner backyards,
    moviehouses' rickety rows, on mountaintops in caves or with gaunt waitresses
    in familiar roadside lonely petticoat upliftings & especially secret gas-station
    solipsisms of johns, & hometown alleys too,
who faded out in vast sordid movies, were shifted in dreams, woke on a sudden
    Manhattan, and picked themselves up out of basements hungover with
    heartless Tokay and horrors of Third Avenue iron dreams & stumbled to
    unemployment offices,
who walked all night with their shoes full of blood on the snowbank docks
    waiting for a door in the East River to open to a room full of steamheat
    and opium,   45
who created great suicidal dramas on the apartment cliff-banks of the Hudson
    under the wartime blue floodlight of the moon & their heads shall be
    crowned with laurel in oblivion,
who ate the lamb stew of the imagination or digested the crab at the muddy
    bottom of the rivers of Bowery,
who wept at the romance of the streets with their pushcarts full of onions and
    bad music,
who sat in boxes breathing in the darkness under the bridge, and rose up to
    build harpsichords in their lofts,
who coughed on the sixth floor of Harlem crowned with flame under the
    tubercular sky surrounded by orange crates of theology,   50
who scribbled all night rocking and rolling over lofty incantations which in
    the yellow morning were stanzas of gibberish,
who cooked rotten animals lung heart feet tail borsht & tortillas dreaming of
    the pure vegetable kingdom,
who plunged themselves under meat trucks looking for an egg,
who threw their watches off the roof to cast their ballot for Eternity outside
    of Time, & alarm clocks fell on their heads every day for the next decade,
who cut their wrists three times successively unsuccessfully, gave up and were
    forced to open antique stores where they thought they were growing old
    and cried,   55
who were burned alive in their innocent flannel suits on Madison Avenue amid
    blasts of leaden verse & the tanked-up clatter of the iron regiments of fashion
    & the nitroglycerine shrieks of the fairies of advertising & the mustard gas of
    sinister intelligent editors, or were run down by the drunken taxicabs of
    Absolute Reality,
who jumped off the Brooklyn Bridge this actually happened and walked away
    unknown and forgotten into the ghostly daze of Chinatown soup alleyways
    & firetrucks, not even one free beer,
who sang out of their windows in despair, fell out of the subway window,
    jumped in the filthy Passaic, leaped on negroes, cried all over the street,
    danced on broken wineglasses barefoot smashed phonograph records of
    nostalgic European 1930's German jazz finished the whiskey and threw
    up groaning into the bloody toilet, moans in their ears and the blast of
    colossal steamwhistles,

who barreled down the highways of the past journeying to each other's
    hotrod-Golgotha jail-solitude watch or Birmingham jazz incarnation,
who drove crosscountry seventytwo hours to find out if I had a vision or you
    had a vision or he had a vision to find out Eternity,   60
who journeyed to Denver, who died in Denver, who came back to Denver &
    waited in vain, who watched over Denver & brooded & loned in Denver
    and finally went away to find out the Time, & now Denver is lonesome for
    her heroes,
who fell on their knees in hopeless cathedrals praying for each other's salvation
    and light and breasts, until the soul illuminated its hair for a second,
who crashed through their minds in jail waiting for impossible criminals with
    golden heads and the charm of reality in their hearts who sang sweet blues
    to Alcatraz,
who retired to Mexico to cultivate a habit, or Rocky Mount to tender Buddha
    or Tangiers to boys or Southern Pacific to the black locomotive or Harvard
    to Narcissus to Woodlawn to the daisychain or grave,
who demanded sanity trials accusing the radio of hypnotism & were left with
    their insanity & their hands & a hung jury,   65
who threw potato salad at CCNY[4] lecturers on Dadaism and subsequently
    presented themselves on the granite steps of the madhouse with shaven heads
    and harlequin speech of suicide, demanding instantaneous lobotomy,
and who were given instead the concrete void of insulin metrasol[5] electricity
    hydrotherapy psychotherapy occupational therapy pingpong & amnesia,
who in humorless protest overturned only one symbolic pingpong table, resting
    briefly in catatonia,
returning years later truly bald except for a wig of blood, and tears and fingers,
    to the visible madman doom of the wards of the madtowns of the East,
Pilgrim State's Rockland's and Greystone's[6] foetid halls, bickering with the
    echoes of the soul, rocking and rolling in the midnight solitude-bench
    dolmen-realms of love, dream of life a nightmare, bodies turned to stone
    as heavy as the moon,   70
with mother finally ******,[7] and the last fantastic book flung out of the
    tenement window, and the last door closed at 4 AM and the last telephone
    slammed at the wall in reply and the last furnished room emptied down to
    the last piece of mental furniture, a yellow paper rose twisted on a wire hanger
    in the closet, and even that imaginary, nothing but a hopeful little bit of
    hallucination—
ah, Carl, while you are not safe I am not safe, and now you're really in the
    total animal soup of time—
and who therefore ran through the icy streets obsessed with a sudden flash of
    the alchemy of the use of the ellipse the catalog the meter & the vibrating
    plane,
who dreamt and made incarnate gaps in Time & Space through images
    juxtaposed, and trapped the archangel of the soul between 2 visual images

---

[4] City College of New York.
[5] A tranquilizing drug.
[6] Pilgrim State, Rockland, and Greystone: state mental hospitals. Carl Solomon was confined in Rockland.
[7] Asterisks replace *fucked*.

and joined the elemental verbs and set the noun and dash of consciousness
   together jumping with sensation of Pater Omnipotens Aeterna Deus[8]
to recreate the syntax and measure of poor human prose and stand before you
   speechless and intelligent and shaking with shame, rejected yet confessing
   out the soul to conform to the rhythm of thought in his naked and endless
   head,   75
the madman bum and angel beat in Time, unknown, yet putting down here
   what might be left to say in time come after death,
and rose reincarnate in the ghostly clothes of jazz in the goldhorn shadow of
   the band and blew the suffering of America's naked mind for love into an
   eli eli lamma lamma sabacthani[9] saxophone cry that shivered the cities down
   to the last radio
with the absolute heart of the poem of life butchered out of their own bodies good to
   eat a thousand years.

1956

A Supermarket in California

What thoughts I have of you tonight, Walt Whitman, for I walked down
the sidestreets under the trees with a headache, self-conscious looking at the
full moon.
   In my hungry fatigue, and shopping for images, I went into the neon fruit supermarket, dreaming of your enumerations!
   What peaches and what penumbras! Whole families shopping at night! Aisles
full of husbands! Wives in the avocados, babies in the tomatoes!—and you, Garcia
Lorca,[1] what were you doing down by the watermelons?

   I saw you, Walt Whitman, childless, lonely old grubber, poking among the
meats in the refrigerator and eyeing the grocery boys.
   I heard you asking questions of each: Who killed the pork chops? What
price bananas? Are you my Angel?   5
   I wandered in and out of the brilliant stacks of cans following you, and
followed in my imagination by the store detective.
   We strode down the open corridors together in our solitary fancy tasting
artichokes, possessing every frozen delicacy, and never passing the cashier.

   Where are we going, Walt Whitman? The doors close in an hour. Which
way does your beard point tonight?

---

[8] Latin, from the Creed: "Omnipotent Father
Eternal God." Ginsberg uses the feminine of
the adjective "aeternus," as does the French
painter Paul Cézanne (1839–1906), from
whose letters Ginsberg borrowed the phrase.
Cézanne meant all of created nature (conventionally imagined as female).

[9] Hebrew: "My God, my God, why hast thou
forsaken me?" These were Jesus' words on
the cross (Matthew 4:26).
[1] Homosexual Spanish poet (1898–1936), shot
by French soldiers in the Spanish Civil War.
He wrote an "Ode to Walt Whitman."

(I touch your book and dream of our odyssey in the supermarket and feel absurd.)

Will we walk all night through solitary streets? The trees add shade to shade, lights out in the houses, we'll both be lonely.   10

Will we stroll dreaming of the lost America of love past blue automobiles in driveways, home to our silent cottage?

Ah, dear father, graybeard, lonely old courage-teacher, what America did you have when Charon[2] quit poling his ferry and you got out on a smoking bank and stood watching the boat disappear on the black waters of Lethe?

1956

America

America I've given you all and now I'm nothing.
America two dollars and twentyseven cents January 17, 1956.
I can't stand my own mind.
America when will we end the human war?
Go fuck yourself with your atom bomb.   5
I don't feel good don't bother me.
I won't write my poem till I'm in my right mind.
America when will you be angelic?
When will you take off your clothes?
When will you look at yourself through the grave?   10
When will you be worthy of your million Trotskyites?[1]
America why are your libraries full of tears?
America when will you send your eggs to India?[2]
I'm sick of your insane demands.
When can I go into the supermarket and buy what I need with my good
      looks?   15
America after all it is you and I who are perfect not the next world.
Your machinery is too much for me.
You made me want to be a saint.
There must be some other way to settle this argument.
Burroughs is in Tangiers[3] I don't think he'll come back it's sinister.   20
Are you being sinister or is this some form of practical joke?
I'm trying to come to the point.
I refuse to give up my obsession.
America stop pushing I know what I'm doing.

---

[2] In mythology Charon is the ferryman who carries souls across the river Styx to Hades, where they drink from the river Lethe, causing them to forget their life before death.
[1] Communist idealists, followers of Leon Trotsky (1879–1940), the opponent of Stalin.

[2] India was suffering a famine, while America had an agricultural surplus.
[3] William Burroughs (b. 1914), a friend of Ginsberg and author of the novel *Naked Lunch* (1959), was living in Morocco.

America the plum blossoms are falling.   25
I haven't read the newspapers for months, everyday somebody goes on trial for
    murder.
America I feel sentimental about the Wobblies.[4]
America I used to be a communist when I was a kid I'm not sorry.
I smoke marijuana every chance I get.
I sit in my house for days on end and stare at the roses in the closet.   30
When I go to Chinatown I get drunk and never get laid.
My mind is made up there's going to be trouble.
You should have seen me reading Marx.[5]
My psychoanalyst thinks I'm perfectly right.
I won't say the Lord's Prayer.   35
I have mystical visions and cosmic vibrations.
America I still haven't told you what you did to Uncle Max after he came over
    from Russia.

I'm addressing you.
Are you going to let your emotional life be run by Time Magazine?
I'm obsessed by Time Magazine.   40
I read it every week.
Its cover stares at me every time I slink past the corner candystore.
I read it in the basement of the Berkeley Public Library.
It's always telling me about responsibility. Businessmen are serious. Movie
    producers are serious. Everybody's serious but me.
It occurs to me that I am America.   45
I am talking to myself again.
Asia is rising against me.
I haven't got a chinaman's chance.
I'd better consider my national resources.
My national resources consist of two joints of marijuana millions of genitals
    an unpublishable private literature that goes 1400 miles an hour and
    twentyfive-thousand mental institutions.   50
I say nothing about my prisons nor the millions of underprivileged who live in
    my flowerpots under the light of five hundred suns.
I have abolished the whorehouses of France, Tangiers is the next to go.
My ambition is to be President despite the fact that I'm a Catholic.

America how can I write a holy litany in your silly mood?
I will continue like Henry Ford my strophes are as individual as his
    automobiles more so they're all different sexes.   55
America I will sell you strophes $2500 apiece $500 down on your old strophe
America free Tom Mooney[6]

4 Nickname for members of the Industrial
    Workers of the World, a revolutionary
    union founded in Chicago in 1905.
5 Karl Marx (1818–1883), German social
    philosopher and author, with Friedrich En-
    gels, of *The Communist Manifesto* (1848).

6 American labor agitator in California, ac-
    cused of bomb killings and sentenced to
    death in 1916 but pardoned in 1939.

America save the Spanish Loyalists[7]
America Sacco & Vanzetti[8] must not die
America I am the Scottsboro boys.[9]   60
America when I was seven momma took me to Communist Cell meetings they
    sold us garbanzos[10] a handful per ticket a ticket costs a nickel and
    the speeches were free everybody was angelic and sentimental about the
    workers it was all so sincere you have no idea what a good thing the party
    was in 1935 Scott Nearing was a grand old man a real mensch Mother Bloor
    made me cry I once saw Israel Amter[11] plain. Everybody must have been a spy.
America you don't really want to go to war.
America it's them bad Russians.
Them Russians them Russians and them Chinamen. And them Russians.
The Russia wants to eat us alive. The Russia's power mad. She wants to take
    our cars from out our garages.   65
Her wants to grab Chicago. Her needs a Red Readers' Digest. Her wants our auto
    plants in Siberia. Him big bureaucracy running our fillingstations.
That no good. Ugh. Him make Indians learn read. Him need big black niggers.
    Hah. Her make us all work sixteen hours a day. Help.
America this is quite serious.
America this is the impression I get from looking in the television set.
America is this correct?   70
I'd better get right down to the job.
It's true I don't want to join the Army or turn lathes in precision parts
    factories, I'm nearsighted and psychopathic anyway.
America I'm putting my queer shoulder to the wheel.
1956

John Ashbery
b. 1927

John Ashbery's poems resemble a score for performance by the reader. Some
experience of interest, depth, and importance is being retold—a journey, a

[7] Those fighting against Franco in the Spanish
  Civil War.
[8] Nicola Sacco and Bartolomeo Vanzetti were
  executed in Massachusetts in 1927 for a
  murder connected with a robbery; sentiment
  ran high against them because of their radical political beliefs.
[9] The "Scottsboro boys" were nine blacks who
  were convicted in Alabama of the rape of
  two white women in 1931. Liberals and radi-

cals believed the conviction to be unproved.
Four years later the sentences were reduced
in four cases and the charges dropped in
five.
[10] Chick peas.
[11] Scott Nearing (1883–1983), Ella ("Mother")
  Bloor (1862–1951), and Israel Amter
  (1881–1954): well-known American Socialists and Communists.

catastrophe, a loss—but we are given the general outline rather than the specific details. Ashbery invites us to involve ourselves in the flow of events, filling in from our own past the appropriate incidents. The disturbances of life, its energies and hates, are transformed into the towers and "lacustrine cities" of art, "things offered," the poet says to his reader, "to your participation." Since the grid of human experience takes on repetitive patterns, Ashbery trusts to an aesthetic of algebraic outline expressed in his masterly syntax and invokes the cooperation of his reader in following his graph. A poem by Ashbery is the occasion for a dazzling unfolding of inventive language, which borrows from popular sources like slang and advertising as well as from intellectual sources like art history and theater. It is impossible to predict what color or shape or tone an Ashbery poem will take on next; the configurations in his kaleidoscope fall into new shapes as the poem turns.

Ashbery's own training centered on language, literature, theater, and the visual arts. His early years were spent on a farm in upstate New York. After preparing at Deerfield Academy, he attended Harvard (B.A., 1949) and then took an M.A. in English at Columbia. Later, a Fulbright scholarship took him to Montpellier and Paris (1955–1957). In 1958, living in Paris, he became the art critic for the *International Herald Tribune* and wrote reviews of art shows for *Art News* and *Arts International*. After his return to America in 1965, he served until 1972 as executive editor of *Art News* and later as the art critic for *Newsweek*. He has taught creative writing at Brooklyn College.

Ashbery's lyrical first volume, *Some Trees* (1956), selected by W. H. Auden for the Yale Younger Poet series, was followed by the unsettling collection *The Tennis Court Oath* (1962), in which many of the poems, notably "Europe," were baffling in their discontinuity, allusiveness, and surreal effects. With *Rivers and Mountains* (1966), Ashbery assumed the cursive, seductive, musical style with which he is now identified. Together with Frank O'Hara (a close friend), he drew poetry away from the deliberateness of Eliot's diction and into the mainstream of urbane American conversational exchange.

Ashbery's poetry has been influenced by our century's experiments in the visual arts, notably cubism and abstraction. Cubism in sculpture suggested that the various forms of the world could be schematized into elementary geometric forms; cubism in painting (as in Picasso's paintings, where we see a profile superimposed on a full face) suggested that any number of perspectives of an object are "true" and that we should attempt to keep all views in mind at once. Ashbery's preference for an elemental outline may be seen as a recourse to a cubist simplicity, while his frequent (and often unsettling) changes of perspective may derive from the multiplicity of perspectives visible, for instance, in Picasso. Other aspects of modern art—the playfulness of Klee, the cartoon sketches of Matisse, the parodic elements of the Dada movement—have all created a revolution that has passed, in linguistic form, into Ashbery's daring loosening of the usual structures of writing. But his liberties with metaphor and pronominal reference (indebted perhaps to the experiments of Gertrude Stein) accompany a deeply traditional sense of the historic genres of poetry in English. Ashbery's use of forms like the sonnet and the sestina; his obedience to the conventions of the elegy, of love poetry, of the ode, and of the landscape poem; and his frequent allusions to his predecessors (especially Keats, Eliot, Stevens, and Auden) establish his homage to the perennial life of poetry.

Ashbery's attention turns frequently to self-reflective poetry, in which he examines the conditions of creation for the contemporary poet. "Our question of a place of origin hangs / Like smoke," he writes; the poet no longer thinks that in creating he imitates the divine freedom of God. Art is a repetitive traditional function but contains an inner freedom:

> So I cradle this average violin that knows
> Only forgotten showtunes, but argues
> The possibility of free declamation anchored
> To a dull refrain.

The function of art is to be a deposit of human physicality, sexuality, and material culture; to affect by its presence the landscape around it; and to serve as a means of self-creation:

> [We] left
> Our trash, sperm and excrement everywhere, smeared
> On the landscape, to make of us what we could.

Art is the "pyrography"—writing (or playing) with fire—undertaken by the artist while life continues its circular journey. In spite of the absence of an origin or goal, life still presents itself to us, Ashbery suggests, as precious and worthy of preservation, so we must "model all these unimportant details" and include them if art is truly to represent the ephemeral truths of culture.

In his love poetry, Ashbery creates compelling sketches of loss, betrayal, and fidelity: Other wagons may go on to the gold rush, "But we stay behind, among them, / The injured, the adored." Lovers keep trying "to get it right," to phrase, in the midst of a night's attrition, their "notes to each other, always repeated, always the same." Ashbery can be brutal as well as tender; his light exploratory tones, his jokes, his parodies often mask the harshness of his vision, as when he imagines life as a damaged carousel constantly climbed onto by blighted supplicants ("Landscapeople"). The end is certain; but at least, like a medieval illuminator, the poet ornaments the black-letter text of life, "filling up the margins of the days / With pictures of fruit, light, colors, music, and vines, / Until it ceases to be a problem."

In recent years, Ashbery has continued his inventiveness, not only in the brilliant prose poems of *Three Poems* (1972) but also in the Pulitzer Prize–winning *Self-portrait in a Convex Mirror* (1975), the lyrics of *Houseboat Days* (1977), the double-column long poem "Litany" in *As We Know* (1979), the unrhymed "sonnets" of *Shadow Train* (1981), and the elegiac title poem of *A Wave* (1984).

Further Reading:

D. Shapiro, *John Ashbery: An Introduction to the Poetry,* 1979.

D. Lehman, ed., *Beyond Amazement: New Essays on John Ashbery,* 1980.

H. Bloom, ed., *John Ashbery,* 1985.

Texts:
"The Painter" from *Some Trees*, 1956.
"These Lacustrine Cities" from *Rivers and Mountains*, 1966.
"Soonest Mended" from *The Double Dream of Spring*, 1970.

"Syringa" from *Houseboat Days*, 1977.
"Landscapeople" from *As We Know*, 1979.

The Painter

Sitting between the sea and the buildings
He enjoyed painting the sea's portrait.
But just as children imagine a prayer
Is merely silence, he expected his subject
To rush up the sand, and, seizing a brush,   5
Plaster its own portrait on the canvas.

So there was never any paint on his canvas
Until the people who lived in the buildings
Put him to work: "Try using the brush
As a means to an end. Select, for a portrait,   10
Something less angry and large, and more subject
To a painter's moods, or, perhaps, to a prayer."

How could he explain to them his prayer
That nature, not art, might usurp the canvas?
He chose his wife for a new subject,   15
Making her vast, like ruined buildings,
As if, forgetting itself, the portrait
Had expressed itself without a brush.

Slightly encouraged, he dipped his brush
In the sea, murmuring a heartfelt prayer: 20
"My soul, when I paint this next portrait
Let it be you who wrecks the canvas."
The news spread like wildfire through the buildings:
He had gone back to the sea for his subject.

Imagine a painter crucified by his subject!   25
Too exhausted even to lift his brush,
He provoked some artists leaning from the buildings
To malicious mirth: "We haven't a prayer
Now, of putting ourselves on canvas,
Or getting the sea to sit for a portrait!"   30

Others declared it a self-portrait.
Finally all indications of a subject
Began to fade, leaving the canvas
Perfectly white. He put down the brush.
At once a howl, that was also a prayer,   35
Arose from the overcrowded buildings.

They tossed him, the portrait, from the tallest of the buildings;
And the sea devoured the canvas and the brush
As though his subject had decided to remain a prayer.
1956

These Lacrustrine* Cities

These lacustrine cities grew out of loathing
Into something forgetful, although angry with history.
They are the product of an idea: that man is horrible, for instance,
Though this is only one example.

They emerged until a tower   5
Controlled the sky, and with artifice dipped back
Into the past for swans and tapering branches,
Burning, until all that hate was transformed into useless love.

Then you are left with an idea of yourself
And the feeling of ascending emptiness of the afternoon   10
Which must be charged to the embarrassment of others
Who fly by you like beacons.

The night is a sentinel.
Much of your time has been occupied by creative games
Until now, but we have all-inclusive plans for you.   15
We had thought, for instance, of sending you to the middle of the desert,

To a violent sea, or of having the closeness of the others be air
To you, pressing you back into a startled dream
As sea-breezes greet a child's face.
But the past is already here, and you are nursing some private project.   20

* Built on stilts in lakes.

The worst is not over, yet I know
You will be happy here. Because of the logic
Of your situation, which is something no climate can outsmart.
Tender and insouciant by turns, you see

You have built a mountain of something,   25
Thoughtfully pouring all your energy into this single monument,
Whose wind is desire starching a petal,
Whose disappointment broke into a rainbow of tears.
1966

Soonest Mended

Barely tolerated, living on the margin
In our technological society, we were always having to be rescued
On the brink of destruction, like heroines in *Orlando Furioso*[1]
Before it was time to start all over again.
There would be thunder in the bushes, a rustling of coils,   5
And Angelica, in the Ingres[2] painting, was considering
The colorful but small monster near her toe, as though wondering whether
    forgetting
The whole thing might not, in the end, be the only solution.
And then there always came a time when
Happy Hooligan[3] in his rusted green automobile   10
Came plowing down the course, just to make sure everything was O.K.,
Only by that time we were in another chapter and confused
About how to receive this latest piece of information.
Was it information? Weren't we rather acting this out
For someone else's benefit, thoughts in a mind   15
With room enough and to spare for our little problems (so they began to
    seem),
Our daily quandary about food and the rent and bills to be paid?
To reduce all this to a small variant,
To step free at last, minuscule on the gigantic plateau—
This was our ambition: to be small and clear and free.   20
Alas, the summer's energy wanes quickly,
A moment and it is gone. And no longer
May we make the necessary arrangements, simple as they are.

[1] Epic (1532) by Lodovico Ariosto (1474–1533), of which the heroine is Angelica.

[2] French painter (1780–1867).
[3] Comic strip character.

Our star was brighter perhaps when it had water in it.
Now there is no question even of that, but only   25
Of holding on to the hard earth so as not to get thrown off,
With an occasional dream, a vision: a robin flies across
The upper corner of the window, you brush your hair away
And cannot quite see, or a wound will flash
Against the sweet faces of the others, something like: 30
This is what you wanted to hear, so why
Did you think of listening to something else? We are all talkers
It is true, but underneath the talk lies
The moving and not wanting to be moved, the loose
Meaning, untidy and simple like a threshing floor.   35
These then were some hazards of the course,
Yet though we knew the course *was* hazards and nothing else
It was still a shock when, almost a quarter of a century later,
The clarity of the rules dawned on you for the first time.
They were the players, and we who had struggled at the game   40
Were merely spectators, though subject to its vicissitudes
And moving with it out of the tearful stadium, borne on shoulders, at last.
Night after night this message returns, repeated
In the flickering bulbs of the sky, raised past us, taken away from us,
Yet ours over and over until the end that is past truth,   45
The being of our sentences, in the climate that fostered them,
Not ours to own, like a book, but to be with, and sometimes
To be without, alone and desperate.
But the fantasy makes it ours, a kind of fence-sitting
Raised to the level of an esthetic ideal. These were moments, years,   50
Solid with reality, faces, namable events, kisses, heroic acts,
But like the friendly beginning of a geometrical progression
Not too reassuring, as though meaning could be cast aside some day
When it had been outgrown. Better, you said, to stay cowering
Like this in the early lessons, since the promise of learning   55
Is a delusion, and I agreed, adding that
Tomorrow would alter the sense of what had already been learned,
That the learning process is extended in this way, so that from this standpoint
None of us ever graduates from college,
For time is an emulsion, and probably thinking not to grow up   60
Is the brightest kind of maturity for us, right now at any rate.
And you see, both of us were right, though nothing
Has somehow come to nothing; the avatars[4]
Of our conforming to the rules and living
Around the home have made—well, in a sense, "good citizens" of us,   65
Brushing the teeth and all that, and learning to accept

---

[4] Embodiments.

The charity of the hard moments as they are doled out,
For this is action, this not being sure, this careless
Preparing, sowing the seeds crooked in the furrow,
Making ready to forget, and always coming back   70
To the mooring of starting out, that day so long ago.
1970

Syringa*

Orpheus[1] liked the glad personal quality
Of the things beneath the sky. Of course, Eurydice was a part
Of this. Then one day, everything changed. He rends
Rocks into fissures with lament. Gullies, hummocks
Can't withstand it. The sky shudders from one horizon   5
To the other, almost ready to give up wholeness.
Then Apollo[2] quietly told him: "Leave it all on earth.
Your lute, what point? Why pick at a dull pavan[3] few care to
Follow, except a few birds of dusty feather,
Not vivid performances of the past." But why not?   10
All other things must change too.
The seasons are no longer what they once were,
But it is the nature of things to be seen only once,
As they happen along, bumping into other things, getting along
Somehow. That's where Orpheus made his mistake.   15
Of course Eurydice vanished into the shade;
She would have even if he hadn't turned around.
No use standing there like a gray stone toga as the whole wheel
Of recorded history flashes past, struck dumb, unable to utter an intelligent
Comment on the most thought-provoking element in its train.   20
Only love stays on the brain, and something these people,
These other ones, call life. Singing accurately
So that the notes mount straight up out of the well of
Dim noon and rival the tiny, sparkling yellow flowers
Growing around the brink of the quarry, encapsulates   25

---

* Flowering bush named from *syrinx*, the
Greek word for panpipe. The nymph Syrinx,
escaping from Pan, was turned into a reed;
Pan in turn formed the reeds into panpipes
and blew through them, creating music.
[1] In myth, a musician married to Eurydice.
After she died, Orpheus descended into
Hades seeking her; he was allowed to repossess her if he promised not to look behind as
he led her out of Hades. He could not refrain
from looking and thus lost Eurydice forever.
[2] God of poets and musicians.
[3] Music for a court dance.

The different weights of the things.
                                  But it isn't enough
To just go on singing. Orpheus realized this
And didn't mind so much about his reward being in heaven
After the Bacchantes[4] had torn him apart, driven
Half out of their minds by his music, what it was doing to them.   30
Some say it was for his treatment of Eurydice.
But probably the music had more to do with it, and
The way music passes, emblematic
Of life and how you cannot isolate a note of it
And say it is good or bad. You must   35
Wait till it's over. "The end crowns all,"
Meaning also that the "tableau"
Is wrong. For although memories, of a season, for example,
Melt into a single snapshot, one cannot guard, treasure
That stalled moment. It too is flowing, fleeting;   40
It is a picture of flowing, scenery, though living, mortal,
Over which an abstract action is laid out in blunt,
Harsh strokes. And to ask more than this
Is to become the tossing reeds of that slow,
Powerful stream, the trailing grasses   45
Playfully tugged at, but to participate in the action
No more than this. Then in the lowering gentian sky
Electric twitches are faintly apparent first, then burst forth
Into a shower of fixed, cream-colored flares. The horses
Have each seen a share of the truth, though each thinks,   50
"I'm a maverick. Nothing of this is happening to me,
Though I can understand the language of birds, and
The itinerary of the lights caught in the storm is fully apparent to me.
Their jousting ends in music much
As trees move more easily in the wind after a summer storm   55
And is happening in lacy shadows of shore-trees, now, day after day."

But how late to be regretting all this, even
Bearing in mind that regrets are always late, too late!
To which Orpheus, a bluish cloud with white contours,
Replies that these are of course not regrets at all,   60
Merely a careful, scholarly setting down of
Unquestioned facts, a record of pebbles along the way.
And no matter how all this disappeared,
Or got where it was going, it is no longer
Material for a poem. Its subject   65
Matters too much, and not enough, standing there helplessly
While the poem streaked by, its tail afire, a bad

---

[4] Female followers of Dionysus, who tore
  Orpheus to pieces.

Comet screaming hate and disaster, but so turned inward
That the meaning, good or other, can never
Become known. The singer thinks   70
Constructively, builds up his chant in progressive stages
Like a skyscraper, but at the last minute turns away.
The song is engulfed in an instant in blackness
Which must in turn flood the whole continent
With blackness, for it cannot see. The singer   75
Must then pass out of sight, not even relieved
Of the evil burthen[5] of the words. Stellification[6]
Is for the few, and comes about much later
When all record of these people and their lives
Has disappeared into libraries, onto microfilm.   80
A few are still interested in them. "But what about
So-and-so?" is still asked on occasion. But they lie
Frozen and out of touch until an arbitrary chorus
Speaks of a totally different incident with a similar name
In whose tale are hidden syllables   85
Of what happened so long before that
In some small town, one indifferent summer.
1977

Landscapeople

Long desired, the journey is begun. The suppliants
Climb aboard the damaged carrousel:
Some have been hacked to death, one has learned
Some new thing, and all are touched
With the same blight, like a snowfall   5
Of moments as they are read back to the monitor
Which only projects.

        Some can decipher it,
The outline of an eddy that traced itself
Before moving on, yet its place had to be,
Such was the appetite of those times. A ring   10
Of places existed around the central one,
And of course these died away eventually.
Everything has turned out for the best,

---

[5] An obsolete spelling of *burden*.
[6] Being turned into a star, or constellation, after death.

The "eggs of the sun" have been returned anonymously,
And the new ways are as simple as the old ones,   15
Only more firmly anchored to the spectacle
Of the madness of the seasons as it unfolds
With iron-clad rigidity, filling the sky with light.
We began in an anonymous sensuality
And lived most of it out before the difference   20
Of time got in the way, filling up the margins of the days
With pictures of fruit, light, colors, music, and vines,
Until it ceases to be a problem.

1979

James Wright
1927–1980

When James Wright died of throat cancer at the early age of fifty-three, he was mourned as the poet who had put the Midwest into verse—its rural despair, its urban poor, its suburban frustration. He was born in Martins Ferry, Ohio, a town he recalled in many poems. Wright's deepest sense of life came to him from his earliest days, when he experienced life as a child of the Depression: "Hundreds of times I must have heard a man returning home after a long day's futile search for work, any work at all, and dispiritedly whispering to his anxious wife, or mumbling absent-mindedly to himself in his baffled loneliness: 'I ain't got a pot to piss in or a window to throw it out of.' " Wright's father worked for fifty years in Wheeling, West Virginia, for the Hazel-Atlas glass factory but was often "laid off," which meant, as Wright said, being "told by the management to just go home and stay there, often for weeks at a time, without being paid." In representing the dark underside of America, Wright follows Whitman's injunction in the preface to *Leaves of Grass* to "stand up for the stupid and crazy."

W. H. Auden chose Wright as Yale Younger Poet for 1957 for the book *The Green Wall*, a book formal in its meters and stanza forms, influenced by Wright's literary studies with John Crowe Ransom at Kenyon College, from which he received an A.B. in 1952, and with Theodore Roethke at the University of Washington, where he took a Ph.D. in 1959. Wright then began, in collaboration with Robert Bly, a series of translations from foreign poets: the Austrian Georg Trakl in 1961 (Wright had been a Fulbright student in Vienna), César Vallejo in 1962, Pablo Neruda in 1968. These translations influenced his own third and fourth books, *The Branch Will Not Break* (1963) and *Shall We Gather at the River* (1968). The stark imagism of Trakl and the uninhibited surrealism of Neruda, combined with the directness and honesty of Vallejo, broke through Wright's formalism and induced in him a new starkness and simplicity of presentation: "I have wasted my life"; "If I stepped out of my body I would break / Into blossom." In subsequent volumes, *Two Citizens* (1973) and *To a Blossoming Pear Tree* (1977), Wright's elegiac plangency threatened to dissolve into sentimentality. Alcoholism sapped his creative energy and induced poems of self-hatred and disgust, of terror at the uncontrolled disintegration of his life. Eventually he gave up alcohol and found a new sweetness in life in America as well as in travel in Europe with his wife, Annie.

Wright's poetry won him a wide following in the late 1960s when the war in Vietnam made readers long for a poetry of direct statement, pity, and elegiac sympathy. During the later years of his life, Wright taught literature at Hunter College in New York, but he remains a poet of "the heart of the heart of the country," that Midwest as yet underrepresented in American verse. Following the example set by Robinson and Frost in their scenes of crabbed rural life in New England, Wright revealed how a transplanted genre could flourish in a new geographic setting, in the flat, despairing tones of Middle America.

Further Reading:

W. S. Saunders, *James Wright: An Introduction*, 1980.
D. Smith, ed., *The Pure Clear Word: Essays on the Poetry of James Wright*, 1982.
D. Dougherty, *James Wright*, 1987.
K. Stein, *James Wright: The Poetry of a Grown Man*, 1989.

P. Stitt and F. Graziano, eds., *James Wright: The Heart of the Light*, 1990.
A. Elkins, *The Poetry of James Wright*, 1991.

Text:

Above the River: The Complete Poems, 1990.

Lament for My Brother on a Hayrake

Cool with the touch of autumn, waters break
Out of the pump at dawn to clear my eyes;
I leave the house, to face the sacrifice
Of hay, the drag and death. By day, by moon,
I have seen my younger brother wipe his face   5
And heave his arm on steel. He need not pass
Under the blade to waste his life and break;

The hunching of the body is enough
To violate his bones. That bright machine
Strips the revolving earth of more than grass;   10
Powered by the fire of summer, bundles fall
Folded to die beside a burlap shroud;
And so my broken brother may lie mown
Out of the wasted fallows, winds return,
Corn-yellow tassels of his hair blow down,   15
The summer bear him sideways in a bale
Of darkness to October's mow of cloud.
1956

A Note Left in Jimmy Leonard's Shack

Near the dry river's water-mark we found
    Your brother Minnegan,
Flopped like a fish against the muddy ground.
Beany, the kid whose yellow hair turns green,
Told me to find you, even in the rain,   5
    And tell you he was drowned.

I hid behind the chassis on the bank,
    The wreck of someone's Ford:
I was afraid to come and wake you drunk:
You told me once the waking up was hard,   10
The daylight beating at you like a board.
    Blood in my stomach sank.

Beside, you told him never to go out
    Along the river-side
Drinking and singing, clattering about.   15
You might have thrown a rock at me and cried
I was to blame, I let him fall in the road
    And pitch down on his side.

Well, I'll get hell enough when I get home
    For coming up this far,   20
Leaving the note, and running as I came.
I'll go and tell my father where you are.
You'd better go find Minnegan before
    Policemen hear and come.

Beany went home, and I got sick and ran,   25
    You old son of a bitch.
You better hurry down to Minnegan;
He's drunk or dying now, I don't know which,
Rolled in the roots and garbage like a fish,
    The poor old man.   30

1959

At the Executed Murderer's Grave

(for J. L. D.)

Why should we do this? What good is it to us? Above all, how can we do such a thing? How can it possibly be done?

Freud

1

My name is James A. Wright, and I was born
Twenty-five miles from this infected grave,
In Martins Ferry, Ohio, where one slave
To Hazel-Atlas Glass became my father.
He tried to teach me kindness. I return   5
Only in memory now, aloof, unhurried,
To dead Ohio, where I might lie buried,
Had I not run away before my time.
Ohio caught George Doty. Clean as lime,
His skull rots empty here. Dying's the best   10
Of all the arts men learn in a dead place.
I walked here once. I made my loud display,
Leaning for language on a dead man's voice.
Now sick of lies, I turn to face the past.
I add my easy grievance to the rest: 15

2

Doty, if I confess I do not love you,
Will you let me alone? I burn for my own lies.
The nights electrocute my fugitive,
My mind. I run like the bewildered mad
At St. Clair Sanitarium, who lurk,   20
Arch and cunning, under the maple trees,
Pleased to be playing guilty after dark.
Staring to bed, they croon self-lullabies.
Doty, you make me sick. I am not dead.
I croon my tears at fifty cents per line.   25

3

Idiot, he demanded love from girls,
And murdered one. Also, he was a thief.
He left two women, and a ghost with child.
The hair, foul as a dog's upon his head,
Made such revolting Ohio animals   30
Fitter for vomit than a kind man's grief.

I waste no pity on the dead that stink,
And no love's lost between me and the crying
Drunks of Belaire, Ohio, where police
Kick at their kidneys till they die of drink.   35
Christ may restore them whole, for all of me.
Alive and dead, those giggling muckers who
Saddled my nightmares thirty years ago
Can do without my widely printed sighing
Over their pains with paid sincerity.   40
I do not pity the dead, I pity the dying.

4

I pity myself, because a man is dead.
If Belmont County killed him, what of me?
His victims never loved him. Why should we?
And yet, nobody had to kill him either.   45
It does no good to woo the grass, to veil
The quicklime hole of a man's defeat and shame.
Nature-lovers are gone. To hell with them.
I kick the clods away, and speak my name.

5

This grave's gash festers. Maybe it will heal,   50
When all are caught with what they had to do
In fear of love, when every man stands still
By the last sea,
And the princes of the sea come down
To lay away their robes, to judge the earth   55
And its dead, and we dead stand undefended everywhere,
And my bodies—father and child and unskilled criminal—
Ridiculously kneel to bare my scars,
My sneaking crimes, to God's unpitying stars.

6

Staring politely, they will not mark my face   60
From any murderer's, buried in this place.
Why should they? We are nothing but a man.

7

Doty, the rapist and the murderer,
Sleeps in a ditch of fire, and cannot hear;
And where, in earth or hell's unholy peace,   65
Men's suicides will stop, God knows, not I.
Angels and pebbles mock me under trees.
Earth is a door I cannot even face.

Order be damned, I do not want to die,
Even to keep Belaire, Ohio, safe.   70
The hackles on my neck are fear, not grief.
(Open, dungeon! Open, roof of the ground!)
I hear the last sea in the Ohio grass,
Heaving a tide of gray disastrousness.
Wrinkles of winter ditch the rotted face   75
Of Doty, killer, imbecile, and thief:
Dirt of my flesh, defeated, underground.
1959

Autumn Begins in Martins Ferry, Ohio

In the Shreve High football stadium,
I think of Polacks[1] nursing long beers in Tiltonsville,
And gray faces of Negroes in the blast furnace at Benwood,
And the ruptured[2] night watchman of Wheeling Steel,
Dreaming of heroes.   5

All the proud fathers are ashamed to go home.
Their women cluck like starved pullets,
Dying for love.

Therefore,
Their sons grow suicidally beautiful   10
At the beginning of October,
And gallop terribly against each other's bodies.
1963

Lightning Bugs Asleep in the Afternoon

These long-suffering and affectionate shadows,
These fluttering jewels, are trying to get
Some sleep in a dry shade beneath the cement
Joists of the railroad trestle.

I did not climb up here to find them.   5
It was only my ordinary solitude

---

[1] Derogatory epithet for Polish-Americans.   [2] i.e., with a hernia supported by a truss.

I was following up here this afternoon.
Last evening I sat here with a girl.

It was a dangerous place to be a girl
And young. But she simply folded her silent   10
Skirt over bare knees, printed with the flowered cotton
Of a meal sack her mother had stitched for her.

Neither of us said anything to speak of.
These affectionate, these fluttering bodies
Signaled to one another under the bridge   15
While the B&O 40-and-8's rattled away.

Now ordinary and alone in the afternoon,
I find this little circle of insects
Common as soot, clustering on dim stone,   20
Together with their warm secrets.

I think I am going to leave them folded
And sleeping in their slight gray wings.
I think I am going to climb back down
And open my eyes and shine.
1982

Philip Levine
b. 1928

Born in Detroit, Philip Levine received B.A. and M.A. degrees from Wayne State
University and an M.F.A. from the University of Iowa. A fellowship in poetry from
Stanford University led him, in 1958, to California, where he eventually settled and
became a professor of English at California State University, Fresno.

Levine's first book, *On the Edge,* was published in 1963, though he had been
appearing in magazines since the mid-fifties. As the title of his second book *Silent in
America: Vivas for Those Who Failed* (1965) would imply, Levine's work champions the
ordinary antiheroic figures who populate the modern (urban) American landscape.
His poetry is marked by an individuality, a natural toughness. He will neither
romanticize our fate nor give in to despair. He has told us that we are

> . . . a people come
> For a new world and a new home
> And what we get is what we bring:
> No fresh start and no bird song
> And no sea and no shore
> That someone hasn't seen before.[1]

[1] From "A New Day," *Not This Pig,*
  Middletown, Conn., 1968.

It is this sense that the everyday contains its own special horror and hope—that the everyday is our arena—that informs poems such as "To a Child Trapped in a Barber Shop" and "Coming Home," while "You Can Have It" displays the highly personal quality of the struggle Levine wages through his verse. Indeed, his protagonists, he has claimed, are those "who live at all cost and come back for more, and who if they bore tattoos—a gesture they don't need—would have them say, 'Don't tread on me' or 'Once more with feeling' or 'No pasarán' or 'Not this pig.' "[2]

A winner of The National Book Award, the National Book Critic's Circle Award, and the American Book Award, Levine's work includes *Not This Pig* (1968), *They Feed They Lion* (1972), *A Walk with Tom Jefferson* (1988), *What Work Is* (1991), *The Simple Truth*, (1994), and *New and Selected Poems* (1995).

Further Reading:

E. Hirsch, "Naming the Lost: The Poetry of Philip Levine," *Michigan Quarterly Review*, Spring 1989.

C. Buckley, ed., *On the Poetry of Philip Levine: Stranger to Nothing*, 1991.

Texts:

"Coming Home" and "They Feed They Lion" from *They Feed They Lion*, 1972.

"You Can Have It" from *7 Years From Somewhere*, 1979.

Coming Home

Detroit, 1968

A winter Tuesday, the city pouring fire,
Ford Rouge sulfurs the sun, Cadillac, Lincoln,
Chevy gray. The fat stacks
of breweries hold their tongues. Rags,
papers, hands, the stems of birches   5
dirtied with words.
        Near the freeway
you stop and wonder what came off,
recall the snowstorm where you lost it all,
the wolverine, the northern bear, the wolf   10
caught out, ice and steel raining
from the foundries in a shower
of human breath. On sleds in the false sun
the new material rests. One brown child
stares and stares into your frozen eyes   15
until the lights change and you go
forward to work. The charred faces, the eyes
boarded up, the rubble of innards, the cry
of wet smoke hanging in your throat,
the twisted river stopped at the color of iron.   20
We burn this city every day.
1972

[2] *Not This Pig*, cover.

They Feed They Lion

Out of burlap sacks, out of bearing butter,
Out of black bean and wet slate bread,
Out of the acids of rage, the candor of tar,
Out of creosote, gasoline, drive shafts, wooden dollies,
They Lion grow.   5
   Out of the gray hills
Of industrial barns, out of rain, out of bus ride,
West Virginia to Kiss My Ass, out of buried aunties,
Mothers hardening like pounded stumps, out of stumps,
Out of the bones' need to sharpen and the muscles' to stretch,   10
They Lion grow.
   Earth is eating trees, fence posts,
Gutted cars, earth is calling in her little ones,
"Come home, Come home!" From pig balls,
From the ferocity of pig driven to holiness,   15
From the furred ear and the full jowl come
The repose of the hung belly, from the purpose
They Lion grow.
   From the sweet glues of the trotters
Come the sweet kinks of the fist, from the full flower   20
Of the hams the thorax of caves,
From "Bow Down" come "Rise Up,"
Come they Lion from the reeds of shovels,
The grained arm that pulls the hands,
They Lion grow.   25
   From my five arms and all my hands,
From all my white sins forgiven, they feed,
From my car passing under the stars,
They Lion, from my children inherit,
From the oak turned to a wall, they Lion,   30
From they sack and they belly opened
And all that was hidden burning on the oil-stained earth
They feed they Lion and he comes.
1972

You Can Have It

My brother comes home from work
and climbs the stairs to our room.
I can hear the bed groan and his shoes drop
one by one. You can have it, he says.

The moonlight streams in the window   5
and his unshaven face is whitened
like the face of the moon. He will sleep
long after noon and waken to find me gone.

Thirty years will pass before I remember
that moment when suddenly I knew each man   10
has one brother who dies when he sleeps
and sleeps when he rises to face this life,

and that together they are only one man
sharing a heart that always labors, hands
yellowed and cracked, a mouth that gasps   15
for breath and asks, Am I gonna make it?

All night at the ice plant he had fed
the chute its silvery blocks, and then I
stacked cases of orange soda for the children
of Kentucky, one gray boxcar at a time   20

with always two more waiting. We were twenty
for such a short time and always in
the wrong clothes, crusted with dirt
and sweat. I think now we were never twenty.

In 1948 in the city of Detroit, founded   25
by de la Mothe Cadillac for the distant purposes
of Henry Ford, no one wakened or died,
no one walked the streets or stoked a furnace,

for there was no such year, and now
that year has fallen off all the old newspapers,   30
calendars, doctors' appointments, bonds,
wedding certificates, drivers licenses.

The city slept. The snow turned to ice.
The ice to standing pools or rivers
racing in the gutters. Then bright grass rose   35
between the thousands of cracked squares,

and that grass died. I give you back 1948.
I give you all the years from then
to the coming one. Give me back the moon
with its frail light falling across a face.   40

Give me back my young brother, hard
and furious, with wide shoulders and a curse
for God and burning eyes that look upon
all creation and say, You can have it.
1979

Anne Sexton
1928–1975

Anne Sexton was born in Newton, Massachusetts, grew up in Wellesley, attended Garland Junior College, and married at twenty. After suffering a mental breakdown, she was urged to write poetry by her therapist. Like Sylvia Plath, she studied with Robert Lowell at Boston University in the 1950s. Sexton's first book, *To Bedlam and Part Way Back* (1960), was published when she was thirty-two, and her third book, *Live or Die* (1967), was awarded the Pulitzer Prize, a recognition that crowned the amazing rise to fame of a woman who a few years before had been a suburban housewife without a college degree. Sexton's poetic talents were a brisk diction, a devastating honesty, a gift for black humor, and a lethal talent for exposing the fraudulence and foolishness of the familial and social world, especially in the socialization of women. Her bold dramatic sense led her, in *Transformations* (1971), to adapt well-known fairy tales (about such heroines as Snow White and Briar Rose) in ways that expose the myths of female acceptability underlying those stories.

At the same time, Sexton's poetry dealt in pathos, often the pathos of the abandoned child. Sexton's capacity to resort to the childlike, even the infantile, in language and then to snap quickly to a disillusioned worldliness gave her poems their linguistic energy. The events of Sexton's life—her breakdown, her time in a mental hospital, her therapy, her troubled marriage (ending in divorce), her affairs, and her relationship with her two daughters—became transparently the stuff of her poetry. Her verse, far more directly than that of Lowell or Plath, can be called confessional poetry (a name first applied in 1959 by the critic M. L. Rosenthal). In her forties, after her marriage had ended in divorce, Sexton, who had been teaching at Boston University, committed suicide by carbon monoxide poisoning, leaving behind manuscripts posthumously published as *The Awful Rowing Toward God* (1975) and *45 Mercy Street* (1976), the volumes following *The Death Notebooks* (1974). Her *Complete Poems* was published posthumously in 1981.

The religious guilt evident in these books may perhaps be traced to Sexton's Roman Catholic upbringing. Her preoccupation with self-abasement, sin, sexual transgression, and bodily disgust worked against the efforts she made in years of therapy to find personal equilibrium. Her good looks and her performing spirit (she had been a fashion model as a girl and later founded her own jazz group, called Anne Sexton and Her Kind) made for gallantry of bearing and a winning insouciance in the poetry. But her last years, complicated by dependence on alcohol, made her become repetitive and self-pitying in the writing and to lose formal control of the poetry. Her surreal images became disconnected; the poems grew overlong. She will be remembered chiefly for her poems of the 1960s, those sharp, observant, satiric vignettes of American life, whether in a mental hospital, in a suburban kitchen, or at a country club dance. Her truthtelling wit and her ruthless self-examination gave her poetry a freshness and candor rarely equaled in domestic poetry.

Further Reading:

L. G. Sexton and L. Ames, eds., *A Self-Portrait in Letters*, 1977.

J. D. McClatchy, *Anne Sexton: The Artist and Her Critics*, 1978.

S. Colburn, ed., *No Evil Star: Selected Essays, Interviews, Prose/Anne Sexton*, 1985.

D. George, *Oedipus Anne: The Poetry of Anne Sexton*, 1987.

C. K. B. Hall, *Anne Sexton*, 1989.

L. Wagner-Martin, ed., *Critical Essays on Anne Sexton*, 1989.

D. Middlebrook, *Anne Sexton: A Biography*, 1991.

Text:

The Complete Poems, 1981.

Her Kind

I have gone out, a possessed witch,
haunting the black air, braver at night;
dreaming evil, I have done my hitch
over the plain houses, light by light:
lonely thing, twelve-fingered,[1] out of mind.   5
A woman like that is not a woman, quite.
I have been her kind.

I have found the warm caves in the woods,
filled them with skillets, carvings, shelves,
closets, silks, innumerable goods;   10
fixed the suppers for the worms and the elves:
whining, rearranging the disaligned.
A woman like that is misunderstood.
I have been her kind.

I have ridden in your cart, driver,   15
waved my nude arms at villages going by,
learning the last bright routes, survivor
where your flames still bite my thigh
and my ribs crack where your wheels wind.[2]
A woman like that is not ashamed to die.   20
I have been her kind.

1960

---

[1] Witches were thought to have six fingers on each hand.

[2] In Europe and America in the seventeenth century, women thought to be witches were often burned at the stake after being tortured on the wheel, which stretched the victim's body till the bones broke.

The Truth the Dead Know

For my mother, born March 1902, died March 1959
and my father, born February 1900, died June 1959

Gone, I say, and walk from church,
refusing the stiff procession to the grave,
letting the dead ride alone in the hearse.
It is June. I am tired of being brave.

We drive to The Cape. I cultivate   5
myself where the sun gutters from the sky,
where the sea swings in like an iron gate
and we touch. In another country people die.

My darling, the wind falls in like stones
from the whitehearted water and when we touch   10
we enter touch entirely. No one's alone.
Men kill for this, or for as much.

And what of the dead? They lie without shoes
in their stone boats. They are more like stone
than the sea would be if it stopped. They refuse   15
to be blessed, throat, eye and knucklebone.
                    1962

Self in 1958

What is reality?
I am a plaster doll; I pose
with eyes that cut open without landfall or nightfall
upon some shellacked and grinning person,
eyes that open, blue, steel, and close.   5
Am I approximately an I. Magnin[1] transplant?
I have hair, black angel,
black-angel-stuffing to comb,
nylon legs, luminous arms
and some advertised clothes.   10

I live in a doll's house
with four chairs,
a counterfeit table, a flat roof
and a big front door.
Many have come to such a small crossroad.   15

---

[1] An expensive department store.

There is an iron bed,
(Life enlarges, life takes aim)
a cardboard floor,
windows that flash open on someone's city,
and little more.   20

Someone plays with me,
plants me in the all-electric kitchen,
Is this what Mrs. Rombauer[2] said?
Someone pretends with me—
I am walled in solid by their noise—   25
or puts me upon their straight bed.
They think I am me!
Their warmth? Their warmth is not a friend!
They pry my mouth for their cups of gin
and their stale bread.   30

What is reality
to this synthetic doll
who should smile, who should shift gears,
should spring the doors open in a wholesome disorder,
and have no evidence of ruin or fears?   35
But I would cry,
rooted into the wall that
was once my mother,
if I could remember how
and if I had the tears.   40

1966

For My Lover, Returning to His Wife

She is all there.
She was melted carefully down for you
and cast up from your childhood,
cast up from your one hundred favorite aggies.[1]

She has always been there, my darling.   5
She is, in fact, exquisite.
Fireworks in the dull middle of February
and as real as a cast-iron pot.

Let's face it, I have been momentary.
A luxury. A bright red sloop in the harbor.   10

---

[2] Author of the cookbook *The Joy of Cooking*.   [1] Agate marbles.

My hair rising like smoke from the car window.
Littleneck clams out of season.

She is more than that. She is your have to have,
has grown you your practical your tropical growth.
This is not an experiment. She is all harmony.   15
She sees to oars and oarlocks for the dinghy,

has placed wild flowers at the window at breakfast,
sat by the potter's wheel at midday,
set forth three children under the moon,
three cherubs drawn by Michelangelo,   20

done this with her legs spread out
in the terrible months in the chapel.
If you glance up, the children are there
like delicate balloons resting on the ceiling.

She has also carried each one down the hall   25
after supper, their heads privately bent,
two legs protesting, person to person,
her face flushed with a song and their little sleep.

I give you back your heart.
I give you permission—   30

for the fuse inside her, throbbing
angrily in the dirt, for the bitch in her
and the burying of her wound—
for the burying of her small red wound alive—

for the pale flickering flare under her ribs,   35
for the drunken sailor who waits in her left pulse,
for the mother's knee, for the stockings,
for the garter belt, for the call—

the curious call
when you will burrow in arms and breasts   40

and tug at the orange ribbon in her hair
and answer the call, the curious call.

She is so naked and singular.
She is the sum of yourself and your dream.
Climb her like a monument, step after step.   45
She is solid.

As for me, I am a watercolor.
I wash off.
1969

Snow White and the Seven Dwarfs

No matter what life you lead
the virgin is a lovely number:
cheeks as fragile as cigarette paper,
arms and legs made of Limoges,[1]
lips like Vin Du Rhone,[2]   5
rolling her china-blue doll eyes
open and shut.
Open to say,
Good Day Mama,
and shut for the thrust   10
of the unicorn.
She is unsoiled.
She is as white as a bonefish.

Once there was a lovely virgin
called Snow White.   15
Say she was thirteen.
Her stepmother,
a beauty in her own right,
though eaten, of course, by age,
would hear of no beauty surpassing her own.   20
Beauty is a simple passion,
but, oh my friends, in the end
you will dance the fire dance in iron shoes.
The stepmother had a mirror to which she
      referred—
something like the weather forecast—   25
a mirror that proclaimed
the one beauty of the land.
She would ask,
Looking glass upon the wall,
who is fairest of us all?   30
And the mirror would reply,
You are fairest of us all.
Pride pumped in her like poison.

Suddenly one day the mirror replied,
Queen, you are full fair, 'tis true,   35
but Snow White is fairer than you.
Until that moment Snow White

---

[1] Fine porcelain made in Limoges, France.   [2] Rhône wine (French).

had been no more important
than a dust mouse under the bed.
But now the queen saw brown spots on her hand   40
and four whiskers over her lip
so she condemned Snow White
to be hacked to death.
Bring me her heart, she said to the hunter,
and I will salt it and eat it.   45
The hunter, however, let his prisoner go
and brought a boar's heart back to the castle.
The queen chewed it up like a cube steak.
Now I am fairest, she said,
lapping her slim white fingers.   50

Snow White walked in the wildwood
for weeks and weeks.
At each turn there were twenty doorways
and at each stood a hungry wolf,
his tongue lolling out like a worm.   55
The birds called out lewdly,
talking like pink parrots,
and the snakes hung down in loops,
each a noose for her sweet white neck.
On the seventh week   60
she came to the seventh mountain
and there she found the dwarf house.
It was as droll as a honeymoon cottage
and completely equipped with
seven beds, seven chairs, seven forks   65
and seven chamber pots.
Snow White ate seven chicken livers
and lay down, at last, to sleep.

The dwarfs, those little hot dogs,
walked three times around Snow White,   70
the sleeping virgin. They were wise
and wattled like small czars.
Yes. It's a good omen,
they said, and will bring us luck.
They stood on tiptoes to watch   75
Snow White wake up. She told them
about the mirror and the killer-queen
and they asked her to stay and keep house.
Beware of your stepmother,
they said.   80
Soon she will know you are here.

While we are away in the mines
during the day, you must not
open the door.

Looking glass upon the wall . . .   85
The mirror told
and so the queen dressed herself in rags
and went out like a peddler to trap Snow White.
She went across seven mountains.
She came to the dwarf house   90
and Snow White opened the door
and bought a bit of lacing.
The queen fastened it tightly
around her bodice,
as tight as an Ace bandage,   95
so tight that Snow White swooned.
She lay on the floor, a plucked daisy.
When the dwarfs came home they undid the lace
and she revived miraculously.
She was as full of life as soda pop.   100
Beware of your stepmother,
they said.
She will try once more.

Looking glass upon the wall . . .
Once more the mirror told   105
and once more the queen dressed in rags
and once more Snow White opened the door.
This time she bought a poison comb,
a curved eight-inch scorpion,
and put it in her hair and swooned again.   110
The dwarfs returned and took out the comb
and she revived miraculously.
She opened her eyes as wide as Orphan Annie.[3]
Beware, beware, they said,
but the mirror told,   115
the queen came,
Snow White, the dumb bunny,
opened the door
and she bit into a poison apple
and fell down for the final time.   120
When the dwarfs returned
they undid her bodice,

---

[3] Comic-strip character.

they looked for a comb,
but it did no good.
Though they washed her with wine   125
and rubbed her with butter
it was to no avail.
She lay as still as a gold piece.

The seven dwarfs could not bring themselves
to bury her in the black ground   130
so they made a glass coffin
and set it upon the seventh mountain
so that all who passed by
could peek in upon her beauty.
A prince came one June day   135
and would not budge.
He stayed so long his hair turned green
and still he would not leave.
The dwarfs took pity upon him
and gave him the glass Snow White—   140
its doll's eyes shut forever—
to keep in his far-off castle.
As the prince's men carried the coffin
they stumbled and dropped it
and the chunk of apple flew out   145
of her throat and she woke up miraculously.

And thus Snow White became the prince's bride.
The wicked queen was invited to the wedding feast
and when she arrived there were
red-hot iron shoes,   150
in the manner of red-hot roller skates,
clamped upon her feet.
First your toes will smoke
and then your heels will turn black
and you will fry upward like a frog,   155
she was told.
And so she danced until she was dead,
a subterranean figure,
her tongue flicking in and out
like a gas jet.   160
Meanwhile Snow White held court,
rolling her china-blue doll eyes open and shut
and sometimes referring to her mirror
as women do.
1971

Martin Luther King, Jr.
1929–1968

Martin Luther King, Jr., was born in Atlanta, Georgia, the son and grandson of Baptist ministers. He attended Morehouse College, and received his Ph.D. in divinity from Boston University. In 1955, he returned South and led a black boycott of the buses in Montgomery, Alabama: a boycott which led to a Supreme Court decision ruling Alabama's segregation laws unconstitutional. In 1957, he founded the Southern Christian Leadership Conference (SCLC) to combat segregation and racism, following Mahatma Gandhi's philosophy of nonviolent civil disobedience. Over the next decade, he helped lead protests throughout the South, and was frequently attacked, arrested and imprisoned. In 1963, he wrote *Letter from a Birmingham Jail,* and later that year delivered his celebrated "I Have a Dream" speech at the Lincoln Memorial during the March on Washington for civil rights. The following year, King won the Nobel Peace Prize, at thirty-five the youngest person to be so honored.

King became the subject of FBI investigations and harassment, due in part to J. Edgar Hoover's conviction that he was a Communist, and in part to King's vocal opposition to the war in Vietnam. He was demonstrating on behalf of striking sanitation workers in Memphis, Tennessee, when he was assassinated in 1968. In 1986, Congress established King's birthday as a federal holiday. In addition to *Letter from a Birmingham Jail,* Martin Luther King's published works include *Our Struggle* (1956), *Stride Toward Freedom* (1958), *Why We Can't Wait* (1964), *Trumpet of Conscience* (1967), and *Where Do We Go from Here: Chaos or Community?* (1967).

Letter from Birmingham Jail

April 16, 1963

My Dear Fellow Clergymen:

While confined here in the Birmingham city jail, I came across your recent statement calling my present activities "unwise and untimely." Seldom do I pause to answer criticism of my work and ideas. If I sought to answer all the criticisms that cross my desk, my secretaries would have little time for anything other than such correspondence in the course of the day, and I would have no time for constructive work. But since I feel that you are men of genuine good will and that your criticisms are sincerely set forth, I want to try to answer your statement in what I hope will be patient and reasonable terms.

I think I should indicate why I am here in Birmingham, since you have been influenced by the view which argues against "outsiders coming in." I have the honor of serving as president of the Southern Christian Leadership Conference, an organization operating in every southern state, with headquarters in Atlanta, Georgia. We have some eighty-five affiliated organizations across the South, and one of them is the Alabama Christian Movement for Human Rights. Frequently we share staff, educational, and financial resources with our affiliates. Several months ago the affiliate here in Birmingham asked us to be on call to engage in a nonviolent direct-action program if such were deemed necessary. We readily consented, and when the hour came we lived up to our promise. So I, along with several members of my staff, am here because I was invited here. I am here because I have organizational ties here.

But more basically, I am in Birmingham because injustice is here. Just as the prophets of the eighth century B.C. left their villages and carried their "thus saith the Lord" far beyond the boundaries of their home towns, and just as the Apostle Paul left his village of Tarsus and carried the gospel of Jesus Christ to the far corners of the Greco-Roman world, so am I compelled to carry the gospel of freedom beyond my own home town. Like Paul, I must constantly respond to the Macedonian call for aid.

Moreover, I am cognizant of the interrelatedness of all communities and states. I cannot sit idly by in Atlanta and not be concerned about what happens in Birmingham. Injustice anywhere is a threat to justice everywhere. We are caught in an inescapable network of mutuality, tied in a single garment of destiny. Whatever affects one directly, affects all indirectly. Never again can we afford to live with the narrow, provincial, "outside agitator" idea. Anyone who lives inside the United States can never be considered an outsider anywhere within its bounds.

You deplore the demonstrations taking place in Birmingham. But your statement, I am sorry to say, fails to express a similar concern for the conditions that brought about the demonstrations. I am sure that none of you would want to rest content with the superficial kind of social analysis that deals merely with effects and does not grapple with underlying causes. It is unfortunate that demonstrations are taking place in Birmingham, but it is even more unfortunate that the city's white power structure left the Negro community with no alternative.

In any nonviolent campaign there are four basic steps: collection of the facts to determine whether injustices exist; negotiation; self-purification; and direct action. We have gone through all these steps in Birmingham. There can be no gainsaying the fact that racial injustice engulfs this community. Birmingham is probably the most thoroughly segregated city in the United States. Its ugly record of brutality is widely known. Negroes have experienced grossly unjust treatment in the courts. There have been more unsolved bombings of Negro homes and churches in Birmingham than in any other city in the nation. There are the hard brutal facts of the case. On the basis of these conditions, Negro leaders sought to negotiate with the city fathers. But the latter consistently refused to engage in good-faith negotiation.

Then, last September, came the opportunity to talk with leaders of Birmingham's economic community. In the course of the negotiations, certain promises were made by the merchants—for example, to remove the stores' humiliating racial signs. On the basis of these promises, the Reverend Fred Shuttlesworth and the leaders of the Alabama Christian Movement for Human Rights agreed to a moratorium on all demonstrations. As the weeks and months went by, we realized that we were the victims of a broken promise. A few signs, briefly removed, returned; the others remained.

As in so many past experiences, our hopes had been blasted, and the shadows of deep disappointment settled upon us. We had no alternative except to prepare for direct action, whereby we would present our very bodies as a means of laying our case before the conscience of the local and the national community. Mindful of the difficulties involved, we decided to undertake a process of self-purification. We began a series of workshops on nonviolence, and we repeatedly asked ourselves: "Are you able to accept blows without retaliating?" "Are you able to endure the ordeal of jail?" We decided to schedule our direct-action program for the Easter season, realizing that except for Christmas, this is the main shopping period of the year. Knowing that a strong economic-withdrawal program would be the by-product of direct action, we felt that this would be the best time to bring pressure to bear on the merchants for the needed change.

Then it occurred to us that Birmingham's mayoral election was coming up in March, and we speedily decided to postpone action until after election day. When we discovered that the Commissioner of Public Safety, Eugene "Bull" Connor, had piled up enough votes to be in the run-off, we decided again to postpone action until the day after the run-off so that the demonstrations could not be used to cloud the issues. Like many others, we waited to see Mr. Connor defeated, and to this end we endured postponement after postponement. Having aided in this community need, we felt that our direct-action program could be delayed no longer.

You may well ask, "Why direct action? Why sit-ins, marches, and so forth? Isn't negotiation a better path?" You are quite right in calling for negotiation. Indeed, this is the very purpose of direct action. Nonviolent direct action seeks to create such a crisis and foster such a tension that a community which has constantly refused to negotiate is forced to confront the issue. It seeks so to dramatize the issue that it can no longer be ignored. My citing the creation of tension as part of the work of the nonviolent resister may sound rather shocking. But I must confess that I am not afraid of the word "tension." I have earnestly opposed violent tension, but there is a type of constructive, nonvioent tension which is necessary for growth. Just as Socrates felt that it was necessary to create a tension in the mind so that individuals could rise from the bondage of myths and half truths to the unfettered realm of creative analysis and objective appraisal, so must we see the need for nonviolent gadflies to create the kind of tension in society that will help men rise from the dark depths of prejudice and racism to the majestic heights of understanding and brotherhood.

The purpose of our direct-action program is to create a situation so crisis-packed that it will inevitably open the door to negotiation. I therefore concur with you in your call for negotiation. Too long has our beloved Southland been bogged down in a tragic effort to live in monologue rather than dialogue.

One of the basic points in your statement is that the action that I and my associates have taken in Birmingham is untimely. Some have asked: "Why didn't you give the new city administration time to act?" The only answer that I can give to this query is that the new Birmingham administration must be prodded about as much as the outgoing one, before it will act. We are sadly mistaken if we feel that the election of Albert Boutwell as mayor will bring the millenniun to Birmingham. While Mr. Boutwell is a much more gentle person than Mr. Connor, they are both segregationists, dedicated to maintenance of the status quo. I have hoped that Mr. Boutwell will be reasonable enough to see the futility of massive resistance to desegregation. But he will not see this without pressure from devotees of civil rights. My friends, I must say to you that we have not made a single gain in civil rights without determined legal and nonviolent pressure. Lamentably, it is an historical fact that privileged groups seldom give up their privileges voluntarily. Individuals may see the moral light and voluntarily give up their unjust posture; but, as Reinhold Niebuhr has reminded us, groups tend to be more immoral than individuals.

We know through painful experience that freedom is never voluntarily given by the oppressor; it must be demanded by the oppressed. Frankly, I have yet to engage in a direct-action campaign that was "well timed" in the view of those who have not suffered unduly from the disease of segregation. For years now I have heard the word "Wait!" It rings in the ear of every Negro with piercing familiarity. This "Wait" has almost always meant "Never." We must come to see, with one of our distinguished jurists, that "justice too long delayed is justice denied."

We have waited for more than 340 years for our constitutional and God-given rights. The nations of Asia and Africa are moving with jet-like speed toward gaining political independence, but we still creep at horse-and-buggy pace toward gaining a cup of coffee at a lunch counter. Perhaps it is easy for those who have never felt the stinging darts of segregation to say, "Wait." But when you have seen vicious mobs lynch your mothers and fathers at will and drown your sisters and brothers at whim; when you have seen hate-filled policemen curse, kick, and even kill your black brothers and sisters; when you see the vast majority of your twenty million Negro brothers smothering in an airtight cage of poverty in the midst of an affluent society; when you suddenly find your tongue twisted and your speech stammering as you seek to explain to your six-year-old daughter why she can't go to the public amusement park that has just been advertised on television, and see tears welling up in her eyes when she is told that Funtown is closed to colored children, and see ominous clouds of inferiority beginning to form in her little mental sky, and see her beginning to distort her personality by developing an unconscious bitterness toward white people; when you have to concoct an answer for a five-year-old son who is asking, "Daddy, why do white people treat colored people so mean?"; when you take a cross-country drive and find it necessary to sleep night after night in the uncomfortable corners of your automobile because no motel will accept you; when you are humiliated day in and day out by nagging signs reading "white" and "colored"; when your first name becomes "nigger," your middle name becomes "boy" (however old you are) and your last name becomes "John," and your wife and mother are never given the respected title "Mrs."; when you are harried by day and haunted by night by the fact that you are a Negro, living constantly at tiptoe stance, never quite knowing what to expect next, and are plagued with inner fears and outer resentments; when you are forever fighting a degenerating sense of "nobodi-ness"—then you will understand why we find it difficult to wait. There comes a time when the cup of endurance runs over, and men are no longer willing to be plunged into the abyss of despair. I hope, sirs, you can understand our legitimate and unavoidable impatience.

You express a great deal of anxiety over our willingness to break laws. This is certainly a legitimate concern. Since we so diligently urge people to obey the Supreme Court's decision of 1954 outlawing segregation in the public schools, at first glance it may seem rather paradoxical for us consciously to break laws. One may well ask: "How can you advocate breaking some laws and obeying others?" The answer lies in the fact that there are two types of laws: just and unjust. I would be the first to advocate obeying just laws. One has not only a legal but a moral responsibility to obey just laws. Conversely, one has a moral responsibility to disobey unjust laws. I would agree with St. Augustine that "an unjust law is no law at all."

Now, what is the difference between the two? How does one determine whether a law is just or unjust? A just law is a man-made code that squares with the moral law or the law of God. An unjust law is a code that is out of harmony with the moral law. To put it in the terms of St. Thomas Aquinas: An unjust law is a human law that is not rooted in eternal law and natural law. Any law that uplifts human personality is just. Any law that degrades human personality is unjust. All segregation statutes are unjust because segregation distorts the soul and damages the personality. It gives the segregator a false sense of superiority and the segregated a false sense of inferiority. Segregation, to use the terminology of the Jewish philosopher Martin Buber, substitues an "I-it" relationship for an "I-thou" relationship and ends up relegating persons to the status of things. Hence segregation is not only politically, economically, and sociologically unsound, it is morally wrong and sinful. Paul Tillich has said that sin is separation. Is not segregation an existential expression of man's tragic separation, his awful estrangement, his terrible sinfullness? Thus it is that I can urge men to obey the 1954 decision of the Supreme Court, for it is morally right; and I can urge them to disobey segregation ordinances, for they are morally wrong.

Let us consider a more concrete example of just and unjust laws. An unjust law is a code that a numerical or power majority group compels a minority group to obey but does not make binding on itself. This is *difference* made legal. By the same token, a just law is a code that a majority compels a minority to follow and that it is willing to follow itself. This is *sameness* made legal.

Let me give another explanation. A law is unjust if it is inflicted on a minority that, as a result of being denied the right to vote, had no part in enacting or devising the law. Who can say that the legislature of Alabama which set up that state's segregation laws was democratically elected? Throughout Alabama all sorts of devious methods are used to prevent Negroes from becoming registered voters, and there are some counties in which, even though Negroes constitute a majority of the population, not a single Negro is registered. Can any law enacted under such circumstances be considered democratically structured?

Sometimes a law is just on its face and unjust in its application. For instance, I have been arrested on a charge of parading without a permit. Now, there is nothing wrong in having an ordinance which requires a permit for a parade. But such an ordinance becomes unjust when it is used to maintain segregation and to deny citizens the First Amendment privilege of peaceful assembly and protest.

I hope you are able to see the distinction I am trying to point out. In no sense do I advocate evading or defying the law, as would the rabid segregationist. That would lead to anarchy. One who breaks an unjust law must do so openly, lovingly, and with a willingness to accept the penalty. I submit that an individual who breaks a law that conscience tells him is unjust, and who willingly accepts the penalty of imprisonment in order to arouse the conscience of the community over its injustice, is in reality expressing the highest respect for law.

Of course, there is nothing new about this kind of civil disobedience. It was evidenced sublimely in the refusal of Shadrach, Meshach, and Abednego to obey the laws of Nebuchadnezzar, on the ground that a higher moral law was at stake. It was practiced superbly by the early Christians, who were willing to face hungry lions and the excruciating pain of chopping blocks rather than submit to certain unjust laws of the Roman Empire. To a degree, academic freedom is a reality today because Socrates practiced civil disobedience. In our own nation, the Boston Tea Party represented a massive act of civil disobedience.

We should never forget that everything Adolf Hitler did in Germany was "legal" and everything the Hungarian freedom fighters did in Hungary was "illegal." It was "illegal" to aid and comfort a Jew in Hitler's Germany. Even so, I am sure that, had I lived in Germany at the time, I would have aided and comforted my Jewish brothers. If today I lived in a Communist country where certain principles dear to the Christian faith are suppressed, I would openly advocate disobeying that country's antireligious laws.

I must make two honest confessions to you, my Christian and Jewish brothers. First, I must confess that over the past few years I have been gravely disappointed with the white moderate. I have almost reached the regrettable conclusion that the Negro's great stumbling block in his stride toward freedom is not the White Citizen's Councilor or the Ku Klux Klanner, but the white moderate, who is more devoted to "order" than to justice, who prefers a negative peace which is the absence of tension to a positive peace which is the presence of justice; who constantly says, "I agree with you in the goal you seek, but I cannot agree with your methods of direct action"; who paternalistically believes he can set the timetable for another man's freedom; who lives by a mythical concept of time and who constantly advises the Negro to wait for a "more convenient season." Shallow understanding from people of good will is more frustrating than absolute misunderstanding from people of ill will. Lukewarm acceptance is much more bewildering than outright rejection.

I had hoped that the white moderate would understand that law and order exist for the purpose of establishing justice and that when they fail in this purpose they become the dangerously structured dams that block the flow of social progress. I had hoped that the white moderate would understand that the present tension in the South is a necessary phase of the transition from an obnoxious negative peace, in which the Negro passively accepted his unjust plight, to a substantive and positive peace, in which all men will respect the dignity and worth of human personality. Actually, we who engage in nonviolent direct action are not the creators of tension. We merely bring to the surface the hidden tension that is already alive. We bring it out in the open, where it can be seen and dealt with. Like a boil that can never be cured so long as it is covered up but must be opened with all its ugliness to the natural medicines of air and light, injustices must be exposed, with all the tension its exposure creates, to the light of human conscience and the air of national opinion, before it can be cured.

In your statement you assert that our actions, even though peaceful, must be condemned because they precipitate violence. But is this a logical assertion? Isn't this like condemning a robbed man because his possession of money precipitated the evil act of robbery? Isn't this like condemning Socrates because his unswerving commitment to truth and his philosophical inquiries precipitated the act by the misguided populace in which they made him drink hemlock? Isn't this like condemning Jesus because his unique God-consciousness and never-ceasing devotion to God's will precipitated the evil act of crucifixion? We must come to see that, as the federal courts have consistently affirmed, it is wrong to urge an individual to cease his efforts to gain his basic constitutional rights because the quest may precipitate violence. Society must protect the robbed and punish the robber.

I had also hoped that the white moderate would reject the myth concerning time in relation to the struggle for freedom. I have just received a letter from a white brother in

Texas. He writes: "All Christians know that the colored people will receive equal rights eventually, but it is possible that you are in too great a religious hurry. It has taken Christianity almost two thousand years to accomplish what it has. The teachings of Christ take time to come to earth." Such an attitude stems from a tragic misconception of time, from the strangely irrational notion that there is something in the very flow of time that will inevitably cure all ills. Actually, time itself is neutral; it can be used either destructively or constructively. More and more I feel that the people of ill will have used time much more effectively than have the people of good will. We will have to repent in this generation not merely for the hateful words and actions of the bad people, but for the appalling silence of the good people. Human progress never rolls in on wheels of inevitability; it comes through the tireless efforts of men willing to be co-workers with God, and without this hard work, time itself becomes an ally of the forces of social stagnation. We must use time creatively, in the knowledge that the time is always ripe to do right. Now is the time to make real the promise of democracy and transform our pending national elegy into a creative psalm of brotherhood. Now is the time to lift our national policy from the quicksand of racial injustice to the solid rock of human dignity.

You speak of our activity in Birmingham as extreme. At first I was rather disappointed that fellow clergymen would see my nonviolent efforts as those of an extremist. I began thinking about the fact that I stand in the middle of two opposing forces in the Negro community. One is a force of complacency made up in part of Negroes who, as a result of long years of oppression, are so drained of self-respect and a sense of "somebodiness" that they have adjusted to segregation; and in part of a few middle-class Negroes who, because of a degree of academic and economic security and because in some ways they profit by segregation, have become insensitive to the problems of the masses. The other force is one of bitterness and hatred, and it comes perilously close to advocating violence. It is expressed in the various black nationalist groups that are springing up across the nation, the largest and best known being Elijah Muhammed's Muslim movement. Nourished by the Negro's frustration over the continued existence of racial discrimination, this movement is made up of people who have lost faith in America, who have absolutely repudiated Christianity, and who have concluded that the white man is an incorrigible "devil."

I have tried to stand between these two forces, saying that we need emulate neither the "do-nothingism" of the complacent nor the hatred and despair of the black nationalist. For there is the more excellent way of love and nonviolent protest. I am grateful to God that, through the influence of the Negro church, the way of nonviolence became an integral part of our struggle.

If this philosophy had not emerged, by now many streets of the South would, I am convinced, be flowing with blood. And I am further convinced that if our white brothers dismiss as "rabble-rousers" and "outside agitators" those of us who employ nonviolent direct action, and if they refuse to support our nonviolent efforts, millions of Negroes will, out of frustration and despair, seek solace and security in black nationalist ideologies—a development that would inevitably lead to a frightening racial nightmare.

Oppressed people cannot remain oppressed forever. The yearning for freedom eventually manifests itself, and that is what has happened to the American Negro. Something within has reminded him of his birthright of freedom, and something without has reminded him that it can be gained. Consciously or unconsciously, he has been caught up by the Zeitgeist, and with his black brothers of Africa and his brown and yellow brothers of Asia, South America, and the Caribbean, the United States Negro is moving with a sense of great urgency toward the promised land of racial justice. If one recognizes this vital urge that has engulfed the Negro community, one should readily understand why public demonstrations are taking place. The Negro has many pent-up resentments and latent frustrations, and he must release them. So let him march; let him make prayer pilgrimages to the city hall, let him go on freedom rides—and try to understand why he must do so. If his repressed emotions are not released in nonviolent ways, they will seek expression through violence; this is not a threat but a fact of history. So I have not said to my people, "Get rid of your discontent." Rather, I have tried to say that this normal and healthy discontent can be channeled into the creative outlet of nonviolent direct action. And now this approach is being termed extremist.

But though I was initially disappointed at being categorized as an extremist, as I continued to think about the matter I gradually gained a measure of satisfaction from the label. Was not Jesus an extremist for love: "Love your enemies, bless them that curse you, do good to them that hate you, and pray for them which despitefully use you, and persecute you." Was not Amos an extremist for justice: "Let justice roll down like waters and righteousness like an ever-flowing stream." Was not Paul an extremist for the Christian gospel: "I bear in my body the marks of the Lord Jesus." Was not Martin Luther an extremist: "Here I stand; I cannot do otherwise, so help me God." And John Bunyan: "I will stay in jail to the end of my days before I make a butchery of my conscience." And Abraham Lincoln: "This nation cannot survive half slave and half free." And Thomas Jefferson: "We hold these truths to be self-evident, that all men are created equal. . . ." So the question is not whether we will be extremists, but what kind of extremists we will be. Will we be extremists for hate for for love? Will we be extremists for the preservation of injustice or for the extension of justice? In that dramatic scene on Calvary's hill three men were crucified. We must never forget that all three were crucified for the same crime—the crime of extremism. Two were extremists for immorality, and thus fell below their environment. The other, Jesus Christ, was an extremist for love, truth, and goodness, and thereby rose above his environment. Perhaps the South, the nation, and the world are in dire need of creative extremists.

I had hoped that the white moderate would see this need. Perhaps I was too optimistic; perhaps I expected too much. I suppose I should have realized that few members of the oppressor race can understand the deep groans and passionate yearnings of the oppressed race, and still fewer have the vision to see that injustice must be rooted out by strong, persistent, and determined action. I am thankful, however, that some of our white brothers in the South have grasped the meaning of this social revolution and committed themselves to it. They are still all too few in quantity, but they are big in quality. Some—such as Ralph McGill, Lillian Smith, Harry Golden, James McBride Dabbs, Ann Braden, and Sarah Patton Boyle—have written about our struggle in eloquent and prophetic terms. Others have marched with us down nameless streets of the South. They have languished in filthy, roach-infested jails, suffering the abuse and brutality of policemen who view them as "dirty nigger-lovers." Unlike so many of their moderate brothers and sisters, they have recognized the urgency of the moment and sensed the need for powerful "action" antidotes to combat the disease of segregation.

Let me take note of my other major disappointment. I have been so greatly disappointed with the white church and its leadership. Of course, there are some notable exceptions. I am not unmindful of the fact that each of you has taken some significant stands on this issue. I commend you, Reverend Stallings, for your Christian stand on this past Sunday, in welcoming Negroes to your worship service on a non-segregated basis. I commend the Catholic leaders of this state for integrating Spring Hill College serveral years ago.

But despite these notable exceptions, I must honestly reiterate that I have been disappointed with the church. I do not say this as one of those negative critics who can always find something wrong with the church. I say this as a minister of the gospel, who loves the church; who was nurtured in its bosom; who has been sustained by its spiritual blessings and who will remain true to it as long as the cord of life shall lengthen.

When I was suddenly catapulted into the leadership of the bus protest in Montgomery, Alabama, a few years ago, I felt we would be supported by the white church. I felt that the white ministers, priests, and rabbis of the South would be among our strongest allies. Instead, some have been outright opponents, refusing to understand the freedom movement and misrepresenting its leaders; all too many others have been more cautious than courageous and have remained silent behind the anesthetizing security of stained-glass windows.

In spite of my shattered dreams, I came to Birmingham with the hope that the white religious leadership of this community would see the justice of our cause and, with deep moral concerns, would serve as the channel through which our just grievances could reach the power structure. I had hoped that each of you would understand. But again I have been disappointed. . . .

There was a time when the church was very powerful—in the time when the early Christians rejoiced at being deemed worthy to suffer for what they believed. In those days the church was not merely a thermometer that recorded the ideas and principles of popular opinion; it was a thermostat that transformed the mores of society. Whenever the early Christians entered a town, the people in power became disturbed and immediately sought to convict the Christians for being "disturbers of the peace" and "outside agitators." But the Christians pressed on, in the conviction that they were "a colony of heaven," called to obey God rather than man. Small in number, they were big in commitment. They were too God intoxicated to be "astronomically intimidated." By their effort and example they brought an end to such ancient evils as infanticide and gladiatorial contests.

Things are different now. So often the contemporary church is a weak, ineffectual voice with an uncertain sound. So often it is an archdefender of the status quo. Far from being disturbed by the presence of the church, the power structure of the average community is consoled by the church's silent—and often even vocal—sanction of things as they are.

But the judgment of God is upon the church as never before. If today's church does not recapture the sacrificial spirit of the early church, it will lose its authenticity, forfeit the loyalty of millions, and be dismissed as an irrelevant social club with no meaning for the twentieth century. Every day I meet young people whose disappointment with the church has turned into outright disgust.

Perhaps I have once again been too optimistic. Is organized religion too inextricably bound to the status quo to save our nation and the world? Perhaps I must turn my faith to the inner spiritual church, the church within the church, as the true ekklesia and the hope of the world. But again I am thankful to God that some noble souls from the ranks of organized religion have broken loose from the paralyzing chains of conformity and joined us as active partners in the struggle for freedom. They have left their secure congregations and walked the streets of Albany, Georgia, with us. They have gone down the highways of the South on torturous rides for freedom. Yes, they have gone to jail with us. Some have been dismissed from their churches, have lost the support of their bishops and fellow ministers. But they have acted in the faith that right defeated is stronger than evil triumphant. Their witness has been the spiritual salt that has preserved the true meaning of the gospel in these troubled times. They have carved a tunnel of hope through the dark mountain of disappointment.

I hope the church as a whole will meet the challenge of this decisive hour. But even if the church does not come to the aid of justice, I have no despair about the future. I have no fear about the outcome of our struggle in Birmingham, even if our motives are at present misunderstood. We will reach the goal of freedom in Birmingham and all over the nation, because the goal of America is freedom. Abused and scorned though we may be, our destiny is tied up with America's destiny. Before the pilgrims landed at Plymouth, we were here. Before the pen of Jefferson etched the majestic words of the Declaration of Independence across the pages of history, we were here. For more than two centuries our forebears labored in this country without wages; they made cotton king; they built the homes of their masters while suffering gross injustice and shameful humiliation—and yet out of a bottomless vitality they continued to thrive and develop. If the inexpressible cruelties of slavery could not stop us, the opposition we now face will surely fail. We will win our freedom because the sacred heritage of our nation and the eternal will of God are embodied in our echoing demands.

Before closing I feel impelled to mention one other point in your statement that has troubled me profoundly. You warmly commended the Birmingham police force for keeping "order" and "preventing violence." I doubt that you would have so warmly commended the police force if you had seen its dogs sinking their teeth into unarmed, non-violent Negroes. I doubt that you would so quickly commend the policemen if you were to observe their ugly and inhumane treatment of Negroes here in the city jail; if you were to watch them push and curse old Negro women and young Negro girls; if you were to see them slap and kick old Negro men and young boys; if you were to observe them, as they did on two occasions, refuse to give us food because we wanted to sing our grace together. I cannot join you in your praise of the Birmingham police department.

It is true that the police have exercised a degree of discipline in handling the demonstrators. In this sense they have conducted themselves rather "nonviolently" in public. But for what purpose? To preserve the evil system of segregation. Over the past few years I have consistently preached that nonviolence demands that the means we use must be as pure as the ends we seek. I have tried to make clear that it is wrong to use immoral means to attain moral ends. But now I must affirm that it is just as wrong, or perhaps even more so, to use moral means to preserve immoral ends. Perhaps Mr. Connor and his policemen have been rather nonviolent in public, as was Chief Pritchett in Albany, Georgia, but they have used the moral means of nonviolence to maintain the immoral end of racial injustice. As T. S. Eliot has said, "The last temptation is the greatest treason: To do the right deed for the wrong reason."

I wish you had commended the Negro sit-inners and demonstrators of Birmingham for their sublime courage, their willingness to suffer, and their amazing discipline in the midst of great provocation. One day the South will recognize its real heroes. They will be the James Merediths, with the noble sense of purpose that enables them to face jeering and hostile mobs, and with the agonizing loneliness that characterizes the life of the pioneer. They will be old, oppressed, battered Negro women, symbolized in a seventy-two-year-old woman in Montgomery, Alabama, who rose up with a sense of dignity and with her people decided not to ride segregated buses, and who responded with ungrammatical profundity to one who inquired about her weariness: "My feets is tired, but my soul is at rest." They will be the young high school and college students, the young ministers of the gospel and a host of their elders, courageously and nonviolently sitting in at lunch counters and willingly going to jail for conscience' sake. One day the South will know that when these disinherited children of God sat down at lunch counters, they were in reality standing up for what is best in the American dream and for the most sacred values in our Judaeo-Christian heritage, thereby bringing our nation back to those great wells of democracy which were dug deep by the founding fathers in their formulation of the Constitution and the Declaration of Independence.

Never before have I written so long a letter. I'm afraid it is much too long to take your precious time. I can assure you that it would have been much shorter if I had been writing from a comfortable desk, but what else can one do when he is alone in a narrow jail cell, other than write long letters, think long thoughts, and pray long prayers?

If I have said anything in this letter that overstates the truth and indicates an unreasonable impatience, I beg you to forgive me. If I have said anything that understates the truth and indicates my having a patience that allows me to settle for anything less than brotherhood, I beg God to forgive me.

I hope this letter finds you strong in the faith. I also hope that circumstances will soon make it possible for me to meet each of you, not as an integrationist or a civil rights leader but as a fellow clergyman and a Christian brother. Let us all hope that the dark clouds of racial prejudice will soon pass away and the deep fog of misunderstanding will be lifted from our fear-drenched communities, and in some not too distant tomorrow the radiant stars of love and brotherhood will shine over our great nation with all their scintillating beauty.

Yours in the cause of Peace and Brotherhood,

Martin Luther King, Jr.

1963

Adrienne Rich
b. 1929

Adrienne Rich was a precocious poet; her first book, *A Change of World* (1951), was selected by W. H. Auden for the Yale Younger Poets series when Rich was still a student at Radcliffe. The daughter of a Jewish doctor and professor of medicine at Johns Hopkins University and a non-Jewish mother, Rich grew up under the intense tutlage of her father. She became estranged from him when, against his assimilationist wishes, she married a Jewish economist, Alfred Conrad, a professor at Harvard. (The family conflicts have been repeatedly examined in Rich's verse.) Rich quickly had three sons; she writes in *Of Woman Born* (1976) of her unhappiness as a wife and mother and of the conflict she felt between those roles, as socially defined, and that of the writer. In 1963, at the age of thirty-four, Rich published *Snapshots of a Daughter-in-Law,* in which the themes of rebellion and disaffection present in masked forms in her first two books became overt. In the 1960s Rich and her husband moved to New York; the marriage dissolved, and Rich's husband committed suicide. Some years later, Rich declared herself to be a lesbian and joined lesbian political action to the other forms of social action in which she had engaged during the 1960s, when she had taught in the open admissions program at the City College of New York and had joined in protests against the Vietnam War.

Rich has lived a politically committed life and has not always escaped the dangers of politically inspired writing—a preference for bluntness over complexity of response, a certain predictability of stance. At the same time, she has been a seismograph of American protest, registering in turn the convulsions of the peace movement, the women's movement, and, later, the gay rights movement.

More recently, Rich has turned to reexamining the traditional life of women in the past, hoping to reconstruct a connection between those older female arts and skills and the inner life of contemporary women. After living for some years in western Massachusetts, she moved to California.

Though Rich's accomplished early verse in *A Change of World* (1951) and *The Diamond Cutters* (1955) imitated the formal patterns she found in Yeats, Auden, and Frost, she moved during the 1960s into free verse and has only rarely returned to formal prosody. She has experimented with the prose poem as well as with forms, such as "jump cuts," borrowed from the cinema and from photography. Her forms seem, however, subordinate to the urgency of the voice that speaks in the poems, whether in rage or in measured attack. It is typical of Rich to utter a theme first in a crude oppositional cartoon, like a political caricaturist, and then more subtly and deeply explore it. *Leaflets* (1969), as its title implies, had the urgency of a set of bulletins from a political strategy center; *The Will to Change* (1971) explored inner personal drama, that drama that Rich has continued to trace in her metaphors of exile, toil, burning, sickness, devastation, rape, imprisonment, nakedness, and struggle. "I am trying to hold in one steady glance / all the parts of my life," she says in "Toward the Solstice," echoing Matthew Arnold's wish "to see life steadily and see it whole."

It is in fact the Victorians whom Rich resembles in her earnestness, her direct gaze at social conditions, and her tone of public moral assertion. But she has never been content simply to be a propagandist. Her drive to make poetry of her autobiography reveals a subjectivity not entirely willing to be absorbed in the role of collective spokesperson. Her books from the late 1970s through the mid-1980s—*The Dream of a Common Language* (1978), *A Wild Patience Has Taken Me This Far* (1981), *The Fact of a Doorframe* (1985), *Your Native Land, Your Life* (1986), and *An Atlas of the Difficult World: Poems 1988–1991* (1991)—show an increasingly complex and searching response to the deprivations and yearning of the human condition. Rich's most recent books include *Time Power: Poems 1985–1988* (1988), *Collected Early Poems, 1950–1970*

(1993), *Dark Fields of the Republic, Poems 1991–1995* (1995), and a book of essays, *What Is Found There: Notebooks on Poetry and Politics,* 1993.

Further Reading:

B. C. Gelpi and A. Gelpi, eds., *Adrienne Rich's Poetry: Text of the Poems; The Poet on Her Work; Reviews and Criticism,* 1975.

C. Altieri, *Self and Sensibility in Contemporary American Poetry,* 1984.

J. R. Cooper, ed., *Reading Adrienne Rich,* 1984.

B. Erkkila, "Dickinson and Rich: Toward a Theory of Female Poetic Influence," *American Literature,* December 1984.

C. Keyes, *The Aesthetics of Power: The Poetry of Adrienne Rich,* 1986.

C. Werner, *Adrienne Rich: The Poet and Her Critics,* 1988.

A. Templeton, *The Dream and The Dialogue: Adrienne Rich's Feminist Poetics,* 1994.

P. Erickson, "Singing America: From Walt Whitman to Adrienne Rich," *Kenyon Review,* Winter 1995.

Text:

Poems Selected and New, 1950–1974, 1975.

Living in Sin

She had thought the studio would keep itself;
no dust upon the furniture of love.
Half heresy, to wish the taps less vocal,
the panes relieved of grime. A plate of pears,
a piano with a Persian shawl, a cat   5
stalking the picturesque amusing mouse
had risen at his urging.
Not that at five each separate stair would writhe
under the milkman's tramp; that morning light
so coldly would delineate the scraps   10
of last night's cheese and three sepulchral bottles;
that on the kitchen shelf among the saucers
a pair of beetle-eyes would fix her own—
envoy from some village in the moldings . . .
Meanwhile, he, with a yawn,   15
sounded a dozen notes upon the keyboard,
declared it out of tune, shrugged at the mirror,
rubbed at his beard, went out for cigarettes;
while she, jeered by the minor demons,
pulled back the sheets and made the bed and found   20
a towel to dust the table-top,
and let the coffee-pot boil over on the stove.
By evening she was back in love again,
though not so wholly but throughout the night

she woke sometimes to feel the daylight coming   25
like a relentless milkman up the stairs.
1955

The Knight

A knight rides into the noon,
and his helmet points to the sun,
and a thousand splintered suns
are the gaiety of his mail.
The soles of his feet glitter   5
and his palms flash in reply,
and under his crackling banner
he rides like a ship in sail.

A knight rides into the noon,
and only his eye is living,   10
a lump of bitter jelly
set in a metal mask,
betraying rags and tatters
that cling to the flesh beneath
and wear his nerves to ribbons   15
under the radiant casque.

Who will unhorse this rider
and free him from between
the walls of iron, the emblems
crushing his chest with their weight?   20
Will they defeat him gently,
or leave him hurled on the green,
his rags and wounds still hidden
under the great breastplate?
1957

Necessities of Life

Piece by piece I seem
to re-enter the world: I first began

a small, fixed dot, still see
that old myself, a dark-blue thumbtack

pushed into the scene,   5
a hard little head protruding

from the pointillist's buzz and bloom.
After a time the dot

begins to ooze. Certain heats
melt it.   10
    Now I was hurriedly

blurring into ranges
of burnt red, burning green,

whole biographies swam up and
swallowed me like Jonah.[1]   15

Jonah! I was Wittgenstein,
Mary Wollstonecraft, the soul

of Louis Jouvet,[2] dead
in a blown-up photograph.

Till, wolfed almost to shreds,   20
I learned to make myself

unappetizing. Scaly as a dry bulb
thrown into a cellar

I used myself, let nothing use me.
Like being on a private dole,   25

sometimes more like kneading bricks in Egypt.[3]
What life was there, was mine,

now and again to lay
one hand on a warm brick

and touch the sun's ghost   30
with economical joy,

[1] Prophet swallowed by a whale (Jonah 1:17).
[2] Wittgenstein: Ludwig Wittgenstein, Austrian philosopher who lived in England (1889–1951); Mary Wollstonecraft: author (1759–1797) of the *Vindication of the Rights of Women* (1792), wife of William Godwin, and mother of Mary Shelley, Louis Jouvet: French stage and film actor (1887–1951).
[3] The work of the Jews before Moses led them out of slavery.

now and again to name
over the bare necessities.

So much for those days. Soon
practice may make me middling-perfect, I'll   35

dare inhabit the world
trenchant in motion as an eel, solid

as a cabbage-head. I have invitations:
a curl of mist steams upward

from a field, visible as my breath,   40
houses along a road stand waiting

like old women knitting, breathless
to tell their tales.
1966

"I Am in Danger—Sir—"*

"Half-cracked" to Higginson, living,
afterward famous in garbled versions,

your hoard of dazzling scraps a battlefield,
now your old snood

mothballed at Harvard[1]   5
and you in your variorum monument
equivocal to the end—
who are you?

Gardening the day-lily,
wiping the wine-glass stems,   10
your thought pulsed on behind
a forehead battered paper-thin,

you, woman, maculine
in single-mindedness,

---

* From Emily Dickinson's letter of June 7,
  1862, to Thomas Wentworth Higginson
  (1823–1911), then editor of the *Atlantic
  Monthly.*
[1] Memorabilia of the Dickinson homestead, as
well as the packets of manuscript poems by
Emily Dickinson, are kept in the Dickinson
Room of the Houghton Library at Harvard
University.

for whom the word was more   15
than a symptom—

a condition of being.
Till the air buzzing with spoiled language
sang in your ears
of Perjury   20

and in your half-cracked way you chose
silence for entertainment,
chose to have it out at last
on your own premises.
1966

Trying to Talk with a Man

Out in this desert we are testing bombs,

that's why we came here.

Sometimes I feel an underground river
forcing its way between deformed cliffs
an acute angle of understanding   5
moving itself like a locus of the sun
into this condemned scenery.

What we've had to give up to get here—
whole LP collections, films we starred in
playing in the neighborhoods, bakery windows 10
full of dry, chocolate-filled Jewish cookies,
the language of love-letters, of suicide notes,
afternoons on the riverbank
pretending to be children

Coming out to this desert   15
we meant to change the face of
driving among dull green succulents
walking at noon in the ghost town
surrounded by a silence

that sounds like the silence of the place   20
except that it came with us
and is familiar
and everything we were saying until now

was an effort to blot it out—
coming out here we are up against it   25

Out here I feel more helpless
with you than without you

You mention the danger
and list the equipment
we talk of people caring for each other   30
in emergencies—laceration, thirst—
but you look at me like an emergency

Your dry heat feels like power
your eyes are stars of a different magnitude
they reflect lights that spell out: EXIT   35
when you get up and pace the floor

talking of the danger
as if it were not ourselves
as if we were testing anything else.
1973

Diving into the Wreck

First having read the book of myths,
and loaded the camera,
and checked the edge of the knife-blade,
I put on
the body-armor of black rubber   5
the absurd flippers
the grave and awkward mask.
I am having to do this
not like Cousteau[1] with his
assiduous team   10
aboard the sun-flooded schooner
but here alone.

---

[1] Jacques Cousteau (1910–1997), French un-
derwater explorer, inventor of the aqualung,
author, and filmmaker.

There is a ladder.
The ladder is always there
hanging innocently   15
close to the side of the schooner.
We know what it is for,
we who have used it.
Otherwise
it's a piece of maritime floss   20
some sundry equipment.

I go down.
Rung after rung and still
the oxygen immerses me
the blue light   25
the clear atoms
of our human air.
I go down.
My flippers cripple me,
I crawl like an insect down the ladder   30
and there is no one
to tell me when the ocean
will begin.

First the air is blue and then
it is bluer and then green and then   35
black I am blacking out and yet
my mask is powerful
it pumps my blood with power
the sea is another story
the sea is not a question of power   40
I have to learn alone
to turn my body without force
in the deep element.

And now: it is easy to forget
what I came for   45
among so many who have always
lived here
swaying their crenellated fans
between the reefs
and besides   50
you breathe differently down here.

I came to explore the wreck.
The words are purposes.

The words are maps.
I came to see the damage that was done   55
and the treasures that prevail.
I stroke the beam of my lamp
slowly along the flank
of something more permanent
than fish or weed   60

the thing I came for:
the wreck and not the story of the wreck
the thing itself and not the myth
the drowned face always staring
toward the sun   65
the evidence of damage
worn by salt and sway into this threadbare beauty
the ribs of the disaster
curving their assertion
among the tentative haunters.   70

This is the place.
And I am here, the mermaid whose dark hair
streams black, the merman in his armored body
We circle silently
about the wreck   75
we dive into the hold.
I am she: I am he
whose drowned face sleeps with open eyes
whose breasts still bear the stress

whose silver, copper, vermeil cargo lies   80
obscurely inside barrels
half-wedged and left to rot
we are the half-destroyed instruments
that once held to a course
the water-eaten log   85
the fouled compass

We are, I am, you are
by cowardice or courage
the one who find our way
back to this scene   90
carrying a knife, a camera
a book of myths
in which
our names do not appear.
1973

Translations

You show me the poems of some woman
my age, or younger
translated from your language

Certain words occur: *enemy, oven, sorrow*
enough to let me know   5
she's a woman of my time

obsessed

with Love, our subject:
we've trained it like ivy to our walls
baked it like bread in our ovens   10
worn it like lead on our ankles
watched it through binoculars as if
it were a helicopter
bringing food to our famine
or the satellite   15
of a hostile power

I begin to see that woman
doing things: stirring rice

ironing a skirt
typing a manuscript till dawn   20

trying to make a call
from a phonebooth

The phone rings unanswered
in a man's bedroom
she hears him telling someone else   25
Never mind. She'll get tired—
hears him telling her story to her sister

who becomes her enemy
and will in her own time
light her own way to sorrow   30

ignorant of the fact this way of grief
is shared, unnecessary
and political
1973

The Ninth Symphony of Beethoven Understood at Last as a Sexual Message

A man in terror of impotence
or infertility, not knowing the difference
a man trying to tell something
howling from the climacteric
music of the entirely   5
isolated soul
yelling at Joy from the tunnel of the ego
music without the ghost
of another person in it, music
trying to tell something the man   10
does not want out, would keep if he could
gagged and bound and flogged with chords of Joy
where everything is silence and the
beating of a bloody fist upon
a splintered table   15
1972

Toni Morrison
b. 1931

Toni Morrison is clear about her major subject: "I'm interested," she says, "in survival—who survives and who does not, and why—and I would like to chart a course that suggests where the dangers are and where the safety might be." Like the medieval cartographers who illustrated their maps with mythic figures of promise and danger, Morrison recognizes the psychic as well as the physical risks of exploration. African American writing, in particular, she feels, lacks the secure sense of closure associated with Western or classical art: "I think about what black writers do as having a quality of hunger and disturbance that never ends." This open-endedness mingles in Morrison's own work with precise, highly controlled use of metaphor, vivid visual images, and an almost baroque allusiveness. But it manifests itself primarily in her ability to draw her readers into active participation in the creative process. "If the life of my novels is long," she says, "then the readers who wish to read my books will know that it is not I who do it: It is they who do."

Morrison grew up in Lorain, Ohio. Since both her parents and her grandparents made great personal sacrifices to ensure good educations for their children, she was exposed early to the rich and varied masterpieces of American and European literature. Yet, as the critic Nellie McKay has noted, Morrison also "tells of a childhood world filled with signs, visitations, and ways of knowing that encompassed more than concrete reality." In 1953 Morrison graduated from Howard University; two years later she received an M.A. from Cornell University. From 1955 to 1957 she was instructor in English at Texas Southern University, and in 1957 she returned to Howard, where she taught until 1964, when she became an editor for Random House. At present, she is Robert F. Goheen Professor, Council of the Humanities, Princeton University. An equally important part of her life has been raising her two sons. "I really only do two things," she reports. "All of my work has to do with books. I teach books, write books, edit books, or talk about books. It is all one thing. And the other thing that I do is to raise my children, which, as you know, I can only do one minute at a time."

All of Morrison's novels deal with "the complexity of how people behave under duress, . . . the qualities they show at the end of an event when their backs are up against the wall." In her first novel, *The Bluest Eye* (1969), Morrison examines the personal and social implications of the American (including African American) ideal of light-skinned beauty. Described by one reviewer as "charged with pain and wonder," the novel not only portrays the lives of those whose dark skin and Negroid features blight their lives; it also explores the human loss that occurs when beauty goes unrecognized. *Sula* (1973), which was nominated for the 1975 National Book Award, depicts a young African American woman whose hard-won independence so threatens her family and neighbors that they scorn and reject her. In *Song of Solomon* (1977), which won the National Book Critics Circle Award, Morrison portrays a young African American man, Macon Dead, as he attempts to come to terms with his heritage. Structured around the African American legend of a flying man, *Song of Solomon* is an especially powerful rendering of African American life—or more precisely, of what Morrison calls "the imaginative combination of the real world, the very shrewd, practical, day-to-day functioning that black people must do, while at the same time encompassing some great supernatural event." In *Tar Baby* (1981), Morrison describes the interaction of a young African American woman named Jadine, who is a Paris model and a graduate student, with an escaped convict named Son, as they try to come to terms simultaneously with their mutual attraction and the vast differences that their heritages impose. Her 1988 novel *Beloved*, which won the Pulitzer Prize for fiction, was followed by *Jazz* (1992). She is also the author of a book of criticism, *Playing in the Dark: Whiteness and the Literary Imagination* (1992). In 1993 she became the first African American writer to receive the Nobel Prize for literature.

Despite the success that Morrison has enjoyed and the recognition that has come with her winning of the Nobel prize, she values most a sense of urgency that can never be totally dispelled. Speaking of African American musicians, she says that "one always has the feeling, whether it is true or not, they may be absolutely parched, but one always has the feeling that there's some more. They have the ability to make you want it, and remember the want. This is a part of what I want to put into my books. They will never fully satisfy—never fully."

Further Reading:

B. Jones and A. Vinson, *The World of Toni Morrison: Explorations in Literary Criticism*, 1985.

N. McKay, *Critical Essays on Toni Morrison*, 1988.

H. L. Gates Jr. and K. A. Appiah, eds., *Toni Morrison: Perspectives Past and Present*, 1993.

J. Furman, *Toni Morrison's Fiction*, 1996.

H. W. Rice, *Toni Morrison and the American Tradition: A Rhetorical Reading*, 1996.

Text:
Playing in the Dark, 1992.

from Playing in the Dark

from **Black Matters**

These chapters put forth an argument for extending the study of American literature into what I hope will be a wider landscape. I want to draw a map, so to speak, of a critical geography and use that map to open as much space for discovery, intellectual adventure, and close exploration as did the original charting of the New World—without the mandate for conquest. I intend to outline an attractive, fruitful, and provocative critical project, unencumbered by dreams of subversion or rallying gestures at fortress walls.

I would like it to be clear at the outset that I do not bring to these matters solely or even principally the tools of a literary critic. As a reader (before becoming a writer) I read as I had been taught to do. But books revealed themselves rather differently to me as a writer. In that capacity I have to place enormous trust in my ability to imagine others and my willingness to project consciously into the danger zones such others may represent for me. I am drawn to the ways all writers do this: the way Homer renders a heart-eating cyclops so that our hearts are wrenched with pity; the way Dostoevsky compels intimacy with Svidrigailov and Prince Myshkin. I am in awe ofthe authority of Faulkner's Benjy, James's Maisie, Flaubert's Emma, Melville's Pip, Mary Shelley's Frankenstein—each of us can extend the list.

I am interested in what prompts and makes possible this process of entering what one is estranged from—and in what disables the foray, for purposes of fiction, into corners of the consciousness held off and away from the reach of the writer's imagination. My work requires me to think about how free I can be as an African-American woman writer in my genderized, sexualized, wholly racialized world. To think about (and wrestle with) the full implications of my situation leads me to consider what happens when other writers work in a highly and historically racialized society. For them, as for me, imagining is not merely looking or looking at; nor is it taking onself intact into the other. It is, for the purposes of the work, *becoming*.

My project rises from delight, not disappointment. It rises from what I know about the ways writers transform aspects of their social grounding into aspects of language, and the ways they tell other stories, fight secret wars, limn out all sorts of debates blanketed in their text. And rises from my certainty that writers always know, at some level, that they do this.

For some time now I have been thinking about the validity or vulnerability of a certain set of assumptions conventionally accepted among literary historians and critics and circulated as "knowledge." This knowledge holds that traditional, canonical American literature is free of, uninformed, and unshaped by the four-hundred-year-old presence of, first, Africans and then African-Americans in the United States. It assumes that this presence—which shaped the body politic, the Constitution, and the entire history of the culture—has had no significant place or consequence in the origin and development of that culture's literature. Moreover, such knowledge assumes that the characteristics of our national literature emanate from a particular "Americanness" that is separate from and unaccountable to this presence. There seems to be a more or less tacit agreement among literary scholars that, because American literature has been clearly the preserve of white male views, genius, and power, those views, genius, and power are without relationship to and removed from the overwhelming presence of black people in the United States. This agreement is made about a population that preceded every American writer of renown and was, I have come to believe, one of the most furtively radical impinging forces on the country's literature. The contemplation of this black presence is central to any understanding of our national literature and should not be permitted to hover at the margins of the literary imagination.

These speculations have led me to wonder whether the major and championed characteristics of our national literature—individualism, masculinity, social engagement versus historical isolation; acute and ambiguous moral problematics; the thematics of innocence coupled with an obsession with figurations of death and hell—are not in fact responses to a dark, abiding, signing Africanist presence. It has occurred to me that the very manner by which American literature distinguishes itself as a coherent entity exists because of this unsettled and unsettling population. Just as the formation of the nation necessitated coded language and purposeful restriction to deal with the racial disingenuousness and moral frailty at its heart, so too did the literature, whose founding characteristics extend into the twentieth century, reproduce the necessity for codes and restriction. Through significant and underscored omissions, startling contradictions, heavily nuanced conflicts, through the way writers peopled their work with the signs and bodies of this presence—one can see that a real or fabricated Africanist presence was crucial to their sense of Americanness. And it shows.

• • •

My curiosity about the origins and literary uses of this carefully observed, and carefully invented, Africanist presence has become an informal study of what I call American Africanism. It is an investigation into the ways in which a nonwhite, Africanlike (or Africanist) presence or persona was constructed in the United States, and the imaginative uses this fabricated presence served. I am using the term "Africanism" not to suggest the larger body of knowledge on Africa that the philosopher Valentine Mudimbe means by the term "Africanism," nor to suggest the varieties and complexities of African people and their descendants who have inhabited this country. Rather I use it as a term for the denotative and connotative blackness that African peoples have come to signify, as well as the entire range of views, assumptions, readings, and misreadings that accompany Eurocentric learning about these people. As a trope, little restraint has been attached to its uses. As a disabling virus within literary discourse, Africanism has become, in the Eurocentric tradition that American education favors, both a way of talking about and a way of policing matters of class, sexual license, and repression, formations and exercises of power, and meditations on ethics and accountability. Through the simple expedient of demonizing and reifying the range of color on a palette, American Africanism makes it possible to say and not say, to inscribe and erase, to escape and engage, to act out and act on, to historicize and render timeless. It provides a way of contemplating chaos and civilization, desire and fear, and a mechanism for testing the problems and blessings of freedom.

The United States, of course, is not unique in the construction of Africanism. South America, England, France, Germany, Spain—the cultures of all these countries have participated in and contributed to some aspect of an "invented Africa." None has been able to persuade itself for long that criteria and knowledge could emerge outside the categories of domination. Among Europeans and the Europeanized, this shared process of exclusion—of assigning designation and value—has led to the popular and academic notion that racism is a "natural," if irritating, phenomenon. The literature of almost all these countries, however, is now subject to sustained critiques of its racialized discourse. The United States is a curious exception, even though it stands out as being the oldest democracy in which a black population accompanied (if one can use that word) and in many cases preceded the white settlers. Here in that nexus, with its particular formulations, and in the absence of real knowledge or open-minded inquiry about Africans and African-Americans, under the pressures of ideological and imperialistic rationales for subjugation, an American brand of Africanism emerged: strongly urged, thoroughly serviceable, companionably ego-reinforcing, and pervasive. For excellent reasons of state—because European sources of cultural hegemony were dispersed but not yet valorized in the new country—the process of organizing American coherence through a distancing Africanism became the operative mode of a new cultural hegemony.

These remarks should not be interpreted as simply an effort to move the gaze of African-American studies to a different site. I do not want to alter one hierarchy in order to institute another. It is true that I do not want to encourage those totalizing approaches to African-American scholarship which have no drive other than the exchange of dominations—dominant Eurocentric scholarship *replaced* by dominant Afrocentric scholarship. More interesting is what makes intellectual domination possible; how knowledge is transformed from invasion and conquest to revelation and choice; what ignites and informs the literary imagination, and what forces help establish the parameters of criticism.

Above all I am interested in how agendas in criticism have disguised themselves and, in so doing, impoverished the literature it studies. Criticism as a form of knowledge is capable of robbing literature not only of its own implicit and explicit ideology but of its ideas as well; it can dismiss the difficult, arduous work writers do to make an art that becomes and remains part of and significant within a human landscape. It is important to see how inextricable Africanism is or ought to be from the deliberations of literary criticism and the wanton, elaborate strategies undertaken to erase its presence from view.

What Africanism became for, and how it functioned in, the literary imagination is of paramount interest because it may be possible to discover, through a close look at literary "blackness," the nature—even the cause—of literary, "whiteness." What is it *for*? What parts do the invention and development of whiteness play in the construction of what is loosely described as "American"? If such an inquiry ever comes to maturity, it may provide access to a deeper reading of American literature—a reading not completely available now, not least, I suspect, because of the studied indifference of most literary criticism to these matters.

One likely reason for the paucity of critical material on this large and compelling subject is that, in matters of race, silence and evasion have historically ruled literary discourse. Evasion has fostered another, substitute language in which the issues are encoded, foreclosing open debate. The situation is aggravated by the tremor that breaks into discourse on race. It is further complicated by the fact that the habit of ignoring race is understood to be a graceful, even generous, liberal gesture. To notice is to recognize an already discredited difference. To enforce its invisibility through silence is to allow the black body a shadowless participation in the dominant cultural body. According to this logic, every well-bred instinct argues *against noticing* and forecloses adult discourse. It is just this concept of literary and scholarly moeurs (which functions smoothly in literary criticism, but neither makes nor receives credible claims in other disciplines) that has terminated the shelf life of some once extremely well-regarded American authors and blocked access to remarkable insights in their works.

These moeurs are delicate things, however, which must be given some thought before they are abandoned. Not observing such niceties can lead to startling displays of scholarly lapses in objectivity. In 1936 an American scholar investigating the use of Negro so-called dialect in the works of Edgar Allan Poe (a short article clearly proud of its racial equanimity) opens this way: "Despite the fact that he grew up largely in the south and spent some of his most fruitful years in Richmond and Baltimore, Poe has little to say about the darky."[1]

Although I know this sentence represents the polite parlance of the day, that "darky" was understood to be a term more acceptable than "nigger," the grimace I made upon reading it was followed by an alarmed distrust of the scholar's abilities. If it seems unfair to reach back to the thirties for samples of the kind of lapse that can occur when certain manners of polite repression are waived, let me assure you equally egregious representations of the phenomenon are still common.

Another reason for this quite ornamental vacuum in literary discourse on the presence and influence of Africanist peoples in American criticism in the pattern of thinking about racialism in terms of its consequences on the victim—of always defining it asymmetrically from the perspective of its impact on the object of racist policy and attitudes. A good deal of time and intelligence has been invested in the exposure of racism and the horrific results on its objects. There are constant, if erratic, liberalizing efforts to legislate these matters. There are also powerful and persuasive attempts to analyze the origin and fabrication of racism itself, contesting the assumption that it is an inevitable, permanent, and eternal part of all social landscapes. I do not wish to disparage these inquiries. It is precisely because of them that any progress at all has been accomplished in matters of racial discourse. But that well-established study should be joined with another, equally important one: the impact of racism on those who perpetuate it. It seems both poignant and striking how avoided and unanalyzed is the effect of racist inflection on the subject. What I propose here is to examine the impact of notions of racial hierarchy, racial exclusion, and racial vulnerability and availability on non-

---

[1] Killis Campbell, "Poe's Treatment of the Negro and of the Negro Dialect," *Studies in English*, 16 (1936), p. 106.

blacks who held, resisted, explored, or altered those notions. The scholarship that looks into the mind, imagination, and behavior of slaves is valuable. But equally valuable is a serious intellectual effort to see what racial ideology does to the mind, imagination, and behavior of masters.

Historians have approached these areas, as have social scientists, anthropologists, psychiatrists, and some students of comparative literature. Literary scholars have begun to pose these questions of various national literatures. Urgently needed is the same kind of attention paid to the literature of the western country that has one of the most resilient Africanist populations in the world—a population that has always had a curiously intimate and unhingingly separate existence within the dominant one. When matters of race are located and called attention to in American literature, critical response has tended to be on the order of a humanistic nostrum—or a dismissal mandated by the label "political." Excising the political from the life of the mind is a sacrifice that has proven costly. I think of this erasure as a kind of trembling hypochondria always curing itself with unnecessary surgery. A criticism that needs to insist that literature is not only "universal" but also "race-free" risks lobotomizing that literature, and diminishes both the art and the artist.

I am vulnerable to the inference here that my inquiry has vested interests, that because I am an African-American and a writer I stand to benefit in ways not limited to intellectual fulfillment from this line of questioning. I will have to risk the accusation because the point is too important: for both black and white American writers, in a wholly racialized society, there is no escape from racially inflected language, and the work writers do to unhobble the imagination from the demands of that language is complicated, interesting, and definitive.

Like thousands of avid but nonacademic readers, some powerful literary critics in the United States have never read, and are proud to say so, *any* African-American text. It seems to have done them no harm, presented them with no discernible limitations in the scope of their work or influence. I suspect, with much evidence to support the suspicion, that they will continue to flourish without any knowledge whatsoeverof African-American literature. What is fascinating, however, is to observe how their lavish exploration of literature manages *not* to see meaning in the thunderous, theatrical presence of black surrogacy—an informing, stabilizing, and disturbing element—in the literature they do study. It is interesting, not surprising, that the arbiters of critical power in American literature seem to take pleasure in, indeed relish, their ignorance of African-American texts. What is surprising is that their refusal to read black texts—a refusal that makes no disturbance in their intellectual life—repeats itself when they reread the traditional, established works of literature worthy of their attention.

It is possible, for example, to read Henry James scholarship exhaustively and never arrive at a nodding mention, much less a satisfactory treatment, of the black woman who lubricates the turn of the plot and becomes the agency of moral choice and meaning in *What Maisie Knew*. Never are we invited to a reading of "The Beast in the Jungle" in which that figuration is followed to what seems to me its logical conclusion. It is hard to think of an aspect of Gertrude Stein's *Three Lives* that has not been covered, except the exploratory and explanatory uses to which she puts the black woman who holds center stage in that work. The urgency and anxiety in Willa Cather's rendering of black characters are liable to be missed entirely; no mention is made of the problem that race causes in the technique and the credibility of her last novel, *Sapphira and the Slave Girl*. These critics see no excitement or meaning in the tropes of darkness, sexuality, and desire in Ernest Hemingway or in his cast of black men. They see no connection between God's grace and Africanist "othering" in Flannery O'Connor. With few exceptions, Faulkner criticism collapses the major themes of that writer into discursive "mythologies" and treats the later works—whose focus is race and class—as minor, superficial, marked by decline.

An instructive parallel to this willed scholarly indifference is the centuries-long, hysterical blindness to feminist discourse and the way in which women and women's issues were read (or unread). Blatant sexist readings are on the decline, and where they still exist they have little effect because of the successful appropriation by women of their own discourse.

National literatures, like writers, get along the best way they can, and with what they can. Yet they do seem to end up describing and inscribing what is really on the national mind. For the most part, the literature of the United States has taken as its concern the architecture of a *new white man.* If I am disenchanted by the indifference of literary criticism toward examining the range of that concern, I do have a lasting resort: the writers themselves.

Writers are among the most sensitive, the most intellectually anarchic, most representative, most probing of artists. The ability of writers to imagine what is not the self, to familiarize the strange and mystify the familiar, is the test of their power. The languages they use and the social and historical context in which these languages signify are indirect and direct revelations of that power and its limitations. So it is to them, the creators of American literature, that I look for clarification about the invention and effect of Africanism in the United States.

My early assumptions as a reader were that black people signified little or nothing in the imagination of white American writers. Other than as the objects of an occasional bout of jungle fever, other than to provide local color or to lend some touch of verisimilitude or to supply a needed moral gesture, humor, or bit of pathos, blacks made no appearance at all. This was a reflection, I thought, of the marginal impact that blacks had on the lives of the characters in the work as well as the creative imagination of the author. To imagine or write otherwise, to situate black people throughout the pages and scenes of a book like some government quota, would be ludicrous and dishonest.

But then I stopped reading as a reader and began to read as a writer. Living in a racially articulated and predicated world, I could not be alone in reacting to this aspect of the American cultural and historical condition. I began to see how the literature I revered, the literature I loathed, behaved in its encounter with racial ideology. American literature could not help being shaped by that encounter. Yes, I wanted to identify those movements when American literature was complicit in the fabrication of racism, but equally important, I wanted to see when literature exploded and undermined it. Still, those were minor concerns. Much more important was to contemplate how Africanist personae, narrative, and idiom moved and enriched the text in self-conscious ways, to consider what the engagement meant for the work of the writer's imagination.

How does literary utterance arrange itself when it tries to imagine an Africanist other? What are the signs, the codes, the literary strategies designed to accommodate this encounter? What does the inclusion of Africans or African-Americans do to and for the work? As a reader my assumption had always been that nothing "happens": Africans and their descendants were not, in any sense that matters, *there;* and when they were there, they were decorative—displays of the agile writer's technical expertise. I assumed that since the author was not black, the appearance of Africanist characters or idiom in a work could never be *about* anything other than the "normal," unracialized, illusory white world that provided the fictional backdrop. Certainly no American text of the sort I am discussing was ever written *for* black people—no more than *Uncle Tom's Cabin* was written for Uncle Tom to read or be persuaded by. As a writer reading, I came to realize the obvious: the subject of the dream is the dreamer. The fabrication of an Africanist persona is reflexive; an extraordinary meditation on the self; a powerful exploration of the fears and desires that reside in the writerly conscious. It is an astonishing revelation of longing, of terror, of perplexity, of shame, of magnanimity. It requires hard work *not* to see this.

It is as if I had been looking at a fishbowl—the glide and flick of the golden scales, the green tip, the bolt of white careening back from the gills; the castles at the bottom, surrounded by pebbles and tiny, intricate fronds of green; the barely disturbed water, the flecks of waste and food, the tranquil bubbles traveling to the surface—and suddenly I saw the bowl, the structure that transparently (and invisibly) permits the ordered life it contains to exist in the larger world. In other words, I began to rely on my knowledge of how books get written, how language arrives; my sense of how and why writers abandon or take on certain aspects of their project. I began to rely on my understanding of what the linguistic struggle requires of writers and what they make of the surprise that is the inevitable concomitant of the act of creation. What became transparent were the self-evident ways that Americans choose to talk about themselves through and within a sometimes allegorical, sometimes metaphorical, but always choked representation of an Africanist presence.

1992

John Updike
b. 1932

John Updike was born on March 18, 1932, in the small town of Shillington, Pennsylvania, where he acquired a sense of place that has continued to yield richly detailed memories—of buildings and pets, scenes and playmates, and above all of family. None of this would be remarkable were Updike's sense of life not inseparable from his sense of place and his sense of art from his sense of life.

Art began for Updike "as a method of riding a thin pencil line out of Shillington, out of time altogether, into an infinity of unseen and even unborn hearts." Yet, having begun as a mode of flight, writing quickly became for him a method of return—or more precisely, a method of transcribing the world he had known: "middleness with all its grits, bumps, and anonymities, in its fullness of satisfaction and mystery." Whether such a thing as transcribing is "possible" or, in view of the world's wild suffering, "worth doing" is a question Updike explicitly puts to himself. "Possibly not," he replies, only to conclude that it is nevertheless necessary since "the horse chestnut trees, the telephone poles, the porches, the green hedges recede to a calm point that in my subjective geography is still the center of the world."

Between his beginnings in Shillington and his emergence as a writer, Updike spent four years at Harvard, from which he was graduated *summa cum laude* in 1954. After studying art for a year in England, Updike returned to the United States in 1955. He worked as a staff reporter for *The New Yorker* for two years and soon began contributing stories there regularly, establishing a relationship with that magazine that has continued to the present. In 1957 he left New York to practice his "solitary trade" in Ipswich, Massachusetts.

In 1959 Updike published a collection of short stories, *The Same Door*, and his first novel—partly inspired by his early reading of Huxley and Orwell—*The Poorhouse Fair*, a futuristic story set in a county home for the elderly poor. The following year Updike published a successful second novel, *Rabbit, Run*, about a former high school basketball star who, nostalgic for a lost past, finds himself continually on the run from the demands of adult responsibility. Updike continued the story of Harry ("Rabbit") Angstrom, taking him through the cultural turmoil of the late 1960s in *Rabbit Redux* (1971) and into upper-middle-class prosperity—though not necessarily peace of mind—in *Rabbit Is Rich* (1981). Updike has frequently connected his themes to classical mythology, a technique that came fully to the surface in his third novel, *The Centaur* (1963), the story of three days in the life of a high school science teacher and his son.

By the mid-1960s it had become clear that one of Updike's dominant subjects was marriage. Many of his short stories—among them "Separating"—deal exclusively with the difficulties of married life in a world where the traditional religious values that once nourished and sanctioned marital love and sex have lost their meaning. In *Of the Farm* (1965) Updike explores the inner dynamics of a marriage during a couple's weekend visit to the husband's dying mother. The problems of marriage in our time are given ritualistic and religious significance in *Couples* (1968), a novel about sexual love and infidelity among ten couples in a small New England community. In *A Month of Sundays* (1975) Updike explores the themes of love and sex, marriage and infidelity within the framework of American Protestant morality. The theme of marriage and infidelity is also at the center of Updike's eighth novel, *Marry Me* (1976), the story of a summer love affair that is also a story of modern morality: We live in "the twilight of the old morality," the book's hero argues, "and there's just enough to torment us, and not enough to hold us in." In 1979 Updike collected his stories about a married couple, the Maples, in *Too Far to Go* and in the same year also published *Problems and Other Stories*, which contains "Separating," another of the Maples stories. His latest collection is *Trust Me: Short Stories*, 1987.

Though continually drawn to the problems of love, sex, and modern domesticity, Updike has nevertheless kept a close eye on literature, culture, and politics. In 1970 he published *Bech: A Book*, a series of linked stories about an American Jewish writer that dealt humorously with the meaning of a literary career; Updike continued the adventures of Henry Bech in another collection of tales, *Bech Is Back* (1982). In 1973 Updike toured Africa as a Fulbright lecturer, and out of his experiences he wrote *The Coup* (1978), a political novel about a violent, imaginary African regime. Updike's enormous output of essays, criticism, and literary reviews have been collected in several volumes: *Assorted Prose* (1965), *Picked-Up Pieces* (1975), *Hugging the Shore* (1983), and *Odd Jobs* (1991). Updike has also written a play and several volumes of poetry. His latest novels are *The Witches of Eastwick* (1984), which uses a contemporary instance of witchcraft as a way of commenting on a modern culture habituated to television and popular media, *Roger's Version* (1986), and *Memories of the Ford Administration* (1992).

Updike's stories, a large number of them set in "Olinger," the small imaginary town that evokes the Shillington of Updike's boyhood and youth, often center on adolescent protagonists. Over the stories hovers a certain nostalgia, a remorse for time. One source of that nostalgia is Updike's feeling for youth itself—for its openness, its honesty, its innocence, its brave sense of immortality. Another source is his feeling for preurban America and the life it spawned. But there is always an edge to Updike's journeys back toward the source, not simply because he is suspicious of nostalgia but also because such journeys always follow lines toward the unseen and the unknown. His larger quest is for some form of work or play or love that can approximate—or some religious experience that can satisfy—our longing for permanence.

Updike's most recent fiction includes *Rabbit at Rest* (1990), *The Afterlife and Other Stories* (1994), and *In the Beauty of the Lilies* (1996). He has also published *Self-Consciousness: Memoirs* (1989) and *Collected Poems, 1953–1993* (1993).

Further Reading:

C. T. Samuels, *John Updike,* 1969.

D. Greiner, *The Other John Updike: Poems, Short Stories, Prose, Plays,* 1981.

W. Macnaughton, ed., *Critical Essays on John Updike,* 1982.

J. H. Campbell, *Updike's Novels: Thorns Spell a Word,* 1987.

M. O'Connell, *Updike and the Patriarchal Dilemma,* 1996.

Text:

"Separating" from *Problems and Other Stories,* 1979.

Separating

The day was fair. Brilliant. All that June the weather had mocked the Maples' internal misery with solid sunlight—golden shafts and cascades of green in which their conversations had wormed unseeing, their sad murmuring selves the only stain in Nature. Usually by this time of the year they had acquired tans; but when they met their elder daughter's plane on her return from a year in England they were almost as pale as she, though Judith was too dazzled by the sunny opulent jumble of her native land to notice. They did not spoil her homecoming by telling her immediately. Wait a few days, let her recover from jet lag, had been one of their formulations, in that string of gray dialogues—over coffee, over cocktails, over Cointreau—that had shaped the strategy of their dissolution, while the earth performed its annual stunt of renewal unnoticed beyond their closed windows. Richard had thought to leave at Easter; Joan had insisted they wait until the four children were at last assembled, with all exams passed and ceremonies attended, and the bauble of summer to console them. So he had drudged away, in love, in dread, repairing screens, getting the mowers sharpened, rolling and patching their new tennis court.

The court, clay, had come through its first winter pitted and windswept bare of red-coat. Years ago the Maples had observed how often, among their friends, divorce followed a dramatic home improvement, as if the marriage were making one last effort to live; their own worst crisis had come amid the plaster dust and exposed plumbing of a kitchen renovation. Yet, a summer ago, as canary-yellow bulldozers gaily churned a grassy, daisy-dotted knoll into a muddy plateau, and a crew of pigtailed young men raked and tamped clay into a plane, this transformation did not strike them as ominous, but festive in its impudence; their marriage could rend the earth for fun. The next spring, waking each day at dawn to a sliding sensation as if the bed were being tipped, Richard found the barren tennis court—its net and tapes still rolled in the barn—an environment congruous with his mood of purposeful desolation, and the crumbling of handfuls of clay into cracks and holes (dogs had frolicked on the court in a thaw; rivulets had eroded trenches) an activity suitably elemental and interminable. In his sealed heart he hoped the day would never come.

Now it was here. A Friday. Judith was re-acclimated; all four children were assembled, before jobs and camps and visits again scattered them. Joan thought they should be told one by one. Richard was for making an announcement at the table. She said, "I think just making an announcement is a cop-out. They'll start quarrelling and playing to each other instead of focusing. They're each individuals, you know, not just some corporate obstacle to your freedom."

"O.K., O.K. I agree." Joan's plan was exact. That evening, they were giving Judith a belated welcome-home dinner, of lobster and champagne. Then, the party over, they, the two of them, who nineteen years before would push her in a baby carriage along Fifth Avenue to Washington Square, were to walk her out of the house, to the bridge across the salt creek, and tell her, swearing her to secrecy. Then Richard Jr., who was going directly from work to a rock concert in Boston, would be told, either late when he returned on the train or early Saturday morning before he went off to his job; he was seventeen and employed as one of a golf-course maintenance crew. Then the two younger children, John and Margaret, could, as the morning wore on, be informed.

"Mopped up, as it were," Richard said.

"Do you have any better plan? That leaves you the rest of Saturday to answer any questions, pack, and make your wonderful departure."

"No," he said, meaning he had no better plan, and agreed to hers, though to him it showed an edge of false order, a hidden plea for control, like Joan's long chore lists and financial accountings and, in the days when he first knew her, her too-copious lecture notes. Her plan turned one hurdle for him into four—four knife-sharp walls, each with a sheer blind drop on the other side.

All spring he had moved through a world of insides and outsides, of barriers and partitions. He and Joan stood as a thin barrier between the children and the truth. Each moment was a partition, with the past on one side and the future on the other, a future containing this unthinkable now. Beyond four knifelike walls a new life for him waited vaguely. His skull cupped a secret, a white face, a face both frightened and soothing, both strange and known, that he wanted to shield from tears, which he felt all about him, solid as the sunlight. So haunted, he had become obsessed with battening down the house against his absence, replacing screens and sash cords, hinges and latches—a Houdini making things snug before his escape.

The lock. He had still to replace a lock on one of the doors of the screened porch. The task, like most such, proved more difficult than he had imagined. The old lock, aluminum frozen by corrosion, had been deliberately rendered obsolete by manufacturers.

Three hardware stores had nothing that even approximately matched the mortised hole its removal (surprisingly easy) left. Another hole had to be gouged, with bits too small and saws too big, and the old hole fitted with a block of wood—the chisels dull, the saw rusty, his fingers thick with lack of sleep. The sun poured down, beyond the porch, on a world of neglect. The bushes already needed pruning, the windward side of the house was shedding flakes of paint, rain would get in when he was gone, insects, rot, death. His family, all those he would lose, filtered through the edges of his awareness as he struggled with screw holes, splinters, opaque instructions, minutiae of metal.

Judith sat on the porch, a princess returned from exile. She regaled them with stories of fuel shortages, of bomb scares in the Underground, of Pakistani workmen loudly lusting after her as she walked past on her way to dance school. Joan came and went, in and out of the house, calmer than she should have been, praising his struggles with the lock as if this were one more and not the last of their long succession of shared chores. The younger of his sons for a few minutes held the rickety screen door while his father clumsily hammered and chiseled, each blow a kind of sob in Richard's ears. His younger daughter, having been at a slumber party, slept on the porch hammock through all the noise—heavy and pink, trusting and forsaken. Time, like the sunlight, continued relentlessly; the sunlight slowly slanted. Today was one of the longest days. The lock clicked, worked. He was through. He had a drink; he drank it on the porch, listening to his daughter. "It was so sweet," she was saying, "during the worst of it, how all the butchers and bakery shops kept open by candlelight. They're all so plucky and cute. From the papers, things sounded so much worse here—people shooting people in gas lines, and everybody freezing."

Richard asked her, "Do you still want to live in England forever?" *Forever:* the concept, now a reality upon him, pressed and scratched at the back of his throat.

"No," Judith confessed, turning her oval face to him, its eyes still childishly far apart, but the lips set as over something succulent and satisfactory. "I was anxious to come home. I'm an American." She was a woman. They had raised her; he and Joan had endured together to raise her, alone of the four. The others had still some raising left in them. Yet it was the thought of telling Judith—the image of her, their first baby, walking between them arm in arm to the bridge—that broke him. The partition between his face and the tears broke. Richard sat down to the celebratory meal with the back of his throat aching; the champagne, the lobster seemed phases of sunshine; he saw them and tasted them through tears. He blinked, swallowed, croakily joked about hay fever. The tears would not stop leaking through; they came not through a hole that could be plugged but through a permeable spot in a membrane, steadily, purely, endlessly, fruitfully. They became, his tears, a shield for himself against these others—their faces, the fact of their assembly, a last time as innocents, at a table where he sat the last time as head. Tears dropped from his nose as he broke the lobster's back; salt flavored his champagne as he sipped it; the raw clench at the back of his throat was delicious. He could not help himself.

His children tried to ignore his tears. Judith, on his right, lit a cigarette, gazed upward in the direction of her too energetic, too sophisticated exhalation; on her other side, John earnestly bent his face to the extraction of the last morsels—legs, tail segments—from the scarlet corpse. Joan, at the opposite end of the table, glanced at him surprised, her reproach displaced by a quick grimace, of forgiveness, or of salute to his superior gift of strategy. Between them, Margaret, no longer called Bean, thirteen and large for her age, gazed from the other side of his pane of tears as if into a shopwindow at something she coveted—at her father, a crystalline heap of splinters and memories. It was not she, however, but John who, in the kitchen, as they cleared the plates and cara-paces away, asked Joan the question: *"Why is Daddy crying?"*

Richard heard the question but not the murmured answer. Then he heard Bean cry, "Oh, no-oh!"—the faintly dramatized exclamation of one who had long expected it.

John returned to the table carrying a bowl of salad. He nodded tersely at his father and his lips shaped the conspiratorial words "She told."

"Told what?" Richard asked aloud, insanely.

The boy sat down as if to rebuke his father's distraction with the example of his own good manners. He said quietly, "The separation."

Joan and Margaret returned; the child, in Richard's twisted vision, seemed dimin-ished in size, and relieved, relieved to have had the bogieman at last proved real. He called out to her—the distances at the table had grown immense—"You knew, you al-ways knew," but the clenching at the back of his throat prevented him from making sense of it. From afar he heard Joan talking, levelly, sensibly, reciting what they had pre-pared: it was a separation for the summer, an experiment. She and Daddy both agreed it would be good for them; they needed space and time to think; they liked each other but did not make each other happy enough, somehow.

Judith, imitating her mother's factual tone, but in her youth off-key, too cool, said, "I think it's silly. You should either live together or get divorced."

Richard's crying, like a wave that has crested and crashed, had become tumultuous; but it was overtopped by another tumult, for John, who had been so reserved, now grew larger and larger at the table. Perhaps his younger sister's being credited with knowing set him off. "Why didn't you *tell* us?" he asked, in a large round voice quite unlike his own. "You should have *told* us you weren't getting along."

Richard was startled into attempting to force words through his tears. "We *do* get along, that's the trouble, so it doesn't show even to us—" *That we do not love each other* was the rest of the sentence; he couldn't finish it.

Joan finished for him, in her style. "And we've always, *especially*, loved our children."

John was not mollified. "What do you care about *us?*" he boomed. "We're just little things you *had*." His sisters' laughing forced a laugh from him, which he turned hard and parodistic: "Ha ha *ha*." Richard and Joan realized simultaneously that the child was drunk, on Judith's homecoming champagne. Feeling bound to keep the center of the stage, John took a cigarette from Judith's pack, poked it into his mouth, let it hang from his lower lip, and squinted like a gangster.

"You're not little things we had," Richard called to him. "You're the whole point. But you're grown. Or almost."

The boy was lighting matches. Instead of holding them to his cigarette (for they had never seen him smoke; being "good" had been his way of setting himself apart), he held them to his mother's face, closer and closer, for her to blow out. Then he lit the whole folder—a hiss and then a torch, held against his mother's face. Prismed by tears, the flame filled Richard's vision; he didn't know how it was extinguished. He heard Mar-garet say, "Oh stop showing off," and saw John, in response, break the cigarette in two and put the halves entirely into his mouth and chew, sticking out his tongue to display the shreds to his sister.

Joan talked to him, reasoning—a fountain of reason, unintelligible. "Talked about it for years . . . our children must help us . . . Daddy and I both want . . ." As the boy listened, he carefully wadded a paper napkin into the leaves of his salad, fashioned a ball of paper and lettuce, and popped it into his mouth, looking around the table for the expected laughter. None came. Judith said, "Be mature," and dismissed a plume of smoke.

Richard got up from this stifling table and led the boy outside. Though the house was in twilight, the outdoors still brimmed with light, the lovely waste light of high summer. Both laughing, he supervised John's spitting out the lettuce and paper and tobacco into the pachysandra. He took him by the hand—a square gritty hand, but for its softness a man's. Yet, it held on. They ran together up into the field, past the tennis court. The raw banking left by the bulldozers was dotted with daisies. Past the court and a flat stretch where they used to play family baseball stood a soft green rise glorious in the sun, each weed and species of grass distinct as illumination on parchment. "I'm sorry, so sorry," Richard cried. "You were the only one who ever tried to help me with all the goddam jobs around this place."

Sobbing, safe within his tears and the champagne, John explained, "It's not just the separation, it's the whole crummy year, I *hate* that school, you can't make any friends, the history teacher's a scud."

They sat on the crest of the rise, shaking and warm from their tears but easier in their voices, and Richard tried to focus on the child's sad year—the weekdays long with homework, the weekends spent in his room with model airplanes, while his parents murmured down below, nursing their separation. How selfish, how blind, Richard thought; his eyes felt scoured. He told his son, "We'll think about getting you transferred. Life's too short to be miserable."

They had said what they could, but did not want the moment to heal, and talked on, about the school, about the tennis court, whether it would ever again be as good as it had been that first summer. They walked to inspect it and pressed a few more tapes more firmly down. A little stiltedly, perhaps trying now to make too much of the moment, Richard led the boy to the spot in the field where the view was best, of the metallic blue river, the emerald marsh, the scattered islands velvety with shadow in the low light, the white bits of beach far away. "See," he said. "It goes on being beautiful. It'll be here tomorrow."

"I know," John answered, impatiently. The moment had closed.

Back in the house, the others had opened some white wine, the champagne being drunk, and still sat at the table, the three females, gossiping. Where Joan sat had become the head. She turned, showing him a tearless face, and asked, "All right?"

"We're fine," he said, resenting it, though relieved, that the party went on without him.

In bed she explained, "I couldn't cry I guess because I cried so much all spring. It really wasn't fair. It's your idea, and you made it look as though I was kicking you out."

"I'm sorry," he said. "I couldn't stop. I wanted to but couldn't."

"You *didn't* want to. You loved it. You were having your way, making a general announcement."

"I love having it over," he admitted. "God, those kids were great. So brave and funny." John, returned to the house, had settled to a model airplane in his room, and kept shouting down to them, "I'm O.K. No sweat." "And the way," Richard went on, cozy in his relief, "they never questioned the reasons we gave. No thought of a third person. Not even Judith."

"That *was* touching," Joan said.

He gave her a hug. "You were great too. Very reassuring to everybody. Thank you." Guiltily, he realized he did not feel separated.

"You still have Dickie to do," she told him. These words set before him a black mountain in the darkness; its cold breath, its near weight affected his chest. Of the four children, his elder son was most nearly his conscience. Joan did not need to add, "That's one piece of your dirty work I won't do for you."

"I know. I'll do it. You go to sleep."

Within minutes, her breathing slowed, became oblivious and deep. It was quarter to midnight. Dickie's train from the concert would come in at one-fourteen. Richard set the alarm for one. He had slept atrociously for weeks. But whenever he closed his lids some glimpse of the last hours scorched them—Judith exhaling toward the ceiling in a kind of aversion, Bean's mute staring, the sunstruck growth in the field where he and John had rested. The mountain before him moved closer, moved within him; he was huge, momentous. The ache at the back of his throat felt stale. His wife slept as if slain beside him. When, exasperated by his hot lids, his crowded heart, he rose from bed and dressed, she awoke enough to turn over. He told her then, "Joan, if I could undo it all, I would."

"Where would you begin?" she asked. There was no place. Giving him courage, she was always giving him courage. He put on shoes without socks in the dark. The children were breathing in their rooms, the downstairs was hollow. In their confusion they had left lights burning. He turned off all but one, the kitchen overhead. The car started. He had hoped it wouldn't. He met only moonlight on the road; it seemed a diaphanous companion, flickering in the leaves along the roadside, haunting his rearview mirror like a pursuer, melting under his headlights. The center of town, not quite deserted, was eerie at this hour. A young cop in uniform kept company with a gang of T-shirted kids on the steps of the bank. Across from the railroad station, several bars kept open. Customers, mostly young, passed in and out of the warm night, savoring summer's novelty. Voices shouted from cars as they passed; an immense conversation seemed in progress. Richard parked and in his weariness put his head on the passenger seat, out of the commotion and wheeling lights. It was as when, in the movies, an assassin grimly carries his mission through the jostle of a carnival—except the movies cannot show the precipitous, palpable slope you cling to within. You cannot climb back down; you can only fall. The synthetic fabric of the car seat, warmed by his cheek, confided to him an ancient, distant scent of vanilla.

A train whistle caused him to lift his head. It was on time; he had hoped it would be late. The slender drawgates descended. The bell of approach tingled happily. The great metal body, horizontally fluted, rocked to a stop, and sleepy teen-agers disembarked, his son among them. Dickie did not show surprise that his father was meeting him at this terrible hour. He sauntered to the car with two friends, both taller than he. He said "Hi" to his father and took the passenger's seat with an exhausted promptness that expressed gratitude. The friends got in the back, and Richard was grateful; a few more minutes' postponement would be won by driving them home.

He asked, "How was the concert?"

"Groovy," one boy said from the back seat.

"It bit," the other said.

"It was O.K.," Dickie said, moderate by nature, so reasonable that in his childhood the unreason of the world had given him headaches, stomach aches, nausea. When the second friend had been dropped off at his dark house, the boy blurted, "Dad, my eyes are killing me with hay fever! I'm out there cutting that mothering grass all day!"

"Do we still have those drops?"

"They didn't do any good last summer."

"They might this." Richard swung a U-turn on the empty street. The drive home took a few minutes. The mountain was here, in his throat. "Richard," he said, and felt the boy, slumped and rubbing his eyes, go tense at his tone, "I didn't come to meet you just to make your life easier. I came because your mother and I have some news for you, and you're a hard man to get ahold of these days. It's sad news."

"That's O.K." The reassurance came out soft, but quick, as if released from the tip of a spring.

Richard had feared that his tears would return and choke him, but the boy's manliness set an example, and his voice issued forth steady and dry. "It's sad news, but it needn't be tragic news, at least for you. It should have no practical effect on your life, though it's bound to have an emotional effect. You'll work at your job, and go back to school in September. Your mother and I are really proud of what you're making of your life; we don't want that to change at all."

"Yeah," the boy said lightly, on the intake of his breath, holding himself up. They turned the corner; the church they went to loomed like a gutted fort. The home of the woman Richard hoped to marry stood across the green. Her bedroom light burned.

"Your mother and I," he said, "have decided to separate. For the summer. Nothing legal, no divorce yet. We want to see how it feels. For some years now, we haven't been doing enough for each other, making each other as happy as we should be. Have you sensed that?"

"No," the boy said. It was an honest, unemotional answer: true or false in a quiz.

Glad for the factual basis, Richard pursued, even garrulously, the details. His apartment across town, his utter accessibility, the split vacation arrangements, the advantages to the children, the added mobility and variety of the summer. Dickie listened, absorbing. "Do the others know?"

"Yes."

"How did they take it?"

"The girls pretty calmly. John flipped out; he shouted and ate a cigarette and made a salad out of his napkin and told us how much he hated school."

His brother chuckled. "He did?"

"Yeah. The school issue was more upsetting for him than Mom and me. He seemed to feel better for having exploded."

"He did?" The repetition was the first sign that he was stunned.

"Yes. Dickie, I want to tell you something. This last hour, waiting for your train to get in, has been about the worst of my life. I hate this. *Hate* it. My father would have died before doing it to me." He felt immensely lighter, saying this. He had dumped the mountain on the boy. They were home. Moving swiftly as a shadow, Dickie was out of the car, through the bright kitchen. Richard called after him, "Want a glass of milk or anything?"

"No thanks."

"Want us to call the course tomorrow and say you're too sick to work?"

"No, that's all right." The answer was faint, delivered at the door to his room; Richard listened for the slam that went with a tantrum. The door closed normally, gently. The sound was sickening.

Joan had sunk into that first deep trough of sleep and was slow to awake. Richard had to repeat, "I told him."

"What did he say?"

"Nothing much. Could you go say goodnight to him? Please."

She left their room, without putting on a bathrobe. He sluggishly changed back into his pajamas and walked down the hall. Dickie was already in bed, Joan was sitting beside him, and the boy's bedside clock radio was murmuring music. When she stood, an inexplicable light—the moon?—outlined her body through the nightie. Richard sat on the warm place she had indented on the child's narrow mattress. He asked him, "Do you want the radio on like that?"

"It always is."

"Doesn't it keep you awake? It would me."

"No."

"Are you sleepy?"

"Yeah."

"Good. Sure you want to get up and go to work? You've had a big night."

"I want to."

Away at school this winter he had learned for the first time that you can go short of sleep and live. As an infant he had slept with an immobile, sweating intensity that had alarmed his babysitters. In adolescence he had often been the first of the four children to go to bed. Even now, he would go slack in the middle of a television show, his sprawled legs hairy and brown. "O.K. Good boy. Dickie, listen. I love you so much, I never knew how much until now. No matter how this works out, I'll always be with you. Really."

Richard bent to kiss an averted face but his son, sinewy, turned and with wet cheeks embraced him and gave him a kiss, on the lips, passionate as a woman's. In his father's ear he moaned one word, the crucial, intelligent word: *Why?*

Why. It was a whistle of wind in a crack, a knife thrust, a window thrown open on emptiness. The white face was gone, the darkness was featureless. Richard had forgotten why.

1975

Sylvia Plath
1932–1963

The intensity, purity, and spareness of Sylvia Plath's last poems have given her short career a weight out of proportion to its brevity. Though they come from a tragic life and often have a tragic subject, these poems are exhilarated, sure, certain of their path. They are poems of cool mastery, of a talent unafraid of its own extremes. It is also a well-schooled talent, one that has assimilated the poetry of D. H. Lawrence, Theodore

Roethke, and Robert Lowell and has added a wild, dark comedy of its own (visible in "Daddy" and "Lady Lazarus") not learned from any of those masters.

Plath worked obsessively at being a poet from childhood; her first published poem appeared in a Boston newspaper when she was eight and a half. By the time she was in college at Smith, she was publishing in *Seventeen* and *Mademoiselle*. As her journals show, she had unlimited ambition and equally unlimited anxiety; cycles of manic planning followed by depressive collapses recurred throughout her life, causing an unsuccessful suicide attempt at nineteen and a successful one at thirty-one. Manic-depressive illness was not well understood at the time, and Plath, like Lowell, underwent electroconvulsive therapy, involuntary confinement in an asylum, and psychiatric therapy. These palliative treatments did not prevent the recurrence of symptoms.

Plath's distress at her own emotional volatility caused her to channel her explosive nature at first into rigidly controlled and conventionally acceptable poems, published in *The Colossus* (1960). With her marriage to the Yorkshire poet Ted Hughes, her expatriation to England, and the birth of her two children, her emotional life deepened and, under the tutelage of Hughes, who approved of the "demonic" forces in poetry, became freer to express itself. She turned savagely against what she regarded as the German oppressiveness of her professor-father (whose academic specialty was bees) and the bourgeois gentility of her mother (who taught secretarial subjects). Her rage turned as well against her husband when she discovered his infidelity; it was after their separation, the coldest London winter in years, that she killed herself by turning on the kitchen gas. Plath's best-selling autobiographical (and pseudonymously published) novel, *The Bell Jar* (1963), has none of the talent of her poetry, but it remains a reference point as one of the changing scenarios of explanation that Plath continuously constructed for her life.

Most of Plath's best poetry—*Ariel* (1966), *Crossing the Water* (1971), and *Winter Trees* (1972)—was published posthumously. It caught the public imagination by the topicality of its subject matter (marriage, childbearing, infidelity, the woman artist), but it also caught the literary imagination by its ardent language, its compression, its violence in metaphor, and its authoritative tone. Plath had studied at Boston University with Robert Lowell, and it was probably his example that she followed in writing her poetry in free verse. Her free verse, however, has none of the loose and low-keyed quality of Lowell's *Life Studies;* rather, it is so firmly supported by internal rhymes, eye rhymes, parallelism, apposition, alliteration, and other binding devices that it seems as fully controlled as any formal verse could be.

Like Emily Dickinson, Plath repudiated the language of conventional female verse for a fierce and daring explicitness. At the same time, her acute and cold self-observation dominated her fiery lines, taming them to form, mediating her tormented states of mind by a high intelligence. Her reputation has grown steadily since her death; *The Collected Poems,* edited by Ted Hughes, was published in 1981 and the *Journals of Sylvia Plath* in 1982. Her short fiction is collected in *Johnny Panic and the Bible of Dreams* (1979), and a selection of her letters, edited with commentary by her mother, Aurelia Schober Plath, was published as *Letters Home* (1975).

Further Reading:
C. Newman, ed., *The Art of Sylvia Plath,* 1970.
G. Lane, ed., *Sylvia Plath: New Views on Poetry,* 1979.
L. Wagner-Martin, ed., *Sylvia Plath: The Critical Heritage,* 1988.

S. G. Axelrod, *Sylvia Plath: The Wound and the Cure of Words,* 1990.

P. Alexander, *Rough Magic: A Biography of Sylvia Plath,* 1991.

R. Hayman, *The Death and Life of Sylvia Plath,* 1991.

T. Saldivar, *Sylvia Plath: Confessing the Fictive Self,* 1992.

S. Van Dyne, *Revising Life: Sylvia Plath's Ariel Poems,* 1993.

Text:
The Collected Poems, 1981.

Black Rook in Rainy Weather

On the stiff twig up there
Hunches a wet black rook
Arranging and rearranging its feathers in the rain.
I do not expect a miracle
Or an accident   5

To set the sight on fire
In my eye, nor seek
Any more in the desultory weather some design,
But let spotted leaves fall as they fall,
Without ceremony, or portent.   10

Although, I admit, I desire,
Occasionally, some backtalk
From the mute sky, I can't honestly complain:
A certain minor light may still
Lean incandescent   15

Out of kitchen table or chair
As if a celestial burning took
Possession of the most obtuse objects now and then—
Thus hallowing an interval
Otherwise inconsequent   20

By bestowing largesse, honor,
One might say love. At any rate, I now walk
Wary (for it could happen
Even in this dull, ruinous landscape); skeptical,
Yet politic; ignorant   25

Of whatever angel may choose to flare
Suddenly at my elbow. I only know that a rook
Ordering its black feathers can so shine
As to seize my senses, haul
My eyelids up, and grant   30

A brief respite from fear
Of total neutrality. With luck,
Trekking stubborn through this season
Of fatigue, I shall
Patch together a content   35

Of sorts. Miracles occur,
If you care to call those spasmodic
Tricks of radiance miracles. The wait's begun again,
The long wait for the angel,
For that rare, random descent.   40

1960

Daddy

You do not do, you do not do
Any more, black shoe
In which I have lived like a foot
For thirty years, poor and white,
Barely daring to breathe or Achoo.   5

Daddy, I have had to kill you.
You died before I had time—
Marble-heavy, a bag full of God,
Ghastly statue with one gray toe[1]
Big as a Frisco seal   10

And a head in the freakish Atlantic
Where it pours bean green over blue
In the waters off beautiful Nauset.
I used to pray to recover you.
Ach, du.[2]   15

In the German tongue, in the Polish town
Scraped flat by the roller
Of wars, wars, wars.
But the name of the town is common.
My Polack[3] friend   20

---

[1] Otto Plath's diabetes caused a gangrenous toe, which led to the septicemia that killed him.

[2] German: "Ah, you." The second-person familiar form is used for intimates.

[3] Derogatory slang for "Polish."

Says there are a dozen or two.
So I never could tell where you
Put your foot, your root,
I never could talk to you.
The tongue stuck in my jaw.   25

It stuck in a barb wire snare.
Ich, ich, ich, ich,[4]
I could hardly speak.
I thought every German was you.
And the language obscene   30

An engine, an engine
Chuffing me off like a Jew.
A Jew to Dachau, Auschwitz, Belsen.[5]
I began to talk like a Jew.
I think I may well be a Jew   35

The snows of the Tyrol,[6] the clear beer of Vienna[7]
Are not very pure or true.
With my gipsy ancestress and my weird luck
And my Taroc pack and my Taroc pack[8]
I may be a bit of a Jew.   40

I have always been scared of *you,*
With your Luftwaffe,[9] your gobbledygoo.
And your neat mustache
And your Aryan[10] eye, bright blue.
Panzer-man, panzer-man,[11] O You———   40

Not God but a swastika[12]
So black no sky could squeak through.
Every woman adores a Fascist,
The boot in the face, the brute
Brute heart of a brute like you.   50

You stand at the blackboard, daddy,[13]
In the picture I have of you,
A cleft in your chin instead of your foot

[4] German: "I, I, I, I."
[5] Nazi concentration camps.
[6] Alpine region of Austria.
[7] Capital of Austria.
[8] Pack of cards used in fortune telling.
[9] The Nazi air force.
[10] Word used by Nazis to characterize those of "pure" or unadulterated German stock.
[11] Man resembling a German armored tank.
[12] Symbol of the Nazi party.
[13] Otto Plath was a professor of biology at Boston University.

But no less a devil for that, no not
Any less the black man who   55

Bit my pretty red heart in two.
I was ten when they buried you.
At twenty I tried to die
And get back, back, back to you.
I thought even the bones would do.   60

But they pulled me out of the sack,
And they stuck me together with glue.
And then I knew what to do.
I made a model of you,
A man in black with a Meinkampf[14] look   65

And a love of the rack and the screw.[15]
And I said I do, I do.
So daddy, I'm finally through.
The black telephone's off at the root,
The voices just can't worm through.   70

If I've killed one man, I've killed two—
The vampire who said he was you
And drank my blood for a year,
Seven years, if you want to know.
Daddy, you can lie back now.   75

There's a stake in your fat black heart[16]
And the villagers never liked you.
They are dancing and stamping on you.
They always *knew* it was you.
Daddy, daddy, you bastard, I'm through.   80
1965

Medusa*

Off that landspit of stony mouth-plugs,
Eyes rolled by white sticks,

---

[14] German: "My struggle," the title of Hitler's
  manifesto.
[15] Rack; screw: instruments of torture.
[16] Traditionally, a vampire was buried at a
  crossroads with a stake through the heart.

* In mythology, the female monster who
  turned all who looked upon her to stone.
  The poem is addressed, from England, to
  Plath's mother in the United States.

Ears cupping the sea's incoherences,
You house your unnerving head—God-ball,
Lens of mercies,

Your stooges
Plying their wild cells in my keel's shadow,
Pushing by like hearts,
Red stigmata[1] at the very center,
Riding the rip tide to the nearest point of departure,   10

Dragging their Jesus hair.
Did I escape, I wonder?
My mind winds to you
Old barnacled umbilicus, Atlantic cable,
Keeping itself, it seems, in a state of miraculous repair.   15

In any case, you are always there,
Tremulous breath at the end of my line,
Curve of water upleaping
To my water rod, dazzling and grateful,
Touching and sucking.   20

I didn't call you.
I didn't call you at all.
Nevertheless, nevertheless
You steamed to me over the sea,
Fat and red, a placenta[2]   25

Paralysing the kicking lovers.
Cobra light
Squeezing the breath from the blood bells
Of the fuchsia. I could draw no breath,
Dead and moneyless,   30

Overexposed, like an X-ray.
Who do you think you are?
A Communion wafer? Blubbery Mary?
I shall take no bite of your body,
Bottle in which I live,   35

Ghastly Vatican.[3]
I am sick to death of hot salt.
Green as eunuchs,[4] your wishes

---

[1] Permanent wounds.
[2] The organ from which nutrients reach the fetus via the umbilical cord.
[3] Residence of the popes.
[4] Castrated men, often used as guardians of the wives of sultans.

Hiss at my sins.
Off, off, eely tentacle!   40

There is nothing between us.
1965

Ariel*

Stasis in darkness.
Then the substanceless blue
Pour of tor[1] and distances.

God's lioness,
How one we grow,   5
Pivot of heels and knees!—The furrow

Splits and passes, sister to
The brown arc
Of the neck I cannot catch,

Nigger-eye   10
Berries cast dark
Hooks———

Black sweet blood mouthfuls,
Shadows.
Something else   15

Hauls me through air———
Thighs, hair;
Flakes from my heels.

White
Godiva,[2] I unpeel———   20
Dead hands, dead stringencies.

And now I
Foam to wheat, a glitter of seas.
The child's cry

---

* Plath's horse.   [2] Lady Godiva, in the legend, rode naked on
[1] High, craggy hill.   her horse.

Melts in the wall.   25
And I
Am the arrow,

The dew that flies
Suicidal, at one with the drive
Into the red   30

Eye, the cauldron of morning.
1965

Lady Lazarus*

I have done it again.
One year in every ten
I manage it———

A sort of walking miracle, my skin
Bright as a Nazi lampshade,[1]   5
My right foot

A paperweight,
My face a featureless, fine
Jew linen.

Peel off the napkin[2]   10
O my enemy.
Do I terrify?———

The nose, the eye pits, the full set of teeth?
The sour breath
Will vanish in a day.   15

Soon, soon the flesh
The grave cave ate will be
At home on me

---

* Lazarus was raised from the dead by Jesus.
[1] The Nazis, in concentration camps, made lampshades of human skin.
[2] According to legend, the veil or napkin with which Veronica wiped Jesus' face, as he bore the Cross, was then impressed with his visage.

And I a smiling woman.
I am only thirty.   20
And like the cat I have nine times to die.

This is Number Three.
What a trash
To annihilate each decade.

What a million filaments.   25
The peanut-crunching crowd
Shoves in to see

Them unwrap me hand and foot————
The big strip tease.
Gentlemen, ladies   30

These are my hands
My knees.
I may be skin and bone,

Nevertheless, I am the same, identical woman.
The first time it happened I was ten.   35
It was an accident.

The second time I meant
To last it out and not come back at all.
I rocked shut

As a seashell.   40
They had to call and call
And pick the worms off me like sticky pearls.

Dying
Is an art, like everything else.
I do it exceptionally well.   45

I do it so it feels like hell.
I do it so it feels real.
I guess you could say I've a call.

It's easy enough to do it in a cell.
It's easy enough to do it and stay put.   50
It's the theatrical

Comeback in broad day
To the same place, the same face, the same brute
Amused shout:

'A miracle!'   55
That knocks me out.
There is a charge

For the eyeing of my scars, there is a charge
For the hearing of my heart————
It really goes.   60

And there is a charge, a very large charge
For a word or a touch
Or a bit of blood

Or a piece of my hair or my clothes.
So, so, Herr Doktor.   65
So, Herr Enemy.

I am your opus,
I am your valuable,
The pure gold baby

That melts to a shriek.   70
I turn and burn.
Do not think I underestimate your great concern.

Ash, ash————
You poke and stir.
Flesh, bone, there is nothing there————   75

A cake of soap,
A wedding ring,
A gold filling.[3]

Herr God, Herr Lucifer
Beware   80
Beware.

---

[3] Items left in the crematoria of the Nazi concentration camps after the bodies of prisoners had been burned. (The rendered fat of the bodies was used to make soap.)

Out of the ash
I rise with my red hair
And I eat men like air.
1965

Death & Co.

Two, of course there are two.
It seems perfectly natural now————
The one who never looks up, whose eyes are lidded
And balled, like Blake's,[1]
Who exhibits   5

The birthmarks that are his trademark————
The scald scar of water,
The nude
Verdigris of the candor.
I am red meat. His beak   10

Claps sidewise: I am not his yet.
He tells me how badly I photograph.
He tells me how sweet
The babies look in their hospital
Icebox, a simple   15

Frill at the neck,
Then the flutings of their Ionian[2]
Death-gowns,
Then two little feet.
He does not smile or smoke.   20

The other does that,
His hair long and plausive.
Bastard
Masturbating a glitter,
He wants to be loved.   25

I do not stir.
The frost makes a flower,
The dew makes a star,

---

[1] The plaster death mask of the English poet William Blake (1757–1827) represents his eyes "lidded and balled."

[2] Greek.

The dead bell,
The dead bell.   30

Somebody's done for.
1965

Fever 103°

Pure? What does it mean?
The tongues of hell
Are dull, dull as the triple

Tongues of dull, fat Cerberus
Who wheezes at the gate. Incapable   5
Of licking clean

The aguey tendon, the sin, the sin.
The tinder cries.
The indelible smell

Of a snuffed candle!   10
Love, love, the low smokes roll
From me like Isadora's scarves, I'm in a fright

One scarf will catch and anchor in the wheel.
Such yellow sullen smokes
Make their own element. They will not rise,   15

But trundle round the globe
Choking the aged and the meek,
The weak

Hothouse baby in its crib,
The ghastly orchid   20
Hanging its hanging garden in the air,

Devilish leopard!
Radiation turned it white
And killed it in an hour.

Greasing the bodies of adulterers   25
Like Hiroshima ash and eating in.
The sin. The sin.

Darling, all night
I have been flickering, off, on, off, on.
The sheets grow heavy as a lecher's kiss.   30

Three days. Three nights.
Lemon water, chicken
Water, water make me retch.

I am too pure for you or anyone.
Your body   35
Hurts me as the world hurts God. I am a lantern————

My head a moon
Of Japanese paper, my gold beaten skin
Infinitely delicate and infinitely expensive.

Does not my heat astound you. And my light.   40
All by myself I am a huge camellia
Glowing and coming and going, flush on flush.

I think I am going up,
I think I may rise—
The beads of hot metal fly, and I, love, I   45

Am a pure acetylene
Virgin
Attended by roses,

By kisses, by cherubim,
By whatever these pink things mean.   50
Not you, nor him

Not him, nor him
(My selves dissolving, old whore petticoats)—
To Paradise.
1965

Philip Roth
b. 1933

Philip Roth was born on March 19, 1933, in Newark, New Jersey, where he grew up, attended high school, and spent his first year at college. In 1951 he transferred to Bucknell University, where he studied English and philosophy and helped found the literary magazine in which he published his first stories. After graduation in 1954 Roth took an M.A. in English at the University of Chicago and in 1955 enlisted in the army. Discharged because of a back injury, Roth returned to Chicago, where he resumed graduate studies, worked as an instructor, and wrote stories, one of which was chosen for inclusion in *The Best American Short Stories of 1956.* With the publication of the award-winning story collection *Goodbye, Columbus* in 1959, Roth left graduate school to concentrate on writing. Roth's first book, still considered one of his best, includes several fine short stories—"Defender of the Faith" and "Conversion of the Jews"—as well as its long title story, which concerns a young man whose love affair with a spoiled, affluent college student discloses the economic and generational conflicts within the urban and suburban Jewish communities to which they respectively belong. Within a year Roth received several grants and fellowships, including a Guggenheim, and was appointed to the faculty of the writer's workshop at the University of Iowa. In his first novel, *Letting Go* (1962), he drew on his academic experiences at both Iowa and Chicago. In 1962 Roth was appointed writer in residence at Princeton University, and in 1965 he began teaching at the University of Pennsylvania.

Through most of his career, Roth has been drawn, as had F. Scott Fitzgerald, toward two rather different realms of experience—what he calls "the aggressive, the crude, and the obscene, at one extreme, and something a good deal more subtle and, in every sense, refined, at the other." To blend these two, Roth strives to master a prose that possesses both the rhythm, diction, and syntax of colloquial American English and the rich evocations of traditional literary prose. Roth's mastery of colloquial speech—the banal, clichéd vernacular that Sinclair Lewis had earlier tried to catch—is amply apparent in his second novel, *When She Was Good* (1967), a story about American puritanical instincts that is steeped in the diction and details of midwestern provincial life. Having flattened his style for *When She Was Good,* however, Roth let it explode into comic rhetorical excess, obscenity, and rage in his next book, *Portnoy's Complaint* (1969), the free-associative narration of a young Jewish intellectual who confides everything about his life—from his masturbatory habits to his father's chronic constipation—to a Jewish analyst. Partly because of its force and partly because of its sensational revelations, *Portnoy's Complaint* threatened to become almost synonymous with the identity of Philip Roth. In response to his new predicament, rather like an actor who feels his identity frozen into a single role, Roth commenced one of the most intense investigations any American writer has yet made into the dynamics of a literary career.

While writing *Portnoy's Complaint,* Roth had been reading and teaching the work of Franz Kafka. "I began reading Kafka seriously in my early thirties," he tells us in a piece called "In Search of Kafka," "at a time when I was enormously dismayed to find myself drifting away, rather than towards, what I had taken to be my goals as a writer and a man—at a time, in other words, when I was unusually sensitized to Kafka's tales of spiritual disorientation and obstructed energies"—and found there "a number of clues as to how to give imaginative expression to preoccupations of my own." Through Kafka, Roth also began to discover new ways of combining social and political satire with absurd, fantastic situations. In 1971, before the Watergate scandal, Roth published *Our Gang,* an attack on the corruptions of the Nixon administration, and a year later he wrote the self-consciously Kafkaesque novella *The Breast,* in which a college professor one day awakens to find that he has been transformed into a woman's breast.

Roth followed up these two literary skits with *The Great American Novel* (1973), a comic baseball story that is actually a burlesque of American literature and a few of its celebrated careers. In his next novel, *My Life as a Man* (1974), he intensified his experimentation with literary parody by probing the relation between fiction and autobiography, a relation that figures as a central issue in his collection of essays, *Reading Myself and Others* (1975). Literature and its connection to life—especially love life—lies at the heart of his next novel, *The Professor of Desire* (1977), in which a college professor tries to become a "rake among scholars, a scholar among rakes." Since then Roth has written a trilogy that penetrates so deeply into the relation between an author's life and his work that it might have been subtitled "My Life as a Book." In *Zuckerman Bound* (1985)—which collects in one volume the novels *The Ghost Writer* (1979), *Zuckerman Unbound* (1981), and *The Anatomy Lesson* (1983) and the story "The Prague Orgy"—he traces the life of a writer from his apprenticeship and search for a mentor through his enormous success and its bizarre consequences to his almost hallucinatory attempt to enter medical school and abandon his literary career. His latest works include *Deception: A Novel* (1990) and *Patrimony: A True Story* (1991).

"My fiction," Roth once remarked, "is about people in trouble." More specifically, Roth focuses on the private lives that individuals must live as social creatures in a world that seems as daunting in its variety and exuberance as it is threatening in its pressures. The conflicts that trouble Roth's characters may be economic, generational, or psychological, and they are often sexual and religious. In portraying them, Roth brings a strong celebratory impulse matched by an equally powerful deflating impulse. Sometimes his playful inventiveness seems to exist almost exclusively for itself. Both "'Sheer Playfulness' and 'Deadly Seriousness,'" he told Joyce Carol Oates in an interview, were among his "closest friends." In his finest fiction, these two friends meet and measure one another in ways that are remarkable.

Roth's most recent books include *The Facts: A Novelist's Autobiography* (1988) and several novels: *The Counterlife* (1986), *Sabbath's Theater* (1995), and *American Pastoral* (1997).

Further Reading:

J. N. McDaniel, *The Fiction of Philip Roth*, 1974.

A. Mibauer and D. Watson, eds., *Reading Philip Roth*, 1988.

M. Baumgarten and B. Gottfried, *Understanding Philip Roth*, 1990.

J. L. Halio, *Philip Roth Revisited*, 1992.

A. Cooper, *Philip Roth and the Jews*, 1996.

Text:
"The Conversion of the Jews" from *Goodbye, Columbus*, 1956.

The Conversion of the Jews

You're a real one for opening your mouth in the first place," Itzie said. "What do you open your mouth all the time for?"

"I didn't bring it up, Itz, I didn't," Ozzie said.

"What do you care about Jesus Christ for anyway?"

"I didn't bring up Jesus Christ. He did. I didn't even know what he was talking about. Jesus is historical, he kept saying. Jesus is historical." Ozzie mimicked the monumental voice of Rabbi Binder.

"Jesus was a person that lived like you and me," Ozzie continued. "That's what Binder said—"

"Yeah? . . . So what! What do I give two cents whether he lived or not. And what do you gotta open your mouth!" Itzie Lieberman favored closed-mouthedness, especially when it came to Ozzie Freedman's questions. Mrs. Freedman had to see Rabbi Binder twice before about Ozzie's questions and this Wednesday at four-thirty would be the third time. Itzie preferred to keep *his* mother in the kitchen; he settled for behind-the-back subtleties such as gestures, faces, snarls and other less delicate barnyard noises.

"He was a real person, Jesus, but he wasn't like God, and we don't believe he is God." Slowly, Ozzie was explaining Rabbi Binder's position to Itzie, who had been absent from Hebrew School the previous afternoon.

"The Catholics," Itzie said helpfully, "They believe in Jesus Christ, that he's God." Itzie Lieberman used "the Catholics" in its broadest sense—to include the Protestants.

Ozzie received Itzie's remark with a tiny head bob, as though it were a footnote, and went on. "His mother was Mary, and his father probably was Joseph," Ozzie said. "But the New Testament says his real father was God."

"His *real* father?"

"Yeah," Ozzie said, "that's the big thing, his father's supposed to be God."

"Bull."

"That's what Rabbi Binder says, that it's impossible—"

"Sure it's impossible. That stuff's all bull. To have a baby you gotta get laid," Itzie theologized. "Mary hadda get laid."

"That's what Binder says: 'The only way a woman can have a baby is to have intercourse with a man.'"

"He said *that*, Ozz?" For a moment it appeared that Itzie had put the theological question aside. "He said that, intercourse?" A little curled smile shaped itself in the lower half of Itzie's face like a pink mustache. "What you guys do, Ozz, you laugh or something?"

"I raised my hand."

"Yeah? Whatja say?"

"That's when I asked the question."

Itzie's face lit up. "Whatja ask about—intercourse?"

"No, I asked the question about God, how if He could create the heaven and earth in six days, and make all the animals and the fish and the light in six days—the light especially, that's what always get me, that He could make the light. Making fish and animals, that's pretty good—"

"That's damn good." Itzie's appreciation was honest but unimaginative: it was as though God had just pitched a one-hitter.

"But making light . . . I mean when you think about it, it's really something," Ozzie said. "Anyway, I asked Binder if He could make all that in six days, and He could *pick* the six days he wanted right out of nowhere, why couldn't He let a woman have a baby without having intercourse."

"You said intercourse, Ozz, to Binder?"

"Yeah."

"Right in class?"

"Yeah,"

Itzie smacked the side of his head.

"I mean, no kidding around," Ozzie said, "that'd really be nothing. After all that other stuff, that'd practically be nothing."

Itzie considered a moment. "What'd Binder say?"

"He started all over again explaining how Jesus was historical and how he lived like you and me but he wasn't God. So I said I under*stood* that. What I wanted to know was different."

What Ozzie wanted to know was always different. The first time he had wanted to know how Rabbi Binder could call the Jews "The Chosen People" if the Declaration of Independence claimed all men to be created equal. Rabbi Binder tried to distinguish for him between political equality and spiritual legitimacy, but what Ozzie wanted to know, he insisted vehemently, was different. That was the first time his mother had to come.

Then there was the plane crash. Fifty-eight people had been killed in a plane crash at La Guardia. In studying a casualty list in the newspaper his mother had discovered among the list of those dead eight Jewish names (his grandmother had nine but she counted Miller as a Jewish name); because of the eight she said the plane crash was "a tragedy." During free-discussion time on Wednesday Ozzie had brought to Rabbi Binder's attention this matter of "some of his relations" always picking out the Jewish names. Rabbi Binder had begun to explain cultural unity and some other things when Ozzie stood up at his seat and said that what he wanted to know was different. Rabbi Binder insisted that he sit down and it was then that Ozzie shouted that he wished all fifty-eight were Jews. That was the second time his mother came.

"And he kept explaining about Jesus being historical, and so I kept asking him. No kidding, Itz, he was trying to make me look stupid."

"So what he finally do?"

"Finally he starts screaming that I was deliberately simple-minded and a wise guy, and that my mother had to come, and this was the last time. And that I'd never get bar-mitzvahed if he could help it. Then, Itz, then he starts talking in that voice like a statue, real slow and deep, and he says that I better think over what I said about the Lord. He told me to go to his office and think it over." Ozzie leaned his body towards Itzie. "Itz, I thought it over for a solid hour, and now I'm convinced God could do it."

Ozzie had planned to confess his latest transgression to his mother as soon as she came home from work. But it was a Friday night in November and already dark, and when Mrs. Freedman came through the door she tossed off her coat, kissed Ozzie quickly on the face, and went to the kitchen table to light the three yellow candles, two for the Sabbath and one for Ozzie's father.

When his mother lit the candles she would move her two arms slowly towards her, dragging them through the air, as though persuading people whose minds were half made up. And her eyes would get glassy with tears. Even when his father was alive Ozzie remembered that her eyes had gotten glassy, so it didn't have anything to do with his dying. It had something to do with lighting the candles.

As she touched the flaming match to the unlit wick of a Sabbath candle, the phone rang, and Ozzie, standing only a foot from it, plucked it off the receiver and held it muffled to his chest. When his mother lit candles Ozzie felt there should be no noise; even breathing, if you could manage it, should be softened. Ozzie pressed the phone to his breast and watched his mother dragging whatever she was dragging, and he felt his own eyes get glassy. His mother was a round, tired, gray-haired penguin of a woman whose gray skin had begun to feel the tug of gravity and the weight of her own history. Even when she was dressed up she didn't look like a chosen person. But when she lit candles she looked like something better; like a woman who knew momentarily that God could do anything.

After a few mysterious minutes she was finished. Ozzie hung up the phone and walked to the kitchen table where she was beginning to lay the two places for the four-course Sabbath meal. He told her that she would have to see Rabbi Binder next Wednesday at four-thirty, and then he told her why. For the first time in their life together she hit Ozzie across the face with her hand.

All through the chopped liver and chicken soup part of the dinner Ozzie cried; he didn't have any appetite for the rest.

On Wednesday, in the largest of the three basement classrooms of the synagogue, Rabbi Marvin Binder, a tall, handsome, broad-shouldered man of thirty with thick strong-fibered black hair, removed his watch from his pocket and saw that it was four o'clock. At the rear of the room Yakov Blotnik, the seventy-one-year-old custodian, slowly polished the large window, mumbling to himself, unaware that it was four o'clock or six o'clock, Monday or Wednesday. To most of the students Yakov Blotnik's mumbling, along with his brown curly beard, scythe nose, and two heel-trailing black cats, made of him an object of wonder, a foreigner, a relic, towards whom they were alternately fearful and disrespectful. To Ozzie the mumbling had always seemed a monotonous, curious prayer; what made it curious was that old Blotnik had been mumbling so steadily for so many years, Ozzie suspected he had memorized the prayers and forgotten all about God.

"It is now free-discussion time," Rabbi Binder said. "Feel free to talk about any Jewish matter at all—religion, family, politics, sports—"

There was silence. It was a gusty, clouded November afternoon and it did not seem as though there ever was or could be a thing called baseball. So nobody this week said a word about that hero from the past, Hank Greenberg—which limited free discussion considerably.

And the soul-battering Ozzie Freedman had just received from Rabbi Binder had imposed its limitation. When it was Ozzie's turn to read aloud from the Hebrew book the rabbi had asked him petulantly why he didn't read more rapidly. He was showing no progress. Ozzie said he could read faster but that he was sure not to understand what he was reading. Nevertheless, at the rabbi's repeated suggestion Ozzie tried, and showed a great talent, but in the midst of a long passage he stopped short and said he didn't understand a word he was reading, and started in again at a drag-footed pace. Then came the soul-battering.

Consequently when free-discussion time rolled around none of the students felt too free. The rabbi's invitation was answered only by the mumbling of feeble old Blotnik.

"Isn't there anything at all you would like to discuss?" Rabbi Binder asked again, looking at his watch. "No questions or comments?"

There was a small grumble from the third row. The rabbi requested that Ozzie rise and give the rest of the class the advantage of his thought.

Ozzie rose. "I forget it now," he said, and sat down in his place.

Rabbi Binder advanced a seat towards Ozzie and poised himself on the edge of the desk. It was Itzie's desk and the rabbi's frame only a dagger's-length away from his face snapped him to sitting attention.

"Stand up again, Oscar," Rabbi Binder said calmly, "and try to assemble your thoughts."

Ozzie stood up. All his classmates turned in their seats and watched as he gave an unconvincing scratch to his forehead.

"I can't assemble any," he announced, and plunked himself down.

"Stand up!" Rabbi Binder advanced from Itzie's desk to the one directly in front of Ozzie; when the rabbinical back was turned Itzie gave it five-fingers off the tip of his nose, causing a small titter in the room. Rabbi Binder was too absorbed in squelching Ozzie's nonsense once and for all to bother with titters. "Stand up, Oscar. What's your question about?"

Ozzie pulled a word out of the air. It was the handiest word. "Religion."

"Oh, now you remember?"

"Yes."

"What is it?"

Trapped, Ozzie blurted the first thing that came to him. "Why can't He make anything He wants to make!"

As Rabbi Binder prepared an answer, a final answer, Itzie, ten feet behind him, raised one finger on his left hand, gestured it meaningfully towards the rabbi's back, and brought the house down.

Binder twisted quickly to see what had happened and in the midst of the commotion Ozzie shouted into the rabbi's back what he couldn't have shouted to his face. It was a loud, toneless sound that had the timbre of something stored inside for about six days.

"You don't know! You don't know anything about God!"

The rabbi spun back towards Ozzie. "What?"

"You don't know—you don't—"

"Apologize, Oscar, apologize!" It was a threat.

"You don't—"

Rabbi Binder's hand flicked out at Ozzie's cheek. Perhaps it had only been meant to clamp the boy's mouth shut, but Ozzie ducked and the palm caught him squarely on the nose.

The blood came in a short, red spurt on to Ozzie's shirt front.

The next moment was all confusion. Ozzie screamed, "You bastard, you bastard!" and broke for the classroom door. Rabbi Binder lurched a step backwards, As though his own blood had started flowing violently in the opposite direction, then gave a clumsy lurch forward and bolted out the door after Ozzie. The class followed after the rabbi's huge blue-suited back, and before old Blotnik could turn from his window, the room was empty and everyone was headed full speed up the three flights leading to the roof.

If one should compare the light of day to the life of man: sunrise to birth; sunset—the dropping down over the edge—to death; then as Ozzie Freedman wiggled through the trapdoor of the synagogue roof, his feet kicking backwards bronco-style at Rabbi Binder's outstretched arms—at that moment the day was fifty years old. As a rule, fifty or fifty-five reflects accurately the age of late afternoons in November, for it is in that month, during those hours, that one's awareness of light seems no longer a matter of seeing, but of hearing: light begins clicking away. In fact, as Ozzie locked shut the trap-door in the rabbi's face, the sharp click of the bolt into the lock might momentarily have been mistaken for the sound of the heavier gray that had just throbbed through the sky.

With all his weight Ozzie kneeled on the locked door; any instant he was certain that Rabbi Binder's shoulder would fling it open, splintering the wood into shrapnel and catapulting his body into the sky. But the door did not move and below him he heard only the rumble of feet, first loud then dim, like thunder rolling away.

A question shot through his brain. "Can this be *me?*" For a thirteen-year-old who had just labeled his religious leader a bastard, twice, it was not an improper question. Louder and louder the question came to him—"Is it me? It is me?"—until he discov-ered himself no longer kneeling, but racing crazily towards the edge of the roof, his eyes crying, his throat screaming, and his arms flying every-whichway as though not his own. "Is it me? Is it me Me ME ME ME! It has to be me—but is it!"

It is the question a thief must ask himself the night he jimmies open his first win-dow, and it is said to be the question with which bridegrooms quiz themselves before the altar.

In the few wild seconds it took Ozzie's body to propel him to the edge of the roof, his self-examination began to grow fuzzy. Gazing down at the street, he became confused as to the problem beneath the question: was it, is-it-me-who-called-Binder-a-bastard? or, is-it-me-prancing-around-on the-roof? However, the scene below settled all, for there is an instant in any action when whether it is you or somebody else is academic. The thief crams the money in his pockets and scoots out the window. The bridegroom signs the hotel register for two. And the boy on the roof finds a streetful of people gap-ing at him, necks stretched backwards, faces up, as though he were the ceiling of the Hayden Planetarium. Suddenly you know it's you.

"Oscar! Oscar Freedman!" A voice rose from the center of the crowd, a voice that, could it have been seen, would have looked like the writing on scroll. "Oscar Freedman, get down from there. Immediately!" Rabbi Binder was pointing one arm stiffly up at him; and at the end of that arm, one finger aimed menacingly. It was the attitude of a dictator, but one—the eyes confessed all—whose personal valet had spit neatly in his face.

Ozzie didn't answer. Only for a blink's length did he look towards Rabbi Binder. In-stead his eyes began to fit together the world beneath him, to sort out people from places, friends from enemies, participants from spectators. In little jagged starlike clus-ters his friends stood around Rabbi Binder, who was still pointing. The topmost point on a star compounded not of angels but of five adolescent boys was Itzie. What a world it was, with those stars below, Rabbi Binder below . . . Ozzie, who a moment earlier hadn't been able to control his own body, started to feel the meaning of the word con-trol: he felt Peace and he felt Power.

"Oscar Freedman, I'll give you three to come down."

Few dictators give their subjects three to do anything; but, as always, Rabbi Binder only looked dictatorial.

"Are you ready, Oscar?"

Ozzie nodded his head yes, although he had no intention in the world—the lower one or the celestial one he'd just entered—of coming down even if Rabbi Binder should give him a million.

"All right then," said Rabbi Binder. He ran a hand through his black Samson hair as though it were the gesture prescribed for uttering the first digit. Then, with his other hand cutting a circle out of the small piece of sky around him, he spoke. "One!"

There was no thunder. On the contrary, at that moment, as though "one" was the cue for which he had been waiting, the world's least thunderous person appeared on the synagogue steps. He did not so much come out the synagogue door as lean out, onto the darkening air. He clutched at the doorknob with one hand and looked up at the roof.

"Oy!"

Yakov Blotnik's old mind hobbled slowly, as if on crutches, and though he couldn't decide precisely what the boy was doing on the roof, he knew it wasn't good—that is, it wasn't-good-for-the-Jews. For Yakov Blotnik life had fractioned itself simply: things were either good-for-the-Jews or no-good-for-the-Jews.

He smacked his free hand to his in-sucked cheek, gently. "Oy, Gut!" And then quickly as he was able, he jacked down his head and surveyed the street. There was Rabbi Binder (like a man at an auction with only three dollars in his pocket, he had just delivered a shaky "Two!"); there were the students, and that was all. So far it-wasn't-so-bad-for-the-Jews. But the boy had to come down immediately, before anybody saw. The problem: how to get the boy off the roof?

Anybody who has ever had a cat on the roof knows how to get him down. You call the fire department. Of first you call the operator and you ask her for the fire department. And the next thing there is great jamming of brakes and clanging of bells and shouting of instructions. And then the cat is off the roof. You do the same thing to get a boy off the roof.

That is, you do the same thing if you are Yakov Blotnik and you once had a cat on the roof.

When the engines, all four of them, arrived, Rabbi Binder had four times given Ozzie the count of three. The big hook-and-ladder swung around the corner and one of the firemen leaped from it, plunging headlong towards the yellow fire hydrant in front of the synagogue. With a huge wrench he began to unscrew the top nozzle. Rabbi Binder raced over to him and pulled at his shoulder.

"There's no fire . . ."

The fireman mumbled back over his shoulder and, heatedly, continued working at the nozzle.

"But there's no fire, there's no fire . . ." Binder shouted. When the fireman mumbled again, the rabbi grasped his face with both hands and pointed it up at the roof.

To Ozzie it looked as though Rabbi Binder was trying to tug the fireman's head out of his body, like a cork from a bottle. He had to giggle at the picture they made: it was a family portrait—rabbi in black skullcap, fireman in red fire hat, and the little yellow hydrant squatting beside like a kid brother, bareheaded. From the edge of the roof Ozzie waved at the portrait, one-handed, flapping, mocking wave; in doing it his right foot slipped from under him. Rabbi Binder covered his eyes with his hands.

Firemen work fast. Before Ozzie had even regained his balance a big, round, yellowed net was being held on the synagogue lawn. The firemen who held it looked up at Ozzie with stern, feelingless faces.

One of the firemen turned his head towards Rabbi Binder. "What, is the kid nuts or something?"

Rabbi Binder unpeeled his hands from his eyes, slowly, painfully, as if they were tape. Then he checked: nothing on the sidewalk, no dents in the net.

"Is he gonna jump, or what?" the fireman shouted.

In a voice not at all like a statue, Rabbi Binder finally answered. "Yes, yes, I think so . . . He's been threatening to . . ."

Threatening to? Why, the reason he was on the roof, Ozzie remembered, was to get away; he hadn't even thought about jumping. He had just run to get away, and the truth was that he hadn't really headed for the roof as much as he'd been chased there.

"What's his name, the kid?"

"Freedman," Rabbi Binder answered. "Oscar Freedman."

The fireman looked up at Ozzie. "What is it with you, Oscar? You gonna jump, or what?"

Ozzie did not answer. Frankly, the question had just arisen.

"Look, Oscar, if you're gonna jump, jump—and if you're not gonna jump, don't jump. But don't waste our time, willya?"

Ozzie looked at the fireman and then at Rabbi Binder. He wanted to see Rabbi Binder cover his eyes one more time.

"I'm going to jump."

And then he scampered around the edge of the roof to the corner, where there was no net below, and he flapped his arms at his sides, swishing the air and smacking his palms to his trousers on the downbeat. He began screaming like some kind of engine, "Wheeeee . . . wheeeeee," and leaning way out over the edge with the upper half of his body. The firemen whipped around to cover the ground with the net. Rabbi Binder mumbled a few words to Somebody and covered his eyes. Everything happened quickly, jerkily, as in a silent movie. The crowd, which had arrived with the fire engines, gave out a long, Fourth-of-July fireworks oooh-aahhh. In the excitement no one had paid the crowd much heed, except, of course, Yakov Blotnik, who swung from the doorknob counting heads. "Fier und tsvansik . . . finf und tsvantsik . . . Oy, Gut!" It wasn't like this with the cat.

Rabbi Binder peeked through his fingers, checked the sidewalk and net. Empty. But there was Ozzie racing to the other corner. The firemen raced with him but were unable to keep up. Whenever Ozzie wanted to he might jump and splatter himself upon the sidewalk, and by the time the firemen scooted to the spot all they could do with their net would be to cover the mess.

"Wheeeee . . . wheeeee . . ."

"Hey, Oscar," the winded fireman yelled, "What the hell is this, a game or something?"

"Wheeeee . . . wheeeee . . ."

"Hey, Oscar—"

But he was off now to the other corner, flapping his wings fiercely. Rabbi Binder couldn't take it any longer—the fire engines from nowhere, the screaming suicidal boy, the net. He fell to his knees, exhausted, and with his hands curled together in front of his chest like a little dome, he pleaded, he pleaded, "Oscar, stop it, Oscar. Don't jump, Oscar. Please come down . . . Please don't jump."

And further back in the crowd a single voice, a single young voice, shouted a lone word to the boy on the roof.

"Jump!"

It was Itzie. Ozzie momentarily stopped flapping.

"Go ahead, Ozz—jump!" Itzie broke off his point of the star and courageously, with the inspiration not of a wise-guy but of a disciple, stood alone. "Jump, Ozz, jump!"

Still on his knees, his hands still curled, Rabbi Binder twisted his body back. He looked at Itzie, then, agonizingly, back to Ozzie.

"Oscar, Don't Jump! Please, Don't Jump . . . please please . . ."

"Jump!" This time it wasn't Itzie but another point of the star. By the time Mrs. Freedman arrived to keep her four-thirty appointment with Rabbi Binder, the whole little upside down heaven was shouting and pleading for Ozzie to jump, and Rabbi Binder no longer pleading with him not to jump, but was crying into the dome of his hands.

Understandably Mrs. Freedman couldn't figure out what her son was doing on the roof. So she asked.

"Ozzie, my Ozzie, what are you doing? My Ozzie, what is it?"

Ozzie stopped wheeeeeing and slowed his arms down to a cruising flap, the kind birds use in soft winds, but he did not answer. He stood against the low, clouded, darkening sky—light clicked down swiftly now, as on a small gear—flapping softly and gazing down at the small bundle of a woman who was his mother.

"What are you doing, Ozzie?" She turned towards the kneeling Rabbi Binder and rushed so close that only a paper-thickness of dusk lay between her stomach and his shoulders.

"What is my baby doing?"

Rabbi Binder gaped up at her but he too was mute. All that moved was the dome of his hands; it shook back and forth like a weak pulse.

"Rabbi, get him down! He'll kill himself. Get him down, my only baby . . ."

"I can't," Rabbi Binder said, "I can't . . ." and he turned his handsome head toward the crowd of boys behind him. "It's them. Listen to them."

And for the first time Mrs. Freedman saw the crowd of boys, and she heard what they were yelling.

"He's doing it for them. He won't listen to me. It's them." Rabbi Binder spoke like one in a trance.

"For them?"

"Yes."

"Why for them?"

"They want him to . . ."

Mrs. Freedman raised her two arms upward as though she were conducting the sky. "For them he's doing it!" And then in a gesture older than pyramids, older than prophets and floods, her arms came slapping down to her sides. "A martyr I have. Look!" She tilted her head to the roof. Ozzie was still flapping softly. "My martyr."

"Oscar, come down, *please*," Rabbi Binder groaned.

In a startlingly even voice Mrs. Freedman called to the boy on the roof. "Ozzie, come down, Ozzie. Don't be a martyr, my baby."

As though it were a litany, Rabbi Binder repeated her words. "Don't be a martyr, my baby. Don't be a martyr."

"Gawhead, Ozz—*be* a Martin!" It was Itzie. "Be a Martin, be a Martin," and all the voices joined in singing for Martindom, whatever *it* was. "Be a Martin, be a Martin . . ."

Somehow when you're on a roof the darker it gets the less you can hear. All Ozzie knew was that two groups wanted two new things: his friends were spirited and musical about what they wanted; his mother and the rabbi were even-toned, chanting, about what they didn't want. The rabbi's voice was without tears now and so was his mother's.

The big net started up at Ozzie like a sightless eye. The big, clouded sky pushed down. From beneath it looked like a gray corrugated board. Suddenly, looking up into that unsympathetic sky, Ozzie realized all the strangeness of what these people, his friends, were asking: they wanted him to jump, to kill himself; they were singing about it now—it made them that happy. And there was an even greater strangeness: Rabbi Binder was on his knees, trembling. If there was a question to be asked now it was not "Is it me?" but rather "Is it us? . . . Is it us?"

Being on the roof, it turned out, was a serious thing. If he jumped would the singing become dancing? Would it? What would jumping stop? Yearningly, Ozzie wished he could rip open the sky, plunge his hands through, and pull out the sun; and on the sun, like a coin, would be stamped JUMP or DON'T JUMP.

Ozzie's knees rocked and sagged a little under him as though they were setting him for a dive. His arms tightened, stiffened, froze, from shoulders to fingernails. He felt as if each part of his body were going to vote as to whether he should kill himself or not— and each part as though it were independent of *him*.

The light took an unexpected click down and the new darkness, like a gag, hushed the friends singing for this and the mother and rabbi chanting for that.

Ozzie Stopped counting votes, and in a curiously high voice, like one who wasn't prepared for speech, he spoke.

"Mamma?"

"Yes, Oscar."

"Mamma, get down on your knees, like Rabbi Binder."

"Oscar—"

"Get down on your knees," he said, "or I'll jump."

Ozzie heard a whimper, then a quick rustling, and when he looked down where his mother had stood he saw the top of a head and beneath that a circle of dress. She was kneeling beside Rabbi Binder.

He spoke again. "Everybody kneel." There was the sound of everybody kneeling.

Ozzie looked around. With one hand he pointed towards the synagogue entrance. "Make *him* kneel."

There was a noise, not of kneeling, but of body-and-cloth stretching. Ozzie could hear Rabbi Binder saying in a gruff whisper, ". . . or he'll *kill* himself," and when next he looked there was Yakov Blotnik off the doorknob and for the first time in his life upon his knees in the Gentile posture of prayer.

As for the firemen—it is not as difficult as one might imagine to hold a net taut while you are kneeling.

Ozzie looked around again; and then he called to Rabbi Binder.

"Rabbi?"

"Yes, Oscar."

"Rabbi Binder, do you believe in God."

"Yes."

"Do you believe God can do Anything?" Ozzie leaned his head out into the darkness. "Anything?"

"Oscar, I think—"

"Tell me you believe God can do Anything."

There was a second's hesitation. Then: "God can do Anything."

"Tell me you believe God can make a child without intercourse."

"He can."

"Tell me!"

"God," Rabbi Binder admitted, "can make a child without intercourse."

"Mamma, you tell me."

"God can make a child without intercourse," his mother said.

"Make *him* tell me." There was no doubt who *him* was.

In a few moments Ozzie heard an old comical voice say something to the increasing darkness about God.

Next, Ozzie made everybody say it. And then he made them all say they believed in Jesus Christ—first one at a time, then all together.

When the catechizing was through it was the beginning of evening. From the street it sounded as if the boy on the roof might have sighed.

"Ozzie?" A woman's voice dared to speak. "You'll come down now?"

There was no answer, but the woman waited, and when a voice finally did speak it was thin and crying, and exhausted as that of an old man who has just finished pulling the bells.

"Mamma, don't you see—you shouldn't hit me. He shouldn't hit me. You shouldn't hit me about God, Mamma. You should never hit anybody about God—"

"Ozzie, please come down now."

"Promise me, promise me you'll never hit anybody about God."

He had asked only his mother, but for some reason everyone kneeling in the street promised he would never hit anybody about God.

Once again there was silence.

"I can come down now, Mamma," the boy on the roof finally said. He turned his head both ways as though checking the traffic lights. "Now I can come down . . ."

And he did, right into the center of yellow net that glowed in the evening's edge like an overgrown halo.

1959

Audre Lorde
1934–1992

Audre Lorde, a self-described "black lesbian feminist warrior poet," was born in Harlem, the child of West Indian immigrants. She graduated from Hunter College, received her M.L.S. from Columbia University, and worked as a teacher and librarian before becoming professor of English at John Jay College of Criminal Justice and Hunter College. She founded the Kitchen Table: Women of Color Press, and received honorary doctorates from several colleges and universities.

Lorde always insisted that the complexity of her self-identification be acknowledged. She wrote committedly as a daughter, a mother, a lesbian, a feminist, a New Yorker, and an African American. As befitted a woman who, in one

questionnaire, concisely entered her religion as "Quaker" and her politics as "Radical,"
Lorde saw her poetry as a political intervention. She told one interviewer: "I loved
poetry, and I loved words. But what was beautiful had to serve the purpose of changing
my life, or I would have died." In 1991, Audre Lorde became the poet laureate of the
state of New York. She died of cancer the following year, on St. Croix in the United
States Virgin Islands. Audre Lorde's books include *The First Cities* (1968), *Cables to
Rage* (1970), *Coal* (1976), *The Black Unicorn* (1978), *The Cancer Journals* (1980), *Zami:
A New Spelling of My Name* (1982), *Our Dead Behind Us* (1986), and *The Marvelous
Arithmetics of Distance: Poems 1987–1992* (1993.)

Texts:
"Walking Our Boundaries" from *The Black Uni-
    corn*, 1978.
"Black Mother Woman," and "Afterimages" from
    Chosen Poems, Old and New, 1982.

"Equinox" from *The Collected Poems of Audre
    Lorde*, 1997.

Black Mother Woman

I cannot recall you gentle
yet through your heavy love
I have become
an image of your once delicate flesh
split with deceitful longings.   5

When strangers come and compliment me
your aged spirit takes a bow
jingling with pride
but once you hid that secret
in the center of furies   10
hanging me
with deep breasts and wiry hair
with your own split flesh
and long suffering eyes
buried in myths of little worth.   15

But I have peeled away your anger
down to the core of love
and look mother
I Am
a dark temple where your true spirit rises   20
beautiful
and tough as chestnut
stanchion against your nightmare of weakness

and if my eyes conceal
a squadron of conflicting rebellions   25
I learned from you
to define myself
through your denials.
1971

Equinox

My daughter marks the day that spring begins.
I cannot celebrate spring without remembering
how the bodies of unborn children
bake in their mothers' flesh like ovens
consecrated by the flame that eats them   5
lit by mobiloil and easternstandard
Unborn children in their blasted mothers
floating like small monuments
in an ocean of oil.

The year my daughter was born   10
Du Bois died in Accra while I
marched into Washington
to the death knell of dreaming
which 250,000 others mistook for a hope
believing only Birmingham's Black children   15
were being pounded into mortar in churches
that year some of us still thought
Vietnam was a suburb of Korea.

Then John Kennedy fell off the roof
of Southeast Asia and shortly afterward   20
my whole house burned down
with nobody in it
and on the following Sunday
my borrowed radio announced
that Malcolm was shot dead   25
and I ran to reread all he had written
because death was becoming such an excellent measure
of prophecy
As I read his words dark mangled children
came streaming out of the atlas   30
Hanoi Angola Guinea-Bissau Mozambique Phnom-Penh
merging into Bedford-Stuyvesant and Hazelhurst Mississippi

haunting my New York tenement that terribly bright summer
while Detroit and Watts and San Francisco were burning
I lay awake in stifling Broadway nights afraid   35
for whoever was growing in my belly
and suppose it started earlier than planned
who would I trust to take care that my daughter
did not eat poisoned roaches
when I was gone?   40

If she did, it doesn't matter
because I never knew it.
Today both children came home from school
talking about spring and peace
and I wonder if they will ever know it   45
I want to tell them that we have no right to spring
because our sisters and brothers are burning
because every year the oil grows thicker
and even the earth is crying
because Black is beautiful but currently   50
going out of style
that we must be very strong
and love each other
in order to go on living.
1969

Walking Our Boundaries

This first bright day has broken
the back of winter.
We rise from war
to walk across the earth
around our house   5
both stunned that sun can shine so brightly
after all our pain
Cautiously we inspect our joint holding.
A part of last year's garden still stands
bracken   10
one tough missed okra pod clings to the vine
a parody of fruit cold-hard and swollen
underfoot
one rotting shingle
is becoming loam.   15

I take your hand beside the compost heap
glad to be alive and still
with you
we talk of ordinary articles
with relief   20
while we peer upward
each half-afraid
there will be no tight buds started
on our ancient apple tree
so badly damaged by last winter's storm   25
knowing
it does not pay to cherish symbols
when the substance
lies so close at hand
waiting to be held   30
your hand
falls off the apple bark
like casual fire
along my back
my shoulders are dead leaves   35
waiting to be burned
to life.

The sun is watery warm
our voices
seem too loud for this small yard   40
too tentative for women
so in love
the siding has come loose in spots
our footsteps hold this place
together   45
as our place
our joint decisions make the possible
whole.
I do not know when
we shall laugh again   50
but next week
we will spade up another plot
for this spring's seeding.
1978

Afterimages*

I

However the image enters
its force remains within
my eyes
rockstrewn caves where dragonfish evolve
wild for life, relentless and acquisitive   5
learning to survive
where there is no food
my eyes are always hungry
and remembering
however the image enters   15
its force remains.
A white woman stands bereft and empty
a black boy hacked into a murderous lesson
recalled in me forever
like a lurch of earth on the edge of sleep   20
etched into my visions
food for dragonfish that learn
to live upon whatever they must eat
fused images beneath my pain.

II

The Pearl River floods through the streets of Jackson   25
A Mississippi summer televised.
Trapped houses kneel like sinners in the rain
a white woman climbs from her roof to a passing boat
her fingers tarry for a moment on the chimney
now awash   30
tearless and no longer young, she holds
a tattered baby's blanket in her arms.
In a flickering afterimage of the nightmare rain
a microphone
thrust up against her flat bewildered words   35
　　　"we jest come from the bank yestiddy
　　　　borrowing money to pay the income tax
　　　　now everything's gone. I never knew
　　　　it could be so hard."

---

* A contemporary poem about the Emmett
Till murder of 1955. Compare it to Gwendolyn Brooks' poem, "A Bronzeville Mother
Loiters in Mississippi . . ." written years before (see page 2380 of this text).

Despair weighs down her voice like Pearl River mud   40
caked around the edges
her pale eyes scanning the camera for help or explanation
unanswered
she shifts her search across the watered street, dry-eyed
       "hard, but not this hard."   45
Two tow-headed children hurl themselves against her
hanging upon her coat like mirrors
until a man with ham-like hands pulls her aside
snarling "She ain't got nothing more to say!"
and that lie hangs in his mouth   50
like a shred of rotting meat.

III

I inherited Jackson, Mississippi.
For my majority it gave me Emmett Till
his 15 years puffed out like bruises
on plump boy-cheeks
his only Mississippi summer   55
whistling a 21 gun salute to Dixie
as a white girl passed him in the street
and he was baptized my son forever
in the midnight waters of the Pearl.

His broken body is the afterimage of my 21st year
when I walked through a northern summer
my eyes averted
from each corner's photographies
newspapers protest posters magazines   65
Police Story, Confidential, True
the avid insistence of detail
pretending insight or information
the length of gash across the dead boy's loins
his grieving mother's lamentation   70
the severed lips, how many burns
his gouged out eyes
sewed shut upon the screaming covers
louder than life
all over   75
the veiled warning, the secret relish
of a black child's mutilated body
fingered by street-corner eyes
bruise upon livid bruise
and wherever I looked that summer   80
I learned to be at home with children's blood
with savored violence

with pictures of black broken flesh
used, crumpled, and discarded
lying amid the sidewalk refuse
like a raped woman's face.   85

A black boy from Chicago
whistled on the streets of Jackson, Mississippi
testing what he'd been taught was a manly thing to do
his teachers   90
ripped his eyes out his sex his tongue
and flung him to the Pearl weighted with stone
in the name of white womanhood
they took their aroused honor
back to Jackson   95
and celebrated in a whorehouse
the double ritual of white manhood
confirmed.

IV

"If earth and air and water do not judge them who are we to refuse a crust of bread?"

Emmett Till rides the crest of the Pearl, whistling
24 years his ghost lay like the shade of a raped woman   95
and a white girl has grown older in costly honor
(what did she pay to never know its price?)
now the Pearl River speaks its muddy judgment
and I can withhold my pity and my bread.
        "Hard, but not this hard."   100
Her face is flat with resignation and despair
with ancient and familiar sorrows
a woman surveying her crumpled future
as the white girl bemirched by Emmett's whistle
never allowed her own tongue   105
without power or conclusion
unvoiced
she stands adrift in the ruins of her honor
and a man with an executioner's face
pulls her away.   110

Within my eyes
the flickering afterimages of a nightmare rain
a woman wrings her hands
beneath the weight of agonies remembered
I wade through summer ghosts   115
betrayed by vision
hers and my own

becoming dragonfish to survive
the horrors we are living
with tortured lungs   120
adapting to breathe blood.

A woman measures her life's damage
my eyes are caves, chunks of etched rock
tied to the ghost of a black boy
whistling   125
crying and frightened
her tow-headed children cluster
like little mirrors of despair
their father's hands upon them
and soundlessly   130
a woman begins to weep.
1981

N. Scott Momaday
b. 1934

N. Scott Momaday, a Kiowa Indian, is a Pulitzer Prize-winning novelist and university professor who believes that the strength of Native American culture rests on its close identification with the land. His grandmother, Aho, typifies for him the Indian experience: "The immense landscape of the continental interior," he says, "lay like memory in her blood." Yet for as long as she lived after witnessing the outlawing of the Sun Dance, the Kiowa ritual of worship, "she bore a vision of deicide," the killing of a god. In his fiction and nonfiction Momaday celebrates the spiritual awareness that his grandmother possessed even as he laments the cultural alienation imposed on her by the United States.

Navarre Scott Momaday, whose Kiowa name is Tsoai-talee, was born on February 27, 1934, near Anadarko, the Oklahoma Kiowa Indian agency. In 1935 his family moved to northern New Mexico, where he grew up on Navajo, Apache, and Jemez Pueblo Indian reservations. He received a B.A. in political science from the University of New Mexico in 1958, an M.A. from Stanford in 1960, and a Ph.D. from Stanford in 1963. Currently on the English and Comparative Literature faculty at Stanford, Momaday has also taught at the Berkeley and Santa Barbara campuses of the University of California and at the Las Cruces campus of New Mexico State University. His scholarly interest is in nineteenth-century American poetry, and he is editor of *The Complete Poems of Frederick Goddard Tuckerman* (1965).

Momaday lives another life, however, as a Kiowa tribal dancer and chronicler of Indian experience in this country. "None but an Indian, I think," he has said, "knows so much what it is like to have existence in two worlds and security in neither." In *House Made of Dawn* (1968), his prizewinning first novel, Momaday recounts the adventures of an Indian named Abel, a man who survives World War II only to discover, as Momaday put it, that he can neither "recover his tribal identity nor . . . escape the cultural context in which he grew up. His is torn, as they say, between two worlds, neither of which he can enter and be a whole man. The story is that of his struggle to survive. . . ." The language of *House Made of Dawn* paradoxically conjoins the lyrical and the violent. Abel and his fellow runners run, we read, "with great dignity and calm, not in hope of anything, but hopelessly; neither in fear nor hatred nor despair of evil, but simply in recognition and with respect. Evil was. Evil was abroad in the night; they must venture out to the confrontation; they must reckon dues and divide the world."

In Momaday's nonfiction the "sacred earth" becomes a redemptive agent in the human quest for knowledge and wholeness. In *The Journey of Tai-me* (1967), the story of the tribal god of the Kiowa whose death his grandmother witnessed at the last Sun Dance, and again in *The Way to Rainy Mountain* (1969), Momaday confronts a world in which experience typically seems fragmentary and inadequate and in which knowledge typically comes as "a moment of truth and exile." But Momaday also writes as one who is convinced that "man's idea of himself" finds "old and essential being in language," in the act of naming and the process of remembering, activities of the mind that are "legendary as well as historical, personal as well as cultural."

Further Reading:

C. Oleson, "The Remembered Earth: Momaday's *House Made of Dawn*," *South Dakota Review*, Spring 1973.

M. S. Trimble, *N. Scott Momaday*, 1973.

A. R. Velie, *Four American Indian Literary Masters*, 1982.

M. Schubnell, *N. Scott Momaday: The Cultural and Literary Background*, 1986.

G. Vizenor, ed., *Narrative Chance: Postmodern Discourse on Native American Indian Literatures*, 1989.

C. Woodward, ed., *Ancestral Voice: Conversations with N. Scott Momaday*, 1989.

S. Scarberry-Garcia, *Landmarks of Healing: A study of* House Made of Dawn, 1990.

R. Nelson, *Place and Vision: The Function of Landscape in Native American Fiction*, 1993.

Text:
From *House Made of Dawn*, 1968.

from House Made of Dawn

from **The Priest of the Sun**

January 26

The Priest of the Sun lived with his disciple Cruz on the first floor of a two-story red-brick building in Los Angeles. The upstairs was maintained as a storage facility by the A. A. Kaul Office Supply Company. The basement was a kind of church. There was a signboard on the wall above the basement steps, encased in glass. In neat, movable white block letters on a black field it read:

LOS ANGELES

HOLINESS PAN-INDIAN RESCUE MISSION

Rev. J. B. B. Tosamah, Pastor & Priest of the Sun

Saturday 8:30 P.M.

"The Gospel According to John"

Sunday 8:30 P.M.

"The Way to Rainy Mountain"

Be kind to a white man today

The basement was cold and dreary, dimly illuminated by two 40-watt bulbs which were screwed into the side walls above the dais. This platform was made out of rough planks of various woods and dimensions, thrown together without so much as a hammer and nails; it stood seven or eight inches above the floor, and it supported the tin firebox and the crescent altar. Off to one side was a kind of lectern, decorated with red and yellow symbols of the sun and moon. In back of the dais there was a screen of purple drapery, threadbare and badly faded. On either side of the aisle which led to the altar there were chairs and crates, fashioned into pews. The walls were bare and gray and streaked with water. The only windows were small rectangular openings near the ceiling, at ground level; the panes were covered over with a thick film of coal oil and dust, and spider webs clung to the frames or floated out like smoke across the room. The air was heavy and stale; odors of old smoke and incense lingered all around. The people had filed into the pews and were waiting silently.

Cruz, a squat, oily man with blue-black hair that stood out like spines from his head, stepped forward on the platform and raised his hands as if to ask for the quiet that already was. Everyone watched him for a moment; in the dull light his skin shone yellow with sweat. Turning slightly and extending his arm behind him, he said, "The Right Reverend John Big Bluff Tosamah."

There was a ripple in the dark screen; the drapes parted and the Priest of the Sun appeared, moving shadow-like to the lectern. He was shaggy and awful-looking in the thin, naked light: big, lithe as a cat, narrow-eyed, suggesting in the whole of his look and manner both arrogance and agony. He wore black like a cleric; he had the voice of a great dog:

" '*In principio erat Verbum.*'[1] Think of Genesis. Think of how it was before the world was made. There was nothing, the Bible says. 'And the earth was without form, and void; and darkness was upon the face of the deep.' It was dark, and there was nothing. There were no mountains, no trees, no rocks, no rivers. There was nothing. But there was darkness all around, and in the darkness something happened. *Something happened!* There was a single sound. Far away in the darkness there was a single sound. Nothing made it, but it was there; and there was no one to hear it, but it was there. It was there, and there was nothing else. It rose up in the darkness, little and still, almost nothing in itself—like a single soft breath, like the wind arising; yes, like the whisper of the wind rising slowly and going out into the early morning. But there was no wind. There was only the sound, little and soft. It was almost nothing in itself, the smallest seed of sound—but it took hold of the darkness and there was light; it took hold of the stillness and there was motion forever; it took hold of the silence and there was sound.

---

[1] Latin: "In the beginning was the Word."
   (See John I:I.)

It was almost nothing in itself, a single sound, a word—a word broken off at the darkest center of the night and let go in the awful void, forever and forever. And it was almost nothing in itself. It scarcely was; but it was, and everything began."

Just then a remarkable thing happened. The Priest of the Sun seemed stricken; he let go of his audience and withdrew into himself, into some strange potential of himself. His voice, which had been low and resonant, suddenly became harsh and flat; his shoulders sagged and his stomach protruded, as if he had held his breath to the limit of endurance; for a moment there was a look of amazement, then utter carelessness in his face. Conviction, caricature, callousness: the remainder of his sermon was a going back and forth among these.

"Thank you *so* much, Brother Cruz. Good evening, blood brothers and sisters, and welcome, welcome. Gracious me, I see lots of new faces out there tonight. *Gracious me!* May the Great Spirit—can we knock off that talking in the back there?—be with you always.

" 'In the beginning was the Word.' I have taken as my text this evening the almighty World itself. Now get this: 'There was a man sent from God, whose name was John. The same came for a witness, to bear witness of the Light, that all men through him might believe.' Amen, brothers and sisters, *Amen.* And the riddle of the Word, 'In the beginning was the Word. . . .' Now what do you suppose old John *meant* by that? That cat was a preacher, and, well, you know how it is with preachers; he had something big on his mind. Oh my, it was big; it was the *Truth,* and it was heavy, and old John hurried to set it down. And in his hurry he said too much. 'In the beginning was the Word, and the Word was with God, and the Word was God.' It was the truth, all right, but it was more than the Truth. The Truth was overgrown with fat, and the fat was God. The fat was *John's* God, and God stood between John and the Truth. Old John, see, he got up one morning and caught sight of the Truth. It must have been like a bolt of lightning, and the sight of it made him blind. And for a moment the vision burned on in back of his eyes, and he *knew* what it was. In that instant he saw something he had never seen before and would never see again. That was the instant of revelation, inspiration, Truth. And old John, he must have fallen down on his knees. Man, he must have been shaking and laughing and crying and yelling and praying—all at the same time—and he must have been drunk and delirious with the Truth. You see, he had lived all his life waiting for that one moment, and it came, and it took him by surprise, and it was gone. And he said, 'In the beginning was the Word. . . .' And, man, right then and there he should have stopped. There was nothing more to say, but he went on. He had said all there was to say, everything, but he went on. 'In the beginning was the Word. . . .' Brothers and sisters, *that* was the Truth, the whole of it, the essential and eternal Truth, the bone and blood and muscle of the Truth. But he went on, old John, because he was a preacher. The perfect vision faded from his mind, and he went on. The instant passed, and then he had nothing but a memory. He was desperate and confused, and in his confusion he stumbled and went on. 'In the beginning was the Word, and the Word was with God, and the Word was God.' He went on to talk about Jews and Jerusalem, Levites and Pharisees, Moses and Philip and Andrew and Peter. Don't you see? Old John *had* to go on. That cat had a whole lot at stake. He couldn't let the Truth alone. He couldn't see that he had come to the end of the Truth, and he went on. He tried to make it bigger and better than it was, but instead he only demeaned and encumbered it. He made if soft and big with fat. He was a preacher, and he made a complex sentence of the Truth, two sentences, three, a paragraph. He made a sermon and theology of the Truth. He imposed his idea of God upon the everlasting Truth. 'In the beginning was the Word. . . .' And that is all there was, and it was enough.

"Now, brothers and sisters, old John was a white man, and the white man has his ways. Oh gracious me, he has his ways. He talks about the Word. He talks through it and around it. He builds upon it with syllables, with prefixes and suffixes and hyphens and accents. He adds and divides and multiplies the Word. And in all of this he sub-tracts the Truth. And, brothers and sisters, you have come here to live in the white man's world. Now the white man deals in words, and he deals easily, with grace and sleight of hand. And in his presence, here on his own ground, you are as children, mere babes in the woods. You must not mind, for in this you have a certain advantage. A child can listen and learn. The Word is sacred to a child.

"My grandmother was a storyteller; she knew her way around words. She never learned to read and write, but somehow she knew the good of reading and writing; she had learned how to listen and delight. She had learned that in words and in language, and there only, she could have whole and consummate being. She told me stories, and she taught me how to listen. I was a child and I listened. She could neither read nor write, you see, but she taught me how to live among her words, how to listen and delight. 'Sto-rytelling; to utter and to hear . . .'' And the simple act of listening is crucial to the concept of language, more crucial even than reading and writing, and language in turn is crucial to human society. There is proof of that, I think, in all the histories and prehistories of human experience. When that old Kiowa woman told me stories, I listened with only one ear. I was a child, and I took the words for granted. I did not know what all of them meant, but somehow I held on to them; I remembered them, and I remember them now. The stories were old and dear; they meant a great deal to my grandmother. It was not until she died that I knew how much they meant to her. I began to think about it, and then I knew. When she told me those old stories, something strange and good and powerful was going on. I was a child, and that old woman was asking me to come di-rectly into the presence of her mind and spirit; she was taking hold of my imagination, giving me to share in the great fortune of her wonder and delight. She was asking me to go with her to the confrontation of something that was sacred and eternal. It was a time-less, *timeless* thing; nothing of her old age or of my childhood came between us.

"Children have a greater sense of the power and beauty of words than have the rest of us in general. And if that is so, it is because there occurs—or reoccurs—in the mind of every child something like a reflection of all human experience. I have heard that the human fetus corresponds in its development, stage by stage, to the scale of evolution. Surely it is no less reasonable to suppose that the waking mind of a child corresponds in the same way to the whole evolution of human thought and perception.

"In the white man's world, language, too—and the way in which the white man thinks of it—has undergone a process of change. The white man takes such things as words and literatures for granted, as indeed he must, for nothing in his world is so com-monplace. On every side of him there are words by the millions, and unending succes-sion of pamphlets and papers, letters and books, bills and bulletins, commentaries and conversations. He has diluted and multiplied the Word, and words have begun to close in upon him. He is sated and insensitive; his regard for language—for the Word itself—as an instrument of creation has diminished nearly to the point of no return. It may be that he will perish by the Word.

"But it was not always so with him, and it is not so with you. Consider for a moment that old Kiowa woman, my grandmother, whose use of language was confined to speech. And be assured that her regard for words was always keen in proportion as she depended upon them. You see, for her words were medicine; they were magic and invisible. They came from nothing into sound and meaning. They were beyond price; they could neither be bought nor sold. And she never threw words away.

"My grandmother used to tell me the story of Tai-me, of how Tai-me came to the Kiowas. The Kiowas were a sun dance culture, and Tai-me was their sun dance doll, their most sacred fetish; no medicine was ever more powerful. There is a story about the coming of Tai-me. This is what my grandmother told me:

Long ago there were bad times. The Kiowas were hungry and there was no food. There was a man who heard his children cry from hunger, and he began to search for food. He walked four days and became very weak. On the fourth day he came to a great canyon. Suddenly there was thunder and lightning. A Voice spoke to him and said, "Why are you following me? What do you want?" The man was afraid. The thing standing before him had the feet of a deer, and its body was covered with feathers. The man answered that the Kiowas were hungry. "Take me with you," the Voice said, "and I will give you whatever you want." From that day Tai-me has belonged to the Kiowas.

"Do you see? There, far off in the darkness, something happened. Do you see? Far, far away in the nothingness something happened. There was a voice, a sound, a word— and everything began. The story of the coming of Tai-me has existed for hundreds of years by word of mouth. It represents the oldest and best idea that man has of himself. It represents a very rich literature, which, because it was never written down, was always but one generation from extinction. But for the same reason it was cherished and revered. I could see that reverence in my grandmother's eyes, and I could hear it in her voice. It was that, I think, that old Saint John had in mind when he said, 'In the beginning was the Word. . . .' But he went on. He went on to lay a scheme about the Word. He could find no satisfaction in the simple fact that the Word was; he had to account for it, not in terms of that sudden and profound insight, which must have devastated him at once, but in terms of the moment afterward, which was irrelevant and remote; not in terms of his imagination, but only in terms of his prejudice.

"Say this: 'In the beginning was the Word. . . .' There was nothing. There was *nothing!* Darkness. There was darkness, and there was no end to it. You look up sometimes in the night and there are stars; you can see all the way to the stars. And you begin to know the universe, how awful and great it is. The stars lie out against the sky and do not fill it. A single star, flickering out in the universe, is enough to fill the mind, but it is nothing in the night sky. The darkness looms around it. The darkness flows among the stars, and beyond them forever. In the beginning that is how it was, but there were no stars. There was only the dark infinity in which nothing was. And something happened. At the distance of a star something happened, and everything began. The Word did not come into being, but *it was.* It did not break upon the silence, but *it was older than the silence and the silence was made of it.*

"Old John caught sight of something terrible. The thing standing before him said, 'Why are you following me? What do you want?' And from that day the Word has belonged to us, who have heard it for what it is, who have lived in fear and awe of it. In the Word was the beginning; '*In the beginning was the Word. . . .*'"

The Priest of the Sun appeared to have spent himself. He stepped back from the lectern and hung his head, smiling. In his mind the earth was spinning and the stars rattled around in the heavens. The sun shone, and the moon. Smiling in a kind of transport, the Priest of the Sun stood silent for a time while the congregation waited to be dismissed.

"Good night," he said, at last, "and get yours." . . .

from January 27

Tosamah, orator, physician, Priest of the Sun, son of Hummingbird, spoke:

"A single knoll rises out of the plain in Oklahoma, north and west of the Wichita range. For my people it is an old landmark, and they gave it the name Rainy Mountain. There, in the south of the continental trough, is the hardest weather in the world. In winter there are blizzards which come down the Williston corridor, bearing hail and sleet. Hot tornadic winds arise in the spring, and in summer the prairie is an anvil's edge. The grass turns brittle and brown, and it cracks beneath your feet. There are green belts along the rivers and creeks, linear groves of hickory and pecan, willow and witch hazel. At a distance in July or August the steaming foliage seems almost to writhe in fire. Great green and yellow grasshoppers are everywhere in the tall grass, popping up like corn to sting the flesh, and tortoises crawl about on the red earth, going nowhere in the plenty of time. Loneliness is there as an aspect of the land. All things in the plain are isolate; there is no confusion of objects in the eye, but one hill or one tree or one man. At the slightest elevation you can see to the end of the world. To look upon that landscape in the early morning, with the sun at your back, is to lose the sense of proportion. Your imagination comes to life, and this, you think, is where Creation was begun.

"I returned to Rainy Mountain in July. My grandmother had died in the spring, and I wanted to be at her grave. She had lived to be very old and at last infirm. Her only living daughter was with her when she died, and I was told that in death her face was that of a child.

"I like to think of her as a child. When she was born, the Kiowas were living the last great moment of their history. For more than a hundred years they had controlled the open range from the Smoky Hill River to the Red, from the headwaters of the Canadian to the fork of the Arkansas and Cimarron. In alliance with the Comanches, they had ruled the whole of the Southern Plains. War was their sacred business, and they were the finest horsemen the world has ever known. But warfare for the Kiowas was pre-eminently a matter of disposition rather that survival, and they never understood the grim, unrelenting advance of the U.S. Cavalry. When at last, divided and ill-provisioned, they were driven onto the Staked Plain in the cold of autumn, they fell into panic. In Palo Duro Canyon they abandoned their crucial stores to pillage and had nothing then but their lives. In order to save themselves, they surrendered to the soldiers at Fort Sill and were imprisoned in the old stone corral that now stands as a military museum. My grandmother was spared the humiliation of those high gray walls by eight or ten years, but she must have known from birth the affliction of defeat, the dark brooding of old warriors.

"Her name was Aho, and she belonged to the last culture to evolve in North America. Her forebears came down from the high north country nearly three centuries ago.

The earliest evidence of their existence places them close to the source of the Yellowstone River in western Montana. They were a mountain people, a mysterious tribe of hunters whose language has never been classified in any major group. In the late seventeenth century they began a long migration to the south and east. It was a journey toward the dawn, and it led to a golden age. Along the way the Kiowas were befriended by the Crows, who gave them the culture and religion of the plains. They acquired horses, and their ancient nomadic spirit was suddenly free of the ground. They acquired Tai-me, the sacred sun dance doll, from that moment the chief object and symbol of their worship, and so shared in the divinity of the sun. Not least, they acquired the sense of destiny, therefore courage and pride. When they entered upon the Southern Plains, they had been transformed. No longer were they slaves to the simple necessity of survival; they were a lordly and dangerous society of fighters and thieves, hunters and priests of the sun. According to their origin myth, they entered the world through a hollow log. From one point of view, their migration was the fruit of an old prophecy, for indeed they emerged from a sunless world.

"I could see that. I followed their ancient way to my grandmother's grave. Though she lived out her long life in the shadow of Rainy Mountain, the immense landscape of the continental interior—all of its seasons and its sounds—lay like memory in her blood. She could tell of the Crows, whom she had never seen, and of the Black Hills, where she had never been. I wanted to see in reality what she had seen more perfectly in the mind's eye.

"I began my pilgrimage on the course of the Yellowstone. There, it seemed to me, was the top of the world, a region of deep lakes and dark timber, canyons and waterfalls. But, beautiful as it is, one might have the sense of confinement there. The skyline in all directions is close at hand, the high wall of the woods and deep cleavages of shade. There is a perfect freedom in the mountains, but it belongs to the eagle and the elk, the badger and the bear. The Kiowas reckoned their stature by the distance they could see, and they were bent and blind in the wilderness.

"Descending eastward, the highland meadows are a stairway to the plain. In July the inland slope of the Rockies is luxuriant with flax and buckwheat, stonecrop and larkspur. The earth unfolds and the limit of the land recedes. Clusters of trees, and animals grazing far in the distance, cause the vision to reach away and wonder to build upon the mind. The sun follows a longer course in the day, and the sky is immense beyond all comparison. The great billowing clouds that sail upon it are shadows that move upon the grass and grain like water, dividing light. Farther down, in the land of the Crows and the Blackfeet, the plain is yellow. Sweet clover takes hold of the hills and bends upon itself to cover and seal the soil. There the Kiowas paused on their way; they had come to the place where they must change their lives. The sun is at home on the plains. Precisely there does it have the certain character of a god. When the Kiowas came to the land of the Crows, they could see the dark lees of the hills at dawn across the Bighorn River, the profusion of light on the grain shelves, the oldest deity ranging after the solstices. Not yet would they veer south to the caldron of the land that lay below; they must wean their blood from the northern winter and hold the mountains a while longer in their view. They bore Tai-me in procession to the east.

"A dark mist lay over the Black Hills, and the land was like iron. At the top of a ridge I caught sight of Devils Tower—the uppermost extremity of it, like a file's end on the gray sky—and then it fell away behind the land. I was a long time then in coming upon it, and I did not see it again until I saw it whole, suddenly there across the valley, as if in the birth of time the core of the earth had broken through its crust and the motion of the world was begun. It stands in motion, like certain timeless trees that aspire too much into the sky, and imposes an illusion on the land. There are things in nature which engender an awful quiet in the heart of man; Devils Tower is one of them. Man must account for it. He must never fail to explain such a thing to himself, or else he is estranged forever from the universe. Two centuries ago, because they could not do otherwise, the Kiowas made a legend at the base of the rock. My grandmother said:

Eight children were there at play, seven sisters and their brother. Suddenly the boy was struck dumb; he trembled and began to run upon his hands and feet. His fingers became claws, and his body was covered with fur. There was a bear where the boy had been. The sisters were terrified; they ran, and the bear after them. They came to the stump of a great tree, and the tree spoke to them. It bade them climb upon it, and as they did so it began to rise into the air. The bear came to kill them, but they were just beyond its reach. It reared against the tree and scored the bark all around with its claws. The seven sisters were borne into the sky, and they became the stars of the Big Dipper.

"From that moment, and so long as the legend lives, the Kiowas have kinsmen in the night sky. Whatever they were in the mountains, they could be no more. However tenuous their well-being, however much they had suffered and would suffer again, they had found a way out of the wilderness.

"The first man among them to stand on the edge of the Great Plains saw farther over land than he had ever seen before. There is something about the heart of the continent that resides always in the end of vision, some essence of the sun and wind. That man knew the possible quest. There was nothing to prevent his going out; he could enter upon the land and be alive, could bear at once the great hot weight of its silence. In a sense the question of survival had never been more imminent, for no land is more the measure of human strength. But neither had wonder been more accessible to the mind nor destiny to the will.

"My grandmother had a reverence for the sun, a certain holy regard which now is all but gone out of mankind. There was a wariness in her, and an ancient awe. She was a Christian in her later years, but she had come a long way about, and she never forgot her birthright. As a child, she had been to the sun dances; she had taken part in that annual rite, and by it she had learned the restoration of her people in the presence of Tai-me. She was about seven years old when the last Kiowa sun dance was held in 1887 on the Washita River above Rainy Mountain Creek. The buffalo were gone. In order to consummate the ancient sacrifice—to impale the head of a buffalo bull upon the Tai-me tree—a delegation of old men journeyed into Texas, there to beg and barter for an animal from the Goodnight herd. She was ten when the Kiowas came together for the last time as a living sun dance culture. They could find no buffalo; they had to hang an old hide from the sacred tree. That summer was known to my grandmother as Ä'poto Etóda-de K'adó, Sun Dance When the Forked Poles Were Left Standing, and it is entered in the Kiowa calendars as the figure of a tree standing outside the unfinished framework of a medicine lodge. Before the dance could begin, a company of armed soldiers rode out from Fort Sill under orders to disperse the tribe. Forbidden without cause the essential act of their faith, having seen the wild herds slaughtered and left to rot upon the ground, the Kiowas backed away forever from the tree. That was July 20, 1890, at the great bend of the Washita. My grandmother was there. Without bitterness, and for as long as she lived, she bore a vision of deicide.

"Now that I can have her only in memory, I see my grandmother in the several postures that were peculiar to her: standing at the wood stove on a winter morning and turning meat in a great iron skillet; sitting at the south window, bent above her beadwork, and afterward, when her vision failed, looking down for a long time into the fold of her hands; going out upon a cane, very slowly as she did when the weight of age came upon her; praying. I remember her most often at prayer. She made long, rambling prayers out of suffering and hope, having seen many things. I was never sure that I had the right to hear, so exclusive were they of all mere custom and company. The last time I saw her, she prayed standing by the side of her bed at night, naked to the waist, the light of a kerosene lamp moving upon her dark skin. Her long black hair, always drawn and braided in the day, lay upon her shoulders and against her breasts like a shawl. I did not always understand her prayers; I believe they were made of an older language than that of ordinary speech. There was something inherently sad in the sound, some slight hesitation upon the syllables of sorrow. She began in a high and descending pitch, exhausting her breath to silence; then again and again—and always the same intensity of effort, of something that is, and is not, like urgency in the human voice. Transported so in the dim and dancing light among the shadows of her room, she seemed beyond the reach of time, as if age could not lay hold of her. But that was illusion; I think I knew then that I should not see her again. . . .

1966

Mary Oliver
b. 1935

"The question asked today is: What does it mean? Nobody says, how does it feel?" says Mary Oliver of today's readers. It would be difficult to appreciate the "mysterious . . . and true spell" that James Dickey has praised in Oliver's work without allowing the body to enter into the act of reading Ms. Oliver's poems. Mary Oliver's spare style guides the reader away from individual concerns toward the vastness, the beauty, and the terror of nature. The journey on which she takes us is not about loss, but about letting go, about feeling our connection to the physical world, and finding life and redemption therein. "When it's over, I want to say: All my life / I was a bride married to amazement. / I was the bridegroom, taking the world into my arms," she writes in "When Death Comes."

Mary Oliver attended Ohio State University and Vassar College. She learned her craft in solitude, reading and writing alone during her childhood and early adulthood, studying and imitating the work of other poets. She describes her first two books, *No Voyage* (1965) and *The River Styx, Ohio* (1972), as "derivative." Influenced by the poetry of James Wright, Robert Frost, Edna St. Vincent Millay, and William Carlos

Williams, her early years were, in her words, "a kind of discipleship. But there is finally a time when you begin to hear something new and different—something of your own—and that's the part of your work you want to cherish, to make strong."

In the books that followed, *Twelve Moons* (1979) and *American Primitive* (1983), "there is one human presence," says Ms. Oliver, "and that is the voice speaking the poem, which should, or can, imaginatively, become the reader's inner voice." In *Dream Work* (1986), a human presence is more dominant. "Everywhere in this world his music / explodes out of itself, as he / could not," she writes of "Robert Schumann"; and she looks at the healing power of love in "A Visitor" and "Dogfish," but the feeling experience is still placed very firmly in the lap of the reader. *House of Light* (1990) and the new poems in *New and Selected Poems* (1992) are, like her other books, but more consistently so, spiritual studies of the human condition through the natural world: "each pond with its blazing lilies / is a prayer heard and answered / lavishly," she writes in "Morning Poem." Throughout, she evokes death and resurrection, risking everything and inviting the reader to do the same: "when death comes / like an iceberg between the shoulder blades, / I want to step through the door full of curiosity, wondering: / what is it going to be like, that cottage of darkness?" she writes in "When Death Comes."

"I am trying in my poems to vanish and have the reader be the experiencer. I do not want to be there. It is not even a walk we take together." She accomplishes this feat with simple language and a commitment to emptiness rooted in Eastern religion. "Make of yourself a light," said the Buddha, before he died," she begins in "The Buddha's Last Instruction," Mary Oliver has mastered the Buddha's lesson in her life's work.

Mary Oliver won the National Book Award for *New and Selected Poems* in 1992, and *American Primitive* was awarded the Pulitzer Prize for Poetry in 1984. Her most recent books are *A Poetry Handbook* (1994), *White Pine* (1994), *Blue Pastures* (1995), a collection of brief prose contemplative works on writing and nature, and *West Wind* (1997), a collection of poems and prose poems. A native of Ohio, Mary Oliver is a long-time resident of Provincetown, Massachusetts.

Further Reading:

J. McNew, "Mary Oliver and the Tradition of Romantic Nature Poetry," *Contemporary Literature* 30:1 (1989), 59–78.

D. Bonds, "The Language of Nature in the Poetry of Mary Oliver," *Women's Studies* 21:1 (1992), 1–16.

V. Graham, "Into the Body of Another: Mary Oliver and the Poetics of Becoming Other," *Papers on Language and Literature* 30:4 (1994), 352–373.

Texts:

"Ghosts," "The Sun," and "When Death Comes" from *New and Selected Poems*, 1992; "Owls" from *Blue Pastures*, 1995.

Ghosts

1

Have you noticed?

2

Where so many millions of powerful bawling beasts
lay down on the earth and died
it's hard to tell now
what's bone, and what merely
was once.

The golden eagle, for instance,
has a bit of heaviness in him;
moreover the huge barns
seem ready, sometimes, to ramble off
toward deeper grass.

3

1805
near the Bitterroot Mountains:
a man named Lewis kneels down
on the prairie watching

a sparrow's nest clearly concealed in the wild hyssop
and lined with buffalo hair. The chicks,
not more than a day hatched, lean
quietly into the thick wool as if
content, after all,

to have left the perfect world and fallen,
helpless and blind
into the flowered fields and the perils
of this one.

4

In the book of the earth it is written:
nothing can die.

In the book of the Sioux it is written:
they have gone away into the earth to hide.
Nothing will coax them out again
but the people dancing.

5

10

15

20

25

30

5

Said the old-timers:
the tongue
is the sweetest meat.

Passengers shooting from train windows
could hardly miss, they were   35
that many.

Afterward the carcasses
stank unbelievably, and sang with flies, ribboned
with slopes of white fat,
black ropes of blood—hellhunks   40
in the prairie heat.

6

Have you noticed? how the rain
falls soft as the fall
of moccasins. *Have you noticed?*
how the immense circles still,   45
stubbornly, after a hundred years,
mark the grass where the rich droppings
from the roaring bulls
fell to the earth as the herd stood
day after day, moon after moon   50
in their tribal circle, outwaiting
the packs of yellow-eyed wolves that are also
have you noticed? gone now.

7

Once only, and then in a dream,
I watched while, secretly   55
and with the tenderness of any caring woman,
a cow gave birth
to a red calf, tongued him dry and nursed him
in a warm corner
of the clear night   60
in the fragrant grass
in the wild domains
of the prairie spring, and I asked them,
in my dream I knelt down and asked them
to make room for me.   65
1972

Owls

Upon the dunes and in the shaggy woodlands of the Provincelands, I have seen plenty of owls. Heard them at twilight and in the dark, and near dawn. Watched them, flying over Great Pond, flying over Rose Tasha's noisy barnyard, flying out of the open fretwork of the spire of the old Methodist Church on Commercial Street, where the pigeons sleep, and disappear one by one. I have seen them in every part of the woods, favoring this or that acreage until the rabbits are scarce and they move to new hunting grounds, and then, in a few seasons, move back.

In January and February I walk in the woods and look for a large nest in a tall tree. In my mind's eye I see the great horned, the early nester, sitting upon her bulk of sticks, like an old woman on a raft.

I look in every part of the Provincelands that is within my walking range. I look by Clapps Pond and Bennet Pond and Round Pond and Oak-Head Pond. I look along the riding trail that borders the landfill—in the old days a likely hunting ground and not one disdained by the owls or much else. I look in the woods close to the airport, so often have I flushed an owl from the pine trees there.

And I look in the woods around Pasture Pond, where, over a century ago, Mr. George Washington Ready, once the Provincetown town crier, saw the six-eyed sea serpent. He witnessed it, he said, emerging from the ocean and slithering across the dunes. Into Pasture Pond it descended, and sank from sight. Every winter I stare into the ice of the pond and think of it—still asleep, I suppose, in the clasp of the lily roots, for no one has ever seen it again.

And I search in the deeper woods, past fire roads and the bike trail, among the black oaks and the taller pines, in the silent blue afternoons, when the sand is still frozen and the snow falls slowly and aimlessly, and the whole world smells like water in an iron cup. And I see, on my way to the owl's nest, many marvelous things: the gray hives of the paper wasps, hidden in summer by the leaves but now apparent on the boughs; nests, including one of the Baltimore oriole, with fishline woven into it, so that it has in the wind a comet's tail of rippling white threads; and pheasants, birds that were released into fall's russet fields but find themselves still alive at the far end of winter, and are glad of it, storming upward from the fields on their bright wings; and great blue herons, thin and melancholy; and deer, in their gray winter coats, bounding through the cold bogs; an owl in a tree with an unexpected face—a barred owl, seen once and once only.

Finally the earth grows softer, and the buds on the trees swell, and the afternoon becomes a wider room to roam in, as the sun moves back from the south and the light grows stronger. The bluebirds come back, and the robins, and the song sparrows, and great robust flocks of blackbirds; and in the fields blackberry hoops put on a soft plum color, a restitution; the ice on the ponds begins to thunder, and between the slices is seen the strokes of its breaking up, a stutter of dark lightning. And then the winter is over, and again I have not found the great horned owl's nest.

But the owls themselves are not hard to find, silent and on the wing, with their ear tufts flat against their heads as they fly and their huge wings alternately gliding and flapping as they maneuver through the trees. Athena's owl of wisdom and Merlin's companion, Archimedes, were screech owls surely, not this bird with the glassy gaze, restless on the bough, nothing but blood on its mind.

When the great horned is in the trees its razor-tipped toes rasp the limb, flakes of bark fall through the air and land on my shoulders while I look up at it and listen to the heavy, crisp, breathy snapping of its hooked beak. The screech owl I can imagine on my wrist, also the delicate saw-whet that flies like a big soft moth down by Great Pond. And I can imagine sitting quietly before the luminous wanderer the snowy owl, and learning, from the white gleam of its feathers, something about the arctic. But the great horned I can't imagine in any such proximity—if one of those should touch me, it would touch to the center of my life, and I must fall. They are the pure wild hunters of our world. They are swift and merciless upon the backs of rabbits, mice, voles, snakes, even skunks, even cats sitting in dusky yards, thinking peaceful thoughts. I have found the headless bodies of rabbits and blue jays, and known it was the great horned owl that did them in, taking the head only, for the owl has an insatiable craving for the taste of brains. I have walked with prudent caution down paths at twilight when the dogs were puppies. I know this bird. If it could, it would eat the whole world.

In the night, when the owl is less than exquisitely swift and perfect, the scream of the rabbit is terrible. But the scream of the owl, which is not of pain and hopelessness and the fear of being plucked out of the world, but of the sheer rollicking glory of the death-bringer, is more terrible still. When I hear it resounding through the woods, and then the five black pellets of its song dropping like stones into the air, I know I am standing at the edge of the mystery, in which terror is naturally and abundantly part of life, part of even the most becalmed, intelligent, sunny life—as, for example, my own. The world where the owl is endlessly hungry and endlessly on the hunt is the world in which I live too. There is only one world.

Sometimes, while I have stood listening to the owl's song drifting through the trees, when it is ten degrees above nothing and life for any small creature is hard enough without *that,* I have found myself thinking of summer fields. Fields full of flowers—poppies or lupines. Or, here, fields where the roses hook into the dunes, and their increase is manyfold. All summer they are red and pink and white tents of softness and nectar, which wafts and hangs everywhere—a sweetness so palpable and excessive that, before it, I'm struck, I'm taken, I'm conquered; I'm washed into it, as though it was a river, full of dreaming and idleness—I drop to the sand, I can't move; I am restless no more; I am replete, supine, finished, filled to the last edges with an immobilizing happiness. And is this not also terrible? Is this not also frightening?

Are the roses not also—even as the owl is—excessive? Each flower is small and lovely, but in their sheer and silent abundance the roses become an immutable force, as though the work of the wild roses was to make sure that all of us, who come wandering over the sand, may be, for a while, struck to the heart and saturated with a simple joy. Let the mind be teased by such *stretches* of the imagination, by such balance. Now I am cringing at the very sound of the owl's dark wings opening over my head—not long ago I could do nothing but lounge on the sand and stare into the cities of the roses.

I have two feathers from the big owl. One I found near Round Pond; the other, on another day, fell as I watched the bird rise from one tree and flap into another. As the owl rose, some crows caught sight of it, and so began another scrimmage in their long battle. The owl wants to sleep, but the crows pursue it and when it settles a second time the crows—now a dozen—gather around and above it, and scream into its face, with open beaks and wagging tongues. They come dangerously close to its feet, which are huge and quick. The caught crow is a dead crow. But it is not in the nature of crows to hide or cower—it is in their nature to gather and to screech and to gamble in the very tree where death stares at them with molten eyes. What fun, to aggravate the old bomber! What joy, to swipe at the tawny feathers even as the bird puffs and hulks and hisses.

But finally the owl rises from the trees altogether and climbs and floats away, over two or three hills, and the crows go off to some other merriment.

And I walk on, over the shoulder of summer and down across the red-dappled fall; and, when it's late winter again, out through the far woodlands of the Provincelands, maybe another few hundred miles, looking for the owl's nest, yes, of course, and looking at everything else along the way.

1995

The Sun

Have you ever seen
anything
in your life
more wonderful

than the way the sun,   5
every evening,
relaxed and easy,
floats toward the horizon

and into the clouds or the hills
or the rumpled sea,   10
and is gone—
and how it slides again

out of the blackness,
every morning,
on the other side of the world,   15
like a red flower

streaming upward on its heavenly oils,
say, on a morning in early summer,
at its perfect imperial distance—
and have you ever felt for anything   20

such wild love—
do you think there is anywhere, in any language,
a word billowing enough
for the pleasure

that fills you,   25
as the sun
reaches out,
as it warms you

as you stand there,
empty-handed—   30
or have you too
turned from this world—

or have you too
gone crazy
for power,   35
for things?
1992

When Death Comes

When death comes
like the hungry bear in autumn;
when death comes and takes all the bright coins from his purse

to buy me, and snaps the purse shut;
when death comes   5
like the measle-pox;

when death comes
like an iceberg between the shoulder blades,

I want to step through the door full of curiosity, wondering:
what is it going to be like, that cottage of darkness?   10

And therefore I look upon everything
as a brotherhood and a sisterhood,
and I look upon time as no more than an idea,
and I consider eternity as another possibility,

and I think of each life as a flower, as common   15
as a field daisy, and as singular,

and each name a comfortable music in the mouth,
tending, as all music does, toward silence,

and each body a lion of courage, and something
precious to the earth.   20

When it's over, I want to say: all my life
I was a bride married to amazement.
I was the bridegroom, taking the world into my arms.

When it's over, I don't want to wonder
if I have made of my life something particular, and real.   25
I don't want to find myself sighing and frightened,
or full of argument.

I don't want to end up simply having visited this world.
1992

Susan Howe
b. 1937

Susan Howe is one of the writers who emerged in the late 1970s as "language" poets.
Among this group which includes Charles Bernstein, David Melnick, and others
published in the journal *L-A-N-G-U-A-G-E* and later in the anthology *In the American
Tree,* Howe has achieved special prominence as a visionary, a woman who aspires to
prophecy.

Although it is difficult to generalize about a "school" of poets that refuses to be
categorized, language poets do tend to be vigorously experimental and "concrete."
They wed what poet Bernstein calls the "factness of the world" to "the factness of the
poem." They emphasize the concreteness of words, the mechanics of syntax. Their
poems are made, wrote Melnick, "of what look like words and phrases but are not."
Their language theory and practice flows from such predecessors as Gertrude Stein,
James Joyce, Louis Zukofsky, and Ludwig Wittgenstein, and was further shaped by
such influences as Charles Olson and John Ashbery.

Howe was born in Boston on June 10, 1937, to an Irish mother and an American
father. They met, she wrote "at a dinner party when her earring dropped into his
soup." By the year of her birth, she continued, "the Nazi dictatorship was well-
established in Germany. . . . I became part of the Ruin." This blurring of the boundary
between personal history and public tragedy informs much of her poetry; she sees
herself as a refugee born into language during wartime, a poet who wishes to
illuminate the condition of those who have been violated and marginalized: spirits,
Native Americans, confused colonizers, women, poets, children, the mad.

A scholar of both literature (Emily Dickinson, especially) and of history (New
England places, in particular), Howe often creates musical riffs off historical texts. In
her *Articulation of Sound Forms in Time,* she chronicles her researches into a myth
from her Massachusetts locale, the story of a seventeenth-century preacher Hope

Atherton who disappeared and years later, reappeared, not entirely coherent.

Howe allows the sound qualities of language to burst through the narrative structure and referential frame—and in the case of "Thorow," through the margins on the printed page and the conventions of the legible line. The resultant poems can have a freshness and freedom of vision that often borders on prophecy.

In the selection "Thorow," Howe also investigates an American place, Lake George. Her project involves the making of an independent American self (here, a "She") and the remaking of an American intellectual tradition that flows as much from preachers Jonathan Edwards and Cotton Mather as from literary sources. Here in the punningly titled "Thorow," as in *Articulation of Sound Forms in Time*, Howe anatomizes an old colonial story, one in which believers "in God and grammar spelled the lake into place."

Further Reading:

M. Perloff, *Poetic License: Essays on Modernist and Postmodernist Lyric*, 1990.

L. Reinfeld, *Language Poetry: Writing as Rescue*, 1992.

Texts:

American Poetry Since 1950, ed. Eliot Weinberger, 1933.

See also *The Europe of Trusts*, Susan Howe, 1990.

Thorow

Author's note: During the winter and spring of 1987 I had a writer-in-residency grant to teach a poetry workshop once a week at the Lake George Arts Project, in the town of Lake George, New York. I rented a cabin off the road to Bolton Landing, at the edge of the lake. The town, or what is left of a town, is a travesty. Scores of two-star motels have been arbitrarily scrambled between gas stations and gift shops selling Indian trinkets, china jugs shaped like breasts with nipples for spouts, American flags in all shapes and sizes, and pornographic bumper-stickers. There are two Laundromats, the inevitable McDonald's, a Howard Johnson, assorted discount leather outlets, video arcades, a miniature golf course, two run-down amusement parks, a fake fort where a real one once stood, a Dairy-Mart, a Donut-land, and a four-star Ramada Inn built over an ancient Indian burial ground. Everything graft, everything grafted. And what is left when spirits have fled from holy places? In winter the Simulacrum is closed for the season.

I went there alone, and until I became friends with some of my students, I didn't know anyone. After I learned to keep out of town, and after the first panic of dislocation had subsided. I moved into the weather's fluctuation. Let myself drift in the rise and fall of light and snow, re-reading re-tracing once-upon

Narrative in Non-Narrative

I thought I stood on the shores of a history of the world where forms of wildness brought up by memory become desire and multiply.

Lake George was a blade of ice to write across not knowing what She.

Interior assembling of forces underneath earth's eye. Yes, she, the Strange, excluded from formalism. I heard poems inhabited by voices.

In the seventeenth century European adventurer-traders burst through the forest to discover this particular long clear body of fresh water. They brought our story to it. Pathfinding believers in God and grammar spelled the lake into *place*. They have re-named it several times since. In paternal colonial systems a positivist efficiency appro-priates primal indeterminacy.

In March 1987, looking for what is looking, I went down to unknown regions of in-differentiation. The Adirondacks *occupied* me.

Gilles Deleuze and Felix Guattari have written in an essay called "May, 1914. One or Several Wolves?": "The proper name (*nom propre*) does not designate an individual: it is on the contrary when the individual opens up to the multiplicities pervading him or her, at the outcome of the most severe operation of depersonalization, that he or she ac-quires his or her true proper name. The proper name is the instantaneous apprehension of a multiplicity. The proper name is the subject of a pure infinitive comprehended as such in a field of intensity."

Thoreau once wrote to a friend: "am glad to see that you have studied out the ponds, got the Indian names straightened out—which means made more crooked—&c. &c."

Sir Humfrey Gilbert wrote in *A New Passage To Cataia:* "To proove that the Indians aforenamed came not by the Northeast, and that there is no thorow passage navigable that way."

Thoreau never visited the Adirondacks. His book about the wilderness and moun-tains in Maine is called *Ktaadn*.

Work penetrated by the edge of author, traverses multiplicities, light letters explod-ing apprehension suppose when individual hearing

Every name driven will be as another rivet in the machine of a universe flux

I

Go on the Scout they say
They will go near Swegachey

I have snow shoes and Indian shoes

Idea of my present
not my silence   5

Surprise is not so much
Hurried and tossed about
that I have not had time

From the Fort but the snow
falling very deep   10
remained a fortnight
Two to view the Fort & get a scalp
domain of transcendental subjectivity
Etymology the this

present in the past now   15
So many thread

Fence blown down in a winter storm

darkened by outstripped possession
Field stretching out of the world

this book is as old as the people   20

There are traces of blood in a fairy tale

The track of Desire

Must see and not see

Must not see nothing

Burrow and so burrow   25

Measuring mastering

When ice breaks up

at the farthest north

of Adirondack peaks

So empty and so empty   30

Go back for your body
Hindge

Dear Seem dear cast out

Sun shall go down and set

Distant monarchs of Europe   35

European grid on the Forest

so many gether togather

were invisible alway Love

at Fort Stanwix the Charrokey
paice   40

only from that Alarm
all those Guards

Constant parties of guards
up & down

Agreseror   45

Bearer law my fathers

Revealing traces
Regulating traces

The true Zeno
the immutable morality   50

Irruptives

thorow out all
the Five Nations

To cut our wete

of the Jentelmen   55

Fort the same
Nuteral

Revealing traces
Regulating traces

To Lake Superior to view   60

that time the Shannas & Dallaways

Home and I hope passage

Begun about the middle next

to Kittaning

Eating nothing but hominey   65

Scribbling the ineffable

See only the tracks of rabbit

A mouse-nest of grass

The German Flatts

Their women old men & children   70

Numerous than I imagined

Singing their War song

I am

Part of their encroachment

Speed & Bleave me &   75

a Good Globe to hang in a hall

with light

To be sent in slays

if we are not careful

To a slightly place   80

no shelter

Let us gether and bury

limbs and leves

Is a great Loast

Cant say for us now   85

Stillest the storm world
Thought

The snow

is still hear

Wood and feld   90

all covered with ise

seem world anew

Only step

as surveyor of the Wood

only Step   95

2

Walked on Mount Vision

New life after the Fall
So many true things

which are not truth itself
We are too finite   100

Barefooted and bareheaded
extended in space

sure of reaching support
Knowledge and foresight
Noah's landing at Ararat   105

Mind itself or life

quicker than thought

slipping back to primordial
We go through the word Forest

Trance of an encampment   110
not a foot of land cleared

The literature of savagism
under a spell of savagism

Nature isolates the Adirondacks

In the machinery of injustice   115
my whole being is Vision

The Source of Snow
the nearness of Poetry

The Captain of Indians
the cause of Liberty   120

Mortal particulars
whose shatter we are

A sort of border life
A single group of trees

Sun on our back   125

Unappropriated land
all the works and redoubts

Young pine in a stand of oak
young oak in a stand of pine

Expectation of Epiphany   130

Not to look off from it
but to look at it

Original of the Otherside
understory of anotherword

Thaw has washed away snow   135
covering the old ice

the Lake a dull crust

Force made desire wander
Jumping from one subject

to another   140
Besieged and besieged

in a chain of Cause
The eternal First Cause

I stretch out my arms
to the author   145

Oh the bare ground

My thick coat and my tent
and the black of clouds

Squadrons of clouds

No end of their numbers   150

Armageddon at Fort William Henry
Sunset at Independence Point

Author the real author
acting the part of a scout

The origin of property   155
that leads here Depth

Indian names lead here

Bars of a social system
Starting for Lost Pond

psychology of the lost   160
First precarious Eden

a scandal of materialism

My ancestors tore off
the first leaves

picked out the best stars   165
Cries accompany laughter

Winter of the great Snow
Life surrounded by snows

The usual loggers camp
the usual bark shelter   170

Fir floor and log benches

Pines seem giant
      phenomena

Child of the Adirondacks
taking notes like a spy   175

Most mysterious river

On the confined brink

Poor storm
all hallows

and palings around cabin   180

Spring-suggesting light

Bustle of embarkation
Guides bewildered

Hunt and not the capture

Underthought draws home   185
Archaism

Here is dammed water

First trails were blazed
lines

Little known place names   190

tossed away as little grave
pivot bravura

Long walk on Erebus

The hell latch Poetry

Ragged rock beside hemlock   195

Mist in deep gulfs

Maps give us some idea
Apprehension as representation

Stood on Shelving Rock

The cold Friday   200
as cold as that was

Flood of light on water
Day went out in storms

Well structure could fall
Preys troop free   205

I have imagined a center

Wilder than this region
The figment of a book

Scarce broken letters
Cold leaden sky   210

Laurentian system of Canada

Tuesday the instant May

Elegiac western Imagination

Mysterious confined enigma
a possible field of work   215

The expanse of unconcealment
so different from all maps

Spiritual typography of elegy

Nature in us as a Nature
the actual one the ideal Self   220

tent tree sere leaf spectre
Unconscious demarkations range

I pick my compass to pieces

Dark here in the driftings
in the spaces of drifting   225

Complicity battling redemption

3.

Cannot be
every
where I
entreat
snapt

R e s o lu t i o n

picked up arrowhead

hieroglyph

battered

Parted with the Otterware

at the three Rivers, & are

Gone to have a Treaty

with the French at Oswego

At this end of the carry   islet

& singing their war song

neck

sheen   The French Hatchet

drisk

Their Plenipo   squall   Messages

disc   coin   splint   cedar

chip   grease   cusk

lily root

a very deep Rabbit

swamp   waveler

of which will not per[mit] of

shrub

fitted to the paper, the Margins

mud

Encampt   Fires by night

Frames should be exactly

wood   waterbug

canoes   c o v er y   Cove

Places to walk out to

Tranquillity of a garrison

Escalade

Traverse canon night siege Constant firing
Traverse canon night siege Constant firing

Gabion
Parapet

Gabion
Parapet

Traverse canon night siege Constant firing
Escalade
Tranquillity of a garrison

Places to walk out to
Cove

waterbug   The Frames should be exactly   wood   canoes

mud   fitted to the paper, the Margins   Fires by night   Encampt

shrub   of which will not per[mit] of

wavelet   a very deep Rabbit   swamp

cusk   lily root
cedar   grease   chip   coin
splint   disc
drisk   Messages   Their plenipo
                                    sheen
neck   The French Hatchet
islet   At this end of the carry
   & singing their war song
battered   The War Belt   hieroglyph
Messengers say   Picked up arrowhead
over the lakes
Of the far nations

You are of me & I of you, I cannot tell

Where you leave off and I begin

          selving

          forfending
              Immeadeat Settlem
but wandering
              Shenks Ferry people
unhoused
              at or naer Mohaxt
elect
              Sacandaga vläie
vision
              Battoes are return
thereafter
              They say
resurgent
              "Where is the path"
laughter

          ankledeep

          answerable   *last*

PASSACAGLIA   Strict counterpoint   *reassemble*
Moon wading through cloud   *Union*

            Stress   *mighty*
       distant   day helter No nd
                 wa
             defiant lenght
         brested   Premis
Awake! top hill demon daunt a
              on
              ce
              first

anthen   uplispth   enend

　　adamap   blue wov   thefthe

folled   floted   keen

Themis

thou sculling me

Thiefth

(1990)

Michael S. Harper
b. 1938

Born in Brooklyn, Michael S. Harper studied in Los Angeles, taking a B.A. and an M.A. at what is now California State University. He then took a second M.A. at the University of Iowa. After leaving Iowa in 1963, he traveled in Mexico and Europe: "Those landscapes," he has said, "broadened my scope and interest in poetry and culture of other countries while I searched my own family and racial history for folklore, history and myth for themes that would give my writing the tradition and context where I could find my own voice." Harper has been a resolutely historical poet, seeking in the narratives of the past explanatory models by which to understand the present. He has studied "the tension between stated moral idealism and brute historical realities," not only to understand American racism and the reality of black life in America but also to understand universal moral questions and perennial human suffering.

　　Harper's underlying music grows out of jazz. "Billie Holiday played piano in my family's house when I was 12," he has said; he has written memorable elegies for her and for John Coltrane, the jazz musician whose name is attached to Harper's first volume, *Dear John, Dear Coltrane* (1970). In that volume, and in subsequent ones such as *Nightmare Begins Responsibility* (1975), *Images of Kin* (1977), and *Healing Song for the Inner Ear* (1985), Harper has sought in language for some equivalent to the syncopations and improvisations of jazz and has disturbed the usual prosody deriving from speech rhythms, from what Frost called "sentence sounds." By writing a deliberately "educated" poetry, Harper has distanced himself from the black poets who write in simple "folk" forms and in black dialect; by writing a deliberately historical poetry, Harper has turned away from the confessional mode that reigned in the 1950s and 1960s. Though Harper's poetry is often autobiographical (as in the poems about his boyhood in Brooklyn or in the elegies for his two sons, his brother, and such fellow poets as Robert Hayden and James Wright), the autobiographical core is never without a meditative enlargement.

Harper has edited (with Robert Stepto) an anthology of black visual art and literature, *Chant of Saints* (1979), and (with Anthony Walton) *Every Shut Eye Ain't Asleep* (1994), an anthology of African American poetry since 1945. His most recent book is *Honorable Amendments: Poems* (1995). Harper is a professor of English at Brown University, where he has directed the writing program.

Further Reading:

J. F. Callahan, "The Testifying Voice in Michael Harper's Images of Kin," *Black American Literature Forum* 13: 89–92 (1979).

J. A. Brown, "Their Long Scars Touch Ours: A Reflection on the Poetry of Michael Harper," *Callaloo* 9: 209–220 (Winter 1986).

Michael S. Harper: American Poet, Special Issue of *Callaloo* 13: 749–829 (Fall 1990).

J. L. Raffa, *Nightmare Begins Responsibility: A study of Michael S. Harper's Poetry,* 1984.

X. Nicholas, ed., "Robert Hayden and Michael Harper: A Literary Friendship," *Callaloo,* Fall 1994.

Texts:

"Dear John, Dear Coltrane" and "American History" from *Dear John, Dear Coltrane,* 1970.

"Nightmare Begins Responsibility" from *Nightmare Begins Responsibility,* 1975.

"Peace on Earth" from *Healing Song for the Inner Ear,* 1985.

Dear John, Dear Coltrane*

a love supreme, a love supreme
a love supreme, a love supreme[1]

Sex fingers toes
in the marketplace
near your father's church
in Hamlet, North Carolina—
witness to this love   5
in this calm fallow
of these minds,
there is no substitute for pain:
genitals gone or going,
seed burned out,   10
you tuck the roots in the earth,
turn back, and move
by river through the swamps,
singing: *a love supreme, a love supreme;*
what does it all mean?   15

---

* John Coltrane (1926–1967), American jazz saxophonist.

[1] "A Love Supreme," one of the songs Coltrane played, contained this chant.

Loss, so great each black
woman expects your failure
in mute change, the seed gone.
You plod up into the electric city—
your song now crystal and   20
the blues. You pick up the horn
with some will and blow
into the freezing night:
a love supreme, a love supreme—

Dawn comes and you cook   25
up the thick sin 'tween
impotence and death, fuel
the tenor sax cannibal
heart, genitals and sweat
that makes you clean—   30
a love supreme, a love supreme—

Why you so black?
cause I am
why you so funky?
cause I am   35
why you so black?
cause I am
why you so sweet?
cause I am
why you so black?   40
cause I am
a love supreme, a love supreme:

So sick
you couldn't play *Naima*,[2]
so flat we ached   45
for song you'd concealed
with your own blood,
your diseased liver gave
out its purity,
the inflated heart
pumps out, the tenor[3] kiss,
tenor love:
a love supreme, a love supreme—
a love supreme, a love supreme—
1970

---

[2] Another song often played by Coltrane.
[3] Allusion to the tenor saxophone, Coltrane's
primary instrument.

American History

Those four black girls blown up
in that Alabama church[1]
remind me of five hundred
middle passage blacks,[2]
in a net, under water   5
in Charleston harbor
so *redcoats*[3] wouldn't find them.
Can't find what you can't see
can you?
1970

Nightmare Begins Responsibility*

I place these numbed wrists to the pane
watching white uniforms whisk over
him in the tube-kept
prison
fear what they will do in experiment   5
watch my gloved stickshifting gasolined hands
breathe *boxcar-information-please* infirmary tubes
distrusting white-pink mending paperthin
silkened end hairs, distrusting tubes
shrunk in his *trunk-skincapped*   10
shaven head, in thighs
distrusting-white-hands-picking-baboon-light
on this son who will not make his second night
of this wardstrewn intensive airpocket
where his father's asthmatic   15
hymns of *night-train,* train done gone
his mother can only know that he has flown

---

[1] One of the white-racist atrocities committed as reprisals against civil rights protests in the South during the 1960s.
[2] Captured blacks en route from Africa to be sold as slaves in the United States.
[3] Epithet for British soldiers.

* A play on the Irish poet William Butler Yeats's epigraph to his volume *Responsibilities* (1913): "In dreams begin responsibilities." The poem is an elegy for Harper's son, who died one day after birth. Another son had also died shortly after birth.

up into essential calm unseen corridor
going boxscarred home, *mamaborn, sweetsonchild*
gonedowntown into *researchtestingwarehouse*
    batteryacid   20
mama-son-done-gone / me telling her 'nother
train tonight, no music, no breathstroked
heartbeat in my infinite distrust of them:

and of my distrusting self
white-doctor-who-breathed-for-him-all-night   25
say it for two sons gone,
say nightmare, say it loud
panebreaking heartmadness:
nightmare begins responsibility.
1975

Peace on Earth

Tunes come to me[1] at morning
prayer, after flax sunflower
seeds jammed in a coffee can;

when we went to Japan
I prayed at the shrine   5
for the war dead broken
at Nagasaki;

the tears on the lip of my soprano
glistened in the sun.

In interviews   10
I talked about my music's
voice of praise to our oneness,

them getting caught up in techniques
of the electronic school

---

[1] John Coltrane

lifting us into assault;   15

in live sessions, without an audience
I see faces on the flues of the piano,
cymbals driving me into ecstacies on my knees,

the demonic angel, Elvin,[2]
answering my prayers on African drum,   20

on *Spiritual*

and on *Reverend King*

we chanted his words
on the mountain, where the golden chalice
came in our darkness.   25
I pursued the songless sound
of embouchures on Parisian thoroughfares,

the coins spilling across the arched
balustrade against my feet;

no high as intense as possessions   30
given up in practice

where the scales came to my fingers

without deliverance,
the light always coming at 4 A.M.

Syeeda's "Song Flute" charts   35
my playing for the ancestors;

how could I do otherwise,

passing so quickly in this galaxy

there is no time for being

to be paid in acknowledgment;   40
all praise to the phrase brought to me:

---

2 Elvin Jones

salaams of becoming:
A LOVE SUPREME:
1985

Joyce Carol Oates
b. 1938

One of the most prolific and popular of recent American writers, Joyce Carol Oates is perhaps best known for the extremities of violence in her fiction. One critic, Marvin Mudrick, has said that "typical activities in Oates's novels are arson, rape, riot, mental breakdown, murder (plain and fancy, with excursions into patricide, matricide, uxoricide, mass filicide), and suicide." For Oates, violence is inseparable from the psychic dislocation she sees as endemic to contemporary society. Like Joan Didion, she professes a strong commitment to family and tradition as defining forces for the individual, and like Didion, she sees modern culture as hostile to the individual. Specific acts of violence thus reflect culture's basic disposition, just as physical danger reflects the psychic risks inherent in our acceptance of modern values. Asked about the preponderance of violence in her fiction, Oates said, "These things do not have to be contrived. This is America."

Joyce Carol Oates was born on June 16, 1938, in Millerport, New York, to working-class, devoutly Catholic parents. A talented student, she won a scholarship to Syracuse University in 1956, and in 1960 she received a B.A. in English, graduating Phi Beta Kappa and valedictorian of her class. The next year she married Raymond Smith, received an M.A. in English literature from the University of Wisconsin, and enrolled in the doctoral program in English at Rice University, only to withdraw soon after one of her stories was listed on the Honor Roll in *Best American Short Stories.* Since publication of her first collection of stories, *By the North Gate,* in 1963, Oates has continued to write, as she puts it, in flurries. Besides numerous collections of short stories, poetry, and critical essays, she has written more than twenty novels over the past twenty-five years—an output that surely places her among the most productive serious writers in the history of American literature.

Her first novel, *With Shuddering Fall* (1964), the story of an intense and violent love affair between an impressionable seventeen-year-old girl and a thirty-year-old stock-car racer, introduced the themes of emotional derangement, tragic love, and compulsive behavior that have characterized much of her fiction. With her second novel, *A Garden of Earthly Delights* (1967), she began an American trilogy that took her from the Arkansas migrant camps of the 1920s to the suburbs of the 1960s and, with *Expensive People* (1968), to the story of a child murderer. The third novel in the trilogy, *Them* (1969), which won the National Book Award, moves from Depression-era Detroit to the shattering violence of the 1967 riots. In *Wonderland* (1971), Oates turned to the region of her childhood with a grisly, obsessive story about a boy who alone survives his insane father's massacre of an entire family. She turned again to childhood trauma in *Do with Me What You Will* (1973), the tale of a woman who as a child had been abducted by her father. In her next two novels, *The Assassins* (1975) and *Childwold* (1976), Oates experimented with intricate narrative techniques to portray the dissolving boundaries of dream and reality, the self and others. In 1978 she published a novel about intense religious experience, *Son of the Morning,* and in the following year turned to a university setting with *Unholy Lives.* In 1980 Oates broke new ground with *Bellefleur,* a novel that combines surrealist elements with a Gothic atmosphere as it traces the story of six generations of an American family in the Adirondack Valley. A year later she published *Angel of Light* (1981), a story of violence and political power whose title comes from Thoreau's description of John Brown. In these and in her latest novels, including *You Must Remember This* (1987), and *Because It Is Bitter, and Because It Is My Heart* (1990), she seems to be simultaneously using and commenting on popular forms of American fiction.

As an artist, Oates allies herself more with D. H. Lawrence than with such experimentalists as James Joyce and Virginia Woolf, though she also insists that she is a committed Anti-Romantic. The individual's desire for autonomy is the primary source of the human moral failure that manifests itself in—and is punished by—the acts of violence that pervade her fiction. One of her recurring themes has to do with "recognizing limits" that are implicit in the conjunction that an individual's history makes with the contours of culture. When her characters attempt to ignore or deny these limits, the givens of their lives, as does the narrator of "How I Contemplated the World," violence and meaninglessness threaten both them and the people around them.

Despite her rejection of Romanticism, Oates mixes realistic settings and characters with surreal and even supernatural experiences, often to disclose some hidden tie between the authors and the victims of violence. Such unexpected connections are important to her for many reasons, the chief one being their potential as a basis for community. In one way or another, her stories center on the importance of establishing a sense of community that is grounded biologically as well as socially, morally, and culturally. To her mind, the great failing of modern literature is its "solipsistic" tendency, its self-indulgent creation of "art forms in which language is arranged and rearranged in such a manner as to give pleasure to the artist and his readers, excluding any referent to an available exterior world." By contrast, her own effort, the only one she finally deems worthy, "is to do no less than attempt the sanctification of the world!"

Oates has continued to publish collections of dramas, essays, and short stories. Her most recent novels include *Black Water* (1992), *Foxfire: Confessions of a Girl Gang* (1993), *What I Lived For* (1995), *We Were the Mulvaneys* (1996), and *Man Crazy: A Novel* (1997).

Further Reading:

L. Wagner, ed., *Critical Essays on Joyce Carol Oates,* 1979.

H. Bloom, ed., *Joyce Carol Oates,* 1987.

J. Creighton, *Joyce Carol Oates: Novels of the Middle Years,* 1992.

B. Daly, *Lavish Self-Divisions: The Novels of Joyce Carol Oates,* 1996.

Text:
"Where Are You Going, Where Have You Been"
  from *Stories of Young America,* 1974.

Where Are You Going, Where Have You Been?

For Bob Dylan

Her name was Connie. She was fifteen and she had a quick, nervous giggling habit of craning her neck to glance into mirrors or checking other people's faces to make sure her own was all right. Her mother, who noticed everything and knew everything and who hadn't much reason any longer to look at her own face, always scolded Connie about it. "Stop gawking at yourself. Who are you? You think you're so pretty?" she would say. Connie would raise her eyebrows at these familiar old complaints and look right through her mother, into a shadowy vision of herself as she was right at that moment: she knew she was pretty and that was everything. Her mother had been pretty once too, if you could believe those old snapshots in the album, but now her looks were gone and that was why she was always after Connie.

"Why don't you keep your room clean like your sister? How've you got your hair fixed—what the hell stinks? Hair spray? You don't see your sister using that junk."

Her sister June was twenty-four and still lived at home. She was a secretary in the high school Connie attended, and if that wasn't bad enough—with her in the same building—she was so plain and chunky and steady that Connie had to hear her praised all the time by her mother and her mother's sisters. June did this, June did that, she saved money and helped clean the house and cooked and Connie couldn't do a thing, her mind was all filled with trashy daydreams. Their father was away at work most of the time and when he came home he wanted supper and he read the newspaper at supper and after supper he went to bed. He didn't bother talking much to them, but around his bent head Connie's mother kept picking at her until Connie wished her mother was dead and she herself was dead and it was all over. "She makes me want to throw up sometimes," she complained to her friends. She had a high, breathless, amused voice that made everything she said sound a little forced, whether it was sincere or not.

There was one good thing: June went places with girl friends of hers, girls who were just as plain and steady as she, and so when Connie wanted to do that her mother had no objections. The father of Connie's best girl friend drove the girls the three miles to town and left them at a shopping plaza so they could walk through the stores or go to a movie, and when he came to pick them up again at eleven he never bothered to ask what they had done.

They must have been familiar sights, walking around the shopping plaza in their shorts and flat ballerina slippers that always scuffed the sidewalk, with charm bracelets jingling on their thin wrists; they would lean together to whisper and laugh secretly if someone passed who amused or interested them. Connie had long dark blond hair that drew anyone's eye to it, and she wore part of it pulled up on her head and puffed out and the rest of it she let fall down her back. She wore a pull-over jersey blouse that looked one way when she was at home and another way when she was away from home. Everything about her had two sides to it, one for home and one for anywhere that was not home: her walk, which could be childlike and bobbing, or languid enough to make anyone think she was hearing music in her head; her mouth, which was pale and smirking most of the time, but bright and pink on these evenings out; her laugh, which was cynical and drawling at home—"Ha, ha, very funny,"—but high-pitched and nervous anywhere else, like the jingling of the charms on her bracelet.

Sometimes they did go shopping or to a movie, but sometimes they went across the highway, ducking fast across the busy road, to a drive-in restaurant where older kids hung out. The restaurant was shaped like a big bottle, though squatter than a real bottle, and on its cap was a revolving figure of a grinning boy holding a hamburger aloft. One night in midsummer they ran across, breathless with daring, and right away someone leaned out a car window and invited them over, but it was just a boy from high school they didn't like. It made them feel good to be able to ignore him. They went up through the maze of parked and cruising cars to the bright-lit, fly-infested restaurant, their faces pleased and expectant as if they were entering a sacred building that loomed up out of the night to give them what haven and blessing they yearned for. They sat at the counter and crossed their legs at the ankles, their thin shoulders rigid with excitement, and listened to the music that made everything so good: the music was always in the background, like music at a church service; it was something to depend upon.

A boy named Eddie came in to talk with them. He sat backwards on his stool, turning himself jerkily around in semicircles and then stopping and turning back again, and after a while he asked Connie if she would like something to eat. She said she would and so she tapped her friend's arm on her way out—her friend pulled her face up into a brave, droll look—and Connie said she would meet her at eleven, across the way. "I just hate to leave her like that," Connie said earnestly, but the boy said that she wouldn't be alone for long. So they went out to his car, and on the way Connie couldn't help but let her eyes wander over the windshields and faces all around her, her face gleaming with a joy that had nothing to do with Eddie or even this place; it might have been the music. She drew her shoulders up and sucked in her breath with the pure pleasure of being alive, and just at that moment she happened to glance at a face just a few feet from hers. It was a boy with shaggy black hair, in a convertible jalopy painted gold. He stared at her and then his lips widened into a grin. Connie slit her eyes at him and turned away, but she couldn't help glancing back and there he was, still watching her. He wagged a finger and laughed and said, "Gonna get you, baby," and Connie turned away again without Eddie noticing anything.

She spent three hours with him, at the restaurant where they ate hamburgers and drank Cokes in wax cups that were always sweating, and then down an alley a mile or so away, and when he left her off at five to eleven only the movie house was still open at the plaza. Her girl friend was there, talking with a boy. When Connie came up, the two girls smiled at each other and Connie said, "How was the movie?" and the girl said, "*You* should know." They rode off with the girl's father, sleepy and pleased, and Connie couldn't help but look back at the darkened shopping plaza with its big empty parking lot and its signs that were faded and ghostly now, and over at the drive-in restaurant where cars were still circling tirelessly. She couldn't hear the music at this distance.

Next morning June asked her how the movie was and Connie said, "So-so."

She and that girl and occasionally another girl went out several times a week, and the rest of the time Connie spent around the house—it was summer vacation—getting in her mother's way and thinking, dreaming about the boys she met. But all the boys fell back and dissolved into a single face that was not even a face but an idea, a feeling, mixed up with the urgent insistent pounding of the music and the humid night air of

July. Connie's mother kept dragging her back to the daylight by finding things for her to do or saying suddenly, "What's this about the Pettinger girl?"

And Connie would say nervously, "Oh, her. That dope." She always drew thick clear lines between herself and such girls, and her mother was simple and kind enough to believe it. Her mother was so simple, Connie thought, that it was maybe cruel to fool her so much. Her mother went scuffling around the house in old bedroom slippers and complained over the telephone to one sister about the other, then the other called up and the two of them complained about the third one. If June's name was mentioned her mother's tone was approving, and if Connie's name was mentioned it was disapproving. This did not really mean she disliked Connie, and actually Connie thought that her mother preferred her to June just because she was prettier, but the two of them kept up a pretense of exasperation, a sense that they were tugging and struggling over something of little value to either of them. Sometimes, over coffee, they were almost friends, but something would come up—some vexation that was like a fly buzzing suddenly around their heads—and their faces went hard with contempt.

One Sunday Connie got up at eleven—none of them bothered with church—and washed her hair so that it could dry all day long in the sun. Her parents and sister were going to a barbecue at an aunt's house and Connie said no, she wasn't interested, rolling her eyes to let her mother know just what she thought of it. "Stay home alone then," her mother said sharply. Connie sat out back in a lawn chair and watched them drive away, her father quiet and bald, hunched around so that he could back the car out, her mother with a look that was still angry and not at all softened through the windshield, and in the back seat poor old June, all dressed up as if she didn't know what a barbecue was, with all the running yelling kids and the flies. Connie sat with her eyes closed in the sun, dreaming and dazed with the warmth about her as if this were a kind of love, the caresses of love, and her mind slipped over onto thoughts of the boy she had been with the night before and how nice he had been, how sweet it always was, not the way someone like June would suppose but sweet, gentle, the way it was in movies and promised in songs; and when she opened her eyes she hardly knew where she was, the back yard ran off into weeds and a fence-like line of trees and behind it the sky was perfectly blue and still. The asbestos "ranch house" that was now three years old startled her—it looked small. She shook her head as if to get awake.

It was too hot. She went inside the house and turned on the radio to drown out the quiet. She sat on the edge of her bed, barefoot, and listened for an hour and a half to a program called XYZ Sunday Jamboree, record after record of hard, fast, shrieking songs she sang along with, interspersed by exclamations from "Bobby King": "An' look here, you girls at Napoleon's—Son and Charley want you to pay real close attention to this song coming up!"

And Connie paid close attention herself, bathed in a glow of slow-pulsed joy that seemed to rise mysteriously out of the music itself and lay languidly about the airless little room, breathed in and breathed out with each gentle rise and fall of her chest.

After a while she heard a car coming up the drive. She sat up at once, startled, because it couldn't be her father so soon. The gravel kept crunching all the way in from the road—the driveway was long—and Connie ran to the window. It was a car she didn't know. It was an open jalopy, painted a bright gold that caught the sunlight opaquely. Her heart began to pound and her fingers snatched at her hair, checking it, and she whispered, "Christ. Christ," wondering how bad she looked. The car came to a stop at the side door and the horn sounded four short taps, as if this were a signal Connie knew.

She went into the kitchen and approached the door slowly, then hung out the screen door, her bare toes curling down off the step. There were two boys in the car and now she recognized the driver: he had shaggy, shabby black hair that looked crazy as a wig and he was grinning at her.

"I ain't late, am I?" he said.

"Who the hell do you think you are?" Connie said.

"Toldja I'd be out, didn't I?"

"I don't even know who you are."

She spoke sullenly, careful to show no interest or pleasure, and he spoke in a fast, bright monotone. Connie looked past him to the other boy, taking her time. He had fair brown hair, with a lock that fell onto his forehead. His sideburns gave him a fierce, embarrassed look, but so far he hadn't even bothered to glance at her. Both boys wore sunglasses. The driver's glasses were metallic and mirrored everything in miniature.

"You wanta come for a ride?" he said.

Connie smirked and let her hair fall loose over one shoulder.

"Don'tcha like my car? New paint job," he said. "Hey."

"What?"

"You're cute."

She pretended to fidget, chasing flies away from the door.

"Don'tcha believe me, or what?" he said.

"Look, I don't even know who you are," Connie said in disgust.

"Hey, Ellie's got a radio, see. Mine broke down." He lifted his friend's arm and showed her the little transistor radio the boy was holding, and now Connie began to hear the music. It was the same program that was playing inside the house.

"Bobby King?" she said.

"I listen to him all the time. I think he's great."

"He's kind of great," Connie said reluctantly.

"Listen, that guy's *great*. He knows where the action is."

Connie blushed a little, because the glasses made it impossible for her to see just what this boy was looking at. She couldn't decide if she liked him or if he was just a jerk, and so she dawdled in the doorway and wouldn't come down or go back inside. She said, "What's all that stuff painted on your car?"

"Can'tcha read it?" He opened the door very carefully, as if he were afraid it might fall off. He slid out just as carefully, planting his feet firmly on the ground, the tiny metallic world in his glasses slowing down like gelatine hardening, and in the midst of it Connie's bright green blouse. "This here is my name, to begin with," he said. ARNOLD FRIEND was written in tarlike black letters on the side, with a drawing of a round, grinning face that reminded Connie of a pumpkin, except it wore sunglasses. "I wanta introduce myself, I'm Arnold Friend and that's my real name and I'm gonna be your friend, honey, and inside the car's Ellie Oscar, he's kinda shy." Ellie brought his transistor radio up to his shoulder and balanced it there. "Now, these numbers are a secret code, honey," Arnold Friend explained. He read off the numbers 33, 19, 17 and raised his eyebrows at her to see what she thought of that, but she didn't think much of it. The left rear fender had been smashed and around it was written, on the gleaming gold background: DONE BY CRAZY WOMAN DRIVER. Connie had to laugh at that. Arnold Friend was pleased at her laughter and looked up at her. "Around the other side's a lot more—you wanta come and see them?"

"No."

"Why not?"

"Why should I?"

"Don'tcha wanta see what's on the car? Don'tcha wanta go for a ride?"

"I don't know."

"Why not?"

"I got things to do."

"Like what?"

"Things."

He laughed as if she had said something funny. He slapped his thighs. He was standing in a strange way, leaning back against the car as if he were balancing himself. He wasn't tall, only an inch or so taller than she would be if she came down to him. Connie liked the way he was dressed, which was the way all of them dressed: tight faded jeans stuffed into black, scuffed boots, a belt that pulled his waist in and showed how lean he was, and a white pull-over shirt that was a little soiled and showed the hard small muscles of his arms and shoulders. He looked as if he probably did hard work, lifting and carrying things. Even his neck looked muscular. And his face was a familiar face, somehow: the jaw and chin and cheeks slightly darkened because he hadn't shaved for a day or two, and the nose long and hawklike, sniffing as if she were a treat he was going to gobble up and it was all a joke.

"Connie, you ain't telling the truth. This is your day set aside for a ride with me and you know it," he said, still laughing. The way he straightened and recovered from his fit of laughing showed that it had been all fake.

"How do you know what my name is?" she said suspiciously.

"It's Connie."

"Maybe and maybe not."

"I know my Connie," he said, wagging his finger. Now she remembered him even better, back at the restaurant, and her cheeks warmed at the thought of how she had sucked in her breath just at the moment she passed him—how she must have looked to him. And he had remembered her. "Ellie and I come out here especially for you," he said. "Ellie can sit in back. How about it?"

"Where?"

"Where what?"

"Where're we going?"

He looked at her. He took off the sunglasses and she saw how pale the skin around his eyes was, like holes that were not in shadow but instead in light. His eyes were like chips of broken glass that catch the light in an amiable way. He smiled. It was as if the idea of going for a ride somewhere, to someplace, was a new idea to him.

"Just for a ride, Connie sweetheart."

"I never said my name was Connie," she said.

"But I know what it is. I know your name and all about you, lots of things," Arnold Friend said. He had not moved yet but stood still leaning back against the side of his jalopy. "I took a special interest in you, such a pretty girl, and found out all about you—like I know your parents and sister are gone somewheres and I know where and how long they're going to be gone, and I know who you were with last night, and your best girl friend's name is Betty. Right?"

He spoke in a simple lilting voice, exactly as if he were reciting the words to a song. His smile assured her that everything was fine. In the car Ellie turned up the volume on his radio and did not bother to look around at them.

"Ellie can sit in the back seat," Arnold Friend said. He indicated his friend with a casual jerk of his chin, as if Ellie did not count and she should not bother with him.

"How'd you find out all that stuff?" Connie said.

"Listen: Betty Schultz and Tony Fitch and Jimmy Pettinger and Nancy Pettinger," he said in a chant. "Raymond Stanley and Bob Hutter—"

"Do you know all those kids?"

"I know everybody."

"Look, you're kidding. You're not from around here."

"Sure."

"But—how come we never saw you before?"

"Sure you saw me before," he said. He looked down at his boots, as if he were a little offended. "You just don't remember."

"I guess I'd remember you," Connie said.

"Yeah?" He looked up at this, beaming. He was pleased. He began to mark time with the music from Ellie's radio, tapping his fists lightly together. Connie looked away from his smile to the car, which was painted so bright it almost hurt her eyes to look at it. She looked at that name, ARNOLD FRIEND. And up at the front fender was an expression that was familiar—MAN THE FLYING SAUCERS. It was an expression kids had used the year before but didn't use this year. She looked at it for a while as if the words meant something to her that she did not yet know.

"What're you thinking about? Huh?" Arnold Friend demanded. "Not worried about your hair blowing around in the car, are you?"

"No."

"Think I maybe can't drive good?"

"How do I know?"

"You're a hard girl to handle. How come?" he said. "Don't you know I'm your friend? Didn't you see me put my sign in the air when you walked by?"

"What sign?"

"My sign." And he drew an X in the air, leaning out toward her. They were maybe ten feet apart. After his hand fell back to his side the X was still in the air, almost visible. Connie let the screen door close and stood perfectly still inside it, listening to the music from her radio and the boy's blend together. She stared at Arnold Friend. He stood there so stiffly relaxed, pretending to be relaxed, with one hand idly on the door handle as if he were keeping himself up that way and had no intention of ever moving again. She recognized most things about him, the tight jeans that showed his thighs and buttocks and the greasy leather boots and the tight shirt, and even that slippery friendly smile of his, that sleepy dreamy smile that all the boys used to get across ideas they didn't want to put into words. She recognized all this and also the singsong way he talked, slightly mocking, kidding, but serious and a little melancholy, and she recognized the way he tapped one fist against the other in homage to the perpetual music behind him. But all these things did not come together.

She said suddenly, "Hey, how old are you?"

His smiled faded. She could see then that he wasn't a kid, he was much older—thirty, maybe more. At this knowledge her heart began to pound faster.

"That's a crazy thing to ask. Can'tcha see I'm your own age?"

"Like hell you are."

"Or maybe a coupla years older. I'm eighteen."

"Eighteen?" she said doubtfully.

He grinned to reassure her and lines appeared at the corners of his mouth. His teeth were big and white. He grinned so broadly his eyes became slits and she saw how thick the lashes were, thick and black as if painted with a black tarlike material. Then, abruptly, he seemed to become embarrassed and looked over his shoulder at Ellie. "*Him*, he's crazy," he said. "Ain't he a riot? He's a nut, a real character." Ellie was still listening to the music. His sunglasses told nothing about what he was thinking. He wore a bright orange shirt unbuttoned halfway to show his chest, which was a pale, bluish chest and not muscular like Arnold Friend's. His shirt collar was turned up all around and the very tips of the collar pointed out past his chin as if they were protecting him. He was pressing the transistor radio up against his ear and sat there in a kind of daze, right in the sun.

"He's kinda strange," Connie said.

"Hey, she says you're kinda strange! Kinda strange!" Arnold Friend cried. He pounded on the car to get Ellie's attention. Ellie turned for the first time and Connie saw with shock that he wasn't a kid either—he had a fair, hairless face, cheeks reddened slightly as if the veins grew too close to the surface of his skin, the face of a forty-year-old baby. Connie felt a wave of dizziness rise in her at this sight and she stared at him as if waiting for something to change the shock of the moment, make it all right again. Ellie's lips kept shaping words, mumbling along with the words blasting in his ear.

"Maybe you two better go away," Connie said faintly.

"What? How come?" Arnold Friend cried. "We come out here to take you for a ride. It's Sunday." He had the voice of the man on the radio now. It was the same voice, Connie thought. "Don'tcha know it's Sunday all day? And honey, no matter who you were with last night, today you're with Arnold Friend and don't you forget it! Maybe you better step out here," he said, and this last was in a different voice. It was a little flatter, as if the heat was finally getting to him.

"No. I got things to do."

"Hey."

"You two better leave."

"We ain't leaving until you come with us."

"Like hell I am—"

"Connie, don't fool around with me. I mean—I mean, don't fool *around*," he said, shaking his head. He laughed incredulously. He placed his sunglasses on top of his head, carefully, as if he were indeed wearing a wig, and brought the stems down behind his ears. Connie stared at him, another wave of dizziness and fear rising in her so that for a moment he wasn't even in focus but was just a blur standing there against his gold car, and she had the idea that he had driven up the driveway all right but had come from nowhere before that and belonged nowhere and that everything about him and even about the music that was so familiar to her was only half real.

"If my father comes and sees you—"

"He ain't coming. He's at a barbecue."

"How do you know that?"

"Aunt Tillie's. Right now they're—uh—they're drinking. Sitting around," he said vaguely, squinting as if he were staring all the way to town and over to Aunt Tillie's back yard. Then the vision seemed to get clear and he nodded energetically. "Yeah. Sitting around. There's your sister in a blue dress, huh? And high heels, the poor sad bitch—nothing like you, sweetheart! And your mother's helping some fat woman with the corn, they're cleaning the corn—husking the corn—"

"What fat woman?" Connie cried.

"How do I know what fat woman, I don't know every goddamn fat woman in the world!" Arnold Friend laughed.

"Oh, that's Mrs. Hornsby. . . . Who invited her?" Connie said. She felt a little light-headed. Her breath was coming quickly.

"She's too fat. I don't like them fat. I like them the way you are, honey," he said, smiling sleepily at her. They stared at each other for a while through the screen door. He said softly, "Now, what you're going to do is this: you're going to come out that door. You're going to sit up front with me and Ellie's going to sit in the back, the hell with Ellie, right? This isn't Ellie's date. You're my date. I'm your lover, honey."

"What? You're crazy—"

"Yes, I'm your lover. You don't know what that is but you will," he said. "I know that too. I know all about you. But look: it's real nice and you couldn't ask for nobody better than me, or more polite. I always keep my word. I'll tell you how it is, I'm always nice at first, the first time. I'll hold you so tight you won't think you have to try to get away or pretend anything because you'll know you can't. And I'll come inside you where it's all secret and you'll give in to me and you'll love me—"

"Shut up! You're crazy!" Connie said. She backed away from the door. She put her hands up against her ears as if she'd heard something terrible, something not meant for her. "People don't talk like that, you're crazy," she muttered. Her heart was almost too big now for her chest and its pumping made sweat break out all over her. She looked out to see Arnold Friend pause and then take a step toward the porch, lurching. He almost fell. But, like a clever drunken man, he managed to catch his balance. He wobbled in his high boots and grabbed hold of one of the porch posts.

"Honey?" he said. "You still listening?"

"Get the hell out of here!"

"Be nice, honey. Listen."

"I'm going to call the police—"

He wobbled again and out of the side of his mouth came a fast spat curse, an aside not meant for her to hear. But even this "Christ!" sounded forced. Then he began to smile again. She watched this smile come, awkward as if he were smiling from inside a mask. His whole face was a mask, she thought wildly, tanned down to his throat but then running out as if he had plastered make-up on his face but had forgotten about his throat.

"Honey—? Listen, here's how it is. I always tell the truth and I promise you this: I ain't coming in that house after you."

"You better not! I'm going to call the police if you—if you don't—"

"Honey," he said, talking right through her voice, "honey, I'm not coming in there but you are coming out here. You know why?"

She was panting. The kitchen looked like a place she had never seen before, some room she had run inside but that wasn't good enough, wasn't going to help her. The kitchen window had never had a curtain, after three years, and there were dishes in the sink for her to do—probably—and if you ran your hand across the table you'd probably feel something sticky there.

"You listening, honey? Hey?"

"—going to call the police—"

"Soon as you touch the phone I don't need to keep my promise and can come inside. You won't want that."

She rushed forward and tried to lock the door. Her fingers were shaking. "But why lock it," Arnold Friend said gently, talking right into her face. "It's just a screen door. It's just nothing." One of his boots was at a strange angle, as if his foot wasn't in it. It pointed out to the left, bent at the ankle. "I mean, anybody can break through a screen door and glass and wood and iron or anything else if he needs to, anybody at all, and specially Arnold Friend. If the place got lit up with a fire, honey, you'd come runnin' out into my arms, right into my arms an' safe at home—like you knew I was your lover and'd stopped fooling around. I don't mind a nice shy girl but I don't like no fooling around." Part of those words were spoken with a slight rhythmic lilt, and Connie somehow recognized them—the echo of a song from last year, about a girl rushing into her boy friend's arms and coming home again—

Connie stood barefoot on the linoleum floor, staring at him. "What do you want?" she whispered.

"I want you," he said.

"What?"

"Seen you that night and thought, that's the one, yes sir. I never needed to look any-more."

"But my father's coming back. He's coming to get me. I had to wash my hair first—" She spoke in a dry, rapid voice, hardly raising it for him to hear.

"No, your daddy is not coming and yes, you had to wash your hair and you washed it for me. It's nice and shining and all for me. I thank you sweetheart," he said with a mock bow, but again he almost lost his balance. He had to bend and adjust his boots. Evidently his feet did not go all the way down; the boots must have been stuffed with something so that he would seem taller. Connie stared out at him and behind him at Ellie in the car, who seemed to be looking off toward Connie's right, into nothing. This Ellie said, pulling the words out of the air one after another as if he were just discovering them, "You want me to pull out the phone?"

"Shut your mouth and keep it shut," Arnold Friend said, his face red from bending over or maybe from embarrassment because Connie had seen his boots. "This ain't none of your business."

"What—what are you doing? What do you want?" Connie said. "If I call the police they'll get you, they'll arrest you—"

"Promise was not to come in unless you touch that phone, and I'll keep that promise," he said. He resumed his erect position and tried to force his shoulders back. He sounded like a hero in a movie, declaring something important. But he spoke too loudly and it was as if he were speaking to someone behind Connie. "I ain't made plans for coming in that house where I don't belong but just for you to come out to me, the way you should. Don't you know who I am?"

"You're crazy," she whispered. She backed away from the door but did not want to go into another part of the house, as if this would give him permission to come through the door. "What do you . . . you're crazy, you. . . ."

"Huh? What're you saying, honey?"

Her eyes darted everywhere in the kitchen. She could not remember what it was, this room.

"This is how it is, honey: you come out and we'll drive away, have a nice ride. But if you don't come out we're gonna wait till your people come home and then they're all going to get it."

"You want that telephone pulled out?" Ellie said. He held the radio away from his ear and grimaced, as if without the radio the air was too much for him.

"I toldja shut up, Ellie," Arnold Friend said, "you're deaf, get a hearing aid, right? Fix yourself up. This little girl's no trouble and's gonna be nice to me, so Ellie keep to yourself, this ain't your date—right? Don't hem in on me, don't hog, don't crush, don't bird dog, don't trail me," he said in a rapid, meaningless voice, as if he were running through all the expressions he'd learned but was no longer sure which of them was in style, then rushing on to new ones, making them up with his eyes closed. "Don't crawl under my fence, don't squeeze in my chipmunk hole, don't sniff my glue, suck my popsicle, keep your own greasy fingers on yourself!" He shaded his eyes and peered in at Connie, who was backed against the kitchen table. "Don't mind him, honey, he's just a creep. He's a dope. Right? I'm the boy for you and like I said, you come out here nice like a lady and give me your hand, and nobody else gets hurt, I mean, your nice old bald-headed daddy and your mummy and your sister in her high heels. Because listen: why bring them in this?"

"Leave me alone," Connie whispered.

"Hey, you know that old woman down the road, the one with the chickens and stuff—you know her?"

"She's dead!"

"Dead? What? You know her?" Arnold Friend said.

"She's dead—"

"Don't you like her?"

"She's dead—she's—she isn't here any more—"

"But don't you like her, I mean, you got something against her? Some grudge or something?" Then his voice dipped as if he were conscious of a rudeness. He touched the sunglasses perched up on top of his head as if to make sure they were still there. "Now, you be a good girl."

"What are you going to do?"

"Just two things, or maybe three," Arnold Friend said. "But I promise it won't last long and you'll like me the way you get to like people you're close to. You will. It's all over for you here, so come on out. You don't want your people in any trouble, do you?"

She turned and bumped against a chair or something, hurting her leg, but she ran into the back room and picked up the telephone. Something roared in her ear, a tiny roaring, and she was so sick with fear that she could do nothing but listen to it—the telephone was clammy and very heavy and her fingers groped down to the dial but were too weak to touch it. She began to scream into the phone, into the roaring. She cried out, she cried for her mother, she felt her breath start jerking back and forth in her lungs as if it were something Arnold Friend was stabbing her with again and again with no tenderness. A noisy sorrowful wailing rose all about her and she was locked inside it the way she was locked inside this house.

After a while she could hear again. She was sitting on the floor with her wet back against the wall.

Arnold Friend was saying from the door, "That's a good girl. Put the phone back."

She kicked the phone away from her.

"No, honey. Pick it up. Put it back right."

She picked it up and put it back. The dial tone stopped.

"That's a good girl. Now, you come outside."

She was hollow with what had been fear but what was now just an emptiness. All that screaming had blasted it out of her. She sat, one leg cramped under her, and deep inside her brain was something like a pinpoint of light that kept going and would not let her relax. She thought, I'm not going to see my mother again. She thought, I'm not going to sleep in my bed again. Her bright green blouse was all wet.

Arnold Friend said, in a gentle-loud voice that was like a stage voice, "The place where you came from ain't there any more, and where you had in mind to go is cancelled out. This place you are now—inside your daddy's house—is nothing but a cardboard box I can knock down any time. You know that and always did know it. You hear me?"

She thought, I have got to think. I have got to know what to do.

"We'll go out to a nice field, out in the country here where it smells so nice and it's sunny," Arnold Friend said. "I'll have my arms tight around you so you won't need to try to get away and I'll show you what love is like, what it does. The hell with this house! It looks solid all right," he said. He ran a fingernail down the screen and the noise did not make Connie shiver, as it would have the day before. "Now, put your hand on your heart, honey. Feel that? That feels solid too but we know better. Be nice to me, be sweet like you can because what else is there for a girl like you but to be sweet and pretty and give in?—and get away before her people come back?"

She felt her pounding heart. Her hand seemed to enclose it. She thought for the first time in her life that it was nothing that was hers, that belonged to her, but just a pounding, living thing inside this body that wasn't really hers either.

"You don't want them to get hurt," Arnold Friend went on. "Now, get up, honey. Get up all by yourself."

She stood.

"Now, turn this way. That's right. Come over here to me.—Ellie, put that away, didn't I tell you? You dope. You miserable creepy dope," Arnold Friend said. His words were not angry but only part of an incantation. The incantation was kindly. "Now, come out through the kitchen to me, honey, and let's see a smile, try it, you're a brave, sweet little girl and now they're eating corn and hot dogs cooked to bursting over an outdoor fire, and they don't know one thing about you and never did and honey, you're better than them because not a one of them would have done this for you."

Connie felt the linoleum under her feet; it was cool. She brushed her hair back out of her eyes. Arnold Friend let go of the post tentatively and opened his arms for her, his elbows pointing in toward each other and his wrists limp, to show that this was an embarrassed embrace and a little mocking, he didn't want to make her self-conscious.

She put out her hand against the screen. She watched herself push the door slowly open as if she were back safe somewhere in the other doorway, watching this body and this head of long hair moving out into the sunlight where Arnold Friend waited.

"My sweet little blue-eyed girl," he said in a half-sung sigh that had nothing to do with her brown eyes but was taken up just the same by the vast sunlit reaches of the land behind him and on all sides of him—so much land that Connie had never seen before and did not recognize except to know that she was going to it.

1974

Raymond Carver
1939–1988

"It's possible," said Raymond Carver, "to write about commonplace things and objects using commonplace but precise language, and to endow these things—a chair, a window curtain, a fork, a stone, a woman's earring—with immense, even startling power. It is possible to write a line of seemingly innocuous dialogue and have it send a chill along the reader's spine." Carver's short stories and poems often turn on just such moments of unexpected revelation of beauty or terror. Like many other contemporary writers, Carver doubts the power of fiction to effect social, political, or even personal change ("perhaps it's different in poetry," he says). Instead, he believes, "it just has to be there for the fierce pleasure we take in doing it, and the different kind of pleasure that's taken in reading something that's durable and made to last, as well as beautiful in and of itself. Something that throws off these sparks—a persistent and steady glow, however dim."

Carver was born on May 25, 1939, in Clatskanie, Oregon, and grew up in the small town of Yakima, Washington, where his father worked as a laborer in a local sawmill. In 1957, at age eighteen, Carver married, but by working evenings he still managed to attend Chico State College, where he studied with the novelist John Gardner. After graduating from Chico State in 1963, he spent a year at the writers' workshop of the University of Iowa and then returned to California, first taking a job as a night janitor at a Sacramento hospital and then as an editor with a textbook publisher in Palo Alto. Carver also lectured in creative writing at the University of California at Santa Cruz and at Berkeley, the University of Texas, the University of Iowa, and Syracuse University.

Deeply influenced, like Sherwood Anderson, by his father's storytelling ability, Carver tried writing stories as a boy. As an undergraduate, he began publishing stories and poems. In 1967 one of his stories, "Will You Please Be Quiet, Please?" was selected for the *Best American Short Stories* anthology; later, in 1976, it became the title story of his first collection of short fiction. Three collections of stories followed—*What We Talk About When We Talk About Love* (1981), *Cathedral* (1983), and *Where I'm Calling From* (1988)—all of which received high critical acclaim. Carver is also the author of several volumes of poetry, including *Near Klamath* (1968), *Winter Insomnia* (1970), *At Night the Salmon Move* (1976), *When Water Comes Together with Other Water* (1985), and *Ultramarine* (1987), and *Fires: Essays, Poems, Stories* (1983).

Widely anthologized, Carver's stories have appeared in numerous literary magazines and have won many awards. Nearly all his stories deal with people living on the fringe of subsistence and articulation. His style is often spare to the point of asceticism, and it characteristically retains a tense, close touch with the diction and rhythm of ordinary speech. "One of Mr. Carver's great gifts," as the critic Michael Wood has noted, "is to make audible the eloquence of the apparently inarticulate. It's not that he lends speech to his characters or talks on their behalf. He hears what they are saying when the words run out."

Further Reading:
A Saltzman, *Understanding Raymond Carver*, 1988.
E. Campbell, *Raymond Carver: A Study of the Short Fiction*, 1992.

K. Nesset, *The Stories of Raymond Carver: A Critical Study*, 1994.
A. Meyer, *Raymond Carver*, 1995.

Text:
What We Talk About When We Talk About Love, 1981.

What We Talk About When We Talk About Love

My friend Mel McGinnis was talking. Mel McGinnis is a cardiologist, and sometimes that gives him the right.

The four of us were sitting around his kitchen table drinking gin. Sunlight filled the kitchen from the big window behind the sink. There were Mel and me and his second wife, Teresa—Terri, we called her—and my wife, Laura. We lived in Albuquerque then. But we were all from somewhere else.

There was an ice bucket on the table. The gin and the tonic water kept going around, and we somehow got on the subject of love. Mel thought real love was nothing less than spiritual love. He said he'd spent five years in a seminary before quitting to go to medical school. He said he still looked back on those years in the seminary as the most important years in his life.

Terri said the man she lived with before she lived with Mel loved her so much he tried to kill her. Then Terri said, "He beat me up one night. He dragged me around the living room by my ankles. He kept saying, 'I love you, I love you, you bitch.' He went on dragging me around the living room. My head kept knocking on things." Terri looked around the table. "What do you do with love like that?"

She was a bone-thin woman with a pretty face, dark eyes, and brown hair that hung down her back. She liked necklaces made of turquoise, and long pendant earrings.

"My God, don't be silly. That's not love, and you know it," Mel said. "I don't know what you'd call it, but I sure know you wouldn't call it love."

"Say what you want to, but I know it was," Terri said. "It may sound crazy to you, but it's true just the same. People are different, Mel. Sure, sometimes he may have acted crazy. Okay. But he loved me. In his own way maybe, but he loved me. There was love there, Mel. Don't say there wasn't."

Mel let out his breath. He held his glass and turned to Laura and me. "The man threatened to kill me," Mel said. He finished his drink and reached for the gin bottle. "Terri's a romantic. Terri's of the kick-me-so-I'll-know-you-love-me school. Terri, hon, don't look that way." Mel reached across the table and touched Terri's cheek with his fingers. He grinned at her.

"Now he wants to make up," Terri said.

"Make up what?" Mel said. "What is there to make up? I know what I know. That's all."

"How'd we get started on this subject, anyway?" Terri said. She raised her glass and drank from it. "Mel always has love on his mind," she said. "Don't you, honey?" She smiled, and I thought that was the last of it.

"I just wouldn't call Ed's behavior love. That's all I'm saying, honey," Mel said. "What about you guys?" Mel said to Laura and me. "Does that sound like love to you?"

"I'm the wrong person to ask," I said. "I didn't even know the man. I've only heard his name mentioned in passing. I wouldn't know. You'd have to know the particulars. But I think what you're saying is that love is an absolute."

Mel said, "The kind of love I'm talking about is. The kind of love I'm talking about, you don't try to kill people."

Laura said, "I don't know anything about Ed, or anything about the situation. But who can judge anyone else's situation?"

I touched the back of Laura's hand. She gave me a quick smile. I picked up Laura's hand. It was warm, the nails polished, perfectly manicured. I encircled the broad wrist with my fingers, and I held her.

"When I left, he drank rat poison," Terri said. She clasped her arms with her hands. "They took him to the hospital in Santa Fe. That's where we lived then, about ten miles out. They saved his life. But his gums went crazy from it. I mean they pulled away from his teeth. After that, his teeth stood out like fangs. My God," Terri said. She waited a minute, then let go of her arms and picked up her glass.

"What people won't do!" Laura said.

"He's out of the action now," Mel said. "He's dead."

Mel handed me the saucer of limes. I took a section, squeezed it over my drink, and stirred the ice cubes with my finger.

"It gets worse," Terri said. "He shot himself in the mouth. But he bungled that too. Poor Ed," she said. Terri shook her head.

"Poor Ed nothing," Mel said. "He was dangerous."

Mel was forty-five years old. He was tall and rangy with curly soft hair. His face and arms were brown from the tennis he played. When he was sober, his gestures, all his movements, were precise, very careful.

"He did love me though, Mel. Grant me that," Terri said. "That's all I'm asking. He didn't love me the way you love me. I'm not saying that. But he loved me. You can grant me that, can't you?"

"What do you mean, he bungled it?" I said.

Laura leaned forward with her glass. She put her elbows on the table and held her glass in both hands. She glanced from Mel to Terri and waited with a look of bewilderment on her open face, as if amazed that such things happened to people you were friendly with.

"How'd he bungle it when he killed himself?" I said.

"I'll tell you what happened," Mel said. "He took this twenty-two pistol he'd bought to threaten Terri and me with. Oh, I'm serious, the man was always threatening. You should have seen the way we lived in those days. Like fugitives. I even bought a gun myself. Can you believe it? A guy like me? But I did. I bought one for self-defense and carried it in the glove compartment. Sometimes I'd have to leave the apartment in the middle of the night. To go to the hospital, you know? Terri and I weren't married then, and my first wife had the house and kids, the dog, everything, and Terri and I were living in this apartment here. Sometimes, as I say, I'd get a call in the middle of the night and have to go in to the hospital at two or three in the morning. It'd be dark out there in the parking lot, and I'd break into a sweat before I could even get to my car. I never knew if he was going to come up out of the shrubbery or from behind a car and start shooting. I mean, the man was crazy. He was capable of wiring a bomb, anything. He used to call my service at all hours and say he needed to talk to the doctor, and when I'd return the call, he'd say, 'Son of a bitch, your days are numbered.' Little things like that. It was scary, I'm telling you."

"I still feel sorry for him," Terri said.

"It sounds like a nightmare," Laura said. "But what exactly happened after he shot himself?"

Laura is a legal secretary. We'd met in a professional capacity. Before we knew it, it was a courtship. She's thirty-five, three years younger than I am. In addition to being in love, we like each other and enjoy one another's company. She's easy to be with.

"What happened?" Laura said.

Mel said, "He shot himself in the mouth in his room. Someone heard the shot and told the manager. They came in with a passkey, saw what had happened, and called an ambulance. I happened to be there when they brought him in, alive but past recall. The man lived for three days. His head swelled up to twice the size of a normal head. I'd never seen anything like it, and I hope I never do again. Terri wanted to go in and sit with him when she found out about it. We had a fight over it. I didn't think she should see him like that. I didn't think she should see him, and I still don't."

"Who won the fight?" Laura said.

"I was in the room with him when he died," Terri said. "He never came up out of it. But I sat with him. He didn't have anyone else."

"He was dangerous," Mel said. "If you call that love, you can have it."

"It was love," Terri said. "Sure, it's abnormal in most people's eyes. But he was willing to die for it. He did die for it."

"I sure as hell wouldn't call it love," Mel said. "I mean, no one knows what he did it for. I've seen a lot of suicides, and I couldn't say anyone ever knew what they did it for."

Mel put his hands behind his neck and tilted his chair back. "I'm not interested in that kind of love," he said. "If that's love, you can have it."

Terri said, "We were afraid. Mel even made a will out and wrote to his brother in California who used to be a Green Beret. Mel told him who to look for if something happened to him."

Terri drank from her glass. She said, "But Mel's right—we lived like fugitives. We were afraid. Mel was, weren't you, honey? I even called the police at one point, but they were no help. They said they couldn't do anything until Ed actually did something. Isn't that a laugh?" Terri said.

She poured the last of the gin into her glass and waggled the bottle. Mel got up from the table and went to the cupboard. He took down another bottle.

"Well, Nick and I know what love is," Laura said. "For us, I mean," Laura said. She bumped my knee with her knee. "You're supposed to say something now," Laura said, and turned her smile on me.

For an answer, I took Laura's hand and raised it to my lips. I made a big production out of kissing her hand. Everyone was amused.

"We're lucky," I said.

"You guys," Terri said. "Stop that now. You're making me sick. You're still on the honeymoon, for God's sake. You're still gaga, for crying out loud. Just wait. How long have you been together now? How long has it been? A year? Longer than a year?"

"Going on a year and a half," Laura said, flushed and smiling.

"Oh, now," Terri said. "Wait awhile."

She held her drink and gazed at Laura.

"I'm only kidding," Terri said.

Mel opened the gin and went around the table with the bottle.

"Here, you guys," he said. "Let's have a toast. I want to propose a toast. A toast to love. To true love," Mel said.

We touched glasses.

"To love," we said.

Outside in the backyard, one of the dogs began to bark. The leaves of the aspen that leaned past the window ticked against the glass. The afternoon sun was like a presence in this room, the spacious light of ease and generosity. We could have been anywhere, somewhere enchanted. We raised our glasses again and grinned at each other like children who had agreed on something forbidden.

"I'll tell you what real love is," Mel said. "I mean, I'll give you a good example. And then you can draw your own conclusions." He poured more gin into his glass. He added an ice cube and a sliver of lime. We waited and sipped our drinks. Laura and I touched knees again. I put a hand on her warm thigh and left it there.

"What do any of us really know about love?" Mel said. "It seems to me we're just beginners at love. We say we love each other and we do, I don't doubt it. I love Terri and Terri loves me, and you guys love each other too. You know the kind of love I'm talking about now. Physical love, that impulse that drives you to someone special, as well as love of the other person's being, his or her essence, as it were. Carnal love and, well, call it sentimental love, the day-to-day caring about the other person. But sometimes I have a hard time accounting for the fact that I must have loved my first wife too. But I did, I know I did. So I suppose I am like Terri in that regard. Terri and Ed." He thought about it and then he went on. "There was a time when I thought I loved my first wife more than life itself. But now I hate her guts. I do. How do you explain that? What happened to that love? What happened to it, is what I'd like to know. I wish someone could tell me. Then there's Ed. Okay, we're back to Ed. He loves Terri so much he tries to kill her and he winds up killing himself." Mel stopped talking and swallowed from his glass. "You guys have been together eighteen months and you love each other. It shows all over you. You glow with it. But you both loved other people before you met each other. You've both been married before, just like us. And you probably loved other people before that too, even. Terri and I have been together five years, been married for four. And the terrible thing, the terrible thing is, but the good thing too, the saving grace, you might say, is that if something happened to one of us—excuse me for saying this—but if something happened to one of us tomorrow, I think the other one, the other person, would grieve for a while, you know, but then the surviving party would go out and love again, have someone else soon enough. All this, all of this love we're talking about, it would just be a memory. Maybe not even a memory. Am I wrong? Am I way off base? Because I want you to set me straight if you think I'm wrong. I want to know. I mean, I don't know anything, and I'm the first one to admit it."

"Mel, for God's sake," Terri said. She reached out and took hold of his wrist. "Are you getting drunk? Honey? Are you drunk?"

"Honey, I'm just talking," Mel said. "All right? I don't have to be drunk to say what I think. I mean, we're all just talking, right?" Mel said. He fixed his eyes on her.

"Sweetie, I'm not criticizing," Terri said.

She picked up her glass.

"I'm not on call today," Mel said. "Let me remind you of that. I am not on call," he said.

"Mel, we love you," Laura said.

Mel looked at Laura. He looked at her as if he could not place her, as if she was not the woman she was.

"Love you too, Laura," Mel said. "And you, Nick, love you too. You know something?" Mel said. "You guys are our pals," Mel said.

He picked up his glass.

Mel said, "I was going to tell you about something. I mean, I was going to prove a point. You see, this happened a few months ago, but it's still going on right now, and it ought to make us feel ashamed when we talk like we know what we're talking about when we talk about love."

"Come on now," Terri said. "Don't talk like you're drunk if you're not drunk."

"Just shut up for once in your life," Mel said very quietly. "Will you do me a favor and do that for a minute? So as I was saying, there's this old couple who had this car wreck out on the interstate. A kid hit them and they were all torn to shit and nobody was giving them much chance to pull through."

Terri looked at us and then back at Mel. She seemed anxious, or maybe that's too strong a word.

Mel was handing the bottle around the table.

"I was on call that night," Mel said. "It was May or maybe it was June. Terri and I had just sat down to dinner when the hospital called. There'd been this thing out on the interstate. Drunk kid, teenager, plowed his dad's pickup into this camper with this old couple in it. They were up in their mid-seventies, that couple. The kid—eighteen, nineteen, something—he was DOA. Taken the steering wheel through his sternum. The old couple, they were alive, you understand. I mean, just barely. But they had everything. Multiple fractures, internal injuries, hemorrhaging, contusions, lacerations, the works, and they each of them had themselves concussions. They were in a bad way, believe me. And, of course, their age was two strikes against them. I'd say she was worse off than he was. Ruptured spleen along with everything else. Both kneecaps broken. But they'd been wearing their seatbelts and, God knows, that's what saved them for the time being."

"Folks, this is an advertisement for the National Safety Council," Terri said. "This is your spokesman, Dr. Melvin R. McGinnis, talking." Terri laughed. "Mel," she said, "sometimes you're just too much. But I love you, hon," she said.

"Honey, I love you," Mel said.

He leaned across the table. Terri met him halfway. They kissed.

"Terri's right," Mel said as he settled himself again. "Get those seatbelts on. But seriously, they were in some shape, those oldsters. By the time I got down there, the kid was dead, as I said. He was off in a corner, laid out on a gurney. I took one look at the old couple and told the ER nurse to get me a neurologist and an orthopedic man and a couple of surgeons down there right away."

He drank from his glass. "I'll try to keep this short," he said. "So we took the two of them up to the OR and worked like fuck on them most of the night. They had these incredible reserves, those two. You see that once in a while. So we did everything that could be done, and toward morning we're giving them a fifty-fifty chance, maybe less than that for her. So here they are, still alive the next morning. So, okay, we move them into the ICU, which is where they both kept plugging away at it for two weeks, hitting it better and better on all the scopes. So we transfer them out to their own room."

Mel stopped talking. "Here," he said, "let's drink this cheapo gin the hell up. Then we're going to dinner, right? Terri and I know a new place. That's where we'll go, to this new place we know about. But we're not going until we finish up this cut-rate, lousy gin."

Terri said, "We haven't actually eaten there yet. But it looks good. From the outside, you know."

"I like food," Mel said. "If I had it to do all over again, I'd be a chef, you know? Right, Terri?" Mel said.

He laughed. He fingered the ice in his glass.

"Terri knows," he said. "Terri can tell you. But let me say this. If I could come back again in a different life, a different time and all, you know what? I'd like to come back as a knight. You were pretty safe wearing all that armor. It was all right being a knight until gunpowder and muskets and pistols came along."

"Mel would like to ride a horse and carry a lance," Terri said.

"Carry a woman's scarf with you everywhere," Laura said.

"Or just a woman," Mel said.

"Shame on you," Laura said.

Terri said, "Suppose you came back as a serf. The serfs didn't have it so good in those days," Terri said.

"The serfs never had it good," Mel said. "But I guess even the knights were vessels to someone. Isn't that the way it worked? But then everyone is always a vessel to someone. Isn't that right? Terri? But what I liked about knights, besides their ladies, was that they had that suit of armor, you know, and they couldn't get hurt very easy. No cars in those days, you know? No drunk teenagers to tear into your ass."

"Vassals," Terri said.

"What?" Mel said.

"Vassals," Terri said. "They were called vassals, not vessels."

"Vassals, vessels," Mel said, "what the fuck's the difference? You knew what I meant anyway. All right," Mel said. "So I'm not educated. I learned my stuff. I'm a heart surgeon, sure, but I'm just a mechanic. I go in and I fuck around and I fix things. Shit," Mel said.

"Modesty doesn't become you," Terri said.

"He's just a humble sawbones," I said. "But sometimes they suffocated in all that armor, Mel. They'd even have heart attacks if it got too hot and they were too tired and worn out. I read somewhere that they'd fall off their horses and not be able to get up because they were too tired to stand with all that armor on them. They got trampled by their own horses sometimes."

"That's terrible," Mel said. "That's a terrible thing, Nicky. I guess they'd just lay there and wait until somebody came along and made a shish kebab out of them."

"Some other vessel," Terri said.

"That's right," Mel said. "Some vassal would come along and spear the bastard in the name of love. Or whatever the fuck it was they fought over in those days."

"Same things we fight over these days," Terri said.

Laura said, "Nothing's changed."

The color was still high in Laura's cheeks. Her eyes were bright. She brought her glass to her lips.

Mel poured himself another drink. He looked at the label closely as if studying a long row of numbers. Then he slowly put the bottle down on the table and slowly reached for the tonic water.

"What about the old couple?" Laura said. "You didn't finish that story you started."

Laura was having a hard time lighting her cigarette. Her matches kept going out.

The sunshine inside the room was different now, changing, getting thinner. But the leaves outside the window were still shimmering, and I stared at the pattern they made on the panes and on the Formica counter. They weren't the same patterns, of course.

"What about the old couple?" I said.

"Older but wiser," Terri said.

Mel stared at her.

Terri said, "Go on with your story, hon. I was only kidding. Then what happened?"

"Terri, sometimes," Mel said.

"Please, Mel," Terri said. "Don't always be so serious, sweetie. Can't you take a joke?"

"Where's the joke?" Mel said.

He held his glass and gazed steadily at his wife.

"What happened?" Laura said.

Mel fastened his eyes on Laura. He said, "Laura, if I didn't have Terri and if I didn't love her so much, and if Nick wasn't my best friend, I'd fall in love with you. I'd carry you off, honey," he said.

"Tell your story," Terri said. "Then we'll go to that new place, okay?"

"Okay," Mel said. "Where was I?" he said. He stared at the table and then he began again.

"I dropped in to see each of them every day, sometimes twice a day if I was up doing other calls anyway. Casts and bandages, head to foot, the both of them. You know, you've seen it in the movies. That's just the way they looked, just like in the movies. Little eye-holes and nose-holes and mouth-holes. And she had to have her legs slung up on top of it. Well, the husband was very depressed for the longest while. Even after he found out that his wife was going to pull through, he was still very depressed. Not about the accident, though. I mean, the accident was one thing, but it wasn't everything. I'd get up to his mouth-hole, you know, and he'd say no, it wasn't the accident exactly but it was because he couldn't see her through his eye-holes. He said that was what was making him feel so bad. Can you imagine? I'm telling you, the man's heart was breaking because he couldn't turn his goddamn head and *see* his goddamn wife."

Mel looked around the table and shook his head at what he was going to say.

"I mean, it was killing the old fart just because he couldn't *look* at the fucking woman."

We all looked at Mel.

"Do you see what I'm saying?" he said.

Maybe we were a little drunk by then. I know it was hard keeping things in focus. The light was draining out of the room, going back through the window where it had come from. Yet nobody made a move to get up from the table to turn on the overhead light.

"Listen," Mel said. "Let's finish this fucking gin. There's about enough left here for one shooter all around. Then let's go eat. Let's go to the new place."

"He's depressed," Terri said. "Mel, why don't you take a pill?"

Mel shook his head. "I've taken everything there is."

"We all need a pill now and then," I said.

"Some people are born needing them," Terri said.

She was using her finger to rub at something on the table. Then she stopped rubbing.

"I think I want to call my kids," Mel said. "Is that all right with everybody? I'll call my kids," he said.

Terri said, "What if Marjorie answers the phone? You guys, you've heard us on the subject of Marjorie? Honey, you know you don't want to talk to Marjorie. It'll make you feel even worse."

"I don't want to talk to Marjorie," Mel said. "But I want to talk to my kids."

"There isn't a day goes by that Mel doesn't say he wishes she'd get married again. Or else die," Terri said. "For one thing," Terri said, "she's bankrupting us. Mel says it's just to spite him that she won't get married again. She has a boyfriend who lives with her and the kids, so Mel is supporting the boyfriend too."

"She's allergic to bees," Mel said. "If I'm not praying she'll get married again, I'm praying she'll get herself stung to death by a swarm of fucking bees."

"Shame on you," Laura said.

"Bzzzzzzz," Mel said, turning his fingers into bees and buzzing them at Terri's throat. Then he let his hands drop all the way to his sides.

"She's vicious," Mel said. "Sometimes I think I'll go up there dressed like a bee-keeper. You know, that hat that's like a helmet with the plate that comes down over your face, the big gloves, and the padded coat? I'll knock on the door and let loose a hive of bees in the house. But first I'd make sure the kids were out, of course."

He crossed one leg over the other. It seemed to take him a lot of time to do it. Then he put both feet on the floor and leaned forward, elbows on the table, his chin cupped in his hands.

"Maybe I won't call the kids, after all. Maybe it isn't such a hot idea. Maybe we'll just go eat. How does that sound?"

"Sounds fine to me," I said. "Eat or not eat. Or keep drinking. I could head right on out into the sunset."

"What does that mean, honey?" Laura said.

"It just means what I said," I said. "It means I could just keep going. That's all it means."

"I could eat something myself," Laura said. "I don't think I've ever been so hungry in my life. Is there something to nibble on?"

"I'll put out some cheese and crackers," Terri said.

But Terri just sat there. She did not get up to get anything.

Mel turned his glass over. He spilled it out on the table.

"Gin's gone," Mel said.

Terri said, "Now what?"

I could hear my heart beating. I could hear everyone's heart. I could hear the human noise we sat there making, not one of us moving, not even when the room went dark.

1981

Bobbie Ann Mason
b. 1940

Of earlier southern writers, such as William Faulkner and Allen Tate, Bobbie Ann Mason says simply that they possessed "a romantic vision." Her own work she describes as "southern Gothic going to the supermarket." The landscape of her fiction, usually rural Kentucky fast being overtaken by urban culture, is dotted with supermarkets, discount stores, video arcades, and vocational training centers. Her characters watch Phil Donahue and Johnny Carson on television; they take up weight training, make zucchini bread, and buy *The Sixties Songbook*. Or they drive trucks, eat "poke salet," and listen to Hank Williams. Caught between the country and the city, they constantly feel, she says, a "tension between their rural traditional past and the modern world." Like the woman who buys *The Sixties Songbook* ten years too late, they often find themselves struggling not to get any further behind.

Mason attributes her own and other contemporary writers' use of popular culture to cultural changes that come so rapidly that "it seems necessary to get a fix on a certain moment—or it may be different by tomorrow." Through a strange blend of colloquialisms and more formal diction, she reflects in the language of her fiction the same cultural gap that she renders in its action.

Reared on a dairy farm in western Kentucky, Mason was encouraged by her parents, neither of whom had finished high school, to continue her education. Unlike most of her friends, she went to high school in the "city"—Mayfield, Kentucky, population 10,725. She is, she now feels, "haunted by the kids I went to grade school with." After high school she went to the University of Kentucky, where she majored in journalism, and then to New York, where she experienced a culture shock so great that it temporarily turned her from a writing career to graduate school.

After receiving an M.A. from the State University of New York at Binghamton and a Ph.D. from the University of Connecticut, Mason became a professor at Mansfield State College (1972–1979). In 1974 she published a study of Vladimir Nabokov's novel *Ada* called *Nabokov's Garden: A Nature Guide to "Ada,"* and in 1975 she published an analysis of fiction especially designed for girls called *The Girl Sleuth: A Feminist Guide to the Bobbsey Twins, Nancy Drew, and Their Sisters*. But it was the writing of fiction that more and more engaged her. In 1980 she published her first story, "Offerings," in *The New Yorker*. Two years later a collection of her stories, *Shiloh and Other Stories*, won the Ernest Hemingway Award for the year's most distinguished first work of fiction and was nominated for the National Book Critics Circle Award. Having received a grant from the National Endowment for the Arts, Mason began work on a novel, *In Country* (1985). Since then she has published a second collection of stories, *Love Life* (1989), several novels, *Spence & Lila* (1988), *Feather Crowns* (1993), and *Christie Couldn't Explain the Queer Lightsomeness Inside Her* (1993).

Out of anonymity, Mason has emerged, according to the writer Anne Tyler and others, as a recognized master of the short story, a sudden transformation that Mason says has left her "absolutely *stunned.*" In "Nancy Culpepper," her own favorite among her stories, the protagonist's mother says, "I guess you think we're just ignorant. The way we talk." "No," Nancy says, "I don't." Like Nancy Culpepper, Mason clearly respects the people she remembers and writes about, perhaps in part because she shares a feeling of kinship with them. "I write," she says, "about people in trapped circumstances. . . . I identify with people who are ambivalent about their situation. And I guess, in my stories, I'm in a way imagining myself as I would have felt if I had not gotten away and gotten a different perspective on things—if, for example, I had gotten pregnant in high school and had to marry a truck driver as the woman did in my story 'Shiloh.' " In her best fiction, Mason offers us not only different perspectives but also new ways of imagining ourselves.

Further Reading:

S. B. Durham, "Women and War: Bobbie Ann Mason's 'In Country,' " *The Southern Literary Journal* 22:2 (1990), 45–53.

D. Booth, "Sam's Quest, Emmett's Wound: Grail Motifs in Bobbie Ann Mason's Portrait of America after Vietnam," *The Southern Literary Journal* 23:2 (1991), 98–110.

S. Lohafer, "Stops on the Way to 'Shiloh': A Special Case for Literary Empiricism," *Style* 27:3 (1993), 395–407.

Y. Krasteva, "The South and the West in Bobbie Ann Mason's 'In Country,' " *The Southern Literary Journal,* 26:2(1994), 77–91.

Text:
Shiloh and Other Stories, 1982.

Shiloh

Leroy Moffitt's wife, Norma Jean, is working on her pectorals. She lifts three-pound dumbbells to warm up, then progresses to a twenty-pound barbell. Standing with her legs apart, she reminds Leroy of Wonder Woman.

"I'd give anything if I could just get these muscles to where they're real hard," says Norma Jean. "Feel this arm. It's not as hard as the other one."

"That's 'cause you're right-handed," says Leroy, dodging as she swings the barbell in an arc.

"Do you think so?"

"Sure."

Leroy is a truckdriver. He injured his leg in a highway accident four months ago, and his physical therapy, which involves weights and a pulley, prompted Norma Jean to try building herself up. Now she is attending a body-building class. Leroy has been collecting temporary disability since his tractor-trailer jackknifed in Missouri, badly twisting his left leg in its socket. He has a steel pin in his hip. He will probably not be able to drive his rig again. It sits in the backyard, like a gigantic bird that has flown home to roost. Leroy has been home in Kentucky for three months, and his leg is almost healed, but the accident frightened him and he does not want to drive any more long hauls. He is not sure what to do next. In the meantime, he makes things from craft kits. He started by building a miniature log cabin from notched Popsicle sticks. He varnished it and placed it on the TV set, where it remains. It reminds him of a rustic Nativity scene. Then he tried string art (sailing ships on black velvet), a macramé owl kit, a snap-together B-17 Flying Fortress, and a lamp made out of a model truck, with a light fixture screwed in the top of the cab. At first the kits were diversions, something to kill time, but now he is thinking about building a full-scale log house from a kit. It would be considerably cheaper than building a regular house, and besides, Leroy has grown to appreciate how things are put together. He has begun to realize that in all the years he was on the road he never took time to examine anything. He was always flying past scenery.

"They won't let you build a log cabin in any of the new subdivisions," Norma Jean tells him.

"They will if I tell them it's for you," he says, teasing her. Ever since they were married, he has promised Norma Jean he would build her a new home one day. They have always rented, and the house they live in is small and nondescript. It does not even feel like a home, Leroy realizes now.

Norma Jean works at the Rexall drugstore, and she has acquired an amazing amount of information about cosmetics. When she explains to Leroy the three stages of complexion care, involving creams, toners, and moisturizers, he thinks happily of other petroleum products—axle grease, diesel fuel. This is a connection between him and Norma Jean. Since he has been home, he has felt unusually tender about his wife and guilty over his long absences. But he can't tell what she feels about him. Norma Jean has never complained about his traveling; she has never made hurt remarks, like calling his truck a "widow-maker." He is reasonably certain she has been faithful to him, but he wishes she would celebrate his permanent homecoming more happily. Norma Jean is often startled to find Leroy at home, and he thinks she seems a little disappointed about it. Perhaps he reminds her too much of the early days of their marriage, before he went on the road. They had a child who died as an infant, years ago. They never speak about their memories of Randy, which have almost faded, but now that Leroy is home all the time, they sometimes feel awkward around each other, and Leroy wonders if one of them should mention the child. He has the feeling that they are waking up out of a dream together—that they must create a new marriage, start afresh. They are lucky they are still married. Leroy has read that for most people losing a child destroys the marriage—or else he heard this on *Donahue*. He can't always remember where he learns things anymore.

At Christmas, Leroy bought an electric organ for Norma Jean. She used to play the piano when she was in high school. "It don't leave you," she told him once. "It's like riding a bicycle."

The new instrument had so many keys and buttons that she was bewildered by it at first. She touched the keys tentatively, pushed some buttons, then pecked out "Chopsticks." It came out in an amplified fox-trot rhythm, with marimba sounds.

"It's an orchestra!" she cried.

The organ had a pecan-look finish and eighteen preset chords, with optional flute, violin, trumpet, clarinet, and banjo accompaniments. Norma Jean mastered the organ almost immediately. At first she played Christmas songs. Then she bought *The Sixties Songbook* and learned every tune in it, adding variations to each with the rows of brightly colored buttons.

"I didn't like these old songs back then," she said. "But I have this crazy feeling I missed something."

"You didn't miss a thing," said Leroy.

Leroy likes to lie on the couch and smoke a joint and listen to Norma Jean play "Can't Take My Eyes Off You" and "I'll Be Back." He is back again. After fifteen years on the road, he is finally settling down with the woman he loves. She is still pretty. Her skin is flawless. Her frosted curls resemble pencil trimmings.

Now that Leroy has come home to stay, he notices how much the town has changed. Subdivisions are spreading across western Kentucky like an oil slick. The sign at the edge of town says "Pop: 11,500"—only seven hundred more than it said twenty years before. Leroy can't figure out who is living in all the new houses. The farmers who used to gather around the courthouse square on Saturday afternoons to play checkers and spit tobacco juice have gone. It has been years since Leroy has thought about the farmers, and they have disappeared without his noticing.

Leroy meets a kid named Stevie Hamilton in the parking lot at the new shopping center. While they pretend to be strangers meeting over a stalled car, Stevie tosses an ounce of marijuana under the front seat of Leroy's car. Stevie is wearing orange jogging shoes and a T-shirt that says CHATTAHOOCHEE SUPER-RAT. His father is a prominent doctor who lives in one of the expensive subdivisions in a new white-columned brick house that looks like a funeral parlor. In the phone book under his name there is a separate number, with the listing "Teenagers."

"Where do you get this stuff?" asks Leroy. "From your pappy?"

"That's for me to know and you to find out," Stevie says. He is slit-eyed and skinny.

"What else you got?"

"What you interested in?"

"Nothing special. Just wondered."

Leroy used to take speed on the road. Now he has to go slowly. He needs to be mellow. He leans back against the car and says, "I'm aiming to build me a log house, soon as I get time. My wife, though, I don't think she likes the idea."

"Well, let me know when you want me again," Stevie says. He has a cigarette in his cupped palm, as though sheltering it from the wind. He takes a long drag, then stomps it on the asphalt and slouches away.

Stevie's father was two years ahead of Leroy in high school. Leroy is thirty-four. He married Norma Jean when they were both eighteen, and their child Randy was born a few months later, but he died at the age of four months and three days. He would be about Stevie's age now. Norma Jean and Leroy were at the drive-in, watching a double feature (*Dr. Strangelove* and *Lover Come Back*), and the baby was sleeping in the back seat. When the first movie ended, the baby was dead. It was the sudden infant death syndrome. Leroy remembers handing Randy to a nurse at the emergency room, as though he were offering her a large doll as a present. A dead baby feels like a sack of flour. "It just happens sometimes," said the doctor, in what Leroy always recalls as a nonchalant tone. Leroy can hardly remember the child anymore, but he still sees vividly a scene from *Dr. Strangelove* in which the President of the United States was talking in a folksy voice on the hot line to the Soviet premier about the bomber accidentally headed toward Russia. He was in the War Room, and the world map was lit up. Leroy remembers Norma Jean standing catatonically beside him in the hospital and himself thinking: Who is this strange girl? He had forgotten who she was. Now scientists are saying that crib death is caused by a virus. Nobody knows anything, Leroy thinks. The answers are always changing.

When Leroy gets home from the shopping center, Norma Jean's mother, Mabel Beasley, is there. Until this year, Leroy has not realized how much time she spends with Norma Jean. When she visits, she inspects the closets and then the plants, informing Norma Jean when a plant is droopy or yellow. Mabel calls the plants "flowers," although there are never any blooms. She always notices if Norma Jean's laundry is piling up. Mabel is a short, overweight woman whose tight, brown-dyed curls look more like a wig than the actual wig she sometimes wears. Today she has brought Norma Jean an off-white dust ruffle she made for the bed; Mabel works in a custom-upholstery shop.

"This is the tenth one I made this year," Mabel says. "I got started and couldn't stop."

"It's real pretty," says Norma Jean.

"Now we can hide things under the bed," says Leroy, who gets along with his mother-in-law primarily by joking with her. Mabel has never really forgiven him for disgracing her by getting Norma Jean pregnant. When the baby died, she said that fate was mocking her.

"What's that thing?" Mabel says to Leroy in a loud voice, pointing to a tangle of yarn on a piece of canvas.

Leroy holds it up for Mabel to see. "It's my needlepoint," he explains. "This is a *Star Trek* pillow cover."

"That's what a woman would do," says Mabel. "Great day in the morning!"

"All the big football players on TV do it," he says.

"Why, Leroy, you're always trying to fool me. I don't believe you for one minute. You don't know what to do with yourself—that's the whole trouble. Sewing!"

"I'm aiming to build us a log house," says Leroy. "Soon as my plans come."

"Like *heck* you are," says Norma Jean. She takes Leroy's needlepoint and shoves it into a drawer. "You have to find a job first. Nobody can afford to build now anyway."

Mabel straightens her girdle and says, "I still think before you get tied down y'all ought to take a little run to Shiloh."

"One of these days, Mama," Norma Jean says impatiently.

Mabel is talking about Shiloh, Tennessee. For the past few years, she has been urging Leroy and Norma Jean to visit the Civil War battleground there. Mabel went there on her honeymoon—the only real trip she ever took. Her husband died of a perforated ulcer when Norma Jean was ten, but Mabel, who was accepted into the United Daughters of the Confederacy in 1975, is still preoccupied with going back to Shiloh.

"I've been to kingdom come and back in that truck out yonder," Leroy says to Mabel, "but we never yet set foot in that battleground. Ain't that something? How did I miss it?"

"It's not even that far," Mabel says.

After Mabel leaves, Norma Jean reads to Leroy from a list she has made. "Things you could do," she announces. "You could get a job as a guard at Union Carbide, where they'd let you set on a stool. You could get on at the lumberyard. You could do a little carpenter work, if you want to build so bad. You could—"

"I can't do something where I'd have to stand up all day."

"You ought to try standing up all day behind a cosmetics counter. It's amazing that I have strong feet, coming from two parents that never had strong feet at all." At the moment Norma Jean is holding on to the kitchen counter, raising her knees one at a time as she talks. She is wearing two-pound ankle weights.

"Don't worry," says Leroy. "I'll do something."

"You could truck calves to slaughter for somebody. You wouldn't have to drive any big old truck for that."

"I'm going to build you this house," says Leroy. "I want to make you a real home."

"I don't want to live in any log cabin."

"It's not a cabin. It's a house."

"I don't care. It looks like a cabin."

"You and me together could lift those logs. It's just like lifting weights."

Norma Jean doesn't answer. Under her breath, she is counting. Now she is marching through the kitchen. She is doing goose steps.

Before his accident, when Leroy came home he used to stay in the house with Norma Jean, watching TV in bed and playing cards. She would cook fried chicken, picnic ham, chocolate pie—all his favorites. Now he is home alone much of the time. In the mornings, Norma Jean disappears, leaving a cooling place in the bed. She eats a cereal called Body Buddies, and she leaves the bowl on the table, with the soggy tan balls floating in a milk puddle. He sees things about Norma Jean that he never realized before. When she chops onions, she stares off into a corner, as if she can't bear to look. She puts on her house slippers almost precisely at nine o'clock every evening and nudges her jogging shoes under the couch. She saves bread heels for the birds. Leroy watches the birds at the feeder. He notices the peculiar way goldfinches fly past the window. They close their wings, then fall, then spread their wings to catch and lift themselves. He wonders if they close their eyes when they fall. Norma Jean closes her eyes when they are in bed. She wants the lights turned out. Even then, he is sure she closes her eyes.

He goes for long drives around town. He tends to drive a car rather carelessly. Power steering and an automatic shift make a car feel so small and inconsequential that his body is hardly involved in the driving process. His injured leg stretches out comfortably. Once or twice he has almost hit something, but even the prospect of an accident seems minor in a car. He cruises the new subdivisions, feeling like a criminal rehearsing for a robbery. Norma Jean is probably right about a log house being inappropriate here in the new subdivisions. All the houses look grand and complicated. They depress him.

One day when Leroy comes home from a drive he finds Norma Jean in tears. She is in the kitchen making a potato and mushroom-soup casserole, with grated-cheese topping. She is crying because her mother caught her smoking.

"I didn't hear her coming. I was standing here puffing away pretty as you please," Norma Jean says, wiping her eyes.

"I knew it would happen sooner or later," says Leroy, putting his arm around her.

"She don't know the meaning of the word 'knock,' " says Norma Jean. "It's a wonder she hadn't caught me years ago."

"Think of it this way," Leroy says. "What if she caught me with a joint?"

"You better not let her!" Norma Jean shrieks. "I'm warning you, Leroy Moffitt!"

"I'm just kidding. Here, play me a tune. That'll help you relax."

Norma Jean puts the casserole in the oven and sets the timer. Then she plays a rag-time tune, with horns and banjo, as Leroy lights up a joint and lies on the couch, laughing to himself about Mabel's catching him at it. He thinks of Stevie Hamilton—a doctor's son pushing grass. Everything is funny. The whole town seems crazy and small. He is reminded of Virgil Mathis, a boastful policeman Leroy used to shoot pool with. Virgil recently led a drug bust in a back room at a bowling alley, where he seized ten thousand dollars' worth of marijuana. The newspaper had a picture of him holding up the bags of grass and grinning widely. Right now, Leroy can imagine Virgil breaking down the door and arresting him with a lungful of smoke. Virgil would probably have been alerted to the scene because of all the racket Norma Jean is making. Now she sounds like a hard-rock band. Norma Jean is terrific. When she switches to a Latin-rhythm version of "Sunshine Superman," Leroy hums along. Norma Jean's foot goes up and down, up and down.

"Well, what do you think?" Leroy says, when Norma Jean pauses to search through her music.

"What do I think about what?"

His mind has gone blank. Then he says, "I'll sell my rig and build us a house." That wasn't what he wanted to say. He wanted to know what she thought—what she *really* thought—about them.

"Don't start in on that again," says Norma Jean. She begins playing "Who'll Be the Next in Line?"

Leroy used to tell hitchhikers his whole life story—about his travels, his hometown, the baby. He would end with a question: "Well, what do you think?" It was just a rhetorical question. In time, he had the feeling that he'd been telling the same story over and over to the same hitchhikers. He quit talking to hitchhikers when he realized how his voice sounded—whining and self-pitying, like some teenage-tragedy song. Now Leroy has the sudden impulse to tell Norma Jean about himself, as if he had just met her. They have known each other so long they have forgotten a lot about each other. They could become reacquainted. But when the oven timer goes off and she runs to the kitchen, he forgets why he wants to do this.

The next day, Mabel drops by. It is Saturday and Norma Jean is cleaning. Leroy is studying the plans of his log house, which have finally come in the mail. He has them spread out on the table—big sheets of stiff blue paper, with diagrams and numbers printed in white. While Norma Jean runs the vacuum, Mabel drinks coffee. She sets her coffee cup on a blueprint.

"I'm just waiting for time to pass," she says to Leroy, drumming her fingers on the table.

As soon as Norma Jean switches off the vacuum, Mabel says in a loud voice, "Did you hear about the datsun dog that killed the baby?"

Norma Jean says, "The word is 'dachshund.' "

"They put the dog on trial. It chewed the baby's legs off. The mother was in the next room all the time." She raises her voice. "They thought it was neglect."

Norma Jean is holding her ears. Leroy manages to open the refrigerator and get some Diet Pepsi to offer Mabel. Mabel still has some coffee and she waves away the Pepsi.

"Datsuns are like that," Mabel says. "They're jealous dogs. They'll tear a place to pieces if you don't keep an eye on them."

"You better watch out what you're saying, Mabel," says Leroy.

"Well, facts is facts."

Leroy looks out the window at his rig. It is like a huge piece of furniture gathering dust in the backyard. Pretty soon it will be an antique. He hears the vacuum cleaner. Norma Jean seems to be cleaning the living room rug again.

Later, she says to Leroy, "She just said that about the baby because she caught me smoking. She's trying to pay me back."

"What are you talking about?" Leroy says, nervously shuffling blueprints.

"You know good and well," Norma Jean says. She is sitting in a kitchen chair with her feet up and her arms wrapped around her knees. She looks small and helpless. She says, "The very idea, her bringing up a subject like that! Saying it was neglect."

"She didn't mean that," Leroy says.

"She might not have *thought* she meant it. She always says things like that. You don't know how she goes on."

"But she didn't really mean it. She was just talking."

Leroy opens a king-sized bottle of beer and pours it into two glasses, dividing it carefully. He hands a glass to Norma Jean and she takes it from him mechanically. For a long time, they sit by the kitchen window watching the birds at the feeder.

Something is happening. Norma Jean is going to night school. She has graduated from her six-week body-building course and now she is taking an adult-education course in composition at Paducah Community College. She spends her evenings outlining paragraphs.

"First you have a topic sentence," she explains to Leroy. "Then you divide it up. Your secondary topic has to be connected to your primary topic."

To Leroy, this sounds intimidating. "I never was any good in English," he says.

"It makes a lot of sense."

"What are you doing this for, anyhow?"

She shrugs. "It's something to do." She stands up and lifts her dumbbells a few times.

"Driving a rig, nobody cared about my English."

"I'm not criticizing your English."

Norma Jean used to say, "If I lose ten minutes' sleep, I just drag all day." Now she stays up late, writing compositions. She got a B on her first paper—a how-to theme on soup-based casseroles. Recently Norma Jean has been cooking unusual foods—tacos, lasagna, Bombay chicken. She doesn't play the organ anymore, though her second paper was called "Why Music Is Important to Me." She sits at the kitchen table, concentrating on her outlines, while Leroy plays with his log house plans, practicing with a set of Lincoln Logs. The thought of getting a truckload of notched, numbered logs scares him, and he wants to be prepared. As he and Norma Jean work together at the kitchen table, Leroy has the hopeful thought that they are sharing something, but he knows he is a fool to think this. Norma Jean is miles away. He knows he is going to lose her. Like Mabel, he is just waiting for time to pass.

One day, Mabel is there before Norma Jean gets home from work, and Leroy finds himself confiding in her. Mabel, he realizes, must know Norma Jean better than he does.

"I don't know what's got into that girl," Mabel says. "She used to go to bed with the chickens. Now you say she's up all hours. Plus her a-smoking. I like to died."

"I want to make her this beautiful home," Leroy says, indicating the Lincoln Logs. "I don't think she even wants it. Maybe she was happier with me gone."

"She don't know what to make of you, coming home like this."

"Is that it?"

Mabel takes the roof off his Lincoln Log cabin. "You couldn't get *me* in a log cabin," she says. "I was raised in one. It's no picnic, let me tell you."

"They're different now," says Leroy.

"I tell you what," Mabel says, smiling oddly at Leroy.

"What?"

"Take her on down to Shiloh. Y'all need to get out together, stir a little. Her brain's all balled up over them books."

Leroy can see traces of Norma Jean's features in her mother's face. Mabel's worn face has the texture of crinkled cotton, but suddenly she looks pretty. It occurs to Leroy that Mabel has been hinting all along that she wants them to take her with them to Shiloh.

"Let's all go to Shiloh," he says. "You and me and her. Come Sunday."

Mabel throws up her hands in protest. "Oh, no, not me. Young folks want to be by theirselves."

When Norma Jean comes in with groceries, Leroy says excitedly, "Your mama here's been dying to go to Shiloh for thirty-five years. It's about time we went, don't you think?"

"I'm not going to butt in on anybody's second honeymoon," Mabel says.

"Who's going on a honeymoon, for Christ's sake?" Norma Jean says loudly.

"I never raised no daughter of mine to talk that-a-way," Mabel says.

"You ain't seen nothing yet," says Norma Jean. She starts putting away boxes and cans, slamming cabinet doors.

"There's a log cabin at Shiloh," Mabel says. "It was there during the battle. There's bullet holes in it."

"When are you going to *shut up* about Shiloh, Mama?" asks Norma Jean.

"I always thought Shiloh was the prettiest place, so full of history," Mabel goes on. "I just hoped y'all could see it once before I die, so you could tell me about it." Later, she whispers to Leroy, "You do what I said. A little change is what she needs."

"Your name means 'the king,'" Norma Jean says to Leroy that evening. He is trying to get her to go to Shiloh, and she is reading a book about another century.

"Well, I reckon I ought to be right proud."

"I guess so."

"Am I still king around here?"

Norma Jean flexes her biceps and feels them for hardness. "I'm not fooling around with anybody, if that's what you mean," she says.

"Would you tell me if you were?"

"I don't know."

"What does *your* name mean?"

"It was Marilyn Monroe's real name."

"No kidding!"

"Norma comes from the Normans. They were invaders," she says. She closes her book and looks hard at Leroy. "I'll go to Shiloh with you if you'll stop staring at me."

On Sunday, Norma Jean packs a picnic and they go to Shiloh. To Leroy's relief, Mabel says she does not want to come with them. Norma Jean drives, and Leroy, sitting beside her, feels like some boring hitchhiker she has picked up. He tries some conversation, but she answers him in monosyllables. At Shiloh, she drives aimlessly through the park, past bluffs and trails and steep ravines. Shiloh is an immense place, and Leroy cannot see it as a battleground. It is not what he expected. He thought it would look like a golf course. Monuments are everywhere, showing through the thick clusters of trees. Norma Jean passes the log cabin Mabel mentioned. It is surrounded by tourists looking for bullet holes.

"That's not the kind of log house I've got in mind," says Leroy apologetically.

"I know *that*."

"This is a pretty place. Your mama was right."

"It's O.K.," says Norma Jean. "Well, we've seen it. I hope she's satisfied."

They burst out laughing together.

At the park museum, a movie on Shiloh is shown every half hour, but they decide that they don't want to see it. They buy a souvenir Confederate flag for Mabel, and then they find a picnic spot near the cemetery. Norma Jean has brought a picnic cooler, with pimiento sandwiches, soft drinks, and Yodels. Leroy eats a sandwich and then smokes a joint, hiding it behind the picnic cooler. Norma Jean has quit smoking altogether. She is picking cake crumbs from the cellophane wrapper, like a fussy bird.

Leroy says, "So the boys in gray ended up in Corinth. The Union soldiers zapped 'em finally. April 7, 1862."

They both know that he doesn't know any history. He is just talking about some of the historical plaques they have read. He feels awkward, like a boy on a date with an older girl. They are still just making conversation.

"Corinth is where Mama eloped to," says Norma Jean.

They sit in silence and stare at the cemetery for the Union dead and, beyond, at a tall cluster of trees. Campers are parked nearby, bumper to bumper, and small children in bright clothing are cavorting and squealing. Norma Jean wads up the cake wrapper and squeezes it tightly in her hand. Without looking at Leroy, she says, "I want to leave you."

Leroy takes a bottle of Coke out of the cooler and flips off the cap. He holds the bottle poised near his mouth but cannot remember to take a drink. Finally he says, "No, you don't."

"Yes, I do."

"I won't let you."

"You can't stop me."

"Don't do me that way."

Leroy knows Norma Jean will have her own way. "Didn't I promise to be home from now on?" he says.

"In some ways, a woman prefers a man who wanders," says Norma Jean. "That sounds crazy, I know."

"You're not crazy."

Leroy remembers to drink from his Coke. Then he says, "Yes, you *are* crazy. You and me could start all over again. Right back at the beginning."

"We *have* started all over again," says Norma Jean. "And this is how it turned out."

"What did I do wrong?"

"Nothing."

"Is this one of those women's lib things?" Leroy asks.

"Don't be funny."

The cemetery, a green slope dotted with white markers, looks like a subdivision site. Leroy is trying to comprehend that his marriage is breaking up, but for some reason he is wondering about white slabs in a graveyard.

"Everything was fine till Mama caught me smoking," says Norma Jean, standing up. "That set something off."

"What are you talking about?"

"She won't leave me alone—*you* won't leave me alone." Norma Jean seems to be crying, but she is looking away from him. "I feel eighteen again. I can't face that all over again." She starts walking away. "No, it *wasn't* fine. I don't know what I'm saying. Forget it."

Leroy takes a lungful of smoke and closes his eyes as Norma Jean's words sink in. He tries to focus on the fact that thirty-five hundred soldiers died on the grounds around him. He can only think of that war as a board game with plastic soldiers. Leroy almost smiles, as he compares the Confederates' daring attack on the Union camps and Virgil Mathis's raid on the bowling alley. General Grant, drunk and furious, shoved the Southerners back to Corinth, where Mabel and Jet Beasley were married years later, when Mabel was still thin and good-looking. The next day, Mabel and Jet visited the battleground, and then Norma Jean was born, and then she married Leroy and they had a baby, which they lost, and now Leroy and Norma Jean are here at the same battleground. Leroy knows he is leaving out a lot. He is leaving out the insides of history. History was always just names and dates to him. It occurs to him that building a house out of logs is similarly empty—too simple. And the real inner workings of a marriage, like most of history, have escaped him. Now he sees that building a log house is the dumbest idea he could have had. It was clumsy of him to think Norma Jean would want a log house. It was a crazy idea. He'll have to think of something else, quickly. He will wad the blueprints into tight balls and fling them into the lake. Then he'll get moving again. He opens his eyes. Norma Jean has moved away and is walking through the cemetery, following a serpentine brick path.

Leroy gets up to follow his wife, but his good leg is asleep and his bad leg still hurts him. Norma Jean is far away, walking rapidly toward the bluff by the river, and he tries to hobble toward her. Some children run past him, screaming noisily. Norma Jean has reached the bluff, and she is looking out over the Tennessee River. Now she turns toward Leroy and waves her arms. Is she beckoning to him? She seems to be doing an exercise for her chest muscles. The sky is unusually pale—the color of the dust ruffle Mabel made for their bed.

1982

Maxine Hong Kingston
b. 1940

"When I write most deeply, fly the highest, reach the furthest, I write like a diarist," asserts Maxine Hong Kingston, as though to remind us that writing begins for her as a private act. "My audience is myself," she says. "I dare to write anything because I can burn my papers at any moment." Using her own life and the lives of her family, Kingston addresses not the experience of being Chinese in America but the experience of being a Chinese American. Her work demands an understanding of three cultures— American, Chinese, and Chinese American. "Some readers," she says, "will just have to do some background reading." At the same time, she continues to believe both in "the timelessness and universality of individual vision" and in the "miracle" of being understood. Of *The Woman Warrior* (1976), from which "No Name Woman" is taken, she says that it is not merely "a family book or an American book or a woman's book but a world book, and, at the same moment, my book."

Born in Stockton, California, on October 27, 1940, Maxine Hong Kingston is a first-generation American. She received a B.A. from the University of California at Berkeley in 1962 and has taught at various high schools in California and Hawaii. From 1970 to 1977 she was on the faculty of the Mid-Pacific Institute in Honolulu, and she currently teaches in the Department of English at the University of California, Berkeley. Meanwhile, her writing has met with consistent critical acclaim. Her first book, *The Woman Warrior: Memoirs of a Girlhood Among Ghosts,* won the National Book Critics Circle Award for nonfiction; her second, *China Men* (1980), won the 1981 American Book Award. Her novel, *Tripmaster Monkey: His Fake Book* was published in 1989. Her short stories, articles, and poems have appeared in such publications as *The New Yorker, New West, Ms.,* and *American Heritage.* Kingston has also received a *Mademoiselle* award (1977), an NEA writing fellowship (1980), and a Guggenheim fellowship (1981).

Given the autobiographical focus of Kingston's fiction, it is fitting that one of her major concerns revolves around the relation between fiction and nonfiction. "My characters are story tellers," she says, "and I suspect that some of them are telling me fiction. So when I write their lives down is it fiction or nonfiction?" The answer, she believes, lies in perspective. Rather than depend solely on verifiable "facts," she also explores impressions, emotions, and interpretations, both her own and those of her characters. At the same time, she carefully delineates the sources on which she has drawn so that her readers can in turn devise interpretations of their own. "When I tell . . . all these versions," she says, "I'm actually giving the culture of these people in a very accurate way. You can see where the people make up these fictions about themselves, and it's not just for fun. It's a terrible necessity." Writing of herself and the mixed world that forms a backdrop for her experiences, Kingston creates a truth that transcends literary and ethnic categories and is as beautiful as it is necessary. Kingston's latest novel is *Tripmaster Monkey: His Fake Book* (1989).

Further Reading:

K. Cheung, *Articulate Silences: Hisaye Yamamoto, Maxine Hong Kingston, Joy Kogawa*, 1993.

M. Wogowitsch, *Narrative Strategies and Multicultural Identity: Maxine Hong Kingston in Context*, 1995.

Y. Gao, *The Art of Parody: Maxine Hong Kingston's Use of Chinese Sources*, 1996.

Text:

The Woman Warrior: Memoirs of a Girlhood Among Ghosts, 1976.

---

from The Woman Warrior

No Name Woman

"You must not tell anyone," my mother said, "what I am about to tell you. In China your father had a sister who killed herself. She jumped into the family well. We say that your father has all brothers because it is as if she had never been born.

"In 1924 just a few days after our village celebrated seventeen hurry-up weddings—to make sure that every young man who went 'out on the road' would responsibly come home—your father and his brothers and your grandfather and his brothers and your aunt's new husband sailed for America, the Gold Mountain. It was your grandfather's last trip. Those lucky enough to get contracts waved goodbye from the decks. They fed and guarded the stowaways and helped them off in Cuba, New York, Bali, Hawaii. 'We'll meet in California next year,' they said. All of them sent money home.

"I remember looking at your aunt one day when she and I were dressing; I had not noticed before that she had such a protruding melon of a stomach. But I did not think, 'She's pregnant,' until she began to look like other pregnant women, her shirt pulling and the white tops of her black pants showing. She could not have been pregnant, you see, because her husband had been gone for years. No one said anything. We did not discuss it. In early summer she was ready to have the child, long after the time when it could have been possible.

"The village had also been counting. On the night the baby was to be born the villagers raided our house. Some were crying. Like a great saw, teeth strung with lights, files of people walked zigzag across our land, tearing the rice. Their lanterns doubled in the disturbed black water, which drained away through the broken bunds. As the villagers closed in, we could see that some of them, probably men and women we knew well, wore white masks. The people with long hair hung it over their faces. Women with short hair made it stand up on end. Some had tied white bands around their foreheads, arms, and legs.

"At first they threw mud and rocks at the house. Then they threw eggs and began slaughtering our stock. We could hear the animals scream their deaths—the roosters, the pigs, a last great roar from the ox. Familiar wild heads flared in our night windows; the villagers encircled us. Some of the faces stopped to peer at us, their eyes rushing like searchlights. The hands flattened against the panes, framed heads, and left red prints.

"The villagers broke in the front and the back doors at the same time, even though we had not locked the doors against them. Their knives dripped with the blood of our animals. They smeared blood on the doors and walls. One woman swung a chicken, whose throat she had slit, splattering blood in red arcs about her. We stood together in the middle of our house, in the family hall with the pictures and tables of the ancestors around us, and looked straight ahead.

"At that time the house had only two wings. When the men came back, we would build two more to enclose our courtyard and a third one to begin a second courtyard. The villagers pushed through both wings, even your grandparents' rooms, to find your aunt's, which was also mine until the men returned. From this room a new wing for one of the younger families would grow. They ripped up her clothes and shoes and broke her combs, grinding them underfoot. They tore her work from the loom. They scattered the cooking fire and rolled the new weaving in it. We could hear them in the kitchen breaking our bowls and banging the pots. They overturned the great waist-high earthenware jugs; duck eggs, pickled fruits, vegetables burst out and mixed in acrid torrents. The old woman from the next field swept a broom through the air and loosed the spirits-of-the-broom over our heads. 'Pig.' 'Ghost.' 'Pig,' they sobbed and scolded while they ruined our house.

"When they left, they took sugar and oranges to bless themselves. They cut pieces from the dead animals. Some of them took bowls that were not broken and clothes that were not torn. Afterward we swept up the rice and sewed it back up into sacks. But the smells from the spilled preserves lasted. Your aunt gave birth in the pigsty that night. The next morning when I went for the water, I found her and the baby plugging up the family well.

"Don't let your father know that I told you. He denies her. Now that you have started to menstruate, what happened to her could happen to you. Don't humiliate us. You wouldn't like to be forgotten as if you had never been born. The villagers are watchful."

Whenever she had to warn us about life, my mother told stories that ran like this one, a story to grow up on. She tested our strength to establish realities. Those in the emigrant generations who could not reassert brute survival died young and far from home. Those of us in the first American generations have had to figure out how the invisible world the emigrants built around our childhoods fit in solid America.

The emigrants confused the gods by diverting their curses, misleading them with crooked streets and false names. They must try to confuse their offspring as well, who, I suppose, threaten them in similar ways—always trying to get things straight, always trying to name the unspeakable. The Chinese I know hide their names; sojourners take new names when their lives change and guard their real names with silence.

Chinese-Americans, when you try to understand what things in you are Chinese, how do you separate what is peculiar to childhood, to poverty, insanities, one family, your mother who marked your growing with stories, from what is Chinese? What is Chinese tradition and what is the movies?

If I want to learn what clothes my aunt wore, whether flashy or ordinary, I would have to begin, "Remember Father's drowned-in-the-well sister?" I cannot ask that. My mother has told me once and for all the useful parts. She will add nothing unless powered by Necessity, a riverbank that guides her life. She plants vegetable gardens rather than lawns; she carries the odd-shaped tomatoes home from the fields and eats food left for the gods.

Whenever we did frivolous things, we used up energy; we flew high kites. We children came up off the ground over the melting cones our parents brought home from work and the American movie on New Year's Day—*Oh, You Beautiful Doll* with Betty Grable one year, and *She Wore a Yellow Ribbon* with John Wayne another year. After the one carnival ride each, we paid in guilt; our tired father counted his change on the dark walk home.

Adultery is extravagance. Could people who hatch their own chicks and eat the embryos and the heads for delicacies and boil the feet in vinegar for party food, leaving only the gravel, eating even the gizzard lining—could such people engender a prodigal aunt? To be a woman, to have a daughter in starvation time was a waste enough. My aunt could not have been the lone romantic who gave up everything for sex. Women in the old China did not choose. Some man had commanded her to lie with him and be his secret evil. I wonder whether he masked himself when he joined the raid on her family.

Perhaps she encountered him in the fields or on the mountain where the daughters-in-law collected fuel. Or perhaps he first noticed her in the marketplace. He was not a stranger because the village housed no strangers. She had to have dealings with him other than sex. Perhaps he worked an adjoining field, or he sold her the cloth for the dress she sewed and wore. His demand must have surprised, then terrified her. She obeyed him; she always did as she was told.

When the family found a young man in the next village to be her husband, she stood tractably beside the best rooster, his proxy, and promised before they met that she would be his forever. She was lucky that he was her age and she would be the first wife, an advantage secure now. The night she first saw him, he had sex with her. Then he left for America. She had almost forgotten what he looked like. When she tried to envision him, she only saw the black and white face in the group photograph the men had had taken before leaving.

The other man was not, after all, much different from her husband. They both gave orders: she followed. "If you tell your family, I'll beat you. I'll kill you. Be here again next week." No one talked sex, ever. And she might have separated the rapes from the rest of living if only she did not have to buy her oil from him or gather wood in the same forest. I want her fear to have lasted just as long as rape lasted so that the fear could have been contained. No drawn-out fear. But women at sex hazarded birth and hence lifetimes. The fear did not stop but permeated everywhere. She told the man, "I think I'm pregnant." He organized the raid against her.

On nights when my mother and father talked about their life back home, sometimes they mentioned an "outcast table" whose business they still seemed to be settling, their voices tight. In a commensal tradition,[1] where food is precious, the powerful older people made wrongdoers eat alone. Instead of letting them start separate new lives like the Japanese, who could become samurais and geishas,[2] the Chinese family, faces averted but eyes glowering sideways, hung on to the offenders and fed them leftovers. My aunt must have lived in the same house as my parents and eaten at an outcast table. My mother spoke about the raid as if she had seen it, when she and my aunt, a daughter-in-

---

[1] One in which all members eat at the same table.

[2] Samurai: member of the Japanese feudal military aristocracy; geisha: Japanese girl trained in singing, dancing, and the art of conversation so as to serve as a hired companion to men.

law to a different household, should not have been living together at all. Daughters-in-law lived with their husbands' parents, not their own; a synonym for marriage in Chinese is "taking a daughter-in-law." Her husband's parents could have sold her, mortgaged her, stoned her. But they had sent her back to her own mother and father, a mysterious act hinting at disgraces not told me. Perhaps they had thrown her out to deflect the avengers.

She was the only daughter; her four brothers went with her father, husband, and uncles "out on the road" and for some years became western men. When the goods were divided among the family, three of the brothers took land, and the youngest, my father, chose an education. After my grandparents gave their daughter away to her husband's family, they had dispensed all the adventure and all the property. They expected her alone to keep the traditional ways, which her brothers, now among the barbarians, could fumble without detection. The heavy, deep-rooted women were to maintain the past against the flood, safe for returning. But the rare urge west had fixed upon our family, and so my aunt crossed boundaries not delineated in space.

The work of preservation demands that the feelings playing about in one's guts not be turned into action. Just watch their passing like cherry blossoms. But perhaps my aunt, my forerunner, caught in a slow life, let dreams grow and fade and after some months or years went toward what persisted. Fear at the enormities of the forbidden kept her desires delicate, wire and bone. She looked at a man because she liked the way the hair was tucked behind his ears, or she liked the question-mark line of a long torso curving at the shoulder and straight at the hip. For warm eyes or a soft voice or a slow walk—that's all—a few hairs, a line, a brightness, a sound, a pace, she gave up family. She offered us up for a charm that vanished with tiredness, a pigtail that didn't toss when the wind died. Why, the wrong lighting could erase the dearest thing about him.

It could very well have been, however, that my aunt did not take subtle enjoyment of her friend, but, a wild woman, kept rollicking company. Imagining her free with sex doesn't fit, though. I don't know any women like that, or men either. Unless I see her life branching into mine, she gives me no ancestral help.

To sustain her being in love, she often worked at herself in the mirror, guessing at the colors and shapes that would interest him, changing them frequently in order to hit on the right combination. She wanted him to look back.

On a farm near the sea, a woman who tended her appearance reaped a reputation for eccentricity. All the married women blunt-cut their hair in flaps about their ears or pulled it back in tight buns. No nonsense. Neither style blew easily into heart-catching tangles. And at their weddings they displayed themselves in their long hair for the last time. "It brushed the backs of my knees," my mother tells me. "It was braided, and even so, it brushed the backs of my knees."

At the mirror my aunt combed individuality into her bob. A bun could have been contrived to escape into black streamers blowing in the wind or in quiet wisps about her face, but only the older women in our picture album wear buns. She brushed her hair back from her forehead, tucking the flaps behind her ears. She looped a piece of thread, knotted into a circle between her index fingers and thumbs, and ran the double strand across her forehead. When she closed her fingers as if she were making a pair of shadow geese bite, the string twisted together catching the little hairs. Then she pulled the thread away from her skin, ripping the hairs out neatly, her eyes watering from the needles of pain. Opening her fingers, she cleaned the thread, then rolled it along her hairline and the tops of her eyebrows. My mother did the same to me and my sisters and herself. I used to believe that the expression "caught by the short hairs" meant a captive held with a depilatory string. It especially hurt at the temples, but my mother said we were lucky we didn't have to have our feet bound when we were seven. Sisters used to sit on their beds and cry together, she said, as their mothers or their slaves removed the bandages for a few minutes each night and let the blood gush back into their veins. I hope that the man my aunt loved appreciated a smooth brow, that he wasn't just a tits-and-ass man.

Once my aunt found a freckle on her chin, at a spot that the almanac said predestined her for unhappiness. She dug it out with a hot needle and washed the wound with peroxide.

More attention to her looks than these pullings of hairs and pickings at spots would have caused gossip among the villagers. They owned work clothes and good clothes, and they wore good clothes for feasting the new seasons. But since a woman combing her hair hexes beginnings, my aunt rarely found an occasion to look her best. Women looked like great sea snails—the corded wood, babies, and laundry they carried were the whorls on their backs. The Chinese did not admire a bent back; goddesses and warriors stood straight. Still there must have been a marvelous freeing of beauty when a worker laid down her burden and stretched and arched.

Such commonplace loveliness, however, was not enough for my aunt. She dreamed of a lover for the fifteen days of New Year's, the time for families to exchange visits, money, and food. She plied her secret comb. And sure enough she cursed the year, the family, the village, and herself.

Even as her hair lured her imminent lover, many other men looked at her. Uncles, cousins, nephews, brothers would have looked, too, had they been home between journeys. Perhaps they had already been restraining their curiosity, and they left, fearful that their glances, like a field of nesting birds, might be startled and caught. Poverty hurt, and that was their first reason for leaving. But another, final reason for leaving the crowded house was the never-said.

She may have been unusually beloved, the precious only daughter, spoiled and mirror gazing because of the affection the family lavished on her. When her husband left, they welcomed the chance to take her back from the in-laws; she could live like the little daughter for just a while longer. There are stories that my grandfather was different from other people, "crazy ever since the little Jap bayoneted him in the head." He used to put his naked penis on the dinner table, laughing. And one day he brought home a baby girl, wrapped up inside his brown western-style greatcoat. He had traded one of his sons, probably my father, the youngest, for her. My grandmother made him trade back. When he finally got a daughter of his own, he doted on her. They must have all loved her, except perhaps my father, the only brother who never went back to China, having once been traded for a girl.

Brothers and sisters, newly men and women, had to efface their sexual color and present plain miens. Disturbing hair and eyes, a smile like no other threatened the ideal of five generations living under one roof. To focus blurs, people shouted face to face and yelled from room to room. The immigrants I know have loud voices, unmodulated to American tones even after years away from the village where they called their friendships out across the fields. I have not been able to stop my mother's screams in public libraries or over telephones. Walking erect (knees straight, toes pointed forward, not pigeon-toed, which is Chinese-feminine) and speaking in an inaudible voice, I have tried to turn myself American-feminine. Chinese communication was loud, public. Only sick people had to whisper. But at the dinner table, where the family members came nearest one another, no one could talk, not the outcasts nor any eaters. Every word that falls from the mouth is a coin lost. Silently they gave and accepted food with both hands. A preoccupied child who took his bowl with one hand got a sideways glare. A complete moment of total attention is due everyone alike. Children and lovers have no singularity here, but my aunt used a secret voice, a separate attentiveness.

She kept the man's name to herself throughout her labor and dying; she did not accuse him that he be punished with her. To save her inseminator's name she gave silent birth.

He may have been somebody in her own household, but intercourse with a man outside the family would have been no less abhorrent. All the village were kinsmen, and the titles shouted in loud country voices never let kinship be forgotten. Any man within visiting distance would have been neutralized as a lover—"brother," "younger brother," "older brother"—one hundred and fifteen relationship titles. Parents researched birth charts probably not so much to assure good fortune as to circumvent incest in a population that has but one hundred surnames. Everybody has eight million relatives. How useless then sexual mannerisms, how dangerous.

As if it came from an atavism deeper than fear, I used to add "brother" silently to boys' names. It hexed the boys, who would or would not ask me to dance, and made them less scary and as familiar and deserving of benevolence as girls.

But, of course, I hexed myself also—no dates. I should have stood up, both arms waving, and shouted out across libraries, "Hey, you! Love me back." I had no idea, though, how to make attraction selective, how to control its direction and magnitude. If I made myself American-pretty so that the five or six Chinese boys in the class fell in love with me, everyone else—the Caucasian, Negro, and Japanese boys—would too. Sisterliness, dignified and honorable, made much more sense.

Attraction eludes control so stubbornly that whole societies designed to organize relationships among people cannot keep order, not even when they bind people to one another from childhood and raise them together. Among the very poor and the wealthy, brothers married their adopted sisters, like doves. Our family allowed some romance, paying adult brides' prices and providing dowries so that their sons and daughters could marry strangers. Marriage promises to turn strangers into friendly relatives—a nation of siblings.

In the village structure, spirits shimmered among the live creatures, balanced and held in equilibrium by time and land. But one human being flaring up into violence could open up a black hole, a maelstrom that pulled in the sky. The frightened villagers, who depended on one another to maintain the real, went to my aunt to show her a personal, physical representation of the break she had made in the "roundness." Misallying couples snapped off the future, which was to be embodied in true offspring. The villagers punished her for acting as if she could have a private life, secret and apart from them.

If my aunt had betrayed the family at a time of large grain yields and peace, when many boys were born, and wings were being built on many houses, perhaps she might have escaped such severe punishment. But the men—hungry, greedy, tired of planting in dry soil, cuckolded—had had to leave the village in order to send food-money home. There were ghost plagues, bandit plagues, wars with the Japanese, floods. My Chinese brother and sister had died of an unknown sickness. Adultery, perhaps only a mistake during good times, became a crime when the village needed food.

The round moon cakes and round doorways, the round tables of graduated size that fit one roundness inside another, round windows and rice bowls—these talismens had lost their power to warn this family of the law: a family must be whole, faithfully keeping the descent line by having sons to feed the old and the dead, who in turn look after the family. The villagers came to show my aunt and her lover-in-hiding a broken house. The villagers were speeding up the circling of events because she was too shortsighted to see that her infidelity had already harmed the village, that waves of consequences would return unpredictably, sometimes in disguise, as now, to hurt her. This roundness had to be made coin-sized so that she would see its circumference: punish her at the birth of her baby. Awaken her to the inexorable. People who refused fatalism because they could invent small resources insisted on culpability. Deny accidents and wrest fault from the stars.

After the villagers left, their lanterns now scattering in various directions toward home, the family broke their silence and cursed her. "Aiaa, we're going to die. Death is coming. Death is coming. Look what you've done. You've killed us. Ghost! Dead ghost! Ghost! You've never been born." She ran out into the fields, far enough from the house so that she could no longer hear their voices, and pressed herself against the earth, her own land no more. When she felt the birth coming, she thought that she had been hurt. Her body seized together. "They've hurt me too much," she thought. "This is gall, and it will kill me." Her forehead and knees against the earth, her body convulsed and then released her onto her back. The black well of sky and stars went out and out and out forever; her body and her complexity seemed to disappear. She was one of the stars, a bright dot in blackness, without home, without a companion, in eternal cold and silence. An agoraphobia rose in her, speeding higher and higher, bigger and bigger; she would not be able to contain it; there would be no end to fear.

Flayed, unprotected against space, she felt pain return, focusing her body. This pain chilled her—a cold, steady kind of surface pain. Inside, spasmodically, the other pain, the pain of the child, heated her. For hours she lay on the ground, alternately body and space. Sometimes a vision of normal comfort obliterated reality: she saw the family in the evening gambling at the dinner table, the young people massaging their elders' backs. She saw them congratulating one another, high joy on the mornings the rice shoots came up. When these pictures burst, the stars drew yet further apart. Black space opened.

She got to her feet to fight better and remembered that old-fashioned women gave birth in their pigsties to fool the jealous, pain-dealing gods, who do not snatch piglets. Before the next spasms could stop her, she ran to the pigsty, each step a rushing out into emptiness. She climbed over the fence and knelt in the dirt. It was good to have a fence enclosing her, a tribal person alone.

Laboring, this woman who had carried her child as a foreign growth that sickened her every day, expelled it at last. She reached down to touch the hot, wet, moving mass, surely smaller than anything human, and could feel that it was human after all—fingers, toes, nails, nose. She pulled it up on to her belly, and it lay curled there, butt in the air, feet precisely tucked one under the other. She opened her loose shirt and buttoned the child inside. After resting, it squirmed and thrashed and she pushed it up to her breast. It turned its head this way and that until it found her nipple. There, it made little snuffling noises. She clenched her teeth at its preciousness, lovely as a young calf, a piglet, a little dog.

She may have gone to the pigsty as a last act of responsibility: she would protect this child as she had protected its father. It would look after her soul, leaving supplies on her grave. But how would this tiny child without family find her grave when there would be no marker for her anywhere, neither in the earth nor the family hall? No one would give her a family hall name. She had taken the child with her into the wastes. At its birth the two of them had felt the same raw pain of separation, a wound that only the family pressing tight could close. A child with no descent line would not soften her life but only trail after her, ghostlike, begging her to give it purpose. At dawn the villagers on their way to the fields would stand around the fence and look.

Full of milk, the little ghost slept. When it awoke, she hardened her breasts against the milk that crying loosens. Toward morning she picked up the baby and walked to the well.

Carrying the baby to the well shows loving. Otherwise abandon it. Turn its face into the mud. Mothers who love their children take them along. It was probably a girl; there is some hope of forgiveness for boys.

"Don't tell anyone you had an aunt. Your father does not want to hear her name. She has never been born." I have believed that sex was unspeakable and words so strong and fathers so frail that "aunt" would do my father mysterious harm. I have thought that my family, having settled among immigrants who had also been their neighbors in the ancestral land, needed to clean their name, and a wrong word would incite the kinspeople even here. But there is more to this silence: they want me to participate in her punishment. And I have.

In the twenty years since I heard this story I have not asked for details nor said my aunt's name; I do not know it. People who can comfort the dead can also chase after them to hurt them further—a reverse ancestor worship. The real punishment was not the raid swiftly inflicted by the villagers, but the family's deliberately forgetting her. Her betrayal so maddened them, they saw to it that she would suffer forever, even after death. Always hungry, always needing, she would have to beg food from other ghosts, snatch and steal it from those whose living descendants give them gifts. She would have to fight the ghosts massed at crossroads for the buns a few thoughtful citizens leave to decoy her away from village and home so that the ancestral spirits could feast unharassed. At peace, they could act like gods, not ghosts, their descent lines providing them with paper suits and dresses, spirit money, paper houses, paper automobiles, chicken, meat, and rice into eternity—essences delivered up in smoke and flames, steam and incense rising from each rice bowl. In an attempt to make the Chinese care for people outside the family, Chairman Mao encourages us now to give our paper replicas to the spirits of outstanding soldiers and workers, no matter whose ancestors they may be. My aunt remains forever hungry. Goods are not distributed evenly among the dead.

My aunt haunts me—her ghost drawn to me because now, after fifty years of neglect, I alone devote pages of paper to her, though not origamied[3] into houses and clothes. I

---

[3] i.e., folded. (Origami is the Japanese art of folding paper into representational or decorative shapes.)

do not think she always means me well. I am telling on her, and she was a spite suicide, drowning herself in the drinking water. The Chinese are always very frightened of the drowned one, whose weeping ghost, wet hair hanging and skin bloated, waits silently by the water to pull down a substitute.

1975

Alice Walker
b. 1944

Alice Walker—novelist, poet, essayist, biographer, and editor—has described herself as "preoccupied with the spiritual survival, the survival *whole* of my people." But Walker was a young African American woman before she became a writer, and she also describes herself as specifically "committed to exploring the oppressions, the insanities, the loyalties, and the triumphs of black women." Too often, Walker believes, African American and female experience, both in life and in literature, has been devalued by a culture that is dominated by white males. She not only sees Zora Neale Hurston as a tragic case of unappreciated—even suppressed—achievement and isolated suffering; she also sees Hurston's neglected achievement as representing a particularly terrible loss to those for whom it should have been an inspiring example. Walker's *In Search of Our Mothers' Gardens* (1984), celebrates the many women who, like Walker's own mother, were left without any traditional outlet for artistic expression and still managed to hand down an abiding "respect for the possibilities [of life]—and the will to grasp them."

Walker learned early the need for indomitable will. Born in 1944 in Eatonton, Georgia—one of her early residences was a shack near Flannery O'Connor's Andalusia Farm—Walker was initially discouraged in her artistic ambition by critics who felt that a poor African American farmer's daughter would face obstacles impossible to overcome. Walker's response was twofold. First, although she agreed that a "shack with only a dozen or so books" was "an unlikely place to discover a young Keats," she was convinced that it was narrow to think of Keats as "the only kind of poet one would want to grow up to be." Second, like the young Richard Wright, Walker began early to broaden her education. Graduating from Sarah Lawrence College in 1965, she began teaching writing and African American literature in Mississippi, at Jackson State College and Tougaloo College. More recently, she has taught at Wellesley College, the University of Massachusetts, and Yale University and has served as a consulting and contributing editor of *Ms.* magazine and *Freedomways,* a quarterly journal of the Black Freedom Movement.

A mother as well as a socially engaged teacher, Walker believes that her maternal experiences as well as her political and educational experiences have enriched her writings. An extremely versatile writer, she has published poetry, short stories, novels, essays, and nonfiction. Her novels include *The Third Life of Grange Copeland* (1970), *Meridian* (1976), *The Color Purple* (1982), and *The Temple of My Familiar* (1988). Her volumes of poetry are: *Once* (1968), *Revolutionary Petunias* (1973), *Good Night, Willie Lee, I'll See You in the Morning* (1979), *Horses Make a Landscape Look More Beautiful* (1984), and a collection, *Her Blue Body Everything We Know: Earthling Poems, 1965–1990* (1991). She has also published two collections of stories, *In Love and Trouble* (1974) and *You Can't Keep a Good Woman Down* (1981), and, besides *In Search of Our Mothers' Gardens,* a second collection of essays, *Living By the Word* (1989). *Possessing the Secret of Joy,* a novel, appeared in 1992. A collection of stories, *Everyday Use* (1994), and a book of essays, *Alice Walker Banned* (1996), are her most recent books. Many of Walker's writings render moments of pain and moments of beauty in the lives of African American women. Individual stories, poems, and essays have appeared in publications as diverse as *Harper's* and *Mother Jones,* and Walker's awards and grants range from a Guggenheim fellowship to a creative writing award from the National Endowment for the Arts and the Front Page Award for best magazine criticism by the Newswomen's Club of New York. Walker currently lives in San Francisco.

Walker's fiction reflects the full range of her interests and experience. From her mother, whose literary heritage derived primarily from the oral tradition of the African American South, Walker inherited not only stories but also an urgent sense that her grandmother's "stories—like her life—must be recorded" if they were not to be lost. From the slave narratives of her ancestors, she gathered a sense that "family relationships are sacred" and that life is a "moral and/or physical struggle, the result of which is expected to be some kind of larger freedom." In her literary models, African American and white, Walker discovered knowledge that "the strength of the artist" consists of the "courage to look at every old thing with fresh eyes." As a result, although she deals primarily with the experiences of poor African American women, she addresses not only those who believe, as Henry James put it, that the house of fiction has many windows but also those who recognize that African American and white writers (and, by extension, male and female writers) are "writing one immense story—the same story, for the most part—with different parts of this immense story coming from a multitude of different perspectives." By exploring the effects of racism and sexism, by giving "voice to centuries not only of silent bitterness and hate but also of neighborly kindness and sustaining love," Walker obviously hopes to enrich the lives of those who share the same race or sex as her most memorable characters. In addition, however, she clearly hopes to touch the lives of those with "different perspectives" who nevertheless can learn from hearing the pained voices she has heard and seeing the troubled gardens she has seen.

Further Reading:
J. Lyons, *Themes in the Novels of Alice Walker:* The Third Life of Grange Copeland, Meridian, and The Color Purple, 1986.
H. Bloom, ed., *Alice Walker,* 1989.

D. Winchell, *Alice Walker,* 1992.
H. L. Gates, Jr. and K. A. Appiah, eds., *Alice Walker: Critical Perspectives Past and Present,* 1993.

Text:
In Love and Trouble, 1974.

Everyday Use

for your grandmama

I will wait for her in the yard that Maggie and I made so clean and wavy yesterday after-noon. A yard like this is more comfortable than most people know. It is not just a yard. It is like an extended living room. When the hard clay is swept clean as a floor and the fine sand around the edges lined with tiny, irregular grooves, anyone can come and sit and look up into the elm tree and wait for the breezes that never come inside the house.

Maggie will be nervous until after her sister goes: she will stand hopelessly in corners, homely and ashamed of the burn scars down her arms and legs, eying her sister with a mixture of envy and awe. She thinks her sister has held life always in the palm of one hand, that "no" is a word the world never learned to say to her.

You've no doubt seen those TV shows where the child who has "made it" is con-fronted, as a surprise, by her own mother and father, tottering in weakly from back-stage. (A pleasant surprise, of course: What would they do if parent and child came on the show only to curse out and insult each other?) On TV mother and child embrace and smile into each other's faces. Sometimes the mother and father weep, the child wraps them in her arms and leans across the table to tell how she would not have made it without their help. I have seen these programs.

Sometimes I dream a dream in which Dee and I are suddenly brought together on a TV program of this sort. Out of a dark and soft-seated limousine I am ushered into a bright room filled with many people. There I meet a smiling, gray, sporty man like Johnny Carson who shakes my hand and tells me what a fine girl I have. Then we are on the stage and Dee is embracing me with tears in her eyes. She pins on my dress a large orchid, even though she has told me once that she thinks orchids are tacky flowers.

In real life I am a large, big-boned woman with rough, man-working hands. In the winter I wear flannel nightgowns to bed and overalls during the day. I can kill and clean a hog as mercilessly as a man. My fat keeps me hot in zero weather. I can work outside all day, breaking ice to get water for washing; I can eat pork liver cooked over the open fire minutes after it comes steaming from the hog. One winter I knocked a bull calf straight in the brain between the eyes with a sledge hammer and had the meat hung up to chill before nightfall. But of course all this does not show on television. I am the way my daughter would want me to be: a hundred pounds lighter, my skin like an uncooked barley pancake. My hair glistens in the hot bright lights. Johnny Carson has much to do to keep up with my quick and witty tongue.

But that is a mistake. I know even before I wake up. Who ever knew a Johnson with a quick tongue? Who can even imagine me looking a strange white man in the eye? It seems to me I have talked to them always with one foot raised in flight, with my head turned in whichever way is farthest from them. Dee, though. She would always look anyone in the eye. Hesitation was no part of her nature.

"How do I look, Mama?" Maggie says, showing just enough of her thin body en-veloped in pink skirt and red blouse for me to know she's there, almost hidden by the door.

"Come out into the yard," I say.

Have you ever seen a lame animal, perhaps a dog run over by some careless person rich enough to own a car, sidle up to someone who is ignorant enough to be kind to him? That is the way my Maggie walks. She has been like this, chin on chest, eyes on ground, feet in shuffle, ever since the fire that burned the other house to the ground.

Dee is lighter than Maggie, with nicer hair and a fuller figure. She's a woman now, though sometimes I forget. How long ago was it that the other house burned? Ten, twelve years? Sometimes I can still hear the flames and feel Maggie's arms sticking to me, her hair smoking and her dress falling off her in little black papery flakes. Her eyes seemed stretched open, blazed open by the flames reflected in them. And Dee. I see her standing off under the sweet gum tree she used to dig gum out of; a look of concentration on her face as she watched the last dingy gray board of the house fall in toward the red-hot brick chimney. Why don't you do a dance around the ashes? I'd wanted to ask her. She had hated the house that much.

I used to think she hated Maggie, too. But that was before we raised the money, the church and me, to send her to Augusta to school. She used to read to us without pity; forcing words, lies, other folks' habits, whole lives upon us two, sitting trapped and ignorant underneath her voice. She washed us in a river of make-believe, burned us with a lot of knowledge we didn't necessarily need to know. Pressed us to her with the serious way she read, to shove us away at just the moment, like dimwits, we seemed about to understand.

Dee wanted nice things. A yellow organdy dress to wear to her graduation from high school; black pumps to match a green suit she'd made from an old suit somebody gave me. She was determined to stare down any disaster in her efforts. Her eyelids would not flicker for minutes at a time. Often I fought off the temptation to shake her. At sixteen she had a style of her own: and knew what style was.

I never had an education myself. After second grade the school was closed down. Don't ask me why: in 1927 colored asked fewer questions than they do now. Sometimes Maggie reads to me. She stumbles along good-naturedly but can't see well. She knows she is not bright. Like good looks and money, quickness passed her by. She will marry John Thomas (who has mossy teeth in an earnest face) and then I'll be free to sit here and I guess just sing church songs to myself. Although I never was a good singer. Never could carry a tune. I was always better at a man's job. I used to love to milk till I was hooked in the side in '49. Cows are soothing and slow and don't bother you, unless you try to milk them the wrong way.

I have deliberately turned my back on the house. It is three rooms, just like the one that burned, except the roof is tin; they don't make shingle roofs any more. There are no real windows, just some holes cut in the sides, like the portholes in a ship, but not round and not square, with rawhide holding the shutters up on the outside. This house is in a pasture, too, like the other one. No doubt when Dee sees it she will want to tear it down. She wrote me once that no matter where we "choose" to live, she will manage to come see us. But she will never bring her friends. Maggie and I thought about this and Maggie asked me, "Mama, when did Dee ever *have* any friends?"

She had a few. Furtive boys in pink shirts hanging about on washday after school. Nervous girls who never laughed. Impressed with her they worshiped the well-turned phrase, the cute shape, the scalding humor that erupted like bubbles in lye. She read to them.

When she was courting Jimmy T she didn't have much time to pay to us, but turned all her faultfinding power on him. He *flew* to marry a cheap city girl from a family of ignorant flashy people. She hardly had time to recompose herself.

When she comes I will meet—but there they are!

Maggie attempts to make a dash for the house, in her shuffling way, but I stay her with my hand. "Come back here," I say. And she stops and tries to dig a well in the sand with her toe.

It is hard to see them clearly through the strong sun. But even the first glimpse of leg out of the car tells me it is Dee. Her feet were always neat-looking, as if God himself had shaped them with a certain style. From the other side of the car comes a short, stocky man. Hair is all over his head a foot long and hanging from his chin like a kinky mule tail. I hear Maggie suck in her breath. "Uhnnnh," is what it sounds like. Like when you see the wriggling end of a snake just in front of your foot on the road. "Uhnnnh."

Dee next. A dress down to the ground, in this hot weather. A dress so loud it hurts my eyes. There are yellows and oranges enough to throw back the light of the sun. I feel my whole face warming from the heat waves it throws out. Earrings gold, too, and hanging down to her shoulders. Bracelets dangling and making noises when she moves her arm up to shake the folds of the dress out of her armpits. The dress is loose and flows, and as she walks closer, I like it. I hear Maggie go "Uhnnnh" again. It is her sister's hair. It stands straight up like the wool on a sheep. It is black as night and around the edges are two long pigtails that rope about like small lizards disappearing behind her ears.

"Wa-su-zo-Tean-o!" she says, coming on in that gliding way the dress makes her move. The short stocky fellow with the hair to his navel is all grinning and he follows up with "Asalamalakim, my mother and sister!" He moves to hug Maggie but she falls back, right up against the back of my chair. I feel her trembling there and when I look up I see the perspiration falling off her chin.

"Don't get up," says Dee. Since I am stout it takes something of a push. You can see me trying to move a second or two before I make it. She turns, showing white heels through her sandals, and goes back to the car. Out she peeks next with a Polaroid. She stoops down quickly and lines up picture after picture of me sitting there in front of the house with Maggie cowering behind me. She never takes a shot without making sure the house is included. When a cow comes nibbling around the edge of the yard she snaps it and me and Maggie *and* the house. Then she puts the Polaroid in the back seat of the car, and comes up and kisses me on the forehead.

Meanwhile Asalamalakim is going through motions with Maggie's hand. Maggie's hand is as limp as a fish, and probably as cold, despite the sweat, and she keeps trying to pull it back. It looks like Asalamalakim wants to shake hands but wants to do it fancy. Or maybe he don't know how people shake hands. Anyhow, he soon gives up on Maggie.

"Well," I say. "Dee."

"No, Mama," she says. "Not 'Dee,' Wangero Leewanika Kemanjo!"

"What happened to 'Dee'?" I wanted to know.

"She's dead," Wangero said. "I couldn't bear it any longer, being named after the people who oppress me."

"You know as well as me you was named after your aunt Dicie," I said. Dicie is my sister. She named Dee. We called her "Big Dee" after Dee was born.

"But who was *she* named after?" asked Wangero.

"I guess after Grandma Dee," I said.

"And who was she named after?" asked Wangero.

"Her mother," I said, and saw Wangero was getting tired. "That's about as far back as I can trace it," I said. Though, in fact, I probably could have carried it back beyond the Civil War through the branches.

"Well," said Asalamalakim, "there you are."

"Uhnnnh," I heard Maggie say.

"There I was not," I said, "before 'Dicie' cropped up in our family, so why should I try to trace it that far back?"

He just stood there grinning, looking down on me like somebody inspecting a Model A car. Every once in a while he and Wangero sent eye signals over my head.

"How do you pronounce this name?" I asked.

"You don't have to call me by it if you don't want to," said Wangero.

"Why shouldn't I?" I asked. "If that's what you want us to call you, we'll call you."

"I know it might sound awkward at first," said Wangero.

"I'll get used to it," I said. "Ream it out again."

Well, soon we got the name out of the way. Asalamalakim had a name twice as long and three times as hard. After I tripped over it two or three times he told me to just call him Hakim-a-barber. I wanted to ask him was he a barber, but I didn't really think he was, so I didn't ask.

"You must belong to those beef-cattle peoples down the road," I said. They said "Asalamalakim" when they met you, too, but they didn't shake hands. Always too busy: feeding the cattle, fixing the fences, putting up salt-lick shelters, throwing down hay. When the white folks poisoned some of the head the men stayed up all night with rifles in their hands. I walked a mile and a half just to see the sight.

Hakim-a-barber said, "I accept some of their doctrines, but farming and raising cattle is not my style." (They didn't tell me, and I didn't ask, whether Wangero (Dee) had really gone and married him.)

We sat down to eat and right away he said he didn't eat collards and pork was unclean. Wangero, though, went on through the chitlins and corn bread, the greens and everything else. She talked a blue streak over the sweet potatoes. Everything delighted her. Even the fact that we still used the benches her daddy made for the table when we couldn't afford to buy chairs.

"Oh, Mamma!" she cried. Then turned to Hakim-a-barber. "I never knew how lovely these benches are. You can feel the rump prints," she said, running her hands underneath her and along the bench. Then she gave a sign and her hand closed over Grandma Dee's butter dish. "That's it!" she said. "I knew there was something I wanted to ask you if I could have." She jumped up from the table and went over in the corner where the churn stood, the milk in it clabber by now. She looked at the churn and looked at it.

"This churn top is what I need," she said. "Didn't Uncle Buddy whittle it out of a tree you all used to have?"

"Yes," I said.

"Uh huh," she said happily. "And I want the dasher, too."

"Uncle Buddy whittle that, too?" asked the barber.

Dee (Wangero) looked up at me.

"Aunt Dee's first husband whittled the dash," said Maggie so low you almost couldn't hear her. "His name was Henry, but they called him Stash."

"Maggie's brain is like an elephant's," Wangero said, laughing. "I can use the churn top as a centerpiece for the alcove table," she said, sliding a plate over the churn, "and I'll think of something artistic to do with the dasher."

When she finished wrapping the dasher the handle stuck out. I took it for a moment in my hands. You didn't even have to look close to see where hands pushing the dasher up and down to make butter and left a kind of sink in the wood. In fact, there were a lot of small sinks; you could see where thumbs and fingers had sunk into the wood. It was beautiful light yellow wood, from a tree that grew in the yard where Big Dee and Stash had lived.

After dinner Dee (Wangero) went to the trunk at the foot of my bed and started rifling through it. Maggie hung back in the kitchen over the dishpan. Out came Wangero with two quilts. They had been pieced by Grandma Dee and then Big Dee and me had hung them on the quilt frames on the front porch and quilted them. One was in the Lone Star pattern. The other was Walk Around the Mountain. In both of them were scraps of dresses Grandma Dee had worn fifty and more years ago. Bits and pieces of Grandpa Jarrell's Paisley shirts. And one teeny faded blue piece, about the size of a penny matchbox, that was from Great Grandpa Ezra's uniform that he wore in the Civil War.

"Mama," Wangero said sweet as a bird. "Can I have these old quilts?"

I heard something fall in the kitchen, and a minute later the kitchen door slammed.

"Why don't you take one or two of the others?" I asked. "These old things was just done by me and Big Dee from some tops your grandma pieced before she died."

"No," said Wangero. "I don't want those. They are stitched around the borders by machine."

"That'll make them last better," I said.

"That's not the point," said Wangero. "These are all pieces of dresses Grandma used to wear. She did all this stitching by hand. Imagine!" She held the quilts securely in her arms, stroking them.

"Some of the pieces, like those lavender ones, come from old clothes her mother handed down to her," I said, moving up to touch the quilts. Dee (Wangero) moved back just enough so that I couldn't reach the quilts. They already belonged to her.

"Imagine!" she breathed again, clutching them closely to her bosom.

"The truth is," I said, "I promised to give them quilts to Maggie, for when she marries John Thomas."

She gasped like a bee had stung her.

"Maggie can't appreciate these quilts" she said. "She'd probably be backward enough to put them to everyday use."

"I reckon she would," I said. "God knows I been saving 'em for long enough with nobody using 'em. I hope she will!" I didn't want to bring up how I had offered Dee (Wangero) a quilt when she went away to college. Then she had told me they were old-fashioned, out of style.

"But they're *priceless!*" she was saying now, furiously; for she has a temper. "Maggie would put them on the bed and in five years they'd be in rags. Less than that!"

"She can always make some more," I said. "Maggie knows how to quilt."

Dee (Wangero) looked at me with hatred. "You just will not understand. The point is these quilts, *these* quilts!"

"Well," I said, stumped. "What would *you* do with them?"

"Hang them," she said. As if that was the only thing you *could* do with quilts.

Maggie by now was standing in the door. I could almost hear the sound her feet made as they scraped over each other.

"She can have them, Mama," she said, like somebody used to never winning anything, or having anything reserved for her. "I can 'member Grandma Dee without the quilts."

I looked at her hard. She had filled her bottom lip with checkerberry snuff and it gave her face a kind of dopey, hangdog look. It was Grandma Dee and Big Dee who taught her how to quilt herself. She stood there with her scarred hands hidden in the folds of her skirt. She looked at her sister with something like fear but she wasn't mad at her. This was Maggie's portion. This was the way she knew God to work.

When I looked at her like that something hit me in the top of my head and ran down to the soles of my feet. Just like when I'm in church and the spirit of God touches me and I get happy and shout. I did something I never had done before: hugged Maggie to me, then dragged her on into the room, snatched the quilts out of Miss Wangero's hands and dumped them into Maggie's lap. Maggie just sat there on my bed with her mouth open.

"Take one or two of the others," I said to Dee.

But she turned without a word and went out to Hakim-a-barber.

"You just don't understand," she said, as Maggie and I came out to the car.

"What don't I understand?" I wanted to know.

"Your heritage," she said. And then she turned to Maggie, kissed her, and said, "You ought to try to make something of yourself, too, Maggie. It's really a new day for us. But from the way you and Mama still live you'd never know it."

She put on some sunglasses that hid everything above the tip of her nose and her chin.

Maggie smiled; maybe at the sunglasses. But a real smile, not scared. After we watched the car dust settle I asked Maggie to bring me a dip of snuff. And then the two of us sat there just enjoying, until it was time to go in the house and go to bed.

1973

Tim O'Brien
b. 1946

William Timothy O'Brien was born in Minnesota, where he graduated from high school and from Macalester College. Immediately after graduating from college, he was drafted into the army as a foot soldier and served in Vietnam, where he was wounded near My Lai. Following his return from Vietnam, he entered Harvard University to begin graduate work in government. O'Brien combined this pursuit, which lasted on and off for several years, with reporting for the *Washington Post* and with writing about the war he could not forget. His first book, *If I Die in a Combat Zone, Box Me Up and Ship Me Home* (1973), consists of a series of sketches based on his experiences in Vietnam. His first novel *Northern Lights* (1974) is set in Minnesota and focuses on the complex relationship between a Vietnam veteran and his brother. Between his first novel and his second, *Going After Cacciato* (1978), parts of which were published separately as prize-winning stories, O'Brien officially ended his work at Harvard in order to concentrate on writing. When *Going After Cacciato* won the National Book Award, it reinforced his reputation as one of the finest fiction writers of his generation, and as its best writer of war fiction.

In *The Things They Carried* (1990), a collection of interrelated stories about a platoon of foot soldiers in Vietnam, O'Brien aggressively works the border between fiction and nonfiction. Running through all of the stories are two recurring themes—the impossibility of seeing anything clearly in a war zone, and the difficulty of seeing and conveying *the* truth under any circumstances—that reinforce our sense of O'Brien's work as fiction grounded in a concerted effort to achieve some larger truthfulness. O'Brien's latest book is a novel, *In the Lake of the Woods* (1994).

Further Reading:

M. J. Bates, "Tim O'Brien's Myth of Courage," *Modern Fiction Studies* 33: 263–279 (Summer 1987).

S. Kaplan, *Understanding Tim O'Brien*, 1995.

M. Kinney, "American Exceptionalism and Empire in Tim O'Brien's *Going after Cacciato*," *American Literary History* 7: 633–653 (Winter 1995).

Text:
The Things They Carried, 1990.

The Things They Carried

First Lieutenant Jimmy Cross carried letters from a girl named Martha, a junior at Mount Sebastian College in New Jersey. They were not love letters, but Lieutenant Cross was hoping, so he kept them folded in plastic at the bottom of his rucksack. In the late afternoon, after a day's march, he would dig his foxhole, wash his hands under a canteen, unwrap the letters, hold them with the tips of his fingers, and spend the last hour of light pretending. He would imagine romantic camping trips into the White Mountains in New Hampshire. He would sometimes taste the envelope flaps, knowing her tongue had been there. More than anything, he wanted Martha to love him as he loved her, but the letters were mostly chatty, elusive on the matter of love. She was a virgin, he was almost sure. She was an English major at Mount Sebastian, and she wrote beautifully about her professors and roommates and midterm exams, about her respect for Chaucer and her great affection for Virginia Woolf. She often quoted lines of poetry; she never mentioned the war, except to say, Jimmy, take care of yourself. The letters weighed 10 ounces. They were signed Love, Martha, but Lieutenant Cross understood that Love was only a way of signing and did not mean what he sometimes pretended it meant. At dusk, he would carefully return the letters to his rucksack. Slowly, a bit distracted, he would get up and move among his men, checking the perimeter, then at full dark he would return to his hole and watch the night and wonder if Martha was a virgin.

The things they carried were largely determined by necessity. Among the necessities or near-necessities were P-38 can openers, pocket knives, heat tabs, wristwatches, dog tags, mosquito repellent, chewing gum, candy, cigarettes, salt tablets, packets of Kool-Aid, lighters, matches, sewing kits, Military Payment Certificates, C rations, and two or three canteens of water. Together, these items weighed between 15 and 20 pounds, depending upon a man's habits or rate of metabolism. Henry Dobbins, who was a big man, carried extra rations; he was especially fond of canned peaches in heavy syrup over pound cake. Dave Jensen, who practiced field hygiene, carried a toothbrush, dental floss, and several hotel-sized bars of soap he'd stolen on R&R in Sydney, Australia. Ted Lavender, who was scared, carried tranquilizers until he was shot in the head outside the village of Than Khe in mid-April. By necessity, and because it was SOP, they all carried steel helmets that weighed 5 pounds including the liner and camouflage cover. They carried the standard fatigue jackets and trousers. Very few carried underwear. On their feet they carried jungle boots—2.1 pounds—and Dave Jensen carried three pairs of socks and a can of Dr. Scholl's foot powder as a precaution against trench foot. Until he was shot, Ted Lavender carried six or seven ounces of premium dope, which for him was a necessity. Mitchell Sanders, the RTO, carried condoms. Norman Bowker carried a diary. Rat Kiley carried comic books. Kiowa, a devout Baptist, carried an illustrated New Testament that had been presented to him by his father, who taught Sunday school in Oklahoma City, Oklahoma. As a hedge against bad times, however, Kiowa also carried his grandmother's distrust of the white man, his grandfather's old hunting hatchet. Necessity dictated. Because the land was mined and booby-trapped, it was SOP for each man to carry a steel-centered, nylon-covered flak jacket, which weighed 6.7 pounds, but which on hot days seemed much heavier. Because you could die so quickly, each man carried at least one large compress bandage, usually in the helmet band for easy access. Because the nights were cold, and because the monsoons were wet, each carried a green plastic poncho that could be used as a raincoat or groundsheet or makeshift tent. With its quilted liner, the poncho weighed almost two pounds, but it was worth every ounce. In April, for instance, when Ted Lavender was shot, they used his poncho to wrap him up, then to carry him across the paddy, then to lift him into the chopper that took him away.

They were called legs or grunts.

To carry something was to hump it, as when Lieutenant Jimmy Cross humped his love for Martha up the hills and through the swamps. In its intransitive form, to hump meant to walk, or to march, but it implied burdens far beyond the intransitive.

Almost everyone humped photographs. In his wallet, Lieutenant Cross carried two photographs of Martha. The first was a Kodacolor snapshot signed Love, though he knew better. She stood against a brick wall. Her eyes were gray and neutral, her lips slightly open as she stared straight-on at the camera. At night, sometimes, Lieutenant Cross wondered who had taken the picture, because he knew she had boyfriends, because he loved her so much, and because he could see the shadow of the picture-taker spreading out against the brick wall. The second photograph had been clipped from the 1968 Mount Sebastian yearbook. It was an action shot—women's volleyball—and

Martha was bent horizontal to the floor, reaching, the palms of her hands in sharp focus, the tongue taut, the expression frank and competitive. There was no visible sweat. She wore white gym shorts. Her legs, he thought, were almost certainly the legs of a virgin, dry and without hair, the left knee cocked and carrying her entire weight, which was just over one hundred pounds. Lieutenant Cross remembered touching that left knee. A dark theater, he remembered, and the movie was *Bonnie and Clyde,* and Martha wore a tweed skirt, and during the final scene, when he touched her knee, she turned and looked at him in a sad, sober way that made him pull his hand back, but he would always remember the feel of the tweed skirt and the knee beneath it and the sound of the gun-fire that killed Bonnie and Clyde, how embarrassing it was, how slow and oppressive. He remembered kissing her good night at the dorm door. Right then, he thought, he should've done something brave. He should've carried her up the stairs to her room and tied her to the bed and touched that left knee all night long. He should've risked it. Whenever he looked at the photographs, he thought of new things he should've done.

What they carried was partly a function of rank, partly of field specialty.

As a first lieutenant and platoon leader, Jimmy Cross carried a compass, maps, code books, binoculars, and a .45-caliber pistol that weighed 2.9 pounds fully loaded. He carried a strobe light and the responsibility for the lives of his men.

As an RTO, Mitchell Sanders carried the PRC-25 radio, a killer, 26 pounds with its battery.

As a medic, Rat Kiley carried a canvas satchel filled with morphine and plasma and malaria tablets and surgical tape and comic books and all the things a medic must carry, including M&M's for especially bad wounds, for a total weight of nearly 20 pounds.

As a big man, therefore a machine gunner, Henry Dobbins carried the M-60, which weighed 23 pounds unloaded, but which was almost always loaded. In addition, Dobbins carried between 10 and 15 pounds of ammunition draped in belts across his chest and shoulders.

As PFCs or Spec 4s, most of them were common grunts and carried the standard M-16 gas-operated assault rifle. The weapon weighed 7.5 pounds unloaded, 8.2 pounds with its full 20-round magazine. Depending on numerous factors, such as topography and psychology, the riflemen carried anywhere from 12 to 20 magazines, usually in cloth bandoliers, adding on another 8.4 pounds at minimum, 14 pounds at maximum. When it was available, they also carried M-16 maintenance gear—rods and steel brushes and swabs and tubes of LSA oil—all of which weighed about a pound. Among the grunts, some carried the M-79 grenade launcher, 5.9 pounds unloaded, a reasonably light weapon except for the ammunition, which was heavy. A single round weighed 10 ounces. The typical load was 25 rounds. But Ted Lavender, who was scared, carried 34 rounds when he was shot and killed outside Than Khe, and he went down under an exceptional burden, more than 20 pounds of ammunition, plus the flak jacket and helmet and rations and water and toilet paper and tranquilizers and all the rest, plus the unweighed fear. He was dead weight. There was no twitching or flopping. Kiowa, who saw it happen, said it was like watching a rock fall, or a big sandbag or something—just boom, then down—not like the movies where the dead guy rolls around and does fancy spins and goes ass over teakettle—not like that, Kiowa said, the poor bastard just flat-fuck fell. Boom. Down. Nothing else. It was a bright morning in mid-April. Lieutenant

Cross felt the pain. He blamed himself. They stripped off Lavender's canteens and ammo, all the heavy things, and Rat Kiley said the obvious, the guy's dead, and Mitchell Sanders used his radio to report one U.S. KIA and to request a chopper. Then they wrapped Lavender in his poncho. They carried him out to a dry paddy, established security, and sat smoking the dead man's dope until the chopper came. Lieutenant Cross kept to himself. He pictured Martha's smooth young face, thinking he loved her more than anything, more than his men, and now Ted Lavender was dead because he loved her so much and could not stop thinking about her. When the dustoff arrived, they carried Lavender aboard. Afterward they burned Than Khe. They marched until dusk, then dug their holes, and that night Kiowa kept explaining how you had to be there, how fast it was, how the poor guy just dropped like so much concrete. Boom-down, he said. Like cement.

In addition to the three standard weapons—the M-60, M-16, and M-79—they carried whatever presented itself, or whatever seemed appropriate as a means of killing or staying alive. They carried catch-as-catch-can. At various times, in various situations, they carried M-14s and CAR-15s and Swedish Ks and grease guns and captured AK-47s and Chi-Coms and RPGs and Simonov carbines and black market Uzis and .38-caliber Smith & Wesson handguns and 66 mm LAWs and shotguns and silencers and blackjacks and bayonets and C-4 plastic explosives. Lee Strunk carried a slingshot; a weapon of last resort, he called it. Mitchell Sanders carried brass knuckles. Kiowa carried his grandfather's feathered hatchet. Every third or fourth man carried a Claymore antipersonnel mine—3.5 pounds with its firing device. They all carried fragmentation grenades—14 ounces each. They all carried at least one M-18 colored smoke grenade—24 ounces. Some carried CS or tear gas grenades. Some carried white phosphorus grenades. They carried all they could bear, and then some, including a silent awe for the terrible power of the things they carried.

In the first week of April, before Lavender died, Lieutenant Jimmy Cross received a good-luck charm from Martha. It was a simple pebble, an ounce at most. Smooth to the touch, it was a milky white color with flecks of orange and violet, oval-shaped, like a miniature egg. In the accompanying letter, Martha wrote that she had found the pebble on the Jersey shoreline, precisely where the land touched water at high tide, where things came together but also separated. It was this separate-but-together quality, she wrote, that had inspired her to pick up the pebble and to carry it in her breast pocket for several days, where it seemed weightless, and then to send it through the mail, by air, as a token of her truest feelings for him. Lieutenant Cross found this romantic. But he wondered what her truest feelings were, exactly, and what she meant by separate-but-together. He wondered how the tides and waves had come into play on that afternoon along the Jersey shoreline when Martha saw the pebble and bent down to rescue it from geology. He imagined bare feet. Martha was a poet, with the poet's sensibilities, and her feet would be brown and bare, the toenails unpainted, the eyes chilly and somber like the ocean in March, and though it was painful, he wondered who had been with her that afternoon. He imagined a pair of shadows moving along the strip of sand where things came together but also separated. It was phantom jealousy, he knew, but he couldn't help himself. He loved her so much. On the march, through the hot days of early April, he carried the pebble in his mouth, turning it with his tongue, tasting sea salt and moisture. His mind wandered. He had difficulty keeping his attention on the war. On occasion he would yell at his men to spread out the column, to keep their eyes open, but then he would slip away into daydreams, just pretending, walking barefoot along the Jersey shore, with Martha, carrying nothing. He would feel himself rising. Sun and waves and gentle winds, all love and lightness.

What they carried varied by mission.

When a mission took them to the mountains, they carried mosquito netting, machetes, canvas tarps, and extra bug juice.

If a mission seemed especially hazardous, or if it involved a place they knew to be bad, they carried everything they could. In certain heavily mined AOs, where the land was dense with Toe Poppers and Bouncing Betties, they took turns humping a 28-pound mine detector. With its headphones and big sensing plate, the equipment was a stress on the lower back and shoulders, awkward to handle, often useless because of the shrapnel in the earth, but they carried it anyway, partly for safety, partly for the illusion of safety.

On ambush, or other night missions, they carried peculiar little odds and ends. Kiowa always took along his New Testament and a pair of moccasins for silence. Dave Jensen carried night-sight vitamins high in carotene. Lee Strunk carried his slingshot; ammo, he claimed, would never be a problem. Rat Kiley carried brandy and M&M's candy. Until he was shot, Ted Lavender carried the starlight scope, which weighed 6.3 pounds with its aluminum carrying case. Henry Dobbins carried his girlfriend's pantyhose wrapped around his neck as a comforter. They all carried ghosts. When dark came, they would move out single file across the meadows and paddies to their ambush coordinates, where they would quietly set up the Claymores and lie down and spend the night waiting.

Other missions were more complicated and required special equipment. In mid-April, it was their mission to search out and destroy the elaborate tunnel complexes in the Than Khe area south of Chu Lai. To blow the tunnels, they carried one-pound blocks of pentrite high explosives, four blocks to a man, 68 pounds in all. They carried wiring, detonators, and battery-powered clackers. Dave Jensen carried ear-plugs. Most often, before blowing the tunnels, they were ordered by higher command to search them, which was considered bad news, but by and large they just shrugged and carried out orders. Because he was a big man, Henry Dobbins was excused from tunnel duty. The others would draw numbers. Before Lavender died there were 17 men in the platoon, and whoever drew the number 17 would strip off his gear and crawl in headfirst with a flashlight and Lieutenant Cross's .45-caliber pistol. The rest of them would fan out as security. They would sit down or kneel, not facing the hole, listening to the ground beneath them, imagining cobwebs and ghosts, whatever was down there—the tunnel walls squeezing in—how the flashlight seemed impossibly heavy in the hand and how it was tunnel vision in the very strictest sense, compression in all ways, even time, and how you had to wiggle in—ass and elbows—a swallowed-up feeling—and how you found yourself worrying about odd things: Will your flashlight go dead? Do rats carry rabies? If you screamed, how far would the sound carry? Would your buddies hear it? Would they have the courage to drag you out? In some respects, though not many, the waiting was worse than the tunnel itself. Imagination was a killer.

On April 16, when Lee Strunk drew the number 17, he laughed and muttered something and went down quickly. The morning was hot and very still. Not good, Kiowa said. He looked at the tunnel opening, then out across a dry paddy toward the village of Than Khe. Nothing moved. No clouds or birds or people. As they waited, the men smoked and drank Kool-Aid, not talking much, feeling sympathy for Lee Strunk but also feeling the luck of the draw. You win some, you lose some, said Mitchell Sanders, and sometimes you settle for a rain check. It was a tired line and no one laughed.

Henry Dobbins ate a tropical chocolate bar. Ted Lavender popped a tranquilizer and went off to pee.

After five minutes, Lieutenant Jimmy Cross moved to the tunnel, leaned down, and examined the darkness. Trouble, he thought—a cave-in maybe. And then suddenly, without willing it, he was thinking about Martha. The stresses and fractures, the quick collapse, the two of them buried alive under all that weight. Dense, crushing love. Kneeling, watching the hole, he tried to concentrate on Lee Strunk and the war, all the dangers, but his love was too much for him, he felt paralyzed, he wanted to sleep inside her lungs and breathe her blood and be smothered. He wanted her to be a virgin and not a virgin, all at once. He wanted to know her. Intimate secrets: Why poetry? Why so sad? Why that grayness in her eyes? Why so alone? Not lonely, just alone—riding her bike across campus or sitting off by herself in the cafeteria—even dancing, she danced alone—and it was the aloneness that filled him with love. He remembered telling her that one evening. How she nodded and looked away. And how, later, when he kissed her, she received the kiss without returning it, her eyes wide open, not afraid, not a virgin's eyes, just flat and uninvolved.

Lieutenant Cross gazed at the tunnel. But he was not there. He was buried with Martha under the white sand at the Jersey shore. They were pressed together, and the pebble in his mouth was her tongue. He was smiling. Vaguely, he was aware of how quiet the day was, the sullen paddies, yet he could not bring himself to worry about matters of security. He was beyond that. He was just a kid at war, in love. He was twenty-four years old. He couldn't help it.

A few moments later Lee Strunk crawled out of the tunnel. He came up grinning, filthy but alive. Lieutenant Cross nodded and closed his eyes while the others clapped Strunk on the back and made jokes about rising from the dead.

Worms, Rat Kiley said. Right out of the grave. Fuckin' zombie.

The men laughed. They all felt great relief.

Spook city, said Mitchell Sanders.

Lee Strunk made a funny ghost sound, a kind of moaning, yet very happy, and right then, when Strunk made that high happy moaning sound, when he went *Ahhooooo*, right then Ted Lavender was shot in the head on his way back from peeing. He lay with his mouth open. The teeth were broken. There was a swollen black bruise under his left eye. The cheekbone was gone. Oh shit, Rat Kiley said, the guy's dead. The guy's dead, he kept saying, which seemed profound—the guy's dead. I mean really.

The things they carried were determined to some extent by superstition. Lieutenant Cross carried his good-luck pebble. Dave Jensen carried a rabbit's foot. Norman Bowker, otherwise a very gentle person, carried a thumb that had been presented to him as a gift by Mitchell Sanders. The thumb was dark brown, rubbery to the touch, and weighed four ounces at most. It had been cut from a VC corpse, a boy of fifteen or sixteen. They'd found him at the bottom of an irrigation ditch, badly burned, flies in his mouth and eyes. The boy wore black shorts and sandals. At the time of his death he had been carrying a pouch of rice, a rifle, and three magazines of ammunition.

You want my opinion, Mitchell Sanders said, there's a definite moral here.

He put his hand on the dead boy's wrist. He was quiet for a time, as if counting a pulse, then he patted the stomach, almost affectionately, and used Kiowa's hunting hatchet to remove the thumb.

Henry Dobbins asked what the moral was.

Moral?

You know. *Moral.*

Sanders wrapped the thumb in toilet paper and handed it across to Norman Bowker. There was no blood. Smiling, he kicked the boy's head, watched the flies scatter, and said, It's like with that old TV show—Paladin. Have gun, will travel.

Henry Dobbins thought about it.

Yeah, well, he finally said. I don't see no moral.

There it *is,* man.

Fuck off.

They carried USO stationery and pencils and pens. They carried Sterno, safety pins, trip flares, signal flares, spools of wire, razor blades, chewing tobacco, liberated joss sticks and statuettes of the smiling Buddha, candles, grease pencils, *The Stars and Stripes,* fingernail clippers, Psy Ops leaflets, bush hats, bolos, and much more. Twice a week, when the resupply choppers came in, they carried hot chow in green mermite cans and large canvas bags filled with iced beer and soda pop. They carried plastic water containers, each with a two-gallon capacity. Mitchell Sanders carried a set of starched tiger fatigues for special occasions. Henry Dobbins carried Black Flag insecticide. Dave Jensen carried empty sandbags that could be filled at night for added protection. Lee Strunk carried tanning lotion. Some things they carried in common. Taking turns, they carried the big PRC-77 scrambler radio, which weighed 30 pounds with its battery. They shared the weight of memory. They took up what others could no longer bear. Often, they carried each other, the wounded or weak. They carried infections. They carried chess sets, basketballs, Vietnamese-English dictionaries, insignia of rank, Bronze Stars and Purple Hearts, plastic cards imprinted with the Code of Conduct. They carried diseases, among them malaria and dysentery. They carried lice and ringworm and leeches and paddy algae and various rots and molds. They carried the land itself—Vietnam, the place, the soil—a powdery orange-red dust that covered their boots and fatigues and faces. They carried the sky. The whole atmosphere, they carried it, the humidity, the monsoons, the stink of fungus and decay, all of it, they carried gravity. They moved like mules. By daylight they took sniper fire, at night they were mortared, but it was not battle, it was just the endless march, village to village, without purpose, nothing won or lost. They marched for the sake of the march. They plodded along slowly, dumbly, leaning forward against the heat, unthinking, all blood and bone, simple grunts, soldiering with their legs, toiling up the hills and down into the paddies and across the rivers and up again and down, just humping, one step and then the next and then another, but no volition, no will, because it was automatic, it was anatomy, and the war was entirely a matter of posture and carriage, the hump was everything, a kind of inertia, a kind of emptiness, a dullness of desire and intellect and conscience and hope and human sensibility. Their principles were in their feet. Their calculations were biological. They had no sense of strategy or mission. They searched the villages without knowing what to look for, not caring, kicking over jars of rice, frisking children and old men, blowing tunnels, sometimes setting fires and sometimes not, then forming up and moving on to the next village, then other villages, where it would always be the same. They carried their own lives. The pressures were enormous. In the heat of early afternoon, they would remove their helmets and flak jackets, walking bare, which was dangerous but which helped ease the strain. They would often discard things along the route of march. Purely for comfort, they would throw away rations, blow their Claymores and grenades, no matter, because by nightfall the resupply choppers would arrive with more of the same, then a day or two later still more, fresh watermelons and crates of ammunition and sunglasses and woolen sweaters—the resources were stunning—sparklers for the Fourth of July, colored eggs for Easter—it was the great American war chest—the fruits of science, the smokestacks, the canneries, the arsenals at Hartford, the Minnesota forests, the machine shops, the vast fields of corn and wheat—they carried like freight trains; they carried it on their backs and shoulders—and for all the ambiguities of Vietnam, all the mysteries and unknowns, there was at least the single abiding certainty that they would never be at a loss for things to carry.

After the chopper took Lavender away, Lieutenant Jimmy Cross led his men into the village of Than Khe. They burned everything. They shot chickens and dogs, they trashed the village well, they called in artillery and watched the wreckage, then they marched for several hours through the hot afternoon, and then at dusk, while Kiowa explained how Lavender died, Lieutenant Cross found himself trembling.

He tried not to cry. With his entrenching tool, which weighed five pounds, he began digging a hole in the earth.

He felt shame. He hated himself. He had loved Martha more than his men, and as a consequence Lavender was now dead, and this was something he would have to carry like a stone in his stomach for the rest of the war.

All he could do was dig. He used his entrenching tool like an ax, slashing, feeling both love and hate, and then later, when it was full dark, he sat at the bottom of his foxhole and wept. It went on for a long while. In part, he was grieving for Ted Lavender, but mostly it was for Martha, and for himself, because she belonged to another world, which was not quite real, and because she was a junior at Mount Sebastian College in New Jersey, a poet and a virgin and uninvolved, and because he realized she did not love him and never would.

Like cement, Kiowa whispered in the dark. I swear to God—boom, down. Not a word.
    I've heard this, said Norman Bowker.
    A pisser, you know? Still zipping himself up. Zapped while zipping.
    All right, fine. That's enough.
    Yeah, but you had to see it, the guy just—
    I *heard,* man. Cement. So why not shut the fuck *up?*
    Kiowa shook his head sadly and glanced over at the hole where Lieutenant Jimmy Cross sat watching the night. The air was thick and wet. A warm dense fog had settled over the paddies and there was the stillness that precedes rain.

After a time Kiowa sighed.

One thing for sure, he said. The lieutenant's in some deep hurt. I mean that crying jag—the way he was carrying on—it wasn't fake or anything, it was real heavy-duty hurt. The man cares.

Sure, Norman Bowker said.

Say what you want, the man does care.

We all got problems.

Not Lavender.

No, I guess not, Bowker said. Do me a favor, though.

Shut up?

That's a smart Indian. Shut up.

Shrugging, Kiowa pulled off his boots. He wanted to say more, just to lighten up his sleep, but instead he opened his New Testament and arranged it beneath his head as a pillow. The fog made things seem hollow and unattached. He tried not to think about Ted Lavender, but then he was thinking how fast it was, no drama, down and dead, and how it was hard to feel anything except surprise. It seemed unchristian. He wished he could find some great sadness, or even anger, but the emotion wasn't there and he couldn't make it happen. Mostly he felt pleased to be alive. He liked the smell of the New Testament under his cheek, the leather and ink and paper and glue, whatever the chemicals were. He liked hearing the sounds of night. Even his fatigue, it felt fine, the stiff muscles and the prickly awareness of his own body, a floating feeling. He enjoyed not being dead. Lying there, Kiowa admired Lieutenant Jimmy Cross's capacity for grief. He wanted to share the man's pain, he wanted to care as Jimmy Cross cared. And yet when he closed his eyes, all he could think was Boom-down, and all he could feel was the pleasure of having his boots off and the fog curling in around him and the damp soil and the Bible smells and the plush comfort of night.

After a moment Norman Bowker sat up in the dark.

What the hell, he said. You want to talk, *talk*. Tell it to me.

Forget it.

No, man, go on. One thing I hate, it's a silent Indian.

For the most part they carried themselves with poise, a kind of dignity. Now and then, however, there were times of panic, when they squealed or wanted to squeal but couldn't, when they twitched and made moaning sounds and covered their heads and said Dear Jesus and flopped around on the earth and fired their weapons blindly and cringed and sobbed and begged for the noise to stop and went wild and made stupid promises to themselves and to God and to their mothers and fathers, hoping not to die. In different ways, it happened to all of them. Afterward, when the firing ended, they would blink and peek up. They would touch their bodies, feeling shame, then quickly hiding it. They would force themselves to stand. As if in slow motion, frame by frame, the world would take on the old logic—absolute silence, then the wind, then sunlight, then voices. It was the burden of being alive. Awkwardly, the men would reassemble themselves, first in private, then in groups, becoming soldiers again. They would repair the leaks in their eyes. They would check for casualties, call in dustoffs, light cigarettes, try to smile, clear their throats and spit and begin cleaning their weapons. After a time someone would shake his head and say, No lie, I almost shit my pants, and someone else would laugh, which meant it was bad, yes, but the guy had obviously not shit his pants, it wasn't that bad, and in any case nobody would ever do such a thing and then go ahead and talk about it. They would squint into the dense, oppressive sunlight. For a few moments, perhaps, they would fall silent, lighting a joint and tracking its passage from man to man, inhaling, holding in the humiliation. Scary stuff, one of them might say. But then someone else would grin or flick his eyebrows and say, Roger-dodger, almost cut me a new asshole, *almost.*

There were numerous such poses. Some carried themselves with a sort of wistful resignation, others with pride or stiff soldierly discipline or good humor or macho zeal. They were afraid of dying but they were even more afraid to show it.

They found jokes to tell.

They used a hard vocabulary to contain the terrible softness. *Greased* they'd say. *Offed, lit up, zapped while zipping.* It wasn't cruelty, just stage presence. They were actors. When someone died, it wasn't quite dying, because in a curious way it seemed scripted, and because they had their lines mostly memorized, irony mixed with tragedy, and because they called it by other names, as if to encyst and destroy the reality of death itself. They kicked corpses. They cut off thumbs. They talked grunt lingo. They told stories about Ted Lavender's supply of tranquilizers, how the poor guy didn't feel a thing, how incredibly tranquil he was.

There's a moral here, said Mitchell Sanders.

They were waiting for Lavender's chopper, smoking the dead man's dope.

The moral's pretty obvious, Sanders said, and winked. Stay away from drugs. No joke, they'll ruin your day every time.

Cute, said Henry Dobbins.

Mind blower, get it? Talk about wiggy. Nothing left, just blood and brains.

They made themselves laugh.

There it is, they'd say. Over and over—there it is, my friend, there it is—as if the repetition itself were an act of poise, a balance between crazy and almost crazy, knowing without going, there it is, which meant be cool, let it ride, because Oh yeah, man, you can't change what can't be changed, there it is, there it absolutely and positively and fucking well *is.*

They were tough.

They carried all the emotional baggage of men who might die. Grief, terror, love, longing—these were intangibles, but the intangibles had their own mass and specific gravity, they had tangible weight. They carried shameful memories. They carried the common secret of cowardice barely restrained, the instinct to run or freeze or hide, and in many respects this was the heaviest burden of all, for it could never be put down, it required perfect balance and perfect posture. They carried their reputations. They carried the soldier's greatest fear, which was the fear of blushing. Men killed, and died, because they were embarrassed not to. It was what had brought them to the war in the first place, nothing positive, no dreams of glory or honor, just to avoid the blush of dishonor. They died so as not to die of embarrassment. They crawled into tunnels and walked point and advanced under fire. Each morning, despite the unknowns, they made their legs move. They endured. They kept humping. They did not submit to the obvious alternative, which was simply to close the eyes and fall. So easy, really. Go limp and tumble to the ground and let the muscles unwind and not speak and not budge until your buddies picked you up and lifted you into the chopper that would roar and dip its nose and carry you off to the world. A mere matter of falling, yet no one ever fell. It was not courage, exactly; the object was not valor. Rather, they were too frightened to be cowards.

By and large they carried these things inside, maintaining the masks of composure. They sneered at sick call. They spoke bitterly about guys who had found release by shooting off their own toes or fingers. Pussies, they'd say. Candyasses. It was fierce, mocking talk, with only a trace of envy or awe, but even so the image played itself out behind their eyes.

They imagined the muzzle against flesh. So easy: squeeze the trigger and blow away a toe. They imagined it. They imagined the quick, sweet pain, then the evacuation to Japan, then a hospital with warm beds and cute geisha nurses.

And they dreamed of freedom birds.

At night, on guard, staring into the dark, they were carried away by jumbo jets. They felt the rush of takeoff. *Gone!* they yelled. And then velocity—wings and engines—a smiling stewardess—but it was more than a plane, it was a real bird, a big sleek silver bird with feathers and talons and high screeching. They were flying. The weights fell off; there was nothing to bear. They laughed and held on tight, feeling the cold slap of wind and altitude, soaring, thinking *It's over, I'm gone!*—they were naked, they were light and free—it was all lightness, bright and fast and buoyant, light as light, a helium buzz in the brain, a giddy bubbling in the lungs as they were taken up over the clouds and the war, beyond duty, beyond gravity and mortification and global entanglements—*Sin loi!* they yelled. *I'm sorry, mother-fuckers, but I'm out of it, I'm goofed, I'm on a space cruise, I'm gone!*—and it was a restful, unencumbered sensation, just riding the light waves, sailing that big silver freedom bird over the mountains and oceans, over America, over the farms and great sleeping cities and cemeteries and highways and the golden arches of McDonald's, it was flight, a kind of fleeing, a kind of falling, falling higher and higher, spinning off the edge of the earth and beyond the sun and through the vast, silent vacuum where there were no burdens and where everything weighed exactly nothing—*Gone!* they screamed. *I'm sorry but I'm gone!*—and so at night, not quite dreaming, they gave themselves over to lightness, they were carried, they were purely borne.

On the morning after Ted Lavender died, First Lieutenant Jimmy Cross crouched at the bottom of his foxhole and burned Martha's letters. Then he burned the two photographs. There was a steady rain falling, which made it difficult, but he used heat tabs and Sterno to build a small fire, screening it with his body, holding the photographs over the tight blue flame with the tips of his fingers.

He realized it was only a gesture. Stupid, he thought. Sentimental, too, but mostly just stupid.

Lavender was dead. You couldn't burn the blame.

Besides, the letters were in his head. And even now, without photographs, Lieutenant Cross could see Martha playing volleyball in her white gym shorts and yellow T-shirt. He could see her moving in the rain.

When the fire died out, Lieutenant Cross pulled his poncho over his shoulders and ate breakfast from a can.

There was no great mystery, he decided.

In those burned letters Martha had never mentioned the war, except to say, Jimmy, take care of yourself. She wasn't involved. She signed the letters Love, but it wasn't love, and all the fine lines and technicalities did not matter. Virginity was no longer an issue. He hated her. Yes, he did. He hated her. Love, too, but it was a hard, hating kind of love.

The morning came up wet and blurry. Everything seemed part of everything else, the fog and Martha and the deepening rain.

He was a soldier, after all.

Half smiling, Lieutenant Jimmy Cross took out his maps. He shook his head hard, as if to clear it, then bent forward and began planning the day's march. In ten minutes, or maybe twenty, he would rouse the men and they would pack up and head west, where the maps showed the country to be green and inviting. They would do what they had always done. The rain might add some weight, but otherwise it would be one more day layered upon all the other days.

He was realistic about it. There was that new hardness in his stomach. He loved her but he hated her.

No more fantasies, he told himself.

Henceforth, when he thought about Martha, it would be only to think that she belonged elsewhere. He would shut down the daydreams. This was not Mount Sebastian, it was another world, where there were no pretty poems or midterm exams, a place where men died because of carelessness and gross stupidity. Kiowa was right. Boom-down, and you were dead, never partly dead.

Briefly, in the rain, Lieutenant Cross saw Martha's gray eyes gazing back at him.

He understood.

It was very sad, he thought. The things men carried inside. The things men did or felt they had to do.

He almost nodded at her, but didn't.

Instead he went back to his maps. He was now determined to perform his duties firmly and without negligence. It wouldn't help Lavender, he knew that, but from this point on he would comport himself as an officer. He would dispose of his good-luck pebble. Swallow it, maybe, or use Lee Strunk's slingshot, or just drop it along the trail. On the march he would impose strict field discipline. He would be careful to send out flank security, to prevent straggling or bunching up, to keep his troops moving at the proper pace and at the proper interval. He would insist on clean weapons. He would confiscate the remainder of Lavender's dope. Later in the day, perhaps, he would call the men together and speak to them plainly. He would accept the blame for what had happened to Ted Lavender. He would be a man about it. He would look them in the eyes, keeping his chin level, and he would issue the new SOPs in a calm, impersonal tone of voice, a lieutenant's voice, leaving no room for argument or discussion. Commencing immediately, he'd tell them, they would no longer abandon equipment along the route of march. They would police up their acts. They would get their shit together, and keep it together, and maintain it neatly and in good working order.

He would not tolerate laxity. He would show strength, distancing himself.

Among the men there would be grumbling, of course, and maybe worse, because their days would seem longer and their loads heavier, but Lieutenant Jimmy Cross reminded himself that his obligation was not to be loved but to lead. He would dispense with love; it was not now a factor. And if anyone quarreled or complained, he would simply tighten his lips and arrange his shoulders in the correct command posture. He might give a curt little nod. Or he might not. He might just shrug and say, Carry on, then they would saddle up and form into a column and move out toward the villages west of Than Khe.

1990

Leslie Marmon Silko
b. 1948

On Tuesday, May 19, 1981, the *New York Times* announced that the MacArthur Foundation had selected twenty-one "exceptionally talented individuals" to receive five-year awards of support. Among these twenty-one American "geniuses" were two writers—Robert Penn Warren, born in Guthrie, Kentucky, in 1905, and Leslie Marmon Silko, born in Albuquerque, New Mexico, in 1948. Of mixed ancestry—part Pueblo Indian, part Mexican, and part white—Silko is today considered one of the best American writers of her generation.

Reared on the Laguna Pueblo, Silko says that her "earliest memories are of my grandmother telling me stories while she watered the morning-glories in her yard. Her stories were about incidents from long ago," Silko continues, "incidents which occurred before she was born but which she told as certainly as if she had been there." Like "Storyteller," included here, all of Silko's finest fiction "captures the essence of the oral tradition." On one side, it possesses an aura of certainty and authenticity: "I will not change the story," says the narrator of "Storyteller." On the other, it possesses a sense of indefiniteness and ambiguity: knowledge has been lost, the narrator's grandmother says; "otherwise I could tell you more."

Silko has written three books, a novel called *Ceremony* (1978); a montage of stories, legends, poems, and photographs called *Storyteller* (1981); and *Almanac of the Dead* (1991). More recent books by Silko are *Yellow Woman* (1993), *Sacred Water: Narratives and Pictures* (1993), *Yellow Woman and a Beauty of the Spirit: Essays on Native American Life Today* (1996), and *Rain* (1996), with Lee Marmon. Also a screenwriter, Silko is the author of the screenplay for Marlon Brando's film *Black Elks*. In addition, her work has appeared in such anthologies as *The Man to Send Rain Clouds, Best Short Stories of 1975,* and *200 Years of Great American Short Stories* as well as in numerous magazines and journals. Besides writing, Silko teaches English at her alma mater, the University of New Mexico, and has been writer in residence at Vassar College.

Silko's numerous, powerful readings have created an enthusiastic audience for her work on many college campuses. From her Pueblo Indian heritage Silko derives many of the concerns that are apparent in *Ceremony* and *Storyteller,* especially concern for injustice, violence, and despair as forces that shape contemporary Native American life. Like Scott Momaday, who has praised her work, Silko explores both the rich heritage of Native Americans and their tragic loss of identity as they find themselves trapped between a culture that no longer exists and a culture that for them is not yet fully available. Also like Momaday, Silko possesses an affinity with "moments of considerable beauty and intensity, moments in which, according to the central tenet of storytelling, language is celebrated." As a result, her chronicle is a celebration as much as it is a lament: To tell the story "the way it must be told, year after year . . . , without lapse or silence" is a victory that Silko—like her ancestors and her characters—creates from defeat.

Further Reading:

P. Seyersted, *Leslie Marmon Silko*, 1980.
A. R. Velie, *Four American Indian Literary Masters:
N. Scott Momaday, James Welch, Leslie Marmon
Silko, and Gerald Vizenor*, 1982.

A. K. Brown, "Pulling Silko's Thread through Time:
An Exploration of Storytelling," *The American Indian Quarterly* 19:2 (1995), 171–180.

Texts:

Storyteller, 1981.
"Lullaby" from *Vietnam Generation*, vol. 3, no. 1,
(n.d.) pp. 125–131.

Storyteller

Every day the sun came up a little lower on the horizon, moving more slowly until one day she got excited and started calling the jailer. She realized she had been sitting there for many hours, yet the sun had not moved from the center of the sky. The color of the sky had not been good lately; it had been pale blue, almost white, even when there were no clouds. She told herself it wasn't a good sign for the sky to be indistinguishable from the river ice, frozen solid and white against the earth. The tundra rose up behind the river but all the boundaries between the river and hills and sky were lost in the density of the pale ice.

She yelled again, this time some English words which came randomly into her mouth, probably swear words she'd heard from the oil drilling crews last winter. The jailer was an Eskimo, but he would not speak Yupik[1] to her. She had watched people in other cells, when they spoke to him in Yupik he ignored them until they spoke English.

He came and stared at her. She didn't know if he understood what she was telling him until he glanced behind her at the small high window. He looked at the sun, and turned and walked away. She could hear the buckles on his heavy snowmobile boots jingle as he walked to the front of the building.

It was like the other buildings that white people, the Gussucks,[2] brought with them: BIA[3] and school buildings, portable buildings that arrived sliced in halves, on barges coming up the river. Squares of metal panelling bulged out with the layers of insulation stuffed inside. She had asked once what it was and someone told her it was to keep out the cold. She had not laughed then, but she did now. She walked over to the small double-pane window and she laughed out loud. They thought they could keep out the cold with stringy yellow wadding. Look at the sun. It wasn't moving; it was frozen, caught in

---

[1] Eskimo-Aleut language spoken across arctic
America from western Alaska to Greenland.
[2] Presumably the Yupik term for "white people."

[3] Bureau of Indian Affairs.

the middle of the sky. Look at the sky, solid as the river with ice which had trapped the sun. It had not moved for a long time; in a few more hours it would be weak, and heavy frost would begin to appear on the edges and spread across the face of the sun like a mask. Its light was pale yellow, worn thin by the winter.

She could see people walking down the snow-packed roads, their breath steaming out from their parka hoods, faces hidden and protected by deep ruffs of fur. There were no cars or snowmobiles that day; the cold had silenced their machines. The metal froze; it split and shattered. Oil hardened and moving parts jammed solidly. She had seen it happen to their big yellow machines and the giant drill last winter when they came to drill their test holes. The cold stopped them, and they were helpless against it.

Her village was many miles upriver from this town, but in her mind she could see it clearly. Their house was not near the village houses. It stood alone on the bank upriver from the village. Snow had drifted to the eaves of the roof on the north side, but on the west side, by the door, the path was almost clear. She had nailed scraps of red tin over the logs last summer. She had done it for the bright red color, not for added warmth the way the village people had done. This final winter had been coming even then; there had been signs of its approach for many years.

She went because she was curious about the big school where the Government sent all the other girls and boys. She had not played much with the village children while she was growing up because they were afraid of the old man, and they ran when her grandmother came. She went because she was tired of being alone with the old woman whose body had been stiffening for as long as the girl could remember. Her knees and knuckles were swollen grotesquely, and the pain had squeezed the brown skin of her face tight against the bones; it left her eyes hard like river stone. The girl asked once what it was that did this to her body, and the old woman had raised up from sewing a sealskin boot, and stared at her.

"The joints," the old woman said in a low voice, whispering like wind across the roof, "the joints are swollen with anger."

Sometimes she did not answer and only stared at the girl. Each year she spoke less and less, but the old man talked more—all night sometimes, not to anyone but himself; in a soft deliberate voice, he told stories, moving his smooth brown hands above the blankets. He had not fished or hunted with the other men for many years, although he was not crippled or sick. He stayed in his bed, smelling like dry fish and urine, telling stories all winter; and when warm weather came, he went to his place on the river bank. He sat with a long willow stick, poking at the smoldering moss he burned against the insects while he continued with the stories.

The trouble was that she had not recognized the warnings in time. She did not see what the Gussuck school would do to her until she walked into the dormitory and realized that the old man had not been lying about the place. She thought he had been trying to scare her as he used to when she was very small and her grandmother was outside cutting up fish. She hadn't believed what he told her about the school because she knew he wanted to keep her there in the log house with him. She knew what he wanted.

The dormitory matron pulled down her underpants and whipped her with a leather belt because she refused to speak English.

"Those backwards village people," the matron said, because she was an Eskimo who had worked for the BIA a long time, "they kept this one until she was too big to learn."

The other girls whispered in English. They knew how to work the showers, and they washed and curled their hair at night. They ate Gussuck food. She lay on her bed and imagined what her grandmother might be sewing, and what the old man was eating in his bed. When summer came, they sent her home.

The way her grandmother had hugged her before she left for school had been a warning too, because the old woman had not hugged or touched her for many years. Not like the old man, whose hands were always hunting, like ravens circling lazily in the sky, ready to touch her. She was not surprised when the priest and the old man met her at the landing strip, to say that the old lady was gone. The priest asked her where she would like to stay. He referred to the old man as her grandfather, but she did not bother to correct him. She had already been thinking about it; if she went with the priest, he would send her away to a school. But the old man was different. She knew he wouldn't send her back to school. She knew he wanted to keep her.

He told her one time, that she would get too old for him faster than he got too old for her; but again she had not believed him because sometimes he lied. He had lied about what he would do with her if she came into his bed. But as the years passed, she realized what he said was true. She was restless and strong. She had no patience with the old man who had never changed his slow smooth motions under the blankets.

The old man was in his bed for the winter; he did not leave it except to use the slop bucket in the corner. He was dozing with his mouth open slightly; his lips quivered and sometimes they moved like he was telling a story even while he dreamed. She pulled on the sealskin boots, the mukluks with the bright red flannel linings her grandmother had sewn for her, and she tied the braided red yarn tassels around her ankles over the gray wool pants. She zipped the wolfskin parka. Her grandmother had worn it for many years, but the old man said that before she died, she instructed him to bury her in an old black sweater, and to give the parka to the girl. The wolf pelts were creamy colored and silver, almost white in some places, and when the old lady had walked across the tundra in the winter, she was invisible in the snow.

She walked toward the village, breaking her own path through the deep snow. A team of sled dogs tied outside a house at the edge of the village leaped against their chains to bark at her. She kept walking, watching the dusky sky for the first evening stars. It was warm and the dogs were alert. When it got cold again, the dogs would lie curled and still, too drowsy from the cold to bark or pull at the chains. She laughed loudly because it made them howl and snarl. Once the old man had seen her tease the dogs and he shook his head. "So that's the kind of woman you are," he said, "in the wintertime the two of us are no different from those dogs. We wait in the cold for someone to bring us a few dry fish."

She laughed out loud again, and kept walking. She was thinking about the Gussuck oil drillers. They were strange; they watched her when she walked near their machines. She wondered what they looked like underneath their quilted goose-down trousers; she wanted to know how they moved. They would be something different from the old man.

The old man screamed at her. He shook her shoulders so violently that her head bumped against the log wall. "I smelled it!" he yelled, "as soon as I woke up! I am sure of it now. You can't fool me!" His thin legs were shaking inside the baggy wool trousers; he stumbled over her boots in his bare feet. His toenails were long and yellow like bird claws; she had seen a gray crane last summer fighting another in the shallow water on the edge of the river. She laughed out loud and pulled her shoulder out of his grip. He stood in front of her. He was breathing hard and shaking; he looked weak. He would probably die next winter.

"I'm warning you," he said, "I'm warning you." He crawled back into his bunk then, and reached under the old soiled feather pillow for a piece of dry fish. He lay back on the pillow, staring at the ceiling and chewed dry strips of salmon. "I don't know what the old woman told you," he said, "but there will be trouble." He looked over to see if she was listening. His face suddenly relaxed into a smile, his dark slanty eyes were lost in wrinkles of brown skin. "I could tell you, but you are too good for warnings now. I can smell what you did all night with the Gussucks."

She did not understand why they came there, because the village was small and so far upriver that even some Eskimos who had been away to school did not want to come back. They stayed downriver in the town. They said the village was too quiet. They were used to the town where the boarding school was located, with electric lights and running water. After all those years away at school, they had forgotten how to set nets in the river and where to hunt seals in the fall. When she asked the old man why the Gussucks bothered to come to the village, his narrow eyes got bright with excitement.

"They only come when there is something to steal. The fur animals are too difficult for them to get now, and the seals and fish are hard to find. Now they come for oil deep in the earth. But this is the last time for them." His breathing was wheezy and fast; his hands gestured at the sky. "It is approaching. As it comes, ice will push across the sky." His eyes were open wide and he stared at the low ceiling rafters for hours without blinking. She remembered all this clearly because he began the story that day, the story he told from that time on. It began with a giant bear which he described muscle by muscle, from the curve of the ivory claws to the whorls of hair at the top of the massive skull. And for eight days he did not sleep, but talked continuously of the giant bear whose color was pale blue glacier ice.

The snow was dirty and worn down in a path to the door. On either side of the path, the snow was higher than her head. In front of the door there were jagged yellow stains melted into the snow where men had urinated. She stopped in the entry way and kicked the snow off her boots. The room was dim; a kerosene lantern by the cash register was burning low. The long wooden shelves were jammed with cans of beans and potted meats. On the bottom shelf a jar of mayonnaise was broken open, leaking oily white clots on the floor. There was no one in the room except the yellowish dog sleeping in the front of the long glass display case. A reflection made it appear to be lying on the knives and ammunition inside the case. Gussucks kept dogs inside their houses with them; they did not seem to mind the odors which seeped out of the dogs. "They tell us we are dirty for the food we eat—raw fish and fermented meat. But we do not live with dogs," the old man once said. She heard voices in the back room, and the sound of bottles set down hard on tables.

They were always confident. The first year they waited for the ice to break up on the river, and then they brought their big yellow machines up river on barges. They planned to drill their test holes during the summer to avoid the freezing. But the imprints and graves of their machines were still there, on the edge of the tundra above the river, where the summer mud had swallowed them before they ever left sight of the river. The village people had gathered to watch the white men, and to laugh as they drove the giant machines, one by one, off the steel ramp into the bogs; as if sheer numbers of vehicles would somehow make the tundra solid. But the old man said they behaved like desperate people, and they would come back again. When the tundra was frozen solid, they returned.

Village women did not even look through the door to the back room. The priest had warned them. The storeman was watching her because he didn't let Eskimos or Indians sit down at the tables in the back room. But she knew he couldn't throw her out if one of his Gussuck customers invited her to sit with him. She walked across the room. They stared at her, but she had the feeling she was walking for someone else, not herself, so their eyes did not matter. The red-haired man pulled out a chair and motioned for her to sit down. She looked back at the storeman while the red-haired man poured her a glass of red sweet wine. She wanted to laugh at the storeman the way she laughed at the dogs, straining against the chains, howling at her.

The red-haired man kept talking to the other Gussucks sitting around the table, but he slid one hand off the top of the table to her thigh. She looked over at the storeman to see if he was still watching her. She laughed out loud at him and the red-haired man stopped talking and turned to her. He asked if she wanted to go. She nodded and stood up.

Someone in the village had been telling him things about her, he said as they walked down the road to his trailer. She understood that much of what he was saying, but the rest she did not hear. The whine of the big generators at the construction camp sucked away the sound of his words. But English was of no concern to her anymore, and neither was anything the Christians in the village might say about her or the old man. She smiled at the effect of the subzero air on the electric lights around the trailers; they did not shine. They left only flat yellow holes in the darkness.

It took him a long time to get ready, even after she had undressed for him. She waited in the bed with the blankets pulled close, watching him. He adjusted the thermostat and lit candles in the room, turning out the electric lights. He searched through a stack of record albums until he found the right one. She was not sure about the last thing he did: he taped something on the wall behind the bed where he could see it while he lay on top of her. He was shriveled and white from the cold; he pushed against her body for warmth. He guided her hands to his thighs; he was shivering.

She had returned a last time because she wanted to know what it was he stuck on the wall above the bed. After he finished each time, he reached up and pulled it loose, folding it carefully so that she could not see it. But this time she was ready; she waited for his fast breathing and sudden collapse on top of her. She slid out from under him and stood up beside the bed. She looked at the picture while she got dressed. He did not raise his face from the pillow, and she thought she heard teeth rattling together as she left the room.

She heard the old man move when she came in. After the Gussuck's trailer, the log house felt cool. It smelled like dry fish and cured meat. The room was dark except for the blinking yellow flame in the mica window of the oil stove. She squatted in front of the stove and watched the flames for a long time before she walked to the bed where her grandmother had slept. The bed was covered with a mound of rags and fur scraps the old woman had saved. She reached into the mound until she felt something cold and solid wrapped in a wool blanket. She pushed her fingers around it until she felt smooth stone. Long ago, before the Gussucks came, they had burned whale oil in the big stone lamp which made light and heat as well. The old woman had saved everything they would need when the time came.

In the morning, the old man pulled a piece of dry caribou meat from under the blankets and offered it to her. While she was gone, men from the village had brought a bundle of dry meat. She chewed it slowly, thinking about the way they still came from the village to take care of the old man and his stories. But she had a story now, about the red-haired Gussuck. The old man knew what she was thinking, and his smile made his face seem more round than it was.

"Well," he said, "what was it?"

"A woman with a big dog on top of her."

He laughed softly to himself and walked over to the water barrel. He dipped the tin cup into the water.

"It doesn't surprise me," he said.

"Grandma," she said, "there was something red in the grass that morning. I remember." She had not asked about her parents before. The old woman stopped splitting the fish bellies open for the willow drying racks. Her jaw muscles pulled so tightly against her skull, the girl thought the old woman would not be able to speak.

"They bought a tin can full of it from the storeman. Late at night. He told them it was alcohol safe to drink. They traded a rifle for it." The old woman's voice sounded like each word stole strength from her. "It made no difference about the rifle. That year the Gussuck boats had come, firing big guns at the walrus and seals. There was nothing left to hunt after that anyway. So," the old lady said, in a low soft voice the girl had not heard for a long time, "I didn't say anything to them when they left that night."

"Right over there," she said, pointing at the fallen poles, half buried in the river sand and tall grass, "in the summer shelter. The sun was high half the night then. Early in the morning when it was still low, the policeman came around. I told the interpreter to tell him that the storeman had poisoned them." She made outlines in the air in front of her, showing how their bodies lay twisted on the sand; telling the story was like laboring to walk through deep snow; sweat shone in the white hair around her forehead. "I told the priest too, after he came. I told him the storeman lied." She turned away from the girl. She held her mouth even tighter, set solidly, not in sorrow or anger, but against the pain, which was all that remained. "I never believed," she said, "not much anyway. I wasn't surprised when the priest did nothing."

The wind came off the river and folded the tall grass into itself like river waves. She could feel the silence the story left, and she wanted to have the old woman go on.

"I heard sounds that night, grandma. Sounds like someone was singing. It was light outside. I could see something red on the ground." The old woman did not answer her; she moved to the tub full of fish on the ground beside the workbench. She stabbed her knife into the belly of a whitefish and lifted it onto the bench. "The Gussuck storeman left the village right after that," the old woman said as she pulled the entrails from the fish, "otherwise, I could tell you more." The old woman's voice flowed with the wind blowing off the river; they never spoke of it again.

When the willows got their leaves and the grass grew tall along the river banks and around the sloughs, she walked early in the morning. While the sun was still low on the horizon, she listened to the wind off the river; its sound was like the voice that day long ago. In the distance, she could hear the engines of the machinery the oil drillers had left the winter before, but she did not go near the village or the store. The sun never left the sky and the summer became the same long day, with only the winds to fan the sun into brightness or allow it to slip into twilight.

She sat beside the old man at his place on the river bank. She poked the smoky fire for him, and felt herself growing wide and thin in the sun as if she had been split from belly to throat and strung on the willow pole in preparation for the winter to come. The old man did not speak anymore. When men from the village brought him fresh fish he hid them deep in the river grass where it was cool. After he went inside, she split the fish open and spread them to dry on the willow frame the way the old woman had done. Inside, he dozed and talked to himself. He had talked all winter, softly and incessantly, about the giant polar bear stalking a lone hunter across Bering Sea ice. After all the months the old man had been telling the story, the bear was within a hundred feet of the man; but the ice fog had closed in on them now and the man could only smell the sharp ammonia odor of the bear, and hear the edge of the snow crust crack under the giant paws.

One night she listened to the old man tell the story all night in his sleep, describing each crystal of ice and the slightly different sounds they made under each paw; first the left and then the right paw, then the hind feet. Her grandmother was there suddenly, a shadow around the stove. She spoke in her low wind voice and the girl was afraid to sit up to hear more clearly. Maybe what she said had been to the old man because he stopped telling the story and began to snore softly the way he had long ago when the old woman had scolded him for telling his stories while others in the house were trying to sleep. But the last words she heard clearly: "It will take a long time, but the story must be told. There must not be any lies." She pulled the blankets up around her chin, slowly, so that her movements would not be seen. She thought her grandmother was talking about the old man's bear story; she did not know about the other story then.

She left the old man wheezing and snoring in his bed. She walked through river grass glistening with frost; the bright green summer color was already fading. She watched the sun move across the sky, already lower on the horizon, already moving away from the village. She stopped by the fallen poles of the summer shelter where her parents had died. Frost glittered on the river sand too; in a few more weeks there would be snow. The predawn light would be the color of an old woman. An old woman sky full of snow. There had been something red lying on the ground the morning they died. She looked for it again, pushing aside the grass with her foot. She knelt in the sand and looked under the fallen structure for some trace of it. When she found it, she would know what the old woman had never told her. She squatted down close to the gray poles and leaned her back against them. The wind made her shiver.

The summer rain had washed the mud from between the logs; the sod blocks stacked as high as her belly next to the log walls had lost their square-cut shape and had grown into soft mounds of tundra moss and stiff-bladed grass bending with clusters of seed bristles. She looked at the northwest, in the direction of the Bering Sea. The cold would come down from there to find narrow slits in the mud, rainwater holes in the outer layer of sod which protected the log house. The dark green tundra stretched away flat and continuous. Somewhere the sea and the land met; she knew by their dark green colors there were no boundaries between them. That was how the cold would come: when the boundaries were gone the polar ice would range across the land into the sky. She watched the horizon for a long time. She would stand in that place on the north side of the house and she would keep watch on the northwest horizon, and eventually she would see it come. She would watch for its approach in the stars, and hear it come with the wind. These preparations were unfamiliar, but gradually she recognized them as she did her own footprints in the snow.

She emptied the slop jar beside his bed twice a day and kept the barrel full of water melted from river ice. He did not recognize her anymore, and when he spoke to her, he called her by her grandmother's name and talked about people and events from long ago, before he went back to telling the story. The giant bear was creeping across the new snow on its belly, close enough now that the man could hear the rasp of its breathing. On and on in a soft singing voice, the old man caressed the story, repeating the words again and again like gentle strokes.

The sky was gray like a river crane's egg; its density curved into the thin crust of frost already covering the land. She looked at the bright red color of the tin against the ground and the sky and she told the village men to bring the pieces for the old man and her. To drill the test holes in the tundra, the Gussucks had used hundreds of barrels of fuel. The village people split open the empty barrels that were abandoned on the river bank, and pounded the red tin into flat sheets. The village people were using the strips of tin to mend walls and roofs for winter. But she nailed it on the log walls for its color. When she finished, she walked away with the hammer in her hand, not turning around until she was far away, on the ridge above the river banks, and then she looked back. She felt a chill when she saw how the sky and the land were already losing their boundaries, already becoming lost in each other. But the red tin penetrated the thick white color of earth and sky; it defined the boundaries like a wound revealing the ribs and heart of a great caribou about to bolt and be lost to the hunter forever. That night the wind howled and when she scratched a hole through the heavy frost on the inside of the window, she could see nothing but the impene-trable white; whether it was blowing snow or snow that had drifted as high as the house, she did not know.

It had come down suddenly, and she stood with her back to the wind looking at the river, its smoky water clotted with ice. The wind had blown the snow over the frozen river, hiding thin blue streaks where fast water ran under ice translucent and fragile as memory. But she could see shadows of boundaries, outlines of paths which were slender branches of solidity reaching out from the earth. She spent days walking on the river, watching the colors of ice that would safely hold her, kicking the heel of her boot into the snow crust, listening for a solid sound. When she could feel the paths through the soles of her feet, she went to the middle of the river where the fast gray water churned under a thin pane of ice. She looked back. On the river bank in the distance she could see the red tin nailed to the log house, something not swallowed up by the heavy white belly of the sky or caught in the folds of the frozen earth. It was time.

The wolverine fur around the hood of her parka was white with the frost from her breathing. The warmth inside the store melted it, and she felt tiny drops of water on her face. The storeman came in from the back room. She unzipped the parka and stood by the oil stove. She didn't look at him, but stared instead at the yellowish dog, covered with scabs of matted hair, sleeping in front of the stove. She thought of the Gussuck's picture, taped on the wall above the bed and she laughed out loud. The sound of her laughter was piercing; the yellow dog jumped to its feet and the hair bristled down its back. The storeman was watching her. She wanted to laugh again because he didn't know about the ice. He did not know that it was prowling the earth, or that it had already pushed its way into the sky to seize the sun. She sat down in the chair by the stove and shook her long hair loose. He was like a dog tied up all winter, watching while the others got fed. He remembered how she had gone with the oil drillers, and his blue eyes moved like flies crawling over her body. He held his thin pale lips like he wanted to spit on her. He hated the people because they had something of value, the old man said, something which the Gussucks could never have. They thought they could take it, suck it out of the earth or cut it from the mountains; but they were fools.

There was a matted hunk of dog hair on the floor by her foot. She thought of the yellow insulation coming unstuffed: their defense against the freezing going to pieces as it advanced on them. The ice was crouching on the northwest horizon like the old man's bear. She laughed out loud again. The sun would be down now; it was time.

The first time he spoke to her, she did not hear what he said, so she did not answer or even look up at him. He spoke to her again but his words were only noises coming from his pale mouth, trembling now as his anger began to unravel. He jerked her up and the chair fell over behind her. His arms were shaking and she could feel his hands tense up, pulling the edges of the parka tighter. He raised his fist to hit her, his thin body quivering with rage; but the fist collapsed with the desire he had for the valuable things, which, the old man had rightly said, was the only reason they came. She could hear his heart pounding as he held her close and arched his hips against her, groaning and breathing in spasms. She twisted away from him and ducked under his arms.

She ran with a mitten over her mouth, breathing through the fur to protect her lungs from the freezing air. She could hear him running behind her, his heavy breathing, the occasional sound of metal jingling against metal. But he ran without his parka or mittens, breathing the frozen air; its fire squeezed the lungs against the ribs and it was enough that he could not catch her near his store. On the river bank he realized how far he was from his stove, and the wads of yellow stuffing that held off the cold. But the girl was not able to run very fast through the deep drifts at the edge of the river. The twilight was luminous and he could still see clearly for a long distance; he knew he could catch her so he kept running.

When she neared the middle of the river she looked over her shoulder. He was not following her tracks; he went straight across the ice, running the shortest distance to reach her. He was close then; his face was twisted and scarlet from the exertion and the cold. There was satisfaction in his eyes; he was sure he could outrun her.

She was familiar with the river, down to the instant ice flexed into hairline fractures, and the cracking bone-sliver sounds gathered momentum with the opening ice until the churning gray water was set free. She stopped and turned to the sound of the river and the rattle of swirling ice fragments where he fell through. She pulled off a mitten and zipped the parka to her throat. She was conscious then of her own rapid breathing.

She moved slowly, kicking the ice ahead with the heel of her boot, feeling for sinews of ice to hold her. She looked ahead and all around herself; in the twilight, the dense white sky had merged into the flat snow-covered tundra. In the frantic running she had lost her place on the river. She stood still. The east bank of the river was lost in the sky; the boundaries had been swallowed by the freezing white. But then, in the distance, she saw something red, and suddenly it was as she had remembered it all those years.

She sat on her bed and while she waited, she listened to the old man. The hunter had found a small jagged knoll on the ice. He pulled his beaver fur cap off his head; the fur inside it steamed with his body heat and sweat. He left it upside down on the ice for the great bear to stalk, and he waited downwind on top of the ice knoll; he was holding the jade knife.

She thought she could see the end of his story in the way he wheezed out the words; but still he reached into his cache of dry fish and dribbled water into his mouth from the tin cup. All night she listened to him describe each breath the man took, each motion of the bear's head as it tried to catch the sound of the man's breathing, and tested the wind for his scent.

The state trooper asked her questions, and the woman who cleaned house for the priest translated them into Yupik. They wanted to know what happened to the storeman, the Gussuck who had been seen running after her down the road onto the river late last evening. He had not come back, and the Gussuck boss in Anchorage was concerned about him. She did not answer for a long time because the old man suddenly sat up in his bed and began to talk excitedly, looking at all of them—the trooper in his dark glasses and the housekeeper in her corduroy parka. He kept saying, "The story! The story! Eh-ya! The great bear! The hunter!"

They asked her again, what happened to the man from the Northern Commercial store. "He lied to them. He told them it was safe to drink. But I will not lie." She stood up and put on the gray wolfskin parka. "I killed him," she said, "but I don't lie."

The attorney came back again, and the jailer slid open the steel doors and opened the cell to let him in. He motioned for the jailer to stay to translate for him. She laughed when she saw how the jailer would be forced by this Gussuck to speak Yupik to her. She liked the Gussuck attorney for that, and for the thinning hair on his head. He was very tall, and she liked to think about the exposure of his head to the freezing; she wondered if he would feel the ice descending from the sky before the others did. He wanted to know why she told the state trooper she had killed the storeman. Some village children had seen it happen, he said, and it was an accident. "That's all you have to say to the judge: it was an accident." He kept repeating it over and over again to her, slowly in a loud but gentle voice: "It was an accident. He was running after you and he fell through the ice. That's all you have to say in court. That's all. And they will let you go home. Back to your village." The jailer translated the words sullenly, staring down at the floor. She shook her head. "I will not change the story, not even to escape this place and go home. I intended that he die. The story must be told as it is." The attorney exhaled loudly; his eyes looked tired. "Tell her that she could not have killed him that way. He was a white man. He ran after her without a parka or mittens. She could not have planned that." He paused and turned toward the cell door. "Tell her I will do all I can for her. I will explain to the judge that her mind is confused." She laughed out loud when the jailer translated what the attorney said. The Gussucks did not understand the story; they could not see the way it must be told, year after year as the old man had done, without lapse or silence.

She looked out the window at the frozen white sky. The sun had finally broken loose from the ice but it moved like a wounded caribou running on strength which only dying animals find, leaping and running on bullet-shattered lungs. Its light was weak and pale; it pushed dimly through the clouds. She turned and faced the Gussuck attorney.

"It began a long time ago," she intoned steadily, "in the summertime. Early in the morning, I remember, something red in the tall river grass. . . ."

The day after the old man died, men from the village came. She was sitting on the edge of her bed, across from the woman the trooper hired to watch her. They came into the room slowly and listened to her. At the foot of her bed they left a king salmon that had been slit open wide and dried last summer. But she did not pause or hesitate; she went on with the story, and she never stopped, not even when the woman got up to close the door behind the village men.

The old man would not change the story even when he knew the end was approaching. Lies could not stop what was coming. He thrashed around on the bed, pulling the blankets loose, knocking bundles of dried fish and meat on the floor. The hunter had been on the ice for many hours. The freezing winds on the ice knoll had numbed his hands in the mittens, and the cold had exhausted him. He felt a single muscle tremor in his hand that he could not stop, and the jade knife fell; it shattered on the ice, and the blue glacier bear turned slowly to face him.

1981

Lullaby

The sun had gone down but the snow in the wind gave off its own light. It came in thick tufts like new wool—washed before the weaver spins it. Ayah reached out for it like her own babies had, and she smiled when she remembered how she had laughed at them. She was an old woman now, and her life had become memories. She sat down with her back against the wide cottonwood tree, feeling the rough bark on her back bones; she faced east and listened to the wind and snow sing a high-pitched Yeibechei song. Out of the wind, she felt warmer, and she could watch the wide fluffy snow fill in her tracks, steadily, until the direction she had come from was gone. By the light of the snow she could see the dark outline of the big arroyo a few feet away. She was sitting on the edge of Cebolleta Creek, where in the springtime the thin cows would graze on grass already chewed flat to the ground. In the wide deep creek bed where only a trickle of water flowed in the summer, the skinny cows would wander, looking for new grass along winding paths splashed with manure.

Ayah pulled the old Army blanket over her head like a shawl. Jimmie's blanket—the one he had sent to her. That was a long time ago and the green wool was faded, and it was unraveling on the edges. She did not want to think about Jimmie. So she thought about the weaving and the way her mother had done it. On the tall wooden loom set into the sand under a tamarack tree for shade. She could see it clearly. She had been only a little girl when her grandma gave her the wooden combs to pull the twigs and burrs from the raw, freshly washed wool. And while she combed the wool, her grandma sat beside her, spinning a silvery strand of yarn around the smooth cedar spindle. Her mother worked at the loom with yarns dyed bright yellow and red and gold. She watched them dye the yarn in boiling black pots full of beeweed petals, juniper berries, and sage. The blankets her mother made were soft and woven so tight that rain rolled off them like birds' feathers. Ayah remembered sleeping warm on cold windy nights, wrapped in her mother's blankets on the hogan's sandy floor.

The snow drifted now, with the northwest wind hurling it in gusts. It drifted up around her black overshoes—old ones with little metal buckles. She smiled at the snow which was trying to cover her little by little. She could remember when they had no black rubber overshoes; only the high buckskin leggings that they wrapped over their elk-hide moccasins. If the snow was dry or frozen, a person could walk all day and not get wet; and in the evenings the beams of the ceiling would hang with lengths of pale buckskin leggings. drying out slowly.

She felt peaceful remembering. She didn't feel cold any more. Jimmie's blanket seemed warmer than it had ever been. And she could remember the morning he was born. She could remember whispering to her mother who was sleeping on the other side of the hogan, to tell her it was time now. She did not want to wake the others. The second time she called to her, her mother stood up and pulled on her shoes; she knew. They walked to the old stone hogan together, Ayah walking a step behind her mother. She waited alone, learning the rhythms of the pains while her mother went to call the old woman to help them. The morning was already warm even before dawn and Ayah smelled the bee flowers blooming and the young willow growing at the springs. She could remember that so clearly, but his birth merged into the births of the other children and to her it became all the same birth. They named him for the summer morning and in English they called him Jimmie.

It wasn't like Jimmie died. He just never came back, and one day a dark blue sedan with white writing on its doors pulled up in front of the boxcar shack where the rancher let the Indians live. A man in a khaki uniform trimmed in gold gave them a yellow piece of paper and told them that Jimmie was dead. He said the Army would try to get the body back and then it would be shipped to them; but it wasn't likely because the helicopter had burned after it crashed. All of this was told to Chato because he could understand English. She stood inside the doorway holding the baby while Chato listened. Chato spoke English like a white man and he spoke Spanish too. He was taller than the white man and he stood straighter too. Chato didn't explain why; he just told the military man they could keep the body if they found it. The white man looked bewildered; he nodded his head and he left. Then Chato looked at her and shook his head. "Goddamn," he said in English, and then he told her "Jimmie isn't coming home anymore," and when he spoke, he used the words to speak of the dead. She didn't cry then, but she hurt inside with anger. And she mourned him as the years passed, when a horse fell with Chato and broke his leg, and the white rancher told them he wouldn't pay Chato until he could work again. She mourned Jimmie because he would have worked for his father then; he would have saddled the big bay horse and ridden the fence lines each day, with wire cutters and heavy gloves, fixing the breaks in the barbed wire and putting the stray cattle back inside again.

She mourned him after the white doctors came to take Danny and Ella away. She was at the shack alone that day when they came. It was back in the days before they hired Navajo women to go with them as interpreters. She recognized one of the doctors. She had seen him at the children's clinic at Cañoncito about a month ago. They were wearing khaki uniforms and they waved papers at her and a black ball point pen, trying to make her understand their English words. She was frightened by the way they looked at the children, like the lizard watches the fly. Danny was swinging on the tire swing in the elm tree behind the rancher's house, and Ella was toddling around the front door, dragging the broomstick horse Chato made for her. Ayah could see they wanted her to sign the papers, and Chato had taught her to sign her name. It was something she was proud of. She only wanted them to go, and to take their eyes away from her children.

She took the pen from the man without looking at his face and she signed the papers in three different places he pointed to. She stared at the ground by their feet and waited for them to leave. But they stood there and began to point and gesture at the children. Danny stopped swinging. Ayah could see his fear. She moved suddenly and grabbed Ella into her arms; the child squirmed, trying to get back to her toys. Ayah ran with the baby toward Danny; she screamed for him to run and then she grabbed him around his chest and carried him too. She ran south into the foothills of juniper trees and black lava rock. Behind her she heard the doctors running, but they had been taken by surprise, and as the hills became steeper and the cholla cactus were thicker, they stopped. When she reached the top of the hill, she stopped too to listen in case they were circling around her. But in a few minutes she heard a car engine start and they drove away. The children had been too surprised to cry while she ran with them. Danny was shaking and Ella's little fingers were gripping Ayah's blouse.

She stayed up in the hills for the rest of the day, sitting on a black lava boulder in the sunshine where she could see for miles all around her. The sky was light blue and cloudless, and it was warm for late April. The sun warmth relaxed her and took the fear and anger away. She lay back on the rock and watched the sky. It seemed to her that she could walk into the sky, stepping through clouds endlessly. Danny played with little pebbles and stones, pretending they were birds, eggs and then little rabbits. Ella sat at her feet and dropped fistfuls of dirt into the breeze, watching the dust and particles of sand intently. Ayah watched a hawk soar high above them, dark wings gliding; hunting or only watching, she did not know. The hawk was patient and he circled all afternoon before he disappeared around the high volcanic peak the Mexicans call Guadalupe.

Late in the afternoon, Ayah looked down at the gray boxcar shack with the paint all peeled from the wood; the stove pipe on the roof was rusted and crooked. The fire she had built that morning in the oil drum stove had burned out. Ella was asleep in her lap now and Danny sat close to her, complaining that he was hungry; he asked when they would go to the house. "We will stay up here until your father comes," she told him, "because those white men were chasing us." The boy remembered then and he nodded at her silently.

If Jimmie had been there he could have read those papers and explained to her what they said. Ayah would have known, then, never to sign them. The doctors came back the next day and they brought a BIA policeman with them. They told Chato they had her signature and that was all they needed. Except for the kids. She listened to Chato sullenly; she hated him when he told her it was the old woman who died in the winter, spitting blood; it was her old grandma who had given the children this disease. "They don't spit blood," she said coldly. "The whites lie." She held Ella and Danny close to her, ready to run to the hills again. "I want a medicine man first," she said to Chato, not looking at him. He shook his head. "It's too late now. The policeman is with them. You signed the paper." His voice was gentle.

It was worse than if they had died; to lose the children and to know that somewhere, in a place called Colorado, in a place full of sick and dying strangers, her children were without her. There had been babies that died soon after they were born, and one that died before he could walk. She had carried them herself, up to the boulders and great pieces of the cliff that long ago crashed down from Long Mesa; she laid them in the crevices of sandstone and buried them in fine brown sand with round quartz pebbles that washed down from the hills in the rain. She had endured it because they had been with her. But she could not bear this pain. She did not sleep for a long time after they took her children. She stayed on the hill where they had fled the first time, and she slept rolled up in the blanket Jimmie had sent her. She carried the pain in her belly and it was fed by everything she saw: the blue sky of their last day together and the dust and pebbles they played with; the swing in the elm tree and broomstick horse choked life from her. The pain filled her stomach and there was no room for food or for her lungs to fill with air. The air and the food would have been theirs.

She hated Chato, not because he let the policeman and doctors put the screaming children in the government car, but because he had taught her to sign her name. Because it was like the old ones always told her about learning their language or any of their ways: it endangered you. She slept alone on the hill until the middle of November when the first snows came. Then she made a bed for herself where the children had slept. She did not lay down beside Chato again until many years later, when he was sick and shivering and only her body could keep him warm. The illness came after the white rancher told Chato he was too old to work for him any more, and Chato and his old woman should be out of the shack by the next afternoon because the rancher had new people to work there. That had satisfied her. To see how the white man repaid Chato's years of loyalty and work. All of Chato's fine-sounding English didn't change things.

II

It snowed steadily and the luminous light from the snow gradually diminished into the darkness. Somewhere in Cebolleta a dog barked and other village dogs joined with it. Ayah looked in the direction she had come, from the bar where Chato was buying the wine. Sometimes he told her to go on ahead and wait; and then he never came. And when she finally went back looking for him, she would find him passed out at the bottom of the wooden steps to Azzie's Bar. All the wine would be gone and most of the money too, from the pale blue check that came to them once a month in a government envelope. It was then that she would look at his face and his hands, scarred by ropes and the barbed wire of all those years, and she would think "this man is a stranger;" for forty years she had smiled at him and cooked his food, but he remained a stranger. She stood up again, with the snow almost to her knees, and she walked back to find Chato.

It was hard to walk in the deep snow and she felt the air burn in her lungs. She stopped a short distance from the bar to rest and readjust the blanket. But this time he wasn't waiting for her on the bottom step with his old Stetson hat pulled down and his shoulders hunched up in his long wood overcoat.

She was careful not to slip on the wooden steps. When she pushed the door open, warm air and cigarette smoke hit her face. She looked around slowly and deliberately, in every corner, in every dark place that the old man might find to sleep. The bar owner didn't like Indians in there, especially Navajos, but he let Chato come in because he could talk Spanish like he was one of them. The men at the bar stared at her, and the bartender saw that she left the door wide open. Snow flakes were flying inside like moths and melting into a puddle on the oiled wood floor. He motioned at her to close the door, but she did not see him. She held herself straight and walked across the room slowly, searching the room with every step. The snow in her hair melted and she could feel it on her forehead. At the far corner of the room, she saw red flames at the mica window of the old stove door; she looked behind the stove just to make sure. The bar got quiet except for the Spanish polka music playing on the jukebox. She stood by the stove and shook the snow from her blanket and held it near the stove to dry. The wet wool reminded her of new-born goats in early March, brought inside to warm near the fire. She felt calm.

In past years they would have told her to get out. But her hair was white now and her face was wrinkled. They looked at her like she was a spider crawling slowly across the room. They were afraid; she could feel the fear. She looked at their faces steadily. They reminded her of the first time the white people brought her children back to her that winter. Danny had been shy and hid behind the thin white woman who brought them. And the baby had not known her until Ayah took her into her arms, and then Ella had nuzzled close to her as she had when she was nursing. The blonde woman was nervous and kept looking at a dainty gold watch on her wrist. She sat on the bench near the small window and watched the dark clouds gather around the mountains; she was worrying about the unpaved road. She was frightened by what she saw inside too: the strips of venison drying on a rope across the ceiling and the children jabbering excitedly in a language she did not know. So they stayed for only a few hours. Ayah watched the government car disappear down the road and she knew they were already being weaned from these lava hills and from this sky. The last time they came was in early June, and Ella stared at her the way the men in the bar were now staring. Ayah did not try to pick her up; she smiled instead and spoke cheerfully to Danny. When he tried to answer her, he could not seem to remember and he spoke English words with the Navajo. But he gave her a scrap of paper that he had found somewhere and carried in his pocket; it was folded in half, and he shyly looked up at her and said it was a bird. She asked Chato if they were home for good this time. He spoke to the white woman and she shook her head. "How much longer," he asked, and she said she didn't know; but Chato saw how she stared at the box car shack. Ayah turned away then. She did not say good-bye.

III

She felt satisfied that the men in the bar feared her. Maybe it was her face and the way she held her mouth with teeth clenched tight, like there was nothing anyone could do to her now. She walked north down the road, searching for the old man. She did this because she had the blanket, and there would be no place for him except with her and the blanket in the old adobe barn near the arroyo. They always slept there when they came to Cebolleta. If the money and the wine were gone, she would be relieved because then they could go home again; back to the old hogan with a dirt roof and rock walls where she herself had been born. And the next day the old man could go back to the few sheep they still had, to follow along behind them, guiding them into dry sandy arroyos where sparse grass grew. She knew he did not like walking behind old ewes when for so many years he rode big quarter horses and worked with cattle. But she wasn't sorry for him; he should have known all along what would happen.

IV

He was walking along the pavement when she found him. He did not stop or turn around when he heard her behind him. She walked beside him and she noticed how slowly he moved now. He smelled strong of woodsmoke and urine. Lately he had been forgetting. Sometimes he called her by his sister's name and she had been gone for a long time. Once she had found him wandering on the road to the white man's ranch, and she asked him why he was going that way; he laughed at her and said "you know they can't run that ranch without me," and he walked on determined, limping on the leg that had been crushed many years before. Now he looked at her curiously, as if for the first time, but he kept shuffling along, moving slowly along the side of the highway. His gray hair had grown long and spread out on the shoulders of the long overcoat. He wore the old felt hat pulled down over his ears. His boots were worn out at the toes and he had stuffed pieces of an old red shirt in the holes. The rags made his feet look like little animals up to their ears in snow. She laughed at his feet; the snow muffled the sound of her laugh. He stopped and looked at her again. The wind had quit blowing and the snow was falling straight down; the southeast sky was beginning to clear and Ayah could see a star.

"Let's rest awhile," she said to him. They walked away from the road and up the slope to the giant boulders that had tumbled down from the red sandrock mesa throughout the centuries of rainstorms and earth tremors. In a place where the boulders shut out the wind, they sat down with their backs against the rock. She offered half of the blanket to him and they sat wrapped together.

The storm passed swiftly. The clouds moved east. They were massive and full, crowding together across the sky. She watched them with the feeling of horses—steely blue-gray horses startled across the sky. The powerful haunches pushed into the distances and the tail hairs streamed white mist behind them. The sky cleared. Ayah saw that there was nothing between her and the stars. The light was crystalline. There was no shimmer, no distortion through earth haze. She breathed the clarity of the night sky; she smelled the purity of the half moon and the stars. He was lying on his side with his knees pulled up near his belly for warmth. His eyes were closed now, and in the light from the stars and the moon, he looked young again.

She could see it descend out of the night sky; an icy stillness from the edge of the thin moon. She recognized the freezing. It came gradually, sinking snow flake by snow flake until the crust was heavy and deep. It had the strength of the stars in Orion, and its journey was endless. Ayah knew that with the wine he would sleep. He would not feel it. She tucked the blanket around him, remembering how it was when Ella had been with her; and she felt the rush so big inside her heart for the babies. And she sang the only song she knew to sing for babies. She could not remember if she had ever sung it to her children, but she knew that her grandmother had sung it and her mother had sung it:

> *The earth is your mother,*
> > *she holds you.*
> *The sky is your father,*
> > *he protects you,*
> *sleep,*
> *sleep.*
> *Rainbow is your sister,*
> > *she loves you.*
> *The winds are your brothers,*
> > *they sing to you.*
> *sleep,*
> *sleep.*
> *We are together always*
> *We are together always*
> *There never was a time*
> *when this*
> *was not so.*

Jorie Graham
b. 1951

Jorie Graham, the daughter of American parents, grew up in Italy. She was sent to a French lycée in Rome and so became trilingual, speaking Italian with friends, English at home, and French in school. (One of her poems retells her bafflement as a child that the chestnut tree had three names.) She attended the Sorbonne for a year (1968) studying philosophy, then came to the United States, where she entered the program in cinema studies (directed by Martin Scorcese) at New York University, and began to write poetry. After her B.A. (1972), she worked for NBC television and attended poetry workshops and seminars at Columbia. She took an M.F.A. at the University of Iowa in 1978, where she is now on the permanent faculty.

Graham was exposed very early to the visual arts (her mother is a painter and sculptor) and to the churches and museums of Italy. Many of her poems meditate on the relation between the expressive possibilities of language and those of the visual arts. They also reflect on the inevitable tension between the damage of life and the beauty of art: "Contained damage makes for beauty," one of the poems ventures to say. How the violent and the sexual are to be handled within the fabric of art; how art can accommodate itself to the infinite shades of nuance that experience demands; how art mends life; how the wish of the spirit to become pure spirit is matched by the wish of the spirit to reenter the body; how time preserves the past in death—all these metaphysical questions are present repeatedly in Graham's work. (Her philosophy studies at the lycée included works of Pascal, Kant, Heidegger, Sartre, and Merleau-Ponty, with weekly papers, as she writes, "on such subjects as 'Reason and Morality," or 'La Passion.'")

Graham's voice tends to move in phrases, recurrent pulses of tentative exploration as she moves over a field of preoccupation, testing its limits, weighing its powers, looking for a way into feeling, "fingering all the stops." In this way the movement of the poem tends to imitate the searchings and depth-soundings of the mind seeking to replicate the starts and questionings of the heart.

"As a young woman," Graham writes, "I read quantities of Baudelaire, Rimbaud, Mallarmé, Apollinaire, and Supervielle; at school we had to bring in huge passages from Racine and Corneille by heart—to this day I hear 'O rage, o désespoir, o vieillesse ennemie, / Ai-je donc tant vécu que pour cette infamie,' etc." She also read, as was inevitable for someone raised in Italy, Dante and Tasso and Petrarch. Among the Americans, besides the modernist poets, Graham read and was attracted to the poetry of Elizabeth Bishop: "I feel strong kinship with her notion of boundaries—the poem as an act of confrontation between two worlds." Graham's musicality and her feeling for etymologies put her poetry in the long tradition of the "pure lyric," stretching from Petrarch and Ronsard to Rilke and Stevens.

Graham's books of poetry include *Hybrids of Plants and of Ghosts* (1980), *Erosion* (1983), *The End of Beauty* (1987), *Region of Unlikeness* (1991), and *Materialism: Poems* (1993). Her poetry has been collected in *Dream of the Unified Field: Selected Poems, 1974–1994* (1995). Her most recent book, *The Errancy*, was published in 1997.

Further Reading:

B. Costello, "Jorie Graham: Art and Erosion," *Contemporary Literature* 32:2 (1992), 373–396.

H. Vendler, *The Breaking of Style: Hopkins, Heaney, Graham*, 1995.

————, *The Given and the Made: Recent American Poets*, 1995.

Texts:

"The Geese," "Over and Over Stitch," and "Mind" from *Hybrids of Plants and Ghosts*, 1980.

"My Garden, My Daylight" from *Erosion*, 1983.

The Geese

Today as I hang out the wash I see them again, a code
as urgent as elegant,
tapering with goals.
For days they have been crossing. We live beneath these geese

as if beneath the passage of time, or a most perfect heading.   5
Sometimes I fear their relevance.
Closest at hand,
between the lines,

the spiders imitate the paths the geese won't stray from,
imitate them endlessly to no avail: 10
things will not remain connected,
will not heal,

and the world thickens with texture instead of history,
texture instead of place.
Yet the small feat of the spiders   15
binds and binds

the pins to the lines, the lines to the eaves, to the pincushion bush,
as if, at any time, things could fall further apart
and nothing could help them
recover their meaning. And if these spiders had their way,   20

chainlink over the visible world,
would we be in or out? I turn to go back in.
There is a feeling the body gives the mind
of having missed something, a bedrock poverty, like falling

without the sense that you are passing through one world,   25
that you could reach another
anytime. Instead the real
is crossing you,

your body an arrival
you know is false but can't outrun. And somewhere in between   30
the geese forever entering and
these spiders turning back,

this astonishing delay, the everyday, takes place.
1980

Over and Over Stitch

Late in the season the world digs in, the fat blossoms
hold still for just a moment longer.
Nothing looks satisfied,
but there is no real reason to move on much further:
this isn't a bad place;   5
why not pretend

we wished for it?
The bushes have learned to live with their haunches.
The hydrangea[1] is resigned
to its pale and inconclusive utterances.   10
Towards the end of the season
it is not bad

to have the body. To have experienced joy
as the mere lifting of hunger
is not to have known it   15
less. The tobacco leaves
don't mind being removed
to the long racks—all uses are astounding

to the used.
There are moments in our lives which, threaded, give us heaven—   20
noon, for instance, or all the single victories
of gravity, or the kudzu vine,[2]
most delicate of manias,
which has pressed its luck

this far this season.   25
It shines a gloating green.

---

[1] Species of flowering bush whose blooms may be either pale pink or pale blue.

[2] Parasitic plant that, in its extremely rapid growth, overwhelms all other vegetation.

Its edges darken with impatience, a kind of wind.
Nothing again will every be this easy, lives
being snatched up like dropped stitches, the dry stalks of daylilies
marking a stillness we can't keep.   30

1980

Mind

The slow overture of rain,
each drop breaking
without breaking into
the next, describes
the unrelenting, syncopated   5
mind. Not unlike
the hummingbirds
imagining their wings
to be their heart, and swallows
believing the horizon   10
to be a line they lift
and drop. What is it
they cast for? The poplars,
advancing or retreating,
lose their stature   15
equally, and yet stand firm,
making arrangements
in order to become
imaginary. The city
draws the mind in streets,   20
and streets compel it
from their intersections
where a little
belongs to no one. It is
what is driven through   25
all stationary portions
of the world, gravity's
stake in things. The leaves,
pressed against the dank
window of November   30
soil, remain unwelcome
till transformed, parts
of a puzzle unsolvable
till the edges give a bit
and soften. See how   35
then the picture becomes clear,

the mind entering the ground
more easily in pieces,
and all the richer for it.
1980

My Garden, My Daylight

My neighbor brings me bottom fish—
      tomcod, rockcod—
a fist of ocean. He comes out
      from the appletrees between us
holding his gift like a tight   5
      spool of thread.

Once a week he brings me fresh-catch,
      boned and skinned
and rolled up like a tongue. I freeze them,
      speechless, angelic   10
instruments. I have a choir of them.
      Alive, they feed

driving their bodies through the mud,
      mud through their flesh.
See how white they become. High above,   15
      the water thins
to blue, then air, then less. . . .
      These aren't as sweet
as those that shine up there,
      quick schools   20
forever trying to slur over, become water.
      But these belong to us
who cannot fall out of this world
      but only deeper
into it, driving it into the white   25
      of our eyes. Muddy
daylight, we utter it, we drown in it.
      You can stay dry
if you can step between the raindrops
      mother's mother   30
said. She's words now you can't hear.
      I try to wind my way

between what's here: chalk, lily, milk,
    titanium, snow—
as far as I can say   35
    those appleblossoms house

five shades of white, and yet
    I know there's more.
Between my held breath its small hot
    death, a garden   40
Whiteness, grows. Its icy fruit
    seems true,

it glows. *For free* he says
    so that I can't refuse.
1983

Rita Dove
b. 1952

Rita Dove went to Miami University as a Presidential Scholar from Ohio and graduated *summa cum laude* in English. She spent 1974 and 1975 studying modern European literature as a Fulbright fellow at the University of Tübingen in Germany, then took an M.F.A. at the Iowa writers' workshop. She is now a professor of English at the University of Virginia, and was the poet laureate of the United States for 1993. She has returned to Germany since her Fulbright year and is planning a book-length sequence on the European experience in World War I of the U.S. 369th Regiment, an African American volunteer regiment under French command. She writes, "I have long been involved with the exploration of lyrical possibilities of the historical poem, with particular emphasis on the history-within-the-history of Blacks in America." Before the book on the African American regiment, Dove worked on a long book, *Thomas and Beulah* (1986) about the history of African Americans who migrated, as her own family did, from the South to the North—in Dove's case, to Akron, Ohio. *Thomas and Beulah* won the Pulitzer Prize for poetry for 1987. She has more recently published *Grace Notes* (1989), *The Island Women of Paris: A Poem* (1990), *Through the Ivory Gate: A Novel* (1993), *Selected Poems* (1993), *Lady Freedom Among Us* (1993), *Adolescence* (1993), *The Poet's World* (1995), *Mother Love: Poems* (1995), *Three Days of a Forest, a River, Free* (1996), and *The Darker Face of the Earth: A Play* (1996).

    Dove's gift as a poet is to compress what is extended over time into a collage of vivid parts. Often, as the parts are assembled, one does not see how they will fit together; there is a piece, and another piece, a tonality, and another tonality; then, toward the end of the poem, the relations are drawn, the pieces slip into place, the tonalities converge, and the whole complex can at last be seen. It is a brilliant technique, in which the visible presence of imaginative restructuring of experience manifests itself as poetic voltage. Though Dove has, as she says, a continuing interest in the interpreting of the African American experience in America and elsewhere, she has written with equal intensity of the life she has seen in Germany and of emotional life (especially that of adolescence). She writes sparely and plainly; her historic sense is strong and vivifying.

Further Reading:

J. Hufstader, *Coming to Consciousness: Lyric Poetry as Social Discourse in the Works of Charles Simic, Seamus Heaney, Tom Paulin, Tony Harrison, and Rita Dove,* 1993.
P. Wallace, "Divided Loyalties: Literal and Literary in the Poetry of Lorna Dee Cervantes, Cathy Song and Rita Dove," *Melus* 18.3 (1993), 3–20.

R. Dove, *The Poet's World,* 1995.
H. Vendler, *The Given and the Made: Recent American Poets,* 1995.

Texts:

"Banneker," "Parsley," "Roast Possum" and "Dusting" from *Selected Poems,* 1993.

"Mississippi" and "In a Neutral City" from *Grace Notes,* 1989.

Banneker

What did he do except lie
under a pear tree, wrapped in
a great cloak, and meditate
on the heavenly bodies?
Venerable, the good people of Baltimore   5
whispered, shocked and more than
a little afraid. After all it was said
he took to strong drink.
Why else would he stay out
under the stars all night   10
and why hadn't he married?

But who would want him! Neither
Ethiopian nor English, neither
lucky nor crazy, a capacious bird
humming as he penned in his mind   15
another enflamed letter
to President Jefferson—he imagined
the reply, polite and rhetorical.
Those who had been to Philadelphia
reported the statue   20
of Benjamin Franklin
before the library

his very size and likeness.
A wife? No, thank you.
At dawn he milked   25
the cows, then went inside
and put on a pot to stew
while he slept. The clock
he whittled as a boy
still ran. Neighbors   30
woke him up
with warm bread and quilts.
At nightfall he took out

his rifle—a white-maned
figure stalking the darkened   35
breast of the Union—and
shot at the stars, and by chance
one went out. Had he killed?
I assure thee, my dear Sir!
Lowering his eyes to fields   40
sweet with the rot of spring, he could see
a government's domed city
rising from the morass and spreading
in a spiral of lights. . . .
1983

Parsley*

1. The Cane Fields

There is a parrot imitating spring
in the palace, its feathers parsley green.
Out of the swamp the cane appears

to haunt us, and we cut it down. El General
searches for a word; he is all the world   5
there is. Like a parrot imitating spring,

we lie down screaming as rain punches through
and we come up green. We cannot speak an R—
out of the swamp, the cane appears

---

* Dove's note: "*Parsley:* On October 2, 1957,
Rafael Trujillo (1891–1961), dictator of the
Dominican Republic, ordered 20,000 blacks
killed because they could not pronounce the
letter "r" in *perejil*, the Spanish word for
parsley."

and then the mountain we call in whispers
   Katalina.[1]   10
The children gnaw their teeth to arrowheads.
There is a parrot imitating spring.

El General has found his word: *perejil.*
Who says it, lives. He laughs, teeth shining
out of the swamp. The cane appears   15

in our dreams, lashed by wind and streaming.
And we lie down. For every drop of blood
there is a parrot imitating spring.
Out of the swamp the cane appears.

2. The Palace

The word the general's chosen is parsley.   20
It is fall, when thoughts turn
to love and death; the general thinks
of his mother, how she died in the fall
and he planted her walking cane at the grave
and it flowered, each spring stolidly forming   25
four-star blossoms. The general

pulls on his boots, he stomps to
her room in the palace, the one without
curtains, the one with a parrot
in a brass ring. As he paces he wonders   30
Who can I kill today. And for a moment
the little knot of screams
is still. The parrot, who has traveled

all the way from Australia in an ivory
cage, is, coy as a widow, practising   35
spring. Ever since the morning
his mother collapsed in the kitchen
while baking skull-shaped candies
for the Day of the Dead,[2] the general
has hated sweets. He orders pastries   40
brought up for the bird; they arrive

dusted with sugar on a bed of lace.
The knot in his throat starts to twitch;
he sees his boots the first day in battle

---

[1] Properly "Katarina."

[2] November 1, Feast of All Souls.

splashed with mud and urine   45
as a soldier falls at his feet amazed—
how stupid he looked!—at the sound
of artillery. *I never thought it would sing*
the soldier said, and died. Now

the general sees the fields of sugar   50
cane, lashed by rain and streaming.
He sees his mother's smile, the teeth
gnawed to arrowheads. He hears
the Haitians sing without R's
as they swing the great machetes: 55
Katalina, they sing, *Katalina*,

mi madle, mi amol en muelte[3] God knows
his mother was no stupid woman; she
could roll an R like a queen. Even
a parrot can roll an R! In the bare room   60
the bright feathers arch in a parody
of greenery, as the last pale crumbs
disappear under the blackened tongue. Someone

calls out his name in a voice
so like his mother's, a startled tear   65
splashes the tip of his right boot.
My mother, my love in death.
The general remembers the tiny green sprigs
men of his village wore in their capes
to honor the birth of a son. He will   70
order many, this time, to be killed

for a single, beautiful word.
1983

Roast Possum

The possum's a greasy critter
that lives on persimmons and what
that Bible calls carrion.
So much from the 1909 Werner
Encyclopedia, three rows of deep green   5

---

[3] "My mother, my love in death." In the
Spanish, the *r*'s have been changed to *l*'s.

along the wall. A granddaughter
propped on each knee,
Thomas went on with his tale—

but it was for Malcolm, little
Red Delicious, that he invented   10
embellishments: *We shined that possum*
with a torch and I shinnied up,
being the smallest,
to shake him down. He glanced at me,
teeth bared like a shark's   15
in that torpedo snout.
Man he was tough but no match
for old-time know-how.

Malcolm hung back, studying them
with his gold hawk eyes. When the girls   20
got restless, Thomas talked horses:
Strolling Jim, who could balance
a glass of water on his back
and trot the village square
without spilling a drop. Who put   25
Wartrace[1] on the map and was buried
under a stone, like a man.

They liked that part.
He could have gone on to tell them
that the Werner admitted Negro children   30
to be intelligent, though briskness
clouded over at puberty, bringing
indirection and laziness. Instead,
he added: *You got to be careful*
with a possum when he's on the ground;   35
he'll turn on his back and play dead
till you give up looking. That's
what you'd call sullin'.

Malcolm interrupted to ask
who owned Strolling Jim,   40
and who paid for the tombstone.
They stared each other down
man to man, before Thomas,
as a grandfather, replied:
                                        Yessir,   45

---

[1] Town in Tennessee, where the character
Thomas was born in 1900.

> *we enjoyed that possum. We ate him*
> *real slow, with sweet potatoes.*
> *1986*

Dusting

Every day a wilderness—no
shade in sight. Beulah
patient among knickknacks,
the solarium a rage
of light, a grainstorm   5
as her gray cloth brings
dark wood to life.

Under her hand scrolls
and crests gleam
darker still. What   10
was his name, that
silly boy at the fair with
the rifle booth? And his kiss and
the clear bowl with one bright
fish, rippling   15
wound!

Not Michael—
something finer. Each dust
stroke a deep breath and
the canary in bloom.   20
Wavery memory: home
from a dance, the front door
blown open and the parlor
in snow, she rushed
the bowl to the stove, watched   25
as the locker of ice
dissolved and he
swam free.

That was years before
Father gave her up   30
with her name, years before
her name grew to mean
Promise, then
Desert-in-Peace.[1]

---

[1] Both translate the name Beulah.

Long before the shadow and   35
sun's accomplice, the tree.

Maurice.
1986

Mississippi

In the beginning was the dark
moan and creak, a sidewheel
moving through. Thicker
then, scent of lilac,
scent of thyme; slight hairs   5
on a wrist lying down in sweat.
We were falling down
river, carnal
slippage and shadow melt.
We were standing on the deck   10
of the New World, before maps:
tepid seizure of a breeze
and the spirit hissing away . . .
1989

In a Neutral City

Someday we'll talk about the day lily,
the puff dandelion aloof on its milky stalk,
wild birds defying notation. Someday
the last sad trickle in a toilet stall
will recall fountains sighing into themselves   5
and ant-freckled stones
swept clean with a breath. In rain
over lunch we will search for a topic
only to remember a hill, a path hushed
in the waxen shade of magnolias.   10
Someday we'll talk because there'll be
little else to say:
and then the cheese and pears will arrive,
and the worms.
1989

Reginald McKnight
b. 1952

"I don't want to be defined as a race man . . . Each individual defines what Blackness is," says Reginald McKnight, fiction writer and professor of English. Although his literary works such as *I Get on the Bus* (1990), *The Kind of Light That Shines on Texas* (1991), and *Moustapha's Eclipse* (1988) deal with African Americans who came of age after the Civil Rights era, he asserts that his writing is not didactic: "If I see that happening, I try to stop it." Instead, McKnight writes to explore the multiple realities of the African American experience. Setting his characters in ever changing locales such as Texas, California, Colorado, and Senegal, McKnight reveals Black Americans' search for self-affirming identities. Notably, McKnight writes in first person to avoid third-person mediation. In his short stories and novel, first-person narration allows McKnight to relinquish his own ideological pursuits and give voice to his protagonists and their individual struggles.

Reginald McKnight grew up in various parts of the United States, traveling with his father who was in the military. After attending Talmudic Research Institute, he worked in Denver Children's Home before returning to graduate school. His graduate school career was spawned by winning the Sloate Award for the short story "Uncle Moustapha's Eclipse." He later received a special citation from the Ernest Hemingway Foundation for the short story collection *Moustapha's Eclipse*. McKnight is the winner of the O. Henry Award, the Whiting Writer's Award, the Kenyon Review Annual Fiction Award, and the Heinz Short Story Prize. He just recently edited *Wisdom of the African World* (1996), a collection of proverbs, poetry, and words of wisdom from the African Diaspora. Reginald McKnight is currently a professor of English at the University of Maryland, College Park.

Further Reading:

R. McKnight, *Moustapha's Eclipse*, 1988.
———, *I Get on the Bus*, 1990.
———, *White Boys*, 1998.

C. Megan, "New Perceptions on Rhythm in Reginald McKnight's Fiction," *The Kenyon Review* 16:2 (1994), 56–63.

Text:

R. McKnight, *The Kind of Light That Shines on Texas*, 1991.

The Kind of Light That Shines on Texas

I never liked Marvin Pruitt. Never liked him, never knew him, even though there were only three of us in the class. Three black kids. In our school there were fourteen classrooms of thirty-odd white kids (in '66, they considered Chicanos provisionally white) and three or four black kids. Primary school in primary colors. Neat division. Alphabet-ized. They didn't stick us in the back, or arrange us by degree of hue, apartheidlike. This was real integration, a ten-to-one ratio as tidy as upper-class landscaping. If it all worked, you could have ten white kids all to yourself. They could talk to you, get the feel of you, scrutinize you bone deep if they wanted to. They seldom wanted to, and that was fine with me for two reasons. The first was that their scrutiny was irritating. How do you comb your hair—why do you comb your hair—may I please touch your hair—were the kinds of questions they asked. This is no way to feel at home. The second rea-son was Marvin. He embarrassed me. He smelled bad, was at least two grades behind, was hostile, dark skinned, homely, close-mouthed. I feared him for his size, pitied him for his dress, watched him all the time. Marveled at him, mystified, astonished, uneasy.

He had the habit of spitting on his right arm, juicing it down till it would glisten. He would start in immediately after taking his seat when we'd finished with the Pledge of Allegiance, "The Yellow Rose of Texas," "The Eyes of Texas Are upon You," and "Mis-tress Shady." Marvin would rub his spit-flecked arm with his left hand, rub and roll as if polishing an ebony pool cue. Then he would rest his head in the crook of his arm, sniff-ing, huffing deep like black-jacket boys huff bagsful of acrylics. After ten minutes or so, his eyes would close, heavy. He would sleep till recess. Mrs. Wickham would let him.

There was one other black kid in our class. A girl they called Ah-so. I never learned what she did to earn this name. There was nothing Asian about this big-shouldered girl. She was the tallest, heaviest kid in school. She was quiet, but I don't think any one of us was subtle or sophisticated enough to nickname our classmates according to any but physical attributes. Fat kids were called Porky or Butterball, skinny ones were called Stick or Ichabod. Ah-so was big, thick, and African. She would impassively sit, sullen, silent as Marvin. She wore the same dark blue pleated skirt every day, the same ruffled white blouse every day. Her skin always shone as if worked by Marvin's palms and fin-gers. I never spoke one word to her, nor she to me.

Of the three of us, Mrs. Wickham called only on Ah-so and me. Ah-so never an-swered one question, correctly or incorrectly, so far as I can recall. She wasn't stupid. When asked to read aloud she read well, seldom stumbling over long words, reading with humor and expression. But when Wickham asked her about Farmer Brown and how many cows, or the capital of Vermont, or the date of this war or that, Ah-so never spoke. Not one word. But you always felt she could have answered those questions if she'd wanted to. I sensed no tension, embarrassment, or anger in Ah-so's reticence. She simply refused to speak. There was something unshakable about her, some core so im-penatrably solid, you got the feeling that if you stood too close to her she could eat your thoughts like a black star eats light. I didn't despise Ah-so as I despised Marvin. There was nothing malevolent about her. She sat like a great icon in the back of the classroom, tranquil, guarded, sealed up, watchful. She was close to sixteen, and it was my guess she'd given up on school. Perhaps she was just obliging the wishes of her family, stick-ing it out till the law could no longer reach her.

There were at least half a dozen older kids in our class. Besides Marvin and Ah-so there was Oakley, who sat behind me, whispering threats into my ear; Varna Willard with the large breasts; Eddie Limon, who played bass for a high school rock band; and Lawrence Ridderbeck, who everyone said had a kid and a wife. You couldn't expect me to know anything about Texan educational practices of the 1960s, so I never knew why there were so many older kids in my sixth-grade class. After all, I was just a boy and had transferred into the school around midyear. My father, an air force sergeant, had been sent to Viet Nam. The air force sent my mother, my sister, Claire, and me to Connolly Air Force Base, which during the war housed "unaccompanied wives." I'd been to so many different schools in my short life that I ceased wondering about their differences. All I knew about the Texas schools is that they weren't afraid to flunk you.

Yet though I was only twelve then, I had a good idea why Wickham never once called on Marvin, why she let him snooze in the crook of his polished arm. I knew why she would press her lips together, and narrow her eyes at me whenever I correctly answered a question, rare as that was. I know why she badgered Ah-so with questions everyone knew Ah-so would never even consider answering. Wickham didn't like us. She wasn't gross about it, but it was clear she didn't want us around. She would prove her dislike day after day with little stories and jokes. "I just want to share with you all," she would say, "a little riddle my daughter told me at the supper table th'other day. Now, where do you go when you injure your knee?" Then one, two, or all three of her pets would say for the rest of us, "We don't know, Miz Wickham," in that skin-chilling way suck-asses speak, "where?" "Why, to Africa," Wickham would say, "where the knee grows."

The thirty-odd white kids would laugh, and I would look across the room at Marvin. He'd be asleep. I would glance back at Ah-so. She'd be sitting still as a projected image, staring down at her desk. I, myself, would smile at Wickham's stupid jokes, sometimes fake a laugh. I tried to show her that at least one of us was alive and alert, even though her jokes hurt. I sucked ass, too, I suppose. But I wanted her to understand more than anything that I was not like her other nigra children, that I was worthy of more than the non-attention and the negative attention she paid Marvin and Ah-so. I hated her, but never showed it. No one could safely contradict that woman. She knew all kinds of tricks to demean, control, and punish you. And she could swing her two-foot paddle as fluidly as a big-league slugger swings a bat. You didn't speak in Wickham's class unless she spoke to you first. You didn't chew gum, or wear "hood" hair. You didn't drag your feet, curse, pass notes, hold hands with the opposite sex. Most especially, you didn't say anything bad about the Aggies, Governor Connolly, LBJ, Sam Houston, or Waco. You did the forbidden and she would get you. It was that simple.

She never got me, though. Never gave her reason to. But she could have invented reasons. She did a lot of that. I can't be sure, but I used to think she pitied me because my father was in Viet Nam and my uncle A.J. had recently died there. Whenever she would tell one of her racist jokes, she would always glance at me, preface the joke with, "Now don't you nigra children take offense. This is all in fun, you know. I just want to share with you all something Coach Gilchrest told me th'other day." She would tell her joke, and glance at me again. I'd giggle, feeling a little queasy. "I'm half Irish," she would chuckle, "and you should hear some of those Irish jokes." She never told any, and I never really expected her to. I just did my Tom-thing. I kept my shoes shined, my desk neat, answered her questions as best I could, never brought gum to school, never cursed, never slept in class. I wanted to show her we were not all the same.

I tried to show them all, all thirty-odd, that I was different. It worked to some degree, but not very well. When some article was stolen from someone's locker or desk, Marvin, not I, was the first accused. I'd be second. Neither Marvin, nor Ah-so nor I were ever chosen for certain classroom honors—"Pledge leader," "flag holder," "noise monitor," "paper passer outer," but Mrs. Wickham once let me be "eraser duster." I was proud. I didn't even care about the cracks my fellow students made about my finally having turned the right color. I had done something that Marvin, in the deeps of his never-ending sleep, couldn't even dream of doing. Jack Preston, a kid who sat in front of me, asked me one day at recess whether I was embarrassed about Marvin. "Can you believe that guy?" I said. "He's like a pig or something. Makes me sick."

"Does it make you ashamed to be colored?"

"No," I said, but I meant yes. Yes, if you insist on thinking us all the same. Yes, if his faults are mine, his weaknesses inherent in me.

"I'd be," said Jack.

I made no reply. I was ashamed. Ashamed for not defending Marvin and ashamed that Marvin even existed. But if it had occurred to me, I would have asked Jack whether he was ashamed of being white because of Oakley. Oakley, "Oak Tree," Kelvin "Oak Tree" Oakley. He was sixteen and proud of it. He made it clear to everyone, including Wickham, that his life's ambition was to stay in school one more year, till he'd be old enough to enlist in the army. "Them slopes got my brother," he would say. "I'mna sign up and git me a few slopes. Gonna kill them bastards deader'n shit." Oakley, so far as anyone knew, was and always had been the oldest kid in his family. But no one contradicted him. He would, as anyone would tell you, "snap yer neck jest as soon as look at you." Not a boy in class, excepting Marvin and myself, had been able to avoid Oakley's pink bellies, Texas titty twisters, moon pie punches, or worse. He didn't bother Marvin, I suppose, because Marvin was closer to his size and age, and because Marvin spent five sixths of the school day asleep. Marvin probably never crossed Oakley's mind. And to say that Oakley hadn't bothered me is not to say he had no intention of ever doing so. In fact, this haphazard sketch of hairy fingers, slash of eyebrow, explosion of acne, elbows, and crooked teeth, swore almost daily that he'd like to kill me.

Naturally, I feared him. Though we were about the same height, he outweighed me by no less than forty pounds. He talked, stood, smoked, and swore like a man. No one, except for Mrs. Wickham, the principal, and the coach, ever laid a finger on him. And even Wickham knew that the hot lines she laid on him merely amused him. He would smile out at the classroom, goofy and bashful, as she laid down the two, five, or maximum ten strokes on him. Often he would wink, or surreptitiously flash us the thumb as Wickham worked on him. When she was finished, Oakley would walk so cool back to his seat you'd think he was on wheels. He'd slide into his chair, sniff the air, and say, "Somethin's burnin. Do y'all smell smoke? I swanee, I smell smoke and fahr back here." If he had made these cracks and never threatened me, I might have grown to admire Oakley, even liked him a little. But he hated me, and took every opportunity during the six-hour school day to make me aware of this. "Some Sambo's gittin his ass broke open one of these days," he'd mumble. "I wanna fight somebody. Need to keep in shape till I git to Nam."

I never said anything to him for the longest time. I pretended not to hear him, pretended not to notice his sour breath on my neck and ear. "Yep," he'd whisper. "Coonies keep y' in good shape for slope killin." Day in, day out, that's the kind of thing I'd pretend not to hear. But one day when the rain dropped down like lead balls, and the cold air made your skin look plucked, Oakley whispered to me, "My brother tells me it rains like this in Nam. Maybe I oughta go out at recess and break your ass open today. Nice and cool so you don't sweat. Nice and wet to clean up the blood." I said nothing for at least half a minute, then I turned half right and said. "Thought you said your brother was dead." Oakley, silent himself, for a time, poked me in the back with his pencil and hissed, "*Yer* dead." Wickham cut her eyes our way, and it was over.

It was hardest avoiding him in gym class. Especially when we played murderball. Oakley always aimed his throws at me. He threw with unblinking intensity, his teeth gritting, his neck veining, his face flushing, his black hair sweeping over one eye. He could throw hard, but the balls were squishy and harmless. In fact, I found his misses more intimidating than his hits. The balls would whizz by, thunder against the folded bleachers. They rattled as though a locomotive were passing through them. I would duck, dodge, leap as if he were throwing grenades. But he always hit me, sooner or later. And after a while I noticed that the other boys would avoid throwing at me, as if I belonged to Oakley.

One day, however, I was surprised to see that Oakley was throwing at everyone else but me. He was uncommonly accurate, too; kids were falling like tin cans. Since no one was throwing at me, I spent most of the game watching Oakley cut this one and that one down. Finally, he and I were the only ones left on the court. Try as he would, he couldn't hit me, nor I him. Coach Gilchrest blew his whistle and told Oakley and me to bring the red rubber balls to the equipment locker. I was relieved I'd escaped Oakley's stinging throws for once. I was feeling triumphant, full of myself. As Oakley and I approached Gilchrest, I thought about saying something friendly to Oakley: Good game, Oak Tree, I would say. Before I could speak, though, Gilchrest said, "All right boys, there's five minutes left in the period. Y'all are so good, looks like, you're gonna have to play like men. No boundaries, no catch outs, and your gotta hit your opponent three times in order to win. Got me?"

We nodded.

"And you're gonna use these," said Gilchrest, pointing to three volleyballs at his feet. "And you better believe they're pumped full. Oates, you start at that end of the court. Oak Tree, you're at th'other end. Just like usual, I'll set the balls at mid-court, and when I blow my whistle I want y'all to haul your cheeks to the middle and th'ow for all you're worth. Got me?" Gilchrest nodded at our nods, then added, "Remember, no boundaries, right"

I at my end, Oakley at his, Gilchrest blew his whistle. I was faster than Oakley and scooped up a ball before he'd covered three quarters of his side. I aimed, threw, and popped him right on the knee. "One-zip!" I heard Gilchrest shout. The ball bounced off his knee and shot back into my hands. I hurried my throw and missed. Oakley bent down, clutched the two remaining balls. I remember being amazed that he could palm each ball, run full out, and throw left-handed or right-handed without a shade of awkwardness. I spun, ran, but one of Oakley's throws glanced off the back of my head. "One–one!" hollered Gilchrest. I fell and spun on my ass as the other ball came sailing at me. I caught it. "He's out!" I yelled. Gilchrest's voice boomed, "No catch outs. Three hits. Three hits." I leapt to my feet as Oakley scrambled across the floor for another ball. I chased him down, leapt, and heaved the ball hard as he drew himself erect. The ball hit him dead in the face, and he went down flat. He rolled around, cupping his hands over his nose. Gilchrest sped to his side, helped him to his feet, asked him whether he was OK. Blood flowed from Oakley's nose, dripped in startlingly bright spots on the floor, his shoes, Gilchrest's shirt. The coach removed Oakley's T-shirt and pressed it against the big kid's nose to stanch the bleeding. As they walked past me toward the office I mumbled an apology to Oakley, but couldn't catch his reply. "You watch your filthy mouth, boy," said Gilchrest to Oakley.

The locker room was unnaturally quiet as I stepped into its steamy atmosphere. Eyes clicked in my direction, looked away. After I was out of my shorts, had my towel wrapped around me, my shower kit in hand, Jack Preston and Brian Nailor approached me. Preston's hair was combed slick and plastic looking. Nailor's stood up like frozen flames. Nailor smiled at me with his big teeth and pale eyes. He poked my arm with a finger. "You fucked up," he said.

"I tried to apologize."

"Won't do you no good," said Preston.

"I swanee," said Nailor.

"It's part of the game," I said. "It was an accident. Wasn't my idea to use volleyballs."

"Don't matter," Preston said. "He's jest lookin for an excuse to fight you."

"I never done nothing to him."

"Don't matter," said Nailor. "He don't like you."

"Brian's right, Clint. He'd jest as soon kill you as look at you."

"I never done nothing to him."

"Look," said Preston, "I know him pretty good. And jest between you and me, it's 'cause you're a city boy—"

"Whadda you mean? I've never—"

"He don't like your clothes—"

"And he don't like the fancy way you talk in class."

"What fancy—"

"I'm tellin him, if you don't mind, Brian."

"Tell him then."

"He don't like the way you say 'tennis shoes' instead of sneakers. He don't like coloreds. A whole bunch a things, really."

"I never done nothing to him. He's got no reason—"

"*And*," said Nailor, grinning, "*and*, he says you're a stuck-up rich kid." Nailor's eyes had crow's-feet, bags beneath them. They were a man's eyes.

"My dad's a sergeant," I said.

"You chicken to fight him?" said Nailor.

"Yeah, Clint, don't be chicken. Jest go on and git it over with. He's whupped pert near ever'body else in the class. It ain't so bad."

"Might as well, Oates."

"Yeah, yer pretty skinny, but yer jest about his height. Jest git 'im in a headlock and don't let go."

"Goddamn," I said, "he's got no reason to—"

Their eyes shot right and I looked over my shoulder. Oakley stood at his locker, turning its tumblers. From where I stood I could see that a piece of cotton was wedged up one of his nostrils, and he already had the makings of a good shiner. His acne burned red like a fresh abrasion. He snapped the locker open and kicked his shoes off without sitting. Then he pulled off his shorts, revealing two paddle stripes on his ass. They were fresh red bars speckled with white, the white speckles being the reverse impression of the paddle's suction holes. He must not have watched his filthy mouth while in Gilchrest's presence. Behind me, I heard Preston and Nailor pad to their lockers.

Oakley spoke without turning around. "Somebody's gonna git his skinny black ass kicked, right today, right after school." He said it softly. He slipped his jock off, turned around. I looked away. Out of the corner of my eye I saw him stride off, his hairy nakedness a weapon clearing the younger boys from his path. Just before he rounded the corner of the shower stalls, I threw my toilet kit to the floor and stammered, "I—I never did nothing to you, Oakley." He stopped, turned, stepped closer to me, wrapping his towel around himself. Sweat steamed down my rib cage. It felt like ice water. "You wanna go at it right now, boy?"

"I never did nothing to you." I felt tears in my eyes. I couldn't stop them even though I was blinking like mad. "Never."

He laughed. "You busted my nose, asshole."

"What about before? What'd I ever do to you?"

"See you after school, Coonie." Then he turned away, flashing his acne-spotted back like a semaphore. "Why?" I shouted, "Why you wanna fight me?" Oakley stopped and turned, folded his arms, leaned against a toilet stall. "Why you wanna fight *me*, Oakley?" I stepped over the bench. "What'd I do? Why me?" And then unconsciously, as if scratching, as if breathing, I walked toward Marvin, who stood a few feet from Oakley, combing his hair at the mirror. "Why not him?" I said. "How come you're after *me* and not *him?*" The room froze. Froze for a moment that was both evanescent and eternal, somewhere between an eye blink and a week in hell. No one moved, nothing happened; there was no sound at all. And then it was as if all of us at the same moment looked at Marvin. He just stood there, combing away, the only body in motion, I think. He combed his hair and combed it, as if seeing only his image, hearing only his comb scraping his scalp. I knew he'd heard me. There's no way he could not have heard me. But all he did was slide the comb into his pocket and walk out the door.

"I got no quarrel with Marvin," I heard Oakley say. I turned toward his voice, but he was already in the shower.

I was able to avoid Oakley at the end of the school day. I made my escape by asking Mrs. Wickham if I could go the rest room.

" 'Rest room,' " Oakley mumbled. "It's a damn toilet, sissy."

"Clinton," said Mrs. Wickham. "Can you *not* wait till the bell rings. It's almost three o'clock."

"No ma'am," I said. "I won't make it."

"Well I should make you wait just to teach you to be more mindful about . . . hygiene . . . uh things." She sucked in her cheeks, squinted. "But I'm feeling charitable today. You may go." I immediately left the building, and got on the bus. "Ain't you a little early?" said the bus driver, swinging the door shut. "Just left the office," I said. The driver nodded, apparently not giving me a second thought. I had no idea why I'd told her I'd come from the office, or why she found it as satisfactory answer. Two minutes later the bus filled, rolled, and shook its way to Connolly Air Base. When I got home, my mother was sitting in the living room, smoking her Slims, watching her soap opera. She absently asked me how my day had gone and I told her fine. "Hear from Dad?" I said.

"No, but I'm sure he's fine." She always said that when we hadn't heard from him in a while. I suppose she thought I was worried about him, or that I felt vulnerable without him. It was neither. I just wanted to discuss something with my mother that we both cared about. If I spoke with her about things that happened at school, or on my weekends, she'd listen with half an ear, say something like, "Is that so?" or "You don't say?" I couldn't stand that sort of thing. But when I mentioned my father, she treated me a bit more like an adult, or at least someone who was worth listening to. I didn't want to feel like a boy that afternoon. As I turned from my mother and walked down the hall I thought about the day my father left for Viet Nam. Sharp in his uniform, sure behind his aviator specs, he slipped a cigar from his pocket and stuck it in mine. "Not till I get back," he said. "We'll have us one when we go fishing. Just you and me, out on the lake all day, smoking and casting and sitting. Don't let Mama see it. Put it in y'back pocket." He hugged me, shook my hand, and told me I was the man of the house now. He told me he was depending on me to take good care of my mother and sister. "Don't you let me down, now, hear?" And he tapped his thick finger on my chest. "You almost as big as me. Boy, you something else." I believed him when he told me those things. My heart swelled big enough to swallow my father, my mother, Claire. I loved, feared, and respected myself, my manhood. That day I could have put all of Waco, Texas, in my heart. And it wasn't till about three months later that I discovered I really wasn't the man of the house, that my mother and sister, as they always had, were taking care of me.

For a brief moment I considered telling my mother about what had happened at school that day, but for one thing, she was deep down in the halls of *General Hospital,* and never paid you much mind till it was over. For another thing, I just wasn't the kind of person—I'm still not, really—to discuss my problems with anyone. Like my father I kept things to myself, talked about my problems only in retrospect. Since my father wasn't around I consciously wanted to be like him, doubly like him, I could say. I wanted to be the man of the house in some respect, even if it had to be in an inward way. I went to my room, changed my clothes, and laid out my homework. I couldn't focus on it. I thought about Marvin, what I'd said about him or done to him—I couldn't tell which. I'd done something to him, said something about him; said something about and done something to myself. *How come you're after* me *and not* him? I kept trying to tell myself I hadn't meant it that way. *That* way. I thought about approaching Marvin, telling him what I really meant was that he was more Oakley's age and weight than I. I would tell him I meant I was no match for Oakley. *See, Marvin, what I meant was that he wants to fight a colored guy, but is afraid to fight you 'cause you could beat him.* But try as I did, I couldn't for a moment convince myself that Marvin would believe me. I meant it *that* way and no other. Everybody heard. Everybody knew. That afternoon I forced myself to confront the notion that tomorrow I would probably have to fight both Oakley and Marvin. I'd have to be two men.

I rose from my desk and walked to the window. The light made my skin look orange, and I started thinking about what Wickham had told us once about light. She said that oranges and apples, leaves and flowers, the whole multicolored world, was not what it appeared to be. The colors we see, she said, look like they do only because of the light or ray that shines on them. "The color of the thing isn't what you see, but the light that's reflected off it." Then she shut out the lights and shone a white light lamp on a prism. We watched the pale splay of colors on the projector screen; some people oohed and aahed.

Suddenly, she switched on a black light and the color of everything changed. The prism colors vanished, Wickham's arms were purple, the buttons of her dress were as orange as hot coals, rather than the blue they had been only seconds before. We were all very quiet. "Nothing," she said, after a while, "is really what it appears to be." I didn't really understand then. But as I stood at the window, gazing at my orange skin. I wondered what kind of light I could shine on Marvin, Oakley, and me that would reveal us as the same.

I sat down and stared at my arms. They were dark brown again. I worked up a bit of saliva under my tongue and spat on my left arm. I spat again, then rubbed the spittle into it, polishing, working till my arm grew warm. As I spat, and rubbed, I wondered why Marvin did this weird, nasty thing to himself, day after day. Was he trying to rub away the black, or deepen it, doll it up? And if he did this weird nasty thing for a hundred years, would he spit-shine himself invisible, rolling away the eggplant skin, revealing the scarlet muscle, blue vein, pink and yellow tendon, white bone? Then disappear? Seen through, all colors, no colors. Spitting and rubbing. Is this the way you do it? I leaned forward, sniffed the arm. It smelled vaguely of mayonnaise. After an hour or so, I fell asleep.

I saw Oakley the second I stepped off the bus the next morning. He stood outside the gym in his usual black penny loafers, white socks, high-water jeans, T-shirt, and black jacket. Nailor stood with him, his big teeth spread across his bottom lip like playing cards. If there was anyone I felt like fighting, that day, it was Nailor. But I wanted to put off fighting for as long as I could. I stepped toward the gymnasium, thinking that I shouldn't run, but if I hurried I could beat Oakley to the door and secure myself near Gilchrest's office. But the moment I stepped into the gym. I felt Oakley's broad palm clap down on my shoulder. "Might as well stay out here, Coonie," he said. "I need me a little target practice." I turned to face him and he slapped me, one-two, with the back, and then the palm of his hand, as I'd seen Bogart do to Peter Lorre in *The Maltese Falcon*. My heart went wild. I could scarcely breathe. I couldn't swallow.

"Call me a nigger," I said. I have no idea what made me say this. All I know is that it kept me from crying. "Call me a nigger, Oakley."

"Fuck you, ya black-ass slope." He slapped me again, scratching my eye. "I don't do what coonies tell me."

"Call me a nigger."

"Outside, Coonie."

"Call me one. Go ahead!"

He lifted his hand to slap me again, but before his arm could swing my way, Marvin Pruitt came from behind me and calmly pushed me aside. "Git out my way, boy," he said. And he slugged Oakley on the side of his head. Oakley stumbled back, stiff-legged. His eyes were big. Marvin hit him twice more, once again to the side of the head, once to the nose. Oakley went down and stayed down. Though blood was drawn, whistles blowing, fingers pointing, kids hollering, Marvin just stood there, staring at me with cool eyes. He spat on the ground, licked his lips, and just stared at me, till Coach Gilchrest and Mr. Calderon tackled him and violently carried him away. He never struggled, never took his eyes off me.

Nailor and Mrs. Wickham helped Oakley to his feet. His already fattened nose bled and swelled so that I had to look away. He looked around, bemused, wall-eyed, maybe scared. It was apparent he had no idea how bad he was hurt. He didn't blink. He didn't even touch his nose. He didn't look like he knew much of anything. He looked at me, looked me dead in the eye, in fact, but didn't seem to recognize me.

That morning, like all other mornings, we said the Pledge of Allegiance, sang "The Yellow Rose of Texas," "The Eyes of Texas Are upon You," and "Mistress Shady." The room stood strangely empty without Oakley, and without Marvin, but at the same time you could feel their presence more intensely somehow. I felt like I did when I'd walk into my mother's room and could smell my father's cigars or cologne. He was more palpable, in certain respects, than when there in actual flesh. For some reason, I turned to look at Ah-so, and just this once I let my eyes linger on her face. She had a very gentle-looking face, really. That surprised me. She must have felt my eyes on her because she glanced up at me for a second and smiled, white teeth, downcast eyes. Such a pretty smile. That surprised me too. She held it for a few seconds, then let it fade. She looked down at her desk, and sat still as a photograph.

1990

Alberto Rios
b. 1952

In Alberto Rios's poetry, the mouth becomes "the final test of all things," and, accordingly, every orifice and pore of his verse lingers over the taste and feel of words. His "cupped tongue" has been described as "both foreign and familiar," and the poems he collects, condensations of the world of the body and the realm of the spirit, truly are "written miracles."

Raised in Arizona, the son of a Mexican American justice of the peace and an English nurse, Alberto Rios says that his background has strongly influenced his writing. Arizona itself informs much of his poetic landscape because he feels that "the work of the place, the work of the times [he is] in, is not yet done there, not yet documented." Rios is also interested in documenting more about the English side of his heritage. While the "Mexican/Chicano aspects" of his writing are very familiar to him, he feels that he knows "almost nothing about [his] mother's side of the family."

Rios attended the University of Arizona, where he received a B.A. in English literature and creative writing in 1974, a B.A. in psychology in 1975, and an M.F.A. in 1979. Currently a professor in the English Department of Arizona State University and co–chair of its Hispanic Research and Development Committee, Rios also has served as artist (1978 to 1983) and consultant (1983–present) to the Artists-in-Education Program sponsored by the Arizona Commission on the Arts. Rios was writer-in-residence at Central Arizona College, Coolidge, from 1980 to 1982, and was a member of the National Advisory Committee to the National Artists-in-Education Program in 1980. He also has served on the Arizona Commission on the Arts and the National Endowment for the Arts Poetry Panel, and has judged the New York City High School Poetry Contest.

Among his numerous honors, Rios won first prize in the 1977 Academy of American Poets Poetry Contest for "A Man Then Suddenly Stops Moving." In 1983, his short story "The Way Spaghetti Feels" placed second in *New Times* annual fiction award competition. Rios has received a fellowship from the Arizona Commission on the Arts, a faculty-in-aid grant from Arizona State University, and a fellowship from the National Endowment for the Arts. He serves as the guest editor of *Poetry Pilot* and *Signal Fire.*

Rios's first two published works, *Elk Heads on the Wall* (1979) and *Sleeping on Fists* (1981) are poetry chapbooks. *Whispering to Fool the Wind* (1982) was awarded the Walt Whitman Award from the Academy of American Poets in 1981, and *The Iguana Killer: Twelve Stories of the Heart* (1984) received the Western States Book Award. Rios has published five volumes of poetry in recent years: *Five Indiscretions* (1985), *The Lime Orchard Woman* (1988). *The Warrington Poems* (1989),*Teodoro Luna's Two Kisses* (1990), and *Pig Cookies and Other Stories* (1995). Rios frequently contributes to a wide range of periodicals, including *American Poetry Review, North American Review, Iowa Review, Ironweed, Black Warrior Review,* and *Prairie Schooner.* His work has been anthologized since 1977, appearing most recently in *Leaving the Bough: Forty-Eight American Poets; Fifty Years of American Poetry; Strings: A Gathering of Family Poems; The Morrow Anthology of Young American Poets, New American Poetry;* and *Strong Measures: Contemporary American Poetry.*

Rios's commitment to language is simultaneously omniverous and fastidious; one truly believes that his characters "eat words" through "two-foot mouths." Yet at the same time, this appetite often serves as an index for desires of a metaphysical sort, of "dreams of farther/ worlds, so different they cannot/ be remembered, cannot be remembered/ because they cannot be described/ or even imagined." From the open mouth of Rios's verse, the reader finds that which satiates the physical hunger of the present as well as that which remembers the satisfactions of the spiritual past.

Further Reading:
A. Rios, *Aqui Poemas,* 1956.   ———, *The Warrington Poems,* 1989.
———, *Elk Heads on the Wall,* 1979.   ———, *Teodoro Luna's Two Kisses,* 1990.

Texts:
"The Good Lunch of Oceans" from *Teodoro Luna's*   All other poetry from *Whispering to Fool the Wind,*
    Two Kisses, 1990.   1982.

Lost on September Trail, 1967

There was a roof over our heads
and that was at least something.
Then came dances.
The energy for them came from

childhood, or before, from the time   5
when only warmth was important.
We had come to the New World
and become part of it.
If the roof would shelter us,
we would keep it in repair.   10
Roof then could be roof,
solid, visible, recognizable,
and we could be whatever it was
that we were at this moment.
Having lost our previous names   15
somewhere in the rocks as we ran,
we could not yet describe ourselves.
For two days the rain had been
steady, and we left the trail
because one of us remembered   20
this place. Once when I was young
I had yielded to the temptation
of getting drunk, and parts of it
felt like this, wet and hot,
timeless, in the care of someone   25
else. After the dances we sat
like cubs, and cried for that
which in another world might be
milk, but none came.
We had only ourselves, side by side   30
and we began a wrestling
that comes, like dances, out of
nowhere and leaves into the night
like sophisticated daughters
painted and in plumes, but young,   35
a night darker than its name.
We gave ourselves over to adoration
of the moon, but we did not call it
moon, the words that came out
were instead noises as we tried   40
to coax it close enough
to where we might jump,
overpower it, and bring it to our
mouths, which is, after all,
the final test of all things.   45
But we could not, it only circled us,
calmly, and we wanted it more.
We called it Carlos, but it did not
come, we called it friend, comrade,
but nothing. We used every word   50

until we fell, exhausted, and slept
with our eyes open, not trusting
each other, dark pushing us even
farther into childhood, into liquid,
making us crave eyelessness,   55
craving so hard we understand
prayer without knowing its name.
At some point failing
ourselves, eyelids fell.
We dreamt the dreams of farther   60
worlds, so different they cannot
be remembered, cannot be remembered
because they cannot be described
or even imagined. We woke
and did not remember, and the night   65
before became part of us
and we did not remember
speaking to the moon.
We got up from the years without numbers
and called   70
each other by name.
Honey, the one that was me said,
drying her tears that were
really the rain from the night
before, which had taken her   75
without me knowing, *honey,*
again, but she did not understand.
She wanted only the sun
because she was cold, she pulled out
hair to offer it, from her head   80
and her arms. She understood me
only when I held her, made her
warm. She reached to her head
and offered now me
more of herself. I took it.   85
I put it to my mouth,
put it to a cupped tongue
and took it in. She moved
and I put my hands on her knees
which looked up at opposite ends   90
of the sky.
1982

Mi Abuelo*

Where my grandfather is is in the ground
where you can hear the future
like an Indian with his ear at the tracks.
A pipe leads down to him so that sometimes
he whispers what will happen to a man   5
in town or how he will meet the best
dressed woman tomorrow and how the best
man at her wedding will chew the ground
next to her. Mi abuelo is the man
who speaks through all the mouths in my house.   10
An echo of me hitting the pipe sometimes
to stop him from saying *my hair is a*
sieve is the only other sound. It is a phrase
that among all others is the best,
he says, and *my hair is a sieve* is sometimes   15
repeated for hours out of the ground
when I let him, which is not often.
An abuelo should be much more than a man
like you! He stops then, and speaks: *I am a man*
who has served ants with the attitude.   20
of a waiter, who has made each smile as only
an ant who is fat can, and they liked me best,
but there is nothing left. Yet I know he ground
green coffee beans as a child, and sometimes
he will talk about his wife, and sometimes   25
about when he was deaf and a man
cured him by mail and he heard groundhogs
talking, or about how he walked with a cane
he chewed on when he got hungry.
At best, mi abuelo is a liar.   30
I see an old picture of him at nani's with an
off-white yellow center mustache and sometimes
that's all I know for sure. He talks best
about these hills, *slowest waves,* and where this man
is going, and I'm convinced his hair is a sieve,   35
that his fever is cooled now underground.
Mi abuelo is an ordinary man.
I look down the pipe, sometimes, and see a
ripple-topped stream in its best suit, in the ground.
1982

* Spanish: my grandfather.

Nani

Sitting at her table, she serves
the sopa de arroz[1] to me
instinctively, and I watch her,
the absolute *mamá*, and eat words
I might have had to say more   5
out of embarrassment. To speak,
now-foreign words I used to speak,
too, dribble down her mouth as she serves
me albondigas.[2] No more
than a third are easy to me.   10
By the stove she does something with words
and looks at me only with her
back. I am full. I tell her
I taste the mint, and watch her speak
smiles at the stove. All my words   15
make her smile. Nani never serves
herself, she only watches me
with her skin, her hair. I ask for more.

I watch the *mamá* warming more
tortillas for me. I watch her   20
fingers in the flame for me.
Near her mouth, I see a wrinkle speak
of a man whose body serves
the ants like she serves me, then more words
from more wrinkles about children, words   25
about this and that, flowing more
easily from these other mouths. Each serves
as a tremendous string around her,
holding her together. They speak
nani was this and that to me   30
and I wonder just how much of me
will die with her, what were the words
I could have been, was. Her insides speak
through a hundred wrinkles, now, more
than she can bear, steel around her,   35
shouting, then, What is this thing she serves?

---

[1] Spanish: rice soup.
[2] Spanish: meatballs; fishballs.

She asks me if I want more.
I own no words to stop her.
Even before I speak, she serves.
1982

The Good Lunch of Oceans

I ate with my father
The avocado
And thought without telling him
The skin of a sidewalk
Dirty with stones. It is the   5
Harbor line of Thrill
And the swim inside.
Scrotum skin,
I could not tell him.
How its feel was of sutures   10
Holding the body together
At its very base.
      Green meat,
Feel of sand completely
Wet, a fragile   15
Lip meat, mouth
Meat of dreams
Two places on her body.
      Green in a garden
Of celeries and the lost   20
Cat-eye marble
That won me everything.
Old Chevrolet paint, green
Virgin of Guadalupe,[1]
That famous painting   25
The color of the Thirties,
From which deep orange
Has also survived. Green
That used to be green.
      Failed ocarina[2]   30

---

[1] Painted image said to result from the appa-
ration of the Virgin Mary, the mother of
Christ, to an Indian convert in 1531 in Mexico City. The incident precipitated widespread conversions of the Indians of Mexico
to Christianity.

[2] Italian: little goose; earthenware globular
flute that sounds one or two soft notes.

Little bear
Shape of an ocean,
I eat our avocado
With my father, play
For its music   35
In my mouth.
1990

Sandra Cisneros
b. 1954

Sandra Cisneros' collection *Woman Hollering Creek and Other Stories* (1991) was the first work by and about Chicanas—that is, Mexican American women—to receive a contract from a major American publishing house, Random House. Cisneros was born in 1954 into a working-class family in Chicago; she is the only daughter in a family of six brothers, a situation she likens to having seven fathers. Her father is Mexican, has close ties to his homeland, and so moved his family back and forth between Chicago apartments and his mother's home in Mexico City. The combination of a transient upbringing and exclusion from her brothers' activities turned Cisneros inward; she spent her childhood in the company of books. Her creative voice emerged in 1974 in a writing class at Loyola University in Chicago, and was further formed at the University of Iowa's Writers Workshop where she discovered her differences from Anglo students, their experiences, and their styles.

Cisneros deals with the serious, painful themes of racism, sexism, and poverty, yet her voice is strong, playful, and often gracefully laced with Spanish words and phrases. She avoids the romantic clichés that have sometimes infected Anglo writing about life in the barrio. Critics have not agreed on what to call her short narratives because, like Jorge Luis Borges, Cisneros blends vivid, lyrical passages that feel poetic into her prose. She has said that while the stories in her collections function individually, they also are joined by a single unifying thread of vision and experience. Many of the stories in *Woman Hollering Creek* feature characters who feel themselves in a triple bind: they are neither Mexican, American, nor male. The theme of education and writing as a means for women to break away from confusion and oppressive traditions is prominent in several of her stories. The narrators change, yet each story is controlled by a determined, sometimes rebellious voice.

The title story of *Woman Hollering Creek* takes an unflinching look at a woman reared in a small town in Mexico whose romantic fantasy—derived from watching soap operas—gets fulfilled when she meets Juan Pedro, a Texan who wants to marry her right away. Life on the other side of the border soon turns from dream to nightmare as Cleofilas finds herself a mother, slapped about by her husband, isolated at home, and soon pregnant again. Eventually she finds the help and the courage to leave. In the whoops of a spirited woman driving her back to Mexico in a pickup truck, she sees what autonomy might look like. In the selection "Barbie Q," a young girl's voice speaks in clipped sentences, in the present tense. As her narrative moves away from scene-setting description of two Barbie doll friends, it gains tension, momentum, and symbolic weight. The girlfriends who own the Barbies clearly live in a run-down neighborhood, have little money, and limited dreams. But when they see new Barbie outfits at a fire sale, their quest takes on urgency and point. Their neighborhood may be smoking, their relationships circumscribed, their toys singed and "stinky," but "inside" the girls are "doing loopity-loops and pirouetting." Clearly the narrator and her friends are survivors; they may be damaged like a doll with a melted foot, yet they're able, for better or worse, to disguise the disfigurement—"if you don't lift her dress, right?–who's to know."

Cisneros has also published three books of poetry (*Bad Boys*, 1980; *My Wicked, Wicked Ways*, 1987; and *Loose Woman*, 1994) and a number of essays on the creative process, especially as it related to being Mexican, female, and what she likes to call "wicked."

Further Reading:
S. Cisneros, *The House on Mango Street*, 1985.　　　　　——, *Loose Woman*, 1994.
——, *My Wicked, Wicked Ways*, 1987.

Text:
Woman Hollering Creek and Other Stories, 1991.

Barbie-Q

from ***Woman Hollering Creek***

Yours is the one with mean eyes and a ponytail. Striped swimsuit, stilettos, sunglasses, and gold hoop earrings. Mine is the one with bubble hair. Red swimsuit, stilettos, pearl earrings, and a wire stand. But that's all we can afford, besides one extra outfit apiece. Yours, "Red Flair," sophisticated A-line coatdress with a Jackie Kennedy pillbox hat, white gloves, handbag, and heels included. Mine, "Solo in the Spotlight," evening elegance in black glitter strapless gown with a puffy skirt at the bottom like a mermaid tail, formal-length gloves, pink chiffon scarf, and mike included. From so much dressing and undressing, the black glitter wears off where her titties stick out. This and a dress invented from an old sock when we cut holes here and here and here, the cuff rolled over for the glamorous, fancy-free, off-the-shoulder look.

Every time the same story. Your Barbie is roommates with my Barbie, and my Barbie's boyfriend comes over and your Barbie steals him, okay? Kiss kiss kiss. Then the two Barbies fight. You dumbbell! He's mine. Oh no he's not, you stinky! Only Ken's invisible, right? Because we don't have money for a stupid-looking boy doll when we'd both rather ask for a new Barbie outfit next Christmas. We have to make do with your mean-eyed Barbie and my bubblehead Barbie and our one outfit apiece not including the sock dress.

Until next Sunday when we are walking through the flea market on Maxwell Street and *there!* Lying on the street next to some tool bits, and platform shoes with the heels all squashed, and a fluorescent green wicker wastebasket, and aluminum foil, and hub-caps, and a pink shag rug, and windshield wiper blades, and dusty mason jars, and a coffee can full of rusty nails. *There!* Where? Two Mattel boxes. One with the "Career Gal" ensemble, snappy black-and-white business suit, three-quarter-length sleeve jacket with kick-pleat skirt, red sleeveless shell, gloves, pumps, and matching hat in-cluded. The other, "Sweet Dreams," dreamy pink-and-white plaid nightgown and matching robe, lace-trimmed slippers, hairbrush and hand mirror included. How much? Please, please, please, please, please, please, please, until they say okay.

On the outside you and me skipping and humming but inside we are doing loopity-loops and pirouetting. Until at the next vendor's stand, next to boxed pies, and bright orange toilet brushes, and rubber gloves, and wrench sets, and bouquets of feather flowers, and glass towel racks, and steel wool, and Alvin and the Chipmunks records, *there!* And *there!* And *there* And *there!* and *there!* and *there!* and *there!* Bendable Legs Barbie with her new page-boy hairdo. Midge, Barbie's best friend. Ken, Barbie's boyfriend. Skipper, Barbie's little sister. Tutti and Todd, Barbie and Skipper's tiny twin sister and brother. Skipper's friends, Scooter and Ricky. Alan, Ken's buddy. And Fran-cie, Barbie's MOD'ern cousin.

Everybody today selling toys, all of them damaged with water and smelling of smoke. Because a big toy warehouse on Halsted Street burned down yesterday—see there?—the smoke still rising and drifting across the Dan Ryan expressway. And now there is a big fire sale at Maxwell Street, today only.

So what if we didn't get our new Bendable Legs Barbie and Midge and Ken and Skip-per and Tutti and Todd and Scooter and Ricky and Alan and Francie in nice clean boxes and had to buy them on Maxwell Street, all water-soaked and sooty. So what if our Bar-bies smell like smoke when you hold them up to your nose even after you wash and wash and wash them. And if the prettiest doll, Barbie's MOD'ern cousin Francie with real eye-lashes, eyelash brush included, has a left foot that's melted a little—so? If you dress her in her new "Prom Pinks" outfit, satin splendor with matching coat, gold belt, clutch, and hair bow included, so long as you don't lift her dress, right?—who's to know.

Louise Erdrich
b. 1954

Karen Louise Erdrich was born in Little Falls, Minnesota, and grew up in Wahpeton, North Dakota, where her father taught at a boarding school run by the Bureau of Indian Affairs. Part Chippewa on her mother's side, Erdrich was encouraged by her parents to write stories while still a child: "My father used to give me a nickel for every story I wrote," she explained to an interviewer, "and my mother wove strips of construction paper together and stapled them into book covers. So at an early age, I felt myself to be a published author earning substantial royalties." While at Dartmouth College, she truly began to publish stories and poems, and after graduating in 1976 she went on to take an M.A. in creative writing at Johns Hopkins University in 1979. For a few years she held various jobs, including waiting on tables and working at a construction site (which helped as background for "Scales"), and for a time she taught at Dartmouth as a writer-in-residence. At Dartmouth, she met the anthropologist and writer, Michael Dorris, who chaired the college's Native American Studies Department. They began collaborating on short fiction in 1980 and were married in 1981.

Erdrich's first book, a collection of fourteen independent yet interconnected short stories, *Love Medicine*, grew out of her collaborative work with her husband and was published in 1984. The title alludes to a Chippewa folk belief, and the stories take place in and around a North Dakota reservation between 1934 and 1984. The book not only became a national bestseller, but won numerous awards, including the National Book Critics Circle Award, the *Los Angeles Times* Award, and the American Academy and Institute of Arts and Letters award for the best first work of fiction. Erdrich has also published two collections of poetry, *Jacklight* (1984) and *Baptism of Desire* (1989). Her other novels are *The Beet Queen* (1986), *Tracks* (1988), and (with Michael Dorris) *The Crown of Columbus* (1991). Throughout most of her fiction Erdrich has creatively documented three generations of Chippewa families in a small region of North Dakota. "I haven't drawn any maps," she claimed, acknowledging her indebtedness to William Faulkner's Yoknapatawpha County, "but I do think it's a certain place that's being imagined more and more completely.

"Lulu's Boys" is one of the interlocking stories of *Love Medicine*.

Text:
Love Medicine, 1984.

Lulu's Boys

On the last day that Lulu Lamartine spent as Henry's widow, her boys were outside drinking beers and shooting plastic jugs. Her deceased husband's brother, Beverly, was sitting across from her at the kitchen table. Having a name some people thought of as feminine had turned Beverly Lamartine to building up his muscles in his youth, and they still bulged, hard as ingots in some places, now lost in others. His plush belly strained open the bottom buttons of his black shirt, and Lulu saw his warm skin peeking through. She also saw how the tattoos he and Henry had acquired on their arms, and which Lulu had always admired, were now deep black and so fuzzy around the edges that she could hardly tell what they were.

Beverly saw her looking at the old tattoos and pushed his sleeves up over his biceps. "Get an eyeful." he grinned. As of old, he stretched his arms across the table, and she gazed at the figures commemorating the two brothers' drunken travels outside her life.

There was a doll, a skull with a knife stuck in it, an eagle, a swallow, and Beverly's name, rank, and serial number. Looking at the arm made Lulu remember her husband's tattoos. Henry's arms had been imprinted with a banner bearing some other woman's name, a rose with a bleeding thorn, two lizards, and like his brother's, with his name, rank, and serial number.

Sometimes Lulu could not help it. She thought of everything so hard that her mind felt warped and sodden as a door that swells up in spring. It would not close properly to keep the troublesome thoughts out.

Right now she thought of those two lizards on either one of Henry's arms. She imagined them clenching together when he put his arms around her. Then she thought of them coupling the same way she and Henry did. She thought of this while looking at Beverly's lone swallow, a bird with outstretched wings deep as ink and bleeding into his flesh. She remembered Beverly's trick: the wings were carefully tattooed on certain muscles, so that when he flexed his arm the bird almost seemed to hover in a dive or swoop.

Lulu hadn't seen her husband's brother since the funeral in 1950, with the casket closed because of how badly Henry had suffered in the car wreck. Drunk, he had started driving the old Northern Pacific tracks and either fallen asleep or passed out, his car straddling the rails. As he'd left the bar that night everyone who had been there remembered his words.

"She comes barreling through, you'll never see me again."

At first they had thought he was talking about Lulu. But even at the time they knew she didn't lose her temper over drinking. It was the train Henry had been talking about. They realized that later when the news came and his casket was sealed.

Beverly Lamartine had shown up from the Twin Cities one hour before his brother's service was held. He had brought along the trophy flag—a black swastika on torn red cloth—that he had captured to revenge the oldest Lamartine, a quiet boy, hardly spoken of now, who was killed early on while still in boot camp.

When the men from the veteran's post had lowered Henry's casket into the grave on ropes, there was a U.S. flag draped across it already. Beverly had shaken out the trophy flag. He'd let it go in the air, and the wind seemed to suck it down, the black arms of the insignia whirling like a spider.

Watching it, Lulu had gone faint. The sudden spokes of the black wheel flashed before her eyes and she'd toppled dizzily, then stumbled over the edge of the grave.

The men were still lowering Henry on ropes. Lulu plunged heavily down with the trophy flag, and the ropes burned out of the pallbearers' hands. The box hit bottom. People screamed and there was a great deal of commotion, during which Beverly jumped down to revive Lulu. All together, the pallbearers tugged and hoisted her out. The black garments seemed to make her even denser than she was. Her round face and chubby hands were a pale dough color, cold and wet with shock. For hours afterward she trembled, uttered senseless vowels, jumped at sounds and touches. Some people, assuming that she had jumped in the grave to be buried along with Henry, thought much better of her for a while.

But most of her life Lulu had been known as a flirt. And that was putting it mildly. Tongues less kind had more indicting things to say.

For instance, besides the fact of Lulu Lamartine's first husband, why did each of the boys currently shooting milk jugs out front of Henry's house look so different? There were eight of them. Some of them even had her maiden name. The three oldest were Nanapushes. The next oldest were Morrisseys who took the name Lamartine, and then there were more assorted younger Lamartines who didn't look like one another, either. Red hair and blond abounded; there was some brown. The black hair on the seven-year-old at least matched his mother's. This boy was named Henry Junior, and he had been born approximately nine months after Henry Senior's death.

Give or take a week, Beverly thought, looking from Henry Junior out the window back to the woman across the table. Beverly was quite certain that he and not his brother, was the father of that boy. In fact, Beverly had come back to the reservation with a hidden purpose.

Beverly Lamartine wanted to claim Henry Junior and take him home.

In the Twin Cities there were great relocation opportunities for Indians with a certain amount of natural stick-to-it-iveness and pride. That's how Beverly saw it. He was darker than most, but his parents had always called themselves French or Black Irish and considered those who thought of themselves as Indians quite backward. They had put the need to get ahead in Beverly. He worked devilishly hard.

Door to door, he'd sold children's after-school home workbooks for the past eighteen years. The wonder of it was that he had sold any workbook sets at all, for he was not an educated man and if the customers had, as they might naturally do, considered him an example of his product's efficiency they might not have entrusted their own children to those pages of sums and reading exercises. But they did buy the workbook sets regularly, for Bev's ploy was to use his humble appearance and faulty grammar to ease into conversation with his hardworking get-ahead customers. They looked forward to seeing the higher qualities, which they could not afford, inculcated in their own children. Beverly's territory was a small-town world of earnest dreamers. Part of Bev's pitch, and the one that usually sold the books, was to show the wife or husband a wallet-size school photo of his son.

That was Henry Junior. The back of the photo was inscribed "To Uncle Bev," but the customer never saw that, because the precious relic was encased in a cardboard-backed sheet of clear plastic. This covering preserved it from thousands of mill-toughened thumbs in the working-class sections of Minneapolis and small towns within its one-hundred-mile radius. Every year or so Beverly wrote to Lulu, requesting another picture. It was sent to him in perfect goodwill. With every picture Beverly grew more familiar with his son and more inspired in the invention of tales he embroidered, day after day, on front porches that were to him the innocent stages for his routine.

His son played baseball in a sparkling-white uniform stained across the knees with grass. He pitched no-hitters every few weeks. Teachers loved the boy for getting so far ahead of the other students on his own initiative. They sent him on to various higher grades, and he was invited to the parties of children in the wealthy suburb of Edina. Henry Junior cleared the hurdles of class and intellect with an ease astonishing to Beverly, who noted to his wistful customers how swiftly the young surpass the older generation.

"Give them wings!" he would urge, flipping softly through the cheap pulp-flecked pages. The sound of the ruffled paper was like the panic of fledglings before they learn how to glide. People usually bought, and only later, when they found themselves rolling up a work-skills book to slaughter a fly or scribbling phone numbers down on the back of *Math Enrichment,* would they realize that their children had absolutely no interest in taking the world by storm through self-enlightenment.

Some days, after many hours of stories, the son became so real in Bev's mind that when he came home to the apartment, he half expected the boy to pounce on him before he put his key in the door. But when the lock turned his son vanished, for Elsa would be there, and she was not particularly interested in children, real or not. She was a typist who changed jobs incessantly. Groomed with exquisite tawdriness, she'd fashioned for Bev the image of a modern woman living the ideal career life. Her salary only fluctuated by pennies from firm to firm, but her importance and value as a knower-of-ropes swelled. She believed herself indispensable, but she heartlessly left employers hanging in their times of worst need to go on to something better.

Beverly adored her.

She was a natural blond with birdlike legs and, true, no chin, but great blue snapping eyes. She smoked exotically, rolling smoke off her tongue, and often told Bev that two weeks from now he might not be seeing her again. Then she would soften toward him. The possibilities she gave up to be with him impressed Bev so much, every time, that it ceased to bother him that Elsa only showed him off to her family in Saint Cloud at the height of summer, when they admired his perfect tan.

The boy, though, who was everywhere in his life and yet nowhere, fit less easily into Bev's fantasy of how he lived. The boy made him ache in hidden, surprising places sometimes at night when he lay next to Elsa, his knuckles resting lightly against her emphatic spine. That was the limit of touching she would tolerate in slumber. She even took her sleeping breath with a certain rigid meanness, holding it stubbornly and releasing it with small explosive sighs. Bev hardly noticed, though, for beside her his mind raced through the ceilings and walls.

One night he saw himself traveling. He was driving his sober green car westward, past the boundaries of his salesman's territory, then over the state line and on across to the casual and lonely fields, the rich, dry violet hills of the reservation. Then he was home where his son really lived. Lulu came to the door. He habitually blotted away her face and body, so that in his thoughts she was a doll of flour sacking with a curly black mop on her head. She was simply glad that he had come at last to take the son she had such trouble providing for off her hands. She was glad Henry Junior would be wafted into a new and better metropolitan existence.

This scenario became so real through the quiet hours he lay beside Elsa that Bev even convinced himself that his wife would take to Henry Junior, in spite of the way she shuddered at children in the streets and whispered "Monkeys!" And then, by the time the next workday was half over, he'd arranged for a vacation and made an appointment to have a once-over done on his car.

Of course, Lulu was not made of flour sacking and yarn. Beverly had realized that in the immediacy of her arms. She grabbed him for a hug when he got out of his car, and, tired by the long trip, his head whirled for a moment in a haze of yellow spots. When she released him, the boys sauntered up, poker-faced and mildly suspicious, to stand in a group around him and await their introductions. There seemed to be so many that at first he was speechless. Each of them was Henry Junior in a different daydream at a different age, and so alike were their flat expressions he couldn't even pick out the one whose picture sold the record number of home workbooks in the Upper Midwestern Regional Divisions.

Henry Junior, of course, was perfectly recognizable after Lulu introduced him. After all, he did look exactly like the picture in Bev's wallet. He put his hand out and shook manfully like his older brothers, which pleased Bev, although he had trouble containing a moment of confusion at the utter indifference in the boy's eyes. He had to remember the boy was meeting him for the first time. In a child's world strange grown-ups are indistinguishable as trees in a forest. Even the writing on the back of those photographs was probably, now that he thought of it, Lulu's.

They went away, started shooting their guns, and then Bev was left with the unexpected problem of the mother of his son, the woman he would just as soon forget. During a moment of adjustment, however, he decided to go through whatever set of manipulations were necessary. He wanted to handle the situation in the ideal, firm, but diplomatic manner. And then, after he'd recovered from the strength of her hug, he had absolutely no doubt that things would go on according to his plan.

"My my my," he said to Lulu now. She was buttering a piece of bread soft as the plump undersides of her arms. "Lot of water under the dam."

She agreed, taking alert nips of her perfectly covered slice. She had sprinkled a teaspoon of sugar over it, carefully distributing the grains. That was how she was. Even with eight boys her house was neat as a pin. The candy bowl on the table sat precisely on its doily. All her furniture was brushed and straightened. Her coffee table held a neat stack of *Fate* and *True Adventure* magazines. On her walls she's hung matching framed portraits of poodles, kittens, and an elaborate embroidered portrait of Chief Joseph. Her windowsills were decorated with pincushions in the shapes of plump little hats and shoes.

"I make these." She cupped a tiny blue sequined pump in her hand. "You have a girl friend? I'll give it to you. Here."

She pushed the little shoe across the table. It skittered over the edge, fell into his lap, and Beverly retrieved it quickly, for he saw that her hand was following. He set the blue slipper between them without addressing her implicit question on his status—girl friend, married, or just looking around. He was intent on bringing up the subject of Henry Junior.

"Remember that time . . ." he started. Then he didn't know what he was going to say. What did come out surprised him. "You and me and Henry were playing cards before you got married and the boys were sleeping?

He could have kicked himself for having blurted that out. Even after all these years he couldn't touch on the memory without running a hand across his face or whistling tunelessly to drive it from his mind. It didn't seem to have bothered her all these years though. She picked up the story smoothly and went on.

"Oh, you men," she laughed chidingly. Her face was so little like Beverly's flour sacking doll he wondered how he had stood imagining her that way all these years. Her mouth was small, mobile, like a puckering flower, and her teeth were unusually tiny and white. He remembered having the urge to lick their smoothness once. But now she was talking.

"I suppose you thought you could take advantage of a poor young woman. I don't know who it was, you or Henry, that suggested after several too many beers that we change our pennyante poker game to strip. Well I still have to laugh. I had you men right down to your boxer shorts in no time flat, and I was sitting there, warm and cozy as you please. I was still in my dress with my shoes on my feet."

"You had them beads on, clip earrings, bangle bracelets, silk stockings," Beverly pouted.

"Garters and other numerous foundation garments. Of course I did. I am a woman of detachable parts. You should know by now. You simply weren't playing in your league with strip poker."

She had the grace to put a hand to her lips as they uncurved, hiding the little gap-toothed smile he'd doted over at the time of that game.

"Want to know something I never told before?" she said "It was after I won your shorts with my pair of deuces and Henry's with my eights, and you were naked, that I decided which one to marry."

Beverly was shocked at this statement, bold even for Lulu. His wind felt knocked out of him for a moment, because her words called up the old times so clearly, the way he felt when she decided to marry his brother. He'd buried the feelings eventually in the knowledge that she wasn't right for him, man of the world that he was becoming. He congratulated himself for years after on getting free of her slack, ambitionless, but mindlessly powerful female clutches. Right now his reasoning had ripped wide open, however, and jealousy kicked him in the stomach.

Lulu cooed. Her voice was like a wind chime rattling. Cheap, sweet, maddening. "Some men react in that situation and some don't," she told him. "It was reaction I looked for, if you know what I mean."

Beverly was silent.

Lulu winked at him with her bold, gleaming blackberry eyes. She had smooth tight skin, wrinkled only where she laughed, always fragrantly powdered. At the time her hair was still dark and thickly curled. Later she would burn it off when her house caught fire, and it would never grow back. Because her face was soft and yet alert, vigilant as some small cat's, plump and tame but with a wildness in its breast, Beverly had always felt exposed, preyed on, undressed around her, even before the game in which she'd stripped him naked and now, as he found, appraised him in his shame.

You got your reaction when you needed it, he wanted to say.

Yet, even in his mounting exasperation, he did not lose control and stoop to discussing what had happened after Henry's wake, when they both went outside to get some air. He rolled his sleeves down and fished a soft pack of Marlboros from her side of the table. She watched his hand as he struck the match, and her eyes narrowed. They were so black the iris sometimes showed within like blue flames. He thought her heartless, suddenly, and wondered if she even remembered the two of them in the shed after Henry's wake. But there was no good way he could think of to ask without getting back down to her level.

Henry Junior came to the window, hungry, and Lulu made a sandwich for him with baloney and hot-dog relish. The boy was seven years old, sturdy, with Lulu's delicate skin and the almost Asian-looking eyes of all the Lamartines. Beverly watched the boy with electrified attention. He couldn't really say if anything about the child reminded him of himself, unless it was the gaze. Beverly had tried to train his gaze like a hawk to use in barroom staredowns during his tour of duty. It came in handy, as well, when he made a sale, although civilian life had long ago taken the edge off his intensity, as it had his muscles, his hero's stubborn, sagging flesh that he could still muster in a crisis. There was a crisis now. The boy seemed to have acquired the staredown technique naturally. Beverly was the first to look away.

"Uncle Bev," Henry Junior said. "I always heard about the bird on your arm. Could you make it fly?"

So Beverly rolled up shirt sleeve once more and forced his blood up. He flexed powerfully, over and over, until the boy was bored, satisfied, and fled back to his brothers. Beverly let his arm down carefully. It was numb. The sound of the .22 reports came thick and fast for a while, then all the boys paused to reload and set the jugs in a line against the fence and argue over whose shot went where.

"They're teaching him to shoot," explained Lulu. "We had two bucks brought down last fall. And pheasants? Those boys will always put meat on my table."

She rambled on about them all, and Bev listened with relief, gathering his strength to pull the conversation back his way again.

One of the oldest boys was going down to Haskell Junior College, while another, Gerry, was testing the limits of the mission school system, at twelve. Lulu pointed Gerry out among the others. Bev could see Lulu most clearly in this boy. He laughed at everything, or seemed barely to be keeping amusement in. His eyes were black, sly, snapping with sparks. He led the rest in play without a hint of effort, just like Lulu, whose gestures worked as subtle magnets. He was a big boy, a born leader, light on his feet and powerful. His mind seemed quick. It would not surprise Bev to hear, after many years passed on, that this Gerry grew up to be both a natural criminal and a hero whose face appeared on the six-o'clock news.

Lulu managed to make the younger boys obey perfectly. Bev noticed, while the older ones adored her to the point that they did not tolerate anything less from anyone else. As her voice swirled on, Bev thought of some Tarzan book he had read. In that book there was a queen protected by bloodthirsty warriors who smoothly dispatched all of her enemies. Lulu's boys had grown into a kind of pack. They always hung together. When a shot went true, their gangling legs, encased alike in faded denim, shifted as if a ripple went through them collectively. They moved in dance steps too intricate for the noninitiated eye to imitate or understand. Clearly they were of one soul. Handsome, rangy, wildly various, they were bound in total loyalty, not by oath but by the simple, unquestioning belongingness of part of one organism.

Lulu had gone silent, suddenly, to fetch something from her icebox. In that quiet moment something about the boys outside struck Beverly as almost dangerous.

He watched them close around Henry Junior in an impenetrable mass of black-and-white sneakers, sweatshirts, baseball hats, and butts of Marlin rifles. Through the chinks between their bodies Beverly saw Gerry, dark and electric as his mother, kneel behind Henry Junior and arm-over-arm instruct him how to cradle, aim, and squeeze-fire the .22. When Henry Junior stumbled, kicked backward by the recoil, missing the jug, the boys dusted him clean and set him back behind the rifle again. Slowly, as he watched, Beverly's uneasy sense of menace gave way to some sweet apprehension of their kinship. He was remembering the way he and Henry and Slick, the oldest of his brothers, used to put themselves on the line for each other in high school. People used to say you couldn't drive a knife edge between the Lamartines. Nothing ever came between them. Nothing ever did or would.

Even while he was thinking that, Beverly knew it wasn't true.

What had come between them was a who, and she was standing across from him now at the kitchen counter. Lulu licked some unseen sweetness from her fingers, having finished her sugared bread. Her tongue was small, flat, and pale as a little cat's. Her eyes had shut in mystery. He wondered if she knew his thoughts.

She padded easily toward him, and he stood up in an odd panic as she approached. He felt his heart knock urgently as a stranger in trouble, and then she touched him through his pants. He was helpless. His mouth fell on hers and kept traveling, through the walls and ceilings, down the levels, through the broad, warm reaches of the years.

The boys came back very late in the afternoon. By then, Beverly had drastically revised his plans for Henry Junior to the point where he had no plans at all. In a dazed, immediate, unhappy bewilderment he sat on the doily-bedecked couch opening and closing his hands in his lap. Lulu was bustling about the kitchen in a calm, automatic frenzy. She seemed to fill pots with food by pointing at them and take things from the oven that she'd never put in. The table jumped to set itself. The pop foamed into glasses, and the milk sighed to the lip. The youngest boy, Lyman, crushed in a high chair, watched eagerly while things placed themselves around him. Everyone sat down. Then the boys began to stuff themselves with a savage and astonishing efficiency. Before Bev had cleaned his plate once, they'd had thirds, and by the time he looked up from desert, they had melted through the walls. The youngest had levitated from his high chair and was sleeping out of sight. The room was empty except for Lulu and himself.

He looked at her. She turned to the sinkful of dishes and disappeared in a cloud of steam. Only the round rear of her blue flowered housedress was visible, so he watched that. It was too late now. He had fallen. He could not help but remember their one night together.

They had gone into the shed while the earth was still damp and the cut flowers in their foam balls still exuded scent over Henry's grave. Beverly had kissed the small cries back onto Lulu's lips. He remembered. Then passion overtook them. She hung on to him like they were riding the tossing ground, her teeth grinding in his ear. He wasn't man or woman. None of that mattered. Yet he was more of a man than he'd ever been. The grief of loss for the beloved made their tiny flames of life so sad and precious it hardly mattered who was what. The flesh was only given so that the flame could touch in a union however less than perfect. Afterward they lay together, breathing the dark in and out. He had wept the one other time in his life besides post combat, and after a while he came into her again, tasting his own miraculous continuance.

Lulu left him sitting on the couch and went back into the sacred domain of her femininity. That was the bedroom with the locking door that she left open just a crack. She pulled down the blue-and-white-checked bedspread, put the pillows aside, and lay down carefully with her hands folded on her stomach. She closed her eyes and breathed deep. She went into herself, sinking through her body as if on a raft of darkness, until she reached the very bottom of her soul where there was nothing to do but wait.

Things had gotten by Beverly. Night came down. His sad dazzlement abated and he tried to avoid thinking of Elsa. But she was there filing her orange nails whichever way he ducked. And then there was the way he was proud of living his life. He wanted to go back and sell word-enrichment books. No one on the reservation would buy them, he knew, and the thought panicked him. He realized that the depth and danger of his situation was great if he had forgotten that basic fact. The moon went black. The bushes seemed to close around the house.

Retrench, he told himself, as the boys turned heavily and mumbled in their invisible cots and all along the floors around him. Retreat if you have to and forget about Henry Junior. He finally faced surrender and knew it was the only thing he could possibly have the strength for.

He planned to get into his car while it was still dark, before dawn, and drive back to Minneapolis without Henry Junior. He would simply have to bolt without saying good-bye to Lulu. But when he rose from the couch, he walked down the hall to her bedroom door. He didn't pause but walked right through. It was like routine he'd built up over time in marriage. The close dark was scented with bath lilac. Glowing green spears told the hour in her side-table clock. The bedclothes rustled. He stood holding the lathed wooden post. And then his veins were full of warm ash and his tongue swelled in his throat.

He lay down in her arms.

Whirling blackness swept through him, and there was nothing else to do.

The wings didn't beat as hard as they used to, but the bird still flew.

1984

Cathy Song
b. 1955

Cathy Song was born in Honolulu, Hawaii, the daughter of a Chinese mother and a Korean father. She received her B.A. from Wellesley in 1977 and an M.A. in creative writing from Boston University in 1981. In addition, she attended the advanced poetry workshop run by Kathleen Spivak. Presently, she teaches creative writing at various North American universities while maintaining a permanent residence in Hawaii.

Song's first book *The Picture Bride* was selected from among 625 entries as the winning manuscript in the Yale Series of Younger Poets in 1983. Prior to *The Picture Bride,* she had published extensively in periodicals such as *Asian-Pacific Literature, The Hawaii Writers' Quarterly,* and *The Greenfield Review.* Her second book of poetry *Frameless Windows, Squares of Light* was published in 1988.

Aptly titled, *The Picture Bride* sought to make connections between poetry and the visual arts. Indeed, the book is divided into four sections, each bearing the title of a different Georgia O'Keeffe painting. Eighteenth-century Japanese printmaker Kitagawa Utamaro provides the inspiration for "Beauty and Sadness," a poem in which Song exquisitely evokes the inhabitants of Utamaro's "floating world," the "hundreds of women/in studies unfolding/like flowers from a fan." It may be said that Song's poetry "unfolds" in much the same manner as Utamaro's images—in rich layers that create complex and intricate relationships between people and places, between old and new worlds, between one generation and another. Each image is wonderfully organic, whether it is that of the daughter bathing her mother in "The Youngest Daughter," or of the young woman smuggling her lover into her home among her "cloth, hair and hands" in "The White Porch." Song's work, informed as it is by English and American literary traditions, is further enriched by her commitment to her Asian-American identity, her willingness to poetically cross oceans and boundaries. "It must be in the blood," she wrote in a poem from her second book, "this notion of returning." Her most recent book is *School Figures* (1994).

Further Reading:

G. K. Fujita-Sato, " 'Third World' as Place and Paradigm in Cathy Song's 'Picture Bride,' " *Melus* 15:1 (1988), 49–73.

P. Wallace, "Divided Loyalties: Literal and Literary in the Poetry of Lorna Dee Cervantes, Cathy Song and Rita Dove," *Melus* 18:3 (1993), 3–20.

C. Song, *School Figures,* 1994.

Text:
The Picture Bride, 1983.

Lost Sister

1

In China,
even the peasants
named their first daughters
Jade—
the stone that in the far fields   5
could moisten the dry season,
could make men move mountains
for the healing green of the inner hills
glistening like slices of winter melon.
And the daughters were grateful: 10
they never left home.
To move freely was a luxury
stolen from them at birth.
Instead, they gathered patience,
learning to walk in shoes   15
the size of teacups,
without breaking—
the arc of their movements
as dormant as the rooted willow,
as redundant as the farmyard hens.   20
But they traveled far
in surviving,
learning to stretch the family rice,
to quiet the demons,
the noisy stomachs.   25

2

There is a sister
who relinquished her name,
diluting jade green
with the blue of the Pacific.   30
Rising with a tide of locusts,
she swarmed with others
to inundate another shore.
In America,
there are many roads   35
and women can stride along with men.

But in another wilderness,
the possibilities,
the loneliness,
can strangulate like jungle vines.   40
The meager provisions and sentiments
of once belonging—
fermented roots, Mah-Jongg[1] tiles and firecrackers—
set but a flimsy household
in a forest of nightless cities.   45
A giant snake rattles above,
spewing black clouds into your kitchen.
Dough-faced landlords
slip in and out of your keyholes,
making claims you don't understand,   50
tapping into your communication systems
of laundry lines and restaurant chains.

You find you need China:
your one fragile identification,
a jade link   55
handcuffed to your wrist.
You remember your mother
who walked for centuries,
footless—
and like her,
you have left no footprints,   60
but only because
there is an ocean in between,
the unremitting space of your rebellion.
1983

---

[1] An Oriental game.

The Youngest Daughter

The sky has been dark
for many years.
My skin has become as damp
and pale as rice paper
and feels the way   5
mother's used to before the drying sun
parched it out there in the fields.

     Lately, when I touch my eyelids,
my hands react as if
I had just touched something   10
hot enough to burn.
My skin, aspirin colored,
tingles with migraine. Mother
has been massaging the left side of my face
especially in the evenings   15
when the pain flares up.

This morning
her breathing was graveled,
her voice gruff with affection
when I wheeled her into the bath.   20
She was in a good humor,
making jokes about her great breasts,
floating in the milky water
like two walruses,
flaccid and whiskered around the nipples.   25
I scrubbed them with a sour taste
in my mouth, thinking:
six children and an old man
have sucked from these brown nipples.

I was almost tender   30
when I came to the blue bruises
that freckle her body,
places where she had been injecting insulin
for thirty years. I soaped her slowly,
she sighed deeply, her eyes closed.   35
It seems it has always
been like this: the two of us
in this sunless room,
the splashing of the bathwater.

In the afternoons   40
when she has rested,
she prepares our ritual of tea and rice,
garnished with a shred of gingered fish,
a slice of pickled turnip,
a token for my white body.   45
We ate in the familiar silence.
She knows I am not to be trusted,
even now planning my escape.
As I toast to her health
with the tea she has poured,   50
a thousand cranes curtain the window,
fly up in a sudden breeze.
1983

The White Porch

I wrap the blue towel
after washing,
around the damp
weight of hair, bulky
as a sleeping cat,   5
and sit out on the porch.
Still dripping water,
it'll be dry by supper,
by the time the dust
settles off your shoes,   10
though it's only five
past noon. Think
of the luxury: how to use
the afternoon like the stretch
of lawn spread before me.   15
There's the laundry.
sun-warm clothes at twilight,
and the mountain of beans
in my lap. Each one,
I'll break and snap   20
thoughtfully in half.

But there is this slow arousal.
The small buttons
of my cotton blouse
are pulling away from my body.   25

I feel the strain of threads,
the swollen magnolias
heavy as a flock of birds
in the tree. Already,
the orange sponge cake   30
is rising in the oven.
I know you'll say it makes
your mouth dry
and I'll watch you
drench your slice of it   35
in canned peaches
and lick the plate clean.

So much hair, my mother
used to say, grabbing
the thick braided rope   40
in her hands while we washed
the breakfast dishes, discussing
dresses and pastries.
My mind often elsewhere
as we did the morning chores together.   45
Sometimes, a few stands
would catch in her gold ring.
I worked hard then,
anticipating the hour
when I would let the rope down   50
at night, strips of sheets,
knotted and tied,
while she slept in tight blankets.
My hair, freshly washed
like a measure of wealth,   55
like a bridal veil.
Crouching in the grass,
you would wait for the signal,
for the movement of curtains
before releasing yourself   60
from the shadow of moths.
Cloth, hair and hands,
smuggling you in.
1983

Beauty and Sadness

for Kitagawa Utamaro

He drew hundreds of women
in studies unfolding
like flowers from a fan.
Teahouse waitresses, actresses,
geishas, courtesans and maids.   5
They arranged themselves
before this quick, nimble man
whose invisible presence
one feels in these prints
is as delicate   10
as the skinlike paper
he used to transfer
and retain their fleeting loveliness.

Crouching like cats,
they purred amid the layers of kimono   15
swirling around them
as though they were bathing
in a mountain pool with irises
growing in the silken sunlit water.
Or poised like porcelain vases,   20
slender, erect and tall; their heavy
brocaded hair was piled high
with sandalwood combs and blossom sprigs
poking out like antennae.
They resembled beautiful iridescent insects,   25
creatures from a floating world.

Utamaro absorbed these women of Edo
in their moments of melancholy
as well as of beauty.
He captured the wisp of shadows,   30
the half-draped body
emerging from a bath; whatever
skin was exposed
was powdered white as snow.
A private space disclosed.   35
Portraying another girl
catching a glimpse of her own vulnerable
face in the mirror, he transposed

the trembling plum lips
like a drop of blood   40
soaking up the white expanse of paper.

At times, indifferent to his inconsolable
eye, the women drifted
through the soft gray feathered light,
maintaining stillness, the moments in between.   45
Like the dusty ash-winged moths
that cling to the screens in summer
and that the Japanese venerate
as ancestors reincarnated;
Utamaro graced these women with immortality   50
in the thousand sheaves of prints
fluttering into the reverent hands of keepers:
the dwarfed and bespectacled painter
holding up to a square of sunlight
what he had carried home beneath his coat   55
one afternoon in winter.

1983

Gish Jen
b. 1955

Lillian Jen adopted the name "Gish"—as in the actress Lillian Gish—while in high
school in Scarsdale, a prosperous, largely Jewish suburb of New York. "It was part of
becoming a writer," she has been quoted, ". . . not becoming the person I was
supposed to be."

Born in Queens, on August 12, 1955, to immigrant parents from Shanghai, China,
Jen was "supposed" to become a math-and-sciences professional and a dutiful
housewife. The second of five children, she was the only one with an insatiable appetite
for books. When the family moved to the more affluent suburb of Scarsdale, New
York, Jen discovered a better-stocked library than the Catholic school collection of her
early childhood. She read voraciously and indiscriminately, yet in school was more
interested in math than in English. By the time she entered Harvard in 1972, however,
she had decided to major in literature. A dutiful daughter, she also took pre-med
classes to satisfy her parents' wish for practicality. In her junior year, she took a writing
class from the famed translator Robert Fitzgerald who immediately recognized her
talent as a poet and storyteller. He helped her get a job in publishing at Doubleday,
which satisfied her family's need for pragmatism, but left her in a kind of no-man's-
land as a writer. She moved on to graduate school in business at Stanford University
where she soon felt out of place. She read more than one hundred novels in her first
year there, and dropped out during her second year. She headed to the University of

Iowa's Writers' Workshop, married the American David O'Connor, and eventually began writing in earnest. Her first story "The Water Faucet Vision" involves a man who throws his wife out the window. "That's the level of frustration I felt," she said.

In 1986 she began publishing her stories regularly in such journals as *Atlantic Monthly*, the *New Yorker*, and the *Yale Review;* many of them have been widely anthologized. Her first novel *Typical American* was published in 1991. It is the often comic, at times tragic story of the Chang family. Ralph comes to the United States for a Ph.D. but finds his American dream in fried-chicken fast food, and later, in a pancake house. His wife Helen lives through glamour magazines while his sister, a doctor, has an affair with a married man. None of the three can make sense of American culture, and each is gradually transformed by forces that also drive them apart.

Mona in the Promised Land, from which the selection "Hot Times at the Hot Line" is taken, is her next novel, the second in a projected trilogy about the Chang family. At the center of the work is Mona, the oldest daughter of Ralph and Helen. The original, tentative title was "Mona Changowitz," because the work chronicles the changes in the teenager Mona Chang, who in 1968 moves with her newly prosperous family to Scarshill, New York, where the Chinese have become "the new Jews." Mona takes their situation literally, even to the point of converting. In this ebullient and inventive novel, Mona attends temple "rap" sessions and falls in love with a "nice Jewish boy" who lives in a tepee. In the lively "Hot Times" segment, Mona and her friend Barbara work for a temple-sponsored help hotline, discuss their relationships to various boys, read philosophers and writers, prepare for the SATs, and solidify their friendship, even though Mona wonders if one boy simply likes her because she is that anomaly, "a Chinese Jew." Jen's wit—intelligent and dry—has been compared to Jane Austen's; her writing takes the much-discussed concept of multculturalism and gives it vivid, particularized life.

Further Reading:
G. Jen, *Typical American*, 1991.

Text:
Mona in the Promised Land, 1996.

---

from Mona in the Promised Land

Hot Times at the Hot Line

This is Mona's theory about her parents: that Ralph thought they should live in their own little world, whereas Helen thought they should belong to society. Even she never intended that they should be a minority, though, and especially an outspoken one. Mona explains this to Rabbi Horowitz as he gravely cracks his knuckles.

"First of all, they don't like the word *minority*," Mona says. "They say they were never a minority when they were in China, why should they be a minority here."

"But there are few of them, and many of everyone else."

"That's what I said. They said they're just as good as anybody, why should they ask for help? Also they do not want to have to riot. I told them they don't have to riot if they don't want to. I told them they can just march in parades and protest. Or else, if they don't want to go outside, they can write letters, like the Jews. I told them that was one of the reasons I turned Jewish, because I thought writing letters was smarter than standing out in the freezing cold, which I knew was not for them, being from Shanghai and everything. I said I knew how much they worried about catching cold, and that I had recently discovered that they were absolutely right when they said people caught cold through their feet. For instance, when they stood on street corners for hours on that cold concrete. I told them writing letters was much warmer, and also that the kind of letters that worked best were the ones that got sent off to big shots. I thought they would like that, writing letters to big shots and not having to get their feet cold."

"But they didn't like it?"

"No. They said they grew up arranging things. Their friends arranged things for them, they arranged things for their friends."

"And what about the poor people? Who did the arranging for them?"

"Got me." Mona shrugs. "I think that's why they had to have a revolution. But my mom said before that nobody yelled. Yelling just meant you had no self-control. She said in fact people knew what other people meant without their hardly saying anything. They understood each other perfectly by what it was that wasn't said."

Rabbi Horowitz clears his throat. "Well, of course, nobody likes to yell," he says. "But your parents want to be Wasps. They are the only ones who do not have to make themselves heard. That is because they do the hearing. And how is that possible?"

"That's what I said. But my mom said it's possible. She said it's all a matter of manners. You have to know how to stand, how to sit. She said people in Shanghai knew who you were right away, you didn't have to open your mouth."

"And is that true?"

"I think you also had to wear a lot of jewelry. Anyway, I said, we are a minority, like it or not, and if you want to know how to be a minority, there's nobody better at it than the Jews. I said it's our job to ask questions now. We can't just accept everything the way they did in China. We can't just go along."

"And what did she say then?"

"She said that as soon as the Communists leave she is going to take me back to Shanghai, where I won't have so much to say."

Naturally, Helen cannot take Mona back to Shanghai; that is the good news. And so Mona continues to be Jewish. Also she takes up the guitar, which involves growing out the nails of her right hand while keeping the left ones short. Helen points out that there are many instruments that do not require asymmetrical nail-growing—for example, how about going back to the piano? Such a nice instrument after all, and you don't have to tune it yourself, a convenience. But in the fashion of the day, Mona is more interested in symbols of wayfaring than in things associated with living rooms and arm protectors and miracle-fiber carpet. How about the harmonica, Mona says, or the mandolin? She has never actually seen a mandolin, but she knows it is anti-orchestra. Helen knows this too. They move diplomatically on to sports, which Helen considers unladylike except for ice-skating and tennis. Does this explain why Mona takes up rock climbing, which she might have otherwise recognized to be, past the rope and carabiners, a form of crawling?

Over Callie's spring break, she journeys out to watch Mona at the Gunks, even though Mona is officially not speaking to her. Callie attempts to patch things up with sisterly concern.

"It just looks so dangerous," she says.

They are perched on a rocky ledge, becoming acquainted with the brevity of life. Callie puts her arm around a tree; she got her ears pierced at college and is wearing large multipart earrings that do not help her balance. Otherwise, she looks more outdoorsy than you'd expect, on account of her also having gotten herself contact lenses. These mean she can now hold her head at funny angles, not to say let her hair swing around as if she's in a hair conditioner ad. "Mom and Dad would have a canary if they knew."

"But of course they're not going to know." Mona surveys the stratosphere.

Callie answers, "Of course not."

The right answer. But then she goes on, by way of changing the topic, to sweetly wonder if that jittering Mona was doing out there on the rock face is what people call sewing-machine knee. Naturally, she is just making conversation. Mona realizes that Callie would just as soon say nothing, except that to say nothing in this case would be to emphasize how big a fight they are having. The silence might fill up with anger and explode, for instance if Mona had a chance to demand whether Callie realized what she was doing when she decided to squeal to the parents like a low-phylum invertebrate; why doesn't she just admit that she has been lusting her whole life to knock Mona off her throne? Instead Callie elects to bravely forge on in a conversational manner, never mind if it means saying the exact wrong thing. For example, How did such a crazy sport become so fashionable? And is it truly intrinsically enjoyable to clutch at nothing for hours, worrying about gravity? Her tone is full of intellectual inquiry. Mona's has the sweet sibilance of a sibling who has learned to use words but atavistically prefers teeth. She insists her interest in climbing is far more than a matter of fashion, and that she finds it spiritually satisfying to pit herself against unyielding nature. She informs Callie that she expects to be climbing as long as her skeletal and muscle groups allow, and that it is a matter of passion she would not expect a milquetoast to quite comprehend.

This is before Mona is treated to a demonstration of the pulley. One day at the Gunks, she sees a climber fall and fall until, just at the point where he's supposed to arrest and dangle, he keeps falling. His partner meanwhile, is also in good-paced motion—going up, you might say, like there's no tomorrow.

A hunch comes to her about then that her G-d-given sport talents are better exercised at the temple than at the cliffs. She accordingly trades in her trusty climbing rope for the Youth Group hot line, thanking G-d Callie will not be home to make Ivy League observations until June. Also Mona thanks G-d that the swap has become possible—an offshoot result of confirmation class. For Rabbi Horowitz has talked so much about I-and-Thou and so on, that many people have been elevated, if not up to his level, then at least a rung or two out of the subbasement. Hitherto sacred distinctions between cool and uncool have thus lost their sanctity. They are all the chosen, or at least the as-good-as-chosen-let-us-not-split-hairs.

Barbara Gugelstein and Mona are thus, through the rigor of the special training course (with its extra-heavy rap sessions, and stress interviews, and mock emergency drills), suddenly friends with all manner of people. Some of these are eminently regular types like Rennie Klingenstein, and Hilary Rothschild, and Aaron Apfelbaum, and Eddie

Levine—kids who've gone skinny-dipping once or twice and are not strangers to the agony of blackheads. But included too are the distinctly higher likes of Danielle Meyers and Chip Weinstein, not to say exquisite Eloise Ingle with the Rapunzel hair, who everyone thought was Wasp, seeing as how she thought so herself until just recently. That was when she discovered the truth about her dead mother's extraction.

Said extraction being a fact her stepmother had been purposefully hiding in the name of sensitivity—said sensitive stepmother having wanted Eloise to feel on a par with her stepsibs. (It was bad enough that they sat so killingly well on their horses and played such cunning games of tennis and got snapped up by Phillips Andover, which she didn't despite alumni pull.) One day in a temple rap session, she reveals how she discovered her identity from a long-lost cousin; and though Rabbi Horowitz is quick to point out that the stepmother meant well, still the group sympathy flows. Indeed, the class stands with Eloise in a solidarity such as bards will someday sing of, and in the meantime, is happy to fill her in on various points she missed as a child—such as the use and meaning of the dreidel, and who is Elijah, and what to make of his drinking habits. Rabbi Horowitz likes to call on Mona most of all for these details; and if Eloise is taken aback by the breath and depth of Mona's knowledge, she is too well bred to let it show, except to ask whether Mona also plays tennis and skis.

"Not really," Mona says.

Her stepbrothers sail, Eloise informs her, and of course they all ride, and they summer on an island in Maine. "Mid-coast," she says.

"You mean you have a summer place?" Mona says.

"A cottage," says Eloise. And this seems to be the match point, because Eloise then graciously affords Mona a glimpse of her orthodontic work, and in conclusion says how splendid to see a Chinese girl turn Jewish. Here they are, two newcomers. She just hopes that Mona feels welcome.

Eloise feels less pressed to extend her welcome to anyone else in the class; and after a few weeks, she has no need at all—having decided to go back to being Wasp. This, even though she is actually still a Jew, according to some people (staunch adherents of the what-the-mother-is-the-child-is rule). Others, though, think how she was brought up determines at least as much who she is, if not more. "Think about what she grew up eating," they say. "That's who she is, you can't deny it." "Like an Eskimo who prefers hamburgers to walrus meat is American," says somebody. "That's assuming walrus is what Eskimos eat," says someone else. "And why can't a person be both?" People nod. Yet another person thinks Eloise can be what she wants. Who are they to say what she is actually, because of her blood or her diet, either? Like the Changowitz, says this person, meaning Mona. People nod again. Should Mona take offense, though, that with this the conversation ends?

Eloise remains friends with a few of the temple crowd—especially Danielle Meyers, but also Barbara Gugelstein, whose father, it turns out, works in the same Wall Street house as Eloise's. That's to say, her ghost lingers hauntingly. For example, Mona notices Barbara start to look down, as if putting away some more pressing matter, before turning her head to answer someone; she does this the exact slow way Eloise Ingle does. In fact, once she takes so long that Mona worries Barbara is not going to respond at all. Not that it is necessarily Mona's business. Mona knows herself to be fatally afflicted with excessive concern, it's because of the parents from China. Still Mona taps her friend on the elbow to remind her to say something. *Oh, he just caught me daydreaming.*

So says Barbara later. But another time, she accuses Mona of being too nice. She says that if there's one thing she learned from Eloise Ingle, it's that she doesn't owe it to people to listen just because they want to talk.

"But it's rude," Mona argues weakly. "What happened to honoring other people as you would have them honor you?"

Barbara replies that she doesn't expect that people should listen just because she wants to talk either. But she doesn't look too sure of this, and when Mona doesn't answer, she goes on to say, nonplussed, "Oh, Mona, you really need to think more like an American. You're too polite."

"Doesn't Eloise have manners? And she's American."

Barbara concedes that Mona's right in a way, but she's wrong in a way too. According to El, Barbara says, manners are not about being nice to everybody. In fact, the whole key to manners is to be aware what set you're talking to.

"Very nice," Mona says. "And what set, pray tell, is she?"

She stomps off in self-righteous fashion, feeling the might of the moral—even though, to be honest, Eloise Ingle's way of thinking is not so different from that of Mona's parents. This Mona admits to Rabbi Horowitz.

"So your parents are snobs. That makes you a snob too?" he says.

"It's more like they'd like to be snobs," Mona clarifies. "The trouble is that here in America, they often can't tell what set they're talking to. And they're not sure what set we are, either."

Rabbi Horowitz listens, working his knuckles as usual, only more sporadically, To appease the temple board of directors, he has recently trimmed his beard, so that his Adam's apple shows; as a result, he from time to time leaves off what he calls his wisecracking, in order to cup his hand over this—his naked compromise.

"With their Chinese friends, it's different. There they can, say, make allowances for So-and-so who's Cantonese but has made something of himself here in America. Which of course they need to do partly because they themselves are from Shanghai, which is sort of like being from New York. People in Peking think they're uncultured and slick." Mona stops. "I've always thought that was so Chinese. I mean, to think like that, everyone looking down on everyone else all the time. I've always thought that was so undemocratic, and un-American, and I've always been glad they at least had redeeming character traits, such as being hardworking. I thought they were the only ones."

"But now you discover what." Rabbi Horowitz, uncharacteristically gloomy, tilts back in his chair. The skeleton rattles behind him.

Barbara is teaching Mona to be cool. The first lesson: When in doubt, act like you couldn't care less.

"But what if you do care?" Mona says.

Barbara doesn't answer. Sometimes when Mona calls these days she finds Barbara's line tied up for hours. Also Barbara now attends concerts without warning. ("El called me up on a whim.") There's a new privacy zone around her; she seems always to be burning incense. Indeed the air is thick enough, that by the time Barbara announces where she is going to sit for the PSATs—namely, next to Eloise—Mona has already lumpenly begun to prepare a defense. Barbara maintains that she would sit next to Mona if their last names were alphabetically closer. But as it happens, Mona is glad enough to be conjoined instead with sweet Rachel Cohen.

Sweet Rachel! Such a true heart she is, sincere and gentle, not to say of a composure you might not predict for a dentist's daughter. She does not sweat. She does not swear. She glides where others lumber, blinks feelingly where others moan. In fact, with her large oval face and sweet limpid eyes, she could almost be the heroine of a long Victorian novel—you would just have to add a little salt—and just as she is, she could no kidding be the heroine's dear sister. Which would make her an ace companion for Mona, except that Rachel is ever-so-gently heavy into making jewelry, and truth to tell (though Mona knows it churlish to say so), she stretches the limits of Mona's interest in solder.

"I notice you didn't like the tiger's eye," says Rachel. "What about these?"

Over Helen's objection, Mona gets her ears pierced like Callie's, and soon they hang noisy with creativity. She sounds like Mr. Bojangles, complete with tambourine. During a math exam, the teacher has to ask her to please stop tinkling, so that other people can think.

"Far out," Rachel says when she hears. "Now for some rings."

After the rings come necklaces, and after the necklaces, bracelets. Rachel is not interested in rap sessions. She takes after her grandfather and great-grandfather—scholars who kept to their small world, and found everything there. They were dreamy people, like her father, a dentist whose life goal is to produce a quartet. (Rachel is the viola.) He will stop in the middle of drilling a tooth to hear how a passage of music develops; also he has been trying to make sense of the new music, though this irritates his clientele. Mutiny! they've threatened (being music lovers themselves). At least one patient has climbed out of the chair, bib and all, to change the tape.

Mona laughs to hear this. How wonderful! She too would like to spend her life among the grace notes—and eventually, maybe she will. For now, though, a callow youth, she's not ready to retire. In truth, she deplores but adores the bloody fray. What would life be without developments?

For example, a cool front happens to blow into Eloise just as the Gugelsteins move to a new house—leaving Mona to help Barbara with the adjustments. Not that the Gugelsteins haven't always lived in something nice. But this house is French provincial to begin with, meaning turrets to house the AC ducts in the Norman style. Also there is a pool, and a tennis court, and a greenhouse with automatic vent flaps; there is a circular driveway, and a two-story, four-bay garage, with servants' quarters up above. There is a screening room for showing movies; there is a library with chestnut paneling; there are six bedrooms, each with its own bathroom. There is a plug-in vacuum system, and an intercom; and instead of regular wallpaper with stripes or birds or flocking, there are in the hallways hand-tinted murals of country scenes in France. Barbara points out the milkmaids for Mona. The scenes begin in the fields and end with wheels of cheese, though there also seem to be a number of rafter-hung hams. Barbara and Mona debate whether hams get dried or smoked, and how many hams a regular rafter can support. Also how many hams one nets per dead pig. They agree that when it comes to production, those milkmaids are an inspiration, Henry Ford himself could probably have picked up a tip. They agree too that the house is some house, and that's not even counting its humanitarian side: Barbara claims that in the basement is a real-life entrance for the Underground Railroad.

"The Underground Railroad was a big deal around here," she says. "That's what the realtor said. It's because this area used to be crawling with Quakers."

"I thought the Underground Railroad wasn't really underground," says Mona.

"Some of it had to be. Otherwise, they'd have called it something else, right?" Barbara retwists her French twist, clamping it into position with a leather-and-stick affair decorated with runes, then goes on to say that according to the realtor, the original house was a colonial. The present house was built on the old foundation plus some, who knows why.

The girls descend the basement stairs. Barbara's head is almost on a level with Mona's, even though she's a step lower; Mona keeps slightly back, so as to avoid being poked by the stick of Barbara's hair affair. More steps. And then, sure enough, in a far corner, behold! A wooden panel the size of a short door, soft with rot. The basement walls are dungeonlike, all ancient rock and hairy mortar, you wouldn't be surprised to find a skeleton built into them. And when Mona and Barbara remove the wooden panel, the rough hole is of a similarly creepy feel. It exhales a cool musty air, though its dirt walls are dry; Mona thinks this must be what catacombs are like, the ones where the early Christians hid to get away from the Romans. Or was it the Jews who hid there to get away from the Christians? Anyway, the hole is just high enough for Mona to stand in; when she steps forward, her hair is teased by the gravel-encrusted ceiling.

"It probably doesn't go very far," Barbara says. "The realtor said the tunnels are mostly blocked off."

"I dare you to go in," says Mona.

But Barbara is chicken; Mona bravely ventures into the tremendous dark alone. One step, two. She's not planning on going far. Hard-packed walls to either side of her; she braces her hands against them. More gravel. "See you later!" she calls. "I'm going to Alabama for to see my Susianna!" Her voice seems sluggishly amplified, as if she is singing in a large padded shower.

"Singing Polly Wolly-doodle all the day?" answers Barbara. Her voice is reassuringly close—right at Mona's back. Two steps more. Now this is the heart of darkness, thinks Mona. But before she can remember who wrote that story, much less what *The horror! The horror!* in it was, she bangs into some kind of metal rack. There is more air beyond this; smooth objects stuck into it. She reemerges, heart thudding, with a pair of bottles.

"Bordeaux!" says Barbara. "Wait until my dad sees these! Are there more?"

"Underground Railroad, wine cellar," mutters Mona. "Very easy to get them mixed up."

Better lit is the last stop of the tour. Barbara's new bedroom, which is so enormous that she's positioned her bed center stage, to take up some of the space. It's the sort of thing you associate with bed-and-bath stores. She's placed a night table next to the bed, and there's a blanket chest at its foot, but all around this island, instead of alluring merchandise, there's just space. For wallpaper she's picked a blue and white sprigged print exactly like the one she had before, in her old room; and her hi-fi too is set up just the way it used to be, with the speakers on either side of the turntable. This, even though she now has the space to separate them for realistic stereophonic sound.

"Where are your records?" Mona asks her.

"Under the bed." This is where she always used to keep them in her old room, in her old house.

"Maybe you should keep them standing up now," says Mona.

But Barbara simply shrugs, digging out her Simon and Garfunkel, her Carole King, her Laura Nyro. "They're warped already anyway," she says. And when she puts them on, you can see that indeed the needle surfs most alarmingly up and down, just the same as ever.

Although the hot line begins as a temple activity, in time Gentile classmates are also encouraged to join, provided that they pass the screening and get trained. And some do, such as Jim Magruder, and Jill Spence, and Georgina Elliott. Also Eloise Ingle. And why shouldn't they be allowed to, after all? The Jews are the Chosen People, but they have always invited outsiders to their Sabbath meals. *You shall love strangers, for strangers you were in Egypt.* Plus they are, Jew and Gentile alike, against suicide–although without an attempt every so often, what will staffers do while on duty but eat fruit leather and gossip? And make out, Barbara says—which Mona would not believe herself, except that Jim Magruder and Aaron Apfelbaum have signed up for every night shift available with Danielle Meyers and Eloise Ingle (who Barbara wishes would sign up with her and Mona, but never does). Also Mona discovers a rubber in the bathroom. Unused, it's true, but as Barbara points out, it could have been used, and why was it there unless someone had ideas?

"You mean as in a Big Idea?" Mona says; and this becomes a joke between them. "What an Idea," they say, and "He was keeping his Idea to himself," and "Now, that's an Idea." Still Mona wonders if Barbara's right. Is there hidden within the circle to which they've been admitted, another, smaller circle? It seems like something out of Nancy Drew: *The Secret of the Temple Hot Line.* Until one day, sure enough, Seth Mandel starts signing up as senior counselor for their shift.

Seth Mandel is a shortish, bright-eyed, pony-tailed guy, with big broad shoulders and the surprise domestic side you associate with primates like the silverback gorilla. Not only is he the type to offer people back rubs of surprising penetration, but he'll pick a piece of lint off your sleeve if he sees it, saying, *Excuse me, I can't help it; I'm driven by early training and the force of neurosis.* And then his eyes will crinkle, and a crack will open in his red-brown beard, and you'll know he's smiling his wide crooked smile. He doesn't laugh much—the enigmatic smile is more his style. But once in a while, he'll let out a guffaw, shocking people, and then he will smile to see their reaction. For this is what he likes more than anything, to conduct little experiments—or as he puts it, to send up balloons. *This is how you see the wind. That is, if you are interested in seeing the wind.* He smiles again.

Seth is the youngest of the senior counselors, meaning that he has graduated from high school, but hasn't from college on account of never having gone. Instead he is taking time off to decide whether college is a socializing force to which he can submit. How this came to pass has been a topic of town debate for some time. To some parents, this is obviously related to the war. Humans are generalizing animals, goes this line of reasoning. Once the kids get the idea they can resist the draft, they start to resist whatever they want. Other parents, though, blame the high school social studies curriculum, and especially advanced placement American history. This everyone knows is taught by a radical extremist in half-glasses. He starts the year by explaining how the Constitution had as much to do with economics as with noble ideals; pretty soon the kids think they know everything, it's only just lucky that this doesn't stop them from going to Ivy League schools if they get in. Seth is the exception, probably because he was the star student, and also because he got in everywhere he applied. That gave him an attitude, say some people. Needless to say too, he'd have gone if he had drawn a lower draft number.

But as it is, Mr. Above-It-All is now more or less educating himself. This is easy enough, since he is the kind of guy who compares translations of Dante for the hell of it, and who goes almost only to foreign films. The exception being *Romeo and Juliet* with Olivia Hussey, which he saw thrice in order to ascertain that (*a*) he doesn't think she is so beautiful, and (*b*) he is personally against girls parting their hair in the middle as if to suggest purity when in fact all they have on their minds is popularity. In other words, he's deep.

Is he interested in Barbara or in Mona? In the beginning it is not so clear, and then it is. He is interested in Mona, partly because of her superlative grade point average, but mostly because she is a phenomenon. A Chinese Jew! He says he sees her sometimes in the pancake house, and that he can't believe she is the same person he sees at temple. What a world-spanner!—a regular Yoko Ono. He takes her, in other words, for a high-wire freethinker, perhaps of his own school—no small compliment since he has, at age nineteen, all but broken away from the small-minded bourgeois thinking of his father, a paper-products mogul and in-the-flesh subscriber to *Pulp* magazine. He does not even live in his father's house anymore, but in a teepee in the backyard, except for when it is really cold. (And of course he helps himself to whatever from the fridge, and leaves his laundry for the maid.) *What do you like to read?* he wants to know. Which inquiry, in truth, Mona finds something of a thrill, seeing it as a level up from *Do you speak Chinese?* and *What do you eat at home?* Her mind, her mind! Someone cares about her mind!

A delicious thought for a closet reader—Mona has never admitted how much she reads, figuring, Why act brainier? It was one thing for JFK to speed-read; it's another for people in the sweet bloom of their youth. As it is, people say things like, *Don't you just hate her?* Meaning her. Last year somebody switched out of Mona's math class, saying he didn't want to be on the same curve as she was, even though Mona wasn't the one pulling down the perfect scores, it was Andy Kaplan. Mona always managed to make some little mistake.

Moreover, as Mona tells Seth, she immediately changed her part from the side to the middle after seeing *Romeo and Juliet;* and she is not interested in being a phenomenon (this being a Feeble excuse for a love affair, it seems to her). In addition, she fails to be charmed when he attempts to woo her with a synopsis of *A Critique of Pure Reason,* even if he did distill it himself from a most hefty original with only a small amount of help from a lecture series he's been listening to on tape. *The Great Thoughts Condensed for the Modern Mind,* this is called; and yes, the reel-to-reel tape machine is indeed installed in his teepee. Likewise, a telephone.

Says Mona, "Why didn't Kant just say, 'Thou shalt not use other people'?"

"Because only G-d can issue commandments," says Seth, gesturing with his hands. (He likes to make a kind of cage with them as he listens, each fingertip lightly touching its comrade on the other hand. When he talks, the cage opens, as if to let the truth flap out.) "And Kant wasn't G-d."

"So why didn't he say it was his suggestion? Why didn't he say it was just his Big Idea?" This is for Barbara's sake. Mona can tell Barbara feels left out by the fact that she's even checked that Kant book out of the library and looked to see how it ends.

Barbara laughs appreciatively.

"Because," sputters Seth.

Another fact, not to be ignored: When Seth is too nonplussed to hold forth any further, Mona feels for him. Is he really so terrible for a pseudointellectual? Plus how can he help but leave Barbara out? After all, he's so in love with Mona, poor fellow.

Still she staunchly defends the status quo that is Barbara and her 4-ever—thereby officially forgiving her friend her E.I.L. (Eloise Ingle lapse). Until after a while, he begins to get the hint. He begins to share with Barbara his synopses and hypotheses and analyses, his assumptions and suppositions. Whereupon, to Mona's confoundment, Barbara goes intellectual. There is suddenly no question like a higher question, and wherefore are there depths to existence, except for to be plumbed?

Creepingly, creepingly, things begin to change. At the outset they all make a show of taking their turn at the phone; and after the calls, they review them as usual. Somehow, though, it begins to transpire that Barbara and Seth happen to have cases requiring extraordinary attention. And so elaborate are the discussions they happen to get involved in while Mona is on the phone, that they are still engrossed in them when the phone rings again; so that it seems only courteous for Mona to answer it. Then it begins to seem only courteous for them to remove themselves and their discussion to the next room, so that they are not disturbing Mona's concentration. And then it seems only courteous that they shut the door.

There being no door between the rooms, they are obliged to move into a large utility closet. This is not such a hospitable place, being full of cleaning supplies and other objects of large utility. Still Mona's friends repair there uncomplainingly, turning out the light so as better to explore the hitherto hidden complexities of this case or that. Every now and then, Mona hears a pail get knocked over, or a mop. And one day, there is a giant crash, which can only be the wet-dry industrial vac. The vac, Mona happens to know, is loaded up with a temple art class project (somebody's still-wet, life-size, papier-mâché armadillo having been sabotaged by felons wielding granola and Gatorade). Is this why the crash is followed by muffled yelling that sounds like "Help! Help!" but could also be "Pulp! Pulp!"? (The latter being a favorite cry in the Mandel household, apparently.)

Mona approaches the closet door but does not knock. "Barbara? Seth? You okay?" The closet door seems to her amazingly wooden.

Silence.

Mona explores with her toe the nub of the indoor-outdoor carpeting. It feels the way it looks, bluish green. "Hey, Kugel Noodle. You vant I should call an ambulance?"

Says Barbara, "I'm fine. But what's that ringing?" Then she says, "Please to go answer it, Polly Wolly," and makes a giggle-like noise.

Was it a giggle? That night, Mona considers this question closely and with tears. "Barbara," Mona says the next time she sees her friend. This is in AP English class. "Barbara."

"That's my name, don't wear it out," she says.

Mona gets up her courage. "What am I, chopped liver, you should do this to me?"

"Wait. What? I'm doing something?"

Mrs. Thompson has left the room. Everyone knows this is because she has a collapsed uterus and needs a bathroom break—during which time, they are supposed to be writing an in-class essay defining irony.

"To you?" Barbara looks honestly puzzled. In fact, so sincerely does she look at Mona with her dewy green eyes, that it is Mona who looks away. Outside the classroom window, the lawn slopes steeply up the road; Mona wonders suddenly who mows that lawn, and whether the person ever feels discouraged. "I thought you didn't want him."

"I didn't, I don't think."

"You were so clear about it, you hurt his feelings. A lot."

"Oh," Mona says, feeling as though she has more to say. But as she doesn't know what it is, she turns her eyes to her page and begins to write.

Mona is waiting, once again, for the hot-line phone to ring. Confirmation class seems for now a light-year away; also Rabbi Horowitz. Mona sees him there at the temple, not preoccupied with his beard length, as he has been of late, but cheerfully snapping one after another of his joints in place. She should shrug too. Instead she thinks about calling him just to say hi, or maybe to ask why it is that now that she's Jewish, she feels like more of a Chinese than ever. Is there some grand explanation—Hegelian perhaps? (Ah, Seth, how you've expanded her wardrobe of trenchant and other thoughts.) All this would tie up the line irresponsibly, though; and so it remains an idle eddying notion, one of life's spin-off ideas that curl to the sides of your mainly rushing existence. It's like wishing that she could call herself up. Or like wishing, when callers are done with themselves, that she could then call them back and tell them how it feels to behold her best friend and erstwhile suitor closeted up with the cleaning appliances. Is this what it means to be your own accounting unit? Mona would ask. And then maybe she would tell them how she's not sure what she thinks about that. In a way she understands that this is how life operates in America, that it's just like the classroom. You have to raise your own hand—no one is going to raise it for you—and then you have to get ready to stand up and give the right answer so that you may gulp down your whole half-cup of approval. But how tempting to stay hunkered down with everyone else, in the comfortable camaraderie of the hungry! After all, you are so tall when you stand up. People look at you with their stomachs rumbling, and you can't help but notice how around you there is so much air.

Of course, this is a foolish way to think. Mona understands that according to the rules, if you don't eat up, someone else will. None of this *nali, nali* Chinese self-effacement. *You've got to look out for number one.* No one sits lumpenly when opportunity knocks—except her, every now and then, and of course Callie, a self-cleaning oven if ever you met one. Is this a matter of their genotypes? Or is it just that other people grew up eating their individual portions from their individual plates; whereas the Changs help themselves from bowls in the middle of the table, and no one can leave until everyone else is done.

A true story: A friend of Helen's comes to visit, some years later, from China. The friend is going to a university, where she will share a room with two other Chinese students. Unfortunately, due to travel and other miseries, she is the last one to arrive. The results: she gets the best bed. No one else would take it! The first to arrive took the worst bed, the second to arrive, the second-worst. And so for an entire year, she is closest to the bathroom and the radiator, farthest from the window opening out onto the fire station. Of course, she tries to make it up to her roommates bit by bit. She brings them fruit, and folding umbrellas, and tickets to the movies. Still she feels the difficulty of her position.

Is this a way to live? Mona ponders the question. Meanwhile, the phone rings—someone calling about her boyfriend. Since he started doing speed, all he will eat is baby food; everything else he suspects. *Trace minerals,* she says he says. *Did you ever think about what they mean by trace minerals?*

The phone rings again. This caller is shook up because in the middle of her parents' divorce, their giant cactus became possessed.

"So I said, Mom, it's moving, I swear, just like in *Rosemary's Baby.* And she said she knew I needed attention, but that she didn't appreciate my trying to get it in this manner, and also that I just wouldn't believe what my papa was putting her through. Even her lawyer had never seen anything like it, and he'd been in the divorce business as long as anybody. Way, way, way before it got popular. So I called up my papa and said, It's moving, I swear. And he said he loved me, but did I have any idea how many times his phone rang an hour? And so the next day, guess what. The whole plant exploded. It turned out it was full of trantulas hatching, and then there were baby tarantulas hatching, and then there were baby tarantulas everywhere, and they attacked my dog, her name was Sheepie, even though she was a beagle, because that was what I wanted originally, a sheep dog. The vet thought that she would live, but she died, and now they want to bury her, but I won't let them. I told them I didn't want my dog buried by her own murderers, especially since all they care about is who's going to pay for the exterminator, and how long my mom and me are going to have to stay in a hundred-dollar-a-night hotel."

The caller is remarkably poised until she describes how in order to bury the dog someplace her parents don't even know exists, she somehow has to first get Sheepie's body back from the veterinarian. Unfortunately, he won't let her have it because she's a minor. "But she's my dog, I told him. I had her since she was a puppy. I raised her up. I taught her tricks. She slept in my bed." She sobs and sobs. Mona tries to say what Rabbi Horowitz would say. She tries to bear in mind what they were taught in training, which is that everyone is calling out of loneliness, and that their job, on some spiritual level, is to take the caller's side. Is it working, though? Suddenly the caller whispers, "Uh oh, it's my ma," and hangs up. Mona waits, hoping she'll call back, but when the phone rings again, it's someone else.

Luckily, none of the day's callers is code red—meaning that none of them is calling from the train tracks, or from the nether reaches of a hallucinogen. Though Mona has been especially trained to deal with drug overdoses, she is first supposed to try to hand such calls over to the capable senior counselor. As for what is the protocol if the capable senior counselor happens to have his hands full, who knows.

Mona tries, between calls, to ignore the loud quiet emanating from the utility closet. Mona tries, between calls, to read an Irish book called *Dubliners.* This is an assignment for English class, meaning that Mona is supposed to be on the lookout for epiphanies. It turns out there is one at the end of each story. The phone rings again. This is no divorce; neither is it a drug-related, or a parent-related, or a school-related call. And it doesn't seem to be Andy Kaplan, either. The boy identifies himself as Japanese, the son of a businessman, and though his English pronunciation is now textbook clear, there is something familiar about his voice.

If he weren't supposed to be in Japan, Mona would almost believe this to be Sherman Matsumoto.

Or is it? Anyway, if this person is in trouble, he won't say what kind. They exchange pleasantries about the weather, and also about how beautiful an area is Westchester, what with the landscaping and lawns. Mona explains about lime, and turf-builder, and preemergent crabgrass control. He replies that he lived in Scarshill some years ago. Now he is living in a neighboring town, near a duck pond with a willow tree. Is he happy to be back? He is enigmatic about this, and about what moved him to call. All he will say is that he is upset because someone trimmed the willow. He had liked the way the branches reached almost all the way down to the water: in the slightest breeze they would touch the pond, and then it would be as if it had been raining just there, right under the tree. The water would be all shivery where it had been touched—as the caller puts it, *full of spirit*—and the bits of light that reflected back up into the undersides of the leaves would toss and dance wildly.

"Crazy in the leaves," he says. "Everywhere else, it is a nice day, sunny. But in just this one tree—monsoon."

"It sounds beautiful." Mona is amazed at how clearly she can picture this private storm, especially the light-in-the-leaves part. It's one of those things you've seen a hundred times without noticing it—how magically the water splatters the sun, like nature's own mirror ball.

"They should not have cut the tree," he says.

"No, they shouldn't have," Mona agrees. "Although did they cut the tree or did they cut the branches?"

"The branches."

"Ah, well. Maybe they'll grow back."

He is suddenly quiet.

"Trees do grow back quickly." Mona tries to take the long view like Rabbi Horowitz, to put things in the comforting context of universal natural principles. "Did they cut a lot or a little?"

Still he says nothing.

"If they cut a lot, it might take a while. If they cut a little, it might be pretty quick."

"It can never grow back," he says with vehemence.

"Are you sure?"

No answer.

"Is there something else you'd like to say?"

The caller hangs up.

Her note in the call log reads this way: *Japanese (?) male calling for (is this preju-diced?) somewhat inscrutable but probably profound reasons. Although who knows, maybe also/just for language practice (English). Good vibes established despite long silences and short sentences. More attention should probably have been paid to drug education. Given caller's depressed state of mind, probably ought also to have explored caller attitude toward hari-kari, even if that's a stereotype. Instead discussed lawn care (fertilizer) and duck pond with tree (willow). Caller disturbed by the pruning of aforementioned tree, which he char-acterized as full of lights like a monsoon and incapable of ever growing back. All this before suddenly hanging up. A hidden message here? Cultural considerations certainly a factor, perhaps major or minor. Still questions remain.*

For instance: Is this Sherman? Sherman! The idea seems at once impossible and pre-ordained. Are they sixteen already? Here he is, as promised. It's kind of young to get married. All the same, Mona studies up on Japan.

An elongated isle, says one book. *Crowded.*

Mona would not have thought she could become Japanese, but here she is, Jewish, right?

She wonders if she is not getting ahead of herself. Why would she want to be Japanese? What if this caller has nothing to do with her at all? The next week, as soon as she comes in, she checks the log to see if he's called, which he hasn't. She waits to see if he calls while she's there. It's amazing how little it matters to her what goes on in the utility closet now. How reoriented she is! So to speak.

The Japanese caller calls again, with about as much to say as last time. They talk about how he's gone down to visit Monticello, in Virginia, with his parents. She's never been there, but he says it's very beautiful, except with too many sides, and he can't understand why Thomas Jefferson had a slave as his mistress.

"Maybe he loved her," Mona says.

"But he is President of whole United States," he says. "Of course, at that time, the United States is only half the size we see now."

"Love is unpredictable."

"That way he makes everyone unhappy."

"But what if he loved her?"

"If he loved her he should leave her alone. When a nail sticks up, people hammer it down."

"But is that right?"

Silence. "That way brings peace and harmony."

"What about right and wrong? Don't you think that's important too?"

No answer at first. Then, "It can't be helped."

"You know," says Mona, "in America, we don't care so much about peace and harmony."

"Oh, really."

"That's right."

"Then why all the time those peace marches?"

"That's different."

He starts to sing: " 'All they are say-ing/is give peace a chance.' "

"Where'd you learn that?"

He hangs up.

The next times he calls, it's about how he walked right under Niagara Falls, which he thought was worth getting soaked—the first thing he's said that they're agreed on. He says this even though as a result of getting wet, he got so sick he ran a fever. Then he calls about Kentucky, and the horse farms there. He does not think these are fundamentally undemocratic. He thinks they are beautiful. Also he says he wouldn't mind being a horse, even if he had to be shot for breaking a leg, and that he wouldn't mind being bred, either.

In short, a pattern has emerged. He calls, always on her shift, offers two or three comments about scenic spots he has visited, then hangs up so abruptly Mona can't help but wonder if there isn't something he doesn't want to go into. For instance, how it is he travels so much. Doesn't his father work? Doesn't he go to school? Is he making it all up about these adventures of his? The last seems unlikely. If she's being read to form *The Scenic Wonders of America*, it must be some special haiku edition. So much is unspoken that when they get to the end of an entry, she doesn't feel nearly so much like saying *Aah* as *Huh?*

What he's holding back may not be trouble—that occurs to her too. Mona wonders if she shouldn't try on some of those wooden platform shoes, see if she can walk in them. She recalls that once she tried stilts and did okay. Also she's a whiz on a pogo stick. And what about the weather in Japan, and do they have mosquitoes? She can almost believe that they don't. For mosquitoes go with cut-offs and camp shirts, who has ever seen a lady in a kimono swat at her pulse points?

She dreams about Sherman, and about what his life is like in Japan, and she finds that in her dreams it is a lot like her life at home, except that her family is like everyone else's. People read each other's minds. They share their food. Everything is simpler. Of course, the Changs also have to eat their fish raw, and sleep on the floor, and wear socks with their sandals; and what with her cowlick, it is not so easy for Mona to get her hair up into that big breakfast-bun style you see the geishas wear. But life is serene. Her family is an interlocking piece of a vast and complex puzzle. There is no Eloise Ingle, and no Seth Mandel; and it is not like China, either, taken over by leather-eating Communists.

Here is the odd thing, though: In her vision, Mona is always fifteen, and never old enough to drive. In fact, she doesn't even have a learner's permit. This is an unreasonable conception, she knows. She knows that people do drive in Japan, although in smaller cars. Still the next time the caller calls, Mona asks, "Do you mind if I ask you a question about driving?"

"Driving?"

"Driving cars," Mona says. "I was just wondering how old you have to be to drive a car in Japan."

He hesitates in a way that makes her wonder if she is being too personal. But how can the driving age in Japan be too personal? "I don't know," he says finally.

She tries to speak more clearly. "I mean, do you have learner's permits there? Here they have learner's permits, and then you have to do the three-point turn, and then you can take the driving test and get your license."

"I see."

"I've been wondering, that's all."

A long silence. So long, Mona wonders if he's hung up. Then he says, "Are you going to Japan?"

"I'd like to. Someday."

"Why?"

"Oh," Mona says. "I guess I've never been there. Why did you go to Monticello?"

"To see the cherry trees. Of course, they are not so nice as the trees in Japan."

"I see."

"Do you like Japan?"

"Oh," Mona says. "I hear it's very interesting."

"I see."

"Very crowded, and with small cars and earthquake trouble," says Mona. "An elongated island. I've never been in an earthquake. Also with volcanoes, I think."

"Mount Fuji," he says politely.

"That's right," Mona says. "Isn't that the one with snow on it?"

"In the wintertime," he says, "snow falls on many mountains. All over. Just like here."

"I see," Mona says. And then, not knowing what else to do, she pretends to knock the phone over. "Whoops," She hangs up. He does not call back.

Seth and Barbara are having a fight. This is because Seth is interested in free love, whereas Barbara is interested in ownership.

"I can't help it," she says. "I do want to be able to say *my* boyfriend, and I just don't see what capitalism and serfs and the Russian Revolution have to do with it." Seth wants her to read *Das Kapital.* She wants him to read Ann Landers. "He has no idea what real love is about," she says. "Him and his Big Idea." She stops.

"Oh, Barbara," Mona says. "You didn't."

Barbara begins to sob.

"You let him give you his tea?"

"We were stoned. And it's just like everyone says—it ruined everything."

Mona takes her friend's backpack for her. She helps her friend sit down on the grass, well away from a pile of dog doo.

"I thought it meant we were definitely going out with each other. But he said we contributed to the social good by reducing world horniness; he doesn't see why that's not enough. He said that all that mattered was if I liked it too, and if I was acting out of my own free will."

"Were you?"

"I was. That's the worst part, except for what he said. Why should he be just my boyfriend, he said."

"What a shithead!"

"It's just what my mother always warned me. What does he really want, a guy like Seth? A guy like Seth, what he really wants is a shiksa."

Nineteen. Eighteen. They count down the days until Barbara's next period while, outside, the dogwood blooms virginal yet again. May! Most merry month. Seventeen. They discuss abortion. First of all, how lucky that it's legal in New York; second of all, what exactly it is. For this information, Mona calls Callie at college. Who else to ask about the special vacuum cleaner, and whether there are nowadays special coat hangers too? Callie looks up the info in *Our Bodies, Ourselves,* which she seems to have sitting right next to the phone; apparently you need it more in college than a dictionary. She does not lecture unduly, except to suggest that Barbara tell her mom. Barbara would sooner throw herself in front of a commuter train.

Sixteen. Seth wonders why the snap freeze. Even pleads, professing concern. Barbara refuses to address His Ignoramus. "Let him use his higher intellect and figure it out himself," she says. "He who reads Nietzsche and can spell it too," agrees Mona. Fifteen. As if Barbara and Mona don't have enough to worry about, they have to take the SATs. They sharpen their number-two pencils together; they try to avoid Eloise Ingle. Mona still sits with Rachel Cohen, though, and so far is this from the G–R section that Mona does not even witness how Barbara breaks down crying in the middle of the test and has to leave the room. Barbara is bravely philosophical about this later. She says she'll try again in the fall, assuming the special vacuum cleaner works.

Fourteen. They try to gain perspective. They discuss whether entertaining a Big Idea was at least fun. Barbara says it wasn't, although it was exciting. Meaning what? Also she says that it was messy and smelly and sticky, and that she dripped for a whole day afterward and had to take about eighty showers to get rid of the smell of him. "Eighty showers?" says Mona. Barbara concedes this to be a manner of speaking. Still the words haunt Mona, rekindling themselves like trick birthday candles. *Eighty showers. Eighty showers.*

Thirteen. Mona lies in bed and wonders: Will Sherman Matsumoto ever make her need to take eighty showers? She feels guilty wondering this. She thinks she should have thoughts only for Kugel Noodle, her friend in need. At the same time, she figures it can't be that bad to wonder, seeing as how there is so little to wonder about. For how should Sherman make her take anything when she hasn't seen him in years? Also the Japanese in general don't seem as if they smell. Maybe this is a stereotype. Maybe if she saw the statistics for deodorant sales in Japan she would be shocked. But what matter, when there is a yet greater misstep in the analytic march of her thinking? For while Mona is antisublimation and can see herself as almost old enough to get married, she finds that she does not see herself as old enough for sex.

How can this be? Mona was the first one in her entire grade to get her period. Plus she surmises by the population problems of the Far East that she is appropriately equipped. But she doesn't look like, say, Barbara. If her friend is a developed nation, Mona is, sure enough, the third world. Barbara's is the body Mona is still waiting to grow into: Her breasts, for example, are veritable colonies of herself, with a distinct tendency toward independence. Whereas Mona's, in contrast, are anything but wayward. A scant handful each, hers are smooth and innocent—the result, you might think, of eating too much ice cream. They meld into the fat under her arms. Even her nipples seem somehow dietary, smallish brownish nubs—areolaless, perhaps, due to inadequate consumption of true adult drinks such as beer and tonic water. Later Mona will realize how in the popular conception Orientals are supposed to be exotically erotic, and all she'll want to say is, But what about my areolaless nubs? Not to say my sturdy short legs—have you ever seen a calf so hammy? And no billowy, Brillo-y bush, alas. How should she have one when she does not even need to shave her legs? This last a convenience of sorts. Although how can she let her legs go natural when they already are natural? Her underarms too—actually she boasts a few wisps there. If only she didn't have to put her hands on her head for anyone to notice! Hair, hair, hair, she thinks. And especially facial hair, body hair. It's different for the sexes, of course. But in general, these are the dead cells that spell wild-side bohemian. She feels condemned to the straight and narrow.

Of course, this whole train of thought will one day prove not her own train at all, but a train set on track by racist sexist imperialists. She will one day discover that it is great to be nonhairy, and what's more that not all Asians are areolaless, just her and some others. Plus that she is yellow and beautiful—baby boobs, hammy calves, and all. She will ask for an extra print when people take her picture. She will come to recognize, with a little squinting, her goddess within.

But for now all Mona can think is, Oh, that subcutaneous fat! So young she looks; so rounded; so unavoidably, irrevocably cute. Oh, to be angular and gaunt! Oh, to be tall! (How she hates the word *petite*.) Oh, to be leggy and buxom like Barbara Gugelstein, and Oh, to have a crisis with Seth Mandel! It seems so awfully glamorous, except when Mona tries to put herself in Barbara's shoes. Then Mona recalls that she would not be in Barbara's shoes. Because if Mona got pregnant, the baby would be mixed. Meaning what? She's not sure, but something complicated, that's certain, and also something for which she's too young.

Twelve. "Ma," Mona says. "Have you ever seen a mixed baby?"

Helen says that she has, yes, two, and the one was beautiful, but the other looked completely Caucasian. That baby had blue eyes and brown hair, and when she grew up she was as big as a horse.

"And what about her legs?"

"Why do you want to know about her legs?" ask Helen, chopping scallions. But then she answers that the girl's legs looked as though there was something the matter with them. "She was still a nice girl. Very smart, and never give her parents any trouble."

"Like me, you mean."

"You!"

"What do you mean, something the matter with them?" Mona asks, after a moment. "What was the matter with her legs?"

"Too long."

"Hmm. I wish my legs were longer."

"Your trouble is not your legs." Helen adds the scallions to the chicken, which is steaming.

"What if I had a mixed baby?" Mona says. "What if I had a mixed baby, and it looked completely Caucasian?"

"Are you having a baby?"

"No. But what if I did, and it looked completely Caucasian? With a big nose and blue eyes and everything."

"Oh, then I would throw it in the garbage," says Helen, turning the heat down.

That night Mona dreams Helen is having a new baby, a boy, which is also the baby that Mona is having, except that Helen doesn't realize it until she notices how long the baby's legs are. Then she shouts, "This baby is Jewish! Throw it in the garbage!" and will not be appeased until Mona throws herself in the garbage instead. The garbage looks to be mostly paper, but turns out to have eggplant at the bottom, which Mona thinks is Italian. Helen insists it's Chinese, though; and when Mona looks again, she sees that her mother is right. There's no mozzarella. She wakes up sweating and feeling like she needs eighty showers.

Eleven. Barbara is friends with Eloise Ingle again, but things so aren't what they were that Barbara doesn't even tell Eloise she might be pregnant. As for Barbara and Mona, they are able to continue working on the hot line as a result of Seth's diplomacy: Knowing an awkward situation when he's engendered one, he graciously cedes his place to an out-of-work comptroller named Mathilde. "You need any help, why, speak right on up," she says, knitting. Her sweater pattern involves chipmunks in a tree full of letters that are going to spell LUV YA.

Barbara wants to quit. Mona, though, explains about the phone calls from Sherman. "Why didn't you tell me?!" says Barbara then. And she's right, Mona should have told her. First of all, because Barbara is telling Mona everything, but also because she knows something Mona doesn't.

"Oh!" she says. "That Andy Kaplan!"

"*Andy Kaplan?*"

They review the evidence. Now that they are discussing it, Mona can recall certain weird moments in her conversations with the Japanese caller. Barbara analyzes these incisively; Mona is suddenly the one who wants to quit the hot line, post-haste. In fact, Mona wouldn't mind quitting town, quitting New York, quitting North America. She wishes she were old enough and had good enough eyes for the space program. Barbara, however, absolutely wants to stay. "Aren't you curious, Watson?" Holding up a pretend monocle, Barbara proposes that Mona let her listen in on the next call. After all, aren't they telling each other everything?

Ten. They wait. Nine.

The mystery caller does not call.

Eight. Barbara Gugelstein's theory (advanced as she taste-tests a can of Diet Dr Pepper) is that Andy Kaplan is afraid to call now because he knows she will catch him out. But how can Andy Kaplan know what Barbara is planning? "He doesn't have ESP," says Mona. Whereupon Barbara, opening a second can for Mona, introduces her to the Theory of Blood Knowledge. Barbara says she believes some people are linked by ancestral memory. She believes that there are genes for ways of thinking, and that if you come from the same gene pool, you are likely to have the same genes.

"I even asked Mr. Ed about it," she says. Mr. Ed is their biology teacher—a horse lover who people say is starting to resemble his favorite ride. "And he said it's possible."

"Possible is only possible."

"Andy Kaplan and I have always been on the same wavelength. Even if he did turn cool before I did."

She says this last because ever since Andy grew his hair and took up the electric guitar, he's been considered the cutest guy in their grade. Not that he rose to this summit without hormones; for a long time he was just like anybody else, only shorter. People noticed that he was golden of aspect and had been to a crack orthodontist, also that he was coordinated and musical, not to say the sort of class-A mimic you would definitely want on your side for charades. But after he suddenly grew eleven inches, he became the sort of guy with whom people liked to claim some connection. His mom worked with their mom on the library committee. They used to be on his paper route. Even Seth claims to play chess with Andy now and then; and Mona sometimes imagines a strange vibe between them, on account of his mom staking her prize chrysanthemums with chopsticks. Also the Kaplans have been to Taiwan and Japan; his father is a professor of East Asian civilization. Around their house, people say, are *belly many Buddhas.*

But of everyone, Barbara feels that she knows Andy best. Not only did they get the same thing for their mothers for Mother's Day, they also have the same hiking boots, the same camping stove, the same Kelty backpack.

"Maybe you should get married," Mona says, sipping away, but Barbara says it would be like marrying her brother. Even going out with him would be like going out with her brother. However, every so often they do smoke pot together, and then it's amazing what they share with each other, the depths of their souls; it's only too bad that the next day she can never remember what they found way down there.

"It's kind of like the tie between you and Sherman Matsumoto," she says. "Now, if you guys end up married, I won't be surprised."

But wouldn't that be like Mona marrying her brother? And what kind of tie is it between her and Sherman Matsumoto if Sherman is not Sherman at all, but actually Andy Kaplan?

Seven. Six. Five. Barbara reports feeling fat. Then, finally—a day early!—her period comes. Hooray! She and Mona celebrate with a ritual egg smash. *O ovum, dear ovum,* they intone. *Be thou ever chary!*

"Chary, or wary?" says Barbara. Mona isn't sure. Still they spend their hot-line shift composing an ode with the rhyme scheme *chary/scary/marry.* They are finagling a way to work in *hari-kari* when, lo and behold, guess who calls?

"Long time no speak," Mona says.

Barbara Gugelstein picks up the other handset. Sherman is talking about a weekend trip to Boston. "Many bricks," he says. "Some of the sidewalks are very hard to walk, and some of the streets have rocks."

No hiking boots? writes Barbara, and passes the note to Mona.

"Those cobblestones," Mona says.

"That's right, cobblestones," he answers, sounding delighted. "All over. Very rough. So hard to drive in Boston! Even we look at the map, we are lost all the time." Still he had fun. He liked the gas lamps, and the swan boats, and the Freedom Trail, although he couldn't understand the Boston Tea Party. Why did the colonists dress up to dump the tea overboard?

"And why they like tea? To drink with their hot dogs?"

Mona explains that in the colonies, there were no hot dogs.

"No hot dogs?" he says, with what seems like real surprise. But then he goes on. "How about hamburgers?"

Ha ha, writes Barbara Gugelstein. *Very funny.*

The caller is generally glad not to have lived through the Revolution. The absence of hot dogs is one reason, but the main reason is that he prefers peace to big fights. On the other hand, he says that he went to Walden Pond and that the man who lived there seemed to him a nut.

He went to Walden Pond too? All in how long?

Mona tries to explain what is a nonconformist.

"Different drummer," Mona explains. "Like in a band."

"If he is in band," the caller says, "the drummer must drum like everyone else."

Get off it! writes Barbara.

The caller goes on to describe how he visited Harvard while he was in Boston, and MIT. (*All in ONE weekend?!*) Both of these he thought very nice, although a little dirty. Also he says the students looked sloppy, and even some of the professors.

"They're just anti-establishment," Mona says.

"What is anti-establishment?"

Mona hesitates. How can he not know what means anti-establishment, when he knows about protest songs?

Ask him what professors wear in Japan, writes Barbara.

"What do professors wear in Japan?"

"What?"

Ask him what he's wearing right now.

"What are you wearing?" Mona asks. "Right now."

"Me? What am I wearing?"

Ask him if he's wearing blue jeans.

"Are you wearing blue jeans?"

How could he not know what he is wearing?

"I am wearing blue jeans," he says finally.

Tell him you are too, with no underwear underneath.

"I'm wearing blue jeans too," Mona says. "Mine have pretty big bells."

More silence. Has he hung up?

"I am so busy these days," he says.

"Schoolwork?" Mona says.

"Sure," he says. "Schoolwork, and sports also."

"Sports!" Mona says. "What sports?"

"Oh," he says. "Some judo, and baseball."

Some judo!!!

"Some judo?" Mona says.

"Judo is very popular sport in Japan."

Did he do it when he lived in America?

"Did you do it when you lived in America?"

"Sure," he says.

Tell him you used to know someone who did judo.

"I used to know someone who did judo," Mona says.

Tell him you were completely in love with him.

"Really," he says.

Tell him you have been saving yourself for him.

"He flipped me on the ground once," Mona says.

"Oh," he says. "You must have done something very bad, that he was so mad at you."

Mona says, "I don't know if it was really that bad."

Now's your chance! Just ask, Do you mind if I ask you a question? Is this Sherman M.?

"Do you mind if I ask you a question?" Mona says.

"Sure," he says.

"I used to know someone named Sherman Matsumoto," Mona says. "Many years ago. Do you know anyone by that name?"

"Sure," he says.

Ask him!

"Are you Sherman?"

Silence.

Or is this Andy Kaplan?

"Or is this Andy Kaplan?"

"Andy?" he says.

"Andy Kaplan," Mona says. "K-A-P-L-A-N."

"Who?" he says. "Kaplan?"

"You heard her," Barbara chimes in. "Give it up!"

"Who's this?" he asks.

"Your friend Barbara," says Barbara.

"Barbara? Not Mona?"

"Also Mona," Mona says.

"Barbara and Mona? What do you mean?"

"Kaplan . . . ," starts Barbara.

"Oh, God. I'm sorry, Sherman," Mona says. "This is Mona. I'm really sorry. It's just that—"

"You will never be Japanese." He hangs up.

Tony Kushner
(b. 1956)

Tony Kushner burst onto the American theatrical scene with a brilliance, exuberance, and political engagement unparalleled since the 1960s. His *Millennium Approaches* won virtually every theatrical award for the 1992 and 1993 theatrical seasons in both England and the United States. Despite its potentially divisive emphasis on gay men and other marginalized communities—socialists, Jews, agnostics, political activists, drag queens, and artists—the play was embraced by academics and mainstream media alike. It proved just as popular and thought-provoking during a nationwide tour when it was paired with its companion *Perestroika* in one, two-part epic called *Angels in America*.

Born in Manhattan in 1956, Kushner grew up in Lake Charles, Louisiana, the son of musician parents of a liberal stripe. As an undergraduate at Columbia University, Kushner saw Richard Foreman's production of Bertolt Brecht's *The Threepenny Opera* for the Public Theater at New York's Lincoln Center. He was "devastated" by the production, saw it six times and became interested in both the political philosophy and the dramaturgy of Brecht from that point on.

There too, he directed his first play, became involved in the anti-apartheid movement, and was a member of a political theater collective, Three P Productions; the three P's stood for popcorn (entertainment), politics (engagement), and poetics (artistic beauty). After college he spent three summers in Louisiana directing youngsters in plays by Shakespeare and Brecht. His interest in Brecht led him to New York University for graduate studies. He also worked at the Repertory Theater of St. Louis, at the New York Theater Workshop, and at the Theater Communications Group before his playwrighting generated enough income for him to write full-time.

Subtitled *A Gay Fantasia on National Themes,* Kushner's epic drama opens with characters whose stage lives begin in 1985. The venal lawyer Roy M. Cohn, based on the red-baiting, real-life attorney, is living high in Washington; he wants to plant young Joe Pitt, an appeals court law clerk from Salt Lake City, in the Justice Department. Pitt's wife Harper is depressed and given to Valium-fuelled hallucinations that take her to Antarctica. She also wonders where Joe goes at night when he leaves her to walk alone. Cohn and Pitt are both closeted homosexuals, and much of *Millennium Approaches* anatomizes the psychic and political costs of living such a lie. But the play's main plot, which meshes with the others, involves Prior Walter and his lover, Louis Ironson who deserts him when he discovers he has AIDS. Walter is haunted by visitations from thirteenth and eighteenth century ancestors who were also born into a time of plague; he also hears an unseen voice which urges him to "prepare the way." When *Millennium Approaches* ends, an angel arrives from above in a blast of music and light which Walter, in Brechtian ironic fashion, calls "Very Steven Spielberg." The angel greets him as a prophet and announces "The Great Work Begins." Kushner never defines the agenda of that "Great Work," but his two-part epic is wide in its thematic reach and highly entertaining as it careens from melodrama to low comedy to high comedy to camp, propelled by a singular combination of intelligence, ebullience, and rage directed at the conservative "revolution" wrought by President Ronald Reagan and his allies.

Kushner has said that anyone interested in exploring alternatives to individualism and the political economy it serves, capitalism, has to be willing to ask tough questions, not only about government, but about the self. The structure of *Millennium Approaches* reflects that kind of questioning as characters often are deployed in two- and three-character scenes for passionate debate.

The production process of *Millennium Approaches* was a long one. The play was commissioned in 1987 by the Eureka Theatre in San Francisco, then had a private, first-draft workshop production at the Mark Taper Forum in Los Angeles, followed a year later by a full production at the Eureka. London's National Theatre next staged a revised *Millennium* in 1992. Later that year *Millennium Approaches* was staged with a still in-process *Perestroika* at the Taper. In the spring of 1993, after its Broadway opening, *Millennium* won the Pulitzer Prize and the Tony Award for best play. Kushner's other works include the early *A Bright Room Called Day*, a later comedy about post-glasnost Russia *Slavs'* and adaptations of Corneille's *The Illusion* and Bertolt Brecht's *The Good Person of Setzuan*.

Further Reading:
R. Vorlicky, ed., *Tony Kushner in Conversation*, 1998.

Text:
T. Kushner, *Plays*, 1992.

Angels in America: Millennium Approaches

THE CHARACTERS

Roy M. Cohn, a successful New York lawyer and unofficial power broker.
Joseph Porter Pitt, chief clerk for Justice Theodore Wilson of the Federal Court of Appeals, Second Circuit.
Harper Amaty Pitt, Joe's wife, an agoraphobic with a mild Valium addiction.
Louis Ironson, a word processor working for the Second Circuit Court of Appeals.
Prior Walter, Louis's boyfriend. Occasionally works as a club designer or caterer, otherwise lives very modestly but with great style off a small trust fund.
Hannah Porter Pitt, Joe's mother, currently residing in Salt Lake City, living off her deceased husband's army pension.
Belize, a former drag queen and former lover of Prior's. A registered nurse. Belize's name was originally Norman Arriaga; Belize is a drag name that stuck.
The Angel, four divine emanations, Fluor, Phosphor, Lumen and Candle; manifest in One: the Continental Principality of America. She has magnificent steel-gray wings.

Other Characters in Part One

Rabbi Isidor Chemelwitz, an orthodox Jewish rabbi, played by the actor playing Hannah.
Mr. Lies, Harper's imaginary friend, a travel agent, who in style of dress and speech suggests a jazz musician; he always wears a large lapel badge emblazoned "IOTA" (The International Order of Travel Agents). He is played by the actor playing Belize.

The Man in the Park, played by the actor playing Prior.

The Voice, the voice of The Angel.

Henry, Roy's doctor, played by the actor playing Hannah.

Emily, a nurse, played by the actor playing The Angel.

Martin Heller, a Reagan Administration Justice Department flackman, played by the actor playing Harper.

Sister Ella Chapter, a Salt Lake City real-estate saleswoman, played by the actor playing The Angel.

Prior 1, the ghost of a dead Prior Walter from the 13th century, played by the actor playing Joe. He is a blunt, gloomy medieval farmer with a guttural Yorkshire accent.

Prior 2, the ghost of a dead Prior Walter from the 17th century, played by the actor playing Roy. He is a Londoner, sophisticated, with a High British accent.

The Eskimo, played by the actor playing Joe.

The Woman in the South Bronx, played by the actor playing The Angel.

Ethel Rosenberg, played by the actor playing Hannah.

PLAYWRIGHT'S NOTES

A Disclaimer: Roy M. Cohn, the character, is based on the late Roy M. Cohn (1927-1986), who was all too real; for the most part the acts attributed to the character Roy, such as his illegal conferences with Judge Kaufmann during the trial of Ethel Rosenberg, are to be found in the historical record. But this Roy is a work of dramatic fiction; his words are my invention, and liberties have been taken.

A Note About the Staging: The play benefits from a pared-down style of presentation, with minimal scenery and scene shifts done rapidly (no blackouts!), employing the cast as well as stagehands—which make for an actor-driven event, as this must be. The moments of magic—the appearance and disappearance of Mr. Lies and the ghosts, the Book hallucination, and the ending—are to be fully realized, as bits of wonderful *theatrical* illusion—which means it's OK if the wires show, and maybe it's good that they do, but the magic should at the same time be thoroughly amazing.

> In a murderous time
> the heart breaks and breaks
> and lives by breaking.
> —Stanley Kunitz
> "The Testing-Tree"

ACT ONE: BAD NEWS

October–November 1985

Scene 1

The last days of October. Rabbi Isidor Chemelwitz alone onstage with a small coffin. It is a rough pine box with two wooden pegs, one at the foot and one at the head, holding the lid in place. A prayer shawl embroidered with a Star of David is draped over the lid, and by the head a yarzheit candle is burning.

Rabbi Isidor Chemelwitz (*He speaks sonorously, with a heavy Eastern European accent, unapologetically consulting a sheet of notes for the family names*): Hello and good morning. I am Rabbi Isidor Chemelwitz of the Bronx Home for Aged Hebrews. We are here this morning to pay respects at the passing of Sarah Ironson, devoted wife of Benjamin Ironson, also deceased, loving and caring mother of her sons Morris, Abraham, and Samuel, and her daughters Esther and Rachel; beloved grandmother of Max, Mark, Louis, Lisa, Maria . . . uh . . . Lesley, Angela, Doris, Luke and Eric. (*Looks more closely at paper*) Eric? This is a Jewish name? (*Shrugs*) Eric. A large and loving family. We assemble that we may mourn collectively this good and righteous woman.

> (*He looks at the coffin*)

This woman. I did not know this woman. I cannot accurately describe her attributes, nor do justice to her dimensions. She was. . . . Well, in the Bronx Home of Aged Hebrews are many like this, the old, and to many I speak but not to be frank with this one. She preferred silence. So I do not know her and yet I know her. She was . . .

> (*He touches the coffin*)

. . . not a person but a whole kind of person, the ones who crossed the ocean, who brought with us to America the villages of Russia and Lithuania—and how we struggled, and how we fought, for the family, for the Jewish home, so that you would not grow up *here*, in this strange place, in the melting pot where nothing melted. Descendants of this immigrant woman, you do not grow up in America, you and your children and their children with the goyische names. You do not live in America. No such place exists. Your clay is the clay of some Litvak shtetl, your air the air of the steppes—because she carried the old world on her back across the ocean, in a boat, and she put it down on Grand Concourse Avenue, or in Flatbush, and she worked that earth into your bones, and you pass it to your children, this ancient, ancient culture and home.

> (*Little pause*)

You can never make that crossing that she made, for such Great Voyages in this world do not any more exist. But every day of your lives the miles that voyage between that place and this one you cross. Every day. You understand me? In you that journey is.

So . . .

She was the last of the Mohicans, this one was. Pretty soon . . . all the old will be dead.

Scene 2

Same day. Roy and Joe in Roy's office. Roy at an impressive desk, bare except for a very elaborate phone system, rows and rows of flashing buttons which bleep and beep and whistle incessantly, making chaotic music underneath Roy's conversations. Joe is sitting, waiting. Roy conducts business with great energy, impatience and sensual abandon: gesticulating, shouting, cajoling, crooning, playing the phone, receiver and hold button with virtuosity and love.

Roy (*Hitting a button*): Hold. (*To Joe*) I wish I was an octopus, a fucking octopus. Eight loving arms and all those suckers. Know what I mean?

Joe: No, I . . .

Roy (Gesturing to a deli platter of little sandwiches on his desk): You want lunch?

Joe: No, that's OK really I just . . .

Roy (Hitting a button): Ailene? Roy Cohn. Now what kind of a greeting is. . . . I thought we were friends, Ai. . . . Look Mrs. Soffer you don't have to get. . . . You're upset. You're yelling. You'll aggravate your condition, you shouldn't yell, you'll pop little blood vessels in your face if you yell. . . . No that was a joke, Mrs. Soffer, I was joking. . . . I already apologized sixteen times for that, Mrs. Soffer, you . . . (*While she's fulminating, Roy covers the mouthpiece with his hand and talks to Joe*) This'll take a minute, *eat* already, what is this tasty sandwich here it's—(*He takes a bite of a sandwich*) Mmmmm, liver or some. . . . Here.

(*He pitches the sandwich to Joe, who catches it and returns it to the platter.*)

Roy (Back to Mrs. Soffer): Uh huh, uh huh. . . . No, I already told you, it wasn't a vacation, it was business, Mrs. Soffer, I have clients in Haiti, Mrs. Soffer, I. . . . Listen, AILENE, YOU THINK I'M THE ONLY GODDAM LAWYER IN HISTORY EVER MISSED A COURT DATE? Don't make such a big fucking. . . . Hold. (*He hits the hold button*) You HAG!

Joe: If this is a bad time . . .

Roy: Bad time? This is a *good* time! (*Button*) Baby doll, get me. . . . Oh fuck, wait . . . (*Button, button*) Hello? Yah. Sorry to keep you holding, Judge Hollins, I. . . . Oh Mrs. Hollins, sorry dear deep voice you got. Enjoying your visit? (*Hand over mouthpiece again, to Joe*) She sounds like a truckdriver and he sounds like Kate Smith, very confusing. Nixon appointed him, all the geeks are Nixon appointees . . . (*To Mrs. Hollins*)Yeah yeah right good so how many tickets dear? Seven. For what, *Cats, 42nd Street,* what? No you wouldn't like *La Cage,* trust me, I know. Oh for godsake. . . . Hold. (*Button, button*) Baby doll, seven for *Cats* or something, anything hard to get, I don't give a fuck what and neither will they. (*Button; to Joe*) You see *La Cage?*

Joe: No I . . .

Roy: Fabulous. Best thing on Broadway. Maybe ever. (*button*) Who? Aw, Jesus H. Christ, Harry, *no,* Harry, Judge John Francis Grimes, Manhattan Family Court. Do I have to do every goddam thing myself? *Touch* the bastard, Harry, and don't call me on this line again, I told you not to . . .

Joe (Starting to get up): Roy, uh, should I wait outside or . . .

Roy (To Joe): Oh sit. (*To Harry*) You hold. I pay you to hold fuck you Harry you jerk. (*Button*) Half-wit dick-brain. (*Instantly philosophical*) I see the universe, Joe, as a kind of sandstrom in outer space with winds of mega-hurricane velocity, but instead of grains of sand it's shards and splinters of glass. You ever feel that way? Ever have one of those days?

Joe: I'm not sure I . . .

Roy: So how's life in Appeals? How's the Judge?

Joe: He sends his best.

Roy: He's a good man. Loyal. Not the brightest man on the bench, but he has manners. And a nice head of silver hair.

Joe: He gives me a lot of responsibility.

Roy: Yeah, like writing his decisions and signing his name.

Joe: Well . . .

Roy: He's a nice guy. And you cover admirably.

Joe: Well, thanks, Roy, I . . .

Roy (Button): Yah? Who is *this*? Well who the fuck are *you*? Hold—(*Button*) Harry? Eighty-seven grand, something like that. Fuck him. Eat me. New Jersey, chain of porno film stores in, uh, Weehawken. That's—Harry, that's the beauty of the law. (*Button*) So, baby doll, what? *Cats*? Bleah. (*Button*) *Cats!* It's about cats. Singing cats, you'll love it. Eight o'clock, the theatre's always at eight. (*Button*) Fucking tourists. (*Button, then to Joe*) Oh live a little, Joe, *eat* something for Christ sake—

Joe: Um, Roy, could you . . .

Roy: What? (*To Harry*) Hold a minute. (*Button*) Mrs. Soffer?
    Mrs. . . . (*Button*) God-fucking-dammit to hell, where is . . .

Joe (Overlapping): Roy, I'd really appreciate it if . . .

Roy (Overlapping): Well she was here a minute ago, baby doll, see if . . .

(*The phone starts making three different beeping sounds, all at once.*)

Roy (Smashing buttons): Jesus fuck this goddam thing . . .

Joe (Overlapping): I really wish you wouldn't . . .

Roy (Overlapping): Baby doll? Ring the *Post* get me Suzy see if . . .

(*The phone starts whistling loudly.*)

Roy: CHRIST!

Joe: Roy.

Roy (Into receiver): Hold. (*Button; to Joe*) What?

Joe: Could you please not take the Lord's name in vain?
    (*Pause*)
    I'm sorry. But please. At least while I'm . . .

Roy (Laughs, then): Right. Sorry. Fuck.
    Only in America. (*Punches a button*) Baby doll, tell 'em all to fuck off. Tell 'em I died. You handle Mrs. Soffer. Tell her it's on the way. Tell her I'm schtupping the judge. I'll call her back. I *will* call her. I *know* how much I borrowed. She's got four hundred times that stuffed up her. . . . Yeah, tell her I said that. (*Button. The phone is silent*)
    So, Joe.

Joe: I'm sorry Roy, I just . . .

Roy: No no no no, principles count, I respect principles, I'm not religious but I like God and God likes me. Baptist, Catholic?

Joe: Mormon.

Roy: Mormon. Delectable. Absolutely. Only in America. So, Joe. Whattya think?

Joe: It's . . . well . . .

Roy: Crazy life.

Joe: Chaotic.

Roy: Well but God bless chaos. Right?

Joe: Ummm . . .

Roy: Huh. Mormons. I knew Mormons, in, um, Nevada.

Joe: Utah, mostly.

Roy: No, these Mormons were in Vegas.

So. So, how'd you like to go to Washington and work for the Justice Department?

Joe: Sorry?

Roy: How'd you like to go to Washington and work for the Justice Department? All I gotta do is pick up the phone, talk to Ed, and you're in.

Joe: In . . . what, exactly?

Roy: Associate Assistant Something Big. Internal Affairs, heart of the woods, something nice with clout.

Joe: Ed . . . ?

Roy: Meese. The Attorney General.

Joe: Oh.

Roy: I just have to pick up the phone . . .

Joe: I have to think.

Roy: Of course.

(*Pause*)

It's a great time to be in Washington, Joe.

Joe: Roy, it's incredibly exciting . . .

Roy: And it would mean something to me. You understand?

(*Little pause.*)

Joe: I . . . can't say how much I appreciate this Roy, I'm sort of . . . well, stunned, I mean. . . . Thanks, Roy. But I have to give it some thought. I have to ask my wife.

Roy: Your wife. Of course.

Joe: But I really appreciate . . .

Roy: Of course. Talk to your wife.

Scene 3

Later that day. Harper at home, alone. She is listening to the radio and talking to herself, as she often does. She speaks to the audience.

Harper: People who are lonely, people left alone, sit talking nonsense to the air, imagining . . . beautiful systems dying, old fixed orders spiraling apart . . .

When you look at the ozone layer, from outside, from a spaceship, it looks like a pale blue halo, a gentle, shimmering aureole encircling the atmosphere encircling the earth. Thirty miles above our heads, a thin layer of three-atom oxygen molecules, product of photosynthesis, which explains the fussy vegetable preference for visible light, its rejection of darker rays and emanations. Danger from without. It's a kind of gift, from God, the crowning touch to the creation of the world: guardian angels, hands linked, make a spherical net, a blue-green nesting orb, a shell of safety for life itself. But everywhere, things are collapsing, lies surfacing, systems of defense giving way. . . . This is why, Joe, this is why I shouldn't be left alone.

(*Little pause*)

I'd like to go traveling. Leave you behind to worry. I'll send postcards with strange stamps and tantalizing messages on the back. "Later maybe." "Nevermore . . ."

(Mr. Lies, a travel agent, appears.)

Harper: Oh! You startled me!

Mr. Lies: Cash, check or credit card?

Harper: I remember you. You're from Salt Lake. You sold us the plane tickets when we flew here. What are you doing in Brooklyn?

Mr. Lies: You said you wanted to travel . . .

Harper: And here you are. How thoughtful.

Mr. Lies: Mr. Lies. Of the International Order of Travel Agents. We mobilize the globe, we set people adrift, we stir the populace and send nomads eddying across the planet. We are adepts of motion, acolytes of the flux. Cash, check or credit card. Name your destination.

Harper: Antarctica, maybe. I want to see the hole in the ozone. I heard on the radio . . .

Mr. Lies (He has a computer terminal in his briefcase): I can arrange a guided tour. Now?

Harper: Soon. Maybe soon. I'm not safe here you see. Things aren't right with me. Weird stuff happens . . .

Mr. Lies: Like?

Harper: Well, like you, for instance. Just appearing. Or last week . . . well never mind.

People are like planets, you need a thick skin. Things get to me, Joe stays away and now. . . . Well look. My dreams are talking back to me.

Mr. Lies: It's the price of rootlessness. Motion sickness. The only cure: to keep moving.

Harper: I'm undecided. I feel . . . that something's going to give. It's 1985. Fifteen years till the third millennium. Maybe Christ will come again. Maybe seeds will be planted, maybe there'll be harvests then, maybe early figs to eat, maybe new life, maybe fresh blood, maybe companionship and love and protection, safety from what's outside, maybe the door will hold, or maybe . . . maybe the troubles will come, and the end will come, and the sky will collapse and there will be terrible rains and showers of poison light, or maybe my life is really fine, maybe Joe loves me and I'm only crazy thinking otherwise, or maybe not, maybe it's even worse than I know, maybe . . . I want to know, maybe I don't. The suspense, Mr. Lies, it's killing me.

Mr. Lies: I suggest a vacation.

Harper (Hearing something): That was the elevator. Oh God, I should fix myself up, I. . . . You have to go, you shouldn't be here . . . you aren't even real.

Mr. Lies: Call me when you decide . . .

Harper: Go!

(The Travel Agent vanishes as Joe enters.)

Joe: Buddy?

Buddy? Sorry I'm late. I was just . . . out. Walking. Are you mad?

Harper: I got a little anxious.

Joe: Buddy kiss.

(They kiss.)

Joe: Nothing to get anxious about.
     So, So how'd you like to move to Washington?

Scene 4

Same day. Louis and Prior outside the funeral home, sitting on a bench, both dressed in funereal finery, talking. The funeral service for Sarah Ironson has just concluded and Louis is about to leave for the cemetery.

Louis: My grandmother actually saw Emma Goldman speak. In Yiddish. But all Grandma could remember was that she spoke well and wore a hat.
     What a weird service. That rabbi . . .
Prior: A definite find. Get his number when you go to the graveyard. I want him to bury me.
Louis: Better head out there. Everyone gets to put dirt on the coffin once it's lowered in.
Prior: Oooh. Cemetery fun. Don't want to miss that.
Louis: It's an old Jewish custom to express love. Here, Grandma, have a shovelful. Latecomers run the risk of finding the grave completely filled.
     She was pretty crazy. She was up there in that home for ten years, talking to herself. I never visited. She looked too much like my mother.
Prior (Hugs him): Poor Louis. I'm sorry your grandma is dead.
Louis: Tiny little coffin, huh
     Sorry I didn't introduce you to. . . . I always get so closety at these family things.
Prior: Butch. You get butch. *(Imitating)* "Hi Cousin Doris, you don't remember me I'm Lou, Rachel's boy." Lou, not Louis, because if you say Louis they'll hear the sibilant S.
Louis: I don't have a . . .
Prior: I don't blame you, hiding. Bloodlines. Jewish curses are the worst. I personally would dissolve if anyone ever looked me in the eye and said "Feh." Fortunately WASPs don't say "Feh." Oh and by the way, darling, cousin Doris is a dyke.
Louis: No.
     Really?
Prior: You don't notice anything. If I hadn't spent the last four years fellating you I'd swear you were straight.
Louis: You're in a pissy mood. Cat still missing

(Little pause.)

Prior: Not a furball in sight. It's your fault.
Louis: It is?
Prior: I warned you, Louis. Names are important. Call an animal "Little Sheba" and you can't expect it to stick around. Besides, it's a dog's name.
Louis: I wanted a dog in the first place, not a cat. He sprayed my books.
Prior: He was a female cat.
Louis: Cats are stupid, high-strung predators. Babylonians sealed them up in bricks. Dogs have brains.

Prior: Cats have intuition.
Louis: A sharp dog is as smart as a really dull two-year-old child.
Prior: Cats know when something's wrong.
Louis: Only if you stop feeding them.
Prior: They know. That's why Sheba left, because she knew.
Louis: Knew what?

(Pause.)

Prior: I did my best Shirley Booth this morning, floppy slippers, housecoat, curlers, can
    of Little Friskies; "Come back, Little Sheba, come back. . . ." To no avail. Le chant,
    elle ne reviendra jamais, jamais . . .
    (He removes his jacket, rolls up his sleeve, shows Louis a dark-purple spot on the under-
side of his arm near the shoulder)
            See.
Louis: That's just a burst blood vessel.
Prior: Not according to the best medical authorities.
Louis: What?
    (Pause)
            Tell me.
Prior: K. S., baby. Lesion number one. Lookit. The wine-dark kiss of the angel of death.
Louis (Very softly, holding Prior's arm): Oh please . . .
Prior: I'm a lesionnaire. The Foreign Lesion. The American Lesion. Lesionnaire's dis-
    ease.
Louis: Stop.
Prior: My troubles are lesion.
Louis: Will you *stop.*
Prior: Don't you think I'm handling this well?
            I'm going to die.
Louis: Bullshit.
Prior: Let go of my arm.
Louis: No.
Prior: Let go.
Louis (Grabbing Prior, embracing him ferociously): No.
Prior: I can't find a way to spare you baby. No wall like the wall of hard scientific fact. K.
    S. Wham. Bang your head on that.
Louis: Fuck you. *(Letting go)* Fuck you fuck you fuck you.
Prior: Now that's what I like to hear. A mature reaction. Let's go see if the cat's come
    home.
            Louis?
Louis: When did you find this?
Prior: I couldn't tell you.
Louis: Why?
Prior: I was scared, Lou.
Louis: Of what?
Prior: That you'll leave me.
Louis: Oh.

(Little pause.)

Prior: Bad timing, funeral and all, but I figured as long as we're on the subject of death . . .
Louis: I have to go bury my grandma.
Prior: Lou?
   (Pause)
         Then you'll come home?
Louis: Then I'll come home.

Scene 5

*Same day, later on. Split scene: Joe and Harper at home; Louis at the cemetery with Rabbi
Isidor Chemelwitz and the little coffin.*

Harper: Washington?
Joe: It's an incredible honor, buddy, and . . .
Harper: I have to think.
Joe: Of course.
Harper: Say no.
Joe: You said you were going to think about it.
Harper: I don't want to move to Washington.
Joe: Well I do.
Harper: It's a giant cemetery, huge white graves and mausoleums everywhere.
Joe: We could live in Maryland. Or Georgetown.
Harper: We're happy here.
Joe: That's not really true, buddy, we . . .
Harper: Well happy enough! Pretend happy. That's better than nothing.
Joe: It's time to make some changes, Harper.
Harper: No changes. Why?
Joe: I've been chief clerk for four years. I make twenty-nine thousand dollars a year.
      That's ridiculous. I graduated fourth in my class and I make less than anyone I
      know. And I'm . . . I'm tired of being a clerk, I want to go where something good is
      happening.
Harper: Nothing good happens in Washington. We'll forget church teachings and buy
      furniture at . . . at *Conran's* and become yuppies. I have too much to do here.
Joe: Like what?
Harper: I *do* have things . . .
Joe: What things?
Harper: I have to finish painting the bedroom.
Joe: You've been painting in there for over a year.
Harper: I know, I. . . . It just isn't done because I never get time to finish it.
Joe: Oh that's . . . that doesn't make sense. You have all the time in the world. You could
      finish it when I'm at work.
Harper: I'm afraid to go in there alone.
Joe: Afraid of what?

Harper: I heard someone in there. Metal scraping on the wall. A man with a knife, maybe.

Joe: There's no one in the bedroom, Harper.

Harper: Not now.

Joe: Not this morning either.

Harper: How do you know? You were at work this morning. There's something creepy about this place. Remember *Rosemary's Baby*?

Joe: Rosemary's Baby?

Harper: Our apartment looks like that one. Wasn't that apartment in Brooklyn?

Joe: No, it was . . .

Harper: Well, it looked like this. It did.

Joe: Then let's move.

Harper: Georgetown's worse. *The Exorcist* was in Georgetown.

Joe: The devil, everywhere you turn, huh, buddy.

Harper: Yeah. Everywhere.

Joe: How many pills today, buddy?

Harper: None. One. Three. Only three.

Louis (Pointing at the coffin): Why are there just two little wooden pegs holding the lid down?

Rabbi Isidor Chemelwitz: So she can get out easier if she wants to.

Louis: I hope she stays put.

I pretended for years that she was already dead. When they called to say she had died it was a surprise. I abandoned her.

Rabbi Isidor Chemelwitz: "Sharfer vi di tson fun a shlang iz an umdankbar kind!"

Louis: I don't speak Yiddish.

Rabbi Isidor Chemelwitz: Sharper than the serpent's tooth is the ingratitude of children. Shakespeare. *Kenig Lear.*

Louis: Rabbi, what does the Holy Writ say about someone who abandons someone he loves at a time of great need?

Rabbi Isidor Chemelwitz: Why would a person do such a thing?

Louis: Because he has to.

Maybe because this person's sense of the world, that it will change for the better with struggle, maybe a person who has this neo-Hegelian positivist sense of constant historical progress towards happiness or perfection or something, who feels very powerful because he feels connected to these forces, moving uphill all the time . . . maybe that person can't, um, incorporate sickness into his sense of how things are supposed to go. Maybe vomit . . . and sores and disease . . . really frighten him, maybe . . . he isn't so good with death.

Rabbi Isidor Chemelwitz: The Holy Scriptures have nothing to say about such a person.

Louis: Rabbi, I'm afraid of the crimes I may commit.

Rabbi Isidor Chemelwitz: Please, mister. I'm a sick old rabbi facing a long drive home to the Bronx. You want to confess, better you should find a priest.

Louis: But I'm not a Catholic, I'm a Jew.

Rabbi Isidor Chemelwitz: Worse luck for you, bubbulah. Catholics believe in forgiveness. Jews believe in Guilt. (*He pats the coffin tenderly*)

Louis: You just make sure those pegs are in good and tight.

Rabbi Isidor Chemelwitz: Don't worry, mister. The life she had, she'll stay put. She's
    better off.
Joe: Look, I know this is scary for you. But try to understand what it means to me. Will
    you try?
Harper: Yes.
Joe: Good. Really try.
        I think things are starting to change in the world.
Harper: But I don't want . . .
Joe: Wait. For the good. Change for the good. America has rediscovered itself. Its sacred
    position among nations. And people aren't ashamed of that like they used to be.
    This is a great thing. The truth restored. Law restored. That's what President Rea-
    gan's done, Harper. He says "Truth exists and can be spoken proudly." And the
    country responds to him. We become better. More good. I need to be part of that, I
    need something big to lift me up. I mean, six years ago the world seemed in decline,
    horrible, hopeless, full of unsolvable problems and crime and confusion and
    hunger and . . .
Harper: But it still seems that way. More now than before. They say the ozone layer is . . .
Joe: Harper . . .
Harper: And today out the window on Atlantic Avenue there was a schizophrenic traffic
    cop who was making these . . .
Joe: Stop it! I'm trying to make a point.
Harper: So am I.
Joe: You aren't even making sense, you . . .
Harper: My point is the world seems just as . . .
Joe: It only seems that way to you because you never go out in the world, Harper, and
    you have emotional problems.
Harper: I do so get out in the world.
Joe: You don't. You stay in all day, fretting about imaginary . . .
Harper: I get out. I do. You don't know what I do.
Joe: You don't stay in all day.
Harper: No.
Joe: Well. . . . Yes you do.
Harper: That's what you think.
Joe: Where do you go?
Harper: Where do *you* go? When you walk.
        (*Pause, then angrily*) And I DO NOT have emotional problems.
Joe: I'm sorry.
Harper: And if I do have emotional problems it's from living with you. Or . . .
Joe: I'm sorry buddy, I didn't mean to . . .
Harper: Or if you do think I do then you should never have married me. You have all
    these secrets and lies.
Joe: I want to be married to you, Harper.
Harper: You shouldn't. You never should.
    (*Pause*)
        Hey buddy. Hey buddy.
Joe: Buddy kiss . . .

(They kiss.)

Harper: I heard on the radio how to give a blowjob.
Joe: What?
Harper: You want to try?
Joe: You really shouldn't listen to stuff like that.
Harper: Mormons can give blowjobs.
Joe: Harper.
Harper (Imitating his tone) : Joe.
It was a little Jewish lady with a German accent. This is a good time. For me to make a
   baby.

(Little pause. Joe turns away.)

Harper: Then they went on to a program about holes in the ozone layer. Over Antarctica. Skin burns, birds go blind, icebergs melt. The world's coming to an end.

Scene 6

*First week of November. In the men's room of the offices of the Brooklyn Federal Court of
Appeals; Louis is crying over the sink; Joe enters.*

Joe: Oh, um. . . . Morning.
Louis: Good morning, counselor.
Joe (He watches Louis cry): Sorry, I. . . . I don't know your name.
Louis: Don't bother. Word processor. The lowest of the low.
Joe (Holding out hand): Joe Pitt. I'm with Justice Wilson . . .
Louis: Oh, I know that. Counselor Pitt. Chief Clerk.
Joe: Were you . . . are you OK?
Louis: Oh, yeah. Thanks. What a nice man.
Joe: Not so nice.
Louis: What?
Joe: Not so nice. Nothing. You sure you're . . .
Louis: Life sucks shit. Life . . . just sucks shit.
Joe: What's wrong?
Louis: Run in my nylons.
Joe: Sorry . . . ?
Louis: Forget it. Look, thanks for asking.
Joe: Well . . .
Louis: I mean it really is nice of you.
        (He starts crying again)
        Sorry, sorry, sick friend . . .
Joe: Oh, I'm sorry.
Louis: Yeah, yeah, well, that's sweet.
        Three of your colleagues have preceded you to this baleful sight and you're the
   first one to ask. The others just opened the door, saw me, and fled. I hope they had
   to pee real bad.

Joe (*Handing him a wad of toilet paper*)*:* They just didn't want to intrude.

Louis: Hah. Reaganite heartless macho asshole lawyers.

Joe: Oh, that's unfair.

Louis: What is? Heartless? Macho? Reaganite? Lawyer?

Joe: I voted for Reagan.

Louis: You did?

Joe: Twice.

Louis: Twice? Well, oh boy. A Gay Republican.

Joe: Excuse me?

Louis: Nothing.

Joe: I'm not . . .

Forget it.

Louis: Republican? Not Republican? Or . . .

Joe: What?

Louis: What?

Joe: Not gay. I'm not gay.

Louis: Oh, Sorry.

(*Blows his nose loudly*) It's just . . .

Joe: Yes?

Louis: Well, sometimes you can tell from the way a person sounds that . . . I mean you *sound* like a . . .

Joe: No I don't. Like what?

Louis: Like a Republican.

(*Little pause. Joe knows he's being teased; Louis knows he knows. Joe decides to be a little brave.*)

Joe (*Making sure no one else is around*)*:* Do I? Sound like a . . . ?

Louis: What? Like a . . . ? Republican, or . . . ? Do *I*?

Joe: Do you what?

Louis: Sound like a . . . ?

Joe: Like a . . . ?

I'm . . . confused.

Louis: Yes.

My name is Louis. But all my friends call me Louise. I work in Word Processing. Thanks for the toilet paper.

(*Louis offers Joe his hand, Joe reaches. Louis feints and pecks Joe on the cheek, then exits.*)

Scene 7

A week later. Mutual dream scene. Prior is at a fantastic makeup table, having a dream, applying the face. Harper is having a pill-induced hallucination. She has these from time to time. For some reason, Prior has appeared in this one. Or Harper has appeared in Prior's dream. It is bewildering.

Prior (*Alone, putting on makeup, then examining the results in the mirror; to the audience*): "I'm ready for my closeup, Mr. DeMille."

One wants to move through life with elegance and grace, blossoming infrequently but with exquisite taste, and perfect timing, like a rare bloom, a zebra orchid. . . . One wants. . . . But one so seldom gets what one wants, does one? No. One does not. One gets fucked. Over. One . . . dies at thirty, robbed of . . . decades of majesty.

Fuck this shit. Fuck this shit.

(*He almost crumbles; he pulls himself together; he studies his handiwork in the mirror*)

I look like a corpse. A corpsette. Oh my queen; you know you've hit rock-bottom when even drag is a drag.

(*Harper appears*)

Harper: Are you. . . . Who are you?

Prior: Who are you?

Harper: What are you doing in my hallucination?

Prior: I'm not in your hallucination. You're in my dream.

Harper: You're wearing makeup.

Prior: So are you.

Harper: But you're a man.

Prior (*Feigning dismay, shock, he mimes slashing his throat with his lipstick and dies, fabulously tragic. Then*): The hands and feet give it away.

Harper: There must be some mistake here. I don't recognize you. You're not. . . . Are you my . . . some sort of imaginary friend?

Prior: No. Aren't you too old to have imaginary friends?

Harper: I have emotional problems. I took too many pills. Why are you wearing makeup?

Prior: I was in the process of applying the face, trying to make myself feel better—I swiped the new fall colors at the Clinique counter at Macy's. (*Showing her*)

Harper: You stole these?

Prior: I was out of cash; it was an emotional emergency!

Harper: Joe will be so angry. I promised him. No more pills.

Prior: These pills you keep alluding to?

Harper: Valium. I take Valium. Lots of Valium.

Prior: And you're dancing as fast as you can.

Harper: I'm not *addicted.* I don't believe in addiction, and I never . . . well, I *never* drink. And I never take drugs.

Prior: Well, smell *you,* Nancy Drew.

Harper: Except Valium.

Prior: Except Valium; in wee fistfuls.

Harper: It's terrible. Mormons are not supposed to be addicted to anything. I'm a Mormon.

Prior: I'm a homosexual.

Harper: Oh! In my church we don't believe in homosexuals.

Prior: In my church we don't believe in Mormons.

Harper: What church do . . . oh! (*She laughs*) I get it.

I don't understand this. If I didn't ever see you before and I don't think I did then I don't think you should be here, in this hallucination, because in my experience the mind, which is where hallucinations come from, shouldn't be able to make up anything that wasn't there to start with, that didn't enter it from experience, from the real world. Imagination can't create anything new, can it? It only recycles bits and pieces from the world and reassembles them into visions. . . . Am I making sense right now?

Prior: Given the circumstances, yes.

Harper: So when we think we've escaped the unbearable ordinariness and, well, untruthfulness of our lives, it's really only the same old ordinariness and falseness rearranged into the appearance of novelty and truth. Nothing unknown is knowable. Don't you think it's depressing?

Prior: The limitations of the imagination?

Harper: Yes.

Prior: It's something you learn after your second theme party: It's All Been Done Before.

Harper: The world. Finite. Terribly, terribly. . . . Well . . . This is the most depressing hallucination I've ever had.

Prior: Apologies. I do try to be amusing.

Harper: Oh, well, don't apologize, you. . . . I can't expect someone who's really sick to entertain me.

Prior: How on earth did you know . . .

Harper: Oh that happens. This is the very threshold of revelation sometimes. You can see things . . . how sick you are. Do you see anything about me?

Prior: Yes.

Harper: What?

Prior: You are amazingly unhappy.

Harper: Oh big deal. You meet a Valium addict and you figure out she's unhappy. That doesn't count. Of course I. . . . Something else. Something surprising.

Prior: Something surprising.

Harper: Yes.

Prior: Your husband's a homo.

(*Pause.*)

Harper: Oh, ridiculous.

(*Pause, then very quietly*)

Really?

Prior(*Shrugs*)*:* Threshhold of revelation.

Harper: Well I don't like your revelations. I don't think you intuit well at all. Joe's a very normal man, he . . .

Oh God. Oh God. He. . . . Do homos take, like, lots of long walks?

Prior: Yes. We do. In stretch pants with lavender coifs. I just looked at you, and there was . . .

Harper: A sort of blue streak of recognition.

Prior: Yes.
Harper: Like you knew me incredibly well.
Prior: Yes.
Harper: Yes.

> I have to go now, get back, something just . . . fell apart.
> Oh God, I feel so sad . . .

Prior: I . . . I'm sorry. I usually say, "Fuck the truth," but mostly, the truth fucks you.
Harper: I see something else about you . . .
Prior: Oh?
Harper: Deep inside you, there's a part of you, the most inner part, entirely free of disease. I can see that.
Prior Is that. . . . That isn't true.
Harper: Threshhold of revelation.

> Home . . .

(She vanishes.)

Prior: People come and go so quickly here . . .

> *(To himself in the mirror)* I don't think there's any uninfected part of me. My heart is pumping polluted blood. I feel dirty.

(He begins to wipe makeup off with his hands, smearing it around. A large gray feather falls from up above. Prior stops smearing the makeup and looks at the feather. He goes to it and picks it up.)

A Voice (It is an incredibly beautiful voice): Look up!
Prior (Looking up, not seeing anyone): Hello?
A Voice: Look up!
Prior: Who is that?
A Voice: Prepare the way!
Prior: I don't see any . . .

(There is a dramatic change in lighting, from above.)

A Voice

> Look up, look up,
> prepare the way
> the infinite descent
> A breath in air
> floating down
> Glory to . . .

(Silence.)

Prior: Hello? Is that it? Helloooo!

> What the fuck . . . ? *(He holds himself)*

Poor me. Poor poor me. Why me? Why poor poor me? Oh I don't feel good right now. I really don't.

Scene 8

That night. Split scene: Harper and Joe at home; Prior and Louis in bed.

Harper: Where were you?

Joe: Out.

Harper: Where?

Joe: Just out. Thinking.

Harper: It's late.

Joe: I had a lot to think about.

Harper: I burned dinner.

Joe: Sorry.

Harper: Not my dinner. My dinner was fine. Your dinner. I put it back in the oven and turned everything up as high as it could go and I watched till it burned black. It's still hot. Very hot. Want it?

Joe: You didn't have to do that.

Harper: I know. It just seemed like the kind of thing a mentally deranged sex-starved pill-popping housewife would do.

Joe: Uh huh.

Harper: So I did it. Who knows anymore what I have to do?

Joe: How many pills?

Harper: A bunch. Don't change the subject.

Joe: I won't talk to you when you . . .

Harper: No. No. Don't do that! I'm . . . I'm fine, pills are not the problem, not our problem, I WANT TO KNOW WHERE YOU'VE BEEN! I WANT TO KNOW WHAT'S GOING ON!

Joe: Going on with what? The job?

Harper: Not the job.

Joe: I said I need more time.

Harper: Not the job!

Joe: Mr. Cohn, I talked to him on the phone, he said I had to hurry . . .

Harper: Not the . . .

Joe: But I can't get you to talk sensibly about anything so . . .

Harper: SHUT UP!

Joe: Then what?

Harper: Stick to the subject.

Joe: I don't know what that is. You have something you want to ask me? Ask me. Go.

Harper: I . . . can't. I'm scared of you.

Joe: I'm tired, I'm going to bed.

Harper: Tell me without making me ask. Please.

Joe: This is crazy, I'm not . . .

Harper: When you come through the door at night your face is never exactly the way I remembered it. I get surprised by something . . . mean and hard about the way you look. Even the weight of you in the bed at night, the way you breathe in your sleep seems unfamiliar.

You terrify me.

Joe (Cold): I know who you are.

Harper: Yes. I'm the enemy. That's easy. That doesn't change.

You think you're the only one who hates sex; I do; I hate it with you; I do. I dream that you batter away at me till all my joints come apart, like wax, and I fall into pieces. It's like a punishment. It was wrong of me to marry you. I knew you . . . (*She stops herself*) It's a sin, and it's killing us both.

Joe: I can always tell when you've taken pills because it makes you red-faced and sweaty and frankly that's very often why I don't want to . . .

Harper: Because . . .

Joe: Well, you aren't pretty. Not like this.

Harper: I have something to ask you.

Joe: Then ASK! ASK! What in hell are you . . .

Harper: Are you a homo?

(*Pause*)

Are you? If you try to walk out right now I'll put your dinner back in the oven and turn it up so high the whole building will fill with smoke and everyone in it will asphyxiate. So help me God I will.

Now answer the question.

Joe: What if I . . .

(*Small pause.*)

Harper: Then tell me, please. And we'll see.

Joe: No. I'm not.

I don't see what difference it makes.

Louis: Jews don't have any clear textual guide to the afterlife; even that it exists. I don't think much about it. I see it as a perpetual rainy Thursday afternoon in March. Dead leaves.

Prior: Eeeugh. Very Greco-Roman.

Louis: Well for us it's not the verdict that counts, it's the act of judgment. That's why I could never be a lawyer. In court all that matters is the verdict.

Prior: You could never be a lawyer because you are oversexed. You're too distracted.

Louis: Not distracted: *ab*stracted. I'm trying to make a point:

Prior: Namely:

Louis: It's the judge in his or her chambers, weighing, books open, pondering the evidence, ranging freely over categories: good, evil, innocent, guilty; the judge in the chamber of circumspection, not the judge on the bench with the gravel. The shaping of the law, not its execution.

Prior: The point, dear, the point . . .

Louis: That it should be the questions and shape of a life, its total complexity gathered, arranged and considered, which matters in the end, not some stamp of salvation or damnation which disperses all the complexity in some unsatisfying little decision—balancing of the scales . . .

Prior: I like this; very zen; it's . . . reassuringly incomprehensible and useless. We who are about to die thank you.

Louis: You are not about to die.

Prior: It's not going well, really . . . two new lesions. My leg hurts. There's protein in my urine, the doctor says, but who knows what the fuck that portends. Anyway it shouldn't be there, the protein. My butt is chapped from diarrhea and yesterday I shat blood.

Louis: I really hate this. You don't tell me . . .

Prior: You get too upset, I wind up comforting you. It's easier . . .

Louis: Oh thanks.

Prior: If it's bad I'll tell you.

Louis: Shitting blood sounds bad to me.

Prior: And I'm telling you.

Louis: And I'm handling it.

Prior: Tell me some more about justice.

Louis: I *am* handling it.

Prior: Well Louis you win Trooper of the Month.

(Louis starts to cry.)

Prior: I take it back. You aren't Trooper of the Month. This isn't working . . .

Tell me some more about justice.

Louis: You are not about to die.

Prior: Justice . . .

Louis: . . . is an immensity, a confusing vastness. Justice is God.

Prior?

Prior: Hmmm?

Louis: You love me.

Prior: Yes.

Louis: What if I walked out on this?

Would you hate me forever?

(Prior kisses Louis on the forehead.)

Prior: Yes.

Joe: I think we ought to pray. Ask God for help. Ask him together . . .

Harper: God won't talk to me. I have to make up people to talk to me.

Joe: You have to keep asking.

Harper: I forgot the question.

Oh yeah. God, is my husband a . . .

Joe (Scary): Stop it. Stop it. I'm warning you.

Does it make any difference? That I might be one thing deep within, no matter how wrong or ugly that thing is, so long as I have fought, with everything I have, to kill it. What do you want from me? What do you want from me, Harper? More than that? For God's sake, there's nothing left, I'm a shell. There's nothing left to kill.

As long as my behavior is what I know it has to be. Decent. Correct. That alone in the eyes of God.

Harper: No, no, not that, that's Utah talk, Mormon talk, I hate it, Joe tell me, say it . . .

Joe: All I will say is that I am a very good man who has worked very hard to become good and you want to destroy that. You want to destroy me, but I am not going to let you do that.

(Pause.)

Harper: I'm going to have a baby.
Joe: Liar.
Harper: You liar.
   A baby born addicted to pills. A baby who does not dream but who hallucinates, who stares up at us with big mirror eyes and who does not know who we are.

(Pause.)

Joe: Are you really . . .
Harper: No. Yes. No. Yes. Get away from me.
   Now we both have a secret.

Prior: One of my ancestors was a ship's captain who made money bringing whale oil to Europe and returning with immigrants—Irish mostly, packed in tight, so many dollars per head. The last ship he captained foundered off the coast of Nova Scotia in a winter tempest and sank to the bottom. He went down with the ship—la Grande Geste—but his crew took seventy women and kids in the ship's only longboat, this big, open rowboat, and when the weather got too rough, and they thought the boat was overcrowded, the crew started lifting people up and hurling them into the sea. Until they got the ballast right. They walked up and down the longboat, eyes to the waterline, and when the boat rode low in the water they'd grab the nearest passenger and throw them into the sea. The boat was leaky, see; seventy people; they arrived in Halifax with nine people on board.
Louis: Jesus.
Prior: I think about that story a lot now. People in a boat, waiting, terrified, while implacable, unsmiling men, irresistibly strong, seize . . . maybe the person next to you, maybe you, and with no warning at all, with time only for a quick intake of air you are pitched into freezing, turbulent water and salt and darkness to drown.
   I like your cosmology, baby. While time is running out I find myself drown to anything that's suspended, that lacks an ending—but it seems to me that it lets you off scot-free.
Louis: What do you mean?
Prior: No judgment, no guilt or responsibility.
Louis: For me.
Prior: For anyone. It was an editorial "you."
Louis: Please get better. Please.
   Please don't get any sicker.

Scene 9

Third week in November. Roy and Henry, his doctor, in Henry's office.

Henry: Nobody knows what causes it. And nobody knows how to cure it. The best theory is that we blame a retrovirus, the Human Immunodeficiency Virus. Its presence is made known to us by the useless antibodies which appear in reaction to its entrance into the bloodstream through a cut, or an orifice. The antibodies are powerless to protect the body against it. Why, we don't know. The body's immune system ceases to function. Sometimes the body even attacks itself. At any rate it's left open to a whole horror house of infections from microbes which it usually defends against.

Like Kaposi's sarcomas. These lesions. Or your throat problem. Or the glands.

We think it may also be able to slip past the blood-brain barrier into the brain. Which is of course very bad news.

And it's fatal in we don't know what percent of people with suppressed immune responses.

(Pause.)

Roy: This is very interesting, Mr. Wizard, but why the fuck are you telling me this?

(Pause.)

Henry: Well, I have just removed one of three lesions which biopsy results will probably tell us is a Kaposi's sarcoma lesion. And you have a pronounced swelling of glands in your neck, groin, and armpits—lymphadenopathy is another sign. And you have oral candidiasis and maybe a little more fungus under the fingernails of two digits on your right hand. So that's why . . .
Roy: This disease . . .
Henry: Syndrome.
Roy: Whatever. It afflicts mostly homosexuals and drug addicts.
Henry: Mostly. Hemophiliacs are also at risk.
Roy: Homosexuals and drug addicts. So why are you implying that I . . .
  (Pause)
  What are you implying, Henry?
Henry: I don't . . .
Roy: I'm not a drug addict.
Henry: Oh come on Roy.
Roy: What, what, come on Roy what? Do you think I'm a junkie, Henry, do you see tracks?
Henry: This is absurd.
Roy: Say it.
Henry: Say what?
Roy: Say, "Roy Cohn, you are a . . ."
Henry: Roy.
Roy: "You are a. . . ." Go on. Not "Roy Cohn you are a drug fiend." "Roy Marcus Cohn, you are a . . ."
  Go on, Henry, it starts with an "H."
Henry: Oh I'm not going to . . .
Roy: *With an* "*H*," Henry, and it isn't "Hemophiliac." Come on . . .
Henry: What are you doing, Roy?
Roy: No, say it. I mean it. Say: "Roy Cohn, you are a homosexual."
  (Pause)
  And I will proceed, systematically, to destroy your reputation and your practice and your career in New York State, Henry. Which you know I can do.

(Pause.)

Henry: Roy, you have been seeing me since 1958. Apart from the facelifts I have treated
you for everything from syphilis . . .

Roy: From a whore in Dallas.

Henry: From syphilis to veneral warts. In your rectum. Which you may have gotten
from a whore in Dallas, but it wasn't a female whore.

(Pause.)

Roy: So say it.

Henry: Roy Cohn, you are . . .

You have had sex with men, many many times, Roy, and one of them, or any
number of them, has made you very sick. You have AIDS.

Roy: AIDS.

Your problem, Henry, is that you are hung up on words, on labels, that you
believe they mean what they seem to mean. AIDS. Homosexual. Gay. Lesbian. You
think these are names that tell you who someone sleeps with, but they don't tell
you that.

Henry: No?

Roy: No. Like all labels they tell you one thing and one thing only: where does an individual so identified fit in the food chain, in the pecking order? Not ideology, or sexual taste, but something much simpler: clout. Not who I fuck or who fucks me, but
who will pick up the phone when I call, who owes me favors. This is what a label
refers to. Now to someone who does not understand this, homosexual is what I am
because I have sex with men. But really this is wrong. Homosexuals are not men
who sleep with other men. Homosexuals are men who in fifteen years of trying
cannot get a pissant antidiscrimination bill through City Council. Homosexuals
are men who know nobody and who nobody knows. Who have zero clout. Does
this sound like me, Henry?

Henry: No.

Roy: No. I have clout. A lot. I can pick up this phone, punch fifteen numbers, and you
know who will be on the other end in under five minutes, Henry?

Henry: The President.

Roy: Even better, Henry, His wife.

Henry: I'm impressed.

Roy: I don't want you to be impressed. I want you to understand. This is not sophistry.
And this is not hypocrisy. This is reality. I have sex with men. But unlike nearly
every other man of whom this is true, I bring the guy I'm screwing to the White
House and President Reagan smiles at us and shakes his hand. Because *what* I am is
defined entirely by *who* I am. Roy Cohn is not a homosexual. Roy Cohn is a heterosexual man, Henry, who fucks around with guys.

Henry: OK, Roy.

Roy: And what is my diagnosis, Henry?

Henry: You have AIDS, Roy.

Roy: No, Henry, no. AIDS is what homosexuals have. I have liver cancer.

(Pause.)

Henry: Well, whatever the fuck you have, Roy, it's very serious, and I haven't got a damn thing for you. The NIH in Bethesda has a new drug called AZT with a two-year waiting list that not even I can get you onto. So get on the phone, Roy, and dial the fifteen numbers, and tell the First Lady you need in on an experimental treatment for liver cancer, because you can call it any damn thing you want, Roy, but what it boils down to is very bad news.

ACT TWO: IN VITRO

December 1985-January 1986

Scene 1

Night, the third week in December. Prior alone on the floor of his bedroom; he is much worse.

Prior: Louis, Louis, please wake up, oh God.

(Louis runs in.)

Prior: I think something horrible is wrong with me I can't breathe . . .
Louis: (Starting to exit): I'm calling the ambulance.
Prior: No, wait, I . . .
Louis: Wait? Are you fucking crazy? Oh God you're on fire, your head is on fire.
Prior: It hurts, it hurts . . .
Louis: I'm calling the ambulance.
Prior: I don't want to go to the hospital, I don't want to go to the hospital please let me lie here, just . . .
Louis: No, no, God, Prior, stand up . . .
Prior: DON'T TOUCH MY LEG!
Louis: We have to . . . oh God this is so crazy.
Prior: I'll be OK if I just lie here Lou, really, if I can only sleep a little . . .

(Louis exits.)

Prior: Louis?
        No! No! Don't call, you'll send me there and I won't come back, please, please Louis I'm begging, baby, please . . .
        (Screams) LOUIS!!
Louis (From off; hysterical): WILL YOU SHUT THE FUCK UP!
Prior (Trying to stand): Aaaah. I have . . . to go to the bathroom. Wait. Wait, just . . . oh. Oh God. *(He shits himself)*
Louis (Entering): Prior? They'll be here in . . .
        Oh my God.
Prior: I'm sorry, I'm sorry.
Louis: What did . . . ? What?

Prior: I had an accident.

(Louis goes to him.)

Louis: This is blood.
Prior: Maybe you shouldn't touch it . . . me. . . . I . . . *(He faints)*
Louis (Quietly): Oh help. Oh help. Oh God oh God oh God help me I can't I can't I can't.

Scene 2

Same night. Harper is sitting at home, all alone, with no lights on. We can barely see her. Joe enters, but he doesn't turn on the lights.

Joe: Why are you sitting in the dark? Turn on the light.
Harper: No. I heard the sounds in the bedroom again. I know someone was in there.
Joe: No one was.
Harper: Maybe actually in the bed, under the covers with a knife.
     Oh, boy. Joe. I, um, I'm thinking of going away. By which I mean: I think I'm going off again. You . . . you know what I mean?
Joe: Please don't. Stay. We can fix it. I pray for that. This is my fault, but I can correct it. You have to try too . . .

(He turns on the light. She turns if off again.)

Harper: When you pray, what do you pray for?
Joe: I pray for God to crush me, break me up into little pieces and start all over again.
Harper: Oh. Please. Don't pray for that.
Joe: I had a book of Bible stories when I was a kid. There was a picture I'd look at twenty times every day: Jacob wrestles with the angel. I don't really remember the story, or why the wrestling—just the picture. Jacob is young and very strong. The angel is . . . a beautiful man, with golden hair and wings, of course. I still dream about it. Many nights. I'm. . . . It's me. In that struggle. Fierce, and unfair. The angel is not human, and it holds nothing back, so how could anyone human win, what kind of a fight is that? It's not just. Losing means your soul thrown down in the dust, your heart torn out from God's. But you can't not lose.
Harper: In the whole entire world, you are the only person, the only person I love or have ever loved. And I love you terribly. Terribly. That's what's so awfully, irreducibly real. I can make up anything but I can't dream that away.
Joe: Are you . . . are you really going to have a baby?
Harper: It's my time, and there's no blood. I don't really know. I suppose it wouldn't be a great thing. Maybe I'm just not bleeding because I take too many pills. Maybe I'll give birth to a pill. That would give a new meaning to pill-popping, huh?
     I think you should go to Washington. Alone. Change, like you said.
Joe: I'm not going to leave you, Harper.
Harper: Well maybe not. But I'm going to leave you.

Scene 3

One AM, *the next morning. Louis and a nurse, Emily, are sitting in Prior's room in the hospital.*

Emily: He'll be all right now.

Louis: No he won't.

Emily: No. I guess not. I gave him something that makes him sleep.

Louis: Deep asleep?

Emily: Orbiting the moons of Jupiter.

Louis: A good place to be.

Emily: Anyplace better than here. You his . . . uh?

Louis: Yes. I'm his uh.

Emily: This must be hell for you.

Louis: It is. Hell. The After Life. Which is not at all like a rainy afternoon in March, by the way, Prior. A lot more vivid than I'd expected. Dead leaves, but the crunchy kind. Sharp, dry air. The kind of long, luxurious dying feeling that breaks your heart.

Emily: Yeah, well we all get to break our hearts on this one. He seems like a nice guy. Cute.

Louis: Not like this.

Yes, he is. Was. Whatever.

Emily: Weird name. Prior Walter. Like, "The Walter before this one."

Louis: Lots of Walters before this one. Prior is an old old family name in an old old family. The Walters go back to the Mayflower and beyond. Back to the Norman Conquest. He says there's a Prior Walter stitched into the Bayeux tapestry.

Emily: Is that impressive?

Louis: Well, it's old. Very old. Which in some circles equals impressive.

Emily: Not in my circle. What's the name of the tapestry?

Louis: The Bayeux tapestry. Embroidered by La Reine Mathilde.

Emily: I'll tell my mother. She embroiders. Drives me nuts.

Louis: Manual therapy for anxious hands.

Emily: Maybe you should try it.

Louis: Mathilde stitched while William the Conqueror was off to war. She was capable of . . . more than loyalty. Devotion.

She waited for him, she stitched for years And if he had come back broken and defeated from war, she would have loved him even more. And if he had returned mutilated, ugly, full of infection and horror, she would still have loved him; fed by pity, by a sharing of pain, she would love him even more, and even more, and she would never, never have prayed to God, please let him die if he can't return to me whole and healthy and able to live a normal life . . . If he had died, she would have buried her heart with him.

So what the fuck is the matter with me?

(*Little pause*)

Will he sleep through the night?

Emily: At least.

Louis: I'm going.

Emily: It's one AM. Where do you have to go at . . .

Louis: I know what time it is. A walk. Night air, good for the. . . . The park.
Emily: Be careful.
Louis: Yeah. Danger.

      Tell him, if he wakes up and you're still on, tell him goodbye, tell him I had to go.

Scene 4

An hour later. Split scene: Joe and Roy in a fancy (straight) bar; Louis and a Man in the Rambles in Central Park, Joe and Roy are sitting at the bar; the place is brightly lit. Joe has a plate of food in front of him but he isn't eating. Roy occasionally reaches over the table and forks small bites off Joe's plate. Roy is drinking heavily, Joe not at all. Louis and the Man are eyeing each other, each alternating interest and indifference.

Joe: The pills were something she started when she miscarried or . . . no, she took some before that. She had a really bad time at home, when she was a kid, her home was really bad. I think a lot of drinking and physical stuff. She doesn't talk about that, instead she talks about . . . the sky falling down, people with knives hiding under sofas. Monsters. Mormons. Everyone thinks Mormons don't come from homes like that, we aren't supposed to behave that way, but we do. It's not lying, or being two-faced. Everyone tries very hard to live up to God's strictures, which are very . . . um . . .
Roy: Strict.
Joe: I shouldn't be bothering you with this.
Roy: No, please. Heart to heart. Want another. . . . What is that, seltzer?
Joe: The failure to measure up hits people very hard. From such a strong desire to be good they feel very far from goodness when they fail.

      What scares me is that maybe what I really love in her is the part of her that's farthest from the light, from God's love; maybe I was drawn to that in the first place. And I'm keeping it alive because I need it.
Roy: Why would you need it?
Joe: There are things. . . . I don't know how well we know ourselves. I mean, what if? I know I married her because she . . . because I loved it that she was always wrong, always doing something wrong, like one step out of step. In Salt Lake City that stands out. I never stood out, on the outside, but inside, it was hard for me. To pass.
Roy: Pass?
Joe: Yeah.
Roy: Pass as what?
Joe: Oh, Well. . . . As someone cheerful and strong. Those who love God with an open heart unclouded by secrets and struggles are cheerful; God's easy simple love for them shows in how strong and happy they are. The saints.
Roy: But you had secrets? Secret struggles . . .
Joe: I wanted to be one of the elect, one of the Blessed. You feel you ought to be, that the blemishes are yours by choice, which of course they aren't. Harper's sorrow, that really deep sorrow, she didn't choose that. But it's there.
Roy: You didn't put it there.
Joe: No.

Roy: You sound like you think you did.

Joe: I am responsible for her.

Roy: Because she's your wife.

Joe: That. And I do love her.

Roy: Whatever. She's your wife. And so there are obligations. To her. But also to yourself.

Joe: She'd fall apart in Washington.

Roy: Then let her stay here.

Joe: She'll fall apart if I leave her.

Roy: Then bring her to Washington.

Joe: I just can't, Roy. She needs me.

Roy: Listen, Joe. I'm the best divorce lawyer in the business.

(Little pause.)

Joe: Can't Washington wait?

Roy: You do what you need to do, Joe. What *you* need. *You.* Let her life go where it
wants to go. You'll both be better for that. *Somebody* should get what they want.

Man: What do you want?

Louis: I want you to fuck me, hurt me, make me bleed.

Man: I want to.

Louis: Yeah?

Man: I want to hurt you.

Louis: Fuck me.

Man: Yeah?

Louis: Hard.

Man: Yeah? You been a bad boy?

(Pause. Louis laughs, softly.)

Louis: Very bad. Very bad.

Man: You need to be punished, boy?

Louis: Yes. I do.

Man: Yes what?

(Little pause.)

Louis: Um, I . . .

Man: Yes *what,* boy?

Louis: Oh. Yes sir.

Man: I want you to take me to your place, boy.

Louis: No, I can't do that.

Man: No *what?*

Louis: No sir, I can't, I . . .
            I don't live alone, sir.

Man: Your lover know you're out with a man tonight, boy?

Louis: No sir, he . . .
          My lover doesn't know.
Man: Your lover know you . . .
Louis: Let's change the subject, OK? Can we go to your place?
Man: I live with my parents.
Louis: Oh.

Roy: Everyone who makes it in this world makes it because somebody older and more powerful takes an interest. The most precious asset in life, I think, is the ability to be a good son. You have that, Joe. Somebody who can be a good son to a father who pushes them farther than they would otherwise go. I've had many fathers, I owe my life to them, powerful, powerful men. Walter Winchell, Edgar Hoover. Joe McCarthy most of all. He valued me because I am a good lawyer, but he loved me because I was and am a good son. He was a very difficult man, very guarded and cagey; I brought out something tender in him. He would have died for me. And me for him. Does this embarrass you?
Joe: I had a hard time with my father.
Roy: Well sometimes that's the way. Then you have to find other fathers, substitutes, I don't know. The father-son relationship is central to life. Women are for birth, beginning, but the father is continuance. The son offers the father his life as a vessel for carrying forth his father's dream. Your father's living?
Joe: Um, dead.
Roy: He was . . . what? A difficult man?
Joe: He was in the military. He could be very unfair. And cold.
Roy: But he loved you.
Joe: I don't know.
Roy: No, no, Joe, he did, I know this. Sometimes a father's love has to be very, very hard, unfair even, cold to make his son grow strong in a world like this. This isn't a good world.

Man: Here, then.
Louis: I. . . . Do you have a rubber?
Man: I don't use rubbers.
Louis: You should. (*He takes one from his coat pocket*) Here.
Man: I don't use them.
Louis: Forget it, then. (*He starts to leave*)
Man: No, wait.
          Put it on me. Boy.
Louis: Forget it, I have to get back. Home. I must be going crazy.
Man: Oh come on please he won't find out.
Louis: It's cold. Too cold.
Man: It's never too cold, let me warm you up. Please?

(*They begin to fuck.*)

Man: Relax.
Louis (*A small laugh*): Not a chance.
Man: It . . .
Louis: What?

Man: I think it broke. The rubber. You want me to keep going? (*Little pause*) Pull out?
Should I . . .

Louis: Keep going.

Infect me.

I don't care. I don't care.

(*Pause. The Man pulls out.*)

Man: I . . . um, look, I'm sorry, but I think I want to go.

Louis: Yeah.

Give my best to mom and dad.

(*The Man slaps him.*)

Louis: Ow!

(*They stare at each other.*)

Louis: It was a joke.

(*The Man leaves.*)

Roy: How long have we known each other?

Joe: Since 1980.

Roy: Right. A long time. I feel close to you, Joe. Do I advise you well?

Joe: You've been an incredible friend, Roy, I . . .

Roy: I want to be family. Familia, as my Italian friends call it. La Familia. A lovely word.
It's important for me to help you, like I was helped.

Joe: I owe practically everything to you, Roy.

Roy: I'm dying, Joe. Cancer.

Joe: Oh my God.

Roy: Please. Let me finish.

Few people know this and I'm telling you this only because. . . . I'm not afraid
of death. What can death bring that I haven't faced? I've lived; life is the worst.
(*Gently mocking himself*) Listen to me, I'm a philosopher.

Joe. You must do this. You must must must. Love; that's a trap. Responsibility;
that's a trap too. Like a father to a son I tell you this: Life is full of horror; nobody
escapes, nobody; save yourself. Whatever pulls on you, whatever needs from you,
threatens you. Don't be afraid; people are so afraid; don't be afraid to live in the
raw wind, naked, alone. . . . Learn at least this: What you are capable of. Let nothing
stand in your way.

Scene 5

*Three days later. Prior and Belize in Prior's hospital room. Prior is very sick but improving.
Belize has just arrived.*

Prior: Miss Thing.

Belize: Ma cherie bichette.

Prior: Stella.

Belize: Stella for star. Let me see. (*Scrutinizing Prior*) You look like shit, why yes indeed you do, comme la merde!

Prior: Merci.

Belize (*Taking little plastic bottles from his bag, handing them to Prior*)*:* Not to despair, Belle Reeve. Lookie! Magic goop!

Prior: (*Opening a bottle, sniffing*): Pooh! What kinda crap is that?

Belize: Beats me. Let's rub it on your poor blistered body and see what it does.

Prior: This is not Western medicine, these bottles . . .

Belize: Voodoo cream. From the botanica 'round the block.

Prior: And you a registered nurse.

Belize (*Sniffing it*)*:* Beeswax and cheap perfume. Cut with Jergen's Lotion. Full of good vibes and love from some little black Cubana witch in Miami.

Prior: Get that trash away from me, I am immune-suppressed.

Belize: I *am* a health professional. I *know* what I'm doing.

Prior: It stinks. Any word from Louis?

(*Pause. Belize starts giving Prior a gentle massage.*)

Prior: Gone.

Belize: He'll be back. I know the type. Likes to keep a girl on edge.

Prior: It's been . . .

(*Pause.*)

Belize (*Trying to jog his memory*)*:* How long?

Prior: I don't remember.

Belize: How long have you been here?

Prior (*Getting suddenly upset*)*:* I don't remember, I don't give a fuck. I want Louis. I want my fucking boyfriend, where the fuck is he? I'm dying, I'm dying, where's Louis?

Belize: Shhhh, shhh . . .

Prior: This is a very strange drug, this drug. Emotional lability, for starters.

Belize: Save a tab or two for me.

Prior: Oh no, not this drug, ce n'est pas pour la joyeux noël et la bonne année, this drug she is serious poisonous chemistry, ma pauvre bichette.

And not just disorienting. I hear things. Voices.

Belize: Voices.

Prior: A voice.

Belize: Saying what?

(*Pause.*)

Prior: I'm not supposed to tell.

Belize: You better tell the doctor. Or I will.

Prior: No no don't. Please. I want the voice; it's wonderful. It's all that's keeping me alive. I don't want to talk to some intern about it.

You know what happens? When I hear it, I get hard.

Belize: Oh my.

Prior: Comme ça. (*He uses his arm to demonstrate*) And you know I am slow to rise.

Belize: My jaw aches at the memory.

Prior: And would you deny me this little solace—betray my concupiscence to Florence Nightingale's storm troopers?

Belize: Perish the thought, ma bébé.

Prior: They'd change the drug just to spoil the fun.

Belize: You and your boner can depend on me.

Prior: Je t'adore, ma belle nègre.

Belize: All this girl-talk shit is politically incorrect, you know. We should have dropped it back when we gave up drag.

Prior: I'm sick, I get to be politically incorrect if it makes me feel better. You sound like Lou.

> (*Little pause*)
>
> Well, at least I have the satisfaction of knowing he's in anguish somewhere. I loved his anguish. Watching him stick his head up his asshole and eat his guts out over some relatively minor moral conundrum—it was the best show in town. But Mother warned me: if they get overwhelmed by the little things . . .

Belize: They'll be belly-up bustville when something big comes along.

Prior: Mother warned me.

Belize: And they do come along.

Prior: But I didn't listen.

Belize: No. (*Doing Hepburn*) Men are beasts.

Prior (Also Hepburn): The absolute lowest.

Belize: I have to go. If I want to spend my whole lonely life looking after white people I can get underpaid to do it.

Prior: You're just a Christian martyr.

Belize: Whatever happens, baby, I will be here for you.

Prior: Je t'aime.

Belize: Je t'aime. Don't go crazy on me, girlfriend, I already got enough crazy queens for one lifetime. For two. I can't be bothering with dementia.

Prior: I promise.

Belize (Touching him; softly): Ouch.

Prior: Ouch. Indeed.

Belize: Why'd they have to pick on you?

> And eat more, girlfriend, you really do look like shit.

(*Belize leaves.*)

Prior (After waiting a beat): He's gone.

> Are you still . . .

Voice: I can't stay. I will return.

Prior: Are you one of those "Follow me to the other side" voices?

Voice: No. I am no nightbird. I am a messenger . . .

Prior: You have a beautiful voice, it sounds . . . like a viola, like a perfectly tuned, tight string, balanced, the truth. . . . Stay with me.

Voice: Not now. Soon I will return, I will reveal myself to you; I am glorious, glorious;
　　my heart, my countenance and my message. You must prepare.

Prior: For what? I don't want to . . .

Voice: No death, no:

　　　　A marvelous work and a wonder we undertake, an edifice awry we sink plumb
　　and straighten, a great Lie we abolish, a great error correct, with the rule, sword
　　and broom of Truth!

Prior: What are you talking about, I . . .

Voice:

　　　　I am on my way; when I am manifest, our Work begins:

　　　　Prepare for the parting of the air,

　　　　The breath, the ascent,

　　　　Glory to . . .

Scene 6

The second week of January. Martin, Roy and Joe in a fancy Manhattan restaurant.

Martin: It's a revolution in Washington, Joe. We have a new agenda and finally a real
　　leader. They got back the Senate but we have the courts. By the nineties the
　　Supreme Court will be block-solid Republican appointees, and the Federal
　　bench—Republican judges like land mines, everywhere, everywhere they turn. Af-
　　firmative action? Take it to court. Boom! Land mine. And we'll get our way on just
　　about everything: abortion, defense, Central America, family values, a live invest-
　　ment climate. We have the White House locked till the year 2000. And beyond. A
　　permanent fix on the Oval Office? It's possible. By '92 we'll get the Senate back,
　　and in ten years the South is going to give us the House. It's really the end of Liber-
　　alism. The end of New Deal Socialism. The end of ipso facto secular humanism.
　　The dawning of a genuinely American political personality. Modeled on Ronald
　　Wilson Reagan.

Joe: It sounds great, Mr. Heller.

Martin: Martin. And Justice is the hub. Especially since Ed Meese took over. He doesn't
　　specialize in Fine Points of the Law. He's a flatfoot, a cop. He reminds me of Teddy
　　Roosevelt.

Joe: I can't wait to meet him.

Martin: Too bad, Joe, he's been dead for sixty years!

(There is a little awkwardness. Joe doesn't respond.)

Martin: Teddy Roosevelt. You said you wanted to. . . . Little joke. It reminds me of the
　　story about the . . .

Roy (Smiling, but nasty): Aw shut the fuck up Martin.

　　　　(To Joe) You see that? Mr. Heller here is one of the mighty, Joseph, in D.C. he
　　sitteth on the right hand of the man who sitteth on the right of The Man. And yet I
　　can say "shut the fuck up" and he will take no offense. Loyalty. He . . .

　　　　Martin?

Martin: Yes, Roy?

Roy: Rub my back.

Martin: Roy . . .

Roy: No no really, a sore spot, I get them all the time now, these. . . . Rub it for me darling, would you do that for me?

(Martin rubs Roy's back. They both look at Joe.)

Roy (To Joe): How do you think a handful of Bolsheviks turned St. Petersburg into Leningrad in one afternoon? *Comrades.* Who do for each other. Marx and Engels. Lenin and Trotsky. Josef Stalin and Franklin Delano Roosevelt.

(Martin laughs.)

Roy: Comrades, right Martin?

Martin: This man, Joe, is a Saint of the Right.

Joe: I know, Mr. Heller, I . . .

Roy: And you see what I mean, Martin? He's special, right?

Martin: Don't embarass him, Roy.

Roy: Gravity, decency, smarts! His strength is as the strength of ten because his heart is pure! *And* he's a Royboy, one hundred percent.

Martin: We're on the move, Joe. On the move.

Joe: Mr. Heller, I . . .

Martin (Ending backrub): We can't wait any longer for an answer.

(Little pause.)

Joe: Oh. Um, I . . .

Roy: Joe's a married man, Martin.

Martin: Aha.

Roy: With a wife. She doesn't care to go to D.C., and so Joe cannot go. And keeps us dangling. We've seen that kind of thing before, haven't we? These men and their wives.

Martin: Oh yes. Beware.

Joe: I really can't discuss this under . . .

Martin: Then *don't* discuss. Say yes, Joe.

Roy: Now.

Martin: Say yes I will.

Roy: Now.

     Now. I'll hold my breath till you do, I'm turning blue waiting. . . . *Now,* goddammit!

Martin: Roy, calm down, it's not . . .

Roy: Aw, fuck it. *(He takes a letter from his jacket pocket, hands it to Joe)* Read. Came today.

(Joe reads the first paragraph, then looks up.)

Joe: Roy. This is . . . Roy, this is terrible.

Roy: You're telling me.

> A letter from the New York State Bar Association, Martin.
> They're gonna try and disbar me.

Martin: Oh my.

Joe: Why?

Roy: Why, Martin?

Martin: Revenge.

Roy: The whole Establishment. Their little rules. Because I know no rules. Because I don't see the Law as a dead and arbitrary collection of antiquated dictums, thou shall, thou shalt not, because, because I know the Law's a pliable, breathing, sweating . . . *organ,* because, because . . .

Martin: Because he borrowed half a million from one of his clients.

Roy: Yeah, well, there's that.

Martin: And he forgot to *return* it.

Joe: Roy, that's. . . . You borrowed money from a client?

Roy: I'm deeply ashamed.

(Little pause.)

Joe (Very sympathetic): Roy, you know how much I admire you. Well I mean I know you have unorthodox ways, but I'm sure you only did what you thought at the time you needed to do. And I have faith that . . .

Roy: Not so damp, please. I'll deny it was a loan. She's got no paperwork. Can't prove a fucking thing.

(Little pause. Martin studies the menu.)

Joe (Handing back the letter, more official in tone): Roy I really appreciate your telling me this, and I'll do whatever I can to help.

Roy (Holding up a hand, then, carefully): I'll tell you what you can do.

> I'm about to be tried, Joe, by a jury that is not a jury of my peers. The disbarment committee: genteel gentleman Brahmin lawyers, country-club men. I offend them, to these men . . . I'm what, Martin, some sort of filthy little Jewish troll?

Martin: Oh well, I wouldn't go so far as . . .

Roy: Oh well I would.

> Very fancy lawyers, these disbarment committee lawyers, fancy lawyers with fancy corporate clients and complicated cases. Antitrust suits. Deregulation. Environmental control. Complex cases like these need Justice Department cooperation like flowers need the sun. Wouldn't you say that's an accurate assessment, Martin?

Martin: I'm not here, Roy. I'm not hearing any of this.

Roy: No. Of course not.

> Without the light of the sun, Joe, these cases, and the fancy lawyers who represent them, will wither and die.
>
> A well-placed friend, someone in the Justice Department, say, can turn off the sun. Cast a deep shadow on my behalf. Make them shiver in the cold. If they overstep. They would fear that.

(Pause.)

Joe: Roy. I don't understand.
Roy: You do.

(*Pause.*)

Joe: You're not asking me to . . .
Roy: Sssshhhh. Careful.
Joe (*A beat, then*): Even if I said yes to the job, it would be illegal to interfere. With the
    hearings. It's unethical. No. I can't.
Roy: Un-ethical.
        Would you excuse us, Martin?
Martin: Excuse you?
Roy: Take a walk, Martin. For real.

(*Martin leaves.*)

Roy: Un-ethical. Are you trying to embarrass me in front of my friend?
Joe: Well it is unethical, I can't . . .
Roy: Boy, you are really something. What the fuck do you think this is, Sunday School?
Joe: No, but Roy this is . . .
Roy: This is . . . this is gastric juices churning, this is enzymes and acids, this is intesti-
    nal is what this is, bowel movement and blood-red meat—this stinks, this is *poli-
    tics,* Joe, the game of being alive. And you think you're. . . . What? Above that?
    Above alive is what? Dead! In the clouds! You're on earth, goddammit! Plant a
    foot, stay a while.
        I'm sick. They smell I'm weak. They want blood this time. I must have eyes in
    Justice. In Justice you will protect me.
Joe: Why can't Mr. Heller . . .
Roy: Grow up, Joe. The administration can't get involved.
Joe: But I'd be part of the administration. The same as him.
Roy: Not the same. Martin's Ed's man. And Ed's Reagan's man. So Martin's Reagan's
    man.
        And you're mine.
        (*Little pause. He holds up the letter*)
        This will never be. Understand me?
        (*He tears the letter up*)
        I'm gonna be a lawyer, Joe, I'm gonna be a lawyer, Joe, I'm gonna be a goddam
    motherfucking legally licensed member of the bar lawyer, just like my daddy was,
    till my last bitter day on earth, Joseph, until the day I die.

(*Martin returns.*)

Roy: Ah, Martin's back.
Martin: So are we agreed?
Roy: Joe?

(*Little pause.*)

Joe: I will think about it.

    (*To Roy*) I will.

Roy: Huh.

Martin: It's the fear of what comes after the doing that makes the doing hard to do.

Roy: Amen.

Martin: But you can almost always live with the consequences.

Scene 7

That afternoon. On the granite steps outside the Hall of Justice, Brooklyn. It is cold and sunny. A Sabrett wagon is selling hot dogs. Louis, in a shabby overcoat, is sitting on the steps contemplatively eating one. Joe enters with three hot dogs and a can of Coke.

Joe: Can I . . . ?

Louis: Oh sure. Sure. Crazy cold sun.

Joe (*Sitting*): Have to make the best of it.

    How's your friend?

Louis: My . . . ? Oh. He's worse. My friend is worse.

Joe: I'm sorry.

Louis: Yeah, well. Thanks for asking. It's nice. You're nice. I can't believe you voted for Reagan.

Joe: I hope he gets better.

Louis: Reagan?

Joe: Your friend.

Louis: He won't. Neither will Reagan.

Joe: Let's not talk politics, OK?

Louis (*Pointing to Joe's lunch*): You're eating *three* of those?

Joe: Well . . . I'm . . . hungry.

Louis: They're really terrible for you. Full of rat-poo and beetle legs and wood shavings 'n' shit.

Joe: Huh.

Louis: And . . . um . . . irridium, I think. Something toxic.

Joe: You're eating one.

Louis: Yeah, well, the shape, I can't help myself, plus I'm *trying* to commit suicide, what's your excuse?

Joe: I don't have an excuse. I just have Pepto-Bismol.

(*Joe takes a bottle of Pepto-Bismol and chugs it. Louis shudders audibly.*)

Joe: Yeah I know but then I wash it down with Coke.

(*He does this. Louis mimes barfing in Joe's lap. Joe pushes Louis's head away.*)

Joe: Are you *always* like this?

Louis: I've been worrying a lot about his kids.

Joe: Whose?

Louis: Reagan's. Maureen and Mike and little orphan Patti and Miss Ron Reagan Jr., the you-should-pardon-the-expression heterosexual.

Joe: Ron Reagan Jr. is *not.* . . . You shouldn't just make these assumptions about people. How do you know? About him? What he is? You don't know.

Louis (*Doing Tallulah*): Well darling he never sucked *my* cock but . . .

Joe: Look, if you're going to get vulgar . . .

Louis: No no really I mean. . . . What's it like to be the child of the Zeitgeist? To have the American Animus as your dad? It's not really a *family,* the Reagans, I read *People,* there aren't any connections there, no love, they don't ever even speak to each other except through their agents. So what's it like to be Reagan's kid? Enquiring minds want to know.

Joe: You can't believe everything you . . .

Louis (*Looking away*): But . . . I think we all know what that's like. Nowadays. No connections. No responsibilities. All of us . . . falling through the cracks that separate what we owe to our selves and . . . and what we owe to love.

Joe: You just. . . . Whatever you feel like saying or doing, you don't care, you just . . . do it.

Louis: Do what?

Joe: It. Whatever. Whatever it is you want to do.

Louis: Are you trying to tell me something?

(*Little pause, sexual. They stare at each other. Joe looks away.*)

Joe: No, I'm just observing that you . . .

Louis: Impulsive.

Joe: Yes, I mean it must be scary, you . . .

Louis (*Shrugs*): Land of the free. Home of the brave. Call me irresponsible.

Joe: It's kind of terrifying.

Louis: Yeah, well, freedom is. Heartless, too.

Joe: Oh you're not heartless.

Louis: You don't know.
       Finish your weenie.

(*He pats Joe on the knee, starts to leave.*)

Joe: Um . . .

(*Louis turns, look at him. Joe searches for something to say.*)

Joe: Yesterday was Sunday but I've been a little unfocused recently and I thought it was Monday. So I came here like I was going to work. And the whole place was empty. And at first I couldn't figure out why, and I had this moment of incredible . . . fear and also. . . . It just flashed through my mind: The whole Hall of Justice, it's empty, it's deserted, it's gone out of business. Forever. The people that make it run have up and abandoned it.

Louis (*Looking at the building*): Creepy.

Joe: Well yes but. I felt that I was going to scream. Not because it was creepy, but because the emptiness felt so *fast.*

And . . . well, good. A . . . happy scream.

I just wondered what a thing it would be . . . if overnight everything you owe anything to, justice, or love, had really gone away. Free.

It would be . . . heartless terror. Yes. Terrible, and . . .

Very great. To shed your skin, every old skin, one by one then walk away, unencumbered, into the morning.

(*Little pause. He looks at the building*)

I can't go in there today.

Louis: Then don't.

Joe (*Not really hearing Louis*): I can't go in, I need . . .

(*He looks for what he needs. He takes a swig of Pepto-Bismol*)

I can't *be* this anymore. I need . . . a change, I should just . . .

Louis (*Not a come-on, necessarily; he doesn't want to be alone*): Want some company? For whatever?

(*Pause. Joe looks at Louis and looks away, afraid. Louis shrugs.*)

Louis: Sometimes, even if it scares you to death, you have to be willing to break the law. Know what I mean?

(*Another little pause.*)

Joe: Yes.

(*Another little pause.*)

Louis: I moved out. I moved out on my . . .

I haven't been sleeping well.

Joe: Me neither.

(*Louis goes up to Joe, licks his napkin and dabs at Joe's mouth.*)

Louis: Antacid moustache.

(*Points to the building*) Maybe the court won't convene. Ever again. Maybe we are free. To do whatever.

Children of the new morning, criminal minds. Selfish and greedy and loveless and blind. Reagan's children.

You're scared. So am I. Everybody is in the land of the free. God help us all.

Scene 8

Late that night. Joe at a payphone phoning Hannah at home in Salt Lake City.

Joe: Mom?

Hannah: Joe?

Joe: Hi.

Hannah: You're calling from the street. It's . . . it must be four in the morning. What's happened?

Joe: Nothing, nothing, I . . .

Hannah: It's Harper. Is Harper. . . . Joe? Joe?

Joe: Yeah, hi. No, Harper's fine. Well, no, she's . . . not fine. How are you, Mom?

Hannah: What's happened?

Joe: I just wanted to talk to you. I, uh, wanted to try something out on you.

Hannah: Joe, you haven't . . . have you been drinking, Joe?

Joe: Yes ma'am. I'm drunk.

Hannah: That isn't like you.

Joe: No. I mean, who's to say?

Hannah: Why are you out on the street at four AM? In that crazy city. It's dangerous.

Joe: Actually, Mom, I'm not on the street. I'm near the boathouse in the park.

Hannah: What park?

Joe: Central Park.

Hannah: CENTRAL PARK! Oh my Lord. What on earth are you doing in Central Park at this time of night? Are you . . .

> Joe, I think you ought to go home right now. Call me from home.
>
> (*Little pause*)
>
> Joe?

Joe: I come here to watch, Mom. Sometimes. Just to watch.

Hannah: Watch what? What's there to watch at four in the . . .

Joe: Mom, did Dad love me?

Hannah: What?

Joe: Did he?

Hannah: You ought to go home and call from there.

Joe: Answer.

Hannah: Oh now really. This is maudlin. I don't like this conversation.

Joe: Yeah, well, it gets worse from here on.

(*Pause.*)

Hannah: Joe?

Joe: Mom. Momma. I'm A homosexual, Momma.

> Boy, did that come out awkward.
>
> (*Pause*)
>
> Hello? Hello?
>
> I'm a homosexual.
>
> (*Pause*)
>
> Please, Momma. Say something.

Hannah: You're old enough to understand that your father didn't love you without being ridiculous about it.

Joe: What?

Hannah: You're ridiculous. You're being ridiculous.

Joe: I'm . . .

> What?

Hannah: You really ought to go home now to your wife. I need to go to bed. This phone call. . . . We will just forget this phone call.

Joe: Mom.

Hannah: No more talk. Tonight. This . . .

(*Suddenly very angry*) Drinking is a sin! A sin! I raised you better than that. (*She hangs up*)

Scene 9

The following morning, early. Split scene: Harper and Joe at home; Louis and Prior in Prior's hospital room. Joe and Louis have just entered. This should be fast and obviously furious; overlapping is fine; the proceedings may be a little confusing but not the final results.

Harper: Oh God. Home. The moment of truth has arrived.

Joe: Harper.

Louis: I'm going to move out.

Prior: The fuck you are.

Joe: Harper. Please listen. I still love you very much. You're still my best buddy; I'm not going to leave you.

Harper: No, I don't like the sound of this. I'm leaving.

Louis: I'm leaving.

I already have.

Joe: Please listen. Stay. This is really hard. We have to talk.

Harper: We are talking. Aren't we. Now please shut up. OK?

Prior: Bastard. Sneaking off while I'm flat out here, that's low.

If I could get up now I'd beat the holy shit out of you.

Joe: Did you take pills? How many?

Harper: No pills. Bad for the . . . (*Pats stomach*)

Joe: You aren't pregnant. I called your gynecologist.

Harper: I'm seeing a new gynecologist.

Prior: You have no right to do this.

Louis: Oh, that's ridiculous.

Prior: No right. It's criminal.

Joe: Forget about that. Just listen. You want the truth. This is the truth.

I knew this when I married you. I've known this I guess for as long as I've known anything, but . . . I don't know, I thought maybe that with enough effort and will I could change myself . . . but I can't . . .

Prior: Criminal.

Louis: There oughta be a law.

Prior: There is a law. You'll see.

Joe: I'm losing ground here, I go walking, you want to know where I walk, I . . . go to the park, or up and down 53rd Street, or places where. . . . And I keep swearing I won't go walking again, but I just can't.

Louis: I need some privacy.

Prior: That's new.

Louis: Everything's new, Prior.

Joe: I try to tighten my heart into a knot, a snarl, I try to learn to live dead, just numb, but then I see someone I want, and it's like a nail, like a hot spike right through my chest, and I know I'm losing.

Prior: Apartment too small for three? Louis and Prior comfy but not Louis and Prior and Prior's disease?

Louis: Something like that.

I won't be judged by you. this isn't a crime, just—the inevitable consequence of people who run out of—whose limitations . . .

Prior: Bang bang bang. The court will come to order.

Louis: I mean let's talk practicalities, schedules; I'll come over if you want, spend nights with you when I can, I can . . .

Prior: Has the jury reached a verdict?

Louis: I'm doing the best I can.

Prior: Pathetic. Who cares?

Joe: My whole life has conspired to bring me to this place, and I can't despise my whole life. I think I believed when I met you I could save you, you at least if not myself, but . . .

I don't have any sexual feelings for you, Harper. And I don't think I ever did.

(Little pause.)

Harper: I think you should go.

Joe: Where?

Harper: Washington. Doesn't matter.

Joe: What are you talking about?

Harper: Without me.

Without me, Joe. Isn't that what you want to hear?

(Little pause.)

Joe: Yes.

Louis: You can love someone and fail them. You can love someone and not be able to . . .

Prior: You *can,* theoretically, yes. A person can, maybe an editorial "you" can love, Louis, but not *you,* specifically you, I don't know, I think you are excluded from that general category.

Harper: You were going to save me, but the whole time you were spinning a lie. I just don't understand that.

Prior: A person could theoretically love and maybe many do but we both know now you can't.

Louis: I do.

Prior: You can't even say it.

Louis: I love you, Prior.

Prior: I repeat. Who cares?

Harper: This is so scary, I want this to stop, to go back . . .

Prior: We have reached a verdict, your honor. This man's heart is deficient. He loves, but his love is worth nothing.

Joe: Harper . . .

Harper: Mr. Lies, I want to get away from here. Far away. Right now. Before he starts talking again. Please, please. . .

Joe: As long as I've known you Harper you've been afraid of . . . of men hiding under the bed, men hiding under the sofa, men with knives.

Prior (*Shattered; almost pleading; trying to reach him*): I'm dying! You stupid fuck! Do you know what that is! Love! Do you know what love means? We lived together four-and-a-half years, you animal, you idiot.

Louis: I have to find some way to save myself.

Joe: Who are these men? I never understood it. Now I know.

Harper: What?

Joe: It's me.

Harper: It is?

Prior: GET OUT OF MY ROOM!

Joe: I'm the man with the knives.

Harper: You are?

Prior: If I could get up now I'd kill you. I would. Go away. Go away or I'll scream.

Harper: Oh God . . .

Joe: I'm sorry . . .

Harper: It is you.

Louis: Please don't scream.

Prior: Go.

Harper: I recognize you now.

Louis: Please . . .

Joe: Oh. Wait, I. . . . Oh!

    (*He covers his mouth with his hand, gags, and removes his hand, red with blood*)
    I'm bleeding.

    (*Prior screams.*)

Harper: Mr. Lies.

Mr. Lies (*Appearing, dressed in antarctic explorer's apparel*): Right here.

Harper: I want to go away. I can't see him anymore.

Mr. Lies: Where?

Harper: Anywhere. Far away.

Mr. Lies: Absolutamento.

(*Harper and Mr. Lies vanish. Joe looks up, sees that she's gone.*)

Prior (*Closing his eyes*): When I open my eyes you'll be gone.

(*Louis leaves.*)

Joe: Harper?

Prior (*Opening his eyes*): Huh. It worked.

Joe (*Calling*): Harper?

Prior: I hurt all over. I wish I was dead.

Scene 10

The same day, sunset. Hannah and Sister Ella Chapter, a real-estate saleswoman, Hannah Pitt's closest friend, in front of Hannah's house in Salt Lake City.

Sister Ella Chapter: Look at that view! A view of heaven. Like the living city of heaven, isn't it, it just fairly glimmers in the sun.

Hannah: Glimmers.

Sister Ella Chapter: Even the stone and brick it just glimmers and glitters like heaven in the sunshine. Such a nice view you get, perched up on a canyon rim. Some kind of beautiful place.

Hannah: It's just Salt Lake, and you're selling the house *for* me, not *to* me.

Sister Ella Chapter: I like to work up an enthusiasm for my properties.

Hannah: Just get me a good price.

Sister Ella Chapter: Well, the market's off.

Hannah: At least fifty.

Sister Ella Chapter: Forty'd be more like it.

Hannah: Fifty.

Sister Ella Chapter: Wish you'd wait a bit.

Hannah: Well I can't.

Sister Ella Chapter: Wish you would. You're about the only friend I got.

Hannah: Oh well now.

Sister Ella Chapter: Know why I decided to like you? I decided to like you 'cause you're the only unfriendly Mormon I ever met.

Hannah: Your wig is crooked.

Sister Ella Chapter: Fix it.

(Hannah straightens Sister Ella's wig.)

Sister Ella Chapter: New York City. All they got there is tiny rooms.

I always thought: People ought to stay put. That's why I got my license to sell real estate. It's a way of saying: Have a house! Stay put! It's a way of saying traveling's no good. Plus I needed the cash. (*She takes a pack of cigarettes out of her purse, lights one, offers pack to Hannah*)

Hannah: Not out here, anyone could come by.

There's been days I've stood at this ledge and thought about stepping over.

It's a hard place, Salt Lake: baked dry. Abundant energy; not much intelligence. That's a combination that can wear a body out. No harm looking someplace else. I don't need much room.

My sister-in-law Libby thinks there's radon gas in the basement.

Sister Ella Chapter: Is there gas in the . . .

Hannah: Of course not. Libby's a fool.

Sister Ella Chapter: 'Cause I'd have to include that in the description.

Hannah: There's no gas, Ella. (*Little pause*) Give a puff. (*She takes a furtive drag of Ella's cigarette*) Put it away now.

Sister Ella Chapter: So I guess it's goodbye.

Hannah: You'll be all right, Ella, I wasn't ever much of a friend.

Sister Ella Chapter: I'll say something but don't laugh, OK?

This is the home of saints, the godliest place on earth, they say, and I think they're right. That mean there's no evil here? No. Evil's everywhere. Sin's everywhere. But this . . . is the spring of sweet water in the desert, the desert flower. Every step a Believer takes away from here is a step fraught with peril. I fear for you, Hannah Pitt, because you are my friend. Stay put. This is the right home of saints.

Hannah: Latter-day saints.

Sister Ella Chapter: Only kind left.

Hannah: But still. Late in the day . . . for saints and everyone. That's all. That's all.

Fifty thousand dollars for the house, Sister Ella Chapter; don't undersell. It's an impressive view.

ACT THREE: *Not-Yet-Conscious, Forward Dawning*

January 1986

Scene I

Late night, three days after the end of Act Two. The stage is completely dark. Prior is in bed in his apartment, having a nightmare. He wakes up, sits up and switches on a nightlight. He looks at his clock. Seated by the table near the bed is a man dressed in the clothing of a 13th-century British squire.

Prior (Terrified): Who are you?

Prior 1: My name is Prior Walter.

(Pause.)

Prior: My name is Prior Walter.

Prior 1: I know that.

Prior: Explain.

Prior 1: You're alive. I'm not. We have the same name. What do you want me to explain?

Prior: A ghost?

Prior 1: An ancestor.

Prior: Not *the* Prior Walter? The Bayeux tapestry Prior Walter?

Prior 1: His great-great grandson. The fifth of the name.

Prior: I'm the thirty-fourth, I think.

Prior 1: Actually the thirty-second.

Prior: Not according to Mother.

Prior 1: She's including the two bastards, then; I say leave them out. I say no room for bastards. The little things you swallow . . .

Prior: Pills.

Prior 1: Pills. For the pestilence. I too . . .

Prior: Pestilence. . . . You too what?

Prior 1: The pestilence in my time was much worse than now. Whole villages of empty houses. You could look outdoors and see Death walking in the morning, dew dampening the ragged hem of his black robe. Plain as I see you now.

Prior: You died of the plague.

Prior 1: The spotty monster. Like you, alone.

Prior: I'm not alone.

Prior 1: You have no wife, no children.

Prior: I'm gay.

Prior 1: So? Be gay, dance in your altogether for all I care, what's that to do with not having children?

Prior: Gay homosexual, not bonny, blithe and . . . never mind.

Prior 1: I had twelve. When I died.

(The second ghost appears, this one dressed in the clothing of an elegant 17th-century Londoner.)

Prior 1: (Pointing to Prior 2) And I was three years younger than him.

(Prior sees the new ghost, screams.)

Prior: Oh God another one.

Prior 2: Prior Walter. Prior to you by some seventeen others.

Prior 1: He's counting the bastards.

Prior: Are you having a convention?

Prior 2: We've been sent to declare her fabulous incipience. They love a well-paved entrance with lots of heralds, and . . .

Prior 1: The messenger come. Prepare the way. The infinite descent, a breath in air . . .

Prior 2: They chose us, I suspect, because of the mortal affinities. In a family as long-descended as the Walters there are bound to be a few carried off by plague.

Prior 1: The spotty monster.

Prior 2: Black Jack. Came from a water pump, half the city of London, can you imagine? His came from fleas. Yours, I understand, is the lamentable consequence of venery . . .

Prior 1: Fleas on rats, but who knew that?

Prior: Am I going to die?

Prior 2: We aren't allowed to discuss . . .

Prior 1: When you do, you don't get ancestors to help you through it. You may be surrounded by children but you die alone.

Prior: I'm afraid.

Prior 1: You should be. There aren't even torches, and the path's rocky, dark and steep.

Prior 2: Don't alarm him. There's good news before there's bad.
   We two come to stew rose petal and palm leaf before the triumphal procession. Prophet. Seer. Revelator. It's a great honor for the family.

Prior 1: He hasn't got a family.

Prior 2: I meant for the Walters, for the family in the larger sense.

Prior (Singing):
   All I want is a room somewhere,
   Far away from the cold night air . . .

Prior 2 (Putting a hand on Prior's forehead): Calm, calm, this is no brain fever . . .

(Prior calms down, but keeps his eyes closed. The lights begin to change. Distant Glorious Music.)

Prior 1 (Low chant):
   Adonai, Adonai,

> Olam ha-yichud,
> Zefirot, Zazahot,
> Ha-adam, ha-gadol
> Daughter of Light,
> Daughter of Splendors,
> Fluor! Phosphor!
> Lumen! Candle!

Prior 2 (Simultaneously):

> Even now,
> From the mirror-bright halls of heaven,
> Across the cold and lifeless infinity of space,
> The Messenger comes
> Trailing orbs of light,
> Fabulous, incipient,
> Oh Prophet,
> To you . . .

Prior 1 and *Prior 2:*

> Prepare, prepare,
> The Infinite Descent,
> A breath, a feather,
> Glory to . . .

(They vanish.)

Scene 2

The next day. Split scene: Louis and Belize in a coffee shop. Prior is at the outpatient clinic at the hospital with Emily, the nurse; she has him on a pentamidine IV drip.

Louis: Why has democracy succeeded in America? Of course by succeeded I mean comparatively, not literally, not in the present, but what makes for the prospect of some sort of radical democracy spreading outward and growing up? Why does the power that was once so carefully preserved at the top of the pyramid by the original framers of the Constitution seem drawn inexorably downward and outward in spite of the best effort of the Right to stop this? I mean it's the really hard thing about being Left in this country, the American Left can't help but trip over all these petrified little fetishes: freedom, that's the worst; you know, *Jeane Kirkpatrick* for God's sake will go on and on about freedom and so what does that mean, the word freedom, when she talks about it, or human rights; you have Bush talking about human rights, and so what are these people talking about, they might as well be talking about the mating habits of Venusians, these people don't begin to know what, ontologically, freedom is or human rights, like they see these bourgeois property-based Rights-of-Man-type rights but that's not enfranchisement, not democracy, not what's implicit, what's potential within the idea, not the idea with blood in it. That's just liberalism, the worst kind of liberalism, really, bourgeois tolerance, and what I think is that what AIDS shows us is the limits of tolerance, that it's not enough to be tolerated, because when the shit hits the fan you find out how much tolerance is worth. Nothing. And underneath all the tolerance is intense, passionate hatred.

Belize: Uh huh.

Louis: Well don't you think that's true?

Belize: Uh huh. It is.

Louis: *Power* is the object, not being tolerated. Fuck assimilation. But I mean in spite of all this the thing about America, I think, is that ultimately we're different from every other nation on earth, in that, with people here of every race, we can't. . . . Ultimately what defines us isn't race, but politics. Not like any European country where there's an insurmountable fact of a kind of racial, or ethnic, monopoly, or monolith, like all Dutchmen, I mean Dutch people, are well, Dutch, and the Jews of Europe were never Europeans, just a small problem. Facing the monolith. But here there are so many small problems, it's really just a collection of small problems, the monolith is missing. Oh, I mean, of course I suppose there's the monolith of White America. White Straight Male America.

Belize: Which is not unimpressive, even among monoliths.

Louis: Well, no, but when the race thing gets taken care of, and I don't mean to minimalize how major it is, I mean I know it is, this is a really, really incredibly racist country but it's like, well, the British. I mean, all these blue-eyed pink people. And it's just weird, you know, I mean I'm not all that Jewish-looking, or . . . well, maybe I am but, you know, in New York, everyone is . . . well, not everyone, but so many are but so but in England, in London I walk into bars and I feel like Sid the Yid, you know I mean like Woody Allen in *Annie Hall,* with the payess and the gabardine coat, like never, never anywhere so much—I mean, not actively despised, not like they're Germans, who I think are still terribly anti-Semitic, and racist too, I mean black-racist, they pretend otherwise but, anyway, in London, there's just . . . and at one point I met this black gay guy from Jamaica who talked with a lilt but he said his family'd been living in London since before the Civil War—the American one—and how the English never let him forget for a minute that he wasn't blue-eyed and pink and I said yeah, me too, these people are anti-Semites and he said yeah but the British Jews have the clothing business all sewed up and blacks there can't get a foothold. And it was an incredibly awkward moment of just. . . . I mean here we were, in this bar that was gay but it was a *pub,* you know, the beams and the plaster and those horrible little, like, two-day-old fish and egg sandwiches—and just so British, so *old,* and I felt, well, there's no way out of this because both of us are, right now, too much immersed in this history, hope is dissolved in the sheer age of this place, where race is what counts and there's no real hope of change—it's the racial destiny of the Brits that matters to them, not their political destiny, whereas in America . . .

Belize: Here in America race doesn't count.

Louis : No, no, that's not. . . . I mean you *can't* be hearing that . . .

Belize: I . . .

Louis: It's—look, race, yes, but ultimately race here is a political question, right? Racists just try to use race here as a tool in a political struggle. It's not really about race. Like the spiritualists try to use that stuff, are you enlightened, are you centered, channeled, whatever, this reaching out for a spiritual past in a country where no indigenous spirits exist—only the Indians, I mean Native American spirits and we killed them off so now, there are no gods here, no ghosts and spirits in America, there are no angels in America, no spiritual past, no racial past, there's only the political, and the decoys and the ploys to maneuver around the inescapable battle of politics, the shifting downwards and outwards of political power to the people . . .

Belize: POWER to the People! AMEN! (*Looking at his watch*) *OH MY GOODNESS!* Will you look at the time. I gotta . . .

Louis: Do you. . . . You think this is, what, racist or naive or something?

Belize: Well it's certainly *something.* Look, I just remembered I have an appointment . . .

Louis: What? I mean I really don't want to, like, speak from some position of privilege and . . .

Belize: I'm sitting here, thinking, eventually he's *got* to run out of steam, so I let you rattle on and on saying about maybe seven or eight things I find really offensive.

Louis: What?

Belize: But I know you, Louis, and I know the guilt fueling this peculiar tirade is obviously already swollen bigger than your hemorrhoids.

Louis: I don't have hemorrhoids.

Belize: I hear different. May I finish?

Louis: Yes, but I don't have hemorrhoids.

Belize: So finally, when I . . .

Louis: Prior told you, he's an asshole, he shouldn't have . . .

Belize: You promised, Louis. Prior is not a subject.

Louis: You brought him up.

Belize: I brought up hemorrhoids.

Louis: So it's indirect. Passive-aggressive.

Belize: Unlike, I suppose, banging me over the head with your theory that America doesn't have a race problem.

Louis: Oh be fair I never said that.

Belize: Not exactly, but . . .

Louis: I said . . .

Belize: . . . but it was close enough, because if it'd been that blunt I'd've just walked out and . . .

Louis: You deliberately misinterpreted! I . . .

Belize: Stop interrupting! I haven't been able to . . .

Louis: Just let me . . .

Belize: NO! What, *talk?* You've been running your mouth nonstop since I got here, yaddadda yaddadda blah blah blah, up the hill, down the hill, playing with your MONOLITH . . .

Louis (*Overlapping*): Well, you could have joined in at any time instead of . . .

Belize (*Continuing over Louis*): . . . and girlfriend it is truly an *awesome* spectacle but I got better things to do with my time than sit here listening to this racist bullshit just because I feel sorry for you that . . .

Louis: I am not a racist!

Belize: Oh come on . . .

Louis: So maybe I am a racist but . . .

Belize: Oh I really hate that! It's no fun picking on you Louis; you're so guilty, it's like throwing darts at a glob of jello, there's no satisfying hits, just quivering, the darts just blop in and vanish.

Louis: I just think when you are discussing lines of oppression it gets very complicated and . . .

Belize: Oh is that a fact? You know, we black drag queens have a rather intimate knowledge of the complexity of the lines of . . .

Louis: *Ex*-black drag queen.

Belize: Actually ex-ex.

Louis: You're doing drag again?

Belize: I don't. . . . Maybe. I don't have to tell you. Maybe.

Louis: I think it's sexist.

Belize: I didn't ask you.

Louis: Well it is. The gay community, I think, has to adopt the same attitude towards drag as black women have to take towards black women blues singers.

Belize: Oh my we *are* walking dangerous tonight.

Louis: Well, it's all internalized oppression, right, I mean the masochism, the stereotypes, the . . .

Belize: Louis, are you deliberately trying to make me hate you?

Louis: No, I . . .

Belize: I mean, are you deliberately transforming yourself into an arrogant, sexual-political Stalinist-slash-racist flagwaving thug for my benefit?

(Pause.)

Louis: You know what I think?

Belize: What?

Louis: You hate me because I'm a Jew.

Belize: I'm leaving.

Louis: It's true.

Belize: You have no basis except your . . .
  Louis, it's good to know you haven't changed; you are still an honorary citizen of the Twilight Zone, and after your pale, pale white polemics on behalf of racial insensitivity you have a flaming *fuck* of a lot of nerve calling me an anti-Semite. Now I really gotta go.

Louis: You called me Lou the Jew.

Belize: That was a joke.

Louis: I didn't think it was funny. It was hostile.

Belize: It was three years ago.

Louis: So?

Belize: You just called yourself Sid and Yid.

Louis: That's not the same thing.

Belize: Sid the Yid is different from Lou the Jew.

Louis: Yes.

Belize: Someday you'll have to explain that to me, but right now . . .
  You hate me because you hate black people.

Louis: I do not. But I do think most black people are anti-Semitic.

Belize: "Most black people." *That's* racist, Louis, and *I* think most Jews . . .

Louis: Louis Farrakhan.

Belize: Ed Koch.

Louis: Jesse Jackson.

Belize: Jackson. Oh really, Louis, this is . . .

Louis: Hymietown! Hymietown!

Belize: Louis, you voted for Jesse Jackson. You send checks to the Rainbow Coalition.

Louis: I'm ambivalent. The checks bounced.

Belize: All your checks bounce, Louis; you're ambivalent about everything.

Louis: What's that supposed to mean?

Belize: You may be dumber than shit but I refuse to believe you can't figure it out. Try.

Louis: I was never ambivalent about Prior. I love him. I do. I really do.

Belize: Nobody said different.

Louis: Love and ambivalence are. . . . Real love isn't ambivalent.

Belize: "Real love isn't ambivalent." I'd swear that's a line from my favorite bestselling paperback novel, *In Love with the Night Mysterious,* except I don't think you ever read it.

(Pause.)

Louis: I never read it, no.

Belize: You ought to. Instead of spending the rest of your life trying to get through *Democracy in America.* It's about this white woman whose Daddy owns a plantation in the Deep South in the years before the Civil War—the American one—and her name is Margaret, and she's in love with her Daddy's number-one slave, and his name is Thaddeus, and she's married but her white slave-owner husband has AIDS: Antebellum Insufficiently Developed Sexorgans. And there's a lot of hot stuff going down when Margaret and Thaddeus can catch a spare torrid ten under the cotton-picking moon, and then of course the Yankees come, and they set the slaves free, and the slaves string up old Daddy, and so on. Historical fiction. Somewhere in there I recall Margaret and Thaddeus find the time to discuss the nature of love; her face is reflecting the flames of the burning plantation—you know, the way white people do—and his black face is dark in the night and she says to him, "Thaddeus, real love isn't ever ambivalent."

(Little pause. Emily enters and turns off IV drip.)

Belize: Thaddeus looks at her; he's contemplating her thesis; and he isn't sure he agrees.

Emily (Removing IV drip from Prior's arm): Treatment number . . . (*Consulting chart*) four.

Prior: Pharmaceutical miracle. Lazarus breathes again.

Louis: Is he. . . . How bad is he?

Belize: You want the laundry list?

Emily: Shirt off, let's check the . . .

(Prior takes his shirt off. She examines his lesions.)

Belize: There's the weight problem and the shit problem and the morale problem.

Emily: Only six. That's good. Pants.

(He drops his pants. He's naked. She examines.)

Belize: And. He thinks he's going crazy.

Emily: Looking good. What else?

Prior: Ankles sore and swollen, but the leg's better. The nausea's mostly gone with the little orange pills. BM's pure liquid but not bloody anymore, for now, my eye doctor says everything's OK, for now, my dentist says "Yuck!" when he sees my fuzzy tongue, and now he wears little condoms on his thumb and forefinger. And a mask. So what? My dermatologist is in Hawaii and my mother . . . well leave my mother out of it. Which is usually where my mother is, out of it. My glands are like walnuts, my weight's holding steady for week two, and a friend died two days ago of bird tuberculosis; bird tuberculosis; that scared me and I didn't go to the funeral today because he was an Irish Catholic and it's probably open casket and I'm afraid of . . . something, the bird TB or seeing him or. . . . So I guess I'm doing OK. Except for of course I'm going nuts.

Emily: We ran the toxoplasmosis series and there's no indication . . .

Prior: I know, I know, but I feel like something terrifying is on its way, you know, like a missile from outer space, and it's plummeting down towards the earth, and I'm ground zero, and . . . I am generally known where I am known as one cool, collected queen. And I am ruffled.

Emily: There's really nothing to worry about. I think that shochen bamromim hamtzeh menucho nechono al kanfey haschino.

Prior: What?

Emily: Everything's fine. Bemaalos k'doshim ut'horim kezohar horokeea mazhirim . . .

Prior: Oh I don't understand what you're . . .

Emily: Es nishmas Prior sheholoch leolomoh, baavur shenodvoo z'dokoh b'ad hazkoras nishmosoh.

Prior: Why are you doing that? Stop it! Stop it!

Emily: Stop what?

Prior: You were just . . . weren't you just speaking in Hebrew or something.

Emily: Hebrew? (*Laughs*) I'm basically Italian-American. No. I didn't speak in Hebrew.

Prior: Oh no, oh God please I really think I . . .

Emily: Look, I'm sorry, I have a waiting room full of. . . . I think you're one of the lucky ones, you'll live for years, probably—you're pretty healthy for someone with no immune system. Are you seeing someone? Loneliness is a danger. A therapist?

Prior: No, I don't need to see anyone, I just . . .

Emily: Well think about it. You aren't going crazy. You're just under a lot of stress. No wonder . . . (*She starts to write in his chart*)

(*Suddenly there is an astonishing blaze of light, a huge chord sounded by a gigantic choir, and a great book with steel pages mounted atop a molten-red pillar pops up from the stage floor. The book opens; there is a large Aleph inscribed on its pages, which bursts into flames. Immediately the book slams shut and disappears instantly under the floor as the lights become normal again. Emily notices none of this, writing. Prior is agog.*)

Emily (*Laughing, exiting*): Hebrew . . .

(*Prior flees.*)

Louis: Help me.

Belize: I beg your pardon?

Louis: You're a nurse, give me something, I . . . don't know what to do anymore, I. . . . Last week at work I screwed up the Xerox machine like permanently and so I . . . then I tripped on the subway steps and my glasses broke and I cut my forehead, here, see, and now I can't see much and my forehead . . . it's like the Mark of Cain, stupid, right, but it won't heal and every morning I see it and I think, Biblical things, Mark of Cain, Judas Iscariot and his silver and his noose, people who . . . in betraying what they love betray what's truest in themselves, I feel . . . nothing but cold for myself, just cold, and every night I miss him, I miss him so much but then . . . those sores, and the smell and . . . where I thought it was going. . . . I could be . . . I could be sick too, maybe I'm sick too. I don't know.

Belize. Tell him I love him. Can you do that?

Belize: I've thought about it for a very long time, and I still don't understand what love is. Justice is simple. Democracy is simple. Those things are unambivalent. But love is very hard. And it goes bad for you if you violate the hard law of love.

Louis: I'm dying.

Belize: He's dying. You just wish you were.

Oh cheer up, Louis. Look at that heavy sky out there.

Louis: Purple.

Belize: Purple? Boy, what kind of a homosexual are you, any way? That's not purple, Mary, that color up there is (*very grand*) mauve.

All day today it's felt like Thanksgiving. Soon, this . . . ruination will be blanketed white. You can smell it—can you smell it?

Louis: Smell what?

Belize: Softness, compliance, forgiveness, grace.

Louis: No . . .

Belize: I can't help you learn that. I can't help you, Louis. You're not my business. (*He exits*)

(*Louis puts his head in his hands, inadvertently touching his forehead.*)

Louis: Ow FUCK! (*He stands slowly, looks towards where Belize is seated*) Smell what?
(*He looks both ways to be sure no one is watching, then inhales deeply, and is surprised*) Huh. Snow.

Scene 3

Same day. Harper in a very white, cold place, with a brilliant blue sky above; a delicate snowfall. She is dressed in a beautiful snowsuit. The sound of the sea, faint.

Harper: Snow! Ice! Mountains of ice! Where am I? I . . . I feel better, I do, I . . . feel better. There are ice crystals in my lungs, wonderful and sharp. And the snow smells like cold, crushed peaches. And there's something . . . some current of blood in the wind, how strange, it has that iron taste.

Mr. Lies: Ozone.

Harper: Ozone! Wow! Where am I?

Mr. Lies: The Kingdom of Ice, the bottommost part of the world.

Harper (*Looking around, then realizing*): Antarctica. This is Antarctica!

Mr. Lies: Cold shelter for the shattered. No sorrow here, tears freeze.

Harper: Antarctica, Antarctica, oh boy oh boy, LOOK at this, I. . . . Wow, I must've really snapped the tether, huh?

Mr. Lies: Apparently . . .

Harper: That's great. I want to stay here forever. Set up camp. Build things. Build a city, an enormous city made up of frontier forts, dark wood and green roofs and high gates made of pointed logs and bonfires burning on every street corner. I should build by a river. Where are the forests?

Mr. Lies: No timber here. Too cold. Ice, no trees.

Harper: Oh details! I'm sick of details! I'll plant them and grow them. I'll live off caribou fat, I'll melt it over the bonfires and drink it from long, curved goat-horn cups.

　　It'll be great. I want to make a new world here. So that I never have to go home again.

Mr. Lies: As long as it lasts. Ice has a way of melting . . .

Harper: No. Forever. I can have anything I want here—maybe even companionship, someone who has . . . desire for me. You, maybe.

Mr. Lies: It's against the by-laws of the International Order of Travel Agents to get involved with clients. Rules are rules. Anyway, I'm not the one you really want.

Harper: There isn't anyone . . . maybe an Eskimo. Who could ice-fish for food. And help me build a nest for when the baby comes.

Mr. Lies: There are no Eskimo in Antarctica. And you're not really pregnant. You made that up.

Harper: Well all of this is made up. So if the snow feels cold I'm pregnant. Right? Here, I can be pregnant. And I can have any kind of a baby I want.

Mr. Lies: This is a retreat, a vacuum, its virtue is that it lacks everything; deep-freeze for feelings. You can be numb and safe here, that's what you came for. Respect the delicate ecology of your delusions.

Harper: You mean like no Eskimo in Antarctica.

Mr. Lies: Correcto. Ice and snow, no Eskimo. Even hallucinations have laws.

Harper: Well then who's that?

(*The Eskimo appears.*)

Mr. Lies: An Eskimo.

Harper: An antarctic Eskimo. A fisher of the polar deep.

Mr. Lies: There's something wrong with this picture.

(*The Eskimo beckons.*)

Harper: I'm going to like this place. It's my own National Geographic Special! Oh! Oh! (*She holds her stomach*) I think . . . I think I felt her kicking. Maybe I'll give birth to a baby covered with thick white fur, and that way she won't be cold. My breasts will be full of hot cocoa so she doesn't get chilly. And if it gets really cold, she'll have a pouch I can crawl into. Like a marsupial. We'll mend together. That's what we'll do; we'll mend.

Scene 4

Same day. An abandoned lot in the South Bronx. A homeless Woman is standing near an oil drum in which a fire is burning. Snowfall. Trash around. Hannah enters dragging two heavy suitcases.

Hannah: Excuse me? I said excuse me? Can you tell me where I am? Is this Brooklyn? Do you know a Pineapple Street? Is there some sort of bus or train or . . . ?

    I'm lost, I just arrived from Salt Lake. City. Utah? I took the bus that I was told to take and I got off—well it was the very last stop, so I had to get off, and I *asked* the driver was this Brooklyn, and he nodded yes but he was from one of those foreign countries where they think it's good manners to nod at everything even if you have no idea what it is you're nodding at, and in truth I think he spoke no English at all, which I think would make him ineligible for employment on public transportation. The public being English-speaking, mostly. Do you speak English?

(The Woman nods.)

Hannah: I was supposed to be met at the airport by my son. He didn't show and I don't wait more than three and three-quarters hours for *anyone.* I should have been patient, I guess, I. . . . Is this . . .

Woman: Bronx.

Hannah: Is that. . . . The *Bronx*? Well how in the name of Heaven did I get to the Bronx when the bus driver said . . .

Woman (Talking to herself): Slurp slurp slurp will you STOP that disgusting slurping! YOU DISGUSTING SLURPING FEEDING ANIMAL! Feeding yourself, just feeding yourself, what would it matter, to you or to ANYONE, if you just stopped. Feeding. And DIED?

(Pause.)

Hannah: Can you just tell me where I . . .

Woman: Why was the Kosciusko Bridge named after a Polack?

Hannah: I don't know what you're . . .

Woman: That was a joke.

Hannah: Well what's the punchline?

Woman: I don't know.

Hannah (Looking around desperately): Oh for pete's sake, is there anyone else who . . .

Woman (Again, to herself): Stand further off you fat loathsome whore, you can't have any more of this soup, slurp slurp slurp you animal, and the—I know you'll just go pee it all away and where will you do that? Behind what bush? It's FUCKING COLD out here and I . . .

    Oh that's right, because it was supposed have been a tunnel!

    That's not very funny.

    Have you read the prophecies of Nostradamus?

Hannah: Who?

Woman: Some guy I went out with once somewhere, Nostradamus. Prophet, outcast, eyes like. . . . Scary shit, he . . .

Hannah: Shut up. Please. Now I want you to stop jabbering for a minute and pull your wits together and tell me how to get to Brooklyn. Because you know! And you are going to tell me! Because there is no one else around to tell me and I am wet and cold and I am very hungry! So I am sorry you're psychotic but just make the effort—take a deep breath—DO IT!

(Hannah and the Woman breathe together.)

Hannah: That's good. Now exhale.

(They do.)

Hannah: Good. Now how do I get to Brooklyn?

Woman: Don't know. Never been. Sorry. Want some soup?

Hannah: Manhattan? Maybe you know . . . I don't suppose you know the location of the Mormon Visitor's . . .

Woman: 65th and Broadway.

Hannah: How do you . . .

Woman: Go there all the time. Free movies. Boring, but you can stay all day.

Hannah: Well. . . . So how do I . . .

Woman: Take the D Train. Next block make a right.

Hannah: Thank you.

Woman: Oh yeah. In the new century I think we will all be insane.

Scene 5

Same day. Joe and Roy in the study of Roy's brownstone. Roy is wearing an elegant bathrobe. He has made a considerable effort to look well. He isn't well, and he hasn't succeeded much in looking it.

Joe: I can't. The answer's no. I'm sorry.

Roy: Oh, well, apologies . . .

    I can't see that there's anyone asking for apologies.

(Pause.)

Joe: I'm sorry, Roy.

Roy: Oh, well, apologies.

Joe: My wife is missing, Roy. My mother's coming from Salt Lake to . . . to help look, I guess. I'm supposed to be at the airport now, picking her up but. . . . I just spent two days in a hospital, Roy, with a bleeding ulcer, I was spitting up blood.

Roy: Blood, huh? Look, I'm very busy here and . . .

Joe: It's just a job.

Roy: A job? A job? *Washington!* Dumb Utah Mormon hick shit!

Joe: Roy . . .

Roy: WASHINGTON! When Washington called me I was younger than you, you think I said "Aw fuck no I can't go I got two fingers up my asshole and a little moral nosebleed to boot!" When Washington calls you my pretty young punk friend you go or you can go fuck yourself sideways 'cause the train has pulled out of the station, and you are *out,* nowhere, out in the cold. Fuck you, Mary Jane, get outta here.

Joe: Just let me . . .

Roy: Explain? Ephemera. You broke my heart. Explain that. Explain that.

Joe: I love you. Roy.

There's so much that I want, to be . . . what you see in me, I want to be a participant in the world, in your world, Roy, I want to be capable of that, I've tried, really I have but . . . I can't do this. Not because I don't believe in you, but because I believe in you so much, in what you stand for, at heart, the order, the decency. I would give anything to protect you, but. . . . There are laws I can't break. It's too ingrained. It's not me. There's enough damage I've already done.

Maybe you were right, maybe I'm dead.

Roy: You're not dead, boy, you're a sissy.

You love me; that's moving, I'm moved. It's nice to be loved. I warned you about her, didn't I, Joe? But you don't listen to me, why, because you say Roy is smart and Roy's a friend but Roy . . . well, he isn't nice, and you wanna be nice. Right? A nice, nice man!

(*Little pause*)

You know what my greatest accomplishment was, Joe, in my life, what I am able to look back on and be proudest of? And I have helped make Presidents and unmake them and more goddam judges than anyone in NYC ever— AND several million dollars, tax-free—and what do you think means the most to me?

You ever hear of Ethel Rosenberg? Huh, Joe, huh?

Joe: Well, yeah, I guess I. . . . Yes.

Roy: Yes. Yes. You have heard of Ethel Rosenberg. Yes. Maybe you even read about her in the history books.

If it wasn't for me, Joe, Ethel Rosenberg would be alive today, writing some personal-advice column for *Ms.* magazine. She isn't. Because during the trial, Joe, I was on the phone every day, talking with the judge . . .

Joe: Roy . . .

Roy: Every day, doing what I do best, talking on the telephone, making sure that timid Yid nebbish on the bench did his duty to America, to history. That sweet unprepossessing woman, two kids, boo-hoo-hoo, reminded us all of our little Jewish mamas—she came this close to getting life; I pleaded till I wept to put her in the chair. Me. I did that. I would have fucking pulled the switch if they'd have let me. Why? Because I fucking hate traitors. Because I fucking hate communists. Was it legal? Fuck legal. Am I a nice man? Fuck nice. They say terrible things about me in the *Nation.* Fuck the *Nation.* You want to be Nice, or you want to be Effective? Make the law, or subject to it. Choose. Your wife chose. A week from today, she'll be back. SHE knows how to get what SHE wants. Maybe I ought to send *her* to Washington.

Joe: I don't believe you.

Roy: Gospel.

Joe: You can't possibly mean what you're saying.

Roy, you were the Assistant United States Attorney on the Rosenberg case, ex-parte communication with the judge during the trial would be . . . censurable, at least, probably conspiracy and . . . in a case that resulted in execution, it's . . .

Roy: What? Murder?

Joe: You're not well is all.

Roy: What do you mean, not well? Who's not well?

(Pause.)

Joe: You said . . .

Roy: No I didn't. I said what?

Joe: Roy, you have cancer.

Roy: No I don't.

(Pause.)

Joe: You told me you were dying.

Roy: What the fuck are you talking about Joe? I never said that. I'm in perfect health. There's not a goddam thing wrong with me.
> (*He smiles*)
> Shake?

(Joe hesitates. He holds out his hand to Roy. Roy pulls Joe into a close, strong clinch.)

Roy (More to himself than to Joe): It's OK that you hurt me because I love you, baby Joe. That's why I'm so rough on you.

(Roy releases Joe. Joe backs away a step or two.)

Roy: Prodigal son. The world will wipe its dirty hands all over you.

Joe: It already has, Roy.

Roy: Now go.

(Roy shoves Joe, hard. Joe turns to leave. Roy stops him, turns him around.)

Roy (Smoothing Joe's lapels, tenderly): I'll always be here, waiting for you . . .
> (*Then again, with sudden violence, he pulls Joe close, violently*)
> What did you want from me, what was all this, what do you want, treacherous ungrateful little . . .

(Joe, very close to belting Roy, grabs him by the front of his robe, and propels him across the length of the room. He holds Roy at arm's length, the other arm ready to hit.)

Roy (Laughing softly, almost pleading to be hit): Transgress a little, Joseph.

(Joe releases Roy.)

Roy: There are so many laws; find one you can break.

(Joe hesitates, than leaves, backing out. When Joe has gone, Roy doubles over in great pain, which he's been hiding throughout the scene with Joe.)

Roy: Ah, Christ . . .
      Andy! Andy! Get in here! Andy!

(The door opens, but it isn't Andy. A small Jewish Woman dressed modestly in a fifties hat and coat stands in the doorway. The room darkens.)

Roy: Who the fuck are you? The new nurse?

(The figure in the doorway says nothing. She stares at Roy. A pause. Roy looks at her carefully, gets up, crosses to her. He crosses back to the chair, sits heavily.)

Roy: Aw, fuck. Ethel.
Ethel Rosenberg *(Her manner is friendly, her voice is ice-cold)*: You don't look good, Roy.
Roy: Well, Ethel. I don't feel good.
Ethel Rosenberg: But you lost a lot of weight. That suits you. You were heavy back then.
      Zaftig, mit hips.
Roy: I haven't been that heavy since 1960. We were all heavier back then, before the
      body thing started. Now I look like a skeleton. They stare.
Ethel Rosenberg: That shit's really hit the fan, huh, Roy?

(Little pause. Roy nods.)

Ethel Rosenberg: Well the fun's just started.
Roy: What is this, Ethel, Halloween? You trying to scare me?

(Ethel says nothing.)

Roy: Well you're wasting your time! I'm scarier than you any day of the week! So beat
      it, Ethel! BOOO! BETTER DEAD THAN RED! Somebody trying to shake me up?
      HAH HAH! From the throne of God in heaven to the belly of hell, you can all fuck
      yourselves and then go jump in the lake because I'M NOT AFRAID OF YOU OR
      DEATH OR HELL OR ANYTHING!
Ethel Rosenberg: Be seeing you soon, Roy. Julius sends his regards.
Roy: Yeah, well send this to Julius!

(He flips the bird in her direction, stands and moves towards her. Halfway across the room he slumps to the floor, breathing laboriously, in pain.)

Ethel Rosenberg: You're a very sick man, Roy.
Roy: Oh God . . . ANDY!
Ethel Rosenberg: Hmmm. He doesn't hear you, I guess. We should call the ambulance.
      (She goes to the phone)
      Hah! Buttons! Such things they got now.
      What do I dial, Roy?

(Pause. Roy looks at her, then:)

Roy: 911.
Ethel Rosenberg (Dials the phone): It sings!
(*Imitating dial tones*) La la la . . .
Huh.
Yes, you should please send an ambulance to the home of Mister Roy Cohn,
the famous lawyer.
What's the address, Roy?
Roy (A beat, then): 244 East 87th.
Ethel Rosenberg: 244 East 87th Street. No apartment number, he's got the whole build-
ing.
My name? (*A beat*) Ethel Greenglass Rosenberg.
(*Small smile*) Me? No I'm not related to Mr. Cohn. An old friend.
(*She hangs up*)
They said a minute.
Roy: I have all the time in the world.
Ethel Rosenberg: You're immortal.
Roy: I'm immortal. Ethel. (*He forces himself to stand*)
I have *forced* my way into history. I ain't never gonna die.
Ethel Rosenberg: (*A little laugh, then*): History is about to crack wide open. Millennium
approaches.

Scene 6

*Late that night. Prior's bedroom. Prior I watching Prior in bed, who is staring back at him,
terrified. Tonight Prior 1 is dressed in weird alchemical robes and hat over his historical
clothing and he carries a long palm-leaf bundle.*

Prior 1: Tonight's the night! Aren't you excited? Tonight she arrives! Right through the
roof! Ha-adam, Ha-gadol . . .
Prior 2 (Appearing similarly attired): Lumen! Phosphor! Fluror! Candle! An unending
billowing of scarlet and . . .
Prior: Look. Garlic. A mirror. Holy water. A crucifix. FUCK OFF! Get the fuck out of
my room! GO!
Prior 1 (To Prior 2): Hard as a hickory knob, I'll bet.
Prior 2: We all tumesce when they approach. We wax full, like moons.
Prior 1: Dance.
Prior: Dance?
Prior 1: Stand up, dammit, give us your hands, dance!
Prior 2: Listen . . .

(*A lone oboe begins to play a little dance tune.*)

Prior 2: Delightful sound. Care to dance?
Prior: Please leave me alone, please just let me sleep . . .
Prior 2: Ah, he wants someone familiar. A partner who knows his steps. (*To Prior*) Close
your eyes. Imagine . . .
Prior: I don't . . .

Prior 2: Hush. Close your eyes.

(Prior does.)

Prior 2: Now open them.

(Prior does. Louis appears. He looks gorgeous. The music builds gradually into a full-blooded, romantic dance tune.)

Prior: Lou.
Louis: Dance with me.
Prior: I can't, my leg, it hurts at night . . .
      Are you . . . a ghost, Lou?
Louis: No. Just spectral. Lost to myself. Sitting all day on cold park benches. Wishing I
   could be with you. Dance with me, babe . . .

(Prior stands up. The leg stops hurting. They begin to dance. The music is beautiful.)

Prior 1 (To Prior 2): Hah. Now I see why he's got no children. He's a sodomite.
Prior 2: Oh be quiet, you medieval gnome, and let them dance.
Prior 1: I'm not interfering, I've done my bit. Hooray, hooray, the messenger's come,
   now I'm blowing off. I don't like it here.

(Prior 1 vanishes.)

Prior 2: The twentieth century. Oh dear, the world has gotten so terribly, terribly old.

(Prior 2 vanishes. Louis and Prior waltz happily. Lights fade back to normal. Louis vanishes.
      Prior dances alone.
      Then suddenly, the sound of wings fills the room.)

Scene 7

   Split scene: Prior alone in his apartment; Louis alone in the park.
   Again, a sound of beating wings.

Prior: Oh don't come in here don't come in . . . LOUIS!!
      No. My name is Prior Walter, I am . . . the scion of an ancient line, I am . . .
   abandoned I . . . no, my name is . . . is . . . Prior and I live . . . *here and now,* and . . .
   in the dark, in the dark, the Recording Angel opens its hundred eyes and snaps the
   spine of the Book of Life and . . . hush! Hush!
      I'm talking nonsense, I . . .
      No more mad scene, hush, hush . . .

(Louis in the park on a bench. Joe approaches, stands at a distance. They stare at each
other, then Louis turns away.)

Louis: Do you know the story of Lazarus?
Joe: Lazarus?

Louis: Lazarus. I can't remember what happens, exactly.

Joe: I don't. . . . Well, he was dead, Lazarus, and Jesus breathed life into him. He brought him back from death.

Louis: Come here often?

Joe: No. Yes. Yes.

Louis: Back from the dead. You believe that really happened?

Joe: I don't know anymore what I believe.

Louis: This is quite a coincidence. Us meeting.

Joe: I followed you.

From work. I . . . followed you here.

(Pause.)

Louis: You followed me.

You probably saw me that day in the washroom and thought: there's a sweet guy, sensitive, cries for friends in trouble.

Joe: Yes.

Louis: You thought maybe I'll cry for you.

Joe: Yes.

Louis: Well I fooled you. Crocodile tears. Nothing . . . (*He touches his heart, shrugs*)

(*Joe reaches tentatively to touch Louis's face.*)

Louis (*Pulling back*): What are you doing? Don't do that.

Joe: (*Withdrawing his hand*): Sorry. I'm sorry.

Louis: I'm . . . just not . . . I think, if you touch me, your hand might fall off or something. Worse things have happened to people who have touched me.

Joe: Please.

Oh, boy . . .

Can I . . .

I . . . want . . . to touch you. Can I please just touch you . . . um, here?

(*He puts his hand on one side of Louis's face. He holds it there*)

I'm going to hell for doing this.

Louis: Big deal. You think it could be any worse than New York City?

(*He puts his hand on Joe's hand. He takes Joe's hand away from his face, holds it for a moment, then*) Come on.

Joe: Where?

Louis: Home. With me.

Joe: This makes no sense. I mean I don't know you.

Louis: Likewise.

Joe: And what you do know about me you don't like.

Louis: The Republican stuff?

Joe: Yeah, well for starters.

Louis: I don't not like that. I *hate* that.

Joe: So why on earth should we . . .

(*Louis goes to Joe and kisses him.*)

Louis: Strange bedfellows. I don't know. I never made it with one of the damned before. I would really rather not have to spend tonight alone.

Joe: I'm a pretty terrible person, Louis.

Louis: Lou.

Joe: No, I really am. I don't think I deserve being loved.

Louis: There? See? We already have a lot in common.

(Louis stands, begins to walk away. He turns, looks back at Joe, Joe follows. They exit.)

(Prior listens. At first no sound, then once again, the sound of beating wings, frighteningly near.)

Prior: That sound, that sound, it. . . . What is that, like birds or something, like a *really* big bird, I'm frightened, I . . . no, no fear, find the anger, find the . . . anger, my blood is clean, my brain is fine, I can handle pressure, I am a gay man and I am used to pressure, to trouble, I am tough and strong and. . . . Oh. Oh my goodness. I . . . *(He is washed over by an intense sexual feeling)* Ooohhhh. . . . I'm hot, I'm . . . so . . . aw Jeez what is going on here I . . . must have a fever I . . .

(The bedside lamp flickers wildly as the bed begins to roll forward and back. There is a deep bass creaking and groaning from the bedroom ceiling, like the timbers of a ship under immense stress, and from above a fine rain of plaster dust.)

Prior: OH!

PLEASE, OH PLEASE! Something's coming in here, I'm scared, I don't like this at all, something's approaching and I. . . . OH!

(There is a great blaze of triumphal music, heralding. The light turns an extraordinary harsh, cold, pale blue, then a rich, brilliant warm golden color, then a hot, bilious green, and then finally a spectacular royal purple. Then silence.)

Prior: (An awestruck whisper): God almighty . . .

Very Steven Spielberg.

(A sound, like a plummeting meteor, tears down from very, very far above the earth, hurtling at an incredible velocity towards the bedroom; the light seems to be sucked out of the room as the projectile approaches; as the room reaches darkness, we hear a terrifying CRASH as something immense strikes earth; the whole building shudders and a part of the bedroom ceiling, lots of plaster and lathe and wiring, crashes to the floor. And then in a shower of unearthly white light, spreading great opalescent gray-silver wings, the Angel descends into the room and floats above the bed.)

Angel:

Greetings, Prophet;

The Great Work begins:

The Messenger has arrived.

(Blackout.)

END OF PART ONE

Li-Young Lee
b. 1957

Li-Young Lee was born in Jakarta, Indonesia of Chinese parents. In 1959, after his father had spent a year in jail as a political prisoner, the family fled Indonesia, arriving in the United States in 1964. Lee has studied at the University of Pittsburgh, the University of Arizona, and SUNY Brockport. Currently, he resides in Chicago, Illinois, with his wife, Donna, and children.

Li-Young Lee's first book of poetry *Rose* was published in 1986 and won the New York University's Delmore Schwartz Memorial Poetry Award. He has received grants from the Illinois Arts Council, the Pennsylvania Council on the Arts, and the National Endowment for the Arts. In 1988 he received a writer's award from the Mrs. Giles Whiting Foundation, and in 1989 was awarded a fellowship by the John Simon Guggenheim Memorial Foundation. His second book of poetry *The City in Which I Love You* was published in 1990 and was the 1990 Lamont Poetry Selection of the Academy of American Poets.

In its use of autobiography, the title poem in the second collection reflects Lee's aesthetic and intellectual struggle with his own constructed positioning as an American poet of Chinese ancestry, born in Indonesia. As he says, "I am recommended by my orphaning,/ . . . my birthplace vanished, my citizenship earned,/ . . . I/enter, without retreat or help from history. . . . " This last line also reflects Lee's selective use of history for a poetic project, which he describes elsewhere as one of "myth-making": "I don't mean I'm telling lies so much as I am telling stories. And that becomes my life. I am the stories that I tell." These "stories," which reflect his suspension between two worlds, also take as their central event or "myth" his understanding of and sympathy for his "heroic" father. These two concerns come together in a poem like "Persimmons," where Lee aims to express the ambiguities which arise when his American world of precise words and his Chinese world of precise textures meet.

Lee's most recent book is "The Winged Seed: A Remembrance" (1995).

Further Reading:

L. Lee, *Rose*, 1986.
———, *Winged Seed/A Remembrance*, 1995.

Z. Xiaojing, "Inheritance and Invention in Li-Young Lee's Poetry," *Melus* 21:1 (1996), 113–133.

Texts:

"The City in Which I Love You" from *The City in Which I Love You*, 1990.

"Eating Together," "The Gift," and "Persimmons" from *Rose*, 1986.

Eating Together

In the steamer is the trout
seasoned with slivers of ginger,
two sprigs of green onion, and sesame oil.
We shall eat it with rice for lunch,
brothers, sister, my mother who will   5
taste the sweetest meat of the head,
holding it between her fingers
deftly, the way my father did
weeks ago. Then he lay down
to sleep like a snow-covered road   10
winding through pines older than him,
without any travelers, and lonely for no one.
1986

Persimmons

In sixth grade Mrs. Walker
slapped the back of my head
and made me stand in the corner
for not knowing the difference
between *persimmon* and *precision*.   5
How to choose

persimmons. This is precision.
Ripe ones are soft and brown-spotted.
Sniff the bottoms. The sweet one
will be fragrant. How to eat: 10
put the knife away, lay down newspaper.
Peel the skin tenderly, not to tear the meat.
Chew the skin, suck it,
and swallow. Now, eat
the meat of the fruit,   15
so sweet,
all of it, to the heart.

Donna undresses, her stomach is white.
In the yard, dewy and shivering
with crickets, we lie naked,   20
face-up, face-down.

I teach her Chinese.
Crickets: *chiu chiu.* Dew: I've forgotten.
Naked: I've forgotten.
Ni, wo: you and me.   25
I part her legs,
remember to tell her
she is beautiful as the moon.

Other words
that got me into trouble were   30
fight and *fright, wren* and *yarn.*
Fight was what I did when I was frightened,
fright was what I felt when I was fighting.
Wrens are small, plain birds,
yarn is what one knits with.   35
Wrens are soft as yarn.
My mother made birds out of yarn.
I loved to watch her tie the stuff;
a bird, a rabbit, a wee man.

Mrs. Walker brought a persimmon to class   40
and cut it up
so everyone could taste
a *Chinese apple.* Knowing
it wasn't ripe or sweet, I didn't eat
but watched the other faces.   45

My mother said every persimmon has a sun
inside, something golden, glowing,
warm as my face.

Once, in the cellar, I found two wrapped in newspaper,
forgotten and not yet ripe.   50
I took them and set both on my bedroom windowsill,
where each morning a cardinal
sang, *The sun, the sun.*

Finally understanding
he was going blind,   55
my father sat up all one night
waiting for a song, a ghost.
I gave him the persimmons,
swelled, heavy as sadness,
and sweet as love.   60

This year, in the muddy lighting
of my parents' cellar, I rummage, looking

for something I lost.
My father sits on the tired, wooden stairs,
black cane between his knees,   65
hand over hand, gripping the handle.

He's so happy that I've come home.
I ask how his eyes are, a stupid question.
All gone, he answers.

Under some blankets, I find a box.   70
Inside the box I find three scrolls.
I sit beside him and untie
three paintings by my father:
Hibiscus leaf and a white flower.
Two cats preening.   75
Two persimmons, so full they want to drop from the cloth.

He raises both hands to touch the cloth,
asks, *Which is this?*
This is persimmons, Father.

Oh, the feel of the wolftail on the silk,
the strength, the tense   80
precision in the wrist.
I painted them hundreds of times
eyes closed. These I painted blind.
Some things never leave a person: 85
scent of the hair of one you love,
the texture of persimmons,
in your palm, the ripe weight.
1986

The City in Which I Love You

I will arise now, and go
about the city in the streets,
and in the broad ways I will seek . . .
whom my soul loveth.
                    Song of Songs 3:2

And when, in the city in which I love you,
even my most excellent song goes unanswered,
and I mount the scabbed streets,

the long shouts of avenues,
and tunnel sunken night in search of you. . . .   5

That I negotiate fog, bituminous
rain ringing like teeth into the beggar's tin,
or two men jackaling a third in some alley
weirdly lit by a couch on fire, that I
drag my extinction in search of you. . . .   10

Past the guarded schoolyards, the boarded-up churches, swastikaed
synagogues, defended houses of worship, past
newspapered windows of tenements, among the violated,
the prosecuted citizenry, throughout this
storied, buttressed, scavenged, policed   15
city I call home, in which I am a guest. . . .

A bruise, blue
in the muscle, you
impinge upon me.
As bone hugs the ache home, so   20

I'm vexed to love you, your body
the shape of returns, your hair a torso
of light, your heat
I must have, your opening
I'd eat, each moment   25
of that soft-finned fruit,
inverted fountain in which I don't see me.

My tongue remembers your wounded flavor.
The vein in my neck
adores you. A sword   30
stands up between my hips,
my hidden fleece sends forth its scent of human oil.

The shadows under my arms,
I promise, are tender, the shadows
under my face. Do not calculate,   35
but come, smooth other, rough sister.
Yet, how will you know me

among the captives, my hair grown long,
my blood motley, my ways trespassed upon?
In the uproar, the confusion   40
of accents and inflections,
how will you hear me when I open my mouth?

Look for me, one of the drab population
under fissured edifices, fractured

artifices. Make my various   45
names flock overhead,
I will follow you.
Hew me to your beauty.

Stack in me the unaccountable fire,
bring on me the iron leaf, but tenderly.   50
Folded one hundred times and
creased, I'll not crack.
Threshed to excellence, I'll achieve you.

But in the city
in which I love you,   55
no one comes, no one
meets me in the brick clefts;
in the wedged dark,

no finger touches me secretly, no mouth
tastes my flawless salt,   60
no one wakens the honey in the cells, finds the humming
in the ribs, the rich business in the recesses;
hulls clogged, I continue laden, translated

by exhaustion and time's appetite, my sleep abandoned
in bus stations and storefront stoops,   65
my insomnia erected under a sky
cross-hatched by wires, branches,
and black flights of rain. Lewd body of wind

jams me in the passageways, doors slam
like guns going off, a gun goes off, a pie plate spins   70
past, whizzing its thin tremolo,
a plastic bag, fat with wind, barrels by and slaps
a chain-link fence, wraps it like clung skin.

In the excavated places,
I waited for you, and I did not cry out.   75
In the derelict rooms, my body needed you,
and there was such flight in my breast.
During the daily assaults, I called to you,

and my voice pursued you,
even backward   80
to that other city
in which I saw a woman
squat in the street

beside a body,
and fan with a handkerchief flies from its face.   85
That woman
was not me. And
the corpse

lying there, lying there
so still it seemed with great effort, as though   90
his whole being was concentrating on the hole
in his forehead, so still
I expected he'd sit up any minute and laugh out loud:

that man was not me;
his wound was his, his death not mine.   95
And the soldier
who fired the shot, then lit a cigarette:
he was not me.

And the ones I do not see
in cities all over the world,   100
the ones sitting, standing, lying down, those
in prisons playing checkers with their knocked-out teeth:
they are not me. Some of them are

my age, even my height and weight;
none of them is me.   105
The woman who is slapped, the man who is kicked,
the ones who don't survive,
whose names I do not know;

they are not me forever,
the ones who no longer live   110
in the cities in which
you are not,
the cities in which I looked for you.

The rain stops, the moon
in her breaths appears overhead.   115
The only sound now is a far flapping.
Over the National Bank, the flag of some republic or other
gallops like water or fire to tear itself away.

If I feel the night
move to disclosures or crescendos,   120
it's only because I'm famished
for meaning; the night
merely dissolves.

And your otherness is perfect as my death.
Your otherness exhausts me,   125
like looking suddenly up from here
to impossible stars fading.
Everything is punished by your absence.

Is prayer, then, the proper attitude
for the mind that longs to be freely blown,   130
but which gets snagged on the barb
called *world,* that
tooth-ache, the actual? What prayer

would I build? And to whom?
Where are you   135
in the cities in which I love you,
the cities daily risen to work and to money,
to the magnificent miles and the gold coasts?

Morning comes to this city vacant of you.
Pages and windows flare, and you are not there.   135
Someone sweeps his portion of sidewalk,
wakens the drunk, slumped like laundry,
and you are gone.

You are not in the wind
which someone notes in the margins of a book.   140
You are gone out of the small fires in abandoned lots
where human figures huddle,
each aspiring to its own ghost.

Between brick walls, in a space no wider than my face,
a leafless sapling stands in mud.   145
In its branches, a nest of raw mouths
gaping and cheeping, scrawny fires that must eat.
My hunger for you is no less than theirs.

At the gates of the city in which I love you,
the sea hauls the sun on its back,   150
strikes the land, which rebukes it.
What ardor in its sliding heft,
a flameless friction on the rocks.

Like the sea, I am recommended by my orphaning.
Noisy with telegrams not received,   155
quarrelsome with aliases,
intricate with misguided journeys,
by my expulsions have I come to love you.

Straight from my father's wrath,
and long from my mother's womb,   160
late in this century and on a Wednesday morning,
bearing the mark of one who's experienced
neither heaven nor hell,

my birthplace vanished, my citizenship earned,
in league with stones of the earth, I   165
enter, without retreat or help from history,
the days of no day, my earth
of no earth, I re-enter

the city in which I love you.
And I never believed that the multitude   170
of dreams and many words were vain.
1990

Cultural Portfolio
Who Is an American Writer?

Teachers and critics of American literature are often confronted with a fundamental question: Who is an American author? For anyone designing an American literature course or putting together an anthology such as this one, the issue becomes especially significant. Which writers should be included in the course or collection and which shouldn't be?

In many cases, the answer is clear: native-born individuals whose literary careers are pursued in the United States and whose work reflects American themes and issues (however broadly defined) indisputably qualify as American writers. Thus, no one questions whether Ralph Waldo Emerson, Mark Twain, Emily Dickinson, Walt Whitman, William Faulkner, Willa Cather, or Langston Hughes should be included in American literature collections and courses.

Yet, many native authors do not comfortably fit this simple criterion. All American literature anthologies, for example, include Henry James and T. S. Eliot, major literary figures who were born and educated in the United States but who lived a good portion of their lives abroad and eventually became British subjects. James, however, consistently explored American subjects and themes, and his decision to become a British subject came only towards the end of his life. Though critics and scholars are fond of identifying "American" images in Eliot's poetry, his best-known work shows very little explicit connection with American experiences; he went to England in 1913, in his mid-twenties, and became a British subject as early as 1927. Eliot made it clear that he aspired to be a "European" poet, so why have his poems and essays always been an integral part of modern American literature courses? Aside from his literary significance and influence, is Eliot regarded as an American author only because of his native roots?

Although collections of American literature often include native-born writers, regardless of their changes in citizenship or permanent expatriate status, they are far less accommodating to foreign-born authors who take up permanent residence here and even become United States citizens. This reluctance to acknowledge someone as an "American writer" is usually tied to an author's foreign origins and "first" language. The great German novelist Thomas Mann (1875–1955) emigrated to the United States in 1938 and eventually settled in Santa Monica, California; he became a citizen in 1944. Though Mann remained in the United States for nearly the rest of his life, he never wrote in English (though several of his novels, including *Dr. Faustus,* were written in America) and never dealt directly with American experience. Despite the fact that he was elected to the American Academy of Arts and Letters (in 1951), it would certainly seem inappropriate to consider Thomas Mann an American novelist.

A somewhat different case involves one of the most distinguished modern French writers, the Belgium-born Marguerite Yourcenar (1903–1987). The first woman author to be elected to the prestigious French Academy, Yourcenar became a United States citizen in 1947. Most of her major publications (all of which were originally composed in French) were written while she was a citizen residing in the United States, where for some forty years (nearly half her life) she lived with her American companion and translator. Yourcenar was also elected to the American Academy of Arts and Letters. The fact that all of her creative writing was done in French apparently disqualifies her as an American author. Her career may be properly compared to a contemporary of hers, the novelist and diarist Julien Green (1900–1998). Born in Paris in 1900 of American parents, Green spent only a few years in the United States (to receive his education at the University of Virginia and to escape the Second World War). Bilingual and also a member of the French Academy, he has written nearly all of his books in French, though several of his major novels are set in the American South. Is Green a French or an American writer? Or is he both?

An even more complex case of national identity is provided by the Russian novelist Vladimir Nabokov (1899–1975). Is a foreign-born writer who settles here, obtains citizenship, begins writing and publishing in English, directly confronts American themes and issues, and achieves an illustrious reputation within the United States to be considered an American author? When asked in 1963 if he felt any sense of national identity, Nabokov, who taught for many years at Cornell (where Thomas Pynchon was one of his students), replied: "I am an American writer, born in Russia and educated in England, where I studied French literature, before spending fifteen years in Germany. I came to America in 1940 and decided to become an American citizen and made America my home." Nabokov had published many books in Russian before he made the leap into English with such critically acclaimed novels as *Bend Sinister* (1947), *Lolita* (1955), *Pnin* (1957), and *Pale Fire* (1962). In many of his latter novels Nabokov uses American settings or—appropriately, given the significance of exile in his work—imaginary countries. To be sure, quite a few readers do regard Nabokov as an American author (and his major novels have recently been published in the prestigious "Library of America" series), but there is still a sufficient number of critics who see him as predominately a Russian author. In early stages of this anthology, for example, some reviewers argued that Nabokov wasn't an American writer and did not belong in the collection.

Another Russian exile who has not received acceptance into the canon of contemporary American literature—also presumably because of a foreign first language—is the Nobel Prize–winning poet, Joseph Brodsky (1940–1996). Brodsky, a former Soviet political prisoner, came to the United States in 1972 and became a citizen five years later. Nearly all of his major volumes of poetry were originally written in Russian, although he began writing essays, criticism, and other nonfiction in English a few years before his untimely death. Brodsky is rarely included in collections of American poetry, even though he held positions at several American colleges, was published principally in the United States, received a MacArthur fellowship, and—most ironically—was named United States Poet Laureate in 1991.

As the critic Susan Sontag, a close friend of Brodsky's reports, Brodsky knew America intimately, although he rarely made it a subject of his work. By becoming an American citizen he believed he was becoming an American. "Does that say something flattering about us?" she asked in 1996 at his memorial service, "that this is a country to which a great foreign writer could emigrate, continuing to write mainly in his own language, and feel quite at home. I doubt it could happen in any other country in the world." But to know America and feel at home here does not necessarily result in an American identity. It seems doubtful that Brodsky's poems and essays will ever be viewed as part of our national literature, especially if literary inclusion depends almost entirely on an American birthplace and the English language.

These two defining factors have played a critical role in excluding a number of important writers who have made the United States home while continuing to publish in their own native languages. Two recent examples are also Nobel Prize winners. Czslaw Milosz, one of the greatest twentieth-century Polish poets, a professor of Slavic languages at Berkeley and a member of the American Academy and Institute of Arts and Letters, was born in Lithuania in 1911 and settled in northern California in 1960. The novelist and short story writer, Isaac Bashevis Singer (1904–1991), emigrated from Poland in 1935. Singer wrote almost exclusively in Yiddish and was the first author in that language to be honored with the Nobel Prize. The first of Singer's tales to make an impact on the American reading public was "Gimpel the Fool," which was translated in 1953 by another Nobel Prize–winning author, the Montreal-born American novelist Saul Bellow. A prolific author, Singer lived in New York City for nearly sixty years and frequently relied on American settings and characters in his later tales. Both writers became naturalized United States citizens, Singer as early as 1943.

In some instances even having English as a first language may not be sufficient if an individual is not native born. How should we identify a major foreign-born poet who (1) speaks English as a native language, (2) resides in the United States for an extended period of time, (3) becomes a citizen early, (4) publishes many of his most celebrated works here, (5) receives major American book awards and critical recognition, and (6) plays a highly influential role in America's literary scene? Such a writer would seem to possess a strong claim to inclusion in American literature courses and collections. Yet one of the twentieth century's major literary figures, W. H. Auden (1907–1973), who emigrated to the United States in 1939, became a citizen as early as 1946, and established the tone of post–World War II American poetry is by and large left out of the American canon. Just as British subject T. S. Eliot has long been a fixture of American literature collections, the British anthologies have never failed to include American citizen W. H. Auden. In both cases, birthplace trumps personal decision.

If Auden finds no entry into American literature even as a citizen, what about other English-speaking writers who reside in the United States, have built their publishing careers here, teach here, have won major American book awards and possess a great deal of literary influence here, but have not become citizens? Both the St. Lucian poet Derek Walcott (who won the Nobel Prize in 1992) and the Antiguan novelist and essayist Jamaica Kincaid were born into the English language and have lived for quite some time in the United States. As natives of the West Indies, both are "American" writers in the larger (and geographically accurate) sense of the word. Their new books are considered important publishing events by the American book reviewing press. They both publish regularly in prominent American literary periodicals. Their works are widely read in the United States and they have in their own ways altered the shape and direction of recent prose and poetry. Do we eliminate from American literature courses and collections such influential English language authors because they have not claimed United States citizenship?

It should be clear that no yardstick exists by which we can consistently and categorically determine who does and who does not qualify for inclusion in an American literature survey. Although this issue may not have seemed so pressing in the past, it has become more urgent today with increased immigration, a broadly diverse population, global markets, and the rise of multicultural studies. Despite an apparent opposition to the legislation of English-only rules in government and society (our constitution stipulates no national language), such rules have indeed applied in the construction of an American canon. Whatever the author's national or cultural background, the assumption appears to be that any piece of writing that requires English translation will by definition be excluded from the American literary tradition. Thus, the probability is that nonnative resident authors who write in a foreign language—even if they become citizens and deal directly with American experience—will not be thought of as American writers. Excluded, too, will be writers born in the United States who chose to write in ancestral languages. Consider bilingual native-born and educated American citizens of foreign parentage who permanently reside in the United States but prefer to write fiction and poetry in Spanish or Chinese or Arabic or Hindi—are they American writers?

Through the eras of exploration, settlement, colonization, independence, territorial expansion and on through several waves of immigration, America became the home of numerous languages. The colonies contained many large communities of European immigrants who continued to speak their native tongues and who frequently published their own newspapers: Dutch and German, for example, were heard widely throughout New York, New Jersey, and Pennsylvania; the Scandanavian languages were commonly spoken in Minnesota and the Dakotas well into the twentieth century, and their accents can still be heard there. Throughout the country, settlers also encountered a variety of indigenous languages, which made their way into English vocabulary and resulted in a great many of our current place names (e.g., Massachusetts, Wyoming, Delaware).

In addition, numerous writers—including travelers, immigrants, and permanent residents—published original poetry, fiction, and drama about American life in languages other than English. Given the taboo on translations, nearly all of these works have vanished from American literature. Recently, to counter the implicit assumption that English is the "official language" of the literature of the United States, scholars at Harvard's Longfellow Institute have been collecting and republishing in bilingual editions American literature in translation. These works include an 1831 Arabic slave narrative set in Fayetteville, North Carolina, a 1927 Norwegian novel about South Dakota farm life, and a 1979 Chinese story dealing with a San Francisco sweatshop.

A national literature, like a modern nation itself, depends on a system of inclusion and exclusion. Although United States citizenship guarantees an individual the right of full social and legal inclusion, citizenship alone, as we have seen, is not sufficient to gain entry into the nation's literature. In a postnational world, however, the very concept of a national literature may be heading towards obsolescence. As social and cultural homogeneity decline throughout the world, and as people feel more comfortable with multiple identities and allegiances, the borders of American literature may become more open to an increasing variety of foreign writers-in-residence, from the naturalized citizen to the totally unassimilated immigrant. If this occurs, the English language may no longer be an insurmountable barrier and all American literature anthologies of the near future may well include a fair number of works in translation.

The following selections are intended to be a small sampling of works written by some prominent foreign-born contemporary writers who have established strong connections with the United States but are rarely represented in American literature courses or collections. Although the writers assembled in this portfolio offer a diversity of cultural and linguistic backgrounds, the selection is not a sampling of contemporary "multiculturalism"—it does not feature American-born writers who have centered their work around ethnic issues and identities (a number of these authors can be found in the main table of contents). They are featured mainly to show a few of the many ways foreign-born writers have participated in the American literary environment.

Vladimir Nabokov
1899–1977

When Vladimir Nabokov was asked in a 1963 interview if he felt any strong sense of national identity, he replied: "I am an American writer, born in Russia and educated in England, where I studied French literature, before spending fifteen years in Germany. I came to America in 1940 and decided to become an American citizen and made America my home." Novelist John Updike responded to Nabokov's mixed identities by calling him "the best writer of English prose at present holding American citizenship."

Born in St. Petersburg, Russia, on April 23, 1899, Nabokov received an excellent education in English and French. In 1919, following the Revolution, his family escaped to Berlin. A scholarship brought Nabokov to Trinity College, Cambridge, where he studied French and Russian literature and proved a gifted soccer and tennis player. After receiving his B.A. in 1922, he returned to Berlin and began supporting his writing by teaching English, French, boxing, tennis, and poetry. In 1923 he published a Russian translation of *Alice in Wonderland,* and soon became a leading contributor of fiction, poetry, criticism and chess columns to Russian émigré journals. He began publishing novels under the pseudonym V. Sirin; by the time he wrote *The Gift* (1937–1938), Nabokov had established himself as a major European novelist. He fled Nazi Germany in 1937 and after a few years in Paris came to the United States with his wife and son in 1940. He taught literature at Stanford, Wellesley, and Cornell between 1941 and 1959. His first novel in English was *The Real Life of Sebastian Knight* (1941); it was followed by *Bend Sinister* (1947), *Lolita* (1955), *Pale Fire* (1962), and *Ada* (1969). His work includes six collections of short stories; and a critical study of Nicolai Gogol (1944); a memoir and a four-volume translation of Aleksandr Pushkin's *Eugene Onegin*. In 1959, following the enormous success of *Lolita*, Nabokov and his wife Vera moved to Montreux, Switzerland, where he died in 1977.

Text:
V. Nabokov, "Terra Incognita," in *A Russian Beauty and Other Stories*, 1973.

Terra Incognita*[1]

The sound of the waterfall grew more and more muffled, until it finally dissolved altogether, and we moved on through the wildwood of a hitherto unexplored region. We walked, and had been walking, for a long time already—in front, Gregson and I; our eight native porters behind, one after the other; last of all, whining and protesting at every step, came Cook. I knew that Gregson had recruited him on the advice of a local hunter. Cook had insisted that he was ready to do anything to get out of Zonraki,[2] where they pass half the year brewing their "von-gho" and the other half drinking it. It remained unclear, however—or else I was already beginning to forget many things, as we walked on and on—exactly who this Cook was (a runaway sailor, perhaps?).

Gregson strode on beside me, sinewy, lanky, with bare, bony knees. He held a long-handled green butterfly net like a banner. The porters, big, glossy-brown Badonians[3] with thick manes of hair and cobalt arabesques[4] between their eyes, whom we had also engaged in Zonraki, walked with a strong, even step. Behind them straggled Cook, bloated, red-haired, with a drooping underlip, hands in pockets and carrying nothing. I recalled vaguely that at the outset of the expedition he had chattered a lot and made obscure jokes, in a manner he had, a mixture of insolence and servility, reminiscent of a Shakespearean clown; but soon his spirits fell and he grew glum and began to neglect his duties, which included interpreting, since Gregson's understanding of the Badonian dialect was still poor.

There was something languorous and velvety about the heat. A stifling fragrance came from the inflorescences[5] of *Vallieria mirifica,*[6] mother-of-pearl in color and resembling clusters of soap bubbles, that arched across the narrow, dry stream bed along which we proceeded. The branches of porphyroferous[7] trees intertwined with those of the Black-Leafed Limia to form a tunnel, penetrated here and there by a ray of hazy light. Above, in the thick mass of vegetation, among brilliant pendulous racemes[8] and strange dark tangles of some kind, hoary monkeys snapped and chattered, while a

---

* The story originally appeared in Russian in 1931. Nabokov's English translation was published in *The New Yorker*, May 18, 1963.
[1] Latin: "unknown land" or "unexplored region."
[2] An imaginary land invented by Nabokov.
[3] An imaginary native people and language invented by Nabokov.
[4] In this usage, an ornament made of geometric, crisscrossing lines worn above the brow.

[5] Clumps of buds or flowers.
[6] A plant invented by Nabokov. Its name is a play on the narrator's name, Vallière, and on the Latin word *mirifica*, meaning "causing awe or wonderment, as in magic."
[7] Producing purplish blooms or leaves.
[8] Cluster or bunch, as in grapes or berries.

cometlike bird flashed like Bengal light,[9] crying out in its small, shrill voice. I kept telling myself that my head was heavy from the long march, the heat, the medley of colors, and the forest din, but secretly I knew that I was ill. I surmised it to be the local fever. I had resolved, however, to conceal my condition from Gregson, and had assumed a cheerful, even merry air, when disaster struck.

"It's my fault," said Gregson. "I should never have got involved with him."

We were now alone. Cook and all eight of the natives, with tent, folding boat, supplies, and collections, had deserted us and vanished noiselessly while we busied ourselves in the thick bush, chasing fascinating insects. I think we tried to catch up with the fugitives—I do not recall clearly, but, in any case, we failed. We had to decide whether to return to Zonraki or continue our projected itinerary, across as yet unknown country, toward the Gurano Hills. The unknown won out. We moved on. I was already shivering all over and deafened by quinine,[10] but still went on collecting nameless plants, while Gregson, though fully realizing the danger of our situation, continued catching butterflies and Diptera[11] as avidly as ever.

We had scarcely walked half a mile when suddenly Cook overtook us. His shirt was torn—apparently by himself, deliberately—and he was panting and gasping. Without a word Gregson drew his revolver and prepared to shoot the scoundrel, but he threw himself at Gregson's feet and, shielding his head with both arms, began to swear that the natives had led him away by force and had wanted to eat him (which was a lie, for the Badonians are not cannibals). I suspect that he had easily incited them, stupid and timorous as they were, to abandon the dubious journey, but had not taken into account that he could not keep up with their powerful stride, and, having fallen hopelessly behind, had returned to us. Because of him invaluable collections were lost. He had to die. But Gregson put away the revolver and we moved on, with Cook wheezing and stumbling behind.

The woods were gradually thinning. I was tormented by strange hallucinations. I gazed at the weird tree trunks, around some of which were coiled thick, flesh-colored snakes; suddenly I thought I saw, between the trunks, as though through my fingers, the mirror of a half-open wardrobe with dim reflections, but then I took hold of myself, looked more carefully, and found that it was only the deceptive glimmer of an acreana bush (a curly plant with large berries resembling plump prunes). After a while the trees parted altogether and the sky rose before us like a solid wall of blue. We were at the top of a steep incline. Below shimmered and steamed an enormous marsh, and, far beyond, one distinguished the tremulous silhouette of a mauve-colored range of hills.

"I swear to God we must turn back," said Cook in a sobbing voice. "I swear to God we'll perish in these swamps—I've got seven daughters and a dog at home. Let's turn back—we know the way. . . ."

He wrung his hands, and the sweat rolled from his fat, red-browed face. "Home, home," he kept repeating. "You've caught enough bugs. Let's go home!"

Gregson and I began to descend the stony slope. At first Cook remained standing above, a small white figure against the monstrously green background of forest; but suddenly he threw up his hands, uttered a cry, and started to slither down after us.

The slope narrowed, forming a rocky crest that reached out like a long promontory into the marshes; they sparkled through the steamy haze. The noonday sky, now freed

---

[9] Bluish light or flare used in theaters or for signaling.

[10] A salt used by explorers to reduce fever.

[11] The largest order of winged insects, of which houseflies, gnats, and mosquitoes are the most common examples.

of its leafy veils, hung oppressively over us with its blinding darkness—yes, its blinding darkness, for there is no other way to describe it. I tried not to look up; but in this sky, at the very verge of my field of vision, there floated, always keeping up with me, whitish phantoms of plaster, stucco curlicues and rosettes, like those used to adorn European celings; however, I had only to look directly at them and they would vanish, and again the tropical sky would bloom, as it were, with even, dense blueness. We were still walking along the rocky promontory, but it kept tapering and betraying us. Around it grew golden marsh reeds, like a million bared swords gleaming in the sun. Here and there flashed elongated pools, and over them hung dark swarms of midges. A large swamp flower, presumably an orchid, stretched toward me its drooping, downy lip, which seemed smeared with egg yolk. Gregson swung his net—and sank to his hips in the brocaded ooze as a gigantic swallowtail, with a flap of its satin wing, sailed away from him over the reeds, toward the shimmer of pale emanations where the indistinct folds of a window curtain seemed to hang. *I must not,* I said to myself, *I must not. . . .* I shifted my gaze and walked on beside Gregson, now over rock, now across hissing and lip-smacking soil. I felt chills, in spite of the greenhouse heat. I foresaw that in a moment I would collapse altogether, that the contours and convexities of delirium, showing through the sky and through the golden reeds, would gain complete control of my consciousness. At times Gregson and Cook seemed to grow transparent, and I thought I saw, through them, wallpaper with an endlessly repeated design of reeds. I took hold of myself, strained to keep my eyes open, and moved on. Cook by now was crawling on all fours, yelling, and snatching at Gregson's legs, but the latter would shake him off and keep walking. I looked at Gregson, at his stubborn profile, and felt, to my horror, that I was forgetting who Gregson was, and why I was with him.

Meanwhile we kept sinking into the ooze more and more frequently, deeper and deeper; the insatiable mire would suck at us; and, wriggling, we would slip free. Cook kept falling down and crawling, covered with insect bites, all swollen and soaked, and, dear God, how he would squeal when disgusting bevies of minute, bright-green hydrotic[12] snakes, attracted by our sweat, would take off in pursuit of us, tensing and uncoiling to sail two yards and then another two. I, however, was much more frightened by something else: now and then, on my left (always, for some reason, on my left), listing among the repetitious reeds, what seemed a large armchair but was actually a strange, cumbersome gray amphibian, whose name Gregson refused to tell me, would rise out of the swamp.

"A break," said Gregson abruptly, "let's take a break."

By a stroke of luck we managed to scramble onto an islet of rock, surrounded by the swamp vegetation. Gregson took off his knapsack and issued us some native patties, smelling of ipecacuanha,[13] and a dozen acreana fruit. How thirsty I was, and how little help was the scanty, astringent juice of the acreana. . . .

"Look, how odd," Gregson said to me, not in English, but in some other language, so that Cook would not understand. "We must get through to the hills, but look, how odd—could the hills have been a mirage?—they are no longer visible."

I raised myself up from my pillow and leaned my elbow on the resilient surface of the rock. . . . Yes, it was true that the hills were no longer visible; there was only the quivering vapor hanging over the marsh. Once again everything around me assumed an

---

[12] Spitting water (in this case, venom).
[13] South American plant used to induce both

expectoration and vomiting. Commonly known as "ipecac."

ambiguous transparency. I leaned back and said softly to Gregson, "You probably can't see, but something keeps trying to come through."

"What are you talking about?" asked Gregson.

I realized that what I was saying was nonsense and stopped. My head was spinning and there was a humming in my ears; Gregson, down on one knee, rummaged through his knapsack, but found no medicine there, and my supply was exhausted. Cook sat in silence, morosely picking at a rock. Through a rent in his shirtsleeve there showed a strange tattoo on his arm: a crystal tumbler with a teaspoon, very well executed.

"Vallière is sick—haven't you got some tablets?" Gregson said to him. I did not hear the exact words, but I could guess the general sense of their talk, which would grow absurd and somehow spherical when I tried to listen more closely.

Cook turned slowly and the glassy tattoo slid off his skin to one side, remaining suspended in mid-air; then it floated off, floated off, and I pursued it with my frightened gaze, but, as I turned away, it lost itself in the vapor of the swamp, with a last faint gleam.

"Serves you right," muttered Cook. "It's just too bad. The same will happen to you and me. Just too bad. . . ."

In the course of the last few minutes—that is, ever since we had stopped to rest on the rocky islet—he seemed to have grown larger, had swelled, and there was now something mocking and dangerous about him. Gregson took off his sun helmet and, pulling out a dirty handkerchief, wiped his forehead, which was orange over the brows, and white above that. Then he put on his helmet again, leaned over to me, and said, "Pull yourself together, please" (or words to that effect). "We shall try to move on. The vapor is hiding the hills, but they are there. I am certain we have covered about half the swamp." (This is all very approximate.)

"Murderer," said Cook under his breath. That tattoo was now again on his forearm; not the entire glass, though, but one side of it—there was not quite enough room for the remainder, which quivered in space, casting reflections. "Murderer," Cook repeated with satisfaction, raising his inflamed eyes. "I told you we would get stuck here. Black dogs eat too much carrion. Mi, re, fa, sol."

"He's a clown," I softly informed Gregson, "a Shakesperean clown."

"Clow, clow, clow," Gregson answered, "clow, clow—clo, clo, clo. . . . Do you hear," he went on, shouting in my ear. "You must get up. We have to move on."

The rock was as white and as soft as a bed. I raised myself a little, but promptly fell back on the pillow.

"We shall have to carry him," said Gregson's faraway voices. "Give me a hand."

"Fiddlesticks," replied Cook (or so it sounded to me). "I suggest we enjoy some fresh meat before he dries up. Fa, sol, mi, re."

"He's sick, he's sick too," I cried to Gregson. "You're here with two lunatics. Go ahead along. You'll make it. . . . Go."

"Fat chance we'll let him go," said Cook.

Meanwhile delirious visions, taking advantage of the general confusion, were quietly and firmly finding their places. The lines of a dim ceiling stretched and crossed in the sky. A large armchair rose, as if supported from below, out of the swamp. Glossy birds flew through the haze of the marsh and, as they settled, one turned into the wooden knob of a bedpost, another into a decanter. Gathering all my will power, I focused my gaze and drove off this dangerous trash. Above the reeds flew real birds with long flame-colored tails. The air buzzed with insects. Gregson was waving away a varicolored fly, and at the same time trying to determine its species. Finally he could contain himself no longer and caught it in his net. His motions underwent curious changes, as if someone kept reshuffling them. I saw him in different poses simultaneously; he was divesting himself of himself, as if he were made of many glass Gregsons whose outlines did not coincide. Then he condensed again, and stood up firmly. He was shaking Cook by the shoulder.

"You are going to help me carry him," Gregson was saying distinctly. "If you were not a traitor, we would not be in this mess."

Cook remained silent, but slowly flushed purple.

"See here, Cook, you'll regret this," said Gregson. "I'm telling you for the last time—"

At this point occurred what had been ripening for a long time. Cook drove his head like a bull into Gregson's stomach. They both fell; Gregson had time to get his revolver out, but Cook managed to knock it out of his hand. Then they clutched each other and started rolling in their embrace, panting deafeningly. I looked at them, helpless. Cook's broad back would grow tense and the vertebrae would show through his shirt, but suddenly, instead of his back, a leg, also his, would appear, covered with coppery hairs, and with a blue vein running up the skin, and Gregson was rolling on top of him. Gregson's helmet flew off and wobbled away, like half of an enormous cardboard egg. From somewhere in the labyrinth of their bodies Cook's fingers wriggled out, clenching a rusty but sharp knife; the knife entered Gregson's back as if it were clay, but Gregson only gave a grunt, and they both rolled over several times; when I next saw my friend's back the handle and top half of the blade protruded, while his hands had locked around Cook's thick neck, which crunched as he squeezed, and Cook's legs were twitching. They made one last full revolution, and now only a quarter of the blade was visible—no, a fifth—no, now not even that much showed: it had entered completely. Gregson grew still after having piled on top of Cook, who had also become motionless.

I watched, and it seemed to me (fogged as my senses were by fever) that this was all a harmless game, that in a moment they would get up and, when they had caught their breath, would peacefully carry me off across the swamp toward the cool blue hills, to some shady place with babbling water. But suddenly, at this last stage of my mortal illness—for I knew that in a few minutes I would die—in these final minutes everything grew completely lucid: I realized that all that was taking place around me was not the trick of an inflamed imagination, not the veil of delirium, through which unwelcome glimpses of my supposedly real existence in a distant European city (the wallpaper, the armchair, the glass of lemonade) were trying to show. I realized that the obtrusive room was fictitious, since everything beyond death is, at best, fictitious: an imitation of life hastily knocked together, the furnished rooms of nonexistence. I realized that reality was here, here beneath that wonderful, frightening tropical sky, among those gleaming swordlike reeds, in that vapor hanging over them, and in the thick-lipped flowers clinging to the flat islet, where, beside me, lay two clinched corpses. And, having realized this, I found within me the strength to crawl over to them and pull the knife from the back of Gregson, my leader, my dear friend. He was dead, quite dead, and all the little bottles in his pockets were broken and crushed. Cook, too, was dead, and his ink-black tongue protruded from his mouth. I pried open Gregson's fingers and turned his body over. His lips were half-opened and bloody; his face, which already seemed hardened, appeared badly shaven; the bluish whites of his eyes showed between the lids. For the last time I saw all this distinctly, consciously, with the seal of authenticity on everything—their skinned knees, the bright flies circling over them, the females of those flies, already seeking a spot for oviposition.[14] Fumbling with my enfeebled hands, I took a thick notebook out of my shirt pocket, but here I was overcome by weakness; I sat

[14] Laying eggs.

down and my head drooped. And yet I conquered this impatient fog of death and looked around. Blue air, heart, solitude. . . . And how sorry I felt for Gregson, who would never return home—I even remembered his wife and the old cook, and his parrots, and many other things. Then I thought about our discoveries, our precious finds, the rare, still undescribed plants and animals that now would never be named by us. I was alone. Hazier flashed the reeds, dimmer flamed the sky. My eyes followed an exquisite beetle that was crawling across a stone, but I had no strength left to catch it. Everything around me was fading, leaving bare the scenery of death—a few pieces of realistic furniture and four walls. My last motion was to open the book, which was damp with my sweat, for I absolutely had to make a note of something; but, alas, it slipped out of my hand. I groped all along the blanket, but it was no longer there.

1931

Isaac Bashevis Singer
1904–1991

In an age when successful authors cultivate their personas, Isaac Bashevis Singer was content to remain in the shadows. This gentle writer was a repository of Jewish folk tales and the most effective advocate for the one-thousand-year-old Yiddish language. In accepting the Nobel Prize for literature in 1978, the self-effacing Singer commented: "Yesterday, a Yiddish writer, today a Nobel Prize winner, tomorrow a Yiddish writer."

He was born in Leoncin, Poland, on July 14, 1904, and moved with his family to Warsaw when he was four years old. His family wanted him to become a rabbi like his father, but he opted to follow in the footsteps of his older brother, novelist Israel Joseph Singer. They grew up amid a vibrant Yiddish culture when Jewish life was basically self-contained. He escaped its destruction at the hands of the Nazis by fleeing to New York in 1935, the same year his first novel *Satan in Goray* was published. He became a United States citizen in 1943.

Settling in an American city teeming with Jewish immigrants, he was able to partially recreate the world of his youth. He married Alma Haimann Wasserman in 1940 and in 1942 joined the staff of the *Jewish Daily Forward,* one of New York's Yiddish newspapers. The publication of *The Family's Moskat* in 1950 and Saul Bellow's masterful translation of "Gimpl Tam" (1945) as "Gimpl the Fool" in 1953 established his reputation among American readers. In his sixties, Singer began writing for children and published extensively in this genre for twenty years. In addition to his fiction, Singer published several autobiographical volumes and several plays.

Singer's fiction often deals with the supernatural, the fantastic, the mystical. "Belief in God and His Providence," Singer has said, "is the very essence of literature. It tells us that causality is nothing but a mask on the face of destiny. Man is constantly watched by powers that seem to know all his desires and complications."

Text:

The Collected Stories of Isaac Bashevis Singer, 1982.

Escape from Civilization

Translated by the author and Ruth Schachner Finkel

I BEGAN to plan my escape from civilization not long after learning the meaning of the word. But the village of Bilgoray, where I lived until I was eighteen, didn't have enough civilization to run away from. Later, when I went to Warsaw, all I could do was run back to Bilgoray. The idea took on substance only after I arrived in New York. It was here that I started to suffer from some kind of allergy—rose fever, hay fever, dust, who knows? I took pills by the bottleful, but they didn't do much good. The heat that early spring was as intense as in August. The furnished room where I lived on the West Side was stifling. I am not one to consult with doctors, but I paid a visit to Dr. Gnizdatka, whom I knew from Warsaw and who faithfully read anything that I managed to get published in the Yiddish press.

Dr. Gnizdatka inserted a speculum into my nostrils and a tongue depressor into my mouth and said, *"Paskudno."* ("Bad.")

"What should I do?"

"Move somewhere near the ocean."

"Where is the ocean?"

"Go to Sea Gate."

The moment Dr. Gnizdatka spoke the name, I realized that the time had finally come to escape from civilization, and that Sea Gate could serve the same purpose as Haiti or Madagascar. The following morning, I went to the bank and withdrew my savings of seventy-eight dollars, checked out of my room, packed all my belongings into a large cardboard suitcase, and walked to the subway. In a cafeteria on East Broadway, someone had told me that it was easy to get a furnished room in Sea Gate. I carried a few books to be my spiritual mainstay while away from civilization: the Bible, Spinoza's *Ethics,* Schopenhauer's *The World as Will and Idea,* as well as a textbook with mathematical formulas. I was then an ardent Spinozist and, according to Spinoza, one can reach immortality only if one meditates upon adequate ideas, which means mathematics.

Because of the heat in New York City, I expected Coney Island to be crowded and the beach lined with bathers. But at Stillwell Avenue, where I got off the train, it was winter. How surprising that in the hour it took me to get from Manhattan to the Island the weather had changed. The sky was overcast, a cold wind blew, and a needle-like rain had begun to fall. The Surf Avenue trolley was empty. At the entrance to Sea Gate there was actually a gate to keep the area private. Two policemen stationed there stopped me and asked who I was and what business I had in Sea Gate. I almost said, "I am running away from civilization," but I answered, "I came to rent a room."

"And you brought your baggage along?"

These interrogations in a country that is supposed to be free insulted me, and I asked, "Is that forbidden?"

One policeman whispered something to the other, and both of them laughed. I received permission to cross the frontier.

The rain intensified. I would have liked to ask someone where I could get a room, but there was no one to ask. Sea Gate looked desolate, still deeply sunk in its winter sleep. For courage I reminded myself of Sven Hedin, Nansen, Captain Scott, Amundsen, and other explorers who left the comforts of the cities to discover the mysteries of the world. The rain pounded on my cardboard suitcase like hail. Perhaps it *was* hailing. The wind tore the hat off my head, and it rolled and flew about like an imp. Suddenly through the downpour I saw a woman beckoning to me from the porch of a house. Her mouth moved, but the wind carried her voice away. She signaled me to come over and find protection from the wild elements. I found myself facing a fancy house with a gabled roof, columns, an ornate door. I walked onto the porch, dropped my suitcase (books and manuscripts can be as heavy as stones), wiped my face with a handkerchief, and was able to see the woman more clearly: a brunette who seemed to me in her thirties, with an olive complexion, black eyes, and classic features. There was something European about her. Her eyebrows were thick. There was no sign of cosmetics on her face. She wore a coat and a beret that reminded me of Poland. She spoke to me in English, but when I answered her and she heard my accent she shifted to Yiddish.

"Who are you looking for? I saw you walking in the rain with that heavy suitcase, and I thought I might . . ."

I told her I had come to rent a room and she smiled, not without irony.

"Is this the way you look for a room? Carrying your luggage? Please come inside. I have a house full of rooms that are to let."

She led me into a parlor, the like of which I had seen only in the movies—Oriental rugs, gold-framed pictures, and an elaborate staircase with carvings and a red velvet bannister. Had I entered an ancient palace? The woman was saying, "Isn't that odd? I've just opened the house this minute. It's been closed for the winter. The weather turned warm and I decided perhaps it's time. As a rule, the season here begins in late May or early June."

"Why is the house closed in the winter?" I asked.

"There's no steam. It's an old building—seventy or eighty years old. It can be heated, but the system is complicated. The heat comes through here." She indicated a brass grate in the floor.

I now realized it was much colder inside than outside. There was a staleness in the air characteristic of places that have been without sun for a long time. We stood silent for a moment. Then she asked, "Are you wanting to move in immediately? The electricity isn't turned on yet and the telephone hasn't been connected. Usually boarders come to make arrangements, pay a deposit, and move in when the weather has become really warm."

"I gave up my room in the city."

The woman looked at me inquisitively and after some hesitation said, "I could swear I've seen your picture in the newspaper."

"Yes, they printed my photograph last week."

"Are you Warshawsky?"

"That's me."

"God in Heaven!"

Darkness had fallen and Esther Royskes lit a candle in a copper candlestick. We were sitting in the kitchen eating supper, like man and wife. She had already told me her whole story: the trouble her ex-husband, a Communist poet, gave her; how she finally divorced him; and how he ran away with his lover to California and left Esther to take care of their two little girls. Two years ago, she had rented this house with the hope that she could earn a living from it, but it did not bring her enough income. People waited until after the Fourth of July and tried to get bargains. Last year, a number of her rooms remained empty.

I put my hand into my pocket, took out the seventy-eight dollars, and offered to give her a down payment, but she protested. "No, you are not going to do that!"

"Why not?"

"First, you have to see what you are taking. It is damp and dark here. You may, God forbid, get a cold. And where will you eat? I would gladly cook for you, but since you tell me you plan to become a vegetarian it may be difficult."

"I will eat in Coney Island."

"You will ruin your stomach. All you get there is hot dogs. A man who packs his valise and comes to Sea Gate without any forethought is not practical. It's a miracle that brought you to me."

"Yes, it is a miracle."

Her black eyes gazed at me half mockingly, and I knew that this was the beginning of a serious relationship. She seemed to be aware of it, too. She spoke to me of things that are usually not told to a stranger. The shadows cast on her face by the candlelight reminded me of a charcoal sketch on a canvas. She said, "Last week I was lying in bed reading your story in the paper. The girls were asleep, but I love to read at night. Who writes about ghosts nowadays, I wondered, and in a Yiddish newspaper to boot! You may not believe me but I thought that I would like to meet you. Isn't that strange?"

"Yes, strange."

"I want to tell you that there is a romantic story connected with this house. A millionaire built it for his mistress. Then Sea Gate was still a place for the rich and American aristocrats. After his death, his mistress remained here until she died. The furnishings are hers—even the library. She seemed not to have left any will, and the bank sold everything intact. For years it remained unoccupied."

"Was she beautiful?"

"Come. I will show you her portrait."

Esther picked up the candlestick. We had to pass through a number of dark rooms to get from the kitchen to the parlor. I stumbled on the thresholds and bumped into rocking chairs. I tripped over a bulge in a rug. Esther took me by the wrist. I felt the warmth of her hand. She asked me, "Are you cold?"

"No. A little."

In the flickering light of the candle, we stood and gazed at the portrait of the mistress. Her hair was arranged in a high pompadour; her low-cut dress exposed her long neck and the upper part of her breasts. Her eyes seemed alive in the semidarkness. Esther said, "Everything passes. I still find pressed flowers and leaves in her books, but there's nothing left of her."

"I'm sure her spirit roams these rooms at night."

The candlestick in Esther's hand trembled and the walls, the pictures, and the furniture shook like stage props in a theater. "Don't say that. I will be afraid to sleep!"

We looked at each other like two mind readers. I remember what I thought then: A situation that a novelist would have to build up slowly, gradually, through a number of chapters, over months or perhaps years, fate has arranged in minutes, in a few strokes. Everything was ready—the characters, the circumstances, the motivations. Well, but in a true drama one can never foresee what will happen the next instant.

The rain had stopped and we were back in the kitchen, drinking tea. I thought it was late, but when I looked at my wristwatch it showed twenty-five past eight. Esther glanced at her watch, too. We sat there for a while, silent. I could see that she was pondering something that required an immediate decision, and I knew what it was. I could almost hear a voice in her mind—perhaps it was the genius of the female species—saying, "It shouldn't come to him so easily. What does a man think when he's able to get a woman so quickly?"

Esther nodded. "The rain has stopped."

"Yes."

"Listen to me," she said. "You can have the best room in this house, and we will not haggle about money. I will be honored and happy to have you here. But it's too early for you to move in. I intended to spend the night here, but now I am going to lock up the house and go home to my children."

"Why don't you want to stay over? Because of me?" I asked, ashamed of my own words.

Esther looked at me questioningly. "Let it be so."

Then she said something that, accordingly to the rules of female diplomacy, she should not have said: "Everything must ripen."

"Very well."

"Where will you sleep now that you've given up your room?"

"I will manage somehow."

"When do you intend to move in?"

"As quickly as possible."

"Will May 15th be too long for you to wait?"

"No, not too long."

"In that case, everything is decided."

And she looked at me with an expression of resentment. Perhaps she expected me to implore her and try to persuade her. But imploring and persuading have never been a part of my male strategy. In the few hours I spent with Esther I had become somewhat surer of myself. I figured that she was about ten years my senior. I had girded myself with the patience necessary to one prepared to give up civilization and its vanities.

Neither of us had removed our coats—it was too cold—so we didn't have to put them on. I took my suitcase, Esther her overnight bag. She blew out the candle. She said, "If you hadn't mentioned her spirit, I might have stayed."

"I'm sure that her spirit is a good one."

"Even good spirits sometimes cause mischief."

We left the house and Esther locked the door. The sky was now clear—light as from an invisible moon. Stars twinkled. The revolving beam from a nearby tower fell on one side of Esther's face. I didn't know why, but I imagined that it was the first night of Passover. I became aware that the house stood apart from other houses and was encircled by lawns. The ocean was only a block away. Because of the howling wind I couldn't hear its sounds earlier, but the winds had subsided and now I heard the waters churning, foaming, like a cosmic stew in a cosmic caldron. In the distance, a tugboat was towing three dark barges. I could barely believe that just an hour away from Manhattan one could reach such quiet.

Esther spoke haltingly. "You wanted to give me an advance before, but I refused to take it. If you are serious about the room, I will accept one, just to make sure that . . ."

"Will twenty dollars be enough?"

"Yes, enough. I ask for it only so that you won't change your mind," she said, and she laughed self-consciously.

In the night light, I counted out twenty dollars. We walked together to the gate. I recognized one of the policemen who had been on duty when I arrived. He looked at us and our suitcases knowingly, as if, like a wizard, he had guessed our secrets. He smiled and winked, and I heard him say, "Are you two going back to civilization?"

Czeslaw Milosz
b. 1911

Czeslaw Milosz was born in Szetejnie, Lithuania, on June 30, 1911, when the country was a part of Poland. Milosz attended high school in the capital city of Vilno, and matriculated in the law department of the Stefan Batory University where he published his first poems in a literary journal in 1929. He received his Masters of Law degree even as he founded literary clubs, published poetry, and won a fellowship to study for a year in France. His second book of poetry, *Three Winters,* earned him a European reputation just before the outbreak of World War II. In 1940 Milosz escaped from Soviet-occupied Vilno to Nazi-occupied Warsaw where he joined the socialist resistance. After the destruction of Warsaw he moved to Cracow and then to New York where he worked in the Polish consulate. In 1949 Milosz visited Poland once more and was shocked by the full dimension of the Soviet system's totalitarianism. In 1951 he asked the French government for political asylum. Milosz has lived in the United States since 1960 and became a naturalized citizen in 1970.

In 1973, his first volume of poetry in English won him a wide American audience and soon a Guggenheim Fellowship. When he was awarded the Nobel Prize for literature in 1980, his poetry was published in Poland for the first time since 1945. In 1981, he held the Eliot Norton chair at Harvard University, gave six public lectures, and began receiving a steady procession of honorary degrees from American universities. He is now a Distinguished Professor Emeritus of Slavic Languages and Literature at the University of California, Berkeley. There he collaborated with poet Robert Hass, now the Poet Laureate of the United States, on English translations of *Unattainable Earth, Provinces,* and his splendid *Collected Poems 1931–1987.*

In his collection of essays, *Visions from San Francisco Bay,* Milosz conducts an imaginary dialogue with the dead, reclusive soul of Robinson Jeffers, the American poet who for years lived in a stone house he built with his own hands in Carmel, California. Jeffers promoted a misanthropic philosophy of "inhumanism," in which he praised the beauty and sacredness of nature over the sick and contaminated human species. "To Robinson Jeffers" accompanied Milosz's essay on the poet.

Text:
C. Milosz, *Visions from San Francisco Bay,* trans. Richard Lourie, 1975.

To Robinson Jeffers

If you have not read the Slavic poets,
so much the better. There's nothing there
for a Scotch-Irish wanderer to seek. They lived in a childhood
prolonged from age to age. For them, the sun
was a farmer's ruddy face, the moon peeped through a cloud,
and the Milky Way gladdened them like a birch-lined road.   5

They longed for the kingdom which is always near,
always right at hand. Then, under apple trees,
angels in homespun linen will come parting the boughs,
and at the white kolkhoz tablecloth 10
cordiality and affection will feast (falling to the ground at times).

And you are from surf-rattled skerries. From the heaths
where, burying a warrior, they broke his bones
so he could not haunt the living. From the sea-night
which your forefathers pulled over themselves, without a word. 15
Above your head, no face, neither the sun's nor the moon's,
only the throbbing of galaxies, the immutable
violence of new beginnings, of new destruction.

All your life listening to the ocean. Black dinosaurs
wade where a purple zone of phosphorescent weeds 20
rises and falls on the waves as in a dream. And Agamemnon
sails the boiling deep to the steps of the palace
to have his blood gush onto marble. Till mankind passes
and the pure and stony earth is pounded by the ocean.

Thin-lipped, blue-eyed, without grace or hope, 25
before God the Terrible, body of the world.
Prayers are not heard. Basalt and granite.
Above them, a bird of prey. The only beauty.

What have I to do with you? From footpaths in the orchards,
from an untaught choir and shimmers of a monstrance, 30
from flower beds of rue, hills by the rivers, books
in which a zealous Lithuanian announced brotherhood, I come.
Oh, consolations of mortals, creeds futile!

And yet you did not know what I know. The earth teaches
more than does the nakedness of elements. No one with impunity 35
gives himself the eyes of a god. So brave, in a void,
you offered sacrifices to daemons; there were Wotan and Thor,
the screech of Erinyes in the air, the terror of dogs
when Hecate with her retinue of the dead draws near.

Better to carve suns and moons on the joints of crosses 40
as was done in my district. To birches and firs
give feminine names. To implore protection
against the mute and treacherous might
than to proclaim, as you did, an inhuman thing.
1963

Louis Simpson
b. 1923

Louis Simpson was raised and educated in Jamaica, West Indies. His father was a lawyer of Scottish descent; his mother was born in Russia. After his father's death, Simpson migrated to the United States in the early 1940s and received his doctorate from Columbia University. His involvement in the United States Army during World War II confirmed his commitment to his new home: "It was as though I had been melted down, new-stamped and cast. I dated my life from the time I had had to defend it," he wrote in his autobiography *North of Jamaica*.

Simpson has been a prolific poet and critic. He has published nine books of poetry beginning with *The Arrivestes: Poems 1940–1949*; he has also written fiction, autobiography, and critical essays on a wide range of modernist, beat, and postmodernist poetry. Simpson's loyalties to North America inspire in his poetry a sharp awareness and a critique of the ways in which the nation has failed to live up to its own, rugged, frontier myth. His poetry also reflects his aesthetic philosophy. As he described his artistic goals, "I have submitted myself to ordinary experiences deliberately, living as most people live, so that I could write poems about it. I wanted to write extraordinary poems about being ordinary." Those poems, as "To the Western World" demonstrates, use traditional poetic resources to transform the mundane into the sublime.

Text:
L. Simpson, *A Dream of Governors*, 1959.

To the Western World

A siren sang, and Europe turned away
From the high castle and the shepherd's crook,
Three caravels went sailing to Cathay
On the strange ocean, and the captains shook
Their banners out across the Mexique Bay.   5

And in our early days we did the same.
Remembering our fathers in their wreck
We crossed the sea from Palos where they came
And saw, enormous to the little deck,
A shore in silence waiting for a name.   10

The treasures of Cathay were never found.
In this America, this wilderness
Where the axe echoes with a lonely sound,
The generations labor to possess
And grave by grave we civilize the ground.   15
1959

American Poetry

Whatever it is, it must have
A stomach that can digest
Rubber, coal, uranium, moons, poems.

Like the shark, it contains a shoe.
It must swim for miles through the desert   5
Uttering cries that are almost human.
1963

Derek Walcott
b. 1930

Derek Walcott's reputation as the finest English-language poet of the Caribbean was confirmed when in 1992 he became the first black poet of the New World to be awarded the Nobel Prize. He was born in St. Lucia, one of the four Windward Islands of the Caribbean, and was educated at St. Mary's College in St. Lucia, and at the University of the West Indies in Jamaica, where he received his B.A. in 1953. He then moved to Trinidad where he directed the Little Carib Theater Workshop, in addition to other activities as an art critic, book reviewer, poet, and playwright. He spent two years studying theater in the United States on a Rockefeller fellowship and since has been awarded the MacArthur Fellowship, commonly referred to as the "genius grant." He has returned often to the United States during the last twenty-five years, to teach and most recently to write the book and lyrics for a musical "The Capeman" with songwriter Paul Simon.

Walcott first published a book of poetry when he was eighteen, with the help of a loan from his mother. Next came the production of his play *Henri Christophe*. In 1962 his first major poetry collection *In a Green Night* was published in England and gained him an international audience. He continued to create poetry, plays, and dramatic adaptations of a high order, taking his place as a citizen of an African diaspora that includes Harlem and the American South as well as the Caribbean. For Walcott, the central issue of the poet's negotiation between two different worlds is further complicated by the violent historical relationship between the two. His connection to both the world of Europe with its ancient classical past, and the once colonized islands of the present-day Caribbean is problematic. As he writes in "A Far Cry from Africa," "I who am poisoned with the blood of both,/ Where shall I turn, divided to the vein?" The violence and slaughter that characterized imperialism are inscribed on the body of the poet; this historical dilemma becomes a quarrel within the isolated self.

Text:

D. Walcott, *Collected Poems, 1948–1984,* 1986.

A Far Cry from Africa

A wind is ruffling the tawny pelt
Of Africa. Kikuyu, quick as flies,
Batten upon the bloodstreams of the veldt.
Corpses are scattered through a paradise.
Only the worm, colonel of carrion, cries: 5
'Waste no compassion on these separate dead!'
Statistics justify and scholars seize
The salients of colonial policy.
What is that to the white child hacked in bed?
To savages, expendable as Jews?   10

Threshed out by beaters, the long rushes break
In a white dust of ibises whose cries
Have wheeled since civilization's dawn
From the parched river or beast-teeming plain.
The violence of beast on beast is read   15
As natural law, but upright man
Seeks his divinity by inflicting pain.
Delirious as these worried beasts, his wars
Dance to the tightened carcass of a drum,
While he calls courage still that native dread   20
Of the white peace contracted by the dead.

Again brutish necessity wipes its hands
Upon the napkins of a dirty cause, again
A waste of our compassion, as with Spain,
The gorilla wrestles with the superman.   25

I who am poisoned with the blood of both,
Where shall I turn, divided to the vein?
I who have cursed
The drunken officer of British rule, how choose
Between this Africa and the English tongue I love?   30
Betray them both, or give back what they give?
How can I face such slaughter and be cool?
How can I turn from Africa and live?
1962

Preparing for Exile

Why do I imagine the death of Mandelstam
among the yellowing coconuts,
why does my gift already look over its shoulder
for a shadow to fill the door
and pass this very page into eclipse?   5

Why does the moon increase into an arc-lamp
and the inkstain on my hand prepare to press thumb-downward
before a shrugging sergeant?
What is this new odour in the air.
that was once salt, that smelt like lime at daybreak,   10
and my cat, I know I imagine it, leap from my path,
and my children's eyes already seem like horizons,
and all my poems, even this one, wish to hide?
1976

Old New England

Black clippers, tarred with whales' blood, fold their sails
entering New Bedford, New London, New Haven.
A white church spire whistles into space
like a swordfish, a rocket pierces heaven
as the thawed springs in icy chevrons race   5
down hillsides and Old Glories flail
the crosses of green farm boys back from 'Nam.
Seasons are measured still by the same
span of the veined leaf and the veined body
whenever the spring wind startles an uproar   10
of marching oaks with memories of a war
that peeled whole counties from the calendar.

The hillside is still wounded by the spire
of the white meetinghouse, the Indian trail
trickles down it like the brown blood of the whale   15
in rowanberries budding like the spoor
on logs burnt black as Bibles by hellfire.
The war whoop is coiled tight in the white owl,
stone-feathered icon of the Indian soul,
and railway lines are arrowing to the far   20
mountainwide absence of the Iroquois.
Spring lances wood and wound, and a spring runs
down tilted birch floors with their splintered suns
of beads and mirrors—broken promises
that helped make this Republic what it is.   25

The crest of our conviction grows as loud
as the spring oaks, rooted and reassured
that God is meek but keeps a whistling sword;
His harpoon is the white lance of the church,
His wandering mind a trial folded in birch,   30
His rage the vats that boiled the melted beast
when the black clippers brought (knotting each shroud
round the crosstrees) our sons home from the East.
1981

Maria Irene Fornes
b. 1930

Maria Irene Fornes was born in Havana and immigrated to New York in 1945, where she became a United States citizen in 1951. She had studied painting in Europe, so that when she began writing plays at the age of thirty, she was influenced less by literary antecedents than by certain styles of painting and by the movies. *Fefu and Her Friends* (1977) is one of her most performed works, a play about eight women who gather to plan an educational event, but distract themselves with talk, lunch, and tea while the audience follows them to four different sites in the theater. Fornes's scenes are often short, and sometimes wordless, simply pictures of characters in moments of stillness or confrontation; yet her plays have a lyricism all out of proportion to the effect of the words on the page. Carefully linking and juxtaposing scenes, Fornes creates theatrical collages with unusually precise visual rhythms. She is a distinctive and subtle director of her own work, able to create both compelling images and a distinctive tone that even in her most solemn plays often draws on an insouciant, irreverent sense of the absurd.

Fornes persistently represents women's lives as shaped by society and culture, yet even in "Sarita" (1984), the heroine who has been victimized and disabled by her obsessive love for Julio lives in a world of vitality and female powers. "Sarita" also deals indirectly with the conflicts erupting when certain aspects of Cuban culture—Voodun religion, music and dance, sexual mores—cannot be assimilated into relationships with Americans. In her plays after 1980, Fornes often moves her female characters toward self-awareness or autonomy, even as they are destroyed by their oppressors, yet Fornes is clear-eyed and never in complicity with the brutality she depicts. In introducing a 1985 anthology of her plays, critic Susan Sontag wrote: "It seems impossible not to connect the truthfulness in Fornes's plays, their alertness of depicting, their unfacile compassionateness, with a certain character, a certain virtue . . . Hers seems to be an admirable temperament, unaffectedly independent, high-minded, ardent." Her awards include six Obies for Off-Broadway achievement, grants from the National Endowment for the Arts and the Rockefeller and Guggenheim foundations.

Text:

Maria Irene Fornes, *Plays,* 1985.

---

from Sarita

Scene 13
1945—Summer Resort

Six months later. A summer resort. Sarita sits on a beach chair. She is sunning herself. There is an empty chair next to her. Mark enters and sits. Through the following speech he takes off his shoes, socks, and shirt. He rolls up his pants and lies back. Sarita wears the skirt of her previous dress and a halter. Mark wears pants and a Hawaiian shirt.

Sarita: What happened?
Mark: Someone passed out.

Sarita: Who?

Mark: A woman.

Sarita: What happened to her?

Mark: I don't know. I couldn't get near her. There was a crowd around her.

Sarita: She probably ate and went in the water.

Mark: (*Surprised.*) That's what they were saying.

Sarita: Maybe that's what happened.

Mark: Why would someone pass out from that?

Sarita: Fron eating and going in the water?

Mark: Yes.

Sarita: You didn't know one could die from that?

Mark: Why would anyone die from that?

Sarita: You must be kidding.

Mark: I'm not kidding. Can you die from that?

Sarita: Sure. You get a congestion and die.

Mark: What is that?

Sarita: A congestion? You don't know what that is?

Mark: No.

Sarita: That's what you get when you go in the water after you eat.

Mark: Come on.

Sarita: You can also die if you drink cold beer or a cold drink after you eat too much on a hot day.

Mark: And what do you call that?

Sarita: Empacho.

Mark: That sounds like a tango. Tango empache.

Sarita: That's apache. Tango apache. I hope you don't catch an empacho and die.

Mark: We don't have empacho in this country.

Sarita: You do. You just don't know what it's called.

Mark: We don't. In English we don't die if we drink cold beer after a meal.

Sarita: You could also die if you take a shower after a meal . . . or a bath. You can kick a leg and that sounds like a conga. You kick your leg when you do a conga. You think empacho sounds like a tango, but kick a leg sounds like a conga.

Mark: You can die from doing a conga?

Sarita: No, you can't die from doing a conga but neither does empacho sound like a tango.

Mark: Well, I don't think she went in the water. She was fully dressed.

Sarita: Maybe she put her feet in the water.

Mark: Maybe. She was wearing shoes though.

Sarita: Well, maybe she fell in.

Mark: Well, maybe.

Sarita: Was she wet?

Mark: I don't know. I didn't see any water.

Sarita: Maybe the water had dried.

Mark: Maybe.

Sarita: Well, if she didn't fall in the water, what did she die of?

Mark: I don't think she died.

Sarita: Well, you don't know how to do a conga, anyway.

Mark: Yes, I do. Anyone can do a conga. (*He moves his feet as if doing a conga.*)

Sarita: Maybe. (*Short pause.*)

Mark: You don't take a shower after a meal?
Sarita: No.
Mark: I do.
Sarita: It's a wonder you're alive.

(Lights fade to black, Music is heard.)

Scene 14
1945—Prayer

A few days later. In Fela's livingroom. Sarita kneels facing front. She looks up. She wears the same dress as in Scene 12.

Sarita: If one has one love in one's lifetime, only one, and one has been true to that love, does one go straight to heaven?—for being true? (*Short pause.*) I hope so. Because here it's hell. (*Short pause.*) I just want to know if you know about this? (*Short pause.*) Is this your idea—Or is the devil doing it? (*Short pause.*) Give me a sign. (*Short pause.*) Say something. (*Short pause.*) Go on. (*Short pause.*) Do something. (*She palms her hand as if there were a small person in it. She lowers her voice.*) Good Lord, child, somebody made a mistake. I put you in for an easy life. You're my favorite kid. Don't worry about a thing, honey. I'll take care of things. (*Using her own voice.*) Oh, God! Thank you God.—God. I am serious. I cannot breathe. I'm burning. I'm turned inside my-self. Do you know what I'm saying?—I feel my life's leaving me. I feel I'm dying. God, I want to love Mark and no one else.

(Lights fade to black. Music is heard.)

Scene 15
1946—I Don't Love You

Sarita's kitchen. Sarita is 20 years old. She sits to the right of the kitchen table. Julio sits on the floor against the right wall. Their clothes are dishevelled.

Sarita: No. I don't love you. I don't love you.
Julio: You don't. Didn't you love me a moment ago? Didn't you?
Sarita: No.
Julio: Oh no. You didn't.

Scene 16
1946—By the Window

A few days later. Fernando sits in Fela's livingroom. The lights are dim. The light of dusk is seen through the windows. Sarita enters. She wears the same dress as in the scene before. Fernando wears pants and a sweater.

Sarita: Fernando . . . (*Pause.*) Why do you sit in the dark?—Should I turn the light on?
Fernando: Oh, no. It's still light outside.
Sarita: Doesn't it bother you to sit in the dark? (*Pause.*) What do you think of when you sit like this?

Fernando: I don't think much. I rest.

Sarita: Won't you rest better lying down?

Fernando: No, I like to sit like this.

Sarita: When I see you sitting in the dark I think you're sad.

Fernando: Oh, no, I'm not.

Sarita: Do you dose off?

Fernando: No.

Sarita: What do you think about? Aren't you thinking anything?

Fernando: I imagine things.

Sarita: What?

Fernando: I imagine that things are peaceful. That people go to work, and come back from work, and they eat, and go to sleep.

Sarita: Is that what you think . . . ?

Fernando: Yes.

Sarita: You are so dear.

Fernando: (*He looks out.*) For many years I didn't think of the people here. I thought of my island—which was beautiful and peaceful. I sat here, but in my mind I was sitting on the porch in my parents' house. Do you do that? Do you spend time in a place that's far away?

Sarita: Yes.

Fernando: In my island nothing bad ever happened. A dog died once. (*He looks out.*) Then, it happened that I didn't think of my island any more. I thought of the people here. That's how I became an American. I thought of the people here. I imagined that you came from school and you did your homework and that you didn't get into fights in the street. Or go out with boys who were mean and disrespectful. That's how I became an American.

Sarita: I wish I could think like you. I think of many things, but never quiet things. My heart is restless and I think of things that hurt me. They frighten me. I feel pain in my chest. I am in danger. Teach me how to be like you. Teach me how to look for peace. My heart won't let me.

(*Lights fade to black. Music is heard.*)

Bharati Mukherjee
b. 1940

Double expatriated, first from India, then from Canada, Bharati Mukherjee now lives in the United States and writes about the immigrant experience from a multiple perspective. Her Indianness becomes metaphor, an emblem for a world experienced through the violence of "broken identities and discarded languages."

She was born into a well-to-do Bengali Braham family in Calcutta and received her early schooling in Great Britain, in Switzerland, and at Loreto Convent School, Calcutta. She received her M.A. in English and ancient Indian culture from the University of Baroda in 1961, an M.F.A. from the Iowa Writers' Workshop in 1963, and a Ph.D. from Iowa in 1969. When she married Clark Blaise, an American writer of Canadian descent, she moved with him for a time to Canada where she taught at McGill University. Other teaching posts have been at Queen's College, New York, and the University of California, Berkeley, where she currently is a distinguished professor of English.

Mukherjee's novels include *The Tiger's Daughter* (1972), *Wife* (1975), and *Jasmine* (1989). She has written two collections of short stories, *Darkness* (1985) and *The Middleman and Other Stories* (1988). She has co-written two books with her husband: *Days and Nights in Calcutta* (1977, 1986) and *The Sorrow and the Terror: The Haunting Legacy of the Air India Tragedy* (1987). She contributes regularly to periodicals.

Mukherjee writes in order to be visible, to be seen as a person rather than as a faceless "type." In her collection, *The Middleman and Other Stories,* this striving finds its perfect setting in America, where Mukherjee is able to refract this desire through a ready-made multicultural lens that addresses the universality of the immigrant quest for recognition. The results of her fictional investigations into this no-man's-land are not always reassuring, but they are startling and vigorous, and must be considered seriously by anyone interested in the words of those whose identities are so fragile and whose language might so easily remain unspoken.

Text:
"Happiness," from *DoubleTake,* Summer 1997.

Happiness

My father was dying of cancer, but he hung in long enough to select a groom for me out of Aunt Flower Garland's short list of three. The night before he passed away, he gave me his last advice and blessing. He said, "In the areas I can control, namely financial security and temperamental compatibility, I have hedged all bets. Happiness in marriage? That, even I can't guarantee."

He rejected the candidacy of a physics professor in Tulsa, Oklahoma, and a dentist in San Leandro, California, in favor of Arjun. The physics professor had a grandfather who had nearly won a Nobel prize in quantum theory, and the dentist's family owned a profitable pharmaceutical company, but Arjun had a Ph.D. in electrical engineering from Columbia University. Columbia was where my father would like to have studied, if his father, so the story went, hadn't died of a ruptured appendix at (even by the local standards) the premature age of twenty-six. My grandmother, two aunts, and father owed their second start in life to the generosity of a maternal uncle, who, being a relative from the maternal side, of course was under no obligation to take them in. This uncle, who had five daughters and three sons of his own, paid for the weddings of my Aunts Flower Garland and Leafy Vine, and, when my father turned seventeen, arranged an apprentice job for him with an engineer friend at a hydroelectric plant an overnight's train ride from the city.

"And as the Calcutta Chamber of Commerce knows," my father was fond of saying, and he said it always in English, "the rest is very much history, isn't it?"

In his anecdotes, he gave his youth Dickensian twists and darkenings, not all of which I believed, probably because by the time I was born he'd made one fortune in lumber up in Assam, and another down in Andhra in steel. In a previous incarnation, Horatio Alger had to have been Bengali.

My father and I were very close, closer than most fathers and daughters in our traditional neighborhood, Mother having died of an overnight fever when I was three. I can't visualize Mother since there are no photographs of her, no likeness for me to have had framed and hung on the wall next to my late grandfather's and grandmother's portraits above the altar of gods in the room of worship, but her presence or absence persists in my brain as a faint stain of melancholy.

A week before my father died, Arjun, whose full name is Arjun Kumar Roy Chowdhury, flew in from New York on a two-week vacation from his job—he was a vice-president in charge of operations research at an electronics company—interviewed the women on the Roy Chowdhury family's short list of bridal candidates that he thought he might survive a lifetime with on the basis of photo, bio, and relatives' preliminary impressions, and picked me. I need to believe that his family's short list was longer than my father's.

Given the long lines for immigrant visas at the U.S. consulate, Arjun was impatient to get the legal formality of marriage over with before he returned to New York at the end of his two-week leave, but we, Ghoses, insisted on letting a respectable time lapse between celebration of funeral and wedding. I don't call it *my* wedding, or Arjun's and my wedding, because the bride and groom played the least assertive roles during the lawyerly dowry negotiations, the by-fax-and-priority-mail transcontinental preparations, and the long, complicated, exhausting pre- and postnupital ceremonies. We fasted when we were told to, we bathed with turmeric paste in Ganges water as prescribed, we played the laid-down games auguring connubial contentment, and when, toward the end of all the chants by the Brahmin priest and the vows in Sanskrit by Arjun and my maternal great-uncle, the dramatic moment came for the veiled bride to lift her head and look into the groom's eyes, we both managed I'm-ready-for-whatever-adventure smiles.

Two days after the wedding, the day known as *bou-bhat,* which I later translated into English for Karin Stein, my neighbor in Upper Montclair, New Jersey, as *the day the bride moves to her husband's house and cooks rice perfect enough for him to eat, because if the rice is too crunchy or too sticky she'll be sent back in disgrace to her parents' house,* Arjun and I boarded an Air India 747, and, strangers safety-belted into side-by-side seats, headed for instant intimacy.

Within a month of making my home in America, I learned how wise my father, the Cheetah of the Calcutta Chamber of Commerce, had been to hedge those bets that he could. At social gatherings, like the Tagore Society evenings in the Bannerjees' split-level in Chappaqua, New York, or at the organizational meetings of the Bengali Heritage Preservation Association in the Dases' condo in Queens, I sniffed out heartache and heard deceit. I picked up words and phrases that I hadn't been taught by Aunts Flower Garland and Leafy Vine: Creedmore, Prozac, shelter for abused women, defenestration.

Comfortable living and decent conduct had been taken for granted by my family. I was grateful that the Ghoses hadn't been deceived by the Roy Chowdhurys. Arjun hadn't lied about his degrees, his salary, his stocks and bonds holdings. He owned the Tudor-style house in Montclair, and the black BMW we had been shown photos of. And he owned things I hadn't seen before: a refrigerator with an ice-water faucet set in its door, a convection oven, an outdoor gas barbecue grill.

The more personal habits and peeves revealed themselves enticingly to me. For instance, every night before coming to bed, he dropped two Alka-Seltzer tablets into a highball glass of water, said, "Plop, plop, fizz, fizz, bottoms up! Prosit!" and gulped the noisy drink down while pinching his nose. I got to look forward to chasing the antacid grains off his lips with my tongue. It made me feel uninhibited. Who cares about long-term happiness when the tongue is tracing, teasing, tormenting, in fulfillment of its own, distinct destiny?

Arjun and I made our voluntary accommodations. At the dinner table, I learned to taste the difference between chardonnay and sauvignon blanc, and pretended preferences for merlots and pinot noirs and contempt for all California cabernets. He cut back on pork and beef. I filled him in on Indian politics: he'd missed so much of which party leaders had defected and why, and which cabinet ministers had been arrested and on what charges among the usual frauds, graft, currency violations, embezzlements. He reciprocated by dictating which senators and Congress representatives I was to trust and explaining the glories and ghastlinesses of the American two-party system. Politics was bedtime story. It didn't matter that I didn't have a vote in this country, that I hadn't voted in any election in any country. I still think of politics as love's foreplay.

Give and take; take and give: that was the flow of our intimacy. Arjun liked to make money, and he liked me to spend it. I did. I drove the BMW—bigger, shinier than in the photos I'd been shown—to the malls, and displayed what money could buy when, late in the New Jersey night, he came through the front door, carrying a briefcaseful of work he had yet to get through. It wasn't about being pliant. My father taught me, through example, that self-worth based on cash-worth is the shortest cut to tragedy.

"Class and conscience," my father said, "go together like a washerman and his donkey. Class is the washerman, but he has to follow the path that his stubborn donkey takes, isn't it?"

My father's analogies were not for me to question. In his adolescent days as apprentice laborer, he'd composed a notebookful of morally uplifting couplets in Bengali, the point of all of which was, cultivate your conscience so that money and rank may not lead you astray.

I have followed his advice by never buying insurance. I wouldn't shed a tear if a burglar broke into the house while Arjun was in the Softron, Inc., offices in Manhattan and I at the cosmetics counter at Bendel's, and made off with a vanload of our belongings. But I have followed his advice for lascivious reasons. Penury neither alarms me nor goads me to covetous ambitiousness. Money, in my marriage to Arjun, was the consensual currency of intimacy. All around me in suburban New York and New Jersey, love was ending in sleeping pills, straitjackets, fatal automobile accidents. Not love, not loyalty, but steel-tipped intimacy, so sharp and thrilling that it has entered and exited before you have touched the wound, felt the pain: that intimacy was our strength. Forget the prenuptial haggling between the Roy Chowdhurys and the Ghoses. To each other we made no promises. We gave and took freely, greedily. We demonstrated large-hearted poor sense instead of self-interest. There should have been time for me to let my father know that before intimacy, happiness in marriage pales.

This is the way that our most special night happened. What does it matter which year, which season. It was a weeknight like any other weeknight in our America life. Arjun came through the front door, which the previous owners, whom Karin Stein remembered as "a moody Middle East type, don't ask me from where exactly, except that he was definitely not from Israel," had fitted with chimes that tinkled out a bar or two of what Karin identified as "It's a Most Beautiful Day"; he dropped his umbrella in its ceramic stand, hung up his all-weather coat in the hall closet; he thrust a cold, heavy bottle of champagne instead of the usual chardonnay against my bosom, grabbed me in a bear hug, and whispered, "Tonight we celebrate!" into the Austrian crystal necklace, which was what I had bought from a just-opened boutique earlier in the day.

"Celebrate what?" I assumed a bonus or promotion, or, for Arjun, more pleasing still would be a stock market coup. My role in our partnership was to draw the answers out of him.

"Who cares what?" He popped the cork right there in the hall, and with the champagne foaming down the sides of the bottle and leaving sticky droplets on the wood floor, dragged me in a bear hug to the kitchen.

A finicky housemaker would have blotted clean the champagne trail while Arjun was reaching for the fluted glasses I'd stuck way in the back of the highest cabinet shelf. They were still in the manufacturer's box. I'd bought them at a going-out-of-business sale in Paramus Mall. Arjun was a Glenfiddich drinker. Wine collecting was a hobby with him. He's made a wine cellar out of what had been the last owner's woodworking shop. "Forget carpentry," Karin scoffed when she came over for our first wine-tasting party, "the guy was making bombs. Don't you hear any funny ticking noises when you're in the basement?"

A women with good sense would have first turned off the gas flames under the pots of Basmati rice and goat vindaloo, then attended to whatever adventure destiny had lassoed.

"Let me guess," I laughed. "I've never seen you this happy, so it has to be something special."

Arjun pulled two champagne flutes out of their box, and held them under the kitchen faucet. I'd forgotten they were etched with a cloudy circlet of leaves and rimmed with a bright, thin band of gold.

"So happy," Arjun retorted, "that I'm not complaining about having to rinse dishes."

"We aren't in Calcutta anymore." I tore off squares of paper towels and held them out to Arjun. Rolls of parch-tongued paper towels, packages of thick, crisp bond paper into which no insect bodies have been processed: those are the American marvels I prize.

"Try telling that to your Chappaqua friends. You think Prafulla Bose comes home at eight and does the dishes?"

He crumpled the dry paper squares and tossed them in the garbage. The track light aimed at the sink caught the bright slitheriness of water coating the inside of each flute.

"You've been nominated Most Valuable Functionary by your CEO."

"Don't even try," Arjun said. He poured the champagne carefully into a glass for me.

I had watched him pour wine before, but I hadn't noticed, really noticed, his wrists. I'd admired his fingers before, told him many times how movingly delicate I found them on a man who claimed to abhor painters and poets. The wrist that rotated with the bottle neck had the showy, arrogant sureness of wrists of the concert pianists I caught by chance on cable channels. "All right, you're a secret gambler, and you've just made a killing." I arced my body to kiss that confident wrist. So what that my head knocked the filled glass out of his surprised grasp.

"A gambler?"

I heard his shoes push aside broken glass. He was thinking of my feet, not his tile floor. I don't wear shoes or slippers at home. I didn't in Calcutta where our floors were of cool marble or stone mosaic, and I didn't in Upper Montclair with its oak, tile, lino, and wool-blend wall-to-wall.

"You don't mind drinking a toast to gambling?" He poured champagne into the second flute.

"Plop, plop, fizz, fizz!" I whispered. "Bottoms up!"

"Prosit!" he whispered back.

I took a gulp, he an assessor's sip. "How much, Arjun?" I was thinking how large a sum I would have to find creative ways for spending.

"Every asshole gambler should be so lucky to have you as a wife?"

Then he whirled me into the living room with strides that resembled waltzers' on colorized, afternoon movies on TV, humming tunes I didn't know and at the same time wriggling out of his suit jacket, stiffening his spine and outstretched arms, tightening his buttocks.

It wasn't natural clumsiness that kept me stepping on his champagne-dampened shoes. Like most young women on my block, I took years of weekends classes in Tagore-style singing and dancing. Aunt Leafy Vine keeps my certificates in the vault compartment of her most secure cabinet, which by the way is made of steel manufactured in one of my father's factories. I am no more and no less physically graceful than the other Tri-State Bengali wives who have volunteered for bit parts in Tagore's drama *Red Oleander,* which the Tagore Society intends to stage next October.

That night I tripped, I kept tripping, stumbling, apologizing, because I couldn't feel the beat to his hummed tune. He rose on the balls of his feet; I thumped with my heels as though I was wearing dance bells on my ankles. He covered the available floor space with wide swoops in circles; I concentrated my energies on the slightest movements of finger joints and neck muscles. I had danced duets as Radha the Milkmaid to a girl-cousin's Krishna the God Biding His Time as Amorous Goatherd in family theatricals. But in those duets, Radha and Krishna never touched. Nobody led, nobody followed. There wasn't any need to. Power was shared by god and mortal. We improvised the depths of the lovers' passion, but never the way their love turned out. That was the trouble, I told myself. I had no way of telling when the humming and the prancing would come to their natural close. There were no scripted roles, no sage-revealed unalterable storyline, no faith that through dance I might discover the simple secret of cosmic chaos.

"It's no good," Arjun said.

He let go of me, suddenly, and I fell back into his favorite chair, a massive leather rocker, embarrassed at my own ungainliness, but thankful the ordeal was over while he hummed, whistled, twirled around the room solo.

"See how easy it is?"

I heard relief, not taunt, in Arjun's question. From the rocker, the posture and the footwork did seem easy. "I think my problem is I'm not hearing what you're hearing. I'm not *feeling* what you're feeling."

"What am I feeling?" He dipped his head back to ask his question, but by the time I answered, "You're feeling good, very good," he'd waltzed away to the farthest corner of the living room.

For another hour I watched, cowering at the unself-conscious celebration of . . . what was it that he was celebrating? What had he gambled on? How destructive could his winnings be? Was I a witness to bliss or lunacy?

When I went to bed that night, he was still dancing.

The next morning he left home at six-thirty as he always did to catch his commuter train. I haven't seen him since. I did find a note, an orange Post-It actually, stuck to the neck of the champagne bottle. It said: *There is another woman, but that's not the reason. Arranged marriages carry no risk. I know you'll react to my leaving, and to a gambler, certainty is boring. Ciao! Have a happy life.*

That was seven years ago. The changes in my life are mostly invisible. I still have the BMW and the house on North Fullerton Street. Karin Stein is still my friend, but she chucked her law practice for a bearded baker somewhere in the Northwest. She sends me postcards with grease stains. Last year I talked myself into starting law school. Night classes, not Harvard or Yale. All the same, it's exciting work, and I am a hardworking student. My father's failure to arrange a lasting marriage has alchemized into new strengths and excitements. Now, for instance, I stay awake nights arguing the legal rights of frozen sperm or defending UFO-borne alien scientists against charges of rape. Are UFO abductions and orifice penetrations punishable crimes in U.S. courts? For amendments to immigration bills, do "UFObacks" fall into the category of undocumenteds? Is Arjun physically as well as legally dead? In American English is self-esteem a synonym for happiness?

Joseph Brodsky
1940–1996

Joseph Brodsky was born in Leningrad in 1940 to a Jewish family. After dropping out of school at fifteen, he worked as a stoker, metal worker, and manual laborer, writing poetry in his spare time. His poetry delighted the Soviet literary underground but angered the Communist authorities. He was accused of "social parasitism" and sent to a forced-labor camp in the Soviet Arctic. International protests led to his early release. After serving eighteen months of a five-year sentence, he was stripped of his Soviet citizenship and kicked out of the country in 1972. Befriended by the Anglo-American poet W. H. Auden, Brodsky moved to the United States, took a poet-in-residence at the University of Michigan and became an American citizen in 1977. His books were banned in his native land until 1987, the same year he won the Nobel Prize in literature. "Reading Brodsky is like standing on top of an existential hill and looking down on two worlds, two empires," the Nobel committee said. Brodsky is not, however, a political writer. His life story has had its political chapters, but not his work, which is both imagistically clear and emotionally intense.

In 1965, while he was in Siberia, Brodsky's first book of poetry, *Verse and Poems*, appeared in the United States. A second book, *A Stop in the Desert* (1970), and the *The End of a Lovely Era*, published in 1977, contained poems written before and after his internal exile. Brodsky compared the lot of an exiled writer to a creature who "survives like a fish in the sand: crawls off into the bush, and getting up on crooked legs, / walks away (his tracks like a line of writing) / into the heart of the continent."

Brodsky's poems and essays have been translated into more than a dozen languages. In 1991, he became the first foreign-born poet laureate to be appointed since the post was created by Congress in 1986. "American poetry to me is a sort of relentless, non-stop sermon of human autonomy," he said at the time of that appointment. "What they are saying is that man can resist the world, that he is not a victim. It's tremendously tempering stuff that gave me resilience and fortitude. That's what made me an American long before I arrived on these shores." Brodsky, who lived in New York City and taught at Mount Holyoke College, died of a heart attack in 1996 at the age of 55.

Texts:

"Letters from the Ming Dynasty" from *A Part of Speech,* 1980.

"May 24, 1980" from *To Urania,* 1988.

Letters from the Ming Dynasty

Translated by Derek Walcott

I

Soon it will be thirteen years since the nightingale
fluttered out of its cage and vanished. And, at nightfall,
the Emperor washes down his medicine with the blood
of another tailor, then, propped on silk pillows, turns on a jeweled bird

that lulls him with its level, identical song.   5
It's this sort of anniversary, odd-numbered, wrong,
that we celebrate these days in our "Land-under-Heaven."
The special mirror that smooths wrinkles even
costs more every year. Our small garden is choked with weeds.
The sky, too, is pierced by spires like pins in the shoulder blades   10
of someone so sick that his back is all we're allowed to see,
and whenever I talk about astronomy
to the Emperor's son, he begins to joke . . .
This letter to you, Beloved, from your Wild Duck
is brushed onto scented rice paper given me by the Empress.   15
Lately there is no rice but the flow of rice paper is endless.

II

"A thousand-li-long road starts with the first step," as
the proverb goes. Pity the road home does
not depend on that same step. It exceeds ten times
a thousand li, especially counting from zeros.   20
One thousand li, two thousand li—
a thousand means "Thou shalt not ever see
thy native place." And the meaninglessness, like a plague,
leaps from words onto numbers, onto zeros especially.

Wild blows us westward like the yellow tares   25

from a dried pod, there where the Wall towers.
Against it man's figure is ugly and stiff as a frightening hieroglyph,

as any illegible scripture at which one stares.
This pull in one direction only has made.
me something elongated, like a horse's head, 30
and all the body should do is spent by its shadow
rustling across the wild barley's withered blade.
1977

May 24, 1980

Translated by the author

I have braved, for want of wild beasts, steel cages,
carved my term and nickname on bunks and rafters,
lived by the sea, flashed aces in an oasis,
dined with the-devil-knows-whom, in tails, on truffles.
From the height of a glacier I beheld half a world, the earthly 5
width. Twice have drowned, thrice let knives rake my nitty-gritty.
Quit the country that bore and nursed me.
Those who forgot me would make a city.
I have waded the steppes that saw yelling Huns in saddles,
worn the clothes nowadays back in fashion in every quarter, 10
planted rye, tarred the roofs of pigsties and stables,
guzzled everything save dry water.
I've admitted the sentries' third eye into my wet and foul
dreams. Munched the bread of exile: it's stale and warty.
Granted my lungs all sounds except the howl; 15
switched to a whisper. Now I am forty.
What should I say about life? That it's long and abhors transparence.
Broken eggs make me grieve; the omelette, though, makes me vomit.
Yet until brown clay has been crammed down my larynx,
only gratitude will be gushing from it. 20
1980

Jamaica Kincaid
b. 1949

Jamaica Kincaid was born in Antigua, a West Indian island that at the time was a British dependency. At sixteen, wishing to escape the provincial life of the island, she left home and came to the United States where she worked as an au pair in New York City and studied photography. Largely self-educated and with an enormous appetite for reading, Kincaid briefly attended Franconia College in New Hampshire; she returned to Manhattan and worked at various jobs until, in the early 1970s, she began writing for the *New Yorker* magazine. Her first nonfiction piece was a description of Brooklyn's annual West Indian Day parade. In 1976 she joined the magazine's staff, and many of her stories and essays have been published there since.

Kincaid's first collection of stories, *At the Bottom of the River,* appeared in 1983 and won the prestigious American Academy and Institute of Arts and Letters' Morton Dauwen Zabel Award. The book was also a critical success, its imagistic, evocative prose establishing Kincaid as one of literature's preeminent stylists. Kincaid's next two works of fiction moved somewhat away from the lyricism of her earlier stories to stronger narrative situations. In 1988, Kincaid published *In a Small Place,* an angry and ironical essay about the effects of colonialism on her native Antiqua. Although much of Kincaid's work is rooted and set in the West Indies, her fiction has nevertheless found a large audience in the United States, where, she has said, "I did find myself and did find my voice."

Text:

J. Kincaid, *At the Bottom of the River,* 1983.

Girl

Wash the white clothes on Monday and put them on the stone heap; wash the color clothes on Tuesday and put them on the clothesline to dry; don't walk barehead in the hot sun; cook pumpkin fritters in very hot sweet oil; soak your little clothes right after you take them off; when buying cotton to make yourself a nice blouse, be sure that it doesn't have gum on it, because that way it won't hold up well after a wash; soak salt fish overnight before you cook it; is it true that you sing benna in Sunday School?; always eat your food in such a way that it won't turn someone else's stomach; on Sundays try to walk like a lady and not like the slut you are so bent on becoming; don't sing benna in Sunday School; you mustn't speak to wharf-rat boys, not even to give directions; don't eat fruits on the street—flies will follow you; *but I don't sing benna on Sundays at all and never in Sunday School;* this is how to sew on a button; this is how to make a buttonhole for the button you have just sewed on; this is how to hem a dress when you see the hem coming down and so to prevent yourself from looking like the slut I know you are so bent on becoming; this is how iron your father's khaki shirt so that it doesn't have a crease; this is how you iron your father's khaki pants so that they don't have a crease; this is how you grow okra—far from the house, because okra tree harbors red ants; when you are growing dasheen, make sure it gets plenty of water or else it makes your throat itch when you are eating it; this is how you sweep a corner; this is how you sweep a whole house; this is how you sweep a yard; this is how you smile to someone you don't like too much; this is how you smile to someone you don't like at all; this is how you smile to someone you like completely; this is how you set a table for tea; this is how you set a table for dinner; this is how you set a table for dinner with an important guest; this is how you set a table for lunch; this is how you set a table for breakfast; this is how to behave in the presence of men who don't know you very well, and this way they won't recognize immediately the slut I have warned you against becoming; be sure to wash every day, even if it is with your own spit; don't squat down to play marbles—you are not a boy, you know; don't pick people's flowers—you might catch something; don't throw stones at blackbirds, because it might not be a blackbird at all; this is how to make a bread pudding; this is how to make doukona; this is how to make pepper pot; this is how to make a good medicine for a cold; this is how to make a good medicine to throw away a child before it even becomes a child; this is how to catch a fish; this is how to throw back a fish you don't like, and that way something bad won't fall on you; this is how to bully a man; this is how a man bullies you; this is how to love a man, and if this doesn't work there are other ways, and if they don't work don't feel too bad about giving up; this is how to spit up in the air if you feel like it, and this is how to move quick so that it doesn't fall on you; this is how to make ends meet; always squeeze bread to make sure it's fresh; *but what if the baker won't let me feel the bread?*; you mean to say that after all you are really going to be a kind of woman who the baker won't let near the bread?

1978

Acknowledgments

Adams, Abigail: "Letter to John Adams" by Abigail Adams from *Adams Family Correspondence, Vol. 1 and 2*, edited by L. H. Butterfield, Cambridge, Mass.: Harvard University Press. Copyright © 1963 by the Massachusetts Historical Society. Reprinted by permission.

Agee, James: Excerpt from *Let Us Now Praise Famous Men* by James Agee and Walker Evans. Copyright 1939, 1940 by James Agee, renewed © 1969 by Mia Fritsch Agee and Walker Evans. Reprinted by permission of Houghton Mifflin. All rights reserved.

Ashbery, John: "Landscapeople" from *As We Know* by John Ashbery. Copyright © 1979 by John Ashbery. Reprinted by permission of Penguin Putnam, Inc. "The Painter" from *Some Trees* by John Ashbery. Copyright © 1956 by John Ashbery, New Haven: Yale University Press. Reprinted by permission of Georges Borchardt, Inc. for the author. "These Lacustrine Cities" from *Rivers and Mountains* by John Ashbery. Copyright © 1962, 1963, 1964, 1966 by John Ashbery, New York: Holt, Rinehart & Winston, 1967. Reprinted by permission of Georges Borchardt, Inc. for the author. "Soonest Mended" from *The Double Dream of Spring* by John Ashbery. Copyright © 1970, 1969, 1968, 1967, 1966 by John Ashbery, New York: Dutton, 1970. Reprinted by permission of Georges Borchardt, Inc. for the author. "Syringa" from *Houseboat Days* by John Ashbery. Copyright © 1975, 1976, 1977 by John Ashbery, New York: Viking, 1977. Reprinted by permission of Georges Borchardt, Inc. for the author.

Baldwin, James: "My Dungeon Shook: Letter to My Nephew on the One-Hundredth Anniversary of the Emancipation" by James Baldwin. Originally published in *The Progressive*. Copyright © 1962 by James Baldwin. Copyright renewed. Collected in *The Fire Next Time*, published by Vintage Books. Reprinted by permission of the James Baldwin Estate. "Sonny's Blues" by James Baldwin originally published in *Parisan Review*. Copyright 1957 by James Baldwin. Copyright renewed. Collected in *Going to Meet the Man* (Vintage Books). Reprinted by permission of the James Baldwin Estate.

Bishop, Elizabeth: "At the Fishhouses," "The Fish," and "In the Waiting Room" "Questions of Travel" "Sestina" "One Art" from *The Complete Poems 1927–1979* by Elizabeth Bishop. Copyright © 1979, 1983 by Alice Helen Methfes-

sel. Reprinted by permission of Farrar, Straus & Giroux, Inc.

Bradford, William: Excerpts from *Plymouth Plantation 1620–1647* by William Bradford, editor Samuel Eliot Morrison. Copyright 1952 by Samuel Eliot Morrison, renewed © 1980 by Emily M. Beck. Reprinted by permission of Alfred A. Knopf Inc.

Brooks, Gwendolyn: "Negro Hero," "Kitchenette Building," "The Blackstone Rangers," "The Last Quatrain of the Ballad of Emmett Till," "Young Afrikans," and "A Bronzeville Mother Loiters in Mississippi" by Gwendolyn Brooks from *Blacks*. Copyright © 1991 by Gwendolyn Brooks. Reprinted by permission of the author. "The Mother" by Gwendolyn Brooks. Copyright by Gwendolyn Brooks. Reprinted by permission of the author.

Brown, Sterling A.: "Ma Rainey" by Sterling A. Brown from *Collected Poems of Sterling A. Brown*, edited by Michael S. Harper. Copyright 1932 by Harcourt Brace & Co. Copyright renewed © 1960 by Sterling A. Brown. Reprinted by permission of HarperCollins Publishers, Inc. "Slim in Hell" by Sterling A. Brown from *Collected Poems of Sterling A. Brown*, edited by Michael S. Harper. Copyright © 1980 by Sterling A. Brown. Reprinted by permission of HarperCollins Publishers, Inc. "Remembering Nat Turner" by Sterling A. Brown from *Collected Poems of Sterling A. Brown*, edited by Michael S. Harper. Copyright 1939 by Sterling A. Brown, renewed © 1980. Reprinted by permission of HarperCollins Publishers, Inc.

Byrd, William: "The Great Dismal Swamp" from *The Prose of William Byrd of Westover* by William Byrd, edited by Louise Wright, Cambridge, Mass: Harvard University Press. Copyright © 1966 by the President and Fellows of Harvard College. Reprinted by permission.

Carver, Raymond: "What We Talk About When We Talk About Love" from *What We Talk About When We Talk About Love* by Raymond Carver. Copyright © 1981 by Raymond Carver. Reprinted by permission of Alfred A. Knopf, Inc.

Cash, W. J.: Excerpt from *The Mind of the South* by W. J. Cash. Copyright 1941 by W. J. Cash. Reprinted by permission of Random House, Inc.

Cather, Willa: "Neighbour Rosicky" from *Obscure Destinies* by Willa Cather. Copyright 1932 by Willa Cather, renewed © 1960 by the Executors of the Estate of Willa Cather. Reprinted by permission of Alfred A. Knopf, Inc.

Columbus, Christopher: Excerpts from *Columbus Journals* by Christopher Columbus, edited by S. E. Morrison. Copyright © 1964 by S. E. Morrison. Reprinted by permission of Curtis Brown, Ltd.

Cisneros, Sandra: "Barbie-Q" from *Woman Hollering Creek* by Sandra Cisneros, pp. 14–16. Copyright © 1991 by Sandra Cisneros. Published by Vintage Books, a division of Random House, Inc., New York and originally in hardcover by Random House, Inc. Reprinted by permission of Susan Bergholz Literary Services, New York. All rights reserved.

Crane, Hart: "Black Tambourine," "Chaplinesque," "At Melville's Tomb," "Voyages I, II, III," and "Brooklyn Bridge" from *Complete Poems of Hart Crane* by Mac Simon, editor. Copyright 1933, © 1958, 1966 by Liveright Publishing Corporation. Copyright © 1986 by Marc Simon. Reprinted by permission of Liveright Publishing Corporation.

Crane, Stephen: "The Open Boat" by Stephen Crane from *The Works of Stephen Crane, Volume 5: Tales of Adventure,* edited by Fedson Bowers (Charlottesville: Virginia, 1990). Used by permission of the University Press of Virginia.

Cullen, Countee: "Yet I Do Marvel," "Incident," and "Heritage" by Countee Cullen from *Color.* Copyright © 1925 Harper & Bros., renewed 1952 by Ida Cullen. Copyrights held by the Amistad Research Center, administered by Thompson and Thompson, NY.

Cummings, E. E.: "In Just-," "the Cambridge ladies who live in furnished souls," "my sweet old etcetera," "I sing of Olaf glad and big," "anyone lived in a pretty how town," "next to of course god america I," and "what a proud dreamhorse pulling (smoothlooming) through" from *Complete Poems: 1904–1962* by E. E. Cummings, edited by George J. Firmage. Copyright 1923, 1925, 1926, 1931, 1935, 1938, 1939, 1940, 1944, 1945, 1946, 1947, 1948, 1949, 1950, 1951, 1952, 1953, 1954, 1955, 1956, 1957, © 1958, 1959, 1960, 1961, 1962, 1963, 1966, 1967, 1968, 1972, 1973, 1974, 1975, 1976, 1977, 1978, 1979, 1980, 1981, 1982, 1983, 1984, 1985, 1986, 1987, 1988, 1989, 1990, 1991 by the Trustees for the E. E. Cummings Trust. Copyright © 1973, 1976, 1978, 1979, 1981, 1983, 1985, 1991 by George James Firmage. Reprinted by permission of Liveright Publishing Corporation.

Dickinson, Emily: Poems #67, 214, 216, 241, 258, 280, 303, 324, 338, 341, 401, 435, 441, 449, 465, 501, 536, 585, 632, 640, 650, 712, 764, 986, 1052, 1071, 1078, 1125, 1129, 1463, 1540, 1624, 1651, 1670, 1732, and 1760 by Emily Dickinson from *The Poems of Emily Dickinson,* Thomas H. Johnson, ed., Cambridge, Mass.: The Belknap Press of Harvard University Press. Copyright © 1951, 1955, 1979, 1983 by the President and Fellows of Harvard College. Reprinted by permissions of the publishers and the Trustees of Amherst College. And from *The Complete Poems of Emily Dickinson,* edited by Thomas H. Johnson, poems 185, 657, 709, 721, 754, and 1545. Copyright 1929, 1935 by Martha Dickinson Bianchi; copyright renewed © 1957, 1963 by Mary L. Hampson. Reprinted by permission of the publishers and the Trustees of Amherst College and Little, Brown and Company. Excerpts from nine letters from *The Letters of Emily Dickinson,* Thomas H. Johnson, ed., Cambridge, Mass.: The Belknap Press of Harvard University Press. Copyright © 1958, 1986 by the President and Fellows of Harvard College. Reprinted by permission.

Doolittle, Hilda: "Sea Rose," "Oread," and "Helen" from *H.D.: Collected Poems, 1912–1944.* Copyright © 1982 by The Estate of Hilda Doolittle. Reprinted by permission of New Directions Publishing Corporation.

Dove, Rita: "Banneker" and "Dusting" from *Museum* (Carnegie-Mellon University Press) by Rita Dove. Copyright © 1983 by Rita Dove. Reprinted by permission of the author. "Parsley" and "Roast Possum" from *Selected Poems,* Vintage Books, 1993 by Rita Dove. Copyright © 1983, 1993 by Rita Dove. Reprinted by permission of the author. "In a Neutral City" and "Mississippi" from *Grace Notes* by Rita Dove, Copyright © 1989 by Rita Dove. Reprinted by permission of the author and W. W. Norton & Company, Inc.

Eliot, T. S.: "The Love Song of J. Alfred Prufrock," "Gerontion," and "The Waste Land" by T. S. Eliot from *Collected Poems: 1909–1962* by T. S. Eliot. Reprinted by permission of Faber and Faber Ltd. "The Hollow Men" from *Collected Poems 1909–1962* by T. S. Eliot. Copyright © 1936 by Harcourt Brace & Company, renewed © 1963, 1964 by T. S. Eliot. Reprinted by permission of Harcourt Brace & Company and Faber and Faber Ltd. "Tradition and the Individual Talent" by T. S. Eliot from *Selected Essays* by T. S. Eliot. Reprinted by permission of Faber and Faber Ltd.

Ellison, Ralph: "Battle Royal" from *Invisible Man* by Ralph Ellison. Copyright 1947, 1948, 1952 by Ralph Ellison. Reprinted by permission of Random House, Inc.

Erdrich, Louise: "Lulu's Boys" from *Love Medicine* by Louise Erdrich, pp. 106–121. Copyright © 1984, 1993 by Louise Erdrich. Reprinted by permission of Henry Holt and Company, Inc.

Evans, Walker: Excerpt from *Let Us Now Praise Famous Men* by James Agee and Walker Evans. Copyright 1939, 1940 by James Agee, renewed © 1969 by Mia Fritsch Agee and Walker Evans. Reprinted by permission of Houghton Mifflin. All rights reserved.

Faulkner, William: "Spotted Horses" by William Faulkner from *Scribner's Magazine.* Copyright 1931 and renewed 1959 by William Faulkner. Reprinted by permission of Random House, Inc. "That Evening Sun" by William Faulkner from *Collected Stories of William Faulkner.* Copyright © 1959 by William Faulkner. Reprinted by permission of Random House, Inc. "Barn Burning" from *Collected Stories of William Faulkner* by William Faulkner. Copyright 1950 by Random House, Inc., renewed © 1977 by Jill Faulkner Summers. Reprinted by permission of Random House, Inc. Excerpt from "April Seventh, 1938" from *The Sound and the Fury* by William Faulkner. Copyright 1929, renewed 1957 by William Faulkner. Reprinted by permission of Random House, Inc.

Fitzgerald, F. Scott: "Winter Dreams" by F. Scott Fitzgerald from *The Short Stories of F. Scott Fitzgerald,* ed. M. J. Bruccoli. Copyright 1931 by The Curtis Publishing Company, renewed © 1959 by Frances Scott Fitzgerald Lanahan. Reprinted by permission of Scribner, a Division of Simon & Schuster.

Fornes, Maria Irene: List of Cast, Scene 13, "1945-Summer Resort," Scene 14, "1945-Prayer," Scene 15, "1946-I Don't Love You" and Scene 16, "1946-By the Window" from "Sarita" from *Maria Irene Fornes Plays* by Maria Irene Fornes, pp. 90, 124–128. Copyright © 1986 by Maria Irene Fornes. Reprinted by permission of PAJ Publications.

Franklin, Benjamin: Excerpt from *The Autobiography of Benjamin Franklin.* Reprinted courtesy of Huntington Library.

Frost, Robert: "Stopping by Woods on a Snowy Evening," "Once by the Pacific," "Desert Places," "Design," "The Most of It," and "Directive" by Robert Frost from *The Poetry of Robert Frost,* edited by Edward Connery Lathem. Copyright 1936, 1942, 1951, © 1956 by Robert Frost. © 1964, 1970, 1975 by Lesley Frost Ballantine. Copyright 1923, 1928, 1939, 1947, © 1967, 1969 by Henry Holt & Co., Inc. Reprinted by permission of Henry Holt & Co., Inc. "The Figure a Poem Makes" by Robert Frost from *Selected Prose of Robert Frost,* edited by Hyde Cox and Edward Connery Lathem. Copyright 1939 by Robert Frost, © 1967 by Henry Holt & Co., Inc. Reprinted by permission of Henry Holt & Co., Inc.

Ginsberg, Allen: "A Supermarket in California" and "Howl!" Part I from *Collected Poems 1947–1980* by Allen Ginsberg. Copyright 1955 by Allen Ginsberg. Reprinted by permission of HarperCollins Publishers, Inc. "America" from *Collected Poems 1947–1980* by Allen Ginsberg. Copyright © 1959 by Allen Ginsberg. Reprinted by permission of HarperCollins Publishers, Inc.

Graham, Jorie: "The Geese," "The Mind," and "Over and Over Stitch" from *Hybrids of Plants and Ghosts* by Jorie Graham. Copyright © 1980 by Princeton University Press. Reprinted by permission of Princeton University Press. "My Garden, My Daylight" from *Erosion* by Jorie Graham. Copyright © 1983 by Princeton University Press. Reprinted by permission of Princeton University Press.

Harper, Michael S.: "Dear John, Dear Coltrane" from *Dear John, Dear Coltrane* by Michael S. Harper. Copyright © 1970 by Michael S. Harper and The University of Illinois Press. Reprinted by permission of the author and the University of Illinois Press. "Peace on Earth" from *Healing Song for the Inner Ear* by Michael S. Harper. Copyright © 1985 by Michael S. Harper. Reprinted by permission of the author and the University of Illinois Press. "American History" from *Images of Kin* by Michael S. Harper. Copyright © 1977 by Michael S. Harper. Reprinted by permission of the author and the University of Illinois Press. "Nightmare Begins Responsibility" by Michael S. Harper. Reprinted by permission of the author and the University of Illinois Press.

Hayden, Robert: "Homage to the Empress of the Blues" and "Those Winter Sundays" by Robert Hayden from *Collected Poems of Robert Hayden* by Frederick Glaysher, editor. Copyright © 1966 by Robert Hayden. Reprinted by permission of Liveright Publishing Corporation. "A Letter from Phillis Wheatley" by Robert Hayden from *Collected Poems of Robert Hayden* by Frederick Glaysher, editor. Copyright © 1978 by Robert Hayden. Reprinted by permission of Liveright Publishing Corporation.

Hemingway, Ernest: "Soldier's Home" from *In Our Time* by Ernest Hemingway. Copyright 1925 by Charles Scribner's Sons, renewed 1953 by Ernest Hemingway. Reprinted by permission of Scribner, a Division of Simon & Schuster.

Howe, Susan: "Thorow" from *Singularities* by Susan Howe, pp. 357–369. Copyright © 1990 by Susan Howe. Originally published by Wesleyan University Press. Reprinted by permission of the University Press of New England.

Hughes, Langston: "The Negro Speaks of Rivers," "The Weary Blues," "I, Too," "Dream Boogie," and "Theme for English B" by Langston Hughes from *Selected Poems of Langston Hughes.* Copyright 1951 by Langston Hughes. Reprinted by permission of Alfred A. Knopf, Inc. Excerpt from "The Negro Artist and the Racial Mountain" by Langston Hughes from *The Nation.* Copyright 1926 by Langston Hughes. Copyright renewed © 1980 by George Houston Bass. Reprinted by permission of Harold Ober Associates Incorporated.

Hurston, Zora Neale: "Sweat," "The Gilded Six-Bits," and "Spunk" from *The Complete Stories* by Zora Neale Hurston. Introduction copyright © 1995 by Henry Louis Gates, Jr. and Sieglinde Lemke. Compilation copyright © 1995 by Vivian Bowden, Lois J. Hurston Gaston, Clifford Hurston, Lucy Ann Hurston, Winifred Hurston Clark, Zora Mack Goins, Edgar Hurston, Sr., and Barbara Hurston Lewis. Afterword and Bibliography copyright © 1995 by Henry Louis Gates. "Sweat" was originally published in *Fire,* November 1926. "Spunk" was originally

published in *Opportunity,* June 1925. "The Gilded Six-Bits" was originally published in *Story,* August 1933. Reprinted by permission of HarperCollins Publishers.

Jarrell, Randall: "The Death of the Ball Turret Gunner" from *The Complete Poems* by Randall Jarrell. Copyright © 1969 by Mrs. Randall Jarrell. Reprinted by permission of Farrar, Straus & Giroux, Inc. "The Woman at the Washington Zoo" by Randall Jarrell reprinted in *The Complete Poems of Randall Jarrell,* Farrar Straus & Giroux, 1989. Copyright © 1960 by Randall Jarrell. Reprinted by permission of Rhoda Weyr Agency, New York.

Jeffers, Robinson: "Boats in a Fog," and "Hurt Hawks" by Robinson Jeffers from *Selected Poetry.* Copyright 1925, 1928 and renewed 1953, 1956 by Robinson Jeffers. Reprinted by permission of Alfred A. Knopf, Inc.

Jefferson, Thomas: "Query V: Cascades (Natural Bridge)," "Query VI: [Productions Mineral, Vegetable, & Animal (Indians and African Slaves)]," and excerpts from *Notes on the State of Virginia* by Thomas Jefferson, edited by William Peden. Copyright © 1954, 1982 by the University of North Carolina Press. Published for the Institute of Early American History and Culture. Reprinted by permission.

Jen, Gish: Chapter 4, "Hot Times at the Hot Line" from *Mona in the Promised Land* by Gish Jen, pp. 52–82. Copyright © 1996 by Gish Jen. Reprinted by permission of Alfred A. Knopf, Inc.

Johnson, Georgia Douglas: "The Heart of a Woman," "Smothered Fires," and "Motherhood" by Georgia Douglas Johnson from *Shadowed Dreams: Women's Poetry of the Harlem Renaissance,* edited by Maureen Honey. Copyright © 1989. Reprinted by permission of Rutger's University Press.

Johnson, Helene: "Sonnet to a Negro in Harlem" and "What Do I Care for Morning" by Helene Johnson from *Caroling Dusk,* edited by Countee Cullen. Copyright 1927 Harper & Bros., renewed 1955 by Ida Cullen. Copyrights held by the Amistad Research Center, Administered by Thompson and Thompson, NY.

Johnson, James Weldon: Excerpt from "Let My People Go" by James Weldon Johnson from *God's Trombones.* Copyright 1927 by The Viking Press, Inc., renewed 1955 by Grace Neil Johnson. Used by permission of Viking Penguin, a division of Penguin Books USA Inc.

Kincaid, Jamaica: "Girl" from *At the Bottom of the River* by Jamaica Kincaid, pp. 468-469. Copyright © 1983 by Jamaica Kincaid. Reprinted by permission of Farrar, Straus & Giroux, Inc.

King, Martin Luther, Jr.: "Letter from Birmingham Jail" by Martin Luther King, Jr. Copyright © 1963 by Martin Luther King, Jr., renewed 1991 by Coretta Scott King. Reprinted by arrangement with the Heirs to the Estate of Martin Luther King, Jr., c/o Writers House, Inc. as agent for the proprietor.

Kingston, Maxine Hong: "No Name Woman" from *The Woman Warrior* by Maxine Hong Kingston. Copyright © 1975, 1976 by Maxine Hong Kingston. Reprinted by permission of Alfred A. Knopf, Inc.

Kushner, Tony: Part One, "Millennium Approaches" from *Angels in America* by Tony Kushner. Copyright © 1992, 1993 by Tony Kushner. Reprinted by permission of Theatre Communications Group.

Lee, Li-Young: "The City in Which I Love You" from *The City in Which I Love You* by Li-Young Lee. Copyright © 1990 by Li-Young Lee. Reprinted by permission of BOA Editions, Ltd., Rochester, NY. "Persimmons" and "Eating Together" from *Rose* by Li-Young Lee. Copyright © 1986 by Li-Young Lee. Reprinted by permission of BOA Editions, Ltd.

1934, 1938 by Ezra Pound. Reprinted by permission of New Directions Publishing Corporation. Excerpts from *Cantos XLV and LXXXI* from *The Cantos of Ezra Pound.* Copyright 1934, 1938 by Ezra Pound. Reprinted by permission of New Directions Publishing Corporation.

Ransom, John Crowe: "Bells for John Whiteside's Daughter," "Piazza Piece," and "The Equilibrists" by John Crowe Ransom from *Selected Poems.* Copyright 1924, 1927 by Alfred A. Knopf, renewed 1952, 1955 by John Crowe Ransom. Reprinted by permission of Alfred A. Knopf, Inc.

Rich, Adrienne: "Living in Sin," "Translations," "The Knight," "I Am in Danger–Sir–," "Necessities of Life," "Trying to Talk with a Man," "Diving into the Wreck," and "The Ninth Symphony of Beethoven Understood at Last as a Sexual Message" from *The Fact of a Doorframe: Poems Selected and New, 1950–1984* by Adrienne Rich. Copyright © 1984 by Adrienne Rich. Copyright © 1975, 1978 by W. W. Norton & Company, Inc. Copyright © 1981 by Adrienne Rich. Reprinted by permission of W. W. Norton & Company, Inc.

Rios, Alberto: "Lost on September Trail, 1967," "Nani," and "Mi Abuelo" from *Whispering to Fool the Wind* by Alberto Rios. Copyright © 1982 by Alberto Rios. Reprinted by permission of the author. "The Good Lunch of Oceans" from *Teodoro Luna's Two Kisses* by Alberto Rios, pp. 22–23. Copyright © 1990 by Alberto Rios. Reprinted by permission of W. W. Norton & Company, Inc.

Robinson, Edwin Arlington: "Richard Cory," "Miniver Cheevy," "Eros Turranos," and "Mr. Flood's Party" from *Collected Poems of Edwin Arlington Robinson* by Edwin Arlington Robinson. Copyright 1937 by Macmillian Publishing Company, renewed © 1965 by Ruth Nivison and Barbara R. Holt. Reprinted by permission of Simon & Schuster.

Roethke, Theodore: "My Papa's Waltz," "Elegy for Jane," "The Lost Son," "Cuttings," "Cuttings (Later)," and "The Waking" by Theodore Roethke from *The Collected Poems of Theodore Roethke.* Copyright 1948, 1950, 1953 by Theodore Roethke. Reprinted by permission of Doubleday, a division of Bantam Doubleday Publishing Group.

Roth, Phillip: "The Conversion of the Jews" from *Goodbye, Columbus* by Phillip Roth. Copyright © 1959, renewed 1987 by Phillip Roth. Reprinted by permission of Houghton Mifflin Co. All rights reserved.

Rowlandson, Mary: "A True History of the Captivity and Restoration of Mrs. Mary Rowlandson" by Mary Rowlandson from *Journeys in New Worlds: Early American Women's Narratives,* ed. William L. Andrews, Sargent Bush Jr., Annette Kolodny, Amy Schrager Lang and Daniel B. Shea. Copyright © 1990 by the University of Wisconsin Press. Reprinted by permission of the University of Wisconsin Press.

Sandburg, Carl: "Chicago" and "Fog" from *Chicago Poems* by Carl Sandburg. Copyright 1916 by Holt, Rinehart and Winston, Inc., renewed 1944 by Carl Sandburg. Reprinted by permission of Harcourt Brace & Company. "Cool Tombs" from *Cornhuskers* by Carl Sandburg. Copyright 1918 by Holt, Rinehart & Winston, Inc., renewed 1946 by Carl Sandburg. Reprinted by permission of Harcourt Brace & Company.

Sewall, Samuel: Excerpts from *The Diary of Samuel Sewall: 1674–1729,* edited by M. Halsey Thomas. Copyright © 1973 by Farrar, Straus & Giroux, Inc.

Sexton, Anne: "Her Kind" from *To Bedlam and Part Way Back* by Anne Sexton. Copyright © 1960 by Anne Sexton, renewed 1988 by Linda G. Sexton. Reprinted by permission of Houghton Mifflin Co. All rights reserved. "The Truth the Dead Know" from *All My Pretty Ones* by Anne Sexton. Copyright © 1962 by Anne Sexton, renewed 1990 by Linda G. Sexton. Reprinted by permission of Houghton

Mifflin Co. All rights reserved. "For My Lover, Returning to His Wife" from *Love Poems* by Anne Sexton. Copyright © 1967, 1968, 1969 by Anne Sexton. Reprinted by permission of Houghton Mifflin Co. All rights reserved. "Self in 1958" from *Live or Die* by Anne Sexton. Copyright © 1966 by Anne Sexton. Reprinted by permission of Houghton Mifflin Company. All rights reserved. "Snow White and the Seven Dwarfs" from *Transformations* by Anne Sexton. Copyright © 1971 by Anne Sexton. Reprinted by permission of Houghton Mifflin Company. All rights reserved.

Silko, Leslie Marmon: "Lullaby" by Leslie Marmon Silko. Copyright © 1981 by Leslie Marmon Silko. Reprinted by permission of The Wylie Agency, Inc. "Storyteller" by Leslie Marmon Silko. Copyright © 1981 by Leslie Marmon Silko. Reprinted by permission of The Wylie Agency, Inc.

Simpson, Louis: "To The Western World" and "American Poetry" from *Caviare at the Funeral* by Louis Simpson. Copyright © 1980 by Louis Simpson. Reprinted by permission of Grolier Publishing Company.

Singer, Isaac Bashevis: "Escape from Civilization" from *The Collected Stories* by Isaac Bashevis Singer, pp. 574–579. Copyright © 1982 by Isaac Bashevis Singer. Reprinted by permission of Farrar, Straus & Giroux.

Song, Cathy: "Lost Sister," "Youngest Daughter," "Beauty and Sadness," and "The White Porch" from *Picture Bride* by Cathy Song. Copyright © 1983 by Cathy Song. Reprinted by permission of Yale University Press.

Stevens, Wallace: "Sunday Morning," "Anecdote of the Jar," "The Emperor of Ice-Cream," and "Thirteen Ways of Looking at a Blackbird" from *Collected Poems* by Wallace Stevens. Copyright 1923, renewed 1951 by Wallace Stevens. Reprinted by permission of Alfred A. Knopf, Inc. "The Idea of Order at Key West" and "The Poem that Took the Place of a Mountain" from *Collected Poems* by Wallace Stevens. Copyright 1936, renewed 1964 by Holly Stevens. Reprinted by permission of Alfred A. Knopf, Inc.

Tate, Allen: "Ode to the Confederate Dead" from *Collected Poems 1919–1976* by Allen Tate. Copyright © 1977 by Allen Tate. Reprinted by permission of Farrar, Straus & Giroux, Inc.

Taylor, Edward: Excerpts from *God's Determinations, Huswifery, and Preparatory Meditations* by Edward Taylor. Copyright © 1960, 1988 by Donald E. Sanford. Reprinted by permission of Donald E. Sanford.

Toomer, Jean: "Blood-Burning Moon" from *Cane* by Jean Toomer. Copyright 1923 by Boni & Liveright, renewed 1951 by Jean Toomer. Reprinted by permissions of Liveright Publishing Corporation.

Twain, Mark: "Fenimore Cooper's Literary Offenses" from *How to Tell a Story* by Mark Twain. Copyright 1923 by the Mark Twain Company, renewed 1951 by the Mark Twain Company. Reprinted by permission of HarperCollins Publishers, Inc. "Corn-Pone Opinions" from *Europe and Elsewhere* by Mark Twain. Copyright 1923 by the Mark Twain Company, renewed 1951 by the Mark Twain Company. Reprinted by permission of HarperCollins Publishers, Inc.

Updike, John: "Separating" from *Problems and Other Stories* by John Updike. Copyright © 1975 by John Updike. Reprinted by permission of Alfred A. Knopf, Inc.

Walcott, Derek: "A Far Cry from Africa," "Preparing for Exile," and "Old New England" from *Collected Poems 1948–1984* by Derek Walcott. Copyright © 1986 by Derek Walcott. Reprinted by permission of Farrar, Straus & Giroux, Inc.

Walker, Alice: "Everyday Use" from *In Love and Trouble: Stories of Black Women* by Alice Walker. Copyright © 1973 by Alice Walker. Reprinted by permission of Harcourt Brace & Company.

Warren, Robert Penn: "Bearded Oaks" from *Selected Poems: 1923–1943* by Robert Penn Warren. Copyright 1943 by Robert Penn Warren. Reprinted by permission of William Morris Agency, Inc. on behalf of the Author.

Welty, Eudora: "Why I Live at the P. O." from *A Curtain of Green and Other Stories* by Eudora Welty. Copyright 1941, renewed © 1968 by Eudora Welty. Reprinted by permission of Harcourt Brace & Company. Excerpt from "A Sweet Devouring" by Eudora Welty from *A Sweet Devouring*. Copyright © 1969 by Eudora Welty. Reprinted by permission of Russell & Volkening as agents for the author.

Wharton, Edith: "The Other Two" from *The Descent of Man*. Copyright under the Berne Convention. Reprinted with the permission of Charles Scribner's Sons.

Wheatley, Phillis: "On the Death of the Rev. Mr. George Whitefield, 1770" "On Being Brought from Africa to America," "To S. M. a Young African Painter," and "To His Excellency General Washington" by Phillis Wheatley from *The Poems of Phillis Wheatley*, revised and enlarged edition, edited by Julian D. Mason, Jr. Copyright © 1989 by the University of North Carolina Press. Used by permission.

Wilbur, Richard: "Love Calls Us to the Things of This World" from *Things of This World* by Richard Wilbur. Copyright 1956, renewed © 1984 by Richard Wilbur. Reprinted by permission of Harcourt Brace & Company. "Playboy" from *Walking to Sleep: New Poems and Translations* by Richard Wilbur. Copyright © 1968 by Richard Wilbur. Reprinted by permission of Harcourt Brace & Company. "The Writer" and "Cottage Street, 1953" from *The Mind-Reader* by Richard Wilbur. Copyright © 1971 by Richard Wilbur. Reprinted by permission of Harcourt Brace & Company.

Williams, Tennessee: *The Glass Menagerie* by Tennessee Williams. Copyright © 1945 by Tennessee Williams and Edwina D. Williams and renewed © 1973 by Tennessee Williams. Reprinted by permission of Random House, Inc.

Williams, William Carlos: "The Yachts," "This is Just to Say," "The Red Wheelbarrow," "Spring and All," and "Queen Anne's Lace" from *Collected Poems: 1909–1939, Volume I* by William Carlos Williams. Copyright © 1938 by New Directions Publishing Corporation. Reprinted by permission of New Directions Publishing Corporation

Winthrop, John: "Christian Charity" by John Winthrop from *A Model of Christian Charity*. Reprinted courtesy Massachussetts Historical Society.

Wright, James: "A Note Left in Jimmy Leonard's Shack" and "At the Executed Murderer's Grave" from *St. Judas* by James Wright. Copyright © 1959 by James Wright. Originally published by Wesleyan University Press. Reprinted by permission of University Press of New England. "Autumn Begins in Martin's Ferry, Ohio" from *The Branch Will Not Break* by James Wright. Copyright © 1963 by James Wright. Originally published by Wesleyan University Press. Reprinted by permission of University Press of New England. "Lament for My Brother on a Hayrake" from *Collected Poems* by James Wright. Copyright © 1971 by James Wright. Originally published by Wesleyan University Press. Reprinted by permission of the University Press of New England. "Lightening Bugs Asleep in the Afternoon" from *This Journey* by James Wright. Copyright © 1977, 1978, 1980, 1981, 1982 by Anne Wright, Executrix of the Estate of James Wright. Reprinted by permission of Random House, Inc.

Wright, Richard: "Long Black Song" by Richard Wright from *Uncle Tom's Cabin* by Richard Wright. Copyright 1938 by Richard Wright, renewed © 1966 by Ellen Wright. Reprinted by permission of HarperCollins Publishers, Inc. Excerpt from chapter 13 of *Black Boy* by Richard Wright. Copyright 1937, 1942, 1944, 1945 by Richard Wright. Copyright renewed © 1973 by Ellen Wright. Reprinted by permission of HarperCollins Publishers, Inc. Excerpt from *American Hunger* by Richard Wright. Copyright 1944 by Richard Wright. Copyright © 1977 by Ellen Wright. Reprinted by permission of HarperCollins Publishers, Inc.

Yezierska, Anzia: "Hester Street" from *Bread Givers* by Anzia Yezierska, pp. 10–14. Copyright © 1970 by Louise Levitas Henriksen. Reprinted by permission of Persea Books, Inc.

From "Yiddish Proverbs," translated by Isadore Goldstick from *A Treasury of Yiddish Stories*, edited by Irving Howe and Eliezer Greenberg, pp. 611-612. Reprinted by permission of Random House, Inc.

Index of Authors, Titles, First Lines of Poetry